COLLINS CONCISE DICTIONARY
OF THE ENGLISH LANGUAGE

COLLINS: LONDON & GLASGOW

Collins Concise English Dictionary is based upon
Webster's New World Dictionary, Second Concise Edition
© 1956, 1975 William Collins + World Publishing Co. Inc.

**Standard
ISBN 0 00 433046 3
Thumb Indexed
ISBN 0 00 433047 1**

Computer typeset by C. R. Barber & Partners, Wrotham, England

Printed and bound by Rand McNally & Company
in the United States of America

for William Collins Sons & Co. Ltd.
P.O. Box, Glasgow G4 0NB

METRICATION TABLES

LINEAR MEASURE (LENGTH)

1 inch	=	25.4mm	1 mm	=	0.039 inches
1 inch	=	2.54 cm	1 cm	=	0.394 inches
1 foot	=	0.3048 m	1 m	=	3.281 feet
1 yard	=	0.9144 m	1 m	=	1.094 yards
1 mile	=	1.609 km	1 km	=	0.621 miles

SQUARE MEASURE (AREA)

1 square inch	=	6.542 cm^2	1 cm^2	=	0.155 square inches
1 square foot	=	0.093 m^2	1 m^2	=	10.76 square feet
1 square yard	=	0.836 m^2	1 m^2	=	1.196 square yards
1 acre	=	0.405 hectare	1 hectare	=	2.471 acres
1 square mile	=	2.59 km^2	1 km^2	=	0.386 square miles

CUBIC MEASURE (VOLUME)

1 cubic inch	=	16.39 cm^3	1 cm^3	=	0.061 cubic inches
1 cubic foot	=	0.028 m^3	1 m^3	=	35.32 cubic feet
1 cubic yard	=	0.765 m^3	1 m^3	=	1.308 cubic yards

LIQUID MEASURE (CAPACITY)

1 fluid ounce	=	0.03 litre	1 litre	=	33.81 fluid ounces
1 pint	=	0.568 litre	1 litre	=	1.76 pints
1 gallon	=	4.546 litre	1 litre	=	0.220 gallons
1 U.S. gallon	=	3.786 litre	1 litre	=	0.264 U.S. gallons

WEIGHTS (MASS)

1 ounce	=	28.35 g	1 g	=	0.0353 ounces
1 pound	=	0.454 kg	1 kg	=	2.205 pounds
1 ton	=	1.016 tonne	1 tonne	=	0.984 ton

TEMPERATURE

Celsius thermometer		Fahrenheit thermometer
0° C	freezing point of water	32° F
100° C	boiling point of water	212° F
36.8°C	body temperature	98.4°F

To find degrees Celsius, subtract 32 from degrees Fahrenheit and divide by 1.8
To find degrees Fahrenheit, multiply degrees Celsius by 1.8 and add 32

CONTENTS

EDITORIAL STAFF

For William Collins + World Publishing Co., Inc.
Editor in Chief
David B. Guralnik

Managing Editor
Samuel Solomon

Associate Editors
Clark C. Livensparger (Supervising)
Thomas Layman, Andrew N. Sparks,
Christopher T. Hoolihan, Paul B. Murry,
Ruth Kimball Kent

For William Collins Sons & Co., Ltd.
Managing Editor
William T. McLeod

Editors
Margaret Martin, Marian Makins,
Pamela Breckenridge, John Morgan

Assistants
Kathleen Cox, Danielle McGrath,
Kay Macpherson, Nancy Marshall

FOREWORD

COLLINS CONCISE DICTIONARY OF THE ENGLISH LANGUAGE is based on the Second Concise Edition of *Webster's New World Dictionary*. This successful dictionary has been thoroughly revised and updated, and is now offered to the many professional and business people, families, pupils, office workers, word-game addicts, learners of English, and others who want a comprehensive and up-to-date dictionary but who have no need for the extensive etymologies, highly technical terms and rarer words and meanings found in larger volumes. For such people COLLINS CONCISE DICTIONARY should prove ideal.

The word stock of this dictionary, over 85 000 vocabulary references, was selected on the basis of frequency of occurrence in publications of general interest. It is one of the major responsibilities of a dictionary to incorporate the developments in vocabulary arising from expanding technology, the mass media, and other forces affecting our culture. Biorhythm, black hole, blow-dry, gulag, Lassa fever, legionnaire's disease, P.L.O., hang gliding, safari park, SIDS (sudden infant death syndrome), reggae, tailback - these and many more are typical of the way the language has been enriched in recent years, and typical of the kind of coinage that the lexicographer must be constantly on the alert to identify, assess, and incorporate if the dictionary is to be a valid ongoing record of language usage. In selecting new words for inclusion we have been careful to choose only those terms that have acquired a stability of form and meaning and show some promise of surviving in the language, at least for a time. We have equally sought to avoid expending space on the merely faddish or ephemeral terms that appear suddenly and then die within a year or two.

Obsolete and archaic terms and senses that are frequently found in the Bible or in standard works of literature have been included. Also, such technical terms and meanings of specialized fields as are encountered in general writings have been entered, usually prefaced by a field label. The abbreviations for these various labels will be found in the List of Abbreviations immediately preceding the first page of the vocabulary. Words which there is reason to believe constitute trademarks have been designated as such. However, the presence or the absence of such designation should not be regarded as affecting the legal status of any trademark.

A great many prefixes, suffixes, and combining forms have been entered, and these will enable the user of this dictionary to determine the meanings of thousands of additional words that are themselves too specialized for entry in a work of this scope. In the interest of conserving space, many words derived from main words, such as nouns ending in *-tion, -er,* or *-ness,* adjectives ending in *-like,* or *-less,* and adverbs ending in *-ly* have been run in at the end of the entry for the base word. Such run-ins are syllabified and, where necessary, pronounced, and irregular inflected forms, if any, are shown. The meaning of any such run-in can easily be determined from the meanings of the base word and the suffix. Any derivative that has an important meaning not readily inferred from its separate parts is entered separately and defined.

Among the words whose spelling offers difficulty to many people are the principal parts of so-called irregular verbs, plurals that are formed in some way other than by adding *-s* or *-es,* and comparisons of adjectives that may or may not double the consonant before adding *-er* and *-est.* Rather than leave these forms to guesswork or to reliance on a number of rules to which many exceptions exist, we have shown them in full or in shortened form immediately after the appropriate part-of-speech label.

To make it easier to use the dictionary all vocabulary items, including abbreviations, affixes, and foreign terms frequently encountered in written and spoken English, have been entered in one alphabetical listing. There is no need to rummage among a number of appendixes in order to find lexical information.

The continuing popular interest in language justifies our decision to include brief etymologies within these entries. The history of the origin and development of a word, in addition to satisfying the curiosity that many people have about the language they speak, can often help one to understand more clearly the current meaning of the word and to remember that meaning when the word is met a second time.

The pronunciations recorded here are those that at present are accepted by most educated speakers of English. Common variants are also shown, as well as native pronunciations of foreign words. Transcription is in a simple, easily read system that avoids a multiplicity of special symbols but is nevertheless remarkably precise. A detailed explanation will be found in the introductory Guide to the Dictionary and inside the front cover of this book.

Through the use of the latest technological advances in composition, this dictionary has been set by computer in modern type that is clear, attractive, and of the largest practicable size. To help the reader find more quickly the information he is seeking, various type faces are used for the different elements within the entry. More than 600 illustrations have been included where it was felt that a picture would help to expand or sharpen the definition. The actual sizes of animals have been given in metres or centimetres and tools and instruments have been shown in use to make even clearer their function and relative size. All measurements in the dictionary are given in metric units, using the International System of Units (SI) as laid down by the General Conference of Weights and Measures. Where non-metric measurements, such as feet and inches, are entered, the metric equivalent has been included.

An important feature of COLLINS CONCISE DICTIONARY is the attention given the vocabulary of American English. American terminology and usage is accurately described for items that are likely to be encountered by non-American users, that are likely to become common in British speech, and that are likely to cause confusion.

To help the user get the full benefit of the language information included in this dictionary, we have prepared a detailed *Guide to the Use of the Dictionary,* which appears on the following pages. You are urged to read it.

GUIDE TO THE USE OF THE DICTIONARY

1. THE MAIN ENTRY WORD

A. Arrangement of Entries

All main entries, including single words, hyphenated and unhyphenated compounds, prefixes, suffixes, and abbreviations, are listed in strict alphabetical order and are set in large, boldface type.

kan·ga·roo (kaŋ′gəroo′) *,n.* ...
kangaroo court ...
kat·a- *same as* CATA-
ka·ty·did (kāt′ē did′) *n.* ...
kau·ri (kou′rē) *n.* ...
kay·o (kā′ō′) *vt.* ...
kc, kc. kilocycle
K.C. King's Counsel

B. Variant Spellings & Forms

When variant spellings of a word are some distance apart in alphabetical listing, the definition appears at the spelling most frequently used. Other spellings of the word are cross-referred to that spelling. Sometimes such a cross-reference indicates that the variant is American, dialectal, slang, obsolete, or the like.

in·sta·ble ... *adj. same as* UNSTABLE
favor ... *n.,vt. U.S. sp. of* FAVOUR
shew ... *n.,vt.,vi. ... archaic sp. of* SHOW

If two variant spellings would appear close to each other in alphabetical order and are used with nearly equal frequency, they are placed together at the head of the entry. Neither spelling is considered to be "more correct," even though the one listed first may be used somewhat more often.

ac·knowl·edg·ment, ac·knowl·edge·ment ... *n.*

If a variant spelling is close in alphabetical order to the main-entry spelling and pronounced exactly like it but is used less often, such a spelling or spellings are given at the end of the entry block or pertinent definition.

lam·baste ... Also sp. **lam·bast′**
blue blood ... : also **blue′blood′** *n.*

When related words with the same meaning would appear in alphabetical order close to each other, the less frequently used word is placed at the end of the entry block or pertinent definition for the more common word.

laud·a·to·ry ... *adj.* ... : also **laud′a·tive**
in·fu·so·ri·an ... *n.* ... *adj.* ... : also **in′fu·so′ri·al**

C. Cross-references

In all entries or senses that consist simply of a cross-reference to another entry having the same meaning, the entry cross-referred to is shown in small capitals.

mon·ied ... *adj. same as* MONEYED
ca·ble ... *n.* 1. ... 2. ... 3. *same as* CABLE LENGTH
air·plane ... *n. U.S. var. of* AEROPLANE
chaunt ... *n.,vt.,vi. archaic var. of* CHANT
mid·den ... *n.* 1. ... 2. *short for* KITCHEN MIDDEN
re·pro ... *n. shortened form of* REPRODUCTION PROOF
lib. ... *n. clipped form of* LIBERATION

D. Homographs

Main entries that are spelled exactly alike but are different in meaning and origin, as **bat** (a club), **bat** (the animal), and **bat** (to wink), are entered in separate blocks and are marked with small, raised numerals just after the boldface spellings.

bat[1] ... *n.* ...
bat[2] ... *n.* ...
bat[3] ... *vt.* ...

Cross-references to such entries are identified by these small, raised numerals

moor·land ... *n. same as* MOOR[1]

E. Foreign Terms

Foreign words and phrases that appear fairly often in English speech and writing but are not yet considered a part of the English vocabulary, are marked with a double dagger (‡) at the beginning of the entry. This mark indicates that such a term is usually printed in italic type.

‡au na·tu·rel .. *[Fr.]* ...

F. Prefixes, Suffixes, & Combining Forms

Prefixes and combining forms used at the beginning of words are indicated in the dictionary by a hyphen placed after the entry form.

re- ... *a prefix meaning:* 1. back *[repay]* 2. again, anew *[reappear]*...

Suffixes and combining forms used at the end of words are indicated in the dictionary by a hyphen placed before the entry form.

-hood ... *a suffix meaning:* 1. state, quality, condition *[childhood]* 2. the whole group of (a specified class, profession, etc.) *[priesthood]*

Many such forms are entered here and make it possible for the reader to work out the meaning of words that are made with these forms but are not entered in the dictionary.

G. Syllabification

Centre dots in the entry words indicate where the words can be divided if they need to be broken at the end of a written or printed line. In actual copy, a hyphen is used in place of the centre dot. For example, **car·niv·o·rous** can be broken at the end of a line in the following ways (*car-* or *carniv-* or *carnivo-*), depending on how much space is available.

If the stress given to the syllables of a word alters when that word is used as another part of speech, the syllabification shown may properly apply only to the use of the word as the first part of speech given. In the case of a word such as *produce,* the writer may wish to change the syllabification from **pro·duce** when the verb is meant to **prod·uce** when the noun is meant; the pronunciation shown for the noun serves as a guide for this change.

All the syllables of a word are marked (for example, **might·y, a·ban·don**) although it is not customary in written or printed matter to break a word after the first syllable or before the last if that syllable consists of only a single letter or generally, in the case of a long word, of only two letters.

II. PRONUNCIATION

A. Introduction

The pronunciations recorded in this dictionary are for the most part those found in the normal, relaxed conversation of educated speakers.

B. Key to Pronunciation

Symbol	Key Words	Symbol	Key Words
a	act, fat, parrot	yōō	use, duty, few
ā	ape, date, play	yoo	united, cure, globule
ä	ah, car, father	oi	oil, point, toy
		ou	out, crowd, plough
e	elf, ten, berry		
ē	even, meet, money	u	up, cut, colour
i	is, hit, mirror, fear	ʉr	urn, fur, deter
ī	ice, bite, high		
		ə	a in ago
o	odd, pot, lorry		e in agent
ō	open, tone, go		i in sanity
ô	all, horn, law		o in comply
ōō	ooze, tool, crew		u in focus
oo	look, pull, moor	ər	perhaps, murder

Guide to the Dictionary

Symbol	Key Words	Symbol	Key Words
b	bed, fable, dub	v	vat, hovel, have
d	dip, beadle, had	w	will, always, swear
f	fall, after, off	y	yet, onion, yard
g	get, haggle, dog	z	zebra, dazzle, haze
h	he, ahead, hotel	ch	chin, butcher, arch
j	joy, agile, badge	sh	she, cushion, dash
k	kill, tackle, bake	th	thin, nothing, truth
l	let, yellow, ball	*th*	*th*en, fa*th*er, la*the*
m	met, camel, trim	zh	azure, leisure
n	not, flannel, ton	ŋ	ring, anger, drink
p	put, apple, tap	'	[see explanatory note
r	red, port, dear		below and also *Foreign*
s	sell, castle, pass		*sounds* below]
t	top, cattle, hat		

The symbols in the key above can be easily understood from the key words in which they are shown, and most speakers of English will automatically read their own pronunciation into any symbol shown here. Explanatory notes on some of these symbols follow.

ä This symbol represents the vowel of *car.* Some words shown with **ä**, such as *fast* (fäst), *bath* (bäth), etc., are heard in the speech of some persons with the vowel sound **a** (fast), (bath). Such variations may be assumed although they are not recorded in this dictionary.

e This symbol represents the vowel of *ten.* It is also used, followed by **r**, to represent the vowel sound of *care* (ker); for this sound, vowels ranging from ā (kār *or* kā′ər) to **a** (kar) are sometimes heard and may be assumed as variants although they are not recorded in this dictionary.

ē This symbol represents the vowel of *meet* and is also used for the vowel in the unstressed final syllable of such words as *lucky* (luk′ē), *pretty* (prit′ē), etc.

i This symbol represents the vowel of *hit* and is also used for the vowel in the unstressed syllables of such words as *village* (vil′ij), *goodness* (good′nis), *preface* (pref′is), *deny* (di nī′), *curate* (kyoor′it), etc. In such unstressed syllables, the schwa (ə) is often heard (vil′əj), (good′nəs), etc. and may be assumed as a variant although not recorded in this dictionary. This symbol is also used, followed by **r**, to represent the vowel sound of *dear* (dir); for this sound, vowels ranging to ē (dēr *or* dē′ər) are sometimes heard and, although not here recorded, may be assumed as variants.

ô This symbol represents the vowel of *all.* When followed by **r**, as in *more* (môr), vowels ranging to ō (mōr *or* mō′ər) are often heard and, although not here recorded, may be assumed as variants.

ur and **ər** These two symbols represent, in order, the stressed and the unstressed vowels heard in the two syllables of *murder* (mur′dər). Where these symbols are shown, some speakers, especially in Scotland and the West Country, will sound the **r** in pronouncing them.

ə This symbol, called the schwa, represents the neutral vowel heard in the unstressed syllables of *ago, agent, focus,* etc. In many words, such as *colitis,* this vowel is sometimes heard as **i** (kō līt′is).

ŋ This symbol represents the nasal sound indicated in spelling by the *ng* of *sing* and occurring also for **n** before the consonants **k** and **g**, as in *drink* (driŋk) and *finger* (fiŋ′gər).

' The apostrophe occurring before **l, m,** and **n** indicates that the following consonant is a syllabic consonant, with little or no vowel sound accompanying it, as in *apple* (ap′′l) or *happen* (hap′′n). Some persons pronounce such words with a vowel sound close to the schwa (ə), as in *happen* (hap′ən), but such variants are not entered in this dictionary.

Foreign Sounds

Most of the symbols in the key above have been used to transcribe pronunciations in foreign languages, although it should be understood that these sounds will vary somewhat from language to language. The additional symbols below will cover those situations that cannot be adequately dealt with using the general key.

à This symbol, representing the *a* in the French *bal* (bàl) can best be described as intermediate between (a) and (ä).

ë This symbol represents the sound of the vowel cluster in French *coeur* (kër) and can be approximated by rounding the lips as for (ô) and pronouncing (e).

ö This symbol variously represents the sound of *eu* in French *feu* (fö) or of *ö* (or *oe*) in German *Göttingen* (gö′tiŋ ən), *Goethe* (gö′tə) and can be approximated by rounding the lips as for (ō) and pronouncing (ā).

ŏ This represents a range of sounds varying from (ō) to (ô) and heard with such varying quality in French *coq* (kŏk),

German *doch* (dŏ kh), Italian *poco* (pŏ′kŏ), Spanish *torero* (tŏ re′rŏ), etc.

ü This symbol variously represents the sound of *u* in French *duc* (dük) and in German *grün* (grün) and can be approximated by rounding the lips as for (ōō) and pronouncing (ē).

kh This symbol represents the sound heard in German *doch* (dŏkh). It can be approximated by arranging the speech organs as for (k) but allowing the breath to escape in a stream, as in pronouncing (h).

H This symbol represents a sound similar to the preceding but formed by friction against the front of the palate, as in German *ich* (iH). It is sometimes misheard, and hence pronounced, by English speakers as (sh).

n This symbol indicates that the vowel sound immediately preceding it is nasalized; that is, the nasal passage is left open so that the breath passes through both the mouth and nose in voicing the vowel, as in French *mon* (mōn).

r This symbol represents any of various sounds used in languages other than English for the consonant *r.* It may represent the tongue-point trill or uvular trill of the *r* in French *reste* (rest) or *sur* (sür), German *Reuter* (roi′tər), Italian *ricotta* (rē kôt′tä), Russian *gorod* (gô′rôd), etc.

' The apostrophe is used after final *l* and *r,* in certain French pronunciations, to indicate that they are voiceless after an unvoiced consonant, as in *lettre* (let′r′). In Russian words the "soft sign" in the Cyrillic spelling is indicated (y′). The sound can be approximated by pronouncing an unvoiced (y) directly after the consonant involved, as in *Sevastopol* (se′väs tô′pəl y′).

C. General Styling of Pronunciation

Pronunciations are given inside parentheses, immediately following the boldface entry. A single space is used between syllables. A primary, or strong, stress is indicated by a heavy stroke (′) immediately following the syllable so stressed. A secondary, or weak, stress is indicated by a lighter stroke (′) following the syllable so stressed. All notes, labels, or other matter inside the parentheses are in italics.

D. Truncation

Variant pronunciations are truncated wherever possible, with only that syllable or those syllables in which change occurs shown. A hyphen after the truncated variant shows that it is the beginning of the word; one before the variant, that it is the end, and hyphens before and after the variant, that it is within the word.

ac·cept (ək sept′, ak-)
dam·son (dam′z'n, -s'n)
dem·a·gog·ic (dem′ə gog′ik, -goj′-)

Truncations of variant pronunciations involving different parts of speech in the same entry block appear as follows:

pre·cip·i·tate (pri sip′ə tāt′: *also, for adj. & n.,* -tit) ...

Truncated pronunciations are also given for a series of words having the same first part, after the pronunciation of this first part has been established.

le·git·i·ma·tize (lə jit′ə mə tīz′)...
le·git·i·mist (-mist)...
le·git·i·mize (-mīz′)...

Similarly, with a series made up of compounds and derived forms:

half-and-half (häf′′n häf′)...
half-back (-bak′)...
half-baked (-bākt′)...
half-beak (-bēk′)...
half binding ...
half-blood (-blud′)...

Full pronunciations are given with words in a series of the following kind when the stress in the first part is changed in some way.

bi·o·as·tro·nau·tics (bī′ō as′trə nô′tiks)...
bi·o·chem·is·try (-kem′is trē)...
bi·o·cide (bī′ə sīd′)...
bi·o·coe·no·sis (bī′ō si nō′sis)...
bi·o·de·grad·a·ble (-di grā′də b'l)...
bi·o·en·gi·neer·ing (-en′jə nir′iŋ)...

E. Variants

Where two or more pronunciations for a single word are given, the order in which they are entered does not necessarily mean that the first is preferred or is more correct. In most cases, the order indicates that on the basis of available information, the form given first is the one more frequent in general educated use. Unless a variant is qualified, as by *now rarely* or *occasionally* or a similar note, it is understood that any pronunciation here entered represents a standard use.

III.   PART-OF-SPEECH LABELS

Part-of-speech labels are generally given for main entries that are solid or hyphenated forms, except for prefixes, suffixes, and abbreviations, The following labels for the parts of speech into which words are classified in traditional English grammar are used in this dictionary. They appear in boldface italic type following the pronunciations.

n.	noun	***prep.***	preposition
vt.	transitive verb	***conj.***	conjunction
vi.	intransitive verb	***pron.***	pronoun
adj.	adjective	***interj.***	interjection
adv.	adverb		

In addition, the following labels are sometimes used:

n.pl.	plural noun
v.aux.	auxiliary verb
v.impersonal	impersonal verb
n.fem.	feminine noun
n.masc.	masculine noun

When an entry word is used as more than one part of speech, long dashes introduce each different part of speech in the entry block and each part-of-speech label appears in boldface italic type.

round¹ ... *adj.* ... —*n.* ... —*vt.* ... —*vi.* ... —*adv.* ... —*prep.* ...

Two or more part-of-speech labels are given jointly for an entry when the definition or definitions, or the cross-reference, will suffice for both or all.

lip-read ... *vt.,vi.* ... to recognize (a speaker's words) by lip reading ...

licht ..... *adj., adv., n., vi., vt. Scot.var. of* LIGHT

It is theoretically possible to use almost any word as whatever part of speech is required. Thus any transitive verb can be used absolutely as an intransitive verb, with the object understood ("Shall I *use* this lotion?" "Yes, but *use* sparingly."). Such absolute uses are entered only when they are relatively common. In the same way nouns used as adjectives (a *cloth* cover; a *family* affair) are indicated only for the most frequent uses.

IV   INFLECTED FORMS

Inflected forms regarded as irregular or offering difficulty in spelling are entered in small boldface immediately following the part-of-speech labels. They are truncated where possible, and syllabified and pronounced where necessary.

A.   Plurals of Nouns

Plurals formed regularly by adding *-s* to the singular (or *-es* after *s, x, z, ch* and *sh*), as *bats, boxes,* are not normally indicated.

Plurals are shown when formed irregularly, as for nouns with a *-y* ending that changes to *-ies,* and for those with an *-o* ending, those inflected by some change within the word, those having variant forms, those having different forms for different meanings, compound nouns, etc.

cit·y ... *n., pl.* **cit′ies** ...
bo·le·ro ... *n., pl.* **-ros** ...
tooth ... *n., pl.* **teeth** (tēth) ...
a·moe·ba ... *n., pl.* **-bas, -bae** (-bē) ...
die² ... *n., pl.,* for 1 **dice** (dīs), for 2 **dies** (dīz)
son-in-law ... *n., pl.* **sons′-in-law′** ...

If an irregular plural is so altered in spelling that it would appear at some distance from the singular form, it is entered additionally in its proper alphabetical place.

lice ... *n. pl. of* LOUSE

B.   Principal Parts

Verb forms regarded as regular and not normally indicated include:

a) present tenses formed by adding *-s* to the infinitive (or *-es* after *s, x, z, ch,* and *sh*), as *waits, searches;*

b) past tenses and past participles formed by simply adding *-ed* to the infinitive with no other changes in the verb form, as *waited, searched;*

c) present participles formed by simply adding *-ing* to the infinitive with no other change in the verb form, as *waiting, searching.*

Principal parts are given for irregular verbs, and for those in which the final *e* is dropped in forming the present participle.

Where two inflected forms are given for a verb, the first is the form for the past tense and the past participle, and the second is the form for the present participle.

make ... *vt.* **made, mak′ing** ...
sip ... *vt., vi.* **sipped, sip′ping**

Where three forms are given, separated from one another by commas, the first represents the past tense, the second the past participle, and the third the present participle.

swim ... *vi.* **swam, swum, swim′ming** ...

Where there are alternative forms for any of the principal parts, these are indicated as follows:

learn .... *vi.* **learned** or **learnt** (lʉrnt), **learn′ing**

If a principal part of a verb is so altered in spelling that it would appear at some distance from the infinitive form, it is entered additionally in its proper alphabetical place.

said ... *pt. & pp. of* SAY

C.   Comparatives & Superlatives of Adjectives & Adverbs

Comparatives and superlatives formed by simply adding *-er* or *-est* to the base, as *taller, tallest,* are not indicated. Those formed irregularly, as by adding *-r* and *-st (rare, rarer, rarest),* by changing final *-y* to *-i- (happy, happier, happiest),* or by some radical change in form *(good, better, best* or *well, better, best),* are indicated with the positive form.

The positive form is also noted at the comparative and superlative forms when these are entered and defined at some distance from it.

best ... *adj. superl. of* GOOD ... —*adv. superl. of* WELL² ...

V.   THE ETYMOLOGY

Brief etymologies, or little histories of the words in this dictionary have been included so that they may help the user to a clearer understanding of these words. The etymology will be found immediately before the definition, set off in heavy brackets. The symbols, as < for "derived from," and the abbreviations of language labels, etc. used in the etymologies are dealt with in full in the list of Abbreviations and Symbols immediately preceding page 1 of the dictionary.

ex·er·cise (ek′sər sīz′) *n.* [< OFr. < L. < pp. of *exercere,* to drive out (farm animals to work) <*ex-,* out + *arcere,* to enclose] **1.** active use or operation ...
es·cape (əskāp′, e-) *vi.* **-caped′, -cap′ing** [< ONormFr. < L. *ex-,* out of + *cappa,* cloak (i.e. leave one's cloak)] **1.** to get free; get away ...

For some words etymologies are shown by means of cross-references (in small capitals) to the elements of which they are formed and which are dealt with separately in the dictionary.

en·dog·a·my (en dog′ə mē) *n.* [ENDO- + -GAMY] **1.** the custom of marrying only within one's own tribe, clan, etc.; inbreeding
ra·don (rā′don) *n.* [RAD(IUM) + -ON] **1.** a radioactive gaseous chemical element ...

No etymology is shown where one is not needed, as when the elements making up the word are immediately apparent to the user (**precondition**) or because the definition that follows clearly explains the derivation (see **bluebottle**)

Where no etymology is known for certain, that fact is indicated by the following: [< ?]

VI.   THE DEFINITIONS

A.   Order of Senses

The definitions, or senses, of a longer entry have been arranged in an order which shows how the word has developed from its etymology and its earliest meanings and how the meanings of the word are related to one another. Senses that need to be labelled as colloquial, slang, obsolete, or the like are given after the general senses. Next, any technical senses are given, arranged in alphabetical order according to their special field labels. Sometimes an obsolete sense may be given first, preceded by "originally" (abbreviated "orig.") or "formerly," to serve as a link between the etymology and the current senses.

B. Numbering & Grouping of Senses

Senses are numbered consecutively within any given part of speech in boldface numerals. A new series of numerals is used for each new part of speech and for each idiomatic phrase.

tap² ... **n. 1.** ... **2.** ... **3.** ... **—vt. 1.** ... **2.** ... **3.** ... **—on tap 1.** ... **2.** ...

Where a primary sense of a word can easily be subdivided into several closely related meanings, this has been done; such meanings are indicated by italicized letters after the pertinent numbered or labelled sense. The words "especially" or "specifically" (abbreviated "esp." and "specif.") are often used after an introductory definition to introduce such a grouping of related senses.

bind·er ... **n. 1.** a person who binds, specif., a bookbinder **2.** a thing that binds, specif., *a)* a band, cord, etc. *b)* a substance, as tar, that binds things together *c)* a detachable cover for holding sheets of paper together **3.** a device attached to a reaper.

C. Capitalization

If a main-entry word is capitalized in all its senses, the entry word itself is printed with a capital letter.

Eur·a·sian (-zhən, -shən) *adj.* **1.** of Eurasia **2.** of mixed European and Asian descent **—n.** a person with one European parent and one Asian parent ...

If a capitalized main-entry word has a sense or senses that are uncapitalized, these are marked with the corresponding lower-case letter enclosed in brackets, sometimes with a qualifying word, such as "usually," "often," "also," etc.

Hel·ot ... **n. 1.** ... **2.** [h-] ...

If a lower-case main-entry word has a sense or senses that are capitalized, these are marked with the corresponding upper-case letter enclosed in brackets, sometimes with a qualifying word, such as "usually," "often," "also," etc.

north ... **n. 1.** ... **2.** ... **3.** [*often* N-] ... **—adj. 1.** ... **2.** ... **3.** [N-] ...

D. Plural Forms

The designation "[*pl.*]" (or "[*often pl.*]," "[*usually pl.*]," etc.) before a definition indicates that it is the plural form of the entry word (or *often* or *usually* the plural form) that has the meaning given in the definition.

lim·it ... **n.** ... **1.** ... **2.** [*pl.*] bounds ...
look ... **vi.** ... **—n. 1.** ... **2.** ... **3.** [Colloq.] *a)* [*usually pl.*] appearance ... *b)* [*pl.*] personal appearance ... esp. of a pleasing nature ...

If such a plural sense is construed as singular, the designation "*with sing. v.*" is added inside the brackets.

dart ... **n.** ... **5.** [*pl., with sing. v.*] a game in which a number of darts (sense 1) are thrown at a target

The note "*usually used in pl.*" at the end of a singular noun definition means that although the definition applies to the given singular form of the entry word, the word is usually used in the plural and with a plural meaning

fa·ther (fä′thər) *n.* ... **7.** any of the leaders of a city, assembly, etc.: *usually used in pl.*

If a plural noun entry is construed as singular, the designation "[*with sing. v.*]" is placed after the *n.pl.* label or, in some cases, with the numbered sense to which it applies.

ger·i·at·rics ... **n.pl.** [*with sing. v.*] ... the branch of medicine that deals with the diseases and hygiene of old age ...
a·cous·tics ... **n.pl. 1.** the qualities of a room, etc. that relate to how clearly sounds can be heard in it **2.** [*with sing. v.*] the branch of physics dealing with sound

E. Prepositions Accompanying Verbs

Where certain verbs are always or usually followed by a specific preposition or prepositions, this has been indicated in the following ways: the preposition has been worked into the definition, italicized and enclosed in parentheses, or a note has been added in parentheses indicating that the preposition is so used.

strike ... **—vi.** ... **9.** to come suddenly (*on* or *upon*) [we *struck* on an idea] ...
hit ... **—vi.** ... **4.** to come by accident or after search (with *on* or *upon*) ...

Note: Such uses of verbs with specific prepositions should not be confused with verb phrases consisting of a verb form with an adverb, which are entered as idiomatic phrases under the key verb (**make out, make over,** and **make up** at the entry **make**).

F. Objects of Transitive Verbs

In definitions of transitive verbs the specific or generalized objects of the verb, where given, are enclosed in parentheses since such objects are not part of the definition.

ob·serve ... **vt.** ... **1.** to adhere to or keep (a law, custom, duty, etc.) **2.** to celebrate (a holiday, etc.) according to custom **3.** *a)* to notice or perceive (something) *b)* to pay special attention to ...

In some cases the transitive verb can be defined jointly with the intransitive verb.

chis·el ... **—vi., vt.** ... **1.** to cut or shape with a chisel ...

G. Additional Information & Notes

Additional information or any note or comment on the definition proper is preceded by a colon.

Di·ves ... **n.** ... any rich man: after the rich man in the parable in Luke's gospel
ma·ture ... **adj.** ... **3.** due: said of a note, bond, etc. ...

If the note or comment applies to all the senses or parts of speech preceding it, it begins with a capital letter and no colon introduces it.

rest² ... **n.** ... **1.** what is left; remainder **2.** [*with pl.v.*] the others Used with *the* ...

H. Illustrative Examples of Entry Words in Context

Examples of a word in use have been given where such examples help make the meaning clearer or show more exactly the differences in meaning among the different senses. Such examples of usage are enclosed in slanted brackets, and the word being defined is set in italics.

spir·it ... **n.** ... **5.** an individual person or personality [a brave *spirit*] **6.** [*usually pl.*] disposition, mood [high *spirits*] **7.** vivacity, courage, enthusiasm, etc. **8.** enthusiasm and loyalty [school *spirit*] **9.** real meaning; true intention [to follow the *spirit* if not the letter of the law] **10.** an essential quality or prevailing tendency [the *spirit* of the Renaissance] **11.** ...

I. Cross-references

Entry words (or tables, illustrations, etc.) to which the reader is being cross-referred are given in small capitals.

cap·i·tal¹ ... **n.** ... **8.** ...: distinguished from LABOUR
ca·tab·o·lism ... **n.** ...: opposed to ANABOLISM
civil disobedience ...: see also NONCOOPERATION, PASSIVE RESISTANCE
clause ... **n.** ... **1.** ...: cf. MAIN CLAUSE, SUBORDINATE CLAUSE **2.** ...
ev·o·lu·tion ... **n.** ... **5.** ...: see DARWINIAN THEORY
Gem·i·ni ...: see ZODIAC, illus.
pipe organ *same as* ORGAN (sense 1)
sol¹ ... **n.** ... *see* MONETARY UNITS, table (Peru)

VII. USAGE LABELS & NOTES

It is generally understood that usage varies among groups of people according to locality, level of education, social environment, occupation, etc. More specifically, usage can vary in the speech of any person depending upon the particular situation in which he is involved and the purpose his language must serve. The language that a scientist uses in preparing a report on his work may be quite different from the language he uses in writing a letter to a friend. What is good usage in a literary essay may not be the best usage in the lyrics of a popular song or in casual conversation. Certain occasions call for language that is more or less formal, and others, language that is more or less informal.

Dictionaries can reasonably be expected to assign usage labels, as, for example, to those terms that the record shows are regularly used in informal or highly informal contexts. The conventional usage labels are so well known that they can be used if their meaning is clearly understood in advance. The labels, and what they are intended to indicate, are given below. If the label, which is placed in brackets (and in some cases abbreviated), occurs directly after a part-of-speech label or after a boldface entry term, it applies to all senses given with that part of speech or that term; if it occurs after a numeral or letter, it applies only to the sense so numbered or lettered.

Colloquial: The term or sense is generally characteristic of conversation and informal writing. It is not to be regarded as substandard or illiterate.

Slang: The term or sense is not generally regarded as conventional or standard usage but is used, even by the best speakers, in highly informal contexts. Slang consists of both coined terms and of new or extended meanings attached to established terms. Slang terms tend either to pass into disuse in time or to move towards standard usage.

Guide to the Dictionary

Obsolete: The term or sense is no longer used but occurs in earlier writings.

Archaic: The term or sense is rarely used today except in certain restricted contexts, as in church ritual, but occurs in earlier writings.

Poetic: The term or sense is used chiefly in poetry, especially in earlier poetry, or in prose where a poetic quality is desired.

Dialect: The term or sense is used regularly only in some geographical areas.

United States (or Australian, etc.): The term or sense is characteristic of United States (or Australian, etc.) English rather than of that spoken in Britain. When preceded by *chiefly*, the label indicates an additional, though less frequent usage elsewhere.

In addition to the above usage labels, additional information is often given after the definition, indicating whether the term or sense is generally regarded as vulgar, substandard, or derogatory, or used for ironic, familiar, or exaggerated effect, etc. Where there are some objections to common usages, that fact is also indicated (for example, **who, whom**).

VIII.   FIELD LABELS

Labels for specialized fields of knowledge and activity appear in italics (in abbreviated form where practical) immediately before the sense involved. In long entry blocks having many general and specialized senses, these labels, arranged in alphabetical or senses, help the user to find quickly the special sense or senses he is seeking.

base[1] ... *n.* .... **8.** *Chem.* ... **9.** *Geom.*... **10.** *Linguis.* ... **11.** *Math.*
...

IX.   IDIOMATIC PHRASES

Idiomatic phrases are run in on an entry block in alphabetical order after the definition or definitions of the main-entry word. The entry for each phrase is set in small boldface with a dash preceding it. Such phrases have been entered wherever possible under the key word.

salt ... *n.* ... **—salt away** (or **down**) ... **—the salt of the earth** ... **—with a grain** (or **pinch**) **of salt** ... **—worth one's salt**

Alternative forms are indicated inside parentheses, as above in **salt away** (or **down**). In the phrase **(at) full tilt** under the entry **tilt**, both the longer phrase, **at full tilt**, and the shorter, **full tilt**, are being recorded.

X.   RUN-IN DERIVED ENTRIES

It is possible in English to form an indefinite number of derived forms simply by adding certain prefixes or suffixes to the base word. This dictionary includes as run-in entries in small boldface type only those words one might reasonably expect to meet in literature or ordinary usage, and then only when the meaning of such derived words can be immediately understood from the meanings of the base word and the affix. Thus, **greatness, liveliness,** and **newness** are run in at the end of the entries for **great, lively,** and **new,** the meanings of the derived forms being understood from the base word and the suffix **-ness,** which is found as a separate entry in this dictionary and means "state, quality, or instance of being." Many words formed with common suffixes such as **-able, -er, -less, -like, -ly, -tion,** etc. are similarly treated as run-in entries with the base word from which they are derived. All such entries are syllabified and either accented to show stress in pronunciation or, where necessary, pronounced in full or in part. Each run-in derived form is preceded by a dash.

If two run-in derived forms have the same meaning and share a part-of-speech label, the more frequently used form appears first and the part-of-speech label is given after the second form. Note the plural form following the first run-in:

prac·ti·cal ... *adj.* ... **prac′ti·cal′i·ty** (-kal′ə tē), *pl.* **-ties, prac′ti·cal·ness** *n.*

When a derived word has a meaning or meanings different from those which can be deduced from the sum of its parts, it has been entered in a block of its own, pronounced, and fully defined (for example, **producer**).

ABBREVIATIONS AND SYMBOLS USED IN THIS DICTIONARY

abbrev. abbreviated; abbreviation
abl. ablative
Abor. Aboriginal (in etym.)
acc. accusative
adj. adjective
admin. administrative
adv. adverb
Aeron. Aeronautics
Afr. African
Afrik. Afrikaans
alt. alternative
Am. American
AmFr. American French
AmInd. American Indian
AmSp. American Spanish
Anat. Anatomy
Anglo-Fr. Anglo-French
Anglo-Ind. Anglo-Indian
Anglo-Ir. Anglo-Irish
Anglo-L. Anglo-Latin
Anglo-N. Anglo-Norse
Anglo-Norm. Anglo-Norman
Ar. Arabic
Aram. Aramaic
Archaeol. Archaeology
Archit. Architecture
Arith. Arithmetic
Arm. Armenian
art. article
assoc. associated
Assyr. Assyrian
Astrol. Astrology
Astron. Astronomy
at. no. atomic number
at. wt. atomic weight
Aust. Australian
A.V. Authorized Version

Bab. Babylonian
Beng. Bengali
Biochem. Biochemistry
Biol. Biology
Bohem. Bohemian
Bot. Botany
Braz. Brazilian
Bret. Breton
Brit. British
Bulg. Bulgarian

C Celsius; Central
c. century (in etym.); circa
Canad. Canadian
CanadFr. Canadian French
cap. capital
Celt. Celtic
cent. century; centuries
cf. compare
Ch. Chaldean; Church
Chem. Chemistry
Chin. Chinese
Chr. Chronicles
cm centimetre(s)
Col. Colossians
comp. compound
compar. comparative
conj. conjunction
contr. contracted; contraction
Cop. Coptic
Cor. Corinthians
Corn. Cornish
Cym. Cymric

Dan. Daniel; Danish
dat. dative
deriv. derivative

Deut. Deuteronomy
Dial., dial. dialectal
dim. diminutive
Du. Dutch

E East; eastern
E. East; English (in etym. & pronun.)
Early ModDu. Early modern Dutch
Early ModG. Early modern German
EC east central
Eccl. Ecclesiastes
Eccles. Ecclesiastical
Ecol. Ecology
Econ. Economics
Educ. Education
e.g. for example
Egypt. Egyptian
Elec. Electricity
Eng. English
Eph. Ephesians
equiv. equivalent
Esk. Eskimo
esp. especially
est. estimated
Esth. Esther
Eth. Ethiopic
etym. etymology
Ex. example; Exodus
exc. except
Ezek. Ezekiel

fem. feminine
ff. following (entry, sense, etc.)
fig. figurative; figuratively
Finn. Finnish
Fl. Flemish
fl. flourished
Fr. French
Frank. Frankish
freq. frequentative
Fris. Frisian
fut. future

g gramme(s)
G. German (in etym. & pronun.)
Gael. Gaelic
Gal. Galatians
Gaul. Gaulish
Gen. Genesis
gen. genitive
Geog. Geography
Geol. Geology
Geom. Geometry
Ger. German
ger. gerund
Gmc. Germanic
Goth. Gothic
Gr. Greek
Gram. Grammar

Hab. Habakkuk
Hag. Haggai
Haw. Hawaiian
Heb. Hebrew; Hebrews
Hort. Horticulture
Hos. Hosea
Hung. Hungarian
hyp. hypothetical

Ice. Icelandic
i.e. that is
imper. imperative
imperf. imperfect
incl. including
Ind. Indian

indic. indicative
inf. infinitive
infl. influenced
intens. intensive
interj. interjection
Ir. Irish
Iran. Iranian
IrGael. Irish Gaelic
irreg. irregular
Isa. Isaiah
It. Italian

Jap. Japanese
Jas. James
Jer. Jeremiah
Josh. Joshua
Judge. Judges

kg kilogramme(s)
km kilometre(s)

l litre(s)
L Late
L. Latin
Lam. Lamentations
Lev. Leviticus
LGr. Late Greek
Linguis. Linguistics
lit. literally
Lith. Lithuanian
LL. Late Latin
LME. Late Middle English
LXX Septuagint

m metre(s)
M Middle; Medieval
Mal. Malachi
Math. Mathematics
Matt. Matthew
MDu. Middle Dutch
ME. Middle English
Mech. Mechanics
Med. Medicine; Medieval
met. metropolitan
Meteorol. Meteorology
Mex. Mexican
MexSp. Mexican Spanish
MFr. Middle French
MGr. Medieval Greek
MHG. Middle High German
Mic. Micah
Mil. Military
ML. Medieval Latin
MLowG. Middle Low German
Mod, Mod. Modern
ModE. Modern English
ModGr. Modern Greek
ModHeb. Modern Hebrew
ModL. Modern Latin
Mongol. Mongolic
Myth. Mythology

N North; northern
N. North
n. noun
Nah. Nahum
Naut., naut. nautical usage
NC north central
NE northeastern
Neh. Nehemiah
neut. neuter
n.fem. feminine form of noun
n.masc. masculine form of noun
nom. nominative
Norm, Norm. Norman

Abbreviations and Symbols *(cont.)*

Norw. Norwegian
n.pl. plural form of noun
n.sing. singular form of noun
N.T. New Testament
Num. Numbers
NW northwestern
N.Z. New Zealand

O Old
Ob. Obadiah
Obs., obs. obsolete
occas. occasionally
OE. Old English
OFr. Old French
OHG. Old High German
OIr. Old Irish
OIt. Old Italian
OL. Old Latin
ON. Old Norse
ONormFr. Old Norman French
orig. origin; originally
OS. Old Saxon
O.T. Old Testament

P Primitive
p. page
part. participle
pass. passive
Per. Persian
perf. perfect
pers. person
Peruv. Peruvian
Pet. Peter
Phil. Philippians
Philem. Philemon
Philos. Philosophy
Phoen. Phoenician
Phonet. Phonetics
Photog. Photography
phr. phrase
Phys. Ed. Physical Education
Physiol. Physiology
PidE. Pidgin English
pl. plural
Poet. Poetic
Pol. Polish
pop. popular; population
Port. Portuguese
poss. possessive

pp. pages; past participle
Pr. Provençal
prec. preceding
prep. preposition
pres. present
prin. pts. principal parts
prob. probably
pron. pronoun
pronun. pronunciation
Prov. Proverbs; Provincial
prp. present participle
Ps. Psalms
pseud. pseudonym
Psychol. Psychology
pt. past tense

R.C.Ch. Roman Catholic Church
redupl. reduplication
refl. reflexive
Rev. Revelation
Rom. Roman; Romans
R.S.F.S.R. Russian Soviet Federated Socialist Republic
RSV Revised Standard Version
Russ. Russian

S South; southern
S. South
Sam. Samuel
Sans. Sanskrit
SC south central
Scand. Scandinavian
Scot, Scot. Scottish
ScotGael. Scottish Gaelic
SE southeastern
Sem. Semitic
Serb. Serbian
sing. singular
Sinh. Sinhalese
Slav. Slavic
S. of Sol. Song of Solomon
Sp. Spanish
sp. spelled; spelling
specif. specifically
S.S.R. Soviet Socialist Republic
subj. subjuncitve
superl. superlative
SW southwestern
Sw. Swedish (in etym. & pronun.)

Swed. Swedish
Syr. Syriac

Tag. Tagalog
Theol. Theology
Thess. Thessalonians
Tim. Timothy
Tit. Titus
transl. translation
Turk. Turkish
TV television

ult. ultimately
UN United Nations
U.S. United States
U.S.S.R. Union of Soviet Socialist Republics

v. verb
var. variant; variety
v.aux. auxiliary verb
Vet. Veterinary Medicine
vi. intransitive verb
VL. Vulgar Latin
voc. vocative
vt. transitive verb
Vulg. Vulgate

W West; western
W. Welsh; West
WAfr. West African
WC west central
WGmc. West Germanic
WInd. West Indian

Yid. Yiddish

Zech. Zechariah
Zeph. Zephaniah
Zool. Zoology

‡   foreign word or phrase
*   hypothetical
\+   plus
<   derived from
?   uncertain; possibly; perhaps
&   and
^{2} squared; square
^{3} cubed; cube

TABLES OF WEIGHTS AND MEASURES

THE METRIC SYSTEM

Linear Measure

1 millimetre	=	0.03937	inch
10 millimetres = 1 centimetre	=	0.3937	inch
10 centimetres = 1 decimetre	=	3.937	inches
10 decimetres = 1 metre	=	39.37	inches or 3.2808 feet
10 metres = 1 decametre	=	393.7	inches
10 decametres = 1 hectometre	=	328.08	feet
10 hectometres = 1 kilometre	=	0.621	mile or 3280.8 feet
10 kilometres = 1 myriametre	=	6.21	miles

Square Measure

1 square millimetre	=	0.00155	square inch
100 square millimetres = 1 square centimetre	=	0.15499	square inch
100 square centimetres = 1 square decimetre	=	15.499	square inches
100 square decimetres = 1 square metre	=	1549.9	square inches or 1.196 square yards
100 square metres = 1 square decametre	=	119.6	square yards
100 square decametres = 1 square hectometre	=	2.471	acres
100 square hectometres = 1 square kilometre	=	0.386	square mile or 247.1 acres

Land Measure

1 square metre = 1 centiare	=	1549.9	square inches
100 centiares = 1 are	=	119.6	square yards
100 ares = 1 hectare	=	2.471	acres
100 hectares = 1 square kilometre	=	0.386	square mile or 247.1 acres

Volume Measure

1000 cubic millimetres = 1 cubic centimetre	=	0.06102	cubic inch
1000 cubic centimetres = 1 cubic decimetre	=	61.023	cubic inches or 0.0353 cubic foot
1000 cubic decimetres = 1 cubic metre	=	35.314	cubic feet or 1.308 cubic yards

Capacity Measure

10 millilitres = 1 centilitre	=	0.338	fluid ounce
10 centilitres = 1 decilitre	=	3.38	fluid ounces or 0.176 pint
10 decilitres = 1 litre	=	1.76	pints
10 litres = 1 decalitre	=	2.199	gallons
10 decalitres = 1 hectolitre	=	21.99	gallons
10 hectolitres = 1 kilolitre	=	219.9	gallons

Weights

10 milligrammes = 1 centigramme	=	0.1543	grain or 0.000353 ounce (avdp.)
10 centigrammes = 1 decigramme	=	1.5432	grains
10 decigrammes = 1 gramme	=	15.432	grains or 0.035274 ounce (avdp.)
10 grammes = 1 decagramme	=	0.3527	ounce
10 decagrammes = 1 hectogramme	=	3.5274	ounces
10 hectogrammes = 1 kilogramme	=	2.2046	pounds
10 kilogrammes = 1 myriagramme	=	22.046	pounds
10 myriagrammes = 1 quintal	=	220.46	pounds
10 quintals = 1 metric ton	=	2204.6	pounds

THE IMPERIAL SYSTEM

Linear Measure

1 mil = 0.001 inch	=	0.0254	millimetre
1 inch = 1000 mils	=	2.54	centimetres
12 inches = 1 foot	=	0.3048	metre
3 feet = 1 yard	=	0.9144	metre
5½ yards or 16½ feet = 1 rod (or pole or perch)	=	5.029	metres
40 rods = 1 furlong	=	201.168	metres
8 furlongs or 1760 yards or 5280 feet = 1 (statute) mile	=	1.6093	kilometres
3 miles = 1 (land) league	=	4.83	kilometres

Square Measure

1 square inch	=	6.452	square centimetres
144 square inches = 1 square foot	=	929.03	square centimetres
9 square feet = 1 square yard	=	0.8361	square metre
30¼ square yards = 1 square rod (or square pole or square perch)	=	25.292	square metres
160 square rods or 4840 square yards or 43 560 square feet = 1 acre	=	0.4047	hectare
640 acres = 1 square mile	=	259.00	hectares or 2.590 square kilometres

Cubic Measure

1 cubic inch = 16.387 cubic centimetres
1728 cubic inches = 1 cubic foot = 0.0283 cubic metre
27 cubic feet = 1 cubic yard = 0.7646 cubic metre

Nautical Measure

6 feet = 1 fathom = 1.829 metres
100 fathoms = 1 cable's length
(In the Royal Navy, 608 feet, or 185.319 metres = 1 cable's length)
10 cables' length = 1 international nautical mile = 1.852 kilometres (exactly)
(6076.11549 feet, by international agreement)
1 international nautical mile = 1.150779 statute miles
(the length of a minute of longitude at the equator)
3 nautical miles = 1 marine league (3.45 statute miles)= 5.56 kilometres
60 nautical miles = 1 degree of a great circle of the earth
= 69.047 statute miles

Liquid and Dry Measure

1 gill = 5 fluid ounces = 9.0235 cubic inches = 0.1480 litre
4 gills = 1 pint = 34.68 cubic inches = 0.568 litre
2 pints = 1 quart = 69.36 cubic inches = 1.136 litres
4 quarts = 1 gallon = 277.4 cubic inches = 4.546 litres
2 gallons = 1 peck = 554.8 cubic inches = 9.092 litres
4 pecks = 1 bushel = 2219.2 cubic inches = 36.37 litres

The U.S. gallon (4 U.S. quarts) = 231 cubic inches = 3.7854 litres.

Apothecaries' Fluid Measure

1 minim = 0.0038 cubic inch = 0.0616 millilitre
60 minims = 1 fluid dram = 0.2256 cubic inch = 3.6966 millilitres
8 fluid drams = 1 fluid ounce = 1.8047 cubic inches = 0.0296 litre
20 fluid ounces = 1 pint = 34.68 cubic inches = 0.568 litre

See table immediately preceding for quart and gallon equivalents.
The U.S. pint = 16 fluid ounces.

Circular (or Angular) Measure

60 seconds (") = 1 minute (')
60 minutes = 1 degree (°)
90 degrees = 1 quadrant or 1 right angle
180 degrees = 2 quadrants or 1 straight angle
4 quadrants or 360 degrees = 1 circle

Avoirdupois Weight

(The grain, equal to 0.0648 gramme, is the same in all three tables of weight.)

1 dram or 27.34 grains = 1.772 grammes
16 drams or 437.5 grains = 1 ounce = 28.3495 grammes
16 ounces or 7000 grains = 1 pound = 453.59 grammes
14 pounds = 1 stone = 6.35 kilogrammes
112 pounds = 1 hundredweight = 50.80 kilogrammes
2240 pounds = 1 (long) ton = 1016.05 kilogrammes
2000 pounds = 1 (short) ton = 907.18 kilogrammes

Troy Weight

(The grain, equal to 0.0648 gramme, is the same in all three tables of weight.)

3.086 grains = 1 carat = 200.00 milligrammes
24 grains = 1 pennyweight = 1.5552 grammes
20 pennyweights or 480 grains = 1 ounce = 31.1035 grammes
12 ounces or 5760 grains = 1 pound = 373.24 grammes

Apothecaries' Weight

(The grain, equal to 0.0648 gramme, is the same in all three tables of weight.)

20 grains = 1 scruple = 1.296 grammes
3 scruples = 1 dram = 3.888 grammes
8 drams or 480 grains = 1 ounce = 31.1035 grammes
12 ounces or 5760 grains = 1 pound = 373.24 grammes

A

A, a (ā) *n.*, *pl.* **A's, a's** 1. the first letter of the English alphabet 2. a sound of *A* or *a* 3. *a symbol for* the first in a sequence or group —**from A to Z** from start to finish; completely

A (ā) *n.* 1. *Cinema* a film which has been classified as suitable for exhibition to adult audiences 2. *Music a*) the sixth tone in the ascending scale of C major *b*) the scale having A as the keynote —*adj.* shaped like *A*

A *Physics the symbol for* ampere

a (ə; *stressed* ā) *adj.*, **indefinite article** [form of AN[1]] 1. one; one sort of 2. each; any one *A* connotes a thing not previously noted or recognized; *the*, a thing previously noted or recognized 3. [orig. a prep. < OE. *an*, in, on, at] to each; in each; per [once *a* day] Before words beginning with a consonant sound or a sounded *h*, *a* is used [*a* child, *a* home, *a* uniform]; before words beginning with a vowel sound or a silent *h*, *an* is used [*an* eye, *an* ultimatum, *an* honour]

a are(s) (metric measure of land)

a-[1] [weakened form of OE. *an*, *on*, in, on, at] *a prefix meaning*: 1. in, into, on, at, to [*abed, ashore*] 2. in the act or state of [*asleep*]

a-[2] *a prefix of various origins and meanings*: 1. [OE. *a-*, out of, up] up, out: now generally an intensive [*awake, arise*] 2. [OE. *of-, af-*] off, of [*akin*] 3. [Gr. *a-, an-*, not] not, without [*atypical*]: before vowels *an-* is used [*anastigmatic*]

Å angstrom unit

A. 1. Absolute 2. ampere 3. angstrom

A., a. *Music* alto

a. 1. acre(s) 2. adjective 3. answer

AA (ā'ā') *n.* *Cinema* a film to which children under fourteen are admitted only if accompanied by an adult

AA, A.A. 1. Alcoholics Anonymous 2. antiaircraft 3. Automobile Association

AAA, A.A.A. Amateur Athletics Association

A1 (ā'wun') 1. a designation of first-class ships as in Lloyd's Register 2. [Colloq.] first-class; excellent

A & R Artist(s) and Repertoire: referring to officials of commercial recording companies who select the performers and supervise the production of recordings

aard·vark (ärd'värk') *n.* [obs. Afrik., earth pig] a burrowing African mammal that feeds on ants and termites: it has a long snout

aard·wolf (-woolf') *n.*, *pl.* **-wolves** (-woolvz') [Afrik., earth wolf] a mammal of S and E Africa resembling the hyena but feeding chiefly on termites and insect larvae

Aar·on's beard (er'ənz) the popular name of various plants, esp. St. John's Wort or Rose of Sharon

Aaron's rod a Eurasian plant with tall, erect spikes of flowers

aas·vo·gel (äs'fō gəl) *n.* [Du. *aas*, carrion + *vogel*, bird] the South African vulture

ab- [L.] *a prefix meaning* away, from, from off, down [*abdicate*]: shortened to *a-* before *m, p,* and *v; often* **abs-** before *c* or *t* [*abstract*]

A.B. 1. able-bodied seaman 2. [ML. *Artium Baccalaureus*] [U.S.] Bachelor of Arts

a·ba (a'bə) *n.* [Ar.] 1. a fabric of wool or hair fibre with a felted finish 2. a loose, sleeveless robe worn by Arabs

a·ba·ca (ab'ə kə) *n.* [Tag.] 1. *same as* MANILA HEMP (sense 1) 2. the Philippine plant yielding Manila hemp

a·back (ə bak') *adv.* 1. [Archaic] backwards; back 2. pressed backwards against the mast, as sails in a wind from ahead —**taken aback** startled and confused

ab·a·cus (ab'ə kəs) *n.*, *pl.* **-cus·es**, **-ci** (-sī') [L. < Gr. *abax*] 1. a frame with beads or balls sliding back and forth on wires or in slots, for doing arithmetic 2. *Archit.* a slab forming the uppermost part of the capital of a column

AARDVARK
(c. 0.6 m high
at shoulder)

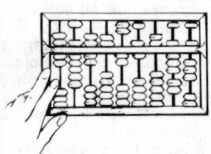

ABACUS

A·bad·don (ə bad'ən) [Heb., destruction] *Bible* 1. hell: Job 26:6 2. the devil: Rev. 9:11

a·baft (ə bäft') *adv.* [< OE. *on*, on + *bæftan* < *be*, by + *æftan*, behind] at or towards the stern of a ship; aft —*prep. Naut.* behind

ab·a·lo·ne (ab'ə lō'nē) *n.* [AmSp. < AmInd.] a sea mollusc with an oval, somewhat spiral shell lined with mother-of-pearl

a·ban·don (ə ban'dən) *vt.* [< OFr. < *mettre a bandon*, to put under (someone else's) ban] 1. to give up (something) completely 2. to forsake; desert 3. to yield (oneself) completely, as to a feeling —*n.* unrestrained freedom of action or emotion —**a·ban'don·ment** *n.*

a·ban·doned (-dənd) *adj.* 1. forsaken; deserted 2. shamefully wicked; immoral 3. unrestrained

a·base (ə bās') *vt.* **a·based'**, **a·bas'ing** [< OFr. *abaissier*, ult. < L. *ad-*, to + LL. *bassus*, low] to humble or humiliate —**a·base'ment** *n.*

a·bash (ə bash') *vt.* [OFr. *esbahir*, to astonish < L. *ex* + *ba*, interj. of surprise] to make ashamed and ill at ease —**a·bashed'** *adj.*

a·bate (ə bāt') *vt.* **a·bat'ed**, **a·bat'ing** [< OFr. *abattre*, to beat down: see AD- & BATTER[1]] 1. to make less in amount, degree, etc. 2. to deduct 3. *Law* to put a stop to; end —*vi.* to become less; subside —**a·bate'ment** *n.*

ab·a·tis, ab·at·tis (ab'ə tis) *n.*, *pl.* **-a·tis, -at·tis** [Fr.: see ABATE] a barricade of felled trees with branches facing the enemy

ab·at·toir (ab'ə twär') *n.* [Fr.: see ABATE] a slaughterhouse

ab·ba·cy (ab'ə sē) *n.*, *pl.* **-cies** an abbot's or abbess's position, jurisdiction, or term of office

ab·ba·tial (ə bā'shəl) *adj.* of an abbot, abbess, or abbey

ab·bé (a'bā; *Fr.* à bā') *n.* [Fr. < LL.: see ABBOT] a French title of respect for a priest, curate, or cleric in minor orders

ab·bess (ab'is, -es) *n.* [< LL.: see ABBOT] a woman who is head of an abbey of nuns

Abbe·vill·i·an (ab vill'ē ər') *adj.* [< *Abbeville*, town in N France] of a lower paleolithic culture characterized by the use of stone axes

ab·bey (ab'ē) *n.* 1. a monastery headed by an abbot or a convent of nuns headed by an abbess 2. the monks or nuns in such a place, collectively 3. a church or building belonging to an abbey

ab·bot (ab'ət) *n.* [< OE. < LL. < Gr. < Aram. *abbā*, father] a man who heads an abbey of monks

abbr., abbrev. 1. abbreviated 2. abbreviation

ab·bre·vi·ate (ə brē'vē āt') *vt.* **-at'ed**, **-at'ing** [< LL. pp. of *abbreviare* < L. < *ad-*, to + *brevis*, short] 1. to make shorter 2. to shorten (a word or phrase) by leaving out or substituting letters —**ab·bre'vi·a'tor** *n.*

ab·bre·vi·a·tion (ə brē'vē ā'shən) *n.* 1. a making shorter 2. the state or fact of being made shorter 3. a shortened form of a word or phrase, as *F.A.* for *Football Association, Mr.* for *Mister*

A B C (ā'bē'sē') *n.*, *pl.* **A B C's** 1. the alphabet 2. the basic elements (*of* a subject); rudiments 3. an alphabetically arranged reference or guide book

ABC Australian Broadcasting Commission

ab·di·cate (ab'də kāt') *vt.*, *vi.* **-cat'ed**, **-cat'ing** [< L. pp. of *abdicare* < *ab-*, off + *dicare*, to proclaim] 1. to give up formally (a high office, etc.) 2. to surrender (a right, responsibility, etc.) —**ab'di·ca'tion** *n.* —**ab'di·ca'tor** *n.*

ab·do·men (ab'də mən, ab dō'-) *n.* [L.] 1. the part of the body between the diaphragm and the pelvis, containing the intestines, etc.; belly 2. in arthropods, the hind part of the body —**ab·dom·i·nal** (ab dom'ə n'l) *adj.*

ab·duct (ab dukt') *vt.* [< L. pp. of *abducere* < *ab-*, away + *ducere*, to lead] 1. to kidnap (a person) 2. to move (a part of the body) away from the median axis of the body —**ab·duc'tion** *n.* —**ab·duc'tor** *n.*

a·beam (ə bēm') *adv.* abreast (*of*) the middle of a ship's side

a·bed (ə bed') *adv.* [Archaic] in bed; on a bed

Ab·er·deen An·gus (ab'ər dēn'aŋ'gəs) any of a breed of black, hornless cattle, originally from Scotland

Aberdeen terrier a prick-eared, long-bodied, wirehaired terrier

ab·er·rant (a ber'ənt) *adj.* [< L. prp. of *aberrare* < *ab-*, from + *errare*, to wander] deviating from what is true, normal, or typical —**ab·er'rance, ab·er'ran·cy** *n.*

ab·er·ra·tion (ab'ər ā'shən) *n.* 1. a departure from what is right, true, etc. 2. a deviation from the normal or typical 3. mental derangement or lapse 4. *Astron.* the apparent displacement of a heavenly body because of the motion of the observer with the earth **5.** *Optics a)* the failure of light rays from one point to converge to a single focus *b)* an error in a lens or mirror causing this

a·bet (əbet′) *vt.* **a·bet′ted, a·bet′ting** [< OFr. *abeter*, to incite < *a-*, to + *beter*, to BAIT] to incite or help, esp. in wrongdoing —**a·bet′ment** *n.* —**a·bet′tor, a·bet′ter** *n.*

a·bey·ance (əbā′əns) *n.* [< Anglo-Fr. < OFr. *abeance*, expectation < *a-*, at + *bayer*, to gape] **1.** temporary suspension, as of an activity or function **2.** *Law* an indeterminate state of ownership, as when the person entitled to an estate has not been ascertained (usually with *in*)

ab·hor (əbhôr′) *vt.* **-horred′, -hor′ring** [< L. *abhorrere* < *ab-*, away, from + *horrere*, to shudder] to shrink from in disgust or hatred; detest

ab·hor·rence (əbhor′əns) *n.* **1.** an abhorring; loathing **2.** a person or thing that is abhorred

ab·hor·rent (-ənt) *adj.* **1.** causing disgust, hatred, etc.; detestable **2.** opposed (*to*) [*abhorrent* to his principles] —**ab·hor′rent·ly** *adv.*

a·bide (əbīd′) *vi.* **a·bode′** or **a·bid′ed, a·bid′ing** [OE. *abidan* < *a-* (intens.) + *bidan*, to remain] **1.** to stand fast; remain **2.** [Archaic] to stay; reside (*in* or *at*) —*vt.* **1.** to await **2.** to submit to; put up with —**abide by 1.** to live up to (a promise, etc.) **2.** to submit to and carry out (a rule, decision, etc.) —**a·bid′ance** *n.*

a·bid·ing (əbīd′iŋ) *adj.* enduring; lasting —**a·bid′ing·ly** *adv.*

a·bil·i·ty (əbil′ətē) *n., pl.* **-ties** [see ABLE] **1.** a being able; power to do **2.** skill or talent; competence

-a·bil·i·ty (əbil′ətē) *pl.* **-ties** [L. *-abilitas*: see -ABLE & -ITY] *a suffix used to form nouns from adjectives ending in* -ABLE [*durability*]

‡**ab in·i·ti·o** (ab′in ish′ē ō′) [L.] from the beginning

ab·i·o·gen·e·sis (ab′ē ō jen′ə sis) *n.* [ModL. < Gr. *a-*, without + BIOGENESIS] *same as* SPONTANEOUS GENERATION

ab·ject (ab′jekt) *adj.* [< L. pp. of *abjicere* < *ab-*, away, from + *jacere*, to throw] **1.** of the lowest degree; miserable [*abject* poverty] **2.** lacking self-respect; servile —**ab′ject·ly** *adv.* —**ab′ject·ness, ab·jec′tion** *n.*

ab·jure (əbjoor′, ab-) *vt.* **-jured′, -jur′ing** [< L. *abjurare* < *ab-*, away, from + *jurare*, to swear] **1.** to give up (rights, allegiance, etc.) on oath; renounce **2.** to give up (opinions) publicly; recant —**ab·ju·ra·tion** (ab′jə rā′shən) *n.* —**ab·jur′er** *n.*

ab·late (ab lāt′) *vt.* **-lat′ed, -lat′ing** [back-formation < *ablation* < LL. < L. *ablatus*: see ff.] **1.** to remove, as by surgery **2.** *Astrophysics* to melt, vaporize, etc. (surface material) during high-speed movement through the atmosphere **3.** *Geol.* to wear away, as by the action of water —*vi.* to become ablated —**ab·la′tion** *n.*

ab·la·tive (ab′lə tiv; *for adj.* 2 ab lāt′iv) *n.* [< L. < *ablatus*, pp. of *auferre* < *ab-*, away + *ferre*, to carry] **1.** the grammatical case in Latin and some other languages expressing removal, deprivation, direction from, or source, cause, etc. **2.** a word in this case —*adj.* **1.** of or in the ablative **2.** *Astrophysics* that ablates

ab·laut (ab′lout G. äp′lout) *n.* [G. < *ab-*, off, from + *Laut*, sound] the change of base vowels in related words to show changes in tense, meaning, etc. (Ex.: drink, drank, drunk) —*adj.* of or characterized by ablaut

a·blaze (əblāz′) *adj.* **1.** flaming; gleaming **2.** greatly excited; eager

a·ble (ā′b'l) *adj.* **a′bler** (-blər), **a′blest** (-blist) [< OFr. < L. *habilis*, handy < *habere*, to have, hold] **1.** having enough power, skill, etc. (*to* do something) **2.** having much power of mind; skilled; talented —**a′bly** *adv.*

-a·ble (ə b'l) [< OFr. < L. *-abilis*] *a suffix meaning:* **1.** able to [*durable*] **2.** capable of being [*drinkable*] **3.** worthy of being [*lovable*] **4.** having qualities of [*comfortable*] **5.** tending or inclined to [*peaceable*]

a·ble-bod·ied (ā′b'l bod′ēd) *adj.* healthy and strong

able-bodied seaman *same as* ABLE RATING

able rating *see* MILITARY RANKS, table

a·bloom (ə bloom′) *adj.* in bloom; in flower

ab·lu·tion (ab loo′shən, əb-) *n.* [< L. *ablutio* < *abluere* < *ab-*, off + *luere*, to LAVE] **1.** a washing of the body, esp. as a religious ceremony **2.** [pl.] [Colloq.] washing facilities

-a·bly (ə blē) *a suffix used to form adverbs from adjectives ending in* -ABLE [*peaceably*]

ABM anti-ballistic missile

ab·ne·gate (ab′nə gāt′) *vt.* **-gat′ed, -gat′ing** [< L. pp. of *abnegare* < *ab-*, away, from + *negare*, to deny] to give up (rights, claims, etc.); renounce —**ab′ne·ga′tion** *n.* —**ab′-ne·ga′tor** *n.*

ab·nor·mal (ab nôr′m'l) *adj.* [earlier *anormal* < Fr. < LL. < Gr. (see ANOMALOUS) infl. by L. *abnormis* < *ab-*, from + *norma*, NORM] **1.** not normal; not average; not typical; irregular, esp. to a considerable degree **2.** relating to, or concerned with, that which is abnormal [*abnormal* psychology] —**ab·nor′mal·ly** *adv.*

ab·nor·mal·i·ty (ab′nôr mal′ə tē) *n.* **1.** the condition of being abnormal **2.** *pl.* **-ties** an abnormal thing

A-bo (a′bō) *n., pl.* **-bos** [clipped form of ABORIGINE or ABORIGINAL] [Aust. slang] an Australian aborigine, or someone of aboriginal descent—*adj.* aboriginal A disparaging term

a·board (ə bôrd′) *adv.* **1.** on board; on, in, or into a ship, aircraft, etc. **2.** alongside —*prep.* on board; on; in —**all aboard!** get on! get in!: a warning that the train, bus, etc. will start soon

a·bode¹ (ə bōd′) *n.* [see ABIDE] a place where one lives or stays; home; residence

a·bode² (ə bōd′) *alt. pt. and pp. of* ABIDE

a·bol·ish (ə bol′ish) *vt.* [< OFr. < L. *abolescere*, to decay < L. *abolere*, to destroy] to do away with; put an end to; annul —**a·bol′ish·ment** *n.*

ab·o·li·tion (ab′ə lish′ən, ab′ō-) *n.* **1.** an abolishing or being abolished; annulment **2.** [*occas.* A-] the abolishing of slavery —**ab′o·li′tion·ar·y** *adj.*

ab·o·li·tion·ist (-ist) *n.* one in favour of abolishing some law, custom, etc.; specif., [*occas.* A-] one who favoured the abolition of slavery —**ab′o·li′tion·ism** *n.*

ab·o·ma·sum (ab′ə mā′səm) *n., pl.* **-ma′sa** (-sə) [ModL. < L. *ab-*, from + *omasum*, paunch] the fourth, or digesting, chamber of the stomach of a cud-chewing animal, as the cow

A-bomb (ā′bom′) *n.* *same as* ATOMIC BOMB —*vt.* to attack with an atomic bomb

a·bom·i·na·ble (ə bom′ə nə b'l) *adj.* [see ABOMINATE] **1.** disgusting; vile; loathsome **2.** disagreeable; very bad —**a·bom′i·na·bly** *adv.*

Abominable Snowman a large, hairy, manlike animal reputed to live in the Himalayas

a·bom·i·nate (ə bom′ə nāt′) *vt.* **-nat′ed, -nat′ing** [< L. pp. of *abominari*, to regard as an ill omen] **1.** to feel hatred and disgust for; loathe **2.** to dislike very much —**a·bom′-i·na′tor** *n.*

a·bom·i·na·tion (ə bom′ə nā′shən) *n.* **1.** hatred and disgust **2.** anything hateful and disgusting

ab·o·rig·i·nal (ab′ə rij′ə n'l, ab′ôr ij′-) *adj.* **1.** existing from earliest days; first; indigenous **2.** of aborigines, esp. [A-] those of Australia —*n.* *same as* ABORIGINE

ab·o·rig·i·ne (ab′ə rij′ə nē′, ab′ô rij′-) *n., pl.* **-nes** [L. < *ab-*, from + *origine*, the beginning] **1.** any of the earliest known inhabitants of a region, esp. [A-] those of Australia **2.** [*pl.*] the native animals or plants of a region

a·bort (ə bôrt′) *vi.* [< L. pp. of *aboriri*, to miscarry] **1.** to have a miscarriage **2.** to fail to be completed or come to maturity —*vt.* **1.** to cause to have an abortion **2.** to check (a disease) before fully developed **3.** to cut short (an operation of an aircraft, missile, etc.)

a·bor·ti·fa·cient (ə bôr′tə fā′shənt) [ABORTI(ON) + -FACIENT] *n.* a drug or device that induces abortion —*adj.* causing abortion

a·bor·tion (ə bôr′shən) *n.* **1.** expulsion of a foetus from the womb before it is viable; miscarriage **2.** deliberate termination of pregnancy **3.** an aborted foetus **4.** anything immature and incomplete **5.** anything grotesquely misshapen

a·bor·tion·ist (-ist) *n.* one who performs an abortion or abortions (sense 2), esp. unlawfully or without medical qualifications

a·bor·tive (ə bôr′tiv) *adj.* **1.** coming to nothing; unsuccessful **2.** *Biol.* rudimentary **3.** *Med.* causing abortion —**a·bor′tive·ly** *adv.*

ABO system the system of classifying human blood types in accordance with their compatibility for transfusion: there are four major types (A, B, AB, and O), determined by the antigens inherited

a·bou·li·a, a·bu·li·a (ə byoo′lē ə, -boo′-) *n.* [< Gr. < *a*, without + *boulē*, will] *Psychol.* loss of the ability to exercise will power and make decisions

a·bound (ə bound′) *vi.* [< OFr. < L. *abundare*, to overflow < *ab-*, away + *undare*, to rise in waves < *unda*, a wave] **1.** to be plentiful **2.** to be rich (*in*) or teem (*with*)

a·bout (ə bout′) *adv.* [< OE. *onbutan*, around, on the outside (of)] **1.** all round [look *about*] **2.** here and there [travel *about*] **3.** near [it is somewhere *about*] **4.** in the opposite direction [turn it *about*] **5.** in succession or rotation [play fair—turn and turn *about*] **6.** approximately [*about* four years old] **7.** [Colloq.] almost [just *about* ready] —*adj.* [*used only in the predicate*] **1.** active [he is up and *about* again] **2.** in the vicinity [typhoid is *about*] —*prep.* **1.** around; on all sides of **2.** here and there in; everywhere in **3.** near to **4.** with; on (one's person) [have your wits *about* you] **5.** attending to [go *about* your business] **6.** intending; on the point of [he is *about* to speak] **7.** having to do with; concerning **8.** in connection with —**how** (or **what) about** [Colloq.] what is your wish or opinion concerning? —**how about that!** [Colloq.] isn't that interesting!

a·bout-turn (ə bout′turn′; *for v.* əbout′turn′) *n.* **1.** a sharp turn to the opposite direction, esp. in response to a military command **2.** a sharp change, as in opinion —*vi.* **-turned′, -turn′ing 1.** to turn or face in the opposite direction **2.** to change one's opinions or policy Also **a·bout′face′**

a·bove (ə buv′) *adv.* [OE. *abufan*] **1.** in, at, or to a higher place; overhead; up **2.** in or to heaven **3.** at a previous place (in a piece of writing) **4.** higher in power, status, etc. —*prep.* **1.** higher than; over **2.** beyond; past [the road *above* the town] **3.** at a point upstream from **4.** better than [*above* the average] **5.** more than [*above* fifty pounds] **6.** too honourable or good for [not *above* cheating] —*adj.* placed, found, mentioned, etc. above or earlier —*n.* something that is above —**above all** most of all; mainly

a·bove·board (-bôrd′) *adv., adj.* without dishonesty or concealment

Abp., abp. archbishop

ab·ra·ca·dab·ra (ab′rə kə dab′rə) *n.* [LL.] **1.** a word supposed to have magic powers, used in incantations, etc. **2.** foolish or meaningless talk

ab·rade (ə brād′) *vt., vi.* -**rad**′**ed**, -**rad**′**ing** [< L. *abradere* < *ab-*, away + *radere*, to scrape] to rub off; wear away by scraping —**ab·rad**′**er** *n.*

a·bran·chi·ate (ā braŋ′kē it, -āt′) *adj.* [< Gr. *a-*, not + *branchia*, gills + -ATE[1]] without gills —*n.* an animal without gills Also **a·bran′chi·al** (-əl)

ab·ra·sion (ə brā′zhən) *n.* **1.** a scraping or rubbing off, as of skin **2.** an abraded spot or area

ab·ra·sive (ə brā′siv, -ziv) *adj.* causing abrasion —*n.* a substance used for grinding, polishing, etc.

ab·re·ac·tion (ab′rē ak′shən) *n.* [AB- + REACTION] *Psychoanalysis* the relieving of a repressed emotion, as by talking about it

a·breast (ə brest′) *adv., adj.* [A-[1] + BREAST] **1.** side by side [walking four *abreast*] **2.** informed (*of*) or conversant (*with*) recent developments

a·bridge (ə brij′) *vt.* **a·bridged′**, **a·bridg′ing** [< OFr. < LL. *abbreviare*: see ABBREVIATE] **1.** to reduce in scope, extent, etc. **2.** to shorten by using fewer words but keeping the main contents **3.** to lessen (rights, authority, etc.) —**a·bridg′a·ble**, **a·bridge′a·ble** *adj.* —**a·bridg′er** *n.*

a·bridg·ment, a·bridge·ment (ə brij′mənt) *n.* **1.** an abridging or being abridged **2.** an abridged form of a book, etc.

a·broad (ə brôd′) *adv.* **1.** broadly; far and wide **2.** circulating [a report is *abroad* that he is ill] **3.** outdoors [to stroll *abroad*] **4.** to or in foreign countries —**from abroad** from a foreign land

ab·ro·gate (ab′rə gāt′) *vt.* -**gat**′**ed**, -**gat**′**ing** [< L. pp. of *abrogare*, to repeal < *ab-*, away + *rogare*, to propose] to cancel or repeal by authority; annul —**ab′ro·ga·ble** (-gə b′l) *adj.* —**ab′ro·ga′tion** *n.* —**ab′ro·ga′tive** *adj.* —**ab′ro·ga′tor** *n.*

a·brupt (ə brupt′) *adj.* [< L. pp. of *abrumpere* < *ab-*, off + *rumpere*, to break] **1.** sudden; unexpected **2.** curt or brusque **3.** very steep **4.** jumping from topic to topic; disconnected **5.** *Geol.* suddenly cropping out [abrupt strata] —**a·brupt′ly** *adv.* —**a·brupt′ness** *n.*

ab·scess (ab′ses) *n.* [< L. *abscedere* < *ab*(s)-, from + *cedere*, to go] a swollen, inflamed area in body tissues, in which pus gathers —*vi.* to form an abscess —**ab′scessed** *adj.*

ab·scis·sa (ab sis′ə) *n.*, *pl.* -**sas**, -**sae** (-ē) [L. *abscissa* (*linea*), (a line) cut off < pp. of *abscindere* < *ab-*, from, off *scindere*, to cut] *Math.* in a system of coordinates, the distance of a point from the vertical axis as measured along a line parallel to the horizontal axis: cf. ORDINATE

ab·scis·sion (ab sizh′ən) *n.* [see prec.] **1.** a cutting off **2.** *Bot.* the normal separation of fruit, leaves, etc. from plants

y·AXIS

ABSCISSA
(x, the abscissa of p;
y, the ordinate of p)

x·AXIS

ab·scond (əb skond′) *vi.* [< L. *abscondere* < *ab*(s)-, from, away + *condere*, to hide] to run away and hide, esp. in order to escape the law —**ab·scond′er** *n.*

ab·seil (ab′sāl, -zīl) *vi.* [< G. *abseilen* < *ab-*, down + *Seil*, rope] *Mountaineering* to descend by means of a double rope secured from above —*n.* *Mountaineering* a descent so made

ab·sence (ab′səns) *n.* **1.** the state of being absent, or away **2.** the time of being away **3.** the fact of being without; lack [in the *absence* of proof]

ab·sent (ab′sənt; *for v.* ab sent′) *adj.* [< OFr. < L. prp. of *abesse* < *ab-*, away + *esse*, to be] **1.** not present; away **2.** not existing; lacking **3.** not attentive; absorbed in thought —*vt.* to keep (oneself) away [he *absents* himself from classes]

ab·sen·tee (ab′sən tē′) *n.* a person who is absent, as from work —*adj.* designating or of a person who lives away from his property, office, etc. [an *absentee* landlord]

ab·sen·tee·ism (-iz′m) *n.* absence from work, school, etc., esp. when deliberate or habitual

ab·sent-mind·ed (ab′sənt mīn′did) *adj.* **1.** so lost in thought as not to pay attention to what is going on around one **2.** habitually forgetful —**ab′sent-mind′ed·ly** *adv.* —**ab′sent-mind′ed·ness** *n.*

ab·sinthe, ab·sinth (ab′sinth) *n.* [< OFr. < L. < Gr. *apsinthion*] **1.** wormwood **2.** a green liqueur with the flavour of wormwood and anise

ab·so·lute (ab′sə lo͞ot′, ab′sə lo͞ot′) *adj.* [< L. pp. of *absolvere*: see ABSOLVE] **1.** perfect; complete [absolute silence] **2.** not mixed; pure **3.** not limited; unrestricted [an *absolute* ruler] **4.** positive; definite **5.** actual; real [an *absolute* truth] **6.** without reference to anything else **7.** *Gram.* a) forming part of a sentence, but syntactically independent [in the sentence "The weather being good, they went," *the weather being good* is an *absolute* construction] b) with no expressed object: said of a verb usually transitive c) used alone, with the noun understood: said of a pronoun or an adjective, such as *ours* and *brave* in the sentence "Ours are the brave." —*n.* something that is absolute —**the Absolute** *Philos.* that which is thought of as existing in and by itself, without relation to anything else —**ab′so·lute′ness** *n.*

ab·so·lute·ly (ab′sə lo͞ot′lē; *for interj.*, ab′sə lo͞ot′lē) *adv.* in an absolute manner —*interj.* yes indeed; definitely

absolute majority 1. a majority of over half **2.** a majority that beats the combined opposition

absolute pitch the ability to identify the pitch of any tone, or to sing a given tone, without having a known pitch sounded beforehand

absolute temperature temperature measured from absolute zero

absolute zero a point of temperature theoretically equal to –273.15° C or –459.67° F: the hypothetical point at which a substance would have no molecular motion and no heat

ab·so·lu·tion (ab′sə lo͞o′shən) *n.* [<OFr. < L. *absolutio* < *absolvere*: see ABSOLVE] **1.** a formal freeing (*from* guilt); forgiveness **2.** a) remission (*of* sin or its penalty); specif., in some churches, such remission formally given by a priest in the sacrament of penance b) the formula stating such remission

ab·so·lut·ism (ab′sə lo͞o′tiz′m) *n.* government in which the ruler has unlimited powers; despotism —**ab′so·lut′ist** *n., adj.*

ab·solve (əb zolv′, əb -solv′) *vt.* -**solved′**, -**solv′ing** [< L. *absolvere* < *ab-*, from + *solvere*, to loose] **1.** to pronounce free from guilt or blame; acquit **2.** a) to give religious absolution to b) to remit (a sin) **3.** to free (someone *from* an obligation) —**ab·solv′ent** *adj., n.* —**ab·solv′er** *n.*

ab·sorb (əb zôrb′, ab-; -sôrb′) *vt.* [< L. *absorbere* < *ab-*, from + *sorbere*, to drink in] **1.** to suck up [sponges *absorb* water] **2.** to take up fully the attention of; engross **3.** to take in and incorporate; assimilate **4.** to take in (a shock, jolt, etc.) with little or no recoil or reaction **5.** to take in and not reflect (light, sound, etc.) —**ab·sorbed′** *adj.* —**ab·sorb′ing** *adj.* —**ab·sorb′ing·ly** *adv.*

ab·sorb·ent (əb zôr′b′nt, ab-; -sôr′-) *adj.* capable of absorbing moisture, light, etc. —*n.* a thing that absorbs moisture, etc. —**ab·sorb′en·cy** *n.*

ab·sorp·tion (əb zôrp′shən, ab-; -sôrp′-) *n.* **1.** an absorbing or being absorbed **2.** great interest; engrossment **3.** *Biol.* the passing of nutrient material into the blood or lymph —**ab·sorp′tive·ly** *adv.*

ab·stain (əb stān′, ab-) *vi.* [< OFr. < L. *abstinere* < *ab*(s)-, from + *tenere*, to hold] **1.** to do without voluntarily; refrain (*from*), esp. alcohol **2.** to choose not to vote on an issue —**ab·stain′er** *n.*

ab·ste·mi·ous (əb stē′mē əs, ab-) *adj.* [< L. < *ab*(s)-, from + root of *temetum*, strong drink] moderate, esp. in eating and drinking; temperate —**ab·ste′mi·ous·ly** *adv.* —**ab·ste′mi·ous·ness** *n.*

ab·sten·tion (əb sten′shən, ab-) *n.* an abstaining; specif., a refraining from voting on some issue

ab·sti·nence (ab′stə nəns) *n.* **1.** an abstaining from some or all food, drink, or other pleasures **2.** an abstaining from alcoholic liquors —**ab′sti·nent** *adj.* —**ab′sti·nent·ly** *adv.*

ab·stract (ab strakt′; *also, and for n.* 1 & *v.* 4 *always,* ab′-strakt) *adj.* [< L. pp. of *abstrahere* < *ab*(s)-, from + *trahere*, to draw] **1.** thought of apart from any particular instances or material objects **2.** expressing a quality so thought of [''beauty'' is an *abstract* word] **3.** not easy to understand; abstruse **4.** theoretical; not practical or applied **5.** designating or of art that seeks to make an effect through form and colour alone —*n.* **1.** a brief statement of the essential thoughts of a book, article, etc.; summary **2.** an abstract thing, condition, etc. —*vt.* **1.** to take away **2.** to steal **3.** to think of (a quality) apart from any particular instance or from any object that has it **4.** to summarize; make an abstract of —**in the abstract** in theory as distinct from practice —**ab·stract′er** *n.* —**ab·stract′ly** *adv.* —**ab·stract′ness** *n.*

ab·stract·ed (ab strak′tid) *adj.* **1.** removed or separated (*from* something) **2.** withdrawn in mind; preoccupied —**ab·stract′ed·ly** *adv.*

abstract expressionism a style of painting popular after

World War II, in which the artist's self-expression is carried out by applying paint freely in compositions that do not represent known objects

ab·strac·tion (ab strak'shən) *n.* **1.** an abstracting or being abstracted **2.** formation of an idea, as of the qualities of a thing, by separating it mentally from any particular instances or material objects **3.** an idea so formed, or a word for it ["honesty" is an *abstraction*] **4.** an unrealistic notion **5.** mental withdrawal; preoccupation **6.** a picture, sculpture, etc. that is wholly or partly abstract —**ab·strac'·tion·ism** *n.* —**ab·strac'tion·ist** *n.*

ab·struse (ab strōōs') *adj.* [< L. pp. of *abstrudere* < *ab*(*s*)-, away + *trudere*, to thrust] hard to understand; deep —**ab·struse'ly** *adv.* —**ab·struse'ness** *n.*

ab·surd (ab surd', ab-; -zurd') *adj.* [< Fr. < L. *absurdus*, not to be heard of < *ab*-, intens. + *surdus*, dull, deaf] **1.** so clearly inconsistent or unreasonable as to be laughable or ridiculous **2.** designating or of the Absurd —**the Absurd** the idea, in philosophy and drama, that human life is essentially pointless —**ab·surd'ly** *adv.* —**ab·surd'ness** *n.*

ab·surd·i·ty (ab sur'də tē, ab-; -zur'-) *n.* **1.** the quality or state of being absurd; foolishness **2.** *pl.* **-ties** an absurd idea or thing

a·bun·dance (ə bun'dəns) *n.* [< OFr. < L. prp. of *abundare*: see ABOUND] **1.** a great supply; more than sufficient quantity **2.** wealth —**a·bun'dant** *adj.* —**a·bun'dant·ly** *adv.*

a·buse (ə byōōz'; *for n.* ə byōōs') *vt.* **a·bused'**, **a·bus'ing** [< OFr. < L. pp. of *abuti*, to misuse < *ab*-, away, from + *uti*, to use] **1.** to use wrongly; misuse **2.** to mistreat **3.** to use insulting language about or to; revile **4.** [Obs.] to deceive —*n.* **1.** wrong or excessive use **2.** mistreatment; injury **3.** a bad or corrupt custom or practice **4.** insulting language —**a·bus'er** *n.*

a·bu·sive (ə byōōs'iv) *adj.* **1.** abusing; mistreating **2.** insulting in language; scurrilous —**a·bu'sive·ly** *adv.* —**a·bu'sive·ness** *n.*

a·but (ə but') *vi.* **a·but'ted**, **a·but'ting** [< OFr. < *a*-, to + *bout*, end] **1.** to touch or lean against end-on, as of walls, buttresses, etc. **2.** to adjoin; to share a common border —*vt.* to border upon

a·but·ment (-mənt) *n.* **1.** an abutting **2.** that part of a support which carries the weight of an arch **3.** the supporting structure at either end of a bridge

a·but·ter (-ər) *n.* the owner of an abutting, or adjacent, piece of land

a·buzz (ə buz') *adj.* **1.** filled with buzzing **2.** full of activity, talk, etc.

a·bysm (ə biz''m) *n.* [Poet.] *same as* ABYSS

a·bys·mal (ə biz'm'l) *adj.* **1.** of or like an abyss; bottomless [*abysmal* poverty] **2.** [Colloq.] immeasurably bad [*abysmal* handwriting] —**a·bys'mal·ly** *adv.*

a·byss (ə bis') *n.* [< L. < Gr. < *a*-, without + *byssos*, bottom] **1.** a deep fissure in the earth; bottomless gulf; chasm **2.** anything too deep for measurement [an *abyss* of shame] **3.** the ocean depths **4.** *Theol.* the primeval chaos before the Creation —**a·bys·sal** (ə bis''l) *adj.*

-ac (ak, ək) [Fr. *-aque* < L. *-acus* < Gr. *-akos* (or directly < any of these)] *a suffix meaning:* **1.** characteristic of [*elegiac*] **2.** of; relating to [*cardiac*] **3.** affected by or having [*maniac*]

Ac *Chem.* actinium

AC, A.C., a.c. alternating current

A.C. aircraft(s)man

A/C, a/c *Bookkeeping* **1.** account **2.** account current

a·ca·cia (ə kā'shə) *n.* [< OFr. < L. < Gr. *akakia*, thorny tree; prob. < *akē*, a point] **1.** a tree or shrub of the legume family, with clusters of yellow or white flowers: some yield gum arabic or dyes **2.** the flower

ac·a·deme (a'kə dēm') *n.* [see ACADEMY] the academic world: often a humorous or disparaging term

ac·a·dem·ic (ak'ə dem'ik) *adj.* [see ACADEMY] **1.** of colleges, universities, etc.; scholastic **2.** having to do with liberal rather than technical or vocational education **3.** following fixed rules; formalistic [an *academic* painter] **4.** merely theoretical [an *academic* question] Also **ac'a·dem'·i·cal** —*n.* a person at university, esp. a teacher or research student —**ac'a·dem'i·cal·ly** *adv.*

academic freedom freedom of a teacher or student to hold and express views without fear of arbitrary interference by officials

a·cad·e·mi·cian (ə kad'ə mish'ən, ak'ə də-) *n.* a member of an academy (sense 3)

a·cad·e·my (ə kad'ə mē) *n., pl.* **-mies** [< Fr. < L. < Gr. *akadēmeia*, the grove of *Akadēmos* (legendary figure), where Plato taught] **1.** a secondary school, esp. in Scotland **2.** a school offering training in a special field [a military *academy*] **3.** an association of scholars, writers, artists, etc., for advancing literature, art, or science

a·can·thus (ə kan'thəs) *n., pl.* **-thus·es**, **-thi** (-thī) [L. < Gr. *akantha*, thorn < *akē*, a point] **1.** a thistlelike

Mediterranean plant with lobed, often spiny leaves **2.** *Archit.* a conventional representation of its leaf, esp. on the capitals of Corinthian columns —**a·can'thine** (-thin) *adj.*

a·ca·pel·la (ä'kə pel'ə, a'-) [It., in chapel style < L. *ad*, to + ML. *capella*, CHAPEL] without instrumental accompaniment: said of choral singing

ac·a·rid (ak'ə rid) *n.* [< Gr. *akari*, mite] any of a large order of small arachnids, including the ticks and mites

a·car·pous (ā kär'pəs) *adj.* [Gr. *akarpos* < *a*-, without + *karpos*, fruit] *Bot.* bearing no fruit; sterile

acc. **1.** accompanied **2.** account **3.** accusative

A.C.C.A. Association of Certified and Corporate Accountants

Ac·ca·di·an (ə kä'dē ən) *n.* *same as* AKKADIAN

ac·cede (ak sēd') *vi.* **-ced'ed**, **-ced'ing** [< L. *accedere* < *ad*-, to + *cedere*, to yield] **1.** to enter upon the duties (of an office); attain (*to*) **2.** to give assent; give in; agree (*to*) **3.** to become a party (*to* a treaty) —**ac·ced'ence** *n.* —**ac·ced'er** *n.*

ac·cel·er·an·do (ak sel'ə ran'dō) *adv., adj.* [It.] *Music* with gradually quickening tempo

ac·cel·er·ate (ək sel'ə rāt', ak-) *vt.* **-at'ed**, **-at'ing** [< L. pp. of *accelerare* < *ad*-, to + *celerare*, to hasten < *celer*, swift] **1.** to increase the speed of **2.** to cause to progress more rapidly **3.** *Physics* to cause a change in the rate of velocity of (a moving body) **4.** to cause to happen sooner —*vi.* to go or progress faster —**ac·cel'er·a'tive** *adj.*

ac·cel·er·a·tion (ək sel'ə rā'shən, ak-) *n.* **1.** an accelerating or being accelerated **2.** change in velocity, or the rate of such change **3.** the power to accelerate [this car has good *acceleration*]

ac·cel·er·a·tor (ək sel'ə rāt'ər, ak-) *n.* **1.** one that accelerates **2.** a device, as the foot throttle of a motor vehicle, for speeding up something **3.** *Chem.* a substance that speeds up a reaction **4.** *Nuclear Physics* a device that accelerates charged particles to high energies

ac·cel·er·om·e·ter (ək sel'ə rom'ə tər, ak-) *n.* [ACCELER(ATE) + -o- + -METER] an instrument for measuring acceleration, as of an aircraft, or for detecting vibrations, as in machinery

ac·cent (ak'sent; *for v. also* ak sent') *n.* [Fr. < L. < *ad*-, to + *cantus*, pp. of *canere*, to sing] **1.** the emphasis given to a particular syllable or word in speaking it **2.** a mark used to show this emphasis, as primary (') and secondary (') accents **3.** *a*) a mark used to distinguish various sounds for the same letter [in French there are acute (´), grave (`), and circumflex (^) accents] *b*) a mark used to distinguish among the various tones in a tonal language **4.** a distinguishing regional or national way of pronouncing **5.** [*pl.*] [Poet.] speech; words [in *accents* mild] **6.** something that lends emphasis, as by contrast with its surroundings **7.** special emphasis [to put the *accent* on safety] **8.** *Music* emphasis or stress on a note or chord **9.** *Prosody* rhythmic stress or beat —*vt.* **1.** to pronounce with special stress **2.** to mark with an accent **3.** to emphasize

ac·cen·tor (ak sen'tər) *n.* [ML. < L. *ad*, to + *cantor*, singer] any of a genus of small songbirds, as the hedge sparrow

ac·cen·tu·al (ak sen'chōō wəl, -tyōō-) *adj.* **1.** of or having to do with accent **2.** having rhythm based on stress, as some poetry —**ac·cen'tu·al·ly** *adv.*

ac·cen·tu·ate (ak sen'chōō wāt', -tyōō-) *vt.* **-at'ed**, **-at'ing** **1.** to pronounce or mark with an accent or stress **2.** to emphasize —**ac·cen'tu·a'tion** *n.*

ac·cept (ək sept', ak-) *vt.* [< OFr. < L. *acceptare* < *accipere* < *ad*-, to + *capere*, to take] **1.** to take (what is offered or given); receive willingly **2.** to receive favourably; approve **3.** to agree or give assent to **4.** to believe in **5.** to understand as having a certain meaning **6.** to reply affirmatively to; say "yes" to [to *accept* an invitation] **7.** *Business* to agree to pay —*vi.* to accept something offered —**ac·cept'er** *n.*

ac·cept·a·ble (ək sep'tə b'l, ak-) *adj.* worth accepting; satisfactory or, sometimes, merely adequate —**ac·cept'a·bil'·i·ty** *n.* —**ac·cept'a·bly** *adv.*

ac·cept·ance (ək sep'təns, ak-) *n.* **1.** an accepting or being accepted **2.** approving reception; approval **3.** belief in; assent **4.** a written order to pay a certain sum at a set future time

ac·cep·ta·tion (ak'sep tā'shən) *n.* the generally accepted meaning (of a word or expression)

ac·cept·ed (ək sep'tid, ak-) *adj.* generally regarded as true, proper, etc.; conventional; approved

ac·cep·tor (ək sep'tər, ak-) *n.* **1.** one who accepts, esp. a bill of exchange **2.** *Electronics* an impurity added to a semiconductor that increases its conductivity

ac·cess (ak'ses) *n.* [< OFr. < L. pp. of *accedere*, ACCEDE] **1.** a coming towards; approach **2.** a means of approaching, using, etc. **3.** the right to enter, approach, or use; admittance **4.** increase **5.** an outburst [an *access* of anger] **6.** the onset (*of* a disease)

ac·ces·sa·ry (ək ses'ər ē, ak-) *adj., n., pl.* **-ries** *same as* ACCESSORY

access broadcasting the provision of time on radio or

television, and of technical advice and assistance, to groups of people who wish to broadcast their own programmes

ac·ces·si·ble (ak ses′ə b'l) *adj.* [see ACCESS] **1.** that can be approached or entered **2.** easy to approach or enter **3.** obtainable **4.** open to the influence of (with *to*) [not *accessible* to pity] —**ac·ces′si·bil′i·ty** *n.* —**ac·ces′si·bly** *adv.*

ac·ces·sion (ak sesh′ən) *n.* [see ACCESS] **1.** the act of attaining (a throne, power, etc.) **2.** formal acceptance of a pact, treaty, etc. **3.** assent **4.** *a)* increase by addition *b)* an item added, as to a library —*vt.* to record (a book, etc.) as a new accession —**ac·ces′sion·al** *adj.*

ac·ces·so·ry (ək ses′ər ē, ak-) *adj.* [< ML. < L. pp. of *accedere*, ACCEDE] **1.** helping in a secondary way; extra; additional **2.** *Law* helping in an unlawful act —*n., pl.* -**ries** **1.** something extra added to help in a secondary way; specif., *a)* an article to complete one's costume, as a handbag, gloves, etc. *b)* a piece of optional equipment for convenience, comfort, etc. **2.** *Law* an accomplice —**accessory before** (or **after**) **the fact** one who, though absent at the commission of a felony, aids the accused before (or after) its commission —**ac·ces·so·ri·al** (ak′sə sôr′ē əl) *adj.*

access time in computers, the time between the moment when information is requested from (or presented for) storage and the moment of its delivery (or storage)

ac·ciac·ca·tu·ra (ə chäk′ə tōōr′ə) *n.* [It. < *acciaccare*, to crush] *Music* a short grace note sounded together with the principal note or chord, but quickly released

ac·ci·dence (ak′sə dəns) *n.* [L. *accidentia*, inessential things, transl. of Gr. *parepomena*, accompanying things; see ff.] the part of grammar dealing with inflection of words

ac·ci·dent (ak′sə dənt) *n.* [< OFr. < L. prp. of *accidere*, happen < *ad-*, to + *cadere*, to fall] **1.** a happening that is not expected, foreseen, or intended **2.** an unintended happening that results in injury, loss, etc. **3.** chance [to meet by *accident*] **4.** an attribute that is not essential

ac·ci·den·tal (ak′sə den′t'l) *adj.* **1.** happening by chance, unexpectedly, or unintentionally **2.** belonging but not essential; incidental —*n.* **1.** a nonessential quality **2.** *Music a)* a sign, as a sharp or flat, placed before a note to show a chromatic change of pitch *b)* the tone of such a note —**ac′ci·den′tal·ly** *adv.*

ac·ci·dent-prone (ak′sə dənt prōn′) *adj.* tending to become involved in accidents

ac·ci·die (ak′sə dē) *n.* same as ACEDIA

ac·claim (ə klām′) *vt.* [< L. *acclamare* < *ad-*, to + *clamare*, to cry out] **1.** to greet with loud applause or strong approval **2.** to announce with much applause or praise; hail [they *acclaimed* him victor] —*n.* loud applause or strong approval

ac·cla·ma·tion (ak′lə mā′shən) *n.* **1.** an acclaiming or being acclaimed **2.** loud applause or strong approval **3.** an enthusiastic approving vote by voice without an actual count —**ac·clam·a·to·ry** (ə klam′ə tər ē) *adj.*

ac·cli·mate (ak′lə māt′, ə klī′mət) *vt., vi.* -**mat′ed**, -**mat′ing** [chiefly U.S.] same as ACCLIMATIZE —**ac′cli·ma′tion** *n.*

ac·cli·ma·tize (ə klī′mə tīz′) *vt., vi.* -**tized′**, -**tiz′ing** [Fr.: see AD- & CLIMATE & -IZE] to accustom or become accustomed to a different climate or environment —**ac·cli′-ma·ti·za′tion** *n.*

ac·cliv·i·ty (ə kliv′ə tē) *n., pl.* -**ties** [< L. < *ad-*, up + *clivus*, hill] an upward slope of ground —**ac·cli·vous** (ə klī′vəs) *adj.*

ac·co·lade (ak′ə lād′) *n.* [Fr. < Pr. < It. pp. of *accollare*, embrace < L. *ad*, to + *collum*, neck] **1.** formerly, an embrace (now, a touch with a sword) used in conferring knighthood **2.** anything done or given as a sign of great respect, appreciation, etc. **3.** *Music* a vertical line joining two or more staffs

ac·com·mo·date (ə kom′ə dāt′) *vt.* -**dat′ed**, -**dat′ing** [< L. pp. of *accommodare* < *ad-*, to + *com-*, with + *modus*, a measure] **1.** to adjust; adapt **2.** to reconcile (differences) **3.** to help by supplying (*with* something) **4.** to do a favour for **5.** to have or find room for —*vi.* to become adjusted, as the lens of the eye in focusing —**ac·com′mo·da′tive** *adj.* —**ac·com′mo·da′tor** *n.*

ac·com·mo·dat·ing (-dāt′iŋ) *adj.* ready to help; obliging —**ac·com′mo·dat′ing·ly** *adv.*

ac·com·mo·da·tion (ə kom′ə dā′shən) *n.* **1.** adaptation (*to* a purpose); adjustment **2.** reconciliation of differences **3.** willingness to do favours **4.** a help or convenience **5.** lodgings or space, as in a hotel, on a ship, etc. **6.** the self-adjustment of the lens of the eye in focusing

accommodation address an address to which letters, etc. may be sent, although the addressee does not live or work there

accommodation bill a bill of exchange signed by one party on behalf of another whose credit is weak

accommodation ladder a ladder hung over a ship's side for access to and from a boat, pier, etc.

ac·com·pa·ni·ment (ə kump′ni mənt, ə kum′pə nē mənt) *n.* **1.** anything that accompanies something else **2.** *Music* a part played as a subsidiary to a song, or to another instrumental part

ac·com·pa·nist (ə kum′pə nist) *n.* a person who plays an accompaniment

ac·com·pa·ny (ə kum′pə nē, ə kump′nē) *vt.* -**nied**, -**ny·ing** [< MFr. < *ac-*, to + OFr. *compagnon*: see COMPANION] **1.** to go or be together with **2.** to supplement [to *accompany* words with acts] **3.** to play an accompaniment for or to

ac·com·plice (ə kum′plis, ə kom′-) *n.* [< A-¹ + OFr. *complice* < LL. *complex*, accomplice: see COMPLEX] a person who knowingly helps another in an unlawful act

ac·com·plish (ə kum′plish, ə kom′-) *vt.* [< OFr. < L. *ad-*, intens. + *complere*: see COMPLETE] to do; succeed in doing; complete —**ac·com′plish·a·ble** *adj.*

ac·com·plished (-plisht) *adj.* **1.** done; completed **2.** skilled; proficient **3.** trained in the social arts or skills; polished

ac·com·plish·ment (-plish mənt) *n.* **1.** an accomplishing or being accomplished; completion **2.** something done successfully; achievement **3.** a social art or skill: *usually used in pl.*

ac·cord (ə kôrd′) *vt.* [< OFr. < L. *ad-*, to + *cor* (gen. *cordis*), heart] **1.** to make agree; reconcile **2.** to grant or concede; bestow —*vi.* to agree or harmonize (*with*) —*n.* **1.** mutual agreement; harmony **2.** an informal agreement, as between nations **3.** harmony of sound, colour, etc. —**of one's own accord** willingly, without being asked —**with one accord** all agreeing

ac·cord·ance (-əns) *n.* agreement; conformity —**ac·cord′-ant** *adj.* —**ac·cord′ant·ly** *adv.*

ac·cord·ing (-iŋ) *adj.* agreeing; in harmony —**according as** **1.** to the degree that **2.** depending on whether; if —**according to** **1.** in agreement with **2.** in the order of [seated *according to* age] **3.** as stated by

ac·cord·ing·ly (-lē) *adv.* **1.** in a way that is fitting and proper **2.** therefore

ac·cor·di·on (ə kôr′dē ən) *n.* [< G., prob. < It. *accordare*, be in tune] a musical instrument with a bellows which is pulled out and pressed together to produce tones by forcing air through metal reeds opened by fingering keys —*adj.* having folds, or folding, like an accordion's bellows [*accordion* pleats] —**ac·cor′-di·on·ist** *n.*

ACCORDION

ac·cost (ə kost′) *vt.* [< Fr. < It. < L. < *ad-*, to + *costa*, rib, side] to approach and speak to, esp. in a bold or forward manner

ac·couche·ment (ə kōōsh′mənt; *Fr.* a kōōsh män′) *n.* [Fr. < OFr. *acoucher*: see AD- & COUCH] confinement for giving birth to a child; childbirth

ac·count (ə kaunt′) *vt.* [< OFr. < *a-*, to + *conter*, to tell < L. *computare*: see COMPUTE] to consider to be; deem —*vi.* **1.** to furnish a reckoning of money received and paid out **2.** to make satisfactory amends (*for*) [made to *account* for his crime] **3.** to give satisfactory reasons or an explanation (*for*) **4.** to be the cause or source of (with *for*) **5.** to put out of action by killing, defeating, etc. (with *for*) —*n.* **1.** *a)* a record of the financial transactions of a person, business, etc. *b)* a statement of money owed for goods or services provided; bill *c)* same as CREDIT ACCOUNT *d)* a business that is a customer or client, esp. on a credit basis **2.** same as BANK ACCOUNT **3.** the period on the Stock Exchange at the end of which settlements are made **4.** worth; importance [a thing of small *account*] **5.** an explanation **6.** a report; description —**by all accounts** according to all opinions —**call to account 1.** to demand an explanation of **2.** to reprimand —**give a good account of oneself** to acquit oneself well —**on account** as partial payment —**on (someone's) account** for (someone's) sake —**on account of** because of —**on no account** under no circumstances —**settle** (or **square**) **accounts with 1.** to pay one's debts, or receive money due to one **2.** to be revenged upon; get even with —**take account of 1.** to allow for **2.** to take notice of —**take into account** to take into consideration —**turn to (good) account** to get use or profit from

ac·count·a·ble (-ə b'l) *adj.* **1.** obliged to account for one's acts; responsible **2.** that can be accounted for; explainable —**ac·count′a·bil′i·ty** *n.* —**ac·count′a·bly** *adv.*

ac·count·an·cy (ə kaunt′ən sē) *n.* the profession or work of an accountant

ac·count·ant (ə kaunt′ənt) *n.* a person whose work is to inspect or keep financial accounts

ac·count·ing (ə kaun′tiŋ) *n.* **1.** the principles or practice of setting up and auditing financial accounts **2.** a settling or balancing of accounts

ac·cou·tre (ə kōōt′ər) *vt.* -**tred**, -**tring** [Fr., prob. < L. *con-*, together + *suere*, to sew] to equip or attire

ac·cou·tre·ments (ə kōō′trə mənts, -kōōt′ər-) *n.pl.* **1.** clothes; dress **2.** equipment; furnishings; trappings

ac·cred·it (ə kred′it) *vt.* [< Fr.: see CREDIT] **1.** to bring into credit or favour **2.** to give credentials to (an ambassador, representative, etc.) **3.** to take as true **4.** to certify as meeting certain standards **5.** to attribute; credit —**ac·cred'·it·a'tion** (-ə tā'shən) *n.*

ac·crete (ə krēt') *vi.* **-cret'ed, -cret'ing** [< L. *accretus*, pp. of *accrescere*, to increase] **1.** to grow by being added to **2.** to grow together —*vt.* to cause to adhere or unite (*to*)

ac·cre·tion (ə krē'shən) *n.* [< L. *accretio* < *accrescere* < *ad-*, to + *crescere*, to grow] **1.** growth in size, esp. by addition or accumulation **2.** a growing together of separate parts **3.** accumulated matter **4.** a part added separately **5.** a whole resulting from such growth —**ac·cre'tive** *adj.*

ac·crue (ə krōō') *vi.* **-crued', -cru'ing** [< OFr. < L.: see ACCRETION] **1.** to come as a natural growth, advantage, or right (*to*) **2.** to be added periodically as an increase: said esp. of interest on money —**ac·cru'al** *n.*

acct. account

ac·cul·tu·rate (ə kul'chə rāt') *vi., vt.* **-rat'ed, -rat'ing** to undergo, or alter by, acculturation

ac·cul·tu·ra·tion (ə kul'chə rā'shən) *n.* [*ac-* (see AD-) + CULTUR(E) + -ATION] **1.** the conditioning of a child to the patterns of a culture **2.** *a)* a becoming adapted to a different culture *b)* the assimilation by one culture of cultural features of another

ac·cu·mu·late (ə kyōōm'yə lāt') *vt., vi.* **-lat'ed, -lat'ing** [< L. pp. of *accumulare* < *ad-*, to + *cumulare*, to pile up or collect, esp. over a period of time —**ac·cu'mu·la·ble** (-lə b'l) *adj.*

ac·cu·mu·la·tion (ə kyōōm'yə lā'shən) *n.* **1.** an accumulating; collection **2.** accumulated or collected material

ac·cu·mu·la·tive (ə kyōōm'yə lāt'iv) *adj.* **1.** resulting from accumulation **2.** tending to accumulate —**ac·cu'mu·la'tive·ly** *adv.* —**ac·cu'mu·la'tive·ness** *n.*

ac·cu·mu·la·tor (-lāt'ər) *n.* **1.** one that accumulates **2.** a storage battery **3.** a device, as in a computer, that stores a quantity and that will add to that quantity others, storing the sum **4.** a bet on several successive races, both the stake and the winnings being carried forward from one race to the next

ac·cu·ra·cy (ak'yoo rə sē) *n.* the quality or state of being accurate; precision

ac·cu·rate (ak'yoo rit) *adj.* [< L. pp. of *accurare*, to take care < *ad-*, to + *cura*, care] **1.** careful and exact **2.** free from errors; precise **3.** adhering closely to a standard —**ac'cu·rate·ly** *adv.* —**ac'cu·rate·ness** *n.*

ac·curs·ed (ə kur'sid, -kurst') *adj.* **1.** under a curse; ill-fated **2.** deserving to be cursed; damnable Also **ac·curst'** (-kurst') —**ac·curs'ed·ly** *adv.* —**ac·curs'ed·ness** *n.*

ac·cu·sa·tion (ak'yoo zā'shən) *n.* **1.** an accusing or being accused **2.** the wrong that one is accused of

ac·cu·sa·tive (ə kyōō'zə tiv) *adj.* [< L. < pp. of *accusare*: see ACCUSE] **1.** designating or in the grammatical case, as in Latin, used for the direct object of a verb and after certain prepositions **2.** accusatory —*n.* **1.** the accusative case **2.** a word in this case —**ac·cu'sa·ti'val** (-tī'v'l) *adj.* —**ac·cu'sa·tive·ly** *adv.*

ac·cu·sa·to·ri·al (ə kyōō zə tôr'ē əl) *adj.* of, or in the manner of, an accuser

ac·cu·sa·to·ry (ə kyōō'zə tər ē) *adj.* making or containing an accusation; accusing

ac·cuse (ə kyōōz') *vt.* **-cused', -cus'ing** [< OFr. < L. *accusare* < *ad-*, to + *causa*, a cause or lawsuit] **1.** to find at fault; blame **2.** to bring formal charges against (*of* breaking the law, etc.) —**the accused** *Law* the person formally charged with committing a crime —**ac·cus'er** *n.* —**ac·cus'ing·ly** *adv.*

ac·cus·tom (ə kus'təm) *vt.* to make used (*to* something) as by custom or regular use; habituate

ac·cus·tomed (-təmd) *adj.* **1.** customary; usual; characteristic **2.** used (*to*); in the habit of

ace (ās) *n.* [< L. *as*, unit] **1.** a playing card, domino, etc. marked with one spot **2.** *a)* a serve, as in tennis, that one's opponent is unable to return *b)* the point thus made **3.** *Golf* a hole in one: see entry HOLE **4.** a combat pilot who has destroyed many enemy aircraft **5.** an expert —*adj.* [Colloq.] first-rate; expert [*an* ace salesman] —**ace up one's sleeve** a hidden and powerful advantage —**within an ace of** on the verge of; very close to

-ace·a (ā'shə, ā'shē ə) [L., neut. pl. of *-aceus*] a plural suffix used in forming zoological names of classes or orders: see -ACEOUS

-ace·ae (ā'si ē') [L., fem. pl. of *-aceus*] a plural suffix used in forming botanical names of families: see -ACEOUS

a·ce·di·a (ə sē'dē ə) *n.* [LL. < Gr. *akēdia* < *a-*, not + *kēdos*, care] spiritual sloth and indifference

-aceous (ā'shəs) [L. *-aceus*] a suffix meaning of the nature of, like, belonging to, producing, etc.: often used to form adjectives corresponding to nouns ending in -ACEA, -ACEAE

a·ceph·a·lous (ā sef'ə ləs) *adj.* [LL. *acephalus* < Gr. *akephalos* < *a-*, without + *kephalē*, head] headless; specif., *Zool.* having no part of the body designated as the head

ac·er·bate (as'ər bāt') *vt.* **-bat'ed, -bat'ing** [< L. pp. of *acerbare*] **1.** to make sour or bitter **2.** to irritate; vex

a·cer·bi·ty (ə sur'bə tē) *n., pl.* **-ties** [< Fr. < L. < *acerbus*,

bitter] **1.** a sour, astringent quality **2.** sharpness or harshness of temper, words, etc. —**a·cer'bic** *adj.*

ac·e·tab·u·lum (as'ə tab'yoo ləm) *n., pl.* **-la** (-lə), **-lums** [L., orig. vinegar cup < *acetum*: see ACETO-] *Anat.* the cup-shaped socket of the hipbone

ac·e·tal (as'ə tal') *n.* [ACET(O)- + -AL] a colourless, volatile liquid used as a hypnotic

ac·et·al·de·hyde (as'ə tal'də hīd') *n.* [ACET(O)- + ALDEHYDE] a colourless, soluble, volatile liquid used as a solvent and in making various organic compounds

ac·et·an·i·lide (as'ə tan'ə līd', -'l id) *n.* [ACET(O)- + ANIL(INE) + -IDE] a white, crystalline organic substance used to lessen pain and fever

ac·e·tate (as'ə tāt') *n.* [ACET(O)- + -ATE²] **1.** a salt or ester of acetic acid **2.** *same as* CELLULOSE ACETATE —**ac'e·tat'ed** *adj.*

a·ce·tic (ə sēt'ik, -set'-) *adj.* [< L. *acetum*: see ACETO-] of, like, containing, or producing acetic acid or vinegar

acetic acid a sour, colourless liquid $C_2H_4O_2$, having a sharp odour: it is found in vinegar

a·cet·i·fy (ə set'ə fī') *vt., vi.* **-fied', -fy'ing** to change into vinegar or acetic acid —**a·cet'i·fi·ca'tion** *n.*

ac·e·to- [< L. *acetum*, vinegar] a combining form meaning of or from acetic acid: also, before a vowel, **ac·et-**

ac·e·tone (as'ə tōn') *n.* [ACET(O)- + -ONE] a colourless, flammable, volatile liquid, C_3H_6O, used as a solvent for certain oils, etc. —**ac·e·ton'ic** (-ton'ik) *adj.*

ac·e·to·phe·net·i·din (ə sēt'ō fə net'ə din) *n.* [ACETO- + PHEN(O)- + ET(HYL) + -ID(E) + -IN¹] a white, crystalline powder used to reduce fever and to relieve headaches and muscular pains; phenacetin

ac·e·tous (as'ə təs, ə sēt'əs) *adj.* of, producing, or like vinegar; sour: also **ac·e·tose'** (-tōs')

a·cet·y·lene (ə set''l ēn') *n.* [ACET(O)- + -YL + -ENE] a colourless, poisonous, highly flammable gaseous hydrocarbon, C_2H_2, used for lighting and, with oxygen, in blowlamps, etc.

ac·e·tyl·sal·i·cyl·ic acid (ə sēt''l sal'ə sil'ik, as'ə t'l-) *same as* ASPIRIN

ace·y-deuc·y (ā'sē dyōō'sē) *n.* [< ACE + DEUCE¹] a variation of backgammon

A·chae·an (ə kē'ən) *adj.* **1.** of Achaea, an ancient province in the Peloponnesus, or its people **2.** loosely, Greek —*n.* **1.** a native or inhabitant of Achaea **2.** loosely, a Greek

A·cha·tes (ə kāt'ēz) *n.* [after the friend of Aeneas in Virgil's *Aeneid*] a loyal friend

ache (āk) *vi.* **ached, ach'ing** [OE. *acan*] **1.** to have or give dull, steady pain **2.** to feel pity, etc. (*for*) **3.** [Colloq.] to yearn or long: with *for* or an infinitive —*n.* a dull, continuous pain

a·chène (ə kēn') *n.* [< ModL. < Gr. *a-*, not + *chainein*, to gape] any small, dry, one-seeded fruit that ripens without bursting —**a·che'ni·al** *adj.*

A·cheu·le·an, A·cheu·li·an (ə shōō'lē ən) *adj.* [< St. Acheul, France, where remains were found] of a lower and middle paleolithic culture characterized by skilfully made stone tools

a·chieve (ə chēv') *vt.* **a·chieved', a·chiev'ing** [< OFr. < *a-*, to + *chief*: see CHIEF] **1.** to succeed in doing; accomplish **2.** to get by exertion; attain; gain —*vi.* to bring about a desired result —**a·chiev'a·ble** *adj.* —**a·chiev'er** *n.*

a·chieve·ment (-mənt) *n.* **1.** an achieving **2.** a thing achieved, esp. by skill, work, etc.; feat

A·chil·les' heel (ə kil'ēz) [after *Achilles*, Gr. hero in the Trojan War, who was killed by an arrow that struck his vulnerable heel] (one's) vulnerable spot

Achilles' tendon the tendon connecting the back of the heel to the muscles of the calf of the leg

ach·ro·mat·ic (ak'rə mat'ik) *adj.* [< Gr. < *a-*, without + *chrōma*, colour + -IC] **1.** colourless **2.** refracting white light without breaking it up into its component colours **3.** forming visual images whose outline is free from prismatic colours [an *achromatic* lens] **4.** *Music same as* DIATONIC —**ach'ro·mat'i·cal·ly** *adv.*

a·chro·mic (ā krō'mik) *adj.* [< Gr. < *a-*, without + *chrōma*, colour + -IC] without colour: also **a·chro'mous** (-məs)

ach·y (ā'kē) *adj.* **ach'i·er, ach'i·est** having an ache, or dull, steady pain

ac·id (as'id) *adj.* [L. *acidus*, sour] **1.** sharp and biting to the taste; sour **2.** sharp or sarcastic in speech, etc. **3.** of or being an acid **4.** having too much acid —*n.* **1.** a sour substance **2.** [Slang] *same as* LSD **3.** *Chem.* any compound that reacts with a base to form a salt, produces hydrogen ions in water solution, and turns blue litmus red —**ac'id·ly** *adv.* —**ac'id·ness** *n.*

a·cid·ic (ə sid'ik) *adj.* **1.** forming acid **2.** acid

a·cid·i·fy (ə sid'ə fī') *vt., vi.* **-fied', -fy'ing** **1.** to make or become sour or acid **2.** to change into an acid —**a·cid'i·fi'a·ble** *adj.* —**a·cid'i·fi·ca'tion** *n.* —**a·cid'i·fi'er** *n.*

a·cid·i·ty (-tē) *n., pl.* **-ties** **1.** *a)* acid quality or condition; sourness *b)* the degree of this **2.** *same as* HYPERACIDITY

ac·i·do·sis (as'ə dō'sis) *n.* *Med.* a condition in which the body's alkali reserve is below normal —**ac′i·dot′ic** (-dot′-ik) *adj.*

acid test [orig., a *test* of gold by *acid*] a crucial, final test of value or quality

a·cid·u·late (ə sid′yoo lāt; -sij′oo-) *vt.* **-lat′ed, -lat′ing** to make somewhat acid or sour —**a·cid′u·la′tion** *n.*

a·cid·u·lous (-las) *adj.* [< L. dim. of *acidus*, sour] **1.** somewhat acid or sour **2.** somewhat sarcastic Also **a·cid′-u·lent** (-lant)

ac·i·nus (as′i nas) *n., pl.* **-ni** (-nī) [L., a grape] **1.** *Anat.* any of the small sacs of a compound gland **2.** *Bot.* a) any of the drupelets in an aggregate fruit, as the blackberry b) any of a collection of berries, as a bunch of grapes —**ac′-i·nar** (-nar), **ac′i·nous** (-nas) *adj.*

-a·cious (ā′shas) [< L. *-ax* (gen. *-acis*) + -OUS] *an adj.* forming suffix meaning characterized by, inclined to, full of [*tenacious*]

-ac·i·ty (as′a tē) a *n.*-forming suffix corresponding to -ACIOUS [*tenacity*]

ack-ack (ak′ak′) *n.* [echoic; prob. expansion of abbrev. *A.A.*, antiaircraft artillery] [Colloq.] an antiaircraft gun or its fire

ac·knowl·edge (ak nol′ij, ak-) *vt.* **-edged, -edg·ing** [< ME. *knowleche* (see KNOWLEDGE): infl. by ME. *aknowen* < OE. *oncnawan*, to understand] **1.** to admit to be true; confess **2.** to recognize the authority or claims of **3.** to recognize and answer (a greeting or introduction) **4.** to express thanks for **5.** to state that one has received (a letter, gift, etc.) **6.** *Law* to certify in legal form [to *acknowledge* a deed] —**ac·knowl′edge·a·ble** *adj.*

ac·knowl·edg·ment, ac·knowl·edge·ment (-mant) *n.* **1.** an acknowledging; admission **2.** something done or given in acknowledging, as thanks **3.** recognition of the authority or claims of **4.** a legal avowal or certificate

a·clin·ic line (a klin′ik) [Gr. *aklinēs* < a-, not + *klinein*, to bend + -IC] an imaginary line round the earth near the equator where a magnetic needle will not dip

ac·me (ak′mē) *n.* [Gr. *akmē*, a point, top] the highest point; peak

ac·ne (ak′nē) *n.* [ModL., ? orig. error for Gr. *akmē*: see prec.] a common skin disease characterized by chronic inflammation of the sebaceous glands, usually causing pimples on the face, etc.

ac·o·lyte (ak′a līt′) *n.* [< ML. < Gr. *akolouthos*, follower] **1.** *R.C.Ch.* a member of the highest of the four minor orders, who serves at Mass **2.** *same as* ALTAR BOY **3.** an attendant **4.** a novice

ac·o·nite (ak′a nīt′) *n.* [< L. < Gr. *akoniton*] **1.** any of a genus of plants of the buttercup family, with blue, purple, or yellow hoodlike flowers: most species are poisonous **2.** a drug made from the dried roots of one species, formerly used in medicine

a·corn (ā′kôrn′) *n.* [< OE. *æcern*, nut] the fruit of the oak tree

a·cous·tic (a kōos′tik) *adj.* [< Fr. < Gr. < *akouein*, to hear] **1.** having to do with hearing or with sound as it is heard **2.** of acoustics **3.** designed to absorb sound [an *acoustic* tile] **4.** detonated by sound vibrations [an *acoustic* mine] **5.** designating a musical instrument whose tones are not electronically altered [an *acoustic* guitar] Also **a·cous′ti·cal** —**a·cous′ti·cal·ly** *adv.*

a·cous·tics (-tiks) *n.pl.* **1.** the qualities of a room, etc. that relate to how clearly sounds can be heard in it **2.** [with *sing. v.*] the branch of physics dealing with sound

ac·quaint (a kwānt′) *vt.* [< OFr. < ML. < L. *ad*, to + *cognitus*, pp. of *cognoscere*, to know thoroughly] **1.** to let know; make aware **2.** to cause to know personally; make familiar (*with*)

ac·quaint·ance (-ans) *n.* **1.** knowledge (of something) gained from personal experience or study **2.** the state of being acquainted (*with* someone) **3.** a person whom one knows only slightly —**make the acquaintance of** to come into social contact with —**ac·quaint′ance·ship** *n.*

ac·qui·esce (ak′wē es′) *vi.* **-esced′, -esc′ing** [< Fr. < L. *acquiescere* < *ad-*, to + *quiescere*: see QUIET] to consent quietly without protest, but without enthusiasm (often with *in*) —**ac′qui·es′cence** *n.* —**ac′qui·es′cent** *adj.* —**ac′qui·es′-cent·ly** *adv.*

ac·quire (a kwīr′) *vt.* **-quired′, -quir′ing** [L. *acquirere* < *ad-*, to + *quaerere*, to seek] **1.** to get or gain by one's own efforts or actions **2.** to get as one's own —**ac·quir′a·ble** *adj.*

acquired characteristic *Biol.* a modification of structure or function caused by environmental factors: now generally regarded as not inheritable

acquired taste 1. a liking for something at first considered unpleasant **2.** the thing so liked

ac·quire·ment (a kwīr′mant) *n.* **1.** an acquiring **2.** something acquired, as a skill, etc.

ac·qui·si·tion (ak′wa zish′an) *n.* **1.** an acquiring or being acquired **2.** something acquired

ac·quis·i·tive (a kwiz′a tiv) *adj.* eager to acquire; good at getting and holding wealth, ideas, etc. —**ac·quis′i·tive·ly** *adv.* —**ac·quis′i·tive·ness** *n.*

ac·quit (a kwit′) *vt.* **-quit′ted, -quit′ting** [< OFr. < ML. *acquitare*, to settle a claim < L. *ad*, to + *quietare*, to quiet] **1.** to release from a duty, etc. **2.** to declare not guilty of a charge; exonerate **3.** to conduct (oneself); behave —**ac·quit′tal** *n.* —**ac·quit′ter** *n.*

ac·quit·tance (-ans) *n.* **1.** a settlement of, or release from, debt or liability **2.** a record of this; receipt

a·cre (ā′kar) *n.* [OE. *æcer*, field; akin to L. *ager*] **1.** a measure of land, 43 560 square feet or 4046 m² **2.** [pl.] specific holdings in land; lands

a·cre·age (ā′kar ij, ā′krij) *n.* acres collectively

ac·rid (ak′rid) *adj.* [< L. *acris*, sharp; form infl. by ACID] **1.** sharp, bitter, or irritating to the taste or smell **2.** bitter or sarcastic in speech, etc. —**a·crid·i·ty** (a krid′a tē, a-), **ac′-rid·ness** *n.* —**ac′rid·ly** *adv.*

ac·ri·dine (ak′ra dēn′) *n.* [ACRID + -INE⁴] a colourless, crystalline compound found in coal tar

ac·ri·fla·vine (ak′ra flā′vēn, -vin) *n.* [ACRI(DINE) + *flavine*, see FLAVIN] a brownish, odourless powder prepared from acridine and used as an antiseptic

ac·ri·mo·ny (ak′ra mō′nē) *n.* [< L. < *acer*, sharp] bitterness or harshness of manner or speech; asperity —**ac′-ri·mo′ni·ous** *adj.*

ac·ro- [< Gr. *akros*, at the end or top] a combining form meaning highest, at the extremities [*acrogen*]

ac·ro·bat (ak′ra bat′) *n.* [< Fr. < Gr. *akrobatos*, walking on tiptoe < *akros* (see prec.) + *bainein*, to go] an expert performer of tricks in tumbling or on the trapeze, tightrope, etc.; skilled gymnast —**ac′ro·bat′ic** *adj.* —**ac′ro·bat′i·cal·ly** *adv.*

ac·ro·bat·ics (ak′ra bat′iks) *n.pl.* [also with *sing. v.*] **1.** the skill or tricks of an acrobat **2.** any activity requiring agility and skill [mental *acrobatics*]

ac·ro·gen (ak′ra jan) *n.* [ACRO- + -GEN] a plant, such as a fern or moss, having a perennial stem with the growing point at the tip —**a·crog·e·nous** (a kroj′a nas), **ac′ro·gen′ic** (-jen′ik) *adj.*

ac·ro·meg·a·ly (ak′rō meg′a lē) *n.* [< Fr.: see ACRO- & MEGALO-] abnormal enlargement of the bones of the head, hands, and feet, resulting from overproduction of growth hormone by the pituitary gland —**ac′ro·me·gal′ic** (-ma gal′-ik) *adj.*

ac·ro·nym (ak′ra nim) *n.* [< ACRO- + Gr. *onyma*, name] a word formed from the first (or first few) letters of a series of words, as *radar*, from *ra*dio *d*etecting *a*nd *r*anging —**ac′-ro·nym′ic** *adj.*

ac·ro·pho·bi·a (ak′ra fō′bē a) *n.* [ACRO- + PHOBIA] an abnormal fear of being in high places

a·crop·o·lis (a krop′′lis) *n.* [< Gr. < *akros* (see ACRO-) + *polis*, city] the fortified upper part of an ancient Greek city, esp. [A-] that of Athens, on which the Parthenon was built

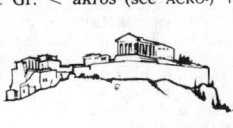

ACROPOLIS

a·cross (a kros′) *adv.* **1.** crossed; crosswise **2.** from one side to the other **3.** on or to the other side —*prep.* **1.** from one side to the other of; so as to cross **2.** on or to the other side of; over **3.** into contact with by chance [he came *across* a friend]

a·cros·tic (a kros′tik) *n.* [< Gr. < *akros* (see ACRO-) + *stichos*, line of verse] a verse or arrangement of words in which certain letters in each line, as the first or last, when taken in order spell out a word, motto, etc. —*adj.* of or like an acrostic —**a·cros′ti·cal·ly** *adv.*

a·cryl·ic fibre (a kril′ik) [ult. < ACR(ID) + -YL + -IC] any of a group of synthetic fibres derived from a compound of hydrogen cyanide and acetylene, and made into fabrics

acrylic resin any of a group of transparent thermoplastic resins, as Perspex

act (akt) *n.* [< Fr. < L. *actus*, a doing, *actum*, thing done, pp. of *agere*, to do] **1.** a thing done; deed **2.** an action; doing **3.** a decision (of a court, legislative body, etc.) **4.** a document formally stating what has been done, etc. **5.** one of the main divisions of a drama or opera **6.** any of the separate performances on a variety programme **7.** insincere behaviour, put on just for effect —*vt.* **1.** to play the part of **2.** to perform in (a play) **3.** to behave like [don't *act* the child] —*vi.* **1.** to perform on the stage; play a role **2.** to behave as though playing a role **3.** to behave; comport oneself **4.** to do something [we must *act* now to save him] **5.** to serve or function **6.** to serve as spokesman (*for*) **7.** to have an effect [acids *act* on metal] **8.** to appear to be —**act on** (or **upon**) to behave in accordance with —**act up** [Colloq.] **1.** to be playful **2.** to misbehave **3.** to become inflamed, painful, etc. —**act′a·ble** *adj.* —**act′a·bil′i·ty** *n.*

A.C.T. Australian Capital Territory

ACTH [< *a*(*dreno*)*c*(*ortico*)*t*(*rophic*) *h*(*ormone*)] a hormone secreted by the anterior lobe of the pituitary gland, that stimulates the growth and hormone production of the adrenal cortex

act·ing (ak'tiŋ) *adj.* **1.** adapted for performance **2.** that acts; functioning **3.** temporarily taking over the duties of a position [the *acting* chairman] —*n.* the art or occupation of performing in plays

acting-lieutenant *see* MILITARY RANKS, table

acting sub-lieutenant *see* MILITARY RANKS, table

ac·tin·i·a (ak tin'ē ə) *n.* [ModL. < Gr. *aktis* (gen. *aktinos*), a ray] any of various sea anemones

ac·tin·ic (ak tin'ik) *adj.* having to do with actinism —**ac·tin'i·cal·ly** *adv.*

actinic rays violet or ultraviolet rays that produce chemical changes, as in photography

ac·ti·nide series (ak'tə nīd') a group of radioactive chemical elements from element 89 (actinium) to element 103 (lawrencium)

ac·tin·ism (ak'tən iz'm) *n.* [< Gr. *aktis* (gen. *aktinos*), ray & -ISM] that property of ultraviolet light, X-rays, etc. by which chemical changes are produced

ac·tin·i·um (ak tin'ē əm) *n.* [ModL. < Gr. *aktis* (gen. *aktinos*), ray] a radioactive chemical element found in pitchblende and other minerals: symbol, Ac; at. wt., 227 (?); at. no., 89

ac·ti·noid (ak'tənoid') *adj.* star-shaped

ac·ti·nom·e·ter (ak'tə nom'ə tər) *n.* [< Gr. *aktis*, (gen. *aktinos*), a ray + -METER] an instrument for measuring the intensity of radiation

ac·ti·no·my·cin (ak'ti nō mī's'n) *n.* [< ModL. *Actinomyces*, a genus of bacteria] any of various antibiotic substances derived from soil bacteria

ac·ti·no·zo·an (ak'ti nō zō'ən) *n.* [< Gr. *aktis* (gen. *aktinos*), ray + *zóion*, animal] same as ANTHOZOAN

ac·tion (ak'shən) *n.* [< OFr. < L. *actio* < pp. of *agere*: see ACT] **1.** the doing of something; a being in motion **2.** an act or thing done **3.** [*pl.*] behaviour; habitual conduct **4.** bold and energetic activity **5.** an effect [the *action* of a drug] **6.** the way of moving, working, etc., as of a machine **7.** the moving parts or mechanism, as of a gun, piano, etc. **8.** the happenings in a story or play **9.** a legal proceeding; lawsuit **10.** military combat **11.** [Colloq.] activity or excitement —**bring action** to start a lawsuit —**out of action** not functioning —**see action** to take part in military combat —**take action 1.** to become active **2.** to start a lawsuit

ac·tion·a·ble (-ə b'l) *adj.* *Law* that gives cause for an action, or lawsuit

action painting a form of abstract expressionism using such methods as the spattering or dripping of paint to create bold, fluid, apparently random compositions

action stations points manned instantly by troops when enemy attack is imminent

ac·ti·vate (ak'tə vāt') *vt.* **-vat'ed, -vat'ing 1.** to make active **2.** to put (an inactive military unit) on an active status **3.** to make radioactive **4.** to make capable of reacting or of accelerating a chemical reaction **5.** to treat (sewage) with air so that aerobes will purify it —**ac'ti·va'·tion** *n.* —**ac'ti·va'tor** *n.*

activated carbon a highly porous carbon that can adsorb gases, vapours, and colloidal particles

activated sludge aerated sewage added to untreated sewage to hasten bacterial decomposition

ac·tive (ak'tiv) *adj.* [< OFr. < L. *activus* < base *act-* as in *actus*: see ACT] **1.** acting, functioning, working, moving, etc. **2.** capable of acting, functioning, etc. **3.** causing motion or change **4.** full of action; lively, busy, quick, etc. [an *active* mind, an *active* boy] **5.** involving action [an *active* role] **6.** necessitating action [*active* sports] **7.** a) in current operation, effect, etc. b) liable to erupt [an *active* volcano] **8.** *Gram.* denoting the voice or form of a verb whose subject is shown as performing the action of the verb —*n.* *Gram.* the active voice —**ac'tive·ly** *adv.*

active list the list of those who can be called on for military duty (**active service**) in the armed forces

ac·tiv·ism (ak'tə viz'm) *n.* the doctrine or policy of taking positive, direct action, esp. for political or social ends —**ac'·tiv·ist** *adj., n.*

ac·tiv·i·ty (ak tiv'ə tē) *n., pl.* **-ties 1.** the state of being active; action **2.** energetic action; liveliness **3.** an active force **4.** any specific action or pursuit [recreational *activities*]

ac·tiv·ize (ak'tə vīz') *vt.* **-ized', -iz'ing** *same as* ACTIVATE

act of God *Law* an occurrence, esp. a disaster, that is caused by the forces of nature and could not reasonably have been prevented

ac·tor (ak'tər) *n.* **1.** a person who does something **2.** a person who acts in plays, films, etc.

ac·tress (ak'tris) *n.* a woman or girl who acts in plays, films, etc.

A.C.T.U. Australian Council of Trade Unions

ac·tu·al (ak'choo wəl) *adj.* [< LL. < L. *actus*: see ACT] **1.** existing in reality or fact; not merely possible, but real **2.** existing at present or at the time

ac·tu·al·i·ty (ak'choo wal'ə tē) *n.* **1.** the state of being actual; reality **2.** *pl.* **-ties** an actual thing or condition; fact

ac·tu·al·ize (ak'choo wə līz') *vt.* **-ized', -iz'ing** to make actual or real —**ac'tu·al·i·za'tion** *n.*

ac·tu·al·ly (ak'choo wəl ē, ak'chə lē) *adv.* as a matter of actual fact; really

ac·tu·ar·y (ak'choo wər ē) *n., pl.* **-ar·ies** *actuarius,* clerk < *actus*: see ACT] a person who calculates risks, premiums, etc. for insurance —**ac·tu·ar·i·al** (ak'choo wer'ē əl) *adj.* —**ac'tu·ar'i·al·ly** *adv.*

ac·tu·ate (ak'choo wāt') *vt.* **-at'ed, -at'ing 1.** to put into action or motion **2.** to cause to take action —**ac'tu·a'tion** *n.* —**ac'tu·a'tor** *n.*

a·cu·i·ty (ə kyōō'ə tē) *n.* [< Fr. < L. *acus,* a needle] keenness, as of thought or vision; acuteness

a·cu·le·us (ə kyōō'lē əs) *n., pl.* **-le·i'** (-ī') [L., dim. of *acus,* needle] **1.** *Bot.* a prickle **2.** *Zool.* a sting —**a·cu'le·ate** (-lē it, -lē āt') *adj.*

a·cu·men (ə kyōō'mən, ak'yoo-) *n.* [L., a point < *acuere,* to sharpen] keenness and quickness of mind

a·cu·mi·nate (ə kyōō'mə nit; *for v.* -nāt') *adj.* [< L. pp. of *acuminare* < *acumen*: see prec.] pointed; tapering to a point —*vt.* **-nat'ed, -nat'ing** to make sharp or pointed —**a·cu'mi·na'tion** *n.*

a·cush·la (ə kōōsh'lə) *n.* [Ir.] darling

a·cute (ə kyōōt') *adj.* [< L. pp. of *acuere:* see ACUMEN] **1.** having a sharp point **2.** keen or quick of mind; shrewd **3.** sensitive [acute hearing] **4.** severe and sharp, as pain, jealousy, etc. **5.** severe but of short duration, as some diseases; not chronic **6.** very serious; critical [an *acute* shortage] **7.** of less than 90° [an *acute* angle] —**a·cute'ly** *adv.* —**a·cute'ness** *n.*

ACUTE ANGLE

acute accent a mark (´) used to show: **1.** the quality or length of a vowel, as in French *idée* **2.** primary stress

-a·cy (ə sē) [variously < Fr. < L. < Gr. *-ateia*] a suffix meaning quality, condition, position, etc. [celibacy, curacy]

ad (ad) *n.* [Colloq.] an advertisement

ad- [L., to, at, towards; akin to AT¹] a prefix meaning variously motion towards, addition to, nearness to [admit, adjoin, adrenal]: assimilated in words of Latin origin to **ac-, af-, ag-, al-, an-, ap-, ar-, as-, at-,** and **a-** before certain consonants

A.D. [L. *Anno Domini,* in the year of the Lord] of the Christian era: used with dates

ad·age (ad'ij) *n.* [Fr. < L. < *ad-,* to + *aio,* I say] an old saying that has been popularly accepted as a truth

a·da·gio (ə dä'jō, -jē ō) *adv.* [It. *ad agio,* lit., at ease] *Music* slowly and leisurely —*adj.* slow —*n., pl.* **-gios 1.** a slow movement in music **2.** a slow ballet dance, esp. by a mixed couple

Ad·am¹ (ad'əm) *Bible* the first man: Gen. 1-5 —**not know (a person) from Adam** not to know (a person) at all —**the old Adam** the evil supposedly inherent in human nature

Ad·am² (ad'əm) *adj.* [after Robert and James *Adam,* 18th c. Brit. architects, its originators] of a style of architecture and furniture based on classical designs

ad·a·mant (ad'ə mənt, -mant') *n.* [OFr. < L. < Gr. *adamas* (gen. *adamantos*) < *a-,* not + *daman,* to subdue] a substance of unbreakable hardness —*adj.* **1.** too hard to be broken **2.** not giving in or relenting; unyielding —**ad'-a·man'tine** (-man'tīn) *adj.* —**ad'a·mant·ly** *adv.*

Adam's ale water: also **Adam's wine**

Adam's apple the projection formed in the front of the throat by the thyroid cartilage, seen chiefly in men

a·dapt (ə dapt') *vt.* [< Fr. < L. *adaptare* < *ad-,* to + *aptare,* to fit] **1.** to make fit or suitable by changing or adjusting **2.** to adjust (oneself) to new or changed circumstances —*vi.* to adjust oneself —**a·dapt'a·bil'i·ty** *n.* —**a·dapt'a·ble** *adj.*

ad·ap·ta·tion (ad'əp tā'shən) *n.* **1.** an adapting or being adapted **2.** a thing resulting from adapting [a film *adaptation* of a novel] **3.** *Biol.* a change in structure, function, etc. of a plant or animal that produces better adjustment to the environment Also **a·dap·tion** (ə dap'shən)

a·dapt·er, a·dap·tor (ə dap'tər) *n.* **1.** a person or thing that adapts **2.** a device for adapting apparatus to new uses or connecting parts that would not otherwise fit **3.** a device for connecting several electrical appliances to a single mains socket

a·dap·tive (ə dap'tiv) *adj.* **1.** showing adaptation **2.** able to adapt —**a·dap'tive·ly** *adv.*

A.D.C., ADC aide-de-camp

add (ad) *vt.* [< L. *addere* < *ad-,* to + *dare,* to give] **1.** to join or unite (*to*) so as to increase the quantity, number, etc. **2.** to state further **3.** to combine (numbers) into a sum or total —*vi.* **1.** to cause an increase (*to*) **2.** to calculate a total —**add in** to include —**add to** to increase —**add up 1.** to find the total of **2.** to seem reasonable —**add up to 1.** to reach a total of **2.** [Colloq.] to mean; signify

ad·dax (ad'aks) *n.* [L. < native Afr. word] a large antelope of N Africa, with long, twisted horns

ad·dend (ăd′end, ə dend′) *n.* [< ff.] a number or quantity to be added to another

ad·den·dum (ə den′dəm) *n.*, *pl.* **-da** (-də) [L., gerundive of *addere:* see ADD] a thing added; esp., an appendix or supplement

ad·der (ad′ər) *n.* [ME. < *nadder* (by faulty separation of *a nadder*) < OE. *nædre*] 1. a small poisonous snake of Europe; common viper 2. any of various other snakes, as the puff adder

ad·der's-tongue (ad′ərz tuŋ′) *n.* a fern with a narrow spike

ad·dict (ə dikt′; *for n.* ad′ikt) *vt.* [< L. pp. of *addicere*, to give assent < *ad-*, to + *dicere*, to say] 1. to give (oneself) up (*to* some strong habit): usually in the passive 2. to make an addict of —*n.* 1. one addicted to some habit, esp. to the use of a narcotic drug 2. [Colloq.] a person extremely or excessively devoted to something [a jazz *addict*] —**ad·dic′tion** *n.* —**ad·dic′tive** *adj.*

Ad·di·son's disease (ad′ə s'nz) [after T. *Addison*, 19th-c. Brit. physician] a disease of the adrenal glands, characterized by weakness, skin discolourations, etc.

ad·di·tion (ə dish′ən) *n.* 1. an adding of numbers to get a number called the sum 2. a joining of a thing to another thing 3. a thing or part added —**in addition (to)** besides; as well (as) —**ad·di′tion·al** *adj.* —**ad·di′tion·al·ly** *adv.*

ad·di·tive (ad′ə tiv) *adj.* 1. showing or relating to addition 2. to be added —*n.* a substance added to another in small quantities for a desired effect, as a preservative added to food

ad·dle (ad′′l) *adj.* [< OE. *adela*, mire, mud] 1. rotten: said of an egg 2. muddled; confused: often in compounds [*addlebrained*] —*vt., vi.* **-dled, -dling** 1. to make or become rotten 2. to make or become muddled or confused

ad·dle·brained (-brānd′) *adj.* having an addle brain; muddled: also **ad′dle·head′ed, ad′dle·pat′ed** (-pāt′id)

ad·dress (ə dres′) *vt.* [< OFr. < *a-*, to + *dresser*, to direct < L. *dirigere:* see DIRECT] 1. to direct (spoken or written words *to*) 2. to speak to or write to 3. to write the destination on (a letter or parcel) 4. to apply (oneself) or direct (one's energies) 5. to take a stance, as in aiming the club at (a golf ball), facing (a target), etc. —*n.* 1. a speech, esp. a formal one 2. the place to which letters, etc. can be sent to one; place where one lives or works 3. the writing on letters or parcels showing their destination 4. the location in a computer's storage compartment of an item of information 5. social skill and tact 6. conversational manner 7. [*pl.*] attentions paid in courting a woman —**ad·dress′er, ad·dres′sor** *n.*

ad·dress·ee (ad′res ē′) *n.* the person to whom a letter, etc., is addressed

ad·duce (ə dyōōs′) *vt.* **-duced′, -duc′ing** [< L. *adducere* < *ad-*, to + *ducere:* see DUCT] to give as a reason or proof; cite —**ad·duc′er** *n.* —**ad·duc′i·ble** *adj.*

ad·duct (a dukt′, ə-) *vt.* [< L. pp. of *adducere:* see prec.] to pull (a part of the body) towards the median axis: said of a muscle —**ad·duc′tor** *n.*

ad·duc·tion (a duk′shən, ə-) *n.* 1. an adducing or citing 2. an adducting

-ade (ād) [ult. < L. *-ata*] a suffix meaning: 1. the act of [*blockade*] 2. the result or product of [*pomade*] 3. participant(s) in an action [*brigade*] 4. [after LEMONADE] drink made from [*limeade*]

ad·e·nine (ad′ən ēn′) *n.* [ADEN(O)- + -INE⁴] a white, crystalline purine base found in nucleic acid in the spleen, pancreas, etc.

ad·e·no- [< Gr. *adēn*, gland] *a combining form meaning* of a gland or glands: also, before a vowel, **aden-**

ad·e·noi·dal (ad′ən oid′′l) *adj.* 1. *a*) glandular *b*) of or like lymphoid tissue: also **ad′e·noid′** 2. having adenoids 3. having the characteristic difficult breathing or nasal tone due to enlarged adenoids

ad·e·noids (ad′ən oidz′) *n.pl.* [< ADEN(O)- & -OID] lymphoid growths in the throat behind the nose: they can swell up and obstruct breathing

ad·e·no·ma (ad′ən ō′mə) *n.* [ADEN(O)- + -OMA] a benign tumour of glandular origin or glandlike cell structure

ADENOIDS

a·den·o·sine (ə den′ə s'n, -sēn′) *n.* [arbitrary blend < ADENINE + RIBOSE] a white crystalline powder obtained from the hydrolysis of yeast nucleic acid: see also ADP¹, ATP

ad·ept (ə dept′; *for n.* ad′ept) *adj.* [< L. pp. of *adipisci* < *ad-*, to + *apisci*, to pursue, attain] highly skilled; expert —*n.* an expert —**ad·ept′ly** *adv.* —**ad·ept′ness** *n.*

ad·e·quate (ad′ə kwət) *adj.* [< L. pp. of *adaequare* < *ad-*, to + *aequare*, to make equal < *aequus*, level] 1. enough or good enough; sufficient; suitable 2. barely satisfactory

—**ad′e·qua·cy** (-kwə sē), **ad′e·quate·ness** *n.* —**ad′e·quate·ly** *adv.*

‡à deux (à dö′) [Fr.] 1. of or for two 2. intimate

ad·here (əd hir′, ad-) *vi.* **-hered′, -her′ing** [< L. *adhaerere* < *ad-*, to + *haerere*, to stick] 1. to stick fast; stay attached 2. to stay firm in supporting or approving; follow closely —**ad·her′er** *n.*

ad·her·ence (əd hir′əns, ad-) *n.* an adhering; attachment or devotion (*to* a person, cause, etc.)

ad·her·ent (-ənt) *adj.* 1. sticking fast; attached 2. *Bot.* grown together —*n.* a supporter or follower (*of* a person, cause, etc.)

ad·he·sion (əd hē′zhən, ad-) *n.* [Fr. < L. *adhaesio* < *adhaerere:* see ADHERE] 1. *a*) a sticking or being stuck together *b*) capacity for sticking 2. devoted attachment; adherence 3. *Med. a*) the joining together, by fibrous tissue, of bodily parts normally separate: usually caused by inflammation *b*) such fibrous tissue 4. *Physics* the force that holds together the molecules of unlike substances in surface contact: distinguished from COHESION

ad·he·sive (əd hē′siv, ad-; -ziv) *adj.* 1. sticking and not coming loose; clinging 2. gummed; sticky —*n.* an adhesive substance, as glue —**ad·he′sive·ly** *adv.* —**ad·he′-sive·ness** *n.*

adhesive tape tape with a sticky substance on one side

ad hoc (ad′hok′) [L., to this] for a special case or purpose only [an ad hoc committee]

ad·i·a·bat·ic (ad′ē ə bat′ik) *adj.* [< Gr. < *a-*, not + *dia*, through + *bainein*, to go] *Physics* involving expansion or compression without loss or gain of heat —*n.* a curve on a graph representing the changes in a system undergoing an adiabatic process —**ad′i·a·bat′i·cal·ly** *adv.*

a·dieu (ə dyōō′; *Fr.* à dyö′) *interj., n., pl.* **a·dieus′**; *Fr.* **a·dieux′** (-dyö′) [Fr. < OFr. < L. *ad*, to + *Deus*, God] goodbye

ad in·fi·ni·tum (ad in′fə nīt′əm) [L., to infinity] endlessly; forever; without limit

ad in·ter·im (ad in′tər im) [L.] 1. in the meantime 2. temporary

a·di·os (a′dē ōs′, ä′-; *Sp.* ä dyôs′) *interj.* [Sp. *adiós* < L. *ad*, to + *Deus*, God] goodbye

ad·i·pose (ad′ə pōs′) *adj.* [< ModL. < L. *adeps* (gen. *adipis*), fat] of, like, or containing animal fat; fatty —*n.* animal fat in the connective tissue —**ad′i·pos′i·ty** (-pos′ə tē) *n.*

ad·it (ad′it) *n.* [< L. pp. of *adire* < *ad-*, to + *ire*, to go] an approach or entrance; specif., an almost horizontal passageway into a mine

adj. 1. adjective 2. adjourned 3. adjutant

ad·ja·cent (ə jā′s'nt) *adj.* [< L. prp. of *adjacere* < *ad-*, to + *jacere*, to lie] near or close (*to* something); adjoining —**ad·ja′cen·cy** *n.* —**ad·ja′cent·ly** *adv.*

adjacent angles two angles having the same vertex and a side in common

ad·jec·tive (aj′ik tiv) *n.* [< L. < pp. of *adjicere*, to add to < *ad-*, to + *jacere*, to throw] any of a class of words used to limit or qualify a noun or other substantive [*good, every*, and *Aegean* are *adjectives*] —*adj.* of, or having the nature or function of, an adjective —**ad′jec·ti′val** (-tī′v'l) *adj.* —**ad′jec·ti′val·ly** *adv.*

ad·join (ə join′) *vt.* [< OFr. < L. *adjungere* < *ad-*, to + *jungere:* see JOIN] to be next to; be contiguous to —*vi.* to be next to each other; be in contact —**ad·join′ing** *adj.*

ad·journ (ə jurn′) *vt.* [< OFr. < *a*, at + *jorn*, day < L. *diurnum*, daily < *dies*, day] to put off or suspend until a future day —*vi.* 1. to close a session or meeting for a time 2. [Colloq.] to go (*to* another place) [let's *adjourn* to the other room] —**ad·journ′ment** *n.*

ad·judge (ə juj′) *vt.* **-judged′, -judg′ing** [< OFr. < L. *adjudicare* < *ad-*, to + *judicare*, to judge < *judex*, JUDGE] 1. to judge or decide by law 2. to declare or order by law 3. to award (costs, etc.) by law 4. [Rare] to regard; deem

ad·ju·di·cate (ə jōō′də kāt′) *vt.* **-cat′ed, -cat′ing** [< L. pp. of *adjudicare:* see prec.] *Law* to hear and decide (a case); adjudge —*vi.* to serve as a judge (*in* or *on* a matter) —**ad·ju′di·ca′tion** *n.* —**ad·ju′di·ca′tive** *adj.* —**ad·ju′di·ca′tor** *n.* —**ad·ju′di·ca·to·ry** (-kā tər ē) *adj.*

ad·junct (aj′uŋkt) *n.* [< L. pp. of *adjungere:* see ADJOIN] 1. a thing added to something else, but secondary 2. a subordinate associate 3. *Gram.* a modifier —*adj.* connected in a subordinate way —**ad·junc′tive** (ə juŋk′tiv) *adj.* —**ad·junc′tive·ly** *adv.* —**ad·junct′ly** *adv.*

ad·jure (ə jōōr′) *vt.* **-jured′, -jur′ing** [< L. *adjurare* < *ad-*, to + *jurare:* see JURY¹] 1. to charge solemnly, often under oath or penalty 2. to entreat earnestly —**ad·ju·ra·tion** (aj′ōō rā′shən) *n.* —**ad·jur′a·to·ry** (-ə tər ē) *adj.* —**ad·jur′er, ad·ju′ror** *n.*

ad·just (ə just′) *vt.* [< OFr. < *a-*, to + *j(o)uster* (see JOUST); infl. by OFr. *juste* < L. *justus*, JUST¹] 1. to change so as to fit, conform, make suitable, etc. 2. to regulate [to *adjust* a watch] 3. to settle or arrange rightly 4. to resolve or bring into accord 5. to decide how much is to be paid on (an insurance claim) —*vi.* to adapt oneself, as to one's surroundings —**ad·just′a·ble** *adj.* —**ad·just′er** *n.*

ad·just·ment (-mənt) *n.* 1. an adjusting or being adjusted 2. a means by which parts are adjusted to one another 3. the settlement of a claim

ad·ju·tant (aj′ə tənt) *n.* [< L. prp. of *adjutare* < *adjuvare* < *ad-*, to + *juvare*, to help] 1. an assistant 2. *Mil.* a staff officer who is an administrative assistant to the commanding officer 3. a large stork of India and Africa

adjutant general *pl.* **adjutants general** 1. an army officer who is the chief administrative assistant of a commanding general 2. the head of a department of general staff 3. [A-G-] *U.S. Army* the general in charge of the department that handles records, correspondence, etc.

Ad·ler·i·an (ad ler′ē ən) *adj.* of or relating to the work of Alfred Adler (1870–1937), Austrian psychiatrist and psychologist —*n.* a follower of Adler

ad·lib (ad′lib′) *vt., vi.* -**libbed′**, -**lib′bing** [< ff.] [Colloq.] to improvise (words, etc. not in the script); extemporize —*n.* [Colloq.] an ad-libbed remark —*adj.* spoken or done extemporaneously —*adv.* 1. [Colloq.] extemporizing freely 2. to any extent; without restriction Also **ad lib**

ad lib·i·tum (ad′lib′i təm) [ML. < L. *ad*, at + *libitum* < *libet*, it pleases] at pleasure; as one pleases: used esp. as a musical direction that a section may be altered to suit the performer

Adm. 1. Admiral 2. Admiralty

ad·man (ad′man′) *n.*, *pl.* -**men** (-men′) a man whose work or business is advertising: also **ad man**

ad·mass (ad′mas) *n.* [AD(VERTISEMENT) + MASS (sense 4)] 1. high pressure advertising directed at a large section of the community by the mass media 2. the section of the community influenced by such advertising —*adj.* 1. characterized by admass 2. influenced by admass

ad·meas·ure (ad me′zhər) *vt.* -**ured**, -**ur·ing** [see AD- & MEASURE] to measure out shares of; apportion —**ad·meas′-ure·ment** *n.*

ad·min (ad′min) *n.* [Colloq.] administration —*adj.* [Colloq.] of or relating to administration

ad·min·is·ter (əd min′ə stər, ad-) *vt.* [< OFr. < L. *administrare* < *ad-*, to + *ministrare*, to serve] 1. to manage or direct 2. to give out or dispense (punishment, etc.) 3. to give or apply (medicine, etc.) 4. to direct the taking of (an oath, pledge, etc.) 5. *Law* to act as executor or administrator of (an estate) —*vi.* 1. to act as manager or administrator 2. to furnish help or be of service —**ad·min′-is·tra·ble** (-ə strə b′l) *adj.* —**ad·min′is·trant** (-ə strənt) *n., adj.*

ad·min·is·trate (əd min′ə strāt′, ad-) *vt.* -**trat′ed**, -**trat′ing** *same as* ADMINISTER

ad·min·is·tra·tion (əd min′ə strā′shən, ad-) *n.* 1. management, specif. of the affairs of a government, business, etc. 2. *a)* the executive officials of a government, business, etc., and their policies *b)* the government 3. the administering (*of* medicine, an oath, etc.) 4. *Law* the management and settling (*of* an estate) —**ad·min′is·tra′tive** *adj.* —**ad·min′is·tra′tive·ly** *adv.*

ad·min·is·tra·tor (əd min′ə strāt′ər, ad-) *n.* 1. one who administers 2. one who has executive ability 3. *Law* one appointed by a court to settle an estate: cf. EXECUTOR —**ad·min′is·tra′trix** (-strā′triks) *n.fem.*, *pl.* -**tra′-tri·ces′** (-tri sēz′), -**trix·es**

ad·mi·ra·ble (ad′mər ə b′l) *adj.* inspiring or deserving admiration or praise; splendid —**ad′mi·ra·bil′i·ty** *n.* —**ad′-mi·ra·bly** *adv.*

ad·mi·ral (ad′mər əl) *n.* [< OFr. < Ar. *amir* a‘ *āli*, high leader; sp. infl. by ADMIRABLE] 1. *see* MILITARY RANKS, table 2. [orig. ADMIRABLE] any of certain colourful butterflies

admiral of the fleet *see* MILITARY RANKS, table

ad·mi·ral·ty (-tē) *n.*, *pl.* -**ties** 1. the rank, position, or authority of an admiral 2. *a)* [often A-] the governmental department for naval affairs, as formerly in Britain *b)* [Colloq.] that part of the Ministry of Defence responsible for naval affairs *c)* maritime law or court

ad·mi·ra·tion (ad′mə rā′shən) *n.* 1. wonder, delight, and pleased approval at anything fine, skilful, beautiful, etc. 2. a thing or person inspiring such feelings

ad·mire (əd mīr′, ad-) *vt.* -**mired′**, -**mir′ing** [< OFr. < L. *admirari* < *ad-*, at + *mirari*, to wonder] 1. to regard with, or express wonder, delight, and approval 2. to have high regard for —**ad·mir′er** *n.* —**ad·mir′ing·ly** *adv.*

ad·mis·si·ble (əd mis′ə b′l, ad-) *adj.* [Fr. < L. pp. of *admittere*, ADMIT] 1. that can be properly accepted or allowed [*admissible* evidence] 2. that ought to be admitted —**ad·mis′si·bil′i·ty** *n.* —**ad·mis′si·bly** *adv.*

ad·mis·sion (əd mish′ən, ad-) *n.* 1. an admitting or being admitted 2. the right to enter 3. an entrance fee 4. a conceding, or granting 5. an acknowledging or confessing 6. a thing conceded, acknowledged, or confessed —**ad·mis′-sive** *adj.*

ad·mit (əd mit′, ad-) *vt.* -**mit′ted**, -**mit′ting** [< L. *admittere* < *ad-*, to + *mittere*, to send] 1. to permit to enter or use 2. to entitle to enter 3. to allow, or leave room for 4. to have room for; hold 5. to concede; grant 6. to

acknowledge or confess 7. to permit to practise [*admitted* to the bar] —*vi.* 1. to give entrance (*to* a place) 2. to allow or warrant (with *of*)

ad·mit·tance (-′ns) *n.* 1. an admitting or being admitted 2. permission or right to enter 3. *Elec.* the reciprocal of impedance

ad·mit·ted·ly (əd mit′id lē) *adv.* by admission or agreement; confessedly [*admittedly* afraid]

ad·mix (ad miks′) *vt., vi.* [< ff.] to mix (a thing) in; mix with something

ad·mix·ture (-chər) *n.* [< L. pp. of *admiscere* < *ad-*, to + *miscere*, to mix + -URE] 1. a mixture 2. a thing or ingredient added in mixing

ad·mon·ish (əd mon′ish, ad-) *vt.* [< OFr. < L. *admonere* < *ad-*, to + *monere*, to warn] 1. to caution against specific faults; warn 2. to reprove mildly 3. to urge or exhort 4. to inform or remind, by way of a warning —**ad·mon′-ish·ing·ly** *adv.* —**ad·mon′ish·ment** *n.*

ad·mo·ni·tion (ad′mə nish′ən) *n.* 1. an admonishing, or warning to correct some fault 2. a mild rebuke; reprimand

ad·mon·i·tor (əd mon′ə tər, ad-) *n.* a person who admonishes —**ad·mon′i·to·ry** (-tər ē) *adj.*

ad nau·se·am (ad′nô′zē əm -sē-) [L., to nausea] to the point of disgust or tedium

a·do (ə do̅o̅′) *n.* [ME. < dial. inf. *at do*, to do] fuss; trouble; excitement

a·do·be (ə dō′bē) *n.* [Sp.] 1. unburnt, sun-dried brick 2. the clay of which such brick is made 3. a building made of adobe

ad·o·les·cence (ad′ə les′′ns) *n.* 1. the state or quality of being adolescent 2. the time of life between puberty and maturity

ad·o·les·cent (-′nt) *adj.* [Fr. < L. prp. of *adolescere*, to mature] 1. developing from childhood to maturity; growing up 2. of or characteristic of adolescence; youthful, exuberant, immature, etc. —*n.* a boy or girl from puberty to adulthood; person in his teens

A·don·is (ə dō′nis) *n.* [after a young man loved by Aphrodite] any very handsome young man —**A·don′ic** (-ik) *adj.*

a·dopt (ə dopt′) *vt.* [< L. *adoptare* < *ad-*, to + *optare*, to choose] 1. to choose and bring into a certain relationship; specif., to take into one's own family by legal process and raise as one's own child 2. to take up and use (an idea, etc.) as one's own 3. to choose and follow (a course) 4. to vote to accept (a motion, candidate, etc.) —**a·dopt′a·ble** *adj.* —**a·dopt′er** *n.* —**a·dop′tion** *n.*

a·dop·tive (ə dop′tiv) *adj.* 1. of adoption 2. having become so by adopting [*adoptive* parents]

a·dor·a·ble (ə dôr′ə b′l) *adj.* 1. [Now Rare] worthy of adoration 2. [Colloq.] delightful; charming —**a·dor′a·bil′-i·ty** *n.* —**a·dor′a·bly** *adv.*

ad·o·ra·tion (ad′ôr ā′shən, ad′ə rā′-) *n.* 1. a worshipping or paying homage 2. great love or devotion

a·dore (ə dôr′) *vt.* **a·dored′**, **a·dor′ing** [< OFr. < L. *adorare* < *ad-*, to + *orare*, to speak] 1. to worship as divine 2. to love or honour greatly; idolize 3. [Colloq.] to like very much —**a·dor′er** *n.* —**a·dor′ing·ly** *adv.*

a·dorn (ə dôrn′) *vt.* [< OFr. < L. *adornare* < *ad-*, to + *ornare*, to deck out] 1. to be an ornament to; add beauty or distinction to 2. to put decorations on; ornament —**a·dorn′-ment** *n.*

ADP¹ [A(DENOSINE) *d(i)p(hosphate)*] a vital substance of all living cells, that is essential to the energy processes of life

ADP² Automatic Data Processing

‡ad rem (ad′rem′) [L.] to the point

ad·re·nal (ə drē′n′l) *adj.* [AD- + RENAL] 1. near the kidneys 2. of or from the adrenal glands —*n.* *same as* ADRENAL GLAND

adrenal gland either of a pair of endocrine organs lying immediately above the kidney and producing a variety of hormones

ad·ren·al·in (ə dren′′l in) [ADRENAL + -IN¹] 1. a hormone secreted by the adrenal gland, that stimulates the heart, increases muscular strength, etc. 2. this substance extracted from animal adrenals or prepared synthetically for therapeutic use Also **ad·ren′al·ine** (-in)

ad·re·no- a combining form meaning: 1. adrenal glands 2. adrenalin Also, before a vowel, **adren-**

a·drift (ə drift′) *adv., adj.* 1. floating freely without being steered; drifting 2. without any particular aim or purpose 3. [Colloq.] wrong; amiss [the project went *adrift*]

a·droit (ə droit′) *adj.* [Fr. à, to + *droit*, right < L. *directus*, pp. of *dirigere*, DIRECT] skilful in a physical or mental way; clever —**a·droit′ly** *adv.* —**a·droit′ness** *n.*

ad·sorb (ad sôrb′, -zôrb′) *vt.* [< AD- + L. *sorbere* (cf. ABSORB)] to collect (a gas, liquid, or dissolved substance) in condensed form on a surface —**ad·sorb′a·ble** *adj.* —**ad·sor′-bent** *adj., n.*

ad·sorp·tion (ad sôrp′shən, -zôrp′-) *n.* adhesion of the molecules of a gas, liquid, or dissolved substance to a surface —**ad·sorp′tive** *adj.*

ad·u·late (ad′yoo lāt′) *vt.* -**lat′ed**, -**lat′ing** [< L. pp. of *adulari*, to fawn upon] to praise or flatter too greatly —**ad′u·la′tion** *n.* —**ad′u·la′tor** *n.* —**ad′u·la·to·ry** (-lə tər ē) *adj.*

a·dult (ə dult′, ad′ult) *adj.* [< L. pp. of *adolescere*: see ADOLESCENT] **1.** grown up; fully developed in size, strength, mind, etc. **2.** of or for adult persons —*n.* **1.** a mature person **2.** a mature animal or plant **3.** a person who has reached the age at which he has full legal rights and responsibilities —**a·dult′hood** *n.* —**a·dult′ness** *n.*

a·dul·ter·ant (ə dul′tər ənt) *n.* a substance used to adulterate something —*adj.* adulterating

a·dul·ter·ate (ə dul′tə rāt′) *vt.* **-at′ed, -at′ing** [< L. pp. of *adulterare*, to falsify < *adulter*, adulterer, counterfeiter < *ad-*, to + *alter*, other] to make inferior, impure, etc. by adding a harmful, inferior, or unnecessary substance —**a·dul′ter·a′tion** *n.* —**a·dul′ter·a′tor** *n.*

a·dul·ter·er (ə dul′tər ər) *n.* a person (esp. a man) who commits adultery —**a·dul′ter·ess** *n.fem.*

a·dul·ter·ine (ə dul′tər in, -tə rīn′) *adj.* **1.** of adultery **2.** of adulteration

a·dul·ter·ous (-əs) *adj.* of, or having committed, adultery —**a·dul′ter·ous·ly** *adv.*

a·dul·ter·y (ə dul′tər ē) *n.,* *pl.* **-ter·ies** [L. *adulterium* < *adulter:* see ADULTERATE] voluntary sexual intercourse between a married person and another not the spouse

ad·um·brate (ad um′brāt, ad′əm brāt′) *vt.* **-brat·ed, -brat·ing** [< L. pp. of *adumbrari* < *ad-*, to + *umbra*, shade] **1.** to outline vaguely; sketch **2.** to foreshadow vaguely **3.** to obscure; overshadow —**ad′um·bra′tion** *n.* —**ad·um′bra·tive** *adj.*

adv. 1. adverb **2.** adverbial **3.** advertisement **4.** advisory **5.** advocate

ad va·lo·rem (ad′və lôr′əm) [L.] in proportion to the value: said of duties levied on imports according to their invoiced value: abbrev. **ad val.**

ad·vance (əd väns′) *vt.* **-vanced′, -vanc′ing** [< OFr. *avancer*, to forward < L. *ab-*, from + *ante*, before] **1.** to bring or move forwards **2.** to raise in rank, importance, etc. **3.** to help; further **4.** to put forward; propose **5.** to cause to happen earlier **6.** to raise the rate of **7.** to pay (money) before due **8.** to lend —*vi.* **1.** to go forward **2.** to improve; progress; develop **3.** to rise in rank, importance, price, etc. —*n.* **1.** a moving forwards **2.** an improvement; progress **3.** a rise in value or cost **4.** [*pl.*] approaches to gain favour, become acquainted, etc. **5.** a payment made before due, as of wages **6.** a loan —*adj.* **1.** in front [*advance* guard] **2.** beforehand [*advance* information] —**in advance 1.** in front **2.** ahead of time

advance copy a copy of a book, etc., sent out before publication

ad·vanced (əd vänst′) *adj.* **1.** in advance; in front **2.** far on in life; old **3.** ahead or beyond in progress, complexity, etc. [*advanced* studies] **4.** considered to be progressive in opinion [*advanced* views] **5.** higher than usual [*advanced* prices]

advanced level a subject taken at the higher standard of the General Certificate of Education, usually by people of about 18

ad·vance·ment (əd väns′mənt) *n.* **1.** an advancing or being advanced **2.** promotion, as to a higher rank **3.** progress or improvement; furtherance

ad·van·tage (əd vän′tij) *n.* [< OFr. < *avant*, before < L. *ab ante*, from before] **1.** a more favourable position; superiority or a better chance **2.** a favourable circumstance, event, etc. **3.** gain or benefit [turn to *advantage*] **4.** *Tennis* the first point scored after deuce —*vt.* **-taged, -tag·ing** to give an advantage to —**take advantage of 1.** to use for one's own benefit **2.** to impose upon the weakness, good nature, etc. of **3.** to seduce —**to advantage** so as to result in a good effect

ad·van·ta·geous (ad′vən tā′jəs) *adj.* favourable; profitable —**ad′van·ta′geous·ly** *adv.*

ad·vec·tion (ad vek′shən) *n.* [AD- + (CON)VECTION] the transference of heat by horizontal currents of air —**ad·vec′tive** *adj.*

Ad·vent (ad′vent) *n.* [< L. pp. of *advenire* < *ad-*, to + *venire*, to come] **1.** the period including the four Sundays just before Christmas **2.** *Theol.* a) Christ's birth b) same as SECOND COMING **3.** [a-] a coming or arrival

Ad·vent·ist (ad′vən tist) *n.* a member of a Christian sect based on the belief that Christ's second coming will soon occur —**Ad′vent·ism** *n.*

ad·ven·ti·tious (ad′ven tish′əs, ad′vən-) *adj.* [< L., coming from abroad: see ADVENT] **1.** added from outside; accidental **2.** *Biol.* occurring in unusual or abnormal places [*adventitious* leaves on a plant] —**ad′ven·ti′tious·ly** *adv.* —**ad′ven·ti′tious·ness** *n.*

ad·ven·tive (ad ven′tiv) *adj.* *Bot.* not native to the environment

ad·ven·ture (əd ven′chər) *n.* [< OFr. < L. *advenire:* see ADVENT] **1.** the encountering of, or a liking for, danger **2.** an exciting and dangerous undertaking **3.** an unusual, stirring experience, often of a romantic nature **4.** a

business venture or speculation —*vt.* **-tured, -tur·ing** to risk or venture —*vi.* **1.** to engage in adventure **2.** to take a risk

adventure playground a playground where children make imaginative use of everyday materials in building, climbing, etc.

ad·ven·tur·er (-ər) *n.* **1.** a person who has or likes to have adventures **2.** same as SOLDIER OF FORTUNE **3.** a financial speculator **4.** a person who seeks to become rich, powerful, etc. by dubious schemes —**ad·ven′tur·ess** *n.fem.*

ad·ven·ture·some (-səm) *adj.* willing to take risks; adventurous

ad·ven·tur·ism (-iz′m) *n.* actions, esp. in international relations, regarded as reckless and risky —**ad·ven′tur·ist** *n., adj.*

ad·ven·tur·ous (-əs) *adj.* **1.** fond of adventure; daring **2.** full of danger; risky —**ad·ven′tur·ous·ly** *adv.* —**ad·ven′·tur·ous·ness** *n.*

ad·verb (ad′vurb) *n.* [< L. *adverbium* < *ad-*, to + *verbum*, a word] any of a class of words used to modify a verb, adjective, or another adverb, by expressing time, place, manner, degree, cause, etc. —**ad·ver′bi·al** *adj., n.* —**ad·ver′·bi·al·ly** *adv.*

ad·ver·sar·y (ad′vər sər ē) *n.,* *pl.* **-sar′ies** [< OFr. < L. < *adversus*, ADVERSE] a person who opposes or fights against another; opponent; enemy

ad·ver·sa·tive (ad vur′sə tiv, əd-) *adj.* [< LL. < L. pp. of *adversari*, to be opposed to] expressing opposition or antithesis —*n.* an adversative word, such as *but, yet, however*

ad·verse (ad′vərs) *adj.* [< OFr. < L. *adversus*, turned opposite to, pp. of *advertere:* see ADVERT[1]] **1.** opposite in position or direction **2.** unfavourable; harmful —**ad·verse′·ly** *adv.*

ad·ver·si·ty (ad vur′sə tē, əd-) *n.* **1.** a state of wretchedness; poverty and trouble **2.** *pl.* **-ties** an instance of misfortune; calamity

ad·vert[1] (ad vurt′, əd-) *vi.* [< OFr. < L. *advertere* < *ad-*, to + *vertere*, to turn: see VERSE] to call attention (*to*); refer or allude

ad·vert[2] (ad′vurt) *n.* [Colloq.] an advertisement, esp. one which is shown on television

ad·vert·ent (-ad vurt′′nt, əd-) *adj.* attentive; heedful —**ad·vert′ence, ad·vert′en·cy** *n.* —**ad·vert′ent·ly** *adv.*

ad·ver·tise (ad′vər tīz′) *vt.* **-tised′, -tis′ing** [< OFr. *advertir*, to call attention to < L. *advertere:* see ADVERT] **1.** to tell about or praise (a product, etc.), as through newspapers, television, or the like, so as to promote sales **2.** to make known —*vi.* **1.** to call the public's attention to things for sale, for rent, etc., as by printed notices **2.** to ask (*for*) publicly by printed notice, etc. [*advertise* for a maid] —**ad′·ver·tis′er** *n.*

ad·ver·tise·ment (əd vur′tiz mənt) *n.* **1.** the act of advertising **2.** a public announcement, usually paid for, as of things for sale, needs, etc.

ad·ver·tis·ing (ad′vər tī′ziŋ) *n.* **1.** printed or spoken matter that advertises **2.** the business or work of preparing and issuing advertisements

ad·ver·tize (ad′vər tīz′) *vt., vi.* **-tized′, -tiz′ing** *U.S. var sp. of* ADVERTISE —**ad·ver·tize·ment** (ad′vər tīz′mənt) *n.*

ad·vice (əd vīs′) *n.* [< OFr. < ML. *advisum* < pp. of *advidere* < L. < *ad-*, at + *videre*, to look] **1.** opinion given as to what to do; counsel **2.** notification of transaction **3.** [*usually pl.*] information or report —**take advice 1.** to act in accordance with advice received **2.** to seek advice from a specialist

ad·vis·a·ble (əd vī′zə b′l) *adj.* proper to be advised or recommended; being good advice —**ad·vis′a·bil′i·ty** *n.* —**ad·vis′a·bly** *adv.*

ad·vise (əd vīz′) *vt.* **-vised′, -vis′ing** [< OFr. < ML. *advisum:* see ADVICE] **1.** to give advice to; counsel **2.** to offer as advice; recommend **3.** to notify; inform —*vi.* **1.** [Chiefly U.S.] to discuss or consult (*with*) **2.** to give advice —**ad·vis′er, ad·vi′sor** *n.*

ad·vised (əd vīzd′) *adj.* showing or resulting from thought or advice: now chiefly in WELL-ADVISED, ILL-ADVISED

ad·vis·ed·ly (əd vī′zid lē) *adv.* with due consideration; deliberately

ad·vi·so·ry (əd vī′zər ē) *adj.* **1.** advising or empowered to advise **2.** relating to, or containing, advice

ad·vo·caat (ad′võ kä′, -kät′; ad′və-) *n.* [Du.] a liqueur with a raw egg base

ad·vo·ca·cy (ad′və kə sē) *n.* an advocating; a speaking or writing in support (*of* something)

ad·vo·cate (ad′və kit, -kāt′; *for v.*-kät′) *n.* [< OFr. < L. *advocatus*, a counsellor < *ad-*, to + *vocare*, to call] **1.** a person who pleads another's cause, esp. in a law court **2.** a person who speaks or writes in support of something —*vt.* **-cat′ed, -cat′ing** to speak or write in support of; be in favour of —**ad′vo·ca′tor** *n.*

ad·vow·son (ad vou′z′n) *n.* [ME. & OFr. *avoueson* < L. *advocatio*, a summoning] the right to name the holder of a benefice

advt. *pl.* **advts.** advertisement

adze (adz) *n.* [OE. *adesa*] an axelike tool for trimming and smoothing wood, etc., with a curved blade at right angles to the handle

AEA, A.E.A. Atomic Energy Authority

A.E.C., AEC [U.S.] Atomic Energy Commission

a·e·des (ā ē′dēz) *n., pl.* **a·e′des** [ModL. < Gr. *aēdēs* < *a*-, not + *hēdys*, sweet] any of a large genus of mosquitoes, esp. one that carries the virus of yellow fever

ADZE

ae·dile (ē′dīl) *n.* [< L. < *aedes*, building] in ancient Rome, an official in charge of buildings, roads, public games, etc.

ae·gis (ē′jis) *n.* [L. < Gr. *aigis*, goatskin] 1. *Gr. Myth.* a shield borne by Zeus and, later, by Athena 2. a protection 3. sponsorship; auspices

ae·gro·tat (ī′grō tat, ē-) *n.* [L., lit., he is ill] 1. a certificate allowing a candidate to pass an examination although he has missed all or part of it through illness 2. an examination pass gained in such circumstances

-ae·mi·a (ē′mē ə) [ModL. < Gr. *haima*, blood] *a suffix* meaning a (specified) condition or disease of the blood [leukaemia]

Ae·ne·id (i nē′əd) a Latin epic poem by Virgil, about the adventures of Aeneas, a Trojan warrior who escaped from ruined Troy and wandered for years before coming to Latium

ae·o·li·an (ē ō′lē ən) *adj.* [after *Aeolus*, in Gr. myth. the god of the winds] of the wind

aeolian harp a boxlike stringed instrument that makes musical sounds when air blows on it

ae·o·lo·trop·ic (ē′ə lə trop′ik) *adj.* [< Gr. *aiolos*, varying + -TROPIC] *same as* ANISTROPIC —**ae′o·lot′ro·py** (-lo′trə pē) *n.*

ae·on (ē′ən, ē′on) *n.* [LL. < Gr. *aiōn*, an age, lifetime] 1. an extremely long, indefinite period of time 2. *Geol.* a period of 10⁹ years

ae·o·ni·an (ē ō′nē ən) *adj.* lasting for aeons; eternal

aer·ate (er′āt′, ā′ər-) *vt.* **-at·ed, -at·ing** [AER(O)- + -ATE¹] 1. to expose to air, or cause air to circulate through 2. to supply oxygen to (the blood) by respiration 3. to charge (liquid) with gas, as in making soda water —**aer′a·tion** *n.* —**aer′a·tor** *n.*

aeri- *same as* AERO-

aer·i·al (er′ē əl; *occas. for adj.* ā ir′ē əl) *adj.* [< L. *aerius* < *aer* (see AIR) + -AL] 1. of, in, or by the air 2. like air; light as air 3. not substantial; unreal; imaginary 4. high up 5. of, for, or by means of aircraft or flying 6. growing in the air instead of in soil or water —*n.* Radio & T.V. an arrangement of wires, metal rods, etc. used in sending and receiving electromagnetic waves —**aer′i·al·ly** *adv.*

aer·i·al·ist (er′ē əl ist) *n.* an acrobat who performs on a trapeze, high wire, etc.

aer·ie (er′ē, ir′ē) *n.* *same as* EYRIE

aer·i·form (er′ə fôrm) *adj.* like air, esp. insubstantial

aer·o (er′ō, ā′ər ō′) *adj.* of or for aeronautics or aircraft

aer·o- [< Gr. *aēr*, air] *a combining form meaning:* 1. air; of the air [*aerolite*] 2. of aircraft or flying [*aerostatics*] 3. of gases [*aerodynamics*]

aer·o·bat·ics (er′ə bat′iks) *n.pl.* [AERO-+ (ACRO)BATICS] spectacular manoeuvres performed in aircraft —**aer′o·bat′-ic** *adj.*

aer·obe (er′ōb) *n.* [< AERO- + Gr. *bios*, life] a microorganism that can live and grow only where free oxygen is present —**aer·o′bic** *adj.*

aer·o·drome (er′ə drōm′) *n.* [AERO-+ -DROME] a landing area for aircraft, with its buildings, etc.; usually smaller than an airport

aer·o·dy·nam·ics (er′ō dī nam′iks) *n.pl.* [with *sing. v.*] the branch of aeromechanics dealing with the forces exerted by air or other gases in motion —**aer′o·dy·nam′ic** *adj.* —**aer′-o·dy·nam′i·cal·ly** *adv.* —**aer′o·dy·nam′i·cist** *n.*

aer·o·em·bo·lism (er′ō em′bə liz′m) *n.* 1. *same as* DECOMPRESSION SICKNESS 2. nitrogen bubbles formed in the blood during decompression sickness

aer·o·en·gine (er′ō en′jin) *n.* an engine for powering an aircraft, esp. a jet engine

aer·o·foil (-foil′) *n.* a part with a flat or curved surface, as a wing, rudder, etc., used to keep an aircraft up or control its movements

aer·o·lite (er′ə līt′) *n.* [AERO- + -LITE] a stony meteorite —**aer′o·lit′ic** (-lit′ik) *adj.*

aer·ol·o·gy (er ol′ə jē) *n.* [AERO- + -LOGY] the branch of meteorology concerned with the study of air, esp. in the upper atmosphere —**aer·o·log′i·cal** (er ə loj′ik′l) *adj.*

aer·o·me·chan·ics (er′ō mə kan′iks) *n.pl.* [with *sing. v.*] the branch of mechanics dealing with air or other gases in motion or equilibrium: it includes aerodynamics and aerostatics —**aer′o·me·chan′ic** *adj.*

aer·o·nau·tics (er′ə nôt′iks) *n.pl.* [with *sing. v.*] [AERO- + Gr. *nautēs*, sailor + -ICS] the science, art, or work of designing, making, and operating aircraft —**aer′o·nau′ti·cal, aer′o·nau′tic** *adj.* —**aer′o·nau′ti·cal·ly** *adv.*

aer·o·pause (er′ō pôz′) *n.* a region at the upper level of the earth's atmosphere, regarded as the boundary between the atmosphere and outer space

aer·o·plane (er′ə plān′) *n.* [Fr. *aéroplane* < *aéro*-, AERO- + base of *planer*, to soar] an aircraft, heavier than air, that is kept aloft by the aerodynamic forces of air upon its wings and is driven forward by a screw propeller, by jet propulsion, etc.

aer·o·sol (-sol′) *n.* [AERO- + SOL³] 1. a suspension of colloidal particles in a gas 2. a spray can dispensing deodorant, paint, etc. under pressure —*adj.* of or dispensed by a container in which gas under pressure is used to aerate liquid and eject it as a spray or foam

aer·o·space (er′ō spās′) *n.* [altered < AIR + SPACE] the earth's atmosphere and the space outside it, considered as one continuous field —*adj.* 1. of aerospace 2. of spacecraft or missiles designed for flight in aerospace

aer·o·stat (-stat′) *n.* [< Fr.: see AERO- & -STAT] a dirigible, balloon, or other airship that is lifted by a contained gas lighter than air

aer·o·stat·ics (er′ō stat′iks) *n.pl.* [with *sing. v.*] the branch of aeromechanics dealing with the equilibrium of air or other gases, and with the equilibrium of solid bodies floating in air or other gases —**aer′o·stat′ic** *adj.*

ae·ru·gi·nous (i roo′ji nəs) *adj.* [L. *aeruginosus* < *aerugo* < *aes*, copper] bluish-green, like verdigris

aer·y (er′ē, ir′ē) *n.* *same as* EYRIE

Aes·chy·le·an (ēs′kə lē′ən) *adj.* of or relating to the works of Aeschylus (525?–456 B.C.), Gr. writer of tragedies

Aes·cu·la·pi·an (ēs′kyoo lā′pē ən) *adj.* [after *Aesculapius,* Rom. god of medicine and healing] of or relating to the art of medicine

aes·the·si·a (es thē′zhə, -zhē ə, zē ə) *n.* [ModL. < Gr. *aisthēsis,* perception] the ability to feel sensations

aes·thete (ēs′thēt′) *n.* [Gr. *aisthētēs,* one who perceives] 1. a person highly sensitive to art and beauty 2. a person who artificially cultivates artistic sensitivity or makes a cult of art and beauty —**aes·thet′i·cism** (es thet′ə siz′m) *n.*

aes·thet·ic (ēs thet′ik) *adj.* 1. of aesthetics 2. of beauty 3. sensitive to art and beauty; artistic Also **aes·thet′i·cal** —*n.* the aesthetic principle —**aes·thet′i·cal·ly** *adv.*

aes·thet·ics (-iks) *n.pl.* [with *sing. v.*] the study or theory of beauty and of the psychological responses to it; specif., the branch of philosophy dealing with art and its forms, effects, etc.

aes·ti·val (es′tə v'l, es tī′v'l) *adj.* [L. *aestivalis* < *aestivus* < *aestas,* summer] of or for summer

aes·ti·vate (ēs′tə vāt′) *vi.* **-vat′ed, -vat′ing** [< L. pp. of *aestivare* < *aestas:* see prec.] 1. to spend the summer 2. to pass the summer in a dormant condition: opposed to HIBERNATE —**aes′ti·va′tion** *n.*

aet., aetat. [L. *aetatis*] at the age of

ae·ther (ē′thər) *n.* earlier var. of ETHER (senses 1 & 3) —**ae·the·re·al** (i thir′ē əl) *adj.*

ae·ti·ol·o·gy (ēt′ē ol′ə jē) *n.* [LL. < Gr. < *aitia,* cause + *logos,* discourse] 1. the philosophy or study of causation 2. *Med.* the study of the causes of diseases

a.f., A.F. audio-frequency

a·far (ə fär′) *adv.* [Poet. or Archaic] at or to a distance —**from afar** from a distance

A.F.C., AFC 1. Air Force Cross 2. Association Football Club 3. automatic frequency control

a·feard, a·feared (ə fird′) *adj.* [< OE. < *a*- (intens.) + *faeran,* to frighten] [Dial. or Archaic] frightened; afraid

af·fa·ble (af′ə b'l) *adj.* [< L. *affabilis* < *ad*-, to + *fari,* to speak] 1. easy to approach and talk to; friendly 2. gentle and kindly [an *affable* smile] —**af′fa·bil′i·ty** *n.* —**af′fa·bly** *adv.*

af·fair (ə fer′) *n.* [< OFr. < *à faire,* to do < L. *ad*-, to + *facere,* to do] 1. a thing to be done; business 2. [*pl.*] matters of business or concern 3. any matter, occurrence, or thing 4. an event arousing public controversy 5. a social gathering 6. a sexual relationship outside marriage

af·fect¹ (ə fekt′; *for n.* af′ekt) *vt.* [< L. *affectare,* to strive after < pp. of *afficere,* to influence < *ad*-, to + *facere,* to do] 1. to have an effect on; influence 2. to move or stir the emotions of —*n.* Psychol. emotion or emotional response

af·fect² (ə fekt′) *vt.* [< OFr. < L. *affectare,* AFFECT¹] 1. to like to have, use, wear, etc. [she *affects* plaid coats] 2. to pretend to have, feel, like, etc.; feign [to *affect* indifference]

af·fec·ta·tion (af′ek tā′shən) *n.* 1. an affecting or pretending to like, have, etc.; show or pretence 2. artificial behaviour meant to impress others

af·fect·ed¹ (ə fek′tid) *adj.* 1. attacked by disease 2. influenced; acted upon 3. emotionally moved

af·fect·ed² (ə fek′tid) *adj.* 1. assumed for effect; artificial 2. behaving in an artificial way to impress people —**af·fect′-ed·ly** *adv.* —**af·fect′ed·ness** *n.*

af·fect·ing (ə fek′tiŋ) *adj.* emotionally touching; causing one to feel pity, sympathy, etc.

af·fec·tion (ə fek′shən) *n.* 1. a tendency or disposition 2.

fond or tender feeling; warm liking **3.** a disease; ailment **4.** an affecting or being affected

af·fec·tion·ate (-it) *adj.* full of affection; tender and loving —**af·fec′tion·ate·ly** *adv.*

af·fec·tive (ə fek′tiv) *adj.* of affects, or feelings; emotional —**af·fec′tive·ly** *adv.* —**af·fec·tiv·i·ty** (af′ek tiv′ə tē) *n.*

af·fer·ent (af′ər ənt) *adj.* [< L. prp. of *afferre* < *ad*-, to + *ferre*, to BEAR¹] *Physiol.* bringing inward to a central part; specif., designating nerves that transmit impulses towards a nerve centre: opposed to EFFERENT

af·fi·ance (ə fī′əns) *vt.* -anced, -anc·ing [< OFr. *afier* < ML. < *ad*-, to + *fidare*, to trust] to pledge, esp. in marriage; betroth

af·fi·da·vit (af′ə dā′vit) *n.* [ML., he has made oath] a written statement made on oath before an authorized person

af·fil·i·ate (ə fil′ē āt′; *for n.* -it) *vt.* -at′ed, -at′ing [< ML. pp. of *affiliare*, to adopt as a son < L. *ad*-, + *filius*, son] **1.** to take in as a member or branch **2.** to connect or associate (oneself *with*) **3.** to trace the origins or source of —*vi.* to associate oneself; join —*n.* an affiliated person or organization —**af·fil′i·a′tion** *n.*

affiliation order a court order that a man judged to be the father of an illegitimate child should contribute to its maintenance

af·fin·i·ty (ə fin′ə tē) *n.*, *pl.* -ties [< OFr. < L. < *affinis*, adjacent < *ad*-, to + *finis*, end] **1.** relationship by marriage **2.** close relationship; connection **3.** a similarity of structure implying common origin **4.** a natural liking; esp., a mutual attraction between a man and a woman **5.** the force that causes the atoms of certain elements to combine and stay combined —**af·fin′i·tive** *adj.*

af·firm (ə furm′) *vt.* [< OFr. < L. *affirmare* < *ad*-, to + *firmare*, to make firm] **1.** to declare positively; assert to be true **2.** to confirm; ratify (a law, decision, or judgment) —*vi.* *Law* to declare solemnly, but not under oath —**af·firm′a·ble** *adj.* —**af·firm′er**, *Law* **af·firm′ant** *n.*

af·fir·ma·tion (af′ər mā′shən) *n.* **1.** an affirming **2.** a positive declaration; assertion **3.** *Law* a solemn declaration, but not under oath, made by one having conscientious objections to taking oaths

af·firm·a·tive (ə fur′mə tiv) *adj.* **1.** answering "yes" **2.** bold or positive, as in asserting —*n.* **1.** a word or expression indicating assent or agreement **2.** an affirmative statement —**af·firm′a·tive·ly** *adv.*

af·fix (ə fiks′; *for n.* af′iks) *vt.* [< L. pp. of *affigere* < *ad*-, to + *figere*, fix] **1.** to fasten; attach **2.** to add at the end —*n.* **1.** a thing affixed **2.** a prefix, suffix, or infix —**af′fix·al** *adj.* —**af·fix′ture** *n.*

af·fla·tus (ə flāt′əs) *n.* [L. < pp. of *afflare* < *ad*-, to + *flare*, to blow] inspiration, as of an artist

af·flict (ə flikt′) *vt.* [< L. *afflictare* < pp. of *affligere* < *ad*-, to + *fligere*, to strike] to cause pain or suffering to; distress very much

af·flic·tion (ə flik′shən) *n.* **1.** an afflicted condition; pain; suffering **2.** anything causing pain or distress; calamity

af·flic·tive (-tiv) *adj.* causing pain or misery —**af·flic′tive·ly** *adv.*

af·flu·ence (af′loo wəns) *n.* [< L < *affluere* < *ad*-, to + *fluere*, to flow] **1.** great plenty; abundance **2.** abundant riches; wealth; opulence

af·flu·ent (-wənt) *adj.* **1.** plentiful; abundant **2.** wealthy; rich —*n.* a stream flowing into a river; tributary —**af′-flu·ent·ly** *adv.*

affluent society a community in which the majority of people are able to enjoy a high standard of living

af·flux (af′luks) *n.* a flow towards a point

af·ford (ə fôrd′) *vt.* [OE. *geforthian*, to advance < *forthian*, to further] **1.** to have enough or the means for; bear the cost of without serious inconvenience: usually with *can* or *be able* **2.** to be able (to do something) with little risk **3.** to give; yield; furnish [it affords much pleasure]

af·for·est (ə for′əst) *vt.* [ML. *afforestare*] to turn (land) into forest; plant many trees on

af·fran·chise (ə fran′chīz) *vt.* -chised′, -chis′ing [< OFr. *afranchir*] to make free

af·fray (ə frā′) *n.* [< OFr. < *esfraer*, to frighten < L. *ex*, out of + Gmc. base *frith*-, peace] a noisy brawl or quarrel; riot

af·fri·cate (af′rə kit) *n.* [< L. pp. of *affricare* < *ad*-, to + *fricare*, to rub] *Phonet.* a sound produced when a slowly released stop consonant is followed immediately by a fricative, as the (ch) in *latch* —**af·fric·a·tive** (ə frik′ə tiv) *n.*, *adj.*

af·fright (ə frīt′) *vt.* [Archaic] to frighten; terrify —*n.* [Archaic] great fright or terror

af·front (ə frunt′) *vt.* [< OFr. *afronter*, to strike in the face < ML. < *ad*-, to + *frons*, forehead] **1.** to insult openly or on purpose **2.** to confront defiantly —*n.* an open or intentional insult

Af·ghan (af′gan, -gən) *n.* **1.** a native of Afghanistan **2.** *former name of* PASHTO (language of Afghanistan) **3.** any of a breed of hunting dog with silky hair and a long, narrow head: also **Afghan hound 4.** [a-] a soft blanket or shawl,

crocheted or knitted, esp. in a geometrical design —*adj.* of Afghanistan, its people, etc.

af·ghan·i (af gan′ē) *n.*, *pl.* -is *see* MONETARY UNITS, table (Afghanistan)

a·fi·cio·na·do (ə fish′ə nä′dō, -fis′ē ə-; *Sp.* ä fē′syô nä′thô) *n.*, *pl.* -dos (-dōz; *Sp.* -thôs) [Sp., pp. of *aficionar*, to be devoted to < L. *affectio*, warm liking] a devoted follower of some sport, art, etc.; fan

a·field (ə fēld′) *adv.* **1.** in, on, or to the field **2.** away (from home) **3.** off the right path; astray

a·fire (ə fīr′) *adv., adj.* **1.** on fire **2.** greatly excited

a·flame (ə flām′) *adv., adj.* **1.** in flames **2.** glowing **3.** greatly excited

a·float (ə flōt′) *adv.* **1.** floating freely **2.** on board ship; at sea **3.** flooded [the deck is *afloat*] **4.** drifting about **5.** in circulation [rumours are *afloat*] **6.** [Colloq.] free of trouble, debt, etc.

a·flut·ter (ə flut′ər) *adv., adj.* in a flutter

A.F.M. Air Force Medal

a·foot (ə foot′) *adv.* **1.** on foot; walking **2.** in motion or operation; in progress; astir

a·fore (ə fôr′) *adv., prep., conj.* [Archaic or Dial. except in compounds and nautical use] before

a·fore·men·tione (ə fôr′men′shənd) *adj.* mentioned before or previously

a·fore·said (-sed′) *adj.* spoken of before; mentioned previously

a·fore·thought (-thôt′) *adj.* thought out beforehand; premeditated

a for·ti·o·ri (ā fôr′tē ôr′ē, -shē ôr′ī) [L., for a stronger (reason)] all the more: said of a conclusion following with even greater logical necessity another already accepted

Afr. **1.** Africa **2.** African

a·fraid (ə frād′) *adj.* [< ME. pp. of *affraien*, to frighten] feeling fear; frightened (with *of, that,* or an infinitive): often used colloquially to indicate regret [I'm afraid I can't go]

a·freet (af′rēt, ə frēt′) *n.* [Ar. '*ifrīt*] *Arabic Myth.* a strong, evil demon: also sp. **af′rit**

a·fresh (ə fresh′) *adv.* again; anew

Af·ri·can (af′ri kən) *adj.* of Africa, its peoples, their cultures, etc. —*n.* **1.** a member of an indigenous ethnic group of Africa **2.** any native or inhabitant of Africa

African violet any of several tropical African plants with violet, pink, or white flowers and hairy, dark-green leaves, often grown as house plants

Af·ri·kaans (af′ri känz′, -käns′, -kanz′) *n.* [Afrik. < *Afrika*, Africa] an official language of South Africa, a development from 17th-cent. Dutch

Af·ri·ka·ner (af′ri kän′ər) *n.* [Du.] a South African of European, esp. Dutch, ancestry; Boer

Af·ro (af′rō) *adj.* [< ff.] designating or of a full, bouffant hair style, orig. modelled on a Negro style

Af·ro- *a combining form meaning:* **1.** Africa **2.** African Also, before a vowel, **Afr-**

Af·ro-A·mer·i·can (af′rō ə mer′ə kən) *adj.* of Negro Americans, their culture, etc. —*n.* a Negro American

af·ror·mos·i·a (af′rôr mōz′ē ə) *n.* [ModL. < AFR(O) + *Ormosia*, a genus of trees] **1.** a tree native to Africa **2.** the wood of this tree, resembling teak

aft (aft) *adv.* [< OE. < *afta*, behind] at, near, or towards the stern of a ship or rear of an aircraft

af·ter (äf′tər) *adv.* [OE. *æfter* < *of,* off + *-ter*, old compar. suffix] behind in place or time; later or next —*prep.* **1.** behind in place **2.** later in time; next **3.** in search of **4.** as a result of [after what has happened, he won't go] **5.** in spite of [after all his bad luck, he is still cheerful] **6.** following next to in rank or importance **7.** in the manner of [a novel after Dickens' style] **8.** for; in honour of [named after his grandfather] **9.** concerning [she asked after you] —*conj.* following the time when —*adj.* **1.** next; later **2.** nearer the rear (esp. of a ship or aircraft) —**after all 1.** when everything is considered [after all, it didn't matter] **2.** nevertheless [he did come after all]

af·ter·birth (-burth′) *n.* the placenta and foetal membranes expelled from the womb after childbirth

af·ter·burn·er (-bur′nər) *n.* **1.** a device for obtaining additional thrust in a jet engine by using the hot exhaust gases to burn extra fuel **2.** a device, as on an incinerator, for burning undesirable exhaust gases

af·ter·care (-ker′) *n.* the supervision given to a a patient recovering from an illness or operation

af·ter·damp (-damp′) *n.* an asphyxiating gas left in a mine after an explosion of firedamp

af·ter·ef·fect (-ə fekt′) *n.* an effect coming later, or as a secondary result

af·ter·glow (-glō′) *n.* **1.** the glow remaining after a light has gone, as after sunset **2.** a pleasant feeling after an enjoyable experience

af·ter·im·age (-im′ij) *n.* a visual image that continues after the external stimulus is withdrawn

af·ter·life (-līf′) *n.* **1.** a life after death **2.** one's later years

af·ter·math (-mäth′,-math′) *n.* [AFTER + dial. *math* < OE. *mæth*, cutting of grass] **1.** a second crop, as of grass that grows after the earlier mowing 2. a result or consequence, esp. an unpleasant one

af·ter·most (-mōst') *adj.* 1. hindmost; last 2. nearest to the stern

af·ter·noon (äf'tər nōon') *n.* the time of day from noon to evening —*adj.* of, in, or for the afternoon

af·ter·noons (-nōonz') *adv.* [Colloq.] during every afternoon or most afternoons

af·ter·pains (äf'tər pānz') *n.pl.* pains from contraction of the uterus following childbirth

af·ters (äf'tərz) *n.pl.* [Colloq.] the sweet course of a meal

af·ter·shave (äf'tər shäv') *n.* a lotion, often perfumed, applied to the face by men after shaving

af·ter·taste (-tāst') *n.* 1. a taste lingering on in the mouth, as after eating 2. the feeling remaining after an experience, often unpleasant

af·ter·thought (-thôt') *n.* 1. an idea, explanation, etc. coming or added later 2. a thought coming too late to be apt, useful, etc.

af·ter·wards (-wərds) *adv.* at a later time; subsequently: also **af'ter·ward**

Ag [L. *argentum*] *Chem.* silver

AG Adjutant General

A.G. Attorney General

a·ga (ä'gə) *n.* [Turk.] in Turkey and other Moslem countries, a title of respect for important officials

a·gain (ə gen', -gān') *adv.* [OE. *ongegn* < *on-*, towards + *gegn*, direct] 1. [Rare] in return [answer *again*] 2. back into a former condition 3. once more; anew 4. besides; further 5. on the other hand —**again and again** often; repeatedly —**as much again** twice as much

a·gainst (ə genst', gänst') *prep.* [ME. *ayeynst*, opposite < OE. *ongegn*: see AGAIN] 1. in opposition to [*against* my will] 2. towards so as to strike [throw the ball *against* the wall] 3. opposite to the direction of [swim *against* the current] 4. in contrast with [green *against* the gold] 5. in contact with [leaning *against* the wall] 6. in preparation for [we provided *against* a poor crop] 7. as a charge on [a bill was entered *against* his account] 8. to the detriment of [the economic situation works *against* small companies] —**over against** 1. opposite to 2. as compared with

a·gam·ic (ə gam'ik) *adj.* [Gr. *agamos* < *a-*, not + *gamos*, marriage] occurring or reproducing without fertilization; asexual

ag·a·mo·gen·e·sis (ag'ə mō jen'ə sis, ə gam'ə-) *n.* [< Gr. *agamos* (see prec.) + -GENESIS] asexual reproduction or development

a·gape[1] (ə gāp') *adv., adj.* [A-[1] + GAPE] 1. with the mouth wide open, as in wonder 2. wide open

ag·a·pe[2] (ag'ə pē) *n.* [< LL. < Gr. *agapē*, love] *Christian Theol.* 1. God's love for man 2. spontaneous, altruistic love 3. a religious meal taken by early Christians

a·gar-a·gar (ä'gər ä'gər) *n.* [Malay] a gelatinous extract of seaweed, used for bacterial cultures, as a laxative, etc.: also **a'gar**

ag·ar·ic (ə ger'ik, ag'ər ik) *n.* [< L. < Gr. *agarikon*] any gill fungus, as the common edible mushroom, etc.

ag·ate (ag'ət) *n.* [OFr. < L. < Gr. *achatēs* < ?] 1. a hard, semiprecious stone, a variety of chalcedony, with striped or clouded colouring 2. a little ball made of this stone or of glass, used in playing marbles

a·ga·ve (ə gä'vē) *n.* [ModL. < Gr. *Agauē*, a proper name, lit., illustrious] any of several American desert plants, as the century plant, having tall flower stalks and fleshy leaves: some agaves yield a rope fibre

a·gaze (ə gāz') *adv., adj.* gazing

age (āj) *n.* [< OFr. < L. *aetas*] 1. the time that a person or thing has existed since birth or beginning 2. the lifetime 3. a stage of life [the awkward *age*] 4. the condition of being old [bent with *age*] 5. a generation 6. a period in history or in prehistoric or geologic time 7. [*often pl.*] [Colloq.] a long time —*vi.* aged, ag'ing or age'ing 1. to grow old or become mature —*vt.* to make old or cause to become mature 2. to show signs of age [she has *aged* greatly since I last saw her] —**(come) of age** (to reach) the age of full legal rights —**under age** not having reached the required or legal age

-age (ij, əj) [OFr. < LL. *-aticum*, belonging to] *a noun-forming suffix meaning:* 1. the act, condition, or result of [*usage*] 2. amount or number of [*acreage*] 3. cost of [*postage*] 4. place of [*steerage*] 5. collection of [*peerage*] 6. home of [*hermitage*]

a·ged (ā'jid *for 1 & 2;* ājd *for 3 & 4*) *adj.* 1. grown old 2. of old age 3. brought to a desired state of aging 4. of the age of [a boy *aged* ten] —**the aged** (ā'jid) old people

age·less (āj'lis) *adj.* 1. seemingly not growing older 2. eternal —**age'less·ly** *adv.*

age·long (-loŋ') *adj.* lasting a very long time

a·gen·cy (ā'jən sē) *n., pl.* **-cies** [see AGENT] 1. action; power 2. means; instrumentality 3. the business or place of business of any person, firm, etc. authorized to act for another 4. an organization offering a particular kind of service [an employment *agency*]

a·gen·da (ə jen'də) *n., pl.* **-das** [L., pl. of *agendum* < *agere*, ACT] programme of things to be done; specif., a list of things to be dealt with at a meeting

a·gent (ā'jənt) *n.* [< L. *agens* (gen. *agentis*), prp. of *agere*, ACT] 1. a person or thing that performs an action 2. a force or substance that produces an effect [chemical *agent*] 3. a person, firm, etc. authorized to act for another [Crown *agent*] 4. [Colloq.] a travelling representative, as for an insurance company —**a·gen·tial** (ā jen'shəl) *adj.*

‡a·gent pro·vo·ca·teur (à zhän' prō vô kà tër') *pl.* **a·gents pro·vo·ca·teurs** (à zhän' prō vô kà tër') [Fr.] a secret agent hired to join some group in order to incite its members to commit unlawful acts to weaken or discredit it

age of consent *Law* the age of a girl, specified by law, before which sexual intercourse with her may be classified as illegal

Age of Reason the 18th cent. in France and Britain

age-old (āj'ōld') *adj.* ages old; ancient

ag·er·a·tum (aj'ə rāt'əm) *n.* [ModL. < Gr. < *agēratos*, not growing old < *a-*, not + *gēras* old age] a plant of the composite family, with small, thick heads of usually bluish flowers

ag·glom·er·ate (ə glom'ə rāt'; *for adj. & n.* -ər it) *vt., vi.* **-at'·ed, -at'ing** [< L. pp. of *agglomerare* < *ad-*, to + *glomerare*, to form into a ball] to gather into a mass or ball —*adj.* gathered into a mass or ball —*n.* 1. a jumbled heap, mass, etc. 2. *Geol.* a mass of fragments of volcanic rock fused by heat —**ag·glom'er·a'tion** *n.* —**ag·glom'er·a'tive** *adj.*

ag·glu·ti·nant (ə glōot'ən ənt) *adj.* [see ff.] sticking together —*n.* a sticky substance

ag·glu·ti·nate (ə glōot'ən it; *for v.* -āt') *adj.* [< L. pp. of *agglutinare* < *ad-*, to + *gluten*, glue] 1. stuck together, as with glue 2. *Linguis.* forming words by agglutination —*vt., vi.* **-nat'ed, -nat'ing** 1. to stick together, as with glue 2. *Linguis.* to form (words) by agglutination 3. *Med. & Bacteriology* to clump, as blood cells, microorganisms, etc. suspended in fluid —**ag·glu'ti·na'tive** *adj.*

ag·glu·ti·na·tion (ə glōot'ən ā'shən) *n.* 1. an agglutinating or being agglutinated 2. a mass of agglutinated parts 3. *Linguis.* the combining of words into compounds without marked change of form or loss of meaning

ag·gran·dize (ə gran'dīz', ag'rən-) *vt.* **-dized', -diz'ing** [< Fr. < *a-*, to + *grandir*, to increase < L. *grandire* < *grandis*, great] 1. to make (esp. oneself) greater, more powerful, richer, etc. 2. to make seem greater —**ag·gran'dize·ment** (-diz mənt) *n.* —**ag·gran'diz'er** *n.*

ag·gra·vate (ag'rə vāt') *vt.* **-vat'ed, -vat'ing** [< L. pp. of *aggravare* < *ad-*, to + *gravis*, heavy] 1. to make worse; make more burdensome, troublesome, etc. 2. [Colloq.] to exasperate; annoy —**ag'gra·va'tion** *n.*

ag·gre·gate (ag'rə gət; *for v.* -gāt') *adj.* [< L. pp. of *aggregare* < *ad-*, to + *gregare*, to herd < *grex* (gen. *gregis*), a herd] gathered into, or considered as, a whole; total —*n.* a group or mass of distinct things gathered into, or considered as, a whole; total —*vt.* **-gat'ed, -gat'ing** 1. to gather into a whole or mass 2. to amount to; total —**in the aggregate** taken all together; on the whole —**ag'gre·ga'tion** *n.* —**ag'gre·ga'tive** *adj.*

ag·gress (ə gres') *vi.* [< L. pp. of *aggredi*, to attack < *ad-*, to + *gradi*, to step] to start a quarrel or be the first to attack

ag·gres·sion (ə gresh'ən) *n.* 1. an unprovoked attack or warlike act 2. the practice or habit of being aggressive, or quarrelsome 3. *Psychiatry* forceful or hostile behaviour

ag·gres·sive (ə gres'iv) *adj.* 1. aggressing or inclined to aggress 2. ready to engage in direct action 3. full of enterprise; bold and active —**ag·gres'sive·ly** *adv.* —**ag·gres'sive·ness** *n.*

ag·gres·sor (-ər) *n.* a person, nation, etc. that is guilty of aggression, or makes an unprovoked attack

ag·grieve (ə grēv') *vt.* **-grieved', -griev'ing** [< OFr. < L. *aggravare*, AGGRAVATE] 1. to cause grief or injury to; offend 2. to injure in one's legal rights

ag·gro (ag'rō) *n.* [clipped form of *aggravation* (see AGGRAVATE) or AGGRESSION] [Slang] aggressive behaviour; trouble-making

a·ghast (ə gäst') *adj.* [< ME. < *a-* (intens.) + *gastan* < OE. *gæstan*, to terrify < *gast*, ghost] feeling great horror or dismay; horrified

ag·ile (aj'īl) *adj.* [Fr. < L. < *agere*, ACT] 1. quick and easy of movement; nimble 2. keen and lively [an *agile* wit] —**ag'ile·ly** *adv.* —**a·gil·i·ty** (ə jil'ə tē) *n.*

ag·in (ə gin') *prep.* [< obs. *again*, AGAINST] [Dial. or Colloq.] against

a·gi·o (aj'ē ō') *n., pl.* **-os'** [< It. *agio*, ease] 1. a fee paid to exchange one kind of money for another or to exchange depreciated money for money of full value 2. money exchange business

ag·i·tate (aj'ə tāt') *vt.* **-tat'ed, -tat'ing** [< L. pp. of *agitare*, to put in motion < *agere*, ACT] 1. to move violently; stir up or shake up 2. to excite or disturb the feelings of 3. to keep discussing so as to stir up support for —*vi.* to stir up support through speeches and writing so as to produce changes [to *agitate* for reform] —**ag′i·tat′ed·ly** *adv.*

ag·i·ta·tion (aj′ə tā′shən) *n.* 1. an agitating or being agitated; violent motion or stirring 2. emotional disturbance 3. discussion meant to stir up people and produce changes

a·gi·ta·to (a′jē tä′tō) *adj., adv.* [It.] *Music* fast and with excitement

ag·i·ta·tor (aj′ə tāt′ər) *n.* 1. a person who tries to stir up people in support of a social or political cause: often used in disapproval 2. an apparatus for shaking or stirring

ag·it·prop (aj′it prop′) *adj.* [< Russ. *agit(atsiya) prop(aganda)*, agitation propaganda] of or for agitating and propagandizing

a·gleam (ə glēm′) *adv., adj.* gleaming

ag·let (ag′lit) *n.* [ME. < OFr. *aiguillette*, dim. of *aiguille* < L. *acula*, dim. of *acus*, a needle] 1. the metal tip at the end of a cord or lace 2. *same as* AIGUILLETTE

a·gley (ə glē′, -gli′, -glā′) *adv.* [Scot.] awry

a·glit·ter (ə glit′ər) *adv., adj.,* glittering

a·glow (ə glō′) *adv., adj.* in a glow (of colour or emotion)

A.G.M. Annual General Meeting

ag·nail (ag′nāl′) *n.* [ME. < OE. *angnægl* < *ange*, pain + *nægl*, nail (metal): because of its nail-head appearance] 1. a sore or swelling round a fingernail or toenail 2. a hangnail

ag·nate (ag′nāt) *n.* [L. *agnatus* < pp. of *agnasci*, to be born in addition to] a relative through male descent or on the father's side —*adj.* 1. related through male descent or on the father's side 2. akin

ag·nos·tic (ag nos′tik) *n.* [< Gr. < *a-*, not + base of *gignōskein*, to know] a person who believes that one cannot know whether there is a God, or an ultimate cause, or anything beyond material phenomena —*adj.* of or characteristic of an agnostic —**ag·nos′ti·cal·ly** *adv.* —**ag·nos′ti·cism** *n.*

Ag·nus De·i (ag′nəs dē′ī; äg′nōos dā′ē) [L., Lamb of God] 1. a representation of Christ as a lamb, often holding a cross or flag 2. *R.C.Ch.* a prayer in the Mass, beginning *Agnus Dei*, or music for it

a·go (ə gō′) *adj.* [< OE. *agan* < *a-*, away + *gan*, go] gone by; past [years *ago*, a month *ago*] —*adv.* in the past [long *ago*]

a·gog (ə gog′) *adv., adj.* [OFr. < *a-*, to + *gogue*, joyfulness] with eager interest or excitement

-a·gogue (ə gog′) [< Gr. prp. of *agein*, to lead] a combining form meaning leading, directing, inciting [demagogue]

a·gon·ic (ə gon′ik, ā-) *adj.* [< Gr. *agōnos* < *a-*, without + *gōnia*, angle] forming no angle

agonic line an imaginary line on the earth's surface joining points of zero magnetic declination; a line on which the magnetic and true north are the same

ag·o·nize (ag′ə nīz′) *vi.* -**nized′**, -**niz′ing** 1. to make convulsive efforts; struggle 2. to be in agony —*vt.* to torture —**ag′o·niz′ing·ly** *adv.*

ag·o·ny (ag′ə nē) *n., pl.* -**nies** [< L. < Gr. *agōnia*, a contest < *agōn*, an assembly < *agein*, to lead] 1. very great mental or physical pain 2. death pangs 3. a convulsive struggle 4. a sudden, strong outburst (*of* emotion)

agony column 1. a section of a newspaper containing advertisements for lost relatives and friends, personal messages, etc. 2. a newspaper feature offering sympathetic advice to readers on their personal problems

ag·o·ra¹ (ag′ə rə,) *n., pl.* -**rae′** (-rē′), -**ras** [Gr. < *ageirein*, to assemble] in ancient Greece, an assembly or a place of assembly, esp. a marketplace

a·go·ra² (ä′gō rä′, ə-) *n., pl.* -**rot′** (-rōt′) [ModHeb. *′āgōrāh*] *see* MONETARY UNITS, table (Israel)

ag·o·ra·pho·bi·a (ag′ər ə fō′bē ə) *n.* [AGORA¹ + -PHOBIA] an abnormal fear of open spaces or public places

a·gou·ti, a·gou·ty (ə gōō′tē) *n., pl.* -**tis**, -**ties**: see PLURAL, II, D, 1 [Fr. < Sp. < Guarani] a rodent related to the guinea pig, found in tropical America

a·grar·i·an (ə grer′ē ən) *adj.* [< L. < *ager*, a field, land] 1. relating to land or to the ownership or division of land 2. of agriculture —*n.* a person who favours a more even division of land among those who work it —**a·grar′i·an·ism** *n.*

a·gree (ə grē′) *vi.* -**greed′**, -**gree′ing** [< OFr. < *a gre*, favourably < L. *ad*, to + *gratus*, pleasing] 1. to consent or accede (*to*) 2. to be in harmony 3. to be of the same opinion; concur (*with*) 4. to arrive at a satisfactory understanding (*about* prices, etc.) 5. to be suitable, healthful, etc. (followed by *with*) [the climate *agrees* with him] 6. *Gram.* to be inflected so as to correspond in number, person, case, or gender —*vt.* to grant or acknowledge [we *agreed* that it was true] —**agree to differ** to accept divergence of opinion

a·gree·a·ble (-ə b′l) *adj.* [see prec.] 1. pleasing or pleasant

AGOUTI
(43-63 cm long)

2. willing or ready to consent 3. conformable; in accord —**a·gree′a·bil′i·ty, a·gree′a·ble·ness** *n.* —**a·gree′a·bly** *adv.*

a·greed (ə grēd′) *adj.* settled by mutual consent [pay the *agreed* price]

a·gree·ment (ə grē′mənt) *n.* 1. an agreeing, or being in harmony 2. an understanding between two or more people, countries, etc. 3. a contract 4. *Gram.* correspondence, as between subject and verb, in number, person, etc.

ag·ri·busi·ness (ag′rə biz′nis) *n.* [AGRI(CULTURE) + BUSINESS] farming and the businesses associated with farming

ag·ri·cul·ture (ag′ri kul′chər) *n.* [Fr. < L. < *ager*, a field + *cultura*, cultivation] the science and art of farming; work of cultivating the soil, producing crops, and raising livestock —**ag′ri·cul′tur·al** *adj.* —**ag′ri·cul′tur·al·ly** *adv.*

ag·ri·cul·tur·ist (ag′ri kul′chər ist) *n.* 1. an expert in agriculture 2. a farmer Also **ag′ri·cul′tur·al·ist**

ag·ri·mo·ny (ag′rə mō′nē) *n., pl.* -**nies** [< OE. & OFr. < L. < Gr. *argemōnē*] a plant of the rose family, having little yellow flowers on spiky stalks and bearing burlike fruits

ag·ro·bi·ol·o·gy (ag′rō bī ol′ə jē) *n.* the science of plant growth and nutrition as applied to improvement of crops and control of soil

a·gron·o·my (ə gron′ə mē) *n.* [< Fr. < Gr. < *agros*, field + *nemein*, to manage] the science and economics of crop production; management of farm land —**ag·ro·nom·ic** (ag′·rə nom′ik), **ag′ro·nom′i·cal** *adj.* —**a·gron′o·mist** *n.*

a·ground (ə ground′) *adv., adj.* on or onto the shore, a reef, etc. [the ship ran *aground*]

agt. agent

a·gue (ā′gyōō) *n.* [< OFr. < ML. (*febris*) *acuta*, violent (fever)] 1. a fever, usually that of malaria, marked by regularly recurring chills 2. a chill; fit of shivering —**a′·gu·ish** *adj.*

ah (ä) *interj.* an exclamation expressing pain, delight, regret, disgust, surprise, etc.

A.H. [L. *Anno Hegirae*] in the year of the Hegira

a·ha (ä hä′, ə hä′) *interj.* an exclamation expressing satisfaction, pleasure, triumph, etc., often mixed with irony or mockery

a·head (ə hed′) *adv., adj.* 1. in or at the front 2. forwards; onwards 3. in advance 4. winning or leading 5. having something as a profit or advantage —**get ahead** to advance socially, financially, etc.

a·hem (ə hem′; *conventionalized pronun.*) *interj.* a cough or similar sound made to get attention, fill a pause, etc.

a·him·sa (ə him′sä) *n.* [< Sans. < *a-*, not + *himsä*, injury] the Buddhist and Hindu principle of not harming any living creature

a·hoy (ə hoi′) *interj.* *Naut.* a call used in hailing [ship *ahoy!*]

a·i (ä′ē) *n., pl.* **a′is** (-ēz) [Tupi *ai hai* < the animal's cry] a S. American sloth with three toes

A.I. artificial insemination

aid (ād) *vt., vi.* [< OFr. < L. *adjutare*: see ADJUTANT] to give help (to); assist —*n.* 1. help; assistance 2. a helper; assistant 3. a helpful device —**in aid of** 1. in support of 2. [Colloq.] for the purpose of

A.I.D. artificial insemination by donor

aide (ād) *n.* [Fr.: see AID] 1. an assistant 2. *same as* AIDE-DE-CAMP

aide-de-camp (ād′də kän′) *n., pl.* **aides-de-camp** [Fr., lit., camp assistant] an officer in the army, navy, etc. serving as assistant and confidential secretary to a superior

ai·grette, ai·gret (ā′gret, ā gret′) *n.* [see EGRET] 1. the long, white plumes of the egret, once worn for ornament by women 2. any ornament like this

ai·guille (ā gwēl′, ā′gwēl) *n.* [Fr.: see AGLET] 1. a peak of rock shaped like a needle 2. an instrument for drilling holes in rocks or masonry

ai·guil·lette (ā′gwi let′) *n.* [Fr.: see AGLET] a gilt cord hung in loops from the shoulder of certain military uniforms

ail (āl) *vt.* [< OE. *eglian*, to afflict with dread, trouble < *egle*, harmful] to be the cause of pain to; trouble —*vi.* to be in poor health; be ill

ai·lan·thus (ā lan′thəs) *n., pl.* -**thus·es** [ModL. < native name in Malacca] a tree, native to Asia, with pointed leaflets, fine-grained wood, and small, greenish flowers with an unpleasant odour

ai·le·ron (ā′lə ron′) *n.* [Fr. < OFr. < *aile* < L. *ala*, wing] a movable hinged section of an aeroplane wing for controlling rolling movements

ail·ing (āl′iŋ) *adj.* in poor health; sickly

ail·ment (āl′mənt) *n.* an illness, esp. a mild one

aim (ām) *vi., vt.* [< OFr. *aesmer* < L. < *ad-*, to + *aestimare*, to estimate] 1. to point (a weapon) or direct (a blow, remark, etc.) 2. to direct (one's efforts) 3. to try or intend (*to* do or be) —*n.* 1. *a*) the act of aiming *b*) the ability to aim 2. the direction of a missile, blow, etc. 3. intention or purpose —**take aim** to point a weapon, as by viewing along a sight

aim·less (ām′ləs) *adj.* having no aim or purpose —**aim′·less·ly** *adv.* —**aim′less·ness** *n.*

ain't (ānt) [early assimilation of *amn't*, contr. of *am not*;

later confused with *a'nt* (are not), *i'nt* (is not), *ha'nt* (has not, have not)] a dialectal or substandard contraction for *am not, is not, are not, has not,* and *have not: ain't* was formerly standard for *am not*

Ai·nu (ī′n$\overline{oo}$) *n.* [Ainu, lit., man] **1.** *pl.* **-nus, -nu** a member of a native, light-skinned people of Japan **2.** their language, unrelated to any other

air (er) *n.* [< OFr. < L. *aer* < Gr. *aēr*, air, mist] **1.** the elastic, invisible mixture of gases (chiefly nitrogen and oxygen, as well as hydrogen, carbon dioxide, etc.) that surrounds the earth; atmosphere **2.** space above the earth; sky **3.** a movement of air; breeze; wind **4.** an outward appearance [an *air* of luxury] **5.** a person's manner or bearing **6.** [*pl.*] affected, superior manners **7.** public expression [give *air* to your opinions] **8.** transportation by aircraft **9.** the medium through which radio signals are transmitted: a figurative use **10.** a song or melody —*adj.* of aircraft, air forces, etc. —*vt.* **1.** to let air into or through **2.** put where air can dry, freshen, etc. **3.** to publicize —*vi.* to become aired, dried, etc. —**in the air 1.** prevalent **2.** not decided —**on** (or **off**) **the air** *Radio & TV* that is (or is not) broadcasting or being broadcast —**take the air** to go outdoors, as for fresh air —**up in the air** not settled or decided —**walk on air** to feel very happy or exalted

air bag a bag of nylon, plastic, etc. that inflates automatically within a motor vehicle at the impact of a collision, to protect riders from being thrown forwards

air base a base of operations for military aircraft

air bladder a sac with air or gas in it, found in most fishes and in some other animals and some plants

air·borne (er′bôrn′) *adj.* **1.** carried by or through the air **2.** aloft or flying

air brake 1. a brake operated by the action of compressed air on a piston **2.** any flap on an aircraft for reducing its speed in flight

air brick a brick with holes in it, put into the wall of a building for ventilation

air·brush (er′brush′) *n.* a kind of atomizer operated by compressed air and used for spraying on paint or other liquid: also **air brush** —**air′brush′** *vt.*

air·bus a short-range or medium-range passenger aircraft

air chamber a cavity or compartment full of air, esp. one used in hydraulics

air chief marshal *see* MILITARY RANKS, table

air commodore *see* MILITARY RANKS, table

air conditioning a method of filtering air and regulating its humidity and temperature in buildings, cars, planes, etc. —**air′con·di′tion** *vt.* —**air conditioner**

air-cooled (er′k$\overline{oo}$ld′) *adj.* cooled by having air passed over, into, or through it —**air′-cool′** *vt.*

air·craft (er′kräft′) *n., pl.* **-craft′** any machine designed for flying, whether heavier or lighter than air; aeroplane, balloon, helicopter, etc.

aircraft carrier a warship that carries aircraft, with a large, flat deck for taking off and landing

air·craft·man (er′kräft mən) *n. see* MILITARY RANKS, table

air·craft·wom·an (er′kräft woom′ən) *n.* a rank in the Women's Royal Air Force corresponding to that of AIRCRAFTMAN

air curtain (or **door**) a downward draught of air at an open entrance for maintaining even temperatures within

air cushion 1. an inflatable cushion **2.** the pocket of air that supports a hovercraft **3.** a form of pneumatic suspension consisting of an enclosed volume of air

air·drome (er′drōm′) *n. U.S. var. of* AERODROME

air·drop (-drop′) *n.* the delivery of supplies or troops by parachute from an aircraft —*vt.* **-dropped′, -drop′ping** to deliver by airdrop

Aire·dale (er′dāl′) *n.* [after *Airedale* in W. Yorkshire] a large terrier having a hard, wiry, tan coat with black markings

air·field (er′fēld′) *n.* a field where aircraft can take off and land

air force the aviation branch of the armed forces

air·frame (er′frām) *n.* the structural framework and covering of an aircraft, rocket, etc.

air gun a gun operated by compressed air

air hole 1. a hole that permits passage of air **2.** an unfrozen or open place in the ice covering a body of water

AIREDALE
(58 cm high at shoulder)

air hostess a stewardess on an airliner or aeroplane

air·i·ly (er′ə lē) *adv.* in an airy or gay, light manner; jauntily; breezily

air·i·ness (-ē nis) *n.* **1.** a being airy, or full of fresh air **2.** gay lightness; jauntiness

air·ing (-in) *n.* **1.** exposure to the air, as for drying **2.** exposure to public knowledge **3.** a walk or ride outdoors

airing cupboard a cupboard in which laundry, etc. is exposed to warm air

air lane a prescribed route for travel by air; .airway

air·less (-lis) *adj.* **1.** without air or without fresh air **2.** without wind or breeze

air letter a single sheet of lightweight paper which may be folded and sealed to form an envelope, and sent cheaply by airmail

air·lift (-lift′) *n.* a system of transporting troops, supplies, etc. by aircraft, as when ground routes are blocked —*vt.* to transport by airlift

air·line (-līn′) *n.* a system or company for moving cargo and passengers by aircraft **3.** a route for travel by air —*adj.* of or on an airline

air·lin·er (-lī′nər) *n.* a large aircraft for carrying passengers

air lock 1. an airtight compartment, with adjustable air pressure, between places that do not have the same air pressure **2.** a blockage, as in a water pipe, caused by trapped air

air·mail (-māl′) *n.* **1.** the system of transporting mail by aircraft **2.** letters, etc. so transported —*vt.* to send by airmail

air·man (-mən) *n., pl.* **-men** an aviator

air marshal *see* MILITARY RANKS, table

air mass *Meteorol.* a large body of air having virtually uniform conditions of temperature and moisture in a horizontal cross section

air·mind·ed (er′mīn′dəd) *adj.* interested in or promoting aviation, aircraft, air power, etc.

air·plane (er′plān′) *n. U.S. var. of* AEROPLANE

air pocket an atmospheric condition that causes an aircraft to make sudden, short drops

air·port (-pôrt′) *n.* a place where aircraft can land and take off, usually with facilities for repair, accommodation for passengers, etc.

air power total capacity of a nation for air war

air pressure the pressure of atmospheric or compressed air

air·proof (-pr$\overline{oo}$f′) *adj.* not penetrable by air —*vt.* to make airproof

air pump a machine for removing or compressing air or for forcing it through something

air raid an attack by aircraft, esp. bombers

air rifle a rifle operated by the force of compressed air

air sac any of the air-filled cavities in a bird's body, having connections to the lungs

air-sea rescue 1. an air rescue at sea **2.** an organisation, including aircraft, lifeboat services, etc., which rescues people from ship or aircraft disasters

air shaft a passage through which fresh air can enter a tunnel, mine, etc.

air·ship (-ship′) *n.* any self-propelled aircraft that is lighter than air and can be steered

air·sick (-sik′) *adj.* unwell or nauseated from travelling in an aircraft —**air′sick′ness** *n.*

air·space (-spās′) *n.* **1.** space for manoeuvring an aircraft **2.** the space above a particular land area

air·speed (-spēd′) *n.* the speed of an aircraft relative to the air rather than to the ground

air·strip (-strip′) *n.* a hard-surfaced area used as a temporary aircraft runway

air terminal a building in a city where transport is available to and from an airport outside the city

air·tight (er′tīt′) *adj.* **1.** too tight for air or gas to enter or escape **2.** [Chiefly U.S.] giving no opening for attack; without weak points [an *airtight* alibi]

air-to-air (er′t$\overline{oo}$ er′) *adj.* operating between aircraft in flight

air vice-marshal *see* MILITARY RANKS, table

air·waves (-wāvz′) *n.pl.* the medium through which radio signals are transmitted

air·way (-wā′) *n.* **1.** *same as:* a) AIR SHAFT b) AIR LANE **2.** a passage for air, as to the lungs

air·wor·thy (-wur′*th*ē) *adj.* fit and safe to fly: said of aircraft —**air′wor′thi·ness** *n.*

air·y (er′ē) *adj.* **air′i·er, air′i·est 1.** in the air; high up **2.** of air **3.** open to the air; breezy **4.** unsubstantial as air; visionary **5.** light as air; delicate; graceful **6.** lighthearted; gay **7.** flippant **8.** [Colloq.] putting on airs; affected

aisle (īl) *n.* [< OFr. *aile:* see AILERON: the *-s-* is through confusion with ISLE] **1.** a part of a church set off by a row of columns or piers **2.** a passageway, as between rows of seats —**aisled** (īld) *adj.*

aitch (āch) *n.* [ME. & OFr. *ache* < LL. *accha, aha*] the letter H, h —**drop one's aitches** to miss off the initial aspiration from words

aitch·bone (āch′bōn′) *n.* [by faulty separation of ME. *nache bone* < OFr. *nache*, buttock] **1.** the rump bone **2.** a cut of beef around the rump bone

a·jar[1] (ə jär′) *adv., adj.* [ME. *on char* < OE. *cier*, a turn: see CHORE] slightly open, as a door

a·jar[2] (ə jär′) *adv., adj.* [A-[1], on + JAR[1] v.] not in harmony

a·kim·bo (ə kim′bō) *adv., adj.* [ME. *in kenebowe*, lit., in keen bow; a folk etym. < ON. < *keng*, bent + *bogi*, a bow] with hands on hips and elbows bent outward [with arms *akimbo*]

a·kin (ə kin′) *adj.* **1.** of one kin; related **2.** having similar qualities; similar

Ak·ka·di·an (ə kăd′ē ən) *n.* an extinct Semitic language of the Mesopotamian region

-al (əl, ′l) [< Fr. < L. *-alis*] **1.** *an adj.-forming suffix meaning* of, like, or suitable for [*comical, hysterical*] **2.** a suffix of nouns originally adjectives [*perennial, annual*] **3.** *a n.-forming suffix meaning* the act or process of [*avowal*] **4.** [AL(DEHYDE)] *Chem. a n.-forming suffix denoting:* a) an aldehyde [*chloral*] b) a barbiturate [*phenobarbital*]

Al *Chem.* aluminium

a·la (ā′lə) *n., pl.* **a′lae** (-lē) [L., a wing] **1.** *Zool.* a wing **2.** a winglike structure, as the ear lobe

à la, a la (ä′lə, -lä; al′ə) [Fr.] **1.** to, in, or at the **2.** in the manner or style of **3.** according to

al·a·bas·ter (al′ə băs′tər, -bas′-) *n.* [ME. & OFr. *alabastre* < Gr. *alabastros*] **1.** a translucent, whitish, fine-grained variety of gypsum **2.** a streaked or mottled variety of calcite —*adj.* of or resembling alabaster —**al′a·bas′trine** (-trin) *adj.*

à la carte (ä′lä kärt′, al′ə-) [Fr., by the bill of fare] with a separate price for each item on the menu: opposed to TABLE D'HOTE

a·lack (ə lak′) *interj.* [A(H) + LACK] [Archaic] an exclamation of regret, surprise, dismay, etc.

a·lac·ri·ty (ə lak′rə tē) *n.* [< OFr. < L. < *alacer*, lively] eager willingness or readiness, often shown by quick, lively action —**a·lac′ri·tous** *adj.*

A·lad·din's cave (ə lad′inz) [after Aladdin in *The Arabian Nights*] an apparently inexhaustible store of riches

à la king (ä′lä kiŋ, al′ə) [lit., in kingly style] diced and served in a sauce containing mushrooms, pimentos, and green peppers

à la mode (ä′lä mōd′, al′ə) [Fr. *à la mode*] **1.** in the fashion; stylish **2.** made or served in a certain style, as (beef) braised with vegetables in sauce

a·lar (ā′lər) *adj.* [< L. < *ala*, a wing] **1.** of or like a wing **2.** having wings

a·larm (ə lärm′) *n.* [< OFr. < It. *all'arme*, to arms] **1.** [Archaic] a sudden call to arms **2.** a signal, sound, etc. to warn of danger **3.** a mechanism designed to warn of danger or trespassing [*a burglar alarm*] **4.** the bell, buzzer, etc. of an alarm clock **5.** fear caused by the sudden realization of danger —*vt.* **1.** to warn of approaching danger **2.** to frighten

alarm clock a clock that can be set to ring or buzz at any particular time, as to awaken a person from sleep

a·larm·ing (-iŋ) *adj.* that alarms, or makes suddenly afraid; frightening —**a·larm′ing·ly** *adv.*

a·larm·ist (-ist) *n.* **1.** one who habitually spreads alarming rumours, etc. **2.** one who is easily frightened and likely to anticipate the worst —*adj.* of or like an alarmist

a·lar·um (ə lar′əm, -lär′-) *n.* archaic var. of ALARM (esp. sense 1) —**alarums and excursions** [< an old stage direction] noisy disturbance; confusion

a·las (ə las′) *interj.* [< OFr. < *a*, ah + *las*, wretched < L. *lassus*, weary] an exclamation of sorrow, pity, regret, etc.

a·late (ā′lāt) *adj.* [< L. < *ala*, a wing] having wings or winglike attachments: also **a′lat·ed**

alb (alb) *n.* [< OE. *albe*, ult. < L. *albus*, white] a long, white linen robe with sleeves tapering to the wrist, worn by a priest at Mass

al·ba·core (al′bə kôr′) *n., pl.* **-cores′, -core′:** see PLURAL, II, D, 1 [Port. < Ar. *al*, the + *bakūrah*, albacore] a fish of the tuna family

al·ba·tross (al′bə tros′) *n., pl.* **-tross′es, -tross′:** see PLURAL, II, D, 1 [< Sp. < Port. < Ar. *al qādūs*, water container < Gr. *kados*, cask; prob. < Heb. *kad*, water jug] any of several large, web-footed sea birds related to the petrel

al·be·do (al bē′dō) *n.* [LL. (Eccles.) < L. *albus*, white] the fraction of the total amount of light incident upon a surface which is reflected from it

al·be·it (ôl bē′it) *conj.* [ME. *al be it*, al(though) it be] although; even though

al·bert (al′bərt) *n.* [after Prince *Albert*, husband of Queen Victoria] a kind of watch chain usually attached to a waistcoat

al·bes·cent (al bes′′nt) *adj.* [< L. prp. of *albescere* < *albus*, white] turning white —**al·bes′cence** *n.*

Al·bi·gen·ses (al′bə jen′sēz) *n.pl.* a religious sect in France c.1020–1250 A.D.: it was suppressed for heresy —**Al′bi·gen′si·an** (-sē ən) *adj., n.*

al·bi·no (al bē′nō) *n., pl.* **-nos** [< Port. < L. *albus*, white] **1.** a person whose skin, hair, and eyes lack normal colouring: albinos have a white skin, whitish hair, and pink eyes **2.** any animal or plant abnormally lacking in colour —**al·bin′ic** (-bin′ik) *adj.* —**al·bi·nism** (al′bə niz′m) *n.*

Al·bi·on (al′bē ən) [Chiefly Poet.] Britain or England

al·bite (al′bīt) *n.* [L. *albus*, white + -ITE] a whitish, glassy mineral of the feldspar family

al·bum (al′bəm) *n.* [L., neut. of *albus*, white] **1.** a book with blank pages for mounting pictures, clippings, stamps, etc., or for collecting autographs **2.** a) a booklike holder for gramophone records b) a set of records in such a holder c) a single long-playing record, not part of a set **3.** an anthology, picture book, or the like

al·bu·men (al′byōō mən) *n.* [L. < *albus*, white] **1.** the white of an egg **2.** the nutritive protein substance in germinating plant and animal cells **3.** *same as* ALBUMIN

al·bu·min (al′byōō mən) *n.* [ALBUM(EN) + -IN¹] any of a class of water-soluble proteins found in milk, egg, muscle, blood, and in many plants

al·bu·mi·nous (al byōō′mə nəs) *adj.* of, like, or containing albumin or albumen

al·bur·num (al bur′nəm) *n.* [< L. < *albus*, white] *same as* SAPWOOD

Al·ca·ic (al kā′ik) *adj.* [after *Alcaeus*, Gr. lyric poet (fl. 600 B.C.)] of Alcaeus or in the form of his verse —*n.* [*usually pl.*] verse by Alcaeus or in his metrical patterns; four-stanza odes, with four lines to a stanza and four feet to a line

al·cal·de (al kal′dē; Sp. äl käl′de) *n.* [Sp. < Ar. < *qada*, to judge] the mayor of a Spanish or Spanish-American town, who also acts as a judge

al·ca·zar (al kə zär′; Sp. äl kä′thär) *n.* [Sp. < Ar. *qasr*, the castle] a palace or fortress of the Moors in Spain; specif., [A-] such a palace in Seville, later used by the Spanish kings

al·che·mist (al′kə mist) *n.* one who practised alchemy —**al′che·mis′tic, al′che·mis′ti·cal** *adj.*

al·che·mize (-mīz′) *vt.* **-mized′, -miz′ing** to change by or as by alchemy

al·che·my (al′kə mē) *n.* [< OFr. < ML. < Ar. *al-kīmiyā* < ? Gr. *cheein*, to pour] **1.** an early form of chemistry studied in the Middle Ages: its chief aims were to change the baser metals into gold and to find the elixir of perpetual youth **2.** a means of transmutation; esp., the seemingly miraculous change of a thing into something better —**al·chem·ic** (al kem′ik), **al·chem′i·cal** *adj.* —**al·chem′i·cal·ly** *adv.*

al·co·hol (al′kə hol′) *n.* [ML. < Ar. *al kuhl*, powder of antimony] **1.** a colourless, volatile, pungent liquid, C_2H_5OH: it can be burned as fuel, is used in industry and medicine, and is the intoxicating element in whisky, wine, beer, etc.: also called *ethyl alcohol* **2.** any intoxicating liquor with this liquid in it **3.** any of a series of similarly constructed organic compounds with a hydroxyl group, as methyl (or wood) alcohol

al·co·hol·ic (al′kə hol′ik) *adj.* **1.** of, containing, or caused by alcohol **2.** suffering from alcoholism —*n.* one who has chronic alcoholism

al·co·hol·ism (al′kə hol′iz′m) *n.* the habitual drinking of alcoholic liquor to excess, or a diseased condition caused by this

al·co·hol·ize (al′kə hol īz′) *vt.* **-ized′, -iz′ing 1.** to saturate or treat with alcohol **2.** to convert into alcohol

al·cove (al′kōv) *n.* [Fr. < Sp. < Ar. < *al*, the + *qubba*, an arch, vault] **1.** a recessed section of a room **2.** a secluded bower in a garden

Al·deb·a·ran (al deb′ər ən) a brilliant red star in the constellation Taurus

al·de·hyde (al′də hīd′) *n.* [< AL(COHOL) + L. *de*, without + HYD(ROGEN)] **1.** a colourless, volatile fluid, CH_3CHO, with a strong, unpleasant odour, obtained from alcohol by oxidation **2.** any of a class of organic compounds containing the CHO group —**al′de·hy′dic** (-hī′dik) *adj.*

al·der (ôl′dər) *n.* [< OE. *alor*] any of a group of trees and shrubs of the birch family, growing in moist regions and having wood that is resistant to underwater rot

al·der·man (ôl′dər mən) *n., pl.* **-men** [< OE. < *eald*, old + *man*, man] **1.** in England and Wales, formerly, a senior member of a county or borough council, elected by the other councillors **2.** in the U.S., Canada, etc. a member of the governing body of a municipality —**al′der·man·ship′** *n.* —**al′-der·man′ic** (-man′ik) *adj.*

Al·der·ney (ôl′dər nē) *n., pl.* **-neys** any of a breed of small dairy cattle originally from Alderney, one of the Channel Islands

ale (āl) *n.* [< OE. *ealu*] **1.** an alcoholic drink made by fermenting a cereal, esp. barley, or a mixture of cereals, originally differing from beer by being unflavoured by hops **2.** [Colloq.] beer

a·le·a·to·ry (ā′lē ə tər ē) *adj.* [< L. < *alea*, chance] depending on chance or luck: also **a′le·a·to′ric**

a·lee (ə lē′) *adv., adj. Naut.* on or towards the lee; leewards

ale·house (āl′hous′) *n.* **1.** [Obs.] a place where ale is sold and served; tavern **2.** [Colloq.] a public house

a·lem·bic (ə lem′bik) *n.* [< OFr. < ML. < Ar. < *al*, the + *anbīq*, a still < Gr. *ambix*, a cup] **1.** an apparatus of glass or metal, formerly used for distilling **2.** anything that refines or purifies

a·leph (ä′lif) *n.* [Heb., lit., ox, leader] the first letter of the Hebrew alphabet

a·lert (ə lurt′) *adj.* [< Fr. < It. *all′ erta*, on the watch] **1.** watchful; vigilantly ready **2.** quick and active; nimble —*n.* **1.** a warning signal, as of an expected air raid **2.** the period when such a warning is in effect —*vt.* to warn to be ready or watchful [the troops were *alerted*] —**on the alert** watchful; vigilant —**a·lert′ly** *adv.* —**a·lert′ness** *n.*

a·leu·rone (al′yə rən, -rōn) *n.* [Gr. *aleuron*, flour + -ONE] finely granulated protein found in seeds generally and forming the outer layer of cereal seeds: also **a′leu·ron**

A·leut (ə lōōt′, al′ōōt) *n.* [< Russ. < ? native name] **1.** *pl.* **A·leuts′, A·leut′** any of a native people of the Aleutian Islands and parts of mainland Alaska **2.** either of their two languages

A·leu·tian (ə lōō′shən) *adj.* **1.** of the Aleutian Islands **2.** of the Aleuts, their culture, etc. —*n.* same as ALEUT

A level same as ADVANCED LEVEL

ale·wife (āl′wīf′) *n.*, *pl.* **-wives′** (-wīvz′) [< ?] an edible N. American fish resembling the herring

al·ex·an·drine (al′ig zan′drin, -drin; -zän′-) *n.* [*occas.* A-] *Prosody* an iambic line having six feet; iambic hexameter —*adj.* of an alexandrine or alexandrines

al·ex·an·drite (al′ig zan′drīt) *n.* [after the Russian czar *Alexander II*] a chrysoberyl that appears dark green in daylight and deep red in artificial light

a·lex·i·a (ə lek′sē ə) *n.* [ModL. < Gr. *a*-, without + *lexis*, speech < *legein*, to speak] a loss of the ability to read, caused by brain injury

al·fal·fa (al fal′fə) *n.* [Sp. < Ar. *al-fasfaṣah*, the best fodder] a deep-rooted plant of the legume family, used for fodder, pasture, and as a cover crop

al fi·ne (al fē′nē) [It.] *Music* to the end (of a repeated section)

al·fres·co (al fres′kō) *adv.* [It. < *al* (for *a il*), in the + *fresco*, fresh, cool] in the open air; outdoors —*adj.* outdoor

Alg. **1.** Algeria **2.** Algerian

alg. algebra

al·gae (al′jē) *n.pl.*, *sing.* **al′ga** (-gə) [pl. of L. *alga*, seaweed] a group of plants, variously one-celled or multicellular, containing chlorophyll and other pigments, and having no true root, stem, or leaf: algae are found in water or damp places and include seaweeds —**al′gal** (-gəl) *adj.*

al·ge·bra (al′jə brə) *n.* [ML. < Ar. < *al*, the + *jabr*, reunion of broken parts] a mathematical system used to generalize certain arithmetical operations by permitting letters or other symbols to stand for numbers: it is used esp. in the solution of polynomial equations —**al′ge·bra′ic** (-brā′ik), **al′ge·bra′-i·cal** *adj.* —**al′ge·bra′i·cal·ly** *adv.* —**al′ge·bra′ist** *n.*

-al·gi·a (al′jə, -jē ə) [< Gr. *algos*, pain] a *n.-forming suffix* meaning pain [*neuralgia*]

al·gid (al′jid) *adj.* [< Fr. < L. *algidus*] cold; chilly —**al·gidi·ty** (al jid′ə tē) *n.*

al·gin·ic acid (al jin′ik) [< ALG(AE) + -IN¹ + -IC] a gelatinous material extracted from brown seaweed or kelp: used in plastics, medicine, etc.

AL·GOL (al′gol) *n.* [Alg(orithmic) O(riented) L(anguage)] a computer programing language designed for mathematical and scientific purposes

Al·gon·qui·an (al goŋ′kē ən, -kwē-) *adj.* designating or of a widespread family of languages used by a number of N. American Indian tribes, —*n.* **1.** this family of languages **2.** a member of any tribe using one of these languages

al·go·rism (al′gər iz′m) *n.* [< ME. & OFr. < ML. *algorismus* < name of 9th-c. Ar. mathematician] **1.** the Arabic, or decimal, system of counting **2.** any method of computing

al·go·rithm (-*ith*′m) *n.* [altered (after ARITHMETIC) < prec.] *Math.* any special method of solving a certain kind of problem; specif., the repetitive calculations used in finding the greatest common divisor of two numbers

a·li·as (ā′lē əs, āl′yəs) *n.*, *pl.* **a′li·as·es** [< L., at another time < *alius*, other] an assumed name; another name —*adv.* otherwise named; called by the assumed name of [*Bell alias Jones*]

al·i·bi (al′ə bī′) *n.*, *pl.* **-bis′** [L., contr. < *alius ibi*, elsewhere] **1.** *Law* the plea or fact that an accused person was elsewhere than at the scene of the crime **2.** [Colloq.] an excuse —*vi.* **-bied′, -bi′ing** [Colloq.] to offer an excuse

al·i·dade (al′ə dād′) *n.* [Fr. < Sp. < Ar. *al 'idādah*, a rule] **1.** a part of an optical or surveying instrument, consisting of the vernier, indicator, etc. **2.** a surveying instrument used in topographic mapping

al·ien (āl′yən, -ē ən) *adj.* [< OFr. < L. *alienus* < *alius*, other] **1.** belonging to another country or people; foreign **2.** not natural; repugnant (*to*) [ideas *alien* to him] **3.** of aliens —*n.* **1.** a foreigner **2.** a foreign-born resident in a country who is not a naturalized citizen **3.** an outsider **4.** in science fiction, a being from another world

al·ien·a·ble (-ə b'l) *adj.* capable of being transferred to a new owner —**al′ien·a·bil′i·ty** *n.*

al·ien·ate (-āt′) *vt.* **-at′ed, -at′ing** **1.** to transfer the ownership of (property) to another **2.** to make unfriendly; estrange [behaviour that *alienated* his friends] **3.** to cause

to be withdrawn or detached, as from society **4.** to cause a transference (of affection) —**al′ien·a′tor** *n.*

al·ien·a·tion (āl′yə nā′shən, -ē ə-) *n.* **1.** an alienating or being alienated **2.** insanity **3.** *Theatre* the objective appraisal of a dramatic work by its audience: in full **alienation effect**

al·ien·ee (āl′yə nē′, āl′ē ə-) *n.* a person to whom property is transferred or conveyed

al·ien·ist (āl′yən ist, āl′ē ən-) *n.* [U.S.] a psychiatrist, esp. one who testifies in a law court

al·ien·or (-ôr′, -ər) *n.* a person from whom property is transferred or conveyed

al·i·form (al′ə fôrm′, ā′lə-) *adj.* [< L. *ala*, a wing + -FORM] shaped like a wing

a·light¹ (ə līt′) *vi.* **a·light′ed** or **a·lit′, a·light′ing** [< ME. < *a*-, out, off + *lihtan*, to dismount] **1.** to get down or off; dismount **2.** to come down after flight **3.** [Rare] to come (*on* or *upon*) accidentally

a·light² (ə līt′) *adj.* lighted up; glowing

a·lign (ə līn′) *vt.* [< Fr. < *a*, to + *ligner* < *ligne*, LINE¹] **1.** to bring into a straight line **2.** to bring (parts, as the wheels of a car) into proper coordination **3.** to bring into agreement, close cooperation, etc. [he *aligned* himself with the liberals] —*vi.* to come into line; line up

a·lign·ment (-mənt) *n.* **1.** an aligning or being aligned; esp., a) arrangement in a straight line b) a condition of close cooperation **2.** a line or lines formed by aligning

a·like (ə līk′) *adj.* [< OE. *gelic*, *onlike*: see A-¹ & LIKE¹] like one another; similar: usually in the predicate —*adv.* **1.** in the same manner; similarly **2.** to the same degree; equally

al·i·ment (al′ə mənt; *for v.* -ment′) *n.* [L. *alimentum* < *alere*, to nourish] **1.** anything that nourishes; food **2.** means of support —*vt.* to nourish —**al′i·men′tal** (-men′t′l) *adj.*

al·i·men·ta·ry (al′ə men′tər ē) *adj.* [see prec.] **1.** connected with food or nutrition **2.** nourishing **3.** furnishing support or sustenance

alimentary canal (or **tract**) the passage in the body through which food passes to be digested: it extends from the mouth to the anus

al·i·men·ta·tion (al′ə men tā′shən) *n.* **1.** nourishment; nutrition **2.** support; sustenance —**al′i·men′ta·tive** (-men′-tə tiv) *adj.*

al·i·mo·ny (al′ə mə nē) *n.* [< L. < *alere*, to nourish] an allowance paid, esp. to a woman, by the spouse or former spouse after a legal separation or divorce

a·line (ə līn′) *vt.*, *vi.* **a·lined′, a·lin′ing** same as ALIGN —**a·line′ment** *n.*

A-line (ā′līn′) *adj.* slightly flared from the waist or shoulders: said of garments

al·i·phat·ic (al′ə fat′ik) *adj.* [< Gr. *aleiphar* (gen. *aleiphatos*), fat + -IC] *Chem.* of or obtained from fat; specif., of a class of carbon compounds in which the carbon atoms are joined in open chains

al·i·quant (al′ə kwənt) *adj.* [< L. < *alius*, other + *quantus*, how much] *Math.* that does not divide a number evenly but leaves a remainder [8 is an *aliquant* part of 25]: cf. ALIQUOT

al·i·quot (al′ə kwət) *adj.* [L. < *alius*, other + *quot*, how many] *Math.* that divides a number evenly and leaves no remainder [8 is an *aliquot* part of 24]: cf. ALIQUANT

a·lit (ə lit′) *alt. pt. & pp. of* ALIGHT¹

a·live (ə līv′) *adj.* [< OE. *on*, in + *life*, life] [usually used in the predicate] **1.** having life; living **2.** in existence, operation, etc. [to keep his memory *alive*] **3.** lively; alert *Alive* is used as an interjection in such phrases as *man alive! sakes alive!* etc. —**alive and kicking** active and in good health —**alive to** fully aware of; perceiving —**alive with** teeming with; full of

a·liz·a·rin (ə liz′ər in) *n.* [G., < Fr. & Sp. *alizari*, dried madder root < Ar. *al aṣārah*, the juice < *aṣara*, to press] a reddish-yellow crystalline compound used in dyes: also **a·liz′a·rine** (-in, -ēn′)

al·ka·li (al′kə lī′) *n.*, *pl.* **-lis′, -lies′** [< Ar. *al*, the + *qili*, ashes (of saltwort)] **1.** any base or hydroxide, as soda, potash, etc., that gives a high concentration of hydroxyl ions in solution **2.** any soluble mineral salt or mixture of salts found in desert soils and capable of neutralizing acids

alkali metals the group of metallic chemical elements consisting of lithium, sodium, potassium, rubidium, caesium, and francium

al·ka·line (al′kə lin, -līn′) *adj.* of, like, or containing an alkali; basic —**al′ka·lin′i·ty** (-lin′ə tē) *n.*

al·ka·line-earth metals (al′kə lin urth′, -līn′-) a group of metallic chemical elements, including calcium, strontium, barium, and sometimes beryllium, magnesium, and radium: the oxides of these metals are called **alkaline earths**

al·ka·lin·ize (al′kə lə nīz′) *vt.* **-ized′, -iz′ing** same as ALKALIZE —**al′ka·lin·i·za′tion** *n.*

al·ka·lize (al′kə līz′) *vt.* **-lized′, -liz′ing** to make alkaline —**al′ka·li·za′tion** *n.*

al·ka·loid (-loid′) *n.* [ALKAL(I) + -OID] any of a number of colourless, bitter, basic organic substances, as caffeine, morphine, quinine, etc., found in certain plants —**al′ka·loid′-al** *adj.*

Al·ko·ran (al′ko rän′,-kô-) *n.* the Koran

al·kyd (al′kid) *n.* [ult. < ALKALI + ACID] any of several synthetic resins used as coatings, and in paints, varnishes, etc.: also **alkyd resin**

al·kyl (al′kil) *n.* [ALK(ALI) + -YL] a hydrocarbon radical with the general formula C_nH_{2n+1}

all (ôl) *adj.* [OE. *eall*] 1. the whole quantity, extent, or number of [*all* the gold, *all* day] 2. every one of [*all* men must eat] 3. the greatest possible [said in *all* sincerity] 4. any; any whatever [true beyond *all* question] 5. every [*all* manner of men] 6. alone; only [life is not *all* pleasure] 7. seeming to be nothing but [he was *all* arms and legs] —*pron.* 1. [with *pl. v.*] everyone [*all* are present] 2. [with *pl. v.*] every one [*all* of us are going] 3. everything [*all* is over between them] 4. every part or bit [*all* of it is eaten] —*n.* 1. everything one has [give your *all*] 2. a totality; whole —*adv.* 1. wholly; entirely [*all* worn out] 2. apiece [a score of thirty *all*] —**after all** nevertheless; in spite of everything —**all but** 1. all except 2. nearly; almost —**all for** [Colloq.] wholeheartedly in support of —**all in** [Colloq.] very tired —**all in all** 1. considering everything 2. as a whole 3. the object of one's attention or interest —**all over** 1. ended 2. everywhere; throughout 3. [Colloq.] typically [that's Mary *all over*] —**all out** to one's maximum speed, effort or capacity —**all round** 1. in every particular 2. to each one —**all the** (**better, worse,** etc.) so much the (better, worse, etc.) —**all the** (**farther, closer,** etc.) [Colloq. or Dial.] as (far, close, etc.) as —**all there** [Colloq.] in possession of all one's mental faculties —**all the same** 1. nevertheless 2. of no importance —**at all** 1. in the least 2. in any way 3. under any conditions —**for all** in spite of —**in all** altogether

all- *a combining form denoting* entirety; comprehensiveness [*all*-electric, *all*-powerful]

al·la bre·ve (äl′a brä′ve) [It.] *Music* the time signature (¢) representing 2/2 time, in which the minim receives the beat

Al·lah (al′a) [Ar. *Allāh* < *al*, the + *ilāh*, god] the Moslem name for GOD

all-A·mer·i·can (ôl′a mer′a kan) *adj.* [U.S.] 1. made up wholly of Americans or of American elements 2. representative of the U.S. as a whole, or chosen as best in the U.S. 3. of all the Americas

al·lan·to·is (a lan′tō wis) *n.*, *pl.* **al·lan·to·i·des** (al′an tō′a dēz′) [ModL. < Gr. *allantoeidēs*, sausage-shaped] a membraneous pouch constituting a breathing apparatus in the embryos of most vertebrates

al·lay (a lā′) *vt.* **-layed′, -lay′ing** [< OE. < a-, down + lecgan, to lay] 1. to put (fears, etc.) to rest; calm 2. to lessen or relieve (pain, etc.)

all-clear (ôl′klir′) *n.* a siren or other signal that an air raid or practice alert is over

al·le·ga·tion (al′a gā′shan) *n.* 1. an alleging 2. something alleged; assertion 3. an assertion made without proof 4. *Law* an assertion which its maker proposes to support with evidence

al·lege (a lej′) *vt.* **-leged′, -leg′ing** [ME. *aleggen*, to produce as evidence < OFr., ult. < L. *ex-*, out of + *litigare*: see LITIGATE] 1. to declare or assert 2. to assert or declare without proof 3. to give as a plea, excuse, etc. —**al·lege′-a·ble** *adj.* —**al·leg′er** *n.*

al·leged (a lejd′, a lej′id) *adj.* 1. so declared, but without proof [the *alleged* assassin] 2. so-called [his *alleged* friends] —**al·leg′ed·ly** *adv.*

al·le·giance (a lē′jans) *n.* [< OFr. a-, to + *ligeance* < *liege*: see LIEGE] 1. the obligation of support and loyalty to one's ruler, government, or country 2. loyalty or devotion, as to a cause, person, etc. —**al·le′giant** (-jant) *adj.*, *n.*

al·le·gor·i·cal (al′a gor′i k'l) *adj.* 1. of or characteristic of allegory 2. that is or contains an allegory Also **al′le·gor′ic** —**al′le·gor′i·cal·ly** *adv.*

al·le·go·rist (al′a gor′ist) *n.* one who writes allegories —**al′-le·go·ris′tic** *adj.*

al·le·go·rize (al′a ga rīz′) *vt.* **-rized′, -riz′ing** 1. to make into or treat as an allegory 2. to interpret in an allegorical sense —*vi.* to make or use allegories —**al′le·go·ri·za′tion** *n.* —**al′le·go·riz′er** *n.*

al·le·go·ry (al′a gor′ē) *n.*, *pl.* **-ries** [< L. < Gr. < *allos*, other + *agoreuein*, to speak < *agora*, AGORA[1]] 1. a story, play, picture, etc. in which people, things, and events have a symbolic meaning: allegories are used for teaching or explaining ideas, moral principles, etc. 2. the presenting of ideas by such symbolism 3. any symbol or emblem

al·le·gret·to (al′a gret′ō) *adj.*, *adv.* [It., dim. of ALLEGRO] *Music* moderately fast; somewhat slower than *allegro* —*n.*, *pl.* **-tos** an allegretto movement or passage

al·le·gro (a leg′rō, -lā′grō) *adj.*, *adv.* [It. < L. *alacer*, brisk] *Music* fast, but not so fast as *presto* —*n.*, *pl.* **-gros** a fast movement or passage

al·lele (a lēl′) *n.* [G. *Allel* < Gr. *allēlōn*, of one another] either of a pair of genes in the same position on both members of a pair of chromosomes and bearing characters inherited alternatively according to Mendelian law: also **al·le·lo·morph** (a lel′a môrf′, a lē′la-) —**al·le′lic** *adj.*

al·le·lu·ia (al′a loo′ya) *interj.*, *n.* same as HALLELUJAH

al·le·mande (al′a mand′) *n.* [Fr. < *allemand*, German] any of various stately German dances 2. music for such a dance 3. a figure in a dance in which a couple join hands and make a turn

al·ler·gen (al′ar jan) *n.* [G. < *Allergie*, ALLERGY + -gen, -GEN] a substance inducing an allergic state or reaction —**al′ler·gen′ic** (-jen′ik) *adj.*

al·ler·gic (a lur′jik) *adj.* 1. of or caused by allergy 2. having an allergy 3. unwilling or not inclined (*to*): a humorous usage [*allergic* to study]

al·ler·gist (al′ar jist) *n.* a doctor who specializes in treating allergies

al·ler·gy (al′ar jē) *n.*, *pl.* **-gies** [< G. < Gr. *allos*, other + -*ergeia*, as in *energeia* (see ENERGY)] 1. abnormal sensitivity to a specific substance (such as a food, pollen, dust, etc.) or condition (as heat or cold) which in like amounts is harmless to most people 2. [Colloq.] a strong dislike

al·le·vi·ate (a lē′vē āt′) *vt.* **-at′ed, -at′ing** [< LL. pp. of *alleviare* < L. < *ad-*, to + *levis*, light] 1. to make less hard to bear; relieve (pain, etc.) 2. to reduce or decrease [to *alleviate* poverty] —**al·le′vi·a′tion** *n.* —**al·le′vi·a′tive** *adj.* —**al·le′vi·a′tor** *n.* —**al·le′vi·a·to·ry** (-a tar ē) *adj.*

al·ley[1] (al′ē) *n.*, *pl.* **-leys** [< OFr. *alee*, a going < *aler* (Fr. *aller*), to go < ML. < L. *ambulare*, to walk] 1. a lane in a garden or park 2. a narrow street or walk; specif., a lane behind a row of buildings 3. *Tenpin Bowling* the long, narrow lane along which the balls are rolled: now usually LANE —**up** (or **down**) **one's alley** [Slang] suited to one's tastes or abilities

al·ley[2] (al′ē) *n.*, *pl.* **-leys** [< *alabaster*, formerly used for marbles] a fine marble used as the shooter in playing marbles: also **al′ly**

al·ley·way (al′ē wä′) *n.* 1. an alley between buildings 2. any narrow passageway

all found including meals, heating, etc. without extra charge

all hail [Archaic] all health: a greeting

All-hal·lows (ôl′hal′ōz) *n.* [< OE. *ealle halgan*: see ALL & HALLOW[1]] [Archaic] same as ALL SAINTS' DAY: also called **All′hal′low·mas** (-hal′ō mas)

al·li·a·ceous (al′ē ā′shas) *adj.* [< L. *allium*, garlic + -ACEOUS] 1. of a group of strong-smelling bulb plants of the lily family, including onion, garlic, etc. 2. tasting or smelling of onions or garlic

al·li·ance (a lī′ans) *n.* [< OFr. < *alier*: see ALLY] 1. an allying or being allied; specif., a union, as of families by marriage 2. a) a close association for a common goal, as of nations, parties, etc. b) the agreement for such an association c) the countries, groups, etc. in such association 3. similarity or relationship in characteristics

al·lied (a līd′; also, esp. for 3, al′īd) *adj.* 1. united by kinship, treaty, etc. 2. closely related [*allied* sciences] 3. [A-] of the Allies

Al·lies (al′īz′, a līz′) *n.pl.* 1. in World War I, the nations allied by treaty against Germany and the other Central Powers; orig., Great Britain, France, and Russia, later joined by the U.S., Italy, Japan, etc. 2. in World War II, the nations associated against the Axis; esp., Great Britain, the Soviet Union, and the U.S.: see UNITED NATIONS

al·li·ga·tor (al′a gāt′ar) *n.* [< Sp. *el*, the + *lagarto* < L. *lacerta*, LIZARD] 1. a large reptile of the crocodile group, found in tropical rivers and marshes of the U.S. and in China 2. a leather made from its hide

alligator pear same as AVOCADO

all-im·por·tant (ôl′im pôr′t'nt) *adj.* essential

all-in (ôl′in′) *adj.* 1. with all expenses included in the price 2. *Wrestling* denoting a style in which any type of hold, throw, or attack is allowed

ALLIGATOR
(2.4-3.6m long)

al·lit·er·ate (a lit′a rāt′) *vi.*, *vt.* **-at′ed, -at′ing** to show or cause to show alliteration

al·lit·er·a·tion (a lit′a rā′shan) *n.* [< ML. < L. *ad-*, to + *littera*, letter] repetition of a beginning sound, usually of a consonant, in two or more words of a phrase, line of poetry, etc. (Ex.: "*S*ing a *s*ong of *s*ixpence")

al·lit·er·a·tive (a lit′a rāt′iv, -a ra tiv) *adj.* of, showing, or using alliteration —**al·lit′er·a′tive·ly** *adv.* —**al·lit′er·a′-tive·ness** *n.*

al·lo- [< Gr. *allos*, other] a combining form signifying variation or reversal [*allotropy*]

al·lo·cate (al′a kāt′) *vt.* **-cat′ed, -cat′ing** [< ML. pp. of *allocare* < L. *ad-*, to + *locus*, a place] 1. to set apart for a specific purpose 2. to distribute in shares; allot 3. to fix the place of; locate —**al′lo·ca·ble** (-ka b'l) *adj.* —**al′lo·ca′-tion** *n.*

al·lo·cu·tion (al'ə kyōō'shən) *n.* [< L. *allocutio* < *alloqui*, to speak to] a formal address

al·lom·er·ism (ə lom'ər iz'm) *n.* [< ALLO- + Gr. *meros*, part + -ISM] variation in chemical makeup without change in crystalline form —**al·lom'er·ous** (-əs) *adj.*

al·lo·morph (al'ə môrf') *n.* [ALLO- + -MORPH] 1. *Linguis.* any of the variant forms of a morpheme as conditioned by position or adjoining sounds 2. *Mineralogy* any of the crystalline forms of a substance existing in more than one such form

al·lo·path (al'ə path') *n.* a person who practises or advocates allopathy: also **al·lop·a·thist** (ə lop'ə thist)

al·lop·a·thy (ə lop'ə thē) *n.* [< G.: see ALLO- & -PATHY] treatment of disease by remedies that produce effects different from those produced by the disease: opposed to HOMEOPATHY —**al·lo·path·ic** (al'ə path'ik) *adj.* —**al'lo·path'i·cal·ly** *adv.*

al·lo·phone (al'ə fōn') *n.* [ALLO- + -PHONE¹] *Linguis.* any of the variant forms of a phoneme

al·lot (ə lot') *vt.* -**lot'ted**, -**lot'ting** [OFr. *aloter* < *a*-, to + *lot*, lot] 1. to distribute by lot or in shares; apportion 2. to give or assign as one's share [each speaker is *allotted* five minutes] —**al·lot'ta·ble** *adj.* —**al·lot'ter** *n.*

al·lot·ment (-mənt) *n.* 1. an allotting or being allotted 2. a thing allotted; portion 3. a plot of land for cultivation rented by an individual from a local council or other body 4. [U.S.] *Mil.* a regular deduction from one's pay, as for one's dependants

al·lo·trope (al'ə trōp') *n.* an allotropic form

al·lo·trop·ic (al'ə trop'ik) *adj.* of or having allotropy: also **al'lo·trop'i·cal** —**al'lo·trop'i·cal·ly** *adv.*

al·lot·ro·py (ə lot'rə pē) *n.* [< Gr. < ALLO- + *tropos*, way, manner] the property that certain chemical elements have of existing in two or more different forms: also **al·lot'ro·pism**

al·lot·tee (ə lot'ē') *n.* a person to whom something is allotted

all-out (ôl'out') *adj.* complete or wholehearted [an *all-out* effort]

al·low (ə lou') *vt.* [< OFr. *alouer* < ML. < L. < *ad*-, to + *locus*, a place: associated with OFr. *alouer* < L. *ad*-, to + *laudare*, to praise] 1. to let do, happen, etc.; permit [*allowed* to rot] 2. to let have [*allowed* no holiday] 3. to let enter [dogs not *allowed*] 4. to admit (a claim or the like); acknowledge as true 5. to provide or allot (an amount, period, etc.) for a purpose [*allow* a little extra for shrinkage] —**allow for** to keep in mind [*allow for* the difference in time] —**allow of** to be subject to

al·low·a·ble (-ə b'l) *adj.* that can be allowed; permissible —**al·low'a·bly** *adv.*

al·low·ance (-əns) *n.* 1. an allowing, permitting, etc. 2. something allowed, as an amount of money, food, etc. given regularly, as to a child, or for a specific purpose 3. a reduction in price in consideration of a large order, a trade-in, etc. —*vt.* -**anced**, -**anc·ing** 1. to put on an allowance 2. to apportion economically —**make allowance** (or **allowances**) to take circumstances into consideration —**make allowance** (or **allowances**) **for** 1. to excuse because of mitigating factors 2. to leave room, time, etc. for

al·low·ed·ly (ə lou'id lē) *adv.* admittedly

al·loy (al'oi; *also, and for* v. *usually*, ə loi') *n.* [< Anglo-Fr. < OFr. < L. *alligare*: see ALLY] 1. a substance that is a mixture of two or more metals, or of a metal and something else 2. a) formerly, a less valuable metal mixed with a more valuable one, often to give hardness b) something that lowers the value of another thing when mixed with it —*vt.* 1. to make (a metal) less pure by mixing with a less valuable metal 2. to mix (metals) to form an alloy 3. to debase by mixing with something inferior

all-pur·pose (ôl'pur'pəs) *adj.* useful in many ways

all right 1. satisfactory; adequate 2. unhurt; safe 3. correct 4. yes; very well 5. [Colloq.] certainly [he's the one, *all right*]

all-round (ôl'round') *adj.* 1. efficient in all respects; versatile [an *all-round* player] 2. comprehensive; many-sided [an *all-round* education]

all-round·er (-ər) *n.* a person who is competent in several activities, esp. in sport; specif., in cricket, one who is both batsman and bowler

All Saints' Day an annual church festival (November 1) in honour of all the saints

All Souls' Day in some Christian churches, a day (usually November 2) of prayer for the dead

all-spice (ôl'spis') *n.* 1. the berry of a West Indian tree of the myrtle family 2. the spice made from this berry: its flavour seems to combine the tastes of several spices 3. the tree itself

all-star (-stär') *adj.* made up entirely of outstanding or star performers

all-time (-tīm') *adj.* unsurpassed up to the present time [an *all-time* record]

al·lude (ə lōōd', ə lyōōd') *vi.* -**lud'ed**, -**lud'ing** [L. *alludere*, to jest < *ad*-, to + *ludere*, to play] to refer to in a casual or indirect way (*to*)

al·lure (ə loor', ə lyoor') *vt., vi.* -**lured'**, -**lur'ing** [< OFr. *a*-, to + *lurer*, to LURE] to tempt with something desirable; attract; entice —*n.* the power of alluring; fascination —**al·lure'ment** *n.* —**al·lur'er** *n.*

al·lur·ing (ə loor'ig, ə lyoor'ig) *adj.* tempting strongly; highly attractive; charming —**al·lur'ing·ly** *adv.*

al·lu·sion (ə lōō'zhən, ə lyōō'zhən) *n.* 1. an alluding 2. an indirect reference; casual mention

al·lu·sive (ə lōōs'iv, ə lyōōs'iv) *adj.* 1. containing an allusion 2. using allusion; full of allusions —**al·lu'sive·ly** *adv.* —**al·lu'sive·ness** *n.*

al·lu·vi·al (ə lōō'vē əl, ə lyōō'vē əl) *adj.* of, composed of, or found in alluvium —*n.* *same as* ALLUVIUM

al·lu·vi·on (ə lōō'vē ən, ə lyōō'-) *n.* 1. the washing of water against a shore or bank 2. an overflowing 3. *same as* ALLUVIUM 4. *Law* a gradual addition to land along a lake, river, etc. by the water's action

al·lu·vi·um (ə lōō'vē əm, ə lyōō'vē əm) *n.* -**vi·ums**, -**vi·a** (-vē ə) [< L. < *alluere* < *ad*-, to + *luere*, to LAVE] sand, clay, etc. gradually deposited by moving water, as along a river bed

al·ly (ə lī'; *also, and for* n. *usually*, al'ī) *vt.* -**lied'**, -**ly'ing** [< OFr. *alier* < L. *alligare* < *ad*-, to + *ligare*, to bind] 1. to unite for a specific purpose, as families by marriage or nations by treaty 2. to relate by similarity of structure, qualities, etc.: usually in the passive [the onion is *allied* to the lily] —*vi.* to become allied —*n.*, *pl.* -**lies** 1. a country or person joined with another for a common purpose 2. [A-] [*pl.*] *see* ALLIES 3. a plant, animal or thing closely related in structure, etc. to another 4. an associate; helper

al·ma ma·ter (al'mə mät'ər, mät'ər) [L., fostering mother] the university or school that one attended

al·ma·nac (ôl'mə nak') *n.* [< ML. < LGr. *almenichiaka*, calendar] 1. a calendar with astronomical data, weather forecasts, etc. 2. a book published annually, containing information, usually statistical, on many subjects

al·might·y (ôl mīt'ē) *adj.* [< OE. < *eal*, all + *mihtig*, mighty] 1. having unlimited power; all-powerful 2. [Slang] great; extreme —*adv.* [Slang] extremely —**the Almighty** God —**al·might'i·ly** *adv.* —**al·might'i·ness** *n.*

al·mond (ä'mənd) *n.* [< OFr. < L. < Gr. *amygdalē*] 1. the edible, nutlike kernel of a small, dry, peachlike fruit 2. the tree bearing this fruit —*adj.* 1. made of, or tasting of, almonds 2. almond-shaped —**al'mond·like'** *adj.*

al·mon·er (al'mən ər, ä'mən-) *n.* 1. one who distributes alms 2. formerly, a hospital social worker responsible, in conjunction with the social services, for the welfare and after-care of patients

al·most (ôl'mōst) *adv.* [OE. *eallmæst*: see ALL & MOST] very nearly; all but

alms (ämz) *n., pl.* **alms** [< OE. *ælmesse* < LL. < Gr. *eleēmosynē*, alms < *eleos*, pity] money, food, etc. given to poor people —**alms'giv'er** *n.*

alms·house (-hous') *n.* a building, endowed by charity for housing the poor

al·oe (al'ō) *n., pl.* -**oes** [< L. < Gr. *aloē*] 1. any of a large genus of South African plants of the lily family, with fleshy, spiny leaves 2. [*pl., with sing.* v.] a laxative drug made from the juice of certain aloe leaves

a·loft (ə loft') *adv.* [ME. *o*, *on*, on + *loft* < ON. *lopt*: see LOFT] 1. high up; up above 2. in the air; flying 3. high above a ship's deck

a·lo·ha (ə lō'ə, ä lō'hä) *n., interj.* [Haw., lit., love] a word used as a greeting or farewell

a·lone (ə lōn') *adj., adv.* [ME. < *al*, ALL + *one*, ONE] 1. apart from anything or anyone else [the hut stood *alone* in the woods] 2. without any other person [to walk *alone*] 3. with nothing more; only [one man *alone* can lift it] 4. without equal or peer —**let alone** 1. to refrain from bothering 2. not to mention [we hadn't a penny, *let alone* a pound] —**let well enough alone** to be content with things as they are —**a·lone'ness** *n.*

a·long (ə log') *prep.* [< OE. *andlang*, along < *and*-, over against + *-lang*, long] 1. on or beside the length of; over or throughout the length of [*along* the wall is a hedge] 2. in conformity with [to think *along* certain lines] —*adv.* 1. in a line; lengthways 2. progressively onwards [he walked *along* by himself] 3. as a companion [come *along* with us] 4. with one [she took her book *along*] —**all along** from the very beginning —**along with** 1. together with 2. in addition to —**be along** [Colloq.] to come or arrive [I'll be *along* soon]

a·long·shore (ə lon'shôr') *adv.* along the shore; near or beside the shore

a·long·side (-sīd') *adv.* at or by the side; side by side —*prep.* at the side of; side by side with —**alongside of** at the side of; beside

a·loof (ə lōōf') *adv.* [a-, on + *loof* < Du. *loef*, LUFF, to windward] at a distance but in view; apart —*adj.* 1. at a distance; removed 2. distant in sympathy, interest, etc. [an *aloof* manner] —**a·loof'ly** *adv.* —**a·loof'ness** *n.*

al·o·pe·ci·a (al'ə pēsh'ē ə, -pēsh'ə) *n.* [L. < Gr. *alōpekia*, fox mange] baldness

a·loud (ə loud′) *adv.* 1. loudly 2. with the normal voice [read the letter *aloud*]

alp (alp) *n.* [< L. *Alpes*, the Alps] a high mountain; esp. [*pl.*] [**A-**] those in Switzerland and adjoining countries

al·pac·a (al̩pak′ə) *n., pl.* **-pac′as, -pac′a :** see PLURAL, II, D, 1 [Sp. < SAmInd. *allpaca*] 1. a domesticated S. American mammal related to the llama, with long, fleecy wool 2. this wool 3. a cloth woven from this wool, often mixed with other fibres 4. a glossy cloth of cotton and wool

al·pen·horn (al′pən hôrn′) *n.* [G., Alpine horn] a curved, wooden, powerful-sounding horn, from 1.5m to 3.5m long, used by Swiss Alpine herdsmen for signalling: also **alp′-horn′**

al·pen·stock (-stok′) *n.* [G., Alpine staff] an iron-pointed staff used by mountain climbers

al·pha (al′fə) *n.* [Gr. < Phoen. name whence Heb. *āleph*: see ALEPH] 1. the first letter of the Greek alphabet (A, α) 2. the beginning of anything 3. the brightest star in a constellation

alpha and omega 1. the first and last letters of the Greek alphabet 2. the beginning and the end

al·pha·bet (al′fə bet′) *n.* [< LL. < LGr. < Gr.: see ALPHA & BETA] 1. the letters of a language, arranged in a traditional order 2. a system of signs or symbols to indicate letters or speech sounds 3. the first elements, as of a subject

al·pha·bet·i·cal (al′fə bet′i k′l) *adj.* 1. of or using an alphabet 2. in the usual order of the alphabet Also **al′-pha·bet′ic** —**al′pha·bet′i·cal·ly** *adv.*

al·pha·bet·ize (al′fə bə tīz′) *vt.* **-ized′, -iz′ing** 1. to arrange in alphabetical order 2. to express by or provide with an alphabet —**al′pha·bet′i·za′tion** (-bet′i zā′shən) *n.*

al·pha·nu·mer·ic (al′fə nyōo mer′ik) *adj.* [ALPHA(BET) + NUMERIC(AL)] having or using both alphabetical and numerical symbols: also **al·pha·mer′ic**

alpha particle a positively charged particle given off by certain radioactive substances: it consists of two protons and two neutrons

alpha ray 1. *same as* ALPHA PARTICLE 2. a stream of alpha particles, less penetrating than a beta ray

Al·pine (al′pīn) *adj.* 1. of the Alps or their inhabitants 2. [**a-**] *a)* of or like high mountains *b)* growing in high altitudes —*n.* [*also* **a-**] a plant that grows at high altitudes

al·read·y (ôl red′ē) *adv.* 1. by or before the given or implied time 2. even now or even then

al·right (ôl rīt′) *adv. var. of* ALL RIGHT: a disputed sp., but in common use

al·sa·tian (al sā′shən) *n.* any of a breed of large, powerful, somewhat wolflike dogs, used in police work, etc.

al·so (ôl′sō) *adv.* [< OE. < *eal*, all + *swa*, so] in addition; too: sometimes used in place of *and*

al·so-ran (-ran′) *n.* 1. a horse that fails to finish first, second, or third in a race 2. [Colloq.] any loser in a race, competition, election, etc.

alt. 1. alternate 2. altitude 3. alto

Alta. Alberta (Canada)

Al·ta·ic (al tā′ik) *adj.* 1. of the Altai Mountains or the people living there 2. designating or of a family of languages including Turkic and Mongolic

al·tar (ôl′tər) *n.* [< OE. & OFr.; both ult. < L. < *altus*, high] 1. a raised platform where sacrifices are made to a god, etc. 2. a table, stand, etc. used for sacred purposes in a place of worship, as the Communion table in Christian churches —**lead to the altar** to marry

altar boy a boy or man who helps a priest, vicar, etc. at religious services, esp. at Mass

al·tar·piece (-pēs′) *n.* an ornamental carving, painting, etc. above and behind an altar

alt·az·i·muth (alt′az′ə məth) *n.* [ALT(ITUDE) + AZIMUTH] an instrument for simultaneously measuring the altitude and azimuth of a star, planet, etc.

al·ter (ôl′tər) *vt.* [< ML. *alterare* < L. *alter*, other] 1. to make different in details; modify 2. to resew (part of) (a garment) for a better fit 3. [Chiefly U.S.] to castrate or spay —*vi.* to become different; change —**al′ter·a·ble** *adj.* —**al′ter·a·bly** *adv.*

al·ter·ant (-ənt) *adj.* causing alteration —*n.* a thing that causes alteration

al·ter·a·tion (ôl′tə rā′shən) *n.* 1. an altering or being altered 2. the result of this; change

al·ter·a·tive (ôl′tə rāt′iv, -rə tiv) *adj.* 1. causing alteration 2. *Med.* gradually altering bodily processes —*n.* an alterative medicine or treatment

al·ter·cate (ôl′tər kāt′) *vi.* **-cat′ed, -cat′ing** [< L. pp. of *altercari*, to dispute < *alter*, other] to argue angrily; quarrel

al·ter·ca·tion (ôl′tər kā′shən) *n.* an angry or heated argument

al·ter e·go (al′tər ē′gō, eg′ō) [L., lit., other I] 1. another aspect of oneself 2. a very close friend or constant companion

al·ter·nate (ôl ter′nit, ol-; *for v.* ôl′tər nāt′) *adj.* [< L. pp. of *alternare*, to do by turns < *alternus*, one after the other < *alter*, other] 1. succeeding each other; first one and then the other 2. every other [*alternate* Fridays] 3. being one

of two or more choices; alternative 4. *Bot.* growing along the stem singly at intervals —*n.* a person chosen to take the place of another if necessary; substitute —*vt.* **-nat′ed, -nat′ing** to do, use, or make happen by turns —*vi.* 1. to act, happen, etc. by turns 2. to take turns 3. to exchange places, etc. regularly 4. *Elec.* to reverse direction periodically: said of a current —**al′ter·nate·ly** *adv.* —**al′-ter·na′tion** *n.*

alternate angles two angles at opposite ends and on opposite sides of a line crossing two others

alternating current an electric current that reverses its direction periodically

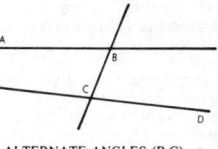

ALTERNATE ANGLES (B,C)

al·ter·na·tive (ôl tur′nə tiv, ol-) *adj.* providing or being a choice between two (or, less strictly, among more than two) things —*n.* 1. a choice between two or more things 2. any of the things to be chosen —**al′ter′na·tive·ly** *adv.*

al·ter·na·tor (ôl′tər nāt′ər, ol′-) *n.* an electric generator or dynamo producing alternating current

al·thae·a (al thē′ə) *n.* [< L. < Gr. *althaia*, wild mallows] 1. any of a genus of plants in the mallow family, as the hollyhock 2. *same as* ROSE OF SHARON (sense 1)

alt·horn (alt′hôrn′) *n.* a brass instrument, the alto saxhorn: also **alto horn**

al·though (ôl thō′) *conj.* [ME. < *all, al*, even (emphatic) + *though*] in spite of the fact that; though

al·tim·e·ter (al′tə mēt′ər) *n.* [< L. *altus*, high + -METER] an instrument for measuring altitude; esp., in aircraft, an aneroid barometer that tells how high the craft is flying —**al·tim′e·try** *n.*

al·ti·tude (al′tə tyōod′) *n.* [< L. < *altus*, high] 1. height; esp., the height of a thing above the earth's surface or above sea level 2. a high place or region: *usually in pl.* 3. a high level, eminence, etc. 4. *Astron.* the angular height of a planet, star, etc. above the horizon 5. *Geom.* the perpendicular distance from the base of a figure to its highest point —**al′ti·tu′di·nal** (-ən əl) *adj.*

al·to (al′tō) *n., pl.* **-tos** [It. < L. *altus*, high] 1. the range of the lowest female voice or, esp. formerly, the highest male voice 2. a voice or singer with such range 3. an instrument with the second highest range within a family of instruments, as the alto saxophone 4. a part for such a voice or instrument —*adj.* of, in, for, or having this range

alto clef *see* C CLEF

al·to·cu·mu·lus (al′tō kyōo′myə ləs) *n.* [< L. *altus*, high + CUMULUS] a cloud formation of many shapes, most commonly rounded, found at intermediate heights

al·to·geth·er (ôl′tə geth′ər, ôl′tə geth′ər) *adv.* [see ALL & TOGETHER] 1. wholly; completely [*altogether* right] 2. in all [he wrote six books *altogether*] 3. on the whole [*altogether* a success] Distinguished from **all together** —**in the altogether** [Colloq.] nude

al·to·stra·tus (al′tō strāt′əs) *n.* [< L. *altus*, high + STRATUS] a cloud formation found at intermediate heights in continuous dense layers or thick patches

al·tri·cial (al trish′əl) *adj.* [< L. *altrix*, a nurse] of birds whose newly hatched young are helpless and dependent on the parents for food

al·tru·ism (al′trōo iz′m) *n.* [< Fr. < It. *altrui*, of or to others < L. *alter*, another] unselfish concern for the welfare of others —**al′tru·ist** *n.*

al·tru·is·tic (al′trōo is′tik) *adj.* of or motivated by altruism —**al′tru·is′ti·cal·ly** *adv.*

al·um (al′əm) *n.* [< OFr. < L. *alumen*] 1. a hydrated double sulphate of a trivalent metal and a univalent metal; esp., a double sulphate of potassium and aluminium, used in medicine and in making dyes, paper, etc. 2. aluminium sulphate: erroneous use

a·lu·mi·na (ə lōo′mi nə) *n.* an oxide of aluminium, Al_2O_3, present in bauxite and clay and found as different forms of corundum, including emery, sapphires, rubies, etc.

al·u·min·i·um (al′yoo min′yəm, -ē əm) *n.* [ModL. < L. *alumen, alum*] a silvery, lightweight, metallic chemical element that is easily worked, resists corrosion, and is found abundantly, but only in combination: symbol, Al; at. wt., 26.9815; at. no., 13 —*adj.* of, containing, or made of aluminium

aluminium oxide *same as* ALUMINA

a·lu·mi·nize (ə lōo′mə nīz′) *vt.* **-nized′, -niz′ing** to cover, or treat, with aluminium

a·lu·mi·nous (-nəs) *adj.* of or containing alum, alumina, or aluminium

a·lu·mi·num (ə lōo′mə nəm) *n. U.S. var. of* ALUMINIUM

a·lum·na (ə lum′nə) *n., pl.* **-nae** (-nē) [L., fem. of ff.] [U.S.] a girl or woman alumnus

a·lum·nus (-nəs) *n., pl.* **-ni** (-nī) [L., foster son < *alere*, to nourish] [U.S.] a person, esp. a boy or man, who has attended or is a graduate of a particular school, college, etc.

al·ve·o·lar (al vē′ə lər) *adj.* 1. of or like an alveolus; socketlike 2. *Anat.* a) of the part of the jaws containing the sockets of the teeth b) designating the ridge of the gums behind the upper front teeth c) of the air pockets in the lungs 3. *Phonet.* formed, as English *t, d, s,* by touching or approaching the alveolar ridge with the tip of the tongue —*n. Phonet.* an alveolar sound

al·ve·o·late (-lit) *adj.* full of small cavities: also **al·ve′o·lat′-ed** (-lāt′id) —**al·ve′o·la′tion** *n.*

al·ve·o·lus (al vē′ə ləs) *n., pl.* **-li** (-lī′) [L., dim. of *alveus,* a cavity < *alvus,* the belly] 1. *Anat., Zool.* a small cavity or hollow, as an air cell of a lung, a tooth socket, etc. 2. [*usually pl.*] the alveolar ridge

al·way (ôl′wā) *adv.* [Archaic] always

al·ways (ôl′wiz, -wāz) *adv.* [see ALL & WAY] 1. in every instance; invariably [he's *always* late] 2. all the time; forever [*always* present in the atmosphere] 3. if need be [you can *always* leave] 4. continually; frequently [the baby's *always* crying]

a·lys·sum (ə′lis əm) *n.* [ModL. < Gr. < *alyssos,* curing madness < *a-,* without + *lyssa,* rage] 1. any of a genus of plants of the cabbage family, with white or yellow flowers 2. same as SWEET ALYSSUM

am (am; *unstressed* əm) [OE. *eom:* see BE] *1st pers. sing., pres. indic.,* of BE

Am *Chem.* americium

AM amplitude modulation

Am. 1. America 2. American

A.M., AM [L. *Artium Magister*] [U.S.] master of arts

A.M., a.m., AM [L. *ante meridiem*] before noon: used to designate the time from midnight to noon

a·mah (ä′mə) *n.* [Anglo-Ind. < Port. *ama*] in the Orient, a woman servant, esp. one who serves as a baby's nurse

a·main (ə mān′) *adv.* [A-¹, on + MAIN¹] [Archaic or Poet.] 1. forcefully; vigorously 2. at or with great speed 3. hastily; suddenly 4. greatly

a·mal·gam (ə mal′gəm) *n.* [< ML., prob. < Ar. < Gr. *malagma,* an emollient < *malassein,* to soften] 1. any alloy of mercury with another metal or metals [silver *amalgam* is used as a dental filling] 2. any mixture or blend

a·mal·ga·mate (-gə māt′) *vt., vi.* **-mat′ed, -mat′ing** 1. to combine in an amalgam 2. to join together into one; unite —**a·mal′ga·ma·ble** (-gəm ə b'l) *adj.* —**a·mal′ga·ma′tion** *n.* —**a·mal′ga·ma′tive** *adj.* —**a·mal′ga·ma′tor** *n.*

a·man·u·en·sis (ə man′yoo wen′sis) *n., pl.* **-ses** (-sēz) [L. < *a-* (*ab*), from + *manus,* a hand + *-ensis,* relating to] an assistant who takes dictation or copies something already written; secretary

am·a·ranth (am′ə ranth′) *n.* [< L. < Gr. *amarantos,* unfading < *a-,* not + *marainein,* to die away] 1. any of a genus of plants, usually with colourful leaves, including love-lies-bleeding, etc. 2. [Poet.] an imaginary flower that never fades or dies 3. a dark purplish red —**am′a·ran′thine** (-ran′thin) *adj.*

am·a·ryl·lis (am′ə ril′əs) *n.* [< L. & Gr.; conventional name for a shepherdess] 1. a bulb plant bearing several white, purple, pink, or red lilylike flowers on a single stem 2. any of several plants closely related to this

a·mass (ə mas′) *vt.* [< Fr. < ML. < *a-,* to + VL. *massare,* to pile up < *massa,* a MASS] 1. to pile up; collect together 2. to accumulate (esp. wealth) —**a·mass′er** *n.* —**a·mass′-ment** *n.*

am·a·teur (am′ə chər, -tər, -tyoor) *n.* [Fr. < L. *amator,* a lover < *amare,* to love] 1. a person who engages in some art, science, sport, etc. for pleasure rather than as a profession; specif., an athlete who is forbidden by rule to profit from his athletic activity 2. a person who does something without professional skill —*adj.* 1. of or done by or as by an amateur or amateurs 2. being an amateur or made up of amateurs

am·a·teur·ish (am′ə choor ish, -tər-, -tyoor-; am′ə tur′ish) *adj.* like an amateur; unskilful; not expert —**am′a·teur′-ish·ly** *adv.* —**am′a·teur′ish·ness** *n.*

am·a·teur·ism (am′ə chər iz′m, -tər-, -tyoor-) *n.* 1. an amateurish method or quality 2. the nonprofessional status of an amateur

am·a·tive (am′ə tiv) *adj.* [< ML. *amativus,* lovable < pp. of L. *amare,* to love] of or inclined to love

am·a·to·ry (am′ə tər ē) *adj.* [< L. pp. of *amare,* to love] of or showing love, esp. sexual love

am·au·ro·sis (am′ô rō′sis) *n.* [ModL. < Gr. < *amauros,* dark] partial or total blindness

a·maze (ə māz′) *vt.* **a·mazed′, a·maz′ing** [< OE. *amasian:* see MAZE] to fill with great surprise or sudden wonder; astonish —*n.* [Poet.] amazement —**a·maz′ed·ly** (-id lē) *adv.* —**a·maz′ing·ly** *adv.*

a·maze·ment (-mənt) *n.* an amazed condition; great wonder; astonishment

am·a·zon (am′ə zən) *n.* [L. < Gr. < ?, but derived by folk

etym. < *a-,* without + *mazos,* breast, hence the story that the Amazons cut off one breast to facilitate archery] a large, strong, or aggressive woman; after a race of female warriors supposed, in Greek mythology, to have lived in Scythia —**am·a·zo·ni·an** (am′ə zō′nē ən) *adj.*

am·bas·sa·dor (am bas′ə dər) *n.* [< MFr. < OIt. < Pr. < hyp. *ambaissa,* task, mission] 1. the highest-ranking diplomatic representative appointed by a government to represent it in another country: an **ambassador extraordinary** is one on a special diplomatic mission; an **ambassador plenipotentiary** has the power to make treaties 2. an official messenger with a special mission 3. a person representing his country informally in sport, culture, etc. —**am·bas′sa·do′ri·al** (-dôr′ē əl) *adj.* —**am·bas′-sa·dor·ship′** *n.* —**am·bas′sa·dress** *n. fem.*

am·bas·sa·dor-at-large (-at lärj) *n.* [U.S.] an ambassador with special duties who may be sent to several governments

am·ber (am′bər) *n.* [< OFr. < Ar. '*anbar,* ambergris] 1. a yellow or brownish-yellow translucent fossil resin used in jewellery, etc. 2. the colour of amber 3. the amber-coloured light between the green and red of traffic lights —*adj.* 1. made of or like amber 2. having the colour of amber

am·ber·gris (-grēs′, -gris′) *n.* [< OFr. < *ambre gris,* grey AMBER] a greyish, waxy substance from the intestines of sperm whales, found floating in tropical seas and used in some perfumes

am·ber·jack (-jak′) *n.* [AMBER + JACK (fish): from its colour] any of several food and game fishes found in warm seas

am·bi- [L. < *ambo,* both] *a combining form meaning* both [*ambidextrous*]

am·bi·ance (am′bē əns) *n.* [Fr.: see AMBIENT] an environment or milieu: also **am′bi·ence**

am·bi·dex·trous (am′bə dek′strəs) *adj.* [< L. AMBI- + *dexter,* right hand + -OUS] 1. able to use both hands with equal ease 2. very skilful or versatile 3. deceitful; double-dealing —**am′bi·dex·ter′i·ty** (-dek ster′ə tē) *n.* —**am′bi·dex′trous·ly** *adv.*

am·bi·ent (am′bē ənt) *adj.* [< L. prp. of *ambire* < *ambi-,* around + *ire,* to go] surrounding; on all sides

am·bi·gu·i·ty (am′bə gyoo′ə tē) *n.* 1. the quality or state of being ambiguous 2. *pl.* **-ties** an ambiguous word, statement, etc.

am·big·u·ous (am big′yoo wəs) *adj.* [< L. < *ambigere,* to wander < *ambi-,* around + *agere,* to act] 1. having two or more possible meanings 2. not clear; indefinite; vague —**am·big′u·ous·ly** *adv.* —**am·big′u·ous·ness** *n.*

am·bit (am′bit) *n.* [L. *ambitus,* a going about < pp. of *ambire:* see AMBIENT] 1. scope; extent 2. boundary; circumference

am·bi·tion (am bish′ən) *n.* [< OFr. < L. *ambitio,* a going around (to solicit votes) < pp. of *ambire:* see AMBIENT] 1. a strong desire for success, fame, power, wealth, etc. 2. the thing so desired

am·bi·tious (-əs) *adj.* 1. full of or showing ambition 2. greatly desirous (*of* something) 3. needing great effort, skill, enterprise, etc. —**am·bi′tious·ly** *adv.* —**am·bi′-tious·ness** *n.*

am·biv·a·lence (am biv′ə ləns) *n.* [AMBI- + VALENCE] simultaneous conflicting feelings towards a person or thing, as love and hate —**am·biv′a·lent** *adj.* —**am·biv′a·lent·ly** *adv.*

am·ble (am′b'l) *vi.* **-bled, -bling** [< OFr. < L. *ambulare,* to walk] 1. to move at a smooth, easy gait by raising first both legs on one side, then both on the other: said of a horse, etc. 2. to walk in a leisurely manner —*n.* 1. a horse's ambling gait 2. a leisurely walking pace —**am′-bler** *n.*

am·bly·o·pi·a (am′blē ōp′ē ə) *n.* [ModL. < Gr. *amblys,* dull + *ōps,* eye] a loss of sharpness of vision, esp. when not traceable to any intrinsic eye disease

am·boy·na (am boi′nə) *n.* [after *Amboyna* in Indonesia] the mottled, curly-grained wood of an Indonesian tree

am·bro·si·a (am brōz′ē ə, -brō′zhə) *n.* [L. < Gr. < *ambrotos* < *a-,* not + *brotos,* mortal] 1. *Gr. & Rom. Myth.* the food of the gods and immortals 2. anything that tastes or smells delicious —**am·bro′sial, am·bro′sian** *adj.*

am·bry (am′brē) *n., pl.* **-bries** [ME. *almerie* < OFr. < L. *armarium,* chest for tools or arms] a recessed cupboard in the wall of a church

am·bu·lance (am′byə ləns) *n.* [< Fr. (*hôpital*) *ambulant* < L. prp. of *ambulare,* to walk] 1. orig., a mobile field hospital 2. a specially equipped vehicle for carrying the sick or wounded

am·bu·lant (am′byə lənt) *adj.* moving; walking

am·bu·late (am′byə lāt′) *vi.* **-lat′ed, -lat′ing** [< L. pp. of *ambulare,* to walk] to move about; walk —**am′bu·la′tion** *n.*

am·bu·la·to·ry (-lə tər ē) *adj.* 1. of or for walking 2. able to walk and not confined to bed 3. moving from one place to another; movable 4. *Law* that can be changed or revoked

—*n.*, *pl.* **-ries** any sheltered place for walking, as in a cloister

am·bus·cade (am'bəs kād') *n.*, *vt.*, *vi.* **-cad'ed, -cad'ing** [< Fr. < OFr. *embuschier:* see ff.] *same as* AMBUSH —**am'·bus·cad'er** *n.*

am·bush (am'boosh) *n.* [< OFr. *embuschier* < ML. *imboscare*, to set an ambush < *in-*, in + *boscus*, woods] **1.** an arrangement of persons in hiding to make a surprise attack **2.** *a)* the persons in hiding *b)* their place of hiding **3.** the act of so lying in wait to attack —*vt.*, *vi.* **1.** to hide in ambush **2.** to attack from ambush —**am'bush·ment** *n.*

a·meer (ə mir') *n.* *same as* AMIR

a·mel·io·rant (ə mēl'yər ənt) *n.* a thing that ameliorates

a·mel·io·rate (ə mēl'yə rāt') *vt.*, *vi.* **-rat'ed, -rat'ing** [< Fr. < OFr. *ameillorer* < *a-*, to + *meillor* < *melior*, better] to make or become better; improve —**a·mel'io·ra·ble** (-yər ə b'l) *adj.* —**a·mel'io·ra'tion** *n.* —**a·mel'io·ra'tive** *adj.* —**a·mel'·io·ra'tor** *n.*

a·men (ā'men', ä'-) *interj.* [< L. < Gr. < Heb. *āmēn*, truly, certainly] may it be so! so it is!: used after a prayer or to express approval —*n.* a speaking or writing of "amen"

a·me·na·ble (ə mē'nə b'l, -men'ə-) *adj.* [Anglo-Fr. < OFr. < *a-*, to + *mener*, to lead < LL. *minare*, to drive (animals) < L. *minare*, to threaten] **1.** responsible or answerable **2.** able to be controlled or influenced; responsive; submissive [*amenable* to suggestion] **3.** that can be tested by (with *to*) [*amenable* to the laws of physics] —**a·me'na·bil'i·ty** *n.* —**a·me'na·bly** *adv.*

a·mend (ə mend') *vt.* [< OFr. < L. *emendare*, to correct: see EMEND] **1.** to make better; improve **2.** to remove the faults of; correct **3.** to change or revise (a legislative bill, a law, etc.) —*vi.* to improve one's conduct —**a·mend'a·ble** *adj.* —**a·mend'a·to·ry** *adj.* —**a·mend'er** *n.*

a·mend·ment (ə mend'mənt) *n.* **1.** a change for the better; improvement **2.** a correction of errors, faults, etc. **3.** a revision or addition proposed or made in a bill, law, constitution, etc.

a·mends (ə mendz') *n.pl.* [< OFr., pl. of *amende*, a fine: see AMEND] [*sometimes with sing. v.*] something given or done to make up for injury, loss, etc. that one has caused [to make *amends* for rudeness by apologizing]

a·men·i·ty (ə men'ə tē, -mē'nə-) *n.*, *pl.* **-ties** [< OFr. < L. *amoenitas* < *amoenus*, pleasant] **1.** pleasant quality; attractiveness **2.** *a)* an attractive or desirable feature, as of a place, climate, etc. *b)* anything that adds to one's comfort; convenience **3.** [*pl.*] the courtesies of polite social behaviour

a·men·or·rhoe·a (ā men'ə rē'ə) *n.* [ModL. < Gr. *a-*, not + *mēn*, month + *rheein*, to flow] abnormal absence or suppression of menstruation

am·ent (am'ənt, ā'mənt) *n.* [< L. *amentum*, thong] *same as* CATKIN —**am·en·ta·ceous** (am'ən tā'shəs) *adj.*

a·men·tia (ā men'shə) *n.* [L., madness < *amens* (gen. *amentis*) < *a-* (ab), away + *mens*, mind] severe congenital mental deficiency: cf. DEMENTIA

a·merce (ə murs') *vt.* **a·merced', a·merc'ing** [< Anglo-Fr. < OFr. *a merci*, at the mercy of] **1.** to punish by imposing an arbitrary fine **2.** to punish generally —**a·merce'ment** *n.*

A·mer·i·can (ə mer'ə kən) *adj.* **1.** of or in America **2.** of, in, or characteristic of the U.S., its people, etc. —*n.* **1.** a native or inhabitant of America **2.** a citizen of the U.S. **3.** the English language spoken in the U.S.

A·mer·i·ca·na (ə mer'ə kä'nə) *n.pl.* [see -ANA] books, papers, objects, etc. having to do with America, its people, and its history

American Indian *same as* INDIAN (*n.* 2)

A·mer·i·can·ism (ə mer'ə kən iz'm) *n.* **1.** a word, phrase or usage originating in or peculiar to American English **2.** a custom, characteristic, or belief of or originating in the U.S. **3.** devotion or loyalty to the U.S., or to its traditions, etc.

A·mer·i·can·ize (-īz') *vt.*, *vi.* **-ized', -iz'ing** to make or become American in character, manners, methods, ideals, etc. —**A·mer'i·can·i·za'tion** *n.*

am·er·ic·i·um (am'ə rish'ē əm, -ris'-) [ModL. < *America*] a chemical element, one of the transuranic elements produced from plutonium: symbol, Am; at. wt., 243.13; at. no., 95

Am·er·ind (am'ə rind') *n.* [AMER(ICAN) + IND(IAN)] an American Indian or Eskimo —**Am'er·in'di·an** *adj.*, *n.* —**Am'·er·in'dic** *adj.*

am·e·thyst (am'ə thist) *n.* [< OFr. < L. < Gr. < *a-*, not + *methystos*, drunken (from the notion that it prevented intoxication)] **1.** a purple or violet variety of quartz, used in jewellery **2.** popularly, a purple corundum, used in jewellery: also called **oriental amethyst 3.** purple or violet —**am'e·thys'tine** (-'tin, -tēn) *adj.*

Am·har·ic (am har'ik) *n.* the Semitic language used officially in Ethiopia

‡a·mi (à mē') *n.*, *pl.* **a·mis'** (-mē') [Fr.] a (man or boy) friend —**a·mie'** *n. fem.*, *pl.* **a·mies'** (-mē')

a·mi·a·ble (ā'mē ə b'l) *adj.* [< OFr. < LL. *amicabilis*, friendly < L. *amicus*, friend] having a pleasant, friendly disposition; good-natured —**a'mi·a·bil'i·ty** *n.* —**a'mi·a·bly** *adv.*

am·i·an·thus (am'ē an'thəs) *n.* [< L. < Gr. *amiantos* (*lithos*), lit., unspotted (stone)] a kind of asbestos with long, silky fibres

am·i·ca·ble (am'i kə b'l) *adj.* [< LL. *amicabilis:* see AMIABLE] friendly in feeling; showing good will; peaceable [an *amicable* discussion] —**am'i·ca·bil'i·ty** *n.* —**am'i·ca·bly** *adv.*

am·ice (am'is) *n.* [< OFr. < L. *amictus*, a cloak] an oblong cloth of white linen worn about the neck and shoulders by a priest at Mass

a·mi·cus cu·ri·ae (ə mī'kəs kyoor'i ē') [L., friend of the court] *Law* a person who offers, or is called in, to advise a court on some legal matter

a·mid (ə mid') *prep.* [ME. < *on*, at + *middan*, middle] in the middle of; among

am·ide (am'īd, -id) *n.* [AM(MONIA) + -IDE] **1.** any of a group of organic compounds containing the CO·NH₂ radical or an acid radical in place of one hydrogen atom of an ammonia molecule **2.** any of the ammono bases in which one hydrogen atom of the ammonia molecule is replaced by a metal —**a·mid·ic** (ə mid'ik) *adj.*

am·i·dol (am'ə dol') *n.* [< AMID(E) + (PHEN)OL] a colourless, crystalline compound used as a developer in photography

a·mid·ships (ə mid'ships) *adv.*, *adj.* in or towards the middle of a ship

a·midst (ə midst') *prep.* *same as* AMID

a·mi·go (ə mē'gō; *Sp.* ä mē'gô) *n.*, *pl.* **-gos** (-gōz; *Sp.* -gôs) [Sp.] a friend

a·mine (ə mēn'; am'ēn, -in) *n.* [AM(MONIA) + -INE⁴] *Chem.* a derivative of ammonia in which hydrogen atoms have been replaced by radicals containing hydrogen and carbon atoms

a·mi·no (ə mē'nō) *adj.* [< prec.] of or containing the NH₂ radical in combination with certain organic radicals

amino acids a group of organic compounds that contain the amino radical and serve as units of structure of the proteins

a·mir (ə mir') *n.* [Ar.] in some Moslem countries, a ruler, prince, or commander: see also EMIR

Am·ish (ä'mish, am'ish) *n.pl.* [after Jacob *Ammann* (or *Amen*), the founder] Mennonites of a sect founded in the 17th cent. —*adj.* of this sect

a·miss (ə mis') *adv.* [ME.: see A-¹ & MISS¹] in a wrong way; astray, wrongly, faultily, etc. —*adj.* wrong, faulty, improper, etc.: used predicatively

a·mi·to·sis (ā'mī tō'sis, am'ə-) *n.* [A-² (sense 3) + MITOSIS] *Biol.* cell division by simple constriction of the nucleus into two halves: opposed to MITOSIS —**am'i·tot'ic** (-tot'ik) *adj.*

am·i·ty (am'ə tē) *n.*, *pl.* **-ties** [< OFr. *amistie* < L. *amicus*, friend] friendly, peaceful relations, as between nations; friendship

am·me·ter (am'mēt'ər) *n.* [AM(PERE) + -METER] an instrument for measuring the strength of an electric current in terms of amperes

am·mo (am'ō) *n.* [Slang] ammunition

am·mo·nia (ə mōn'ē ə, -yə) *n.* [< (SAL) AMMONIAC] **1.** a colourless, pungent gas, NH₃, used in fertilizers, cleaning fluids, etc. **2.** a water solution of this gas: in full, **ammonia water** —**am·mo·ni·a·cal** (am'ə nī'ə k'l) *adj.*

am·mo·ni·ac (ə mō'nē ak') *n.* [< L. < Gr. *ammōniakon*, gum resin said to come from near the temple of Jupiter *Ammon*, in Libya] an Asian gum resin formerly used in perfumes, porcelain cements, etc.

am·mo·ni·ate (ə mō'nē āt'; *for n.* -it) *vt.* **-at'ed, -at'ing** to mix or combine with ammonia —*n.* any of several compounds containing ammonia —**am·mo'ni·a'tion** *n.*

am·mo·ni·fi·ca·tion (ə mō'nə fi kā'shən, -mon'ə-) *n.* **1.** an ammoniating **2.** the forming of ammonia by bacterial action in the decay of nitrogenous organic matter —**am·mo'·ni·fy'** *vt.*, *vi.* **-fied', -fy'ing**

am·mo·nite (am'ə nīt') *n.* [< L. (*cornu*) *Ammonis*, (horn) of *Ammon*] any of the coiled fossil shells of a Mesozoic mollusc

am·mo·ni·um (ə mō'nē əm) *n.* the radical NH₄, present in salts produced by the reaction of ammonia with an acid

ammonium chloride a white, crystalline compound, NH₄Cl: it is used in medicine, and also in dry cells, dyes, etc.: also called **sal ammoniac**

ammonium hydroxide an alkali, NH₄OH, formed by dissolving ammonia in water

ammonium sulphate an ammonium salt, (NH₄)₂SO₄, used in making fertilizers, in treating water, etc.

am·mo·no (am'ə nō') *adj.* of, containing, or derived from ammonia

am·mu·ni·tion (am'yoo nish'ən) *n.* [< Fr., by faulty separation of *la munition:* see MUNITIONS] **1.** anything hurled by a weapon or exploded as a weapon, as bullets, shells, bombs, grenades, etc. **2.** any means of attack or defence *[*the fact served as *ammunition* for his argument*]*

am·ne·si·a (am nē′zē ə) *n.* [ModL. < Gr. < a-, not + mnasthai, to remember] partial or total loss of memory caused by brain injury, or by shock, repression, etc. —**am·ne′si·ac′** (-zē ak′), **am·ne′sic** (-sik, -zik) *adj., n.*

am·nes·ty (am′nəs tē) *n., pl.* **-ties** [< Fr. < L. < Gr. amnēstia, a forgetting: see prec.] a general pardon, esp. for political offences —*vt.* **-tied, -ty·ing** to grant amnesty to; pardon

am·ni·on (am′nē ən, -on′) *n., pl.* **-ni·ons, -ni·a** (-ə) [Gr., dim. of amnos, lamb] the innermost membrane of the sac enclosing the embryo of a mammal, reptile, or bird: it is filled with a watery fluid (**amniotic fluid**) —**am′ni·ot′ic** (-ot′ik) *adj.*

a·moe·ba (ə mē′bə) *n., pl.* **-bas, -bae** (-bē) [ModL. < Gr. amoibē < ameibein, to change] a microscopic, one-celled animal found usually in stagnant water: it moves by making continual changes in its shape and multiplies by fission **a·moe·bic** (-bik) *adj.* **1.** of or like an amoeba or amoebas **2.** caused by amoebas Also **a·moe′ban** (-bən) **amoebic dysentery** *same as* DYSENTERY

NUCLEUS

VACUOLE

PSEUDOPODIUM

AMOEBA

a·mok (ə muk′) *adj., adv.* [Malay amoq] in a frenzy to kill; in a violent rage —**run** (or **go) amok 1.** to rush about in a frenzy to kill **2.** to lose control of oneself and attempt violence

a·mong (ə muŋ′) *prep.* [OE. on gemang, in the company (of) < on, in + gemang, a crowd < gemengan, to mingle] **1.** in the company of; surrounded by *[*among friends*]* **2.** from place to place in *[*pass among the crowd*]* **3.** in the group or class of *[*fairest among women*]* **4.** by or with many of *[*rebellion among the youth*]* **5.** as compared with *[*one among thousands*]* **6.** with a share for each of *[*divided among us*]* **7.** with one another *[*talking among ourselves*]* **8.** by the joint action of *[*settle it among yourselves*]*

a·mongst (ə muŋst′) *prep. same as* AMONG

a·mon·til·la·do (ə mon′tə lä′dō) *n.* [Sp. < Montilla, a town in Spain] a pale, rather dry sherry

a·mor·al (ā mor′əl) *adj.* **1.** not to be judged by moral values; neither moral nor immoral **2.** without moral sense or principles —**a·mor·al·i·ty** (ā′mə ral′ə tē) *n.* —**a·mor′al·ly** *adv.*

am·o·rist (am′ər ist) *n.* [L. amor, love + -IST] a person much occupied with love or love-making

am·o·rous (am′ər əs) *adj.* [< OFr. < LL. amorosus < L. amor, love < amare, to love] **1.** fond of making love **2.** in love; enamoured or fond (of) **3.** full of or showing love or sexual desire *[*amorous words*]* **4.** of sexual love or lovemaking —**am′o·rous·ly** *adv.* —**am′o·rous·ness** *n.*

a·mor·phous (ə môr′fəs) *adj.* [< ModL. < Gr. < a-, without + morphē, form] **1.** without definite form; shapeless **2.** indefinite, unorganized, vague, etc. **3.** *Biol.* without specialized structure **4.** *Chem., Mineralogy* not crystalline —**a·mor′phism** *n.* —**a·mor′phous·ly** *adv.* —**a·mor′phous·ness** *n.*

a·mor·tize (ə môr′tīz) *vt.* **-tized, -tiz·ing** [< OFr. amortir, to extinguish < ML. < L. ad, to + mors, death] **1.** to put money aside at intervals, as in a sinking fund, for gradual payment of (a debt, etc.) **2.** *Accounting* to write off (expenditures) by prorating over a fixed period —**am′or·tiz′·a·ble** *adj.* —**am′or·ti·za′tion** *n.*

a·mount (ə maunt′) *vi.* [< OFr. amonter < amont, upward < a- (L. ad), to + mont < L. mons, mountain] **1.** to add up; total *[*the bill amounts to £5*]* **2.** to be equal in meaning, value, or effect *[*her reply amounts to a refusal*]* —*n.* **1.** the sum of two or more quantities; total **2.** a principal sum plus its interest **3.** a quantity; degree

a·mour (ə moor′) *n.* [Fr. < Pr. < L. amor, love] a love affair, esp. one that is illicit or secret

‡**a·mour-pro·pre** (à moor prô′pr′) *n.* [Fr.] self-respect

amp. 1. amperage **2.** ampere(s)

am·pe·lop·sis (am′pə lop′sis) *n.* [ModL. < Gr. ampelos, vine + opsis, appearance] a climbing shrub of a genus in the grape family

am·per·age (am′pər ij) *n.* the strength of an electric current, measured in amperes

am·pere (am′per) *n.* [after A. M. Ampère (1775–1836), Fr. physicist] the SI unit of electric current, defined as the intensity of a constant current which, maintained in two parallel, rectilinear conductors of infinite length and negligible cross-section placed one metre apart, produces a force between the conductors equal to 2×10^{-7} newton per metre of length

ampere turn the amount of magnetomotive force produced

by an electric current of one ampere flowing round one turn of a wire coil

am·per·sand (am′pər sand′) *n.* [< and per se and, lit., (the sign) & by itself (is) and] a sign (&) meaning and

am·phet·a·mine (am fet′ə mēn′, -min) *n.* [alpha-methyl-beta-phenyl-ethyl-amine] a compound used as a drug to overcome depression, fatigue, etc. and to lessen the appetite

am·phi- [< Gr.] a prefix meaning: **1.** on both sides or ends **2.** of both kinds **3.** around; about

am·phib·i·an (am fib′ē ən) *n.* [see ff.] **1.** any of a class of vertebrates, including frogs, toads, salamanders, etc., that usually begin life in the water as tadpoles with gills, and later develop lungs: they are coldblooded and scaleless **2.** any amphibious animal or plant **3.** an aircraft that can take off from and come down on either land or water **4.** a vehicle that can travel on either land or water —*adj.* **1.** of the amphibians **2.** *same as* AMPHIBIOUS

am·phib·i·ous (am fib′ē əs) *adj.* [< Gr. < amphi-, AMPHI- + bios, life] **1.** that can live both on land and in water **2.** that can operate on both land and water **3.** of or for a military operation involving the landing of troops from seaborne transports —**am·phib′i·ous·ly** *adv.*

am·phi·bole (am′fə bōl′) *n.* [Fr. < LL. amphibolus, ambiguous < Gr. amphiballein, to be uncertain < amphi-, AMPHI- + ballein, to throw] any of a group of rock-forming minerals, as hornblende or asbestos, composed largely of silica, calcium, iron, and magnesium —**am′phi·bol′ic** (-bol′-ik) *adj.*

am·phi·bol·o·gy (am′fi bol′ə jē) *n.* [< Gr. amphibolos, ambiguous] an ambiguity caused by grammatical construction

am·phic·ty·o·ny (am fik′tē ə nē) *n.* [< Gr. amphiktiones, neighbours] in ancient Greece, a confederation of states established round a religious centre —**am·phic′ty·on′ic** (-on′ik) *adj.*

am·phi·mix·is (am fə mik′sis) *n.* [ModL. < AMPHI- + Gr. mixis, a mixing] *Biol.* the uniting of male and female germ cells from two individuals in reproduction

am·phi·ox·us (am′fē ok′səs) *n.* [< AMPHI- + Gr. oxys, sharp] *same as* LANCELET

am·phi·pod (am′fə pod′) *n.* [AMPHI- + -POD] any of several crustaceans with one set of feet for jumping or walking and another set for swimming

am·phi·pro·style (am′fə prō′stīl, am fip′rə stīl′) *adj.* [< L. < Gr.: see AMPHI- & PROSTYLE] *Archit.* having rows of columns only at the front and back —*n.* an amphiprostyle building

am·phi·the·a·tre (am′fə thē′ə tər) *n.* [< L. < Gr.: see AMPHI- & THEATRE] **1.** a round or oval building with an open space (arena) surrounded by rising rows of seats **2.** a scene of contest **3.** a level place surrounded by rising ground **4.** a gallery in a theatre

am·pho·ra (am′fər ə) *n., pl.* **-rae** (-ē), **-ras** [L. < Gr. < amphi-, AMPHI- + pherein, to bear] a tall jar with a narrow neck and base and two handles, used by the ancient Greeks and Romans

am·pho·ter·ic (am′fə ter′ik) *adj.* [< Gr. < amphō, var. of AMPHI-] *Chem.* having both acid and basic properties

am·ple (am′p'l) *adj.* **-pler, -plest** [OFr. < L. amplus] **1.** large in size, extent, etc. **2.** more than enough; abundant **3.** enough; adequate —**am′ple·ness** *n.*

am·plex·i·caul (am plek′sə kôl′) *adj.* [< L. pp. of amplectari, to twine around + caulis, stem] *Bot.* growing directly from the main stem and encircling it

am·pli·fi·ca·tion (am′plə fi kā′shən) *n.* **1.** an amplifying or being amplified **2.** additional details **3.** something added to a statement, etc.

am·pli·fi·er (am′plə fī′ər) *n.* **1.** a person or thing that amplifies **2.** *Electronics* a device used to increase electrical signal strength

am·pli·fy (am′plə fī′) *vt.* **-fied′, -fy′ing** [< OFr. < L. amplificare < amplus, AMPLE + facere, to make] **1.** to make stronger; increase (power, authority, etc.) **2.** to develop more fully, as with details, examples, etc. **3.** *Electronics* to strengthen (an electrical signal) by means of an amplifier —*vi.* to speak or write at length; expatiate

am·pli·tude (am′plə tyōōd′) *n.* [< L. < amplus, AMPLE] **1.** extent; largeness **2.** abundance; fullness **3.** scope or breadth, as of mind **4.** the extreme range of a fluctuating quantity, from the average or mean to the extreme

amplitude modulation the changing of the amplitude of the transmitting radio wave in accordance with the signal being broadcast: distinguished from FREQUENCY MODULATION

am·ply (am′plē) *adv.* to an ample degree

am·poule (am′pool, -pul) *n.* [Fr. < L. ampulla, AMPULLA] a small, sealed glass container for one dose of a medicine to be injected hypodermically: also **am′pule** (-pyool), **am′pul** (-pool)

am·pul·la (am pul′ə, -pool′ə) *n., pl.* **-pul′lae** (-ē) [< OE. < L. ampulla, dim. of AMPHORA] **1.** a nearly round bottle with two handles, used by the ancient Greeks and Romans **2.** a container used in churches for holy oil, consecrated wine, etc.

am·pu·tate (am'pyσσtāt') *vt.* **-tat'ed, -tat'ing** [< L. pp. of *amputare* < *am-*, for AMBI- + *putare*, to prune] to cut off (an arm, leg, etc.), esp. by surgery —**am'pu·ta'tion** *n.* —**am'pu·ta'tor** *n.*

am·pu·tee (am'pyσσtē') *n.* [see -EE] a person who has had a limb or limbs amputated

amt. amount

amu, AMU atomic mass unit

a·muck (əmuk') *adj., adv.* same as AMOK

am·u·let (am'yσσlit) *n.* [< Fr. < L.] something worn on the body as a charm against evil

a·muse (əmyσσz') *vt.* **a·mused', a·mus'ing** [< Fr. < à, at + OFr. *muser*, to stare fixedly] **1.** to keep pleasantly occupied; entertain **2.** to make laugh, smile, etc. by being humorous —**a·mus'a·ble** *adj.* —**a·mus'er** *n.*

a·muse·ment (-mənt) *n.* **1.** the condition of being amused **2.** something that amuses or entertains

amusement park an outdoor place with devices for entertainment, as side shows, roundabouts, etc.

a·mus·ing (əmyσσ'zin) *adj.* **1.** entertaining; diverting **2.** causing laughter —**a·mus'ing·ly** *adv.*

a·myg·da·lin (əmig'dəlin) *n.* [< L. *amygdala*, almond + -IN¹] a glucoside present in bitter almonds

am·yl (am'il) *n.* [AM(YLUM) + -YL] any of various isomeric forms of the monovalent radical C₅H₁₁ —**a·myl'ic** (əmil'ik) *adj.*

am·y·la·ceous (am'əlā'shəs) *adj.* [< AMYLUM + -ACEOUS] of or like starch

am·yl·ase (am'əlās') *n.* an enzyme that helps change starch into sugar: it is found in saliva, pancreatic juice, etc.: see also DIASTASE

am·y·loid (am'əloid') *n.* a starchy substance

am·y·lop·sin (am'əlop'sin) *n.* [< ff. + TRYPSIN] the enzyme (amylase) of pancreatic juice

am·y·lum (am'ələm) *n.* [< L. < Gr.] *Chem.* a technical name for STARCH

an¹ (ən; stressed an) *adj., indefinite article* [weakened variant of ONE < OE. *an*, the numeral one] **1.** one; one sort of [an apple pie] **2.** each; any one [pick an apple] **3.** to each; in each; for each; per [two an hour] See also A. *adj.*

an², an' (an) *conj.* [< and] [Archaic] if

an- same as A² (not, without): used before vowels

-an (ən, 'n) [< L. *-anus*] an *adj.*-forming and *n.*-forming suffix meaning: **1.** (one) belonging to or having some relation to [diocesan] **2.** (one) born in or living in [American] **3.** (one) believing in or following [Mohammedan]

an. **1.** [L. *anno*] in the year **2.** anonymous

an·a- [L. < Gr. *ana*, up, on, again] a prefix meaning: **1.** up [anadromous] **2.** back, backwards [anagram] **3.** again [Anabaptist] **4.** throughout [analysis] **5.** according to, similar to [analogy]

-ana (ā'nə, ä'nə) [neut. pl. of L. *-anus*] a *n.*-forming suffix meaning sayings, writings, anecdotes, facts, or small articles of [Victoriana]

An·a·bap·tist (an'əbap'tist) *n.* [< LL. < Gr. < *ana-*, again + *baptizein*, to baptize] a member of a 16th-cent. Swiss sect of the Reformation, that rejected infant baptism and practised baptism of adults —*adj.* of this sect —**An'a·bap'tism** *n.*

an·a·bas (an'əbas') *n.* [ModL. < Gr. < *anabainein*, to go up: so named from its habit of climbing] any of several freshwater fishes which can live for a long time out of water

a·nab·a·sis (ə nab'ə sis) *n.,* pl. **-ses'** (sēz') [Gr. < *anabainein*, to go up < *ana-*, up + *bainein*, to go] any large military expedition: after the unsuccessful expedition (401-400 B.C.) of Cyrus the Younger to overthrow Artaxerxes II

an·a·bat·ic (an'əbat'ik) *adj.* [Gr. *anabatikos:* see prec.] moving upwards: said of air currents

an·a·bi·o·sis (an'əbī ō'sis) *n.* [ModL. < Gr. < *anabioein*, to come to life again] a state of suspended animation, as in certain arthropods when desiccated —**an'a·bi·ot'ic** (-ot'ik) *adj.*

a·nab·o·lism (ə nab'ə liz'm) *n.* [< Gr. *anabolē*, a rising up + -ISM] the process in a plant or animal by which food is changed into living tissue; constructive metabolism: opposed to CATABOLISM —**an·a·bol·ic** (an'ə bol'ik) *adj.*

a·nach·ro·nism (ə nak'rə niz'm) *n.* [< MGr. *anachronizein*, to refer to a wrong time < *ana-*, against + *chronos*, time] **1.** the representation of something as existing or occurring at other than its proper time **2.** anything out of its proper time in history —**a·nach'ro·nis'tic, a·nach'ro·nous** (-nəs) *adj.* —**a·nach'ro·nis'ti·cal·ly** *adv.*

an·a·co·lu·thon (an'ə kə lōō'thon) *n.,* pl. **-tha** (-thə), **-thons** [Gr. < *anakolouthos*, inconsequent < *an-*, not + *akolouthos*, following] a change from one grammatical construction to another within the same sentence, sometimes as a rhetorical device —**an'a·co·lu'thic** *adj.*

an·a·con·da (an'ə kon'də) *n.* [< ? Singhalese *henakandayā*, whip snake] a long, heavy S. American snake of the boa family

an·a·cru·sis (an'ə krōōs'is) *n.* [ModL. < Gr. < *anakrouein*, to push back] **1.** one or more unstressed syllables at the beginning of a line of verse that are not counted as part of the first foot **2.** *Music* same as UPBEAT

a·nad·ro·mous (ə nad'rə məs) *adj.* [< Gr. < *ana-*, upward + *dramein*, to run] going up rivers to spawn: said of salmon, shad, etc.

a·nae·mi·a (ə nē'mē ə, -myə) *n.* [ModL. < Gr. < *a-, an*, without + *haima*, blood] **1.** a condition in which there is a reduction of the number of red blood corpuscles or of haemoglobin (or of both) in the bloodstream

ANACONDA (to 9 m long)

a·nae·mic (-mik) *adj.* **1.** relating to or suffering from anaemia **2.** pale; lacking vitality

an·aer·obe (an er'ōb, an'ə rōb') *n.* [< Gr. *an-*, AN- + *aero-*, AERO- + *bios, life*] a microorganism that can live and grow where there is no free oxygen: also **an'aer·o'bi·um** —**an·aer·o·bic** (an'er ō'bik, -ə rō'-) *adj.*

an·aes·the·sia (an'əs thē'zē ə, -zhə) *n.* [< Gr. < *an*, without + *aisthesis*, feeling] **1.** partial or total loss of the sense of pain, temperature, touch, etc., produced by disease **2.** a loss of sensation induced by an anaesthetic and limited to a specific area (**local anaesthesia**) or producing unconsciousness (**general anaesthesia**)

an·aes·the·si·ol·o·gy (an'əs thē'zē ol'ə jē) *n.* the science of anaesthesia and anaesthetics —**an'aes·the·si·ol'o·gist** *n.*

an·aes·thet·ic (an'əs thet'ik) *adj.* **1.** of or with anaesthesia **2.** producing anaesthesia —*n.* a drug, gas, etc. used to produce anaesthesia, as before surgery —**an'aes·thet'i·cal·ly** *adv.*

an·aes·the·tist (ə nēs'thə tist) *n.* a person who administers anaesthetics

an·aes·the·tize (-tīz') *vt.* **-tized', -tiz'ing** to cause anaesthesia in, as by giving an anaesthetic —**an·aes'the·ti·za'tion** *n.*

an·a·glyph (an'ə glif') *n.* [Gr. *anaglyphē* < *ana-*, up + *glyphein*, to carve] **1.** ornament, as a cameo, carved in low relief **2.** a photograph composed of two views of the same subject: when viewed through coloured filters, the picture seems three-dimensional

an·a·gram (an'ə gram') *n.* [< ModL. < Gr. *anagrammatizein*, to transpose letters < *ana-*, back + *gramma*, letter] **1.** a word or phrase made from another by rearranging its letters (Ex.: *now — won*) **2.** [*pl.*, with sing. *v.*] a game in which players seek to form words by arranging letters drawn at random from a stock of them —**an'a·gram·mat'ic** (-grə mat'ik), **an'a·gram·mat'i·cal** *adj.* —**an'a·gram·mat'i·cal·ly** *adv.*

an·a·gram·ma·tize (an'ə gram'ə tīz') *vt.* **-tized', -tiz'ing** to make an anagram of

a·nal (ā'n'l) *adj.* **1.** of or near the anus **2.** *Psychoanalysis* of an early stage of psychosexual development focusing on excretory functions —**a'nal·ly** *adv.*

an·a·lects (an'ə lekts') *n.pl.* [< L. < Gr. *analegein*, to collect < *ana-*, up + *legein*, to gather] collected literary excerpts: also **an'a·lec'ta** (-lek'tə) —**the Analects** a collection of Confucius' teachings

an·a·lep·tic (an'ə lep'tik) *adj.* [< Gr. < *analambanein*, to recover < *ana-*, up + *lambanein*, to take] *Med.* restorative —*n.* an analeptic drug

an·al·ge·si·a (an''l jē'zē ə, -sē ə) *n.* [ModL. < Gr. *an-*, without + *algēsia*, pain] a state of not feeling pain although fully conscious

an·al·ge·sic (-zik, -sik) *adj.* of or causing analgesia —*n.* a drug producing analgesia

an·a·log·i·cal (an'ə loj'i k'l) *adj.* of, expressing, or based upon analogy —**an'a·log'i·cal·ly** *adv.*

a·nal·o·gize (ə nal'ə jīz') *vi.* **-gized', -giz'ing** to use, or reason by, analogy —*vt.* to explain or liken by analogy —**a·nal'o·gist** (-jist) *n.*

a·nal·o·gous (ə nal'ə gəs) *adj.* [see ANALOGY] **1.** similar or comparable in certain respects **2.** *Biol.* similar in function but not in origin and structure —**a·nal'o·gous·ly** *adv.*

an·a·logue, an·a·log (an'ə log') *adj.* of or by means of an analogue computer

an·a·logue (an'ə log') *n.* a thing or part that is analogous

analogue computer an electronic computer that uses voltages to represent the numerical data of physical quantities: cf. DIGITAL COMPUTER

a·nal·o·gy (ə nal'ə jē) *n.,* pl. **-gies** [< ME. & OFr. < L. < Gr. *analogia*, proportion < *ana-*, according to + *logos*, ratio: see LOGIC] **1.** similarity in some respects; partial resemblance **2.** a comparing of something point by point with something similar **3.** *Biol.* similarity in function but not in origin and structure **4.** *Linguis.* the formation of new words based on the pattern of older (often unrelated) ones [*energize* is formed from *energy* by *analogy* with *apologize* from *apology*] **5.** *Logic* the inference that because one idea, thing, etc. resembles another in certain respects it does in other respects

a·nal·y·sand (ə nal'ə sand') *n.* a person who is undergoing psychoanalysis

an·a·lyse (an'ə līz') *vt.* -lysed', -lys'ing [< Fr. < *analyse*, ANALYSIS] **1.** to separate into parts so as to find out their nature, function, etc. **2.** to examine in detail so as to determine the nature or tendencies of **3.** to psychoanalyse —**an'a·lys'a·ble** *adj.* —**an'a·lys'er** *n.*

a·nal·y·sis (ə nal'ə sis) *n., pl.* -ses' (-sēz') [ML. < Gr., a dissolving < *ana-*, up, throughout + *lysis*, a loosing < *lyein*, to loose] **1.** *a)* a breaking up of any whole into its parts so as to find out their nature, function, etc. *b)* a statement of these findings **2.** *same as* PSYCHOANALYSIS **3.** *Chem.* the separation of compounds and mixtures into their constituent substances to determine the nature (*qualitative analysis*) or the proportion (*quantitative analysis*) of the constituents

an·a·lyst (an'ə list) *n.* **1.** a person who analyses **2.** *same as* PSYCHOANALYST

an·a·lyt·ic (an'ə lit'ik) *adj.* **1.** *Linguis.* using word order rather than inflection to express syntactic relationships **2.** *same as* ANALYTICAL

an·a·lyt·i·cal (-i k'l) *adj.* **1.** of analysis or analytics **2.** skilled in or using analysis **3.** *same as* ANALYTIC (sense 1) —**an'a·lyt'i·cal·ly** *adv.*

an·a·lyt·ics (-iks) *n.pl.* [*with sing. v.*] the part of logic having to do with analysing

an·a·lyze (an'ə līz') *vt.* -lyzed', -lyz'ing *U.S. sp. of* ANALYSE

an·an·drous (an an'drəs) *adj.* [< Gr. < *an-*, not + *anēr* (gen. *ardros*), man] *Bot.* having no stamens

an·a·paest (an'ə pest') *n.* [< L. < Gr. < *ana-*, back + *paiein*, to strike] a metrical foot consisting of two unaccented syllables followed by an accented one, as in English verse (Ex.: "And thĕ shĕen/ŏf thĕir spĕars/wăs līke stărs/ŏn thĕ sĕa") —**an'a·paes'tic** *adj.*

a·naph·o·ra (ə naf'ər ə) *n.* [L. < Gr. < *ana-*, up, back + *pherein*, to BEAR[1]] **1.** the repetition of a word or phrase at the beginning of successive clauses or sentences as a rhetorical device **2.** *Linguis.* the use of pronouns, etc., to refer back to earlier words or phrases in a text: cf. CATAPHORA

an·aph·ro·dis·i·ac (an af'rə diz'ē ak) *adj.* that lessens sexual desire —*n.* a drug, etc. that lessens sexual desire

an·ap·tyx·is (an'ap tik'sis) *n.* [ModL. < Gr. *anaptyxis*, an opening < *ana-*, up + *ptyssein*, to fold] *Linguis.* the insertion of an extra vowel into a consonant group, esp. to make it more easily pronounceable, as in a three-syllable pronunciation of *athlete* (ath'ə lēt')

an·ar·chic (an är'kik) *adj.* **1.** of, like, or promoting anarchy **2.** without controls; lawless Also **an·ar'chi·cal** —**an·ar'-chi·cal·ly** *adv.*

an·ar·chism (an'ər kiz'm) *n.* [ANARCH(Y) + -ISM] **1.** the theory that all forms of government interfere unjustly with individual liberty and should be replaced by a system of voluntary cooperation **2.** resistance, sometimes by terrorism, to government

an·ar·chist (-kist) *n.* **1.** a person who believes in or advocates anarchism **2.** a person who promotes anarchy —**an'ar·chis'tic** *adj.*

an·ar·chy (-kē) *n., pl.* -chies [< Gr. < *an-*, without + *archos*, leader] **1.** the complete absence of government **2.** political disorder and violence **3.** disorder in any sphere of activity

an·as·tig·mat·ic (an as'tig mat'ik, an'ə stig-) *adj.* free from, or corrected for, astigmatism

a·nas·to·mose (ə nas'tə mōz') *vt., vi.* -mosed', -mos'ing to join by anastomosis

a·nas·to·mo·sis (ə nas'tə mō'sis) *n., pl.* -ses (-sēz) [ModL. < Gr. *anastomōsis*, opening < *ana-*, again + *stoma*, mouth] **1.** interconnection as between blood vessels or veins of a leaf **2.** a surgical joining of one hollow or tubular organ to another

a·nas·tro·phe (ə nas'trə fē) *n.* [Gr. < *ana-*, back + *strephein*, to turn] reversal of the usual word order of a sentence (Ex.: "Came the dawn")

anat. **1.** anatomical **2.** anatomist **3.** anatomy

a·nath·e·ma (ə nath'ə mə) *n., pl.* -mas [LL. < Gr., thing devoted to evil < *anatithenai*, to dedicate < *ana-*, up *tithenai*, to set] **1.** a thing or person accursed **2.** a thing or person greatly detested **3.** a formal curse, as in excommunicating a person from a church **4.** any strong curse

a·nath·e·ma·tize (ə nath'ə mə tīz') *vt., vi.* -tized', -tiz'ing to utter an anathema (against); curse —**a·nath'e·ma·ti·za'-tion** *n.*

an·a·tom·i·cal (an'ə tom'i k'l) *adj.* **1.** of or connected with

anatomy **2.** structural Also **an'a·tom'ic** —**an'a·tom'i·cal·ly** *adv.*

a·nat·o·mist (ə nat'ə mist) *n.* **1.** a person skilled in anatomy **2.** a person who anatomizes

a·nat·o·mize (-mīz') *vt., vi.* -mized', -miz'ing [see ff.] **1.** to dissect (an animal or plant) in order to examine the structure **2.** to analyse in great detail —**a·nat'o·mi·za'-tion** *n.*

a·nat·o·my (ə nat'ə mē) *n., pl.* -mies [< ME. & OFr. < LL. < Gr. < *ana-*, up + *temnein*, to cut] **1.** the dissecting of an animal or plant in order to study its structure **2.** the science of the structure of animals or plants **3.** the structure of an organism **4.** a detailed analysis

anc. **1.** ancient **2.** anciently

-ance (əns, 'ns) [< Fr. < L. *-antia*, *-entia*, or directly < L.] a suffix meaning: **1.** the act of [*utterance*] **2.** the quality or state of being [*vigilance*] **3.** a thing that [*conveyance*] **4.** a thing that is [*dissonance*, *inheritance*]

an·ces·tor (an'səs'tər) *n.* [< ME. & OFr. < L. *antecessor*, one who goes before < *ante-*, before + *cedere*, to go] **1.** any person from whom one is descended; forebear **2.** an early type of animal from which later kinds have evolved **3.** a precursor or predecessor **4.** *Law* the person from whom an estate has been inherited —**an'ces'tress** (-trəs) *n.fem.*

an·ces·tral (an ses'trəl) *adj.* of or inherited from ancestors —**an·ces'tral·ly** *adv.*

an·ces·try (an'səs trē) *n., pl.* -tries **1.** family descent or lineage **2.** ancestors collectively

an·chor (aŋ'kər) *n.* [< OE. < L. < Gr. *ankyra*, a hook] **1.** a heavy object, usually a shaped iron weight with flukes, lowered to the bottom of water by cable or chain to keep a ship from drifting **2.** any device that holds something else secure **3.** anything regarded as giving stability or security —*vt.* to hold secure by or as by an anchor —*vi.* **1.** to lower the anchor overboard **2.** to be or become fixed —**at anchor** anchored —**drop** (or **cast**) **anchor 1.** to lower the anchor overboard **2.** to settle (*in* a place) —**weigh anchor 1.** to raise the anchor **2.** to leave; go away

ANCHOR

an·chor·age (aŋ'kər ij) *n.* **1.** money charged for the right to anchor **2.** an anchoring or being anchored **3.** a place to anchor **4.** something that can be relied on

an·cho·rite (aŋ'kə rīt') *n.* [< OFr. < LL. < Gr. *anachōrētēs* < *ana-*, back + *chōrein*, to retire] a person who lives alone for religious meditation; hermit: also **an'cho·ret** (-rit) —**an'cho·ress** *n.fem.* —**an'cho·rit'ic** (-rit'ik), **an'cho·ret'ic** (-ret'ik) *adj.*

anchor man 1. the final contestant, as on a relay team **2.** *Radio & TV* that member of a team of broadcasters who coordinates various items

an·cho·vy (an'chō'vē, -chə-; an'chō'vē) *n., pl.* -vies, -vy: see PLURAL, II, D, 1 [< Port. *anchova*, perhaps ult. < Gr. *aphyē*, small fry] a very small, herringlike fish: anchovies are usually tinned in oil or made into a salty paste

an·chu·sa (aŋ kyōō'sə) *n.* [< Gr. *anchousa*] any of several plants of the borage family

an·chy·lose (aŋ'kə lōs') *vt., vi.* -losed', -los'ing *same as* ANKYLOSE —**an'chy·lo'sis** (-lō'sis) *n.*

‡**an·cien ré·gime** (än syan rā zhēm') [Fr., old order] the former social and political system, esp. that in France before the Revolution of 1789

an·cient (ān'shənt) *adj.* [< OFr., ult. < L. *ante*, before] **1.** of times long past; esp., of the time before the end of the Western Roman Empire in 476 A.D. **2.** very old **3.** antiquated —*n.* **1.** a person who lived in ancient times **2.** an aged person —**the ancients** the people who lived in ancient times; esp., the classical writers and artists of Graeco-Roman times —**an'cient·ness** *n.*

an·cient·ly (-lē) *adv.* in ancient times

an·cil·lar·y (an sil'ər ē) *adj.* [< L. < *ancilla*, maidservant] **1.** subordinate (*to*) **2.** auxiliary

an·con (aŋ'kon) *n., pl.* **an·co·nes** (aŋ kō'nēz) [L. < Gr. < *ankos*, a bend] a bracketlike projection supporting a cornice

-an·cy (ən sē, 'n sē) *same as* -ANCE

and (and, ən, 'n; *stressed* and) *conj.* [OE.] **1.** also; in addition; as well as: used to join elements of equal grammatical value [apples *and* pears, to beg *and* borrow] **2.** plus [6 *and* 2 equals 8] **3.** as a result [he told her *and* she wept] **4.** [Colloq.] to [try *and* get it] **5.** [Archaic] then [*and* it came to pass] **6.** [Obs.] if

an·dan·te (an dan'tē) *adj., adv.* [It., prp. of *andare*, to walk] *Music* moderate in tempo —*n.* an andante movement or passage

an·dan·ti·no (an'dan tē'nō) *adj., adv.* [It., dim. of *andante*] *Music* slightly faster than andante —*n., pl.* -nos an andantino movement or passage

and·i·ron (an'dī'ərn) *n.* [< OFr. *andier* (with ending altered after IRON)] either of a pair of metal supports with front uprights, used to hold the wood in a fireplace

and/or either *and* or *or*, according to what is meant [personal *and/or* real property]

an·dro- [< Gr. *anēr* (gen. *andros*), man] *a combining form meaning:* 1. man, male, masculine 2. anther, stamen

an·droe·ci·um (an drē'shē əm, -sē-) *n., pl.* -ci·a (-ə) [ModL. < ANDRO- + Gr. *oikos*, house] *Bot.* the stamens and the parts belonging to them, collectively

ANDIRONS

an·dro·gen (an'drə jən) *n.* [ANDRO- + -GEN] a male sex hormone that can give rise to masculine characteristics —**an'dro·gen'ic** (-jen'ik) *adj.*

an·drog·y·nous (an droj'ə nəs) *adj.* [< L. < Gr. < *anēr* (gen. *andros*), man + *gynē*, woman] 1. hermaphroditic 2. *Bot.* bearing both staminate and pistillate flowers in the same cluster —**an·drog'y·ny** (-ə nē) *n.*

an·droid (an'droid) *n.* [ANDR(O)- + -OID] in science fiction, a) an automaton that looks human b) an artificially created human being

An·drom·e·da (an drom'ə də) 1. *Gr. Myth.* an Ethiopian princess whom Perseus rescued from a sea monster and then married 2. *Astron.* a N constellation just south of Cassiopeia

an·dros·ter·one (an dros'tə rōn') *n.* [ANDRO- + STER(OL) + -ONE] a steroid that is a male sex hormone

-an·drous (an'drəs) [< also *see* ANDRO-] *a suffix meaning* having stamens [monandrous]

-ane (ān) [arbitrary formation] *a suffix denoting* a hydrocarbon of the paraffin series [methane]

a·near (ə nir') *adv., prep.* [Dial. or Poet.] near

an·ec·dote (an'ik dōt') *n.* [Fr. < ML. < Gr. *anekdotos*, unpublished < *an-*, not + *ek-*, out + *didonai*, to give] a short, entertaining account of some happening, usually personal or biographical —**an·ec·dot·al** (an'ik dōt'l) *adj.* —**an'ec·dot'ist** (-dōt'ist) *n.*

an·e·cho·ic (an'e kō'ik) *adj.* [AN- + ECHOIC] free from echoes [an anechoic recording chamber]

a·ne·mi·a (ə nē'mē ə, -myə) *n.* *U.S. var. sp. of* ANAEMIA

a·nem·o·graph (ə nem'ə graf') *n.* [< Gr. *anemos*, the wind + -GRAPH] an instrument for recording the velocity and direction of the wind

an·e·mom·e·ter (an'ə mom'ə tər) *n.* [< Gr. *anemos*, the wind + -METER] a gauge for determining the force or speed of the wind, and sometimes its direction —**an'e·mo·met'ric** (-mō met'rik) *adj.* —**an'e·mom'e·try** *n.*

a·nem·o·ne (ə nem'ə nē') *n.* [L. < Gr., infl. by *anemos*, wind] 1. any of various plants of the buttercup family, with cup-shaped flowers, usually white, purple, or red 2. *same as* SEA ANEMONE

an·e·moph·i·lous (an'ə mof'ə ləs) *adj.* [< Gr. *anemas*, wind + *-philos*, loving] pollinated by the wind

a·nent (ə nent') *prep.* [< OE. *on efen*, lit., on even (with), level (with)] [Archaic or Scot.] concerning; as regards

an·er·oid (an'ər oid) *adj.* [< Gr. *a-*, without + *nēros*, liquid + -OID] not using liquid —*n.* *same as* ANEROID BAROMETER

aneroid barometer a barometer consisting of a box in which a partial vacuum is maintained: changes in atmospheric pressure cause its elastic top to bend in or out, thus moving a pointer

an·es·the·sia (an'es thē'zē ə, -zhə, -zhē ə) *n.* *U.S. var. sp. of* ANAESTHESIA —**an·es·thet·ic** (-thet'ik) *adj., n.* —**an·es·the·tist** (ən es'thə tist) *n.* —**an·es'the·tize'** *vt.* -tized', -tiz'ing

an·eu·rysm, an·eu·rism (an'yər iz'm) *n.* [ModL. < Gr. < *ana-*, up + *eurys*, broad] a sac formed when the wall of an artery, weakened by disease or injury, becomes enlarged —**an'eu·rys'mal, an'eu·ris'mal** (-yə riz'm'l) *adj.*

a·new (ə nyo͞o') *adv.* 1. once more; again 2. in a new manner or form

an·ga·ry (aŋ'gə rē) *n.* [L. *angaria*, enforced service < Gr. < *angaros*, a mounted courier] *International Law* the right of a belligerent to use or destroy a neutral's property if necessary, provided that indemnification is made

an·gel (ān'j'l) *n.* [< OFr. or OE. < L. *angelus* < Gr. *angelos*, messenger] 1. *Theol.* a) a messenger of God b) a supernatural being, either good or bad, of more than human power, intelligence, etc. 2. a guiding spirit [one's good angel] 3. a conventionalized image of a figure in human form with wings and a halo 4. a person regarded as beautiful, good, etc. 5. a former English gold coin with the imprint of the Archangel Michael and the dragon 6. a radar echo whose origin has not been found 7. [Colloq.] a supporter who provides money, as for producing a play —*vt.* [Slang] to support with money

angel cake a light, spongy, white cake made with egg whites and no fat: also **angel food cake**

an·gel·fish (ān'j'l fish') *n., pl.* **-fish'**, **-fish'es:** see FISH 1. a shark with winglike pectoral fins 2. any of a number of brightly coloured tropical fishes with spiny fins

an·gel·ic (an jel'ik) *adj.* 1. of an angel or the angels 2. like an angel in beauty, goodness, etc. Also **an·gel'i·cal** —**an·gel'i·cal·ly** *adv.*

an·gel·i·ca (an jel'i kə) *n.* [ML. (*herba*) *angelica*, lit., the angelic (herb)] 1. any of a number of related plants with roots and fruit used in flavouring, medicine, etc. 2. its candied stems, used in cookery for flavouring and decoration

An·ge·lus (an'jə ləs) *n.* [L.: see ANGEL] [*also* a-] *R.C.Ch.* 1. a prayer said at morning, noon, and evening in commemoration of the Incarnation 2. a bell rung to announce the time for this

an·ger (aŋ'gər) *n.* [ON. *angr*, distress, sorrow] a feeling of displeasure and hostility resulting from injury, mistreatment, opposition, etc. —*vt.* to make angry; enrage

An·ge·vin, An·ge·vine (an'jə vin) *adj.* [Fr.] of Anjou or the Plantagenets —*n.* 1. a native of Anjou 2. any of the Plantagenets

an·gi·na (an jī'nə,) *n.* [L., quinsy < Gr. < *anchein*, to squeeze] 1. any inflammatory disease of the throat, esp. one characterized by fits of suffocation 2. a localized spasm of pain 3. *same as* ANGINA PECTORIS —**an·gi'nal, an·gi·nose** (an'jə nōs'), **an·gi·nous** (-nəs) *adj.*

angina pec·to·ris (pek'tər is) [L., angina of the breast] a condition marked by recurrent pain in the chest and left arm, caused by a sudden decrease of blood supply to the heart

an·gi·o·ma (an'jē ō'mə) *n., pl.* -ma·ta (-mə tə), -mas [< Gr. *angeion*, vessel + -OMA] a tumour made up mainly of blood vessels and lymph vessels

an·gi·o·sperm (an'jē ə spurm') *n.* [< Gr. *angeion*, capsule + -SPERM] any flowering plant having the seeds enclosed in an ovary

Angl. 1. Anglican 2. Anglicized

an·gle[1] (aŋ'g'l) *n.* [ME. & OFr. < L. *angulus*, a corner < Gr. *ankylos*, bent] 1. a) the shape made by two straight lines or plane surfaces that meet b) the space between such lines or surfaces c) the degrees of difference in direction between them 2. a sharp corner 3. a) point of view [consider this from all *angles*] b) the direction from which something is seen [from this *angle*, the house looks different] 4. [Colloq.] a selfish motive or tricky plan —*vt., vi.* -gled, -gling 1. to move or bend at an angle 2. [Colloq.] to give a specific point of view to (a story, report, etc.)

an·gle[2] (aŋ'g'l) *vi.* -gled, -gling [OE. *angul*, fishhook] 1. to fish with a hook and line 2. to use tricks to get something [angling for attention]

angle iron an angled piece of iron or steel used for joining or reinforcing two beams, girders, etc.

angle of incidence the angle that a light ray or electromagnetic wave striking a surface makes with a line perpendicular to the surface

an·gler (aŋ'glər) *n.* [< ANGLE[2]] 1. a fisherman 2. a saltwater fish that feeds on other fish attracted by a filament on its head

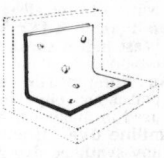

ANGLE IRON

An·gles (aŋ'g'lz) *n.pl.* a Germanic people that settled in NE and E England in the 5th cent. A.D. —**An'gli·an** (-glē ən) *adj., n.*

an·gle·worm (aŋ'g'l wurm') *n.* an earthworm: so called because used as fishing bait

An·gli·can (aŋ'gli kən) *adj.* [< ML. < *Anglicus*, of England, of the Angles] of the Church of England or any related church with the same faith and forms —*n.* a member of an Anglican church —**An'gli·can·ism** *n.*

An·gli·cism (aŋ'glə siz'm) *n.* 1. a word or idiom peculiar to English, esp. British English 2. a typically English trait, custom, etc. 3. the quality of being English

An·gli·cize (aŋ'glə sīz') *vt., vi.* -cized', -ciz'ing [*also* a-] to change to English idiom, pronunciation, customs, etc. —**An'gli·ci·za'tion** *n.*

an·gling (aŋ'gliŋ) *n.* the act or skill of fishing with hook and line

An·glo- [< L. *Anglus*, sing. of *Angli*, ANGLES] *a combining form meaning* English [Anglophile]

An·glo-A·mer·i·can (aŋ'glō ə mer'ə kən) *adj.* English and American —*n.* an American of English birth or ancestry

An·glo-French (-french') *adj.* English and French —*n.* the French spoken in England from the Norman Conquest through the Middle Ages: see NORMAN FRENCH

An·glo-In·di·an (-in'dē ən) *adj.* 1. of England and India 2. of Anglo-Indians or their English speech —*n.* 1. a person of British and Indian ancestry 2. a British citizen who lives or has lived in India, esp. when it was part of the British empire 3. words taken into English from the languages of India

An·glo·ma·ni·a (-mā'nē ə) *n.* an exaggerated liking for and imitation of English customs, manners, institutions, etc. —**An'glo·ma'ni·ac'** (-ak') *n.*

An·glo-Nor·man (-nôr'mən) *adj.* English and Norman —*n.*

1. a Norman settler in England after the Norman Conquest
2. the Anglo-French dialect spoken by such settlers

An·glo·phil·i·a (aŋ'glə fil'ē ə) *n.* [often a-] extreme admiration for England, its people, customs, etc. —**An'·glo·phile'** (-fīl') *n.*

An·glo·pho·bi·a (aŋ'glə fō'bē ə) *n.* [often a-] hatred or fear of England, its people, customs, etc. —**An'glo·phobe'** (-fōb') *n.* —**An'glo·pho'bic** (-fō'bik) *adj.*

an·glo·phone (aŋ'glə fōn') *n.* a person who speaks English, esp in a country where English is not the sole official language —*adj.* speaking English

An·glo-Sax·on (aŋ'glō sak's'n) *n.* [< ML.: see ANGLES & SAXON] 1. a member of the Germanic peoples (Angles, Saxons, and Jutes) living in England at the time of the Norman Conquest 2. *same as* OLD ENGLISH 3. [Colloq.] plain, blunt language 4. a person of English nationality or descent —*adj.* 1. of the Anglo-Saxons or their language 2. of their descendants; English

An·go·ra (aŋ gôr'ə, an-) *n.* [former name of *Ankara*] 1. a kind of cat with long, silky fur 2. *a*) a kind of goat raised for its long, silky hair *b*) a cloth made from this hair 3. *a*) a long-eared rabbit, raised for its long, silky hair *b*) a soft yarn made from this hair Also **angora** for senses 2*b*, 3*b*

an·gos·tu·ra (bark) (aŋ'gəs tyoor'ə) [after *Angostura*, former name of Ciudad Bolivar, in Venezuela] a bitter bark used as a tonic and as a flavouring in bitters

an·gry (aŋ'grē) *adj.* **-gri·er, -gri·est** 1. feeling, showing, or resulting from anger 2. wild and stormy 3. inflamed and sore —**an'gri·ly** (-grə lē) *adv.* —**an'gri·ness** (-grē nis) *n.*

ang·strom (aŋ'strəm) *n.* [after A. J. *Angström*, 19th-c. Swed. physicist] one hundred-millionth of a centimetre, a unit formerly used in measuring the length of light waves: also **angstrom unit**

an·guine (aŋ'win) *adj.* [< L. *anguīnus* < *anguis*, snake] of, or similar to, a snake

an·guish (aŋ'gwish) *n.* [< OFr. < L. *angustia*, tightness < *angustus*, narrow] great suffering, as from grief or pain; agony —*vi., vt.* to feel or make feel anguish —**an'guished** (-gwisht) *adj.*

an·gu·lar (aŋ'gyə lər) *adj.* 1. having or forming an angle or angles; having sharp corners 2. measured by an angle [angular distance] 3. lean; bony; gaunt 4. without ease or grace; awkward [an angular stride] —**an'gu·lar·ly** *adv.*

an·gu·lar·i·ty (aŋ'gyə lar'ə tē) *n., pl.* **-ties** 1. the quality of being angular 2. [*pl.*] angular forms; angles

an·hy·dride (an hī'drīd) *n.* [< Gr. *anhydros* (see ff.) + -IDE] 1. an oxide that reacts with water to form an acid or a base 2. any compound formed by the removal of water, usually from an acid

an·hy·drous (-drəs) *adj.* [Gr. *anhydros* < *an-*, without + *hydōr*, water] 1. without water 2. *Chem.* having no water of crystallization

an·il (an'il) *n.* [Fr. < Port. < Ar. *al*, the + *nīl*, indigo] 1. a West Indian shrub from which indigo is made 2. *same as* INDIGO

an·i·line (an'il in, -ēn', -īn') *n.* [prec. + -INE⁴] a colourless, poisonous, oily liquid, $C_6H_5NH_2$, a derivative of benzene, used in making dyes, synthetic resins, rocket fuel, etc.

aniline dye 1. any dye made from aniline 2. commonly, any synthetic dye made from coal tar

an·i·ma (an'ə mə) *n.* [L.] 1. life principle; soul 2. *Psychol. a*) the inner personality; true self *b*) the feminine principle in the male unconscious

an·i·mad·ver·sion (an'ə mad vur'zhən, -shən) *n.* [see ff.] 1. a critical, esp. unfavourable, comment (on or upon something) 2. the act of criticizing adversely

an·i·mad·vert (-vurt') *vi.* [< L. < *animus*, mind + *advertere*, to turn: see ANIMUS & ADVERT] to comment (on or upon), esp. with disapproval; criticize adversely

an·i·mal (an'ə m'l) *n.* [L. < *anima*, animus, breath, life principle, soul] 1. any living organism except a plant or bacterium: most animals can move about voluntarily and are unable to make their own food by photosynthesis, as plants do 2. any such organism other than a human being, esp. a mammal or, sometimes, any four-footed creature 3. a brutish or inhuman person —*adj.* 1. of, like, or from an animal 2. gross, bestial, sensual, etc. —**an'i·mal·ly** *adv.*

an·i·mal·cule (an'ə mal'kyool) *n.* [< ModL., dim. of prec.] a very small or microscopic animal: also **an'i·mal'cu·lum** (-kyə ləm) *n., pl.* **-la** (-lə) —**an'i·mal'cu·lar** (-kyə lər) *adj.*

animal husbandry the raising of domesticated animals, as cattle, sheep, horses, etc.

an·i·mal·ism (an'ə m'l iz'm) *n.* 1. the activity, appetites, nature, etc. of animals 2. the doctrine that man is a mere animal with no soul —**an'i·mal·ist** *n.* —**an'i·mal·is'tic** *adj.*

an·i·mal·i·ty (an'ə mal'ə tē) *n.* 1. animal characteristics or nature 2. the animal kingdom; animal life 3. the animal instincts or nature in man

an·i·mal·ize (an'ə mə līz') *vt.* **-ized', -iz'ing** 1. to change into animal form 2. to make (a person) resemble a beast; brutalize; dehumanize —**an'i·mal·i·za'tion** *n.*

animal magnetism 1. *old term for* HYPNOTISM 2. the power to attract others in a sensual way

animal spirits healthy, lively vigour

an·i·mate (an'ə māt'; *for adj.* -mit) *vt.* **-mat'ed, -mat'ing** [< L. pp. of *animare*, to make alive < *anima:* see ANIMAL] 1. to give life to; bring to life 2. to make gay or spirited; enliven 3. to cause to act; inspire 4. to give motion to [a breeze *animating* the leaves] 5. to make move so as to seem lifelike [to *animate* puppets] 6. to produce as an animated cartoon —*adj.* 1. living; having life, esp. animal life 2. lively; spirited —**an'i·ma'tor** *n.*

an·i·mat·ed (-māt'id) *adj.* 1. alive or seeming alive; living 2. lively; spirited —**an'i·mat'ed·ly** *adv.*

animated cartoon a film made by photographing a series of drawings, each slightly changed from the one before, so that the figures in them seem to move when the film is projected

an·i·ma·tion (an'ə mā'shən) *n.* 1. an animating or being animated 2. life 3. vivacity; liveliness 4. the making of animated cartoons 5. *same as* ANIMATED CARTOON

a·ni·ma·to (ä'nē mä'tô) *adj., adv.* [It.] *Music* with animation

an·i·mé (an'ə mā', -mē') *n.* [Fr. < Port. or Sp. *anime*, prob. < native (Tupi) name] any of various resins obtained from certain tropical trees and used in making varnish

an·i·mism (an'ə miz'm) *n.* [< Fr. & Gr. < L. *anima:* see ANIMAL & -ISM] 1. the doctrine that all life is produced by a spiritual force 2. the belief that all natural objects and phenomena have souls 3. a belief in the existence of spirits, demons, etc. —**an'i·mist** *n.* —**an'i·mis'tic** *adj.*

an·i·mos·i·ty (an'ə mos'ə tē) *n., pl.* **-ties** [< L. *animositas*, spirit < *animus:* see ff.] ill will; hostility

an·i·mus (an'ə məs) *n.* [L., soul, mind, passion: see ANIMAL] 1. an animating force; intention 2. a feeling of ill will; animosity 3. *Psychol.* the masculine principle in the female unconscious

an·i·on (an'ī'ən) *n.* [< Gr. neut. prp. of *anienai*, to go up < *ana-*, up + *ienai*, to go] a negatively charged ion: in electrolysis, anions move towards the anode —**an·i·on·ic** (an'ī on'ik) *adj.*

an·ise (an'is) *n.* [< ME. & OFr. < L. < Gr. *anēson*] a plant with fragrant seeds used for flavouring

an·i·seed (an'ə sēd') *n.* the seed of anise

an·i·sette (an'ə set', -zet') *n.* [Fr., dim. < *anis:* see ANISE] a sweet, anise-flavoured liqueur

an·i·so·trop·ic (an'ī'sə trop'ik) *adj.* [AN- + ISOTROPIC] 1. *Bot.* having unequal responses to external stimuli 2. *Physics* having properties that vary according to the direction in which they are measured

ankh (aŋk) *n.* [Egypt., life, soul] a cross with a loop at the top, an ancient Egyptian symbol of life

an·kle (aŋ'k'l) *n.* [OE. *ancleow*] 1. the joint that connects the foot and the leg 2. the part of the leg between the foot and calf

an·kle·bone (-bōn') *n.* the bone of the ankle; talus

an·klet (aŋ'klit) *n.* anything worn around the ankle as an ornament or fetter

an·ky·lose (aŋ'kə lōs') *vt., vi.* **-losed', -los'ing** to stiffen or join by ankylosis

an·ky·lo·sis (aŋ'kə lō'sis) *n.* [Gr. < *ankyloun*, to stiffen < *ankylos*, bent] *Med.* an abnormal growing together and stiffening of a joint —**an·ky·lot'ic** (-lot'ik) *adj.*

an·na (an'ə) *n.* [Hindi *ānā*] a former coin of India, Pakistan, and Burma, equal to 1/16 of a rupee

an·nal·ist (an'l ist) *n.* a writer of annals —**an'nal·is'tic** *adj.*

an·nals (an'lz) *n.pl.* [< L. < *annus*, year] 1. a written account of events year by year in chronological order 2. historical records; history 3. any journal containing reports of a society, etc.

an·nates (an'āts) *n.pl.* [< Fr. *annate* < ML. < L. *annus*, year] *Eccles.* the first year's revenue of a see, benefice, etc., paid to the Pope

an·nat·to (ə nat'ō) *n.* [of W Ind. origin] a reddish-yellow dye made from pulp round the seeds of a tropical tree

an·neal (ə nēl') *vt.* [OE. *anælan*, to burn < *an-*, on + *ælan*, to burn < *æl*, fire] 1. to heat (glass, metals, etc.) and then cool slowly to prevent brittleness 2. to temper (the mind, will, etc.) —**an·neal'er** *n.*

an·ne·lid (an'ə lid) *n.* [< Fr. < L. *annellus*, dim. of *anulus*, ring: see ANNULAR] a worm with a body made of joined segments, as the earthworm —*adj.* of such worms

an·nex (ə neks') *vt.* [< OFr. < L. pp. of *annectere* < *ad-*, to + *nectere*, to tie, bind] 1. to add on or attach, esp. to something larger 2. to add as a condition, consequence, etc. 3. to incorporate into a state, etc. the territory of (another state, etc.) 4. to take, esp. without asking —*n.* something added on; specif., *a*) an addition to a document *b*) *same as* ANNEXE —**an·nex'a·ble** *adj.* —**an·nex·a·tion** (an'-ek sā'shən) *n.* —**an'nex·a'tion·ist** *n.*

an·nexe (an'eks) *n.* 1. a wing added to a building 2. a nearby building used as an addition to the main building

an·ni·hi·late (ə nī'ə lāt') *vt.* **-lat'ed, -lat'ing** [< L. pp. of *annihilare*, to bring to nothing < *ad-*, to + *nihil*, nothing] 1. to destroy completely; demolish 2. to kill 3. to conquer decisively —**an·ni'hi·la·ble** (-lə b'l) *adj.* —**an·ni'hi·la'tion** *n.* —**an·ni'hi·la'tive** *adj.* —**an·ni'hi·la'tor** *n.*

an·ni·ver·sa·ry (an'ə vur'sər ē) *n., pl.* **-ries** [< L. < *annus*, year + pp. of *vertere*, to turn] 1. the date on which some event occurred in an earlier year 2. the celebration of such a date —*adj.* of, being, or connected with an anniversary
‡**an·no Do·mi·ni** (an'ō dom'ə nī) [L., lit., in the year of the Lord] in the (given) year since the beginning of the Christian Era —*n.* [Colloq.] old age
an·no·tate (an'ə tāt', -ō-) *vt., vi.* **-tat'ed, -tat'ing** [< L. pp. of *annotare* < *ad*-, to + *notare*, to mark < *nota*: see NOTE] to provide critical or explanatory notes for (a literary work, etc.) —**an'no·ta'tive** *adj.* —**an'no·ta'tor** *n.*
an·no·ta·tion (an'ə tā'shən, -ō-) *n.* 1. an annotating or being annotated 2. a critical or explanatory note or notes
an·nounce (ə nouns') *vt.* **-nounced', -nounc'ing** [< OFr. < L. *annuntiare* < *ad*-, to + *nuntiare*, to report < *nuntius*, messenger] 1. to give notice of publicly; proclaim 2. to say or tell 3. to make known the arrival, etc. of 4. *Radio & TV* to be an announcer for —*vi.* 1. to serve as an announcer, as on radio —**an·nounce'ment** *n.*
an·nounc·er (-ər) *n.* a person who announces; specif., one who introduces radio or television programmes, identifies the station or channel, reads the news, etc.
an·noy (ə noi') *vt.* [< OFr. < VL. < *in odio habere*, to have in hate: see ODIUM] 1. to irritate, bother, or make somewhat angry 2. to harm by repeated attacks; harass —*vi.* to be annoying —**an·noy'er** *n.* —**an·noy'ing** *adj.* —**an·noy'ing·ly** *adv.*
an·noy·ance (-əns) *n.* 1. an annoying or being annoyed 2. a thing or person that annoys
an·nu·al (an'yoo wəl) *adj.* [< ME. & OFr. < L. < *annus*, year] 1. of or measured by a year 2. happening once a year; yearly 3. for a year's time, work, etc. [an *annual* wage] 4. living for only one year or season —*n.* 1. a yearly publication 2. a plant that lives only one year or season —**an'nu·al·ly** *adv.*
annual ring any of the concentric rings seen in cross-sections of the stems of most trees and shrubs: each ring is a layer of wood that is a year's growth
an·nu·i·tant (ə nyoo'ə tənt) *n.* a person receiving an annuity
an·nu·i·ty (ə nyoo'ə tē) *n., pl.* **-ties** [< ME. & OFr. < ML. < L. *annus*, year] 1. a payment of a fixed sum of money at regular intervals, esp. yearly 2. an investment yielding such payments
an·nul (ə nul') *vt.* **-nulled', -nul'ling** [< OFr. < LL. *annullare*, to bring to nothing < *ad*-, + *nullum*, nothing: see NULL] 1. to do away with 2. to invalidate; cancel —**an·nul'la·ble** *adj.*
an·nu·lar (an'yoo lər) *adj.* [< L. < *anulus*, a ring] of, like, or forming a ring —**an'nu·lar'i·ty** (-lar'ə tē) *n.* —**an'·nu·lar·ly** *adv.*
annular eclipse an eclipse in which a ring of sunlight can be seen around the disc of the moon
annular ligament the ligament surrounding the ankle joint or wrist joint
an·nu·late (an'yoo lit, -lāt') *adj.* [see ANNULAR] marked with, or made up of, rings: also **an'nu·lat'ed** —**an'nu·la'tion** *n.*
an·nu·let (an'yoo lət) *n.* [< L. *anulus*, a ring + -ET] 1. a small ring 2. *Archit.* a ringlike moulding near the top of a column
an·nul·ment (ə nul'mənt) *n.* 1. an annulling or being annulled 2. an invalidation, as of a marriage, by the decree of a court, the Pope, etc.
an·nu·lus (an'yoo ləs) *n., pl.* **-li'** (-lī'), **-lus·es** [L. *anulus*] any ringlike part or mark
an·nun·ci·ate (ə nun'sē āt', -shē-) *vt.* **-at'ed, -at'ing** [< L. pp. of *annuntiare*] to announce
an·nun·ci·a·tion (ə nun'sē ā'shən) *n.* 1. an announcing or being announced 2. [A-] *a)* the angel Gabriel's announcement to Mary that she was to give birth to Jesus: Luke 1:26-38 *b)* the church festival (March 25) commemorating this
an·nun·ci·a·tor (ə nun'sē āt'ər, -shē-) *n.* 1. a person or thing that announces 2. an electric indicator, as in hotels, to show the source of calls
a·no·a (ə nō'ə) *n.* [from native name in Celebes] a wild ox, the smallest of the cattle tribe
an·ode (an'ōd) *n.* [< Gr. < *ana*-, up + *hodos*, way] 1. a positively charged electrode, as in an electrolytic cell, electron tube, etc. 2. the negative electrode in a battery supplying current
an·o·dize (an'ə dīz') *vt.* **-dized', -diz'ing** to put a protective oxide film on (a light metal) by an electrolytic process in which the metal serves as the anode
an·o·dyne (an'ə dīn') *adj.* [< L. < Gr. < *an*-, without + *odynē*, pain] relieving or lessening pain —*n.* anything that relieves pain or soothes —**an'o·dyn'ic** (-din'ik) *adj.*
a·noint (ə noint') *vt.* [< OFr. < L. *inungere* < *in*-, on + *ungere*, to smear] 1. to rub oil or ointment on 2. to put oil on in a ceremony of consecration —**a·noint'er** *n.* —**a·noint'-ment** *n.*
Anointing of the Sick *R.C.Ch.* the sacrament in which a priest prays for and anoints a person dying or critically ill

a·nom·a·lis·tic (ə nom'ə lis'tik) *adj.* 1. tending to be anomalous 2. of an anomaly
a·nom·a·lous (ə nom'ə ləs) *adj.* [< L. < Gr. < *an*-, not + *homalos* < *homos*, the same] 1. deviating from the general rule; abnormal 2. being, or seeming to be, inconsistent or improper —**a·nom'a·lous·ly** *adv.* —**a·nom'a·lous·ness** *n.*
a·nom·a·ly (-lē) *n., pl.* **-lies** [< L. < Gr. *anōmalia*, inequality: see prec.] 1. departure from the regular arrangement or usual method; abnormality 2. anything anomalous 3. *Astron.* a planet's angular distance from its perihelion, viewed as if measured from the sun
an·o·mie, an·o·my (an'ə mē) *n.* [< Fr. < Gr. < *a*-, without + *nomos*, law] lack of purpose, identity, or ethical values in a person or in a society; rootlessness —**a·nom·ic** (ə nom'-ik) *adj.*
a·non (ə non') *adv.* [OE. *on an*, in one, straightaway] [Archaic or Lit.] 1. soon; shortly; at another time 2. at once —**ever and anon** now and then
anon. anonymous
an·o·nym (an'ə nim) *n.* [Fr. < Gr.: see ANONYMOUS] 1. a person whose name is not known 2. a pseudonym
an·o·nym·i·ty (an'ə nim'ə tē) *n.* the condition or fact of being anonymous
a·non·y·mous (ə non'ə məs) *adj.* [< Gr. < *an*-, without + *onyma*, name] 1. with no name known or acknowledged 2. given, written, etc. by a person whose name is withheld or unknown 3. lacking in distinctive features —**a·non'-y·mous·ly** *adv.*
a·noph·e·les (ə nof'ə lēz') *n.* [ModL. < Gr. *anōphelēs*, harmful < *an*-, without + *ophelēs*, use] the mosquito that can carry the malaria parasite and transmit the disease —**a·noph'e·line'** (-līn', -lin) *adj.*
an·o·rex·i·a (an'ə rek'sē ə) *n.* [ModL. < Gr. *an*-, without + *orexis*, desire] chronic lack of appetite for food —**an'o·ret'-ic** (ret'ik) *adj.*
an·os·mi·a (an oz'mē ə, -os'-) *n.* [ModL. < Gr. *an*-, without + *osmē*, smell] loss of the sense of smell —**an·os'mic** (-mik) *adj.*
an·oth·er (ə nuth'ər) *adj.* [ME. *an other*] 1. one more; an additional 2. a different 3. one of the same kind as [*another* Caesar] —*pron.* 1. one additional 2. a different one 3. one of the same kind
an·ox·i·a (an ok'sē ə) *n.* [AN- + OX(YGEN) + -IA] the condition of not having enough oxygen in the body tissues —**an·ox'ic** (-sik) *adj.*
ans. answer
an·schluss (än'shloos) *n.* [G.] union, esp. [A-] the political union of Germany and Austria (1938)
an·ser·ine (an'sər īn', -in) *adj.* [< L. < *anser*, goose] 1. of or like a goose 2. stupid; foolish
an·swer (an'sər) *n.* [< OE. < *and*-, against + *swerian*, to SWEAR] 1. something said or written in return to a question, letter, etc. 2. any act in response or retaliation 3. a solution to a problem —*vi.* 1. to reply in words, by an action, etc. 2. to respond (*to*) [the horse *answered* to its rider's touch] 3. to be sufficient 4. to be responsible (*to* a person *for* an action, etc.) 5. to correspond (*to*) [he *answers* to the description] —*vt.* 1. to reply to in some way 2. to respond to the signal of (a telephone, doorbell, etc.) 3. to comply with; serve [to *answer* a purpose] 4. to refute (an accusation, criticism, etc.) 5. to suit [he *answers* the description] —**answer back** [Colloq.] to reply rudely or impertinently
an·swer·a·ble (-ə b'l) *adj.* 1. responsible; accountable 2. that can be answered or shown to be wrong [an *answerable* argument]
ant (ant) *n.* [OE. *æmete*] any of a family of insects, generally wingless, that live in colonies with a complex division of labour
-ant (ənt, 'nt) [Fr. < L. *-antem* or *-entem*, acc. prp. ending] *a suffix meaning:* 1. that has, shows, or does [*defiant, radiant*] 2. a person or thing that [*occupant, accountant*]
ant·ac·id (ant'as'id) *adj.* counteracting acidity —*n.* an antacid substance

WORKER ANT

an·tag·o·nism (an tag'ə niz'm) *n.* [see ANTAGONIZE] 1. the state of being opposed or hostile to another or to each other; opposition or hostility 2. an opposing force, principle, etc.; specif., a mutually opposing action between organisms, muscles, drugs, etc.
an·tag·o·nist (-nist) *n.* 1. an adversary; opponent 2. a muscle, drug, etc. that counteracts another
an·tag·o·nis·tic (an tag'ə nis'tik) *adj.* showing antagonism; acting in opposition —**an·tag'o·nis'ti·cal·ly** *adv.*
an·tag·o·nize (an tag'ə nīz') *vt.* **-nized', -niz'ing** [< Gr. < *anti*-, against + *agōn*, a contest: see AGONY] 1. to oppose or counteract 2. to incur the dislike of; make an enemy of
ant·al·ka·li (ant al'kə lī') *n., pl.* **-lis', -lies'** a substance that counteracts alkalinity
ant·arc·tic (ant ärk'tik, -är'-) *adj.* [< OFr. < L. < Gr. <

anti, opposite + *arktikos*, arctic] of or near the South Pole or the region around it

Antarctic Circle [*also* a- c-] an imaginary circle parallel to the equator, 66°33′ south of it

ant bear a large anteater of tropical S. America

an·te (an′tē) *n.* [L., before] 1. *Poker* the stake that each player must put into the pot before receiving cards 2. [Colloq.] the amount one must pay as one's share, esp. in advance —*vt., vi.* -**ted** or -**teed**, -**te·ing** 1. *Poker* to put in (one's stake) 2. [Colloq.] to pay (one's share) —**ante up** to ante one's stake or share

an·te- [< L. *ante*, before] a prefix meaning: 1. before, prior (to) [*antecedent, ante*-Victorian] 2. before, in front (of) [*anteroom*]

ant·eat·er (ant′ēt′ər) *n.* any of several mammals that feed mainly on ants: anteaters have a long, sticky tongue and a long snout

an·te·bel·lum (an′ti bel′əm) *adj.* [L.] before the war; specif., before the American Civil War

an·te·cede (an′tə sēd′) *vt., vi.* -**ced′ed**, -**ced′ing** [< L. *antecedere* < *ante*, before + *cedere*, to go] to go before; precede

an·te·ced·ence (-sēd′əns) *n.* [see prec.] a being prior; precedence: also **an′te·ced′en·cy** (-ən sē)

an·te·ced·ent (-sēd′ənt) *adj.* [see ANTECEDE] prior; previous —*n.* 1. any thing prior to another 2. anything logically preceding 3. [*pl.*] one's ancestry, past life, etc. 4. *Gram.* the word, phrase, or clause to which a pronoun refers 5. *Logic* the conditional part of a hypothetical proposition —**an′te·ced′ent·ly** *adv.*

an·te·cham·ber (an′ti chām′bər) *n.* [< Fr.: see ANTE- & CHAMBER] a smaller room leading into a larger or main room

an·te·date (-dāt′) *vt.* -**dat′ed**, -**dat′ing** 1. to put a date on that is earlier than the actual date 2. to come before 3. to set an earlier date for

an·te·di·lu·vi·an (an′ti də lōō′vē ən) *adj.* [< ANTE- + L. *diluvium*, a flood + -AN] 1. of the time before the Biblical Flood 2. very old or old-fashioned —*n.* an antediluvian person or thing

an·te·lope (an′tə lōp′) *n., pl.* -**lopes′**, -**lope′**: see PLURAL, II, D, 1 [< ME. & OFr. < ML. < MGr. *antholops*, deer] 1. any of a group of swift, cud-chewing, hollow-horned, deerlike animals related to oxen, sheep, and goats 2. leather made from an antelope's hide

an·te me·ri·di·em (an′tē mə rid′ē əm) [L.] before noon: abbrev. **A.M., a.m., AM**

an·te·na·tal (an′tē nā′t′l) *adj.* before birth

antenatal clinic a clinic that advises pregnant women on their health, diet, etc.

an·ten·na (an ten′ə) *n.* [< L. < *antemna*, sail yard] 1. *pl.* -**nae** (-ē), -**nas** either of a pair of movable sense organs on the head of an insect, crab, etc.; feeler 2. *pl.* -**nas** *Radio & TV same as* AERIAL

ANTELOPE
(to 1·8m high at shoulder)

an·te·pen·di·um (an′ti pen′dē əm) *n., pl.* -**di·a** (-ə), -**di·ums** [ML. < L. *ante*, before + *pendere*, to hang] a screen or veil hanging from the front of an altar, pulpit, etc.

an·te·pe·nult (an′ti pi nult′) *n.* [see ANTE-& PENULT] the third last syllable in a word, as -*lu*- in *an·te·di·lu·vi·an*

an·te·pe·nul·ti·mate (-pi nul′tə mit) *adj.* third last; third from the end —*n.* 1. anything third from the end 2. an antepenult

an·te·ri·or (an tir′ē ər) *adj.* [L., compar. of *ante*, before] 1. at or towards the front; forward: opposed to POSTERIOR 2. coming before in time, order, etc.; earlier —**an·te′ri·or·ly** *adv.*

an·te·room (an′ti rōōm′, -rōōm′) *n.* a room leading to a larger one; waiting room

an·the·li·on (an thē′lē ən) *n. pl.* -**li·a** (-ē·ə) -**li·ons** [ModL. < Gr. < *anti*, against + *hēlios*, sun] a halo round an object's shadow cast by the sun on a cloud or bank of mist at high altitudes or in polar regions

an·them (an′thəm) *n.* [< OE. *antefn* < ML. < Gr. *antiphōnos*, sounding back < *anti*-, over against + *phōnē*, voice] 1. a religious choral song usually based on words from the Bible 2. a song of praise or devotion [*national anthem*]

an·ther (an′thər) *n.* [< Fr. < ModL. < Gr. *anthēros*, blooming < *anthos*, a flower] the part of a stamen that contains the pollen

an·ther·id·i·um (an′thə rid′ē əm) *n., pl.* -**id′i·a** (-ə) [ModL. < prec. + Gr. dim. suffix -*idion*] in flowerless and seedless plants, the organ in which the male sex cells are developed —**an′ther·id′i·al** *adj.*

ant·hill (ant′hil′) *n.* the soil carried by ants from their underground nest and heaped around its entrance

an·thol·o·gize (an thol′ə jīz′) *vi.* -**gized′**, -**giz′ing** to make

anthologies —*vt.* to make an anthology of or include in an anthology —**an·thol′o·gist** *n.*

an·thol·o·gy (an thol′ə jē) *n., pl.* -**gies** [< Gr. *anthologia*, a garland < *anthos*, flower + *legein*, to gather] a collection of poems, stories, etc. —**an·tho·log·i·cal** (an·thə loj′i k′l) *adj.*

an·tho·zo·an (an′thə zō′ən) *n.* [< ModL. < Gr. *anthos*, flower + *zōion*, animal + -AN] any of a class of sea organisms, comprising corals, sea anemones, etc. —*adj.* of the anthozoans

an·thra·cene (an′thrə sēn′) *n.* [< Gr. *anthrax*, coal + -ENE] a crystalline hydrocarbon, a product of coal-tar distillation used in making dyes and as a radiation detector

an·thra·cite (-sīt′) *n.* [< Gr. < *anthrax*, coal] hard coal, which gives much heat but little flame and smoke —**an′thra·cit′ic** (-sit′ik) *adj.*

an·thrax (an′thraks) *n.* [L. < Gr., (burning) coal, hence carbuncle] 1. an infectious disease of wild and domesticated animals, esp. cattle and sheep, that can be transmitted to man: it is characterized by black pustules 2. any such pustule

an·thro·po- [< Gr. *anthrōpos*, man] a combining form meaning man, human [*anthropology*]: also, before a vowel, **anthrop-**

an·thro·po·cen·tric (an′thrə pə sen′trik) *adj.* [prec. + -CENTRIC] 1. that considers man as the central fact, or final aim, of the universe 2. viewing everything in terms of human values

an·thro·po·gen·e·sis (-jen′ə sis) *n.* the study of man's origin and development: also **an′thro·pog′e·ny** (-poj′ə nē) —**an′thro·po·ge·net′ic** (-jə net′ik) *adj.*

an·thro·poid (an′thrə poid′) *adj.* [ANTHROP(O)- + -OID] 1. resembling man; manlike; esp., designating or of any of the most highly developed apes, as the chimpanzee and gorilla 2. apelike —*n.* any anthropoid ape —**an′thro·poi′dal** *adj.*

an·thro·pol·o·gist (an′thrə pol′ə jist) *n.* a student of or specialist in anthropology

an·thro·pol·o·gy (-pol′ə jē) *n.* [ANTHROPO- + -LOGY] the study of man, esp. of the variety, distribution, characteristics, cultures, etc. of mankind —**an′thro·po·log′i·cal** (-pə loj′i k′l), **an′thro·po·log′ic** *adj.* —**an′thro·po·log′i·cal·ly** *adv.*

an·thro·pom·e·try (-pom′ə trē) *n.* [ANTHROPO- + -METRY] the science dealing with measurement of the human body in comparing individual and group differences —**an′thro·po·met′ric** (-pə met′rik), **an′thro·po·met′ri·cal** *adj.* —**an′thro·po·met′ri·cal·ly** *adv.*

an·thro·po·mor·phic (-pə môr′fik) *adj.* of, characterized by, or resulting from anthropomorphism —**an′thro·po·mor′phi·cal·ly** *adv.*

an·thro·po·mor·phism (-pə môr′fiz′m) *n.* [ANTHRO-POMORPH(OUS) + -ISM] the attributing of human shape or characteristics to a god, animal, or inanimate thing —**an′thro·po·mor′phist** *n.*

an·thro·po·mor·phous (-pə môr′fəs) *adj.* [< Gr. < *anthrōpos*, a man + *morphē*, form, shape] having human shape and appearance

an·thro·poph·a·gi (-pof′ə gī′) *n.pl., sing.* -**a·gus** (-ə gəs) [L. < Gr. < *anthrōpos*, man + *phagein*, to eat] cannibals

an·thro·poph·a·gy (-pof′ə jē) *n.* [see prec.] cannibalism —**an′thro·poph′a·gous** (-gəs), **an′thro·po·phag′ic** (-pə faj′-ik) *adj.*

an·thu·ri·um (an thoor′ē əm) *n.* [ModL. < Gr. *anthos*, flower + *oura*, tail] a tropical American plant having a long spike with a flaring, heart-shaped spathe around its base

an·ti (an′ti, -tē) *n., pl.* -**tis** [< ff.] [Colloq.] a person opposed to some policy, proposal, etc. —*prep.* [Colloq.] opposed to; against

an·ti- (an′ti; *also variously* -tē, -tī, -tə) [< Gr. < *anti*, against] a prefix meaning: 1. against; hostile to [*anticlerical*] 2. that operates against [*antiaircraft*] 3. that prevents, cures, or neutralizes [*antitoxin*] 4. opposite; reverse [*antimatter*] 5. rivalling [*antipope*]

an·ti·air·craft (an′tē er′kräft) *adj.* used for defence against hostile aircraft [*antiaircraft gun*]

an·ti·ar (an′tē är′) *n.* [Javanese *antjar*] 1. the upas tree of Java 2. a poison made from its gum resin

an·ti·bac·te·ri·al (-bak tir′ē əl) *adj.* that checks the growth or effect of bacteria

an·ti·bal·lis·tic missile (-bə lis′tik) a ballistic missile intended to intercept and destroy another ballistic missile in flight

an·ti·bi·o·sis (-bī ō′sis) *n.* [ModL. < ANTI- + Gr. *biōsis*, way of life < *bios*, life] *Biol.* an association between organisms which is harmful to one of them

an·ti·bi·ot·ic (-bī ot′ik) *adj.* 1. of antibiosis 2. destroying, or stopping the growth of, bacteria and other microorganisms —*n.* an antibiotic substance produced by various microorganisms, as by bacteria or fungi

an·ti·bod·y (an′ti bod′ē) *n., pl.* -**bod′ies** a protein produced in the body in response to contact of the body with an antigen, serving to neutralize the antigen, thus creating immunity

an·tic (an'tik) *adj.* [< It. < L. *antiquus*: see ANTIQUE] 1. [Archaic] fantastic and queer 2. odd and funny —*n.* 1. a playful or silly act, trick, etc.; caper 2. [Archaic] a clown or buffoon —*vi.* **-ticked, -tick·ing** to perform antics; caper

an·ti·cath·ode (an'ti kath'ōd) *n.* in an X-ray tube, the piece opposite the cathode; the target for the cathode's discharge

an·ti·christ (an'ti krīst') *n.* an opponent of Christ —[A-] *Bible* great antagonist of Christ expected to rule the world but be conquered at Christ's second coming: I John 2:18

an·tic·i·pant (an tis'ə pənt) *adj.* expecting; anticipating (with *of*) —*n.* a person who anticipates

an·tic·i·pate (an tis'ə pāt') *vt.* **-pat'ed, -pat'ing** [< L. pp. of *anticipare* < *ante-*, before + *capere*, to take] 1. to look forward to; expect 2. to prevent by action in advance; forestall [to *anticipate* an opponent's blows] 3. to foresee and take care of in advance [to *anticipate* a request] 4. to use or enjoy in advance [to *anticipate* a legacy] 5. to be ahead of in doing or achieving something —**an·tic'i·pa'tor** *n.*

an·tic·i·pa·tion (an tis'ə pā'shən) *n.* 1. an anticipating or being anticipated 2. something anticipated or expected 3. foreknowledge; presentiment

an·tic·i·pa·tive (an tis'ə pāt'iv) *adj.* of or full of anticipation —**an·tic'i·pa'tive·ly** *adv.*

an·tic·i·pa·to·ry (-pə tər ē) *adj.* of or expressing anticipation —**an·tic'i·pa·to·ri·ly** *adv.*

an·ti·cler·i·cal (an'ti kler'ə k'l, -tī-) *adj.* opposed to the influence of the clergy or church, esp. in public affairs —*n.* a person of anticlerical views —**an'ti·cler'i·cal·ism** *n.*

an·ti·cli·max (-klī'maks) *n.* 1. a sudden drop from the dignified or important to the commonplace or trivial 2. a final event which is in disappointing contrast to those coming before —**an'ti·cli·mac'tic** (-mak'tik) *adj.*

an·ti·cline (an'ti klīn') *n.* [< ANTI- + Gr. *klinein*, to incline] *Geol.* a fold of stratified rock in which the strata slope downward in opposite directions from the central axis: opposed to SYNCLINE —**an'ti·cli'nal** *adj.*

an·ti·clock·wise (an'ti klok'wīz) *adj., adv.* in a direction opposite to that in which the hands of a clock move

an·ti·co·ag·u·lant (an'ti kō ag'yə lənt) *n.* a drug or substance that delays or prevents the clotting of blood

an·ti·cy·clone (-sī'klōn) *n.* an extensive atmospheric condition of high barometric pressure, with the winds at the edge blowing outwards —**an'ti·cy·clon'ic** (-klon'ik) *adj.*

an·ti·de·pres·sant (-di pres'ənt) *adj.* designating or of any drug used to treat emotional depression —*n.* an antidepressant drug

an·ti·dote (an'tə dōt') *n.* [ME. & OFr. < L. < Gr. < *anti-*, against + *dotos*, given < *didonai*, to give] 1. a remedy to counteract a poison 2. anything that works against an evil or unwanted condition —**an'ti·dot'al** *adj.*

an·ti·freeze (an'ti frēz') *n.* a substance of low freezing point added esp. to the water in car radiators to prevent freezing

an·ti·gen (an'tə jən) *n.* [ANTI- + -GEN] an enzyme, toxin, etc. to which the body reacts by producing antibodies —**an'ti·gen'ic** (-jen'ik) *adj.*

an·ti·he·ro (an'ti hir'ō) *n.* the main character of a novel, play, etc. who lacks the virtues of a traditional hero

an·ti·his·ta·mine (an'ti his'tə mēn',-mən) *n.* any drug used to minimize the action of histamine in allergic conditions such as hay fever —**an'ti·his'ta·min'ic** (-min'ik) *adj.*

an·ti·knock (an'ti nok') *n.* a substance added to the fuel of internal-combustion engines to do away with noise caused by too rapid combustion

an·ti·log·a·rithm (an'ti log'ə rith'm) *n.* the number corresponding to a given logarithm [the *antilogarithm* of 1 is 10]: also **an·ti·log**

an·til·o·gy (an til'ə jē) *n., pl.* **-gies** [Gr. *antilogia* < *anti*, against & *legein*, to speak] a contradiction in ideas, statements or terms

an·ti·ma·cas·sar (an'ti mə kas'ər) *n.* [ANTI- + *macassar* (*oil*), a former hair oil] a small cover to protect the back or arms of a chair, etc. from soiling

an·ti·mag·net·ic (an'ti mag net'ik) *adj.* made of metals that resist magnetism [an *antimagnetic* watch]

an·ti·ma·lar·i·al (-mə ler'ē əl) *adj.* preventing or relieving malaria —*n.* an antimalarial drug

an·ti·masque, an·ti·mask (an'ti mäsk') *n.* a comic sketch, often a burlesque, between the acts of a masque

an·ti·mat·ter (an'ti mat'ər) *n.* a form of matter in which the electrical charge or other property of each constituent particle is the reverse of that in the usual matter of our universe

an·ti·mis·sile (-mis'īl) *adj.* designed as a defence against ballistic missiles

an·ti·mo·ny (an'tə mə'nē) *n.* [< OFr. < ML. *antimonium*] a silvery-white, brittle, metallic chemical element, found only in combination: used to harden alloys, etc.: symbol, Sb; at. wt., 121.75; at. no., 51 —**an'ti·mo'nic** *adj.*

an·ti·no·mi·an (an'ti nō'mē ən) *n.* [< ANTINOMY + -AN] [*also* A-] *Christian Theol.* a believer in the doctrine that faith alone, not obedience to the moral law, is necessary for salvation —*adj.* of this doctrine —**an'ti·no'mi·an·ism** *n.*

an·tin·o·my (an tin'ə mē) *n., pl.* **-mies** [L. < Gr. *antinonua* < *anti*, against + *nonau* < *normas*, law] 1. the opposition of one law, regulation, etc. to another 2. a contradiction or inconsistency between two apparently reasonable principles or laws

an·ti·nov·el (an'ti nov'l) *n.* [transl. of Fr. *anti-roman*, term coined by Sartre] a work of prose fiction in which the author's intention is to violate such traditional aspects of the novel as plot, concept of a hero, etc.

an·ti·par·ti·cle (an'ti pär'tə k'l) *n.* any of the constituent particles of antimatter

an·ti·pas·to (an'ti pas'tō, -päs'-) *n.* [It. < *anti-* (L. *ante*), before + *pasto* < L. *pastus*, food] a dish of salted fish, meat, olives, etc. served as an appetizer

an·ti·pa·thet·ic (an'ti pə thet'ik) *adj.* 1. having antipathy 2. opposed or antagonistic in character, tendency, etc. Also **an'ti·pa·thet'i·cal** —**an'ti·pa·thet'i·cal·ly** *adv.*

an·tip·a·thy (an tip'ə thē) *n., pl.* **-thies** [< L. < Gr. < *anti-*, against + *patheia* < *pathein*, to feel] 1. a strong dislike 2. the object of such dislike

an·ti·per·son·nel (an'ti pur'sə nel') *adj.* directed against, or intended to destroy, people rather than material objects [*antipersonnel* mines]

an·ti·per·spir·ant (-pur'spər ənt) *n.* a substance applied to the skin to reduce perspiration

an·ti·phlo·gis·tic (-flə jis'tik) *adj.* counteracting inflammation —*n.* an antiphlogistic substance

an·ti·phon (an'tə fon') *n.* [< ML. < Gr.: see ANTHEM] a hymn, psalm, etc. chanted or sung in responsive, alternating parts —**an·tiph'o·nal** (-tif'ə n'l), **an'ti·phon'ic** *adj.*

an·tiph·o·nar·y (an tif'ə nər ē) *n., pl.* **-nar·ies** a book of antiphons

an·tiph·o·ny (an tif'ə nē) *n., pl.* **-nies** 1. antiphonal chanting or singing 2. any response or echo

an·ti·pode (an'tə pōd') *n.* [back-formation of ff.] an exact opposite

an·tip·o·des (an tip'ə dēz') *n.pl.* [ML. < L. < Gr., pl. of *antipous* < *anti-*, opposite + *pous*, foot] 1. any two places directly opposite each other on the earth 2. [*with pl. or sing. v.*] a place on the opposite side of the earth: in British usage, New Zealand and Australia 3. two opposite or contrary things —**an·tip'o·dal** *adj.* —**an·tip'o·de'an** (-dē'ən) *adj., n.*

an·ti·pope (an'ti pōp') *n.* a pope set up against the one chosen by church laws, as in a schism

an·ti·py·ret·ic (an'ti pī ret'ik) *adj.* [ANTI- + PYRETIC] reducing fever —*n.* anything that reduces fever

antiq. 1. antiquarian 2. antiquity; antiquities

an·ti·quar·i·an (an'tə kwer'ē ən) *adj.* 1. of antiques or antiquities 2. of antiquaries 3. of, or dealing in, rare old books —*n.* an antiquary

an·ti·quar·y (an'tə kwər ē) *n., pl.* **-quar·ies** one who collects or studies antiquities and ancient art

an·ti·quate (-kwāt.') *vt.* **-quat'ed, -quat'ing** [< L. pp. of *antiquare* < *antiquus*: see ANTIQUE] to make old or obsolete; cause to become old-fashioned —**an'ti·quat'ed** *adj.* —**an'ti·qua'tion** *n.*

an·tique (an tēk') *adj.* [Fr. < L. *antiquus*, ancient < *ante*, before] 1. of ancient times; ancient 2. out-of-date; old-fashioned 3. in the style of classical antiquity 4. of, or in the style of, a former period 5. dealing in antiques —*n.* 1. an ancient relic 2. the ancient style, esp. of Greek or Roman sculpture, etc. 3. a piece of furniture, silverware, etc. of a former period 4. *Printing* a variety of boldface type having all lines of nearly equal thickness —*vt.* **-tiqued', -tiqu'ing** to make look antique —**an·tique'ly** *adv.* —**an·tique'ness** *n.*

an·tiq·ui·ty (an tik'wə tē) *n., pl.* **-ties** [see prec.] 1. the early period of history, esp. before the Middle Ages 2. great age; oldness [a statue of great *antiquity*] 3. the people of ancient times 4. [*pl.*] a) relics, monuments, etc. of the distant past b) ancient manners, customs, etc.

an·tir·rhi·num (an'ti rī'nəm) *n.* [L. < Gr. *antirrhinon* < *anti-*, like + *rhis* (gen *rhinos*), nose] any of a genus of plants with two-lipped flowers, esp. the snapdragon

an·ti·scor·bu·tic (an'ti skôr byōō'tik) *adj.* that cures or prevents scurvy

an·ti·Se·mit·ic (-sə mit'ik) *adj.* 1. having or showing prejudice against Jews 2. discriminating against or persecuting Jews —**an'ti·Sem'ite** (-sem'īt, -sē'mīt) —**an'ti·Sem'i·tism** (-sem'ə tiz'm) *n.*

an·ti·sep·sis (-sep'sis) *n.* [ANTI + SEPSIS] 1. the technique of preventing infection, the growth of microorganisms, etc. 2. the condition of being antiseptic 3. the use of antiseptics

an·ti·sep·tic (-sep'tik) *adj.* 1. preventing infection, decay, etc. by inhibiting the action of microorganisms 2. using antiseptics **3.** free from infection; sterile **4.** untouched by life, its problems, etc. —*n.* any antiseptic substance —**an'-ti·sep'ti·cal·ly** *adv.* —**an'ti·sep'ti·cize'** *vt.* -**cized'**, -**ciz'ing**

an·ti·se·rum (an'ti sir'əm) *n.* a serum with antibodies in it

an·ti·so·cial (-sō'shəl) *adj.* **1.** unsociable **2.** harmful to the welfare of the people generally

an·ti·spas·mod·ic (-spaz mod'ik) *adj.* relieving spasms —*n.* an antispasmodic drug

an·ti·stat·ic (-stat'ik) *adj.* reducing static electric charges, as on textiles, polishes, etc.

an·tis·tro·phe (an tis'trə fē) *n.* [L. < Gr. < *anti-*, opposite + *strephein*, to turn] **1.** *a)* the return movement, left to right, made by the chorus of an ancient Greek play in answering a strophe *b)* the part of a choric song performed during this **2.** a stanza following a strophe, often in the same form —**an·ti·stroph·ic** (an'tə strof'ik) *adj.*

an·ti·tank (an'ti taŋk') *adj.* for use against tanks in war

an·tith·e·sis (an tith'ə sis) *n.*, *pl.* -**ses'** (-sēz') [L. < Gr. < *anti-*, against + *tithenai*, to place] **1.** a contrast of thoughts, usually in two phrases, clauses, etc. (Ex.: "Man proposes God disposes") **2.** a contrast or opposition **3.** the exact opposite [joy is the *antithesis* of sorrow] —**an'ti·thet'ic** (an'ti thet'ik), —**an'ti·thet'i·cal** *adj.* —**an'ti·thet'-i·cal·ly** *adv.*

an·ti·tox·in (an'ti tok'sin) *n.* **1.** an antibody formed by the body to act against a specific toxin **2.** a serum containing an antitoxin: taken from the blood of an immunized animal, such a serum is injected into a person to prevent a specific disease, such as diphtheria or tetanus —**an'ti·tox'ic** *adj.*

an·ti·trades (an'ti trādz') *n.pl.* winds that blow above and opposite to the trade winds

an·ti·trust (an'ti trust') *adj.* [Chiefly U.S.] opposed to, or regulating trusts, or business monopolies

an·ti·type (an'ti tīp') *n.* [< LL. < Gr. *antitypos* < *anti, typos*, form] **1.** that which is corresponding to + *typos*, form] **1.** that which is represented by a type **2.** an opposite type

an·ti·ven·in (-ven'ən) *n.* [ANTI- + VEN(OM) + -IN¹] **1.** an antitoxin for venom, as of snakes, produced by gradually increased injections of the specific venom **2.** a serum containing this antitoxin

an·ti·viv·i·sec·tion (-viv'ə sek'shən) *n.* opposition to medical research on living animals —**an'ti·viv'i·sec'tion·ist** *n.*, *adj.*

ant·ler (ant'lər) *n.* [< OFr. *antoillier* < ?] **1.** the branched, deciduous horn of any animal of the deer family **2.** any branch of such a horn —**ant'lered** *adj.*

ant lion **1.** the large-jawed larva of certain winged insects that digs a pit for trapping ants, etc. on which it feeds **2.** the adult insect

an·to·no·ma·si·a (an'tə nə mā'zē ə) *n.* [L. < Gr. *antonomazein*, to call by another name] **1.** the use of an epithet or title in place of a name, as in calling a judge *his honour* **2.** the use of a proper name to denote a class, as in calling a philanderer a *Don Juan*

an·to·nym (an'tə nim') *n.* [< Gr. < *anti-*, opposite + *onyma*, name] a word that is opposite in meaning to another word ["sad" is an *antonym* of "happy"] —**an·ton·y·mous** (an ton'ə məs) *adj.*

ANTLERS
A, roe deer; B, red deer; C, fallow deer

an·trum (an'trəm) *n.*, *pl.* -**tra** (-trə), -**trums** [L. < Gr. *antron*, cave] *Anat.* a cavity; esp., either of a pair of sinuses in the upper jaw

an·u·re·sis (an'yoo rē'sis) *n.* [ModL. < AN- + Gr. *ourēsis*, urination] the condition of being unable to pass one's urine

a·nus (ā'nəs) *n.*, *pl.* **a'nus·es, a'ni** (-nī) [L., a ring] the opening at the lower end of the alimentary canal

an·vil (an'vəl) *n.* [< OE. *anfilt* < *an-*, on + hyp. *filtan*, to beat] **1.** an iron or steel block on which metal objects are hammered into shape **2.** the incus, one of the three bones of the middle ear

anx·i·e·ty (aŋ zī'ə tē) *n.*, *pl.* -**ties** [see ff.] **1.** a state of being uneasy or worried about what may happen **2.** an eager but often uneasy desire [*anxiety* to do well]

anx·ious (aŋk'shəs, aŋ'-) *adj.* [L. *anxius* < *angere*, to choke] **1.** uneasy in mind; worried **2.** causing or full of anxiety [an *anxious* hour] **3.** eagerly wishing —**anx'ious·ly** *adv.* —**anx'ious·ness** *n.*

an·y (en'ē) *adj.* [< OE. *ænig* < *an*, ONE] **1.** one, no matter which, of more than two [*any* pupil may answer] **2.** some, no matter what amount or kind [he hasn't *any* food] **3.** without limit [enter *any* number of times] **4.** every [*any* child can do it] —**pron. sing. & pl.** any one or ones; any amount or number —*adv.* to any degree or extent; at all [is he *any* better?]

an·y·bod·y (-bod'ē) *pron.* **1.** any person; anyone **2.** a person of fame, importance, etc.

an·y·how (-hou') *adv.* **1.** no matter in what way **2.** in any case **3.** carelessly

any more now; nowadays: in standard use, only in negative constructions [he doesn't live here *any more*]

an·y·one (-wun') *pron.* any person; anybody

any one any single (person or thing)

an·y·place (en'ē plās') *adv.* [U.S. Colloq.] in, at, or to any place; anywhere

an·y·thing (-thiŋ') *pron.* any object, event, fact, etc. —*n.* a thing, no matter of what kind —*adv.* in any way; at all —**anything but** not at all

an·y·way (-wā') *adv.* **1.** in any manner or way **2.** at least; anyhow **3.** haphazardly; carelessly

an·y·where (-wer', -hwer') *adv.* in, at, or to any place —**get anywhere** [Colloq.] to have any success

an·y·wise (-wīz') *adv.* in any manner; at all

An·zac (an'zak') *n.* [an acronym formed from the title] **1.** a soldier in the Australian and New Zealand Army Corps **2.** any Australian or New Zealand soldier

A/O, a/o account of

A.O.B., a.o.b. any other business

a·o·rist (ā'ə rist, er'ist) *n.* [Gr. *aoristos*, indefinite < *a-*, without + *horizein*, to define] a past tense of Greek verbs, denoting an action without indicating whether completed, continued or repeated —*adj.* designating or in this tense

a·or·ta (ā ôr'tə) *n.*, *pl.* -**tas, -tae** (-tē) [ModL. < Gr. < *aeirein*, to raise] the main artery of the body carrying blood from the left ventricle of the heart to arteries in all organs and parts —**a·or'tic, a·or'tal** *adj.*

a·ou·dad (ä'oo dad') *n.* [Fr. < Moorish *audad*] a wild North African sheep with large, curved horns and a heavy growth of hair on the chest

a·pace (ə pās') *adv.* at a fast pace; swiftly

A·pach·e (ə pach'ē) *n.* [AmSp., prob. < Zuñi *ápachu*, enemy] **1.** *pl.* **A·pach'es, A·pach'e** any member of a group of tribes of Indians of N Mexico and the SW U.S. **2.** any of their Athapascan languages

a·pache (ə pash', -päsh'; *Fr.* ä päsh') *n.*, *pl.* **a·pach'es** (-iz; *Fr.* ä päsh') [Fr., lit., APACHE] a gangster of Paris —*adj.* designating a dance which represents an apache handling his girl brutally

a·part (ə pärt') *adv.* [< OFr. < L. *ad*, to, at + *partem*, acc. of *pars*, a part, side] **1.** to one side; aside **2.** *a)* away in place or time *b)* secluded **3.** separately in function, use, etc. [viewed *apart*] **4.** in or to pieces **5.** aside; notwithstanding [all joking *apart*] —*adj.* [used only in the predicate] separated —**apart from** **1.** other than; besides **2.** with the exception of —**take apart** **1.** to reduce (a whole) to its parts **2.** to investigate fully, esp. in order to find something or some fact —**tell apart** to distinguish one from another

a·part·heid (ə pärt'hāt, -hīt) *n.* [Afrik., apartness] in South Africa, the policy of strict racial segregation and discrimination imposed on Negroes and other coloured peoples

a·part·ment (ə pärt'mənt) *n.* [< Fr. < It. < *appartare*, to separate < *parte*, PART] **1.** a room in a building **2.** [U.S.] same as FLAT² **3.** [*pl.*] a set of rented rooms; lodgings

apartment house [U.S.] a block of flats: also **apartment building**

ap·a·thet·ic (ap'ə thet'ik) *adj.* [< APATHY, after PATHETIC] **1.** feeling no emotion; unmoved **2.** not interested; indifferent —**ap'a·thet'i·cal·ly** *adv.*

ap·a·thy (ap'ə thē) *n.*, *pl.* -**thies** [< Fr. < L. < Gr. < *a-*, without + *pathos*, emotion] **1.** lack of emotion **2.** lack of interest; indifference

ap·a·tite (ap'ə tīt') *n.* [< Gr. *apatē*, deceit + -ITE: so named from being mistaken for other minerals] any of a group of minerals consisting essentially of calcium phosphate, and varying in colour

ape (āp) *n.* [OE. *apa*] **1.** any of a family of large, tailless monkeys; specif., a chimpanzee, gorilla, orangutan, or gibbon **2.** any monkey **3.** a person who imitates; mimic —*vt.* **aped, ap'ing** to imitate or mimic —**ape'like'** *adj.*

ape-man (-man') *n.* any of several extinct primates, with structural characteristics between those of man and the higher apes

‡**a·per·çu** (ap'ər syoo') *n.*, *pl.*, -**cus** (-sooz') [Fr.] **1.** a quick impression or insight **2.** a brief digest or survey

a·pe·ri·ent (ə pir'ē ənt) *adj., n.* [< L. prp. of *aperire*: see APERTURE] same as LAXATIVE

a·pe·ri·od·ic (ā'pir ē əd'ik) *adj.* **1.** occurring irregularly **2.** *Physics* without periodic vibrations

a·pe·ri·tif (ə per'i tēf) *n.* [< Fr. < L. *apertus*: see ff.] an alcoholic drink, esp. a wine, taken before meals to stimulate the appetite

ap·er·ture (ap'ər chər, -tyoor) *n.* [< L. < *apertus*, pp. of *aperire*, to open] **1.** an opening; hole; gap **2.** the diameter of the opening in a camera, etc., through which light passes into the lens

a·pet·a·lous (ā pet'əl əs) *adj.* *Bot.* without petals

a·pex (ā'peks) *n.*, *pl.* **a'pex·es, ap'i·ces** (ap'ə sēz', ā'pə-)

[L., a point] **1.** the highest point; peak; vertex **2.** the pointed end; tip **3.** a climax

a·phaer·e·sis, a·pher·e·sis (ə fer'ə sis) *n.* [< L. < Gr. < *aphairein*, to take away] the dropping of a letter or syllable at the beginning of a word (Ex.: *'cause* for *because*)

a·pha·si·a (ə fā'zhə, -zhē ə) *n.* [ModL. < Gr. < *a-*, not + *phanai*, to speak] a total or partial loss of the power to use or understand words —**a·pha'sic** (-zik), **a·pha'-si·ac'** (-zē ak') *adj., n.*

a·phe·li·on (ə fē'lē ən) *n., pl.* **-li·ons, -li·a** (-ə) [ModL. < Gr. *apo*, from + *hēlios*, sun] the point farthest from the sun in the orbit around it of a planet, comet, or man-made satellite: cf. PERIHELION

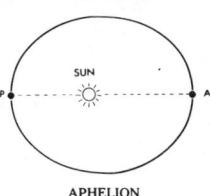

APHELION
(planet at aphelion A and at perihelion P)

aph·e·sis (af'ə sis) *n.* [Gr. a letting go] loss of a short unaccented vowel at the beginning of a word (Ex.: *squire* for *esquire*) —**a·phet'ic** *adj.*

a·phid (ā'fid, af'id) *n.* [ModL. *aphis* < ?] any of a group of small insects that suck the juice from plants; greenfly —**a·phid·i·an** (ə fid'ē ən) *adj., n.*

a·phis (ā'fis, af'is) *n., pl.* **aph·i·des** (af'ə dēz') an aphid; specif., one of a widespread genus of small insects

a·pho·ni·a (ā fō'nē ə) *n.* [ModL. < *aphōnia* < *a-*, without + *phōnē*, sound] loss of voice caused by an organic or functional disorder: also **a·pho·ny** (a'fə nē)

aph·o·rism (af'ə riz'm) *n.* [< Fr. < Gr. < *aphorizein*, to divide < *apo-*, from + *horizein*, to bound: see HORIZON] **1.** a short, concise statement of a principle **2.** a maxim or adage —**aph'o·rist** *n.* —**aph'o·ris'tic** *adj.* —**aph'o·ris'ti·cal·ly** *adv.*

a·phyl·lous (ā'fil'əs) *adj.* [Gr. *aphyllos* < *a-*, without + *phyllon*, a leaf] lacking leaves as most cactuses

a·pi·an (ā'pē ən) *adj.* [< L. < *apis*, bee] of a bee or bees

a·pi·a·rist (ā'pē ə rist, -pyer ist) *n.* a person who keeps bees —**a·pi·ar'i·an** (ā'pē ar'ē ən)

a·pi·ar·y (ā'pyər ē, ā'pē ər'ē) *n., pl.* **-ar·ies** [< L. < *apis*, bee] a place where bees are kept for their honey

ap·i·cal (ap'i k'l, ā'pi-) *adj.* of, at, or constituting the apex

ap·i·ces (ap'ə sēz', ā'pə-) *n.* alt. pl. of APEX

a·pi·cul·ture (ā'pə kul'chər) *n.* [< L. *apis*, bee + CULTURE] the raising and care of bees; beekeeping —**a·pi·cul'tur·al** *adj.* —**a·pi·cul'tur·ist** *n.*

a·piece (ə pēs') *adv.* [see A & PIECE] for each one

ap·ish (āp'ish) *adj.* **1.** like an ape **2.** foolishly imitative **3.** silly, affected, mischievous, etc. —**ap'ish·ly** *adv.* —**ap'ish·ness** *n.*

a·plen·ty (ə plen'tē) *adj., adv.* [Colloq.] in abundance

a·plomb (ə plom') *n.* [Fr., lit., perpendicularity < *à*, to + *plomb*, a PLUMB[1]] self-possession; poise

ap·noe·a (ap nē'ə, ap'nē ə) *n.* [ModL. < Gr. < *a-*, without + *pnoiē* wind] stopping of breathing

ap·o- [< Gr. *apo*, off] a prefix meaning off, from, or away from [*apogee*]

Apoc. 1. Apocalypse **2.** Apocrypha

a·poc·a·lypse (ə pok'ə lips') *n.* [< L. < Gr. < *apokalyptein*, to disclose] **1.** any of various religious writings depicting symbolically the end of evil and the triumph of good; specif., [A-] the last book of the New Testament; book of Revelation **2.** any prophetic disclosure; revelation —**a·poc'-a·lyp'tic** (-lip'tik), **a·poc'a·lyp'ti·cal** *adj.* —**a·poc'a·lyp'ti·cal·ly** *adv.*

a·po·car·pous (ap'ə kär'pəs) *adj. Bot.* having separate or partially joined carpels

a·poc·o·pe (ə pok'ə pē') *n.* [< Gr. < *apo-*, from + *koptein*, to cut off] the dropping of a sound or sounds at the end of a word (Ex.: *mos'* for *most*)

a·poc·ry·pha (ə pok'rə fə) *n.pl.* [< LL. < Gr. *apokryphos*, hidden, obscure < *apo-*, away + *kryptein*, to hide] **1.** any writings, anecdotes, etc. of doubtful authenticity or authorship **2.** [A-] fourteen books of the Septuagint that are rejected in Judaism and regarded by Protestants as not canonical: eleven are fully accepted in the Roman Catholic canon

a·poc·ry·phal (-f'l) *adj.* **1.** of doubtful authorship or authenticity **2.** not genuine; false; counterfeit **3.** [A-] of or like the Apocrypha **4.** invented: said usually of a story about a living person

ap·o·dal (ap'ə d'l) *adj.* [< Gr. *apous, apodos* < *a-*, without + *pous*, foot + -AL] *Zool.* **1.** lacking feet or legs, as snakes, **2.** lacking pelvic fins: also **ap'o·dous** (-dəs)

a·pod·o·sis (ə pod'ə sis) *n., pl.* **-ses** (-sēz') [Gr., a giving back] the clause expressing result in a conditional sentence: opposed to PROTASIS

ap·o·gee (ap'ə jē') *n.* [< Fr. < L. < Gr. < *apo-*, from + *gē*, earth] **1.** the point farthest from the earth, the moon, or another planet, in the orbit of a satellite or spacecraft around it: opp. to PERIGEE **2.** the highest or farthest point —**ap'o·ge'an** (-jē'ən), **ap'o·ge'al** *adj.*

EARTH

APOGEE
(moon at apogee A and at perigee P)

a·po·lit·i·cal (ā'pə lit'ə k'l) *adj.* not concerned with political matters —**a'po·lit'-i·cal·ly** *adv.*

a·pol·o·get·ic (ə pol'ə jet'ik) *adj.* making apology; esp., showing realization of and regret for a fault, wrong, etc.: also **a·pol'o·get'i·cal** —**a·pol'-o·get'i·cal·ly** *adv.*

a·pol·o·get·ics (-iks) *n.pl.* [*with sing. v.*] [see APOLOGY] the branch of theology dealing with the defence and proofs of Christianity

ap·o·lo·gi·a (ap'ə lō'jē ə) *n.* an apology, esp. a formal defence of an idea, religion, etc.

a·pol·o·gist (ə pol'ə jist) *n.* a person who writes or speaks in defence or justification of a doctrine, faith, action, etc.

a·pol·o·gize (ə pol'ə jīz') *vi.* **-gized', -giz'ing** to make an apology; esp., to state that one is aware of and regrets a fault, wrong, etc.

ap·o·logue (ap'ə log') *n.* [Fr. < L. < Gr.] a short allegorical story with a moral; fable

a·pol·o·gy (ə pol'ə jē) *n., pl.* **-gies** [< LL. < Gr. *apologia*, a speaking in defence < *apo-*, from + *logos*, word] **1.** a formal spoken or written defence of some idea, doctrine, etc. **2.** an acknowledgment of some fault, wrong, etc., with an expression of regret **3.** an inferior substitute [he is a poor *apology* for an actor]

ap·o·phthegm (ap'ə thəm') *n.* [< Gr. < *apo-*, from + *phthengesthai*, to utter] a short, pithy saying (Ex.: "Brevity is the soul of wit") —**ap'o·phtheg·mat'ic** (-theg mat'ik), **ap'-o·phtheg·mat'i·cal** *adj.*

ap·o·plec·tic (ap'ə plek'tik) *adj.* **1.** of, like, or causing apoplexy **2.** having apoplexy **3.** [Colloq.] seemingly about to have apoplexy [*apoplectic* with rage] Also **ap'o·plec'-ti·cal** —*n.* a person having or likely to have apoplexy —**ap'-o·plec'ti·cal·ly** *adv.*

ap·o·plex·y (ap'ə plek'sē) *n.* [< ME. & OFr. < L. < Gr. < *apo-*, down + *plēssein*, to strike] sudden paralysis with some loss of consciousness and feeling, caused when a blood vessel in the brain breaks or becomes clogged; stroke

a·port (ə pôrt') *adv. Naut.* on or to the left, or port, side

a·pos·ta·sy (ə pos'tə sē) *n., pl.* **-sies** [< LL. < Gr. < *apo-*, away + *stasis*, a standing] an abandoning of something that one once believed in, as a faith, cause, etc.

a·pos·tate (-tāt', -tit) *n.* a person guilty of apostasy; renegade —*adj.* guilty of apostasy

a·pos·ta·tize (-tə tīz') *vi.* **-tized', -tiz'ing** to become an apostate

a pos·te·ri·o·ri (ā'pos tir'ē ôr'ī, -ôr'ē) [ML., lit., from what comes later] **1.** from effect to cause, or from particular instances to a generalization; inductive or inductively **2.** based on observation or experience; empirical Opposed to A PRIORI

a·pos·tle (ə pos''l) *n.* [< OE. & OFr. < LL. < Gr. *apostolos*, one sent forth < *apo-*, from + *stellein*, to send] **1.** a person sent out on a special mission; specif., [*usually* A-] any of the twelve disciples sent out by Jesus to teach the gospel **2.** the first Christian missionary in a place **3.** any of a group of early Christian missionaries **4.** an early advocate or leader, as of a reform movement **5.** any of the twelve administrative officials of the Mormon Church —**a·pos'tle·ship'** *n.*

Apostles' Creed an early statement of belief in the basic Christian doctrines, formerly thought to have been composed by the twelve Apostles

a·pos·to·late (ə pos'tə lit, -lāt') *n.* the office, duties, or period of activity of an apostle

ap·os·tol·ic (ap'əs tol'ik) *adj.* **1.** of an apostle **2.** of the Apostles, their teachings, work, or times **3.** held to derive from the Apostles in a direct line of succession **4.** [*often* A-] of the Pope; papal Also **ap'os·tol'i·cal**

Apostolic See *R.C.Ch.* the Pope's see at Rome

a·pos·tro·phe[1] (ə pos'trə fē) *n.* [L. < Gr. *apostrophē*, a turning away to address one person < *apo-*, from + *strephein*, to turn] words addressed to a person or thing, whether absent or present —**ap·os·troph·ic** (ap'ə strof'ik) *adj.*

a·pos·tro·phe[2] (ə pos'trə fē) *n.* [Fr. < LL. < Gr. *apostrophos* (*prosōdia*), averted (accent): see prec.] the mark (') used:

1. to show the omission of a letter or letters from a word (Ex.: *it's* for *it is*) **2.** to indicate the possessive case (Ex.: *Mary's* dress, the *girls'* club) **3.** in forming some plurals, as of figures and letters (Ex.: five *6's,* dot the *i's*)

a·pos·tro·phize (-fīz′) *vt., vi.* **-phized′, -phiz′ing** to speak or write an apostrophe (to)

apothecaries' measure a system of units used in measuring liquids in pharmacy: see TABLES OF WEIGHTS AND MEASURES in the Supplements

apothecaries' weight formerly, a system of weights used in pharmacy: see TABLES OF WEIGHTS AND MEASURES in the Supplements

a·poth·e·car·y (ə poth′ə kər ē) *n., pl.* **-car·ies** [< OFr. < ML. < L. < Gr. *apothēkē,* storehouse < *apo-,* away + *tithenai,* to put] **1.** [*Archaic*] a chemist **2.** a chemist licensed by the Society of Apothecaries to prescribe, prepare, and sell drugs

ap·o·thegm (ap′ə them′) *n.* same as APOPHTHEGM

ap·o·them (ap′ə them′) *n.* [ModL. < APO-+ Gr. *thema:* see THEME] *Math.* the perpendicular from the centre of a regular polygon to any one of its sides

a·poth·e·o·sis (ə poth′ē ō′sis) *n., pl.* **-ses** (-sēz′) [L. < Gr. < *apotheoun,* to deify < *apo-,* from + *theos,* a god] **1.** the act of raising a person to the status of a god; deification **2.** the glorification of a person or thing **3.** an ideal or exact type [she is the *apotheosis* of beauty]

a·poth·e·o·size (ə poth′ē ə sīz′) *vt.* **-sized′, -siz′ing** [APOTHEOS(IS) + -IZE] **1.** to deify **2.** to glorify; idealize

app. **1.** appendix **2.** appointed **3.** approved

ap·pal (ə pôl′) *vt.* **-palled′, -pal′ling** [< OFr. *apalir* < *a-,* to + *palir,* to grow pale < L. *pallidus,* pale] to fill with horror or dismay; shock

ap·pal·ling (-iŋ) *adj.* **1.** causing horror, shock, or dismay **2.** [Colloq.] very bad —**ap·pal′ling·ly** *adv.*

ap·pa·loo·sa (ap′ə loo͞′sə) *n.* [altered < *a palouse,* after the *Palouse* Indians of the NW U.S.] any of a sturdy breed of saddle horses with spotted markings on the rump and loins, orig. from the W U.S.

ap·pa·nage (ap′ə nij) *n.* [< Fr. < ML. < L. *ad,* to + *panis,* bread] **1.** money, land, etc. set aside by a monarch for the support of his younger children **2.** a benefit that is a perquisite or adjunct Also **a′pa·nage**

ap·pa·ra·tus (ap′ə rāt′əs) *n., pl.* **-ra′tus, -ra′tus·es** [L., a making ready < *apparare* < *ad-,* to + *parare,* to prepare] **1.** the instruments, equipment, etc. for a specific use **2.** any complex device or system **3.** *Physiol.* a set of organs having a specific function [the digestive *apparatus*]

ap·par·el (ə par′əl) *n.* [< OFr., ult. < L. *apparare:* see prec.] clothing; attire —*vt.* **-elled, -el·ling** **1.** to clothe; dress **2.** to adorn; bedeck

ap·par·ent (ə par′ənt) *adj.* [< OFr. < L. prp. of *apparere,* APPEAR] **1.** readily seen; visible **2.** readily understood; obvious **3.** appearing to be real or true; seeming See also HEIR APPARENT —**ap·par′ent·ly** *adv.* —**ap·par′ent·ness** *n.*

ap·pa·ri·tion (ap′ə rish′ən) *n.* [< OFr. < ML. < L. *apparere:* see APPEAR] **1.** anything that appears unexpectedly or remarkably **2.** a ghost; phantom **3.** the act of appearing —**ap′pa·ri′tion·al** *adj.*

ap·peal (ə pēl′) *vt.* [< OFr. < L. *appellare,* to accost, appeal < *ad-,* to *pellere:* see COMPEL] to make a request to a higher court for the rehearing of (a case) —*vi.* **1.** to apply (to a higher court) for the alteration of a decision made by a lower one **2.** to make an urgent request (*to a person for* help, sympathy, etc.) **3.** to resort (*to*) for decision, etc. **4.** to be attractive, interesting, etc. **5.** *Cricket* to ask the umpire to declare a batsman out —*n.* **1.** a call upon some authority for a decision, etc. **2.** an urgent request for help, etc. **3.** a quality that arouses interest, sympathy, etc.; attraction **4.** *Cricket* a request to the umpire to declare a batsman out **5.** *Law a)* the review by a higher court of the decision of a lower tribunal *b)* the right to request this —**ap·peal′a·ble** *adj.* —**ap·peal′ing** *adj.* —**ap·peal′ing·ly** *adv.*

ap·pear (ə pir′) *vi.* [< OFr. < L. *apparere* < *ad-,* to + *parere,* to come forth] **1.** to come into sight **2.** to come into being **3.** to become understood [it *appears* he left] **4.** to seem; look **5.** to present oneself formally, as in court **6.** to act as counsel in a court of law **7.** to come before the public [he *appeared* in Hamlet] **8.** to be published

ap·pear·ance (-əns) *n.* **1.** an appearing **2.** the outward aspect of anything **3.** an outward show; pretence **4.** [*pl.*] the way things seem to be —**keep up appearances** to try to give the impression of being proper, well-off, etc. —**put in an appearance** to be present for a short time, as at a party

ap·pease (ə pēz′) *vt.* **-peased′, -peas′ing** [< OFr. < *a-,* to + *pais* < L. *pax,* PEACE] **1.** to make peaceful or quiet, esp. by giving in to the demands of **2.** to satisfy or relieve [water *appeases* thirst] —**ap·peas′a·ble** *adj.* —**ap·peas′er** *n.*

ap·pease·ment (-mənt) *n.* **1.** an appeasing or being

appeased **2.** the policy of giving in to demands of a hostile power in an attempt to keep peace

ap·pel·lant (ə pel′ənt) *adj.* *Law* relating to appeals; appealing —*n.* a person who appeals, esp. to a higher court

ap·pel·late (-it) *adj.* [< L. pp. of *appellare,* APPEAL] *Law* relating to, or having jurisdiction to review, appeals [an *appellate* court]

ap·pel·la·tion (ap′ə lā′shən) *n.* [< L. < pp. of *appellare,* APPEAL] **1.** the act of calling by a name **2.** a name or title; designation

ap·pel·la·tive (ə pel′ə tiv) *adj.* of appellation; naming —*n.* **1.** a name or title **2.** a common noun: earlier usage —**ap·pel′la·tive·ly** *adv.*

ap·pend (ə pend′) *vt.* [< OFr. < L. *appendere* < *ad-,* to + *pendere,* to suspend] to attach or affix; add as a supplement or appendix

ap·pend·age (ə pen′dij) *n.* **1.** anything appended; adjunct **2.** *Biol.* any secondary, external organ or part, as a tree branch or a dog's tail

ap·pend·ant (-dənt) *adj.* [Fr.: see APPEND] **1.** attached or added **2.** associated with as a consequence —*n.* an appendage

ap·pen·di·cec·to·my (ə pen′di sek′tə mē) *n., pl.* **-mies** [APPENDIX + -ECTOMY] the surgical removal of the vermiform appendix: also **ap·pen·dec·to·my** (ap′ən dek′-tə mē)

ap·pen·di·ci·tis (ə pen′də sīt′əs) *n.* [< ff. + -ITIS] inflammation of the vermiform appendix

ap·pen·dix (ə pen′diks) *n., pl.* **-dix·es, -di·ces′** (-də sēz′) [L.: see APPEND] **1.** additional material at the end of a book **2.** *Anat.* an outgrowth of an organ; esp., a small sac (**vermiform appendix**) extending from the caecum of the large intestine

ap·per·ceive (ap′ər sēv′) *vt.* **-ceived′, -ceiv′ing** [< OFr. < L. *ad,* to + *percipere,* PERCEIVE] *Psychol.* to assimilate and interpret (a new perception) by the help of past experience

ap·per·cep·tion (ap′ər sep′shən) *n.* [< Fr. < *apercevoir,* APPERCEIVE] **1.** an apperceiving **2.** the state of the mind in being conscious of its own consciousness —**ap′per·cep′tive** *adj.*

ap·per·tain (ap′ər tān′) *vi.* [< OFr. < L. *appertinere* < *ad-,* to + *pertinere:* see PERTAIN] to belong properly as a function, part, etc.; pertain

ap·pe·ten·cy (ap′ə tən sē) *n., pl.* **-cies** [< L. prp. of *appetere:* see ff.] **1.** a strong desire **2.** a propensity **3.** an affinity Also **ap′pe·tence**

ap·pe·tite (ap′ə tīt′) *n.* [< ME. & OFr. < L. *appetitus,* pp. of *appetere* < *ad-,* + *petere,* to seek] a desire or craving, esp. for food or for a specific food —**ap′pe·ti′tive** (-tīt′iv, tət′iv) *adj.*

ap·pe·tiz·er (-tī′zər) *n.* a small portion of a tasty food or a drink to stimulate the appetite at the beginning of a meal

ap·pe·tiz·ing (-tī′ziŋ) *adj.* **1.** stimulating the appetite **2.** savoury; tasty —**ap′pe·tiz′ing·ly** *adv.*

ap·plaud (ə plôd′) *vt., vi.* [L. *applaudere* < *ad-,* to + *plaudere,* to clap hands] **1.** to show approval (of) by clapping the hands, cheering, etc. **2.** to praise; approve —**ap·plaud′er** *n.*

ap·plause (ə plôz′) *n.* approval or praise, esp. as shown by clapping hands, cheering, etc.

ap·ple (ap′'l) *n.* [OE. *æppel*] **1.** *a)* a round, firm, fleshy, edible fruit with a red, yellow, or green skin and a seed core, growing on any of a genus of trees in temperate regions *b)* any of these trees **2.** any of various apple-like fruits, as the crab apple

apple green a bright, light green or moderate yellowish-green

apple of one's eye **1.** the pupil of one's eye **2.** any person or thing that one cherishes

apple-pie bed (ap′'l pī′) a bed in which the sheets are so folded that one cannot stretch one's legs

ap·ple-pie order [Colloq.] neat order

ap·pli·ance (ə plī′əns) *n.* a device or machine for a specific task, esp. one worked mechanically or by electricity

ap·pli·ca·ble (ap′li kə b'l, əp lik′ə b'l) *adj.* that can be applied; appropriate; suitable —**ap′pli·ca·bil′i·ty** *n.* —**ap′-pli·ca·bly** *adv.*

ap·pli·cant (ap′li kənt) *n.* a person who applies, as for employment, help, etc.

ap·pli·ca·tion (ap′lə kā′shən) *n.* **1.** the act or a way of applying or being applied **2.** anything applied, esp. a remedy **3.** a request, or the form completed in making a request [an *application* for employment] **4.** continued effort; diligence **5.** relevance or practicality [this idea has no *application* to the case]

ap·pli·ca·tor (ap′lə kāt′ər) *n.* any device for applying medicine or paint, polish, etc.

ap·pli·ca·to·ry (-kə tər ē) *adj.* that can be applied or used; practical: also **ap′pli·ca′tive** (-kāt′iv)

ap·plied (ə plīd′) *adj.* used in actual practice or to work out practical problems [applied science]

ap·pli·qué (ap′lə kā′) *n.* [Fr. < L. *applicare:* see ff.] a decoration made of one material attached by sewing, etc. to another —*adj.* applied as such a decoration —*vt.* **-quéd′, -qué′ing** 1. to decorate with appliqué 2. to put on as appliqué

APPLIQUÉ

ap·ply (ə plī′) *vt.* **-plied′, -ply′ing** [< OFr. < L. *applicare,* to attach to < *ad-,* to + *plicare,* to fold] 1. to put on [to *apply* salve] 2. to use practically [to *apply* one's knowledge] 3. to refer to a person or thing with (an epithet, etc.) 4. to concentrate (one's faculties); employ (oneself) diligently —*vi.* 1. to make a formal request 2. to be suitable or relevant [this rule *applies* to everyone] —**ap·pli′er** *n.*

ap·pog·gia·tu·ra (ə poj′ə toor′ə) *n.* [It. < *appoggiare,* to lean, ult. < L. *ad-,* to + *podium,* PODIUM] *Music* an auxiliary note like a grace note but rhythmically more prominent than the melodic note that it precedes

ap·point (ə point′) *vt.* [< OFr. *apointer,* to make ready, ult. < L. *ad,* to + *punctum,* a POINT] 1. to set (a date, place, etc.); decree 2. to name for an office, etc. [to *appoint* a chairman] 3. to furnish and arrange: now usually in *well-appointed,* etc. —**ap·point·ee** (ə poin′tē′) *n.*

ap·point·ive (ə poin′tiv) *adj.* [Chiefly U.S.] to which one is appointed, not elected [an *appointive* office]

ap·point·ment (ə point′mənt) *n.* 1. an appointing or being appointed; specif., a naming for an office, etc. 2. a person so named 3. an office held in this way 4. an arrangement to meet a person; engagement 5. [*pl.*] furnishings

ap·por·tion (ə pôr′shən) *vt.* [< OFr.: see AD- & PORTION] to divide and distribute in shares according to a plan —**ap·por′tion·ment** *n.*

ap·pose (ə pōz′) *vt.* **-posed′, -pos′ing** [< Fr. < L. *appositus,* pp. of *apponere* < *ad-,* near + *ponere,* to put] to put side by side, next, or near —**ap·pos′a·ble** *adj.*

ap·po·site (ap′ə zit) *adj.* [see prec.] appropriate; apt —**ap′·po·site·ly** *adv.* —**ap′po·site·ness** *n.*

ap·po·si·tion (ap′ə zish′ən) *n.* 1. an apposing or being apposed 2. the position resulting from this 3. *Gram. a)* the placing of a word or expression beside another so that the second explains and has the same grammatical construction as the first *b)* the relationship between such terms [*"my cousin"* is in *apposition* with "Mary" in "Mary, my cousin, is here"] —**ap′po·si′tion·al** *adj.*

ap·pos·i·tive (ə poz′ə tiv) *adj.* of or in apposition —*n.* a word, phrase, or clause in apposition —**ap·pos′i·tive·ly** *adv.*

ap·prais·al (ə prā′z'l) *n.* 1. an appraising 2. an appraised value; esp., an expert valuation as for sale Also **ap·praise′·ment**

ap·praise (ə prāz′) *vt.* **-praised′, -prais′ing** [< OFr. < LL. *appretiare* < L. *ad,* to + *pretium,* PRICE; Eng. sp. infl. by PRAISE] 1. to set a price for; decide the value of, esp. officially 2. to estimate the quantity or quality of —**ap·prais′a·ble** *adj.* —**ap·prais′er** *n.* —**ap·prais′ing·ly** *adv.*

ap·pre·ci·a·ble (ə prē′shə b'l, -shē ə-) *adj.* enough to be perceived; noticeable; measurable [an *appreciable* difference] —**ap·pre′ci·a·bly** *adv.*

ap·pre·ci·ate (ə prē′shē āt′) *vt.* **-at′ed, -at′ing** [< LL. pp. of *appretiare,* APPRAISE] 1. to think well of; enjoy; esteem 2. to recognize gratefully 3. to estimate the quality or worth of 4. to be fully or sensitively aware of 5. to raise the price of: opposed to DEPRECIATE —*vi.* to rise in value —**ap·pre′ci·a′tor** *n.* —**ap·pre′ci·a·to·ry** (-shə tər ē, -shē ə-) *adj.*

ap·pre·ci·a·tion (ə prē′shē ā′shən) *n.* 1. an appreciating; specif., *a)* proper estimation *b)* grateful recognition, as of a favour *c)* sensitive awareness or enjoyment, as of art *d)* an evaluation 2. a rise in value or price

ap·pre·ci·a·tive (ə prē′shə tiv, -shē ə-) *adj.* feeling or showing appreciation —**ap·pre′ci·a·tive·ly** *adv.* —**ap·pre′·ci·a·tive·ness** *n.*

ap·pre·hend (ap′rə hend′) *vt.* [< L. *apprehendere,* to take hold of < *ad-,* to + *prehendere,* to seize] 1. to take into custody; arrest 2. to perceive or understand 3. to anticipate with anxiety; dread

ap·pre·hen·si·ble (-hen′sə b'l) *adj.* that can be apprehended —**ap′pre·hen′si·bil′i·ty** *n.*

ap·pre·hen·sion (-hen′shən) *n.* 1. capture or arrest 2. perception or understanding 3. anxiety or dread

ap·pre·hen·sive (-hen′siv) *adj.* 1. perceptive 2. uneasy or fearful about the future —**ap′pre·hen′sive·ly** *adv.* —**ap′·pre·hen′sive·ness** *n.*

ap·pren·tice (ə pren′tis) *n.* [< OFr. < *aprendre,* to teach < L. *apprehendere,* APPREHEND] 1. a person under legal agreement to work a specified length of time for a master craftsman in a craft or trade in return for instruction and, formerly, support 2. a person learning a trade, etc. under specified conditions 3. any learner or beginner —*vt.* **-ticed, -tic·ing** to place or accept as an apprentice —**ap·pren′·tice·ship′** *n.*

ap·prise¹, ap·prize¹ (ə prīz′) *vt.* **-prised′** or **-prized′, -pris′-ing** or **-priz′ing** [< Fr. pp. of *apprendre,* to teach, inform < L. *apprehendere,* APPREHEND] to inform or notify

ap·prize², ap·prise² (ə prīz′) *vt.* **-prized′** or **-prised′, -priz′-ing** or **-pris′ing** *same as* APPRAISE

ap·pro (ap′rō) *n.* [Colloq.] approval: chiefly in the phrase **on appro**

ap·proach (ə prōch′) *vi.* [< OFr. < LL. *appropiare* < L. *ad,* to + *propius,* compar. of *prope,* near] to come closer or draw nearer —*vt.* 1. to come near or nearer to 2. to be similar to; approximate 3. to bring near (*to* something) 4. to make advances, a proposal, or a request to 5. to begin dealing with [to *approach* a task] —*n.* 1. a coming closer 2. an approximation 3. an advance or overture (*to* someone): *often used in pl.* 4. a way of getting to a person, place, or thing; path; road; access 5. *Aeron.* the act of bringing an aircraft into position for landing, bombing a target, etc. 6. *Golf* a shot to drive the ball from the fairway onto the putting green —**ap·proach′a·bil′i·ty** *n.* —**ap·proach′a·ble** *adj.*

ap·pro·ba·tion (ap′rə bā′shən) *n.* [< L. < *approbare,* APPROVE] official approval, permission, or praise —**ap′·pro·ba′tive, ap·pro·ba·to·ry** (ə prō′bə tər ē) *adj.*

ap·pro·pri·ate (ə prō′prē āt′; *for adj.* -it) *vt.* **-at′ed, -at′ing** [< LL. pp. of *appropriare* < L. < *ad-,* to + *proprius,* one's own] 1. to take for one's own use 2. to take improperly, as without permission 3. to set aside for a specific use —*adj.* right for the purpose; suitable —**ap·pro′pri·ate·ly** (-it lē) *adv.* —**ap·pro′pri·ate·ness** *n.* —**ap·pro′pri·a′tive** (-āt′-iv) *adj.* —**ap·pro′pri·a′tor** *n.*

ap·pro·pri·a·tion (ə prō′prē ā′shən) *n.* 1. an appropriating or being appropriated 2. a thing appropriated; esp., money set aside for a specific use

ap·prov·al (ə prōō′v'l) *n.* 1. an approving 2. favourable attitude or opinion 3. formal consent or permission —**on approval** for the customer to examine and decide whether to buy or return

ap·prove (ə prōōv′) *vt.* **-proved′, -prov′ing** [< OFr. < L. *approbare* < *ad-,* to + *probare,* to try, test < *probus,* good] 1. to give one's consent to; sanction 2. to be favourable towards; judge to be good, satisfactory, etc. —*vi.* to have a favourable opinion (*of*) —**ap·prov′er** *n.* —**ap·prov′ing·ly** *adv.*

approved school formerly, an institution for the care and education of young people who broke the law or who were considered to be in need of care and protection

approx. 1. approximate 2. approximately

ap·prox·i·mate (ə prok′sə mit; *for v.* -māt′) *adj.* [< LL. pp. of *approximare* < L. *ad,* to + *proximus,* superl. of *prope,* near] 1. near in position 2. much like; resembling 3. not exact, but almost so —*vt.* **-mat′ed, -mat′ing** 1. to come near to; be almost the same as [a painting that *approximates* reality] 2. to bring near (*to* something) —*vi.* to come near; be almost the same —**ap·prox′i·mate·ly** *adv.*

ap·prox·i·ma·tion (ə prok′sə mā′shən) *n.* 1. an approximating 2. a fairly close estimate, etc.

ap·pur·te·nance (ə pur′tin əns) *n.* [< Anglo-Fr. < OFr. < L. prp. of *appertinere,* APPERTAIN] 1. something added to a more important thing; adjunct 2. [*pl.*] accessories 3. *Law* an additional, subordinate right or privilege —**ap·pur′·te·nant** *adj., n.*

Apr. April

a·prax·i·a (ə prak′sē ə) *n.* [ModL. < Gr. *apraxia,* nonaction] loss of memory of how to perform complex muscular movements, resulting from brain damage —**a·prax′ic** (-prak′sik), **a·prac′tic** (-prak′tik) *adj.*

a·près (a′prā′; *Fr.* ȧ pre′) *prep.* [Fr.] after: often in hyphenated compounds [an *après*-ski party]

a·pri·cot (āp′rə kot′) *n.* [< Fr. < Port. < Ar. < MGr. < L. *praecoquus,* early matured (fruit)] 1. a small, yellowish-orange fruit related to the peach 2. the tree it grows on 3. yellowish orange

A·pril (ā′prəl) *n.* [< OFr. < L. *Aprilis*] the fourth month of the year, having 30 days: abbrev. **Apr.**

April fool a victim of jokes on April Fools' Day

April Fools' Day April 1, All Fools' Day, when practical jokes are traditionally played

a pri·o·ri (ā′ prē ôr′ē, ā′ prī ôr′ī) [L., from something prior] 1. from cause to effect or from a generalization to particular instances; deductive or deductively 2. based on theory instead of on experience or experiment 3. before examination or analysis Opposed to A POSTERIORI

a·pron (ā′prən) *n.* [by faulty separation < ME. *a napron* < OFr. *naperon* < *nape,* a cloth < L. *mappa,* a napkin] 1. a garment worn over the front part of the body, usually to protect one's clothes 2. a similar covering worn as part of official dress, as by a bishop 3. anything like an apron; specif., *a)* a protective covering for or edging on a structure, machine, etc. *b)* the hard-surfaced area in front of a hangar *c)* the part of a stage in front of the curtain 4. a continuous conveyor belt —*vt.* to put an apron on or provide an apron for

apron string a string for tying an apron on —**tied to one's**

mother's (or **wife's**, etc.) **apron strings** dominated by one's mother (or wife, etc.)

ap·ro·pos (ap'rə pō') *adv.* [Fr. *à propos*, to the purpose] 1. at the right time; opportunely 2. by the way; used to introduce a remark —*adj.* relevant; apt —**apropos of** with regard to

apse (aps) *n.* [< L. < Gr. *hapsis*, an arch, fastening < *haptein*, to fasten] a semicircular or polygonal projection of a building, esp. one at the east end of a church, with a domed or vaulted roof —**ap'si·dal** (ap'sid'l) *adj.*

ap·sis (ap'sis) *n., pl.* **-si·des'** (-sə dēz') [L. *apsis*, an arch] that point in the orbit of the moon, a planet, etc. nearest to (**lower apsis**), or that farthest from (**higher apsis**), the centre of attraction

apt (apt) *adj.* [< ME. & OFr. < L. *aptus*, pp. of *apere*, to fasten] 1. appropriate; fitting [an apt remark] 2. tending or inclined; likely [apt to rain] 3. quick to learn or understand [an apt student] —**apt'ly** *adv.* —**apt'ness** *n.*

ap·ter·ous (ap'tər əs) *adj.* [< Gr. < a-, without + *pteron*, a wing] *Biol.* having no wings; wingless

ap·ter·yx (ap'tər iks) *n.* [< Gr. a-, without + *pteryx*, wing] *same as* KIWI

ap·ti·tude (ap'tə tyōōd') *n.* [< ML. < L. *aptus*: see APT] 1. the quality of being appropriate; fitness 2. a natural tendency, inclination, or ability 3. quickness to learn or understand

aq·ua (ak'wə) *n., pl.* **aq'uas, aq'uae** (-wē) [L.] water; esp., *Pharm.* a solution of a substance in water —*adj.* [< AQUAMARINE] bluish-green

aq·ua·cul·ture (ak'wə kul'chər) *n.* [prec. + CULTURE] cultivation of water plants and animals for human use —**aq'·ua·cul'tur·al** *adj.*

aqua for·tis (fôr'təs) [L., strong water] *same as* NITRIC ACID

aq·ua·lung (ak'wə luŋ') *n.* [AQUA + LUNG] a kind of self-contained underwater breathing apparatus: see SCUBA —*adj.* of or using an aqualung —*vi.* to dive, etc. using an aqualung

aq·ua·ma·rine (ak'wə mə rēn') *n.* [L. *aqua marina*, sea water] 1. a transparent, pale bluish-green variety of beryl, used in jewellery 2. its colour —*adj.* bluish-green

aq·ua·naut (ak'wə nôt') *n.* [AQUA + (ASTRO)NAUT] 1. any of a group of persons using a watertight underwater chamber as a base for oceanographic experiments 2. *same as* skin diver (see SKIN DIVING)

aq·ua·plane (ak'wə plān') *n.* [AQUA + PLANE⁴] a board on which one rides standing up as it is pulled over water by a motorboat —*vi.* **-planed', -plan'ing** 1. to ride on such a board as a sport 2. to skim uncontrollably over a road surface on a thin film of water: said of a motor vehicle

aqua re·gi·a (rē'jē ə) [L., lit., kingly water: it dissolves the "noble metals," gold and platinum] a mixture of nitric and hydrochloric acids

a·quar·ist (ə kwer'ist) *n.* the keeper of an aquarium

a·quar·i·um (ə kwer'ē əm) *n., pl.* **-i·ums, -i·a** (-ē ə) [L., neut. of *aquarius*, of water < *aqua*, water] 1. a tank, usually with glass sides, or a pool, bowl, etc., for keeping live water animals and water plants 2. a building where such collections are exhibited

A·quar·i·us (ə kwer'ē əs) [L., the water carrier] 1. a large S constellation 2. the eleventh sign of the zodiac: see ZODIAC, illus.

a·quat·ic (ə kwat'ik, -kwot'-) *adj.* [< L. < *aqua*, water] 1. growing or living in or upon water 2. done in or upon the water [aquatic sports] —*n.* 1. an aquatic plant or animal 2. [pl., often with sing. v.] aquatic sports or performances —**a·quat'i·cal·ly** *adv.*

aq·ua·tint (ak'wə tint') *n.* [< Fr. < It. *acqua tinta*, dyed water] 1. a process by which spaces rather than lines are etched with acid to produce an etching that looks like a water colour 2. such an etching —*vt.* to etch in this way

aqua vi·tae (vīt'ē) [L., water of life] 1. *Alchemy* alcohol 2. brandy or other strong drink

aq·ue·duct (ak'wə dukt') *n.* [< L. < *aqua*, water + pp. of *ducere*, to lead] 1. a large pipe or conduit for bringing water from a distant source 2. a bridgelike structure for carrying a water conduit or canal across a river or valley 3. *Anat.* a passage or canal

a·que·ous (ā'kwē əs, ak'wē-) *adj.* [see AQUA & -OUS] 1. of, like, or containing water; watery 2. *Geol.* formed by the action of water

aqueous humour a watery fluid in the space between the cornea and the lens of the eye

aq·ui·cul·ture (ak'wi kul'chər) *n. same as* AQUACULTURE —**aq'ui·cul'tur·al** *adj.*

aq·ui·fer (ak'wə fər) *n.* [see AQUA & -FER] an underground layer of porous rock, sand, etc. containing water

aq·ui·line (ak'wə līn') *adj.* [< L. < *aquila*, eagle] 1. of or like an eagle 2. curved or hooked like an eagle's beak [an aquiline nose]

-ar (ər) [< ME. < OFr. < L. *-aris* or *-arius*; or directly < L.] 1. *a suffix meaning* of, relating to, like, of the nature of [singular, polar] 2. *a suffix denoting* agency [bursar, vicar]

Ar *Chem.* argon

Ar. 1. Arabic 2. Aramaic

ar. 1. arrival 2. arrives

Ar·ab (ar'əb) *n.* 1. a native or inhabitant of Arabia 2. any of a Semitic people originating in Arabia; commonly, a Bedouin 3. any of a breed of swift, graceful horses native to Arabia 4. loosely, any member of an Arabic-speaking tribe —*adj. same as* ARABIAN

ar·a·besque (ar'ə besk') *n.* [Fr. < It. < *Arabo*, Arab < Ar. '*arab*: with reference to Moorish designs] 1. an elaborate design of intertwined flowers, foliage, geometrical patterns, etc. 2. *Ballet* a position in which one leg is extended backwards and the arms are extended, usually one backwards and one forwards 3. *Music* a light, whimsical composition —*adj.* of or done in arabesque; fantastic and elaborate

ARABESQUE

A·ra·bi·an (ə rā'bē ən) *adj.* of Arabia or the Arabs —*n. same as* ARAB (senses 1 & 3)

Ar·a·bic (ar'ə bik) *adj.* 1. of Arabia 2. of the Arabs, their language, culture, etc. —*n.* the Semitic language of the Arabs, spoken in Arabia, Syria, Jordan, Iraq, northern Africa, etc.

Arabic numerals the figures 1, 2, 3, 4, 5, 6, 7, 8, 9, and the 0 (zero), orig. used in India

ar·ab·ist (ar'ə bist) *n.* a student or expert in Arabic culture, language, etc.

ar·a·ble (ar'ə b'l) *adj.* [Fr. < L. < *arare*, to plough] suitable for ploughing and producing crops —*n.* arable land —**ar'a·bil'i·ty** *n.*

Ar·a·by (ar'ə bē) [Archaic or Poet.] Arabia

a·rach·nid (ə rak'nid) *n.* [ModL. < Gr. *arachnē*, spider] any of a large group of arthropods, including spiders, scorpions, and mites, with four pairs of legs and with breathing tubes or lunglike sacs —**a·rach'ni·dan** (-ni dən) *adj., n.*

a·rach·noid (-noid) *adj.* [< Gr. *arachnē*, spider + -OID] 1. *Anat.* designating the middle of three membranes covering the brain and the spinal cord 2. *Bot.* of, or covered with, fine hairs or fibres —*n.* 1. *Anat.* the arachnoid membrane 2. *Zool.* an arachnid

ar·ak (ar'ək) *n. same as* ARRACK

Aram. Aramaic

Ar·a·mà·ic (ar'ə mā'ik) *n.* a group of northwestern Semitic languages of Biblical times, including that of Palestine

ar·au·car·i·a (ar'ô ker'ē ə) *n.* [ModL. < *Arauco*, province in Chile] any of several trees of a coniferous genus, as the monkey puzzle

ar·ba·lest, ar·ba·list (är'bə list) *n.* [< OFr. < L. < *arcus*, a bow + *ballista*, BALLISTA] a medieval crossbow with a steel bow

ar·bi·ter (är'bə tər) *n.* [L.] 1. a person selected to judge a dispute; umpire; arbitrator 2. a person fully authorized to judge or decide 3. a person having control (of something) [an arbiter of fashion] —**ar'bi·tral** (-trəl) *adj.* —**ar'bi·tress** *n.fem.*

ar·bi·tra·ble (är'bə trə b'l) *adj.* that can be arbitrated; subject to arbitration

ar·bit·ra·ment (är bit'rə mənt) *n.* 1. arbitration 2. an arbitrator's verdict or award

ar·bi·trar·y (är'bə trər ē) *adj.* [< L. < *arbiter*, ARBITER] 1. not fixed by rules but left to one's own choice 2. based on one's whim or notion; capricious 3. absolute; despotic —**ar'bi·trar·i·ly** *adv.* —**ar'bi·trar·i·ness** *n.*

ar·bi·trate (är'bə trāt') *vt.* **-trat'ed, -trat'ing** [< L. pp. of *arbitrari*, to give a decision < *arbiter*, ARBITER] 1. to give to an arbitrator to decide 2. to decide (a dispute) as an arbitrator —*vi.* 1. to act as an arbitrator (in a dispute, between persons) 2. to submit a dispute to arbitration

ar·bi·tra·tion (är'bə trā'shən) *n.* settlement of a dispute by someone chosen to hear both sides and come to a decision —**ar'bi·tra'tion·al** *adj.*

ar·bi·tra·tor (är'bə trāt'ər) *n.* a person chosen to arbitrate a dispute

ar·bor¹ (är'bər) *n.* U.S. sp. of ARBOUR

ar·bor² (är'bər) *n., pl.* **ar'bo·res'** (-bə rēz') [L.] *Bot.* a tree

ar·bor³ (är'bər) *n.* [< Fr. *arbre* < L. *arbor*, tree, beam] *Mech.* 1. a shaft; beam 2. a spindle; axle 3. a bar that holds cutting tools

ar·bo·ra·ceous (är'bə rā'shəs) *adj.* 1. of or like a tree 2. wooded

Arbor Day a tree-planting day observed in the U.S., Australia, and some other countries

ar·bo·re·al (är bôr'ē əl) *adj.* 1. of or like a tree 2. living in trees

ar·bo·res·cent (är'bə res'ənt) *adj.* treelike in form or growth; branching —**ar'bo·res'cence** *n.*

ar·bo·re·tum (är'bə rēt'əm) *n., pl.* **-tums, -ta** (-ə) [L.] a place where many kinds of trees and shrubs are grown for exhibition or study

ar·bo·ri·cul·ture (är′bər kul′chər) *n.* [< L. *arbor,* tree + *cultura,* culture] the scientific cultivation of trees and shrubs —**ar′bo·ri·cul′tur·ist** *n.*

ar·bor·vi·tae (är′bər vīt′ē) *n.* [L., tree of life] any of several evergreen trees related to the cypress, with flattened sprays of scalelike leaves

ar·bour (är′bər) *n.* [< OFr. < LL. *herbarium,* HERBARIUM] a place shaded by trees, climbing plants, etc., esp. when trained over a trellis; bower —**ar′boured** *adj.*

ar·bu·tus (är byōōt′əs) *n.* [L., wild strawberry tree] any of a genus of trees or shrubs with dark-green leaves and berries like strawberries

arc (ärk) *n.* [OFr. < L. *arcus,* a bow, arch] **1.** a bowlike curved line or object **2.** *Elec.* the band of sparks or incandescent light formed when an electric discharge is conducted from one electrode or conducting surface to another **3.** *Geom. a)* any part of a curve, esp. of a circle *b)* the angular measurement of this —*vi.* **arced** or **arcked, arc′-ing** or **arck′ing** **1.** to move in a curved course **2.** *Elec.* to form an arc

ar·cade (är kād′) *n.* [Fr. < Pr. < ML. < L. *arcus,* bow, arch] **1.** a covered passageway, as through a building, often with an arched roof; esp., such a passage with shops along the sides **2.** a line of arches and their supporting columns —*vt.* **-cad′ed, -cad′ing** to make into or provide with an arcade

Ar·ca·di·an (är kā′dē ən) *adj.* [after *Arcadia,* a pastoral district of ancient Greece] ideally rustic —*n.* a person who leads a simple rural life

ar·cane (är kān′) *adj.* [see ff.] **1.** hidden or secret **2.** understood by only a few; esoteric

ar·ca·num (-kā′nəm) *n., pl.* **-na** (-nə), **-nums** [L., hidden < *arcere,* to shut up] a secret; mystery

arch¹ (ärch) *n.* [< OFr. < ML. < L. *arcus,* a bow, arch] **1.** a curved structure, as of masonry, that supports the weight of material over an open space, as in a bridge, doorway, etc. **2.** the form of an arch **3.** anything shaped like an arch [the *arch* of the foot] —*vt.* **1.** to provide with an arch or arches **2.** to form into an arch —*vi.* **1.** to form an arch **2.** to span as an arch

arch² (ärch) *adj.* [< ff.] **1.** main; chief **2.** gaily mischievous; pert —**arch′ly** *adv.* —**arch′ness** *n.*

arch- [< OE. < L. < Gr. *archos,* ruler] *a prefix meaning* main, chief [*archbishop, archduke*]

-arch (ärk; *occas.* ərk) [< Gr. *archos,* ruler] *a suffix meaning* ruler [*matriarch*]

ARCHES
(A, semicircular; B, horseshoe; C, pointed)

arch. **1.** archaic **2.** archaism **3.** archipelago **4.** architect **5.** architectural **6.** architecture

Ar·chae·an (är kē′ən) *adj.* [< Gr. *archaios,* ancient < *archē,* beginning] *Geol.* of the oldest period of geological time: also [Chiefly U.S.] **Ar·che′an**

ar·chae·ol·o·gy (är′kē ol′ə jē) *n.* [< Gr. *archaios,* ancient < *archē,* the beginning + -LOGY] the scientific study of the life and culture of ancient peoples, as by excavation of ancient cities, artifacts, etc. —**ar′chae·o·log′i·cal** (-ə loj′i k′l) *adj.* —**ar′chae·o·log′i·cal·ly** *adv.* —**ar′chae·ol′o·gist** *n.*

ar·chae·op·ter·yx (-op′tər iks) *n.* [< Gr. *archaias,* ancient + *pteryx,* wing] an extinct, reptilelike bird which had teeth, a lizardlike tail, and well-developed wings

ar·cha·ic (är kā′ik) *adj.* [< Gr. *archaios,* ancient] **1.** ancient **2.** antiquated; old-fashioned **3.** that is now seldom used except in poetry, church ritual, etc., as the word *thou* —**ar·cha′i·cal·ly** *adv.*

ar·cha·ism (är′kā iz′m) *n.* **1.** the use or imitation of archaic words, technique, etc. **2.** an archaic word, usage, etc. —**ar′-cha·ist** *n.* —**ar′cha·is′tic** *adj.* —**ar′cha·is′ti·cal·ly** *adv.*

arch·an·gel (ärk′ān′j′l) *n.* a chief angel

arch·bish·op (ärch′bish′əp) *n.* a chief bishop, who presides over an archbishopric or archdiocese

arch·bish·op·ric (-bish′ə prik′) *n.* the office, rank, term, or church district of an archbishop

arch·dea·con (ärch′dē′k′n) *n.* [see ARCH- & DEACON] a church official ranking just below a bishop, as in the Anglican Church —**arch′dea′con·ry** *n.*, *pl.* **-ries**

arch·di·o·cese (ärch′dī′ə sis, -sēs′) *n.* the diocese of an archbishop —**arch′di·oc′e·san** (-dī os′ə sən) *adj.*

arch·du·cal (-dyōōk′′l) *adj.* of an archduke or archduchy

arch·duch·ess (-duch′is) *n.* **1.** the wife or widow of an archduke **2.** a princess of the former Austrian royal family

arch·duch·y (-duch′ē) *n., pl.* **-ies** the territory of an archduke or of an archduchess

arch·duke (-dyōōk′) *n.* a chief duke, esp. a prince of the former Austrian royal family

ar·che·go·ni·um (är′kə gō′nē əm) *n., pl.* **-ni·a** (-nē ə) [ModL. < Gr. < *archos,* first + *gonos,* offspring] the flask-shaped female reproductive organ in mosses, ferns, etc. —**ar′che·go′ni·al** *adj.*

arch·en·e·my (ärch′en′ə mē) *n., pl.* **-mies** a chief enemy —**the archenemy** Satan

arch·er (är′chər) *n.* [< ME. & OFr. < VL. < L. < *arcus,* a bow] a person who shoots with bow and arrow; bowman —[A-] the constellation Sagittarius

arch·er·y (är′chər ē) *n.* **1.** the practice, art, or sport of shooting with bow and arrow **2.** an archer's equipment **3.** archers collectively

arch·e·type (är′kə tīp′) *n.* [< L. < Gr. < *archos,* first + *typos:* see TYPE, *n.*] **1.** the original pattern or model of something; prototype **2.** a perfect example of a type or group —**ar′che·typ′al** (-tīp′əl), **ar′che·typ′i·cal** (-tip′i k′l) *adj.*

arch·fiend (ärch′fēnd′) *n.* a chief fiend —**the archfiend** Satan

ar·chi·di·ac·o·nal (är′kə dī ak′ə n′l) *adj.* of an archdeacon or archdeaconry —**ar′chi·di·ac′o·nate** (-nit) *n.*

ar·chi·e·pis·co·pal (är′kē ə pis′kə p′l) *adj.* of an archbishop or archbishopric —**ar′chi·e·pis′co·pate** (-pət, -pāt′) *n.*

ar·chi·man·drite (är′kə man′drīt′) *n.* [< LL. (Eccles.) *archimandrita* < LGr. < *archos,* chief + *mandra,* monstery] *Orthodox Eastern Ch.* the head of a monastery or of a number of monasteries

ar·chi·pel·a·go (är′kə pel′ə gō′) *n., pl.* **-goes′, -gos′** [< It. < MGr. < Gr. *archi-,* chief + *pelagos,* sea] **1.** a sea with many islands **2.** such a group of islands —**ar′chi·pe·lag′ic** (-pə laj′ik) *adj.*

ar·chi·tect (är′kə tekt′) *n.* [< L. < Gr. < *archi-,* chief + *tektōn,* carpenter] **1.** a person whose profession is designing plans for buildings, bridges, etc. and generally administering construction **2.** any planner, builder, or creator

ar·chi·tec·ton·ic (är′kə tek ton′ik) *adj.* [see prec.] **1.** of architecture or architectural methods, etc. **2.** having structure or design like that of architecture **3.** *Philos.* having to do with the systematizing of knowledge —*n. same as* ARCHITECTONICS

ar·chi·tec·ton·ics (-ton′iks) *n.pl.* [*with sing. v.*] **1.** the science of architecture **2.** structural design, as of a symphony **3.** *Philos.* the science of systematizing knowledge

ar·chi·tec·ture (är′kə tek′chər) *n.* [Fr. < L. *architectura:* see ARCHITECT] **1.** the science, art, or profession of designing and constructing buildings, etc. **2.** a building, or buildings collectively **3.** a style of construction [modern *architecture*] **4.** design and construction **5.** any framework, system, etc. —**ar′chi·tec′tur·al** *adj.* —**ar′-chi·tec′tur·al·ly** *adv.*

ar·chi·trave (är′kə trāv′) *n.* [Fr. < It. < L. *archi-,* first + *trabs,* a beam] *Archit.* **1.** the lowest part of an entablature, a beam resting directly on the tops of the columns **2.** the moulding around a doorway, window, etc.

ar·chives (är′kīvz) *n.pl.* [Fr. < L. < Gr. *archeion,* town hall < *archē,* the beginning] **1.** a place where public records, documents, etc. are kept **2.** the public records, documents, etc. kept there —**ar·chi·val** (är kī′v′l) *adj.*

ar·chi·vist (är′kə vist) *n.* a person having charge of archives

ar·chon (är′kon′) *n.* [< Gr. < *archein,* to be first, rule] one of the nine chief magistrates of ancient Athens

arch·priest (ärch′prēst′) *n.* a chief priest

arch·way (ärch′wā′) *n.* a passage under an arch

-ar·chy (är kē, ər kē) [< Gr. < *archein,* to rule] *a suffix meaning* a ruling, or that which is ruled [*matriarchy, monarchy*]

arc lamp a lamp in which the light is produced by an arc between electrodes; also **arc light**

arc·tic (ärk′tik, är′-) *adj.* [< OFr. < L. < Gr. *arktikos,* lit., of the (constellation of the) Bear (Gr. *arktos*), northern] **1.** of, characteristic of, or near the North Pole or the region around it **2.** very cold —**the Arctic** the region around the North Pole

Arctic Circle [*also* a- c-] an imaginary circle parallel to the equator, 66°33′north of it

Arc·tu·rus (ärk choor′əs, -tyoor′-) [L. < Gr. *Arktouros* < *arktos,* a bear + *ouros,* a guard] a giant red star of the first magnitude, the brightest in the constellation Boötes

ar·cu·ate (är′kyōō wit, -wāt′) *adj.* [L. *arcuatus,* pp. of *arcuare,* to arch] curved like a bow; arched

arc welding the welding of metal parts using the extreme heat of an electric arc

-ard (ərd) [OFr. < MHG. *hart,* bold] *a suffix denoting* one who carries an action too far or has too much of some quality [*sluggard, drunkard*]

ar·dent (är′dənt) *adj.* [< L. prp. of *ardere,* to burn] **1.** warm or intense in feeling; passionate **2.** intensely enthusiastic or devoted; zealous **3.** glowing; radiant **4.** burning; aflame —**ar′den·cy** (-dən sē) *n.* —**ar′dent·ly** *adv.*

ar·dor (är′dər) *n. U.S. sp. of* ARDOUR

ar·dour (är′dər) *n.* [< OFr. < L. < *ardere,* to burn] **1.** emotional warmth; passion **2.** enthusiasm; zeal **3.** intense heat; fire

ar·du·ous (är′dyo̅o̅ wəs, -əs) *adj.* [L. *arduus,* steep] **1.** difficult to do; laborious **2.** using much energy; strenuous **3.** steep; hard to climb —**ar′du·ous·ly** *adv.* —**ar′du·ous·ness** *n.*

are[1] (är; *unstressed* ər) [OE. (Northumbrian) *aron*] *pl. & 2nd pers. sing., pres. indic., of* BE

are[2] (er, är) *n.* [Fr. < L. *area:* see ff.] a unit of surface measure in the metric system, equal to 100 square metres

ar·e·a (er′ē ə) *n.* [L., vacant place, courtyard] **1.** orig., a level surface **2.** a part of the earth's surface; region **3.** the size of a surface, in square units **4.** a sunken space outside the basement of a building **5.** a part of a house, district, city, etc. having a specific use or character [*dining area,* slum *area*] **6.** a part of any surface **7.** scope or extent, as of an operation, a discussion, etc. —**ar′e·al** *adj.*

a·re·na (ə rē′nə) *n.* [L., sand, sandy place, arena] **1.** the central part of an ancient Roman amphitheatre, for gladiatorial contests **2.** any place like this **3.** any sphere of struggle

ar·e·na·ceous (ar′ə nā′shəs) *adj.* [L. *arenaceus:* see ARENA] **1.** sandy **2.** growing in sand

arena theatre *same as* THEATRE-IN-THE-ROUND

aren't (ärnt) are not: also, a contraction of *am not* in questions: see also AIN'T

a·re·o·la (ə rē′ə lə) *n., pl.* **-lae′** (-lē′), **-las** [L., dim. of *area:* see AREA] **1.** a small space, as between the veins of a leaf **2.** *Anat.* a small, surrounding area, as the dark ring around a nipple Also **ar·e·ole** (ar′ē ōl′) —**a·re′o·lar** (-lər) *adj.* —**a·re′o·late** (-lit) *adj.* —**ar·e·o·la·tion** (ar′ē ə lā′shən, ə rē′ə-) *n.*

a·rête (ə ret′, -rāt′) *n.* [Fr., lit., fish skeleton, ridge] a sharp, narrow ridge or crest of a mountain

ar·ga·li (är′gə lē) *n., pl.* **-lis, -li:** see PLURAL, II, D, 1 [Mongol.] a wild sheep of Asia, with large, curved horns

ar·gent (är′jənt) *n.* [Fr. < L. *argentum,* silver] [Archaic or Poet.] silver —*adj.* [Poet.] of silver: also **ar·gen′tal** (-jen′t'l)

ar·gen·tif·er·ous (är′jən tif′ər əs) *adj.* [see prec. & -FEROUS] containing silver, as ore

ar·gen·tine (är′jən tin, -tīn′, -tēn′) *adj.* of or like silver —*n.* silver or a silvery substance

ar·gil·la·ceous (är′jə lā′shəs) *adj.* [< L. *argilla,* clay < Gr. < *argos,* white] like or containing clay

Ar·give (är′gīv, -jīv) *adj., n.* Greek

ar·gol (är′g'l) *n.* [ME. *argoile* < Anglo-Fr.] tartar in its crude form

ar·gon (är′gon) *n.* [Gr., inert < *a-,* without + *ergon,* work] one of the chemical elements, an inert, odourless, colourless gas forming nearly one percent of the atmosphere: it is used in radio tubes, welding, etc.: symbol, Ar; at. wt., 39.948; at. no., 18

ar·go·sy (är′gə sē) *n.,* **-sies** [earlier *ragusy* < It. *(nave) Ragusea,* (vessel of) Ragusa, ancient Dalmatian port; sp. infl. by *Argo,* the name of the ship on which Jason sailed to find the Golden fleece] [Poet.] **1.** a large ship **2.** a fleet of such ships

ar·got (är′gō) *n.* [Fr. < ?] the specialized vocabulary and idioms of a particular group, as the secret jargon of criminals

ar·gue (är′gyo̅o̅) *vi.* **-gued, -gu·ing** [< OFr. < L. *argutare,* to prattle, freq. of *arguere,* to prove] **1.** to give reasons (*for* or *against* a proposal, etc.) **2.** to have a disagreement; quarrel —*vt.* **1.** to give reasons for and against; debate **2.** to try to prove by giving reasons; contend **3.** to give evidence of; indicate **4.** to persuade (*into* or *out of* an action, etc.) by giving reasons —**ar′gu·a·ble** *adj.* —**ar′gu·a·bly** *adv.* —**ar′gu·er** *n.*

ar·gu·fy (är′gyə fī′) *vt., vi.* **-fied′, -fy′ing** [< ARGU(E) + -FY] [Colloq. or Dial.] to argue, esp. merely for the sake of arguing

ar·gu·ment (är′gyə mənt) *n.* **1.** a reason or reasons offered for or against something **2.** the offering of such reasons; reasoning **3.** discussion in which there is disagreement; dispute; debate **4.** a short statement of subject matter; summary **5.** *Math.* an independent variable whose value determines that of a function

ar·gu·men·ta·tion (är′gyə men tā′shən) *n.* **1.** the process of arguing **2.** debate; discussion

ar·gu·men·ta·tive (-men′tə tiv) *adj.* **1.** controversial **2.** apt to argue Also **ar′gu·men′tive** -**ar′gu·men′ta·tive·ly** *adv.* —**ar′gu·men′ta·tive·ness** *n.*

Ar·gus (är′gəs) *n.* [after a giant in Gr. myth. with a hundred eyes] an alert watchman

Ar·gus-eyed (-īd′) *adj.* keenly observant; vigilant

ar·gy-bar·gy (är′jē bär′jē) *n.* [< Scot. < dial. *argle* < ? ARGUE] [Colloq.] a wrangling argument

a·ri·a (är′ē ə) *n.* [It. < L. *aer,* AIR] an air or melody in an opera, cantata, or oratorio, esp. for solo voice with instrumental accompaniment

-a·ri·a (er′ē ə, ā′rē ə) [ModL. < L. *-arius*] *Biol.* a plural suffix used in names of taxonomic groups

Ar·i·an[1] (er′ē ən, ar′-) *n., adj. same as* ARYAN

Ar·i·an[2] (er′ē ən, ar′-) *adj.* of Arius or Arianism —*n.* a believer in Arianism

-ar·i·an (er′ē ən) [L. *-arius* + *-anus*] a suffix denoting: **1.** age [*octogenarian*] **2.** sect [*Unitarian*] **3.** social belief [*utilitarian*] **4.** occupation [*antiquarian*]

Ar·i·an·ism (er′ē ə niz′m) *n.* the doctrines of Arius, who taught that Jesus was not of the same substance as God

ar·id (ar′id) *adj.* [< L. < *arere,* to be dry] **1.** dry and barren **2.** not interesting; dull —**a·rid·i·ty** (ə rid′ə tē), **ar′-id·ness** *n.* —**ar′id·ly** *adv.*

Ar·i·es (er′ēz, ar′-; -i ēz′) [L., the Ram] **1.** a N constellation **2.** the first sign of the zodiac: see ZODIAC, illus.

a·right (ə rīt′) *adv.* in a right way; correctly

ar·il (ar′il) *n.* [ModL. *arillus* < ML., dried grape] an additional covering that forms on certain seeds after fertilization —**ar′il·late** (-ə lāt′) *adj.*

a·ri·o·so (är′ē ō′sō, ar′-) *adj., adv.* [It. < *aria,* ARIA] like an aria —*n.* an arioso composition

a·rise (ə rīz′) *vi.* **a·rose′, a·ris′en** (-riz′'n), **a·ris′ing** [OE. < *a-,* out + *risan,* to rise] **1.** to get up, as from sleeping or sitting; rise **2.** to move upwards; ascend **3.** to come into being; originate **4.** to result or spring (*from* something)

ar·is·toc·ra·cy (ar′ə stok′rə sē) *n., pl.* **-cies** [< L. < Gr. < *aristos,* best + *kratein,* to rule] **1.** orig., government by the best citizens **2.** government by a privileged minority, usually of inherited wealth and social position **3.** a country with such government **4.** *a)* a privileged ruling class *b)* the hereditary nobility **5.** those considered the best in some way

a·ris·to·crat (ar′is tə krat′, ə ris′-) *n.* **1.** a member of the aristocracy; nobleman **2.** a person with the manners, beliefs, etc. of the upper class **3.** a supporter of aristocracy in government

a·ris·to·crat·ic (ar′is tə krat′ik, ə ris′-) *adj.* **1.** of or favouring aristocracy in government **2.** of an aristocracy or upper class **3.** like an aristocrat —**a·ris′to·crat′i·cal·ly** *adv.*

Ar·is·to·te·li·an (ar′is tə tēl′yən, -tē′lē ən) *adj.* of Aristotle or his philosophy —*n.* **1.** a follower of Aristotle **2.** a person who is empirical or practical in his thinking —**Ar′is·to·te′li·an·ism** *n.*

a·rith·me·tic (ə rith′mə tik; *for adj.* ar′ith met′ik) *n.* [OFr. < L. < Gr. < *arithmein,* to count < *arithmos,* number] **1.** the science of computing by positive, real numbers, specif. by adding, subtracting, multiplying, and dividing **2.** skill in this science —*adj.* of or using arithmetic: also **ar′ith·met′-i·cal** —**ar′ith·met′i·cal·ly** *adv.*

a·rith·me·ti·cian (ar′ith mə tish′ən, ə rith′mə-) *n.* a person skilled in arithmetic

arithmetic mean the average obtained by dividing a sum by the number of its addends

arithmetic progression a sequence of terms each of which, after the first, is derived by adding to or subtracting from the preceding one a constant quantity (Ex.: 5, 9, 13)

ark (ärk) *n.* [< OE. *earc* < L. *arca* < *arcere,* to enclose] **1.** *Bible* the huge boat in which Noah, his family, and two of every kind of creature survived the Flood: Gen. 6:9 **2.** formerly, a large, flat-bottomed river boat **3.** a place of refuge *same as* ARK OF THE COVENANT

ark of the covenant *Bible* the chest in which the stone tablets inscribed with the Ten Commandments were kept: Ex. 25:10

arm[1] (ärm) *n.* [OE. *earm*] **1.** an upper limb of the human body **2.** anything like this in structure or function; esp., *a)* the forelimb of a vertebrate animal *b)* any limb of an octopus, starfish, etc. *c)* a branch of a tree **3.** anything commonly in contact with the human arm; esp., *a)* a sleeve *b)* a for the arm, as on a chair **4.** anything armlike, esp. in being connected with something larger [an *arm* of the sea] **5.** power to seize, control, etc. [the *arm* of the law] —**arm in arm** with arms interlocked —**at arm's length 1.** at a distance; aloof **2.** with each side having the power to bargain independently: said of negotiations —**with open arms** in a warm and friendly way —**arm′less** *adj.* —**arm′-like′** *adj.*

arm[2] (ärm) *n.* [< OFr. *armes,* pl. < L. *arma,* implements, weapons] **1.** any weapon: *usually used in pl.:* see also SMALL ARMS **2.** [*pl.*] warfare; fighting **3.** [*pl.*] heraldic insignia: see COAT OF ARMS **4.** any combatant branch of the military forces —*vt.* **1.** to provide with weapons, tools, etc. **2.** to prepare for or against attack **3.** to equip with needed

ARGALI (0.9-1.2m high at shoulder)

parts —vi. to equip oneself with weapons, etc., esp. for war —**bear arms** 1. to carry weapons 2. to serve in the armed forces 3. to possess a coat of arms —**take up arms** 1. to go to war 2. to enter a dispute —**to arms!** get ready to fight! —**under arms** equipped with weapons —**up in arms** 1. prepared to fight (with *against*) 2. indignant (with *about*)

ar·ma·da (är mä′də) *n.* [Sp. < L. *armata*, fem. pp. of *armare*, to arm < *arma*: see ARM²] 1. *a)* a fleet of warships *b)* [A-] such a fleet sent against England by Spain in 1588 but destroyed: also **Spanish Armada** 2. a fleet of military aircraft

ar·ma·dil·lo (är′mə dil′ō) *n.,* *pl.* -los [Sp., dim. of *armado* < L. *armatus*, pp. of *armare*: see prec.] any of a family of burrowing, chiefly nocturnal mammals of the S U.S. and South America, having an armourlike covering of bony plates

Ar·ma·ged·don (är′mə ged′′n) *Bible* the place described as the scene of the last, deciding battle between good and evil: Rev. 16:16

ar·ma·ment (är′mə mənt) *n.* [< L. < *armare*: see ARMADA] 1. [*often pl.*] all the military forces and equipment of a nation 2. a combat force 3. all the military equipment of a warship, fortification, etc. 4. an arming or being armed for war 5. anything serving to protect or defend

ar·ma·ture (är′mə chər) *n.* [< L. *armatura*, arms, equipment < pp. of *armare*: see ARMADA] 1. any protective covering; armour 2. any part of an animal useful for offence or defence 3. a soft iron bar placed across the poles of a magnet 4. *a)* the laminated iron core wound around with wire, usually a revolving part, in a generator or motor *b)* the vibrating part in an electric relay, bell, etc. 5. *Sculpture* a framework for supporting the clay, etc. in modelling

arm·chair (ärm′cher′) *n.* a chair with supports at the sides for one's arms or elbows

armed (ärmd) *adj.* 1. provided with arms (weapons), armour, etc. 2. having arms (limbs) of a specified kind [*long-armed*]

armed forces all the military, naval, and air forces of a country or group of countries

arm·ful (ärm′fool) *n.,* *pl.* -fuls as much as the arms or one arm can hold

arm·hole (-hōl′) *n.* an opening for the arm in a garment

Ar·min·i·an·ism (är min′ē ən izm) *n.* the doctrines of Arminius, which stress man's free will as against Calvinistic predestination —**Ar·min′i·an** *adj., n.*

ar·mi·stice (är′mə stis) *n.* [Fr. < L. *arma*, arms + *sistere*, to cause tò stand] a temporary stopping of warfare by mutual agreement; truce

Armistice Day November 11, the anniversary of the armistice of World War I in 1918: see REMEMBRANCE DAY

arm·let (ärm′lit) *n.* 1. a band worn for ornament around the upper arm 2. a small inlet of the sea

ar·moire (är mwär′) *n.* [Fr. < OFr. < L. *armarium*, chest for arms] a large cupboard or clothespress

ar·mor (är′mər) *n., vi., vt. U.S. sp. of* ARMOUR

ar·mo·ri·al (är môr′ē əl) *adj.* of coats of arms; heraldic

ar·mour (är′mər) *n.* [< OFr. < L. *armatura*: see ARMATURE] 1. covering worn to protect the body against weapons 2. any defensive or protective covering, as the shell of a turtle or the metal plating on warships 3. armoured forces, as tanks 4. a quality, etc. serving as a defence difficult to penetrate —*vt., vi.* to put armour on

ar·mour·bear·er (-ber′ər) *n.* a person who carried the armour or weapons of a warrior

ar·moured (är′mərd) *adj.* 1. covered with armour or armour plate 2. equipped with tanks and other armoured vehicles

ar·mour·er (är′mər ər) *n.* 1. formerly, one who made or repaired armour 2. a maker of firearms 3. *Mil.* a man in charge of small arms

armour plate a protective covering of steel plates, as on a tank —**ar′mour plat′ed** *adj.*

ar·mour·y (är′mər ē) *n.* *pl.* -mour·ies [< OFr. < *arme*: see ARM²] 1. a storehouse for weapons; arsenal 2. weapons or resources collectively

arm·pit (ärm′pit′) *n.* the hollow under the arm where it joins the shoulder; axilla

arm·rest (-rest′) *n.* a support for one's arm

ar·my (är′mē) *n.,* *pl.* -mies [< OFr. < L. *armata*: see ARMADA] 1. a large, organized body of soldiers for waging war 2. a military unit of two or more corps, with auxiliary troops; field army 3. [*often* A-] a large organization of persons for a specific cause [the Salvation *Army*] 4. any large number of persons, animals, etc.

army ant any of certain ants that travel in large groups and devour insects and animals

army of occupation an army that goes into a defeated country to enforce peace terms, keep order, etc.

army worm any of the larvae of certain moths that travel in large groups, ruining crops

ar·ni·ca (är′ni kə) *n.* [ModL.] 1. any of a number of plants bearing bright yellow flowers 2. a preparation made from certain of these plants, formerly used for treating sprains, bruises, etc.

a·roint (ə roint′) *vt.* [< ?] [Obs.] begone!: used in the imperative, usually followed by *thee*

a·ro·ma (ə rō′mə) *n.* [LL. < Gr. *arōma*, sweet spice] 1. a pleasant, often spicy odour; fragrance, as of a plant, cooking, etc. 2. a characteristic quality or atmosphere

ar·o·mat·ic (ar′ə mat′ik) *adj.* 1. of or having an aroma 2. *Chem.* containing one or more benzene rings in the molecule —*n.* an aromatic plant, substance, or chemical —**ar′·o·mat′i·cal·ly** *adv.*

a·ro·ma·tize (ə rō′mə tīz′) *vt.* -tized′, -tiz′ing to make aromatic —**a·ro′ma·ti·za′tion** *n.*

a·rose (ə rōz′) *pt. of* ARISE

a·round (ə round′) *adv.* [ME. < *a-*, on + *round*: all senses derive from "circling, within a circle"] 1. round; esp. *a)* in every direction [he looked *around* carefully] *b)* in various places [to shop *around*] 2. [Colloq.] nearby [stay *around*] —*prep.* 1. round; esp., *a)* so as to encircle or envelop [the air *around* us] *b)* on the border of *c)* on all sides of *d)* in various places in or on 2. [Chiefly U.S.] close to; about [*around* 1890] —*adj.* [*used only in the predicate*] 1. on the move; about [he's up and *around* now] 2. [Colloq.] existing [when dinosaurs were *around*] —**have been around** [Colloq.] to have had wide experience; be sophisticated

a·rouse (ə rouz′) *vt.* **a·roused′**, **a·rous′ing** [< *a-* (sense 1) + ROUSE] 1. to awaken, as from sleep 2. to stir, as to action 3. to bring forth or work up (some action or feeling); excite —*vi.* to become aroused —**a·rous′al** *n.*

ar·peg·gio (är pej′ō, -pej′ē ō) *n.,* *pl.* -gios [It. < *arpeggiare*, to play on a harp < *arpa*, a harp] 1. the playing of the notes of a chord in quick succession instead of simultaneously 2. a chord so played

ar·que·bus (är′kwə bəs) *n. same as* HARQUEBUS

arr. 1. arranged 2. arrival

ar·rack (ar′ək) *n.* [< Fr. < Ar. ʼaraq, sweat, liquor] in the Orient, strong alcoholic drink, esp. that made from rice or coconut milk

ar·raign (ə rān′) *vt.* [< OFr. < ML. < L. *ad*, to + *ratio*, reason] 1. to bring before a law court to hear and answer charges 2. to call to account; accuse —**ar·raign′er** *n.* —**ar·raign′ment** *n.*

ar·range (ə rānj′) *vt.* -ranged′, -rang′ing [< OFr. < *a-*, to + *renc*, rank: see RANGE] 1. to put in the correct or suitable order 2. to classify 3. to prepare or plan 4. to settle or adjust (matters) 5. *Music* to adapt (a composition) to other instruments or voices than those for which it was written, or to the style of a certain band or orchestra —*vi.* 1. to come to an agreement (*with* a person, *about* a thing) 2. to make plans 3. *Music* to write arrangements —**ar·range′a·ble** *adj.* —**ar·rang′er** *n.*

ar·range·ment (-mənt) *n.* 1. an arranging or being arranged 2. the way in which something is arranged 3. something made by arranging parts in a particular way 4. [*usually pl.*] a plan or preparation [*arrangements* for the party] 5. a settlement or adjustment 6. *Music* an adaptation of a composition for other instruments, voices, etc.

ar·rant (ar′ənt) *adj.* [var. of ERRANT] that is plainly such; out-and-out [an *arrant* fool] —**ar′rant·ly** *adv.*

ar·ras (ar′əs) *n.* [after *Arras*, city in France, where it was made] 1. an elaborate kind of tapestry 2. a wall hanging, esp. of tapestry

ar·ray (ə rā′) *vt.* [< OFr. < ML. *arredare*, to put in order < *ad-*, to + Gmc. base *raid-*, order] 1. to put in the proper order; marshal (troops, etc.) 2. to dress in finery; adorn 3. *Law* to empanel (a jury) —*n.* 1. an orderly grouping, esp. of troops 2. a military force so grouped 3. an impressive display of persons or things 4. fine clothes 5. *Law a)* the formation of a jury *b)* a panel of jurors —**ar·ray′al** *n.* —**ar·ray′er** *n.*

ar·rear·age (ə rir′ij) *n.* arrears or the state of being in arrears

ar·rears (ə rirz′) *n.pl.* [< OFr. *ariere*, backwards < VL. < L. *ad*, to + *retro*, behind] 1. overdue debts 2. unfinished work, etc. —**in arrears** (or **arrear**) behind in paying a debt, in one's work, etc.

ar·rest (ə rest′) *vt.* [< OFr. < L. *ad-*, to + *restare*, to stop] 1. to stop or check 2. to seize or take into custody by authority of the law 3. to catch and keep (one's attention, etc.) —*n.* an arresting or being arrested —**under arrest** in legal custody, as of the police —**ar·rest′er, ar·res′tor** *n.*

ar·rest·ing (-in) *adj.* attracting attention; interesting; striking —**ar·rest′ing·ly** *adv.*

ar·rhyth·mi·a (ə rith′mē ə) *n.* [ModL. < Gr. < *a-*, without + *rhythmos*, measure] any irregularity in the rhythm of the heart's beating —**ar·rhyth′mic, ar·rhyth′mi·cal** *adj.* —**ar·rhyth′mi·cal·ly** *adv.*

‡**ar·rière-pen·sée** (à ryer′pän sā′) *n.* [Fr., lit., a backthought] a mental reservation; ulterior motive

ar·ris (ar'əs) *n.* [< OFr. < L. *arista*, awn of grain] the edge made by two surfaces coming together at an angle, as in a moulding

ar·riv·al (ərī'v'l) *n.* 1. the act of arriving 2. a person or thing that arrives or has arrived

ar·rive (ərīv', -rived', -riv'ing [< OFr. < L. *ad-*, to + *ripa*, shore] 1. to reach one's destination; come to a place 2. to come [the time has *arrived*] 3. to attain fame, etc. —**arrive at** 1. to reach by travelling 2. to reach by thinking, etc.

‡**ar·ri·ve·der·ci** (ä rē've der'chē) *interj.* [It.] until we meet again; goodbye

‡**ar·ri·viste** (á rēvēst') *n.* [Fr. < *arriver* (see ARRIVE) + -*iste*, -IST] same as PARVENU

ar·ro·gance (ar'əgəns) *n.* [see ff.] overbearing pride or self-importance: also **ar'ro·gan·cy**

ar·ro·gant (-gənt) *adj.* [OFr. < L. prp. of *arrogare*, ARROGATE] full of or due to arrogance; overbearing; haughty —**ar'ro·gant·ly** *adv.*

ar·ro·gate (-gāt') *vt.* -**gat'ed**, -**gat'ing** [< L. pp. of *arrogare* < *ad-*, for + *rogare*, to ask] 1. to claim or seize without right 2. to ascribe or attribute without reason —**ar'ro·ga'tion** *n.*

‡**ar·ron·disse·ment** (á rõn dēs män') *n.*, *pl.* -**ments'**(-män') [Fr. < *arrondir*, to make round] 1. the largest subdivision of a department 2. a municipal subdivision, as of Paris

ar·row (ar'ō) *n.* [OE. *earh*, *arwe*] 1. a slender shaft, usually pointed at one end and feathered at the other, for shooting from a bow 2. anything like an arrow in form, etc. 3. a sign (→) used to indicate direction —**ar'row·y** *adj.*

ar·row·head (-hed') *n.* 1. the pointed tip of an arrow 2. anything shaped like an arrowhead, as an indicating mark 3. a marsh plant with arrow-shaped leaves and small, white flowers

ar·row·root (-r̅o̅o̅t') *n.* [from its use as an antidote for poisoned arrows] 1. a tropical American plant with starchy roots 2. the edible starch made from its roots

ar·roy·o (əroi'ō) *n.*, *pl.* -**os** [Sp. < L. *arrugia*, mine shaft] [U.S.] 1. a dry gully 2. a rivulet or stream

arse (ärs) *n.* [< OE. *ærs*] the buttocks; rump: usually considered a vulgar term

ar·se·nal (är's'nəl, -snəl) *n.* [It. *arsenale*, a dock < Ar. *dâr* (*ês*) *sinâ'a*, wharf, workshop] 1. a place for making or storing weapons and other munitions 2. a store or collection [an *arsenal* of facts used in a debate]

ar·se·nate (är's'n ät', -it) *n.* [ARSEN(IC) + -ATE²] a salt or ester of arsenic acid

ar·se·nic (är's'n ik, -snik; *for adj.* är sen'ik) *n.* [OFr. < L. < Gr. *arsenikon*, a yellow sulphide of arsenic; ult. < Per. *zar*, gold] 1. a silvery-white, brittle, very poisonous chemical element, compounds of which are used in making insecticides, medicines, etc.: symbol, As; at. wt., 74.9216; at. no., 33 2. loosely, arsenic trioxide, a poisonous, tasteless, white powder, used to exterminate insects and rodents —*adj.* of or containing arsenic, esp. with a valence of five

arsenic acid a white, poisonous, crystalline compound, used in insecticides, etc.

ar·sen·i·cal (är sen'ə k'l) *adj.* of or containing arsenic —*n.* an arsenical drug, insecticide, etc.

ar·se·ni·ous (är sē'nē əs) *adj.* of or containing arsenic, esp. with a valence of three: also **ar·se·nous** (är's'n əs)

ar·son (är's'n) *n.* [OFr. < L. pp. of *ardere*, to burn] the crime of purposely setting fire to a building or property —**ar'son·ist** *n.*

art¹ (ärt) *n.* [< OFr. < L. *ars* (gen. *artis*), art] 1. human creativity 2. skill 3. any specific skill or its application 4. any craft or profession, or its principles [the cobbler's *art*] 5. a making or doing of things that have form and beauty; creative work: see also FINE ART 6. any branch of creative work, esp. painting, drawing, sculpture, etc. 7. products of creative work; paintings, statues, etc. 8. a branch of learning; specif., [*pl.*] the liberal arts as distinguished from the sciences 9. cunning 10. trick; wile: *usually used in pl.* —*adj.* of or for works of art or artists

art² (ärt) archaic 2nd pers. sing., pres. indic., of BE: used with thou

-**art** (ərt) *same as* -ARD

art. 1. article 2. artificial

art dec·o (dek'ō) a decorative style of the late 1920's and the 1930's, based generally on geometric forms, and applied to furnishings, textiles, graphic arts, etc.

ar·te·fact (är'tə fakt') *n.* var. sp. of ARTIFACT

ar·tel (är tel') *n.* [Russ.] a group of people, esp. in the Soviet Union, working collectively and sharing the income and liability

ar·te·ri·al (är tir'ē əl) *adj.* 1. of or like an artery or arteries 2. designating or of the bright-red, oxygenated blood in the arteries 3. of or being a main road with many branches —**ar·te'ri·al·ly** *adv.*

ar·te·ri·al·ize (-īz') *vt.* -**ized'**, -**iz'ing** to change (venous

blood) into arterial blood by oxygenation —**ar·te'ri·al·i·za'tion** *n.*

ar·te·ri·ole (är tir'ē ōl') *n.* a small artery

ar·te·ri·o·scle·ro·sis (är tir'ē ō sklərō'sis) *n.* [see ff. & SCLEROSIS] a thickening, and loss of elasticity, of the walls of the arteries, as in old age —**ar·te'ri·o·scle·rot'ic** (-rot'ik) *adj.*

ar·ter·y (är'tər ē) *n.*, *pl.* -**ter·ies** [< L. < Gr.; prob. < *aeirein*, to raise] 1. any of the system of tubes carrying blood from the heart to all parts of the body: cf. VEIN 2. a main road or channel

ar·te·sian well (är tē'zhən, -zē ən) [Fr. *artésien*, lit., of Artois, former Fr. province] a well in which ground water is forced up by hydrostatic pressure

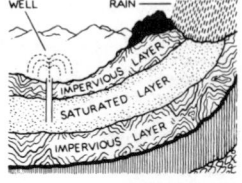

ARTESIAN WELL

art form 1. an accepted mode of artistic composition, as the novel 2. a recognized vehicle of artistic expression

art·ful (ärt'fəl) *adj.* 1. skilful or clever, esp. in achieving a purpose 2. sly or cunning —**art'ful·ly** *adv.* —**art'ful·ness**

ar·thral·gia (är thral'jə) *n.* [see ff. & -ALGIA] neuralgic pain in a joint or joints

ar·thri·tis (är thrīt'əs) *n.* [Gr. < *arthron*, a joint + -ITIS] inflammation of a joint or joints —**ar·thrit'ic** (-thrit'ik) *adj.* —**ar·thrit'i·cal·ly** *adv.*

ar·thro·pod (är'thrə pod') *n.* [< Gr. *arthron*, a joint + -POD] any member of a large group of invertebrate animals with jointed legs and a segmented body, as insects, crustaceans, arachnids, etc. —**ar·throp·o·dal** (är throp'ə d'l), **ar·throp'o·dous** (-dəs) *adj.*

ar·tic (är tik') *n.* [Colloq.] an articulated lorry

ar·ti·choke (är'tə chōk') *n.* [< It. < Sp. < Ar. *al-harsûf*] 1. a thistlelike plant 2. its flower head, cooked as a vegetable 3. *short for* JERUSALEM ARTICHOKE

ar·ti·cle (är'ti k'l) *n.* [OFr. < L. *articulus*, dim. of *artus*, a joint] 1. any of the sections of a written document, as of a treaty 2. a complete piece of writing that is part of a newspaper, magazine, or book 3. a separate item [an *article* of luggage] 4. a commodity 5. *Gram.* any one of the words *a*, *an*, or *the* (and their equivalents in other languages), used as adjectives —*vt.* -**cled**, -**cling** to bind by the articles of an agreement or contract

ar·tic·u·lar (är tik'yə lər) *adj.* [< L. < *articulus*: see prec.] of a joint or joints [an *articular* inflammation]

ar·tic·u·late (är tik'yə lit; *for v.* -lāt') *adj.* [< L. pp. of *articulare*, to disjoint < *articulus*: see ARTICLE] 1. jointed: usually **ar·tic'u·lat'ed** 2. made up of distinct syllables or words that have meaning 3. able to speak 4. expressing oneself easily and clearly 5. well formulated —*vt.* -**lat'ed**, -**lat'ing** 1. to put together by joints 2. to pronounce carefully; enunciate 3. to express clearly —*vi.* 1. to speak distinctly 2. to be jointed —**ar·tic'u·late·ly** *adv.* —**ar·tic'u·late·ness** *n.* —**ar·tic'u·la'tive** *adj.* —**ar·tic'u·la'tor** *n.*

articulated lorry a large lorry made in two sections connected by a pivoted bar so that the two parts can be at an angle to each other when turning

ar·tic·u·la·tion (är tik'yə lā'shən) *n.* 1. a jointing or being jointed 2. the way in which parts are joined together 3. enunciation 4. a spoken sound 5. a joint between bones or similar parts 6. *Bot.* a node, or a space between two nodes

ar·ti·fact (är'tə fakt') *n.* [< L. *ars* (gen. *artis*), ART¹ + *factum*, thing made (see FACT)] any object made by human work; esp., a primitive tool, etc.

ar·ti·fice (är'tə fis) *n.* [Fr. < L. < *ars*, ART¹ + *facere*, to make] 1. skill or ingenuity 2. trickery or craft 3. a sly or artful trick

ar·tif·i·cer (är tif'ə sər) *n.* [see prec. & -ER] 1. a skilled craftsman 2. an inventor 3. a military mechanic

ar·ti·fi·cial (är'tə fish'əl) *adj.* [< OFr. < L.: see ARTIFICE] 1. made by human work or art; not natural 2. made in imitation of something natural; simulated [*artificial* teeth] 3. unnatural in an affected way [an *artificial* smile] —**ar'ti·fi·ci·al'i·ty** (-fish'ē al'ə tē) *n.*, *pl.* -**ties** —**ar'ti·fi'cial·ly** *adv.* —**ar'ti·fi'cial·ness** *n.*

artificial insemination the impregnation of a female by the introduction of semen without sexual intercourse

artificial respiration the artificial maintenance of breathing, as by forcing breath into the mouth

ar·til·ler·y (är til'ər ē) *n.* [< OFr. *artillerie* < *artillier*, to arm] 1. heavy mounted guns, as cannon or missile launchers 2. the science of guns; gunnery —**the artillery** the military branch specializing in the use of artillery —**ar·til'ler·ist**, **ar·til'ler·y·man** (-mən) *n.*, *pl.* -**men**

ar·ti·san (är'tə zən, är'tə zan') *n.* [Fr. < It.; ult. < L. *ars*, ART¹] a skilled workman; craftsman

art·ist (är′tist) *n.* [ML. *artista*, craftsman < L. *ars,* ART¹] 1. a person who is skilled in any of the fine arts, esp. in painting, sculpture, etc. 2. a person who does anything very well, with a feeling for form, etc. 3. *same as* ARTISTE

ar·tiste (är tēst′) *n.* [Fr.] 1. a professional in any of the performing arts 2. a person very skilled in his work: often humorous or facetious

ar·tis·tic (är tis′tik) *adj.* 1. of art or artists 2. proficient in art 3. done skilfully and tastefully 4. keenly sensitive to aesthetic values —**ar·tis′ti·cal·ly** *adv.*

art·ist·ry (är′tis trē) *n.* artistic work or skill

art·less (ärt′lis) *adj.* 1. lacking skill or art 2. uncultured; ignorant 3. simple; natural 4. without guile or deceit; ingenuous —**art′less·ly** *adv.* —**art′less·ness** *n.*

‡**art nou·veau** (är noo vō′) [Fr., lit., new art] an art movement of the late 19th and early 20th cent., emphasizing stylized curvilinear designs

art paper paper given a very smooth surface with a coating of china clay, etc.

art·y (ärt′ē) *adj.* **art′i·er, art′i·est** [Colloq.] showing artistic pretensions —**art′i·ness** *n.*

art·y-craft·y (ärt′ē kräft′ē) *adj.* [Colloq.] of arts and crafts: usually a disparaging term connoting faddishness, amateurishness, etc.

ar·um (er′əm) *n.* [L. < Gr. *aron*] any of a family of plants bearing small flowers on a fleshy spike enclosed by a hoodlike leaf, as the cuckoopint

-ar·y (ər ē) [L. *-arius, -aria, -arium*] 1. a suffix meaning: a) related to; connected with [*auxiliary*] b) a person or thing connected with [*missionary*] c) a place for [*granary*] 2. [L. *-aris*] a suffix meaning like; of the same kind [*military*]

Ar·y·an (er′ē ən, ar′-) *adj.* [< Sans. *ārya*, noble, lord (used as a tribal name)] 1. *earlier term for* INDO-EUROPEAN 2. *same as* INDO-IRANIAN 3. of the Aryans —*n.* 1. formerly, the hypothetical language from which all Indo-European languages are supposed to be descended 2. a person belonging to, or supposed to be a descendant of, the prehistoric peoples who spoke this language 3. loosely, esp. in Nazi usage, a non-Jewish Caucasoid, a Nordic, etc.

as¹ (az; *unstressed* əz) *adv.* [weakened form of ALSO < OE. *ealswa*, quite so, just as: see ALSO] 1. to the same amount or degree; equally [*he's just as happy at home*] 2. for instance; thus [*a card game, as bridge*] 3. when related in a specified way [*romanticism as contrasted with classicism*] —*conj.* 1. to the same amount or degree that [*it flew straight as an arrow*] 2. in the same manner that [*do as he does*] 3. at the same time that [*she wept as she spoke*] 4. because [*as you object, we won't go*] 5. that the consequence is [*a question so obvious as to need no reply*] 6. though [*full as he was, he kept eating*] —*pron.* 1. a fact that [*he is tired, as anyone can see*] 2. that (preceded by *such* or *the same*) [*the same colour as yours (is)*] —*prep.* 1. in the role, function, capacity, or sense of [*he poses as a friend*] 2. like [*the same as mine*] —**as . . . as** a correlative construction used to indicate the equality or sameness of two things [*as large as, as many as,* etc.] —**as for** with reference to; concerning —**as if** (or **though**) 1. as it (or one) would if 2. that [*it seems as if she's never home*] —**as it were** as if it were so; so to speak —**as of** on or from (a specified time) [*as of Friday, he'll be retired*] —**as to** 1. concerning 2. as if to

as² (as) *n., pl.* **as′ses** (-əz, -ēz) [L.] 1. an ancient Roman unit of weight equal to about 350 grammes 2. an ancient Roman coin of copper alloy

As *Chem.* arsenic

AS., A.S., A.-S. Anglo-Saxon

A.S.A. Amateur Swimming Association

as·a·foet·i·da (as′ə fet′ə də, -fēt′-) *n.* [ML. *asa* < Per. *āzā*, gum + L *foetida,* FETID] a bad-smelling gum resin obtained from various Asiatic plants formerly used in folk medicine to repel disease

as·bes·tos (as bes′təs, az-) *n.* [< L. < Gr. *asbestos,* inextinguishable < *a-,* not + *sbennynai,* to extinguish] a greyish mineral, esp. an amphibole, that separates into long, threadlike fibres: some varieties resist heat and chemicals and are used in fireproof curtains, roofing, etc.

as·ca·rid (as′kə rid) *n.* [< Gr. *askaris*] a roundworm that is a parasite in mammals

as·cend (ə send′) *vi.* [< OFr. < L. < *ad-,* to + *scandere,* to climb] 1. to go up; move upwards; rise 2. to slope or lead upwards —*vt.* 1. to move upwards along; climb 2. to succeed to (a throne) —**as·cend′i·ble, as·cend′a·ble** *adj.*

as·cend·an·cy, as·cend·en·cy (-ən sē) *n.* a position of control or power; supremacy; domination: also **as·cend′-ance, as·cend′ence**

as·cend·ant, as·cend·ent (-ənt) *adj.* 1. rising; ascending 2. in control; dominant; superior —*n.* 1. a dominating position; ascendancy 2. *Astrol.* the sign of the zodiac just above the eastern horizon at any given moment —**in the ascendant** at or approaching the height of power, fame, etc.

as·cend·er (-ər) *n.* 1. a person or thing that ascends 2.

Typography the extension or upward stroke of any of the tall lower-case letters, as *b, d, k,* etc. 3. any of these letters

as·cen·sion (ə sen′shən) *n.* 1. an ascending; ascent 2. [A-] *same as* ASCENSION DAY —**the Ascension** *Bible* the bodily ascent of Jesus into heaven on the fortieth day after the Resurrection: Acts 1:9 —**as·cen′sion·al** *adj.*

Ascension Day the fortieth day after Easter, celebrating the Ascension

as·cent (ə sent′) *n.* 1. an ascending or rising 2. an advancement, as in rank, fame, etc. 3. a) a way leading up b) the degree of an upward slope 4. a going back in time or genealogy

as·cer·tain (as′ər tān′) *vt.* [< OFr. < a-, to + *certain,* CERTAIN] to find out with certainty —**as·cer·tain′a·ble** *adj.* —**as·cer·tain′ment** *n.*

as·cet·ic (ə set′ik) *adj.* [< Gr. < *askein,* to train the body] of or characteristic of ascetics or their way of life; self denying; austere: also **as·cet′i·cal** —*n.* a person who leads a life of contemplation and rigorous self-denial, esp. for religious purposes —**as·cet′i·cal·ly** *adv.* —**as·cet′i·cism** *n.*

as·cid·i·an (ə sid′ē ən) *n.* [< Gr. *askidion:* see ff.] any of a class of sea animals that are sac-shaped and have a tough outer covering

as·cid·i·um (-əm) *n., pl.* **-i·a** (-ə) [ModL. < Gr. dim. of *askos,* a bag, bladder] *Bot.* a pitcherlike leaf or structure, as of the pitcher plant

as·co·my·cete (as′kə mī sēt′) *n.* [< Gr. *askos,* bladder + *mykēs,* fungus] any of a class of fungi, including the mildews, yeasts, etc., that develop spores in a saclike structure —**as′co·my·ce′tous** *adj.*

a·scor·bic acid (ə skôr′bik) [A.² (sense 3) + SCORB(UTIC) + -IC] a water-soluble vitamin occurring in citrus fruits, tomatoes, etc.: it prevents and cures scurvy; vitamin C

as·cribe (ə skrīb′) *vt.* **-cribed′, -crib′ing** [< OFr. < L. < *ad-,* to + *scribere,* to write] 1. to put down (*to* a supposed cause); attribute 2. to regard as belonging (*to*) or coming from someone [*poems ascribed to Homer*] —**as·crib′a·ble** *adj.*

as·crip·tion (ə skrip′shən) *n.* 1. the act of ascribing 2. a statement that ascribes

-ase (ās, āz) [< (DIAST)ASE] a suffix denoting an enzyme, esp. one of vegetable origin [*amylase*]

a·sep·sis (ā sep′sis, ə-) *n.* 1. the condition of being aseptic 2. aseptic treatment or technique

a·sep·tic (-tik) *adj.* 1. not septic 2. designed to ensure freedom from microorganisms that cause disease 3. surgically sterilized —**a·sep′ti·cal·ly** *adv.*

a·sex·u·al (ā sek′shoo wəl) *adj.* 1. having no sex or sexual organs; sexless 2. of reproduction without the union of male and female germ cells —**a·sex′u·al′i·ty** (-wal′ə tē) *n.* —**a·sex′u·al·ly** *adv.*

ash¹ (ash) *n.* [OE. *æsce*] 1. the white or greyish powder left after something has been thoroughly burned 2. fine, volcanic lava 3. the silvery-grey colour of wood ash See also ASHES

ash² (ash) *n.* [OE. *æsc*] 1. a timber and shade tree of the olive family, having tough, elastic, straight-grained wood 2. the wood

a·shamed (ə shāmd′) *adj.* 1. feeling shame 2. feeling humiliated or embarrassed 3. reluctant because fearing shame beforehand —**a·sham·ed·ly** (ə shā′mid lē) *adv.*

ash·can (ash′kan′) *n.* [U.S.] a dustbin

ash·en¹ (ash′ən) *adj.* 1. of ashes 2. like ashes, esp. in colour; pale; pallid

ash·en² (ash′ən) *adj.* [Archaic] of the ash tree or its wood

ash·es (ash′iz) *n.pl.* 1. the unburned particles and greyish powder left after a thing has been burned 2. human remains, esp. after cremation 3. the ruins or remains of something destroyed 4. [A-] [< mock *In memoriam* newspaper notice of England's test match defeat (1882) by Australia] *Cricket* the mythical trophy for which England and Australia compete in test matches

Ash·ke·naz·im (ash′kə näz′im) *n.pl., sing.* **-naz′, -naz′i** (-ē) [Heb.: cf. Jer. 51:27] the Jews who settled in C and N Europe after the Diaspora, or their descendants: cf. SEPHARDIM —**Ash′ke·naz′ic** *adj.*

ash·lar, ash·ler (ash′lər) *n.* [< OFr. < L. *assis,* board] 1. a square, hewn stone used in building 2. a thin, dressed, square stone used for facing masonry walls 3. masonry made of either kind of ashlar

a·shore (ə shôr′) *adv., adj.* 1. to or on the shore 2. to or on land

ash pan a removable receptacle for ashes under a grate

ash·ram (ash′rəm) *n.* [< Sans. < *ā,* towards + *srama,* fatigue, penance] a secluded place for a community of Hindus leading a life of religious meditation

ash·tray (ash′trā′) *n.* a container for smokers' tobacco ashes: also **ash tray**

Ash Wednesday the first day of Lent: from the putting of ashes on the forehead in penitence

ash·y (ash′ē) *adj.* **ash′i·er, ash′i·est** 1. of, like, or covered with ashes 2. of ash colour; pale

A·sian (ā′zhən, -shən) *adj.* of Asia —*n.* an inhabitant of Asia Also **A·si·at·ic** (ā′zhē at′ik)

Asian influenza a widespread influenza caused by a strain of virus first isolated in Singapore in 1957: also **Asian flu**

Asiatic cholera *same as* CHOLERA

a·side (ə sīd′) *adv.* 1. on or to one side 2. away; in reserve [put this *aside* for me] 3. out of the way; out of one's mind 4. apart; notwithstanding [joking *aside*, I mean it] —*n.* an actor's words spoken as to the audience and supposedly not heard by the other actors

as·i·nine (as′ə nīn′) *adj.* [< L. < *asinus*, ass] like an ass; esp., having qualities thought of as asslike; stupid, silly, obstinate, etc. —**as′i·nine′ly** *adv.* —**as′i·nin′i·ty** (-nin′ə tē) *n., pl.* **-ties**

ask (äsk) *vt.* [OE. *ascian*] 1. to use words in seeking the answer to (a question); inquire about 2. to put a question to (a person); inquire of 3. to request; solicit; beg 4. to demand or expect as a price 5. to be in need of or call for (a thing) 6. to invite —*vi.* 1. to make a request (*for*) 2. to inquire (*about, after,* or *for*) 3. to behave so as to appear to be looking (*for* trouble, etc.) —**ask′er** *n.* —**ask′ing** *n.*

a·skance (ə skans′, ə skäns′) *adv.* [< ?] 1. with a sideways glance; obliquely 2. with suspicion, disapproval, etc. Also [Archaic or Poet.] **a·skant′**

a·skew (ə skyoō′) *adv.* to one side; awry; crookedly —*adj.* on one side; awry

asking price the price asked by a seller, esp. when he will accept less after bargaining

a·slant (ə slänt′) *adv.* on a slant; slantingly —*prep.* on a slant across —*adj.* slanting

a·sleep (ə slēp′) *adj.* [used only in the predicate] 1. in a condition of sleep; sleeping 2. inactive; dull; sluggish 3. numb except for a prickly feeling [my arm is *asleep*] 4. dead —*adv.* into a sleeping or inactive condition

A.S.L.E.F. Associated Society of Locomotive Engineers and Firemen

a·slope (ə slōp′) *adv., adj.* at a slant

a·so·cial (ā sō′shəl) *adj.* 1. not social; characterized by withdrawal from others 2. selfish

asp (asp) *n.* [< OFr. < L. < Gr. *aspis*] any of several small, poisonous snakes of Africa and Europe, as the horned viper

as·par·a·gus (ə spar′ə gəs) *n.* [L. < Gr. *asparagos*, a sprout] 1. a plant of the lily family, with small, scalelike leaves and many needlelike branches 2. the tender shoots of this plant, eaten as a cooked vegetable

a·spar·kle (ə spär′k'l) *adj.* sparkling

as·pect (as′pekt) *n.* [< L. pp. of *aspicere* < ad-, to, at + *specere*, to look] 1. the way a person or thing appears or looks to another; appearance 2. the appearance of an idea, problem, etc. regarded from a specific viewpoint 3. a facing in a given direction 4. a side facing in a given direction [the eastern *aspect* of the house] 5. *Astrol.* the position of stars in relation to each other or to the observer, as it supposedly influences human affairs

aspect ratio 1. *Aeron.* the ratio of the span of an aerofoil to its mean chord 2. *Television* the ratio of the width of a televised picture to its height

as·pen (as′pən) *n.* [OE. *æspe*] a kind of poplar tree with leaves that flutter in the least breeze —*adj.* of or like an aspen; esp., fluttering; trembling

as·per·i·ty (as per′ə tē) *n., pl.* **-ties** [ME. & OFr. < L. < *asper*, rough] 1. roughness or harshness, as of surface, sound, etc. 2. sharpness of temper

as·perse (ə spurs′) *vt.* **-persed′, -pers′ing** [< L. pp. of *aspergere* < ad-, to + *spargere*, to sprinkle] to spread false or damaging rumours about; slander —**as·pers′er** *n.*

as·per·sion (ə spur′shən) *n.* 1. a defaming 2. a damaging or disparaging remark; slander

as·phalt (as′falt) *n.* [< ML. < Gr.] 1. a brown or black tarlike substance, a variety of bitumen, found in a natural state or obtained by evaporating petroleum 2. a mixture of this with sand or gravel, for paving, roofing, etc. —*vt.* to pave, roof, etc. with asphalt —**as·phal′tic** *adj.*

as·phal·tum (as fal′təm) *n. same as* ASPHALT

as·pho·del (as′fə del′) *n.* [< L. < Gr. *asphodelos*] 1. a plant of the lily family, having fleshy roots and white or yellow flowers 2. *Gr. Myth.* the immortal flower growing in the Elysian fields

as·phyx·i·a (as fik′sē ə) *n.* [ModL. < Gr., a stopping of the pulse < a-, not + *sphyzein*, to throb] loss of consciousness as a result of too little oxygen and too much carbon dioxide in the blood: suffocation causes asphyxia —**as·phyx′i·ant** *adj., n.*

as·phyx·i·ate (-āt′) *vt.* **-at′ed, -at′ing** 1. to cause asphyxia in 2. to suffocate —*vi.* to undergo asphyxia —**as·phyx′i·a′tion** *n.* —**as·phyx′i·a′tor** *n.*

as·pic (as′pik) *n.* [Fr. < OFr. *aspe*, ASP] 1. [Archaic] an asp 2. [Fr., ? from its asplike colourfulness] a jelly of

meat juice, tomato juice, etc., moulded, often with meat, seafood, etc., and eaten as a relish

as·pi·dis·tra (as′pə dis′trə) *n.* [ModL. < Gr. *aspis*, a shield + *astron*, a star] a plant of the lily family, with stiff, glossy evergreen leaves

as·pir·ant (as′pər ənt, ə spīr′ənt) *adj.* aspiring —*n.* a person who aspires, as after honours, etc.

as·pi·rate (as′pə rāt′; *for n. & adj.* -pər it) *vt.* **-rat′ed, -rat′ing** [< L. pp. of *aspirare*: see ASPIRE] 1. to begin (a word or syllable) with the sound of English *h* 2. to follow (a consonant) with a puff of suddenly released breath 3. to suck in or draw in, as by inhaling 4. *Med.* to remove (fluid or gas), as from a body cavity, by suction —*n.* 1. the speech sound represented by English *h* 2. an expiratory breath puff —*adj.* preceded or followed by an aspirate: also **as′pi·rat′ed**

as·pi·ra·tion (as′pə rā′shən) *n.* 1. *a*) strong desire or ambition, as for honour, etc. *b*) the thing so desired 2. an aspirating 3. an aspirate

as·pi·ra·tor (as′pə rāt′ər) *n.* a suction apparatus for removing air, fluids, etc. as from a body cavity

as·pir·a·to·ry (ə spīr′ə tər ē) *adj.* of or suited for breathing or suction

as·pire (ə spīr′) *vi.* **-pired′, -pir′ing** [< L. *aspirare* < ad-, to + *spirare*, to breathe] 1. to be ambitious (*to get* or do something lofty); yearn or seek (*after*) 2. [Archaic] to rise high; tower —**as·pir′er** *n.* —**as·pir′ing·ly** *adv.*

as·pi·rin (as′pər in, as′prin) *n.* [G. < *a(cetyl)* + *Spir(säure)*, salicylic acid + -IN′] a white, crystalline powder, acetylsalicylic acid, used for reducing fever, relieving headaches, etc.

a·squint (ə skwint′) *adv., adj.* [ME. < ? Du. *schuinte*, a slant] with a squint; out of the corner of the eye

ass (as) *n.* [OE. *assa* < L. *asinus*] 1. an animal related to the horse but having longer ears and a shorter mane: donkeys are domesticated asses 2. a stupid or silly person; fool

as·sa·foet·i·da (as′ə fet′ə də, -fēt′-) *n. same as* ASAFOETIDA

‡as·sa·i (äs sä′ē) *adv.* [It.] *Music* very: used in indicating tempo [adagio *assai*]

as·sail (ə sāl′) *vt.* [< OFr. < L. *assilire* < ad, to + *salire*, to leap] 1. to attack physically and violently 2. to attack with arguments, etc. 3. to begin working on (a task, etc.) with vigour 4. to have a forceful effect on —**as·sail′a·ble** *adj.* —**as·sail′er** *n.* —**as·sail′ment** *n.*

as·sail·ant (-ənt) *n.* a person who assails; attacker

as·sas·sin (ə sas′in) *n.* [Fr. < Ar. *hash-shāshīn*, hashish users < *hashish*, hemp] 1. [A-] a member of a secret cult of Moslems who killed Crusaders, supposedly while under the influence of hashish 2. a murderer who strikes suddenly; esp., the killer of a politically important person

as·sas·si·nate (-āt′) *vt.* **-nat′ed, -nat′ing** 1. to murder (esp. a politically important person) 2. to harm or ruin (a reputation, etc.), as by slander —**as·sas′si·na′tion** *n.*

as·sault (ə sôlt′) *n.* [< OFr. < L. *ad*, to + *saltare*, to leap] 1. a violent attack, either physical or verbal; sometimes, specif., rape 2. *Law* an unlawful threat or unsuccessful attempt to physically harm another —*vt., vi.* 1. to make an assault (upon) 2. to rape —**as·sault′ive** *adj.*

assault and battery *Law* the carrying out of threatened physical harm or violence

as·say (as′ā, a sā′; *for v.* a sā′, ə-) *n.* [OFr. *essai*, trial, test < L. *exagium*, a weighing < *ex-*, out + *agere*, to ACT] 1. an examination or testing 2. the analysis of an ore, etc. to find out the nature and proportion of the ingredients 3. a substance to be analysed in this way 4. the result or report of such analysis —*vt.* 1. to make an assay of; test; analyse 2. to try; attempt —**as·say′er** *n.*

as·se·gai, as·sa·gai (as′ə gī′) *n.* [Port *azagaia* < Ar. *az-zaghayāh* < *az*, for *al*, the + *zaghāyah*, spear, of Berber origin] 1. a slender spear with an iron tip, used in southern Africa 2. a tree of the dogwood family, whose hard wood is used to make such spears

as·sem·blage (ə sem′blij) *n.* 1. an assembling or being assembled 2. a group of persons or things gathered together; assembly 3. a form of art in which a number of unrelated objects are arranged together to form a kind of sculptural collage

as·sem·ble (ə sem′b'l) *vt., vi.* **-bled, -bling** [< OFr. < L. < *ad-*, to + *simul*, together] 1. to gather into a group; collect 2. to fit or put together the parts of —**as·sem′bler** *n.*

as·sem·bly (ə sem′blē) *n., pl.* **-blies** 1. an assembling or being assembled 2. a group of persons gathered together, as for a meeting 3. a legislative body 4. *a*) a fitting together of parts to form a complete unit *b*) such parts 5. a call, as by bugle or drum, for soldiers to assemble in ranks

assembly line in many factories, an arrangement by which each worker does a single operation in assembling the work as it is passed along, often on a slowly moving belt or track

as·sem·bly·man (ə sem′blē mən) *n., pl.* **-men** (-mən, -men′) a member of a legislative assembly

as·sent (ə sent') *vi.* [< OFr. < L. < *assentire* < *ad-*, to + *sentire*, to feel] to express acceptance of an opinion, proposal, etc.; agree (*to*); concur —*n.* consent or agreement —**as·sent'er** *n.*

as·sen·ta·tion (as'en tā'shən) *n.* immediate and usually flattering or hypocritical assent

as·sert (ə surt') *vt.* [< L. pp. of *asserere* < *ad-*, to + *serere*, to join] 1. to state positively; declare 2. to insist on or defend (one's rights, a claim, etc.) —**assert oneself** to insist on one's rights, or on being recognized —**as·sert'er, as·ser'tor** *n.*

as·ser·tion (ə sur'shən) *n.* 1. an asserting 2. a positive statement; declaration

as·ser·tive (-tiv) *adj.* positive or confident in a dogmatic way —**as·ser'tive·ly** *adv.* —**as·ser'tive·ness** *n.*

as·sess (ə ses') *vt.* [< OFr. < ML. *assessare*, to set a rate < L. pp. of *assidere*, to to sit beside, assist < *ad-*, to + *sedere*, to sit] 1. to set an estimated value on (property, etc.) for taxation 2. to set the amount of (damages, a fine, etc.) 3. to impose a fine, tax, etc. on (a person or property) 4. to impose (an amount) as a fine, tax, etc. 5. to estimate the importance or value of

as·sess·ment (-mənt) *n.* 1. an assessing 2. an amount assessed

as·ses·sor (-ər) *n.* 1. a person who assesses property, etc. for taxation 2. a person called in to advise a court on a matter requiring specialist knowledge 3. a person who estimates the value of damage to property for insurance purposes —**as·ses·so·ri·al** (as'ə sôr'ē əl) *adj.* —**as·ses'sor·ship'** *n.*

as·set (as'et) *n.* [< Anglo-Fr. *assetz*, enough < OFr.; ult. < L. *ad*, to + *satis*, enough] 1. anything owned that has exchange value 2. a valuable or desirable thing [charm is her chief *asset*] 3. [*pl.*] *a) Accounting* the entries on a balance sheet showing all the resources of a person or business, as accounts and notes receivable, cash, property, etc. *b) Law* property, as of a bankrupt

as·sev·er·ate (ə sev'ə rāt') *vt.* -at'ed, -at'ing [< L. pp. of *asseverare* < *ad-*, to + *severus*, earnest] to state seriously or positively; assert —**as·sev'er·a'tion** *n.*

as·sib·i·late (ə sib'ə lāt') *vt.* -lat'ed, -lat'ing to substitute a sibilant sound for in pronouncing

as·si·du·i·ty (as'ə dyōō'ə tē) *n.,* pl. -ties 1. the quality or condition of being assiduous; diligence 2. [*pl.*] constant personal attention

as·sid·u·ous (ə sid'yoo wəs) *adj.* [< L. < *assidere:* see ASSESS] working with constant and careful attention; diligent; persevering —**as·sid'u·ous·ly** *adv.* —**as·sid'·u·ous·ness** *n.*

as·sign (ə sīn') *vt.* [< OFr. < L. *assignare*, to allot < *ad-*, to + *signare*, SIGN] 1. to set apart or mark for a specific purpose; designate 2. to place at some task or duty 3. to give out as a task; allot 4. to ascribe (a motive, reason, etc.) 5. *Law* to transfer (a claim, property, etc.) to another —*vi. Law* to transfer property, etc. to another —*n.* [usually *pl.*] an assignee —**as·sign'a·bil'i·ty** *n.* —**as·sign'·a·ble** *adj.* —**as·sign'or**, *Law* **as·sign'or** (-ər, -ôr') *n.*

as·sig·na·tion (as'ig nā'shən) *n.* 1. an assigning 2. anything assigned 3. an appointment to meet, esp. one made secretly by lovers; rendezvous

as·sign·ee (ə sī'nē') *n. Law* a person to whom a claim, property, etc. is transferred

as·sign·ment (ə sīn'mənt) *n.* 1. an assigning or being assigned 2. anything assigned, as a task, etc. 3. *Law a)* a transfer of a claim, property, etc. *b)* a deed, etc. authorizing this

as·sim·i·late (ə sim'ə lāt') *vt.* -lat'ed, -lat'ing [< L. pp. of *assimilare* < *ad-*, to + *similare*, make similar to < *similis*, like] 1. to absorb (food) into the body 2. to absorb and incorporate into one's thinking 3. to absorb (groups of different cultures) into the main culture 4. to make like or alike (with *to*) —*vi.* to become assimilated —**as·sim'·i·la·bil'i·ty** *n.* —**as·sim'i·la·ble** *adj.* —**as·sim'i·la'tor** *n.*

as·sim·i·la·tion (ə sim'ə lā'shən) *n.* 1. an assimilating or being assimilated; specif., *a)* the absorption of a minority group into the main culture *b) Phonet.* the process by which a sound tends to become like a neighbouring sound [the *p* in *cupboard* has been lost by assimilation to *b*] *c) Physiol.* the change of digested food into the protoplasm of an animal; also, the absorption of nutritive elements by plants

as·sim·i·la·tive (ə sim'ə lāt'iv, -lət-) *adj.* of or causing assimilation; assimilating: also **as·sim·i·la·to·ry** (ə sim''l-ə tər ē)

as·sist (ə sist') *vt.* [< OFr. < L. *assistere* < *ad-*, to + *sistere*, to make stand < *stare*, to stand] 1. to give help to; aid 2. to work as an assistant to —*vi.* to give help; aid —**assist at** to be present at; attend

as·sis·tance (ə sis'təns) *n.* the act of assisting or the help given; aid

as·sis·tant (-tənt) *adj.* assisting; helping —*n.* 1. a person who assists another or serves in a lower position; helper 2. a thing that aids 3. *same as* SHOP ASSISTANT

as·size (ə sīz') *n.* [< OFr. < L. *assidere:* see ASSESS] 1. [*pl.*] formerly, *a)* court sessions held periodically in each county of England and Wales to try civil and criminal cases *b)* the time or place of these 2. [Archaic] *a)* a law regulating standards of weight, price, measure, etc. for goods to be sold *b)* these standards as formerly prescribed

assn. association

assoc. 1. associate 2. associated 3. association

as·so·ci·ate (ə sō'shē āt', -sē-; *for n. &adj., usually* -it) *vt.* -at'ed, -at'ing [< L. pp. of *associare* < *ad-*, to + *sociare*, to join < *socius*, companion] 1. to join together; connect; combine 2. to bring into relationship as companion, partner, friend, etc. 3. to connect in the mind [to *associate* rain with grief] —*vi.* 1. to join (*with*) as a companion, partner, friend, etc. 2. to join together; unite —*n.* 1. a friend, partner, fellow worker, etc. 2. a member of less than full status, as of a society 3. anything joined with another thing or things —*adj.* 1. joined with others, as in some work 2. of less than full status

as·so·ci·a·tion (ə sō'shē ā'shən, -sē-) *n.* 1. the act of associating 2. companionship; fellowship; partnership 3. an organization of persons having the same interests, purposes, etc.; society 4. a connection in the mind between ideas, feelings, etc. 5. *Chem.* the joining of molecules of the same or different substances into a larger aggregate 6. *Ecol.* a group of similar plants that grow in a uniform environment —**as·so'ci·a'tion·al** *adj.*

association football a game in which two teams of eleven players try to kick or propel a ball into their opponents' goal, only the goalkeepers being allowed to touch the ball with their hands

as·so·ci·a·tive (ə sō'shē āt'iv, -sē-; -shə tiv) *adj.* 1. of, characterized by, or causing association 2. *Math.* of an operation, as multiplication of three numbers, in which the result is the same regardless of the way the elements are grouped

as·so·nance (as'ə nəns) *n.* [Fr. < L. prp. of *assonare* < *ad-*, to + *sonare*, to sound] 1. likeness of sound, as in a series of words or syllables 2. a partial rhyme in which the stressed vowel sounds are alike but the consonant sounds are unlike, as in *late* and *make* —**as'so·nant** *adj., n.*

as·sort (ə sôrt') *vt.* [< OFr. < *a-* (L. *ad*), to + *sorte*, SORT] 1. to separate into classes according to sorts or kinds; classify 2. to supply with an assortment of goods —*vi.* to match or harmonize (*with*) —**as·sort'a·tive** *adj.* —**as·sort'·er** *n.*

as·sort·ed (-id) *adj.* 1. of different sorts; miscellaneous 2. sorted into groups according to kind 3. matched [a poorly *assorted* pair]

as·sort·ment (-mənt) *n.* 1. an assorting or being assorted; classification 2. an assorted, or miscellaneous, group or collection; variety

ASSR, A.S.S.R. Autonomous Soviet Socialist Republic

asst. assistant

as·suage (ə swāj') *vt.* -suaged', -suag'ing [< OFr. < L. *ad*, to + *suavis*, sweet] 1. to lessen (pain, distress, etc.); allay 2. to calm (passion, anger, etc.); pacify 3. to satisfy or slake (thirst, etc.) —**as·suage'ment** *n.* —**as·suag'er** *n.*

as·sume (ə syōōm') *vt.* -sumed', -sum'ing [< L. *assumere*, to claim < *ad-*, to + *sumere*, to take] 1. to take on or put on (the appearance, form, role, etc. of) 2. to seize; usurp [to *assume* control] 3. to take upon oneself; undertake 4. to take for granted; suppose 5. to pretend to have; feign —**as·sum'a·ble** *adj.* —**as·sum'a·bly** *adv.* —**as·sum'ed·ly** *adv.* —**as·sum'er** *n.*

as·sum·ing (ə syōō'miŋ) *adj.* taking too much for granted; presumptuous

as·sump·tion (ə sump'shən) *n.* 1. the act of assuming 2. anything taken for granted; supposition 3. presumption; impudence 4. [A-] *R.C.Ch. a)* the taking up of the body and soul of the Virgin Mary into heaven after her death *b)* a church festival on August 15 celebrating this —**as·sump'tive** *adj.*

as·sur·ance (ə shoor'əns) *n.* 1. the act of assuring 2. a being assured; sureness; confidence 3. something that inspires confidence, as a promise, positive statement, etc.; guarantee 4. self-confidence 5. impudent forwardness; presumption 6. insurance, esp. providing for events that are certain to occur, as death

as·sure (ə shoor') *vt.* -sured', -sur'ing [< OFr. < ML. *assecurare* < L. *ad*, to + *securus*, SECURE] 1. to make (a person) sure of something; convince 2. to give confidence to 3. to declare to or promise confidently 4. to make (a doubtful thing) certain; guarantee 5. to insure against loss, esp. of life —**as·sur'er** *n.*

as·sured (ə shoord') *adj.* 1. made sure; certain 2. confident 3. insured —*n.* 1. the person to whom a life insurance policy is payable 2. the person whose life is insured —**as·sur·ed·ly** (ə shoor'id lē) *adv.* —**as·sur'ed·ness** *n.*

As·syr·i·an (ə sir′ē ən) *adj.* of Assyria, its people, language, etc. —*n.* **1.** a native or inhabitant of Assyria **2.** the Semitic language of the Assyrians

a·stat·ic (ā stat′ik) *adj.* [Gr. *astatos*, unstable] **1.** unstable **2.** *Physics* not taking a definite position or direction [an *astatic* needle is not affected by the earth's magnetism]

as·ta·tine (as′tə tēn) *n.* [< Gr. *astatos*, unstable + -INE⁴] a radioactive chemical element formed from bismuth bombarded by alpha particles: symbol, At; at. wt., 210 (?); at. no., 85

as·ter (as′tər) *n.* [L. < Gr. *astēr*, star] a plant of the composite family, with purplish, pink, or white daisylike flowers

-as·ter (as′tər) [L. dim. suffix] *a suffix meaning* inferior or worthless [*poetaster*]

as·ter·isk (as′tər isk) *n.* [< LL. < Gr. dim. of *astēr*, a star] a starlike sign (*) used in printing to indicate footnote references, omissions, etc. —*vt.* to mark with this sign

as·ter·ism (as′tər iz'm) *n.* [< Gr. < *astēr*, star] *Astron.* a group or cluster of stars

a·stern (ə sturn′) *adv.* **1.** behind a ship or aircraft **2.** at or towards the back of a ship or aircraft **3.** backwards; in a reverse direction

as·ter·oid (as′tə roid′) *adj.* [< Gr. < *astēr*, star + -OID] like a star or starfish —*n.* **1.** any of the many small planets with orbits between those of Mars and Jupiter; planetoid **2.** a starfish

as·the·ni·a (as thēn′ē ə) *n.* [ML. < Gr. < *a-*, without + *sthenos*, strength] bodily weakness —**as·then′ic** (-then′ik) *adj.*

asth·ma (as′mə) *n.* [Gr.] a chronic disorder characterized by wheezing, coughing, difficulty in breathing, and a suffocating feeling

asth·mat·ic (as mat′ik) *adj.* of or having asthma: also **asth·mat′i·cal** —*n.* a person who has asthma —**asth·mat′i·cal·ly** *adv.*

as·tig·mat·ic (as′tig mat′ik) *adj.* **1.** of or having astigmatism **2.** correcting astigmatism **3.** having a distorted view or judgment —**as′tig·mat′i·cal·ly** *adv.*

a·stig·ma·tism (ə stig′mə tiz'm) *n.* [< Gr. *a-*, without + *stigma*, a mark + -ISM] **1.** an irregularity in the curvature of a lens, esp. of the eye, so that light rays do not meet in a single focal point and images are distorted **2.** a distorted view or judgment, as because of prejudice

a·stir (ə stur′) *adv., adj.* **1.** in motion; in excited activity **2.** out of bed

A.S.T.M.S. Association of Scientific, Technical and Managerial Staff

as·ton·ish (ə ston′ish) *vt.* [< OFr. < L. < *ex-*, emphatic + *tonare*, to thunder] to fill with sudden wonder or great surprise; amaze —**as·ton′ish·ing** *adj.* —**as·ton′ish·ing·ly** *adv.*

as·ton·ish·ment (-mənt) *n.* **1.** a being astonished; great amazement **2.** anything that astonishes

as·tound (ə stound′) *vt.* [< ME. pp. of *astonien*, ASTONISH] to astonish greatly; amaze —**as·tound′ing** *adj.* —**as·tound′ing·ly** *adv.*

a·strad·dle (ə strad′'l) *adv.* in a straddling position

as·tra·gal (as′trə g'l) *n.* [L. *astragalus* < Gr. *astragalos*, anklebone, vertebra, moulding] **1.** *Anat.* same as ASTRAGALUS **2.** *Archit.* a small, convex moulding

as·trag·a·lus (ə strag′ə ləs) *n.,* pl. **-li′** (-lī′) [L., ASTRAGAL] **1.** a member of a genus of leguminous plants **2.** *Anat.* older term for the anklebone **3.** *Archit.* same as ASTRAGAL

as·tra·khan (as′trə kan′) *n.* **1.** a loosely curled fur from the pelt of very young lambs orig. bred near Astrakhan **2.** a wool fabric made to look like this Also sp. **as′tra·chan′**

as·tral (as′trəl) *adj.* [< L. < Gr. *astron*, star = *astēr*, star] **1.** of, from, or like the stars **2.** *Theosophy* of a substance supposedly existing at a level just beyond normal human perception

a·stray (ə strā′) *adv.* **1.** off the right path **2.** so as to be in error

a·stride (ə strīd′) *adv.* **1.** with a leg on either side; astraddle **2.** with legs far apart —*prep.* **1.** with a leg on either side of (a horse, etc.) **2.** extending over or across

as·trin·gent (ə strin′jənt) *adj.* [< L. prp. of *astringere*, to contract < *ad-*, to + *stringere*, to draw] **1.** that contracts body tissues and checks secretions, capillary bleeding, etc. **2.** *a)* having a harsh, biting quality *b)* severe; stern; austere —*n.* an astringent substance —**as·trin′gen·cy** *n.* —**as·trin′gent·ly** *adv.*

as·tro- [< Gr. *astron*: see ASTRAL] *a combining form meaning* of a star or stars [*astrophysics*]

as·tro·dome (as′trə dōm′) *n.* a transparent dome on top of an aircraft fuselage for the navigator

astrol. **1.** astrologer **2.** astrology

as·tro·labe (as′trə lāb′) *n.* [< OFr. < ML. < Gr. < *astron*, a star + *lambanein*, to take] an instrument once used to find the altitude of stars, etc.

as·trol·o·gy (ə strol′ə jē) *n.* [< L. & Gr. *astron*, star + -*logia*, -LOGY] **1.** orig., primitive astronomy **2.** a study based on the belief that the positions of the moon, sun, and planets affect human affairs and that one can foretell the future by studying the planets, etc. —**as·trol′o·ger** *n.* —**as·tro·log·i·cal** (as′trə loj′i k'l) *adj.* —**as′tro·log′i·cal·ly** *adv.*

astron. **1.** astronomer **2.** astronomy

as·tro·naut (as′trə nôt′) *n.* [< Fr.: see ff.] a person trained to make rocket flights in outer space

as·tro·nau·tics (as′trə nôt′iks) *n.pl.* [with sing. v.: see ASTRO- & AERONAUTICS] the science that deals with spacecraft and with travel in outer space —**as′tro·nau′ti·cal** *adj.*

as·tro·nom·i·cal (as′trə nom′i k'l) *adj.* **1.** of or having to do with astronomy **2.** extremely large, as the numbers or quantities used in astronomy Also **as′tro·nom′ic** —**as′tro·nom′i·cal·ly** *adv.*

astronomical unit a unit of length equal to the mean radius of the earth's orbit (c. 150 million km) used in measuring distances in astronomy

as·tron·o·my (ə stron′ə mē) *n.* [< ME. & OFr. < L. < Gr. < *astron*, star + *nomos*, system of laws < *nemein*, to arrange] the science of the stars, planets, and all other heavenly bodies, dealing with their composition, motion, relative position, size, etc. —**as·tron′o·mer** *n.*

as·tro·phys·ics (as′trō fiz′iks) *n.pl.* [with sing. v.] the science of the physical properties and phenomena of the stars, planets, etc. —**as′tro·phys′i·cal** *adj.* —**as′tro·phys′i·cist** (-ə sist) *n.*

as·tute (ə styoot′) *adj.* [< L. < *astus*, craft, cunning] having or showing a clever or shrewd mind; keen —**as·tute′ly** *adv.* —**as·tute′ness** *n.*

a·sun·der (ə sun′dər) *adv.* [see SUNDER] **1.** into parts or pieces **2.** apart or separate

a·sy·lum (ə sī′ləm) *n.* [L. < Gr. *asylon*, asylum < *a-*, without + *sylē*, right of seizure] **1.** formerly, a sanctuary, as a temple, where criminals, etc. were safe from arrest **2.** any refuge **3.** the protection given by one country to refugees from another; also **political asylum** **4.** [Obs.] a place for the care of the mentally ill, or of the aged, poor, etc.

a·sym·me·try (ā sim′ə trē, ə sim′-) *n.* lack of symmetry —**a·sym·met·ri·cal** (ā′sə met′ri k'l), **a′sym·met′ric** *adj.* —**a′sym·met′ri·cal·ly** *adv.*

as·ymp·tote (as′im tōt′) *n.* [ModL. < Gr. < *a-*, not + *syn-*, together + *piptein*, to fall] a straight line always approaching but never meeting a curve —**as′ymp·tot′ic** (-tot′ik), **as′ymp·tot′i·cal** *adj.*

ASYMPTOTE
(A, asymptote of curve C)

at¹ (at; *unstressed* ət) *prep.* [OE. *æt*] **1.** on; in; near; by [at the office] **2.** to or towards [look at her] **3.** through [enter at the gate] **4.** from [get the facts at their source] **5.** attending [at the party] **6.** occupied in; busy with [at work] **7.** in a state of [at war] **8.** in the manner of [at a trot] **9.** because of [terrified at the sight] **10.** according to [at his discretion] **11.** with reference to [good at tennis] **12.** in the amount, degree, price, etc. of [at five pounds each] **13.** from an interval of [visible at fifty metres] **14.** on or close to the time or age of [at five o'clock] **15.** during the period of [to happen at night]

at² (ät, at) *n.,* pl. **at** see MONETARY UNITS, table (Laos)

At *Chem.* astatine

at. **1.** atmosphere **2.** atomic

At·a·brine (at′ə brin, -brēn′) [G. *Atebrin*] a trademark for a synthetic drug used in treating malaria and other diseases —*n.* [a-] this drug

at·a·rac·tic (at′ə rak′tik) *n.* [< Gr. < *ataraxia*, calmness < *a-*, not + *tarassein*, to disturb] a tranquillizing drug —*adj.* of tranquillizing drugs or their effects Also **at′a·rax′ic** (-rak′sik)

at·a·rax·i·a (at′ə rak′sē ə) *n.* [Gr. < *a-*, not + *tarassein*, to disturb] calmness of the mind and emotions; also **at′a·rax′y** (-rak′se)

at·a·vism (at′ə viz'm) *n.* [< Fr. < L. *atavus*, ancestor < *at-*, beyond + *avus*, grandfather] **1.** the appearance in an individual of a characteristic found in an early ancestor but not in more recent ones **2.** reversion to a former type —**at′a·vis′tic** *adj.* —**at′a·vis′ti·cal·ly** *adv.*

a·tax·i·a (ə tak′sē ə) *n.* [Gr., disorder < *a-*, not + *tassein*, to arrange] inability to coordinate voluntary muscular movements —**a·tax′ic** *adj., n.*

A.T.C. **1.** Air Traffic Control **2.** Air Training Corps

ate (et, āt) *pt. of* EAT

-ate¹ (āt for 1; āt for 2 & 3) [< L. *-atus*, pp. ending] **1.** a suffix meaning: a) to become [maturate] b) to cause to become [sublimate] c) to produce [salivate] d) to provide or treat with [vaccinate] e) to put in the form of [triangulate] f) to arrange for [orchestrate] g) to combine or treat with [oxygenate] **2.** a suffix meaning: a) of or characteristic of [roseate] b) having or filled with [*passionate*] c) *Biol.* having or characterized by [*spatulate*] **3.** *a suffix roughly equivalent to the past participial ending -ed* [*animate* (*animated*)]

-ate² (āt, it) [L. *-atus*, a noun ending] *a suffix denoting:* **1.** a function, agent, or official [*directorate, potentate*] **2.** [L. *-atum*, neut. of *-atus*] *Chem.* a salt made from (an acid with a name ending in *-ic*) [*acetate, nitrate*]

at·el·ier (at′əl yā′; a tel′yā, -ē ā) *n.* [Fr., ult. < L. *assula*, dim. of *assis*, board] a studio or workshop

a tem·po (ä tem′pō) [It.] *Music* in time: a direction to return to the original tempo

Ath·a·na·sian (ath′ə nā′zhən) *adj.* **1.** of Athanasius (296?-373 A.D.), Alexandrian bishop who opposed Arianism **2.** of the creed formerly attributed to him

Ath·a·pas·can, Ath·a·pas·kan (ath′ə pas′kən) *adj.* [< Cree *athap-askaw*, lit., grass here and there] designating or of the most widely scattered linguistic family of N. American Indians, including the Navahos and Apaches —*n.* an Athapascan Indian or language Also **Ath′a·bas′can, Ath′-a·bas′kan** (-bas′-)

a·the·ism (ā′thē iz′m) *n.* [< Fr. < Gr. < *a-*, without + *theos*, god] the belief that there is no God —**a′the·ist** (-ist) *n.* —**a′the·is′tic, a′the·is′ti·cal** *adj.*

ath·e·nae·um (ath′ə nē′əm) *n.* [after the temple of Athena at Athens, where writers and scholars met] **1.** an institution for the promotion of learning, as a literary or scientific society **2.** a building containing a reading room or library, esp. one used by such an institution

ath·er·o·scle·ro·sis (ath′ər ō sklə rō′sis) *n.* [ModL. < Gr. *athērōma*, tumour filled with grainy matter + SCLEROSIS] a thickening, and loss of elasticity, of the walls of arteries, with the formation of fatty nodules —**ath′er·o·scle·rot′ic** (-rot′ik) *adj.*

a·thirst (ə thurst′) *adj.* **1.** thirsty **2.** eager; longing [*athirst for knowledge*]

ath·lete (ath′lēt′) *n.* [< L. < Gr. < *athlein*, to contest for a prize < *athlon*, a prize] a person trained in exercises, games, or contests requiring physical strength, skill, speed, etc.

athlete's foot a common fungous infection of the skin of the feet; ringworm of the feet

ath·let·ic (āth let′ik) *adj.* **1.** of, like, or proper to athletes or athletics **2.** physically strong, skilful, muscular, etc. —**ath·let′i·cal·ly** *adv.*

ath·let·i·cism (-ə siz′m) *n.* **1.** addiction to athletics **2.** an athletic quality

ath·let·ics (-iks) *n.pl.* [*sometimes with sing. v.*] the practice of, or contests in, track and field events

at-home (ət hōm′) *n.* an informal reception at one's home, usually in the afternoon

a·thwart (ə thwôrt′) *prep.* **1.** from one side to the other of; across **2.** in opposition to; against **3.** *Naut.* across the course or length of —*adv.* **1.** crosswise **2.** so as to block or thwart

-at·ic (at′ik) [< Fr. or L. < Gr. *-atikos*] *a suffix meaning* of, of the kind of [*lymphatic, chromatic*]

a·tilt (ə tilt′) *adj., adv.* tilted

a·tin·gle (ə tiŋ′g'l) *adj.* tingling; excited

-a·tion (ā′shən) [< Fr. or L.] *a suffix meaning:* **1.** the act of [*alteration*] **2.** the condition of being [*gratification*] **3.** the result of [*compilation*]

-a·tive (ə tiv, āt′iv) [< Fr. or L.] *a suffix meaning* of or relating to, serving to, tending to [*demonstrative, informative, talkative*]

At·lan·te·an (at′lan tē′ən; ət lan′tē ən, at-) *adj.* **1.** of or like Atlas, in Gr. myth. a Titan forced to hold the heavens on his shoulders; strong **2.** of Atlantis

at·lan·tes (ət lan′tēz) *n.pl., sing.* **at·las** (at′ləs) [L. < Gr. pl. of *Atlas*: see ATLAS] supporting columns in the form of standing or kneeling figures of men

At·lan·tic (ət lan′tik, at-) *adj.* [< L. *Atlanticum* (*mare*), Atlantic (Ocean)] of, in, on, or near the ocean touching Europe and Africa to the east and the American continents to the West

At·lan·tis (ət lan′tis, at-) legendary island or continent west of Gibraltar, supposed to have sunk in the Atlantic

at·las (at′ləs) *n.* [L. < Gr.: after *Atlas*, in Gr. myth. a Titan forced to hold the heavens on his shoulders] **1.** a book of maps **2.** a book of tables, charts, etc. on a specific subject **3.** *Anat.* the topmost vertebra of the neck

atm. **1.** atmosphere **2.** atmospheric

at·man (ät′mən) *n.* [Sans., breath, soul] *Hinduism* **1.** the individual soul or ego **2.** [A-] the universal soul; source of all individual souls

at·mos·phere (at′məs fir′) *n.* [< ModL. < Gr. *atmos*, vapour + *sphaira*, sphere] **1.** all the air surrounding the earth, consisting of oxygen, nitrogen, and other gases **2.** the gaseous mass surrounding any star, etc. **3.** the air in any given place **4.** the general feeling or spirit of a place; mood **5.** [Colloq.] an interesting effect produced by

decoration, etc. **6.** *Physics* a unit of pressure equal to 101 325 pascals

at·mos·pher·ic (at′məs fer′ik) *adj.* **1.** of or in the atmosphere **2.** caused or produced by the atmosphere **3.** creating an atmosphere, or mood Also **at′mos·pher′i·cal** —**at′mos·pher′i·cal·ly** *adv.*

at·mos·pher·ics (-iks) *n.pl.* *same as* STATIC (*n.* 1)

at. no. atomic number

at·oll (a′tol) *n.* [< Maldive Is. term] a ring-shaped coral island nearly or completely surrounding a lagoon

ATOLL

at·om (at′əm) *n.* [< OFr. < L. < Gr. *atomos*, uncut < *a-*, not + *temnein*, to cut] **1.** orig., any of the tiny particles that ancient philosophers imagined as the basic component of all matter **2.** a tiny particle; jot **3.** *Chem. & Physics* any of the smallest particles of an element that combine with similar particles of other elements to produce compounds: atoms consist of electrons revolving about a positively charged nucleus —**the atom** *same as* ATOMIC ENERGY

atom bomb *same as* ATOMIC BOMB —**at′om-bomb′** *vt.*

a·tom·ic (ə tom′ik) *adj.* **1.** of an atom or atoms; esp. in an uncombined form **2.** of or using atomic energy or atomic bombs —**a·tom′i·cal·ly** *adv.*

atomic bomb an extremely destructive type of bomb, the power of which comes from the very great quantity of energy that is suddenly released when a chain reaction of nuclear fission is set off

atomic clock a highly accurate clock regulated by the unvarying vibrational frequency of the atoms or molecules of certain substances

atomic energy the energy released from an atom in nuclear fission or nuclear fusion, or by radioactive decay

at·o·mic·i·ty (at′ə mis′ə tē) *n.* **1.** the state of being made up of atoms **2.** *Chem.* a) the number of atoms in a molecule b) *same as* VALENCE

atomic mass unit a unit of mass, exactly one twelfth of the mass of an atom of the most common isotope of carbon

atomic number *Chem.* a number representing the relative position of an element in the periodic table; number representing the number of protons in the nucleus of the atom of an element

atomic pile *early name for* NUCLEAR REACTOR

atomic theory the theory that all material objects and substances are composed of atoms, and that various phenomena are explained by the properties and interactions of these atoms

atomic weight *Chem.* a number representing the weight of one atom of an element as compared with an arbitrary number representing the weight of one atom of another element taken as the standard (now usually carbon at 12)

at·om·ize (at′ə mīz′) *vt.* **-ized′, -iz′ing** **1.** to separate into atoms **2.** to reduce (a liquid) to a fine spray **3.** to separate into fragments **4.** [Chiefly U.S.] to destroy by atomic weapons —**at′om·i·za′tion** *n.*

at·om·iz·er (-mī′zər) *n.* a device used to shoot out a fine spray, as of medicine or perfume

atom smasher *same as* ACCELERATOR (sense 3)

a·ton·al (ā tōn′'l) *adj.* having atonality —**a·ton′al·ism** *n.* —**a·ton′al·ist** *n.* —**a·ton·al·is′tic** *adj.* —**a·ton′al·ly** *adv.*

a·to·nal·i·ty (ā′tō nal′ə tē) *n.* *Music* lack of tonality through intentional disregard of key; also, use of chromatic tones without relation to a central keynote

a·tone (ə tōn′) *vi.* **a·toned′, a·ton′ing** to make amends (*for wrongdoing*, etc.) —**a·ton′er** *n.*

a·tone·ment (-mənt) *n.* [ME. *at-onement*, in harmony] **1.** an atoning **2.** satisfaction given for wrongdoing, etc.; expiation **3.** [A-] *Theol.* the reconciliation of God to man by means of Jesus' sufferings and death

a·ton·ic (ā ton′ik, ə-) *adj.* [< Gr. *atonia* < *a-*, not + *tonos*, tone] **1.** lacking bodily tone or muscle tone **2.** unaccented: said of a word or syllable —*n.* an unaccented syllable or word

a·top (ə top′) *adv.* on the top; at the top —*prep.* on the top of

-a·to·ry (ə tər ē) [< L. *-atorius*] *a suffix meaning* of, characterized by, produced by [*accusatory*]

ATP [A(DENOSINE) t(ri)p(hosphate)] a vital substance found in all living cells: it is the immediate source of muscular energy

at·ra·bil·ious (a′trə bil′yəs) *adj.* [< L. *atra bilis*, black bile: cf. MELANCHOLY] melancholy, morose, cross, etc.: also **at′-ra·bil′iar** (-yər)

a·tri·um (ā′trē əm) *n.*, *pl.* **a′tri·a** (-ə), **a′tri·ums** [L.] **1.** the main room of an ancient Roman house **2.** a hall or entrance court **3.** *Anat.* a chamber or cavity, esp. either of the upper chambers of the heart —**a′tri·al** (-əl) *adj.*

a·tro·cious (ə trō′shəs) *adj.* [< L. *atrox* (gen. *atrocis*), fierce < *ater*, black + -OUS] **1.** very cruel, evil, etc. **2.** appalling or dismaying **3.** [Colloq.] very bad, offensive, inferior, etc. —**a·tro′cious·ly** *adv.* —**a·tro′cious·ness** *n.*

a·troc·i·ty (ə tros′ə tē) *n., pl.* **-ties** **1.** atrocious behaviour; brutality, etc. **2.** an atrocious act **3.** [Colloq.] a very offensive thing

at·ro·phy (at′rə fē) *n.* [< Fr. < L. < Gr. < *a*-, not + *trephein*, to nourish] a wasting away, or the failure to grow, of an organ, etc., because of insufficient nutrition —*vi.* **-phied, -phy·ing** to waste away or fail to develop —*vt.* to cause atrophy in —**a·troph·ic** (ə trof′ik) *adj.*

at·ro·pine (at′rə pēn′, -pin) *n.* [< ModL. < Gr. *Atropos*, name of that one of the three Fates who cuts the thread of life, + -INE⁴] a poisonous, crystalline alkaloid obtained from belladonna and similar plants, used to relieve spasms or to dilate the pupil of the eye: also **at′ro·pin** (-pin)

att. **1.** attention **2.** attorney

at·tach (ə tach′) *vt.* [< OFr. < *estachier*, to fasten] **1.** to fasten by tying, etc. **2.** to join (often used reflexively) [he *attached* himself to us] **3.** to connect by ties of affection, etc. **4.** to affix (a signature, etc.) **5.** to ascribe **6.** to appoint by order **7.** *Law* to take (property or a person) into custody by writ **8.** *Mil.* to join (troops, etc.) temporarily to another unit —*vi.* to be joined; belong —**at·tach′a·ble** *adj.*

at·ta·ché (ə tash′ā; *Fr.* à tà shā′) *n.* [Fr., pp. of *attacher*, ATTACH] a person with special duties on the staff of an ambassador or minister

attaché case a flat, rectangular case for carrying documents, papers, etc.

at·tach·ment (ə tach′mənt) *n.* **1.** the act of attaching something **2.** anything that attaches; fastening **3.** devotion **4.** anything attached **5.** an accessory for an electrical appliance, etc. **6.** *Law* a taking of a person, property, etc. into custody, or a writ for this

at·tack (ə tak′) *vt.* [< Fr. < It. < OFr. *atachier*] **1.** to use force against in order to harm **2.** to speak or write against **3.** to begin working on energetically **4.** to begin acting upon harmfully —*vi.* to make an assault —*n.* **1.** an attacking; onslaught **2.** an onset or recurrence of a disease **3.** a beginning of a task, undertaking, etc. **4.** *Music* promptness and precision in beginning a passage —**at·tack′er** *n.*

at·tain (ə tān′) *vt.* [< OFr. < L. *attingere* < *ad*-, to + *tangere*, to touch] **1.** to gain through effort; achieve **2.** to reach or come to; arrive at —*vi.* to succeed in reaching or coming (*to* a goal) —**at·tain′a·bil′i·ty, at·tain′a·ble·ness** *n.* —**at·tain′a·ble** *adj.*

at·tain·der (ə tān′dər) *n.* [OFr. *ataindre*, to attain] the loss of a person's civil rights and property because he has been sentenced to death or outlawed: see BILL OF ATTAINDER

at·tain·ment (ə tān′mənt) *n.* **1.** an attaining or being attained **2.** anything attained, as a skill

at·taint (ə tānt′) *vt.* to punish by attainder —*n.* an attainder

at·tar (at′ər) *n.* [< Per. < Ar. 'itr, perfume] a perfume made from the petals of flowers, esp. of damask roses (**attar of roses**)

at·tempt (ə tempt′) *vt.* [< OFr. < L. *attemptare* < *ad*-, to + *temptare*, to try] to try to do, get, etc.; endeavour —*n.* **1.** a try; endeavour **2.** an attack, as on a person's life —**attempt the life of** to try to kill —**at·tempt′a·ble** *adj.*

at·tend (ə tend′) *vt.* [< OFr. < L. *attendere*, to give heed to < *ad*-, to + *tendere*, to stretch] **1.** [Now Rare] to take care or charge of **2.** *a)* to wait on; serve *b)* to serve as doctor to during an illness **3.** to go with **4.** to accompany as a result [success *attended* his efforts] **5.** to be present at —*vi.* **1.** to pay attention **2.** to wait (*on* or *upon*) **3.** to devote oneself (*to*) **4.** to give the required care or attention (*to*)

at·tend·ance (ə ten′dəns) *n.* **1.** an attending **2.** the number of persons attending **3.** the degree of regularity in attending

attendance officer an official dealing with school children who play truant

at·tend·ant (-dənt) *adj.* **1.** attending or serving **2.** being present **3.** accompanying [*attendant* difficulties] —*n.* **1.** one who attends or serves **2.** a person present **3.** an accompanying thing

at·ten·tion (ə ten′shən) *n.* **1.** *a)* the act of keeping one's mind closely on something; concentration *b)* readiness for concentration **2.** notice **3.** care or consideration **4.** *a)* thoughtful consideration for others *b)* an act of consideration, courtesy, etc.: *usually used in pl.* **5.** *Mil. a)* the erect, motionless posture of soldiers in readiness for a command *b)* a command to assume this posture

at·ten·tive (ə ten′tiv) *adj.* **1.** paying attention **2.** courteous, devoted, etc. —**at·ten′tive·ly** *adv.* —**at·ten′tive·ness** *n.*

at·ten·u·ate (ə ten′yoo wāt′) *vt.* **-at′ed, -at′ing** [< L. pp. of

attenuare < *ad*-, to + *tenuare* < *tenuis*, thin] **1.** to make slender or thin **2.** to dilute; rarefy **3.** to lessen or weaken —*vi.* to become thin, weak, etc. —**at·ten′u·a·ble** *adj.* —**at·ten′u·a′tion** *n.*

at·test (ə test′) *vt.* [< Fr. < L. *attestari* < *ad*-, to + *testari*, to bear witness < *testis*, a witness] **1.** to declare to be true or genuine **2.** to certify, as by oath **3.** to serve as proof of —*vi.* to bear witness; testify (*to*) —**at·tes·ta·tion** (at′- es tā′shən) *n.* —**at·test′er, at·tes′tor** *n.*

at·test·ed (-əd) certified to be free of a disease, esp. tuberculosis; said of cattle, etc.

At·tic (at′ik) *adj.* **1.** of Attica **2.** Athenian **3.** classical in a simple, restrained way [an *Attic* style] —*n.* **1.** the Greek dialect of Attica, the literary language of ancient Greece **2.** an Athenian

at·tic (at′ik) *n.* [< Fr. < prec.] **1.** a low wall or storey above the cornice of a classical façade **2.** the room or space just below the roof of a house; garret

At·ti·cism (at′ə siz′m) *n.* [*also* a-] **1.** an Attic idiom, style, custom, etc. **2.** an elegant, simple phrase —**At′- ti·cize′** (-sīz′) *vt., vi.* **-cized′, -ciz′ing**

Attic salt, Attic wit graceful, piercing wit

at·tire (ə tīr′) *vt.* **-tired′, -tir′ing** [< OFr. *atirier*, put in order < *a* (L. *ad*), to + *tire*, row, order] to dress, esp. in fine garments; clothe; array —*n.* clothes, esp. rich apparel; finery

at·ti·tude (at′ə tyood′) *n.* [Fr. < It. < LL. *aptitudo* < L. *aptus*, APT] **1.** the posture of the body in connection with an action, mood, etc. **2.** a way of acting, feeling, or thinking; one's disposition, outlook, etc. **3.** the position of an aircraft or spacecraft in relation to a given line or plane —**at′ti·tu′di·nal** *adj.*

at·ti·tu·di·nize (at′ə tyood′ən īz) *vi.* **-nized′, -niz′ing** to pose for effect

attn. attention

at·to- [< Dan. *atten*, eighteen] a combining form meaning one trillionth (10⁸) [*attosecond*]

at·tor·ney (ə tur′nē) *n., pl.* **-neys** [< OFr. < *a*- (L. *ad*), to + *torner*: see TURN] **1.** any person having the legal power to act for another **2.** [U.S.] a lawyer: also **attorney at law**

attorney general *pl.* **attorneys general, attorney generals** the chief law officer of a government

at·tract (ə trakt′) *vt.* [< L. pp. of *attrahere* < *ad*-, to + *trahere*, to draw] **1.** to draw to itself or oneself [a magnet *attracts* iron] **2.** to get the admiration, attention, etc. of; allure —*vi.* to be attractive —**at·tract′a·ble** *adj.* —**at·trac′- tor** *n.*

at·trac·tion (ə trak′shən) *n.* **1.** an attracting or the power of attracting; esp., charm or fascination **2.** anything that attracts **3.** *Physics* the mutual action by which bodies or particles of matter tend to draw together or cohere: opposed to REPULSION

at·trac·tive (-tiv) *adj.* that attracts or has the power to attract; esp., charming, pretty, etc. —**at·trac′tive·ly** *adv.* —**at·trac′tive·ness** *n.*

attrib. **1.** attribute **2.** attributive

at·trib·ute (ə trib′yoot; *for n.* ə trib′yoot′) *vt.* **-ut·ed, -ut·ing** [< L. pp. of *attribuere* < *ad*-, to + *tribuere*, to assign < *tribus*: see TRIBE] **1.** to think of as belonging to or coming from a particular person or thing; assign or ascribe (*to*) **2.** to ascribe as a characteristic or quality —*n.* **1.** a characteristic or quality of a person or thing **2.** an object used in the arts as a symbol for a person, office, etc. **3.** a word or phrase used as an adjective —**at·trib′ut·a·ble** *adj.* —**at′tri·bu′tion** *n.*

at·trib·u·tive (ə trib′yoo tiv) *adj.* **1.** attributing **2.** of or like an attribute **3.** *Gram.* joined directly to the substantive it modifies, esp., in English, coming just before it: said of an adjective —*n.* an attributive adjective, as *black* in *black cat* —**at·trib′u·tive·ly** *adv.*

at·tri·tion (ə trish′ən) *n.* [< L. < pp. of *atterere*, to wear < *ad*-, to + *terere*, to rub] **1.** a wearing away by friction **2.** any gradual wearing, or weakening, esp. to the point of exhaustion [war of *attrition*]

at·tune (ə tyoon′) *vt.* **-tuned′, -tun′ing** **1.** to tune **2.** to bring into harmony or agreement

A.T.V. Associated Television

at. wt. atomic weight

a·typ·i·cal (ā tip′i k′l) *adj.* not typical; not characteristic: also **a·typ′ic** —**a·typ′i·cal·ly** *adv.*

Au [L. *aurum*] *Chem.* gold

au·ber·gine (ō′bər zhēn′) *n.* [Fr. < Catalan *albergina* < Ar. *al-bādhinjān* < Per. *badindjan*] **1.** the fruit of the eggplant, used as a vegetable **2.** the colour of this vegetable, a dark purple

au·brie·tia (ô brē′shə) *n.* [ModL. < Claude *Aubriet*, 18th-c. Fr. painter of flowers and animals] any of a genus of plants with flowers in a range of pink and purple shades, often grown in rock gardens

au·burn (ô′bərn) *adj., n.* [< OFr. < L. *alburnus* < *albus*, white; meaning infl. by ME. *brun,* brown] reddish brown, esp. of hair

‡**au cou·rant** (ō kōō rän′) [Fr., lit., with the current] fully informed; up-to-date

auc·tion (ôk′shən, ok′-) *n.* [< L. < pp. of *augere,* to increase] 1. a public sale at which each item is sold to the highest bidder 2. *same as* AUCTION BRIDGE 3. the bidding in bridge —*vt.* to sell at auction

auction bridge a variety of the game of bridge in which the players bid for the right to say what suit shall be trumps or to declare no-trump

auc·tion·eer (ôk′shə nir′, ok′-) *n.* one whose work is selling things at auction —*vt.* to auction

auc·to·ri·al (ôk tôr′ē əl) *adj.* [< L. *auctor,* author] of or by an author

aud. 1. audit 2. auditor

au·da·cious (ô dā′shəs) *adj.* [< L. < *audax,* bold < *audere,* to dare] 1. bold or daring; fearless 2. rudely bold; brazen; insolent —**au·da′cious·ly** *adv.* —**au·da′cious·ness** *n.*

au·dac·i·ty (ô das′ə tē) *n.* 1. bold courage; daring 2. brazen boldness; insolence 3. *pl.* **-ties** an audacious act or remark

au·di·ble (ô′də b′l) *adj.* [< ML. < L. *audire,* to hear] loud enough to be heard —**au′di·bil′i·ty** *n.* —**au′di·bly** *adv.*

au·di·ence (ô′dē əns) *n.* [ME. & OFr. < L. *audientia,* a hearing < prp. of *audire,* to hear] 1. a group assembled to see and hear a play, concert, etc. 2. those who are tuned in to a certain radio or TV programme or who read a certain book 3. those who pay attention to what one writes or says 4. the act or state of hearing 5. a chance to be heard; hearing 6. a formal interview with one in high position

au·di·o (ô′dē ō) *adj.* [< L. *audire,* hear] 1. of frequencies corresponding to sound waves that are normally audible 2. of or relating to sound reproduction

au·di·o-fre·quen·cy (ô′dē ō frē′kwən sē) *adj.* of the band of audible sound frequencies or corresponding electric current frequencies, from about 20 to 20 000 hertz

au·di·ol·o·gy (ô′dē ol′ə jē) *n.* the science of hearing; esp., evaluation of hearing defects and rehabilitation of those who have such defects —**au′di·o·log′i·cal** (-ə loj′i k′l) *adj.* —**au′di·ol′o·gist** *n.*

au·di·om·e·ter (ô′dē om′ə tər) *n.* an instrument for measuring hearing

au·di·o·phile (ô′dē ə fīl′) *n.* a devotee of high-fidelity sound reproduction

au·di·o·typ·ist (ô′dē ō tī′pist) *n.* a typist trained to type from a dictating machine

au·di·o·vis·u·al (ô′dē ō vizh′ōō wəl) *adj.* involving both hearing and sight; used esp. of teaching aids

au·dit (ô′dit) *n.* [< L. pp. of *audire,* to hear] 1. a formal, often periodic examination and checking of accounts or financial records 2. a settlement or adjustment of accounts 3. an account thus examined and adjusted, or a statement of this —*vt., vi.* to examine and check (accounts, claims, etc.)

au·di·tion (ô dish′ən) *n.* 1. the act or sense of hearing 2. a hearing to test the ability or fitness of an actor, musician, etc. —*vt.* to give an audition to —*vi.* to perform in an audition

au·di·tor (ô′də tər) *n.* 1. a hearer or listener 2. a person who is authorized to audit accounts

au·di·to·ri·um (ô′də tôr′ē əm) *n.* 1. the area of a concert hall, theatre, etc. in which the audience sits 2. [U.S.] a room or hall for speeches, concerts, etc.

au·di·to·ry (ô′di tôr′ē) *adj.* of hearing or the sense of hearing —**au′di·to′ri·ly** *adv.*

A.U.E.W. Amalgamated Union of Engineering Workers

au fait (ō fā′) [Fr.] 1. acquainted with the facts; well-informed 2. proficient; expert

au fond (ō fôn′) [Fr.] at bottom; basically

‡**auf ′Wie·der·se·hen** (ouf vē′dər zā′ ən) [G.] till we see each other again; goodbye

Aug. August

Au·ge·an (ô jē′ən) *adj.* 1. *Gr. Myth.* of King Augeas or his large, filthy stable, which Hercules cleaned in one day 2. very filthy

au·ger (ô′gər) *n.* [by faulty separation of ME. *a nauger* < OE. *nafu,* nave (of a wheel) + *gar,* a spear] 1. a tool for boring holes in wood 2. a similar but larger tool, as for boring in the earth

aught (ôt) *n.* [OE. *awiht* < *a,* one + *wiht,* a creature, WIGHT] 1. anything whatever [for *aught* I know] 2. [< *a naught* (see NAUGHT), wrongly divided *an aught*] a zero —*adv.* [Archaic] to any degree

aug·ment (ôg ment′) *vt., vi.* [< OFr. < L. *augmentare* < *augere,* to increase] to make or become greater; increase —**aug·ment′a·ble** *adj.* —**aug·ment′er** *n.*

aug·men·ta·tion (ôg′men tā′shən) *n.* 1. an augmenting or being augmented 2. an addition; increase

aug·men·ta·tive (ôg men′tə tiv) *adj.* augmenting —*n.* an intensifying word or affix

au gra·tin (ō grat′ən) [Fr., lit., with scrapings] made with a lightly browned crust of bread crumbs and grated cheese

au·gur (ô′gər) *n.* [L., orig., a priest at rituals of fertility] 1. in ancient Rome, any of a group of officials who interpreted omens as favourable or unfavourable for an undertaking 2. a fortuneteller; soothsayer —*vt., vi.* 1. to foretell or prophesy 2. to be an omen (of) —**augur ill** (or **well**) to be a bad (or good) omen —**au′gur·al** (ô′gər al) *adj.*

au·gu·ry (ô′gyər ē) *n., pl.* **-ries** 1. the rite conducted by an augur 2. an omen; indication

Au·gust (ô′gəst) *n.* [L. < *Augustus* (Caesar)] the eighth month of the year, having 31 days: abbrev. **Aug.**

au·gust (ô gust′) *adj.* [L. *augustus,* orig., prob. "consecrated by the augurs"] 1. inspiring awe and reverence; imposing 2. worthy of respect; venerable —**au·gust′ly** *adv.* —**au·gust′ness** *n.*

Au·gus·tan (ô gus′tən) *adj.* 1. of or characteristic of Augustus Caesar, his reign (27 B.C.-14 A.D.), or the literary achievements of his times 2. of or like any similar literary period, esp. the first half of the 18th cent. in England; classical; elegant —*n.* a writer living in an Augustan age

Au·gus·tin·i·an (ô′gəs tin′ē ən) *adj.* 1. of Saint Augustine of Hippo or his doctrines 2. designating or of a religious order following the rule composed by him —*n.* 1. a follower of St. Augustine of Hippo 2. a member of an Augustinian religious order

auk (ôk) *n.* [dial. *alk* < ON. *alka*] any of a number of related diving birds of the northern seas, with webbed feet and short wings used as paddles

‡**au lait** (ō lā′) [Fr.] with milk

auld (ôld) *adj.* [Dial. & Scot.] old

auld lang syne (ôld′laŋ′zīn′, sīn′) [Scot., lit., old long since] old times; the good old days

aum·bry (ôrm′brē) *n. same as* AMBRY

‡**au na·tu·rel** (ō nä tü rel′) [Fr.] 1. in the natural state 2. naked 3. prepared simply

aunt (änt) *n.* [< ME. & OFr. < L. *amita,* paternal aunt] 1. a sister of one's mother or father 2. the wife of one's uncle 3. [Colloq.] a term used by children for an unrelated woman friend of the family

GREAT AUK
(to 75 cm high)

aunt·ie, aunt·y (än′tē) *n.* aunt: a familiar or affectionate form

Aunt Sally 1. a figure of an old woman used as a target in a fairground game 2. any person or thing that is a target for insults or criticism

‡**au pair** (ō per′) [Fr., lit., as an equal] designating an arrangement by which services are exchanged without money payment; used esp. of the system whereby a girl receives board and lodging with a family, usually in a foreign country, in return for household help —*n.* such a girl

au·ra (ôr′ə) *n., pl.* **-ras, -rae** (-ē) [L. < Gr., a breeze] 1. an invisible emanation 2. a particular atmosphere or quality that seems to arise from and surround a person or thing

au·ral (ôr′əl) *adj.* [< L. *auris,* ear + -AL] of or received through the ear or the sense of hearing —**au′ral·ly** *adv.*

au·re·ate (ôr′ē it) *adj.* [< LL. < L. *aureus* < *aurum,* gold] 1. golden; gilded 2. splendid or brilliant, often affectedly so

au·re·ole (ôr′ē ōl′) *n.* [< L. *aureola* (*corona*), golden (crown) < L. *aureus:* see AUREATE] 1. a halo 2. the sun's corona Also **au·re·o·la** (ô rē′ə lə)

au re·voir (ō′rə vwär′) [Fr.] until we meet again; goodbye

au·ric (ôr′ik) *adj.* [< L. *aurum,* gold] 1. of or containing gold 2. *Chem.* designating or of compounds in which the gold has a valence of three

au·ri·cle (ôr′ə k′l) *n.* [< L. *auricula,* dim. of *auris,* ear] 1. *Anat. a)* the external part of the ear; pinna *b)* an atrium of the heart 2. *Biol.* an earlike part or organ

au·ric·u·la (ô rik′yōō lə) *n., pl.* **-las, -lae** (-lē′) [see prec.] 1. a species of primrose with leaves shaped like a bear's ear 2. *same as* AURICLE

au·ric·u·lar (ô rik′yōō lər) *adj.* 1. of or near the ear, or having to do with the sense of hearing 2. spoken directly into the ear 3. ear-shaped 4. *Anat.* of an auricle —**au·ric′u·lar·ly** *adv.*

au·rif·er·ous (ô rif′ər əs) *adj.* [< L. < *aurum,* gold + *ferre,* to BEAR¹ + -OUS] bearing or yielding gold

au·ri·form (ôr′ə fôrm′) *adj.* ear-shaped

Au·rig·na·cian (ô′rig nā′shən) *adj.* [after *Aurignac,* village in S France, in whose caves artifacts were discovered] of a late paleolithic culture, characterized by bone artifacts and the appearance of primitive artistic designs

au·rochs (ô′roks) *n., pl.* **au′rochs** [G. *Auerochs* < OHG. *urohso* < *uro,* aurochs + *ohso,* ox] 1. the wild ox of Europe, now extinct 2. the nearly extinct European bison

au·ro·ra (ô rôr′ə, ə-) *n., pl.* **-ras, rae** (-ē) [L., lit., dawn] 1. the dawn 2. *same as* AURORA AUSTRALIS or AURORA BOREALIS —**au·ro′ral, au·ro′re·an** (-ē ən) *adj.*

aurora aus·tra·lis (ô strā′lis) [L.: see prec. & AUSTRAL] luminous bands of light like the aurora borealis, but in the Southern Hemisphere

aurora bo·re·a·lis (bôr'ē al'is) [L. < AURORA & *Boreas*, in Gr. myth. the god of the north wind] luminous bands or streamers of light sometimes appearing in the night sky of the Northern Hemisphere; northern lights

aus·cul·ta·tion (ôs'kəl tā'shən) *n.* [< pp. of L. *auscultare*, to listen] **1.** a listening **2.** a listening, often with a stethoscope, to sounds in the chest, abdomen, etc., as in diagnosis —**aus'cul·tate'** *vt., vi.* -**tat'ed, -tat'ing** —**aus'cul·ta'tor** *n.*

aus·pice (ôs'pis) *n., pl.* -**pi·ces'** (-pə sēz') [Fr. < L. *auspicium,* omen] **1.** an omen, esp. a favourable one **2.** [*pl.*] guiding sponsorship; patronage

aus·pi·cious (ôs pish'əs) *adj.* **1.** of good omen; favourable **2.** favoured by fortune; successful —**aus·pi'cious·ly** *adv.* —**aus·pi'cious·ness** *n.*

Aus·sie (os'ē, oz'-) *adj., n.* [Slang] Australian

aus·tere (ô stir', o-) *adj.* [< OFr. < L. < Gr. *austēros* < *auos,* dry] **1.** having a stern manner; forbidding **2.** showing strict self-discipline; ascetic **3.** very plain —**aus·tere'ly** *adv.* —**aus·tere'ness** *n.*

aus·ter·i·ty (ô ster'ə tē, o-) *n., pl.* -**ties 1.** an austere quality, state, act, or practice **2.** tightened economy, as from shortages of goods

Aus·tin (os'tin, ôs-) *adj., n. same as* AUGUSTINIAN

aus·tral (ôs'trəl) *adj.* [< L. < *auster,* the south] **1.** southern; southerly **2.** [A-] Australian

Aus·tral·a·sian (os'trə lā'zhən, -shən, ôs-) *adj.* of the islands of the SW Pacific; Australia, New Zealand, and adjacent islands

Aus·tral·i·an (o strāl'ē ən, ô-) *adj.* of Australia —*n.* an inhabitant of Australia

Aus·tra·loid (os'trə loid') *adj.* [AUSTRAL(IA) + -OID] designating or of an ethnic group of mankind that includes the Australian aborigines —*n.* any member of this group

Aus·tro-¹ *a combining form meaning* Austria

Aus·tro-² [< L. *auster,* south] *a combining form meaning* South, Southern

Aus·tro-A·si·at·ic (os'trō ā'shē at'ik, -zhē-) *adj.* of a family of languages widely scattered throughout SE Asia, including Vietnamese

au·tar·chy (ô'tär kē) *n., pl.* -**chies** [< Gr. < *autarchos,* absolute ruler < *autos,* self + *archos,* first, ruler] **1.** absolute rule; autocracy **2.** a country under such rule —**au·tar'chic, au·tar'chi·cal** *adj.*

au·tar·ky (ô'tär kē) *n.* [Gr. *autarkeia* < *autos,* self + *arkein,* to suffice] economic self-sufficiency as a national policy —**au·tar'kic, au·tar'ki·cal** *adj.*

auth. 1. author **2.** authority **3.** authorized

au·then·tic (ô then'tik) *adj.* [< OFr. < LL. < Gr. *authentikos* < *authentēs,* one who does things himself] **1.** that can be believed; reliable [an *authentic* report] **2.** genuine; real [an *authentic* antique] **3.** legally executed, as a deed —**au·then'ti·cal·ly** *adv.* —**au·then·tic·i·ty** (ô'thən tis'ə tē) *n.*

au·then·ti·cate (-tə kāt') *vt.* -**cat'ed, -cat'ing** to establish as authentic, or true, valid, genuine, etc. —**au·then'ti·ca'tion** *n.* —**au·then'ti·ca'tor** *n.*

au·thor (ô'thər) *n.* [< OFr. < L. *auctor* < *augere,* to increase] **1.** one who makes or originates something; creator **2.** the writer (*of* a book, article, etc.) —*vt.* to be the author of —**au'thor·ess** [Now Rare] *n.fem.* —**au·tho·ri·al** (ô thôr'ē əl) *adj.*

au·thor·i·tar·i·an (ô thor'ə ter'ē ən) *adj.* believing in or characterized by unquestioning obedience to authority rather than individual freedom —*n.* a person who believes in or enforces such obedience —**au·thor'i·tar'i·an·ism** *n.*

au·thor·i·ta·tive (ô thor'ə tāt'iv, ə-) *adj.* **1.** having authority; official **2.** reliable because coming from an authority or expert **3.** asserting authority; dictatorial —**au·thor'i·ta'tive·ly** *adv.* —**au·thor'i·ta'tive·ness** *n.*

au·thor·i·ty (ô thor'ə tē, ə-) *n., pl.* -**ties** [< OFr. < L. *auctoritas* < *auctor:* see AUTHOR] **1.** a) the power or right to give commands, enforce obedience, take action, or make final decisions; jurisdiction *b*) the position of one having such power [the man in *authority*] *c*) such power as delegated; authorization **2.** power or influence resulting from knowledge, prestige, etc. **3.** a writing, decision, etc. cited in support of an opinion, action, etc. **4.** a) [*pl.*] persons, esp. in government, having the power to enforce orders, laws, etc. *b*) an elected or appointed body with powers to make and enforce bylaws, levy rates, etc. in a given area [a local *authority*] *c*) [U.S.] a government agency that administers a project **5.** evidence or testimony [we have it on his *authority*] **6.** an expert whose opinion is considered reliable **7.** self-assurance based on expertness

au·thor·ize (ô'thə rīz) *vt.* -**ized', -iz'ing 1.** to give official approval to or permission for **2.** to give power or authority to; empower; commission **3.** to give justification for; warrant —**au'thor·i·za'tion** *n.* —**au'thor·iz'er** *n.*

Authorized Version the revised English translation of the Bible published in England in 1611 with the authorization of King James I: also called *King James Version*

au·thor·ship (ô'thər ship') *n.* **1.** the profession of a writer **2.** the origin (of a book, idea, etc.) with reference to its author or originator [a story of unknown *authorship*]

au·tism (ô'tiz'm) *n.* [AUT(O)- + -ISM] *Psychol.* a state of mind characterized by self-absorption, fantasy, and a disregard of external reality —**au·tis'tic** *adj.*

au·to (ôt'ō) *n., pl.* -**tos** [U.S.] a motor car

au·to- [Gr. *autos,* self] *a combining form meaning:* **1.** of or for oneself; self [*autobiography*] **2.** by oneself or itself [*automobile*] Also, before a vowel, **aut-**

‡**Au·to·bahn** (ou'tō bän'; *E.* ôt'ə bän') *n., pl.* -**bahn'en** (-bä'nən); *E.* -**bahns** [G.] in Germany, a motorway

au·to·bi·og·ra·phy (ôt'ō bī og'rə fē) *n., pl.* -**phies** the story of one's own life written or dictated by oneself —**au'·to·bi·og'ra·pher** *n.* —**au'to·bi'o·graph'i·cal** (-bī'ə graf'i k'l), **au'to·bi'o·graph'ic** *adj.* —**au'to·bi'o·graph'i·cal·ly** *adv.*

au·to·ceph·a·lous (-sef'ə ləs) *adj.* [see AUTO- & -CEPHALOUS] self-governing; independent: said of certain churches within the communion of the Orthodox Eastern Church

au·toch·thon (ô tok'thən) *n., pl.* -**thons, -tho·nes'** (-thə nēz') [< Gr. *autochthōn* < *autos,* self & *chthōn,* earth] **1.** any of the earliest known inhabitants of a place; aborigine **2.** any indigenous animal or plant —**au·toch'tho·nous** (-thə nəs) *adj.*

au·to·clave (ôt'ə klāv') *n.* [Fr. < *auto-,* AUTO- + L. *clavis,* a key] a container for sterilizing, cooking, etc. by superheated steam under pressure —*vt.* -**claved', -clav'ing** to sterilize, etc. in this

au·toc·ra·cy (ô tok'rə sē) *n., pl.* -**cies** [< Gr. < *autokratēs:* see ff.] **1.** a government in which one person has supreme power; dictatorship **2.** unlimited power or authority over others

au·to·crat (ôt'ə krat') *n.* [< Fr. < Gr. *autokratēs,* absolute ruler < *autos,* self + *kratos,* power] **1.** a ruler with absolute power; dictator; despot **2.** anyone having unlimited power over others **3.** any domineering, self-willed person —**au'to·crat'ic, au'to·crat'i·cal** *adj.* —**au'to·crat'i·cal·ly** *adv.*

au·to·da·fé (ôt'ō də fā') *n., pl.* **au'tos-da-fé'** [Port., lit., act of the faith] **1.** the public ceremony in which the Inquisition judged and sentenced those tried as heretics **2.** the execution of the sentence; esp., the public burning of a heretic

au·tog·a·my (ô tog'ə mē) *n.* [AUTO- + -GAMY] self fertilization, in a flower receiving pollen from its own stamens —**au·tog'a·mous** *adj.*

au·tog·e·nous (ô toj'ə nəs) *adj.* [Gr. *autogenēs,* (< *autos,* self + *genesis,* birth) + -OUS] **1.** self-generated or self-generating **2.** produced in or obtained from one's own body [an *autogenous* vaccine]

au·to·gi·ro, au·to·gy·ro (ôt'ə jī'rō) *n., pl.* -**ros** [orig. a trademark < AUTO- + Gr. *gyros,* a circle] an early kind of aircraft having both a propeller and a large horizontal rotor

au·to·graph (ôt'ə graf') *n.* [< L. < Gr. *autographos* < *autos,* self + *graphein,* to write] **1.** a person's own signature or handwriting **2.** a thing written in one's own handwriting; holograph —*vt.* **1.** to write (something) with one's own hand **2.** to write one's signature on or in —**au'to·graph'ic** *adj.* —**au'to·graph'i·cal·ly** *adv.*

au·to·hyp·no·sis (ôt'ō hip nō'sis) *n.* a hypnotizing of oneself or the state of being so hypnotized

au·to·in·tox·i·ca·tion (-in tok'sə kā'shən) *n.* poisoning by toxic substances (**autotoxins**) formed within the body —**au'·to·tox'ic** *adj.*

au·tol·y·sis (ô tol'ə sis) *n.* [AUTO- + -LYSIS] the destruction of cells or tissues by enzymes within them, as after death or in some diseases —**au·to·lyt·ic** (ôt'ə lit'ik) *adj.*

au·to·mat (ôt'ə mat') *n.* [see AUTOMATIC] [Chiefly U.S.] a restaurant in which patrons get food from small compartments opened by putting coins into slots

au·to·mate (ôt'ə māt') *vt.* -**mat'ed, -mat'ing** [back-formation < AUTOMATION] **1.** to convert (a factory, process, etc.) to automation **2.** to use the techniques of automation in

au·to·mat·ic (ôt'ə mat'ik) *adj.* [Gr. *automatos,* selfmoving] **1.** done without conscious thought or volition, as if mechanically, or from force of habit **2.** involuntary or reflex, as some muscle action **3.** a) moving, operating, etc. by itself [*automatic* machinery] *b*) done with automatic equipment **4.** occurring as a necessary consequence; inevitable [such action incurs *automatic* dismissal] **5.** *Firearms* using the force of the explosion of a shell to eject, reload, and fire again, so that shots continue in rapid succession with one trigger pull: cf. SEMIAUTOMATIC —*n.* **1.** an automatic pistol, rifle, etc. **2.** any automatic machine **3.** a motor vehicle having automatic transmission —**au'·to·mat'i·cal·ly** *adv.*

automatic pilot a gyroscopic instrument that automatically keeps an aircraft, missile, etc. to a predetermined course and altitude

automatic tranmission a transmission system in a motor vehicle in which the gears can be set to change automatically

au·to·ma·tion (-mā'shən) *n.* [AUTOMA(TIC) + -TION] 1. in manufacturing, a system or method in which many or all of the processes are automatically performed or controlled by machinery, electronic devices, etc. 2. any system using equipment to replace people 3. the state of being automated

au·tom·a·tism (ô tom'ə tiz'm) *n.* 1. the quality or condition or being automatic 2. automatic action 3. *Physiol.* action independent of outside stimulus or of conscious control

au·tom·a·tize (-tīz') *vt.* -tized', -tiz'ing 1. to make automatic 2. *same as* AUTOMATE

au·tom·a·ton (ô tom'ə ton', -tən) *n.*, *pl.* -tons', -ta (-tə) [Gr., neut. of *automatos*: see AUTOMATIC] 1. anything that can move or act of itself 2. an apparatus that works or moves by responding to preset controls or computerized instructions 3. a person acting in a mechanical way

au·to·mo·bile (ôt'ə mə bēl') *n.* [Fr.: see AUTO- & MOBILE] [Chiefly U.S.] a motor car

au·to·mo·tive (ôt'ə mōt'iv) *adj.* [AUTO- + -MOTIVE] 1. moving by its own power; self-moving 2. of or having to do with motor vehicles

au·to·nom·ic (-nom'ik) *adj.* 1. of or controlled by the autonomic nervous system 2. *Biol.* resulting from internal causes —**au'to·nom'i·cal·ly** *adv.*

autonomic nervous system the divisions of the nervous system that control the motor functions of the heart, lungs, intestines, smooth muscles, glands, etc.

au·ton·o·mous (ô ton'ə məs) *adj.* [< Gr. < *autos*, self + *nomos*, law] 1. of an autonomy 2. *a)* having selfgovernment *b)* functioning independently 3. *Biol.* functioning independently of other parts

au·ton·o·my (-mē) *n.* 1. self-government 2. *pl.* -mies any state that governs itself

au·to·pi·lot (ôt'ō pī'lət) *n.* *same as* AUTOMATIC PILOT

au·top·sy (ô'top'sē) *n.*, *pl.* -sies [< ML. & Gr. *autopsia*, a seeing with one's own eyes < *autos*, self + *opsis*, a sight] an examination and dissection of a dead body to discover the cause of death, damage done by a disease, etc.; post mortem

au·to·route (ôt'ō rōōt') *n.* [Fr.] in France, a motorway

au·to·stra·da (-mē) *n.* [It.] in Italy, a motorway

au·to·sug·ges·tion (ôt'ō sag jes'chən) *n.* suggestion to oneself arising within oneself and having effects on one's thinking and bodily function

au·tot·o·my (ô tot'ə mē) *n.* [AUTO- + -TOMY] the reflex action by which a leg, claw, tail, etc., as of a lobster, starfish or lizard, is dropped off from the body when the part is damaged or the animal is under attack

au·to·troph·ic (ôt'ə trof'ik) *adj.* [< Gr. *autos*, self & *trophē*, food] making its own food by photosynthesis, as a green plant, or by chemosynthesis, as some bacteria

au·tumn (ôt'əm) *n.* [< OFr. < L. *autumnus*] 1. the season that comes between summer and winter 2. any period of maturity or of incipient decline —*adj.* of, in, characteristic of, or like autumn —**au·tum·nal** (ô tum'nəl) *adj.* —**au·tum'·nal·ly** *adv.*

aux. auxiliary

aux·a·nom·e·ter (ôks'ə nom'ə tər) *n.* [< Gr. *auxanein*, to increase + -METER] an instrument that measures the linear growth of plant shoots

aux·il·ia·ry (ôg zil'yər ē, -zil'ər-) *adj.* [< L. < *auxilium*, aid < pp. of *augere*, AUGMENT] 1. giving help or aid; assisting 2. acting in a subsidiary, or subordinate, capacity 3. additional; supplementary; reserve —*n.*, *pl.* -ries 1. an auxiliary person or thing 2. [*pl.*] foreign troops aiding a country at war 3. a supplementary group or organization [a women's *auxiliary*]

auxiliary verb a verb that helps to form tenses, moods, or voices of other verbs, as *have*, *be*, *may*, *can*, *must*, *do*, *shall*, *will*

aux·in (ôk'sin) *n.* [< Gr. *auxein*, to increase + -IN¹] an organic compound that promotes plant growth

Av., av. avenue

av. average

A.V. Authorized Version (of the Bible)

a·vail (ə vāl') *vi.*, *vt.* [< OFr. *a* (L. *ad*), to + *valoir*, to be worth < L. *valere*, to be strong] to be of use, help, worth, or advantage (to), as in accomplishing an end —*n.* effective use or help; advantage [of no *avail*] —**avail oneself of** to take advantage of (an opportunity, etc.)

a·vail·a·ble (ə vā'lə b'l) *adj.* 1. that can be used 2. that can be got, had, or reached; accessible —**a·vail'a·bil'i·ty** *n.* —**a·vail'a·bly** *adv.*

av·a·lanche (av'ə länsh', -länch') *n.* [Fr. (altered after *avaler*, to descend) < *lavanche* < LL. < L. *labi*, to slip, glide down] 1. a large mass of loosened snow, earth, rocks, etc. suddenly and swiftly sliding down a mountain 2. anything that comes suddenly in overwhelming number [an

avalanche of letters] —*vi.*, *vt.* -lanched', -lanch'ing to come down (on) like an avalanche

a·vant-garde (a voŋ'gärd'; *Fr.* á vän gàrd') *n.* [Fr., lit., advance guard] the leaders in new or unconventional movements, esp. in the arts; vanguard —*adj.* of such movements, ideas, etc. —**a·vant'-gard'ism** *n.* —**a·vant'-gard'ist** *n.*

av·a·rice (av'ər is) *n.* [< OFr. < L. < *avarus*, greedy < *avere*, to desire] too great a desire to have wealth; greed for riches; cupidity —**av·a·ri·cious** (av'ə rish'əs) *adj.* —**av'·a·ri'cious·ly** *adv.* —**av'a·ri'cious·ness** *n.*

a·vast (ə väst') *interj.* [< Du. *houd vast*, hold fast] *Naut.* stop! cease! halt!

av·a·tar (av'ə tär') *n.* [Sans. *avatāra*, descent] 1. *Hinduism* a god's coming down in bodily form to the earth; incarnation 2. any embodiment

a·vaunt (ə vônt') *interj.* [< OFr. < L. *ab*, from + *ante*, before] [Archaic] begone! go away!

avdp. avoirdupois

a·ve (ä'vä, ä'vē) *interj.* [L., imperative of *avere*, to be well] 1. hail! 2. farewell! —*n.* 1. the salutation *ave* 2. [A-] the prayer AVE MARIA

Ave., ave. avenue

A·ve Ma·ri·a (ä'vä mə rē'ə, -vē) [L. (Luke 1:28)] 1. "Hail, Mary," the first words of a prayer to the Virgin Mary used in the Roman Catholic Church 2. this prayer 3. a musical setting of this

a·venge (ə venj') *vt.*, *vi.* a·venged', a·veng'ing [< OFr. < *a-* (L. *ad*) to + *vengier* < L. *vindicare*, to claim: see VINDICATE] 1. to get revenge for (an injury, wrong, etc.) 2. to take vengeance on behalf of, as for a wrong —**a·veng'·er** *n.*

av·ens (av'inz) *n.* [ME. & OFr. *avence*] any of a genus of small plants of the rose family

a·ven·tu·rine (ə ven'tyoor in) *n.* [Fr. < It.] 1. a kind of glass flecked with spangles, as from copper filings or bits of chromic oxide 2. a translucent quartz shot through with sparkling bits of mica, etc.

av·e·nue (av'ə nyōō') *n.* [Fr. < L. *advenire*: see ADVENT] 1. a road, path, or drive, often bordered with trees 2. a way of approach to something 3. a street, esp. a wide, principal one

a·ver (ə vur') *vt.* a·verred', a·ver'ring [< OFr. *averrer* < L. *ad*, to + *verus*, true] 1. to declare to be true; affirm 2. *Law* to state or declare formally; assert; allege —**a·ver'·ment** *n.*

av·er·age (av'rij, -ər ij) *n.* [< Fr. *avarie*, damage to ship < It. < Ar. *'awar*, damaged goods; sense development from *n.* 4] 1. the numerical result obtained by dividing the sum of two or more quantities by the number of quantities; an arithmetic mean 2. any similar value 3. the usual or normal kind, amount, quality, etc. 4. *Marine Law a)* a loss incurred by damage to a ship or its cargo *b)* the equitable division of such a loss among the interested parties —*adj.* 1. being a numerical average 2. usual; normal; ordinary —*vi.* -aged, -ag·ing 1. to be or amount to on the average 2. to buy or sell more shares, goods, etc. at intervals so as to get a better average price —*vt.* 1. to calculate the average or mean of 2. to do, take, etc. on the average 3. to divide proportionately among more than two —**on the** (or **an**) **average** as an average quantity, rate, etc. —**av'er·age·ness** *n.* —**average out** to arrive at an average eventually

a·verse (ə vurs') *adj.* [< L. pp. of *avertere*: see AVERT] not willing; reluctant; opposed (*to*) —**a·verse'ly** *adv.* —**a·verse'·ness** *n.*

a·ver·sion (ə vur'shən, -zhən) *n.* 1. a strong or definite dislike; antipathy; repugnance 2. the object arousing such dislike

a·vert (ə vurt') *vt.* [< L. *avertere* < *a-* (*ab-*), from + *vertere*, to turn] 1. to turn away [to *avert* one's eyes] 2. to keep from happening; avoid; prevent [to *avert* a catastrophe] —**a·vert'i·ble** *adj.*

A·ves·ta (ə ves'tə) *n.* [< Per.] the sacred writings of Zoroastrianism, in an ancient Iranian language —**A·ves'tan** *adj.*, *n.*

avg. average

a·vi·an (ā'vē ən) *adj.* [< L. *avis*, bird + -AN] of or having to do with birds

a·vi·ar·y (ā'vē ər ē, āv'yər-) *n.*, *pl.* -ar·ies [< L. < *avis*, bird] a large cage or building for keeping many birds

a·vi·a·tion (ā'vē ā'shən) *n.* [Fr. < L. *avis*, bird] 1. the art or science of flying aircraft 2. the development and operation of heavier-than-air craft

a·vi·a·tor (ā'vē āt'ər) *n.* an aeroplane pilot; flier —**a'vi·a'·trix** (-ā'triks) *n.fem.*

av·id (av'id) *adj.* [L. *avidus* < *avere*, to desire] 1. having an intense desire or craving; greedy [*avid* for power] 2. eager and enthusiastic [an *avid* reader] —**a·vid·i·ty** (ə vid'ə tē) *n.* —**av'id·ly** *adv.*

a·vi·fau·na (ā'və fô'nə) *n.* [< L. *avis*, bird + FAUNA] the birds of a specified region or time

a·vi·on·ics (ā′vē on′iks) *n.pl.* [AVI(ATION) + (ELECTR)ONICS] [*with sing. v.*] the branch of electronics dealing with the use of electronic equipment in aviation and astronautics —a′·vi·on′ic *adj.*

a·vi·ta·min·o·sis (ā′vit ə mi nō′sis) *n.* [A-² + VITAMIN + -OSIS] any disease caused by a deficiency of vitamins

av·o·ca·do (av′ə kä′dō) *n.,* pl. **-dos** [Sp. < MexSp. *aguacate* < Nahuatl *ahuacatl*] 1. a thick-skinned, pear-shaped tropical fruit, yellowish green to purplish black, with a single large seed and yellow, buttery flesh, used in salads; alligator pear 2. the tree that it grows on

av·o·ca·tion (av′ə kā′shən) *n.* [< L. pp. of *avocare* < *ab-*, away + *vocare*, to call] something one does in addition to one's regular work, and usually for pleasure; hobby —av′·o·ca′tion·al *adj.*

av·o·cet (av′ə set′) *n.* [< Fr. < It.] a long-legged wading bird with webbed feet and a slender bill that curves upwards

A·vo·ga·dro's Law (av′ə ga′drō) [after A. *Avogadro* (1776-1856), It. chemist & physicist] the theory that equal volumes of all gases under identical conditions of temperature and pressure contain equal numbers of molecules

a·void (ə void′) *vt.* [< Anglo-Fr. < OFr. *esvuidier,* to empty < *es-* (< L. *ex*), out + *vuidier:* see VOID] 1. to make void; annul, invalidate, or quash (a plea, etc. in law) 2. to keep away from; shun [to *avoid* crowds] 3. to keep from happening [to *avoid* breakage] —a·void′a·ble *adj.* —a·void′a·bly *adv.* —a·void′ance *n.*

av·oir·du·pois (av′ər də poiz′) *n.* [< OFr. *aveir de peis,* goods having weight] 1. *same as* AVOIRDUPOIS WEIGHT 2. [Colloq.] heaviness or weight, esp. of a person

avoirdupois weight a system of weights based on a pound of 16 ounces: see TABLES OF WEIGHTS AND MEASURES in Supplements

a·vouch (ə vouch′) *vt.* [< OFr. *avochier* < L. *advocare:* see ADVOCATE] 1. to vouch for; guarantee 2. to declare the truth of; affirm 3. to acknowledge openly; avow —a·vouch′ment *n.*

a·vow (ə vou′) *vt.* [< OFr. *avouer* < L. *advocare:* see ADVOCATE] 1. to declare openly or admit frankly 2. to acknowledge or claim (oneself) to be [he *avowed* himself a patriot] —a·vowed′ *adj.* —a·vow·ed·ly (ə vou′id lē) *adv.* —a·vow′er *n.*

a·vow·al (-əl) *n.* open acknowledgment or declaration; frank admission

a·vun·cu·lar (ə vuŋ′kyə lər) *adj.* [< L. *avunculus,* maternal uncle, dim. of *avus,* ancestor] of, like, or in the relationship of, an uncle

a·wait (ə wāt′) *vt.* [< ONormFr. < *a-* (L. *ad*), to + *waitier,* WAIT] 1. to wait for; expect 2. to be in store for; be ready for —*vi.* to wait

a·wake (ə wāk′) *vt.* **a·woke′** or **a·waked′, a·woke′** or **a·wok′en, a·waked′, a·wak′ing** [< OE. *awacan* (*on- + wacan,* to arise, awake) & OE. *awacian* (*on- + wacian,* to be awake, watch)] 1. to rouse from sleep; wake 2. to rouse from inactivity; stir up 3. to call forth (memories, etc.) —*vi.* 1. to come out of sleep; wake 2. to become active 3. to become aware (with *to*) —*adj.* [*used only in the predicate*] 1. not asleep 2. active or alert

a·wak·en (ə wāk′'n) *vt., vi.* to awake; wake up; rouse —a·wak′en·er *n.*

a·wak·en·ing (-iŋ) *n., adj.* 1. (a) waking up 2. (an) arousing, as of impulses, interest, etc.

a·ward (ə wôrd′) *vt.* [< Anglo-Fr. < ONormFr. < *es-* (< L. *ex*) + Gmc. hyp. *wardon:* see GUARD] 1. to give by the decision of a law court or arbitrator 2. to give as the result of judging, as in a contest [*award* prizes] —*n.* 1. a decision, as by a judge or arbitrator 2. something awarded; prize

a·ware (ə wer′) *adj.* [< OE. *gewær* < *wær,* cautious] 1. orig., on one's guard 2. knowing or realizing; conscious; informed —a·ware′ness *n.*

a·wash (ə wosh′) *adv., adj.* 1. just above the surface of the water and washed over by it 2. floating on the water 3. flooded with water

a·way (ə wā′) *adv.* [< OE. *aweg* < *on,* on + *weg,* way] 1. from any given place; off [to run *away*] 2. in another place, esp. the proper place [put tools *away*] 3. in another direction [look *away*] 4. far [*away* behind] 5. off; aside [to clear snow *away*] 6. from one's possession [give it *away*] 7. out of existence [to fade *away*] 8. at once [fire *away*] 9. without stopping [to work *away* all night] 10. into action [*away* we go!] —*adj.* 1. absent; gone [he is *away*] 2. at a distance [a mile *away*] 3. *Sport* played on an opponent's ground [an *away* match] —*n. Sport* a match or game played on an opponent's ground —*interj.* 1. begone! 2. let's go! —**do away with** 1. take away 2. go or come away —**away with** 1. take away 2. go or come away —**do away with** 1. to get rid of 2. to kill

awe (ô) *n.* [< ME. < ON. *agi*] a mixed feeling of reverence, fear, and wonder, caused by something sublime, etc. —*vt.* **awed, aw′ing** to inspire awe in; fill with awe —**stand** (or **be**) **in awe of** to respect and fear —**awe′less, aw′less** *adj.*

a·weigh (ə wā′) *adj. Naut.* clearing the bottom; being weighed: said of an anchor

awe·some (ô′səm) *adj.* 1. inspiring awe 2. showing awe —awe′some·ly *adv.* —awe′some·ness *n.*

awe-struck (ô′struk′) *adj.* filled with awe or wonder: also **awe′-strick′en** (-strik′ən)

aw·ful (ô′fəl) *adj.* [see AWE & -FUL] 1. inspiring awe 2. causing fear; terrifying 3. [Colloq.] *a)* very bad, unpleasant, etc. [an *awful* joke] *b)* great [an *awful* bore] —aw′ful·ness *n.*

aw·ful·ly (ô′fə lē, ô′flē) *adv.* 1. in a way to inspire awe 2. [Colloq.] badly or offensively [to behave *awfully*] 3. [Colloq.] very; extremely

a·while (ə wīl′, -hwīl′) *adv.* for a while; for a short time

awk·ward (ôk′wərd) *adj.* [< ON. *ǫfugr,* turned backwards + OE. *-weard,* -WARD] 1. not having grace or skill; clumsy; bungling 2. hard to handle and use; unwieldy 3. inconvenient; uncomfortable [an *awkward* position] 4. embarrassed or embarrassing [an *awkward* remark] 5. not easy to deal with; requiring tact [an *awkward* situation, an *awkward* customer] —awk′ward·ly *adv.* —awk′ward·ness *n.*

awl (ôl) *n.* [< OE. *æl, awel*] a small, pointed tool for making holes in wood, leather, etc.

awn (ôn) *n.* [ON. *ǫgn,* chaff] any of the bristly fibres on a head of barley, oats, etc., or, usually, such fibres collectively; beard —**awned** *adj.* —**awn′less** *adj.*

awn·ing (ô′niŋ) *n.* [< ? MFr. *auvans,* pl. of *auvent,* window shade] a structure of canvas, metal, etc. extended before a window or door or over a patio, deck, etc. as a protection from sun or rain

a·woke (ə wōk′) *alt. pt. & occas. pp. of* AWAKE

a·wok·en (ə wōk′'n) *occas. pp. of* AWAKE

A·WOL, a·wol (ā′wol′) *adj.* [*a(bsent) w(ith)o(ut) l(eave)*] *Mil.* absent without leave, but without intention of deserting

a·wry (ə rī′) *adv., adj.* [see A-¹ (sense 1) & WRY] 1. with a twist to a side; askew 2. wrong; amiss [our plans went *awry*]

axe (aks) *n., pl.* **ax′es** [OE. *eax, æx*] 1. a tool with a long handle and a bladed head, for chopping trees and splitting wood 2. any similar tool or weapon, as a battle-axe —*vt.* **axed, ax′ing** 1. to trim, split, etc. with an axe 2. to get rid of; dismiss (employees) *b)* to handle; restrict (expenditure, services, etc.) —**get the axe** [Colloq.] 1. to be beheaded 2. to be discharged from one's job —**have an axe to grind** [Colloq.] to have an object of one's own to promote

ax·es¹ (ak′siz) *n. pl. of* AXE

ax·es² (ak′sēz) *n. pl. of* AXIS¹

ax·i·al (ak′sē əl) *adj.* 1. of, like, or forming an axis 2. round or along an axis —ax′i·al·ly *adv.*

ax·il (ak′sil) *n.* [L. *axilla:* see ff.] the upper angle between a leaf, twig, etc. and the stem from which it grows

ax·il·la (ak sil′ə) *n., pl.* **-lae** (-ē), **-las** [L., armpit] 1. the armpit 2. *Bot.* an axil

ax·il·lar (ak′sə lər) *adj. same as* AXILLARY —*n.* any of the stiff feathers on the underside of a bird's wing where it joins the body

ax·il·la·ry (ak sil′ər ē) *adj.* 1. *Anat.* of or near the axilla 2. *Bot.* of, in, or growing from an axil —*n., pl.* **-ries** *same as* AXILLAR

ax·i·om (ak′sē əm) *n.* [< Fr. < L. < Gr. *axiōma,* authority < *axios,* worthy] 1. a statement widely accepted as true; truism 2. an established principle or law of a science, art, etc. 3. *Logic, Math.* a statement that needs no proof because its truth is obvious; self-evident proposition

ax·i·o·mat·ic (ak′sē ə mat′ik) *adj.* 1. of or like an axiom; self-evident 2. full of axioms; aphoristic —ax′i·o·mat′·i·cal·ly *adv.*

ax·is¹ (ak′sis) *n., pl.* **ax′es** (-sēz) [L.] 1. a real or imaginary straight line on which an object rotates or is regarded as rotating [the earth's *axis*] 2. a real or imaginary straight line around which the parts of a thing, system, etc. are symmetrically or evenly arranged 3. a straight line for reference or measurement, as in a graph [x-axis, y-axis] 4. *Bot., Zool.* any of various axial or central parts, as the main stem of a plant —**the Axis** Germany and Italy (**Rome-Berlin Axis**), and later Japan, etc. (**Rome-Berlin-Tokyo Axis**), as allies in World War II

ax·is² (ak′sis) *n.* [L.] any of a subgenus of small, white-spotted deer of India and S Asia

ax·le (ak′s'l) *n.* [< ff.] 1. a rod on which a wheel turns, or one connected to a wheel so that they turn together 2. a bar connecting opposite wheels, as of a motor car

ax·le·tree (-trē′) *n.* [< ON. < *ǫxull,* axle + *tre,* tree, beam] a bar connecting two opposite wheels of a carriage, wagon, etc.

Ax·min·ster (aks′min stər) *n.* [< *Axminster,* town in Devon] a type of carpet with a cut pile

ax·o·lotl (ak′sə lot′'l) *n.* [< Nahuatl, lit., water toy] a salamander of Mexico and the W U.S. that matures sexually while remaining in the larval stage

ax·on (ak'son) *n.* [ModL. < Gr. *axōn*, axis] that part of a nerve cell through which impulses travel away from the cell body

ay·ah (ī'yə) *n.* [< Hindi < Port. *aia*, governess] a native nursemaid or lady's maid in India, esp. formerly

aye¹ (ā) *adv.* [ON. *ei*] [Poet.] always; ever: also sp. **ay**

aye² (ī) *adv.* [< ? prec.] yes; yea —*n.* an affirmative vote or voter Also sp. **ay**

aye-aye (ī'ī') *n.* [Fr. < Malagasy: prob. echoic of its cry] a lemur of Madagascar, with shaggy fur, large ears, fingerlike claws, and a long, bushy tail

Ayr·shire (er'shər) *n.* [after the former Scot. county where the breed originated] any of a breed of brown and white dairy cattle

a·za·le·a (ə zāl'ē ə, -yə) *n.* [ModL.< Gr. fem. of *azaleos*, dry: because it thrives in dry soil] 1. any of several shrubs of the heath family, allied to the rhododendron, having variously coloured flowers and leaves that are usually shed in the autumn 2. the flower of any of these plants

AYE-AYE
(85-100 cm long,
including tail)

a·ze·o·trope (ə zē'ə trōp') *n.* [< A-² + Gr. *zein*, to boil + *tropos*, turning] a liquid mixture that maintains a constant boiling point and that produces a vapour of the same composition as the mixture —**a·ze·o·trop·ic** (ā'zē ə trop'ik) *adj.*

A·zil·i·an (ə zil'ē ən) *adj.* [< Mas d'*Azil*, cavern in the French Pyrenees, where traces were found] denoting or of a stage of prehistoric culture between the paleolithic and the neolithic periods in Europe

az·i·muth (az'ə məth) *n.* [< OFr. < Ar. *as-sumūt* < *al*, the + *sumūt*, pl. of *samt*, way, path] *Astron.*, *Surveying*, etc. distance in angular degrees in a clockwise direction from the north point or, in the Southern Hemisphere, south point —**az'i·muth'al** (-muth'əl) *adj.*

az·o (az'ō, ā'zō) *adj.* [< *azote*, obs. name for nitrogen] containing the nitrogen radical -N:N- [*azo* dyes]: used also as a prefix, **az·o-**

Az·tec (az'tek) *n.* [< Nahuatl *Aztatlán*, name of their legendary place of origin] 1. *pl.* -tecs, -tec a member of a people who lived in Mexico and had an advanced civilization before the conquest of Mexico by Cortés in 1519 2. their Uto-Aztecan language, usually called Nahuatl —*adj.* of the Aztecs, their language, culture, etc.: also **Az'tec·an**

az·ure (azh'ər) *adj.* [OFr. *azur* < Ar. < Per. *lāzhuward*, lapis lazuli] of or like the colour of a clear sky; sky-blue —*n.* 1. sky blue or any similar blue 2. [Poet.] the blue sky

az·u·rite (azh'ə rīt') *n.* [AZUR(E) + -ITE] 1. a brilliant blue mineral, 2CuCO₃·Cu(OH)₂, an ore of copper 2. a semiprecious gem cut from it

az·y·gous (az'i gəs) *adj.* [Gr.] not one of a pair; unpaired; odd

B

B, b (bē) *n.*, *pl.* **B's, b's** 1. the second letter of the English alphabet 2. the sound of *B* or *b* 3. *a symbol for* the second in a sequence or group

B (bē) *n.* 1. *Cinema* designating a supporting film [a *B* film] 2. *Music* a) the seventh tone in the ascending scale of C major b) the scale having B as the keynote

B 1. *Chess* bishop 2. *Chem.* boron

B- [U.S.] bomber

B. 1. Bible 2. British 3. Brotherhood

B., b. 1. bachelor 2. bacillus 3. *Music* bass 4. bay 5. book 6. born 7. brother

b. *Cricket* 1. bowled 2. bye

Ba *Chem.* barium

B.A. [*L. Baccalaureus Artium*] Bachelor of Arts

baa (bä) *n.* [echoic] the cry of a sheep or goat —*vi.* to make this cry; bleat

B.A.A. British Airports Authority

Ba·al (bā'əl, bāl) *n.*, *pl.* **Ba·al·im** (-im) 1. among some ancient Semitic peoples, any of several fertility gods; later, a chief god 2. a false god; idol —**Ba'al·ism** *n.* —**Ba'al·ist, Ba'al·ite'** (-īt') *n.*

baas (bäs) *n.* [Afrik. < Du., master] master; sir: term of address used in South Africa by non-whites speaking to a white man

baas·skap (bäs'skäp') *n.* [BAAS + MDu. -*scap*, -SHIP] the policy of domination of non-whites by whites in South Africa

ba·ba (bä'bä) *n.* [Fr.] a sponge cake saturated in spirits and served as a dessert [a rum *baba*]

bab·bitt (bab'it) *n.* *same as* BABBITT METAL —*vt.* to line or cover with Babbitt metal

Bab·bitt (bab'it) *n.* [after the title character of a novel by Sinclair Lewis (1922)] [also b-] a smugly conventional person interested chiefly in business and social success and indifferent to cultural values —**Bab'bitt·ry** *n.*

Babbitt metal [after Isaac *Babbitt* (1799-1862), U.S. inventor] a soft alloy of tin, copper, and antimony, used to reduce friction in bearings, etc.

bab·ble (bab''l) *vi.* -bled, -bling [of echoic origin] 1. to make incoherent sounds, as a baby does; prattle 2. to talk foolishly or too much 3. to make a low, bubbling sound [a babbling brook] —*vt.* 1. to say indistinctly or incoherently 2. to reveal secrets; blab —*n.* 1. confused, incoherent vocal sounds 2. foolish or meaningless talk 3. a low, bubbling sound —**bab'bler** *n.*

babe (bāb) *n.* 1. a baby 2. a naive, gullible, or helpless person: also **babe in the woods** 3. [Chiefly U.S. Slang] a girl or young woman

ba·bel (bā'b'l) *n.* [after the city where people tried to build a tower to the sky and were stopped by God, who caused them suddenly to speak in different languages: Gen. 11:1-9] [also **B-**] 1. a confusion of voices, languages, or sounds; tumult 2. a place of such confusion

bab·i·ru·sa, bab·i·rous·sa, bab·i·rus·sa (bab'ə rōōs'ə, bä'ba-) *n.* [Malay *bābī*, hog + *rūsa*, deer] a wild hog of the East Indies, with large, curving tusks: the upper pair grow through the skin of the snout and curve backwards

Bab·ism (bäb'iz'm) *n.* a Persian religion founded c. 1844: cf. BAHAISM

ba·boon (ba bōōn') *n.* [< OFr. *babuin*, ape, fool < *baboue*, lip (of animals) < *bab*, echoic] any of various large and fierce, short-tailed monkeys of Africa and Arabia, having a doglike snout, cheek pouches, and bare calluses on the rump —**ba·boon'er·y** *n.* —**ba·boon'ish** *adj.*

ba·bu, ba·boo (bäb'ōō) *n.* [Hindi *bābu*] 1. a Hindu title equivalent to *Mr.* or *Sir* 2. formerly, a native clerk in India who could write English

ba·bush·ka (bə bōōsh'kə) *n.* [Russ., grandmother] a scarf worn on the head by a woman or girl and tied under the chin

BABOON
(90-150 cm long,
including tail)

ba·by (bā'bē) *n.*, *pl.* -bies [ME. *babi*] 1. a very young child; infant 2. a person who behaves like an infant 3. a very young animal 4. the youngest or smallest in a group 5. [Slang] a) a girl or young woman b) any person or thing 6. [Colloq.] favourite scheme; concern; responsibility [it's your *baby*] —*adj.* 1. of or for an infant 2. extremely young 3. small of its kind 4. infantile or childish —*vt.* -bied, -by·ing to treat like a baby; pamper; coddle —**be left holding the baby** to be left to take the responsibility —**ba'by·hood'** *n.* —**ba'by·ish** *adj.* —**ba'by·ish·ly** *adv.* —**ba'by·like'** *adj.*

baby carriage [U.S.] a perambulator: also **baby buggy**

baby grand a small grand piano

Bab·y·lon (bab'ə lən, -lon') *n.* [after the ancient capital of Babylonia] any city of great wealth, luxury, and vice

Bab·y·lo·ni·an (bab'ə lō'nē ən) *n.* 1. an inhabitant of ancient Babylon or Babylonia 2. the extinct language of Babylonia —*adj.* 1. of ancient Babylon or Babylonia 2. decadent; depraved

ba·by's breath (bā'bēz breth') 1. any of several plants of the pink family, having small, delicate, white or pink flowers 2. any of several other plants with small, sweetly scented flowers: also **ba'bies' breath**

ba·by-sit (bā'bē sit') *vi.*, *vt.* -sat', -sit'ting to act as a baby sitter (to)

baby sitter a person who takes care of a child or children, as when parents are away for an evening

baby snatcher a person who marries or becomes romantically attached to someone much younger
baby walker a frame on castors to support a child learning to walk
B.A.C. British Aircraft Corporation
bac·ca·lau·re·ate (bak'ə lôr'ē it) *n.* [< ML. < *baccalaris*, young nobleman seeking to become a knight] the degree of Bachelor of Arts (or Science, etc.)
bac·ca·rat, bac·ca·ra (bak'ə rä') *n.* [Fr. < ?] a gambling game played with cards
bac·cate (bak'āt) *adj.* [L. < *bacca*, berry] 1. like a berry, as in form 2. bearing berries
bac·cha·nal (bak'ə nəl, -nal'; bak'ə nal') *n.* [L., place devoted to Bacchus] 1. a worshipper of Bacchus 2. a drunken carouser 3. [*pl.*] the Bacchanalia 4. a drunken party; orgy —*adj.* 1. of Bacchus or his worship 2. carousing
Bac·cha·na·li·a (bak'ə nāl'yə, -nā'lē ə) *n.pl.* 1. an ancient Roman festival honouring Bacchus 2. [b-] a drunken party; orgy —**bac'cha·na'li·an** *adj., n.*
bac·chant (bak'ənt) *n., pl.* **-chants, -chan'tes** (bə kan'tēz) 1. a priest or worshipper of Bacchus 2. a drunken carouser —*adj.* 1. worshipping Bacchus 2. given to carousing —**bac·chan·te** (bə kan'tē, -kant') *n.fem.* —**bac·chan'tic** *adj.*
Bac·chic (bak'ik) *adj.* [< *Bacchus*, ancient Gr. & Rom. god of wine and revelry] *same as* BACCHANAL
bac·cy (bak'ē) *n. Colloq.* clipped form of TOBACCO
bach (bach) *vi.* [< BACHELOR] [Slang] to live alone or keep house for oneself, as a bachelor: usually in phr. **bach it** —*n.* [Slang] a bachelor
bach·e·lor (bach'əl ər, bach'lər) *n.* [< OFr. < ML. *baccalaris*: see BACCALAUREATE] 1. orig., a young knight who served under another's banner 2. a man who has not married 3. a person who is a BACHELOR OF ARTS (or SCIENCE, etc.) —*adj.* of or for a bachelor —**bach'·e·lor·hood** *n.*
bachelor flat a small flat suitable for a person living alone
bachelor girl an unmarried young woman who leads an independent life
Bachelor of Arts (or **Science,** etc.) 1. a degree given by a college or university to one who has usually completed a three- or four-year course in the humanities (or in science, etc.) 2. one who has this degree
bachelor's button any of several plants of the composite family, as the cornflower or buttercup, having flowers shaped somewhat like buttons
bac·il·lar·y (bas'ə lər ē, bə sil'ər ē) *adj.* [ModL. *bacillarius*: see ff.] 1. rod-shaped: also **ba·cil·li·form** (bə sil'ə fôrm') 2. consisting of rodlike structures 3. of, like, characterized by, or caused by bacilli Also **ba·cil·lar** (bə sil'ər)
ba·cil·lus (bə sil'əs) *n., pl.* **-cil'li** (-ī) [ModL. < LL. < L. dim. of *baculus*, a stick] 1. any of the rod-shaped bacteria 2. [*usually pl.*] loosely, any of the bacteria, esp. those causing disease
back (bak) *n.* [< OE. *bæc*] 1. the part of the body opposite to the front; in man and other animals, the part from the nape of the neck to the end of the spine 2. the backbone 3. the part of a chair that supports one's back 4. the part of a garment that fits on the back 5. the rear part of anything 6. the part or side that is less often used, seen, etc. 7. the part of a book where the sections are fastened together 8. *Sports* a mainly defensive player or position in many different games, esp. football —*adj.* 1. at the rear; behind 2. of or for a time in the past [*back* pay] 3. backward; reversed 4. *Phonet.* with the tongue towards the back of the mouth —*adv.* 1. at, to, or towards the rear 2. to or towards a former position 3. into or towards a previous condition 4. to or towards an earlier time 5. in concealment [to hold *back* information] 6. in return [to pay one *back*] —*vt.* 1. to cause to move backwards (often with *up*) 2. to stand behind 3. to support or help 4. to bet on 5. to get on the back of; mount 6. to provide with a back or backing 7. to form the back of —*vi.* 1. to go backwards 2. to shift anticlockwise: said of the wind 3. to have the back facing —**at the back of** 1. behind 2. encouraging, guiding, etc., often secretly —**at the back of one's mind** dimly recalled but not receiving one's conscious attention —**back and forth** to and fro —**back down** to withdraw from a position, etc.—**back mark** [Slang] to outdistance competitors in a game or race —**back out (of)** 1. to withdraw from an enterprise 2. to break a promise or engagement —**back up** 1. to support 2. to go backwards: also **back away, back out,** etc. 3. [Chiefly U.S.] to accumulate as the result of a stoppage [traffic *backed up*] —**be (flat) on one's back** to be ill, bedridden, etc. —**behind one's back** without one's knowledge or consent —**to get off (or have on) one's back** [Slang] to stop (or have someone) nagging or harassing one —**get (or put) one's back up** to make or be obstinate —**go back on** [Colloq.] 1. to betray 2. to fail to keep (a promise), etc. —**put one's back into it** apply oneself energetically to a task —**turn one's back on** to desert; fail —**with one's back to the wall** in a desperate position

back·bench·er (bak'ben'chər) *n.* a member of parliament who is not a leader in his party
back·bite (-bīt') *vt., vi.* -**bit'**, -**bit'ten** or -**bit'**, -**bit'ing** to slander (an absent person) —**back'bit'er** *n.*
back-blocks (-bloks') *n.pl.* the far interior of Australia and New Zealand
back·board (-bôrd') *n.* 1. a board that forms or supports the back of something 2. a board worn to straighten or support a person's back 3. *Basketball* a board or flat surface just behind the basket
back boiler a tank or pipes behind a fireplace for heating water
back·bone (-bōn') *n.* 1. the column of bones (vertebrae) along the centre of the back; spine 2. main support 3. a main ridge of mountains 4. willpower, courage, etc.
back·break·ing (-brāk'iŋ) *adj.* very tiring
back chat (Colloq.) saucy or insolent retorts
back-comb (-kōm') *vt.* to fluff (the hair) by brushing or combing the hair ends towards the scalp
back country [Aust.] remote and sparsely inhabited areas
back court *Tennis* the area from the service line to the base line on either side of the net
back·date (-dāt') *vt.* -**dat'ed**, -**dat'ing** to date or put into effect from before the actual date [a *backdated* pay rise]
back·door (bak'dôr') *adj.* 1. of a rear entrance 2. secret; underhand; surreptitious
back·down (-doun') *n.* [Colloq.] a backing down; withdrawal from a position, claim, etc.
back·drop (-drop') *n.* a curtain hung at the back of a stage, often a painted scene: also **backcloth**
backed (bakt) *adj.* having a (specified kind of) back [canvas-*backed*]
back·er (bak'ər) *n.* 1. a patron; supporter 2. a person who bets on a contestant
back·fill (-fil') *vt.* to refill (an excavation), as with earth previously removed
back·fire (-fir') *n.* 1. a premature explosion in a cylinder of an internal-combustion engine 2. an explosive force towards the breech of a firearm 3. [Aust.] a fire started to stop a forest fire by creating a burned area in its path —*vi.* -**fired'**, -**fir'ing** 1. to explode as a backfire 2. to go awry; boomerang [his plan *backfired*] 3. [Aust.] to use or set a backfire
back-for·ma·tion (-fôr mā'shən) *n.* 1. a word formed from, but looking as if it were the base of, another word (Ex.: *burgle* from *burglar*) 2. the forming of such a word
back·gam·mon (-gam'ən) *n.* [BACK + GAMMON²] a game played on a special board by two people, with pieces moved according to the throw of dice
back·ground (-ground') *n.* 1. the part of a scene or picture towards the back 2. surroundings behind something, providing harmony or contrast 3. an unimportant position 4. the whole of one's study, training, and experience 5. events or conditions leading up to or surrounding something, helping to explain it 6. any of various constant, interfering effects occurring in electronic apparatus, as static in radio, etc.
background music sound effects or music accompanying action, as in films
back·hand (-hand') *n.* 1. handwriting that slants backwards, up to the left 2. a stroke, as in tennis, with the back of the hand turned forward —*adj.* 1. done with the back of the hand 2. done or performed with a backhand —*adv.* with a backhand
back·hand·ed (-han'did) *adj.* 1. *same as* BACKHAND 2. indirect or sarcastic; equivocal [a *backhanded* compliment] 3. *Sports* performed by hitting the ball with a backhand —*adv.* with a backhand
back·hand·er (-han'dər) *n.* 1. a blow with the back of the hand 2. a bribe
back·ing (-iŋ) *n.* 1. something forming a back for support or strength 2. support given to a person or cause 3. those giving such support 4. [Slang] a musical accompaniment

BACKHAND STROKE

back·lash (-lash') *n.* 1. a quick, sharp recoil 2. a sudden, strong reaction, as to a political or social movement or development 3. a snarl in a reeled fishing line, from an imperfect cast 4. the jarring reaction of loose or worn parts of machinery
back·log (-log') *n.* 1. a reserve 2. an accumulation of unfilled orders, etc. 3. [U.S.] a large log at the back of a fireplace —*vi., vt.* -**logged'**, -**log'ging** to accumulate as a backlog
back·mark·er (-mä'kər) *n.* 1. a competitor in a game or race who concedes a start or initial advantage to his opponents 2. a competitor who is behind the others at any stage in a contest
back number 1. an old issue of a periodical 2. [Colloq.] an old-fashioned person or thing
back order an order not yet completed

back·ped·al (-ped´´l) *vi.* **-ped´alled, -ped´al·ling** 1. to press backwards on bicycle pedals in braking 2. to move backwards quickly in boxing to avoid a blow 3. to retreat from a previously held opinion

back projection the projection of pictures onto the back of a translucent screen for viewing from the front

back·room (-room´) *adj.* doing important research without any publicity and often in secret

back seat a secondary or inconspicuous position

back-seat driver (-sēt´) a passenger in a motor car who offers unwanted advice about driving

back·sheesh, back·shish (bak´shēsh´) *n.* *same as* BAKSHEESH

back·side (bak´sīd´) *n.* 1. the back or hind part 2. the rump; buttocks

back·slide (-slīd´) *vi.* **-slid´, -slid´, -slid´ing** to slide backwards in morals or religious enthusiasm —**back´slid´er** *n.*

back·space (-spās´) *vi.* **-spaced´, -spac´ing** to move a typewriter carriage back a space at a time by depressing a certain key (**backspacer**)

back·spin (-spin´) *n.* a backward spin given to a propelled ball, wheel, etc. that causes it, upon hitting a surface, to change, esp. to reverse, its normal direction

back·stage (-stāj´) *adv.* in the wings or dressing rooms of a theatre —*adj.* 1. situated backstage 2. of the life of people in show business

back·stairs (-sterz´) *adj.* involving intrigue or scandal: also **back´stair´**

back·stay (-stā´) *n.* a stay or rope extending aft from a masthead to the side or stern of the ship

back·stretch (-strech´) *n.* the part of a race track farthest from the grandstand

back·stroke (-strōk´) *n.* 1. a backhand stroke 2. a stroke made by a swimmer lying face upwards, stretching the arms alternately over the head —*vi.* **-stroked´, -strok´ing** to perform a backstroke —*vt.* to hit with a backstroke

back-to-back (bak´tə bak´) *adj.* 1. of or designating houses or terraces built with backs adjoining 2. [Colloq.] one after another; consecutive

back·track (-trak´) *vi.* 1. to return by the same path 2. to withdraw from a position, etc.

back·up, back-up (-up´) *adj.* 1. alternate or auxiliary [a backup pilot] 2. supporting [a backup effort] —*n.* the act or result of backing up; specif., a) an accumulation because of a stoppage b) a support or help

back·veld (-velt´, -velt´) *n.* [S. Afr.] a sparsely inhabited, remote, rural area

back·ward (-wərd) *adv.* 1. towards the back; behind 2. with the back or rear foremost 3. in reverse 4. in a way contrary to normal 5. into the past 6. from a better to a worse state Also **back´wards** —*adj.* 1. turned or directed towards the rear or in the opposite way 2. hesitant or shy, as in meeting people 3. late in developing; retarded —**bend** (or **lean**) **over backwards** 1. to try earnestly (to please, pacify, etc.) 2. to offset a tendency, bias, etc. by an effort in the opposite direction —**back´ward·ly** *adv.* —**back´ward·ness** *n.*

back·wash (-wosh´) *n.* 1. water moved backwards, as by a ship, an oar, etc. 2. a backward current, as of air from an aircraft propeller

back·wa·ter (-wôt´ər) *n.* 1. water moved backwards or held back by a dam, etc. 2. stagnant water in a stream 3. a place or condition where there is no progress or growth —*adj.* stagnant; backward

back·woods (-woodz´) *n.pl.* [*occas. with sing. v.*] 1. heavily wooded areas far from centres of population 2. any remote, thinly populated place —*adj.* in, from, or like the backwoods: also **back´wood´** —**back´woods´man** *n.,* pl. **-men**

back·yard (-yärd´) *n.* 1. a yard or area of enclosed ground behind a house 2. somewhere within easy reach [in one's own *backyard*]

ba·con (bāk´'n) *n.* [OFr. < OS. *baco,* side of bacon] cured meat from the back or sides of a pig —**bring home the bacon** [Colloq.] 1. to earn a living 2. to succeed; win

Ba·co·ni·an (bā kō´nē ən) *adj.* of Francis Bacon, 16th cent. Eng. philosopher, or his inductive system of philosophy —*n.* 1. an adherent of the Baconian philosophy 2. one who believes Bacon was the writer of the plays attributed to Shakespeare

bac·te·ri·a (bak tir´ē ə) *n.pl., sing.* **-ri·um** (-əm) [ModL. < Gr. dim. of *baktron,* a staff] typically one-celled microorganisms which have no chlorophyll, multiply by simple division, and occur in various forms, chiefly as cocci, bacilli, and spirilla: some bacteria cause diseases, but others are necessary for fermentation, nitrogen fixation, etc. —**bac·te´ri·al** *adj.* —**bac·te´ri·al·ly** *adv.*

bac·te·ri·cide (bak tir´ə sīd´) *n.* [BACTERI(O)- + -CIDE] an agent that destroys bacteria —**bac·te´ri·ci´dal** *adj.*

bac·te·ri·o- a combining form meaning of bacteria

bac·te·ri·ol·o·gy (bak tir´ē ol´ə jē) *n.* the study of bacteria, as in medicine, or for food processing, agriculture, etc.

—**bac·te´ri·o·log´ic** (-ē ə loj´ik), **bac·te´ri·o·log´i·cal** *adj.* —**bac·te´ri·o·log´i·cal·ly** *adv.* —**bac·te´ri·ol´o·gist** *n.*

bac·te·ri·o·phage (bak tir´ē ə fāj´) *n.* [BACTERIO- + -PHAGE] any virus that is parasitic upon certain bacteria, disintegrating them

bac·te·ri·um (-əm) *n.* *sing. of* BACTERIA

Bac·tri·an camel (bak´trē ən) [< *Bactria,* ancient country in W Asia] a camel with two humps, native to C Asia, shorter and hairier than the dromedary

bad¹ (bad) *adj.* **worse, worst** [ME.] 1. not good; not as it should be 2. defective in quality 3. unfit; unskilled 4. not pleasant; unfavourable [*bad* news] 5. rotten; spoiled 6. incorrect; faulty [*bad* spelling] 7. *a)* wicked; immoral *b)* mischievous 8. causing injury; harmful 9. severe [a *bad* storm] 10. ill; in poor health 11. *Law* not valid —*n.* 1. anything bad; bad quality or state 2. wickedness —**not bad** [Colloq.] good; fairly good: also **not half bad, not so bad** —**bad´ness** *n.*

bad² (bad) *archaic pt. of* BID

bad blood a feeling of (mutual) enmity

bad debt a debt which is unpaid and not collectable

bade (bad; *occas.* bād) *alt. pt. of* BID

bad egg [Slang] a mean or dishonest person: also **bad actor, bad apple, bad hat, bad lot,** etc.

badge (baj) *n.* [ME. *bage*] 1. a token, emblem, or sign worn to show rank, membership, etc. 2. any distinguishing mark or symbol

badg·er (baj´ər) *n.,* pl. **-ers, -er:** see PLURAL, II, D, 1 [< ? obs. *n.* & personal name *badger,* grain dealer] 1. a carnivorous, burrowing mammal with thick, short legs, and long claws on the forefeet 2. its fur —*vt.* to nag at

bad·i·nage (bad´ə näzh´) *n.* [Fr. < *badiner,* to jest < Pr. < ML. *badare,* to gape] playful, teasing talk; banter —*vt.* **-naged´, -nag´ing** to tease with playful talk

bad·lands (bad´landz´) *n.pl.* any section of barren land where deep erosion has cut the dry soil or soft rocks into strange shapes, esp. [B-] as found in South Dakota, U.S.: also **Bad Lands**

bad·ly (bad´lē) *adv.* 1. in a bad manner 2. [Colloq.] very much; greatly Also used informally as an adjective meaning "sorry" or "distressed" [he feels *badly* about it]

bad·min·ton (bad´min tən) *n.* [after *Badminton,* estate of the Duke of Beaufort] a game in which a feathered cork (*shuttlecock*) is batted back and forth with light rackets across a net

bad-tem·pered (bad´tem´pərd) *adj.* having a bad temper or ill-humoured disposition; irritable

Bae·de·ker (bā´də kər) *n.* 1. any of a series of guidebooks to foreign countries first published in Germany by Karl Baedeker (1801-59) 2. loosely, any guidebook

baf·fle (baf´'l) *vt.* **-fled, -fling** [16th-c. Scot.; prob. respelling of obs. Scot. *bauchle*] 1. to confuse so as to keep from understanding or solving; puzzle; confound 2. to hinder; impede 3. to check the interference of (sound waves) by a baffle —*n.* 1. a baffling or being baffled 2. a wall or screen to deflect the flow of liquids, gases, etc.: also **baf´fle·plate´** 3. a mounting that checks the transmission of sound waves between the front and rear of a loudspeaker —**baf´fle·ment** *n.* —**baf´fler** *n.* —**baf´fling** *adj.*

bag (bag) *n.* [ON. *baggi*] 1. a nonrigid container made of fabric, paper, leather, etc., with an opening at the top that can be closed; sack 2. the amount a bag holds 3. a piece of hand luggage 4. a woman's handbag 5. *a)* a container for game *b)* the amount of game caught or killed 6. anything shaped or bulging like a bag [*bags* under the eyes] 7. an udder or sac 8. [pl.] [Colloq.] plenty [*bags* of room] 9. [< BAGGAGE, 3a] [Slang] an unattractive woman —*vt.* **bagged, bag´ging** 1. to make bulge 2. to enclose within a bag 3. to capture 4. to kill in hunting 5. [Slang] to get —*vi.* 1. to swell 2. to hang loosely —**bag and baggage** [Colloq.] 1. with all one's possessions 2. entirely —(**whole**) **bag of tricks** all one's resources —**in the bag** [Slang] having its success assured —**bags** (I)! [Slang] I claim it! it's mine!: used esp. by children [*bags* I first!] —**bag´ful´** *n.,* pl. **-fuls´**

ba·gasse (bə gas´) *n.* [Fr. < Pr. *bagasso,* refuse from processing grapes, etc. < L. *baca,* berry] the part of sugar cane left after the juice has been extracted, or the residue of certain other processed plants: used for making fibreboard, etc.

bag·a·telle (bag´ə tel´) *n.* [Fr. < It. *bagatella,* dim. < ML. *baga,* chest, bag] 1. something of little value; trifle 2. a game, somewhat like billiards, played with nine balls on a table 3. a short musical composition, esp. for the piano

bag·gage (bag´ij) *n.* [< OFr. < *bagues,* baggage < ML. *baga,* chest] 1. the bags and other equipment of a traveller 2. the supplies and gear of an army 3. *a)* [Fr. *bagasse,* harlot, ult. < Ar. *bagīja,* adulteress: infl. by "army baggage," i.e., "camp follower"] formerly, a prostitute *b)* a saucy girl

bag·gy (bag´ē) *adj.* **-gi·er, -gi·est** 1. puffed in a baglike way 2. hanging loosely [*baggy* trousers] —**bag´gi·ly** *adv.* —**bag´gi·ness** *n.*

bag·man (bag′mən) *n.,* *pl.* **-men** 1. a travelling salesman 2. [Aust.] a tramp

bagn·io (bän′yō) *n.,* *pl.* **-ios** [< It. < L. < Gr. *balaneion,* bath] a house of prostitution; brothel

bag·pipe (bag′pīp′) *n.* [*often pl.*] a shrill-toned musical instrument with a double-reed, fingered pipe and drone pipes, all sounded by air forced from a leather bag: now chiefly Scottish —**bag′pip′-er** *n.*

ba·guette, ba·guet (ba get′) *n.* [< Fr. < It. < L. *baculum,* a staff] 1. a gem, etc. cut in the shape of a narrow oblong 2. this shape 3. *Archit.* a small, convex moulding

bah (bä, ba) *interj.* an exclamation expressing contempt, scorn, or disgust

Ba·hai (bə hī′, bə hä′ē) *n.,* *pl.* **Ba·hais′** 1. a believer in Bahaism 2. same as BAHAISM —*adj.* of Bahaism or a Bahai Also written Baha'i

BAGPIPE

Ba·ha·ism (bə hä′iz'm, -hī′-) *n.* [Ar. *ba-hā,* splendour + -ISM] a modern religion, developed orig. in Iran from Babism, that advocates universal brotherhood, social equality, etc. —**Ba·ha′ist** *n.,* *adj.*

baht (bät) *n., pl.* **bahts, baht** [Thai *bāt*] see MONETARY UNITS, table (Thailand)

bail[1] (bāl) *n.* [OFr., power, control < *baillir,* keep in custody < L. *bajulare,* bear a burden < *bajulus,* porter] 1. money or credit deposited with the court to obtain the release of an arrested person until his trial 2. the release thus brought about 3. the person giving bail —*vt.* 1. to set (an arrested person) free on bail or have (an arrested person) set free by giving bail (often with *out*) 2. to help out of financial or other difficulty (often with *out*) —**go bail for** to furnish bail for —**bail′a·ble** *adj.*

bail[2] (bāl) *n.* [< OFr. < VL. hyp. *bajula,* vessel < *bajulare:* see prec.] a bucket, etc. for removing water from a boat —*vi., vt.* 1. to remove water from (a boat) as with a bail 2. to ladle out (water, etc.) as with a bail —**bail out** 1. to make a parachute jump from an aircraft 2. [Colloq.] to help out or rescue —**bail′er** *n.*

bail[3] (bāl) *n.* [< ON. *beygla* < *beygja,* to bend] 1. a hoop-shaped support, as for a canopy 2. a hoop-shaped handle for a bucket, etc. 3. a bar on a typewriter to hold the paper against the platen

bail[4] (bāl) *n.* [< OFr., ult. < L. *bajulus,* porter] 1. [*pl.*] formerly, an outer fortification made of stakes 2. *Cricket* either of two pieces of wood laid across the three stumps to form a wicket

bai·ley (bā′lē) *n.* [ME. *baili,* var. of *baile,* BAIL[4]] the outer wall or court of a medieval castle: term still kept in some proper names, as in OLD BAILEY

Bai·ley bridge (bā′lē) [after Sir D. C. Bailey (1901-), Brit. inventor] *Mil. Engineering* a portable bridge consisting of a series of prefabricated steel sections

bai·lie (bā′lē) *n.* [Scot. < OFr. < *bailif:* see ff.] in Scotland, a municipal councillor who serves as a magistrate

bai·liff (bā′lif) *n.* [OFr. *bailif* < *baillir:* see BAIL[1]] 1. a deputy sheriff who serves processes, etc. 2. [Chiefly U.S.] a court officer who guards jurors, keeps order in the courtroom, etc. 3. formerly, an administrative official of a district 4. an overseer or steward of an estate

bai·li·wick (bā′lə wik) *n.* [ME. < *bailif,* BAILIFF + *wik* < OE. *wic,* village] 1. a bailiff's district 2. [Chiefly U.S.] one's particular area of activity, authority, etc.

bails·man (bālz′mən) *n., pl.* **-men** a person who acts as surety or gives bail for another

bain-ma·rie (ban′má rē′) *n., pl.* **bains-marie** [Fr. < ML. *balneum Mariae,* lit., bath of Maria] a double boiler or an open pan of hot water in which other containers are placed to warm or cook the contents

Bai·ram (bī räm′) *n.* [Turk. *bairam*] either of two Moslem festivals following the fast of Ramadan

bairn (bern) *n.* [< OE. *bearn* < *beran,* to BEAR[1]] [Scot.] a son or daughter; child

bait (bāt) *vt.* [ON. *beita,* to make bite, caus. < *bīta,* to bite] 1. to set attacking dogs against for sport [to *bait* bears] 2. to torment or harass with unprovoked, repeated attacks 3. to tease or goad 4. to put food, etc. on (a hook or trap) so as to lure animals or fish 5. to lure; tempt; entice —*n.* 1. food, etc. put on a hook or trap to lure fish or animals 2. any lure; enticement —**bait′er** *n.*

baize (bāz) *n.* [< OFr. pl. of *baie* < L. *badius,* chestnut-brown] a feltlike, thick woollen cloth, often green, used to cover billiard tables, etc.

bake (bāk) *vt.* **baked, bak′ing** [OE. *bacan*] 1. to cook (food) by dry heat, esp. in an oven 2. to dry and harden (esp. glazed stoneware) by heat —*vi.* 1. to bake bread, etc. 2. to become baked —*n.* 1. a baking 2. a product of baking —**bake blind** to bake an empty pastry case by filling it with dried peas, breadcrumbs, etc. to keep its shape

baked Alaska a dessert consisting of cake and ice cream covered with meringue

baked beans cooked haricot beans in tomato sauce

bake·house (bāk′hous′) *n.* a place where bread, cakes, etc. are baked

Ba·ke·lite (bā′kə līt′) [after L. H. *Baekeland* (1863–1944), U.S. chemist] *a trademark for* a synthetic resin and plastic —*n.* [b-] this resin

bak·er (bāk′ər) *n.* one whose work or business is baking bread, etc.

baker's dozen thirteen

bak·er·y (bāk′ər ē) *n., pl.* **-er·ies** a place where bread, cakes, etc. are baked or sold

baking powder a leavening agent containing baking soda and an acid substance, such as cream of tartar, which together produce carbon dioxide in the presence of water

baking soda sodium bicarbonate, $NaHCO_3$, used as a leavening agent and as an antacid

bak·sheesh, bak·shish (bak′shēsh) *n.* [via Turk. or Ar. < Per. < *bakhshidan,* to give] in Turkey, Egypt, India, etc., a tip, gratuity, or alms

bal. balance

Bal·a·kla·va helmet (bal′ə klä′və) a woollen covering for the whole head, leaving only the face exposed

bal·a·lai·ka (bal′ə lī′kə) *n.* [Russ.] a Russian stringed instrument somewhat like a guitar, but with a triangular body

bal·ance (bal′əns) *n.* [OFr. < ML. < LL. *bilanx,* having two scales < L. *bis,* twice + *lanx,* a scale] 1. an instrument for weighing, esp. one with two matched pans hanging from either end of a poised lever; scales 2. a state of equilibrium or equipoise; equality in weight, value, importance, etc. 3. bodily equilibrium [he kept his *balance* on the tightrope] 4. mental or emotional stability 5. the pleasing harmony of various elements in a work of art; harmonious proportion 6. a weight, force, etc. that counteracts another or causes equilibrium 7. the point along an object's length at which there is equilibrium: in full, **balance point** 8. a) equality of debits and credits in an account b) the difference between credits and debits 9. the amount still owed after a partial settlement 10. a remainder 11. a balancing 12. same as BALANCE WHEEL —*vt.* **-anced, -anc·ing** 1. to weigh in or as in a balance 2. to compare as to relative importance, value, etc. 3. to counterpoise or counteract; offset 4. to put or keep in a state of equilibrium; poise 5. to bring into proportion, harmony, etc. 6. to make or be equal to in weight, force, etc. 7. a) to find any difference between the debit and credit sides of (an account); also, to equalize the debit and credit sides of (an account) b) to settle (an account) —*vi.* 1. to be in equilibrium 2. to be equal in value, weight, etc. 3. to have the credit and debit sides equal 4. to waver slightly —**in the balance** in a critical, undecided state —**on balance** considering everything; all in all —**bal′ance·a·ble** *adj.* —**bal′anc·er** *n.*

balance of (international) payments a balance estimated for a given period showing an excess or deficit in total payments of all kinds between one country and another country or other countries

balance of power an even distribution of military and economic power among nations that keeps any one of them from being too strong or dangerous

balance of trade the difference in value between the imports and exports of a country

balance sheet a summarized statement showing the financial status of a business

balance wheel a wheel that swings back and forth to regulate the movement of a timepiece, etc.

bal·a·ta (bal′ə tə, bal ä′tə) *n.* [Sp. < Tupi] 1. a tropical American tree 2. its dried milky sap, a rubberlike gum used commercially

bal·bo·a (bal bō′ə) *n.* [after Vasco Núñez de *Balboa,* Sp. explorer] see MONETARY UNITS, table (Panama)

bal·brig·gan (bal brig′ən) *n.* [after *Balbriggan,* town in Ireland] a knitted cotton material used for hosiery, underwear, etc.

bal·co·ny (bal′kə nē) *n., pl.* **-nies** [< It. < Gmc., akin to OHG. *balcho,* a beam] 1. a platform projecting from a building and enclosed by a balustrade 2. an upper floor of rows of seats in a theatre, etc., often jutting out over the main floor —**bal′co·nied** *adj.*

bald (bôld) *adj.* [ME. *balled* < ?] 1. having white fur or feathers on the head, as some animals and birds 2. having no hair on all or part of the scalp 3. not covered by natural growth [*bald* hills] 4. plain; unadorned 5. frank and blunt —**bald′ly** *adv.* —**bald′ness** *n.*

bal·da·chin, bal·da·quin (bal′də kin, bô′-) *n.* [It. *Baldacco,* Baghdad, where cloth was manufactured] 1. a rich brocade 2. a canopy carried in church processions or placed over an altar or throne

bald eagle a large, strong eagle of N. America, with a white-feathered head and neck

bal·der·dash (bôl′dər dash′) *n.* [orig., a senseless mixture of liquids] nonsensical talk or writing

bald·head (-hed′) *n.* **1.** a person who has a bald head **2.** a bald (sense 1) bird —**bald′head′ed** *adj.*
bald·ing (bôl′diŋ) *adj.* becoming bald
bald·pate (bôld′pāt′) *n.* **1.** a baldheaded person **2.** a N. American duck with a white crown
bal·dric (bôl′drik) *n.* [< OFr., ult. < L. *balteus*, a girdle] a belt worn over one shoulder and across the chest to support a sword, etc.
bale¹ (bāl) *n.* [OFr. < OHG. *balla*, a ball] a large bundle, esp. a standardized quantity, as of cotton, hay, or straw, compressed and bound —*vt.* **baled, bal′ing** to make into bales —**bal′er** *n.*
bale² (bāl) *n.* [OE. *bealu*] [Poet.] **1.** evil; disaster; harm **2.** sorrow; woe
bale³ (bāl) *n., vi., vt.* same as BAIL²
ba·leen (bə lēn′) *n.* [< OFr. < L. *ballaena*, a whale] same as WHALEBONE
bale·ful (bāl′fəl) *adj.* harmful or evil; sinister —**bale′ful·ly** *adv.* —**bale′ful·ness** *n.*
balk (bôk) *n.* [OE. *balca*, a bank, ridge] **1.** a ridge of unploughed land between furrows **2.** a roughly hewn piece of timber **3.** a check, hindrance, disappointment, etc. —*vt.* **1.** to miss or let slip by **2.** to obstruct or thwart; foil —*vi.* **1.** to stop and obstinately refuse to move or act **2.** to hesitate or recoil (*at*) —**balk′er** *n.*
Bal·kan (bôl′kən) *adj.* of the countries of the Balkan Peninsula in SE Europe, their people, etc.
balk·line (bôk′līn′) *n.* a line across one end of a billiard table, from behind which opening shots are made
balk·y (bôk′ē) *adj.* **balk′i·er, balk′i·est** stubbornly refusing to move or act —**balk′i·ness** *n.*
ball¹ (bôl) *n.* [ME. *bal*, akin to OHG. *balla*] **1.** any round object; sphere; globe **2.** a planet or star, esp. the earth **3.** a round or egg-shaped object used in various games **4.** a throw or pitch of a ball [a fast *ball*] **5.** a solid missile for a cannon or firearm **6.** a rounded part of the body [the *ball* of the foot] **7.** [*pl.*] [Slang] the testicles: usually considered a vulgar term —*vi., vt.* to form into a ball —*interj.* [*pl.*] a vulgar expression of contempt or annoyance —**balls up** [Slang] to muddle or confuse —**be on the ball** [Slang] to be alert; be efficient —**get** (or **keep**) **the ball rolling** [Colloq.] to start (or maintain) some action —**have the ball at one's feet** [Colloq.] to have everything in one's favour —**play ball** [Colloq.] to cooperate
ball² (bôl) *n.* [Fr. *bal* < OFr. < LL. *ballare*, to dance < Gr. *ballein*, to throw] **1.** a formal social dance **2.** [Slang] an enjoyable time or experience
bal·lad (bal′əd) *n.* [< OFr. *ballade*, dancing song, ult. < LL. *ballare*: see prec.] **1.** a romantic or sentimental song with the same melody for each stanza **2.** a song or poem, usually of unknown authorship and handed down orally, that tells a story in short stanzas and simple words, with repetition, refrain, etc. **3.** a slow, sentimental popular song —**bal′lad·eer′** *n.* —**bal′lad·ry** *n.*
bal·lade (bə läd′) *n.* [Fr.: see prec.] **1.** a verse form with three stanzas of eight or ten lines each and an envoy of four or five lines **2.** a romantic musical composition
ball-and-sock·et joint (bôl′'n sok′it) a joint, as that of the hip, formed by a ball in a socket, allowing limited movement in any direction
bal·last (bal′əst) *n.* [LowG. < ODan. *barlast* < *bar*, bare + *last*, a load] **1.** anything heavy carried in a ship, aircraft, or vehicle to give stability or in an airship or balloon to help control altitude **2.** anything giving stability and firmness to character, human relations, etc. **3.** crushed rock or gravel, as that used to make a firm bed for railway sleepers —*vt.* **1.** to furnish with ballast; stabilize **2.** to fill in (a railway bed, etc.) with ballast
ball bearing 1. a bearing in which the moving parts revolve on freely rolling metal balls so that friction is reduced **2.** any of these balls
ball boy *Sport* a person who retrieves balls, esp. in tennis
ball cock an automatic device in a cistern which controls the flow of water by means of a floating ball and valve
bal·le·ri·na (bal′ə rē′nə) *n.* [It. < LL. *ballare*: see BALL²] a woman ballet dancer
bal·let (bal′ā, ba lā′) *n.* [< Fr. < It. *balletto*, dim. < *ballo*, a dance: see BALL²] **1.** an intricate group dance (or dancing) using pantomime and conventionalized movements to tell a story **2.** a company of such dancers —**bal·let·ic** (ba let′ik) *adj.*
bal·let·o·mane (ba let′ə mān′) *n.* [BALLET + Fr. *manie*, mania] a person enthusiastic about ballet —**bal′let·o·ma′-ni·a** (-mā′nē ə) *n.*
ball·game (bôl′gām) *n.* **1.** [Chiefly U.S.] any of several games played with a ball, esp. baseball **2.** [Colloq.] scene of action **3.** [Colloq.] set of circumstances; situation [a different *ballgame*]

bal·lis·ta (bə lis′tə) *n., pl.* **-tae** (-tē) [L. < Gr. *ballein*, to throw] a device used in ancient warfare to hurl heavy stones, etc.
ballistic missile a long-range missile guided automatically in the first part of its flight, but free-falling as it approaches its target
bal·lis·tics (bə lis′tiks) *n.pl.* [with sing. v.] **1.** the science dealing with the motion and impact of projectiles, such as bullets, rockets, bombs, etc. **2.** the study of the effects of firing on a firearm or bullet, etc. —**bal·lis′tic** *adj.* —**bal·lis·ti·cian** (bal′əs tish′ən) *n.*
bal·locks (bol′loks) *n.pl.* [< OE. *beallucas*, testicles] [Slang] the testicles —*interj.* [Slang] nonsense! Usually considered a vulgar term
bal·loon (bə lōōn′) *n.* [< Fr. < It. *pallone* < *palla*, a ball] **1.** a large, airtight bag that rises above the earth when filled with a gas lighter than air **2.** a bag of this sort with an attached car for passengers or instruments **3.** a small, inflatable rubber bag, used as a toy **4.** the outline enclosing spoken words in a comic strip —*vt.* to cause to swell like a balloon —*vi.* **1.** to ride in a balloon **2.** to swell; expand —*adj.* like a balloon —**bal·loon′ist** *n.*
bal·lot (bal′ət) *n.* [It. *ballotta, pallotta*, dim. of *palla*, a ball] **1.** orig. a ball, now a ticket, paper, etc., by which a vote is registered: in full, **ballot paper 2.** act or method of voting, esp. secret voting by the use of ballots **3.** the total number of votes cast in an election —*vi.* to decide by means of the ballot; vote —**bal′lot·er** *n.*
ballot box a sealed container into which completed ballot papers are inserted
ball·park (bôl′pärk) *n.* [U.S.] a stadium for playing baseball
ball point pen a pen having instead of a point a small ball bearing that rolls over an ink reservoir: also **ball′-point′, ball′point′** *n.*
ball·room (-rōōm′) *n.* a large hall for dancing
ballroom dancing dancing in which two people dance as partners to a waltz, fox trot, etc.
balls-up (bôlz′up) *n.* [Slang] a muddle or confusion: often considered a vulgar term
bal·ly (bal′ē) *adj., adv.* a euphemism for BLOODY (adj. 5, adv.)
bal·ly·hoo (bal′ē hōō′) *n.* [< ?] **1.** loud talk; uproar **2.** loud or sensational advertising or propaganda —*vt., vi.* **-hooed′, -hoo′ing** [Colloq.] to advertise or promote by sensational methods —**bal′ly·hoo′er** *n.*
balm (bäm) *n.* [< OFr. < L. < Gr. *balsamon*] **1.** an aromatic gum resin obtained from certain trees and plants and used as medicine; balsam **2.** any fragrant ointment or oil **3.** anything healing or soothing, esp. to the mind or temper **4.** any of several aromatic herbs **5.** pleasant odour; fragrance
balm of Gil·e·ad (gil′ē əd) **1.** *a)* a small evergreen tree native to Asia and Africa *b)* an aromatic ointment formerly prepared from its resin **2.** anything healing or soothing **3.** same as BALSAM FIR
bal·mor·al (bal mor′əl) *n.* [< *Balmoral* Castle, royal residence in Scotland] **1.** a round, flat Scottish cap **2.** a petticoat **3.** a long laced boot
balm·y (bäm′ē) *adj.* **balm′i·er, balm′i·est 1.** having the qualities of balm; soothing, mild, pleasant, etc. **2.** [var. of BARMY] [Slang] crazy or foolish —**balm′i·ly** *adv.* —**balm′-i·ness** *n.*
bal·ne·ol·o·gy (bal′nē ol′ə jē) *n.* [< L. *balneum*, bath + -LOGY] the study of the therapeutic use of various sorts of bathing
ba·lo·ney (bə lō′nē) *n.* [altered < ? *bologna*, sausage] [Slang] nonsense —*interj.* [Slang] nonsense!
B.A.L.P.A. British Airline Pilots' Association
bal·sa (bôl′sə) *n.* [Sp.] **1.** a tropical American tree that yields an extremely light and buoyant wood used for rafts, etc. **2.** the wood **3.** a raft, esp. one made up of a frame on cylindrical floats
bal·sam (bôl′səm) *n.* [OE. < L.: see BALM] **1.** any of various aromatic resins obtained from certain trees **2.** any of various aromatic, resinous oils or fluids **3.** any aromatic preparation made with balsam, as certain medical dressings **4.** anything healing or soothing; balm **5.** any of various trees that yield balsam, as the balsam fir **6.** any of various species of the impatiens —**bal·sam·ic** (bôl sam′ik) *adj.*
balsam fir an evergreen tree of Canada and the northern U.S. with a soft wood used for pulpwood
Bal·tic (bôl′tik) *adj.* **1.** of the Baltic Sea **2.** of the Baltic States, the former independent countries of Latvia, Lithuania, & Estonia **3.** of a branch of the Indo-European language family that includes Lithuanian, Latvian, and Old Prussian —*n.* the Baltic Sea
Bal·ti·more oriole (bôl′tə môr′) [from the colours of the coat of arms of Lord *Baltimore*] a N. American oriole that has an orange body with black on the head, wings, and tail
bal·us·ter (bal′əs tər) *n.* [< Fr. < It. < Gr. *balaustion*,

BALL-AND-SOCKET JOINT

flower of the wild pomegranate: from some resemblance in shape] any of the small posts supporting a railing, as on a staircase

bal·us·trade (bal'ə strād') *n.* a railing held up by balusters

bam·bi·no (bam bē'nō) *n., pl.* **-nos, -ni** (-nē) [It., dim. of *bambo*, childish] 1. a child; baby 2. any image of the infant Jesus

bam·boo (bam bōō') *n.* [Malay *bambu*] any of a number of treelike, semitropical or tropical grasses with springy, jointed, often hollow stems, sometimes growing to heights of 37 metres: the stems are used for furniture, canes, etc., and the young shoots of some species are eaten

bamboo curtain [often **B- C-**] the barrier of political and ideological differences that separate China from the West

bam·boo·zle (bam bōō'z'l) *vt.* **-zled, -zling** [< ?] 1. to deceive or cheat by trickery 2. to confuse or puzzle —**bam·boo'zle·ment** *n.* —**bam·boo'zler** *n.*

ban[1] (ban) *vt.* **banned, ban'ning** [OE. *bannan*, to summon] to prohibit or forbid, as by official order —*n.* [< the *v.*; also < OFr. *ban*, decree < OHG. *bann*] 1. an excommunication or condemnation by church authorities 2. a curse 3. an official prohibition 4. strong public disapproval 5. a sentence of outlawry

ban[2] (bän) *n., pl.* **ba·ni** (bä'nē) *see* MONETARY UNITS, table (Rumania)

ba·nal (bə näl'; bā'nəl) *adj.* [Fr. < *ban*: see BAN[1]] dull or stale because of overuse; trite; hackneyed —**ba·nal·i·ty** (bə nal'ə tē) *n., pl.* **-ties** —**ba'nal·ly** *adv.*

ba·nan·a (bə nän'ə) *n.* [Sp. & Port. < native name in W Africa] 1. any of a genus of treelike, tropical plants, with long, broad leaves and large clusters of edible fruit 2. the fruit: it is narrow and somewhat curved, and has a sweet, creamy flesh covered by a yellow or reddish skin

ba·nan·a·land (bə nän'ə land') [Aust. Colloq.] Queensland —**ba·nan'a·land'er** *n.*

banana oil a colourless liquid acetate with a bananalike odour, used in flavourings, in making lacquers, etc.

banana republic any small country, esp. in C America, whose economy is controlled by foreign capital

BANANA

Ban·bur·y cake (ban'bər ē) [after *Banbury*, a town in Oxfordshire] a small pie filled with currants, mixed peel, etc.

band[1] (band) *n.* [ON.; also (in meaning "thin strip") < Fr. *bande* < OFr. < ML. < Goth. *binda* < *bindan*, to bind] 1. something that binds, ties together, restrains, etc. 2. a strip or ring of wood, metal, rubber, etc. fastened round something to bind or tie it together 3. a stripe 4. a narrow strip of cloth used to line, decorate, etc. [hatband] 5. [usually *pl.*] two strips hanging in front from the neck, as part of certain academic, legal, or clerical dress 6. a division on a long-playing gramophone record containing an individual selection 7. a specific range of wavelengths or frequencies, as in radio broadcasting or sound or light transmission 8. a belt to drive wheels or pulleys in machinery —*vt.* 1. to put a band on or round, as in tying or in marking for identification 2. to put schoolchildren into groups according to ability

band[2] (band) *n.* [Fr. *bande*, a troupe (orig., prob., those following the same sign) < It. *banda* < Goth. *bandwa*, sign] 1. a group of people united for a common purpose [a band of thieves] 2. a group of musicians playing together, esp. upon wind and percussion instruments [a dance band] —*vi., vt.* to unite for a common purpose (usually with *together*)

band·age (ban'dij) *n.* [Fr. < *bande*, BAND[1]] a strip of cloth or other dressing used to bind or cover an injured part of the body —*vt.* **-aged, -ag·ing** to put a bandage on

ban·dan·na, ban·dan·a (ban dan'ə) *n.* [Hindi *bāndhnū*, method of dyeing] a large, coloured handkerchief, usually with a printed pattern

B & B, b. and b. bed and breakfast

band·box (band'boks') *n.* a light box of wood or pasteboard to hold hats, collars, etc.

ban·deau (ban dō', ban'dō) *n., pl.* **-deaux'** (-dōz', -dōz) [Fr.] a narrow ribbon, esp. one worn around the head to hold the hair in place

ban·de·role, ban·de·rol (ban'də rōl') *n.* [Fr. < It. dim. of *bandiera*, banner] 1. a narrow flag or pennant, as one attached to a lance 2. a ribbonlike scroll, or a sculptured representation of one, carrying an inscription or symbol

ban·di·coot (ban'di kōōt') *n.* [< Telugu *pandikokku*, pig rat] 1. a very large rat found esp. in India and Ceylon 2. a ratlike animal of Australia that carries its young in a pouch

ban·dit (ban'dit) *n., pl.* **-dits, ban·dit·ti** (ban dit'ē) [It. *bandito* < *bandire*, to outlaw, akin to OHG. *bann* (see BAN[1], n.)] 1. a robber, esp. one who robs travellers on the road; brigand 2. anyone who cheats, steals, etc. —**ban'dit·ry** *n.*

band·mas·ter (band'mäs'tər) *n.* the leader or conductor of a band, esp. a military or brass band

Band of Hope a society founded to promote temperance, esp. among the young

ban·do·leer, ban·do·lier (ban'də lir') *n.* [< Fr. < Sp. < *banda*, a scarf] a broad shoulder belt with pockets for carrying ammunition, etc.

band saw a power saw consisting of an endless, toothed steel belt running over pulleys

bands·man (bandz'mən) *n., pl.* **-men** a member of a band of musicians

band·stand (band'stand') *n.* 1. an outdoor, usually roofed platform for a band or orchestra 2. any platform for a musical band, as in a ballroom

band·wag·on (band'wag'ən) *n.* a wagon for the band to ride in, as in a parade —**on the bandwagon** [Colloq.] on the popular or apparently winning side, as in an election

band·width (-width') *n.* the range of frequencies within a radiation band needed to transmit a particular signal

ban·dy[1] (ban'dē) *vt.* **-died, -dy·ing** [? Fr. *bander*, to bandy (a tennis)] 1. to toss or hit (a ball, etc.) back and forth 2. to pass (gossip, etc.) about carelessly 3. to exchange (words), as in arguing

ban·dy[2] (ban'dē) *adj.* [? < Fr. pp. of *bander*, to bend (as a bow)] bent or curved outwards

ban·dy·leg·ged (-leg'id, -legd') *adj.* having bandy legs; bowlegged

bane (bān) *n.* [OE. *bana*, slayer] 1. [Poet.] ruin 2. the cause of distress, death, or ruin 3. deadly poison: now obs. except in *ratsbane*, etc.

bane·ber·ry (bān'bər ē) *n., pl.* **-ries** 1. any of a genus of plants of the buttercup family, with clusters of berries, some of which are poisonous 2. the berry of any of these plants

bane·ful (-fəl) *adj.* causing distress, death, or ruin —**bane'ful·ly** *adv.*

bang[1] (baŋ) *vt.* [ON. *banga*, to pound] 1. to hit hard and noisily 2. to shut (a door, etc.) noisily 3. to handle violently 4. [Slang] to have sexual intercourse (with) —*vi.* 1. to make a sharp, loud noise 2. to strike sharply (*against, into*, etc.) —*n.* 1. a hard blow or loud knock 2. a sudden, loud noise 3. [Colloq.] a display of enthusiasm or vigour [to start with a *bang*] —*adv.* 1. hard and noisily 2. suddenly or exactly —**bang off** [Slang] immediately —**bang on** [Slang] absolutely right

bang[2] (baŋ) *vt.* [< ?] [Chiefly U.S.] to cut (hair) short and straight across —*n.* [Chiefly U.S.] [usually *pl.*] a fringe cut short and straight across the forehead

bang·er (baŋ'ər) *n.* [< BANG[1]] [Colloq.] 1. a sausage [bangers and mash] 2. a noisy old car 3. a firework that explodes loudly

ban·gle (baŋ'g'l) *n.* [Hindi *bangrī*, glass bracelet] a decorative bracelet, armlet, or anklet

bang·tail (baŋ'tāl') *n.* a horse whose tail has been cut straight across

bang-up (baŋ'up') *adj.* [Colloq.] excellent

ban·ian[1] (ban'yən) *n.* same as BANYAN

ban·ian[2] (ban'yən) *n.* [Port., ult. < Sans. *vaṇij*, merchant] a Hindu merchant

ban·ish (ban'ish) *vt.* [< extended stem of OFr. *banir* < *ban*: see BAN[1]] 1. to send into exile 2. to send or put away; dismiss —**ban'ish·ment** *n.*

ban·is·ter (ban'əs tər) *n.* [altered < BALUSTER] 1. [often *pl.*] a railing and the balusters supporting it, as on a staircase 2. the railing itself

ban·jo (ban'jō) *n., pl.* **-jos, -joes** [< U.S. pronunciation of *bandore*, ult < Gr. *pandoura*, a musical instrument] a stringed musical instrument having a long neck and a circular body covered with taut skin —**ban'jo·ist** *n.*

BANJO

bank[1] (baŋk) *n.* [< Fr. < It. *banca*, orig. a (moneylender's) table < OHG. *bank*, bench: see ff.] 1. *a)* an establishment for receiving, lending, or, sometimes, issuing money *b)* its building 2. same as PIGGY BANK 3. the fund held, as by the dealer, in some gambling games 4. *Med. a)* any place for gathering and distributing blood for transfusions or body parts for transplantation *b)* any reserve thus gathered —*vi.* 1. to put money in or do business with a bank 2. to manage a bank 3. to keep the bank, as in some gambling games —*vt.* to deposit (money) in a bank —**bank on** [Colloq.] to depend on; rely on —**bank′a·ble** *adj.*

bank² (baŋk) *n.* [ME. *banke* < ON.] 1. a long mound or heap; ridge 2. a steep slope, as of a hill 3. a stretch of rising land at the edge of a stream, etc. 4. a shoal or shallow place, as in a sea 5. the sloping of an aircraft laterally to avoid slipping sideways on a turn 6. the sloping of a road laterally along a curve —*vt.* 1. to cover (a fire) with ashes and fuel so that it will burn longer 2. to pile up so as to form a bank 3. to construct (a curve in a road, etc.) so that it slopes up from the inside edge 4. to slope (an aircraft) laterally on a turn 5. *Billiards* to stroke (a ball) so that it recoils from a cushion —*vi.* 1. to form a bank or banks 2. to bank an aircraft

bank³ (baŋk) *n.* [< OFr. < OHG. *bank:* see prec.] 1. a bench for rowers in a galley 2. a row of oars 3. a row or tier of objects 4. a row of keys in a keyboard or console —*vt.* to arrange in a bank

bank account money deposited in a bank and subject to withdrawal by the depositor

bank bill a bill of exchange drawn by one bank on another

bank·book (baŋk′book′) *n.* the book in which the account of a depositor in a bank is recorded

bank card *same as* CHEQUE CARD

bank·er¹ (baŋ′kər) *n.* 1. one who owns or manages a bank 2. the keeper of the bank in some gambling games

bank·er² *n.* [< BANK²] [Aust.] a flooded river

bank holiday a day on which banks are closed by law and which is usually a general holiday

bank·ing (-kiŋ) *n.* the business of a bank

bank manager the head of a local branch of a bank

bank note a promissory note issued by a bank, payable on demand: it is a form of paper money

Bank of England the government bank responsible for keeping the country's gold reserves and for the issue of bank notes in England

bank rate the official rate at which the Bank of England will discount approved bills of exchange

bank·rupt (baŋk′rupt′, -rəpt) *n.* [< Fr. < It. < *banca,* bench (see BANK¹) + *rotta,* broken < L. pp. of *rumpere,* to break] a person legally declared unable to pay his debts: his property is divided among his creditors —*adj.* 1. that is a bankrupt 2. lacking in some quality [morally *bankrupt*] 3. that has failed completely [a *bankrupt* foreign policy] —*vt.* ·to make bankrupt

bank·rupt·cy (-rupt′sē, -rəp sē) *n., pl.* **-cies** 1. the state or an instance of being bankrupt 2. complete failure; ruin; destitution

ban·ner (ban′ər) *n.* [< OFr. *baniere* (< WGmc. *banda,* a sign), altered after *banir,* to announce (see BANISH)] 1. a piece of cloth bearing a design, motto, etc. 2. a flag

banner headline a headline extending across a newspaper page

ban·nis·ter (ban′əs tər) *n. same as* BANISTER

ban·nock (ban′ək) *n.* [< OE. *bannuc,* a cake] [Scot.] a flat cake of oatmeal or barley meal

banns (banz) *n.pl.* [see BAN¹] the proclamation, generally made in church on three successive Sundays, of an intended marriage

ban·quet (baŋ′kwit, ban′-) *n.* [Fr. < It. *banchetto,* dim. of *banca:* see BANK¹] 1. a feast 2. a formal dinner, usually with speeches —*vt.* to honour with a banquet —*vi.* to dine at a banquet —**ban′quet·er** *n.*

ban·quette (baŋ ket′) *n.* [Fr., dim. < Norm. *banque,* earthwork < Du. *bank,* BANK²] 1. a platform along the inside of a trench or parapet 2. an upholstered bench along a wall

ban·shee (ban′shē) *n.* [< Ir. < *bean,* woman + *sith,* fairy] *Ir. & Scot. Folklore* a female spirit believed to wail outside a house to warn of an impending death in the family

ban·tam (ban′təm) *n.* [after *Bantam,* former Du. residency in Java] 1. [*often* B-] any of various dwarf varieties of breeds of domestic fowl 2. a small but aggressive person —*adj.* like a bantam; small and aggressive

ban·tam·weight (-wāt′) *n. see* BOXING AND WRESTLING WEIGHTS, table

ban·ter (ban′tər) *vt.* [17th-c. slang < ?] to tease in a playful way —*vi.* to exchange banter (*with* someone) —*n.* good-natured teasing or joking —**ban′ter·er** *n.* —**ban′·ter·ing·ly** *adv.*

bant·ling (bant′liŋ) *n.* [< G. *Bänkling,* bastard < *Bank,* a bench] [Archaic] a young child; brat

Ban·tu (ban′tōō) *n.* [Bantu *ba-ntu,* mankind] 1. *pl.* **-tus,** **-tu** any member of a large group of Negroid tribes of equatorial and southern Africa 2. any of the group of languages of these peoples —*adj.* of the Bantus or their languages

Ban·tu·stan (ban′tōō stan′) *n.* [BANTU + Per. *stän,* a place] any of several territories in S. Africa set aside as reserves for native black peoples, supposedly with self-government

ban·yan (ban′yən) *n.* [from a tree of this kind under which

the *banians* (see BANIAN²) had built a pagoda] an East Indian fig tree whose branches take root and become new trunks

ban·zai (ban′zī′) *interj.* a Japanese greeting or shout, meaning "May you live ten thousand years!"

ba·o·bab (bā′ō bab′) *n.* [prob. EAfr. native name] a tall tree of Africa and India, with a thick trunk and gourdlike, edible fruit

B.A.O.R. British Army of the Rhine

bap (bap) *n.* [< ?] [Chiefly Scot.] a soft bread roll

bap·tism (bap′tiz′m) *n.* [< OFr. < L. < Gr. < *baptizein,* to immerse] 1. the rite or sacrament of admitting a person into a Christian church by dipping him in water or sprinkling water on him 2. any experience that initiates, tests, or purifies —**bap·tis′mal** (-tiz′m′l) *adj.*

baptism of fire [trans. of Gr. *baptisma pyros* (see Matt. 3:11)] 1. the first time that troops are under fire or in combat 2. any experience that tests one's courage, strength, etc. for the first time

bap·tist (bap′tist) *n.* 1. a person who baptizes; specif., [B-] John the Baptist 2. [B-] a member of a Protestant denomination holding that baptism should be given only after confession of faith and only by immersion

bap·tis·ter·y (bap′tis trē, -tis tər ē) *n., pl.* **-ter·ies** a place, esp. a part of a church, used for baptizing: also **bap′tis·try** (-trē), *pl.* **-tries**

bap·tize (bap tīz′) *vt.* **-tized′, -tiz′ing** 1. to administer baptism to 2. to purify; initiate 3. to christen —*vi.* to administer baptism —**bap·tiz′er** *n.*

bar¹ (bär) *n.* [OFr. *barre* < ML. *barra,* barrier] 1. any piece of wood, metal, etc. longer than it is wide or thick, often used as a barrier, lever, etc. 2. *a)* an oblong piece [bar of soap] *b)* a metal strip added to a medal indicating a second award 3. anything that obstructs, hinders, or prevents: cf. SAND BAR 4. a strip, band, or broad line 5. the part of a law court where prisoners are brought to trial 6. *a)* a law court *b)* any place of judgment 7. *a)* lawyers collectively *b)* the legal profession 8. *a)* a counter at which alcoholic drinks are served *b)* a place with such a counter 9. a handrail held onto while doing ballet exercises: also **barre** 10. the mouthpiece of a horse's bit 11. a part of a shop that offers a particular item or service [heel bar] 12. a dividing line in the House of Commons beyond which only members are allowed to go 13. *Heraldry* a horizontal stripe on a shield or bearing 14. *Music a)* any of the vertical lines across a staff *b)* the notes or rests, or both, contained between two such lines on the staff —*vt.* **barred, bar′ring** 1. to fasten with or as with a bar 2. to obstruct; shut off; close 3. to oppose, prevent, or forbid 4. to keep out; exclude 5. to set aside [barring certain possibilities] 6. to mark with stripes —*prep.* 1. excluding; excepting [the best, *bar* none] 2. *Betting* the rest; excluding those already mentioned [10 to 1 *bar*] —**be called to the bar** to be admitted as a barrister —**behind bars** in prison

BARS

bar² (bär) *n.* [G. < Gr. *baros,* weight] a unit of pressure equivalent to 100 000 pascals

bar. 1. barometer 2. barrel 3. barrister

barb¹ (bärb) *n.* [< OFr. < L. *barba,* a beard] 1. a beardlike growth near the mouth of certain animals 2. a sharp point projecting away from the main point of a fishhook, arrow, etc. 3. a cutting remark 4. any of the hairlike projections from the shaft of a feather —*vt.* to provide with a barb or barbs —**barbed** *adj.*

barb² (bärb) *n.* [< Fr. < It. < Ar. *Barbar,* Berber] 1. a horse of a breed native to Barbary 2. a breed of pigeon similar to the carrier pigeon

bar·bar·i·an (bär ber′ē ən) *n.* [see BARBAROUS] 1. orig., a foreigner; esp., a non-Greek or non-Roman 2. a member of a people with a civilization regarded as primitive, etc. 3. a person who lacks culture 4. a coarse or unmannerly person; boor 5. a savage, cruel person; brute —*adj.* of or like a barbarian; esp., uncivilized, cruel, rude, etc. —**bar·bar′i·an·ism** *n.*

bar·bar·ic (bär bar′ik) *adj.* 1. of or like barbarians; uncivilized; primitive 2. wild, crude, and unrestrained —**bar·bar′i·cal·ly** *adv.*

bar·ba·rism (bär′bər iz′m) *n.* 1. *a)* the use of words and expressions not standard in a language *b)* a word or expression of this sort (Ex.: "youse" for "you") 2. the state of being primitive or uncivilized 3. a barbarous act, custom, etc.

bar·bar·i·ty (bär bar′ə tē) *n., pl.* **-ties** 1. cruel or brutal behaviour 2. a cruel or brutal act 3. a crude or coarse taste, manner, etc.

bar·ba·rize (bär′bə rīz′) *vt., vi.* **-rized′, -riz′ing** to make or become barbarous —**bar′ba·ri·za′tion** *n.*

bar·ba·rous (-bər əs) *adj.* [< L. < Gr. *barbaros,* foreign;

prob. < echoic word describing unintelligible speech] **1.** orig., foreign or alien; esp., in the ancient world, non-Greek or non-Roman **2.** characterized by substandard usages in speaking or writing **3.** uncivilized **4.** uncultured, crude, coarse, etc. **5.** cruel; brutal —**bar′ba·rous·ly** *adv.* —**bar′-ba·rous·ness** *n.*

Bar·ba·ry ape (bär′bər ē) a tailless, apelike monkey of North Africa and Gibraltar

bar·bate (bär′bāt) *adj.* [< L. < *barba*, a beard] bearded

bar·be·cue (bär′bə kyōō′) *n.* [< Sp. < Haitian Creole *barbacoa*, framework] **1.** orig., a framework for smoking, drying, or grilling meat **2.** a pig, ox, etc. roasted whole over an open fire **3.** any meat grilled over an open fire **4.** a party or picnic at which such meat is served **5.** a portable outdoor grill —*vt.* **-cued′, -cu′ing 1.** to prepare (meat) outdoors by roasting on a spit or over a grill **2.** to cook (meat) with a highly seasoned sauce (**barbecue sauce**)

barbed wire twisted wire with sharp points all along it, used for barriers

bar·bel (bär′b'l) *n.* [OFr., ult. < L. *barba*, a beard] **1.** a threadlike growth from the jaws of certain fishes: it is an organ of touch **2.** any of several large European freshwater fishes with such growths

bar·bell (bär′bel′) *n.* [BAR[1] + (DUMB)BELL] a metal bar to which discs of varying weights are attached at each end, used for weight-lifting exercises: also **bar bell, bar-bell**

bar·ber (bär′bər) *n.* [OFr. barbour, ult. < L. *barba*, a beard] a person whose work is cutting hair, shaving and trimming beards, etc. —*vt.* to cut the hair of, shave, etc.

bar·ber·ry (bär′bər ē) *n.,* pl. **-ries** [< ML. *barberis* < Ar. *barbārīs*] **1.** a spiny shrub with sour, red berries **2.** the berry

bar·ber·shop (bär′bər shop′) *n.* [Chiefly U.S.] a barber's place of business —*adj.* [Chiefly U.S. Colloq.] designating, characterized by, or like the close harmony of male or female voices [a *barbershop* quartet]

barber's pole a pole with spiral stripes of red and white, a symbol of the barber's trade

bar·bi·can (bär′bi kən) *n.* [< OFr., prob. < Per. *barbar-khānah*, house on a wall] a fortification at the gate or bridge leading into a town or castle

bar·bi·cel (bär′bə sel′) *n.* [< ModL. < L. *barba*, a beard] any of the tiny, hairlike extensions growing from the barbules of a feather

bar·bi·tal (bär′bi tal) *n.* *U.S. var. of* BARBITONE

bar·bi·tone (bär′bi tōn) *n.* [BARBIT(URIC ACID) + -ONE] a drug, in the form of a white powder, used to induce sleep

bar·bi·tu·rate (bär bich′ər it) *n.* any salt or ester of barbituric acid, used as a sedative or to induce sleep

bar·bi·tu·ric acid (bär′bə tyoor′ik) [< G. *Barbitursäure* + -IC] a crystalline acid, derivatives of which are used to induce sleep

bar·bule (bär′byool) *n.* [< L. *barba*, a beard] **1.** a very small barb **2.** any of the threadlike parts fringing each barb of a feather

barb·wire (bärb′wīr′) *n.* *same as* BARBED WIRE

bar·ca·role, bar·ca·rolle (bär′kə rōl′) *n.* [Fr. < It. < *barca*, boat] **1.** a song sung by Venetian gondoliers **2.** a piece of music imitating this

bar chart *same as* BAR GRAPH

bard (bärd) *n.* [Gael. & Ir.] **1.** an ancient Celtic poet **2.** any poet —**bard′ic** *adj.*

Bard of Avon William Shakespeare: so called from his birthplace, Stratford-on-Avon

bare[1] (ber) *adj.* [OE. *bær*] **1.** *a)* without the customary covering [*bare* floors] *b)* without clothing; naked **2.** without equipment or furnishings; empty **3.** simple; plain [the *bare* truth] **4.** without tools or weapons [to use one's *bare* hands] **5.** threadbare **6.** mere [a *bare* wage] —*vt.* **bared, bar′ing** to make bare; uncover; strip —**lay bare** to uncover; expose —**bare′ness** *n.*

bare[2] (ber) *archaic pt. of* BEAR[1]

bare·back (ber′bak′) *adv., adj.* on a horse with no saddle

bare·faced (-fāst′) *adj.* **1.** with the face uncovered or beardless **2.** unconcealed; open **3.** shameless; brazen; audacious —**bare′fac′ed·ly** (-fās′id lē) *adv.* —**bare′fac′-ed·ness** *n.*

bare·foot (-foot′) *adj., adv.* without shoes and stockings —**bare′foot′ed** *adj.*

bare·hand·ed (-han′did) *adj., adv.* **1.** with hands uncovered **2.** without weapons or other means

bare·head·ed (-hed′id) *adj., adv.* wearing no hat or other head covering

bare·leg·ged (-leg′id, -legd′) *adj., adv.* with the legs bare; without stockings on

bare·ly (ber′lē) *adv.* **1.** openly; plainly **2.** only just; scarcely **3.** scantily [*barely* furnished]

bar·gain (bär′gin) *n.* [< OFr. < *bargaignier*, to haggle < Frank.] **1.** a mutual agreement between parties on what should be given or done by each **2.** such an agreement in terms of its worth to one of the parties [a bad *bargain*] **3.**

something sold at a price favourable to the buyer —*vi.* **1.** to talk over a transaction, contract, etc., trying to get the best possible terms **2.** to make a bargain —*vt.* to barter —**bargain for 1.** to try to get cheaply **2.** to expect; count on: also **bargain on** —**into the bargain** in addition —**bar′-gain·er** *n.*

barge (bärj) *n.* [< OFr. < ML. *barga*] **1.** a large, flatbottomed boat for carrying freight on rivers, etc. **2.** a large pleasure boat, used for pageants, etc. **3.** a flagship's boat for use by flag officers —*vt.* **barged, barg′ing** to carry by barge —*vi.* **1.** to move slowly and clumsily **2.** to come or go (*in* or *into*) in a rude, abrupt way **3.** to collide (*into*)

bar·gee (bä jē′) *n.* [BARG(E) + EE] a man who operates, or works aboard, a barge

barge pole a long pole used to propel a barge —**not touch with a barge pole** to refuse to have anything to do with (something or someone)

bar graph a graph with parallel bars representing in proportional lengths the figures given in the data

bar·ite (ber′īt) *n.* *same as* BARYTES

bar·i·tone (bar′ə tōn) *n.* [< It. < Gr. < *barys*, deep + *tonos*, tone] **1.** the range of a male voice between bass and tenor **2.** a voice or singer with such a range **3.** any wind instrument with a similar range **4.** a part for such a voice or instrument —*adj.* of, in, for, or having this range

bar·i·um (ber′ē əm) *n.* [ModL. < Gr. *barys*, heavy] a silver-white, metallic chemical element: symbol, Ba; at. wt., 137.34; at. no., 56

barium meal a thick mixture containing barium sulphate which is opaque to X-rays: it is used for examination of the stomach and intestines

bark[1] (bärk) *n.* [ON. *bọrkr*] the outside covering of the stems and roots of trees and woody plants —*vt.* **1.** to tan (hides) with a bark infusion **2.** to take the bark off (a tree) **3.** [Colloq.] to scrape some skin off [to *bark* one's shin]

bark[2] (bärk) *vi.* [OE. *beorcan:* echoic] **1.** to make the sharp, abrupt cry of a dog **2.** to make a sound like this [the engine *barked*] **3.** to speak or shout sharply; snap **4.** [Colloq.] to cough —*vt.* to say with a bark or a shout —*n.* a sound made in barking —**bark up the wrong tree** to misdirect one's attack, energies, etc.

bark[3] (bärk) *n.* *same as* BARQUE

bar·keep·er (bär′kēp′ər) *n.* **1.** an owner or manager of a bar **2.** a bartender

bark·en·tine (bär′kən tēn′) *n.* *same as* BARQUENTINE

bar·ley (bär′lē) *n.* [< OE. PLURAL, II, D, 3 [< OE. *bærlic*, adj. < *bere*, barley] **1.** a cereal grass **2.** its grain, used in making malts, in soups, and as a feed for animals

bar·ley·corn (-kôrn′) *n.* **1.** barley or a grain of barley: see also JOHN BARLEYCORN **2.** an obs. unit of length (c. 8.5 mm)

barley sugar a clear, hard sweet made by melting sugar, formerly with a barley extract added

barley water a drink made by boiling barley in water

barm (bärm) *n.* [OE. *beorma*] the foamy yeast that appears on the surface of fermenting malt liquors

bar·maid (bär′mād′) *n.* a waitress who serves alcoholic drinks in a bar

bar·man (-mən) *n.,* pl. **-men** a bartender

bar mitz·vah, bar miz·vah (bär mits′və) [Heb. *bar mitswāh*, son of the commandment] [*also* B- M-] **1.** a Jewish boy who has arrived at the age of religious responsibility, thirteen years **2.** the ceremony celebrating this event

barm·y (bär′mē) *adj.* **-i·er, -i·est 1.** full of barm; foamy **2.** [Slang] silly; idiotic

barn (bärn) *n.* [< OE. *bern, berern* < *bere*, barley + *ærn*, building] **1.** a farm building for sheltering harvested crops, livestock, etc. **2.** [arbitrary use, from phr. *as big as a barn*] *Nuclear Physics* a unit of measure of the degree of probability that a nuclear reaction will occur: 1 barn = 10^{-24} cm² per nucleus

bar·na·cle (bär′nə k'l) *n.* [< Fr. *bernicle* & Bret. *bernik,* kind of shellfish] **1.** any of a number of saltwater shellfish that attach themselves to rocks, ship bottoms, etc. **2.** a person or thing hard to get rid of —**bar′na·cled** *adj.*

barnacle goose a species of wild goose, once widely believed to have sprung from barnacles

barn dance 1. a lively country dance **2.** [U.S.] a party, orig. held in a barn, at which people dance square dances

barn·ey (bär′nē) *n.* [< ? Dial.] [Colloq.] **1.** a fight **2.** a noisy quarrel

barn owl a species of brown and grey owl with a spotted white breast, commonly found in barns

barn·storm (bärn′stôrm′) *vi., vt.* [BARN + STORM, *vi.* 3: from occas. use of barns as auditoriums] **1.** to tour in small towns and rural districts, performing plays **2.** [U.S.] to tour rural areas making political speeches —**barn′storm′er** *n.* —**barn′storm′ing** *adj., n.*

barn·yard (bärn′yärd′) *n.* the yard or ground near a barn —*adj.* **1.** of a barnyard **2.** like or fit for a barnyard; earthy, smutty, etc.

bar·o- [< Gr. *baros*, weight] *a prefix meaning* of pressure, esp. atmospheric pressure [*barograph*]

bar·o·gram (bar′ə gram′) *n.* the linear record traced by a barograph

bar·o·graph (-gräf′, -graf′) *n.* a barometer that records variations in atmospheric pressure automatically on a revolving cylinder —**bar′o·graph′ic** *adj.*

ba·rom·e·ter (bə rom′ə tər) *n.* [BARO- + -METER] **1.** an instrument for measuring atmospheric pressure, as by a graduated glass tube (**mercury barometer**) in which a column of mercury rises or falls as the pressure changes (see also ANEROID BAROMETER): barometers are used in forecasting the weather or finding height above sea level **2.** anything that indicates change —**bar·o·met·ric** (bar′ə met′- rik), **bar′o·met′ri·cal** *adj.* —**bar′o·met′ri·cal·ly** *adv.*

barometric pressure the pressure of the atmosphere as indicated by a barometer: in a mercury barometer it averages 760 mm at sea level

bar·on (bar′ən) *n.* [OFr. < Frank. hyp. *baro*, freeman, man] **1.** a member of the lowest rank of the British hereditary peerage **2.** a European or Japanese nobleman of like rank **3.** a powerful businessman or industrialist; magnate —**ba·ro·ni·al** (bə rō′nē əl) *adj.*

bar·on·age (bar′ə nij) *n.* **1.** barons as a class **2.** the peerage **3.** the rank, title, etc. of a baron

bar·on·ess (-nis, -nes) *n.* **1.** a baron's wife or widow **2.** a lady with a barony in her own right

bar·on·et (-nit, -net′) *n.* a man holding the lowest hereditary British title, below a baron but above a knight —**bar′on·et·cy** (-sē) *n., pl.* **-cies**

ba·ro·ni·al (bə rō′nē əl) *adj.* of or fit for a baron [a baronial mansion]

baron of beef a joint of meat consisting of both sides of the back; a double sirloin

bar·on·y (bar′ə nē) *n., pl.* **-on·ies 1.** a baron's domain **2.** the rank or title of a baron **3.** a division of a county in Ireland **4.** a large freehold estate in Scotland

ba·roque (bə rōk′, -rok′) *adj.* [Fr. < Port. *barroco*, imperfect pearl] **1.** a) of or like a style of art and architecture with much ornamentation and curved rather than straight lines b) of or like a style of music with highly embellished melodies and fugal or contrapuntal forms **2.** of the period in which these styles flourished (c. 1550–1750) **3.** *same as* ROCOCO **4.** overdecorated, or too ornate **5.** irregular in shape: said of pearls —*n.* baroque style, baroque art, etc.

bar·o·scope (bar′ə skōp′) *n.* [BARO- + -SCOPE] an instrument indicating but not measuring changes in atmospheric pressure —**bar′o·scop′ic** (-skop′ik) *adj.*

ba·rouche (bə rōōsh′) *n.* [< G. < It. < LL. *birotus* < *bi-*, two + *rota*, a wheel] a four-wheeled carriage with a collapsible hood, two double seats opposite each other, and a driver's seat in front

barque (bärk) *n.* [< Fr. < It. & L. *barca* < Gr. < Coptic *bari*, small boat] **1.** [Poet.] any boat, esp. a small sailing boat **2.** a sailing vessel with its two forward masts square-rigged and its rear mast rigged fore-and-aft

bar·quen·tine (bär′kən tēn′) *n.* [< BARQUE after BRIGANTINE] a sailing vessel with its foremast square-rigged and its other two masts rigged fore-and-aft

bar·rack¹ (bar′ək) *n.* [< Fr. < Sp. < *barro*, clay < VL. hyp. *barrum*, clay] [*pl.*, *often with sing. v.*] **1.** a building or group of buildings for housing soldiers, workmen, etc. **2.** a large, plain building —*vt., vi.* to house in barracks

bar·rack² (bar′ək) *vi., vt.* [< Abor. *borak*, banter] to shout and cheer in chorus with the aim of encouraging or discouraging one of the players in a game, as in cricket —**bar′rack·ing** *n., adj.*

bar·ra·cu·da (bar′ə kōō′də) *n., pl.* **-da, -das:** see PLURAL, II, D, 2 [Sp., prob. < native WInd. name] a fierce, pikelike fish of tropical seas

bar·rage (bə räzh′) *n.* [Fr. < *barrer*, to stop < *barre*, BAR¹] **1.** a curtain of artillery fire laid down to keep enemy forces from moving, or to cover one's own forces, esp. in attack **2.** a prolonged attack of words, blows, etc. **3.** a man-made barrier in a river; dam —*vi., vt.* **-raged, -rag·ing** to lay down a barrage (against)

barrage balloon any of a number of anchored balloons with cables or nets attached for entangling low-flying attacking aircraft

bar·ra·tor, bar·ra·ter (bar′ə tər) *n.* [< OFr. *barater*, to cheat < *barate*, fraud < ? ON. *baratta*, quarrel] a person guilty of barratry

bar·ra·try (-trē) *n.* [see prec.] **1.** the criminal offence of habitually bringing about quarrels or lawsuits **2.** fraud or negligence on the part of a ship's officers or crew that results in a loss to the owners —**bar′ra·trous** *adj.*

‡barre (bär) *n.* [Fr.] the practice bar in a ballet studio

barred (bärd) *adj.* **1.** having bars or stripes **2.** closed off with bars **3.** forbidden or excluded

bar·rel (bar′əl) *n.* [< OFr. *baril* < ML. *barillus* < ?] **1.** a large, wooden, cylindrical container with slightly bulging sides and flat ends, made usually of staves bound together with hoops **2.** the capacity of a barrel (c. 136-182 litres) **3.** any somewhat similar cylinder, drum, etc. [the *barrel* of a windlass] **4.** the tube of a gun, through which the projectile is fired **5.** the trunk of a four-legged animal —*vt.* **-relled, -rel·ling** to put or pack in a barrel or barrels —**have (someone) over a barrel** [Slang] to have (someone) completely at one's mercy, esp. financially

bar·rel-chest·ed (-ches′tid) *adj.* having an especially broad, deep chest for one's height

barrel organ a mechanical musical instrument having a revolving cylinder studded with pins which open pipe valves, producing a tune

barrel roll a complete revolution made by an aircraft around its longitudinal axis while in flight

barrel vault *Archit.* a vault shaped like half a cylinder

bar·ren (bar′ən) *adj.* [< OFr. *baraigne*, orig. used of land] **1.** that cannot produce offspring; sterile **2.** not producing crops or fruit; having little or no vegetation **3.** unproductive; unprofitable **4.** lacking appeal, interest, or meaning; dull; boring **5.** empty; devoid [*barren* of creative spirit] —*n.* [U.S.] **1.** an area of unproductive land **2.** [*usually pl.*] land with shrubs, brush, etc. and sandy soil —**bar′ren·ly** *adv.* —**bar′ren·ness** *n.*

bar·ri·cade (bar′ə kād′; *also, esp. for v.*, bar′ə kād′) *n.* [Fr. < It. pp. of *barricare*, to fortify] **1.** a barrier thrown up hastily for defence **2.** any barrier or obstruction —*vt.* **-cad′- ed, -cad′ing 1.** to shut in or keep out with a barricade **2.** to put up barricades in; obstruct

bar·ri·er (bar′ē ər) *n.* [< OFr. < *barre*, BAR¹] **1.** an obstruction, as a fence or wall **2.** anything that holds apart or separates [racial *barriers*]

barrier cream a cream used to protect the skin from dirt, harmful substances, etc.

barrier reef a long ridge of coral parallel to the coastline, separated from it by a lagoon

bar·ring (bär′iŋ) *prep.* unless there should be; excepting [*barring* rain, we leave tonight]

bar·ris·ter (bar′is tər) *n.* [< BAR¹ (*n.* 6) + *-ister*, as in MINISTER] a member of the legal profession qualified to plead cases in the higher courts: distinguished from SOLICITOR

bar·row¹ (bar′ō) *n.* [< OE. < *beran*, BEAR¹] **1.** *same as:* a) HANDBARROW b) WHEELBARROW **2.** a small cart with two wheels, pushed by hand; pushcart

bar·row² (bar′ō) *n.* [OE. *beorg*, hill] a heap of earth or rocks marking an ancient grave

bar sinister *same as* BEND SINISTER

Bart. Baronet

bar·tend·er (bär′ten′dər) *n.* a man who mixes and serves alcoholic drinks at a bar

bar·ter (bär′tər) *vi.* [< OFr. *barater:* see BARRATOR] to trade by exchanging goods or services without using money —*vt.* to exchange (goods, etc.); trade —*n.* **1.** the act or practice of bartering **2.** anything bartered —**bar′ter·er** *n.*

bar·ti·zan (bär′tə zan, bär′tə zan′) *n.* [altered < ME. *bretasce*, a parapet < OFr., prob. < OHG. *bret*, a board] a small, overhanging turret on a tower or battlement

bar·y·on (bar′ē on′) *n.* [< Gr. *barys*, heavy + (ELECTR)ON] one of a class of heavy atomic particles, including the proton and neutron

ba·ry·ta (bə rīt′ə) *n.* [ModL. < ff.] **1.** barium oxide **2.** barium hydroxide —**ba·ryt′ic** (-rit′ik) *adj.*

ba·ry·tes (bə rīt′ēz) *n.* [< Gr. *barys*, weighty] a white, crystalline mineral composed mainly of barium sulphate

bar·y·tone (bar′ə tōn′) *adj., n. same as* BARITONE

bas·al (bā′s'l) *adj.* **1.** of, at, or forming the base **2.** basic; fundamental —**bas′al·ly** *adv.*

basal metabolism the quantity of energy used by any organism at rest, measured by the rate (**basal metabolic rate**) at which heat is given off by the organism

ba·salt (bas′sôlt, bə sôlt′) *n.* [< L. *basaltes*, a dark marble] a dark, tough, fine-grained to dense, volcanic rock —**ba·sal′- tic** *adj.*

bas·cule (bas′kyōōl) *n.* [Fr.] any device balanced like a seesaw

bascule bridge a drawbridge counterweighted so that it can be raised and lowered easily

base¹ (bās) *n., pl.* **bas′es** (-əz) [< OFr. *bas* < L. *basis*, BASIS] **1.** the thing or part on which something rests; foundation **2.** the main part, as of a plan, system, etc., on which the rest depends **3.** the principal or essential ingredient [paint with an oil *base*] **4.** a basis **5.** a goal or place of safety in certain games, as rounders **6.** the point of attachment of a part of the body **7.** a centre of operations or source of supply; headquarters **8.** *Chem.* any compound that reacts with an acid to form a salt, produces hydroxyl ions in water solutions, and turns red litmus blue **9.** *Geom.* the line or plane upon which a figure is thought of as resting **10.** *Linguis.* any morpheme to which prefixes, suffixes, etc. are added; root **11.** *Math. a)* the number that is raised to various powers to produce the main counting units of a number system [10 is the *base* of the decimal system] **b)** the number that when raised to the logarithm of a given number produces the given number *c)* in business, etc., figure or sum upon which certain calculations are made —*adj.* forming a base —*vt.* **based, bas'ing 1.** to make a base for **2.** to put or rest (*on*) as a base or basis **3.** to place or station (*in* or *at* a base)

base² (bās) *adj.* [< OFr. < VL. *bassus,* low] **1.** with little or no honour, courage, or decency; mean; contemptible **2.** of a menial or degrading kind **3.** inferior in quality **4.** of comparatively low worth [iron is a *base* metal, gold a precious one] **5.** debased or counterfeit **6.** [Archaic] of servile or humble birth —**base'ly** *adv.* —**base'ness** *n.*

base·ball (bās'bôl') *n.* **1.** a game played, chiefly in the U.S., with a leather-covered ball and a bat by two opposing teams of nine players each, on a field with four bases forming a diamond **2.** the ball used in this game

base·born (-bôrn') *adj.* **1.** of humble birth or origin **2.** of illegitimate birth **3.** mean or ignoble

base·less (bās'lis) *adj.* having no basis in fact; unfounded —**base'less·ness** *n.*

base line 1. a line serving as a base **2.** *Tennis* the line at the back at either end of a court

base·ment (bās'mənt) *n.* [BASE¹ + -MENT] **1.** the lower part of a wall or structure **2.** the lowest storey of a building, below the main floor and wholly or partly below the surface of the ground

ba·sen·ji (bə sen'jē) *n.* [Bantu < *ba-,* plural prefix + *senji* < Fr. *singe,* a monkey] any of an African breed of small dog with a reddish-brown coat

bas·es¹ (bās'ez) *n.* *pl.* of BASE¹

ba·ses² (bā'sēz) *n.* *pl.* of BASIS

bash (bash) *vt.* [echoic] [Colloq.] to strike with a violent blow; smash (*in* or *into*) —*n.* **1.** [Colloq.] a violent blow **2.** [Slang] a gala event or party —**have a bash at** [Slang] to make an attempt at

bash·ful (bash'fəl) *adj.* [(A)BASH + -FUL] **1.** timid, shy, and easily embarrassed **2.** showing an embarrassed timidity —**bash'ful·ly** *adv.* —**bash'ful·ness** *n.*

BA·SIC (bā'sik) *n.* [B(*eginner's*) A(*ll-purpose*) S(*ymbolic*) I(*nstruction*) C(*ode*)] a computer language that uses common English terms

bas·ic (bā'sik) *adj.* **1.** of, at, or forming a base; fundamental **2.** introductory or elementary **3.** a minimum rate or amount exclusive of additions [*basic* pay] **4.** *Chem.* of, having the nature of, or containing a base; alkaline —*n.* a basic principle, factor, etc.: *usually used in pl.* —**bas'i·cal·ly** *adv.*

Basic English a copyrighted simplified form of English for international communication and for first steps into full English, devised by C. K. Ogden (1889–1957)

basic industry an industry that is fundamental to a country's economy

ba·sic·i·ty (bə sis'ə tē) *n.* *Chem.* the capacity of an acid to react with a base, measured by the number of chemical equivalents of a base with which one gramme molecular weight of the acid reacts

basic slag a by-product in the manufacture of steel, now widely used as a fertilizer

ba·sid·i·o·my·cete (bə sid'ē ō mī'sēt, -mī sēt') *n.* [< ModL. < Gr. *basis,* base + ModL. dim. suffix *-idium* + -MYCETE] any of a class of fungi, including the mushrooms, rusts, etc., that reproduce through spores borne on a club-shaped structure

bas·il (baz'¹l) *n.* [< OFr. < ML. < Gr. *basilikon* (*phyton*), lit., royal (plant) < *basileus,* king] a fragrant herb whose leaves are used for flavouring in cooking

bas·i·lar (bas'ə lər) *adj.* of or at the base, esp. of the skull: also **bas'i·lar·y** (-lər ē)

ba·sil·i·ca (bə sil'i kə) *n.* [L. < Gr. *basilikē* (*stoa*), royal (portico)] **1.** in ancient Rome, a rectangular building with a broad nave flanked by colonnaded aisles, used as a courtroom, etc. **2.** a Christian church in this style —**ba·sil'·i·can** *adj.*

bas·i·lisk (bas'ə lisk', baz-) *n.* [< L. < Gr. dim. of *basileus,* king] **1.** a mythical, lizardlike monster with fatal breath and glance **2.** a tropical American lizard with a crest on its back and tail

ba·sin (bās'¹n) *n.* [< OFr. < VL. < *bacca,* water vessel] **1.** *a)* a wide, shallow container, as for liquid *b)* its contents or capacity **2.** a washbowl or sink **3.** any shallow, esp. water-filled hollow, as a pond **4.** a bay or harbour **5.** all the land drained by a river and its branches **6.** a depression in the earth's surface **7.** *Geol.* a wide, depressed area in which the rock layers all incline towards a centre

ba·sis (bā'sis) *n.,* *pl.* **ba'ses** (-sēz) [L. < Gr., a base, pedestal] **1.** the base or foundation of anything **2.** a principal constituent **3.** the basic principle or theory, as of a system of knowledge

bask (bask) *vi.* [ME. *basken,* to wallow (in blood) < ?] **1.** to warm oneself pleasantly, as in sunlight **2.** to enjoy any pleasant or warm feeling [he *basked* in her favour]

bas·ket (bäs'kit) *n.* [ME. < ?] **1.** a container made of interwoven cane, strips of wood, etc. **2.** the amount that a basket will hold **3.** anything used or shaped like a basket **4.** the structure hung from a balloon to carry persons, etc. **5.** [Slang] *a euphemism for* BASTARD (*n.* 3) **6.** *Basketball a)* the goal, a round net open at the bottom and hanging from a metal ring *b)* a score made by tossing the ball through this net

bas·ket·ball (-bôl') *n.* **1.** a game played by two teams of five players each, in a zoned floor area: points are scored by tossing a ball through a basket at the opponent's end of the court **2.** the large, round, inflated ball used in this game

basket chair a chair that is made of basketwork

bas·ket·ry (bäs'kə trē) *n.* **1.** the craft of making baskets **2.** *same as* BASKETWORK

basket weave a weave of fabrics resembling the weave used in basketwork

bas·ket·work (bäs'kit wurk') *n.* work that is interlaced or woven like a basket

basking shark a large shark that feeds on plankton: often found basking on the surface in northern seas

ba·so·phile (bā'sə fīl', -fil') *n.* [< BASIC + -PHILE] a cell or tissue that is readily stained with basic dyes: also **ba'·so·phil'** (-fil') —**ba'so·phil'ic** *adj.*

Basque (bask, bäsk) *n.* **1.** any member of a certain people living in the W Pyrenees **2.** their unique language —*adj.* of the Basques, their language, etc.

basque (bask, bäsk) *n.* [Fr. < Pr. *basto* < ?] a woman's tightfitting bodice or tunic

bas-re·lief (bä'rə lēf', bäs'rə lēf') *n.* [Fr. < It. *basso-rilievo:* see BASSO & RELIEF] sculpture in which figures are carved in a flat surface so that they project only a little from the background

bass¹ (bās) *n.* [ME. *bas,* BASE²] **1.** the range of the lowest male voice **2.** a voice or singer with such a range **3.** an instrument of the lowest range; specif., *same as* DOUBLE BASS **4.** a part for such a voice or instrument —*adj.* of, in, for, or having this range

bass² (bas) *n.,* *pl.* **bass, bass'es:** see PLURAL, II, D, 2 [< OE. *bærs*] a spiny-finned food and game fish of fresh or salt water

bass³ (bas) *n.* *same as:* **1.** BAST **2.** BASSWOOD

bass clef *Music* a sign on a staff, indicating the position of F below middle C on the fourth line

bass drum (bās) the largest and lowest-toned of the double-headed drums

bas·set (bas'it) *n.* [OFr., orig., dim. of *bas,* BASE²] a kind of hunting hound with a long body, short legs, and long, drooping ears: also **basset hound**

basset horn a rich-toned wind instrument, similar to a clarinet in tone and fingering

bass horn (bās) an old musical instrument like a tuba

bas·si·net (bas'ə net') *n.* [< Fr. *bercelonnette,* dim. of *berceau,* cradle] an infant's basketlike bed, often hooded and set on a stand having casters

bass·ist (bās'ist) *n.* a person who plays the double bass

bas·so (bas'ō; *It.*bäs'sō) *n., pl.* **bas'sos;** *It.* **bas'si** (-sē) [It. < VL. *bassus,* low] a bass voice or singer

bas·soon (bə sōōn') *n.* [Fr. *basson* < It. < prec.] a double-reed woodwind instrument having a long, curved stem attached to the mouthpiece —**bas·soon'ist** *n.*

bas·so-re·lie·vo (bas'ō rə lē'vō) *n., pl.* **-vos** *same as* BAS-RELIEF

bass viol (bās) *same as* VIOLA DA GAMBA

bass·wood (bas'wood') *n.* **1.** any of several trees of the U.S. and Canada, with fragrant, yellowish flowers and light, soft wood **2.** the wood

BASSOON

bast (bast) *n.* [OE. *bæst*] **1.** *same as* PHLOEM **2.** fibre obtained from phloem, for making ropes, etc.

bas·tard (bäs'tərd, bas'-) *n.* [< OFr. < ?] **1.** a person born of parents not married to each other **2.** anything spurious, inferior, or varying from standard **3.** a person regarded with contempt, hatred, pity, etc. or, sometimes, with playful affection: a vulgar usage **4.** [S.Afr.] a person with mixed white and coloured parents: also **bastaard** —*adj.* **1.** of illegitimate birth or uncertain origin **2.** of a size or shape not standard **3.** not genuine or authentic; inferior; spurious —**bas'tard·ly** *adj.* —**bas'tard·y** *n., pl.* **-ies**

bas·tard·ize (bäs'tər dīz', bas'-) *vt.* **-ized', -iz'ing 1.** to make, declare, or show to be a bastard **2.** to make corrupt or inferior —**bas'tard·i·za'tion** *n.*

baste¹ (bāst) *vt.* **bast'ed, bast'ing** [< OFr. < OHG. *bastjan,* to sew with bast] to sew with long, loose stitches so as to keep the parts together until properly sewed —**bast'er** *n.*

baste² (bāst) *vt.* **bast'ed, bast'ing** [? < OFr. < *bassiner,* to moisten < *bassin,* BASIN] to moisten (meat) with melted butter, drippings, etc. during roasting —**bast'er** *n.*

baste[3] (bāst) *vt.* **bast′ed, bast′ing** [prob. < ON. *beysta*] 1. to beat soundly 2. to attack with words; abuse
bas·tille, bas·tile (bas tēl′) *n.* [Fr. < OFr. *bastir*, to build: see BASTION] a prison —**the Bastille** a state prison in Paris until destroyed (July 14, 1789) in the French Revolution
bas·ti·na·do (bas′tə nā′dō, -nā′dō) *n., pl.* **-does** [< Sp. < *bastón*, a stick] 1. a beating with a stick, usually on the soles of the feet, esp. as a punishment 2. a rod or stick Also **bas′ti·nade′** (-nād′) —*vt.* **-doed, -do·ing** to inflict a bastinado on
bast·ing (bās′tiŋ) *n.* 1. the act of sewing with loose, temporary stitches 2. loose, temporary stitches or the thread used for them
bas·tion (bas′chən, -tē ən) *n.* [Fr. < It. < *bastire*, to build < Gmc. *bastjan*, to make with bast, build] 1. a projection from a fortification 2. any strong defence or bulwark —**bas′tioned** *adj.*
bat[1] (bat) *n.* [< OE. *batt*, cudgel (prob. < W. *bat*) & < OFr. *battre*, BATTER[1]] 1. any stout club or stick 2. a club used to strike the ball in baseball and cricket 3. a disc with a short handle used to strike the ball in table tennis, etc. 4. a similar object used by a person guiding an aircraft on the ground 5. a turn at batting 6. a batsman at cricket 7. [Colloq.] a blow or hit 8. [Old Slang] a spree —*vt.* **bat′ted, bat′ting** to strike with or as with a bat —*vi.* to take a turn at batting —**bat around** [Slang] to travel or roam about —**carry one's bat** to be "not out" at the end of an innings at cricket —**off one's own bat** alone; without any assistance or guidance
bat[2] (bat) *n.* [altered < ME. *bakke* < Scand.] a mouselike mammal with a furry body and membranous wings, usually seen flying at night —**blind as a bat** quite blind —**have bats in the** (or one's) **belfry** [Slang] to be insane; have crazy ideas —**like a bat out of hell** [Slang] at great speed
bat[3] (bat) *vt.* **bat′ted, bat′ting** [ME. *baten*, to flap (wings) < OFr. *battre*, BATTER[1]] [Colloq.] to wink; blink; flutter —**not bat an eye** (or **eyelid**) [Colloq.] 1. not show surprise 2. not sleep
batch (bach) *n.* [OE. *bacan*, to bake] 1. the amount (of bread, etc.) produced at one baking 2. the quantity of anything needed for or made in one operation or lot 3. a number of things or persons taken as a group —*vt.* to arrange or handle in batches
bate (bāt) *vt., vi.* **bat′ed, bat′ing** [< ABATE] to abate or lessen —**with bated breath** with the breath held in because of fear, excitement, etc.
ba·teau (ba tō′) *n., pl.* **-teaux′** (-tōz′) [Fr. < OFr. *batel* < OE. *bat*, boat] a lightweight, flat-bottomed river boat with tapering ends
bath (bäth) *n., pl.* **baths** (bäth̲z, bäths) [OE. *bæth*] 1. a washing or dipping of a thing, esp. the body, in water or other liquid, steam, etc. 2. water or other liquid for bathing, or for dipping, soaking, regulating temperature, etc. 3. a container for such liquid 4. a bathtub 5. [usually *pl.*] a building or set of rooms for bathing or swimming 6. [often *pl.*] a resort where bathing is part of the medical treatment —*vt.* to give a bath to; wash —*vi.* to take a bath
Bath bun (bäth) [after the city in SW England] a rich, sweet bun containing dried fruit and often coated with sugar
Bath chair a hooded wheelchair of a kind used at Bath
bath cube a soluble cube that scents or softens water
bathe (bāth) *vt.* **bathed, bath′ing** [OE. *bathian* < *bæth*, bath] 1. to put into a liquid; immerse 2. to wet or moisten 3. to cover as if with a liquid [trees *bathed* in moonlight] —*vi.* 1. to go into or be in water so as to swim, cool oneself, etc. 2. to soak oneself in some substance or influence —*n.* a swim or dip —**bath′er** *n.*
bath·house (bäth′hous′) *n.* formerly, a public building where people could take baths
bathing cap a tightfitting cap of rubber, etc., worn to keep the hair dry as while swimming
bathing suit a garment worn for swimming
bath·mat (bäth′mat′) *n.* a mat used in or next to a bathtub, as to prevent slipping
bath·o· (bath′ə, -ō) [< Gr. *bathos*, depth] a *combining form* meaning depth [*bathometer*]
bath·o·lith (bath′ə lith′) *n.* [BATHO-+ -LITH] a large, deep-seated rock intrusion, usually granite, often forming the base of a mountain range, and uncovered only by erosion: also **bath′o·lite′** (-līt′)
ba·thom·e·ter (bə thom′ə tər) *n.* [BATHO-+ -METER] an instrument for measuring water depths
ba·thos (bā′thos) *n.* [Gr., depth] 1. an abrupt change from the lofty to the ordinary or trivial in writing or speech; anticlimax 2. false pathos; sentimentality 3. triteness —**ba·thet·ic** (bə thet′ik) *adj.* —**ba·thet′i·cal·ly** *adv.*
bath·robe (bäth′rōb′) *n.* a long, loose coat for wear before or after a bath, swimming, etc.
bath·room (-rōōm′) *n.* a room with a bathtub and usually a toilet, washbasin, etc.
bath salts a substance which is added to bath water to scent or soften it

bath·tub (-tub′) *n.* a tub, now usually a bathroom fixture, in which to take a bath
bath·y·scaph (bath′ə skaf′) *n.* [Fr. < Gr. *bathys*, deep + *skaphē*, boat] a deep-sea diving compartment for reaching great depths without a cable
bath·y·sphere (bath′ə sfir′) *n.* [< Gr. *bathys*, deep + -SPHERE] a round, watertight observation chamber lowered by cables into sea depths
ba·tik (bat′ik, bə tēk′) *n.* [Malay] 1. a method of dyeing designs on cloth by coating with removable wax the parts not to be dyed 2. cloth so decorated or a design made in this way —*adj.* of or like batik
ba·tiste (ba tēst′, bə-) *n.* [Fr. < OFr. *baptiste*: after the supposed original maker, *Baptiste* of Cambrai] a fine, thin cloth of cotton, linen, rayon, etc.
bat·man (bat′mən) *n., pl.* **-men** (-mən) [< Fr. *bat*, packsaddle + MAN] 1. orig., a groom in charge of an officer's horse: now an officer's personal servant 2. a person who guides aircraft into position on the ground
bat mitz·vah, bat miz·vah (bät mits′və) [Heb. *bat mitswāh*, daughter of the commandment] [*also* B- M-] 1. a Jewish girl who undergoes a ceremony analogous to that of a bar mitzvah 2. the ceremony itself
ba·ton (bat′ən) *n.* [Fr. < OFr. < VL. hyp. *basto*, a stick] 1. a staff serving as a symbol of office 2. slender stick used by a conductor in directing an orchestra, choir, etc. 3. a hollow metal rod twirled in a showy way, as by a drum majorette 4. the short rod passed from one runner to the next in a relay race
ba·tra·chi·an (bə trā′kē ən) *adj.* [< ModL. < Gr. < *batrachos*, frog] of, like, or concerning amphibians without tails, as frogs and toads —*n.* an amphibian without a tail; frog or toad
bats (bats) *adj.* [Slang] insane; crazy
bats·man (bats′mən) *n., pl.* **-men** the batter in cricket
bat·tal·ion (bə tal′yən) *n.* [< Fr. < It. < VL. *battalia*, BATTLE] 1. a large group of soldiers arrayed for battle 2. any large group joined together in some activity 3. *Mil.* a tactical and administrative unit of infantry made up of two or more companies
bat·ten[1] (bat′'n) *n.* [var. of BATON] 1. a sawed strip of wood, flooring, etc. 2. a strip of wood put over a seam between boards as a fastening or covering 3. a strip used to fasten canvas over a ship's hatchways —*vt.* to fasten or supply with battens —**batten down the hatches** to fasten canvas over the hatches, esp. in preparing for a storm
bat·ten[2] (bat′'n) *vi.* [ON. *batna*, to improve] to grow fat; thrive —*vt.* [Obs.] to fatten up; overfeed —**batten on** to thrive, esp. at the expense of someone else
bat·ter[1] (bat′ər) *vt.* [OFr. *batre, battre* < VL. < L. *battuere*, to beat; also, in part, freq. of BAT[1], v.] 1. to beat or strike with blow after blow; pound 2. to injure by pounding, hard wear, or use —*vi.* to pound noisily and repeatedly
bat·ter[2] (bat′ər) *n.* the player whose turn it is to bat, esp. in baseball
bat·ter[3] (bat′ər) *n.* [< OFr., prob. < *batre*: see BATTER[1]] a flowing mixture of flour, milk, eggs, etc. for making cakes, pancakes, etc.
battered baby a young child with serious physical injuries caused by a parent or other adult
bat·ter·ing ram (bat′ər iŋ ram′) 1. an ancient military machine having a heavy wooden beam for battering down gates, walls, etc. 2. any bar, log, etc. used like this to force entrance
bat·ter·y (bat′ər ē, bat′rē) *n., pl.* **-ter·ies** [< Fr. < *battre*: see BATTER[1]] 1. a battering or beating 2. a group of similar things arranged, connected, or used together; set or series 3. a large number of cages for the intensive rearing of poultry, cattle, etc. 4. *Elec.* a connected group of cells (or popularly, a single cell) storing an electrical charge and capable of furnishing a current 5. *Law* any illegal beating or touching of another person: see ASSAULT AND BATTERY 6. *Mil. a)* an emplacement or fortification equipped with heavy guns *b)* a set of heavy guns, rockets, etc. *c)* the men who operate such a set: usually the basic unit of artillery —*adj.* of poultry or cattle reared in cages [*battery* hens]
bat·ting (bat′iŋ) *n.* [< BAT[1]] fibre of cotton, wool, etc., wadded into sheets and used in bandages, quilts, etc.
bat·tle (bat′'l) *n.* [< OFr. < VL. hyp. *battalia* < L. < *battuere*: see BATTER[1]] 1. a large-scale fight between armed forces 2. armed fighting; combat or war 3. any fight or struggle; conflict —*vt., vi.* **-tled, -tling** to oppose, fight, or struggle —**give** (or **do**) **battle** to engage in battle; fight —**bat′tler** *n.*
bat·tle-axe (-aks′) *n.* 1. a heavy axe formerly used as a weapon of war 2. [Colloq.] a woman who is harsh, domineering, etc.
battle cruiser a large warship with longer range and greater speed than a battleship, but less heavily armoured
battle cry a cry or slogan used to encourage those in a battle, struggle, contest, etc.
bat·tle·dore (bat′'l dôr′) *n.* [< ? Pr. *batedor*, beater] 1. a

bat or racket used to hit a shuttlecock back and forth in a game (called **battledore and shuttlecock**) like badminton **2.** this game

battle dress the standard everyday uniform of a soldier

battle fatigue *same as* COMBAT FATIGUE

bat·tle·field (bat′'l fēld′) *n.* **1.** the place where a battle is fought or was fought **2.** any area of conflict Also **bat′-tle·ground′**

bat·tle·ment (-mənt) *n.* [< OFr. *batailler*, to fortify] **1.** a low wall, as on top of a tower, with open spaces for shooting **2.** an architectural decoration like this —**bat′tle·ment′ed** (-men′tid) *adj.*

battle royal *pl.* **battles royal 1.** a fight involving many contestants; free-for-all **2.** a bitterly fought battle **3.** a heated dispute

bat·tle·ship (-ship′) *n.* any of a class of large warships with the biggest guns and very heavy armour

bat·ty (bat′ē) *adj.* **-ti·er, -ti·est** [< BAT² + -y²] [Slang] **1.** insane; crazy **2.** odd; eccentric

bat·wom·an (bat′woom′ən) *n.* [cf. BATMAN] the personal servant of a female officer, esp. in the army

BATTLEMENTS

bau·ble (bô′b'l) *n.* [< OFr. *baubel*, plaything] **1.** a showy but worthless thing; trinket, trifle, etc. **2.** [Archaic] a jester's stick with an ornament at the end

Bau·haus (bou′hous′) [G. < *bauen*, to build + *Haus*, a house] the architectural school of Walter Gropius, founded in Germany, 1919

baulk (bôk) *n., vt., vi.* *same as* BALK

baux·ite (bôk′sīt, bō′zīt) *n.* [Fr. < (*Les*) *Baux*, town in SE France] the claylike ore from which aluminium is obtained

bawd (bôd) *n.* [< ? OFr. *baud*, gay, licentious (< Frank. *bald*, bold)] [Now Literary] **1.** a person, esp. a woman, who keeps a brothel **2.** a prostitute

bawd·y (bô′dē) *adj.* **bawd′i·er, bawd′i·est** [see prec.] characterized by references to sex, esp. in a humorous way —**bawd′i·ly** *adv.* —**bawd′i·ness** *n.*

bawd·y·house (-hous′) *n.* a house of prostitution

bawl (bôl) *vi., vt.* [< ML. *baulare*, to bark & ? ON. *baula*, to low like a cow] **1.** to shout or call out noisily; bellow **2.** to weep loudly —**bawl out** [Slang] to scold angrily —**bawl′-er** *n.*

bay¹ (bā) *n.* [< OFr. < ML. *baia*] **1.** a part of a sea or lake, indenting the shoreline; wide inlet **2.** any land feature resembling a bay

bay² (bā) *n.* [< OFr. *baer* < VL. *batare*, to gape] **1.** *a*) an opening or alcove marked off by columns, etc. *b*) a recess in a wall, as for a window *c*) *same as* BAY WINDOW **2.** a wing of a building **3.** a compartment or space: cf. BOMB BAY **4.** *same as* SICK BAY **5.** a recess in a railway station forming the terminus of a branch line or siding

bay³ (bā) *vi.* [< OFr., ult. < VL. *batare*, to gape] to bark in long, deep tones —*vt.* **1.** to bark at **2.** to bring to or hold at bay —*n.* **1.** the sound of baying **2.** the situation of or as of a hunted animal forced to turn and fight —**at bay 1.** with escape cut off; cornered **2.** held off [the bear kept the hunters *at bay*] —**bring to bay** to force into a situation that makes escape impossible

bay⁴ (bā) *n.* [< OFr. < L. *baca*, berry] **1.** *same as* LAUREL (*n.* 1) **2.** [*pl.*] *a*) a wreath of bay leaves, a classical token of honour given to poets and conquerors *b*) honour; fame

bay⁵ (bā) *adj.* [< OFr. < L. *badius*] reddish-brown: said esp. of horses —*n.* **1.** a horse, etc. of this colour **2.** reddish brown

bay·ber·ry (bā′bər ē) *n., pl.* **-ries 1.** *same as* WAX MYRTLE **2.** a tropical American tree yielding an aromatic oil used in bay rum

bay leaf the aromatic leaf of the laurel, dried and used as a herb

bay·o·net (bā′ə nit, -net′; bā′ə net′) *n.* [< Fr. < *Bayonne*, city in France] a detachable, daggerlike blade put on the muzzle end of a rifle, for hand-to-hand fighting —*vt., vi.* **-net′ed, -net′ing** to stab, prod, or kill with a bayonet

bayonet fitting a plug or joint that is fixed in place by a push and twist movement

bay·ou (bī′yōō) *n.* [AmFr. < Choctaw *bayuk*, small stream] in the southern U.S., a marshy inlet or outlet of a lake, river, etc.

bay rum an aromatic liquid formerly obtained from leaves of a bayberry tree, now made of certain oils, water, and alcohol: it is used in medicines and cosmetics

bay window 1. a window or set of windows jutting out from the wall of a building **2.** [Colloq.] a large, protruding belly

ba·zaar (bə zär′) *n.* [Per. *bāzār*] **1.** in Oriental countries, a market or street of shops **2.** a shop for selling various

kinds of goods **3.** a sale of various articles, usually to raise money for a club, church, etc.

ba·zoo·ka (bə zōōk′ə) *n.* [term orig. coined for a comic musical horn] a weapon of metal tubing, for aiming and launching electrically fired, armour-piercing rockets

BB 1. Boys' Brigade **2.** double black (of pencil lead)

BBC British Broadcasting Corporation

bbl. *pl.* **bbls.** barrel

B.C. before Christ

B.C.E. before the Common Era

bch. *pl.* **bchs.** bunch

bd. *pl.* **bds. 1.** board **2.** bond **3.** bound

B/D bank draft

B.D. Bachelor of Divinity

bdel·li·um (del′ē əm) *n.* [< Gr. *bdellion*, of Oriental origin] **1.** a myrrhlike gum resin **2.** *Bible* a jewel variously interpreted as being a carbuncle, a crystal, or a pearl

bd. ft. board foot (or feet)

bdl. *pl.* **bdls.** bundle

B.D.S. Bachelor of Dental Surgery

be (bē; *unstressed* bi) *vi.* **was** or **were, been, be′ing** [OE. *beon*] **1.** to exist; live [Caesar *is* no more] **2.** to happen or occur [the party *is* tonight] **3.** to remain or continue [will he *be* here long?] **4.** to come to; belong [peace *be* with you] **5.** to have a place or position in space or time [the door *is* on your left] **6.** to pay a visit; go [have you *been* to Blackpool?]: only used as a past participle Note: *be* is often used to link its subject to a predicate nominative, adjective, or pronoun and is sometimes equivalent to the mathematical sign (=) (Ex.: he *is* brave, that hat *is* ten pounds, let x *be* y); *be* is also used as an auxiliary: (1) with the past participle of a transitive verb to form the passive voice [he will *be* paid] (2) with the past participle of certain intransitive verbs to form an archaic perfect tense [Christ *is* risen] (3) with the present participle of another verb to express continuation [the motor *is* running] (4) with the present participle or infinitive of another verb to express futurity, possibility, obligation, intention, etc. [he *is* going next week, she *is* to wash the dishes] *Be* is conjugated in the present indicative: (I) *am*, (he, she, it) *is*, (we, you, they) *are*; in the past indicative: (I, he, she, it) *was*, (we, you, they) *were*; archaic forms are (thou) *art, wert, wast*; the present subjunctive is *be*, the past subjunctive *were* —**be off** go away —**be that as it may** without taking that into account; even so

be- [OE. < *be, bi*, about, near] *a prefix used variously with verbs, nouns, and adjectives to mean:* **1.** around [besprinkle, beset] **2.** completely; thoroughly [bedeck, besmear] **3.** away [bereave, betake] **4.** about [bethink, bemoan] **5.** make [besot, bepretty] **6.** furnish with; affect by [befriend, bedizen, becloud] **7.** covered with; furnished with (to excess) [bemedalled, bewhiskered]

Be *Chem.* beryllium

B/E, b.e. bill of exchange

B.E. Bachelor of Engineering

beach (bēch) *n.* [< ?] **1.** a nearly level stretch of pebbles and sand beside a sea, lake, etc.; sandy shore **2.** an area of shore as for swimmers, sunbathers, etc. —*vt., vi.* to ground (a boat) on a beach —**on the beach 1.** not aboard a ship; ashore **2.** unemployed

beach·comb·er (-kō′mər) *n.* **1.** a long wave rolling ashore; comber **2.** a man who loafs on beaches or wharves, living on what he can beg or find

beach·head (-hed′) *n.* **1.** a position established by invading troops on an enemy shore **2.** a position secured as a starting point for any action

bea·con (bēk′'n) *n.* [OE. *beacen*] **1.** a signal fire, esp. one on a hill, pole, etc. **2.** a hill suitable for such a fire **3.** any light for warning or guiding **4.** a lighthouse **5.** a radio transmitter that sends out signals for guiding aircraft, as at night **6.** a person or thing that warns, offers guidance, etc. **7.** *same as* BELISHA BEACON —*vt.* **1.** to light up (darkness, etc.) **2.** to provide or mark with beacons —*vi.* to shine or serve as a beacon

bead (bēd) *n.* [ME. *bede*, prayer bead < OE. *bed* < *biddan*, to pray] **1.** a small, usually round piece of glass, wood, metal, etc., pierced for stringing **2.** [*pl.*] *a*) a string of beads; necklace *b*) a rosary **3.** any small, round object, as the front sight of a rifle **4.** a drop or bubble **5.** foam, as on beer **6.** the inner edge of a rubber tyre where it fits on the rim **7.** a narrow, half-round moulding —*vt.* **1.** to decorate or string with beads **2.** to string like beads —*vi.* to form a bead or beads —**draw a bead on** to take careful aim at —**say** (or **tell** or **count**) **one's beads** to say prayers with a rosary —**bead′ed** *adj.*

bead·ing (-iŋ) *n.* **1.** beads or decorative work in beads **2.** a moulding or edge resembling a row of beads **3.** a narrow, half-round moulding **4.** *a*) a narrow trimming of lacelike loops *b*) an openwork trimming through which a ribbon can be run

bea·dle (bē′d'l) *n.* [< OFr. < Frank. hyp. *bidal*, messenger] formerly, a minor parish officer in the Church of England, who was concerned with parish matters, as keeping order in church, etc.

beads·man (bēdz'mən) *n.*, *pl.* **-men** [see BEAD] **1.** a person who prays for another's soul, esp. one hired to do so **2.** a person in a poorhouse —**beads'wom'an** *n.fem.*, *pl.* **-wom'en**

bead·y (bē'dē) *adj.* **bead'i·er**, **bead'i·est 1.** small, round, and glittering like a bead [the *beady* eyes of a snake] **2.** decorated with beads

bea·gle (bē'g'l) *n.* [< ? Fr. *bégueule*, wide-throat] a small hound with a smooth coat, short legs, and drooping ears

beak (bēk) *n.* [< OFr. < L. *beccus* < Gaul.] **1.** a bird's bill, esp. the large, sharp, horny bill of a bird of prey **2.** the beaklike mouthpart of various insects, fishes, etc. **3.** the spout of a jug **4.** the metal-covered ram projecting from the prow of an ancient warship **5.** [Colloq.] the nose **6.** [Slang] a magistrate or schoolteacher —**beaked** (bēkt) *adj.* —**beak'less** *adj.* —**beak'-like'** *adj.*

BEAGLE
(33-38 cm high at shoulder)

beak·er (bē'kər) *n.* [< ON. *bikarr*, a cup < VL. < LL. *bacarium*, wine glass] **1.** *a)* a large or ornate cup; goblet *b)* a cup having a wide mouth and often made of unbreakable material [a plastic *beaker*] **2.** a jarlike container of glass or metal with a lip for pouring, used by scientists **3.** its contents or capacity

Beaker folk a Bronze Age people named after the bell-shaped beakers found in graves

be-all and end-all 1. a thing or person regarded as incapable of improvement; acme; ultimate **2.** chief or all-important element

beam (bēm) *n.* [< OE., akin to G. *Baum*, a tree] **1.** a long, thick piece of wood, or of metal or stone, esp. one used as a horizontal support for a ceiling **2.** the part of a plough to which the handles, share, etc. are attached **3.** the crossbar of a balance, or the balance itself **4.** any of the heavy, horizontal crosspieces of a ship **5.** a ship's breadth at its widest point **6.** the side of a ship or the direction out sideways from a ship **7.** a slender shaft of light or other radiation, as of X-rays **8.** a radiant look, smile, etc. **9.** a stream of radio or radar signals sent continuously in one direction as a guide for aircraft or ships **10.** [Colloq.] the width of the hips [she's broad in the *beam*] **11.** *Mech.* a lever that is moved back and forth by a piston rod and transmits its motion to the crank, etc. —*vt.* **1.** to give out (shafts of light); radiate **2.** to direct or aim (a radio signal, programme, etc.) —*vi.* **1.** to shine brightly **2.** to smile warmly —**off the beam 1.** not following a guiding beam, as an aeroplane **2.** [Colloq.] wrong; incorrect —**on the beam 1.** at right angles to the ship's keel **2.** following a guiding beam, as an aircraft **3.** [Colloq.] working or functioning well; alert, keen, quick, etc. —**beam'ing** *adj.* —**beam'ing·ly** *adv.*

beamed (bēmd) *adj.* having exposed beams [a *beamed* ceiling]

beam-ends (bēm'endz') *n.pl.* the ends of a ship's beams —**on her beam-ends** tipping so far to the side as to be in danger of overturning —**on one's beam-ends** at the end of one's resources, money, etc.

beam·y (-ē) *adj.* **beam'i·er**, **beam'i·est 1.** sending out beams of light; radiant **2.** beamlike; broad

bean (bēn) *n.* [OE. *bean*] **1.** any of various plants of the legume family, with edible, smooth, kidney-shaped seeds **2.** any such seed **3.** a pod with such seeds, eaten as a vegetable when still unripe **4.** any of various beanlike seeds [coffee *beans*] **5.** [Colloq.] the head or brain —*vt.* [Colloq.] to hit on the head —**full of beans** [Colloq.] lively; ebullient —**not a bean** [Colloq.] no money at all —**spill the beans** [Colloq.] to divulge secret information —**bean'-like'** *adj.*

bean·bag (bēn'bag') *n.* a small cloth bag filled with beans, and thrown in some games

bean-feast (bēn'fēst') *n.* [BEAN (*n.* 3) + FEAST] **1.** an annual dinner or outing given by an employer to his workers **2.** any celebration or festivity

bean·ie (bē'nē) *n.* [Colloq.] any of various kinds of skullcap worn by children, etc.

bean·o (bēn'ō) *n.* [Slang] any celebration or party

bean·pole (bēn'pōl') *n.* **1.** a tall pole for bean plants to climb on **2.** [Colloq.] a tall, lean person

bean·stalk (-stôk') *n.* the main stem of a bean plant

bear¹ (ber) *vt.* **bore** or archaic **bare**, **borne** or **born** (see *vt.* 3), **bear'ing** [OE. *beran*, akin to L. *ferre*, Gr. *pherein*] **1.** to carry; transport **2.** to have or show [the letter *bore* his

signature] **3.** to give birth to: the passive past participle in this sense is **born** when *by* does not follow **4.** to produce or yield [fruit-*bearing* trees] **5.** to support or sustain **6.** to sustain the burden of [to *bear* the cost] **7.** to put up with; tolerate [to *bear* pain] **8.** to call for; require [his actions *bear* watching] **9.** to carry or conduct (oneself) **10.** to carry over or hold (a sentiment) [to *bear* a grudge] **11.** to bring and tell (a message, tales, etc.) **12.** to move or push as if carrying [the crowd *bore* us along] **13.** to give or supply [to *bear* witness] —*vi.* **1.** to be productive [the tree *bears* well] **2.** *a)* to lie or move in a given direction *b)* to point towards (with *on* or *upon*) **3.** to have bearing (*on*); have a relation [his story *bears* on the crime] **4.** to tolerate; put up patiently (*with*) **5.** to be oppressive; weigh [grief *bears* heavily on her] —**bear arms** to serve as a soldier —**bear away** (**the bell**) to win; take the prize —**bear down 1.** to press or push down **2.** to make a strong effort —**bear down on 1.** to exert pressure on **2.** to make a strong effort towards accomplishing **3.** to approach —**bear out** to support or confirm —**bear up** to endure, as under a strain —**bring to bear on** (or **upon**) to cause to have an effect on

bear² (ber) *n.*, *pl.* **bears**, **bear**: see PLURAL, II, D, 1 [OE. *bera*] **1.** a large, heavy mammal with shaggy fur and a very short tail, native to temperate and arctic zones **2.** [B-] either of two N constellations, the **Great Bear** and the **Little Bear 3.** a person who is clumsy, rude, etc. **4.** one who sells stock-market shares, etc. in the expectation of buying them later at a lower price —*adj.* falling in price [a *bear* market] —**like a bear with a sore head** [Colloq.] aggressively bad-tempered —**bear'like'** *adj.*

bear·a·ble (-ə b'l) *adj.* that can be borne or endured; tolerable —**bear'a·bly** *adv.*

beard (bird) *n.* [OE., akin to G. *Bart*] **1.** the hair growing on the lower part of a man's face; whiskers **2.** any beardlike part, as of certain animals **3.** a hairy outgrowth on the head of certain grains, etc.; awn **4.** anything that projects like a beard; barb or hook —*vt.* **1.** to face or oppose courageously, as if grasping by the beard; defy **2.** to provide with a beard —**beard'ed** *adj.*

beard·ie, **beard·y** (bird'ē) *n.* [Colloq.] a man with a beard

beard·less (bird'lis) *adj.* **1.** having no beard **2.** too young to have a beard **3.** young, callow, etc.

bear·er (ber'ər) *n.* **1.** a person or thing that bears, carries, or supports **2.** a plant or tree that bears fruit **3.** a person presenting for payment a cheque, note, money order, etc. —*adj.* made out to the bearer [*bearer* bonds]

bear garden 1. orig. a place for bearbaiting **2.** any rough, noisy, rowdy place

bear hug a tight embrace

bear·ing (ber'iŋ) *n.* **1.** way of carrying and conducting oneself; carriage; manner **2.** a support or supporting part **3.** *a)* the act, power, or period of producing young, fruit, etc. *b)* that which is produced, as a crop **4.** endurance **5.** *a)* [*sometimes pl.*] direction or position with reference to the compass, some known points, etc. *b)* [*pl.*] awareness of one's position or situation [to lose one's *bearings*] **6.** relevant meaning; application; relation [the evidence has no *bearing* on the case] **7.** *Heraldry* any figure in a coat of arms **8.** *Mech.* any part of a machine in or on which another part revolves, slides, etc. —*adj.* that bears, or supports weight

bear·ish (ber'ish) *adj.* **1.** bearlike; rough, surly, etc. **2.** directed towards or causing a lowering of prices in the stock exchange —**bear'ish·ly** *adv.* —**bear'ish·ness** *n.*

bear·skin (ber'skin') *n.* **1.** the pelt or hide of a bear **2.** a rug, coat, etc. made of this **3.** a tall fur hat worn as part of some uniforms

beast (bēst) *n.* [< OFr. < L. *bestia*] **1.** orig., any animal except man **2.** any large, four-footed animal **3.** a person who is brutal, gross, vile, etc. **4.** qualities or impulses like those of an animal [the *beast* in him]

beast·ly (bēst'lē) *adj.* **-li·er**, **-li·est 1.** of or like a beast; bestial, brutal, etc. **2.** [Colloq.] disagreeable; unpleasant —*adv.* [Colloq.] very [*beastly* bad news] —**beast'li·ness** *n.*

beast of burden any animal used for carrying things

beast of prey any animal that hunts and kills other animals for food

beat (bēt) *vt.* **beat**, **beat'en**, **beat'ing** [OE. *beatan*] **1.** to strike repeatedly; pound **2.** to punish by so striking; flog **3.** to dash repeatedly against [waves *beat* against the shore] **4.** to form (a path, etc.) by repeated treading or riding **5.** to shape by hammering; forge **6.** to mix by stirring or striking repeatedly with a utensil; whip **7.** to move (esp. wings) up and down; flap **8.** to drive game out of cover **9.** to make or force, as by flailing or pounding [to *beat* one's way through a crowd] **10.** *a)* to defeat in a contest or struggle *b)* to outdo or surpass *c)* to act, arrive, or finish before **11.** to mark (time) by tapping, etc. **12.** to sound or signal, as by a drumbeat **13.** [Colloq.] to baffle or puzzle —*vi.* **1.** to strike repeatedly 2. to move or sound rhythmically; throb, pulsate, etc. 3. to hunt through woods, etc. for game 4. to take a beating or stirring [this cream doesn't *beat* well] 5. to make a sound by being struck, as a drum 6. *Naut.* to progress by tacking into the wind —*n.* 1. a beating, as of the heart 2. any of a series of blows or strokes 3. a pulsating movement or sound; throb 4. a habitual route [a policeman's *beat*] 5. *a*) the unit of musical rhythm [four *beats* to a bar] *b*) the accent in the rhythm of verse or music *c*) the gesture of the hand, baton, etc. used to mark this 6. *Acoustics* the regular recurring amplification of sound produced by two simultaneous tones of nearly equal frequency —*adj.* 1. [Slang] tired out; exhausted 2. of or belonging to a group of alienated young persons, esp. of the 1950's, rebelling against conventional attitudes, dress, speech, etc. [the *beat* generation] —**beat about** to hunt or look through or around —**beat back** to force to retreat —**beat down** 1. to shine with dazzling light and intense heat 2. to put down; suppress 3. [Colloq.] to force to a lower price —**beat it!** [Slang] go away! —**beat off** to drive back; repel —**to beat the band** (or **hell, the devil,** etc.) [Slang] vigorously; fast and furiously —**beat up** [Slang] to give a beating to; thrash

beat·en (bēt´'n) *adj.* 1. struck with repeated blows; whipped 2. shaped by hammering 3. flattened by treading [a *beaten* path] 4. *a*) defeated *b*) crushed in spirit by defeat 5. tired out —**off the beaten track** (or **path**) unusual, unfamiliar, etc.

beat·er (bēt´ər) *n.* 1. a person or thing that beats 2. an implement or utensil for beating 3. a person who drives game from cover in a hunt

be·a·tif·ic (bē´ə tif´ik) *adj.* [see BEATIFY] 1. making blissful or blessed 2. full of bliss or joy [a *beatific* smile] —**be´a·tif´i·cal·ly** *adv.*

be·at·i·fi·ca·tion (bē at´ə fi kā´shən) *n.* [see ff.] *R.C.Ch.* the process of declaring a certain dead person to be among the blessed in heaven: he is then entitled to public veneration

be·at·i·fy (bē at´ə fī´) *vt.* -**fied´**, -**fy´ing** [< Fr. < LL. *beatificare* < L. *beatus*, happy + *facere*, to make] 1. to make blissfully happy 2. *R.C.Ch.* to pronounce the beatification of by papal decree

beat·ing (bēt´iŋ) *n.* 1. the act of one that beats 2. a whipping 3. a throbbing 4. a defeat

be·at·i·tude (bē at´ə tyōōd´) *n.* [< Fr. < L. < *beatus*, happy] perfect blessedness or happiness —**the Beatitudes** the blessings on the meek, the peacemakers, etc. in the Sermon on the Mount: Matt. 5: 3-12

beat·nik (bēt´nik) *n.* [BEAT, *adj.* 2 + Russ. (via. Yid.) -*nik*, equiv. to -ER] a member of the beat generation

beau (bō) *n., pl.* **beaus, beaux** (bōz) [Fr. < *beau*, pretty < L. *bellus*, pretty] 1. a dandy 2. [Chiefly U.S.] boyfriend; suitor

Beau·fort scale (bō´fərt) [after Sir Francis *Beaufort* (1774-1857), Brit. naval officer] *Meteorol.* a scale of wind velocities ranging from 0 (calm) to 17 (hurricane)

‡**beau geste** (bō zhest´) *pl.* **beaux gestes** (bō zhest´) [Fr.] 1. a fine gesture 2. an act or offer that seems fine, noble, etc., but is empty

beau i·de·al (ī dē´al) [Fr.] 1. ideal beauty 2. the perfect type or conception (*of* something)

Beau·jo·lais (bō´zhə lā´) *n.* a rich red wine from the region of Beaujolais near Burgundy, France

beau monde (bō´mônd´) [Fr.] fashionable society

beaut (byōōt) *n.* [Slang] one that is beautiful or superlative in some way: often used ironically —*adj.* [Aust. Colloq.] good or excellent: an expression of approval

beau·te·ous (byōō´tē əs) *adj. same as* BEAUTIFUL —**beau´·te·ous·ly** *adv.*

beau·ti·cian (byōō tish´ən) *n.* a person who does hair styling, manicuring, etc. in a beauty salon

beau·ti·ful (byōō´tə fəl) *adj.* having beauty; very pleasing to the eye, ear, mind, etc. —**beau´ti·ful·ly** *adv.* —**beau´·ti·ful·ness** *n.*

beau·ti·fy (byōō´tə fī´) *vt., vi.* -**fied´**, -**fy´ing** to make or become beautiful or more beautiful —**beau´ti·fi·ca´tion** *n.* —**beau´ti·fi´er** *n.*

beau·ty (byōōt´ē) *n., pl.* -**ties** [< OFr. < L. *bellus*, pretty] 1. the quality attributed to whatever pleases the senses or mind, as by line, colour, form, tone, behaviour, etc. 2. a thing having this quality 3. good looks 4. a very good-looking woman 5. any very attractive feature [that's the *beauty* of the scheme]

beauty queen a woman who has won a beauty contest

beauty salon (or **shop** or **parlour**) a place where women go for hair styling, manicuring, etc.

beauty sleep [Colloq.] 1. sleep before midnight, popularly thought to be most restful 2. any extra sleep

beauty spot 1. a tiny black patch formerly applied by women to the face or back to emphasize whiteness of skin 2. a natural mark or mole on the skin 3. any place noted for its beauty

beauty treatment the use of cosmetics to improve a person's appearance

beaux (bōz; *Fr.* bō) *n. alt. pl. of* BEAU

‡**beaux-arts** (bō zàr´) *n.pl.* [Fr.] the fine arts

bea·ver[1] (bē´vər) *n.* [OE. *beofor*] 1. *pl.* -**vers, -ver:** see PLURAL, II, D, 1 *a*) a large rodent with soft, brown fur, webbed hind feet, and a flat, broad tail: it can live on land or in water *b*) its fur 2. a hat made of this fur 3. a heavy cloth of felted wool —**beaver away** to work hard and steadily

bea·ver[2] (bē´vər) *n.* [OFr. *baviere*, ult. < *bave*, saliva] 1. orig., a piece of armour to protect the mouth and chin 2. later, the visor of a helmet

BEAVER
(81-120 cm long, including tail)

Bea·ver·board (-bôrd´) *a trademark for* artificial board made of wood fibre, used for walls, etc.—*n.* [**b-**] fibreboard of this kind

be-bop (bē´bop´) *n. orig. name for* BOP

be·calm (bi käm´) *vt.* 1. to make calm 2. to make (a sailing ship) motionless from lack of wind

be·came (bi kām´) *pt. of* BECOME

be·cause (bi koz´, -kôz´) *conj.* [< ME. *bi*, by + *cause*] for the reason or cause that; since —**because of** by reason of; on account of

bé·cha·mel (bāsh´əmel´) *n.* [Fr. < Louis de *Béchamel*, steward to Louis XIV] a rich white sauce

‡**bêche-de-mer** (besh də mer´) *n.* [Fr., worm of the sea < Port. *bicho do mar*, sea slug] 1. *pl.* **bêches-de-mer´** (besh-) *same as* TREPANG 2. a pidgin English spoken in island areas of the SW Pacific

Bech·u·a·na (bech´ōō wän´ə) *n.* 1. *pl.* -**nas, -na** a member of a Bantu-speaking people living in Botswana 2. their language

beck[1] (bek) *n.* [< BECKON] a beckoning gesture of the hand, head, etc. —*vt., vi.* [Archaic] to beckon —**at the beck and call of** at the service of

beck[2] (bek) *n.* [ME. *bek* < ON. *bekkr*, a brook] a little stream, esp. one with a rocky bottom

beck·on (bek´'n) *vi., vt.* [OE. *beacnian* < *beacen*, a beacon] 1. to call or summon by a gesture 2. to attract; lure —*n.* a summoning gesture

be·cloud (bi kloud´) *vt.* to cloud over; obscure

be·come (bi kum´) *vi.* -**came´**, -**come´**, -**com´ing** [OE. *becuman*: see BE- & COME] 1. to come to be [to *become* ill] 2. to grow to be [the tadpole *becomes* a frog] —*vt.* to be right for or suitable to [that hat *becomes* you] —**become of** to happen to; be the fate of

be·com·ing (bi kum´iŋ) *adj.* 1. that is suitable or appropriate; fit 2. suitable to the wearer [a *becoming* gown] —**be·com´ing·ly** *adv.*

bec·que·rel (bek´ə rel´) [after A. H. *Becquerel* (1852-1908), Fr. physicist] the SI unit of activity of a radioactive source

bed (bed) *n.* [OE.] 1. a piece of furniture for sleeping or resting on, consisting typically of a bedstead, springs, mattress, and bedding 2. *same as* BEDSTEAD 3. any place or thing used for sleeping or reclining, or for sexual intercourse 4. *a*) a plot of soil where plants are raised *b*) such plants 5. *a*) the bottom of a river, lake, etc. *b*) a place on the ocean floor where things grow [oyster *bed*] 6. rock, etc. in which something is embedded 7. any flat surface used as a base or support 8. a pile or heap resembling a bed 9. a geological layer [a *bed* of coal] —*vt.* **bed´ded, bed´ding** 1. to provide with a sleeping place 2. to put to bed 3. to have sexual intercourse with 4. to embed 5. *a*) to plant in a bed of earth: also **bed out** *b*) to make (earth) into a bed for plants 6. to arrange in layers —*vi.* 1. to go to bed; rest 2. to form in layers —**bed and board** 1. sleeping accommodation and meals 2. the married state —**bed down** to prepare and use a sleeping place —**get up on the wrong side of the bed** to be cross or grouchy —**put to bed** 1. to get a (child, etc.) ready for sleep 2. [Slang] to get (a newspaper, etc.) ready for the press —**take to one's bed** to go to bed because of illness, etc.

B.Ed. Bachelor of Education

bed and breakfast overnight accommodation and breakfast, as offered by a hotel or boarding house, etc.

be·daub (bi dôb´) *vt.* 1. to make daubs on; smear over 2. to overdecorate

be·daz·zle (bi daz´'l) *vt.* -**zled, -zling** to dazzle thoroughly; bewilder; confuse

bed·bug (bed´bug´) *n.* a small, wingless, reddish-brown, bloodsucking insect that infests beds, etc.

bed·cham·ber (-chăm´bər) *n.* [Archaic] *same as* BEDROOM

bed·clothes (-klōz´, -klōthz´) *n.pl.* sheets, blankets, quilts, etc. used on a bed

bed·ding (-iŋ) *n.* 1. mattresses and bedclothes 2. straw, hay, etc., used to bed animals 3. a bottom layer 4. *Geol.* stratification

bedding plant a plant for a garden bed

be·deck (bi dek´) *vt.* to decorate; adorn

be·dev·il (bi dev´'l) *vt.* -**illed, -il·ling** 1. to plague diabolically; torment 2. to bewitch 3. to confuse completely; muddle 4. to corrupt; spoil —**be·dev´il·ment** *n.*

be·dew (bi dyōō′) *vt.* to make wet with or as if with drops of dew

bed·fast (bed′fäst′) *adj.* *same as* BEDRIDDEN

bed·fel·low (-fel′ō) *n.* 1. a person who shares one's bed 2. an associate, ally, etc.

be·dight (bi dīt′) *adj.* [pp. of obs. *bedight* < ME. < *bi-*, BE- + *dighten*, to set in order < OE. *dihtan*, to compose < L. *dictare*: see DICTATE] [Archaic or Poet.] bedecked; arrayed

be·dim (bi dim′) *vt.* **-dimmed′, -dim′ming** to make (the eyes or vision) dim; darken or obscure

be·di·zen (bi dī′z'n, -diz′'n) *vt.* [BE- + DIZEN] to dress in a cheap, showy way —**be·di′zen·ment** *n.*

bed jacket a woman's short, loose upper garment sometimes worn in bed over a nightgown

bed·lam (bed′lam) *n.* [< *Bedlam*, altered < (St. Mary of) *Bethlehem*, old insane asylum in London] 1. [Archaic] an insane asylum 2. any place or condition of noise and confusion —**bed′lam·ite′** (-īt′) *n.*

bed linen bed sheets, pillowcases, etc.

bed of roses [Colloq.] a situation or position of ease and luxury

Bed·ou·in (bed′ōō win) *n.,* *pl.* **-ins, -in** [< Fr. < Ar. *badāwīn,* dwellers in the desert] [*also* **b-**] 1. an Arab of any of the nomadic desert tribes of Arabia, Syria, or N Africa 2. any wanderer or nomad —*adj.* of or like the Bedouins

bed·pan (bed′pan′) *n.* 1. *same as* WARMING PAN 2. a shallow pan for use as a toilet by a person confined to bed

be·drag·gle (bi drag′'l) *vt.* **-gled, -gling** to make wet, limp, and dirty, as by dragging through mud —**be·drag′gled** *adj.*

bed·rid·den (bed′rid′'n) *adj.* having to stay in bed, usually for a long period, because of illness, infirmity, etc.: also **bed′rid′**

bed·rock (-rok′) *n.* 1. solid rock beneath the soil and superficial rock 2. a secure foundation 3. the very bottom 4. basic principles

bed·roll (-rōl′) *n.* [Chiefly U.S.] a portable roll of bedding, generally for sleeping outdoors

bed·room (-rōōm′) *n.* a room to sleep in —*adj.* dealing with sex or sexual affairs [a *bedroom* farce]

Beds. Bedfordshire

bed·side (-sīd′) *n.* the side of a bed; space beside a bed —*adj.* 1. beside a bed 2. as regards patients [a doctor's *bedside* manner]

bed-sitting room (bed′sit′iŋ) furnished accommodation consisting of a combined bedroom and sitting room: also **bed′sit′ter, bed′sit′n.**

bed·sore (-sôr′) *n.* a sore on the body of a bedridden person, caused by chafing or pressure

bed·spread (-spred′) *n.* a cover spread over the blanket on a bed, mainly for ornament

bed·stead (-sted′) *n.* a framework for supporting the springs and mattress of a bed

bed·straw (-strô′) *n.* [from its former use as straw for beds] a small plant of the madder family, with whorled leaves and small, white or coloured flowers

bed·time (-tīm′) *n.* one's usual time for going to bed

Bed·u·in (bed′ōō win) *n.* *alt. sp. of* BEDOUIN

bed-wet·ting (-wet′iŋ) *n.* urinating in bed

bee¹ (bē) *n.* [OE. *beo*] 1. a four-winged, hairy insect that gathers pollen and make honey 2. some bees live in organized colonies and make honey 2. a busy person —**have a bee in one's bonnet** 1. to be preoccupied or obsessed by an idea 2. to be not quite sane

bee² (bē) *n.* [ult. < OE. *ben,* compulsory service] [U.S.] a meeting of people to work together or to compete [a sewing *bee,* spelling *bee*]

beeb (bēb) *n.* [Colloq.] British Broadcasting Corporation

bee·bread (-bred′) *n.* a yellowish-brown mixture of pollen and honey, made and eaten by some bees

beech (bēch) *adj.* [OE. *boece, bece*] designating a family of trees including the beeches, oaks, and chestnuts —*n.* 1. a tree of the beech family, with smooth bark, hard wood, dark-green leaves, and edible nuts 2. its wood —**beech′en** *adj.*

beech·mast (bēch′mäst′) *n.* beechnuts, esp. as they lie on the ground: also **beech mast**

beech·nut (-nut′) *n.* the small, three-cornered, edible nut of the beech tree

beef (bēf) *n.,* *pl.* **beeves**; also, and for 5 always, **beefs** [< OFr. *boef* < L. *bovis,* gen. of *bos,* ox] 1. a full-grown ox, cow, or bull, esp. one bred for meat 2. meat from such an animal; specif., a dressed carcass 3. such animals collectively 4. [Colloq.] *a)* human flesh or muscle *b)* strength; brawn 5. [Slang] a complaint —*vi.* [Slang] to complain —**beef up** [Colloq.] to strengthen by addition, reinforcement, etc.

beef·burg·er (bēf′bur′gər) *n.* *same as* HAMBURGER

beef·cake (bēf′kāk) *n.* [Slang] display of the male figure, as in some magazine photographs: cf. CHEESECAKE (sense 2)

beef cattle cattle bred and fattened for meat

beef·eat·er (-ēt′ər) *n.* 1. an eater of beef, typified as portly,

ruddy, etc. 2. *same as* YEOMAN OF THE GUARD 3. a guard at the Tower of London

beef·steak (-stāk′) *n.* a thick slice of beef for grilling or frying

beef tea a drink made from beef extract or by boiling lean strips of beef

beef·y (bēf′ē) *adj.* **beef′i·er, beef′i·est** fleshy and solid; very muscular; brawny —**beef′i·ness** *n.*

bee·hive (bē′hīv′) *n.* 1. a box or other shelter for a colony of bees, where they make and store honey 2. a place of great activity

bee·keep·er (-kēp′ər) *n.* a person who keeps bees for producing honey —**bee′keep′ing** *n.*

bee·line (-līn′) *n.* a straight, direct route —**make a beeline for** [Colloq.] to go straight towards

Be·el·ze·bub (bē el′zə bub′) [< L. < Gr. *Beelzeboub* < Heb. *Ba'al zebūb,* lit., god of flies] *Bible* the chief devil; Satan: also **Be·el′ze·bul′** (-bōōl′)

bee moth a moth whose larvae, hatched in beehives, eat the wax of the honeycomb

been (bēn) *pp. of* BE —**been (and gone) and** [Colloq.] an expression of surprise or annoyance, etc. [see what he's *been (and gone) and* done!]

beep (bēp) *n.* [echoic] 1. the brief, high-pitched sound of a horn, as on a motor vehicle 2. a brief, high-pitched electronic signal, used in warning, direction-finding, etc. —*vi., vt.* to make or cause to make such a sound

beep·er (-ər) *n.* [see prec.] an instrument that gives out a beep

beer (bir) *n.* [OE. *beor*] 1. an alcoholic, fermented beverage made from grain, esp. malted barley, and flavoured with hops 2. a drink of this 3. any of various soft drinks made from root and plant extracts [ginger *beer*]

beer and skittles a time of pleasure and amusement

beer·gar·den (bir′gär′d'n) *n.* an open-air enclosure where beer and other drinks are served

beer·y (bir′ē) *adj.* **beer′i·er, beer′i·est** 1. of or like beer 2. showing the effects of drinking beer; drunken, maudlin, etc. —**beer′i·ness** *n.*

bee's knees [Colloq.] a person or thing of exceptional excellence

beest·ings (bēs′tiŋz) *n.pl.* [often with sing. v.] [OE. *bysting* < *beost,* beestings] the first milk of a cow after having a calf

bees·wax (bēz′waks′) *n.* 1. wax secreted and used by bees to build their honeycomb: see WAX¹ (sense 1) 2. a polish made from this

bees·wing (-wiŋ′) *n.* a gauzy film that forms in some old wines, esp. port

beet (bēt) *n.* [< OE. < L. *beta*] a plant with edible leaves and a thick, fleshy, white or red root

bee·tle¹ (bēt′'l) *n.* [OE. *bitela* < *bitan,* to bite] 1. an insect with biting mouthparts and hard front wings that cover the membranous hind wings when these are folded 2. any insect resembling a beetle —**beetle off** [Colloq.] to scurry away like a beetle

bee·tle² (bēt′'l) *n.* [OE. *betel,* ult. connected with BEAT] 1. a heavy, wooden mallet 2. a household mallet or pestle for mashing or beating —*vt.* **-tled, -tling** to pound with a beetle

bee·tle³ (bēt′'l) *vi.* **-tled, -tling** [prob. < ff.] to project or jut; overhang —*adj.* jutting; overhanging: also **bee′tling**

bee·tle-browed (bēt′'l broud′) *adj.* [ME. < ? *bitel,* sharp + *brouwe,* BROW] 1. having bushy or overhanging eyebrows 2. frowning; scowling

beet·root (bēt′rōōt) *n.* a variety of beet: its dark red root is eaten as a vegetable

beet sugar sugar extracted from sugar beets

beeves (bēvz) *n.* *alt. pl. of* BEEF

B.E.F. British Expeditionary Force

be·fall (bi fôl′) *vi.* **-fell′, -fall′en, -fall′ing** [< OE. < *be-* + *feallan,* to fall] to come to pass; happen —*vt.* to happen to [what *befell* them?]

be·fit (bi fit′) *vt.* **-fit′ted, -fit′ting** to be suitable or proper for —**be·fit′ting·ly** *adv.*

be·fog (bi fog′) *vt.* **-fogged′, -fog′ging** 1. to cover with fog; make foggy 2. to make obscure or muddled; confuse [to *befog* an issue]

be·fore (bi fôr′) *adv.* [< OE. < *be-,* by + *foran,* before] 1. ahead; in front 2. in the past; previously [I've seen him *before*] 3. earlier; sooner [come at ten, not *before*] —*prep.* 1. ahead of in time, space, rank, or importance 2. just in front of [he paused *before* the door] 3. in the sight, notice, presence, etc. of [to stand *before* a judge] 4. being considered, judged, or decided by [the bill *before* the assembly] 5. earlier than [he left *before* noon] 6. in preference to [death *before* dishonour] 7. under the force of [*before* the enemy] —*conj.* 1. earlier than the time that [drop in *before* you go] 2. rather than [I'd die *before* I'd tell]

before Christ in the (given) year before the beginning of the Christian Era: it is fixed by counting backwards from 1 A.D.

be·fore·hand (-hand') *adv., adj.* 1. ahead of time; in advance 2. in anticipation

be·foul (bifoul') *vt.* to dirty or sully; foul

be·friend (-frend') *vt.* to act as a friend to; help

be·fud·dle (-fud''l) *vt.* **-dled, -dling** 1. to fuddle or confuse (the mind, a person, etc.) 2. to stupefy with alcoholic drink —**be·fud'dle·ment** *n.*

beg (beg) *vt.* **begged, beg'ging** [< Anglo-Fr. < OFr. *begard,* beggar < MDu. *beggaert*] 1. to ask for as charity 2. to ask for earnestly as a kindness or favour —*vi.* 1. to ask for alms; be a beggar 2. to entreat —**beg off** to ask to be released from —**beg the question** 1. to use an argument that assumes as proved the very thing one is trying to prove 2. loosely, to evade the issue —**go (a-)begging** to be unwanted

be·gan (bi gan') *pt. of* BEGIN

be·get (bi get') *vt.* **-got'** or archaic **-gat'**(-gat'), **-got'ten** or **-got', -get'ting** [< OE. *begitan,* to acquire: see BE- & GET] 1. to be the father of; procreate 2. to bring into being; produce [*tyranny begets* rebellion] —**be·get'ter** *n.*

beg·gar (beg'ər) *n.* [< OFr. *begard:* see BEG] 1. a person who begs; esp., one who lives by begging 2. a very poor person; pauper 3. [Colloq.] a person; fellow —*vt.* 1. to make a beggar of; make poor 2. to make seem inadequate or useless [*her beauty beggars* description] —**beg'gar·dom** (-dəm) *n.*

beg·gar·ly (-lē) *adj.* like or fit for a beggar; very poor, inadequate, etc. —**beg'gar·li·ness** *n.*

beg·gar-my-neigh·bour (beg'ər mī nā'bər) *n.* a card game which lasts until one player obtains all the cards

beg·gar·y (beg'ər ē) *n.* 1. extreme poverty 2. the act of begging

be·gin (bi gin') *vi.* **be·gan', be·gun', be·gin'ning** [< OE. *beginnan*] 1. to start doing something; get under way 2. to come into being; arise 3. to have a first part [the Bible *begins* with Genesis] 4. to be or do in the slightest degree [they don't *begin* to compare] —*vt.* 1. to cause to start; commence 2. to bring into being; originate 3. to do or be the first part of —**to begin with** in the first place

be·gin·ner (-ər) *n.* 1. one who begins anything 2. one just beginning to do or learn a thing; novice

beginner's luck the exceptional luck that is believed to accompany beginners

be·gin·ning (-iŋ) *n.* 1. a starting or commencing 2. the time or place of starting; birth; origin; source 3. the first part [the *beginning* of a book] 4. [usually *pl.*] an early stage —**beginning of the end** the last stage

be·gird (bi gurd') *vt.* **-girt'** or **-gird'ed, -girt', -gird'ing** 1. to bind around; gird 2. to encircle

be·gone (bi gôn') *interj., vi.* (to) be gone; go away; get out

be·gon·ia (bi gōn'yə) *n.* [after M. *Bégon* (1638–1710), Fr. governor of the Dominican Republic] a plant with showy flowers and ornamental leaves

be·got (bi got') *pt. & alt. pp. of* BEGET

be·got·ten (-'n) *alt. pp. of* BEGET

be·grime (bi grīm') *vt.* **-grimed', -grim'ing** to cover with grime; make dirty; soil

be·grudge (bi gruj') *vt.* **-grudged', -grudg'ing** 1. to feel ill will or resentment at the possession or enjoyment of (something) by another [to *begrudge* another's fortune] 2. to give with ill will or reluctance [he *begrudges* her every penny] —**be·grudg'ing·ly** *adv.*

be·guile (bi gīl') *vt.* **-guiled', -guil'ing** 1. to mislead by guile; deceive 2. to deprive (*of* or *out of*) by deceit; cheat 3. to pass (time) pleasantly; while away [he *beguiled* his day with reading] 4. to charm or delight —**be·guile'ment** *n.* —**be·guil'er** *n.* —**be·guil'ing·ly** *adv.*

be·guine (bi gēn') *n.* [< Fr. *béguin,* infatuation] a native dance of Martinique or its music

be·gum (bē'gəm) *n.* [< Hindi *begam,* lady] in India, a Moslem princess or lady of high rank

be·gun (bi gun') *pp. of* BEGIN

be·half (bi häf') *n.* [< OE. *be,* by + *healf,* side, half] support, interest, side, etc. [speak on his *behalf*] —**on behalf of** 1. in the interest of; for 2. speaking for; representing

be·have (bi hāv') *vt., vi.* **-haved', -hav'ing** [see BE- & HAVE] 1. to conduct (oneself or itself) or act in a specified way 2. to conduct (oneself) properly; do what is right

be·hav·ior (bi hāv'yər) *n. U.S. sp. of* BEHAVIOUR

be·hav·iour (bi hāv'yər) *n.* 1. the way a person behaves or acts; conduct 2. an organism's observable responses to stimulation 3. the way a machine, element, etc. acts or functions —**be·hav'iour·al** *adj.* —**be·hav'iour·al·ly** *adv.*

behavioural science any of the sciences, as sociology, psychology, or anthropology, that study human behaviour

be·hav·iour·ism (bi hāv'yər iz'm) *n.* the doctrine that observed behaviour provides the only valid data of psychology: it rejects the concept of mind —**be·hav'iour·ist** *n., adj.* —**be·hav'iour·is'tic** *adj.*

behaviour therapy the treatment of a psychological disorder by training a patient to react normally

be·head (bi hed') *vt.* to cut off the head of

be·held (bi held') *pt. & pp. of* BEHOLD

be·he·moth (bi hē'məth, bē'ə-) *n.* [Heb. *behēmōth,* intens. pl. of *behēmāh,* beast] 1. *Bible* a huge animal, assumed to be the hippopotamus: Job 40:15-24 2. any huge animal or thing

be·hest (bi hest') *n.* [OE. *behæs,* a vow] an order, command, or earnest request

be·hind (bi hīnd') *adv.* [OE. *behindan:* see BE- & HIND¹] 1. in or to the rear or back [walk *behind*] 2. in a former time, place, condition, etc. [the girl he left *behind*] 3. into a retarded state [to drop *behind* in one's studies] 4. into arrears [to fall *behind* in one's dues] 5. slow in time; late —*prep.* 1. remaining after [the sons he left *behind* him] 2. at the back of [sit *behind* her] 3. lower in rank, achievement, etc. 4. later than [*behind* schedule] 5. on the other or farther side of [*behind* the hill] 6. gone by or ended for [his schooling is *behind* him] 7. supporting or advocating [the committee is *behind* the plan] 8. hidden by; not yet revealed [the story *behind* the news] —*adj.* that follows [the person *behind*] —*n.* [Colloq.] the buttocks

be·hind·hand (-hand') *adv., adj.* 1. behind in paying debts, rent, etc. 2. behind time; late 3. behind or slow in progress, advancement, etc.

be·hold (bi hōld') *vt.* **-held', -held'** or archaic **-hold'en, -hold'ing** [OE. *bihealdan,* to hold: see BE- & HOLD¹] to hold in view; look at; regard —*interj.* look! see! —**be·hold'er** *n.*

be·hold·en (-ən) *adj.* obliged to feel grateful; owing thanks; indebted

be·hoof (bi hōōf') *n.* [OE. *behof,* profit] [Now Rare] behalf, benefit, interest, advantage, sake, etc.

be·hoove (-hōōv') *vt.* **-hooved', -hoov'ing** chiefly *U.S. var. of* BEHOVE

be·hove (-hōv') *vt.* **-hoved', -hov'ing** [OE. *behofian* to need] to be necessary or fitting for; incumbent upon [it *behoves* you to do this]

beige (bāzh) *n.* [Fr.] 1. a soft, unbleached and undyed, wool fabric 2. its characteristic sandy colour; greyish tan —*adj.* greyish-tan

be·ing (bē'iŋ) *n.* [see BE] 1. existence; life 2. basic or essential nature 3. one that lives or exists, or is assumed to do so [a human *being,* a divine *being*] —**being as** (or **that**) [Dial. or Colloq.] since; because —**for the time being** for now

be·jab·bers (bi jab'ərz) *interj.* [< *by Jesus*] an exclamation used to express surprise, pleasure, anger, etc.: also **be·ja'bers** (-jā'bərz), **be·je'sus** (-jē'zəs)

be·jew·el (bi jōō'əl) *vt.* **-elled, -el·ling** to decorate with or as with jewels

bel (bel) *n.* [after A. G. *Bell* (1847-1922), U.S. inventor] *Physics* a unit for comparing two power levels, equal to 10 decibels: cf. DECIBEL

be·la·bour (-lā'bər) *vt.* 1. to beat severely 2. to attack verbally 3. *popularly, same as* LABOUR. *vt.*

be·lat·ed (-lāt'id) *adj.* late or too late; tardy —**be·lat'ed·ly** *adv.* —**be·lat'ed·ness** *n.*

be·lay (-lā') *vt., vi.* **-layed', -lay'ing** [< OE. < *be-* + *lecgan,* to lay] 1. to make (a rope) secure by winding round a pin (**belaying pin**), cleat, etc. 2. [Naut. Colloq.] to hold; stop [*belay* there!] 3. to secure (a person or thing) by a rope —*n.* action, method, or place of securing a hold for a rope in mountain climbing

bel can·to (bel'kän'tō) [It., lit., beautiful song] a style of singing with brilliant vocal display and purity of tone

belch (belch) *vi., vt.* [OE. *bealcian*] 1. to expel (gas) through the mouth from the stomach 2. to utter (curses, etc.) violently 3. to throw forth (its contents) violently [the volcano *belched* flame] —*n.* 1. a belching 2. a thing belched

bel·dam, bel·dame (bel'dəm) *n.* [*bel-* < Fr. *belle* (see BELLE) + DAME] [Obs.] an old woman; esp., a hideous old woman; hag

be·lea·guer (bi lē'gər) *vt.* [Du. *belegeren* < *legeren,* to camp < *leger,* a camp] 1. to besiege by encircling, as with an army 2. to beset; harass

bel·fry (bel'frē) *n., pl.* **-fries** [altered (after BELL¹) < OFr. *berfroi* < OHG. < *bergen,* to protect + *frid,* peace] 1. a bell tower 2. the part of a steeple that holds the bell or bells —**bel'fried** *adj.*

Belg. 1. Belgian 2. Belgium

Bel·gium hare (bel'jəm) a large, reddish-brown domestic rabbit

Be·li·al (bē'lē əl, bēl'yəl) *n.* [< LL. < Heb. *belīya'al,* worthlessness] *Bible* wickedness as an evil force (in the New Testament, personified as Satan)

be·lie (bi lī') *vt.* **-lied', -ly'ing** 1. to give a false idea of; misrepresent [his smile *belies* his anger] 2. to leave unfulfilled [war *belied* hopes for peace] 3. to show to be untrue [her cruelty *belied* her kind words] —**be·li'er** *n.*

be·lief (bə lēf') *n.* [ME. < *bi-,* BE- + *-leve* < OE. *geleafa,* belief] 1. the state of believing; conviction 2. faith, esp. religious faith 3. trust or confidence [I have *belief* in his ability] 4. anything believed or accepted as true; esp., a creed, tenet, etc. **5.** an opinion; expectation [my *belief* is that he'll come]

be·lieve (bə lēv′) *vt.* **-lieved′, -liev′ing** [ME. < *bi-*, BE- + *-leven* < OE. *geliefan*, believe] **1.** to take as true, real, etc. **2.** to have confidence in a statement or promise of (another person) **3.** to suppose or think *—vi.* **1.** to have trust or confidence (*in*) **2.** to have religious faith **3.** to suppose or think **—be·liev′a·bil′i·ty** *n.* **—be·liev′a·ble** *adj.* **—be·liev′-a·bly** *adv.* **—be·liev′er** *n.*

be·like (bi līk′) *adv.* [Archaic] quite likely; probably

Be·li·sha beacon (bə lē′shə) [< *Hore-Belisha*, Minister of Transport when first introduced] a flashing orange light mounted on a post and marking a pedestrian crossing

be·lit·tle (bi lit′'l) *vt.* **-tled, -tling** to make seem little, less important, etc.; depreciate **—be·lit′tle·ment** *n.* **—be·lit′tler** *n.*

bell¹ (bel) *n.* [OE. *belle*] **1.** a hollow object, usually cuplike and of metal, which rings when struck **2.** *a)* the sound made by a bell *b)* this sound made to mark the beginning or end of a period of time, as in boxing **3.** anything shaped like a bell, as a flower, the flare of a horn, etc. **4.** *Naut. a)* a bell rung every half hour to mark the periods of the watch *b)* any of these periods *—vt.* **1.** to attach a bell to **2.** to shape like a bell *—vi.* to flare out like a bell **—bell, book, and candle** instruments used formerly in excommunications in the R.C. Church **—bell the cat** to hazard one's safety for the sake of others, by challenging a superior in any way **—sound as a bell** in perfect condition

bell² (bel) *n., vi., vt.* [< OE. *bellan*] bellow; roar; bay

bel·la·don·na (bel′ə dän′ə) *n.* [ModL. < It. *bella donna*, beautiful lady] **1.** a poisonous plant with purplish, bell-shaped flowers and black berries; deadly nightshade: it yields atropine **2.** *same as* ATROPINE

bell-bot·tom (bel′bät′əm) *adj.* designating trousers flaring at the ankles: also **bell′-bot′tomed**

bell·boy (-boi′) *n.* [U.S.] a page or porter in a hotel, club, etc.

bell buoy a buoy with a warning bell rung by the motion of the waves

belle (bel) *n.* [Fr., fem. of *beau*: see BEAU] a pretty woman or girl; often, one who is the prettiest or most popular [the *belle* of the ball]

‡belle é·poque (be lä pôk′) an era of elegance and gaiety for the well-off preceding World War I

belles-let·tres (bel let′rə) *n.pl.* [Fr.] literature as a fine art; fiction, poetry, drama, etc. as distinguished from technical and scientific writings **—bel·let·rist** (bel let′rist) *n.* **—bel′-le·tris′tic** (-lə tris′tik) *adj.*

bell·flow·er (bel′flou′ər) *n.* any of a large genus of plants, with showy, bell-shaped flowers of white, pink, or blue

bell·foun·der (bel′foun′dər) *n.* a person who casts bells in a foundry

bel·li·cose (bel′ə kōs′) *adj.* [< L. < *bellicus*, of war < *bellum*, war] of a quarrelsome or hostile nature; eager to fight; warlike **—bel′li·cose′ly** *adv.* **—bel·li·cos·i·ty** (bel′ə kos′ə tē) *n.*

bel·lied (bel′ēd) *adj.* having a belly, esp. of a specified kind [yellow-*bellied*]

bel·lig·er·ence (bə lij′ər əns) *n.* belligerent or aggressively hostile attitude or quality

bel·lig·er·en·cy (-ən sē) *n.* **1.** the state of being at war or of being recognized as a belligerent **2.** *same as* BELLIGERENCE

bel·lig·er·ent (bə lij′ər ənt) *adj.* [< L. prp. of *belligerare* < *bellum*, war + *gerere*, to carry on] **1.** recognized under international law as being engaged in a war; at war **2.** of war; of fighting **3.** warlike **4.** showing readiness to fight or quarrel *—n.* a belligerent person or nation **—bel·lig′-er·ent·ly** *adv.*

bell jar a bell-shaped container or cover made of glass, used to keep gases, air, moisture, etc. in or out: also **bell glass**

bell·man (bel′mən) *n.*, *pl.* **-men** *same as* TOWN CRIER

bell metal an alloy of copper and tin used in bells

bel·low (bel′ō) *vi.* [OE. *bylgan*] **1.** to roar with a reverberating sound, as a bull **2.** to cry out loudly, as in anger or pain *—vt.* to utter loudly or powerfully *—n.* a bellowing sound; roar

bel·lows (bel′ōz, -əz) *n.sing. & pl.* [ME. *belwes*, orig. pl. of *beli*: see BELLY] **1.** a device that produces a stream of air through a narrow tube when its sides are pumped together: used for blowing fires, in pipe organs, etc. **2.** anything like a bellows, as the folding part of some cameras

bell-pull (bel′pool′) *n.* a handle or cord pulled to operate a bell

bell-push (bel′poosh′) *n.* a button that operates an electric bell

bell-ring·er (bel′riŋ′ər) *n.* **1.** a person who rings church bells **2.** a performer on musical handbells

bell-weth·er (bel′weth′ər) *n.* a male sheep, usually wearing a bell, that leads the flock

bel·ly (bel′ē) *n.*, *pl.* **-lies** [ME. *beli* < OE. *belg*, leather bag, bellows] **1.** the lower front part of the human body between the chest and thighs; abdomen **2.** the underside of an animal's body **3.** the abdominal cavity **4.** the stomach **5.** an appetite for food **6.** the deep interior [the *belly* of a ship] **7.** any part, surface, or section that curves outwards or bulges *—vt., vi.* **-lied, -ly·ing** to swell out; bulge

bel·ly·ache (-āk′) *n.* pain in the abdomen or bowels *—vi.* **-ached′, -ach′ing** [Slang] to complain or grumble **—bel′-ly·ach′er** *n.*

bel·ly·band (-band′) *n.* a girth around an animal's belly for keeping a saddle, etc. in place

bel·ly·but·ton (-but′'n) *n.* [Colloq.] the navel: also **belly button**

belly dance a dance of eastern Mediterranean origin characterized by a twisting of the abdomen, sinuous hip movements, etc. **—bel′ly-dance′** *vi.* **-danced′, -danc′ing —belly dancer**

bel·ly·flop (-fläp′) *vi.* **-flopped′, -flop′ping** [Colloq.] **1.** to dive awkwardly, with the belly striking flat against the water *—n.* such a dive

bel·ly·ful (-fool′) *n.* **1.** enough or more than enough to eat **2.** [Colloq.] all that one can bear

bel·ly-land·ing (-lan′diŋ) *n.* the landing of an aircraft with the undercarriage up, esp. in an emergency

belly laugh [Colloq.] a hearty laugh

be·long (bi lôŋ′) *vi.* [ME. < *be-*, intens. + OE. *langian*, belong] **1.** to have a proper or fitting place [the book *belongs* on his desk] **2.** to be part of; be related (*to*) **3.** to be a member (with *to*) **4.** to be owned (with *to*) **5.** [Colloq.] to be the owner (with *to*) [who *belongs* to this hat?]

be·long·ing (-iŋ) *n.* **1.** [*pl.*] possessions; property **2.** close relationship; affinity [a sense of *belonging*]

be·lov·ed (bi luv′id, -luvd′) *adj.* dearly loved *—n.* a dearly loved person

be·low (bi lō′) *adv., adj.* [see BE- & LOW¹] **1.** in or to a lower place; beneath **2.** in a lower place on the page or on a later page (of a book, etc.) **3.** in hell **4.** on earth **5.** on or to a lower floor or deck **6.** in or to a lesser rank, function, etc. *—prep.* **1.** lower than, as in position, rank, worth, etc. **2.** unworthy of [it is *below* her to do that]

bel pa·e·se (bel pä ā′zē) [It.] a mild and creamy Italian cheese

belt (belt) *n.* [OE., ult. < L. *balteus*, a belt] **1.** a band of leather, etc., worn about the waist to hold clothing up, support tools, etc., or as an ornament or sign of rank or proficiency: see also SAFETY BELT **2.** any encircling thing like this **3.** an endless band for transferring motion from one wheel or pulley to another, or for carrying things **4.** an area or zone with some distinctive feature [the green *belt*] **5.** [Slang] a hard blow; cuff *—vt.* **1.** to surround or encircle as with a belt **2.** to fasten or attach as with a belt **3.** to hit hard, as with a belt **4.** [Colloq.] to sing (*out*) lustily *—vi.* [Colloq.] to move at high speed **—below the belt** unfair(ly); foul **—belt up** **1.** [Colloq.] to become silent; stop talking **2.** to fasten a safety belt **—tighten one's belt** to live more thriftily **—under one's belt** [Colloq.] as part of one's experience [ten years at sea *under his belt*]

Bel·tane (bel′tān) *n.* [Scot. < Gael. *Bealtainn*] **1.** May 1 (Old Style) **2.** an ancient Celtic festival observed about May 1

belt·ed (bel′tid) *adj.* **1.** wearing a belt, esp. as a mark of distinction **2.** marked by a band or stripe

belt·ing (-tiŋ) *n.* **1.** material for making belts **2.** belts collectively **3.** [Slang] a beating

be·lu·ga (bə loo′gə) *n.*, *pl.* **-ga, -gas:** see PLURAL, II, D, 2 [< Russ. < *byeli*, white] **1.** a large, white sturgeon of the Black and Caspian seas **2.** a large, white dolphin of northern seas; white whale

bel·ve·dere (bel′və dir′, bel′və dir′) *n.* [It., beautiful view] a summerhouse, or an open, roofed gallery in an upper storey, built to give a view of the scenery

B.E.M. British Empire Medal

be·mire (bi mīr′) *vt.* **mired′, mir′ing** **1.** to dirty as with mire **2.** to cause to bog down in mud

be·moan (bi mōn′) *vt., vi.* to moan about or lament (a loss, grief, etc.) [to *bemoan* one's fate]

be·muse (bi myooz′) *vt.* **-mused′, -mus′ing** [BE- + MUSE] to muddle, confuse, or stupefy **—be·muse′ment** *n.*

be·mused (-myoozd′) *adj.* **1.** confused; stupefied **2.** plunged in thought; preoccupied

ben¹ (ben) *n.* [Scot. < Gael. *beann*, a peak] [Scot. & Ir.] a mountain peak [Ben Nevis]

ben² (ben) *adv., prep* [OE. *be-* + *innan*, in] [Scot.] within; inside *—n.* [Scot.] the inner room or living room of a cottage

bench (bench) *n.* [OE. *benc* (cf. BANK²)] **1.** a long, hard seat for several persons, with or without a back **2.** the place where judges sit in a court **3.** [*sometimes* B-] the status or office of a judge *b)* judges collectively *c)* a law court **4.** a stand for exhibiting a dog at a dog show **5.** a strong table on which work with tools is done; worktable **6.** a shelf in rock or mine workings *—vt.* **1.** to provide with benches **2.** to place on a bench, esp. an official one **—on the bench** **1.** presiding in a law court; serving as a judge or magistrate

bench·er (ben'chər) *n. Law* a senior member of the Inns of Court

bench mark 1. a surveyor's mark made on a permanent landmark for use as a reference point in determining other altitudes **2.** a standard in judging quality, value, etc. Also **bench'mark'** *n.*

bench warrant an order issued by a judge or law court for the arrest of a person

bend¹ (bend) *vt.* **bent** or archaic **bend'ed, bend'ing** [OE. *bendan*, to bind with a string; hence, to bend (a bow)] **1.** to force (an object) into a curved or crooked form, or (*back*) to its original form **2.** to turn from a straight line [to bend one's steps from a path] **3.** to make (someone) submit or give in, as to one's will **4.** to turn or direct (one's attention, etc. *to*) **5.** to incline or tend (*to* or *towards*) **6.** *Naut.* to fasten (sails or ropes) into position —*vi.* **1.** to turn or be turned as from a straight line **2.** to yield by curving or crooking, as from pressure **3.** to crook or curve the body; stoop (*over* or *down*) **4.** to give in; yield [he bent to her wishes] —*n.* **1.** a bending or being bent **2.** a bending or curving part, as of a river —**round the bend** [Colloq.] crazy, mad, insane, etc. —**bend'a·ble** *adj.*

bend² (bend) *n.* [ME. < prec.] any of various knots used in tying ropes —**the bends** [Colloq.] *same as* DECOMPRESSION SICKNESS

bend³ (bend) *n.* [< OFr. < Goth. *bindan*, to bind] *Heraldry* a band or stripe on a coat of arms, from the upper left to the lower right corner

bend·er (ben'dər) *n.* **1.** a person or thing that bends **2.** [Slang] a drinking bout; spree

bend sinister *Heraldry* a band or stripe on a coat of arms, from the upper right to the lower left corner: a sign of bastardy in the family line

be·neath (bi nēth') *adv.* [< OE. < *be-*+ *neothan*, down] **1.** in a lower place **2.** just below something; underneath —*prep.* **1.** lower than; below **2.** directly under; underneath **3.** inferior to in rank, quality, worth, etc. **4.** unworthy of [it is beneath him to cheat]

ben·e·dic·i·te (ben'ə dis'ə tē'; *for n 2 usually* bā'nā dē'-chē tā') *interj.* [L.] bless you! —*n.* **1.** the invocation of a blessing **2.** [B-] the canticle that begins with the word *Benedicite*

ben·e·dict (ben'ə dikt') *n.* [< *Benedick*, a bachelor in Shakespeare's *Much Ado About Nothing*] a newly married man, esp. one who seemed to be a confirmed bachelor

Ben·e·dic·tine (ben'ə dik'tin; *also, and for n. 2 usually,* -tēn) *adj.* **1.** of Saint Benedict **2.** designating or of the monastic order based on his teachings —*n.* **1.** a Benedictine monk or nun **2.** [b-] a liqueur, orig. made by Benedictine monks

ben·e·dic·tion (ben'ə dik'shən) *n.* [< L. < *bene*, well + *dicere*, to speak] **1.** a blessing **2.** an invocation of divine blessing, esp. ending a religious service **3.** blessedness —**ben'e·dic'to·ry** *adj.*

ben·e·fac·tion (ben'ə fak'shən, ben'ə fak'shən) *n.* [< LL. < L. *benefacere* < *bene*, well + *facere*, to do] **1.** the act of doing good or helping those in need **2.** money or help freely given

ben·e·fac·tor (ben'ə fak'tər) *n.* a person who has given help, esp. financial help; patron —**ben'e·fac'tress** (-tris) *n.fem.*

ben·e·fice (ben'ə fis) *n.* [OFr. < L. *beneficium*, a kindness: see BENEFACTION] **1.** an endowed church office providing a living for a vicar, rector, etc. **2.** its income —*vt.* **-ficed, -fic·ing** to provide with a benefice

be·nef·i·cence (bə nef'ə səns) *n.* [< L.: see BENEFACTION] **1.** the fact or quality of being kind or doing good **2.** a charitable act or generous gift

be·nef·i·cent (-sənt) *adj.* **1.** showing beneficence; doing good **2.** resulting in benefit Also **be·nef·ic** (bə nef'ik) —**be·nef'i·cent·ly** *adv.*

ben·e·fi·cial (ben'ə fish'əl) *adj.* **1.** producing benefits; advantageous; favourable **2.** *Law* entitled to the use or profit of property, etc. —**ben'e·fi'cial·ly** *adv.*

ben·e·fi·ci·ar·y (ben'ə fish'ē ər ē, -fish'ər ē) *adj.* of or holding a benefice —*n., pl.* **-ar·ies 1.** a holder of a benefice **2.** anyone receiving benefit **3.** a person named to receive the income or inheritance from a will, insurance policy, trust, etc.

ben·e·fit (ben'ə fit) *n.* [< OFr. < L.: see BENEFACTION] **1.** [Archaic] a charitable act **2.** anything helping to improve conditions; advantage **3.** [often *pl.*] payments made by an insurance company, public agency, etc., as during sickness or retirement **4.** a public performance, dance, etc. whose proceeds go to help a certain person, cause, etc. —*vt.* **-fit·ed, -fit·ing** to do good to or for; aid —*vi.* to receive advantage; profit —**give someone the benefit of the doubt** to assume a person is innocent rather than guilty

benefit of clergy 1. the exemption which the medieval clergy had from trial or punishment except in a church court **2.** the rites or approval of the church [marriage without *benefit of clergy*]

benefit society *same as* FRIENDLY SOCIETY

be·nev·o·lence (bə nev'ə ləns) *n.* [ME. & OFr. < L. < *bene*, well + *volens*, prp. of *velle*, to wish] **1.** an inclination to do good; kindliness **2.** a kindly, charitable act or gift; beneficence

be·nev·o·lent (-lənt) *adj.* **1.** doing or inclined to do good; kindly; charitable **2.** characterized by benevolence —**be·nev'o·lent·ly** *adv.*

Beng. Bengali

Ben·gal·i (ben gôl'ē, beŋ-) *n.* **1.** a native of Bengal **2.** the Indo-European, Indic language of Bengal —*adj.* of Bengal, its people, or their language

ben·ga·line (beŋ'gə lēn', beŋ'gə lēn') *n.* [Fr. < *Bengal*] a corded cloth of silk, rayon, etc. and either wool or cotton

Ben·gal light (ben gôl', beŋ-) a firework or flare with a steady blue light, used, esp. formerly, as a signal, etc.

be·night·ed (bi nīt'id) *adj.* **1.** surrounded by darkness or night **2.** intellectually or morally backward; unenlightened —**be·night'ed·ness** *n.*

be·nign (bi nīn') *adj.* [OFr. < L. < *bene*, well + *genus*, birth] **1.** good-natured; kindly **2.** favourable; beneficial **3.** *Med.* doing little or no harm; not malignant —**be·nign'ly** *adv.*

be·nig·nant (bi nig'nənt) *adj.* [< prec., by analogy with MALIGNANT] **1.** kindly or gracious, sometimes in a patronizing way **2.** favourable; beneficial —**be·nig'nan·cy** *n., pl.* **-cies**

be·nig·ni·ty (-nə tē) *n., pl.* **-ties 1.** benignancy; kindliness **2.** a kind act; favour

ben·i·son (ben'ə z'n, -s'n) *n.* [< OFr. < L.: see BENEDICTION] a blessing; benediction

bent¹ (bent) *pt. and pp. of* BEND¹ —*adj.* **1.** made curved or crooked; not straight **2.** strongly determined (with *on*) [she is *bent* on going] **3.** set in a course; bound [westward *bent*] **4.** [Slang] dishonest; corrupt —*n.* **1.** an inclining; tendency **2.** a mental leaning; propensity [a *bent* for art] —**to** (or **at**) **the top of one's bent** to (or at) the limit of one's ability

bent² (bent) *n.* [OE. *beonot*] **1.** any of various wiry, low-growing grasses much used for lawns and golf greens: also called **bent'grass' 2.** the stiff flower stalk of certain grasses **3.** a heath; moor

Ben·tham·ism (ben'thəm iz'm) *n.* the utilitarian philosophy of Jeremy Bentham (1748-1832), Brit. philosopher and economist, which holds that the greatest happiness of the greatest number should be the ultimate goal of society —**Ben'tham·ite'** (-īt') *n.*

ben·ton·ite (ben'tə nīt') *n.* [after Fort *Benton*, Montana, U.S., where found] a porous clay, formed by the decomposition of volcanic ash

bent·wood (bent'wood') *adj.* designating furniture made of wood permanently bent into various forms by heat, moisture, and pressure

be·numb (bi num') *vt.* **1.** to make numb **2.** to deaden the mind, will, or feelings of

Ben·ze·drine (ben'zə drēn') a trademark for AMPHETAMINE —*n.* [b-] this drug

ben·zene (ben'zēn, ben zēn') *n.* [BENZ(OIC) + -ENE] a clear, flammable, poisonous liquid, C_6H_6, obtained from coal tar and used as a solvent for fats and in making varnishes, dyes, etc.

BENTWOOD CHAIR

benzene ring a structural unit thought to exist in the molecules of benzene and derivatives of benzene, consisting of a ring of six carbon atoms with alternate double bonds between them

ben·zine (ben'zēn, ben zēn') *n.* [BENZ(OIC) + -INE⁴] a colourless, flammable liquid obtained in the fractional distillation of petroleum and used as a motor fuel, a solvent in dry cleaning, etc.

ben·zo·ate (ben'zō āt') *n.* a salt or ester of benzoic acid

ben·zo·caine (ben'zō kān') *n.* [BENZO(IN) + (CO)CAINE] a white, odourless powder, used in ointments as an anaesthetic and to protect against sunburn

ben·zo·ic (ben zō'ik) *adj.* [BENZO(IN) + -IC] of or derived from benzoin

benzoic acid a white, crystalline organic acid, C_6H_5COOH, used as an antiseptic, preservative, etc.

ben·zo·in (ben'zō in, -zoin) *n.* [< Fr. < It. *benzoino* < Ar. *lubān jāwi*, incense of Java] the balsamic resin from certain tropical Asiatic trees, used in medicine and perfumery and as incense

ben·zol (ben'zōl, -zol) *n.* [BENZ(OIN) + -OL¹] *same as* BENZENE: sometimes, a mixture distilling below 100° C that is 70 percent benzene

be·queath (bi kwēth', -kwēth') *vt.* [OE. *becwethan*, to give by will < *be-* + *cwethan*, to say: see QUOTH] **1.** to leave (property) to another by last will and testament **2.** to hand down; pass on —**be·queath'a·ble** *adj.* —**be·queath'al** (-əl) *n.*

be·quest (-kwest') *n.* [< *be-* + OE. *cwis* < *cwethan*: see prec.] **1.** a bequeathing **2.** anything bequeathed

be·rate (bi rāt') *vt.* **-rat'ed, -rat'ing** [BE- + RATE²] to scold or rebuke severely

Ber·ber (bur'bər) *n.* **1.** any of a Moslem people living in N

Africa **2.** their language —*adj.* of the Berbers, their culture, or their language

ber·ceuse (*Fr.* bersöz') *n., pl.* **-ceuses** (*Fr.* -söz') [Fr. < *bercer*, to rock] **1.** a lullaby **2.** a piece of instrumental music that has a rocking or lulling effect

be·reave (bi rēv') *vt.* **-reaved'** or **-reft'** (-reft'), **-reav'ing** [OE. *bereafian* < *be-* + *reafian*, to rob] **1.** to deprive or rob: now usually in the pp. (**bereft**) [*bereft* of hope] **2.** to leave in a sad or lonely state, as by death —**the bereaved** the survivors of a recently deceased person —**be·reave'-ment** *n.*

be·ret (ber'ā) *n.* [< Fr. < Pr. < LL.: see BIRETTA] a flat, round cap of felt, wool, etc.

berg (burg) *n.* **1.** *same as* ICEBERG **2.** in South Africa, a hill or mountain

ber·ga·mot (bur'gə mot') *n.* [< Fr. < It. < ? Turk. *beg-armūdī*, prince's pear] **1.** *a)* a pear-shaped citrus fruit grown in S Europe for its oil, used in perfumery *b)* this oil **2.** an aromatic herb

berg-schrund (burk'shrunt) *n.* [G., lit., mountain cleft] a crevasse at the head of a glacier

BERET

ber·i·ber·i (ber'ē ber'ē) *n.* [Singh. *beri*, weakness] a deficiency disease caused by lack of thiamine (vitamin B₁) in the diet and characterized by nerve disorders, body swelling, etc.

berk (burk) *n.* [< *Berkshire Hunt*, rhyming slang for cunt] [Slang] a stupid person; fool

berke·li·um (bur'klē əm) *n.* [< University of California at *Berkeley*, where first isolated] a radioactive chemical element: symbol, Bk; at. wt., 248 (?); at. no., 97

ber·lin (bər lin', bur'lin) *n.* [after *Berlin* in Germany] **1.** a four-wheeled, closed carriage with a footman's platform behind **2.** [*sometimes* B-] a fine, soft wool yarn: also called Berlin wool

berm, berme (burm) *n.* [Fr. < MDu. *baerm*] a ledge or shoulder, as along the edge of a paved road

Ber·mu·da grass (bər myōō'də) a creeping perennial grass widely grown in warm climates for lawns or pasture

Bermuda shorts short trousers extending to just above the knee

ber·ret·ta (bə ret'ə) *n. same as* BIRETTA

ber·ry (ber'ē) *n., pl.* **-ries** [OE. *berie*] **1.** any small, juicy, fleshy fruit, as a raspberry, blackberry, etc. **2.** the dry seed or kernel of various plants, as a coffee bean **3.** an egg of a lobster, crayfish, etc. **4.** *Bot.* a fleshy fruit with a soft wall and thin skin, as the tomato, grape, etc. —*vi.* **-ried, -ry·ing** **1.** to bear berries **2.** to look for and pick berries —**ber'-ry·like'** *adj.*

ber·serk (bər surk', -zurk') *n.* [ON. *berserkr*, warrior in bearskin < *ber*, a bear + *serkr*, coat] *Norse Legend* a frenzied warrior: also **ber·serk'er** —*adj., adv.* in or into a state of violent or destructive rage or frenzy

berth (burth) *n.* [< base of BEAR¹] **1.** *Naut. a)* enough space to keep clear of another ship, the shore, etc. *b)* space for anchoring *c)* a place of anchorage **2.** a position, office, job, etc. **3.** *a)* a built-in bed or bunk on a ship, train, etc. *b)* any sleeping place —*vt.* **1.** to put into a berth **2.** to furnish with a berth —*vi.* to come into or occupy a berth —**give a wide berth to** to stay well away from

ber·tha (bur'thə) *n.* [Fr. *berthe*, < *Berthe*, Bertha, a feminine name] a woman's wide collar, often of lace, usually extending over the shoulders

ber·yl (ber'əl) *n.* [< OFr. < L. < Gr. *bēryllos*] beryllium aluminium silicate, a very hard, crystalline mineral: emerald and aquamarine are two gem varieties of beryl

be·ryl·li·um (bə ril'ē əm) *n.* [ModL. < prec.] a hard, rare, metallic chemical element: symbol, Be; at. wt., 9.0122; at. no., 4

be·seech (bi sēch') *vt.* **-sought'** or **-seeched', -seech'ing** [< OE. *besecan*: see BE- & SEEK] **1.** to ask (someone) earnestly; implore **2.** to ask for earnestly; beg for —**be·seech'ing·ly** *adv.*

be·seem (bi sēm') *vi.* to be suitable or appropriate (to)

be·set (bi set') *vt.* **-set', -set'ting** [< OE. *besettan*: see BE- & SET] **1.** to set thickly with; stud **2.** to attack from all sides; harass or besiege **3.** to surround or hem in —**be·set'ment** *n.*

be·set·ting (-iŋ) *adj.* constantly harassing or attacking [a *besetting* temptation]

be·shrew (bi shrōō') *vt.* [< ME.: see BE- & SHREW] [Archaic] to curse: used mainly in mild oaths

be·side (bi sīd') *prep.* [ME.: see BY & SIDE] **1.** by or at the side of; alongside; near **2.** in comparison with [*beside* yours, my share seems small] **3.** in addition to; besides **4.** other than; aside from [*beside* him, who is going?] **5.** not pertinent to [*beside* the point] —*adv.* [Archaic] in addition —**beside oneself** wild with fear, rage, etc.

be·sides (-sīdz') *adv.* [ME. < prec. + adv. gen. -(e)s] **1.** in addition; as well **2.** except for that mentioned; else **3.** moreover; furthermore —*prep.* **1.** in addition to; as well as **2.** other than; except

be·siege (bi sēj') *vt.* **-sieged', -sieg'ing** [ME. < *be-* + *segen*,

to lay siege to < *sege*, SIEGE] **1.** to hem in with armed forces, esp. for a sustained attack **2.** to close in on; crowd around **3.** to overwhelm or beset [*besieged* with queries] —**be·sieg'er** *n.*

be·smear (bi smir') *vt.* to smear over; soil

be·smirch (bi smurch') *vt.* [BE- + SMIRCH] **1.** to make dirty; soil **2.** to bring dishonour to; sully

be·som (bē'zəm, bi'-) *n.* [< OE. *besma*, broom, rod] **1.** a broom, esp. one made of twigs tied to a handle **2.** a troublesome woman or girl; hussy

be·sot (bi sot') *vt.* **-sot'ted, -sot'ting** **1.** to make a sot of; stupefy, as with alcoholic drink **2.** to make silly or foolish —**be·sot'ted** *adj.*

be·sought (bi sôt') *alt. pt. and pp. of* BESEECH

be·span·gle (bi spaŋ'g'l) *vt.* **-gled, -gling** to cover with or as with spangles

be·spat·ter (bi spat'ər) *vt.* to spatter, as with mud or slander; soil or sully by spattering

be·speak (bi spēk') *vt.* **-spoke'** (-spōk') or archaic **-spake** (-spāk'), **-spo'ken** or **-spoke', -speak'ing** **1.** to speak for or engage in advance; reserve **2.** to be indicative of; show [a mansion that *bespeaks* wealth] **3.** to foreshadow; point to **4.** [Archaic or Poet.] to speak to; address

be·spec·ta·cled (bi spek'tə k'ld) *adj.* wearing eyeglasses

be·spoke (bi spōk') *pl. and alt. pp. of* BESPEAK —*adj.* custom-made; making or made to order

be·spread (bi spred') *vt.* **-spread', -spread'ing** to spread over or cover

be·sprin·kle (bi spriŋ'k'l) *vt.* **-kled, -kling** to sprinkle over (*with* something)

Bes·se·mer process (bes'ə mər) [after Sir Henry *Bessemer* (1813-98), Brit. inventor] a method of making steel by blasting air through molten pig iron in a large container (**Bessemer converter**) to burn away the carbon and other impurities

best (best) *adj. superl. of* GOOD [OE. *betst*] **1.** of the most excellent sort; above all others in worth or ability **2.** most suitable, most desirable, etc. **3.** being almost the whole; largest [the *best* part of an hour] —*adv. superl. of* WELL² **1.** in the most excellent or most suitable manner **2.** in the highest degree; most —*n.* **1.** the person or people, thing, condition, action, etc. of the greatest excellence, worth, suitability, etc. **2.** the utmost [to do one's *best*] **3.** one's finest clothes —*vt.* defeat or outdo —**all for the best** **1.** turning out to be fortunate after all **2.** with good intentions —**as best one can** as well as one can —**at best** **1.** under the most favourable conditions **2.** at most —**at one's best** in one's best mood, form, health, etc. —**get** (or **have**) **the best of** **1.** to outdo or defeat **2.** to outwit —**give someone best** to concede a person's superiority —**had best** ought to —**make the best of** to do as well as one can with

be·stead (bi sted') *adj.* [< ME. < *bi-*, be + *stad*, placed < ON. *staddr*, prp. of *stethja*, to place] [Archaic] situated; placed —*vt.* **-stead'ed, -stead', -stead'ing** [Archaic] to help; avail

bes·tial (bes'tē əl, -tyəl) *adj.* [OFr. < LL. *bestialis*] **1.** of beasts **2.** like a beast; brutish, savage, vile, etc. —**bes·ti·al·i·ty** (bes'tē al'ə tē) *n., pl.* **-ties** —**bes'tial·ly** *adv.*

bes·tial·ize (bes'tē ə līz', -tyə-) *vt.* **-ized', -iz'ing** to make bestial; brutalize

bes·ti·ar·y (bes'tē ər ē) *n., pl.* **-aries** [< ML. < L. < *bestia*, beast] a type of medieval natural history book with moralistic or religious fables about real and mythical animals

be·stir (bi stur') *vt.* **-stirred', -stir'ring** to stir to action; exert or busy (oneself)

best man the principal attendant of the bridegroom at a wedding

be·stow (bi stō') *vt.* [see BE- & STOW] **1.** to give or present as a gift (often with *on* or *upon*) **2.** to apply; devote **3.** [Archaic] to put or place, as in storage **4.** [Obs.] to give in marriage —**be·stow'al** *n.*

be·strew (bi strōō') *vt.* **-strewed', -strewed'** or **-strewn', -strew'ing** **1.** to cover over (a surface); strew **2.** to scatter or lie scattered over or about

be·stride (bi strīd') *vt.* **-strode'** (-strōd'), **-strid'den** (-strid''n), **-strid'ing** **1.** to sit on, mount, or stand over with a leg on each side; straddle **2.** [Archaic] to stride over

best seller a book, gramophone record, etc. currently outselling most others

bet (bet) *n.* [prob. < ABET] **1.** an agreement between two persons that the one proved wrong about the outcome of something will do or pay what is stipulated; wager **2.** *a)* the thing or sum thus staked *b)* the thing, contestant, etc. that something is staked on **3.** a person, thing, or action likely to bring about a desired result [he's the best *bet* for the job] —*vt.* **bet** or **bet'ted, bet'ting** **1.** to declare in or as in a bet [I bet he'll be late] **2.** to stake (money, etc.) in a bet **3.** to wager with (someone) —*vi.* to make a bet —**you bet** (you)! [Colloq.] certainly!

be·ta (bēt'ə) *n.* [L. < Gr. *bēta* < Heb. *bēth*, lit., house; of Phoen. origin] **1.** the second letter of the Greek alphabet (B, β) **2.** the second of a group or series

be·take (bi tāk') *vt.* **-took', -tak'en, -tak'ing** **1.** to go (used reflexively) [he *betook* himself to his castle] **2.** to direct or devote (oneself)

beta particle an electron or positron ejected at high velocity from the nucleus of an atom undergoing radioactive disintegration

beta ray **1.** *same as* BETA PARTICLE **2.** a stream of beta particles

be·ta·tron (bēt′ə tron′) *n.* [BETA (RAY) + (ELEC)TRON] an electron accelerator that uses a rapidly changing magnetic field to accelerate the particles to high velocities

be·tel (bēt′′l) *n.* [Port. < Malay *vettilai*] a tropical Asian climbing plant of the pepper family, whose leaf is chewed by some Asians

Be·tel·geuse, Be·tel·geux (bet′′l jōōz′, bēt′-) [< Fr. < Ar. *bayt al jauza*] a very large, red, first-magnitude star, second brightest in the constellation Orion

betel nut the fruit of the betel palm, chewed together with lime and leaves of the betel (plant) by some Asians

betel palm a palm grown in SE Asia

bête noire (bāt′nwär′) *pl.* **bêtes noires** (bāt′nwär′) [Fr., lit., black beast] a person or thing feared, disliked, and avoided

beth (bāth, beth; Heb. bāt, bās) *n.* [Heb. *bēth*: see BETA] the second letter of the Hebrew alphabet

beth·el (beth′əl) *n.* [LL. < Heb. *bēth 'ēl*, house of God] **1.** a holy place **2.** a church or other place of worship for seamen **3.** a nonconformist chapel: also **be·thes′da**

be·think (bi thiŋk′) *vt.* **-thought′, -think′ing** to bring (oneself) to think of, consider, or recollect; remind (oneself)

be·tide (bi tīd′) *vi., vt.* **-tid′ed, -tid′ing** [< ME. < *be-* + OE. *tidan*, to happen < *tid*, time] to happen (to); befall

be·times (bi tīmz′) *adv.* [ME. < *bi-*, by + *time*, TIME + adv. gen. *-(e)s*] **1.** early or early enough **2.** [Archaic] promptly or quickly

be·to·ken (bi tō′k'n) *vt.* [< ME. < *be-* + *toknen* < OE. *tacnian*, to mark < *tacen*, TOKEN] **1.** to be a token or sign of; show **2.** to show beforehand

bet·o·ny (bet′ə nē) *n.* [< OF. < L. *betonica*] any of several related plants formerly used for dyeing and in medicine

be·tray (bi trā′) *vt.* [< ME. < *be-* + *traien*, betray < OFr. < L. *tradere*, to hand over] **1.** to help the enemy of (one's country, cause, etc.); be a traitor to **2.** to break faith with; fail to uphold [to *betray* a trust] **3.** to lead astray; specif., to seduce and then desert **4.** to reveal unknowingly **5.** to reveal or show signs of **6.** to disclose (secret information, etc.) —**be·tray′al** *n.* —**be·tray′er** *n.*

be·troth (bi trōth′, -trôth′) *vt.* [< ME. < *be-* + *treuthe* < OE. *treowth*, truth] **1.** to promise in marriage **2.** [Archaic] to promise to marry

be·troth·al (-əl) *n.* a betrothing or being betrothed; mutual pledge to marry; engagement

be·trothed (-trōthd′, -trôtht′) *adj.* engaged to be married —*n.* the person to whom one is betrothed

bet·ta (bet′ə) *n.* [ModL.] a brightly coloured, tropical, freshwater fish of SE Asia: some species are kept in aquariums

bet·ted (bet′id) *alt. pt. and pp. of* BET

bet·ter (bet′ər) *adj. compar. of* GOOD [< OE. *betera*] **1.** superior; above another or others in worth or ability **2.** more suitable, more desirable, etc. **3.** being more than half; larger [the *better* part of an hour] **4.** improved in health or disposition —*adv. compar. of* WELL[2] **1.** in a more excellent or more suitable manner **2.** in a higher degree **3.** more [it took *better* than an hour] —*n.* **1.** a person superior in authority, position, etc. **2.** the thing, condition, etc. that is more excellent, etc. —*vt.* **1.** to outdo; surpass **2.** to make better; improve —*vi.* to become better —**better off** in more favourable circumstances, esp. financially —**for the better** to a better condition —**get** (or **have**) **the better of** **1.** to outdo **2.** to outwit —**had better** would be wise; ought to

better half [Colloq.] one's wife or, less often, one's husband

bet·ter·ment (-mənt) *n.* **1.** a making or being made better; improvement **2.** *Law* an improvement, other than repairs, that increases the value of property

betting shop a licensed off-course bookmaker's premises

bet·tor, bet·ter (bet′ər) *n.* a person who bets

be·tween (bi twēn′) *prep.* [< OE. < *be*, by + *tweon(um)*, by twos, in pairs] **1.** in or through the space that separates (two things) **2.** in or of the time, amount, or degree that separates (two things); intermediate to **3.** that connects or relates to [a bond *between* friends] **4.** along a course that connects [a road *between* here and there] **5.** by the joint action of [*between* them they landed the fish] **6.** in or into the combined possession of [they had fifty pounds *between* them] **7.** from one or the other of [choose *between* love and duty] **8.** because of the combined effect of [*between* work and study he has no time left] *Between* is sometimes used of more than two, if the relationship is thought of as individual with each of the others [a treaty *between* four powers] —*adv.* in an intermediate space, position, or function —**between ourselves** in confidence; as a secret:

also **between you and me** —**in between** in an intermediate position

be·tween·times (-tīmz′) *adv.* in the intervals: also **be·tween′whiles′**

be·twixt (bi twikst′) *prep., adv.* [< OE. *betwix* < *be-* + a form related to *twegen*, TWAIN] between: now archaic except in **betwixt and between,** neither altogether one nor altogether the other

BeV (bev) *n.* [B(ILLION) + E(LECTRON-) V(OLTS)] a unit of energy equal to one billion electron-volts

bev·a·tron (bev′ə tron′) *n.* [< BeV + (CYCLO)TRON] *Physics* a synchrotron used to accelerate atomic particles

bev·el (bev′'l) *n.* [prob. < OFr. hyp. *baivel*, dim. < *baif*, gaping: see BAY[2]] **1.** a tool that is a rule with a movable arm, for measuring or marking angles, etc.: also **bevel square** **2.** an angle other than a right angle **3.** a sloping edge between parallel surfaces —*adj.* sloped; bevelled —*vt.* **-elled, -el′ling** to cut to an angle other than a right angle —*vi.* to slope at an angle

bevel gear a gearwheel meshed with another so that their shafts are at an angle

bev·er·age (bev′rij, -ər ij) *n.* [< OFr. < *bevre* < L. *bibere*, IMBIBE] any liquid for drinking, esp. other than plain water

bev·y[1] (bev′ē) *n., pl.* **bev′ies** [< ?] **1.** a group, esp. of girls or women **2.** a flock: now chiefly of quail

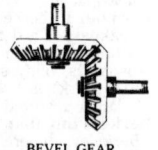

bev·y[2] (bev′ē) *n.* [< BEVERAGE] [Slang] a drink, esp. beer: also **bev·vy**

be·wail (bi wāl′) *vt.* to wail over or complain about; lament; mourn —**be·wail′er** *n.*

BEVEL GEAR

be·ware (bi wer′) *vi., vt.* [prob. < OE. < *be-* + *warian*, to be wary] to be wary or careful (of); be on one's guard (against): used only in inf. and imper.

be·wil·der (bi wil′dər) *vt.* [BE- + archaic *wilder*, to lose one's way] to confuse hopelessly, as by something complicated; befuddle; puzzle —**be·wil′dered** *adj.* —**be·wil′der·ing·ly** *adv.* —**be·wil′der·ment** *n.*

be·witch (bi wich′) *vt.* [< ME. < *be-* + *wicchen* < OE. < *wicca*: see WITCH[1]] **1.** to cast a spell over **2.** to enchant; fascinate; charm —**be·witch′ing** *adj.* —**be·witch′ing·ly** *adv.*

be·witch·ment (-mənt) *n.* **1.** power to bewitch **2.** a bewitching or being bewitched **3.** a spell that bewitches Also **be·witch′er·y** (-ər ē), *pl.* **-er·ies**

be·wray (bi rā′) *vt.* [< ME. < *be-* + OE. *wregan*, to accuse] [Archaic] to divulge; reveal; betray

bey (bā) *n.* [Turk. *bey, beg*] **1.** in the Ottoman Empire, the governor of a Turkish province **2.** a Turkish title of respect and former title of rank **3.** the former native ruler of Tunis

be·yond (bi yond′) *prep.* [< OE. < *be-* + *geond*, yonder] **1.** on or to the far side of; farther on than **2.** later than [*beyond* noon] **3.** outside the reach or understanding of [*beyond* help] **4.** more or better than; exceeding [success *beyond* one's hopes] —*adv.* **1.** farther away **2.** in addition —**the** (**great**) **beyond** whatever follows death

bez·el (bez′'l) *n.* [< OFr. hyp. *bisel* (Fr. *biseau*), sloping edge] **1.** a sloping surface, as the cutting edge of a chisel **2.** the slanting faces of a cut jewel, esp. those of the upper half **3.** the groove and flange holding a gem or a watch crystal in place

be·zique (bi zēk′) *n.* [Fr. *bésigue*] a card game for two players using two packs from which all cards under seven are omitted

bf, b.f. boldface

B/F, b.f. brought forward

b.f. bloody fool

bhang (baŋ) *n.* [Hindi < Sans. *bhaṅgā*, hemp] **1.** the hemp plant **2.** its dried leaves and flowers, or a preparation, such as hashish, made from these and used for its intoxicating properties

bhin·di (bin′dē) *n.* [Hindi] the Indian name for okra

b.h.p. brake horsepower

bi- (bī) [L. *bi-* < OL. *dui-*] a prefix meaning: **1.** having two [biangular] **2.** doubly [biconvex] **3.** happening every two [biweekly] **4.** happening twice during every [bimonthly]: in this sense, now usually *semi-* or *half-* **5.** using two or both [bilabial] **6.** joining or involving two [bilateral] **7.** *Chem.* having twice as many atoms or chemical equivalents for a definite weight of the other constituent of the compound [sodium *bicarbonate*]: in organic compounds, usually replaced by *di-*

Bi *Chem.* bismuth

bi·an·gu·lar (bī aŋ′gyoo lər) *adj.* having two angles

bi·an·nu·al (-an′yoo wəl, -yool) *adj.* coming twice a year; semiannual: see also BIENNIAL —**bi·an′nu·al·ly** *adv.*

bi·as (bī′əs) *n., pl.* **bi′as·es** [Fr. *biais*, a slant] **1.** a slanting or diagonal line, cut or sewn across the weave of cloth **2.** a mental leaning; partiality; prejudice; bent **3.** *Bowls* the weight in the side of the ball that causes it to roll in a curve **4.** *Math.* the difference between the estimated value and the true value of a statistic obtained by random sampling —*adj.* slanting; diagonal —*adv.* diagonally —*vt.* **-ased** or **-assed,**

-as·ing or **-as·sing** to cause to have a bias; prejudice —**on the bias** diagonally
bias binding a strip of material cut on the bias and used for binding hems or for decoration
bi·ath·lon (bī ath'lən, -lon) *n.* [BI- + Gr. *athlon*, a contest] an event combining two sports, as skiing and shooting in the winter Olympics
bi·ax·i·al (bī ak'sē əl) *adj.* having two axes, as some crystals —**bi·ax'i·al·ly** *adv.*
bib[1] (bib) *vt., vi.* bibbed, bib'bing [< L. *bibere*, to drink] [Archaic] to drink; imbibe —*n.* 1. an apronlike cloth tied under a child's chin at meals 2. the front upper part of an apron or overalls
bib[2] (bib) *n., pl.* bib, bibs: see PLURAL, II, D, 2 [< ?] a food fish related to the cod, found in the North Sea and the Arctic
Bib. 1. Bible 2. Biblical
bib and tucker [Colloq.] an outfit of clothes
bib·cock (bib'kok') *n.* a tap whose nozzle is bent downwards
‡**bi·be·lot** (bē blō') *n.* [Fr. < OFr. < *belbel*, BAUBLE] a small object whose value lies in its beauty or rarity
Bibl., bibl. 1. Biblical 2. bibliographical
Bi·ble (bī'b'l) *n.* [< OFr. < ML. < Gr. *biblia*, collection of writings, pl. of *biblion*, book < *biblos*, papyrus] 1. the sacred book of Christianity; Old Testament and New Testament 2. the Holy Scriptures of Judaism, identical with the Old Testament of Christianity 3. any collection of writings sacred to a religion [the Koran is the Moslem *Bible*] 4. [b-] any book regarded as authoritative See also AUTHORIZED VERSION, REVISED STANDARD VERSION, DOUAI BIBLE, VULGATE, SEPTUAGINT, APOCRYPHA
Bi·ble-thump·er (-thum'pər) *n.* a clergyman or other person who is a vigorous exponent of his beliefs: also **Bi'-ble-pound'er, Bi'ble-punch'er**
Bib·li·cal (bib'li k'l) *adj.* [*also* b-] 1. of or in the Bible 2. in keeping with or according to the Bible; like that in the Bible —**Bib'li·cal·ly** *adv.*
Bib·li·cist (-sist) *n.* 1. a person who takes the words of the Bible literally 2. a specialist in Biblical literature —**Bib'-li·cism** *n.*
bib·li·o- [< Gr. *biblion*: see BIBLE] *a combining form* meaning: 1. book; of books [*bibliophile*] 2. of the Bible [*bibliomancy*]
bib·li·og·ra·phy (bib'lē og'rə fē) *n., pl.* **-phies** [< Gr.: see BIBLE & -GRAPHY] 1. the study of the editions, dates, authorship, etc. of books and other writings 2. a list of writings on a given subject, by a given author, etc. 3. a list of the books, articles, etc. referred to by an author —**bib'-li·og'ra·pher** *n.* —**bib'li·o·graph'ic** (-ə graf'ik), **bib'-li·ograph'i·cal** *adj.* —**bib'li·o·graph'i·cal·ly** *adv.*
bib·li·o·man·cy (bib'lē ə man'sē) *n.* [BIBLIO- + -MANCY] prediction based on a phrase taken from a book, esp. a Bible, opened at random
bib·li·o·ma·ni·a (bib'lē ə mā'nē ə, -nyə) *n.* [BIBLIO- + -MANIA] a craze for collecting books, esp. rare ones —**bib'li·o·mane'** (-mān') *n.* —**bib'li·o·ma'ni·ac** *n., adj.*
bib·li·o·phile (bib'lē ə fīl') *n.* [BIBLIO- + -PHILE] 1. one who loves or admires books, esp. for their style of binding, printing, etc. 2. a book collector Also **bib'li·o·phil'**(-fil'), **bib·li·oph·i·list** (bib'lē of'ə list) —**bib'li·o·phil'ic** (-ə fil'ik) *adj.* —**bib'li·oph'i·lism** (-of'ə liz'm), **bib'li·oph'i·ly** (-of'-ə lē) *n.*
bib·li·o·pole (-pōl') *n.* [< L. < Gr. < *biblion*, a book + *pōlein*, to sell] a bookseller, esp. one dealing in rare works: also **bib·li·op·o·list** (bib'lē op'ə list) —**bib'li·o·pol'ic** (-ə pol'ik) *adj.* —**bib'li·op'o·lism** (-op'ə liz'm), **bib'li·op'o·lism** *n.*
bib·u·lous (bib'yoo ləs) *adj.* [< L. < *bibere*, to drink] 1. highly absorbent 2. addicted to or fond of alcoholic drink —**bib'u·lous·ly** *adv.* —**bib'u·lous·ness** *n.*
bi·cam·er·al (bī kam'ər əl) *adj.* [< BI- + L. *camera*, a chamber] made up of or having two legislative or other chambers —**bi·cam'er·al·ism** *n.*
bi·carb (bī kärb') *n.* [Colloq.] *short for* SODIUM BICARBONATE
bi·car·bon·ate (bī kär'bə nit, -nāt') *n.* an acid salt of carbonic acid containing the radical HCO_3
bicarbonate of soda *same as* SODIUM BICARBONATE
bic·cy (bik'ē) *n., pl.* **-cies** [Colloq.] *clipped form of* BISCUIT (sense 1)
bice (bīs) *n.* [OFr. *bis*, dusky, dark] a greyish-blue or green pigment made from smalt or azurite
bi·cen·te·nar·y (bī'sen ten'ər ē) *adj., n., pl.* **-nar·ies** *same as* BICENTENNIAL
bi·cen·ten·ni·al (bī'sen ten'ē əl) *adj.* 1. happening once in a period of 200 years 2. lasting for 200 years —*n.* a 200th anniversary or its celebration
bi·ceph·a·lous (bī sef'ə ləs) *adj.* [BI- + -CEPHALOUS] two-headed: also **bi·ce·phal·ic** (bī se fal'ik)
bi·ceps (bī'seps) *n., pl.* **-ceps** [L. < *bis*, two + *caput*, head] 1. a muscle having two heads, or points of origin; esp., the large muscle in the front of the upper arm or the corresponding muscle at the back of the thigh 2. strength or muscular development, esp. of the arm
bi·chlo·ride (bī klôr'īd) *n.* 1. a binary compound containing

two atoms of chlorine for each atom of another element 2. *same as* MERCURIC CHLORIDE
bichloride of mercury *same as* MERCURIC CHLORIDE
bi·chro·mate (bī krō'māt) *n.* *same as* DICHROMATE
bick·er (bik'ər) *vi.* [ME. *bikeren*] 1. to have a petty quarrel; squabble 2. to flicker, twinkle, etc. —*n.* a petty quarrel —**bick'er·er** *n.*
bi·col·our (bī'kul'ər) *adj.* of two colours: also **bi'col'oured**
bi·con·cave (bī'kon kāv', bī kon'kāv) *adj.* concave on both surfaces [a *biconcave* lens]
bi·con·vex (bī'kon veks', bī kon'veks) *adj.* convex on both surfaces [a *biconvex* lens]
bi·cus·pid (bī kus'pid) *adj.* [< BI- + L. *cuspis*, pointed end] having two points [a *bicuspid* tooth]: also **bi·cus'pi·date** (-pi dāt') —*n.* any of eight adult teeth with two-pointed crowns

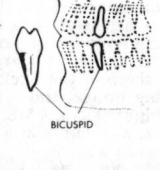

BICUSPID

bi·cy·cle (bī'si k'l) *n.* [Fr.: see BI- & CYCLE] a vehicle consisting of a metal frame mounted on two wheels, one behind the other, and equipped with handlebars, a saddlelike seat and foot pedals —*vi., vt.* **-cled, -cling** to ride on a bicycle —**bi'cy·clist, bi'cy·cler** *n.*
bid (bid) *vt.* **bade** or **bid** or archaic **bad, bid'den** or **bid, bid'ding**; for vt. 2, 6, & for vi., the pt. & pp. are always **bid** [< OE. *biddan*, to urge & OE. *beodan*, to command] 1. to command, ask, or tell 2. to offer (a certain amount) as the price that one will pay or accept 3. to declare openly [to *bid* defiance] 4. to express in greeting or taking leave [to *bid* farewell] 5. [Archaic or Dial.] to invite 6. *Card Games* to state (the number of tricks one expects to take) and declare (a suit or no-trump) —*vi.* to make a bid —*n.* 1. a bidding of an amount 2. the amount bid 3. a chance to bid 4. an attempt or try [a *bid* for fame] 5. *Card Games* a) the act of bidding b) the number of tricks stated c) a player's turn to bid —**bid fair** to seem likely —**bid up** to raise the amount bid —**bid'der** *n.*
bid·da·ble (bid'ə b'l) *adj.* 1. obedient; docile 2. worth bidding on [a *biddable* bridge hand]
bid·ding (bid'iŋ) *n.* 1. a command or request 2. an invitation or summons 3. the bids or the making of bids in a card game or auction
bid·dy (bid'ē) *n., pl.* **-dies** 1. a hen 2. [Slang] a woman, esp. an elderly, gossipy one
bide (bīd) *vi.* **bode** or **bid'ed, bid'ed, bid'ing** [OE. *bidan*] [Archaic or Dial.] 1. to stay; continue 2. to dwell; reside 3. to wait —*vt.* [Archaic or Dial.] to endure or tolerate —**bide one's time** *pt.* **bid'ed** to wait patiently for an opportunity
bi·den·tate (bī den'tāt) *adj.* having two teeth or toothlike parts
bi·det (bē'dā) *n.* [Fr.] a low, bowl-shaped bathroom fixture equipped with running water, used for washing the genitals
bi·en·ni·al (bī en'ē əl) *adj.* [< L. < *bis*, twice + *annus*, year + -AL] 1. happening every two years 2. lasting for two years —*n.* 1. a biennial event 2. *Bot.* a plant that lasts two years, usually producing flowers and seed the second year —**bi·en'ni·al·ly** *adv.*
bier (bir) *n.* [OE. *bær*, a bed] 1. a portable framework on which a coffin or corpse is placed 2. a coffin and its supporting platform
biest·ings (bēs'tiŋz) *n.pl.* *same as* BEESTINGS
biff (bif) *n.* [prob. echoic] [Colloq.] a blow; strike; hit —*vt.* [Colloq.] to strike; hit
bi·fid (bī'fid) *adj.* [< L. < *bis*, twice + *findere*, to cleave] divided into two equal parts by a cleft; forked —**bi·fid'i·ty** (-ə tē) *n.* —**bi'fid·ly** *adv.*
bi·fo·cal (bī fō'k'l) *adj.* adjusted to two different focal lengths —*n.* a lens with one part ground to adjust the eyes for close focus, and the rest ground for distant focus
bi·fo·cals (bī'fō'k'lz) *n.pl.* a pair of glasses with bifocal lenses
bi·fur·cate (bī'fər kāt', bī fur'kāt; *for adj. also* -kit) *adj.* [< ML. < L. < *bi-* + *furca*, FORK] having two branches; forked —*vt., vi.* **-cat'ed, -cat'ing** to divide into two branches —**bi'fur·cate'ly** *adv.* —**bi'fur·ca'tion** *n.*
big (big) *adj.* **big'ger, big'gest** [ME. < ?] 1. a) of great size, extent, or capacity; large b) great in force or intensity [a *big* wind] 2. a) full-grown b) elder [his *big* sister] 3. a) far advanced in pregnancy (*with*) b) filled or swelling (*with*) 4. loud 5. important or outstanding [to do *big* things] 6. boastful; extravagant; ambitious [*big* talk] 7. generous; noble [a *big* heart] *Big* is much used in combination to form adjectives [*big*-bodied, *big*-souled] —*adv.* [Colloq.] 1. pompously; boastfully [to talk *big*] 2. impressively 3. in a broad way; showing imagination [think *big*!] —**too big for one's boots** pompous; conceited —**big'ness** *n.*
big·a·my (big'ə mē) *n., pl.* **-mies** [< OFr. < LL. < *bis*, twice + Gr. *gamos*, marriage] the act of marrying a second time while a previous marriage is still legally in

effect: when done knowingly, it is a criminal offence —**big′-a·mist** n. —**big′a·mous** adj. —**big′a·mous·ly** adv.

big-bang theory a theory of cosmology holding that the expansion of the universe began with a gigantic explosion

Big Ben 1. the great bell in the Parliament clock tower in London 2. the clock itself

Big Brother [< concept in Brit. novelist G. Orwell's *1984*] a person or organization with total control over others, esp. of a dictatorial or paternalistic nature

big dipper 1. *same as* SWITCHBACK (sense 2) 2. [B-D-] [U.S.] the constellation of Ursa Major (Great Bear)

big end the crankpin end of a connecting rod at its point of attachment in an internal-combustion engine

big game large wild animals hunted for sport, as lions, tigers, etc.

big·head (big′hed′) n. [Colloq.] a conceited person; egotist

big·heart·ed (big′här′tid) adj. generous or magnanimous —**big′heart′ed·ly** adv.

big·horn (-hôrn′) n., pl. **-horns′, -horn′**: see PLURAL, II, D, 1 an animal with large horns, esp. a large, wild, shaggy-haired sheep of the Rocky Mountains

big house, the [Slang] a prison

bight (bīt) n. [ME. *byht*] 1. a loop or slack part in a rope 2. a) a curve in a river, coastline, etc. b) a bay formed by such a curve

big lie, the 1. a gross distortion of facts, constantly repeated to make it seem credible 2. a propaganda technique using this device

big money [Colloq.] very high pay or large profit

big mouth [Slang] a noisy, indiscreet, or boastful person

big·no·ni·a (big nō′nē ə) n. [after the Abbé *Bignon*, 18th-c. Fr. librarian] a tropical American plant with trumpet-shaped flowers

big·ot (big′ət) n. [Fr. < OFr., a term of insult used of Normans] a narrow-minded person who is intolerant of other creeds, opinions, races, etc. —**big′ot·ed** adj. —**big′-ot·ed·ly** adv. —**big′ot·ry** (-ə trē) n., pl. **-ries**

big shot [Chiefly U.S. Slang] an important, influential person: also **big noise, big wheel**, etc.

big smoke, the a large town or city, esp. London

big stick [< use of term by T. Roosevelt] [also B- S-] a policy of acting or negotiating from a position backed by a show of strength

big time [Colloq.] 1. [U.S.] formerly, vaudeville of the top-ranking theatrical circuits 2. the highest level in any profession, etc. —**big′-time′** adj.

big top [Colloq.] 1. the main tent of a circus 2. the life or work of circus performers

big·wig (big′wig′) n. [Colloq.] a person of great importance or influence

bi·jou (bē′zhōō) n., pl. **-joux** (-zhōōz, -zhōō) [Fr. < Bret. *bizou*, a ring < *biz*, a finger] 1. a jewel 2. an exquisite trinket

bi·ju·gate (bī′joo gāt′, bī jōō′git) adj. [BI- + JUGATE] having two pairs of leaflets, as some pinnate leaves: also **bi′ju·gous** (-gəs)

bike (bīk) n., vt., vi. biked, bik′ing [< BICYCLE] [Colloq.] 1. bicycle 2. motorcycle

bi·ki·ni (bi kē′nē) n. [< *Bikini*, atoll in the Marshall Islands] an extremely brief two-piece bathing suit for women

bik·ky (bik′ē) n., pl. **-kies** [Colloq.] *same as* BICCY

bi·la·bi·al (bī lā′bē əl) adj. 1. *same as* BILABIATE 2. *Phonet.* made by stopping or constricting the airstream with the lips, as the English stops *p* and *b* —n. a bilabial sound

bi·la·bi·ate (-bē it, -āt′) adj. [BI- + LABIATE] *Bot.* having two lips, as the corolla of some flowers

bi·lat·er·al (bī lat′ər əl) adj. [BI- + LATERAL] 1. of, on, or having two sides, factions, etc. 2. affecting both sides equally; reciprocal [a *bilateral* trade pact] 3. symmetrical on both sides of an axis —**bi·lat′er·al·ism** n. —**bi·lat′-er·al·ly** adv.

BIKINI

bil·ber·ry (bil′bər ē) n., pl. **-ries** [ult. < ON. *bollr*, BALL¹ + *ber*, berry] 1. a) a European plant having pink flowers and edible blue or blackish berries b) the berry of this plant: also called **blaeberry, whortleberry**

bil·bo (bil′bō) n., pl. **-boes** [after *Bilbao*, seaport in N Spain] 1. [pl.] a long iron bar with shackles, for fettering a prisoner's feet 2. [Archaic] a sword

‡**Bil·dungs·ro·man** (bil′doonz rō män′) n., pl. **-ma·ne** (-mä′-nə) [G.] a novel that details the psychological development of the principal character

bile (bīl) n. [Fr. < L. *bilis*] 1. the bitter, yellow-brown or greenish fluid secreted by the liver and found in the gall bladder: it helps in digestion, esp. of fats 2. ill health due to faulty secretion of this fluid 3. [< ancient belief in bile as the humour causing anger] bitterness of spirit; anger

bilge (bilj) n. [var. of BULGE] 1. the bulge of a cask 2. the

rounded, lower part of a ship's hold 3. stagnant, dirty water that gathers there: also **bilge water** 4. [Slang] worthless talk or writing; nonsense —vt. **bilged, bilg′ing** to break open in the bilge: said of a ship —vi. to spring a leak in the bilge

bil·i·ar·y (bil′ē ə rē, bil′yər ē) adj. [Fr. *biliaire*] 1. of or involving the bile 2. bile-carrying 3. bilious

bi·lin·gual (bī liŋ′gwəl) adj. [< L. < *bis*, two + *lingua*, tongue] 1. of or in two languages 2. capable of using two languages, esp. with equal facility —n. a bilingual person —**bi·lin′gual·ism** n. —**bi·lin′gual·ly** adv.

bil·i·ous (bil′ē əs, -yəs) adj. 1. of the bile 2. having, appearing to have, or resulting from some ailment of the bile or the liver 3. bad-tempered; cross —**bil′ious·ly** adv. —**bil′ious·ness** n.

bilk (bilk) vt. [? altered < BALK] 1. to cheat or swindle; defraud 2. to evade paying (a debt, etc.) 3. to elude —n. 1. a bilking or being bilked 2. a cheat or swindler —**bilk′-er** n.

bill¹ (bil) n. [< Anglo-L. *billa*, altered < ML. *bulla*, sealed document < L. *bulla*, knob] 1. a statement of charges for goods or services; invoice 2. a list, as a menu, theatre programme, ship's roster, etc. 3. a poster or handbill, esp. one announcing a circus, show, etc. 4. the entertainment offered in a theatre 5. a draft of a law proposed to a lawmaking body 6. a bill of exchange 7. any promissory note 8. [U.S.] a bank note or piece of paper money 9. *Law* a declaration of certain facts in legal proceedings —vt. 1. to make out a bill of (items); list 2. to present a statement of charges to 3. a) to advertise by bills or posters b) to book (a performer or performance) —**fill the bill** [Colloq.] to meet the requirements —**bill′a·ble** adj.

bill² (bil) n. [OE. *bile*] 1. the horny jaws of a bird, usually pointed; beak 2. a beaklike mouthpart, as of a turtle 3. a narrow promontory —vi. 1. to touch bills together 2. to caress lovingly: now only in **bill and coo**, to kiss, talk softly, etc. in a loving way

bill³ (bil) n. [OE. *bill*] 1. an ancient weapon having a hook-shaped blade with a spike at the back 2. *same as* BILLHOOK

bill·a·bong (bil′ə boŋ′) n. [Abor. < *billa*, water + ?] in Australia, a backwater channel that forms a lagoon or pool

bill·board (bil′bôrd′) n. [U.S.] a hoarding

bil·let¹ (bil′it) n. [< Anglo-Fr., dim. of *bille*, BILL¹] 1. a) a written order to provide lodging for military personnel, as in private buildings b) the quarters thus occupied c) the sleeping place assigned to a sailor on ship 2. a position or job —vt. to assign to lodging by billet —vi. to be billeted or quartered

bil·let² (bil′it) n. [OFr. *billette*, dim. of *bille*, tree trunk] 1. a) a short, thick piece of firewood b) [Obs.] a wooden club 2. an unfinished metal bar, esp. of iron or steel

bil·let-doux (bil′ē dōō′, bil′ā-; Fr. bē ye dōō′) n., pl. **bil·lets-doux** (bil′ē dōōz′; Fr. bē ye dōō′) [Fr., lit., sweet letter] a love letter

bill·head (-hed′) n. a letterhead used for statements of charges

bill·hook (-hook′) n. a tool with a curved or hooked blade at one end, for pruning and cutting

bil·liard (bil′yərd) adj. of or for billiards

bil·liards (-yərdz) n. [Fr. *billard*; orig., a cue < *bille*: see BILLET²] any of several games played with hard balls on an oblong table covered with cloth and having raised, cushioned edges: a cue is used to hit and move the balls

bill·ing (bil′iŋ) n. the listing or the order of listing of actors' names on a programme, poster, etc.

bil·lings·gate (bil′iŋz gāt′) n. [after a fish market in London] foul, vulgar, abusive talk

bil·lion (bil′yən) n. [Fr. contr. < *bi-*, BI- + *million*] 1. in Great Britain and Germany, a million millions (1 000 000 000 000) 2. in the U.S. and France, a thousand millions (1 000 000 000) 3. an indefinite but very large number —adj. amounting to one billion in number —**bil′-lionth** adj., n.

bil·lion·aire (bil′yə ner′) n. one whose wealth comes to at least a billion pounds, dollars, etc.

bill of attainder formerly, a legislative enactment pronouncing a person guilty, without a trial, of an alleged crime (esp. treason) and declaring him to be attainted and his property forfeited

bill of exchange a written order to pay a certain sum of money to the person named; draft

bill of fare 1. a list of the foods served; menu 2. a programme

bill of health a certificate stating whether there is infectious disease aboard a ship or in the port sailed from —**clean bill of health** 1. a bill of health certifying the absence of infectious disease 2. [Colloq.] a good record; favourable report, as after an investigation

bill of lading a contract issued by the master of a ship listing the goods received for shipment and promising their delivery

bill of quantities a description of labour and material required for a job on the basis of which a building contractor prepares a tender for a contract

bill of rights 1. a list of the rights and freedoms regarded as essential to a people 2. [**B- R-**] the first ten amendments to the Constitution of the U.S., which guarantee certain rights to the people, as freedom of speech, assembly, and worship

bill of sale a written statement transferring the ownership of something by sale

bil·low (bil′ō) **n.** [ON. *bylgja*: see BELLY] 1. a large wave; great swell of water 2. any large, swelling mass or surge, as of smoke, sound, etc. —**vi., vt.** to surge, swell, or cause to swell like or in a billow

bil·low·y (bil′ō wē) **adj.** -low·i·er, -low·i·est swelling in or as in a billow —**bil′low·i·ness n.**

bill·stick·er (bil′stik′ər) **n.** a person hired to paste advertisements or notices on walls, hoardings, etc.: also **bill′post′er**

bil·ly (bil′ē) **n.,** *pl.* **-lies** [< Abor. *billa*, water] [Aust.] a can or kettle used in outdoor cooking: also **billycan**

bil·ly goat (bil′ē) [< *Billy*, pet name for *William*, a masculine name]

bi·lo·bate (bī lō′bāt) **adj.** having or divided into two lobes: also **bi·lo′bat·ed, bi′lobed**

bil·tong (bil′toŋ) **n.** [Afrik. < *bil*, rump (from which it is cut) + *tong*, tongue (from the shape)] in South Africa, sun-dried strips of meat

B.I.M. British Institute of Management

bi·man·u·al (bī man′yoo wəl) **adj.** using or requiring both hands —**bi·man′u·al·ly adv.**

bi·me·tal·lic (bī′mə tal′ik) **adj.** 1. containing or using two metals, often two metals bonded together 2. of or based on bimetallism

bi·met·al·lism (bī met′l iz′m) **n.** the use of two metals, usually gold and silver, as the monetary standard, with fixed values in relation to each other —**bi·met′al·list n.**

bi·month·ly (bī munth′lē) **adj., adv.** 1. once every two months 2. twice a month; semimonthly —**n.,** *pl.* **-lies** a publication appearing once every two months or twice a month

bin (bin) **n.** [OE., manger, crib] 1. a box or enclosed space, esp. for storing foods or other things 2. a container for rubbish —**vt. binned, bin′ning** to store in a bin

bi·na·ry (bī′nər ē) **adj.** [< L. < *bini*, two by two < *bis*, double] 1. made up of two parts or things; twofold; double 2. designating or of a number system that has 2 as its base 3. *Chem.* composed of two elements or radicals or of one element and one radical —**n.,** *pl.* **-ries** 1. something made up of two parts or things 2. *same as* BINARY STAR

binary star two stars revolving around a common centre of gravity; double star

bi·nate (bī′nāt) **adj.** [see BINARY] *Bot.* occurring in pairs [*binate* leaves] —**bi′nate·ly adv.**

bin·au·ral (bin nôr′əl, bi-) **adj.** [see BI- & AURAL] 1. having two ears 2. of or involving the use of both ears 3. of sound reproduction or transmission using at least two sources of sound to give a stereophonic effect —**bin·au′·ral·ly adv.**

bind (bīnd) **vt. bound, bind′ing** [< OE. *bindan*] 1. to tie together; make fast, as with a rope 2. to hold or restrain as if tied [*bound* by convention] 3. to gird or encircle with a belt, etc. 4. to bandage (often with *up*) 5. to make stick together; make cohere 6. to constipate 7. to strengthen or ornament the edges of by a band, as of tape 8. to fasten together printed sheets of (a book) and enclose within a cover 9. to secure or make firm (a bargain, contract, etc.) 10. to obligate, as by duty 11. to compel, as by oath or legal restraint 12. to make an apprentice of (often with *out* or *over*) 13. to unite or hold, as by loyalty or love —**vi.** 1. to do the act of binding 2. to grow hard or stiff 3. to be constricting or restricting 4. to be obligatory —**n.** 1. anything that binds 2. [Colloq.] an annoyance; a bore —**bind over** to put under legal bond to abstain from committing some offence or to do some particular act, as appear before a law court

bind·er (bīn′dər) **n.** 1. a person who binds; specif., a bookbinder 2. a thing that binds; specif., *a)* a band, cord, etc. *b)* a substance, as tar, that binds things together *c)* a detachable cover for holding sheets of paper together 3. a device attached to a reaper, for tying grain in bundles 4. *Law* a temporary memorandum of a contract, in effect pending execution of the final contract

bind·er·y (bīn′dər ē, -drē) **n.,** *pl.* **-er·ies** a place where books are bound

bind·ing (-diŋ) **n.** 1. the action of one that binds 2. a thing that binds, as *a)* the fastenings on a ski for the boot *b)* a band or bandage *c)* tape used in sewing for strengthening seams, edges, etc. *d)* the covers and backing of a book 3. a cohesive substance for binding a mixture —**adj.** that binds; esp., that holds one to an agreement, etc.; obligatory —**bind′ing·ly adv.**

bind·weed (bīnd′wēd′) **n.** a plant with twining stems; convolvulus

bine (bīn) **n.** [dial. form of BIND] any climbing, twining stem, as of the hop

Bi·net-Si·mon test (bi nă′sē mon′) [after its Fr. devisers, A. *Binet* (1857–1911) and T. *Simon* (1873-1961)] any of a series of tests seeking to measure intelligence in children: also **Binet test**

binge (binj) **n.** [? < dial. *binge*, to soak] [Colloq.] a drunken or unrestrained spree

bin·go (biŋ′gō) **n.** [< ?] a gambling game, like lotto, usually with many players

bin·na·cle (bin′ə k'l) **n.** [formerly *bittacle* < Port. < L. *habitaculum*, dwelling place < *habitare*, to inhabit] the case enclosing a ship's compass, usually located near the helm

bin·oc·u·lar (bī nok′yə lər; *also, esp. for n.,* bi-) **adj.** [< L. *bini*, double + *oculus*, an eye] using, or for the use of, both eyes at the same time —**n.** [*usually pl.*] a binocular instrument, as field glasses or opera glasses —**bin·oc′u·lar′i·ty** (-lar′ə tē) **n.** —**bin·oc′u·lar·ly adv.**

bi·no·mi·al (bī nō′mē əl) **n.** [< LL. < *bi-* + Gr. *nomos*, part + -AL] 1. a mathematical expression consisting of two terms connected by a plus or minus sign 2. a two-word scientific name of a plant or animal —**adj.** 1. composed of two terms 2. of binomials

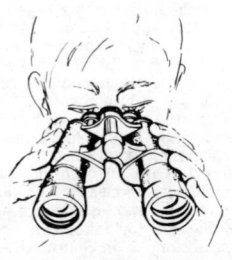

BINOCULARS

binomial theorem a general formula expressing any power of a binomial as a sum each of whose terms is a multiple of the product of a power of the first term of the binomial and a power of the second (Ex.: $(a + b)^2 = a^2 + 2ab + b^2$)

bint (bint) **n.** [Ar., lit., daughter] [Slang] a girl or woman: often a derogatory usage

bin·tu·rong (bin′too roŋ′) **n.** [Malay] a variety of civet of SE Asia, with tufted ears and a long tail

bi·o- [Gr. < *bios*, life] *a combining form meaning* life, of living things, biological [*biography*]

bi·o·as·tro·nau·tics (bī′ō as′trə nô′tiks) **n.pl.** [with *sing. v.*] the science dealing with the effects of space travel upon living organisms

bi·o·chem·is·try (-kem′is trē) **n.** the branch of chemistry that deals with plants and animals and their life processes —**bi′o·chem′i·cal adj.** —**bio′chem′i·cal·ly adv.** —**bi′o·chem′·ist n.**

bi·o·cide (bī′ə sīd′) **n.** [BIO- + -CIDE] any substance that can kill living organisms

bi·o·coe·no·sis (bī′ō si nō′sis) **n.** [ModL. < BIO- + Gr. *koinōsis*, a mingling] a community of biologically integrated and interdependent plants and animals

bi·o·de·grad·a·ble (bī′ō di grā′də b'l) **adj.** [BIO- + DEGRAD(E) + -ABLE] that can be readily decomposed by biological, esp. bacterial, action, as some detergents

bi·o·en·gi·neer·ing (-en′jə nir′iŋ) **n.** a science dealing with the application of engineering science to problems of biology and medicine

bi·o·feed·back (-fēd′bak′) **n.** a technique of seeking to control emotional states, as anxiety, by training oneself, with the aid of electronic devices, to modify involuntary body functions, as blood pressure

biog. 1. biographer 2. biographical 3. biography

bi·o·gen·e·sis (bī′ō jen′ə sis) **n.** [BIO- + GENESIS] 1. the principle that living organisms derive only from other similar organisms 2. such generation of organisms —**bi′o·ge·net′ic** (-jə net′ik), **bi′o·ge·net′i·cal adj.** —**bi′o·ge·net′·i·cal·ly adv.**

bi·og·ra·phy (bī og′rə fē) **n.** [< Gr.: see BIO- & -GRAPHY] 1. *pl.* **-phies** an account of a person's life written by another 2. such writings, collectively, as a branch of literature —**bi·og′ra·pher n.** —**bi·o·graph·i·cal** (bī′ə graf′i k'l), **bi′o·graph′ic adj.** —**bi′o·graph′i·cal·ly adv.**

biol. 1. biological 2. biologist 3. biology

bi·o·log·i·cal (bī′ə loj′i k'l) **adj.** 1. of or connected with biology; of plants and animals 2. of the nature of living matter 3. used in or produced by practical biology Also **bi′o·log′ic** —**n.** a biological product —**bi′o·log′i·cal·ly adv.**

biological clock any of various rhythm patterns in organisms, associated with recurrent natural cycles, as of tides, days and nights, seasons, etc.

biological control the control of destructive organisms, esp. insects, by various, usually nonchemical means, as by introducing natural enemies

biological warfare the use of disease-spreading microorganisms, toxins, etc. as a weapon of war

bi·ol·o·gy (bī ol′ə jē) **n.** [BIO- + -LOGY] 1. the science that deals with the origin, history, life processes, structure, etc. of plants and animals: it includes botany, zoology, and their subdivisions 2. animal and plant life, as of a given area —**bi·ol′o·gist** *n.*

bi·o·lu·mi·nes·cence (bī′ō lōō′mə nes′əns) *n.* the production of light by living organisms, as by glow-worms

bi·o·med·i·cine (bī′ō med′ə s'n) *n.* a branch of medicine that is combined with research in biology and that studies the effects of abnormal environmental stress, esp. that produced by space travel —**bi′o·med′i·cal** *adj.*

bi·o·met·rics (-met′riks) *n.pl.* [*with sing. v.*] that branch of biology which deals with its data statistically —**bi′o·met′-ric, bi′o·met′ri·cal** *adj.* —**bi′o·met′ri·cal·ly** *adv.*

bi·on·ic (bī on′ik) *adj.* 1. designating a living organism, parts of which are artificial [the *bionic* woman] 2. [Colloq.] very strong; superhuman

bi·on·ics (bī on′iks) *n.pl.* [*with sing. v.*] [< Gr. *bion*, living + -ICS] the science of designing instruments or systems modelled after living organisms

bi·o·nom·ics (bī′ō nom′iks) *n.pl.* [*with sing. v.*] [BIO- + Gr. *nomos*, law] *same as* ECOLOGY

bi·o·phys·ics (bī′ō fiz′iks) *n.pl.* [*with sing. v.*] the study of biological phenomena in relation to physics —**bi′o·phys′-i·cal** *adj.* —**bi′o·phys′i·cist** *n.*

bi·op·sy (bī′op′sē) *n.,* pl. **-sies** [see BIO- & -OPSIS] the removal of bits of living tissue, fluids, etc. from the body for diagnostic examination

bi·o·rhythm (bī′ō rith′′m, -rith′əm) *n.* any of three separate biological cycles which are held to affect a person's physical, emotional, and intellectual energy levels

bi·o·scope (bī′ə skōp′) *n.* [BIO- + -SCOPE] 1. an early film projector 2. in South Africa, a cinema

bi·os·co·py (bī os′kə pē) *n.* [BIO- + -SCOPY] a medical examination to find out whether life is present

-bi·o·sis (bī ō′sis, bē-) [< Gr. *biōsis*, way of life < *bios*, life] *a combining form meaning* way of living [symbiosis]

bi·o·sphere (bī′ə sfir′) *n.* [BIO- + SPHERE] that portion of the earth and its atmosphere which contains living organisms

bi·o·syn·the·sis (bī′ō sin′thə sis) *n.* the formation of chemical compounds by living organisms, as in photosynthesis —**bi′o·syn·thet′ic** (-sin thet′ik) *adj.*

-bi·ot·ic (bī ot′ik) *a combining form meaning* of or having a (specified) way of living [symbiotic]

bi·o·tin (bī′ə tin) *n.* [< Gr. *bios*, life + -IN[1]] a bacterial growth factor, one of the vitamin B group, found in liver, egg yolk, and yeast

bi·par·ti·san (bī′pär tə zan′, bī pär′ti zan′) *adj.* of or representing two parties —**bi·par′ti·san·ship′** *n.*

bi·par·tite (bī pär′tīt) *adj.* [< L. < *bi-*, two + *partire*, to divide] 1. having two (corresponding) parts 2. with two involved 3. Bot. divided in two nearly to the base, as some leaves —**bi·par′tite·ly** *adv.* —**bi′par·ti′tion** (-tish′ən) *n.*

bi·ped (bī′ped) *n.* [< L. < *bi-* + *pedis*, gen. of *pes*, foot] any two-footed animal —*adj.* two-footed: also **bi·ped′al**

bi·pet·al·ous (bī pet′'l əs) *adj.* having two petals

bi·pin·nate (bī pin′āt, -it) *adj.* having pinnate leaflets on stems that grow opposite each other on a main stem —**bi·pin′nate·ly** *adv.*

bi·plane (bī′plān′) *n.* an aircraft with two sets of wings, one above the other

bi·po·lar (bī pō′lər) *adj.* 1. of or having two poles 2. of or involving both of the earth's polar regions 3. characterized by two opposed opinions, natures, etc. —**bi·po·lar·i·ty** (bī′-pō lar′ə tē) *n.*

bi·pro·pel·lant (bī′prə pel′ənt) *n.* a rocket propellant consisting of a fuel and oxidizer that are brought together only in the combustion chamber

bi·quad·rat·ic (bī′kwod rat′ik) *adj.* Math. of or involving the fourth power of a quantity —*n.* 1. the fourth power 2. an algebraic equation of the fourth power

bi·ra·cial (bī rā′shəl) *adj.* consisting of or involving two races, esp. Negroes and whites

birch (burch) *n.* [OE. *beorc*] 1. a tree having smooth bark easily peeled off in thin sheets, and hard, closegrained wood 2. this wood 3. a birch rod or bunch of twigs used for whipping —*vt.* to beat with a birch —*adj.* of birch: also **birch′en**

bird (burd) *n.* [OE. *bridd*, young bird] 1. any of a class of warmblooded, two-legged, egg-laying vertebrates with feathers and wings 2. a small game bird 3. same as CLAY PIGEON 4. a shuttlecock 5. [Slang] a person, esp. a mildly eccentric one 6. [Slang] a young woman 7. [Slang] a rocket or guided missile 8. [Slang] prison or a term in prison —*vi.* 1. to shoot or catch birds 2. to engage in bird watching —**bird in the hand** something sure because already in one's possession: opposed to **bird in the bush**, something unsure, etc. —**birds of a feather** people with the same characteristics or tastes —**for the birds** [Slang] ridiculous, worthless, etc. —**get the bird** to be rudely dismissed; booed —**bird′er** *n.*

bird·bath (-bäth′) *n.* a basinlike garden ornament for birds to bathe in

bird·brain (-brān′) *n.* [Colloq.] a stupid or silly person

bird·call (-kôl′) *n.* 1. the sound or song of a bird 2. an imitation of this 3. a device for imitating bird sounds

bird·ie (bur′dē) *n.* 1. a small bird: child's word 2. *Golf* a score of one stroke under par for a hole

bird·lime (burd′līm′) *n.* 1. a sticky substance spread on twigs to catch birds 2. anything that snares —*vt.* **-limed′, -lim′ing** to catch with birdlime

bird of paradise 1. any of a number of brightly coloured birds found in and near New Guinea 2. a tropical plant with brilliant orange and blue flowers in a form resembling a bird in flight

bird of passage 1. any migratory bird 2. anyone who travels or roams about constantly

bird of peace the dove

bird of prey any bird, as the hawk, owl, etc., that kills and eats mammals and other birds

bird·seed (-sēd′) *n.* seed for feeding caged birds

bird's-eye (burdz′ī′) *n.* a cotton or linen cloth with a woven pattern of small, diamond-shaped figures —*adj.* 1. a) seen from above b) general; cursory 2. having markings like birds' eyes

bird's-foot (-foot′) *n.,* pl. **-foots** any of various plants whose leaves or flowers resemble a bird's foot

bird·shot (burd′shot′) *n.* small shot for shooting birds

bird watching the hobby of observing wild birds in their habitat —**bird watcher**

bi·re·frin·gence (bī′ri frin′jəns) *n.* [< BI- + L. prp. of *refringere*: see REFRACT] the splitting of a light ray, generally by a crystal, into two components which travel at different velocities within the crystal —**bi′re·frin′gent** *adj.*

bi·reme (bī′rēm) *n.* [< L. < *bi-* + *remus*, oar] a galley having two rows of oars on each side

bi·ret·ta (bə ret′ə) *n.* [< It. < LL. dim. of L. *birrus*, a hood, cloak] a square cap with three projections, worn by Roman Catholic clergy

birl (burl) *vt., vi.* [? echoic, after *whirl, purl,* etc.] [Scot] to spin with a whirring sound, as a coin

birl·ing (-iŋ) *n.* [U.S.] a competition among loggers in which each tries to keep his balance while revolving a floating log with his feet —**birl′er** *n.*

Bi·ro (bī′rō) *a trademark for* a kind of ballpoint pen —*n.* [**b-**] *pl.* **-os** such a pen

birth (burth) *n.* [< OE. *byrde* < *beran*, to BEAR[1]] 1. the act of bringing forth offspring 2. the act of being born 3. origin or descent [a Spaniard by *birth*] 4. the beginning of anything 5. an inherited or natural inclination or talent [an actor by *birth*] —*vi., vt.* [Dial.] to give birth (to) —**give birth to** 1. to bring forth (offspring) 2. to be the cause of; originate

birth certificate an official document stating the date and place of a person's birth

birth control control of how many children a woman will have, as by contraception

birth·day (-dā′) *n.* 1. the day of a person's birth or a thing's beginning 2. the anniversary of this

birth·mark (-märk′) *n.* a skin blemish present at birth

birth·place (-plās′) *n.* 1. the place of one's birth 2. the place where something originated

birth·rate (-rāt′) *n.* the number of births per year per thousand of population in a given group: sometimes other units of time or population are used

birth·right (-rīt′) *n.* the rights that a person has because he was born in a certain family, nation, etc., or because he was the firstborn son

birth·stone (-stōn′) *n.* a precious or semiprecious gem symbolizing the month of one's birth

bis·cuit (bis′kit) *n.,* pl. **-cuits, -cuit** [OFr. *bescuit* < ML. < L. *bis*, twice + *coctum*, pp. of *coquere*, to cook] 1. a small, crisp, flat cake, often sweetened 2. light brown; tan 3. pottery after the first firing and before glazing

‡**bise** (bēz) *n.* [Fr. < Frank. *bisa*] a cold north or northeast wind blowing down from the Swiss Alps

bi·sect (bī sekt′) *vt.* [< ML. pp. of *bisecare* < L. *bi-* + *secare*, to cut] 1. to cut in two 2. *Geom.* to divide into two equal parts —*vi.* to divide; fork —**bi·sec′tion** *n.* —**bi·sec′tion·al** *adj.* —**bi·sec′tor** *n.*

bi·sex·u·al (bī sek′shoo wəl) *adj.* 1. of both sexes 2. having both male and female organs; hermaphroditic 3. sexually attracted to both sexes —*n.* one that is bisexual —**bi·sex′-u·al′i·ty** (-wal′ə tē), **bi·sex′u·al·ism** *n.* —**bi·sex′u·al·ly** *adv.*

bish·op (bish′əp) *n.* [< OE. *bisceop* < LL. < Gr. *episkopos*, overseer < *epi-*, upon + *skopein*, to look] 1. a high-ranking Christian clergyman usually supervising a diocese 2. a chessman that can move only diagonally 3. a hot drink made of red wine, oranges and sugar

bish·op·ric (bish′ə prik) *n.* the diocese, office, authority, or rank of a bishop

bis·muth (biz′məth) *n.* [< G. *Wismut* < ?] a hard,

BIRETTA

brittle, metallic chemical element used in low-melting alloys, medical compounds, etc.: symbol, Bi; at. wt., 208.980; at. no., 83

bi·son (bī's'n, -z'n) *n.*, *pl.* **bi'sons** [Fr. < L. < Gmc. hyp. *wisunt*] any of several four-legged bovine mammals with a shaggy mane, short, curved horns, and a humped back, as the European wisent or the American buffalo

bisque[1] (bisk) *n.* [Fr.] a rich, thick, creamy soup usually made from shellfish

bisque[2] (bisk) *n.* 1. biscuit ceramic ware left unglazed in the finished state 2. a light brown or red-yellow colour

bisque[3] (bisk) *n.* [Fr.] a handicap of one point per set in tennis, one turn per game in croquet, or one or more strokes per game at match play in golf

BISON
(1.6-1.8 m high at shoulder)

bis·tort (bis'tôrt) *n.* [L. *bis*, twice + *tortus*, twisted] any of several plants with twisted roots and small pink flowers

bis·tre (bis'tər) *n.* [Fr. *bistre*] 1. a yellowish-brown to dark-brown pigment made from the soot of burned wood 2. a colour in this range

bis·tro (bis'trō, bēs'-) *n.*, *pl.* **-tros** [Fr.] a small restaurant or bar

bi·sul·phate (bī sul'fāt) *n.* an acid sulphate; compound containing the monovalent HSO₄- radical

bi·sul·phide (bī sul'fid) *n.* same as DISULPHIDE

bit[1] (bit) *n.* [< OE. *bite*, a bite < *bitan*, to bite] 1. the metal mouthpiece on a bridle, used for controlling the horse 2. anything that curbs or controls 3. the part of a key that actually turns the lock 4. the cutting part of any tool 5. a drilling or boring tool for use in a brace, drill press, etc. —*vt.* **bit'ted**, **bit'ting** to put a bit into the mouth of (a horse) —**take the bit between one's teeth** to be beyond control

bit[2] (bit) *n.* [< OE. *bita*, a piece < *bitan*, to bite] 1. *a)* a small piece or quantity *b)* a limited degree: used with *a* and having adverbial force [a *bit* bored] *c)* a short time .2. [U.S. Colloq.] an amount equal to 12¹/₂ cents 3. a small part, as in a play —*adj.* very small [a *bit* role] —**bit by bit** little by little; gradually —**do one's bit** to do one's share —**every bit** altogether; entirely

bit[3] (bit) *n.* [b(*inary*) (*dig*)it] Computers a single character in a binary number system; specif., a unit of information equal to the amount of information obtained by learning which of two equally likely events occurred

bitch (bich) *n.* [< OE. *bicce*] 1. the female of the dog, wolf, etc. 2. a bad-tempered, malicious, or promiscuous woman: a coarse term of contempt 3. [Slang] anything especially unpleasant or difficult —*vi.* [Slang] to complain —**bitch'·i·ness** *n.* —**bitch'y** *adj.* **bitch'i·er**, **bitch'i·est**

bite (bīt) *vt.* **bit** (bit), **bit·ten** (bit''n) or **bit**, **bit'ing** [< OE. *bitan*] 1. to seize or cut with or as with the teeth 2. to cut into, as with a sharp weapon 3. to sting, as an insect 4. to hurt in a sharp, stinging way 5. to eat into; corrode 6. to seize or possess [*bitten* by a lust for fame] —*vi.* 1. *a)* to press or snap the teeth (*into, at,* etc.) *b)* to have a tendency to do this 2. to cause a biting sensation 3. to press hard; grip [the tyres *bit* into the snow] 4. to seize a bait 5. to be caught, as by a trick —*n.* 1. the act of biting 2. biting quality; sting 3. a wound or sting from biting 4. *a)* a mouthful *b)* a light meal or snack 5. a tight hold or grip 6. the way the upper and lower teeth meet 7. [Colloq.] an amount removed —**bit'er** *n.*

bit·ing (bit'iŋ) *adj.* 1. cutting; sharp 2. sarcastic —**bit'ing·ly** *adv.*

bitt (bit) *n.* [< ?] *Naut.* any of the deck posts, usually in pairs, around which ropes or cables are fastened —*vt.* to wind around a bitt

bit·ter (bit'ər) *adj.* [< OE. < base of *bitan*, to bite] 1. having a sharp, often unpleasant taste; acrid 2. causing or showing sorrow, pain, etc. 3. sharp; harsh; piercing 4. characterized by hatred, resentment, etc. —*adv.* in a bitter way —*n.* 1. something bitter [take the *bitter* with the sweet] 2. bitter, strongly hopped beer: cf. BITTERS —**to the bitter end** *a)* until the end, however difficult or distressing *b)* until death —**bit'ter·ly** *adv.* —**bit'ter·ness** *n.*

bit·tern (bit'ərn) *n.*, *pl.* **-terns**, **-tern**: see PLURAL, II, D, 1 [< OFr. *butor*, prob. < L. *butio*] a wading bird of the heron family, the male of which has a resounding call

bit·ters (bit'ərz) *n.pl.* a drink containing bitter herbs, roots, etc. and usually alcohol, used as a tonic and for flavouring in some cocktails

bit·ter·sweet (bit'ər swēt') *n.* 1. *same as* WOODY NIGHTSHADE 2. a N. American woody plant bearing clusters of orange fruits which open to expose the red seeds —*adj.* 1. both bitter and sweet 2. pleasant with sad overtones

bit·ty (bit'ē) *adj.* lacking unity; disjointed

bi·tu·men (bi'tyōō mən) *n.* [L. < Celt.] 1. any of several substances obtained as asphaltic residue in the distillation of

coal tar, petroleum, etc., or occurring as natural asphalt 2. [Aust. Colloq.] a tarred road —**bi·tu'mi·nize'** (-mə nīz') *vt.* **-nized'**, **-niz'ing** —**bi·tu'mi·nous** *adj.*

bituminous coal coal that yields pitch or tar when it burns; soft coal

bi·va·lent (bī vā'lənt, biv'ə-) *adj.* 1. having two valences 2. having a valence of two —**bi·va'lence, bi·va'len·cy** *n.*

bi·valve (bī'valv') *n.* any mollusc having a shell of two parts, or valves, hinged together, as a mussel, clam, etc. —*adj.* having such a shell: also **bi'valved'**

biv·ou·ac (biv'wak, -wäk') *n.* [Fr. < OHG. *biwacht*, outpost < *bi-*, by + *wacht*, a guard] a temporary encampment (esp. of soldiers) in the open, with only improvised shelter —*vi.* **-acked, -ack·ing** to encamp in the open

bi·week·ly (bī wēk'lē) *adj., adv.* 1. once every two weeks 2. twice a week; semiweekly —*n.*, *pl.* **-lies** a publication that appears once every two weeks or twice a week

bi·year·ly (bī yir'lē) *adj., adv.* 1. once every two years; biennial(ly) 2. twice a year; biannual(ly)

biz (biz) *n.* [Slang] business [show *biz*]

bi·zarre (bi zär') *adj.* [Fr. < It. < Sp. *bizarro*, bold < Basque *bizar*, a beard] 1. odd in manner, appearance, etc.; grotesque; queer; eccentric 2. unexpected and unbelievable; fantastic —**bi·zarre'ly** *adv.* —**bi·zarre'ness** *n.*

Bk *Chem.* berkelium

bk. *pl.* **bks.** 1. bank 2. book

bkg. banking

bkt. basket(s)

bl. 1. bale(s) 2. barrel(s) 3. black

B/L, b/l *pl.* **BS/L, bs/l** bill of lading

B.L. Bachelor of Law

blab (blab) *vt., vi.* **blabbed, blab'bing** [ME. *blabben*: see ff.] 1. to give away (a secret) in idle chatter 2. to chatter; prattle —*n.* 1. loose chatter; gossip 2. a person who blabs

blab·ber (-ər) *vt., vi.* [ME. *blabberen*, freq. of *blabben*, of echoic origin] [Dial. or Colloq.] to blab or babble —*n.* a person who blabs: also [Colloq.] **blab'ber·mouth'** (-mouth')

black (blak) *adj.* [OE. *blæc*] 1. opposite to white; of the colour of coal: see COLOUR 2. having dark-coloured skin and hair; esp., Negro 3. *a)* totally without light; in complete darkness *b)* very dark 4. without cream, milk, etc.: said of coffee 5. soiled; dirty 6. wearing black clothing 7. evil; wicked 8. disgraceful 9. sad; dismal 10. sullen or angry 11. without hope [a *black* future] 12. humorous or satirical in a morbid or cynical way [*black* comedy] —*n.* 1. *a)* black colour *b)* a black pigment, dye, etc. 2. black clothes, esp. when worn in mourning 3. a person with dark-coloured skin; esp., a Negro 4. complete darkness —*vt.* 1. to blacken 2. to polish with blacking 3. to boycott cargo, work, etc. as a form of industrial action —**black out** 1. to cover (writing, etc.) as with black pencil marks 2. to cause a blackout in 3. to lose consciousness —**in the black** operating at a profit —**black'ish** *adj.* —**black'ly** *adv.* —**black'ness** *n.*

black·a·moor (-ə moor') *n.* [BLACK + MOOR] [Archaic] a dark-skinned person; specif., an African Negro

black-and-blue (-ən bloo') *adj.* discoloured from congestion of blood under the skin, as a bruise

Black and Tans the unofficial name for the semimilitary force sent to Ireland in 1920 to combat Sinn Fein activities

black and white writing or print [to put an agreement down in *black and white*]

black art *same as* BLACK MAGIC

black·ball (-bôl') *n.* a secret ballot or vote against a person or thing —*vt.* 1. to vote against; esp., to vote to exclude 2. to ostracize

black bass (bas) any of various freshwater game fishes of N. America

black bear 1. the common N American bear 2. any of several dark-coloured bears of Asia

black belt a black-coloured belt awarded to an expert in judo or karate

black·ber·ry (-bər ē) *n.*, *pl.* **-ries** 1. the fleshy, purple or black, edible fruit of various brambles of the rose family 2. a bush bearing this fruit

black·bird (-bɜrd') *n.* a songbird of the thrush family the male of which is almost entirely black

black·board (-bôrd') *n.* a smooth, usually dark surface, originally of slate, on which to write or draw with chalk

black·bod·y (-bod'ē) *n.* an ideal surface or body that can absorb all radiation striking it

black book a book with the names of those blacklisted

black box *a popular term for* FLIGHT RECORDER

black·cap (-kap') *n.* a small songbird, the male of which has a black head

black·cock (-kok') *n.*, *pl.* **-cocks', -cock'**: see PLURAL, II, D, 1 the male of the black grouse

Black Country, the heavily industrialized region of the Midlands of England

black·cur·rant (-kur'ənt) *n.* 1. the small black fruit of a garden shrub 2. the shrub itself

black·damp (-damp') *n.* a suffocating gas, a mixture of carbon dioxide and nitrogen, found in mines

Black Death a deadly disease, probably bubonic plague, which devastated Europe and Asia in the 14th cent.

black·en (blak''n) *vi.* to become black or dark —*vt.* 1. to make black; darken 2. to slander; defame —**black'en·er** *n.*

black eye a discolouration of the skin surrounding an eye, resulting from a sharp blow or contusion

black-eyed Susan a N. American flower with yellow ray flowers about a dark, cone-shaped centre

black·face (blak'fās') *n.* 1. black makeup used by performers to imitate Negroes, as in minstrel shows 2. a variety of sheep with a black face

black flag the flag of piracy, usually with a white skull and crossbones on a black background

Black Forest heavily wooded, mountainous region in SW Germany

Black Friar a Dominican Friar

black grouse a large grouse of Europe and Asia: the male is almost entirely black

black·guard (blag'ard, -ärd) *n.* [BLACK + GUARD] a scoundrel; villain —*adj.* vulgar, abusive, etc. —*vt.* to abuse with words; revile —**black'guard·ly** *adj., adv.*

black·head (blak'hed') *n.* 1. any of various birds black about the head 2. a black-tipped plug of dried fatty matter clogging a skin pore

black·heart·ed (-här'tid) *adj.* wicked; evil

black hole a hypothetical body in space, supposed to be an invisible collapsed star so condensed that neither light nor matter can escape its gravitational field

black·ing (-iŋ) *n.* a black polish, as for shoes

black·jack (-jak') *n.* [see JACK] [Chiefly U.S.] 1. a small, leather-covered bludgeon with a flexible handle 2. the card game VINGT-ET-UN —*vt.* 1. to hit with a blackjack 2. to coerce by threatening

black lead graphite, as used in lead pencils, etc.

black·leg (-leg) *n.* a worker who refuses to join a strike —*vi.* to work during a strike —*vt.* to take the place of a striking worker

black light ultraviolet or infrared radiation used for fluorescent effects, photography, etc. in the dark

black·list (-list') *n.* a list of censured persons being discriminated against, refused employment, etc. —*vt.* to put on a blacklist

black magic magic with an evil purpose; sorcery

black·mail (-māl') *n.* [lit., black rent < OE. *mal*, lawsuit < ON. *mal*, discussion; infl. by OFr. *maille*, a coin] 1. payment extorted to prevent disclosure of information that could bring disgrace 2. extortion of such payment —*vt.* 1. to get or try to get blackmail from 2. to coerce (*into* doing something) as by threats —**black'mail·er** *n.*

Black Ma·ri·a (mə rī'ə) a police van used to transport prisoners

black mark an unfavourable item in one's record

black market a place or system for selling goods illegally, esp. in violation of rationing —**black marketeer**

Black Mass [*also* b- m-] 1. a Requiem Mass, at which the clergy are dressed in black 2. a parody of the Mass by worshippers of Satan

Black Monk a Benedictine Monk

Black Muslim [Chiefly U.S.] a member of a militant Islamic sect of American Negroes that advocates racial separation: members of the sect call themselves simply "Muslims"

black nightshade a poisonous plant with white, star-shaped flowers and black berries

black·out (-out') *n.* 1. the extinguishing of all stage lights to end a play or scene 2. a concealing of all lights that might be visible to enemy air raiders at night 3. a temporary loss of consciousness or vision 4. a loss of memory of an event 5. suppression or concealment, as of news by censorship

black pepper a hot seasoning made by grinding the whole dried, black berries of the pepper plant

black power [*also* B- P-] political and economic power sought by Negroes in the struggle for civil rights

black pudding a sausage made of blood, suet, and seasoning

Black Rod the chief usher to the Order of the Garter and the House of Lords

black sheep a person regarded as not so respectable as the rest of his family or group

Black Shirt a member of any fascist organization (specif., of the Italian Fascist party) having a black-shirted uniform: also **Black'shirt'** *n.*

black·smith (blak'smith') *n.* a smith who works in iron, making and fitting horseshoes, etc.

black·snake (-snāk') *n.* 1. a harmless, black or dark-coloured snake of the U.S. 2. a very poisonous Australian snake

black spot a dangerous place, esp. a part of a road where there are many accidents

black tea tea withered and fermented before being dried by heating

black·thorn (-thôrn') *n.* 1. a thorny shrub with blue-black, plumlike fruit; sloe 2. a walking stick made of its stem

black tie 1. a black bow tie, properly worn with a dinner jacket 2. a dinner jacket and the proper accessories

black·top (blak'top') *n.* a bituminous mixture, usually asphalt, used as a surface for roads, etc. —*vt.* -topped', -top'ping to cover with blacktop

black velvet a drink made of stout and champagne

Black Watch a Highland regiment, so called from the dark colour of the tartan

black widow an American spider the female of which has a black body with red markings underneath, and a very poisonous bite: so called because the female sometimes eats its mate

Black·wood (-wood) *n.* [after E. F. *Blackwood,* U.S. bridge player] *Bridge* a conventional bidding sequence whereby players show each other how many aces and kings they hold

blad·der (blad'ər) *n.* [OE. *blæddre*] 1. a bag of membranous tissue in the bodies of many animals, that inflates to receive and contain liquids or gases; esp., the **urinary bladder** in the pelvic cavity, which holds urine flowing from the kidneys 2. a bag, etc. resembling this 3. an air sac, as in some water plants —**blad'der·y** *adj.*

blad·der·wort (-wurt') *n.* a plant growing in or near water and having leaves with bladders on them that trap small insects and crustaceans

blad·der·wrack (-rak) *n.* any of various seaweeds having branched brown fronds and air sacs

blade (blād) *n.* [OE. *blæd*] 1. *a)* the leaf of a plant, esp. of grass *b)* the flat, expanded part of a leaf; lamina 2. a broad, flat surface, as of an oar 3. a flat bone [the shoulder *blade*] 4. the cutting part of a knife, tool, etc. 5. the metal runner of an ice skate 6. a sword or a swordsman 7. a gay, dashing young man 8. *Phonet.* the flat part of the tongue, behind the tip —*adj.* designating or of various cuts of meat from the shoulder blade section —**blad'ed** *adj.*

blae·ber·ry (blā'bər ē) *n.* [< Dial. *bla*, bluish + BERRY] same as BILBERRY

blah (blä) *n., interj.* [Slang] nonsense —*adj.* [Slang] 1. unappetizing 2. dull, lifeless, etc.

blain (blān) *n.* [< OE. *blegen*] a pustule or blister

blam·a·ble, blame·a·ble (blām'ə b'l) *adj.* that deserves blame; culpable —**blam'a·bly** *adv.*

blame (blām) *vt.* **blamed, blam'ing** [< OFr. < LL. *blasphemare,* BLASPHEME] 1. to accuse of being at fault; condemn (*for* something) 2. to find fault with 3. to put the responsibility of (an error, fault, etc. *on*) —*n.* 1. a blaming; condemnation 2. responsibility for a fault or wrong 3. [Archaic] fault —**be to blame** to be blamable —**blame'ful** *adj.* —**blame'ful·ly** *adv.* —**blame'ful·ness** *n.* —**blame'less** *adj.* —**blame'less·ly** *adv.* —**blame'less·ness** *n.*

blame·wor·thy (blām'wur'thē) *adj.* deserving to be blamed —**blame'wor'thi·ness** *n.*

blanch (blänch) *vt.* [OFr. *blanchir* < *blanc:* see BLANK] 1. to make white; bleach 2. to make pale 3. to scald (vegetables, almonds, etc.), as for removing the skins 4. to bleach (leeks, celery, etc.) by earthing up or covering so as to keep away light —*vi.* to turn white or pale —**blanch'-er** *n.*

blanc·mange (blə mänzh', -mônzh') *n.* [Fr. < *blanc*, white + *manger,* to eat] a sweet, moulded, jellylike dessert made with starch or gelatin, milk, etc.

bland (bland) *adj.* [< L. *blandus,* mild] 1. pleasantly smooth; agreeable; suave 2. *a)* mild and soothing; not sharp, harsh, etc. *b)* tasteless, insipid, dull, etc. —**bland'ly** *adv.* —**bland'ness** *n.*

blan·dish (blan'dish) *vt., vi* [< OFr. < L. *blandiri,* to flatter < prec.] to flatter or coax in persuading; cajole —**blan'-dish·er** *n.* —**blan'dish·ment** *n.*

blank (blaŋk) *adj.* [OFr. *blanc,* white < Frank.] 1. *a)* not written on; not marked [a *blank* paper] *b)* having empty spaces to be filled in 2. having an empty or vacant look 3. empty of thought [a *blank* mind] 4. utter; complete [a *blank* denial] 5. lacking certain elements or characteristics, as a wall without an opening —*n.* 1. an empty space, esp. one to be filled out in a printed form 2. such a printed form 3. an empty place or time; void 4. a piece of metal, etc. to be finished by stamping or marking 5. a lottery ticket that fails to win 6. a powder-filled cartridge without a bullet: in full, **blank cartridge** 7. a mark, often a dash, written in place of a word, esp. a swearword —**blank out** to cancel or obscure as by covering over —**draw a blank** [Colloq.] 1. to be unsuccessful in an attempt 2. to be unable to remember a particular thing —**blank'ly** *adv.* —**blank'ness** *n.*

blank cheque a cheque carrying a signature only and allowing the bearer to fill in any amount

blan·ket (blaŋ'kit) *n.* [< OFr. dim. of *blanc,* white] 1. a large, soft piece of cloth used for warmth, esp. as a bed cover 2. anything like a blanket [a *blanket* of leaves] —*adj.* covering a group of conditions or items [a *blanket* insurance policy] —*vt.* 1. to cover, as with a blanket 2. to suppress; obscure [a powerful radio station *blankets* a weaker one]

blanket stitch a kind of wide buttonhole stitch used to reinforce the edges of blankets and other thick material

blan·ke·ty-blank (blaŋ'ka tē blaŋk') *adj., adv.* [see BLANK *n.*7] a humorous euphemism for any vulgar term

blank verse unrhymed verse; esp., unrhymed verse having five iambic feet per line

blan·quette (blän ket') *n.* [Fr.] a stew made from white meat, esp. veal, and having a white sauce

blare (bler) *vt., vi.* **blared, blar'ing** [ME. *bleren,* to bellow] 1. to sound out with loud, trumpetlike tones 2. to exclaim loudly —*n.* a loud, brassy sound

blar·ney (blär'nē) *n.* [after the stone in Blarney Castle in Cork county, Ireland, supposed to give the gift of flattery to those who kiss it] smooth talk used in flattering or coaxing —*vt., vi.* **-neyed, -ney·ing** to use blarney (on)

bla·sé (blä'zā) *adj.* [Fr., pp. of *blaser,* to satiate] having indulged in pleasure so much as to be unexcited by it; satiated and bored

blas·pheme (blas fēm') *vt.* **-phemed', -phem'ing** [< OFr. < LL. < Gr. *blasphēmein,* to speak evil of] 1. to speak irreverently or profanely of or to (God or sacred things) 2. to curse or revile —*vi.* to utter blasphemy —**blas·phem'·er** *n.*

blas·phe·my (blas'fə mē) *n., pl.* **-mies** [see prec.] 1. words or action showing disrespect or scorn for God or anything held sacred 2. any irreverent or disrespectful remark or action —**blas'phe·mous** *adj.* —**blas'phe·mous·ly** *adv.*

blast (bläst) *n.* [< OE. *blæst*] 1. a gust of wind; strong rush of air 2. the sound of a sudden rush of air or gas, as through a trumpet 3. the steady current of air forced into a blast furnace 4. an abrupt and damaging influence; blight 5. *a)* an explosion, as of dynamite *b)* a charge of explosive causing this 6. a strong, sudden outburst, as of criticism 7. [U.S. Slang] a gay, hilarious time; esp., a wild party —*vi.* 1. to make a loud, harsh sound 2. to set off explosives, gunfire, etc. 3. to suffer from a blight —*vt.* 1. to damage or destroy by or as if by a blight; wither 2. to blow up with an explosive; explode 3. [Colloq.] to criticize sharply —**blast off** to take off with explosive force and begin its flight, as a rocket —**(at) full blast** at full speed or capacity —**blast'er** *n.*

-blast (blast) [< Gr. *blastos,* a sprout] *a combining form meaning* formative, embryonic

blast·ed (bläs'tid) *adj.* 1. blighted; withered; destroyed 2. damned; confounded

blast furnace a smelting furnace into which a blast of air is forced from below for intense heat

blast-off, blast-off (bläst'of) *n.* the launching of a rocket, space vehicle, etc.

blas·tu·la (blas'tyoo lə) *n., pl.* **-las, -lae** (-lē') [ModL. dim. < Gr. *blastos,* a germ, sprout] an embryo at the stage of development in which it consists typically of a single layer of cells around a central cavity —**blas'tu·lar** *adj.*

bla·tant (blāt'ənt) *adj.* [coined by E. Spenser; prob. < L. *blaterare,* to babble] 1. disagreeably loud; noisy 2. glaringly conspicuous or obtrusive —**bla'tan·cy** *n., pl.* **-cies** —**bla'tant·ly** *adv.*

blath·er (blath'ər) *n., vi., vt.* same as BLETHER

blath·er·skite (-skīt') *n.* same as BLETHERSKITE

blaze¹ (blāz) *n.* [< OE. *blæse*] 1. a brilliant burst of flame; strongly burning fire 2. any very bright light or glare 3. a sudden or spectacular outburst [a *blaze* of oratory] 4. a brightness; vivid display 5. [*pl.*] hell: a euphemism, esp. in the phrase **go to blazes!** —*vi.* **blazed, blaz'ing** 1. to burn rapidly or brightly 2. to give off a strong light; glare 3. to be deeply stirred, as with anger —**blaze away** 1. to fire a gun rapidly several times 2. [Colloq.] to work energetically

blaze² (blāz) *n.* [< ON. *blesi*] 1. a white spot on an animal's face 2. a mark made on a tree by cutting off a piece of bark —*vt.* **blazed, blaz'ing** to mark (a tree or trail) with blazes —**blaze a way** (or **path,** etc.) to pioneer in

blaze³ (blāz) *vt.* **blazed, blaz'ing** [ME. *blasen,* to blow < OE. or ON.] to make known publicly

blaz·er (blā'zər) *n.* [< BLAZE¹ + -ER] a lightweight jacket, often striped or in the colours of a sports club or school

bla·zon (blā'z'n) *n.* [OFr. *blason,* a shield] a coat of arms —*vt.* 1. to make widely known; proclaim (often with *forth, out,* or *abroad*) 2. to describe or portray (coats of arms) 3. *a)* to portray in colours *b)* to adorn colourfully or showily —**bla'zon·er** *n.* —**bla'zon·ment** *n.* —**bla'zon·ry** *n., pl.* **-ries**

bldg. building

bleach (blēch) *vt., vi.* [OE. *blæcan* < *blac,* pale] to make or become white or colourless by means of chemicals or by exposure to sunlight —*n.* 1. a bleaching 2. a substance used for bleaching —**bleach'er** *n.*

bleach·ers (-ərz) *n.pl.* [< prec., in reference to the effects of exposure] [U.S.] seats or benches in tiers without a roof, for spectators at sporting events

bleaching powder chloride of lime or any other powder used in bleaching

bleak¹ (blēk) *adj.* [< ON. *bleikr,* pale] 1. exposed to wind and cold; unsheltered 2. cold and cutting; harsh 3. not cheerful or hopeful; gloomy —**bleak'ly** *adv.* —**bleak'ness** *n.*

bleak² (blēk) *n.* [< ON. *bleikr,* pale] a small, silvery European fish of the carp family

blear (blir) *adj.* [< ME. *bleren,* to have watery eyes] 1. made dim by tears, mucus, etc.: said of eyes 2. blurred; dim —*vt.* 1. to dim (the eyes) with tears, mucus, etc. 2. to blur

blear·y (-ē) *adj.* **blear'i·er, blear'i·est** 1. dim or blurred 2. having blurred vision —**blear'i·ly** *adv.* —**blear'i·ness** *n.*

blear·y-eyed (-id') *adj.* having bleary eyes or blurred vision: also **blear'eyed'**

bleat (blēt) *vi.* [< OE. *blætan*] 1. to make the cry of a sheep, goat, or calf 2. to make a sound like this cry —*vt.* to say in a bleating voice —*n.* a bleating cry or sound —**bleat'er** *n.*

bleb (bleb) *n.* [echoic] 1. a small swelling on the skin or on plants; blister 2. an air bubble, as in water or glass

bleed (blēd) *vi.* **bled** (bled), **bleed'ing** [< OE. *bledan* < *blod,* blood] 1. to emit or lose blood 2. to suffer wounds or die in a battle or cause 3. to feel pain, grief, or sympathy; suffer [my heart *bleeds*] 4. to ooze sap, juice, etc., as bruised plants 5. to run together, as dyes in wet cloth 6. to come through a covering coat of paint 7. to be printed so that text, illustrations, etc. run off the edge of the trimmed page —*vt.* 1. to draw blood from 2. to ooze (sap, juice, etc.) 3. to empty of liquid, air, or gas 4. to take sap or juice from 5. [Colloq.] to extort money from —**bleed like a pig** to bleed profusely

bleed·er (-ər) *n.* 1. a person who bleeds profusely; haemophiliac 2. [Slang] a person, esp. an unpleasant one

bleed·ing (-iŋ) *adj., adv.* a euphemism for BLOODY (*adj.*5, *adv.*): often considered a vulgar usage

bleeding heart 1. a plant with fernlike leaves and drooping clusters of pink, heart-shaped flowers 2. a person regarded as too sentimental or too liberal in his approach to social problems

bleep (blēp) *n., vi.* [echoic] same as BEEP —*vt.* to censor (something said), as in a broadcast, by substituting a beep

blem·ish (blem'ish) *vt.* [< OFr. *blesmir,* to injure] to mar, as by some flaw or fault —*n.* 1. a mark that mars the appearance, as a stain or nick 2. any flaw, defect, or shortcoming

blench (blench) *vi.* [< OE. *blencan,* to deceive] to shrink back, as in fear; flinch

blend (blend) *vt.* **blend'ed** or **blent, blend'ing** [< OE. *blendan* & ON. *blanda,* to mix] 1. to mix or mingle (varieties of tea, tobacco, etc.) 2. to mix or fuse thoroughly, so the parts are no longer distinct —*vi.* 1. to mix or merge 2. to shade gradually into each other, as colours 3. to go well together; harmonize —*n.* 1. a blending 2. a mixture of varieties [a *blend* of coffee] 3. Linguis. a word formed by combining parts of other words (Ex.: *smog*) —**blend'er** *n.*

blende (blend) *n.* [G. < *blenden,* to blind, deceive] sphalerite or any of certain other sulphides

blended whisky a blend of grain and malt whisky

blen·ny (blen'ē) *n., pl.* **-nies, -ny:** see PLURAL, II, D, 1 [< L. < Gr. < *blenna,* slime] any of a number of small ocean fishes having long dorsal fins and a tapering body covered with a slimy substance —**blen'ni·oid'** (-ē oid') *adj.*

bleph·a·ri·tis (blef'ə rīt'əs) *n.* [< Gr. *blepharon,* eyelid + -ITIS] inflammation of the eyelids

bles·bok (bles'bok) *n., pl.* **-bok, -boks** see PLURAL, II, D, 2 [Afrik. < *bles,* BLAZE² + *bok,* BUCK¹] a South African antelope that has a large, white mark on its face

bless (bles) *vt.* **blessed** or **blest, bless'ing** [< OE. *bletsian,* to consecrate with blood < *blod,* blood] 1. to make holy; hallow 2. to ask divine favour for 3. to favour or endow (with) [*blessed* with health] 4. to make happy or prosperous 5. to praise or glorify 6. to make the sign of the cross over or upon 7. to protect from evil, harm, etc. —**bless me** (or **you, him,** etc.)! an exclamation of surprise, dismay, etc. —**bless you!** an exclamation originally supposed to protect a person from illness: said to someone who has just sneezed

bless·ed (bles'id; *occas.* blest) *adj.* 1. holy; sacred 2. blissful; fortunate 3. of or in eternal bliss: a title applied to one who has been beatified 4. bringing joy 5. cursed: an ironical oath —**bless'ed·ly** *adv.* —**bless'ed·ness** *n.*

bless·ing (-iŋ) *n.* 1. an invocation or benediction 2. a grace said before or after eating 3. the gift of divine favour 4. good wishes or approval 5. a special benefit or favour [a *blessing* in disguise]

blest (blest) *alt. pt. & pp. of* BLESS —*adj.* blessed

bleth·er (bleth'ər) *n.* [ON. *blathr*] 1. foolish talk 2. a person who chatters foolishly —**bleth'er·er** *n.*

bleth·er·skite (-skīt') *n.* a talkative, foolish person

blew (blōō) *pt. of* BLOW¹ & BLOW³

blight (blīt) *n.* [? < ON. *blikja,* turn pale] 1. any parasite, insect, etc. that destroys or stunts plants 2. any of several plant diseases, as mildew 3. anything that destroys, prevents growth, frustrates, etc. 4. an area of decay and neglect, esp. in a city —*vt.* 1. to wither 2. to destroy 3. to frustrate —*vi.* to suffer blight

blight·er (-ər) *n.* 1. a person or thing that blights 2. a contemptible or annoying person

blight·y (-ē) *n.* [< Hindi *bilāyatī,* foreign land] [Mil. Slang] 1. [*often* B-] Britain; home 2. a wound involving a return to Britain: also **a blighty one**

bli·mey (blī′mē) *interj.* [contr. < (*God*) *blind me*] [Colloq.] an exclamation of surprise, wonder, etc.

blimp (blimp) *n.* [echoic coinage] 1. a soundproof cover for a cine camera 2. [Colloq.] a small, nonrigid or semirigid airship 3. [< Col. *Blimp,* creation of Brit. cartoonist David Low] a person, esp. a military officer, who is stupidly complacent and highly conservative: also **Colonel Blimp**

blind (blīnd) *adj.* [OE.] 1. without the power of sight; sightless 2. of or for sightless persons 3. not able or willing to notice or understand 4. done without adequate directions or knowledge [*a blind search*] 5. disregarding evidence, sound logic, etc. [*blind faith*] 6. reckless; unreasonable 7. hard to see; hidden [*a blind corner*] 8. dense; impenetrable [*a blind hedge*] 9. closed at one end 10. not controlled by intelligence [*blind destiny*] 11. [Slang] drunk 12. *Aeron.* by the use of instruments only [*blind flying*] 13. *Archit.* having no opening 14. *Bookbinding* without gilding or colouring [*blind tooling*] —*vt.* 1. to make sightless 2. to dazzle 3. to deprive of the power of insight or judgment 4. to make dim; obscure 5. to hide —*n.* 1. anything that obscures or prevents sight 2. a) a screen for a window, esp. one of stiffened cloth on a spring roller b) *same as* VENETIAN BLIND 3. a person or thing used to deceive or mislead —*adv.* 1. blindly 2. recklessly 3. sight unseen [*to buy a thing blind*] —**the blind** blind people —**blind′ly** *adv.* —**blind′ness** *n.*

blind alley 1. a lane shut off at one end 2. any undertaking, idea, etc. that leads to nothing

blind date [Colloq.] 1. a social engagement arranged for a man and a woman previously unacquainted 2. either of these persons

blind·er (blīn′dər) *n.* [U.S.] *same as* BLINKER (sense 2)

blind·fold (blīnd′fōld′) *vt.* [altered (after FOLD¹) < ME. *blindfeld,* struck blind: see BLIND & FELL²] to cover the eyes of, as with a cloth —*n.* something used to cover the eyes —*adj.* 1. with the eyes covered 2. reckless

blind gut *same as* CAECUM

blind·man's buff (blīnd′manz buf′) [*buff,* contr. < BUFFET¹] a game in which a blindfolded player has to catch and identify another

blind spot 1. the small area, insensitive to light, in the retina of the eye where the optic nerve enters 2. an area where vision is obscured 3. a prejudice, or area of ignorance, that one has but is often unaware of

blind·worm (-wurm) *n.* *same as* SLOWWORM

blink (bliŋk) *vi.* [ME. *blenken* (see BLENCH)] 1. to wink quickly one or more times 2. to flash on and off; twinkle 3. to look with eyes half shut and winking —*vt.* to cause (eyes, light, etc.) to wink or blink —*n.* 1. a blinking 2. a glimmer —**blink at** to ignore or condone (a mistake) —**on the blink** [Colloq.] not working properly; out of order

blink·er (-ər) *n.* 1. a flashing light, as a motor car indicator 2. either of two flaps on a horse's bridle that shut out the side view

blink·ing (-iŋ) *adj., adv.* a euphemism for BLOODY (*adj.*5, *adv.*)

blip (blip) *n.* [echoic of a brief sound] 1. a luminous image, as on an oscilloscope, or radar screen 2. a quick, sharp sound —*vt.* **blipped, blip′ping** *same as* BLEEP

bliss (blis) *n.* [OE. *bliths* < *blithe,* BLITHE] 1. great joy or happiness 2. spiritual joy —**bliss′ful** *adj.* —**bliss′ful·ly** *adv.* —**bliss′ful·ness** *n.*

blis·ter (blis′tər) *n.* [< ? Du. *bluister* or OFr. *blestre* < ON. *blastr*] 1. a raised patch of skin filled with watery matter and caused by burning or rubbing 2. anything resembling a blister —*vt.* 1. to raise blisters on 2. to lash with words —*vi.* to have or form blisters —**blis′ter·y** *adj.*

blithe (blīth) *adj.* [OE.] gay; cheerful; carefree —**blithe′ly** *adv.* —**blithe′ness** *n.*

blith·er·ing (blith′ər iŋ) *adj.* [*blither,* var. of BLETHER] talking without sense; jabbering

blithe·some (blīth′səm) *adj.* blithe; gay —**blithe′some·ly** *adv.* —**blithe′some·ness** *n.*

B.Litt., B.Lit. [L. *Baccalaureus Lit(t)erarum*] Bachelor of Letters (or Literature)

blitz (blits) *n.* [< ff.] 1. a sudden, overwhelming attack 2. [B-] the German air raids on Britain during 1940 (preceded by *the*) —*vt.* to subject to a blitz; overwhelm

blitz·krieg (-krēg′) *n.* [G. < *Blitz,* lightning + *Krieg,* war] 1. sudden, swift, large-scale offensive warfare intended to win a quick victory 2. any sudden, overwhelming attack

bliz·zard (bliz′ərd) *n.* [U.S. dial. *bliz,* violent blow (? akin to G. *Blitz,* lightning) + -ARD] a violent storm with driving snow and very cold winds

blk. 1. black 2. block 3. bulk

bloat¹ (blōt) *vt., vi* [< ON. *blautr,* soaked] 1. to swell, as with water or air 2. to puff up, as with pride

bloat² (blōt) *vt.* [< ME. *blote,* soft with moisture < ON. *blautr:* see prec.] to cure (herring, etc.) by soaking in salt water and smoking

bloat·ed (-id) *adj.* 1. cured by salting and smoking: said of fish 2. swollen, as with pride, self-indulgence, great wealth, etc. [*a bloated plutocrat*]

bloat·er (-ər) *n.* a fat herring or mackerel that has been bloated, or cured

blob (blob) *n.* [echoic] 1. a small drop or mass 2. something of indefinite form

bloc (blok) *n.* [Fr. & OFr. < LowG. *block,* log] a bipartisan group of legislators, or a group of nations, acting together in some common cause

block (blok) *n.* [< MDu. or OFr. < LowG. *block:* see prec.] 1. any large, solid piece of wood, stone, or metal 2. a blocklike stand for chopping, beheading, mounting a horse from, etc. 3. a large building divided into offices, flats, etc. 4. a mould upon which hats, etc. are shaped 5. an obstruction or hindrance 6. an interruption of a normal body function 7. a pulley in a frame 8. a large, hollow building brick 9. a child's wooden or plastic toy brick 10. any number of things regarded as a unit 11. [Chiefly U.S.] a) a group of buildings bounded by intersecting streets b) the area or distance between such streets 12. [Colloq.] a person's head 13. *Printing* a piece of engraved wood, etc. with a design or picture 14. *Psychiatry* an interruption in speech or thought processes, resulting from emotional conflict, repression, etc. 15. *Sports* a legal thwarting of an opponent's play or movement —*vt.* 1. to impede the passage or progress of; obstruct 2. to stand in the way of; hinder 3. to shape or mould on a block 4. to strengthen or support with blocks 5. to sketch with little detail (often with *out*) 6. *Cricket* to play (a ball) defensively 7. *Med.* to deaden (a nerve), esp. by anaesthesia 8 *Sports* to hinder (an opponent or his play) —**block up** to shut in; enclose —**block′age** *n.* —**block′er** *n.*

block·ade (blo kād′) *n.* [BLOCK + -ADE] 1. a shutting off of a port or region by hostile troops or ships to prevent passage 2. the troops or ships so used 3. any strategic barrier —*vt.* **-ad′ed, -ad′ing** to subject to a blockade —**run the blockade** to go through a blockade —**block·ad′er** *n.*

blockade runner a ship or person that tries to go through or past a blockade

block and tackle pulley blocks and ropes or cables, used for hoisting large, heavy objects

block·bust·er (blok′bus′tər) *n.* [Colloq.] 1. a large, highly destructive aerial bomb 2. a successful, heavily promoted film, novel, etc.

block·head (-hed′) *n.* a stupid person

block·house (-haus′) *n.* 1. [U.S.] formerly, a strong wooden fort with a projecting second storey and openings in the walls to shoot from 2. any building of squared timber or logs 3. *Mil.* a small structure of concrete for defence or observation

block·ish (-ish) *adj.* stupid; dull —**block′ish·ly** *adv.* —**block′-ish·ness** *n.*

BLOCKHOUSE

block letter 1. a plain capital letter used in writing for its legibility 2. *Printing* a letter that is simple in form, as sans-serif

block release the release of employees from work, usually for a session of several weeks, to enable them to attend a training course

block system a system of dividing a railway line into sections, ensuring by signals that only one train can be in the section at a time

block vote a vote in which a delegate's influence is in accordance with the number of people he represents

block·y (-ē) *adj.* 1. like a block 2. stocky; chunky —**block′-i·ness** *n.*

bloke (blōk) *n.* [< ?] [Colloq.] a fellow; chap

blond (blond) *adj.* [Fr. < ? Gmc.] 1. having yellow or yellowish-brown hair, often with fair skin and blue or grey eyes 2. yellow or yellowish-brown: said of hair —*n.* a blond person —**blond′ness** *n.*

blonde (blond) *adj.* *same as* BLOND —*n.* a blond woman or girl

blood (blud) *n.* [< OE. *blod*] 1. *a*) the fluid, usually red, circulating in the heart, arteries, and veins of vertebrates *b*) a similar fluid in invertebrates 2. the spilling of blood; murder 3. the essence of life; lifeblood 4. the sap or juice of anything, esp. if red 5. passion, temperament, or disposition 6. parental heritage; family line; lineage; ancestry 7. kinship; family relationship 8. descent from nobility 9. a descent from purebred stock 10. people, esp. youthful people [*new blood in the firm*] 11. [Now Rare] a dandy —*vt.* 1. to let (a hunting dog) taste or see the blood of its prey 2. to initiate (a person) in any new experience

—bad blood anger; hatred **—in cold blood** 1. with cruelty; unfeelingly 2. dispassionately; deliberately **—in one's blood** to be a natural or inherited characteristic or talent **—make one's blood boil** to make one angry **—make one's blood run cold** to terrify one

blood bank 1. a place where whole blood or plasma is stored for future use in transfusion 2. any reserve of such blood

blood bath a massacre; slaughter

blood brother 1. a brother by birth 2. a person bound to one by the ceremony of mingling his blood with one's own **—blood brotherhood**

blood count the number of red corpuscles and white corpuscles in a given volume of blood

blood·cur·dling (-kurd'liŋ) *adj.* very frightening; causing terror or horror

blood·ed (blud'id) *adj.* 1. having (a specified kind of) blood [hot-*blooded*] 2. of fine stock or breed

blood group any of several groups into which human blood is classified

blood heat the normal temperature of human blood, approximately 36.8° C (98.4° F)

blood·hound (-hound') *n.* any of a breed of large, keen-scented dogs used in tracking fugitives, etc.

blood·less (-las) *adj.* 1. without blood 2. without bloodshed 3. anaemic or pale 4. having little energy or vitality 5. unfeeling; cruel **—blood'less·ly** *adv.* **—blood'-less·ness** *n.*

blood·let·ting (-let'iŋ) *n.* 1. the opening of a vein to remove blood; bleeding 2. *same as* BLOODSHED

blood money 1. money paid to a hired killer 2. money paid as compensation for a murder 3. money obtained ruthlessly through others' suffering

blood orange a variety of orange with a red pulp

blood poisoning any of various diseases in which the blood contains microorganisms, their toxins, or other poisonous matter; septicaemia

blood pressure the pressure exerted by the blood against the inner walls of the blood vessels: it varies with age, physical condition etc.

blood pudding *same as* BLACK PUDDING

blood relation a person related by birth rather than by marriage

blood·shed (-shed') *n.* the shedding of blood; killing

blood·shot (-shot') *adj.* red because the small blood vessels are swollen or broken: said of an eye

blood sport any pastime, as fox-hunting, in which killing is involved

blood·stained (-stānd') *adj.* 1. soiled or discoloured with blood 2. guilty of murder

blood·stone (-stōn') *n.* a dark-green variety of quartz spotted with red jasper, used as a gem

blood·stream (-strēm') *n.* the blood flowing through the circulatory system of a body

blood·suck·er (-suk'ər) *n.* 1. an animal that sucks blood, esp. a leech 2. a person who extorts from others all that he can **—blood'suck'ing** *adj., n.*

blood·thirst·y (-thur'stē) *adj.* eager to kill; murderous; cruel **—blood'thirst'i·ly** *adv.* **—blood'thirst'i·ness** *n.*

blood type *same as* BLOOD GROUP

blood typing the classification of blood to determine compatible blood groups for transfusion

blood vessel a tube through which the blood circulates in the body; artery, vein, or capillary

blood·y (blud'ē) *adj.* **blood'i·er, blood'i·est** 1. of, like, or containing blood 2. covered or stained with blood 3. involving bloodshed 4. bloodthirsty 5. [Slang] cursed; damned: a vulgar usage **—***adv.* [Slang] very: a vulgar usage **—***vt.* **blood'ied, blood'y·ing** to cover or stain with blood **—blood'i·ly** *adv.* **—blood'i·ness** *n.*

Bloody Mary a drink of vodka with tomato juice

blood·y-mind·ed (-mīnd'id) *adj.* [Colloq.] intentionally awkward or uncooperative **—blood'y-mind'ed·ness** *n.*

bloom¹ (blōōm) *n.* [< ON. *blomi*, flowers] 1. a flower; blossom 2. flowers collectively, as of a plant 3. the state or time of flowering 4. the state or time of most health, vigour, etc. 5. a youthful, healthy glow, as of the cheeks 6. *a)* the powdery coating on some fruits or leaves *b)* a similar coating, as on new coins 7. a dull area on a varnished surface **—***vi.* 1. to bear flowers; blossom 2. to be in one's prime; flourish 3. to glow as with health **—bloom'ing** *adj.*

bloom² (blōōm) *n.* [OE. *bloma*, lump of metal] an oblong mass of metal in an intermediate stage of manufacture

bloom·er¹ (blōō'mər) *n.* 1. a plant with reference to its blooming [an early *bloomer*] 2. [Slang] a stupid mistake

bloom·er² (blōō'mər) *n.* [after Amelia J. *Bloomer* (1818–94), U.S. feminist who advocated it] 1. formerly, a woman's costume consisting of a short skirt and loose trousers gathered at the ankles 2. [*pl.*] *a)* baggy trousers gathered at the knee, formerly worn by women for athletics *b)* an undergarment somewhat like this

blos·som (blos'əm) *n.* [< OE. *blostma*] 1. a flower or

bloom, esp. of a fruit-bearing plant 2. a state or time of flowering **—***vi.* 1. to have or open into blossoms; bloom 2. to begin to thrive or flourish; develop **—blos'som·y** *adj.*

blot (blot) *n.* [< ?] 1. a spot or stain, esp. of ink 2. anything that spoils or mars something 3. a moral stain; disgrace **—***vt.* **blot'ted, blot'ting** 1. to spot; stain 2. to erase or get rid of [memories *blotted* from one's mind] 3. to dry, as with blotting paper **—***vi.* 1. to make blots 2. to become blotted 3. to be absorbent **—blot one's copybook** to spoil one's reputation as by a mistake or indiscretion **—blot out** 1. to darken or obscure 2. to destroy

blotch (bloch) *n.* [? extension of BLOT] 1. a discoloured patch or blemish on the skin 2. any large blot or stain **—***vt.* to mark with blotches **—blotch'y** *adj.* **blotch'i·er, blotch'-i·est**

blot·ter (blot'ər) *n.* 1. a piece of blotting paper 2. [U.S.] a book for recording events as they occur [a police *blotter*]

blotting paper a thick, soft, absorbent paper used to dry a surface freshly written on in ink

blot·to (-ō) *adj.* [< ? BLOT] [Slang] very drunk; unconscious because of drinking too much

blouse (blouz, blous) *n.* [Fr., workman's or peasant's smock] 1. a loose, shirtlike garment extending to the waist, worn by women and children 2. the coat or jacket of a military uniform **—***vi., vt.* **bloused, blous'ing** to gather in and drape at the waistline

blous·on (blōō'zon) *adj.* [Fr., extended < *blouse*] styled with a long, full, bloused top **—***n.* a blouson dress, top, etc., esp. one with a drawstring waist

blow¹ (blō) *vi.* **blew, blown, blow'ing** [< OE. *blawan*] 1. to move with some force: said of the wind 2. to send forth air, as with the mouth 3. to pant; be breathless 4. to sound by blowing or being blown 5. to spout water and air, as whales do 6. to be carried by the wind [the paper *blew* away] 7. to be stormy 8. to burst suddenly, as a tyre, or melt, as a fuse (often with *out*) 9. to lay eggs: said of flies 10. [Aust. & U.S. Colloq.] to brag; boast 11. [Slang] to go away **—***vt.* 1. to force air from (a bellows, etc.) 2. to send out (breath, etc.) from the mouth 3. to force air onto, into, or through 4. to drive by blowing 5. *a)* to sound (a wind instrument) by blowing *b)* to make (a sound) by blowing 6. to shape or form by blown air or gas 7. to clear by blowing through 8. to burst by an explosion 9. to cause (a horse) to pant 10. to melt (a fuse, etc.) 11. [Colloq.] to spend (money) freely 12. [Slang] go away from 13. [Slang] to bungle and fail in **—***n.* 1. a blowing 2. a blast of air **—***interj.* [Colloq.] damn! **—blow hot and cold** to be favourable towards and then opposed to; vacillate **—blow in** [Slang] to arrive **—blow one's top** (or lid) [Slang] to lose one's temper **—blow one's mind** [Slang] to be exhilarating; stimulating **—blow one's own trumpet** to boast of one's achievements **—blow out** 1. to put out or be put out by blowing 2. to blow (*vi.* 8) 3. to dispel (itself) after a time: said of a storm **—blow over** 1. to move away, as rain clouds 2. to be forgotten **—blow up** 1. to fill with air or gas 2. to explode 3. to arise and become intense, as a storm 4. to enlarge (a photograph) 5. to exaggerate (an incident, etc.) 6. [Colloq.] to lose one's temper **—blow'-er** *n.*

blow² (blō) *n.* [ME. *blowe*, akin to G. *bleuen*, to strike] 1. a hard hit or stroke, as with the fist 2. a sudden attack or forcible effort 3. a sudden calamity or misfortune; shock **—at a** (or **one**) **blow** by one action **—come to blows** to begin fighting

blow³ (blō) *vi.* **blew, blown, blow'ing** [OE. *blowan*] [Poet.] to bloom; blossom **—***n.* 1. a mass of blossoms 2. any splendid display

blow-by-blow (-bī'blō') *adj.* told in great detail [a *blow-by-blow* description]

blow-dry (-drī') *vt.* **-dried', -dry'ing** to dry (wet hair) with an electric device (**blow'-dry'er**) that sends out a powerful stream of heated air **—***n.* the act of blow-drying the hair

blow·fish (-fish') *n., pl.* **-fish', -fish'es:** see FISH *same as* PUFFER (sense 2)

blow·fly (-flī') *n., pl.* **-flies'** [BLOW¹ (*vi.* 9) + FLY²] any of various two-winged flies that deposit eggs in meat, open wounds, etc.

blow·gun (-gun') *n. same as* BLOWPIPE

blow·hole (-hōl') *n.* 1. a nostril in the top of the head of whales, etc., used for breathing 2. a hole through which gas or air can escape 3. a hole in the ice to which seals, etc. come for air

blow·lamp (-lamp') *n.* a small burner that shoots out a hot flame intensified by a blast of air: used to melt metal, remove old paint, etc.

blown (blōn) *pp.* of BLOW¹ & BLOW³ **—***adj.* 1. swollen or bloated 2. out of breath, as from exertion 3. made by blowing or by using a blowpipe, etc.

blow·out (blō'out') *n.* 1. the bursting of a tyre 2. the melting of an electric fuse 3. the uncontrolled escape of oil or gas from an oil or gas well 4. [Slang] a very large meal

blow·pipe (-pīp') *n.* 1. a tube for forcing air or gas into a flame to increase its heat 2. a metal tube used in blowing glass **3.** a long, tubelike weapon through which darts or pellets are blown

blow·torch (-tôrch′) *n.* [U.S.] a blowlamp

blow·up (-up′) *n.* **1.** an explosion **2.** an enlarged photograph **3.** [Colloq.] a hysterical outburst

blow·y (-ē) *adj.* **blow′i·er, blow′i·est** windy

blowz·y (blou′zē) *adj.* **blowz′i·er, blowz′i·est** [< obs. *blouze*, wench] **1.** fat, ruddy, and coarse-looking **2.** slovenly; sloppy Also **blows′y**

bls. **1.** bales **2.** barrels

blub (blub) *vi.* **blubbed, blub′bing** [< BLUBBER²] to cry and sob; blubber

blub·ber¹ (blub′ər) *n.* [ME. *blober*, a bubble; prob. echoic] **1.** the fat of the whale and other sea mammals **2.** [Colloq.] unsightly fat on the human body

blub·ber² (blub′ər) *vi.* [ME. *bloberen*, to bubble (see prec.)] to weep loudly, like a child —*vt.* to say while blubbering —*n.* loud weeping —*adj.* thick or swollen —**blub′ber·er** *n.*

blub·ber·y (-ər ē) *adj.* **1.** of, full of, or like blubber **2.** swollen, as by blubbering

blu·cher (bloō′chər, -kər) *n.* [after G. L. von *Blücher* (1742–1819), Prussian field marshal] a strong leather half-boot or high shoe

bludg·eon (bluj′′n) *n.* [? altered < MFr. dim. of *bouge*, a club] a short club with a thick, heavy, or loaded end —*vt., vi.* **1.** to strike with or as with a bludgeon **2.** to bully or coerce

blue (bloō) *adj.* [< OFr. *bleu* < Frank. *blao*] **1.** having the colour of the clear sky or the deep sea **2.** having a blue tinge through cold or anger: said of the skin **3.** sad and gloomy; depressed or depressing **4.** [Colloq.] indecent; risqué —*n.* **1.** the colour of the clear sky or the deep sea **2.** any blue pigment or dye **3.** anything coloured blue **4.** a blue liquid or powder used in rinsing white fabrics to prevent yellowing **5.** a supporter of a particular political party, esp. the British Conservative party **6.** *a)* a sportsman who has represented his university, esp. at Oxford or Cambridge *b)*.the badge awarded to him **7.** *a)* [often **B-**] one who wears a blue uniform *b)* [pl.] a sailor's blue uniform **8.** [pl.] [Colloq.] a depressed, unhappy feeling (with *the*) **9.** [pl., also with sing. v.] *a)* Negro folk music, or the jazz evolved from it, with minor harmonies, slow tempo, and melancholy words (often with *the*) *b)* a song in this style —*vt.* **blued, blu′ing** or **blue′ing** **1.** to make blue **2.** to use laundering blue on or in —*vi.* to become blue —**once in a blue moon** very seldom —**out of the blue** as if from the sky; unexpected —**the blue** **1.** the sky **2.** the sea —**blue′ness** *n.*

blue baby a baby born with cyanosis

Blue·beard (-bird′) *n.* [after *Bluebeard*, legendary character in European folk tales] a man who murders several wives or commits other monstrous deeds

blue·bell (-bel′) *n.* any of various plants with blue, bell-shaped flowers

blue·ber·ry (-bər ē) *n., pl.* **-ries** **1.** a shrub bearing small, edible, blue-black berries with tiny seeds **2.** any of the berries

blue·bird (-burd′) *n.* any of several small N. American songbirds: the male has a blue or bluish back and an orange or reddish breast

blue blood **1.** descent from nobility or royalty **2.** a person of such descent; aristocrat: also **blue′blood** *n.* —**blue′-blood′ed** *adj.*

blue·bon·net (-bon′it) *n.* **1.** a blue woollen cap, formerly worn in Scotland **2.** a Scotsman **3.** [Chiefly Scot.] a cornflower with blue blossoms Also **blue bonnet**

blue book [also **B- B-**] an official government publication, often having a blue cover

blue·bot·tle (-bot′′l) *n.* **1.** any of several plants with blue, bottle-shaped flowers, as the cornflower, grape hyacinth, etc. **2.** a large blowfly with a steel-blue abdomen and a hairy body **3.** [Old Slang] a policeman

blue cheese a cheese in which a blue mould has been intentionally produced, as Roquefort, Danish Blue, etc.

blue-chip (-chip′) *adj.* [after the high-value *blue chips* of poker] **1.** designating a high-priced stock with a good record of earnings and price stability **2.** [Colloq.] excellent, valuable, etc.

blue-col·lar (-kol′ər) *adj.* [from the colour of many work shirts] designating or of industrial workers, esp. the semiskilled and unskilled

blue-eyed boy (-id) [Colloq.] a favourite who cannot do wrong; pet

blue·fish (-fish′) *n., pl.* **-fish′, -fish′es:** see FISH a bluish food fish, common along the Atlantic coast of N. America

blue fox **1.** a mutant of the arctic fox, having a bluish or smoky-grey fur **2.** this fur

blue·gill (-gil′) *n.* a bluish, freshwater sunfish

blue·grass (-gräs′) *n.* [U.S.] **1.** any of various forage grasses, esp. **Kentucky bluegrass** **2.** [often **B-**] Southern U.S. string-band folk music

blue ground [S.Afr.] a decomposed soil which sometimes contains diamonds; kimberlite

blue gum a large Australian tree with aromatic leaves and a smooth bark that peels off in strips

blue·ish (-ish) *adj.* *same as* BLUISH

blue·jack·et (-jak′it) *n.* a sailor in the British or U.S. navy

blue jay a noisy, often crested, American bird with a bluish upper part: also **blue′jay′** *n.*

blue mould a fungus that produces bluish masses of spores on cheese, bread, etc.

blue-pen·cil (-pen′s′l) *vt.* **-cilled, -cil·ling** to edit, cross out, etc. with or as with a blue pencil

blue peter [also **B- P-**] a blue signal flag with a white square in the centre, displayed on a vessel about to leave port

blue·print (-print′) *n.* **1.** a photographic reproduction in white on a blue background, as of architectural plans **2.** any exact or detailed plan or outline —*vt.* to make a blueprint of

blue-rib·bon (-rib′ən) *adj.* [Colloq.] outstanding of its kind

blue ribbon first prize in a competition

blue·stock·ing (-stok′iŋ) *n.* [from the blue stockings worn at literary meetings in 18th-c. London] a learned, bookish, or pedantic woman

blue·stone (-stōn′) *n.* **1.** a blue-grey sandstone **2.** *same as* COPPER SULPHATE

blue tit a common European tit having a blue crown, wings and tail and yellow underparts

blue whale a whalebone whale with a dark blue-grey body: probably the largest animal that has ever lived

bluff¹ (bluf) *vt., vi.* [prob. < Du. *bluffen*, to baffle] **1.** to mislead by a false, bold front **2.** to frighten by threats that cannot be made good **3.** to manage to get (one's way) by bluffing —*n.* **1.** a bluffing **2.** a person who bluffs —**call someone's bluff** to challenge someone to give proof of his claims —**bluff′er** *n.*

bluff² (bluf) *adj.* [< Du. *blaf*, flat] **1.** having a broad, flat front that slopes steeply **2.** having a rough, frank, but affable manner —*n.* a high, steep bank or cliff —**bluff′ly** *adv.* —**bluff′ness** *n.*

blu·ish (-ish) *adj.* somewhat blue

blun·der (blun′dər) *vi.* [< ON. *blunda*, to shut the eyes] **1.** to move clumsily or carelessly; flounder; stumble **2.** to make a foolish mistake —*vt.* **1.** to say stupidly or confusedly; blurt (*out*) **2.** to do clumsily or poorly; bungle —*n.* a foolish mistake —**blun′der·er** *n.* —**blun′der·ing·ly** *adv.*

blun·der·buss (-bus′) *n.* [Du. *donderbus*, thunder box: altered after prec.] an obsolete short gun with a broad muzzle

blunge (blunj) *vt.* **blunged, blung′ing** [< ? PLUNGE] *Ceramics* to mix (clay) with water —**blung′er** *n.*

blunt (blunt) *adj.* [< ?] **1.** slow to perceive; dull **2.** having a dull edge or point **3.** plain-spoken and abrupt —*vt.* **1.** to make dull or insensitive **2.** to make less effective —*vi.* to become dull —**blunt′ly** *adv.* —**blunt′ness** *n.*

blur (blur) *vt., vi.* **blurred, blur′ring** [? akin to BLEAR] **1.** to smear or smudge **2.** to make or become less distinct or clear **3.** to dim or dull —*n.* **1.** the state of being blurred **2.** an obscuring stain or blot **3.** anything indistinct to the sight or mind —**blur′ri·ness** *n.* —**blur′ry** *adj.*

blurb (blurb) *n.* [arbitrary coinage (c. 1907) by Gelett Burgess (1866–1951), U.S. humorist] [Colloq.] an exaggerated advertisement, as on a book jacket

blurt (blurt) *vt.* [prob. echoic] to say suddenly, without stopping to think (with *out*)

blush (blush) *vi.* [< OE. *blyscan*, to shine] **1.** to become red in the face from shame, embarrassment, etc. **2.** to be ashamed or embarrassed (*at* or *for*) **3.** to be or become rosy —*n.* **1.** a reddening of the face, as from shame **2.** a rosy colour [the *blush* of youth] —*adj.* rosy [*blush*-pink] —**at first blush** at first sight; without further thought —**blush′er** *n.* —**blush′ful** *adj.* —**blush′ing·ly** *adv.*

blus·ter (blus′tər) *vi.* [< or akin to LowG. *blüstern*] **1.** to blow stormily: said of wind **2.** to speak or behave in a noisy, swaggering, or bullying way —*vt.* **1.** to force by blustering **2.** to say noisily and aggressively —*n.* **1.** noisy commotion **2.** noisy swaggering or bullying talk —**blus′ter·er** *n.* —**blus′ter·ing·ly** *adv.* —**blus′ter·y, blus′ter·ous** *adj.*

blvd. boulevard

BM bench mark

B.M. **1.** Bachelor of Medicine **2.** British Museum

B.M.A. British Medical Association

B.Mus. Bachelor of Music

Bn., bn. battalion

BO, B.O. **1.** [Colloq.] body odour **2.** box office

b.o. **1.** back order **2.** branch office

bo·a (bō′ə) *n.* [L.] **1.** any of a number of tropical snakes that crush their prey in their coils, as the anaconda **2.** a woman's long, fluffy scarf, as of feathers

boa constrictor a species of boa which reaches a length of 3 to 4.5 metres

boar (bôr) *n., pl.* **boars, boar:** see PLURAL, II, D 1 [OE. *bar*]

1. an uncastrated male pig **2.** a wild pig of Europe, Africa, and Asia

board (bôrd) *n.* [< OE. *bord,* plank & OFr. *bord,* side of a ship] **1.** a long, broad, flat piece of sawn wood ready for use **2.** a flat piece of wood or other material for some special use [a notice *board,* diving *board*] **3.** *a)* a construction material made in thin, flat, rectangular sheets [*fibreboard*] *b)* pasteboard or stiff paper, often used in book covers **4.** *a)* a table for meals *b)* food served at a table; esp., meals provided regularly for pay **5.** a council table **6.** *a)* a group of administrators; council *b)* a group of examiners or interviewers **7.** [Chiefly U.S.] a stock exchange or its listings **8.** the side of a ship [*overboard*] **9.** a rim or border [*seaboard*] —*vt.* **1.** to cover or close (*up*) with boards **2.** to provide with meals, or room and meals, regularly for pay **3.** to come onto the deck of (a ship) **4.** to get on (an aircraft, bus, etc.) —*vi.* to receive meals, or room and meals, regularly for pay —**across the board** including all classes or groups —**board out** to arrange for someone, esp. a child, to receive food and lodging away from home —**go by the board 1.** to be swept overboard **2.** to be got rid of, lost, etc. —**on board** on or in a ship, aircraft, bus, etc. —**the boards** the stage (of a theatre)

board·er (bôr′dər) *n.* **1.** one who boards at a boarding house, boarding school, etc. **2.** one who boards ship, etc.

board foot *pl.* **board feet** a unit of measure of timber (**board measure**), equal to a board one foot square (0.09 m²) and one inch (2.54 cm) thick

board·ing (bôr′diŋ) *n.* **1.** a structure or covering of boards **2.** boards collectively

board·ing·house (-haus′) *n.* a house where meals, or room and meals, can be had for pay: also **boarding house**

boarding school a school providing lodging and meals for the pupils

Board of Trade a British government department supervising commerce and industry

board·room (bôrd′rōōm) *n.* a room in which a board of administrators, directors, etc. regularly holds meetings

board·walk (bôrd′wôk′) *n.* [U.S.] a walk made of boards, esp. one elevated and placed along a beach

boast (bōst) *vi.* [< Anglo-Fr.] **1.** to talk about deeds, abilities, etc. with too much pride and satisfaction; brag **2.** to be vainly proud; exult —*vt.* **1.** to brag about **2.** to glory in having or doing (something); be proud of —*n.* **1.** the act of one who boasts **2.** anything boasted of —**boast′er** *n.* —**boast′ing·ly** *adv.*

boast·ful (-fəl) *adj.* inclined to brag; boasting —**boast′ful·ly** *adv.* —**boast′ful·ness** *n.*

boat (bōt) *n.* [OE. *bat*] **1.** a small, open vessel or watercraft propelled by oars, sails, or engine **2.** a large vessel; ship: landsman's term **3.** a boat-shaped dish [a gravy *boat*] —*vt.* to lay or carry in the boat [*boat* the oars] —*vi.* to row, sail, or cruise in a boat —**in the same boat** in the same unfavourable situation —**miss the boat** [Colloq.] to fail to make the most of an opportunity —**rock the boat** [Colloq.] to disturb the status quo

boat·er (bōt′ər) *n.* a stiff straw hat with a flat crown and brim and a wide hatband

boat·hook (-hook′) *n.* a long pole with a metal hook on one end for manoeuvring boats

boat·house (bōt′hous′) *n.* a building for storing a boat or boats

boat·ing (-iŋ) *n.* rowing, sailing, or cruising

boat·load (-lōd′) *n.* **1.** all the cargo or passengers that a boat can carry or contain **2.** the load carried by a boat

boat·man (-mən) *n.,* *pl.* **-men** a man who operates, works on, rents, or sells boats

boat·swain (bō′s′n) *n.* a ship's warrant officer or petty officer in charge of the deck crew, the rigging, anchors, etc.

boat train a train scheduled to take passengers to or from a particular ship

bob[1] (bob) *n.* [ME. *bobbe,* hanging cluster; senses 4 & 5 < the *v.*] **1.** a knoblike weight hanging as at the end of a plumb line **2.** a docked tail, as of a horse **3.** a woman's or girl's short haircut **4.** a quick, jerky motion **5.** a bobsleigh —*vt.* **bobbed, bob′bing** [ME. *bobben,* to knock against] **1.** to move, esp. up and down, with short, jerky motions **2.** to cut (hair, a tail, etc.) short —*vi.* **1.** to move with short, jerky motions **2.** to try to catch hanging or floating fruit with the teeth (with *for*) **3.** to ride on a bobsleigh —**bob up** to appear unexpectedly or suddenly

bob[2] (bob) *n.,* *pl.* **bob** [< ?] [Slang] a shilling

bob·bin (bob′in) *n.* [Fr. *bobine*] a reel or spool for thread or yarn, used in spinning, weaving, machine sewing, etc.

bob·ble (bob′'l) *n.* [< BOB[1]] a small tufted ball for decoration, as on a woollen hat

bob·by (bob′ē) *n.,* *pl.* **-bies** [after Sir Robert (*Bobby*) Peel (1788-1850), who reorganized the London police force] [Colloq.] a policeman

bob·by-daz·zler (-daz′lər) *n.* [< DAZZLE] [Colloq.] anything that is outstanding, striking, showy, etc., esp. an attractive or smartly-dressed girl

bobby pin [from use with *bobbed* hair] a hairgrip

bobby socks (or **sox**) [< BOB[1] (*vt.* 2)] [U.S. Colloq.] girls' socks that reach just above the ankle

bob·cat (bob′kat′) *n., pl.* **-cats′, -cat′**: see PLURAL, II, D, 1 [< its short tail] a wild cat of temperate N America: also **bay lynx**

bob·o·link (bob′ə liŋk′) *n.* [echoic, after its call] a migratory songbird of N. America

bob·sled (-sled′) *n.* same as BOBSLEIGH

bob·sleigh (-slā′) *n.* a long sledge with two sets of runners one behind the other, steering apparatus, and brakes: it is ridden by a team of four or two men in races down a prepared run —*vi.* to ride or race on a bobsleigh

bob·stay (-stā′) *n.* a rope or chain for tying down a bowsprit to keep it from bobbing

BOBSLEIGH

bob·tail (-tāl′) *n.* **1.** a tail cut short; docked tail **2.** a horse or dog with a bobtail —*adj.* **1.** having a bobtail **2.** cut short; abbreviated —*vt.* **1.** to dock the tail of **2.** to cut short; curtail

Boche (bosh) *n.* [Fr. slang, contr. < *tête de caboche,* hard head, head of cabbage] [*also* **b-**] a German, esp. a German soldier in World War I: a derogatory term

bock (bok) *n.* [G. < *Bockbier* < *Einbecker bier* < *Einbeck,* Hanover, where first brewed] a dark German beer: also **bock beer**

bod (bod) *n.* [< BODY] [Colloq.] a person

bode[1] (bōd) *vt.* **bod′ed, bod′ing** [< OE. < *boda,* messenger] to be an omen of; presage —**bode ill** (or **well**) to be a bad (or good) omen —**bode′ful** *adj.*

bode[2] (bōd) *alt. pt. of* BIDE

bo·de·ga (bə dē′gə) *n.* [Sp. < L. < Gr. *apothēkē,* storehouse] a wine shop, esp. in Spanish-speaking countries

bodge (boj) *vt.* [Colloq.] same as BOTCH

bo·dhi·satt·va (bō di sat′və) *n.* [Sans. *bodhi,* enlightenment + *sattva,* being, essence] *Buddhism* a person worthy of nirvana, esp. one who remains on the human plane in order to assist suffering mankind

bod·ice (bod′is) *n.* [altered < *bodies,* pl. of *body*] **1.** the upper part of a woman's dress **2.** a kind of vest for women and girls, usually laced in front and worn as an undergarment or over a blouse or dress

bod·ied (bod′ēd) *adj.* having a body or substance, esp. of a specified kind [able-*bodied*]

bod·i·less (-ē lis) *adj.* without a body; having no material substance; incorporeal

bod·i·ly (-ə lē) *adj.* of, in, by, or to the body —*adv.* **1.** in person; in the flesh **2.** as a single body; in entirety

bod·kin (bod′kən) *n.* [ME. *boidekyn* < ?] **1.** a pointed instrument for making holes in cloth **2.** a long, ornamental hairpin **3.** a thick, blunt needle **4.** [Obs.] a dagger

bod·y (bod′ē) *n.,* *pl.* **bod′ies** [< OE. *bodig,* trunk, orig. sense "cask"] **1.** the whole physical substance of a person, animal, or plant **2.** *a)* the trunk or torso of a man or animal *b)* the part of a garment that covers the trunk **3.** a dead person; corpse **4.** the flesh, as opposed to the spirit **5.** [Colloq.] a person **6.** a group of people or things regarded as a unit [an advisory *body*] **7.** the main or central part of anything **8.** a portion or mass of matter [a *body* of water] **9.** density or consistency, as of a liquid, fabric, etc. **10.** richness of tone or flavour —*vt.* **bod′ied, bod′y·ing** to give a body or substance to —**in a body** as a single unit, esp. to show shared opinion or purpose —**keep body and soul together** to stay alive

bod·y·guard (-gärd′) *n.* a person or persons, usually armed, assigned to guard someone

body-line bowling *Cricket* fast bowling at the batsman's body instead of at the wicket

body politic the people who collectively constitute a political unit under a government

body snatcher a person who steals corpses from graves, as formerly to sell them for anatomical dissection

body stocking a tightfitting garment, usually of one piece, that covers the torso and, sometimes, the legs

bod·y·surf (-surf′) *vi.* to engage in the sport of surfing, lying prone on the wave without the use of a surfboard

Boe·o·tian (bē ō′shən) *adj.* of or like Boeotia or its people, who were reputed to be dull and stupid —*n.* **1.** a native or inhabitant of Boeotia **2.** a dull, stupid person

Boer (bôr, boor, bō′ər) *n.* [Du. *boer,* peasant: see BOOR] a South African whose ancestors were Dutch colonists

bof·fin (bof′in) *n.* [< ?] [Colloq.] a scientist, esp. one engaged in military or government research

Bo·fors gun (bō′fôrz) [< *Bofors,* Sweden, where first made] an automatic double-barrelled antiaircraft gun

bog (bog) *n.* [< Gael. & Ir. *bog,* soft, moist] **1.** wet, spongy ground; a small marsh or swamp **2.** [Slang] a lavatory —*vt., vi.* **bogged, bog′ging** to sink or become stuck in or as in a bog (often with *down*); mire —**bog′gi·ness** *n.* —**bog′gy** *adj.* **bog′gi·er, bog′gi·est**

bog·bean (-bēn′) *n. same as* BUCKBEAN
bo·gey (bō′gē) *n., pl.* **-geys** 1. *same as* BOGY 2. [after Colonel *Bogey,* imaginary first-rate golfer] *Golf* par or, now usually, one stroke more than par on a hole —*vt.* **-geyed, -gey·ing** *Golf* to score one over par on (a hole)
bog·gle (bog′'l) *vi.* **-gled, -gling** [< Scot. *bogle,* spectre; now associated with BUNGLE] 1. to be startled or frightened (*at*); shy away 2. to hesitate (*at*); have scruples 3. to equivocate; quibble (with *at*) —*vt.* [Rare] to bungle; botch —*n.* a boggling
bo·gie¹ (bō′gē) *n., pl.* **-gies** *same as* BOGY
bo·gie² (bō′gē) *n., pl.* **-gies** [< Dial.] 1. an undercarriage on a railway carriage 2. any of the wheels supporting the tread of an armoured tank 3. a small, low, swivelling truck
bo·gle (bō′g'l) *n.* [see BOGGLE] a bogy, or goblin
bog oak oak or other wood preserved in peat bogs
bog·trot·ter (bog′trot′ər) *n.* 1. a person who lives in a boggy country 2. an Irishman Often a derogatory usage
bo·gus (bō′gəs) *adj.* [< ?] not genuine; spurious; counterfeit
bo·gy (bō′gē) *n., pl.* **-gies** [see BOGGLE] 1. an imaginary evil spirit; goblin 2. anything causing great, often needless, fear; bugbear
bo·gy·man, bo·gey·man (bō′gē man′) *n., pl.* **-men′** (-men′) an imaginary frightful being, esp. one used as a threat in disciplining children
bo·hea (bō hē′) *n.* [< *Wu-i Shan,* hills in China where tea was grown] an inferior kind of black tea
Bo·he·mi·an (bō hē′mē ən) *n.* 1. a native or inhabitant of Bohemia 2. *same as* CZECH (*n.* 2) 3. a gypsy 4. [often **b-**] an artist, poet, etc. who lives in an unconventional, nonconforming way —*adj.* 1. of Bohemia, its people, or their language; Czech 2. [often **b-**] like or characteristic of a Bohemian (*n.* 4) —**Bo·he′mi·an·ism** *n.*
boil¹ (boil) *vi.* [< OFr. < L. < *bulla,* a bubble] 1. to bubble up and vaporize by being heated 2. to seethe like boiling liquids 3. to be agitated, as with rage 4. to cook in boiling water or other liquid —*vt.* 1. to heat to the boiling point 2. to cook or process in boiling water, etc. —*n.* the act or state of boiling —**boil away** to evaporate by boiling —**boil down** 1. to lessen in quantity by boiling 2. to condense; summarize —**boil down to** to amount to; to come to as a final outcome —**boil over** 1. to come to a boil and spill over the rim 2. to lose one's temper
boil² (boil) *n.* [< OE. *byl*] an inflamed, painful, pus-filled swelling on the skin, caused by infection
boil·er (boi′lər) *n.* 1. a container in which things are boiled or heated 2. a tank in which water is turned to steam for heating or power 3. a tank for heating water and storing it
boil·er·mak·er (-mā′kər) *n.* a worker who makes or repairs boilers
boiler suit a one-piece suit worn for dirty work, often over ordinary clothes
boiling point 1. the temperature at which a specified liquid boils: water at sea level boils at 100°C or 212°F 2. state of high excitement or anger
bois·ter·ous (bois′tər əs) *adj.* [ME. *boistreous,* crude, coarse < *boistous,* violent] 1. rough and stormy 2. *a)* noisy and unruly *b)* loud and exuberant —**bois′ter·ous·ly** *adv.* —**bois′ter·ous·ness** *n.*
bo·la (bō′lə) *n.* [Sp., a ball < L. *bulla,* a bubble] a S American weapon made of a long cord or thong with heavy balls at the ends, used for throwing at and entangling cattle, etc.: also **bo′las** (-ləs)
bold (bōld) *adj.* [< OE. *beald*] 1. daring; fearless 2. taking liberties; impudent 3. steep or abrupt 4. prominent and clear [to write a *bold* hand] —**make bold** to dare (*to*) —**bold′ly** *adv.* —**bold′ness** *n.*
bold·face (bōld′fās′) *n.* a printing type with a heavy, dark face (Ex.: **face**)
bold·faced (-fāst′) *adj.* impudent; forward
bole (bōl) *n.* [ON. *bolr*] a tree trunk
bo·le·ro (bə ler′ō; *for 3 also* bol′ər ō) *n., pl.* **-ros** [Sp.] 1. a Spanish dance in 3/4 time 2. music for this 3. a sleeveless or sleeved jacket that ends at the waist and is open in front
bo·lí·var (bō lē′vär, bol′ə vər) *n., pl.* **bo·lí·var·es** (bō′li vä′res), **bo·lí′vars** [after Simón *Bolívar* (1783-1830), S American revolutionary] see MONETARY UNITS, table (Venezuela)
boll (bōl) *n.* [< OE. *bolla,* a bowl] the roundish seed pod of a plant, esp. of cotton or flax
bol·lard (bol′ərd, -ärd) *n.* [< ? BOLE + ARD] 1. a strong post on a ship or wharf for securing ropes 2. a post used *a)* to mark a traffic island *b)* to close a path, road, etc. to vehicles
bol·locks (bol′loks) *n.pl. same as* BALLOCKS
boll weevil a small, greyish weevil whose larvae destroy the cotton bolls in which they are hatched
bo·lo (bō′lō) *n., pl.* **-los** [Sp. < native name] a large, single-edged knife used in the Philippines
bo·lo·gna (bə lō′nē, -nyə, -nə) *n.* [after *Bologna,* city in NC Italy] a large smoked sausage of various meats: also **bologna sausage**

bo·lom·e·ter (bō lom′ə tər) *n.* [< Gr. *bolē,* ray < *ballein,* to throw + -METER] *Physics* an instrument for measuring minute differences of radiant heat —**bo·lo·met·ric** (bō′lə met′rik) *adj.*
Bol·she·vik (bol′shə vik′) *n., pl.* **-viks′, Bol′she·vi′ki** (-vē′kē) [Russ. < *bolshe,* the majority] [*also* **b-**] 1. orig., a member of a majority faction of the Social Democratic Party of Russia, which formed the Communist Party after seizing power in the 1917 Revolution 2. a Communist, esp. of the Soviet Union 3. loosely, any radical: hostile usage —*adj.* [*also* **b-**] of or like the Bolsheviks or Bolshevism —**Bol′she·vism** *n.* —**Bol′she·vist** *n., adj.* —**Bol′she·vize′** (-vīz′) *vt.* **-vized′, -viz′ing**
Bol·shie, Bol·shy (bol′shē) *adj.* [contr. < BOLSHEVIK] [*also* **b-**] [Colloq.] 1. difficult to manage; rebellious 2. bad-tempered 3. left wing; radical: a hostile usage —*n.* a Bolshevik
bol·ster (bōl′stər) *n.* [OE.] 1. a long, narrow cushion or pillow 2. a soft pad 3. any bolsterlike object or support 4. *Masonry* a bricklayer's cutting chisel —*vt.* to prop up as with a bolster; support (often with *up*) —**bol′ster·er** *n.*
bolt¹ (bōlt) *n.* [OE.] 1. an arrow with a thick, blunt head, shot from a crossbow 2. a flash of lightning 3. a sudden dash or movement 4. a sliding bar for locking a door, etc. 5. a similar bar in a lock, moved by a key 6. a metal rod with a head, threaded and used with a nut to hold parts together 7. a roll (*of* cloth, paper, etc.) of a given length 8. *Firearms* a sliding bar that pushes the cartridge into place and extracts the empty cartridge case after firing —*vt.* 1. [Archaic] to shoot (an arrow, etc.) 2. to say suddenly; blurt (*out*) 3. to swallow (food) hurriedly; gulp down 4. to fasten as with a bolt 5. to roll (cloth, etc.) into bolts —*vi.* 1. to dash or spring away suddenly; dart 2. *Horticulture* to produce seed prematurely —*adv.* straight; erectly [to sit *bolt* upright] —**bolt from the blue** a sudden, unforeseen occurrence, often an unfortunate one —**shoot one's bolt** to exhaust one's capabilities —**bolt′er** *n.*
bolt² (bōlt) *vt.* [< OFr. *buleter* < ?] 1. to sift (flour, grain, etc.) so as to separate and grade 2. to examine closely —**bolt′er** *n.*
bolt·rope (bōlt′rōp′) *n.* [BOLT¹ + ROPE] a rope sewn into the edge seam of a sail to prevent tearing
bo·lus (bō′ləs) *n., pl.* **bo′lus·es** [L. < Gr. *bōlos,* a lump] 1. a small, round lump or mass, as of chewed food 2. *Vet.* a large pill
bomb (bom) *n.* [< Fr. < It. < L. < Gr. *bombos,* hollow sound] 1. a container filled with an explosive, incendiary, or other chemical, for dropping or hurling, or for detonating by a timing mechanism 2. a sudden, surprising occurrence 3. a shielded device containing radioactive material, used in radiotherapy [a cobalt *bomb*] 4. [often **B-**] the atom bomb or similar nuclear device (preceded by *the*) 5 [Slang] *a)* a success: said esp. of a performance or show *b)* [U.S.] a complete failure 6. [Slang] a large sum of money 7. *Geol.* a globular mass of lava ejected from a volcano —*vt.* to attack or destroy with a bomb or bombs —*vi.* [Slang] to have a complete failure —**like a bomb** [Colloq.] with great speed or success
bom·bard (bom bärd′; *for n.* bom′bärd) *vt.* [< Fr. < *bombarde,* mortar < *bombe,* BOMB] 1. to attack with or as with artillery or bombs 2. to keep attacking with questions, suggestions, etc. 3. to direct a stream of particles, as neutrons, against —*n.* an early type of cannon, hurling stones —**bom·bard′ment** *n.*
bom·bar·dier (bom′bə dir′, -bər-) *n.* 1. a noncommissioned rank in the Royal Artillery 2. [U.S.] person who releases the bombs in a bomber
bom·bast (bom′bast) *n.* [< OFr. < ML. < *bambax,* cotton] pompous, high-sounding talk or writing —**bom·bas′tic** *adj.* —**bom·bas′ti·cal·ly** *adv.*
Bom·bay duck (bom′bā′) any of various dried fishes that are eaten as a relish with curry dishes
bom·ba·zine (bom′bə zēn′, bom′bə zēn′) *n.* [< Fr. < ML. < *bambax,* cotton] a twilled cloth of silk or rayon with worsted, often dyed black
bomb bay a compartment in the fuselage of a bomber that can be opened to drop bombs
bomb·er (bom′ər) *n.* 1. an aircraft designed for dropping bombs 2. a person who uses bombs as for illegal purposes
bomb·proof (bom′proof′) *adj.* capable of withstanding the force of ordinary bombs
bomb·shell (-shel′) *n. same as* BOMB (*n.* 1, 2)
bomb·sight (-sīt′) *n.* an instrument on a bomber for aiming the bombs
bo·na fi·de (bō′nə fīd′, bō′nə fī′dē) [L.] in good faith; without fraud or deceit
bo·nan·za (bə nan′zə, bō-) *n.* [Sp., prosperity, ult. < Gr. *malakia,* a calm at sea] 1. a rich vein of ore 2. any source of wealth or profits
bon·bon (bon′bon′) *n.* [Fr. *bon,* good] a name for various sweets
bonce (bons) *n.* [< ?] 1. a large playing-marble 2. [Slang] the head

bond[1] (bond) *n.* [ME. *bond, band:* see BAND[1]] 1. anything that binds, fastens, or unites; specif., glue, solder, etc. 2. [*pl.*] *a*) fetters; shackles *b*) [Archaic] imprisonment 3. a binding or uniting force 4. a binding agreement; covenant 5. the status of goods kept in a warehouse until taxes are paid 6. *same as* BOND PAPER 7. *Chem.* the means by which atoms or groups of atoms are combined in molecules 8. *Finance* an interest-bearing certificate issued by a government or business, promising to pay the holder a specified sum on a specified date 9. *Law a*) a written obligation to pay specified sums, do or not do specified things, etc. *b*) [Archaic] a bondsman 10. *Masonry* an overlapping arrangement of bricks or stones to provide strength, as in a wall —*vt.* 1. to fasten or unite as with a bond 2. to place (goods) under bond 3. to issue bonds (sense 8) on; mortgage 5. to put under bonded debt —*vi.* to hold together by or as by a bond —**bottled in bond** bottled and stored in bonded warehouses for the length of time stated on the label, as some whisky —**bond'a·ble** *adj.* —**bond'er** *n.*

bond[2] (bond) *n.* [see ff.] [Obs.] a serf or slave —*adj.* in serfdom or slavery

bond·age (bon'dij) *n.* [< Anglo-L. < OE. *bonda* < ON. *bonde* < *bua*, to inhabit] 1. serfdom; slavery 2. subjection to some force or influence

bond·ed (-did) *adj.* 1. subject to or secured by a bond or bonds 2. placed in a government-certified, or bonded, warehouse pending payment of taxes

bond·hold·er (bond'hōl'dər) *n.* an owner of bonds issued by a company, government, or person

bond·man (-mən) *n., pl.* **-men** 1. a feudal serf 2. a man or boy bondservant Also **bondsman** —**bond'maid'** *n.fem.* —**bond'wom'an** *n.fem., pl.* **-wom'en**

bond paper a strong, superior stock of paper, esp. of rag pulp, used for documents, letterheads, etc.

bond·ser·vant (-sur'vənt) *n.* 1. a person bound to service without pay 2. a slave

bond washing a series of illegal deals in bonds made with the intention of avoiding taxation

bone (bōn) *n.* [OE. *ban*] 1. any of the pieces of hard tissue forming the skeleton of most vertebrate animals 2. this hard tissue 3. [*pl.*] *a*) the skeleton *b*) the body 4. a bonelike substance or part 5. a thing made of bone, plastic, etc.; specif., *a*) a corset stay *b*) [*pl.*] [Colloq.] dice 6. [*pl.*] *a*) flat sticks used as clappers in minstrel shows *b*) [with *sing. v.*] an end man in a minstrel show —*vt.* **boned, bon'·ing** 1. to remove the bones from 2. to put whalebone, etc. into 3. [Slang] to steal —*vi.* [U.S. Slang] to study hard and hurriedly; cram (usually with *up*) —**feel in one's bones** to be certain without any real reason —**have a bone to pick** to have something to quarrel about —**make no bones about** [Colloq.] to make no attempt to hide; admit freely —**to the bone** to the bare essentials; minimum —**bone'like' adj.**

bone china translucent china made with white clay to which bone ash or calcium phosphate has been added

bone-dry (bōn'drī') *adj.* dry as bone; very dry

bone·head (-hed') *n.* [Slang] a stupid person

bone·less (-lis) *adj.* without bones; specif., with the bones removed

bone meal crushed or finely ground bones, used as feed for stock or as fertilizer

bon·er (bōn'ər) *n.* [Chiefly U.S. Slang] a stupid blunder

bone-shak·er (bōn'shā'kər) *n.* 1. an early kind of bicycle with solid tyres 2. [Slang] any old or rickety vehicle

bon·fire (bon'fīr') *n.* [ME. *banefyre*, bone fire] a large fire built outdoors

Bonfire Night the fifth of November, the anniversary of the unsuccessful attempt made by Guy Fawkes to blow up Parliament in 1605: it is celebrated by bonfires and fireworks displays

bong (boŋ) *n.* [echoic] a deep, ringing sound, as of a large bell —*vi.* to make this sound

bon·go[1] (bon'gō) *n., pl.* **-gos** [native African name] any of various large African antelopes, having a reddish-brown coat with white stripes

bon·go[2] (boŋ'gō) *n., pl.* **-gos, -goes** [AmSp. < ?] either of a pair of small joined drums, of different pitch, struck with the fingers: in full, **bongo drum**

bon·ho·mie, bon·hom·mie (bon'ə mē'; Fr. bô nô mē') *n.* [Fr. < *bon*, good + *homme*, man] good nature; pleasant, affable manner; amiability

bo·ni·to (bə nēt'ō) *n., pl.* **-tos, -toes, -to:** see PLURAL, II, D, 1 [Sp.] any of several saltwater fishes of the mackerel family, related to the tuna

‡**bon jour** (bon zhōōr') [Fr.] good day; hello

bonk·ers (boŋk'ərz) *adj.* [< ?] [Slang] mad; crazy

bon mot (bon'mō'; Fr. bon mō') *pl.* **bons mots** (bon'-mōz'; Fr. bon mō') [Fr., lit., good word] an apt, clever, or witty remark

bon·net (bon'it) *n.* [OFr. *bonet*] 1. a flat, brimless cap, worn by men and boys in Scotland 2. *a*) a hat with a ribbon, worn by babies or girls *b*) [Colloq.] any hat for a woman or girl 3. *a*) a metal covering, as over a fireplace *b*) a hinged metal cover over the engine of a motor vehicle 4. *Naut.* a strip of canvas fastened by lacing to the bottom of a sail to increase its area —*vt.* to put a bonnet on

bon·ny, bon·nie (bon'ē) *adj.* **-ni·er, -ni·est** [< Fr. *bon*, good < L. *bonus*] [Now Chiefly Scot. or Eng. Dial.] 1. handsome or pretty, with a healthy, cheerful glow 2. fine; pleasant —**bon'ni·ly** *adv.* —**bon'ni·ness** *n.*

bon·sai (bon sī') *n.* [Jap., lit., planted in a tray] *n.* 1. the art of dwarfing and shaping trees, shrubs, etc. 2. *pl.* **bon·sai'** such a tree or shrub

‡**bon soir** (bon swär') [Fr.] good evening

bo·nus (bō'nəs) *n., pl.* **bo'nus·es** [L., good] 1. anything given or paid in addition to the customary or required amount as an incentive, reward, etc. 2. an extra dividend allotted to shareholders out of profits 3. a dividend paid to insurance policyholders

bon vi·vant (bon'vi vänt'; Fr. bon vē vän') *pl.* **bons vi·vants** (bon'vi vänts'; Fr. bon vē vän') [Fr.] one who enjoys good food and other luxuries

bon voy·age (bon'voi äzh'; Fr. bon vwá yàzh') [Fr.] pleasant journey: a farewell to a traveller

bon·y (bō'nē) *adj.* **bon'i·er, bon'i·est** 1. of or like bone 2. having many bones 3. having protruding bones 4. thin; emaciated —**bon'i·ness** *n.*

bonze (bonz) *n.* [Fr. < Port. *bonzo* < Jap. *bonsō*, prob. < Chin. *fan seng*, religious person] a Buddhist monk

boo (bōō) *interj., n., pl.* **boos** [echoic] a prolonged sound made to show disapproval, scorn, etc., or, more abruptly, to startle —*vi., vt.* **booed, boo'ing** to make this sound (at)

boob (bōōb) *n.* [Slang] 1. a booby; foolish person 2. an embarrassing mistake; blunder 3. a female breast: sometimes considered a vulgar usage —*vi.* [Slang] to make a blunder

boo-boo, boo·boo (bōō'bōō') *n., pl.* **-boos'** [Slang] a stupid or foolish mistake

boo·by (bōō'bē) *n., pl.* **-bies** [prob. < Sp. *bobo*, stupid] 1. a stupid or foolish person 2. a tropical, diving sea bird related to the gannet 3. the one doing worst in a game, contest, etc.

booby prize a prize, usually ridiculous, given in fun to whoever has done worst in a game, race, etc.

booby trap 1. any device for tricking a person unawares 2. a mine set to be exploded by some action of the unsuspecting victim —**boo'by-trap'** *vt.* **-trapped'**, **-trap'ping**

boo·dle (bōō'd'l) *n.* [< Du. *boedel*, property] 1. something given as a bribe 2. the loot taken in a robbery

boo·gie-woo·gie (bōōg'ē wōōg'ē) *n.* [? echoic of the characteristic "walking" bass] a style of jazz piano playing in which repeated bass figures in 8/8 rhythm accompany the melodic variations

boo·hoo (bōō'hōō') *vi.* **-hooed', -hoo'ing** [echoic] to weep noisily —*n., pl.* **-hoos'** noisy weeping

book (bōōk) *n.* [OE. *boc*, pl. *bec*, akin to OE. *bece*, beech: runes were first carved on beech tablets] 1. *a*) a number of sheets of paper, etc. with writing or printing on them, fastened together along one edge, usually between protective covers *b*) a relatively long literary work, scientific writing, etc. 2. a main division of a literary work 3. *a*) a number of blank or ruled sheets or printed forms bound together [an account *book*] *b*) a record or account kept in this 4. the words of an opera, etc.; libretto 5. a booklike package, as of matches or tickets 6. a record of bets, as on horse races 7. something regarded as a subject for study [the *book* of life] 8. the facts or characteristics connected with a person or subject, esp. as being understandable [an open *book*] or obscure, finished with, etc. [a closed *book*] 9. *Bridge*, etc. a specified number of tricks that must be won before scoring can take place —*vt.* 1. to record in a book; list 2. to engage (rooms, performers, etc.) ahead of time 3. to record charges against on a police record —*adj.* in, from, or according to books or accounts —**book in** 1. to make a reservation or appointment 2. to register at a hotel —**bring to book** 1. to force to explain 2. to reprimand —**by the book** according to the rules —**close the books** *Bookkeeping* to make no further entries —**in one's book** in one's opinion —**in someone's good** (or bad) **books** in (or out of) someone's favour, or good graces —**keep books** to keep a record of business transactions —**know like a book** to know well or fully —**make a book** [Slang] to make or accept bets —**on the books** 1. recorded 2. enrolled —**the Book** the Bible —**throw the book at** [Slang] 1. to place all possible charges against (an accused person) 2. to give the maximum punishment to —**book'er** *n.*

book·bind·ing (-bīn'diŋ) *n.* the art, trade, or business of binding books —**book'bind'er** *n.* —**book'bind'er·y** *n., pl.* **-er·ies**

book·case (-kās') *n.* a set of shelves or a cabinet for holding books

book club an organization that sells books, usually at reduced prices, to members who undertake to buy a minimum number of them annually

book·end (-end') *n.* an ornamental weight or bracket at the end of a row of books to keep them upright

book·ie (-ē) *n.* [Colloq.] *same as* BOOKMAKER (sense 2)

book·ing (-iŋ) *n.* **1.** a reservation of a room, seat, berth, etc. **2.** an engagement, as for a lecture, performance, etc.

book·ish (-ish) *adj.* **1.** of books **2.** inclined to read and study; scholarly **3.** having mere book learning; pedantic; stodgy —**book′ish·ness** *n.*

book·keep·ing (-kēp′iŋ) *n.* the work of keeping a systematic record of business transactions —**book′keep′-er** *n.*

book learning knowledge gained from reading or formal education rather than from practical experience: also **book′-lore′** (-lôr′) *n.*

book·let (-lit) *n.* a small, often paper-covered book

book·mak·er (-māk′ər) *n.* **1.** a maker of books **2.** a person in the business of taking bets, as on horse races —**book′-mak′ing** *n.*

book·mark (-märk′) *n.* anything slipped between the pages of a book to mark a place

Book of Common Prayer the official book of services and prayers used in Anglican churches

book·plate (-plāt′) *n.* a label pasted in a book to identify its owner

book·rest (-rest′) *n.* *same as* BOOKSTAND (sense 1)

book review an article or talk in which a book is discussed and critically analysed

book·sell·er (-sel′ər) *n.* the owner or manager of a bookshop

book·shelf (-shelf′) *n.*, *pl.* **-shelves** a shelf on which books are kept

book·shop (-shop′) *n.* a shop where books are sold

book·stack (-stak′) *n.* a series of bookshelves, one over the other, as in a library

book·stall (-stôl′) *n.* a stand, booth, or counter, often one outdoors, where books are sold

book·stand (-stand′) *n.* **1.** a stand for holding a book open before a reader **2.** *same as* BOOKSTALL

book value the value as shown in account books; specif., the value of the capital stock of a business as shown by the excess of assets over liabilities

book·worm (-wurm′) *n.* **1.** an insect or insect larva that harms books by feeding on the binding, paste, etc. **2.** one who reads or studies much

Bool·e·an algebra (boo′lē ən) [after G. Boole (1815-64), Brit. mathematician] a mathematical structure, orig. devised to show the homomorphism between arithmetic and symbolic logic: it now forms the basis of the algebraic theory of sets

boom¹ (boom) *vi.* [echoic] to make a deep, hollow, resonant sound —*vt.* to utter with such a sound —*n.* a booming sound, as of thunder, heavy guns, etc.

boom² (boom) *n.* [Du., a tree, beam] **1.** a spar extending from a mast to hold the bottom of a sail outstretched **2.** a long beam extending as from an upright to lift and guide something [a microphone *boom*] **3.** a barrier of chains or timbers to keep ships out or to keep floating logs in —*vt.* **1.** to stretch out (sails) with a boom **2.** to place a boom in (a river, etc.) —*vi.* to sail or move at top speed (usually with *along*)

boom³ (boom) *vi.* [< ? prec. *vi.*; later associated with BOOM¹] to increase suddenly or grow swiftly; flourish [business *boomed*] —*vt.* **1.** to cause to flourish **2.** to promote vigorously —*n.* a period of business prosperity, etc. —*adj.* of or resulting from a boom in business [a *boom* town]

boom·er·ang (boom′ə raŋ) *n.* [Abor.] **1.** a flat, curved stick that can be thrown so that it will return to the thrower: used as a weapon by Australian aborigines **2.** something that goes contrary to the expectation of its originator and results in his disadvantage or harm —*vi.* to act as a boomerang

boon¹ (boon) *n.* [ON. *bon*, a petition] **1.** a welcome benefit; blessing **2.** [Archaic] a request or favour

boon² (boon) *adj.* [< OFr. < L. *bonus*, good] **1.** [Archaic or Poet.] kind, generous, pleasant, etc. **2.** merry; convivial: now only in **boon companion**

boon·docks (boon′doks′) *n.pl.* [orig. military slang < Tag. *bundok*, mountain] [U.S. Colloq.] **1.** a wild, heavily wooded area; wilderness **2.** any remote rural region; hinterland Used with *the*

boor (boor) *n.* [Du. *boer* < MDu. *gheboer*, fellow dweller < *ghe-*, with, co- + *bouwen*, to cultivate] **1.** orig., a peasant or farm worker **2.** a rude, awkward, or ill-mannered person —**boor′ish** *adj.* —**boor′ish·ly** *adv.* —**boor′ish·ness** *n.*

boost (boost) *vt.* [< ?] **1.** to raise by or as by a push from behind or below **2.** to urge others to support; promote **3.** to increase in amount, power, etc. —*n.* **1.** a push to help a person or thing upwards or forwards **2.** an act that helps or promotes **3.** an increase in amount, power, etc.

boost·er (boos′tər) *n.* **1.** one who boosts; ardent supporter **2.** any device providing added power, thrust, etc. **3.** any of the early stages of a multistage rocket; also, a rocket system that launches a spacecraft, etc.: also **booster rocket**

booster shot (or **injection**) a later injection of a vaccine for maintaining immunity

boot¹ (boot) *n.* [OFr. *bote*] **1.** a protective covering of leather, rubber, etc. for the foot and part of the leg **2.** boot-shaped instrument of torture **3.** the luggage compartment of a motor car **4.** [Colloq.] a kick —*vt.* **1.** to put boots on **2.** to kick **3.** [Slang] to dismiss (often with *out*) —**die with one's boots on** to die in action —**lick the boots of** to be servile towards —**put the boot in** **1.** to kick a person when he is already down **2.** to torment a person who is already overcome —**the boot** [Slang] dismissal; discharge

boot² (boot) *n.*, *vt.*, *vi.* [< OE. *bot*, advantage] [Archaic] profit —**to boot** besides; in addition

boot·black (-blak′) *n.* *Chiefly U.S. var. of* SHOEBLACK

boot·ee (boot′ē, boo tē′) *n.* **1.** a short boot or light overshoe worn by women and children **2.** a baby's soft, knitted or cloth shoe

Bo·ö·tes (bō ō′tēz) [L. < Gr. *boōtēs*, lit., ploughman] a N constellation including the star Arcturus

booth (booth) *n.*, *pl.* **booths** (boothz) [< ON. *buth*, temporary dwelling < *bua*, to dwell, akin to BONDAGE] **1.** a stall for the sale or display of goods, as at a market **2.** a small structure or enclosure for telephoning, voting, etc. **3.** a small, partially enclosed compartment with a table and seats, as in some restaurants

boot·jack (boot′jak′) *n.* a device to grip a boot heel, for helping a person to pull off boots

boot·leg (-leg′) *vt.*, *vi.* **-legged′**, **-leg′ging** [in allusion to concealing objects in the leg of a boot] to make, carry, or sell (esp. alcoholic liquor) illegally —*adj.* bootlegged; illegal —**boot′leg′ger** *n.*

boot·less (-lis) *adj.* [BOOT² + -LESS] useless —**boot′less·ly** *adv.* —**boot′less·ness** *n.*

boot·lick·er (-lik′ər) *n.* [Colloq.] a person who tries to gain favour with someone by fawning, servility, etc.

boot·strap (-strap′) *n.* **1.** a strap on a boot for pulling it on **2.** *Computers* a technique for loading the first few program instructions into a computer and using these to enable the rest of the program to be introduced from an input device —*adj.* undertaken without others' help [a *bootstrap* operation] —**lift** (or **raise**) **oneself by the** (or **one's own**) **bootstraps** to achieve success by one's own unaided efforts

boo·ty (boot′ē) *n.*, *pl.* **-ties** [< MLowG. *bute*; infl. by BOOT²] **1.** spoils of war **2.** any loot **3.** any valuable gain; prize: a humorous usage

booze (booz) *vi.* **boozed, booz′ing** [< Du. *buizen*] [Colloq.] to drink too much alcoholic liquor —*n.* [Colloq.] alcoholic liquor —**booz′y** *adj.* **-i·er, -i·est**

booz·er (booz′ər) *n.* [Colloq.] **1.** a person who is fond of drinking alcohol **2.** a public house or bar

bop (bop) *n.* [< earlier *be-bop* < ?] a style of jazz with complex rhythms and harmonies, etc.

bo·ra (bôr′ə) *n.* [It. dial. for *borea* < L. *boreas*, Boreas, god of the north wind] a fierce, cold northeasterly wind of the Adriatic sea

bo·rac·ic (bə ras′ik) *adj.* *same as* BORIC

bor·age (bor′ij, bur′-) *n.* [< OFr. < ML. < ? *burra*, coarse hair] an annual plant with brilliant blue flowers and hairy leaves

bo·rate (bôr′āt) *n.* a salt or ester of boric acid —*vt.* **-rat·ed**, **-rat·ing** to treat or mix with borax or boric acid —**bo′-rat·ed** *adj.*

bo·rax (bôr′aks) *n.* [< OFr. < ML. < Ar. < Per. *būrah*] a white, crystalline salt, Na₂B₄O₇, used as a flux and in glass, soaps, etc.

bo·ra·zon (bôr′ə zən) *n.* [BOR(ON) + AZ(O)- + -ON] a crystalline modification of boron nitride, harder and more heat-resistant than diamond

bor·bo·ryg·mus (bô′bə rig′mus) *n.* [Gr.] the rumbling noise caused by gas in the intestines

Bor·deaux (bôr dō′) *n.* red or white wine from the region around Bordeaux

Bordeaux mixture a mixture of lime, water and copper sulphate, used as a spray on trees and plants to kill insects and fungi

bor·der (bôr′dər) *n.* [< OFr. < OHG. *bord*, margin] **1.** an edge or a part near an edge; margin **2.** a dividing line between countries, etc.; frontier **3.** a narrow, ornamental strip along an edge —*vt.* **1.** to provide with a border **2.** to bound —*adj.* of, forming, or near a border —**border on** (or **upon**) **1.** to be next to **2.** to be like; be nearly —**the Borders** the district on or near the boundary between Scotland and England —**bor′dered** *adj.*

bor·der·er (bôr′dər ər) *n.* a person living near a border

bor·der·land (-land′) *n.* **1.** land forming or near a border **2.** a vague, uncertain condition

bor·der·line (-līn′) *n.* a boundary —*adj.* on the boundary of what is acceptable, normal, etc.

bore¹ (bôr) *vt.* **bored, bor′ing** [< OE. < *bor*, auger] **1.** to make a hole in or through with a drill, etc. **2.** to make (a hole, tunnel, etc.) as by drilling **3.** to force (one's way), as through a crowd —*vi.* to bore a hole or passage —*n.* **1.** a hole made by or as by boring **2.** *a)* the hollow part of a tube, gun barrel, etc. *b)* its inside diameter; calibre

bore² (bôr) *n.* [< ON. *bara*, a billow] a high, abrupt tidal wave in a narrow channel

bore³ (bôr) *vt.* **bored, bor'ing** [< ?] to weary by being dull or monotonous —*n.* a tiresome, dull person or thing

bore⁴ (bôr) *pt. of* BEAR¹

bo·re·al (bôr'ē əl) *adj.* [LL. after *Boreas*, in Gr. myth. the god of the north wind] 1. northern 2. of the northern zone of plant and animal life lying just below the tundra

bore·dom (bôr'dəm) *n.* the condition of being bored or uninterested; ennui

bor·er (bôr'ər) *n.* 1. a tool for boring 2. an insect or worm that bores holes in trees, fruit, etc.

bo·ric (bôr'ik) *adj.* of or containing boron

boric acid a white, crystalline, weakly acid compound, H_3BO_3, used as a mild antiseptic

born (bôrn) *alt. pp. of* BEAR¹ —*adj.* 1. brought into life or being 2. by birth [French-*born*] 3. natural [a *born* athlete] 4. [Colloq.] since birth [in all my *born* days] —**not born yesterday** not naive or lacking in experience

borne (bôrn) *alt. pp. of* BEAR¹

bo·ron (bôr'on) *n.* [< BOR(AX) + -*on* as in (CARB)ON] a non-metallic chemical element occurring only in combination, as with sodium and oxygen in borax: symbol, B; at. wt., 10.811; at. no., 5

boron carbide a compound of boron and carbon, B_4C, almost as hard as diamond: used as an abrasive and in control rods for nuclear reactors

bor·ough (bur'ə) *n.* [< OE. *burg*, town, fortress] 1. a town with a municipal corporation granted by royal charter 2. a town that sends representatives to Parliament 3. in the United States a) a self-governing, incorporated town b) any of the five administrative units of New York City

bor·row (bor'ō) *vt., vi.* [< OE. *borgian*, to borrow, lend] 1. to take or receive (something) with the understanding that one will return it or an equivalent 2. to adopt (something) as one's own [to *borrow* a theory] 3. to adopt (a word) from another language 4. *Arith.* in subtraction, to take from the next higher denomination in the minuend and add to the next lower —**borrowed plumes** 1. wearing finery not belonging to oneself to make a display 2. any disguise or camouflage intended to deceive —**borrow trouble** to worry prematurely —**bor'row·er** *n.*

borsch (bôrsh, bôrshch) *n.* [Russ. *borshch*] a Russian beetroot soup, served hot or cold, usually with sour cream: also **bortsch**

Bor·stal (bôr'stəl) *n.* [< *Borstal*, town in England] [*also* b-] a treatment centre for young offenders (c. 15-21 years old)

bort (bôrt) *n.* [< ? OFr. *bourt*, bastard] a poorly crystallized variety of diamond used as an abrasive in industry: also **boart**

bor·zoi (bôr'zoi) *n.* [Russ., swift] any of a breed of large dog with a narrow head, long legs, and silky coat

bos·cage (bos'kij) *n.* [OE. < Frank. *busk*, forest] a natural growth of trees or shrubs

bosh (bosh) *n., interj.* [Turk., empty, worthless] [Colloq.] nonsense

bosk (bosk) *n.* [ME. *bosk*, BUSH¹] a small wooded place; thicket

bosk·y (bos'kē) *adj.* covered with trees or shrubs

bo's'n (bōs'n) *n.* contracted form of BOATSWAIN

bos·om (booz'əm, boo'zəm) *n.* [OE. *bosm*] 1. the human breast; specif., a woman's breasts 2. a thing thought of as like this [the *bosom* of the sea] 3. the breast regarded as the source of feelings 4. the enclosing space formed by the breast and arms in embracing 5. the midst [in the *bosom* of one's family] 6. the part of a garment that covers the breast —*vt.* 1. to embrace 2. to conceal —*adj.* close; intimate [a *bosom* friend]

bos·om·y (-ē) *adj.* having large breasts

bos·on (bō'sən) *n.* [after Sir J. C. *Bose* (1858-1937), Ind. physicist] a subatomic particle, as a photon or any of certain mesons, that does not obey the Pauli exclusion principle

boss¹ (bos) *n.* [Du. *baas*, a master] 1. a person in authority over employees, as an employer or supervisor 2. [U.S.] a person who controls a political organization —*vt.* 1. to act as boss of 2. [Colloq.] to order (a person) about —*adj.* [Colloq.] chief

boss² (bos) *n.* [< OFr. *boce*, a swelling] 1. a raised part on a flat surface; esp., a decorative knob, stud, etc. 2. *Geol.* a rounded mass of igneous rock laid bare by erosion 3. *Mech.* the enlarged part of a shaft —*vt.* to decorate with knobs, studs, etc.

bos·sa no·va (bos'ə nō'və) [Port., lit., new bump, new tendency < *bossa*, a bump + *nova* new] 1. jazz samba music originating in Brazil 2. a dance for couples performed to this music

boss·y (bos'ē) *adj.* **boss'i·er, boss'i·est** [BOSS¹ + -Y²] [Colloq.] domineering or dictatorial —**boss'i·ly** *adv.* —**boss'i·ness** *n.*

Bos·ton terrier (bos'tən) any of a breed of small dog having a smooth, dark coat with white markings

bo·sun (bōs'n) *n.* same as BOATSWAIN

bot (bot) *n.* [< ? Gael. < *boiteag*, maggot] the larva of the botfly

bot. 1. botanical 2. botanist 3. botany 4. bottle

bo·tan·i·cal (bə tan'i k'l) *adj.* [< ML. < Gr. < *botanē*, a plant] 1. of plants and plant life 2. of or connected with the science of botany Also **bo·tan'ic** —*n.* a vegetable drug prepared from bark, roots, herbs, etc. —**bo·tan'i·cal·ly** *adv.*

bot·a·nize (bot'ə nīz') *vi.* **-nized', -niz'ing** 1. to gather plants for botanical study 2. to study plants, esp. in their natural environment —*vt.* to investigate the plant life of (a region)

bot·a·ny (bot'ə nē) *n.* [BOTAN(ICAL) + -Y³] 1. the science, a branch of biology, that deals with plants, their life, structure, growth, etc. 2. the plant life of an area 3. the characteristics of a plant or plant group —**bot'a·nist** *n.*

botch (boch) *vt.* [ME. *bocchen*, to repair < ? Du. *botsen*, to patch] 1. to repair or patch clumsily 2. to bungle —*n.* 1. a badly patched place or part 2. a bungled piece of work —**botch'er** *n.* —**botch'y** *adj.*

bot·fly (bot'flī') *n., pl.* **-flies'** [see BOT] a fly whose larvae are parasitic in horses, sheep, etc.

both (bōth) *adj., pron.* [< OE. *ba tha*, both these] the two (of them) [*both* (birds) sang] —*conj., adv.* together; equally; as well: used correlatively with *and* [*both* tired *and* sick]

both·er (both'ər) *vt., vi.* [prob. Anglo-Ir. for POTHER] 1. to worry, trouble, annoy, etc. 2. to bewilder 3. to concern or trouble (oneself) —*n.* 1. worry; trouble 2. a person who gives trouble —*interj.* an expression of annoyance, etc.

both·er·a·tion (both'ə rā'shən) *n., interj.* [Colloq.] same as BOTHER

both·er·some (both'ər səm) *adj.* causing bother; annoying; troublesome; irksome

both·y, both·ie (both'ē) *n.* [< BOOTH] [Scot.] 1. a small roughly-built shelter or outhouse 2. a poorly-finished dwelling for farm workers

bo tree (bō) [Sinh. *bo* < Pali *bodhi*, wisdom + *taru*, tree] a fig tree sacred to Buddhists as the tree under which Buddha received enlightenment, and to Hindus as the tree under whose leaves Vishnu was born

bott (bot) *n.* same as BOT

bot·tle (bot'l) *n.* [< OFr. < ML. *butticula*, a bottle < LL. *buttis*, a cask] 1. a container, esp. for liquids, usually of glass or plastic, with a relatively narrow neck 2. the amount that a bottle holds 3. milk from an infant's nursing bottle —*vt.* **-tled, -tling** 1. to put into a bottle or bottles 2. to store under pressure in a cylinder, etc. [*bottled* gas] —**bottle up** 1. to shut in (enemy troops, etc.) 2. to hold in or suppress (emotions) —**hit the bottle** [Slang] to drink much alcoholic liquor —**bot'tle·ful** *n., pl.* **-fuls'** —**bot'tler** *n.*

bottle green a dark green colour

bot·tle·neck (-nek') *n.* 1. a place, as a narrow road, where traffic is slowed down or halted 2. any point at which progress is slowed down

bot·tle·nose (-nōz') *n.* a kind of dolphin, grey or greenish, with a bottle-shaped snout

bottle party a party to which guests bring drink with them

bottle tree any of a genus of Australian trees, some of which have a swollen, bottle-shaped trunk

bot·tom (bot'əm) *n.* [< OE. *botm, bodan*, ground] 1. the lowest part 2. the lowest or last position 3. the farthest part [the *bottom* of the lane] 4. the part on which something rests; base 5. the side or end that is underneath 6. the seat of a chair 7. the ground beneath a body of water 8. low land through which a river flows; flood plain 9. a) a ship's keel b) a ship 10. basic meaning or cause; source 11. stamina 12. [Colloq.] the buttocks —*adj.* of, at, or on the bottom; lowest, last, etc. —*vt.* 1. to provide (a chair, etc.) with a bottom 2. to understand; fathom 3. to place or base (*on* or *upon*) —*vi.* 1. to reach the bottom 2. to be based —**at bottom** fundamentally; actually —**be at the bottom of** to be the real reason for —**bottom out** to level off at a low point, as prices —**bottoms up!** [Colloq.] drink deep!: a toast

bottom drawer a woman's collection of linen, clothing, etc., made in preparation for marriage

bot·tom·less (-lis) *adj.* 1. having no bottom 2. very deep, endless, etc.

bot·tom·ry (-rē) *n.* [< BOTTOM, *n.* 8 b, after Du. *bodomerij*, bottomry] a contract by which a shipowner borrows money for equipment, repairs, etc. pledging the ship as security

bot·u·lism (bot'yŏŏ liz'm) *n.* [< G. < L. *botulus*, sausage + -*ismus*, -ISM: from early German cases involving sausages] poisoning resulting from the toxin produced by a certain bacillus sometimes found in foods improperly tinned or preserved

bou·clé (boō klā) *n.* [Fr., pp. of *boucler*, to buckle, curl] 1.

a curly yarn that gives the fabric made from it a tufted or knotted texture **2.** fabric made from this yarn

bou·doir (bōōd'wär) *n.* [Fr., lit., pouting room < *bouder*, to pout, sulk] a woman's bedroom, dressing room, or private sitting room

bouf·fant (bōō fän') *adj.* [Fr., prp. of *bouffer*, to puff out] **1.** having extra height and width through backcombing, as some hairstyles **2.** puffed out; full, as some skirts

bou·gain·vil·lae·a, bou·gain·vil·le·a (bōō'gən vil'ē ə) *n.* [ModL., after L. A. de *Bougainville* (1729–1811), Fr. explorer] a woody tropical plant having flowers with large, showy, purple or red bracts

bough (bou) *n.* [OE. *bog*, shoulder, hence branch] a branch of a tree, esp. a main branch

bought (bôt) *pt. & pp. of* BUY

bou·gie (bōō'zhē) *n.* [Fr., wax candle < *Bougie*, Algerian seaport from which wax was exported] **1.** a wax candle **2.** *Med.* a slender instrument introduced into a body canal, esp. the uretha or rectum, as for dilating it

bouil·la·baisse (bōōl'yə bās'; *Fr.* bōō yä bes') *n.* [Fr. < Pr. < *bouli*, to boil + *abaissa*, to settle] a soup made with several kinds of fish

bouil·lon (bool'yon; -yən; *Fr.* bōō yōn') *n.* [Fr. < *bouillir*, to boil] a clear broth, esp. of beef

boul·der (bōl'dər) *n.* [< ME. *bulderstan* < Scand., as in Sw. *bullersten*, lit., noisy stone] any large rock worn smooth and round by weather and water

boulder clay unstratified material left by a glacier, consisting of fine clay, boulders and pebbles

bou·le[1] (bōō'lē) *n.* [Gr. *boule*] **1.** the ancient Greek senate **2.** the modern Greek parliament

boule[2] (bōōl) *n.* [Fr., ball] **1.** [*usually pl.*] a French game similar to bowls **2.** a gambling game like roulette **3.** a small rounded mass, as of synthetic ruby, produced by the fusion of alumina

boule[3], **boulle** *n.* same as BUHL

boul·e·vard (bōōl'ə värd') *n.* [Fr. < MDu. *bolwerc*, bulwark] a broad street, often lined with trees, plots of grass, etc.

boult (bōlt) *vt.* same as BOLT[2]

bounce (bouns) *vt.* **bounced, bounc'ing** [akin to Du. *bonzen* & LowG. *bunsen*, to thump] **1.** orig., to bump or thump **2.** to cause to hit against a surface so as to spring back **3.** [Slang] to put (a person) out by force —*vi.* **1.** to spring back after striking a surface; rebound **2.** to jump; leap [*bounce* out of bed] **3.** to boast **4.** [Slang] to be returned to the payee by a bank: said of a worthless cheque —*n.* **1.** *a*) a bouncing; rebound *b*) a leap or jump **2.** capacity for bouncing **3.** impudence; bluster **4.** [Colloq.] energy; zest —**bounce back** [Colloq.] to recover strength, spirits, etc. quickly —**bounc'y** *adj.*

bounc·er (boun'sər) *n.* **1.** [Slang] a man hired to remove disorderly people from a nightclub, etc. **2.** [Colloq.] an outrageous or barefaced lie

bounc·ing (-siŋ) *adj.* big, healthy, strong, etc.

bouncing Bet (bet) a perennial plant with clusters of pinkish flowers; soapwort

bound[1] (bound) *vi.* [Fr. *bondir*, to leap, orig., to echo < LL. < L. *bombus*, a humming (see BOMB)] **1.** to move with a leap or series of leaps **2.** to bounce or rebound, as a ball —*n.* **1.** a jump; leap **2.** a bounce

bound[2] (bound) *pt. & pp. of* BIND —*adj.* **1.** tied **2.** closely connected **3.** certain; destined [*bound* to win] **4.** obliged [legally *bound* to pay] **5.** constipated **6.** provided with a binding, as a book —**bound up in** (or **with**) **1.** devoted to **2.** involved in

bound[3] (bound) *adj.* [ME. < *boun*, ready < ON. *buinn*, pp. of *bua*: see BONDAGE] going; headed [*bound* for home]

bound[4] (bound) *n.* [< OFr. < ML. *bodina*, boundary] **1.** a boundary; limit **2.** [*pl.*] a place near or enclosed by a boundary —*vt.* **1.** to limit; confine **2.** to be a limit or boundary to —*vi.* to have a boundary (*on* another country, etc.) —**beat the bounds** to walk or ride ceremoniously around the boundaries of a parish or town —**out of bounds 1.** beyond the boundaries or limits **2.** forbidden

-bound (bound) a combining form meaning going or headed in (a specified direction) [*southbound*]

bound·a·ry (boun'drē, -dər ē) *n., pl.* **-ries** [altered after BOUND[4] < ML. *bunnarium*] **1.** any line or thing marking a limit; bound; border **2.** *Cricket a*) the marked limit of the playing area *b*) a stroke that hits the ball beyond this limit, scoring four or six runs

boundary rider [Aust & N.Z.] an employee on a sheep or cattle farm whose job is to maintain fences in good repair, etc.

bound·en (boun'dən) *adj.* [old pp. of BIND] **1.** under obligation **2.** obligatory [*bounden* duty]

bound·er (-dar) *n.* [BOUND[1] + -ER] [Colloq.] an ill-mannered fellow; cad

bound·less (bound'lis) *adj.* having no bounds; unlimited —**bound'less·ly** *adv.* —**bound'less·ness** *n.*

boun·te·ous (boun'tē əs) *adj.* [< OFr. *bontive*: see BOUNTY]

same as BOUNTIFUL —**boun'te·ous·ly** *adv.* —**boun'te·ous·ness** *n.*

boun·ti·ful (-tə f'l) *adj.* **1.** giving freely and graciously; generous **2.** abundant; plentiful —**boun'ti·ful·ly** *adv.* —**boun'ti·ful·ness** *n.*

boun·ty (-tē) *n., pl.* **-ties** [< OFr. < L. < *bonus*, good] **1.** generosity **2.** a generous gift **3.** a reward or premium, as one given by a government for the performance of certain services

bou·quet (bō kā'; *also, & for 2 usually,* bōō-) *n.* [Fr.] **1.** a bunch of cut flowers **2.** a fragrant smell or aroma, esp. of a wine or brandy **3.** a compliment

‡**bouquet gar·ni** (gär nē') a bunch of herbs tied together and used for flavouring soups, stews, etc.

bour·bon (bur'bən, boor'-) *n.* [< *Bourbon* County, Kentucky, U.S.] [U.S.] [*sometimes* B-] a whisky made from a mash of at least 51% maize and aged for not less than two years —*adj.* of or made with such whisky

bour·don (bōōr'dən) *n.* [Fr. < ML. *burdo*, drone (bee), wind instrument] **1.** a bass stop on the organ **2.** the drone of a bagpipe

bour·geois (boor zhwä', boor'zhwä) *n., pl.* **-geois'** [Fr. < OFr. < ML. < LL. *burgus*, castle] **1.** a shopkeeper **2.** a member of the bourgeoisie **3.** a person whose beliefs, attitudes, etc. are middle-class —*adj.* of or characteristic of the bourgeoisie; middle-class, conventional, smug, materialistic, etc. —**bour·geoise'** (-zhwäz') *n.fem.*

bour·geoi·sie (boor'zhwä zē') *n.* [with *sing. or pl. v.*] **1.** the social class between the aristocracy or very wealthy and the working class; middle class **2.** in Marxist doctrine, capitalists as a social class antithetical to the proletariat

bour·geon (bur'jən) *n., vt., vi.* same as BURGEON

bourn[1], **bourne**[1] (bôrn, boorn) *n.* [OE. *burna*, a stream] a brook or stream

bourn[2], **bourne**[2] (bôrn, boorn) *n.* [< Fr. < OFr. < ML. *bodina*: see BOUND[4]] [Archaic] **1.** a limit; boundary **2.** a goal; objective **3.** a domain

bour·rée (bōō rā') *n.* [Fr. < ? *bourrir*, to whir] **1.** a lively, 17th-cent. French dance in duple time **2.** music for this

bourse (boors) *n.* [Fr., a purse < OFr. < ML. *bursa*, a bag < Gr. *byrsa*, a hide] a stock exchange; specif., [B-] the stock exchange of Paris

bou·stro·phe·don (bōō'strə fēd'ən) *adj.* [Gr., lit., turning like an ox in ploughing < *bous*, ox + *strephein*, to turn] designating or of an ancient form of writing in which the lines run alternately from right to left and left to right

bout (bout) *n.* [for earlier *bought* < ME. *bught*] **1.** a struggle; contest or match **2.** a period of time taken up by some activity, illness, etc.

bou·tique (bōō tēk') *n.* [Fr. < Gr. *apothēkē*: see APOTHECARY] a small shop, or a part of a department store, selling fashionable, expensive items

bou·ton·niere, bou·ton·nière (bōōt'on ir', -yer') *n.* [Fr. *boutonnière*, a buttonhole] [U.S.] a buttonhole (sense 2)

bou·zou·ki (bōō zōō'kē) *n.* [< ModGr., prob. < Turk.] a stringed musical instrument of Greece, somewhat like a mandolin

bo·vine (bō'vīn, -vin, -vēn) *adj.* [< LL. < L. *bovis*, gen. of *bos*, ox] **1.** of an ox or cow **2.** slow, dull, stupid, stolid, etc.

Bov·ril (bov'ril) *a trademark for* a concentrated extract of beef used as a drink and for gravies, etc. —*n.* [b-] this substance

bow[1] (bou) *vi.* [< OE. *bugan*, to bend] **1.** [Dial.] to bend or stoop **2.** to bend the head or body in respect, greeting, agreement, etc. **3.** to yield, as to authority —*vt.* **1.** [Dial.] to bend **2.** to bend (the head) in respect, prayer, shame, etc. **3.** to indicate (agreement, thanks, etc.) by bowing **4.** to weigh (*down*); overwhelm —*n.* a bending of the head or body, as in respect, greeting, etc. —**bow and scrape** to be too polite and ingratiating —**bow out 1.** to leave or retire formally **2.** (or **in**) to usher out (or in) with a bow —**take a bow** to acknowledge applause, etc. as by bowing

bow[2] (bō) *n.* [< OE. *boga* < *bugan*, BOW[1]] **1.** anything curved or bent [a *rainbow*] **2.** a curve; bend **3.** a device for shooting arrows, a flexible, curved strip of wood, etc. with a taut cord connecting the two ends **4.** an archer **5.** a slender stick strung along its length with horsehairs, drawn across the strings of a violin, cello, etc. to play it **6.** a decorative knot, usually with two loops, untied by pulling the ends —*vt., vi.* **1.** to bend in the shape of a bow **2.** to play (a violin, etc.) with a bow

bow[3] (bou) *n.* [< LowG. or Scand.] **1.** the front part of a ship, etc.; prow **2.** the oarsman nearest the bow —*adj.* of or near the bow

bow compasses a pair of drawing compasses whose legs are joined together by a flexible steel band instead of a hinge

bowd·ler·ize (boud'lə rīz', bōd'-) *vt.* **-ized', -iz'ing** [after Thomas *Bowdler*, who in 1818 published an expurgated Shakespeare] to expurgate —**bowd'ler·ism** *n.* —**bowd'- ler·i·za'tion** *n.*

bow·el (bou'əl, boul) *n.* [< OFr. < ML. < L. *botellus*, dim. of *botulus*, sausage] **1.** an intestine of a human being;

gut; entrail: *usually used in pl.* **2.** [*pl.*] the inner part [the *bowels* of the earth] **3.** [*pl.*] [Archaic] tender emotions —*vt.* **-elled, -el·ling** to disembowel —**move one's bowels** to pass waste matter from the large intestine; defecate

bowel movement **1.** the act of defecating **2.** defecated matter; faeces

bow·er¹ (bou′ər) *n.* [< OE. *bur*, a dwelling] **1.** a place enclosed as by leafy boughs; arbour **2.** [Archaic] a boudoir —*vt.* to enclose in a bower —**bow′er·y** *adj.*

bow·er² (bou′ər) *n.* [< BOW³] the heaviest anchor of a ship, normally carried at the bow

bow·er·bird (-bʉrd′) *n.* any of certain brightly-coloured birds of Australia and New Guinea: the male builds a decorated mating bower to attract the female

bow·fin (bō′fin′) *n.* a primitive freshwater fish of E N. America, with a rounded tail fin

bow·head (-hed′) *n.* a whale with a very large head and an arched upper jaw, found in arctic seas

bow·ie knife (bōō′ē, bō′ē) [after Col. J. *Bowie*, Am. frontiersman] a long sheath knife with a single edge, orig. carried by American frontiersmen

bowl¹ (bōl) *n.* [< OE. *bolla*] **1.** a deep, hollow, rounded dish **2.** a large drinking cup **3.** convivial drinking **4.** a thing or part shaped like a bowl, as the hollowed-out part of a smoking pipe, a hollow land formation, or an amphitheatre **5.** the contents of a bowl —**bowl′like**′ *adj.*

bowl² (bōl) *n.* [< OFr. < L. *bulla*, a bubble] **1.** a heavy ball used in the game of bowls **2.** a roll of the ball in bowling or bowls —*vi., vt.* **1.** to roll (a ball) or participate in bowling or bowls **2.** to move or cause to move swiftly and smoothly, as on wheels (often with *along*) **3.** *Cricket a*) to throw (a ball) to the batsman *b*) to dismiss a batsman by delivering a ball that knocks down the wicket (often with *out*) —**bowl over** **1.** to knock over **2.** [Colloq.] to astonish and confuse —**bowl′er** *n.*

bowl·der (bōl′dər) *n.* *same as* BOULDER

bow·leg (bō′leg′) *n.* a leg that is bowed or curved outwards —**bow′leg′ged** (-leg′id, -legd′) *adj.*

bowl·er (bōl′ər) *n.* [< *Bowler*, name of 19th-c. London hat manufacturer] a stiff felt hat with a rounded crown and narrow curved brim

bow·line (bō′lin) *n.* [ME. *bouleine*, prob. < Scand.] **1.** a rope used to keep the sail taut when sailing into the wind **2.** a knot used to tie off a loop: also **bowline knot**

bowl·ing (bōl′iŋ) *n.* **1.** a game in which a heavy ball is bowled along a wooden lane (**bowling alley**) in an attempt to knock over wooden pins, now usually ten, set upright at the far end **2.** *same as* BOWLS **3.** the playing of either game

bowls (bōlz) *n.* **1.** a game played on a smooth lawn (**bowling green**) with wooden balls which are rolled in an attempt to make them stop near a target ball (the *jack*) **2.** ninepins, tenpins, or skittles

bow·man (bō′mən) *n.*, *pl.* **-men** an archer

bow·shot (-shot′) *n.* the distance an arrow can travel when shot from a bow

bow·sprit (bō′sprit) *n.* [prob. < Du. < *boeg*, BOW³ + *spriet*, SPRIT] a large, tapered spar extending forwards from the bow of a sailing vessel

BOWSPRIT

bow·string (bō′striŋ′) *n.* a cord stretched from one end of an archer's bow to the other

bow tie (bō) a small necktie tied in a bow

bow window a curved, bay window

bow-wow (bou′wou′; bou′wou′) *n.* [echoic] **1.** the bark of a dog or a sound imitating this **2.** a child's word for dog —*vi.* to to bark as or like a dog

box¹ (boks) *n.* [OE. < ML. *buxis* < L. < Gr. *pyxos*, boxwood] **1.** any of various kinds of containers, usually lidded, made of cardboard, wood, or other stiff material; case; carton **2.** the contents of a box **3.** [< the tool *box* under the seat] the driver's seat on a coach **4.** any boxlike thing, as *a*) a small, enclosed group of seats in a theatre, stadium, etc. *b*) a small booth *c*) a large, enclosed stall, for a horse, etc.: in full, **box stall** *d*) a space for a certain person or group [a jury *box*] **5.** a short newspaper article enclosed in borders **6.** *same as* HORSE-BOX **7.** a small country house used by sportsmen **8.** [often **B-**] [Colloq.] television (preceded by *the*) **9.** *Mech.* a protective casing for a part [a journal *box*] **10.** *Sport* a shaped device of light, tough material worn by men to protect the genitals, as in boxing or cricket —*vt.* **1.** to provide with a box **2.** to put into a box —*adj.* **1.** shaped or made like a box **2.** packed in a box —**box in** (or *up*) to shut in or keep in —**box the compass** **1.** to name the thirty-two points of the compass in order: compasses were kept in boxes **2.** to make a complete circuit —**box′like**′ *adj.*

box² (boks) *n.* [< ?] a blow struck with the hand or fist, esp. on the ear —*vt.* **1.** to strike such a blow **2.** to fight in a boxing match with —*vi.* to fight with the fists; engage in boxing —**box clever** [Colloq.] behave in a clever or cunning manner

box³ (boks) *n.* [OE. < L. *buxus* < Gr. *pyxos*] an evergreen shrub or small tree with small, leathery leaves

box camera a simple camera shaped like a box and having a fixed focus and, usually, a single shutter speed

Box·er (bok′sər) *n.* a member of a Chinese society that led an unsuccessful uprising (the **Boxer Rebellion**, 1900) against foreigners in China

box·er (bok′sər) *n.* **1.** a man who boxes; pugilist; prizefighter **2.** a medium-sized dog with a sturdy body and a smooth, fawn or brindle coat

box girder a girder that is hollow and square or rectangular in shape

box·ing (-siŋ) *n.* [< BOX²] the skill or sport of fighting with the fists, esp. in padded leather mittens (**boxing gloves**)

Boxing Day [from the custom of giving Christmas boxes to milkmen, postmen, etc. on this day] the first day after Christmas (26th December), observed as a holiday

box junction a junction marked by yellow cross-hatching painted on the road: drivers may only enter the junction if their exit is clear

box kite a kite with an oblong, box-shaped framework open at both ends

box number a number given to newspaper advertisements to which replies may be sent

box office **1.** a place where admission tickets are sold, as in a theatre **2.** [Colloq.] the power of a show or performer to attract an audience

box pleat a double pleat with the under edges folded towards each other

box·room (-rōōm) *n.* a small room or cubbyhole used for storing articles that are not immediately required

box seat a seat in a box at a theatre, etc.

box spanner a tool used for turning nuts inaccessible to an ordinary spanner, consisting of a long tube shaped at the end to fit the nut

box spring a coiled spring contained in a boxlike frame,

BOXING AND WRESTLING WEIGHTS

PROFESSIONAL BOXING			OLYMPIC BOXING			FREESTYLE WRESTLING		
FLYWEIGHT	under	50.8 kg	LIGHT FLYWEIGHT	under	48 kg	LIGHT FLYWEIGHT	under	48 kg
BANTAMWEIGHT	„	53.5 kg	FLYWEIGHT	„	51 kg	FLYWEIGHT	„	52 kg
FEATHERWEIGHT	. „	57.2 kg	BANTAMWEIGHT	„	54 kg	BANTAMWEIGHT	„	57 kg
JUNIOR LIGHTWEIGHT	„	59.0 kg	FEATHERWEIGHT	„	57 kg	FEATHERWEIGHT	„	62 kg
LIGHTWEIGHT	„	61.2 kg	LIGHTWEIGHT	„	60 kg	LIGHTWEIGHT	„	68 kg
JUNIOR WELTERWEIGHT	„	63.5 kg	LIGHT WELTERWEIGHT	„	63.5 kg	WELTERWEIGHT	„	74 kg
WELTERWEIGHT	„	66.7 kg	WELTERWEIGHT	„	67 kg	MIDDLEWEIGHT	„	82 kg
JUNIOR MIDDLEWEIGHT	„	70.0 kg	LIGHT MIDDLEWEIGHT	„	71 kg	LIGHT HEAVYWEIGHT	„	90 kg
MIDDLEWEIGHT	„	72.3 kg	MIDDLEWEIGHT	„	75 kg	MID HEAVYWEIGHT	„	100 kg
LIGHT HEAVYWEIGHT	„	79.4 kg	LIGHT HEAVYWEIGHT	„	81 kg	HEAVYWEIGHT	over	100 kg
HEAVYWEIGHT	over	79.4 kg	HEAVYWEIGHT	over	81 kg			

used as a base for mattresses, chairs, etc.

box·wood (boks'wood') *n.* 1. the wood of the box (shrub or tree) 2. the box (shrub or tree)

box·y (bok'sē) *adj.* **-i·er, -i·est** like a box, as in squarish form, confining quality, etc.

boy (boi) *n.* [ME. *boie*] 1. a male child from birth to physical maturity 2. an immature or callow man 3. any man; fellow: familiar term 4. a man servant, porter, etc.: a patronizing term 5. [Colloq.] a son —*interj.* [Slang] an exclamation of pleasure, surprise, etc.: often **oh, boy!** —**boy'ish** *adj.* —**boy'ish·ly** *adv.* —**boy'ish·ness** *n.*

boy·cott (boi'kot) *vt.* [after Captain C. C. *Boycott*, Irish land agent so treated in 1880] 1. to join together in refusing to deal with, so as to punish, coerce, etc. 2. to refuse to buy, sell, or use (something) —*n.* the act of boycotting

boy·friend (boi'frend') *n.* 1. a sweetheart, or escort of a girl or woman 2. a boy who is one's friend

boy·hood (-hood') *n.* [see -HOOD] 1. the time or state of being a boy 2. boys collectively

Boyle's Law (boilz) [after R. *Boyle* (1627-91), Brit. chemist and physicist] the principle that the pressure of a gas varies inversely with its volume when the temperature is kept constant

boy scout a member of the **Boy Scouts,** a worldwide boys' organization that stresses outdoor life and service to others

boy·sen·ber·ry (boi'z'n ber'ē) *n., pl.* **-ries** [after Rudolph *Boysen,* U.S. horticulturist] a large, purple berry, a cross of the raspberry, loganberry, and blackberry

Bp. bishop

B/P, BP, b.p. bills payable

B.P. 1. British Petroleum 2. British Pharmacopoeia

b.p. 1. below proof 2. birthplace: also **bpl.** 3. boiling point

B.P.C. British Pharmaceutical Codex

Bq *Physics the symbol for* becquerel

Br *Chem.* bromine

Br. 1. Breton 2. Britain 3. British

br. 1. branch 2. bronze 3. brother 4. brown

B/R, BR, b.r. bills receivable

B.R., BR British Rail

bra (brä) *n.* [< BRA(SSIÈRE)] an undergarment worn by women to support and shape the breasts

brace (brās) *vt.* **braced, brac'ing** [< OFr. < L. *brachia,* pl. of *brachium,* an arm] 1. to tie or bind on firmly 2. to tighten, esp. by stretching 3. to strengthen or make firm by supporting the weight of, etc.; prop up 4. to equip with braces 5. to make ready for an impact, shock, etc. 6. to stimulate 7. to get a firm hold with (the hands or feet) —*n.* 1. a couple; pair 2. a device that clasps or connects; fastener 3. [*pl.*] a pair of straps passed over the shoulders to hold up trousers 4. a device for maintaining tension, as a guy wire 5. either of the signs { }, used to connect words, lines, or staves of music 6. a device, as a beam, used as a support, to resist strain, etc.; prop 7. *a)* any of various devices for supporting a weak or deformed part of the body *b)* a device, usually consisting of metal bands and wires, for correcting the position of irregular teeth 8. a tool for holding and rotating a drilling bit —**brace up** [Colloq.] to call forth one's courage, etc.

brace and bit a tool for boring, consisting of a removable drill (*bit*) in a rotating handle (*brace*)

brace·let (brās'lit) *n.* [< OFr. < L. < *brachium,* an arm] 1. an ornamental band or chain worn about the wrist or arm 2. [Colloq.] a handcuff: *usually used in pl.* —**brace'let·ed** *adj.*

brac·er (brā'sər) *n.* 1. a person or thing that braces 2. [Slang] an alcoholic drink

bra·chi·ate (brāk'ē āt', brak'-; *also for adj.,* -it) *adj.* [BRACHI(O)- + -ATE[1]] having widely spreading branches, alternately arranged —*vi.,* **-at'ed, -at'ing** to swing arm over arm from one hold to the next, as certain apes and monkeys do —**bra'chi·a'tion** *n.*

BRACE AND BIT

bra·chi·o- [< L. < Gr. *brachiōn,* an arm] *a combining form meaning* of an arm or the arms [*brachiopod*]: also **bra'chi-**

bra·chi·o·pod (brā'kē ə pod', brak'ē-) *n.* [prec. + -POD] any of a number of related marine animals with hinged upper and lower shells and two armlike parts with tentacles

bra·chi·o·sau·rus (brak'ē ə sôr'əs) *n., pl.* **-sau'rus·es, -sau'-ri** (-ī) [BRACHIO- + -SAURUS] a large dinosaur with long forelegs: also **brach'i·o·saur** (-sôr')

bra·chi·um (brā'kē əm, brak'ē-) *n., pl.* **-chi·a** (-ə) [L.] 1. the part of the arm from the shoulder to the elbow 2. *Biol.* any armlike part —**bra'chi·al** *adj.*

brach·y- [< Gr. *brachys,* short] *a combining form meaning* short [*brachycephalic*]

brach·y·ce·phal·ic (brak'i sə fal'ik) *adj.* [BRACHY- + -CEPHALIC] having a relatively short or broad head: also **brach'y·ceph'a·lous** (-sef'ə ləs): see CEPHALIC INDEX —**brach'y·ceph'a·ly** (-sef'ə lē) *n.*

brac·ing (brās'iŋ) *adj.* invigorating; stimulating —*n.* 1. a device that braces 2. braces

brack·en (brak''n) *n.* [< ON.] 1. a large, coarse fern, as the brake 2. a growth of such ferns

brack·et (brak'it) *n.* [< Fr. dim. of *brague,* knee pants, ult. < Gaul. *braca,* pants] 1. an architectural support projecting from a wall 2. any angle-shaped support, esp. one in the form of a right-angled triangle 3. a wall shelf held up by brackets 4. a wall fixture, as for a small electric lamp 5. either of the signs [ ], or ( ) used to enclose words, figures, etc. 6. the part of a classified grouping that falls within specified limits [a £5 to £10 price *bracket*] 7. *a)* the interval between the ranges of two rounds of artillery fire, one over and the other short of the target, used to find the correct range *b)* such a pair of rounds —*vt.* 1. to support with brackets 2. to enclose in brackets 3. to classify together 4. to fire a bracket of artillery rounds at (a target)

brack·ish (brak'ish) *adj.* [earlier Scot. *brack* < MDu. *brak,* salty + -ISH] 1. somewhat salty, as water in some marshes near the sea 2. having an unpleasant taste; nauseating —**brack'ish·ness** *n.*

bract (brakt) *n.* [L. *bractea,* thin metal plate] a modified leaf, usually small and scalelike, growing at the base of a flower or on its stalk —**brac·te·al** (brak'tē əl) *adj.* —**brac'-te·ate** (-it) *adj.*

bract·let (-lit) *n.* a secondary bract at the base of a flower: also **brac·te·ole** (brak'tē ōl')

brad (brad) *n.* [ON. *broddr,* a spike] a thin wire nail with a small or off-centre head —*vt.* **brad'ded, brad'ding** to fasten with brads

brad·awl (-ôl) *n.* a small hand-boring tool with a chisel edge

Brad·shaw (brad'shô) *n.* [after G. *Bradshaw* (1801-53), its original publisher] a British railway timetable published annually 1839-1961

brae (brā) *n.* [ON. *bra,* eyelid, brow] [Scot.] a sloping bank; hillside

brag (brag) *vt., vi.* **bragged, brag'ging** [prob. < OFr. *braguer;* ? akin to BRAY] to boast —*n.* 1. boastful talk or manner 2. [Colloq.] anything boasted of; boast 3. a braggart 4. an old card game, much like poker —**brag'-ger** *n.*

brag·ga·do·ci·o (brag'ə dō'shē ō, -dō'shō) *n., pl.* **-os** [coined by Spenser < BRAG + It. ending] 1. a braggart 2. noisy boasting or bragging

brag·gart (brag'ərt) *n.* [< OFr.: see BRAG] an offensively boastful person —*adj.* boastful

Brah·ma (brä'mə; *for n.* brä'-) [Hindi < Sans. *brahman,* worship] *Hinduism* the supreme essence or spirit of the universe —*n. same as* BRAHMAN (sense 2)

Brah·man (brä'mən; *for 2* brä'-) *n., pl.* **-mans** [see prec.] 1. a member of the priestly Hindu caste, the highest 2. a breed of domestic cattle developed from the zebu of India —**Brah·man·ic** (brä man'ik), **Brah·man'i·cal** *adj.*

Brah·man·ism (-iz'm) *n.* the religious doctrines and system of the Brahmans

Brah·min (brä'mən) *n.* 1. *same as* BRAHMAN (sense 1) 2. [U.S.] a cultured upper-class person regarded as haughty or conservative —**Brah·min·ic** (brä min'ik), **Brah·min'i·cal** *adj.*

Brah·min·ism (-iz'm) *n.* 1. *same as* BRAHMANISM 2. the characteristic attitude, etc. of Brahmins

braid (brād) *vt.* [< OE. *bregdan,* to move quickly] 1. to plait (hair, straw, etc.) 2. to trim or bind with braid —*n.* 1. a band or strip formed by braiding 2. a length of braided hair; plait 3. a woven band of tape, ribbon, etc. used to bind or decorate clothing —**braid'er** *n.* —**braid'ing** *n.*

Braille (brāl) *n.* [after L. *Braille* (1809–52), Fr. teacher who devised it] [*also* b-] 1. a system of printing and writing for the blind, using raised dots felt by the fingers 2. the characters used in this system —*vt.* **Brailled, Brail'ling** [*also* b-] to print or write in such characters

brain (brān) *n.* [OE. *brægen*] 1. the mass of nerve tissue in the cranium of vertebrate animals: it is the centre of thought and receives and transmits impulses: cf. GREY MATTER, WHITE MATTER 2. *a)* [*often pl.*] intelligence; mental ability *b)* [Colloq.] a person of great intelligence *c)* [Colloq.] the main organizer of a group activity *d)* [Colloq.] an electronic device able to perform some of the functions of a human brain, as computation —*vt.* 1. to dash out the brains of 2. [Slang] to hit hard on the head —**beat** (or **rack, cudgel,** etc.) **one's brains** to try hard to remember, understand, etc. —**have on the brain** to be obsessed by

brain·case (-kās') *n. same as* BRAINPAN

brain·child (-child') *n.* [Colloq.] an idea, plan, etc. regarded as produced by one's mental labour

brain drain [Colloq.] depletion of the intellectual or professional resources of a country, etc., esp. through emigration

brain fever inflammation of the brain or its covering membranes

brain·less (-lis) *adj.* foolish or stupid —**brain'less·ly** *adv.* —**brain'less·ness** *n.*

brain·pan (-pan') *n.* the part of the cranium containing the brain

brain·pow·er (-pou′ər) *n.* mental ability

brain·storm (-stôrm′) *n.* 1. a sudden attack of insanity 2. [Colloq.] a mental aberration 3. *U.S. var. of* BRAINWAVE (sense 2)

brains trust a group of knowledgeable or famous people who answer questions of current or topical interest in public, esp. on radio or television

brain teaser a difficult problem or puzzle, esp. one intended to be solved for entertainment

brain trust [U.S.] a group of experts acting as administrative advisers —**brain truster**

brain·wash (-wosh′) *vt.* [Colloq.] to indoctrinate so intensively and thoroughly as to effect a radical transformation of beliefs —**brain′wash′ing** *n.*

brain·wave (-wāv) *n.* 1. rhythmic electric impulses given off by nerve centres in the brain 2. [Colloq.] a sudden inspiration or idea

brain·y (-ē) *adj.* **brain′i·er, brain′i·est** [Colloq.] intelligent; mentally bright —**brain′i·ness** *n.*

braise (brāz) *vt.* **braised, brais′ing** [Fr. *braiser* < *braise* (< Gmc. *brasa*), live coals] to cook (meat) by browning in fat and then simmering in a covered pan with a little liquid

brake[1] (brāk) *n.* [prob. taken as sing. of BRACKEN] a large, coarse fern, a variety of bracken

brake[2] (brāk) *n.* [< MLowG. *brake* or ODu. *braeke* < *breken*, to break] 1. a device for beating flax or hemp so that the fibre can be separated 2. any device for slowing or stopping the motion of a vehicle or machine, as by causing a block or band to press against a moving part 3. a hindrance [a *brake* on new developments] 4. a heavy harrow for breaking up clods of earth —*vt.* **braked, brak′-ing** 1. to break up (flax, etc.) into smaller pieces 2. to slow down or stop as with a brake —*vi.* 1. to operate a brake 2. to be slowed down or stopped by a brake —**brake′less** *adj.*

brake[3] (brāk) *n.* [< or akin to MLowG. *brake*, stumps] a clump of brushwood, briers, etc.

brake[4] (brāk) *archaic pt. of* BREAK

brake band a band with a lining (**brake lining**) of asbestos, fine wire, etc., that creates friction when tightened about the drum of a brake

brake horsepower the rate at which an engine does work measured according to the force needed to brake it

brake shoe a block curved to fit the shape of a wheel and forced against it to act as a brake

brakes·man (brāks′mən) *n., pl.* **-men** a worker who operates the brakes on railway rolling stock

brake van the railway carriage from which the guard applies the brakes

bram·ble (bram′b'l) *n.* [< OE. *bræmel* < *brom*, broom] 1. any prickly shrub of the rose family, as the raspberry, blackberry, etc. 2. any prickly shrub 3. [Scot.] a blackberry (sense 1) —**bram′bly** *adj.* **-bli·er, -bli·est**

bram·bling (-bliŋ) *n.* [earlier *bramline*, prob. < prec.] a brightly coloured finch of Europe and Asia, similar to the chaffinch

bran (bran) *n.* [OFr. *bren*] the skin or husk of grains of wheat, rye, oats, etc. separated from the flour, as by sifting

branch (bränch) *n.* [< OFr. *brance* < LL. *branca*, a paw] 1. any woody extension from the trunk or main stem, or from a main limb, of a tree or shrub 2. anything like a branch, as a tine of a deer's antler 3. any of the streams into which a river may divide or which flow into it 4. *a)* a division of a body of learning *b)* a division of a family *c)* a separately located unit of an organization [a *branch* of a library] —*vi.* 1. to put forth or divide into branches; ramify 2. to come out (*from* the trunk or stem) as a branch —*vt.* to separate into branches —**branch off** 1. to separate into branches; fork 2. to go off in another direction; diverge —**branch out** 1. to put forth branches 2. to extend the scope of interests, activities, etc. —**branched** *adj.* —**branch′-like′** *adj.*

bran·chi·ae (braŋ′ki ē′) *n.pl., sing.* **-chi·a** (-ə) [< L. < Gr. *branchia*, fins] the gills of a fish —**bran′chi·al** *adj.* —**bran′-chi·ate** (-kē it) *adj.*

brand (brand) *n.* [< OE., flame, sword < base of *biernan, vi.*, to burn] 1. a stick that is burning or partially burned 2. *a)* a mark burned on the skin with a hot iron, formerly used to punish and identify criminals, now used on cattle to show ownership *b)* the iron thus used 3. a mark of disgrace; stigma 4. *a)* an identifying mark or label on products; trademark *b)* the kind or make of a commodity [a *brand* of cigars] *c)* a special kind [a *brand* of nonsense] 5. a fungal disease of plants characterized by brown spots on the leaves 6. [Archaic] a sword —*vt.* 1. to mark with or as with a brand [a scene *branded* in his memory] 2. to mark as disgraceful —**brand′er** *n.*

bran·died (bran′dēd) *adj.* flavoured, mixed or preserved with brandy

bran·dish (bran′dish) *vt.* [< OFr. < Gmc. *brand:* see BRAND] to wave or shake menacingly or exultantly; flourish —*n.* a brandishing of something

brand·ling (brand′liŋ) *n.* [BRAND, *n.* + -LING[1]] a small, red or yellowish worm used for fish bait

brand name the name by which a brand or make of commodity is known —**brand′name′** *adj.*

brand-new (brand′nyo͞o′) *adj.* [orig., fresh from the fire: see BRAND] 1. entirely new; recently made 2. recently acquired

bran·dy (bran′dē) *n., pl.* **-dies** [earlier *brandywine* < Du. *brandewijn*, lit., burnt (i.e., distilled) wine] 1. an alcoholic spirit distilled from wine 2. a similar spirit distilled from fermented fruit juice [cherry *brandy*]

brandy butter a sauce made from butter, sugar and brandy; it is often served with Christmas pudding

brandy snap a crisp, ginger-flavoured biscuit, rolled and usually filled with cream

brant (brant) *n., pl.* **brants, brant:** see PLURAL, II, D, 1 [< ?] *Chiefly U.S. var. of* BRENT

bran tub a lucky dip in which parcels are concealed in bran

brash[1] (brash) *adj.* [< ?] 1. reckless; rash 2. bold, presumptuous, impudent, etc. —**brash′ly** *adv.* —**brash′-ness** *n.*

brash[2] (brash) *n.* [Fr. < OHG. *brecha*, fragment < *brehhan*, to break] loose fragments, as of rock, ice, hedge clippings, etc.

bra·sier (brā′zhər) *n. same as* BRAZIER

brass (bräs) *n., pl.* **brass′es:** see PLURAL, II, D, 3 [OE. *bræs*] 1. a yellowish metal that is essentially an alloy of copper and zinc 2. things made of brass 3. the brass instruments of an orchestra 4. a brass memorial tablet, as in a church and often bearing an effigy of the deceased 5. [Colloq.] bold impudence; effrontery 6. [Colloq.] money 7. [often with *pl. v.*] [Slang] *a)* military officers of high rank: see BRASS HAT *b)* any high officials —*adj.* made of brass

bras·sard (brə särd′, bras′ärd) *n.* [Fr., ult. < *bras*, an arm] 1. armour for the upper arm: also **bras·sart** (bras′ärt) 2. an identifying arm band or badge

brass band a band of brass and percussion instruments

brass hat [< the gold braid on the cap] [Slang] 1. a military officer of high rank 2. any high official

bras·si·ca (bras′i kə) *n.* [L., lit., cabbage] a plant of the cabbage and turnip family

brass·ie (bras′ē) *n.* [orig. made with a *brass* sole] a golf club with a wooden head, used for long fairway shots: now usually called *number 2 wood*

bras·sière (bras′ē ər, braz′-) *n.* [Fr., orig. arm guard < *bras*, an arm] *same as* BRA

brass tacks [Colloq.] basic facts; practical details: usually in **get** (or **come**) **down to brass tacks**

brass·ware (bräs′wer′) *n.* articles made of brass

brass·y (-ē) *adj.* **brass′i·er, brass′i·est** 1. of or decorated with brass 2. like brass 3. cheap and showy 4. loud and blaring 5. impudent; brazen —**brass′i·ly** *adv.* —**brass′-i·ness** *n.*

brat (brat) *n.* [OE. *bratt*, a cloak < Gael. *bratt*, a cloth, rag < ?] a child, esp. an impudent, unruly child: scornful or playful term —**brat′tish·ness** *n.* —**brat′tish** *adj.*

brat·tice (brat′is) *n.* [ME. *bretice* < OFr. < ML. prob. < OHG. *bret*, board] 1. formerly, a temporary breastwork or parapet put up during a siege 2. *Mining* a partition of wood, cloth, etc. used to form ventilation passages

bra·va·do (brə vä′dō) *n.* [< Sp. *bravada* < *bravo*, BRAVE] pretended courage or defiant confidence

brave (brāv) *adj.* [Fr. < It. *bravo*, brave, fine, orig., wild, savage < L. *barbarus*, BARBAROUS] 1. not afraid; having courage; valiant 2. fine; splendid [*brave* new world] —*n.* 1. any brave man 2. [< 17th-c. NAmFr.] a N. American Indian warrior —*vt.* **braved, brav′ing** 1. to face with courage 2. to defy; dare —**brave′ly** *adv.* —**brave′ness** *n.*

brav·er·y (brā′vər ē) *n.* 1. courage; valour 2. fine appearance, show, or dress

bra·vo[1] (brä′vō) *interj.* [It.: see BRAVE, *adj.*] well done! very good! excellent! —*n., pl.* **-vos** a shout of "bravo!"

bra·vo[2] (brä′vō) *n., pl.* **-voes, -vos;** It. **-vi** (-vē) [It.: see BRAVE] a hired killer; assassin

bra·vu·ra (brə vyoor′ə, -voor′-) *n.* [It., spirit < *bravo*, BRAVE] 1. a display of daring; dash 2. *Music a)* a brilliant passage or piece that displays the performer's skill and technique *b)* brilliant technique —*adj.* characterized by bravura

braw (brô) *adj.* [< BRAVE] [Scot.] 1. finely dressed 2. fine; excellent

brawl (brôl) *vi.* [< ? Du. *brallen*, to boast] 1. to quarrel or fight noisily 2. to flow noisily over rapids, falls, etc.: said of water —*n.* 1. a noisy quarrel or fight; row 2. [Slang] a noisy party —**brawl′er** *n.*

brawn (brôn) *n.* [< OFr. *braon*, muscular part < Frank. *brado*, meat, calf (of leg)] 1. strong, well-developed muscles 2. muscular strength 3. a loaf of jellied, seasoned meat made from parts of the head and feet of a pig or calf —**brawn′i·ness** *n.* —**brawn′y** *adj.* **brawn′i·er, brawn′i·est**

bray (brā) *vi.* [< OFr. < VL. *bragire*, to cry out] to make the loud, harsh cry of a donkey, or a sound, esp. a laugh, like this—*vt.* to utter loudly and harshly —*n.* the loud, harsh cry of a donkey, or a sound like this

braze¹ (brāz) *vt.* **brazed, braz′ing** [Fr. *braser*, to solder, var. of *braiser*, BRAISE] to solder with a metal having a high melting point, esp. with an alloy of zinc and copper —**braz′-er** *n.*

braze² (brāz) *vt.* **brazed, braz′ing** [< OE. *bræsian* < *bræs*, BRASS] 1. to make of, or coat with, brass 2. to make hard like brass —**braz′er** *n.*

bra·zen (brā′z'n) *adj.* [OE. *bræsen* < *bræs*, BRASS] 1. of brass 2. like brass in colour, etc. 3. showing no shame; bold; impudent 4. harsh and piercing —**brazen it out** to act boldly as if one need not be ashamed —**bra′zen·ly** *adv.* —**bra′zen·ness** *n.*

bra·zier¹ (brā′zhər) *n.* [Fr. *brasier* < *braise*: see BRAISE] a metal pan, bowl, etc. to hold burning coals or charcoal

bra·zier² (brā′zhər) *n.* [see BRASS] a person who works in brass

Bra·zil nut (brə zil′) 1. a hard-shelled, three-sided, oily edible seed of a tall S. American tree 2. this tree, on which the seeds grow clustered in capsules

bra·zil·wood (brə zil′wood′) *n.* [< *Brazil*, S. America] a reddish wood obtained from several tropical American trees; it yields a red dye and is also used in making furniture and violin bows

BRAZIL NUTS

B.R.C.S. British Red Cross Society

breach (brēch) *n.* [< OE. < *brecan*, to break] 1. orig., a breaking or being broken 2. a failure to observe a law, a contract, etiquette, public peace, etc. 3. an opening made by breaking through a wall, defence, etc. 4. a break in friendly relations —*vt.* to make a breach in; break through —**step into the breach** to take on a responsibility, give help, etc., in an emergency

breach of promise a breaking of a promise to marry

bread (bred) *n.* [OE. *bread*, crumb, morsel] 1. a food baked from a leavened, kneaded dough made with flour or meal, water, yeast, etc. 2. any baked food like bread 3. food generally 4. one's livelihood 5. [Slang] money —*vt.* to cover with bread crumbs before cooking —**bread and butter** one's means of subsistence; livelihood —**break bread** 1. to partake of food; eat 2. to take Holy Communion —**cast one's bread upon the waters** to do good deeds without expecting something in return —**know which side one's bread is buttered on** to know what is to one's (economic) interest —**take the bread out of someone's mouth** to deprive someone of his means of livelihood

bread-and-but·ter (-'n but′ər) *adj.* 1. of the product, work, etc. basically relied on for earnings 2. basic, commonplace, everyday, etc. 3. expressing thanks, as a letter to one's host after a visit

bread·bas·ket (-bäs′kit) *n.* 1. a region supplying much grain 2. [Slang] the stomach or abdomen

bread·board (-bôrd′) *n.* 1. a board on which bread is sliced 2. a board, usually portable, on which experimental electronic circuits or diagrams can be laid out

bread·fruit (-frōōt′) *n.* 1. a large, round fruit with a starchy pulp, that is like bread when baked 2. the tropical tree on which it grows

bread line [U.S.] a line of poor people waiting to be given food —**on the bread line** very poor; living at subsistence level

bread·stuff (-stuf′) *n.* 1. ground grain or flour for making bread 2. bread

breadth (bredth) *n.* [OE. *brædu* < *brad*, broad + -TH¹] 1. the distance from side to side of a thing; width 2. lack of narrowness or of restriction [*breadth* of knowledge] 4. *Art* an effect of unity and inclusiveness achieved as by subordinating details

breadth·ways (-wāz′) *adv., adj.* in the direction of the breadth: also **breadth′wise′** (-wīz′)

bread·win·ner (bred′win′ər) *n.* a person who supports dependants by his earnings

break (brāk) *vt.* **broke, bro′ken, break′ing** [OE. *brecan*] 1. to cause to come apart by force; smash; burst 2. to cut open the surface of (soil, the skin, etc.) 3. to cause the failure of by force [to *break* a strike] 4. to make inoperative by cracking, disrupting, etc. 5. to tame with or as with force 6. *a)* to cause to get rid (*of* a habit) *b)* to get rid of (a habit) 7. to lower in rank or grade; demote 8. *a)* to reduce to poverty or bankruptcy *b)* to wreck the health, spirit, etc. of 9. to surpass (a record) 10. to violate (a law, agreement, etc.) 11. to escape from by force [to *break* prison] 12. to disrupt the order or completeness of [to *break* ranks] 13. to interrupt (a journey, electric circuit, etc.) 14. to reduce the force of by interrupting (a fall, etc.) 15. to bring to a sudden end [to *break* a tie] 16. to penetrate (silence, darkness, etc.) 17. to make known; disclose 18. to decipher (a code, etc.) 19. to make (a will)

invalid 20. to prove (an alibi) false 21. to begin; open 22. to exchange (a bill or coin) for smaller units 23. to fracture (a bone) in (a limb, etc) —*vi.* 1. to split into pieces; come apart; burst 2. to scatter; disperse [*break* and run] 3. to force one's way (*through*) 4. to stop associating (*with*) 5. to become inoperative 6. to rise, fall, turn, shift, etc. suddenly [the weather *broke*] 7. to move away suddenly 8. to begin suddenly to perform, etc. [*break* into song] 9. to come into being, evidence, or general knowledge [the story *broke*] 10. *a)* to fall apart slowly; disintegrate *b)* to dash apart, as a wave on the shore 11. to change in tone [his voice *broke*] 12. *Boxing and Wrestling* to separate, as from a clinch 13. *Cricket* to change direction on bouncing; spin: said of a ball —*n.* 1. a breaking; breach; fracture 2. *a)* a breaking in, out, or forth *b)* a sudden move; rush; dash 3. a broken place; separation; crack 4. a beginning or appearance [*break* of day] 5. an interruption of something regular 6. a gap; interval; omission 7. a breach in friendly relations 8. a sudden change 9. an escape, as from prison 10. a lowering or drop, as of prices 11. a short rest between periods of work, as in an office or school 12. [Colloq.] an improper or untimely action or remark 13. *Cricket* a chance piece of luck, specif. of good luck 13. *Cricket* a change in direction of a ball on bouncing 14. *Music a)* the point where one register changes to another *b)* a transitional phrase in a piece of jazz music —**break away** 1. to leave suddenly; escape 2. to become detached 3. to secede 4. to start too soon, as in a race —**break down** 1. to go out of working order 2. to give way to tears or emotion 3. to have a physical or nervous collapse 4. to analyse 5. to crush or overcome (opposition, etc.) —**break even** to make neither a profit nor a loss —**break in** 1. to enter forcibly 2. to interrupt 3. to train (a beginner) 4. to work the stiffness out of (new equipment) —**break off** 1. to stop abruptly 2. to stop being friendly —**break out** 1. to begin suddenly 2. to escape 3. to become covered with pimples or a rash —**break service** *Tennis* to win a game in which an opponent is serving —**break the back of** to get through the greater or worst part of —**break the bank** to overstrain the financial resources —**break up** 1. to disperse: also, esp. as a command, **break it up** 2. to take apart 3. to put a stop to 4. to begin holidays, as at the end of a school term 5. [Colloq.] to end a relationship 6. [Colloq.] to laugh or make laugh uncontrollably —**break′a·ble** *adj.*

break·age (-ij) *n.* 1. a breaking 2. things or quantity broken 3. loss or damage due to breaking, or the sum allowed for this

break·a·way (-ə wā′) *adj.* of that which has seceded

break·down (-doun′) *n.* a breaking down; specif., *a)* a failure to function properly *b)* a failure of health *c)* decomposition *d)* a separating into parts; analysis

break·er (-ər) *n.* a person or thing that breaks; specif., a wave that breaks into foam

break·even (brāk′ē′vən) *adj.* designating that point, as in a commercial venture, at which profits and losses are equal

break·fast (brek′fəst) *n.* the first meal of the day —*vi.* to eat breakfast —*vt.* to give breakfast to —**break′fast·er** *n.*

break·front (brāk′frunt′) *adj.* having a front with a projecting section —*n.* a breakfront cabinet

breaking and entering unauthorized entry into a building with intent to commit a crime

breaking point the point at which material, or one's endurance, etc., collapses under strain

break·neck (brāk′nek′) *adj.* likely to cause an accident; highly dangerous [*breakneck* speed]

break·out (-out′) *n.* a sudden, forceful escape, as from prison

break·through (-thrōō′) *n.* 1. the act or place of breaking through against resistance 2. a strikingly important advance or discovery

break·up (-up′) *n.* a breaking up; specif., *a)* a dispersion *b)* a disintegration or decay *c)* a collapse *d)* a stopping or ending

break·wa·ter (-wôt′ər) *n.* a barrier to break the impact of waves, as before a harbour

bream¹ (brēm) *n., pl.* **bream, breams:** see PLURAL, II, D, 2 [< OFr. *bresme* < Frank. *brahsima*] 1. a European freshwater fish related to the minnows 2. any of various saltwater fishes

bream² (brēm) *vt.* [< ? Du. *brem*, furze: burning furze was orig. used in process] to clean (a ship's bottom) by applying heat and then scraping

breast (brest) *n.* [OE. *breost*] 1. either of two milk-secreting glands at the upper, front part of a woman's body 2. a corresponding gland in other animals 3. the upper, front part of the body; chest 4. the part of a garment, etc. that is over the breast 5. the breast regarded as the centre of emotions or as a source of nourishment 6. anything likened to the breast [the *breast* of the sea] —*vt.* 1. to face, esp. firmly 2. to reach the top of (a hill) —**beat one's breast** to make an exaggerated display of feeling, as of guilt —**make a clean breast of** to confess (guilt, etc.) fully

breast·bone (-bōn´) *n.* *same as* STERNUM
breast-feed (-fēd´) *vt.* **-fed´** (-fed´), **-feed´ing** to feed (a baby) milk from the breast; suckle
breast·pin (-pin´) *n.* an ornamental pin or brooch worn on a dress or in a tie
breast·plate (-plāt´) *n.* a piece of armour for the breast
breast stroke a swimming stroke in which both arms are simultaneously brought out sideways from a position close to the chest
breast·work (-wurk´) *n.* a low wall put up quickly as a defence, esp. to protect gunners
breath (breth) *n.* [OE. *bræth*, odour, exhalation] 1. air taken into the lungs and then let out 2. breathing; respiration 3. the power to breathe easily 4. life or spirit 5. air carrying fragrance or odour 6. a puff or whiff, as of air; slight breeze 7. moisture produced by a condensing of the breath, as in cold air 8. a whisper or murmur 9. the time taken by a single respiration; moment 10. a slight pause or rest 11. a faint hint or indication 12. *Phonet.* a voiceless exhalation of the airstream, as in pronouncing (s) or (p) —**below** (or **under**) **one's breath** in a whisper or murmur —**catch one's breath** 1. to gasp or pant 2. to pause or rest —**in the same breath** almost simultaneously —**out of breath** breathless, as from exertion —**save one's breath** not to waste one's time by trying to convince —**take one's breath away** to overwhelm with awe, surprise, horror, etc.
Breath·a·lyz·er, Breath·a·lys·er (breth´ə līz´ er) [*breath* (*an*)*alyser*] a *trademark for* a device that tests exhaled breath to measure the amount of alcohol in the body —*n.* [b-] such a device
breathe (brēth) *vi., vt.* **breathed, breath´ing** [< ME. < *breth*, BREATH] 1. to take (air) into the lungs and let it out again; inhale and exhale 2. to live 3. to take in or give out (air, an odour) 4. to instil [to *breathe* confidence] 5. to blow softly 6. to speak or sing softly; whisper 7. to give or take time to breathe; rest 8. to pant or cause to pant, as from exertion —**breathe again** (or **freely**) to have a feeling of relief or reassurance —**breathe one's last** to die —**breath·a·ble** (brē´thə b'l) *adj.*
breath·er (brē´thər) *n.* 1. one who breathes in a certain way 2. a small vent, as for releasing moisture 3. [Colloq.] a pause as for rest
breath·ing (brē´thiŋ) *adj.* that breathes; living; alive —*n.* 1. respiration 2. a single breath or the time taken by this 3. the sound of *h* in *hit, hope,* etc.; aspirate
breath·less (breth´lis) *adj.* 1. without breath 2. no longer breathing; dead 3. out of breath; gasping 4. unable to breathe easily because of excitement, fear, etc. 5. still and heavy, as the air —**breath´less·ly** *adv.* —**breath´less·ness** *n.*
breath·tak·ing (-tāk´iŋ) *adj.* 1. that takes one's breath away 2. very exciting; thrilling —**breath´tak´ing·ly** *adv.*
breath test a chemical test of a driver's breath to determine the amount of alcohol in his blood
breath·y (-ē) *adj.* with too much, audible letting out of breath —**breath´i·ly** *adv.* —**breath´i·ness** *n.*
brec·ci·a (brech´ē ə) *n.* [It.] rock consisting of sharp-cornered bits cemented together by sand, clay, or lime —**brec´ci·a·ted** *adj.*
bred (bred) *pt. & pp. of* BREED
breech (brēch; *for vt. 1, usually* brich) *n.* [< OE. *brec,* pl. of *broc*] 1. the buttocks; rump 2. the lower or back part of a thing 3. the part of a gun behind the barrel —*vt.* 1. to clothe with breeches 2. to provide (a gun) with a breech
breech birth the birth of a baby with the feet or buttocks appearing first: also **breech delivery**
breech·es (brich´iz) *n.pl.* [see BREECH] 1. trousers reaching to the knees 2. [Colloq.] any trousers —**too big for one's breeches** too forward, presumptuous, etc. for one's position or status
breech·es buoy (brēch´iz) a device for rescuing people at sea, consisting of a pair of short canvas breeches suspended from a life buoy that is run along a rope from ship to shore or to another ship
breech·ing (brich´iŋ, brēch´-) *n.* a harness strap around a horse's hindquarters
breech·load·er (brēch´lōd´ər) *n.* any gun loaded at the breech —**breech´-load´ing** *adj.*
breed (brēd) *vt.* **bred, breed´ing** [< OE. *bredan* < *brod,* a hatching, foetus] 1. to bring forth (offspring) 2. to be the source of; produce [ignorance *breeds* prejudice] 3. to cause to reproduce; raise [to *breed* dogs] 4. to bring up or train 5. to produce (fissionable material) in a breeder reactor —*vi.* 1. to be produced; originate 2. to reproduce —*n.* 1. a stock of animals or plants descended from common ancestors 2. a kind; sort; type —**breed´er** *n.*
breeder reactor a nuclear reactor that produces more fissionable material than it consumes
breed·ing (-iŋ) *n.* 1. the producing of young 2. the rearing of young 3. good upbringing or training 4. the producing of plants and animals, esp. so as to develop new or better types

BREECH-
ES

breeze¹ (brēz) *n.* [< Fr. *brise,* prob. < EFris. *brisen,* to blow fresh and strong] 1. a wind, esp. a gentle wind 2. [Colloq.] commotion 3. [Colloq.] a thing easy to do 4. *Meteorol.* a wind of force 2 to 6 on the Beaufort scale (c. 6-49 km/h) —*vi.* **breezed, breez´ing** [Colloq.] to move or go quickly, jauntily, etc. (often with *along, in*)
breeze² (brēz) *n.* [Fr. *braise,* live coals: see BRAISE] a substance left when coke, coal, or charcoal is burned
breeze block a building block, usually hollow, made of concrete and fine cinders
breeze·way (-wā´) *n.* a covered passageway, as between a house and garage
breez·y (brē´zē) *adj.* **breez´i·er, breez´i·est** 1. slightly windy 2. lively and carefree [breezy manner] —**breez´i·ly** *adv.* —**breez´i·ness** *n.*
brems·strah·lung (brem´shträ lŏŏŋ) *n.* [G., lit., braked radiation < *Bremse,* a brake + *Strahlung,* radiation] the electromagnetic radiation given off by a high-energy particle, as an electron, when suddenly accelerated or retarded by another charged particle, as an atomic nucleus
Bren (gun) (bren) [< *Br*no, Czechoslovakia, where first made + *En*field, England, where manufactured for the Brit. army] a light, fast, gas-operated machine gun used by the British army in World War II
brent (brent) *n., pl.* **brents, brent:** see PLURAL, II, D, 1 [?] any of a number of related small, dark wild geese of Europe and N America
breth·ren (breth´rən) *n.pl.* brothers: now chiefly in religious use
Bret·on (bret´'n) *adj.* [Fr., ult. same word as BRITON] of Brittany, its people, or their language —*n.* 1. a native or inhabitant of Brittany 2. the Celtic language of the Bretons
breve (brēv) *n.* [It. < L. *brevis,* brief] 1. a mark (‿) put over a short vowel or short or unstressed syllable 2. *Music* a note (▯) equal to two semibreves 3. *R.C.Ch.* an episcopal letter from the Pope
bre·vet (brev´it) *n.* [< OFr., a note < ML. *breve,* letter < L. *brevis,* brief] *Mil.* a commission giving an officer a higher honorary rank without more pay —*adj.* held by brevet —*vt.* **-vet´ted** or **-vet´ed, -vet´ting** or **-vet´ing** to give a brevet to —**bre·vet´cy** *n., pl.* **-cies**
bre·vi·ar·y (brē´vē ər ē, brēv´yər ē) *n., pl.* **-ar·ies** [< ML. *brevarium,* abridgment, ult. < L. *brevis,* brief] *R.C.Ch.* a book of the daily prayers, hymns, etc. prescribed for priests and other clerics
brev·i·ty (brēv´ə tē) *n.* [< L. < *brevis,* brief] 1. briefness of time 2. conciseness; terseness
brew (brōŏ) *vt.* [< OE. *breowan*] 1. to make (beer, ale, etc.) from malt and hops by steeping, boiling, and fermenting 2. to make (tea, coffee, etc.) by steeping or boiling 3. to plan (mischief, trouble, etc.); plot —*vi.* 1. to brew beer, ale, etc. 2. to infuse 3. to begin to form: said of a storm, trouble, etc. —*n.* 1. a brewed beverage 2. an amount brewed —**brew up** to make tea —**brew´er** *n.*
brew·er·y (brōŏ´ər ē) *n., pl.* **-er·ies** an establishment where beer, ale, etc. are brewed
brew·ing (brōŏ´iŋ) *n.* 1. the preparation of a brew 2. the amount of brew made at one time
bri·ar¹ (brī´ər) *n.* *same as* BRIER¹ —**bri´ar·y** *adj.*
bri·ar² (brī´ər) *n.* 1. *same as* BRIER² 2. a tobacco pipe made of brierroot
bri·ar·root (-rōŏt´, -root´) *n.* *same as* BRIERROOT
bri·ar·wood (-wood´) *n.* *same as* BRIERWOOD
bribe (brīb) *n.* [< OFr., morsel of bread given to beggars < *briber,* to beg] 1. anything given or promised to induce a person to do something illegal or wrong 2. anything given or promised as an inducement —*vt.* **bribed, brib´ing** 1. to offer or give a bribe to 2. to get or influence by bribing —*vi.* to give bribes —**brib´a·ble** *adj.* —**brib´er** *n.*
brib·er·y (brī´bər ē) *n., pl.* **-er·ies** the giving, offering, or taking of bribes
bric-a-brac (brik´ə brak´) *n.* [< Fr.] small, rare, or artistic objects, or knickknacks, placed about a room for ornament
brick (brik) *n.* [< MDu. *bricke* & OFr. *brique,* a fragment] 1. a substance made from clay moulded into oblong blocks and baked, used in building, etc. 2. any of these blocks 3. bricks collectively 4. anything shaped like a brick 5. [Colloq.] a loyal and dependable person —*adj.* 1. built or paved with brick 2. like brick [brick red] —*vt.* to build or pave with brick —**drop a brick** [Colloq.] to make a tactless or indiscreet remark —**like a ton** (or **load**) **of bricks** [Colloq.] with great force; heavily [he came down on me like a ton of bricks] —**brick up** (or **in**) to wall in with brick
brick·bat (-bat´) *n.* 1. a piece of brick used as a missile 2. an unfavourable or critical remark
brick·ie, brick·y (brik´ē) *n.* [Slang] a bricklayer or his assistant
brick·lay·ing (-lā´iŋ) *n.* the act or work of building with bricks —**brick´lay´er** *n.*
brick red yellowish or brownish red —**brick´-red´** *adj.*
brick·work (-wurk´) *n.* anything built of bricks
brick·yard (-yärd´) *n.* a place where bricks are made or sold

brid·al (brīd''l) *n.* [< OE. *bryd ealo*, marriage feast < *bryd*, bride + *ealo*, ale] a wedding —*adj.* **1.** of a bride **2.** of a wedding

bridal wreath a cultivated shrub of the rose family, with many small, white double flowers

bride (brīd) *n.* [OE. *bryd*] a woman who has just been married or is about to be married

bride·groom (brīd'grōom', -groom') *n.* [< OE. *brydguma*, suitor < *bryd*, bride + *guma*, man; altered by folk etym. after GROOM] a man who has just been married or is about to be married

bride price in some societies, money or property given by a bridegroom to the bride's family

brides·maid (brīdz'mād') *n.* any of the young women who attend the bride at a wedding

bridge[1] (brij) *n.* [< OE. *brycge*] **1.** a structure built over a river, railway, etc. to provide a way across for vehicles or pedestrians **2.** a thing that provides connection or contact **3.** *a*) the upper, bony part of the nose *b*) the curved bow of a pair of glasses fitting over the nose **4.** the thin, arched piece over which the strings are stretched on a violin, etc. **5.** a raised platform on a ship for the commanding officer **6.** *Billiards* a support for the cue **7.** *Dentistry* a fixed or removable mounting for false teeth, attached to real teeth **8.** *Elec.* a circuit for measuring electrical quantities **9.** *Music* a connecting passage —*vt.* **bridged, bridg'ing 1.** to build a bridge on or over **2.** to provide a connection, transition, etc. across or between —**burn one's bridges (behind one)** to commit oneself to a course from which there is no retreat —**bridge'a·ble** *adj.*

bridge[2] (brij) *n.* [earlier *biritch*, "Russian whist," altered after prec.; ? of Russ. origin] any of various card games that developed from whist: see AUCTION BRIDGE, CONTRACT BRIDGE

bridge·head (-hed') *n.* **1.** a fortified position established by an attacking force on the enemy's side of a bridge, river, etc. **2.** *same as* BEACHHEAD (sense 2)

bridge roll a finger-shaped, soft bread roll

bridge·work (-wʉrk') *n.* a dental bridge or bridges

bri·dle (brīd''l) *n.* [< OE. < *bregdan*, to pull] **1.** a head harness for guiding a horse: it consists of headstall, bit, and reins **2.** anything that controls or restrains **3.** *Naut.* a Y-shaped cable or chain for holding, towing, etc. —*vt.* **-dled, -dling 1.** to put a bridle on **2.** to curb as with a bridle —*vi.* **1.** to pull one's head back quickly with the chin drawn in, as in showing anger, scorn, etc. **2.** to take offence (*at*)

BROW BAND
CHEEK STRAP
NOSE BAND
BIT   REINS
BRIDLE

bridle path a path for horseback riding

Brie (cheese) (brē) [after *Brie*, region in N France] a ripened soft, white cheese

brief (brēf) *adj.* [< OFr. *bref* < L. *brevis*] **1.** of short duration or extent **2.** terse; concise **3.** curt or abrupt —*n.* **1.** a summary or abstract **2.** a concise statement of the main points of a law case, as prepared by a solicitor for a counsel **3.** [*pl.*] closefitting, legless underpants or panties **4.** *R.C.Ch.* a papal letter less formal than a bull —*vt.* **1.** [Obs.] to summarize **2.** to supply with all the pertinent instructions or information **3.** *a*) to furnish with a legal brief *b*) to hire as counsel —**hold a brief for 1.** to be retained as counsel for **2.** to argue for or be in favour of —**in brief** in a few words —**brief'ing** *n.* —**brief'ly** *adv.* —**brief'ness** *n.*

brief·case (-kās') *n.* a flat, flexible case, usually of leather, for carrying papers, etc.

brief·less (-lis) *adj.* without clients: said of a lawyer

bri·er[1] (brī'ər) *n.* [< OE. *brer*] **1.** any thorny bush, as a bramble, wild rose, etc. **2.** a growth of such bushes —**bri'er·y** *adj.*

bri·er[2] (brī'ər) *n.* [Fr. *bruyère*, white heath] **1.** a heath native to S Europe **2.** its root, or a tobacco pipe made from the root: usually sp. **bri'ar**

bri·er·root (-rōot') *n.* the root wood of the brier, or a pipe made of this

bri·er·wood (-wood') *n.* *same as* BRIERROOT

brig[1] (brig) *n.* [< BRIGANTINE] a two-masted ship with square sails

brig[2] (brig) *n.* *Scot. & N Eng.* var. of BRIDGE[1]

Brig. 1. Brigade **2.** Brigadier

bri·gade (bri gād') *n.* [Fr. < It. *brigata*, troop < *brigare*, to contend < *briga*, strife] **1.** a large unit of soldiers **2.** *Mil.* a unit composed of two or more battalions **3.** a group of people organized to function as a unit in some work [a fire brigade] —*vt.* **-gad'ed, -gad'ing** to organize into a brigade

brig·a·dier (brig'ə dir') *n.* see MILITARY RANKS, *table*

brig·and (brig'ənd) *n.* [< OFr. < It. *brigante* < *brigare*: see

BRIGADE] a bandit, usually one of a roving band —**brig'and·age** (-ən dij) *n.*

brig·an·tine (brig'ən tēn') *n.* [< Fr. < It. *brigantino*, pirate vessel: see BRIGAND] a two-masted ship with the foremast square-rigged and a fore-and-aft mainsail

bright (brīt) *adj.* [OE. *bryht*, earlier *beorht*] **1.** shining with light that is radiated or reflected; full of light **2.** clear or brilliant in colour or sound; vivid or intense **3.** lively; vivacious; cheerful **4.** mentally quick; clever **5.** *a*) full of happiness or hope *b*) favourable; auspicious **6.** glorious or splendid; illustrious —*adv.* in a bright manner —**bright'ly** *adv.* —**bright'ness** *n.*

Bright's disease (brīts) [after R. *Bright* (1789-1858), Brit. physician] chronic nephritis

bril·liance (bril'yəns) *n.* great brightness, radiance, splendour, intelligence, etc.: also **bril'lian·cy**

bril·liant (-yənt) *adj.* [< Fr. prp. of *briller* < It. *brillare*, to sparkle] **1.** shining brightly; sparkling **2.** vivid; intense **3.** very splendid or distinguished **4.** highly intelligent, talented, or skilful —*n.* a gem, esp. a diamond, cut with many facets to increase its sparkle —**bril'liant·ly** *adv.*

bril·lian·tine (bril'yən tēn') *n.* [Fr.: see prec. + -INE[4]] an oily dressing for grooming the hair

brim (brim) *n.* [MHG. *brem*, edge] **1.** the topmost edge of a cup, bowl, etc. **2.** a projecting rim or edge, as of a hat —*vt., vi.* **brimmed, brim'ming** to fill up or be full to the brim —**brim over** overflow —**brim'less** *adj.*

brim·ful (brim'fool') *adj.* full to the brim

brim·stone (-stōn') *n.* [< OE. *brynstan*: see BURN[1] & STONE] *same as* SULPHUR

brimstone butterfly a species of yellow butterfly

brin·dle (brin'd'l) *adj. same as* BRINDLED —*n.* **1.** a brindled colour **2.** a brindled animal

brin·dled (-d'ld) *adj.* [prob. < ME. *brended* < *brennen*, to burn] grey or tawny, streaked or spotted with a darker colour [a *brindled* cow]

brine (brīn) *n.* [OE.] **1.** water full of salt **2.** *a*) the water of the sea *b*) the sea; ocean —*vt.* **brined, brin'ing** to soak in or treat with brine

bring (briŋ) *vt.* **brought, bring'ing** [OE. *bringan*] **1.** to carry or lead (a person or thing) to the place thought of as "here" or to a place the speaker will be **2.** to cause to be, happen, appear, etc. [war *brings* death] **3.** to lead, persuade, or influence along a course of action or belief **4.** to sell for [to *bring* a high price] **5.** *Law a*) to present in a law court [to *bring* charges] *b*) to advance (evidence, etc.) —**bring about 1.** to make happen; effect **2.** to turn (a ship) around —**bring down 1.** to cause to come down or fall **2.** to wound or kill —**bring forth 1.** to produce (offspring, fruit, etc.) **2.** to make known; disclose —**bring forward 1.** to introduce; show **2.** *Bookkeeping* to transfer (a figure) to the top of the next page or column; carry over —**bring home to** to prove; make realise —**bring in 1.** to import **2.** to produce (income or revenue) **3.** to introduce or put forward **4.** to give (a verdict) —**bring off** to accomplish —**bring on** to cause to be, happen, or appear —**bring out 1.** to reveal; make clear **2.** to publish (a book), produce (a play), etc. **3.** to introduce (a girl) formally to society —**bring over** to convince or persuade —**bring round 1.** to persuade by arguing, urging, etc. **2.** to bring back to consciousness —**bring to 1.** to revive (an unconscious person) **2.** to cause (a ship) to stop —**bring up 1.** to take care of during childhood; raise; rear **2.** to introduce, as into discussion **3.** to cough up **4.** to vomit **5.** to stop abruptly **6.** to cause someone to face a charge in court —**bring'er** *n.*

bring-and-buy sale a bazaar, often in aid of charity, to which people bring items for sale and buy those brought by others

brink (briŋk) *n.* [< MLowG. or Dan., shore, bank] the edge, esp. at the top of a steep place; verge: often used figuratively [on the *brink* of war]

brink·man·ship (briŋk'mən ship') *n.* [BRINK + -MANSHIP] the policy of pursuing a hazardous course of action to the brink of catastrophe before withdrawing: also **brinks'·man·ship'** (briŋks'-)

brin·y (brīn'ē) *adj.* **brin'i·er, brin'i·est** of or like brine; very salty —**the briny** [Slang] the ocean —**brin'i·ness** *n.*

bri·o (brē'ō) *n.* [It.] animation; zest

bri·oche (brē osh') *n.* [Fr.] a light, rich roll made with flour, butter, eggs, and yeast

bri·quette, bri·quet (bri ket') *n.* [< Fr. dim. of *brique*, brick] a brick made of compressed coal dust, etc., used for fuel or kindling

brisk (brisk) *adj.* [< ? Fr. *brusque*, BRUSQUE] **1.** quick in manner; energetic **2.** cool, dry, and bracing [*brisk* air] **3.** active; busy [*brisk* trading] —*vt., vi.* to make brisk; enliven (often with *up*) —**brisk'ly** *adv.* —**brisk'ness** *n.*

brisk·en (brisk'ən) *vt., vi.* to make or become brisk (often with *up*)

bris·ket (bris'kit) *n.* [ME. *brusket*, akin to Dan. *bryske*] **1.** the breast of an animal **2.** meat cut from this part

bris·ling (bris'liŋ, briz'-) *n.* [Norw. dial. < older Dan. *bretling*] *same as* SPRAT (sense 1)

bris·tle (bris′'l) *n.* [< OE. *byrst*] 1. any short, stiff, prickly hair of an animal or plant 2. *a*) any of the hairs of a pig or other animal, used for brushes *b*) such a hair, or an artificial hair like it, in a brush —*vi.* -tled, -tling 1. to become stiff and erect, like bristles 2. to have the bristles become erect, as in fear 3. to become tense with fear, anger, etc. 4. to be thickly covered or filled (*with*) [bristling with difficulties] —*vt.* 1. to make stand up like bristles 2. to make bristly

bris·tly (bris′lē) *adj.* -tli·er, -tli·est 1. having bristles; rough with bristles 2. bristlelike; prickly —bris′tli·ness *n.*

Bris·tol board (bris′t'l) [after *Bristol* in SW England] a fine, smooth pasteboard used by artists, painters, etc

Bristol fashion *Naut.* in good order; neat and tidy

bris·tols (bris′t'lz) *n.pl.* [contr. < *Bristol Cities*, rhyming slang for *titties*, breasts] [Slang] a woman's breasts

Brit (brit) *n.* [Colloq.] a British person

Brit. 1. Britain 2. Britannia 3. British

Bri·tan·ni·a (bri tan′yə, -tan′ē ə) 1. *Roman name for* Great Britain, esp. the southern part 2. the personification of Britain as a helmeted female warrior with trident and shield

britannia metal [*also* B-] an alloy of tin, copper, and antimony, used in tableware, like pewter

Bri·tan·nic (bri tan′ik) *adj.* of Britain; British

britch·es (brich′iz) *n.pl.* [Colloq.] *same as* BREECHES (sense 2)

Brit·i·cism (brit′ə siz'm) *n.* a word, phrase, or idiom peculiar to or characteristic of British English: also **Brit′·ish·ism**

Brit·ish (brit′ish) *adj.* [< OE. *Bryttisc* < *Bret*, a Celt. inhabitant of Britain < Celt.] 1. of Great Britain or its people 2. of the British Commonwealth 3. of the English language as spoken and written in Britain —**the British** the people of Great Britain

Brit·ish·er (-ər) *n.* Chiefly U.S. name for a native of Great Britain, esp. an Englishman

British Legion *former title of the* ROYAL BRITISH LEGION

British Lion the personification of Britain as a lion

British thermal unit the quantity of heat required to raise the temperature of one pound of water one degree Fahrenheit: SI equivalent 1055.06 joules

Brit·on (brit′'n) *n.* [< OFr. < ML. *Britto*; *of* Celt. origin: see BRITISH] 1. a member of an early Celtic people living in S Britain at the time of the Roman invasion 2. a native or inhabitant of Great Britain, esp. an Englishman

brit·tle (brit′'l) *adj.* [< OE. *breotan*, to break] 1. easily broken or shattered because hard and inflexible; fragile 2. having a sharp, hard quality [brittle tones] 3. stiff and unbending in manner —*n.* a brittle, crunchy sweet with nuts in it [peanut brittle] —brit′tle·ly, brit′tly *adv.* —brit′tle·ness *n.*

bro. *pl.* **bros.** brother

broach¹ (brōch) *n.* [< OFr. < ML. *brocca*, a spike < L. *broccus*, with projecting teeth] 1. a spit for roasting meat 2. a tapered bit for enlarging or shaping holes —*vt.* 1. to make a°hole in so as to let out liquid 2. to start a discussion of; bring up 3. to open in order to begin to use —broach′·er *n.*

broach² (brōch) *vi., vt* [< ?] *Naut.* to turn or swing so that the beam faces the waves and wind and there is a danger of swamping or capsizing

B road a second-class road

broad (brôd) *adj.* [< OE. *brad*] 1. of large extent from side to side; wide 2. spacious [a broad plain] 3. clear; open; full [broad daylight] 4. plain to the mind; obvious [a broad hint] 5. strongly marked [a broad accent] 6. coarse or ribald [a broad joke] 7. tolerant; liberal [a broad view] 8. wide in range; not limited [a broad survey] 9. main or general; not detailed [in broad outline] 10. *Phonet.* pronounced with the tongue held low and flat in the mouth; open, esp. as the (ä) of father —*n.* 1. the broad part of anything 2. [U.S. Slang] a woman: a vulgar term —**the Broads** in East Anglia, a group of shallow navigable lakes, connected by a network of rivers —broad′ly *adv.* —broad′·ness *n.*

broad arrow 1. an arrow with a broad, barbed head 2. an identification mark in the form of a broad arrow formerly used on British government property, as on prison uniforms

broad bean a plant of the legume family, bearing large, broad pods with flat, edible seeds

broad·cast (-käst′) *vt.* -cast′ or, in radio, occas. -cast′ed, -cast′ing 1. to scatter (seed) widely 2. to spread (information, etc.) widely 3. to transmit by radio or TV —*vi.* to broadcast radio or TV programmes —*adj.* 1. widely scattered 2. of, for, or by radio or TV broadcasting —*n.* 1. a broadcasting 2. a radio or TV programme —*adv.* far and wide —broad′cast′er *n.*

Broad Church that part of the Anglican Church holding a doctrinal position between High Church and Low Church —Broad′-Church′ *adj.*

broad·cloth (-kloth′) *n.* 1. a fine, smooth woollen cloth: it originally was made on broad looms 2. a fine, smooth cotton or silk cloth, used for shirts, pyjamas, etc.

broad·en (-'n) *vt., vi.* to widen; expand

broad gauge a railway track with a greater distance between the lines than the standard gauge of 56.5 inches (c. 1.44 metres) —broad′-gauge′, broad′-gauged′ *adj.*

broad-leaved (-lēvd′) *adj.* denoting trees other than conifers; having broad rather than needle-shaped leaves

broad·loom (-lōōm′) *adj.* woven on a broad loom, as a carpet

broad-mind·ed (-mīn′did) *adj.* tolerant of others' opinions and behaviour; not bigoted; liberal —broad′-mind′ed·ly *adv.* —broad′-mind′ed·ness *n.*

broad·sheet (-shēt′) *n.* a large sheet of paper printed only on one side, as with a political message, advertising, or, formerly, a popular ballad

broad·side (-sīd′) *n.* 1. the entire side of a ship above the waterline 2. *a*) all the guns that can be fired from one side of a ship *b*) their simultaneous firing 3. an abusive attack in words 4. *same as* BROADSHEET —*adv.* 1. with the length turned (*to* an object) 2. directly in the side

broad-spec·trum (-spek′trəm) *adj.* effective against a wide variety of microorganisms

broad·sword (-sôrd′) *n.* a sword with a broad blade, for slashing rather than thrusting

broad·tail (-tāl′) *n.* 1. *same as* KARAKUL (sense 1) 2. the glossy, wavy pelt of the karakul lamb, esp. of one prematurely born

Broad·way (brôd′wā′) street in New York City, the axis of the city's entertainment section

Brob·ding·nag (brob′diŋ nag′) in Swift's *Gulliver's Travels*, a land of giants —Brob′ding·nag′i·an *adj., n.*

bro·cade (brō kād′) *n.* [Sp. *brocado* < It. pp. of *broccare*, to embroider: see BROACH¹] a rich cloth with a raised design, as of silk, velvet, gold, or silver, woven into it —*vt.* -cad′ed, -cad′ing to weave a raised design into (cloth)

broc·co·li (brok′ə lē) *n.* [It., pl. of *broccolo*, a sprout, dim. of *brocco*: see BROACH¹] a plant related to the cauliflower but bearing tender shoots with greenish buds, cooked as a vegetable

bro·chette (brō shet′) *n.* [Fr., dim. of *broche*: see BROACH¹] a small spit, as for grilling kebabs

bro·chure (brō shoor′, -shyoor′; brō′shər) *n.* [Fr. < *brocher*, to stitch] a pamphlet

bro·de·rie an·glaise (brō drē än glez′) [Fr., lit., English embroidery] fine eyelet embroidery, usually white, used on women's garments and linens

brogue¹ (brōg) *n.* [prob. < Ir. *barróg*, a hold, grip (esp. on the tongue)] dialectal pronunciation, esp. that of English as spoken by the Irish

brogue² (brōg) *n.* [Gael. & Ir. *brōg*, a shoe] 1. a coarse shoe of untanned leather, formerly worn in Ireland 2. a sturdy walking shoe, usually with decorative perforations

broil¹ (broil) *vt.* [OFr. *bruillir*, prob. by confusion of *bruir*, to burn & *usler*, to singe] [Chiefly U.S.] to grill —*vi.* 1. to be grilled 2. to become heated or angry

broil² (broil) *n.* [ME. *broilen*, to quarrel < OFr. *brouillier*, to dirty] a noisy or violent quarrel; brawl —*vi.* to take part in a broil

broil·er (broil′ər) *n.* 1. a pan, grill, etc. for broiling 2. a young chicken suitable for roasting 3. a very hot day

broke (brōk) *pt. & archaic pp. of* BREAK —*adj.* [Colloq.] having no money; bankrupt —**go broke** [Colloq.] to become bankrupt

bro·ken (brō′k'n) *pp. of* BREAK —*adj.* 1. splintered, fractured, burst, etc. 2. not in working condition 3. violated [a broken promise] 4. disrupted as by divorce [a broken home] 5. sick, weakened, or beaten 6. bankrupt 7. not even; interrupted 8. intermittent [broken sunshine] 9. imperfectly spoken, esp. with reference to grammar and syntax [broken English] 10. subdued and trained; tamed For phrases, see BREAK —bro′ken·ly *adv.* —bro′ken·ness *n.*

broken chord *same as* ARPEGGIO

bro·ken-down (-doun′) *adj.* 1. sick or worn out, as by old age or disease 2. out of order; useless

bro·ken-heart·ed (-här′tid) *adj.* crushed by sorrow, grief, or disappointment; inconsolable

bro·ken-wind·ed (-wind′əd) *adj.* gasping with or as with the heaves

bro·ker (brō′kər) *n.* [< ONormFr. < OFr. *brochier*, to broach, tap; orig. sense "wine dealer"] 1. a person hired to act as an agent in making contracts or sales 2. *same as* STOCKBROKER 3. a dealer in second-hand goods

bro·ker·age (-ij) *n.* 1. the business of a broker 2. a broker's fee

brol·ly (brol′ē) *n.* [altered < (UM)BRELLA] 1. [Colloq.] an umbrella 2. [Slang] a parachute

bro·mide (brō′mīd) *n.* [BROM(INE) + -IDE] 1. a compound of bromine with another element or with a radical 2. potassium bromide, KBr, used in medicine as a sedative 3. *a*) a trite saying or remark; platitude *b*) a person who says trite things

bromide paper a type of photographic paper coated with an emulsion of silver bromide

bro·mid·ic (brō mid′ik) *adj.* [see BROMIDE] using or containing a trite remark or remarks; dull

bro·mine (brō′mēn) *n.* [Fr. *brome* < Gr. *brōmos*, stench + -INE⁴] a chemical element, usually a reddish-brown, corrosive liquid volatilizing to form an irritating vapour: symbol, Br; at. wt., 79.909; at. no., 35
bron·chi (broŋ′kī) *n. pl. of* BRONCHUS
bron·chi·al (-kē əl) *adj.* of the bronchi or bronchioles
bronchial tubes the bronchi and the tubes branching from them
bron·chi·ole (broŋ′kē ōl′) *n.* any of the small subdivisions of the bronchi
bron·chi·tis (broŋ kīt′əs) *n.* [BRONCH(O)- + -ITIS] an inflammation of the mucous lining of the bronchial tubes —**bron·chit·ic** (-kit′ik) *adj.*
bron·cho- [< Gr. *bronchos*, windpipe] *a combining form* meaning having to do with the bronchi [*bronchoscope*]: also, before a vowel, **bronch-**
bron·cho·scope (broŋ′kə skōp′) *n.* [BRONCHO- + -SCOPE] an instrument for examining the bronchi, or for removing foreign bodies from them
bron·chus (broŋ′kəs) *n., pl.* **-chi** (-kī) [ModL. < Gr. *bronchos*, windpipe] either of the two main branches of the trachea, or windpipe
bron·co (broŋ′kō) *n., pl.* **-cos** [MexSp. < Sp., rough] a wild or partially tamed horse or pony of the western U.S.: also sp. **bron′cho,** pl. **-chos**
bron·to·sau·rus (bron′tə sôr′əs) *n., pl.* **-sau′rus·es, -sau′ri** (-ī) [ModL. < Gr. *brontē*, thunder + -SAURUS] a huge, plant-eating dinosaur common in N America in the late Jurassic Period: also **bron′-to·saur′** (-sôr′)
bronze (bronz) *n.* [Fr. < It. *bronzo*] 1. an alloy consisting chiefly of copper and tin 2. an article, esp. a sculpture, made of bronze 3. a reddish-brown colour like that of bronze 4. an award given to mark the attainment of an intermediate

BRONTOSAURUS
(to 23 m long)

standard in certain sports, dancing, etc —*adj.* of or like bronze —*vt.* **bronzed, bronz′ing** to give a bronze colour to —**bronz′y** *adj.*
Bronze Age a phase of human culture (c. 3500–1000 B.C.) characterized by bronze tools and weapons
bronze medal a medal awarded to an entrant who is placed third in a competition
brooch (brōch) *n.* [see BROACH¹] a large ornamental pin with a clasp
brood (brōōd) *n.* [< OE. *brod*] 1. a group of birds or fowl hatched at one time and cared for together 2. [Colloq.] all the children in a family 3. a group of a particular breed or kind —*vt.* 1. to sit on and hatch (eggs) 2. to hover over or protect (offspring, etc.) —*vi.* 1. to brood eggs or offspring 2. to keep thinking about something in a troubled way; worry (often with *on, over,* or *about*) —*adj.* kept for breeding [a *brood* mare] —**brood′ing·ly** *adv.*
brood·er (-ər) *n.* 1. one that broods 2. a heated shelter for raising young fowl
brood·y (-ē) *adj.* **brood′i·er, brood′i·est** 1. ready to brood, as poultry 2. inclined to dwell moodily on one's own thoughts —**brood′i·ly** *adv.* —**brood′i·ness** *n.*
brook¹ (brook) *n.* [OE. *broc*] a small stream, usually not so large as a river
brook² (brook) *vt.* [OE. *brucan,* to use] to put up with; endure [he will *brook* no interference]
brook·let (-lit) *n.* a little brook
brook·lime (-līm) *n.* a variety of speedwell that often grows in brooks and ditches
broom (brōōm, broom) *n.* [OE. *brom,* brushwood] 1. a shrub of the legume family, with many, usually yellow, flowers 2. *a)* a bundle of long, stiff fibres or straws (orig. twigs of broom) fastened to a long handle and used for sweeping *b)* any long-handled sweeping brush —*vt.* to sweep as with a broom
broom·rape (-rāp) *n.* [BROOM + RAPE²] any of a genus of leafless, fleshy, parasitic plants growing on the roots of other plants
broom·stick (-stik′) *n.* the handle of a broom
bros. brothers
brose (brōz) *n.* [Scot., alt. < ME. *broues,* broth] [Scot.] a thin porridge eaten with butter, cream, or milk
broth (broth, brôth) *n.* [OE.] a clear, thin soup made by boiling meat, etc. in water
broth·el (broth′əl) *n.* [ME., wretched person < OE. pp. of *breothan,* to go to ruin] a house of prostitution
broth·er (bruth′ər) *n., pl.* **broth′ers;** chiefly religious, **breth′ren** [OE. *brothor*] 1. a male as he is related to the other children of his parents 2. a close friend who is like a brother 3. a fellow man 4. a fellow member of the same race, creed, profession, organization, etc. 5. a member of a men's religious order —*vt.* to treat or address as a brother
broth·er·hood (-hood′) *n.* 1. the state of being a brother or

brothers 2. an association of men united in a common interest, work, creed, etc.
broth·er-in-law (-in lô′) *n., pl.* **broth′ers-in-law′** 1. the brother of one's husband or wife 2. the husband of one's sister 3. the husband of the sister of one's wife or husband
broth·er·ly (-lē) *adj.* 1. of or like a brother 2. friendly, kind, loyal, etc. —**broth′er·li·ness** *n.*
brougham (brōōm; brōō′əm, brō′-) *n.* [after Lord *Brougham* (1778–1868), Brit. statesman] 1. a closed carriage with the driver's seat outside 2. any of various early styles of motor car
brought (brôt) *pt. & pp. of* BRING
brou·ha·ha (brōō′hä hä) *n.* [Fr.] a noisy stir or wrangle; uproar
brow (brou) *n.* [< OE. *bru*] 1. the eyebrow 2. the forehead 3. the facial expression [an angry *brow*] 4. a projecting edge, as of a cliff 5. the rounded top of a hill

BROUGHAM

brow·beat (-bēt′) *vt.* **-beat′, -beat′en, -beat′ing** to intimidate with harsh, stern looks and talk
brown (broun) *adj.* [< OE. *brun*] 1. having the colour of chocolate or coffee, a mixture of red, black, and yellow 2. tanned or dark-skinned —*n.* 1. a brown colour 2. a brown pigment or dye —*vt., vi.* to make or become brown, as by exposure to sunlight or heat —**browned off** [Colloq.] disheartened or resentful —**brown′ish** *adj.* —**brown′ness** *n.*
brown bet·ty (bet′ē) [*also* b- B-] a baked apple pudding made with bread crumbs, butter, etc.
brown bread any bread made of dark flour
brown coal *same as* LIGNITE
Brown·i·an movement (broun′ē ən) [after R. *Brown* (1773–1858), Brit. botanist who described it] the constant, random, zigzag movement of small particles dispersed in a fluid medium, caused by collision with molecules of the fluid
brown·ie (broun′ē) *n.* 1. a small, helpful, brown elf or goblin in folk tales 2. [B-] a Girl Guide of the youngest group, those seven to eleven years old
brown·ing (broun′iŋ) *n.* a preparation for colouring and thickening gravy
brown paper coarse wrapping paper made from unbleached material
brown rice rice that has not been polished
brown shirt 1. [*often* B- S-] a storm trooper in Nazi Germany 2. any Nazi
brown·stone (-stōn′) *n.* [U.S.] 1. a reddish-brown sandstone, used for building 2. a house with a façade of brownstone
brown study [< early sense of BROWN, gloomy] deep absorption in thought; reverie
brown sugar soft sugar prepared so that the crystals retain a brown coating of dark syrup
browse (brouz) *n.* [< OFr. < OS. *brustian,* to sprout] 1. leaves, twigs, and young shoots of trees or shrubs, which animals feed on 2. the act of browsing —*vt.* **browsed, brows′ing** 1. to nibble at 2. to graze on 3. to examine casually —*vi.* 1. to nibble at leaves, twigs, etc. 2. to glance through a book, etc. casually 3. to look casually over articles for sale —**brows′er** *n.*
B.R.S. British Road Services
bru·cel·lo·sis (brōō′sə lō′sis) *n.* [after Sir David *Bruce* (1855–1931), Scot. physician + -OSIS] a disease, esp. in man and cattle, caused by bacteria: see UNDULANT FEVER
Bru·in (brōō′ən) [Du., brown] [*also* b-] a name for the bear in fable and folklore
bruise (brōōz) *vt.* **bruised, bruis′ing** [ME. *bruisen* (infl. by OFr. *bruisier,* to break) < OE. *brysan,* to crush] 1. to injure (body tissue) without breaking the skin but causing discolouration 2. to injure the surface of (fruit, etc.) 3. to crush as with a pestle in a mortar 4. to hurt (the feelings, spirit, etc.) —*vi.* to be or become bruised —*n.* 1. a bruised area of tissue, of a surface, etc. 2. an injury to one's feelings, etc.
bruis·er (brōōz′ər) *n.* a strong, pugnacious man; specif., a professional boxer
bruit (brōōt) *vt.* [< OFr. < *bruire,* to rumble, prob. < L. *rugire,* to roar] [Archaic or U.S.] to spread (*about*) a rumour of
brum·by (brum′bē) *n.* [Aust.] a wild horse, esp. one that is descended from runaway stock
brume (brōōm) *n.* [Fr. < L. *bruma,* winter] mist; fog —**bru·mous** (brōō′məs) *adj.*
brunch (brunch) *n.* [BR(EAKFAST) + (L)UNCH] [Colloq.] a meal combining breakfast and lunch
bru·nette (brōō net′) *n.* [< OFr., dim. of *brun* < OHG. *brun,* brown] a girl or woman with dark brown hair —*adj.* of a dark brown colour [*brunette* hair]
brunt (brunt) *n.* [< ?] 1. the shock (of an attack) or impact (of a blow) 2. the heaviest or hardest part
brush¹ (brush) *n.* [< OFr. *broce,* bush < VL. *bruscia* < Gmc.] 1. *same as* BRUSHWOOD 2. *a)* sparsely settled, scrubby country *b)* in Australia, a thickly forested area 3. *a)* a device for cleaning, polishing, painting, etc., having

bristles, hairs, or wires fastened into a back, with or without a handle *b*) a device of wires spread from a handle, used as on drums for a swishing effect **4.** the act of brushing **5.** a light, grazing stroke **6.** a bushy tail, esp. that of a fox **7.** a brief encounter, esp. an unpleasant or unfriendly one **8.** [Aust. Slang] a woman or women collectively **9.** *Elec.* a piece or bundle of carbon, copper, etc. used as a conductor between an external circuit and a revolving part —*vt.* **1.** to clean, polish, paint, etc. with a brush **2.** to apply, remove, etc. with a stroke or strokes as of a brush **3.** to touch or graze in passing —*vi.* to graze past something —**brush aside** (or **away**) to dismiss from consideration —**brush off** [Slang] to dismiss or get rid of abruptly —**brush up 1.** to clean up **2.** to refresh one's memory or skill (often with *on*)
brush² (brush) *vi.* [ME. *bruschen* < ?] to move with a rush; hurry —*n.* a short, quick fight or quarrel
brush discharge a visible, brushlike electric discharge as in the air surrounding a wire at high potential
brushed (brusht) *adj.* processed by brushing so as to raise the nap, as some fabrics or leather
brush fire 1. a fire in brushwood **2.** a flare-up that threatens to intensify unless controlled
brush-off (-of') *n.* [Slang] an abrupt dismissal: esp. in the phrase **give** (or **get**) **the brushoff**
brush turkey any of several Australian birds with black plumage that lay their eggs in a mound of sand
brush-up (-up') *n.* the act or instance of tidying one's appearance, esp. in the phrase **wash and brush-up**
brush·wood (-wood') *n.* **1.** chopped-off tree branches **2.** a thick growth of small trees and shrubs
brush·work (-wurk') *n.* **1.** work done with a brush **2.** a characteristic way of putting on paint with a brush [Renoir's *brushwork*]
brush·y (-ē) *adj.* **brush'i·er, brush'i·est 1.** rough and bristly **2.** covered with brushwood or underbrush
brusque (brusk) *adj.* [Fr. < It. *brusco* < ML. *bruscus*, brushwood] rough and abrupt in manner or speech; curt —**brusque'ly** *adv.* —**brusque'ness** *n.*
Brus·sels carpet (brus''lz) a kind of carpet with a thick-looped pile
Brussels lace a lace made by sewing completed patterns on a machine-made net
Brussels sprouts 1. a plant of the cabbage family that bears miniature cabbagelike heads on an erect stem **2.** these edible heads
bru·tal (broot''l) *adj.* **1.** like a brute; savage, violent, ruthless, etc. **2.** very harsh [a *brutal* winter] **3.** plain and direct, but disturbing [*brutal* facts] —**bru'tal·ly** *adv.*
bru·tal·i·ty (broo tal'ə tē) *n.* **1.** the quality of being brutal **2.** *pl.* **-ties** a brutal act
bru·tal·ize (broot'əl īz') *vt.* **-ized', -iz'ing 1.** to make brutal **2.** to treat brutally —*vi.* to become brutal —**bru'tal·i·za'tion** *n.*
brute (broot) *adj.* [OFr. *brut* < L. *brutus*, irrational] **1.** lacking the ability to reason [a *brute* beast] **2.** lacking consciousness [the *brute* force of nature] **3.** of or like an animal; brutal, cruel, sensual, stupid, etc. —*n.* **1.** an animal **2.** a person who is brutal or stupid, sensual, etc.
brut·ish (broot'ish) *adj.* of or like a brute; savage, stupid, sensual, etc. —**brut'ish·ly** *adv.* —**brut'ish·ness** *n.*
bry·ol·o·gy (brī ol'ə jē) *n.* [< Gr. *bryon*, moss + -LOGY] the branch of botany dealing with bryophytes —**bry'o·log'i·cal** (-ə loj'i k'l) *adj.* —**bry·ol'o·gist** *n.*
bry·o·ny (brī'ə nē) *n., pl.* **-nies** [< L. < Gr. < *bryein*, to swell] a climbing plant with large, fleshy roots and greenish flowers
bry·o·phyte (-fīt') *n.* [< Gr. *bryon*, moss + -PHYTE] any moss or liverwort —**bry'o·phyt'ic** (-fit'ik) *adj.*
Bry·thon·ic (bri thon'ik) *adj., n.* [W., ult. < same word as BRITON] *see* CELTIC
B/s, b/s 1. bags **2.** bales **3.** bill of sale
B.S., BS 1. balance sheet **2.** British Standard
B.Sc. [L. *Baccalaureus Scientiae*] Bachelor of Science
B.S.I. British Standards Institution
Bs/L bills of lading
B.S.T. British Summer Time
Bt. Baronet
btry battery (of artillery)
B.t.u. British thermal unit(s): also **B.Th.U., B.T.U., b.t.u., Btu, btu**
bu. bushel(s)
bub·ble (bub''l) *n.* [echoic] **1.** a very thin film of liquid forming a ball around air or gas [soap *bubbles*] **2.** a tiny ball of air or gas in a liquid or solid **3.** anything shaped like a bubble, sphere, or hemisphere **4.** any scheme, etc. that seems plausible but proves to be worthless **5.** the act or sound of bubbling —*vi.* **-bled, -bling 1.** to rise in bubbles; boil; foam **2.** to make a bubbling sound; burble —*vt.* to form bubbles in; make bubble —**bubble over 1.** to overflow, as boiling liquid **2.** to be unrestrained in one's enthusiasm, etc.
bubble and squeak a dish of cabbage and potatoes, and sometimes meat, fried together

bubble bath 1. a bath perfumed and softened by a solution, crystals, or powder that forms surface bubbles **2.** such a solution, powder, etc.
bubble car a small car with a transparent, bubble-shaped top
bubble chamber a device that enables the tracks of ionizing particles to become visible as a row of bubbles —*vi.* a superheated liquid
bubble gum a kind of chewing gum that can be blown into large bubbles
bub·bly (bub'lē) *adj.* **1.** full of bubbles **2.** like a bubble —*n.* [Colloq.] champagne
bu·bo (byōo'bō) *n., pl.* **-boes** [< ML. < Gr. *boubōn*, groin] an inflamed swelling of a lymph gland, esp. in the groin —**bu·bon'ic** (-bon'ik) *adj.*
bubonic plague a contagious disease characterized by buboes, fever, and delirium: fleas from infected rats are the carriers
buc·cal (buk''l) *adj.* [L. *bucca*, cheek + -AL] **1.** of the cheek or cheeks **2.** of the mouth
buc·ca·neer (buk'ə nir') *n.* [Fr. *boucanier*, user of a *boucan*, native Brazilian grill for roasting meat; orig. applied to Fr. hunters in Haiti] a pirate, or sea robber —*vi.* to act as or like a buccaneer —**buc'ca·neer'ing** *n.*
buck¹ (buk) *n.* [< OE. *bucca*, male goat] **1.** *pl.* **bucks, buck:** see PLURAL, II, D, 1 a male deer, goat, etc. **2.** the act of bucking **3.** [Colloq.] a young man —*vi.* to rear upwards quickly in an attempt to throw off a rider: said of a horse, etc. —*vt.* to throw by bucking —*adj.* male —**buck up** [Colloq.] **1.** to cheer up **2.** to hurry up —**buck'er** *n.*
buck² (buk) *n.* [prob. < BUCKHORN: a knife with a buckhorn handle was used as a counter] **1.** *Poker* a counter placed before a player as a reminder to deal next, etc. **2.** [U.S. & Aust. Slang] a dollar —**pass the buck** [Colloq.] to seek to make someone else take the blame or responsibility
buck·bean (-bēn') *n.* [after Du. *boksboon*, lit., goat's bean] a bog plant of the gentian family with pink or white flowers resembling those of the hyacinth
buck·board (buk'bord') *n.* [< ?] [U.S.] a four-wheeled, open carriage with the seat carried on a flooring of long, flexible boards whose ends rest directly on the axles
buck·et (buk'it) *n.* [< Anglo-Fr. *buket*, dim. of OE. *buc*, pitcher] **1.** a container with a handle, for carrying water, coal, etc.; pail **2.** the amount held by a bucket: also **buck'et·ful', *pl.* -fuls' 3.** a thing like a bucket, as a scoop on a mechanical shovel **4.** [*pl.*] [Colloq.] large amounts [she wept *buckets*] —*vt., vi.* **1.** to carry or lift in a bucket **2.** to move or drive rapidly or bumpily **3.** to rain heavily (often with *down*) —**kick the bucket** [? < obs. *bucket,* beam on which a slaughtered pig was hung] [Slang] to die

BUCKBOARD

bucket seat a single contoured seat whose back can often be tipped forwards, as in some sports cars
bucket shop an unregistered firm of stockbrokers engaging in highly speculative transactions
buck·eye (buk'ī') *n.* [BUCK¹ + EYE: from the appearance of the seed] [U.S.] **1.** a tree of the horse-chestnut family, with large, spiny capsules enclosing shiny brown seeds **2.** the seed
buck·horn (-hôrn') *n.* the horn of a buck, used for knife handles, etc.
buck·le¹ (buk''l) *n.* [< OFr. < LL. < L. *buccula*, cheek strap of a helmet, dim. of *bucca*, cheek] **1.** a clasp for fastening a strap, belt, etc. **2.** a clasplike ornament, as for shoes —*vt., vi.* **-led, -ling** to fasten with a buckle —**buckle down** to apply oneself energetically
buck·le² (buk''l) *vt., vi.* **-led, -ling** [prob. < Du. *bukken,* to bend] to bend, warp, or crumple —*n.* a bend, bulge, kink, etc. —**buckle under** to give in; yield; submit
buck·ler (buk'lər) *n.* [OFr. *bocler* < *bocle*, the boss, in its centre] **1.** a small, round shield worn on the arm **2.** any protection or defence
buck·o (buk'ō) *n., pl.* **-oes** [< BUCK¹] a bully
buck·pass·er (-päs'ər) *n.* [Colloq.] a person who regularly seeks to shift blame or responsibility to someone else —**buck'-pass'ing** *n.*
buck·ram (buk'rəm) *n.* [< OFr., prob. < *Bokhara,* in Asia Minor] a coarse cloth stiffened with glue or other size, for use in bookbinding, for lining clothes, etc. —*adj.* of or like buckram
buck·shee (buk'shē', buk'shē') *n.* [< BAKSHEESH] something free; gratuity —*adj.* free of charge; unexpected but welcome
buck·shot (buk'shot') *n.* a large lead shot for shooting deer and other large game
buck·skin (-skin') *n.* **1.** a soft, usually napped, yellowish-grey leather made from the skins of deer or sheep

2. [*pl.*] clothes or shoes made of buckskin **3.** a strong cotton or woollen fabric —*adj.* made of buckskin

buck·thorn (-thôrn') *n.* [BUCK¹ + THORN] a tree or shrub with small, greenish flowers and purple berries formerly used as a purgative

buck·tooth (-tōōth') *n., pl.* -teeth' [BUCK¹ + TOOTH] a projecting front tooth —**buck'toothed'** *adj.*

buck·wheat (-hwēt', -wēt') *n.* [< ME. *bok-* (< OE. *boc-*), BEECH + WHEAT: from the beechnut-shaped seeds] **1.** a plant grown for its black, tetrahedral grains **2.** the grain of this plant, from which a dark flour is made **3.** this flour

bu·col·ic (byōōkol'ik) *adj.* [< L. < Gr. < *boukolos*, herdsman < *bous*, ox] **1.** of shepherds; pastoral **2.** of country life; rustic —*n.* a pastoral poem —**bu·col'i·cal·ly** *adv.*

bud¹ (bud) *n.* [ME. *budde*, seedpod] **1.** *a*) a small swelling on a plant, from which a shoot, cluster of leaves, or flower develops *b*) a partly opened flower **2.** any immature person or thing **3.** an asexually produced outgrowth or swelling in simple organisms, as the hydra, that develops into a new individual —*vi.* **bud'ded, bud'ding 1.** to put forth buds **2.** to begin to develop **3.** to be young, promising, etc. —*vt.* **1.** to cause to bud **2.** to graft by inserting a bud of (a plant) into the bark of another sort of plant —**nip in the bud** to check at the earliest stage —**bud'der** *n.* —**bud'like'** *adj.*

bud² (bud) *n.* [U.S. Slang] *short for* BUDDY: used in addressing a man or boy

Bud·dhism (bood'iz'm) *n.* a religion of central and eastern Asia, founded in India by Buddha: it teaches that right living and self-denial will enable the soul to reach Nirvana, a divine state of release from bodily pain and sorrow —**Bud'dhist** *n., adj.* —**Bud'dhis'tic** *adj.*

bud·dle·ia (bud'lē'ə) *n.* [after Adam *Buddle*, 18th-c. Brit. botanist] any of a genus of shrubs and trees of the logania family with purple or orange blossoms

bud·dy (bud'ē) *n., pl.* -dies [< ? Brit. dial. *butty*, companion] [Chiefly U.S. Colloq.] a companion; comrade

budge (buj) *vt., vi.* **budged, budg'ing** [Fr. *bouger*, to move, ult. < L. *bulla*: see BOIL¹] **1.** to move even a little **2.** to yield or cause to yield

budg·er·i·gar (buj'əri gär') *n.* [Abor., lit., good cockatoo] an Australian parakeet with a greenish-yellow body and bright blue on the cheeks and tail feathers

budg·et (buj'it) *n.* [< OFr. *bougette*, dim. of *bouge*, a bag < L. *bulga*, leather bag] **1.** a collection of items; stock **2.** a plan adjusting expenses to the expected income during a certain period **3.** the estimated cost of living, operating, etc. **4.** the amount of money needed for a specific use **5.** an estimate of revenue and expenditure for a country or organization, usually prepared annually —*vt.* **1.** to put on or in a budget **2.** to plan in detail; schedule [*budget* your time] —*vi.* **1.** to make a budget **2.** to make provision (with *for*) —**budg'et·ar·y** *adj.* —**budg'et·er** *n.*

budg·ie (buj'ē) *n.* [Colloq.] *same as* BUDGERIGAR

buff¹ (buf) *n.* [earlier *buffe*, buffalo < It. *bufalo*, BUFFALO] **1.** a heavy, soft, brownish-yellow leather made from the skin of a buffalo or from other animal hides **2.** a military coat made of this leather **3.** a stick, small block, or wheel (**buff-wheel**) covered with leather or cloth used for cleaning or shining **4.** a dull brownish yellow **5.** [Colloq.] a devotee; fan [a jazz *buff*] —*adj.* **1.** made of buff **2.** of the colour buff —*vt.* to shine with a buff —**in the buff** naked

buff² (buf) *n.* [OFr. *buffe*: see BUFFET¹] a blow: now only in BLINDMAN'S BUFF

buf·fa·lo (buf'əlō') *n., pl.* -loes', -los', -lo': see PLURAL II, D, 1 [It. *bufalo* < LL. < Gr. < *bous*, ox] **1.** any of various wild oxen, sometimes domesticated, as the water buffalo of India, Cape buffalo of Africa, etc. **2.** popularly, the American bison

buffalo grass [U.S.] a low, creeping prairie grass used for forage

buff·er¹ (buf'ər) *n.* [BUFF¹, *v.* + -ER] a person or thing that buffs or polishes

buff·er² (buf'ər) *n.* [BUFF² + -ER] **1.** a device to lessen the shock of collision, esp. of railway vehicles **2.** any person or thing that serves to lessen shock, as between antagonistic forces **3.** a substance that tends to stabilize the hydrogen ion concentration in a solution by neutralizing an added acid or alkali **4.** *Computing* a memory device for temporarily storing data

buff·er³ (buf'ər) *n.* [< ? ME. *buffer*, stammerer] [Colloq.] a stupid or bumbling man, esp. one who is elderly or pompous: also **old buffer**

buffer state a small country located between two antagonistic powers and regarded as lessening the possibility of conflict between them

WATER BUFFALO
(1.4-1.8 m high
at shoulder)

buf·fet¹ (buf'it) *n.* [< OFr. < *buffe*, a blow] **1.** a blow with the hand or fist **2.** any blow or shock —*vt.* **1.** to punch or slap **2.** to thrust about **3.** to struggle against —*vi.* to struggle

buf·fet² (bōō'fā; *for 1 usually* buf'it) *n.* [Fr. < OFr. *buffet*, a bench] **1.** a piece of furniture with drawers and cupboards for dishes, table linen, silver, etc. **2.** a counter where refreshments are served, or a restaurant with such a counter **3.** a meal at which guests serve themselves as from a buffet

buffet car a railway coach where light meals or snacks are served

buf·fet·ing (buf'itiŋ) *n.* [< BUFFET¹] **1.** a blow or blows with the hand **2.** the act of jostling, shoving, etc. **3.** *Aeron.* an irregular oscillation of an aircraft caused by air eddies

‡**buf·fo** (bōōf'fō; E. bōō'fō) *n., pl.* -fi (-fē) [It., comic: see ff.] an opera singer, generally a bass, who plays a comic role

buf·foon (bəfōōn') *n.* [< Fr. < It. < *buffare*, to jest] a person who is always clowning and trying to be funny —**buf·foon'er·y** *n.* —**buf·foon'ish** *adj.*

bug (bug) *n.* [prob. < W. *bwg*, hobgoblin] **1.** any of various insects with sucking mouthparts and with forewings thickened toward the base **2.** [Colloq.] any insect or small, insectlike animal, specif. one regarded as a pest **3.** [Colloq.] a germ or virus **4.** [Slang] a tiny microphone hidden to record conversation secretly **5.** [Slang] a defect, as in a machine **6.** [Slang] an enthusiast; devotee —*vt.* **bugged, bug'ging** [Slang] **1.** to hide a microphone in (a room, etc.) for secretly recording conversation **2.** to annoy, anger, etc.

bug·a·boo (bug'əbōō') *n., pl.* -boos' a bugbear

bug·bear (-ber') *n.* [BUG + BEAR²] **1.** an imaginary hobgoblin or terror **2.** anything causing seemingly needless or excessive fear or anxiety

bug·ger (bug'ər) *n.* [ME. *bougre* < OFr. < ML. *Bulgarus*, lit., a Bulgarian; orig., 11th-c. Bulgarian heretic] **1.** a sodomite **2.** [Slang] a contemptible or unpleasant person or thing: often considered a vulgar usage **3.** [Slang] a person; chap: often used humorously or affectionately —*vt.* **1.** to commit sodomy with **2.** [Slang] to ruin; complicate (often with *up*) **3.** [Slang] to tire; make weary —*interj.* [Slang] a strong exclamation of annoyance or disappointment —**bugger about** (or **around**) [Slang] **1.** to fool about; waste time **2.** to create difficulties —**bugger off** [Slang] to go away; depart —**bug'ger·y** *n.*

bug·gy¹ (bug'ē) *n., pl.* -gies [< ?] a light, one-horse carriage with one seat

bug·gy² (bug'ē) *adj.* -gi·er, -gi·est infested or swarming with bugs

bu·gle (byōō'g'l) *n.* [< OFr. < L. *buculus*, young ox, dim. of *bos*, ox] a brass instrument like a trumpet but smaller, and usually without keys or valves: used chiefly for military calls —*vi., vt.* **-gled, -gling** to call or signal by blowing a bugle —**bu'gler** *n.*

bu·gloss (byōō'glos) *n.* [ME & OFr. *buglosse* < L. < Gr. *bouglossos*, oxtongue] any of various Eurasian plants having hairy stems and leaves with clusters of blue flowers

bug·shah (bug'shə, -shô) *n., pl.* -shah, -shahs see MONETARY UNITS, table (Yemen Arab Rep.)

buhl (bōōl) *n.* [after Charles André *Boulle* (1642-1732), Fr. cabinetmaker] **1.** decoration of furniture with designs of tortoise shell, brass, silver, etc. inlaid in wood **2.** furniture so decorated Also **buhl'work'**

build (bild) *vt.* **built** or archaic **build'ed, build'ing** [< OE. *byldan* < base of *bold*, a house] **1.** to make, or direct the making of, by putting together materials, parts, etc.; construct **2.** to make a basis for; establish [to *build* a theory on facts] **3.** to create, develop, promote, strengthen, etc. —*vi.* **1.** *a*) to put up buildings *b*) to have a house, etc. built **2.** to grow or intensify —*n.* form or figure [a stocky *build*]

build·er (bil'dər) *n.* **1.** one that builds **2.** a person in the business of constructing buildings

build·ing (-diŋ) *n.* **1.** anything that is built with walls and a roof **2.** the act, process, work, or business of constructing houses, ships, etc.

building society a cooperative banking enterprise financed by deposits on which interest is paid and from which mortgage loans are advanced on homes and real estate

build·up, build-up (bild'up') *n.* [Colloq.] **1.** favourable publicity or praise **2.** growth or expansion [a military *buildup*] **3.** a gradual preparation for, or approach to, a climax, as in a novel or film

built-in (bilt'in') *adj.* **1.** made as part of the building [a *built-in* wardrobe] **2.** intrinsic; inherent

built-up (-up') *adj.* **1.** made higher, stronger, etc. by the addition of parts **2.** having many buildings on it: said of an area

bulb (bulb) *n.* [< L. < Gr. *bolbos*] **1.** an underground bud that sends down roots and has a very short stem covered with leafy scales, as in a lily, onion, etc. **2.** a corm, tuber, or tuberous root resembling a bulb, as in a crocus **3.** a plant that grows from a bulb   4. anything shaped like a bulb [an electric light *bulb*] —**bul·bar** (bul′bər) *adj.* —**bulbed** *adj.*

bul·ba·ceous (bəl bā′shəs) *adj.*   *same as* BULBOUS

bul·bous (bul′bəs) *adj.*   1. of, having, or growing from bulbs   2. shaped like a bulb

bulge (bulj) *n.* [ME., var. of *bouge*: see BUDGET]   1. an outward swelling; protuberance   2. a projecting part   3. [Colloq.] a sudden increase —*vi., vt.* **bulged, bulg′ing**   to swell or bend outwards; protrude —**bulg′y** (-ē) *adj.*

bulk (bulk) *n.* [ON. *bulki*, a heap, cargo]   1. size, mass, or volume, esp. if great   2. the main mass or body; largest part [the *bulk* of one's fortune]   3. soft, bulky matter that passes through the intestines unabsorbed —*vi.*   1. to form into a mass   2. to increase in size, importance, etc.   3. to have size or importance —*vt.*   to cause to bulk; give more bulk to —*adj.*   1. total; aggregate   2. not put up in individual packets —**in bulk**   1. not put up in individual packets   2. in large amounts

bulk buying   the purchase of large quantities of a commodity, often on preferential terms

bulk·head (bulk′hed′) *n.* [< ON. *balkr*, partition + HEAD]   1. any of the upright partitions separating parts of a ship, aircraft, etc. as for protection against fire or leakage   2. a wall or embankment for holding back earth, fire, water, etc.

bulk·y (bul′kē) *adj.* **bulk′i·er, bulk′i·est**   1. *a)* having great bulk; large; massive *b)* relatively large for its weight   2. awkwardly large; big and clumsy —**bulk′i·ly** *adv.* —**bulk′-i·ness** *n.*

bull¹ (bool) *n.* [< OE. *bula*, a steer]   1. the adult male of any bovine animal, as the ox, buffalo, etc.   2. the adult male of certain other large animals, as the elephant, moose, walrus, whale, etc.   3. a person who buys stocks, etc. expecting, or seeking to bring about, a rise in their prices   4. a person regarded as like a bull in size, strength, etc.   5. *a)* the central mark of a target *b)* a direct hit   6. [Slang] foolish or insincere talk; nonsense —[B-]   *same as* TAURUS —*vt.*   to make (one's way) with force —*adj.*   1. male   2. like a bull in size, strength, etc.   3. rising in price [a *bull* market] —**like a bull in a china shop**   in an outrageous, clumsy, or tactless manner —**take the bull by the horns**   to deal boldly with a danger or difficulty —**bull′ish** *adj.* —**bull′ish·ly** *adv.* —**bull′ish·ness** *n.*

bull² (bool) *n.* [< OFr. < LL. *bulla*, a seal (L., bubble)]   an official document or decree from the Pope

bull³ (bool) *n.* [ult. < L. *bulla*, bubble]   a mistake in statement that is ludicrous in a ludicrous way

bull- [< BULL¹]   *a combining form meaning:*   1. of a bull or bulls [*bullfight*]   2. like a bull or bull's [*bullhead*]   3. large or male [*bullfrog*]

bull·dog (bool′dog′) *n.* [BULL- + DOG]   a short-haired, square-jawed, heavily built dog noted for its strong, stubborn grip —*adj.*   like or characteristic of a bulldog

bulldog ant   a large and very ferocious Australian insect

bulldog clip   a strong clip consisting of two metal clamps held in place by a spring and used for holding papers together

bull·doze (-dōz′) *vt.* **-dozed′, -doz′ing** [< ? *bull* (Botany Bay slang), a flogging of 75 lashes + DOSE]   1. [Colloq.] to force or frighten by threatening; intimidate   2. to move, make level, dig out, etc. with a bulldozer

bull·doz·er (-dō′zər) *n.*   1. a person who bulldozes   2. a tractor with a large, shovellike blade on the front, for pushing or moving earth, debris, etc.

bul·let (bool′it) *n.* [Fr. *boulette*, dim. of *boule*, a ball < L. *bulla*: see BULL²]   1. a small, shaped piece of lead, metal alloy, etc. to be shot from a firearm   2. anything like a bullet in shape, action, etc.

bul·le·tin (bool′ə tin) *n.* [Fr. < It. dim. of LL. *bulla*: see DULL²]   1. a brief statement of the latest news   2. a regular publication, as for members of a society —*vt.*   to announce in a bulletin

bulletin board   [U.S.] a notice board

bul·let·proof (bool′it proof′) *adj.*   that bullets cannot pierce —*vt.*   to make bulletproof

bull·fight (bool′fīt′) *n.*   a public show in which a bull is first provoked in various ways and then usually killed with a sword by a matador —**bull′fight′er** *n.* —**bull′fight′ing** *n.*

bull·finch (-finch′) *n.* [BULL- + FINCH]   1. a European songbird with a black head and, in the male, a bright red throat and breast   2. any of various other small songbirds

bull·frog (-frog′) *n.* [BULL- + FROG]   a large N. American frog with a deep, loud croak

bull·head·ed (-hed′id) *adj.*   blindly stubborn —**bull′head′-ed·ly** *adv.* —**bull′head′ed·ness** *n.*

bull·horn (-hôrn′) *n.* [BULL- + HORN]   *U.S. var. of* LOUD-HAILER

bul·lion (bool′yən) *n.* [< Du. < OFr. *billon*, small coin < *bille*, a stick: see BILLET²]   1. gold and silver regarded as raw material   2. bars of gold or silver, as before coinage

bull-necked (-nekt′) *adj.*   having a short, thick neck

bull·ock (bool′ək) *n.* [< OE. *bulluc*, dim. of *bula*: see BULL¹]   a castrated bull; steer

bull·ring (-riŋ′) *n.*   an arena for bullfighting

bull-roar·er (-rôr′ər) *n.*   a flat piece of wood at the end of a string, which makes a roaring noise when whirled

bull's-eye (boolz′ī′) *n.*   1. a thick, circular glass in a roof, ship's deck, etc., for admitting light   2. *same as* BULL¹ (n.5)   3. *a)* a convex lens for concentrating light *b)* a lantern with such a lens   4. the glass boss at the centre of a plate of glass   5. a hard, round sweet

bull·shit (-shit) *n.* [Slang] foolish talk; nonsense: a vulgar term

bull terrier   a strong, lean, white dog, developed by crossing the bulldog and the terrier

bul·ly¹ (bool′ē) *n., pl.* **-lies** [orig., sweetheart < Du. < MHG. *buole* (G. *Buhle*), lover; later infl. by BULL¹]   a person who hurts, frightens, or browbeats those who are smaller or weaker —*vt., vi.* **-lied, -ly·ing**   to behave like a bully (towards) —*adj.* [Colloq.] fine; very good —*interj.* [Colloq.] good! well done!

bul·ly² (bool′ē) *n.* [< Fr. < *bouillir*, to boil]   tinned or corned beef: also **bully beef**

bul·ly³ (bool′ē) *n. Hockey*   the method of starting or restarting play in which two opposing players alternately strike their sticks together and against the ground three times before trying to hit the ball: also **bully-off** —*vi.*   to start or restart play by a bully: also **bully off**

bul·ly·rag (-rag′) *vt.* **-ragged′, -rag′ging** [see BULLY¹, *vt.* & RAG², *vt.*] [Dial. or Colloq.] to bully or intimidate

bul·rush (bool′rush′) *n.* [< OE. *bol*, BOLE + *risc*, a rush]   1. a marsh plant of the sedge family   2. a tall marsh plant with reedlike leaves and long, brown, fuzzy, cylindrical flower spikes: also **cat's tail**   3. the papyrus or other aquatic plant like a bulrush: cf. Ex. 2:3

bul·wark (bool′wərk, bul′-) *n.* [< MDu. *bolwerc*: see BOLE & WORK]   1. an earthwork or defensive wall; rampart   2. a defence or protection   3. [usually pl.] a ship's side above the deck —*vt.*   1. to provide bulwarks for   2. to be a bulwark to

bum¹ (bum) *n.* [prob. < G. *Bummler*, loafer < *bummeln*, to go slowly] [U.S. Colloq.]   1. a vagrant, tramp, beggar, or derelict   2. any shiftless or irresponsible person —*vi.* **bummed, bum′ming** [U.S. Colloq.]   1. to live as a bum   2. to live by sponging on people —*vt.* [U.S. Slang] to get by sponging; cadge —*adj.* **bum′mer, bum′mest** [U.S. Slang] poor in quality —**bum steer** [U.S. Slang] false or invalid information —**bum′mer** *n.*

bum² (bum) *n.* [ME. *bom* < ?] [Colloq.] the buttocks

bum-bail·iff (bum′bā′lif) *n.* [< ? BUM² + BAILIFF: ? because the officer was often close behind]   a sheriff's officer employed to collect debts and arrest debtors

bum·ble·bee (bum′b'l bē′) *n.* [altered (after ME. *bomblen*, to buzz) < ME. *humbul-be*, bumblebee]   a large, hairy, yellow-and-black social bee

bum·bling (bum′bliŋ) *adj.* [prp. of bumble, buzz: see prec.]   self-important in a blundering way

bumf, bumph (bumf) *n.* [contr. < *bumfodder*, lit., toilet paper < BUM² + FODDER] [Colloq.] official documents, publicity material, etc. regarded disparagingly

bump (bump) *vt.* [echoic] to hit against; collide lightly with —*vi.*   1. to collide with a jolt   2. to move with jolts —*n.*   1. a light blow or jolt   2. a swelling or lump, esp. one caused by a blow   3. a collision   4. one of the protuberances on the skull, said by phrenologists to give an indication of mental qualities, character, etc.   5. *Cricket* a ball that bounces up high when bowled —**bump into** [Colloq.] to meet unexpectedly —**bump off** [Slang] to murder —**bump up** to increase (prices, etc.)

bump·er¹ (bum′pər) *n.*   a device for absorbing some of the shock of a collision; specif., a metal bar across the front or back of a motor car

bump·er² (bum′pər) *n.* [prob. < obs. *bombard*, leather jug, altered after BUMP]   1. a cup or glass filled to the brim   2. [Colloq.] anything unusually large of its kind —*adj.* unusually abundant [a *bumper* crop]

bump·kin (bump′kən, bum′-) *n.* [prob. < MDu. *bommekijn*, small cask]   an awkward or simple person from the country

bump·tious (bump′shəs) *adj.* [prob. < BUMP]   disagreeably conceited, arrogant, or forward —**bump′tious·ly** *adv.* —**bump′tious·ness** *n.*

bump·y (bum′pē) *adj.* **bump′i·er, bump′i·est**   full of bumps; rough —**bump′i·ly** *adv.* —**bump′i·ness** *n.*

bun (bun) *n.* [ME. *bunne*, wheat cake, prob. < OFr. *buigne*, a swelling]   1. a small roll or cake usually somewhat sweetened and often spiced   2. hair worn in a roll or knot

bunch (bunch) *n.* [ult. < Fl. *boudje*, dim. of *boud*, bundle]   1. a cluster of things growing together [a *bunch* of grapes]   2. a collection of things of the same kind fastened, grouped, or thought of together [a *bunch* of keys]   3. [Colloq.] a group of people —*vt., vi.*   to gather together in a mass or in loose folds, wads, etc. (often with *up*) —**bunch′i·ness** *n.* —**bunch′y** *adj.*

bun·combe (buŋ′kəm) *n.* [< *Buncombe* county, N. Carolina, U.S., whose Congressman (1819-21) regularly made "a speech for Buncombe"] [Colloq.] talk that is empty, insincere, or merely for effect; humbug

bund, Bund (boond; *G.* boont) *n., pl.* **bunds**; *G.* **Bun·de** (bün′də) [G.] a league or confederation

bun·dle (bun′d'l) *n.* [prob. < MDu. *bondel* < *binden*, BIND] 1. a number of things tied or wrapped together 2. a package or parcel 3. a bunch, collection, or group 4. [Slang] a large amount of money 5. *same as* VASCULAR BUNDLE 6. *Biol.* an anatomic unit consisting of a number of separate nerve fibres, muscles, etc. closely banded together —*vt.* **-dled, -dling** 1. to make into a bundle; wrap or tie together 2. to send hastily (*away, off, out*, or *into*) —*vi.* 1. to move or go hastily; bustle 2. to lie in the same bed with one's sweetheart without undressing: a former courting custom, esp. in Wales —**bundle up** to put on plenty of warm clothing —**bun′dler** *n.*

bun·fight (—) *n.* [Colloq.] a social gathering; tea party

bung (buŋ) *n.* [< MDu. *bonge*] 1. a cork or other stopper for the hole in a barrel, cask, or keg 2. a bunghole —*vt.* 1. to close (a bunghole) with a stopper 2. to stop up 3. [Slang] to fling; throw

bun·ga·low (buŋ′gə lō′) *n.* [< Hindi *bānglā*, thatched house, lit., Bengalese] a small house or cottage, usually of one storey and an attic

bung·hole (buŋ′hōl′) *n.* a hole in a barrel or keg through which liquid can be drawn out

bun·gle (buŋ′g'l) *vt.* **-gled, -gling** [< ? Sw. *bangla*, to work ineffectually] to spoil by clumsy work; botch —*vi.* to do things badly or clumsily —*n.* 1. a bungling, or clumsy, act 2. a bungled piece of work —**bun′gler** *n.* —**bun′gling·ly** *adv.*

bun·ion (bun′yən) *n.* [prob. < ME. *boni*, swelling, boil < OFr. *buigne*: see BUN] an inflammation and swelling on the foot, esp. on the big toe

bunk[1] (buŋk) *n.* [prob. < Scand. cognate of BENCH] 1. a shelf-like bed or berth built into or against a wall, as in a ship 2. [Colloq.] any sleeping place, as a narrow bed —*vi.* 1. to sleep in a bunk 2. [Colloq.] to use a makeshift sleeping place

bunk[2] (buŋk) *n.* [Slang] *same as* BUNCOMBE

bunk[3] (buŋk) *n.* [< ?] a hurried departure, esp. under suspicious circumstances: only in **do a bunk**

bunk bed a pair of twin beds linked one above the other, often with a detachable ladder

bunk·er (buŋ′kər) *n.* [Scot. < ?] 1. a large bin or tank, as for a ship's fuel 2. a weapon emplacement of steel and concrete in an underground fortification system 3. a sand trap or mound of earth serving as an obstacle on a golf course —*vt.* *Golf* to hit (a ball) into a bunker

bun·kum (buŋ′kəm) *n.* *same as* BUNCOMBE

bun·ny (bun′ē) *n., pl.* **-nies** [dim. of dial. *bun*, rabbit] a rabbit: pet name used by children

Bun·sen burner (bun′s'n) [after R. W. Bunsen, 19th-c. Ger. chemist] a small, tubular gas burner that produces a hot, blue flame

bun·ting[1] (bun′tiŋ) *n.* [< ? ME. *bonting*, sifting (cloth)] 1. a thin cloth used in making flags, etc. 2. flags, or strips of cloth in the colours of the flag, used as decorations 3. [U.S.] a baby's garment of soft, warm cloth

bun·ting[2] (bun′tiŋ) *n.* [< ?] any of various small birds having a stout bill

bunt·line (bunt′lin, -līn′) *n.* [*bunt*, middle part of a sail + LINE[1]] one of the ropes attached to the foot of a square sail to prevent the sail from bellying when drawn up to be furled

bun·ya (bun′yə) *n.* [Abor.] an Australian coniferous tree with large edible seeds: also **bun·ya-bun·ya**

bun·yip (bun′yip) *n.* [Abor.] [Aust.] a mythical monster supposed to haunt swamps

buoy (boi) *n.* [< OFr. *buie*, chain < L. *boia*, fetter: prob. first applied to the chain anchoring the float] 1. a floating object anchored in water to warn of rocks, shoals, etc. or to mark a channel 2. *short for* LIFE BUOY —*vt.* 1. to mark or provide with a buoy 2. to keep afloat: usually with *up* 3. to lift or keep up in spirits; encourage: usually with *up*

buoy·an·cy (boi′an sē) *n.* [< ff.] 1. the ability or tendency to float or rise in liquid or air 2. the power to keep something afloat 3. lightness of spirit; cheerfulness 4. the ability to recover quickly after a setback; resilience

buoy·ant (-ant, -yant) *adj.* [< ? Sp. < *boyar*, to float] having or showing buoyancy —**buoy′ant·ly** *adv.*

bur (bur) *n.* [ME. *burre* < Scand.] 1. the rough, prickly seedcase or fruit of certain plants 2. a weed or other plant with burs 3. anything that clings like a bur 4. *Dentistry* a cutting or drilling bit 5. *same as* BURR[1] & BURR[2] —*vt.* **burred, bur′ring** 1. to remove burs from 2. to burr

bur. bureau

bur·ble (bur′b'l) *vi.* **-bled, -bling** [echoic] 1. to make a gurgling or bubbling sound 2. to babble as a child does 3. [Colloq.] to be verbose (often with *on* or *away*)

bur·bot (bur′bət) *n., pl.* **-bot, -bots**: see PLURAL, II, D, 2 [< OFr. *borbote*, ult. < L. *barba*, a beard] a freshwater fish of the cod family, with barbels on the nose and chin

bur·den[1] (burd′'n) *n.* [< OE. *byrthen* < base of *beran*: see BEAR[1]] 1. anything that is carried; load 2. a heavy load, as of work, responsibility, sorrow, etc. 3. the carrying of loads [a beast of *burden*] 4. the carrying capacity of a ship, or the weight of its cargo —*vt.* to put a burden on; load; oppress

bur·den[2] (burd′'n) *n.* [< OFr. *bourdon*, a humming < ML. *burdo*, DRONE[1], wind instrument] 1. a chorus or refrain of a song 2. a repeated, central idea; theme [the *burden* of a speech]

burden of proof the obligation to prove what is asserted and in dispute

bur·den·some (-səm) *adj.* hard to bear; heavy; oppressive —**bur′den·some·ly** *adv.*

bur·dock (bur′dok′) *n.* [BUR + DOCK[3]] a plant of the composite family, with large leaves, and purple-flowered heads covered with hooked prickles

bu·reau (byoor′ō) *n., pl.* **-reaus, -reaux** (-ōz) [Fr., desk < OFr. *burel*, coarse cloth (as table cover) < LL. *burra*, ragged (woollen) garment] 1. a desk with drawers for papers 2. [U.S.] a chest of drawers, often with a mirror, for clothing, etc. 3. an agency providing specified services for clients [a travel *bureau*] 4. [U.S.] a government department or a subdivision of this

bu·reau·cra·cy (byoo ro′krə sē) *n., pl.* **-cies** [< Fr. < *bureau* + *-cratie*, -CRACY] 1. the administration of government through departments managed by officials following an inflexible routine 2. the officials collectively 3. governmental officialism or inflexible routine 4. concentration of authority in a complex structure of administrative bureaus

bu·reau·crat (byoor′ə krat′) *n.* an official in a bureaucracy, esp. one who follows a routine strictly, insisting on proper forms, petty rules, etc. —**bu′reau·crat′ic** *adj.* —**bu′reau·crat′i·cal·ly** *adv.*

bu·reau·cra·tize (byoo ro′krə tīz′) *vt., vi.* **-tized′, -tiz′ing** to make or become bureaucratic —**bu·reau′cra·ti·za′tion** *n.*

bu·rette (byoo ret′) *n.* [Fr. < OFr. dim. of *buire*, flagon] a graduated glass tube with a stopcock at the bottom, for measuring small quantities of liquid or gas

burg (burg) *n.* [var. of BOROUGH] 1. orig., a fortified town 2. [U.S. Colloq.] a city, town, or village, esp. one regarded as quiet, unexciting, etc.

bur·geon (bur′jən) *vi.* [< OFr. < *burjon*, a bud] 1. to put forth buds, shoots, etc. 2. to grow or develop rapidly; flourish [the *burgeoning* suburbs]

bur·gess (bur′jis) *n.* [OFr. *burgeis*: see BOURGEOIS] 1. an inhabitant, citizen or freeman of a borough 2. formerly, a member of parliament representing a borough, corporate town or university

burgh (bu′rə) *n.* [Scot. var. of BOROUGH] in Scotland, a chartered town —**burgh·al** (bur′g'l) *adj.*

burgh·er (bur′gər) *n.* 1. a citizen or inhabitant of a corporate town, esp. on the continent 2. [S. Afr.] formerly, a citizen of a Boer republic

bur·glar (bur′glər) *n.* [< Anglo-L. *burglator*, altered after L. *latro*, thief < OFr. *burgeor*, burglar] a person who commits burglary

bur·glar·i·ous (bər gler′ē əs) *adj.* of, given to, or being burglary —**bur·glar′i·ous·ly** *adv.*

bur·gla·ry (bur′glər ē) *n., pl.* **-ries** [BURGLAR + -Y[4]] the act of breaking into a house or other building to commit theft or other felony

bur·gle (bur′g'l) *vt., vi.* **-gled, -gling** [< BURGLAR] to commit burglary (in)

bur·go·mas·ter (bur′gə mäs′tər) *n.* [< MDu. < *burg*, town + *meester*, master] the mayor or head magistrate of a city or town in the Netherlands, Flanders, Austria, or Germany

bur·i·al (ber′ē əl) *n.* the burying of a dead body; interment —*adj.* of or connected with burial

burial ground a cemetery; graveyard

bu·rin (byoor′in) *n.* [Fr. < It. < Gmc. *boro*, borer] a pointed cutting tool used by engravers or marble workers

burk, burke (burk) *n.* *same as* BERK

burl (burl) *n.* [< OFr. < VL. < LL. *burra*: see BUREAU] a knot in wool, thread, yarn, etc. that gives a knobbly appearance to cloth —*vt.* to finish (cloth) by taking out the burls, etc. —**burled** *adj.*

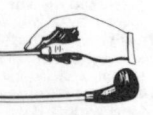

BURIN

bur·lap (bur′lap) *n.* [< ? ME. *borel*, coarse cloth (< OFr. *burel*: see BUREAU) + *lappa*, LAP[1]] a coarse cloth made of jute or hemp, used for making sacks, etc.

bur·lesque (bər lesk′) *n.* [Fr. < It. < *burla*, a jest] 1. any broadly comic or satirical imitation; parody 2. [U.S.] a sort of variety show characterized by low comedy, striptease acts, etc. —*adj.* 1. comically imitating;

parodying **2.** of or connected with burlesque (sense 2) —*vt.*, *vi.* **-lesqued'**, **-lesqu'ing** to imitate comically or derisively; parody

bur·ly (bur'lē) *adj.* **-li·er**, **-li·est** [ME. *borlich*, excellent, handsome < ? OE. *borlice*, very, excellently] **1.** big and strong; heavy and muscular **2.** rough and hearty in manner —**bur'li·ness** *n.*

burn[1] (burn) *vt.* **burned** or **burnt**, **burn'ing** [< ON. & OE.: ON. *brenna*, to burn, light; OE. *biernan*] **1.** to set on fire or subject to combustion **2.** to destroy by fire **3.** to injure or damage by fire, heat, friction, or acid; scorch, scald, etc. **4.** to consume as fuel **5.** to transform into energy by metabolism **6.** to sunburn **7.** to cauterize **8.** to harden or glaze (bricks, pottery, etc.) by fire; fire **9.** to cause by fire, heat, etc. [to *burn* a hole in a coat] **10.** to cause a sensation of heat in [horseradish *burns* the throat] —*vi.* **1.** to be on fire; flame; blaze **2.** to undergo combustion **3.** to give out light or heat; shine; glow **4.** to be destroyed by fire or heat **5.** to be injured or damaged by or as by fire or heat **6.** to feel hot **7.** to be excited or inflamed, as with anger or desire —*n.* **1.** an injury caused by fire, heat, wind, etc. **2.** the process or result of burning **3.** a single firing of a rocket or thruster on a space vehicle **4.** [Slang] a cigarette —**burn down** to burn to the ground —**burn one's boats** (or **bridges**) to embark on a course of action from which there can be no retreat —**burn oneself out** to exhaust oneself by too much work or dissipation —**burn one's fingers** [Colloq.] to suffer from having meddled or interfered —**burn the midnight oil** to stay up late at night, reading or working —**burn up** to burn completely

burn[2] (burn) *n.* [see BOURN[1]] [Scot. & North Eng.] a brook

burn·a·ble (-ə b'l) *adj.* that can be burned —*n.* something, esp. refuse, that can be burned

burn·er (bur'nər) *n.* the part of a stove, furnace, etc. from which the flame comes

burn·ing (bur'niŋ) *adj.* **1.** that burns **2.** intense; critical [a *burning* issue]

burning bush [after the Biblical burning bush: cf. Ex. 3] any of various shrubs with red flowers, red fruit or bright red autumnal foliage

burning glass a convex lens for focusing the sun's rays so as to set fire to something

bur·nish (bur'nish) *vt.*, *vi.* [< OFr. *brunir*, to make brown < *brun*, brown] to make or become shiny by rubbing; polish —*n.* a gloss or polish —**bur'nish·er** *n.*

bur·noose, **bur·nous** (bər nōōs') *n.* [< Fr. < Ar. *burnus*, prob. < Gr. *birros*, a cloak] a long cloak with a hood, worn by Arabs and Moors

burnt (burnt) *alt. pt. and pp. of* BURN[1]

burnt offering 1. an animal, food, etc. burned at an altar as an offering or sacrifice to a god **2.** [Colloq.] food that has been overcooked or allowed to burn

burnt sienna *see* SIENNA

burnt umber *see* UMBER

burp (burp) *n.*, *vi.* [echoic] [Colloq.] belch —*vt.* to cause (a baby) to relieve itself of stomach gas, as by patting its back

burr[1] (bur) *n.* [var. of BUR] **1.** a rough edge left on metal, etc. by cutting or drilling **2.** *same as* BUR (senses 1, 2, 3, 4)

burr[2] (bur) *n.* [prob. echoic] **1.** the trilling of *r*, with uvula or tongue [a Scottish *burr*] **2.** a whirring sound —*vi.* **1.** to speak with a burr **2.** to make a whir —*vt.* to pronounce with a burr

bur·row (bur'ō, -ə) *n.* [see BOROUGH] **1.** a hole dug in the ground by an animal **2.** any similar hole for shelter, etc. —*vi.* **1.** to make a burrow **2.** to live or hide in or as in a burrow **3.** to delve or search, as if by digging —*vt.* **1.** to make burrows in **2.** to make by burrowing —**bur'row·er** *n.*

bur·ry[1] (bur'ē) *adj.* **-ri·er**, **-ri·est 1.** full of burs **2.** like a bur or burs; prickly

bur·ry[2] (bur'ē) *adj.* **-ri·er**, **-ri·est** having a burr in speech

bur·sa (bur'sə) *n.*, *pl.* **-sae** (-sē), **-sas** [ML., a bag < Gr. *byrsa*, a hide] *Anat.* a sac or cavity, esp. one containing a fluid that reduces friction, as between a tendon and bone —**bur'sal** *adj.*

bur·sar (bur'sər) *n.* [ML. *bursarius* < *bursa*: see prec.] **1.** a treasurer, as of a college **2.** the holder of a scholarship at school or university

bur·sa·ry (bur'sər ē) *n.* [ML. *bursaria* < *bursarius*: see BURSAR] **1.** a treasury, esp. of a college **2.** a scholarship or grant, esp. one awarded in a Scottish school or university —**bur·sar·i·al** (bər ser'ē əl) *adj.*

bur·si·tis (bər sīt'əs) *n.* [< BURSA + -ITIS] inflammation of a bursa

burst (burst) *vi.* **burst**, **burst'ing** [< OE. *berstan* & ON. *bresta*] **1.** to come apart suddenly and violently; break open or out; explode **2.** to give sudden expression to some feeling; break (*into* tears, laughter, etc.) **3.** to go, come, start, etc. suddenly and with force [he *burst* into the room] **4.** *a)* to be as full or crowded as possible *b)* to be filled (*with* anger, pride, etc.) —*vt.* to cause to burst —*n.* **1.** a bursting; explosion **2.** the result of a bursting; break **3.** a

sudden, violent display of feeling **4.** a sudden action; spurt [a *burst* of speed] **5.** a single series of shots from an automatic firearm —**burst'er** *n.*

bur·then (bur'thən) *n.*, *vt.* archaic var. of BURDEN[1]

bur·ton (bur'tən) *n.* [< Burton, Staffordshire, renowned for its beer] [Colloq.] a drink —**go for a burton** [Colloq.] **1.** to be or become broken or irretrievably lost **2.** to die

bur·y (ber'ē) *vt.* **bur'ied**, **bur'y·ing** [OE. *byrgan*, akin to *beorgan*, conceal] **1.** to put (a dead body) into the earth, a tomb, the sea, etc.; inter **2.** *a)* to hide (something) in the ground *b)* to cover up so as to conceal **3.** to put away [to *bury* a feud] **4.** to involve oneself deeply in [to *bury* oneself in one's work] —**bury the hatchet** to stop fighting and become reconciled

bur·y·ing-ground (ber'ē iŋ ground') *n.* a cemetery: also **burying-place**

bus (bus) *n.*, *pl.* **bus'es** [< (OMNI)BUS] **1.** a large motor coach for carrying many passengers, usually along a regular route; omnibus **2.** *same as* BUSBAR **3.** [Colloq.] any vehicle, as a motor car or aeroplane —*vt.* **bussed**, **bus'sing** to transport by bus, esp. to achieve racial integration in schools —*vi.* to go by bus —**miss the bus** to miss an opportunity

bus. business

bus·bar (bus'bär) *n.* *Elec.* a bar or heavy wire forming a common junction between two or more electrical circuits

bus·by (buz'bē) *n.*, *pl.* **-bies** [prob. < the name *Busby*] a tall fur hat worn by hussars, guardsmen in the British army, etc.

bush[1] (boosh) *n.* [ME., of WGmc. orig.] **1.** a woody plant having many stems branching out near ground level instead of one main stem; shrub **2.** anything resembling a bush; esp., a thickly furred tail **3.** shrubby woodland or uncleared country **4.** a bunch of ivy as a symbol for wine, formerly used on tavern signs —*vi.* to grow thickly or spread out like a bush —**beat about the bush** to talk around a subject without getting to the point

bush[2] (boosh) *n.* [MDu. *busse*, box < ML. *buxis*: see BOX[1]] a removable metal sleeve for reducing the effect of friction on a bearing or for decreasing the diameter of a hole —*vt.* to fit with a bush

bush baby any of various nocturnal lemurlike mammals of African forests, with a long, bushy tail and large eyes

bushed (boosht) *adj.* **1.** [Aust.] bewildered, as by being lost in the bush **2.** [U.S. & Canad.] very tired; exhausted

bush·el (boosh'l) *n.* [< OFr. *boissel* < *boisse*, grain measure] **1.** a unit of dry measure for grain, fruit, liquids, etc., equal to 4 pecks or 8 gallons (c. 36.4 litres) **2.** a container holding one bushel **3.** [Colloq.] a large amount Abbrev. **bu.** —**bush'el·bas'ket** *n.*

Bu·shi·do (boo'shē dō') *n.* [Jap., way of the warrior] [also **b-**] the chivalric code of the samurai of feudal Japan

bush·man (boosh'mən) *n.*, *pl.* **-men 1.** a person who lives in the Australian bush **2.** a backwoodsman **3.** [B-] [transl. of obs. Afrik. *boschjesman*] a member of a nomadic people of SW Africa

bush·mas·ter (-mäs'tər) *n.* a large, poisonous snake of Central and South America

bush·rang·er (-rān'jər) *n.* [< BUSH[1] (*n.* 3) + RANGER] **1.** a person who lives in the bush **2.** in Australia, an outlaw who makes the bush his hide-out

bush telegraph [Colloq.] the informal but rapid means by which news is spread throughout a community

bush·whack (-hwak', -wak') *vi.* [prob. < BUSH[1] + WHACK] [Chiefly U.S.] **1.** to beat or cut one's way through bushes **2.** to engage in guerrilla fighting, attacking from ambush —*vt.* to ambush —**bush'whack'er** *n.* —**bush'whack'ing** *n.*

bush·y (boosh'ē) *adj.* **bush'i·er**, **bush'i·est 1.** covered or overgrown with bushes **2.** thick and spreading out like a bush —**bush'i·ness** *n.*

bus·i·ly (biz'ə lē) *adv.* in a busy manner

busi·ness (biz'nis) *n.* [OE. *bisignes*: see BUSY & -NESS] **1.** one's work, occupation, or profession **2.** rightful concern or responsibility **3.** a matter, affair, activity, etc. **4.** the buying and selling of goods and services; commerce; trade **5.** a commercial or industrial establishment; shop, factory, etc. **6.** action in a drama to take up a pause in dialogue, etc. —*adj.* of or for business —**business is business** sentiment, friendship, etc. cannot be allowed to interfere with profit making —**do business with 1.** to engage in commerce with **2.** to have dealings with —**mean business** [Colloq.] to be in earnest —**mind one's own business** to refrain from interfering in the affairs of others

business college (or **school**) a school offering instruction in secretarial skills, business administration, etc.

busi·ness·like (-līk') *adj.* efficient, methodical, etc.

busi·ness·man (-man') *n.*, *pl.* **-men** (-men') a man in business, esp. as an owner or executive —**busi'ness·wom'an** *n.fem.*, *pl.* **-wom'en**

busk·er (bus'kər) *n.* [< Slang *busk*, to be a strolling entertainer, orig., to seek < MFr. *busquer* to seek] a street singer or strolling entertainer, esp. in London

bus·kin (bus′kin) *n.* [< ? OFr. < MDu. *brosekin,* small leather boot] 1. a boot reaching to the calf or knee, worn long ago 2. *a)* the high, thick-soled, laced boot worn by actors in ancient Greek and Roman tragedy *b)* tragic drama; tragedy **—bus′-kined** *adj.*

bus·man (bus′mən) *n., pl.* **-men** the driver of a bus

busman's holiday a holiday in which one's recreation is very similar to one's daily work

buss (bus) *n., vt., vi.* [? akin to G. dial. (or W. & Gael.) *bus*] [Archaic or Dial.] kiss

bust[1] (bust) *n.* [< Fr. < It. *busto*] 1. a piece of sculpture representing a person's head, shoulders, and upper chest 2. a woman's bosom

BUSKINS

bust[2] (bust) *vt., vi.* [orig., dial. var. of BURST] [Slang] 1. to burst or break 2. to make or become penniless or bankrupt 3. to demote or become demoted 4. to arrest **—n.** [Slang] 1. a financial collapse 2. a punch 3. a spree 4. an arrest **—adj.** bankrupt **—bust up** [Colloq.] 1. to put an end to a friendship; quarrel 2. to disrupt a meeting, esp. violently **—go bust** to become bankrupt

bus·tard (bus′tərd) *n.* [< OFr., ult. < L. *avis tarda,* lit., slow bird] a large, long-legged, old-world game bird of Europe, Asia and Africa

bus·tle[1] (bus′l) *vi., vt.* **-tled, -tling** [< ME. *busken,* to prepare < ON.] to hurry busily or with much fuss and bother **—n.** busy and noisy activity **—bus′tling·ly** *adv.*

bus·tle[2] (bus′l) *n.* [late 18th c. < ? G. *Buschel,* a bunch, pad] a framework or padding worn at the back by women to puff out the skirt

bust-up (bust′up) *n.* [Colloq.] 1. a quarrel 2. a disturbance or brawl

bus·y (biz′ē) *adj.* **bus′i·er, bus′i·est** [< OE. *bisig*] 1. occupied; at work; not idle 2. full of activity 3. in use at the moment, as a telephone line 4. meddlesome 5. displeasingly crowded with detail, colours, etc. **—vt. bus′-ied, bus′y·ing** to make or keep busy **—bus′y·ness** *n.*

bus·y·bod·y (-bod′ē) *n., pl.* **-bod′ies** one who pries into other people's affairs; meddler

busy Lizzie a pot plant with fast-growing drooping stems

but[1] (but; *unstressed* bət) *prep.* [< OE. *butan,* without < *be,* by + *utan,* out < *ut,* out] 1. except; save [nobody came *but* me]: sometimes regarded as a conjunction [nobody came *but* I (came)] 2. other than [we cannot choose *but* (to) stay] **—conj.** 1. yet; still; however [he is bad, *but* he has some virtues] 2. on the contrary [I am old, *but* you are young] 3. unless [it never rains *but* it pours] 4. that [I don't question *but* you're right] 5. that . . . not [I never think of London *but* I think of fog] **—adv.** 1. only [if I had *but* known] 2. merely [he is *but* a child] 3. just [I heard it *but* now] **—pron.** who . . . not; which . . . not [not a man *but* felt it] **—n.** an objection [ifs and *buts*] **—vt.** to raise an objection **—but for** if it were not for **—but that** 1. about the fact that [I've no doubt *but that* he'll come] 2. that there isn't some chance that [we can't be sure *but that* he's right]

but[2] (but) *adj.* [akin to prec.] [Scot.] outside; outer **—n.** [Scot.] the outer room, esp. the kitchen of a cottage **—but and ben** [Scot.] a two-room cottage consisting of an outer and an inner room

bu·ta·di·ene (byōōt′ə dī′ēn) *n.* [BUTA(NE) + DI-[1] + -ENE] a hydrocarbon, C₄H₆, used to make buna, a synthetic rubber

bu·tane (byōō′tān) *n.* [BUT(YL) + -ANE] either of two hydrocarbons in the methane series, with the formula C₄H₁₀, used as a fuel, etc.

bu·ta·nol (byōō′tə nol′) *n.* [BUTAN(E) + -OL[1]] same as BUTYL ALCOHOL

butch (booch) *adj.* [prob. < *Butch,* nickname for a boy] [Slang] masculine in appearance, manner, etc.; mannish **—n.** [Chiefly U.S. Slang] 1. a tough or rugged man or boy: chiefly a term of address 2. a lesbian with noticeably masculine characteristics

butch·er (booch′ər) *n.* [< OFr. < *bouc,* he-goat < Frank. *bukk*] 1. one whose work is killing animals or dressing their carcasses for meat 2. one who cuts up meat for sale 3. anyone who kills as if slaughtering animals **—vt.** 1. to kill or dress (animals) for meat 2. to kill brutally or in large numbers; slaughter 3. to botch; mangle

butch·er·bird (-bûrd′) *n.* a shrike which, after killing prey, impales it on thorns

butch·er·y (-ē) *n., pl.* **-er·ies** 1. a slaughterhouse 2. the work or business of a butcher 3. brutal bloodshed 4. the act or result of botching

but·ler (but′lər) *n.* [< OFr. < *bouteille,* BOTTLE] a manservant, now usually the head servant of a household, in charge of wines, pantry, etc.

butler's pantry a serving pantry between the kitchen and the dining room

but·ler·y (but′lər ē) *n., pl.* **-ler·ies** the butler's pantry; buttery

butt[1] (but) *n.* [< ? OFr. *bout,* end, or < ? ON. *būtr,* block of wood] 1. the thick end of anything 2. a stub or stump, as of a partially smoked cigarette 3. *a)* [? infl. by Fr. *butte,* mound] a mound of earth behind a target for receiving fired rounds *b)* a target *c)* [*pl.*] a target range *d)* an open hide for grouse shooters 4. an object of ridicule or criticism 5. [Slang] a cigarette **—vt., vi.** to join end to end

butt[2] (but) *vt.* [< OFr. *buter* (< Frank. *botan*), to thrust against] 1. to ram with the head 2. to strike against 3. to abut on **—vi.** 1. to make a butting motion 2. to project 3. to abut **—n.** a thrust with the head or horns **—butt in** (or **into**) [Slang] to interfere in (another's business, a conversation, etc.)

butt[3] (but) *n.* [< OFr. *botte* < ML. < LL. *bottis,* cask] a large barrel or cask, as for wine or beer

but·ter (but′ər) *n.* [< OE. < L. *butyrum* < Gr. *boutyron* < *bous,* ox, cow + *tyros,* cheese] 1. the solid, yellowish, edible fat obtained by churning cream or whole milk 2. a substance somewhat like butter; specif., *a)* any of certain other spreads for bread [*peanut butter*] *b)* any of certain vegetable oils that are solid at ordinary temperatures [*cocoa butter*] *c)* any of certain metallic chlorides [*butter* of antimony] 3. [Colloq.] flattery **—vt.** 1. to spread with butter 2. [Colloq.] to flatter (often with *up*) **—look as if butter would not melt in one's mouth** to look innocent or demure

butter bean a large, dried haricot bean

but·ter·bur (-bûr′) *n.* a plant of the composite family with large rhubarb-like leaves formerly used for wrapping butter

but·ter·cup (-kup′) *n.* any of a genus of yellow-flowered plants, common in meadows and wet places **—adj.** designating a large family of plants, including the peony, aconite, larkspur, etc.

but·ter·fat (-fat′) *n.* the fatty part of milk, from which butter is made

but·ter·fin·gers (-fiŋ′gərz) *n.* one who often fumbles and drops things **—but′ter·fin′gered** *adj.*

but·ter·fish (-fish′) *n., pl.* **-fish′, -fish′es:** see FISH any of various slippery-coated fishes

but·ter·fly (-flī′) *n., pl.* **-flies′** [< OE. *buttorfleoge*] 1. any of a large group of insects active by day, having a sucking mouthpart, slender body, and four broad, usually brightly coloured wings 2. a person, esp. a woman, thought of as flighty, frivolous, etc. 3. [*pl.*] [Colloq.] a nervous sensation, esp. in the stomach

butterfly nut same as WING NUT

butterfly stroke *Swimming* a stroke in which the arms are plunged forward together in large circular movements to pull the swimmer through the water

butter knife a small, dull-edged knife for cutting or spreading butter

but·ter·milk (-milk′) *n.* the sour liquid left after churning butter from milk

butter muslin a thin, loosely-woven cotton fabric formerly used for wrapping butter, backing maps, etc.

but·ter·scotch (-skoch′) *n.* a hard, sticky sweet made with brown sugar, butter, etc. **—adj.** having the flavour of butterscotch

but·ter·wort (-wûrt) *n.* any of a genus of small, stemless plants with flat, sticky leaves on which insects are trapped

but·ter·y[1] (but′ər ē, but′rē) *n., pl.* **-ter·ies** [< OFr. < ML. *buteria:* see BUTT[3]] 1. a storeroom for food and wine 2. in some universities, a bar run for students

but·ter·y[2] (but′ər ē) *adj.* 1. like butter 2. containing or spread with butter 3. adulatory

but·tock (but′ək) *n.* [< OE. *buttuc,* end] 1. either of the two fleshy, rounded parts at the back of the hips 2. [*pl.*] the rump

but·ton (but′'n) *n.* [OFr. *boton,* a button < *buter:* see BUTT[2]] 1. any small disc or knob used as a fastening, ornament, etc. on a garment 2. anything small and shaped like a button; specif., *a)* a small emblem worn in the lapel, etc. *b)* a small knob for operating a doorbell, electric lamp, etc. *c)* a small mushroom *d)* a guard on the tip of a fencing foil 3. [Slang] [*pl.*] one's full senses [to have all of one's *buttons*] **—vt., vi.** to fasten with buttons **—not worth a button** of little or no value **—but′ton·er** *n.* **—but′ton·less** *adj.*

but·ton-down (-doun′) *adj.* designating a collar with points fastened down by small buttons

but·ton·hole (-hōl′) *n.* 1. a slit or loop through which a button can be fastened 2. a flower or spray worn pinned to the lapel or in the buttonhole, esp. at weddings **—vt. -holed′, -hol′ing** 1. to make buttonholes in 2. to make (a person) listen to one, as if by grasping his coat by a buttonhole **—but′ton·hol′er** *n.*

but·ton·hook (-hook′) *n.* a hook for pulling buttons through buttonholes, as in some shoes

but·tress (but′ris) *n.* [< OFr. < *buter:* see BUTT[2]] 1. a projecting structure built against a wall to support or reinforce it 2. a support; prop **—vt.** 1. to support or reinforce with a buttress 2. to prop up; bolster

but·ty¹ (but′ē) *n.* [< ? BOOTY] [Colloq.] a friend or workmate, esp. in a mine

but·ty² (but′ē) *n.* [< *buttered bread*] [N Eng. Dial] a sandwich; slice of bread and butter

bu·tut (bōō tōōt′) *n., pl.* -tut [native term, lit., small] *see* MONETARY UNITS, table (Gambia)

bu·tyl (byōōt′′l) *n.* [< L. *butyrum* (see BUTTER) + -YL] any of the four isomeric organic radicals C₄H₉

butyl alcohol any of four isomeric alcohols, C₄H₉OH, used as solvents and in organic synthesis

bu·tyr·ic (byōō tir′ik) *adj.* [< L. *butyrum* (see BUTTER) + -IC] 1. of or obtained from butter 2. of or pertaining to butyric acid

butyric acid a fatty acid, C₃H₇CO₂H, with a rancid odour, found in butter, etc.

bux·om (buk′səm) *adj.* [ME., humble, obedient < base of *bouen*, to BOW¹ + -*sum*, -SOME¹] healthy, comely, plump, jolly, etc.; specif. now, having a shapely, full-bosomed figure: said of a woman or girl —**bux′om·ly** *adv.* —**bux′-om·ness** *n.*

buy (bī) *vt.* **bought, buy′ing** [< OE. *bycgan*] 1. to get by paying money; purchase 2. to get by any exchange or sacrifice 3. to be the means of purchasing [all that money can *buy*] 4. to bribe 5. [Slang] to accept as valid, agreeable, etc. —*vi.* to buy things; be a buyer —*n.* 1. a buying 2. anything bought or buyable —**buy into** (or in) to pay money so as to get shares of, membership in, etc. —**buy off** to appease by bribery —**buy out** to buy all the stock, rights, etc. of —**buy up** to buy all that is available of —**buy′a·ble** *adj.*

buy·er (-ər) *n.* 1. one who buys; consumer 2. one whose work is to buy merchandise for a retail store

buzz (buz) *vi.* [echoic] 1. to hum like a bee 2. to talk excitedly 3. to gossip 4. to move with a buzzing sound 5. to be filled with noisy activity or talk —*vt.* 1. to tell (rumours, etc.) in a buzzing manner 2. to make (wings, etc.) buzz 3. to fly an aircraft low over 4. to signal with a buzzer 5. [Colloq.] to telephone —*n.* 1. a sound like a bee's hum 2. a confused sound, as of many voices 3. noisy activity 4. a signal on a buzzer 5. [Colloq.] a telephone call 6. [Colloq.] a rumour —**buzz about** (or **around**) to scurry about —**buzz off** [Colloq.] to hurry away

buz·zard (buz′ərd) *n.* [< OFr. *busart* < *buse* (< L. *buteo*, kind of hawk) + -*art*, -ARD] any of various hawks that are slow and heavy in flight

buzz·er (buz′ər) *n.* an electrical device that makes a buzzing sound as a signal

B.V.M. [L. *Beata Virgo Maria*] Blessed Virgin Mary

bwa·na (bwä′nə) *n.* [Swahili < Ar. *abūna*, our father] [*often* **B-**] master; sir: native respectful term of address used in parts of Africa

B.W.I. British West Indies

bx. *pl.* **bxs.** box

by (bī) *prep.* [< OE. *be* (unstressed), *bi* (stressed)] 1. near or beside; at [stand *by* the wall] 2. a) in or during [to travel *by* night] b) for a fixed time [to work *by* the hour] c) not later than [be back *by* noon] 3. a) via b) past; beyond [to march *by* the reviewing stand] c) towards [north *by* west] 4. on behalf of [he did well *by* me] 5. through the means, work, or operations of [made *by* hand] 6. a) according to [*by* the book] b) in [to grow dark *by* degrees] c) following in series [march two *by* two] 7. with the sanction of [*by* your leave] 8. a) in or to the amount or degree of [apples *by* the kilo] b) and in another dimension [two *by* four] c) using (the given number) as multiplier or divisor —*adv.* 1. close at hand; near [stand *by*] 2. away; aside [put money *by*] 3. past [cars sped *by*] —*adj., n.* same as BYE —**by and by** after a while —**by and large** considering everything —**by oneself** 1. alone 2. unaided —**by the by** incidentally

by- a prefix meaning: 1. close by; near [*bystander*] 2. secondary [*byproduct*]

by-and-by (bī′′n bī′) *n.* a future time

bye (bī) *n.* [see BY] 1. something incidental 2. in sports in which competitors are paired, the status of the extra man, who advances to the next round without playing 3. *Cricket* a run scored off a ball not struck by the batsman 4. *Golf* any holes left unplayed at the end of a match —*adj.* incidental —**by the bye** incidentally

bye-bye (bī′bī′, bī′bī′) *n., interj.* goodbye

bye-byes (bī′bīz) *n.* sleep; bed: a child's word, esp. in the phrase **go to bye-byes**

bye·law (bī′lô′) *n. same as* BYLAW

by-e·lec·tion (bī′i lek′shən) *n.* a special election held between general elections to fill a vacant parliamentary seat

by·gone (bī′gon′) *adj.* gone by; past —*n.* anything that is gone or past —**let bygones be bygones** to let past offences be forgotten

by·law (bī′lô′) *n.* [< ME. < *bi*, town (< ON. *byr* < *būa*, to dwell) + *laue*, LAW: meaning infl. by BY] any of a set of rules made by a local authority or by an organization for governing its own affairs

by·line (-līn′) *n.* a line at the head of a newspaper or magazine article, telling who wrote it

by·pass (-päs′) *n.* 1. a way, path, pipe, channel, etc. between two points that avoids or is auxiliary to the main way; detour 2. a main road built to avoid a city or other congested area 3. *Elec. same as* SHUNT (n. 3) —*vt.* 1. to go around instead of through 2. to furnish with a bypass 3. to ignore, avoid, fail to consult, etc.

by·path, by-path (-päth′) *n.* a side path; byway

by·play (-plā′) *n.* action, gestures, etc. going on aside from the main action, as in a play

by·prod·uct, by-prod·uct (-prod′əkt) *n.* anything produced, as from residues, in the course of making another thing; secondary product or result

byre (bīr) *n.* [OE., hut] a cowshed

by·road (bī′rōd′) *n.* a side road; byway

By·ron·ic (bī ron′ik) *adj.* of, like, or characteristic of Byron or his writings; romantic, passionate, cynical, ironic, etc. —**By·ron′i·cal·ly** *adv.*

by·stand·er (bī′stan′dər) *n.* a person who stands near but does not participate; onlooker

by·way (bī′wā′) *n.* 1. a path or road that is not a main road, esp. one not used very much 2. a secondary activity, line of study, etc.

by·word (-wʉrd′) *n.* 1. a familiar saying; proverb 2. a person or thing proverbial for some specific characteristic [this name was a *byword* for cruelty] 3. a favourite or pet word or phrase

By·zan·tine (biz′′n tēn′, -tīn′; bi zan′tīn, bī-) *adj.* 1. of or like Byzantium or the Byzantine Empire, its culture, etc. 2. of or pertaining to the Orthodox Eastern Church 3. *Archit.* designating or of a style developed in Byzantium, characterized by domes, round arches, mosaics, etc. —*n.* a native or inhabitant of Byzantium

C

C 1. *Chem.* carbon 2. *Physics* capacitance 3. *Physics the symbol for* coulomb

C, c (sē) *n., pl.* **C's, c's** 1. the third letter of the English alphabet 2. a sound of *C* or *c* 3. *a symbol for* the third in a sequence or group

C (sē) *n.* 1. a Roman numeral for 100 2. *Music a)* the first tone in the scale of C major *b)* the scale having this tone as the keynote

C, C. 1. Celsius or centigrade 2. Conservative

C, c copyright

C. 1. Catholic 2. Church

C., c. 1. cathode 2. century 3. *pl.* **CC.** chapter 4. contralto

c. 1. carat 2. cent 3. circa 4. *Cricket* caught

Ca *Chem.* calcium

ca. 1. cathode 2. circa

C.A. 1. Central America 2. Chartered Accountant

CAA, C.A.A. Civil Aviation Authority

Caa·ba (kä′bə) *same as* KAABA

cab (kab) *n.* [< CABRIOLET] 1. a horse-drawn carriage, esp. one for public hire 2. *clipped form of* TAXICAB 3. the place in a locomotive, lorry, crane, etc. where the operator sits

ca·bal (kə bal′) *n.* [Fr., intrigue < ML. *cabbala*, CABALA] 1. a small group of persons joined in a secret intrigue; junta 2. the intrigues of such a group; plot —*vi.* **-balled′, -bal′ling** to join in a cabal; plot

cab·a·la (kab′ə lə, kə bäl′ə) *n.* [< ML. < Heb. *qabbālāh*, received lore < *qābal*, to receive] 1. an occult rabbinical philosophy, based on a mystical interpretation of the

Scriptures **2.** any esoteric or secret doctrine; occultism Also sp. **cab′ba·la** —**cab′a·lism** n. —**cab′a·list** n. —**cab′a·lis′tic** adj. —**cab′a·lis′ti·cal·ly** adv.

ca·bal·le·ro (kab′ə ler′ō, -əl yer′ō; Sp. kä′bä lye′rō) n., pl. **-ros** (-ōz; Sp. -rōs) [Sp. < LL. < L. caballus, horse] **1.** a Spanish gentleman **2.** [Southwest U.S.] a horseman

ca·ba·na (kə bän′ə, -bän′ya; -ban′-) n. [Sp. cabaña < LL. capanna, hut] [U.S.] **1.** a cabin or hut **2.** a small shelter for swimmers at a beach, pool, etc.

cab·a·ret (kab′ə rā′, kab′ə rā′) n. [Fr., tavern] **1.** a restaurant or café with dancing, singing, etc. as entertainment **2.** such entertainment

cab·bage (kab′ij) n. [OFr. caboche, ult. < ? L. caput, the head] **1.** a common vegetable with thick leaves formed into a round, compact head on a short stalk **2.** [Colloq.] same as VEGETABLE (n. 3)

cabbage palm any of several palms with terminal buds used as a vegetable: also **cabbage tree**

cabbage white a common white butterfly whose green larvae feed on cabbage and related plants

cab·driv·er (kab′drīv′ər) n. a person who drives a cab: also [Colloq.] **cab′by, cab′bie** (-ē), pl. **-bies**

ca·ber (kā′bər) n. [Gael. cabar] a long, heavy pole tossed as a test of muscular strength in the Highland Games

cab·in (kab′in) n. [< OFr. < Pr. < LL. capanna, hut] **1.** a small house, built simply or crudely **2.** any simple, small structure designed for a brief stay **3.** a private room on a ship, as a bedroom or office **4.** a roofed section of a small boat **5.** an enclosed section for passengers in an aircraft —vt. to confine in or as in a cabin; cramp

cabin boy a boy whose work is to serve and run errands for officers and passengers aboard a ship

cabin cruiser a motorboat with a cabin and the necessary equipment for living on board

cab·i·net (kab′ə nit, kab′nit) n. [Fr., dim. of cabine; origin obscure] **1.** a case with drawers or shelves for holding or storing things **2.** a boxlike enclosure for a record player, radio, television, etc. **3.** formerly, a private council room **4.** [often C-] a) the body of senior ministers in a government b) [U.S.] the heads of certain governmental departments —adj. **1.** of a kind usually kept in a cabinet **2.** of a political cabinet

cab·i·net·mak·er (-māk′ər) n. a workman who makes fine furniture, etc. —**cab′i·net·mak′ing** n.

cab·i·net·work (-wurk′) n. **1.** articles made by a cabinetmaker **2.** the work or art of a cabinetmaker

ca·ble (kā′b'l) n. [OFr. < LL. capulum < L. capere, to take hold] **1.** a thick, heavy rope, now often of wire **2.** a ship's anchor chain **3.** same as CABLE LENGTH **4.** a bundle of insulated wires through which an electric current can be passed **5.** same as CABLEGRAM —vt. **-bled, -bling** **1.** to fasten with a cable **2.** to transmit by undersea cable **3.** to send a cablegram to —vi. to send a cablegram

cable car a car drawn by a moving cable

ca·ble·gram (-gram′) n. a message sent by undersea cable

cable length a unit of nautical measure: in Britain, one tenth of a nautical mile (185.2m); in the U.S., 120 fathoms (219.5m): also **cable's length**   CABLES

cable television a television service transmitted to subscribers by cable

ca·bob (kə bob′) n. same as KEBAB

ca·bo·chon (kab′ə shon; Fr. kȧ bō shōn′) n. [Fr. < caboche, head: see CABBAGE] any precious stone cut in convex shape, polished but not faceted

ca·boo·dle (kə bōō′d'l) n. [< ? KIT + BOODLE] [Colloq.] lot; group [the whole caboodle]

ca·boose (kə bōōs′) n. [< MDu. kabuys, kambuis (< ?), cabin house, ship's galley] **1.** a ship's galley or kitchen **2.** [U.S.] guard's van on a goods train, usually at the rear

cab·o·tage (kab ə täzh′) n. [Fr. < caboter, to sail along the coast < Sp. cabo, cape] **1.** coastal navigation and trade, esp. between ports within a country **2.** the practice of using lorries registered in one country to transport goods in another, in order to avoid payment of taxes and licence-fees

cab·ri·ole (kab′rē ōl′) n. [Fr.: see ff.] a leg of a table, chair, etc. that curves outwards and then tapers inwards, popular in the early 18th c.

cab·ri·o·let (kab′rē ə lā′) n. [Fr., dim. of cabriole, a leap < It. capriola] **1.** a light, two-wheeled carriage, usually with a hood that folds, drawn by one horse **2.** a former style of motor car with a folding top

cab·stand (kab′stand′) n. [U.S.] same as TAXI RANK

ca·ca·o (kə kā′ō, -kä′-) n., pl. **-ca′os** [Sp. < Nahuatl cacauatl, cacao seed] **1.** a tropical American tree, bearing large, elliptical seedpods **2.** the seeds (**cacao beans**) of this tree, from which cocoa and chocolate are made

cach·a·lot (kash′ə lot′, -lō′) n. [Fr. < Sp. < ? Port. cachola, big head] same as SPERM WHALE

cache (kash) n. [Fr. < cacher, conceal < L. coactare,

constrain] **1.** a place in which stores of food, supplies, etc. are hidden **2.** a safe place for hiding things **3.** anything so hidden —vt., cached, cach′ing to hide or store in a cache

cache-pot (kash′pot, -pō) n. [Fr., lit., hide-pot < cacher, to hide + pot, pot] a decorative pot, jar, etc., esp. for house plants: also **cache pot**

ca·chet (kash′ā, ka shā′) n. [Fr. < cacher: see CACHE] **1.** a seal or stamp on an official letter **2.** a) a mark indicating genuine or superior quality b) prestige **3.** a commemorative design, slogan, etc. stamped on letters, etc.

ca·chex·i·a (kə kek′sē ə) n. [ModL. < Gr. kachexia, bad habit of body < kakos, bad + hexis, habit] a generally weakened, emaciated condition of the body, esp. as associated with a chronic illness: also **ca·chex′y** —**ca·chec′tic** (-kek′tik) adj.

cach·in·nate (kak′ə nāt) vi. **-nat′ed, -nat′ing** [< L. pp. of cachinnare, prob. echoic] to laugh loudly or too much —**cach′in·na′tion** n. —**cach′in·na′to·ry** adj.

ca·chou (ka shōō′) n. [Fr. < Malay kachu] **1.** same as CATECHU **2.** a lozenge for sweetening the breath

ca·cique (kə sēk′) n. [Sp. < native word] **1.** in Latin America, an Indian chief **2.** in Latin America and Spain, a local political boss

cack-hand·ed (kak′han′did) adj. [< ? cack, excrement + HANDED] **1.** [Dial.] left-handed **2.** [Colloq.] clumsy; awkward

cack·le (kak′'l) vi. **-led, -ling** [akin to Du. kokkelen, of echoic origin] **1.** to make the shrill, broken, vocal sounds of a hen **2.** to laugh or chatter with similar sounds —vt. to utter in a cackling manner —n. **1.** a cackling **2.** cackling laughter or chatter —**cut the cackle** [Slang] come to the point

cac·o- [< Gr. kakos, bad, evil] a combining form meaning bad, poor, harsh [cacography]: also, before a vowel, **cac-** **2.** to laugh or chatter with similar sounds —vt. to utter in a cackling manner —n. **1.** a cackling **2.** cackling laughter or chatter —**cut the cackle** [Slang] come to the point

ca·co·e·thes (kak′ō ē′thēz) n. [L. < Gr. kakoethes < kakos, bad + ēthos, habit, custom] an itch (to do something); mania

ca·cog·ra·phy (kə kog′rə fē) n. [CACO- + -GRAPHY] **1.** bad handwriting **2.** incorrect spelling —**cac·o·graph·ic** (kak′ə graf′ik) adj.

ca·coph·o·ny (kə kof′ə nē) n., pl. **-nies** [< ModL. < Gr. < kakos, bad + phōnē, voice] harsh, jarring sound; dissonance —**ca·coph′o·nous** adj. —**ca·coph′o·nous·ly** adv.

cac·tus (kak′təs) n., pl. **-tus·es, -ti** (-tī) [L. < Gr. kaktos, kind of thistle] any of various desert plants found in N and S America with fleshy stems, reduced or spinelike leaves, and often showy flowers

ca·cu·mi·nal (kə kyōō′mə n'l) adj. [L. cacuminis, gen. of cacumen, top + -AL] Phonet. pronounced with the tip of the tongue turned backwards and upwards against or towards the hard palate — a cacuminal sound

cad (kad) n. [< CADDIE & CADET] a man or boy whose behaviour is considered to be ungentlemanly

ca·dav·er (kə dāv′ər, dav′-) n. [L., prob. < cadere, to fall] a dead body, esp. of a person; corpse, as for dissection

ca·dav·er·ous (kə dav′ər əs) adj. of or like a cadaver; esp., pale, ghastly, or gaunt and haggard —**ca·dav′er·ous·ly** adv.

cad·die (kad′ē) n. [Scot. form of Fr. cadet: see CADET] **1.** a person who attends a golfer, carrying his clubs, etc. **2.** a small, wheeled cart used by golfers —vi. **-died, -dy·ing** to act as a caddie

cad·dis fly (kad′is) [< ?] a small, mothlike insect with two pairs of wings, a soft body, and long legs

cad·dish (kad′ish) adj. like or characteristic of a cad; ungentlemanly —**cad′dish·ly** adv. —**cad′dish·ness** n.

cad·dis worm (kad′is) the wormlike aquatic larva of the caddis fly that lives in a case made of twigs, grains of sand, etc. cemented together with its secreted silk: used as bait by anglers

cad·dy¹ (kad′ē) n., pl. **-dies** [< Malay kati, weight equivalent to c. 500g.] **1.** a small container used for tea **2.** any of various devices for holding or storing certain articles

cad·dy² (kad′ē) n., vi. same as CADDIE

-cade (kād) [< (CAVAL)CADE] a suffix meaning procession, parade [motorcade]

ca·dence (kād′'ns) n. [ult. < L. prp. of cadere, to fall] **1.** fall of the voice in speaking **2.** inflection or modulation in tone **3.** a rhythmic flow of sound **4.** measured movement, as in marching, or the beat of such movement **5.** Music the harmonic ending, final trill, etc. of a phrase or movement Also **ca′den·cy** —**ca′denced** adj.

ca·den·za (kə den′zə) n. [It.: see prec.] **1.** an elaborate, often improvised musical passage played by the solo instrument in a concerto, usually near the end of the first movement **2.** any brilliant flourish in an aria or solo passage

ca·det (kə det′) n. [Fr. < Gascon capdet, chief < Pr. < LL. dim. of L. caput: see CAPTAIN] **1.** a younger son or brother **2.** a student at an armed forces or police academy **3.**

[N.Z.] a young man undergoing training on a farm away from home —**ca·det′ship′** *n.*

cadge (kaj) *vt., vi.* **cadged, cadg′ing** [< ?] to beg or get by begging; sponge —**cadg′er** *n.*

ca·di (kä′dē, kä′-) *n.* [Ar. *qādi*] a Moslem magistrate or judge

Cad·me·an victory (kad mē′ən) [after *Cadmus*, in Gr. myth, who killed a dragon and sowed its teeth, from which many armed men rose and fought, five surviving to help him build Thebes] a victory won with great losses to the victors

cad·mi·um (kad′mē əm) *n.* [ModL. < L. *cadmia*, zinc ore < Gr. *kadmeia*] a blue-white, malleable, ductile, metallic chemical element occurring in zinc ores: it is used in some alloys, electroplating, etc.: symbol, Cd; at. wt., 112.40; at. no., 48 —**cad′mic** (-mik) *adj.*

ca·dre (kä′də, käd′rē) *n.* [Fr. < L. *quadrum*, a square] 1. a framework 2. a nucleus of trained men around which a military or political unit can be built 3. a member of such a nucleus

ca·du·ce·us (kə dyōō′sē əs) *n., pl.* **-ce·i′** (-sē ī′) [L.] 1. the staff of an ancient herald; esp., the winged staff with two serpents twined about it, carried by Mercury 2. a staff like this twined with one or two serpents, used as an emblem of the medical profession —**ca·du′ce·an** *adj.*

ca·du·cous (kə dyōō′kəs) *adj.* [L. *caducus*, falling < *cadere*, to fall] *Biol.* falling off early, as some organs and leaves —**ca·du′ci·ty** *n.*

cae·cil·i·an (sē sil′ē ən, -sil′yən) *n.* [L. *caecilia*, kind of lizard < *caecus*, blind] any of a family of legless, tropical amphibians resembling worms

cae·cum (sē′kəm) *n., pl.* **-ca** (-kə) [< L. (*intestinum*) *caecum*, blind (intestine)] the pouch that is the beginning of the large intestine —**cae′-cal** *adj.*

Cae·no·zo·ic (kī′nō zō′ik) *adj. same as* CAINOZOIC

Caer·phil·ly (ker fil′ē) *n.* [after the town in SE Wales, where orig. made] a creamy-white, mild cheese

Cae·sar (sē′zər) *n.* [after the family name of Gaius Julius *Caesar* (100? - 44 B.C.), Rom. general & statesman] 1. the title of the Roman emperors from Augustus to Hadrian 2. any emperor or dictator —**Cae′sar·ism** *n.*

Cae·sar·e·an, Cae·sar·i·an (si zer′ē ən) *adj.* of Julius Caesar or the Caesars —*n. same as* CAESAREAN SECTION

Caesarean section [after Julius *Caesar*, supposedly born in this way] [*also* **c- s-**] a surgical operation for delivering a baby by cutting through the mother's abdominal and uterine walls

cae·si·um (sē′zē əm) *n.* [ModL., neut. of L. *caesius*, bluish-grey] a soft, silver-white, ductile, metallic element, used in photoelectric cells: symbol, Cs; at. wt., 132.905; at. no., 55

cae·su·ra (si zyoor′ə, -zhoor′ə) *n., pl.* **-ras, -rae** (-ē) [L., a cutting < pp. of *caedere*, to cut] 1. a break or pause in a line of verse: in Greek and Latin verse, the caesura falls within the metrical foot; in English verse, it is usually about the middle of the line 2. a pause showing rhythmic division of a melody —**cae·su′ral** *adj.*

ca·fé, ca·fe (ka fā′, kə-) *n.* [Fr. café, COFFEE] a small or inexpensive restaurant or coffee bar, serving light meals and refreshments

‡**ca·fé au lait** (kȧ fā ō lā′) [Fr.] 1. coffee with hot milk 2. pale brown

‡**ca·fé noir** (kȧ fā nwȧr′) [Fr.] black coffee

caf·e·te·ri·a (kaf′ə tir′ē ə) *n.* [AmSp., coffee shop] a restaurant in which food is displayed on counters and patrons serve themselves

caff (kaf) *n.* [Colloq.] *clipped form of* CAFE

caf·feine (kaf′ēn, -ē in) *n.* [< G., ult. < It. *caffè*, COFFEE + *-in*, -INE⁴] an alkaloid present in coffee, tea, and coca cola: it is a stimulant to the heart and central nervous system

caf·tan (kaf′tən, kaf tän′) *n.* [Turk. *qaftān*] 1. a long-sleeved robe with a girdle, worn in eastern Mediterranean countries 2. a similar garment worn in western countries

cage (kāj) *n.* [OFr. < L. *cavea*, hollow place < *cavus*, hollow] 1. a box or structure of wires, bars, etc. for confining birds or animals 2. an openwork structure, as some lift compartments 3. *Basketball* the basket —*vt.* **caged, cag′ing** to put or confine, as in a cage

ca·gey, ca·gy (kā′jē) *adj.* **ca′gi·er, ca′gi·est** [< ?] [Colloq.] 1. not open or frank; wary 2. careful not to get caught or fooled —**ca′gi·ly** *adv.* —**ca′gi·ness** *n.*

ca·goule (kə gōōl′) *n.* [Fr., a monk's hood] a form of very light anorak that packs away into a small space

ca·hoots (kə hōōts′) *n.pl.* [< ?] [Colloq.] partnership; league: chiefly in the phrase **in cahoots** in league: usually applied to questionable dealing

cai·man (kā′mən) *n., pl.* **-mans** *same as* CAYMAN

Cain (kān) *n.* [after *Cain*, eldest son of Adam and Eve: he killed his brother Abel: Gen 4] any murderer —**raise Cain** [Colloq.] to cause a great commotion or much trouble

Cai·no·zo·ic (kī′nō zō′ik, kā′-) *adj.* [< Gr. *kainos*, recent +

zo- + -ic] designating or of the geologic era following the Mesozoic and including the present —**the Cainozoic** the Cainozoic Era or its rocks: see GEOLOGY, chart

ca·ique, ca·ïque (kī ēk′) *n.* [Fr. < It. < Turk. *qayiq*] 1. a light rowing boat used on the Bosporus 2. a sailing vessel used esp. in the eastern Mediterranean

cairn (kern) *n.* [Scot. < Gael. *carn*, an elevation] a conical heap of stones built as a monument or landmark —**cairned** *adj.*

cairn·gorm (kern′gôrm) *n.* [after the *Cairngorms*, mountain range in NE Scotland] a yellow or brown variety of quartz, used as a gem

cairn terrier [said to be so named from its burrowing in cairns] a small, shaggy Scottish terrier

cais·son (kā′son, kās′'n) *n.* [Fr. < It. < *cassa* < L. *capsa*, a box, CASE²] 1. a chest for holding ammunition 2. a two-wheeled wagon for transporting ammunition 3. a watertight enclosure inside which men can do construction work under water 4. a watertight box for raising sunken ships

caisson disease *same as* DECOMPRESSION SICKNESS

cai·tiff (kāt′if) *n.* [OFr. *caitif*, a captive < L. *captivus*, CAPTIVE] [Archaic] a mean, evil, or cowardly person —*adj.* mean, evil, or cowardly

ca·jole (kə jōl′) *vt., vi.* **-joled′, -jol′ing** [< Fr. < ? blend of OFr. *cage*, CAGE + *jaole, gaole*, prison: see JAIL] to coax with flattery and insincere talk; wheedle —**ca·jole′ment, ca·jol′er·y** *n.* —**ca·jol′er** *n.* —**ca·jol′ing·ly** *adv.*

cake (kāk) *n.* [< ON. *kaka*] 1. a mixture of flour, eggs, milk, sugar, etc. baked as in a loaf and often covered with icing 2. a shaped, usually rounded and flattened, portion of a food mixture, baked or fried [an *oatcake*] 3. a shaped, solid mass, as of soap, ice, etc. 4. a hard crust or deposit —*vt., vi.* **caked, cak′ing** to form into a hard mass or a crust —**have one's cake and eat it** to benefit from opposing courses of action —**piece of cake** (something) very easy to accomplish —**take the cake** [Colloq.] to win the prize; excel: ironic usage —**cak′y** *adj.*

cakes and ale the good things of life

cake·walk (-wôk′) *n.* 1. formerly, a competition among Negroes in the S U.S. for the prize of a cake, judged on the elegance of a promenade to music 2. a dance-step developed from this 3. anything very easily accomplished —*vi.* to do a cakewalk

Cal. large calorie(s)

cal. 1. calendar 2. calibre 3. small calorie(s)

cal·a·bash (kal′ə bash′) *n.* [< Sp. *calabaza* < ?] 1. a tropical American tree or its large, gourdlike fruit 2. *a)* a tropical plant bearing white flowers, or its bottle-shaped gourd *b)* a large smoking pipe made from the neck of this gourd 3. the dried, hollow shell of a calabash, used as a bowl, cup, etc.

cal·a·boose (kal′ə bōōs′) *n.* [Sp. *calabozo*] [U.S. Slang] a prison; jail

ca·la·di·um (kə lā′dē əm) *n.* [ModL. < Malay *kélādy*, kind of plant] a tropical American plant of the arum family, with brilliantly coloured leaves

cal·a·man·der (kal′ə man′dər) *n.* [< ? *Coromandel* coast in SE India] the hard, heavy, black wood of an East Indian tree of the ebony family

cal·a·mar·y (kal′ə mər ē) *n., pl.* **-mar·ies** [L. *calamarius*, of a writing reed < *calamus*, a reed, pen] a squid: so called from its pen-shaped skeleton

cal·a·mine (kal′ə mīn′) *n.* [Fr. < ML. *calamina* < L. *cadmia*: see CADMIUM] a pink powder consisting of zinc oxide mixed with a little ferric oxide, used in skin lotions and ointments

cal·a·mint (kal′ə mint′) *n.* [< OFr. *calamente* < *calaminthe* Gr. *kalaminthē*] any of a genus of plants related to mint and thyme

ca·lam·i·tous (kə lam′ə təs) *adj.* bringing or causing calamity —**ca·lam′i·tous·ly** *adv.* —**ca·lam′i·tous·ness** *n.*

ca·lam·i·ty (-tē) *n., pl.* **-ties** [< Fr. < L. *calamitas*] 1. deep trouble or misery 2. any extreme misfortune; disaster

cal·a·mus (kal′ə məs) *n., pl.* **-mi′** (-mī′) [L. < Gr. *kalamos*, a reed] 1. *same as* SWEET FLAG 2. the quill of a feather

ca·lan·do (kə lan′dō) *adj., adv.* [It., decreasing] *Music* with gradually decreasing speed and volume; fading away

ca·lan·dri·a (kə lan′drē ə) *n.* [< Sp. *calandria*, lark] a sealed vessel used as a heat-exchanger in the core of certain nuclear reactors

ca·lash (kə lash′) *n.* [Fr. *calèche* < G. < Czech *kolésa*; prob. < *kolo*, a wheel] 1. a light, low-wheeled carriage, usually with a folding top 2. a folding top of a carriage 3. a folding hood or bonnet, worn by women in the 18th cent.

cal·ca·ne·um (kal kā′nē əm) *n., pl.* **-ne·a** (-nē ə) [LL. < *calx*, the heel] the heel bone —**cal·ca′ne·al** *adj.*

cal·car·e·ous (kal ker′ē əs) *adj.* [< L. < *calx*, lime] of, like, or containing calcium carbonate, calcium, or lime —**cal·car′-e·ous·ness** *n.*

cal·ces (kal′sēz) *n. alt. pl. of* CALX

cal·ci- [< L. *calx* (gen. *calcis*), lime] *a combining form meaning* calcium or lime [*calcify*]

cal·cif·er·ol (kal sif′ə rol′) *n.* [CALCIF(EROUS) + (ERGOST)EROL] vitamin D₂: it is a crystalline alcohol

cal·cif·er·ous (-ər əs) *adj.* [CALCI- + -FEROUS] producing or containing calcite

cal·ci·fy (kal′sə fī′) *vt., vi.* -fied′, -fy′ing [CALCI- + -FY] to change into a hard, stony substance by the deposit of lime or calcium salts —**cal′ci·fi·ca′tion** *n.*

cal·ci·mine (-mīn′, -min) *n.* [< L. *calx*, lime] a white or tinted liquid of whiting or zinc white, glue, and water, used as a wash for plastered surfaces —*vt.* -mined′, -min′ing to cover with calcimine

cal·cine (kal′sīn, kal′sin) *vt., vi.* -cined, -cin·ing [< OFr. < ML. *calcinare* (an alchemists′ term)] 1. to change to calx or powder by heat 2. to burn to ashes or powder —**cal·ci·na·tion** (kal′sə nā′shən) *n.*

cal·cite (kal′sīt) *n.* crystalline calcium carbonate, CaCO₃, a mineral found as limestone, chalk, and marble

cal·ci·um (kal′sē əm) *n.* [ModL. < L. *calx*, lime] a soft, silver-white, metallic chemical element found in limestone, marble, chalk, etc.: symbol, Ca; at. wt., 40.08; at. no., 20

calcium carbide a dark-grey, crystalline compound, CaC₂, used to produce acetylene, etc.

calcium carbonate a white powder or colourless, crystalline compound, CaCO₃, found mainly in limestone, marble, and chalk, and in bones, teeth, shells, and plant ash: used in making lime

calcium chloride a white, crystalline compound, CaCl₂, used in making ice, for dehydrating, etc.

calcium hydroxide slaked lime, Ca(OH)₂, a white, crystalline compound, used in making alkalis, bleaching powder, etc.

calcium oxide a white, soft, caustic solid, CaO, prepared by heating calcium carbonate; lime: used in mortar and plaster, in ceramics, etc.

calcium phosphate any of a number of phosphates of calcium found in bones, teeth, etc.

calc·spar (kalk′spär′) *n. same as* CALCITE

cal·cu·la·ble (kal′kyoo lə b′l) *adj.* that can be calculated —**cal′cu·la·bil′i·ty** *n.* —**cal′cu·la·bly** *adv.*

cal·cu·late (kal′kyoo lāt′) *vt.* -lat′ed, -lat′ing [< L. pp. of *calculare*, to reckon < *calculus*, pebble used in counting, dim. of *calx*, limestone] 1. to determine by using mathematics; compute 2. to determine by reasoning; estimate 3. to plan or intend 4. [U.S. Colloq.] to think; suppose —*vi.* 1. to make a computation 2. to rely or count (on)

cal·cu·lat·ed (-lāt′id) *adj.* 1. undertaken after the probable results have been estimated [*calculated* risk] 2. deliberately planned [*calculated* cruelty] 3. apt or likely [behaviour *calculated* to anger him] —**cal′cu·lat′ed·ly** *adv.*

cal·cu·lat·ing (-iŋ) *adj.* shrewd or scheming

cal·cu·la·tion (kal′kyoo lā′shən) *n.* 1. a calculating 2. something deduced by calculating; estimate; plan 3. careful planning or forethought, esp. with selfish motives —**cal′·cu·la′tive** *adj.*

cal·cu·la·tor (kal′kyoo lāt′ər) *n.* 1. a person who calculates 2. a device, now usually electronic, for doing rapid mathematical calculations 3. a set of arithmetical tables

cal·cu·lous (kal′kyoo ləs) *adj. Med.* caused by or having a calculus or calculi

cal·cu·lus (kal′kyoo ləs) *n., pl.* -li (-lī′), -lus·es [L.: see CALCULATE] 1. any abnormal stony mass or deposit formed in the body, as in a kidney 2. *Math.* a) a method of calculation using symbols b) a method of mathematical analysis using the combined methods of DIFFERENTIAL CALCULUS and INTEGRAL CALCULUS

cal·de·ra (kal der′ə, kôl′də rə) *n.* [Sp. < LL. *caldaria*, cauldron] a broad, craterlike basin of a volcano, formed by an explosion or by collapse of the cone

cal·dron (kôl′drən) *n. same as* CAULDRON

ca·lèche (kə lesh′) *n. same as* CALASH

Cal·e·do·ni·a (kal′ə dō′nē ə) [L.] poet name for Scotland

Cal·e·do·ni·an (kal′ə dō′nē ən) *adj.* 1. Scottish; of or designating the Scottish Highlands [the *Caledonian* Canal] 2. *Geol.* of or designating the pre-Devonian mountains running NE-SW from Norway to Ireland, or the period in which they were built —*n.* a Scot

cal·e·fa·cient (kal′ə fā′shənt) *adj.* [L. *calefaciens*, prp. of *calefacere* < *calere*, to be warm + *facere*, to make] making warm; heating —*n. Med.* a substance applied to the body to give a sensation of heat

cal·en·dar (kal′ən dər) *n.* [L. *kalendarium*, account book < *kalendae*, CALENDS] 1. a system of determining the beginning, length, and divisions of a year and for arranging it into days, weeks, and months 2. a table or chart that shows such an arrangement, usually for a single year 3. a list or schedule, as of pending court cases —*adj.* that appears on popular calendars [*calendar* art] —*vt.* to enter in a calendar; schedule

calendar year the period of time from Jan. 1 to Dec. 31: distinguished from FINANCIAL YEAR

cal·en·der (kal′ən dər) *n.* [< Fr. < ML. < L. *cylindrus*, CYLINDER] a machine with rollers between which paper,

cloth, etc. is run, to give it a smooth or glossy finish —*vt.* to process (paper, etc.) in a calender —**cal′en·der·er** *n.*

cal·ends (-əndz) *n.pl.* [often with sing. v.] [< L. *kalendae* < *calare*, to proclaim < Gr. *kalein*] the first day of each month in the ancient Roman calendar: also **kalends**

ca·len·du·la (kə len′dyoo lə) *n.* [ModL. < L. *kalendae*, calends: the connection is unclear] any of a genus of plants of the composite family, with yellow or orange flowers

calf¹ (käf) *n., pl.* **calves** [< OE. *cealf* & ON. *kalfr*] 1. a young cow or bull 2. the young of some other large animals, as the elephant, whale, hippopotamus, seal, etc. 3. leather from the hide of a calf; calfskin 4. a piece of ice broken off from an iceberg or coastal glacier 5. [Colloq.] an awkward or silly youth —**in calf** pregnant: said of a cow —**kill the fatted calf** to make a feast of welcome: Luke 15:23

calf² (käf) *n., pl.* **calves** [ON. *kalfi*] the fleshy back part of the leg below the knee

calf′s-foot jelly (käfs′foot′) an edible gelatin made by boiling calves′ feet

calf·skin (käf′skin′) *n.* 1. the skin of a calf 2. a soft, flexible leather made from this

cal·i·brate (kal′ə brāt′) *vt.* -brat′ed, -brat′ing [see ff.] 1. to determine the calibre of 2. to fix, check, or correct the scale of (a measuring instrument, as a thermometer) —**cal′·i·bra′tion** *n.* —**cal′i·bra′tor** *n.*

cal·i·bre (kal′ə bər) *n.* [< Fr. & Sp. < *calibo* < Ar. *qālib*, a mould] 1. the size of a bullet or shell as measured by its diameter 2. the diameter of the bore of a gun measured in hundredths of an inch or in millimetres 3. the diameter of a cylindrical body or of its hollowed interior 4. quality or ability Also, U.S. sp., **cal′i·ber**

ca·li·ces (kal′ə sēz, kā′lə-) *n. pl.* of CALIX

cal·i·co (kal′ə kō′) *n., pl.* -coes′, -cos′ [< Calicut (now Kozhikode), city in India where first obtained] 1. a plain, white or unbleached cotton fabric 2. [U.S.] a coarse, printed cotton fabric —*adj.* 1. of calico 2. [U.S.] spotted like calico [a *calico* cat]

cal·i·for·ni·um (kal′ə fôr′nē əm) *n.* [< University of *California*] a radioactive chemical element produced by intense neutron irradiation of plutonium or curium: symbol, Cf; at. wt., 251 (?); at. no., 98

cal·i·pash (kal′ə pash′) *n.* [W Ind. < ? Sp. *carapacho* a shell] a greenish, gelatinous, edible substance under the upper shell of a turtle

cal·i·pee (kal′ə pē) *n.* [var. of prec.] a yellowish, gelatinous, edible substance inside the lower shell of a turtle

cal·i·per (kal′ə pər) *n. same as* CALLIPER

ca·liph (kā′lif, kal′if) *n.* [< OFr. < Ar. *khalīfa*] supreme ruler: the title taken by Mohammed′s successors as heads of Islam: also **calif, khalif**

cal·iph·ate (kal′ə fāt′, -fit) *n.* the rank, reign, or dominion of a caliph: also **cal′if·ate′**

cal·is·then·ics (kal′ə sthen′iks) *n.pl. same as* CALLISTHENICS —**cal′is·then′ic, cal′is·then′i·cal** *adj.*

ca·lix (kā′liks, kal′iks) *n., pl.* **ca·li·ces** (kal′ə sēz′, kā′lə-) [L.] a cup; chalice

calk¹ (kôk) *vt. same as* CAULK —**calk′er** *n.*

calk² (kôk) *n.* [OE. *calc*, shoe < L. *calx*, a heel] 1. the part of a horseshoe that projects downwards to prevent slipping 2. [Chiefly U.S.] a metal plate with spurs, fastened to the sole of a shoe to prevent slipping —*vt.* to fasten calks on the sole of a shoe to prevent slipping

call (kôl) *vt.* [< OE. *ceallian* & (or <) ON. *kalla*] 1. to say or read in a loud tone; shout; announce 2. to ask to come; summon 3. to summon to a specific duty, etc. [the army *called* him] 4. to convoke [to *call* a meeting] 5. to give or apply a name to [*call* the baby Ann] 6. to consider or declare to be as specified [I *call* it silly] 7. to awaken [*call* me at six] 8. to communicate with by telephone 9. to give orders for [to *call* a strike] 10. to demand payment of (a loan or bond issue) 11. to utter directions for (a square dance) 12. in pool, to describe (the shot one plans to make) 13. *Bridge* to name (a suit) 14. a) *Poker* to require (a player) to show his hand by equalling his bet b) to force to account for something said or done c) to expose (someone′s bluff) by such action 15. *Sports* to give a decision on [the linesman *called* the shot out] —*vi.* 1. to speak in a loud tone; shout 2. to utter its characteristic cry, as a bird or animal 3. to visit for a short while 4. to telephone 5. *Poker* to require a player to show his hand by equalling his bet —*n.* 1. an act or instance of calling 2. a loud utterance; shout 3. the distinctive cry of an animal or bird, or a device imitating this 4. a summons to a meeting, etc. 5. a signal on a bugle, etc. 6. an economic demand, as for a product 7. an inner urging towards a certain action or profession, esp. to be a priest, minister, etc. 8. power to attract [the *call* of the wild] 9. need; occasion [no *call* for tears] 10. an order or demand for payment 11. a brief visit, esp. a formal or professional visit 12. *Bridge* a bid or right to bid 13. *Poker* a demand for a player′s hand to be shown 14. *Sports* an official′s decision —**call back** 1. to ask or command to come back 2. to telephone again or in return —**call down** 1. to invoke 2. [U.S. Colloq.] to scold sharply —**call for** 1. to demand 2. to come and get; stop for 3. to need (this *calls for* action) —**call forth** to bring into play —**call in** 1. to summon for help or consultation 2. to take out of circulation, as coin 3. to demand payment of (a loan, etc.) 4. [Colloq.] to pay a short visit: also **call in on** —**call in question** to raise doubts about; dispute —**call off** 1. to order away 2. to read aloud in order from a list 3. to cancel (a scheduled event) —**call on** 1. to visit briefly 2. to ask (a person) to speak —**call out** 1. to shout 2. to summon into action 3. to challenge, as to a duel —**call over** to read aloud in order from a list —**call round** to visit informally —**call up** 1. to make one remember 2. to summon, esp. for military duty 3. to telephone —**call (up)on** 1. to summon 2. to invite (a person) to speak, perform a service, etc. —**on call** 1. available when summoned 2. payable on demand —**within call** in hearing distance

cal·la (kal'ə) *n.* [ModL. (named by Linnaeus)] any of several plants of the arum family, with a conspicuous spathe surrounding a yellow spadix: also **calla lily**

call-box (kôl'boks') *n.* a soundproof kiosk containing a public telephone

call-boy (-boi') *n.* a boy who calls actors when it is time for them to go on the stage

cal·er¹ (-ər) *n.* 1. a person or thing that calls, esp. for a square dance 2. a person who makes a short visit

cal·ler² (kal'ər) *adj.* [MScot.; ? var. of *calver*, fresh] [Scot.] 1. fresh: said of food 2. fresh and cool: said of the weather, a breeze, etc.

cal·lig·ra·phy (kə lig'rə fē) *n.* [< Gr. < *kallos*, beauty + *graphein*, to write] 1. beautiful handwriting 2. handwriting —**cal·lig'ra·pher, cal·lig'ra·phist** *n.* —**cal·i·graph·ic** (kal'ə graf'ik) *adj.*

cal·ing (kôl'iŋ) *n.* 1. the action of one that calls 2. one's occupation, profession, or trade 3. an inner urging towards some profession or activity, esp. the Christian ministry; vocation

calling card [U.S.] *same as* VISITING CARD

Cal·li·o·pe (kə lī'ə pē; for *n.*, *also* kal'ē ōp') [L. < Gr. *Kalliopē* < *kallos*, beauty + *ops*, voice] *Gr. Myth.* the Muse of eloquence and epic poetry —*n.* [c-] [U.S.] a keyboard instrument like an organ, having a series of steam whistles

cal·li·per (kal'ə pər) *n.* [var. of CALIBRE] 1. [*usually pl.*] an instrument consisting of a pair of movable, curved legs fastened together at one end, used to measure the thickness or diameter of something: there are **inside callipers** and **outside callipers** 2. a splint of metal used to support the leg 3. same as CALLIPER RULE —*vt., vi.* to measure with callipers

calliper rule a graduated rule with one sliding jaw and one that is stationary

cal·lis·then·ics (kal'as then'iks) *n.pl.* [< Gr. *kallos*, beauty + *sthenos*, strength] 1. exercises to develop a strong, trim body; simple gymnastics 2. [*with sing. v.*] the art of developing bodily strength and gracefulness by such exercises —**cal'lis·then'ic, cal'lis·then'ic·al** *adj.*

call loan a loan that must be repaid on demand

call money 1. money borrowed as a call loan 2. money available for call loans

cal·lop (kal'əp) *n.* [< Abor.] [Aust.] the golden perch

cal·los·i·ty (ka los'ə tē) *n.* *pl.* -ties a hardened, thickened place on skin or bark; callus

cal·lous (kal'əs) *adj.* [< L. < *callum*, hard skin] 1. *a)* having calluses *b)* thick and hardened 2. lacking pity, mercy, etc.; unfeeling; insensitive —*vt., vi.* to make or become callous —**cal'lous·ly** *adv.* —**cal'lous·ness** *n.*

call-over (kôl'ōvər) *n.* the reading aloud (in betting shops, etc.) of betting prices

cal·low (kal'ō) *adj.* [< OE. *calu*, bald] 1. [Rare] still lacking the feathers needed for flying 2. young and inexperienced; immature —**cal'low·ness** *n.*

call-sign (-sīn') *n.* the letters and numbers that identify a radio transmitting station

cal·lus (kal'əs) *n.,* *pl.* -lus·es [L., var. of *callum*, hard skin] 1. a hardened, thickened place on the skin 2. the hard substance that forms initially at the break in a fractured bone so as to reunite the parts 3. a mass of undifferentiated cells that develops over cuts or wounds on plants —*vi., vt.* to develop or cause to develop a callus

calm (käm) *n.* [< OFr. < It. < LL. *cauma*, heat of the day (hence, in It., time to rest: cf. SIESTA) < Gr. *kauma*, heat] 1. lack of wind or motion; stillness 2. lack of excitement; tranquillity; serenity —*adj.* 1. without wind or motion; still; quiet 2. not excited; tranquil —*vt., vi.* to make or become calm (often with *down*) —**calm'at·ive** *adj.* —**calm'ly** *adv.* —**calm'ness** *n.*

cal·o·mel (kal'ə mel', -məl) *n.* [Fr. < Gr. *kalos*, beautiful + *melas*, black] mercurous chloride, HgCl, a white, tasteless powder, formerly used as a cathartic, for intestinal worms, etc.

cal·or gas (kal'ər) a *trademark* for butane gas liquefied under pressure in containers for cooking, heating, etc.

ca·lor·ic (kə lor'ik, kal'ə rik) *n.* [< Fr. < L. *calor*, heat]

[Archaic] heat —*adj.* 1. of heat 2. of or pertaining to calories —**ca·lor'i·cal·ly** *adv.*

cal·o·rie (kal'ə rē) *n.* [Fr. < L. *calor*, heat] 1. the amount of heat needed to raise the temperature of one gramme of water from 14.5 °C to 15.5 °C, equivalent to 4.1855 joules: also **small calorie** 2. the International Table calorie, 4.1868 joules 3. [C-] the amount of heat needed to raise the temperature of one kilogramme of water by one degree Celsius, 4185.5 joules: also **large calorie** 4. unit equal to the large calorie, used for measuring energy produced by food when oxidized in the body Also sp. **cal'o·ry,** *pl.* -ries

cal·o·rif·ic (kal'ə rif'ik) *adj.* [< Fr. < L. < *calor*, heat + *facere*, to make] producing or relating to heat

cal·o·rim·e·ter (kal'ə rim'ə tər) *n.* [< L. *calor*, heat + -METER] an apparatus for measuring amounts of heat, as in chemical combination, friction, etc.

cal·o·rim·e·try (kal'ə rim'ə trē) *n.* [< L. *calor*, heat + -METRY] measurement of the quantity of heat —**cal·o·ri·met·ric** (kal'ə ri met'rik), **cal'o·ri·met'ri·cal** *adj.*

calque (kalk) *n.* [Fr., an imitation, tracing < *calquer*, to trace < It. *caleare*, to press, trample < L., to trade] *Linguis.* a borrowing by which a specialized meaning of a word or phrase in one language is transferred to another language by a literal translation (Ex: *masterpiece* from German *Meisterstück*)

cal·u·met (kal'yə met', kal'yə met') *n.* [Fr.; ult. < L. *calamus*, a reed] a long-stemmed ceremonial pipe, smoked by N. American Indians as a token of peace

ca·lum·ni·ate (kə lum'nē āt') *vt., vi.* -at'ed, -at'ing [< L. pp. of *calumniari*, to slander < *calumnia*, CALUMNY] to spread false and harmful statements about; slander —**ca·lum'ni·a'tion** *n.* —**ca·lum'ni·a'tor** *n.*

CALUMET

ca·lum·ni·ous (kə lum'nē əs) *adj.* full of calumnies; slanderous —**ca·lum'ni·ous·ly** *adv.*

cal·um·ny (kal'əm nē) *n.,* *pl.* -nies [< Fr. < L. *calumnia*, trickery, slander] 1. a false and malicious statement meant to hurt someone's reputation 2. the uttering of such a statement; slander —*vt. same as* CALUMNIATE

Cal·va·dos (kal'və dos') *n.* [< *Calvados*, department in NW France, where chiefly distilled] a French brandy distilled from apple cider

Cal·va·ry (kal'vər ē) [< LL. < L. *calvaria*, skull; transl. of Aram. *gūlgulthā*, Golgotha, lit., skull] *Bible* the place near Jerusalem where the crucifixion of Jesus took place: Luke 23:33, Matt. 27:33

calve (käv) *vi., vt.* **calved, calv'ing** [< OE. *cealfian*] 1. to give birth to (a calf) 2. to release (a mass of ice into water): said of a glacier or an iceberg

calves (kävz) *n.* *pl. of* CALF

Cal·vin·ism (-iz'm) *n.* the theological system of John Calvin and his followers, which emphasizes the doctrines of predestination and salvation solely by God's grace: associated, in practice, with a stern moral code —**Cal'vin·ist** *n., adj.* —**Cal'vin·is'tic, Cal'vin·is'ti·cal** *adj.* —**Cal'vin·is'ti·cal·ly** *adv.*

calx (kalks) *n.,* *pl.* **calx'es, cal·ces** (kal'sēz) [L., small stone, lime] the ashy powder left after a metal or mineral has been calcined

ca·lyp·so (kə lip'sō) *n.* [< ? *Calypso*, in Homer's *Odyssey* a sea nymph] 1. a W Indian, esp. Trinidadian, style of singing, with improvised, often satirical words, and syncopated rhythm 2. a song or dance in calypso style

ca·lyx (kā'liks, kal'iks) *n.,* *pl.* **ca'lyx·es, ca·ly·ces** (kā'lə sēz', kal'ə-) [L., outer covering, pod < Gr. *kalyx*] 1. the outer whorl of protective leaves, or sepals, of a flower, usually green 2. *same as* CALIX

cam (kam) *n.* [Du. *cam*, orig., comb] a wheel, projection on a wheel, etc. which gives an eccentric or reciprocating motion to another wheel, a shaft, etc., or receives such motion from it

Cam. Cambridgeshire

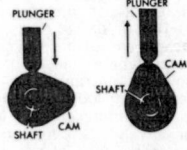

ca·ma·ra·de·rie (kam'ə räd'ər ē) *n.* [Fr. < *camarade*, comrade] loyalty and warm, friendly feeling among comrades; comradeship

cam·a·ril·la (kam'ə ril'ə; *Sp.* kä'mä rēl'yä) *n.* [Sp. dim. of *camara*, chamber < L. *camera*, a vault] a group of secret or confidential advisers; cabal

cam·ber (kam'bər) *n.* [OFr., dial. var. of *chambre*, bent < L. *camur*, arched] 1. a slight convex curve of a surface, as of a road, a beam, etc. 2. a slight tilt given to each of a pair of motor vehicle wheels by aligning them so that the bottoms are closer together than the tops **3.** *Aeron.* the arching curve of an aerofoil —*vt., vi.* to arch slightly

cam·bi·um (kam′bē əm) *n.* [LL., change] a layer of formative cells between the wood and bark in woody plants: the cells increase by division and differentiate to form new wood and bark

Cam·bri·an (kam′brē ən) *adj.* designating or of the first geological period in the Paleozoic Era —**the Cambrian** the Cambrian Period or its rocks: see GEOLOGY, chart

cam·bric (kām′brik) *n.* [< *Kambryk*, Fl. name of *Cambrai*, city in N France] **1.** a very fine, thin linen **2.** a cotton cloth like this

Cambs. Cambridgeshire

came (kām) *pt.* of COME

cam·el (kam′'l) *n.* [< OE. or OFr. < L. *camelus* < Gr. *kamēlos* < Heb. *gāmāl* (or) < Egypt. *kamál*] **1.** either of two species of large, domesticated, cud-chewing mammals with a humped back, long neck, and large, cushioned feet: capable of storing water in its body tissue, the camel is the common beast of burden in Asian and African deserts: see BACTRIAN CAMEL and DROMEDARY **2.** a watertight cylinder used to raise sunken ships

cam·el·eer (kam′ə lir′) *n.* a camel driver

ca·mel·li·a (kə mēl′yə, -mē′lē ə) *n.* [after G. J. *Kamel* (1661–1706), Jesuit missionary to the Far East] **1.** any of a genus of Asian evergreen trees and shrubs with glossy evergreen leaves and waxy, roselike flowers **2.** the flower

ca·mel·o·pard (kə mel′ə pärd′) *n.* [< LL. < L. < Gr. < *kamēlos*, camel + *pardalis*, leopard: from its camellike neck and leopardlike spots] *early name for the* GIRAFFE

camel's hair 1. the hair of the camel **2.** cloth made of this hair, sometimes mixed with wool, etc. —**cam′el's-hair′, cam′el-hair′** *adj.*

camel's-hair brush an artist's small brush, made of hair from a squirrel's tail

Cam·em·bert (cheese) (kam′əm ber′) [from *Camembert*, in Normandy] a soft, creamy, rich French cheese

cam·e·o (kam′ē ō′) *n., pl.* **-os**′ [< It. < ML. *camaeus* < ?] **1.** a carving in relief on certain stratified gems or shells so that the raised design, often a head in profile, is usually in a layer of different colour from its background: opposed to INTAGLIO **2.** a gem, shell, etc. so carved **3.** *a)* a small but creative part in a film or play, esp. when played by a notable actor *b)* a fine piece of descriptive writing

cam·er·a (kam′ər ə, kam′rə) *n., pl.* **-er·as**; also for 1, **-er·ae**′ (-ə rē′) [L., a vault < Gr. *kamara*, vaulted chamber] **1.** a chamber; specif., the private office of a judge **2.** a device for taking photographs, consisting essentially of a closed box containing a sensitized plate or film on which an image is formed when light enters the box through a lens **3.** *TV* that part of the transmitter which consists of a lens and a special cathode-ray tube containing a plate on which the image to be televised is projected for transformation into electrical signals —**in camera** in privacy or secrecy

cam·er·a·man (-man′, -mən) *n., pl.* **-men**′ (-men′, -mən) an operator of a camera, esp. of a cinema or television camera

cam·er·a-shy (-shī′) *adj.* unwilling to be photographed

cam·i·knick·ers (kam′ē nik′ərz) *n. pl.* [CAMI(SOLE) + KNICKERS] a one-piece undergarment for women, consisting of knickers attached to a camisole top

cam·i·sole (kam′ə sōl′) *n.* [Fr. < Sp. dim. of *camisa*, shirt: see CHEMISE] **1.** a woman's sleeveless underbodice, orig. a corset cover **2.** a woman's short negligée

cam·o·mile (kam′ə mil′, -mēl′) *n.* [< OFr. < L. < Gr. *chamaimēlon* < *chamai*, on the ground + *mēlon*, apple] any of several plants with strong-smelling foliage; esp., a plant whose dried, daisylike flower heads have been used in a medicinal tea

cam·ou·flage (kam′ə fläzh′, kam′ōō-) *n.* [Fr. < *camoufler*, to disguise] **1.** the disguising of troops, ships, guns, etc. to conceal them from the enemy, as by the use of paint, nets, leaves, etc. in patterns merging with the background **2.** a disguise or concealment of this kind **3.** any device or action used to conceal or mislead; deception —*vt., vi.* **-flaged**′, **-flag**′**ing** to disguise or conceal by camouflage —**cam′-ou·flag′er** *n.*

camp¹ (kamp) *n.* [< Fr. < It. < L. *campus*, a field] **1.** *a)* a place where tents, huts, barracks, etc. are put up, as for soldiers in training or in bivouac *b)* military life **2.** any temporary lodging composed of tents, huts etc. [a holiday *camp*, mining *camp*] **3.** *a)* a group of people who support or advance a common cause or ideology *b)* the position taken by such a group, esp. when strongly defended —*vi.* **1.** to set up a camp **2.** to live or stay in or as if in a camp (often with *out*) —*vt.* to put into a camp —**break camp** to pack up camping equipment and go away

camp² (kamp) *adj.* [< ?] **1.** affectedly theatrical **2.** effeminate; homosexual **3.** of a deliberately assumed banality or mediocrity —*n.* camp behaviour —*vi.* **1.** to act in an exaggerated or bizarre manner **2.** to parade one's homosexuality —**camp′y** *adj.*

cam·paign (kam pān′) *n.* [Fr. *campagne*, open country < It. < LL. < L. *campus*, a field] **1.** a series of military operations with a particular objective in a war **2.** a series of organized, planned actions for a particular purpose, as for electing a candidate —*vi.* to participate in, or go on, a campaign —**cam·paign′er** *n.*

cam·pa·ni·le (kam′pə nē′lē, -lā) *n., pl.* **-les, -li** (-lē) [It. < LL. *campana*, a bell] a bell tower, esp. one that stands apart from another building

cam·pa·nol·o·gy (kam′pə nol′ə jē) *n.* [< L. *campana*, a bell + -LOGY] **1.** the study of bells **2.** the art of bellringing —**cam′pa·nol′o·gist** *n.*

cam·pan·u·la (kam pan′yōō lə) *n.* [ModL. < LL., dim. of *campana*, a bell] any of a genus of plants with bell-shaped flowers; bellflower

camp bed a portable, folding bed used in camping, etc.

camp chair a lightweight folding chair

camp·er (kamp′ər) *n.* **1.** a person who camps out on holiday **2.** [Chiefly U.S.] any of various motor vehicles or trailers equipped for camping out

camp·fire (kamp′fīr′) *n.* an outdoor fire at a camp

camp follower 1. a civilian who goes along with an army, esp. as a vendor of goods and services or as a prostitute **2.** a non-member who is associated with a certain group

cam·phor (kam′fər) *n.* [< OFr. < LL. < Ar. < Sans. *karpurah*, camphor tree] a volatile, crystalline substance, $C_{10}H_{16}O$, with a strong characteristic odour, derived chiefly from the wood of an Asian laurel (**camphor tree**): used as a moth repellent, in making cellulose plastics, and in medicine as an irritant, etc. —**cam·phor′ic** (-fôr′ik) *adj.*

cam·phor·ate (kam′fə rāt′) *vt.* **-at**′**ed, -at**′**ing** to put camphor in or on [*camphorated* oil]

camphor ball *same as* MOTHBALL

camphor ice an ointment made of white wax, camphor, spermaceti, and castor oil, used for dry, chapped skin

camphor-wood (-wood) *n.* any of several Australian trees with sweet smelling wood

cam·pi·on (kam′pē ən) *n.* [< ?] any of various flowering plants of the pink family, with white or pink flowers

camp·site (kamp′sīt′) *n.* **1.** any site for a temporary camp **2.** an area set aside for camping, often equipped with water, toilets, picnic stoves, etc.

camp·stool (-stool′) *n.* a light folding stool

cam·pus (kam′pəs) *n., pl.* **-pus·es** [L., a field] the grounds, sometimes including the buildings, of a college or university —*adj.* **1.** on or of the campus **2.** of a college or university [*campus* politics]

Cams. Cambridgeshire

cam·shaft (kam′shäft′) *n.* a shaft to which a cam is fastened

can¹ (kan; *as an auxiliary, usually* kən, k'n) *vi. pt.* **could** [< OE. < *cunnan*, to know, be able] **1.** to know how to **2.** to be able to **3.** to be likely to [*can* it be true?] **4.** to have the right to **5.** [Colloq.] to be permitted to; may —**can but** can only

can² (kan) *n.* [< OE. *canne*, a cup] **1.** a container of various kinds, usually made of metal with a separate cover [a milk *can*, a petrol *can*] **2.** *same as* TIN (*n.* 3) **3.** [Chiefly U.S. Slang] *a)* a prison *b)* a toilet —*vt.* **canned, can′ning 1.** to put in airtight cans for preservation **2.** [Slang] to make a recording of —**carry the can** to take the responsibility (*for*) —**can′ner** *n.*

Can. 1. Canada **2.** Canadian **3.** Canon

Ca·naan (kā′nən) Promised Land of the Israelites, between the Jordan & the Mediterranean

Ca·naan·ite (-īt′) *n.* **1.** one of the original inhabitants of Canaan **2.** their Semitic language —**Ca′naan·it′ish** (-it′ish), **Ca′naan·it′ic** (-it′ik) *adj.*

Canad. Canadian

Can·a·da balsam (kan′ə də) a thick, yellow, resinous fluid from the balsam fir

Canada goose a large wild goose of Canada and the northern U.S., grey, with black head and neck: introduced into Britain and now a common resident

Ca·na·di·an (kə nā′dē ən) *adj.* of Canada or its people —*n.* a native or inhabitant of Canada

Ca·na·di·an·ism (-iz'm) *n.* **1.** a custom, belief, etc. originating in Canada **2.** a word or phrase originating in or peculiar to Canadian English

ca·naille (kə nī′, *Fr.* kȧ nä′y) *n.* [Fr. < It. *canaglia* < L. *canis*, a dog] the mob; rabble

ca·nal (kə nal′) *n.* [< OFr. < L. *canalis*, a channel < *canna*, a reed] **1.** an artificial waterway for transportation or irrigation **2.** *Anat.* a tubular passage or duct —*vt.* **-nalled**′, **-nal′ling** to build a canal through or across

ca·nal·boat (-bōt′) *n.* a long, narrow boat, used on canals: also **canal boat**

can·a·lic·u·lus (kan′ə lik′yōō ləs) *n., pl.* **-li** (-lī) [L., dim. of *canalis*, a groove] *Anat., Bot., Zool.* a very small groove, as in bone —**can′a·lic′u·late** (-lit, -lāt′) *adj.*

ca·nal·i·za·tion (kan′′l ī zā′shən) *n.* **1.** a canalizing **2.** a system of canals or channels

ca·nal·ize (kan'ə līz') *vt.* -ized', -iz'ing 1. to make a canal through 2. to change into or make like a canal 3. to provide an outlet for, esp. by directing into a specific channel

ca·na·pé (kan'ə pē, -pā') *n.* [Fr.] a small piece of bread, toast, etc. spread with spiced meat, fish, cheese, etc., served as an appetizer

ca·nard (kə närd', ka'närd) *n.* [Fr., a duck, hoax] a false, malicious report, fabricated as by a newspaper

ca·nar·y (kə ner'ē) *n., pl.* -nar'ies [< *Canary Islands*] 1. a small, yellow songbird of the finch family 2. a light yellow: also **canary yellow** 3. a sweet wine like madeira, of the Canary Islands

ca·nas·ta (kə nas'tə) *n.* [Sp., basket] a card game for two to six players played with two packs

can·as·ter (kan'əs tər) *n.* [< Sp. *canastro*, a basket: named from the container in which it was packed: see CANISTER] a type of coarse tobacco

canc. 1. cancel 2. cancelled 3. cancellation

can·can (kan'kan') *n.* [Fr.] a lively dance with much high kicking performed by women entertainers, orig. in Paris music halls in the late 19th cent.

can·cel (kan's'l) *vt.* -celled, -cel·ling [< Anglo-Fr. < L. *cancellare*, to draw latticelike lines across < *cancer*, lattice] 1. to cross out with lines or mark over, as in deleting written matter or marking a postage stamp, cheque, etc. as used 2. to make invalid; annul 3. to do away with; abolish, withdraw, etc. [to *cancel* an order] 4. to neutralize or balance; offset (often with *out*) 5. to call off (a meeting etc.) 6. *Math.* to remove (a common factor from both terms of a fraction, equivalents on opposite sides of an equation, etc.) —*vi.* to offset or cancel each other (with *out*) —*n.* a cancellation —**can'cel·ler** *n.*

can·cel·la·tion (kan'sə lā'shən) *n.* 1. the act of cancelling 2. something cancelled 3. the mark showing that something is cancelled

can·cel·lous (kan'səl əs) *adj.* [< L. *cancelli*: see CANCEL] 1. *Anat.* having a porous or spongy structure: said of bones 2. *Bot.* having a close network of veins: said of certain leaves Also **can'cel·late** (-sə lit, -lāt'), **can'cel·lat·ed**

can·cer (kan'sər) [< L., a crab; later, malignant tumour] 1. [C-] a N constellation 2. [C-] the fourth sign of the zodiac: see ZODIAC. illus. —*n.* 1. a malignant new growth, or tumour, anywhere in the body: cancers tend to spread: see CARCINOMA, SARCOMA 2. anything bad or harmful that spreads and destroys —**can'cer·ous** *adj.*

can·croid (kaŋ'kroid) *adj.* [< L. *cancer* (gen. *cancri*), CANCER + -OID] 1. like a crab 2. like cancer —*n.* a skin cancer, esp. of a mild sort

can·de·la (kan dē'lə) *n.* [L., candle] the SI unit of luminous intensity, defined as the luminous intensity in a perpendicular direction of a surface of 1/600000 square metre of a black body at the temperature of solidifying platinum under a pressure of 101325 newtons per square metre

can·de·la·brum (kan'də lä'brəm) *n., pl.* -bra (-brə), -brums [L.: see CHANDELIER] a large branched candlestick: also **can'de·la'bra,** *pl.* -bras

can·des·cent (kan des''nt) *adj.* [< L. prp. of *candescere* < *candere*, to shine] glowing; incandescent —**can·des'-cence** *n.*

can·did (kan'did) *adj.* [L. *candidus*, white, sincere < *candere*: see prec.] 1. free from bias; fair; impartial 2. very honest or frank in speech or writing —**can'did·ly** *adv.* —**can'did·ness** *n.*

can·di·da·cy (kan'də də sē) *n., pl.* -cies the fact or state of being a candidate: also **can'di·da·ture** (-di chər, -dā'chər)

can·di·date (kan'də dāt', -dit) *n.* [L. *candidatus*, white-robed < *candidus* (see CANDID): office seekers in Rome wore white gowns] 1. a person who seeks, or has been proposed for, an office, an award, etc. 2. a person entered for an examination 3. a person or thing apparently destined for a certain end [a *candidate* for fame]

candid camera a camera, usually small, with a fast lens, used to take informal, unposed pictures

can·died (kan'dēd) *adj.* 1. cooked in or with sugar or syrup, esp. to preserve, glaze, or encrust 2. crystallized into sugar

can·dle (kan'd'l) *n.* [< OE. < L. *candela*, a torch < *candere*, to shine] 1. a cylinder of tallow or wax with a wick through its centre, which gives light when burned 2. anything like this in form or use 3. *same as* CANDELA —*vt.* -dled, -dling to examine (eggs) for freshness, fertilization, etc. by holding in front of a light —**burn the candle at both ends** to work or, esp., play too much so that one's energy is dissipated —**not hold a candle to** to be not nearly so good as —**not worth the candle** not worth doing —**can'-dler** *n.*

can·dle·ber·ry (-bər ē) *n., pl.* -ries *same as:* 1. WAX MYRTLE 2. CANDLENUT

can·dle·light (-līt') *n.* 1. subdued light given by or as by candles 2. twilight; evening

Can·dle·mas (kan'd'l məs) *n.* [< OE.: see CANDLE & MASS]

1. a church feast, Feb. 2, commemorating the purification of the Virgin Mary: candles for sacred uses are blessed then: also **Candlemas Day** 2. a Scottish Quarter Day

can·dle·nut (kan'd'l nut') *n.* 1. a tree growing in the Pacific Islands, whose fruit the natives burn as candles 2. its fruit

can·dle·pow·er (-pou'ər) *n.* the luminous intensity of a light source, now expressed in candelas

can·dle·stick (-stik') *n.* a cupped or spiked holder for a candle or candles

can·dle·wick (-wik') *n.* a thick, soft cotton yarn —*adj.* designating or of a muslin fabric, bedspread, etc. patterned with tufts of soft cotton yarn

can·dour (kan'dər) *n.* [L., whiteness, openness < *candere*: see CANDESCENT] 1. the quality of being fair and unprejudiced 2. sharp honesty in expressing oneself

can·dy (kan'dē) *n., pl.* -dies [< *sugar candy* < OFr. < It. < Ar. < Per. *qand*, cane sugar] 1. crystallized sugar made by evaporating boiled cane sugar, syrup, etc. 2. [Chiefly U.S.] a sweet —*vt.* -died, -dy·ing 1. to cook in or with sugar or syrup, esp. to preserve, glaze, or encrust 2. to crystallize into sugar 3. to sweeten; make pleasant —*vi.* to become candied (in senses 1 & 2)

can·dy-floss (-flos) *n.* a light, fluffy confection consisting of threadlike fibres of melted sugar spun around a stick or paper cone

can·dy-striped (-strīpt') *adj.* having diagonal, coloured stripes

cane (kān) *n.* [< OFr. < It. < L. *canna* < Gr. *kanna*] 1. the slender, jointed, usually flexible stem of any of certain plants, as bamboo, rattan, etc. 2. any plant with such a stem, as sugar cane, etc. 3. the woody stem of a fruiting plant, as the blackberry 4. a stick used for flogging 5. *same as* WALKING STICK 6. split rattan, used in weaving chair seats, etc. —*vt.* caned, can'ing 1. to flog with a cane 2. to make or furnish (chairs, etc.) with cane —**can'er** *n.*

cane-brake (kān'brāk') *n.* [CANE + BRAKE³] a dense growth of cane plants

cane sugar sugar (*sucrose*) from sugar cane

cangue (kaŋ) *n.* [Fr. < Port. *canga*, a yoke < Vietnamese] a large wooden yoke formerly fastened about the neck in China, as a punishment for petty crime

ca·nine (kā'nīn) *adj.* [L. *caninus* < *canis*, a dog] 1. of or like a dog 2. of the family of animals that includes dogs, wolves, jackals, and foxes —*n.* 1. a dog or other canine animal 2. a sharp-pointed tooth on either side of the upper jaw and lower jaw, between the incisors and the bicuspids: in full, **canine tooth**

Ca·nis Ma·jor (kān'is mā'jər) [L., the Greater Dog] a S constellation southeast of Orion, containing the Dog Star, Sirius

Canis Mi·nor (mī'nər) [L., the Lesser Dog] a N constellation east of Orion, containing the bright star Procyon

can·is·ter (kan'is tər) *n.* [< L. *canistrum*, wicker basket < Gr. *kanistron* < *kanna*, a reed] 1. a small box or can for coffee, tea, etc. 2. *same as* CANISTER SHOT 3. the part of a gas mask with chemicals for filtering the air

canister shot formerly, lead or iron shot in a container that scattered its contents when fired

can·ker (kaŋ'kər) *n.* [< OFr. < L. *cancer*: see CANCER] 1. an ulcerlike sore, esp. in the mouth, that spreads 2. a disease of plants that causes decay 3. anything that corrupts —*vt.* 1. to attack or infect with canker 2. to infect or debase with corruption —*vi.* to become cankered —**can'ker·ous** *adj.*

can·ker·worm (-wurm') *n.* any of several moth larvae harmful to fruit trees

can·na (kan'ə) *n.* [L., a reed] any of a genus of broad-leaved tropical plants, often grown for its striking foliage and brilliant flowers

can·na·bis (kan'ə bis) *n.* [L., hemp < Gr. *kannabis*] 1. *same as* HEMP (sense 1) 2. the female flowering tops of the hemp

canned (kand) *adj.* 1. preserved in cans 2. [Slang] recorded for reproduction, as on radio [*canned* commercials] 3. [Slang] intoxicated

can·nel (coal) (kan''l) [< ? *candle coal*] a variety of bituminous coal that burns with a bright flame and has a high volatile content

can·nel·lo·ni (kan'ə lō'nē; *It.* kän'nel lō'nē) *n.* [It., pl. of *cannellone*, hollow noodle] tubular casings of pasta filled with minced meat, baked, and served in a tomato sauce

can·ner·y (kan'ər ē) *n., pl.* -ner·ies a factory where foods are canned

can·ni·bal (kan'ə b'l) *n.* [Sp. *canibal*, a savage (term used by Columbus) < *Caniba*, a cannibal people, prob. < Carib *galibi*, lit., strong men] 1. a person who eats human flesh 2. an animal that eats its own kind —*adj.* of, resembling, or having the habits of, cannibals —**can'ni·bal·ism** *n.* —**can'-ni·bal·is'tic** *adj.*

can·ni·bal·ize (-īz') *vt., vi.* -ized, -iz'ing 1. to strip (old or worn equipment) of parts for use in other units 2. to take personnel or components from (one organization) for use in building up another **3.** to devour (another of the same kind): used figuratively —**can'ni·bal·i·za'tion** *n.*

can·ni·kin (kan'ə k'n) *n.* [prob. < Du. *kanneken:* cf CAN², -KIN] **1.** a small can **2.** [Dial.] a wooden bucket

can·ning (kan'iŋ) *n.* the act, process, or work of putting food in cans for preservation

can·non (kan'ən) *n.,* *pl.* **-nons, -non:** see PLURAL, II, D, 4 [< OFr. < It. < L. *canna:* see CANE] **1.** *a)* a large, mounted piece of artillery; sometimes, specif., a large gun with a relatively short barrel, as a howitzer *b)* an automatic gun, now usually of 20-mm. calibre, mounted on an aircraft **2.** a heavy cylinder free to revolve on a shaft **3.** *same as* CANNON BONE **4.** *Billiards* a shot in which the cue ball strikes both object balls —*vt.* to cannonade —*vi.* **1.** to cannonade **2.** to collide (with *into*)

can·non·ade (kan'ə näd') *n.* a continuous firing of artillery —*vi., vt.* **-ad'ed, -ad'ing** to fire artillery (at)

can·non·ball (kan'ən bôl') *n.* a heavy ball, esp. of iron, formerly used as a projectile in cannon: also **cannon ball** —*adj.* [Slang] fast; rapid —*vi.* [Slang] to move very rapidly

cannon bone the bone between hock or knee and fetlock in a four-legged, hoofed animal

can·non·eer (kan'ə nir') *n.* formerly, an artilleryman

cannon fodder soldiers, sailors, etc. thought of as being expended (i.e., killed or maimed) or expendable in war

can·non·ry (kan'ən rē) *n.,* *pl.* **-ries** **1.** cannons collectively; artillery **2.** cannon fire

can·not (kan'ot, -ət; kə not') can not

can·ny (kan'ē) *adj.* **-ni·er, -ni·est** [< CAN¹] **1.** careful and shrewd in one's actions and dealings; clever and cautious **2.** wise and well-informed **3.** careful with money; thrifty —**can'ni·ly** (-'l ē) *adv.* —**can'ni·ness** (-ē nis) *n.*

ca·noe (kə nōō') *n.* [< Sp. *canoa* < the Carib name] a narrow, light boat with its sides meeting in a sharp edge at each end: it is moved by paddles —*vi.* **-noed', -noe'ing** to paddle, or go in, a canoe —*vt.* to transport by canoe —**ca·noe'ist** *n.*

can·on¹ (kan'ən) *n.* [< OE. & OFr. < L., a rule < Gr. *kanōn,* rod, bar < *kanna:* see CANE] **1.** a law or body of laws of a church **2.** *a)* an established or basic rule, principle, or criterion [the *canons* of good taste] *b)* a body of rules, principles, criteria, etc. **3.** *a)* a list of sacred books officially accepted as genuine *b)* a list of the genuine works of an author [the Shakespearean *canon*] **4.** *a)* [often C-] *Eccles.* the fundamental part of the Mass, between the Preface and the Communion *b)* a list of recognized saints as in the Roman Catholic Church **5.** *Music* a polyphonic composition in which a melody is repeated at delayed intervals in the same or a related key

can·on² (kan'ən) *n.* [< OE. & OFr. < LL. *canonicus,* one living by the canon: see prec.] **1.** a member of a clerical group living according to a canon, or rule **2.** a clergyman serving in a cathedral or collegiate church

ca·ñon (kan'yən; *Sp.* kä nyôn') *n.* *same as* CANYON

ca·non·i·cal (kə non'i k'l) *adj.* **1.** of, according to, or ordered by church canon **2.** authoritative; accepted **3.** belonging to a scriptural canon **4.** of a canon (clergyman) —**ca·non'i·cal·ly** *adv.*

canonical hour any of the seven periods of the day assigned to prayer and worship

ca·non·i·cals (-k'lz) *n.pl.* the clothes prescribed by canon for a clergyman when conducting services

can·on·ic·i·ty (kan'ə nis'ə tē) *n.* *Eccles.* the fact or condition of being canonical

can·on·ist (kan'ən ist) *n.* an expert in canon law —**can'-on·is'tic** *adj.*

can·on·ize (kan'ə nīz') *vt.* **-ized', -iz'ing** [< LL. *canonizare:* see CANON¹ + -IZE] **1.** to declare (a dead person) a saint in formal church procedure **2.** to glorify **3.** to put into a scriptural canon **4.** to give church sanction to —**can'-on·i·za'tion** *n.*

canon law the laws governing the ecclesiastical affairs of a Christian church

can·on·ry (kan'ən rē) *n.,* *pl.* **-ries** **1.** the benefice or office of a canon **2.** canons collectively

ca·noo·dle (kə nōō'd'l) *vi.* **-dled, -dling** [< ?] to caress or cuddle (with)

Ca·no·pic urn (kə nō'pik) [< L. *Canopicus,* of Canopus: town in ancient Egypt] an urn used in ancient Egypt to hold and preserve the internal organs of the mummified dead: also **canopic jar** (or **vase**)

can·o·py (kan'ə pē) *n.,* *pl.* **-pies** [< ML. < L. < Gr. *kōnōpeion,* bed with mosquito nets, dim. of *kōnōps,* gnat] **1.** a covering of cloth, etc. fastened above a bed, throne, etc. or held on poles over a person or sacred thing **2.** a canvas structure forming a sheltered walk to a building entrance **3.** anything that covers or seems to cover like a canopy, as the sky **4.** the transparent hood over an aeroplane cockpit **5.** the part of a parachute that opens up and catches the air

6. a rooflike projection over a door, pulpit, etc. —*vt.* **-pied, -py·ing** to place or form a canopy over; cover; shelter

canst (kanst; *unstressed* kənst) *archaic 2nd pers. sing., pres. indic., of* CAN¹: *used with* thou

cant¹ (kant) *n.* [< L. *cantus:* see CHANT] **1.** whining, singsong speech, esp. as used by beggars **2.** the secret slang of beggars, thieves, etc.; argot **3.** the special words and phrases used by those in a certain sect, occupation, etc.; jargon **4.** insincere, trite talk, esp. when pious or moral —*vi.* to use cant; speak in cant —*adj.* of, or having the nature of, cant —**cant'er** *n.*

cant² (kant) *n.* [< OFr. < LL. < L. *cant(h)us,* tyre of a wheel < Celt.] **1.** a corner or outside angle **2.** a slanting surface; bevelled edge **3.** a sudden movement that causes tilting, turning, or overturning **4.** the tilt, turn, or slant thus caused —*vt.* **1.** to give a sloping edge to; bevel **2.** to tilt or overturn **3.** to pitch; toss —*vi.* **1.** to tilt or turn over **2.** to slant —*adj.* **1.** with canted sides or corners **2.** slanting

can't (känt) cannot

Cantab. Cantabrigian

can·ta·bi·le (kan tä'bi lā') *adj., adv.* [< It. < L. < *cantare:* see CHANT] *Music* in any easy, flowing manner; songlike —*n.* music in this style

Can·ta·brig·i·an (kan'tə brij'ē ən, -brij'ən) *adj.* [< ML. *Cantabrigia,* Cambridge] of Cambridge, or Cambridge University —*n.* **1.** a student or graduate of Cambridge University **2.** any inhabitant of Cambridge

can·ta·loupe, can·ta·loup (kan'tə lōōp') *n.* [< Fr. < It.< *Cantalupo,* near Rome, where first grown in Europe] **1.** melon with a hard, ribbed rind and sweet, juicy, orange flesh **2.** any of several other melons

can·tan·ker·ous (kan taŋ'kər əs) *adj.* [prob. < ME. *contakour,* a troublemaker (< *contek,* strife) + -OUS] bad-tempered; quarrelsome —**can·tan'ker·ous·ly** *adv.* —**can·tan'ker·ous·ness** *n.*

can·ta·ta (kən tät'ə) *n.* [< It. pp. of *cantare:* see CHANT] a musical composition with vocal solos, choruses, etc., telling a story that is sung but not acted

can·teen (kan tēn') *n.* [< Fr. < It. *cantina,* wine cellar] **1.** a shop providing luxuries, spirits, etc. to the personnel of a military camp **2.** *a)* a place where refreshments can be obtained, as by employees or visitors *b)* [U.S.] such a place serving as a social centre [a youth *canteen*] **3.** a place where cooked food is dispensed to people in distress, as in a disaster area **4.** *a)* a box containing cutlery *b)* a set of cutlery **5.** a small flask for carrying drinking water

can·ter (kan'tər) *n.* [contr. < *Canterbury gallop,* the riding pace of the medieval Canterbury pilgrims] a smooth, easy pace like a moderate gallop —*vi., vt.* to ride or move at a canter

Can·ter·bur·y bells (kan'tər bar ē) a cultivated bellflower with white, pink, or blue, cuplike flowers

can·thar·i·des (kan thär'ə dēz') *n.pl.* [L., pl. of *cantharis,* kind of beetle, Spanish fly < Gr. *kantharis,* blistering beetle] a preparation of powdered, dried Spanish flies, formerly used internally as a diuretic and genitourinary stimulant, and externally as a skin irritant

cant hook [see CANT²] a pole with a movable hooked arm at or near one end, for catching hold of logs and rolling them

can·thus (kan'thəs) *n.,* *pl.* **-thi** (-thī) [ModL. < Gr. *kanthos*] either corner of the eye, where the eyelids meet

can·ti·cle (kan'ti k'l) *n.* [< L. dim. of *canticum,* song < *cantus*] **1.** a song or chant **2.** a non-metrical liturgical hymn with words from the Bible

can·ti·le·na (kan'tə lē'nə) *n.* [It. < L., a song < *cantare,* to sing] a smooth, flowing, lyrical passage of vocal, or sometimes instrumental, music

can·ti·le·ver (kan'tə lē'vər) *n.* [? < CANT² + LEVER] **1.** a large bracket or block projecting from a wall to support a balcony, cornice, etc. **2.** a projecting beam or structure supported only at one end, which is anchored as to a pier or wall —*vt.* to support by means of cantilevers —**can'ti·le'-vered** *adj.*

cantilever bridge a bridge whose span is formed by two cantilevers projecting towards each other

CANTILEVER

can·til·la·tion (kan'tə lā'shən) *n.* [< L. *cantillare,* to hum < *cantare:* see CHANT] in Jewish liturgy, a chanting with certain prescribed musical phrases indicated by notations —**can'til·late'** (-āt') *vt., vi.* **-lat'ed, -lat'ing**

can·tle (kan't'l) *n.* [< OFr. < ML. dim. of L. *cantus:* see CANT²] the upward-curving rear part of a saddle

can·to (kan'tō) *n.,* *pl.* **-tos** [It. < L. *cantus:* see CHANT] any of the chapterlike divisions of certain long poems

can·ton¹ (kan'tən, -ton, kan ton') *n.* [Fr. < It. < LL. *cantus,* corner: see CANT²] any of the political divisions of a country or territory; specif., any of the states in the Swiss Republic —*vt.* to divide into cantons —**can'ton·al** *adj.*

can·ton² (kan tōōn′) *vt.* [< ? prec.] to assign quarters to (troops, etc.)

Can·ton·ese (kan′tə nēz′) *adj.* of Canton, China, or its people —*n.* **1.** *pl.* **-ese** a native or inhabitant of Canton **2.** the Chinese dialect spoken in and around Canton

can·ton·ment (kan tōōn′mənt) *n.* [Fr. *cantonnement*: see CANTON] **1.** the assigning of quarters to troops **2.** a permanent military camp in British India

can·tor (kan′tôr) *n.* [L., singer < *canere:* see CHANT] **1.** a church choir leader **2.** a singer of liturgical solos in a synagogue, who leads the congregation in prayer —**can·to′ri·al** (-tôr′ē əl) *adj.*

Ca·nuck (kə nuk′) *n.* [< ?] [U.S. & Canad. Colloq.] a Canadian; sometimes specif., a French Canadian —**Ca·nuck′** *adj.*

can·vas (kan′vəs) *n.* [< OFr. < It. < L. *cannabis*, hemp] **1.** a closely woven, coarse cloth of hemp, cotton, or linen, used for tents, sails, etc. **2.** a sail or set of sails **3.** *a)* a specially prepared piece of canvas on which an oil painting is made *b)* such a painting **4.** a tent or tents, esp. circus tents **5.** any loosely woven, coarse cloth for embroidery, etc. —**the canvas** the canvas-covered floor of a boxing or wrestling ring —**under canvas 1.** in tents **2.** with sails unfurled

can·vas·back (-bak′) *n., pl.* **-backs′, -back′:** see PLURAL, II, D,1 a large, N. American wild duck with a brownish-red head and dark back

can·vass (kan′vəs) *vt.* [< *canvas:* ? because used for sifting] **1.** to examine or discuss in detail **2.** to go through (places) or among (people) asking for (votes, opinions, orders, etc.) —*vi.* to try to get votes, orders, etc. —*n.* the act of canvassing, esp. in an attempt to estimate the outcome of an election, sales campaign, etc. —**can′vass·er** *n.*

can·yon (kan′yən) *n.* [Sp. *cañon*, a canyon, tube < L. *canna*, a reed: see CANE] a long, narrow valley between high cliffs, often containing a stream

caou·tchouc (kou chōōk′) *n.* [Fr. < obs. Sp. *cauchuc* < Quechua] crude, natural rubber

cap (kap) *n.* [OE. *cæppe* < LL. *cappa*, a cloak] **1.** any closefitting head covering, brimless or visored **2.** *a)* a head covering worn as a mark of occupation, rank, etc. [a nurse's *cap*] *b)* a mortarboard (sense 2) **3.** a caplike part or thing; cover or top **4.** *same as* PERCUSSION CAP **5.** *Sport* a hat awarded to a player selected for his country or national team —*vt.* **capped, cap′ping 1.** to put a cap on **2.** *a)* to present with a cap, as in sport [to *cap* a player] *b)* [U.S., N.Z.] to present with an academic cap at a graduation ceremony **3.** to cover the top or end of [snow *capped* the hills] **4.** to match, surpass, or top **5.** to bring to a high point; climax —**cap in hand** in a humble or submissive manner —**cap it all** to give the finishing touch —**if the cap fits** [Colloq.] take it how you please: an expression used to a person who takes a general remark personally

cap. 1. capacity **2.** *pl.* **caps.** capital **3.** capitalize **4.** capitalized

ca·pa·bil·i·ty (kā′pə bil′ə tē) *n., pl.* **-ties 1.** the quality of being capable; practical ability **2.** a capacity for being used or developed **3.** [pl.] abilities, features, etc. not yet developed

ca·pa·ble (kā′pə b'l) *adj.* [Fr. < LL. *capabilis* < L. *capere*, to take] having ability; able; skilled; competent —**capable of 1.** admitting of; open to **2.** having the ability or qualities necessary for [capable of telling a lie] —**ca′pa·ble·ness** *n.* —**ca′pa·bly** *adv.*

ca·pa·cious (kə pā′shəs) *adj.* [< L. *capax* (gen. *capacis*) < *capere*, to take + -OUS] able to contain or hold much; roomy; spacious —**ca·pa′cious·ly** *adv.* —**ca·pa′cious·ness** *n.*

ca·pac·i·tance (kə pas′ə təns) *n.* [CAPACIT(Y) + -ANCE] *Elec.* the quantity of electric charge that can be stored in a capacitor, expressed, in farads, as the ratio of the charge to the potential difference between the plates —**ca·pac′i·tive** *adj.*

ca·pac·i·tor (-tər) *n.* *Elec.* a device consisting of two or more conducting plates separated by insulating material and used for storing an electric charge; condenser

ca·pac·i·ty (kə pas′ə tē) *n., pl.* **-ties** [< OFr. < L. < *capax:* see CAPACIOUS] **1.** the ability to contain, absorb, or receive **2.** the amount of space that can be filled; content or volume **3.** mental ability **4.** aptitude; capability; potentiality **5.** maximum output or producing ability [operating at *capacity*] **6.** position, function, status, etc. [acting in the *capacity* of adviser] **7.** *Elec.* formerly, *same as* CAPACITANCE **8.** *Law* legal authority or competence

cap and bells a fool's cap with little bells on it

cap-a-pie, cap-à-pie (kap′ə pē′) *adv.* [< OFr. < L. *caput*, head + *pes*, foot] from head to foot

ca·par·i·son (kə par′ə s'n) *n.* [< Fr. < Pr. *caparasso*, large cloak < ff.] **1.** an ornamented covering for a horse; trappings **2.** clothing, equipment, and ornaments; outfit —*vt.* to adorn, as with trappings or rich clothing

cape¹ (kāp) *n.* [Fr. < Pr. *capa* < LL. *cappa*, mantle, cloak] a sleeveless garment fastened at the neck and hanging over the back and shoulders

cape² (kāp) *n.* [OFr. < ML. < *caput*, head] a piece of land projecting into a body of water —**the Cape** the Cape of Good Hope

ca·per¹ (kā′pər) *vi.* [prob. < CAPRIOLE] to skip about in a playful manner —*n.* **1.** a gay, playful jump or leap **2.** a wild, foolish action or prank **3.** [Slang] a criminal act, esp. a robbery —**cut a caper** (or **capers**) **1.** to caper **2.** to play tricks

ca·per² (kā′pər) *n.* [< L. < Gr. *kapparis*] **1.** a prickly, trailing Mediterranean bush whose green flower buds are pickled and used to flavour sauces, etc. **2.** any of these buds

cap·er·cail·lie (kap′ər kāl′yē) *n.* [< Gael. *capull*, horse + *coille*, forest] the largest species of European grouse: also **cap·er·cail′zie** (-yē, -zē)

cap·ful (kap′fool′) *n., pl.* **-fuls′** as much as the cap of the bottle can hold

ca·pi·as (kā′pē əs, kap′ē-) *n.* [< ML. < L., 2nd pers. sing., pres. subj., of *capere*, to take] *Law* a writ issued by a court directing an officer to arrest the person named

cap·il·lar·i·ty (kap′ə lar′ə tē) *n.* **1.** capillary state **2.** the property of exerting or having capillary attraction **3.** *same as* CAPILLARY ATTRACTION

cap·il·lar·y (kə pil′ə rē) *adj.* [< L. < *capillus*, hair] **1.** of or like a hair; very slender **2.** having a very small bore **3.** in or of capillaries —*n., pl.* **-lar·ies 1.** a tube with a very small bore: also **capillary tube 2.** any of the tiny blood vessels connecting the arteries with the veins

capillary attraction a phenomenon that results from the adhesion, cohesion, and surface tension in liquids which are in contact with solids, as in a capillary tube, causing the liquid surface to rise or be depressed in the tube: also **capillary action**

cap·i·tal¹ (kap′ət'l) *adj.* [< OFr. < L. < *caput*, head] **1.** involving or punishable by death [a *capital* offence] **2.** most important or most serious; principal; chief [a *capital* virtue] **3.** being the seat of government [a *capital* city] **4.** of or having to do with capital, or wealth **5.** first-rate; excellent [a *capital* idea] See also CAPITAL LETTER —*n.* **1.** *same as* CAPITAL LETTER **2.** a city or town that is the official seat of government of a state, nation, etc. **3.** a city where a certain industry, etc. is centred [the rubber *capital*] **4.** money or property owned or used in business by a person, company, etc. **5.** an accumulation of such wealth, or its value **6.** wealth used to produce more wealth **7.** any source of benefit **8.** [often **C-**] capitalists collectively: distinguished from LABOUR —**make capital of** to make the most of; exploit

cap·i·tal² (kap′ət'l) *n.* [< OFr. < L. dim. of *caput*, head] the top part of a column or pilaster

capital gain profit resulting from the sale of capital investments, as stock, property, etc.

capital goods commodities for use in production, as raw materials, machinery, etc.; producer's goods as distinguished from consumer's goods

cap·i·tal·ism (-iz'm) *n.* **1.** the economic system in which the means of production and distribution are privately owned and operated for profit **2.** the principles, power, etc. of capitalists

cap·i·tal·ist (-ist) *n.* **1.** a person who has capital; owner of wealth used in business **2.** an upholder of capitalism —*adj.* capitalistic

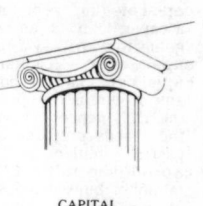

CAPITAL

cap·i·tal·is·tic (kap′ət'l is′tik) *adj.* **1.** of or characteristic of capitalists or capitalism **2.** upholding, preferring, or practising capitalism —**cap′i·tal·is′ti·cal·ly** *adv.*

cap·i·tal·i·za·tion (-ī zā′shən) *n.* **1.** the act or process of converting something into capital **2.** the total capital funds of a company, represented by stock, undivided profit, etc. **3.** the total par value of the stock outstanding of a company **4.** the act or system of using capital letters in writing and printing

cap·i·tal·ize (kap′ət'l īz′) *vt.* **-ized′, -iz′ing 1.** to use as capital; convert into capital **2.** to establish the capital stock of (a business firm) at a certain figure **3.** to supply capital to or for (an enterprise) **4.** to print or write (a word or words) in capital letters **5.** to begin (a word) with a capital letter —**capitalize on** (**something**) to use (something) to one's own advantage

capital letter a large letter of a kind used to begin a sentence or proper name, as A, B, C

capital levy a tax on individual or corporate capital levied in addition to income tax

cap·i·tal·ly (kap′ət'l ē) *adv.* in an excellently or admirable manner; very well

capital punishment penalty of death for a crime
capital ship formerly, an armoured war vessel carrying guns exceeding a calibre of a specified size
capital stock 1. the capital of a company, divided into negotiable shares 2. the total par or stated value of the issued shares of stock
cap·i·ta·tion (kap'ə tā'shən) n. [< LL. < L. caput, the head] a tax or fee of so much per head
ca·pit·u·late (kə pi'tyo͞o lāt') vi. -lat'ed, -lat'ing [< LL. pp. of capitulare, to draw up in heads or chapters] 1. to give up (to an enemy) on prearranged conditions 2. to give up; surrender
ca·pit·u·la·tion (kə pi'tyo͞o lā'shən) n. 1. [Rare] a statement of the main parts of a subject 2. a conditional surrender 3. a document containing terms of surrender, etc.; treaty
ca·pit·u·lum (kə pit'yo͞o ləm) n., pl. -la (-lə) [L., dim. of caput, the head] 1. Anat., Zool. a knoblike part, as at the end of a bone in a joint 2. Bot. the flattened or rounded flower-head of a composite, as the dandelion
ca·po (ka'pō) n., pl. -pos [short for capotasto < It., lit. chief key < capo, chief, head + tasto, key] a device fastened over the fingerboard of an instrument, as the guitar, to shorten the strings uniformly and facilitate a change of key
ca·pon (kā'pon, -pən) n. [< OE. & OFr. < L. capo] a castrated cock fattened for eating —ca'pon·ize' (-pə nīz') vt. -ized', -iz'ing
ca·pote (kə pōt') n. [Fr., dim. of cape, CAPE¹] a long cloak, usually with a hood
cap·puc·ci·no (kap'ə chē'nō) n., pl. -ni [It., lit., CAPUCHIN (in allusion to the brown habit worn by the friars)] espresso coffee served with thick cream or hot milk
ca·pric·ci·o (kə prē'chē ō; It. kä prēt'chō) n., pl. -ci·os; It. -pric'ci (-chē) [It.: see ff.] 1. a whim; caprice 2. a lively musical composition of irregular form
ca·pric·ci·o·so (kə prich'ē ō'sō; It. kä prēt chō'sō) adv. [It., CAPRICIOUS] Music in a light, free whimsical style
ca·price (kə prēs') n. [Fr. < It. capriccio < capo, head + riccio, curl, lit., hedgehog] 1. a sudden, impulsive change in thought or action; freakish notion; whim 2. a capricious quality or nature 3. Music same as CAPRICCIO
ca·pri·cious (kə prish'əs) adj. subject to caprices; erratic; flighty —ca·pri'cious·ly adv. —ca·pri'cious·ness n.
Cap·ri·corn (kap'rə kôrn') [< OFr. < L. < caper, goat + cornu, a horn] 1. a S constellation 2. the tenth sign of the zodiac: see ZODIAC, illus.
cap·ri·fi·ca·tion (kap'rə fi kā'shən) n. [< L. < caprificare, to ripen figs by caprification] the pollination of certain cultivated figs through the transfer to them of pollen from the wild fig by a species of gall wasp
ca·prine (ka'prēn) adj. [ME. < L. caprinus < caper (gen. capri), goat] of, like, or designating a goat
cap·ri·ole (kap'rē ōl') n. [Fr. < It., ult. < L. caper, goat] 1. a caper; leap 2. an upward leap made by a horse without going forward —vi. -oled', -ol'ing to make a capriole
caps. capitals (capital letters)
cap·si·cum (kap'sə kəm) n. [ModL. < L. capsa, a box] 1. any of various red peppers whose pungent, fleshy pods are the chili peppers, cayenne peppers, etc. of commerce 2. these pods prepared as condiments, or, in medicine, as a gastric stimulant
cap·sid (kap'sid) n. [ModL. < L. capsa, case] 1. any of a family of bugs that feed on plant tissues 2. the outer case of some viruses
cap·size (kap sīz') vt., vi. -sized', -siz'ing [? < Sp. cabezar, lit., to sink by the head] to overturn or upset: said esp. of a boat
cap·stan (kap'stən) n. [Fr. & Pr. cabestan < L. capistrum < capere, to take] 1. an apparatus, mainly on ships, consisting of an upright cylinder around which cables or hawsers are wound, by machinery or by hand, for hoisting anchors, etc. 2. a rotating spindle on a tape-recorder that drives the tape past the head
capstan bar any of the poles inserted in a capstan and used as levers in turning it by hand
capstan lathe a lathe fitted with a rotating turret to which tools are attached: also **turret lathe**
cap·stone (-stōn') n. same as COPESTONE (sense 1)
cap·sule (kap'syo͞ol) n. [Fr. < L. dim. of capsa, chest] 1. a small, soluble gelatin container for enclosing a dose of medicine 2. a) the ejectable cockpit of an aeroplane b) a detached, closed compartment to hold and protect men, instruments, etc. in a space vehicle: in full, **space capsule** 3. Anat. a sac or membrane enclosing a part 4. Bot. a case, pod, or fruit containing seeds, spores, or carpels, esp.

CAPSTAN

one that bursts when ripe —adj. in a concise form [a capsule biography] —vt. -suled, -sul·ing to condense —cap'su·lar adj. —cap'su·late', cap'su·lat'ed adj.
cap·sul·ize (-īz') vt. -ized', -iz'ing 1. to enclose in a capsule 2. to condense
Capt. Captain
cap·tain (kap'tən) n. [< OFr. < LL. < L. caput, the head] 1. a chief or leader 2. see MILITARY RANKS, table 3. a) the commander or master of a ship b) the pilot of a commercial aircraft c) the leader of a team, as in sports —vt. to be captain or leader of —cap'tain·cy (-sē), pl. -cies, cap'-tain·ship' n.
cap·tion (kap'shən) n. [< OFr. < L. < pp. of capere, to take] 1. a heading, as of a newspaper article, or a legend, as under an illustration 2. same as SUBTITLE (n. 2) —vt. to supply a caption for
cap·tious (-shəs) adj. [< L. captiosus < prec.] 1. made for the sake of argument or faultfinding; sophistical 2. quick to find fault; quibbling —cap'tious·ly adv. —cap'tious·ness n.
cap·ti·vate (kap'tə vāt') vt. -vat'ed, -vat'ing [< LL., ult. < L. captivus, CAPTIVE] 1. orig., to take captive 2. to capture the attention or affection of; charm —cap'ti·vat'ing·ly adv. —cap'ti·va'tion n. —cap'ti·va'tor n.
cap·tive (kap'tiv) n. [L. captivus < pp. of capere, to take] a person or animal caught and held, as a prisoner, or captivated, as by love —adj. 1. a) taken or held prisoner b) unable to act independently c) forced to listen or act in a certain way [a captive audience, a captive market] 2. restrained or limited [a captive balloon] 3. captivated 4. of captivity
cap·tiv·i·ty (kap tiv'ə tē) n., pl. -ties the condition or time of being captive; imprisonment
cap·tor (kap'tər) n. [L.] a person who captures or holds captive
cap·ture (kap'chər) n. [Fr. < L. captura < pp. of capere, to take] 1. a taking or being taken by force, surprise, or skill 2. that which is thus taken 3. the absorption of a bombarding particle by an atomic nucleus, often causing radiation —vt. -tured, -tur·ing 1. to take or seize by force, surprise, or skill 2. a) to represent (something immaterial, etc.) in more or less permanent form [to capture her charm on canvas] b) to describe or account for (in a theory) 3. to effect the capture of (a subatomic particle)
Cap·u·chin (kap'yo͞o shin, -chin) n. [< Fr. < It. cappuccio, a cowl] 1. a monk of a branch of the Franciscan order cloak with a hood 3. [c-] a S. American monkey with a hoodlike crown of hair
cap·y·ba·ra (kap'ə bär'ə) n. [Port. capibara < Tupi kapigwara, lit., one who eats grass] a tailless, partly webfooted S. American animal found in and around lakes and streams: the largest extant rodent, reaching a length of over 1m
car (kär) n. [< ONormFr. < LL. < L. carrus, two-wheeled chariot < OCelt. carros] 1. orig., any vehicle on wheels 2. [Poet.] a chariot 3. a name given to certain types of railway carriage [dining car, sleeping car] 4. [U.S.] a) any vehicle that moves on rails b) the cage of a lift [elevator car] 5. same as MOTOR CAR 6. the part of a balloon or airship for carrying people and equipment
car·a·bi·neer, car·a·bi·nier (kar'ə bə nir') n. [Fr. carabinier] 1. a soldier armed with a carbine 2. a light cavalryman
car·a·bi·ner (kar'ə bē'nər) n. same as KARABINER
car·a·cal (kar'ə kal') n. [Fr. < Turk. kara kulak < kara, black + kulak, ear] 1. a reddish-brown lynx of SW Asia and E Africa, with black-tipped ears. 2. the fur of this animal
car·a·ca·ra (kär'ə kär'ə) n. [Sp. < Tupi] a large, vulturelike hawk of S. America
car·a·cole (kar'ə kōl') n. [Fr. < Wal. < Sp. caracol, shell of a snail] a half turn to the right or left made by a horse with a rider —vi. -coled', -col'ing to make a caracole or caracoles
car·a·cul (kar'ə kəl) n. same as KARAKUL
ca·rafe (kə räf') n. [Fr. < It. caraffa, prob. < Ar. gharafa, to draw water] a bottle of glass or metal for water, coffee, etc.
car·a·mel (kar'ə m'l, -mel') n. [Fr. < OFr., ult. < L. canna mellis, sugar cane] 1. burnt sugar used to colour or flavour food 2. a toffee made from sugar, milk, etc.
car·a·mel·ize (-mə līz') vt., vi. -ized', -iz'ing to turn into caramel
car·a·pace (kar'ə pās') n. [Fr. < Sp. carapacho] an upper case or shell, as of the turtle
car·at (kar'ət) n. [Fr. < It. < Ar. < Gr. keration, carat, dim. of keras, horn] 1. a unit of weight for precious stones, equal to 200 milligrammes 2. one 24th part (of pure gold) [14-carat gold is 14 parts pure gold and 10 parts alloy]
car·a·van (kar'ə van') n. [< Fr. < OFr. < Per. kārwān, caravan] 1. a company of merchants, pilgrims, etc. travelling together for safety, as through a desert 2. a number of vehicles travelling together 3. a) a large covered

vehicle, esp. when horsedrawn [a gypsy *caravan*] b) a closed vehicle designed to be pulled by a motor vehicle and equipped as a place to live or work in —*vi.* **-vanned′, -van′-ning** to go on holiday in or with a caravan

car·a·van·se·rai (kar′ə van′sə rē) *n.,* [< Fr. < Per. < *kärwän,* caravan + *sarāī,* palace] in the Orient, a kind of inn with a large central court, where caravans stop for the night

caravan site an area, usually with piped water, electricity, etc. designed to accommodate caravans (*n.* 3b): also **caravan park**

car·a·vel (kar′ə vel′) *n.* [< Fr. < Port. < LL. < Gr. *karabos,* kind of light ship] a fast, small sailing ship used in the 16th cent.

car·a·way (kar′ə wā′) *n.* [< Ar. *karawiyā′* < ? Gr. *karon,* caraway] 1. a herb with spicy, strong-smelling seeds 2. the seeds, used to flavour bread, cakes, cheese, etc.

car·bide (kär′bīd) *n.* [CARB(O)- + -IDE] a compound of an element, usually a metal, with carbon; esp., calcium carbide

car·bine (kär′bīn, -bēn) *n.* [< Fr., ult. < *scarabée,* a beetle] 1. a rifle with a short barrel 2. [U.S.] a semiautomatic or automatic .30-calibre rifle

car·bi·neer (kär′bə nir′) *n.* *same as* CARABINEER

car·bo- a *combining form meaning* carbon: also, before a vowel, **carb-**

car·bo·hy·drate (kär′bō hī′drāt, -bə-) *n.* [CARBO- + HYDRATE] any of a group of organic compounds, including the sugars and starches, composed of carbon, hydrogen, and oxygen: carbohydrates form an important class of foods

car·bo·lat·ed (kär′bō lāt′id, -bə-) containing or treated with carbolic acid

car·bol·ic acid (kär bol′ik) [CARB(O)- + -OL¹ + -IC] *same as* PHENOL

car·bon (kär′bən) *n.* [< Fr. < L. *carbo,* charcoal] 1. a nonmetallic chemical element found in many inorganic compounds and all organic compounds: diamond and graphite are pure carbon; carbon is also present in coal, coke, etc.: symbol, C; at. wt., 12.01115; at. no., 6: a radioactive isotope (**carbon 14**) is used in biochemical research and in dating archaeological specimens, etc. 2. a sheet of carbon paper 3. a copy, as of a letter, made with carbon paper: in full, **carbon copy** 4. *Elec.* a) a stick of carbon used in an arc lamp b) a carbon plate or rod used in a battery —*adj.* of carbon

car·bo·na·ceous (kär′bə nä′shəs) *adj.* 1. of, consisting of, or containing carbon 2. resembling coal or carbon

car·bo·na·do (kär bə nä′dō) *n., pl.* **-dos** [Port., lit., carbonated] a massive form of diamond characterized by opacity and dark colour, used for drills

car·bon·ate (kär′bə nit; *also, and for v. always,* -nāt′) *n.* a salt or ester of carbonic acid —*vt.* **-at′ed, -at′ing** 1. to charge with carbon dioxide [*carbonated* drinks] 2. to form into a carbonate —**car′bon·a′tion** *n.*

carbon black finely divided carbon produced by the incomplete burning of oil or gas, used esp. in rubber and ink

car·bon-date (kär′bən dāt′) *vt.* **-dat′ed, -dat′ing** to establish the approximate age of by carbon dating

carbon dating the determination of the approximate age of (fossils, etc.) by measuring the carbon 14 content

carbon dioxide a colourless, odourless gas, CO_2: it passes out of the lungs in respiration, and is absorbed by plants in photosynthesis

car·bon·ic (kär bon′ik) *adj.* of, containing, or obtained from carbon or carbon dioxide

carbonic acid a weak, colourless acid, H_2CO_3, formed by the solution of carbon dioxide in water

car·bon·if·er·ous (kär′bə nif′ər əs) *adj.* [< CARBON + -FEROUS] 1. producing or containing carbon or coal 2. [C-] designating or of a great coal-making period of the Paleozoic Era: the warm, damp climate produced great forests, which later formed rich coal seams —**the Carboniferous** 1. the Carboniferous Period, divided into the **Upper Carboniferous** period and the **Lower Carboniferous** period 2. the rock and coal strata formed then See GEOLOGY, chart

car·bon·ize (kär′bə nīz′) *vt.* **-ized′, -iz′ing** 1. to change into carbon, as by partial burning 2. to treat, cover, or combine with carbon —*vi.* to become carbonized —**car′-bon·i·za′tion** *n.*

carbon monoxide a colourless, odourless, highly poisonous gas, CO, produced by the incomplete combustion of carbon

carbon paper very thin paper coated on one side with a carbon preparation: placed between sheets of paper, it is used to make copies of letters, etc.

carbon tet·ra·chlo·ride (tet′rə klôr′īd) a nonflammable, colourless liquid, CCl_4, used in fire extinguishers, cleaning mixtures, etc.

Car·bo·run·dum (kär′bə run′dəm) [CARB(ON) + (C)ORUN-dum] a trademark for a very hard, abrasive substance, esp. silicon carbide, used in grindstones, abrasives, etc.

car·box·yl (kär boks′il) *n.* [CARB(O)- + OX(YGEN) + -YL] the univalent radical COOH, occurring in the fatty acids and most other organic acids —**ca′box·yl′ic** (-sil′ik) *adj.*

car·boy (kär′boi) *n.* [< Per. *qarābah*] a large glass bottle enclosed in basketwork or in a wooden crate: used as a container for corrosive liquids

car·bun·cle (kär′buŋ k′l) *n.* [< OFr. < L. dim. of *carbo,* coal] 1. a smooth, convex-cut garnet 2. a painful, pus-bearing inflammation of the tissue beneath the skin, more severe than a boil and having several openings —**car·bun′cu·lar** (-kyoo lər) *adj.*

car·bu·rate (kä′byoo rāt′, kär′bə-) *vt.* [< obs. *carburet,* carbide] 1. to combine chemically with carbon 2. mix or charge (gas or air) with volatile carbon compounds —**car′-bu·ra′tion** *n.*

car·bu·ret·tor, car·bu·ret·ter (kär′bə ret′ər, -byoo-) *n.* a device in which air is mixed with vaporized petrol to make an explosive mixture in an internal-combustion engine: U.S. sp. **car′bu·ret′or**

car·ca·jou (kär′kə joo̅, -zhoo̅′) *n.* [CanadFr. < Algonquian] *same as* WOLVERINE

car·case, car·cass (kär′kəs) *n.* [< OFr. & Fr. < ?] 1. the dead body of an animal, often specif. of a slaughtered animal dressed as meat 2. the human body, living or dead: scornful or humorous usage 3. the worthless remains of something 4. a framework or shell

car·cin·o·gen (kär sin′ə jən, kär′sin ə jen′) *n.* [< ff. + -GEN] any substance that produces cancer —**car·ci·no·gen·e·sis** (kär′sə nō jen′ə sis) *n.* —**car′ci·no·gen′ic** *adj.*

car·ci·no·ma (kär′sə nō′mə) *n., pl.* **-mas, -ma·ta** (-mə tə) [L. < Gr. *karkinōma,* cancer < *karkinos,* a crab] a cancerous growth made up of epithelial cells —**car′ci·nom′-a·tous** (-nōm′ə təs) *adj.*

car coat a short overcoat, mid-thigh in length, esp. for use on car journeys

card¹ (kärd) *n.* [< OFr. < L. *charta* < Gr. *chartēs,* leaf of paper] 1. a flat, stiff piece of thick paper or thin pasteboard, usually rectangular; specif., a) one of a pack of playing cards: see also CARDS b) a piece of pasteboard with small articles attached for sale [a *card* of buttons] c) *same as* VISITING CARD, COMPASS CARD, POSTCARD, SCORE CARD d) a card bearing a message or greeting [a birthday *card*] e) a card to advertise or announce f) a card identifying person as an agent, member, patron, etc. g) any of a series of cards on which information is recorded [an index *card*] h) [pl.] [Colloq.] formerly, an employee's insurance card, tax form etc., kept by his employer 2. a series of events making up a programme, as in horse-racing 3. [Colloq.] an eccentric or entertaining person —*vt.* 1. to provide with a card 2. to put or list on a card or cards —**ask for one's cards** [Colloq.] to resign from one's job —**card up one's sleeve** a plan or resource kept secret or in reserve —**get one's cards** [Colloq.] to be dismissed from one's job —**in** (or **on**) **the cards** likely or seemingly destined to happen —**play one's cards (well)** to act carefully or cleverly —**put** (or **lay**) **one's cards on the table** to reveal frankly, as one's intentions

card² (kärd) *n.* [< Fr. < Pr. < L. *carere,* to card; sp. infl. by L. *carduus,* thistle] 1. a metal comb or wire brush for raising nap or combing fibres of wool, cotton, etc. 2. a machine with rollers covered with wire teeth, used to brush, clean, and straighten such fibres —*vt.* to use a card on (fibres) in preparation for spinning —**card′er** *n.* —**card′ing** *n., adj.*

car·da·mom (kär′də məm) *n.* [< L. < Gr. < *kardamon,* cress + *amōmon,* spice plant] 1. an Asiatic plant with aromatic seeds 2. its seeds, used in medicine and as a spice Also **car′da·mon** (-mən)

card·board (kärd′bôrd′) *n.* stiff, thick paper, or pasteboard, used for cards, boxes, etc.

card-car·ry·ing (-kar′ē iŋ) *adj.* owning a membership card in a specified organization [a *card-carrying* communist]

car·di·ac (kär′dē ak′) *adj.* [< Fr. < L. < Gr. < *kardia,* the heart] 1. of, near, or affecting the heart 2. relating to the part of the stomach connected with the oesophagus —*n.* a person with a heart disorder

car·di·gan (kär′di gən) *n.* [after 7th Earl of *Cardigan* (1797-1868)] a sweater or jacket, usually knitted, that opens down the front

car·di·nal (kär′din əl) *adj.* [< OFr. < L. *cardinalis,* chief < *cardo,* hinge] 1. of main importance; principal; chief 2. deep red —*n.* 1. one of the Roman Catholic officials appointed by the Pope to his council 2. bright red 3. a deep red, crested American songbird: in full, **cardinal bird** 4. *same as* CARDINAL NUMBER —**car′di·nal·ly** *adv.*

CARDIGAN

car·di·nal·ate (-āt′) *n.* the position, dignity, or rank of a cardinal: also **cardinalship**

cardinal flower 1. the bright-red flower of a N. American plant that grows in damp, shady places or in shallow water 2. this plant

cardinal number _Math._ 1. any number used in counting or showing how many (e.g., two, forty, 627, etc.): distinguished from ORDINAL NUMBER 2. the number of elements in a set

cardinal points the four principal points of the compass; north, south, east, and west

cardinal virtues the basic virtues taught in ancient Greek philosophy: justice, prudence, fortitude, and temperance: see also THEOLOGICAL VIRTUES

card index cards containing data or records, arranged systematically: also **card catalogue, card file**

car·di·o- [< Gr. _kardia_, heart] _a combining form meaning_ of the heart: also, before a vowel, **cardi-**

car·di·o·gram (kär'dē ō gram') _n._ _same as_ ELECTROCARDIOGRAM —**car'di·o·graph'** (-graf') _n._ —**car'di·og'·ra·phy** (-og'rə fē) _n._

car·di·ol·o·gy (kär'dē ol'ə jē) _n._ the branch of medicine dealing with the heart, its functions, and its diseases —**car'di·ol'o·gist** _n._

car·di·o·vas·cu·lar (kär'dē ō vas'kyoo lər) _adj._ of the heart and the blood vessels as a system

cards (kärdz) _n.pl._ 1. a game or games played with a pack or packs of cards, as bridge, rummy, poker, etc. 2. the playing of such games; card playing

card·sharp (kärd'shärp') _n._ [Colloq.] a professional cheater at cards: also **card'sharp'er**

card table a table at which card games are played, esp. a small, square table with folding legs

card vote _same as_ BLOCK VOTE

care (ker) _n._ [< OE. _caru_, sorrow] 1. _a)_ worry or concern _b)_ a cause of this 2. close attention or careful heed 3. a liking or regard (_for_) 4. charge; protection; custody 5. something to watch over or attend to —_vi._ **cared, car'ing** 1. to have objection, worry, regret, etc.; mind 2. to feel concern or interest 3. to feel love or a liking (_for_) 4. to look after; provide (_for_) 5. to wish (_for_); want —**care of** at the address of —**have a care** to be careful: also **take care** —**take care of** 1. to be responsible for; attend to 2. to provide for

ca·reen (kə rēn') _vt._ [< Fr. < It. < L. _carina_, keel] 1. to cause (a ship) to lean or lie on one side, as for repairs or cleaning 2. to cause to lean sideways; tip; tilt —_vi._ 1. to lean sideways 2. to lurch from side to side —_n._ a careening

ca·reer (kə rir') _n._ [Fr. _carrière_, racecourse < It. < _carro_, CAR] 1. a swift course 2. one's progress through life or in a particular vocation 3. a profession or occupation —_adj._ pursuing a normally temporary activity as a lifework [a _career_ soldier] —_vi._ to move at full speed; rush wildly —**in full career** at full speed

career girl (or **woman**) a woman who follows a professional or business career

ca·reer·ist (-ist) _n._ a person interested chiefly in success in his own career, to the neglect of other things —**ca·reer'·ism** _n._

care·free (ker'frē') _adj._ free from troubles or worry

care·ful (-fəl) _adj._ 1. acting or working in a thoughtful, painstaking way 2. cautious or wary 3. [Colloq. or Dial] unwilling to spend money 4. accurately or thoroughly done [a _careful_ analysis] —**care'ful·ly** _adv._ —**care'ful·ness** _n._

care·less (-lis) _adj._ 1. carefree; untroubled 2. not paying enough attention;· not thinking before one acts or speaks; inconsiderate 3. done without enough attention, precision, etc. —**care'less·ly** _adv._ —**care'less·ness** _n._

ca·ress (kə res') _vt._ [< Fr. < It., ult. < L. _carus_, dear] to touch or stroke lovingly or gently; also, to embrace or kiss —_n._ an affectionate touch or gesture —**ca·ress'er** _n._ —**ca·ress'ing·ly** _adv._ —**ca·res'sive** _adj._ —**ca·res'sive·ly** _adv._

car·et (kar'it) _n._ [L., lit., there is lacking] a mark (∧) used in writing or in correcting proof, to show where something is to be added

care·tak·er (ker'tāk'ər) _n._ a person employed to take care of something, as a house, estate, etc. —_adj._ holding office temporarily [a _caretaker_ government]

care·worn (-wôrn') _adj._ showing the effects of troubles and worry; haggard

car·go (kär'gō) _n._, _pl._ **-goes** [< Sp. < _cargar_, to load < VL. _carricare_: see CHARGE] the load of goods carried by a ship, aircraft, lorry, etc.; freight

Car·ib (kar'ib) _n._ [< Sp. _caribal_, altered < _canibal_: see CANNIBAL] 1. a member of an Indian people of the S West Indies and the N coast of S. America 2. the family of languages of the Caribs —**Car'ib·an** _adj._, _n._

Car·ib·be·an (kar'ə bē'ən, kə rib'ē ən) _adj._ 1. of the Caribs, their language, culture, etc. 2. of the Caribbean Sea, its islands, etc. —_n._ 1. _same as_ CARIB (sense 1) 2. the Caribbean Sea

ca·ri·be (kə rē'bā) _n._ [AmSp., lit., Carib (see CANNIBAL)] _same as_ PIRANHA

car·i·bou (kar'ə bōō') _n._, _pl._ **-bous', -bou'**: SEE PLURAL, II, D, 1 [CanadFr. < Algonquian name] the N. American reindeer

car·i·ca·ture (kar'i kə tyōōr', -chər) _n._ [Fr. < It. < _caricare_, to load, exaggerate] 1. a picture or imitation of a person, literary style, etc. that exaggerates certain features or mannerisms for satirical effect 2. the art of making caricatures 3. a ridiculously poor imitation —_vt._ **-tured', -tur'ing** to depict as in a caricature —**car'i·ca·tur'ist** _n._

CARIBOU
(1-1.4 m high
at shoulder)

car·ies (ker'ēz, -ē ēz) _n._ [L., decay] decay of bones, or, esp., of teeth

car·il·lon (kə ril'yən, kar'əl yən) _n._ [Fr., chime of (orig. four) bells, ult. < L. _quattuor_, four] 1. a set of stationary bells, each producing one tone of the chromatic scale 2. a melody played on such bells 3. an organ stop producing a carillonlike sound

ca·ri·na (kə rē'nə) _n._, _pl._ **-nae** (-nē), **-nas** [L., a keel] _Biol._ a structure or part resembling a keel or ridge, as the projection on the breastbone of a bird —**ca·ri'nal** _adj._

car·i·nate (kar'ə nāt', -nit) _adj._ [L. _carinatus_ < _carina_, a keel] 1. with a keeled breastbone: said of a bird 2. _Biol._ having a ridge down the middle; keel-shaped

car·i·o·ca (kar'ē ō'kə) _n._ [Braz. Port. < Tupi _cari_, white + _oca_, house] 1. a native of Rio de Janeiro 2. a dance, similar to the samba 3. music for this dance

car·i·ole (kar'ē ōl') _n._ [< Fr. < It. dim. of _carro_, CAR] 1. a small carriage drawn by one horse 2. a light, covered cart

car·i·ous (ker'ē əs) _adj._ [L. _cariosus_] having caries; decayed —**car'i·os'i·ty** (-os'ə tē) _n._

cark (kärk) _vt._, _vi._ [< ONormFr. var. of OFr. _chargier_: see CHARGE] [Archaic] to worry or be worried —_n._ [Archaic] distress; anxiety

carl, carle (kärl) _n._ [OE. < ON. _karl_] [Archaic or Obs.] a peasant, bondman, or villein

Car·lo·vin·gi·an (kär'lō vin'jē ən) _adj._, _n._ _same as_ CAROLINGIAN

car·ma·gnole (kär'mən yōl') _n._ [Fr., altered < older _carmignole_, kind of cap] 1. the costume worn by French Revolutionaries (1792) 2. a song and dance popular during the French Revolution

Car·mel·ite (kär'mə lit') _n._ a friar or nun of the order of Our Lady of Mount Carmel, founded in Syria about 1160 —_adj._ of this order

car·min·a·tive (kär min'ə tiv, kär'mə nāt'iv) _adj._ [ModL. < L. pp. of _carminare_, to card, cleanse] causing gas to be expelled from the stomach and intestines —_n._ a medicine to relieve flatulence

car·mine (kär'min, -mīn) _n._ [< Fr. < ML. _carminium_ < Ar. _qirmiz_, crimson] 1. a red or purplish-red pigment obtained mainly from cochineal 2. its colour —_adj._ red or purplish-red; crimson

car·nage (kär'nij) _n._ [< Fr. < It., ult. < L. _caro_ (gen. _carnis_), flesh] bloody and extensive slaughter, esp. in battle; massacre; bloodshed

car·nal (-n'l) _adj._ [OFr. < LL. _carnalis_ < L. _caro_: see prec.] 1. in or of the flesh; material or worldly, not spiritual 2. sensual; sexual —**car·nal·i·ty** (kär nal'ə tē) _n._, _pl._ **-ties** —**car'nal·ly** _adv._

carnal knowledge [Archaic] sexual intercourse

car·na·tion (kär nā'shən) _n._ [Fr. < LL. _carnatio_ < _caro_: see CARNAGE] 1. rosy pink 2. a plant of the pink family, with white, pink, or red flowers that smell like cloves

car·nau·ba (kär na ōō'bə, -nou'-) _n._ [Braz. Port. < Tupi native name] a Brazilian palm yielding a hard wax used in polishes, lipsticks, etc.

car·nel·ian (kär nēl'yən, -ē ən) _n._ _same as_ CORNELIAN

car·net (kär'nā; Fr. kär ne') _n._ [Fr.] an official document, as a camping permit, motor vehicle certificate, book of tickets, etc.

car·ni·val (kär'nə vəl) _n._ [< Fr. or It. < ML. < hyp. _carnem levare_, to remove meat] 1. the period of feasting and revelry just before Lent 2. a revelling; festivity; merrymaking 3. [Chiefly U.S.] a travelling entertainment with fairground rides, games, etc. 4. a programme of contests, etc. [sports _carnival_]

car·ni·vore (-vôr') _n._ [Fr.: see ff.] 1. any of an order of fanged, flesh-eating mammals, including the dog, wolf, cat, lion, bear, seal, etc.: opposed to HERBIVORE 2. any animal or plant that feeds on animals

car·niv·o·rous (kär niv'ə rəs) _adj._ [< L. < _caro_ (see CARNAGE) + _vorare_, to eat] 1. _a)_ flesh-eating; opposed to HERBIVOROUS _b)_ insect-eating, as certain plants 2. of the carnivores —**car·niv'o·rous·ly** _adv._ —**car·niv'o·rous·ness** _n._

car·ob (kar'əb) _n._ [Fr. _caroube_ < It. _carrubo_ < Ar. _kharrub_, bean pod] 1. a leguminous tree of the E Mediterranean, bearing long flat, brown pods 2. such a pod, used as fodder and sometimes human food

car·ol (kar′əl) *n.* [< OFr. < L. < Gr. < *choros*, dance + *aulein*, to play on the flute] a song of joy or praise; esp., a Christmas song —*vi.* **-olled, -ol·ling** 1. to sing in joy; warble 2. to sing carols, esp. Christmas carols, in unison —*vt.* 1. to sing (a tune, etc.) 2. to praise in song —**car′ol·er** *n.*

Car·o·le·an (kar′ə lē′ən) *adj.* [L. *Carolus*, Charles] 1. of or relating to Charles I or Charles II of England, their reign or period 2. of or relating to any other king called Charles Also **Car·o·line**

Car·o·lin·gi·an (kar′ə lin′jē ən) *adj.* [< ML. *Carolingi*, pl. of *Carolingus* < *Carolus*, Charles + Gmc. -*ing*, patronymic suffix + -AN] designating or of the second Frankish dynasty, founded (751 A.D.) by Pepin the Short, son of Charles Martel —*n.* a member of this dynasty

car·om (kar′əm) *n.* [< Fr. < Sp. *carambola*] [U.S.] same as CANNON (sense 4)

car·o·tene (kar′ə tēn′) *n.* [< L. *carota*, CARROT + -ENE] any of three red or orange-coloured isomeric hydrocarbons found in carrots and some other vegetables, and changed into vitamin A in the body: also **car′o·tin** (-tin)

ca·rot·e·noid, ca·rot·i·noid (kə rot′ən oid′) *n.* any of several red and yellow pigments related to and including carotene —*adj.* 1. of or like carotene 2. of the carotenoids

ca·rot·id (kə rot′id) *adj.* [Gr. *karōtides*, the carotids < *karoun*, to plunge into sleep: compression of these arteries causes unconsciousness] designating, of, or near either of the two principal arteries, one on each side of the neck, which convey the blood to the head —*n.* a carotid artery

ca·rous·al (kə rou′zəl) *n.* same as CAROUSE

ca·rouse (kə rouz′) *vi.* **-roused′, -rous′ing** [< Fr. < G. *gar aus*(*trinken*), (to drink) quite out] to drink heavily, esp. along with others having a noisy, merry time —*n.* a noisy, merry drinking party —**ca·rous′er** *n.*

car·ou·sel (kar′ə sel′) *n.* [Fr. < It. dial. *carusiello*, prob. < *carro*, CAR] same as MERRY-GO-ROUND

carp¹ (kärp) *n.,* pl. **carp, carps:** see PLURAL, II, D, 2 [OFr. *carpe* < Gmc.] 1. any of a group of edible freshwater fishes living in ponds 2. any of various similar fishes, as the goldfish

carp² (kärp) *vi.* [< ON. *karpa*, to brag] to find fault in a petty or nagging way —**carp′er** *n.*

-carp (kärp) [< Gr. *karpos*, fruit] a terminal combining form meaning fruit [endocarp]

car·pal (kär′pəl) *adj.* [ModL. *carpalis*] of the carpus —*n.* a bone of the carpus: also **car·pa′le** (-pā′lē), pl. **-li·a** (-ə)

car park a building or piece of land designed for the parking of cars

‡**car·pe di·em** (kär′pe dē′em, dī′-) [L., lit., seize the day] make the most of present opportunities

car·pel (kär′pəl) *n.* [ModL. dim. < Gr. *karpos*, fruit] 1. a simple pistil, regarded as a single ovule-bearing leaf or modified leaflike structure 2. any of the segments of a compound pistil —**car′pel·lar·y** (-pə lər ē) *adj.* —**car′-pel·late′** (-pə lāt′) *adj.*

car·pen·ter (kär′pən tər) *n.* [Anglo-Fr. < LL. *carpentarius* < L. *carpentum*, a cart < Gaul.] a workman who builds and repairs wooden articles, buildings, etc. —*vi.* to do a carpenter's work —*vt.* to make or repair as by carpentry

car·pen·try (-trē) *n.* the work or trade of a carpenter

car·pet (kär′pit) *n.* [< OFr. < ML. *carpita*, woollen cloth < L. pp. of *carpere*, to card] 1. a heavy fabric for covering a floor, stairs, etc. 2. anything like a carpet [a *carpet* of snow] —*vt.* to cover as with a carpet —**on the carpet** 1. under consideration 2. being, or about to be, reprimanded —**sweep under the carpet** to conceal from sight or knowledge, esp. something unpleasant

car·pet·bag (-bag′) *n.* an old-fashioned type of travelling bag, made of carpeting —*vi.* **-bagged′, -bag′ging** to act as a carpetbagger

car·pet·bag·ger (-bag′ər) *n.* [U.S.] 1. a Northern politician or adventurer who went South to take advantage of unsettled conditions after the American Civil War: contemptuous term 2. any candidate for office without local connections

carpet beetle a small beetle whose larvae feed on furs and woollens, esp. carpets

car·pet·ing (-iŋ) *n.* carpets or carpet fabric

carpet shark an Australian species of shark with a carpetlike pattern on its back

carpet-snake a large Australian snake with a patterned skin

carpet sweeper a hand-operated device with a revolving brush for sweeping carpets and rugs

-car·pic (kär′pik) same as -CARPOUS

carp·ing (kär′piŋ) *adj.* tending to carp, or find fault; captious —**carp′ing·ly** *adv.*

car·po- [< Gr. *karpos*, fruit] a combining form meaning fruit, seeds

car pool an arrangement by a group to rotate the use of their cars, as for going to work

car·port (kär′pôrt′) *n.* a shelter for a motor car, consisting of a roof supported on posts

-car·pous (kär′pəs) [< Gr. *karpos*, fruit] a terminal combining form meaning fruited, having fruit

car·pus (kär′pəs) *n.,* pl. **-pi** (-pī) [ModL. < Gr. *karpos*, wrist] the wrist, or the wrist bones

car·rack (kar′ək) *n.* [< OFr. < Sp. < Ar. pl. of *qurqūr*, merchant ship] an armed merchantman of the 15th and 16th cent.

car·ra·geen, car·ra·gheen (kar′ə gēn′) *n.* [< *Carragheen*, near Waterford, Eire] a purplish, edible seaweed found on rocky shores of N Europe and N America Also called **Irish moss**

car·rel, car·rell (kar′əl) *n.* [< ML. *carula*, small study in a cloister] a small enclosure in a library, for study or reading

car·riage (kar′ij) *n.* [< Anglo-Fr. < *carier*, CARRY] 1. a carrying; transportation 2. the cost of carrying 3. manner of carrying the head and body; posture 4. a four-wheeled passenger vehicle, usually horse-drawn 5. a wheeled support [a gun *carriage*] 6. a moving part (as on a typewriter) for supporting and shifting something 7. a passenger coach on a railway train

carriage clock a portable clock, usually with a case, capable of being carried in any position

carriage forward with the cost of transport to be paid by the consignee

carriage paid with the cost of transport paid by the sender

car·riage·way (-wā) *n.* 1. the part of the road designated for use by vehicles, as distinct from the pavement, etc. 2. part of a road intended for use by vehicles passing in one direction only [a dual *carriageway*]

car·ri·er (kar′ē ər) *n.* 1. a person or thing, as a messenger or a train, that carries something 2. a person or company hired or licensed to carry passengers 3. something in or on which something else is carried or conducted, as on a bicycle 4. same as AIRCRAFT CARRIER 5. a person or animal that carries and transmits disease germs, esp. a person immune to the germs 6. *Electronics* the steady transmitted wave whose amplitude, frequency, or phase is modulated by the signal: also **carrier wave**

carrier bag a large paper or plastic bag with handles, used for shopping, etc.

carrier pigeon a homing pigeon trained to carry a written message fastened to its leg

car·ri·ole (kar′ē ōl′) *n.* same as CARIOLE

car·ri·on (kar′ē ən) *n.* [< Anglo-Fr., ult. < L. *caro*, flesh] 1. the decaying flesh of a dead body 2. anything very repulsive —*adj.* 1. of or like carrion 2. feeding on carrion

carrion crow a black European crow with a thick, black bill, which feeds on carrion and small creatures

car·rot (kar′ət) *n.* [< Fr. < L. < Gr. *karōton*] 1. an umbelliferous plant with a fleshy, orange-red root, eaten as a vegetable 2. the root

car·rot·y (-ē) *adj.* 1. orange-red, like carrots 2. having red hair; redheaded

car·ry (kar′ē) *vt.* **-ried, -ry·ing** [< Anglo-Fr. *carier* < VL. *carricare:* see CHARGE] 1. to hold or support while moving 2. to take from one place to another; transport, as in a vehicle 3. to hold, and direct the motion of [a pipe *carrying* water] 4. to lead or impel 5. to transmit [air *carries* sound] 6. to transfer or extend [to *carry* the fight to the enemy] 7. to transfer (a figure, entry, etc.) from one column, time, etc. to the next 8. to bear the weight of 9. to be pregnant with 10. to have as a quality, consequence, etc. [to *carry* a guarantee] 11. to keep with one [to *carry* a watch] 12. to hold or conduct (oneself) in a specified way 13. to include as part of its contents or programme: said of a newspaper, TV service, etc. 14. to have or keep on a list or register 15. to capture (a fortress, etc.) 16. to win over or influence (a group) 17. *a)* to win (an election, argument, etc.) *b)* to gain a majority of the votes in (a district, constituency, etc.) 18. *Commerce a)* to keep in stock *b)* to keep on one's account books, etc. 19. *Music* to sing the notes of (a melody or part) accurately —*vi.* 1. to act as a bearer, conductor, etc. 2. to have or cover a range [his voice *carries* well] 3. to have an intended effect 4. to win approval [the motion *carried*] 5. [Slang] to carry a gun or illicit drugs on one's person —*n.,* pl. **-ries** 1. the range or distance covered by a gun, golf ball, etc. 2. a portage between two navigable bodies of water 3. a carrying —**be (or get) carried away** to be moved to unreasoning enthusiasm —**carry forward** to take over to the next page, accounting period, etc.: said of accounts —**carry off** 1. to kill [disease *carries off* many] 2. to win (a prize, etc.) 3. to handle (a situation), esp. with success —**carry on** 1. to engage in; conduct 2. to continue as before 3. [Colloq.] to behave in a wild or childish way 4. [Colloq.] to engage in an illicit love affair —**carry out** 1. to put (plans, etc.) into practice 2. to get done; accomplish —**carry over** 1. to have or be remaining 2. to transfer or hold over 3. to postpone; continue —**carry through** 1. to get done; accomplish 2. to sustain

car·ry·all (-ôl′) *n.* [Chiefly U.S.] same as HOLDALL

car·ry-cot (-kot´) *n.* a child's portable cot, made of canvas and fitted with handles

car·ry·ings-on (kar´ē iŋz on´) *n.pl.* [Colloq.] wild, extravagant, or amorous behaviour

car·ry·out (kar´ē out´) *adj. same as* TAKEAWAY

car·ry-o·ver (-ō´vər) *n.* something carried over, as a remainder of crops or goods

carse (kärs) *n.* [< ?] [Scot.] a stretch of low fertile land along the banks of a river

car·sick (kär´sik´) *adj.* affected with nausea from riding in a motor car, bus, etc. **—car´sick´ness** *n.*

cart (kärt) *n.* [< ON. *kartr*] 1. a small, strong, two-wheeled vehicle drawn by a horse, etc. 2. a small, wheeled vehicle, drawn or pushed by hand **—vt., vi.** to carry or deliver, as in a cart, truck, etc. **—cart off** to carry away **—in the cart** in trouble **—put the cart before the horse** to do things backwards **—cart´er** *n.*

cart·age (kär´tij) *n.* 1. the act or work of carting 2. the charges made for carting

carte blanche (kärt´blänsh´) [Fr., lit., white (i.e., blank) card] 1. full authority 2. freedom to do as one thinks best

car·tel (kär tel´) *n.* [Fr. < It. *cartello*, dim. of *carta*, CARD¹] 1. a written challenge, as to a duel 2. a written agreement between nations at war, esp. as to exchange of prisoners 3. [G. *Kartell* < Fr.] an agreement among apparently competing firms to fix prices etc.

Car·te·sian (kär tē´zhən, -zən) *adj.* [< *Cartesius*, Latinized form of *Descartes*, 17th-c. Fr. mathematician] of Descartes or his philosophical or mathematical ideas **—n.** a follower of Descartes **—Car·te´sian·ism** *n.*

Cartesian coordinates a set of numbers that locate a point by its distances from axes intersecting at right angles

cart·horse *n.* 1. a horse for pulling carts 2. any strong, heavy horse

Car·thu·sian (kär thyoo´zhən, -thoo´-) *n.* [< ML. < L. name for Chartreuse] a monk or nun of a very strict order founded at Chartreuse, France, in 1084 **—adj.** of the Carthusians

car·ti·lage (kär´til ij, kärt´´l ij) *n.* [OFr. < L. *cartilago*] 1. a tough, elastic, whitish tissue forming part of the skeleton; gristle 2. a part or structure consisting of cartilage

car·ti·lag·i·nous (kärt´il aj´ə nəs) *adj.* 1. of or like cartilage; gristly 2. having a skeleton made up mainly of cartilage

cart·load (kärt´lōd´) *n.* as much as a cart holds

car·to·gram (kär´tə gram´) *n.* [Fr. *cartogramme* < *carte*, chart, map + -*gramme*, -GRAM] a map giving statistical data by means of lines, dots, shaded areas, etc.

car·tog·ra·phy (kär tog´rə fē) *n.* [< ML. *carta* (see CARD¹) + -GRAPHY] the art or work of making maps or charts **—car·tog´ra·pher** *n.* **—car·to·graph·ic** (kär´tə graf´ik), **car´·to·graph´i·cal** *adj.*

car·ton (kärt´´n) *n.* [Fr. < It. *cartone* < *carta*: see CARD¹] 1. a cardboard box or container 2. a full carton or its contents 3. *Shooting* a white disc placed within the bull of a target

car·toon (kär toon´) *n.* [Fr. *carton* < It. *cartone*: see prec.] 1. a drawing that caricatures, often satirically, some situation or person 2. a full-size sketch of a design or picture to be copied in a fresco, tapestry, etc. 3. *a)* a humorous drawing, often with a caption *b) same as* COMIC STRIP 4. *same as* ANIMATED CARTOON **—vt.** to draw a cartoon of **—vi.** to draw cartoons **—car·toon´ist** *n.*

car·touche (kär toosh´) *n.* [Fr. < It. *cartoccio*, cartridge, roll of paper < *carta*, paper: see CARD¹] 1. a scroll-like ornament or tablet, esp. as an architectural feature 2. on Egyptian monuments, an oval or oblong figure containing the name of a ruler or deity

car·tridge (kär´trij) *n.* [altered < Fr. *cartouche* < It. < *carta*: see CARD¹] 1. a cylindrical case of cardboard, metal, etc. containing the charge and primer, and usually the projectile, for a firearm 2. a small container holding a supply of material for insertion into a larger device 3. a protected roll of camera film 4. a replaceable stylus unit in a gramophone pickup 5. a continuous loop of magnetic tape wound on spools and encased for insertion in a tape recorder

cartridge belt a belt with pockets or loops for cartridges

cartridge clip a metal container for cartridges, inserted in certain types of firearms

cartridge paper a heavy, unbleached drawing or printing paper

cartwheel (kärt´wēl´) *n.* 1. the large, spoked wheel of a cart 2. anything resembling this, as a large coin or hat 3. a kind of handspring performed sideways

car·un·cle (kar´əŋ k´l, kə ruŋ´k´l) *n.* [Fr. *caroncule* < L. *caruncula*, dim. of *caro*, flesh] 1. an outgrowth of flesh, as the comb and wattles of a fowl. 2. a swelling at or near the hilum of a seed **—ca·run´cu·lar** (kə ruŋ´kyoo lər), **ca·run´·cu·lous** (-ləs), **ca·run·cu·late** (-lit) *adj.*

carve (kärv) *vt.* carved, carv´ing [< OE. *ceorfan*] 1. to make or shape by or as by cutting, chipping, etc. [carve a statue, *carve* a career] 2. to decorate the surface of with

cut designs 3. to divide by cutting; slice **—vi.** 1. to carve statues or designs 2. to carve meat **—carve out** 1. to take a piece from 2. to appropriate (land, position, etc.) **—carve up** to divide; share out **—carv´er** *n.*

car·vel (kär´vəl) *n. same as* CARAVEL

car·vel-built (-bilt´) *adj. Shipbuilding* with the hull planks laid edge to edge to form a smooth surface: distinguished from CLINKER-BUILT

carv·en (kär´v´n) *adj.* [Archaic or Poet.] carved

carve-up (kärv´up) *n.* [Slang] 1. a division, esp. of illicit gains 2. a swindle 3. a secret agreement to share out jobs, privileges, etc.

carv·ing (kär´viŋ) *n.* 1. the work or art of a person who carves 2. a carved figure or design

carving knife a large knife for carving meat, used with a large, two-tined fork **(carving fork)**

car·wash (kär´wosh´) *n.* a facility for washing and polishing motor cars

car·y·at·id (kar´ē at´id) *n., pl.* -ids, -i·des´ (-ə dēz´) [< L. < Gr. *karyatides*, priestesses at Karyai, in Macedonia] a supporting column that has the form of a draped female figure

ca·sa·ba (kə sä´bə) *n.* [< *Kassaba*, town near Smyrna, Asia Minor] a cultivated melon with a hard, yellow rind and sweet, usually white flesh

Ca·sa·no·va (kas´ə nō´və) *n.* [after Giovanni *Casanova* (1725-98), It. adventurer] a libertine; rake

cas·bah (kaz´bä) *n.* [Fr. < Ar. dial. *qaṣba* < Ar. *qaṣaba*, fortress] 1. in N Africa, a fortress 2. the old, crowded quarter of a N African city, esp. [C-] of Algiers

cas·cade (kas käd´) *n.* [Fr. < It. *cascata* < L. *cadere*, to fall] 1. a small, steep waterfall, esp. one of a series 2. a shower of sparks, or rippling fall of lace, etc. 3. a consecutive series of steps in a chemical process or electrical apparatus **—vt., vi.** -cad´ed, -cad´ing to fall or drop in a cascade

cas·car·a (kas kär´ə) *n.* [Sp. *cáscara*, bark] 1. a small buckthorn of the U.S. Pacific coast 2. a laxative made from its bark: in full, **cascara sa·gra·da** (sə grä´də)

case¹ (kās) *n.* [< OFr. *cas*, an event < L. *casus*, an accident, pp. of *cadere*, to fall] 1. an example or instance [a *case* of measles] 2. a person being treated or helped, as by a doctor or social worker 3. any matter undergoing observation, study, etc. 4. a statement of the facts, as in a law court 5. convincing arguments [he has no *case*] 6. a lawsuit 7. [Colloq.] a peculiar person 8. *Gram. a)* an inflected form taken by a noun, pronoun, or adjective to show syntactic relationship *b)* such relationship **—vt.** cased, cas´ing [Slang] to look over carefully, esp. for an intended robbery **—in any case** no matter what **—in case** 1. in the event that 2. as a precaution against some eventuality **—in case of** in the event of **—in no case** by no means; never

case² (kās) *n.* [< ONormFr. < L. *capsa*, a box < *capere*, to hold] 1. a container, as a box, sheath, etc. 2. a protective cover [a *watchcase*] 3. a full box or its contents 4. a set or pair [a *case* of pistols] 5. a frame, as for a window 6. the hard cover of a book 7. *Printing* a shallow tray in which type is kept: the **upper case** is for capitals, the **lower case** for small letters **—vt.** cased, cas´ing 1. to put in a container 2. to cover or enclose 3. to bind (a book) in hard covers

ca·se·fy (kā´sə fī´) *vt., vi.* -fied´, -fy´ing [< L. *caseus*, CHEESE¹ + -FY] to make or become cheeselike

case·hard·en (kās´här´d´n) *vt.* 1. *Metallurgy* to form a hard, thin surface on (an iron alloy) 2. to make callous or unfeeling **—case´hard´ened** *adj.*

case history (or **study**) collected information about an individual or group, for use in sociological, medical, or psychiatric studies

ca·se·in (kā´sē in, kā´sēn) *n.* [< L. *caseus*, CHEESE¹ + -IN¹] a protein that is one of the chief constituents of milk and the basis of cheese

case law law based on previous judicial decisions, or precedents: distinguished from STATUTE LAW

case·load (kās´lōd´) *n.* the number of cases being handled by a court, a social or welfare agency, a caseworker, probation officer, etc.

case·mate (kās´māt´) *n.* [Fr. < It. < Gr. *chasmata*, pl. of *chasma*, CHASM, fused with It. *casa*, house] a shellproof or armoured enclosure with openings for guns, as in a fortress or on a warship **—case´mat´ed** *adj.*

case·ment (kās´mənt) *n.* [< OFr. *encassement*, a frame: see CASE²] 1. a hinged window frame that opens outwards: a **casement window** often has two such frames, opening like French doors 2. a casing; covering **—case´ment·ed** *adj.*

ca·se·ous (kā´sē əs) *adj.* [< L. *caseus*, cheese] of or like cheese

ca·sern, ca·serne (kə zurn´) *n.* [< Fr. < Pr. *cazerna*, small hut < LL. *quaterna*, four each < *quattuor*, four] formerly, a military barracks or temporary quarters in a fortified town

CARY-
ATID

case·work (kās′wʉrk′) *n.* social work in which the worker, gives guidance or assistance on the basis of a study of individual and family background —**case′work′er** *n.*

cash[1] (kash) *n.* [< Fr. *caisse*, money box < Pr. < L. *capsa*: see CASE[2]] 1. money that a person actually has; esp., ready money 2. notes and coins 3. money or a cheque paid at the time of purchase —*vt.* to obtain cash for —*adj.* of, for, or requiring cash [a cash sale] —**cash in** to turn into cash —**cash in on** to get profit or profitable use from

cash[2] (kash) *n., pl.* **cash** [Port. *caixa* < Tamil *kasu* < Sans. *karṣa*] any of several Chinese or Indian coins of small value

cash-and-car·ry (kash′ən kar′ē) *adj.* with cash payments and no deliveries

cash·book (-book′) *n.* a book in which all receipts and payments of money are entered

cash crop a crop grown for sale, rather than for subsistence

cash discount a discount allowed a purchaser paying within a specified period

cash·ew (kash′ōō, kə shōō′) *n.* [< Fr. < Port. < Tupi *acajú*] 1. a tropical tree bearing edible, kidney-shaped nuts 2. the nut: also **cashew nut**

cash flow the total amount of money that moves in and out of a business over a given period

cash·ier[1] (ka shir′) *n.* [< Fr. *caissier*] a person in charge of cash transactions for a bank, shop, etc.

cash·ier[2] (ka shir′) *vt.* [< MDu. < OFr. < LL. *cassare* (see QUASH[1]) & L. *quassare* (see QUASH[2])] to dismiss, esp. with dishonour, from a position of command, trust, etc.

cash·mere (kash′mir) *n.* [< *Cashmere*, former sp. of *Kashmir* in Asia] 1. a fine wool from goats of Kashmir 2. a soft, twilled cloth of this or similar wool 3. a cashmere shawl, sweater, coat, etc.

cash on delivery payment in cash when a purchase or shipment is delivered

cash register a business machine, usually with a money drawer, that registers visibly the amount of each sale

cas·ing (kās′iŋ) *n.* 1. a protective covering; specif., *a)* a membrane used to encase processed meats *b)* a pneumatic rubber tyre exclusive of an inner tube and often of the tread *c)* the steel pipe used to line an oil or gas well 2. a frame, as of a window or door

ca·si·no (kə sē′nō) *n., pl.* **-nos** [It., dim. of *casa*, house < L., hut] 1. a room or building for dancing, or, esp., gambling 2. *same as* CASSINO

cask (käsk) *n.* [< Fr. *casque* < Sp. *casco* a helmet] 1. a barrel of any size, made of staves, esp. one for liquids 2. the contents of a full cask; barrelful

cas·ket (käs′kit) *n.* [prob. < OFr. dim. of *casse* (see CASE[2])] 1. a small box or chest, as for valuables 2. [Chiefly U.S.] a coffin

casque (kask) *n.* [Fr.: see CASK] a helmet —**casqued** (kaskt) *adj.*

cas·sa·ba (kə sä′bə) *n. same as* CASABA

Cas·san·dra (kə san′drə) *n.* [after *Cassandra*, daughter of Priam: Apollo gave her prophetic power but decreed no one should believe her prophecies] a person whose warnings of misfortune are disregarded

cas·sa·va (kə sä′və) *n.* [< Fr. < Sp. < native Indian *casávi*] 1. any of several tropical American plants with edible starchy roots 2. a starch taken from the root, used to make bread and tapioca

cas·se·role (kas′ə rōl′) *n.* [Fr., dim. of *casse*, a bowl < Pr. < VL. < Gr. dim. of *kyathos*, a bowl] 1. a baking dish of earthenware or heat resistant glass, often with a cover, in which food can be cooked and served 2. the food cooked in such a dish —*vt.* to cook in a casserole

cas·sette (ka set′, kə-) *n.* [Fr., dim. < ONormFr. *casse*, a CASE[2]] 1. a case with roll film in it, for loading a camera quickly and easily 2. a similar case with magnetic tape, for use in a tape recorder

cas·si·a (ka′sē ə, kash′ə) *n.* [< L. < Gr. *kasia*, kind of cinnamon < Heb. *qeṣī′āh*] 1. *a)* the bark (**cassia bark**) of a tree native to SE Asia: used as an alternative source of cinnamon *b)* this tree 2. *a)* any of a genus of herbs, shrubs, etc. of the legume family, common in tropical countries: the pods (**cassia pods**) of some of these plants have a mildly laxative pulp (**cassia pulp**); from others the drug senna is extracted *b)* cassia pods *c)* cassia pulp

cas·si·mere (kas′ə mir′) *n.* [var. of CASHMERE] a woollen cloth, twilled or plain, used for men's suits

cas·si·no (kə sē′nō) *n.* [see CASINO] a simple card game for two to four players

Cas·si·o·pe·ia (kas′ē ə pē′ə) [after *Cassiopeia*, mother of Andromeda in Gr. Myth.] a N constellation near Andromeda

Cassiopeia's Chair five stars in the constellation Cassiopeia, supposedly outlining a chair

cas·sis (ka sēs′, -sē′; Fr. kȧ sēs′, -sē′) *n.* [Fr.] 1. blackcurrant syrup, esp. as flavouring in drinks 2. a liqueur made from blackcurrants

cas·sit·er·ite (kə sit′ə rīt′) *n.* [Gr. *kassiteros*] native tin

dioxide, SnO_2, the chief ore of tin: it is brown or black and very hard and heavy Also **tin·stone**

cas·sock (kas′ək) *n.* [< Fr. < Per. *kazhāghand*, a jacket < *kazh*, raw silk] a long, closefitting vestment, usually black, worn as an outer garment or under the surplice by clergymen, choristers, etc.

cas·so·war·y (kas′ə wər ē) *n., pl.* **-war·ies** [Malay *kasuārī*] any of a genus of large, flightless birds of Australia and New Guinea, somewhat like the emu, but smaller

cast (käst) *vt.* **cast**, **cast′ing** [< ON. *kasta*, to throw] 1. to throw with force; fling; hurl 2. to deposit (a ballot or vote) 3. *a)* to cause to fall or turn; direct [to *cast* one's eyes on a thing] *b)* to give forth [to *cast* light, gloom, etc.] 4. to throw out or drop (a net, anchor, etc.) at the end of a rope or cable 5. to throw out (a fly, etc.) at the end of a fishing line 6. to draw (lots) or shake (dice) out of a container 7. to throw off; shed [the snake *casts* its skin] 8. to throw (into prison) 9. to calculate (a horoscope, tides, etc.) 10. to formulate 11. *a)* to form (molten metal, plastic, etc.) by pouring or pressing into a mould *b)* to make by such a method 12. *a)* to choose actors for (a play or film) *b)* to select (an actor) for (a role) —*vi.* 1. to throw dice 2. to throw out a fly, etc. on a fishing line 3. to eject (bones, feathers, etc.) from the crop: said of birds of prey —*n.* 1. a casting; a throw; specif., *a)* a throw of dice; also, the number thrown *b)* a turn of the eye; glance; look *c)* a throw of a fishing line, net, etc. 2. a quantity or thing cast in a certain way; specif., *a)* something formed in a mould, as a statue; also, the mould *b)* a mould taken of an object *c)* a plaster form to immobilize a broken arm, leg, etc. *d)* the set of actors in a play or film 3. the form in which a thing is cast; specif., *a)* an appearance, as of features *b)* kind; quality *c)* a tinge; shade [a reddish *cast*] *d)* a turn or twist to one side *e)* a slight turning in or out of the eye 4. *a)* a pellet ejected from the crop of a bird of prey *b)* same as WORMCAST —**cast about** 1. to search (for) 2. to devise (means for doing something) —**cast aside** (or **away**) to discard —**cast back** to refer to something past —**cast down** 1. to turn downwards 2. to sadden; discourage —**cast in a heroic mould** having a heroic character —**cast off** 1. to discard; disown 2. to set free 3. to free a ship from a dock, quay, etc., as by releasing the lines 4. *Knitting* to make the last row of stitches —**cast on** *Knitting* to make the first row of stitches —**cast out** to expel —**cast up** 1. to throw up 2. to turn upwards 3. to total 4. to construct by digging [to *cast up* earthworks]

cas·ta·nets (kas′tə nets′) *n.pl.* [< Fr. < Sp. *castañeta*, dim. < L. *castanea*, chestnut: from the shape] a pair of small, hollowed pieces of hard wood, ivory, etc. held in the hand and clicked together in time to music, esp. in Spanish dances

cast·a·way (käs′tə wā′) *n.* 1. a person or thing cast out or off, esp. an outcast 2. a shipwrecked person —*adj.* 1. thrown away; discarded 2. cast adrift or stranded, as by shipwreck

CASTANETS

caste (käst) *n.* [Fr. < Port. *casta*, a breed < L. *castus*, pure] 1. any of the distinct, hereditary Hindu social classes, each by tradition, but no longer officially, excluded from social dealings with the others 2. any exclusive social or occupational class or group 3. rigid class distinction based on birth, wealth, etc., operating as a social system or principle 4. any of the differentiated types of social insects in a colony —**lose caste** to lose social status or rank

cas·tel·lan (kas′tə lən) *n.* [ME. & Anglo-Fr. *castellain* < ML. *castellanus*, keeper of a castle < L. *castellum*, CASTLE] the warden or governor of a castle

cas·tel·lat·ed (kas′tə lāt′id) *adj.* [< ML. < L. *castellum*, CASTLE] 1. built with turrets and battlements, like a castle 2. *same as* crenellated (see CRENELLATE) —**cas′tel·la′tion** *n.*

cast·er (käs′tər) *n.* 1. a person or thing that casts 2. a small bottle or container with a perforated top for serving sugar, salt, etc. at the table 3. a wheel or freely rolling ball set in a frame and attached to each leg, bottom corner, etc. of a piece of furniture, etc. so that it can be moved easily

cas·ti·gate (kas′tə gāt′) *vt.* **-gat′ed**, **-gat′ing** [< L. pp. of *castigare*, to purify, chastise < *castus*, pure] to punish or rebuke severely, esp. by public criticism —**cas′ti·ga′tion** *n.* —**cas′ti·ga′tor** *n.* —**cas′ti·ga·to·ry** (-ge tə rē) *adj.*

Cas·tile soap (kas tēl) [< *Castile*, where first made] [also **c- s-**] a fine, mild, hard soap made from olive oil and sodium hydroxide

Cas·til·ian (kas til′yən) *adj.* of Castile, its people, language, or culture —*n.* 1. a native or inhabitant of Castile 2. the dialect spoken in Castile, now the standard form of Spanish

cast·ing (käs′tiŋ) *n.* 1. the action of one that casts 2. anything, esp. of metal, that has been cast in a mould 3. *same as* CAST (*n.* 4)

casting vote the deciding vote cast by a chairman in the event of a deadlock in a committee, board meeting, etc.: also **casting voice**

cast·i·ron (käst'ī'ərn) *adj.* 1. made of cast iron 2. very hard, rigid, strong, healthy, etc. 3. impregnable [a cast-iron alibi]

cast iron a hard, unmalleable alloy of iron made by casting: it has a high proportion of carbon

cas·tle (käs'l) *n.* [< OE. & Anglo-Fr. < L. *castellum*, dim. of *castrum*, fort] 1. a large building or group of buildings fortified with thick walls, turrets, and often a moat: castles were strongholds for noblemen in the Middle Ages 2. any massive dwelling like this 3. a safe, secure place 4. Chess same as ROOK² —*vt.* -**tled, -tling** 1. to furnish with a castle 2. Chess to move (a king) two squares to either side and then, in the same move, place the castle on the square passed over by the king —*vi.* Chess 1. to castle a king 2. to be castled: said of a king

castle in the air an imaginary scheme unlikely to be realized; daydream: also **castle in Spain**

cast·off (käst'ôf) *adj.* thrown away; discarded —*n.* a person or thing cast off

cas·tor¹ (käs'tər) *n.* [Fr. < L. < Gr. *kastōr*, beaver] 1. a strong-smelling, oily substance obtained from the beaver, used in perfumery: also **cas·to·re·um** (kas'tôr'ē əm) 2. a hat of beaver or rabbit fur

cas·tor² (käs'tər) *n.* same as CASTER (senses 2 & 3)

cas·tor-oil plant (käs'tər oil') a tropical plant with large, beanlike seeds (**castor beans**) from which oil (**castor oil**) is extracted: this oil is used as a cathartic and lubricant

castor sugar finely ground white sugar, used as a decoration or sweetening: also **cas·ter sugar**

cas·trate (kas trāt') *vt.* -**trat·ed, -trat·ing** [< L. *castratus*, pp. of *castrare*] 1. to remove the testicles of; emasculate; geld 2. to deprive of real vigour or meaning by mutilation, expurgation, etc.; emasculate —**cas·tra'tion** *n.*

cas·tra·to (kas trä'tō) *n.* pl. -**ti** (-ē) [It. < L. *castratus*, pp. of *castrare*, CASTRATE] formerly, esp. in the 18th cent., a singer castrated as a boy to preserve the soprano or contralto range of his voice

cast steel steel formed by casting, not by rolling or forging —**cast'-steel'** *adj.*

cas·u·al (kazh'yŏŏ wəl) *adj.* [< OFr. < LL. *casualis*, by chance < L. *casus*, chance] 1. happening or governed by chance; not planned [a casual visit] 2. happening, active, etc. at irregular intervals; occasional [a casual worker] 3. slight or superficial [a casual acquaintance] 4. careless or nonchalant 5. a) informal or relaxed [a casual atmosphere] b) designed for informal occasions or use [casual clothes] —*n.* 1. one who does something only occasionally or temporarily, esp. a casual worker 2. [pl.] shoes, clothes, etc. for informal occasions —**cas'u·al·ly** *adv.* —**cas'·u·al·ness** *n.*

cas·u·al·ty (kazh'yŏŏ wəl tē, -əl tē) *n.,* pl. -**ties** [see prec.] 1. an accident, esp. a fatal one 2. a member of the armed forces killed, wounded, captured, etc. 3. anyone hurt or killed in an accident 4. anything lost, destroyed, or made useless by some unfortunate or unforeseen happening

ca·su·a·ri·na (kaz'yŏŏ wə rē'nə) *n.* [< Malay *kasuāri*, lit., CASSOWARY: so named from the similarity of the branches to the bird's feathers] any of several Australian trees with jointed, green branchlets

cas·u·ist (kaz'yŏŏ wist) *n.* [< Fr. < L. *casus*, CASE¹] a person expert in, or apt to resort to, casuistry —**cas'u·is'tic, cas'u·is'ti·cal** *adj.* —**cas'u·is'ti·cal·ly** *adv.*

cas·u·ist·ry (kaz'yŏŏ wis trē) *n.,* pl. -**ries** [prec. + -RY] 1. the solving of specific cases of right and wrong in conduct by applying general principles of ethics 2. subtle but misleading or false reasoning, esp. about moral issues; sophistry

‡**ca·sus bel·li** (kä'zəs bel'ē, kä'səs bel'ī) pl. **casus belli** [L.] an event provoking war or used as a pretext to make war

cat (kat) *n.* [OE.] 1. any of a family of flesh-eating, predacious mammals, including the lion, tiger, leopard, etc.; specif., a small, lithe, soft-furred animal of this family, often kept as a pet or for killing mice 2. a person regarded as a cat in some way, esp. a woman who makes spiteful remarks 3. same as CAT-O'-NINE-TAILS 4. [C-] same as CATERPILLAR (tractor) 5. [Slang] a) a jazz musician or enthusiast b) any person, esp. a man 6. Naut. tackle to hoist an anchor to the cathead —*vt.* **cat'ted, cat'ting** to hoist (an anchor) to the cathead —**let the cat out of the bag** to let a secret be found out —**like a cat on hot bricks** excessively nervous —**set the cat among the pigeons** to stir up trouble —**the cat's pyjamas** (or **whiskers**) [Colloq.] the very best —**cat'like** *adj.*

cat. 1. catalogue 2. catechism

cat·a- (kat'ə) [< Gr. *kata*, down] a prefix meaning: 1. down, downwards [catabolism] 2. away, completely [catalysis] 3. against [catapult] Also, before a vowel, **cat-**

ca·tab·o·lism (kə tab'ə liz'm) *n.* [< CATA- + Gr. *bolē*, to throw + -ISM] the process in a plant or animal by which living tissue is changed into waste products of a simpler composition; destructive metabolism: opposed to ANABOLISM —**cat·a·bol·ic** (kat'ə bol'ik) *adj.* —**cat'a·bol'i·cal·ly** *adv.*

ca·tab·o·lize (-līz') *vi., vt.* -**lized', -liz'ing** to change by catabolism

cat·a·chre·sis (kat'ə krē'sis) *n.,* pl. -**ses** (-sēz) [L. < Gr. < *kata-*, against + *chrēsthai*, to use] incorrect use of a word or words —**cat'a·chres'tic** (-kres'tik), **cat'a·chres'ti·cal** *adj.* —**cat'a·chres'ti·cal·ly** *adv.*

cat·a·clysm (kat'ə kliz'm) *n.* [< L. < Gr. < *kata-*, down + *klyzein*, to wash] 1. a great flood; deluge 2. any great upheaval or sudden, violent change, as an earthquake, war, etc.—**cat'a·clys'mic** (-kliz'mik), **cat'a·clys'mal** *adj.*

cat·a·comb (kat'ə kōōm', -kōm') *n.* [< LL. *catacumba* < L. < *cata* (< Gr. *kata*), down + *tumba*, TOMB] any of a series of galleries in an underground burial place: usually used in pl.

ca·tad·ro·mous (kə tad'rə məs) *adj.* [CATA- + Gr. *dromos* < *dramein*, to run] going back to or towards the sea to spawn: said of certain freshwater fishes, as the eel

cat·a·falque (kat'ə falk') *n.* [Fr. < It. < L. *cata* (< Gr. *kata*), by + *fala*, a scaffold] a wooden framework, usually draped, on which the body in a coffin awaiting burial lies in state

Cat·a·lan (kat'ə lan', ə lən) *adj.* of Catalonia, its people, or their language —*n.* 1. a native or inhabitant of Catalonia 2. the Romance language of Catalonia, closely akin to Provençal

cat·a·lep·sy (kat'ə lep'sē) *n.* [< LL. < Gr. *katalēpsis*, a seizing < *kata-*, down + *lambanein*, to seize] a condition in which consciousness and feeling are suddenly and temporarily lost, and the muscles become rigid —**cat'a·lep'-tic** *adj.,* *n.*

cat·a·logue (kat'ə log') *n.* [Fr. < LL. *catalogus*, list < Gr. < *kata*, down + *legein*, to collect] a complete list; esp., a) an alphabetical card index, as of the books in a library b) a list of things exhibited, articles for sale, etc., usually with comments and illustrations c) a book or pamphlet with such a list —*vt., vi.* 1. to enter in a catalogue 2. to make a catalogue of —**cat'a·logu'er, cat'a·logu'ist** *n.*

‡**ca·ta·logue rai·son·né** (kà tà lôg' re zô nä') [Fr., lit., reasoned catalogue] a catalogue of books (esp. in a bibliography), paintings, etc. arranged by subject and with explanatory notes

ca·tal·pa (kə tal'pə) *n.* [< AmInd. (Creek) *kutuhlpa*] a tree of America and Asia with large, heart-shaped leaves, showy trumpet-shaped flowers, and slender, beanlike pods

cat·a·lyse (kat'ə līz') *vt.* -**lysed', -lys'ing** to change or bring about as a catalyst —**cat'a·lys'er** *n.*

ca·tal·y·sis (kə tal'ə sis) *n.,* pl. -**ses'** (-sēz') [Gr. *katalysis*, dissolution < *kata-*, down + *lyein*, to loosen] the speeding up of the rate of a chemical reaction by the addition of some substance which itself undergoes no permanent chemical change thereby

cat·a·lyst (kat'ə list) *n.* 1. any substance serving as the agent in catalysis 2. a person or thing that is a stimulus in producing or hastening results —**cat'a·lyt'ic** *adj., n.* —**cat'·a·lyt'i·cal·ly** *adv.*

cat·a·ma·ran (kat'ə mə ran') *n.* [Tamil *kattumaram* < *kattu*, tie + *maram*, log, tree] 1. a narrow log raft or float propelled by sails or paddles 2. a boat with two parallel hulls

cat·a·mount (kat'ə mount') *n.* [< CAT + obs. *a*, of + MOUNT(AIN)] any of various wild cats; esp., a) the puma; cougar b) the lynx

ca·taph·o·ra (kə taf'ər ə) *n.* [CATA- + (ANA)PHORA] Linguis. the use of pronouns, etc., to refer back to later words or phrases in a text: cf. ANAPHORA

cat·a·plex·y (kat'ə pleks'ē) *n.* [CATA- + Gr. *plexis* < *plessein*, to strike] a state of immovability, esp. of animals feigning death

cat·a·pult (kat'ə pult', -poolt') *n.* [< L. < Gr. *katapeltēs* < *kata-*, down + *pallein*, to hurl] 1. an ancient military device for throwing or shooting stones, spears, etc. 2. a weapon for shooting stones, consisting of a piece of strong elastic fixed at each end to a forked stick 3. a mechanism for launching an aeroplane, rocket, etc., as from a ship's deck —*vt.* to shoot from or as from a catapult; hurl —*vi.* to be catapulted; leap

CATAPULT

cat·a·ract (kat'ə rakt') *n.* [< L. *cataracta* < Gr. *katarrhaktēs*, a waterfall] 1. a large waterfall 2. any strong flood or rush of water 3. a) an eye disease in which the crystalline lens or its capsule becomes opaque, causing partial or total blindness b) the opaque area

ca·tarrh (kə tär') *n.* [< Fr. < LL. < Gr. < *kata-*, down + *rhein*, to flow] inflammation of a mucous membrane, esp.

of the nose or throat, causing an increased flow of mucus —**ca·tarrh′al, ca·tarrh′ous** adj.

cat·ar·rhine (kat′ə rīn′) adj. [ModL. catarrhinus < Gr. katarrin, long-nosed < kata- (see CATA-) + rhis (gen. rhinos), nose] having a slender nose with the nostrils placed close together —n. a catarrhine creature, as man or certain other primates

ca·tas·tro·phe (kə tas′trə fē) n. [< L. < Gr. katastrophē, an overthrowing < kata-, down + strephein, to turn] 1. the culminating event of a drama, esp. of a tragedy, by which the plot is resolved 2. a disastrous end 3. any great and sudden disaster 4. a total failure; fiasco —**cat·a·stroph·ic** (kat′ə strof′ik) adj. —**cat′a·stroph′i·cal·ly** adv.

cat·a·to·ni·a (kat′ə tō′nē ə) n. [CATA- + Gr. tonos, tension] a syndrome, esp. of schizophrenia, marked by stupor or muscular rigidity alternating with phases of excitement —**cat′a·ton′ic** adj.

cat·bird (kat′bʉrd′) n. 1. a N. American songbird 2. any of several Australian birds whose cry resembles the mew of a cat

cat·boat (-bōt′) n. a catrigged sailing boat, usually having a centreboard

cat brier a thorny climbing plant of the lily family, with oval leaves and black berries

cat burglar [Slang] a burglar who climbs up to upper windows, roofs, etc. to enter

cat·call (-kôl′) n. a shrill shout or whistle expressing derision or disapproval, as of a speaker, actor, etc. —vt., vi. to make catcalls (at)

catch (kach) vt. **caught, catch′ing** [< Anglo-Fr. cachier < VL. < L. captare, to try to seize < pp. of capere, to take] 1. to seize and hold, as after a chase; capture 2. to take by or as by a trap, snare, etc. 3. to deceive; ensnare 4. to surprise in the act [to be caught stealing] 5. to hit [the blow caught him in the eye] 6. to get to in time [to catch a train] 7. to lay hold of; grab [to catch a ball] 8. a) to get as by chance or quickly [to catch a glimpse] b) [Colloq.] to manage to see, hear, etc. [to catch a broadcast] 9. to get as by exposure to others infected [to catch the mumps] 10. a) to understand; apprehend b) to show an understanding of by depicting [the statue catches her beauty] 11. to captivate; charm 12. to cause to be entangled [to catch one's heel in a rug] 13. to attract or arrest [to catch someone's eye] 14. [Colloq.] to hear [I didn't catch what he said] 15. Cricket to dismiss (a batsman) by catching the ball before it touches the ground —vi. 1. to become held, fastened, or entangled 2. to take fire or start burning 3. to take and keep hold, as a lock —n. 1. the act of catching 2. a thing that catches or holds, esp. a lock 3. the person or thing caught 4. the amount caught 5. a person worth catching, esp. as a husband or wife 6. a snatch, scrap, or bit [catches of old tunes] 7. an emotional break in the voice 8. a simple game of throwing and catching a ball 9. [Colloq.] a hidden qualification; difficult condition [a catch in his offer] 10. Cricket the dismissal of a batsman by a fielder catching the ball before it touches the ground 11. Music a round for three or more voices —adj. 1. designed to trick; deceptive [a catch question on an exam] 2. attracting or meant to attract attention or interest —**catch as catch can** with any hold, approach, etc.: orig. said of a style of wrestling —**catch at** 1. to try to catch 2. to reach for eagerly —**catch it** [Colloq.] to receive a scolding or other punishment —**catch me!** [Colloq.] you won't find me (doing that) —**catch on** 1. to understand 2. to become fashionable, popular, etc. —**catch oneself** to hold oneself back abruptly from saying or doing something —**catch out** 1. to discover (someone) in the act of committing a crime, making an error, etc. 2. Cricket to dismiss (a batsman) by making a catch —**catch up** 1. to take up suddenly; snatch 2. to come up even, as by hurrying or by extra work 5. to fasten in loops —**catch up on** to engage in more (work, sleep, etc.) so as to compensate for earlier neglect —**catch′er** n.

catch·fly (-flī′) n., pl. **-flies′** same as CAMPION

catch·ing (-iŋ) adj. 1. contagious; infectious 2. attractive; catchy

catch·ment (-mənt) n. 1. the catching or collecting of water, esp. rainfall 2. a reservoir or other basin for catching water 3. the water thus caught 4. all those served by a school, hospital, etc. in a particular catchment area

catchment area 1. the area draining into a river, reservoir, etc. 2. the area served by a school, hospital, etc.

catch·pen·ny (-pen′ē) adj. cheap and flashy; worthless —n., pl. **-nies** a catchpenny commodity

catch phrase a phrase that catches or is meant to catch popular attention by repetition

Catch-22 (-twen′tē tōō′) n. [from the novel Catch-22 (1961) by J. Heller] a paradox in a law, regulation, or practice that makes one victim of its provisions no matter what one does

catch-weight (kach′wāt′) adj., adv. with no restrictions being set on the weight of the contestants [a catchweight wrestling contest]

catch·word (kach′wʉrd′) n. 1. a word placed to catch attention and be a guide, as either of the words at the top of this page 2. a word or phrase repeated so often that it becomes a slogan

catch·y (-ē) adj. **catch′i·er, catch′i·est** 1. catching attention; arousing interest 2. easily taken up and remembered [a catchy tune] 3. meant to trick 4. spasmodic —**catch′i·ness** n.

cat·e·chet·i·cal (kat′ə ket′i k'l) adj. 1. of or like a catechism 2. teaching by questions and answers Also **cat′e·chet′ic** —**cat′e·chet′i·cal·ly** adv.

cat·e·chism (kat′ə kiz'm) n. [< LL. < Gr. < katēchizein, to catechize < kata-, thoroughly + ēchein, to sound] 1. a handbook of questions and answers for teaching the principles of a religion 2. any similar handbook for teaching the fundamentals of a subject 3. a series of questions; close questioning —**cat′e·chis′mal** adj. —**cat′e·chis′tic** (-kis′tik), **cat′e·chis′ti·cal** adj.

cat·e·chist (-kist) n. a person who catechizes

cat·e·chize (-kīz′) vt. **-chized′, -chiz′ing** [see CATECHISM] 1. to teach (esp. religion) by the use of questions and answers 2. to question searchingly (on one's beliefs, actions, etc.) Also sp. **cat′e·chise** —**cat′e·chi·za′tion** n. —**cat′e·chiz′er** n.

cat·e·chu (kat′ə chōō′) n. [Malay kachu] a water-soluble, astringent substance obtained from several Asiatic trees: used in dyeing, tanning, etc.

cat·e·chu·men (kat′ə kyōō′mən) n. [< LL. < Gr. katēchoumenos: see CATECHISM] a person, esp. an adult, being instructed in the fundamentals of Christianity before baptism or confirmation

cat·e·gor·i·cal (kat′ə gôr′i k'l) adj. 1. unqualified; unconditional; absolute; positive: said of a statement, theory, etc. 2. of, as, or in a category Also **cat′e·gor′ic** —**cat′e·gor′i·cal·ly** adv.

cat·e·go·rize (kat′ə gə rīz′) vt. **-rized′, -riz′ing** to place in a category —**cat′e·go·ri·za′tion** n.

cat·e·go·ry (kat′ə gôr ē) n., pl. **-ries** [< LL. < Gr. < katēgorein, to accuse < kata-, against + agoreuein, to declaim] 1. a class or division in a scheme of classification 2. Philos. one of a fundamental set of concepts, modes of being, etc.

ca·te·na (kə tē′nə) n., pl. **-nae** (-nē) [L., a chain] a linked or connected series, as of excerpted writings, esp. comments on scripture by the Fathers of the Churches

cat·e·nate (kat′ə nāt′) vt. **-nat′ed, -nat′ing** [< L. < catena, chain] to form into a chain or series; link —**cat′e·na′tion** n.

ca·ter (kā′tər) vi. [< OFr. < acater, to buy, ult. < L. ad-, to + capere, to take] 1. to provide food; act as a caterer 2. to take pains to gratify another's needs or desires (with to or for) —vt. to serve as caterer for (a banquet, party, etc.)

cat·er-cor·nered (kat′ə kôr′nərd) adj. [ME. cater, four (ult. < L. quattuor, FOUR) + cornered, see CORNER] [U.S.] diagonal —adv. diagonally Also **cat′er-cor′ner**

ca·ter·er (kāt′ər ər) n. one who caters; esp., one whose business is providing food and service as for parties

cat·er·pil·lar (kat′ər pil′ər, kat′ə-) n. [< ONormFr. catepelose < L. catta pilosa, hairy cat] the wormlike larva of various insects, esp. of a butterfly or moth —[C-] a trademark for a tractor having on each side an endless roller belt over cogged wheels, to move over rough or muddy ground

cat·er·waul (kat′ər wôl′) vi. [ME. cater (prob. < MDu. kater, tomcat) + w(r)awlen, v., prob. echoic] to make a shrill, howling sound like that of a cat; wail; scream —n. such a sound

cat·fish (kat′fish′) n., pl. **-fish′, -fish′es**: see FISH any of a group of scaleless fishes with long barbels about the mouth

cat·gut (-gut′) n. [CAT + GUT: reason for cat unc.] a tough string or thread made from the dried intestines of sheep, horses, etc. and used for surgical sutures, musical instruments, etc.

cath- (kath) same as CATA-: used before an aspirate

Cath. 1. Catholic 2. [also c-] cathedral

Cath·ar (kath′är, -ər) n., pl. **-ars, -ar·i** (-ər ē) a member of a medieval Christian sect (12th-13th cent.) that stressed the opposition of the material and spiritual worlds

ca·thar·sis (kə thär′sis) n. [ModL. < Gr. katharsis < katharos, pure] 1. purgation, esp. of the bowels 2. the purifying or relieving of the emotions, esp. by art 3. Psychiatry the relieving of fears, problems, etc. by bringing them to consciousness or giving them expression

ca·thar·tic (-tik) adj. of or effecting catharsis; purging: also **ca·thar′ti·cal** —n. a medicine to stimulate evacuation of the bowels

Ca·thay (ka thā′, kə-) poet. or archaic name of China

cat·head (kat′hed′) n. a projecting beam near the bow of a ship, to which the anchor is fastened

ca·the·dra (kə thē′drə, kath′i-) n. [LL. < L. < Gr. kathedra, a seat < kata-, down + hedra, a seat] 1. the bishop's throne in a cathedral **2.** the episcopal see See also EX CATHEDRA

ca·the·dral (kə thē′drəl) **n.** **1.** the main church of a bishop's see, containing the cathedra **2.** loosely, any large, imposing church —**adj.** **1.** of, like, or containing a cathedra **2.** of or like a cathedral

Cath·er·ine wheel (kath′rin) [orig. a spiked wheel symbolizing the instrument of torture involved in the martyrdom of St. *Catherine* of Alexandria] [*also* **c- w-**] **1.** a firework in the shape of a wheel, that spins and throws out coloured lights **2.** *same as* CARTWHEEL (sense 3)

cath·e·ter (kath′ə tər) **n.** [LL. < Gr. *kathetēr* < *kata-*, down + *hienai*, to send] a slender tube inserted into a body passage, etc. for passing fluids, making examinations, etc., esp. for draining urine from the bladder

cath·e·ter·ize (-īz′) **vt.** **-ized′, -iz′ing** to insert a catheter into —**cath′e·ter·i·za′tion n.**

cath·ode (kath′ōd) **n.** [< Gr. *kathodos*, descent < *kata-*, down + *hodos*, way] **1.** in an electrolytic cell, the negative electrode, from which current flows: opposed to ANODE **2.** in a vacuum tube, the negatively charged electron emitter **3.** the positive terminal of a battery —**ca·thod·ic** (ka thod′-ik) **adj.**

cathode rays a stream of electrons projected from the surface of a cathode: cathode rays produce X-rays when they strike solids

cathode-ray tube a vacuum tube in which the electrons can be focused on a fluorescent screen, producing a visible pattern on the exterior face: used as oscilloscopes, television picture tubes, etc.

cath·o·lic (kath′ə lik, kath′lik) **adj.** [L. *catholicus*, universal < Gr. < *kata-*, completely + *holos*, whole] **1.** of general scope or value; all inclusive; universal **2.** broad in sympathies, tastes, etc.; liberal **3.** [*often* **C-**] of the universal Christian church **4.** [**C-**] of the Christian church headed by the Pope; Roman Catholic —**n.** **1.** [*often* **C-**] a member of the universal Christian church **2.** [**C-**] *same as* ROMAN CATHOLIC —**ca·thol·i·cal·ly** (kə thol′i k'l ē, -ik lē) **adv.**

Ca·thol·i·cism (kə thol′ə siz′m) **n.** the doctrine, faith, practice, and organization of a Catholic church, esp. of the Roman Catholic Church

cath·o·lic·i·ty (kath′ə lis′ə tē) **n.** **1.** broadness of taste, sympathy, etc.; liberality, as of ideas **2.** universality

ca·thol·i·cize (kə thol′ə sīz′) **vt., vi.** **-cized′, -ciz′ing** **1.** to make or become catholic **2.** [**C-**] to convert or be converted to Catholicism

cat·i·on (kat′ī′ən) **n.** [coined by Faraday < Gr. < *kata*, down + *ion*, prp. of *ienai*, to go] a positive ion: in electrolysis, cations move towards the cathode —**cat·i·on·ic** (kat′ī on′ik) **adj.**

cat·kin (kat′kin) **n.** [< Du. dim. of *katte*, cat] a drooping, scaly spike of unisexual flowers without petals, as on willows, hazels etc.

cat·mint (-mint′) **n.** *same as* CATNIP

cat·nap (kat′nap′) **n.** a short, light sleep; doze —**vi.** **-napped′, -nap′ping** to take a catnap

cat·nip (-nip′) **n.** [CAT + *nip* (dial. for *catnip*) < L. *nepeta*] a labiate plant with downy leaves and bluish flowers: cats like its odour Also, **cat′mint′**

cat-o′-nine-tails (kat′ə nīn′tālz′) **n.,** *pl.* **-tails′** a whip made of nine knotted cords attached to a handle, formerly used for flogging

cat rig a rig, esp. of a catboat, consisting of one large sail on a mast well forward in the bow —**cat′rigged′** (-rigd′) **adj.**

cat's cradle a child's game in which a string looped over the fingers is transferred back and forth on the hands of the players to form designs

cat's-eye (kats′ī′) **n.** **1.** any gem, stone, etc. that reflects light in a way suggestive of a cat's eye, as a child's marble, a glass reflector, etc. **2.** a glass marker stud set in a road so as to reflect light from headlights

cat's-paw (kats′pô′) **n.** **1.** a person used by another to do distasteful or unlawful work; dupe **2.** a light breeze rippling the surface of water

CAT'S CRADLE

cat·sup (kech′əp, kach′-; kat′səp) **n.** [U.S.] *same as* KETCHUP

cat·tish (kat′ish) **adj.** **1.** like a cat; feline **2.** *same as* CATTY —**cat′tish·ly adv.** —**cat′tish·ness n.**

cat·tle (kat′'l) **n.** [< Anglo-Fr. *catel* < ML. *captale*, property < L. < *caput*, the head] **1.** [Archaic] farm animals **2.** domesticated bovine animals collectively; cows, bulls, steers, or oxen **3.** people in the mass: contemptuous term

cat·tle-cake (-kāk′) **n.** a concentrated, high-protein food for cattle, pressed into cakes

cat·tle-grid (-grid′) **n.** a device to prevent cattle, etc. from straying, consisting of a shallow pit crossed by parallel bars

cat·tle·man (-mən) **n.,** *pl.* **-men** a cattle farmer, esp. on a large scale

cat·ty (kat′ē) **adj.** **-ti·er, -ti·est** **1.** of or like a cat **2.** spiteful, mean, malicious, etc. —**cat′ti·ly adv.** —**cat′ti·ness n.**

cat·walk (kat′wôk′) **n.** a high, narrow walk, as along the edge of a bridge or over an engine room

Cau·ca·sian (kô kā′zē ən, -zhən) **adj.** **1.** of the Caucasus, its people, their languages, etc. **2.** *same as* CAUCASOID Also **Cau·cas′ic** (-kas′ik) —**n.** **1.** a native of the Caucasus **2.** *same as* CAUCASOID **3.** the Caucasian languages; Circassian, Georgian, etc.

Cau·ca·soid (kôk′ə soid′, -zoid) **adj.** [from the erroneous notion that the original home of the hypothetical Indo-Europeans was the Caucasus] designating or of one of the major groups of mankind that includes the native peoples of Europe, North Africa, the Near East, India, etc.: loosely called the *white race*, although skin colour varies —**n.** a member of the Caucasoid group

cau·cus (kôk′əs) **n.** [< ? Algonquin *caucausu*, adviser] **1.** a private meeting of leaders or a committee of a political party or faction to decide on policy, candidates, etc., esp. prior to an open meeting **2.** a local faction or organization of a political party —**vi.** **-cused, -cus·ing** to hold, or take part in, a caucus

cau·dal (kôd′'l) **adj.** [< L. *cauda*, tail] **1.** of or like a tail **2.** at or near the tail —**cau′dal·ly adv.**

cau·date (kô′dāt) **adj.** [< L. *cauda*, tail] having a tail or taillike part: also **cau′dat·ed**

cau·dil·lo (kou dē′lyō) **n.,** *pl.* **-los** [Sp. < LL. *capitellum*, dim. of *caput*, head, chief] in Spanish-speaking countries, a leader, esp. a military dictator

cau·dle (kôd′'l) **n.** [< Anglo-Fr., ult. < L. *cal(i)dus*, warm] a warm drink for invalids; esp., a spiced and sugared gruel with wine or ale added

caught (kôt) **pt. & pp.** *of* CATCH

caul (kôl) **n.** [OE. *cawl*, basket, net] a membrane sometimes enveloping the head of a child at birth

caul·dron (kôl′drən) **n.** [< OFr. < L. *caldaria*, warm bath < *calidus*, warm] a large pot used for boiling, usually with a hooped handle

cau·li·flow·er (kol′ə flou′ər) **n.** [< It. *cavolfiore*, after L. *caulis*, cabbage] **1.** a variety of cabbage with a compact white head of fleshy flower stalks **2.** the head of this plant, eaten as a vegetable

cauliflower ear an ear permanently deformed by injuries from repeated blows, as in boxing

caulk (kôk) **vt.** [< OFr. < L. *calcare*, to tread < *calx*, heel] **1.** to make (a boat, etc.) watertight by filling the seams or cracks with oakum, tar, etc. **2.** to stop up (cracks of window frames, etc.) with a filler —**caulk′er n.**

caus·al (kôz′'l) **adj.** **1.** of, like, or being a cause **2.** relating to cause and effect **3.** expressing a cause or reason —**caus′al·ly adv.**

cau·sal·i·ty (kô zal′ə tē) **n.,** *pl.* **-ties** **1.** causal quality or agency **2.** the interrelation or principle of cause and effect

cau·sa·tion (kô zā′shən) **n.** **1.** the act of causing **2.** causality

caus·a·tive (kôz′ə tiv) **adj.** **1.** producing an effect; causing **2.** expressing causation, as the verb *fell* (to cause to fall) —**n.** a causative word or form —**caus′a·tive·ly adv.**

cause (kôz) **n.** [< OFr. (or) < L. *causa*] **1.** anything producing an effect or result **2.** a person or thing that brings about an effect or result **3.** a reason, motive, or ground for some action, feeling, etc.; esp., sufficient reason [*cause* for complaint] **4.** any objective or movement that a person or group is interested in and supports, esp. one involving social reform **5.** *Law* an action or question to be resolved by a court of law —**vt. caused, caus′ing** to be the cause of; bring about; effect —**make common cause with** to join forces with —**caus′a·ble adj.** —**cause′less adj.**

‡**cause cé·lè·bre** (kōz′sä leb′r′; E. kôz′sə leb′rə) [Fr.] a celebrated law case, trial, or controversy

cau·se·rie (kō′zə rē′) **n.** [Fr. < *causer*, to chat < VL. < L. *causari*, to plead < *causa*, cause] **1.** an informal talk; chat **2.** a short, conversational piece of writing

cause·way (kôz′wā′) **n.** [< Brit. dial. *causey*, ult. < L. *calx*, limestone + WAY] **1.** a raised path or road, as across a marsh **2.** a paved way or road

caus·tic (kôs′tik) **adj.** [< L. < Gr. *kaustikos* < *kaiein*, to burn] **1.** that can burn or destroy tissue by chemical action; corrosive **2.** cutting or sarcastic in utterance —**n.** any caustic substance —**caus′ti·cal·ly adv.** —**caus·tic′i·ty** (-tis′ə tē) **n.**

caustic potash *same as* POTASSIUM HYDROXIDE

caustic soda *same as* SODIUM HYDROXIDE

cau·ter·ize (kôt′ər īz′) **vt.** **-ized, -iz′ing** [< LL. < Gr. < *kautērion*, branding iron < *kaiein*, to burn] to burn with a hot iron or needle, or with a caustic substance, so as to destroy dead tissue, etc. —**cau′ter·i·za′tion n.**

cau·ter·y (kôt′ər ē) **n.,** *pl.* **-ter·ies** **1.** an instrument or substance for cauterizing: also **cau′ter·ant** **2.** the act of cauterizing

cau·tion (kô'shən) *n.* [< L. *cautio* < same base as *cavere*, to take heed] **1.** a warning; admonition, esp. *Law* a warning given to a person suspected of an offence, that his words will be taken down and may be used in evidence **2.** a word, sign, etc. by which warning is given **3.** the act or practice of being cautious; wariness **4.** [Colloq.] a person or thing provoking notice, surprise, etc. *[*he's a proper *caution] —vt.* **1.** to urge to be cautious; warn; admonish **2.** to warn (a person arrested) that he need not speak, but that if he does so, his words may be taken down in writing

cau·tion·ar·y (ər ē) *adj.* urging caution; warning

cau·tious (kô'shəs) *adj.* full of caution; careful to avoid danger; circumspect; wary **—cau'tious·ly** *adv.* **—cau'tious·ness** *n.*

cav·al·cade (kav''l kād', kav''l kād') *n.* [Fr. < It. < *cavalcare*, to ride < VL. < L. *caballus*, horse, nag] **1.** a procession of horsemen or carriages **2.** *a)* any procession *b)* a sequence of events, etc.

cav·a·lier (kav'ə lir') *n.* [Fr. < It. *cavaliere* < LL. < L. *caballus*, horse, nag] **1.** an armed horseman; knight **2.** a gallant gentleman, esp. one serving as a lady's escort **3.** [C-] a partisan of Charles I of England in his struggles with Parliament (1641-49); Royalist **—adj. 1.** [C-] of the Cavaliers **2.** *a)* free and easy; gay *b)* casual or indifferent towards matters of some importance *c)* haughty; arrogant; supercilious **—cav'a·lier'ly** *adv., adj.* **—cav'a·lier'ness** *n.*

cav·al·ry (kav'əl rē) *n., pl.* **-ries** [< Fr. < It. < *cavaliere*: see CAVALIER] combat troops mounted originally on horses but now often on motorized armoured vehicles **—cav'-al·ry·man** (-mən) *n., pl.* **-men**

cave[1] (kāv) *n.* [< OFr. < L. < *cavus*, hollow] a hollow place inside the earth; cavern **—vt. caved, cav'ing** to make a hollow in **—vi. 1.** to cave in **2.** to explore caves **—cave in 1.** to collapse **2.** to make collapse **3.** [Colloq.] to give way; give in; yield **—cav'er** *n.*

ca·ve[2] (kä'vē) *interj.* [L. *cave*, imper. of *cavere*, to beware] watch out! **—keep cave** keep a lookout

ca·ve·at (kä'vē at', kav'ē-) *n.* [L., let him beware] **1.** *Law* a notice that an interested party files with the proper officers directing them to stop an action until he can be heard **2.** a warning

caveat emp·tor (emp'tôr) [L.] let the buyer beware (i.e., one buys at one's own risk)

cave-in (kāv'in') *n.* **1.** a caving in **2.** a place where the ground, a mine, etc. has caved in

cave man 1. a prehistoric human being of the Stone Age who lived in caves: also **cave dweller 2.** a man who is rough and crudely direct, esp. in his approach to women

cav·en·dish (kav'ən dish) *n.* [prob. after proper name] leaf tobacco, sweetened as with treacle, and pressed into plugs or cakes

cav·ern (kav'ərn) *n.* [< Fr. < L. *caverna* < *cavus*, hollow] a cave, esp. a large cave **—vt. 1.** to enclose in or as in a cavern **2.** to hollow (*out*)

cav·ern·ous (kav'ər nəs) *adj.* **1.** full of caverns **2.** full of cavities; porous **3.** like a cavern; deep-set, hollow, etc. **—cav'ern·ous·ly** *adv.*

cav·i·ar, cav·i·are (kav'ē är', kav'ē är') *n.* [Fr. < It. < Turk. < Per. *khāviyār*] the salted eggs of sturgeon, salmon, etc. eaten as an appetizer

cav·il (kav'əl) *vi.* **-illed, -il·ling** [< OFr. < L. *cavillari* < *cavilla*, a jest] to object when there is little reason; resort to trivial faultfinding; carp (*at* or *about*) **—n.** a trivial objection; quibble **—cav'il·er** *n.*

cav·i·ty (kav'ə tē) *n., pl.* **-ties** [< Fr. < LL. *cavitas* < L. *cavus*, hollow] **1.** a hole or hollow place, as in a tooth **2.** a natural hollow place within the body *[*the abdominal *cavity]*

cavity wall a double wall containing an air-space, for insulation or to prevent damp

ca·vort (kə vôrt') *vi.* [< ?] **1.** to leap about; prance or caper **2.** to romp about happily; frolic

ca·vy (kā'vē) *n., pl.* **-vies** [< Carib *cabiai*] any of several short-tailed S. American rodents, as the guinea pig

caw (kô) *n.* [echoic] the harsh, strident cry of a crow or raven **—vi.** to make this sound

cay (kā, kē) *n.* [Sp. *cayo*: see KEY[2]] a low island, coral reef, or sandbank off a mainland

cay·enne (kī en', kā-) *n.* [< Tupi *kynnha*] a very hot red pepper made from the dried fruit of a pepper plant, esp. of the capsicum: also **cayenne pepper**

cay·man (kā'mən) *n., pl.* **-mans** [Sp. < Carib native name] a reptile of Central and South America similar to the alligator

Cb *Chem.* columbium

CBC Canadian Broadcasting Corporation

cc. chapters

cc., c.c. cubic centimeter(s)

C.C., c.c. carbon copy

C clef *Music* a sign on a staff indicating that C is the note on the third line (*alto clef*) or on the fourth line (*tenor clef*)

Cd *Chem.* cadmium

CD, C.D. Civil Defence

cd. cord(s)

cd *Physics the symbol for* candela

Cdr. Commander

Ce *Chem.* cerium

C.E. 1. Church of England **2.** Civil Engineer

cease (sēs) *vt., vi.* **ceased, ceas'ing** [< OFr. < L. *cessare* < *cedere*, to yield] to end; stop; discontinue **—n.** a ceasing: chiefly in **without cease**

cease-fire (sēs'fīr') *n.* a temporary cessation of warfare by mutual agreement of the participants; truce

cease·less (-lis) *adj.* unceasing; continual **—cease'less·ly** *adv.*

ce·cum (sē'kəm) *n., pl.* **-ca** (-kə) [U.S.] *same as* CAECUM **—ce'cal** *adj.*

ce·dar (sē'dər) *n.* [< OFr. < L. < Gr. *kedros*] **1.** any of certain coniferous trees of the pine family, having durable, fragrant wood, as the **cedar of Lebanon 2.** any of various trees like this **3.** the wood of any of these **—adj.** of cedar

cede (sēd) *vt.* **ced'ed, ced'ing** [< Fr. < L. *cedere*, to yield] **1.** to give up one's rights in; surrender **2.** to transfer the title or ownership of **3.** to admit or allow, as an argument

ce·di (sā'dē) *n., pl.* **-dis** [< native word *sedie*, cowrie, formerly used as money] *see* MONETARY UNITS, table (Ghana)

ce·dil·la (si dil'ə) *n.* [< Fr. < Sp. *cedilla*, dim. of *zeda* (< Gr. *zēta*, zeta)] a hooklike mark placed under *c* in some French and Portuguese words (Ex.: *façade*, *ração*) to show the sound of *s* rather than *k*, and other letters in other languages, as Turkish *s*

ceil (sēl) *vt.* [see CEILING] **1.** to build a ceiling in or over **2.** to cover (the ceiling or walls of a room) with plaster or boards

ceil·idh (kā'lē) *n.* [Gael., lit., visit] [Scot. & Ir.] a gathering, usually in a private house, to sing, play music, tell stories, etc.

ceil·ing (sēl'iŋ) *n.* [< ? L. *celare*, to hide + -ING] **1.** the inside top part of a room, opposite the floor **2.** an upper limit set on anything *[*a *ceiling* on prices*]* **3.** *Aeron. a)* a cloud cover limiting vertical visibility, or the height of its lower surface *b)* the maximum height at which an aircraft can normally fly **—hit the ceiling** [Slang] to lose one's temper

cel·an·dine (sel'ən dīn', -dēn') *n.* [< OFr. < L. < Gr. *chelidōn*, a swallow] **1.** a plant related to the poppy, with yellow flowers: also, **greater celandine 2.** a plant of the buttercup family, with yellow flowers: also, **lesser celandine**

-cele (sēl) [< Gr. *kēlē*] **1.** *a combining form meaning* tumour, hernia, or swelling **2.** *same as* -COELE

cel·e·brant (sel'ə brənt) *n.* [see ff.] **1.** a person who performs a religious rite, as the priest officiating at the Eucharist **2.** a celebrator

cel·e·brate (-brāt') *vt.* **-brat'ed, -brat'ing** [< L. pp. of *celebrare*, to frequent, honour < *celeber*, populous] **1.** to perform (a ritual, etc.) publicly and formally; solemnize **2.** to commemorate (an anniversary, etc.) with ceremony or festivity **3.** to honour or praise publicly **4.** to mark (a happy occasion) with a pleasurable activity **—vi. 1.** to observe a holiday, anniversary, etc. with festivities **2.** to perform a religious ceremony **3.** [Colloq.] to have a good time **—cel'e·bra'tor** *n.* **—cel'e·bra'to·ry** *adj.*

cel·e·brat·ed (-id) *adj.* famous; renowned

cel·e·bra·tion (sel'ə brā'shən) *n.* **1.** the act or an instance of celebrating **2.** that which is done to celebrate

ce·leb·ri·ty (sə leb'rə tē) *n.* **1.** wide recognition; fame **2.** *pl.* **-ties** a celebrated person

ce·le·ri·ac (sə ler'ē ak') *n.* [altered < CELERY + -ac, of unknown origin] a variety of celery with an edible, turniplike root

ce·ler·i·ty (sə ler'ə tē) *n.* [< Fr. < L. *celeritas* < *celer*, swift] swiftness in acting or moving

cel·er·y (sel'ər ē) *n.* [Fr. *céleri* < It. < LL. < Gr. *selinon*, parsley] an umbelliferous plant with long, crisp leafstalks eaten as a vegetable

celery salt a seasoning made of celery seed and salt

ce·les·ta (sə les'tə) *n.* [< Fr. < *céleste*, celestial] a small keyboard instrument with hammers that strike metal plates to make bell-like tones

ce·leste (sə lest') *n.* **1.** *same as* CELESTA **2.** an organ-stop with a soft, vibrant quality

ce·les·tial (sə les'chəl) *adj.* [OFr. < L. *caelestis* < *caelum*, heaven] **1.** of the heavens, or sky **2.** *a)* of heaven; divine *[celestial* beings*]* *b)* highest; perfect *[celestial* bliss*]* **—ce·les'tial·ly** *adv.*

celestial equator the great circle of the celestial sphere formed by projecting the plane of the earth's equator on the celestial sphere

celestial sphere an imaginary sphere of infinite diameter containing the whole universe and on which all celestial bodies appear to be projected

ce·li·ac (sē'lē ak') *adj. same as* COELIAC

cel·i·ba·cy (sel'ə bə sē) *n.* [see ff.] **1.** the state of being unmarried, esp. that of one under a vow not to marry **2.** complete sexual abstinence

cel·i·bate (sel'ə bət) *adj.* [< L. *caelebs*, unmarried] of or in a state of celibacy **—n.** a celibate person

cell (sel) *n.* [< OFr. *celle* < L. *cella*] 1. a small room or cubicle, as in a convent or prison 2. a very small hollow, cavity, or enclosed space, as in a honeycomb, or in a plant ovary 3. any of the smallest organizational units of a group or movement, as of a Communist party 4. *Biol.* a small unit of protoplasm, usually with a nucleus, cytoplasm, and an enclosing membrane : all plants and animals are made up of one or more cells 5. *Elec.* a receptacle used either for generating electricity by chemical reactions or for decomposing compounds by electrolysis —**celled** *adj.*

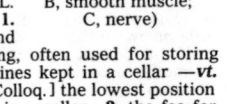

CELLS
(A, epithelial;
B, smooth muscle;
C, nerve)

cel·lar (sel'ər) *n.* [< OFr. < L. *cellarium* < *cella*, small room] 1. a room or rooms below ground level and usually under a building, often used for storing fuel, wines, etc. 2. a stock of wines kept in a cellar —*vt.* to store in a cellar —**the cellar** [Colloq.] the lowest position
cel·lar·age (-ij) *n.* 1. space of or in a cellar 2. the fee for storage in a cellar
cel·lar·er (-ar) *n.* a person in charge of a cellar or provisions, as in a monastery
cel·lar·et (sel'ə ret') *n.* [CELLAR + -ET] a cabinet for bottles of wine
cel·lo (chel'ō) *n., pl.* **-los, -li** (-ē) [< VIOLONCELLO] an instrument of the violin family, between the viola and double bass in size and pitch; violoncello also sp. **'cel'lo** —**cel'list** *n.*
cel·lo·phane (sel'ə fān') *n.* [< CELLULOSE + Gr. *phainein*, appear] a thin, transparent material made from cellulose, used as moistureproof wrapping for foods, etc.
cel·lu·lar (sel'yoo lar) *adj.* of, like, or containing a cell or cells —**cel'lu·lar'i·ty** (-lar'ə tē) *n.*
cel·lule (sel'yōōl) *n.* [L. *cellula*, dim of *cella*, CELL] a very small cell
cel·lu·lite (sel'yoo līt') *n.* [CELLUL(E) + -ITE] permanent deposits of subcutaneous fat
Cel·lu·loid (sel'yoo loid') [CELLUL(OSE) + -OID] *a trademark for* a flammable substance made from pyroxylin and camphor, used for toilet articles, etc. and, formerly, for photographic films —*n.* [**c-**] this substance
cel·lu·lose (sel'yoo lōs') *n.* [Fr.: see CELLULE & -OSE[1]] the chief substance composing the cell walls or fibres of all plant tissue: used in the manufacture of paper, textiles, explosives, etc. —**cel'lu·los'ic** (-lō'sik) *adj., n.*
cellulose acetate a cellulose resin used in making acetate fibre, plastics, lacquers, etc.
Cel·si·us (sel'sē əs) *adj.* [after A. *Celsius* (1701–44), Swed. astronomer] designating or of a thermometer on which 0° is the freezing point and 100° is the boiling point of water; centigrade: abbrev. **C**
Celt (kelt, selt) *n.* [< Fr. < L. *Celta*, pl. *Celtae* (Gr. *Keltoi*), the Gauls] 1. a person who speaks a Celtic language : the Bretons, Irish, Welsh, and Highland Scots are Celts 2. an ancient Gaul or Briton
celt (selt) *n.* [ML. *celtis* < LL. hyp. *celtis* inferred < Vulgate *vel celte sculpantur in silice* (Job 19:24); prob. ghost word (*certe* in other mss.) adopted as genuine by archeologists] a prehistoric tool of stone or metal, resembling a chisel or axe head
Cel·tic (kel'tik, sel'-) *adj.* of the Celts, their languages, culture, etc. —*n.* an Indo-European subfamily of languages with a Goidelic branch (Irish Gaelic, Scottish Gaelic, Manx) in Ireland, the Scottish Highlands, and the Isle of Man, and a Brythonic branch (Welsh, Breton, and Cornish) in Wales, Brittany, and esp. formerly, Cornwall
Celtic cross a cross having a wheellike circle around the intersection of the limbs
Celtic fringe a name sometimes used to refer to the Highlands of Scotland, Wales, Cornwall, and Ireland as distinct from the rest of Britain
ce·ment (si ment') *n.* [< OFr. < L. *caementum*, rough stone < *caedere*, to cut] 1. a powdered substance made of burned lime and clay, mixed with water and sand to make mortar or with water, sand, and gravel to make concrete: the mixture hardens like stone when it dries 2. any soft substance that fastens things together firmly when it hardens, as glue 3. a cementlike substance used in dentistry as to fill cavities 4. anything that joins together or unites; bond 5. *same as* CEMENTUM —*vt.* 1. to join or unite as with cement 2. to cover with cement —*vi.* to become cemented —**ce·men·ta·tion** (sē'men tā'shən) *n.* —**ce·ment'er** *n.* —**ce·ment'like**' *adj.*
ce·men·tum (si men'təm) *n.* [< L.: see prec.] the hard, bony outer tissue of the root of a tooth
cem·e·ter·y (sem'ə tər ē, trē) *n., pl.* **-ter·ies** [< LL. < Gr. *koimētērion* < *koiman*, to put to sleep] a place for the burial of the dead, esp. one not attached to a church

cen·o·bite (sen'ə bīt', sē'nə-) *n. same as* COENOBITE
cen·o·taph (sen'ə taf') *n.* [< Fr. < L. < Gr. < *kenos*, empty + *taphos*, a tomb] a monument honouring a dead person whose body is somewhere else —**the Cenotaph** a monument in Whitehall, London, commemorating the dead of World War I and World War II
Ce·no·zo·ic (sē'nə zō'ik, sen'ə-) *adj. U.S. sp. of* CAINOZOIC
cen·ser (sen'sər) *n.* [< OFr. < *encens*: see INCENSE[1]] a container in which incense is burned
cen·sor (sen'sər) *n.* [L. < *censere*, to tax, value] 1. one of two Roman magistrates appointed to take the census and, later, to supervise public morals 2. an official with the power to examine publications, films, mail, etc. and to remove or prohibit anything considered obscene, objectionable, etc. —*vt.* to subject (a book, letter, writer, etc.) to censorship —**cen·so'ri·al** (sen sôr'ē əl) *adj.*
cen·so·ri·ous (sen sôr'ē əs) *adj.* [see prec.] inclined to find fault; harshly critical —**cen·so'ri·ous·ly** *adv.* —**cen·so'ri·ous·ness** *n.*
cen·sor·ship (sen'sər ship') *n.* 1. the act or a system of censoring 2. the work or position of a censor
cen·sure (sen'shər) *n.* [L. *censura* < *censor*, CENSOR] 1. a condemning as wrong; strong disapproval 2. an official expression of disapproval, specif. as passed by a legislature —*vt.* **-sured, -sur·ing** to express strong disapproval of; condemn as wrong —**cen'sur·a·ble** *adj.* —**cen'sur·a·bly** *adv.* —**cen'sur·er** *n.*
cen·sus (sen'səs) *n.* [L., orig. pp. of *censere*: see CENSOR] 1. in ancient Rome, a count of the people and evaluation of their property for taxation 2. an official, usually periodic, count of population and recording of economic status, age, sex, etc.
cent (sent) *n.* [< OFr. < L. *centum*, a hundred] 1. a 100th part of a dollar, or a coin of this value: symbol, ¢ 2. a 100th part of a rupee, piastre, etc.: see MONETARY UNITS, table
cent. 1. centigrade 2. centimetre 3. central 4. century
cen·tare (sen'ter, -tär) *n. same as* CENTIARE
cen·taur (sen'tôr) *n.* [< L. < Gr. *Kentauros*] *Gr. Myth.* any of a race of monsters with a man's head, trunk, and arms, and a horse's body and legs
cen·tau·ry (sen'tôr ē) *n., pl.* **-ries** [< ML. *centauria* < L. *centaureum* < Gr. *kentaureion* < *Kentauros*, centaur: the centaur Chiron was said to have discovered the medicinal properties of the plant] any of a genus of small plants of the gentian family, with flat clusters of red and rose flowers
cen·ta·vo (sen tä'vō) *n., pl.* **-vos** [Sp. < L. *centum*, a hundred] a unit of currency equal to 1/100 of a peso in Mexico, the Philippines, etc. and to 1/100 of a Brazilian cruzeiro, a Portuguese escudo, etc.: see MONETARY UNITS, table
cen·te·nar·i·an (sen'tə ner'ē ən) *adj.* 1. of 100 years; of a centenary 2. of a centenarian —*n.* a person at least 100 years old
cen·te·nar·y (sen tēn'ər ē) *adj.* [< L. < *centum*, a hundred] 1. of a century, or period of 100 years 2. of a centennial —*n., pl.* **-nar·ies** 1. a century; period of 100 years 2. *same as* CENTENNIAL
cen·te·nier (sen'tə nir') *n.* [Fr. < L. *centenarius* < *centeni*, a hundred each < *centum*, a hundred] a policeman on Jersey
cen·ten·ni·al (sen ten'ē əl) *adj.* [< L. *centum*, a hundred + *annus*, year + -AL] 1. of 100 years 2. happening once in 100 years 3. 100 years old 4. of a 100th anniversary —*n.* a 100th anniversary or its celebration —**cen·ten'ni·al·ly** *adv.*
cen·ter (sen'tər) *n. U.S. sp. of* CENTRE
cen·tes·i·mal (sen tes'ə məl) *adj.* [< L. *centesimus* < *centum*, a hundred] 1. hundredth 2. of or divided into hundredths —**cen·tes'i·mal·ly** *adv.*
cen·tes·i·mo (sen tes'ə mō'; *Sp.* -ē mō'; *It.* chen te'sē mō') *n., pl.* **-mos'** (-mōz'; *Sp.* -môs'; *It.* -mi' (-mē') [It. & Sp. < L.: see prec.] a unit of currency equal to 1/100th of an Italian lira, a Uruguayan peso, etc.: see MONETARY UNITS, table
centi- [L. < *centum*] a combining form meaning: 1. hundred or hundredfold 2. a 100th part of
cen·ti·are (sen'tē er', -är') *n.* [Fr.: see CENTI- & ARE[2]] a 100th part of an are (unit of land measure)
cen·ti·grade (sen'tə grād') *adj.* [Fr. < L. *centum*, a hundred + *gradus*, a degree] 1. consisting of or divided into 100 degrees 2. *same as* CELSIUS: the preferred term until the international adoption of *Celsius* in 1948
cen·ti·gramme, cen·ti·gram (-gram') *n.* [Fr.: see CENTI- & GRAMME] a unit of weight, equal to 1/100 gramme: abbrev. **cg**
cen·ti·li·tre (sen'tə lēt'ər) *n.* [Fr.: see CENTI- & LITRE] a unit of capacity, equal to 1/100 litre: abbrev. **cl**
cen·time (sän'tēm; *Fr.* sän tēm') *n.* [Fr. < L.: see CENTESIMAL] the 100th part of a franc, an Algerian dinar, etc.: see MONETARY UNITS, table
cen·ti·me·tre (sen'tə mēt'ər) *n.* [< Fr.: see CENTI- & METRE] a unit of measure, equal to 1/100 metre: abbrev. **cm**
cen·ti·me·tre-gramme-sec·ond (-gram'sek'ənd) *adj.* designating or of a system of measurement in which the

centimetre, gramme, and second are used as the units of length, mass, and time, respectively

cen·ti·mo (sen'tə mō') *n., pl.* **-mos'** [see CENTIME] the 100th part of a Spanish peseta, a Venezuelan bolívar, etc.: see MONETARY UNITS, table

cen·ti·pede (sen'tə pēd') *n.* [Fr. < L. < *centum*, a hundred + *pes* (gen. *pedis*), a foot] a many-segmented arthropod with a pair of legs to each segment

cen·to (sen'tō) *n., pl.* **-tos** [L., patchwork garment] a literary or musical composition made up of passages from other compositions

CENTO (sen'tō) Central Treaty Organization

cen·tral (sen'trəl) *adj.* [L. *centralis*] 1. in, at, or near the centre 2. of or forming the centre 3. equally distant or accessible from various points 4. main; basic; principal 5. of or having to do with a single source that controls all activity in an organization or system 6. designating or of that part of the nervous system consisting of the brain and spinal cord (of a vertebrate) —**cen·tral'i·ty** (-tral'ə tē) *n.* —**cen'tral·ly** *adv.*

Central America part of N. America between Mexico and S. America —**Central American**

central bank a national bank that controls credit, issues banknotes, and acts as the government's banker

central heating a form of heating for buildings in which a central heat source is linked to radiators or air ducts in each room

cen·tral·ism (-iz'm) *n.* the principle or system of centralizing power or authority —**cen'tral·ist** *adj., n.* -**cen'tral·is'tic** *adj.*

cen·tral·ize (sen'trə līz') *vt.* **-ized', -iz'ing** 1. to make central; bring to or focus on a centre; gather together 2. to organize under one control —*vi.* to become centralized —**cen'tral·i·za'tion** *n.* —**cen'tral·iz'er** *n.*

central reservation the strip of land that separates the two sides of a motorway or dual carriageway

cen·tre (sen'tər) *n.* [< OFr. < L. *centrum* < Gr. *kentron*, sharp point] 1. a point equally distant from all points on the circumference of a circle or surface of a sphere 2. the point around which anything revolves; pivot 3. a place at which an activity or complex of activities is carried on [a shopping *centre*], from which ideas, influences, etc. emanate [Paris, the fashion *centre*], or to which many people are attracted [a *centre* of interest] 4. the approximate middle point, place, or part of anything 5. a group of nerve cells regulating a particular function 6. in some sports, a player near the centre of the line or playing area, who often puts the ball or puck into play 7. *Mil.* that part of an army between the flanks 8. [often C-] *Politics* a position or party between the left and right —*vt.* 1. to place in, at, or near the centre 2. to draw or gather to one place 3. to furnish with a centre —*vi.* 1. to be centred; be concentrated or focussed 2. *Football* to pass the ball from the wing to the centre of the field

cen·tre·board (-bôrd') *n.* a movable, keellike board that is lowered through a slot in the floor of a sailing boat to prevent drifting to leeward

cen·tre·fold (-fōld') *n.* the central facing pages of a magazine, often with one or more extra folds, devoted to a photograph or other graphic display

cen·tre·for·ward (-fôr'wərd) *n.* the central position in the forward line of a football team, etc.

cen·tre·half (-häf) *n.* the central position in the half-back line of a football team etc.

centre of gravity that point in a body or system around which its weight is evenly distributed or balanced and may be assumed to act

cen·tre·piece (sen'tər pēs') *n.* 1. an ornament, bowl of flowers, etc. for the centre of a table 2. the most important item, as in a display

centre spread 1. the middle pages of a newspaper, magazine, etc. 2. same as CENTREFOLD

cen·tri- same as CENTRO-

cen·tric (sen'trik) *adj.* 1. in, at, or near the centre; central 2. of or having a centre 3. of or originating from a nerve centre Also **cen'tri·cal** —**cen'tri·cal·ly** *adv.* —**cen·tric'i·ty** (-tris'ə tē) *n.*

-cen·tric (sen'trik) a combining form meaning: 1. having a centre or centres (of a specified kind or number) [polycentric] 2. having (a specified thing) as its centre [geocentric]

cen·trif·u·gal (sen trif'yə gəl, sen'tri fyōō'gəl) *adj.* [< ModL. < CENTRI- + L. *fugere*, to flee + -AL] 1. moving or tending to move away from a centre 2. using or acted on by centrifugal force —*n.* a centrifuge —**cen·trif'u·gal·ly** *adv.*

centrifugal force the force tending to pull a thing outwards when it is rotating rapidly around a centre

cen·trif·u·gal·ize (-iz') *vt.* **-ized', -iz'ing** to subject to or as to the action of a centrifuge —**cen·trif'u·gal·i·za'tion** *n.*

cen·tri·fuge (sen'trə fyōōj') *n.* a machine using centrifugal force to separate particles of varying density, as cream from milk, or to subject human beings, animals, etc. to high

acceleration —*vt.* **-fuged', -fug'ing** to subject to the action of a centrifuge

cen·tring (sen'triŋ) *n.* a temporary frame to support an arch or vault during construction

cen·trip·e·tal (sen trip'ət 'l, sen'tri pēt''l) *adj.* [< ModL. < CENTRI- + L. *petere*, to seek + -AL] 1. moving or tending to move towards a centre 2. using or acted on by centripetal force —**cen·trip'e·tal·ly** *adv.*

centripetal force the force tending to pull a thing inwards when it is rotating rapidly around a centre

cen·trist (sen'trist) *n.* a member of a political party of the centre

cen·tro- [< L. *centrum*, CENTRE] a combining form meaning centre

cen·tro·some (sen'trə sōm') *n.* [CENTRO- + -SOME³] a very small body near the nucleus in most animal cells: it divides in mitosis —**cen'tro·som'ic** (-som'ik, -sōm'-) *adj.*

cen·tu·ple (sen'tyōōp 'l) *adj.* [Fr. < LL. *centuplus* < L. *centuplex*, hundredfold < *centum*, hundred + -*plex* (< *plicare*, fold)] a hundred times as much or as many; hundredfold —*n.* a hundredfold amount —*vt.* **-pled, -pling** to multiply by a hundred

cen·tu·ri·on (sen tyoor'ē ən) *n.* [< L. *centuria*: see ff.] the commanding officer of a Roman century

cen·tu·ry (sen'chər ē, -tyoo rē) *n., pl.* **-ries** [L. *centuria* < *centum*, a hundred] 1. any period of 100 years, esp. as reckoned from the beginning of the Christian Era 2. in ancient Rome *a)* a military unit, originally made up of 100 men *b)* a subdivision of the people made for voting purposes 3. *Sports* a score of 100, esp. 100 runs in cricket —**cen·tu·ri·al** (sen tyoor'ē əl) *adj.*

cep (sep) *n.* [< Fr. *cèpe*, boletus < Gascon dial. *cep*, treetrunk < L. *cippus*, stake] a brown edible fungus with a rich flavour

ce·phal·ic (sə fal'ik) *adj.* [< L. < Gr. < *kephalē*, the head] 1. of the head, skull, or cranium 2. in, on, near, or towards the head —**ce·phal'i·cal·ly** *adv.*

-ce·phal·ic (sə fal'ik) a combining form meaning head or skull [dolichocephalic]

cephalic index a measure of the human head computed by dividing its maximum breadth by its maximum length and multiplying by 100

ceph·a·lo- [see CEPHALIC] a combining form meaning the head, skull, or brain: also, before a vowel, **cephal-**

ceph·a·lo·pod (sef'ə lə pod') *n.* [prec. + -POD] any of a class of molluscs having a distinct head with a beak, and muscular tentacles about the mouth, as the octopus, squid, and cuttlefish

ceph·a·lo·tho·rax (sef'ə lə thôr'aks) *n.* the head and thorax united as a single part, in certain crustaceans and arachnids

-ceph·a·lous (sef'əl əs) [see CEPHALIC] a combining form meaning -headed [microcephalous]

ceph·e·id variable (sef'ē id, sē'fē id) [after *Delta Cephei*, a star in the N constellation *Cepheus* + -ID] any of a class of stars whose light varies in brightness in regular periods

ce·ram·ic (sə ram'ik) *adj.* [< Gr. *keramos*, clay, pottery] 1. of pottery, earthenware, tile, porcelain, etc. 2. of ceramics —*n.* 1. [pl., with sing. v.] the art or work of making objects of baked clay 2. such an object —**ce·ram·ist** (sə ram'ist, ser'ə mist), **ce·ram'i·cist** (-ə sist) *n.*

cere (sir) *n.* [< Fr. < L. < Gr. *kēros*, wax] a waxy, fleshy area at the base of the beak of some birds, as the parrot, eagle, etc. —*vt.* **cered, cer'ing** to wrap in a cerecloth

ce·re·al (sir'ē əl) *adj.* [< L. *Cerealis*, of Ceres] of grain or the grasses producing grain —*n.* 1. any grain used for food, as wheat, oats, etc. 2. any grass producing such grain 3. food made from grain, esp. breakfast food, as porridge

cer·e·bel·lum (ser'ə bel'əm) *n., pl.* **-lums, -la** (-ə) [L., dim. of *cerebrum*, the brain] the section of the brain behind and below the cerebrum: it is the coordinating centre for muscular movement

cer·e·bral (ser'ə brəl, sə rē'-) *adj.* of the brain or the cerebrum —**cer·e'bral·ly** *adv.*

cerebral palsy any of several disorders of the central nervous system resulting from brain damage and characterized by spastic paralysis

cer·e·brate (ser'ə brāt') *vi.* **-brat'ed, -brat'ing** [< L. *cerebrum* (see CEREBELLUM) + -ATE¹] to use one's brain; think —**cer'e·bra'tion** *n.*

cer·e·bro- [< L. *cerebrum*, the brain] a combining form meaning the brain (and); cerebrum (and)

cer·e·bro·spi·nal (ser'ə brō spī'n'l, sə rē'brō-) *adj.* of or affecting the brain and the spinal cord

cer·e·brum (ser'ə brəm, sə rē'-) *n., pl.* **-brums, -bra** (-brə) [L.: see CEREBELLUM] the upper, main part of the brain of vertebrate animals, consisting of two equal hemispheres and, in man, controlling conscious and voluntary processes

cere·cloth (sir'klôth') *n.* [< *cered cloth*: see CERE] cloth treated with wax or a similar substance, formerly used to wrap a dead person for burial

cere·ment (sir′mənt) *n.* [see CERE] 1. a cerecloth; shroud 2. [*usually pl.*] any burial clothes

cer·e·mo·ni·al (ser′ə mō′nē əl, -nyəl) *adj.* of, for, or consisting of ceremony; ritual; formal —*n.* 1. an established system of rites or formal actions connected with an occasion; ritual 2. a rite or ceremony 3. *Eccles.* a book detailing a prescribed set or order of rites —**cer′e·mo′-ni·al·ism** *n.* —**cer′e·mo′ni·al·ist** *n.* —**cer′e·mo′ni·al·ly** *adv.*

cer·e·mo·ni·ous (-nē əs, -nyəs) *adj.* 1. ceremonial 2. full of ceremony 3. characterized by conventional usages or formality 4. especially or excessively polite or formal —**cer′e·mo′ni·ous·ly** *adv.* —**cer′e·mo′ni·ous·ness** *n.*

cer·e·mo·ny (ser′ə mə nē) *n., pl.* **-nies** [L. *caerimonia*] 1. a formal act or set of formal acts established as proper to a special occasion, such as a wedding, religious rite, etc. 2. a conventionally courteous act 3. behaviour that follows rigid etiquette 4. formality or formalities 5. empty or meaningless formality —**stand on ceremony** to behave with or insist on formality

ce·rise (sə rēs′, -rēz′) *n., adj.* [Fr.: see CHERRY] bright red; cherry red

ce·ri·um (sir′ē əm) *n.* [after the asteroid *Ceres*] a grey, metallic chemical element: symbol, Ce; at. wt., 140.12; at. no., 58

cer·met (sur′met) *n.* [CER(AMIC) + MET(AL)] a bonded mixture of ceramic material and a metal, that is tough and heat-resistant: used in gas turbines, nuclear reactor mechanisms, rocket motors, etc.

CERN *C(entre) E(uropéen pour la) R(echerche) N(ucléaire)* a co-operative European nuclear research organization centred in Geneva, Switzerland

ce·ro- [< L. < Gr. *kēros*, wax] a combining form meaning wax

ce·rog·ra·phy (sir og′rə fē) *n.* [CERO- + -GRAPHY] the process of engraving on a wax-covered metal plate from which a printing surface is prepared by electrotyping

ce·ro·plas·tic (sir′ə plas′tik) *adj.* [< Gr. < *kēros*, wax + *plassein*, to mould] 1. having to do with wax modelling 2. modelled in wax

cert (surt) *n.* [Slang] a clipped form of CERTAINTY —**a dead cert** something certain to happen, succeed, etc.

cert. 1. certificate 2. certified

cer·tain (surt′n) *adj.* [< OFr. < L. *certus*, determined < *cernere*, to decide] 1. fixed, settled, or determined 2. inevitable 3. not to be doubted [the evidence is *certain*] 4. reliable; dependable [a *certain* cure] 5. controlled; unerring [his *certain* aim] 6. convinced; positive [I'm *certain* he's here] 7. not named or described, though definite [a *certain* person] 8. some, but not very much; appreciable [to a *certain* extent] —**for certain** without doubt

cer·tain·ly (-lē) *adv.* beyond a doubt; surely

cer·tain·ty (-tē) *n.* 1. the quality, state, or fact of being certain 2. *pl.* **-ties** anything certain; definite fact

cer·tes (sur′tēz) *adv.* [< OFr. < L. *certus*, CERTAIN] [Archaic] certainly; verily

cer·tif·i·cate (sur tif′ə kit; *for v.* -kāt′) *n.* [< OFr. < ML. < LL. pp. of *certificare*, CERTIFY] a written or printed statement testifying to a fact, qualification, ownership, etc. —*vt.* **-cat′ed, -cat′ing** to attest by a certificate; issue a certificate to —**cer·tif′i·ca′tor** *n.* —**cer·tif′i·ca·to·ry** (-kə tər ē, trē) *adj.*

Certificate of Secondary Education an examination taken in secondary schools, usually at the age of 16, and of a lower standard than the GENERAL CERTIFICATE OF EDUCATION

cer·ti·fi·ca·tion (sur′tə fi kā′shən) *n.* 1. a certifying or being certified 2. a certified statement

cer·ti·fied (sur′tə fīd′) *adj.* 1. vouched for; guaranteed 2. having or attested to by, a certificate 3. formerly, officially declared insane

certified cheque a cheque certified by a bank as genuine, on which it guarantees payment

cer·ti·fy (sur′tə fī′) *vt.* **-fied′, -fy′ing** [< OFr. < LL. *certificare* < L. *certus*, CERTAIN + *facere*, to make] 1. to declare (a thing) true, accurate, certain, etc. by formal statement; verify 2. formerly, to declare officially insane 3. to guarantee; vouch for 4. to issue a certificate to 5. [Archaic] to assure; make certain —*vi.* to testify (*to*) —**cer′ti·fi′a·ble** *adj.* —**cer′ti·fi′a·bly** *adv.* —**cer′ti·fi′er** *n.*

cer·ti·o·ra·ri (sur′shē ə rer′ē, sur′tē ə rār′ē) *n.* [LL., to be made more certain] *Law* a writ from a higher court to a lower one, or to a board or official with judicial power, requesting the record of a case for review

cer·ti·tude (sur′tə tyood′) *n.* [< OFr. < LL. *certitudo*] 1. a feeling absolutely sure 2. inevitability

ce·ru·le·an (sə roo′lē ən) *adj.* [< L., prob. < *caelum*, heaven] sky-blue; azure

ce·ru·men (sə roo′mən) *n.* [< L. *cera*, wax, after ALBUMEN] *same as* EARWAX —**ce·ru′min·ous** *adj.*

cer·ve·lat (sur və lät′) *n.* [OFr. < It. *cervellata*] a type of smoked sausage, of pork and sometimes beef

cer·vi·cal (sur′vi kəl) *adj.* of the neck or cervix

cer·vine (sur′vīn) *adj.* [L. *cervinus* < *cervus*, deer] of or like a deer

cer·vix (sur′viks) *n., pl.* **-vi·ces′** (sur′və sēz′, sər vī′-), **-vix·es** [L., the neck] 1. the neck, esp. the back of the neck 2. a necklike part, esp. of the uterus

ce·si·um (sē′zē əm) *U.S. spelling of* CAESIUM

cess (ses) *n.* [prob. < ASSESS] [Archaic] an assessment; tax —**bad cess to** [Ir.] bad luck to

ces·sa·tion (se sā′shən) *n.* [< L. < pp. of *cessare*, CEASE] a ceasing, either final or temporary; stop

ces·sion (sesh′ən) *n.* [OFr. < L. < pp. of *cedere*, to yield] a ceding or giving up (of rights, territory, etc.) to another

ces·sion·ar·y (sesh′ə nər ē) *n., pl.* **-ar·ies** *Law* same as ASSIGNEE

cess·pit (ses′pit′) *n.* [back formation from ff. + PIT²] same as CESSPOOL

cess·pool (ses′pool′) *n.* [< OF. *souspirail*, air vent, altered after POOL¹] 1. a tank or deep hole in the ground to receive drainage or sewage from the sinks, toilets, etc. of a house 2. a centre of moral filth and corruption

ces·toid (ses′toid) *adj.* [< L. *cestus* < Gr. *kestos*, a girdle] ribbonlike, as a tapeworm

ces·tus (ses′təs) *n.* [L. *caestus* < *caedere*, to strike] a device of leather straps, sometimes weighted with metal, worn on the hand by boxers in ancient Rome

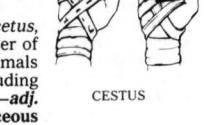

CESTUS

ce·su·ra (si zhoor′ə, -zyoor′ə) *n., pl.* **-ras, -rae** (-ē) *same as* CAESURA

ce·ta·cean (si tā′shən) *n.* [L. *cetus*, whale < Gr. *kētos*] any of an order of nearly hairless, fishlike water mammals with paddlelike forelimbs, including whales, porpoises, and dolphins —*adj.* of the cetaceans: also **ce·ta′ceous** (-shəs)

ce·tane (sē′tān) *n.* [< L. *cetus*, whale + -ANE] a saturated hydrocarbon of the methane family, found as a colourless oil in petroleum

cetane number a number representing the ignition properties of diesel engine fuel oils: the higher the number, the better the ignition quality

Cf *Chem.* californium

cf. [L. *confer*] compare

cg centigram(me)(s)

cgs, c.g.s., C.G.S. centimetre-gramme-second

Ch. 1. Chaldean 2. China 3. Chinese

Ch., ch. 1. chain 2. champion 3. chapter 4. child; children 5. church

cha (chä) *n.* [< Hindi *cā* < Chin. *ch'a*] [Slang] tea

Cha·blis (shab′lē; *Fr.* shà blē′) *n.* a dry, white wine from the region of Chablis, in Burgundy

cha-cha (chä′chä) *n.* [AmSp., of echoic orig.] a ballroom dance of Latin American origin, with a recurrent triple beat Also **cha′-cha′-cha′**

cha·conne (shä kon′) *n.* [Fr. < Sp. *chacona*] 1. a slow, stately dance of 17th- and 18th-cent. Europe 2. a musical form developed from the music for this dance; specif., *a)* a series of variations based on a short harmonic progression *b)* an expanded rondo form

chafe (chāf) *vt.* **chafed, chaf′ing** [< OFr. *chaufer*, to warm < L. < *calere*, to be warm + *facere*, to make] 1. to rub so as to make warm 2. to wear away by rubbing 3. to make sore by rubbing 4. to annoy; irritate —*vi.* 1. to rub (*on* or *against*) 2. to be or become irritated or impatient —*n.* an injury or irritation caused by rubbing —**chafe at the bit** to be impatient

chaf·er (chāf′ər) *n.* [OE. *ceafor*] any of various large, heavy beetles

chaff (chäf) *n.* [OE. *ceaf*] 1. threshed or winnowed husks of wheat or other grain 2. anything worthless 3. good-natured teasing; banter 4. strips of metal foil released in the air to deflect radar signals —*vt., vi.* to tease or ridicule in a good-natured way —**chaff′y** *adj.* **chaff′i·er**, **chaff′i·est**

chaf·fer (chaf′ər) *vi.* [< OE. *ceapfaru* < *ceap*, a purchase + *faru*, a journey] [Now Rare] to haggle over price; bargain —**chaf′fer·er** *n.*

chaf·finch (chaf′finch′) *n.* [OE. *ceaffinc*: see CHAFF + FINCH: it eats chaff] a small European songbird, with black and white wings: the male has a reddish body and blue-grey head

chaf·ing dish (chāf′iŋ) [see CHAFE] a pan with a heating apparatus beneath it, to cook food at the table or to keep food hot

cha·grin (sha′grin, shə grēn′) *n.* [Fr., grief, prob. < OFr. *graignier*, to sorrow < Gmc. *gram*, sorrow] a feeling of embarrassment and distress caused by failure or disappointment —*vt.* **-grined′, -grin′ing** to cause to feel chagrin

chain (chān) *n.* [OFr. *chaine* < L. *catena*, a chain] 1. a flexible series of joined links, usually of metal 2. [*pl.*] *a)* bonds, fetters, etc. *b)* captivity; bondage 3. a chainlike measuring instrument, or its measure of length: a *surveyor's chain* is 66 feet (20.12m); an *engineer's chain* is 100 feet (30.48m) **4.** a connected series of things or events **5.** a number of stores, restaurants, etc. owned by one company **6.** *Chem.* a linear bonding of atoms in a molecule **7.** *Geog.* a series of mountains or parallel mountain ranges —*vt.* **1.** to fasten or shackle with chains **2.** to hold down, restrain, confine, etc.

chain gang a gang of prisoners chained together, as when working

chain letter a letter to be circulated among many people by being copied and passed to others

chain mail flexible armour made of metal links

chain-re·act (-rē akt′) *vi.* to be involved in or subjected to a chain reaction

chain reaction 1. a self-sustaining series of chemical or nuclear reactions in which the products of the reaction contribute directly to the propagation of the process **2.** any sequence of events, each of which results in the following

chain saw a portable power saw with an endless chain that carries cutting teeth

chain-smoke (-smōk′) *vt., vi.* **-smoked′, -smok′ing** to smoke (cigarettes) one straight after the other —**chain smoker, chain′-smok′er** *n.*

chain stitch a fancy stitch in which the loops are connected in a chainlike way, as in crocheting —**chain′-stitch′** *vt.*

chain store any of a chain of retail shops

chair (cher) *n.* [OFr. *chaiere* < Ł. *cathedra*: see CATHEDRA] **1.** a piece of furniture for one person to sit on, having a back and, usually, four legs **2.** a seat of authority or dignity **3.** an important or official position, as a full professorship **4.** a person who presides over a meeting; chairman **5.** *same as:* a) SEDAN CHAIR b) ELECTRIC CHAIR —*vt.* **1.** to place in a chair; seat **2.** to place in authority **3.** to preside over as chairman **4.** to carry aloft in, or as in a chair, as a mark of respect [the candidate was *chaired* from the hall] —**take the chair** to preside as chairman

chair-lift (-lift′) *n.* a line of seats suspended from a power-driven endless cable, used esp. to carry skiers up a mountain slope

chair·man (-mən) *n., pl.* **-men** a person who presides at a meeting or heads a committee, board, etc. Also, **chair′per′son** —**chair′man·ship′** *n.* —**chair′wom′an** *n.fem., pl.* **-wom′en**

chaise (shāz) *n.* [Fr., var. of *chaire*, CHAIR] **1.** any of certain lightweight carriages, some with a collapsible top, having two or four wheels **2.** *same as* CHAISE LONGUE

chaise longue (shāz′lon′) *pl.* **chaise** (or **chaises**) **longues** (shāz′lonz′) [Fr., lit., long chair] a couchlike chair with a support for the back and a seat long enough to support the outstretched legs

cha·la·za (kə lā′zə) *n., pl.* **-zae** (-zē), **-zas** [ModL. < Gr. *chalaza*, hailstone] either of the spiral bands of dense albumen extending from the yolk towards the lining membrane at each end of a bird's egg

chal·ced·o·ny (kal sed′ən ē, kal′sə dō′nē) *n., pl.* **-nies** [< OFr. < LL. < Gr. *chalkēdōn*, a precious stone < ?] a kind of quartz with the lustre of wax, variously coloured

chal·dron (chôl′drən) *n.* [ME. < OFr. *chaudron*: see CAULDRON] an old unit of dry measure equal to 36 bushels (1.309 m³)

cha·let (shal′ā) *n.* [Swiss-Fr.] **1.** a herdsman's hut or cabin in the Swiss Alps **2.** a) a type of Swiss house, with balconies and overhanging eaves b) any building in this style **3.** a hut or cabin in a holiday camp

chal·ice (chal′is) *n.* [OFr. < L. *calix*, a cup] **1.** a cup; goblet **2.** the cup for the wine of Holy Communion **3.** a cup-shaped flower —**chal′iced** *adj.*

chalk (chôk) *n.* [OE. *cealc* < L. *calx*, limestone] **1.** a white or whitish limestone that is soft and easily pulverized, composed mainly of minute seashells **2.** any substance like chalk **3.** a piece of chalk, often coloured, used for writing on a blackboard, etc. —*adj.* made or drawn with chalk —*vt.* **1.** to rub or smear with chalk **2.** to make pale **3.** to write, draw, or mark with chalk —*vi.* to become chalky or powdery —**as different as chalk from cheese** totally different —**by a long chalk** by a long way —**chalk out 1.** to mark out as with chalk **2.** to outline; plan —**chalk up 1.** to score, get, or achieve **2.** to charge or credit —**chalk′-i·ness** *n.* —**chalk′y** *adj.* **chalk′i·er, chalk′i·est**

chal·lenge (chal′ənj) *n.* [< OFr. < L. *calumnia*, CALUMNY] **1.** a demand for identification [a sentry gave the *challenge*] **2.** a calling into question [a *challenge* to an assertion] **3.** a call or dare to take part in a duel, contest, etc. **4.** anything that calls for special effort or dedication **5.** *Law* a formal objection or exception to a person chosen as a prospective juror —*vt.* **-lenged, -leng·ing 1.** to call to a halt for identification **2.** a) to call to account b) to make an objection to; call into question **3.** to call or dare to take part in a duel, contest, etc.; defy **4.** to call for; make demands on [to *challenge* the imagination] **5.** to take

formal exception to (a prospective juror) —*vi.* to issue or offer a challenge —**chal′lenge·a·ble** *adj.* —**chal′leng·er** *n.*

chal·lis (shal′ē) *n.* [< ?] a soft, lightweight, usually printed fabric of wool, cotton, etc.

cha·lyb·e·ate (kə lib′ē at, -āt′) *adj.* [< L. *chalybs* < Gr. *chalyps*, steel] **1.** containing salts of iron **2.** tasting like iron —*n.* a chalybeate liquid

cham·ber (chām′bər) *n.* [< OFr. < LL. *camera*: see CAMERA] **1.** [Archaic] a room in a house, esp. a bedroom **2.** [*pl.*] a suite of rooms used by one person **3.** [*pl.*] a) a place where judicial business not requiring to be done in open court is transacted b) the set of rooms where a barrister conducts business **4.** an assembly hall **5.** a legislative or judicial body or division [the *Chamber* of Deputies] **6.** a council or board [a *chamber* of commerce] **7.** an enclosed space or cavity **8.** a compartment; specif., the part of a gun that holds the charge or cartridge **9.** *same as* CHAMBER POT —*vt.* to provide a chamber or chambers for —**cham′bered** *adj.*

cham·ber·lain (-lin) *n.* [< OFr. < OHG. < *chamara* (< L. *camera*) + dim. suffix *-linc*: see CAMERA & -LING¹] **1.** an officer in charge of the household of a ruler or lord; steward **2.** a high official in certain royal courts **3.** formerly, a treasurer esp. of a municipality

cham·ber·maid (-mād′) *n.* a woman whose work is taking care of bedrooms, as in hotels

chamber music music for performance by a small group, as a string quartet, orig. in a small hall

chamber of commerce an association established to further the business interests of its community

chamber pot a portable container kept in a bedroom and used as a toilet

cham·bray (sham′brā) *n.* [var. of CAMBRIC] a smooth fabric of cotton, made by weaving white or unbleached threads across a coloured warp

cha·me·le·on (kə mēl′yən, -mē′lē ən) *n.* [< L. < Gr. < *chamai*, on the ground + *leōn*, lion] **1.** any of various lizards that can change the colour of their skin **2.** a changeable or fickle person —**cha·me′le·on′ic** (-mē′lē on′ik) *adj.*

cham·fer (cham′fər) *n.* [< OFr. < Fr. < L. *cantum frangere*: see CANT² & FRAGILE] a bevelled edge or corner, esp. one cut at a 45° angle —*vt.* **1.** to cut a chamfer on; bevel **2.** to make a groove or fluting in

cham·ois (sham′wä; for 1b, sham′ē) *n., pl.* **-ois** [Fr. < VL. *camox*] **1.** a small, goatlike antelope of the mountains of Europe and the Caucasus **2.** a) a soft leather made from the skin of chamois, or of sheep, deer, goats, etc. b) a piece of this leather, used as a polishing cloth: also

CHAMELEON
(to 60 cm long, including tail)

cham·my (sham′ē), *pl.* **-mies** —*adj.* **1.** made of chamois **2.** yellowish-brown —*vt.* **cham′oised** (-ēd), **cham′ois·ing** (-ē iŋ) to polish with a chamois skin

cham·o·mile (kam′ə mīl′, -mēl′) *n.* *same as* CAMOMILE

champ¹ (champ) *vt., vi.* [earlier *cham*: prob. echoic] to chew hard and noisily; munch —*n.* the act of champing —**champ at the bit 1.** to bite upon its bit repeatedly and restlessly: said of a horse **2.** to be restless

champ² (champ) *n.* [Slang] *same as* CHAMPION

cham·pagne (sham pān′) *n.* **1.** orig., any of various wines produced in Champagne, a region in NE France **2.** now, any effervescent white wine: a symbol of luxury **3.** pale, tawny yellow

cham·pers (sham′pərz) *n.* [Slang] champagne

cham·per·ty (cham′pər tē) *n., pl.* **-ties** [ME. *champartie* < OFr. *champart*, the lord's share in the crop of a tenant's land < L. *campi pars* < *campi*, gen. of *campus*, a field + *pars*, a part] *Law* an act by which a person not concerned in a lawsuit makes a bargain with one of the litigants to help maintain the costs of the suit in return for a share in any proceeds: illegal in England

cham·pi·on (cham′pē ən) *n.* [< OFr. < LL. *campio*, combatant < L. *campus*, a field] **1.** a person who fights for another or for a cause; defender; supporter **2.** a winner of first place in a competition —*adj.* **1.** winning first place; excelling over all others **2.** [Colloq.] first-rate; excellent —*vt.* to fight for; defend; support

cham·pi·on·ship (-ship′) *n.* **1.** a championing **2.** the position or title of a champion **3.** a contest to find an overall winner

cham·ple·vé (shän lə vā′) *adj.* [Fr.] designating or of a kind of enamel work in which furrows or hollows cut in a metal surface, usually copper, are filled with vitreous powders and then fired —*n.* champlevé enamel

Chan., Chanc. 1. Chancellor **2.** Chancery

chan. channel

chance (chäns) *n.* [< OFr. < ML. < L. prp. of *cadere*, to fall] **1.** the happening of events without apparent cause; fortuity; luck **2.** an unpredictable event or accidental happening **3.** a risk or gamble **4.** an opportunity [a *chance* to go] **5.** a possibility or probability [a *chance* that he will live] **6.** *Cricket* a missed catch —*adj.* happening by chance; accidental —*vi.* **chanced, chanc'ing 1.** to have the fortune (*to*) **2.** [Archaic] to happen by chance —*vt.* to risk [let's *chance* it] —**by chance** accidentally —**chance on** (or **upon**) to find by chance —**chance one's arm** to risk possible failure —**on the off chance** relying on the (remote) possibility —**stand a chance** to have some likelihood of succeeding

chan·cel (chän's'l) *n.* [< OFr. < LL. < L. *cancelli,* pl., lattices: see CANCEL] that part of a church around the altar, reserved for the clergy and the choir: it is sometimes set off by a railing

chan·cel·ler·y (chän'sə lə rē, -slə rē) *n., pl.* **-ler·ies 1.** the position, staff, residence or rank of a chancellor **2.** the political section of an embassy **3.** a consulate or consular building Also sp. **chan'cel·lor·y**

chan·cel·lor (-lər) *n.* [< OFr. < LL. *cancellarius,* keeper of the barrier: see CANCEL] **1.** [usually C-] any of several high officials in the British government **2.** the honorary head of a university **3.** the prime minister in W Germany and Austria **4.** the chief secretary of an embassy **5.** *R.C.Ch.* the priest in charge of a chancery —**chan'cel·lor·ship'** *n.*

Chancellor of the Exchequer the cabinet minister responsible for finance, taxation, etc.

chance-med·ley (chäns'med'lē) *n.* [see CHANCE & MEDDLE] **1.** a criminal act committed largely, but not wholly, by accident, esp. homicide **2.** haphazard action

chan·cer·y (chän'sər ē) *n., pl.* **-cer·ies** [< OFr. < ML. *cancellaria:* see CHANCELLOR] **1.** a division of the High Court of Justice in England and Wales **2.** same as CHANCELLERY **3.** *R.C.Ch. a)* the diocesan office in charge of certain documents, secretarial services, etc. for the bishop *b)* the department of the Curia responsible for issuing bills, etc. **4.** *Wrestling* a hold in which a wrestler's head is held under his opponent's arm —**in chancery 1.** in process of litigation in the court of chancery **2.** in a helpless situation

chan·cre (shaŋ'kər) *n.* [Fr.: see CANCER] a venereal sore or ulcer; primary lesion of syphilis —**chan'crous** (-krəs) *adj.*

chan·croid (-kroid) *n.* [CHANCR(E) + -OID] a nonsyphilitic venereal ulcer: also called **soft chancre**

chanc·y (chän'sē) *adj.* **chanc'i·er, chanc'i·est** risky; uncertain

chan·de·lier (shan'də lir') *n.* [Fr. < OFr. < L. *candelabrum* < *candela,* CANDLE] a lighting fixture hanging from a ceiling, with branches for candles, electric bulbs, etc.

chan·dler (chän'dlər) *n.* [< OFr. < L. *candela,* CANDLE] **1.** a maker or seller of candles **2.** a retailer of supplies, equipment, etc. of a certain kind [ship's *chandler*] —**chan'dler·y** (-ē) *n., pl.* **-dler·ies**

change (chānj) *vt.* **changed, chang'ing** [< OFr. < LL. < L. *cambire,* to barter < Celt.] **1.** to put or take (a thing) in place of something else; substitute [to *change* one's clothes] **2.** to exchange [let's *change* seats] **3.** *a)* to make different; alter *b)* to undergo a variation of [leaves *change* colour] **4.** to give or receive the equivalent of (a coin or banknote) in currency of lower denominations or in foreign money **5.** to put a fresh covering, as a nappy, on —*vi.* **1.** *a)* to alter; vary [the scene *changes*] *b)* to undergo alteration or replacement **2.** to become lower in range, as the male voice at puberty **3.** to leave one train, bus, etc. and board another **4.** to put on other clothes **5.** to make an exchange —*n.* **1.** the act or process of substitution, alteration, or variation **2.** variety **3.** something of the same kind but new or fresh **4.** another set of clothes **5.** *a)* money returned as the difference between the purchase price and the larger sum given in payment *b)* a number of coins or banknotes whose total value equals a single larger coin or note *c)* small coins **6.** a place where merchants meet to do business; exchange: also **'change 7.** [usually pl.] *Bell Ringing* any order in which the bells may be rung —**change down** to change to a lower gear —**change up** to change to a higher gear —**get no change out of** [Slang] **1.** to fail to gain information, help, etc. from **2.** to fail to outwit —**ring the changes 1.** to ring a set of bells with all possible variations **2.** to do or say a thing in many and various ways —**change'ful** *adj.* —**change'ful·ly** *adv.* —**change'ful·ness** *n.* —**chang'er** *n.*

change·a·ble (chān'jə b'l) *adj.* **1.** that can change or be changed; alterable **2.** having a changing appearance or colour —**change'a·bil'i·ty, change'a·ble·ness** *n.* —**change'·a·bly** *adv.*

change·less (chānj'lis) *adj.* unchanging; immutable —**change'less·ly** *adv.* —**change'less·ness** *n.*

change·ling (-liŋ) *n.* a child secretly put in the place of another, esp., in folk tales, by fairies

change of life same as MENOPAUSE

change·o·ver (-ō'vər) *n.* **1.** a complete change, as in goods produced, equipment, etc. **2.** a change of situation, job, etc. [a *changeover* of shifts]

change ringing the art of ringing a series of unrepeated changes on a set of bells tuned together

changing room a room where persons can change their clothes, as at a sports ground, clothing shop, etc.

chan·nel (chan'l) *n.* [< OFr.: see CANAL] **1.** the bed of a river, etc. **2.** the deeper part of a river, harbour, etc. **3.** a body of water joining two larger bodies of water **4.** a tubelike passage for liquids **5.** any means of passage or transmission **6.** [pl.] the proper or official course of action [to make a request through army *channels*] **7.** a long groove or furrow **8.** a frequency band within which a radio or television transmitting station must keep its signal **9.** *a)* the path of an electric signal [a four-*channel* audio system] *b)* a strip along a recording tape, computer tape, etc. on which a message can be recorded —**the Channel** the English Channel —*vt.* **-nelled, -nel·ling 1.** to make a channel in **2.** to send through or direct into a channel

chan·nel-bill (-bil') *n.* a large Australian cuckoo with a groove along its bill

‡**chan·son** (shän sôn') *n., pl.* **-sons'** (-sôn'; *E.* -sənz) [Fr.] a song, esp. as sung in a cabaret

‡**chan·son de geste** (shän sôn'də zhest') [Fr., song of heroic acts] any of the Old French epic poems of the 11th to 13th centuries, esp. of the type of the *Chanson de Roland* (Song of Roland)

chant (chänt) *n.* [Fr. < L. *cantus,* song < the *v.*] **1.** a song; melody **2.** *a)* a simple liturgical song in which a series of syllables or words is sung to each tone *b)* words, as of a psalm, to be sung in this way **3.** a singsong way of speaking **4.** a rhythmic or repetitious slogan —*vi.* [< OFr. < L. *cantare,* freq. of *canere,* to sing] **1.** to sing a chant; intone **2.** to speak monotonously **3.** to intone rhythmically or repetitiously —*vt.* **1.** to sing **2.** to celebrate in song **3.** to say monotonously **4.** to intone —**chant'er** *n.*

chan·te·relle (shän'tə rel', chan'-) *n.* [Fr., dim. < L. *cantharus,* drinking cup < Gr. *kantharos*] any of a genus of yellow or orange mushrooms with forking gills and funnel-shaped caps, esp. an edible species

chan·teuse (shän töz') *n.* [Fr.] a woman singer

chan·ty (shan'tē) *n., pl.* **-ties** [< ? Fr.: see CHANT] same as SHANTY²

chan·ti·cleer (chan'tə klir') *n.* [< OFr.: see CHANT & CLEAR] a cock: name used in fable and folklore

chan·try (chän'trē) *n., pl.* **-tries** [ME & OFr. *chanterie:* see CHANT] *R.C.Ch.* **1.** an endowment to pay for the saying of Masses and prayers for the soul of a specified person, often the endower **2.** a chapel or altar endowed, esp. in the Middle Ages, for this purpose

cha·os (kā'os) *n.* [L. < Gr. *chaos,* space, chaos (sense 1)] **1.** the disorder of formless matter and infinite space, supposed to have existed before the ordered universe **2.** extreme confusion or disorder

cha·ot·ic (kā ot'ik) *adj.* in a state of chaos; in a completely confused or disordered condition —**cha·ot'i·cal·ly** *adv.*

chap¹ (chap) *n.* [< ?] same as CHOP²

chap² (chap) *n.* [< CHAPMAN] [Colloq.] a man or boy; fellow

chap³ (chap) *vt., vi.* **chapped, chap'ping** [ME. *chappen,* var. of *choppen* (see CHOP¹)] to crack open or roughen, as the skin from exposure to cold —*n.* a chapped place in the skin

chap. **1.** chaplain **2.** chapter

cha·pa·re·jos, cha·pa·ra·jos (chap'ə rā'hōs, shap'-) *n.pl.* [MexSp.] [U.S.] same as CHAPS¹

chap·ar·ral (chap'ə ral', shap'-) *n.* [Sp. < *chaparro,* evergreen oak] [U.S.] a thicket of shrubs, thorny bushes, etc., orig. of evergreen oaks

cha·pat·ti, cha·pa·ti (chə pä'tē) *n., pl.* **-tis, -ties** [< Hindi *capati* < Sans. *carpati,* a thin, flat loaf < *carpata,* flat] a flat, unleavened bread from India

chap·book (chap'book') *n.* [< CHAP(MAN): chapmen peddled such books] a small book or pamphlet of poems, ballads, religious tracts, etc.

cha·peau (sha pō') *n., pl.* **-peaux', -peaus'** (-pōz') [Fr. < OFr. < VL. *capellus,* dim. of LL. *cappa:* see CAPE¹] a hat

chap·el (chap''l) *n.* [< OFr. < ML. < VL. (see prec.): orig. sanctuary in which cloak of St. Martin was preserved] **1.** a room or building used as a place of worship, as in a school **2.** a small room in a church, having its own altar **3.** a religious service, as in a chapel **4.** any place of worship for those who are not members of an established church **5.** the members, or a meeting of the members of, a trade union in a publishing house, printing works, etc.

chap·er·on, chap·er·one (shap'ə rōn') *n.* [Fr. < OFr., hood (hence, protector) < *chape,* COPE²] a person, esp. an older or married woman, who accompanies young unmarried people in public or attends their parties, etc. for propriety or to supervise their behaviour —*vt., vi.* **-oned', -on'ing** to act as chaperon (to) —**chap'er·on·age** *n.*

chap·fall·en (chap'fô'lən) *adj.* [< *chap,* jaw + FALLEN] **1.** having the lower jaw hanging down, as from fatigue **2.** disheartened, depressed, or humiliated

chap·lain (chap'lən) *n.* [< OFr. < ML.: see CHAPEL] **1.** a clergyman attached to a chapel, as of a royal court **2.** a minister, priest, or rabbi serving in a religious capacity with the armed forces or in a prison, hospital, etc. **3.** a clergyman with spiritual charge of a bishop, monarch, etc. —**chap′lain·cy,** *pl.* **-cies, chap′lain·ship′** *n.*

chap·let (chap′lit) *n.* [< OFr. dim. of *chapel* < VL. *capellus:* see CHAPEAU] **1.** a garland for the head **2.** *a)* a string of prayer beads one third the length of a full rosary *b)* the prayers said with such beads **3.** any string of beads —**chap′let·ed** *adj.*

chap·man (chap′mən) *n.,* *pl.* **-men** [< OE. < *ceap,* trade + *man*] [Archaic] a pedlar; hawker

chap·pie, chap·py (chap′ē) *n.* [CHAP² + -y¹] *same as* CHAP²

chaps¹ (chaps, shaps) *n.pl.* [< CHAPAREJOS] leather trousers without a seat, worn over ordinary trousers by cowboys to protect their legs

chaps² (chaps) *n.pl.* *same as* CHOPS

chap·ter (chap′tər) *n.* [< OFr. *chapitre* < L. *capitulum,* dim. of *caput,* head] **1.** a main division, as of a book **2.** a thing like a chapter; part; episode **3.** *a)* a formal meeting of canons of a church or of the members of a religious order *b)* the group of such canons, etc. **4.** a local branch of a club, society, etc. —**vt.** to divide into chapters —**chapter and verse 1.** the exact Scriptural reference **2.** authority cited (for a statement, belief, etc.) **3.** detailed information —**chapter of accidents** a chain of unexpected and unfortunate events

char¹ (chär) *vt., vi.* **charred, char′ring** [< CHARCOAL] **1.** to burn to charcoal **2.** to scorch —*n.* anything charred

char² (chär) *n.* [< CHARWOMAN] a charwoman —*vi.* **charred, char′ring** to work as a charwoman

char³ (chär) *n.,* *pl.* **chars, char:** see PLURAL, II, D, 1 [< ?] any of a genus of trout with small scales and a red belly Also sp. **charr**

char⁴ (chä) *n.* *same as* CHA

char·a·banc, char-à-banc (shar′ə baŋ′) *n.* [Fr., lit., car with bench] a sightseeing bus

char·ac·ter (kar′ik tər) *n.* [< OFr. < L. < Gr. *charaktēr,* an engraving instrument < *charassein,* to engrave] **1.** a distinctive mark **2.** any figure, letter, or symbol used in writing and printing **3.** a distinctive trait or quality **4.** nature; kind or sort **5.** the pattern of behaviour or personality found in an individual or group **6.** moral strength; self-discipline, fortitude, etc. **7.** *a)* reputation *b)* good reputation **8.** status; position **9.** a personage [great *characters* in history] **10.** a person in a play, novel, etc. **11.** [Colloq.] an odd, eccentric, or noteworthy person **12.** *Biol.* any attribute, as colour, shape, etc., caused by the action of one or more genes —**in** (or **out of**) **character** consistent with (or inconsistent with) the role or general character —**char′ac·ter·less′** *adj.*

character actor an actor who specializes in the roles of persons with pronounced or eccentric characteristics

char·ac·ter·is·tic (kar′ik tə ris′tik) *adj.* of or constituting the special character; typical; distinctive —*n.* **1.** a distinguishing trait, feature, or quality **2.** the whole number, or integral part, of a logarithm, as 4 in the logarithm 4.7193: cf. MANTISSA —**char′ac·ter·is′ti·cal·ly** *adv.*

char·ac·ter·ize (kar′ik tə rīz′) *vt.* **-ized′, -iz′ing 1.** to describe or portray the particular qualities or traits of **2.** to be the distinctive character of; distinguish —**char′-ac·ter·i·za′tion** *n.*

cha·rade (shə rād′) *n.* [Fr. < Pr. *charrada* < *charrar,* to gossip] **1.** [often *pl.*] a game in which a word or phrase to be guessed is acted out in pantomime, syllable by syllable or as a whole **2.** a mockery; farce

char·coal (chär′kōl) *n.* [ME. *char cole,* prob. < *charren,* to turn + *cole,* coal] **1.** a form of carbon produced by partially burning wood or other organic matter in large kilns from which air is excluded **2.** a pencil made of this substance **3.** a drawing made with such a pencil **4.** a very dark grey or brown, almost black —*vt.* to draw with charcoal

chard (chärd) *n.* [Fr. *carde* < L. *carduus,* thistle] a kind of beet whose large leaves and thick stalks are used as food

charge (chärj) *vt.* **charged, charg′ing** [< OFr. *chargier* < VL. *carricare,* to load < L. *carrus,* car, wagon] **1.** to load or fill with the required material [*charged* with gunpowder] **2.** to saturate with another substance [air *charged* with steam] **3.** to add carbon dioxide to (water, etc.) **4.** to add an electrical charge to (a battery, etc.) **5.** to give as a task, duty, etc. to **6.** to give instructions to or command authoritatively **7.** to accuse of wrongdoing; censure [he *charged* her with negligence] **8.** to make liable for (an error, etc.) **9.** to ask as a price or fee [to *charge* £20 for labour] **10.** to record as a debt against a person or his account [to *charge* a purchase] **11.** to rush forward and attack —*vi.* **1.** to ask payment (for) [to *charge* for a service] **2.** to attack vigorously or move forward as if

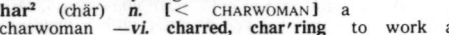

CHAPS

attacking —*n.* **1.** the amount, as of fuel, gunpowder, etc., used to load or fill something **2.** *a)* the amount of chemical energy stored in a battery and dischargeable as electrical energy *b)* a change from the condition of electrical neutrality by the accumulation of electrons (*negative charge*) or by the loss of electrons (*positive charge*) **3.** responsibility or duty (*of*) **4.** care or custody (*of*) **5.** a person or thing entrusted to someone's care **6.** instruction or command, esp. instructions given by a judge to a jury **7.** accusation; indictment [*charges* of cruelty] **8.** the cost or price of an article, service, etc. **9.** a financial obligation **10.** *a)* an attack or onrush, as by troops *b)* the signal for this **11.** *Heraldry* a bearing —**charge off 1.** to regard as a loss **2.** to ascribe —**in charge** having the responsibility or control —**take charge** to assume responsibility or control

charge·a·ble (chär′jə b'l) *adj.* **1.** that can be charged **2.** that may become a public charge

charge account *same as* CREDIT ACCOUNT

char·gé d'af·faires (shär′zhā da fer′) *pl.* **char·gés d'af·faires** (shär′zhā da fer′) [Fr.] **1.** a diplomat temporarily substituting for a minister or ambassador **2.** a diplomat in charge of a minor diplomatic mission

charge·hand (chärj′hand′) *n.* a workman in charge of a process or section, below a foreman

charge nurse a nurse with responsibility for a ward, etc.

charg·er¹ (chär′jər) *n.* **1.** one that charges **2.** a horse ridden in battle or on parade **3.** an apparatus for charging storage batteries

charg·er² (chär′jər) *n.* [ME. *chargeour*] [Archaic] a large, flat dish; platter

charge sheet in a police station, a daily record of charges made against suspected criminals

char·i·ly (cher′ə lē) *adv.* in a chary manner

char·i·ness (-ē nis) *n.* the quality of being chary

char·i·ot (char′ē ət) *n.* [< OFr. < VL. *carricare:* see CHARGE] a horse-drawn, two-wheeled cart used in ancient times for war, racing, etc. —*vt., vi.* to drive or ride in a chariot

char·i·ot·eer (char′ē ə tir′) *n.* a chariot driver

cha·ris·ma (kə riz′mə) *n.,* *pl.* **-ma·ta** (-mə tə) [< Gr., favour, grace] **1.** *Christian Theol.* a divinely inspired gift or talent, as for prophesying **2.** a special quality of leadership that inspires great popular allegiance Also **char·ism** (kar′iz′m) —**char·is·mat·ic** (kar′iz mat′ik) *adj.*

CHARIOT

charismatic movement a cross-denominational religious movement characterized by a belief in the charismatic gifts of speaking in tongues, healing, etc.

char·i·ta·ble (char′i tə b'l) *adj.* **1.** kind and generous in giving help to those in need **2.** of or for charity **3.** kind and forgiving in judging others —**char′i·ta·ble·ness** *n.* —**char′i·ta·bly** *adv.*

char·i·ty (char′ə tē) *n.,* *pl.* **-ties** [< OFr. < L. *caritas,* affection < *carus,* dear] **1.** *Christian Theol.* the love of God for man or of man for his fellow men **2.** an act of good will **3.** benevolence **4.** kindness in judging others **5.** a voluntary giving of money, etc. to those in need **6.** a welfare institution, organization, etc.

cha·ri·va·ri (shä′rē vä′rē) *n.* [Fr. < LL. < Gr. *karēbaria,* heavy head] **1.** a mock serenade, as to newlyweds, with kettles, horns, etc. **2.** a loud noise; hubbub

char·la·dy (chä′lā dē) *n.,* *pl.* **-dies** *same as* CHARWOMAN

char·la·tan (shär′lə t'n) *n.* [Fr. < It. *ciarlatano*] one who pretends to have expert knowledge or skill that he does not have; fake; mountebank —**char′la·tan·ism, char′la·tan·ry,** *pl.* **-ries** *n.*

Charles's Wain (chärl′ziz) *same as* PLOUGH

charles·ton (chärl′stən) *n.* [< *Charleston,* a port in S. Carolina, U.S.] [also C-] a lively dance in 4/4 time, characterized by a twisting step

char·ley horse (chär′lē) [U.S. Colloq.] a cramp in the leg or arm muscles, caused by strain

char·lie (chär′lē) *n.* [dim. of *Charles,* a masculine name] [Colloq.] a fool

char·lock (chär′lək) *n.* [OE. *cerlic*] a weed of the cabbage family, with yellow flowers

char·lotte (shär′lət) *n.* [Fr. <*Charlotte,* feminine name] a dessert made of fruit, gelatin, custard, etc. in a mould lined with strips of bread, cake, etc.

charlotte russe (r̄o̅o̅s) [Fr., lit., Russian charlotte] a dessert made of whipped cream, custard, etc. in a mould lined with spongecake

charm (chärm) *n.* [< OFr. < L. *carmen,* song, charm] **1.** a chanted word or verse, an action, or an object assumed to have magic power to help or hurt **2.** a trinket on a bracelet, watch chain, etc. **3.** a quality or feature that attracts or delights —*vt.* **1.** to act on as though by magic **2.** to attract or please greatly; fascinate; delight —*vi.* to be charming —**like a charm** perfectly —**charm′er** *n.*

charm·ing (chärm′iŋ) *adj.* attractive; fascinating; delightful —**charm′ing·ly** *adv.*

char·nel (chär′n'l) *n.* [OFr. < LL. *carnale*, graveyard; neut. of *carnalis*, CARNAL] a building or place where corpses or bones are deposited: in full, **charnel house** —*adj.* of, like, or fit for a charnel

Cha·ron (ker′ən) *Gr. Myth.* the boatman who ferried dead souls across the river Styx to Hades

chart (chärt) *n.* [OFr. < ML. < L. *charta*: see CARD[1]] 1. a map, esp. one for marine or air navigation 2. an outline map on which special information, as of weather, is plotted geographically 3. *a)* a group of facts set up in the form of a diagram, graph, etc. *b)* such a diagram, graph, etc., or a sheet with diagrams, etc. 4. [*chiefly pl.*] a list of the currently most popular gramophone records, books, etc. —*vt.* 1. to make a chart of 2. to plan (a course of action) 3. to show by, on, or as by, a chart —**chart′less** *adj.*

char·ter (chär′tər) *n.* [< OFr. < L. dim. of *charta*: see CARD[1]] 1. a franchise or written grant of specified rights given by a monarch or legislature to a person, corporation, university, etc. 2. *a)* a document setting forth the aims and principles of a united group, as of nations *b)* a document embodying a city constitution 3. a document authorizing the organization of a local chapter of a society 4. the hire or lease of a ship, bus, etc. —*vt.* 1. to grant a charter to 2. to hire for exclusive use —**char′ter·er** *n.*

char·tered accountant (chär′tərd) an accountant certified by the Institute of Chartered Accountants

Chart·ism (chär′tiz'm) *n.* a movement for democratic social and political reform in England (1838-48), or its principles set forth in the People's Charter (1838) —**Chart′ist** *n., adj.*

char·treuse (shär trʉrz′; *Fr.* shár tröz′) *n.* [Fr., Carthusian] 1. a yellow, pale-green, or white liqueur made by Carthusian monks 2. pale, yellowish green

char·wom·an (chär′woom′ən) *n., pl.* **-wom′en** [see CHORE] a woman who does cleaning or scrubbing, as in office buildings

char·y (cher′ē) *adj.* **char′i·er, char′i·est** [OE. *cearig* < *cearu*, care] 1. not taking chances; cautious 2. not giving freely; sparing

Cha·ryb·dis (kə rib′dis) whirlpool off the NE coast of Sicily: see SCYLLA

chase[1] (chās) *vt.* **chased, chas′ing** [< OFr. *chacier, cachier*: see CATCH] 1. to follow quickly or persistently so as to catch or harm 2. to run after; follow 3. to make run away; drive 4. to hunt 5. [Slang] to court in an unsubtle manner —*vi.* 1. to go in pursuit 2. [Colloq.] to go hurriedly; rush —*n.* 1. a chasing; pursuit 2. *a)* the hunting of game for sport *b)* anything hunted; quarry 3. same as FOREST (sense 2) 4. *Clipped form of* STEEPLECHASE —**give chase** to chase

chase[2] (chās) *n.* [OFr. < L. *capsa*: see CASE[2]] 1. a groove; furrow 2. a rectangular metal frame in which pages or columns of type are locked —*vt.* **chased, chas′ing** to make a groove or furrow in; indent

chase[3] (chās) *vt.* **chased, chas′ing** [< Fr. *enchâsser*, enshrine] to ornament (metal) by engraving, embossing, etc.

chas·er (chā′sər) *n.* 1. one that chases or hunts 2. [Colloq.] a horse for steeplechasing 3. [Colloq.] a drink taken after another, as beer after spirits

chasm (kaz′'m) *n.* [L. & Gr. *chasma* < Gr. *chainein*, to gape] 1. a deep crack in the earth's surface; abyss; gorge 2. any break or gap 3. a wide divergence of feelings, interests, etc.; rift —**chas′mal** (-m'l), **chas′mic** (-mik) *adj.*

chas·seur (sha sʉr′) *n.* [Fr.] 1. a hunter 2. a soldier, esp. one of certain French troops, trained for rapid action 3. a uniformed attendant —*adj.* designating meat or game cooked in a sauce of white wine and mushrooms

chas·sis (shas′ē) *n., pl.* **-sis** (-ēz) [Fr. *châssis*: see CHASE[2]] 1. the frame of a motor vehicle, but not the body and engine 2. *a)* the frame supporting the body of an aircraft *b)* the landing gear of an aircraft 3. *Radio & TV a)* the framework to which the parts of a receiver, amplifier, etc. are attached *b)* the assembled frame and parts 4. [Slang] the body; figure, esp. of a woman

chaste (chāst) *adj.* [OFr. < L. *castus*, pure: see CASTE] 1. not indulging in extramarital sexual activity; virtuous: said esp. of women 2. sexually abstinent; celibate 3. pure; decent; modest 4. restrained and simple in style —**chaste′ly** *adv.* —**chaste′ness** *n.*

chas·ten (chās′'n) *vt.* [< OFr. < L. *castigare*, to punish < *castus*, pure + *agere*, to lead] 1. to punish so as to correct; chastise 2. to restrain from excess; subdue 3. to refine in style —**chas′ten·er** *n.*

chas·tise (chas tīz′) *vt.* **-tised′, -tis′ing** [see prec.] 1. to punish, esp. by beating 2. to scold or condemn sharply —**chas·tise′ment** *n.* —**chas·tis′er** *n.*

chas·ti·ty (chas′tə tē) *n.* [see CHASTE] the quality or state of being chaste; specif., *a)* virtuousness *b)* sexual abstinence *c)* decency *d)* simplicity of style

chas·u·ble (chaz′yoo b'l) *n.* [OFr. < ML. *casubla*, hooded garment] a sleeveless outer vestment worn over the alb by priests at Mass

chat (chat) *vi.* **chat′ted, chat′ting** [< CHATTER] to talk or converse in a light, easy, informal way —*n.* 1. a light, easy, informal conversation 2. any of various birds with a chattering call —**chat up** [Colloq.] to draw into conversation, esp. with the aim of gaining some advantage

CHASUBLE

châ·teau (sha′tō, sha tō′) *n., pl.* **-teaux′** (-tōz′, -tō′), **-teaus′** [Fr. < OFr. < L. *castellum*, CASTLE] 1. a French feudal castle 2. a large country house, esp. in France Also **cha·teau′**

cha·teau·bri·and (shá tō brē än′) *n.* [after F. R. de *Chateaubriand* (1768-1848), Fr. statesman] a thick beef fillet cut from the centre

chat·e·laine (shat′ə lān′) *n.* [Fr., ult. < L. *castellum*, CASTLE] 1. the mistress of a castle or of any large household 2. a woman's ornamental chain or clasp, esp. for the waist, with keys, a watch, etc. fastened to it

chat·tel (chat′'l) *n.* [OFr. *chatel*: see CATTLE] 1. *a)* a movable item of personal property, as a piece of furniture: in full, **chattel personal** *b)* any interest in land less than a freehold: in full, **chattel real** 2. [Archaic] a slave

chat·ter (chat′ər) *vi.* [echoic] 1. to make short, indistinct sounds in rapid succession, as birds, apes, etc. 2. to talk fast, incessantly, and foolishly 3. to click together rapidly, as the teeth do from fright or cold 4. to vibrate irregularly, as a drill against metal —*vt.* to utter with a chattering sound —*n.* 1. the act or sound of chattering 2. rapid, foolish talk —**chat′ter·er** *n.*

chat·ter·box (-boks′) *n.* an incessant talker

chat·ty (chat′ē) *adj.* **-ti·er, -ti·est** 1. fond of chatting 2. light, familiar, and informal: said of talk —**chat′ti·ly** *adv.* —**chat′ti·ness** *n.*

chauf·feur (shō′fər, shō fʉr′) *n.* [Fr., lit., stoker < *chauffer*, to heat: see CHAFE] a person hired to drive a private car for someone else —*vt.* to act as chauffeur to

chaunt (chônt) *n., vt., vi.* archaic var. of CHANT

chau·vin·ism (shō′və niz'm) *n.* [< Fr. < N. *Chauvin*, Napoleonic soldier, notorious for his fanatical patriotism] 1. militant, boastful, and fanatical patriotism 2. unreasoning devotion to one's race, sex, etc., with contempt for other races, the opposite sex, etc. —**chau′vin·ist** *n., adj.* —**chau′vin·is′tic** *adj.* —**chau′vin·is′ti·cal·ly** *adv.*

cheap (chēp) *adj.* [< *good cheap*, good bargain < OE. *ceap*, a bargain] 1. low in price; not expensive 2. charging low prices 3. spending little 4. worth more than the price 5. easily got 6. of little or no value 7. contemptible 8. available at low interest rates: said of money—*adv.* at low cost —**on the cheap** cheaply —**cheap′ly** *adv.* —**cheap′ness** *n.*

cheap·en (chēp′'n) *vt., vi.* to make or become cheap or cheaper —**cheap′en·er** *n.*

cheap-jack (-jak′) *n.* [CHEAP + JACK] a seller of cheap, inferior articles —*adj.* cheap, inferior, base, etc.

cheap·skate (-skāt′) *n.* [Colloq.] a miserly person

cheat (chēt) *n.* [< ME. *eschete*: see ESCHEAT] 1. a fraud; deception 2. one who deceives or defrauds others; swindler —*vt.* 1. to defraud; swindle 2. to deceive by trickery; fool 3. to foil or escape by tricks or good luck [to *cheat* death] —*vi.* 1. to practise fraud or deception 2. [Slang] to be sexually unfaithful (often with *on*) —**cheat′er** *n.* —**cheat′ing·ly** *adv.*

check (chek) *n.* [OFr. *eschec*, a check at chess < ML. *scaccus* < Per. *shāh*, king] 1. a sudden stop 2. any restraint or control of action 3. one that restrains or controls 4. a supervision of accuracy, efficiency, etc. 5. *a)* a test, comparison, etc. to see if something is as it should be *b)* a standard or sample used for this 6. [Chiefly U.S.] a tick (√) to show approval or verification or to call attention to something 7. [Chiefly U.S.] an identification token enabling one to re-claim an item [a hat *check*] 8. [U.S.] one's bill at a restaurant or bar 9. *U.S. sp. of* CHEQUE 10. *a)* a pattern of small squares like that of a chessboard *b)* one of these squares 11. a fabric with such a pattern 12. a small split or crack, as in timber 13. *Chess* the condition of a king that is in danger and must be put into a safe position 14. *Hunting* the loss of a quarry's scent by the hounds 15. *Ice Hockey* a blocking of an opponent's play or movement —*interj.* 1. [Chiefly U.S. Colloq.] agreed! right! OK! 2. *Chess* a call indicating that the opponent's king is in check —*vt.* 1. to make stop suddenly 2. to hold back; restrain 3. to rebuff, repulse, or rebuke 4. to test, measure, verify, or control by investigation or comparison 5. [Chiefly U.S.] to mark with a check (√) 6. to mark with a pattern of squares 7. [Chiefly U.S.] to deposit or receive for deposit temporarily, as in a left-luggage office **8.** to get (esp. luggage) cleared for shipment **9.** to make chinks or cracks in **10.** *Chess* to place (an opponent's king) in check **11.** *Ice Hockey* to block the play or movement of (an opponent) —*vi.* **1.** to agree with one another, item for item [the accounts *check*] **2.** to investigate so as to determine the condition, validity, etc. of something (often with *on*) **3.** to crack in small checks, as paint **4.** *Chess* to place an opponent's king in check **5.** *Hunting* to lose the scent of the quarry: said of hounds —*adj.* **1.** used to check or verify **2.** having a crisscross pattern; checked —**check in 1.** to register at a hotel, airport, etc. **2.** [Colloq.] to report, as by presenting oneself [*check in* at the office] —**check off** to mark as verified, examined, etc. —**check out 1.** to settle one's bill and leave a hotel, etc. **2.** to add up the prices of (purchases) and collect the total: said of a cashier, as in a supermarket **3.** to examine and verify or approve **4.** to prove to be accurate, sound, etc. upon examination —**check up on** to examine or investigate —**in check** in restraint; under control

checked (chekt) *adj.* having a pattern of squares

check·er[1] (chek'ər) *n.* a variant sp. of CHEQUER

check·er[2] (chek'ər) *n.* **1.** a person who examines or verifies **2.** [Chiefly U.S.] a person who checks hats, luggage, etc. **3.** [U.S.] a cashier, as in a supermarket

check·er·board (-bôrd') *n.* [U.S.] *same as* DRAUGHTBOARD

check·ered (-ərd) *adj.* *same as* CHEQUERED

check·ers *n.pl.* [U.S.] *same as* DRAUGHTS

check·list (-list') *n.* a list of things to be checked off or referred to: also **check list**

check·mate (-māt') *n.* [OFr. *eschec mat*, ult. < Per. *shāh māt*, lit., the king is dead] **1.** *Chess* a) the winning move that checks the opponent's king so that it cannot be put into safety b) the king's position after this move **2.** complete defeat, frustration, etc. —*interj.* *Chess* a call indicating checkmate —*vt.* -**mat·ed, -mat·ing** to subject to checkmate

check·out (-out') *n.* **1.** the act or place of checking out purchases, as in a supermarket **2.** the time by which one must check out of a hotel, etc. **3.** a testing, esp. of a machine, as for accuracy Also **check'-out'**

check·point (-point') *n.* a place where traffic is stopped by authorities, as for inspection

check·up (-up') *n.* an examination or investigation, esp. a general medical examination

Ched·dar (cheese) (ched'ər) [< *Cheddar*, Avon, where orig. made] [often c-] a variety of hard, smooth cheese

cheek (chēk) *n.* [OE. *ceoke*, jaw, jawbone] **1.** either side of the face, below the eye **2.** either of two sides of a thing, as the jaws of a vice: *usually used in pl.* **3.** either of the buttocks **4.** [Colloq.] sauciness; impudence —*vt.* to speak insolently to —**cheek by jowl** close together; intimately —(with) **tongue in cheek** in a humorously ironic or insincere way

cheek·bone (-bōn') *n.* the bone of the upper cheek, just below the eye

cheek·y (-ē) *adj.* **cheek'i·er, cheek'i·est** [CHEEK + -Y[2]] [Colloq.] saucy; impudent; insolent —**cheek'i·ly** *adv.* —**cheek'i·ness** *n.*

cheep (chēp) *n.* [echoic] the short, faint, shrill sound of a young bird; peep —*vt., vi.* to make, or utter with, such a sound —**cheep'er** *n.*

cheer (chir) *n.* [< OFr. *chiere* < LL. *cara*, the head < Gr. *kara*] **1.** state of mind or of feeling; spirit: now in **be of good cheer, with good cheer,** etc. **2.** gladness; joy **3.** festive food or entertainment **4.** encouragement **5.** a) a shout of welcome, approval, encouragement, etc. b) a slogan, etc. shouted in unison in supporting a team —*vt.* **1.** to fill with joy and hope; gladden; comfort (often with *up*) **2.** to urge on or encourage by cheers **3.** to greet or applaud with cheers —*vi.* **1.** to be or become cheerful; feel encouraged (usually with *up*) **2.** to shout cheers

cheer·ful (-fəl) *adj.* **1.** full of cheer; joyful **2.** filling with cheer; bright and attractive [a *cheerful* room] **3.** willing; ready [a *cheerful* helper] —**cheer'ful·ly** *adv.* —**cheer'·ful·ness** *n.*

cheer·i·o (-ē ō') *interj., n., pl.* -**os'** [Colloq.] **1.** goodbye **2.** good health: a toast

cheer·lead·er (-lē'dər) *n.* [Chiefly U.S.] one who leads others in cheering for a team, etc.

cheer·less (-lis) *adj.* not cheerful; dismal —**cheer'less·ly** *adv.* —**cheer'less·ness** *n.*

cheers (chirz) *interj.* [Colloq.] good health: a toast

cheer·y (chir'ē) *adj.* **cheer'i·er, cheer'i·est** cheerful —**cheer'i·ly** *adv.* —**cheer'i·ness** *n.*

cheese[1] (chēz) *n.* [OE. *cyse*, akin to L. *caseus*] **1.** a food made from curds of soured milk pressed together to form a solid, variously hardened, ripened, etc. **2.** a shaped mass of this **3.** anything like or of the consistency of cheese [lemon *cheese*]

cheese[2] (chēz) *n.* [prob. < Hindi *chīz* (< Per. *čīz*), thing] [Slang] an important person or thing: also **big cheese**

cheese[3] (chēz) *vt.* [< ?] [Slang] to stop; leave off —**cheese it!** stop it!; give up! —**cheesed off** bored; fed up (*with*)

cheese·burg·er (chēz'bur'gər) *n.* [CHEESE[1] + (HAM)BURGER] a hamburger topped with melted cheese

cheese·cake (-kāk') *n.* **1.** a kind of cake made of cottage cheese or cream cheese, eggs, sugar, etc. **2.** [Slang] photographs, etc. of women displayed for their sex appeal

cheese·cloth (-kloth') *n.* [from use as cheese wrapping] a thin cotton cloth with a loose weave

cheese·par·ing (-per'iŋ) *n.* **1.** anything as worthless as a paring of cheese rind **2.** miserly handling of money —*adj.* stingy; miserly

cheese·wood (-wood') *n.* **1.** either of two Australian trees **2.** the yellowish wood obtained from these trees

chees·y (-ē) *adj.* **chees'i·er, chees'i·est 1.** like cheese in consistency, smell, etc. **2.** [Slang] inferior; poor —**chees'·i·ness** *n.*

chee·tah (chēt'ə) *n.* [Hindi *chītā* < Sans. *citra*, spotted] a swift, leopardlike animal of Africa and S Asia, with a small head, long legs, and a black-spotted, tawny coat: it can be trained to hunt

chef (shef) *n.* [Fr. < *chef de cuisine*, lit., head of the kitchen: see CHIEF] **1.** a head cook, as in a restaurant **2.** any cook

‡**chef-d'oeu·vre** (shā dē'vr') *n., pl.* **chefs-d'oeu'vre** (shā dē'-vr') [Fr., principal work] a masterpiece, as in art or literature

che·la[1] (kē'lə) *n., pl.* -**lae** (-lē) [ModL. < Gr. *chēlē*, claw] a pincerlike claw of a crab, lobster, scorpion, etc.

che·la[2] (chā'lə) *n.* [Hindi *celā* < Sans. *cela*, a servant] a novice or disciple of a religious teacher, esp. in Hinduism and Buddhism

che·late (kē'lāt) *adj.* resembling or having chelae —*n. Chem.* a compound in which a central atom (usually a metal ion) is attached to at least two other atoms by bonds so as to form a ring structure —*vt.* -**lat·ed, -lat·ing** to cause (a metal ion) to react with another molecule to form a chelate —**che·la'tion** *n.*

che·lic·er·a (kə lis'ə rə) *n., pl.* -**er·ae** (-ə rē') [ModL. < Gr. *chēlē*, claw + *keras*, horn] either of the first pair of appendages of spiders and other arachnids, used for grasping —**che·lic·er·ate** (-ə rāt', -ə rit) *adj.*

Che·loid (kē'loid) *n.* same as KELOID

che·lo·ni·an (ki lō'nē ən) *adj.* [< ModL. *Chelonia* < Gr. *chelōnē*] of, like, or being a turtle or tortoise —*n.* a turtle or tortoise

Chel·sea Pensioner (chel'sē) an inmate of the Chelsea Royal Hospital for old soldiers

chem. 1. chemical(s) **2.** chemist **3.** chemistry

chem·i·cal (kem'i k'l) *adj.* **1.** of or having to do with chemistry **2.** involving the use of chemicals —*n.* any substance used in or obtained by a chemical process —**chem'i·cal·ly** *adv.*

chemical engineering the science or profession of applying chemistry to industrial uses

chemical warfare warfare using poisonous gases, flame throwers, defoliants etc.

chem·i·lu·mi·nes·cence (kem'i loo'mə nes'əns) *n.* visible light chemically produced without heat —**chem'i·lu'mi·nes'-cent** *adj.*

che·min de fer (shə man'də fer') [Fr., a railway] a kind of baccarat, a gambling game

che·mise (shə mēz') *n.* [OFr. < VL. *camisia*, shirt < Gaul.] **1.** a woman's undergarment somewhat like a loose, short slip **2.** a straight, loose dress

chem·ist (kem'ist) *n.* [< (AL)CHEMIST] **1.** an expert or specialist in chemistry **2.** a pharmacist **3.** one who sells medicines, toiletries, etc.

chem·is·try (kem'is trē) *n., pl.* -**tries** [prec. + -RY] **1.** the science dealing with the composition and properties of substances, and with the reactions by which substances are produced from or converted into other substances **2.** the application of this to a specified subject or field of activity **3.** the chemical properties, composition, reactions, and uses of a substance **4.** any process of synthesis or analysis similar to that used in chemistry [the *chemistry* of wit]

chem·o- a combining form meaning of, with, or by chemicals or chemistry [chemotherapy]

chem·o·re·cep·tor (kem'ō ri sep'tər) *n.* a nerve ending or sense organ responsive to chemical stimuli, as a taste bud—**chem'o·re·cep'tion** *n.*

chem·o·ther·a·py (-ther'ə pē) *n.* the prevention or treatment of infection or disease by doses of chemical drugs: also **chem'o·ther'a·peu'tics** (-ther'ə pyoot'iks) —**chem'o·ther'a·peu'tic** *adj.* —**chem'o·ther'a·peu'ti·cal·ly** *adv.* —**chem'o·ther'a·pist** *n.*

chem·ur·gy (kem'ər jē) *n.* [CHEM(O)- + -URGY] the branch of chemistry dealing with the industrial use of organic products, esp. from farms (e.g., the use of soya beans as a base for plastics) —**chem·ur·gic** (kem ur'jik) *adj.*

che·nille (shi nēl') *n.* [Fr., lit., hairy caterpillar < L. *canicula*, little dog] **1.** a tufted, velvety yarn used for trimming, embroidery, etc. **2.** a fabric filled or woven with this, as for rugs

cheong·sam, cheong-sam (choŋ'sam') *n.* [< Cantonese < Mandarin Chin., a long jacket] a high-necked, closefitting Chinese dress with the skirt slit part way up the sides

cheque (chek) *n.* [see CHECK] **1.** a written order to a bank to pay the stated amount from one's account **2.** in Scotland, a restaurant bill

cheque card a card issued by a bank to an account-holder to guarantee payment of a cheque up to a stated limit

cheq·uer (chek'ər) *n.* [OFr. *eschekier,* a chessboard < *eschec: see* CHECK] **1.** a small square, as on a chessboard **2.** a pattern of such squares **3.** [*pl. with sing. v.*] *a) same as* DRAUGHTS *b)* a game played by 2-6 players with marbles or pegs on a board: also **Chinese chequers 4.** *same as* DRAUGHTSMAN (sense 4) —*vt.* **1.** to mark off in squares, or in patches of colour **2.** to break the uniformity of, as with varied features, changes in fortune, etc.

cheq·uered (-ərd) *adj.* **1.** having a pattern of squares **2.** varied in colour and shading **3.** marked by diversified features or by varied events [a *chequered* career]

cher·ish (cher'ish) *vt.* [< OFr. < *cher,* dear < L. *carus*] **1.** to hold dear; feel or show love for **2.** to take good care of; protect; foster [to *cherish* one's rights] **3.** to cling to the idea of

che·root (shə rōōt') *n.* [< Tamil *churuṭṭu,* a roll] a cigar with both ends cut square

cher·ry (cher'ē) *n., pl.* **-ries** [Anglo-Fr. *cherise* < OFr. < VL. < Gr. *kerasion* < *kerasos,* cherry tree] **1.** a small, fleshy fruit, yellow to dark red, with a smooth, hard stone **2.** any tree of the rose family which bears this fruit, or its wood **3.** the bright-red colour of certain cherries **4.** [Slang] virginity —*adj.* **1.** bright-red **2.** of cherry wood **3.** made with cherries

chert (chərt) *n.* [< ?] a very fine-grained, tough rock composed mainly of silica —**chert'y** (-ē) *adj.* **chert'i·er, chert'i·est**

cher·ub (cher'əb) *n., pl.* **-ubs;** for 1-3 usually **-u·bim** (-ə bim, -yōō bim) *or* (AV) **-u·bims** [< LL. < Heb. *kerūbh*] **1.** *Bible* one of certain winged heavenly beings: Ezek. 10 **2.** *Christian Theol.* any of the second order of angels, just below the seraphim **3.** a representation of a cherub, now usually as a chubby, rosy-faced child with wings **4.** a person, esp. a child, with a sweet, innocent face —**che·ru·bic** (chə rōō'bik) *adj.* —**che·ru'bi·cal·ly** *adv.*

cher·vil (chər'vəl) *n.* [< OE. < L. < Gr. < *chairein,* to rejoice + *phyllon,* leaf] an aromatic plant, with leaves used to flavour soups, etc.

Chesh·ire cat (chesh'ir, -ər) a proverbial grinning cat from Cheshire, esp. one described in Lewis Carroll's *Alice's Adventures in Wonderland*

chess (ches) *n.* [< OFr. *esches,* pl. of *eschec: see* CHECK] a game for two, each with 16 pieces moved variously on a chessboard in alternation, the object being to checkmate the opponent's king

chess·board (-bôrd') *n.* a board with 64 squares of two alternating colours, for chess and draughts

chess·man (-man', -mən) *n., pl.* **-men** (-men', -mən) any of the pieces used in chess

chest (chest) *n.* [< OE. < L. < Gr. *kistē,* a box] **1.** a box with a lid and, often, a lock, for storing or shipping things **2.** *same as* CHEST OF DRAWERS **3.** a cabinet for medicines, toiletries, etc. **4.** *a)* the part of the body enclosed by the ribs; thorax *b)* the outside front of this —**get (something) off one's chest** [Colloq.] to unburden oneself of (some trouble, etc.) by talking about it

chest·ed (-id) *adj.* having a (specified kind of) chest, or thorax [hollow-*chested*]

ches·ter·field (ches'tər feld') *n.* [after a 19th-c. Earl of *Chesterfield*] **1.** a single-breasted overcoat for men, usually with a velvet collar **2.** a sofa with upright ends

chest·nut (ches'nut', -nət) *n.* [< OFr. < L. < Gr. *kastaneia*] **1.** the smooth-shelled, sweet, edible nut of certain trees of the beech family **2.** one of these trees, or the wood **3.** *same as* HORSE CHESTNUT **4.** reddish brown **5.** a reddish-brown horse **6.** [Colloq.] *a)* an old, stale joke or phrase; cliché *b)* a familiar story, piece of music, etc., repeated too often —*adj.* reddish-brown

chest of drawers a set of drawers within a frame, as for keeping clothing in a bedroom

chest·y (ches'tē) *adj.* **chest'i·er, chest'i·est** [Colloq.] **1.** having a large chest, or thorax **2.** bosomy **3.** inclined to or having a disease of the chest

che·val glass (shə val') [Fr. *cheval,* horse, support + GLASS] a full-length mirror on swivels in a frame

chev·a·lier (shev'ə lir'; *for 1, often* shə val'yā') *n.* [see CAVALIER] **1.** a member of the lowest rank of the French Legion of Honour **2.** a cavalier; gallant

Chev·i·ot (chev'ē ət, chēv'-, shev'-) *n.* [after the *Cheviot Hills,* between England and Scotland] **1.** any of a breed of sheep with short, dense wool **2.** [*usually* c-] *a)* a rough wool fabric in a twill weave *b)* a cotton cloth resembling this

chev·ron (shev'rən) *n.* [< OFr., rafter (from its shape), ult. < L. *capra,* she-goat] any V-shaped pattern or device, esp. *a)* a bar or bars worn on the sleeve, as of a military uniform, to show rank or service *b) Heraldry* an inverted V-shaped charge on a shield

chevron board a board on the roadside marked with horizontal chevrons indicating the direction of a sharp bend in the road

chev·y (chev'ē) *n., pl.* **chev'ies** [< hunting cry *chivy,* in the ballad of *Chevy Chase*] a hunt; chase —*vt., vi.* **chev'ied, chev'y·ing 1.** to hunt; chase; run about **2.** to worry; fret; chivvy

CHEVRON

chew (chōō) *vt.* [< OE. *ceowan*] **1.** to bite and crush with the teeth **2.** *a)* to think over *b)* to discuss (often with *over*) **3.** [Slang] to rebuke severely (often with *out*) —*vi.* **1.** to do chewing **2.** [Colloq.] to chew tobacco —*n.* **1.** a chewing **2.** something chewed or for chewing, as a portion of tobacco —**chew the rag** (or **fat**) [Slang] to converse idly —**chew'er** *n.*

chew·ing gum (chōō'iŋ) chicle or other gummy substance, flavoured and sweetened for chewing

chew·y (chōō'ē) *adj.* **chew'i·er, chew'i·est** needing much chewing —**chew'i·ness** *n.*

‡chez (shā) *prep.* [Fr.] by; at; at the home of

chg. *pl.* **chgs.** charge

chgd. charged

chi (kī) *n.* [Gr.] the 22nd letter of the Greek alphabet (X, χ)

Chi·an·ti (kē an'tē, -än'-) *n.* [It.] a red or white wine, orig. made in Tuscany

chi·a·ro·scu·ro (kē är'ə skyoor'ō) *n., pl.* **-ros** [It. < L. *clarus,* clear + *obscurus,* dark] **1.** the treatment of light and shade in a painting, drawing, etc., as to produce an illusion of depth **2.** a style or a painting, etc. emphasizing this

chic (shēk) *n.* [Fr. < *schick,* order, skill] smart elegance of style and manner —*adj.* **chic·quer** (shēk'ər), **chic'quest** (-ist) smartly stylish

chi·cane (shi kān') *n.* [Fr. < *chicaner,* to quibble < MLowG. *schikken,* to arrange] **1.** *same as* CHICANERY **2.** *Bridge, Whist* a hand without trumps **3.** *Motor Racing* an artificial barrier designed to reduce speeds before a bend, etc. —*vi.* **-caned', -can'ing** to use chicanery —*vt.* **1.** to trick **2.** to get by chicanery

chi·can·er·y (-ər ē) *n., pl.* **-er·ies 1.** the use of clever but deceptive talk or action to deceive, evade, etc. **2.** an instance of this

Chi·ca·no (chə kä'nō) *n., pl.* **-nos** [altered < AmSp. (*Mé)jicano,* a Mexican] [*also* c-] [U.S.] a U.S. citizen or inhabitant of Mexican descent

chi·chi, chi-chi (shē'shē) *adj.* [Fr.] affectedly or showily stylish in looks or behaviour —*n.* anything chichi

chick (chik) *n.* [< CHICKEN] **1.** a young chicken **2.** any young bird **3.** a child: term of endearment **4.** [Slang] a young woman

chick·a·dee (chik'ə dē') *n.* [echoic of its note] **1.** any of various small N. American birds closely related to the tits, with black, grey, and white feathers **2.** [Chiefly U.S.] a term of endearment

chick·en (chik'ən) *n.* [< OE. *cycen,* lit., little cock] **1.** a common farm bird raised for its edible eggs or flesh; hen or rooster, esp. a young one **2.** its flesh **3.** a young or inexperienced person **4.** [Slang] a timid or cowardly person —*adj.* **1.** of chicken **2.** [Slang] timid or cowardly —*vi.* [Slang] to lose courage and abandon a plan, action, etc. (usually with *out*)

chicken feed [Slang] a petty sum of money

chick·en-heart·ed (-här'tid) *adj.* timid; cowardly: also **chick'en-liv'ered**

chicken pox an acute, contagious virus disease, usually of young children, with fever and a series of skin eruptions

chicken wire light, pliable wire fencing, used esp. for enclosing chicken runs

chick·pea (chik'pē') *n.* [for *chich pea,* ult. < L. *cicer,* pea] **1.** a bushy annual plant of the legume family, with short, hairy pods containing usually two seeds **2.** the edible seed

chick·weed (-wēd') *n.* any of several low-growing plants of the pink family, often found as weeds

chic·le (chik''l) *n.* [AmSp. < Nahuatl *chictli*] a gumlike substance made from the milky juice of the sapodilla tree, used in making chewing gum

chic·o·ry (chik'ə rē) *n., pl.* **-ries** [< OFr. < L. < Gr. *kichorion*] **1.** a plant of the composite family, with blue flowers: the leaves are used for salad **2.** its root, roasted and ground for mixing with coffee or for use as a coffee substitute

chide (chīd) *vt., vi.* **chid'ed** *or* **chid** (chid), **chid'ed** *or* **chid** *or* **chid·den** (chid'n), **chid'ing** [OE. *cidan*] to scold; now, usually, to reprove mildly —**chid'er** *n.* —**chid'ing·ly** *adv.*

chief (chēf) *n.* [< OFr. < L. *caput,* the head] **1.** the head or leader of a group of people, specif., *a)* a tribe *b)* [Colloq.] a company or department **2.** the appointed or elected official in charge of a district: term used in parts of Africa **3.** [Colloq.] *same as* CHIEF PETTY OFFICER **4.** *Heraldry* the upper part of a shield —*adj.* **1.** highest in rank, office, etc. **2.** main; principal —*adv.* [Archaic] chiefly —**in chief 1.** in the chief position **2.** [Archaic] chiefly

chief·dom (-dəm) *n.* the office or territory of a chief (*n.* 1*a*)

chief justice 1. *same as* LORD CHIEF JUSTICE **2.** in some countries, the judge presiding over the supreme court **3.** [U.S.] the presiding judge of a court made up of several members

chief·ly (-lē) *adv.* **1.** most of all; above all **2.** mainly; mostly —*adj.* of or like a chief

Chief of Staff 1. the senior staff officer and principal adviser to the commander of a major military unit **2.** the senior officer of each branch of the armed forces

chief petty officer *see* MILITARY RANKS, table

chief·tain (-tən) *n.* [< OFr. < LL. < L. *caput*, the head] a leader, esp. of a clan or tribe —**chief′tain·cy,** *pl.* **-cies, chief′tain·ship′** *n.*

chief technician *see* MILITARY RANKS, table

chiff·chaff (chif′chaf′) *n.* [echoic] a small, olive-green and brown warbler, feeding mainly on insects and spiders

chif·fon (shi fon′, shif′on) *n.* [Fr., dim. of *chiffe*, a rag] **1.** a sheer, lightweight fabric of silk, nylon, etc. **2.** [*pl.*] ribbons, laces, etc. used as accessories to a woman's dress —*adj.* **1.** made of chiffon **2.** *Cooking* made light and porous as by adding beaten egg whites

chif·fo·nier, chif·fon·ier (shif′ə nir′) *n.* [Fr., orig., rag-picker < prec.] a narrow, high cabinet or chest of drawers, often with a mirror

chig·ger (chig′ər) *n.* [of Afr. origin] *same as* CHIGOE

chi·gnon (shēn′yon, -yōn) *n.* [Fr. < OFr. < L. *catena*, a chain] a knot or coil of hair sometimes worn at the back of the neck by women

chig·oe (chig′ō) *n.,* *pl.* **-oes** (-ōz) [? via Fr. *chique* < WInd. native name] a flea of tropical S. America and Africa: the female burrows into the skin, causing painful sores

Chi·hua·hua (chi wä′wä) *n.* [after *Chihuahua*, state of Mexico] any of an ancient Mexican breed of very small dog with large, pointed ears

chil·blain (chil′blān′) *n.* [CHIL(L) + BLAIN] a painful swelling or sore on the foot or hand, caused by exposure to cold —**chil′blained′** *adj.*

child (chīld) *n.,* *pl.* **chil′dren** [< OE. *cild,* pl. *cildru*] **1.** an infant; baby **2.** an unborn offspring **3.** a boy or girl in the period before puberty **4.** a son or daughter **5.** a descendant **6.** a person like a child; immature or childish adult **7.** a person or thing viewed as produced by a certain place, time, source, etc. [*a child* of the Renaissance] —**with child** pregnant —**child′less** *adj.* —**child′less·ness** *n.*

child·bear·ing (-ber′iŋ) *n.* the act of giving birth to children; parturition

child·bed (-bed′) *n.* the condition of a woman giving birth to a child

child·birth (-bʉrth′) *n.* the act of giving birth to a child; parturition

child·hood (-hood′) *n.* the time or state of being a child; period from infancy to puberty

child·ish (-ish) *adj.* **1.** of or like a child **2.** not fit for an adult; immature; silly —**child′ish·ly** *adv.* —**child′ish·ness** *n.*

child·like (-līk′) *adj.* like a child, esp. in being innocent, trusting, etc. —**child′like′ness** *n.*

child·mind·er (-mīn′dər) *n.* a person employed to look after young childern

chil·dren (chil′drən) *n.* pl. of CHILD

child's play (chīldz) anything simple to do

chil·e con car·ne (chil′ē kən kär′nē) *same as* CHILI CON CARNE

Chile pine *same as* MONKEY PUZZLE

Chile saltpetre native sodium nitrate

chil·i (chil′ē) *n.,* *pl.* **chil′ies** [MexSp. < Nahuatl *chilli*] **1.** the dried pod of red pepper, a very hot seasoning **2.** the tropical American plant, of the nightshade family, that bears this pod

chil·i·ad (kil′ē ad′) *n.* [L. *chilias* (gen. *chiliadis*) < Gr. *chilias* < *chilioi*, a thousand] **1.** a group of 1000 **2.** a thousand years

chil·i con car·ne (chil′ē kən kär′nē) [< MexSp., lit., red pepper with meat] a highly seasoned dish with minced or chopped beef, chilies or chili powder, beans, and often tomatoes

chili powder a powder of dried chili pods, herbs, etc.

chili sauce a spiced sauce of chopped tomatoes, green and red sweet peppers, onions, etc.

chill (chil) *n.* [OE. *ciele*] **1.** a feeling of coldness that makes one shiver **2.** a moderate coldness **3.** a discouraging influence **4.** a feeling of sudden fear **5.** unfriendliness **6.** a feverish cold —*adj.* *same as* CHILLY —*vi.* **1.** to become cool or cold **2.** to shiver from cold, fear, etc. —*vt.* **1.** to make cool or cold **2.** to cause a chill in **3.** to check (enthusiasm, etc.) **4.** to depress; dispirit **5.** *Metallurgy* to harden (metal) on the surface by rapid cooling —**chill′er** *n.* —**chill′ing·ly** *adv.* —**chill′ness** *n.*

chill factor [Chiefly U.S.] the combined effect of low temperature and high winds on loss of body heat

chil·li (chil′ē) *n.,* *pl.* **-lies** *same as* CHILI

chill·y (chil′ē) *adj.* **chill′i·er, chill′i·est 1.** moderately cold; uncomfortably cool **2.** chilling **3.** cool in manner; unfriendly **4.** depressing; dispiriting —**chill′i·ly** *adv.* —**chill′i·ness** *n.*

Chil·tern Hundreds (chil′tərn) a nominal office under the British crown, the holding of which debars one from membership of the House of Commons: appointment to it formally circumvents the rule against resignation from Parliament In full, **Stewardship of the Chiltern Hundreds**

Chi·mae·ra (ki mir′ə, kī-) *same as* CHIMERA —*n.* [c-] a chimera

chime¹ (chīm) *n.* [< OFr. < L. *cymbalum,* CYMBAL] **1.** [usually *pl.*] *a*) a tuned set of bells or metal tubes *b*) the sounds produced by these **2.** a single bell in a clock, etc. **3.** harmony; agreement —*vi.* chimed, chim′ing **1.** to sound as a chime **2.** to sound in harmony, as bells **3.** to harmonize; agree —*vt.* **1.** to ring (a chime or chimes) **2.** to indicate (time) by chiming —**chime in 1.** to join in or interrupt, as talk **2.** to agree —**chim′er** *n.*

chime² (chīm) *n.* [ME. *chimb* < OE. *cimb-* (only in compounds)] the extended rim at each end of a cask or barrel

Chi·me·ra (ki mir′ə, kī-) *n.* [< OFr. < L. < Gr. *chimaira,* she-goat] *Gr. Myth.* a fire-breathing monster with a lion's head, goat's body, and serpent's tail —*n.* [c-] **1.** any similar unreal monster **2.** an impossible or foolish fancy

chi·mer·i·cal (ki mer′i k'l, -mer′-; kī-) *adj.* [see prec.] **1.** imaginary; unreal **2.** absurd; impossible **3.** visionary Also **chi·mer′ic** —**chi·mer′i·cal·ly** *adv.*

chim·ney (chim′nē) *n.,* *pl.* **-neys** [< OFr. < LL. *caminata,* fireplace < L. *caminus* < Gr. *kaminos,* oven] **1.** the passage through which smoke escapes from a fire; flue **2.** a structure containing a flue and extending above the roof **3.** a glass tube around the flame of a lamp, etc. **4.** a fissure or vent, as in a cliff or volcano

chimney pot a short pipe on a chimney top to carry the smoke off and increase the draught

chimney sweep a person whose work is cleaning the soot from chimneys

chimp (chimp) *n.* [Colloq.] a chimpanzee

chim·pan·zee (chim′pan zē′) *n.* [< Fr. < Bantu *kampenzi*] an anthropoid ape of Africa, with black hair and large ears: it is smaller than a gorilla and is noted for its intelligence

CHIMPANZEE
(90-150 cm high)

chin (chin) *n.* [OE. *cin*] the part of the face below the lower lip; projecting part of the lower jaw —*vt.* **chinned, chin′ning** to pull (oneself) up, while hanging by the hands from a horizontal bar, until the chin is just above the level of the bar —*vi.* **1.** to chin oneself **2.** [Slang] to chat, gossip, etc. —**keep one's chin up** to bear up bravely —**take it on the chin** [Slang] to suffer defeat, hardship, etc.

Chin. 1. China **2.** Chinese

chi·na (chī′nə) *n.* **1.** *a*) porcelain, orig. from China *b*) vitrified ceramic ware like porcelain **2.** dishes, etc. of this **3.** any earthenware dishes or crockery

china clay *same as* KAOLIN

chi·na·graph (chī′nə graf′) *n.* [CHINA +-GRAPH] a kind of pencil used to write on china, plastic, etc.

Chi·na·man (-man) *n.,* *pl.* **-men** (-mən) **1.** [Archaic] a native of China **2.** *Cricket* an off-break or googly bowled by a left-handed bowler to a right-handed batsman, spinning from off to leg

Chi·na·town (-toun′) *n.* the Chinese quarter of a city

chi·na·ware (-wer′) *n.* *same as* CHINA

chin·chil·la (chin chil′ə) *n.* [Sp., prob. dim. of *chinche* < L. *cimex,* bug] **1.** a small rodent of the Andes, bred extensively for its fur **2.** its expensive, soft, pale-grey fur **3.** a heavy, nubby wool cloth

chin-chin (chin′chin′) *interj.* [PidE. < Chin. *ch'ing ch'ing,* lit., please please] a greeting or toast

Chin·dit (chin′dit) *n.* [Burmese *chinthé,* a mythological creature] a member of a group of Allied guerilla fighters behind the Japanese lines in Burma (1943-45)

chine¹ (chīn) *n.* [< OFr. *eschine* < Frank. *skina,* small bone, shin bone] **1.** the backbone; spine **2.** a cut of meat containing part of the backbone **3.** a ridge —*vt.* **chined, chin′ing** to cut along or across the backbone of (a meat carcass)

chine² (chīn) *n.* [ME. < OE. *cine,* fissure, akin to *cinan,* to burst open] [S Eng. Dial.] a rocky ravine or deep fissure in a cliff

Chi·nese (chī nēz′; *for adj., often* chī′nēz′) **1.** *pl.* **-nese′** *a* native of China or a person of Chinese descent **2.** the standard language of the Chinese; Mandarin **3.** any Chinese language —*adj.* of China, its people, etc.

Chinese cabbage any of several vegetables with long, narrow leaves in loose, cylindrical heads and a cabbagelike taste

Chinese chequers [< ?] same as CHEQUER (sense 3b)

Chinese gooseberry a vine of New Zealand and the Pacific, bearing large, edible fruit

Chinese lantern a lantern of brightly coloured paper, made so that it can be folded up

Chin·ese-lan·tern plant (-lan′tərn) a perennial herb of the nightshade family, with a bladderlike red calyx

Chinese puzzle any intricate puzzle

Chinese red a brilliant orange-red

Chink (chiŋk) *n.* [altered < CHINESE] *a derogatory name for a Chinese*

chink[1] (chiŋk) *n.* [OE. *cine*] a crack; fissure

chink[2] (chiŋk) *n.* [echoic] a sharp, clinking sound, as of coins striking together —*vi., vt.* to make or cause to make a sharp, clinking sound

chin·less wonder (chin′lis) [Colloq.] a weak, ineffectual, or cowardly person

chin·oi·se·rie (shin′wä′zə rē) *n.* [Fr. < *Chinois*, Chinese + *-erie*, -ERY] **1.** an ornate decorative style based on Chinese motifs **2.** articles, designs, etc. in this style

chi·nook salmon (chi nook) the largest Pacific salmon

chintz (chints) *n.* [earlier a pl. form < Hindi *chhīnt* < Sans. *citra*, spotted, bright] a cotton cloth printed in colours and usually glazed

chintz·y (-ē) *adj.* chintz′i·er, chintz′i·est **1.** like chintz **2.** of or designating a style of furnishing typified by chintz curtains, furniture coverings, etc. **3.** [U.S. Colloq.] cheap, stingy, etc.

chin·wag (chin′wag′) *n.* [Colloq.] a talk; chat —*vi.* to talk

chip (chip) *vt.* **chipped, chip′ping** [< OE. hyp. *cippian*] **1.** *a)* to break or cut a small piece or thin slice from *b)* to break or cut off (a small piece or pieces) **2.** to shape by cutting or chopping —*vi.* to break off into small pieces —*n.* **1.** a small, thin piece of wood, etc. cut or broken off **2.** a place where a small piece has been chipped off **3.** wood, palm leaf, or straw split and woven into baskets, etc. **4.** a fragment of dried animal dung, sometimes used for fuel **5.** [U.S.] a worthless thing **6.** a small, round disc used in poker, etc. as a money token; counter **7.** [U.S.] *same as* CRISP (n. 2) **8.** a slice or strip of potato fried in deep fat **9.** *Electronics a)* a semiconductor body for an integrated circuit *b) same as* INTEGRATED CIRCUIT —**chip in** [Colloq.] **1.** to share in giving money or help **2.** to add one's comments —**chip off the old block** a person much like his father —**chip on one's shoulder** [Colloq.] an inclination to fight —**have had one's chips** [Colloq.] to be defeated, dead, etc. —**let the chips fall where they may** [Colloq.] whatever the consequences —**when the chips are down** [Colloq.] when something is really at stake

chip-board (-bôrd′) *n.* a wood substitute made from compressed wood chips or shavings bonded in resin and formed into sheets or planks

chip·munk (-muŋk′) *n.* [of Algonquian origin] a small, striped N. American squirrel: it lives mainly on the ground

chip·o·la·ta (chip′ō lä′tə) *n.* [Fr. < It. *cipollata* < *cipolla*, onion < L. *cepa*, onion: from the onions used as flavouring] a small sausage, esp. of pork sausagemeat

Chip·pen·dale (chip′n dāl′) *adj.* [after T. *Chippendale* (1718?–79), Brit. cabinetmaker] designating or of an 18th-cent. Brit. style of furniture with graceful lines and, often, rococo ornamentation

chip·per (chip′ər) *adj.* [< N Brit. *kipper*] [U.S. Colloq.] in good spirits; lively

chip shot *Golf* a short, lofted shot, made esp. from just off the green

chi·ro- [< Gr. *cheir*, the hand] *a combining form meaning* hand [*chiromancy*]

chi·rog·ra·phy (kī rog′rə fē) *n.* [CHIRO- + -GRAPHY] handwriting; penmanship —**chi·rog′ra·pher** *n.* —**chi·ro·graph·ic** (kī′rə graf′ik), **chi′ro·graph′i·cal** *adj.*

chi·ro·man·cy (kī′rə man′sē) *n.* [CHIRO- + -MANCY] *same as* PALMISTRY —**chi′ro·man′cer** *n.*

chi·rop·o·dy (kə rop′ə dē, kī-) *n.* [CHIRO- + -POD + -Y³] the profession dealing with the care of the feet and with the treatment of foot disorders —**chi·rop′o·dist** *n.*

chi·ro·prac·tic (kī′rə prak′tik, kī′rə prak′tik) *n.* [< CHIRO- + Gr. *praktikos*, practical] a method of treating disease by manipulation of the body joints, esp. of the spine —**chi′·ro·prac′tor** *n.*

chirp (chʉrp) *vi.* [echoic] **1.** to make the short, shrill sound of some birds or insects **2.** to speak in a lively, shrill way —*vt.* to utter in a sharp, shrill tone —*n.* a short, shrill sound —**chirp′er** *n.*

chirp·y (chʉrp′ē) *adj.* [CHIRP + -Y²] [Colloq.] cheerful; merry —**chirp′i·ly** *adv.* —**chirp′i·ness** *n.*

chirr (chʉr) *n.* [echoic] a shrill, trilled sound, as of some insects or birds —*vi.* to make such a sound

chir·rup (chir′əp) *vi.* [var. of CHIRP] to chirp repeatedly —*n.* a chirruping sound

chis·el (chiz′'l) *n.* [ONormFr. < VL. < L. pp. of *caedere*, to cut] a sharp-edged tool for cutting or shaping wood, stone, or metal —*vi., vt.* **-elled, -el·ling 1.** to cut or shape with a chisel **2.** [Colloq.] to take advantage of (someone) or get (something) by cheating, sponging, etc. —**chis′el·ler** *n.*

chi-square (kī′skwer′) *n.* a statistical method used to test whether the classification of data can be ascribed to chance or to some underlying law

chit[1] (chit) *n.* [ME. *chitte*, prob. var. of *kitte*, for kitten] **1.** a child **2.** an immature, slender or childish girl

chit[2] (chit) *n.* [< Hindi < Sans. *citra*, spotted] **1.** a memorandum **2.** a voucher of a small sum owed for drink, food, etc. **3.** [Colloq.] an invoice, etc.

CHISELS
(A, cold;
B, wood)

chit·chat (chit′chat′) *n.* [< CHAT] **1.** light, familiar, informal talk; small talk **2.** gossip

chi·tin (kīt′'n) *n.* [Fr. *chitine* < Gr.: see CHITON] a tough, horny substance forming the outer covering of insects, crustaceans,etc. —**chi′tin·ous** *adj.*

chi·ton (kīt′'n, kī′ton) *n.* [Gr. *chitōn*, garment, tunic < Sem.] a loose garment similar to a tunic, worn by both men and women in ancient Greece

chit·ter·lings (chit′ər liŋz) *n.pl.* [ME. *chiterling* < Gmc. base] the small intestines of pigs, etc., used for food

chiv·al·ric (shiv′'l rik, shi val′rik) *adj.* of chivalry

chiv·al·rous (shiv′'l rəs) *adj.* **1.** having the attributes of an ideal knight; gallant, courteous, honourable, etc. **2.** of chivalry —**chiv′al·rous·ly** *adv.* —**chiv′al·rous·ness** *n.*

chiv·al·ry (shiv′'l rē) *n.* [< OFr. *chivalerie* < *chevaler*, a knight: doublet of CAVALRY] **1.** a group of knights or gallant gentlemen **2.** the medieval system of knighthood **3.** the noble qualities a knight was supposed to have, such as courage, honour, and a readiness to help the weak and protect women **4.** the demonstration of any of these qualities

chives (chīvz) *n.pl.* [< OFr. < L. *cepa*, onion] [often with sing. v.] a plant of the lily family, with small, hollow leaves having a mild onion odour: used to flavour soups, stews, etc.

chiv·y, chiv·vy (chiv′ē) *n., pl.* **chiv′ies** or **chiv′vies** *same as* CHEVY —*vt., vi.* **chiv′ied** or **chiv′vied, chiv′y·ing** or **chiv′vy·ing 1.** to fret; worry; nag **2.** to manipulate **3.** *same as* CHEVY

chiz, chizz (chiz) *n.* [< CHISEL] [Slang] a swindle

chlo·ral (klôr′əl) *n.* [CHLOR(O)- + AL(COHOL)] **1.** a thin, oily, colourless liquid, CCl₃CHO, with a pungent odour, prepared by the action of chlorine on alcohol **2.** *same as* CHLORAL HYDRATE

chloral hydrate a colourless, crystalline compound used chiefly as a sedative

chlor·am·phen·i·col (klôr′am fen′ə kol′) *n.* [CHLOR(O)- + AM(IDE) + PHEN(O)- + NI(TRO)- + (GLY)COL] an antibiotic drug used against a wide variety of bacterial and rickettsial diseases and against some viruses

chlo·rate (klôr′āt, -it) *n.* a salt of chloric acid

chlor·dane (klôr′dān) *n.* [CHLOR(O)- + (*in*)*dane*, a coal-tar derivative] a poisonous, volatile oil used as an insecticide: also **chlor′dan** (-dan)

chlo·ric (klôr′ik) *adj.* **1.** of or containing chlorine with a higher valency than in corresponding chlorous compounds **2.** designating or of a colourless acid, HClO₃, whose salts are chlorates

chlo·ride (-īd) *n.* a compound in which chlorine is combined with another element or radical (e.g., a salt of hydrochloric acid)

chloride of lime a white powder, CaOCl₂, obtained by treating slaked lime with chlorine and used for disinfecting and bleaching: also, **bleaching powder**

chlo·ri·nate (klôr′ə nāt′) *vt.* **-nat′ed, -nat′ing** to treat or combine (a substance) with chlorine; esp., to pass chlorine into (water or sewage) for purification —**chlo′ri·na′tion** *n.* —**chlo′ri·na′tor** *n.*

chlo·rine (klôr′ēn, -in) *n.* [CHLOR(O)- + -INE⁴] a greenish-yellow, poisonous, gaseous chemical element with a disagreeable odour, used in bleaching, water purification, etc.: symbol, Cl; at. wt., 35.453; at. no., 17

chlo·rite (-īt) *n.* a salt of chlorous acid

chlo·ro- [< Gr. *chlōros*, pale green] *a combining form meaning:* **1.** green [*chlorophyll*] **2.** having chlorine in the molecule [*chloroform*] Also, before a vowel, **chlor-**

chlo·ro·form (klor′ə fôrm′) *n.* [see CHLORO- & FORM(IC) + -YL] a sweetish, colourless, volatile liquid, CHCl₃, used as a general anaesthetic and as a solvent —*vt.* **1.** to anaesthetize with chloroform **2.** to kill with chloroform

Chlo·ro·my·ce·tin (klôr′ə mī sēt′'n) [CHLORO- + -MYCET(E) + -IN¹] *a trademark for* CHLORAMPHENICOL

chlo·ro·phyll (klôr'ə fil') *n.* [< Fr. < Gr. *chlōros*, green + *phyllon*, a leaf] the green pigment of plants: it is involved in photosynthesis —**chlo'ro·phyl'lose** (-ōs), **chlo'ro·phyl'lous** (-əs) *adj.*

chlo·ro·plast (klôr'ə plast') *n.* [CHLORO- + Gr. *plastos*, formed] an oval, chlorophyll-bearing body found in the cytoplasm in cells of green plants

chlo·rous (klôr'əs) *adj.* **1.** of or containing chlorine with a lower valency than in corresponding chloric compounds **2.** designating or of an unstable acid, $HClO_2$, a strong oxidizing agent whose salts are chlorites

chlor·prom·a·zine (klôr prom'ə zēn') *n.* a synthetic drug used as a tranquillizer

chlor·tet·ra·cy·cline (-tet'rə sī'klēn, -klin) *n.* a yellow antibiotic used against a wide variety of bacterial and rickettsial infections and certain viruses

chm., chmn. chairman

chock (chok) *n.* [ONormFr. *choque*, a block] **1.** a block or wedge placed under a wheel, barrel, etc. to prevent motion **2.** *Naut.* a block with two hornlike projections curving inwards, through which a rope may be run —*vt.* to provide or wedge fast as with chocks —*adv.* as close or tight as can be

chock·a·block (-ə blok') *adj.* **1.** pulled so tight as to have the blocks touching: said of a hoisting tackle **2.** crowded —*adv.* tightly together

chock-full (chok'fool') *adj.* as full as possible; filled to capacity

choc·o·late (chok'lət, -ə lət) *n.* [< Fr. < Sp. < Nahuatl *chocolatl*] **1.** a paste, powder, etc. made from cacao seeds that have been roasted and ground **2.** a drink made of chocolate, hot milk or water, and sugar **3.** a sweet made of or coated with chocolate **4.** reddish brown —*adj.* **1.** made of or flavoured with chocolate **2.** reddish-brown

choc·o·late-box (-boks') *adj.* [Colloq.] of or designating a style of painting that is pretty or attractive in a stereotyped, sentimental way

choice (chois) *n.* [< OFr. < *choisir*, to choose < Goth. *kausjan*, to taste] **1.** a choosing; selection **2.** the right or power to choose; option **3.** a person or thing chosen **4.** the best part **5.** a variety from which to choose **6.** a supply well chosen **7.** an alternative **8.** care in choosing —*adj.* **choic'er, choic'est** **1.** of special excellence **2.** carefully chosen —**choice'ly** *adv.* —**choice'ness** *n.*

choir (kwīr) *n.* [< OFr. *cuer* < ML. *chorus*, choir < L.: see CHORUS] **1.** a group of singers trained to sing together, esp. in a church **2.** the part of a church they occupy **3.** an instrumental section of an orchestra

choke (chōk) *vt.* **choked, chok'ing** [< OE. *aceocian*] **1.** to prevent from breathing by blocking the windpipe; strangle; suffocate **2.** to block up; obstruct by clogging **3.** to hinder the growth or action of **4.** to fill up **5.** to cut off some air from the carburettor of (a petrol engine) so as to make a richer petrol mixture **6.** to hold (a ball, golf club, etc.) towards the middle of the handle —*vi.* **1.** to be suffocated **2.** to be blocked up; be obstructed —*n.* **1.** the act or sound of choking **2.** the valve that chokes a carburettor —**choke back** to hold back (feelings, sobs, etc.) —**choke down** to swallow with difficulty —**choke off** to bring to an end; end the growth of —**choke up** **1.** to block up; clog **2.** to fill too full **3.** [Colloq.] to be unable to speak, act efficiently, etc., as because of fear, tension, etc.

choke·bore (-bôr') *n.* **1.** a shotgun bore that tapers towards the muzzle to keep the shot closely bunched **2.** a gun with such a bore

chok·er (chōk'ər) *n.* **1.** a person or thing that chokes **2.** a closely fitting necklace

chok·y¹ (-ē) *adj.* **chok'i·er, chok'i·est** **1.** inclined to choke **2.** suffocating; stifling Also sp. **chok'ey**

chok·y² (-ē) *n.* [< Hindi *caukī*, shed] [Slang] prison: also **chok'ey**

chol·e- same as CHOLO-: also, before a vowel, **chol-**

chol·er (kol'ər) *n.* [< OFr. < L. *cholera*: see ff.] **1.** [Obs.] bile: in medieval times yellow bile was considered the source of anger and irritability **2.** [Now Rare] anger or ill humour

chol·er·a (kol'ər ə) *n.* [L., jaundice < Gr. *cholera*, nausea < *cholē*, bile] any of several intestinal diseases; esp., Asiatic cholera, an acute, infectious disease characterized by severe diarrhoea, cramps, and loss of water from the body —**chol'·e·ra'ic** (-ə rā'ik) *adj.*

chol·er·ic (kol'ər ik, kə ler'ik) *adj.* [see CHOLER] showing a quick temper or irascible nature

cho·les·ter·ol (kə les'tə rol') *n.* [< CHOLE- + Gr. *stereos*, solid + -OL¹] a crystalline fatty alcohol found esp. in animal fats, blood, nerve tissue, and bile

cho·line (kō'lēn) *n.* [CHOL(O)- + -INE⁴] a viscous liquid found in many animal and vegetable tissues: a vitamin of the B complex

chol·o- [< Gr. *cholē*, bile] a combining form meaning bile, gall

chomp (chomp) *vt., vi.* [dial. var. of CHAMP¹] **1.** to chew

hard and noisily **2.** to bite down (*on*) repeatedly and restlessly —*n.* the act or sound of chomping —**chomp'er** *n.*

chon·drite (kon'drīt) *n.* [< G. *Chondrit* < Gr. *chondros*, granule] a stony meteorite that contains silicates in the form of small rounded masses

choose (chōōz) *vt.* **chose, cho'sen** or obs. **chose, choos'ing** [OE. *ceosan*] **1.** to pick out; take as a choice; select **2.** to decide or prefer [to *choose* to remain] —*vi.* **1.** to make one's selection **2.** to have the desire or wish —**choos'er** *n.*

choos·y, choos·ey (chōō'zē) *adj.* **choos'i·er, choos'i·est** [Colloq.] very careful or fussy

chop¹ (chop) *vt.* **chopped, chop'ping** [ME. *choppen*, prob. < OFr. *c(h)oper*, to cut] **1.** to cut by blows with an axe or other sharp tool **2.** to cut into small bits **3.** to say in an abrupt way **4.** to hit with a short, sharp stroke —*vi.* **1.** to make quick, cutting strokes with a sharp tool **2.** to act with a quick, jerky motion —*n.* **1.** the act of chopping **2.** a short, sharp blow or stroke **3.** a piece chopped off **4.** a slice of lamb, pork, veal, etc. cut from the rib, loin, or shoulder **5.** a short, broken movement of waves **6.** [N.Z.] a woodchopping contest —**get the chop** [Slang] to be dismissed from one's job

chop² (chop) *n.* [var. of *chap*, jaw] **1.** a jaw **2.** a cheek See CHOPS

chop³ (chop) *vi.* **chopped, chop'ping** [OE. *ceapian*, to bargain] to shift or veer suddenly, as the wind; change direction —**chop and change** to change (one's plans, ideas, etc.) constantly —**chop logic** to argue

chop⁴ (chop) *n.* [Hindi *chāp*] **1.** a brand, or trademark **2.** [Colloq.] quality; grade; brand

chop-chop (chop'chop') *adv., interj.* [PidE. < Chin.] quickly

chop·house (-hous') *n.* a restaurant that specializes in chops and steaks

chop·per (chop'ər) *n.* **1.** a person or thing that chops **2.** a small hand-axe or cleaver, esp. for chopping firewood **3.** [pl.] [Slang] a set of teeth, esp. false teeth **4.** [Colloq.] a helicopter

chop·py¹ (-ē) *adj.* **-pi·er, -pi·est** [< CHOP³ + -Y²] shifting constantly and abruptly, as the wind —**chop'pi·ness** *n.*

chop·py² (-ē) *adj.* **-pi·er, -pi·est** [< CHOP¹ + -Y²] **1.** rough with short, broken waves, as the sea **2.** making abrupt starts and stops; jerky —**chop'pi·ly** *adv.* —**chop'pi·ness** *n.*

chops (chops) *n.pl.* [var. of *chap*, jaw] **1.** the jaws **2.** the mouth and lower cheeks —**lick one's chops** to experience or show pleasure in the anticipation of something

chop·sticks (chop'stiks') *n.pl.* [PidE. for Chin. *k'wai-tsze*, the quick ones] two small sticks held together in one hand and used in some Asian countries to lift food to the mouth

chop su·ey (chop'sōō'ē) [altered < Chin. *tsa-sui*, lit., various pieces] a Chinese-American dish of meat, bean sprouts, celery, mushrooms, etc. cooked together in a sauce and served with rice

cho·ral (kôr'əl) *adj.* [Fr.] of, for, sung by, or recited by a choir or chorus —**cho'ral·ly** *adv.*

cho·rale, cho·ral (kə räl') *n.* [< G. *Choral* (*gesang*), choral (song)] **1.** a hymn tune **2.** a choral composition based on such a tune **3.** a group of singers; choir

chord¹ (kôrd) *n.* [altered (after L. *chorda*) < CORD] **1.** a feeling or emotion thought of as being played on like the string of a harp [to strike a sympathetic *chord*] **2.** *Anat.* same as CORD (sense 5) **3.** *Engineering* a principal horizontal member in a rigid framework, as of a bridge **4.** *Geom.* a straight line joining any two points on an arc, curve, or circumference

CHORDS (AC, AO)

chord² (kôrd) *n.* [< *cord*, contr. < ACCORD] *Music* a combination of three or more tones sounded together in harmony —*vi., vt.* **1.** to harmonize **2.** to play chords on —**chord'al** *adj.*

chore (chôr) *n.* [< OE. *cierr*] **1.** a small routine task; odd job: *often used in pl.* **2.** a hard or unpleasant task

cho·re·a (ko rē'ə) *n.* [ModL. < L. < Gr. *choreia*, choral dance] a nervous disorder characterized by jerking movements caused by involuntary muscular contractions; Saint Vitus' dance

chor·e·o·graph (kor'ē ə gräf') *vt., vi.* [< ff.] to design or plan the movements of (a dance, esp. a ballet) —**chor'e·og'ra·pher** (-og'rə fər) *n.*

chor·e·og·ra·phy (kor'ē og'rə fē) *n.* [Gr. *choreia*, dance + -GRAPHY] **1.** dancing, esp. ballet dancing **2.** the arrangement of the movements of a dance **3.** the art of devising dances, esp. ballets —**chor'e·o·graph'ic** (-ə graf'ik) *adj.* —**chor'e·o·graph'i·cal·ly** *adv.*

cho·ric (kor'ik) *adj.* of, for, or like a chorus, esp. in an ancient Greek play

chor·is·ter (kor'is tər) *n.* [< OFr. *cueristre*: see CHOIR] a member of a choir, esp. a boy singer

cho·roid (kôr'oid) *adj.* [< Gr. < *chorion*, leather + *eidos*, form] designating of or certain vascular membranes —*n.*

the dark, vascular membrane between the sclera and retina of the eye Also **cho′ri·oid′** (-ē ɔid′)

chor·tle (chôr′t'l) *vi., vt.* **-tled, -tling** [coined by Lewis Carroll, prob. < CHUCKLE + SNORT] to make, or utter with, a gleeful chuckling or snorting sound —*n.* such a sound —**chor′tler** *n.*

cho·rus (kôr′əs) *n.* [L. < Gr. *choros*, a dance, chorus] 1. in ancient Greek drama, a group whose singing, dancing, and narration supplement the main action 2. a group of dancers and singers performing together as in an opera 3. the part of a drama, song, etc. performed by a chorus 4. a group trained to sing or speak something together simultaneously 5. a simultaneous utterance by many [a *chorus* of protest] 6. music written for group singing 7. a) the refrain of a song following each verse b) the main tune, as of a jazz piece, following the introduction —*vt., vi.* to sing, speak, or say in unison —**in chorus** in unison

chorus girl (or **boy**) a woman (or man) singing or dancing in the chorus of a musical show

chose (chōz) *pt. & obs. pp. of* CHOOSE

cho·sen (chō′z'n) *pp. of* CHOOSE —*adj.* picked out by preference; selected

chough (chuf) *n.* [ME.] a European bird of the crow family, with red legs and beak and -glossy black feathers

choux pastry (shōō) [< Fr. (*pâte*) *choux*, lit., cabbage (dough)] a very light pastry made with eggs, used esp. for cream puffs, éclairs, etc.

chow (chou) *n.* [< Chin. dial. form akin to Cantonese *kaú*, a dog] 1. any of a breed of medium-sized dog, originally from China, with a compact, muscular body and thick coat of brown or black: official name **chow chow** 2. [Slang] food

chow·chil·la (chou′chil′ə) [< echoic] [Aust.] a small Australian bird with a piercing, repetitive callnote

chow·chow (chou′chou′) *n.* [PidE. < Chin.] chopped pickles in a highly seasoned mustard sauce

chow·der (chou′dər) *n.* [Fr. *chaudière*, a pot < LL. *caldaria*: see CAULDRON] [Chiefly U.S.] a thick soup of onions, potatoes, and salt pork, sometimes sweetcorn, tomatoes, etc. and often, specif., clams and milk

chow mein (chou mān′) [Chin. *ch'ao*, to fry + *mien, flour*] a Chinese-American dish consisting of a thick stew of meat, celery, bean sprouts, etc., served with fried noodles and usually soy sauce

Chr. 1. Christ 2. Christian 3. Chronicles

chrism (kriz′'m) *n.* [< OE. < LL. < Gr. *chrisma* < *chriein*, to anoint] consecrated oil used in baptism and other sacraments —**chris′mal** *adj.*

Christ (krīst) [< LL. < Gr. *christos*, the anointed (in NT., MESSIAH) < *chriein*, to anoint] Jesus of Nazareth, regarded by Christians as the Messiah prophesied in the Old Testament

Chris·ta·del·phi·an (kris′tə del′fē ən) *n.* [CHRIST + Gr. *adelphos*, brother + -AN] a member of a Christian unitarian sect believing in eternal life only for the just

chris·ten (kris′'n) *vt.* [OE. *cristnian*] 1. to take into a Christian church by baptism; baptize 2. to give a name to at baptism 3. to give a name to (a ship being launched, etc.) 4. [Colloq.] to make use of for the first time —**chris′tening** *n.*

Chris·ten·dom (-dəm) *n.* 1. Christians collectively 2. those parts of the world where most of the inhabitants profess Christianity

Chris·tian (kris′tē an, -tyən) *n.* [OE. *cristen*, ult. < Gr. *christos*: see CHRIST] 1. a person professing belief in Jesus as the Christ, or in the religion based on the teachings of Jesus 2. [Colloq.] a decent, respectable person —*adj.* 1. of Jesus Christ or his teachings 2. of or professing the religion based on these teachings 3. having the qualities demonstrated and taught by Jesus Christ, as love, kindness, etc. 4. of or representing Christians or Christianity 5. [Colloq.] humane, decent, etc. —**Chris′tian·ly** *adj., adv.*

Christian Era the era beginning with the year formerly thought to be that of the birth of Jesus Christ

Chris·ti·an·i·ty (kris′tē an′ə tē) *n.* 1. Christians collectively 2. the Christian religion 3. a particular Christian religious system 4. the state of being a Christian

Chris·tian·ize (kris′tē ə nīz′) *vt.* **-ized′, -iz′ing** 1. to convert to Christianity 2. to cause to conform with Christian character or precepts —**Chris′tian·i·za′tion** *n.* —**Chris′tian·iz′er** *n.*

Christian name the baptismal name as distinguished from the surname or family name

Christian Science a religion and system of healing founded by Mary Baker Eddy c. 1866: official name, *Church of Christ, Scientist* —**Christian Scientist**

chris·tie, chris·ty (kris′tē) *n., pl.* **-ties** [< *Christiania*, former name of Oslo] *Skiing* any of various high-speed turns to change direction, stop, etc., made by shifting weight, with skis usually kept parallel

Christ·like (krīst′līk′) *adj.* like Jesus Christ, esp. in character or spirit —**Christ′like′ness** *n.*

Christ·ly (-lē) *adj.* of Jesus Christ; Christlike —**Christ′·li·ness** *n.*

Christ·mas (kris′məs) *n.* [OE. *Cristesmæsse*: see CHRIST & MASS] 1. a holiday on Dec. 25 celebrating the birth of Jesus Christ: also **Christmas Day** 2. *same as* CHRISTMASTIDE

Christmas box a sum of money or other present given at Christmas to tradesmen, employees, etc.

Christmas Eve the evening before Christmas Day

Christmas pudding *same as* PLUM PUDDING

Christmas rose *same as* HELLEBORE

Christ·mas·tide (-tīd′) *n.* Christmas time, from Christmas Eve to New Year's Day or to Epiphany (Jan. 6)

Christmas tree an evergreen or artificial tree hung with ornaments and lights at Christmas time

chro·ma (krō′mə) *n.* [Gr. *chrōma*, colour] *same as* SATURATION (sense 2)

chro·mate (krō′māt) *n.* a salt of chromic acid

chro·mat·ic (krō mat′ik) *adj.* [< LL. < Gr. < *chrōma*, colour] 1. of or having colour or colours 2. highly coloured 3. *Music* a) using or progressing by semitones [a *chromatic* scale] b) using tones not in the key of a work —*n.* *Music* a tone modified by an accidental —**chro·mat′i·cal·ly** *adv.* —**chro·mat′i·cism** (-ə siz′m), **chro′ma·tic′i·ty** (-tis′ə tē) *n.*

chromatic aberration a property of lenses that causes the various colours in a beam of light to be focused at different points, thus causing a margin of colours to appear around the edges of the image

chro·mat·ics (krō mat′iks) *n.pl.* [*with sing. v.*] the scientific study of colours

chromatic scale the musical scale made up of thirteen successive semitones to the octave

chro·ma·tin (krō′mə tin) *n.* [< Gr. *chrōma* (gen. *chrōmatos*), colour + -IN¹] a protoplasmic substance in the nucleus of living cells that readily takes a deep stain: chromatin forms the chromosomes

chro·ma·to- [< Gr. *chrōma*: see prec.] *a combining form meaning:* 1. colour or pigmentation 2. chromatin Also, before a vowel, **chromat-**

chro·ma·tog·ra·phy (krō′mə tog′rə fē) *n.* [CHROMATO- + -GRAPHY] the process of separating constituents of a mixture by running a solution of it through an adsorbent on which the different substances are separated into bands or spots

chrome (krōm) *n.* [Fr. < Gr. *chrōma*, colour] 1. chromium or chromium alloy, esp. as plating 2. any of certain salts of chromium, used in dyeing and tanning 3. a chromium pigment —*vt.* **chromed, chrom′ing** 1. to plate with chromium 2. to treat with a salt of chromium, as in dyeing

-chrome (krōm) [< Gr. *chrōma*, colour] *a suffix meaning:* 1. colour or colouring agent 2. chromium

chrome steel *same as* CHROMIUM STEEL

chrome yellow a neutral lead chromate, $PbCrO_4$, used as a yellow pigment

chro·mic (krō′mik) *adj.* designating or of compounds containing trivalent chromium

chromic acid an acid, H_2CrO_4, existing only in solution or known in the form of its salts

chro·mite (krō′mīt) *n.* a black mineral, $FeCr_2O_4$, with a metallic sheen and an uneven fracture: it is the chief ore of chromium

chro·mi·um (krō′mē əm) *n.* [CHROM(E) + -*ium*] a very hard, metallic chemical element with a high resistance to corrosion: symbol, Cr; at. wt., 51.996; at. no., 24

chromium plate a thin coating of chromium, esp. on steel, deposited by electrolysis —**chro′mi·um-plat′ed** *adj.*

chromium steel a very strong, hard alloy steel containing chromium: also **chrome steel**

chro·mo (krō′mō) *n., pl.* **-mos** a chromolithograph

chro·mo- [< Gr. *chrōma*, colour] *a combining form meaning* colour or pigment [*chromosome*]: also, before a vowel, **chrom-**

chro·mo·lith·o·graph (krō′mō lith′ə graf′) *n.* a coloured picture printed by the lithographic process from a series of stone or metal plates —**chro′mo·li·thog′ra·pher** (-li thog′·rə fər) *n.* —**chro′mo·lith′o·graph′ic** (-lith′ə graf′ik) *adj.* —**chro′mo·li·thog′ra·phy** *n.*

chro·mo·some (krō′mə sōm′) *n.* [CHROMO- + -SOME³] any of the microscopic rod-shaped bodies into which the chromatin of a cell nucleus separates during mitosis: they carry the genes, which convey hereditary characteristics, and are constant in number for each species —**chro′mo·so′·mal** *adj.*

chro·mo·sphere (-sfir′) *n.* [CHROMO- + -SPHERE] the reddish layer of gases around the sun between the photosphere and the corona —**chro′mo·spher′ic** (-sfer′ik) *adj.*

chro·mous (krō′məs) *adj.* designating or of compounds containing bivalent chromium

Chron. Chronicles

chron. 1. chronological 2. chronology

chron·ic (kron′ik) *adj.* [< Fr. < L. < Gr. < *chronos*, time]

1. lasting a long time or recurring often: said of a disease, and distinguished from ACUTE 2. having had an ailment for a long time 3. perpetual; constant [a chronic worry] 4. habitual 5. [Colloq.] a) pitifully bad; of very poor quality [her singing was chronic] b) very serious, esp. of illness, psychological state, etc. —n. a chronic patient —**chron'-i·cal·ly** adv. —**chro·nic·i·ty** (krə nis'ə tē) n.

chron·i·cle (kron'i k'l) n. [< Anglo-Fr. < OFr. < L. < Gr. chronika, annals: see prec.] 1. a historical record of events in the order in which they happened 2. a narrative; history —vt. **-cled, -cling** to tell or write the history of; put into a chronicle —**chron'i·cler** (-klər) n.

chro·no- [Gr. < chronos, time] a combining form meaning time: also, before a vowel, **chron-**

chron·o·graph (kron'ə graf') n. [CHRONO- + -GRAPH] an instrument for measuring and recording brief, precisely spaced intervals of time, as a stopwatch —**chron'o·graph'ic** adj. —**chro·nog·ra·phy** (krə nog'rə fē) n.

chron·o·log·i·cal (kron'ə loj'i k'l) adj. 1. arranged in the order of occurrence 2. relating to a narrative or history Also **chron'o·log'ic** —**chron'o·log'i·cal·ly** adv.

chro·nol·o·gy (krə nol'ə jē) n., pl. **-gies** [CHRONO- + -LOGY] 1. the science of measuring time and of dating events in proper order 2. an arrangement or list of events, dates, etc. in the order of occurrence —**chro·nol'o·gist, chro·nol'o·ger** n.

chro·nom·e·ter (-nom'ə tər) n. [CHRONO- + -METER] an instrument for measuring time precisely; highly accurate kind of clock or watch —**chron·o·met·ric** (kron'ə met'-rik, krō'nə-), **chron'o·met'ri·cal** adj. —**chron'o·met'ri·cal·ly** adv.

chro·nom·e·try (krə nom'ə trē) n. the scientific measurement of time

chro·non (krō'non) n. [< CHRON(O)- + -ON] a hypothetical particle of time, equivalent to the ratio of the diameter of an electron to the velocity of light

-chro·ous (krō əs) [Gr. chrōs, chroos, colour] a terminal combining form meaning coloured

chrys·a·lid (kris'ə lid') n. same as CHRYSALIS.—adj. of a chrysalis

chrys·a·lis (kris'ə lis') n., pl. **chry·sal·i·des** (kri sal'ə dēz'), **chrys·a·lis·es** [< L. < Gr. chrysallis, golden-coloured chrysalis < chrysos, gold] 1. the pupa of a butterfly, when it is in a case or cocoon 2. the case or cocoon 3. anything in a formative or undeveloped stage

chrys·an·the·mum (kri san'thə məm) n. [L. < Gr. < chrysos, gold + anthemon, a flower] 1. any of a genus of late-blooming plants of the composite family, cultivated for their showy flowers, in a wide variety of colours 2. the flower

chrys·o·ber·yl (kris'ə ber'əl) n. [Gr. chrysos, gold + BERYL] beryllium aluminate, BeAl₂O₄, a yellowish or greenish mineral used as a semiprecious stone

chrys·o·lite (kris'ə līt') n. [< OFr. < L. < Gr. chrysos, gold + lithos, stone] same as OLIVINE

chrys·o·prase (-prāz') n. [< OFr. < L. < Gr. chrysos, gold + prason, leek] a light-green variety of chalcedony sometimes used as a semiprecious stone

chtho·ni·an (thō'nē ən) adj. [Gr. chthonios, in the earth < chthōn, the earth] Gr. Myth. designating or of the underworld of the dead and its gods or spirits —**chthon·ic** (thon'ik) adj.

chub (chub) n., pl. **chubs, chub:** see PLURAL, II, D, 1 [ME. chubbe] a small, freshwater fish related to the carp

chub·by (chub'ē) adj. **-bi·er, -bi·est** [< prec.] round and plump —**chub'bi·ness** n.

chuck¹ (chuk) vt. [< ? Fr. choquer, to strike against] 1. to tap or pat gently, esp. under the chin, as a playful gesture 2. to throw with a quick, short movement; toss 3. [Slang] a) to discard; get rid of b) to give up (often with in) —n. 1. a light tap or squeeze under the chin 2. a toss —**chuck it!** stop!; give it up! —**chuck out** [Colloq.] to evict; throw out

chuck² (chuk) n. [prob. var. of CHOCK] 1. a cut of beef including the parts around the neck and the shoulder blade 2. a clamplike device, as on a lathe, by which the tool or work is held

chuck·er-out (-ər out') n. same as BOUNCER

chuck·le (chuk'l) vi. **-led, -ling** [prob. <chuck, to cluck] 1. to laugh softly in a low tone, as in mild amusement 2. to cluck, as a hen —n. a soft, low-toned laugh —**chuck'ler** n.

chuck·le·head (-hed') n. [Colloq.] a stupid person

chuff (chuf) vi., n. [echoic] same as CHUG

chuff·ed (chuft) adj. [< ?] [Slang] 1. pleased; gratified 2. displeased; fed up

chug (chug) n. [echoic] any of a series of abrupt, puffing or explosive sounds, as of a locomotive —vi. **chugged, chug'ging** to make, or move with, such sounds

chuk·ka (boot) (chuk'ə) [< CHUKKER] a man's ankle-high bootlike shoe, often fleece-lined, orig. worn for the game of polo

chuk·ker, chuk·kar (chuk'ər) n. [Hindi chakar < Sans.

CHUCK
(of a
drill)

cakra, wheel] any of the periods of play, 7 ¹/₂ minutes each, of a polo match

chum (chum) n. [17th-c. slang; prob. < chamber in chamber mate] [Colloq.] a close friend —vi. **chummed, chum'ming** [Colloq.] to be close friends

chum·my (chum'ē) adj. **-mi·er, -mi·est** [Colloq.] intimate; friendly —**chum'mi·ly** adv. —**chum'mi·ness** n.

chump (chump) n. [< ? CHUCK² or CHUNK + LUMP¹] 1. a heavy block of wood 2. a thick, blunt end 3. [Colloq.] a foolish, stupid, or gullible person —**off one's chump** [Colloq.] insane

chunk (chunk) n. [< ? CHUCK²] 1. a short, thick piece, as of meat, wood, etc. 2. a considerable portion

chunk·y (chun'kē) adj. **chunk'i·er, chunk'i·est** 1. short and thick 2. stocky; thickset 3. containing chunks —**chunk'-i·ness** n.

chun·ter (chun'tər) vi. [echoic] [Colloq.] 1. to mutter, esp. discontentedly 2. to talk in a rambling or incoherent fashion

church (church) n. [< OE. cirice, ult. < Gr. kyriakē (oikia), Lord's (house) < kyros, supreme power] 1. a building for public worship, esp. one for Christian worship 2. public worship; religious service 3. [usually C-] a) all Christians collectively b) a particular sect or denomination of Christians 4. ecclesiastical government, or its power, as opposed to secular government 5. the profession of the clergy 6. a group of worshippers —adj. of a church or of organized Christian worship —vt. to bring (a woman after childbirth) to church for a service of thanksgiving —**church'less** adj.

Church Army an Anglican evangelistic and welfare organization modelled on the Salvation Army

Church Commissioners the administrative body responsible for the property of the Church of England

church·go·er (-gō'ər) n. a person who attends church, esp. regularly —**church'go'ing** n., adj.

church·ly (church'lē) adj. of, fit for, or belonging to, a church —**church'li·ness** n.

church·man (-mən) n., pl. **-men** 1. a clergyman 2. a member of a church

Church of Christ, Scientist see CHRISTIAN SCIENCE

Church of England the episcopal church of England; Anglican Church: it is an established church with the Sovereign as its head

Church of Jesus Christ of Latter-day Saints see MORMON

church·ward·en (-wôr'd'n) n. 1. one of two lay officers elected annually by the congregation of a Church of England parish to perform certain secular functions 2. a type of long-stemmed tobacco pipe made of clay

church·wom·an (-woom'ən) n., pl. **-wom'en** (-wim'in) a woman member of a church

church·yard (-yärd') n. the land adjoining a church, often used as a place of burial

chu·rin·ga (choo rin'gə) n. [< Abor.] a carved stone or piece of wood, sacred to some Aboriginal tribes; amulet

churl (churl) n. [OE. ceorl, freeman] 1. a peasant 2. a surly, ill-bred, or miserly person —**churl'ish** adj. —**churl'-ish·ly** adv. —**churl'ish·ness** n.

churn (churn) n. [OE. cyrne] 1. a container or contrivance in which milk or cream is beaten and shaken to form butter 2. a large vessel for containing milk —vt. 1. to beat and shake (milk or cream) in a churn 2. to make (butter) in a churn 3. to stir up vigorously 4. to make (foam, etc.) by stirring vigorously —vi. 1. to use a churn in making butter 2. to move as if in a churn; seethe —**churn out** to produce in great numbers, as from a production line

churr (chur) n. a low, trilled or whirring sound made by some birds —vi. to make such a sound

chute¹ (shoot) n. [Fr., a fall, ult. < L. cadere, to fall] 1. a waterfall or rapids in a river 2. an inclined or vertical trough or passage down which something may slide or be slid or dropped

chute² (shoot) n. colloq. clipped form of PARACHUTE —**chut'-ist** n.

chut·ney (chut'nē) n., pl. **-neys** [Hindi chatnī] a relish made of fruits, spices, and herbs: also sp. **chut'nee**

chyle (kīl) n. [< LL. < Gr. chylos < cheein, to pour] a milky fluid composed of lymph and emulsified fats: it is formed from chyme in the small intestine and is passed into the blood through the thoracic duct —**chy·la·ceous** (kī lā'shəs), **chy'lous** adj.

chyme (kīm) n. [< LL. < Gr. chymos, juice < cheein, to pour] the semifluid mass resulting from gastric digestion of food: see CHYLE —**chy'mous** adj.

chyp·re (shē'prə) n. [Fr., of Cyprus] a perfume made from sandalwood

C.I. Channel Islands

CIA, C.I.A. Central Intelligence Agency

‡**ciao** (chou) interj. [It.] an informal expression of greeting or farewell

ci·bo·ri·um (si bôr'ē əm) n., pl. **-ri·a** (-ə) [ML. < L., a cup < Gr. kibōrion, seed vessel of the Egyptian waterlily, hence, a cup] 1. a canopy covering an altar 2. a covered cup for holding the consecrated wafers of the Eucharist

ci·ca·da (si kä'də) *n., pl.* **-das, -dae** (-dē) [L.] a large flylike insect with transparent wings: the male makes a loud, shrill sound by vibrating a special organ on its underside

cic·a·trix (sik'ə triks) *n., pl.* **cic·a·tri·ces** (si kat'rə sēz', sik'ə trī'sēz) [L.] 1. *Med.* the contracted fibrous tissue at the place where a wound has healed; scar 2. *Bot.* the scar left where a branch, leaf, seed, etc. was once attached or where a wound has healed Also **cic'a·trice** (-tris) —**cic'·a·tri'cial** (-trish'əl) *adj.*

cic·a·trize (-trīz') *vt., vi.* **-trized', -triz'ing** to heal with the formation of a scar —**cic'a·tri·za'tion** *n.*

cic·e·ly (sis'ə lē) *n.* [ME. *seseli* < L. *seselis* < Gr.] a European perennial plant similar to chervil, used as a herb: in full, **sweet cicely**

ci·ce·ro·ne (sis'ə rō'nē; *It.* chē che rô'ne) *n., pl.* **-nes;** *It.* **-ni** (-nē) [It. < L. *Cicero,* the orator] a well-informed guide for sightseers

C.I.D. Criminal Investigation Department

-cide (sīd) [< Fr. *-cide* or L. *-cida* < L. *caedere,* to kill] a suffix meaning: 1. killer [*pesticide*] 2. killing [*genocide*]

ci·der (sī'dər) *n.* [< OFr. < LL. < Gr. *sikera* < Heb. *shēkār,* strong drink] 1. an alcoholic beverage made from fermented apple juice 2. [Chiefly U.S.] the juice pressed from apples, used as a beverage or for making vinegar

C.I.F., c.i.f. cost, insurance, and freight

ci·gar (si gär') *n.* [Sp. *cigarro,* prob. < Maya *sicar,* to smoke < *sic,* tobacco] a compact roll of tobacco leaves for smoking

cig·a·rette (sig'ə ret') *n.* [Fr., dim. of *cigare,* cigar] a small roll of finely cut tobacco wrapped in thin paper for smoking

cigarette card a picture card formerly given away in cigarette packets and collected in sets

cig·a·ril·lo (sig'ə ril'ō) *n., pl.* **-los** [Sp., dim. of *cigarro,* CIGAR] a small, thin cigar

cil·i·a (sil'ē ə) *n.pl., sing.* **-i·um** (-əm) [L.] 1. the eyelashes 2. *Bot.* small hairlike processes, as on the edges of some leaves 3. *Zool.* hairlike outgrowths of certain cells, capable of rhythmic beating that can produce locomotion, as in protozoans or certain small worms —**cil'i·ate** (-it, -āt'), **cil'i·at'ed** *adj.*

cil·i·ar·y (sil'ē ər ē) *adj.* of, like, or having cilia

cill (sil) *n. same as* SILL

cim·ba·lom, cym·ba·lom (sim'bə ləm) *n.* [< Hung. < L. *cymbalum,* cymbal] a type of large dulcimer associated with Hungarian folk music

C.-in-C. Commander-in-Chief

cinch (sinch) *n.* [< Sp. < L. *cingulum,* a girdle < *cingere,* to encircle] 1. a saddle or pack girth 2. [Colloq.] a sure or easy thing —*vt.* 1. to gird with a cinch 2. [U.S. Colloq.] to make sure of

cin·cho·na (sin kō'nə, siŋ-) *n.* [ModL., after the Countess del *Chinchón,* wife of a 17th-c. Peruv. viceroy, who was treated with the bark] 1. a tropical S. American tree from the bark of which quinine is obtained 2. the bitter bark of this tree —**cin·chon'ic** (-kon'ik) *adj.*

cin·cho·nize (sin'kə nīz') *vt.* **-nized', -niz'ing** to treat with cinchona, quinine, etc.

cinc·ture (siŋk'chər) *n.* [L. *cinctura,* a girdle: see CINCH] 1. an encircling or girding 2. anything that encircles, as a belt or girdle —*vt.* **-tured, -tur·ing** to encircle with or as with a cincture

cin·der (sin'dər) *n.* [OE. *sinder*] 1. slag, as from the smelting of ores 2. any matter, as coal or wood, burned but not reduced to ashes 3. a minute piece of such matter 4. a coal that is still burning but not flaming 5. [*pl.*] ashes from coal or wood —**cin'der·y** *adj.*

Cin·der·el·la (sin'də rel'ə) *n.* [after a character in a fairy tale] 1. a young girl who finds fame and happiness after humble beginnings 2. any poor or obscure person, organization, etc.

cin·e·ma (sin'ə mə) *n.* [< CINEMA(TOGRAPH)] a film theatre —**the cinema** 1. the art or business of making films 2. films —**cin'e·mat'ic** (-mat'ik) *adj.* —**cin'e·mat'i·cal·ly** *adv.*

cin·e·mat·o·graph (sin'ə mat'ə graf') *n.* [< Fr. < Gr. *kinēma,* motion + *graphein,* to write] a film projector, camera, theatre, etc. —*adj.* of or designating films or the film industry

cin·e·ma·tog·ra·pher (sin'ə mə tog'rə fər) *n.* a film cameraman

cin·e·ma·tog·ra·phy (-fē) *n.* the art of photography in making film —**cin'e·mat'o·graph'ic** (-mat'ə graf'ik), **cin'·e·mat'o·graph'i·cal** *adj.* —**cin'e·mat'o·graph'i·cal·ly** *adv.*

‡**cin·é·ma vér·i·té** (sē nä mä'vä rē tā') [Fr., lit., truth cinema] a form of documentary film in which a small camera and unobtrusive techniques are used to record or simulate scenes as naturally as possible

cin·e·rar·i·a (sin'ə rer'ē ə) *n.* [ModL. < L. < *cinis,* ashes: the leaves have an ash-coloured down] a common hothouse plant of the composite family, with heart-shaped leaves and colourful flowers

cin·e·rar·i·um (-ē əm) *n., pl.* **-rar'i·a** (-ə) [L. < *cinis,* ashes] a place to keep the ashes of cremated bodies —**cin'e·rar·y** *adj.*

cin·er·a·tor (sin'ə rāt'ər) *n.* [< CINERARIUM] [Chiefly U.S.] a furnace for cremation

cin·na·bar (sin'ə bär') *n.* [< L. < Gr. *kinnabari* < ? Per. *šangarf*] 1. mercuric sulphide, HgS, a heavy, bright-red mineral, the principal ore of mercury 2. artificial mercury sulphide, used as a red pigment 3. brilliant red; vermilion 4. a large red and black moth of Europe

cin·na·mon (sin'ə mən) *n.* [< OFr. < L. < Gr. < Heb. *qinnāmōn*] 1. the yellowish-brown spice made from the dried inner bark of a laurel tree or shrub native to the East Indies and SE Asia 2. this bark 3. any tree or shrub from which it is obtained 4. yellowish brown —*adj.* 1. yellowish-brown 2. made or flavoured with cinnamon

cinque (siŋk) *n.* [< Fr. *cinq,* five < L. *quinque*] a five at dice or on a playing card

cin·que·cen·to (chiŋ'kwə chen'tō) *n.* [It., (*mille*) *cinquecento,* (one thousand) five hundred] the 16th cent. as a period in Italian art and literature

cinque·foil (siŋk'foil') *n.* [< OFr. < It. < L. < *quinque,* five + *folium,* leaf] 1. a plant of the rose family with a fruit like a dry strawberry: some species have compound leaves with five leaflets 2. *Archit.* a circular design of five converging arcs

Cinque Ports a group of ports in SE England, originally five in number, which until 1685 provided the Crown with ships in return for certain privileges

ci·on (sī'ən) *n. same as* SCION (sense 1)

CINQUEFOIL

C.I.P.F.A. Chartered Institute of Public Finance and Accountancy

ci·pher (sī'fər) *n.* [< OFr. < ML. < Ar. *ṣifr,* nothing < *ṣafare,* to be empty] 1. the symbol 0, indicating a value of nought; zero 2. a person or thing of no importance or value; nonentity 3. *a*) a system of secret writing based on a key *b*) a message in such writing *c*) the key to such a system See also CODE 4. a monogram 5. an Arabic numeral —*vt., vi.* 1. [Now Rare] to do, or solve by, arithmetic 2. to write in cipher, or secret writing

cir., circ. 1. circa 2. circulation 3. circumference

cir·ca (sʉr'kə) *prep.* [L.] about: used before an approximate date, figure, etc. [*circa* 1650]

cir·ca·di·an (sər kā'dē ən) *adj.* [coined < L. *circa,* about + acc. sing. of *dies,* day] designating or of certain biological rhythms associated with the 24-hour daily cycles, as, in man, the regular metabolic, glandular, and sleep rhythms

cir·cle (sʉr'k'l) *n.* [< OFr. < L. *circulus,* dim. of *circus:* see CIRCUS] 1. a plane figure bounded by a single curved line every point of which is equally distant from the point at the centre 2. the line bounding such a figure; circumference 3. anything shaped like a circle, as a ring, crown, etc. 4. the orbit of a heavenly body 5. a section of seats in a theatre, as in a balcony [*the dress circle*] 6. a complete or recurring series, usually ending as it began; cycle; period 7. a group of people bound together by common interests; group; coterie 8. range or extent, as of influence or interest; scope —*vt.* **-cled, -cling** 1. to form a circle around; encompass; surround 2. to move round, as in a circle —*vi.* to go round in a circle; revolve —**come full circle** to return to an original position or state after going through a series or cycle —**cir'cler** *n.*

cir·clet (sʉr'klit) *n.* 1. a small circle 2. a circular band worn as an ornament, esp. on the head

circs (sʉrks) *n.pl. colloq. clipped form of* circumstances (see CIRCUMSTANCE)

cir·cuit (sʉr'kit) *n.* [OFr. < L. *circuitus* < *circum,* around + *ire,* to go] 1. the line or the length of the line forming the boundaries of an area 2. the area bounded 3. a going round something; course or journey around 4. *a*) the regular journey through a fixed district of a person performing his duties, as of a minister of religion *b*) such a district 5. a chain or group of theatres, resorts, etc. at which plays, films, entertainers, etc. appear in turn 6. a motor racing track 7. *Elec. a*) a complete or partial path over which current may flow *b*) a hookup that is connected into this path 8. *Sport a*) a series of sporting events, usually involving the same players [*the international golf circuit*] *b*) the players taking part in such a circuit —*vi.* to go in a circuit —*vt.* to make a circuit about —**cir'cuit·al** *adj.*

circuit breaker a device that automatically interrupts the flow of an electric current

cir·cu·i·tous (sər kyoo̅'ə təs) *adj.* [see CIRCUIT] roundabout; devious —**cir·cu'i·tous·ly** *adv.* —**cir·cu'i·ous·ness, cir·cu'i·ty** *n., pl.* **-ties**

cir·cuit·ry (sʉr'kə trē) *n.* the scheme, system, or components of an electric circuit

cir·cu·lar (sur′kyə lər) *adj.* [L. *circularis*] **1.** in the shape of a circle; round **2.** relating to a circle **3.** moving in a circle or spiral **4.** roundabout; circuitous **5.** intended for circulation among a number of people **6.** *Logic* of or designating an argument whose premises presuppose its conclusion —*n.* a circular advertisement, letter, etc. —**cir′·cu·lar′i·ty** (-lə′rə tē) *n.* —**cir′cu·lar·ly** *adv.*

cir·cu·lar·ize (-lə riz′) *vt.* **-ized′, -iz′ing 1.** to make circular **2.** to send circulars to **3.** to canvass —**cir′cu·lar·i·za′tion** *n.* —**cir′cu·lar·iz′er** *n.*

circular saw a saw in the form of a disc with a toothed edge, rotated at high speed by a motor

cir·cu·late (sur′kyə lāt′) *vi.* **-lat′ed, -lat′ing** [< L. pp. of *circulari*, to form a circle] **1.** to move in a circle or circuit and return to the same point, as the blood **2.** to go from person to person or from place to place; specif., *a)* to move about freely, as air *b)* to move about in society, at a party, etc. *c)* to be made widely known *d)* to be distributed to a mass of readers —*vt.* to cause to circulate —**cir′cu·la′tor** *n.* —**cir′cu·la·to·ry** (-lə tər ē), **cir′cu·la′tive** (-lā′tiv) *adj.*

circulating library a library from which books can be borrowed, sometimes for a subscription

cir·cu·la·tion (sur′kyə lā′shən) *n.* **1.** a circulating or moving round, often specif. in a complete circuit, as of air in ventilating or of blood through the arteries and veins **2.** the passing of something, as money, news, etc., from person to person **3.** *a)* the distribution of newspapers, magazines, etc. *b)* the average number of copies of a magazine or newspaper sold in a given period —**in circulation 1.** current; in use **2.** participating in activities, society, etc.

cir·cum- [< L. *circum*, around, about] *a prefix meaning* round, about, surrounding, on all sides

cir·cum·am·bi·ent (sur′kəm am′bē ənt) *adj.* [CIRCUM- + AMBIENT] extending all around; surrounding —**cir′cum·am′·bi·ence, cir′cum·am′bi·en·cy** *n.*

cir·cum·cise (sur′kəm siz′) *vt.* **-cised′, -cis′ing** [< OFr. < L. pp. of *circumcidere* < *circum-*, around + *caedere*, to cut] to cut off all or part of the foreskin or clitoris of —**cir′·cum·ci′sion** (-sizh′ən) *n.*

cir·cum·fer·ence (sər kum′fər əns) *n.* [< L. prp. of *circumferre* < *circum-*, around + *ferre*, to carry] **1.** the line bounding a circle or other rounded surface or area **2.** the distance measured by this line —**cir·cum′fer·en′tial** (-fə ren′shəl) *adj.* —**cir·cum′fer·en′tial·ly** *adv.*

cir·cum·flex (sur′kəm fleks′) *n.* [< L. pp. of *circumflectere* < *circum-*, around + *flectere*, to bend] a mark (^ ⌢) used over certain vowels in some languages to indicate a specific sound or pitch, or as a diacritical mark in some phonetic systems: also **circumflex accent** —*adj.* **1.** of or marked by a circumflex **2.** bending around; curved —*vt.* **1.** to bend round; curve **2.** to write with a circumflex —**cir′·cum·flex′ion** *n.*

cir·cum·flu·ent (sər kum′floo wənt) *adj.* [< L. prp. of *circumfluere* < *circum-*, around + *fluere*, to flow] flowing round; surrounding: also **cir·cum′flu·ous** —**cir·cum′flu·ence** *n.*

cir·cum·fuse (sur′kəm fyooz′) *vt.* **-fused′, -fus′ing** [< L. pp. of *circumfundere* < *circum-*, around + *fundere*, to pour] **1.** to pour or spread (a fluid) round; diffuse **2.** to surround (*with* a fluid); suffuse (*in*) —**cir′cum·fu′sion** *n.*

cir·cum·lo·cu·tion (sur′kəm lō kyoo′shən) *n.* [< L.: see CIRCUM- & LOCUTION] a roundabout, indirect, or lengthy way of expressing something —**cir′cum·loc′u·to·ry** (-lok′yə tər ē) *adj.*

cir·cum·nav·i·gate (-nav′ə gāt′) *vt.* **-gat′ed, -gat′ing** [< L. pp. of *circumnavigare:* see CIRCUM- & NAVIGATE] to sail or fly around (the earth, an island, etc.) —**cir′cum·nav′i·ga′·tion** *n.* —**cir′cum·nav′i·ga′tor** *n.*

cir·cum·scribe (sur′kəm skrib′, sur′kəm skrib′) *vt.* **-scribed′, -scrib′ing** [< L. < *circum-*, around + *scribere*, to write] **1.** to trace a line around; encircle **2.** *a)* to limit; confine *b)* to restrict **3.** *Geom. a)* to draw a figure around (another figure) so as to touch it at as many points as possible without intersection *b)* to be thus drawn around —**cir′cum·scrib′a·ble** *adj.* —**cir′cum·scrib′er** *n.* —**cir′·cum·scrip′tion** (-skrip′shən) *n.*

cir·cum·spect (sur′kəm spekt′) *adj.* [< L. pp. of *circumspicere* < *circum-*, around + *specere*, to look] careful to consider all related circumstances before acting, deciding, etc.; cautious —**cir′cum·spec′tion** *n.* —**cir′·cum·spect′ly** *adv.*

cir·cum·stance (-stans′, -stəns) *n.* [< OFr. < L. < *circum-*, around + *stare*, to stand] **1.** a fact or event, esp. one accompanying another, either incidentally or as a determining factor **2.** [*pl.*] conditions affecting a person, esp. financial conditions **3.** chance; luck **4.** ceremony; show [pomp and *circumstance*] **5.** *a)* surrounding detail *b)* fullness of detail —*vt.* **-stanced′, -stanc′ing** to place in certain circumstances —**under no circumstances** under no conditions; never —**under the circumstances** conditions being what they are or were —**cir′cum·stanced′** *adj.*

cir·cum·stan·tial (sur′kəm stan′shəl) *adj.* **1.** having to do with, or depending on, circumstances **2.** incidental **3.** full

or complete in detail —**cir′cum·stan′ti·al′i·ty** (-shē al′ə tē) *n., pl.* **-ties** —**cir′cum·stan′tial·ly** *adv.*

circumstantial evidence *Law* evidence offered to prove certain circumstances from which the existence of the fact at issue may be inferred

cir·cum·stan·ti·ate (-stan′shē āt′) *vt.* **-at′ed, -at′ing** to give detailed proof or support of —**cir′cum·stan′ti·a′tion** *n.*

cir·cum·val·late (-val′āt) *vt.* **-lat·ed, -lat·ing** [< L. pp. of *circumvallare* < *circum-*, around + *vallare*, to wall] to surround with or as with a wall or trench —*adj.* surrounded by a wall, trench, etc. —**cir′cum·val·la′tion** *n.*

cir·cum·vent (sur′kəm vent′) *vt.* [< L. pp. of *circumvenire* < *circum-*, around + *venire*, to come] **1.** to surround or circle round **2.** to surround with evils, enmity, etc.; entrap **3.** to get the better of or prevent from happening by craft or ingenuity —**cir′cum·ven′tion** *n.*

cir·cus (sur′kəs) *n.* [L. < or akin to Gr. *kirkos*, a circle] **1.** in ancient Rome, an oval or oblong arena with tiers of seats around it, used for games, races, etc. **2.** a similar arena for a travelling show of acrobats, trained animals, clowns, etc. **3.** such a show or the performance of such a show **4.** [Colloq.] any riotously entertaining person, event, etc. **5.** [Colloq.] any group of persons who habitually travel together, as politicians, technical experts, sportsmen, etc. **6.** an open space, usually circular, where streets converge

ci·ré (sə rā′) *adj.* [Fr., lit., waxed, ult. < Gr. *kēros*, wax] having a smooth, glossy finish as by treatment with wax —*n.* a ciré silk, straw, etc.

cirque (surk) *n.* [Fr. < L. *circus:* see CIRCUS] *Geol.* a steep, hollow depression on a mountainside, made by glacial erosion

cir·rho·sis (sə rō′sis) *n.* [ModL. < Gr. *kirrhos*, tawny + -OSIS: after the yellowish colour of the diseased liver] a degenerative disease in a bodily organ, esp. the liver, marked by excess formation of connective tissue and the subsequent contraction of the organ —**cir·rhot′ic** (-rot′ik) *adj.*

cir·ri- [< L. *cirrus*] *a combining form meaning* curl, ringlet: also **cir′ro-, cir′rhi-, cir′rho-**

cir·ri·ped (sir′ə ped′) *n.* [< ModL. *cirripedia* < prec. + L. *pes.* (gen. *pedis*), foot] any of a subclass of crustaceans including the barnacles: also **cir′ri·pede′** (-pēd′)

cir·ro·cu·mu·lus (sir′ō kyoo′myə ləs) *n.* a high formation of clouds in small, white puffs, flakes, or streaks

cir·ro·stra·tus (-strāt′əs, -strāt′-) *n.* a high formation of clouds in a thin, whitish veil

cir·rus (sir′əs) *n., pl.,* for 1 **-ri** (-ī); for 2 **-rus** [L., a curl] **1.** *a)* a plant tendril *b)* a flexible, threadlike appendage, as a feeler in certain organisms *c)* a cluster of fused cilia as in some infusorians **2.** a high formation of clouds in wispy filaments or feathery tufts —**cir′rose, cir′rous** *adj.*

cis- [< L. *cis*, on this side] *a prefix meaning:* **1.** on this side of **2.** subsequent to

cis·al·pine (sis al′pin, -pin) *adj.* on this (the Roman, or southern) side of the Alps

cis·lu·nar (sis loo′nər) *adj.* on this side of the moon, between the moon and the earth

cis·sy (sis′ē) *n.* same as SISSY

cist[1] (sist, kist) *n.* [W. < L. *cista* < Gr. *kistē*, chest] a prehistoric tomb made of stone slabs or hollowed out of rock

cist[2] (sist) *n.* [< L. *cista* < Gr. *kistē*, chest] in ancient times, a box, esp. one containing sacred utensils

Cis·ter·cian (sis tur′shən) *adj.* [< OFr. < ML. *Cistercium* (now *Cîteaux*, France)] designating or of a monastic order following the Benedictine rule strictly —*n.* a Cistercian monk or nun

cis·tern (sis′tərn) *n.* [< OFr. < L. < *cista*, CHEST] **1.** a tank for the storage of water, specif., *a)* in the roofspace of a house *b)* above a W.C., for flushing **2.** an underground reservoir for the storage of liquid, esp. rain water **3.** *Anat.* a sac or cavity containing a natural body fluid: also **cis·tern′a** (-tur′nə)

cit·a·del (sit′ə d′l, -del′) *n.* [< Fr. < It. dim. of *cittade*, city < L. *civitas*, CITY] **1.** a fortress on a commanding height for defence of a city **2.** a fortified place; stronghold **3.** a place of safety; refuge **4.** a Salvation Army meeting house

ci·ta·tion (sī tā′shən) *n.* [< OFr. < L. pp. of *citare:* see ff.] **1.** a summons to appear before a court of law **2.** a citing; quoting **3.** a passage cited; quotation **4.** a reference to a legal statute, a previous law case, etc. **5.** *a)* official honourable mention for meritorious service in the armed forces *b)* a formal statement honouring a person —**ci·ta′tor** *n.* —**ci·ta·to·ry** (sī tā′tər ē) *adj.*

cite (sīt) *vt.* **cit′ed, cit′ing** [< OFr. < L. *citare*, to summon < *ciere*, to rouse] **1.** to summon to appear before a court of law **2.** to quote (a passage, book, writer, etc.) **3.** to refer to or mention by way of example, proof, etc. **4.** to mention in a citation (sense 5) —**cit′a·ble, cite′a·ble** *adj.*

cith·a·ra (sith′ə rə) *n.* [L. < Gr. *kithara*] an ancient musical instrument somewhat like a lyre

cith·er (sith′ər) *n.* [< Fr. < prec.] same as CITTERN: also **cith′ern** (-ərn)

cit·i·fied (sit′i fīd′) *adj.* having the manners, dress, etc. attributed to city people

cit·i·zen (sit′ə zən) *n.* [Anglo-Fr. *citizein* < OFr. < *cite*: see CITY] 1. formerly, an inhabitant of a town or city 2. a member of a state or nation who owes allegiance to it by birth or naturalization and is entitled to full civil rights 3. a civilian, as distinguished from a soldier, policeman, etc.

cit·i·zen·ry (-rē) *n.* all citizens as a group

cit·i·zen·ship (-ship′) *n.* 1. the status or condition of a citizen, or his duties, rights, and privileges 2. one's conduct as a citizen

cit·rate (si′trāt) *n.* [CITR(US) + -ATE²] a salt or ester of citric acid

cit·ric (si′trik) *adj.* [CITR(US) + -IC] 1. of or from lemons, oranges, or similar fruits 2. designating or of an acid, $C_6H_8O_7$, obtained from such fruits, used in making dyes, citrates, etc.

cit·ri·cul·ture (-trə kul′chər) *n.* the cultivation of citrus fruits

cit·rine (-trin, -trēn, -trīn) *adj.* [< OFr. < ML. < L. *citrus*, CITRUS] of the yellow colour of a lemon —*n.* 1. lemon yellow 2. a yellow quartz

cit·ron (-trən) *n.* [Fr., lemon < It. *citrone* < L. *citrus*, CITRUS] 1. a yellow, thick-skinned fruit resembling a lemon but larger and less acid 2. the semitropical tree bearing this fruit 3. the candied peel of this fruit, used in cakes, etc.

cit·ron·el·la (si′trə nel′ə) *n.* [ModL. < prec.] 1. a volatile, sharp-smelling oil used in perfume, soap, insect repellents, etc.: also **citronella oil** 2. a grass of S Asia from which it is derived

cit·rus (si′trəs) *n.* [L., citron tree (whence Gr. *kitron*)] 1. any of a genus of trees and shrubs that bear oranges, lemons, limes, or other such fruit —*adj.* of these trees or shrubs: also **cit′rous** (-trəs)

cit·tern (sit′ərn) *n.* [< CITHER, prob. infl. by ME. *giterne*, GITTERN] a stringed instrument of the guitar family, popular in the 16th & 17th cent.

cit·y (sit′ē) *n.,* *pl.* **cit′ies** [< OFr. *cite* < L. *civitas*, orig. citizenship < *civis*, citizen] 1. a centre of population larger or more important than a town or village 2. in Britain, a large town that has been granted a charter from the Crown: usually the seat of a bishop 3. in the U.S., an incorporated municipality whose boundaries and powers of self-government are defined by a charter from its state 4. in Canada, a large urban municipality within a province 5. all the people of a city —*adj.* of or in a city —**the City** 1. the City of London, esp. the financial and commercial institutions located there 2. finance and the financial world in general

city editor 1. the editor of a newspaper, responsible for financial news 2. [Chiefly U.S.] the editor in charge of local news

city fathers the important officials of a city

city manager [Chiefly U.S.] a chief municipal administrator appointed by a city council on a professional basis, with tenure free from public elections

cit·y·scape (sit′ē skāp′) *n.* [CITY + (LAND)SCAPE] 1. a painting, photograph, etc. of a section of a city 2. a view of a section of a city, esp. of buildings silhouetted against the horizon

cit·y-state (-stāt′) *n.* a state made up of an independent city and the territory directly controlled by it, as in ancient Greece

civ. 1. civil 2. civilian

civ·et (siv′it) *n.* [< Fr. < It. *zibetto* < Ar. *zabād*] 1. a yellowish substance with a musklike scent, secreted by a gland of the civet cat and used in making some perfumes 2. the civet cat or its fur

civet cat a catlike, flesh-eating mammal of Africa and S Asia, with spotted, yellowish fur

civ·ic (siv′ik) *adj.* [L. *civicus* < *civis*: see CITY] 1. of a city; municipal 2. of citizens or citizenship —**civ′i·cal·ly** *adv.*

civic centre a complex of buildings serving the administrative, social, and recreational needs of a town

civ·ics (siv′iks) *n.pl.* [*with sing. v.*] the branch of political science dealing with civic affairs and the duties and rights of citizenship

civ·il (siv′'l) *adj.* [OFr. < L. *civilis* < *civis*: see CITY] 1. of a citizen or citizens [*civil* rights] 2. of a community of citizens, their government, or their interrelations 3. civilized 4. polite or courteous, esp. in a merely formal way 5. not military or religious [*civil* marriage] 6. *Law* relating to private rights and legal actions involving these

civil defence a system of warning devices, air-raid or fallout shelters, civilian volunteers, etc. for defence of a population against enemy attack

civil disobedience nonviolent opposition to a government policy or law by refusing to comply with it, on the grounds of conscience: see also NONCOOPERATION, PASSIVE RESISTANCE

civil engineering the branch of engineering dealing with the design and construction of roads, bridges, harbours, etc. —**civil engineer**

ci·vil·ian (sə vil′yən) *n.* [< OFr. < L.: see CIVIL] a person not an active member of the armed forces or of an official force having police power —*adj.* of or for civilians; nonmilitary

ci·vil·i·ty (-ə tē) *n.,* *pl.* **-ties** 1. politeness, esp. of a merely formal kind 2. a civil act or utterance

civ·i·li·za·tion (siv′ə lī′zā′shən, -li′-) *n.* 1. a civilizing or becoming civilized 2. the condition of being civilized; social organization of a high order 3. the total culture of a people, nation, period, etc. 4. the countries and peoples considered to have reached a high stage of social and cultural development 5. intellectual and cultural refinement 6. the comforts of civilized life

civ·i·lize (siv′ə līz′) *vt.* **-lized′,** **-liz′ing** [< Fr. < L.: see CIVIL & -IZE] 1. to bring out of a primitive or savage condition and into a state of civilization 2. to improve in habits or manners; refine —**civ′i·liz′a·ble** *adj.* —**civ′i·lized′** *adj.*

civil law 1. the body of codified law developed from Roman law 2. the body of law that an individual nation or state has established for itself 3. the body of law concerning private rights

civil liberties liberties guaranteed to the individual by law and custom; rights of thinking, speaking, and acting as one likes without hindrance except in the interests of the public good

civil list in Britain, the annual amount fixed by Parliament for the household expenses of members of the royal family

civ·il·ly (siv′il ē) *adv.* 1. with civility; politely 2. in relation to civil law, civil rights, etc.

civil marriage a marriage performed by a public official, not by a clergyman

civil rights 1. the rights of a citizen as a private individual, esp. in relation to the state 2. [Colloq.] the rights of minorities or disadvantaged groups within a society

civil service all those employed in government work except those in the armed forces, legislature and judicature —**civil servant**

civil war war between different sections or factions of the same nation

civ·vies (siv′ēz) *n.pl.* [Colloq.] civilian clothes, as distinguished from a military uniform; mufti

Civ·vy Street (siv′ē) [Colloq.] civilian life, as opposed to military

C.J. Chief Justice

ck. *pl.* **cks.** cask

Cl *Chem.* chlorine

cl centilitre(s)

cl. 1. claim 2. class 3. clause

cla·chan (klakh′'n) *n.* [Gael. < *clach*, stone] [Scot. & Ir.] a hamlet; small village

clack (klak) *vi.* [prob. < ON. *klaka*, of echoic origin] 1. to make a sudden, sharp sound [high heels *clacking*] 2. to chatter —*vt.* to cause to make a sudden, sharp sound —*n.* 1. a clacking sound 2. chatter 3. a simple non-return valve, as in a pump: also **clack valve** —**clack′er** *n.*

clad (klad) *alt. pt. & pp. of* CLOTHE —*adj.* 1. clothed; dressed 2. having a layer of another metal or of an alloy bonded to it [*clad* steel]

clad·ding (-iŋ) *n.* [see prec.] 1. a layer of some metal or alloy bonded to another 2. any material, as wood, stone, etc., used as an external facing for buildings 3. the process of attaching such materials

claim (klām) *vt.* [< OFr. < L. *clamare*, to cry out] 1. to demand as rightfully belonging to one; assert one's right to (a title, etc. that should be recognized) 2. to call for; require; deserve [problems *claiming* our attention] 3. to assert; maintain —*n.* 1. a demand for something rightfully due 2. a right or title to something 3. something claimed, as land staked out by a settler 4. an assertion —**claim′a·ble** *adj.* —**claim′er** *n.*

claim·ant (klā′mənt) *n.* one who makes a claim

clair·voy·ance (kler voi′əns) *n.* [Fr. < ff.] 1. the supposed ability to perceive things that are not in sight or that cannot be seen 2. keen perception or insight

clair·voy·ant (-ənt) *adj.* [Fr. < *clair*, clear + prp. of *voir*, to see] 1. of or apparently having clairvoyance 2. having keen insight —*n.* a clairvoyant person —**clair·voy′ant·ly** *adv.*

clam (klam) *n.,* *pl.* **clams, clam:** see PLURAL, II, D, 1 [< OE. *clamm*, fetter, in reference to the action of the shells] 1. any of certain hard-shelled, bivalve molluscs living in the shallows of the sea or in fresh water 2. the soft, edible part of these molluscs —*vi.* to dig, or go digging, for clams —**clam up** [Colloq.] to refuse to talk

clam·ber (klam′bər) *vi.,* *vt.* [ME. *clambren*] to climb clumsily or with effort, using both hands and feet —*n.* a hard or clumsy climb —**clam′ber·er** *n.*

clam·my (klam′ē) *adj.* **-mi·er,** **-mi·est** [prob. < OE. *clam,* clay] unpleasantly moist, cold, and sticky —**clam′mi·ly** *adv.* —**clam′mi·ness** *n.*

clam·our (klam′ər) *n.* [< OFr. < L. < *clamare*, to cry out] 1. a loud outcry; uproar 2. a strong, insistent public demand or complaint **3.** a loud, sustained noise —*vi.* to make a clamour; cry out, demand, or complain noisily —*vt.* to express with clamour Also, U.S. sp., **clam'or** —**clam'or·ous** (-əs) *adj.* —**clam'or·ous·ly** *adv.* —**clam'or·ous·ness** *n.*

clamp[1] (klamp) *n.* [< MDu. *klampe*] a device for clasping or fastening things together; esp., an appliance with two parts brought together to grip something —*vt.* **1.** to grip, fasten, or brace with a clamp **2.** to impose forcefully —**clamp down** (**on**) to become more strict (with)

clamp[2] (klamp) *n.* [< MDu. *klamp, heap*] a pile, esp. of potatoes, stored under earth or straw —*vt.* to keep in a clamp

clan (klan) *n.* [Gael. & Ir. *clann*, offspring < L. *planta*, offshoot] **1.** a social group, as in the Scottish Highlands, composed of several families descended from a common ancestor **2.** a group of people with interests in common **3.** [Colloq.] family (sense 3)

CLAMP

clan·des·tine (klan des'tin) *adj.* [< Fr. < L. *clandestinus* < *clam*, secretly] kept secret or hidden, esp. for some illicit purpose; surreptitious —**clan·des'tine·ly** *adv.*

clang (klaŋ) *vi., vt.* [echoic, or akin to L. *clangere*: see CLANGOUR] to make or cause to make loud, sharp, ringing sound, as by striking metal —*n.* a clanging sound or cry

clang·er (klaŋ'ər) *n.* [< prec.] [Colloq.] a mistake, esp. a social blunder [he dropped a *clanger*]

clan·gour (klaŋ'ər) *n.* [L. < *clangere*, to clang] a clanging sound, esp. a continued clanging —*vi.* to make a clangour Also, U.S. sp., **clan'gor** —**clan'gor·ous** *adj.* —**clan'gor·ous·ly** *adv.*

clank (klaŋk) *n.* [echoic] a sharp, metallic sound, not so resonant as a clang —*vi.* to make, or move with, a clank —*vt.* to cause to clank

clan·nish (klan'ish) *adj.* **1.** of a clan **2.** tending to associate closely and to avoid others —**clan'nish·ly** *adv.* —**clan'nish·ness** *n.*

clans·man (klanz'mən) *n.,* pl. **-men** a member of a clan —**clans'wom'an** *n.fem.,* pl. **-wom'en**

clap[1] (klap) *vi.* **clapped** or archaic **clapt, clap'ping** [OE. *clæppan*, to beat] **1.** to make a sudden, explosive sound, as of two flat surfaces being struck together **2.** to strike the hands together, as in applauding —*vt.* **1.** to strike together briskly and loudly **2.** to strike with an open hand **3.** to put, move, etc. swiftly [*clapped* into jail] **4.** to put together hastily —*n.* **1.** the sound of clapping [*clap* of thunder] **2.** the act of striking the hands together **3.** a sharp slap, as in hearty greeting —**clap eyes on** [Colloq.] to catch sight of; see —**clap hold of** [Colloq.] to seize; grasp —**clapped out** [Colloq.] **1.** worn out; dilapidated **2.** exhausted; fatigued

clap[2] (klap) *n.* [< ME. *claper*, brothel, orig. rabbit burrow < OFr. *clapier*] [Slang] gonorrhoea: with *the*

clap·board (klap'bôrd', klab'ərd) *n.* [partial transl. of MDu. *klapholt* < *klappen*, to fit + *holt*, wood] [Chiefly U.S.] same as WEATHERBOARD

clap·per (klap'ər) *n.* **1.** a person who claps **2.** a thing that makes a clapping noise, as the tongue of a bell or, facetiously, that of a person —**like the clappers** [Colloq.] very fast

clap·per·board (-bôrd) *n.* Cinema a pair of hinged boards struck together before and after a film sequence to aid in synchronizing sound and picture

clap·trap (klap'trap') *n.* [CLAP[1] + TRAP[1]] showy, insincere, empty talk, etc. intended only to get applause or attention —*adj.* showy and cheap

claque (klak) *n.* [Fr. < *claquer*, to clap] **1.** a group of people paid to go to a play, opera, etc. and applaud **2.** a group of fawning followers —**claqu'eur** *n.*

clar·ence (klar'əns) *n.* [< the Duke of *Clarence*, later William IV] a closed, four-wheeled carriage

clar·et (klar'it) *n.* [< OFr. dim. of *cler* < L. *clarus*, clear] **1.** a red wine, esp. red Bordeaux **2.** purplish red: also **claret red** —*adj.* purplish-red

clar·i·fy (klar'ə fī) *vt., vi.* **-fied', -fy'ing** [< OFr. < L. < *clarus*, clear + *facere*, to make] **1.** to make or become clear and free from impurities: said esp. of fat **2.** to make or become easier to understand [*clarify* your meaning] —**clar'i·fi·ca'tion** *n.* —**clar'i·fi'er** *n.*

clar·i·net (klar'ə net') *n.* [Fr. *clarinette*, dim. of *clarine*, little bell < ML. *clario*: see ff.] a single-reed, woodwind instrument with a long wooden or metal tube and a flaring bell, played by means of holes and keys —**clar'i·net'tist** *n.*

clar·i·on (klar'ē ən) *n.* [OFr. < ML. *clario* < L. *clarus*, clear] **1.** a trumpet of the Middle Ages producing clear, sharp, shrill tones **2.** [Poet.] a sound of or like a clarion —*adj.* clear, sharp, and ringing [a *clarion* call] —*vt.* to announce forcefully or loudly

clar·i·ty (klar'ə tē) *n.* [OFr. *clarte* < L. *claritas* < *clarus*, clear] a being clear; clearness

clash (klash) *vi.* [echoic] **1.** to collide with a loud, harsh, metallic noise **2.** *a)* to conflict; disagree *b)* to fail to harmonize [the colours *clashed*] —*vt.* to strike together, shut, etc. with a loud, harsh noise —*n.* **1.** the sound of clashing **2.** *a)* conflict *b)* lack of harmony —**clash'er** *n.*

clasp (kläsp) *n.* [ME. *claspe*] **1.** a fastening, as a hook or catch, to hold two things or parts together **2.** a grasping; embrace **3.** a grip of the hand **4.** a metal bar attached to the ribbon of a military decoration to show a subsequent award of the same medal or to specify the type or place of service —*vt.* **1.** to fasten with a clasp **2.** to grasp firmly; embrace **3.** to grip with the hand **4.** to cling to —**clasp'er** *n.*

clasp-knife (-nīf') *n.* a large pocketknife with one or more folding blades, secured by a catch when open

class (kläs) *n.* [< Fr. < L. *classis*, prob. akin to *calare*, to call] **1.** a number of people or things grouped together because of certain likenesses; kind; sort **2.** a group of people of the same social or economic status [the middle *class*] **3.** high social rank or caste **4.** the division of society into ranks or castes **5.** *a)* a group of pupils or students taught together *b)* a meeting of such a group *c)* [U.S.] a group of students graduating together **6.** grade or quality [travel first *class*] **7.** [Colloq.] excellence, as of style **8.** Biol. a group of animals or plants ranking below a phylum and above an order —*vt.* to put in a class; classify —*vi.* to be classed —**in a class by itself** (or **oneself**) unique

class. **1.** classic; **2.** classical; **3.** classification; **4.** classified

class consciousness an awareness of belonging to a certain economic class in the social order —**class'-con'scious** *adj.*

clas·sic (klas'ik) *adj.* [L. *classicus*, superior < *classis*, CLASS] **1.** of the highest class; being a model of its kind; standard **2.** *a)* of the art, literature, and culture of the ancient Greeks or Romans, or their writers, artists, etc. *b)* derived from their literary and artistic standards **3.** balanced, formal, objective, restrained, regular, etc. **4.** famous as traditional or typical **5.** [Colloq.] simple in style and continuing in fashion: said of an article of apparel —*n.* **1.** a writer, artist, etc., or a literary or artistic work, recognized as excellent, authoritative, etc. **2.** a famous traditional event **3.** [Colloq.] a suit, dress, etc. that is classic (sense 5) **4.** [Colloq.] any remarkable, excellent or unique thing or occurrence [his mistake was a *classic*] **5.** Horse Racing any of the five principal races in the flat racing calendar: One Thousand Guineas, Two Thousand Guineas, Derby, Oaks, and St. Leger —**the classics** literature regarded as classic (senses 1, 2)

clas·si·cal (-i k'l) *adj.* **1.** same as CLASSIC (senses 1, 2, 3) **2.** versed in and devoted to Greek and Roman culture, literature, etc. **3.** designating or of the form of language used in standard literary works [*classical* Arabic, *classical* Chinese] **4.** designating or of music that conforms to certain established standards of form, complexity, musical literacy, etc.: distinguished from POPULAR, ROMANTIC **5.** standard and traditionally authoritative, not new and experimental [*classical* economics] —**clas'si·cal·i·ty** (-kal'ə tē), **clas'si·cal·ness,** *n.* —**clas'si·cal·ly** *adv.*

clas·si·cism (klas'ə siz'm) *n.* **1.** the aesthetic principles or qualities of ancient Greece and Rome: generally contrasted with ROMANTICISM **2.** adherence to such principles **3.** knowledge of the literature and art of ancient Greece and Rome **4.** *a)* a Greek or Latin idiom or expression *b)* a modern form of language modelled on a classical form Also **clas'si·cal·ism** —**clas'si·cist** *n.*

clas·si·cize (-sīz') *vt.* **-cized', -ciz'ing** to make classic —*vi.* to employ or imitate a classic style

clas·si·fi·ca·tion (klas'ə fi kā'shən) *n.* **1.** an arrangement according to some systematic division into classes or groups **2.** such a class or group **3.** Biol. same as TAXONOMY —**clas·si·fi·ca·to·ry** (klas'ə fi kā'tər ē) *adj.*

classified advertising advertising, as in newspaper columns, under such listings as *situations vacant, for sale,* etc.

clas·si·fy (klas'ə fī') *vt.* **-fied', -fy'ing** **1.** to arrange in classes according to some system or principle **2.** to place in a category **3.** to designate (government documents, etc.) as secret or confidential —**clas'si·fi'a·ble** *adj.* —**clas'si·fi'er** *n.*

class·less (kläs'lis) *adj.* **1.** having no distinct social or economic classes [a *classless* society] **2.** not belonging to a social class [a *classless* individual]

class list a list of examination results, esp. at a university

class·mate (-māt') *n.* a member of the same class in a school

class·room (-room') *n.* a room in a school in which classes are taught

class·y (-ē) *adj.* **class'i·er, class'i·est** [Colloq.] first-class, esp. in style or manner —**class'i·ness** *n.*

clat·ter (klat'ər) *vi.* [ME. *clateren*] **1.** to make, or move with, a rapid succession of loud, sharp noises, as dishes rattling **2.** to chatter noisily —**vt.** to cause to clatter —**n. 1.** a rapid succession of loud, sharp noises **2.** a tumult; hubbub **3.** noisy chatter —**clat'ter·er** n. —**clat'ter·ing·ly** adv.

clause (klôz) n. [OFr. < ML. clausa < L. pp. of claudere, to close] **1.** a group of words containing a subject and predicate, usually forming part of a compound or complex sentence: cf. MAIN CLAUSE, SUBORDINATE CLAUSE **2.** a particular article, stipulation, or provision in a formal or legal document —**claus'al** adj.

claus·tro·pho·bi·a (klôs'trə fō'bē ə) n. [< L. claustrum (see CLOISTER) + -PHOBIA] an abnormal fear of being in an enclosed or confined place —**claus'tro·pho'bic** adj.

cla·vate (klā'vāt) adj. [< L. clava, a club + -ATE¹] club-shaped —**cla'vate·ly** adv. —**cla·va'tion** n.

clave¹ (klāv) archaic pt. of CLEAVE¹ & CLEAVE²

clave² (kläv) n. [Sp. < L. clavis, key] one of a pair of wooden sticks used as a percussion instrument

clav·i·chord (klav'ə kôrd') n. [< ML. < L. clavis, a key + chorda, a string] a stringed musical instrument with a keyboard, predecessor of the piano

clav·i·cle (klav'ə k'l) n. [< Fr. < L. clavicula, dim. of clavis, a key] a bone connecting the breastbone with the shoulder blade; collarbone —**cla·vic·u·lar** (klə vik'yoo lər) adj.

cla·vi·er (klə vir'; for 1, also klav'ē ər) n. [Fr., keyboard < L. clavis, a key] **1.** the keyboard of an organ, piano, etc. **2.** any stringed instrument that has a keyboard

CLAVICLES

claw (klô) n. [OE. clawu] **1.** a sharp, hooked nail on the foot of a bird and of many reptiles and mammals **2.** a foot with such nails **3.** a pincer, or chela, of a lobster, crab, etc. **4.** anything regarded as or resembling a claw, as a hammer (**claw hammer**) with one end forked and curved, used to pull nails —**vt., vi.** to scratch, clutch, pull, dig, or tear with or as with claws —**clawed** adj.

clay (klā) n. [OE. clæg] **1.** a firm, plastic earth, used in the manufacture of bricks, pottery, etc. **2.** a) earth b) the human body —**clay'ey** adj. **clay'i·er, clay'i·est** —**clay'ish** adj.

clay·more (klā'môr') n. [Gael. claidheamhmor, great sword] **1.** a large, two-edged broadsword formerly used by Scottish Highlanders **2.** a broadsword with a basket hilt worn by Highland regiments

clay pigeon a disc as of baked clay, tossed into the air from a trap as a target in trapshooting

clean (klēn) adj. [OE. clæne] **1.** free from dirt or impurities; unsoiled; unstained **2.** producing little immediate fallout: said of nuclear weapons **3.** recently laundered; fresh **4.** a) morally or ritually pure b) not obscene or indecent **5.** sportsmanlike **6.** keeping oneself or one's surroundings neat and tidy **7.** shapely or trim [clean lines] **8.** skilful; deft [a clean stroke] **9.** having no obstructions or flaws; clear **10.** complete; thorough **11.** empty **12.** [Slang] a) innocent of any crime b) not in possession of weapons, drugs, etc. —**adv. 1.** in a clean manner **2.** [Colloq.] completely —**vt. 1.** to make clean **2.** to remove (dirt, impurities, etc.) **3.** to empty or clear **4.** to prepare (fish, fowl, etc.) for cooking **5.** [Slang] to take away or use up the money, etc. of (often with out) —**vi.** to undergo or perform the act of cleaning —**clean out 1.** to empty so as to make clean **2.** to empty —**clean sheet** (or slate) a new start, esp. when free of earlier mistakes, crimes, etc. —**clean up 1.** to make clean or neat **2.** to get washed, combed, etc. **3.** [Colloq.] to finish **4.** [Slang] to make much profit —**clean up on** [Slang] to make a large profit from —**come clean** [Slang] to confess; tell the truth —**make a clean breast of** [Colloq.] to confess —**clean'a·ble** adj. —**clean'-ness** n.

clean-cut (-kut') adj. **1.** clearly and sharply outlined **2.** well-formed **3.** distinct; clear **4.** good-looking, trim, neat, etc.

clean·er (-ər) n. a person or thing that cleans; specif., a) one who cleans offices, homes, etc. b) one who dry-cleans c) a preparation for removing dirt, stains, etc.

clean·ly¹ (klēn'lē) adj. -li·er, -li·est **1.** keeping oneself or one's surroundings clean **2.** always kept clean —**clean'li·ly** adv. —**clean'li·ness** n.

clean·ly² (klēn'lē) adv. in a clean manner

cleanse (klenz) vt. cleansed, cleans'ing [OE. clænsian] to make clean, pure, etc.; purge

cleans·er (klen'zər) n. a preparation for cleansing, esp. a powder for scouring pots, sinks, etc.

clean-shav·en (klēn'shā'v'n) adj. having all the hairs shaved off, esp. from the face

clean-up (klēn'up') n. **1.** a cleaning up **2.** elimination of crime, vice, etc. **3.** [Slang] profit; gain

clear (klir) adj. [< OFr. < L. clarus] **1.** free from clouds or mist; bright; light **2.** transparent; not turbid **3.** having no blemishes [a clear skin] **4.** easily seen; sharply defined; distinct **5.** perceiving acutely; keen **6.** serene and calm **7.** not obscure; easily understood **8.** obvious **9.** certain; positive **10.** free from guilt; innocent **11.** free from charges or deductions; net **12.** free from debt or encumbrance **13.** absolute; complete **14.** free from obstruction; open **15.** emptied of freight or cargo —**adv. 1.** in a clear manner **2.** [Colloq.] all the way; completely [it sank clear to the bottom] **3.** out of the way [stand clear of the gates] —**vt. 1.** to make clear or bright **2.** to free from impurities, muddiness, blemishes, etc. **3.** a) to make intelligible or lucid b) to decode or decipher **4.** to rid of obstructions; open **5.** to get rid of; remove **6.** to empty or unload **7.** to free (a person or thing) of or from something **8.** to free from guilt or blame **9.** to pass over, under, by, etc. with space to spare **10.** to discharge (a debt) by paying it **11.** to give or get clearance for **12.** to be passed or approved by **13.** to make (a given amount) as profit; net **14.** Banking to pass (a cheque, etc.) through a clearinghouse —**vi. 1.** to become clear, unclouded, etc. **2.** to pass away; vanish **3.** to get clearance, as a ship leaving port **4.** Banking to exchange cheques, etc., and balance accounts, through a clearinghouse —**n. 1.** a clear space **2.** ordinary language; not cipher [the message was in clear] —**clear away 1.** to take away so as to leave a cleared space **2.** to go away —**clear off 1.** to clear away **2.** to remove things from (a surface) **3.** [Colloq.] to depart —**clear out 1.** to clear by emptying **2.** [Colloq.] to depart —**clear the air** (or atmosphere) to get rid of emotional tensions, etc. —**clear up 1.** to make or become clear **2.** to make orderly **3.** to explain **4.** to cure or become cured —**in the clear 1.** in the open **2.** [Colloq.] free from suspicion, guilt, etc. —**clear'a·ble** adj. —**clear'er** n. —**clear'ly** adv. —**clear'-ness** n.

clear·ance (-əns) n. **1.** a making clear **2.** the clear space between things, or between a moving object and that which it passes by, through, over, under, etc. **3.** a) the removal of property, furniture, etc. from a building b) the demolition of buildings in an area [slum clearance] **4.** official authorization to see classified documents, work on secret projects, enter an area, etc. **5.** Banking the adjustment of accounts in a clearinghouse **6.** Naut. a certificate authorizing a ship to enter or leave port: also called **clearance papers**

clear-cut (-kut') adj. **1.** clearly and sharply outlined **2.** distinct; definite; certain

clear·head·ed (-hed'id) adj. having a clear mind —**clear'-head'ed·ly** adv. —**clear'head'ed·ness** n.

clear·ing (klir'iŋ) n. **1.** a making clear or being cleared **2.** an area of land cleared of trees **3.** Banking a) same as CLEARANCE b) [pl.] the amount of the balances settled in clearing

clearing bank any of the principal British banks, esp. those that are members of the central clearinghouse in London

clear·ing·house (-hous') n. **1.** an office maintained by a group of banks as a centre for exchanging cheques, balancing accounts, etc. **2.** a central office for getting and giving information, etc.

clear·sight·ed (klir'sīt'id) adj. **1.** seeing clearly **2.** understanding or thinking clearly —**clear'sight'ed·ly** adv. —**clear'sight'ed·ness** n.

clear·sto·ry (-stôr'ē) n., pl. -ries same as CLERESTORY

clear·way (-wā') n. a stretch of road, not a motorway, where motorists may not stop

cleat (klēt) n. [< OE. hyp. cleat, a lump] **1.** a piece of wood or metal, often wedge-shaped, fastened to something to strengthen it or give secure footing **2.** a small triangular nail without a head, used to secure a pane of glass in a frame **3.** Naut. a small piece of wood or metal with projecting ends on which a rope can be fastened —**vt.** to fasten to or with a cleat

cleav·age (klē'vij) n. **1.** a cleaving, splitting, or dividing **2.** the manner in which a thing splits **3.** a cleft; fissure **4.** the hollow between a woman's breasts, as exposed by a low-cut neckline **5.** Biol. cell division that transforms the fertilized ovum into the earliest embryonic stage

cleave¹ (klēv) vt. cleaved or cleft or clove, cleaved or cleft or clo'ven, cleav'ing [OE. cleofan] **1.** to divide by a blow, as with an axe; split **2.** to pierce **3.** to sever; disunite —**vi. 1.** to split; separate **2.** to make one's way by or as by cutting —**cleav'a·ble** adj.

cleave² (klēv) vi. cleaved, cleav'ing [OE. cleofian] **1.** to adhere; cling (to) **2.** to be faithful (to)

cleav·er (-ər) n. a heavy cleaving tool with a broad blade, used by butchers

cleav·ers (-ərz) n., pl. -ers [< CLEAVE²] a plant of the madder family, with stalkless leaves, clusters of small flowers, and prickly stems

clef (klef) *n.* [Fr. < L. *clavis*, a key] a symbol used in music to indicate the pitch of the notes on the staff: there are three clefs: G (treble), F (bass), and C (tenor or alto)

G CLEF   F CLEF

cleft[1] (kleft) *n.* [< OE. hyp. *clyft* < *cleofan*, CLEAVE[1]] **1.** an opening made by or as by cleaving; crack; crevice **2.** a hollow between two parts

cleft[2] *alt. pt. & pp.* of CLEAVE[1] —*adj.* split; divided

cleft palate a congenital fissure from front to back along the roof of the mouth, often associated with a harelip

cleg (kleg) *n.* [< ON. *kleggi*] *same as* HORSEFLY

clem·a·tis (klem′ə tis, klə māt′is) *n.* [L. < Gr. < *klēma*, vine, twig] a perennial plant or woody climbing plant of the buttercup family, with brightly coloured flowers

C CLEFS

TYPES OF CLEF

clem·en·cy (klem′ən sē) *n., pl.* -cies [< L. < *clemens*, merciful] **1.** forbearance, leniency, or mercy **2.** mildness, as of weather

clem·ent (klem′ənt) *adj.* [L. *clemens*] **1.** lenient; merciful **2.** mild, as weather —**clem′ent·ly** *adv.*

clem·en·tine (klem′ən tēn′) *n.* [< Fr. *clémentine* < ? L. fem. of *Clement*, a masculine name] a kind of small orange, similar to the tangerine

clench (klench) *vt.* [< OE. -*clencan* (in *beclencan*), lit., to make cling] **1.** to clinch, as a nail **2.** to bring together tightly; close (the teeth or fist) firmly **3.** to grip tightly —*n.* **1.** a firm grip **2.** a device that clenches —**clench′er** *n.*

clep·sy·dra (klep′si drə) *n., pl.* -dras or -drae′ (-drē′) [L. < Gr. < *kleptein*, to steal + *hydōr*, water] *same as* WATER CLOCK

clep·to·ma·ni·a (klep′tə mā′nē ə) *n. same as* KLEPTOMANIA

clere·sto·ry (klir′stôr′ē) *n., pl.* -ries [< ME. < *cler*, clear + *storie*, STOREY] **1.** the wall of a church rising above the roofs of the flanking aisles and containing windows for lighting the central part of the structure **2.** any similar windowed wall

cler·gy (klur′jē) *n., pl.* -gies [< OFr. < LL. *clericus*: see CLERK] men ordained for religious service; ministers, priests, rabbis, etc. collectively

cler·gy·man (-mən) *n., pl.* -men a member of the clergy; minister, priest, rabbi, etc.

cler·ic (kler′ik) *n.* [LL. *clericus*: see CLERK] a clergyman —*adj.* of a clergyman or the clergy

cler·i·cal (kler′i k′l) *adj.* [LL. *clericalis* < *clericus*: see CLERK] **1.** relating to a clergyman or the clergy **2.** relating to office clerks or their work **3.** favouring clericalism —*n.* **1.** a clergyman **2.** [*pl.*] clergymen's garments **3.** one who favours clericalism —**cler′i·cal·ly** *adv.*

clerical collar a stiff, white collar buttoned at the back, worn by certain clergymen

cler·i·cal·ism (-iz′m) *n.* political influence or power of the clergy —**cler′i·cal·ist** *n.*

cler·i·hew (kler′ə hyōō′) *n.* [after *Clerihew* Bentley (1875-1956), Brit. author] a humorous, quasi-biographical poem with two rhyming couplets in irregular metre

clerk (klärk) *n.* [< OFr. & OE. < LL. *clericus* < Gr. *klērikos*, priest] **1.** a layman who has minor duties in a church **2.** an office worker who keeps records, types letters, does filing, etc. **3.** an official in charge of records, etc. of a court **4.** [Chiefly U.S.] a hotel receptionist **5.** [Archaic] *a)* a clergyman *b)* a scholar —*vi.* to work as a clerk —**clerk′ly** *adj., adv.* —**clerk′ship** *n.*

clerk of (the) works the agent or overseer responsible for supervising work on a building site, etc.

clev·er (klev′ər) *adj.* [< ?] **1.** skilful in doing something; adroit; dexterous **2.** intelligent, quick-witted, witty, facile, etc. **3.** showing quick, sometimes superficial, intelligence [a *clever* book] **4.** [Colloq.] in good health —**clev′er·ly** *adv.* —**clev′er·ness** *n.*

clev·is (klev′is) *n.* [ult. akin to CLEAVE[2]] a U-shaped piece of iron with holes in the ends through which a pin is run to attach one thing to another

clew (klōō) *n.* [< OE. *cliwen*] **1.** a ball of thread or yarn **2.** *same as* CLUE **3.** *Naut. a)* a lower corner of a square sail *b)* the lower corner aft of a fore-and-aft sail *c)* a metal loop in the corner of a sail —*vt.* **1.** to wind (*up*) into a ball **2.** *same as* CLUE —**clew down** (or **up**) to lower (or raise) a sail by the clews

cli·ché (klē′shā) *n.* [Fr. < *clicher*, to sterotype] **1.** a stereotype printing plate **2.** a trite expression or idea

click (klik) *n.* [echoic] **1.** a slight, sharp sound like that of a door latch snapping into place **2.** a mechanical device, as a catch or pawl, that clicks into position **3.** *Phonet.* a sound made by drawing the breath into the mouth and clicking the tongue —*vi.* **1.** to make a click **2.** [Colloq.] *a)* to be suddenly comprehensible *b)* to work or get along together successfully *c)* to be a success —*vt.* to cause to click —**click′er** *n.*

cli·ent (klī′ənt) *n.* [OFr. < L. *cliens*, follower] **1.** a person or company for whom a lawyer, accountant, social worker, etc. is acting **2.** a customer —*adj.* depending upon another for help [a *client* state] —**cli·en·tal** (klī ən′t′l) *adj.*

cli·en·tele (klē′ on tel′) *n.* [< Fr. < L. *clientela*] all one's clients or customers, collectively: also **cli·ent·age** (klī′ən tij)

cliff (klif) *n.* [OE. *clif*] a high, steep face of rock, esp. one on a coast; precipice —**cliff′y** *adj.*

cliff·hang·er, cliff-hang·er (-haŋ′ər) *n.* any highly suspenseful story, situation, etc. as in an early type of serialized film with an episode which ends with the hero hanging from a cliff —**cliff′hang′ing, cliff′-hang′ing** *adj.*

cli·mac·ter·ic (klī mak′tər ik, klī′mak ter′ik) *n.* [< L. < Gr. < *klimax*, ladder] **1.** a period in a person's life when an important physiological change occurs, esp. the menopause **2.** any crucial period —*adj.* of or resembling a climacteric: also **cli′mac·ter′i·cal**

cli·mac·tic (klī mak′tik) *adj.* of or constituting a climax: also **cli·mac′ti·cal** —**cli·mac′ti·cal·ly** *adv.*

cli·mate (klī′mət) *n.* [< OFr. < L. < Gr. *klima*, region] **1.** the prevailing weather conditions of a place, as determined by the temperature and meteorological changes over a period of years **2.** any prevailing conditions affecting life, activity, etc. **3.** a region with certain prevailing weather conditions [move to a warm *climate*] —**cli·mat·ic** (klī mat′ik) *adj.* —**cli·mat′i·cal·ly** *adv.*

cli·ma·tol·o·gy (klī′mə tol′ə jē) *n.* the science dealing with climate and climate phenomena —**cli′ma·to·log′i·cal** (-tə loj′-i k′l) *adj.* —**cli′ma·tol′o·gist** *n.*

cli·max (klī′maks) *n.* [L. < Gr. *klimax*, ladder] **1.** formerly, an arrangement of ideas, images, etc. with the most forceful last **2.** the final, culminating element or event in a series; highest point, as of interest, excitement, etc.; specif., *a)* the decisive turning point of the action, as in drama *b)* an orgasm **3.** *Ecol.* a state of equilibrium with its surroundings reached by a plant or animal community —*vi., vt.* to reach, or bring to, a climax

climb (klīm) *vi., vt.* **climbed** or archaic **clomb, climb′ing** [OE. *climban*] **1.** to go up by using the feet and often the hands **2.** to rise or ascend gradually; mount **3.** to move (*down, over, along,* etc.) using the hands and feet **4.** to rise socially **5.** *Bot.* to grow upwards on by winding round or adhering with tendrils —*n.* **1.** a climbing; rise; ascent **2.** a thing or place to be climbed —**climb down** to withdraw from a position, argument, etc. —**climb′a·ble** *adj.*

climb·down (-doun′) *n.* a withdrawal or retreat from a position, argument, opinion, etc.

climb·er (-ər) *n.* **1.** one that climbs, specif., a mountaineer **2.** [Colloq.] one who constantly tries to advance himself socially or in business **3.** *Bot.* a climbing plant

clime (klīm) *n.* [L. *clima*: see CLIMATE] [Poet.] a region, esp. with reference to its climate

cli·nah (klī′nə) *n.* [< ?] [Aust. Slang] a girl; girl-friend: also **cli′ner**

clinch (klinch) *vt.* [var. of CLENCH] **1.** to fasten (a nail, bolt, etc. driven through something) by bending or flattening the projecting end **2.** to fasten together by this means **3.** *a)* to settle (an argument, deal, etc.) definitely *b)* to win conclusively —*vi.* **1.** *Boxing* to grip the opponent's body with the arms **2.** [Slang] to embrace —*n.* **1.** *a)* a clinching, as with a nail *b)* a clinched nail, bolt, etc. *c)* the part clinched **2.** *Boxing* an act of clinching **3.** [Slang] an embrace

clinch·er (-ər) *n.* **1.** a tool for clinching nails **2.** a decisive point, argument, act, etc.

cling (kliŋ) *vi.* **clung, cling′ing** [OE. *clingan*] **1.** to hold fast by or as by embracing, entwining, or sticking; adhere **2.** *a)* to be or stay near *b)* to be emotionally attached —*adj., n. same as* CLINGSTONE —**cling′er** *n.* —**cling′ing·ly** *adv.* —**cling′y** *adj.*

cling·stone (-stōn′) *adj.* having a stone that clings to the fleshy part: said of some peaches —*n.* a peach of this sort

clin·ic (klin′ik) *n.* [L. *clinicus*, physician who attends bedridden persons < Gr. *klinikos*, of a bed < *klinē*, a bed] **1.** a place where patients are treated by specialist physicians or surgeons **2.** a department of a hospital or medical school where outpatients are treated **3.** a private hospital or nursing home **4.** an organization that offers some kind of advice, treatment, or instruction

clin·i·cal (-i k′l) *adj.* **1.** of or connected with a clinic **2.** having to do with the treatment and observation of patients, as distinguished from experimental or laboratory study **3.** scientifically impersonal **4.** austere, antiseptic, etc., like a medical clinic —**clin′i·cal·ly** *adv.*

clinical thermometer a thermometer with which the body temperature is measured

cli·ni·cian (kli nish′ən) *n.* an expert in or practitioner of clinical medicine, psychology, etc.

clink[1] (kliŋk) *vi., vt.* [< MDu. *klinken*: echoic] to make or cause to make a slight, sharp sound, as of glasses striking together —*n.* such a sound

clink² (kliŋk) *n.* [< name of an 18th c. London prison] [Colloq.] a jail; prison

clink·er (-ər) *n.* [Du. *klinker*, vitrified brick < *klinken*, to ring] a hard mass of fused stony matter formed in a furnace, as from impurities in the coal —*vi.* to form clinkers in burning

clink·er-built (-bilt´) *adj.* [*clinker* < *clink*, dial. var. of CLINCH] built with overlapping boards or plates, as a boat

cli·nom·e·ter (klī nom´ə tər) *n.* [< Gr. < *klinein*, to slope + -METER] an instrument for measuring angles of slope or inclination —**cli·no·met·ric** (klī´nə met´rik), **cli´no·met´-ri·cal** *adj.* —**cli·nom´e·try** (-ə trē) *n.*

Cli·o (klī´ō) [L. < Gr. < *kleos*, fame] *Gr. Myth.* the Muse of history

clip¹ (klip) *vt.* **clipped, clip´ping** [< ON. *klippa*] **1.** to cut or cut off as with shears **2.** to cut (an item) out of (a newspaper, etc.) **3.** *a*) to cut short *b*) to shorten by omitting syllables, etc. **4.** to cut the hair of **5.** [Colloq.] to hit with a quick, sharp blow **6.** [Slang] to cheat, esp. by overcharging —*vi.* **1.** to clip something **2.** to move rapidly —*n.* **1.** the act of clipping **2.** a thing clipped; specif., *a*) the amount of wool clipped from sheep at one time *b*) a sequence clipped from a film **3.** a rapid pace **4.** [Colloq.] a quick, sharp blow **5.** *same as* CLIPPED FORM

clip² (klip) *vi., vt.* **clipped, clip´ping** [OE. *clyppan*, to embrace] to grip tightly; fasten —*n.* **1.** any device that clips or fastens things together **2.** *same as* CARTRIDGE CLIP **3.** a brooch or other piece of jewellery fitted with a clip **4.** *same as* HAIR-GRIP

clip·board (-bôrd´) *n.* a portable writing board with a hinged clip at the top to hold papers

clip joint [Slang] a nightclub, etc. that charges excessive prices

clipped form (or **word**) a shortened form of a word, as *phone* (for *telephone*) or *fan* (for *fanatic*)

clip·per (klip´ər) *n.* [ME. < *clippen*, CLIP¹] **1.** a person who cuts, trims, etc. **2.** [usually pl.] a tool for cutting or trimming **3.** [for sense, cf. CUTTER] a sharp-bowed, narrow-beamed sailing ship built for great speed

clip·pie (klip´ē) *n.* [< CLIP¹] [Slang] a bus conductress

clip·ping (-iŋ) *n.* **1.** something cut out or trimmed off **2.** an item clipped from a newspaper, magazine, etc.

clique (klēk, klik) *n.* [Fr. < *cliquer*, to make a noise] a small, exclusive circle of people; snobbish or narrow coterie —**cliqu´ish, cliqu´ey, cliqu´y** *adj.* —**cliqu´ish·ly** *adv.* —**cliqu´ish·ness** *n.*

CLIPPER SHIP

clit·o·ris (klit´ə ris) *n.* [ModL. < Gr. < *kleitys*, hill] a small, sensitive, erectile organ at the upper end of the vulva: it corresponds to the penis in the male —**clit´o·ral** (-ər əl), **cli·tor·ic** (klī tôr´ik) *adj.*

clk. clerk

Cllr. Councillor

clo·a·ca (klō ā´kə) *n., pl.* **-cae** (-sē, -kē), **-cas** [L. < *cluere*, to cleanse] **1.** a sewer or cesspool **2.** *Zool.* the cavity into which the intestinal and genitourinary tracts empty in reptiles, birds, amphibians, and many fishes —**clo·a´cal** *adj.*

cloak (klōk) *n.* [< OFr. < ML. *clocca* (see CLOCK¹), a bell, cloak: so called from its bell-like appearance] **1.** a loose, usually sleeveless outer garment **2.** something that covers or conceals —*vt.* **1.** to cover as with a cloak **2.** to conceal; hide

cloak-and-dag·ger (-ən dag´ər) *adj.* **1.** dealing in a melodramatic way with spies and spying **2.** [Colloq.] of or given to intrigues

cloak·room (-rōōm´) *n.* a room where hats, coats, umbrellas, etc. can be left temporarily

clob·ber¹ (klob´ər) *n.* [< ?] [Colloq.] personal belongings, esp. clothes

clob·ber² (klob´ər) *vt.* [< ?] [Slang] **1.** to beat or hit repeatedly; maul **2.** to defeat decisively

cloche (klosh, klōsh) *n.* [Fr. < ML. *clocca*, bell < Celt.] **1.** a bell-shaped glass or plastic cover for delicate plants **2.** a closefitting, bell-shaped hat for women

clock¹ (klok) *n.* [ME. *clokke*, orig., clock with bells < ML. *clocca*, bell < Celt.] **1.** a device for measuring and indicating time, as by pointers moving over a dial: clocks, unlike watches, are not carried on one's person **2.** [Colloq.] any device for recording or measuring, specif. *a*) TIME CLOCK *b*) SPEEDOMETER *c*) TAXIMETER **3.** [Slang] the face —*vt.* **1.** to measure or record the time of (a race, runner, etc.) with a stopwatch, etc. **2.** to register (an amount, etc.) on a meter **3.** [Slang] to punch or strike, esp. in the face —**clock in** (or **on**) to report for work, esp. by punching a timeclock —**clock off** to go off duty —**clock up** **1.** to reach a given speed, time, etc. in competition **2.** to

work a given number of hours, days, etc. —**round the clock** day and night, without stopping

clock² (klok) *n.* [< ? prec., because orig. bell-shaped] a woven or embroidered ornament on the side of a sock or stocking, going up from the ankle —**clocked** *adj.*

clock radio a radio with a built-in clock that can be set to turn the radio on or off

clock·wise (-wīz´) *adv., adj.* in the direction in which the hands of a clock rotate

clock·work (-wurk´) *n.* **1.** the mechanism of a clock **2.** any similar mechanism, consisting of springs and geared wheels, as in some mechanical toys —**like clockwork** very regularly and precisely

clod (klod) *n.* [OE.] **1.** a lump, esp. of earth, clay, loam, etc. **2.** earth; soil **3.** a dull, stupid fellow; dolt —**clod´dish** *adj.* —**clod´dish·ly** *adv.* —**clod´dish·ness** *n.* —**clod´dy** *adj.*

clod·hop·per (-hop´ər) *n.* [CLOD + HOPPER] a ploughman **2.** a clumsy, stupid fellow; lout **3.** a coarse, heavy shoe

clog (klog) *n.* [ME. *clogge*, a lump of wood] **1.** a weight fastened to an animal's leg to hinder motion **2.** anything that hinders or obstructs **3.** a wooden shoe **4.** a shoe with a thick, usually wooden sole **5.** *same as* CLOG DANCE —*vt.* **clogged, clog´ging 1.** to hinder; impede **2.** to fill with obstructions or with thick, sticky matter; stop up —*vi.* **1.** to become stopped up **2.** to do a clog dance —**clog´gi·ness** *n.* —**clog´gy** *adj.*

clog dance a dance in which clogs are worn to beat out the rhythm —**clog dancer** —**clog dancing**

cloi·son·né (klòi´za nā´) *adj.* [Fr., lit., partitioned] denoting a kind of enamel work in which the surface decoration is set in hollows formed by thin strips of wire welded to a metal plate in a complex pattern —*n.* cloisonné enamel

clois·ter (klòis´tər) *n.* [< OFr. < L. *claustrum*, bolt, place shut in < pp. of *claudere*, to close] **1.** a place of religious seclusion; monastery or convent **2.** monastic life **3.** any place where one may lead a secluded life **4.** a covered walk along the inside walls of a monastery, college, etc., with a columned opening along one side —*vt.* **1.** to seclude or confine as in a cloister **2.** to furnish with a cloister —**clois´-tered** *adj.* —**clois´tral** *adj.*

clomb (klōm) *archaic pt. & pp. of* CLIMB

clomp (klomp) *vi.* to walk heavily or noisily; clump

clone (klōn) *n.* [< Gr. *klōn*, a twig] *Biol.* all the descendants derived asexually from a single individual —*vi., vt.* to propagate as a clone Also **clon** (klōn, klon)

clonk (kloŋk) *n., vi., vt. same as* CLUNK

clo·nus (klō´nəs) *n.* [ModL. < Gr. *klonos*, turmoil] a series of muscle spasms —**clon·ic** (klon´ik) *adj.* —**clo·nic·i·ty** (klə nis´ə tē) *n.* —**clo´nism** *n.*

clop (klop) *n.* [echoic] a sharp, clattering sound, like hoofbeats on a pavement —*vi.* **clopped, clop´ping** to make, or move with, such a sound

close¹ (klōs) *adj.* **clos´er, clos´est** [< OFr. *clos*, pp. of *clore*: see ff.] **1.** shut; not open **2.** enclosed or enclosing; shut in **3.** confined or confining **4.** carefully guarded [*close* custody*]* **5.** hidden; secluded **6.** secretive; reserved **7.** miserly; stingy **8.** restricted, as in membership **9.** oppressively warm and stuffy, as stale air **10.** not readily available [*credit* is *close*] **11.** with little space between; near together **12.** compact; dense [a *close* weave] **13.** fitting tightly **14.** *a*) down or near to the surface [a *close* haircut] *b*) nearby [a *close* neighbour] **15.** very near in interests, affection, etc.; intimate [a *close* friend] **16.** varying little from the original [a *close* translation] **17.** strict; thorough; careful [*close* attention] **18.** *a*) concise *b*) accurate; precise **19.** nearly equal or alike [*close* in age] **20.** nearly even [a *close* contest] —*adv.* in a close manner —**close to the wind** **1.** *Naut.* heading as closely as possible in the direction from which the wind blows **2.** [Colloq.] almost breaking the law or a moral code —**close´-ly** *adv.* —**close´ness** *n.*

close² (klōz) *vt.* **closed, clos´ing** [< OFr. < L. *claudere*, to close] **1.** to shut **2.** to block up or stop (an opening, passage, etc.) **3.** to bring together; unite [*close* forces] **4.** to bring to an end; finish **5.** to stop or suspend the operation of (a school, business, etc.) **6.** to complete or make final (a sale, agreement, etc.) —*vi.* **1.** to undergo shutting **2.** to come to an end **3.** to end or suspend operations; specif., in the stock exchange, to show an indicated price level at day's end **4.** to become joined together **5.** to come together **6.** to take hold **7.** to throng closely **8.** to lessen an intervening distance **9.** to come close in order to fight —*n.* **1.** a closing or being closed **2.** the final part; end —**close down** **1.** to shut or stop entirely **2.** to settle down (on), as darkness or fog —**close in** to surround, cutting off escape —**close out** to sell out (goods), as in ending a business —**close up** **1.** to draw nearer together **2.** to shut or stop up entirely **3.** to heal, as a wound does —**clos´er** *n.*

close³ (klōs) *n.* [< OFr. *clos* < L. *clausum*, neut. pp. of *claudere*: see prec.] **1.** an enclosed place **2.** enclosed grounds around or beside a building [a cathedral *close*] **3.**

a quiet residential street, esp. one closed at one end **4.** [Scot.] the entrance to a tenement building

closed (klōzd) *adj.* **1.** not open; shut **2.** covered over or enclosed **3.** functioning independently **4.** not open to new ideas, discussion, etc. **5.** restricted; exclusive **6.** *Math. a)* of a curve whose ends are joined *b)* of a surface whose plane sections are closed curves *c)* of a set in which a given operation on other members always produces a member of the set **7.** *Phonet.* ending in a consonant sound [a *closed* syllable]

closed chain the structural form of certain molecules, graphically represented as a ring of atoms

closed circuit a system of television transmission by cables to a limited number of receivers on a circuit —**closed'-cir'cuit** *adj.*

closed shop a factory, business, etc. operating under an agreement with a trade union by which only members of the union may be employed

close-fist·ed (klōs'fis'tid) *adj.* stingy; miserly

close-fit·ting (-fit'iŋ) *adj.* fitting tightly, esp. so as to show the contours of the body

close harmony (klōs) *Music* **1.** harmony consisting of chords having all four tones within the compass of an octave **2.** a style of singing employing this

close-hauled (klōs'hôld') *adj.* with the sails set for heading as nearly as possible into the wind

close-mouthed (-mouthd', -moutht') *adj.* not talking much; taciturn: also **close'lipped'** (-lipt')

close punctuation punctuation characterized by the use of many commas and other marks

close quarters a confined space or position —**at close quarters** in close proximity; very near together

close season the period during which it is not permitted to kill certain game or fish

close shave a shave very close to the surface of the skin **2.** [Colloq.] a narrow escape from danger: also **close call, close thing**

clos·et (kloz'it) *n.* [OFr., dim. of *clos:* see CLOSE³] **1.** a small room or cupboard for clothes, supplies, etc. **2.** a small, private room for reading, consultation, etc. **3.** *same as* WATER CLOSET —*vt.* to shut up in a private room for confidential discussion

close-up (klōs'up') *n.* a photograph, or a film or TV shot, made at very close range

clo·sure (klō'zhər) *n.* [OFr. < L. *clausura* < pp. of *claudere*, CLOSE²] **1.** a closing or being closed **2.** a finish; end; conclusion **3.** anything that closes **4.** the parliamentary procedure by which debate is closed and the measure put to an immediate vote —*vt.* **-sured, -sur·ing** to apply the closure to (a bill, debate, etc.)

clot (klot) *n.* [OE. *clott*] **1.** a soft, thickened area or lump formed on or within a liquid [a blood *clot*] **2.** [Colloq.] a fool; stupid person —*vt., vi.* **clot'ted, clot'ting** to thicken or form into a clot or clots; coagulate

cloth (kloth, klôth) *n., pl.* **cloths** (kloths, klôths) [OE. *clath*] **1.** a woven, knitted, or pressed fabric of fibrous material, as cotton, wool, silk, hair, synthetic fibres, etc. **2.** a piece of such fabric for a special use [tablecloth, dishcloth] —*adj.* made of cloth —**the cloth** the clergy collectively

clothe (klōth) *vt.* **clothed** or **clad, cloth'ing** [OE. *clathian* < prec.] **1.** to put clothes on; dress **2.** to provide with clothes **3.** to cover over as if with a garment

clothes (klōthz, klōz) *n.pl.* [OE. *clathas*, pl. of *clath*, CLOTH] **1.** articles, usually of cloth, to cover the body; apparel; garments **2.** *same as* BEDCLOTHES

clothes·horse (-hôrs') *n.* **1.** a frame on which to hang clothes, etc. for airing or drying **2.** [Colloq.] one who pays too much attention to clothes

clothes·line (-līn') *n.* a rope or wire on which clothes, etc. are hung for airing or drying

clothes·peg (-peg') *n.* a small clip, as of wood or plastic, for fastening clothes on a line

clothes·press (-pres') *n.* a cupboard, wardrobe, or chest in which to keep clothes

cloth·ier (klōth'yər, klō'thē ər) *n.* a person who makes or sells clothes, esp. for men

cloth·ing (klō'thiŋ) *n.* **1.** wearing apparel; clothes; garments **2.** a covering

Clo·tho (klō'thō) *Gr. & Rom. Myth.* one of the three Fates, spinner of the thread of human life

clotted cream thick cream made from scalded milk

clo·ture (klō'chər) *n.* [Fr. < OFr. < ML. < L. *clausura:* see CLOSURE] [U.S.] *same as* CLOSURE (sense 4)

cloud (kloud) *n.* [OE. *clud*, mass of rock] **1.** a visible mass of condensed water vapour suspended in the atmosphere **2.** a mass of smoke, dust, steam, etc. **3.** a great number of moving things close together [a *cloud* of locusts] **4.** a murkiness or dimness, as in a liquid **5.** a dark marking, as in marble **6.** anything that darkens, obscures, or makes gloomy —*vt.* **1.** to cover with clouds **2.** to make muddy or foggy **3.** to darken; obscure **4.** to make gloomy or troubled **5.** to sully (a reputation, etc.) —*vi.* **1.** to become cloudy **2.** to become gloomy or troubled —**in the clouds 1.**

high up in the sky **2.** fanciful; impractical **3.** in a reverie or daydream —**under a cloud 1.** under suspicion of wrongdoing **2.** troubled; depressed —**cloud'less** *adj.* —**cloud'less·ly** *adv.* —**cloud'less·ness** *n.*

cloud·burst (-burst') *n.* a sudden, very heavy rain

cloud chamber *Physics* a chamber supersaturated with water vapour for tracking the path of charged particles

cloud-cuck·oo-land (-kōō'kōō land') *n.* [transl. of Gr. *nephelokokkygia* < *nephele*, cloud + *kokkyx*, cuckoo] a realm or mental state of dreams and fantasies

cloud nine [Colloq.] a state of euphoria

cloud·y (-ē) *adj.* **cloud'i·er, cloud'i·est 1.** covered with clouds; overcast **2.** of or like clouds **3.** streaked, as marble **4.** opaque, muddy, or foggy [a *cloudy* liquid] **5.** obscure; vague **6.** troubled; gloomy —**cloud'i·ly** *adv.* —**cloud'·i·ness** *n.*

clough (kluf) *n.* [< OE. *clōh*] a steep valley, esp. in N England

clout (klout) *n.* [OE. *clut*] **1.** [Archaic or Dial.] a piece of cloth [a *dishclout*] **2.** a blow, as with the hand; rap **3.** [Colloq.] power or influence; esp., political power **4.** a short nail with a large, flat head —*vt.* **1.** [Colloq.] to strike, as with the hand; hit hard **2.** [Slang] to hit (a ball) a far distance

clove¹ (klōv) *n.* [OFr. *clou* < L. *clavus*, nail: from its shape] **1.** the dried flower bud of a tropical evergreen tree of the myrtle family: it is used as a pungent, fragrant spice **2.** the tree

clove² (klōv) *n.* [OE. *clufu*, akin to *cleofan*, CLEAVE¹] a segment of a bulb, as of garlic

clove³ (klōv) *alt. pt. of* CLEAVE¹

clove hitch a kind of knot for fastening a rope around a spar, pole, or another rope

clo·ven (klō'v'n) *alt. pp. of* CLEAVE¹ —*adj.* divided; split

cloven foot (or **hoof**) a foot divided by a cleft, as in the ox, deer, and sheep: used as a symbol of the Devil, usually pictured with such hoofs —**clo'ven-foot'ed, clo'-ven-hoofed'** *adj.*

clo·ver (klō'vər) *n.* [< OE. *clafre*] **1.** any of a genus of low-growing leguminous herbs with leaves of three leaflets and small flowers in dense heads **2.** any similar plant: cf. SWEET CLOVER —**in clover** living in ease and luxury

clo·ver·leaf (-lēf') *n., pl.* **-leafs'** a motorway interchange in the form of a four-leaf clover, which, by means of an overpass with curving ramps, permits traffic to move or turn in any of four directions with little interference —*adj.* in the shape of a leaf of clover

clown (kloun) *n.* [< ?] **1.** orig., a peasant; rustic **2.** a clumsy, boorish person **3.** a performer who entertains, as in a circus, by antics, jokes, tricks, etc. **4.** a buffoon —*vi.* **1.** to perform as a clown **2.** to play practical jokes, act in a silly manner, etc. —**clown'er·y** *n.* —**clown'ish** *adj.* —**clown'ish·ly** *adv.* —**clown'ish·ness** *n.*

CLOVERLEAF

cloy (kloi) *vt., vi.* [< OFr. *encloyer*, to fasten with a nail, hinder, ult. < L. *clavus*, nail] to surfeit by too much of something, esp. something sweet, rich, etc. —**cloy'ing·ly** *adv.*

club (klub) *n.* [< ON. *klumba*, mass of something, clump] **1.** *a)* a heavy stick, usually thinner at one end, used as a weapon *b)* anything used to threaten **2.** any stick or bat used to strike a ball in a game [a golf *club*] **3.** *same as* INDIAN CLUB **4.** a group of people associated for a common purpose **5.** the room, building, etc. used by such a group **6.** *same as* NIGHTCLUB **7.** *a)* [pl.] a suit of playing cards marked with a black cloverleaf figure (♣) *b)* a card of this suit —*vt.* **clubbed, club'bing 1.** to strike as with a club **2.** to unite for a common purpose **3.** to pool (resources, etc.) —*vi.* to unite or combine for a common purpose —**in the club** [Slang] pregnant

club·foot (-foot') *n.* **1.** a congenital deformity of the foot, often with a clublike appearance; talipes **2.** *pl.* **-feet'** a foot so deformed —**club'foot'ed** *adj.*

club·house (-hous') *n.* a building occupied by a club

club·man (-mən, -man') *n., pl.* **-men** (-mən, -men') a man who is a member of, or spends much time at, a private club or clubs —**club'wom'an** *n.fem., pl.* **-wom'en**

club soda *same as* SODA WATER

cluck (kluk) *vi.* [< OE. *cloccian:* orig. echoic] to make a low, sharp, clicking sound, as of a hen calling her chickens —*vt.* to utter with such a sound —*n.* the sound of clucking

clue (klōō) *n.* something that leads out of a maze or perplexity or helps to solve a problem —*vt.* **clued, clu'ing 1.** to indicate by or as by a clue **2.** [Colloq.] to provide with necessary information (often with *in*) —**not have a clue 1.** to be completely baffled **2.** to be incompetent

clue·less (-lis) *adj.* [Colloq.] helpless; stupid

clump (klump) *n.* [< Du. *klomp* or LowG. *klump*] **1.** a lump; mass **2.** a cluster, as of trees **3.** the sound of heavy footsteps —*vi.* **1.** to tramp heavily **2.** to form clumps —*vt.* **1.** to group together in a cluster **2.** to cause to form clumps —**clump′ish** *adj.* —**clump′y** *adj.* **clump′i·er, clump′i·est**

clum·sy (klum′zē) *adj.* **-si·er, -si·est** [ME. *clumsid*, numb with cold < ON. base] **1.** lacking grace or skill; awkward **2.** awkwardly shaped or made; ill-constructed **3.** inelegant [a *clumsy* style] —**clum′si·ly** *adv.* —**clum′si·ness** *n.*

clung (kluŋ) *pt. & pp. of* CLING

clunk (kluŋk) *n.* [echoic] **1.** a dull, metallic sound **2.** [Colloq.] a heavy blow —*vi.* to move with a clunk or clunks

clus·ter (klus′tər) *n.* [OE. *clyster*] **1.** a number of things of the same sort gathered or growing together; bunch **2.** a number of persons or animals grouped together **3.** *Linguis.* two or more consecutive consonants —*vi., vt.* to gather or grow in a cluster or clusters —**clus′ter·y** *adj.*

clutch[1] (kluch) *vt.* [OE. *clyccan*, to clench] **1.** to grasp or snatch with a hand or claw **2.** to grasp or hold eagerly or tightly —*vi.* to snatch or seize (*at*) —*n.* **1.** a claw or hand in the act of seizing **2.** [*usually pl.*] power; control **3.** *a*) a clutching *b*) a grasp; grip **4.** *a*) a mechanical device, as in a motor car, for engaging or disengaging the engine *b*) the lever or pedal that operates this **5.** a device for gripping

clutch[2] (kluch) *n.* [< ME. *clekken* (< ON. *klekja*), to hatch] **1.** a nest of eggs **2.** a brood of chicks **3.** a cluster of persons, animals, or things

clut·ter (klut′ər) *n.* [< CLOT] **1.** a number of things scattered in disorder; jumble **2.** *dial. var. of* CLATTER **3.** the interfering traces on a radarscope caused by hills, buildings, etc. —*vt.* to put into disorder; jumble (often with *up*) —*vi.* [Dial.] to make a clatter —**clut′ter·y** *adj.*

Clydes·dale (klīdz′dāl′) *n.* [orig. from *Clydesdale,* Scotland] any of a breed of strong draught horse

clyp·e·ate (klip′ē it, -āt′) *adj.* [< L. < *clypeus*, a shield] *Biol.* **1.** shaped like a round shield **2.** having a shieldlike process Also **clyp′e·at′ed**

clys·ter (klis′tər) *n.* [< L. < Gr. *klystēr* < *klyzein*, to wash] [Archaic] *same as* ENEMA

Cm *Chem.* curium

cm centimetre; centimetres

cmdg. commanding

Cmdr. Commander

C.M.G. Companion (of the Order) of St. Michael and St. George

cml. commercial

CND, C.N.D. Campaign for Nuclear Disarmament

co- **1.** *a prefix shortened from* COM- *meaning: a*) together with [*cooperation*] *b*) joint [*co*-owner] *c*) equally [*coextensive*] **2.** *a prefix meaning* complement of [*cosine*]

Co *Chem.* cobalt

Co. *pl.* **Cos. 1.** company **2.** county

C/O, co. 1. care of **2.** carried over

C.O., CO 1. Commanding Officer **2.** conscientious objector

coach (kōch) *n.* [< Fr. < G. < Hung. *kocsi (szekér),* (carriage of) Kócs, village in Hungary] **1.** a large, covered, four-wheeled carriage with an open, raised seat in front for the driver; stagecoach **2.** a railway carriage **3.** a single-decker bus, esp. one used for travel over long distances **4.** a private tutor who prepares a student as for an examination **5.** an instructor or trainer, as of athletes, singers, etc. **6.** *Sports* a person in charge of a team or of some aspect of team play or practice —*vt.* **1.** to instruct by private tutoring **2.** to instruct and train (athletes, actors, etc.) —*vi.* to act as a coach

coach·build·er (-bil′dər) *n.* a person or company that builds motor vehicle bodies, esp. to a high standard of craftsmanship

coach dog *same as* DALMATIAN

coach·man (-mən) *n., pl.* **-men** the driver of a coach or carriage

co·ad·ju·tor (kō aj′ə tər) *n.* [< OFr. < L. < *co-*, together + *adjuvare*, to help] **1.** an assistant; helper **2.** a bishop appointed to assist a bishop

co·ag·u·la·ble (kō ag′yoo lə b'l) *adj.* that can be coagulated —**co·ag′u·la·bil′i·ty** *n.*

co·ag·u·late (kō ag′yoo lāt′) *vt.* **-lat′ed, -lat′ing** [< L. pp. of *coagulare* < *coagulum*, coagulating agent < *cogere*, to curdle: see COGENT] to cause (a liquid) to become a soft, semisolid mass; curdle; clot —*vi.* to become coagulated —**co·ag′u·lant** *n.* —**co·ag′u·la′tion** *n.* —**co·ag′u·la′tive** *adj.* —**co·ag′u·la′tor** *n.*

coal (kōl) *n.* [OE. *col*, a live coal, charcoal] **1.** a black, combustible, mineral solid resulting from the partial decomposition of vegetable matter away from air and under high heat and great pressure over millions of years: used as a fuel and in the production of coke and many coal-tar compounds **2.** a piece or, collectively, pieces of this

substance **3.** an ember **4.** charcoal —*vt.* to provide with coal —*vi.* to take in a supply of coal —**carry** (or **send**) **coals to Newcastle 1.** to take things to a place where they are plentiful **2.** to do an unnecessary thing —**haul** (or **rake, drag, call**) **over the coals** to criticize sharply; censure —**heap coals of fire on (someone's) head** to cause (someone) to feel remorse by returning good for his evil —**coal′y** *adj.*

coal-bunk·er (-buŋ′kər) *n.* a large receptacle for storing coal, as in a garden, on board ship, etc.

coal·er (-ər) *n.* a ship that transports or supplies coal

co·a·lesce (kō′ə les′) *vi.* **-lesced′, -lesc′ing** [< L. *coalescere* < *co-*, together + *alescere*, to grow up] **1.** to grow together **2.** to unite or merge into a single body, group, or mass —**co′a·les′cence** *n.* —**co′a·les′cent** *adj.*

coal·face (-fās′) *n.* the exposed seam of coal in a mine

coal·field (-fēld′) *n.* an area rich in coal deposits

coal gas 1. a gas produced by the distillation of bituminous coal: used for lighting and heating **2.** a poisonous gas given off by burning coal

co·a·li·tion (kō′ə lish′ən) *n.* [< ML. < LL., orig. pp. of *coalescere:* see COALESCE] **1.** a combination; union **2.** a temporary alliance of political parties, nations, etc. for some specific purpose —**co′a·li′tion·ist** *n.*

coal measures coal beds or strata

coal scuttle a metal container for storing and carrying coal for domestic use

coal tar a black, thick, opaque liquid obtained by the distillation of bituminous coal: many synthetic compounds have been developed from it, including dyes, medicines, explosives, and perfumes

coal-tit (-tit′) *n.* a small European songbird with a black head and dark upper parts, and a white patch on the nape: also **coal′mouse′** (-mous′)

coam·ing (kō′miŋ) *n.* [< ?] a raised border around a hatchway, etc. to keep out water

coarse (kôrs) *adj.* [var. of COURSE in sense of "ordinary or usual order," as in *of course*] **1.** of inferior or poor quality; common **2.** consisting of rather large particles [*coarse* sand] **3.** not fine in texture, form, etc.; rough [*coarse* cloth] **4.** for rough work or results [a *coarse* file] **5.** lacking in refinement; vulgar [a *coarse* joke] **6.** obscene [*coarse* language] —**coarse′ly** *adv.* —**coarse′ness** *n.*

coarse fish any freshwater fish not of the salmon family, and caught other than by fly-fishing

coarse-grained (-grānd′) *adj.* **1.** having a coarse texture **2.** lacking in refinement; crude

coars·en (-'n) *vt., vi.* to make or become coarse

coast (kōst) *n.* [< OFr. < L. *costa*, a rib, side] **1.** land beside the sea; seashore **2.** [< CanadFr., hillside, slope] [Chiefly Canad. & U.S.] *a*) an incline down which a slide is taken *b*) a slide or ride down, as on a sledge —*vi.* **1.** to sail near or along a coast **2.** [Chiefly Canad. & U.S.] to go down an incline on a sledge **3.** to continue in motion on momentum after propelling power has stopped **4.** to let one's past efforts carry one along —*vt.* to sail along or near the coast of —**the coast is clear** there is no apparent danger or hindrance

coast·al (-'l) *adj.* of, at, near, or along a coast

coast·er (kōs′tər) *n.* **1.** a person or thing that coasts **2.** a ship that travels from port to port along a coast **3.** a sledge or wagon for coasting **4.** a small tray, mat, disc, etc. placed under a glass or bottle to protect a table or other surface

coast guard 1. a governmental force employed to defend a nation's coasts, prevent smuggling, aid vessels in distress, etc. **2.** a member of a coast guard —**coast guards′man** *pl.* **-men**

coast·land (kōst′land′) *n.* land along a coast

coast·line (-līn′) *n.* the outline of a coast

coast·wards (-wərdz) *adj., adv.* towards the coast

coat (kōt) *n.* [< OFr. < ML. *cot(t)a*, a tunic < Frank. hyp. *kotta*, coarse cloth] **1.** a sleeved outer garment opening down the front, as a suit jacket or an overcoat **2.** the natural covering of an animal, as of fur, wool, etc. **3.** any outer covering, as of a plant **4.** a layer of some substance, as paint, over a surface —*vt.* **1.** to provide or cover with a coat **2.** to cover with a layer of something —**coat′ed** *adj.* —**coat′less** *adj.*

co·a·ti (kō ät′ē) *n., pl.* **-tis** [Tupi < *cua*, a belt + *tim*, the nose] a small, flesh-eating, tree-dwelling mammal of Mexico and Central and South America, like the raccoon but with a long, flexible snout: also **co·a′ti-mun′di, co·a′ti-mon′-di** (-mun′dē)

coat·ing (kōt′iŋ) *n.* **1.** a coat or layer over a surface **2.** cloth for making coats

coat of arms [after Fr. *cotte d'armes*, light garment worn over armour, and blazoned with one's heraldic arms] a group of emblems and figures (heraldic bearings) usually arranged on and around a shield and used as the insignia of a family, etc.

coat of mail *pl.* **coats of mail** a suit of armour made of linked metal rings or overlapping plates

coat·tail (-tāl´) *n.* the back part of a coat below the waist; esp., either half of this part when divided —**ride** (or **hang,** etc.) **on** (**someone's**) **coattails** to have one's success dependent on that of someone else

co·au·thor (kō ô´thər) *n.* a joint author —*vt.* to be a coauthor (of)

coax (kōks) *vt.* [< obs. slang *coax, cokes,* a fool] **1.** to persuade or urge by soothing words, flattery, etc.; wheedle **2.** to get by coaxing —*vi.* to use gentle persuasion, urging, etc. —**coax'er** *n.* —**coax'ing** *adj., n.* —**coax'ing·ly** *adv.*

co·ax·i·al (kō ak´sē əl) *adj.* [CO- + AXIAL] **1.** having a common axis: also **co·ax'al 2.** designating a compound loudspeaker consisting of a smaller unit mounted within and connected with a larger one on a common axis **3.** designating a high-frequency transmission cable or line for telephone, telegraph, television, etc.: its outer conductor tube surrounds an insulated, solid or stranded central conductor

cob (kob) *n.* [prob. < LowG.] **1.** [Dial.] *a*) a lump *b*) a leader; chief **2.** a hazelnut: also **cob'nut' 3.** a round loaf of bread **4.** a head of maize **5.** a male swan **6.** a short, thickset horse

co·balt (kō´bôlt) *n.* [G. *Kobalt* < *Kobold,* goblin, demon of the mines] a hard, lustrous, steel-grey, ductile metallic chemical element, used in alloys, inks, paints, etc.: symbol Co; at. wt., 58.9332; at. no., 27: a radioactive isotope (**cobalt 60**) is used in the treatment of cancer, in research, etc. —**co·bal'tic** *adj.* —**co·bal'tous** *adj.*

cobalt blue 1. a dark blue pigment made from cobalt and aluminium oxides **2.** dark blue

cob·ber (kob´ər) *n.* [< ?] [Aust. & N.Z. Colloq.] a friend; mate

cob·ble¹ (kob´'l) *vt.* -**bled, -bling** [prob. akin to COB] **1.** to mend (shoes, etc.) **2.** to mend or put together clumsily or crudely

cob·ble² (kob´'l) *n.* [prob. < COB] *same as* COBBLESTONE —*vt.* -**bled, -bling** to pave with cobblestones

cob·bler¹ (-lər) *n.* [of U.S. orig. < ?] an iced drink of wine, whisky, or rum, an orange or lemon slice, sugar, etc.

cob·bler² (-lər) *n.* **1.** a person whose work is mending shoes **2.** [Archaic] a clumsy workman

cob·blers (-lərz) *n.* [< *cobbler's awls,* rhyming slang for balls] [Slang] **1.** the testicles **2.** nonsense —*interj.* nonsense!

cob·ble·stone (kob´'l stōn´) *n.* [COBBLE² + STONE] a rounded stone of a kind formerly much used for paving streets

cob coal coal in large, rounded lumps

co·bel·lig·er·ent (kō´bə lij´ər ənt) *n.* a nation associated but not formally allied with another or others in waging war

co·bi·a (kō´bē ə) *n.* [< ?] a large, voracious game fish of warm seas

CO·BOL (kō´bol) *n.* [CO(mmon) B(usiness) O(riented) L(anguage)] a computer programming language for general commercial use

co·bra (kō´brə, ko´-) *n.* [< Port. *cobra* (*de capello*), serpent (of the hood)] a very poisonous snake of Asia and Africa: loose skin around the neck expands into a hood when the snake is excited

cob·web (kob´web´) *n.* [< ME. *coppe,* spider + WEB] **1.** a web spun by a spider **2.** a single thread of such a web **3.** anything flimsy, gauzy, or ensnaring, like a spider's web **4.** [*pl.*] stickiness of the eyelids experienced upon first awakening —*vt.* -**webbed'**, -**web'bing** to cover as with cobwebs —**blow** (or **sweep**) **away the cobwebs 1.** to clear away accumulated dirt, etc. **2.** to get rid of obscurities, antiquated ideas, etc. —**cob'web'by** *adj.*

INDIAN COBRA
(to 2 m long)

co·ca (kō´kə) *n.* [Quechuan *cuca*] **1.** any of certain S. American shrubs, esp. a species whose dried leaves are the source of cocaine and some other alkaloids **2.** these dried leaves

co·caine, co·cain (kō kān´, kə kān´) *n.* [COCA + -INE⁴] a crystalline alkaloid obtained from dried coca leaves: it is a narcotic and local anaesthetic

-coc·cal (kok´'l) *a combining form meaning* of or produced by a (specified kind of) coccus [*staphylococcal*]: also **-coc'·cic** (-sik)

coc·cus (kok´əs) *n., pl.* **coc·ci** (kok´sī) [ModL. < Gr. *kokkos,* a berry] a bacterium of a spherical shape —**coc'·coid** (-oid) *adj.*

-coc·cus (kok´əs) *a combining form meaning* coccus: used in names of various bacteria [*gonococcus*]

coc·cyx (kok´siks) *n., pl.* **coc·cy·ges** (kok sī´jēz) [L. < Gr. *kokkyx,* cuckoo: from its shape like a cuckoo's beak] a small, triangular bone at the lower end of the vertebral column —**coc·cyg'e·al** (-sij´ē əl) *adj.*

coch·i·neal (koch´ə nēl´, koch´ə nēl´) *n.* [< Fr. < It. < L.

coccinus, scarlet-coloured < *coccum,* a berry] a red dye made from the dried bodies of female cochineal insects: used, esp. formerly, in colouring foods and cosmetics and as a dye

cochineal insect a scale insect having a brilliant red body fluid and feeding on cactus: found chiefly in Mexico and used as a source of cochineal

coch·le·a (kok´lē ə) *n., pl.* -**le·ae'** (-ē´), -**le·as** [L. < Gr. *kochlias,* snail] the spiral-shaped part of the internal ear, containing the auditory nerve endings —**coch'le·ar** *adj.*

coch·le·ate (-it, -āt´) *adj.* [< L.: see prec.] shaped like a snail shell: also **coch'le·at'ed**

cock¹ (kok) *n.* [OE. *coc*] **1.** *a*) the male of the chicken; rooster *b*) the male of certain other birds *c*) the male of other creatures, as the lobster and salmon **2.** a weathercock **3.** a leader or chief **4.** a tap or valve for regulating the flow of liquid or gas **5.** the hammer of a firearm, or the position of the hammer set for firing **6.** a jaunty, erect position [the *cock* of a hat] **7.** [Colloq.] a friend; fellow: used as a term of address **8.** [Slang] the penis —*vt.* **1.** to set (a hat, etc.) jauntily on one side **2.** to raise; erect [a dog *cocks* his ears] **3.** to turn (the eye or ear) towards something **4.** *a*) to set the hammer of (a gun) in firing position *b*) to set (a tripping device, as for a camera shutter) **5.** to draw back (one's fist, etc.) ready to strike —*vi.* to assume an upright or tilted position —**at half cock** before full preparations have been made —**cock up** [Colloq.] to make a mess of; bungle

cock² (kok) *n.* [ME. *cokke*] a small, cone-shaped pile, as of hay —*vt.* to pile in cocks

cock·ade (ko kād´) *n.* [Fr. *cocarde* < *coq,* a cock] a rosette, knot of ribbon, etc. worn on the hat as a badge —**cock·ad'ed** *adj.*

cock-a-doo·dle-doo (kok´ə dōō´d'l dōō´) *n.* [echoic] a conventional term for the crow of a cock

cock-a-hoop (kok´ə hōōp´) *adj.* [Fr. *coq à huppe,* cock with a crest] **1.** in very high spirits; elated **2.** boastful; conceited

cock-a-leek·ie (kok´ə lē´kē) *n.* [var. of *cocky-leeky* < *cocky,* dim. of COCK¹ + *leeky,* dim of LEEK] [Scot.] a soup made by boiling chicken with leeks

cock·a·lo·rum (kok´ə lôr´əm) *n.* [pseudo L. extension of COCK¹] **1.** a little man with an exaggerated idea of his own importance **2.** boastful talk

cock-and-bull story (kok´'n bool´) [< Fr. *coq à l'âne*] an absurd, improbable story

cock·a·teel, cock·a·tiel (kok´ə tēl´) *n.* [< Du. dim. of *kaketoe:* see ff.] a small, crested, Australian parrot with a long tail and yellow head

cock·a·too (kok´ə tōō´, kok´ə tōō´) *n., pl.* -**toos'** [Du. *kaketoe* < Malay *kakatua;* prob. echoic] a crested parrot of Australia and the East Indies, with white plumage tinged with yellow or pink

cock·a·trice (kok´ə tris´) *n.* [< OFr. < L. *calcare,* to tread < *calx,* the heel] a legendary serpent supposedly hatched from a cock's egg and having power to kill by a look

cock·boat (kok´bōt´) *n.* [< ME. < *cok,* ship's boat + *bote,* BOAT] a small boat, esp. one used as a ship's tender

cock·chaf·er (-chāf´ər) *n.* [COCK¹ (? because of size) + CHAFER] a large European beetle whose grubs feed on the roots of plants

cock·crow (-krō´) *n.* the time when cocks begin to crow; dawn: also **cock'crow'ing**

cocked hat 1. a three-cornered hat with a turned-up brim **2.** a peaked hat pointed in front and at the back —**knock into a cocked hat** [Slang] to damage or spoil completely; ruin

cock·er·el (kok´ər əl, kok´ral) *n.* [dim. of COCK¹] a young cock, less than a year old

cock·er (**spaniel**) (kok´ər) [from its use in hunting woodcock] a small spaniel with a compact body, long, silky hair, and long, drooping ears

cock·eye (kok´ī´) *n.* [COCK¹, *vi.* + EYE] a squinting eye

cock·eyed (-īd´) *adj.* **1.** cross-eyed **2.** [Colloq.] *a*) tilted; crooked; awry *b*) silly; foolish *c*) drunk

cock·fight (-fīt´) *n.* a fight between gamecocks, usually wearing metal spurs —**cock'fight'ing** *n.*

cock·horse (-hôrs´) *n.* [16th c., toy horse] *same as* ROCKING HORSE (sense 1) or HOBBYHORSE (sense 1)

cock·le¹ (kok´'l) *n.* [< OFr. *coquille,* a shell < L. < Gr. < *konchē,* CONCH] **1.** an edible shellfish with two heart-shaped, radially ridged shells **2.** a cockleshell **3.** a wrinkle; pucker —*vi., vt.* -**led, -ling** to wrinkle; pucker —**cockles of one's heart** one's deepest feelings or emotions

cock·le² (kok´'l) *n.* [< OE. *coccel,* tares] any of various weeds that grow in grainfields

cock·le·bur (-bur´) *n.* a coarse plant of the composite or daisy family, bearing burs, that grows as a weed

cock·le·shell (-shel´) *n.* **1.** the shell of a cockle **2.** loosely, a scallop shell, etc. **3.** a small boat

cock·ney (kok´nē) *n., pl.* -**neys** [ME. *cokenei,* spoiled child; understood as *coken-ey,* lit., cock's egg; ? infl. by Fr.

acoquiné, ıdle < *coquin,* rascal] [*often* C-] **1.** a native of London, esp. of the East End: traditionally one born within sound of the bells of St. Mary-le-Bow church (Bow Bells) **2.** the urban dialect of London, esp. the East End —*adj.* [*often* C-] of or like cockneys or their dialect —**cock′·ney·ish** *adj.* —**cock′ney·ism** *n.*

cock of the walk a dominating person in any group, esp. an overbearing one

cock·pit (kok′pit′) *n.* **1.** an enclosed space for cockfighting **2.** in small decked vessels, a sunken space towards the stern used by the steersman, etc. **3.** the space in a small aeroplane for the pilot and, sometimes, passengers, or in a large aeroplane for the pilot and copilot or crew **4.** any place that has been much fought over

cock·roach (-rōch′) *n.* [Sp. *cucaracha,* altered after COCK[1] + ROACH[1]] an insect with long feelers, and a flat, soft body: a household pest

cocks·comb (koks′kōm′) *n.* **1.** the red, fleshy growth on the head of a cock **2.** *same as* COXCOMB **3.** a plant related to the amaranth, with red or yellow flower heads

cock·shy (kok′shī′) *n.* [COCK[1] + SHY[2]] **1.** a target in throwing games **2.** a throw in such a game **3.** an object of criticism or ridicule; butt

cock·sure (-shoor′) *adj.* [COCK[1] (cf. COCKY[1]) + SURE] **1.** absolutely sure **2.** self-confident and overbearing —**cock′sure′ness** *n.*

cock·tail (-tāl′) *n.* [< ?] **1.** an alcoholic drink, usually iced, made of a spirit mixed with a wine, fruit juice, etc. **2.** an appetizer, as fruit juice, diced fruits, or seafood

cock·y[1] (kok′ē) *adj.* **cock′i·er, cock′i·est** [COCK[1] + -Y[2]] [Colloq.] jauntily conceited; self-confident in an aggressive or swaggering way —**cock′i·ly** *adv.* —**cock′i·ness** *n.*

cock·y[2] (kok′ē) *n.* [COCK(ATOO) + -Y[1]] [Aust. & N.Z.] **1.** a cockatoo **2.** a small farmer

co·co (kō′kō) *n., pl.* **-cos** [Sp. & Port. < ? L. *coccum,* a seed < Gr. *kokkos,* a berry] **1.** *same as* COCONUT PALM **2.** its fruit; coconut —*adj.* made of the fibre from coconut husks

co·coa (kō′kō) *n.* [Sp. & Port. *cacao* < Nahuatl *cacauatl*] **1.** powder made from cacao seeds that have been roasted and ground **2.** a drink made by adding sugar and hot water or milk to this powder **3.** a reddish-yellow brown

cocoa butter a yellowish fat prepared from cacao seeds: used in pharmacy and in cosmetics

co·co·nut, co·coa·nut (kō′kə nut′) *n.* **1.** the fruit of the coconut palm, a thick, brown, oval husk enclosing a layer of edible white meat: the hollow centre is filled with a sweet, milky fluid called **coconut milk** **2.** the meat of the coconut, often dried and shredded for use in confectionery **3.** [Old Slang] the head

coconut matting matting woven from the fibre of coconut husks

coconut oil oil obtained from the dried meat of coconuts, used for making soap, etc.

coconut palm (or **tree**) a tall tropical palm tree that bears coconuts: also **coco palm**

co·coon (kə koon′) *n.* [< Fr. < Pr. *coucoun,* egg shell, ult. < ML. *coco,* shell] **1.** the silky case which the larvae of certain insects spin about themselves for shelter during the pupa stage **2.** any protective cover like this —*vt.* to wrap in or protect by or as if by a cocoon

co·cotte (kə kot′, kō′kot′) *n.* [Fr., orig., hen < *coq,* cock] **1.** a prostitute **2.** any sexually promiscuous woman **3.** a small fireproof dish in which food is cooked and served individually

cod[1] (kod) *n., pl.* **cod, cods:** see PLURAL, II, D. 2 [ME.] an important food fish, with firm flesh and soft fins, found in northern seas

cod[2] (kod) *n.* [< ?] a hoax; prank —*vt., vi.* **cod′ded, cod′ding** **1.** to make fun of **2.** to make a fool of; hoax

cod[3] (kod) *n.* [ME. < OE. *codd,* bag] **1.** [Dial.] a husk or pod, esp. a pea pod **2.** [Archaic] the scrotum

C.O.D., c.o.d. cash (or collect) on delivery

co·da (kō′də) *n.* [It. < L. *cauda,* a tail] *Music* a passage formally ending a composition or section

cod·dle (kod′'l) *vt.* **-dled, -dling** [prob. < CAUDLE] **1.** to cook (esp. eggs) gently in water not quite boiling **2.** to treat tenderly; pamper

code (kōd) *n.* [< OFr. < L. *codex,* wooden tablet for writing, orig., tree trunk] **1.** a body of laws of a nation, city, etc. arranged systematically for easy reference **2.** any set of principles [a moral *code*] **3.** *a)* a set of signals for sending messages, as by telegraph, flags, etc. *b)* any set of signals, as that (**genetic code**) in the chromosomes determining the pattern of growth, etc. **4.** *a)* a system of secret writing, information processing, etc., in which letters, figures, etc. are given certain meanings *b)* the symbols used —*vt.* **cod′ed, cod′ing** to put in the form or symbols of a code —*vi.* to represent in a coded form (with *for*) —**cod′er** *n.*

co·deine (kō′dēn, -dē in) *n.* [< Gr. *kōdeia,* poppy head + -INE[4]] an alkaloid derived from opium and resembling morphine: used for the relief of pain and in cough medicines: also **co′dein, co·de·ia** (kō dē′ə)

co·dex (kō′deks) *n., pl.* **co·di·ces** (kō′də sēz′, kod′ə-) [L.: see CODE] **1.** orig., a code, or body of laws **2.** a manuscript volume, esp. of the Scriptures or of a classic text

cod·fish (kod′fish′) *n., pl.* **-fish′, -fish′es:** see FISH same as COD[1]

codg·er (koj′ər) *n.* [prob. var. of *cadger,* see CADGE] [Colloq.] an eccentric, esp. elderly, fellow

cod·i·cil (kod′i s'l, -sil′) *n.* [< L. dim. of *codex:* see CODE] **1.** *Law* an addition to a will to change, revoke, or add provisions **2.** an appendix or supplement —**cod′i·cil′la·ry** *adj.*

cod·i·fy (kō′də fī′, kod′ə-) *vt.* **-fied′, -fy′ing** [see CODE & -FY] to arrange (laws, etc.) systematically —**cod′i·fi·ca′tion** *n.* —**cod′i·fi′er** *n.*

cod·ling[1] (kod′liŋ) *n., pl.* **-ling, -lings:** see PLURAL, II, D, 2 a young cod

cod·ling[2] (kod′liŋ) *n.* [ult. < Fr. *coeur de lion,* lit., heart of lion] **1.** a variety of elongated apple **2.** a small, unripe apple Also **cod′lin**

codling (or **codlin**) **moth** a small moth whose larva destroys apples, pears, quinces, etc.

cod-liv·er oil (kod′liv′ər) oil obtained from the liver of the cod and related fishes: it is rich in vitamins A and D

cod·piece (kod′pēs′) *n.* [COD[3] + PIECE] a bag or flap fastened over the front opening in the tight breeches worn by men in the 15th and 16th cent.

cods·wal·lop (kodz′wol′əp) *n.* [< ?] [Slang] pretentious nonsense

co·ed, co·ed (kō′ed′) *adj.* *clipped form of* coeducational (see COEDUCATION) —*n.* **1.** [Colloq.] a coeducational school or college **2.** [Chiefly U.S. Colloq.] a girl attending a coeducational college or university

co·ed·u·ca·tion (kō′ed yoo kā′shən) *n.* [CO- + EDUCATION] the educational system in which students of both sexes attend classes together —**co′ed·u·ca′tion·al** *adj.* —**co′ed·u·ca′tion·al·ly** *adv.*

co·ef·fi·cient (kō′ə fish′ənt) *n.* [CO- + EFFICIENT] **1.** a factor that contributes to produce a result **2.** *Math.* a number, symbol, etc. used as a multiplier **3.** *Physics* a number, constant for a given substance, used as a multiplier in measuring the change in some property of the substance under given conditions

coe·la·canth (sē′lə kanth′) *n.* [ModL. < Gr. *koilos,* hollow + *akantha,* spine] any of a group of primitive, almost entirely extinct fishes that were possibly ancestors to land animals

-coele, -coel (sēl) [< Gr. *koilia,* body cavity < *koilos,* hollow] a combining form meaning cavity, chamber of the body

coe·len·ter·ate (si len′tə rāt′, -tər it) *n.* [ult. < Gr. *koilos* (see prec.) + *enteron,* intestine] any of a large group of marine animals, as the hydroids, jellyfishes, corals, etc., in which the characteristic structure is a large central cavity with a single opening

coe·li·ac (sē′lē ak′) *adj.* [L. *coeliacus* < Gr. < *koilos*] of or in the abdominal cavity

coe·lom (sē′lom) *n.* [< Gr. < *koilos:* see -COELE] the main body cavity of most higher animals, in which the visceral organs are suspended

coe·no- [< Gr. *koinos,* common] a combining form meaning common: also, before a vowel, **coen-**

coe·no·bite (sē′nə bīt′) *n.* [< LL. *coenobita* < Gr. < *koinos,* common + *bios,* life] a member of a religious order in a monastery or convent —**coe′no·bit′ic** (-bit′ik), **coe′no·bit′i·cal** *adj.* —**coe′no·bit·ism** (-bit iz′m) *n.*

co·e·qual (kō ē′kwəl) *adj., n.* equal —**co′e·qual′i·ty** (-i kwol′ə tē) *n.* —**co·e′qual·ly** *adv.*

co·erce (kō urs′) *vt.* **-erced′, -erc′ing** [< OFr. < L. *coercere* < *co-,* together + *arcere,* to confine] **1.** to restrain or constrain by force; curb **2.** to force; compel **3.** to enforce —**co·erc′er** *n.* —**co·er′ci·ble** *adj.* —**co·er′ci·bly** *adv.*

co·er·cion (kō ur′shən) *n.* **1.** the act or power of coercing **2.** government by force

co·er·cive (-siv) *adj.* of coercion or tending to coerce —**co·er′cive·ly** *adv.* —**co·er′cive·ness** *n.*

co·e·val (kō ē′v'l) *adj.* [< LL. < L. *co-,* together + *aevum,* age + -AL] of the same age or period; contemporary —*n.* a contemporary —**co·e′val·ly** *adv.* —**cole·val′i·ty** *n.*

co·ex·ec·u·tor (kō′ig zek′yoo tər) *n.* a person acting as executor jointly with another

co·ex·ist (-ig zist′) *vi.* **1.** to exist together, at the same time, or in the same place **2.** to live together without hostility or conflict despite differences, as in political systems —**co′ex·ist′ence** *n.* —**co′ex·ist′ent** *adj.*

co·ex·tend (-ik stend′) *vt., vi.* to extend equally in space or time —**co′ex·ten′sion** *n.* —**co′ex·ten′sive** *adj.* —**co′ex·ten′sive·ly** *adv.*

C. of C. Chamber of Commerce

C. of E. Church of England

cof·fee (kof′ē) *n.* see PLURAL, II, D. 3 [< It. < Turk. *kahve* < Ar. *qahwa,* orig., wine] **1.** a dark-brown, aromatic drink made by brewing in water the roasted and ground beanlike seeds of a tall tropical shrub of the madder family **2.** these seeds: also **coffee beans 3.** the shrub **4.** the colour of coffee with milk or cream in it; brown

coffee bar a snack bar, esp. one serving espresso coffee

coffee break a brief respite from work when coffee or other refreshment may be taken

coffee cup a small cup for serving coffee

cof·fee·house (-hous′) *n.* a place where coffee and other refreshments are served and, formerly, people gathered for conversation, entertainment, etc.

coffee mill a small machine for grinding roasted coffee beans: also **coffee grinder**

cof·fee·pot (-pot′) *n.* a container with a lid and spout, for making and serving coffee

coffee shop [Chiefly U.S.] an informal restaurant, as in a hotel, where light refreshments or meals are served

coffee table a low table, usually in a living room, for serving refreshments

cof·fer (kof′ər) *n.* [< OFr. < L. *cophinus:* see COFFIN] **1.** a chest or strongbox for keeping valuables **2.** [*pl.*] a treasury; funds **3.** a decorative sunken panel in a vault, dome, etc. **4.** a cofferdam —*vt.* **1.** to enclose in a coffer **2.** to furnish with coffers (*n.* 3)

cof·fer·dam (-dam′) *n.* [prec. + DAM¹] **1.** a watertight temporary structure in a river, lake, etc. to keep the water from an enclosed area that has been pumped dry so that dams, etc. may be constructed **2.** a watertight box attached to the side of a ship so that repairs can be made below the waterline

cof·fin (kof′in) *n.* [< OFr. < L. *cophinus* < Gr. *kophinos,* basket] **1.** the case or box in which a dead person is buried **2.** the horny part of a horse's hoof —*vt.* to put into or as if into a coffin —**a nail in one's coffin** anything that brings, or appears to bring, one's death closer

coffin nail [Old Slang] a cigarette

cof·fle (kof′'l) *n.* [Ar. *qâfila,* caravan] a group of animals or slaves fastened together in a line, or driven along together

C. of S. Church of Scotland

cog¹ (kog) *n.* [< Scand.] **1.** *a)* any of a series of teeth on the rim of a wheel, for transmitting or receiving motion by fitting between the teeth of another wheel; gear tooth *b)* a cogwheel **2.** [Colloq.] a person thought of as one small part in the working of a business, etc. —**cogged** *adj.*

cog² (kog) *n.* [altered (after prec.) < earlier *cock,* to secure] a projection on a beam that fits into a corresponding groove or notch in another beam, making a joint —*vt., vi.* **cogged, cog′ging** to join by a cog or cogs

co·gent (kō′jənt) *adj.* [< L. prp. of *cogere,* to collect < *co-,* together + *agere,* to drive] forceful and to the point, as a reason or argument; compelling —**co′gen·cy** *n.* —**co′gent·ly** *adv.*

cog·i·tate (koj′ə tāt′) *vi., vt.* **-tat′ed, -tat′ing** [< L. pp. of *cogitare,* to ponder] to think seriously and deeply about); ponder; consider —**cog′i·ta·ble** *adj.* —**cog′i·ta′tion** *n.* —**cog′i·ta′tive** *adj.* —**cog′i·ta′tor** *n.*

co·gnac (kon′yak) *n.* [Fr.] **1.** a French brandy distilled from wine near Cognac, France **2.** loosely, any brandy

cog·nate (kog′nāt) *adj.* [L. *cognatus < co-,* together + pp. of (g)*nasci,* to be born] **1.** related by family; specif., descended from a common maternal ancestor **2.** derived from a common original form [French and Italian are *cognate* languages] **3.** having the same nature or quality —*n.* **1.** a person related to another through common ancestry **2.** a cognate word, language, or thing —**cog′-nate·ness, cog·na′tion** *n.*

cog·ni·tion (kog nish′ən) *n.* [L. *cognito,* knowledge < pp. of *cognoscere < co-,* together + (g)*noscere,* to know] **1.** the process of knowing in the broadest sense, including perception, memory, judgment, etc. **2.** the result of such a process; perception, etc. —**cog·ni′tion·al** *adj.* —**cog′ni·tive** *adj.*

cog·ni·za·ble (kog′ni zə b'l, kog nī′-; *occas.* kon′ə-) *adj.* **1.** that can be known or perceived **2.** *Law* within the jurisdiction of a court Also, **cog′ni·sa·ble**

cog·ni·zance (kog′nə zəns, kon′ə-) *n.* [< OFr. *conoissance,* knowledge < L. *cognoscere:* see COGNITION] **1.** perception or knowledge; esp., the range of knowledge possible through observation **2.** official observation **3.** *Heraldry* a distinguishing crest or mark **4.** *Law a)* a court hearing *b)* the right or power of dealing with a matter judicially —**take cognizance of** to notice or recognize

cog·ni·zant (-zənt) *adj.* having cognizance; aware or informed (*of* something)

cog·no·men (kog nō′mən) *n., pl.* **-no′mens, -nom′i·na** (-nom′i na) [L. < *co-,* with + *nomen,* name] **1.** the third or family name of an ancient Roman **2.** any family name; surname **3.** any name; esp., a nickname —**cog·nom′i·nal** (-nom′i n'l) *adj.*

co·gno·scen·te (kon′yō shen′tā) *n., pl.* **-ti** (-tē) [It., orig. prp. of *conoscere,* to know < L. *cognoscere: see* COGNITION] [*usually pl.*] a person with special knowledge in some field, esp. in the fine arts; connoisseur

cog·wheel (kog′wēl′, -hwēl′) *n.* a wheel with a rim notched into teeth which mesh with those of another wheel or of a rack to transmit or receive motion

COGWHEELS

co·hab·it (kō hab′it) *vi.* [< LL. < L. *co-,* together + *habitare,* to dwell] **1.** to live together as husband and wife, esp. when not legally married **2.** [Archaic] to live together —**co·hab′it·ant** *n.* —**co·hab′i·ta′-tion** *n.*

co·heir (kō′er′) *n.* a person who inherits jointly with another or others —**co′heir′ess** *n.fem.*

co·here (kō hir′) *vi.* **-hered′, -her′ing** [< L. < *co-,* together + *haerere,* to stick] **1.** to stick together, as parts of a mass **2.** to be connected naturally or logically **3.** to be in accord

co·her·ence (kō hir′əns) *n.* **1.** the condition of cohering **2.** the quality of being logically consistent and intelligible Also **co·her′en·cy**

co·her·ent (-ənt) *adj.* **1.** sticking together; having cohesion **2.** showing logical consistency or intelligibility **3.** *Physics* having the same frequency and constant phase difference [*coherent* light] —**co·her′ent·ly** *adv.*

co·he·sion (kō hē′zhən) *n.* **1.** the act or condition of cohering; tendency to stick together **2.** *Bot.* the union of like flower parts **3.** *Physics* the force by which the molecules of a substance are held together: distinguished from ADHESION —**co·he′sive** (-hēs′iv) *adj.* —**co·he′sive·ly** *adv.* —**co·he′sive·ness** *n.*

co·ho (kō′hō) *n., pl.* **-ho, -hos:** see PLURAL, II, D, 2 [< ?] a small Pacific salmon: also **coho salmon, silver salmon**

co·hort (kō′hôrt) *n.* [< L. *cohors,* enclosure, crowd] **1.** an ancient Roman military unit, one tenth of a legion **2.** a band of soldiers **3.** any group or band **4.** an associate, colleague, or supporter

C.O.I. Central Office of Information

coif (koif; *for n. 2 & vt. 2, usually* kwäf) *n.* [< OFr. < LL. *cofea,* a cap, hood] **1.** a cap that fits the head closely, as that once worn under a hood of mail **2.** [< COIFFURE] a style of arranging the hair —*vt.* **coifed, coif′ing;** also, and for 2 usually, **coiffed, coif′fing 1.** to cover as with a coif **2.** *a)* to style (the hair) *b)* to give a coiffure to

coif·feur (kwä fur′; *Fr.* kwä fër′) *n.* [Fr. < *coiffer,* to dress the hair < prec.] a male hairdresser —**coif·feuse′** (-föz′) *n. fem.*

coif·fure (kwä fyoor′, -fyur′; *Fr.* kwä für′) *n.* [Fr. < *coiffe,* COIF] **1.** a headdress **2.** a style of arranging the hair —*vt.* **-fured′, -fur′ing** to coif (sense 2)

coign of vantage (koin) [archaic var. of *coin* (QUOIN)] an advantageous position

coil¹ (koil) *vt.* [< OFr. < L. *colligere:* see COLLECT²] to wind or gather (rope, etc.) into a circular or spiral form —*vi.* **1.** to wind round and round **2.** to move in a winding course —*n.* **1.** anything wound into a series of rings or a spiral **2.** such a series of rings or a spiral **3.** a single turn of a coiled figure **4.** a series of connected pipes in rows or coils **5.** a contraceptive device consisting of a loop of wire or plastic inserted in the womb **6.** *Elec.* a spiral of wire, etc. used as an inductor, heating element, etc.

coil² (koil) *n.* [Early ModE. < ?] [Archaic] commotion; turmoil —**mortal coil** the activities and troubles of life

coin (koin) *n.* [< OFr. < L. *cuneus,* a wedge] **1.** archaic var. of QUOIN **2.** *a)* a piece of metal with a distinctive stamp, issued by a government as money *b)* such pieces collectively —*vt.* **1.** *a)* to make (coins) by stamping metal *b)* to make (metal) into coins **2.** to invent (a new word or phrase) —*vi.* to make coins —**coin money** [Colloq.] to earn money rapidly —**false coin** anything sham or spurious —**pay (someone) back in his own coin** to treat (a person) in the same way that he treated others

coin·age (koi′nij) *n.* **1.** the act or process of coining **2.** metal money **3.** a system of metal currency **4.** an invented word or expression

co·in·cide (kō′in sīd′) *vi.* **-cid′ed, -cid′ing** [< Fr. < ML. < L. *co-,* together + *incidere,* to fall upon] **1.** to take up the same place in space **2.** to occur at the same time **3.** to hold equivalent positions, as on a scale **4.** to be identical; correspond exactly **5.** to be in accord; agree

co·in·ci·dence (kō in′sə dəns) *n.* **1.** the fact or condition of coinciding **2.** an accidental and remarkable occurrence of events, ideas, etc. at the same time, with no apparent causal relationship

co·in·ci·dent (-dənt) *adj.* **1.** occurring at the same time **2.** in the same position in space at the same time **3.** in agreement; identical [desire *coincident* with need] —**co·in′-ci·dent·ly** *adv.*

co·in·ci·den·tal (kō in′sə den′t'l) *adj.* characterized by coincidence —**co·in′ci·den′tal·ly** *adv.*

coin·er (koi′nər) *n.* one who makes false coinage; counterfeiter

Coin·treau (kwän′trō′) *n.* a trademark for an orange-flavoured French liqueur

coir (koir) *n.* [< Port., ult. < Tamil *kayaru,* to be twisted] the prepared fibre of the husks of coconuts, used to make rope, etc.

co·i·tus (kō′it əs) *n.* [L. < *co-*, together + *ire*, to go] sexual intercourse: also **co·i·tion** (kō ish′ən) —**co′i·tal** *adj.*

coitus in·ter·rup·tus (in′tə rup′təs) [L.] a method of avoiding conception by withdrawing the penis from the vagina before ejaculation

Coke (kōk) *n.* *a trademark for* a type of cola drink: in full, **Co·ca-Co·la** (kō′kə kō′lə)

coke¹ (kōk) *n.* [< ME. *colke*, core, charcoal] coal from which most of the gases have been removed by heating: it burns with intense heat and little smoke, and is used as an industrial fuel —*vt., vi.* **coked, cok′ing** to change into coke

coke² (kok) *n.* *Colloq. clipped form of* COCAINE

Col. 1. Colombia 2. Colonel 3. Colorado 4. Colossians

col (kol) *n.* [Fr. < L. *collum*, neck] 1. a gap between peaks in a mountain range, used as a pass 2. *Meteorol.* a low-pressure area between two anticyclones

col. 1. collected 2. collector 3. colony 4. colour(ed) 5. column

co·la (kō′lə) *n.* [< WAfr. name] 1. an African tree whose nuts yield an extract with caffeine, used in soft drinks and medicine 2. a sweet, carbonated soft drink flavoured with this extract

col·an·der (kul′ən dər) *n.* [prob. ult. < L. *colare*, to strain < *colum*, strainer] a vessel with a perforated bottom to drain off liquids

col·chi·cine (kol′chə sēn′, -ki sin) *n.* [< ff. + -INE⁴] a poisonous alkaloid extracted from colchicum, used to treat gout and to produce chromosome doubling in plants

col·chi·cum (-kəm) *n.* [L. < Gr. *kolchikon*, plant with a poisonous root] 1. a plant of the lily family, with crocuslike flowers usually blooming in the autumn 2. its dried seeds or corm

COLANDER

cold (kōld) *adj.* [OE. *cald*] 1. of a temperature much lower than that of the human body; very chilly; frigid 2. without the proper heat or warmth [this soup is *cold*] 3. dead 4. feeling chilled 5. without warmth of feeling; not cordial [a *cold* personality] 6. sexually frigid 7. depressing or saddening [the *cold* truth] 8. not involving one's feelings; detached [*cold* logic] 9. designating or having colours that suggest cold, as tones of blue, green, or grey 10. faint or stale [a *cold* scent] 11. [Colloq.] far from the object of a search or the correct answer in a guessing game 12. [Colloq.] with little or no preparation [to enter a game *cold*] 13. [Slang] unconscious [knocked *cold*] 14. *Metallurgy* of or designating a process in which metal is worked below the annealing temperature —*n.* 1. *a)* absence of heat; lack of warmth: often thought of as an active force *b)* a low temperature; esp., one below freezing 2. the sensation produced by a loss or absence of heat 3. cold weather 4. an acute inflammation of the mucous membranes of the nose and throat, thought to be caused by a virus and characterized by nasal discharge, malaise, etc. —**catch** (a) **cold** 1. to become ill with a cold 2. to encounter unexpected difficulties 3. to suffer a financial loss —**cold comfort** little or no comfort —**have** (or **get**) **cold feet** [Colloq.] to be (or become) timid or fearful —**in cold blood** without feeling pity or remorse; ruthlessly —**leave** (**someone**) **cold** to fail to inspire or excite (someone) —**out in the cold** ignored; neglected —**throw cold water on** to discourage —**cold′ish** *adj.* —**cold′ly** *adv.* —**cold′ness** *n.*

cold·blood·ed (-blud′id) *adj.* 1. having a body temperature approximating to that of the surrounding air, land, or water, as fishes and reptiles 2. easily affected by cold 3. without pity; cruel —**cold′blood′ed·ly** *adv.* —**cold′blood′ed·ness** *n.*

cold cathode *Electronics* a cathode from which electrons are emitted without the cathode being heated

cold chisel a hardened and tempered steel chisel for cutting or chipping cold metal

cold cream a creamy, soothing preparation for softening and cleansing the skin

cold cuts slices of cooked meat served cold

cold feet [Colloq.] lack or loss of confidence; timidity

cold frame an unheated, boxlike, glass-covered structure for protecting young plants

cold front *Meteorol.* the edge of a cold air mass advancing into a warmer air mass

cold·heart·ed (-här′tid) *adj.* lacking sympathy or kindness; unfeeling —**cold′heart′ed·ly** *adv.* —**cold′heart′ed·ness** *n.*

cold pack a process of preserving foodstuffs in which the raw products are placed in tins or jars first and then subjected to heat —**cold′-pack′** *vt.*

cold shoulder [Colloq.] deliberate indifference; slight or snub: often with *the* —**cold′-shoul′der** *vt.*

cold sore *same as* HERPES SIMPLEX

cold storage 1. storage of perishable foods, furs, etc. in a very cold place, esp. in a refrigerating chamber 2. a state

of temporary disuse or suspension [put a scheme into *cold storage*]

cold sweat [Colloq.] a physical reaction to fear, anxiety, etc., characterized by chill and moist skin

cold turkey [U.S. Slang] 1. the abrupt, total withdrawal of drugs from an addict 2. in a frank, blunt way [to talk *cold turkey*]

cold war sharp conflict in diplomacy, economics, etc. between states, without actual warfare

cold wave 1. a period of weather colder than is normal 2. a permanent wave in which the hair is set with a liquid preparation instead of heat

cole (kōl) *n.* [OE. *cal* < L. *caulis, colis*, a cabbage] any of various plants of the cabbage family, used as a vegetable or for fodder; esp., rape

co·le·op·ter·on (kol′ē op′tər on′) *n., pl.* **-ter·a** (-ə) any coleopterous insect: also **co′le·op′ter·an** (-ən)

co·le·op·ter·ous (-əs) *adj.* [< Gr. *koleos*, sheath + *pteron*, wing + -OUS] belonging to an order of insects, including beetles and weevils, with the front wings forming a horny covering for the membranous hind wings, which are usually functional

cole·slaw (kōl′slô′) *n.* [< Du. *kool*, cabbage (akin to COLE) + *sla*, for *salade*, salad] a salad made of shredded raw cabbage dressed with mayonnaise, etc.: also **cole slaw**

cole·tit (-tit′) *n.* *same as* COAL-TIT

co·le·us (kō′lē əs) *n.* [ModL. < Gr. *koleos*, a sheath] a labiate plant grown for its showy, brightly coloured leaves

cole·wort (kōl′wurt′) *n.* [COLE + WORT²] any cabbage whose leaves do not form a compact head

col·ey (kō′lē) *n.* [< ? *coal-fish*, saithe] any of several edible deep-water fish, esp. the saithe

col·ic (kol′ik) *n.* [< OFr. < L. < Gr. < *kolon*, colon] acute abdominal pain caused by various abnormal conditions in the bowels —*adj.* 1. of colic 2. of the colon —**col′ick·y** *adj.*

co·li·form (kō′lə fôrm′, kol′ə-) *adj.* designating, of, or like the aerobic bacillus normally found in the colon: a coliform count is an indicator of faecal contamination of water supplies

col·i·se·um (kol′ə sē′əm) *n.* [after the *Colosseum*, an amphitheatre in Rome] a large building or stadium for sports events, shows, etc.: also **col·os·se′um**

co·li·tis (ko lit′is, kō-) *n.* [ModL. < Gr. *kolon*, colon + -ITIS] inflammation of the large intestine

coll. 1. collect 2. collection 3. college 4. colloquial

col·lab·o·rate (kə lab′ə rāt′) *vi.* **-rat′ed, -rat′ing** [< L. pp. of *collaborare* < *com-*, with + *laborare*, to work] 1. to work together, esp. in some literary, artistic, or scientific undertaking 2. to cooperate with an enemy invader —**col·lab′o·ra′tion** *n.* —**col·lab′o·ra′tive** *adj.* —**col·lab′o·ra′tor** *n.*

col·lab·o·ra·tion·ist (kə lab′ə rā′shən ist) *n.* a person who cooperates with an enemy invader

col·lage (kə läzh′) *n.* [Fr. < *colle*, paste < Gr. *kolla*] 1. an art form in which bits of objects, as newspaper, cloth, leaves, etc., are pasted together on a surface 2. a composition so made —**col·lag′ist** *n.*

col·la·gen (kol′ə jen′) *n.* [< Gr. *kolla*, glue + -GEN] a fibrous protein found in connective tissue, bone, and cartilage —**col′la·gen′ic** *adj.*

col·lap·sar (kol ap′sär) *n.* [COLLAPS(E) + (QUAS)AR] *same as* BLACK HOLE

col·lapse (kə laps′) *vi.* **-lapsed′, -laps′ing** [< L. pp. of *collabi* < *com-*, together + *labi*, to fall] 1. to fall down or fall to pieces; cave in 2. to break down suddenly; fail; give way 3. *a)* to break down suddenly in health *b)* to fall down, as from a blow or exhaustion *c)* to fall or drop drastically, as in value, force, etc. 4. to fold or come together compactly —*vt.* to cause to collapse —*n.* the act of collapsing; a falling in or together; failure or breakdown, as in business, health, etc. —**col·laps′i·bil′i·ty** *n.* —**col·laps′i·ble** *adj.*

col·lar (kol′ər) *n.* [< OFr. < L. < *collum*, the neck] 1. the part of a garment that encircles the neck 2. a cloth band attached to the neck of a garment 3. a band of leather or metal for the neck of a dog, cat, etc. 4. the part of the harness that fits over the neck of a horse 5. a ring or flange, as on rods or pipes, to prevent sideways motion, connect parts, etc. 6. a band of contrasting colour, etc. on an animal's neck —*vt.* 1. to put a collar on 2. to seize by or as by the collar 3. [Colloq.] to arrest —**hot under the collar** 1. angry 2. excited 3. embarrassed; ill at ease —**col′lared** *adj.*

col·lar·bone (-bōn′) *n.* a slender bone joining the breastbone to the shoulder blade; clavicle

col·lard (kol′ərd) *n.* [contr. < COLEWORT] a kind of kale whose coarse leaves are borne in tufts

collat. collateral

col·late (ko lāt′, kə-) *vt.* **-lat′ed, -lat′ing** [< L. *collatus*, pp. of *conferre* < *com-*, together + *ferre*, to bring] 1. to compare (texts, data, etc.) critically in order to note points of agreement and disagreement **2.** *a)* to gather (the sections of a book) together in proper order for binding *b)* to examine (such sections) to see that all pages are present and in proper order —**col·la'tor** *n.*

col·lat·er·al (kə lat'ər əl) *adj.* [< ML. *collateralis* < L. *com-*, together + *lateralis*, LATERAL] **1.** side by side; parallel **2.** accompanying the main thing in a subordinate or corroborative way **3.** of the same ancestors but in a different line **4.** *a)* designating or of security given as a pledge for the fulfilment of an obligation *b)* secured by stocks, property, etc. [a collateral loan] —*n.* **1.** a collateral relative **2.** stocks, bonds, etc. used for collateral security —**col·lat'er·al·ly** *adv.*

col·la·tion (ko lā'shən, kə-) *n.* **1.** the act, process, or result of collating **2.** a light meal **3.** a description of the physical make-up of a book

col·league (kol'ēg) *n.* [< Fr. < L. *collega* < *com-*, with + *legare*, to appoint as deputy] a fellow worker in the same profession; associate in office

col·lect¹ (kə lekt') *vt.* [< OFr. < L. *collectus*: see ff.] **1.** to gather together; assemble **2.** to gather (stamps, books, etc.) for a hobby **3.** to call for and receive (money) for (rent, a fund, taxes, bills, etc.) **4.** to call for and take away [the parcel may be *collected* from the railway station] **5.** to regain control of (oneself or one's wits) —*vi.* **1.** to gather; assemble [a crowd *collected*] **2.** to accumulate [water *collects* in the basement] **3.** to collect payments, etc. —*adj., adv.* [U.S.] with payment to be made by the receiver [to telephone *collect*] —**col·lect'a·ble, col·lect'i·ble** *adj.*

col·lect² (kol'ekt) *n.* [< OFr., ult. < L. *collectus*, pp. of *colligere* < *com-*, together + *legere*, to gather] [*also* **C-**] a short prayer used in certain church services

col·lect·ed (kə lek'tid) *adj.* **1.** gathered together; assembled **2.** in control of oneself; calm —**col·lect'ed·ly** *adv.* —**col·lect'-ed·ness** *n.*

col·lec·tion (-shən) *n.* **1.** the act or process of collecting, specif., *a)* post for dispatch *b)* rubbish for disposal **2.** things collected [a *collection* of stamps] **3.** a mass or pile; accumulation **4.** money collected, as during a church service **5.** [*pl.*] a college examination or report to assess a student's progress at Oxford University

col·lec·tive (-tiv) *adj.* **1.** formed by collecting; gathered into a whole **2.** of or as a group; of or by the individuals in a group acting together [the *collective* effort of the students] **3.** designating or of any enterprise in which people work together as a group, esp. under a system of collectivism [a *collective* farm] **4.** *Gram.* designating a noun which is singular in form but denotes a collection of individuals (e.g., *army, crowd*) —*n.* **1.** *a)* any collective enterprise; specif., a collective farm *b)* the people involved in such enterprise **2.** *Gram.* a collective noun —**col·lec'tive·ly** *adv.* —**col'lec·tiv'-i·ty** *n.*

collective bargaining negotiation between organized workers and their employer or employers concerning wages, hours, and working conditions

collective ownership the ownership of land, an enterprise, etc. by the community or state for the benefit of all

collective unconscious *Psychol.* in the theories of C.G. Jung, the aspect of the unconscious mind incorporating memories and experiences common to all mankind

col·lec·tiv·ism (kə lek'tə viz'm) *n.* the principle of ownership and control of the means of production and distribution by the people collectively —**col·lec'tiv·ist** *n., adj.* —**col·lec'tiv·is'tic** *adj.*

col·lec·tiv·ize (-tə vīz') *vt.* -ized', -iz'ing to establish or organize under a system of collective ownership —**col·lec'-ti·vi·za'tion** *n.*

col·lec·tor (kə lek'tər) *n.* **1.** a person or thing that collects; specif., *a)* a person whose work is collecting taxes, overdue bills, etc. *b)* a person who collects stamps, etc. as a hobby **2.** *Electronics* the region of a transistor that absorbs charge carriers

collector's item any rare or beautiful object thought worthy of collection

col·leen (kol'ēn, kə lēn') *n.* [< Ir., dim. of *caile*, girl] [Irish] a girl

col·lege (kol'ij) *n.* [< OFr. < L. *collegium*, a society, guild < *collega*, COLLEAGUE] **1.** an association of individuals having certain powers, duties, etc. [the electoral *college*] **2.** an autonomous academic institution within a university [a Cambridge *college*] **3.** any institution of higher education not designated as a university [a *college* of arts and technology] **4.** an institution set up by a profession as for the training or supervision of its members [the Royal *College* of Surgeons] **5.** a school offering specialized instruction in some occupation [a secretarial *college*] **6.** a name given to some private secondary schools **7.** the buildings, students, staff, members, or administrators of a college

College of Cardinals the cardinals of the Roman Catholic Church, serving as a privy council to the Pope and electing his successor: also, **Sacred College**

College of Education a training college for school teachers

college pudding a steamed suet pudding containing dried fruit

col·le·gi·al (kə lē'jē əl) *adj.* **1.** with authority shared equally among colleagues **2.** *same as* COLLEGIATE

col·le·gi·al·i·ty (kə lē'jē al'ə tē) *n.* **1.** the sharing of authority among colleagues **2.** *R. C. Ch.* the principle that authority is shared by the Pope and the bishops

col·le·gian (kə lē'jən) *n.* a member of a college

col·le·giate (-jət, -jē ət) *adj.* **1.** of or like a college or college students **2.** made up of colleges, as some universities

collegiate church 1. a church with a chapter of canons although it is not a bishop's see **2.** [Scot.] a church under joint pastorate

col·let (kol'it) *n.* [Fr., dim. of *col*, neck < L. *collum*] **1.** a metal band or ring such as is used in a watch to support the end of a hairspring **2.** a metal sleeve used to secure a shaft in a socket **3.** *Jewellery* a flange holding an individual stone

col·lide (kə līd') *vi.* -lid'ed, -lid'ing [L. *collidere* < *com-*, together + *laedere*, to strike] **1.** to come into violent contact; strike violently against each other; crash **2.** to come into conflict; clash

col·lie (kol'ē) *n.* [< ? *coaly*, from black coat of earlier collies] a silky-haired dog with a long, narrow head: first bred in Scotland to herd sheep

col·lier (kol'yər) *n.* [see COAL & -IER] **1.** a coal miner **2.** *a)* a ship for carrying coal *b)* a member of its crew

col·lier·y (-ē) *n., pl.* -lier·ies a coal mine and its buildings, equipment, etc.

col·li·mate (kol'ə māt') *vt.* -mat'ed, -mat'ing [< false reading of L. *collineare* < *com-*, with + *lineare*, to make straight < *linea*, a line] **1.** to make (beams of radiation) parallel **2.** to adjust the line of sight of (a telescope, etc.) —**col'li·ma'tion** *n.*

COLLIE
(58-66 cm high at shoulder)

col·li·ma·tor (-māt'ər) *n.* [see prec.] **1.** a device for collimating beams of radiation **2.** a small telescope with cross hairs at its focus, fixed to another telescope, surveying instrument, etc. for adjusting the line of sight

col·lin·e·ar (ko lin'ē ər) *adj.* [*col-*, COM- + LINEAR] in the same straight line

Col·lins (kol'inz) *n.* an iced drink made with gin (*Tom Collins*), or vodka, rum, whisky, etc., mixed with soda water, lime or lemon juice, and sugar

col·li·sion (kə lizh'ən) *n.* **1.** a colliding, or coming together with sudden, violent force **2.** a clash or conflict of opinions, interests, etc.

collision course 1. *Naut.* a course bound to end in collision **2.** any plan or course of action destined to produce conflict

col·lo·cate (kol'ə kāt') *vt.* -cat'ed, -cat'ing [< L. pp. of *collocare*: see LOCATE] to arrange or place together, esp. side by side

col·loc·u·tor (kol'ə kyōō tər, kə lok'yə tər) *n.* *same as* INTERLOCUTOR

col·lo·di·on (kə lō'dē ən) *n.* [< Gr. < *kolla*, glue + *eidos*, form] a highly flammable solution of pyroxylin in alcohol and ether that dries quickly, forming a tough, elastic film: used to protect wounds, in photographic films, etc. Also, **col·lo'di·um** (-əm)

col·logue (kə lōg') *vi.* -logued', -lo'guing [< Fr. < L.: see COLLOQUY] **1.** to confer privately **2.** conspire

col·loid (kol'oid) *n.* [< Gr. *kolla*, glue + -OID] **1.** a solid, liquid, or gaseous substance made up of insoluble, nondiffusible particles (as single large molecules or masses of smaller molecules) that remain suspended in a solid, liquid, or gaseous medium of different matter **2.** a gelatinous material that holds the hormonal secretions of the thyroid gland —**col·loi'dal** *adj.*

col·lop (kol'əp) *n.* [ME. < Scand.] a small slice of meat, esp. of bacon

colloq. 1. colloquial(ly) **2.** colloquialism

col·lo·qui·al (kə lō'kwē əl) *adj.* [see COLLOQUY] **1.** having to do with or like conversation **2.** designating or of the words, phrases, and idioms characteristic of informal speech and writing; informal: the label [Colloq.] is used throughout this dictionary in this sense, and does not indicate substandard or illiterate usage —**col·lo'qui·al·ly** *adv.* **-col·lo'qui·al·ness** *n.*

col·lo·qui·al·ism (-iz'm) *n.* **1.** colloquial quality, style, or usage **2.** a colloquial word or expression

col·lo·qui·um (kə lō'kwē əm) *n., pl.* -quia (-ə), -qui·ums [L.: see ff.] an organized conference or seminar on some subject, involving a number of scholars or experts

col·lo·quy (kol'ə kwē) *n., pl.* -quies [L. *colloquium*, conversation < *com-*, together + *loqui*, to speak] a conversation, esp. a formal discussion; conference —**col′-lo·quist** *n.* —**col′lo·quize′** *vi.*

col·lude (kə lōōd′) *vi.* **-lud′ed, -lud′ing** [< L. < *com-*, with + *ludere*, to play] to act in collusion or conspire, esp. for a fraudulent purpose —**col·lud′er** *n.*

col·lu·sion (kə lōō′zhən) *n.* [see prec.] a secret agreement for fraudulent or illegal purpose; conspiracy —**col·lu′sive** (-siv) *adj.* —**col·lu′sive·ly** *adv.*

col·ly·wob·bles (kol′ē wob′′lz) *n.pl.* [*often with sing v.*] [prob. < COLIC + WOBBLE] [Colloq.] **1.** pain in the abdomen; stomach-ache **2.** extreme nervousness; apprehension

col·o·bus (kol′ə bəs) *n.* [ModL. < Gr. *kolobos*, curtailed: so named prob. because of the absent or rudimentary thumbs] any of three species of leaf-eating, long-haired African monkeys

co·logne (kə lōn′) *n.* *same as* EAU DE COLOGNE

co·lon[1] (kō′lən) *n.* [L. < Gr. *kōlon*, member, limb] a mark of punctuation (:) used before an extended quotation, explanation, example, series, etc., and for certain other purposes, as to show ratio [10:1]

co·lon[2] (kō′lən) *n., pl.* **-lons, -la** (-lə) [L. < Gr. *kolon*] that part of the large intestine extending from the caecum to the rectum —**co·lon·ic** (kə lon′ik) *adj.*

co·lon[3] (kə lon′; Sp. kô lôn′) *n., pl.* **-lons′,** Sp. **-lon′es** (-lô′-nes) [AmSp. *colón* < Sp. *Colón,* Columbus] *see* MONETARY UNITS, table (Costa Rica, El Salvador)

colo·nel (kur′n'l) *n.* [earlier *coronel* < Fr. < It. < *colonna,* (military) column < L. *columna*] **1.** *see* MILITARY RANKS, table **2.** [U.S.] an honorary, nonmilitary title in some southern or western states —**colo′nel·cy** (-sē) *n., pl.* **-cies**

co·lo·ni·al (kə lō′nē əl) *adj.* **1.** of or living in, or designating a colony or colonies, **2.** [*often* C-] of or relating to any or all of the colonies of the British Empire **3.** of or characteristic of the thirteen British colonies that became the U.S., or of their period, architecture, etc. **4.** made up of or having colonies **5.** *Ecology* established as a community: said of animals and plants in a new environment —*n.* an inhabitant of a colony —**co·lo′ni·al·ly** *adv.*

co·lo·ni·al·ism (-iz′m) *n.* the system or policy by which a country maintains foreign colonies, esp. in order to exploit them economically —**co·lo′ni·al·ist** *n., adj.*

col·o·nist (kol′ə nist) *n.* **1.** any of the original settlers of a colony **2.** an inhabitant of a colony

col·o·nize (kol′ə nīz′) *vt., vi.* **-nized′, -niz′ing 1.** to found or establish a colony or colonies (in) **2.** to settle in a colony —**col′o·ni·za′tion** *n.* —**col′o·niz′er** *n.*

col·on·nade (kol′ə nād′) *n.* [Fr. < It. < L. *columna,* column] **1.** *Archit.* a series of columns set at regular intervals, usually supporting a roof or series of arches **2.** an avenue of trees —**col′on·nad′ed** *adj.*

col·o·ny (kol′ə nē) *n., pl.* **-nies** [< L. < *colonus,* farmer < *colere,* to cultivate] **1.** *a)* a group of people who settle in a distant land but under the jurisdiction of their native land *b)* the region thus settled **2.** a territory distant from the state having jurisdiction over it **3.** any subject state or territory **4.** [C-] [*pl.*] the colonies and, loosely, the dominions, of the British Empire **5.** [C-] [*pl.*] the thirteen British colonies in N. America that became the U.S. **6.** a community of people of the same nationality or pursuits concentrated in a particular place [an artists' *colony*] **7.** *Bacteriology* a group of similar bacteria growing in a culture medium **8.** *Biol.* a group of similar plants or animals living or growing together **7.** *Zool.* a compound organism of incompletely separated individuals, as in corals, hydroids, etc.

COLONNADE

col·o·phon (kol′ə fon′, -fən) *n.* [LL. < Gr. *kolophōn,* summit, top, end] **1.** a note in a book giving facts about its production, formerly printed at the end **2.** the distinctive emblem of the publisher

col·o·pho·ny (kol′ə nē, kə-) *n.* [ME. *colofonie* < L. < Gr. *kolophonia (rhētinē),* lit., Colophonian (resin)] *same as* ROSIN

col·or (kul′ər) *n.* *U.S. sp. of* COLOUR

col·o·rad·o (kol′ə räd′ō) *adj.* [Sp., red] of medium strength and colour: said of cigars

Colorado beetle a widely distributed black-and-yellow beetle that is a destructive pest of potatoes and other plants

col·or·ant (kul′ər ənt) *n.* [Fr. < prp. of *colorer,* to colour] anything used to give colour to something else; pigment, dye, etc.

col·o·ra·tu·ra (kol′ər ə toor′ə, -tyoor′-) *n.* [It. < L. pp. of *colorare,* to colour] **1.** brilliant runs, trills, etc., used to display a singer's skill **2.** music containing such ornamentation **3.** a soprano who sings such music: in full, **coloratura soprano**

col·or·if·ic (kol′ə rif′ik, kul-) *adj.* **1.** producing or imparting colour **2.** of colour

col·or·im·e·ter (-rim′ə tər) *n.* [< L. *color,* COLOUR + -METER] an instrument for determining the intensity and hue of a colour, as of a solution in chemical analysis, by comparing it with standard colours

co·los·sal (kə los′'l) *adj.* **1.** like a colossus in size; huge; gigantic **2.** [Colloq.] extraordinary [a *colossal* fool] —**co·los′sal·ly** *adv.*

co·los·sus (kə los′əs) *n., pl.* **-los′si** (-ī) **-los′sus·es** [L. < Gr. *kolossos*] **1.** a gigantic statue; esp., [C-] that of Apollo set at the entrance to the harbour of Rhodes c. 280 B.C. **2.** any huge or important person or thing

co·los·to·my (kə los′tə mē) *n., pl.* **-mies** [COLO(N)[2] + -STOMY] the surgical operation of forming an artificial opening in the colon

co·los·trum (kə los′trəm) *n.* [L., beestings] the first fluid, rich in protein, secreted by the mammary glands for several days after the birth of the young

co·lot·o·my (kə lot′ə mē) *n.* [COLO(N)[2] + -TOMY] surgical incision into the colon

col·our (kul′ər) *n.* [< OFr. < L. *color* < OL. *colus,* orig., a covering] **1.** the sensation resulting from stimulation of the retina of the eye by light waves of particular wavelengths **2.** the property of reflecting light of a particular wavelength: the distinct colours of the spectrum are red, orange, yellow, green, blue, indigo, and violet; the *primary colours* of the spectrum are red, green, and blue **3.** any colouring matter; dye; pigment; paint: the *primary colours* (red, yellow, and blue) and *secondary colours* formed from these (green, orange, purple, etc.) are sometimes distinguished from black, white, and grey (*achromatic colours*) **4.** colour of the face; esp. a healthy rosiness or a blush **5.** the colour of the skin of a Negro or other nonwhite person **6.** [*usually pl.*] a coloured badge, costume, etc. that identifies the wearer **7.** [*pl.*] *a)* a flag of a country, regiment, etc. *b)* the armed forces of a country, symbolized by its flag [to serve with the *colours*] *c)* *Sport* a badge or cap denoting membership of a team, esp. at school or college [he won his first-team *colours*] **8.** [*pl.*] one's postion, opinion, or true nature [stick to your *colours*] **9.** outward appearance **10.** appearance of truth; semblance; justification or plausibility [the news lent *colour* to the rumour] **11.** general nature; character [the *colour* of his mind] **12.** vividness or authenticity, as in a literary work [local *colour*] **13.** *Art* the way of using colour **14.** *Music a)* timbre *b)* variety of tone and expression —*vt.* **1.** to give colour to; paint; stain; dye **2.** to change the colour of **3.** to alter or influence, as by distortion [prejudice *coloured* his views] **4.** to give a convincing or plausible aspect to, esp. a story or report —*vi.* **1.** to become coloured **2.** to change in colour **3.** to become red in the face, as when embarrassed or angered; blush; flush —**call to the colours** call or order to serve in the armed forces —**change colour 1.** to become pale **2.** to blush or flush —**colour up** to blush or flush —**lose colour** to become pale —**nail one's colours to the mast** to commit oneself to a particular course of action —**off colour 1.** unwell; out of sorts **2.** in bad taste —**under colour of** under the pretext of —**under false colours** deceitfully; as an impostor —**with flying colours** triumphantly —**col′our·er** *n.*

col·our·a·ble (-ə b'l) *adj.* **1.** capable of being coloured **2.** apparently plausible, but actually specious; deceptive

col·our·a·tion, col·or·a·tion (kul′ə rā′shən) *n.* **1.** a being coloured **2.** the way a thing, esp. a living creature, is coloured **3.** the technique of using colours

colour atlas a chart showing shades of colour, as of paints, dyes, etc.

colour bar a barrier of social, political, and economic restrictions imposed on Negroes or other nonwhites; racial discrimination

col·our·blind (kul′ər blīnd′) *adj.* unable to perceive colours or to distinguish between certain colours, as red and green —**col′our·blind′ness** *n.*

colour code a system of colours used to distinguish or identify components, electrical circuits, etc.

col·oured (kul′ərd) *adj.* **1.** having colour **2.** of a (specified) colour **3.** [*sometimes* C-] of a group of mankind other than the Caucasoid; nonwhite; specif., Negro **4.** [C-] in South Africa, of racially mixed parentage **5.** alterd, distorted, or exaggerated; with a strong element of fixation or fantasy [a highly *coloured* account] —*n.* **1.** [*usually* C-] a person who is not white; specif., a Negro **2.** [C-] in South Africa, a person of racially mixed parentage

col·our·fast (kul′ər fäst′) *adj.* that will keep its colour without fading or running: said of fabrics —**col′our·fast′-ness** *n.*

col·our·ful (-fəl) *adj.* **1.** full of vivid colours **2.** full of interest or variety; distinctive in style, detail, imagery, etc.; picturesque —**col′our·ful·ly** *adv.* —**col′our·ful·ness** *n.*

colour guard a military escort for a flag or regimental colours

col·our·ing (kul′ər iŋ) *n.* **1.** the act, process, or art of applying colours **2.** anything applied to impart colour; pigment, dye, stain, etc. **3.** *same as* COLOURATION **4.** skin colour **5.** specious or false appearance **6.** alteration or influence **7.** characteristic style or flavour, as of a literary work

col·our·ist (-ist) *n.* **1.** a person who uses colours **2.** an artist skilful in using colours **3.** one who applies colour to photographs, black and white prints, etc.

col·our·less (-lis) *adj.* **1.** without colour **2.** dull in colour; grey or pallid; drab **3.** lacking interest or life; dull —**col'·our·less·ly** *adv.* —**col'our·less·ness** *n.*

colour line *same as* COLOUR BAR

colour sergeant *see* MILITARY RANKS. table

colour supplement a magazine printed in colour given away with a newspaper

-co·lous (kə ləs) [< base of L. *colere*, to inhabit + -OUS] a combining form meaning growing (or living) in or among

colt (kōlt) *n.* [OE.] **1.** a young horse, donkey, zebra, etc.; specif., a male racehorse four years of age or under **2.** a young, inexperienced person **3.** *Sport a)* a young or inexperienced player *b)* a member of a junior team

col·ter (kōl'tər) *n.* *chiefly U.S. sp. of* COULTER

colt·ish (kōl'tish) *adj.* of or like a colt; esp., frisky, frolicsome, etc. —**colt'ish·ly** *adv.*

colts·foot (kōlts'foot') *n.,* *pl.* **-foots** a plant of the composite family, with yellow flowers and large leaves suggesting the print of a colt's foot

col·u·brine (kol'yoo brīn') *adj.* [L. *colubrinus* < *coluber*, serpent] **1.** of, characteristic of, or like a snake **2.** of any of a large family of nonpoisonous snakes, including the grass snake

Col·um·bine (kol'əm bīn') [It. *Columbina* < L. *columbina*, fem. of *columbinus*: see ff.] the sweetheart of Harlequin in early pantomime

col·um·bine (kol'əm bīn') *n.* [OFr. < ML. < L. *columbinus*, dovelike < *columba*, dove] a plant of the buttercup family, with showy, spurred flowers of various colours

col·umn (kol'əm) *n.* [< OFr. < L. *columna*] **1.** a slender upright structure, generally a cylindrical shaft with a base and a capital; pillar: it is usually a supporting or ornamental member in a building **2.** anything like a column in shape or function [the spinal column] **3.** a cylindrical body of· fluid, as mercury or air **4.** a formation of troops, ships, etc. in a file **5.** any of the vertical sections of printed matter lying side by side on a page and separated by a rule or blank space **6.** a vertical arrangement of numbers, as in a ledger **7.** a series of feature articles under a fixed title in a newspaper or magazine, written by a special writer or devoted to a certain subject —**co·lum·nar** (kə lum'nər), **col'·umned** *adj.*

co·lum·ni·a·tion (kə lum'nē ā'shən) *n.* the architectural use or arrangement of columns

CAPITAL

SHAFT

BASE

COLUMN

column inch a quantity of printed·matter one inch deep and one column wide

col·um·nist (kol'əm nist, -ə mist) *n.* a person who writes or conducts a column, as in a newspaper

col·za (kol'zə) *n.* [Fr. < Du. < *kool*, a cabbage + *zaad*, a seed] **1.** any of several plants of the cabbage family, esp. rape, whose seeds yield an oil used in lubricants, etc. **2.** this oil: in full, **colza oil**

com- [L. *com-* < OL. *com* (L. *cum*), with] a prefix meaning with or together [*combine*]: also used as an intensive [*command*]: assimilated to **col-** before *l* ; **cor-** before *r* ; **con-** before *c, d, g, j, n, q, s, t,* and *v*; and **co-** before *h, w,* and all vowels

Com. **1.** Commander **2.** Commission(er) **3.** Committee **4.** Commodore **5.** Communist

com. **1.** commerce **2.** common **3.** communication

co·ma¹ (kō'mə) *n.* [ModL. < Gr. *koma*, deep sleep] **1.** a state of deep and prolonged unconsciousness caused by injury or disease **2.** a condition of stupor or lethargy

co·ma² (kō'mə) *n.,* *pl.* **-mae** (-mē) [L. < Gr. *komē*, hair] **1.** *Astron.*,a globular, cloudlike mass around the nucleus of a comet **2.** *a)* a bunch of branches, as on the top of some palms *b)* a tuft of hairs at the end of certain seeds —**co'·mate** (-māt) *adj.*

co·ma·tose (kō'mə tōs') *adj.* **1.** of, like, or in a coma or stupor **2.** as if in a coma; torpid

comb (kōm) *n.* [OE. *camb*] **1.** a thin strip of plastic, metal, etc. with teeth, passed through the hair to arrange or clean it, or set in the hair to hold it in place **2.** anything like a comb in form or function; specif., *a)* a currycomb *b)* a tool for cleaning and straightening wool, flax, etc. *c)* a red, fleshy outgrowth on the top of the head, as of a cock *d)* a thing like a cock's comb in position or appearance, as a helmet crest **3.** a honeycomb —*vt.* **1.** to clean or arrange with a comb **2.** to remove with or as with a comb; separate

(often with *out*) **3.** to search thoroughly; look everywhere in —*vi.* to roll over; break: said of waves

com·bat (*for v.,* kam bat', kom'bat; *for n.* & *adj.,* kom'bat) **-bat'ed, -bat'ing** [< Fr. < VL. < L. *com-*, with + *battuere*, to beat] to fight, contend, or struggle —*vt.* to fight or struggle against; oppose; resist; or seek to get rid of —*n.* **1.** armed fighting; battle **2.** any struggle or conflict; strife —*adj.* *Mil.* of or for combat

com·bat·ant (kom'bə tənt) *adj.* **1.** fighting **2.** ready or prepared to fight —*n.* a person who engages in combat; fighter

combat fatigue a neurotic condition characterized by anxiety, irritability, depression, etc., often occurring after prolonged combat in warfare

com·bat·ive (kom'bə tiv) *adj.* ready or eager to fight; pugnacious —**com·bat'ive·ly** *adv.* —**com·bat'ive·ness** *n.*

combe (koom) *n.* *same as* COOMB

comb·er (kō'mər) *n.* **1.** one that combs wool, flax, etc. **2.** a large wave that breaks on a beach, reef, etc.

com·bi·na·tion (kom bə nā'shən) *n.* **1.** a combining or being combined **2.** a thing formed by combining **3.** an association of persons, firms, political parties, etc. for a common purpose **4.** the series of numbers or letters used in opening a combination lock **5.** [*pl.*] a one-piece undergarment for body and legs **6.** a motorcycle with sidecar attached **7.** *Chess* a series of moves involving several pieces in a concerted attack **8.** *Math.* any of the various groupings, or subsets, into which a number, or set, of units may be arranged without regard to order —**com'·bi·na'tion·al, com'bi·na'tive** *adj.*

combination lock a lock operated by a dial that is turned to a set series of numbers or letters to work the mechanism that opens it

combination room at Cambridge University, a common room

com·bine (kəm bīn'; *for n.* & *v.* 3, kom'bīn) *vt., vi.* **-bined', -bin'ing** [< OFr. < LL. *combinare* < L. *com-*, together + *bini*, two by two: see BI-] **1.** to come or bring into union; act or mix together; unite; join **2.** to unite to form a chemical compound **3.** to harvest and thresh with a combine —*n.* **1.** a machine for harvesting and threshing grain: also **combine harvester** **2.** an association of persons, corporations, etc. for commercial or political, often unethical, purposes —**com·bin'a·ble** *adj.* —**com·bin'er** *n.*

comb·ings (kō'miŋz) *n.pl.* loose hair, wool, etc. removed in combing

combining form a word form that occurs only in compounds or derivatives, and that can combine with other such forms or with affixes to form a word (Ex.: *cardio-* and *-logy* in *cardiology*)

com·bo (kom'bō) *n.,* *pl.* **-bos** [Colloq.] a combination; specif., a small jazz ensemble

com·bus·ti·ble (kəm bus'tə b'l) *adj.* [see ff.] **1.** that catches fire and burns easily; flammable **2.** easily aroused; fiery —*n.* a flammable substance —**com·bus'ti·bil'i·ty** *n.* —**com·bus'ti·bly** *adv.*

com·bus·tion (-chən) *n.* [< OFr. < LL. < L. pp. of *comburere* < *com-*, intens. + *urere*, to burn] **1.** the act or process of burning **2.** rapid chemical combination accompanied by heat and, usually, light **3.** slow oxidation accompanied by relatively little heat and no light **4.** violent excitement; tumult —**com·bus'tive** (-tiv) *adj.*

com·bus·tor (-tər) *n.* the chamber in a jet engine, gas turbine, etc. in which combustion occurs

Comdr. Commander

Comdt. Commandant

come (kum) *vi.* **came, come, com'ing** [OE. *cuman*] **1.** to move from a place thought of as "there" to a place thought of as "here" **2.** to approach by moving towards **3.** to arrive or appear [help will *come*] **4.** to extend; reach **5.** to take place; befall [success *came* to him] **6.** to take form in the mind [her name *came* to him] **7.** to occur in a certain place or order [after 9 *comes* 10] **8.** to become actual; evolve; develop [will peace *come*?] **9.** to arrive at a particular state [*come* to grief] **10.** to be brought (to an awareness, understanding, etc.) [he *came* to regret what he had done] **11.** *a)* to be derived or descended *b)* to be a resident or former resident (with *from*) **12.** to be caused; result **13.** to happen [how did he *come* to hear of it?] **14.** to be due or owed (*to*): used in the participle [to get what is *coming* to one] **15.** to pass as by inheritance **16.** to get to be; become [it *came* loose] **17.** to be available [this dress *comes* in four sizes] **18.** to amount; add up [to] **19.** to germinate: said of grain **20.** [Slang] to have a sexual orgasm *Come* is often used in the subjunctive, with the subject inverted, to mean "when (a specified time or event) occurs" [*come* evening] —*vt.* [Colloq.] to play the part of; pretend to be [don't *come* the innocent with me] —*interj.* look! see here! stop! —**as good** (or **tough, strong,** etc.) **as they come** extremely good (or tough, strong, etc.) —**come about** **1.** to happen; occur **2.** to turn about —**come across** **1.** to find by chance **2.** [Colloq] to be effective, etc. **3.** [Slang] to give, do, or say what is wanted —**come again?** [Colloq.] what did you say? —**come at** **1.** to reach; attain **2.** to approach angrily or swiftly —**come back** **1.** to return **2.** [Colloq.] to make a comeback —**come between** to estrange; divide —**come by** **1.** to get; gain **2.** to pay a visit —**come clean** to make a confession; reveal the truth —**come down** **1.** to suffer loss in status, wealth, etc. **2.** to leave university —**come down on** (or **upon**) to scold; criticize harshly —**come down with** to catch (a disease) —**come in** **1.** to enter **2.** to come into fashion **3.** to finish in a contest [he came in fifth] **4.** [Colloq.] to prove to be [the money came in very useful] **5.** Cricket a) to start one's innings as a batsman b) to bat in a certain position in the order [he comes in at number five] **6.** Radio to answer a call or signal —**come in for** [Colloq.] to get; acquire —**come into** **1.** to enter into **2.** to inherit —**come it** [Slang] **1.** to pretend; act a part **2.** to exaggerate —**come off** **1.** to become detached **2.** to occur **3.** [Colloq.] to prove successful, etc. —**come off it!** [Colloq.] I don't believe you! —**come on** **1.** to make progress **2.** to find **3.** to appear, make an entrance, etc. **4.** to begin: said of rain, snow, etc. —**come on!** [Colloq.] **1.** get started! hurry! **2.** stop behaving like that! —**come one's way** **1.** to yield or become agreeable **2.** to come to one's notice, into one's possession, etc. —**come out** **1.** to be disclosed **2.** to go on strike **3.** to make a debut **4.** to end up; turn out **5.** to be published **6.** [Slang] to declare openly one's homosexuality —**come out for** to support; endorse —**come out with** **1.** to disclose **2.** to say; publish **3.** to offer for public sale, etc. —**come over** **1.** to pay a visit from some distance **2.** a) to change sides or one's opinions b) to defect **3.** to make an impression [the Prime Minister came over badly] **4.** [Colloq.] to feel [he came over faint] —**come round** **1.** to revive; recover **2.** to make a turn **3.** to visit casually **4.** to concede or yield —**come through** **1.** to complete or endure something successfully **2.** [Slang] to do or give what is wanted —**come to** **1.** to recover consciousness **2.** to anchor —**come up** **1.** to arise, as in discussion **2.** to rise, as in status **3.** to be put forward, as for a vote **4.** to begin a term at university —**come upon** to find —**come up to** **1.** to reach to **2.** to equal —**come up with** to propose, produce, find, etc. —**how come?** [Colloq.] how is it that? why? —**to come** in the future

come·back (kum'bak') n. [Colloq.] **1.** a return to a previous state or position, as of success **2.** a witty answer **3.** a complaint or retaliatory action in response to something done or said

Com·e·con (kom'i kon') Council for Mutual Economic Assistance: a trade organization of Soviet-oriented Communist nations

co·me·di·an (kə mē'dē ən) n. **1.** an actor who plays comic parts **2.** an entertainer who tells jokes, sings comic songs, etc. **3.** a person who amuses others by behaving in a comic way: often used ironically

co·me·di·enne (kə mē'dē en') n. **1.** a woman comedian **2.** an actress in comedy

com·e·do (kom'ə dō') n., pl. **com'e·do·nes** (-dō'nēz), **com'·e·dos'** [< L. < comedere: see COMESTIBLE] same as BLACKHEAD (sense 2)

come·down (kum'daun) n. a fall to a lower status or position, as of power, wealth, etc.

com·e·dy (kom'ə dē) n., pl. **-dies** [< OFr. < L. < Gr. kōmōidia < kōmōs, festival + aeidein, to sing] **1.** orig., a drama or narrative with a happy ending or nontragic theme **2.** a) any of various types of play or film with a humorous treatment of characters and situation and a happy ending b) the branch of drama having to do with such plays **3.** a novel or any narrative having a comic theme, tone, etc. **4.** the comic element in a literary work, or in life—**cut the comedy** [Chiefly U.S. Slang] to stop joking —**co·me·dic** (kə mē'dik, -med'ik) adj. —**com'e·dist** n.

comedy of manners a type of comedy satirizing the manners and customs of fashionable society

come-hith·er (kum'hith'ər) adj. [Colloq.] flirtatious or inviting [a come-hither look]

come·ly (kum'lē) adj. **-li·er, -li·est** [OE. cymlic < cyme, delicate, orig., feeble] **1.** pleasant to look at; attractive **2.** [Archaic] seemly; proper —**come'li·ness** n.

come-on (kum'on') n. [Slang] **1.** an inviting look or gesture **2.** an inducement **3.** a swindler

com·er (-ər) n. **1.** a person who comes [a contest open to all comers] **2.** [Chiefly U.S. Colloq.] a person or thing that shows promise of being a success

co·mes·ti·ble (kə mes'tə b'l) adj. [Fr. < L. pp. of comedere < com-, intens. + edere, to eat] [Rare] eatable; edible —n. [usually pl.] food

com·et (kom'ət) n. [< OE. < L. cometa < Gr. < komē, hair] a heavenly body having a solid nucleus with a luminous mass (coma) around it, and, usually, a long, luminous tail: comets move in ecliptical or nearly parabolic orbits round the sun —**com'e·tar·y** (-ə tər ē), **co·met·ic** (ko met'ik) adj.

come-up·pance (kum'up''ns) n. [< COME + UP + -ANCE] [Colloq.] deserved punishment; retribution

com·fit (kum'fit) n. [< OFr. < L. conficere: see CONFECT] a sugar-coated sweet, often with a nut, fruit, etc. in the centre

com·fort (kum'fərt) vt. [< OFr. < LL. < L. com-, intens. + fortis, strong] **1.** to soothe in distress or sorrow; console **2.** to give a sense of ease to —n. **1.** aid; encouragement: now only in **aid and comfort** **2.** relief from distress, grief, etc. **3.** a person or thing that comforts **4.** a state of, or thing that provides, ease and quiet enjoyment —**com'fort·ing** adj. —**com'fort·ing·ly** adv. —**com'fort·less** adj.

com·fort·a·ble (kumf'tər b'l, kum'fər tə b'l) adj. **1.** providing comfort [comfortable shoes] **2.** at ease in body or mind; contented **3.** [Colloq.] sufficient to satisfy [a comfortable salary] —**com'fort·a·ble·ness** n. —**com'·fort·a·bly** adv.

com·fort·er (kum'fər tər, -fə tər) n. **1.** a person or thing that comforts **2.** a woollen neckscarf **3.** a baby's dummy **4.** [U.S.] a quilted bed covering —**the Comforter** Bible the Holy Spirit: John 14:26

com·frey (kum'frē) n., pl. **-freys** [< OFr. confirie < L. conferva, a water plant < confervere, to heal: from its use in medicine to congeal wounds] any of several European plants of the borage family, with rough hairy leaves and small blue, purplish, or yellow flowers

com·fy (kum'fē) adj. **-fi·er, -fi·est** [contr. < COMFORTABLE] [Colloq.] comfortable; snug

com·ic (kom'ik) adj. [< L. < Gr. kōmikos] **1.** of or having to do with comedy **2.** amusing; humorous; funny **3.** of comic strips or cartoons —n. **1.** a comedian **2.** the humorous element in art or life **3.** a) a magazine or booklet containing comic strips, esp. for children b) a similar booklet for adults, often macabre or horrific in content

com·i·cal (kom'i k'l) adj. causing amusement; humorous; funny; droll —**com'i·cal'i·ty** (-kal'ə tē), **com'i·cal·ness** n. —**com'i·cal·ly** adv.

comic opera opera with humorous situations, a story that ends happily, and some spoken dialogue

comic strip a series of cartoons, as in a newspaper, telling a humorous or adventurous story

Com·in·form (kom'in fôrm') n. [< Com(munist) Inform(ation)] the Communist Information Bureau, an association of various European Communist parties (1947–56)

com·ing (kum'iŋ) adj. **1.** approaching; next [this coming Tuesday] **2.** showing promise of being successful, etc. [the coming thing] —n. arrival; advent —**have it** (or something) **coming** to one **1.** to deserve or merit (something) **2.** [Colloq.] to deserve punishment, etc.

Com·in·tern (kom'in turn') n. [< Com(munist) Intern(ational)] an international organization (Third International) of Communist parties (1919–43)

com·i·ty (kom'ə tē) n., pl. **-ties** [< L. comitas < comis, polite, kind] **1.** courteous behaviour; politeness **2.** agreement among Christian denominations to avoid duplication of churches, missions, etc. in specific areas

comity of nations the respect of peaceful nations for each other's laws and institutions

comm. **1.** commander **2.** commission **3.** committee

Comm. **1.** Commonwealth **2.** Communist

com·ma (kom'ə) n. [L. < Gr. komma, clause, that which is cut off < koptein, to cut off] a mark of punctuation (,) used to indicate a slight separation of sentence elements, as in setting off nonrestrictive or parenthetical elements, quotations, items in a series, etc.

comma bacillus the bacillus causing Asiatic cholera

com·mand (kə mänd') vt. [< OFr. < VL. < L. com-, intens. + mandare: see MANDATE] **1.** to give an order to; direct with authority **2.** to have authority over; control **3.** to have ready for use [to command a large vocabulary] **4.** to deserve and get; require as due [to command respect] **5.** to control or overlook from a higher position —vi. to exercise authority; be in control; act as commander —n. **1.** an order; direction; mandate **2.** authority to command **3.** power to control by position **4.** range of view **5.** ability to use; mastery **6.** a military or naval force, organization, or district, under a specified authority [Strategic Air Command] **7.** the post where the person in command is stationed

com·man·dant (kom'ən dant') n. a commanding officer of a fort, prisoner of war camp, etc.

com·man·deer (kom'ən dir') vt. [< Du. or Afrik. < Fr. commander, to command] **1.** to force into military service **2.** to seize (property) for military or governmental use **3.** [Colloq.] to take forcibly

com·mand·er (kə män'dər) n. **1.** a person who commands; leader **2.** same as COMMANDING OFFICER **3.** a member of the higher class of some orders of chivalry [Knight Commander of Royal Victorian Order] **4.** an officer with responsibility for a district of the Metropolitan Police **5.** see MILITARY RANKS, table —**com·mand'er·ship'** n.

commander in chief *pl.* **commanders in chief** 1. the supreme commander of the armed forces of a nation 2. an officer in command of all armed forces in a certain theatre of war

com·mand·ing (kə mänd′iŋ) *adj.* 1. being in command 2. having the presence, authority, bearing, etc. of one in command; authoritative 3. dominating 4. from which the surrounding countryside may be seen [a *commanding* position]

commanding officer the officer in command of any of certain military units or installations

com·mand·ment (kə mänd′mənt) *n.* an authoritative command or order; mandate; precept; specif., any of the Ten Commandments

command module that part of a manned space vehicle which functions as control room and living quarters, and which returns to earth

com·man·do (kə mān′dō) *n.,* *pl.* **-dos, -does** [Afrik. < Port., lit., party commanded] 1. orig., in South Africa, a force of Boer troops 2. a tactical and administrative unit of the Royal Marines 3. *a)* a small raiding force trained to operate inside enemy territory *b)* a member of such a group

command paper a government document presented to Parliament by, or as by, royal command, as a white paper

command performance a performance of a play, film, etc. for, or as for, a ruler by command or request

command post the field headquarters of a military unit, where the commander directs operations

com·me·dia del·l'ar·te (kôm mä′dyä del lär′te) [It., lit., comedy of art] a type of Italian comedy of the 16th century, having a stereotyped plot, improvised dialogue, and stock characters

‡**comme il faut** (kô mēl fō′) [Fr.] as it should be; proper; fitting

com·mem·o·rate (kə mem′ə rāt′) *vt.* **-rat′ed, -rat′ing** [< L. pp. of *commemorare* < *com-*, intens. + *memorare*, to remind] 1. to honour the memory of, as by a ceremony 2. to serve as a memorial to —**com·mem′o·ra′tion** *n.* —**com·mem′o·ra·tive** (-ər ə tiv, -ə rāt′iv), **-com·mem′o·ra·to·ry** *adj.* —**com·mem′o·ra·tive·ly** *adv.* —**com·mem′o·ra′tor** *n.*

com·mence (kə mens′) *vi., vt.* **-menced′, -menc′ing** [< OFr. < L. *com-*, together + *initiare*, to INITIATE] to begin; start; originate —**com·menc′er** *n.*

com·mence·ment (-mənt) *n.* 1. the act or time of commencing; beginning; start 2. the ceremonies at which degrees are conferred at some universities

com·mend (kə mend′) *vt.* [< L. *commendare:* see COMMAND] 1. to put in the care of another; entrust 2. to mention as worthy; recommend 3. to express approval of; praise —**com·mend′a·ble** *adj.* —**com·mend′a·bly** *adv.*

com·men·da·tion (kom′ən dā′shən) *n.* a commending; esp., recommendation or praise

com·men·da·to·ry (kə men′də tər ē) *adj.* 1. expressing praise or approval 2. recommending

com·men·sal (kə men′səl) *adj.* [ME. < ML. *commensalis* < L. *com-*, with + *mensa*, table] 1. eating together 2. *Biol.* of or designating either of two different species of plant or animal life that live in close association (as by sharing food) without interdependence —*n.* 1. a companion at meals 2. *Biol.* a commensal plant or species —**com·men′sal·ly** *adv.* —**com·men′sal·ism** *n.*

com·men·su·ra·ble (kə men′shər ə b'l, -syoor-) *adj.* [LL. *commensurabilis* < L. *com-*, together + *mensurare:* see ff.] measurable by the same standard or measure —**com·men′su·ra·bil′i·ty** *n.* —**com·men′su·ra·bly** *adv.*

com·men·su·rate (-shər it, -syoor-) *adj.* [< LL. < *com-*, with + pp. of *mensurare*, to measure < L. *mensura*, MEASURE] 1. equal in measure or size; coextensive 2. corresponding in extent or degree; proportionate 3. commensurable —**com·men′su·rate·ly** *adv.* —**com·men′su·ra′tion** (-ā′shən) *n.* —**com·men′su·rate·ness** *n.*

com·ment (kom′ent) *n.* [OFr. < L. < pp. of *comminisci*, to contrive < *com-*, intens. + base of *meminisse*, to remember] 1. a note or notes in explanation or criticism of something written or said; annotation 2. a remark or observation made as in criticism 3. talk; gossip —*vi.* [< OFr. < L. *commentari*, to consider thoroughly] to make a comment or comments (*on* or *upon*); make remarks —**no comment** I have nothing to say on the matter

com·men·ta·ry (kom′ən tər ē) *n., pl.* **-tar·ies** 1. a series of explanatory notes or annotations 2. a series of remarks or observations; specif., *a)* an analysis of current events *b)* a description, as for radio or TV, of a sporting event, ceremony, etc. 3. something having the force of a comment or remark 4. [*usually pl.*] a memoir —**com′men·tar′i·al** (-ter′ē əl) *adj.*

com·men·tate (-tāt′) *vt.* **-tat′ed, -tat′ing** [back-formation from ff.] to give a commentary on —*vi.* to perform as a commentator (sense 2)

com·men·ta·tor (-ər) *n.* 1. a person who gives a commentary 2. a person who reports and analyses etc. 3.

a person who describes and comments upon sporting events, etc., as on radio or TV

com·merce (kom′ərs) *n.* [Fr. < L. *commercium* < *com-*, together + *merx* (gen. *mercis*), merchandise] 1. the buying and selling of goods, as between cities, states, or countries; trade 2. social intercourse 3. [Rare] sexual intercourse

com·mer·cial (kə mur′shəl) *adj.* 1. of or connected with commerce or trade 2. of or having to do with shops, office buildings, etc. 3. of a lower grade, or for use in large quantities in industry 4. *a)* made or done primarily for profit, esp. when to the detriment of other values *b)* designed to have wide popular appeal 5. offering training in business skills, etc. —*n.* *Radio & TV* a paid advertisement —**com·mer′cial·ly** *adv.*

commercial art the use of graphic art in advertising, packaging, product design, etc.

commercial broadcasting radio and TV financed by advertising and generally run to make a profit

com·mer·cial·ism (-iz′m) *n.* the practices and spirit of commerce or business, esp. in seeking profits —**com·mer′cial·ist** *n.* —**com·mer′cial·is′tic** *adj.*

com·mer·cial·ize (-īz′) *vt.* **-ized′, -iz′ing** 1. to apply commercial or business methods to 2. to make use of or exploit mainly for profit, esp. at the expense of quality 3. to imbue with commercialism —**com·mer′cial·i·za′tion** *n.*

commercial paper [U.S.] a short-term negotiable document, such as a bill of exchange, promissory note, etc.

commercial traveller a representative of a commercial firm who visits customers to solicit business, take orders, etc.

commercial vehicle any vehicle used in business, to transport goods, paying passengers, etc.

Com·mie (kom′ē) *adj., n.* [*sometimes* **c-**] [Chiefly U.S. Colloq.] Communist: a derogatory usage

com·mi·na·tion (kom′ə nā′shən) *n.* [ME. < L. *comminatio* < *comminatus*, pp. of *comminari*, to threaten] 1. a threat or warning, esp. of divine punishment 2. in the Church of England, a recital of judgment against sinners in the liturgy for Ash Wednesday and certain other days —**com·mi·na·to·ry** (kom′i nə trē, -tər ē) *adj.*

com·min·gle (kə miŋ′g'l, kom′iŋ g'l) *vt., vi.* **-gled, -gling** to mingle together; intermix; blend

com·mi·nute (kom′ə nyoot′) *vt.* **-nut′ed, -nut′ing** [< L. pp. of *comminuere* < *com-*, intens. + *minuere*, to make small] 1. to reduce to powder or minute particles; pulverize 2. to splinter or break (a bone) into small pieces 3. to subdivide (land, etc.) into small parcels —**com′mi·nu′tion** *n.*

com·mis (kom′ē, -ēs) *n., pl.* **-mis** (-ēz) [Fr., orig pp. of *committre*, commit] 1. [Rare] an agent or deputy 2. a junior or apprentice waiter or chef

com·mis·er·ate (kə miz′ə rāt′) *vt.* **-at′ed, -at′ing** [< L. pp. of *commiserari* < *com-*, intens. + *miserari*, to pity] to feel or show sorrow or pity for —*vi.* to condole or sympathize (*with*) —**com·mis′er·a′tion** *n.* —**com·mis′er·a·tive** (-ə rāt′iv, -ər ə tiv) *adj.* —**com·mis′er·a·tive·ly** *adv.*

com·mis·sar (kom′ə sär′) *n.* [< Russ. < ML. *commissarius:* see COMMISSARY] the head of a commissariat (sense 2): since 1946, called *minister*

com·mis·sar·i·at (kom′ə ser′ē ət) *n.* 1. the branch of an army which provides food and supplies for the troops 2. formerly, a government department in the U.S.S.R.: since 1946, called *ministry*

com·mis·sar·y (kom′ə sər ē) *n., pl.* **-sar·ies** [ML. *commissarius* < L. pp. of *committere:* see COMMIT] 1. a deputy assigned to some duty 2. formerly, an army officer in charge of providing food and supplies 3. [Chiefly U.S.] a store in a lumber camp, army camp, etc. handling food and supplies —**com′mis·sar′i·al** (-ser′ē əl) *adj.*

com·mis·sion (kə mish′ən) *n.* [OFr. < ML. < L. pp. of *committere:* see COMMIT] 1. an authorization to perform certain duties or to take on certain powers 2. a document giving such authorization or instruction 3. the state of being so authorized 4. authority to act for another 5. that which one is authorized to do for another 6. a committing or perpetration, as of a crime 7. *a)* a group of people officially appointed to perform specified duties *b)* a government department or board set up for a specific purpose [the *Price Commission*] *c)* a group of people empowered to inquire into some particular matter: in full, **commission of inquiry** 8. *a)* a percentage or fee paid to an agent for services *b)* a percentage of the money taken by a shop, etc., paid to a sales assistant 9. *Mil. a)* an official document conferring a rank of officer *b)* the rank conferred —*vt.* 1. to give a commission to 2. to authorize; empower 3. to give an order to make or do 4. *Naut.* to put (a vessel) into service —**in** (or **out of**) **commission** 1. in (or not in) use 2. in (or not in) working order

commission agent *same as* BOOKMAKER

com·mis·sion·aire (kə mish′ə ner′) *n.* [Fr.] a uniformed doorman at a hotel, cinema, office block, etc., esp. one of a group of ex-servicemen (**Corps of Commissionaires**)

commissioned officer an officer in the armed forces holding rank by a commission

com·mis·sion·er (kə mish′ə nər) *n.* **1.** a member of a commission (sense 7) **2.** an official in charge of a government agency, police department, etc. **3.** a senior civil servant appointed to administer a territory

Commissioner for Oaths a solicitor empowered to administer an oath to one making a sworn statement, affidavit, etc.

com·mit (kə mit′) *vt.* **-mit′ted, -mit′ting** [L. *committere* < *com-*, together + *mittere*, to send] **1.** to give in charge or trust; consign [we *commit* his fame to posterity] **2.** to put officially in custody or confinement esp. before and during a trial [*committed* to prison] **3.** to set apart for some purpose **4.** to do or perpetrate (an offence or crime) **5.** to bind as by a promise; pledge [*committed* to the struggle] **6.** to make known the opinions or views of [to *commit* oneself on an issue] **7.** to refer (a bill, etc.) to a committee to be considered **—commit to memory** to learn by heart; memorize **—commit to paper** (or **writing**) to write down **—com·mit′ta·ble** *adj.*

com·mit·ment (-mənt) *n.* **1.** a committing or being committed **2.** official consignment by court order of a person to prison, to a mental hospital, etc. **3.** a pledge or promise **4.** any obligation or engagement that curtails one's choice of action

com·mit·tal (-t′l) *n.* same as COMMITMENT (senses 1, 2, and 3)

com·mit·tee (kə mit′ē) *n.* [< Anglo-Fr. < L. *committere*: see COMMIT] **1.** a group of people chosen, as in a legislature or club, to consider or act on some matter **2.** group of people organized to support some cause **3.** [C-] the House of Commons when sitting as a Committee of the whole house **—in committee** under consideration by a committee, as a resolution or bill

com·mit·tee·man (-mən) *n.,* pl. **-men** a member of a committee **—com·mit′tee·wom′an** *n.fem.,* pl. **-wom′en**

Committee of Supply the House of Commons when sitting as a Committee of the whole house to discuss public expenditure estimates

com·mode (kə mōd′) *n.* [Fr. < L. *commodus*, suitable: see COM- & MODE] **1.** a chest of drawers **2.** a small, low table with drawers or cabinet space: also **commode table 3.** a movable washstand **4.** a chair enclosing a chamber pot

com·mo·di·ous (kə mō′dē əs) *adj.* [ME., convenient: see prec.] spacious; roomy **—com·mo′di·ous·ly** *adv.* **—com·mo′di·ous·ness** *n.*

com·mod·i·ty (kə mod′ə tē) *n.,* pl. **-ties** [< OFr. < L. < *commodus*: see COMMODE] **1.** any useful thing **2.** anything bought and sold, as in commerce

com·mo·dore (kom′ə dôr′) *n.* [prob. via Du. *kommandeur* < Fr. *commander*: see COMMAND] **1.** a courtesy title, as of the president of a yacht club **2.** the senior captain of a merchant shipping line **3.** see MILITARY RANKS, table

com·mon (kom′ən) *adj.* [< OFr. < L. *communis*, shared by all or many] **1.** belonging equally to, or shared by all **2.** belonging or relating to the community at large; public **3.** widely existing; general; prevalent **4.** notorious [a *common* criminal] **5.** familiar; usual **6.** not of the upper classes; of the masses [the *common* people] **7.** having no rank [a *common* soldier] **8.** below ordinary; inferior **9.** vulgar; low; coarse **10.** *Gram. a)* designating a noun that refers to any of a group or class, as *book, apple, street*: opposed to PROPER *b)* either masculine or feminine [the word *child* is of *common* gender] **11.** *Math.* belonging equally to two or more quantities [a *common* denominator] **—n. 1.** [sometimes pl.] land owned or used by all the inhabitants of a place **2.** the right of a person to pasture animals, etc., on another's land **3.** [Slang] common sense **—common or garden** of the usual kind; ordinary **—in common** equally with, or shared by, another or all concerned **—com′mon·ly** *adv.* **—com′mon·ness** *n.*

com·mon·age (-ij) *n.* **1.** the right to pasture on common land **2.** the state of being held in common **3.** public or common land **—com′mon·a·ble** *adj.*

com·mon·al·i·ty (kom′ə nal′ə tē) *n.* **1.** the common people **2.** a sharing of common features, etc.

com·mon·al·ty (kom′ən əl tē) *n.,* pl. **-ties 1.** the common people **2.** a general body or group **3.** a corporation or its membership

common carrier a person or company in the business of transporting people or goods for a fee

common cold same as COLD (*n.* 4)

com·mon·er (-ər) *n.* **1.** one who is not of the nobility **2.** at some universities, a student who is not supported by a university or college scholarship **3.** one who has rights of common

common fraction a fraction whose numerator and denominator are both whole numbers

common knowledge knowledge shared, or believed to be shared, by all

common law the law of a country or state based on

custom, usage, and the decisions of law courts: separate from STATUTE LAW

com·mon-law marriage (kom′ən lô′) *Law* a marriage not solemnized by religious or civil ceremony but effected by agreement to live together as husband and wife and by the fact of such cohabitation

common market an association of countries formed to effect a closer economic union; specif., [C- M-] the European Economic Community

com·mon·place (-plās′) *n.* **1.** a trite or obvious remark; truism; platitude **2.** anything common or ordinary **—adj.** neither new nor interesting; obvious or ordinary **—com′mon·place′ness** *n.*

common room a sitting-room in schools, colleges, etc. for the use of students or staff

com·mons (kom′ənz) *n.pl.* **1.** the common people **2.** [often with sing. v.] [C-] same as HOUSE OF COMMONS **3.** [often with sing. v.] food provided for meals in common for a whole group, or a dining room where such food is served, as at a college **—short commons** a reduced diet

common sense ordinary good sense or sound practical judgment **—com′mon-sense′, com′mon-sen′si·cal** (-sen′si k'l) *adj.*

common time *Music* a metre of four beats to the bar; 4/4 time: also **common measure**

com·mon·weal (kom′ən wēl′) *n.* [Archaic] the public good; the general welfare

Com·mon·wealth (-welth′) *n.* **1.** an association of British-ruled territories, now sovereign states, and British dependencies, that recognize the reigning British sovereign as titular head **2.** the republican government of England under the Cromwells (1649-60) **3.** the official designation of the federated states of Australia

com·mon·wealth (-welth′) *n.* **1.** the people of a state viewed politically; body politic **2.** a state in which the people are taken as sovereign; democracy **3.** *a)* a republic *b)* [U.S.] loosely, any state of the U.S., strictly, Kentucky, Massachusetts, Pennsylvania, or Virginia **5.** same as COMMONWEAL

Commonwealth Day the anniversary of Queen Victoria's birth, May 24: the Queen's official birthday, celebrated as a public holiday in some Commonwealth countries

com·mo·tion (kə mō′shən) *n.* [< L. pp. of *commovere* < *com-*, together + *movere*, to move] **1.** violent motion; turbulence **2.** confusion; bustle

com·mu·nal (kom′yoon 'l, kə myoon′'l) *adj.* **1.** of a commune or communes **2.** of or belonging to the community; public **3.** designating or of social or economic organization in which there is common ownership of property **—com·mu′nal·ly** *adv.*

com·mu·nal·ism (kom′yoon'l iz'm) *n.* **1.** a theory or system of government in which communes or local communities have virtual autonomy within a federated state **2.** communal organization; loosely, socialism **—com·mu′nal·ist** *n., adj.* **—com·mu′nal·is′tic** *adj.*

com·mu·nal·ize (-īz′) *vt.* **-ized′, -iz′ing** to make communal **—com·mu′nal·i·za′tion** *n.*

com·mune¹ (kə myoon′; for n. kom′yoon) *vi.* **-muned′, -mun′ing** [< OFr. *comuner*, to share < *comun* (see COMMON)] **1.** to talk together intimately **2.** to be in close rapport [to *commune* with nature] **—n.** [Poet.] intimate conversation **—commune with oneself** to ponder

com·mune² (kom′yoon) *n.* [< OFr., ult. < L. *communis*, COMMON] **1.** a community; specif., the smallest administrative district of local government in France, Belgium, and some other European countries **2.** a collective farm, as in China **3.** a small group of people living communally and sharing in work, earnings, etc. **—the Commune** the revolutionary government of Paris from 1792 to 1794 or in 1871

com·mu·ni·ca·ble (kə myoo′ni kə b'l) *adj.* **1.** that can be communicated, as an idea **2.** that can be transmitted, as a disease **—com·mu′ni·ca·bil′i·ty** *n.* **—com·mu′ni·ca·bly** *adv.*

com·mu·ni·cant (-kənt) *n.* a person who receives Holy Communion or belongs to a church celebrating this sacrament

com·mu·ni·cate (-kāt′) *vt.* **-cat′ed, -cat′ing** [< L. pp. of *communicare* < *communis*, COMMON] **1.** to pass along; impart; transmit (heat, motion, a disease, etc.) **2.** to make known; give (information, etc.) **—vi. 1.** to receive Holy Communion **2.** *a)* to give or exchange information, etc., as by talk, writing, etc. *b)* to have a sympathetic personal relationship **3.** to be connected, as by a door [*communicating* rooms] **—com·mu′ni·ca′tor** *n.*

com·mu·ni·ca·tion (kə myoo′nə kā′shən) *n.* **1.** a transmitting **2.** *a)* a giving or exchanging of information, etc. by talk, writing, etc. *b)* the information so given **3.** close, sympathetic relationship **4.** a means of communicating; specif., *a)* [pl.] a system for sending and receiving messages, as by telephone or radio *b)* [pl.] a system for moving troops and materiel *c)* a passage for getting from one place to another **5.** [often pl., with sing.

v.] *a)* the art of expressing ideas *b)* the science of transmitting information

communication cord a device in a train, orig. a cord but now usually a handle, enabling a passenger to stop the train in an emergency

com·mu·ni·ca·tive (kə myōō′ni kə tiv) *adj.* 1. giving information readily; talkative 2. of communication —**com·mu′ni·ca·tive·ly** *adv.* —**com·mu′ni·ca·tive·ness** *n.*

com·mun·ion (kə myōōn′yən, -ē ən) *n.* [OFr. < L. < *communis,* COMMON] 1. a sharing; possession in common 2. a sharing of one's thoughts and emotions 3. an intimate relationship with deep understanding 4. a Christian denomination 5. [C-] a sharing in, or celebrating, of, Holy Communion

com·mu·ni·qué (kə myōō′nə kā′) *n.* [Fr.] an official communication or bulletin

com·mu·nism (kom′yə niz′m) *n.* [< Fr.: see COMMON & -ISM] 1. a theory or system based on the ownership of all property by the community as a whole 2. [*often* C-] a) a hypothetical stage of socialism, as formulated by Marx, Engels, Lenin, etc., to be characterized by a classless and stateless society and the equal distribution of economic goods *b)* the form of government in the U.S.S.R., China, etc., professing to be working towards this stage 3. [*often* C-] a) a political movement for establishing a communist system *b)* the doctrines, methods, etc. of the Communist parties 4. loosely, communalism See also SOCIALISM

com·mu·nist (-nist) *n.* 1. an advocate or supporter of communism 2. [C-] a member of a Communist Party —*adj.* 1. of, characteristic of, or like communism or communists 2. advocating or supporting communism 3. [C-] designating or of a political party advocating Communism —**com′mu·nis′tic** *adj.* —**com′mu·nis′ti·cal·ly** *adv.*

com·mu·ni·ty (kə myōō′nə tē) *n.,* pl. **-ties** [< OFr. < L. *communitas* < *communis,* COMMON] 1. a) all the people living in a particular district, city, etc. *b)* the district, city, etc. where they live 2. a group of people living together as a smaller social unit within a larger one, and having interests, work, etc. in common [a college *community*] 3. any group of people sharing a religion, profession, culture, etc. 4. a group of nations associated because of common traditions or for mutual advantage 5. society; the public 6. ownership or participation in common 7. similarity; likeness [a *community* of tastes] 8. friendly association 9. *Ecology* a group of animals and plants living together and having close interactions

community centre a meeting place in a community for cultural, recreational, or social activities

community chest (or **fund**) [U.S.] a fund collected annually in many cities and towns by private contributions for certain local welfare agencies

community home a residential centre for the instruction and rehabilitation of young people who have committed an offence or are deemed to be in need of care and protection

com·mu·nize (kom′yə nīz′) *vt.* **-nized′, -niz′ing** 1. to subject to communal ownership and control 2. to make communistic —**com′mu·ni·za′tion** *n.*

com·mu·tate (kom′yə tāt′) *vt.* **-tat′ed, -tat′ing** [back-formation < ff.] 1. to change the direction of (an electric current) 2. to change (alternating current) to direct current; rectify

com·mu·ta·tion (kom′yə tā′shən) *n.* [< OFr. < L. < pp. of *commutare,* COMMUTE] 1. an exchange; substitution 2. the substitution of one kind of payment for another 3. *Elec.* change of the direction of a current by a commutator 4. *Law* a change of a sentence or punishment to one that is less severe

com·mu·ta·tive (kom′yə tə tiv; kə myōōt′ə tiv) *adj.* 1. of or involving interchange or substitution 2. *Math.* of or designating an operation, etc. that is unchanged by altering the order of symbols [addition of numbers is *commutative*]

com·mu·ta·tor (kom′yə tāt′ər) *n.* 1. a device for commutating an electric current 2. in a dynamo or motor, a revolving rotary part that collects the current from, or distributes it to, the brushes

com·mute (kə myōōt′) *vt.* **-mut′ed, -mut′ing** [< L. *commutare* < *com-,* intens. + *mutare,* to change] 1. to exchange; substitute; transform 2. to change (an obligation, punishment, etc.) to one that is less severe —*vi.* 1. to be a substitute 2. to travel as a commuter —**com·mut′a·ble** *adj.*

com·mut·er (kə myōōt′ər) *n.* a person who travels daily or regularly, esp. by train, bus, etc., between two points at some distance

co·mose (kō′mōs) *adj.* [L. *comosus* < *coma,* hair] *Bot.* having a tuft of hairs; hairy

comp (komp) *vi.* [< (AC)COMP(ANY)] [Colloq.] to play an accompaniment, esp. in jazz or popular music —*vt.* [Colloq.] to accompany —*n.* [Colloq.] an accompaniment

comp. 1. comparative 2. compare 3. compiled 4. composition 5. compositor 6. compound

com·pact (kəm pakt′; *also for adj., and for n. always,* kom′-pakt) *adj.* [< L. pp. of *compingere* < *com-,* together + *pangere,* to fasten] 1. closely and firmly packed; dense; solid 2. taking little space 3. not wordy; terse 4. composed (*of*) —*vt.* 1. to pack or join firmly together 2. to make by putting together 3. to condense —*n.* 1. a small cosmetic case, usually containing face powder and a mirror 2. [< L. pp. of *compacisci,* to agree together] an agreement; covenant —**com·pact′ly** *adv.* —**com·pact′ness** *n.* —**com·pact′or** *n.*

com·pan·ion¹ (kəm pan′yən) *n.* [< OFr. < hyp. VL. *companio,* messmate < L. *com-,* with + *panis,* bread] 1. one who associates with or accompanies another or others; associate; comrade 2. a person employed to live or travel with another 3. a thing that matches another in sort, colour, etc. 4. [C-] a member of the lowest rank in an order of knighthood 5. a guidebook or handbook 6. *Astron.* the smaller or fainter element in a double star —*vt.* [Archaic] to accompany —**com·pan′ion·ship′** *n.*

com·pan·ion² (kəm pan′yən) *n.* [< Du. < OFr. < It. (*camera della*) *compagna,* (room of the) company, crew] *Naut.* 1. a skylight on the upper deck of a ship, to let light into the cabin below 2. the covering at the head of a companionway 3. a companionway

com·pan·ion·a·ble (-ə b'l) *adj.* having the qualities of a good companion; sociable —**com·pan′ion·a·bil′i·ty, com·pan′ion·a·ble·ness** *n.* —**com·pan′ion·a·bly** *adv.*

com·pan·ion·ate (-it) *adj.* of or characteristic of companions

com·pan·ion·way (-wā′) *n.* a stairway leading from the deck of a ship to the cabins or space below

com·pa·ny (kum′pə nē) *n.,* pl. **-nies** [< OFr. < VL. hyp. *compania,* lit., group sharing bread: see COMPANION¹] 1. companionship; society 2. a group of people; specif., a) a group gathered for social purposes *b)* a group associated for some purpose [a business *company,* a theatrical *company*] 3. the partners whose names are not given in the title of a firm [John Smith and *Company*] 4. a guest or guests; visitor or visitors 5. a habitual associate or associates 6. *Mil.* a body of troops, as of infantry, normally composed of two or more platoons commanded by a major or captain 7. *Naut.* the whole crew of a ship, including the officers: in full, **ship's company** —**keep (a person) company** to stay with (a person) and provide companionship —**keep company** 1. to associate (*with*) 2. to court —**part company** 1. to stop associating (*with*) 2. to separate and go in different directions

company sergeant major *see* WARRANT OFFICER

compar. 1. comparative 2. comparison

com·pa·ra·ble (kom′pər ə b'l) *adj.* 1. that can be compared 2. worthy of comparison —**com′pa·ra·bil′i·ty, com′-pa·ra·ble·ness** *n.* —**com′pa·ra·bly** *adv.*

com·par·a·tive (kəm par′ə tiv) *adj.* 1. that compares; involving comparison as a method [*comparative* linguistics] 2. relative [*comparative* joy] 3. *Gram.* designating or of the second degree of comparison of adjectives and adverbs: usually indicated by the suffix *-er* (*harder*) or by the use of *more* (*more beautiful*) —*n. Gram.* 1. the comparative degree 2. a word or form in this degree —**com·par′a·tive·ly** *adv.* —**com·par′a·tive·ness** *n.*

com·pare (kəm per′) *vt.* **-pared′, -par′ing** [< OFr. < L. *comparare* < *com-,* with + *par,* equal] 1. to regard as similar or equal; liken (*to*) 2. to examine in order to observe similarities or differences (often followed by *with*) 3. *Gram.* to form the positive, comparative, and superlative degrees of (an adjective or adverb) —*vi.* 1. to be worthy of comparison (*with*) 2. to be regarded as similar —*n.* [Poet.] comparison —**beyond** (or **past** or **without**) **compare** without equal —**compare notes** to exchange views, opinions, impressions, etc.

com·par·i·son (kəm par′ə s'n) *n.* 1. a comparing or being compared; estimation of similarities and differences 2. likeness; similarity [no *comparison* between the two] 3. *Gram.* change in an adjective or adverb to show the positive, comparative, and superlative degrees (Ex.: *long, longer, longest; good, better, best; slowly, more slowly, most slowly*) —**bear** (or **stand**) **comparison** to be capable of being compared with, esp. favourably —**in comparison with** compared with

com·part·ment (kəm pärt′mənt) *n.* [< Fr. < It. < LL. < L. *com-,* intens. + *partiri,* to divide < *pars,* a part] 1. any of the divisions into which a space is partitioned off 2. a separate section, part, division, or category 3. a division of a railway carriage 4. a small storage space [the glove *compartment* of a car] —*vt.* same as COMPARTMENTALIZE —**com·part′men′tal** (-men′t'l) *adj.* —**com·part′ment·ed** *adj.*

com·part·men·tal·ize (kəm pärt′men′tə līz′, kom′pärt-) *vt.* **-ized′, -iz′ing** to put or separate into detached compartments, divisions, or categories —**com·part′men′-tal·i·za′tion** *n.*

com·pass (kum′pəs) *vt.* [< OFr., ult. < L. *com-*, together + *passus*, a step]
1. to go round 2. to surround; encircle 3. to understand; comprehend 4. to achieve; accomplish 5. to plot or contrive (something harmful) —*n.* 1. [*often pl.*] an instrument consisting of two pivoted legs, used for drawing arcs or circles or for taking measurements: also called **pair of compasses**

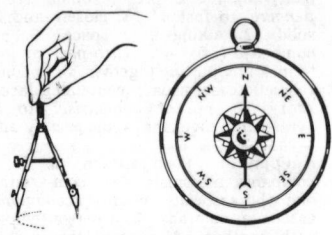

DRAWING COMPASS
DIRECTIONAL COMPASS

2. a boundary; circumference 3. an enclosed area 4. full extent or range; reach; scope; specif., range of tones, as of a voice 5. an instrument for showing direction, esp. one consisting of a magnetic needle swinging freely on a pivot and pointing to the magnetic north —**com′pass·able** —*adj.*

compass card the circular card mounted on a free pivot inside a compass and marked with points of direction and, often, the degrees of the circle

com·pas·sion (kəm pash′ən) *n.* [OFr. < LL. *compassio*, ult. < L. *com-*, together + *pati*, to suffer] sorrow for the sufferings or trouble of another, with the urge to help; deep sympathy; pity

com·pas·sion·ate (-it; *for v.* -āt′) *adj.* 1. feeling or showing compassion; sympathizing deeply 2. given out of compassion [*compassionate* leave] —*vt.* -at′ed, -at′ing [Obs.] to pity —**com·pas′sion·ate·ly** *adv.*

compass rose a conventional design showing the principal directions, as on a compass card or chart

compass saw a narrow saw for making a curved cut

com·pat·i·ble (kəm pat′ə b'l) *adj.* [Fr. < LL.: see COMPASSION] 1. capable of living together harmoniously or getting along well together; in agreement 2. consistent [his behaviour is not *compatible* with his position] 3. *a)* that can be used together: said of equipment [speakers *compatible* with the amplifier] *b)* that can be taken in combination: said of drugs, etc. 4. *TV* designating or of a system of colour transmission producing satisfactory black and white pictures —**com·pat′i·bil′i·ty, com·pat′i·ble·ness** *n.* —**com·pat′i·bly** *adv.*

com·pa·tri·ot (kəm pat′rē ət, -pā′trē-) *n.* [< Fr. < LL. *compatriota*: see COM- & PATRIOT] a fellow countryman —*adj.* of the same country —**com·pa′tri·ot·ism** *n.*

com·peer (kom′pir, kəm pir′) *n.* [< OFr. < L. *com-*, with + *par*, equal] 1. an equal; peer 2. a companion; comrade

com·pel (kəm pel′) *vt.* -pelled′, -pel′ling [< OFr. < L. *compellere* < *com-*, together + *pellere*, to drive] 1. to force or constrain, as to do something 2. to get or bring about by force —**com·pel′la·ble** *adj.* —**com·pel′ler** *n.*

com·pel·ling (-iŋ) *adj.* strongly attractive, desirable, etc. —**com·pel′ling·ly** *adv.*

com·pen·di·ous (kəm pen′dē əs) *adj.* [L. *compendiosus*: see ff.] containing all the essentials in a brief form; concise but comprehensive —**com·pen′di·ous·ly** *adv.* —**com·pen′di·ous·ness** *n.*

com·pen·di·um (-əm) *n.*, *pl.* -di·ums, -di·a (-ə) [L., an abridgment < *com-*, together + *pendere*, to weigh] 1. a summary containing the essential information in a brief form; concise but comprehensive treatise: also **com·pend** (kom′pend) 2. a collection or selection, as of board games, in one container

com·pen·sate (kom′pən sāt′) *vt.* -sat′ed, -sat′ing [< L. pp. of *compensare* < *com-*, with + *pensare*, freq. of *pendere*, to weigh] 1. to make up for; counterbalance in weight, force, etc. 2. to make equivalent return to; recompense —*vi.* 1. to make or serve as compensation or amends (*for*) 2. to attempt to make up for inadequacy in one area by exaggerating successes or achievements in another —**com·pen·sa·tive** (kom′pən sāt′iv, kəm pen′sə tiv) *adj.* —**com′pen·sa′tor** *n.* —**com·pen·sa·to·ry** (kom′pən sā′tər ē, kəm pen′sə tər ē) *adj.*

com·pen·sa·tion (kom′pən sā′shən) *n.* 1. a compensating or being compensated 2. *a)* anything given as an equivalent, or to make amends for a loss, etc. *b)* [Chiefly U.S.] payment for services; esp., wages 3. the counterbalancing of a defect by a greater activity or development of some other part, quality, etc. 4. *Psychol.* a mechanism by which an individual seeks to make up for a real or imagined psychological defect by developing or exaggerating a psychological strength —**com′pen·sa′tion·al** *adj.*

com·père (kom′per) *n.* [Fr., lit., godfather < ML. L. *com-*, with + *pater*, father] a master of ceremonies, esp. in a variety show —*vt.* to act as a compere; to introduce (a variety show, etc.) —**com·mère** (kom′mer′) *n.fem.*

com·pete (kəm pēt′) *vi.* -pet′ed, -pet′ing [< L. *competere* < *com-*, together + *petere*, to seek] to enter into or be in rivalry; contend; vie (*in* a contest, etc.)

com·pe·tence (kom′pə təns) *n.* [< Fr. < L. < prp. of *competere*: see prec.] 1. sufficient means for one's needs 2. ability; fitness 3. legal capability, power, or jurisdiction Also **com′pe·ten·cy**

com·pe·tent (-tənt) *adj.* [< OFr. < L. prp. of *competere*: see COMPETE] 1. well qualified; capable; fit 2. sufficient; adequate 3. *Law* legally qualified or fit —**com′pe·tent·ly** *adv.*

com·pe·ti·tion (kom′pə tish′ən) *n.* 1. a competing; rivalry 2. a contest or match 3. rivalry in business, as for customers or markets 4. the person or persons against whom one competes

com·pet·i·tive (kəm pet′ə tiv) *adj.* of, involving, or based on competition: also **com·pet′i·to·ry** (-tər ē) —**com·pet′i·tive·ly** *adv.* —**com·pet′i·tive·ness** *n.*

com·pet·i·tor (-tər) *n.* a person, team, company, etc. that competes

com·pile (kəm pīl′) *vt.* -piled′, -pil′ing [< OFr. < L. *compilare* < *com-*, together + *pilare*, to compress] 1. to gather together (statistics, facts, etc.) in an orderly form 2. to compose (a book, etc.) of materials gathered from various sources 3. *Computers* to use a compiler to produce (instructions in machine language) for a computer —**com·pi·la·tion** (kom′pə lā′shən) *n.*

com·pil·er (-ər) *n.* 1. one who compiles 2. *Computers* a unit that transforms a high-level programing language into machine language that can be read by a computer

com·pla·cen·cy (kəm plās′'n sē) *n.* [< LL. < L.: see ff.] quiet satisfaction; contentment; often, self-satisfaction, or smugness: also **com·pla′cence**

com·pla·cent (-ənt) *adj.* [< L. prp. of *complacere* < *com-*, intens. + *placere*, please] self-satisfied; smug —**com·pla′cent·ly** *adv.*

com·plain (kəm plān′) *vi.* [< OFr. < VL. *complangere* < L. *com-*, intens. + *plangere*, to strike (the breast)] 1. to express pain, displeasure, etc. 2. to find fault 3. to state a grievance, esp. in a court of law —**com·plain′er** *n.* —**com·plain′ing·ly** *adv.*

com·plain·ant (-ənt) *n.* *Law* one who states a grievance or makes a complaint in court; plaintiff

com·plaint (kəm plānt′) *n.* 1. a complaining; utterance of pain, displeasure, annoyance, etc. 2. a subject or cause for complaining 3. an illness; ailment 4. *Law* a statement initiating a civil action

com·plai·sant (kəm plā′zənt) *adj.* [< Fr. prp. of *complaire* < L. *complacere*: see COMPLACENT] willing to please; affably agreeable; obliging —**com·plai′sance** *n.* —**com·plai′sant·ly** *adv.*

com·ple·ment (kom′plə mənt; *for v.* -ment′) *n.* [L. *complementum* < *complere*: see COMPLETE] 1. that which completes or brings to perfection 2. the amount needed to fill or complete 3. a complete set; entirety 4. either of two parts that complete each other 5. the officers and crew needed to man a ship 6. *Gram.* a word or words that complete the meaning of the predicate (Ex.: *foreman* in *make him foreman, paid* in *he expects to get paid*) 7. *Immunology* any of a group of heat-sensitive proteins in blood serum that destory bacteria or foreign proteins 8. *Logic* the class of all things that are not members of a given class 9. *Math.* the number of degrees added to an angle or arc to make it equal 90 degrees —*vt.* to make complete; be a complement to

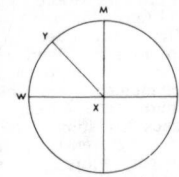

COMPLEMENT
(arc YM, complement of arc WY; angle YXM, complement of angle WXY)

com·ple·men·ta·ry (kom′plə men′tər ē) *adj.* 1. acting as a complement; completing 2. mutually making up what is lacking Also **com′ple·men′tal** —**com′ple·men·tar′i·ty** (-tar′ə tē) *n.*

complementary angle either of two angles that together form a 90° angle

complementary colours any two colours of the spectrum that combine to form white light

com·plete (kəm plēt′) *adj.* [< OFr. < L. pp. of *complere* < *com-*, intens. + *plere*, to fill] 1. lacking no component part; entire 2. ended; finished 3. thorough; absolute [a *complete* scoundrel] —*vt.* -plet′ed, -plet′ing 1. to end; finish 2. to make whole, full, or perfect —**com·plete′ly** *adv.* —**com·plete′ness** *n.*

com·ple·tion (kəm plē′shən) *n.* 1. a completing, or finishing 2. the state of being completed

com·plex (kom′pleks) *adj.* [< L. pp. of *complecti* < *com-*, with + *plectere*, to weave] 1. consisting of two or more related parts 2. not simple; complicated —*n.* 1. a group of related ideas, activities, things, etc. that form, or are viewed as forming, a single whole **2.** *Psychoanalysis a)* a group of largely unconscious impulses, ideas, and emotions related to a particular object, activity, etc., strongly influencing the individual's behaviour *b)* popularly, any strong dislike, fear or obsession —**com·plex′ly** *adv.* —**com·plex′ness** *n.*

complex fraction   a fraction with a fraction in its numerator or denominator, or in both

com·plex·ion (kəm plek′shən) *n.* [OFr. < L. < *complexus*: see COMPLEX] **1.** one's temperament or disposition **2.** the colour, texture, etc. of the skin, esp. of the face **3.** general appearance or nature; character; aspect —**com·plex′ion·al** *adj.*

com·plex·ioned (-shənd) *adj.*   having a (specified) complexion [light-*complexioned*]

com·plex·i·ty (kəm plek′sə tē) *n.* **1.** a complex condition or quality **2.** *pl.* **-ties** anything complex or intricate; complication

complex number   any number expressed as the formal sum of a real number and a multiple of the imaginary square root of -1

complex sentence   a sentence consisting of a main clause and one or more subordinate clauses

com·pli·ance (kəm plī′əns) *n.* **1.** a complying, or giving in to a request, demand, etc. **2.** a tendency to give in readily to others Also **com·pli′an·cy** —**in compliance with** complying with

com·pli·ant (-ənt) *adj.*   complying; yielding; submissive —**com·pli′ant·ly** *adv.*

com·pli·cate (kom′plə kāt′) *vt.*, *vi.* **-cat′ed, -cat′ing** [< L. pp. of *complicare* < *com-*, together + *plicare*, to fold] to make or become intricate, difficult, or involved —*adj. Biol.* folded on itself, as some leaves and insects' wings

com·pli·cat·ed (-kāt′id) *adj.*   intricately involved; hard to untangle, solve, analyse, etc. —**com′pli·cat′ed·ly** *adv.* —**com′pli·cat′ed·ness** *n.*

com·pli·ca·tion (kom′plə kā′shən) *n.* **1.** a complicating **2.** a complicated condition or structure **3.** a complicating factor, as in the plot of a story **4.** *Med.* a second disease or abnormal condition occurring as a consequence of, or in addition to, a primary disease

com·plic·i·ty (kəm plis′ə tē) *n.*, *pl.* **-ties** [< Fr. < L. *complex* (gen. *complicis*): see COMPLEX] the fact or state of being an accomplice in wrongdoing

com·pli·ment (kom′plə mənt; *for v.* -ment′) *n.* [Fr. < It., ult. < L. *complere*, to COMPLETE] **1.** a formal act of courtesy **2.** something said in praise **3.** [*pl.*] formal greetings; respects —*vt.* **1.** to pay a compliment to **2.** to present something to (a person) to show respect

com·pli·men·ta·ry (kom′plə men′tər ē) *adj.* **1.** paying or containing a compliment **2.** given free as a courtesy [a *complimentary* ticket] —**com′pli·men′tar·i·ly** (-men′tər ə lē) *adv.*

com·pline, com·plin (kom′plin) *n.* [< OFr. < L. *completus*: see COMPLETE] *Eccles.* [*often* C-] the last of the seven canonical hours: also **com′plines, com′plins** (-plinz)

com·ply (kəm plī′) *vi.* **-plied′, -ply′ing** [< OFr. < L. *complere*: see COMPLETE] to act in accordance (*with* a request, order, rule, etc.) —**com·pli′er** *n.*

com·po¹ (kom′pō) *n.*, *pl.* **-pos** [< COMPOSITION] any material used as a surfacing or filling agent, as plaster, mortar, etc.

com·po² (kom′pō) *n.* [< COMPENSATION] [Aust. Colloq.] compensation, esp. for injury at work

com·po·nent (kəm pō′nənt) *adj.* [< L. prp. of *componere*: see COMPONE] serving as one of the parts of a whole —*n.* **1.** an element or ingredient **2.** an individual part of a mechanism, as of a motor car **3.** *Electronics* any device with distinct electrical characteristics that may be connected with others in a circuit **4.** *Math.* any of the elements into which a vector quality may be resolved on analysis

com·port (kəm pôrt′) *vt.* [< OFr. < L. *comportare* < *com-*, together + *portare*, to bring] to behave (oneself) in a specified manner —*vi.* to agree or accord (*with*) —**com·port′ment** *n.*

com·pose (kəm pōz′) *vt.* **-posed′, -pos′ing** [< OFr. *composer* < *com-*, with + *poser*, to place] **1.** to make up; constitute **2.** to put in proper order or form **3.** to create (a musical or literary work) **4.** to adjust or settle [to *compose* differences] **5.** to calm (oneself, one's mind, etc.); allay **6.** *Printing* to set (type) —*vi.* **1.** to create musical or literary works **2.** to set type

com·posed (-pōzd′) *adj.*   calm; tranquil; self-possessed —**com·pos′ed·ly** (-pō′zid lē) *adv.* —**com·pos′ed·ness** *n.*

com·pos·er (-pō′zər) *n.*   a person who composes, esp. one who composes music

com·po·site (kom′pə zit′; *for v. also* -zīt′) *adj.* [< L. pp. of *componere* < *com-*, together + *ponere*, to put] **1.** formed of distinct parts; compound **2.** designating a large family of plants, as the daisy, chrysanthemum, etc., having flower heads composed of dense clusters of small flowers **3.** [C-] *Archit.* designating the classic order which combines features of the Ionic and Corinthian capitals —*n.* **1.** a thing

of distinct parts **2.** a composite plant **3.** a material, such as fibreglass, composed of two or more distinct substances in combination —*vt.* to combine (motions, resolutions, etc.) into one for voting or discussion —**com′po·site·ly** *adv* —**com′po·site·ness** *n.*

composite photograph   a photograph made by superimposing one or more photographs on another

com·po·si·tion (kom′pə zish′ən) *n.* **1.** a composing; specif., *a)* the art of writing *b)* the creation of musical works **2.** the makeup of a thing or person; constitution **3.** that which is composed; specif., *a)* a mixture of several parts or ingredients *b)* a work of music, literature, or art *c)* an exercise in writing **4.** an aesthetically unified arrangement of parts **5.** an agreement, or settlement, often by compromise, esp. one made between a debtor and his creditors **6.** *Printing* the work of setting type —**com′-po·si′tion·al** *adj.*

com·pos·i·tor (kəm poz′ə tər) *n.*   a person who sets type; typesetter

‡**com·pos men·tis** (kom′pəs men′tis) [L.] of sound mind; sane

com·post (kom′post) *n.* [< OFr. < L.: see COMPOSITE] **1.** a compound **2.** a mixture of decomposing vegetation, manure, etc. for fertilizing soil

com·po·sure (kəm pō′zhər) *n.* [COMPOS(E) + -URE] calmness; tranquillity; self-possession

com·pote (kom′pōt) *n.* [Fr.: see COMPOST] a dish of fruits stewed in a syrup

com·pound¹ (kom pound′, kəm-; *for n. and, usually,* kom′pound) *vt.* [< OFr. < L. *componere*: see COMPOSITE] **1.** to mix or combine **2.** to make by combining parts **3.** to settle by mutual agreement **4.** to settle (a debt) by compromise payment **5.** to intensify by adding new elements [to *compound* a problem] **6.** to compute (interest) as compound interest —*vi.* to agree or compromise —*adj.* made up of two or more separate parts or elements —*n.* **1.** a thing formed by the combination of parts **2.** a substance containing two or more elements chemically combined in fixed proportions: distinguished from MIXTURE in that a compound has characteristics different from those of its constituents **3.** a word composed of two or more existing words or from existing words and affixes —**compound a felony** (or **crime**) to agree, for payment, not to inform about or prosecute for a felony (or crime) —**com·pound′a·ble** *adj.*

com·pound² (kom′pound) *n.* [Anglo-Ind. < Malay *kampong*] **1.** in the Orient, an enclosed space with a building or group of buildings in it, esp. if occupied by foreigners **2.** [S Afr.] an enclosure in which Bantu workers are housed, esp. miners **3.** any similar enclosed area, as in a prison

compound eye   an eye made up of numerous simple eyes functioning collectively, as in insects

compound fraction   same as COMPLEX FRACTION

compound fracture   a bone fracture in which broken ends of bone have pierced the skin

compound interest   interest paid on both the principal and the accumulated unpaid interest

compound leaf   a leaf divided into two or more leaflets with a common leafstalk

compound number   a quantity expressed in two or more sorts of related units (Ex.: 2 hours 35 minutes)

compound sentence   a sentence consisting of two or more independent, coordinate clauses

compound time   *Music* a time in which each beat in the bar is divisible into three, as 6/4, 9/8, etc.

com·pre·hend (kom′prə hend′) *vt.* [< L. *comprehendere* < *com-*, with + *prehendere*, to seize] **1.** to grasp mentally; understand **2.** to include; comprise —**com′pre·hend′ing·ly** *adv.*

com·pre·hen·si·ble (-hen′sə b'l) *adj.* that can be comprehended; intelligible —**com′pre·hen′si·bil′i·ty** *n.* —**com′pre·hen′si·bly** *adv.*

com·pre·hen·sion (-hen′shən) *n.* **1.** the fact of including or comprising; inclusiveness **2.** the act of or capacity for understanding

com·pre·hen·sive (-hen′siv) *adj.* **1.** including much; inclusive **2.** able to comprehend fully **3.** of or relating to comprehensive schools or an education system including comprehensive schools —*n.* same as COMPREHENSIVE SCHOOL —**com′prehen′sive·ly** *adv.* —**com′pre·hen′sive·ness** *n.*

comprehensive school   a secondary school serving the educational needs of all the children in an area

com·press (kəm pres′; *for n.* kom′pres) *vt.* [< OFr. < LL. < L. pp. of *comprimere* < *com-*, together + *premere*, to press] to press together; make more compact as by pressure —*n.* a pad of folded cloth, often medicated or wet, for applying pressure, heat, cold, etc. to a part of the body —**com·pressed′** *adj.* —**com·pres′si·bil′i·ty** *n.* —**com·pres′-si·ble** *adj.* —**com·pres′sive** *adj.* —**com·pres′sive·ly** *adv.*

compressed air   air held under pressure in a container: its expansive force can operate machines

com·pres·sion (kəm presh′ən) *n.* **1.** a compressing or being compressed **2.** the compressing of a working fluid in an engine, as of the mixture in an internal-combustion engine just before ignition

com·pres·sor (-pres′ər) *n.* **1.** one that compresses **2.** a muscle that compresses a part **3.** a machine for compressing air, gas, etc. **4.** *Electronics* a device for reducing the variation in signal amplitude in a transmission system

com·prise (-prīz′) *vt.* **-prised′, -pris′ing** [< OFr. pp. of *comprendre*: see COMPREHEND] **1.** to include; contain **2.** to consist of [a set *comprising* twelve volumes] —**com·pris′-a·ble** *adj.* —**com·pris′al** *n.*

com·pro·mise (kom′prə mīz′) *n.* [< OFr. < LL. < L. pp. of *compromittere* < *com-*, together + *promittere*, to PROMISE] **1.** a settlement in which each side makes concessions **2.** the result of such a settlement **3.** something midway between two other things **4.** *a)* exposure, as of one's reputation, to danger, suspicion, or disrepute *b)* a weakening, as of one's principles —*vt.* **-mised′, -mis′ing 1.** to settle by concessions on both sides **2.** to lay open to danger, suspicion, or disrepute **3.** to weaken (one's principles, etc.) —*vi.* to make a compromise —**com′-pro·mis′er** *n.*

‡**compte ren·du** (kônt′ rän dü′) [Fr.] a report; account

Comp·tom·e·ter (komp′tom′ə tər) *a trademark for* a high-speed mechanical calculating machine

comp·trol·ler (kən trō′lər) *n.* [altered (after Fr. *compte*, an account) < CONTROLLER] *same as* CONTROLLER (sense 1) —**comp·trol′ler·ship′** *n.*

com·pul·sion (kəm pul′shən) *n.* [< LL. < L. pp. of *compellere*] **1.** a compelling or being compelled; coercion **2.** a driving force **3.** *Psychol.* an irresistible, repeated, irrational impulse to perform some act, often against one's will

com·pul·sive (-siv) *adj.* **1.** of, having to do with, or resulting from compulsion **2.** acting as if under a compulsion [a *compulsive* liar] —*n. Psychol.* one who is subject to a compulsion —**com·pul′sive·ly** *adv.* —**com·pul′-sive·ness** *n.*

com·pul·so·ry (-sər ē) *adj.* **1.** obligatory; required **2.** compelling; coercive —**com·pul′so·ri·ly** *adv.* —**com·pul′-so·ri·ness** *n.*

compulsory purchase the enforced purchase of land, etc., as by a local authority

com·punc·tion (kəm puŋk′shən) *n.* [< OFr. < LL. *compunctio*, a pricking (of conscience) < L. *com-*, intens. + *pungere*, to prick] **1.** a sharp feeling of uneasiness brought on by a sense of guilt; remorse **2.** a feeling of slight regret for something done —**com·punc′tious** *adj.* —**com·punc′-tious·ly** *adv.*

com·pu·ta·tion (kom′pyoo tā′shən) *n.* **1.** a computing; calculation, esp. involving numbers **2.** a method of computing **3.** a computed amount —**com′pu·ta′tion·al** *adj.*

com·pute (kəm pyoot′) *vt., vi.* **-put′ed, -put′ing** [L. *computare* < *com-*, with + *putare*, to reckon] **1.** to determine (an amount, etc.) by reckoning; calculate **2.** to use a computer —**com·put′a·bil′i·ty** *n.* —**com·put′a·ble** *adj.*

com·put·er (kəm pyoot′ər) *n.* a person or thing that computes; specif., an electronic machine that performs rapid, often complex calculations or compiles, correlates, and selects data: see ANALOGUE COMPUTER, DIGITAL COMPUTER

com·put·er·ize (-īz′) *vt.* **-ized′, -iz′ing** to equip with, or operate, produce, control, etc. by or as if by means of, an electronic computer —**com·put′er·i·za′tion** *n.*

com·rade (kom′rād, -rəd) *n.* [< Fr. < Sp. *camarada*, room mate < L. *camera*: see CAMERA] **1.** a friend; close companion **2.** one who shares interests and activities in common with others; associate **3.** a fellow-member of a political party, esp. a fellow communist or socialist: used esp. as a term of address —**com′rade·ly** *adj.* —**com′-rade·ship′** *n.*

comrade in arms a fellow soldier

coms (komz) *n. Colloq. clipped form of* COMBINATION (sense 5)

com·sat (kom′sat) *n.* [*com*(munications) *sat*(ellite)] an artificial satellite used for relaying TV and radio signals, telephone communications, etc.

‡**comte** (kônt) *n.* [Fr.] *same as* COUNT[2] —**com·tesse** (kôn tes′) *n.fem.*

con[1] (kon) *adv.* [contr. < L. *contra*, against] against; in opposition [to argue pro and *con*] —*n.* a reason, vote, position, etc. in opposition

con[2] (kon) *vt.* **conned, con′ning** [ME. *connen*, to be able: see CAN[1]] to peruse or learn carefully

con[3] (kon) *vt.*, **conned, con′ning** [< OFr. < L. *conducere*, conduct] *Naut.* to direct the course of (a vessel) —*n.* the act of conning

con[4] (kon) *adj.* [Slang] confidence [a *con* man] —*vt.* **conned, con′ning** [Slang] **1.** to swindle (a victim) by first gaining his confidence **2.** to trick or fool, esp. by glib, persuasive talk

con[5] (kon) *n.* [Slang] a convict

con. **1.** concerto **2.** conclusion **3.** consolidated

con a·mo·re (kon′ə môr′e; *It.* kôn′ä mô′re) [It.] with love; tenderly: a direction in music

con bri·o (kon brē′ō, kon-) [It.] with spirit; spiritedly: a direction in music

con·cat·e·nate (kon kat′ə nāt′, kən-) *adj.* [< LL. pp. of *concatenare* < L. < *com-*, together + *catenare* < *catena*, a chain] linked together; connected —*vt.* **-nat′ed, -nat′ing** to link or join, as in a chain

con·cat·e·na·tion (kon kat′ə nā′shən, kən-) *n.* **1.** a linking together or being linked together **2.** a series of things or events regarded as causally connected

con·cave (kon kāv′; *also, and for n. usually,* kon′kāv) *adj.* [< OFr. < L. < *com-*, intens. + *cavus*, hollow] hollow and curved like the inside half of a hollow ball —*n.* a concave surface, line, object, etc. —*vt.* **-caved′, -cav′ing** to make concave —**con·cave′ly** *adv.* —**con·cave′ness** *n.*

con·cav·i·ty (kon kav′ə tē) *n.* **1.** the quality or condition of being concave **2.** *pl.* **-ties** a concave surface, line, etc.

con·ca·vo-con·cave (kon kā′vō kon kāv′) *adj.* concave on both sides, as some lenses

con·ca·vo-con·vex (-kon veks′) *adj.* concave on one side and convex on the other

con·ceal (kən sēl′) *vt.* [< OFr. < L. *concelare* < *com-*, together + *celare*, to hide] **1.** to put out of sight; hide **2.** to keep secret —**con·ceal′ment** *n.*

con·cede (kən sēd′) *vt.* **-ced′ed, -ced′ing** [L. *concedere* < *com-*, with + *cedere*, to yield] **1.** to admit as true; acknowledge **2.** to admit as certain **3.** to grant as a right —*vi.* **1.** to make a concession **2.** to acknowledge defeat in an election, sporting competition, etc. —**con·ced′er** *n.*

con·ceit (kən sēt′) *n.* [see CONCEIVE] **1.** orig., an idea **2.** an exaggerated opinion of oneself, one's merits, etc.; vanity **3.** a fanciful or witty expression or notion **4.** a flight of imagination

con·ceit·ed (-id) *adj.* having an exaggerated opinion of oneself, one's merits, etc.; vain —**con·ceit′ed·ly** *adv.* —**con·ceit′ed·ness** *n.*

con·ceiv·a·ble (kən sē′və b′l) *adj.* that can be conceived, understood, imagined, or believed —**con·ceiv′a·bil′i·ty** *n.* —**con·ceiv′a·bly** *adv.*

con·ceive (kən sēv′) *vt.* **-ceived′, -ceiv′ing** [< OFr. < L. *concipere*, to receive < *com-*, together + *capere*, to take] **1.** to become pregnant with **2.** to form in the mind **3.** to think; imagine **4.** to understand **5.** to express in words —*vi.* **1.** to become pregnant **2.** to form an idea (*of*)

con·cel·e·brate (kon sel′ə brāt′) *vt.* **-brat′ed, -brat′ing** [< L. pp. of *concelebrare*: see COM- & CELEBRATE] to celebrate (the Eucharist) jointly: said of two or more priests —**con′-cel·e·bra′tion** *n.* —**con·cel′e·brant** *n.*

con·cen·trate (kon′sən trāt′) *vt.* **-trat′ed, -trat′ing** [< CONCENTRE + -ATE[1]] **1.** to bring to a common centre **2.** to focus (one's thoughts, efforts, etc.) **3.** to increase the strength, density, purity, or intensity of —*vi.* **1.** to come to a common centre **2.** to fix one's attention (*on* or *upon*) —*n.* a substance that has been concentrated —**con′cen·tra′tive** *adj.* —**con′cen·tra′tor** *n.*

con·cen·tra·tion (kon′sən trā′shən) *n.* **1.** a concentrating or being concentrated **2.** close or fixed attention **3.** strength or density, as of a solution **4.** a concentrated substance, etc.

concentration camp a prison camp in which political dissidents, etc. are confined, esp. under conditions of extreme hardship

con·cen·tre (kon sen′tər) *vt., vi.* [< Fr. < L. < *com-*, together + *centrum*, CENTRE] to bring or come to a common centre; concentrate or converge

con·cen·tric (kon sen′trik) *adj.* [< OFr. < ML. < L. *com-*, together + *centrum*, CENTRE] having a centre in common [*concentric* circles] : also **con·cen′tri·cal** —**con·cen′tri·cal·ly** *adv.* —**con·cen·tric·i·ty** (kon′sen tris′ə tē) *n.*

con·cept (kon′sept) *n.* [< L. pp. of *concipere*: see CONCEIVE] an idea or thought, esp. a generalized idea of a class of objects; abstract notion

con·cep·tion (kən sep′shən) *n.* **1.** a conceiving or being conceived in the womb **2.** an embryo or foetus **3.** the beginning of some process, etc. **4.** the formulation of ideas **5.** a mental impression; concept **6.** an original idea, design, plan, etc. —**con·cep′tion·al** *adj.* —**con·cep′tive** *adj.*

con·cep·tu·al (kən sep′choo wəl) *adj.* of conception or concepts —**con·cep′tu·al·ly** *adv.*

con·cep·tu·al·ize (-īz′) *vt.* **-ized′, -iz′ing 1.** to form a concept or idea of; conceive **2.** to think about in concepts —**con·cep′tu·al·i·za′tion** *n.*

con·cern (kən surn′) *vt.* [< ML. < LL. *concernere* < L. *com-*, with + *cernere*, to sift] **1.** to have a relation to; deal with **2.** to involve; be a proper affair of; affect **3.** to make uneasy or anxious —*n.* **1.** a matter of importance to one; affair **2.** interest in or regard for a person or thing **3.** relation; reference **4.** worry; anxiety **5.** a business firm —**as concerns** in regard to —**concern oneself 1.** to busy oneself (*with, about, over, in* something) **2.** to be worried or anxious —**to whom it may concern** a way of addressing a letter, testimonial, etc., that has no individual addressee

con·cerned (-surnd′) *adj.* 1. involved or interested (often with *in*) 2. uneasy or anxious 3. [Colloq.] interested in or anxious about contemporary social or political matters

con·cern·ing (-sur′niŋ) *prep.* relating to; having to do with; in regard to; about —*adj.* worrying

con·cern·ment (-surn′mənt) *n.* [Rare] concern; specif., a) an affair; matter b) importance c) worry

con·cert (kən surt′; *for n. & adj.* kon′sərt) *vt., vi.* [Fr. < It. < L. *concertare* < *com-*, with + *certare*, to strive] to arrange by mutual understanding; plan together; devise —*n.* 1. mutual agreement; concord 2. musical consonance 3. a programme of vocal or instrumental music —*adj.* of or for concerts —**in concert** in unison; together

con·cert·ed (kən sur′tid) *adj.* 1. mutually arranged or agreed upon; done together 2. *Music* arranged in parts —**con·cert′ed·ly** *adv.*

concert grand (piano) the largest size of grand piano, for concert performance

con·cer·ti·na (kon′sər tē′nə) *n.* [CONCERT + -INA: a coinage] a small musical instrument similar to an accordion, with buttons instead of a keyboard —*vi.* to fold or crumple like a concertina

con·cert·mas·ter (kon′sərt mäs′tər) *n.* [transl. of G. *Konzertmeister*] [U.S.] *same as* LEADER (sense 9): also **con′-cert·meis′ter** (-mīs′-)

con·cer·to (kən cher′tō) *n., pl.* **-tos, -ti** (-tē) [It.: see CONCERT] a composition, usually in three movements in symphonic form, for one or more solo instruments and an orchestra

CONCERTINA

concert pitch *Music* 1. a pitch, slightly higher than the usual pitch, to which concert instruments are turned to achieve an increased brilliance of quality 2. the standard pitch, in which A above middle C has a frequency of 440 hertz

con·ces·sion (kən sesh′ən) *n.* 1. a conceding 2. a thing conceded; acknowledgment, as of an argument 3. [Chiefly U.S. & Canad.] a privilege granted by a government, company, etc.; esp., a) the right to/use land b) the right to sell food, parking space, etc. on the lessor's premises —**con·ces′sive** (-ses′iv) *adj.*

con·ces·sion·aire (kən sesh′ə ner′) *n.* [Fr. *concessionnaire*] the holder of a concession granted by a government, company, etc.: also **con·ces·sion·naire′**

con·ces·sion·ar·y (kən sesh′ə nər ē) *adj.* of a concession —*n., pl.* **-ar·ies** a concessionaire

conch (koŋk, konch) *n., pl.* **conchs** (koŋks), **conch·es** (kon′chəz) [< L. < Gr. *konchē*] 1. the spiral, one-piece shell of various sea molluscs 2. such a mollusc, often edible

con·chie, con·chy (kon′chē, -shē) *n.* Colloq. clipped form of CONSCIENTIOUS OBJECTOR

con·chol·o·gy (koŋ kol′ə jē) *n.* [see CONCH & -LOGY] the branch of zoology that deals with molluscs and shells —**con·chol′o·gist** *n.*

con·ci·erge (kon′sē erzh′; *Fr.* kōn syerzh′) *n.* [Fr.] a caretaker or doorkeeper of a block of flats, offices, etc., esp. in France

con·cil·i·ar (kən sil′ē ər) *adj.* [< L. *concilium*, COUNCIL] of, from, or by means of a council, esp. an ecclesiastical one

con·cil·i·ate (-āt′) *vt.* **-at′ed, -at′ing** [< L. pp. of *conciliare* < *concilium*, COUNCIL] 1. to win over; make friendly; placate 2. to gain (regard, good will, etc.) by friendly acts or concessions 3. [Archaic] to reconcile; make consistent —**con·cil′i·a·ble** *adj.* —**con·cil′i·a′tion** *n.* —**con·cil′i·a′tor** *n.*

con·cil·i·a·to·ry (-ə tər ē) *adj.* tending to conciliate or reconcile: also **con·cil′i·a·tive** (-tiv)

con·cise (kən sīs′) *adj.* [< L. pp. of *concidere* < *com-*, intens. + *caedere*, to cut] brief and to the point; short and clear —**con·cise′ly** *adv.* —**con·cise′ness, con·ci′sion** (-sizh′ən) *n.*

con·clave (kon′klāv, koŋ′-) *n.* [OFr. < L., a room, closet < *com-*, with + *clavis*, a key] 1. R.C.Ch. a) the private meeting of the cardinals to elect a pope b) the cardinals collectively 2. any private or secret meeting

con·clude (kən klōōd′) *vt.* **-clud′ed, -clud′ing** [< L. *concludere* < *com-*, together + *claudere*, to shut] 1. to bring to a close; end; finish 2. to decide by reasoning; infer; deduce 3. to decide (*to* do something); determine 4. to settle; come to an agreement about —*vi.* 1. to come to a close; end; finish 2. to come to an agreement

con·clu·sion (kən klōō′zhən) *n.* 1. the end or last part; as, a) the last division of a discourse b) the last step in a reasoning process; judgment or opinion formed after thought c) the last of a chain of events; outcome 2. concluding (*of a* treaty, etc.) —**in conclusion** lastly; in closing

con·clu·sive (-siv) *adj.* that settles a question; final; decisive —**con·clu′sive·ly** *adv.* —**con·clu′sive·ness** *n.*

con·coct (kən kokt′, kon-) *vt.* [< L. pp. of *concoquere* < *com-*, together + *coquere*, to cook] 1. to make by combining ingredients 2. to devise; plan —**con·coct′er** *n.* —**con·coc′tion** *n.* —**con·coc′tive** *adj.*

con·com·i·tance (kən kom′ə tans) *n.* the fact of being concomitant: also **con·com′i·tan·cy**

con·com·i·tant (-kom′ə tənt) *adj.* [< L. prp. of *concomitari* < *com-*, together + *comitari*, to accompany < *comes*, companion] accompanying; attendant —*n.* an accompanying or attendant condition, circumstance, or thing —**con·com′i·tant·ly** *adv.*

con·cord (kon′kôrd, koŋ′-) *n.* [< OFr. < L. < *concors* (gen. *concordis*), of the same mind < *com-*, together + *cor*, heart] 1. agreement; harmony 2. a) peaceful relations, as between nations b) a treaty establishing this 3. *Gram.* same as AGREEMENT 4. musical consonance

con·cord·ance (kən kôr′dəns, kon-) *n.* [see prec.] 1. agreement; harmony 2. an alphabetical list of the principle words of a book or author, with references to the passages in which they occur

con·cord·ant (-dənt) *adj.* agreeing; consonant; harmonious —**con·cord′ant·ly** *adv.*

con·cor·dat (kon kôr′dat) *n.* [Fr. < ML. < L. pp. of *concordare*, to agree < *concors*: see CONCORD] 1. a compact; formal agreement 2. an agreement between a pope and a government concerning church affairs

con·course (kon′kôrs, koŋ′-) *n.* [< OFr. < L. < *concurrere*: see CONCUR] 1. a coming or flowing together 2. a crowd; throng 3. a large open space where crowds gather, as in a railway station or airport terminal

con·crete (kon krēt′; *also, and for n. & vt.* 2 *usually,* kon′-krēt, koŋ′-) *adj.* [< L. pp. of *concrescere* < *com-*, together + *crescere*, to grow] 1. formed into a solid mass; coalesced 2. having a material, perceptible existence; real; actual 3. specific, not general or abstract 4. made of concrete 5. *Gram.* designating a thing or class of things that can be perceived by the senses; not abstract —*n.* 1. a concrete thing, idea, etc. 2. a building material made by mixing cement, sand aggregate, and water, which hardens as it dries —*vt.* **-cret′ed, -cret′ing** 1. to form into a mass; solidify 2. to make of or cover with concrete —*vi.* to solidify —**con·crete′ly** *adv.* —**con·crete′ness** *n.*

concrete music a form of music constructed out of edited, and often distorted, recordings of natural sounds

concrete poetry poetry that employs visual means, as the arrangement of words on the page, to make an effect

con·cre·tion (kon krē′shən) *n.* [see CONCRETE] 1. a solidifying or being solidified 2. a solidified mass —**con·cre′tion·ar·y** (-ər ē) *adj.*

con·cre·tize (kon′krə tīz′, koŋ′-) *vt.* **-tized′, -tiz′ing** to make (something) concrete; make specific

con·cu·bine (koŋ′kyə bīn′, kon′-) *n.* [< L. < *concumbere* < *com-*, with + *cubare*, to lie down] 1. a woman who cohabits with a man although not legally married to him 2. in certain polygamous societies, a secondary wife, of inferior social and legal status —**con·cu·bi·nage** (kon kyōō′bə nij) *n.*

con·cu·pis·cence (kon kyōō′pə səns) *n.* [OFr. < LL. < L. prp. of *concupiscere* < *com-*, intens. + *cupere*, to desire] strong or abnormal desire or appetite, esp. sexual desire; lust —**con·cu′pis·cent** *adj.*

con·cur (kən kur′) *vi.* **-curred′, -cur′ring** [< L. *concurrere* < *com-*, together + *currere*, to run] 1. to occur at the same time; coincide 2. to combine in having an effect; act together 3. to agree (*with*); be in accord (*in an* opinion, etc.)

con·cur·rence (-kur′əns) *n.* 1. a coming or happening together 2. a combining to bring about something 3. agreement; accord Also **con·cur′ren·cy**

con·cur·rent (-ənt) *adj.* 1. occurring or existing at the same time 2. meeting in the same point 3. acting together 4. in agreement 5. *Law* exercised equally over the same area [*concurrent* jurisdiction] —**con·cur′rent·ly** *adv.*

con·cuss (kən kus′) *vt.* to give a concussion to

con·cus·sion (kən kush′ən) *n.* [L. *concussio* < pp. of *concutere* < *com-*, together + *quatere*, to shake] 1. a violent shaking; agitation; shock, as from impact 2. *Med.* a condition of impaired functioning, esp. of the brain, as a result of a violent blow or impact —**con·cus′sive** (-kus′iv) *adj.*

con·demn (kən dem′) *vt.* [< OFr. < L. *condemnare* < *com-*, intens. + *damnare*, to harm, condemn] 1. to disapprove of strongly; censure 2. a) to declare guilty of wrongdoing; convict b) to inflict a penalty upon c) to doom 3. a) to declare (property) unfit for habitation b) to declare unfit for use or service —**con·dem′na·ble** (-dem′nə b'l, -ə b'l) *adj.* —**con·demn′er** *n.*

con·dem·na·tion (kon′dem nā′shən, -dəm-) *n.* 1. a condemning or being condemned 2. a cause for condemning —**con·dem·na·to·ry** (kən dem′nə tər ē) *adj.*

con·den·sate (kon′dən sāt′, kən den′sāt) *n.* a product of condensation

con·den·sa·tion (kon′dən sā′shən) *n.* 1. a condensing or being condensed 2. anything condensed

condensation trail a visible trail of condensed vapour left by an aircraft flying at high altitude: also called **vapour trail**

con·dense (kən dens′) *vt.* **-densed′, -dens′ing** [< Fr. < L. < *com-*, intens. + *densus*, dense] 1. to make more dense or compact; compress 2. to express in fewer words; make concise; abridge 3. to change (a substance) to a denser form, as from a gas to a liquid —*vi.* to become condensed —**con·dens′a·bil′i·ty, con·dens′i·bil′i·ty** *n.* —**con·dens′a·ble, con·dens′i·ble** *adj.*

condensed milk a thick milk made by evaporating part of the water from cow's milk and adding sugar

con·dens·er (kən den′sər) *n.* a person or thing that condenses; specif., *a*) an apparatus for converting gases or vapours to a liquid state *b*) a lens or series of lenses for concentrating light rays on an area *c*) *Elec.* same as CAPACITOR

con·de·scend (kon′də send′) *vi.* [< OFr. < LL. *condescendere* < L. *com-*, together + *descendere*, DESCEND] 1. to descend voluntarily to the level, regarded as lower, of the person that one is dealing with; deign 2. to deal with others in a patronizing manner —**con′de·scend′ing** *adj.* —**con′de·scend′ing·ly** *adv.* —**con′de·scen′sion** (-sen′shən), **con′de·scend′ence** *n.*

con·dign (kən dīn′) *adj.* [< OFr. < L. *condignus* < *com-*, intens. + *dignus*, worthy] deserved; suitable: said esp. of punishment —**con·dign′ly** *adv.*

con·di·ment (kon′də mənt) *n.* [< OFr. < L. *condimentum*, a spice < *condire*, to pickle] a seasoning or relish for food, as pepper, mustard, sauces, etc.

con·di·tion (kən dish′ən) *n.* [< OFr. < L. *condicio*, agreement < *com-*, together + *dicere*, to speak] 1. anything required before the performance or completion of something else; provision; stipulation 2. prerequisite 3. anything that modifies the nature of something else [good business *conditions*] 4. manner or state of being [the human *condition*] 5. *a*) state of health [the patient's *condition*] *b*) [Colloq.] an illness; ailment [a lung *condition*] 6. a proper or healthy state [athletes out of *condition*] 7. social position; rank; station 8. *Law* a clause in a contract, will, etc. that revokes or modifies a stipulation on certain contingencies —*vt.* 1. [Now Rare] to set as a requirement; stipulate 2. to impose a condition or conditions on 3. to be a condition of; determine 4. to affect, modify, or influence 5. to bring into a proper or desired condition 6. *Psychol. a*) to develop a conditioned reflex or behaviour pattern in *b*) to cause to become accustomed (*to*) —**on condition that** provided that —**con·di′tion·er** *n.*

con·di·tion·al (-′l) *adj.* 1. containing or dependent on a condition; qualified [a *conditional* award] 2. expressing a condition [a *conditional* clause] —*n.* *Gram.* the mood expressing a condition —**con·di′tion·al′i·ty** (-al′ə tē) *n.* —**con·di′tion·al·ly** *adv.*

conditioned reflex (or **response**) a reflex in which the response (e.g., secretion of saliva in a dog) is occasioned by a secondary stimulus (e.g., the ringing of a bell) repeatedly associated with the primary stimulus (e.g., the sight of meat)

con·dole (kən dōl′) *vi.* **-doled′, -dol′ing** [< LL. *condolere* < L. *com-*, with + *dolere*, to grieve] to express sympathy; mourn in sympathy —**con·do′la·to·ry** (-dō′lə tər ē) *adj.* —**con·dol′er** *n.*

con·do·lence (kən dō′ləns) *n.* expression of sympathy with another in grief: also **con·dole′ment**

con·dom (kon′dəm) *n.* [< ?] a thin sheath, esp. of rubber, for the penis, used to prevent venereal disease or as a contraceptive

con·do·min·i·um (kon′də min′ē əm) *n.,* pl. **-i·ums, -i·a** (-ə) [ModL. < L. *com-*, together + *dominium*, dominion] 1. joint rule by two or more states 2. a territory ruled in this manner 3. [U.S.] a block of flats or multiple-unit dwelling in which each tenant holds full title to his unit and joint ownership in the common grounds

con·done (kən dōn′) *vt.* **-doned′, -don′ing** [< L. *condonare* < *com-*, intens. + *donare*, to give] to forgive, pardon, or overlook (an offence) —**con·don′a·ble** *adj.* —**con·do·na·tion** (kon′dō nā′shən, -də-) *n.* —**con·don′er** *n.*

con·dor (kon′dər) *n.* [Sp. < Quechua *cuntur*] 1. a very large vulture of the S. American Andes, with a bare head and a neck ruff of downy white feathers 2. a similar vulture of S California 3. *pl.* **con·dor·es** (kən dô′res) any of various S. American gold coins

con·dot·tie·re (kon′də tyer′ē; *It.* kôn′dôt tye′re) *n.,* pl. **-ri** (-ē; *It.* -rē) [It. < *condotto*, one hired] 1. a leader of mercenary soldiers in Italy from the 13th to the 16th cents. 2. any professional mercenary soldier

con·duce (kən dyōōs′) *vi.* **-duced′, -duc′ing** [< L. *conducere*

CONDOR
(wingspread to 3.5 m.)

< *com-*, together + *ducere*, to lead] to tend or lead (*to* an effect); contribute

con·du·cive (-dyōō′siv) *adj.* conducing; tending or leading (*to*) —**con·du′cive·ness** *n.*

con·duct (kon′dukt′; *for v.* kən dukt′) *n.* [< L. pp. of *conducere:* see CONDUCE] 1. management; handling 2. the way that one acts; behaviour —*vt.* 1. to lead; guide; escort 2. to manage, control, or direct 3. to act as conductor of (an orchestra, choir, etc.) 4. to behave (oneself) 5. to be able to transmit [copper *conducts* electricity] —*vi.* 1. to lead 2. to act as a conductor —**con·duct′i·bil′i·ty** *n.* —**con·duct′i·ble** *adj.*

con·duct·ance (kən duk′təns) *n.* the ability of a component to conduct electricity, measured by the ratio of the current to applied electromotive force

con·duc·tion (kən duk′shən) *n.* 1. a conveying, as of liquid through a channel 2. the transmission of nerve impulses 3. *Physics a*) transmission (*of* electricity, heat, etc.) by the passage of energy from particle to particle *b*) same as CONDUCTIVITY: see also CONVECTION, RADIATION

con·duc·tive (-tiv) *adj.* having conductivity

con·duc·tiv·i·ty (kon′duk tiv′ə tē) *n.* the property of conducting heat, electricity, etc.

con·duc·tor (kən duk′tər) *n.* 1. a person who conducts; leader; guide 2. one who controls and directs the performance of music by an orchestra or choir, esp. by indicating tempo, expression, etc. 3. one who has charge of the passengers and collects fares on a public passenger vehicle 4. a thing that conducts electricity, heat, etc. —**con·duc·to·ri·al** (kən duk′tôr′ē əl) *adj.* —**con·duc′tor·ship′** *n.* —**con·duc′tress** *n.fem.*

conductor rail an extra rail used to transmit electric current to a railway train

con·duit (kon′dit, -dyōō wit) *n.* [< OFr. < L. pp. of *conducere:* see CONDUCE] 1. a pipe or channel for conveying fluids 2. a tube or protected trough for electric wires

con·dyle (kon′dil, -dil) *n.* [Fr. < L. < Gr. *kondylos*, knuckle] a rounded process at the end of a bone —**con′dy·lar** (-də lər) *adj.* —**con′dy·loid** (-də loid) *adj.*

cone (kōn) *n.* [< L. < Gr. *kōnos*] 1. *a*) a solid with a circle for its base and a curved surface tapering evenly to a point *b*) a surface described by a moving straight line passing through a fixed point and tracing a fixed curve, as a circle or ellipse, at another point 2. any object shaped like a cone, as a shell or wafer for holding ice cream, the peak of a volcano, etc. 3. a reproductive structure of certain lower plants, with an elongated central axis bearing overlapping scales, bracts, etc. which produce pollen, spores, or ovules 4. *Zool.* any of the flask-shaped cells in the retina, sensitive to light and colour —*vt.* **coned, con′ing** to shape like a cone

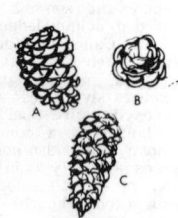

CONES
(A, maritime pine;
B, Japanese larch;
C, blue spruce)

co·ney (kō′nē) *n.,* *pl.* **-neys** same as CONY

conf. 1. conference 2. confessor

con·fab (kon′fab′) *n.* [Colloq.] a confabulation; chat —*vi.* **-fabbed′, -fab′bing** [Colloq.] to confabulate

con·fab·u·late (kən fab′yə lāt′) *vi.* **-lat′ed, -lat′ing** [< L. pp. of *confabulari* < *com-*, together + *fabulari*, to talk: see FABLE] 1. to talk together informally; chat 2. *Psychol.* to fill in gaps in the memory with imaginary remembered experiences believed to be true —**con·fab′u·la′tion** *n.*

con·fect (kən fekt′) *vt.* [< L. pp. of *conficere* < *com-*, with + *facere*, to make, do] to prepare or make, esp. by mixing or combining

con·fec·tion (kən fek′shən) *n.* 1. a confecting 2. any sweetmeat or other sweet preparation, as ice cream 3. a frivolous piece of work 4. an elaborate or fashionable article of women's clothing —**con·fec′tion·ar·y** *adj.*

con·fec·tion·er (-ər) *n.* one whose work or business is making or selling confectionery

con·fec·tion·er·y (-ər ē) *n.,* *pl.* **-er·ies** 1. confections or sweets, collectively 2. the business, work, or shop of a confectioner

con·fed·er·a·cy (kən fed′ər ə sē) *n.,* *pl.* **-cies** [see ff.] 1. people, nations, etc. united for some common purpose 2. a league or alliance formed by such a union; federation 3. a conspiracy

con·fed·er·ate (kən fed′ər it; *for v.* -ə rāt′) *adj.* [< LL. pp. of *confoederare*, to unite by a league < *foedus*, a league] united in a confederacy or league —*n.* 1. a person, group, or state united with another or others for a common purpose; ally 2. an associate in crime; accomplice 3. [C-] any supporter of the Confederate States of America during the American Civil War —*vt., vi.* **-at′ed, -at′ing** to unite in a confederacy; ally

con·fed·er·a·tion (kən fed′ə rā′shən) *n.* **1.** a uniting or being united in a league or alliance **2.** nations or states joined in a league, esp. permanently, as for common defence [the Swiss *Confederation*] **—con·fed′er·al** *adj.* **—con·fed′er·a′tive** *adj.*

con·fer (kən fur′) *vt.* **-ferred′, -fer′ring** [< L. *conferre* < *com-*, together + *ferre*, to BEAR¹] to give, grant, or bestow **—vi.** to have a conference; meet for discussion **—con·fer′ment, con·fer′ral** *n.* **—con·fer′ra·ble** *adj.* **—con·fer′rer** *n.*

con·fer·ee (kon′fə rē′) *n.* **1.** a participant in a conference **2.** a person on whom an honour, degree, favour, etc. is conferred

con·fer·ence (kon′fər əns, -frəns) *n.* **1.** a conversing or consulting on a serious matter **2.** a formal meeting of a group for discussion or consultation, as of states to reconcile differences **3** [*often* C-] the governing body of some churches **—in conference** occupied in discussion **—con·fer·en·tial** (kon′fə ren′shəl) *adj.*

con·fess (kən fes′) *vt.* [< OFr. < L. pp. of *confiteri* < *com-*, together + *fateri*, to acknowledge] **1.** *a*) to admit (a fault, crime, etc.) *b*) to acknowledge (an opinion, etc.) **2.** to declare one's faith in **3.** *Eccles. a*) to tell (one's sins) to God or a priest *b*) to hear the confession of (a person): said of a priest **—vi.** **1.** to admit a fault or crime **2.** *a*) to make one's confession *b*) to hear confessions: said of a priest **—confess to** to admit or admit having **—stand confessed as** to be revealed as

con·fess·ed·ly (-id lē) *adv.* admittedly

con·fes·sion (kən fesh′ən) *n.* **1.** a confessing; admission of guilt or sin; specif., a confessing of sins in the sacrament of penance **2.** something confessed **3.** *a*) a statement of religious beliefs: in full, **confession of faith** *b*) a church having such a confession; communion **—con·fes′sion·ar·y** *adj.*

con·fes·sion·al (-'l) *n.* a small, enclosed place in a church, where a priest hears confessions **—adj.** of or for a confession

con·fes·sor (kən fes′ər) *n.* **1.** one who confesses **2.** *R.C.Ch.* a male saint who was not a martyr **3.** a priest authorized to hear confessions

con·fet·ti (kən fet′ē) *n.pl.* [with sing. v.] [It., pl. of *confetto*, sweetmeat: sweets were formerly so scattered] pieces of coloured paper scattered about at weddings and other celebrations

con·fi·dant (kon′fə dant′; kon′fə dant′) *n.* a close, trusted friend to whom one confides personal secrets **—con′fi·dante′** *n.fem.*

con·fide (kən fīd′) *vi.* **-fid′ed, -fid′ing** [L. *confidere* < *com-*, intens. + *fidere*, to trust] to trust (in someone), esp. by sharing secrets or discussing private affairs **—vt.** **1.** to tell or talk about as a secret [to *confide* one's troubles to a friend] **2.** to entrust (a duty, person, etc.) *to* someone **—con·fid′er** *n.*

con·fi·dence (kon′fə dəns) *n.* **1.** firm belief; trust; reliance **2.** certainty; assurance **3.** belief in one's own abilities; self-confidence **4.** a relationship as confidant [take me into your *confidence*] **5.** the belief that another will keep a secret [told in strict *confidence*] **6.** something told as a secret

confidence trick a swindle effected by one **(confidence man)** who first gains the confidence of his victim

con·fi·dent (-dənt) *adj.* full of confidence; specif., *a*) assured; certain [*confident* of victory] *b*) sure of oneself; self-confident; bold [a *confident* boy] **—n.** same as CONFIDANT **—con′fi·dent·ly** *adv.*

con·fi·den·tial (kon′fə den′shəl) *adj.* **1.** told in confidence; secret **2.** of or showing confidence **3.** entrusted with private or secret matters [a *confidential* agent] **—con′fi·den′tial·ly** *adv.* **—con·fi·den′ti·al·i·ty** (-shē al′ə tē) *n.*

con·fid·ing (kon′fīd′iŋ) *adj.* trustful or inclined to trust **—con·fid′ing·ly** *adv.*

con·fig·u·ra·tion (kən fig′yoo rā′shən) *n.* [< L. *configurare* < *com-*, together + *figurare*: see FIGURE] **1.** arrangement of parts **2.** form, outline, or structure as determined by the arrangement of parts **—con·fig′u·ra′tion·al** *adj.* **—con·fig′u·ra′tive** *adj.*

con·fine (kən fīn′; *for n.* kon′fīn′) *n.* [< OFr. < L. *confinium*, boundary < *com-*, with + *finis*, an end, limit] [*usually pl.*] a boundary or bounded region; border; limit **—vt.** **-fined′, -fin′ing** **1.** to keep within limits; restrict [to *confine* a talk to ten minutes] **2.** to keep shut up, as in prison, in bed because of illness, indoors, etc. **—be confined** to be undergoing childbirth **—con·fin′a·ble, -a·ble** *adj.*

con·fine·ment (kən fīn′mənt) *n.* a confining or being confined; specif., *a*) imprisonment *b*) restriction; restraint *c*) childbirth; lying-in

con·firm (kən furm′) *vt.* [< OFr. < L. *confirmare* < *com-*, intens. + *firmare* < *firmus*, firm] **1.** to make firm; strengthen; establish **2.** to make valid by formal approval; ratify **3.** to prove the truth or validity of; verify **4.** to cause to undergo religious confirmation **—con·firm′a·ble** *adj.*

con·fir·ma·tion (kon′fər mā′shən) *n.* **1.** a confirming or being confirmed; ratification; verification **2.** something that confirms or proves **3.** *a*) a Christian ceremony admitting a person to full church membership *b*) a Jewish ceremony in which young people reaffirm their belief in Judaism

con·firm·a·to·ry (kən fur′mə tər ē) *adj.* confirming or tending to confirm: also **con·firm′a·tive**

con·firmed (-furmd′) *adj.* **1.** firmly established, as in a habit or condition [a *confirmed* liar] **2.** corroborated **3.** having accepted religious confirmation **—con·firm′ed·ly** *adv.*

con·fis·cate (kon′fə skāt′) *vt.* **-cat′ed, -cat′ing** [< L. pp. of *confiscare*, to lay up in a chest < *com-*, together + *fiscus*, money chest, treasury] **1.** to seize (private property) for the public treasury, usually as a penalty **2.** to seize as by authority; appropriate **—con·fis′ca·ble** *adj.* **—con′fis·ca′tion** *n.* **—con′fis·ca′tor** *n.*

con·fis·ca·to·ry (kən fis′kə tər ē) *adj.* **1.** of, constituting, or effecting confiscation **2.** confiscating

con·fit·e·or (kən fit′ē ôr′) *n.* [< LL., I confess] a formal prayer in which sins are confessed

con·fla·gra·tion (kon′flə grā′shən) *n.* [< L. < pp. of *conflagrare* < *com-*, intens. + *flagrare*, to burn] a big, destructive fire

con·flate (kən flāt′) *vt.* [< ME. < L. *conflare*, to blow together] to combine (texts, propositions, etc.) to form a whole

con·flict (kən flikt′; *for n.* kon′flikt) *vi.* [< L. pp. of *configere* < *com-*, together + *fligere*, to strike] **1.** orig., to fight **2.** to be antagonistic, incompatible, or contradictory; clash **—n.** **1.** a fight or struggle **2.** sharp disagreement or opposition, as of interests or ideas **3.** emotional disturbance resulting from opposing impulses **—con·flic′tion** *n.* **—con·flic′tive** *adj.*

con·flu·ence (kon′floo əns) *n.* [OFr. < LL. < L. prp. of *confluere* < *com-*, together + *fluere*, to flow] **1.** a flowing together, esp. of two or more streams **2.** the place where they join, or a stream formed in this way **3.** a coming together as of people; crowd; throng **—con′flu·ent** *adj.*

con·form (kən fôrm′) *vt.* [< OFr. < L. *conformare* < *com-*, together + *formare*, to FORM] **1.** to make the same or similar **2.** to bring into harmony or agreement; adapt **—vi.** **1.** to be or become the same or similar **2.** to be in accord or agreement **3.** to accept without question customs, traditions, prevailing opinion, etc. **—con·form′er** *n.* **—con·form′ism** *n.* **—con·form′ist** *n.*

con·form·a·ble (-fôr′mə b'l) *adj.* **1.** that conforms; specif., *a*) similar *b*) in harmony or agreement *c*) suited; adapted **2.** quick to conform; obedient; submissive **—con·form′a·bil′i·ty** *n.* **—con·form′a·bly** *adv.*

con·for·mal (-fôr′m'l) *adj.* [< LL. < L.: see CONFORM] designating or of a map projection in which shapes at any point are true, but areas become increasingly exaggerated

con·form·ance (-fôr′məns) *n.* same as CONFORMITY

con·for·ma·tion (kon′fôr mā′shən) *n.* **1.** a symmetrical formation and arrangement of the parts of a thing **2.** the structure or form of a thing as determined by the arrangement of its parts

con·form·i·ty (kən fôr′mə tē) *n.*, *pl.* **-ties** **1.** the condition or fact of being in harmony or agreement; correspondence; similarity **2.** action in accordance with customs, rules, popular opinion, etc.

con·found (kən found′, kon-; *for 3, usually* kon′ found′) *vt.* [< OFr. < L. *confundere* < *com-*, together + *fundere*, to pour] **1.** to mix up or lump together indiscriminately; confuse **2.** to make feel confused; bewilder **3.** to damn: used as a mild oath **4.** [Archaic] to defeat or destroy **—con·found′ed** (-id) *adj.* **1.** confused; bewildered **2.** damned: a mild oath **—con·found′ed·ly** *adv.*

con·fra·ter·ni·ty (kon′frə tur′nə tē) *n.*, *pl.* **-ties** [< ML.: see COM- & FRATERNITY] **1.** brotherhood **2.** a group of men associated for some purpose, often religious

con·frere (kon′frer) *n.* [OFr. *confrère*] a fellow member or worker; colleague

con·front (kən frunt′) *vt.* [Fr. < ML. *confrontare* < L. *com-*, together + *frons*, forehead, front] **1.** to stand or meet face to face **2.** to face or oppose boldly or defiantly **3.** to bring face to face (*with*) [to *confront* one with the facts] **—con·fron·ta·tion** (kon′frən tā′shən), **con·front′al** *n.*

Con·fu·cian·ism (kən fyoo′shən iz'm) *n.* the ethical teachings of Confucius (551?-479? B.C.), Chinese philosopher, emphasizing devotion to parents, ancestor worship, and the maintenance of justice and peace **—Con·fu′cian·ist** *n., adj.*

con·fuse (kən fyooz′) *vt.* **-fused′, -fus′ing** [< OFr. < L. pp. of *confundere*: see CONFOUND] **1.** to mix up; jumble together; put into disorder **2.** to mix up mentally; specif., *a*) to bewilder; perplex *b*) to embarrass; disconcert *c*) to fail to distinguish between; mistake the identity of **—con·fus′ed·ly** (-fyooz′id lē) *adv.* **—con·fus′ed·ness** *n.* **—con·fus′ing** *adj.* **—con·fus′ing·ly** *adv.*

con·fu·sion (kən fyoo′zhən) *n.* a confusing or being confused; specif., *a*) state of disorder *b*) bewilderment *c*) embarrassment *d*) failure to distinguish between things **—covered with confusion** greatly embarrassed **—con·fu′sion·al** *adj.*

con·fute (kən fyōōt′) *vt.* **-fut′ed, -fut′ing** [L. *confutare*] to prove (a person, statement, etc.) to be in error or false; overcome by argument or proof —**con·fu·ta·tion** (kon′-fyōō tā′shən) *n.* —**con·fu′ta·tive** *adj.* —**con·fut′er** *n.*

con·ga (koŋ′gə) *n.* [AmSp., ult. < *Congo*, former name of Zaire in Africa] **1.** a Latin American dance in which the dancers form a winding line **2.** music for this dance, in 4/4 syncopated time —*vi.* to dance the conga

con·gé (kon′zhā; *Fr.* kôn zhä′) *n.* [Fr. < OFr. < L. < *com-*, intens. + *meare*, to go] **1.** a dismissal **2.** permission to leave **3.** a formal farewell

con·geal (kən jēl′) *vt., vi.* [< OFr. < L. *congelare* < *com-*, together + *gelare*, to freeze] **1.** to solidify or thicken by cooling or freezing **2.** to thicken; coagulate; jell —**con·geal′-a·ble** *adj.* —**con·geal′ment** *n.*

con·ge·la·tion (kon′jə lā′shən) *n.* **1.** a congealing or being congealed **2.** something congealed

con·gen·er (kon′jə nər) *n.* [L. < *com-*, together + *genus* (gen. *generis*), race, kind] a person or thing of the same kind, class, genus, etc. —**con′gen·er′ic** (-ner′ik), **con·gen·er·ous** (kən jen′ər əs) *adj.*

con·gen·ial (kən jēn′yəl, -ē əl) *adj.* [see COM- & GENIAL[1]] **1.** kindred; compatible **2.** having the same tastes and temperament; sympathetic [*congenial* friends] **3.** suited to one's needs or disposition; agreeable [*congenial* work] —**con·ge′ni·al′i·ty** (-jēn′ē al′ə tē) *n.* —**con·gen′ial·ly** *adv.*

con·gen·i·tal (kən jen′ə t'l) *adj.* [< L.: see COM- & GENITAL] existing as such at birth; resulting from one's prenatal environment [a *congenital* disease] —**con·gen′i·tal·ly** *adv.*

con·ger (eel) (koŋ′gər) [< OFr. < L. < Gr. *gongros*] a large, edible saltwater eel

con·ge·ries (kon′jə rēz′, kon jir′ēz) *n., pl.* **con′ge·ries′** [see ff.] a collection of things or parts massed together; heap; pile

con·gest (kən jest′) *vt.* [< L. pp. of *congerere*, to pile up < *com-*, together + *gerere*, to carry] **1.** to cause too much blood to accumulate in the vessels of (a part of the body) **2.** to fill to excess; overcrowd; clog [a *congested* road] —*vi.* to become congested —**con·ges′tion** (-jes′chən) *n.* —**con·ges′tive** (-tiv) *adj.*

con·glom·er·ate (kən glom′ə rāt′; *for adj.* & *n.* -ər it) *vt., vi.* **-at′ed, -at′ing** [< L. pp. of *conglomerare* < *com-*, together + *glomerare* < *glomus*, a ball] to form or collect into a rounded or compact mass —*adj.* **1.** formed into a rounded or compact mass; clustered **2.** made up of separate substances collected into a single mass **3.** *Geol.* made up of rock fragments or pebbles cemented together by clay, silica, etc.: also **con·glom′er·at′-ic** (-ə rat′ik), **con·glom′er·it′ic** (-ə rit′-ik) —*n.* **1.** a conglomerate mass; cluster **2.** a large corporation formed by merging many diverse companies **3.** *Geol.* a conglomerate rock —**con·glom′er·a′tion** *n.*

CONGLOMERATE ROCK

con·grats (kən gratz′) *interj.* [Colloq.] congratulations

con·grat·u·late (kən grat′yə lāt′) *vt.* **-lat′ed, -lat′ing** [< L. pp. of *congratulari* < *com-*, together + *gratulari*, to wish joy < *gratus*, agreeable] to express to (a person) one's pleasure at his good fortune, success, etc. —**congratulate oneself** to consider oneself clever or fortunate —**con·grat′-u·la′tor** *n.* —**con·grat′u·la·to·ry** (-lə tər ē) *adj.*

con·grat·u·la·tion (kən grat′yə lā′shən) *n.* **1.** a congratulating **2.** [pl.] expressions of pleasure and good wishes at another's fortune or success

con·gre·gate (koŋ′grə gāt′; *for adj.* -git) *vt., vi.* **-gat′ed, -gat′-ing** [< L. pp. of *congregare* < *com-*, together + *gregare*, to gather < *grex*, a flock] to gather into a mass or crowd; collect; assemble —*adj.* **1.** assembled; collected **2.** collective —**con′gre·ga′tive** *adj.* —**con′gre·ga′tor** *n.*

con·gre·ga·tion (koŋ′grə gā′shən) *n.* **1.** a congregating or being congregated **2.** a gathering of people or things; assemblage **3.** an assembly of people for religious worship **4.** the members of a particular place of worship **5.** an assembly of members of a university **6.** *R.C.Ch.* a religious community not necessarily under solemn vows but bound by a common rule

con·gre·ga·tion·al (-'l) *adj.* **1.** of or like a congregation **2.** [C-] of Congregationalism or Congregationalists

con·gre·ga·tion·al·ism (-'l iz'm) *n.* **1.** a form of church organization in which each local congregation is self-governing **2.** [C-] the faith and form of organization of a Protestant denomination in which each member church is self-governing —**Con′gre·ga′tion·al·ist** *n., adj.*

con·gress (koŋ′grəs) *n.* [< L. pp. of *congredi* < *com-*, together + *gradi*, to walk < *gradus*, a step] **1.** a coming together; meeting **2.** an association or society **3.** an assembly or conference **4.** any of various legislatures, esp. [C-] the legislature of the U.S., consisting of the Senate and the House of Representatives **5.** [C-] in India, a major political party: also **Congress Party**

con·gres·sion·al (kən gresh′ən 'l) *adj.* **1.** of a congress **2.** [C-] of Congress —**con·gres′sion·al·ly** *adv.*

con·gress·man (koŋ′grəs mən) *n., pl.* **-men** [*often* C-] in the U.S., a member of Congress, esp. of the House of Representatives

con·gru·ence (koŋ′grōō wəns) *n.* [see ff.] **1.** the state or quality of being in agreement; harmony **2.** *Math.* the relation between two numbers each of which, when divided by a third, leaves the same remainder Also **con′gru·en·cy**

con·gru·ent (-wənt, -ənt) *adj.* [< L. prp. of *congruere*, to come together, agree] **1.** in agreement; harmonious **2.** *Geom.* of the same shape and size **3.** *Math.* in congruence [*congruent* numbers] —**con′gru·ent·ly** *adv.*

con·gru·i·ty (kən grōō′ə tē) *n., pl.* **-ties** **1.** the condition or fact of being congruous or congruent; specif., a) agreement; harmony b) appropriateness c) *Geom.* exact coincidence (of two or more figures) **2.** an instance of agreement

con·gru·ous (koŋ′grōō wəs) *adj.* **1.** *same as* CONGRUENT **2.** corresponding to what is right, proper, or reasonable; fitting; suitable; appropriate —**con′gru·ous·ly** *adv.* —**con′-gru·ous·ness** *n.*

con·ic (kon′ik) *adj. same as* CONICAL —*n. same as* CONIC SECTION

con·i·cal (-i k'l) *adj.* **1.** of a cone **2.** resembling or shaped like a cone —**con′i·cal·ly** *adv.*

conic section a curve, as an ellipse, circle, parabola, or hyperbola, produced by the intersection of a plane with a right-angled circular cone

co·nid·i·um (kə nid′ē əm) *n., pl.* **-i·a** (-ə) [ModL. < Gr. *konis*, dust] a small asexual spore of certain fungi —**co·nid′i·al, co·nid′i·an** *adj.*

co·ni·fer (kon′ə fər, kō′nə-) *n.* [L. < *conus*, a cone + *ferre*, to BEAR[1]] any of an order of cone-bearing trees and shrubs, mostly evergreens, as the pine, spruce, fir, cedar, yew, etc. —**co·nif·er·ous** (kə nif′ər əs) *adj.*

conj. **1.** conjugation **2.** conjunction

con·jec·tur·al (kən jek′chər əl) *adj.* **1.** based on or involving conjecture **2.** inclined to make conjectures —**con·jec′-tur·al·ly** *adv.*

con·jec·ture (kən jek′chər) *n.* [< L. *conjectura* < pp. of *conjicere*, to guess < *com-*, together + *jacere*, to throw] **1.** an inferring, theorizing, or predicting from incomplete evidence; guesswork **2.** an inference, theory, or prediction based on guesswork; guess —*vt., vi.* **-tured, -tur·ing** to arrive at or propose (something) by conjecture; guess —**con·jec′tur·a·ble** *adj.* —**con·jec′tur·er** *n.*

con·join (kən join′) *vt., vi.* [< OFr. < L. *conjungere* < *com-*, together + *jungere*, to join] to join together; unite; combine —**con·join′er** *n.*

con·joint (-joint′) *adj.* [see prec.] **1.** joined together; united; combined **2.** of or involving two or more in association; joint —**con·joint′ly** *adv.*

con·ju·gal (kon′jə gəl) *adj.* [< L. < *conjunx*, spouse < *com-*, together + base akin to *jugum*, yoke] of marriage or the relation between husband and wife; matrimonial —**con′-ju·gal′i·ty** (-jə gal′ə tē) *n.* —**con′ju·gal·ly** *adv.*

con·ju·gate (kon′jə gāt′; *also, and for v. always,* -gət′) *adj.* [< L. pp. of *conjugare* < *com-*, together + *jugare*, to join < *jugum*, a yoke] **1.** joined together, esp. in a pair; coupled **2.** *Gram.* derived from the same base and, usually, related in meaning **3.** *Math.* reciprocally related and interchangeable as to properties, as two points, lines, etc. —*n.* a conjugate word —*vt.* **-gat′ed, -gat′ing** **1.** [Archaic] to join together; couple **2.** *Gram.* to inflect (a verb) systematically, according to voice, mood, tense, number, and person —*vi. Gram.* **1.** to conjugate a verb **2.** to be conjugated —**con′ju·ga′tive** *adj.* —**con′ju·ga′tor** *n.*

con·ju·ga·tion (kon′jə gā′shən) *n.* **1.** a conjugating or being conjugated; union **2.** *Gram.* a) a methodical presentation or arrangement of the inflectional forms of a verb b) a class of verbs with similar inflectional forms —**con′ju·ga′tion·al** *adj.* —**con′ju·ga′tion·al·ly** *adv.*

con·junc·tion (kən juŋk′shən) *n.* [see CONJOIN] **1.** a joining together or being joined together; union; combination **2.** coincidence **3.** *Astrol., Astron.* a) the apparent closeness of two or more heavenly bodies b) the condition of being in the same celestial longitude [planets in *conjunction*] **4.** *Gram.* an uninflected word used to connect words, phrases, clauses, or sentences; connective: conjunctions may be coordinating (e.g., *and, but, or*), subordinating (e.g., *if, when, as, because, though*), or correlative (e.g., *either . . . or, both . . . and*) —**con·junc′tion·al** *adj.* —**con·junc′tion·al·ly** *adv.*

con·junc·ti·va (kon′əŋk tī′və, kən juŋk′ti və) *n., pl.* **-vas, -vae** (-vē) [< ModL. (*membrana*) *conjunctiva*, connecting (membrane)] the mucous membrane lining the inner surface of the eyelids and covering the front part of the eyeball —**con′junc·ti′val** *adj.*

con·junc·tive (kən juŋk′tiv) *adj.* **1.** serving to join together; connective **2.** united; combined; joint **3.** *Gram.* used as a conjunction [a *conjunctive* adverb] —*n. Gram.* a conjunctive word; esp., a conjunction —**con·junc′tive·ly** *adv.*

con·junc·ti·vi·tis (kən juŋk′tə vīt′is) *n.* [see -ITIS] inflammation of the conjunctiva

con·junc·ture (kən junk'chər) *n.* [< ML.: see CONJOIN] 1. [Rare] a joining or being joined together 2. a combination of events or circumstances, esp. one creating a critical situation; crisis

con·ju·ra·tion (kon'jə rā'shən) *n.* 1. [Obs.] a conjuring; invocation 2. a magic spell; incantation

con·jure (kun'jər; *for vt.* 1 kən joor') *vi.* **-jured, -jur·ing** [< OFr. < L. *conjurare* < *com-*, together + *jurare*, to swear] 1. to summon a demon, spirit, etc. by a magic spell 2. to practise magic —*vt.* 1. to appeal to or entreat solemnly 2. to summon (a devil, etc.) by a magic spell —**conjure up** 1. to cause to appear as by magic 2. to call to mind [the music *conjured up* memories]

con·jur·er, con·jur·or (kun'jər ər; *for* 1 kən joor'ər) *n.* 1. one who solemnly entreats someone 2. a 'magician 3. one skilled in legerdemain

conk (konk) *n.* [< ? CONCH] [Slang] a blow on the head —*vt.* [Slang] to hit on the head —**conk out** [Slang] 1. to fail suddenly in operation 2. to become very tired and, usually, fall asleep

con·ker (-ər) *n.* [< dial. *conker*, snail shell, orig. used in the game] 1. the horse chestnut 2. [*pl.*] a children's game in which a horse chestnut, threaded on a string, is knocked against another to try to break it

con man [Slang] *same as* confidence man (see CONFIDENCE TRICK)

con mo·to (kon mō'tō) [It.] *Music* with animated movement

conn (kon) *vt., n. same as* CON³

con·nate (kon'āt) *adj.* [LL. *connatus*, pp. of *connasci*, to be born at the same time] 1. inborn; innate 2. coexisting since birth or the beginning 3. having the same origin

con·nect (kə nekt') *vt.* [< L. *connectere* < *com-*, together + *nectere*, to fasten] 1. to join (two things together, or one thing *with* or *to* another); link; couple 2. to show or think of as related; associate 3. to plug into an electrical circuit —*vi.* 1. to be joined or be related 2. to meet so that passengers can change to another bus, aeroplane, etc. 3. [Colloq.] *Sports* to hit a ball, target, etc. solidly —**con·nect'·i·ble, con·nect'a·ble** *adj.* —**con·nec'tor, con·nect'er** *n.*

connecting rod a rod connecting by reciprocating motion two or more moving parts of a machine

con·nec·tion, con·nex·ion (kə nek'shən) *n.* 1. a joining or being joined; coupling; union 2. a thing that joins; means of joining 3. a relation; association; coherence 4. *a*) a relative, esp. by marriage *b*) a business associate, friend, etc., esp. an influential one: *usually used in pl.* 5. [*usually pl.*] the act or means of transferring from one bus, aeroplane, etc. to another 6. a group of people associated in politics, business, etc. —**in connection with** 1. together with 2. with reference to —**con·nec'tion·al** *adj.*

con·nec·tive (kə nek'tiv) *adj.* connecting or serving to connect —*n.* something that connects, esp. a word that connects words, phrases, or clauses, as a conjunction or relative pronoun —**con·nec'tive·ly** *adv.* —**con·nec·tiv·i·ty** (kon'ek tiv'ə tē) *n.*

connective tissue body tissue that connects and supports other tissues and organs in the body

conn·ing tower (kon'iŋ) [prp. of CON³] 1. an armoured pilothouse on the deck of a warship 2. on submarines, a low observation tower serving also as an entrance to the interior

con·niv·ance (kə nī'vəns) *n.* a conniving; esp., passive cooperation, as by consent or pretended ignorance, esp. in wrongdoing

con·nive (kə nīv') *vi.* **-nived', -niv'ing** [< L. *conivere*, to wink, connive] 1. to pretend not to see or look (*at* something wrong or evil), thus giving tacit consent or cooperation 2. *a*) to cooperate secretly (*with* someone), esp. in wrongdoing *b*) to scheme underhandedly —**con·niv'·er** *n.*

con·nois·seur (kon'ə sur') *n.* [< Fr. < OFr. < L. *cognoscere*, to know: see COGNITION] one who has expert knowledge and keen discrimination in some field, esp. in the fine arts —**con'nois·seur'ship** *n.*

con·no·ta·tion (kon'ə tā'shən) *n.* 1. the act or process of connoting 2. an idea suggested by or associated with a word, phrase, etc. in addition to its explicit meaning —**con·no·ta·tive** (kon'ə tāt'iv, kə nōt'ə tiv), **con'no·ta'·tion·al** *adj.* —**con'no·ta'tive·ly** *adv.*

con·note (kə nōt') *vt.* **-not'ed, -not'ing** [< ML. *connotare* < L. *com-*, together + *notare*, to mark: see NOTE] 1. to suggest or convey (associations, overtones, etc.) in addition to the explicit, or denoted, meaning 2. to imply or involve

con·nu·bi·al (kə nyoo'bē əl) *adj.* [< L. *conubium*, marriage < *com-*, together + *nubere*, to marry] of marriage or the state of being married; conjugal —**con·nu'·bi·al'i·ty** (-bē al'ə tē) *n.* —**con·nu'bi·al·ly** *adv.*

co·noid (kō'noid) *adj.* cone-shaped: also **co·noi'dal** *n.* a cone-shaped thing

con·quer (koŋ'kər) *vt.* [< OFr. < VL. *conquarere* < L. *com-*, intens. + *quaerere*, to seek] 1. to get possession or control of by or as by winning a war 2. to overcome by

physical, mental, or moral force; defeat —*vi.* to be victorious; win —**con'quer·a·ble** *adj.*

con·quer·or (-ər) *n.* one who conquers —**the Conqueror** William I of England

con·quest (koŋ'kwest, kon'-) *n.* [< OFr. < ML. < L. pp. of *conquirere*, to procure] 1. the act of conquering 2. something conquered 3. *a*) a winning of someone's love *b*) one whose love has been won —**the (Norman) Conquest** the conquering of England by the Normans under William the Conqueror in 1066

con·quis·ta·dor (kon kwis'tə dôr', -kēs'-; koŋ-) *n. pl.* **-dors', -dores'** [Sp., conqueror] any of the Spanish conquerors of Mexico, Peru, or other parts of America in the 16th century

Cons. Conservative

cons. 1. consolidated 2. consonant 3. consulting

con·san·guin·e·ous (kon'saŋ gwin'ē əs, -san-) *adj.* [see COM- & SANGUINE] having the same ancestor; closely related: also **con·san'guine** (-saŋ'gwin) —**con'san·guin'e·ous·ly** *adv.* —**con'san·guin'i·ty** *n.*

con·science (kon'shəns) *n.* [OFr. < L. < prp. of *conscire* < *com-*, with + *scire*, to know] a knowledge or sense of right and wrong, with a compulsion to do right; moral judgment that keeps one from violating one's ethical principles —**in (all) conscience** in fairness —**on one's conscience** causing one to feel guilty —**con'science·less** *adj.*

conscience clause a clause (in a law) exempting those whose religious or moral principles forbid compliance

conscience money money one pays to relieve one's conscience, as for some former dishonesty

con·science-strick·en (-strik'ən) *adj.* feeling guilty or remorseful because of having done some wrong

con·sci·en·tious (kon'shē en'shəs) *adj.* [see CONSCIENCE] 1. governed by, or done according to, what one knows is right; scrupulous 2. showing care and precision; painstaking —**con'sci·en'tious·ly** *adv.* —**con'sci·en'tious·ness** *n.*

conscientious objector a person who for reasons of conscience refuses to take part in warfare

con·scious (kon'shəs) *adj.* [< L. *conscius* < *conscire*: see CONSCIENCE] 1. having a feeling or knowledge (*with of* or *that*); aware; cognizant 2. able to feel and think; in the normal waking state 3. aware of oneself as a thinking being 4. *same as* SELF-CONSCIOUS 5. intentional [*conscious* humour] 6. known to or felt by oneself [*conscious* guilt] 7. interested in; concerned with [fashion-*conscious*] —**con'scious·ly** *adv.*

con·scious·ness (-nis) *n.* 1. the state of being conscious; awareness of one's own feelings, what is happening around one, etc. 2. the totality of one's thoughts, feelings, and impressions; conscious mind

con·script (kən skript'; *for adj. & n.* kon'skript) *vt.* to enrol for compulsory service in the forces or other national service —*adj.* conscripted —*n.* a conscripted person

con·scrip·tion (kən skrip'shən) *n.* [< L. *conscriptio*, enrolment < *com-*, with + *scribere*, to write] compulsory military or other national service

con·se·crate (kon'sə krāt') *vt.* **-crat'ed, -crat'ing** [< L. pp. of *consecrare* < *com-*, together + *sacrare*, to make holy < *sacer*, sacred] 1. to set apart as holy; make or declare sacred for religious use 2. to devote entirely; dedicate [to *consecrate* one's life to art] 3. to cause to be revered; hallow [ground *consecrated* by their martyrdom] —**con'·se·cra'tor** *n.* —**con'se·cra·to·ry** (-krə tər ē) *adj.*

con·se·cra·tion (kon'sə krā'shən) *n.* 1. a consecrating or being consecrated 2. a ceremony for this 3. the ordaining of someone to the office of bishop

con·sec·u·tive (kən sek'yə tiv) *adj.* [< Fr. < ML. < pp. of L. *consequi*: see CONSEQUENCE] 1. following in order, without interruption; successive 2. proceeding from one part or idea to the next in logical order —**con·sec'u·tive·ly** *adv.* —**con·sec'u·tive·ness** *n.*

con·sen·su·al (kən sen'shoo wəl) *adj.* [CONSENSUS + -AL] 1. *Law* existing by mutual consent, as a contract 2. *Physiol.* acting in sympathetic response to voluntary movements

con·sen·sus (kən sen'səs) *n.* [L. < pp. of *consentire*: see ff.] 1. an opinion held by all or most 2. general agreement

con·sent (kən sent') *vi.* [< OFr. < L. *consentire* < *com-*, with + *sentire*, to feel] 1. to agree (*to* do something) 2. to give permission or approval (*to* something) —*n.* 1. permission, approval, or assent 2. agreement [by common *consent*] —**con·sent'er** *n.*

con·se·quence (kon'sə kwəns) *n.* [OFr. < L. < prp. of *consequi* < *com-*, with + *sequi*, to follow] 1. a result of an action, process, etc.; effect 2. a logical result or conclusion; inference 3. importance as a cause [a matter of slight *consequence*] 4. importance in rank; influence [a person of *consequence*] —**in consequence (of)** as a result (of) —**take the consequences** to accept the results of one's actions

con·se·quent (-kwənt) *adj.* 1. following as a result; resulting 2. proceeding in logical sequence —*n.* anything that follows —**consequent on** (or **upon**) 1. following as a result of 2. inferred from

con·se·quen·tial (kon'sə kwen'shəl) *adj.* 1. following as an effect **2.** important **—con'se·quen'ti·al'i·ty** (-shē al'ə tē) **—con'se·quen'tial·ness** *n.* **—con'se·quen'tial·ly** *adv.*

con·se·quent·ly (kon'sə kwənt'lē) *adv.* as a result; by logical inference; therefore

con·ser·van·cy (kən sur'vən sē) *n.* **1.** a commission with jurisdiction over a river or port **2.** conservation of natural resources

con·ser·va·tion (kon'sər vā'shən) *n.* **1.** a conserving; protection from loss, waste, etc. **2.** the official care and protection of natural resources, as forests **—con'ser·va'·tion·al** *adj.* **—con'ser·va'tion·ist** *n.*

conservation of energy the principle that energy is never consumed but only changes form, and that the total energy in the universe remains fixed

conservation of matter (or **mass**) the principle that matter is neither created nor destroyed during any physical or chemical change

con·ser·va·tism (kən sur'və tiz'm) *n.* the principles and practices of a conservative person or party

con·ser·va·tive (-tiv) *adj.* **1.** conserving or tending to conserve; preservative **2.** tending to preserve established institutions or methods and to resist or oppose any changes in these **3.** [C-] designating or of the major right-wing political party of Great Britain or of Canada **4.** [C-] designating or of a movement in Judaism accepting moderate adaptation of religious ritual, etc. to modern conditions **5.** moderate; cautious; safe **—n.** **1.** a conservative person **2.** [C-] a member of a Conservative party **—con'ser·va·tive·ly** *adv.* **—con'ser·va·tive·ness** *n.*

con·ser·va·toire (kən sur'və twär') *n.* [Fr.] a school or academy of music or art

con·ser·va·tor (kon'sər vāt'ər, kən sur'və tər) *n.* [see CONSERVE] a protector, guardian, or custodian

con·ser·va·to·ry (kən sur'və tər ē, -trē) *n., pl.* **-ries** [see ff.] **1.** a room enclosed in glass, for growing and showing plants; noncommercial greenhouse **2.** *same as* CONSERVATOIRE

con·serve (kən surv') *vt.* **-served', -serv'ing** [< OFr. < L. *conservare* < *com-*, with + *servare*, to guard] **1.** to keep from being damaged, lost, or wasted **2.** to preserve (a foodstuff, esp. fruit) with sugar **—n.** [*often pl.*] fruit, etc., preserved with sugar **—con·serv'a·ble** *adj.* **—con·serv'er** *n.*

con·sid·er (kən sid'ər) *vt.* [< OFr. < L. *considerare*, to observe < *com-*, with + *sidus*, a star] **1.** to think about in order to understand or decide; ponder **2.** to keep in mind; take into account **3.** to be thoughtful of (others, their feelings, etc.) **4.** to regard as; think to be [I *consider* him an expert] **—vi.** to think carefully; reflect

con·sid·er·a·ble (-ə b'l) *adj.* **1.** worth considering; important **2.** much or large **—con·sid'er·a·bly** *adv.*

con·sid·er·ate (-it) *adj.* [see CONSIDER] having or showing regard for others and their feelings; thoughtful **—con·sid'·er·ate·ly** *adv.* **—con·sid'er·ate·ness** *n.*

con·sid·er·a·tion (kən sid'ə rā'shən) *n.* **1.** the act of considering; deliberation **2.** *a)* thoughtful or sympathetic regard for others *b)* esteem **3.** something considered in making a decision **4.** a thought or opinion produced by considering **5.** a recompense, as for a service rendered; fee; compensation **—in consideration of 1.** because of **2.** in return for **—take into consideration** to keep in mind; take into account **—under consideration** being thought over

con·sid·ered (kən sid'ərd) *adj.* arrived at after careful thought

con·sid·er·ing (-ər iŋ) *prep.* in view of; taking into account **—adv.** [Colloq.] all things considered

con·sign (kən sīn') *vt.* [L. *consignare*, to seal < *com-*, together + *signare* < *signum*, a sign] **1.** to hand over; deliver **2.** to put in the care of another; entrust **3.** to assign to an undesirable position or place; relegate **4.** to send or deliver (goods) **—con·sign'a·ble** *adj.* **—con·sign·ee** (kon'sī nē', kən sī'nē') *n.* **—con·sign'or** *or* **con·sign'er** *n.*

con·sign·ment (-mənt) *n.* **1.** a consigning or being consigned **2.** something consigned; esp., a shipment of goods sent to an agent for sale or safekeeping

con·sist (kən sist') *vi.* [L. *consistere* < *com-*, together + *sistere*, to stand] **1.** to be formed or composed (*of*) **2.** to be contained or inherent (*in*) as a cause, characteristic, etc. **3.** to exist in harmony (*with*)

con·sis·ten·cy (-ən sē) *n., pl.* **-cies 1.** *a)* firmness or thickness, as of a liquid *b)* degree of this **2.** agreement; harmony **3.** conformity with previous practice or principle Also **con·sis'tence**

con·sis·tent (-ənt) *adj.* [see CONSIST] **1.** [Rare] firm; solid **2.** in agreement or harmony; compatible **3.** holding always to the same principles or practice **—con·sis'tent·ly** *adv.*

con·sis·to·ry (kən sis'tər ē) *n., pl.* **-ries** [< OFr. < L. *consistorium*, place of assembly < *consistere*: see CONSIST] **1.** a church council or court, as the papal senate **2.** a session of such a body **—con·sis·to·ri·al** (kon'sis tôr'ē əl) *adj.*

con·so·la·tion (kon'sə lā'shən) *n.* **1.** a consoling or being consoled; solace **2.** a person or thing that consoles

consolation prize a prize given to a contestant who does well but does not win

con·sol·a·to·ry (kən sol'ə tər ē, -sōl'-) *adj.* consoling or tending to console; comforting

con·sole¹ (kən sōl') *vt.* **-soled', -sol'ing** [< Fr. < L. *consolari* < *com-*, with + *solari*, to solace] to make feel less sad or disappointed; comfort **—con·sol'a·ble** *adj.* **—con·sol'ing·ly** *adv.*

con·sole² (kon'sōl) *n.* [Fr.] **1.** an ornamental bracket for supporting a shelf, bust, cornice, etc. **2.** the desklike frame containing the keys, stops, pedals, etc. of an organ **3.** a radio, television, or cabinet designed to stand on the floor **4.** an instrument panel or unit, containing the controls for operating aircraft, computers, etc.

CONSOLE
(of an organ)

console table a small table with legs resembling consoles, placed against a wall

con·sol·i·date (kən sol'ə dāt') *vt., vi.* **-dat'ed, -dat'ing** [< L. pp. of *consolidare* < *com-*, together + *solidare* < *solidus*, solid] **1.** to combine into a single whole; merge; unite **2.** to make or become strong, stable, etc. [the troops *consolidated* their position] **3.** to make or become solid or compact **—con·sol'i·da'tion** *n.* **—con·sol'i·da'tor** *n.*

con·sols (kon'solz, kon solz') *n.pl.* [< *consolidated annuities*] British government securities

con·som·mé (kon'səm ā) *n.* [Fr., orig. pp. of *consommer*, CONSUMMATE, confused with *consumer*, CONSUME] a clear soup made by boiling meat, and sometimes vegetables, in water and straining

con·so·nance (kon'sə nəns) *n.* [OFr. < L. < prp. of *consonare* < *com-*, with + *sonare*, to sound < *sonus*, a sound] **1.** harmony or agreement of elements or parts; accord **2.** harmony of musical tones Also **con'so·nan·cy**

con·so·nant (kon'sə nənt) *adj.* [see prec.] **1.** in harmony or agreement; in accord **2.** harmonious in tone: opposed to DISSONANT **3.** consonantal **—n.** **1.** any speech sound produced by obstructing the breath stream in any of various ways, as the sounds of p, t, k, m, l, f, etc. **2.** a letter or symbol representing such a sound **—con'so·nant·ly** *adv.*

con·so·nan·tal (kon'sə nant''l) *adj.* of, being, or having a consonant or consonants

con·sort¹ (kon'sôrt; *for v.* kən sôrt') *n.* [< OFr. < L. *consors* (gen. *consortis*) < *com-*, with + *sors*, a share] **1.** orig., a partner; companion **2.** a wife or husband; spouse, esp. of a reigning king or queen **3.** a ship that travels with another **—vi.** **1.** to keep company; associate **2.** to agree; be in accord **—vt.** to associate; join

con·sort² (kon'sôrt) *n.* [altered < CONCERT] **1.** harmony of sounds **2.** an ensemble of musicians

con·sor·ti·um (kən sôr'tē əm) *n., pl.* **-ti·a** (-ə) [L., community of goods: see CONSORT¹] **1.** an alliance, as of two or more business firms in some venture **2.** an international banking agreement or association

con·spec·tus (kən spek'təs) *n.* [L., a view, pp. of *conspicere*: see ff.] **1.** a general view; survey **2.** a summary; synopsis; digest

con·spic·u·ous (kən spik'yōō wəs) *adj.* [< L. < *conspicere*, to look at < *com-*, intens. + *specere*, to see] **1.** easy to see or perceive; obvious **2.** attracting attention by being outstanding; striking [*conspicuous* bravery, *conspicuous* folly] **—con·spic'u·ous·ly** *adv.* **—con·spic'u·ous·ness** *n.*

con·spir·a·cy (kən spir'ə sē) *n., pl.* **-cies 1.** a conspiring, esp. in an unlawful or harmful plot **2.** such a plot **3.** the group taking part in such a plot **4.** a combining or working together [the *conspiracy* of events]

conspiracy of silence an agreement not to mention a specific subject

con·spir·a·tor (-tər) *n.* a person who takes part in a conspiracy **—con·spir·a·to·ri·al** (kən spir'ə tôr'ē əl) *adj.* **—con·spir'a·to'ri·al·ly** *adv.*

con·spire (kən spīr') *vi.* **-spired', -spir'ing** [< OFr. < L. *conspirare* < *com-*, together + *spirare*, to breathe] **1.** to plan and act together secretly, esp. in order to commit a crime **2.** to combine or work together for any purpose or effect [events *conspired* to ruin him]

con spi·ri·to (kon spir'i tō') [It.] *Music* with spirit; with vigour

con·sta·ble (kun'stə b'l, kon'-) *n.* [< OFr. < LL. *comes stabuli*, lit., count of the stable] **1.** in the Middle Ages, the highest ranking official of a royal household, court, etc. **2.** formerly, a peace officer in a town or village **3.** the keeper or governor of a royal castle **4.** a policeman

con·stab·u·lar·y (kən stab'yə lər ē) *n., pl.* **-ies** the police force of a town or district **—adj.** of constables or a constabulary: also **con·stab'u·lar** (-lər)

con·stant (kon'stənt) *adj.* [< OFr. < L. prp. of *constare* < *com-*, together + *stare*, to stand] **1.** not changing; remaining the same; specif., *a)* remaining firm in purpose; resolute *b)* loyal; faithful *c)* regular; stable; unvarying **2.**

going on all the time; continual; persistent [*constant* interruptions] —*n.* 1. anything that does not change or vary 2. *Math., Physics a*) a quantity that always has the same value *b*) a quantity or factor assumed to have one value throughout a particular discussion or investigation: symbol, c (or k): opposed to VARIABLE —**con′stan·cy** *n.* —**con′stant·ly** *adv.*

con·stel·late (kon′stə lāt′) *vi., vt.* -**lat′ed, -lat′ing** to unite in a constellation; cluster

con·stel·la·tion (kon′stə lā′shən) *n.* [< OFr. < LL. < L. *com-*, with + pp. of *stellare*, to shine < *stella*, a star] 1. a) an arbitrary group of fixed stars, usually named after some object, animal, or mythological being that they supposedly suggest in outline *b*) the part of the heavens occupied by such a group 2. any brilliant cluster, gathering, or collection 3. a group of related ideas, feelings, etc. —**con′stel·la·to·ry** (kən stel′ə tər ē) *adj.*

con·ster·nate (kon′stər nāt′) *vt.* -**nat′ed, -nat′ing** to overcome with consternation; dismay

con·ster·na·tion (kon′stər nā′shən) *n.* [< L. < *consternare*, to throw into confusion; terrify] great fear or shock that makes one feel helpless or bewildered

con·sti·pate (kon′stə pāt′) *vt.* -**pat′ed, -pat′ing** [< L. pp. of *constipare* < *com-*, together + *stipare*, to cram] to cause constipation in

con·sti·pa·tion (kon′stə pā′shən) *n.* [see prec.] a condition in which the faeces are hard and elimination from the bowels is infrequent and difficult

con·stit·u·en·cy (kən stich′ oo wən sē) *n., pl.* -**cies** [< CONSTITUENT + -CY] 1. all the people, esp. voters, served by a particular elected official 2. the district of such a group of voters, etc.

con·stit·u·ent (-oo wənt) *adj.* [< L. prp. of *constituere*: see ff.] 1. necessary in forming a whole; component [a *constituent* part] 2. that can appoint or elect 3. authorized to make or revise a constitution or establish a government [a *constituent* assembly] —*n.* 1. a person who appoints another as his representative 2. a member of a constituency 3. a necessary part or element; component

con·sti·tute (kon′stə tyoot′) *vt.* -**tut′ed, -tut′ing** [< L. pp. of *constituere* < *com-*, together + *statuere*, to set] 1. to establish (a law, government, institution, etc.) 2. to set up (an assembly, proceeding, etc.) in a legal form 3. to give a certain office or function to [we *constitute* you our spokesman] 4. to make up; form; compose

con·sti·tu·tion (kon′stə tyoo′shən) *n.* 1. a constituting; establishment, appointment, or formation 2. structure; organization; makeup 3. the physical makeup of a person 4. *a*) the system of fundamental laws and principles of a government, state, society, etc. *b*) a document in which these are written down

con·sti·tu·tion·al (-əl) *adj.* 1. of or in the constitution of a person or thing; basic; essential 2. for improving a person's constitution 3. of or in accordance with the constitution of a nation, society, etc. [*constitutional* right, *constitutional* monarchy] 4. upholding the constitution —*n.* a walk or other exercise taken for one's health —**con′sti·tu′tion·al′i·ty** (-shə nal′ə tē) *n.* —**con′sti·tu′tion·al·ly** *adv.*

con·sti·tu·tion·al·ism (-əl iz′m) *n.* 1. government according to a constitution 2. adherence to constitutional principles or government —**con′sti·tu′tion·al·ist** *n.*

con·sti·tu·tive (kon′stə tyoot′iv) *adj.* 1. having power to establish, appoint, or enact 2. making a thing what it is; basic 3. forming a part (*of*); constituent —**con′sti·tu′tive·ly** *adv.*

con·strain (kən strān′) *vt.* [< OFr. < L. *constringere* < *com-*, together + *stringere*, to draw tight] 1. to force into, or hold in, close bounds; confine 2. to hold back or in by force or strain; restrain 3. to compel [*constrained* to agree]

con·strained (-strānd′) *adj.* 1. compelled; obliged 2. forced and unnatural [a *constrained* laugh] —**con·strain′ed·ly** (-strā′nid lē) *adv.*

con·straint (-strānt′) *n.* 1. a constraining or being constrained; specif., *a*) confinement or restriction *b*) compulsion or coercion 2. a forced, unnatural manner

con·strict (kən strikt′) *vt.* [< L. pp. of *constringere*: see CONSTRAIN] 1. to make smaller or narrower by binding, squeezing, etc.; contract 2. to hold in; limit —**con·stric′tive** *adj.*

con·stric·tion (-strik′shən) *n.* 1. a constricting or being constricted 2. a feeling of tightness or pressure, as in the chest 3. something that constricts 4. a constricted part

con·stric·tor (-strik′tər) *n.* that which constricts; specif., *a*) a muscle that contracts an opening or compresses an organ *b*) a snake that kills by coiling around its prey and squeezing

con·struct (kən strukt′; *for n.* kon′strukt) *vt.* [< L. pp. of *construere* < *com-*, together + *struere*, to pile up] 1. to build, form, or devise by fitting parts or elements together systematically 2. *Geom.* to draw (a figure) so as to meet the specified requirements —*n.* something built or put together systematically —**con·struc′tor, con·struct′er** *n.*

con·struc·tion (kən struk′shən) *n.* 1. the act or process of constructing 2. the way in which something is constructed

3. something constructed; structure; building 4. an explanation or interpretation, as of a statement 5. the arrangement and relation of words in a phrase, clause, or sentence 6. a three-dimensional work of art of various materials —**con·struc′tion·al** *adj.* —**con·struc′tion·al·ly** *adv.*

con·struc·tive (kən struk′tiv) *adj.* 1. helping to construct; leading to improvements [*constructive* criticism] 2. of construction or structure 3. inferred or implied by legal or judicial interpretation —**con·struc′tive·ly** *adv.* —**con·struc′tive·ness** *n.*

con·struc·tiv·ism (-iz′m) *n.* a movement in sculpture, painting, etc. characterized by abstract and geometric design and massive structural form

con·strue (kən stroo′) *vt.* -**strued′, -stru′ing** [< L. *construere*: see CONSTRUCT] 1. to analyse (a sentence, clause, etc.) so as to show its syntactical construction and meaning 2. to translate 3. to explain or deduce the meaning of; interpret [her silence was *construed* as agreement] 4. *Gram.* to combine in syntax [the verb "let" unlike "permit" is *construed* with an infinitive omitting the "to"]

con·sub·stan·tial (kon′sub stan′shəl) *adj.* [ME. < LL. (Eccles.) *consubstantialis*] having the same substance or essential nature —**con′sub·stan′ti·al′i·ty** (-shē al′ə tē) *n.*

con·sub·stan·ti·a·tion (-stan′shē ā′shən) *n.* [ML. (Eccles.) *consubstantio*] *Theol.* the doctrine that the substance of the bread and wine of the Eucharist exists, after consecration, together with the substance of the body and blood of Christ but is not changed into it: cf. TRANSUBSTANTIATION

con·sue·tude (kon′swi tyood′) *n.* [ME. < OFr. < L. *consuetudo*: see CUSTOM] established custom or usage

con·sul (kon′s'l) *n.* [< OFr. < L. < *consulere*, to deliberate] 1. either of the two chief magistrates of the ancient Roman republic 2. any of the three highest officials of the French republic from 1799 to 1804 3. a government official appointed to live in a foreign city and serve his country's citizens and business interests there —**con′sul·ar** (kon′-syool ər) *adj.* —**con′sul·ship′** *n.*

con·sul·ate (kon′syool it) *n.* 1. the position, powers, and duties of a consul 2. the office or residence of a consul 3. the term of office of a consul 4. government by consuls; specif., [C-] the government of France from 1799 to 1804

consul general *pl.* **consuls general, consul generals** a consul in a principal commercial city, who supervises other consuls within his district

con·sult (kən sult′) *vi.* [L. *consultare* < pp. of *consulere*, to deliberate] to talk things over in order to decide something; confer —*vt.* 1. *a*) to ask the advice of *b*) to refer to, esp. for information 2. to show regard for; consider [*consult* your own wishes in the matter] —**con·sult′er** *n.*

con·sult·ant (kən sul′tənt) *n.* 1. a person who consults with another 2. a specialist physician who examines a patient to confirm a diagnosis made by another physician 3. an expert called on for professional or technical advice or opinions —**con·sul′tan·cy** *n.*

con·sul·ta·tion (kon′s'l tā′shən) *n.* 1. the act of consulting 2. a meeting to discuss, decide, or plan something —**con·sul·ta·tive** (kən sul′tə tiv), **con·sul′ta·to·ry** (-tər ē) *adj.*

con·sult·ing (kən sult′in) *adj.* acting in an advisory capacity on professional matters [a *consulting* engineer]

consulting room a room used by a doctor when examining patients

con·sume (kən syoom′) *vt.* -**sumed′, -sum′ing** [< OFr. < L. *consumere* < *com-*, together + *sumere*, to take < *sub-*, under + *emere*, to buy] 1. to destroy, as by fire 2. to use up; spend or waste (time, energy, money, etc.) 3. to eat or drink; devour 4. to engross or obsess [*consumed* with envy] —**con·sum′a·ble** *adj.*

con·sum·ed·ly (-id lē) *adv.* [Now Rare] extremely or excessively

con·sum·er (kən syoo′mər) *n.* a person or thing that consumes; specif., a person who buys goods or services for his own needs and not for resale or to use in the production of other goods for resale: opposed to PRODUCER

consumer goods goods required for personal needs rather than for the production of other goods or services

con·sum·er·ism (-iz′m) *n.* 1. the movement for consumer protection in connection with defective and unsafe products, misleading business practices, etc. 2. the consumption of goods and services

consumer research research conducted to discover the needs and desires of consumers

con·sum·mate (kən sum′it; *for v.* kon′sə māt′, -syoo-) *adj.* [< L. pp. of *consummare*, to sum up < *com-*, together + *summa*, a SUM] 1. complete or perfect 2. highly expert [a *consummate* liar] —*vt.* -**mat′ed, -mat′ing** 1. to bring to completion or fulfilment; finish 2. to make (a marriage) actual by sexual intercourse —**con·sum′mate·ly** *adv.* —**con·sum·ma·tive** (kon′sə māt iv), **con·sum′ma·to·ry** (-ə tər ē) *adj.* —**con′sum·ma′tor** *n.*

con·sum·ma·tion (kon'sə mā'shən) *n.* 1. a consummating or being consummated 2. an end; outcome

con·sump·tion (kən sump'shən) *n.* 1. *a)* a consuming or being consumed; specif., the using up of goods or services *b)* the amount consumed 2. a disease causing wasting away of the body; esp., tuberculosis of the lungs

con·sump·tive (-tiv) *adj.* 1. consuming or tending to consume; destructive; wasteful 2. *Med.* of, having, or relating to tuberculosis of the lungs —*n.* a person who has tuberculosis of the lungs —**con·sump'tive·ly** *adv.*

cont. 1. containing 2. contents 3. continent(al) 4. continue 5. continued

con·tact (kon'takt) *n.* [< L. pp. of *contingere* < *com-*, together + *tangere*, to touch] 1. the act of touching or meeting 2. the state or fact of being in touch, communication, or association (*with*) 3. *a)* an acquaintance, esp. one who is influential *b)* a connection with such a person 4. a person who has been exposed to a contagious disease and who may transmit it 5. *Elec. a)* a connection between two conductors in a circuit *b)* a device for opening and closing such a connection —*vt.* 1. to place in contact 2. to get in touch with —*vi.* to be in or come into contact —*adj.* of, involving, or relating to contact

contact lens a tiny, thin correctional lens of glass or plastic placed in the fluid over the cornea of the eye

con·ta·gion (kən tā'jən) *n.* [L. *contagio*, a touching < *contingere:* see CONTACT] 1. the spreading of disease by contact 2. a contagious disease 3. the causative agent of a communicable disease 4. *a)* the spreading of an emotion, idea, etc. from person to person *b)* the emotion, idea, etc. so spread

con·ta·gious (-jəs) *adj.* [< OFr. < LL. *contagiosus*] 1. spread by contact: said of diseases 2. carrying the causative agent of such a disease 3. spreading from person to person —**con·ta'gious·ly** *adv.* —**con·ta'gious·ness** *n.*

con·tain (kən tān') *vt.* [< OFr. < L. *continere* < *com-*, together + *tenere*, to hold] 1. to have in it; hold, enclose, or include 2. to have the capacity for holding 3. to hold back or within fixed limits; specif., *a)* to restrain (one's feelings, oneself, etc.) *b)* to check the power or expansion of 4. to be divisible by, esp. without a remainder [10 *contains* 5 and 2] —**con·tain'a·ble** *adj.*

con·tain·er (-ər) *n.* 1. a thing for containing something; box, tin, jar, etc. 2. a reusable, standardized receptacle for carrying cargo

con·tain·er·ize (-īz') *vt.* -ized', -iz'ing to pack (general cargo) in large, standardized containers for more efficient shipment —**con·tain'er·i·za'tion** *n.*

container ship a ship which has been designed to carry containerized cargo

con·tain·ment (-mənt) *n.* the policy of attempting to prevent the influence of an opposing nation or political system from spreading

con·tam·i·nant (kən tam'ə nənt) *n.* a substance that contaminates another substance, the air, water, etc.

con·tam·i·nate (-ə nāt') *vt.* -nat'ed, -nat'ing [< L. pp. of *contaminare*, to defile < *contamen*, contact < *com-*, together + base of *tangere*, to touch] to make impure, infected, corrupt, radioactive, etc. by contact with or addition of something; pollute; defile; sully; taint —**con·tam'i·na'tion** *n.* —**con·tam'i·na'tive** *adj.* —**con·tam'i·na'tor** *n.*

con·tan·go (kən tan'gō) *n., pl.* -gos [19th-c. < ?] 1. a postponement of payment for and delivery of stocks or shares from one account day to the next 2. the fee paid for such a postponement

contd. continued

conte (kônt) *n.* [Fr.] a short story, esp. of adventure

con·temn (kən tem') *vt.* [< OFr. < L. *contemnere* < *com-*, intens. + *temnere*, to scorn] to treat with contempt; scorn —**con·temn'er, con·tem'nor** (-tem'ər, -tem'nər) *n.*

con·tem·plate (kon'təm plāt') *vt.* -plat'ed, -plat'ing [< L. pp. of *contemplari*, to observe (orig., in augury, to mark out a space for observation) < *com-*, intens. + *templum*, TEMPLE[1]] 1. to look at intently; gaze at 2. to think about intently; study carefully; consider 3. to expect or intend —*vi.* to meditate or muse —**con'tem·pla'tion** *n.* —**con'-tem·pla'tor** *n.*

con·tem·pla·tive (kən tem'plə tiv, kon'təm plāt'iv) *adj.* 1. of or inclined to contemplation; thoughtful; meditative 2. designating any of several religious orders dedicated to prayer and meditation —*n.* a member of a contemplative religious order —**com·tem'pla·tive·ly** *adv.* —**con·tem'-pla·tive·ness** *n.*

con·tem·po·ra·ne·ous (kən tem'pə rā'nē əs) *adj.* [< L. < *com-*, with + *tempus* (gen. *temporis*), time] existing or happening at the same time —**con·tem'po·ra·ne'i·ty** (-pər ə nē'ə tē), **con·tem'po·ra'ne·ous·ness** *n.* —**con·tem'-po·ra'ne·ous·ly** *adv.*

con·tem·po·rar·y (kən tem'pə rer ē) *adj.* [< L. *com-*, with + *temporarius* < *tempus*, time] 1. living or happening in the same period 2. of about the same age 3. of or in the style of the present or recent times; modern —*n., pl.* -ries a person or thing of the same period or about the same age as another or others

con·tem·po·rize (kən tem'pə rīz') *vt., vi.* -rized', -riz'ing to make or become contemporary

con·tempt (kən tempt') *n.* [OFr. < L. pp. of *contemnere:* see CONTEMN] 1. the feeling of a person towards someone or something he considers worthless or beneath notice; scorn 2. the condition of being despised or scorned 3. *Law* a showing disrespect for the dignity of a court: in full, **contempt of court**

con·tempt·i·ble (kən temp'tə b'l) *adj.* deserving contempt or scorn; despicable —**con·tempt'i·bil'i·ty, con·tempt'-i·ble·ness** *n.* —**con·tempt'i·bly** *adv.*

con·temp·tu·ous (kən temp'tyoo wəs) *adj.* full of contempt; scornful; disdainful —**con·temp'tu·ous·ly** *adv.* —**con·temp'-tu·ous·ness** *n.*

con·tend (kən tend') *vi.* [< L. *contendere* < *com-*, together + *tendere*, to stretch] 1. to strive in combat; fight 2. to strive in debate; argue 3. to strive in competition; compete; vie —*vt.* to hold to be a fact; assert —**con·tend'er** *n.*

con·tent¹ (kən tent') *adj.* [< OFr. < L. pp. of *continere:* see CONTAIN] 1. happy enough with what one has or is; satisfied 2. willing; assenting —*vt.* to make content; satisfy —*n.* contentment

con·tent² (kon'tent) *n.* [< L. pp. of *continere:* see CONTAIN] 1. [usually pl.] *a)* all that is contained in something *b)* all that is dealt with in a writing or speech [a table of *contents*] 2. *a)* all that is dealt with in an area of study, work of art, discussion, etc. *b)* meaning; substance 3. the amount contained [iron with a high carbon *content*]

con·tent·ed (kən ten'tid) *adj.* having or showing no desire for something more or different; satisfied —**con·tent'ed·ly** *adv.* —**con·tent'ed·ness** *n.*

con·ten·tion (kən ten'shən) *n.* [see CONTEND] 1. the act of contending; strife, struggle, controversy, dispute, quarrel, etc. 2. a statement or point that one argues for as true or valid

con·ten·tious (-ten'shəs) *adj.* 1. quarrelsome 2. of or characterized by contention —**con·ten'tious·ly** *adv.* —**con·ten'tious·ness** *n.*

con·tent·ment (kən tent'mənt) *n.* the state, quality, or fact of being contented

con·ter·mi·nous (kən tur'mə nəs, kon-) *adj.* [< L. < *com-*, together + *terminus*, an end] 1. having a common boundary; contiguous 2. contained within the same boundaries or limits —**con·ter'mi·nous·ly** *adv.*

con·tes·sa (kon tes'ə) *n.* [It.] an Italian countess

con·test (kən test'; *for n.* kon'test) *vt.* [< Fr. < L. *contestari* < *com-*, together + *testari*, to bear witness < *testis*, a witness] 1. to try to disprove or invalidate (something); dispute [to *contest* a will] 2. to fight for; struggle to win or keep —*vi.* to struggle (*with* or *against*); contend —*n.* 1. a fight, struggle, or controversy 2. any race, game, etc. in which individuals or teams compete to determine the winner —**con·test'a·ble** *adj.* —**con·test'er** *n.*

con·test·ant (kən tes'tant) *n.* [Fr.] 1. one that competes in a contest 2. one who contests a claim, decision, etc.

con·text (kon'tekst) *n.* [< L. pp. of *contexere* < *com-*, together + *texere*, to weave] the parts of a sentence, paragraph, etc. immediately next to or surrounding a specified word or passage and determining its exact meaning [to quote a remark out of *context*] —**con·tex·tu·al** (kən teks'tyoo wəl) *adj.* —**con·tex'tu·al·ly** *adv.*

con·ti·gu·i·ty (kon'tə gyoo'ə tē) *n., pl.* -ties the state of being contiguous; nearness or contact

con·tig·u·ous (kən tig'yoo wəs) *adj.* [< L. *contiguus* < base of *contingere:* see CONTACT] 1. in physical contact; touching along all or most of one side 2. near, next, or adjacent —**con·tig'u·ous·ly** *adv.* —**con·tig'u·ous·ness** *n.*

con·ti·nence (kon'tin əns) *n.* [see ff.] 1. self-restraint; moderation 2. self-restraint in sexual activity; esp., total abstinence 3. the ability to control urination and defecation

con·ti·nent (-ənt) *adj.* [< OFr. < L. prp. of *continere:* see CONTAIN] 1. self-restrained; temperate 2. characterized by self-restraint, esp. by total abstinence, in sexual activity 3. able to control urination and defecation —*n.* any of the main large land areas of the earth (Africa, Asia, Australia, Europe, N. America, S. America, and, sometimes, Antarctica) —**the Continent** all Europe except the British Isles —**con'ti·nent·ly** *adv.*

con·ti·nen·tal (kon'tin en't'l) *adj.* 1. of a continent 2. [*sometimes* C-] European 3. [C-] of the American colonies at the time of the War of American Independence —*n.* 1. [*usually* C-] a European 2. [C-] a soldier of the American army during the War of American Independence —**con'-ti·nen'tal·ly** *adv.*

continental breakfast a breakfast consisting of coffee, rolls or bread, and jam, etc.

continental climate the type of climate experienced in the centres of continents, characterized by extremes of temperature

continental drift the hypothetical drifting of continents caused by currents in the earth's mantle

continental quilt *same as* DUVET
continental shelf the submerged, gradually sloping shelf of land that borders a continent and ends in a steep descent (**continental slope**) to the deep sea
con·tin·gen·cy (kən tin′jən sē) *n., pl.* **-cies** 1. a contingent quality or condition; esp., dependence on chance or uncertain conditions 2. a possible, unforeseen, or accidental occurrence 3. some thing or event which depends on or is incidental to another Also **con·tin′gence**
con·tin·gent (-jənt) *adj.* [< L. prp. of *contingere*: see CONTACT] 1. that may or may not happen; possible 2. happening by chance; accidental 3. unpredictable because dependent on chance 4. dependent (*on* or *upon* an uncertainty); conditional —*n.* 1. a chance happening 2. a share or quota, as of troops, labourers, etc. 3. a group forming part of a larger group —**con·tin′gent·ly** *adv.*
con·tin·u·al (kən tin′yoo wəl) *adj.* 1. repeated often; going on in rapid succession 2. going on uninterruptedly; continuous —**con·tin′u·al·ly** *adv.*
con·tin·u·ance (-yoo wəns) *n.* 1. the act or process of continuing 2. the time during which an action or state lasts; duration 3. the fact of remaining (*in* a place or condition); stay 4. an unbroken succession 5. [Rare] a sequel
con·tin·u·ant (-yoo wənt) *n.* a speech sound that can be prolonged as long as the breath lasts, as *f, m, l*
con·tin·u·a·tion (kən tin′yoo wā′shən) *n.* 1. a keeping up or going on without stopping 2. a beginning again after an interruption; resumption 3. a part or thing by which something is continued; extension, supplement, sequel, etc.
con·tin·ue (kən tin′yoo, -yoo) *vi.* **-ued, -u·ing** [< OFr. < L. *continuare*, to join < *continere*: see CONTAIN] 1. to last; endure 2. to go on in a specified course of action or condition; persist 3. to go on or extend 4. to stay 5. to go on again after an interruption; resume —*vt.* 1. to go on with; carry on; keep up 2. to extend 3. to resume 4. to cause to remain; retain —**con·tin′u·a·ble** *adj.* —**con·tin′·u·er** *n.*
con·ti·nu·i·ty (kon′tə nyoo′ə tē) *n., pl.* **-ties** 1. a continuous state or quality 2. an unbroken, coherent whole 3. continuous duration 4. the script or scenario for a film, radio or television programme, etc. 5. a series of comments connecting the parts of a radio or television programme
continuity girl one who sees that details of dress, properties, etc. in a film are consistent from scene to scene
con·tin·u·o (kən tin′yoo wō′) *n.* [It., orig., continuous] *Music* a continuous base accompaniment played as on a harpsichord or organ
con·tin·u·ous (kən tin′yoo wəs) *adj.* [L. *continuus*: see CONTINUE] going on or extending without interruption or break; unbroken; connected —**con·tin′u·ous·ly** *adv.*
con·tin·u·um (-yoo wəm) *n., pl.* **-u·a** (-wə), **-u·ums** [L.] a continuous whole, quantity, or series
con·tort (kən tôrt′) *vt., vi.* [< L. pp. of *contorquere* < *com-*, together + *torquere*, to twist] to twist or wrench out of its usual form into one that is grotesque; distort violently —**con·tor′tion** *n.* —**con·tor′tive** *adj.*
con·tor·tion·ist (kən tôr′shən ist) *n.* a person who can twist his body into unnatural positions
con·tour (kon′toor) *n.* [Fr. < It. < LL. *contornare* < L. *com-*, intens. + *tornare*, to turn: see TURN] the outline of a figure, land, etc. —*vt.* 1. to represent in contour 2. to shape or mould to the contour of something —*adj.* 1. made so as to conform to the shape of something 2. characterized by the making of furrows along the natural contour lines so as to avoid erosion [*contour* ploughing]
contour map a map with lines (**contour lines**) connecting all points of the same elevation
contr. 1. contract 2. contraction 3. contrary
con·tra- [< L. *contra*, against] a prefix meaning: 1. against, opposite, opposed to 2. lower in musical pitch [*contrabassoon*]
con·tra·band (kon′trə band′) *n.* [< Sp. < It. < *contra-*, against + *bando* < VL. *bannum* (akin to BAN¹)] 1. unlawful or prohibited trade 2. smuggled goods, forbidden by law to be imported and exported 3. *same as* CONTRABAND OF WAR —*adj.* forbidden by law to be imported or exported —**con′·tra·band′ist** *n.*
contraband of war war materiel which, by international law, may be seized by a belligerent when shipped to the other one by a neutral
con·tra·bass (kon′trə bās′) *adj.* [see CONTRA- & BASS¹] having its pitch an octave lower than the normal bass —*n.* *same as* DOUBLE BASS —**con′tra·bass′ist** *n.*
con·tra·bas·soon (kon′trə bə soon′) *n.* the double bassoon, which is larger than the ordinary bassoon and an octave lower in pitch
con·tra·cep·tion (kon′trə sep′shən) *n.* [CONTRA- + (CON)CEPTION] intentional prevention of the fertilization of the human ovum, as by special devices, drugs, etc. —**con′·tra·cep′tive** *adj., n.*
con·tract (kon′trakt for n. & usually for vt. 1 & vi. 1; kən trakt′ for v. generally) *n.* [OFr. < L. pp. of *contrahere* <

com-, together + *trahere*, to draw] 1. an agreement to do something, esp. a written one enforceable by law 2. a formal agreement of marriage or betrothal 3. a document containing the terms of an agreement 4. *Bridge a)* the number of tricks bid by the highest bidder *b) same as* CONTRACT BRIDGE —*vt.* 1. to enter upon, or undertake, by contract 2. *a)* to get, acquire, or incur *b)* to catch (a disease) 3. to reduce in size; draw together; shrink 4. to narrow in scope; restrict 5. *Gram.* to shorten (a word or phrase) by the omission of a letter or sound (*I'm, e'er*) —*vi.* 1. to make a contract 2. to become reduced in size or bulk —**contract out** to agree not to participate in something, esp. the state pension scheme —**con·tract′i·bil′i·ty** *n.* —**con·tract′i·ble** *adj.*
con·tract bridge (kon′trakt) a form of auction bridge: only the tricks bid may be counted towards a game
con·trac·tile (kən trak′tīl) *adj.* 1. having the power of contracting 2. producing contraction —**con·trac·til·i·ty** (kon′trak til′ə tē) *n.*
con·trac·tion (-shən) *n.* 1. a contracting or being contracted 2. the drawing up and thickening of a muscle in action 3. *Gram. a)* the shortening of a word or phrase *b)* a word form resulting from this (Ex.: *aren't* for *are not*) —**con·trac′·tion·al** *adj.* —**con·trac′tive** (-tiv) *adj.*
con·trac·tor (kən trak′tər, kon′trak-) *n.* 1. one of the parties to a contract 2. one who contracts to supply certain materials or do certain work for a stipulated sum; esp. one who does so in the building trades 3. a muscle that contracts
con·trac·tu·al (kən trak′tyoo wəl) *adj.* of, or having the nature of, a contract —**con·trac′tu·al·ly** *adv.*
con·tra·dance (kon′trə däns′) *n.* *same as* CONTREDANSE
con·tra·dict (kon′trə dikt′) *vt.* [< L. pp. of *contradicere* < *contra-*, against + *dicere*, to speak] 1. *a)* to assert the opposite of (a statement) *b)* to deny the statement of (a person) 2. to be contrary or opposed to; go against —**con′·tra·dict′a·ble** *adj.* —**con′tra·dic′tor, con′tra·dict′er** *n.*
con·tra·dic·tion (-dik′shən) *n.* 1. a contradicting or being contradicted 2. a statement in opposition to another; denial 3. a condition in which things tend to be contrary to each other; inconsistency; discrepancy
con·tra·dic·tious (-dik′shəs) *adj.* 1. inclined to contradict; contentious 2. [Archaic] contradictory
con·tra·dic·to·ry (-dik′tər ē) *adj.* 1. involving a contradiction; inconsistent 2. inclined to contradict or deny Also **con′tra·dic′tive** —**con′tra·dic′to·ri·ly** *adv.* —**con′·tra·dic′to·ri·ness** *n.*
con·tra·dis·tinc·tion (-dis tiŋk′shən) *n.* distinction by contrast —**con′tra·dis·tinc′tive** *adj.* —**con′tra·dis·tinc′·tive·ly** *adv.*
con·trail (kon′trāl′) *n.* clipped form of CONDENSATION TRAIL
con·tral·to (kən tral′tō) *n., pl.* **-tos, -ti** (-tē) [It.: see CONTRA- & ALTO] 1. the range of the lowest female voice 2. a voice or singer with such range 3. a part for this voice —*adj.* of or for a contralto
con·trap·tion (kən trap′shən) *n.* [< ?] [Colloq.] a contrivance or gadget
con·tra·pun·tal (kon′trə pun′t'l) *adj.* [< It. *contrappunto* (see COUNTERPOINT) + -AL] 1. of or characterized by counterpoint 2. according to the principles of counterpoint —**con′tra·pun′tal·ly** *adv.* —**con′tra·pun′tist** *n.*
con·tra·ri·e·ty (kon′trə rī′ə tē) *n.* 1. the condition or quality of being contrary 2. *pl.* **-ties** anything that is contrary; inconsistency
con·tra·ri·wise (kon′trər ē wīz′; *for 3, often* kən trer′-) *adv.* 1. on the contrary; from the opposite point of view 2. in the opposite way, order, direction, etc. 3. perversely
con·tra·ry (kon′trər ē; *for adj. 4, often* kən trer′ē) *adj.* [< OFr. < L. *contrarius* < *contra*, against] 1. in opposition 2. opposite in nature, order, direction, etc.; altogether different 3. unfavourable [*contrary* winds] 4. inclined to oppose stubbornly; perverse —*n., pl.* **-ries** the opposite; thing that is the opposite of another —*adv.* in a contrary way —**on the contrary** as opposed to what has been said —**to the contrary** to the opposite effect —**con′trar·i·ly** *adv.* —**con′trar·i·ness** *n.*
con·trast (kən träst′; *for n.* kon′träst) *vt.* [< Fr. < It. < L. *contra*, against + *stare*, to stand] to compare so as to point out the differences; set off against one another —*vi.* to show differences when compared —*n.* 1. a contrasting or being contrasted 2. a difference, esp. a striking difference, between things being compared 3. a person or thing showing differences when compared with another —**con·trast′a·ble** *adj.* —**con·trast′ive** *adj.*
con·tra·vene (kon′trə vēn′) *vt.* **-vened′, -ven′ing** [< Fr. < LL. < L. *contra*, against + *venire*, to come] 1. to go against; oppose; violate 2. to disagree with; contradict —**con′tra·ven′er** *n.*
con·tra·ven·tion (-ven′shən) *n.* violation; infringement —**in contravention of** infringing, violating: said esp. of laws, etc.
con·tre·danse (kon′trə däns′) *n.* [Fr., altered (after *contre*, opposite) < COUNTRY-DANCE] a country dance with the partners in two facing lines

con·tre·temps (kōn´trə tän´) *n.*, *pl.* **-temps'** (-tän´) [Fr., ult. < OFr. prp. of *contrester*, CONTRAST] an inopportune happening causing embarrassment

con·trib·ute (kən trib´yōōt) *vt.*, *vi.* **-ut·ed**, **-ut·ing** [< L. pp. of *contribuere*: see COM- & TRIBUTE] **1.** to give jointly with others to a common fund **2.** to write (an article, poem, etc.) for a magazine, newspaper, etc. **3.** to furnish (ideas, etc.) —**contribute to** to have a share in bringing about —**con·trib'u·tive** *adj.* —**con·trib'u·tor** *n.*

con·tri·bu·tion (kon´trə byōō´shən) *n.* **1.** a contributing **2.** something contributed **3.** [Archaic] a special levy or tax

con·trib·u·to·ry (kən trib´yōō tər ē) *adj.* **1.** contributing **2.** involving a contribution —*n.*, *pl.* **-ries** a person or thing that contributes

con·trite (kən trīt´, kon´trīt) *adj.* [OFr. < LL. < L. pp. of *conterere*, to grind < *com-*, together + *terere*, to rub] **1.** feeling deep sorrow or remorse for having sinned or done wrong **2.** resulting from remorse or guilt —**con·trite'ly** *adv.* —**con·trite'ness**, **con·tri'tion** (-trish´ən) *n.*

con·triv·ance (kən trī´vəns) *n.* **1.** the act, way, or power of contriving **2.** something contrived, as an invention, mechanical device, plan, etc.

con·trive (kən trīv´) *vt.* **-trived'**, **-triv'ing** [< OFr. *controver*, to find out < ML. *contropare*, to compare] **1.** to devise; plan **2.** to construct skilfully or ingeniously; fabricate **3.** to bring about, as by a scheme —*vi.* to form plans; scheme —**con·triv'a·ble** *adj.* —**con·triv'er** *n.*

con·trived (-trīvd´) *adj.* not spontaneous

con·trol (kən trōl´) *vt.* **-trolled'**, **-trol'ling** [< Anglo-Fr. < Fr. < ML. *contrarotulus*, a duplicate register < L. *contra*, against + *rotulus*: see ROLL] **1.** to regulate (financial affairs) **2.** to exercise authority over; direct; command **3.** to curb; restrain —*n.* **1.** power to direct or regulate **2.** the condition of being directed; restraint **3.** a means of controlling; check **4.** a standard of comparison for checking the findings of an experiment **5.** [*usually pl.*] an apparatus to regulate a mechanism **6.** a spirit supposed to direct the actions and speech of a spiritualistic medium —**con·trol'la·bil'i·ty** *n.* —**con·trol'la·ble** *adj.*

control experiment an experiment in which one factor after another is varied while the other factors are controlled

con·trol·ler (kən trōl´ər) *n.* **1.** a person in charge of expenditures or finances, as in a business, government (usually sp. **comptroller**), etc. **2.** a person or device that controls —**con·trol'ler·ship'** *n.*

control panel the array of instruments in front of a pilot, technician, etc.

control tower a tower at an airport, from which air traffic is directed

con·tro·ver·sial (kon´trə vur´shəl) *adj.* of, subject to, or stirring up controversy; debatable —**con'tro·ver'sial·ist** *n.* —**con'tro·ver'sial·ly** *adv.*

con·tro·ver·sy (kon´trə vur´sē, kən tro´-) *n.*, *pl.* **-sies** [< L. < *contra*, against + pp. of *vertere*, to turn] **1.** a discussion of a question in which opposing opinions clash; debate **2.** a quarrel or dispute

con·tro·vert (kon´trə vurt´) *vt.* [backformation < prec.] **1.** to argue or reason against; dispute **2.** to argue about; debate —**con'tro·vert'i·ble** *adj.* —**con'tro·vert'i·bly** *adv.*

con·tu·ma·cious (kon´tyōō mā´shəs) *adj.* [< ff.] obstinately resisting authority; disobedient —**con'tu·ma'cious·ly** *adv.*

con·tu·ma·cy (kon´tyōō mə sē) *n.*, *pl.* **-cies** [< L. *contumax*, stubborn < *com-*, intens. + *tumere*, to swell up] stubborn refusal to submit to authority; disobedience

con·tu·me·ly (kon´tyōō mə lē) *n.*, *pl.* **-lies** [< OFr. < L. *contumelia*, reproach, prob. akin to prec.] **1.** haughty rudeness; humiliating treatment **2.** a scornful insult —**con'·tu·me'li·ous** (-mē´lē əs) *adj.*

con·tuse (kən tyōōz´) *vt.* **-tused'**, **-tus'ing** [< L. pp. of *contundere* < *com-*, intens. + *tundere*, to beat] to bruise without breaking the skin

con·tu·sion (-tyōō´zhən) *n.* a bruise

co·nun·drum (kə nun´drəm) *n.* [16th-c. < ?] **1.** a riddle whose answer contains a pun **2.** any puzzling question or problem

con·ur·ba·tion (kon´ər bā´shən) *n.* [< *con-*, see COM- + L. *urbs*, city + -ATION] a densely populated urban area, including suburbs and towns around a large city

con·va·lesce (kon´və les´) *vi.* **-lesced'**, **-lesc'ing** [< L. *convalescere* < *com-*, intens. + *valescere* < *valere*, to be strong] to recover gradually from illness; regain strength and health

con·va·les·cence (-les´əns) *n.* [see prec.] **1.** a gradual recovery of health after illness **2.** the period of such recovery —**con'va·les'cent** *adj.*, *n.*

convalescent home a home or hospital for convalescents, usually with medical staff on duty: also **convalescent hospital**

con·vec·tion (kən vek´shən) *n.* [< L. < pp. of *convehere* < *com-*, together + *vehere*, to carry] **1.** a transmitting or conveying **2.** *a)* the movement of parts of a fluid within the fluid because of differences in the density, temperature, etc.

of the parts *b)* the transference of heat by such movement —**con·vec'tion·al** *adj.* —**con·vec'tive** *adj.* —**con·vec'tive·ly** *adv.*

con·vec·tor (-ər) *n.* a heating device which transmits heat to the air by convection

con·vene (kən vēn´) *vi.*, *vt.* **-vened'**, **-ven'ing** [< OFr. < L. *convenire* < *com-*, together + *venire*, to come] to assemble for a meeting

con·ven·er (kən vēn´ər) *n.* a person who convenes or chairs a meeting, committee, etc., esp. one elected to do this [*convener* of shop stewards]: also **con·ven'or**

con·ven·i·ence (kən vēn´ē əns, -yəns) *n.* [< L. < *convenire*, CONVENE] **1.** the quality or condition of being convenient **2.** personal comfort **3.** anything that adds to one's comfort or saves work **4.** a lavatory, esp. a public one —**at one's convenience** at a time, place, etc. that suits one —**at your earliest convenience** as soon as possible

convenience food food, often tinned or frozen, that is bought precooked or otherwise made ready so as to require little preparation

con·ven·i·ent (-ē ənt, -yənt) *adj.* **1.** favourable to one's comfort; easy to do, use, or get to; handy **2.** [Colloq.] easily accessible (*for*); near (*for*) —**con·ven'ient·ly** *adv.*

con·vent (kon´vənt, -vent) *n.* [< OFr. < L. *conventus*, assembly, orig. pp. of *convenire*, CONVENE] **1.** a community of nuns or, sometimes, monks, living under strict religious vows **2.** the building or buildings occupied by such a group

con·ven·ti·cle (kən ven´ti k'l) *n.* [< OFr. < L. dim. of prec.] **1.** a religious assembly, esp. an illegal or secret one **2.** a place where such an assembly meets

con·ven·tion (kən ven´shən) *n.* **1.** an assembly, often periodical, or the delegates to it [a trade union *convention*, lawyers' *convention*] **2.** *a)* an agreement between persons, nations, etc. *b)* general agreement on the usages and practices of social life *c)* *Card Games* a play or bid established as having a certain meaning between partners **3.** a customary practice, rule, method, etc.

con·ven·tion·al (-'l) *adj.* **1.** having to do with a convention **2.** of, sanctioned by, or growing out of custom or usage; customary **3.** *a)* conforming to accepted rules or standards; formal; not natural, original, or spontaneous *b)* not unusual; ordinary **4.** stylized; conventionalized **5.** nonnuclear [*conventional* weapons] —**con·ven'tion·al·ism** *n.* —**con·ven'tion·al·ist** *n.* —**con·ven'tion·al·ly** *adv.*

con·ven·tion·al·i·ty (kən ven´shə nal´ə tē) *n.*, *pl.* **-ties** **1.** the quality, fact or condition of being conventional **2.** conventional behaviour or act **3.** a conventional form, usage, or rule

con·ven·tion·al·ize (kən ven´shən 'l īz´) *vt.* **-ized'**, **-iz'ing** **1.** to make conventional **2.** *Art* to treat in a conventional manner —**con·ven'tion·al·i·za'tion** *n.*

con·ven·tu·al (kən ven´tyōō wəl) *adj.* of or like a convent —*n.* a member of a convent

con·verge (kən vurj´) *vi.* **-verged'**, **-verg'ing** [< LL. *convergere* < L. *com-*, together + *vergere*, to turn] to come together or tend to come together at a point —*vt.* to cause to converge

con·ver·gence (-vur´jəns) *n.* **1.** the act, fact, or condition of converging **2.** the point at which things converge Also **con·ver'gen·cy**, *pl.* **-cies** —**con·ver'gent** *adj.*

con·vers·a·ble (kən vur´sə b'l) *adj.* **1.** easy to talk to; affable **2.** liking to converse or talk

con·ver·sant (kən vur´s'nt, kon´vər-) *adj.* [see CONVERSE¹] familiar or acquainted (*with*), esp. as a result of study or experience; versed (*in*) —**con·ver'sance**, **con·ver'san·cy** *n.* —**con·ver'sant·ly** *adv.*

con·ver·sa·tion (kon´vər sā´shən) *n.* [see CONVERSE¹] a talking together; specif., familiar talk; verbal exchange of ideas, opinions, etc.

con·ver·sa·tion·al (-'l) *adj.* **1.** of, like, or for conversation **2.** given to conversation; liking to converse —**con'ver·sa'tion·al·ist**, **con'ver·sa'tion·ist** *n.* —**con'ver·sa'tion·al·ly** *adv.*

conversation piece **1.** a type of painting which shows a group of people in an appropriate setting **2.** an unusual article of furniture, bric-a-brac, etc. that attracts attention or invites comment

con·verse¹ (kən vurs´; for *n.* kon´vurs) *vi.* **-versed'**, **-vers'-ing** [< OFr. < L. *conversari*, to live with, ult. < *convertere*: see CONVERT] to hold a conversation; talk —*n.* informal talk; conversation —**con·vers'er** *n.*

con·verse² (kon´vurs; also, for *adj.*, kən vurs´) *adj.* [< L. pp. of *convertere*: see CONVERT] reversed in position, order, etc.; opposite; contrary —*n.* a thing related in a converse way; the opposite —**con·verse'ly** *adv.*

con·ver·sion (kən vur´zhən, -shən) *n.* a converting or being converted; specif., *a)* a change from lack of faith to religious belief or from one religion to another *b)* *Rugby* an additional score made after a try by kicking the ball over the crossbar from a place kick —**con·ver'sion·al**, **con·ver'sion·ar·y** *adj.*

con·vert (kən vurt´; for *n.* kon´vərt) *vt.* [< OFr. < L. *convertere* < *com-*, together + *vertere*, to turn] **1.** to change from one form or use to another; transform [*convert* grain into flour] **2.** to cause to change from one belief, religion, etc. to another **3.** to exchange for something equal in value **4.** *Finance* to change (a security, currency, etc.) into an equivalent of another form **5.** *Law* to take and use (another's property) unlawfully —*vi.* **1.** to be converted **2.** *Logic* to change (a proposition) by transposing the subject and the predicate **3.** *Rugby* to score the extra point or points after a try —*n.* a person converted, as to a religion

con·vert·er (kən vur'tər) *n.* a person or thing that converts; specif., *a*) a furnace for converting pig iron into steel *b*) *Elec.* a device for converting alternating current into direct current: cf. INVERTER *c*) *Radio & TV* any device for adapting a receiver to added frequencies or modulations Also sp. **con·ver'tor**

converter reactor a nuclear reactor that produces less fissionable material than it consumes

con·vert·i·ble (kən vur'tə b'l) *adj.* that can be converted —*n.* **1.** a thing that can be converted **2.** a motor car with a top that can be folded back —**con·vert'i·bil'i·ty** *n.* —**con·vert'i·bly** *adv.*

con·vex (kon'veks; *also, & for n. usually,* kon veks') *adj.* [< L. *convexus,* pp. of *convehere* < *com-,* together + *vehere,* to bring] curving outwards like the surface of a sphere —*n.* a convex surface, line, object, etc. —**con·vex'i·ty** *n.,* *pl.* **-ties** —**con·vex'ly** *adv.*

con·vex·o·con·cave (kən vek'sō kon kāv') *adj.* convex on one side and concave on the other

con·vex·o·con·vex (-kon veks') *adj.* convex on both sides, as some lenses

con·vex·o·plane (-plān') *adj.* same as PLANO-CONVEX

CONVEX LENSES (A, plano-convex; B, convexo-concave; C, convexo-convex)

con·vey (kən vā') *vt.* [< Anglo-Fr. *conveier,* to escort < L. *com-,* together + *via,* way] **1.** to take from one place to another; transport; carry **2.** to seve as a channel or medium for; transmit **3.** to make known; communicate **4.** to transfer, as a title to property, to another person —**con·vey'a·ble** *adj.*

con·vey·ance (-əns) *n.* **1.** a conveying **2.** a means of conveying, esp. a vehicle **3.** *a*) the transfer of the ownership of real property from one person to another *b*) a document by which this is effected; deed —**con·vey'anc·er** *n.* —**con·vey'anc·ing** *n.*

con·vey·or, con·vey·er (-ər) *n.* one that conveys; esp., a mechanical contrivance, as a continuous chain or belt (**conveyor belt**)

con·vict (kən vikt'; *for n.* kon'vikt) *vt.* [< L. pp. of *convincere*: see CONVINCE] **1.** to prove (a person) guilty [*convicted by the evidence*] **2.** to judge and find guilty of an offence charged —*n.* **1.** one found guilty of a crime and sentenced by a court **2.** one serving a sentence in prison

con·vic·tion (kən vik'shən) *n.* **1.** a convicting or being convicted **2.** the state or appearance of being convinced, as of the truth of a belief [*to speak with conviction*] **3.** a strong belief —**carry conviction** to be convincing —**con·vic'tive** *adj.* —**con·vic'tive·ly** *adv.*

con·vince (kən vins') *vt.* -**vinced'**, -**vinc'ing** [L. *convincere* < *com-,* intens. + *vincere,* to conquer] to overcome the doubts of; persuade by argument or evidence; make feel sure —**con·vinc'er** *n.* —**con·vinc'i·ble** *adj.* —**con·vinc'ing·ly** *adv.*

con·viv·i·al (kən viv'ē əl) *adj.* [< L. < *convivium,* a feast < *com-,* together + *vivere,* to live] **1.** having to do with a feast or festive activity **2.** fond of eating, drinking, and good company; sociable; jovial —**con·viv'i·al·ist** *n.* —**con·viv'i·al'i·ty** *n.* —**con·viv'i·al·ly** *adv.*

con·vo·ca·tion (kon'və kā'shən) *n.* **1.** a convoking **2.** a group that has been convoked; esp. *a*) *Church of England* either of the two provincial synods of the provinces of Canterbury and York *b*) in some universities, a legislative assembly composed of the university's graduates —**con'·vo·ca'tion·al** *adj.*

con·voke (kən vōk') *vt.* -**voked'**, -**vok'ing** [< Fr. < L. *convocare* < *com-,* together + *vocare,* to call] to call together; summon to assemble; convene —**con·vok'er** *n.*

con·vo·lute (kon'və lōōt') *adj.* [< L. pp. of *convolvere*: see CONVOLVE] rolled up in a spiral with the coils falling one upon the other; coiled —*vt., vi.* -**lut'ed**, -**lut'ing** to wind around; coil —**con'vo·lute'ly** *adv.*

con·vo·lut·ed (-id) *adj.* **1.** having convolutions; coiled **2.** involved; intricate; complicated

con·vo·lu·tion (kon'və lōō'shən) *n.* **1.** a twisting, coiling, or winding together **2.** a convoluted condition **3.** a fold, twist, or coil of something convoluted; specif., any of the irregular folds or ridges on the surface of the brain

con·volve (kən volv') *vt., vi.* -**volved'**, -**volv'ing** [< L. *convolvere* < *com-,* together + *volvere,* to roll] to roll, coil, or twist together

con·vol·vu·lus (kən vol'vyə ləs) *n.,* *pl.* **-lus·es, -li'** (-lī') [L., bindweed: see prec.] any of a genus of trailing or twining plants related to the morning glory

con·voy (kon'voi) *vt.* [< OFr. *convoier,* CONVEY] to go with as an escort, esp. in order to protect —*n.* **1.** the act of convoying **2.** a protecting escort, as for ships or troops **3.** a group of ships, vehicles, etc. travelling together for mutual protection

con·vulse (kən vuls') *vt.* -**vulsed'**, -**vuls'ing** [< L. *convulsus,* pp. of *convellere* < *com-,* together + *vellere,* to pluck] **1.** to shake or disturb violently; agitate **2.** to cause convulsions, or spasms, in **3.** to cause to shake with laughter, rage, grief, etc. —**con·vul'sive** *adj.* —**con·vul'sive·ly** *adv.*

con·vul·sion (-vul'shən) *n.* **1.** a violent, involuntary contraction or spasm of the muscles: *often used in pl.* **2.** a violent fit of laughter **3.** any violent disturbance —**con·vul'·sion·ar·y** *adj.*

co·ny (kō'nē) *n.,* *pl.* **-nies** [< OFr. < L. *cuniculus,* rabbit] **1.** a rabbit **2.** rabbit fur **3.** *Bible* a small animal, probably the hyrax **4.** same as PIKA Also sp. **co'ney**

coo (kōō) *vi.* [echoic] **1.** to make the soft, murmuring sound of pigeons or doves or a sound like this **2.** to speak gently and lovingly: see BILL², *vi.* 2 —*vt.* to express lovingly, as with a coo —*n.* a cooing sound —**coo'ing·ly** *adv.*

coo·ee (kōō'ē) *interj.* a call designed to attract attention, esp. a loud, high-pitched call on two notes used in the Australian bush —*vi.* **coo'eed** or **coo'eyed, coo'ee·ing** or **coo'ey·ing** to utter the call of cooee

cook (kook) *n.* [OE. *coc* < L. < *coquere,* to cook] a person who prepares food for eating —*vt.* **1.** to prepare (food) for eating by boiling, baking, frying, etc. **2.** to subject to heat or a treatment suggestive of this **3.** [Colloq.] to alter or falsify [*to cook the books*] **4.** [Slang] to spoil —*vi.* **1.** to act as a cook **2.** to undergo cooking —**cook someone's goose** [Colloq.] **1.** to impede or spoil someone's plans **2.** to bring about someone's ruin, downfall, etc. —**cook up** [Colloq.] to concoct; devise —**what's cooking?** [Slang] what's happening?

cook·er (-ər) *n.* **1.** an apparatus used for cooking food; stove **2.** a fruit, esp. an apple, that is more suitable for cooking than for eating raw

cook·er·y (-ər ē) *n.* the art, practice, or work of cooking

cookery book a book with recipes and other information about preparing food: also **cook'book** *n.*

cook·gen·er·al (-jen'ər al) *n.* formerly, a servant who did the housework and cooked

cook·ie, cook·y (-ē) *n.,* *pl.* **-ies** [prob. Du. *koekje,* dim. of *koek,* a cake] [U.S.] **1.** a small, sweet cake, usually flat; biscuit **2.** [Chiefly U.S. Slang] a person, esp. one qualified as "tough, smart, etc."

Cook's tour [after Thomas *Cook* & Son, Brit. travel agents] any guided sightseeing tour, esp. if rapid and extensive

cool (kōōl) *adj.* [OE. *col*] **1.** moderately cold; neither warm nor very cold **2.** tending to reduce discomfort in hot weather [*cool* clothes] **3.** *a*) not excited; calm; composed *b*) restrained [*cool* jazz] *c*) [Slang] emotionally uninvolved; dispassionate **4.** showing dislike or indifference **5.** calmly impudent or bold **6.** not suggesting warmth: said of blue-green colours **7.** [Colloq.] without exaggeration [*a cool* thousand] **8.** [U.S. Slang] pleasing; excellent —*adv.* in a cool manner —*n.* **1.** a cool place, time, thing, etc. **2.** [Chiefly U.S. Slang] cool, dispassionate attitude or manner [keep one's *cool*] —*vt., vi.* to make or become cool —**cool off** **1.** to calm down **2.** to lose enthusiasm, interest, etc. —**cool one's heels** to wait or be kept waiting, esp. as a result of discourtesy —**play it cool** [Slang] to stay aloof —**cool'ish** *adj.* —**cool'ly** *adv.* —**cool'ness** *n.*

coo·la·bar (kōō'la bär') *n.* [Abor.] an Australian eucalyptus that grows along rivers: also **coo'la·bah**

cool·ant (kōōl'ənt) *n.* a substance, usually a fluid, used to remove heat as from a nuclear reactor, an internal-combustion engine, etc.

cool·er (-ər) *n.* **1.** a device, container, or room for cooling things or keeping them cool **2.** anything that cools **3.** [Slang] a jail

coo·lie (kōō'lē) *n.* [Hindi *qūlī,* hired servant] an unskilled native labourer, esp. formerly, in China, India, etc.

coomb, coombe (kōōm) *n.* [ME. < OE. *cumb* < Celt.: cf. CWM] **1.** a deep, narrow valley **2.** same as CWM (sense 2)

coon (kōōn) *n.* clipped form of RACCOON

coon·skin (-skin') *n.* the skin of a raccoon, used as a fur —*adj.* made of coonskin

coop (kōōp) *n.* [ult. < L. *cupa,* tub, cask] **1.** a small cage, pen, or building for poultry, etc. **2.** any place of confinement **3.** a wicker basket for catching fish —*vt.* to confine in or as in a coop —**fly the coop** [U.S. Slang] to escape, as from a jail

co-op (kō'op) *n.* [Colloq.] **1.** a cooperative **2.** a shop run by a cooperative society

co-op., coop. cooperative

coop·er (kōōp'ər) *n.* [< MDu. < LL. *cuparius* < L. *cupa,* a cask] a person whose work is making or repairing barrels and casks —*vt., vi.* to make or repair (barrels and casks)

coop·er·age (-ij) *n.* **1.** the work or workshop of a cooper: also **coop'er·y,** *pl.* **-ies** **2.** the price for such work

co·op·er·ate, co-op·er·ate (kō ŏp'ə rāt') *vi.* -at'ed, -at'ing [< LL. pp. of *cooperari* < L. *co-*, with + *operari*, to work < *opus*, work] to act or work together with another or others —**co·op'er·a'tor, co-op'er·a'tor** *n.*

co·op·er·a·tion, co-op·er·a·tion (kō ŏp'ə rā'shən) *n.* 1. a cooperating; joint effort or operation 2. the association of a number of people in an enterprise for mutual benefits or profits —**co·op'er·a'tion·ist, co-op'er·a'tion·ist** *n.*

co·op·er·a·tive, co-op·er·a·tive (kō ŏp'ər ə tiv, -op'rə tiv) *adj.* 1. cooperating or inclined to cooperate 2. designating or of an organization (as for the production or marketing of goods), shop, etc. owned collectively by members who share in its benefits —*n.* a cooperative society, shop, etc. —**co·op'er·a·tive·ly, co-op'er·a·tive·ly** *adv.* —**co·op'er·a·tive·ness, co-op'er·a·tive·ness** *n.*

cooperative shop a shop or store run by a cooperative society

cooperative society a commercial enterprise owned and managed by customers or workers, usually providing them with commodities or work on advantageous terms, esp. a chain of shops in which profits are distributed to members of the society

co-opt (kō opt') *vt.* [< L. < *co-*, with + *optare*, to choose] to add (a person or persons) to a group by a vote or action of those already members —**co'-op·ta'tion, co-op'tion** *n.* —**co-op'ta·tive, co-op'tive** *adj.*

co·or·di·nate, co-or·di·nate (kō ôr'də nit; *also, and for v.* *always,* -də nāt') *adj.* [< ML. pp. of *coordinare* < L. *co-*, with + *ordinare*, to arrange < *ordo* (gen. *ordinis*), order] 1. of equal order or importance 2. of or involving coordination or coordinates 3. *Gram.* being of equal structural rank [*coordinate* clauses] —*n.* 1. a coordinate person or thing 2. [*pl.*] articles of women's clothing that harmonize or contrast in colour, texture, etc. 3. *Math.* any of two or more magnitudes used to define the position of a point, line, curve, or plane —*vt.* -nat'ed, -nat'ing 1. to make coordinate 2. to bring into proper order or relation; adjust various parts so that they harmonize —*vi.* 1. to become coordinate 2. to work together, esp. harmoniously —**co·or'di·nate·ly, co-or'di·nate·ly** *adv.* —**co·or'di·na·tive, co-or'di·na·tive** (-nə tiv, -nāt'iv) *adj.* —**co·or'di·na'tor, co-or'di·na'tor** *n.*

coordinating conjunction a conjunction that connects coordinate words, phrases, or clauses (Ex.: *and, but, for, or, nor, yet*)

co·or·di·na·tion, co-or·di·na·tion (kō ôr'də nā'shən) *n.* 1. a coordinating or being coordinated 2. harmonious adjustment or action, as of muscles

coot (kōōt) *n., pl.* **coots:** *also for* 1 & 2 **coot:** see PLURAL, II, D, 1 [< ? MDu. *koet*] 1. a ducklike, freshwater bird of the rail family with unwebbed toes 2. [Colloq.] a foolish, stupid, or senile person

cop¹ (kop) *vt.* **copped, cop'ping** [< obs. *cap*, to seize; ? ult. < L. *capere*, to take] [Slang] 1. to seize, capture, win, steal, etc. 2. to suffer, esp. a punishment [to *cop* a clout] —*n.* [Slang] 1. a policeman 2. an arrest, esp. in a **fair cop** —**cop it** to get into trouble and be punished —**cop out** [U.S. Slang] 1. to confess to the police 2. *a*) to back down; renege *b*) to give up; quit

cop² (kop) *n.* [ME. & OE. *cop*, summit] 1. [Dial.] the top or crest, as of a hill 2. a cone-shaped roll of thread or yarn coiled round a spindle

cop³ (kop) *n.* [< COP¹] [Slang] worth or value: usually used in negative [not much *cop*, no *cop*]

co·pal (kō'pəl, -pal) *n.* [Sp. < Nahuatl *copalli*, resin] a hard resin from tropical trees

co·part·ner (kō pärt'nər) *n.* a partner, or associate —**co·part'ner·ship'** *n.*

cope¹ (kōp) *vi.* **coped, cop'ing** [OFr. *couper*, to strike < *coup*, COUP] 1. to fight or contend (*with*) successfully or on equal terms 2. to deal with problems, troubles, etc.

cope² (kōp) *n.* [< ML. *capa*, var. of *cappa*: see CAP] 1. a large, capelike vestment worn by priests at certain ceremonies 2. anything that covers like a cope, as a canopy —*vt.* **coped, cop'ing** to cover with a cope or coping

cope³ (kōp) *vt.* **coped, cop'ing** [< COPING] to cut so as to fit against a coping or moulding with curves, angles, etc.

co·peck (kō pek) *n. same as* KOPECK

cop·er (kō'pər) *n.* [< obs. *cope*, to barter < MDu. *koopen*, to trade] a horse-dealer

Co·per·ni·can system (kō pur'ni kən) the theory of Copernicus that the planets revolve around the sun and that the earth rotates.

cope·stone (kōp'stōn') *n.* 1. the top stone of a wall; stone in a coping 2. a finishing touch; *also* **coping stone**

cop·i·er (kop'ē ər) *n.* 1. one who copies; imitator, transcriber, etc. 2. a duplicating machine

co·pi·lot (kō'pī'lət) *n.* the assistant pilot of an aircraft, who aids or relieves the pilot

cop·ing (kō'piŋ) *n.* [< fig. use of COPE²] the top layer of a masonry wall, usually sloped

coping saw a saw with a narrow blade in a U-shaped frame, esp. for cutting curved outlines

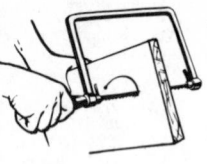

COPING SAW

co·pi·ous (kō'pē əs) *adj.* [< L. < *copia*, abundance] 1. plentiful; abundant 2. wordy; profuse or diffuse 3. full of information —**co'pi·ous·ly** *adv.* —**co'pi·ous·ness** *n.*

co·pla·nar (kō plā'nər) *adj. Math.* in the same plane: said of figures

cop-out (kop'out') *n.* [Chiefly U.S. Slang] a copping out, as by confessing, backing down, quitting, etc.

cop·per¹ (kop'ər) *n.* see PLURAL, II, D, 3 [OE. *coper* < LL. *cuprum*, contr. < *Cyprium* (*aes*), Cyprian (metal) < Gr. *Kyprios*, Cyprus, noted for its copper mines] 1. a reddish-brown, malleable, ductile, metallic element that is an excellent conductor of electricity and heat: symbol, Cu; at. wt., 63.546; at. no., 29 2. a copper coin, as an old penny 3. the colour of copper; reddish brown 4. large vessel, formerly made of copper, used esp. for boiling washing —*adj.* 1. of copper 2. reddish-brown —*vt.* to coat with copper —**cop'per·y** *adj.*

cop·per² (kop'ər) *n.* [prob. < COP¹] [Slang] a policeman

cop·per·as (-əs) *n.* [< OFr. < ML. (*aqua*) *cuprosa*, lit., copper (water)] ferrous sulphate, a green, crystalline compound used in dyeing, the making of ink, etc.

copper beech a variety of beech tree with coppery-coloured leaves

copper belt the area of central Africa that is rich in copper

cop·per-bot·tom·ed (-bot'əmd) *adj.* 1. having the bottom sheathed with copper: said esp. of sailing ships 2. financially reliable

cop·per·head (-hed') *n.* a poisonous N. American pit viper with a copper-coloured head

cop·per·plate (-plāt') *n.* 1. a sheet of copper etched or engraved for printing 2. a print made from this 3. copperplate printing or engraving 4. a fine style of handwriting based on that used for captioning copperplate engravings

copper pyrites a yellow sulphide of copper and iron, an important copper ore

cop·per·smith (-smith') *n.* a person whose work is making utensils, etc. out of copper

copper sulphate a blue, crystalline substance, $CuSO_4 5H_2O$: used in making pigments, batteries, etc.

cop·pice (kop'is) *n.* [< OFr. *copeis* < *couper*, to cut: see COUP] *same as* COPSE

co·pra (kop'rə) *n.* [Port. < Malayalam < Hindi *khoprā*] dried coconut kernel, the source of coconut oil

copse (kops) *n.* [< COPPICE] a thicket of small trees, undergrowth, and shrubs; coppice

cop shop [Slang] a police station

Copt (kopt) *n.* 1. a native of Egypt descended from the ancient inhabitants of that country 2. a member of the Coptic Church

Cop·tic (kop'tik) *adj.* [< ModL. < Ar. *Quft*, the Copts < Gr. *Aigyptios*, Egyptian] 1. of the Copts, their language, etc. 2. of the Coptic Church —*n.* the Afro-Asiatic language of the Copts, derived from ancient Egyptian

Coptic Church the native Christian church of Egypt and of Ethiopia

cop·u·la (kop'yə lə) *n., pl.* **-las** [L., a link < *co-*, together + *apere*, to join] something that connects or links together; specif., *same as* LINKING VERB —**cop'u·lar** *adj.*

cop·u·late (-lāt') *vi.* -lat'ed, -lat'ing [< L. pp. of *copulare*, to couple < *copula*: see prec.] to have sexual intercourse —**cop'u·la'tion** *n.* —**cop'u·la·to·ry** (-lə tər ē) *adj.*

cop·u·la·tive (-lāt'iv, -lə tiv) *adj.* 1. coupling 2. *Gram. a*) connecting coordinate words, phrases, or clauses *b*) involving connected words or clauses *c*) being a copula [a *copulative* verb] 3. of or for copulating —*n.* a copulative word —**cop'u·la'tive·ly** *adv.*

cop·y (kop'ē) *n., pl.* **cop'ies** [< OFr. < ML. *copia*, copious transcript < L. *copia*, plenty] 1. a thing made just like another; imitation 2. any of a number of books, magazines, engravings, etc. having the same printed matter 3. a manuscript or illustration to be set in type or printed 4. subject matter for a writer 5. the words of an advertisement —*vt., vi.* **cop'ied, cop'y·ing** 1. to make a copy or copies of; reproduce 2. to imitate

cop·y·book (-book') *n.* a book with models of handwriting, formerly used in teaching penmanship —*adj.* ordinary; trite [*copybook* maxims]

cop·y·cat (-kat') *n.* a person who habitually imitates or mimics: a child's term

cop·y·hold (-hōld') *n. Law* tenure of property less than a freehold proved by a written transcript or record in the rolls of a manorial court —**cop'y·hold'er** *n.*

cop·y·ist (-ist) *n.* 1. a person who makes written copies; transcriber 2. a person who imitates

cop·y·read·er (-rē'dər) *n.* a person whose work is editing articles or other copy for publication

cop·y·right (-rīt') *n.* [COPY + RIGHT] the exclusive right to the publication, production, or sale of a literary, musical, or artistic work, granted by law for a specified period of time to an author, composer, etc. —*vt.* to protect (a book, etc.) by copyright —*adj.* protected by copyright —**cop'y·right'-a·ble** *adj.* —**cop'y·right'er** *n.*

copy typist a typist who types from copy (sense 3)

cop·y·writ·er (-rīt'ər) *n.* a writer of copy for advertising or promotional material

co·quet (kō ket', ko-) *vi.* -**quet'ted**, -**quet'ting** [< Fr. < dim. of *coq*, a cock: see COCK[1]] **1.** to behave as.a coquette; flirt **2.** to trifle or dally (*with* an idea, offer, etc.) —*adj.* coquettish —**co·quet'ry** (kōk'ə trē, kok-) *n.*, *pl.* -**ries**

co·quette (kō ket', ko-) *n.* [Fr.: see prec.] a girl or woman flirt —*vi.* -**quet'ted**, -**quet'ting** to behave as a coquette; flirt —**co·quet'tish** *adj.* —**co·quet'tish·ly** *adv.* —**co·quet'-tish·ness** *n.*

cor (kôr) *interj.* [earlier *Gor* < GOD] [Slang] an exclamation of surprise, admiration, irritation, etc.

Cor. 1. Corinthians **2.** Coroner

cor. 1. corner **2.** cornet **3.** correct **4.** correction **5.** correlative **6.** correspondence

cor·a·cle (kor'ə k'l) *n.* [< W. < *corwg*, orig., leather-covered boat] a small boat of waterproof material stretched over a wooden frame

cor·a·coid (kor'ə koid') *adj.* [< Gr. < *korax*, raven + *eidos*, form] designating or of a bony process extending from the shoulder blade towards the breastbone —*n.* this bony process

cor·al (kor'əl) *n.* [OFr. < L. < Gr. *korallion* < ? Heb. *gôrāl*, pebble] **1.** the hard, stony skeleton of some marine polyps, often in masses forming reefs and atolls in tropical seas **2.** any of such polyps, living singly or in large colonies **3.** a piece of coral **4.** yellowish red or yellowish pink: also **coral red** or **coral pink** —*adj.* **1.** made of coral **2.** coral-red or coral-pink

coral reef a reef made up chiefly of coral

CORAL
(A, organ-pipe; B, reef; C, mushroom; D, Bermuda)

cor·al·root (-rōōt') *n.* a brownish orchid with corallike rootstocks and no leaves

cor an·glais (kôr äṅ'glä) *pl.* **cors anglais** [Fr.] a double-reed instrument of the woodwind family, similar to the oboe but larger and a fifth lower in pitch

cor·bel (kôr'bəl) *n.* [OFr. < L. *corvus*, raven] a bracket of stone, wood, etc. projecting from a wall to support a cornice, etc. —*vt.* -**belled**, -**bel·ling** to provide or support with a corbel or corbels

cor·bie (kôr'bē) *n.*, *pl.* -**bies** [see prec.] [Scot.] a crow or raven

cor·bie-step (-step') *n.* [CORBIE + STEP] [Scot.] one of a series of steps at the upper end wall of some gables: also **crow-step**

COR ANGLAIS

cord (kôrd) *n.* [< OFr. < L. < Gr. *chordē*] **1.** (a) thick string or thin rope **2.** any force acting as a tie or bond **3.** [from cord used in measuring] a measure of wood cut for fuel (128 cubic feet, c. 3.6m³) **4.** *a)* a rib on the surface of a fabric *b)* corduroy *c)* [*pl.*] corduroy trousers **5.** *Anat.* any part like a cord [the spinal *cord*]: also CHORD[1] **6.** *Elec. U.S. var.* of FLEX[2] —*vt.* **1.** to fasten or provide with a cord or cords **2.** to stack (wood) in cords

cord·age (-ij) *n.* **1.** cords and ropes collectively, esp. the ropes in a ship's rigging **2.** the amount of wood, in cords, in a given area

cor·date (kôr'dāt) *adj.* [< ModL. < L. *cor* (gen. *cordis*), heart] heart-shaped —**cor'date·ly** *adv.*

cord·ed (kôr'did) *adj.* **1.** fastened with cords **2.** made of cords **3.** that looks like a tight cord, as a muscle **4.** having a ribbed surface, as corduroy **5.** stacked in cords, as wood

cor·di·al (kôr'dē əl) *adj.* [< ML. < L. *cor* (gen. *cordis*), heart] **1.** [Rare] invigorating **2.** warm and friendly; hearty; sincere —*n.* **1.** [Rare] a stimulating medicine, food, or drink **2.** an aromatic, alcoholic drink; liqueur —**cor'-dial·ly** *adv.* —**cor'dial·ness** *n.*

cor·di·al·i·ty (kôr'dē al'ə tē) *n.* **1.** a cordial quality; warm, friendly feeling **2.** *pl.* -**ties** a cordial act or remark

cor·dil·le·ra (kôr'dil yer'ə, kôr dil'ər ə) *n.* [Sp. < dim. of *cuerda*, rope < L. *chorda*, CORD] a chain of mountains; esp., the principal mountain range of a continent —**cor'-dil·le'ran** *adj.*

cord·ing (kôr'diŋ) *n.* the ribbed surface of corded cloth

smokeless explosive made of nitroglycerin, guncotton, petroleum jelly, and acetone

cord·less (kôrd'lis) *adj.* operated by batteries rather than by current from an outlet

cór·do·ba (kôr'də bə) *n.* [after F. F. de *Córdoba*, 16th-cent. Sp. explorer] *see* MONETARY UNITS, table (Nicaragua)

cor·don (kôr'd'n) *n.* [Fr., dim. of *corde*: see CORD] **1.** a line or circle of police, ships, etc. stationed around an area to guard it **2.** a cord, ribbon, or braid worn as a decoration or badge —*vt.* to encircle or shut (*off*) with a cordon

‡**cor·don bleu** (kôr dôn blö') [Fr.] **1.** *a)* formerly, a blue ribbon worn in France by the Knights of the Holy Ghost *b)* a person wearing this ribbon **2.** any very high distinction, esp. in cookery —*adj.* of, relating to, or denoting food prepared to a very high standard

cor·do·van (kôr'də vən) *adj.* [< Sp. < *Cordoba*, city in Spain] made of cordovan —*n.* a fined-grained, coloured leather, usually of split horsehide

cor·du·roy (kôr'də roi') *n.* [prob. < CORD + obs. *duroy*, a coarse fabric] **1.** a heavy cotton fabric with a velvety surface, ribbed vertically **2.** [*pl.*] trousers made of this —*adj.* **1.** made of, or ribbed like, corduroy **2.** made of logs laid crosswise [a *corduroy* road]

cord·wain·er (kôrd'wān'ər) *n.* [ME. *cordwaner* < Sp. *cordobán*, CORDOVAN] [Archaic] a shoemaker or worker in cordovan leather

cord·wood (kôrd'wood') *n.* wood stacked or sold in cords

core (kôr) *n.* [< OFr., prob. < L. *cor*, heart] **1.** the central part of an apple, pear, etc., containing the seeds **2.** the central part of anything **3.** the most important part; essence; pith **4.** in foundry work, that part of a mould forming the interior of a hollow casting **5.** a sample section of the earth's strata from underground, obtained with a hollow drill **6.** the centre of a nuclear reactor that contains the fissionable fuel **7.** *Chem.* the nucleus of an atom with its electron shells **8.** *Computers* a ferrite ring used to store one bit of information **9.** *Elec. a)* the inner strand of a cable, etc. *b)* a mass of iron inside a wire coil: it increases the magnetic field —*vt.* **cored**, **cor'ing** to remove the core of —**cor'er** *n.*

co·re·li·gion·ist (kō'ri lij'ə nist) *n.* a person of the same religion or religious denomination

co·re·op·sis (kor'ē op'sis) *n.* [ModL. < Gr. *koris*, bug + *opsis*, appearance: from the shape of the fruit] a plant of the composite family, with showy flowers of yellow, crimson, or maroon

co·re·spond·ent (kō'ri spon'dənt) *n.* [CO- + RESPONDENT] *Law* a person charged with having committed adultery with the wife or husband from whom a divorce is being sought —**co're·spond'en·cy** *n.*

corf (kôrf) *n.*, *pl.* **corves** (kôrvz) [ME. < MDu. & MLowG. < L. *corbis*, a basket] a basket or small cart, as for carrying coal, ore, etc. in mines

cor·gi (kôr'gē) *n.* [W. *corgi* < *cor(r)*, dwarf + *ci*, dog] either of two breeds of short-legged dog with a foxlike head, orig. from Wales

co·ri·an·der (kor'ē an'dər) *n.* [< OFr. < L. < Gr. *koriandron*] **1.** an umbelliferous European herb **2.** its strong-smelling, seedlike fruit, used in flavouring food and liqueurs

Co·rin·thi·an (kə rin'thē ən) *adj.* **1.** of Corinth, its people, or culture **2.** dissolute and loving luxury, as the people of Corinth were said to be **3.** designating or of the most elaborate of the three orders of Greek architecture, distinguished by a bell-shaped capital with a design of acanthus leaves: cf. DORIC, IONIC —*n.* a native or inhabitant of Corinth

CORINTHIAN CAPITAL

Cor·i·o·lis force (ko'rē ō'lis) [after G. de *Coriolis*, 19th-c. Fr. mathematician] the apparent force, caused by the earth's rotation, that produces the deflection (**Coriolis effect**) of a moving body to the right in the Northern Hemisphere and to the left in the Southern

cork (kôrk) *n.* [< Sp. *corcho*, ult. via ? L. *quercus*, oak] **1.** the light, thick, elastic outer bark of an oak tree, the **cork oak**, of the Mediterranean area **2.** a piece of cork; esp., a stopper for a bottle, cask, etc. **3.** any stopper, as one of rubber, etc. **4.** the outer bark of the stems of woody plants —*adj.* made of cork —*vt.* **1.** to stop with a cork **2.** to restrain; check **3.** to blacken with burnt cork

cork·age (-ij) *n.* [CORK + -AGE] a charge made at a restaurant, club, etc. for serving bottles of wine or other alcoholic drink, esp. those bought off the premises

corked (kôrkd) *adj.* **1.** stopped up with a cork **2.** tainted by the cork: said esp. of wine

cork·er (kôr'kər) *n.* **1.** a worker or device that corks bottles **2.** [Slang] *a)* a remarkable person or thing *b)* an argument, statement, or circumstance that appears conclusive *c)* a preposterous lie

cork·screw (kôrk'skroō') *n.* a spiral-shaped device for pulling corks out of bottles —*adj.* shaped like a corkscrew —*vi., vt.* to move in a spiral; twist

cork·y (kôr′kē) *adj.* **cork′i·er, cork′i·est** 1. of or like cork 2. tasting of the cork: said of wine

corm (kôrm) *n.* [< Gr. *kormos*, a lopped tree trunk < *keirein*, to cut off] the fleshy, scaly, underground stem of certain plants, as the gladiolus

cor·mo·rant (kôr′mə rənt) *n.* [< OFr. < L. < *corvus*, raven + *marinus*, MARINE] 1. a large, voracious, diving bird with webbed toes: used by fishermen in the Orient to catch fish 2. a greedy person

corn[1] (kôrn) *n.* see PLURAL, II, D, 3 [OE.] 1. a small, hard seed, esp. a seed or grain of a cereal grass; kernel: chiefly in compounds [*peppercorn*] 2. the seeds of all cereal grasses; grain 3. the leading cereal crop, as wheat in England or oats in Scotland and Ireland 4. [U.S.] maize 5. [Colloq.] ideas, music, etc. considered old-fashioned, trite, sentimental, etc. —*vt.* to preserve or pickle (meat, etc.) with salt granules or in brine

corn[2] (kôrn) *n.* [< OFr. < L. *cornu*, a horn] a hard, thick, painful growth of skin, esp. on a toe

corn borer [U.S.] a moth larva that feeds esp. on maize

corn bread [U.S.] a bread made with maize meal

corn bunting a small, brown bird of the finch family, with a stout, yellow bill and yellow legs: also **common bunting**

corn·cob (-kob′) *n.* 1. the woody core of an ear of maize 2. a tobacco pipe with a bowl made of a hollowed, dried piece of such a core: in full, **corncob pipe**

corn cockle a tall weed of the pink family, with pink flowers, often found in grainfields

corn-crake (-krāk′) *n.* [see CRAKE] a brown, short-billed rail often found in cornfields

cor·ne·a (kôr′nē ə) *n.* [< ML. < L. cornea (tela), horny (tissue) < *cornu*, a horn] the transparent outer coat of the eyeball, covering the iris and pupil —**cor′ne·al** *adj.*

corned (kôrnd) *adj.* preserved with salt or brine [*corned beef*]

cor·nel (kôr′n'l, -nel) *n.* [< OFr. < VL. < L. *cornus*] any of a genus of shrubs and small trees with very hard wood, including the dogwoods, cornelian cherries, etc.

cor·nel·ian (kôr nēl′yən, -ē ən) *n.* [< OFr. *corneola*, prob. < VL. *cornea* < L. *cornu*, a horn] a red variety of chalcedony, used in jewellery

cor·ner (kôr′nər) *n.* [< OFr. < ML. < *cornu*, a horn] 1. the point or place where lines or surfaces join and form an angle 2. the space within the angle formed at the joining of lines or surfaces 3. the tip of any angle formed at a street intersection 4. something used to form, mark, protect, or decorate a corner 5. a remote or secluded spot 6. region; quarter [*every corner of the world*] 7. an awkward position from which escape is difficult 8. a monopoly acquired on a stock or commodity to raise the price 9. *Sports* a free kick taken from the corner of the field in football and hockey when a defender puts the ball over his goal line: also **corner kick, corner hit** —*vt.* 1. to force into a corner or awkward position, so that escape is difficult 2. to get a monopoly on (a stock or commodity) —*vi.* to turn corners: said of a vehicle —*adj.* 1. at or on a corner 2. used in a corner —**around the corner** very near or imminent —**cut corners** to economize on time, effort, etc., esp. at the expense of quality —**turn the corner** to get safely past the critical point —**cor′nered** *adj.*

cor·ner·stone (-stōn′) *n.* 1. a stone laid in the corner of a building, esp. at a ceremony for beginning a building 2. the basic part; foundation

cor·net (kôr′nət) *n.* [< OFr. < L. *cornu*, a horn] 1. *a)* a brass musical instrument similar to the trumpet *b)* a person who plays the cornet 2. *a)* a cone-shaped wafer for holding ice cream *b)* a cone-shaped pastry 3. formerly, a cavalry officer of the lowest commissioned rank —**cor·net′ist** *n.*

corn exchange 1. a place where grain is sold by samples 2. the building where grain was formerly sold

corn·flakes (kôrn′flāks′) *n.pl.* a breakfast cereal of crisp flakes made from hulled maize

corn·flour (-flour′) *n.* a finely ground starchy flour made from maize, corn, etc.; used esp. for thickening sauces

corn·flow·er (-flou′ər) *n.* a plant of the composite family, with white, pink, or blue flowers

cor·nice (kôr′nis) *n.* [Fr. < It. < L. < Gr. *korōnis*, a wreath] 1. a horizontal moulding projecting along the top of a wall, building, etc. 2. the top part of an entablature 3. a decorative strip above a window for hiding a curtain rod —*vt.* **-niced, -nic·ing** to top as with a cornice

cor·niche (kôr′nish) *n.* [Fr., lit., a cornice] a road that winds along a cliff or steep slope

Cor·nish (kôr′nish) *adj.* of Cornwall, its people, or culture —*n.* 1. the Brythonic Celtic language spoken in Cornwall until c. 1800: efforts are now being made to revive it 2. *pl.* **Cor′nish** *a)* a British breed of chicken *b)* a breed of chicken crossbred from these and Plymouth Rocks: also **Cornish hen** or **Rock Cornish (hen)**

Cornish pasty same as PASTY[2]

corn·meal (kôrn′mēl′) *n.* meal made from maize

corn salad *same as* LAMB'S LETTUCE

corn-starch (-stärch′) *n.* [U.S.] cornflour

cor·nu·co·pi·a (kôr′nyōō kō′pē ə) *n.* [L. *cornu copiae*, horn of plenty] 1. a representation in painting, sculpture, etc. of a horn overflowing with fruits, flowers, and grain; horn of plenty 2. an abundance 3. any cone-shaped container

corn whiskey [U.S.] whisky made from maize

corn·y (kôr′nē) *adj.* **corn′i·er, corn′i·est** 1. of corn 2. [Colloq.] unsophisticated, old-fashioned, trite, sentimental, etc. —**corn′i·ness** *n.*

corol., coroll. corollary

co·rol·la (kə rol′ə) *n.* [L., dim. of *corona*, CROWN] the petals, or inner floral leaves, of a flower —**cor·ol·late** (kor′ə lāt′), **cor′ol·lat′ed** *adj.*

CORNUCOPIA

cor·ol·lar·y (kə rol′ər ē) *n.,* *pl.* **-lar·ies** [< LL. *corollarium*, a deduction < L., a gift < *corolla*: see prec.] 1. a proposition that follows from another that has been proved 2. an inference or deduction 3. anything that follows as a normal result

co·ro·na (kə rō′nə) *n.,* *pl.* **-nas, -nae** (-nē) [L., CROWN] 1. a crown or something like a crown 2. a long cigar with blunt ends 3. *Anat.* the upper part of a tooth, of a skull, etc. 4. *Archit.* the top projection of a cornice 5. *Astron. a)* the outermost part of the sun's atmosphere, seen during a total eclipse *b)* a ring of coloured light seen around a luminous body, as the sun or moon, as a result of diffraction by mist, dust, etc. 6. *Bot.* the cuplike part on the inner side of the corolla of certain flowers, as the daffodil 7. *Elec.* a sometimes visible electric discharge around a conductor at high potential —**cor·o′nal** *adj.*

co·ro·nach (kor′ə nəkh) *n.* [Ir. & ScotGael. < *comh-*, together + *ranach*, outcry] a dirge or lamentation for the dead

cor·o·nar·y (kor′ə nər ē) *adj.* [see CORONA] 1. of, or in the form of, a crown 2. *Anat.* designating or of either of two arteries branching from the aorta and supplying blood directly to the heart muscle —*n.,* *pl.* **-nar·ies** same as CORONARY THROMBOSIS

coronary thrombosis the formation of an obstructing clot in a coronary artery: also **coronary occlusion**

cor·o·na·tion (kor′ə nā′shən) *n.* [< OFr. < L. pp. of *coronare* < *corona*, CROWN] the act or ceremony of crowning a sovereign

cor·o·ner (kor′ə nər) *n.* [ME., officer of the crown < Anglo-Fr. < L. *corona*, CROWN] a public officer whose chief duty is to determine by inquest before a jury the causes of any deaths not obviously due to natural causes —**cor′o·ner·ship** *n.*

cor·o·net (kor′ə net′) *n.* [< OFr. dim. of *corone*, CROWN] 1. a small crown worn by princes and others of high rank 2. an ornamental band, as of gold, jewels, or flowers, worn around the head —**cor′o·net′ed** *adj.*

corp., corpn. corporation

cor·po·ral[1] (kôr′pər əl) *n.* [< Fr. < It. < *capo*, chief < L. *caput*, the head: sp. infl. by *corps* or ff.] *see* MILITARY RANKS, table

cor·po·ral[2] (kôr′pər əl) *adj.* [< L. *corporalis* < *corpus*, body] of the body; bodily —**cor′po·ral′i·ty** (-pə ral′ə tē) *n.* —**cor′po·ral·ly** *adv.*

cor·po·ral[3] (kôr′pə rəl) *n.* [OFr. < ML. *corporalis* (*palla*), body (cloth): see prec.] *Eccles.* a small, linen altar cloth on which the bread and chalice are placed for the Eucharist

corporal punishment punishment inflicted directly on the body, as flogging

cor·po·rate (kôr′pər it) *adj.* [< L. pp. of *corporare*, to make into a body < *corpus*, body] 1. incorporated 2. of a corporation 3. shared by all in a group [*corporate blame*] —**cor′po·rate·ly** *adv.*

cor·po·ra·tion (kôr′pə rā′shən) *n.* 1. a group of people with a charter granting them as a body certain of the legal powers, rights, and liabilities of an individual 2. a group of people, as the municipal authorities of a town or city, legally authorized to act as an individual 3. [U.S.] a business company 4. [Colloq.] a pot belly —**cor′po·ra·tive** *adj.* —**cor′po·ra′tor** *n.*

cor·po·re·al (kôr pôr′ē əl) *adj.* [< L. < *corpus* (gen. *corporis*), body] 1. of or for the body; bodily 2. material; physical; tangible —**cor·po′re·al·i·ty** (-al′ə tē), **cor′po·re′i·ty** (-pə rē′ə tē) *n.* —**cor·po′re·al·ly** *adv.*

corps (kôr) *n.,* *pl.* **corps** (kôrz) [< OFr. *corps, cors* < L. *corpus*, body] 1. a body of people associated in some work, organization, etc. 2. *Mil. a)* a branch of the armed forces with some specialized function [*Signal Corps*] *b)* a tactical subdivision of an army, composed of two or more divisions

corps de bal·let (kôr′də ba lā′) [Fr.] the members of a ballet company who dance together in a group, as opposed to the soloists

corps dip·lo·ma·tique (dip′lō ma tēk′) the body of diplomatic officials accredited to foreign governments; diplomatic corps

corpse (kôrps) *n.* [var. of CORPS] 1. a dead body, esp. of a person 2. something lifeless and of no use

cor·pu·lence (kôr′pyoo ləns) *n.* [OFr. < L. < *corpus*, body] fatness or stoutness of body; obesity: also **cor′pu·len·cy** —**cor′pu·lent** *adj.* —**cor′pu·lent·ly** *adv.*

cor·pus (kôr′pəs) *n.*, *pl.* **cor′po·ra** (-pər ə) [L.] 1. a human or animal body; esp., a dead one: now mainly a facetious usage 2. a complete collection, as of laws or writings of a specified type 3. the main body or substance of anything

Corpus Christ·i (kris′tē) [L., Body of Christ] *R.C.Ch.* a festival celebrated on the Thursday after Trinity Sunday, in honour of the Eucharist

cor·pus·cle (kôr′pus′'l) *n.* [< L. dim. of *corpus*, body] 1. a very small particle 2. *Anat.* a protoplasmic particle with a special function; esp., any of the erythrocytes (**red corpuscles**) or leucocytes (**white corpuscles**) that float in the blood, lymph, etc. of vertebrates: also **cor·pus·cule** (kôr pus′-kyool) —**cor′pus·cu·lar** (-kyoo lər) *adj.*

corpus de·lic·ti (di lik′tī) [ModL., lit., body of the crime] 1. the facts constituting or proving a crime 2. loosely, the body of a murder victim

corpus ju·ris (joor′is) [L., body of law] a collection of all the laws of a nation or district

corpus lu·te·um (loo′tē əm) *pl.* **cor·po·ra lu·te·a** (kôr′-pər ə loo′tē ə) [ModL., lit., yellow body] a mass of yellow tissue, formed in the ovary after ovulation, that secretes progesterone if fertilization occurs

corr. 1. corrected 2. correspondence

cor·ral (kə räl′) *n.* [Sp. < *corro*, a circle < L. *currere*, to run] an enclosure for holding or capturing horses, cattle, etc.; pen —*vt.* **-ralled′, -ral′ling** 1. to drive into or confine in a corral 2. to surround or capture; round up

cor·ra·sion (kə rä′zhən) *n.* [< L. *corradere*, to scrape together] *Geol.* the erosion of rock by the action of running water or glacial ice

cor·rect (kə rekt′) *vt.* [< L. pp. of *corrigere* < *com-*, together + *regere*, to lead straight] 1. to make right; change from wrong to right 2. to mark the errors or faults of 3. to make conform to a standard 4. to scold or punish so as to cause to rectify faults 5. to cure or counteract (a fault, disease, etc.) —*vi.* to make corrections or an adjustment to compensate (*for* an error, etc.) —*adj.* 1. conforming to an established standard; proper 2. conforming to fact or logic; true; accurate; right 3. equal to the required number, amount, etc. —**cor·rect′a·ble** *adj.* —**cor·rect′ly** *adv.* —**cor·rect′ness** *n.* —**cor·rec′tor** *n.*

cor·rec·tion (kə rek′shən) *n.* 1. a correcting or being corrected 2. a change that corrects a mistake; rectification 3. punishment or scolding to correct faults —**cor·rec′tion·al** *adj.*

cor·rec·tive (-tiv) *adj.* tending or meant to correct or improve; remedial —*n.* something corrective; remedy —**cor·rec′tive·ly** *adv.*

corrector of the press a proof reader

cor·re·late (kor′ə lāt′) *n.* [*cor-* (see COM-) + L. *relatus*: see RELATE] either of two interrelated things —*adj.* closely and naturally related —*vi.* **-lat′ed, -lat′ing** to be mutually related (*to* or *with*) —*vt.* to bring (a thing) into mutual relation (*with* another); calculate or show the relation between

cor·re·la·tion (kor′ə lā′shən) *n.* [see prec.] 1. a mutual relationship or connection 2. the degree of relative correspondence between two sets of data 3. a correlating or being correlated —**cor′re·la′tion·al** *adj.*

cor·rel·a·tive (kə rel′ə tiv) *adj.* 1. having a mutual relationship; reciprocally dependent 2. *Gram.* expressing mutual relation and used in pairs [*neither . . . nor* are *correlative* conjunctions] —*n.* 1. a correlate 2. a correlative word —**cor·rel′a·tive·ly** *adv.* —**cor·rel′a·tiv′i·ty** *n.*

cor·re·spond (kor′ə spond′) *vi.* [< Fr. < ML. *correspondere* < L. *com-*, together + *respondere*, to answer] 1. to be in agreement (*with* something); conform (*to* something); match 2. to be similar, analogous, or equal (*to* something) 3. to communicate (*with* someone) by letters —**cor′re·spond′ing·ly** *adv.*

cor·re·spond·ence (-spon′dəns) *n.* [see CORRESPOND] 1. agreement; conformity 2. similarity; analogy 3. *a*) communication by exchange of letters *b*) the letters written or received

correspondence school a school that gives courses of instruction (**correspondence courses**) by post

cor·re·spond·ent (kor ə spon′dənt) *adj.* corresponding —*n.* 1. a thing that corresponds 2. a person who exchanges letters with, or writes a letter to, another 3. a person hired as by a newspaper to send news regularly from a distant place or write on a special subject

corresponding member an honorary member of a learned society who has no voice in the decisions made

‡**cor·ri·da** (kō rē′thä; E. kə rēd′ə) *n.* [Sp. *corrida* (*de toros*), (bull-) baiting] a bullfight

cor·ri·dor (kor′ə dôr′,-dər) *n.* [Fr. < It. < L. *currere*, to run] 1. a long passageway or hall 2. a strip of land providing passage through foreign-held land, as from a country to its seaport 3. a passageway running the length of a railway carriage, connecting all the compartments

corridors of power the Civil Service, etc. considered as a source of influence in administrative decisions

cor·rie (kor′ē) *n.* [< ScotGael. *coire*, cauldron] [Scot.] a round hollow in a hillside; cirque

cor·ri·gen·dum (kor′ə jen′dəm) *n.*, *pl.* **-da** (-də) [L., gerundive of *corrigere*: see CORRECT] an error to be corrected in a printed work, or [*pl.*] a list of such errors inserted in the work

cor·ri·gi·ble (kor′i jə b'l) *adj.* [< OFr. < ML. < L. *corrigere*: see CORRECT] capable of being corrected, improved, or reformed —**cor′ri·gi·bil′i·ty** *n.* —**cor′ri·gi·bly** *adv.*

cor·rob·o·rate (kə rob′ə rāt′) *vt.* **-rat′ed, -rat′ing** [< L. pp. of *corroborare* < *com-*, intens. + *roborare* < *robur*, strength] to confirm; bolster; support —**cor·rob′o·ra′tion** *n.* —**cor·rob′o·ra′tor** *n.*

cor·rob·o·ra·tive (kə rob′er ə tiv) *adj.* corroborating; confirmatory: also **cor·rob′o·ra·to·ry** (-ər ə tər ē) —**cor·rob′-o·ra·tive·ly** *adv.*

cor·rob·o·ree (kə rob′ə rē) *n.* [Abor.] [Aust.] 1. an Aboriginal festival or ceremony 2. any noisy gathering or celebration

cor·rode (kə rōd′) *vt.* **-rod′ed, -rod′ing** [< OFr. < L. *corrodere* < *com-*, intens. + *rodere*, to gnaw] to eat into or wear away gradually, as by rusting or by the action of chemicals —*vi.* to become corroded —**cor·rod′i·ble** *adj.*

cor·ro·sion (kə rō′zhən) *n.* 1. a corroding or being corroded 2. a substance formed by corroding

cor·ro·sive (kə rōs′iv) *adj.* [< OFr. < ML. *corrosivus*] causing corrosion —*n.* something causing corrosion —**cor·ro′sive·ly** *adv.* —**cor·ro′sive·ness** *n.*

corrosive sublimate *same as* MERCURIC CHLORIDE

cor·ru·gate (kor′ə gāt′, -yoo-) *vt.*, *vi.* **-gat′ed, -gat′ing** [< L. pp. of *corrugare* < *com-*, intens. + *rugare*, to wrinkle] to shape into parallel grooves and ridges; make wrinkles in; furrow [*corrugated* iron, *corrugated* paper]

CORRUGATED SURFACE

cor·ru·ga·tion (kor′ə gā′shən, -yoo-) *n.* 1. a corrugating or being corrugated 2. any ridge or groove of a corrugated surface

cor·rupt (kə rupt′) *adj.* [< L. pp. of *corrumpere*, to ruin < *com-*, together + *rumpere*, to break] 1. orig., spoiled; rotten 2. morally debased; evil; depraved 3. taking bribes 4. containing alterations, foreign admixtures, or errors [a *corrupt* text] —*vt.*, *vi.* to make or become corrupt —**cor·rupt′er, cor·rup′tor** *n.* —**cor·rup′tive** *adj.* —**cor·rupt′-ly** *adv.* —**cor·rupt′ness** *n.*

cor·rupt·i·ble (kə rup′tə b'l) *adj.* that can be corrupted, esp. morally —**cor·rupt′i·bil′i·ty** *n.* —**cor·rupt′i·bly** *adv.*

cor·rup·tion (kə rup′shən) *n.* 1. a making, becoming, or being corrupt 2. depravity 3. bribery 4. decay; rottenness 5. something corrupted

cor·sage (kôr säzh′) *n.* [Fr.: see CORPS & -AGE] 1. the bodice of a dress 2. a small bouquet for a woman to wear, as at the waist or shoulder

cor·sair (kôr′ser) *n.* [< Fr. < Pr. < It. < L. *cursus*, a COURSE] 1. a privateer 2. a pirate 3. a pirate ship

corse (kôrs) *n.* [Archaic or Poet.] a corpse

corse·let (kôrs′lət; *for 2* kôr′sə let′) *n.* [see ff.] 1. a medieval piece of body armour: also sp. **cors′let** 2. a woman's lightweight corset: also sp. **cor′se·lette′**

cor·set (kôr′sit) *n.* [OFr., dim. of *cors*: see CORPS] [*sometimes pl.*] a closefitting undergarment, often reinforced with stays, worn, chiefly by women, to give support to or shape the torso —*vt.* to dress in, or fit with, a corset —**cor′set·ry** *n.*

cor·tège (kôr tāzh′) *n.* [Fr. < It. *corteggio*, retinue < L. *cohors*: see COURT] 1. a group of attendants; retinue. 2. a ceremonial procession, as at a funeral

cor·tex (kôr′teks) *n.*, *pl.* **-ti·ces** (-tə sēz′) [L., bark of a tree] 1. *a*) the outer part of an internal organ, as of the kidney *b*) the outer layer of grey matter over most of the brain 2. a layer of tissue under the epidermis in plant roots and stems 3. the bark or rind of a plant —**cor′ti·cal** (-ti k'l) *adj.* —**cor′ti·cal·ly** *adv.*

cor·ti·cate (kôr′ti kit, -kāt′) *adj.* [L. *corticatus* < CORTEX] covered with bark: also **cor′ti·cat′ed, cor′ti·cose′** (-kōs′)

cor·ti·sone (kôrt′ə sōn′, -zōn′) *n.* [< *corticosterone*, a hormone] an adrenal-gland hormone used in treating adrenal insufficiency and various inflammatory and allergic diseases

co·run·dum (kə run′dəm) *n.* [Tamil *kurundam* < Sans. *kuruvinda*, ruby] a hard mineral, aluminium oxide, Al_2O_3, used for grinding and polishing: the ruby, sapphire, etc. are precious varieties

cor·us·cate (kor′əs kāt′) *vt.* **-cat′ed, -cat′ing** [< L. pp. of

coruscare < *coruscus*, vibrating] to emit flashes of light; glitter; sparkle —**co·rus·cant** (kə rus′kənt) *adj.* —**cor′us·ca′-tion** *n.*

cor·vée (kôr′vā′) *n.* [< MFr. < LL. *corrogata*, to make a request] *History* **1.** the enforced and unpaid labour of a peasant for his feudal lord **2.** forced labour exacted by a government, as for the construction of roads, bridges, etc.

corves (kôrvz) *n.* *pl. of* CORF

cor·vette (kôr vet′) *n.* [Fr., prob. ult. < L. *corbita* (*navis*), cargo (ship) < *corbis*, basket] **1.** formerly, a sailing warship smaller than a frigate **2.** a small, fast warship used for antisubmarine and convoy duty

cor·vine (kôr′vīn) *adj.* [< L. < *corvus*, a raven] of or like a crow or raven

cor·y·bant (kor′ə bant′) *n.*, *pl.* -**bants**, **cory′y·ban′tes** (-ban′tēz) [after the attendant of the goddess Cybele in Gr. myth.] a reveller —**cor′y·ban′tic**, **cor′y·ban′tian** (-ban′shən) *adj.*

cor·ymb (kor′im, -imb) *n.* [< Fr. < L. *corymbus*, flower cluster < Gr. *korymbos*] a broad, flat cluster of flowers in which the outer stems are long and those towards the centre progressively shorter —**co·rym·bose** (kə rim′bōs), **co·rym′-bous** *adj.* —**co·rym′bose·ly** *adv.*

co·ry·za (kə rī′zə) *n.* [ModL. < LL. < Gr. *koryza*, catarrh] a cold in the head; acute nasal congestion

cos[1] cosine

cos[2] (kos) *n.* [after Aegean island of Cos whence orig. imported] a kind of lettuce with long leaves that form a cylindrical or conical head: also **cos lettuce**

'cos (kos) *conj.* [Colloq.] because: also **cos**

Cos., cos. **1.** companies **2.** counties

cosec cosecant

co·se·cant (kō sē′kənt) *n.* *Trigonometry* the ratio between the hypotenuse and the side opposite a given acute angle in a right-angled triangle

cosh[1] (kosh) *n.* [< Romany < *koshter*, a skewer, stick] [Slang] a blunt weapon, often made from hard rubber; bludgeon —*vt.* [Slang] to strike with a cosh

cosh[2] (kosh) hyperbolic cosine

co·sign (kō′sīn′) *vt., vi.* **1.** to sign (a promissory note) in addition to the maker, thus becoming responsible for the obligation if the maker should default **2.** to sign jointly —**co′sign′er** *n.*

co·sig·na·to·ry (kō sig′nə tər ē) *adj.* signing jointly —*n.*, *pl.* -**ries** one of two or more joint signers

co·sine (kō′sīn) *n.* *Trigonometry* the ratio between the side adjacent to a given acute angle in a right-angled triangle and the hypotenuse

cos·met·ic (koz met′ik) *adj.* [< Gr. *kosmētikos*, skilled in arranging < *kosmos*, order] **1.** designed to beautify the complexion, hair, etc. **2.** for improving the appearance by correcting deformities, esp. of the face **3.** having no other function than to embellish or beautify [the house had some *cosmetic* repairs done] —*n.* any cosmetic preparation for the skin, hair, etc. —**cos·met′i·cal·ly** *adv.*

cos·me·tol·o·gy (koz′mə tol′ə jē) *n.* the work of applying cosmetics to, or performing plastic surgery on, women —**cos′me·tol′o·gist** *n.*

cos·mic (koz′mik) *adj.* [Gr. *kosmikos* < *kosmos*, order] **1.** of the cosmos; relating to the universe as a whole **2.** vast —**cos′mi·cal·ly** *adv.*

cosmic dust small particles falling from interstellar space to the earth

cosmic rays streams of highly penetrating charged particles that bombard the earth from outer space

cos·mo- [see COSMOS[1]] *a combining form meaning* world, universe [*cosmology*]

cos·mog·o·ny (koz mog′ə nē) *n.* [< Gr. < *kosmos*, universe + *gignesthai*, to produce] **1.** the origin of the universe **2.** *pl.* -**nies** a theory or account of this —**cos′mo·gon′ic** (-mə gon′ik), **cos′mo·gon′i·cal**, **cos·mog′o·nal** *adj.* —**cos·mog′o·nist** *n.*

cos·mog·ra·phy (-rə fē) *n.* [< LL. < Gr.: see COSMO- & -GRAPHY] the science dealing with the structure of the universe as a whole —**cos·mog′ra·pher** *n.* —**cos′mo·graph′-ic** (-mə graf′ik), **cos′mo·graph′i·cal** *adj.* —**cos′mo·graph′-i·cal·ly** *adv.*

cos·mol·o·gy (koz mol′ə jē) *n.* [COSMO- + -LOGY] the study of the universe as a whole and of its form, nature, etc. as a physical system —**cos′mo·log′i·cal** (-mə loj′ə k'l) *adj.* —**cos′mo·log′i·cal·ly** *adv.* —**cos·mol′o·gist** *n.*

cos·mo·naut (koz′mə nôt′) *n.* [Russ. *kosmonaut* < *kosmo-*, COSMO- + -*naut* < Gr. *nautēs*, sailor (see NAUTICAL)] an astronaut, esp. a Russian astronaut

cos·mo·pol·i·tan (koz′mə pol′ə t'n) *adj.* [COSMOPOLIT(E) + -AN] **1.** representative of all or many parts of the world **2.** not bound by local or national prejudices; at home in all countries or places —*n.* a cosmopolitan person —**cos′-mo·pol′i·tan·ism** *n.*

cos·mop·o·lite (koz mop′ə līt′) *n.* [< Gr. < *kosmos*, world + *politēs*, citizen < *polis*, city] **1.** a cosmopolitan person **2.** a plant or animal common to all or most parts of the world

cos·mos[1] (koz′məs) *n.* [Gr. *kosmos*, universe, harmony] **1.** the universe considered as a harmonious and orderly system **2.** any complete and orderly system

cos·mos[2] (koz′məs) *n.*, *pl.* **cos′mos** [ModL. < Gr. *kosmos*, ornament] a tropical American plant of the composite family, with white, pink, or purple flower heads

COSPAR Committee on Space Research

Cos·sack (kos′ak, -ək) *n.* [Russ. *kazak* < Turk.] a member of a people of southern Russia, famous as horsemen —*adj.* of the Cossacks

cos·set (kos′it) *n.* [< ? OE. *cot-sæta*, cot dweller] a pet lamb, or any small pet —*vt.* to make a pet of; pamper

cost (kost) *vt.* **cost** or, for 2, **cost′ed**, **cost′ing** [< OFr. < ML. *costare* < L. < *com-*, together + *stare*, to stand] **1.** *a)* to be obtained or obtainable for (a certain price) *b)* to require the expenditure, loss, or experience of **2.** *Business* to estimate the cost of producing (often with *out*) —*n.* **1.** *a)* the amount asked or paid for a thing *b)* the amount spent in producing a commodity **2.** *a)* the amount of money, effort, etc. required to achieve an end *b)* loss; sacrifice **3.** [*pl.*] *Law* court expenses of a lawsuit —**at all costs** regardless of the cost or difficulty involved: also **at any cost**

cost accounting *Accounting* **1.** a system for recording, analysing, and allocating production and distribution costs **2.** the keeping of such records —**cost accountant**

cos·tal (kos′t'l) *adj.* [Fr. < ML. < L. *costa*, a rib] of or near a rib or the ribs

cost·ed (-id) *adj.* having the price fixed or estimated

cos·ter·mon·ger (kos′tər mung′gər) *n.* [< *costard*, a kind of apple + MONGER] a person who sells fruit or vegetables from a barrow: also **cos′ter**

cos·tive (kos′tiv) *adj.* [< OFr. pp. of *costever* < L. *constipare*: see CONSTIPATE] constipated or constipating —**cos′tive·ly** *adv.* —**cos′tive·ness** *n.*

cost·ly (kost′lē) *adj.* -**li·er**, -**li·est** **1.** *a)* costing much; expensive; dear *b)* at the cost of great effort, damage, etc. **2.** magnificent; sumptuous —**cost′li·ness** *n.*

cost of living the average cost of the necessities of life, as food, shelter, and clothes

cost-plus (kost′plus′) *adj.* with the price for goods or services set at the cost of materials, labour, etc. plus a specified amount of profit

cos·tume (kos′tyōōm) *n.* [< Fr. < It. < L. *consuetudo*, CUSTOM] **1.** *a)* the style of dress typical of a certain period, people, etc. *b)* a set of such clothes as worn in a play or at a masquerade **2.** a set of outer clothes for some occasion, esp. one worn by a woman —*vt.* -**tumed**, -**tum·ing** to provide with a costume

costume jewellery relatively inexpensive jewellery worn for show

cos·tum·i·er (-ē ər) *n.* one who makes, sells, or rents costumes, as for masquerades, theatres, etc.: also **cos·tum·er** (kos tyōōm′yər)

co·sy (kō′zē) *adj.* -**si·er**, -**si·est** [Scot. < ?] warm and comfortable; snug —*n.,pl.* -**sies** a knitted or padded cover to keep a teapot or egg hot —**co′si·ly** *adv.* —**co′si·ness** *n.*

cot[1] (kot) *n.* [Anglo-Ind. < Hindi *khāṭ* < Sans.] **1.** a narrow, collapsible bed, as one made of canvas on a folding frame **2.** a small bed with high sides for a baby

cot[2] (kot) *n.* [OE.] **1.** [Poet.] a cottage **2.** a cote **3.** a sheath, as for a hurt finger

cot cotangent

co·tan·gent (kō tan′jənt) *n.* *Trigonometry* the ratio between the side adjacent to a given acute angle in a right-angled triangle and the side opposite

cot death the unexplained sudden death of an infant during sleep: also **sudden infant death syndrome**

cote (kōt) *n.* [ME., COT[2]] a small shelter for sheep, doves, etc.

co·ten·ant (kō ten′ənt) *n.* one of two or more tenants who share a place —**co·ten′an·cy** *n.*

co·te·rie (kōt′ər ē) *n.* [Fr., orig., organization of feudal tenants < OFr. *cotier*, COTTER[1]] a close circle of friends with common interests; clique

co·ter·mi·nous (kō tur′mə nəs) *adj.* *same as* CONTERMINOUS: also **co·ter′mi·nal** —**co·ter′mi·nous·ly** *adv.*

co·til·lion (kə til′yən, ko-) *n.* [Fr. *cotillon*, orig., petticoat < OFr. *cotte*, a COAT] **1.** a lively dance of French origin, for eight persons **2.** [U.S.] a formal ball, esp. one at which debutantes are presented Also sp. **co·til′lon**

cot·tage (kot′ij) *n.* [< ML. *cotagium* < OFr. *cote* or ME. *cot*, hut] **1.** a small house in a rural area **2.** a small house in the country or at the seaside used for holidays **3.** [Aust.] a one-storey house

cottage cheese a soft, white cheese made by straining and seasoning the curds of sour milk

cottage hospital a small hospital in a rural area, often without resident medical staff

cottage industry an industry in which employees work in their own homes, often using their own equipment

cottage pie *same as* SHEPHERD'S PIE

cot·tag·er (-ər) *n.* **1.** a person who lives in a cottage **2.** a farm labourer

cot·ter¹, cot·tar (kot'ər) *n.* [< OFr. *cotier* < OE. *cot*, COT²] **1.** a cottager **2.** [Scot.] a farm-worker who occupies a cottage belonging to his employer, rent-free

cot·ter² (kot'ər) *n.* [< ?] **1.** a bolt or wedge put through a slot to hold together parts of machinery **2.** *same as* COTTER PIN

cotter pin a split pin used as a cotter, fastened in place by spreading apart its ends after it is inserted

cot·ton (kot'n) *n.* [< Ar. *qutun*] **1.** the soft, white seed hairs filling the seedpods of various shrubby plants of the mallow family **2.** a plant or plants producing this material **3.** the crop of such plants **4.** thread or cloth made of cotton —*adj.* of cotton —**cotton on to** [Colloq.] **1.** to take a liking to **2.** to become aware of (a situation) —**cotton up to** [Colloq.] to try to make friends with —**cot'ton·y** *adj.*

COTTER PIN

cotton gin [see GIN²] a machine for separating cotton fibres from the seeds

cot·ton-pick·ing (-pik''n) *adj.* [U.S. Slang] worthless, damned, hateful, etc.

cot·ton·seed (-sēd') *n.* the seed of the cotton plant, from which an oil (**cottonseed oil**) is pressed for use in margarine, cooking oil, etc.

cot·ton·tail (-tāl') *n.* a common American rabbit with a short, fluffy tail

cot·ton·wood (-wood') *n.* **1.** a poplar that has seeds covered with cottony hairs **2.** its wood

cotton wool 1. raw cotton **2.** fluffy absorbent cotton, used for surgical dressings, etc.

cot·y·le·don (kot'əlēd''n) *n.* [L. < Gr. < *kotylē*, a cavity] the first single leaf or either of the first pair of leaves produced by the embryo of a flowering plant —**cot'y·le'-don·ous, cot'y·le'don·al** *adj.*

couch (kouch) *n.* [< OFr.: see the *v.*] **1.** an article of furniture on which one may sit or lie down; sofa **2.** any resting place —*vt.* [< OFr. *coucher*, to lie down < L. *collocare* < *com-*, together + *locare*, to place] **1.** to lay as on a couch: now usually used reflexively or in the passive voice **2.** to bring down; esp., to lower (a spear, etc.) to an attacking position **3.** to put in words; express —*vi.* **1.** to lie down on a bed; recline **2.** to lie in hiding or ambush

couch·ant (-ənt) *adj.* [see prec.] *Heraldry* lying down

cou·chette (kōō shet') *n.* a berth in a railway carriage or on a ship

couch grass (kouch) [var. of QUITCH] a weedy grass that spreads rapidly by its underground stems

cou·gar (kōō'gər, -gär) *n.*, *pl.* **-gars, -gar:** see PLURAL, II, D, 1 [< Fr. < Port. *çuçuarana* < Tupi] *same as* PUMA

cough (kof) *vi.* [ME. *coughen*] to expel air suddenly and noisily from the lungs through the glottis —*vt.* to expel by coughing —*n.* **1.** a coughing **2.** a condition, as of the lungs or throat, causing frequent coughing —**cough up 1.** to bring up (phlegm, etc.) by coughing **2.** [Slang] to hand over (money, etc.) —**cough'er** *n.*

cough drop a small, flavoured, medicated tablet for the relief of coughs, hoarseness, etc.

cough mixture a liquid medicine for the relief of coughs, etc.

could (kood) *v.* [< OE. *cuthe*, pt. of *cunnan:* see CAN¹] **1.** *pt. of* CAN¹ **2.** an auxiliary in verbal phrases with present or future sense, generally equivalent to *can* in meaning and use, expressing esp. a shade of doubt or a smaller degree of possibility [it *could* be so]

could·n't (-'nt) could not

couldst (koodst) *archaic or poetic 2nd pers. sing., past indic., of* CAN¹: *used with* thou

cou·lee (kōō'lē) *n.* [Fr. < *couler*, to flow < L. < *colum*, a strainer] **1.** a stream or sheet of lava **2.** [Northwest U.S.] a deep gulch or ravine, usually dry in summer

cou·lomb (kōō'lom) *n.* [after C. A. de *Coulomb* (1736-1806), Fr. physicist] the SI unit of electric charge; charge transported through a conductor by a current of one ampere flowing for one second

coul·ter (kōl'tər) *n.* [< OFr. or OE., both < L. *culter*, ploughshare] a blade or disc on a plough, for making vertical cuts in the soil

coun·cil (koun's'l) *n.* [< OFr. < L. *concilium*, meeting < *com-*, with + *calere*, to call] **1.** a group of people called together for consultation, advice, etc. **2.** a group of people chosen as an administrative or legislative assembly **3.** the legislative body of a city or town **4.** a church assembly to discuss points of doctrine, etc. **5.** any of various organizations or societies

council chamber the room in which a council meets, esp. a local government council

council estate a group of houses or flats built for a council

council house a dwelling built by a local council and often let at a subsidized rent

coun·cil·man (-mən) *n.*, *pl.* **-men** a member of a council —**coun'cil·man'ic** (-man'ik) *adj.*

coun·cil·lor (koun'sə lər) *n.* [< COUNSELLOR] a member of a council, esp. of a city or town —**coun'cil·lor·ship'** *n.*

coun·sel (koun's'l) *n.* [< OFr. < L. *consilium*] **1.** a mutual exchange of ideas, opinions, etc.; discussion **2.** a) advice resulting from such an exchange b) any advice **3.** a) a lawyer or group of lawyers giving legal advice or acting for clients b) a barrister —*vt.* **-selled, -sel·ling 1.** to give advice to; advise **2.** to urge the acceptance of (a plan, etc.) —*vi.* to give or take advice —**keep one's own counsel** to keep one's thoughts, plans, etc. to oneself —**take counsel** to consult; exchange advice, opinions, etc.

coun·sel·lor (-ər) *n.* **1.** a person who counsels; adviser **2.** a senior British diplomatic officer **3.** [U.S.] a lawyer, esp. one who conducts cases in court: in full, **counsellor-at-law coun'sel·lor·ship'** *n.*

Counsellor of State someone appointed as a temporary regent during the sovereign's absence

count¹ (kount) *vt.* [< OFr. < L. *computare*, COMPUTE] **1.** to name numbers in regular order to (a certain number) [to *count* five] **2.** to add up, one by one, by units or groups, so as to get a total **3.** to check by numbering off; inventory **4.** to take account of; include [ten, *counting* you] **5.** to believe to be; consider [to *count* oneself lucky] —*vi.* **1.** to name numbers or items in order **2.** to be taken into account; have importance, value, etc. **3.** to have a specified value (often with *for*) **4.** to rely or depend (*on* or *upon*) —*n.* **1.** a counting, or adding up **2.** the number or a total reached by counting **3.** a reckoning or accounting **4.** to end a Parliamentary sitting when there is not a quorum of members present **5.** *Boxing* ten seconds counted to give a fallen boxer time to rise before he loses the match **6.** *Law* any of the charges in an indictment, each of which is sufficient for prosecution —**count in** to include —**count out 1.** to disregard; omit **2.** *Boxing* to declare (a boxer) defeated when he has remained down for a count of ten —**out for the count** unconscious, esp. because of exhaustion —**count'a·ble** *adj.*

count² (kount) *n.* [< OFr. < L. *comes* (gen. *comitis*), companion < *com-*, with + *ire*, to go] a European nobleman equal in rank to an English earl

count·down (-doun') *n.* the schedule of operations just before the firing of a rocket, etc.; also, the counting backwards of units of time in such a schedule

coun·te·nance (koun'tə nəns) *n.* [< OFr. < L. *continentia*, bearing < *continere*, CONTAIN] **1.** the look on a person's face that shows his nature or feelings **2.** the face; facial features **3.** a) a look of approval b) approval; support **4.** calm control; composure esp. in **keep** (or **lose**) one's **countenance** —*vt.* **-nanced, -nanc·ing** to give support to; approve —**put out of countenance** to disconcert

count·er¹ (koun'tər) *n.* [see COUNT¹] **1.** a person or thing that counts or keeps count **2.** a small piece of metal, wood, etc., used in some games, esp. for keeping score **3.** an imitation coin, or token **4.** a long table, board, etc., as in a shop or kitchen for the display of goods, serving of food, etc. **5.** a person or thing that may be used or manipulated, esp. in a negotiation —**over the counter** sold directly, not through a stock exchange —**under the counter** in a surreptitious manner: said of illegal sales

coun·ter² (koun'tər) *adv.* [< Fr. < L. *contra*, against] in a contrary direction, manner, etc.; opposite —*adj.* acting in opposition or in an opposite direction —*n.* **1.** the opposite; contrary **2.** an opposing action **3.** a stiff leather piece around the heel of a shoe **4.** the part of a ship's stern between the waterline and the curved part **5.** *Boxing, Fencing,* etc. a) a blow or parry given while parrying an opponent's blow b) a giving of such a blow or parry —*vt., vi.* **1.** to oppose or check (a person or thing) **2.** to say or do (something) in reply or retaliation **3.** *Boxing* to strike one's opponent while parrying (his blow)

coun·ter- [< Fr. < L. *contra-*, against] a combining form meaning: **1.** opposite, contrary to [counterculture] **2.** in retaliation or return [counterplot] **3.** complementary [counterpart]

coun·ter·act (koun'tər akt') *vt.* to act against; neutralize the effect of with opposing action —**coun'ter·ac'tion** *n.* —**coun'ter·ac'tive** *adj., n.*

coun·ter·at·tack (koun'tər ə tak'; for v., usually koun'-tər ə tak') *n.* an attack made in opposition to another attack —*vt., vi.* to attack so as to offset the enemy's attack

coun·ter·bal·ance (koun'tər bal'əns; for v., usually koun'-tər bal'əns) *n.* **1.** a weight used to balance another weight **2.** any force or influence that balances or offsets another —*vt.* **-anced, -anc·ing** to be a counterbalance to; offset

coun·ter·blast (-bläst') *n.* an aggressive retort or response to a verbal attack

coun·ter·check (koun'tər chek'; for v., usually koun'tər chek') *n.* **1.** anything that checks, restrains, etc. **2.** a double-check to be sure —*vt.* **1.** to check or counteract **2.** to check again to be sure

coun·ter·claim (koun'tər klām'; for v., usually koun'-tər klām') *n.* an opposing claim to offset another —*vt., vi.* to make a counterclaim (of) —**coun'ter·claim'ant** *n.*

coun·ter·clock·wise (koun'tər klok'wīz) *adj., adv.* [U.S.] anticlockwise

coun·ter·es·pi·on·age (koun'tər es'pē ə näzh', -nij) *n.* actions to prevent or thwart enemy espionage

coun·ter·feit (koun'tər fit) *adj.* [< OFr. pp. of *contrefaire,* to imitate < *contre-,* counter- + *faire* (< L. *facere*), to make] 1. made in imitation of something genuine so as to defraud; forged [*counterfeit* money] 2. pretended; sham; feigned —*n.* 1. an imitation made to deceive 2. something so much like something else as to mislead —*vt., vi.* 1. to make an imitation of (money, pictures, etc.) in order to defraud 2. to pretend 3. to resemble (something) closely —**coun'ter·feit'er** *n.*

coun·ter·foil (-foil') *n.* [COUNTER- + FOIL[2]] the stub of a cheque, receipt, etc. kept by the issuer as a record

coun·ter·in·sur·gen·cy (koun'tər in sur'jən sē) *n.* military and political action carried on to defeat an insurgency

coun·ter·in·tel·li·gence (-in tel'ə jəns) *n.* actions to counter enemy intelligence or espionage activity, prevent sabotage, etc.

coun·ter·ir·ri·tant (-ir'ə tənt) *n.* anything used to produce a slight irritation to relieve more serious inflammation elsewhere

coun·ter·mand (koun'tər mänd'; *also, and for n. always,* koun'tər mänd') *vt.* [< OFr. < L. *contra,* against + *mandare:* see MANDATE] 1. to cancel or revoke (a command or order) 2. to call back or order back by a contrary order —*n.* a command or order cancelling another

coun·ter·march (koun'tər märch'; *for v., also* koun'tər märch') *n.* a march back or in the opposite direction —*vi., vt.* to march back

coun·ter·meas·ure (koun'tər mezh'ər) *n.* action taken to oppose, neutralize, or retaliate against some other action

coun·ter·move (koun'tər mōōv') *n.* a move made in opposition or retaliation

coun·ter·of·fen·sive (koun'tər ə fen'siv) *n.* an attack in force by troops who have been defending a position

coun·ter·pane (koun'tər pān') *n.* [altered < ME. *countrepoint,* quilt < OFr. < L. *culcita puncta,* pricked (i.e., embroidered) quilt] a bedspread

coun·ter·part (-pärt') *n.* 1. a person or thing that corresponds to or closely resembles another 2. a thing that completes or complements another 3. a copy or duplicate, as of a lease

coun·ter·plot (koun'tər plot'; *for v., also* koun'tər plot') *n.* a plot to defeat another plot —*vt., vi.* -plot'ted, -plot'ting to plot against (a plot); defeat (a plot) with another

coun·ter·point (-point') *n.* [< Fr. < It. *contrappunto,* lit., pointed against: see COUNTER- & POINT, *n.*] 1. a melody accompanying another melody note for note 2. *a)* the art of adding related but independent melodies to a basic melody, in accordance with the fixed rules of harmony *b)* this kind of composition

coun·ter·poise (-poiz') *n.* [< ONormFr.: see COUNTER[2] & POISE] 1. *same as* COUNTERBALANCE 2. a state of balance or equilibrium —*vt.* -poised', -pois'ing *same as* COUNTERBALANCE

coun·ter·pro·duc·tive (-prə duk'tiv) *adj.* bringing about effects or results that are contrary to those intended

coun·ter·pro·po·sal (-prə pō'z'l) *n.* a proposal in response to one regarded as unsatisfactory

Counter-Reformation the reform movement in the Roman Catholic Church in the 16th cent., following in reaction to the Protestant Reformation

coun·ter·rev·o·lu·tion (koun'tər rev'ə lōō'shən) *n.* 1. a political movement or revolution against a government or social system set up by a previous revolution 2. a movement to combat revolutionary tendencies —**coun'ter·rev'o·lu'tion·ar·y** *adj., n.* —**coun'ter·rev'o·lu'tion·ist** *n.*

coun·ter·shaft (koun'tər shäft') *n.* an intermediate shaft that transmits motion from the main shaft of a machine to a working part

coun·ter·sign (koun'tər sīn'; *for v., also* koun'tər sīn') *n.* 1. a signature added to a previously signed document for confirmation 2. *Mil.* a secret word or signal which must be given to a sentry by someone wishing to pass —*vt.* to confirm (a previously signed document) by signing —**coun'ter·sig'na·ture** (-sig'nə chər) *n.*

coun·ter·sink (koun'tər siŋk'; *for v., also* koun'tər siŋk') *vt.* -sunk', -sink'ing 1. to enlarge the top part of (a hole in metal, wood, etc.) to make the head of a bolt, screw, etc. fit into it 2. to sink (a bolt, screw, etc.) into such a hole —*n.* 1. a tool for countersinking holes 2. a countersunk hole

coun·ter·spy (-spī') *n.* a spy in counterespionage

coun·ter·ten·or (-ten'ər) *n.* 1. the range of the highest mature male voice, above tenor 2. a voice, singer, or part with such a range

coun·ter·vail (koun'tər vāl') *vt.* [< OFr. < *contre* (see COUNTER[2]) + *valoir,* to avail < L. *valere,* to be strong] 1. to make up for; compensate 2. to counteract; avail against —*vi.* to avail (*against*)

coun·ter·weigh (-wā') *vt.* *same as* COUNTERBALANCE —**coun'ter·weight'** *n.*

counter word any word freely used as a general term of approval or disapproval without reference to its more exact meaning, as *nice* or *terrible*

count·ess (koun'tis) *n.* 1. the wife or widow of a count or earl 2. a noblewoman whose rank is equal to that of a count or earl

count·ing·house (koun'tiŋ hous') *n.* [Now Rare] an office where a firm keeps accounts, etc.

count·less (kount'lis) *adj.* too many to count; innumerable; myriad

coun·tri·fied (kun'tri fīd') *adj.* 1. rural; rustic 2. having the appearance, actions, etc. attributed to country people Also sp. **coun'try·fied'**

coun·try (kun'trē) *n., pl.* -tries [< OFr. < ML. *contrata,* that which is beyond < L. *contra,* opposite] 1. an area of land; region [*wooded country*] 2. the whole territory of a nation 3. the people of a nation 4. the land of a person's birth or citizenship 5. land with farms and small towns; rural region 6. the area associated with a poet, novelist, etc. [Burns *country*] —*adj.* 1. of, in, or from a rural district 2. like that of the country; rustic —**across country** to travel not using roads, lanes, etc. —**go to the country** to dissolve Parliament and hold an election

country and western a 20th-cent. variation of country music, including the type of song supposedly sung by cowboys

country club a social club in the country or on the outskirts of a city, equipped with a clubhouse, golf course, etc.

coun·try-dance (-däns') *n.* an English folk dance, esp. one in which partners form two facing lines

country house a residence in the country, esp. of someone who also owns a residence in town

coun·try·man (-mən) *n., pl.* -men 1. a man who lives in the country; rustic 2. a man of one's own country; compatriot —**coun'try·wom'an** *n.fem., pl.* -wom'en

country music rural folk music, esp. a commercialized variety deriving from the folk music of the South-Eastern U.S.

coun·try·seat (-sēt') *n.* a rural mansion or estate

coun·try·side (-sīd') *n.* a rural region or its inhabitants

coun·ty (koun'tē) *n., pl.* -ties [< OFr. < ML. *comitatus,* jurisdiction of a count < L. *comes:* see COUNT[2]] 1. a small administrative district; esp., *a)* any of the chief administrative and judicial districts into which Great Britain and Ireland were divided *b)* since 1974, a unit of local government in England and Wales *c)* the largest local administrative unit of most states in the U.S. 2. the people in a county, esp. the upper-class families

county council the governing body composed of the elected representatives of the ratepayers of a county

county cricket the level of cricket at which teams representing counties compete against each other

county town a town or city that is the seat of government of a county

coup (kōō) *n., pl.* **coups** (kōōz; *Fr.* kōō) [Fr. < VL. < L. *colaphus,* a blow < Gr. *kolaphos*] 1. literally, a blow 2. a sudden, successful move or action; brilliant stroke 3. *same as* COUP D'ÉTAT

‡**coup de grâce** (kōō də gräs') [Fr., lit., stroke of mercy] 1. the blow, shot, etc. that brings death to a sufferer 2. a finishing stroke

‡**coup de main** (man') [Fr., lit., stroke of hand] a surprise attack or movement, as in war

‡**coup d'é·tat** (dā tä') [Fr., lit., stroke of state] a sudden, forceful stroke in politics, esp. the sudden, forcible overthrow of a government

coupe (kōōp) *n.* [< Fr., lit., a goblet] 1. a dessert of fruit and ice cream 2. the dish or stemmed glass bowl in which this dessert is usually served

cou·pé (kōō pā') *n.* [Fr., pp. of *couper,* to cut] 1. a closed carriage seating two passengers, with a seat outside for the driver 2. a closed, two-door motor car, usually with a sloping back

cou·ple (kup''l) *n.* [< OFr. < L. *copula:* see COPULA] 1. anything joining two things together; bond; link 2. two things or persons of the same sort that are somehow associated 3. a man and a woman who are engaged, married, or partners in a dance, etc. 4. [Colloq.] a few; several [a *couple* of drinks] 5. *Mech.* two equal forces producing rotation by moving in parallel but opposite directions —*vt.* -pled, -pling to join together; link; connect —*vi.* 1. to come together; unite 2. to copulate

cou·pler (kup'lər) *n.* a person or thing that couples; specif., a device on an organ connecting two keyboards or keys an octave apart so that they can be played together

cou·plet (kup'lit) *n.* [Fr. dim.: see COUPLE] 1. two successive lines of poetry, esp. two of the same length that rhyme 2. [Rare] a couple

cou·pling (kup′liŋ) *n.* 1. a joining together 2. a mechanical device for joining parts together 3. a device for joining railway carriages 4. a method or device for joining two electric circuits to transfer energy from one to the other

cou·pon (koo′pon) *n.* [Fr. < *couper,* to cut] 1. a detachable printed statement on a bond, specifying the interest due at a given time 2. a certificate or ticket entitling the holder to a specified right, as reduced purchase price 3. a part of a printed advertisement for use in ordering goods, etc. 4. the entry form for various competitions, esp. the football pools

cour·age (kur′ij) *n.* [< OFr. < L. *cor,* heart] a willingness to face and deal with danger, trouble, or pain; fearlessness; bravery; valour —**the courage of one's convictions** the courage to do what one thinks is right

cou·ra·geous (kə rā′jəs) *adj.* having or showing courage; brave —**cou·ra′geous·ly** *adv.* —**cou·ra′geous·ness** *n.*

cour·gette (koor′zhet′) *n.* a variety of marrow that is green-skinned and shaped somewhat like a cucumber

cou·ri·er (koor′ē ər) *n.* [< OFr., ult. < L. *currere,* to run] 1. a messenger sent in haste or on a regular schedule with important or urgent messages 2. a person who makes arrangements for, or accompanies, a group of travellers on a journey or tour

course (kôrs) *n.* [< OFr. *cours* < L. pp. of *currere,* to run] 1. an onward movement; progress 2. a way, path, or channel of movement; specif., *same as:* a) RACECOURSE b) GOLF COURSE 3. the direction taken, as by a ship or plane [a *course* due south] 4. a) a regular manner of procedure [the law must take its *course*] b) a way of behaving; mode of conduct 5. a) a series of like things in some regular order b) a particular succession of events or actions 6. natural development [the *course* of true love] 7. a part of a meal served at one time 8. a horizontal layer, as of bricks, in the face of a building 9. *Educ.* a complete series of lectures, etc. leading to a degree, etc. —*vt.* coursed, cours′ing 1. to pursue 2. to cause (esp. hunting hounds) to chase 3. to traverse —*vi.* 1. to run or race 2. to hunt with hounds —**in due course** in the usual or proper sequence (of events) —**in the course of** in the process of; during —**of course** 1. as is or was to be expected; naturally 2. certainly —**on** (or **off**) **course** moving (or not moving) in the intended direction

cours·er (kôr′sər) *n.* [see prec.] 1. [Poet.] a graceful, spirited, or swift horse 2. a person that engages in the sport of coursing

cours·ing (-siŋ) *n.* 1. the action of a person or thing that courses 2. hunting with dogs trained to follow game, esp. hares, by sight rather than by scent

court (kôrt) *n.* [OFr. < LL. < L. *cohors:* see COHORT] 1. an uncovered space wholly or partly surrounded by buildings or walls 2. a short street, often closed at one end 3. a) a block of flats b) a mansion or country house 4. a) an area for playing any of several ball games b) a part of such an area 5. [U.S.] a motel: in full, **motor court** 6. a) the palace of a sovereign b) the family, advisers, etc. of a sovereign, as a group c) a sovereign and his councillors as a governing body d) any formal gathering held by a sovereign 7. attention paid to someone in order to get something 8. courtship; wooing 9. a) a person or persons appointed to try law cases, make investigations, etc.; judge or judges b) a place where trials are held, investigations made, etc. c) a judicial assembly; also, a regular session of such an assembly —*vt.* 1. to pay attention to (a person) in order to get something 2. to try to get the love of; woo 3. to try to get; seek [to *court* favour] 4. to make oneself open to [to *court* insults] —*vi.* to woo —*adj.* of or fit for a court —**go to court** to initiate legal action —**hold court** to officiate or preside over a group of one's admirers —**laugh out of court** to ridicule completely —**out of court** without a trial —**pay court to** to court, as for favour or love —**court′er** *n.*

court bouillon a stock made from wine and root vegetables: used esp. for poaching fish

court card any king, queen or jack in a pack of cards

court circular the official, daily report of the affairs and actions of the royal family

cour·te·ous (kur′tē əs) *adj.* [< OFr. *courteis* < *court:* see COURT & -EOUS] polite and gracious; considerate of others; well-mannered —**cour′te·ous·ly** *adv.* —**cour′te·ous·ness** *n.*

cour·te·san (kôr′tə zan) *n.* [< Fr. < It. *cortigiana,* court lady < *corte,* COURT] a prostitute; esp., formerly, a mistress of a king, nobleman, etc.: also **cour′te·zan**

cour·te·sy (kur′tə sē) *n., pl.* **-sies** [< OFr. *curteisie:* see COURTEOUS] 1. courteous behaviour; gracious politeness 2. a polite or considerate act or remark 3. an act or usage intended to honour or compliment [a title of *courtesy*] —**by courtesy** by consent of (someone)

courtesy light the small light in a car that is switched on automatically when the door is opened

courtesy title a title with no legal significance, as that borne by children of certain peers

court·house (kôrt′hous′) *n.* 1. a building in which law courts are held 2. [U.S.] a building that houses the offices of a county government

cour·ti·er (kôr′tē ər, -tyər) *n.* 1. an attendant at a royal court 2. a person who courts favour by flattery, etc.

court·ly (kôrt′lē) *adj.* **-li·er, -li·est** 1. suitable for a king's court; dignified, elegant, etc. 2. flattering, esp. in an obsequious or humble way —*adv.* in a courtly manner —**court′li·ness** *n.*

court-mar·tial (-mär′shəl) *n., pl.* **courts′-mar′tial;** for 2, now often **court′-mar′tials** 1. a court of personnel in the armed forces to try offences against military law 2. a trial by a court-martial —*vt.* **-tialled, -tial·ling** to try by a court-martial

Court of Appeal 1. a court to which appeals are taken from the High Court and the county courts

Court of St. James [< *St. James Palace,* former royal residence] the British royal court

court plaster [from former use by court ladies for beauty spots] cloth covered with an adhesive material, formerly used to protect minor skin wounds

court·room (kôrt′room′) *n.* a room in which a law court is held

court·ship (-ship′) *n.* the act, process, or period of courting, or wooing

court shoe a woman's low-cut shoe without straps or laces

court·yard (-yärd′) *n.* a space enclosed by walls, adjoining or in a large building

cous·cous (koos′koos) *n.* [Fr. < Berber < Ar. < *kaskasa,* to grind] a N African dish of crushed grain, usually steamed and served with meat

cous·in (kuz′'n) *n.* [< OFr. < L. < *com-,* with + *sobrinus,* maternal cousin < *soror,* sister] 1. the son or daughter of one's uncle or aunt: also **cous′in-ger′man** (-jur′mən), **first** (or **full**) **cousin** 2. loosely, any relative by blood or marriage 3. a person thought of as related to another 4. a title of address used by one sovereign to another or to a nobleman —**cous′in·ly** *adj., adv.* —**cous′in·ship′** *n.*

couth (kooth) *adj.* [back formation < UNCOUTH] sophisticated; cultured: usually used facetiously

cou·ture (koo toor′) *n.* [Fr., sewing < L. pp. of *consuere* < *com-,* together + *suere,* to sew] the work or business of designing new fashions in women's clothes

‡**cou·tu·rier** (koo tü ryā′; E. koo toor′ē ä′) *n.* [Fr.] a man engaged in couture —**cou·tu·rière** (-tü ryer′; E. -toor′ē er′) *n.fem.*

co·va·lence (kō vā′ləns) *n.* the number of pairs of electrons an atom can share with neighbouring atoms —**co·va′lent** *adj.*

cove[1] (kōv) *n.* [< OE. *cofa,* cave, cell] 1. a sheltered nook or recess, as in cliffs 2. a small bay or inlet 3. [U.S.] a small valley 4. a concave moulding —*vt., vi.* **coved, cov′-ing** to curve concavely

cove[2] (kōv) *n.* [< ? Romany *covo,* that man] [Slang] a boy or man; chap; fellow

cov·en (kuv′ən) *n.* [< OFr. < L. *convenire,* CONVENE] a gathering or meeting, esp. of witches

cov·e·nant (kuv′ə nənt) *n.* [< OFr. < L. *convenire,* CONVENE] 1. a binding agreement made by two or more individuals, parties, etc. to do or keep from doing a specified thing; compact 2. *Law* a) a formal, sealed contract b) an agreement in writing under seal, as to pay a given stated annual sum to a charity 3. *Theol.* the promises made by God to man, as recorded in the Bible —*vt., vi.* to promise by or in a covenant —**cov′e·nan′tal** (-nant′l) *adj.* —**cov′e·nant·er, cov′e·nan·tor** (-nan tər) *n.*

cov·e·nant·ed (-əd) *adj.* obliged or bound by a covenant

cov·e·nant·er (kuv′ə nan tər) *n.* 1. a person who enters into a covenant 2. [C-] a person who supported either of the Scottish Presbyterian Covenants in the 17th cent.

Cov·en·try (kov′ən trē) *n.* [after *Coventry,* city in W Midlands] ostracism [to send a person to *Coventry*]

cov·er (kuv′ər) *vt.* [< OFr. < L. < *co-,* intens. + *operire,* to hide] 1. to place something on, over, or in front of 2. to extend over; overlay 3. to mate with (a mare): said of a stallion 4. to clothe 5. to coat, sprinkle, etc. thickly 6. to sit on (eggs); brood 7. to conceal by hiding or screening 8. to protect as by shielding 9. to take into account 10. a) to protect against financial loss, or make up for (a loss, etc.), as by insurance b) to be sufficient for payment of (a debt, etc.) c) to buy stock to replace (shares borrowed from a broker to effect a short sale) 11. to accept (a bet) 12. to travel over [to *cover* a distance] 13. to be responsible for (an area or range of activity) 14. to deal with [to *cover* a subject] 15. to point a firearm at 16. *Journalism* to get news, pictures, etc. of [to *cover* a train crash] 17. *Sports* to guard or obstruct (an opponent, position, etc.) —*vi.* 1. to spread over a surface, as a liquid 2. to put on a cap, hat, etc. 3. to provide an alibi or excuse (*for* another) —*n.* 1.

anything that covers, as a binding, lid, top, etc. **2.** *a)* a protective shelter or a hiding place *b)* a pretext, disguise, or false identity **3.** a tablecloth and a place setting for one person **4.** *same as* COVER-UP **5.** *a)* an envelope, wrapping, etc. for post *b)* an entire envelope and stamp that has been postmarked for the collection of a philatelist **6.** *Cricket same as* COVER POINT —**break cover** to come out of protective shelter —**cover up 1.** to cover entirely **2.** to keep blunders, crimes, etc. from being known —**take cover** to seek protective shelter —**under cover** in secrecy or concealment —**cov′er·er** *n.*

cov·er·age (-ij) *n.* **1.** the amount, extent, etc. covered by something **2.** *Insurance* all the risks covered by an insurance policy

cover charge a fixed charge added to the cost of food and drink, as at a nightclub or restaurant

cover crop a crop, as vetch or clover, grown to protect soil from erosion and to keep it fertile

cover drive *Cricket* a stroke by the batsman sending the ball past cover point

covered wagon a large wagon with an arched cover of canvas, used by American pioneers

cover girl [Colloq.] a girl model whose picture is often put on magazine covers, etc.

cov·er·ing (kuv′ər iŋ) *n.* anything that covers

covering letter (or **note**) a letter (or note) sent with a parcel, another letter, etc. as an explanation

cov·er·let (kuv′ər lit) *n.* [< Anglo-Fr. < OFr. *covrir*, COVER + *lit*, a bed < L. *lectus*] **1.** a bedspread **2.** any covering

cover note a certificate from an insurance company that provides proof of the existence of an insurance policy

cover point *Cricket* **1.** a fielding position at right angles to the pitch on the off side and about halfway to the boundary **2.** a fielder in this position

cov·ert (kuv′ərt) *adj.* [OFr., pp. of *covrir*, COVER] concealed, hidden, or disguised —*n.* **1.** a covered or protected place; shelter **2.** a hiding place for game **3.** any of the small feathers covering the bases of the larger feathers of a bird's wing and tail —**cov′ert·ly** *adv.* —**cov′ert·ness** *n.*

covert (**cloth**) a smooth, twilled, lightweight cloth, usually of wool, used for suits, topcoats, etc.

cov·er·ture (kuv′ər chər) *n.* **1.** a covering **2.** a refuge **3.** a concealment or disguise

cov·er-up (kuv′ər up′) *n.* something used for hiding one's real activities, intentions, etc.

cov·et (kuv′it) *vt., vi.* [< OFr. < L. *cupiditas*: see CUPIDITY] to want ardently (esp., something that another has) —**cov′et·a·ble** *adj.* —**cov′et·er** *n.*

cov·et·ous (-əs) *adj.* greedy; avaricious —**cov′et·ous·ly** *adv.* —**cov′et·ous·ness** *n.*

cov·ey (kuv′ē) *n., pl.* **-eys** [< OFr. < *cover*, to hatch < L. *cubare*, to lie down] **1.** a small flock of birds, esp. partridges or quail **2.** a small group of people or, sometimes, things

cow[1] (kou) *n., pl.* **cows**; archaic **kine** (kīn) [OE. *cu*] **1.** the mature female of domestic cattle, valued for its milk, or of certain other animals, as the buffalo, elephant, etc.: the male of such animals is called a *bull* **2.** loosely, any domestic bovine animal, whether a bull, cow, or calf **3.** [Colloq.] a woman, esp. one considered to be disagreeable **4.** [Aust. Slang] something objectionable, esp. in **a fair cow**

cow[2] (kou) *vt.* [< ON. *kūga*, to subdue] to make timid and submissive by filling with fear or awe

cow·age (kou′ij) *n.* [< Hindi] a tropical climbing plant with blackish pods covered with fine barbed hairs

cow·ard (kou′ərd) *n.* [< OFr. < *coe* < L. *cauda*, tail] one who lacks courage or suffers from cowardice —*adj.* cowardly

cow·ard·ice (-is) *n.* lack of courage; esp., shamefully excessive fear of danger, difficulty, etc.

cow·ard·ly (-lē) *adj.* of or typical of a coward; shamefully fearful —*adv.* in the manner of a coward —**cow′ard·li·ness** *n.*

cow·ard·y custard (-dē) [Colloq.] *a children's taunt meaning* very cowardly: also **cowardy, cowardy custard**

cow·bell (kou′bel′) *n.* a bell hung from a cow's neck so she can be found by its clanging

cow·ber·ry (-ber′ē) *n., pl.* **-ries 1.** a low creeping shrub with white or pink flowers and dark-red, acid berries **2.** its berry

cow·boy (-boi′) *n.* [U.S.] **1.** a ranch worker who rides horseback on his job of herding cattle: also **cow′hand′ 2.** a performer in a rodeo **3.** a conventionalized character in films, books, etc., typically one who rides a horse, carries pistols, sings ballads, etc. —**cow′girl′** *n.fem.*

cow·catch·er (-kach′ər) *n.* [U.S.] a metal frame on the front of a locomotive to remove obstructions from the railway line

cow·er (kou′ər) *vi.* [ME. *couren*, prob. < ON.] **1.** to crouch or huddle up, as from fear **2.** to shrink and tremble, as from someone's anger, threats, or blows; cringe —**cow′er·ing·ly** *adv.*

cow·herd (kou′hurd′) *n.* a tender of grazing cattle

cow·hide (-hīd′) *n.* **1.** the hide of a cow **2.** leather made from it **3.** a whip made of this

cowl (koul) *n.* [< OE. < LL. < L. *cucullus*, hood] **1.** *a)* a monk's hood *b)* a monk's cloak with a hood **2.** something shaped like a cowl; esp., *a)* a cover for the top of a chimney, to increase the draught *b)* the top front part of a motor car body, to which the windscreen and dashboard are fastened *c)* a cowling —*vt.* to cover as with a cowl —**cowled** *adj.*

cow·lick (kou′lik) *n.* [< the idea that it looks as if it has been licked by a cow] a tuft of hair on the head that cannot easily be combed flat

cowl·ing (kou′liŋ) *n.* [see COWL] a detachable metal covering for an aircraft engine, etc.

cow·man (kou′mən) *n., pl.* **-men 1.** a cowherd **2.** [U.S.] the owner or operator of a cattle ranch

co-work·er (kō′wur′kər) *n.* a fellow worker

cow parsley an umbelliferous plant, found in the hedgerows of Europe and Asia

cow·pea (kou′pē′) *n.* **1.** a bushlike annual forage plant of the legume family, with seeds in slender pods **2.** its edible seed

cow·pox (kou′poks′) *n.* a contagious disease of cows that causes pustules on the udders: smallpox vaccine is made from the virus

cow·punch·er (-pun′chər) *n.* [from the prodding of animals in herding] [U.S. Colloq.] a cowboy

cow·rie, cow·ry (kou′rē) *n., pl.* **-ries** [< Hindi < Sans. *kaparda*] **1.** any of certain gastropods of warm seas, with brightly coloured shells **2.** the shell of such a mollusc, esp. of the **money cowrie**, formerly used as currency in parts of Africa and S Asia

cow·shed (kou′shed′) *n.* a shelter for cows

cow·slip (-slip′) *n.* [< OE., lit., cow dung < *cu*, cow + *slyppe*, paste] **1.** a European primrose with yellow flowers **2.** [U.S.] *same as* MARSH MARIGOLD

cox (koks) *n., pl.* **cox′es** [Colloq.] a coxswain —*vt., vi.* to be coxswain for (a boat or crew)

cox·a (kok′sə) *n., pl.* **cox′ae** (-sē) [L.] **1.** the hip or hip joint **2.** the basal segment of an arthropod leg —**cox′al** *adj.*

cox·al·gi·a (kok sal′jē ə, -jə) *n.* [see prec. & -ALGIA] pain in, or disease of, the hip or hip joint: also **cox·al′gy** (-jē) —**cox·al′gic** *adj.*

cox·comb (koks′kōm′) *n.* [for *cock's comb*] **1.** a cap topped with a notched strip of red cloth like a cock's comb, formerly worn by jesters **2.** a silly, vain, foppish fellow; dandy —**cox·comb·i·cal** (koks kō′mi k'l, -kom′i-) *adj.* —**cox·comb′i·cal·ly** *adv.* —**cox′comb′ry** (-kōm′rē) *n., pl.* **-ries**

cox·swain (kok′sən, -swān′) *n.* [< COCK(BOAT) + SWAIN] **1.** a person in charge of a ship's boat and acting as its steersman **2.** the steersman of a racing shell, calling out the stroke rhythm —*vi.,vt.* to act as a coxswain

coy (koi) *adj.* [< OFr. < LL. < L. *quietus*: see QUIET] **1.** bashful; shy **2.** affecting innocence or shyness, esp. playfully or coquettishly **3.** reticent in making a commitment —**coy′ly** *adv.* —**coy′ness** *n.*

Coy. *Mil.* Company

coy·o·te (kī ōt′ē, kī′ōt) *n., pl.* **coy·o′tes, coy·o′te:** see PLURAL, II, D, 1 [AmSp. < Nahuatl *coyotl*] a small wolf of western N. American prairies

coy·pu (koi′pōo) *n., pl.* **-pus, -pu:** see PLURAL, II, D, 1 [< AmSp. < native name] **1.** a S American water-rat similar to the beaver **2.** the fur of this animal Also **nutria**

coz (kuz) *n.* [Colloq.] cousin

coz·en (kuz′'n) *vt., vi.* [< ME. *cosin*, fraud < ?] to cheat, defraud, or deceive —**coz′en·age** *n.*

co·zy (kō′zē) *adj.* **-zi·er, -zi·est** [U.S.] *same as* COSY

COYOTE
(to 1.20 m long, including tail)

cp, c.p. candlepower

cp. compare

C.P. 1. Cape Province **2.** Common Pleas **3.** Common Prayer **4.** Communist Party **5.** Country Party (in Australia)

CPA critical path analysis

cpd. compound

Cpl, Cpl. Corporal

cpm, c.p.m. cycles per minute

CPO, C.P.O. Chief Petty Officer

cps, c.p.s. cycles per second

CQ amateur radio operators' signal inviting a reply

Cr *Chem.* chromium

cr. 1. credit **2.** creditor **3.** crown

crab[1] (krab) *n.* [< OE. *crabba*] **1.** any of various crustaceans with four pairs of legs, one pair of pincers, a flattish shell, and a short, broad abdomen folded under its thorax **2.** any of several similar animals **3.** *same as* CRAB LOUSE **4.** a machine for hoisting heavy weights —[C-]

Cancer, the constellation and zodiac sign —*vi.* **crabbed,** **crab′bing** to fish for or catch crabs —**catch a crab** *Rowing* to unbalance the boat by a faulty stroke —**crab′-** **ber** *n.*

crab² (krab) *n.* [akin ? to Scot. *scrabbe,* Sw. dial. *scrabba,* wild apple] 1. *same as* CRAB APPLE 2. a sour-tempered person —*adj.* of a crab apple —*vi.* **crabbed,** **crab′bing** [Colloq.] to complain peevishly —**crab′ber** *n.* —**crab′like** *adj.*

crab apple 1. a small, very sour apple, used for jellies, jams, etc. 2. a tree bearing crab apples: also **crab tree**

crab·bed (krab′id) *adj.* [< CRAB (APPLE)] 1. peevish; cross 2. hard to understand; intricate 3. hard to read; illegible —**crab′bed·ly** *adv.* —**crab′bed·ness** *n.*

crab·by (-ē) *adj.* **-bi·er, -bi·est** [see prec.] peevish; cross —**crab′bi·ly** *adv.* —**crab′bi·ness** *n.*

crab louse a louse, somewhat crablike in shape, infesting the pubic regions, armpits, etc.

crab·wise (-wīz′) *adv.* moving sideways like a crab

crack (krak) *vi.* [< OE. *cracian,* to resound] 1. to make a sudden, sharp breaking noise 2. to break or split, usually without complete separation of parts 3. to become rasping or change pitch suddenly, as the voice 4. [Colloq.] to break down [to *crack* under the strain] —*vt.* 1. to cause to make a sharp, sudden noise 2. to cause to break or split 3. to destroy or impair 4. to subject (as petroleum) to cracking: see CRACKING² 5. to hit or strike with a sudden, sharp blow or impact 6. to manage to solve [to *crack* a code] 7. [Colloq.] to break open or into 8. [Slang] to make (a joke) —*n.* 1. a sudden, sharp noise 2. *a)* a break, usually partial *b)* a flaw 3. a chink; fissure 4. an abrupt, erratic shift of vocal tone 5. a moment; instant [the *crack* of dawn] 6. [Colloq.] a sudden, sharp blow or impact 7. [Colloq.] an attempt; try 8. [Slang] a joke or gibe 9. [Slang] a person that excels —*adj.* [Colloq.] excelling in skill; first-rate [*crack* troops] —**crack a bottle** [Colloq.] to drink —**crack a smile** [Slang] to relax or unbend enough to smile —**crack down (on)** to become strict or stricter (with) —**cracked up to be** [Colloq.] alleged or believed to be —**(fair) crack of the whip** [Colloq.] a fair chance or opportunity —**crack up** [Colloq.] 1. to break down physically or mentally 2. to break into a fit of laughter or tears

crack·brain (-brān′) *n.* a crazy person

crack·brained (-brānd′) *adj.* crazy

crack·down (-doun′) *n.* a resorting to strict or stricter measures of discipline or punishment

cracked (krakt) *adj.* 1. broken, usually without complete separation of parts 2. harsh [a *cracked* voice] 3. [Colloq.] crazy

cracked wheat coarsely milled wheat particles

crack·er (krak′ər) *n.* 1. one that cracks 2. a firework 3. a little paper roll used as a Christmas toy: it contains sweets, mottos, etc. and pops open when the ends are pulled 4. a thin, crisp, unsweetened biscuit 5. [Slang] a person of notable qualities or abilities, esp. an attractive girl

crack·er·jack (krak′ər jak′) *adj.* [extension of CRACK, adj. + *Jack,* masculine name] [Slang] excellent —*n.* [Slang] an excellent person or thing

crack·ers (krak′ərz) *adj.* [altered < CRACKED] [Slang] crazy

crack·ing¹ (krak′iŋ) *adj.* [Colloq.] excellent; fine —*adv.* [Colloq.] very —**get cracking** [Colloq.] to start doing something, esp. vigorously and energetically

crack·ing² (krak′iŋ) *n.* the process of breaking down heavier hydrocarbons, as by heat and pressure, into lighter hydrocarbons, as in producing petrol

crack·jaw (krak′jô) *n.* [Colloq.] a word that is difficult to pronounce

crack·le (krak′'l) *vi.* **-led, -ling** [freq. of CRACK] 1. to make slight, sharp popping sounds, as of dry wood burning 2. to be bursting with vivacity, etc. 3. to develop a finely cracked surface —*vt.* 1. to crush or break with crackling sounds 2. to produce a finely cracked surface on —*n.* 1. crackling sounds 2. fine, irregular surface cracks, as on old oil paintings 3. crackleware

crack·le·ware (krak′'l wer′) *n.* pottery, porcelain, etc. with a finely cracked surface

crack·ling (krak′liŋ) *n.* 1. the production of slight, sharp popping sounds 2. *a)* the browned, crisp rind of roast pork *b)* [pl.] crisp bits left when pig fat is rendered 3. [Slang] an attractive girl, esp. in phrase **a bit of crackling**

crack·ly (-lē) *adj.* that crackles; crackling

crack·pot (-pot′) *n.* [Colloq.] a crazy or eccentric person —*adj.* [Colloq.] crazy or eccentric

crack·up (krak′up′) *n.* [Colloq.] a mental or physical collapse

-cra·cy (krə sē) [< Fr. < ML. < Gr. *-kratia* < *kratos,* rule] *a combining form meaning* a (specified) type of government; rule by [*autocracy*]

cra·dle (krā′d'l) *n.* [OE. *cradol*] 1. a baby's small bed, usually on rockers 2. infancy 3. the place of a thing's

beginning 4. anything cradlelike; specif., *a)* a framework to hold or lift a boat, etc. being built or repaired *b)* the support for the handset of a telephone (**cradle telephone**) *c)* *Agric.* a frame on a scythe (**cradle scythe**) for laying the grain evenly as it is cut *d)* *Mining* a boxlike device on rockers for washing out gold —*vt.* **-dled, -dling** 1. to place, rock, or hold in or as in a cradle 2. *Mining* to wash (sand) in a cradle

cradle snatcher *same as* BABY SNATCHER

cra·dle·song (-soŋ′) *n.* a lullaby

craft (kräft) *n.* [OE. *cræft,* strength, power] 1. a special skill or art 2. an occupation requiring this; esp., any manual art 3. the members of a skilled trade 4. skill in deceiving; guile 5. *pl.* **craft** a boat, ship, or aircraft —*vt.* to make with skill or artistry: usually in pp.

-craft (kräft) [< prec.] *a combining form meaning* the work, skill, or practice of [*handicraft*]

crafts·man (kräfts′mən) *n., pl.* **-men** 1. a skilled workman 2. a skilful artist or one having only technical skill —**crafts′-** **man·ship′** *n.*

craft·y (kräf′tē) *adj.* **craft′i·er, craft′i·est** sly; cunning —**craft′i·ly** *adv.* —**craft′i·ness** *n.*

crag (krag) *n.* [< Celt.] a steep, rugged rock rising above others or projecting from a rock mass

crag·gy (-ē) *adj.* **-gi·er, -gi·est** having many crags: also **crag′ged** (-id) —**crag′gi·ness** *n.*

crake (krāk) *n., pl.* **crakes, crake:** see PLURAL, II. D. 1 [< ON. *kraka,* crow] any of several rails with long legs and a short bill

cram (kram) *vt.* **crammed, cram′ming** [OE. *crammian,* to stuff] 1. to pack full or too full 2. to stuff; force 3. to feed to excess 4. to prepare (a student) or review (a subject) for an examination in a hurried, intensive way —*vi.* 1. to eat too much or too quickly 2. to study a subject in a hurried, intensive way, for an examination —*n.* 1. a crowded condition 2. a cramming

cram·bo (kram′bō) *n.* [< ? L. *crambe,* cabbage (as in *crambe repetita,* lit., cabbage repeatedly served, hence old tale)] a word game in which players find rhymes for words or lines of verse given by each other

cram·mer (kram′ər) *n.* a person or institution that prepares students for examinations, esp. by cramming them

cramp¹ (kramp) *n.* [< OFr. *crampe,* bent, twisted < OHG] 1. a sudden, painful, involuntary contraction of a muscle from chill, strain, etc. 2. partial local paralysis, as from excessive use of muscles [writer's *cramp*] 3. [U.S.] [usually *pl.*] abdominal spasms and pain —*vt.* to cause a cramp in

cramp² (kramp) *n.* [MDu. *krampe,* lit., bent in] 1. a metal bar bent at each end at a right angle, for holding together timbers, etc.: also **cramp iron** 2. a clamp 3. anything that confines or hampers —*vt.* 1. to fasten as with a cramp 2. to confine or hamper —**cramp one's style** [Slang] to hamper one's skill, confidence, etc. in doing something

cramped (krampt) *adj.* 1. confined; restricted 2. irregular and crowded, as some handwriting

cram·pon (kram′pən) *n.* [Fr., akin to CRAMP²] 1. either of a pair of iron hooks for raising heavy weights 2. either of a pair of spiked iron plates fastened on shoes to prevent slipping

cran·ber·ry (kran′bər ē) *n., pl.* **-ries** [< Du. *kranebere,* LowG. *kraanbere,* lit., crane berry] 1. a firm, sour, edible, red berry of an evergreen shrub of the heath family 2. this shrub

crane (krān) *n.* [OE. *cran*] 1. *pl.* **cranes, crane:** see PLURAL, II. D. 1 *a)* a large wading bird with very long legs and neck, and a long, straight bill *b)* popularly, any of various herons or storks 2. a machine for lifting or moving heavy weights by means of a movable projecting arm or a horizontal travelling beam 3. any device with a swinging arm fixed on a vertical axis, as to hold a kettle —*vt., vi.* **craned, cran′ing** 1. to raise or move as by a crane 2. to stretch (the neck) in trying to see over something

crane fly any of various two-winged, slender flies with very long legs; daddy long-legs

cranes·bill, crane's-bill (krānz′bil′) *n.* a popular name for GERANIUM (sense 1)

cra·ni·al (krā′nē əl) *adj.* of or from the cranium

cranial index the ratio of the greatest length to the greatest width of the human skull, multiplied by 100

cranial nerve any of the pairs of nerves, twelve in man, connected directly with the brain

cra·ni·ate (krā′nē it, -āt′) *adj.* having a cranium, as mammals —*n.* a craniate animal

cra·ni·o- [Gr. *kranio-* < *kranion,* skull] *a combining form meaning* of the head, cranial

cra·ni·ol·o·gy (krā′nē ol′ə jē) *n.* the scientific study of skulls, esp. human skulls

cra·ni·om·e·try (-om′ə trē) *n.* the science of measuring skulls; cranial measurement

cra·ni·ot·o·my (-ot′ə mē) *n., pl.* **-mies** the surgical operation of opening the skull

cra·ni·um (krā′nē əm) *n., pl.* **-ni·ums, -ni·a** (-ə) [ML. < Gr. *kranion*] 1. the skull 2. the bones forming the enclosure of the brain

crank (kraŋk) *n.* [< OE. *cranc-*, as in *crancstæf*, yarn comb] 1. a handle or arm at right angles to a shaft of a machine, to transmit or change motion, as to start a motor car engine 2. [Colloq.] *a)* an eccentric person *b)* [U.S.] an irritable, complaining person —*vt.* to start or operate by a crank —*vi.* to turn a crank —**crank up** 1. to start an engine by using a starting handle 2. [Colloq] to get started or begin moving faster

crank·case (kraŋk′kās′) *n.* the metal casing of the crankshaft of an internal-combustion engine

crank·pin (-pin′) *n.* a cylindrical bar or pin, as part of a crankshaft, to which a connecting rod is attached: also **crank pin**

crank·shaft (-shäft′) *n.* a shaft having one or more cranks for transmitting motion

crank·y (kraŋ′kē) *adj.* **crank′i·er, crank′i·est** 1. out of order; loose 2. irritable; cross 3. queer; eccentric —**crank′i·ly** *adv.* —**crank′i·ness** *n.*

cran·nog (kran′əg) *n.* [Ir. < *crann*, a tree, mast] an ancient Irish or Scottish lake dwelling

cran·ny (kran′ē) *n., pl.* **-nies** [OFr. *cran* < Olt. < LL. *crena*, a notch] a small, narrow opening; crevice —**cran′-nied** (-ēd) *adj.*

crap[1] (krap) *n.* [see CRAPS] [U.S.] 1. *same as* CRAPS 2. a losing throw at craps —**crap out** 1. to make a losing throw at craps 2. [Slang] to fail, give up, etc. because of exhaustion, etc.

crap[2] (krap) *n.* [< OFr., ordure] [Slang] 1. nonsense, insincerity, etc. 2. trash; junk 3. faeces —*vi.* to defecate Usually a vulgar term, esp. n. 3 and vi. —**crap′py** *adj.* **-pi·er, -pi·est**

crape (krāp) *n.* [Fr. *crêpe*: see CRÊPE] 1. *same as* CRÊPE (sense 1) 2. a piece of black crêpe as a sign of mourning

crape fern a New Zealand fern with dark-green fronds

craps (kraps) *n.pl.* [with sing. v.] [Fr. *crabs, craps* < obs. E. *crabs*, lowest throw at hazard, two aces] [U.S.] a gambling game played with two dice, in which, for example, a first throw of seven or eleven wins —**crap′shoot′er** *n.* —**crap′shoot′ing** *n.*

crap·u·lence (krap′yōō ləns) *n.* [see ff.] 1. sickness from excess in drinking or eating 2. gross intemperance, esp. in drinking —**crap′u·lent** *adj.*

crap·u·lous (-ləs) *adj.* [< LL. < L. *crapula*, drunkenness < Gr. *kraipalè*, drunken headache] 1. intemperate, esp. in drinking 2. sick from such intemperance

crash[1] (krash) *vi.* [ME. *crashen*, prob. echoic var. of *craken*, CRACK] 1. to fall, collide, or break with force and with a loud, smashing noise, as one car with another 2. *a)* to make this noise *b)* to move with such a noise 3. to fall and be damaged or destroyed: said of aircraft 4. to collapse, as a business —*vt.* 1. to break into pieces; smash 2. to cause (a motor car, etc.) to crash 3. to force or impel with a crashing noise (with *in, out*, etc.) 4. [Colloq.] to get into (a party, etc.) without an invitation, etc. —*n.* 1. a loud, smashing noise 2. a crashing 3. a sudden collapse —*adj.* [Colloq.] using all possible resources, effort, and speed [a *crash* course]

crash[2] (krash) *n.* [prob. < Russ. *krashenina*, coloured linen] a coarse cloth of plain, loose weave

crash barrier a barrier, usually made of steel, erected round race tracks, along central reservations of motorways, etc., for safety purposes

crash dive a sudden submergence of a submarine to escape from attack —**crash′-dive′vi. -dived′, -div′ing**

crash helmet a thickly padded, protective helmet worn by motorcyclists, aviators, etc.

crash·ing (-iŋ) *adj.* [Colloq.] thorough; complete [a *crashing* bore]

crash-land (krash′land′) *vt., vi.* to bring (an aeroplane) down in a forced landing, with some damage —**crash landing**

crass (kras) *adj.* [L. *crassus*, gross] grossly stupid, dull, or obtuse —**crass′ly** *adv.* —**crass′ness, cras′-si·tude′** (-ə tyōod′) *n.*

-crat (krat) [< Fr. < Gr. -*kratēs* < *kratos*, rule] a combining form meaning participant in or supporter of (a specified kind of) government or ruling body [democrat, aristocrat]

crate (krāt) *n.* [L. *cratis*, wickerwork] 1. a box or case made of wood slats, for shipping or storing things 2. [Slang] an old, decrepit motor car or aeroplane —*vt.* **crat′-ed, crat′ing** to pack in a crate —**crat′er** *n.*

cra·ter (krāt′ər) *n.* [L. < Gr. *kratēr*] 1. in ancient Greece, a kind of bowl or jar 2. a bowl-shaped cavity, as at the mouth of a volcano or on the moon 3. any pit like this, as one made by an exploding bomb

cra·vat (krə vat′) *n.* [< Fr. < *Cravate*, Croat: referring to scarves worn by Croatian soldiers] 1. a neckerchief or scarf 2. a necktie

crave (krāv) *vt.* **craved, crav′ing** [OE. *crafian*] 1. to ask for

earnestly; beg 2. to long for; desire strongly 3. to need greatly —*vi.* to have a longing or strong desire (*for*) —**crav′er** *n.*

cra·ven (krā′vən) *adj.* [< OFr. < L. *crepare*, to burst] very cowardly —*n.* a complete coward —**cra′ven·ly** *adv.* —**cra′ven·ness** *n.*

crav·ing (krā′viŋ) *n.* an intense desire or longing, as for affection or a food, drug, etc.

craw (krô) *n.* [ME. *craue*] 1. the crop of a bird or insect 2. the stomach of any animal —**to stick in the** (or one's) **craw** to be unacceptable to one

craw·fish (krô′fish′) *n., pl.* **-fish′, -fish′es**: see FISH *same as* CRAYFISH

crawl[1] (krôl) *vi.* [< ON. *krafla*] 1. to move slowly by drawing the body along the ground, as a worm 2. to go on hands and knees 3. to move slowly or laboriously 4. to act abjectly 5. to swarm (*with* crawling things) 6. to feel as if insects were crawling on the skin 7. to swim the crawl —*n.* 1. a crawling 2. an overarm swimming stroke, face downwards —**crawl′er** *n.*

crawl[2] (krôl) *n.* [WIndDu. *kraal* < Sp. *corral*: see CORRAL] an enclosure made in shallow water for confining fish, turtles, etc.

crawl space a narrow space, as under a roof or floor, allowing access to wiring, plumbing, etc.

crawl·y (krôl′ē) *adj.* **crawl′i·er, crawl′i·est** *same as* CREEPY

cray·fish (krā′fish′) *n., pl.* **-fish′, -fish′es** see FISH [< OFr. *crevice* < OHG.] 1. any of certain small, lobster-shaped freshwater crustaceans 2. *same as* SPINY LOBSTER

cray·on (krā′ən, -on′) *n.* [Fr. < *craie*, chalk < L. *creta*] 1. a small stick of chalk, charcoal, or coloured wax, used for drawing, colouring, or writing 2. a crayon drawing —*vt.* to draw or colour with crayons —**cray′on·ist** *n.*

craze (krāz) *vt.* **crazed, craz′ing** [ME. *crasen*, to crack < Scand.] 1. to make mentally ill or insane 2. to produce small cracks in the surface or glaze of (pottery, etc.) —*vi.* to become finely cracked, as pottery glaze —*n.* 1. a mania 2. a fad 3. a crack in the glaze of pottery, etc.

cra·zy (krā′zē) *adj.* **-zi·er, -zi·est** [< CRAZE] 1. flawed, cracked, or rickety 2. mentally unbalanced or insane 3. [Colloq.] foolish, wild, fantastic, etc. 4. [Colloq.] very enthusiastic or eager —**cra′zi·ly** *adv.* —**cra′zi·ness** *n.*

crazy paving a form of paving made from irregular shaped stones fitted together

crazy quilt a quilt made of pieces of cloth of various colours, patterns, shapes, and sizes

creak (krēk) *vi., vt.* [ME. *creken*, akin to CROAK] to make, cause to make, or move with a harsh, shrill, grating, or squeaking sound, as rusted hinges —*n.* such a sound

creak·y (-ē) *adj.* **creak′i·er, creak′i·est** creaking —**creak′-i·ly** *adv.* —**creak′i·ness** *n.*

cream (krēm) *n.* [OFr. *cresme*, prob. a blend of LL. *chrisma* (see CHRISM) & VL. *crama*, cream] 1. the oily, yellowish part of milk 2. any food made of cream or having a creamy consistency 3. a creamy cosmetic or emulsion 4. the best part 5. yellowish white —*adj.* of, with, or like cream; creamy, cream-coloured etc. —*vi.* to form cream or a creamy foam —*vt.* 1. to take cream from 2. to add cream to 3. to make creamy by beating, etc. —**cream of** creamed purée of [cream of tomato soup] —**cream off** to remove the best of (something), leaving a remainder

cream cheese a soft, white cheese made of cream or of milk enriched with cream

cream·er (-ər) *n.* 1. a device for separating cream from milk 2. [U.S.] a small jug for cream

cream·er·y (-ər ē) *n., pl.* **-er·ies** 1. a place where milk and cream are pasteurized, separated, and bottled, and butter and cheese are made 2. a shop where dairy products are sold

cream of tartar a white, acid, crystalline substance used in baking powder

cream puff a round shell of pastry filled with whipped cream or custard

cream soda a soft drink flavoured with vanilla

cream tea an afternoon tea with bread, jam, and clotted cream, served esp. in Devon and Cornwall in the summer

cream·y (-ē) *adj.* **cream′i·er, cream′i·est** 1. full of cream 2. like cream in consistency or colour —**cream′i·ness** *n.*

crease[1] (krēs) *n.* [earlier *creaste*, lit., ridge < ME. *creste*, crest < OFr. *creste*: see CREST] 1. a line, mark, or ridge made by folding and pressing cloth, paper, etc. 2. a fold or wrinkle [creases in a jowl] 3. *Cricket* any of three lines marking positions for the bowler or batsman —*vt.* 1. to make a crease in 2. to graze with a bullet —*vi.* to become creased —**creas′er** *n.* —**creas′y** *adj.*

crease[2] (krēs) *n. same as* KRIS

cre·ate (krē āt′) *vt.* **-at′ed, -at′ing** [< L. pp. of *creare*] 1. to bring into being; originate, design, invent, etc. 2. to bring about; cause 3. to invest with a new rank, function, etc. 4. *Theatre* to be the first to portray (a role) —*vi.* [Slang] to make a fuss or cause an uproar

cre·a·tion (-ā′shən) *n.* 1. a creating or being created 2. *a)* the whole universe *b*) all living creatures   **3.** anything created; esp., an original design, etc. —**the Creation** *Theol.* God's creating of the world

cre·a·tive (-āt′iv) *adj.* **1.** creating or able to create **2.** productive (*of*) **3.** imaginative and inventive **4.** stimulating the inventive powers —**cre·a′tive·ly** *adv.* —**cre·a′tive·ness,** *n.* —**cre·a·tiv·i·ty** (krē′ā tiv′ə tē) *n.*

cre·a·tor (-āt′ər) *n.* **1.** one who creates **2.** [C-] God

crea·ture (krē′chər) *n.* [< OFr. < L. *creatura*] **1.** anything created, animate or inanimate **2.** a living being; esp., *a*) a domestic animal *b*) a human being: often used endearingly, patronizingly, or contemptuously **3.** one completely dominated by or dependent on another —**crea′tur·al, crea′·ture·ly** *adj.*

crèche (kresh, krāsh) *n.* [Fr. < Frank. hyp. *kripja,* crib] **1.** a display of a stable with figures, representing a scene at the birth of Jesus **2.** a day nursery for babies and very young children

cre·dal (krēd′'l) *adj.* of a creed

cre·dence (krēd′əns) *n.* [< OFr. < ML. < L. prp. of *credere:* see CREED] **1.** belief, esp. in another's reports or testimony **2.** credentials: now only in **letter of credence 3.** *Eccles.* a small side table for the Eucharistic wine, etc.

cre·den·tial (kri den′shəl) *n.* **1.** that which entitles to credit, confidence, etc. **2.** [*usually pl.*] a letter or certificate showing that one has a right to a certain position or authority

cre·den·za (kri den′zə) *n.* [It.] a type of buffet, or sideboard

credibility gap 1. an apparent disparity between what is said and the actual facts **2.** the disbelief or tendency to disbelieve produced by such disparity

cred·i·ble (kred′ə b'l) *adj.* [< L. < *credere:* see CREED] that can be believed; believable —**cred′i·bil′i·ty, cred′·i·ble·ness** *n.* —**cred′i·bly** *adv.*

cred·it (kred′it) *n.* [< Fr. < It. < L. pp. of *credere:* see CREED] **1.** belief or trust; confidence **2.** *a*) good reputation *b*) one's influence based on one's reputation **3.** praise to which one is entitled **4.** a source of approval or honour [a *credit* to the team] **5.** acknowledgment of work done or help given; specif., [*pl.*] a list of such acknowledgments in a film, TV programme, etc. **6.** *a*) the amount in a bank account, etc. *b*) a sum made available by a bank for withdrawal by someone specified **7.** *Accounting a*) acknowledgment of a payment by entry of the amount in an account *b*) the right-hand side of an account, for such entries *c*) an entry, or the sum of entries, there *d*) a deduction from a debt or an addition (as to a bank account) in making an adjustment **8.** *Business a*) trust in one's ability to make payments when due *b*) time allowed for payment **9.** *Educ. a*) certification of a successfully completed unit or course of study *b*) a distinction awarded to an examination candidate who performs well —*vt.* **1.** to believe in the truth, reliability, etc. of; trust **2.** to give credit to or deserved commendation for **3.** to give credit in a bank account, etc. **4.** *Accounting* to enter on the credit side —**credit one with** to ascribe to one —**do credit to** to bring approval or honour to —**give credit to 1.** to trust **2.** to commend —**give one credit for 1.** to commend one for **2.** to believe or recognize that one has —**on credit** with agreement on future payment —**to one's credit** bringing approval or honour to one

cred·it·a·ble (-ə b'l) *adj.* **1.** praiseworthy **2.** ascribable (*to*) —**cred′it·a·bil′i·ty, cred′it·a·ble·ness** *n.* —**cred′it·a·bly** *adv.*

credit account a business arrangement by which a customer may buy things or services and pay for them within a specified future period

credit card a card issued by banks, business enterprises, etc., enabling the holder to obtain goods and services on credit

cred·i·tor (-ər) *n.* a person who extends credit or to whom money is owed

credit rating the rating of an individual or firm as a credit risk, based on past records of debt repayment, financial status, etc.

cre·do (krē′dō, krā′dō) *n.,* *pl.* **-dos** [L., I believe: see CREED] **1.** *same as* CREED **2.** [*usually* C-] the Apostles' Creed or the Nicene Creed

cre·du·li·ty (krə dyoo′lə tē) *n.* a tendency to believe too readily

cred·u·lous (kred′yoo ləs) *adj.* [L. *credulus* < *credere:* see CREED] **1.** tending to believe too readily **2.** resulting from or indicating credulity —**cred′u·lous·ly** *adv.* —**cred′·u·lous·ness** *n.*

creed (krēd) *n.* [< OE. < L. *credo,* lit., I believe < *credere,* to trust] **1.** a brief statement of religious belief; esp. as accepted by a church **2.** any statement of belief, opinions, etc. —**creed′al** *adj.*

creek (krēk) *n.* [ME. *creke* < ON. *-kriki,* a winding] **1.** a narrow inlet or bay **2.** [U.S. & Aust.] a small stream, somewhat larger than a brook —**up the creek** [Slang] **1.** in trouble **2.** crazy

creel (krēl) *n.* [< OFr. *grail:* see GRIDDLE] a wicker basket for fishermen to carry fish caught

creep (krēp) *vi.* **crept, creep′ing** [OE. *creopan*] **1.** to move along with the body close to the ground, as on hands and knees **2.** to come on or move slowly, gradually, stealthily, etc. **3.** to grow along the ground, etc., as some plants **4.** to change position or shape slightly **5.** to dredge the bottom of a river, pond, etc. with a creeper (sense 3) —*n.* **1.** a creeping **2.** [Slang] a person regarded as very annoying, etc. **3.** *Geol.* the slow movement of loose rock and soil down a slope —**make one's flesh** (or **skin**) **creep** to make one fearful, etc., as if insects were creeping on one's skin —**the creeps** [Colloq.] a feeling of fear, repugnance, etc.

CREEL

creep·age (-ij) *n.* a gradual creeping movement

creep·er (-ər) *n.* **1.** a person, animal, or thing that creeps **2.** a plant whose stem puts out tendrils or rootlets for creeping along a surface **3.** an instrument for dragging a river, etc.; grapnel **4.** any of various birds that feed on insects found in tree crevices, as the tree creeper **5.** [Slang] a pair of thick, crepe-soled shoes; gym shoes

creep·y (krēp′ē) *adj.* **creep′i·er, creep′i·est 1.** creeping; moving slowly **2.** having or causing fear or disgust, as if insects were creeping on one's skin —**creep′i·ly** *adv.* —**creep′i·ness** *n.*

creep·y-crawl·y (-krô′lē) *n.* [Colloq.] a small, crawling creature; insect —*adj.* [Colloq.] feeling or causing a sensation of repulsion, horror, etc., as of creatures crawling on the skin

creese (krēs) *n. same as* KRIS

cre·mate (kri māt′) *vt.* **-mat′ed, -mat′ing** [< L. pp. of *cremare,* to burn] to burn up; esp., to burn (a dead body) to ashes —**cre·ma′tion** *n.* —**cre′ma·tor** *n.*

cre·ma·to·ri·um (krem′ə tôr′ē əm) *n.,* *pl.* **-ri·ums, -ri·a** (-ə) **1.** a furnace for cremating **2.** a building with such a furnace in it

cre·ma·to·ry (krem′ə tər ē) *n.,* *pl.* **-ries** *same as* CREMATORIUM —*adj.* of or for cremation: also **crematorial**

crème (krem, krām) *n.* [Fr.] **1.** cream **2.** a thick liqueur

‡crème de la crème (krem də lá krem′) [Fr., lit., cream of the cream] the very best

crème de menthe (də mänt′, menth′) [Fr.] a sweet, mint-flavoured liqueur, green or colourless

Cre·mo·na (kri mō′nə) *n.* any famous violin formerly made in Cremona, Italy, as by Stradivari

cre·nate (krē′nāt) *adj.* [< ModL. < VL. *crena,* a notch] having a scalloped edge, as certain leaves: also **cre′nat·ed** —**cre′nate·ly** *adv.* —**cre·na′tion** *n.*

cren·el (kren′'l) *n.* [OFr. < VL. *crena,* a notch] an indentation in the top of a battlement or wall: also **cre·nelle** (kri nel′) —*vt.* **-elled, -el·ling** to crenelate

cren·el·late (kren′'l āt′) *vt.* **-el·lat′ed, -el·lat′ing** to furnish with crenels or with squared notches —**cren′el·la′tion** *n.*

Cre·ole, cre·ole (krē′ōl) *n.* [< Fr. < Sp. *criollo* < Port. < *criar,* to rear < L. *creare,* to create] **1.** orig., a person of European parentage born in Latin America or the Gulf States of the U.S. **2.** *a*) a descendant of such persons *b*) a person of mixed Creole and Negro descent **3.** French as spoken by Creoles —*adj.* **1.** of Creoles or their languages **2.** [*usually* c-] made with sautéed tomatoes, green peppers, onions, etc.

cre·o·sol (krē′ə sol′) *n.* [CREOS(OTE) + -OL¹] a colourless, oily, antiseptic liquid obtained esp. from beech tar

cre·o·sote (krē′ə sōt′) *n.* [< Gr. *kreas,* flesh + *sōzein,* to save] a transparent, pungent, oily liquid distilled from wood tar or coal tar: used as an antiseptic and a wood preservative —*vt.* **-sot′ed, -sot′ing** to treat with creosote

crêpe, crepe (krāp; *for 3, also* krep) *n.* [Fr. *crêpe* < L. *crispus:* see CRISP] **1.** a thin, crinkled cloth, as of silk or wool; crape **2.** *same as: a*) CRAPE (sense 2) *b*) CREPE PAPER *c*) CREPE RUBBER **3.** a very thin pancake, generally rolled up or folded with a filling: usually **crêpe**

crêpe de Chine (krāp′ de shēn′) [Fr., lit., crepe of China] a soft, thin, crêpe cloth, usually of silk

crepe paper thin paper crinkled like crepe

crepe rubber soft rubber in sheets with a wrinkled surface, used for some shoe soles

crêpes su·zette (krāp′ soo zet′; *Fr.* krep sü-) [Fr.] crêpes in a hot, orange-flavoured sauce, usually served in flaming brandy

crep·i·tate (krep′ə tāt′) *vi.* **-tat′ed, -tat′ing** [< L. pp. of *crepitare,* freq. of *crepare,* to creak] to crackle —**crep′·i·tant** *adj.* —**crep′i·ta′tion** *n.*

crept (krept) *pt.* & *pp. of* CREEP

cre·pus·cu·lar (kri pus′kyoo lər) *adj.* [< L. *crepusculum,* twilight < *creper,* dark] of, like, or active at, twilight

Cres. Crescent

cre·scen·do (krə shen′dō) *adj., adv.* [It. < L. *crescere:* see

ff.] *Music* gradually getting louder: symbol < **—n.,** *pl.*
-dos 1. a gradual increase in loudness or intensity 2. a
passage played crescendo **—vi. -doed, -do·ing** to get louder
cres·cent (kres′'nt) *n.* [< OFr. < L. *crescere,* to grow] 1.
the moon in its first or last quarter, when it appears
concavo-convex 2. a figure of or like this 3. anything of
similar shape, as a curved roll 4. a street that curves in a
crescent shape 5. [*also* C-] [< the Turkish crescent
emblem] Turkish or Moslem power **—adj.** 1. [Poet.]
increasing; growing 2. shaped like a crescent **—cres·cen′-**
tic (krə sen′tik) *adj.*
cre·sol (krē′sol) *n.* [< CREOSOTE + -OL¹] any of three
colourless, oily liquids or solids distilled from coal tar: used
in disinfectants, etc.
cress (kres) *n.* [OE. *cressa,* lit., ? creeper] a plant of the
mustard family, as watercress, with pungent leaves used in
salads and as garnishes
cres·set (kres′it) *n.* [< OFr.] a metal container for burning
oil, wood, etc., used as a torch or lantern
crest (krest) *n.* [< OFr. < L. *crista*] 1. a comb, tuft, etc. on
the heads of some animals or birds 2. a plume or emblem
on a helmet 3. a helmet 4. a heraldic device above the
shield in a coat of arms or used on silverware, note paper,
etc. 5. top; ridge 6. the highest point or level **—vt.** 1. to
provide with a crest 2. to reach the top of **—vi.** to form or
reach a crest **—crest′ed** *adj.*
crest·fall·en (krest′fôl′ən) *adj.* 1. with drooping crest or
bowed head 2. dejected or humbled
cre·ta·ceous (kri tā′shəs) *adj.* [< L. < *creta*: see CRAYON]
1. of, like, or containing chalk 2. [C-] designating or of the
third geological period of the Mesozoic Era **—the**
Cretaceous the Cretaceous Period or its rocks: see
GEOLOGY, chart
Cre·tan (krēt′ən) *adj.* of the island of Crete or its
inhabitants **—n.** a native or inhabitant of Crete
cre·tin (kret′in, krēt-) *n.* [< Fr. dial. form of *chrétien,*
Christian, hence human being] 1. a person suffering from
cretinism 2. [Colloq.] an idiot **—cre′ti·nous** *adj.*
cre·tin·ism (-iz′m) *n.* [see prec.] a congenital thyroid
deficiency with resulting deformity and idiocy
cre·tonne (kre′ton, kre ton′) *n.* [Fr. < *Creton,* village in
Normandy] a heavy, unglazed, printed cotton or linen
cloth, for curtains, etc.
cre·vasse (kri vas′) *n.* [Fr. < OFr. *crevace,* CREVICE] 1. a
deep crack or fissure, esp. in a glacier 2. [U.S.] a break in
an embankment, as of a river **—vt. -vassed′, -vas′sing** to
make crevasses
crev·ice (krev′is) *n.* [< OFr. < L. *crepare,* to creak] a
narrow opening caused by a crack or split; fissure; cleft
—crev′iced *adj.*
crew¹ (krōō) *n.* [OFr. *creue,* growth < L. *crescere,* to grow]
1. a group of people associating or working together or
classed together; company, set, gang, etc. 2. the personnel
of a ship, usually excepting the officers, or of an aircraft 3.
a rowing team **—vt., vi.** to serve (on) as a crew member
—crew′man (-mən) *n., pl.* **-men**
crew² (krōō) *alt. pt. of* CROW² (sense 1)
crew cut a man's style of close-cropped haircut
crew·el (krōō′əl) *n.* [LME. *crule* < ?] a fine worsted yarn
used in fancywork and embroidery **—crew′el·work′** *n.*
crew neck a round, closefitting neckline
crib (krib) *n.* [OE.] 1. a rack, trough, or box for fodder;
manger 2. a small, crude house or room 3. [U.S.] a baby's
cot 4. a framework of bars for support or strengthening, as
in a mine 5. a representation of the manger in which the
infant Jesus was laid at birth 6. a structure anchored under
water, serving as a pier, water intake, etc. 7. [Colloq.] *a)* a
plagiarism *b)* a translation or other aid used, often
dishonestly, in doing schoolwork 8. [Colloq.] the game of
cribbage 9. [Colloq.] *Cribbage* the discard pile, which belongs to the
dealer **—vt. cribbed, crib′bing** 1. to confine 2. to provide
with a crib 3. [Colloq.] *a)* to steal *b)* to plagiarize **—vi.**
[Colloq.] to do schoolwork dishonestly, as by using a crib
—crib′ber *n.*
crib·bage (krib′ij) *n.* [< prec. + -AGE] a card game in
which the object is to form various combinations that count
for points: score is kept on a board (**cribbage board**) with
holes for pegs
crib biting a habit some horses have of biting the feeding
trough and swallowing air **—crib′-bite′** *vi.* **-bit′, -bit′ten**
or -bit′, -bit′ing
crick (krik) *n.* [< ? ON.] a painful cramp in the neck, back,
etc. **—vt.** to cause a crick in
crick·et¹ (krik′it) *n.* [< OFr. < *criquer,* to creak] a leaping
insect, usually with long antennae, related to the locusts and
grasshoppers: the males make a chirping noise with their
forewings
crick·et² (krik′it) *n.* [< OFr. < ?] 1. an outdoor game
played by two teams of eleven men each, in which a ball,
bats, and wickets are used 2. [Colloq.] fair play;
sportsmanship **—vi.** to play cricket **—crick′et·er** *n.*
crick·et³ (krik′it) *n.* [< ?] a wooden footstool
cri·coid (krī′koid) *adj.* [Gr. *krikoeidēs,* ring-shaped] of the
ring-shaped cartilage forming the lower part of the larynx
—n. this cartilage
cried (krīd) *pt. & pp. of* CRY
cri·er (krī′ər) *n.* 1. a person who cries 2. a person who
shouts out news, proclamations, etc.
crime (krīm) *n.* [OFr. < L. *crimen,* verdict, offence] 1. an
act committed or omitted in violation of a law 2. an
offence against morality; sin 3. criminal acts, collectively
4. [Colloq.] something deplorable; shame
crim·i·nal (krim′ə n'l) *adj.* 1. having the nature of crime;
being a crime 2. relating to or dealing with crime 3. guilty
of crime 4. [Colloq.] deplorable **—n.** a person guilty of, or
convicted of, a crime **—crim′i·nal′i·ty** (-ə nal′ə tē) *n., pl.*
-ties —crim′i·nal·ly *adv.*
criminal conversation *Law* adultery
criminal law law dealing with crime
crim·i·nate (krim′ə nāt′) *vt.* **-nat′ed, -nat′ing** [< L. pp. of
criminari < *crimen*: see CRIME] 1. to accuse of a crime 2.
to incriminate **—crim′i·na′tion** *n.* **—crim′i·na′tive,**
crim′i·na·to·ry (-nə tər ē) **—crim′i·na′tor** *n.*
crim·i·nol·o·gy (krim′ə nol′ə jē) *n.* [< L. *crimen* (gen.
criminis): see CRIME & -LOGY] the scientific study and
investigation of crime **—crim′i·no·log′i·cal** (-nə loj′i k'l)
adj. **—crim′i·no·log′i·cal·ly** *adv.* **—crim′i·nol′o·gist** *n.*
crimp¹ (krimp) *vt.* [< OE. (*ge*)*crympan,* to curl & MDu.
crimpen, to wrinkle] 1. to press into narrow, regular folds;
pleat 2. to make (hair, etc.) wavy or curly 3. to pinch
together 4. [Colloq.] to hamper **—n.** 1. a crimping 2.
anything crimped or crimpy 3. crimpy condition **—put a**
crimp in [U.S. Colloq.] to hamper **—crimp′er** *n.*
crimp² (krimp) *n.* [< prec.] a person who gets men by
force or trickery to serve as sailors or soldiers **—vt.** to get
(men) thus into such service
crimp·y (krim′pē) *adj.* **crimp′i·er, crimp′i·est** [< CRIMP¹]
curly; wavy; frizzly **—crimp′i·ness** *n.*
crim·son (krim′z'n) *n.* [< ML., ult. < Ar. *qirmiz*: see
CARMINE] 1. deep red 2. deep-red colouring matter **—adj.**
1. deep-red 2. bloody **—vt., vi.** to make or become crimson
cringe (krinj) *vi.* **cringed, cring′ing** [OE. *cringan,* to fall (in
battle)] 1. to draw back, crouch, etc., as when afraid;
cower 2. to act servilely; fawn **—n.** a cringing **—cring′-**
er *n.*
crin·gle (kriŋ′g'l) *n.* [< ON. *kringla,* circle, or MDu. *kringel,*
ring] a small ring or loop of rope or metal on the edge of a
sail, for inserting a rope
crin·kle (kriŋ′k'l) *vi., vt.* **-kled, -kling** [OE. *crincan,* var. of
cringan: see CRINGE] 1. to be or make full of wrinkles or
ripples 2. to rustle, as paper when crushed **—n.** 1. a
wrinkle, twist, or ripple 2. a rustling sound **—crin′kly** *adj.*
-kli·er, -kli·est
cri·noid (krī′noid, krin′oid) *adj.* [< Gr. < *krinon,* lily +
-eidēs, -OID] 1. lily-shaped 2. designating or of a class of
marine animals that are flowerlike and anchored by a stalk
or that are free-swimming **—n.** such an animal
crin·o·line (krin′əl in, -ə lēn) *n.* [Fr. < It. < L. *crinis,* hair +
linum, thread] 1. a coarse, stiff, heavily sized cloth, orig. of
horsehair and linen, used as lining to stiffen garments 2. a
petticoat of this, to puff out a skirt 3. *same as* HOOP SKIRT
crip·ple (krip′'l) *n.* [< OE. < base of *creopan,* to creep] a
person or animal that is lame or disabled in a way
preventing normal movement **—vt. -pled, -pling** to lame or
disable **—crip′pler** *n.*
cri·sis (krī′sis) *n., pl.* **-ses** (-sēz) [L. < Gr. < *krinein,* to
decide] 1. the turning point in a disease, indicating either
imminent recovery or death 2. a turning point in the course
of anything 3. a time of great danger or trouble
crisp (krisp) *adj.* [OE. < L. *crispus,* curly] 1. easily broken
or crumbled; brittle 2. fresh and firm, as celery 3. fresh
and tidy, as a uniform 4. sharp and clear [a *crisp* analysis]
5. lively, as talk 6. invigorating [*crisp* air] 7. closely
curled and wiry 8. rippled; wavy **—n.** 1. something crisp
2. a very thin slice of potato fried and eaten cold, esp. as a
snack **—vt., vi.** to make or become crisp **—crisp′ly** *adv.*
—crisp′ness *n.*
crisp bread (-bred) *n.* any of various thin, crisp, usually
rectangular biscuits made of rye, etc.
crisp·er (-ər) *n.* a compartment in a refrigerator for storing
salads, vegetables, etc., to keep them fresh
crisp·y (kris′pē) *adj.* **crisp′i·er, crisp′i·est** *same as* CRISP
—crisp′i·ness *n.*
criss·cross (kris′kros′) *n.* [earlier Christ's cross, for the
symbol X, abbrev. of Christ] 1. a mark made of two
crossed lines (X) 2. a pattern of crossed lines 3. a being
confused **—adj.** marked with or moving in crossing lines
—vt., vi. 1. to mark with crossing lines 2. to cross back
and forth **—adv.** 1. crosswise 2. awry
crit (krit) *n.* [Colloq.] 1. criticism 2. critique
cri·te·ri·on (krī tir′ē ən) *n., pl.* **-i·a** (-ē ə), **-i·ons** [< Gr. <
kritēs, judge: see ff.] a standard, rule, or test by which
something can be judged
crit·ic (krit′ik) *n.* [< L. < Gr. *kritikos,* orig., able to discern,
akin to *krinein*: see CRISIS] 1. a person who forms and
expresses judgments of people or things; specif., one who

writes judgments of books, plays, music, etc. professionally **2.** a person given to faultfinding and censure
crit·i·cal (krit′i k'l) *adj.* **1.** tending to find fault; censorious **2.** characterized by careful analysis **3.** of critics or criticism **4.** of or forming a crisis; decisive **5.** dangerous or risky **6.** designating or of the point at which a change of character, property, or condition is effected, or at which a nuclear chain reaction becomes self-sustaining —**crit′i·cal′i·ty** (-kal′ə tē), **crit′i·cal·ness** *n.* —**crit′i·cal·ly** *adv.*
critical mass the minimim amount of fissionable material that can sustain nuclear chain reaction under a given set of conditions
critical path analysis a technique for determining which mode of operation of a particular project involves the lowest cost, least time, etc.
critical temperature that temperature above which a given gas cannot be liquified
crit·i·cise (krit′ə sīz′) *vi., vt.* -cised′, -cis′ing *same as* CRITICIZE —**crit′i cis′er** *n.*
crit·i·cism (krit′ə siz'm) *n.* **1.** the act, art, or principles of criticizing, esp. of criticizing literary or artistic work **2.** a comment, review, article, etc. expressing this **3.** faultfinding; disapproval
crit·i·cize (-sīz′) *vi., vt.* -cized′, -ciz′ing **1.** to analyze and judge as a critic **2.** to find fault (with) —**crit′i·ciz′a·ble** *adj.* —**crit′i·ciz′er** *n.*
cri·tique (kri tēk′) *n.* [Fr.] **1.** a critical analysis or evaluation **2.** the art of criticizing
croak (krōk) *vi.* [< OE. < cræcettan, of echoic origin] **1.** to make a deep, hoarse sound, as that of a frog **2.** to talk dismally; grumble **3.** [Slang] to die —*vt.* **1.** to utter in deep, hoarse tones **2.** [Slang] to kill —*n.* a croaking sound —**croak′y** (-ē) *adj.* **croak′i·er, croak′i·est**
croak·er (-ər) *n.* **1.** an animal or fish that makes croaking sounds **2.** a foreteller of evil; grumbler
Cro·at (krō′at, -ət) *n.* **1.** a native or inhabitant of Croatia **2.** *same as* CROATIAN (n. 2) —*adj. same as* CROATIAN
Cro·a·tian (krō ā′shən) *adj.* of Croatia, its people, language, etc. —*n.* **1.** a Croat **2.** the South Slavic language of the Croats: see SERBO-CROATIAN
cro·chet (krō′shā) *n.* [Fr., small hook: see CROTCHET] needlework in which loops of thread or yarn are interwoven with a hooked needle (**crochet hook**) —*vi., vt.* **-cheted** (-shād), **-chet·ing** to do crochet or make by crochet —**cro·chet′er** *n.*
crock¹ (krok) *n.* [OE. *crocca*] an earthenware pot or jar
crock² (krok) *n.* [< ON. *kraki*, bent object] [Slang] anyone or anything worthless or useless, as from age
crock·er·y (krok′ər ē) *n.* [CROCK¹ + -ERY (sense 5)] earthenware pots, jars, dishes, etc.
crock·et (krok′it) *n.* [ME. *croket* < OFr. *crochet*, small hook] a carved ornament, as a curved leaf, decorating the edges of spires, pinnacles, etc., esp. in Gothic architecture
croc·o·dile (krok′ə dil′) *n.* [< OFr. < ML. < L. < Gr. *krokodilos* < ? *krokē*, pebble + *drilos*, worm] **1.** a large, flesh-eating, lizardlike reptile of tropical streams, with a thick, horny skin, long tail, and long, narrow head with massive jaws **2.** leather made from a crocodile's hide **3.** a party of people, esp. schoolchildren, walking in double file
crocodile clip a type of clasp, used for holding electrical wires, etc., with two interlocking, serrated edges

CROCODILE
(to 6 m long)

crocodile tears insincere tears or a hypocritical show of grief
croc·o·dil·i·an (krok′ə dil′ē ən) *adj.* **1.** of or like a crocodile **2.** of a group of reptiles including the crocodile, alligator, cayman, and gavial —*n.* any reptile of this group
cro·cus (krō′kəs) *n., pl.* **cro′cus·es, cro′ci** (-kē) [L. < Gr. *krokos*, saffron, via Sem. ult. < Sans.] any of a genus of spring-blooming plants with fleshy corms and a yellow, purple, or white flower
Croe·sus (krē′səs) *n.* [after *Croesus*, fl. 6th c. B.C.; last king of Lydia and noted for his great wealth] a very rich man
croft (kroft) *n.* [OE.] **1.** a small enclosed field **2.** a small farm, esp. one in Scotland or N England —**croft′er** *n.*
crois·sant (krwä′son) *n.* [Fr., lit., CRESCENT] a rich, flaky bread roll in the shape of a crescent
‡croix de guerre (krwä də ger′) [Fr., cross of war] a French military decoration for bravery
Cro-Ma·gnon (krō mag′nən, -man′yən) *adj.* [after *Cro-Magnon* cave in SW France, where remains were found] belonging to a prehistoric, Caucasoid type of man, tall and erect, who lived on the European continent —*n.* a member of this group
crom·lech (krom′lek) *n.* [W. < *crom*, bent + *llech*, flat stone] **1.** *same as* DOLMEN **2.** an ancient monument of monoliths, arranged in a circle around a mound or dolmen

crone (krōn) *n.* [< Anglo-Fr. *carogne* (cf. CARRION) or via MDu. *kronje*, old ewe] an ugly, withered old woman; hag
cro·ny (krō′nē) *n., pl.* **-nies** [university slang < ? Gr. *chronios*, long-continued (hence "old friend")] a close companion
crook (krook) *n.* [< ON. *krōkr*, hook] **1.** a hooked, bent, or curved thing or part; hook **2.** *a)* a shepherd's staff *b)* a crosier **3.** a bend or curve **4.** [Colloq.] a swindler or thief —*adj.* [Aust. & N.Z. Colloq.] **1.** unwell; ill **2.** of poor quality **3.** dishonest; untrustworthy **4.** unpleasant; bad-tempered —*vt., vi.* **crooked** (krookt), **crook′ing** to bend or curve —**go crook** [Aust. Colloq.] to become angry; reproach; upbraid (sometimes with *on*)
crook·ed (krookt; *for 2 & 3* krook′id) *adj.* **1.** having a crook or hook **2.** not straight; bent; curved **3.** dishonest; swindling —**crook′ed·ly** *adv.* —**crook′ed·ness** *n.*
croon (kroon) *vi., vt.* [< MDu. *cronen*, to growl] **1.** to sing or hum in a low, gentle tone **2.** to sing (popular songs) in a soft, sentimental manner —*n.* a low, gentle singing or humming —**croon′er** *n.*
crop (krop) *n.* [OE. *croppa*, cluster, flower, crop of bird] **1.** a saclike enlargement of a bird's gullet, in which food is stored before digestion; craw **2.** any agricultural product, growing or harvested, as wheat, fruit, etc. **3.** the yield of any product in one season or place **4.** a group or collection **5.** the handle or butt of a whip **6.** *same as* RIDING CROP **7.** hair cut close to the head **8.** an earmark on an animal, made by clipping —*vt.* **cropped, crop′ping 1.** to cut off or bite off the tops or ends of **2.** to grow or harvest as a crop **3.** to cut short —*vi.* **1.** to plant, grow, or bear crops **2.** to feed by grazing —**crop out** to appear at the surface, as a rock formation —**crop up 1.** to appear or happen unexpectedly **2.** *same as* CROP OUT
crop-dust·ing (-dust′iŋ) *n.* the spraying of growing crops with pesticides from an aircraft —**crop′-dust′** *vi., vt.* —**crop′-dust′er** *n.*
crop-eared (-ird′) *adj.* **1.** having the ears cropped **2.** having the hair cut short, so that the ears show
crop·per (-ər) *n.* **1.** a person or thing that crops **2.** a sharecropper —**come a cropper** [Colloq.] **1.** to fall heavily or headlong **2.** to fail
crop rotation a system of growing successive crops that have different food requirements, to prevent soil depletion, break up a disease cycle, etc.
cro·quet (krō′ka′, -kē) *n.* [Fr., dial. form of *crochet*: see CROTCHET] an outdoor game in which the players use mallets to drive a wooden ball through a series of hoops placed in the ground
cro·quette (krō ket′) *n.* [Fr. < *croquer*, to crunch] a small cake or roll of chopped meat, fish, etc., coated with crumbs and fried in deep fat
cro·sier (krō′zhər) *n.* [< OFr. < *croce* < ML. *crocia*] a staff with a crook at the top, carried by or before a bishop or abbot as a symbol of his office
cross (kros) *n.* [< OE. *cros* & ON. *kross*, both < OIr. *cros* < L. *crux* (gen. *crucis*), a cross] **1.** an upright post with a bar across it near the top, on which the ancient Romans fastened convicted persons to die **2.** a representation of a cross, used as a badge, ornament, etc. **3.** *a)* a monument in the shape of a cross *b)* the place in a town or village where such a cross has been set up **4.** a representation of a cross as a symbol of the crucifixion of Jesus, and hence of the Christian religion **5.** any trouble or affliction that one has to bear or that thwarts one **6.** any mark made by intersecting lines or surfaces **7.** such a mark (X) made as a signature by one who cannot write **8.** *a)* a crossing of varieties or breeds; hybridization *b)* the result of such mixing; hybrid **9.** something that combines the qualities of two different things or types **10.** [Slang] a double-cross —*vt.* **1.** to make the sign of the cross over or upon **2.** to place across or crosswise [*cross* your fingers] **3.** to lie or cut across; intersect **4.** *a)* to draw a line or lines across [*cross* your t's] *b)* to draw two parallel lines across (a cheque) and so make it payable only into a bank account **5.** to pass over; go across **6.** to carry or lead across **7.** to extend across [the bridge *crosses* a river] **8.** to bring into contact, causing electrical interference [the wires were *crossed*] **9.** to thwart; oppose **10.** to interbreed (animals or plants); hybridize —*vi.* **1.** to intersect **2.** to go or extend from one side to the other **3.** to pass each other while moving in opposite directions **4.** to interbreed —*adj.* **1.** lying or passing across; crossing; transverse **2.** going counter; contrary; opposed **3.** ill-tempered; cranky; irritable **4.** involving reciprocation **5.** of mixed variety or breed; hybrid —*adv.* crosswise —**cross off** (or **out**) to cancel by or as by drawing lines across —**cross one's fingers**

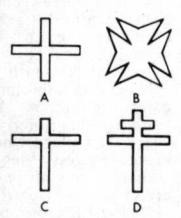

CROSSES
(A, Greek; B,
Maltese; C, Latin;
D, Patriarchal)

to fold one finger over another in the hope of bringing good luck —**cross one's mind** to come suddenly or briefly to one's mind —**cross one's palm** to pay one money —**cross one's path** to meet one —**cross swords (with)** to enter into argument, disagreement or rivalry (with someone) —**the Cross 1.** the cross on which Jesus was put to death **2.** the suffering and death or Atonement of Jesus **3.** Christianity or Christendom —**cross'a·ble** adj. —**cross'ly** adv. —**cross'ness** n.

cross·bar (kros'bär') n. a bar, line, or stripe placed crossways, specif., a) the horizontal bar on a man's bicycle b) the horizontal beam across a pair of goalposts —vt. **-barred', -bar'ring** to furnish with crossbars

cross·beam (-bēm') n. a beam placed across another or from one wall to another

cross·bench (-bench) n. in the British parliament, a bench reserved for members who belong to neither the government nor the opposition —**cross·bench'er** n.

cross·bill (-bil') n. a finch having a bill with curving points that cross

cross·bones (-bōnz') n. see SKULL AND CROSSBONES

cross·bow (-bō') n. a medieval weapon consisting of a bow set transversely on a wooden stock: the stock was grooved to direct an arrow or stone —**cross'bow'man** n., pl. **-men**

cross·bred (-bred') adj. produced by the interbreeding of different varieties or breeds —n. a hybrid; mongrel

cross·breed (-brēd') vt., vi. **-bred** (-bred), **-breed'ing** same as HYBRIDIZE —n. same as HYBRID (sense 1)

cross·check (-chek') vi., vt. to verify (a statement, report, etc.) by consulting other sources —n. an act or instance of crosschecking

cross·coun·try (-kun'trē) adj., adv. **1.** across open country or fields, not by roads **2.** across a country —n. a cross-country race

cross·cur·rent (-kur'ənt) n. **1.** a current flowing at an angle to the main current **2.** an opposing opinion, influence, or tendency

cross·cut (-kut') adj. **1.** made or used for cutting across [a crosscut saw] **2.** cut across —n. **1.** a cut across **2.** something that cuts across **3.** Mining a cutting made across a vein —vt., vi. **-cut', -cut'ting** to cut across

crosse (kros) n. [Fr.: see CROSIER] the pouched racket used in playing lacrosse

cross·ex·am·ine (kros'ig zam'in) vt., vi. **-ined, -in·ing 1.** to question closely **2.** Law to question (a witness already questioned by the opposing side) to determine the validity of his testimony —**cross'-ex·am'i·na'tion** n. —**cross'-ex·am'in·er** n.

cross·eye (kros'ī') n. an abnormal condition in which the eyes are turned towards each other; convergent strabismus —**cross'-eyed'** (-īd') adj.

cross·fer·ti·lize (-furt'il īz') vt., vi. **-lized', -liz'ing** to fertilize or be fertilized by pollen from another plant or variety of plant —**cross'-fer'ti·li·za'tion** n.

cross fire 1. Mil. a firing at an objective from two or more positions so that the lines of fire cross **2.** any complex of opposing forces, opinions, etc.

cross-grained (-grānd') adj. **1.** having an irregular or transverse grain: said of wood **2.** contrary; perverse; cantankerous

cross·hatch (-hach') vt., vi. to shade with two sets of crossing parallel lines

cross·ing (-iŋ) n. **1.** the act of passing across, thwarting, interbreeding, etc. **2.** an intersection, as of lines, streets, etc. **3.** a place where a street, river, etc. may be crossed

cross-leg·ged (-leg'id, -legd') adj., adv. with ankles crossed, or with one leg crossed over the other

cross·patch (-pach') n. [CROSS + dial. patch, fool] [Colloq.] a cross, bad-tempered person

cross·piece (-pēs') n. a piece lying across another

cross-ply (-pli) adj. having the fabric cords in the outer casing running diagonally to stiffen the sidewalls: said of a tyre

cross-pol·li·nate (kros'pol'ə nāt') vt., vi. **-nat'ed, -nat'ing** to transfer pollen from the anther of (one flower) to the stigma of (another) —**cross'-pol'li·na'tion** n.

cross-pur·pose (kros'pur'pəs) n. a contrary or conflicting purpose —**be at cross-purposes** to talk, act, etc. along different lines without either party realising it

cross-ques·tion (-kwes'chən) vt. to cross-examine —n. a question asked in cross-examination

cross-re·fer (-ri fur') vt., vi. **-ferred', -fer'ring** to refer from one part to another

cross-ref·er·ence (-ref'ər əns, -ref'rəns) n. a reference from one part of a book, catalogue, index, etc. to another part —vt., vi. **-enced, -enc·ing 1.** to provide (an index, reference book, etc.) with systematic cross-references **2.** same as CROSS-REFER

cross·road (-rōd') n. **1.** a road that crosses another **2.** a road that connects main roads **3.** [usually pl.] the place where roads intersect —**at the crossroads** at the point where one must choose between different courses of action

cross·ruff (-ruf') n. Card Games a sequence of plays in

which each of two partners in turn leads a card which the other can trump

cross section 1. a) a cutting through something, esp. at right angles to its axis b) a piece so cut off c) a drawing of a plane surface as exposed by such a cutting **2.** a sample with enough of each kind to show what the whole is like —**cross'-sec'tion** vt. —**cross'-sec'tion·al** adj.

cross-stitch (-stich') n. **1.** a stitch made by crossing two stitches diagonally in the form of an X **2.** needlework made with this stitch —vt., vi. to sew or embroider with this stitch

cross·talk (-tôk') n. **1.** rapid, witty dialogue; repartee **2.** conversation in which two or more people are talking at once **3.** Radio etc. undesired sounds heard on a receiving channel

cross·trees (-trēz') n.pl. two short, horizontal bars across a ship's masthead, which spread the rigging that supports the mast

cross·wise (-wīz') adv. so as to cross; across: also **cross'ways'** (-wāz')

cross·word puzzle (-wurd') an arrangement of numbered squares to be filled in with words, a letter to each square: numbered synonyms, definitions, etc. are given as clues for the words

crotch (kroch) n. [ME. croche, var. of crucche, CRUTCH] **1.** a pole forked on top **2.** a forked place, as where a tree trunk divides into two branches **3.** the place where the legs fork from the human body **4.** the place where the legs of a pair of trousers, etc. meet —**crotched** adj.

crotch·et (kroch'it) n. [OFr. crochet, dim. < croc, hook] **1.** a peculiar whim or stubborn idea **2.** Music a note having the tune value of one quarter of a semibreve: see NOTE, illus.

crotch·et·y (-ē) adj. full of peculiar whims or stubborn ideas —**crotch'et·i·ness** n.

cro·ton (krōt''n) n. [ModL. < Gr. kroton] any of a large, mostly tropical genus of shrubs and trees of the spurge family: one species yields an oil (**croton oil**) formerly used in medicine

crouch (krouch) vi. [< OFr. crochir < croc, a hook] **1.** to stoop low with the limbs close to the body, as an animal ready to pounce or cowering **2.** to cringe or bow in a servile manner —n. the act or position of crouching

croup[1] (krōōp) n. [< obs. or dial. croup, to speak hoarsely, of echoic origin] an inflammation of the respiratory passages, with laboured breathing and hoarse coughing —**croup'y** adj.

croup[2] (krōōp) n. [OFr. croupe] the rump of a horse, etc.

crou·pi·er (krōō'pē ər, -pē ā') n. [Fr., orig., one who rides on the croup: see prec.] a person in charge of a gambling table, who rakes in and pays out the money

crou·ton (krōō'ton) n. [< Fr. < croûte < L. crusta: see CRUST] a small piece of toasted or fried bread, often served in soup or salads

crow[1] (krō) n. [OE. crawa] a large bird with glossy black plumage and a typical harsh call: the raven, rook, and jackdaw are crows —**as the crow flies** in a direct line —**eat crow** [U.S. Colloq.] to undergo the humiliation of admitting an error, etc.

crow[2] (krō) vi. **crowed** or, for 1, **crew** (krōō), **crowed, crow'ing** [OE. crawan] **1.** to make the shrill cry of a cock **2.** to boast in triumph; exult **3.** to make a sound expressive of pleasure, as a baby does —n. a crowing sound

crow·bar (krō'bär') n. a long metal bar, chisellike at one end, used as a lever for prying, etc.

crowd[1] (kroud) vi. [OE. crudan] **1.** to press, push, or squeeze **2.** to push one's way (forward, into, etc.) **3.** to throng —vt. **1.** to press, push, or shove **2.** to press closely together; cram **3.** to fill too full **4.** to be or press very near to **5.** [Colloq.] to put (a person) under pressure, as by dunning —n. **1.** a large number of people or things gathered closely together **2.** the common people; the masses **3.** [Colloq.] a set or clique —**crowd out** to exclude because of insufficient space or time —**crowd'ed** adj.

crowd[2] (kroud) n. [W. crwth] an old Celtic musical instrument like a violin but with a shallow, broad body

crow·foot (krō'foot') n., pl. **-foots'** a plant of the buttercup family, with leaves resembling a crow's foot

crown (kroun) n. [< OFr. < L. corona, a garland < Gr. korōnē, wreath] **1.** a garland or wreath worn on the head as a sign of honour, victory, etc. **2.** a reward or honour given for merit; specif., a sports championship **3.** the emblematic headdress of a monarch **4.** [often C-] a) the power or dominion of a monarch b) the monarch as head of the state **5.** anything serving to adorn or honour like a crown **6.** a thing like a crown in shape, position, etc., as the top of the head, of a hat, etc. **7.** a) orig., any coin bearing the figure of a crown b) a former British coin equal to five shillings (25p) **8.** a) the highest point, as of an arch b) the centre part of a road, esp. when it is cambered **9.** the highest quality, state, etc. of anything **10.** a) the part of a tooth projecting beyond the gum line b) an artificial substitute for this **11.** the lowest point of an anchor, between the arms —*vt.* 1. *a*) to put a crown on the head of *b*) to enthrone 2. to honour or reward as with a crown 3. to be the crown or highest part of 4. to put the finishing touch on 5. to cover (a tooth) with an artificial crown 6. [Slang] to hit on the head 7. *Draughts* to make a king of —**crown'er** *n.*

crown colony a British colony directly under the control of the home government in London

crown court a court of criminal jurisdiction holding sessions throughout England and Wales

Crown Derby a type of fine china

crown glass a very clear optical glass

crown jewels the jewellery, including the regalia, used by the sovereign on a state occasion

crown prince the male heir apparent to a throne

crown princess 1. the wife of a crown prince 2. a female heir presumptive to a throne

crow's-foot (krōz'foot') *n.*, *pl.* **-feet'** any of the wrinkles that often develop at the outer corners of the eyes: *usually used in pl.*

crow's-nest (-nest') *n.* 1. a small, partly enclosed platform close to the top of a ship's mast, used by the lookout 2. any platform like this

cro·zier (krō'zhər) *n.* *same as* CROSIER

cru·ces (krōō'sēz) *n.* *alt. pl. of* CRUX

cru·cial (krōō'shəl) *adj.* [Fr. < L. *crux*, CROSS] of supreme importance; decisive; critical —**cru'cial·ly** *adv.*

cru·ci·ble (krōō'sə b'l) *n.* [< ML. *crucibulum*, lamp] 1. a container made of a heat-resistant substance, as graphite, for melting ores, metals, etc. 2. a severe test or trial

cru·ci·fix (krōō'sə fiks') *n.* [< OFr. or ML., orig. pp. of LL. *crucifigere*, CRUCIFY] 1. a representation of a cross with the figure of Jesus crucified on it 2. the cross as a Christian symbol

cru·ci·fix·ion (krōō'sə fik'shən) *n.* 1. a crucifying or being crucified 2. [C-] the crucifying of Jesus, or a representation of this in painting, statuary, etc.

cru·ci·form (krōō'sə fôrm') *adj.* [< L. *crux*, CROSS + -FORM] cross-shaped —**cru'ci·form'ly** *adv.*

cru·ci·fy (krōō'sə fī') *vt.* **-fied'**, **-fy'ing** [< OFr. < LL. *crucificare*, for *crucifigere* < L. *crux*, CROSS + *figere*, FIX] 1. to execute by nailing or binding to a cross and leaving to die of exposure 2. to torment; torture 3. [Colloq.] to defeat, ridicule, suppress, etc., totally [the critics *crucified* his performance] —**cru'ci·fi'er** *n.*

crud (krud) *vt.*, *vi.* **crud'ded**, **crud'ding** [ME. *crud*: see CURD] [Dial.] to curdle —*n.* [Chiefly U.S. Slang] 1. any coagulated substance, caked deposit, dregs, filth, etc. 2. a worthless, disgusting, or contemptible person or thing —**crud'dy** *adj.* **-di·er**, **-di·est**

crude (krōōd) *adj.* [L. *crudus*, raw, rough] 1. in a raw or natural condition; not refined or processed 2. lacking grace, style etc. [*crude* furnishings] 3. not carefully made or done; rough 4. stark [*crude* reality] 5. [Colloq.] vulgar; tasteless [a *crude* remark] —**crude'ly** *adv.* —**crude'ness** *n.*

cru·di·ty (krōō'də tē) *n.* 1. a crude condition or quality 2. *pl.* **-ties** a crude remark, etc.

cru·el (krōō'əl) *adj.* [OFr. < L. *crudelis* < *crudus*: see CRUDE] 1. enjoying others' suffering; merciless 2. causing, or of a kind to cause, pain, distress, etc. —**cru'el·ly** *adv.* —**cru'el·ness** *n.*

cru·el·ty (-tē) *n.* 1. the quality of being cruel; inhumanity; hardheartedness 2. *pl.* **-ties** a cruel action, remark, etc. 3. *Law* wilful mistreatment seriously harmful to life or to health

cru·et (krōō'it) *n.* [< Anglo-Fr. dim. of OFr. *crue*, earthen pot < Gmc.] 1. a small glass bottle, as for holding vinegar, oil, etc., for the table 2. a stand for holding such bottles, pepper pots, mustard pots, etc.

cruise (krōōz) *vi.* **cruised**, **cruis'ing** [< Du. *kruisen*, to cross < *kruis* < L. *crux*, CROSS] 1. to sail from place to place, as for pleasure or in search of something 2. to go or drive about in a similar manner, as a taxi 3. to move at the most efficient speed for sustained travel —*vt.* to sail, journey, or move over or about —*n.* the action of cruising; esp., a cruising voyage

cruis·er (-ər) *n.* 1. one that cruises 2. a fast warship somewhat smaller than a battleship and having less armour and fire power 3. *same as* CABIN CRUISER 4. [Aust. Colloq.] a large glass for beer

cruis·er·weight (krōōz'ər wāt') *n.* *Boxing* a light heavyweight: see BOXING and WRESTLING WEIGHTS, table

crumb (krum) *n.* [OE. *cruma*] 1. a small piece broken off something, as of bread, or cake 2. any bit or scrap [*crumbs* of knowledge] 3. the soft, inner part of bread 4. [Slang] a worthless or despicable person —*vt.* 1. to break into small

fragments; crumble 2. *Cooking* to cover or thicken with crumbs

crum·ble (krum'b'l) *vt.* **-bled**, **-bling** [freq. of prec.] to break into crumbs or small pieces —*vi.* to fall to pieces; decay —*n.* a baked pudding consisting of a crumbly topping over stewed fruit

crum·bly (-blē) *adj.* **-bli·er**, **-bli·est** apt to crumble; easily crumbled —**crum'bli·ness** *n.*

crum·by (krum'ē) *adj.* **crum'bi·er**, **crum'bi·est** 1. full of crumbs 2. soft, as the inner part of bread 3. [Slang] same as CRUMMY —**crum'bi·ness** *n.*

crum·my (krum'ē) *adj.* **-mi·er**, **-mi·est** [< CRUM(B) + -Y²] [Slang] 1. dirty, cheap, etc. 2. inferior, worthless, contemptible, etc. —**crum'mi·ness** *n.*

crum·pet (krum'pit) *n.* [17th c. < ?] a light, soft cake baked on a griddle: it is usually toasted before serving 2. [Slang] sexually attractive womanhood

crum·ple (krum'p'l) *vt.*, *vi.* **-pled**, **-pling** [ME. *crumplen*, var. of *crimplen*, to wrinkle, freq. of *crimpen*, CRIMP¹] 1. to crush or become crushed together into wrinkles 2. to break down; collapse Sometimes with *up* —*n.* a crease or wrinkle —**crum'ply** *adj.*

crunch (krunch) *vi.*, *vt.* [echoic origin] 1. to chew with a noisy, crackling sound 2. to press, grind, tread, etc. with a noisy, crushing sound —*n.* 1. the act or sound of crunching 2. [Colloq.] *a*) a showdown *b*) a tight situation

crunch·y (-ē) *adj.* **crunch'i·er**, **crunch'i·est** making a crunching sound, as when chewed; crisp —**crunch'i·ness** *n.*

crup·per (krup'ər) *n.* [< OFr. *cropiere*, crope, rump] 1. a leather strap attached to a saddle or harness and passed under the horse's tail 2. a horse's rump; croup

cru·sade (krōō sād') *n.* [< Sp. *cruzada* & Fr. *croisade*, both < ML. pp. of *cruciare*, to mark with a cross < L. *crux*, CROSS] 1. [*sometimes* C-] any of the military expeditions which Christians undertook from the 11th to the 13th cent. to recover the Holy Land from the Moslems 2. any church-sanctioned war or expedition like this 3. vigorous, concerted action for some cause or against some abuse —*vi.* **-sad'ed**, **-sad'ing** to engage in a crusade —**cru·sad'er** *n.*

cruse (krōōz, krōōs) *n.* [OE. *cruse*] [Obs.] a small container for water, oil, honey, etc.

crush (krush) *vt.* [< OFr. *croisir*, to break < Frank. *krostjan*, to gnash] 1. to press between opposing forces so as to break or put out of shape; crumple 2. to grind or pound into small particles 3. to subdue; overwhelm [a *crushing* retort] 4. to oppress 5. to extract by pressing or squeezing —*vi.* 1. to be or become crushed 2. to crowd (*into*, etc.) —*n.* 1. a crushing; severe pressure 2. a crowded mass of people 3. a drink prepared by crushing fruit 4. [Colloq.] *a*) an infatuation *b*) the object of an infatuation —**crush'a·ble** *adj.* —**crush'er** *n.*

crush barrier a barrier erected to separate or restrain large crowds

Cru·soe (krōō'sō), **Robinson** *see* ROBINSON CRUSOE

crust (krust) *n.* [< OFr. *crouste* or < L. *crusta*] 1. *a*) the hard, outer part of bread *b*) a piece of this *c*) any dry, hard piece of bread 2. the pastry covering of a pie 3. any hard surface layer, as of snow, soil, etc. 4. *same as* SCAB (*n.* 1) 5. [Slang] audacity; insolence 6. *Geol.* the solid outer shell of the earth —*vt.*, *vi.* 1. to cover or become covered with a crust 2. to harden into a crust —**crus'tal** (krus't'l) *adj.* —**crust'ed** *adj.*

crus·ta·cean (krus tā'shən) *n.* [< ModL. < *crustaceus*, having a crust < L. *crusta*, crust] any of a class of arthropods, including shrimps, crabs, barnacles, and lobsters, that usually live in water and breathe through gills: they have a hard outer shell and jointed appendages and bodies —*adj.* of crustaceans: also **crus·ta'ceous**

crust·y (krus'tē) *adj.* **crust'i·er**, **crust'i·est** 1. having, forming, or resembling a crust 2. rudely abrupt or surly; bad-tempered —**crust'i·ly** *adv.* —**crust'i·ness** *n.*

crutch (kruch) *n.* [OE. *crycce*, staff] 1. a staff with a hand grip and a crosspiece on top that fits under the armpit, used by lame people as an aid in walking 2. anything relied on for support; prop 3. any device that resembles a crutch —*vt.* to support with or as with a crutch; prop up

crux (kruks) *n.*, *pl.* **crux'es**, **cru·ces** (krōō'sēz) [L., CROSS] 1. a difficult problem; puzzling thing 2. the essential or deciding point

cru·zei·ro (krōō zā'rō; *Port.* krōō zā'rōō) *n.*, *pl.* **-ros** [Port.< *cruz*, a cross < L. *crux*, CROSS] *see* MONETARY UNITS, table (Brazil)

cry (krī) *vi.* **cried**, **cry'ing** [OFr. *crier* < L. *quiritare*, to wail] 1. to make a loud vocal sound or utterance, as for help 2. to sob and shed tears in expressing sorrow, pain, etc.; weep 3. *a*) to plead or clamour (*for*) *b*) to show a great need (*for*) [problems *crying* for solution] 4. to utter its characteristic call: said of an animal or bird —*vt.* 1. to plead or beg for [to *cry* quarter] 2. to utter loudly; shout 3. to call out (wares for sale, etc.) —*n.*, *pl.* **cries** 1. a loud vocal sound expressing pain, anger, etc. 2. any loud utterance; shout 3. an announcement called out publicly 4. an urgent appeal; plea 5. popular report; rumour; rallying call 6. the

CROW'S-NEST

current opinion or fashion **7.** public outcry **8.** a slogan **9.** a fit of weeping **10.** the characteristic vocal sound of an animal or bird **11.** the baying of hounds in the chase **—a far cry** a great distance or difference **—cry down** to belittle; disparage **—cry for the moon** to long for what is unobtainable **—cry off** to withdraw from an agreement or undertaking **—cry one's eyes out** to weep much and bitterly **—cry out 1.** to shout; yell **2.** to complain loudly **—cry up** to praise highly **—in full cry** in eager pursuit

cry·ba·by (-bā′bē) *n., pl.* **-bies 1.** a child who cries often or with little cause **2.** a person who complains when he fails to win or get his own way

cry·ing (-iŋ) *adj.* **1.** that cries **2.** demanding immediate notice **—for crying out loud** [Colloq.] an exclamation of annoyance, surprise, etc.

cry·o- [< Gr. *kryos*, cold, frost] *a combining form meaning* cold or freezing [*cryolite*]

cry·o·gen (krī′ə jən) *n.* [CRYO- + -GEN] a refrigerant

cry·o·gen·ics (krī′ə jen′iks) *n.pl.* [with *sing. v.*] [CRYOGEN + -ICS] the science that deals with the effects of very low temperatures on the properties of matter

cry·o·lite (krī′ə līt′) *n.* [CRYO- + -LITE] a fluoride of sodium and aluminium used in the production of aluminium

cry·o·stat (krī′ə stat′) *n.* [CRYO- + -STAT] an apparatus for maintaining a constant, low temperature

cry·o·sur·ger·y (krī′ə sur′jə rē) *n.* [CRYO- + SURGERY] surgery in which tissues are destroyed by freezing: also **cryogenic surgery**

crypt (kript) *n.* [< L. < Gr. < *kryptein*, to hide] an underground chamber; esp., a vault under the main floor of a church, used as a burial place

crypt·a·nal·y·sis (kript′ə nal′ə sis) *n.* [CRYPT(OGRAM) ANALYSIS] the act or science of deciphering codes

cryp·tic (krip′tik) *adj.* [< LL. < Gr.: see CRYPT] **1.** having a hidden meaning; mysterious **2.** obscure and curt Also **cryp·ti·cal** **—cryp·ti·cal·ly** *adv.*

cryp·to- *a combining form meaning:* **1.** secret or hidden **2.** being such secretly Also, before a vowel, **crypt-**

cryp·to·gam (krip′tə gam′) *n.* [< Fr. < Gr. *kryptos*, hidden + *gamos*, marriage] a plant that bears no flowers or seeds but propagates by means of spores, as algae, mosses, ferns, etc. **—cryp·to·gam·ic, cryp·tog·a·mous** (-tog′ə məs) *adj.*

cryp·to·gram (krip′tə gram′) *n.* [CRYPTO- + -GRAM] something written in code or cipher: also **cryp′·to·graph′**(-gräf′) **—cryp·to·gram′mic** *adj.*

cryp·tog·ra·phy (krip tog′rə fē) *n.* [CRYPTO- + -GRAPHY] **1.** the art of writing or deciphering messages in code **2.** a code system **—cryp·tog′ra·pher, cryp·tog′ra·phist** *n.* **—cryp·to·graph·ic** (krip′tə graf′ik) *adj.* **—cryp′to·graph′·i·cal·ly** *adv.*

cryst. 1. crystalline **2.** crystallized

crys·tal (kris′t'l) *n.* [< OE. & OFr. < L. < Gr. *krystallos*, ice < *kryos*, frost] **1.** *a)* a clear, transparent quartz *b)* a piece of this cut in the form of an ornament **2.** *a)* a very clear, brilliant glass *b)* an article or articles made of such glass, as goblets, bowls, etc. **3.** the transparent covering over the face of a watch **4.** anything clear and transparent like crystal **5.** a solidified form of a substance made up of plane faces in three dimensions in a symmetrical arrangement **6.** *Radio* a piezoelectric material, as quartz, used to produce and control very precisely a desired frequency, as in transmitters, etc. **—adj. 1.** of or composed of crystal **2.** like crystal; transparent **3.** *Radio* using a crystal

CRYSTALS
(A, isometric; B, monoclinic; C, triclinic)

crystal detector *Radio* a semiconductor rectifier used, esp. in early radio receivers, for demodulation

crystal gazing the practice of gazing into a large glass ball **(crystal ball)** and professing to see images, esp. of future events **—crystal gazer**

crys·tal·line (kris′tə lin) *adj.* **1.** consisting or made of crystal or crystals **2.** like crystal; clear and transparent **3.** having the character or structure of a crystal

crystalline lens the lens of the eye, serving to focus light on the retina

crys·tal·lize (kris′tə līz′) *vt.* **-lized′, -liz′ing 1.** to cause to form crystals **2.** to give a definite form to **3.** to coat with sugar **—vi. 1.** to become crystalline in form **2.** to take on a definite form **—crys·tal·liz′a·ble** *adj.* **—crys′tal·li·za′-tion** *n.*

crys·tal·lo- [< Gr. *krystallos*, CRYSTAL] *a combining form meaning* crystal Also **crys·tall-**

crys·tal·log·ra·phy (kris′tə log′rə fē) *n.* [prec. + -GRAPHY] the science of the form, structure, properties, and classification of crystals **—crys′tal·log′ra·pher** *n.* **—crys′·tal·lo·graph′ic** (-lə graf′ik) **—crys′tal·lo·graph′i·cal** *adj.*

crys·tal·loid (kris′tə loid′) *adj.* **1.** like a crystal **2.** having the nature of a crystalloid **—n.** a substance, usually crystallizable, which, when in solution, readily passes

through vegetable and animal membranes **—crys′tal·loi′dal** *adj.*

crystal pickup a piezoelectric vibration pickup, used on some gramophones

crystal set an early type of radio receiver with a crystal, instead of an electron tube, detector

Cs *Chem.* caesium

cs. case; cases

C.S. 1. chartered surveyor **2.** Christian Science

C.S., c.s. 1. capital stock **2.** civil service

csc cosecant

C.S.C. Civil Service Commission

C.S.E. Certificate of Secondary Education

C.S. gas [after B. *C(arson)* & R. *S(taughton)*, its U.S. inventors] a gas causing tears, salivation and painful breathing, used in chemical warfare and civil disturbances

C.S.I.R.O. [Aust.] Commonwealth Scientific and Industrial Research Organization

ct. 1. carat **2.** *pl.* **cts.** cent **3.** court

cten·o·phore (ten′ə fôr) *n.* [< Gr. *kteis* (gen. *ktenos*), comb & -PHORE] a sea animal with a transparent, jellylike body bearing eight rows of comblike teeth that aid in swimming

ctn 1. carton: also **ctn. 2.** cotangent

ctr. centre

Cu [L. *cuprum*] *Chem.* copper

cu. cubic

cub (kub) *n.* [< ? OIr. *cuib*, whelp] **1.** the young of certain mammals, as the fox, bear, lion, whale, etc. **2.** an inexperienced or callow person, esp. a novice reporter **—vt., vi.** to give birth to (cubs) **—cub′bish** *adj.* **—cub′bish·ness** *n.*

cub·by·hole (kub′ē hōl′) *n.* [< dial. *cub*, little shed + HOLE] a small, enclosed space or room

cube (kyoob) *n.* [Fr. < L. < Gr. *kybos*, a cube, die] **1.** a solid with six equal, square sides **2.** anything having more or less this shape [an ice *cube*] **3.** the product obtained by multiplying a given number or quantity by its square; third power [the *cube* of 3 is 27 (3 x 3 x 3)] **—vt. cubed, cub′ing 1.** to raise to the third power **2.** to cut or shape into cubes **—cub′er** *n.*

cu·beb (kyoo′beb) *n.* [< Fr. < ML. < Ar. *kabāba*] the spicy berry of an East Indian shrub, formerly used medicinally in cigarettes

cube root the number or quantity of which a given number or quantity is the cube [the *cube root* of 8 is 2]

cu·bic (kyoo′bik) *adj.* **1.** having the shape of a cube **2.** having three dimensions, or having the volume of a cube whose length, width, and depth each measure the given unit [a *cubic* metre] **3.** relating to the cubes of numbers or quantities **—cu′bi·cal** (-bi k'l) *adj.* **—cu′bi·cal·ly** *adv.*

cu·bi·cle (kyoo′bi k'l) *n.* [L. *cubiculum* < *cubare*, to lie down] **1.** a small sleeping compartment, as in a dormitory **2.** any small compartment

cubic measure a system of measuring volume in cubic units, esp. that in which 1,728 cubic inches = 1 cubic foot and 1,000 cubic millimetres = 1 cubic centimetre: see TABLE OF WEIGHTS AND MEASURES in Supplement

cu·bi·form (kyoo′bə fôrm′) *adj.* cube-shaped

cub·ism (kyoo′biz′m) *n.* a movement in art, esp. of the early 20th century, characterized by the use of cubes and other geometric forms in abstract arrangements rather than by a realistic representation of nature **—cub′ist** *n., adj.* **—cu·bis′tic** *adj.*

cu·bit (kyoo′bit) *n.* [< OE. < L. *cubitum*, the elbow, cubit] an ancient measure of length, about 50 cm; orig., the length of the arm from the end of the middle finger to the elbow

cu·boid (kyoo′boid) *adj.* cube-shaped: also **cu·boi′dal —n.** a six-sided figure with all faces rectangular

Cub Scout a member of a division of the Boy Scouts for boys eight to ten years old

cuck·ing stool (kuk′iŋ) [ME. < *coken*, to defecate] a seat in which disorderly women, cheats, etc. were exposed to public ridicule or, sometimes, ducked

cuck·old (kuk′'ld, -öld) *n.* [< OFr. *cucuault* < *cucu:* see ff.] a man whose wife has committed adultery **—vt.** to make a cuckold of **—cuck′old·ry** (-rē) *n.*

cuck·oo (koo′koo′, kook′oo) *n., pl.* **cuck′oos** [< OFr. *coucou, cucu,* echoic of its cry] **1.** any of a family of greyish-brown birds with a long, slender body: the European species lays eggs in the nests of other birds **2.** the call of a cuckoo, which sounds somewhat like its name **3.** an imitation of this **4.** [Slang] a crazy or foolish person **—vi.** to utter the call of a cuckoo **—adj.** [Slang] crazy; silly

cuckoo clock a clock with a toy bird that pops out and cuckoos to mark intervals of time

cuck·oo·pint (koo′koo pint′) *n.* a wild flower with arrow-shaped leaves and a purple spadix: also called **lords-and-ladies**

cuckoo spit (or spittle) a froth produced on plants by the larvae of certain insects

cu·cul·late (kyoo′kə lāt′, kyoo kul′it) *adj.* [< L. *cucullus*, hood] shaped like a hood: also **cu′cul·lat′ed**

cu·cum·ber (kyoo′kum bər) *n.* [< OFr. < L. *cucumis* (gen.

cucumeris)] **1.** an annual creeping plant of the gourd family, grown for its edible fruit **2.** the long fruit, with a green rind and firm, white flesh, used in salads or preserved as pickles —**cool as a cucumber 1.** comfortably cool **2.** calm and self-possessed

cud (kud) *n.* [OE. *cudu*] a mouthful of swallowed food regurgitated from the first stomach of cattle and other ruminants and chewed slowly a second time —**chew the cud** to ruminate; ponder

cud·dle (kud′'l) *vt.* **-dled, -dling** [? < ME. hyp. *couthelen* < *couth*, known, hence comfortable with + -*le*, freq. suffix] to hold lovingly and gently in one's arms; embrace and fondle —*vi.* to lie close and snug; nestle —*n.* **1.** a cuddling **2.** an embrace; hug —**cud′dle·some** (-səm), **cud′dly** *adj.* -**dli·er, -dli·est**

cud·dy (kud′ē) *n.*, *pl.* **-dies** [< ?] **1.** a small cabin on a ship **2.** the cook's galley on a small ship

cudg·el (kuj′əl) *n.* [OE. *cycgel*] a short, thick stick or club —*vt.* **-elled, -el·ling** to beat with a cudgel —**cudgel one's brains** to think hard —**take up the cudgels (for)** to come to the defence (of)

cue[1] (kyoo) *n.* [prob. < *q*, *Q* (? for L. *quando*, when) found in 16th-c. plays to mark actors' entrances] **1.** a short piece of dialogue, action, or music that is a signal for an actor's entrance or speech, or for lights, sound effects, etc. **2.** anything serving as a signal to do something **3.** an indirect suggestion; hint —*vt.* **cued, cu′ing** or **cue′ing** to give a cue to

cue[2] (kyoo) *n.* [var. of QUEUE] **1.** a pigtail **2.** a long, tapering rod used in billiards, etc. to strike the cue ball —*vt.* **cued, cu′ing** or **cue′ing** to strike (a cue ball, etc.) with a cue

cue ball the ball, usually white, that a player strikes with his cue in billiards, etc.

cues·ta (kwes′tə) *n.* [Sp. < L. *costa*, side, rib] a ridge or hill with a steep incline on one side and a gentle slope on the other

cuff[1] (kuf) *n.* [< ME. *cuffe*, glove] **1.** a fixed or detachable band or fold at the end of a sleeve **2.** a trouser turnup **3.** a handcuff —*vt.* to put a cuff on —**off the cuff** [Colloq.] improvised; impromptu

cuff[2] (kuf) *vt.* [< ? CUFF[1] (in orig. sense "glove")] to strike, esp. with the open hand; slap —*n.* a slap or blow

cuff link a pair of linked buttons or any similar small device for keeping a shirt cuff closed

‡**cui bo·no** (kwē bō′nō, bo′-) [L., to whom (is it) a benefit?] **1.** for whose benefit? **2.** to what purpose?

cui·rass (kwi ras′) *n.* [< Fr. < It. < L. (*vestis*) *coriacea*, leather (clothing) < *corium*, leather] **1.** a piece of closefitting armour for protecting the breast and back **2.** the breastplate of such armour —*vt.* to cover as with a cuirass

cui·ras·sier (kwi′rə sir′) *n.* [Fr.] a cavalryman wearing a cuirass

Cui·se·naire rod (kwē′zə ner′) *a trademark for* any of a set of rods of various colours and lengths representing different numbers that are used to teach children arithmetic

cui·sine (kwi zēn′) *n.* [Fr. < LL. *coquina*, kitchen < L. *coquere*, to cook] **1.** style of cooking or preparing food **2.** the food prepared, as at a restaurant

cuisse (kwis) *n.* [< OFr. < L. *coxa*, hip] a piece of armour to protect the thigh: also **cuish** (kwish)

cul-de-sac (kul′də sak′, kool′-; *Fr.* küt såk′) *n.*, *pl.* **cul-de-sacs;** *Fr.* **culs-de-sac** (küt säk′) [Fr., lit., bottom of a sack] a passage or position with only one outlet; blind alley

-cule (kyool, kyool) [< Fr. or L.] *a suffix meaning* small

cu·lex (kyoo′leks) *n.* [L., a gnat] any of a large genus of mosquitoes including many of the most common species found in Europe and N. America

cu·li·nar·y (ku′lə nər ē) *adj.* [< LL. < L. *culina*, kitchen] of the kitchen or of cooking

cull (kul) *vt.* [< OFr. < L. *colligere*: see COLLECT[2]] **1.** to pick out; select and gather **2.** to examine carefully so as to select or reject **3.** to take out (inferior or surplus animals) from a herd or flock —*n.* **1.** something picked out; select, something rejected as not being up to standard **2.** an inferior or surplus animal taken from a herd or flock

culm[1] (kulm) *n.* [< ME. *colme* < ? OE. *col*, coal] waste material from coal screenings or washings

culm[2] (kulm) *n.* [L. *culmus*, a stem] the jointed stem of various grasses, usually hollow —*vi.* to grow or develop into a culm

cul·mi·nate (kul′mə nāt′) *vi.* **-nat′ed, -nat′ing** [< ML. pp. of *culminare* < L. *culmen* (gen. *culminis*), peak] to reach its highest point or climax —*vt.* to bring to its climax —**cul′mi·nant** *adj.*

cul·mi·na·tion (kul′mə nā′shən) *n.* **1.** a culminating **2.** the highest point; climax

cu·lotte (kyoo lot′) *n.* [Fr. < *cul*, posterior < L. *culus*] [*often pl.*] trousers made full in the legs to resemble a skirt, worn by women and girls

cul·pa·ble (kul′pə b'l) *adj.* [< OFr. < L. < *culpa*, fault,

blame] deserving blame; blameworthy —**cul′pa·bil′i·ty** *n.* —**cul′pa·bly** *adv.*

cul·prit (kul′prit) *n.* [< Anglo-Fr. *cul.*, contr. for *culpable*, guilty + *prit*, ready (i.e., to prove guilt)] **1.** a person accused of a crime or offence, as in a court **2.** a person guilty of a crime or offence; offender

cult (kult) *n.* [< L. *cultus*, care, orig. pp. of *colere*, to till] **1.** a system of religious worship or ritual **2.** *a)* devoted attachment to, or admiration for, a person, principle, etc. *b)* the object of such attachment **3.** a group of followers; sect —**cult′ic** *adj.* —**cult′ism** *n.* —**cult′ist** *n.*

cul·ti·va·ble (kul′tə və b'l) *adj.* that can be cultivated: also **cul′ti·vat′a·ble** (-vāt′ə b'l) —**cul′ti·va·bil′i·ty** *n.*

cul·ti·vate (kul′tə vāt′) *vt.* **-vat′ed, -vat′ing** [< ML. < LL. *cultivus*, tilled < L. *cultus*: see CULT] **1.** to prepare and use (land) for growing crops; till **2.** to break up the surface soil around (plants) in order to aerate it, destroy weeds, etc. **3.** to grow (plants or crops) **4.** to develop (plants) by various horticultural techniques **5.** to develop or improve by care, training, etc.; refine [to *cultivate* one's mind] **6.** to seek to become familiar with —**cul′ti·vat′ed** *adj.*

cul·ti·va·tion (kul′tə vā′shən) *n.* **1.** the act of cultivating (in various senses) **2.** refinement, or culture

cul·ti·va·tor (kul′tə vāt′ər) *n.* **1.** one who cultivates **2.** a tool or machine for loosening the earth and destroying weeds around growing plants

cul·tur·al (kul′chər əl) *adj.* **1.** of culture **2.** obtained by breeding —**cul′tur·al·ly** *adv.*

cul·ture (kul′chər) *n.* [< L. *cultura* < *colere*: see CULT] **1.** cultivation of the soil **2.** development or improvement of a particular plant or animal **3.** a growth of bacteria, etc. in a specially prepared nourishing substance (**culture medium**) **4.** *a)* development, improvement, or refinement of the mind, manners, taste, etc. *b)* the result of this **5.** development or improvement of physical qualities by special training or care [*body culture*] **6.** the ideas, customs, skills, arts, etc. of a given people in a given period; civilization —*vt.* **-tured, -tur·ing** to cultivate —**the two cultures** science and the humanities —**cul′tur·ist** *n.*

cul·tured (-chərd) *adj.* **1.** produced by cultivation **2.** refined in speech, behaviour, etc.

cultured pearl a pearl induced to grow in the shell of a mollusc by the insertion of a foreign body

culture shock the feelings of isolation, disorientation, etc. experienced by a person or group from one culture when brought into sudden contact with another

culture vulture [Colloq.] a person who is enthusiastic about the arts, esp. one who is excessively so

cul·tus (kul′təs) *n.* [L.] a religious cult

cul·ver·in (kul′vər in) *n.* [< Fr. < L. *colubra*, a snake] **1.** a musket used in the Middle Ages **2.** a long cannon of the 16th and 17th centuries

cul·vert (kul′vərt) *n.* [< ?] a conduit, esp. a drain, under a road, through an embankment, etc.

cum (kum) *prep.* [L.] with; combined with [a *kitchen-cum-dining* room]

cum·ber (kum′bər) *vt.* [< OFr. *encombrer* < *en-* (see EN) + *combre*, obstruction] **1.** to hinder by obstruction or interference; hamper **2.** to burden in a troublesome way

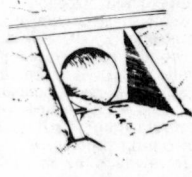

CULVERT

cum·ber·some (kum′bər səm) *adj.* burdensome; unwieldy; clumsy —**cum′ber·some·ly** *adv.* —**cum′-ber·some·ness** *n.*

cum·brance (kum′brəns) *n.* a troublesome burden

Cum·bri·an (kum′brē ən) *adj.* **1.** of the ancient British kingdom of Cumbria **2.** of the former English county of Cumberland **3.** of the modern English county of Cumbria —*n.* a native or inhabitant of Cumbria or Cumberland

cum·brous (-brəs) *adj.* *same as* CUMBERSOME —**cum′-brous·ly** *adv.* —**cum′brous·ness** *n.*

cum·in (kum′in) *n.* [< OFr. < L. < Gr. < Sem., as in Heb. *kammōn*, Ar. *kammūn*] a small umbelliferous plant **2.** its aromatic fruits, used for flavouring pickles, soups, etc. Also sp. **cum′min**

cum·mer·bund (kum′ər bund′) *n.* [Hindi & Per. *kamarband*, loin band] a wide sash worn as a waistband, esp. with men's formal dress

cum·quat (kum′kwot) *n.* *same as* KUMQUAT

cu·mu·late (kyoo′m′yə lāt′) *vt.*, *vi.* **-lat′ed, -lat′ing** [< L. pp. of *cumulare*, to heap up < *cumulus*, a heap] *same as* ACCUMULATE —**cu′mu·la′tion** *n.*

cu·mu·la·tive (kyoo′m′yə lə tiv) *adj.* [see prec.] increasing in effect, size, quantity, etc. by successive additions; accumulated [*cumulative* interest is interest added to the principal and drawing additional interest] —**cu′mu·la′-tive·ly** *adv.*

cu·mu·lo·nim·bus (kyoo′m′yoo lō nim′bəs) *n.* a towering cloud type, usually producing heavy rain

cu·mu·lus (-yə ləs) *n.*, *pl.* **-li′** (-lī′) [L., a heap] **1.** a heap

2. a thick cloud type with a dark, horizontal base and upper parts resembling domes —**cu'mu·lous** *adj.*

cu·ne·ate (kyōō'nē it, -āt') *adj.* [< L. < *cuneus*, a wedge] wedge-shaped; tapering, as some leaves: also **cu'ne·al, cu'ne·at'ed** (-āt'id), **cu'ne·at'ic** (-at'ik)

cu·ne·i·form (kyōō'nē ə fôrm, kyōō'nē fôrm) *adj.* [< L. *cuneus* (see prec.) + -FORM] wedge-shaped; esp., designating the characters used in ancient Assyrian, Babylonian, and Persian inscriptions, or such inscriptions —*n.* cuneiform characters or inscriptions

cun·ni·lin·gus (kun'ə lin'gəs) *n.* [< L. < *cunnus*, vulva + *lingere*, to lick] a sexual activity involving oral contact with the female genitals: also **cun·ni·linc'tus**

cun·ning (kun'iŋ) *adj.* [ME. < prp. of *cunnen*, to know: see CAN[1]] **1.** [Now Rare] skilful or clever **2.** skilful in deception; sly; crafty **3.** made or done with skill or ingenuity **4.** [U.S.] pretty in a delicate way; quaint —*n.* **1.** [Now Rare] skill **2.** skill in deception; slyness; craftiness —**cun'ning·ly** *adv.* —**cun'ning·ness** *n.*

cunt (kunt) *n.* [ME.] **1.** the female genitals. **2.** a despicable person Usually considered a vulgar term

cup (kup) *n.* [OE. *cuppe* < LL. *cuppa* < L. *cupa*, tub] **1.** a small, bowl-shaped container for beverages, often with a handle **2.** the bowl part of a drinking vessel **3.** a cup and its contents **4.** the amount a cup holds; cupful **5.** anything shaped like a cup **6.** an ornamental cup given as a prize **7.** the wine chalice at Communion; also, the wine **8.** one's portion or allotment **9.** something served in a cup **10.** *Golf* the hole in each putting green —*vt.* **cupped, cup'ping 1.** to shape like a cup **2.** to take in or put into a cup **3.** *Med.* to subject to cupping —**in one's cups** drunk —**cup'like'** *adj.*

C.U.P. Cambridge University Press

cup·bear·er (-ber'ər) *n.* a person who fills and serves the wine cups, as in a king's palace

cup·board (kub'ərd) *n.* a piece of furniture or a recessed area of a room, with a door concealing storage space, often with shelves, hooks, etc.

cupboard love a pretended affection assumed in the hope of a gain

cup·cake (kup'kāk') *n.* a little cake for one person, baked in a cup-shaped mould

cu·pel (kyōō'pəl) *n.* [Fr. *coupelle* < ML.< L. *cupa*, tub] **1.** a small cup used in assaying gold, silver, etc. **2.** a hearth for refining metals —*vt.* **-pelled, -pel·ling** to assay or refine in a cupel

Cup Final 1. the annual final of the F.A. Cup soccer competition **2.** [often **C- F-**] the final of any cup competition

Cu·pid (kyōō'pid) [< OFr. < L. < *cupido*, desire] the Roman god of love, son of Venus: identified with the Greek god Eros —*n.* [**c-**] a representation of Cupid as a naked, winged cherub with bow and arrow

cu·pid·i·ty (kyōō pid'ə tē) *n.* [< Anglo-Fr. < L. < *cupere*, to desire] strong desire for wealth; greed

cup of tea [Colloq.] a favourite thing, activity, person, etc. [golf isn't his *cup of tea*]

cu·po·la (kyōō'pə lə) *n.* [It. < L. dim. of *cupa*, a tub] **1.** a rounded roof or ceiling **2.** a small dome or similar structure on a roof **3.** a small furnace for melting metals **4.** an armour-plated, dome-shaped turret to protect a gun, esp. on a ship —**cu'po·laed** (-ləd) *adj.*

cup·pa (kup'ə) *n.* [Colloq.] a cup of tea: also **cup'per**

cup·ping (kup'iŋ) *n.* the use of a glass cup (**cupping glass**) from which the air has been exhausted, to draw blood to the surface of the skin: used, esp. formerly, in medicine —**cup'per** *n.*

cu·pre·ous (kyōō'prē əs) *adj.* [< L.: see COPPER[1]] of, like, or containing copper

cu·pric (kyōō'prik) *adj.* [CUPR(O)- + -IC] *Chem.* of or containing copper with a valence of two

cu·prif·er·ous (kyōō prif'ər əs) *adj.* [*cupri*- (see CUPRO-) + -FEROUS] containing copper

cu·pro- [< L. *cuprum*: see COPPER[1]] *a combining form meaning* copper (and): also **cu·pri-, cupr-**

cu·pro·nick·el (kyōō'prō nik'l) *n.* an alloy of copper and nickel, used in condenser tubes, some coins, etc.

cu·prous (kyōō'prəs) *adj.* [CUPR(O)- + -OUS] *Chem.* of or containing copper with a valence of one

cu·pule (kyōō'pyool) *n.* [ME. < L. *cupula*, dim. of *cupa*, a tub] *Bot.* a cuplike structure, as the part of an acorn that holds the nut

cur (kur) *n.* [prob. < ON. *kurra* or MLowG. *korren*, to growl] **1.** a dog of mixed breed; mongrel **2.** a mean, contemptible, or cowardly person

cur. **1.** currency **2.** current

cur·a·ble (kyoor'ə b'l) *adj.* that can be cured —**cur'a·bil'i·ty** *n.*

cu·ra·çao (kyoor'ə sō') *n.* [after *Curaçao*, island in the Caribbean, where originally made] a liqueur flavoured with orange peel

cu·ra·cy (kyoor'ə sē) *n.,* *pl.* **-cies** the position, office, or work of a curate

cu·ra·re, cu·ra·ri (kyoo rä'rē) *n.* [< Port. or Sp. < native (Tupi) name] **1.** a black, resinous substance prepared from the juices of certain S. American plants, used as an arrow poison by some Indians and in medicine to relax muscles **2.** any of the plants from which this is prepared

cu·rate (kyoor'it) *n.* [< ML. < L. pp. of *curare:* see CURATOR] a clergyman who assists a vicar or rector

curate's egg something that is bad but may be euphemistically described as being only partly so

cur·a·tive (kyoor'ə tiv) *adj.* curing or having the power to cure —*n.* a thing that cures; remedy

cu·ra·tor (kyoo rāt'ər) *n.* [< L. < *curare*, take care of < *cura*, care] a person in charge of a museum, art gallery etc. —**cu·ra·to·ri·al** (kyoor'ə tôr'ē əl) *adj.* —**cu·ra'tor·ship'** *n.*

curb (kurb) *n.* [< OFr. < L. *curvus*, bent] **1.** a chain or strap passed around a horse's lower jaw and attached to the bit, used to check the horse **2.** anything that checks, restrains, or subdues **3.** a raised margin along an edge, to strengthen or confine **4.** *same as* KERB **5.** [U.S.] a market dealing in stocks and bonds not listed on the stock exchange —*vt.* **1.** to restrain; check; control **2.** to provide with a curb

curb bit a horse's bit with a curb

cur·cu·li·o (kər kyōō'lē ō') *n.,* *pl.* **-li·os'** [L., weevil] any of a family of weevils with long snouts: some are harmful to fruit

cur·cu·ma (kur'kyoo mə) *n.* [ModL. < *kurkum*, saffron] any of a genus of tropical plants of the ginger family that yield starch and turmeric

curd (kurd) *n.* [< ME. *crud*, orig., any coagulated substance] [*often pl.*] the coagulated part of milk, from which cheese is made: it is formed when milk sours and is distinguished from whey, the watery part —*vt., vi.* to curdle —**curd'y** *adj.*

cur·dle (kur'd'l) *vt., vi.* **-dled, -dling** [< CURD + -*le*, freq. suffix] to form into curd; coagulate; congeal —**curdle one's blood** to horrify or terrify one

cure (kyoor) *n.* [OFr. < L. *cura*, care] **1.** a healing or being healed **2.** a medicine or treatment for restoring health; remedy· **3.** a method or course of treating a disease, ailment, etc. **4.** *same as* CURACY **5.** a process for curing meat, fish, tobacco, etc. —*vt.* **cured, cur'ing 1.** to restore to health or a sound condition; heal **2.** to get rid of (an ailment, evil, etc.) **3.** to get rid of an undesirable condition in (with *of*) [*cured* him of lying] **4.** *a*) to preserve (meat, fish, etc.), as by salting or smoking *b*) to process (tobacco, leather, etc.), as by drying or aging **5.** to vulcanize (rubber) **6.** to assist the hardening of (concrete, etc.) by keeping it moist —*vi.* **1.** to bring about a cure **2.** to undergo curing, preserving, or processing —**cure'less** *adj.* —**cur'er** *n.*

cu·ré (kyoo'rā) *n.* [Fr.] in France, a parish priest

cure-all (kyoor'ôl') *n.* something supposed to cure all ailments or evils; panacea

cu·ret, cu·rette (kyoo ret') *n.* [Fr. < *curer*, to cleanse] a spoon-shaped surgical instrument for the removal of tissue from the walls of body cavities —*vt.* **-ret'ted, -ret'ting** to clean or scrape with a curet

cu·ret·tage (kyoor'ə täzh', kyoo ret'ij) *n.* [Fr.: see prec.] the process of curetting

cur·few (kur'fyōō) *n.* [< OFr. *covrefeu* < *covrir*, to COVER + *feu*, fire] **1.** *a*) in the Middle Ages, the ringing of a bell every evening as a signal for people to cover fires, put out lights, and retire *b*) the bell *c*) the time at which it was rung **2.** *a*) a time in the evening set as a deadline beyond which people may not appear on the streets *b*) the regulation establishing this time

cu·ri·a (kyoor'ē ə) *n.,* *pl.* **-ri·ae** (-ē') [L.] **1.** a medieval judicial court held in the king's name **2.** [**C-**] the administrative body of the Roman Catholic Church, consisting of various departments, courts, officials, etc. functioning under the authority of the Pope: in full, **Curia Ro·ma·na** (rō mä'nə) —**cu'ri·al** *adj.*

cu·rie (kyoor'ē) *n.* [after Marie *Curie* (1867-1934), Pol. chemist & physicist in France, and her husband Pierre *Curie* (1859-1906)] a unit used in measuring radioactivity

cu·ri·o (kyoor'ē ō') *n.,* *pl.* **-os'** [contr. of CURIOSITY] any unusual or rare article

cu·ri·os·i·ty (kyoor'ē os'ə tē) *n.,* *pl.* **-ties** [< OFr. < L. *curiositas* < *curiosus:* see CURIOUS] **1.** a desire to learn or know **2.** a desire to learn about things that do not properly concern one **3.** anything curious, rare, or fascinating

cu·ri·ous (kyoor'ē əs) *adj.* [OFr. < L. *curiosus*, careful] **1.** eager to learn or know **2.** unnecessarily inquisitive; prying **3.** arousing attention or interest because unusual or strange —**cu'ri·ous·ly** *adv.* —**cu'ri·ous·ness** *n.*

cu·ri·um (kyoor'ē əm) *n.* [ModL., after Marie & Pierre *Curie:* see CURIE] a radioactive chemical element of the actinide series: symbol, Cm; at. wt., 247 (?); at. no., 96

curl (kurl) *vt.* [ME. *curlen < crul*, curly] **1.** to wind (esp. hair) into ringlets or coils **2.** to cause to bend round **3.** to raise the upper corner of (the lip), as in showing scorn —*vi.* **1.** to become curled **2.** to form, or move in, a spiral or curve **3.** to play the game of curling —*n.* **1.** a ringlet of hair **2.** anything with a curled shape; coil **3.** a curling or being curled —**curl up 1.** to gather into spirals or curls **2.** to sit or lie with the legs drawn up **3.** [Colloq.] to be embarrassed or disgusted **4.** [Colloq.] to give in; collapse —**in curl** curled

curl·er (-ər) *n.* a person or thing that curls, specif., a pin, clasp, etc. into or around which hair is rolled to make it curl

cur·lew (kur'lyōō) *n., pl.* **-lews, -lew:** see PLURAL, II, D, 1 [< OFr. *corlieu*, of echoic origin] a large, brownish wading bird with long legs

curl·i·cue (kur'li kyōō') *n.* [< CURLY + CUE²] a fancy curve, flourish, etc., as in a design

curl·ing (kur'liŋ) *n.* a game played on ice by sliding a heavy disc (**curling stone**) towards a target circle

curling iron (or **irons**) a metal rod heated for curling or waving hair rolled around it

curling tongs tongs which are heated and used to set the hair in curls

CURLEW

(length to 48 cm; wingspread to 84 cm)

curl·y (kur'lē) *adj.* **curl'i·er, curl'i·est 1.** curling or tending to curl **2.** having curls **3.** having a wavy grain, as certain woods —**curl'i·ness** *n.*

cur·mudg·eon (kər muj'ən) *n.* [< ?] a surly, ill-mannered person; cantankerous fellow

cur·rach, cur·ragh (kur'əkh, kur'ə) *n.* [Gael.] [Ir. & Scot.] SAME AS CORACLE

cur·rant (kur'ənt) *n.* [< Anglo-Fr. (*raisins de*) *Corauntz*, lit., (raisins of) Corinth] **1.** a small, seedless raisin from the Mediterranean region **2.** *a)* the red, white, or black berry of several species of hardy shrubs, used for jellies and jams *b)* a shrub bearing this fruit

cur·ren·cy (kur'ən sē) *n., pl.* **-cies** [< L. *currens:* see ff.] **1.** a continual passing from hand to hand; circulation **2.** the money in circulation in any country **3.** common acceptance or use; prevalence

cur·rent (kur'ənt) *adj.* [< OFr. < L. *currere,* to run] **1.** *a)* now in progress [his *current* job] *b)* contemporary [*current* fashions] *c)* of most recent date [the *current* edition] **2.** passing from person to þerson; circulating **3.** commonly used or accepted; prevalent —*n.* **1.** a flow of water or air in a definite direction **2.** a general tendency or drift; course **3.** *Elec.* the flow or rate of flow of electric charge in a conductor —**cur'rent·ly** *adv.*

current account a bank account that usually carries no interest and against which the holder may draw cheques at any time

cur·ri·cle (kur'i k'l) *n.* [L. *curriculum:* L.: see ff.] a two-wheeled carriage drawn by two horses abreast

cur·ric·u·lum (kə rik'yə ləm) *n., pl.* **-u·la** (-lə), **-u·lums** [L., a course, race < *currere,* to run] **1.** a course of study in a particular subject at a school, college, etc. **2.** all the courses, collectively, offered in a school, college, etc. —**cur·ric'u·lar** *adj.*

curriculum vi·tae (vē'tī) [L., course of life] a summary of one's personal, educational and professional history, usually prepared for job applications

cur·rish (kur'ish) *adj.* like a cur; mean; ill-bred —**cur'rish·ly** *adv.*

cur·ry¹ (kur'ē) *vt.* **-ried, -ry·ing** [< OFr. *correier,* to put in order] **1.** to rub down and clean the coat of (a horse, etc.) with a currycomb or brush **2.** to prepare (tanned leather) by soaking, cleaning, beating, etc. —**curry favour** to try to win favour by flattery, fawning, etc. —**cur'ri·er** *n.*

cur·ry² (kur'ē) *n., pl.* **-ries** [Tamil *kari,* sauce] **1.** *same as* CURRY POWDER **2.** a sauce made with curry powder **3.** a kind of stew prepared with curry —*vt.* **-ried, -ry·ing** to prepare with curry powder

cur·ry·comb (kur'ē kōm') *n.* a comb with teeth or ridges, to curry a horse —*vt.* to curry with this

curry powder a seasoning prepared from turmeric and various spices and herbs

curse (kurs) *n.* [Late OE. *curs, n., cursian, v.*] **1.** a calling on God or the gods to send evil or injury to some person or thing **2.** a profane or blasphemous oath, imprecation, etc. **3.** a thing cursed **4.** evil or injury that seems to come in answer to a curse **5.** any cause of evil or injury **6.** [Colloq.] menstruation (preceded by *the*) —*vt.* **cursed** or **curst, curs'ing 1.** to call evil or injury down on; damn **2.** to swear at **3.** to bring evil or injury on; afflict —*vi.* to swear; blaspheme —**be cursed with** to suffer from —**curs'er** *n.*

curs·ed (kur'sid, kurst) *adj.* **1.** under a curse **2.** deserving to be cursed; specif., *a)* evil; wicked *b)* hateful —**curs'ed·ly** *adv.* —**curs'ed·ness** *n.*

cur·sive (kur'siv) *adj.* [ML. *cursivus* < L. *cursus:* see

CURRYCOMB

COURSE] designating or of writing in which the letters are joined in each word —*n.* **1.** a cursive character **2.** *Printing* a typeface that looks like handwriting —**cur'sive·ly** *adv.* —**cur'sive·ness** *n.*

cur·sor (kur'sə) *n.* [L., runner] the sliding part of a measuring instrument, as on a slide rule

cur·so·ri·al (kər sôr'ē əl) *adj.* [< CURSORY + -AL] *Zool.* adapted for running

cur·so·ry (kur'sər ē) *adj.* [< L. < *cursor,* runner < *cursus:* see COURSE] hasty, and usually superficial —**cur'so·ri·ly** *adv.* —**cur'so·ri·ness** *n.*

curt (kurt) *adj.* [L. *curtus*] **1.** orig., short or shortened **2.** so brief as to be rude; terse; brusque [a *curt* reply] —**curt'ly** *adv.* —**curt'ness** *n.*

cur·tail (kər tāl') *vt.* [< OFr. *curtald,* shortened < L. *curtus,* short] to cut short; reduce; abridge —**cur·tail'er** *n.* —**cur·tail'ment** *n.*

cur·tain (kur't'n) *n.* [< OFr. < LL. *cortina,* circle of a theatre < L. *cohors,* a COURT] **1.** a piece of cloth, etc., often one that can be drawn up or sideways, hung, as at a window, to decorate, cover, or conceal **2.** anything that covers, conceals, or shuts off **3.** *Theatre a)* the screen at the front of the stage, which is drawn up or aside to reveal the stage *b)* the opening or the closing of the curtain for a play, act, or scene **4.** [*pl.*] [Slang] death; the end —*vt.* to provide or shut off as with a curtain —**draw** (or **drop**) **the curtain on 1.** to end **2.** to conceal —**lift** (or **raise**) **the curtain on 1.** to begin **2.** to reveal

curtain call 1. a call, usually by continued applause, for the performers to return to the stage **2.** such a return, acknowledging the applause

curtain lecture a wife's private reprimand to her husband: so called from the curtained beds in which such reproofs were conventionally given

curtain raiser 1. a short play or skit presented before a longer production **2.** any brief preliminary event

curtain wall an independently supported outer wall bearing only its own weight

curt·sy (kurt'sē) *n., pl.* **-sies** [var. of COURTESY] a gesture of greeting, respect, etc. made, esp. formerly, by girls and women and characterized by a bending of the knees and a slight lowering of the body —*vi.* **-sied, -sy·ing** to make a curtsy Also sp. **curt'sey**

cur·va·ceous (kər vā'shəs) *adj.* [CURV(E) + -ACEOUS] [Colloq.] having a full, shapely figure: said of a woman

cur·va·ture (kur'və chər) *n.* **1.** a curving or being curved **2.** a curve; curved part of anything

curve (kurv) *n.* [L. *curvus,* bent] **1.** a line having no straight part; bend with no angles **2.** a thing or part with the shape of a curve **3.** a curving, or the extent of this **4.** a curved line indicating variations, as in prices **5.** a line representing data, esp. statistical data, on a graph **6.** *Math.* a one-dimensional continuum of points in a space of two or more dimensions —*vt., vi.* **curved, curv'ing 1.** to form a curve by bending **2.** to move in a curve

cur·vet (kur'vit; *for v., usually* kər vet') *n.* [< It. dim. < *corvo* < L. *curvus,* bent] an upward leap by a horse, raising its hind legs just before its forelegs come down again —*vi.* **-vet'ted** or **-vet'ed, -vet'ting** or **-vet'ing 1.** to make a curvet **2.** to leap; frolic —*vt.* to cause to curvet

cur·vi·lin·e·ar (kur'və lin'ē ər) *adj.* consisting of or enclosed by a curved line or lines: also **cur'vi·lin'e·al**

curv·y (kur'vē) *adj.* **curv'i·er, curv'i·est 1.** having curves or a curve **2.** [Colloq.] curvaceous

cu·sec (kyōō'sek') *n.* [CU(BIC) + SEC(OND)²] a unit for measuring volume of flow, equal to 1 cubic foot per second

cush·at (koosh'ət) *n.* [ME.] *same as* WOOD PIGEON

cush·ion (koosh'ən) *n.* [< OFr. *coissin* < ML. *coxinum* (infl. by L. *coxa,* hip) < L. *culcita*] **1.** a pillow or pad for sitting or kneeling on, or reclining against **2.** a thing like this in shape or use **3.** anything serving to absorb shock, as air or steam in some machines, the elastic inner rim of a billiard table, or a soft, padded insole **4.** anything that relieves distress, provides comfort, etc. —*vt.* **1.** to provide with a cushion **2.** to seat or set on a cushion **3.** to absorb (shock or noise) **4.** to act as a cushion as in protecting from injury, relieving distress, etc. —**cush'ion·y** *adj.*

Cush·it·ic (kush it'ik) *adj.* [< Cush, ancient land in the Nile valley] designating or of a group of languages spoken in Ethiopia and E Africa —*n.* this group of languages

cush·y (koosh'ē) *adj.* **cush'i·er, cush'i·est** [orig. army slang < Hindi *khush,* pleasant < Per.] [Colloq.] easy; comfortable [a *cushy* job] —**cush'i·ly** *adv.* —**cush'i·ness** *n.*

cusp (kusp) *n.* [L. *cuspis,* a point] **1.** a pointed end; peak **2.** any of the elevations on the chewing surface of a tooth **3.** any triangular fold of a heart valve **4.** either horn of a crescent, as of the moon **5.** *Geom.* a corner point formed by two tangent branches of a curve

cus·pid (kus'pid) *n.* a canine tooth: see CANINE

cus·pi·date (kus'pə dāt') *adj.* **1.** having a cusp or cusps **2.** having a short, abrupt point, as some leaves Also **cus'pi·dat'ed**

cus·pi·dor (kus'pə dôr') *n.* [< Port. < *cuspir,* to spit < L.

< *com-*, intens. + *spuere,* to spit out] [U.S.] *same as* SPITTOON

cuss (kus) *n.* [< CURSE] [Colloq.] **1.** a curse **2.** a person or animal regarded as queer or annoying —*vt., vi.* [Colloq.] to curse —**cuss'er** *n.*

cuss·ed (kus'id) *adj.* [Colloq.] **1.** cursed **2.** perverse; stubborn —**cuss'ed·ly** *adv.* —**cuss'ed·ness** *n.*

cus·tard (kus'tərd) *n.* [< L. *crusta,* a crust] **1.** a mixture of eggs, milk, flavouring, and, often, sugar, either boiled or baked **2.** a sauce made of milk, sugar, and cornflour

cus·tard-ap·ple (-ap''l) *n.* **1.** any of several tropical trees with edible, heart-shaped fruits **2.** the fruit

cus·tard-pie (-pī) *adj.* denoting an unsubtle form of comedy that relies on horseplay; slapstick

cus·to·di·an (kəs·tō'dē ən) *n.* one who has the custody or care of something, esp. a public building; keeper —**cus·to'di·an·ship'** *n.*

cus·to·dy (kus'tə dē) *n., pl.* **-dies** [< L. < *custos,* a guard] a guarding or keeping safe; care —**in custody** in the keeping of the police; under arrest —**take into custody** to arrest —**cus·to'di·al** (-tō'dē əl) *adj.*

cus·tom (kus'təm) *n.* [< OFr. < L. *consuetudo* < *com-,* intens. + *suere,* to be accustomed] **1.** a usual practice or habitual way of behaving; habit **2.** *a)* a social convention carried on by tradition *b)* such practices, collectively **3.** [pl.] *a)* duties or taxes imposed by a government on imported goods *b)* [often **C-**] [*with sing. v.*] the department in charge of collecting these duties **4.** *a)* the regular patronage of a business establishment *b)* customers collectively **5.** *Law* such usage as by common consent and long-established practice has taken on the force of law —*adj.* [U.S.] made or done to order or as if to order

cus·tom·ar·y (kus'tə mər ē) *adj.* **1.** in keeping with custom, or usage; usual; habitual **2.** *Law* holding or held by custom —*n.* a collection of the laws established by custom for a manor, region, etc. —**cus'tom·ar·i·ly** *adv.* —**cus'tom·ar·i·ness** *n.*

cus·tom-built (kus'təm bilt') *adj.* built to order, according to the customer's specifications

cus·tom·er (kus'tə mər) *n.* [see CUSTOM] **1.** a person who buys, esp. one who patronizes an establishment regularly **2.** [Colloq.] any person with whom one has dealings [a rough *customer*]

cus·tom·house (kus'təm hous') *n.* a building or office where customs or duties are paid, and ships cleared for entering or leaving: also **cus'toms·house'**

cus·tom·ize (-īz') *vt., vi.* **-ized', -iz'ing** [CUSTOM + -IZE] to make or build according to individual specifications —**cus'tom·iz'er** *n.*

cus·tom-made (-mād') *adj.* made to order, according to the customer's specifications

cut (kut) *vt.* **cut, cut'ting** [ME. *cutten*] **1.** to make an opening in as with a sharp-edged instrument; pierce; gash **2.** to pierce sharply so as to hurt **3.** to hurt the feelings of **4.** to grow (a new tooth making its way through the gum) **5.** to divide into parts with a sharp-edged instrument; sever **6.** to carve (meat) **7.** to fell; hew **8.** to mow or reap **9.** to pass through or across; intersect **10.** to divide (a pack of cards) at random before dealing **11.** to stop photographing (a film scene) **12.** to reduce; lessen; curtail [to *cut* salaries] **13.** to make shorter by trimming (hair, branches, etc.) **14.** to dissolve the fat globules of [lye *cuts* grease] **15.** to make or do by or as by cutting; specif., *a)* to make (an opening, clearing, channel, etc.) *b)* to type or otherwise mark (a stencil) for mimeographing *c)* to cut cloth so as to form (a garment) *d)* to perform [to *cut* a caper] *e)* to hit, drive, or throw (a ball) so that it spins or is deflected *f)* to cause (a wheel) to turn sharply *g)* to edit (film) as by deleting scenes *h)* to make a recording of (a speech, music, etc.) on (a gramophone record) **16.** [Colloq.] to pretend not to see or know (a person) **17.** [Colloq.] to stay away from without being excused **18.** [Slang] to stop; discontinue —*vi.* **1.** to do the work of a sharp-edged instrument; pierce, sever, gash, etc. **2.** to work as a cutter **3.** to take cutting [pine *cuts* easily] **4.** to use an instrument that cuts **5.** to cause pain by sharp, piercing strokes [the wind *cut* through his coat] **6.** to swing a bat, etc. (*at* a ball) **7.** to move swiftly **8.** to make a sudden shift to another scene, as in a film —*adj.* **1.** that has been cut **2.** made or formed by cutting **3.** reduced; lessened —*n.* **1.** a cutting or being cut **2.** a stroke or blow with a sharp-edged instrument, whip, etc. **3.** a stroke taken at a ball **4.** an opening, wound, etc. made by a sharp-edged instrument **5.** the omission of a part **6.** a piece or part cut off or out, as from a meat animal **7.** *a)* the amount cut *b)* a reduction; decrease **8.** the shortest way across: usually **short cut 9.** a passage or channel cut out or worn away **10.** the style in which a thing is cut; fashion [a stylish *cut*] **11.** an act, remark, etc. that hurts one's feelings **12.** a block or plate engraved for printing, or the impression made from it **13.** [Colloq.] the act of snubbing or ignoring **14.** [Slang] a share, as of profits or loot —**a cut above** [Colloq.] somewhat better than —**cut across** to take a shorter course by going straight across —**cut a figure**

to attract attention or make a (certain) impression —**cut and dried 1.** arranged beforehand; not allowing any alteration **2.** lifeless; dull; boring —**cut back 1.** to make shorter by cutting off the end **2.** to reduce or discontinue (production, etc.) —**cut dead** [Colloq.] to snub completely —**cut down 1.** to make fall by cutting **2.** to kill **3.** to reduce; lessen —**cut in 1.** to draw in front of another vehicle leaving too little space, esp. when overtaking: said of a driver, motor car, etc. **2.** to interrupt **3.** to interrupt a couple dancing in order to dance with one of them **4.** to make a connection, as in an electrical circuit **5.** to give a share to —**cut it fine** [Colloq.] **1.** to make exact calculations or distinctions **2.** to leave only a minimum reserve of time, resources, etc. —**cut it out** [Colloq.] to stop what one is doing —**cut loose** [Colloq.] to act without restraint —**cut no ice** [Colloq.] to make no impression —**cut off 1.** to sever **2.** to stop abruptly **3.** to shut off **4.** to interrupt **5.** to intercept **6.** to disinherit —**cut one's losses** to abandon any further attempt to make good one's losses —**cut out 1.** to remove by cutting **2.** to remove; omit **3.** to eliminate and take the place of (a rival) **4.** to make or form as by cutting **5.** [Colloq.] *a)* to discontinue; stop *b)* cease to function —**cut out for** suited for —**cuts both ways** [Colloq.] results in both good and bad effects —**cut short** to stop abruptly before the end —**cut up 1.** to cut into pieces **2.** [Colloq.] *a)* to criticize harshly *b)* to cause to be dejected **3.** [U.S. Slang] to clown, joke, etc. to attract attention —**cut up rough** [Colloq.] to react with anger, resentment, etc.

cu·ta·ne·ous (kyoo tā'nē əs) *adj.* [< ML. < L. *cutis,* the skin] of, on, or affecting the skin

cut·a·way (kut'ə wā') *n.* a man's formal daytime coat with the front of the skirt cut so as to curve back to the tails: also **cutaway coat** —*adj.* designating or of a diagram or model having outer parts cut away so as to show the inside

cut·back (kut'bak') *n.* a cutting back; specif., a reduction, as of production, personnel, etc.

cute (kyoot) *adj.* **cut'er, cut'est** [< ACUTE] [Colloq.] **1.** clever; sharp; shrewd **2.** [U.S.] pretty, esp. in a dainty way **3.** [U.S.] straining for effect; artificial —**cute'ly** *adv.* —**cute'ness** *n.*

cut glass glass, esp. flint glass, shaped or ornamented by grinding and polishing —**cut'-glass'** *adj.*

cu·ti·cle (kyoot'i k'l) *n.* [L. *cuticula,* skin, dim. < *cutis,* skin] **1.** *same as* EPIDERMIS **2.** hardened skin accumulating at the base and sides of a fingernail or toenail **3.** *Bot.* a delicate, waxy layer over the outer surface of the epidermis of plants **4.** *Zool.* the tough, nonliving outer structure secreted by the epidermis in many invertebrates —**cu·tic·u·lar** (kyoo tik'-yoo lər) *adj.*

cu·tin·i·za·tion (kyoot'ən ə zā'shən) *n.* [< L. *cutis,* skin] a process in which the outermost plant cells become thickened and covered with a varnishlike material (**cutin**), making them waterproof —**cu'tin·ize'** (-īz') *vi., vt.* **-ized', -iz'ing**

cu·tis (kyoot'is) *n.* [L.] **1.** the vertebrate skin, including both its layers, the dermis and the epidermis **2.** the dermis only

cut·lass (kut'ləs) *n.* [< Fr. < It. < L. < *culter,* a knife] a short, thick, curved sword with a single cutting edge, formerly used esp. by sailors

cut·ler (kut'lər) *n.* [< Anglo-Fr. < OFr. < ML. < L. < *culter,* a knife] a person who makes, sells, or repairs knives and other cutting tools

cut·ler·y (kut'lər ē) *n.* **1.** the work or business of a cutler **2.** cutting instruments, such as knives and scissors; often, specif., such implements used in preparing food **3.** any implements used for eating, as knives, forks, spoons, etc.

cut·let (kut'lit) *n.* [< Fr. *côtelette* < OFr. dim. of *coste,* a rib < L. *costa*] **1.** a small slice of meat from the ribs or leg, often breaded and fried, etc. **2.** a small, flat croquette of chopped meat or fish

cut·off (kut'of') *n.* **1.** the act of cutting off; esp., the limit set for a process, activity, etc. **2.** the act of stopping steam, etc. from entering the cylinder of an engine **3.** any device for cutting off the flow of a fluid, a connection, etc. **4.** [U.S.] a road or passage that is a short cut

cutoff point the point at which something is halted; limit [the *cutoff point* for financial aid]

cut·out (-out') *n.* **1.** a device for breaking or closing an electric circuit **2.** a device for letting the exhaust gases of an internal-combustion engine pass directly into the air instead of through a silencer **3.** a design cut out or to be cut out, as from cardboard

cut-price (-prīs) *adj.* **1.** available at a lower price than the standard or recommended rate **2.** offering cut-price goods or services Also **cut-rate**

cut·purse (-purs') *n.* **1.** orig., a thief who cut purses from belts **2.** a pickpocket

cut·ter (kut'ər) *n.* **1.** a device for cutting **2.** a person whose work is cutting, as the sections of a garment **3.** a small, swift vessel; specif., *a)* a boat carried by large ships as a communications tender: also **ship's cutter** *b)* an armed sailing vessel, formerly used to pursue smugglers, etc.: also **revenue cutter** c) a single-masted sailing boat with a mainsail and two foresails **4.** [U.S.] a small, light sleigh, usually drawn by one horse

cut·throat (kut′thrōt′) *n.* **1.** a murderer **2.** a razor with a long, unguarded blade that usually folds into the handle —*adj.* **1.** murderous **2.** merciless; ruthless **3.** three-handed: said of certain card games

cut·ting (kut′iŋ) *n.* **1.** the act of one that cuts **2.** a piece cut off **3,** a newspaper clipping: also **press cutting 4.** a shoot cut away from a plant for rooting or grafting **5.** an excavation for a railway line, road, etc. through high ground —*adj.* **1.** that cuts; sharp **2.** chilling or piercing **3.** sarcastic; harsh —**cut′ting·ly** *adv.*

cut·tle·bone (kut′′l bōn′) *n.* the internal shell of cuttlefish, used as food for caged birds and, when powdered, as a polishing agent

cut·tle·fish (-fish′) *n.,* *pl.* **-fish′**, **-fish′es:** see FISH [OE. *cudele*] a squidlike sea mollusc with ten sucker-bearing arms and a hard internal shell: when in danger, some cuttlefish eject an inky fluid: also **cuttle**

cut·wa·ter (-wôt′ər) *n.* the fore part of a ship's prow

cut·worm (-wurm′) *n.* any of a number of caterpillars that feed on young plants of cabbage, maize, etc., cutting them off at ground level

Cwlth. Commonwealth

cwm (kōōm) *n.* [W.] **1.** [Welsh] a valley **2.** *Geol.* a hollow on a mountainside worn by glacial action; cirque

C.W.O., c.w.o. cash with order

cwt. hundredweight (senses 1 and 2)

-cy (sē, si) [< OFr. *-cie*, L. *-cia*, Gr. *-kia*] a suffix meaning: **1.** quality, condition, state, or fact of being [*hesitancy*] **2.** position, rank, or office of [*curacy*]

cy·an (sī′ən) *n.,* *adj.* [< Gr. *kyanos*] greenish-blue

cy·a·nate (sī′ə nāt′) *n.* a salt of cyanic acid

cy·an·ic (sī an′ik) *adj.* **1.** of or containing cyanogen **2.** blue

cyanic acid a colourless, poisonous acid, HOCN

cy·a·nide (sī′ə nīd′) *n.* a compound containing the cyanogen radical, —CN; esp., potassium cyanide, KCN, or sodium cyanide, NaCN, highly poisonous compounds with many industrial uses

cy·an·o·gen (sī an′ə jən) *n.* [< Gr. *kyanos*, blue + -GEN] **1.** a colourless, poisonous, flammable gas, C_2N_2 **2.** the univalent radical —CN, in cyanides

cy·a·no·sis (sī′ə nō′sis) *n.* [ModL. < Gr. < *kyanos*, blue] a bluish colouration of the skin caused by lack of oxygen in the blood —**cy′a·not′ic** (-not′ik) *adj.*

cy·ber·na·tion (sī′bər nā′shən) *n.* [CYBERN(ETICS) + -ATION] the use of computers in connection with automation —**cy′ber·nate′** *vt.* **-nat′ed, -nat′ing**

cy·ber·net·ics (sī′bər net′iks) *n.pl.* [*with sing. v.*] [< Gr. *kybernētēs*, helmsman + -ICS] a science dealing with the comparative study of the operations of complex electronic computers and the human nervous system —**cy′ber·net′ic** *adj.*

cy·cad (sī′kad) *n.* [ModL. *Cycas* < Gr. *kykas*, erroneous pl. of *koïx*, a palm] any of an order of tropical shrubs and trees resembling thick-stemmed palms, with crowns of leathery, fernlike leaves

cy·cla·mate (sī′klə māt′, sik′lə-) *n.* a complex organic compound with an extremely sweet taste

cyc·la·men (si′klə mən) *pl.* **-mens** [< L. < Gr. *kyklaminos*] a plant of the primrose family, having heart-shaped leaves and white, pink, or red flowers with reflexed petals

cy·cle (sī′k′l) *n.* [< LL. *cyclus* < Gr. *kyklos*, a circle] **1.** a) a period of time within which a round of regularly recurring events is completed b) a complete set or series of such events **2.** a very long period of time; an age **3.** all the traditional poems, songs, etc. connected with a hero or an event **4.** a series of poems or songs on the same theme **5.** a bicycle, tricycle, etc. **6.** *Elec.* one complete period of the reversal of an alternating current —*vi.* **-cled, -cling 1.** to occur in cycles; pass through a cycle **2.** to ride a bicycle, tricycle, etc.

cy·clic (sī′klik, sik′lik) *adj.* **1.** of, or having the nature of, a cycle; moving or occurring in cycles **2.** *Chem.* arranged in a ring or closed-chain structure: said of atoms Also **cy′cli·cal** —**cy′cli·cal·ly** *adv.*

cy·clist (sī′klist) *n.* a person who rides a bicycle

cy·cli·zine (sī′klə zēn′) *n.* an antihistamine, used to treat nausea and travel sickness

cy·clo- [< Gr. *kyklos*, a circle] a combining form meaning of a circle or wheel, circular: also, before a vowel, **cycl-**

cy·cloid (sī′kloid) *adj.* [< Gr. < *kyklos*, a circle + *eidos*, form] circular —*n.* *Geom.* a curve traced by a point in a circle when the circle revolves along a straight line

cy·clom·e·ter (sī klom′ə tər) *n.* [CYCLO- + -METER] an instrument that records the revolutions of a wheel, for measuring distance travelled

cy·clone (sī′klōn) *n.* [< Gr. < *kykloein*, to whirl < *kyklos*, a circle] **1.** loosely, a violent, whirling windstorm; tornado or hurricane **2.** *Meteorol.* a storm with strong winds

rotating about a moving centre of low atmospheric pressure —**cy·clon·ic** (sī klon′ik) *adj.* —**cy·clon′i·cal·ly** *adv.*

Cy·clo·pe·an (sī′klə pē′ən) *adj.* **1.** of the Cyclopes **2.** [c-] huge; gigantic; enormous

cy·clo·pe·di·a, cy·clo·pae·di·a (sī′klə pē′dē ə) *n.* same as ENCYCLOPEDIA —**cy′clo·pe′dic, cy′clo·pae′dic** *adj.* —**cy′clo·pe′dist, cy′clo·pae′dist** *n.*

Cy·clops (sī′klops) *n., pl.* **Cy·clo·pes** (sī klō′pēz) [L. < Gr. < *kyklos*, a circle + *ōps*, an eye] *Gr. Myth.* any of a race of giants who had only one eye, centred in the forehead

cy·clo·ra·ma (sī′klə räm′ə) *n.* [CYCLO- + Gr. *horama*, sight] **1.** a series of large pictures, as of a landscape, put on the wall of a circular room so as to suggest natural perspective to a viewer **2.** a large, curved curtain or screen used as a background for stage sets —**cy′clo·ram′ic** (-ram′-, -räm′-) *adj.*

cy·clo·stome (sī′klə stōm) *n.* [CYCLO- + -STOME] any of a class of eellike, parasitic fishes, including the lamprey, with a circular, sucking mouth

cy·clo·style (sī′klə stīl′) *n.* [CYCLO- + STYLE] an apparatus for making copies of written material, using a pen with a small, toothed wheel which cuts holes in a prepared stencil —*vt.* to duplicate (written material) in this way

cy·clo·tron (sī′klə tron′) *n.* [CYCLO- + (ELEC)TRON] an apparatus for giving high energy to particles, usually protons and deuterons, so as to produce transmutations or radioactivity in a target element

cy·der (sī′dər) *n.* same as CIDER

cyg·net (sig′nət) *n.* [< Fr. *cygne*, swan < VL. < Gr. *kyknos*, swan] a young swan

cyl. **1.** cylinder **2.** cylindrical

cyl·in·der (sil′an dər) *n.* [< Fr. < L. < Gr. < *kylindein*, to roll] **1.** *Geom.* a solid figure described by the edge of a rectangle rotated around the parallel edge as axis: the ends of a cylinder are parallel and equal circles **2.** anything, hollow or solid, with the shape of a cylinder; specif., a) the turning part of a revolver, containing chambers for cartridges b) the chamber in which the piston moves in a reciprocating engine c) the barrel of a pump

cy·lin·dri·cal (sə lin′dri k′l) *adj.* **1.** having the shape of a cylinder **2.** of a cylinder Also **cy·lin′dric** —**cy·lin′dri·cal′-i·ty** (-kal′ə tē) *n.* —**cy·lin′dri·cal·ly** *adv.*

Cym. Cymric

cym·bal (sim′b′l) *n.* [< OFr. & OE. < L. < Gr. < *kymbē*, hollow of a vessel] a circular, slightly concave brass plate used as a percussion instrument: it is struck with a drumstick, brush, etc. or used in pairs which are struck together to produce a crashing, ringing sound —**cym′bal·ist** *n.*

cym·bid·i·um (sim bid′ē əm) *n., pl.* **-i·ums, -i·a** (-ə) [ModL. < L. *cymba*, a boat (< Gr. *kymbē*) + ModL. *-idium*, dim. suffix] any of various tropical Asiatic orchids with sprays of white, pink, yellow, or maroon flowers

CYMBALS

cyme (sīm) *n.* [< L. < Gr. *kyma*, swelling] a flat-topped flower cluster in which the central flower blooms first, followed by the outer ones —**cy·mose** (sī′mōs, sī mōs′) *adj.*

Cym·ric (kim′rik; *occas.* sim′-) *adj.* [< W. < *Cymru,* Wales] **1.** of the Celtic people of Wales **2.** of their language —*n.* Brythonic: see CELTIC

Cym·ry (-rē) *n.pl.* the Cymric Celts; the Welsh

cyn·ic (sin′ik) *n.* [see ff.] **1.** [C-] a member of a school of ancient Greek philosophers who held virtue to be the only good, and stressed independence from worldly needs and pleasures: they became critical of materialistic social values **2.** a cynical person *adj.* **1.** [C-] of or like the Cynics or their doctrines **2.** same as CYNICAL

cyn·i·cal (sin′i k′l) *adj.* [< L. < Gr. *kynikos,* canine < *kyōn,* dog] **1.** denying the sincerity of people's motives and actions, or the value of living **2.** sarcastic, sneering, etc. **3.** [C-] same as CYNIC —**cyn′i·cal·ly** *adv.* —**cyn′i·cal·ness** *n.*

cyn·i·cism (sin′ə siz′m) *n.* **1.** [C-] the philosophy of the Cynics **2.** the attitude or beliefs of a cynical person **3.** a cynical remark, idea, or action

cy·no·sure (sī′nə shoor′, sin′ə-) [L. < Gr. *kynosoura,* dog's tail] [C-] an old name for: **1.** URSA MINOR **2.** NORTH STAR —*n.* any person or thing that is a centre of attention or interest

cy·pher (sī′fər) *n., vt., vi.* same as CIPHER

cy·press (sī′prəs) *n.* [< OFr. < L. *cupressus* < Gr. *kyparissos*] **1.** any of a group of dark-foliaged, cone-bearing evergreens, native to Europe, Asia, and N. America **2.** any of a number of related trees **3.** the wood of any of these **4.** cypress branches used as a symbol of mourning

cyp·ri·noid (sip′rə noid′) *adj.* [< Gr. *kyprinos,* carp + -OID] of or like the fishes of the carp family —*n.* any of a family of freshwater fishes, including the carps, minnows, dace, etc. Also **cyp′ri·nid** (-nid)

Cyp·ri·ot (sip′rē ət) *adj.* of or designating Cyprus —*n.* a native or inhabitant of Cyprus Also **Cyp′ri·ote** (-ōt)

cyp·ri·pe·di·um (sip′rə pē′de əm) *n., pl.* **-di·ums, -di·a** (-ə) [ModL. < Gr. *Kypris,* Venus + *podion,* slipper] *same as* LADY-SLIPPER

Cy·re·na·ic (sir′ə nā′ik, sī′rə-) *adj.* of the Greek school of philosophy founded by Aristippus of Cyrene, who considered individual sensual pleasure the greatest good —*n.* a follower of this school

Cy·ril·lic (sə ril′ik) *adj.* designating or of the Slavic alphabet attributed to Saint Cyril, 9th-cent. apostle to the Slavs: it is used in Russia, Bulgaria, and other Slavic countries

cyst (sist) *n.* [ModL. *cystis* < Gr. *kystis,* sac] 1. any of certain saclike structures in plants or animals; specif., such a structure when abnormal and filled with fluid or diseased matter 2. a protective membrane surrounding certain organisms in a resting stage —**cyst′ic** *adj.* —**cyst′oid** *adj., n.*

-cyst (sist) [see prec.] *a suffix meaning* sac, pouch, bladder [*encyst*]

cys·ti·cer·cus (sis′tə sur′kəs) *n., pl.* **-cer′ci** (-sī) [ModL. < *cysti-* (see CYSTO-) + Gr. *kerkos,* tail] the larva of certain tapeworms having the head and neck partly enclosed in a cyst

cystic fibrosis a congenital disease of children, characterized by fibrosis and malfunctioning of the pancreas, and frequent respiratory infections

cys·ti·tis (sis tīt′is) *n.* [CYST- + -ITIS] an inflammation of the urinary bladder

cys·to- [see CYST] *a combining form meaning* of or like a bladder or sac: also **cyst-, cysti-**

cys·to·scope (sis′tə skōp′) *n.* [CYSTO- + -SCOPE] an instrument for visually examining the interior of the urinary bladder —*vt.* **-scoped′, -scop′ing** to examine with a cystoscope —**cys′to·scop′ic** (-skop′ik) *adj.* **-cys·tos′co·py** (-tos′kə pē) *n.*

-cyte (sīt) [< Gr. *kytos,* a hollow] *a combining form meaning* a cell [*lymphocyte*]

cy·to- [see -CYTE] *a combining form meaning* of a cell or cells: also, before a vowel, **cyt-**

cy·to·ge·net·ics (sīt′ō jə net′iks) *n.pl.* [with *sing. v.*] the science correlating cytology and genetics with regard to heredity and variation —**cy′to·ge·net′ic, cy′to·ge·net′i·cal** *adj.* —**cy′to·ge·net′i·cal·ly** *adv.* —**cy′to·ge·net′i·cist** *n.*

cy·tol·o·gy (sī tol′ə jē) *n.* [CYTO- + -LOGY] the branch of biology dealing with the structure, function, pathology, and life history of cells —**cy·to·log·ic** (sī′tə loj′ik), **cy′to·log′i·cal** *adj.* —**cy′to·log′i·cal·ly** *adv.* —**cy·tol′o·gist** *n.*

cy·to·plasm (sīt′ə plaz′m) *n.* [CYTO- + -PLASM] the protoplasm of a cell, exclusive of the nucleus: also **cy′to·plast′** —**cy′to·plas′mic** *adj.*

cy·to·sine (sīt′ə sēn′) *n.* [G. *zytosin*] a nitrogenous base, $C_4H_5N_3O$, a constituent of various nucleic acids

czar (zär) *n.* [< Russ. < OSlav. via Goth. < L. *Caesar*] 1. an emperor: title of any of the former emperors of Russia 2. an absolute ruler; despot —**czar′dom** *n.* —**czar′ism** *n.* —**czar′ist** *adj., n.*

czar·das (chär′dəsh, -däsh) *n.* [Hung. *csárdás*] 1. a Hungarian dance with fast and slow sections 2. music for this dance

czar·e·vitch (zär′ə vich′) *n.* [< Russ.] the eldest son of a czar of Russia

cza·ri·na (zä rē′nə) *n.* [< G. < Russ. *tsaritsa*] the wife of a czar; empress of Russia: also **cza·rit′za** (-rit′sə)

Czech (chek) *n.* 1. a Bohemian, Moravian, or Silesian Slav of Czechoslovakia 2. the West Slavic language of the Czechs —*adj.* of Czechoslovakia, its people, or their language: also **Czech′ish**

Czech·o·slo·vak (chek′ə slō′vak) *adj.* of Czechoslovakia or its people —*n.* a Czech or Slovak living in Czechoslovakia Also **Czech′o·slo·vak′i·an** (-slō va′kē ən)

D

D, d (dē) *n., pl.* **D's, d's** 1. the fourth letter of the English alphabet 2. the sound of D or d 3. *a symbol for* the fourth in a sequence or group

D (dē) *n.* 1. a Roman numeral for 500 2. *Music a)* the second tone in the ascending scale of C major *b)* the scale having this tone as the keynote

D *Chem.* deuterium

D. 1. [Chiefly U.S.] Democrat(ic) 2. Dutch 3. *Music* Deutsch (in numbering Schubert's works)

d. 1. daughter 2. day(s) 3. dead 4. delete 5. diameter 6. died 7. dose 8. [L. *pl. denarii*] penny; pence (in former Brit. currency)

'd 1. *contracted auxiliary form of* had or would [*I'd, they'd*] 2. *contraction of* -ed [*foster'd*]

da deca-

dab¹ (dab) *vt., vi.* **dabbed, dab′bing** [ME. *dabben,* to strike] 1. to touch lightly and quickly 2. to pat with something soft or moist 3. to put on (paint, etc.) with light, quick strokes —*n.* 1. a light, quick stroke; tap; pat 2. a bit, esp. of a soft or moist thing [a *dab* of rouge] 3. [*pl.*] [Slang] fingerprints —**dab′ber** *n.*

dab² (dab) *n.* [ME. *dabbe* < ?] 1. any of several flounders of coastal waters 2. any small flatfish

dab³ (dab) *n.* [< ?] [Colloq.] an expert

dab·ble (dab′'l) *vt.* **-bled, -bling** [Du. *dabbelen,* freq. of *dabben,* to strike, DAB¹] 1. to dip lightly in and out of a liquid 2. to spatter or splash —*vi.* 1. to play in water, as with the hands 2. to do something superficially (with *in* or *at*) [to *dabble* in art] —**dab′bler** *n.*

dab·chick (dab′chik′) *n.* [< OE. *dop,* to dive + CHICK] either of two small grebes of Europe and the Americas

dab hand someone who is skilled at some activity; expert

‡**da ca·po** (dä kä′pō) [It.] *Music* from the beginning: a direction to repeat

dace (dās) *n., pl.* **dace, dac′es:** see PLURAL, II, D, 2 [< OFr. *dars,* dart] a small freshwater fish of the carp family

‡**da·cha** (dä′chə) *n.* [Russ.] a country house or cottage used as a summer home

dachs·hund (daks′hoond) *n.* [G. *Dachs,* a badger + *Hund,* a dog] a small dog of German breed, with a long body and short legs

DACHSHUND
(20-25 cm high at shoulder)

Da·cron (dak′ron) [arbitrary coinage, after (NYL)ON] a trademark for a synthetic polyester fibre or a washable, wrinkle-resistant fabric made from it —*n.* [*also* d-] this fibre or fabric

dac·tyl (dak′təl) *n.* [< L. < Gr. *daktylos,* a finger or (by analogy with a finger's three joints) a dactyl] a metrical foot of three syllables, the first accented and the others unaccented, as in English verse (Ex.: "táke hĕr ŭp/ténderlỳ") **dac·tyl·ic** (dak til′ik) *adj.* of or made up of dactyls —*n.* a dactylic verse

dad (dad) *n.* [< child's cry *dada*] [Colloq.] father: also **dad·dy** (dad′ē), *pl.* **-dies**

da·da (dä′dä, -də) *n.* [Fr., lit., hobbyhorse < baby talk] [*also* D-] a nihilistic movement (1916-22) in art and literature characterized by fantastic, abstract, or incongruous creations: also **da′da·ism** —**da′da·ist** *adj., n.* —**da′da·is′tic** *adj.*

dad·dy-long-legs (dad′ē loŋ′legz′) *n., pl.* **-long′-legs′** *same as:* 1. CRANE FLY 2. HARVESTMAN (sense 2)

da·do (dā′dō) *n., pl.* **-does** [< It. < L. *datum,* a die] 1. the part of a pedestal between the cap and the base 2. the lower part of the wall of a room if decorated differently from the upper part —*vt.* **-doed, -do·ing** to furnish with a dado

dae·dal (dē′d'l) *adj.* [< L. *daedalus* < Gr. *daidalein,* to work skilfully] [Chiefly Poet.] 1. skilfully made 2. intricate; complex

dae·mon (dē′mən) *n.* [L. < Gr. *daimōn*] **1.** *Gr. Myth.* any of the secondary divinities ranking below the gods **2.** a guardian spirit **3.** *same as* DEMON —**dae·mon·ic** (di mon′ik) *adj.*

daff (daf) *n.* [Colloq.] a daffodil

daf·fa·down·dil·ly, daf·fy·down·dil·ly (daf′ə dɔun dil′ē) *n.*, *pl.* **-lies** [Dial.] a daffodil: also **daf′fo·dil′ly, daf′fa·dil′ly,** *pl.* **-lies**

daf·fo·dil (daf′ə dil′) *n.* [< ML. < L. < Gr. *asphodelos*] **1.** any of several hardy kinds of narcissus, typically having a single, yellow flower and a large, trumpetlike central crown **2.** the flower, one of the Welsh national emblems

daf·fy (daf′ē) *adj.* **-fi·er, -fi·est** [see ff.] [Colloq.] crazy; silly; frolicsome —**daf′fi·ness** *n.*

daft (däft) *adj.* [< OE. (ge)*dæfte*, mild, gentle] **1.** silly; foolish **2.** insane; crazy —**daft′ly** *adv.* —**daft′ness** *n.*

dag·ger (dag′ər) *n.* [< ME. *daggere* < ?] **1.** a weapon with a short, pointed blade, used for stabbing **2.** *Printing* a reference mark (†) —*vt.* **1.** to stab with a dagger **2.** to mark with a dagger —**look daggers at** to look at with anger —**at daggers drawn** in a state of open hostility

da·go (dā′gō) *n.* [< Sp. *Diego*, James] [Slang] a foreigner, esp. a Spaniard, Portuguese, or Italian: a derogatory term

da·guerre·o·type (də ger′ə tīp′) *n.* [after L. J. M. *Daguerre* (1789-1851), Fr. inventor] **1.** a photograph made by an early method on a plate of chemically treated metal or glass **2.** this method —*vt.* **-typed′, -typ′ing** to photograph by this method —**da·guerre′o·typ′y** *n.*

dahl·ia (dāl′yə, -ē ə) *n.* [after A. *Dahl*, 18th-c. Swed. botanist] **1.** a perennial plant of the composite family, with tuberous roots and large, showy flowers **2.** the flower

Dail Eir·eann (doil′er′ən) [Ir. *dáil*, assembly + *Eireann*, gen. of *Eire*, Ireland] the lower house of the legislature of the Republic of Ireland

dai·ly (dā′lē) *adj.* **1.** relating to, done, happening, or published every day or every weekday **2.** calculated by the day [*daily* rate] —*n.*, *pl.* **-lies 1.** a daily newspaper **2.** a charwoman —*adv.* every day; day after day

dai·mon (dī′mon) *n.* [< Gr.] *same as* DAEMON —**dai·mon′ic** (-mon′ik) *adj.*

dain·ty (dān′tē) *n.*, *pl.* **-ties** [< OFr. *deinté*, worth, delicacy < L. *dignitas*, worth, dignity] a choice food; delicacy —*adj.* **1.** delicious and choice **2.** delicately pretty or lovely **3.** *a)* of or showing delicate and refined taste *b)* excessively fastidious; squeamish —**dain′ti·ly** *adv.* —**dain′ti·ness** *n.*

dai·qui·ri (dak′ər ē, dīk′-) *n.* [after *Daiquirī*, village in Cuba] a cocktail made of rum, sugar, and lime or lemon juice

dair·y (der′ē) *n.*, *pl.* **dair′ies** [ME. *daierie* < *daie*, dairymaid < OE. *dæge*, breadmaker] **1.** a room, building, etc. where milk and cream are kept and butter, cheese, etc. are made **2.** *a)* a commercial establishment that processes and distributes milk and milk products *b)* a retail shop where these are sold —*adj.* of milk, cream, butter, cheese, etc.

dairy cattle cows raised mainly for their milk

dairy farm a farm that specializes in producing milk and milk products

dair·y·ing (-iŋ) *n.* the business of producing or selling dairy products

dair·y·maid (-mād′) *n.* a girl or woman who milks cows or works in a dairy

dair·y·man (-mən) *n.*, *pl.* **-men** a man who works in or for a dairy or who owns a dairy

dairy products milk, cream, cheese, butter, etc.

da·is (dā′is, dās) *n.*, *pl.* **da′is·es** [< OFr. < ML. *discus*, table < L. *discus*, DISCUS] a platform raised above the floor at one end of a hall or room, as for seats of honour, a speaker's stand, etc.

dai·sy (dā′zē) *n.*, *pl.* **-sies** [< OE. *dæges eage*, lit., day's eye] **1.** a plant of the composite family, bearing flowers with white rays around a yellow disc **2.** any similar member of the composite family **3.** the flower of any of these plants —**push up (the) daisies** [Slang] to be dead and buried

dai·sy-cut·ter (dā′zē kut′ər) *n.* *Sports* a ball that skims along close to the ground after being hit, kicked, etc.

Da·lai La·ma (da′lī lä′mə) [Mongol. *dalai*, ocean + *blama*: see LAMA] the traditional high priest of the Lamaist religion: see LAMAISM

da·la·si (da′lä sē) *n.*, *pl.* **-si** [native term, lit., complete] *see* MONETARY UNITS, table (Gambia)

dale (dāl) *n.* [OE. *dæl*] a valley

dales·man (dālz′mən) *n.*, *pl.* **-men** (-mən) a person living in a dale, specif. in northern England

dal·li·ance (dal′ē əns) *n.* the act of dallying; flirting, trifling, etc.

dal·ly (dal′ē) *vi.* **-lied, -ly·ing** [< OFr. *dalier*, to converse, trifle] **1.** to make love in a playful way **2.** to deal lightly or carelessly (*with*); trifle; toy **3.** to waste time; loiter —**dally away** to waste (time) in trifling activities

Dal·ma·tian (dal mā′shən) *adj.* of Dalmatia or its people

—*n.* **1.** a native of Dalmatia **2.** a large, short-haired dog with dark spots on a white coat

‡**dal se·gno** (dal se′nyô) [It.] *Music* from the sign: a direction to return and repeat from the sign (𝄋)

Dal·ton·ism (dôl′tən iz′m) *n.* [< Fr. *daltonisme*, after John *Dalton* (1766-1844), Brit. chemist] colour-blindness, esp. red-green blindness

dam¹ (dam) *n.* [ME. < Gmc. base seen in ON. *dammr*, to stop up] **1.** a barrier built to hold back flowing water **2.** the water thus kept back **3.** any barrier like a dam —*vt.* **dammed, dam′ming 1.** to build a dam in **2.** to keep back or confine as by a dam (usually with *up*)

dam² (dam) *n.* [ME., var. of *dame*, DAME] **1.** the female parent of any four-legged animal **2.** [Archaic] a mother

dam·age (dam′ij) *n.* [OFr. < L. *damnum*, loss, injury] **1.** injury or harm resulting in a loss in soundness, value, etc. **2.** [*pl.*] *Law* money claimed by, or ordered paid to, a person to compensate for injury, loss, etc. that is another's fault **3.** [Colloq.] cost or expense —*vt.* **-aged, -ag·ing** to do damage to —*vi.* to incur damage —**dam′age·a·ble** *adj.*

Dam·a·scene (dam′ə sēn′,   dam′ə sēn′) *adj.* [L. *Damascenus*, of Damascus] **1.** of Damascus, its people, etc. **2.** [d-] of damascening or damask —*n.* **1.** a native or inhabitant of Damascus **2.** [d-] damascened work —*vt.* **-scened′, -scen′ing** [d-] to decorate (steel, etc.) with wavy markings or with inlaid patterns of gold or silver

Da·mas·cus steel (də mas′kəs) a hard, flexible steel decorated with wavy lines, orig. made in Damascus and used for sword blades: also **damask steel**

dam·ask (dam′ask) *n.* [< It. < L. *Damascus* (the city)] **1.** a durable, lustrous, reversible fabric as of silk or linen, in figured weave, used for table linen, upholstery, etc. **2.** *a) same as* DAMASCUS STEEL *b)* the wavy markings of such steel **3.** deep pink or rose —*adj.* **1.** orig., of or from Damascus **2.** made of damask **3.** like damask **4.** deep-pink or rose —*vt.* **1.** to ornament with flowered designs or wavy lines **2.** to make deep-pink or rose

damask rose a very fragrant rose important as a source of attar of roses

dame (dām) *n.* [OFr. < L. *domina*, lady, fem. of *dominus*, a lord] **1.** orig., a title given to the mistress of a household **2.** a lady **3.** an elderly woman **4.** [D-] *a)* the legal title of the wife of a knight or baronet *b)* the title of a woman who has received an order of knighthood **5.** the role of a comic old woman in a pantomime, usually played by a man **6.** [Chiefly U.S. Slang] a woman or girl

dam·fool (dam′fd′) *n.* [Colloq.] a damned fool —*adj.* [Colloq.] of or like a damned fool

dam·mit (dam′it) *interj.* [Slang] damn it

damn (dam) *vt.* **damned, damn′ing** [< OFr. < L. *damnare*, to condemn < *damnum*, loss] **1.** *a)* to condemn to an unhappy fate; doom *b)* *Theol.* to condemn to endless punishment **2.** to condemn as bad, inferior, etc. **3.** to criticize adversely **4.** to cause the ruin of; make fail **5.** to swear at by saying "damn" —*vi.* to swear or curse; say "damn," etc. —*n.* the saying of "damn" as a curse —*adj.*, *adv.* [Colloq.] *clipped form of* DAMNED —*interj.* an expression of anger, annoyance, etc. —**damn all** [Slang] nothing whatever —**damn with faint praise** to condemn by praising mildly —**not give (or care) a damn** [Colloq.] not care at all —**not worth a damn** [Colloq.] worthless

dam·na·ble (dam′nə b'l) *adj.* deserving to be damned; outrageous; execrable —**dam′na·bly** *adv.*

dam·na·tion (dam nā′shən) *n.* a damning or being damned —*interj.* an expression of anger, annoyance, etc.

dam·na·to·ry (dam′nə tər ē) *adj.* **1.** threatening with damnation; damning **2.** condemning [*damnatory* evidence]

damned (damd) *adj.* **1.** condemned or deserving condemnation **2.** [Colloq.] deserving cursing, outrageous: now often a mere intensive [a *damned* shame] —*adv.* [Colloq.] very [a *damned* good job] —**do (or try) one's damnedest** [Colloq.] to do or try one's utmost —**the damned** *Theol.* souls doomed to eternal punishment

damn·ing (dam′iŋ) *adj.* proving or indicative of guilt [*damning* evidence]

dam·oi·selle, dam·o·sel, dam·o·zel (dam′ə zel′) *n.* [Archaic or Poet.] a damsel

damp (damp) *n.* [MDu., vapour] **1.** a slight wetness; moisture **2.** any harmful gas in a mine; firedamp, blackdamp, etc. —*adj.* somewhat moist or wet; humid —*vt.* **1.** to make damp; moisten **2.** to reduce or check (energy, action, etc., as fire in a furnace or the vibration of a piano string) —**damp′ish** *adj.* —**damp′ly** *adv.* —**damp′ness** *n.*

damp course a layer of impervious material in a brick wall that prevents damp from rising: also **dampproof course**

damp·en (dam′pən) *vt.* **1.** to make damp; moisten **2.** to deaden, depress, reduce, or lessen —*vi.* to become damp —**damp′en·er** *n.*

damp·er (-pər) *n.* [see DAMP] 1. anything that deadens or depresses 2. a movable plate or valve in the flue of a stove or furnace, for controlling the draught 3. a device to check vibration in the strings of a piano, etc. 4. a device for lessening the oscillation of a magnetic needle, a moving coil, etc.

dam·sel (dam'z'l) *n.* [< OFr. *dameisele* < L. *domina:* see DAME] [Archaic or Poet.] a girl; maiden

dam·son (dam'z'n) *n.* [< OFr. < L. *Damascenus,* (plum) of Damascus] 1. a variety of small, purple plum 2. the tree on which it grows —*adj.* of the colour of the damson plum

DAMPER

dan (dan) *n.* [Jap.] any of the grades to which experienced judo competitors are assigned

Dan. 1. Daniel 2. Danish

dance (däns) *vi.* **danced, danc'ing** [< OFr. *danser*] 1. to move the body and feet in rhythm, ordinarily to music 2. to move lightly, rapidly, or gaily about, as leaves in a wind 3. to bob up and down —*vt.* 1. to take part in or perform (a dance) 2. to cause to dance —*n.* 1. rhythmic movement of the body and feet, ordinarily to music 2. a particular kind of dance, as the waltz, tango, etc. 3. the art of dancing 4. one round of a dance 5. a party to which people come to dance 6. a piece of music for dancing 7. rapid, lively movement —**dance attendance on** to be always near so as to lavish attentions on —**dance to another tune** to alter one's actions or opinions as a result of changed conditions —**danc'er** *n.*

dance hall a public hall where dancing takes place, for entry to which an admission fee is usually charged

dancing girl a professional dancer, esp. one who is part of a group

D and C dilatation (of the cervix) and curettage (of the uterus)

dan·de·li·on (dan'də li'ən) *n.* [< OFr. *dent de lion* < L. *dens* (gen. *dentis*), tooth + *de,* of + *leo,* lion] a common weed with jagged leaves, often used as greens, and yellow flowers

dan·der (dan'dər) *n.* [< ?] tiny particles, as from feathers, skin, or hair, that may cause allergies —**get one's dander up** [Chiefly U.S. Colloq.] to become or make angry

dan·di·fy (dan'də fī') *vt.* **-fied', -fy'ing** to dress up like a dandy —**dan'di·fi·ca'tion** *n.*

dan·dle (dan'd'l) *vt.* **-dled, -dling** [< ? OIt. *dandolare,* to dally] 1. to dance (a child) up and down on the knee or in the arms 2. to fondle; pet

dan·druff (dan'drəf) *n.* [< ? earlier *dandro* (< ?) + dial. *hurf,* scab] little scales or flakes of dead skin formed on the scalp —**dan'druff·y** *adj.*

dan·dy (dan'dē) *n., pl.* **-dies** [< ? Scot. var. of *Andy* < *Andrew*] 1. a man excessively attentive to his clothes and appearance; fop 2. [U.S. Colloq.] something very good or first-rate —*adj.* **-di·er, -di·est** [U.S. Colloq.] very good; first-rate —**dan·di'a·cal** (dan dī'ə kəl) *adj.* —**dan'dy·ish** *adj.* —**dan'dy·ism** *n.*

Dane (dān) *n.* a native or inhabitant of Denmark

Dane·geld (-geld') *n.* [ME. < ON. *Dana,* Dane + *gjald,* payment] a tax levied in the 10th cent. to buy off the Danes or to subsidize a military force to prevent their landing

Dane·law, Dane·lagh (-lô') *n.* the law code enforced in NE England by Danish invaders in the 9th and 10th cent. A.D.; also, this part of England

dan·ger (dān'jər) *n.* [< OFr. < L. < *dominus,* a master] 1. liability to injury, damage, loss, or pain 2. a thing that may cause injury, pain, etc.

danger money extra money paid to compensate for the risks involved in certain dangerous jobs

dan·ger·ous (-əs) *adj.* full of danger; unsafe; perilous —**dan'ger·ous·ly** *adv.* —**dan'ger·ous·ness** *n.*

dan·gle (dan'g'l) *vi.* **-gled, -gling** [< Scand.] 1. to hang swinging loosely 2. to be a hanger-on; follow (*after*) —*vt.* to cause to dangle —**dan'gler** *n.*

Dan·ish (dā'nish) *adj.* of Denmark, the Danes, or their language —*n.* the language of the Danes

Danish blue a soft, blue-veined cheese originally made in Denmark

Danish pastry [*also* d- p-] a rich, yeast pastry filled with fruit, jam, etc. and usually topped with icing

dank (daŋk) *adj.* [ME., akin to ON.] disagreeably damp; moist and chilly —**dank'ly** *adv.* —**dank'ness** *n.*

dan·seuse (dän surz'; *Fr.* dä söz') *n., pl.* **-seus'es** (-surz'əz; *Fr.* -söz') [Fr.] a girl or woman dancer, esp. a ballet dancer

daph·ne (daf'nē) *n.* [L. < Gr. *daphnē,* the laurel tree] any of various small evergreen shrubs with fragrant flowers

dap·per (dap'ər) *adj.* [< ? MDu. *dapper,* nimble] 1. small and active 2. trim, neat, or smart in appearance —**dap'per·ly** *adv.* —**dap'per·ness** *n.*

dap·ple (dap''l) *adj.* [< ? ON. *depill,* a spot] marked or variegated with spots; mottled: also **dap'pled** —*n.* 1. a spotted condition 2. an animal whose skin is spotted —*vt., vi.* **-pled, -pling** to cover or become covered with spots

dap·ple-grey (-grā') *adj.* grey spotted with darker grey —*n.* a dapple-grey horse

dar·bies (där'bēz) *n.pl.* [< *Father Derby's bonds,* a rigid agreement between moneylender & client] [Slang] handcuffs

Dar·by and Joan (där'bē ən jōn') [< ? an 18th-cent. song] an old married couple devoted to each other

Darby and Joan Club a club esp. for elderly people

dare (der) *vi.* **dared** or archaic **durst** (durst), **dared, dar'ing;** 3rd pers. sing., pres. **dare** or **dares** [< OE. *dear,* 1st pers. sing. of *durran,* to dare] to have enough courage or audacity for some act; be fearless —*vt.* 1. to have courage for; venture upon 2. to oppose and defy [he *dared* the wrath of the tyrant] 3. to test the courage of (someone) with a dare —*n.* a challenge to do a hard, dangerous, or rash thing as a test —**dare say** to think likely or probable; suppose —**dar'er** *n.*

dare·dev·il (-dev''l) *adj.* bold and reckless —*n.* a bold, reckless person —**dare'dev'il·ry, dare'dev'il·try** *n.*

dar·ing (der'iŋ) *adj.* having or showing a bold willingness to take risks, etc.; fearless —*n.* bold courage —**dar'ing·ly** *adv.*

Dar·jee·ling (där jē'liŋ) *n.* a fine variety of tea from Darjeeling, a district in NE India

dark (därk) *adj.* [< OE. *deorc*] 1. entirely or partly without light 2. neither giving nor receiving light 3. *a)* almost black *b)* not light in colour; deep in shade 4. not fair in complexion; brunette 5. hidden; secret 6. not easily understood 7. gloomy; dismal 8. angry or sullen 9. evil; sinister 10. ignorant; unenlightened —*n.* 1. the state of being dark 2. night; nightfall 3. a dark colour or shade —**in the dark** uninformed; ignorant —**keep dark** to keep secret or hidden —**dark'ish** *adj.* —**dark'ly** *adv.* —**dark'ness** *n.*

Dark Ages, dark ages 1. the Middle Ages; esp., the early part from 476 A.D. to the late 10th cent.: so called because of the idea that there was cultural decline in Europe at this time 2. any period like this

Dark Continent Africa: because it was little known until the late 19th cent.

dark·en (där'kən) *vt., vi.* to make or become dark or darker —**not darken one's door** (or **doorway**) not come to one's home —**dark'en·er** *n.*

dark horse [Colloq.] 1. an unexpected, almost unknown winner, as in a horse race 2. a person who reveals unexpected talents

dark lantern a lantern with a shutter that can hide the light

dark·ling (därk'liŋ) *adv.* [DARK + -LING²] [Poet.] in the dark —*adj.* [Poet.] dark, dim, obscure, etc.

dark·room (därk'rōōm') *n.* a room from which all actinic rays are excluded, so that photographs can be developed in it

dark·some (-səm) *adj.* [Poet.] 1. dark; darkish 2. dismal; gloomy

dar·ling (där'liŋ) *n.* [OE. *deorling,* dim. of *deore,* DEAR] 1. a person much loved by another 2. a favourite or a lovable person —*adj.* very dear; beloved

darn¹ (därn) *vt., vi.* [< ? MFr. dial. *darner,* to mend] to mend (cloth, etc.) or repair (a hole in cloth) by sewing a network of stitches across the gap —*n.* a darned place in fabric —**darn'er** *n.*

darn² (därn) *vt., vi., n., adj., adv., interj.* [Colloq.] a euphemism for DAMN (the curse) —**darned** *adj., adv.*

dar·nel (där'n'l) *n.* [< Fr. dial. *darnelle*] a weedy rye grass often found in cornfields: a certain fungus can make the seeds poisonous

darn·ing (där'niŋ) *n.* 1. a mending with interlaced stitches 2. things to be darned

darning needle a large needle for darning

dart (därt) *n.* [< OFr.] 1. a small, pointed missile for throwing or shooting 2. anything resembling this 3. a sudden, quick movement 4. a short, tapered, stitched fold to make a garment fit more closely 5. [*pl., with sing.* v.] a game in which a number of darts (sense 1) are thrown at a target —*vt., vi.* 1. to throw, shoot, send out, etc. suddenly and fast 2. to move suddenly and fast

dart·board (-bôrd') *n.* a circular piece of wood, cork, etc. used as a target in the game of darts

dart·er (-ər) *n.* 1. a thing or animal that darts 2. a tropical diving bird with a long, pointed bill and a long neck 3. any of various small, brightly coloured freshwater fishes of N America

Dart·ford warbler (därt'fərd) a small, dark brown, moorland warbler with a dark grey head and yellow legs

dar·tle (där''l) *vt., vi.* **-tled, -tling** to dart about

Dart·moor pony (därt'moor) a breed of small, strong ponies, originally from Dartmoor

Dar·win·i·an theory (där win'ē ən) Darwin's theory of evolution, which holds that all species of plants and animals developed from earlier forms by hereditary transmission of slight variations in successive generations, those forms surviving which are best adapted to the environment (*natural selection*): also called **Dar'win·ism —Dar'win·ist** *adj., n.* **—Dar'win·is'tic** *adj.*

dash (dash) *vt.* [< Scand., as in Sw. *daska*, to slap] **1.** to throw so as to break; smash **2.** to strike violently (*against*) **3.** to throw, thrust, etc. (with *away, down,* etc.) **4.** to splash (liquid) on (someone or something) **5.** to mix with a little of another substance **6.** to destroy; frustrate [to *dash* one's hopes] **7.** to depress; discourage **8.** to put to shame; abash **9.** [Colloq.] a *euphemism for* DAMN —*vi.* **1.** to strike violently (*against* or *on*) **2.** to move swiftly; rush —*n.* **1.** the sound of splashing **2.** a bit of something added **3.** a sudden rush **4.** vigour; verve **5.** showy appearance **6.** the mark (—), used in printing and writing to indicate a break in a sentence, a parenthetical element, an omission, etc. **7.** *Telegraphy* a long sound or signal, as in Morse code: cf. DOT[1] **—dash off 1.** to do, write, etc. hastily **2.** to rush away **—dash'er** *n.*

dash·board (-bôrd') *n.* **1.** a screen at the front or side of a carriage, boat, etc., for protection against splashing **2.** a panel with instruments and gauges on it, as in a motor car; facia

dash·ing (-iŋ) *adj.* **1.** full of dash or spirit; lively **2.** showy; stylish **—dash'ing·ly** *adv.*

dash light a light to illuminate a dashboard (sense 2)

das·tard (däs'tard) *n.* [ME., prob. < Scand. base] a mean, cowardly evildoer

das·tard·ly (-lē) *adj.* [see prec.] mean, base, cowardly, etc. **—das'tard·li·ness** *n.*

das·y·ure (das'ē yoor') *n.* [< Gr. *dasys*, hairy + *oura*, tail] a small tree-dwelling marsupial of Australia

dat. dative

da·ta (dāt'ə, dät'ə) *n.pl.* [*often with sing. v.*] [L., things given < pp. of *dare*, to give] things known or assumed; facts or figures from which conclusions can be inferred; information: the sing. form is **datum**

data bank information stored in a form that can be directly retrieved by a computer

data processing the recording and handling of information by means of mechanical or electronic equipment

date[1] (dāt) *n.* [< OFr. < L. *data*, as in *data Romae*, etc., lit., given at Rome, etc., formula used in letters for place and date] **1.** a statement on a writing, coin, etc. of when it was made **2.** the time at which a thing happens or is done **3.** the time that anything lasts **4.** the day of the month **5.** *a)* an appointment for a set time; specif., a social engagement with a person of the opposite sex *b)* the person with whom one has such an engagement —*vt.* **dat'ed, dat'ing 1.** to mark (a letter, etc.) with a date **2.** to find out or give the date of **3.** to assign a date to **4.** *a)* to show or reveal as typical of a certain period or age *b)* to make seem old-fashioned or out of date **5.** to refer to as a starting point **6.** to have a social engagement with —*vi.* to belong to, or have origin in, a definite period in the past (usually with *from* or *back to*) **—out of date** no longer in use; old-fashioned **—to date** until now; as yet **—up to date** in or into agreement with the latest facts, ideas, styles, etc. **—dat'a·ble, date'a·ble** *adj.* **—dat'er** *n.*

date[2] (dāt) *n.* [< OFr. < L. < Gr. *daktylos*, a date, lit., a finger] **1.** the sweet, fleshy fruit of a cultivated palm (**date palm**) **2.** the tree itself

date·less (-lis) *adj.* **1.** without a date **2.** without limit or end **3.** too old for its date to be fixed **4.** still good or interesting though old **—date'less·ness** *n.*

date·line (-līn') *n.* **1.** the date and place of writing or issue, as given in a line in a newspaper, a dispatch, etc. **2.** *same as* DATE LINE —*vt.* **-lined', -lin'ing** to furnish with a dateline

date line an imaginary line drawn north and south through the Pacific Ocean, largely along the 180th meridian: at this line, by international agreement, each calendar day begins at midnight, so that when it is Sunday just west of the line, it is Saturday just east of it

date stamp 1. a rubber stamp with figures that can be adjusted to show the date **2.** the mark made by this

da·tive (dāt'iv) *adj.* [L. *dativus*, of giving < *datus*, pp. of *dare*, to give] designating, of, or in that case of a noun, pronoun, or adjective which expresses the indirect object of a verb and, in many languages, approach towards something —*n.* **1.** the dative case: in English, the dative is expressed by *to* or by word order (Ex.: I gave the book *to* him, I gave *him* the book) **2.** a word or phrase in the dative case **—da·ti·val** (dā tī'v'l) *adj.* **—da'tive·ly** *adv.*

da·tum (dāt'əm, dät'-) *n.* *sing.* of DATA

dau. daughter

daub (dôb) *vt., vi.* [< OFr. < L. *dealbare*, to whitewash < *de-*, intens. + *albus*, white] **1.** to cover or smear with sticky, soft matter, such as plaster, grease, etc. **2.** to smear on (grease, etc.) **3.** to paint coarsely and unskilfully —*n.* **1.** anything daubed on **2.** a daubing stroke or splash **3.** a poorly painted picture **—daub'er** *n.*

daugh·ter (dôt'ər) *n.* [< OE. *dohtor*] **1.** a girl or woman as she is related to either or both parents: sometimes also used of animals **2.** a female descendant **3.** *a)* a daughter -in-law *b)* a stepdaughter **4.** a female thought of as if in the relation of child to parent [a *daughter* of France] **5.** anything thought of as like a daughter in relation to its origin **—daugh'ter·li·ness** *n.* **—daugh'ter·ly** *adj.*

daugh·ter-in-law (-in lô') *n., pl.* **daugh'ters-in-law'** the wife of one's son

daunt (dônt) *vt.* [< OFr. < L. < *domare*, to tame] to make afraid or discouraged; intimidate; dishearten

daunt·less (-lis) *adj.* that cannot be daunted, intimidated, or discouraged; fearless **—daunt'less·ly** *adv.* **—daunt'less·ness** *n.*

dau·phin (dô'fin; *Fr.* dō faⁿ') *n.* [Fr., lit., DOLPHIN: used as a proper name by the counts of Vienne, and hence as a title by the oldest son of the king after the province of *Dauphiné* was ceded to the crown] the eldest son of the king of France: a title used from 1349 to 1830 **—dau'phine, dau'phin·ess** *n. fem.*

dav·en·port (dav'ən pôrt') *n.* [< ?] **1.** a small writing desk with a hinged writing surface **2.** [U.S.] a large sofa, sometimes one convertible into a bed

dav·it (dav'it) *n.* [< OFr. dim. of *David*] either of a pair of uprights projecting over the side of a ship for suspending, lowering, or raising a boat

Da·vy Jones (dā'vē jōnz') the spirit of the sea: humorous name given by sailors

Davy Jones's locker (jōn'ziz, jōnz') the bottom of the sea; grave of those drowned or buried at sea

Davy lamp [after Sir Humphrey *Davy* (1778-1829), Brit. chemist, its inventor] an early safety lamp for miners, with the flame enclosed by wire gauze

daw (dô) *n.* [ME. *dawe*] *same as* JACKDAW

DAVITS

daw·dle (dôd''l) *vi., vt.* **-dled, -dling** [< ?] to waste (time) in trifling or by being slow; loiter (often with *away*) —*n.* **1.** a dawdling **2.** someone who dawdles **—daw'dler** *n.*

dawn (dôn) *vi.* [< OE. < *dagian*, to become day < *dæg*, DAY] **1.** to begin to be day; grow light **2.** to begin to appear, develop, etc. **3.** to begin to be understood or felt (usually with *on* or *upon*) [the meaning *dawned* on me] —*n.* **1.** daybreak **2.** the beginning (of something)

dawn chorus the singing of many birds at daybreak

day (dā) *n.* [< OE. *dæg*] **1.** *a)* the period of light between sunrise and sunset *b)* daylight *c)* sunshine **2.** *a)* the time (24 hours) that it takes the earth to revolve once on its axis: the civil day is from midnight to midnight *b)* *Astron.* the time that it takes any celestial body to revolve once on its axis **3.** [*often* D-] a particular or specified day [Christmas *Day*] **4.** [*also pl.*] a period of time; era [the best writer of his *day*, in *days* of old] **5.** a time of power, glory, success, etc. [he has had his *day*] **6.** the time one works each day [an eight-hour *day*] **7.** [*pl.*] one's lifetime [to spend one's *days* in study] **—all in a** (or **the**) **day's work** part of the usual course of events **—call it a day** [Colloq.] **1.** to stop working for the day **2.** to decide to stop doing (something) [the boxing champion *called it a day* and retired] **—day after day** every day **—day by day** each day **—day in, day out** every day **—from day to day 1.** from one day to the next **2.** without particular concern about the future **—if he's** (or **she's**) **a day** at least: said of someone's age

Day·ak (dī'ak) *n.* *same as* DYAK

day·bed (dā'bed') *n.* a couch that can also be used as a bed

day·book (-book') *n.* **1.** a diary or journal **2.** *Bookkeeping* a book used for recording the transactions of each day as they occur

day·boy (dā'boi') *n.* a child who attends a boarding school by day and returns home each night **—day'girl** *n.fem.*

day·break (-brāk') *n.* the time in the morning when light first appears; dawn

day·dream (-drēm') *n.* **1.** a pleasant, dreamlike thinking or wishing; reverie **2.** a pleasing but visionary notion —*vi.* to have daydreams **—day'dream'er** *n.*

day labourer an unskilled worker paid by the day

day·light (-līt') *n.* **1.** the light of day; sunlight **2.** dawn; daybreak **3.** daytime **4.** full understanding or knowledge of something hidden or obscure **5.** the approaching end of a task, etc. [to see *daylight*] **6.** [*pl.*] [Slang] orig., the eyes; hence, consciousness: often used hyperbolically, as in **scare** (or **beat, knock,** etc.) **the daylights out of**

daylight robbery blatant overcharging

day·light-sav·ing time (-sā'viŋ) time that is one hour later than standard time, generally used in the summer to give an hour more of daylight at the end of the usual working day

day·long (dā'loŋ') *adj., adv.* during the whole day

day nursery a room for children during the daytime **2.** *same as* NURSERY SCHOOL

day release a system of vocational training for employees during working hours, usually one day a week

day return a ticket, esp. for a railway journey, allowing travel from one place to another and back at a reduced rate

day room a room for recreation, reading, etc., as in a barracks, institution, or the like

days (dāz) *adv.* on every day or most days

day school 1. a school that has classes only in the daytime 2. a school whose pupils live at home and attend classes daily

day·time (dā′tīm′) *n.* the period of daylight

day-to-day (dā′tə dā′) *adj.* everyday; daily

day·work (dā′wurk′) *n.* work done (esp. by a domestic worker) and paid for on a daily basis

daze (dāz) *vt.* **dazed, daz′ing** [< ON. *dasast*, to become weary < *dasi*, tired] to stun or bewilder, as by a shock or blow —*n.* a dazed condition; bewilderment —**daz′ed·ly** *adv.*

daz·zle (daz′'l) *vt.* **daz′zled, daz′zling** [freq. of DAZE] 1. to overpower or dim the vision of with very bright light or moving lights 2. to surprise or overpower with brilliant qualities, display, etc. —*vi.* 1. to be overpowered by glare 2. to arouse admiration by brilliant display —*n.* 1. a dazzling 2. something that dazzles —**daz′zle·ment** *n.* —**daz′zler** *n.* —**daz′zling·ly** *adv.*

db decibel; decibels

D.B.E. Dame Commander of the Order of the British Empire

D.Bib. Douai Bible

dbl. double

DC, D.C., d.c. direct current

D.C.B. Dame Commander of the Order of the Bath

D.C.M. Distinguished Conduct Medal

dd., d/d delivered

D.D. 1. demand draft: also **D/D** 2. [L. *Divinitatis Doctor*] Doctor of Divinity

D-day (dē′dā′) *n.* the day for beginning a military operation; specif., June 6, 1944, the day Allied forces invaded W Europe in World War II

D.D.S. Doctor of Dental Surgery

DDT a powerful insecticide effective upon contact

de- [< Fr. *dé-* or L. *de* < L. *dis-*: see DIS-] a prefix meaning: 1. away from, off [*derail*] 2. down [*decline*] 3. wholly, entirely [*defunct*] 4. reverse the action of; undo [*defrost, decode*]

dea·con (dēk′'n) *n.* [OE. < LL. < Gr. *diakonos*, servant] 1. a cleric ranking just below a priest in the Roman Catholic and Anglican churches 2. in certain other Christian churches, a church officer who helps the clergyman, esp. in secular matters —**dea′con·ate** *n.*

dea·con·ess (dēk′'n is) *n.* a woman in early and modern Christian Churches who performs similar work to that performed by a deacon

de·ac·ti·vate (dē ak′tə vāt′) *vt.* **-vat′ed, -vat′ing** to make (an explosive, chemical, etc.) inactive or inoperative —**de·ac′ti·va′tion** *n.*

dead (ded) *adj.* [OE.] 1. no longer living; having died 2. without life; inanimate [*dead* stones] 3. deathlike 4. lacking vitality, interest, variety, warmth, brilliance, etc. 5. without feeling, motion, or power 6. a) extinguished b) extinct [a *dead* volcano] 7. slack, stagnant, etc. 8. no longer resilient 9. no longer used or significant; obsolete [*dead* languages] 10. barren or unprofitable [*dead* soil] 11. unerring; sure [a *dead* shot] 12. exact; precise [*dead* centre] 13. complete; absolute [a *dead* stop] 14. [Colloq.] very tired; exhausted 15. *Elec.* a) without current [a *dead* line] b) uncharged [a *dead* battery] 16. *Sports* no longer in play [a *dead* ball] —*n.* the time of greatest darkness, most intense cold, etc. [the *dead* of night, the *dead* of winter] —*adv.* 1. completely; absolutely [*dead* right] 2. directly [*dead* ahead] —**dead from the neck up** [Colloq.] extremely stupid; brainless —**the dead** those who have died —**dead′ness** *n.*

dead·beat (-bēt′) *n.* [Slang] 1. a person who is moneyless or exhausted 2. [Chiefly U.S.] a person who evades paying his debts, etc. 3. a lazy, idle person —*adj.* [Slang] 1. moneyless 2. exhausted

dead cert [Colloq.] 1. a horse considered to be certain to win 2. anything that is considered as a certainty [it's a *dead cert* that he'll be late on Monday]

dead duck [Colloq.] a person or thing doomed to death, failure, etc., esp. because of a mistake

dead·en (ded′'n) *vt.* 1. to lessen the vigour or intensity of 2. to make numb 3. to make soundproof —*vi.* to become as if dead; lose vigour, etc.

dead-end (-end′) *adj.* 1. having only one exit [a *dead-end* street] 2. giving no opportunity for progress [a *dead-end* job]

dead end 1. an end of a street, etc. that has no regular exit 2. an impasse

dead·eye (-ī′) *n.* 1. a round, flat wooden block with three holes in it for the lanyard, used on a ship to fasten the shrouds 2. [Chiefly U.S. Slang] an accurate marksman

dead·fall (-fôl′) *n.* [Chiefly U.S.] a trap arranged so that a heavy weight is dropped on the prey

dead·head (-hed′) *n.* 1. a person who uses a free ticket to go to the theatre, etc. 2. [U.S. & Aust.] a vehicle travelling without cargo or passengers 3. [Slang] a boring person —*vt.,* 1. to drive (a vehicle) as a deadhead 2. to remove dead flower heads —*vi.* to travel as a deadhead

dead heat a race in which two or more contestants reach the finishing line at exactly the same time; tie

dead letter 1. a law, practice, etc. no longer enforced or operative but not formally done away with 2. a letter that cannot be delivered or returned, as because incorrectly addressed

dead·line (-līn′) *n.* 1. a boundary which it is forbidden to cross 2. the latest time by which something must be done or completed

dead·lock (-lok′) *n.* 1. a standstill resulting from the action of equal and opposed forces 2. a tie between opponents 3. a type of springless lock that can be locked or unlocked only with a key —*vt., vi.* to bring or come to a deadlock

dead loss 1. a loss for which no compensation is payable 2. [Colloq.] a worthless person or thing

dead·ly (-lē) *adj.* **-li·er, -li·est** 1. causing or likely to cause death 2. to the death; mortal or implacable [*deadly* combat] 3. typical of death [*deadly* pallor] 4. very harmful 5. extreme or excessive [*deadly* silence] 6. oppressively tiresome [a *deadly* bore] 7. perfectly accurate [*deadly* aim] 8. *Theol.* causing spiritual death —*adv.* 1. as if dead [to lie *deadly* still] 2. extremely or excessively [*deadly* serious] —**dead′li·ness** *n.*

deadly nightshade *same as* BELLADONNA (sense 1)

deadly sins *Theol.* the seven sins regarded as causing spiritual death (pride, covetousness, lust, anger, gluttony, envy, and sloth)

dead man's handle a device in trains that requires constant pressure to maintain the power supply: also **dead man's pedal**

dead march funeral music in slow march tempo

dead men [Slang] emptied bottles

dead·pan (-pan′) *adj., adv.* [Colloq.] without expression [*deadpan* humour]

dead reckoning [< ? *ded* (for *deduced*) *reckoning*] the finding of a ship's position by an estimate based on data recorded in the log, such as the time spent on a specified course, speed, etc., rather than by taking astronomical observations

dead set 1. the stance of a dog when pointing at game 2. a resolute attack or effort —*adv.* absolutely and uncompromisingly [he was *dead set* against moving house]

dead weight 1. the weight of an inert person or thing 2. the weight of a vehicle without a load

dead·wood (-wood′) *n.* 1. dead wood on trees 2. a useless or burdensome person or thing

deaf (def) *adj.* [OE.] 1. totally or partially unable to hear 2. unwilling to hear or listen [*deaf* to her pleas] —*deaf′ly* *adv.* —**deaf′ness** *n.*

deaf-and-dumb (-'n dum′) *adj.* 1. deaf-mute 2. of or for deaf-mutes [*deaf-and-dumb* alphabet]

deaf·en (-'n) *vt.* 1. to make deaf 2. to overwhelm with noise 3. to soundproof with insulation —**deaf′en·ing** *adj., n.* —**deaf′en·ing·ly** *adv.*

deaf-mute (-myōot′) *n.* a person who is deaf, esp. from birth, and unable to speak: most deaf-mutes have the necessary vocal organs and can be taught to speak —*adj.* of or being a deaf-mute

deal[1] (dēl) *vt.* **dealt, deal′ing** [OE. *dælan*] 1. to portion out or distribute 2. to give or administer (a blow) —*vi.* 1. to have to do (*with*) [*books dealing* with fish] 2. to act or conduct oneself (followed by *with*) [*deal* fairly with others] 3. to consider or attend to; cope (*with*) [to *deal* with a problem] 4. to do business; trade (*with* or *in*) [to *deal* in haberdashery] 5. to distribute playing cards to the players —*n.* 1. a) the act of distributing playing cards b) cards dealt c) a player's turn to deal d) the playing of one deal of cards 2. a business transaction 3. a bargain or agreement, esp. when secret or underhanded 4. a) [Colloq.] behaviour or conduct towards another; treatment [a square *deal*] b) a particular plan, policy, etc. [the New *Deal*] —**big deal** [Colloq.] a very important or impressive thing —**raw** (or **rough**) **deal** very unfair treatment —**deal′er** *n.*

deal[2] (dēl) *n.* [OE. *dæl*, a part] an indefinite or considerable amount [a *deal* of trouble] —**a good** (or **great**) **deal** 1. a large amount 2. very much

deal[3] (dēl) *n.* [MDu. *dele*] 1. a fir or pine board 2. fir or pine wood —*adj.* made of deal

deal·ing (dēl′iŋ) *n.* 1. distribution 2. way of acting towards others 3. [*usually pl.*] transactions or relations, usually of business

dealt (delt) *pt. and pp. of* DEAL[1]

dean[1] (dēn) *n.* [< OFr. < LL. *decanus*, head of ten soldiers or monks < L. *decem*, ten] 1. a) the presiding official of a cathedral or collegiate church b) R.C.Ch. a priest chosen by his bishop to supervise a number of parishes within the diocese 2. a) a university official in charge of a faculty b) a fellow of a college with responsibility for undergraduate discipline 3. [Chiefly U.S.] doyen —**dean′ship** *n.*

dean² (dēn) *n.* [< OE. *denu,* a small valley] a narrow wooded valley
dean·er·y (dēn′ər ē) *n., pl.* **-er·ies** 1. the rank or authority of a dean 2. The residence of a dean 3. the group of parishes presided over by a rural dean
dear (dir) *adj.* [OE. *deore*] 1. much loved; beloved 2. much valued; esteemed: a polite form of address [*Dear* Sir] 3. *a*) high-priced *b*) charging high prices 4. earnest [our *dearest* wish] 5. valued; cherished; precious [he ran for *dear* life] —*adv.* 1. with deep affection 2. at a high cost —*n.* a loved or endearing person: also **dear′est** —*interj.* an expression of surprise, pity, etc.: also **dear dear! dear me!** —**dear′ly** *adv.* —**dear′ness** *n.*
dearth (durth) *n.* [see DEAR & -TH¹] 1. scarcity of food; famine 2. any scarcity or lack
dear·y, dear·ie (dir′ē) *n., pl.* **-ies** [Colloq.] dear; darling: now often ironic or humorous —**dearie me** an expression of surprise, regret, etc.: also **dear me**
death (deth) *n.* [OE.] 1. the act or fact of dying; final ending of life 2. [D-] the personification of death, usually as a skeleton holding a scythe 3. the state of being dead 4. any end resembling dying [the *death* of fascism] 5. any experience thought of as like dying or being dead 6. the cause of death 7. murder or bloodshed —**at death's door** nearly dead —**be the death of** cause or likely to cause the death of —**catch one's death** to catch a bad cold, chill, etc. —**put to death** to kill; execute —**to death** very much [worried *to death*] —**to the death** 1. to the very end of (a struggle, etc.) 2. always —**death′like′** *adj.*
death·bed (-bed′) *n.* the bed on which a person dies or spends his last hours of life —*adj.* done or made in one's last hours of life [a *deathbed* will]
death·blow (-blō′) *n.* 1. a blow that kills 2. a thing destructive or fatal (*to* something)
death certificate a document stating the cause of death and signed by a doctor
death cup a deadly mushroom with a white cap and a cuplike structure around the base of the stalk: also **death cap**
death duty a tax levied on property inheritances
death·less (-lis) *adj.* that cannot die; immortal —**death′-less·ly** *adv.* —**death′less·ness** *n.*
death·ly (-lē) *adj.* 1. causing death; deadly 2. like or characteristic of death —*adv.* 1. in a deathlike way 2. extremely [*deathly* ill]
death mask a cast of a dead person's face
death rate the number of deaths per year per thousand of population: sometimes other units of time or population are used
death's-head (deths′hed′) *n.* a human skull or a representation of it, symbolizing death
death's-head moth a large, dark-coloured, European hawk moth with markings that resemble a skull on its back
death·trap (deth′trap′) *n.* 1. an unsafe building, vehicle, etc. 2. any very dangerous place or situation
death warrant 1. an official order to put a person to death 2. anything that makes inevitable the destruction or end of a person or thing
death·watch (-woch′) *n.* 1. a vigil kept beside a dead or dying person 2. a guard set over a person soon to be executed 3. any of various beetles that bore into wood and make a tapping sound as a mating call: also **deathwatch beetle**
deb (deb) *n.* [Colloq.] *short for* DÉBUTANTE
deb. debenture
de·ba·cle (dā bäk′'l) *n.* [< Fr. < *débâcler,* to break up] 1. a breaking up of ice in a river, etc. 2. a rush of debris-filled waters 3. an overwhelming defeat or rout 4. a total, often ludicrous, collapse or failure
de·bag (dē bag′) *vt.* **-bagged′, -bag′ging** [Slang] to remove the trousers from (someone) by force
de·bar (dē bär′) *vt.* **-barred′, -bar′ring** [< Anglo-Fr. *debarrer:* see DE- & BAR¹] 1. to exclude (*from* something); bar 2. to prevent or prohibit —**de·bar′ment** *n.*
de·bark (di bärk′) *vt., vi.* [< Fr. *débarquer:* see DE- & BARQUE] to disembark —**de·bar·ka·tion** (dē′-bär kā′shən) *n.*
de·base (di bās′) *vt.* **-based′, -bas′ing** [DE- + (A)BASE] to make lower in value, quality, character, dignity, etc.; cheapen —**de·base′ment** *n.* —**de·bas′er** *n.*
de·bate (di bāt′) *vi.* **-bat′ed, -bat′ing** [< OFr. *debatre,* to fight: see DE- & BATTER¹] 1. to discuss opposing reasons; argue 2. to take part in a formal discussion or a debate (*n.* 2) —*vt.* 1. to dispute about, esp. in a meeting or legislature 2. to argue (a question) or argue with (a person) formally 3. to consider reasons for and against (*with* oneself or *in* one's own mind) —*n.* 1. discussion of opposing reasons; argument 2. *a*) the discussion of a bill, motion, etc. in Parliament *b*) a formal contest in reasoned argument by two opposing teams 3. the art or study of formal debate —**de·bat′a·ble** *adj.* —**de·bat′er** *n.*
debating society a society that holds meetings for debates: also **debating club**
de·bauch (di bôch′) *vt.* [< Fr. < OFr. *desbaucher,* to

seduce] to lead astray morally; corrupt —*vi.* to indulge in debauchery; dissipate —*n.* 1. debauchery 2. an orgy —**de·bauch′ed·ly** (-id lē) *adv.* —**de·bauch′er** *n.* —**de·bauch′-ment** *n.*
deb·au·chee (deb′ô chē′) *n.* one who indulges in debauchery; dissipated person
de·bauch·er·y (di bôch′ər ē) *n., pl.* **-er·ies** 1. extreme indulgence of one's appetites; dissipation 2. [*pl.*] orgies 3. a leading astray morally
de·ben·ture (di ben′chər) *n.* [< ML. < L. *debentur,* there are owing < *debere:* see DEBT] 1. a voucher acknowledging that a debt is owed by the signer 2. an interest-bearing bond issued by a company or governmental agency, often without security
debenture stock shares issued by a company, which guarantee a fixed return at regular intervals
de·bil·i·tate (di bil′ə tāt′) *vt.* **-tat′ed, -tat′ing** [< L. pp. of *debilitare,* to weaken < *debilis,* weak] to make weak; enervate —**de·bil′i·ta′tion** *n.*
de·bil·i·ty (-tē) *n., pl.* **-ties** [< OFr. < L. *debilitas* < *debilis,* weak] bodily weakness; feebleness
deb·it (deb′it) *n.* [< OFr. < L. *debitum,* what is owing; neut. pp. of *debere:* see DEBT] 1. an entry on the left-hand side of an account, giving rise to an increase in an asset account or decrease in a liability or net worth account 2. the total of such entries —*vt.* 1. to enter as a debit or debits
deb·o·nair (deb′ə ner′) *adj.* [< OFr. < *de bon aire,* lit., of good breed] 1. friendly in a cheerful way; genial; affable 2. carefree in manner; jaunty 3. suave; urbane —**deb′-o·nair′ly** *adv.*
de·bouch (di boōsh′-boush′) *vi.* [< Fr. < *dé-,* DE- + *bouche,* the mouth < L. *bucca,* cheek] 1. *Mil.* to come forth from a narrow or shut-in place into open country 2. to come forth; emerge —**de·bouch′ment** *n.*
Debrett (də bret′) *n.* a shortened form of Debrett's Peerage, the "Who's Who" of the aristocracy
de·brief (dē brēf′) *vt.* [DE- + BRIEF] to question and instruct (a pilot, emissary, etc.) following a flight or mission —**de·brief′ing** *n.*
de·bris, dé·bris (dā′brē, de′-) *n.* [Fr. < OFr. *desbrisier,* to break apart] 1. broken pieces of stone, wood, etc., as after destruction; rubble 2. bits of rubbish; litter 3. a heap of rock fragments, as from a glacier
debt (det) *n.* [< OFr. < L. *debitum,* neut. pp. of *debere,* to owe < *de-,* from + *habere,* to have] 1. something owed by one person to another 2. an obligation or liability to pay or return something 3. the condition of owing [to be in *debt*] 4. *Theol.* formerly, a sin
debt collector someone who collects debts on behalf of creditors
debt of honour a gambling or betting debt
debt·or (-ər) *n.* one that owes a debt
de·bug (dē bug′) *vt.* **-bugged′, -bug′ging** [DE- + BUG] 1. [Colloq.] to remove insects from 2. [Slang] to find and correct defects, faults, etc. in 3. [Slang] to find and remove hidden electronic listening devices from (a room, etc.)
de·bunk (di bunk′) *vt.* [DE- + BUNK²] [Colloq.] to expose the false or exaggerated claims, pretensions, glamour, etc. of —**de·bunk′er** *n.*
dé·but (dā′byoō, de′-) *n.* [Fr. < *débuter,* to lead off < (*jouer*) *de but,* (to play) for the mark] 1. the first appearance before the public, as of an actor 2. the formal introduction of a girl into society 3. the beginning of a career, course, etc.
déb·u·tante (deb′yoō tänt′) *n.* [< Fr. *débutant,* prp. of *débuter,* to make a DEBUT] a girl making a debut into society
Dec. December
dec. 1. deceased 2. declension 3. declination 4. decrease
dec·a- [< Gr. *deka,* ten] *a combining form meaning* ten [*decagon, decametre*]: also, before a vowel, **dec-**
dec·ade (dek′ād) *n.* [< OFr. < L. < Gr. < *deka,* ten] 1. a group of ten 2. a period of ten years
dec·a·dence (dek′ə dəns) *n.* [< Fr. < ML. < prp. of VL. *decadere* < L. *de-,* from + *cadere,* to fall] a process, condition, or period of decline, as in morals, art, literature, etc.; deterioration; decay
dec·a·dent (-dənt) *adj.* in a state of decline; characterized by decadence —*n.* a decadent person, esp. a decadent writer or artist —**dec′a·dent·ly** *adv.*
de·caf·fein·ate (dē kaf′ə nāt′) *vt.* to remove caffeine, esp. from coffee
dec·a·gon (dek′ə gon′) *n.* [see DECA- & -GON] a plane figure with ten sides and ten angles —**de·cag·o·nal** (di kag′ə nəl) *adj.*
dec·a·gramme, dec·a·gram (-gram′) *n.* [see DECA- & GRAMME] a measure of weight, equal to 10 grammes
dec·a·he·dron (dek′ə hē′drən) *n., pl.* **-drons, -dra** (-drə) [see DECA- & -HEDRON] a solid figure with ten plane surfaces —**dec′a·he′dral** (-drəl) *adj.*
de·cal (di kal′, dē′kal) *n.* *same as* DECALCOMANIA
de·cal·ci·fy (dē kal′sə fī′) *vt.* **-fied′, -fy′ing** to remove

calcium or lime from (bones, etc.) —**de·cal'ci·fi·ca'tion** *n.* —**de·cal'ci·fi'er** *n.*

de·cal·co·ma·ni·a (di kal'kə mā'nē ə) *n.* [< Fr. < *dé-*, DE- + *calquer*, to copy + *manie*, mania] **1.** the process of transferring decorative pictures or designs from specially prepared paper onto glass, wood, etc. **2.** a picture or design of this kind

dec·a·li·tre (dek'ə lēt'ər) *n.* [see DECA- & LITRE] a measure of capacity, equal to 10 litres: also, U.S., **dec'a·li'ter** (-lēt'ər)

Dec·a·logue (dek'ə log') *n.* [< LL. < Gr. *dekalogos:* see DECA- & -LOGUE] [*sometimes* d-] *same as* TEN COMMANDMENTS

dec·a·me·tre (dek'ə mēt'ər) *n.* [see DECA- & METRE] a measure of length, equal to 10 metres: also, U.S., **dec'a·me'ter** (-mēt'ər)

de·camp (di kamp') *vi.* [< Fr.: see DE- & CAMP¹] **1.** to break or leave camp **2.** to go away suddenly and secretly; run away —**de·camp'ment** *n.*

dec·a·nal (də kā'n'l) *adj.* [< LL.(Eccles.) *decanus*, dean + -AL] of a dean or deanery

de·cant (di kant') *vt.* [< Fr. < ML. < L. *de-*, from + *canthus*, rim, edge] to pour off (a liquid, esp. wine) gently without stirring up the sediment —**de·can·ta·tion** (dē'kan tā'shən) *n.*

de·cant·er (-ər) *n.* a decorative glass bottle, used for serving wine, etc.

de·cap·i·tate (di kap'ə tāt') *vi.* -tat'ed, -tat'ing [< Fr. < ML. pp. of *decapitare* < L. *de-*, off + *caput* the head] to cut off the head of; behead —**de·cap'i·ta'tion** —**de·cap'i·ta'tor** *n.*

dec·a·pod (dek'ə pod') *adj.* [see DECA- & -POD] ten-legged —*n.* **1.** any crustacean with ten legs, as a lobster, shrimp, crab, etc. **2.** any cephalopod with ten arms, as a squid —**de·cap·o·dal** (di kap'ə d'l), **de·cap'o·dous** (-dəs) *adj.* —**de·cap'o·dan** (-dən) *adj., n.*

de·car·bon·ate (dē kär'bə nāt') *vt.* -at'ed, -at'ing to remove carbon dioxide or carbonic acid from —**de·car'bon·a'tion** *n.*

DECANTER

de·car·bon·ize (-nīz') *vt.* -ized', -iz'ing to remove carbon from: also **de·car'bu·rize** (-byoo rīz') -rized', -riz'ing —**de·car'bon·i·za'tion** *n.*

dec·a·syl·la·ble (dek'ə sil'ə b'l) *n.* a line of verse with ten syllables —**dec'a·syl·lab'ic** (-si lab'ik) *adj.*

de·cath·lon (di kath'lon, -lən) *n.* [DEC(A)-+ Gr. *athlon*, contest] an athletic contest consisting of ten events: the contestant receiving the highest total of points wins

de·cay (di kā') *vi.* [< Anglo-Fr. & OFr. < LL. *decadere:* see DECADENCE] **1.** to lose strength, soundness, prosperity, etc. gradually; deteriorate **2.** to rot **3.** to undergo spontaneous radioactive disintegration —*vt.* to cause to decay —*n.* **1.** a gradual decline; deterioration **2.** a rotting **3.** *a)* rottenness *b)* rotted matter **4.** *a)* the spontaneous disintegration of radioactive atoms with a resulting decrease in their number *b)* the spontaneous disintegration of a particle or nucleus, as a meson, with the formation of a more stable state

de·cease (di sēs') *n.* [< OFr. < L. *decessus*, pp. of *decedere* < *de-*, from + *cedere*, to go] death —*vi.* -ceased', -ceas'ing to die

de·ceased (di sēst') *adj.* dead —**the deceased** the dead person or persons

de·ceit (di sēt') *n.* [< OFr. pp. of *deceveir:* see DECEIVE] **1.** the act of deceiving or lying **2.** a dishonest action or trick; lie **3.** the quality of being deceitful

de·ceit·ful (-fəl) *adj.* **1.** tending to deceive; apt to lie or cheat **2.** intended to deceive; deceptive; false —**de·ceit'ful·ly** *adv.* —**de·ceit'ful·ness** *n.*

de·ceive (di sēv') *vt.* -ceived', -ceiv'ing [< OFr. *deceveir* < L. *decipere*, to ensnare < *de-*, from + *capere*, to take] to make (a person) believe what is not true; mislead —*vi.* to use deceit —**deceive oneself** to delude or fool oneself —**de·ceiv'a·ble** *adj.* —**de·ceiv'er** *n.* —**de·ceiv'ing·ly** *adv.*

de·cel·er·ate (dē sel'ə rāt') *vt., vi.* -at'ed, -at'ing [DE- + (AC)CELERATE] to slow down —**de·cel'er·a'tion** *n.* —**de·cel'er·a'tor** *n.*

De·cem·ber (di sem'bər) *n.* [< OFr. < L. < *decem*, ten: the early Romans reckoned from March] the twelfth and last month of the year, having 31 days: abbrev. **Dec.**

de·cem·vir (di sem'vər) *n., pl.* **-virs, -vir·i** (-və rī') [L. < *decem*, ten + *vir*, a man] a member of a council of ten magistrates in ancient Rome

de·cen·cy (dē'sən sē) *n., pl.* **-cies 1.** a being decent; propriety; proper behaviour, modesty, good taste, etc. **2.** [*pl.*] socially proper actions **3.** [*pl.*] things needed for a comfortable standard of living

de·cen·ni·al (di sen'ē əl) *adj.* [< L. *decem*, ten + *annus*, year + -AL] **1.** of or lasting ten years **2.** occurring every ten years —*n.* a tenth anniversary —**de·cen'ni·al·ly** *adv.*

de·cent (dē'sənt) *adj.* [< L. prp. of *decere*, to befit] **1.** proper and fitting **2.** not immodest; not obscene **3.**

conforming to approved social standards; respectable **4.** reasonably good; adequate [*decent* wages] **5.** fair and kind **6.** [Colloq.] adequately clothed for propriety —**de'cent·ly** *adv.*

de·cen·tral·ize (dē sen'trə līz') *vt.* -ized', -iz'ing to break up a concentration of (governmental authority, etc.) in a main centre and distribute more widely —**de·cen'tral·i·za'tion** *n.*

de·cep·tion (di sep'shən) *n.* [< OFr. < L. pp. of *decipere*] **1.** a deceiving or being deceived **2.** something that deceives, as an illusion, or is meant to deceive, as a fraud

de·cep·tive (-tiv) *adj.* deceiving or meant to deceive —**de·cep'tive·ly** *adv.* —**de·cep'tive·ness** *n.*

deci- [Fr. < L. < *decem*, ten] a combining form meaning one tenth [*decigramme*]

dec·i·bel (des'ə bel') *n.* [DECI- + *bel* (after A. G. *Bell*)] a numerical expression of the relative loudness of a sound or of the relative power level of an electrical signal

de·cide (di sīd') *vt.* -cid'ed, -cid'ing [< L. *decidere* < *de-*, off + *caedere*, to cut] **1.** to end (a contest, dispute, etc.) by giving one side the victory **2.** to reach a decision about **3.** to cause to reach a decision **4.** to influence definitely the outcome of (a contest or question) —*vi.* to arrive at a judgment or decision —**de·cid'a·ble** *adj.* —**de·cid'er** *n.*

de·cid·ed (di sīd'id) *adj.* **1.** definite; clear-cut **2.** unhesitating; determined —**de·cid'ed·ly** *adv.*

de·cid·u·ous (di sid'yoo wəs) *adj.* [L. *deciduus* < *de-*, off + *cadere*, to fall] **1.** falling off at a certain season or stage of growth, as some leaves, antlers, etc. **2.** shedding leaves annually: opposed to EVERGREEN —**de·cid'u·ous·ly** *adv.* —**de·cid'u·ous·ness** *n.*

dec·i·gramme, dec·i·gram (des'ə gram') *n.* [see DECI- & GRAMME] a metric weight, equal to 1/10 gramme

dec·i·li·tre (des'ə lēt'ər) *n.* [see DECI- & LITRE] a metric measure of volume, equal to 1/10 litre: also, chiefly U.S., **dec'i·li'ter**

de·cil·lion (di sil'yən) *n.* [< *dec-* (see DECA-) + (M)ILLION] **1.** in Britain and Germany, the number written as 1 followed by 60 zeros **2.** in the U.S. and France, the number written as 1 followed by 33 zeros —*adj.* amounting to one decillion in number

dec·i·mal (des'ə m'l) *adj.* [OFr. < ML. *decimalis* < L. < *decem*, ten] of or based on the number 10; progressing by tens —*n.* a fraction with an unwritten denominator of 10 or some power of ten, indicated by a point (**decimal point**) before the numerator (Ex.: ·5 = 5/10): in full, **decimal fraction** —**dec'i·mal·ly** *adv.*

decimal classification *same as* DEWEY DECIMAL SYSTEM

decimal currency a system of currency in which the monetary units are parts or powers of ten: also **decimal coinage**

dec·i·mal·ize (des'ə mə līz') *vt.* -ized', -iz'ing **1.** to adopt a decimal system for (currency, etc.) **2.** to change into a decimal or decimals —**dec'i·mal·i·za'tion** *n.*

decimal system a system of computation based on the number ten

dec·i·mate (des'ə māt') *vt.* -mat'ed, -mat'ing [< L. pp. of *decimare* < *decem*, ten] **1.** orig., to select by lot and kill every tenth one of **2.** to destroy or kill a large part of —**dec'i·ma'tion** *n.* —**dec'i·ma'tor** *n.*

dec·i·me·tre (des'ə mēt'ər) *n.* [see DECI- & METRE] a metric measure of length, equal to 1/10 metre: also, U.S., **dec'i·me'ter**

de·ci·pher (di sī'fər) *vt.* [DE- + CIPHER] **1.** to translate (a message in cipher or code) into ordinary language; decode **2.** to make out the meaning of (ancient inscriptions, a scrawl, etc.) —**de·ci'pher·a·ble** *adj.* —**de·ci'pher·ment** *n.*

de·ci·sion (di sizh'ən) *n.* **1.** the act of deciding something **2.** a judgment or conclusion reached or given **3.** determination; firmness of mind [a man of *decision*] **4.** *Boxing* a victory on points instead of by a knockout —**de·ci'sion·al** *adj.*

de·ci·sive (di sī'siv) *adj.* **1.** that settles a dispute, question, etc.; conclusive **2.** critically important; crucial **3.** showing decision or determination —**de·ci'sive·ly** *adv.* —**de·ci'sive·ness** *n.*

deck¹ (dek) *n.* [prob. < MLowG. *verdeck* (< *ver-*, prefix + *decken*, to cover)] **1.** a roof over a section of a ship's hold, serving as a floor **2.** any platform or floor like a ship's deck **3.** [Chiefly U.S.] a pack of playing cards —**clear the decks** to get ready for action —**hit the deck** [Colloq.] **1.** to get out of bed **2.** to get ready for action **3.** to throw oneself to the ground, as to avoid injury **4.** to be knocked down —**on deck** [Colloq.] ready; on hand

deck² (dek) *vt.* [MDu. *decken*, to cover] **1.** to cover with finery or ornaments; adorn **2.** to furnish (a ship, etc.) with a deck

deck chair a folding chair, usually with a canvas seat

-deck·er (dek'ər) a combining form meaning having (a specified number of) decks, layers, etc.

deck·hand (dek'hand') *n.* a common sailor

deck·le (dek''l) *n.* [< G. *Decke*, a cover] **1.** a wooden frame used as a mould in paper-making **2.** the strap that fixes the width of paper on a paper-making machine

deck·le edge (dek''l) a rough, irregular edge sometimes given to a sheet of paper

de·claim (di klām') *vi., vt.* [< L. < *de-*, intens. + *clamare*, to shout] **1.** to recite (a speech, poem, etc.) with artificial eloquence **2.** to speak or utter in a pompous way **3.** to deliver a tirade (*against*) —**de·claim'er** *n.*

dec·la·ma·tion (dek'lə mā'shən) *n.* [< L. *declamatio* < pp. of prec.] **1.** the act or art of declaiming **2.** a speech, poem, etc. that is or can be declaimed —**de·clam·a·to·ry** (di klam'ə tər ē) *adj.*

de·clar·a·ble (di kler'ə b'l) *adj.* that can be or must be declared for taxation

dec·la·ra·tion (dek'lə rā'shən) *n.* **1.** the act of declaring; announcement **2.** a thing declared **3.** a formal statement **4.** a statement of taxable goods **5.** the winning bid in a game of bridge **6.** *Cricket* the voluntary closing of an innings before all ten wickets have fallen

declaration of the poll the official announcement of the result of an election for public office

de·clar·a·tive (di kler'ə tiv, -klar'-) *adj.* making a statement or assertion: also **de·clar·a·to·ry** (-ə tər ē) —**de·clar'a·tive·ly** *adv.*

de·clare (di kler') *vt.* -**clared'**, -**clar'ing** [< OFr. < L. < *de-*, intens. + *clarare* < *clarus*, clear] **1.** to make clearly known; announce openly, formally, etc. **2.** to show or reveal **3.** to say emphatically **4.** to make a statement of (taxable goods), as at customs **5.** to authorize payment of (a dividend, etc.) **6.** *Card Games* to establish (trump or no-trump) by a successful bid —*vi.* **1.** to make a declaration **2.** to state openly a choice, opinion, etc. (*for* or *against*) **3.** *Cricket* to close an innings voluntarily before all ten wickets have fallen —**declare oneself** **1.** to state strongly one's opinion **2.** to reveal one's true character, etc. —**I declare!** I am surprised, startled, etc. —**de·clar'er** *n.*

de·clas·si·fy (dē klas'ə fī') *vt.* -**fied'**, -**fy'ing** to remove (governmental documents, reports, etc.) from secret or restricted classifications and make available to the public

de·clen·sion (di klen'shən) *n.* [< OFr. < L. < pp. of *declinare*: see DECLINE] **1.** a sloping; descent **2.** a declining; deterioration **3.** *Gram.* a) a class of nouns, pronouns, or adjectives having the same or a similar system of inflections to show case b) their inflection —**de·clen'sion·al** *adj.*

dec·li·na·tion (dek'lə nā'shən) *n.* **1.** a bending or sloping downwards **2.** an oblique variation from a definite direction **3.** the angle formed by a magnetic needle with the line pointing to true north **4.** a polite refusal **5.** *Astron.* the angular distance of a heavenly body north or south from the celestial equator

de·cline (di klīn') *vi.* -**clined'**, -**clin'ing** [< OFr. < L. < *de-*, from + *-clinare*, to bend] **1.** to bend or slope downwards or aside **2.** to sink, as the setting sun **3.** to approach the end; wane **4.** to deteriorate; decay **5.** to descend to base or immoral behaviour **6.** to refuse to do something —*vt.* **1.** to cause to bend or slope downwards or aside **2.** to refuse, esp. politely **3.** *Gram.* to give the inflected forms of (a noun, pronoun, or adjective) —*n.* **1.** a declining; deterioration; decay **2.** a failing of health, etc. **3.** a period of decline **4.** the last part **5.** a wasting disease, esp. tuberculosis of the lungs **6.** a downward slope —**de·clin'a·ble** *adj.* —**de·clin'er** *n.*

DECLINATION
(CP, celestial poles; CE, celestial equator; O, observer, or centre of earth; DS, or angle DOS, declination of star S)

de·cliv·i·tous (di kliv'ə təs) *adj.* fairly steep

de·cliv·i·ty (-tē) *n., pl.* -**ties** [< L. < *de-*, down + *clivus*, a slope] a downward slope of the ground

de·clutch (di kluch') *vi.* to disengage the clutch which connects the engine and transmission of a motor vehicle

de·coct (di kokt') *vt.* [< L. pp. of *decoquere* < *de-*, down + *coquere*, to cook] to extract the essence, flavour, etc. of by boiling —**de·coc'tion** *n.*

de·code (dē kōd') *vt.* -**cod'ed**, -**cod'ing** to translate (a coded message) into ordinary, understandable language —**de·cod'er** *n.*

de·coke (dē kōk') *vt. same as* DECARBONIZE

dé·col·le·tage (dā kol'ə täzh') *n.* [Fr.] a low-cut dress or neckline

dé·col·le·té (dā kol'ə tā; *Fr.* dā kôl tā') *adj.* [Fr., ult. < L. *de*, from + *collum*, the neck] **1.** cut low so as to bare the neck and shoulders **2.** wearing a décolleté dress, etc.

de·co·lo·ni·za·tion (dē kol'ə nī zā'shən) *n.* a freeing or being freed from colonialism or colonial status —**de·col'o·nize** (-nīz') *vt., vi.* -**nized'**, -**niz'ing**

de·com·pose (dē'kəm pōz') *vt., vi.* -**posed'**, -**pos'ing** [<

Fr.: see DE- & COMPOSE] **1.** to break up into components components or parts **2.** to rot —**de'com·pos'a·ble** *adj.* —**de'com·po·si'tion** (-kom pə zish'ən)

de·com·press (dē'kəm pres') *vt.* to free from pressure —**de'com·pres'sion** *n.* —**de'com·pres'sor** *n.*

decompression sickness a condition caused by the formation of nitrogen bubbles in the blood or body tissues as a result of a sudden lowering of air pressure, resulting in collapse in severe cases

de·con·gest·ant (dē'kən jes'tənt) *n.* a drug, etc. that relieves congestion, as in the nasal passages

de·con·se·crate (dē kon'si krāt) *vt.* to secularize, esp. to use a church, etc., for secular purposes

de·con·tam·i·nate (-tam'ə nāt') *vt.* -**nat'ed**, -**nat'ing** to rid of a harmful substance, as radioactive products —**de'·con·tam'i·na'tion** *n.*

de·con·trol (-trōl') *vt.* -**trolled'**, -**trol'ling** to free from controls —*n.* withdrawal of controls

dé·cor (dā'kôr) *n.* [Fr.] **1.** decoration **2.** the decorative scheme of a room, stage set, etc.

dec·o·rate (dek'ə rāt') *vt.* -**rat'ed**, -**rat'ing** [< L. pp. of *decorare* < *decus*, an ornament] **1.** to adorn; ornament **2.** to plan and arrange the colours, furnishings, etc. of **3.** to paint or wallpaper **4.** to give a medal or similar token of honour to —**dec·o·ra·tive** (dek'ər ə tiv, dek'rə-) *adj.* —**dec'·o·ra·tive·ly** *adv.* —**dec'o·ra·tive·ness** *n.* —**dec'o·ra'tor** *n.*

decorated style a richly ornamented style of 14th cent. Gothic architecture

dec·o·ra·tion (dek'ə rā'shən) *n.* **1.** the act of decorating **2.** anything used for decorating; ornament **3.** a medal, badge, or similar token of honour

dec·or·ous (dek'ər əs, di kôr'əs) *adj.* [L. *decorus*, becoming] characterized by or showing decorum, good taste, etc. —**dec'o·rous·ly** *adv.* —**dec'o·rous·ness** *n.*

de·co·rum (di kôr'əm) *n.* [L., neut. of *decorus*: see prec.] **1.** whatever is suitable or proper; propriety **2.** propriety and good taste in behaviour, speech, dress, etc. **3.** an act or requirement of polite behaviour: *often used in pl.*

dé·cou·page (dā'kōō päzh') *n.* [Fr., a cutting up] the mounting of decorative paper cutouts on a surface

de·coy (di koi'; *for n. also* dē'koi) *n.* [< Du. *de kooi*, the cage < L. *cavea*, CAGE] **1.** a place in which wild ducks, etc. are lured for capture **2.** an artificial or trained bird or animal used to lure game to a place where it can be shot **3.** a thing or person used to lure into a trap —*vt., vi.* to lure or be lured into a trap, danger, etc.

de·crease (di krēs'; *also, & for n. usually,* dē'krēs) *vi., vt.* -**creased'**, -**creas'ing** [< OFr. < L. < *de-*, from + *crescere*, to grow] to become or cause to become gradually less, smaller, etc.; diminish —*n.* **1.** a decreasing; lessening **2.** amount of decreasing —**on the decrease** decreasing —**de·creas'ing·ly** *adv.*

de·cree (di krē') *n.* [< OFr. < L. *decretum* < *de-*, from + *cernere*, to see, judge] **1.** an official order or decision, as of a government **2.** something that is or seems to be foreordained —*vt.* -**creed'**, -**cree'ing** to order, decide, or appoint by decree —*vi.* to issue a decree

dec·re·ment (dek'rə mənt) *n.* **1.** a decreasing or decrease; loss **2.** amount lost by decrease

de·crep·it (di krep'it) *adj.* [< OFr. < L. < *de-*, intens. + pp. of *crepare*, to creak] broken down or worn out by old age, illness, or long use —**de·crep'it·ly** *adv.*

de·crep·i·tude (di krep'ə tyōod') *n.* a decrepit condition; feebleness or infirmity

de·cre·scen·do (dē'krə shen'dō) *adj., adv.* [It.] *Music* with a gradual decrease in loudness —*n., pl.* -**dos** *Music* **1.** a gradual decrease in loudness; symbol < **2.** a decrescendo passage

de·cres·cent (di kres'nt) *adj.* [L. < *decrescere*, decrease] decreasing; waning: said of the moon in its final quarter

de·cre·tal (di krēt''l) *adj.* [< LL. *decretalis*] of or containing a decree —*n.* **1.** a decree **2.** *R.C.Ch.* a decree issued by the Pope on some matter of ecclesiastical discipline

de·crim·i·nal·ize (di krim'ə nə liz) *vt.* -**ized'**, -**iz'ing** to remove the legal penalties from (an action, etc.) [to *decriminalize* the possession of marijuana]

de·cry (di krī') *vt.* -**cried'**, -**cry'ing** [< Fr. < OFr. *descrier*: see DE- & CRY] **1.** to speak out against strongly and openly; denounce **2.** to depreciate (money, etc.) officially —**de·cri'·al** *n.* —**de·cri'er** *n.*

de·cum·bent (di kum'bənt) *adj.* [< L. prp. of *decumbere* < *de-*, down + *-cumbere, cubare*, to recline] **1.** lying down **2.** *Bot.* trailing on the ground and rising at the tip, as some stems —**de·cum'ben·cy** *n.*

ded·i·cate (ded'ə kāt') *vt.* -**cat'ed**, -**cat'ing** [< L. pp. of *dedicare* < *de-*, intens. + *dicare*, to proclaim < *dicere*, to speak] **1.** to devote to a sacred purpose **2.** to devote to some work, duty, etc. **3.** to address (a book, artistic performance, etc.) to someone as a sign of honour or affection —**ded'i·ca'tor** *n.*

ded·i·ca·ted (ded'ə kāt'əd) *adj.* devoted; single-minded [a *dedicated* footballer]

ded·i·ca·tion (ded'ə kā'shən) *n.* **1.** a dedicating or being dedicated **2.** an inscription, as in a book, dedicating it to someone **3.** wholehearted devotion —**ded'i·ca·to·ry, ded'·i·ca'tive** *adj.*

de·duce (di dyoōs') *vt.* **-duced', -duc'ing** [< L. < *de-*, down + *ducere*, to lead] **1.** to trace the course or derivation of **2.** to infer by logical reasoning; conclude from known facts or general principles —**de·duc'i·ble** *adj.*

de·duct (di dukt') *vt.* [L. *deductus*, pp. of *deducere*: see prec.] to take away or subtract (a quantity)

de·duct·i·ble (-ə b'l) *adj.* **1.** that can be deducted **2.** that is allowed as a deduction in computing income tax —**de·duct'·i·bil'i·ty** *n.*

de·duc·tion (di duk'shən) *n.* **1.** a deducting or being deducted; subtraction **2.** the amount deducted **3.** *Logic* reasoning from the general to the specific, or from a premise to a logical conclusion; also, a conclusion so deduced: opposed to INDUCTION —**de·duc'tive** *adj.* —**de·duc'·tive·ly** *adv.*

deed (dēd) *n.* [OE. *ded, dæd*] **1.** a thing done; act **2.** a feat of courage, skill, etc. **3.** action; actual performance **4.** *Law* a document under seal which, when delivered, transfers a present interest in property —*vt.* [Chiefly U.S.] to transfer (property) by such a document —**in deed** in fact; really

deed box a strong box used to hold documents

deed poll *Law* a deed made by one party only, esp. one by which a person changes his name

dee·jay (dē'jā') *n.* [D(ISC) J(OCKEY)] [Colloq.] same as DISC JOCKEY

deem (dēm) *vt., vi.* [OE. *deman*, to judge < base of *dom*, DOOM] to think, believe, or judge

de·em·pha·size (dē em'fə sīz') *vt.* **-sized', -siz'ing** to lessen the importance or prominence of —**de·em'pha·sis** (-sis) *n.*

deem·ster (dēm'stər) *n.* the title of either of the two chief judges of the Isle of Man: also **demp'ster**

deep (dēp) *adj.* [OE. *deop*] **1.** extending far downwards from the top, inwards from the surface, or backwards from the front **2.** extending down, back, or in a specified distance [two feet *deep*] **3.** *a)* located far down or back *b)* coming from or going far down or back **4.** hard to understand; abstruse **5.** extremely grave or serious [in *deep* trouble] **6.** strongly felt **7.** intellectually profound **8.** *a)* devious and sly *b)* carefully guarded [a *deep* secret] **9.** dark and rich [a *deep* red] **10.** absorbed in [deep in thought] **11.** *a)* intense *b)* heavy and unbroken [a *deep* sleep] **12.** of low pitch [a *deep* voice] —*n.* **1.** a deep place **2.** the middle part; part that is darkest, etc. [the *deep* of the night] **3.** *Cricket* the area of the field relatively far from the wicket —*adv.* in a deep way; far down, far back, far on, etc. —**go off the deep end** [Colloq.] to become angry or excited —**in deep water** in trouble or difficulty —**the deep** [Poet.] the sea or ocean —**deep'ly** *adv.* —**deep'ness** *n.*

deep·en (-'n) *vt., vi.* to make or become deep or deeper

deep-freeze (-frēz') **1.** storage in a deep freezer **2.** a condition of suspended activity —*vt.* **-froze'-fro'zen** or **-freezed'-freez'ing** **1.** to subject (foods) to sudden freezing so as to preserve and store **2.** to store in a deep freezer

deep freezer any freezer for quick-freezing and storing food

deep-fry (-frī') *vt.* **-fried', -fry'ing** to fry in a deep pan of boiling fat or oil

deep-laid (-lād') *adj.* carefully worked out and kept secret [deep-laid plans]

deep-root·ed (-rōōt'id) *adj.* **1.** having deep roots **2.** firmly fixed; hard to remove

deep-seat·ed (-sēt'id) *adj.* **1.** placed or originating far beneath the surface **2.** firmly fixed

deep-set (-set') *adj.* **1.** deeply set **2.** firmly fixed

deep space same as OUTER SPACE

deer (dir) *n., pl.* **deer** [OE. *deor*, wild animal] any of a family of hoofed, cud-chewing animals, including the elk, reindeer, red deer, etc., the males of which usually bear antlers that are shed annually

deer forest a stretch of wild land reserved for deer

deer·skin (-skin') *n.* **1.** the hide of a deer **2.** leather or a garment made from this

deer·stalk·er (-stôk'ər) *n.* **1.** someone who stalks deer **2.** a hat with peaks in front and behind and ear flaps

de·es·ca·late (dē es'kə lāt') *vi., vt.* **-lat'ed, -lat'ing** to reduce or lessen in scope, magnitude, etc. —**de·es'ca·la'·tion** *n.*

def. **1.** defence **2.** defendant **3.** deferred **4.** defined **5.** definite **6.** definition

de·face (dē fās') *vt.* **-faced', -fac'ing** [< OFr. *desfacier*: see DE- & FACE] to spoil or mar the surface or appearance of —**de·face'ment** *n.* —**de·fac'er** *n.*

de fac·to (dē fak'tō, dā-) [L.] existing in actual fact though not by official recognition, etc. [a de facto government]: cf. DE JURE

de·fal·cate (dē'fal kāt') *vi.* **-cat·ed, -cat·ing** [< ML. pp. of *defalcare*, to cut off < L. *de-*, from + *falx* (gen. *falcis*), sickle] to steal or misuse funds entrusted to one's care;

embezzle —**de·fal·ca·tion** (dē'fal kā'shən) *n.* —**de·fal·ca·tor** *n.*

de·fame (di fām') *vt.* **-famed', -fam'ing** [< OFr. or ML. < L. < *dis-*, from + *fama*, FAME] to attack the reputation of; slander or libel —**def·a·ma·tion** (def'ə mā'shən) *n.* —**de·fam·a·to·ry** (di fam'ə tər ē) *adj.* —**de·fam'er** *n.*

de·fault (di fôlt') *n.* [< OFr. *defaute* < L. *de-*, away + *fallere*, to fail, deceive] failure to do or appear as required; specif., *a)* failure to pay money due *b)* failure to appear in court to defend or prosecute a case *c)* failure to take part in or finish a contest —*vi.* **1.** to fail to do or appear as required; specif., *a)* to fail to make payment when due *b)* to fail to appear in court *c)* to fail to take part in or finish a contest **2.** to lose by default —*vt.* **1.** to fail to do, pay, finish, etc. (something) when required **2.** to lose (a contest, etc.) by default —**go by default** to occur because of absence, lack of action, etc. —**de·fault'er** *n.*

de·feat (di fēt') *vt.* [< OFr. < ML. < L. *dis-*, from + *facere*, to do] **1.** to win victory over; overcome; beat **2.** to bring to nothing; frustrate **3.** to make null and void —*n.* a defeating or being defeated

de·feat·ist (-ist) *n.* a person who too readily accepts or expects defeat —*adj.* of or like a defeatist —**de·feat'ism** *n.*

def·e·cate (def'ə kāt') *vt.* **-cat'ed, -cat'ing** [< L. pp. of *defaecare* < *de-*, from + *faex* (gen. *faecis*), dregs] to remove impurities from; refine —*vi.* **1.** to become free from impurities **2.** to excrete waste matter from the bowels Also **def'ae·cate** —**def'e·ca'tion** *n.* —**def'e·ca'tor** *n.*

de·fect (dē'fekt; *also, and for v. always,* di fekt') *n.* [< L. pp. of *deficere*, to fail < *de-*, from + *facere*, to do] **1.** lack of something necessary for completeness; shortcoming **2.** an imperfection; fault; blemish —*vi.* to forsake a party, cause, etc.; desert —**de·fec'tor** *n.*

de·fec·tion (di fek'shən) *n.* **1.** abandonment of loyalty, duty, etc.; desertion **2.** a failure

de·fec·tive (-tiv) *adj.* **1.** having a defect or defects; faulty **2.** *Gram.* lacking some of the usual grammatical forms **3.** subnormal in intelligence —*n.* a person with some bodily or mental defect —**de·fec'tive·ly** *adv.* —**de·fec'tive·ness** *n.*

de·fence (di fens') *n.* [OFr. < L. pp. of *defendere*] **1.** a defending against attack or danger **2.** a being defended **3.** means of protection **4.** justification or support by speech or writing **5.** self-protection, as by boxing **6.** the side that is defending in any contest **7.** *a)* the arguments of the defendant in contesting a case *b)* the defendant and his lawyer or lawyers, collectively —**de·fence'less** *adj.* —**de·fence'less·ly** *adv.* —**de·fence'less·ness** *n.*

defence mechanism *Psychiatry* any behaviour unconsciously used by an individual to protect himself against painful feelings, impulses, etc.

de·fend (di fend') *vt.* [< OFr. < L. *defendere* < *de-*, away + *fendere*, to strike] **1.** to guard from attack; protect **2.** to support, maintain, or justify **3.** *Law a)* to oppose (an action, etc.) *b)* to act as lawyer for (an accused) —*vi.* to make a defence —**de·fend'a·ble** *adj.* —**de·fend'er** *n.*

de·fend·ant (di fen'dənt) *adj.* defending —*n.* *Law* the person sued or accused: opposed to PLAINTIFF

de·fen·es·tra·tion (dē fen'ə strā'shən) *n.* [DE- + L. *fenestra*, window + -TION] a tossing out through a window

de·fense (di fens') *n.* *U.S.* spelling of DEFENCE

de·fen·si·ble (di fen'sə b'l) *adj.* that can be defended or justified —**de·fen'si·bil'i·ty, de·fen'si·ble·ness** *n.* —**de·fen'·si·bly** *adv.*

de·fen·sive (-siv) *adj.* **1.** defending **2.** of or for defence **3.** *Psychol.* feeling under attack and hence quick to justify one's actions —*n.* a position of defence: chiefly in the phrase **on the defensive**, in a position that makes defence necessary —**de·fen'sive·ly** *adv.* —**de·fen'sive·ness** *n.*

de·fer[1] (di fur') *vt., vi.* **-ferred', -fer'ring** [< OFr. *differer*: see DIFFER] to put off; postpone; delay —**de·fer'ment, de·fer'ral** *n.* —**de·fer'rer** *n.*

de·fer[2] (di fur') *vi.* **-ferred', -fer'ring** [< OFr. < L. < *de-*, down + *ferre*, to bear] to give in or yield to the wish or judgment of another

def·er·ence (def'ər əns) *n.* **1.** a yielding in opinion, judgment, etc. **2.** courteous regard or respect —**in deference to** out of regard for (a person, his wishes, etc.)

def·er·en·tial (def'ə ren'shəl) *adj.* showing deference; very respectful; also **def·er·ent** (def'ər ənt) —**def'er·en'tial·ly** *adv.*

de·fi·ance (di fī'əns) *n.* **1.** a defying; open, bold resistance to authority or opposition **2.** a challenge —**bid defiance to** to defy —**in defiance of** **1.** defying; running counter to **2.** in spite of —**de·fi'ant** *adj.* —**de·fi'ant·ly** *adv.*

de·fib·ril·late (di fib'rə lāt') *vt.* **-lat'ed, -lat'ing** to stop fibrillation of the heart, as by electric current —**de·fib'ril·la'·tion** *n.* —**de·fib'ril·la'tor** *n.*

de·fi·cien·cy (di fish'ən sē) *n.* **1.** the quality or state of being deficient; absence of an essential; incompleteness **2.** *pl.* **-cies** *a)* a shortage *b)* the amount of shortage; deficit

deficiency disease a disease, as rickets, caused by lack of vitamins, minerals, etc. in the diet

de·fi·cient (di fish'ənt) *adj.* [< L. *deficiens*, prp. of *deficere*:

see DEFECT] **1.** lacking in some essential; incomplete; defective **2.** inadequate in amount, quality, degree, etc. —*n.* a deficient person or thing —**de·fi′cient·ly** *adv.*

def·i·cit (def′ə sit) *n.* [L., it is lacking < *deficere*, to lack] the amount by which a sum of money is less than the required amount, as an excess of expenditure over income

deficit spending government spending in excess of revenues, used esp. to remedy unemployment

de·fi·er (di fī′ər) *n.* a person who defies

de·file¹ (di fīl′) *vt.* **-filed′, -fil′ing** [< OFr. *defouler,* to tread underfoot (infl. by OE. *fylan,* make foul)] **1.** to make filthy; pollute **2.** to corrupt **3.** to profane or sully (a person's name, etc.) **4.** [Archaic] to violate the chastity of —**de·file′ment** *n.* —**de·fil′er** *n.*

de·file² (di fīl′, dē′fīl) *vi.* **-filed′, -fil′ing** [< Fr. < *dé-* (L. *de*), from + *filer,* to form a line] to march in single file or by files —*n.* **1.** a narrow passage through which troops must defile **2.** any narrow valley or mountain pass

de·fine (di fīn′) *vt.* **-fined′, -fin′ing** [< OFr. < L. *definire,* to limit < *de-,* from + *finis,* boundary] **1.** to determine the boundaries of **2.** to determine the extent and nature of **3.** to state the meaning or meanings of (a word, etc.) —*vi.* to prepare definitions —**de·fin′a·ble** *adj.* —**de·fin′er** *n.*

def·i·nite (def′ə nit) *adj.* [< L. pp. of *definire:* see prec.] **1.** having exact limits **2.** precise and clear in meaning; explicit **3.** certain; positive **4.** *Gram.* limiting or specifying [*"the"* is the *definite* article] —**def′i·nite·ly** *adv.* —**def′i·nite·ness** *n.*

def·i·ni·tion (def′ə nish′ən) *n.* **1.** a defining or being defined **2.** a statement of the meaning of a word, phrase, etc. **3.** *a)* a putting or being in clear, sharp outline *b)* a making or being definite or explicit **4.** the power of a lens to show (an object) in clear, sharp outline **5.** *Radio & TV* the clearness with which sounds or images are reproduced —**def′i·ni′tion·al** *adj.*

de·fin·i·tive (di fin′ə tiv) *adj.* **1.** decisive; conclusive **2.** most nearly complete and accurate **3.** serving to define precisely **4.** *Biol.* fully developed —**de·fin′i·tive·ly** *adv.* —**de·fin′i·tive·ness** *n.*

def·la·grate (def′lə grāt′) *vi., vt.* **-grat′ed, -grat′ing** [< L. pp. of *deflagrare,* to burn] to burn rapidly, with intense heat and dazzling light —**def′la·gra′tion** *n.*

de·flate (di flāt′) *vt., vi.* **-flat′ed, -flat′ing** [DE- + (IN)FLATE] **1.** to collapse by letting out air or gas **2.** to make or become smaller or less important **3.** to cause deflation of (currency, prices, etc.) Opposed to INFLATE —**de·fla′tor** *n.*

de·fla·tion (di flā′shən) *n.* **1.** a deflating or being deflated **2.** a lessening of the amount of money in circulation, causing a rise in its value and a fall in prices —**de·fla′tion·ar·y** *adj.*

de·flect (di flekt′) *vt., vi.* [< L. < *de-,* from + *flectere,* to bend] to bend or turn to one side; swerve —**de·flec′tion, de·flex′ion** *n.* —**de·flec′tive** *adj.* —**de·flec′tor** *n.*

de·flow·er (di flou′ər) *vt.* [see DE- & FLOWER] **1.** to deprive of virginity: said esp. of women **2.** to ravage or spoil **3.** to remove flowers from (a plant) —**def·lo·ra·tion** (def′lə rā′shən) *n.*

de·fo·li·ant (dē fō′lē ənt) *n.* a chemical spray that strips growing plants of their leaves

de·fo·li·ate (-āt′) *vt.* **-at′ed, -at′ing** [< LL. pp. of *defoliare* < L. *de-,* from + *folium,* a leaf] **1.** to strip (trees, etc.) of leaves **2.** to use defoliants on —**de·fo′li·a′tion** *n.* —**de·fo′li·a′tor** *n.*

de·for·est (dē for′ist) *vt.* to clear (land) of forests or trees —**de·for′est·a′tion** *n.*

de·form (di fôrm′) *vt.* [< OFr. < L. < *de-,* from + *forma,* form] **1.** to impair the form or shape of **2.** to make ugly; disfigure **3.** *Physics* to change the shape of by pressure or stress —*vi.* to become deformed —**de·form′a·ble** *adj.* —**de·for·ma·tion** (dē′fôr mā′shən, def′ər-) *n.* —**de′for·ma′tion·al** *adj.*

de·formed (di fôrmd′) *adj.* changed as in form or shape, esp. so as to be misshapen, ugly, etc.

de·form·i·ty (di fôr′mə tē) *n., pl.* **-ties** **1.** the condition of being deformed **2.** a deformed or disfigured part of the body **3.** ugliness or depravity **4.** anything deformed or disfigured

de·fraud (di frôd′) *vt.* [< OFr. < L. *defraudare* < *de-,* from + *fraus,* FRAUD] to take or hold back property, rights, etc. from by fraud; cheat —**de·frau·da·tion** (dē′frô dā′shən) *n.*

de·fray (di frā′) *vt.* [< Fr. < OFr., prob. < L. *de,* from + *fractum,* neut. pp. of *frangere,* to break] to pay (the cost or expenses) —**de·fray′a·ble** *adj.* —**de·fray′al, de·fray′ment** *n.*

de·frock (dē frok′) *vt.* same as UNFROCK (sense 2)

de·frost (di frost′) *vt.* **1.** to remove frost or ice from by thawing **2.** to cause (frozen foods) to become unfrozen —*vi.* to become defrosted

de·frost·er (-ər) *n.* [U.S.] a demister

deft (deft) *adj.* [see DAFT] skilful in a quick, sure, and easy way —**deft′ly** *adv.* —**deft′ness** *n.*

de·funct (di funkt′) *adj.* [< L. *defunctus,* pp. of *defungi,* to finish, die < *de-,* from, off + *fungi,* to perform] no longer living or existing; dead or extinct

de·fuse (dē fyōōz′) *vt.* **-fused′, -fus′ing** **1.** to remove the

fuse from (a bomb, etc.) **2.** to remove the cause of tension from (a crisis, etc.) **3.** to render harmless

de·fy (di fī′) *vt.* **-fied′, -fy′ing** [< OFr. *defier* < L. *dis-,* from + *fidus,* faithful] **1.** to resist or oppose boldly or openly **2.** to resist completely in a baffling way **3.** to dare (someone) to do or prove something

deg. degree; degrees

de·gauss (dē gous′) *vt.* [DE- + GAUSS] to demagnetize (as a ship) by passing an electric current through a coil along or around the edge in order to neutralize the surrounding magnetic field —**de·gauss′er** *n.*

de·gen·er·a·cy (di jen′ər ə sē) *n.* **1.** the state of being degenerate **2.** degenerate behaviour

de·gen·er·ate (-ər it; *for v.* -ə rāt′) *adj.* [L. pp. of *degenerare,* ult. < *de-,* from + *genus,* race] **1.** having sunk below a former or normal condition, etc.; deteriorated **2.** morally corrupt; depraved —*n.* a degenerate person, esp. one who is morally depraved —*vi.* **-at′ed, -at′ing** **1.** to lose former normal or higher qualities **2.** to become debased morally, culturally, etc. **3.** *Biol.* to undergo degeneration —**de·gen′er·ate·ly** *adv.* —**de·gen′er·ate·ness** *n.* —**de·gen′er·a·tive** *adj.* —**de·gen′er·a·tive·ly** *adv.*

de·gen·er·a·tion (di jen′ə rā′shən) *n.* **1.** the process of degenerating **2.** a degenerate condition **3.** *Biol.* deterioration or loss of a function or structure in the course of evolution **4.** *Med.* deterioration in structure or function of cells, tissues, or organs, as in disease or aging

de·grade (di grād′) *vt.* **-grad′ed, -grad′ing** [< OFr. < LL. *degradare* < L. *de-,* down + *gradus:* see GRADE] **1.** to lower in rank or status; demote **2.** to lower or corrupt in quality, moral character, etc. **3.** to bring into dishonour or contempt **4.** *Chem.* to convert (an organic compound) into a simpler compound **5.** *Geol.* to lower (a land surface) by erosion —*vi.* **1.** to degenerate **2.** *Chem.* to decompose —**de·grad′a·ble** *adj.* —**deg·ra·da·tion** (deg′rə dā′shən) *n.* —**de·grad′er** *n.*

de·grad·ed (-id) *adj.* disgraced, debased, depraved, etc. —**de·grad′ed·ly** *adv.* —**de·grad′ed·ness** *n.*

de·grad·ing (-iŋ) *adj.* that degrades; debasing —**de·grad′ing·ly** *adv.*

de·gree (di grē′) *n.* [< OFr. < LL. *degradare:* see DEGRADE] **1.** any of the successive steps or stages in a process or series **2.** a step in the direct line of descent **3.** social or official rank **4.** relative condition; manner or respect **5.** extent, amount, or relative intensity [hungry to a slight *degree*] **6.** *Algebra* rank as determined by the sum of a term's exponents [a^3c^2 and x^5 are each of the fifth *degree*] **7.** *Educ.* a rank given by a college or university to a student who has completed a course of study, or to a distinguished person as an honour **8.** *Gram.* a grade of comparison of adjectives and adverbs [the superlative *degree* of "good" is "best"] **9.** *Law* [Chiefly U.S.] the seriousness of a crime [murder in the first *degree*] **10.** *Math., Astron., Geog.,* etc. a unit of measure for angles or arcs, 1/360 of the circumference of a circle **11.** *Music* a note with respect to its position relative to the other notes in that scale **12.** *Physics* a unit of measure on a scale, as for temperature —**by degrees** step by step; gradually —**to a degree** somewhat

de·hisce (di his′) *vi.* **-hisced′, -hisc′ing** [< L. < *de-,* off + *hiscere,* to gape] to burst or split open, as a seedpod —**de·his′cence** *n.* —**de·his′cent** *adj.*

de·horn (dē hôrn′) *vt.* to remove the horns from

de·hu·man·ize (dē hyōō′mə nīz′) *vt.* **-ized′, -iz′ing** to deprive of human qualities; make inhuman or machinelike —**de·hu′man·i·za′tion** *n.*

de·hu·mid·i·fy (dē′hyōō mid′ə fī′) *vt.* **-fied′, -fy′ing** to remove moisture from (the air, etc.) —**de′hu·mid′i·fi·ca′tion** *n.* —**de′hu·mid′i·fi′er** *n.*

de·hy·drate (dē hī′drāt) *vt.* **-drat·ed, -drat·ing** to remove water from (a compound, body tissues, etc.); dry —*vi.* to lose water; become dry —**de′hy·dra′tion** *n.* —**de·hy′dra·tor** *n.*

de·hy·dro·gen·ate (dē hī′drə jə nāt′) *vt.* **-at′ed, -at′ing** to remove hydrogen from: also **de·hy′dro·gen·ize′** (-nīz′) **-ized′, -iz′ing** —**de·hy′dro·gen·a′tion** *n.*

de·ice (dē īs′) *vt.* **-iced′, -ic′ing** to melt ice from or keep free of ice —**de·ic′er** *n.*

deic·tic (dīk′tik) *adj.* [Gr. < *deiktos,* capable of proof] **1.** *Gram.* demonstrative **2.** *Logic* proving by direct argument

de·i·fy (dē′ə fī′) *vt.* **-fied′, -fy′ing** [< OFr. < LL. < L. *deus,* god + *facere,* to make] **1.** to make a god of; rank among the gods **2.** to look upon or worship as a god —**de·if′ic** (-if′-ik) *adj.* —**de′i·fi·ca′tion** (-ə fi kā′shən) *n.* —**de′i·fi′er** *n.*

deign (dān) *vi.* [< OFr. < L. *dignare* < *dignus,* worthy] to think it not beneath one's dignity (to do something); condescend

de·i·on·ize (dē ī′ə nīz′) *vt.* **-ized′, -iz′ing** **1.** to remove ions from (water, etc.) **2.** to restore ionized gas, etc. to its former condition

de·ism (dē′iz'm) *n.* [< Fr. < L. *deus,* god] **1.** belief in the existence of God based on reason rather than revelation **2.** the additional doctrine that God created the world but takes

no further part in its functioning —**de'ist** *n.* —**de·is'tic,**
de·is'ti·cal *adj.* —**de·is'ti·cal·ly** *adv.*

de·i·ty (dē'ə tē) *n.*, *pl.* **-ties** [< OFr. < LL. < L. *deus*, god]
1. the state of being a god; divine nature 2. a god or goddess —**the Deity** God

‡**dé·jà vu** (dā zhà vü') [Fr., lit., already seen] 1. *Psychol.*
the illusion that one has previously experienced something actually new to one 2. anything which is hackneyed, unoriginal, etc.: said esp. of the arts

de·ject (di jekt') *vt.* [< L. pp. of *dejicere* < *de-*, down + *jacere*, to throw] to dishearten; depress

de·ject·ed (di jek'tid) *adj.* in low spirits; depressed; disheartened —**de·ject'ed·ly** *adv.* —**de·ject'ed·ness** *n.*

de·jec·tion (di jek'shən) *n.* lowness of spirits; depression

de ju·re (dē joor'ē, dā) [L.] by right or legal establishment [*de jure* government]: cf. DE FACTO

dek·a- *same as* DECA-: also, before a vowel, **dek-**

dek·ko (dek'ō) *n.* [Hindi. *dekho* < *deknā*, to see] [Colloq.] a look; glance

del. 1. delegate 2. delegation 3. delete

de·lay (di lā') *vt.* [< OFr. < *de-*, intens. + *laier*, to leave, let < L. *laxare*: see RELAX] 1. to put off; postpone 2. to make late; detain —*vi.* to stop for a while; linger —*n.* 1. a delaying or being delayed 2. the period of time for which something is delayed —**de·lay'er** *n.*

de·le (dē'lē) *vt.* **-led, -le·ing** [L., imperative sing. of *delere*: see DELETE] *Printing* to take out (a letter, word, etc.); delete: usually in the imperative and expressed by the mark ✄, indicating the matter to be deleted —*n.* this mark

de·lec·ta·ble (di lek'tə b'l) *adj.* [< L. < *delectare*: see DELIGHT] very pleasing; delightful; delicious —**de·lec'ta·bil'i·ty, de·lec'ta·ble·ness** *n.* —**de·lec'ta·bly** *adv.*

de·lec·ta·tion (dē'lek tā'shən, di lek'-) *n.* [OFr. < L. < *delectare*: see DELIGHT] delight; entertainment

del·e·gate (del'ə gāt'; *also for n.* -git) *n.* [< L. pp. of *delegare* < *de-*, from + *legare*, to send] a person authorized to act for others; representative, as at a conference —*vt.* **-gat'ed, -gat'ing** 1. to send or appoint as a representative or deputy 2. to entrust (authority, power, etc.) to a person acting as one's representative

del·e·ga·tion (del'ə gā'shən) *n.* 1. a delegating or being delegated 2. a body of delegates Also **del·e·ga·cy** (del'ə gə sē) *pl.* **-cies**

de·lete (di lēt') *vt.* **-let'ed, -let'ing** [< L. *deletus*, pp. of *delere*, to destroy] to take out (a printed or written letter, word, etc.); cross out —**de·le'tion** *n.*

del·e·te·ri·ous (del'ə tir'ē əs) *adj.* [Gr. *dēlētērios* < *dēleisthai*, to injure] harmful to health, well-being, etc.; injurious —**del'e·te'ri·ous·ly** *adv.* —**del'e·te'ri·ous·ness** *n.*

delft·ware (delft'wer') *n.* 1. glazed earthenware, usually blue and white, which originated in Delft, a city in W Netherlands 2. any similar ware Also **delft, delf** (delf)

de·lib·er·ate (di lib'ər it; *for v.* -āt') *adj.* [< L. pp. of *deliberare* < *de-*, intens. + *librare*, to weigh < *libra*, a scales] 1. carefully thought out and formed, or done on purpose 2. careful in considering; not rash or hasty 3. unhurried and methodical [*deliberate* aim] —*vi.* **-at'ed, -at'ing** to think or consider carefully and fully; esp., to consider reasons for and against in order to make up one's mind —*vt.* to consider carefully —**de·lib'er·ate·ly** *adv.* —**de·lib'er·ate·ness** *n.* —**de·lib'er·a'tor** *n.*

de·lib·er·a·tion (di lib'ər ā'shən) *n.* 1. a deliberating, or considering carefully 2. [*often pl.*] consideration and discussion before reaching a decision 3. carefulness; slowness

de·lib·er·a·tive (di lib'ər ə tiv) *adj.* 1. of or for deliberating [a *deliberative* assembly] 2. characterized by deliberation —**de·lib'er·a'tive·ly** *adv.* —**de·lib'er·a'tive·ness** *n.*

del·i·ca·cy (del'i kə sē) *n.*, *pl.* **-cies** 1. a delicate quality 2. graceful slightness, softness, etc.; fineness 3. weakness of constitution or health 4. a need for careful and deft handling 5. fineness of feeling or appreciation 6. fineness of touch, skill, etc. 7. a fine regard for the feelings of others 8. a sensitive distaste for what is considered improper or offensive 9. a choice food

del·i·cate (del'i kit) *adj.* [L. *delicatus*, delightful] 1. pleasing in its lightness, mildness, etc. 2. beautifully fine in texture, workmanship, etc. 3. slight and subtle 4. easily damaged, disordered, spoiled, etc. 5. frail in health 6. *a)* needing careful handling, tact, etc. [a *delicate* situation] *b)* showing tact, consideration, etc. 7. finely sensitive [a *delicate* gauge] 8. finely skilled 9. having a sensitive distaste for what is considered offensive or improper —**del'i·cate·ly** *adv.* —**del'i·cate·ness** *n.*

del·i·ca·tes·sen (del'i kə tes''n) *n.* [G. pl. < Fr. *délicatesse*, delicacy] 1. prepared cooked meats, smoked fish, cheeses, salads, relishes, etc., collectively 2. a shop where such foods are sold

de·li·cious (di lish'əs) *adj.* [< OFr. < L. < *deliciae*, delight] 1. very enjoyable; delightful 2. very pleasing to taste or smell —*n.* [**D-**] a sweet, red or green winter apple —**de·li'cious·ly** *adv.* —**de·li'cious·ness** *n.*

de·light (di līt') *vt.* [< OFr. < L. < *delicere* < *de-*, from +

lacere, to entice] to give great pleasure to —*vi.* 1. to give great pleasure 2. to be highly pleased —*n.* 1. great pleasure 2. something giving great pleasure —**de·light'ed** *adj.* —**de·light'ed·ly** *adv.* —**de·light'ed·ness** *n.*

de·light·ful (-fəl) *adj.* giving delight; very pleasing; charming: also [Archaic] **de·light'some** (-səm) —**de·light'·ful·ly** *adv.* —**de·light'ful·ness** *n.*

De·li·lah (di lī'lə) *n.* [Heb. *delīlāh*, lit., delicate] a seductive, treacherous woman: after the mistress of Samson, in the Bible, who betrayed him to the Philistines

de·lim·it (di lim'it) *vt.* to set the limits or boundaries of: also **de·lim'i·tate'-tat'ed, -tat'ing** —**de·lim'i·ta'tion** *n.* —**de·lim'i·ta'tive** *adj.*

de·lin·e·ate (di lin'ē āt') *vt.* **-at'ed, -at'ing** [< L. < *de-*, from + *linea*, LINE¹] 1. to trace the outline of 2. to draw; depict 3. to depict in words; describe —**de·lin'e·a'tion** *n.* —**de·lin'·e·a'tive** *adj.* —**de·lin'e·a'tor** *n.*

de·lin·quen·cy (di lin'kwən sē) *n.*, *pl.* **-cies** 1. failure or neglect to do what duty or law requires 2. a fault; misdeed 3. antisocial or illegal behaviour esp. by the young: see JUVENILE DELINQUENCY

de·lin·quent (-kwənt) *adj.* [< L. *delinquens*, prp. of *delinquere* < *de-*, from + *linquere*, to leave] failing or neglecting to do what duty or law requires —*n.* a delinquent person; esp., a juvenile delinquent —**de·lin'·quent·ly** *adv.*

del·i·quesce (del'ə kwes') *vi.* **-quesced', -quesc'ing** [< L. *deliquescere* < *de-*, from + *liquere*, to be liquid] 1. to melt away 2. to become liquid by absorbing moisture from the air —**del'i·ques'cence** *n.* —**del'i·ques'cent** *adj.*

de·lir·i·ous (di lir'ē əs) *adj.* 1. in a state of delirium 2. of or caused by delirium 3. wildly excited —**de·lir'i·ous·ly** *adv.* —**de·lir'i·ous·ness** *n.*

de·lir·i·um (-ē əm) *n.*, *pl.* **-i·ums, -i·a** (-ə) [L. < *delirare*, to rave, lit., to turn the furrow awry in ploughing < *de-*, from + *lira*, a line] 1. a temporary state of extreme mental excitement, marked by confused speech and hallucinations: it sometimes occurs during a fever, in some forms of insanity, etc. 2. uncontrollably wild excitement

delirium tre·mens (trē'mənz) [ModL., lit., trembling delirium] a violent delirium resulting chiefly from chronic alcoholism

de·liv·er (di liv'ər) *vt.* [< OFr. < LL. < L. *de-*, from + *liberare*, to free < *liber*, free] 1. to set free or save from evil, danger, etc. 2. to assist at the birth of (offspring) 3. to express in words; utter [*deliver* a speech] 4. to hand over; transfer 5. to distribute [*deliver* the post] 6. to strike (a blow) 7. to throw (a ball, etc.) —*vi.* 1. to make deliveries, as of merchandise 2. [Colloq.] to produce the expected, or promised, results —**be delivered of** to give birth to —**deliver oneself of** to express; utter —**deliver the goods** [Colloq.] to produce what has been promised or is expected —**de·liv'er·a·ble** *adj.* —**de·liv'er·er** *n.*

de·liv·er·ance (-əns) *n.* 1. a freeing or being freed 2. an opinion, etc. publicly expressed

de·liv·er·y (-ē) *n.*, *pl.* **-er·ies** 1. a handing over; transfer 2. a distributing, as of the post 3. a giving birth; childbirth 4. any giving forth 5. the act or manner of giving a speech, striking a blow, throwing a ball, etc. 6. something delivered

dell (del) *n.* [OE. *dell*] a small, secluded valley or glen, usually a wooded one

de·louse (dē lous', -louz') *vt.* **-loused', -lous'ing** to rid of lice —**de·lous'er** *n.*

Del·phic (del'fik) *adj.* 1. of Delphi 2. designating or of the oracle of Apollo at Delphi in ancient times Also **Del'phi·an** (-fē ən)

del·phin·i·um (del fin'ē əm) *n.* [< Gr. *delphin*, dolphin: its nectary resembles a dolphin] a plant bearing spikes of spurred, irregular flowers, usually blue, on tall stalks: some are poisonous

del·phi·noid (del'fin oid') *adj.* [< Gr. *delphin*, dolphin] of or like a dolphin —*n.* the family of animals including dolphins, porpoises, etc.

del·ta (del'tə) *n.* [< Gr.] 1. the fourth letter of the Greek alphabet (Δ, δ) 2. a deposit of sand and soil, usually triangular, formed at the mouth of some rivers —**del·ta·ic** (del tā'ik) *adj.*

delta ray an electron ejected by the passage of a primary ionizing particle through matter

delta wing the triangular shape of certain kinds of jet aircraft —**del'ta-wing', del'·ta-winged'** *adj.*

del·ti·ol·o·gy (del'ti ol'ə jē) *n.* [< Gr. *deltion* dim. of *deltos*, a writing tablet + -LOGY] the collection and study of postcards

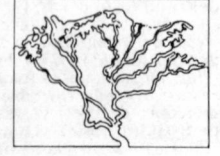

DELTA

del·toid (del'toid) *adj.* 1. shaped like a delta; triangular 2. designating or of a large, triangular muscle of the shoulder —*n.* the deltoid muscle

de·lude (di lōōd′, -lyōōd′) *vt.* **-lud′ed, -lud′ing** [< L. < *de-*, from + *ludere*, to play] to mislead; deceive; trick —**de·lud′er** *n.*

del·uge (del′yōōj) *n.* [< OFr. < L. *diluvium* < *dis-*, off + *lavere*, to wash] **1.** a great flood **2.** a heavy rainfall **3.** an overwhelming, floodlike rush of anything —*vt.* **-uged, -ug·ing 1.** to flood **2.** to overwhelm —**the Deluge** *Bible* the great flood in Noah's time: Gen. 7

de·lu·sion (di lōō′zhən) *n.* **1.** a deluding or being deluded **2.** a false belief or opinion **3.** *Psychiatry* a false, persistent belief not substantiated by sensory or objective evidence —**de·lu′sion·al** *adj.*

de·lu·sive (di lōōs′iv) *adj.* **1.** tending to delude; misleading **2.** unreal Also **de·lu′so·ry** (-lōō′sə rē) —**de·lu′sive·ly** *adv.* —**de·lu′sive·ness** *n.*

de·luxe (di luks′, -looks′, -lōōks′) *adj.* [Fr., lit., of luxury] of extra fine quality; luxurious; elegant —*adv.* in a deluxe manner

delve (delv) *vi.* **delved, delv′ing** [OE. *delfan*] **1.** [Archaic] to dig with a spade **2.** to investigate for information; search (*into* books, the past, etc.) —**delv′er** *n.*

Dem. [U.S.] **1.** Democrat **2.** Democratic

de·mag·net·ize (dē mag′nə tīz′) *vt.* **-ized′, -iz′ing** to deprive of magnetism —**de·mag′net·i·za′tion** *n.* —**de·mag′·net·iz′er** *n.*

dem·a·gog·ic (dem′ə gog′ik, -goj′-) *adj.* of, like, or characteristic of a demagogue or demagogy: also **dem′·a·gog′i·cal** —**dem′a·gog′i·cal·ly** *adv.*

dem·a·gogue (dem′ə gog′) *n.* [< Gr. < *dēmos*, the people + *agōgos*, leader < *agein*, to lead] a person who tries to stir up the people by appeals to emotion, prejudice, etc. in order to win them over quickly and so gain power

dem·a·gog·y (dem′ə gog′ē, go′jē) *n.* the methods or practices of a demagogue: also **dem′a·gog′uer·y** (-gog′ər ē)

de·mand (di mänd′) *vt.* [< OFr. < L. < *de-*, from + *mandare*, to entrust: see MANDATE] **1.** to ask for boldly or urgently **2.** to ask for as a right or with authority **3.** to ask to know or be informed of **4.** to require *[the work demands time]* —*vi.* to make a demand —*n.* **1.** a demanding **2.** a thing demanded **3.** a strong request **4.** an urgent requirement or claim **5.** *a)* the desire for a commodity along with ability to pay for it *b)* the amount of a commodity, etc. that people are prepared to buy at a given price: cf. SUPPLY (*n.* 5) —**in demand** asked for —**on demand** when presented for payment —**de·mand′a·ble** *adj.* —**de·mand′er** *n.*

de·mand·ing (-iŋ) *adj.* making demands on one's patience, energy, etc. —**de·mand′ing·ly** *adv.*

de·mar·cate (dē′mär kāt′) *vt.* **-cat′ed, -cat′ing** [< ff.] **1.** to mark the limits of **2.** to distinguish; separate

de·mar·ca·tion, de·mar·ka·tion (dē′mär kā′shən) *n.* [Sp. < *de-* (L. *de*), from + *marcar*, to mark] **1.** the act of setting and marking boundaries **2.** a limit or boundary **3.** a separation

dé·marche (dā märsh′) *n.* [Fr.: see DE- & MARCH¹] a line of action; manoeuvre, ploy

de·ma·te·ri·al·ize (dē′mə tir′ē ə līz′) *vi., vt.* **-ized, -iz′ing** to lose or cause to lose material from

deme (dēm) *n.* [< Gr. *dēmos*, people, district] **1.** any of the hundred townships of ancient Attica. **2.** *Biol.* a particular interbreeding population within a species

de·mean¹ (di mēn′) *vt.* [DE- & MEAN², after DEBASE] to degrade; humble *[to demean oneself by lying]*

de·mean² (di mēn′) *vt.* [see ff.] to behave or conduct (oneself)

de·mean·our (-ər) *n.* [< OFr. < *de-* (L. *de*), from + *mener*, to lead < LL. *minare*, to drive (animals) < L. *minari*, to threaten] outward behaviour; conduct; deportment: also, U.S. sp., **de·mean′or**

de·ment·ed (di ment′id) *adj.* [< L. < *demens* (gen. *dementis*), mad: see ff.] mentally deranged; insane —**de·ment′ed·ly** *adv.*

de·men·tia (di men′shə) *n.* [L. < *de-*, out from + *mens*, the mind] loss or impairment of mental powers from organic causes: cf. AMENTIA

dementia prae·cox (prē′koks) [ModL.: see prec. & PRECOCIOUS] *former term for* SCHIZOPHRENIA

dem·e·rar·a (dem′ə rer′ə) *n.* [< *Demerara*, in Guyana] brown crystallized cane sugar from the West Indies

de·mer·it (di mer′it) *n.* [< OFr. < ML. < L. *demerere*, to deserve well, with intens. prefix *de-* mistaken as negative in ML.] **1.** a fault; defect **2.** [U.S.] a mark recorded against a student, trainee, etc. for poor conduct or work —**de·mer′·i·to′ri·ous** *adj.*

de·mesne (di mān′, -mēn′) *n.* [OFr. *demeine* < L. *dominium*: see DOMAIN] **1.** *Law* possession of (real estate) in one's own right **2.** the land around a mansion **3.** a region or domain: also used figuratively

dem·i- [OFr. < L. < *dis-*, apart + *medius*, middle] *a prefix meaning:* **1.** half *[demisemiquaver]* **2.** less than usual in size, power, etc. *[demigod]*

dem·i·god (dem′ē god′) *n.* **1.** *Myth.* a) a minor deity b) the offspring of a human being and a god or goddess **2.** a godlike person

dem·i·john (-jon′) *n.* [Fr. *dame-jeanne*] a large bottle of glass or earthenware, with a narrow neck and a wicker casing and handle

de·mil·i·ta·rize (dē mil′ə tə rīz′) *vt.* **-rized′, -riz′ing** to free from military control or activity, or from militarism —**de·mil′·i·ta·ri·za′tion** *n.*

dem·i·mon·daine (dem′ē mon dān′) *n.* [Fr.] a woman of the demimonde

DEMIJOHN

dem·i·monde (dem′ē mond′) *n.* [Fr. < *demi-*, DEMI- + *monde* (< L. *mundus*), world] formerly, the class of women who have lost social standing because of sexual promiscuity

de·mise (di mīz′) *n.* [< Fr. fem. pp. of *démettre*, to dismiss < L. < *de-*, down + *mittere*, to send] **1.** *Law* a transfer of an estate by lease **2.** the transfer of sovereignty by death or abdication **3.** death —*vt.* **-mised′, -mis′ing 1.** to give or transfer (an estate) by lease **2.** to transfer (sovereignty) by death or abdication

dem·i·sem·i·qua·ver (dem′ē sem′ē kwā′vər) *n.* *Music* a note having 1/32 of the duration of a semibreve: see NOTE, illus.

de·mist·er (dē mist′ər) *n.* a device for melting ice and frost, as on a windscreen

dem·i·tasse (dem′ē tas′) *n.* [Fr. < *demi-*, DEMI- + *tasse*, a cup] a small cup of or for after-dinner black coffee

dem·i·urge (dem′ē urj′) *n.* [Gr. *dēmiourgos*, skilled workman, creator] [*often* D-] **1.** in Plato's philosophy, the deity as creator of the universe **2.** in Gnostic philosophy, the creator of the universe who is subordinate to the supreme deity

dem·o (dem′ō) *n.* [Colloq.] *same as* DEMONSTRATION (sense 5)

de·mob (dē mob′) *vt.* **-mobbed′, -mob′bing** [Colloq.] to demobilize

de·mo·bi·lize (dē mō′bə līz′) *vt.* **-lized′, -liz′ing 1.** to disband (troops) **2.** to discharge (a person) from the armed forces —**de·mo′bi·li·za′tion** *n.*

de·moc·ra·cy (di mok′rə sē) *n.*, *pl.* **-cies** [< Fr. < ML. *democratia* < Gr. < *dēmos*, the people + *kratein*, to rule] **1.** government in which the people hold the ruling power either directly or through elected representatives **2.** a country, state, etc. with such government **3.** majority rule **4.** the principle of equality of rights, opportunity, etc., or the practice of this principle

dem·o·crat (dem′ə krat′) *n.* **1.** a person who believes in and upholds government by the people **2.** a person who believes in and practises the principle of equality of rights, opportunity, etc. **3.** [U.S.] [**D-**] a member of the Democratic Party

dem·o·crat·ic (dem′ə krat′ik) *adj.* **1.** of, belonging to, or upholding (a) democracy **2.** of or for all or most people **3.** treating people of all classes in the same way —**dem′o·crat′·i·cal·ly** *adv.*

de·moc·ra·tize (di mok′rə tīz′) *vt., vi.* **-tized′, -tiz′ing** to make or become democratic —**de·moc′ra·ti·za′tion** *n.*

de·mod·u·late (dē mod′yoo lāt′) *vt.* **-lat′ed, -lat′ing** to cause to undergo demodulation —**de·mod′u·la′tor** *n.*

de·mod·u·la·tion (dē mod′yoo lā′shən) *n.* *Radio* the recovery, at the receiver, of a signal that has been modulated on a carrier wave

de·mog·ra·phy (di mog′rə fē) *n.* [< Gr. *dēmos*, the people + -GRAPHY] the statistical science dealing with the distribution, vital statistics, etc. of populations —**de·mog′·ra·pher** *n.* —**de·mo·graph·ic** (dē′mə graf′ik, dem′ə-) *adj.* —**de′mo·graph′i·cal·ly** *adv.*

dem·oi·selle (dem′wä zel′) *n.* [Fr.] **1.** a damsel; young lady **2.** a small crane of Africa, Asia, and Europe

de·mol·ish (di mol′ish) *vt.* [< Fr. < L. *demoliri*, to destroy < *de-*, down + *moliri*, to build < *moles*, a mass] **1.** to tear down or smash to pieces (a building, etc.) **2.** to destroy; ruin —**de·mol′ish·er** *n.* —**de·mol′ish·ment** *n.*

dem·o·li·tion (dem′ə lish′ən, dē′mə-) *n.* a demolishing or being demolished; often, specif., destruction by explosives

de·mon (dē′mən) *n.* [L. *daemon*: see DAEMON] **1.** *same as* DAEMON **2.** a devil; evil spirit **3.** a person or thing regarded as evil, cruel, etc. **4.** a person who has great energy or skill —**de·mon·ic** (di mon′ik) *adj.* —**de·mon′i·cal·ly** *adv.*

de·mon·e·tize (dē mun′ə tīz′) *vt.* **-tized′, -tiz′ing 1.** to deprive (currency) of its standard value **2.** to stop using (silver or gold) as a monetary standard —**de·mon·e·ti·za′tion** *n.*

de·mo·ni·ac (di mō′nē ak′) *adj.* **1.** possessed or influenced by a demon **2.** of a demon or demons **3.** like or characteristic of a demon; fiendish Also **de·mo·ni·a·cal** (dē′·mə nī′ə k′l) —*n.* a person supposedly possessed by a demon —**de′mo·ni′a·cal·ly** *adv.*

de·mon·ism (dē′mən iz′m) *n.* belief in the existence and powers of demons —**de′mon·ist** *n.*

de·mon·o- *a combining form meaning* demon: also, before a vowel, **demon-**

de·mon·ol·a·try (dē'mə nol'ə trē) *n.* worship of demons —**de'mon·ol'a·ter** *n.*

de·mon·ol·o·gy (-jē) *n.* the study of demons or of beliefs about them —**de'mon·ol'o·gist** *n.*

de·mon·stra·ble (dem'ən strə b'l, di mon'-) *adj.* that can be demonstrated, or proved —**de·mon'stra·bil'i·ty** *n.* —**de·mon'stra·bly** *adv.*

dem·on·strate (dem'ən strāt') *vt.* **-strat'ed, -strat'ing** [< L. pp. of *demonstrare* < *de-*, from + *monstrare*, to show] **1.** to show by reasoning; prove **2.** to explain by using examples, experiments, etc. **3.** to show the operation or working of **4.** to show (feelings) plainly —*vi.* **1.** to show one's feelings or views by taking part in a public meeting, parade, etc. **2.** to show military power **3.** to act as a demonstrator of machines, etc.

dem·on·stra·tion (dem'ən strā'shən) *n.* **1.** a making evident or proving **2.** an explanation by example, experiment, etc. **3.** a practical showing of how something works or is used **4.** a display or outward show **5.** a public show of opinion, etc., as by a mass meeting **6.** a show of military force

de·mon·stra·tive (di mon'strə tiv) *adj.* **1.** giving convincing evidence or proof (usually with *of*) **2.** having to do with demonstration **3.** showing feelings openly and frankly **4.** *Gram.* pointing out ["this" is a *demonstrative* pronoun] —*n.* *Gram.* a demonstrative word —**de·mon'stra·tive·ly** *adv.* —**de·mon'stra·tive·ness** *n.*

dem·on·stra·tor (dem'ən strāt'ər) *n.* [L.] one that demonstrates; specif., *a)* a person who takes part in a public demonstration *b)* a person who explains the uses of machinery, products, etc., as at a trade exhibition

de·mor·al·ize (di mor'ə līz') *vt.* **-ized', -iz'ing** **1.** [Now Rare] to corrupt the morals of **2.** to lower the morale of **3.** to throw into confusion —**de·mor'al·i·za'tion** *n.* —**de·mor'al·iz'er** *n.*

de·mote (di mōt') *vt.* **-mot'ed, -mot'ing** [DE- + (PRO)MOTE] to reduce to a lower grade; lower in rank —**de·mo'tion** *n.*

de·mot·ic (di mot'ik) *adj.* [< ML. < Gr. < *dēmotes*, one of the people < *dēmos*, the people] **1.** of the people; popular; specif., vernacular (sense 2) **2.** designating or of a simplified system of ancient Egyptian writing

de·mul·cent (di mul's'nt) *adj.* [< L. prp. of *demulcere* < *de-*, down + *mulcere*, to stroke] soothing —*n.* a medicine or ointment that soothes irritated mucous membrane

de·mur (di mur') *vi.* **-murred', -mur'ring** [OFr. *demorer* < L. < *de-*, from + *morari*, to delay < *mora*, a delay] **1.** to be unwilling because of doubts or objections; object **2.** *Law* to enter a demurrer —*n.* **1.** a demurring **2.** an objection raised or exception taken Also **de·mur'ral** *n.* —**de·mur'ra·ble** *adv.*

de·mure (di myoor') *adj.* [< ME. < *de-* (prob. intens.) + *mur* < OFr. *mēur*, ripe < L. *maturus*, mature] **1.** modest; reserved **2.** affectedly modest or shy; coy —**de·mure'ly** *adv.* —**de·mure'ness** *n.*

de·mur·rage (di mur'ij) *n.* [< OFr. < *demorer*: see DEMUR] **1.** the delaying of a ship, railway wagon, etc., as by failure to load, unload, or sail within the time allowed **2.** the compensation paid for this

de·mur·rer (-ər) *n.* [OFr. *demorer*, to DEMUR] **1.** a plea for the dismissal of a lawsuit on the grounds that even if the statements of the opposition are true, they do not sustain the claim **2.** an objection; demur **3.** a person who demurs

de·mys·ti·fy (dē mis'tə fī') *vt.* **-fied', -fy'ing** to make clear; remove the mystery from

de·my·thol·o·gize (dē mi thol'ə jīz') *vt.* **-gized', -giz'ing** **1.** to eliminate mythical elements from a (given piece of writing, esp. the Bible) **2.** to restate (a religious message) in rational terms

den (den) *n.* [OE. *denn*] **1.** the cave or other lair of a wild animal **2.** a retreat or headquarters, as of thieves **3.** a small, cosy room where a person can be alone to read, work, etc. —*vi.* **denned, den'ning** to live or hide as in a den

Den. Denmark

de·nar·i·us (di när'ē əs, -ner'-) *n.*, *pl.* **-nar'i·i'** (-ī') [< L. < *deni*, by tens < *decem*, ten] **1.** an ancient Roman silver coin, the penny of the New Testament **2.** an ancient Roman gold coin

den·a·ry (dē'nər ē) *adj.* [see prec.] of the number ten; decimal

de·na·tion·al·ize (dē nash'ən'l īz') *vt.* **-ized', -iz'ing** **1.** to deprive of national rights or status **2.** to place (a government-controlled industry) under private ownership —**de·na'tion·al·i·za'tion** *n.*

de·nat·u·ral·ize (dē nach'rə līz') *vt.* **-ized', -iz'ing** **1.** to make unnatural **2.** to take citizenship away from —**de·nat'-u·ral·i·za'tion** *n.*

de·na·ture (dē nā'chər) *vt.* **-tured, -tur·ing** **1.** to change the nature of **2.** to make (alcohol, etc.) unfit for human consumption without spoiling for other uses **3.** to change the composition of (a protein) by heat, acids, etc. —**de·na'-tur·a'tion** *n.*

den·drite (den'drīt) *n.* [< Gr. < *dendron*: see ff.] **1.** the branched part of a nerve cell that carries impulses towards the cell body **2.** a mineral with tree or plant-like markings —**den·drit'ic** (-drit'ik), **den·drit'i·cal** *adj.* —**den·drit'i·cal·ly** *adv.*

den·dro- [< Gr. *dendron*, a tree] *a combining form meaning* tree: also **dendri-** or before a vowel, **dendr-**

den·drol·o·gy (den drol'ə jē) *n.* the scientific study of trees —**den'dro·log'ic** (-drə loj'ik), **den'dro·log'i·cal** *adj.* —**den·drol'o·gist** *n.*

-dendron (den'drən) [see DENDRO-] *a combining form meaning* tree or treelike structure

dene¹ (dēn) *n.* [akin to DUNE] a low dune or sandy tract near a seashore

dene² (dēn) *n.* same as DEAN²

den·gue (den'gē) *n.* [WIndSp. < Swahili *dinga*, a cramp, infl. by Sp. *dengue*, affected contortion] an infectious tropical disease transmitted by mosquitoes and characterized by severe pain in the joints and back, fever, and rash

de·ni·a·ble (di nī'ə b'l) *adj.* that can be denied

de·ni·al (di nī'əl) *n.* **1.** a denying; saying "no" (to a request, etc.) **2.** a statement in opposition to another **3.** a disowning; repudiation [the *denial* of one's family] **4.** a refusal to believe or accept (a doctrine, etc.) **5.** same as SELF-DENIAL

de·nier¹ (den'yər) *n.* [< OFr. < L. *denarius*, DENARIUS] a unit of weight for measuring the fineness of threads of silk, nylon, etc.

de·ni·er² (di nī'ər) *n.* a person who denies

den·i·grate (den'ə grāt') *vt.* **-grat'ed, -grat'ing** [< L. pp. of *denigrare* < *de-*, intens. + *nigrare*, to blacken < *niger*, black] to belittle; depreciate; defame; speak ill of someone's character or reputation —**den'i·gra'tion** *n.* —**den'i·gra·tor** *n.* —**den'i·gra·to·ry** (-grə tôr'ē) *adj.*

den·im (den'əm) *n.* [< Fr. (*serge*) *de Nîmes*, (serge) of Nîmes, Fr. town] a coarse, twilled cotton cloth used for overalls, jeans, uniforms, etc.

den·i·zen (den'i zən) *n.* [< Anglo-Fr. < OFr. *denzein* < *denz*, within < L. *de intus*, from within] **1.** *a)* an inhabitant *b)* a frequenter of a particular place **2.** an animal, plant, etc. that has become naturalized —*vt.* to naturalize

de·nom·i·nate (di nom'ə nāt') *vt.* **-nat'ed, -nat'ing** [< L. pp. of *denominare* < *de-*, intens. + *nominare*: see NOMINATE] to give a specified name to; call

de·nom·i·na·tion (di nom'ə nā'shən) *n.* **1.** the act of denominating **2.** a name, esp. of a class of things **3.** a class or kind with a specific name or value [coins of different *denominations*] **4.** a particular religious sect or body

de·nom·i·na·tion·al (-'l) *adj.* of, or under the control of, a religious denomination —**de·nom'i·na'tion·al·ism** *n.* —**de·nom'i·na'tion·al·ly** *adv.*

de·nom·i·na·tive (di nom'ə nə tiv) *adj.* **1.** denominating; naming **2.** *Gram.* formed from a noun or adjective stem

de·nom·i·na·tor (-nāt'ər) *n.* [ML.] the term below the line in a fraction, indicating the number of equal parts into which the whole is divided

de·no·ta·tion (dē'nō tā'shən) *n.* **1.** a denoting **2.** the explicit meaning or reference of a word or term: cf. CONNOTATION **3.** an indication or sign

de·note (di nōt') *vt.* **-not'ed, -not'ing** [< Fr. < L. < *de-*, down + *notare*, to mark < *nota*, NOTE] **1.** to be a sign of; indicate **2.** to signify or refer to explicitly; mean: cf. CONNOTE —**de·not'a·ble** *adj.* —**de·no·ta·tive** (dē'nō tāt'iv) *adj.*

de·noue·ment, dé·noue·ment (dā nōō'män; Fr. dā nōō- män') *n.* [Fr. < *dé-* (L. *dis-*), out + *nouer*, to tie < L. < *nodus*: see NODE] **1.** the outcome, solution, or unravelling of a plot in a drama, story, etc. **2.** any final revelation or outcome

de·nounce (di nouns') *vt.* **-nounced', -nounc'ing** [< OFr. < L. *denuntiare*: see DENUNCIATION] **1.** to accuse publicly; inform against **2.** to condemn strongly as evil; censure **3.** to give formal notice of the ending of (a treaty, armistice, etc.) —**de·nounce'ment** *n.* —**de·nounc'er** *n.*

‡**de no·vo** (dē nō'vō) [L.] once more; anew

dense (dens) *adj.* **dens'er, dens'est** [L. *densus*, compact] **1.** packed tightly together; compact **2.** difficult to get through, penetrate, etc. **3.** stupid **4.** *Photog.* opaque, with good contrast in light and shade: said of a negative —**dense'ly** *adv.* —**dense'ness** *n.*

den·si·ty (den'sə tē) *n.*, *pl.* **-ties** **1.** the quality or condition of being dense **2.** quantity or number per unit, as of area [the *density* of population] **3.** *Physics* the ratio of the mass of an object to its volume

dent (dent) *n.* [ME., var. of DINT] **1.** a slight hollow made in a surface by a blow or pressure **2.** an appreciable effect [to make a *dent* in our resources] —*vt.* to make a dent in —*vi.* to become dented

den·tal (den't'l) *adj.* [ModL. < L. *dens* (gen. *dentis*), a tooth] **1.** of or for the teeth or dentistry **2.** *Phonet.*

formed by placing the tip of the tongue against or near the upper front teeth —*n.* *Phonet.* a dental consonant (th, *th*)

dental floss thin, strong thread for removing food particles from between the teeth

dental surgeon *same as* DENTIST

den·tate (den'tāt) *adj.* [< L. < *dens:* see DENTAL] having teeth or toothlike projections; toothed or notched —**den'·tate·ly** *adv.* —**den·ta'tion** *n.*

den·ti- [< L. *dens:* see DENTAL] *a combining form meaning* tooth or teeth: also **dento-** or, before a vowel, **dent-**

den·ti·frice (den'tə fris) *n.* [< L. < *dens* (see DENTAL) + *fricare*, to rub] any preparation for cleaning teeth, as a powder, paste, or liquid

den·til (den'til) *n.* [< MFr. < L. *dens:* see DENTAL] *Archit.* any of a series of small rectangular blocks projecting like teeth, as from under a cornice

den·tine (den'tēn) *n.* [< L. *dens:* see DENTAL] the hard, calcareous tissue forming the body of a tooth, under the enamel

den·tist (den'tist) *n.* [< Fr. < ML. < L. *dens:* see DENTAL] one whose profession is the care of teeth and surrounding tissues, the replacement of missing teeth with artificial ones, etc.

den·tist·ry (-rē) *n.* the profession or work of a dentist

den·ti·tion (den tish'ən) *n.* [< L. < *dentire*, to cut teeth < *dens:* see DENTAL] 1. the teething process 2. the number and kind of teeth and their arrangement

den·ture (den'chər) *n.* [Fr. < L. *dens:* see DENTAL] a fitting for the mouth, with artificial teeth

de·nu·cle·ar·ize (dē nyoo'klē ə rīz) *vt.* **-ized'**, **-iz'ing** to prohibit the possession of nuclear weapons in —**de·nu'·cle·ar·i·za'tion** *n.*

de·nu·date (di nyoo'dāt) **-dat·ed**, **-dat·ing** [< L. pp. of *denudare* < *de-*, off + *nudare*, to strip] *same as* DENUDE —**de·nu·da·tion** (dē'nyoo dā'shən) *n.*

de·nude (di nyood') *vt.* **-nud'ed**, **-nud'ing** [see prec.] 1. to make bare; strip 2. to destroy all life in (an area) 3. to lay bare as by erosion

de·nu·mer·a·ble (di nyoo'mər ə b'l) *adj.* *Math* countable: said of a set whose elements can be put into one-to-one correspondence with the positive integers

de·nun·ci·ate (di nun'sē āt') *vt.* **-at'ed**, **-at'ing** *same as* DENOUNCE —**de·nun'ci·a'tor** *n.*

de·nun·ci·a·tion (di nun'sē ā'shən) *n.* [< L. pp. of *denuntiare* < *de-*, intens. + *nuntiare*, ANNOUNCE] the act of denouncing —**de·nun'ci·a·to·ry** (-ə tər ē), **de·nun'ci·a'tive** (-āt'iv) *adj.*

de·ny (di nī') *vt.* **-nied'**, **-ny'ing** [< OFr. < L. < *de-*, intens. + *negare*, to deny] 1. to declare (a statement) untrue 2. to refuse to accept as true or right 3. to refuse to acknowledge as one's own; repudiate 4. to refuse access to 5. to refuse to give 6. to refuse the request of —**deny oneself** to do without desired things

deoch an do·ris (dokh'ən do'ris) [Gael., lit., drink at the door] a stirrup cup; any drink taken at parting

de·o·dar (dē'ə där') *n.* [Hindi < Sans. *dēvadāru*, lit., tree of the gods] 1. a Himalayan cedar with fragrant, light-red wood 2. the wood

de·o·dor·ant (dē ō'dər ənt) *adj.* that prevents, destroys, or masks undesired odours —*n.* any deodorant preparation, esp. one used on the body

de·o·dor·ize (dē ō'də rīz') *vt.* **-ized'**, **-iz'ing** to remove or mask the odour of or in —**de·o'dor·i·za'tion** *n.* —**de·o'·dor·iz'er** *n.*

de·on·tic (dē on'tik) *adj.* [< Gr. *deon*, duty] of duty, esp. the branch of logic that deals with concepts of moral obligation [*deontic* logic]

de·ox·i·dize (dē ok'sə dīz') *vt.* **-dized'**, **-diz'ing** to remove oxygen, esp. chemically combined oxygen, from —**de·ox'·i·diz'er** *n.*

de·ox·y·gen·ate (-jə nāt') *vt.* **-at'ed**, **-at'ing** to remove oxygen, esp. free oxygen, from (water, air, etc.)

de·ox·y·ri·bo·nu·cle·ic acid (dē ok'si rī'bō nyoo klē'ik) an essential component of all living matter and a basic material in the chromosomes of the cell nucleus: it contains the genetic code and transmits the hereditary pattern

dep. 1. department 2. deposed 3. deposit 4. deputy

de·part (di pärt') *vi.* [< OFr. *departir* < L. < *dis-*, apart + *partire*, to divide < *pars*, a PART] 1. to go away (*from*); leave 2. to set out; start 3. to die 4. to turn aside (*from* something) [to *depart* from custom] —*vt.* to leave: now only in **depart this life**, to die

de·part·ed (-id) *adj.* 1. gone away; past 2. dead —**the departed** the dead person or persons

de·part·ment (-mənt) *n.* [see DEPART] 1. a separate part or division, as of a government, business, or school 2. a field of knowledge or activity 3. an administrative district in France or in certain Latin American countries —**de·part·men·tal** (di pärt'men't'l) *adj.* —**de·part'men'·tal·ly** *adv.*

de·part·men·tal·ize (di pärt'men'tə līz') *vt.* **-ized'**, **-iz'ing** to organize into departments

department store a retail store for the sale of many kinds of goods arranged in departments: also **departmental store**

de·par·ture (di pär'chər) *n.* 1. a departing, or going away 2. a starting out, as on a journey or new course of action 3. a deviation or turning aside (*from* something) 4. [Archaic] death

de·pend (di pend') *vi.* [< OFr. < L. < *de-*, down + *pendere*, to hang] 1. to be influenced or determined by something else; be contingent (*on*) 2. to be sure of; rely (*on*) 3. to rely (*on*) for support or aid 4. [Archaic] to hang down

de·pend·a·ble (di pen'də b'l) *adj.* that can be depended on; reliable —**de·pend'a·ble·ness**, —**de·pend'a·bil'i·ty** *n.* —**de·pend'a·bly** *adv.*

de·pend·ant (-dənt) *n.* a person who depends on someone else for support, etc.: also sp. **de·pend'ent**

de·pend·ence (-dəns) *n.* 1. the condition or fact of being dependent; specif., *a*) a being influenced or determined by something else *b*) reliance (*on* another) for support or aid *c*) subordination 2. reliance; trust Also U.S. sp. **de·pend'ance**

de·pend·en·cy (-dən sē) *n.,* *pl.* **-cies** 1. *same as* DEPENDENCE 2. something dependent or subordinate 3. a land or territory geographically distinct from the country governing it

de·pend·ent (-dənt) *adj.* 1. hanging down 2. influenced or determined by something else 3. relying (*on* another) for support or aid 4. subordinate

dependent clause *same as* SUBORDINATE CLAUSE

de·per·son·al·ize (dē pur's'n ə līz') *vt.* **-ized'**, **-iz'ing** 1. to deprive of individuality; treat impersonally 2. to cause to lose one's sense of personal identity —**de·per'son·al·i·za'·tion** *n.*

de·pict (di pikt') *vt.* [< L. pp. of *depingere* < *de-*, intens. + *pingere*, to paint] 1. to represent in a drawing, sculpture, etc. 2. to picture in words; describe —**de·pic'tion** *n.* —**de·pic'tive** *adj.* —**de·pic'tor** *n.*

dep·i·late (dep'ə lāt') *vt.* **-lat'ed**, **-lat'ing** [< L. pp. of *depilare* < *de-*, from + *pilus*, hair] to remove hair from —**dep'i·la'tion** *n.*

de·pil·a·to·ry (di pil'ə tər ē) *adj.* serving to remove unwanted hair —*n.,* *pl.* **-ries** a depilatory agent, as in cream form

de·plane (dē plān') *vi.* **-planed'**, **-plan'ing** to get out of an aircraft after it lands

de·plete (di plēt') *vt.* **-plet'ed**, **-plet'ing** [< L. pp. of *deplere* < *de-*, from + *plere*, to fill] 1. to make less by gradually using up (funds, energy, etc.) 2. to empty wholly or partly —**de·ple'tion** *n.*

de·plor·a·ble (di plôr'ə b'l) *adj.* 1. that can or should be deplored; lamentable 2. very bad; wretched —**de·plor'a·bly** *adv.*

de·plore (di plôr') *vt.* **-plored'**, **-plor'ing** [< Fr. < L. < *de-*, intens. + *plorare*, to weep] 1. to be regretful or sorry about; lament 2. to regard as unfortunate or wretched

de·ploy (dē ploi') *vt.,* *vi.* [< Fr. < OFr. *desployer* < L. *displicare*, to scatter, unfold: see DISPLAY] [Chiefly *Mil.*] 1. to spread out (troops, etc.) so as to form a wider front 2. to station or move in accordance with a plan —**de·ploy'ment** *n.*

de·po·lar·ize (dē pō'lə rīz') *vt.* **-ized'**, **-iz'ing** to destroy or counteract the polarization of —**de·po'lar·i·za'tion** *n.*

de·pon·ent (di pō'nənt) *adj.* [< L. prp. of *deponere*, to set down: see DEPOSIT] *L. & Gr. Gram.* denoting a verb with a passive voice form and an active meaning —*n.* 1. a deponent verb 2. *Law* a person who gives written testimony under oath

de·pop·u·late (dē pop'yə lāt') *vt.* **-lat'ed**, **-lat'ing** to reduce the population of, esp. by violence, pestilence, etc. —**de·pop'u·la'tion** *n.* —**de·pop'u·la'tor** *n.*

de·port (di pôrt') *vt.* [< OFr. < L. < *de-*, from + *portare*, to carry] 1. to behave (oneself) in a specified way 2. to carry or send away; specif., to expel (an alien) from a country by official order

de·por·ta·tion (dē'pôr tā'shən) *n.* expulsion, as of an undesirable alien, from a country

de·por·tee (dē'pôr tē') *n.* a deported person, or one sentenced to deportation

de·port·ment (di pôrt'mənt) *n.* the manner of conducting oneself; behaviour

de·pose (di pōz') *vt.* **-posed'**, **-pos'ing** [< OFr. < *de-* (L. *de*), from + *poser* < L. *pausare*, to cease: confused with L. *deponere*: see ff.] 1. to remove from office or a position of power, esp. from a throne; oust 2. *Law* to state under oath but out of court —*vi.* to bear witness —**de·pos'al** *n.*

de·pos·it (di poz'it) *vt.* [< L. *depositus*, pp. of *deponere*, to put down < *de-*, down + *ponere*, to put] 1. to place or entrust, as for safekeeping [to *deposit* money in a bank] 2. to give as a pledge or partial payment 3. to put or set down 4. to leave (sediment, etc.) lying —*n.* 1. something placed for safekeeping; specif., money put in a bank, esp. to earn interest 2. a pledge or part payment 3. a depository 4. something left lying, as sand or clay deposited by the action of wind, water, etc. —**on deposit** placed or entrusted for safekeeping

deposit account an account in a bank, post office, etc. which pays interest on depositors' savings

de·pos·i·tar·y (di poz'ə tər ē) *n., pl.* **-tar·ies** 1. a person, firm, etc. entrusted with something for safekeeping; trustee 2. a storehouse; depository

dep·o·si·tion (dep'ə zish'ən) *n.* 1. a deposing or being deposed, as from office 2. a testifying 3. a depositing or being deposited 4. something deposited 5. *Law* the written testimony of a witness, made under oath, to be used in court

de·pos·i·tor (di poz'ə tər) *n.* a person who deposits something, esp. money in a bank

de·pos·i·to·ry (di poz'ə tər ē) *n., pl.* **-ries** 1. a place where things are put for safekeeping; storehouse 2. a trustee; depositary

de·pot (dep'ō) *n.* [Fr. *dépôt,* a storehouse < L. *depositum:* see DEPOSIT] 1. a storehouse; warehouse 2. a bus station 3. *Mil.* a) a storage place for supplies b) a centre for assembling recruits or combat replacements

de·prave (di prāv') *vt.* **-praved', -prav'ing** [< OFr. < L. < *de-,* intens. + *pravus,* crooked] to make morally bad; corrupt **—dep·ra·va·tion** (dep'rə vā'shən) *n.* **—de·praved'** *adj.* **—de·prav'er** *n.*

de·prav·i·ty (di prav'ə tē) *n.* 1. a depraved condition; corruption; wickedness 2. *pl.* **-ties** a depraved act or practice

dep·re·cate (dep'rə kāt') *vt.* **-cat'ed, -cat'ing** [< L. pp. of *deprecari* < *de-,* off + *precari,* PRAY] 1. to feel and express disapproval of 2. to depreciate; belittle **—dep're·cat'ing·ly** *adv.* **—dep're·ca'tion** *n.* **—dep're·ca'tor** *n.*

dep·re·ca·to·ry (-kə tər ē) *adj.* deprecating; disapproving, belittling, etc. Also **dep're·ca'tive** (-kāt'iv) **—dep're·ca·to·ri·ly** *adv.*

de·pre·ci·ate (di prē'shē āt') *vt.* **-at'ed, -at'ing** [< L. pp. of *depretiare* < *de-,* from + *pretiare,* to value < *pretium,* a PRICE] 1. to reduce in value or price 2. to belittle; disparage **—vi.** to drop in value or price **—de·pre'ci·a·to·ry** (-shə tər ē) *adj.*

de·pre·ci·a·tion (di prē'shē ā'shən) *n.* 1. a decrease in value of property through wear, deterioration, etc. 2. a decrease in the purchasing power of money 3. a belittling; disparagement

dep·re·da·tion (dep'rə dā'shən) *n.* [< LL. pp. of *depraedari* < L. *de-,* intens. + *praedari,* to plunder < *praeda,* PREY] a robbing, plundering, or laying waste

de·press (di pres') *vt.* [< OFr. < L. *depressus,* pp. of *deprimere* < *de-,* down + *premere,* to PRESS¹] 1. to press down; lower 2. to lower in spirits; make gloomy; sadden 3. to decrease the activity of; weaken 4. to lower in value, price, or amount **—de·press'ing** *adj.* **—de·press'ing·ly** *adv.*

de·pres·sant (-ənt) *adj.* lowering the rate of muscular or nervous activity **—n.** a depressant medicine, drug, etc.; sedative

de·pressed (di prest') *adj.* 1. pressed down 2. lowered in position, intensity, amount, etc. 3. flattened or hollowed, as if pressed down 4. gloomy; dejected; sad 5. characterized by widespread unemployment, poverty, etc. [a depressed area] 6. *Bot.* flattened vertically, as if from downward pressure

de·pres·sion (di presh'ən) *n.* 1. a depressing or being depressed 2. a depressed part or place; hollow or low place 3. low spirits; dejection 4. a decrease in force, activity, amount, etc. 5. a period marked by slackening business activity, much unemployment, falling prices and wages, etc., esp. [D-] the period beginning in 1929 with the Wall Street crash 6. *Psychol.* an emotional condition characterized by feelings of hopelessness, inadequacy, etc.

de·pres·sive (di pres'iv) *adj.* 1. tending to depress 2. characterized by psychological depression **—de·pres'sive·ly** *adv.* **—de·pres'sive·ness** *n.*

de·pres·sor (-ər) *n.* 1. one that depresses 2. a muscle that draws down a part of the body 3. an instrument for pressing a protruding part out of the way, as during a medical examination

de·pres·sur·ize (dē presh'ər īz') *vt.* to cause a drop in pressure, esp. in an aircraft cabin

dep·ri·va·tion (dep'rə vā'shən) *n.* a depriving or being deprived

de·prive (di prīv') *vt.* **-prived', -priv'ing** [< ML. < L. *de-,* intens. + *privare,* to separate] 1. to take something away from forcibly; dispossess 2. to keep from having, using, or enjoying [deprived of his rights]

dept. department

depth (depth) *n.* [ME. *depthe:* see DEEP & -TH¹] 1. a) the distance from the top downwards, or from front to back b) perspective, as in a painting 2. the condition of being deep; deepness; specif., a) intensity, as of colours, emotion, etc. b) profundity of thought c) lowness of pitch 3. the middle part [the *depth* of winter] 4. [usually pl.] the inmost part [the *depths* of a wood] 5. [usually pl.] the deep or deepest part, as of the sea 6. [usually pl.] the extreme degree, as of despair **—in depth** in a thorough way **—out of** (or **beyond**)

one's depth 1. in water too deep for one 2. past one's ability or understanding

depth charge (or **bomb**) an explosive charge that explodes under water: used esp. against submarines

depth perception ability to perceive perspective

depth psychology any system of psychology, as psychoanalysis, dealing with the unconscious

dep·u·ta·tion (dep'yoo tā'shən) *n.* 1. a deputing or being deputed 2. a group of persons, or one person, appointed to represent others; delegation

de·pute¹ (di pyoot') *vt.* **-put'ed, -put'ing** [< OFr. < L. < *de-,* from + *putare,* to consider] 1. to give (authority, etc.) to someone else as deputy 2. to appoint as one's substitute, agent, etc.

de·pute² (dep'yoot) *n.* [< DEPUTY] [Scot.] a deputy

dep·u·tize (dep'yə tīz') *vt.* **-tized', -tiz'ing** to appoint as deputy **—vi.** to act as deputy

dep·u·ty (-tē) *n., pl.* **-ties** [see DEPUTE¹] 1. a person appointed to substitute for, or to assist, another 2. a member of a legislature called a Chamber of Deputies **—adj.** acting as deputy

deputy lieutenant the person who acts as the deputy of the Lord Lieutenant of a county

der. 1. derivation 2. derivative 3. derived

de·rac·i·nate (di ras'ə nāt') *vt.* **-nat'ed, -nat'ing** [< Fr. < *dé-* (L. *dis-),* from + *racine,* a root < < LL. *radix*] 1. to pull up by or as by the roots; uproot; eradicate **—de·rac'i·na'·tion** *n.*

de·rail (di rāl') *vi., vt.* to go or cause to go off the rails: said of a train, etc. **—de·rail'ment** *n.*

de·range (di rānj') *vt.* **-ranged', -rang'ing** [< Fr. < *des-* (L. *dis-),* apart + *rengier:* see RANGE] 1. to upset the order or working of 2. to make insane **—de·ranged'** *adj.* **—de·range'ment** *n.*

Der·by (där'bē) *n., pl.* **-bies** 1. an annual race for three-year-old horses at Epsom Downs, begun by the Earl of Derby in 1780 2. any similar horse race 3. any local sporting event, esp. a game between two local football teams

der·e·lict (der'ə likt') *adj.* [< L. pp. of *derelinquere* < *de-,* intens. + *relinquere:* see RELINQUISH] 1. deserted by the owner; abandoned 2. [U.S.] neglectful of duty; negligent **—n.** 1. a property abandoned by the owner; esp., a ship deserted at sea 2. a destitute person with no home or job

der·e·lic·tion (der'ə lik'shən) *n.* 1. an abandoning or being abandoned 2. a neglect of, or failure in, duty; a being remiss

de·re·strict (dē'ri strikt') *vt.* to remove a restriction from, esp. the speed restriction on motor vehicles in built-up areas **—de·re·strict'ed** *adj.* **—de·re·stric'tion** *n.*

de·ride (di rīd') *vt.* **-rid'ed, -rid'ing** [< L. < *de-,* down + *ridere,* to laugh] to laugh at in contempt or scorn; ridicule **—de·rid'er** *n.* **—de·rid'ing·ly** *adv.*

‡de ri·gueur (də rē gёr') [Fr.] 1. required by etiquette; according to good form 2. fashionable

de·ri·sion (di rizh'ən) *n.* a deriding or being derided; contempt or ridicule

de·ri·sive (di rī'siv) *adj.* showing or provoking derision: also **de·ri'so·ry** (-sər ē) **—de·ri'sive·ly** *adv.* **—de·ri'·sive·ness** *n.*

deriv. 1. derivation 2. derivative 3. derived

der·i·va·tion (der'ə vā'shən) *n.* 1. a deriving or being derived 2. something derived 3. a) the source or origin of something b) the etymology of a word 4. the forming of words from bases, as by adding affixes **—der'i·va'tion·al** *adj.*

de·riv·a·tive (də riv'ə tiv) *adj.* 1. derived 2. not original **—n.** 1. something derived 2. a word formed by derivation 3. *Chem.* a substance derived from another by chemical change 4. *Math.* the instantaneous rate of change of one variable with respect to another **—de·riv·a·tive·ly** *adv.*

de·rive (di rīv') *vt.* **-rived', -riv'ing** [< OFr. < L. *derivare,* to divert a stream < *de-,* from + *rivus,* a stream] 1. to get or receive (from a source) 2. to deduce or infer 3. to trace from or to a source; show the derivation of 4. *Chem.* to obtain (a compound) from another compound by replacing one element with one or more other elements **—vi.** to come (from a source) **—de·riv'a·ble** *adj.*

-derm (durm) [see ff.] *a suffix meaning skin or covering* [endoderm]

der·ma (dur'mə) *n.* [ModL. < Gr. *derma,* the skin] same as DERMIS **—der'mal, der'mic** *adj.*

der·ma·ti·tis (dur'mə tīt'is) *n.* [ff. + -ITIS] inflammation of the skin

der·ma·to- [Gr. < *derma* (gen. *dermatos*)] *a combining form meaning skin:* also **dermat-, dermo-**

der·ma·tol·o·gy (dur'mə tol'ə jē) *n.* [DERMATO- + -LOGY] the branch of medicine dealing with the skin and its diseases **—der'ma·to·log'i·cal** (-tə loj'ə k'l) *adj.* **—der'·ma·tol'o·gist** *n.*

der·mis (dur'mis) *n.* [ModL. < LL. *epidermis,* EPIDERMIS] the layer of skin just below the epidermis

der·o·gate (der'ə gāt') *vt., vi.* **-gat'ed, -gat'ing** [< L. pp. of *derogare* < *de-,* from + *rogare,* to ask] 1. [Archaic] to take away (*from*) so as to impair 2. [Rare] to disparage —**der′o·ga′tion** *n.*

de·rog·a·to·ry (di rog′ə tər ē) *adj.* 1. tending to lessen or impair 2. disparaging; belittling Also **de·rog′a·tive** —**de·rog′a·to·ri·ly** *adv.*

der·rick (der′ik) *n.* [orig., a gallows, after T. *Derrick*, 17th-c. London hangman] 1. a large apparatus with tackle and beams, for lifting and moving heavy objects 2. a tall, tapering framework, as over an oil well, to support drilling machinery, etc.

der·ri·ère (der′ē er′) *n.* [Fr., back part < LL. < L. *de*, from + *retro*, back] the buttocks

der·ring-do (der′iŋ dōō′) *n.* [ME. *derrynge do*, daring to do] daring action; reckless courage

der·rin·ger (der′in jər) *n.* [after H. *Deringer*, 19th-c. U.S. gunsmith] a small, short-barrelled pistol of large calibre

DERRICK (for oil well)

der·ry (der′ē) *n.* [< ? song refrain] [Aust.] a dislike or prejudice

derv (durv) *n.* [< *d(iesel) e(ngine) r(oad) v(ehicle)*] diesel oil, esp. when used for road transport

der·vish (dur′vish) *n.* [Turk. < Per. *darvêsh*, beggar] a member of any of various Moslem orders dedicated to poverty and chastity: some dervishes practise whirling, howling, etc. as religious acts

de·sal·i·na·tion (dē sal′ə nā′shən) *n.* [DE- + SALIN(E) + -ATION] the removal of salt, esp. from sea water to make it drinkable: also **de·sal′i·ni·za′tion** —**de·sal′i·nate′** *vt.* -nat′ed, -nat′ing

desc. descendant

des·cant (des′kant; *for vi., also* des kant′) *n.* [< Anglo-Fr. < L. *dis-*, apart + *cantus*, song] 1. *Music* a) singing in which there is a fixed melody and a subordinate melody added above b) this added melody 2. a comment; discourse —*vi.* 1. to discourse (*on* or *upon*) 2. to sing or play a descant 3. to sing —*adj.* of the highest member of a family of instruments [*descant* recorder]

de·scend (di send′) *vi.* [< OFr. < L. < *de-*, down + *scandere*, to climb] 1. to move from a higher to a lower place; come or go down 2. to pass from an earlier to a later time, from general to particular, etc. 3. to slope downwards 4. to come down (*from* a source) [he is *descended* from pioneers] 5. to pass by inheritance or heredity 6. to stoop (*to* some act) 7. to make a sudden visit or attack (*on* or *upon*) 8. *Astron.* to move towards the horizon *Music* to move down the scale —*vt.* to move down, down along, or through —**de·scend′i·ble** *adj.*

de·scend·ant (-ənt) 1. one who is an offspring, however remote, of a certain ancestor, family, group, etc. 2. something derived from an earlier form

de·scend·ent (-ənt) *adj.* descending

de·scend·er (-ər) *n.* 1. a person or thing that descends 2. *Typography* a) the part of a letter, such as *g* or *y*, that extends below the line b)) such a letter

de·scent (di sent′) *n.* 1. a descending; coming or going down 2. lineage; ancestry 3. one generation (in a specified lineage) 4. a downward slope 5. a way down 6. a sudden raid or attack (*on* or *upon*) 7. a decline; fall 8. a stooping (*to* an act) 9. *Law* transference (of property) to heirs

de·school (dē′skōōl′, dē′skool′) *vt.* to remove traditional methods and places of teaching and learning, as schools, etc., from [to *deschool* society]

de·scribe (di skrīb′) *vt.* -scribed′, -scrib′ing [< OFr. < L. < *de-*, from + *scribere*, to write] 1. to tell or write about 2. to picture in words 3. to trace the outline of —**de·scrib′a·ble** *adj.*

de·scrip·tion (di skrip′shən) *n.* 1. the act, process, or technique of describing 2. a statement or passage that describes 3. sort or variety [books of every *description*] —**answers** (or **fits**) **the description** corresponds to a given description

de·scrip·tive (-tiv) *adj.* of or characterized by description —**de·scrip′tive·ly** *adv.* —**de·scrip′tive·ness** *n.*

de·scry (di skrī′) *vt.* -scried′, -scry′ing [< OFr. *descrier*, to proclaim < *des-*, from + *crier*: see CRY] 1. to catch sight of (distant or obscure objects) 2. to look for and discover; detect

des·e·crate (des′ə krāt′) *vt.* -crat′ed, -crat′ing [DE- + (CON)SECRATE] to violate the sacredness of; profane —**des′e·crat′er, des′e·cra′tor** *n.* —**des′e·cra′tion** *n.*

de·seg·re·gate (dē seg′rə gāt′) *vt., vi.* -gat′ed, -gat′ing to abolish racial segregation in (schools, etc.) —**de·seg′re·ga′tion** *n.*

de·sen·si·tize (dē sen′sə tīz′) *vt.* -tized′, -tiz′ing to make insensitive or less sensitive [desensitized to an allergen] —**de·sen′si·ti·za′tion** *n.* —**de·sen′si·tiz′er** *n.*

de·sert¹ (di zurt′) *vt.* [< Fr. < LL. *desertare* < L. pp. of

deserere < *de-*, from + *serere*, to join] 1. to forsake (someone or something that one ought not to leave); abandon 2. to leave (one's post, etc.) without permission 3. to fail (someone) when most needed —*vi.* to leave one's post, etc. without permission and with no intent to return or, in war, to avoid hazardous duty —**de·sert′er** *n.*

des·ert² (dez′ərt) *n.* [< OFr. < LL. *desertum*, a desert < L. pp. of *deserere*: see prec.] 1. an uncultivated region without inhabitants; wilderness 2. a dry, sandy region with little plant life 3. any place considered to lack certain qualities [a cultural *desert*] —*adj.* 1. of a desert 2. wild and uninhabited

de·sert³ (di zurt′) *n.* [< OFr. < *deservir*, DESERVE] 1. the fact of deserving reward or punishment 2. [*often pl.*] deserved reward or punishment

desert boot a suede, ankle-length boot

de·ser·tion (di zur′shən) *n.* a deserting or being deserted

desert rat 1. a North African jerboa 2. a soldier in World War II who served in an armoured division in North Africa

de·serve (di zurv′) *vt.* -served′, -serv′ing [< OFr. *deservir* < L. < *de-*, intens. + *servire*, to SERVE] to be worthy of (reward, punishment, etc.); merit —*vi.* to be worthy

de·served (-zurvd′) *adj.* rightfully earned or merited; just —**de·serv′ed·ly** (-zur′vid lē) *adv.*

de·serv·ing (-zur′viŋ) *adj.* having merit; worthy (*of* help, reward, etc.) —**de·serv′ing·ly** *adv.*

dés·ha·bil·lé (dāz′a bē′ā) *n.* same as DISHABILLE

des·ic·cant (des′i kant) *adj.* [see ff.] drying —*n.* a substance used as a drying agent

des·ic·cate (-kāt) *vt.* -cat′ed, -cat′ing [< L. pp. of *desiccare* < *de-*, intens. + *siccare* < *siccus*, dry] 1. to dry completely 2. to preserve (food) by drying —*vi.* to become completely dry —**des′ic·ca′tion** *n.* —**des′ic·ca′tor** *n.*

de·sid·er·ate (di sid′ə rāt′) *vt.* -at′ed, -at′ing [< L. pp. of *desiderare*: see DESIRE] to want; need —**de·sid′er·a′tion** *n.* —**de·sid′er·a′tive** *adj.*

de·sid·er·a·tum (di sid′ə rāt′əm, -zid′-; -rät′-) *n., pl.* -ta (-ə) [L., neut. pp. of *desiderare*: see DESIRE] something needed and wanted

de·sign (di zīn′) *vt.* [< L. < *de-*, out + *signare* < *signum*, a mark] 1. to make preliminary sketches of; plan 2. to form (plans, etc.) in the mind; contrive 3. to plan and work out (something) creatively; devise 4. to plan to do; intend 5. to intend for some purpose —*vi.* to make original plans, patterns, etc. —*n.* 1. a plan; scheme; project 2. purpose; intention; aim 3. [*pl.*] a secret, usually dishonest or selfish, scheme (often with *on* or *upon*) 4. a plan or sketch to work from; pattern 5. the art of making designs or patterns 6. the arrangement of parts, form, colour, etc. so as to produce an artistic unit 7. a finished artistic work or decoration —**by design** purposely

des·ig·nate (dez′ig nāt′; *for adj., also* -nit) *adj.* [see prec.] named for an office, etc. but not yet in possession of it —*vt.* -nat′ed, -nat′ing 1. to point out; indicate; specify 2. to refer to by a distinguishing name, title, etc.; name 3. to name for an office or duty; appoint —**des′ig·na′tive** *adj.* —**des′ig·na′tor** *n.*

des·ig·na·tion (dez′ig nā′shən) *n.* 1. a pointing out or marking out 2. appointment to an office, post, etc. 3. a distinguishing name, title, etc.

de·sign·ed·ly (di zīn′id lē) *adv.* purposely

de·sign·er (di zī′nər) *n.* a person who designs, or makes original sketches, patterns, etc.

de·sign·ing (-niŋ) *adj.* 1. that designs or makes plans, patterns, etc. 2. scheming; crafty —*n.* the art or work of creating designs, patterns, etc. —**de·sign′ing·ly** *adv.*

de·sir·a·ble (di zīr′ə b'l) *adj.* worth wanting or having; pleasing, excellent, etc. —**de·sir′a·bil′i·ty, de·sir′a·ble·ness** *n.* —**de·sir′a·bly** *adv.*

de·sire (di zīr′) *vt.* -sired′, -sir′ing [< OFr. < L. *desiderare* < *de-*, from + *sidus* (gen. *sideris*), a star] to wish or long for; crave 2. to ask for; request 3. to want sexually —*vi.* to have a desire —*n.* 1. a strong wish or craving 2. sexual appetite 3. a request 4. anything desired

de·sir·ous (di zīr′əs) *adj.* desiring; having or characterized by desire

de·sist (di zist′, -sist′) *vi.* [< OFr. < L. < *de-*, from + *sistere*, to cause to stand < *stare*, to stand] to cease (*from* an action); stop —**de·sis′tance** *n.*

desk (desk) *n.* [ML. *desca*, a table, ult. < L. *discus*, DISCUS] 1. a kind of table with drawers and with a flat or sloping top for writing, etc. 2. a musician's stand in an orchestra 3. a table or counter at which public services are carried out [information *desk*, registration *desk*] 4. an editorial section of a newspaper [the city *desk*]

desk-bound (-bound′) *adj.* of or designating a job, etc., performed while sitting at a desk

des·o·late (des′ə lit; *for v.* -lāt′) *adj.* [< L. pp. of *desolare* < *de-*, intens. + *solare*, to make lonely < *solus*, alone] 1. lonely; solitary 2. uninhabited; deserted 3. made uninhabitable; laid waste 4. forlorn; wretched —*vt.* -lat′ed, -lat′ing 1. to rid of inhabitants 2. to lay waste; devastate

3. to forsake; abandon **4.** to make forlorn, wretched, etc. —**des′o·late·ly** *adv.* —**des′o·late·ness** *n.* —**des′o·la·tor, des′-o·lat′er** *n.*

des·o·la·tion (des′ə lā′shən) *n.* **1.** a making desolate **2.** a desolate condition **3.** lonely grief; misery **4.** loneliness **5.** a desolate place

de·spair (di sper′) *vi.* [< OFr. < L. < *de-*, without + *sperare*, to hope < *spes*, hope] to lose hope; be without hope (usually with *of*) —*n.* **1.** a despairing; loss of hope **2.** a person or thing causing despair

de·spair·ing (-iŋ) *adj.* feeling or showing despair; hopeless —**de·spair′ing·ly** *adv.*

des·patch (di spach′) *vt., n.* var. sp. of DISPATCH

des·per·a·do (des′pə rä′dō, -rä′-) *n.*, pl. **-does, -dos** [OSp. < L. *desperare*: see DESPAIR] a dangerous, reckless criminal; bold outlaw

des·per·ate (des′pər it) *adj.* [< L. pp. of *desperare*: see DESPAIR] **1.** rash or violent because of despair **2.** having a very great desire, need, etc. [*desperate* for affection] **3.** causing despair; extremely dangerous or serious **4.** extreme; drastic [in *desperate* need] —**des′per·ate·ly** *adv.*

des·per·a·tion (des′pə rā′shən) *n.* **1.** the state of being desperate **2.** recklessness caused by despair

des·pi·ca·ble (des′pik ə b′l, di spik′-) *adj.* deserving to be despised; —**des·pi·ca·bly** (des′pik ə blē, di spik′-) *adv.*

de·spise (di spiz′) *vt.* **-spised′, -spis′ing** [< OFr. < L. *despicere* < *de*, down + *specere*, to look at] **1.** to look down on with contempt and scorn **2.** to regard with extreme dislike

de·spite (di spit′) *n.* [< OFr. < L. pp. of *despicere*: see prec.] **1.** malice; spite **2.** [Archaic] contempt; scorn —*prep.* in spite of; notwithstanding —**in despite of** in spite of

de·spoil (di spoil′) *vt.* [< OFr. < L. < *de-*, intens. + *spoliare*, to plunder: see SPOIL] to deprive (*of* something) by force; rob; plunder —**de·spoil′er** *n.* —**de·spoil′ment** *n.*

de·spo·li·a·tion (di spō′lē ā′shən) *n.* a despoiling or being despoiled; pillage

de·spond (di spond′) *vi.* [L. *despondere*, to give up < *de*, from + *spondere*, to promise] to lose courage or hope; become disheartened —*n.* despondency: now chiefly in **slough of despond** —**de·spond′ing·ly** *adv.*

de·spond·en·cy (di spon′dən sē) *n.* [see prec.] loss of courage or hope; dejection: also **de·spond′ence** —**de·spond′ent** (-dənt) *adj.* filled with despondency; dejected —**de·spond′ent·ly** *adv.*

des·pot (des′pot, -pət) *n.* [< OFr. < Gr. *despotēs*, a master] **1.** an absolute ruler; autocrat **2.** anyone in charge who acts like a tyrant

des·pot·ic (de spot′ik) *adj.* of or like a despot; autocratic; tyrannical —**des·pot′i·cal·ly** *adv.*

des·pot·ism (des′pə tiz′m) *n.* **1.** rule by a despot; autocracy **2.** the methods of a despot; tyranny

des·sert (di zɜrt′) *n.* [< OFr. < *desservir*, to clear the table < *des-* (L. *de*), from + *servir* < L. *servire*, to serve] **1.** a sweet course, as of pie, ice cream, etc., served at the end of a meal **2.** uncooked fruit and nuts served after the sweet course

des·sert·spoon (-spσσn′) *n.* a spoon between a teaspoon and tablespoon in size

de·sta·bi·lize (dē stā′bə liz′) *vt.* **-lized′, -liz′ing** to upset the stability of; unbalance

des·ti·na·tion (des′tə nā′shən) *n.* **1.** the end for which something or someone is destined **2.** the place towards which someone or something is going or sent

des·tine (des′tin) *vt.* **-tined, -tin·ing** [< OFr. < L. *destinare*, to secure, fix < *de-*, intens. + base of *stare*, to stand] **1.** to predetermine, as by fate [he seemed *destined* to succeed] **2.** to set apart for a certain purpose; intend —**destined for 1.** bound for **2.** intended for

des·ti·ny (des′tə nē) *n.*, pl. **-ies** [see prec.] **1.** the seemingly inevitable or necessary succession of events **2.** what will necessarily happen to any person or thing; (one's) fate **3.** that which determines events

des·ti·tute (des′tə tyσσt′) *adj.* [< L. pp. of *destituere*, to forsake < *de-*, down + *statuere*, to set] **1.** not having; lacking (with *of*) [*destitute* of trees] **2.** living in complete poverty

des·ti·tu·tion (des′tə tyσσ′shən) *n.* the state of being destitute; esp., abject poverty

des·tri·er (des′trē ər) *n.* [ME < OFr., ult. < L. *dextra*, right hand: because the squire led the knight's horse with his right hand] [Archaic] a war horse

de·stroy (di stroi′) *vt.* [< OFr. < L. < *de-*, down + *struere*, to build] **1.** to tear down; demolish **2.** to spoil completely; ruin **3.** to put an end to **4.** to kill **5.** to neutralize the effect of **6.** to make useless —*vi.* to bring about destruction

de·stroy·er (-ər) *n.* **1.** a person or thing that destroys **2.** a small, fast, heavily armed warship

de·struct (di strukt′) *n.* [back-formation < DESTRUCTION] the deliberate destruction of a malfunctioning missile,

rocket, etc. after its launch —*vi.* to be automatically destroyed

de·struct·i·ble (di struk′tə b′l) *adj.* that can be destroyed —**de·struct′i·bil′i·ty** *n.*

de·struc·tion (di struk′shən) *n.* [< OFr. < L. pp. of *destruere*: see DESTROY] **1.** a destroying or being destroyed **2.** the cause or means of destroying

de·struc·tive (di struk′tiv) *adj.* **1.** tending or likely to cause destruction **2.** causing destruction; destroying **3.** merely negative; not helpful [*destructive* criticism] —**de·struc′tive·ly** *adv.* —**de·struc′tive·ness, de·struc′tiv′i·ty** *n.*

destructive distillation the decomposition of coal, wood, etc. by heat in the absence of air, and the recovery of the volatile products of the decomposition by condensation or other means

de·struc·tor (di struk′tər) *n.* [LL. < *destructus*, pp. of *destruere*, to destroy] an incinerator for rubbish

des·ue·tude (de syσσ′ə tyσσd′) *n.* [< L. < pp. of *desuescere* < *de-*, from + *suescere*, to be accustomed] disuse [laws fallen into *desuetude*]

de·sul·phur·ize (dē sul′fə rīz′) *vt.* **-ized′, -iz′ing** to remove sulphur from: also **de·sul′phur**

des·ul·to·ry (des′′l tər ē) *adj.* [< L. < *desultor*, vaulter < pp. of *desilire* < *de-*, from + *salire* to leap] **1.** passing from one thing to another in an aimless way; disconnected; not methodical **2.** random [a *desultory* observation] —**des′ul·tori·ly** *adv.* —**des′ul·tori·ness** *n.*

de·tach (di tach′) *vt.* [< Fr. < OFr. < *de-*, off + *estachier*, to ATTACH] **1.** to unfasten or separate and remove; disconnect **2.** to send (troops, ships, etc.) on a special mission —**de·tach′a·bil′i·ty** *n.* —**de·tach′a·ble** *adj.*

de·tached (di tacht′) *adj.* **1.** not connected; separate [a *detached* house] **2.** disinterested; impartial; aloof —**de·tach′ed·ly** (-tach′id lē) *adv.* —**de·tach′ed·ness** *n.*

de·tach·ment (di tach′mənt) *n.* **1.** a detaching; separation **2.** *a)* the sending of troops or ships on special service *b)* a unit of troops assigned to some special task **3.** the state of being disinterested, impartial, or aloof

de·tail (dē′tāl) *n.* [< Fr. < dé-(L. *de*), from + *tailler*, to cut] **1.** a dealing with things item by item **2.** a minute account [to go into *detail*] **3.** an item or particular **4.** a small part of a whole structure, design, etc. **5.** *a)* one or more soldiers, sailors, etc. chosen for a particular task *b)* the task itself —*vt.* **1.** to give the particulars of; tell, item by item **2.** to choose for a particular task [*detail* a man for sentry duty] —**in detail** item by item; with particulars —**de′tailed** *adj.*

de·tain (di tān′) *vt.* [< OFr. < L. < *de-*, off + *tenere*, to hold] **1.** to keep in custody; confine **2.** to keep from going on; hold back —**de·tain·ee′** *n.* —**de·tain′er** *n.* —**de·tain′ment** *n.*

de·tect (di tekt′) *vt.* [< L. *detectus*, pp. of *detegere* < *de-*, from + *tegere*, to cover] **1.** to catch or discover, as in a misdeed **2.** to discover (something hidden or not easily noticed) **3.** *Radio* same as DEMODULATE —**de·tect′a·ble, de·tect′i·ble** *adj.*

de·tec·tion (di tek′shən) *n.* **1.** a finding out or being found out **2.** same as DEMODULATION

de·tec·tive (-tiv) *adj.* **1.** of or for detection **2.** of detectives and their work [a *detective* story] —*n.* a person, usually on a police force, whose work is investigating crimes, getting secret information, etc.

de·tec·tor (-tər) *n.* **1.** a person or thing that detects **2.** *Radio* a device used in demodulation

de·tent (di tent′) *n.* [< Fr.] *Mech.* a part that stops or releases a movement

dé·tente (dā tänt′) *n.* [Fr.] a lessening of tension or hostility, esp. between nations

de·ten·tion (di ten′shən) *n.* a detaining or being detained; specif., *a)* a keeping in custody; confinement *b)* an enforced delay

detention centre a place where young persons may be detained for short periods, by a court order

de·ter (di tur′) *vt.* **-terred′, -ter′ring** [< L. < *de-*, from + *terrere*, to frighten] to keep or discourage (a person) from doing something by instilling fear, anxiety, doubt, etc. —**de·ter′ment** *n.*

de·terge (di turj′) *vt.* **-terged′, -terg′ing** [< L. < *de-*, off + *tergere*, to wipe] to cleanse, as a wound —**de·ter′gen·cy, de·ter′gence** *n.*

de·ter·gent (di tur′jənt) *adj.* [see prec.] cleansing —*n.* a cleansing substance that is like soap but is made synthetically and not from fats and lye

de·te·ri·o·rate (di tir′ē ə rāt′) *vt., vi.* **-rat′ed, -rat′ing** [< LL. pp. of *deteriorare* < L. *deterior*, worse] to make or become worse; depreciate —**de·te′ri·o·ra′tion** *n.* —**de·te′ri·o·ra′tive** *adj.*

de·ter·mi·na·cy (di tur′mi nə sē) *n.* **1.** the state or quality of being determinate **2.** the condition of being determined, as in being caused or in having predictable results

de·ter·mi·nant (-nənt) *adj.* determining —*n.* **1.** a thing or factor that determines **2.** *Maths* the sum of the products formed, following certain rules, from a square array of numbers

de·ter·mi·nate (-nit) *adj.* [see DETERMINE] 1. having exact limits; definite; fixed 2. settled; conclusive 3. *Bot.* having a flower at the end of the primary axis and of each secondary axis —**de·ter'mi·nate·ly** *adv.* —**de·ter'-mi·nate·ness** *n.*

de·ter·mi·na·tion (di tur'mə nā'shən) *n.* 1. a determining or being determined 2. a firm intention 3. firmness of purpose

de·ter·mi·na·tive (di tur'mə nə tiv) *adj.* determining —*n.* a thing that determines —**de·ter'mi·na'tive·ly** *adv.* —**de·ter'-mi·na'tive·ness** *n.*

de·ter·mine (di tur'mən) *vt.* **-mined, -min·ing** [< OFr. < L. < *de-*, from + *terminare*, to set bounds < *terminus*, an end] 1. to set limits to; bound; define 2. to settle conclusively; decide 3. to reach a decision about; decide upon 4. to establish or affect the nature, kind, or quality of [genes *determine* heredity] 5. to find out exactly; calculate precisely 6. to give a definite aim to; direct —*vi.* 1. to decide; resolve 2. *Law* to come to an end —**de·ter'-mi·na·ble** *adj.* —**de·ter'min·er** *n.*

de·ter·mined (-mənd) *adj.* 1. having one's mind made up; resolved 2. resolute; unwavering —**de·ter'mined·ly** *adv.* —**de·ter'mined·ness** *n.*

de·ter·min·ism (-mə niz'm) *n.* the doctrine that everything, esp. one's choice of action, is determined by a sequence of causes independent of one's will —**de·ter'min·ist** *n., adj.* —**de·ter'min·is'tic** *adj.*

de·ter·rent (di ter'ənt) *adj.* deterring or tending to deter —*n.* a thing or factor that deters; hindrance —**de·ter'rence** *n.*

de·test (di test') *vt.* [< Fr. < L. *detestari*, to curse by calling the gods to witness < *de-*, down + *testis*, a witness] to dislike intensely; hate; abhor —**de·test'er** *n.*

de·test·a·ble (di tes'tə b'l) *adj.* that is or should be detested; hateful; odious —**de·test'a·bil'i·ty, de·test'a·ble·ness** *n.* —**de·test'a·bly** *adv.*

de·tes·ta·tion (dē'tes tā'shən) *n.* 1. intense dislike or hatred; loathing 2. a detested person or thing

de·throne (dē thrōn') *vt.* **-throned', -thron'ing** to remove from a throne; depose —**de·throne'ment** *n.* —**de·thron'er** *n.*

det·o·nate (det'ən āt') *vi., vt.* **-nat'ed, -nat'ing** [< L. pp. of *detonare* < *de-*, intens. + *tonare*, to thunder] to explode noisily —**det'o·na'tion** *n.*

det·o·na·tor (-āt'ər) *n.* 1. a fuse, percussion cap, etc. for setting off explosives 2. an explosive

de·tour (dē'toor) *n.* [< Fr. < *détourner*, to turn aside < OFr. < *des-* (L. *dis-*) + *tourner*: see TURN] 1. a roundabout way 2. a route used when the regular route is closed to traffic —*vi., vt.* to go or cause to go by way of a detour

de·tox·i·fy (dē tok'sə fī') *vt.* **-fied'-fy'ing** [DE- + TOXI(N) + -FY] to remove a poison or poisonous effect from, esp. that produced by alcohol —**de·tox'i·fi·ca'tion** *n.*

de·tract (di trakt') *vt.* [< L. pp. of *detrahere* < *de-*, from + *trahere*, to draw] to take or draw away —*vi.* to take something desirable away (from) [frowning *detracts* from her beauty] —**de·trac'tion** *n.* —**de·trac'tive** *adj.* —**de·trac'-tor** *n.*

de·train (dē trān') *vi., vt.* to get off or remove from a railway train —**de·train'ment** *n.*

det·ri·ment (det'rə mənt) *n.* [OFr. < L. *detrimentum,* damage < pp. of *deterere* < *de-*, off + *terere*, to rub] 1. damage; injury; harm 2. anything that causes damage or injury —**det'ri·men'tal** (-men't'l) *adj.* —**det'ri·men'tal·ly** *adv.*

de·tri·tus (di trīt'əs) *n.* [L., pp. of *deterere*: see prec.] fragments of rock, etc. produced by disintegration or wearing away; debris

‡de trop (də trō') [Fr.] too much; superfluous

de·tu·mes·cence (dē'tyōō mes'əns) *n.* [< L. *detumescere*, to stop swelling] a subsidence, or lessening of a swelling

deuce[1] (dyōōs) *n.* [< OFr. < L. acc. of *duo*, two] 1. a playing card with two spots 2. the side of a die bearing two spots, or a throw of the dice totalling two 3. *Tennis* a score of 40 each (or five games each) after which one side must get two successive points (or games) to win the game (or set)

deuce[2] (dyōōs) *n., interj.* [< OFr. *dieu* & L. *deus*, God: also infl. by DEUCE[1] in reference to low score at dice] bad luck, the devil, etc.: a mild oath or exclamation of annoyance, surprise, etc.

deu·ced (dyōō'sid; dyōōst) *adj.* 1. devilish; confounded 2. extreme Used in mild oaths —*adv.* extremely; very: also **deu'ced·ly**

‡De·us (dā'oos, dē'əs) [L.] God

‡de·us ex ma·chi·na (eks'mak'i nə) [L., god from a machine] 1. in ancient Greek and Roman plays a deity brought in by stage machinery to intervene in the action 2. any unconvincing character or event brought artificially into the plot of a story, play, etc. to settle an involved situation

3. anyone who unexpectedly intervenes to change the course of events

Deut. Deuteronomy

deu·te·ri·um (dyōō tir'ē əm) *n.* [ModL. < Gr. *deuteros*, second] the hydrogen isotope having an atomic weight of 2.0141 and boiling point of -249.7 C; heavy hydrogen: symbol, D

deu·ter·o-, deu·ter- [< Gr. *deuteros*, second] a combining form meaning second, secondary

deu·ter·on (dyōōt'ər on') *n.* the nucleus of an atom of deuterium

deut·sche mark (doi'chə) *pl.* **mark,** Eng. **marks** *see* MONETARY UNITS, table (West Germany)

de·val·ue (dē val'yōō) *vt.* **-ued, -u·ing** 1. to lessen the value of 2. to lower the exchange value of (a currency) in relation to other currencies Also **de·val'u·ate'** (-yōō wāt') **-at'ed, -at'ing** —**de·val'u·a'tion** *n.*

De·va·na·ga·ri (dā'və nä'gər ē) *n.* [Sans. *devanāgarī*, city writing of the gods] the alphabet in which Sanskrit and most northern Indic languages are written

dev·as·tate (dev'ə stāt') *vt.* **-tat'ed, -tat'ing** [< L. pp. < *de-*, intens. + *vastare*, to make empty < *vastus*, empty] 1. to lay waste; make desolate; ravage; destroy 2. to make helpless; overwhelm —**dev'as·tat'ing·ly** *adv.* —**dev'as·ta'-tion** *n.* —**dev'as·ta'tor** *n.*

de·vel·op (di vel'əp) *vt.* [< Fr. < *dé-* (L. *dis-*), apart + OFr. *voloper*, to wrap] 1. to cause to become gradually fuller, larger, better, stronger, etc. 2. to bring (an idea, plan, etc.) into activity or reality 3. to cause (a bud, etc.) to evolve gradually 4. to make (housing, roads, etc.) more available or extensive 5. *Music* to elaborate (a theme) 6. *Photog.* a) to put (an exposed film, plate, or printing paper) in various chemical solutions in order to make the picture visible b) to make (a picture) thus 7. to show or work out by degrees; make known gradually; reveal 8. to explain more clearly 9. to begin to experience, express, etc. [*develop* tuberculosis, *develop* a wobble] —*vi.* 1. to come into being or activity 2. to become larger, fuller, better, etc.; make progress; grow or evolve 3. to be disclosed —**de·vel'op·a·ble** *adj.*

de·vel·op·er (-ər) *n.* a person or thing that develops; esp., *Photog.* a chemical used to develop film, plates, etc.

developing country a country that is in the process of becoming industrialized

de·vel·op·ment (-mənt) *n.* 1. a developing or being developed 2. a stage in growth, advancement, etc. 3. an event or happening 4. a thing that is developed, as a tract of land —**de·vel'op·men'tal** (-men't'l) *adj.* —**de·vel'-op·men'tal·ly** *adv.*

development area an area in which the government encourages industrial expansion because of unemployment

de·vi·ant (dē'vē ənt) *adj.* [< LL. prp. of *deviare*: see ff.] deviating, esp. from what is considered normal, established, etc. —*n.* a person whose behaviour is deviant —**de'-vi·an·cy, de'vi·ance** *n.*

de·vi·ate (dē'vē āt'; *for adj. & n.* -it) *vi., vt.* **-at'ed, -at'ing** [< LL. pp. of *deviare* < *de-*, from + *via*, road] to turn aside (*from* a course, direction, standard, etc.) —*adj.* same as DEVIANT —*n.* a deviant; esp., one with deviant sexual behaviour —**de'vi·a'tor** *n.*

de·vi·a·tion (dē'vē ā'shən) *n.* 1. a deviating or being deviant, as in behaviour, political ideology, etc. 2. *Statistics* the difference between a particular number in a set and some fixed value, usually the mean —**de'vi·a'tion·al** *adj.* —**de'vi·a'tion·ism** *n.* —**de'vi·a'tion·ist** *adj., n.*

de·vice (di vīs') *n.* [< OFr. *devis*, division < *deviser*: see DEVISE] 1. a thing devised; esp., a underhanded scheme; trick 2. a mechanical invention or contrivance 3. something used for artistic effect [rhetorical *devices*] 4. an ornamental figure or design 5. a design or emblem on a coat of arms 6. any motto or emblem —**leave to one's own devices** to allow to do as one wishes

dev·il (dev''l) *n.* [OE. *deofol* < LL. < Gr. *diabolos*, slanderous (in N.T., devil) < *dia-*, across + *ballein*, to throw] 1. [often D-] *Theol. a)* the chief evil spirit; Satan (with *the*): typically depicted as a man with horns, a tail, and cloven feet *b)* any demon of hell 2. a wicked or malevolent person 3. one who is mischievous, reckless, etc. 4. an unlucky, unhappy person [that poor *devil*] 5. something difficult, annoying etc. 6. any machine for tearing paper, rags, etc. to bits 7. a literary hack 8. a printer's devil 9. *Law* a junior barrister who works without a fee in order to gain experience —*vt.* **-illed, -il·ling** 1. to prepare (food, often finely chopped) with hot seasoning 2. [Chiefly U.S.] to annoy; torment; tease —*vi.* to work for a lawyer, author, etc. without pay or recognition —**a devil of a** an extreme example of a —**between the devil and the deep (blue) sea** between equally unpleasant alternatives —**give the devil his due** to acknowledge the good qualities of even a wicked person —**go to the devil** to fall into bad habits —**play the devil with** 1. to ruin; cause havoc 2. to upset; make worse —**the devil!** [Colloq.] an exclamation of anger, surprise, etc. —**the devil to pay** trouble as a consequence

dev·il·fish (-fish') *n.*, *pl.* **-fish'**, **-fish'es**: see FISH 1. a large ray whose pectoral fins are hornlike when rolled up 2. an octopus

dev·il·ish (dev'əl ish, dev'lish) *adj.* 1. of, like, or characteristic of a devil; diabolical 2. mischievous; reckless 3. [Colloq.] *a)* extremely bad *b)* extreme —*adv.* [Colloq.] extremely; very —**dev'·il·ish·ly** *adv.* —**dev'il·ish·ness** *n.*

DEVILFISH
(to 6 m across)

dev·il-may-care (dev''l mā ker') *adj.* reckless or careless; happy-go-lucky

dev·il·ment (dev'''l mənt) *n.* 1. [Archaic] evil behaviour 2. mischief or mischievous action

dev·il·ry (-rē) *n.*, *pl.* **-ries** 1. witchcraft 2. evil behaviour 3. *same as* DEVILTRY

devil's advocate 1. *R.C.Ch.* an official selected to raise objections in the case of one named for beatification or canonization 2. one who upholds the wrong side, as for argument's sake

devil's coach horse a large rove beetle, common in most parts of Britain

dev·il's-darn·ing-nee·dle (dev''lz där'nin nē'd'l) *n.* same as DRAGONFLY

dev·il's-food cake (dev''lz food') a rich, chocolate cake

dev·il·try (dev''l trē) *n.*, *pl.* **-tries** 1. reckless mischief, fun, etc. 2. *same as* DEVILRY

de·vi·ous (dē'vē əs) *adj.* [< L. *devius* < *de-*, off, from + *via*, road] 1. roundabout; winding 2. going astray 3. not straightforward or frank; deceiving —**de'vi·ous·ly** *adv.* —**de'vi·ous·ness** *n.*

de·vise (di vīz') *vt., vi.* **-vised'**, **-vis'ing** [< OFr. *deviser*, to distribute, direct < L. pp. of *dividere*, to divide] 1. to work out (something) by thinking; plan; invent 2. *Law* to bequeath (real property) by will —*n.* *Law* 1. a gift of real property by will 2. a will, or clause in a will, granting such a gift —**de·vis'a·ble** *adj.* —**de·vis'er** *n.*

de·vi·tal·ize (dē vīt'əl īz') *vt.* **-ized'**, **-iz'ing** to lower in vitality —**de·vi'tal·i·za'tion** *n.*

de·void (di void') *adj.* [< OFr. < *des-* (L. *dis-*), from + *vuidier*: see VOID] completely without; empty (*of*)

de·voir (dev'wär) *n.* [< OFr. < L. *debere*, to owe] 1. duty 2. [*pl.*] acts of due respect or courtesy

de·vol·ute (dēv ə loot') *vt.* 1. to delegate work to others 2. to tranfer authority; to devolve

dev·o·lu·tion (dē'və loo'shən, dev'-) *n.* the act of devolving, specif., a transfer of authority from a central to a regional government

de·volve (di volv') *vt., vi.* **-volved'**, **-volv'ing** [< L. < *de-*, down + *volvere*, to roll] to pass (*on*) to another: said of duties, responsibilities, etc. —**de·volve'ment** *n.*

De·vo·ni·an (di vō'nē ən) *adj.* [after *Devonshire*, county of SW England] *Geol.* designating or of the period after the Silurian in the Paleozoic Era —**the Devonian** the Devonian Period or its rocks: see GEOLOGY. chart

Devonshire split a kind of yeast bun split open and served with clotted cream and jam: also **split**

de·vote (di vōt') *vt.* **-vot'ed**, **-vot'ing** [< L. *devotus*, pp. < *de-*, from + *vovere*, to vow] 1. to set apart for a special use or service; dedicate 2. to give up (oneself or one's time, energy, etc.) to some purpose, activity, or person

de·vot·ed (-id) *adj.* 1. dedicated; consecrated 2. very loving, loyal, or faithful —**de·vot'ed·ly** *adv.* —**de·vot'ed·ness** *n.*

dev·o·tee (dev'ə tē') *n.* a person strongly devoted to someone or to something, as a religion

de·vo·tion (di vō'shən) *n.* 1. a devoting or being devoted 2. piety 3. religious worship 4. [*pl.*] prayers 5. loyalty or deep affection —**de·vo'tion·al·ly** *adv.*

de·vour (di vour') *vt.* [< OFr. < L. < *de-*, intens. + *vorare*, to swallow whole] 1. to eat (up) hungrily or voraciously 2. to consume; destroy; devastate 3. to take in greedily with the eyes, ears, or mind [to *devour* novels] 4. to engross [*devoured* by curiosity] 5. to swallow up; engulf —**de·vour'er** *n.*

de·vout (di vout') *adj.* [< OFr. < L. *devotus*: see DEVOTE] 1. very religious; pious 2. showing reverence 3. earnest; sincere; heartfelt —**de·vout'ly** *adv.* —**de·vout'ness** *n.*

dew (dyoo) *n.* [OE. *deaw*] 1. the moisture that condenses after a warm day and appears during the night in little drops on cool surfaces 2. anything regarded as refreshing, pure, etc., like dew 3. any moisture in small drops —*vt.* to wet as with drops of dew

dew·ber·ry (dyoo'ber'ē) *n.*, *pl.* **-ries** 1. any of various trailing blackberry plants of the rose family 2. the fruit of any of these plants

dew·claw (-klô') *n.* 1. a functionless digit on the foot of some animals, as on the inner side of a dog's leg 2. the claw or hoof on such a digit

dew·drop (-drop') *n.* a drop of dew

Dew·ey Decimal System (dyoo'ē) a library system of classifying books by use of numbers with decimals

dew·lap (-lap') *n.* [< ME. < *dew*, prob. dew + *lappe*, a fold < OE. *læppa*] 1. a loose fold of skin hanging from the throat of cattle and certain other animals 2. a similar loose fold under the chin of an elderly person —**dew'lapped'** (-lapt') *adj.*

DEWLAP

DEW line (dyoo) [D(istant) E(arly) W(arning)] a line of radar stations near the 70th parallel in N America

dew point the temperature at which dew starts to form or vapour to condense into liquid

dew pond an artificial pond usually on the chalk downs in S England, fed by condensation

dew·y (-ē) *adj.* **dew'i·er**, **dew'i·est** 1. wet or damp with dew 2. of dew 3. [Poet.] dewlike; refreshing, etc. —**dew'i·ly** *adv.* —**dew'i·ness** *n.*

dex·ter (dek'stər) *adj.* [L., right] of or on the right-hand side (on a coat of arms, the left of the viewer)

dex·ter·i·ty (dek ster'ə tē) *n.* [< L. < *dexter*: see prec.] 1. skill in using one's hands or body; adroitness 2. skill in using one's mind; cleverness

dex·ter·ous (dek'strəs, -stər əs) *adj.* [see prec.] 1. having or showing skill in the use of the hands or body 2. having or showing mental skill —**dex'ter·ous·ly** *adv.* —**dex'·ter·ous·ness** *n.*

dex·tral (dek'strəl) *adj.* [< L. *dextra*, right-hand side] 1. on the right-hand side; right 2. right-handed —**dex·tral'i·ty** (-stral'ə tē) *n.* —**dex'tral·ly** *adv.*

dex·tran (dek'stran, -strən) *n.* [< L. *dexter*, right] a chainlike polymer of glucose produced by certain strains of bacteria acting on sucrose

dex·trin (dek'strin) *n.* [< Fr. < L. *dexter*, right: it turns the plane of polarized light to the right] a soluble, gummy substance obtained from starch and used as adhesive, sizing, etc.: also **dex'trine** (-strēn, -strən)

dex·tro- (dek'strō) [< L. *dexter*, right] *a combining form meaning* towards or on the right hand side

dex·trorse (dek'strôrs) *adj.* [< L. < *dexter*, right + *versus*, pp. of *vertere*, to turn] *Bot.* twining upwards to the right, as the stem of the hop

dex·trose (dek'strōs) *n.* [ult. < L. *dexter*: cf. DEXTRIN] a glucose, $C_6H_{12}O_6$, found in plants and animals

dex·trous (-strəs) *adj.* *same as* DEXTEROUS

DF, D/F, D.F. *Radio* direction finder

D.F. Defender of the Faith

D.F.C., DFC Distinguished Flying Cross

D.F.M., DFM Distinguished Flying Medal

dg. decigramme(s)

dhal (dä) *n.* [Hindi] 1. an Asian and African shrub of the legume family 2. the split pulse that is the seed of this shrub Also **dal**

‡**dhar·ma** (dʉr'mə, där'-) *n.* [Sans., law] *Hinduism, Buddhism* 1. cosmic order or law, including the natural and moral principles that apply to all beings and things 2. observance of this law in one's life

dhow (dou) *n.* [Ar. *dāwa*] a single-masted ship with a lateen sail, used along the Indian Ocean coasts

di-[1] [Gr. *di-* < *dis*, twice] *a prefix meaning:* 1. twice, double, twofold 2. *Chem.* having two atoms, molecules, radicals, etc. Also **dis-**

di-[2] *same as* DIS-

di-[3] *same as* DIA-

di., dia. diameter

di·a- [< Gr.] *a prefix meaning:* 1. through, across [*diaphragm, diagonal*] 2. apart, between [*diagnose*]

di·a·be·tes (dī'ə bēt'is, -ēz) *n.* [L. < Gr. *diabētēs*, a siphon < *dia-*, through + *bainein*, to go] any of various diseases characterized by an excessive discharge of urine; esp., DIABETES MELLITUS

diabetes mel·li·tus (mə līt'is) [ModL., lit., honey diabetes] a chronic form of diabetes involving an insulin deficiency and characterized by excess of sugar in the blood and urine, hunger, thirst, etc.

di·a·bet·ic (dī'ə bet'ik) *adj.* 1. of or having diabetes 2. prepared specially for diabetics —*n.* a person who has diabetes

di·a·bol·ic (dī'ə bol'ik) *adj.* [< Fr. < LL. < Gr. *diabolos*: see DEVIL] 1. of the Devil or devils 2. very wicked or cruel; fiendish Also **di·a·bol'i·cal** —**di·a·bol'i·cal·ly** *adv.*

di·ab·o·lism (dī ab'ə liz'm) *n.* 1. sorcery or witchcraft 2. belief in or worship of the Devil; diabolical behaviour

di·ab·o·lo (dē ab'ə lō') *n.* [< ? It. *diavolo*, a devil] a toy consisting of a spinning top that is caught on a cord fastened between two sticks that are held in the hand

di·a·chron·ic (dī'ə kron'ik) *adj.* [DIA- + Gr. *chronos*, time] of the study of changes occurring over a period of time, as in language, morals, etc.

di·ac·o·nal (dī ak'ə n'l) *adj.* of a deacon or deacons
di·ac·o·nate (-nit) *n.* 1. the rank, office, or tenure of a deacon 2. a group of deacons
di·a·crit·ic (dī'ə krit'ik) *adj.* [Gr. *diakritikos* < *dia-*, across + *krinein*, to separate] *same as* DIACRITICAL —*n.* *same as* DIACRITICAL MARK
di·a·crit·i·cal (-i k'l) *adj.* 1. serving to distinguish 2. able to distinguish —**di′a·crit′i·cal·ly** *adv.*
diacritical mark a mark, as a macron or a cedilla, added to a letter or symbol to show its pronunciation or to distinguish it in some way
di·a·dem (dī'ə dem', -dəm) *n.* [< OFr. < L. < Gr. *diadēma* < *dia-*, through + *dein*, to bind] 1. a crown 2. a jewelled headband or circlet worn as a crown 3. royal power or authority —*vt.* to crown
di·aer·e·sis (dī er'ə sis) *n.*, *pl.* **-ses′** (-sēz′) [LL. < Gr. *diairesis*, division < *dia-*, apart + *hairein*, to take] a mark (··) placed over the second of two consecutive vowels to show that it is pronounced in a separate syllable: now usually replaced by a hyphen (*reënter*, *re-enter*), or simply omitted (*cooperate*, *naive*) The mark is also used, as in this dictionary, to show a certain pronunciation of a vowel (ä) —**di·ae·ret·ic** (dī'ə ret'ik) *adj.*
diag. 1. diagonal 2. diagram
di·ag·nose (dī'əg nōz', -nōs') *vt.*, *vi.* **-nosed′-nos′ing** to make a diagnosis of (a disease, etc.)
di·ag·no·sis (dī'əg nō'sis) *n.*, *pl.* **-ses** (-sēz) [ModL. < Gr. < *dia-*, between + *gignōskein*, to know] 1. the act or process of deciding the nature of a diseased condition by examination of the symptoms 2. a careful analysis of the facts meant to explain something 3. a decision based on such an examination or analysis —**di′ag·nos′tic** (-nos'tik) *adj.* —**di′ag·nos′ti·cal·ly** *adv.* —**di′ag·nos·ti′cian** (-nos tish'ən) *n.* —**di′ag·nos′tics** *n.pl.*
di·ag·o·nal (dī ag'ə n'l) *adj.* [L. *diagonalis* < Gr. < *dia-*, through + *gōnia*, an angle] 1. extending slantingly between opposite corners, as of a rectangle 2. having a slanting direction or slanting markings, lines, etc. —*n.* 1. *a*) a diagonal line or plane *b*) *same as* VIRGULE 2. any diagonal course, line, part, etc. —**di·ag′o·nal·ly** *adv.*
di·a·gram (dī'ə gram') *n.* [Gr. *diagramma* < *dia-*, across + *graphein*, to write] a drawing, plan, or chart that explains a thing, as by outlining its parts and their relationships, workings, etc. —*vt.* **-grammed′**, **-gram′ming** to make diagram of —**di′a·gram·mat′ic** (-grə mat'ik), **di′a·gram·mat′i·cal** *adj.* —**di′a·gram·mat′i·cal·ly** *adv.*

DIAGONAL (AB)

di·al (dī'əl) *n.* [< ML. *dialis*, daily < L. *dies*, day] 1. a sundial 2. the face of a watch or clock 3. the face of a meter, gauge, etc. on which a pointer indicates an amount, degree, etc. 4. a graduated disc or strip on a radio or television set, for tuning in stations or channels 5. a rotating disc on a telephone, used in making connections automatically 6. [Slang] the face —*vt.*, *vi.* **-alled**, **-al·ling** 1. to measure, regulate, etc. with a dial 2. to call on a telephone by using a dial or other automatic device
dial. 1. dialect(al) 2. dielectric(al)
di·a·lect (dī'ə lekt') *n.* [< L. < Gr. *dialektos*, discourse < *dia-*, between + *legein*, to talk] 1. the sum total of local characteristics of speech 2. any form of speech that differs from a real or imaginary standard speech 3. the form of a spoken language peculiar to a region, community, social group, occupational group, etc. 4. any language as a member of a group or family of languages [English is a West Germanic *dialect*] —*adj.* of or in dialect —**di′a·lec′tal** *adj.* —**di′a·lec′tal·ly** *adv.*
di·a·lec·tic (dī'ə lek'tik) *n.* [< OFr. < L. < Gr. < *dialektikos*: see prec.] 1. [*often pl.*] the art or practice of examining ideas logically, often by question and answer, so as to determine their validity 2. logical argumentation 3. [*often pl.*] a method logic used by Hegel in which opposites are reconciled in a synthesis; it was adapted by Marx to observable social and economic processes —*adj.* *same as* DIALECTICAL
di·a·lec·ti·cal (-ti k'l) *adj.* 1. of or using dialectic or dialectics 2. of or characteristic of a dialect; dialectal —**di′a·lec′ti·cal·ly** *adv.*
dialectical materialism the philosophy stemming from Marx and Engels which applies Hegel's dialectical method to observable social processes
di·a·lec·ti·cian (dī'ə lek tish'ən) *n.* 1. an expert in dialectic; logician 2. a specialist in dialects
dialling tone a low, purring sound indicating to the user of a telephone that the line is open and a number may be dialled
di·a·logue (dī'ə lòg') *n.* [OFr. < L. < Gr. *dialogos* < *dialegein*: see DIALECT] 1. a talking together; conversation 2. open and frank discussion of ideas, as in seeking mutual understanding 3. a written work in the form of a conversation 4. the passages of talk in a play, story, etc. —**di·al·o·gist** (dī al'ə jist, dī'ə log'ist)
di·a·lyse (dī'ə līz') *vt.* **-lysed**, **-lys′ing** to apply dialysis to or separate by dialysis —*vi.* to undergo dialysis —**di′a·lys′-er** *n.*
di·al·y·sis (dī al'ə sis) *n.*, *pl.* **-ses′** (-sēz′) [L. < Gr. < *dia-*, apart + *lyein*, to loose] the separation of crystalloids from colloids in solution by the greater diffusibility of the smaller molecules through a semipermeable membrane —**di·a·lyt·ic** (dī'ə lit'ik) *adj.* —**di′a·lyt′i·cal·ly** *adv.*
diam. diameter
di·a·mag·net·ic (dī'ə mag net'ik) *adj.* having diamagnetism —*n.* a diamagnetic substance, as bismuth: also **di′a·mag′-net**
di·a·mag·net·ism (-mag'nə tiz'm) *n.* the property that certain substances have of being repelled by both poles of a magnet
di·a·man·té (dē'ə mán'tā) *adj.* [Fr.] decorated with rhinestones or other glittering bits of material —*n.* glittering ornamentation
di·am·e·ter (dī am'ət ər) *n.* [< OFr. < ML. < L. < Gr. < *dia-*, through + *metron*, a measure] 1. a straight line passing through the centre of a circle, sphere, etc. from one side to the other 2. the length of such a line
di·a·met·ri·cal (dī'ə met'ri k'l) *adj.* 1. of or along a diameter 2. designating an opposite, a difference, etc. that is wholly so [*diametrical* opposites]: also **di′a·met′ric** —**di′-a·met′ri·cal·ly** *adv.*
di·a·mond (dī'mənd, -ə mənd) *n.* [< OFr. < ML. *diamas* (gen. *diamantis*) < L. < Gr. *adamas*, ADAMANT] 1. a mineral consisting of nearly pure carbon in crystalline form: it is the hardest mineral known and has great brilliance: unflawed stones are cut into precious gems; less perfect forms are used for gramophone-needle tips, cutting tools, abrasives, etc. 2. a gem cut from this mineral 3. *a*) a lozenge-shaped plane figure (♦) *b*) a red mark like this on a suit of playing cards *c*) [*pl.*] this suit *d*) a card of this suit —*adj.* of, like, or set with a diamond —*vt.* to decorate with or as with diamonds
diamond anniversary the sixtieth, or sometimes seventy-fifth, anniversary: also **diamond jubilee**
di·a·mond·back (-bak') *adj.* having diamond-shaped markings on the back —*n.* 1. a large, poisonous rattlesnake native to the S U.S. 2. an edible turtle found in coastal salt marshes on the Atlantic coast of the U.S. in full, **diamondback terrapin** 3. a small, brown and white moth
diamond snake an Australian snake with diamond markings
diamond wedding a sixtieth, or sometimes seventy-fifth, wedding anniversary
di·an·thus (dī an'thəs) *n.* [ModL. < Gr. *dios*, divine + *anthos*, a flower] any of a genus of flowers, including sweet williams, pinks, and carnations
di·a·pa·son (dī'ə pāz''n, -pās'-) *n.* [< L. < Gr. contr. < *dia*, through + *pasōn*, gen. pl. of *pas*, all (notes)] 1. the entire range of a musical instrument or voice 2. one of the principal stops of an organ covering the instrument's complete range 3. a swelling burst of harmony
di·a·per (dī'pər, dī'ə pər) *n.* [MF. *diaspre* < ML. < MGr. *diaspros*, pure white] 1. *a*) orig., cloth or fabric with a pattern of repeated small figures, such as diamonds *b*) such a pattern, as in art 2. [U.S.] a baby's napkin or nappy —*vt.* to give a diaper design to
di·aph·a·nous (dī af'ə nəs) *adj.* [< ML. < Gr. < *dia-*, through + *phainein*, to show] so fine or gauzy in texture as to be transparent or translucent [*diaphanous* cloth] —**di·aph′a·nous·ly** *adv.*
di·a·pho·re·sis (dī'ə fə rē'sis) *n.* [LL. < Gr. < *dia-*, through + *pherein*, to bear] perspiration, esp. when profuse —**di′-a·pho·ret′ic** (-ret'ik) *adj.*
di·a·phragm (dī'ə fram') *n.* [< LL. < Gr. < *dia-*, through + *phragma*, a fence < *phrassein*, enclose] 1. the partition of muscles and tendons between the chest cavity and the abdominal cavity; midriff 2. any separating membrane or device 3. a device to regulate the amount of light entering a camera lens, etc. 4. a thin, vibrating disc or cone that produces electrical signals, as in a microphone, or sound waves, as in a loudspeaker 5. a contraceptive device placed over the mouth of the cervix —**di′a·phrag·mat′ic** (-frag mat'ik) *adj.* —**di′a·phrag·mat′i·cal·ly** *adv.*
di·aph·y·sis (dī af'ə sis) *n.*, *pl.* **-ses′** (-sēz′) [ModL. < Gr. < *dia-*, through + *phyein*, to produce] the shaft of a long bone —**di·a·phys·e·al, di·a·phys·i·al** (dī'ə fiz'ē əl) *adj.*
di·a·pos·i·tive (dī'ə poz'ə tiv) *n.* [DIA- + POSITIVE] *Photog.* a positive transparency, as a slide on film or glass
di·a·rist (dī'ə rist) *n.* a person who keeps a diary —**di·a·rize** *vt.*
di·ar·rhoe·a (dī'ə rē'ə) *n.* [< OFr. & LL. < Gr. < *dia-*, through + *rhein*, to flow] excessive frequency and looseness of bowel movements —**di′ar·rhoe′al, di′ar·rhoe′-ic** *adj.*
di·a·ry (dī'ə rē) *n.*, *pl.* **-ries** [L. *diarium* < *dies*, day] 1. a

daily written record, esp. of the writer's own experiences, thoughts, etc. **2.** a book for this

Di·as·po·ra (dī as′pə rə) *n.* [< Gr. < *dia-*, across + *speirein*, to sow] **1.** *a)* the dispersion of the Jews after the Babylonian exile *b)* these Jews **2.** [**d-**] any scattering of people with a common origin, background, beliefs, etc.

di·a·stase (dī′ə stās′) *n.* [Fr. < Gr. *diastasis*, separation < *dia-*, apart + *histanai*, to stand] an enzyme, occurring in the seed of grains and malt, that changes starches into maltose and later into dextrose —**di′a·stat′ic** (-stat′ik) *adj.*

di·as·to·le (dī as′tə lē′) *n.* [LL. < Gr. *diastolē*, expansion < *dia-*, apart + *stellein*, to put] the usual rhythmic dilatation of the heart, esp. of the ventricles, during which the chambers fill with blood —**di·a·stol·ic** (dī′ə stol′ik) *adj.*

di·as·tro·phism (dī as′trə fiz′m) *n.* [< Gr. < *dia-*, aside + *strephein*, to turn + -ISM] the process by which the earth's surface is reshaped by rock movements —**di·a·stroph·ic** (dī′ə strof′ik) *adj.*

di·a·ther·man·cy (dī′ə thur′man sē) *n.* [Fr. < Gr. *dia-*, through + *thermansis*, a heating] the property of transmitting infrared or heat rays

di·a·ther·my (dī′ə thur′mē) *n.* [ModL. < Gr. *dia-*, through + *thermē*, heat] medical treatment in which heat is produced in the tissues beneath the skin by a high-frequency electric current —**di′a·ther′mic** *adj.*

di·a·tom (dī′ət əm, -ə tom′) *n.* [ModL. < Gr. < *dia-*, through + *temnein*, to cut] any of a number of related microscopic algae whose cell walls contain silica: diatoms are a source of food for marine life —**di·a·to·ma·ceous** (dī′ət ə mā′shəs, dī at′ə-) *adj.*

di·a·tom·ic (dī′ə tom′ik) *adj.* **1.** having two atoms in the molecule **2.** having two radicals in the molecule

di·a·ton·ic (dī′ə ton′ik) *adj.* [Fr. < LL. < Gr. *diatonikos*, stretched through (the notes) < *dia-*, through + *teinein*, to stretch] *Music* designating, of, or using any standard major or minor scale of eight tones without the chromatic intervals —**di′a·ton′i·cal·ly** *adv.*

di·a·tribe (dī′ə trīb′) *n.* [Fr. < L. < Gr. *diatribē*, a wearing away < *dia-*, through + *tribein*, to rub] a bitter, abusive criticism or denunciation

di·a·zo (dī a′zō) *adj.* [DI-¹ + AZO] **1.** having a group of two nitrogen atoms combining directly with one hydrogen radical **2.** designating a paper sensitive to ultraviolet light

di·bas·ic (dī bās′ik) *adj.* denoting or of an acid with two hydrogen atoms which may be replaced by basic radicals or atoms to form a salt

dib·ble (dib′'l) *n.* [ME. *dibbel*, prob. < *dibben*, to dip] a pointed tool used to make holes in the soil for seeds, bulbs, or young plants: also called **dib′ber** —*vt.* **-bled, -bling** **1.** to make a hole in (the soil) with a dibble **2.** to plant with a dibble —*vi.* to use a dibble

dibs (dibz) *n.pl.* [< *dibstone*, a jack in a children's game] **1.** a children's game similar to jacks **2.** [Slang] money

dice (dīs) *n.pl., sing.* **die** or **dice** [ME. *dis*, pl.: see DIE²] **1.** small cubes of bone, plastic, etc. marked on each side with from one to six spots and used, usually in pairs, in games of chance **2.** [*with sing. v.*] a gambling game played with dice **3.** any small cubes —*vi.* **diced, dic′ing** **1.** to play or gamble with dice **2.** to take a chance or risk[to *dice* with death] —*vt.* to cut (vegetables, etc.) into small cubes —**no dice** **1.** no: used in refusing a request **2.** no success, luck, etc. —**dic′er** *n.*

dice·y (dī′sē) *adj.* [Colloq.] hazardous; risky

di·chlo·ride (dī klôr′īd) *n.* any chemical compound in which two atoms of chlorine are combined with an element or radical

di·chot·o·my (dī kot′ə mē) *n., pl.* **-mies** [< Gr. < *dicha*, in two + -TOMY] **1.** division into two usually opposed parts or groups **2.** *Biol., Bot.* a dividing or branching into two parts, esp. when repeated —**di·chot′o·mize′** (-mīz′) *vt.* **-mized′, -miz′ing** —**di·chot′o·mous** (-məs) *adj.*

di·chro·mate (dī krō′māt) *n.* any salt of dichromic acid

di·chro·mat·ic (dī′krō mat′ik) *adj.* [DI-¹ + CHROMATIC] **1.** having two colours **2.** *Biol.* having two varieties of colouration that are independent of sex or age —**di·chro′ma·tism** *n.*

di·chro·mic (dī krō′mik) *adj.* **1.** *same as* DICHROMATIC **2.** *Chem.* designating a hypothetical acid, with two chromium atoms from which dichromates are formed

dick (dik) *n.* [< *Richard*, proper name] **1.** a fellow or person **2.** [Slang] a detective —**clever dick** [Colloq.] an opinionated person; a know-all

dick·ens (dik′'nz) *n., interj.* [prob. < nickname for *Richard*] [Colloq.] devil; deuce: a mild oath

Dick·en·si·an (di ken′zē ən) *adj.* [after Charles *Dickens* (1812-70), Brit. novelist] **1.** of Dickens or his writings **2.**

resembling the situations, characters, etc. described by Dickens

dick·er (dik′ər) *vi., vt.* [< *dicker*, ten, ten hides (as a unit of barter), ult. < L. *decem*, ten] to trade by bargaining, esp. on a small scale; barter; haggle —*n.* the act of bargaining or haggling

dick·y (dik′ē) *adj.* **dick′i·er, dick′i·est** [? < *Dick*, a man's name] [Colloq.] diseased; unsound; shaky

di·cli·nous (dī klī′nəs) *adj.* [< DI-¹ + Gr. *klinē*, bed + -OUS] *Bot.* having the stamens and pistils in separate flowers —**di·cli·nism** (dī′kli niz′m), **di′cli·ny** (-nē) *n.*

di·cot·y·le·don (dī′ kot əl ēd′'n, dī kot′'l-) *n.* a flowering plant with two seed leaves (cotyledons) —**di·cot′y·le′don·ous** *adj.*

di·cou·ma·rin (dī kōō′mər in) *n.* [DI-¹ + *coumarin*, a plant extract] a compound used as an anticoagulant

dict. **1.** dictator **2.** dictionary

dic·ta (dik′tə) *n.* *alt. pl. of* DICTUM

Dic·ta·phone (dik′tə fōn′) [DICTA(TE) + -PHONE] a *trademark for* a machine that records spoken words so that they can be played back later for typed transcripts, etc. —*n.* this machine

dic·tate (dik′tāt; *also for v.* dik tāt′) *vt., vi.* **-tat·ed, -tat·ing** [< L. pp. of *dictare*, freq. of *dicere*, to speak] **1.** to speak or read (something) aloud for someone else to write down **2.** to command expressly **3.** to impose or give (orders) with authority or arbitrarily —*n.* **1.** an authoritative command **2.** a guiding principle [the *dictates* of conscience]

dic·ta·tion (dik tā′shən) *n.* **1.** the dictating of words for another to write down **2.** the words so spoken or read **3.** the giving of authoritative orders or commands —**dic·ta′tion·al** *adj.*

dic·ta·tor (dik tāt′ər) *n.* **1.** a ruler with absolute power and authority, esp. a tyrant or despot **2.** a person who is domineering or arbitrary in giving orders, etc. **3.** one who dictates words for another to write down —**dic·ta′tor·ship′** *n.*

dic·ta·to·ri·al (dik′tə tôr′ē əl) *adj.* of, like, or characteristic of a dictator; autocratic; tyrannical; domineering —**dic′·ta·to′ri·al·ly** *adv.*

dic·tion (dik′shən) *n.* [< L. pp. of *dicere*, to say] **1.** manner of expression in words; choice of words **2.** enunciation

dic·tion·ar·y (dik′shə nə rē) *n., pl.* **-ar·ies** [ML. *dictionarium* < L. *dictio*: see prec.] **1.** a book of alphabetically listed words in a language, with definitions, etymologies, pronunciations, etc.; lexicon **2.** such a book of words in one language with their equivalents in another **3.** any alphabetically arranged list of words or articles relating to a special subject [a medical *dictionary*]

dic·tum (dik′təm) *n., pl.* **-tums, -ta** (-tə) [L., neut. pp. of *dicere*, to speak] a formal statement of fact, opinion, principle, etc.; pronouncement

did (did) *pt. of* DO¹

di·dac·tic (di dak′tik, dī-) *adj.* [Gr. *didaktikos* < *didaskein*, to teach] **1.** used or intended for teaching or instruction **2.** morally instructive **3.** too much inclined to teach others; boringly pedantic or moralistic Also **di·dac′ti·cal** —**di·dac′ti·cal·ly** *adv.* —**di·dac′ti·cism** (-tə siz′m) *n.*

di·dac·tics (-tiks) *n.pl.* [*usually with sing. v.*] the art or science of teaching; pedagogy

did·dle¹ (did′'l) *vi., vt.* **-dled, -dling** [Eng. dial. *duddle, diddle,* to totter] [U.S. Colloq.] to move back and forth jerkily; jiggle —**did′dler** *n.*

did·dle² (did′'l) *vt., vi.* **-dled, -dling** [< ?] [Colloq.] **1.** to cheat or swindle **2.** [U.S.] to waste (time) in trifling —**did′-dler** *n.*

did·ger·i·doo (di′jer ē dōō′) *n.* [Abor.] [Aust.] a musical instrument made from a bamboo pipe or hollow sapling

did·n't (did′'nt) did not

di·do (dī′dō) *n., pl.* **-does, -dos** [< ?] [U.S. Colloq.] a mischievous trick; prank; caper

didst (didst) *archaic 2nd pers. sing., past indic., of* DO¹: used with *thou*

di·dym·i·um (dī dim′ē əm) *n.* [< Gr. *didymos*, twin] a mixture of two rare-earth elements, formerly considered a single element

die¹ (dī) *vi.* **died, dy′ing** [ME. *dien* < ON. *deyja*] **1.** to stop living; become dead **2.** to suffer the agony of, or like that of, death **3.** to cease existing or stop functioning; end **4.** to lose force or activity **5.** to fade or wither away **6.** to pine away, as with desire **7.** [Colloq.] to wish intensely; yearn [she's *dying* to tell] **8.** *Theol.* to suffer spiritual death —**die away** (or **down**) to become weaker and cease gradually —**die back** (or **down**) to wither to the roots or woody part —**die hard** to resist to the last —**die off** to die one by one until all are gone —**die (of) laughing** to be overcome with mirth —**die out** to go out of existence

die² (dī) *n., pl.,* for 1 **dice** (dīs); for 2 **dies** (dīz) [< OFr. *de* < L. pp. of *dare*, to give] **1.** a small, marked cube used in games of chance: see also DICE **2.** any of various tools or devices for moulding, stamping, cutting, or shaping —*vt.* **died, die′ing** to mould, stamp, cut, or shape with a die —**the die is cast** the irrevocable decision has been made

die casting **1.** the process of making a casting by forcing

DIBBLE

molten metal into a metallic mould, or die, under pressure **2.** a casting so made —**die caster**

dief·fen·bach·i·a (dēf''n bak'ē ə) *n.* [ModL. < E. *Dieffenbach* (19th-c. Ger. botanist)] a tropical plant of the arum family, with large leaves

die-hard, die·hard (dī'härd') *adj.* extremely stubborn in resistance; unwilling to give in —*n.* a stubborn or resistant person, esp. an extreme conservative

diel·drin (dēl'drin) *n.* a highly toxic, long-lasting insecticide

di·e·lec·tric (dī'ə lek'trik) *n.* [< DI(A)- + ELECTRIC] a material, as rubber, glass, etc., that does not conduct electricity and that can sustain an electric field: used in capacitors, etc. —*adj.* having the properties or function of a dielectric

di·er·e·sis (dī er'ə sis) *n., pl* **-ses'** (-sēz') Chiefly U.S. *sp.* of DIAERESIS

die·sel (dē'z'l, -s'l) *n.* [after R. *Diesel* (1858–1913), Ger. inventor] [often D-] **1.** a type of internal-combustion engine that burns fuel oil: the ignition is brought about by heat resulting from air compression, instead of by an electric spark as in a petrol engine: also **diesel engine** (or **motor**) **2.** a train, lorry, etc. with such an engine **3.** short for DIESEL FUEL

die·sel-e·lec·tric (-i lek'trik) *n.* a locomotive driven by an electric generator powered by a diesel engine —*adj.* of or relating to such a locomotive

diesel fuel a heavy oil, distilled from petroleum, used by diesel engines: also **diesel oil**

die·sink·er (dī'siŋ'kər) *n.* a maker of dies that are used in stamping or shaping —**die'sink'ing** *n.*

‡**Di·es I·rae** (dē'āz ir'ā) [L., Day of Wrath] a medieval Latin hymn about Judgment Day, beginning *Dies Irae*, a part of the Requiem Mass

di·e·sis (dī'ə sis) *n., pl.* **-ses'** (-sēz') [L. < Gr. < *diienai*, to send through] a reference mark (‡) used in printing: also called DOUBLE DAGGER

di·et[1] (dī'ət) *n.* [< OFr. < ML. < L. < Gr. *diaita*, way of life] **1.** *a)* what a person or animal usually eats and drinks; daily fare *b)* figuratively, what a person regularly reads, listens to, does, etc. **2.** a regimen of special or limited food and drink, chosen or prescribed for health or to gain or lose weight —*vi.* to eat special or limited food, esp. for losing weight —**di'et·er** *n.*

di·et[2] (dī'ət) *n.* [< OFr. < ML. < L. *dies*, day] **1.** a formal assembly, as formerly of princes, electors, etc. of the Holy Roman Empire **2.** in some countries, a national or local legislative assembly **3.** *Scots Law* a sitting of a law court

di·e·tar·y (dī'ə tər ē), *n., pl.* **-ies** **1.** a system of diet **2.** daily food allowance or ration —*adj.* **1.** of diet **2.** of a dietary

di·e·tet·ic (dī'ə tet'ik) *adj.* of, relating to, or designed for a particular diet of food and drink: also **di'e·tet'i·cal** —**di'·e·tet'i·cal·ly** *adv.*

di·e·tet·ics (-iks) *n.pl.* [with sing. v.] the study of the kinds and quantities of food needed for health

di·e·ti·tian, di·e·ti·cian (dī'ə tish'ən) *n.* an expert in dietetics; specialist in planning meals or diets

dif- same as DIS-: used before *f*

dif·fer (dif'ər) *vi.* [< OFr. < L. *differre* < *dis-*, apart + *ferre*, to bear] **1.** to be unlike; be not the same (often with *from*) **2.** to be of opposite or unlike opinions; disagree

dif·fer·ence (dif'ər əns, dif'rəns) *n.* [see prec.] **1.** condition or quality of being different **2.** the way in which people or things are different **3.** the state of holding a differing opinion; disagreement; also, the point at issue; point of disagreement **4.** a dispute; quarrel **5.** *Math.* the amount by which one quantity is greater or less than another —**make a difference** **1.** to have an effect; matter **2.** to change the situation —**split the difference** **1.** to share equally what is left over **2.** to make a compromise —**what's the difference?** [Colloq.] what does it matter?

dif·fer·ent (dif'ər ənt, dif'rənt) *adj.* [see DIFFER] **1.** not alike; dissimilar (with *from* or *to*) **2.** not the same; distinct; separate; other **3.** various **4.** unlike most others; unusual —**dif'fer·ent·ly** *adv.*

dif·fer·en·ti·a (dif'ə ren'shē ə) *n., pl.* **-ti·ae** (-shi ē') a distinguishing characteristic

dif·fer·en·tial (-shəl) *adj.* **1.** of, showing, or depending on a difference **2.** constituting a specific difference; distinguishing **3.** having different effects or making use of differences [a *differential* gear] **4.** *Math.* of or involving differentials —*n.* **1.** a differentiating amount, degree, factor, etc. [differentials in salary] **2.** *Math.* dy and dx, where y is a function of the variable x and, in the notation introduced by Leibnitz, dy/dx is its derivative **3.** *Mech.* same as DIFFERENTIAL GEAR —**dif'fer·en'tial·ly** *adv.*

differential calculus the branch of higher mathematics which deals with derivatives and their applications

differential gear (or **gearing**) an arrangement of gears connecting two axles in the same line and allowing one axle to turn faster than the other: used in the rear axles of motor cars to permit a difference in axle speeds while turning curves

dif·fer·en·ti·ate (-shē āt') *vt.* **-at'ed, -at'ing** **1.** to constitute a difference in or between **2.** to make unlike **3.** to perceive or express the difference in; distinguish between **4.** *Math.* to work out the derivative of —*vi.* **1.** to become different or differentiated **2.** to perceive or express a difference —**dif'·fer·en'ti·a'tion** *n.*

dif·fi·cult (dif'i kəlt) *adj.* **1.** hard to do, make, manage, understand, etc. **2.** hard to satisfy, persuade, please, etc. —**dif'fi·cult·ly** *adv.*

dif·fi·cul·ty (dif'i kəl'tē) *n., pl.* **-ties** [< OFr. < L. *difficultas* < *dis-*, not + *facilis*, easy] **1.** the condition or fact of being difficult **2.** something difficult; an obstacle or objection **3.** trouble or distress **4.** a disagreement or quarrel —**in difficulties** in distress, esp. financially

dif·fi·dent (dif'ə dənt) *adj.* [< L. prp. of *diffidere* < *dis-*, not + *fidere*, to trust] lacking confidence in oneself; hesitant to assert oneself; timid; shy —**dif'fi·dence** *n.* —**dif'fi·dent·ly** *adv.*

dif·fract (di frakt') *vt.* [< L. pp. of *diffringere* < *dis-*, apart + *frangere*, to break] to break into parts; specif., to subject to diffraction

dif·frac·tion (di frak'shən) *n.* **1.** the breaking up of a ray of light into dark and light bands or into the colours of the spectrum, as when it is deflected at the edge of an opaque object **2.** a similar breaking up of other waves, as of sound or electricity —**dif·frac'tive** (-tiv) *adj.* —**dif·frac'tive·ly** *adv.*

dif·fuse (di fyōos'; *for v.* -fyōoz') *adj.* [< L. pp. of < *dis-*, apart + *fundere*, to pour] **1.** spread out; not concentrated **2.** using more words than are needed —*vt., vi.* **-fused', -fus'·ing** **1.** to pour or disperse in every direction; spread or scatter widely **2.** *Physics* to mix by diffusion, as gases, liquids, etc. —**dif·fuse'ly** *adv.* —**dif·fuse'ness** *n.* —**dif·fus'er, dif·fu'sor** (-fyōo'zər) *n.* —**dif·fus'i·bil'i·ty** *n.* —**dif·fus'i·ble** *adj.*

dif·fu·sion (di fyōo'zhən) *n.* **1.** a diffusing or being diffused; specif., *a)* a dissemination, as of news *b)* a scattering of light rays, as by reflection; also, the dispersion and softening of light, as by using frosted glass *c)* an intermingling of the molecules of liquids, gases, etc. **2.** wordiness

dif·fu·sive (-siv) *adj.* **1.** tending to diffuse **2.** characterized by diffusion **3.** diffuse —**dif·fu'sive·ly** *adv.* —**dif·fu'·sive·ness** *n.*

dig (dig) *vt.* **dug** or archaic & poet. **digged, dig'ging** [< ? OFr. *digue*, dike < Du. *dijk*] **1.** to break and turn up or remove (ground, etc.) with a spade or other tool, or with hands, claws, etc. **2.** to make (a hole, cellar, etc.) as by doing this **3.** to get from the ground in this way [to *dig* potatoes] **4.** to find out, as by careful study; unearth (usually with *up* or *out*) [to *dig* out the truth] **5.** to jab or prod **6.** [Slang] *a)* to understand *b)* to approve of or like —*vi.* **1.** to dig the ground **2.** to make a way by or as by digging (*through, into, under*) **3.** [Colloq.] to have rooms or lodgings **4.** [U.S. Colloq.] to work or study hard —*n.* **1.** the act of digging **2.** [Colloq.] *a)* a poke, nudge, etc. *b)* a sarcastic comment **3.** an archaeological excavation **4.** [*pl.*, often with sing. v.] [Colloq.] living quarters —**dig in** **1.** to dig trenches for cover **2.** to entrench oneself **3.** [Colloq.] *a)* to begin to work hard *b)* to begin eating —**dig into** **1.** to penetrate by digging **2.** [Colloq.] to begin eating —**dig one's heels** (or **toes**) **in** to refuse to move or be persuaded

di·gest (dī'jest; *for v.* di jest', dī-) *n.* [< L. pp. of *digerere*, to separate < *di-*, apart + *gerere*, to bear] **1.** a collection of condensed, systematic information; summary or synopsis, as of legal material **2.** a book, periodical, etc. consisting of such summaries **3.** [D-] the Roman laws compiled by order of the Emperor Justinian —*vt.* **1.** *a)* to arrange systematically, usually in condensed form *b)* to condense and summarize (a piece of writing) **2.** to change (food), esp. in the stomach and intestines, so that it can be absorbed by the body **3.** to aid the digestion of (food) **4.** to think over and absorb **5.** to soften or dissolve soluble material in, esp. with liquid —*vi.* **1.** to be digested **2.** to digest food —**di·gest'er** *n.*

di·gest·i·ble (di jes'tə b'l) *adj.* that can be digested —**di·gest'i·bil'i·ty** *n.* —**di·gest'i·bly** *adv.*

di·ges·tion (-chən) *n.* **1.** the act or process of digesting food **2.** the ability to digest food **3.** the absorption of ideas **4.** decomposition of sewage by bacteria

di·ges·tive (-tiv) *adj.* of, for, or aiding digestion —*n.* any substance or drink that aids digestion —**di·ges'tive·ly** *adv.* —**di·ges'tive·ness** *n.*

digestive biscuit a semisweet biscuit made from wholemeal flour

dig·ger (dig'ər) *n.* **1.** a person or thing that digs **2.** a tool or machine for digging **3.** same as DIGGER WASP **4.** [D-] [Slang] an Australian or New Zealander

digger wasp any of various wasps that dig a nest in the ground

dig·gings (dig'iŋz) *n.pl.* **1.** materials dug out **2.** [often with sing. v.] a place where digging or mining is carried on **3.** [Slang] one's lodgings

dight (dīt) *vt.* **dight** or **dight'ed, dight'ing** [< OE. *dihtan*, to arrange < L. *dictare:* see DICTATE] [Archaic or Poet.] **1.** to adorn **2.** to equip

dig·it (dij′it) *n.* [L. *digitus*, a finger, toe] **1.** a finger or toe **2.** any numeral from 0 to 9

dig·it·al (-′l) *adj.* **1.** of, like, or constituting a digit **2.** having digits **3.** performed with the finger **4.** using numbers that are digits to represent all the variables involved in calculation —*n.* **1.** a finger **2.** a key played with a finger, as on the piano —**dig′it·al·ly** *adv.*

digital clock (or **watch**) a timepiece that shows the time in digits rather than by hands on a dial

digital computer a computer that uses numbers to perform calculations, usually in a binary system

dig·i·tal·in (dij′ə tāl′in) *n.* [< ff. + -IN¹] a poisonous glucoside obtained from digitalis and used in treating heart disease

dig·i·tal·is (dij′ə tāl′is) *n.* [ModL. < L.: see DIGIT: from its flowers] **1.** any of a genus of plants of the figwort family, with long spikes of thimblelike flowers **2.** the dried leaves of the purple foxglove **3.** a medicine made from these leaves, used as a heart stimulant

dig·i·tate (dij′ə tāt′) *adj.* [see DIGIT] **1.** having separate fingers or toes **2.** fingerlike **3.** *Bot.* having fingerlike divisions, as some leaves Also **dig′i·tat′ed** —**dig′i·tate′ly** *adv.* —**dig′i·ta′tion** *n.*

dig·ni·fied (dig′nə fīd′) *adj.* having or showing dignity or stateliness —**dig′ni·fied′ly** *adv.*

dig·ni·fy (dig′nə fī′) *vt.* -**fied′**, -**fy′ing** [< OFr. < ML. < L. *dignus*, worthy + *facere*, to make] to give dignity to; make worthy of esteem; honour; exalt

dig·ni·tar·y (-ter ē) *n.*, *pl.* -**tar·ies** [< L. *dignitas*, dignity .+ -ARY] a person holding a high, dignified position or office —*adj.* of a dignitary

dig·ni·ty (-tē) *n.*, *pl.* -**ties** [< OFr. < L. < *dignus*, worthy] **1.** the quality of being worthy of esteem or honour **2.** high repute; honour **3.** the degree of worth, repute, or honour **4.** a high position, rank, or title **5.** loftiness of appearance or manner; stateliness **6.** proper pride and self-respect

di·graph (dī′grăf) *n.* [DI-¹ + -GRAPH] a combination of two letters to express a simple sound (Ex.: re*ad*, *sh*ow, gra*ph*ic) —**di·graph′ic** *adj.*

di·gress (di gres′, dī-) *vi.* [< L. pp. of *digredi* < *dis-*, apart + *gradi*, to go, step] to depart temporarily from the main subject in talking or writing —**di·gres′sion** (-gresh′ən) *n.*

di·gres·sive (-gres′iv) *adj.* given to digression —**di·gres′-sive·ly** *adv.* —**di·gres′sive·ness** *n.*

di·he·dral (dī hē′drəl) *adj.* [< DI-¹ + Gr. *hedra*, a seat] **1.** having or formed by two intersecting plane faces [a *dihedral* angle] **2.** *a)* inclined to each other at a dihedral angle, as some aircraft wings *b)* having such wings —*n.* a dihedral angle

dik-dik (dik′dik′) *n.* [< the Ethiopian native name] any of several small antelopes found in E Africa

dike (dīk) *n.* [< OE. *dic* & ON. *diki*] **1.** a ditch or watercourse **2.** an embankment or dam made to prevent flooding as by the sea **3.** a protective barrier **4.** a low wall, often made of stone **5.** *Geol.* igneous rock solidified as a tabular body in a vertical fissure —*vt.* **diked**, **dik′ing** **1.** to protect or enclose with a dike **2.** to drain by a ditch Also **dyke** —**dik′er** *n.*

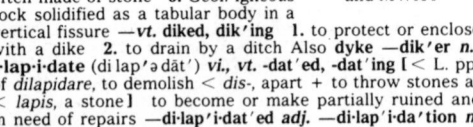

DIHEDRAL ANGLE
(angle formed by planes MWON and MWXY

di·lap·i·date (di lap′ə dāt′) *vi.*, *vt.* -**dat′ed**, -**dat′ing** [< L. pp. of *dilapidare*, to demolish < *dis-*, apart + to throw stones at < *lapis*, a stone] to become or make partially ruined and in need of repairs —**di·lap′i·dat′ed** *adj.* —**di·lap′i·da′tion** *n.*

dil·a·ta·tion (dil′ə tā′shən, dī′lə-) *n.* same as DILATION —**dil′a·ta′tion·al** *adj.*

di·late (dī lāt′, di-) *vt.* -**lat′ed**, -**lat′ing** [L. *dilatare* < *dis-*, apart + *latus*, wide] to make wider or larger; cause to expand or swell —*vi.* **1.** to become wider or larger; swell **2.** to speak or write in detail (*on* or *upon* a subject) —**di·lat′-a·bil′i·ty** *n.* —**di·lat′a·ble** *adj.* —**di·lat′ive** *adj.* —**di·la′tor** *n.*

di·la·tion (dī lā′shən, di-) *n.* **1.** a dilating or being dilated **2.** a dilated part

dil·a·to·ry (dil′ə tər ē) *adj.* [< LL. < L. < *dilatus*, pp. of *differre*, DEFER¹] **1.** causing or tending to cause delay **2.** inclined to delay; slow; tardy —**dil′a·to·ri·ly** *adv.* —**dil′-a·to·ri·ness** *n.*

dil·do (dil′dō) *n.*, *pl.* -**dos**, **does** [< ?] a device, usually made of rubber, used as a penis substitute

di·lem·ma (di lem′ə, dī-) *n.* [LL. < LGr. < *di-*, two + *lēmma*, proposition] **1.** an argument or a situation in which one must choose between unpleasant alternatives **2.** a problem or predicament —**dil·em·mat′ic** (dil′ə mat′ik) *adj.*

dil·et·tante (dil′ə tan′tē) *n.*, *pl.* -**tantes′**, -**tan′ti** (-tan′tē) [It. < prp. of *dilettare* < L. *delectare*, to delight] **1.** a person who loves the fine arts **2.** a person who dabbles in an art or science in a superficial way —*adj.* of or

characteristic of a dilettante —**dil′et·tant′ish** *adj.* —**dil′-et·tant′ism, dil′et·tan′te·ism** *n.*

dil·i·gence¹ (dil′ə jəns) *n.* a being diligent; constant, careful effort; perseverance; industry

dil·i·gence² (dil′ə jəns; *Fr.* dē lē zhäns′) *n.* [Fr.] a public stagecoach, esp. as formerly used in France

dil·i·gent (dil′ə jənt) *adj.* [OFr. < L. prp. of *diligere*, to esteem highly < *di-*, apart + *legere*, to choose] **1.** persevering and careful in work; industrious **2.** done with careful, steady effort; painstaking —**dil′i·gent·ly** *adv.*

dill (dil) *n.* [OE. *dile*] **1.** a plant of the parsley family, with bitter seeds and aromatic leaves, used to flavour pickles, etc. **2.** the seeds or leaves

dill pickle a cucumber pickle flavoured with dill

dil·ly (dil′ē) *n.*, *pl.* -**lies** [< ? DEL(IGHTFUL) + -Y¹] **1.** [Slang] a surprising or remarkable person or thing **2.** [Aust.] *a)* a bag made of twisted grass or fibre *b)* any small bag carrying personal belongings: also **dilly bag**

DILL

dil·ly·dal·ly (dil′ē dal′ē) *vi.* -**lied**, -**ly·ing** [redupl. form of DALLY] [Colloq.] to waste time in hesitation; loiter or dawdle

di·lute (di lōōt′) *vt.* -**lut′ed**, -**lut′ing** [< L. pp. of *diluere* < *dis-*, off + *-luere* < *lavare*, to wash] **1.** to thin down or weaken by mixing with water or other liquid **2.** to change or weaken (in brilliance, force, effect, etc.) by mixing with something else —*vi.* to become diluted —*adj.* diluted —**di·lute′ness** *n.* —**di·lut′er, di·lu′tor** *n.*

di·lu·tion (-lōō′shən) *n.* **1.** a diluting or being diluted **2.** something diluted

di·lu·vi·al (di lōō′vē əl, dī-) *adj.* [< LL. < L. *diluvium*, a deluge] of or caused by a flood, esp. the Deluge Also **di·lu′-vi·an**

dim (dim) *adj.* **dim′mer**, **dim′mest** [OE. *dimm*] **1.** not bright; somewhat dark; dull **2.** not clear or distinct; lacking definition, strength, etc. **3.** not clearly seen, heard, or understood; vague **4.** not clearly seeing, hearing, or understanding **5.** not likely to turn out well [dim prospects] **6.** [Colloq.] stupid; slow to understand —*vt.*, *vi.* **dimmed**, **dim′ming** to make or grow dim —*n.* [Poet.] dim light; dusk —**take a dim view of** to view sceptically, etc. —**dim′ly** *adv.* —**dim′mish** *adj.* —**dim′ness** *n.*

dim., dimin. **1.** diminuendo **2.** diminutive

dime (dim) *n.* [< OFr. < L. *decimus*, a tenth < *decem*, ten] a coin of the U.S. and of Canada equal to ten cents; tenth of a dollar —**a dime a dozen** [U.S. Colloq.] very abundant or cheap

di·men·hy·dri·nate (dī′men hi′drə nāt′) *n.* a white, crystalline solid used to control nausea and vomiting, as in travel sickness

dime novel [U.S.] a very cheap, melodramatic novel

di·men·sion (də men′shən, di-) *n.* [L. *dimensio* < pp. of *dimetiri* < *dis-*, off + *metiri*, to MEASURE] **1.** any measurable extent, as length, width, depth, etc.: see also FOURTH DIMENSION **2.** [*pl.*] measurements in length and width, and often depth **3.** [*often pl.*] *a)* extent or size *b)* scope or importance —**di·men′sion·al** *adj.* —**di·men′-sion·al·ly** *adv.* —**di·men′sion·less** *adj.*

di·min·ish (də min′ish) *vt.* [a blend of ME. *diminuen* (ult. < L. *deminuere*, to make smaller) & *minishen* (ult. < L. *minutus*, MINUTE²)] **1.** to make, or make seem, smaller; reduce in size, degree, importance, etc. **2.** *Music* to reduce (a minor interval) by a semitone —*vi.* to become smaller or less —**di·min′ish·a·ble** *adj.* —**di·min′ished** *adj.*

diminished responsibility *Law* a plea in which mental derangement is submitted as demonstrating lack of criminal responsibility

di·min·u·en·do (də min′yoo wen′dō) *adj.*, *adv.*, *n.*, *pl.* -**dos** [It. < L. *diminuere*, make smaller] same as DECRESCENDO

dim·i·nu·tion (dim′ə nyoo′shən) *n.* a diminishing or being diminished; lessening; decrease

di·min·u·tive (də min′yoo tiv) *adj.* **1.** very small; tiny **2.** *Gram.* expressing smallness or diminution [a *diminutive* suffix] —*n.* **1.** a very small person or thing **2.** *a)* a word or name formed from another by the addition of a suffix expressing smallness and, sometimes, endearment or condescension, as *ringlet, Jackie, sonny* *b)* such a suffix —**di·min′u·tive·ly** *adv.* —**di·min′u·tive·ness** *n.*

dim·is·so·ry (di mis′ər ē, di mis-) *adj.* sending away; granting official leave to depart

dim·i·ty (dim′ə tē) *n.*, *pl.* -**ties** [< ML. < MGr. *dimitos*, double-threaded < *dis-*, two + *mitos*, a thread] a thin, often corded or patterned cotton cloth, used for curtains, dresses, etc.

dim·mer (dim′ər) *n.* **1.** a person that dims **2.** a device for dimming an electric light, as in theatre stage lights

dim·out (-out′) *n.* a dimming or reduction of the night lighting in a city, etc., to make it less easily visible, as to enemy aircraft

dim·ple (dim'p'l) *n.* [ME. *dimpel*] 1. a small, natural hollow spot, as on the cheek or chin 2. any little hollow, as on water —*vt.* **-pled, -pling** to make dimples in —*vi.* to show or form dimples

dim·wit (dim'wit') *n.* [Colloq.] a stupid person; simpleton —**dim'wit'ted** *adj.* —**dim'wit'ted·ly** *adv.* —**dim'wit'·ted·ness** *n.*

din (din) *n.* [OE. *dyne*] a loud, continuous noise; confused clamour or uproar —*vt.* **dinned, din'ning** 1. to beset with a din 2. to repeat insistently or noisily [to *din* an idea into one's ears] —*vi.* to make a din

di·nar (di när') *n.* [< Ar. < L. *denarius*: see DENARIUS] the monetary unit of Algeria, Iraq, Jordan, Libya, Tunisia, etc., and a coin of Iran: see MONETARY UNITS, table

dine (dīn) *vi.* **dined, din'ing** [< OFr. *disner*, ult. < L. *dis-*, away + *jejunus*, fasting] to eat dinner —*vt.* to provide a dinner for, or entertain at dinner —**dine out** to dine away from home

din·er (dī'nər) *n.* 1. a person eating dinner 2. *same as* DINING CAR 3. [U.S.] a small restaurant

din·ette (dī net') *n.* 1. an alcove or small, partitioned space used as a dining room 2. a set of tables and chairs for such a space [a 5-piece *dinette*]

ding (diŋ) *vi.* [< Scand. (as in ON. *dengja*, to hammer)] 1. to make a sound like that of a bell; ring 2. to speak repetitiously and tiresomely —*vt.* to repeat insistently or tiresomely; din —*n.* the sound of a bell

ding-a-ling, ding·a·ling (diŋ'ə liŋ') *n.* [U.S. Slang] a person who seems crazy, silly, eccentric, etc.

ding-dong (-doŋ') *n.* [echoic] 1. the sound of a bell struck repeatedly 2. a heated argument —*adj.* [Colloq.] vigorously contested —*vi.* to sound with a ding-dong

din·ghy (diŋ'gē) *n.,* pl. **-ghies** [Hindi *dīngī*] 1. orig., a rowing boat used on the rivers of India 2. any small boat used as a tender to a yacht, etc. 3. a small, undecked, single-masted racing boat 4. an inflatable life raft Also sp. **din'gey**

din·gle (diŋ'g'l) *n.* [ME. *dingel*, abyss] a small, deep, wooded valley; dell

din·go (diŋ'gō) *n.,* pl. **-goes** [Abor.] the Australian wild dog

ding·us (diŋ'əs) *n.* [Du. *dinges* (or G. *Dings*), orig. gen. of *Ding*, thing] [Colloq.] any device; contrivance; gadget: humorous substitute for a name not known or temporarily forgotten

din·gy (din'jē) *adj.* **-gi·er, -gi·est** [orig. dial. var. of *dungy*: see DUNG] 1. dirty-coloured; not bright or clean 2. dismal; shabby —**din'gi·ly** *adv.* —**din'gi·ness** *n.*

dining car a railway carriage equipped to serve meals to passengers

dining room a room where meals are eaten

din·kum (diŋ'kəm) *adj.* [? < dial. (Lincolnshire), a fair share of work] [Aust.Slang] genuine; true; real —**dinkum oil** [Aust. Colloq.] the truth

din·ky (diŋ'kē) *adj.* **-ki·er, -ki·est** [< Scot. *dink*, trim + -Y²] [Colloq.] small and neat; dainty

din·ner (din'ər) *n.* [< OFr. *disner*, inf. used as n.: see DINE] 1. the chief meal of the day, whether eaten in the evening or about noon 2. a banquet in honour of some person or event

dinner dance an evening event consisting of a dinner followed by a dance, usually formal

dinner jacket a man's tailless jacket for semiformal evening wear, orig. black

di·no·saur (dī'nə sôr') *n.* [< Gr. *deinos*, terrible + *sauros*, lizard] any of a large group of extinct, four-limbed reptiles of the Mesozoic Era, including some almost 30 m long —**di'·no·sau'ri·an** *adj.*

dint (dint) *n.* [OE. *dynt*, a blow] 1. force; exertion: now chiefly in **by dint of** 2. a dent —*vt.* 1. to dent 2. to drive in with force

dioc. 1. diocesan 2. diocese

di·oc·e·san (dī os'ə s'n) *adj.* of a diocese —*n.* the bishop of a diocese

di·o·cese (dī'ə sis) *n.* [< OFr. < L. < Gr. *dioikēsis*, administration < *dioikein*, to keep house < *dia-*, through *oikos*, a house] the district under a bishop's jurisdiction

di·ode (dī'ōd) *n.* [DI-¹ + -ODE] an electron tube or semiconductor device having two terminals and conducting electricity in only one direction

di·oe·cious (dī ē'shəs) *adj.* [< DI-¹ + Gr. *oikos*, a house + -OUS] *Biol.* having the male reproductive organs in one individual and the female organs in another —**di·oe'cious·ly** *adv.* —**di·oe'cism** (-siz'm) *n.*

Di·o·ny·sian (dī'ə nizh'ən) *adj.* [< *Dionysus*, the Greek god of wine & revelry] wild, frenzied, and sensuous

Di·o·phan·tine equation (dī'ō fan'tin) *Math.* an equation in more than one variable for which integral solutions are sought

di·op·tre (dī op'tər) *n.* [< L. < Gr. *dioptra*, levelling instrument < *dia-*, through + base of *opsis*, sight] a unit of 1 measure of the power of a lens: the reciprocal of its focal length in metres —**di·op'tral** *adj.*

di·o·ra·ma (dī'ə räm'ə) *n.* [DI(A)- + (PAN)ORAMA] 1. a picture painted on a set of transparent curtains and looked at through a small opening 2. a miniature scene depicting three-dimensional figures in a naturalistic setting 3. a museum display of a preserved or reconstructed specimen, as of wildlife in a simulated habitat

di·ox·ide (dī ok'sīd) *n.* an oxide containing two atoms of oxygen per molecule

dip (dip) *vt.* **dipped dip'ping** [OE. *dyppan*] 1. to put into liquid for a moment and then quickly take out 2. to dye in this way 3. to baptize by immersion 4. to wash and clean (sheep or pigs) in disinfectant 5. to make (a candle) by putting a wick repeatedly in melted tallow or wax 6. to take out as by scooping up with a container, the hand, etc. 7. to lower and immediately raise again [dip the flag in salute] 8. to switch car headlights from main to lower beam —*vi.* 1. to plunge into a liquid and quickly come out 2. to sink or seem to sink suddenly [the sun *dips* into the sea] 3. to undergo a slight decline [sales *dipped* in May] 4. to slope down 5. to lower a container, the hand, etc. into liquid, a receptacle, etc., esp. in order to take something out: often figurative [to *dip* into one's savings] 6. to read or study casually or superficially (with *into*) [to *dip* into a book] 7. *Aeron.* to drop suddenly before climbing —*n.* 1. a dipping or being dipped 2. *a)* a brief plunge into a liquid *b)* a brief swim 3. a liquid into which something is dipped, as for dyeing 4. whatever is removed by dipping 5. a candle made by dipping 6. *a)* a downward slope or inclination or a deviation *b)* the amount of this 7. a slight hollow 8. a short downward plunge, as of an aircraft 9. *a)* a sweet liquid sauce for desserts *b)* a thick, creamy sauce into which one dips crisps or other appetizers 10. [Slang] a pickpocket

Dip., dip. Diploma

Dip. A.D. Diploma in Art and Design

Dip. Ed. Diploma in Education

diph·the·ri·a (dif thir'ē ə, dip-) *n.* [ModL. < Fr. < Gr. *diphthera*, leather < *dephein*, to tan hides] an acute infectious disease caused by a bacterium and characterized by weakness, high fever, and the formation in the air passages of a membrane-like obstruction to breathing —**diph·the'ri·al** *adj.* —**diph'the·rit'ic** (-thə rit'ik), **diph·ther'·ic** *adj.*

diph·thong (dif'thoŋ, dip'-) *n.* [< LL. < Gr. < *di-*, two + *phthongos*, sound] *Phonet.* a complex vowel sound made by gliding continuously from the position for one vowel to that for another within the same syllable, as (ou) in *down*, (oi) in *boy* —**diph·thon'gal** (-thoŋ'g'l) *adj.*

diph·thong·ize (-īz') *vt.* **-ized', -iz'ing** to pronounce (a simple vowel) as a diphthong —*vi.* to become a diphthong —**diph'thong·i·za'tion** *n.*

dip·loid (dip'loid) *adj.* [< Gr. *diploos*, double + -OID] 1. twofold or double 2. *Biol.* having twice the number of chromosomes normally occurring in a mature germ cell: most somatic cells are diploid: see HAPLOID —**dip·loi'dy** (-loi'dē) *n.*

di·plo·ma (di plō'mə) *n.* [L. < Gr. *diplōma*, folded letter < *diploos*, double] 1. a certificate conferring honours, privileges, etc. 2. a certificate conferring a degree from a college or university

di·plo·ma·cy (di plō'mə sē) *n.,* pl. **-cies** [< Fr.: see ff.] 1. (skill in) conducting relations between nations 2. tact in dealing with people

dip·lo·mat (dip'lə mat') *n.* [< Fr., ult. < L. *diploma*, DIPLOMA] 1. a representative of a government who conducts relations with another government in the interests of his own country 2. a tactful person Also **di·plo·ma·tist** (di plō'mə tist)

dip·lo·mat·ic (dip'lə mat'ik) *n.* 1. of or connected with diplomacy 2. tactful and adroit in dealing with people —**dip'lo·mat'i·cal·ly** *adv.*

diplomatic bag the bag or container for the official mail from an embassy, consulate, etc.

diplomatic immunity exemption from local taxes, court action, etc. in a foreign country, granted to all members of diplomatic service

di·pole (dī'pōl') *n.* 1. *Physics* any system having two equal but opposite electric charges or magnetic poles separated by a small distance 2. an antenna usually separated at the centre by an insulator and fed by a balanced transmission line: in full, **dipole antenna** —**di·po'·lar** *adj.*

dip·per (dip'ər) *n.* 1. a person whose work is dipping something in liquid 2. a container for dipping; esp., a long-handled cup 3. any of a genus of songbirds, as the water ouzel, which wade and submerge in streams in search of insects, etc. —**dip'per·ful'** *n.,* pl. **-fuls'**

dip·py (dip'ē) *adj.* **-pi·er, -pi·est** [< ?] [Slang] crazy;

dip·so (dip'sō) *n.* [Colloq.] a dipsomaniac

dip·so·ma·ni·a (dip'sə mā'nē ə, -nyə) *n.* [ModL. < Gr. *dipsa*, thirst + -MANIA] an abnormal and insatiable craving for alcoholic drink —**dip'so·ma'ni·ac'** (-ak') *n.* —**dip'so·ma·ni'·a·cal** (-mə nī'ə k'l) *adj.*

dip·stick (dip′stik′) *n.* a graduated rod for measuring the depth of a substance in its container, as oil in a car engine
dip switch a switch which dips a motor vehicle's headlights
dipt (dipt) *occas. pt. & pp. of* DIP
dip·ter·an (dip′tər ən) *n.* [see ff.] any of a large order of insects, including the housefly, gnat, etc., having two pairs of wings, one pair usually vestigial
dip·ter·ous (-əs) *adj.* [<ModL. < Gr. < *di-*, two + *pteron*, a wing] 1. having two wings or two winglike appendages 2. of the dipterans
dip·tych (dip′tik) *n.* [< LL. < Gr. < *di-*, twice + *ptychē*, a fold] 1. an ancient writing tablet made up of a hinged pair of wooden or ivory pieces 2. a picture painted or carved on two hinged tablets
dire (dīr) *adj.* **dir′er, dir′est** [L. *dirus*] 1. arousing terror; dreadful 2. urgent [a *dire* need] —**dire′ly** *adv.* —**dire′-ness** *n.*
di·rect (di rekt′, dī-) *adj.* [< L. pp. of *dirigere*, to lay straight < *dis-*, apart + *regere*, to rule] 1. by the shortest way; not roundabout; straight [a *direct* route] 2. honest and straightforward; frank 3. with nothing or no one between; immediate [*direct* contact] 4. in an unbroken line of descent; lineal 5. exact; complete [the *direct* opposite] 6. in the exact words of the speaker [a *direct* quotation] 7. by action of the people through popular vote instead of through representatives —*vt.* 1. to manage the affairs or action of; guide; conduct 2. to order or command with authority 3. to turn or point (a person or thing) towards an object or goal; aim; head 4. to tell (a person) the way to a place 5. to address (words, etc.) to a specific person or persons 6. to write the name and address on (a letter, etc.) 7. to plan and supervise the action of (a play, film, etc.) or of (the actors, etc.) —*vi.* 1. to give directions 2. to be a director —*adv.* directly —**di·rect′ness** *n.*
direct current an electric current flowing in one direction
direct-grant school a grammar school or day public school that receives a government grant for its non-fee paying pupils
di·rec·tion (də rek′shən, dī-) *n.* 1. the act of directing; management; supervision 2. [*usually pl.*] instructions for doing, using, etc. 3. an authoritative order or command 4. the point towards which one faces or line along which one moves or lies 5. an aspect, way, trend, etc. [research in new *directions*]
di·rec·tion·al (-′l) *adj.* 1. of, aimed at, or indicating (a specific) direction 2. designed for radiating or receiving radio signals most effectively in one or more particular directions [a *directional* antenna] 3. designed to pick up or send out sound most efficiently in one direction —**di·rec′-tion·al′i·ty** *n.* —**di·rec′tion·al·ly** *adv.*
direction finder a device for finding out the direction from which radio waves or signals are coming
di·rec·tive (də rek′tiv, dī-) *adj.* 1. directing 2. indicating direction —*n.* a general instruction or order issued authoritatively
di·rect·ly (-rekt′lē) *adv.* 1. in a direct way or line; straight 2. with nothing coming between [*directly* responsible] 3. exactly [*directly* opposite] 4. right away —*conj.* [Colloq.] as soon as
direct object the word or words denoting the thing or person that receives the action of a transitive verb (Ex.: *ball* in *he hit the ball*)
di·rec·tor (di rek′tər) *n.* a person or thing that directs; specif., *a*) a person who supervises the affairs of an institution, trust, etc. *b*) a member of a board chosen to direct the affairs of a company or institution *c*) a person who directs the staging, etc. of a film, etc. *d*) [Chiefly U.S.] *Music* a conductor —**di·rec·to·ri·al** (də rek′tôr′ē əl, dī-) *adj.* —**di·rec′tor·ship** *n.* —**di·rec′tress** (-tris) *n.fem.*
di·rec·tor·ate (-it) *n.* 1. the position of director 2. a board of directors
director general the chief administrator, as of the B.B.C.
director of public prosecutions an official who, under the direction of the Attorney General, institutes, undertakes, or conducts criminal proceedings
di·rec·to·ry (də rek′tər ē, dī-) *adj.* directing or advising —*n., pl.* **-ries** 1. a book of directions 2. a book listing the names, addresses, etc. of a specific group of persons 3. a directorate
direct primary election [U.S.] a preliminary election at which candidates for public office are chosen by direct vote of the people
direct speech the reporting of what was said using the exact words and quotation marks
direct tax a tax levied directly on the person who is to pay it, as an income tax or property tax
dire·ful (dīr′fəl) *adj.* dreadful; terrible —**dire′ful·ly** *adv.* —**dire′ful·ness** *n.*
dirge (durj) *n.* [< L. *dirige* (imper. of *dirigere*, to direct), first word of an antiphon in the Office of the Dead] 1. a funeral hymn 2. a slow, sad song, poem, etc. expressing grief or mourning
dir·ham (dir ham′) *n.* [Ar. < L. *drachma*, DRACHMA] *see*

MONETARY UNITS, table (Morocco, Qatar, United Arab Emirates)
dir·i·gi·ble (dir′i jə b′l, də rij′ə-) *adj.* [ML. *dirigibilis*: see DIRECT & -IBLE] that can be directed or steered —*n.* same *as* AIRSHIP
dirk (durk) *n.* [earlier *dork, durk* < ?] a short, straight dagger —*vt.* to stab with a dirk
dirn·dl (durn′d′l) *n.* [G., dial. dim. of *Dirne*, girl] 1. a kind of dress with a full skirt, gathered waist, and closefitting bodice 2. the skirt of such a dress: also **dirndl skirt**
dirt (durt) *n.* [ME. < *drit* < ON. *dritr*, excrement] 1. any unclean matter, as mud, etc.; filth 2. earth or garden soil 3. dirtiness, corruption, etc. 4. obscene writing, speech, etc. 5. malicious talk or gossip 6. *Gold Mining* the gravel, soil, etc. from which gold is separated by washing or panning —*adj.* surfaced with compacted earth [a *dirt* track] —**do one dirt** [Slang] to harm one —**hit the dirt** [Slang] to drop to the ground
dirt-cheap (-chēp′) *adj.* [Colloq.] as cheap as dirt; very inexpensive
dirt track a track of levelled cinders, loose earth, etc. used for motor-cycle racing
dirt·y (-ē) *adj.* **dirt′i·er, dirt′i·est** 1. soiled or soiling with dirt; unclean 2. muddy or clouded [a *dirty* green] 3. obscene; pornographic [*dirty* jokes] 4. mean; nasty; vile [a *dirty* coward] 5. unfair; dishonest [a *dirty* player] 6. producing much fallout: said of nuclear weapons 7. [Colloq.] showing dislike, anger, irritation, etc. [a *dirty* look] 8. *Naut.* squally; rough [*dirty* weather] —*vt., vi.* **dirt′ied, dirt′y·ing** to make or become dirty; soil; stain —*adv.* [Slang] extremely; very (with *big* or *great*) [a *dirty* big hole] —**a dirty shame** a very unfortunate circumstance —**dirty linen** private matters that could cause gossip —**do the dirty on** to behave meanly or unkindly towards —**dirt′-i·ly** *adv.* —**dirt′i·ness** *n.*
dis- [< OFr. or L.; OFr. *des-* < L. *dis-*: cf. DE-] 1. a *v.-forming prefix meaning: a*) away, apart [*dismiss*] *b*) deprive of, expel from [*disbar*] *c*) cause to be the opposite of [*disable*] *d*) fail, cease, refuse to [*dissatisfy*] or do the opposite of [*disjoin*] 2. *an adj.-forming prefix meaning* not, un-, the opposite of [*dishonest*] 3. *a n.-forming prefix meaning* opposite of, lack of [*disunion*]
dis·a·bil·i·ty (dis′ə bil′ə tē) *n., pl.* **-ties** 1. a disabled condition 2. that which disables, as an illness or injury 3. a legal disqualification 4. a limitation or disadvantage
dis·a·ble (dis ā′b′l) *vt.* **-bled, -bling** 1. to make unable, unfit, or ineffective; cripple; incapacitate 2. to disqualify legally —**dis·a′ble·ment** *n.*
dis·a·buse (dis′ə byōoz′) *vt.* **-bused′, -bus′ing** to rid of false ideas; undeceive
dis·ad·van·tage (-əd vän′tij) *n.* 1. an unfavourable situation or circumstance; drawback; handicap 2. harm or detriment to one's interests —*vt.* **-taged, -tag·ing** to act to the disadvantage of —**at a disadvantage** in an unfavourable situation
dis·ad·van·taged (-tijd) *adj.* deprived of a decent standard of living, education, etc. by poverty and a lack of opportunity; underprivileged
dis·ad·van·ta·geous (dis ad′vən tā′jəs) *adj.* causing disadvantage; unfavourable; adverse —**dis·ad′van·ta′-geous·ly** *adv.*
dis·af·fect (dis′ə fekt′) *vt.* to make unfriendly, discontented, or disloyal, as towards the government —**dis′-af·fect′ed** *adj.* —**dis′af·fec′tion** *n.*
dis·af·fil·i·ate (-ə fil′ē āt′) *vt., vi.* **-at′ed, -at′ing** to end an affiliation (with) —**dis′af·fil′i·a′tion** *n.*
dis·af·for·est (-ə for′ist) *vt.* *Law* to reduce from the legal status of a forest to that of ordinary land
dis·a·gree (-ə grē′) *vi.* **-greed′, -gree′ing** 1. to fail to agree; be different 2. to differ in opinion; often, specif., to quarrel or dispute 3. to give distress [cheese *disagrees* with me]
dis·a·gree·a·ble (-ə b′l) *adj.* 1. not to one's taste; unpleasant; offensive 2. hard to get along with; quarrelsome —**dis′a·gree′a·ble·ness** *n.* —**dis′a·gree′a·bly** *adv.*
dis·a·gree·ment (-mənt) *n.* 1. refusal to agree 2. failure to agree; difference; discrepancy 3. difference of opinion 4. a quarrel or dispute
dis·al·low (dis′ə lou′) *vt.* to refuse to allow; reject as invalid or illegal —**dis′al·low′ance** *n.*
dis·ap·pear (-ə pir′) *vi.* 1. to cease to be seen; go out of sight 2. to cease being; become lost or extinct —**dis′-ap·pear′ance** *n.*
dis·ap·point (-ə point′) *vt.* 1. to fail to satisfy the hopes or expectations of; leave unsatisfied 2. to frustrate (hopes, etc.) —**dis′ap·point′ing·ly** *adv.*
dis·ap·point·ment (-mənt) *n.* 1. a disappointing or being disappointed 2. a person or thing that disappoints
dis·ap·pro·ba·tion (-ap′rə bā′shən) *n.* disapproval
dis·ap·prov·al (-ə prōov′l) *n.* 1. failure or refusal to approve 2. unfavourable opinion
dis·ap·prove (-ə prōov′) *vt.* **-proved′, -prov′ing** 1. to have or express an unfavourable opinion of 2. to refuse to

approve; reject —*vi.* to feel or express disapproval (*of*)
—**dis′ap·prov′ing·ly** *adv.*

dis·arm (dis ärm′) *vt.* **1.** to take away weapons or armaments from **2.** to make harmless **3.** to overcome the hostility of —*vi.* **1.** to lay down arms **2.** to reduce or do away with armed forces and armaments

dis·ar·ma·ment (-är′mə mənt) *n.* **1.** the act of disarming **2.** the reduction of armed forces and armaments, as to a limitation set by treaty

dis·arm·ing (-är′miŋ) *adj.* removing suspicions, fears, or hostility —**dis·arm′ing·ly** *adv.*

dis·ar·range (dis′ə rānj′) *vt.* **-ranged′, -rang′ing** to upset the order or arrangement of; make less neat; disorder —**dis′-ar·range′ment** *n.*

dis·ar·ray (-ə rā′) *vt.* **1.** to throw into disorder or confusion; upset **2.** [Archaic] to undress —*n.* **1.** disorder; confusion **2.** a state of disorderly or insufficient dress

dis·as·sem·ble (-ə sem′b'l) *vt.* **-bled, -bling** to take apart —**dis′as·sem′bly** *n.*

dis·as·so·ci·ate (-ə sō′shē ãt′, -sē-) *vt.* **-at′ed, -at′ing** to sever association with; separate; dissociate —**dis′as·so′ci·a′tion** *n.*

dis·as·ter (di zäs′tər) *n.* [< OFr. < It. < L. *dis-* + *astrum* < Gr. *astron,* a star: cf. ILL-STARRED] any happening that causes great harm or damage; serious or sudden misfortune; calamity

dis·as·trous (-trəs) *adj.* of the nature of a disaster; causing great harm, damage, grief, etc.; calamitous —**dis·as′trous·ly** *adv.*

dis·a·vow (dis′ə vou′) *vt.* to deny any knowledge or approval of, or responsibility for; disclaim; disown —**dis′-a·vow′al** *n.*

dis·band (dis band′) *vt.* **1.** to break up (an association or organization) **2.** to dismiss (a military force) from service —*vi.* to cease to exist as an organization; scatter; disperse —**dis·band′ment** *n.*

dis·bar (-bär′) *vt.* **-barred′, -bar′ring** to expel (a lawyer) from the bar; deprive of the right to practise law —**dis·bar′-ment** *n.*

dis·be·lief (dis′bə lēf′) *n.* refusal to believe; absence of belief

dis·be·lieve (-lēv′) *vt.* **-lieved′, -liev′ing** to reject as untrue —*vi.* to refuse to believe (*in*) —**dis′be·liev′er** *n.*

dis·bur·den (dis bur′d'n) *vt.* to relieve of a burden or of anything burdensome

dis·burse (-burs′) *vt.* **-bursed′, -burs′ing** [< OFr. *desbourser:* see DIS- & BOURSE] to pay out; expend —**dis·burs′a·ble** *adj.* —**dis·burs′al, —dis·burse′ment** *n.* —**dis·burs′er** *n.*

disc (disk) *n.* [< L. *discus,* DISCUS] **1.** any flat, circular thing **2.** anything with the appearance of a disc [the moon's *disc*] **3.** *a*) a gramophone record *b*) a thin, flat, circular plate coated with ferromagnetic particles, on which computer data can be stored **4.** any of the sharp, circular blades on a disc harrow **5.** *Biol.* any disc-shaped part or structure; specif., *a*) the disc-shaped centre of certain composite flowers *b*) a layer of fibrous connective tissue, with some cartilage, occurring between vertebrae

disc. **1.** discount **2.** discovered

dis·card (dis kärd′; *for n.* dis′kärd) *vt.* [< OFr.: see DIS- & CARD[1]] **1.** *Card Games a*) to remove (a card or cards) from the hand dealt *b*) to play (a card not a trump and not in the suit led) **2.** to get rid of as no longer valuable or useful —*vi. Card Games* to make a discard —*n.* **1.** a discarding or being discarded **2.** something discarded **3.** *Card Games* the card or cards discarded

disc brake a brake, as on a motor vehicle, that causes two friction pads to press on either side of a disc rotating with the wheel

dis·cern (di surn′, -zurn′) *vt.* [< OFr. < L. *dis-,* apart + *cernere,* to separate] **1.** to recognize as separate or different **2.** to perceive or recognize; make out clearly —*vi.* to perceive or recognize the difference —**dis·cern′i·ble** *adj.* —**dis·cern′i·bly** *adv.*

dis·cern·ing (-iŋ) *adj.* having or showing good judgment or understanding —**dis·cern′ing·ly** *adv.*

dis·cern·ment (-mənt) *n.* **1.** a discerning **2.** keen perception or judgment; insight; acumen

disc flower any of the tubular flowers in the central disc of the flower head of a composite plant

dis·charge (dis chärj′; *for n.* usually dis′chärj) *vt.* **-charged′, -charg′ing** [< OFr. < L. *dis-,* from + *carrus,* wagon, CAR] **1.** to relieve of or release from something that burdens or confines; specif., *a*) to remove the cargo of (a ship) *b*) to release the charge of (a gun) *c*) to release (a soldier, jury, etc.) from duty *d*) to dismiss from employment *e*) to release (a prisoner) from jail, (a defendant) from suspicion, (a debtor or bankrupt) from obligations, etc. **2.** to release or remove (that by which one is burdened or confined); specif., *a*) to unload (a cargo) *b*) to shoot (a projectile) **3.** to relieve oneself or itself of (a burden, load, etc.); specif., *a*) to throw off; emit [to *discharge* pus] *b*) to pay (a debt) or perform (a duty) **4.** *Elec.* to remove stored energy from (a battery

or capacitor) —*vi.* **1.** to get rid of a burden, load, etc. **2.** to be released or thrown off **3.** to go off: said of a gun, etc. **4.** to emit waste matter: said of a wound, etc. —*n.* **1.** a discharging or being discharged **2.** that which discharges, as a certificate of dismissal from military service, etc. **3.** that which is discharged, as pus from a sore **4.** a flow of electric current across a gap, as in a spark or arc —**dis·charge′a·ble** *adj.* —**dis·charg′er** *n.*

discharge tube a device in which a gas or metal vapour conducting an electric discharge is the source of light

disc harrow a harrow with sharp, revolving circular blades used to break up the soil for sowing

dis·ci·ple (di sī′p'l) *n.* [< OFr. & OE., both < L. *discipulus,* pupil < *discere,* to learn] **1.** a pupil or follower of any teacher or school **2.** an early follower of Jesus, esp. one of the Apostles —**dis·ci′ple-ship′** *n.*

dis·ci·pli·nar·i·an (dis′ə pli ner′ē ən) *n.* one who believes in or enforces strict discipline

dis·ci·pli·nar·y (dis′ə pli nər ē) *adj.* **1.** of or having to do with discipline **2.** that enforces discipline by punishing or correcting

DISC HARROW

dis·ci·pline (dis′ə plin) *n.* [< OFr. < L. *disciplina* < *discipulus:* see DISCIPLE] **1.** a branch of knowledge or learning **2.** *a*) training that develops self-control or orderliness and efficiency *b*) strict control to enforce obedience **3.** the result of such training or control; orderly conduct, obedience, etc. **4.** a system of rules, as for a monastic order **5.** treatment that corrects or punishes —*vt.* **-plined, -plin·ing** **1.** to subject to discipline; train; control **2.** to punish —**dis′ci·plin·a·ble** *adj.* —**dis′ci·plin·al** *adj.* —**dis′-ci·plin·er** *n.*

disc jockey a person who conducts a radio programme of recorded music, interspersed with chatter, etc.

dis·claim (dis klām′) *vt.* **1.** to give up any claim to or connection with **2.** to refuse to acknowledge or admit; repudiate —*vi.* to make a disclaimer —**dis·cla·ma·tion** (dis′-klə mā′shən) *n.*

dis·claim·er (-ər) *n.* **1.** a disclaiming or renunciation, as of a claim, title, etc. **2.** a disavowing

dis·close (-klōz′) *vt.* **-closed′, -clos′ing** **1.** to bring into view; uncover **2.** to reveal; make known —**dis·clos′er** *n.*

dis·clos·ure (-klō′zhər) *n.* **1.** a disclosing or being disclosed **2.** a thing disclosed; revelation

dis·co (dis′kō) *n.* *clipped form of* DISCOTHEQUE

dis·cob·o·lus (dis kob′ə ləs) *n.* [L. < Gr. < *diskos,* discus + *ballein,* to throw] a discus thrower

dis·cog·ra·phy (dis kog′rə fē) *n., pl.* **-phies** [< L. *discus,* a disc + (BIBLIO)GRAPHY] **1.** the systematic cataloguing of gramophone records **2.** a list of the recordings of a particular performer, composer, composition, etc. —**dis·cog′ra·pher** *n.*

dis·coid (dis′koid) *adj.* [< LL. < Gr. < *diskos,* a disc + *eidos,* form] shaped like a disc: also **dis·coi′dal** —*n.* anything shaped like a disc

dis·col·our (dis kul′ər) *vt., vi.* to change in colour by fading, streaking, or staining —**dis·col′our·a′tion, dis·col′-or·a′tion** *n.*

dis·com·bob·u·late (dis′kəm bob′yoo lāt′) *vt.* **-lat′ed, -lat′-ing** [prob. whimsical alteration of ff.] [Chiefly U.S. Colloq.] to upset the composure of; disconcert

dis·com·fit (dis kum′fit) *vt.* [< OFr. < L. *dis-* + *conficere:* see CONFECT] **1.** orig., to defeat **2.** to frustrate the plans or expectations of **3.** to make uneasy; disconcert —**dis·com′-fi·ture** (-fi chər) *n.*

dis·com·fort (dis kum′fərt) *n.* **1.** lack of comfort; uneasiness; inconvenience **2.** anything causing this —*vt.* to cause discomfort to; distress

dis·com·mode (dis′kə mōd′) *vt.* **-mod′ed, -mod′ing** [< DIS- + L. *commodare,* to make suitable] to cause bother to; inconvenience —**dis′com·mo′di·ous** *adj.*

dis·com·pose (-kəm pōz′) *vt.* **-posed′, -pos′ing** **1.** to disturb the calm or poise of; fluster; disconcert **2.** [Now Rare] to disturb the order of; disarrange —**dis′com·po′sure** (-pō′zhər) *n.*

dis·con·cert (-kən surt′) *vt.* **1.** to upset or frustrate (plans, etc.) **2.** to upset the composure of —**dis′con·cert′ing** *adj.* —**dis′con·cert′ing·ly** *adv.* —**dis′con·cer′tion** *n.*

dis·con·firm (-kən furm′) *vt.* to tend to falsify a theory, hypothesis, etc.

dis·con·nect (-kə nekt′) *vt.* to break or undo the connection of; separate, detach, unplug, etc. —**dis′con·nec′-tion** *n.*

dis·con·nect·ed (-nek′tid) *adj.* **1.** separated, detached, etc. **2.** broken up into unrelated parts; incoherent —**dis′-con·nect′ed·ly** *adv.* —**dis′con·nect′ed·ness** *n.*

dis·con·so·late (dis kon′sə lit) *adj.* [< ML. < L.: see DIS- & CONSOLE[1]] **1.** so unhappy that nothing will console;

dejected **2.** causing dejection; cheerless —**dis·con′so·late·ly** *adv.* —**dis·con′so·late·ness, dis·con′so·la′tion** (-lā′shən) *n.*

dis·con·tent (dis′kən tent′) *adj.* *same as* DISCONTENTED —*n.* lack of contentment; dissatisfaction: also **dis′con·tent′ment** —*vt.* to make discontented

dis·con·tent·ed (-id) *adj.* not contented; wanting something more or different —**dis′con·tent′ed·ly** *adv.* —**dis′con·tent′ed·ness** *n.*

dis·con·tin·ue (dis′kən tin′yōō) *vt.* -**ued, -u·ing 1.** to stop using, doing, etc.; cease; give up **2.** *Law* to stop (a suit) prior to trial —*vi.* to stop; end —**dis′con·tin′u·ance** (-yōō wəns), **dis′con·tin′u·a′tion** (-yōō wā′shən) *n.*

dis·con·tin·u·ous (-yōō wəs) *adj.* not continuous; broken; intermittent —**dis·con·ti·nu·i·ty** (dis kon′tə nyōō′ə tē) *n.* —**dis′con·tin′u·ous·ly** *adv.*

dis·co·phile (dis′kə fil′) *n.* [< L. *discus*, disc + -PHILE] an expert on, or collector of, gramophone records

dis·cord (dis′kôrd; *for v., usually* dis kôrd′) *n.* [< OFr. < L. < *discors* (gen. *discordis*), discordant < *dis-*, apart + *cor*, heart] **1.** lack of concord; disagreement **2.** a harsh or confused noise, as the sound of battle **3.** *Music* a lack of harmony in tones sounded together —*vi.* to disagree; clash

dis·cord·ant (dis kôr′d'nt) *adj.* **1.** not in accord; disagreeing; conflicting **2.** not in harmony; dissonant; clashing —**dis·cord′ance, dis·cord′an·cy** *n.* —**dis·cord′ant·ly** *adv.*

dis·co·thèque (dis′kə tek) *n.* [Fr. < *disque*, record + *bibliothèque*, library] a nightclub or other public place for dancing to recorded popular music

dis·count (dis′kount; *for v., also* dis kount′) *n.* [< OFr. < ML. *discomputare*: see DIS- & COMPUTE] **1.** *a)* a reduction from a usual or list price *b)* a deduction from a debt, allowed for prompt or cash payment **2.** the interest deducted in advance by one who lends money on a promissory note, etc. **3.** the rate of interest (**discount rate**) charged for this **4.** a discounting —*vt.* **1.** to pay or receive the value of (a promissory note, etc.), minus the discount (sense 2) **2.** to deduct an amount or percent from (a bill, price, etc.) **3.** to sell at less than the regular price **4.** *a)* to take (a story, etc.) at less than face value, allowing for exaggeration, bias, etc. *b)* to disbelieve or disregard entirely **5.** to reckon with in advance —**at a discount 1.** below the regular price **2.** worth little —**dis′count·a·ble** *adj.*

dis·coun·te·nance (dis koun′tə nəns) *vt.* -**nanced, -nanc·ing 1.** to make ashamed or embarrassed; disconcert **2.** to refuse approval or support to

discount house 1. a finance organization which lends funds to both public and private enterprises **2.** [Chiefly U.S.] a retail store that sells goods for less than regular or list prices

dis·cour·age (dis kur′ij) *vt.* -**aged, -ag·ing** [OFr. *descoragier*] **1.** to deprive of courage; dishearten **2.** to advise or persuade (a person) to refrain **3.** to prevent or try to prevent by disapproving —*vi.* to become discouraged —**dis·cour′age·ment** *n.* —**dis·cour′ag·ing** *adj.* —**dis·cour′ag·ing·ly** *adv.*

dis·course (dis′kôrs; *also, and for v. usually,* dis kôrs′) *n.* [< OFr. < L. pp. < *dis-*, from + *currere*, to run] **1.** communication of ideas, information, etc., esp. by talking; conversation **2.** a formal treatment of a subject, in speech or writing **3.** [Archaic] ability to reason —*vi.* **-coursed′, -cours′ing 1.** to converse; talk **2.** to speak or write (*on* or *upon* a subject) formally —*vt.* [Archaic] to utter or tell —**dis·cours′er** *n.*

dis·cour·te·ous (dis kur′tē əs) *adj.* not courteous; impolite; ill-mannered —**dis·cour′te·ous·ly** *adv.* —**dis·cour′te·ous·ness** *n.*

dis·cour·te·sy (-tə sē) *n.* **1.** lack of courtesy; impoliteness; rudeness **2.** *pl.* **-sies** a rude or impolite act or remark

dis·cov·er (dis kuv′ər) *vt.* [< OFr. < LL. *discooperire*: see DIS- & COVER] **1.** to be the first to find, see, or know about **2.** to find out; learn of the existence of **3.** [Archaic] *a)* to reveal *b)* to uncover —**dis·cov′er·a·ble** *adj.* —**dis·cov′er·er** *n.*

dis·cov·er·y (-ər ē) *n.,* *pl.* **-er·ies 1.** a discovering **2.** anything discovered **3.** [Archaic] a revealing **4.** *Law* any disclosure that a defendant is compelled to make

disc parking a parking system in which cars display discs showing time of arrival

dis·cred·it (dis kred′it) *vt.* **1.** to reject as untrue **2.** to cast doubt on **3.** to damage the reputation of; disgrace —*n.* **1.** loss of belief or trust; doubt **2.** damage to one's reputation; disgrace **3.** something that causes disgrace —**dis·cred′it·a·ble** *adj.* —**dis·cred′it·a·bly** *adv.*

dis·creet (dis krēt′) *adj.* [< OFr. < L. pp. of *discernere*: see DISCERN] **1.** careful about what one says or does; prudent; esp., preserving confidences when necessary **2.** unobtrusively tasteful —**dis·creet′ly** *adv.* —**dis·creet′ness** *n.*

dis·crep·an·cy (dis krep′ən sē) *n.,* *pl.* **-cies** [< OFr. < L. < prp. of *discrepare*, to sound differently < *dis-*, from + *crepare*, to rattle] lack of agreement, or an instance of this; difference; inconsistency —**dis·crep′ant** *adj.* —**dis·crep′ant·ly** *adv.*

dis·crete (dis krēt′) *adj.* [< L.: see DISCREET] **1.** separate and distinct; not attached to others; unrelated **2.** made up of distinct parts; discontinuous —**dis·crete′ly** *adv.* —**dis·crete′ness** *n.*

dis·cre·tion (dis kresh′ən) *n.* **1.** the freedom or authority to make decisions and choices **2.** the quality of being discreet; prudence —**at one's discretion** as one wishes —**years (or age) of discretion** maturity

dis·cre·tion·ar·y (-ər ē) *adj.* left to one's discretion: also **dis·cre′tion·al**

dis·crim·i·na·ble (dis krim′ə nə b'l) *adj.* that can be discriminated or distinguished

dis·crim·i·nate (dis krim′ə nāt′; *for adj.* -nit) *vt.* -**nat′ed, -nat′ing** [< L. pp. of *discriminare* < *discrimen*, division < *discernere*: see DISCERN] **1.** to constitute a difference between; differentiate **2.** to recognize the difference between; distinguish —*vi.* **1.** to see the difference (*between* things); distinguish **2.** to be discerning **3.** to show partiality (*in favour of*) or prejudice (*against*) —*adj.* distinguishing carefully —**dis·crim′i·nat′ing** *adj.* —**dis·crim′i·nat′ing·ly** *adv.* —**dis·crim′i·na′tive** (-nāt′iv, -nə tiv) *adj.* —**dis·crim′i·na′tor** *n.*

dis·crim·i·na·tion (dis krim′ə nā′shən) *n.* **1.** the act of discriminating, or distinguishing differences **2.** the ability to do this **3.** a showing of partiality or prejudice in treatment; specif., policies directed against the welfare of minority groups

dis·crim·i·na·to·ry (-krim′ə nə tər ē) *adj.* **1.** practising discrimination, or showing prejudice **2.** discriminating, or distinguishing

dis·cur·sive (dis kur′siv) *adj.* [< ML. < L.: see DISCOURSE] **1.** wandering from one topic to another; rambling; digressive **2.** *Philos.* going from premises to conclusions in a series of logical steps —**dis·cur′sive·ly** *adv.* —**dis·cur′sive·ness** *n.*

dis·cus (dis′kəs) *n.,* *pl.* **dis′cus·es, dis·ci** (dis′kī) [L. < Gr. *diskos*] **1.** a heavy disc of metal and wood, orig. often of stone, thrown for distance in competition **2.** such a contest

dis·cuss (dis kus′) *vt.* [< L. pp. of *discutire* < *dis-*, apart + *quatere*, to shake] to talk or write about; consider and argue the pros and cons of —**dis·cuss′a·ble, dis·cuss′i·ble** *adj.* —**dis·cuss′ant, dis·cuss′er** *n.*

dis·cus·sion (dis kush′ən) *n.* talk or writing in which the pros and cons or various aspects of a subject are considered —**under discussion** being discussed

DISCUS THROWER

dis·dain (dis dān′) *vt.* [< OFr. < L. *dis-*, not + *dignari*, DEIGN] to regard as beneath one's dignity; specif., to refuse or reject with aloof contempt or scorn —*n.* aloof contempt or scorn —**dis·dain′ful** *adj.* —**dis·dain′ful·ly** *adv.* —**dis·dain′ful·ness** *n.*

dis·ease (di zēz′) *n.* [OFr. *desaise* < *des-*, DIS- + *aise*, EASE] **1.** any departure from health; illness in general **2.** a particular destructive process in an organ or organism; specific illness **3.** a harmful condition, as of society —*vt.* -**eased′, -eas′ing** to cause disease in; infect —**dis·eased′** *adj.*

dis·em·bark (dis′im bärk′) *vt.* to unload (passengers or goods) from a ship, aircraft, etc. —*vi.* to go ashore from a ship or leave an aircraft, etc. —**dis·em·bar·ka·tion** (dis′-em bär kā′shən) *n.*

dis·em·bar·rass (-im bar′əs) *vt.* to rid or relieve of something embarrassing, annoying, entangling, perplexing, or burdensome

dis·em·bod·y (-im bod′ē) *vt.* -**bod′ied, -bod′y·ing** to free from bodily existence; make incorporeal —**dis′em·bod′ied** *adj.* —**dis′em·bod′i·ment** *n.*

dis·em·bogue (-im bōg′) *vt., vi.* -**bogued′, -bogu′ing** [< Sp.] to pour out (its water) at the mouth; empty itself: said of a stream, etc.

dis·em·bow·el (-im bou′əl) *vt.* -**elled, -el·ling** to take out the bowels, or entrails, of; eviscerate —**dis′em·bow′el·ment** *n.*

dis·en·chant (-in chänt′) *vt.* to set free from an enchantment or illusion —**dis′en·chant′ment** *n.*

dis·en·cum·ber (-in kum′bər) *vt.* to relieve of a burden; free from a hindrance or annoyance

dis·en·fran·chise (-in fran′chīz) *vt.* -**chised, -chis·ing** *same as* DISFRANCHISE —**dis′en·fran′chise·ment** *n.*

dis·en·gage (-in gāj′) *vt.* -**gaged′, -gag′ing** to release or loosen from something that binds, holds, entangles, etc.; unfasten; detach —*vi.* to release oneself or itself —**dis′en·gage′ment** *n.*

dis·en·gaged (-in gājd′) *adj.* **1.** at leisure **2.** set loose; detached **3.** out of gear

dis·en·tan·gle (-in taŋ′g'l) *vt.* -**gled, -gling 1.** to free from something that entangles, confuses, etc.; extricate **2.** to straighten out (anything tangled, confused, etc.); untangle —*vi.* to get free from a tangle —**dis'en·tan'gle·ment** *n.*

dis·e·qui·lib·ri·um (dis ē'kwə lib'rē əm) *n., pl.* -**ri·ums, -ri·a** (-ə) lack or destruction of equilibrium, esp. in the economy

dis·es·tab·lish (dis'ə stab'lish) *vt.* 1. to deprive of the status of being established 2. to deprive (a state church) of official sanction and support by the government —**dis'·es·tab'lish·ment** *n.*

dis·es·teem (-ə stēm') *vt.* to hold in low esteem; dislike; slight —*n.* lack of esteem; disfavour

dis·fa·vour (dis fā'vər) *n.* 1. an unfavourable opinion; dislike; disapproval 2. the state of being disliked or disapproved of 3. an unkind act; disservice —*vt.* to regard or treat unfavourably; slight

dis·fig·ure (-fig'ər) *vt.* -**ured, -ur·ing** to hurt the appearance or attractiveness; deface; mar —**dis·fig'ure·ment, dis·fig'·u·ra'tion** *n.*

dis·fran·chise (-fran'chīz) *vt.* -**chised, -chis·ing** 1. to deprive of the rights of citizenship, esp. of the right to vote 2. to deprive of a privilege, right, or power —**dis·fran'·chise·ment** *n.*

dis·gorge (-gôrj') *vt., vi.* -**gorged', -gorg'ing** [< OFr.: see DIS- & GORGE] 1. to vomit 2. to give up (something) against one's will 3. to pour forth (its contents)

dis·grace (-grās') *n.* [< Fr. < It. < *dis-* (L. *dis-*), not + *grazia,* favour < L. *gratia:* see GRACE] 1. a being in disfavour as because of bad conduct 2. loss of respect; public dishonour; shame 3. a person or thing that brings shame (*to* one) —*vt.* -**graced', -grac'ing** to bring shame or dishonour upon; be a discredit to —**dis·grac'er** *n.*

dis·grace·ful (-fəl) *adj.* causing or characterized by disgrace; shameful —**dis·grace'ful·ly** *adv.* —**dis·grace'·ful·ness** *n.*

dis·grun·tle (-grun't'l) *vt.* -**tled, -tling** [DIS- + obs. *gruntle,* freq. of GRUNT] to make peevishly discontented —**dis·grun'tle·ment** *n.*

dis·guise (-gīz') *vt.* -**guised', -guis'ing** [< OFr.: see DIS- & GUISE] 1. to make appear, sound, etc. different from usual so as to be unrecognizable 2. to hide the real nature of —*n.* 1. any clothes, equipment, manner, etc. used for disguising 2. the state of being disguised 3. the act or practice of disguising —**dis·guis'ed·ly** *adv.* —**dis·guis'er** *n.*

dis·gust (-gust') *n.* [< MFr. < *des-* (see DIS-) + L. *gustus,* taste] a sickening distaste or dislike; deep aversion; repugnance —*vt.* to cause to feel disgust; be sickening or repulsive to —**dis·gust'ed** *adj.* —**dis·gust'ed·ly** *adv.* —**dis·gust'ing** *adj.* —**dis·gust'ing·ly** *adv.*

dish (dish) *n.* [OE. *disc,* dish, ult. < L. *discus,* DISCUS] 1. *a)* any container, generally shallow and concave, for food *b)* [*pl.*] plates, bowls, cups, etc., collectively 2. *a)* the food in a dish *b)* a particular kind of food 3. a dishful 4. a dish-shaped object or concavity 5. [Slang] *a)* a pretty girl or woman *b)* a favourite thing —*vt.* 1. to serve (food) in a dish (usually with *up* or *out*) 2. to make concave 3. [Slang] to ruin or spoil —*vi.* to be or become dish-shaped; cave in —**dish out** to distribute; share or give out, esp. carelessly

dis·ha·bille (dis'ə bēl') *n.* [< Fr. < *dés-* (see DIS-) + *habiller,* to dress] the state of being dressed only partially or in night clothes

dish antenna a radio transmitting or receiving antenna with a dish-shaped reflector

dis·har·mo·ny (dis här'mə nē) *n.* lack of harmony; discord —**dis'har·mo'ni·ous** (-mō'nē əs) *adj.*

dish·cloth (dish'klôth') *n.* a cloth for washing dishes

dis·heart·en (dis härt'n) *vt.* to discourage; depress —**dis·heart'en·ing** *adj.* —**dis·heart'en·ing·ly** *adv.* —**dis·heart'en·ment** *n.*

di·shev·el (di shev'l) *vt.* -**elled, -el·ling** [< OFr. < *des-,* DIS- + *chevel,* hair < L. *capillus*] 1. to cause (hair, clothing, etc.) to become disarranged and untidy; rumple 2. to cause the hair or clothes of (a person) to become disarranged —**di·shev'elled** *adj.* —**di·shev'el·ment** *n.*

dish·ful (dish'fool') *n., pl.* -**fuls'** as much as a dish holds

dis·hon·est (dis on'ist) *adj.* not honest; lying, cheating, etc. —**dis·hon'est·ly** *adv.*

dis·hon·es·ty (-ist ē) *n.* 1. the quality of being dishonest 2. *pl.* -**ties** a dishonest act or statement; fraud, lie, etc.

dis·hon·our (dis on'ər) *n.* 1. *a)* loss of honour, respect, etc. *b)* state of shame; disgrace 2. a cause of dishonour; discredit 3. a refusal or failure to pay a cheque, draft, etc. —*vt.* 1. to treat disrespectfully 2. to disgrace 3. to refuse or fail to pay (a cheque, draft, etc.)

dis·hon·our·a·ble (-ə b'l) *adj.* causing or deserving dishonour; shameful; disgraceful —**dis·hon'our·a·ble·ness** *n.* —**dis·hon'our·a·bly** *adv.*

dish·rag (dish'rag') *n.* same as DISHCLOTH

dish·wash·er (-wosh'ər) *n.* 1. a machine for washing dishes, etc. 2. a person whose job is to wash dishes, cutlery, etc. 3. the water wagtail 4. [Aust.] the restless flycatcher

dish·water (-wôt'ər) *n.* 1. water in which dishes, etc. have been washed 2. something resembling this

dish·y (dish'ē) *adj.* [Slang] good-looking; attractive

dis·il·lu·sion (dis'i loo'zhən) *vt.* 1. to free from illusion or false ideas 2. to take away the idealism of and make disappointed, bitter, etc. —*n.* a disillusioning or being disillusioned: also **dis'il·lu'sion·ment**

dis·in·cen·tive (dis'in sen'tiv) *n.* a thing or factor that keeps one from doing something; deterrent

dis·in·cli·na·tion (dis in'klə nā'shən) *n.* a dislike or unwillingness; aversion; reluctance

dis·in·cline (dis'in klīn') *vt.* -**clined', -clin'ing** to make unwilling

dis·in·fect (-in fekt') *vt.* to destroy the harmful bacteria, viruses, etc. in or on —**dis'in·fec'tion** *n.*

dis·in·fect·ant (-ənt) *adj.* disinfecting —*n.* anything that disinfects

dis·in·fla·tion (-in flā'shən) *n. Econ.* a reduction of price levels, planned to increase purchasing power but control deflation —**dis'in·fla'tion·ar·y** *adj.*

dis·in·gen·u·ous (-in jen'yoo wəs) *adj.* not straightforward; not candid; insincere —**dis'in·gen'u·ous·ly** *adv.* —**dis'·in·gen'u·ous·ness** *n.*

dis·in·her·it (-in her'it) *vt.* 1. to deprive of an inheritance or the right to inherit 2. to deprive of any right or privilege —**dis'in·her'it·ance** *n.*

dis·in·te·grate (dis in'tə grāt') *vt., vi.* -**grat'ed, -grat'ing** 1. to separate into parts or fragments; break up 2. to undergo or cause to undergo a nuclear transformation —**dis·in'·te·gra'tion** *n.* —**dis·in'te·gra'tive** *adj.* —**dis·in'te·gra'tor** *n.*

dis·in·ter (dis'in tur') *vt.* -**terred', -ter'ring** 1. to remove from a grave, tomb, etc.; dig up; exhume 2. to bring to light —**dis'in·ter'ment** *n.*

dis·in·ter·est (dis in'trist, -tər ist) *n.* 1. lack of personal or selfish interest 2. lack of interest

dis·in·ter·est·ed (-id) *adj.* 1. not influenced by personal interest or selfish motives; impartial 2. uninterested: a revival of an obsolete meaning —**dis·in'ter·est·ed·ly** *adv.* —**dis·in'ter·est·ed·ness** *n.*

dis·join (-join') *vt.* to separate or detach

dis·joint (-joint') *vt.* 1. to put out of joint; dislocate 2. to dismember 3. to destroy the unity, connections, or orderliness of —*vi.* to come apart at the joints

dis·joint·ed (-id) *adj.* 1. out of joint 2. dismembered 3. incoherent: said esp. of speech —**dis·joint'ed·ly** *adv.* —**dis·joint'ed·ness** *n.*

dis·junc·tion (-juŋk'shən) *n.* 1. a disjoining or being disjoined; separation: also **dis·junc'ture** (-chər) 2. *Logic a)* the relation between alternatives of a disjunctive proposition *b)* a disjunctive proposition

dis·junc·tive (-tiv) *adj.* 1. disjoining; separating or causing to separate 2. *Gram.* indicating a contrast or an alternative between words, clauses, etc. ["or" and "but" are *disjunctive* conjunctions] 3. *Logic* presenting alternatives [a *disjunctive* proposition] —*n.* 1. *Gram.* a disjunctive conjunction 2. *Logic* a disjunctive proposition —**dis·junc'·tive·ly** *adv.*

disk (disk) *n.* var. sp. of DISC

disk harrow same as DISC HARROW

disk jockey same as DISC JOCKEY

dis·like (dis līk') *vt.* -**liked', -lik'ing** to have a feeling of not liking; feel aversion to —*n.* a feeling of not liking; distaste; aversion —**dis·lik'a·ble, dis·like'a·ble** *adj.*

dis·lo·cate (dis'lō kāt') *vt.* -**cat'ed, -cat'ing** 1. to put out of place; specif., to displace (a bone) from its proper position at a joint 2. to disarrange; disrupt —**dis'lo·ca'tion** *n.*

dis·lodge (dis loj') *vt., vi.* -**lodged', -lodg'ing** to force or be forced from a position or place where lodged, hiding, etc. —**dis·lodg'ment** *n.*

dis·loy·al (-loi'əl) *adj.* not loyal or faithful; faithless —**dis·loy'al·ly** *adv.*

dis·loy·al·ty (-tē) *n.* 1. the quality of being disloyal 2. *pl.* -**ties** a disloyal act

dis·mal (diz'm'l) *adj.* [ME., orig. n., evil days < OFr. < ML. *dies mali*] 1. causing gloom or misery 2. dark and gloomy; bleak; dreary 3. depressed; miserable —**dis'mal·ly** *adv.*

dis·man·tle (dis man't'l) *vt.* -**tled, -tling** [< OFr. *desmanteller:* see DIS- & MANTLE] 1. to strip of covering 2. to strip (a house, ship, etc.) of furniture, equipment, etc. 3. to take apart; disassemble —**dis·man'tle·ment** *n.*

dis·may (-mā') *vt.* [< Anglo-Fr. < OFr. *des-,* intens. + *esmayer,* to deprive of power] to make discouraged at the prospect of trouble; fill with alarm; daunt —*n.* a loss of courage at the prospect of trouble

dis·mem·ber (-mem'bər) *vt.* [< OFr.: see DIS- & MEMBER] 1. to remove the limbs of by cutting or tearing 2. to pull or cut to pieces; divide up or mutilate —**dis·mem'ber·ment** *n.*

dis·miss (-mis') *vt.* [< ML. pp. of *dimittere,* for L. *dimittere < dis-,* from + *mittere,* to send] 1. to send away; cause or allow to leave 2. to remove or discharge from an office, employment, etc. 3. to put out of one's mind 4.

Cricket to put (a batsman or team) out as by being bowled, caught, etc. **5.** *Law* to reject (a claim or action) —**dis·miss'·al** *n.* —**dis·miss'i·ble** *adj.* —**dis·mis'sive** *adj.*

dis·mount (-mount') *vi.* to get off, as from a horse or bicycle —*vt.* **1.** to remove (a thing) from its mounting or setting **2.** to cause to dismount **3.** to take apart —*n.* a dismounting

dis·o·be·di·ence (dis'ə bē'dē əns) *n.* refusal to obey; failure to follow commands; insubordination —**dis'o·be'di·ent** *adj.* —**dis'o·be'di·ent·ly** *adv.*

dis·o·bey (dis'ə bā') *vt., vi.* to refuse or fail to obey

dis·o·blige (-ə blīj') *vt.* -**bliged'**, -**blig'ing 1.** to refuse to oblige, or do a favour for **2.** to slight; offend —**dis'o·blig'ing** *adj.* —**dis'o·blig'ing·ly** *adv.*

dis·or·der (dis ôr'dər) *n.* **1.** a lack of order; confusion **2.** a breach of public peace; riot **3.** a disregard of system; irregularity **4.** an upset of normal function; ailment —*vt.* **1.** to throw into disorder; disarrange **2.** to upset the normal functions or health of —**dis·or'dered** *adj.*

dis·or·der·ly (-lē) *adj.* **1.** not orderly; untidy; unsystematic **2.** unruly; riotous **3.** *Law* violating public peace, safety, or order —**dis·or'der·li·ness** *n.*

dis·or·gan·ize (dis ôr'gə nīz') *vt.* -**ized'**, -**iz'ing** to break up the order, arrangement, or system of; throw into disorder —**dis·or'gan·i·za'tion** *n.*

dis·o·ri·ent (-ôr'ē ent') *vt.* **1.** to cause to lose one's bearings **2.** to confuse mentally Also **dis·o'·ri·en·tate'**(-ən tāt') -**tat'ed**, -**tat'ing** —**dis·o'ri·en·ta'tion** *n.*

dis·own (-ōn') *vt.* to refuse to acknowledge as one's own; repudiate; cast off

dis·par·age (-par'ij) *vt.* -**aged**, -**ag'ing** [< OFr. *desparagier,* to marry one of inferior rank < *des-* (see DIS-) + *parage,* rank < *per,* PEER[1]] **1.** to lower in esteem; discredit **2.** to speak slightingly of; belittle —**dis·par'age·ment** *n.* —**dis·par'ag·ing** *adj.* —**dis·par'ag·ing·ly** *adv.*

dis·pa·rate (dis'pər it) *adj.* [< L. pp. of *disparare* < *dis-,* apart, not + *parare,* to make equal < *par,* equal] distinct or different in kind; unequal —**dis'pa·rate·ly** *adv.* —**dis'·pa·rate·ness** *n.*

dis·par·i·ty (dis par'ə tē) *n., pl.* -**ties 1.** inequality or difference, as in quality **2.** incongruity

dis·pas·sion·ate (-pash'ən it) *adj.* free from passion, emotion, or bias; calm; impartial —**dis·pas'sion** *n.* —**dis·pas'sion·ate·ly** *adv.*

dis·patch (-pach') *vt.* [< Sp. & It. < OFr. *despeechier, pedica,* a fetter ult. < L. *dis-,* not + LL. *impedicare,* to entangle < L. ?] **1.** to send off or out promptly on a specific errand or official business; specif., to send out (trains, buses, etc.) according to a schedule **2.** to kill **3.** to finish quickly or promptly —*n.* **1.** a sending out or off **2.** a killing **3.** efficient speed; promptness **4.** a message, esp. an official message **5.** a news story sent to a newspaper, TV company, etc., as by a special reporter or news agency —**mentioned in dispatches** to be commended for bravery in action —**dis·patch'er** *n.*

dispatch case a case used for carrying papers, documents, etc.

dispatch rider a soldier, originally on horseback, now on a motorcycle, who carries dispatches

dis·pel (-pel') *vt.* -**pelled'**, -**pel'ling** [< L. *dispellere* < *dis-,* away + *pellere,* to drive] to scatter and drive away; disperse

dis·pen·sa·ble (-pen'sə b'l) *adj.* **1.** that can be dispensed or dealt out **2.** that can be dispensed with —**dis·pen'sa·bil'·i·ty** *n.*

dis·pen·sa·ry (-sər ē) *n., pl.* -**ries 1.** a room or place, as in a school or factory, where medicines and first aid are available **2.** an outpatient's department

dis·pen·sa·tion (dis'pen sā'shən) *n.* **1.** a dispensing; distribution **2.** anything distributed **3.** an administrative system; management **4.** a release from an obligation **5.** *R.C.Ch.* an exemption from a specific church law **6.** *Theol.* a) the ordering of events under divine authority b) any religious system —**dis'pen·sa'tion·al** *adj.*

dis·pen·sa·to·ry (dis pen'sə tər ē) *n., pl.* -**ries** a handbook on medicines; pharmacopoeia

dis·pense (-pens') *vt.* -**pensed'**, -**pens'ing** [< OFr. < L. *dispensare* < pp. of *dispendere* < *dis-,* out + *pendere,* to weigh] **1.** to give or deal out; distribute **2.** to prepare and give out (medicines, prescriptions, etc.) [a *dispensing* chemist] **3.** to administer [to *dispense* the law] **4.** to exempt; excuse —**dispense with 1.** to get rid of **2.** to do without

dis·pens·er (-pen'sər) *n.* one that dispenses, as a container designed to dispense its contents in handy units or portions

dis·perse (-purs') *vt.* -**persed'**, -**pers'ing** [< L. pp. of *dispergere* < *dis-,* out + *spargere,* to strew] **1.** to break up and scatter in all directions; distribute widely **2.** to dispel (mist, etc.) **3.** to break up (light) into its component coloured rays —*vi.* to move in different directions —**dis·per'sal** *n.* —**dis·pers'er** *n.* —**dis·pers'i·ble** *adj.* —**dis·per'sive** (-pur'siv) *adj.*

dis·per·sion (dis pur'zhən, -shən) *n.* **1.** a dispersing or being dispersed **2.** the breaking up of light into component coloured rays, as by a prism **3.** a colloidal system with its dispersed particles and the medium in which these are suspended

dis·pir·it (di spir'it) *vt.* to depress; deject —**dis·pir'it·ed** *adj.* —**dis·pir'it·ed·ly** *adv.*

dis·place (dis plās') *vt.* -**placed'**, -**plac'ing 1.** to move from its usual or proper place **2.** to remove from office **3.** to replace [a ship *displaces* a certain amount of water]

displaced person a person forced from his country, esp. in war, and left homeless elsewhere

dis·place·ment (-mənt) *n.* **1.** a displacing or being displaced **2.** a) the weight or volume of a fluid displaced by a floating object; specif., the weight of water displaced by a ship b) the volume displaced by a piston

dis·play (-plā') *vt.* [< OFr. < L. *displicare* < *dis-,* apart + *plicare,* to fold] **1.** to unfold; spread out **2.** to put or spread out to be seen; exhibit **3.** to disclose; reveal —*n.* **1.** a displaying; exhibition **2.** anything displayed; exhibit **3.** showy exhibition; ostentation **4.** a) a manifestation [a *display* of courage] b) a mere show; sham [a *display* of pity] **5.** *Zool.* a pattern of behaviour in birds, fishes, etc., by which the male attracts attention while it is courting the female, defending its territory, etc. —*adj.* designating printing types used for headings, advertisements, etc. —**dis·play'er** *n.*

dis·please (-plēz') *vt., vi.* -**pleased'**, -**pleas'ing** to fail to please; annoy; offend —**dis·pleas'ing** *adj.* —**dis·pleas'ing·ly** *adv.*

dis·pleas·ure (-plezh'ər) *n.* **1.** the fact or feeling of being displeased; dissatisfaction, annoyance, etc. **2.** [Archaic] discomfort, trouble, etc.

dis·port (-pôrt') *vi.* [< OFr. < *des-* (see DIS-) + *porter* < L. *portare,* to carry] to play; frolic —*vt.* to amuse or divert (oneself)

dis·pos·a·ble (-pō'zə b'l) *adj.* **1.** that can be discarded **2.** that can be disposed as one wishes —*n.* something that is designed for disposal —**dis·pos'a·bil'i·ty** *n.*

dis·pos·al (-pō'z'l) *n.* **1.** a disposing; specif., a) arrangement in a particular order b) a dealing with matters; settling of affairs c) a giving away; transfer d) a getting rid of **2.** the power to dispose —**at one's disposal** available to be used as one wishes

dis·pose (-pōz') *vt.* -**posed'**, -**pos'ing** [< OFr. < L. pp. of *disponere:* see DIS- & POSITION] **1.** to place in a certain order; arrange **2.** to arrange (matters); settle (affairs) **3.** to make willing **4.** to make susceptible or liable —*vi.* to have the power to arrange or settle affairs —**dispose of 1.** to deal with; settle **2.** to give away or sell **3.** to get rid of **4.** to eat or drink up **5.** to refute an argument —**dis·pos'er** *n.*

dis·po·si·tion (dis'pə zish'ən) *n.* **1.** proper or orderly arrangement **2.** management or settlement of affairs **3.** a selling, giving away, etc. of something **4.** the power to dispose; control **5.** an inclination or tendency **6.** one's nature or temperament

dis·pos·sess (-pə zes') *vt.* to deprive of the possession of land, a house, etc.; oust —**dis'pos·ses'sion** (-zesh'ən) *n.* —**dis'pos·ses'sor** *n.*

dis·praise (dis prāz') *vt.* -**praised'**, -**prais'ing** to speak of with disapproval; disparage; censure —*n.* a dispraising; blame —**dis·prais'ing·ly** *adv.*

dis·proof (-proof') *n.* **1.** a disproving; refutation **2.** evidence that disproves

dis·pro·por·tion (dis'prə pôr'shən) *n.* lack of proportion; lack of symmetry —*vt.* to cause to be disproportionate —**dis'pro·por'tion·al** *adj.* —**dis'pro·por'tion·al·ly** *adv.*

dis·pro·por·tion·ate (-it) *adj.* not proportionate; not in proportion —**dis'pro·por'tion·ate·ly** *adv.*

dis·prove (dis proov') *vt.* -**proved'**, -**prov'ing** to prove to be false or in error —**dis·prov'a·ble** *adj.*

dis·pu·ta·ble (dis pyoot'ə b'l, dis'pyoo tə b'l) *adj.* that can be disputed; debatable —**dis·pu'ta·bil'i·ty** *n.* —**dis·pu'ta·bly** *adv.*

dis·pu·tant (dis pyoot''nt, dis'pyoo tənt) *adj.* disputing —*n.* one who disputes, or debates

dis·pu·ta·tion (dis'pyoo tā'shən) *n.* **1.** a disputing; dispute **2.** a debatelike discussion

dis·pu·ta·tious (-shəs) *adj.* inclined to dispute; fond of arguing: also **dis·pu·ta·tive** (dis pyoot'ə tiv) —**dis'pu·ta'·tious·ly** *adv.* —**dis'pu·ta'tious·ness** *n.*

dis·pute (dis pyoot') *vi.* -**put'ed**, -**put'ing** [< OFr. < L. *disputare* < *dis-,* apart + *putare,* to think] **1.** to argue; debate **2.** to quarrel —*vt.* **1.** to argue or debate (a question) **2.** to question the truth of; doubt **3.** to oppose in any way; resist **4.** to fight for; contest —*n.* **1.** a disputing; argument; debate **2.** a quarrel —**beyond dispute 1.** not open to dispute; settled **2.** indisputably —**in dispute** not settled —**dis·put'er** *n.*

dis·qual·i·fy (-kwol'ə fī') *vt.* -**fied'**, -**fy'ing 1.** to make unfit or unqualified **2.** to make or declare ineligible, as to participate further in a sport, for breaking rules —**dis·qual'·i·fi·ca'tion** (-fi kā'shən) *n.*

dis·qui·et (-kwī'ət) *vt.* to make anxious or restless; disturb —*n.* restlessness; anxiety —**dis·qui'et·ing** *adj.* —**dis·qui'·et·ing·ly** *adv.*

dis·qui·e·tude (-kwī'ə tyōōd') *n.* a disturbed or uneasy condition; restlessness; anxiety

dis·qui·si·tion (dis'kwə zish'ən) *n.* [< L. < pp. of *disquirere* < *dis-*, apart + *quaerere*, to seek] a formal discussion of some subject; treatise

dis·re·gard (dis'ri gärd') *vt.* 1. to pay little or no attention to 2. to treat without due respect; slight —*n.* 1. lack of attention 2. lack of due regard or respect —**dis're·gard'ful** *adj.*

dis·re·mem·ber (-ri mem'bər) *vt.* [Dial. or Colloq.] to forget; be unable to remember

dis·re·pair (-ri per') *n.* the condition of needing repairs; state of neglect; dilapidation

dis·rep·u·ta·ble (dis rep'yoo tə b'l) *adj.* 1. not reputable; having or causing a bad reputation 2. not fit to be seen; shabby, dirty, etc. —**dis·rep'u·ta·bly** *adv.*

dis·re·pute (dis'ri pyōōt') *n.* lack or loss of repute; bad reputation; disgrace; disfavour

dis·re·spect (-ri spekt') *n.* lack of respect or esteem; discourtesy —*vt.* to have or show a lack of respect for —**dis're·spect'ful** *adj.* —**dis're·spect'ful·ly** *adv.* —**dis'·re·spect'ful·ness** *n.*

dis·robe (dis rōb') *vt., vi.* -robed', -rob'ing to undress —**dis·rob'er** *n.*

dis·rupt (-rupt') *vt., vi.* [< L. pp. of *disrumpere* < *dis-*, apart + *rumpere*, to break] 1. to break apart; rend asunder 2. to interrupt the orderly course of (a meeting, etc.) —**dis·rupt'er, dis·rup'tor** *n.* —**dis·rup'tion** *n.* —**dis·rup'tive** *adj.*

dis·sat·is·fac·tion (dis sat'is fak'shən) *n.* the condition of being dissatisfied; discontent

dis·sat·is·fac·to·ry (-tər ē) *adj.* not satisfactory

dis·sat·is·fy (dis sat'is fī') *vt.* -fied', -fy'ing to fail to satisfy; discontent; displease

dis·sect (di sekt', dī-) *vt.* [< L. pp. of *dissecare* < *dis-*, apart + *secare*, to cut] 1. to cut apart piece by piece; separate into parts, as a body for purposes of study 2. to examine or analyse closely —**dis·sec'tion** *n.* —**dis·sec'tor** *n.*

dis·sect·ed (-id) *adj.* 1. cut up into parts 2. *Bot.* consisting of many lobes and segments, as some leaves 3. *Geol.* cut by erosion into valleys and hills

dis·sem·ble (di sem'b'l) *vt.* -bled, -bling [< OFr. < *des-*, DIS- + *sembler* < L. *simulare*, SIMULATE] 1. to conceal under a false appearance [to *dissemble* fear by smiling] 2. to make a false show of; feign [to *dissemble* innocence] —*vi.* to conceal the truth, or one's true feelings, motives, etc., by pretence —**dis·sem'blance** *n.* —**dis·sem'bler** *n.*

dis·sem·i·nate (di sem'ə nāt') *vt.* -nat'ed, -nat'ing [< L. pp. of *disseminare* < *dis-*, apart + *seminare*, to sow < *semen*, seed] to scatter far and wide; spread abroad; promulgate widely —**dis·sem'i·na'tion** *n.* —**dis·sem'i·na'tive** *adj.* —**dis·sem'i·na'tor** *n.*

dis·sen·sion (di sen'shən) *n.* a dissenting in opinion; disagreement or, esp., violent quarrelling or wrangling

dis·sent (di sent') *vi.* [< L. *dissentire* < *dis-*, apart + *sentire*, to feel] 1. to differ in belief or opinion; disagree 2. to reject the doctrines and forms of an established church —*n.* a dissenting; specif., a) a minority opinion in the decision of a law case b) religious nonconformity —**dis·sent'ing** *adj.*

dis·sent·er (-ər) *n.* a person who dissents; specif., [D-] a Protestant who refuses to conform to the established church in England or Scotland

dis·sen·tient (di sen'shənt) *adj.* dissenting, esp. from the majority opinion —*n.* one who dissents

dis·ser·ta·tion (dis'ər tā'shən) *n.* [< L. < pp. of *dissertare*, to discuss, freq. of *disserere* < *dis-*, apart + *serere*, to join] a formal and lengthy discourse or treatise; thesis

dis·serve (dis surv') *vt.* -served', -serv'ing to do a disservice to; harm

dis·serv·ice (dis sur'vis) *n.* harmful action; injury

dis·sev·er (di sev'ər) *vt.* 1. to sever; separate 2. to divide into parts —*vi.* to separate; disunite —**dis·sev'er·ance, dis·sev'er·ment** *n.*

dis·si·dence (dis'ə dəns) *n.* [< L. < prp. of *dissidere* < *dis-*, apart + *sidere*, to sit] disagreement; dissent, esp. from a government —**dis'si·dent** *adj., n.* —**dis'si·dent·ly** *adv.*

dis·sim·i·lar (di sim'ə lər) *adj.* not similar or alike; different —**dis·sim'i·lar'i·ty** *n.*, *pl.* -ties —**dis·sim'i·lar·ly** *adv.*

dis·sim·i·late (di sim'ə lāt') *vt.* -lat'ed, -lat'ing [DIS- + (AS)SIMILATE] 1. to make dissimilar 2. to cause to undergo dissimilation —*vi.* to become dissimilar

dis·sim·i·la·tion (di sim'ə lā'shən) *n.* 1. a making or becoming dissimilar 2. *Linguis.* the replacement or disappearance of a phoneme when it recurs in the same word (Ex.: Eng. ma*r*ble < OFr. ma*r*bre)

dis·si·mil·i·tude (dis'si mil'ə tyōōd') *n.* dissimilarity; difference

dis·sim·u·late (di sim'yə lāt') *vt., vi.* -lat'ed, -lat'ing [< L. pp. of *dissimulare*: see DIS- & SIMULATE] to hide (one's feelings, motives, etc.) by pretence; dissemble —**dis·sim'·u·la'tion** *n.* —**dis·sim'u·la'tor** *n.*

dis·si·pate (dis'ə pāt') *vt.* -pat'ed, -pat'ing [< L. pp. of *dissipare* < *dis-*, apart + *supare*, to throw] 1. to scatter; disperse 2. to drive completely away; make disappear 3. to waste or squander —*vi.* 1. to be dispelled; vanish 2. to indulge in pleasure to the point of harming oneself —**dis'·si·pat'er, dis'si·pa'tor** *n.* —**dis'si·pa'tive** *adj.*

dis·si·pat·ed (-id) *adj.* 1. scattered 2. squandered or wasted 3. dissolute; debauched

dis·si·pa·tion (dis'ə pā'shən) *n.* a dissipating or being dissipated; dispersion, squandering, dissoluteness, etc.

dis·so·ci·ate (di sō'shē āt', -sē-) *vt.* -at'ed, -at'ing [< L. pp. of *dissociare* < *dis-*, apart + *sociare*, to join < *socius*, companion] 1. to break the ties between; sever association with; separate; disunite 2. to cause to undergo dissociation —*vi.* 1. to stop associating 2. to undergo dissociation —**dissociate oneself from** to repudiate any connection with

dis·so·ci·a·tion (di sō'sē ā'shən, -shē-) *n.* 1. a dissociating or being dissociated 2. *Chem.* the breaking up of a compound into simpler components 3. *Psychol.* a split in the individual consciousness in which a group of mental activities functions as a separate unit —**dis·so'ci·a'tive** *adj.*

dis·sol·u·ble (di sol'yoo b'l) *adj.* that can be dissolved —**dis·sol'u·bil'i·ty** *n.*

dis·so·lute (dis'ə lōōt') *adj.* [< L. pp. of *dissolvere*: see DISSOLVE] dissipated and immoral; debauched —**dis'·so·lute'ly** *adv.* —**dis'so·lute'ness** *n.*

dis·so·lu·tion (dis'ə lōō'shən) *n.* a dissolving or being dissolved; specif., *a)* a breaking up or into parts; disintegration *b)* the termination, as of a business or marriage *c)* death *d)* the dismissal of an assembly, esp. of parliament before a general election or adjournment of a meeting

dis·solve (di zolv') *vt., vi.* -solved', -solv'ing [< L. *dissolvere* < *dis-*, apart + *solvere*, to loosen: see SOLVE] 1. to make or become liquid; melt 2. to merge with a liquid; pass or make pass into solution 3. to break up; decompose 4. to end as by breaking up; terminate 5. to disappear or make disappear 6. *Cinema & TV* to fade or be faded out by means of a lap dissolve —*n.* *Cinema & TV* same as LAP DISSOLVE —**dissolved in tears** weeping —**dis·solv'a·ble** *adj.* —**dis·solv'er** *n.*

dis·so·nance (dis'ə nəns) *n.* [< LL. < L. prp. of *dissonare* < *dis-*, apart + *sonare* to SOUND[1]] 1. an inharmonious combination of sounds; discord 2. any lack of harmony or agreement; incongruity 3. *Music* a chord that sounds harsh and incomplete

dis·so·nant (-nənt) *adj.* 1. characterized by or constituting a dissonance 2. opposing in opinion, temperament, etc.; incompatible —**dis'so·nant·ly** *adv.*

dis·suade (di swād') *vt.* -suad'ed, -suad'ing [L. *dissuadere* < *dis-*, away + *suadere*, to persuade] to turn (a person) aside (*from* a course, etc.) by persuasion or advice —**dis·suad'er** *n.* —**dis·sua'sion** *n.* —**dis·sua'sive** *adj.* —**dis·sua'sive·ly** *adv.*

dis·syl·la·ble (dis'sil'ə b'l) *n.* same as DISYLLABLE —**dis·syl·lab·ic** (dis'si lab'ik) *adj.*

dis·sym·me·try (dis sim'ə trē) *n.*, *pl.* -tries 1. a lack or deficiency of symmetry 2. the symmetry of two objects with one the mirror image of the other, as a pair of hands —**dis·sym·met·ri·cal** (dis'si·met'ri k'l) *adj.*

dist. 1. distance 2. distinguish 3. district

dis·taff (dis'täf) *n.* [< OE. < *dis-*, flax + *stæf*, a staff] a staff on which flax, wool, etc. is wound for use in spinning —*adj.* female, or designating the maternal side of a family

dis·tal (dis't'l) *adj.* [DIST(ANT) + -AL] *Anat.* farthest from the centre or the point of attachment or origin —**dis'·tal·ly** *adv.*

dis·tance (dis'təns) *n.* [< OFr. < L. < prp. of *distare* < *dis-*, apart + *stare*, to stand] 1. the fact or condition of being separated in space or time; remoteness 2. a space between two points 3. an interval between two points in time 4. the length of a line between two points 5. a remoteness in relationship or in behaviour 6. a remote point in space or time —*vt.* -tanced, -tanc·ing to leave behind; outdistance —**go the distance** to last through an activity, specif., to complete a boxing match without being knocked out —**keep at a distance** to treat aloofly —**keep one's distance** to be aloof

DISTAFF

dis·tant (-tənt) *adj.* 1. having a space between; separated

2. widely separated; far apart in space or time 3. away [ten kilometres *distant*] 4. far apart in relationship [a *distant* cousin] 5. cool in manner; aloof 6. from or at a distance 7. faraway or dreamy [a *distant* look] —**dis'tant·ly** *adv.*

dis·taste (dis tāst') *n.* dislike or aversion (*for*)

dis·taste·ful (-fəl) *adj.* 1. unpleasant to taste 2. causing distaste; unpleasant; disagreeable —**dis·taste'ful·ly** *adv.* —**dis·taste'ful·ness** *n.*

dis·tem·per[1] (dis tem'pər) *vt.* [< OFr. < ML. *distemperare,* to disorder < L. *dis-,* apart + *temperare,* to mix in proportion] to upset the functions of; derange; disorder —*n.* 1. a mental or physical disorder; disease 2. an infectious virus disease of young dogs 3. civil disorder

dis·tem·per[2] (dis tem'pər) *n.* [< OFr. < ML. < L. *dis-,* intens. + *temperare:* see prec.] any of various water-based paints, as for walls, etc. —*vt.* to paint (walls, etc.) with distemper

dis·tend (dis tend') *vt., vi.* [< L. *distendere* < *dis-,* apart + *tendere,* to stretch] 1. to stretch out 2. to expand; make or become swollen —**dis·ten'si·ble** *adj.* —**dis·ten'tion, dis·ten'sion** *n.*

dis·tich (dis'tik) *n.* [< L. < Gr. < *di-,* two + *stichos,* a row] two successive lines of verse regarded as a unit; couplet

dis·til (dis til') *vi.* -**tilled'**, -**till'ing** [< OFr. < L. *destillare* < *de-,* down + *stillare,* to drip < *stilla,* a drop] 1. to fall in drops; drip 2. to undergo distillation 3. to be produced as the essence of something —*vt.* 1. to let fall in drops 2. to subject to distillation 3. to remove, extract, etc. by distillation 4. to purify, refine, or concentrate as by distillation

dis·til·late (dis'tə lāt') *n.* 1. a liquid obtained by distilling 2. the essence of anything

dis·til·la·tion (dis'tə lā'shən) *n.* 1. a distilling 2. the process of heating a mixture to separate the more volatile from the less volatile parts, and condensing the resulting vapour to produce a more nearly pure substance 3. a distillate

dis·till·er (dis til'ər) *n.* 1. a person or apparatus that distils 2. a person, company, etc. in the business of distilling whisky, gin, etc.

dis·till·er·y (-til'ər ē) *n., pl.* -**er·ies** a place where distilling is carried on

dis·tinct (-tiŋkt') *adj.* [OFr. < L. pp. of *distinguere:* see DISTINGUISH] 1. not alike; different 2. separate; individual 3. clearly marked off; plain 4. well-defined; unmistakable —**dis·tinct'ly** *adv.* —**dis·tinct'ness** *n.*

dis·tinc·tion (-tiŋk'shən) *n.* 1. the act of making or keeping distinct 2. the condition of being different 3. a quality, mark, or feature that differentiates 4. fame; eminence 5. the quality that makes one seem superior 6. a mark or sign of honour

dis·tinc·tive (-tiŋk'tiv) *adj.* distinguishing from others; characteristic —**dis·tinc'tive·ly** *adv.* —**dis·tinc'tive·ness** *n.*

dis·tin·gué (dis taŋ gā') *adj.* [Fr.] having an air of distinction; distinguished: also, **dis·tin·guée'** *fem.*

dis·tin·guish (dis tiŋ'gwish) *vt.* [< L. *distinguere* < *dis-,* apart + *-stinguere,* to prick, pierce] 1. to perceive or show the difference in; differentiate 2. to characterize 3. to recognize plainly by any of the senses 4. to separate and classify 5. to make famous or eminent —*vi.* to make a distinction (*between* or *among*) —**dis·tin'guish·a·ble** *adj.* —**dis·tin'guish·a·bly** *adv.*

dis·tin·guished (-gwisht) *adj.* 1. celebrated; famous 2. having an air of distinction

dis·tort (dis tôrt') *vt.* [< L. pp. of *distorquere* < *dis-,* intens. + *torquere,* to twist] 1. to twist out of the usual shape, form, or appearance 2. to misrepresent; pervert 3. to modify (a sound, etc.) so as to produce an unfaithful reproduction —**dis·tort'er** *n.* —**dis·tor'tion** *n.* —**dis·tor'tion·less** *adj.*

distr. 1. distributed 2. distribution

dis·tract (dis trakt') *vt.* [< L. pp. of *distrahere* < *dis-,* apart + *trahere,* to draw] 1. to draw (the mind, etc.) away in another direction; divert 2. to create conflict and confusion in —**dis·tract'ed** *adj.* —**dis·tract'ed·ly** *adv.* —**dis·tract'i·ble** *adj.* —**dis·tract'ing** *adj.* —**dis·tract'ing·ly** *adv.*

dis·trac·tion (-trak'shən) *n.* 1. a distracting or being distracted; confusion 2. anything that distracts; specif., *a)* a cause of mental confusion *b)* anything that gives mental relaxation 3. great mental distress —**to distraction** almost insanely —**dis·trac'tive** *adj.*

dis·train (dis trān') *vt., vi.* [< OFr. < ML. *distringere* < L. < *dis-,* apart + *stringere,* to draw tight] *Law* to seize and hold (property) as security or indemnity for a debt —**dis·train'a·ble** *adj.* —**dis·train'er, dis·trai'nor** *n.* —**dis·train'ment** *n.* —**dis·traint'** *n.*

dis·trait (-trā') *adj.* [< OFr. < L. *distrahere:* see DISTRACT] absent-minded; inattentive

dis·traught (-trôt') *adj.* [var. of prec.] 1. very troubled or confused 2. driven mad; crazed

dis·tress (dis tres') *vt.* [< OFr. < ML. < L. pp. of *distringere:* see DISTRAIN] 1. to cause sorrow, misery, or suffering to; pain; trouble 2. to weaken with strain —*n.* 1. the state of being distressed; pain, suffering, etc. 2. anything that distresses; affliction 3. a state of danger or trouble 4. *Law a)* distraint *b)* the property distrained —**dis·tress'ful** *adj.* —**dis·tress'ful·ly** *adv.* —**dis·tress'ing** *adj.* —**dis·tress'ing·ly** *adv.*

dis·tressed (-trest') *adj.* 1. full of distress; troubled, etc. 2. given an antique appearance, as by having the finish marred [*distressed* walnut] 3. designating an area in which there is much poverty, unemployment, etc. 4. in financial straits; poor [*distressed* gentlewoman]

distress signal a signal given by a ship in need of immediate aid

dis·trib·ute (dis trib'yoot, dis'trib-) *vt.* -**ut·ed**, -**ut·ing** [< L. pp. of *distribuere* < *dis-,* apart + *tribuere,* to allot] 1. to divide and give out in shares; allot 2. to scatter or spread out, as over a surface 3. to classify 4. to put (things) in various distinct places —**dis·trib'ut·a·ble** *adj.*

dis·tri·bu·tion (dis'trə byoo'shən) *n.* 1. a distributing or being distributed; specif., *a)* apportionment by law (*of funds,* etc.) *b)* the process by which commodities get to consumers *c)* frequency of occurrence or extent of existence 2. anything distributed; portion; share 3. *Statistics* the arrangement of a set of numbers classified according to some property, as frequency, or to some other criterion, as time or location—**dis'tri·bu'tion·al** *adj.*

dis·trib·u·tive (dis trib'yoo tiv) *adj.* 1. distributing or tending to distribute 2. relating to distribution 3. *Gram.* referring to each member of a group regarded individually ["each" is a *distributive* word] 4. *Math.* of the principle in multiplication that allows the multiplier to be used separately with each term of the multiplicand —*n.* a distributive word —**dis·trib'u·tive·ly** *adv.*

dis·trib·u·tor (-tər) *n.* a person or thing that distributes; specif., *a)* an agent or business firm that distributes goods to consumers or dealers *b)* a device for distributing electric current to sparking plugs

dis·trict (dis'trikt) *n.* [Fr. < ML. < L. pp. of *distringere:* see DISTRAIN] 1. a geographical or political division made for a specific purpose [an urban *district*] 2. any region; part of a country, city, etc.

district attorney [U.S.] a lawyer serving in a specified judicial district as a prosecutor for the State or Federal government in criminal cases

district nurse a nurse appointed by a local authority to attend patients within a district

dis·trust (dis trust') *n.* a lack of trust or of confidence; doubt; suspicion —*vt.* to have no trust or confidence in; doubt; suspect —**dis·trust'ful** *adj.* —**dis·trust'ful·ly** *adv.* —**dis·trust'ful·ness** *n.*

dis·turb (dis turb') *vt.* [< OFr. < L. *disturbare* < *dis-,* intens. + *turbare,* to disorder < *turba,* a mob] 1. to break up the quiet or calm of; agitate 2. to make uneasy or anxious 3. to break up the settled order of 4. to break in on; interrupt 5. to inconvenience —**dis·turb'er** *n.*

dis·turb·ance (-əns) *n.* 1. *a)* a disturbing or being disturbed *b)* any departure from normal 2. anything that disturbs 3. commotion; disorder

di·sul·phide (dī sul'fīd) *n.* a chemical compound of two sulphur atoms united with a single radical or with a single atom of an element

dis·un·ion (dis yoon'yən, -ē ən) *n.* 1. the ending of union; separation 2. lack of unity; discord

dis·u·nite (dis'yoo nīt') *vt.* -**nit'ed**, -**nit'ing** to destroy the unity of; separate —*vi.* to become separated or divided —**dis·u'ni·ty** (-yoo'nə tē) *n.*

dis·use (dis yooz'; *for n.* -yoos') *vt.* -**used'**, -**us'ing** to stop using —*n.* lack of use

di·syl·la·ble (di sil'ə b'l, dī'-) *n.* [< Fr. < L. < Gr. < *di-,* two + *syllabē,* SYLLABLE] a word of two syllables —**di·syl·lab·ic** (di'si lab'ik, dī'-) *adj.*

ditch (dich) *n.* [OE. *dic*] a long, narrow channel dug into the earth, as a trough for drainage or irrigation —*vt.* 1. to make a ditch in 2. to cause (a car, etc.) to go into a ditch 3. to set (a disabled aircraft) down on water and abandon it 4. [Slang] to get rid of or get away from —*vi.* 1. to dig a ditch 2. to ditch a disabled aircraft

ditch·water (-wôt'ər) *n.* stagnant water, esp. in the phrase **as dull as ditchwater**

dith·er (dith'ər) *vi.* [prob. akin to ME. *daderen,* DODDER] to be nervously excited or confused —*n.* a nervously excited or confused condition [all of a *dither*] —**dith'er·y**

dith·y·ramb (dith'ə ram', -ramb') *n.* [< L. < Gr. *dithyrambos*] 1. in ancient Greece, a wild choric hymn in honour of Dionysus 2. any wildly emotional speech or writing —**dith'y·ram'bic** *adj., n.*

dit·ta·ny (dit'ə nē) *n., pl.* -**nies** [ME. *ditane,* < OFr. < L. < Gr. *diktamnon* < ? *Dikte,* Mount Dicte, in Crete, where it grew] a creeping, woolly herb of the labiate family, native to Greece

dit·to (dit'ō) *n., pl.* -**tos** [It. < L. *dictum,* a saying: see

DICTUM] 1. the same (as something stated above or before) 2. a duplicate 3. *same as* DITTO MARK —*adv.* as said before; likewise —*vt.* -toed, -to·ing 1. to duplicate 2. to indicate repetition by ditto marks 3. to repeat

ditto mark a mark (") used in lists or tables to show that the item above is to be repeated

dit·ty (dit'ē) *n.,* *pl.* -ties [< OFr. < L. pp. of *dictare:* see DICTATE] a short, simple song

ditty bag (or **box**) [< ?] a small bag (or box) used as by sailors for carrying sewing equipment, toilet articles, etc.

di·u·ret·ic (dī'yoo ret'ik) *adj.* [< LL. < Gr. < *dia-*, through + *ourein*, to urinate] increasing the secretion and flow of urine —*n.* a diuretic drug or other substance —**di'u·ret'·i·cal·ly** *adv.*

di·ur·nal (dī ʉr'n'l) *adj.* [< L. < *diurnus* < *dies*, day] 1. happening each day; daily 2. of or in the daytime: opposed to NOCTURNAL —**di·ur'nal·ly** *adv.*

div. 1. dividend 2. division 3. divorced

di·va (dē'vä) *n., pl.* -vas; It. -ve (-ve) [It. < L., goddess] a prima donna in grand opera

di·va·gate (dī'və gāt') *vi.* -gat'ed, -gat'ing [< LL. < L. *dis-*, from + *vagari*, to wander] 1. to wander about 2. to digress —**di'va·ga'tion** *n.*

di·va·lent (di vā'lənt) *adj.* *Chem. same as* BIVALENT

di·van (di van', dī van') *n.* [< Turk. *dīwān* < Per.] 1. a) a large, low couch or sofa, usually without armrests or back b) a bed resembling such a couch 2. formerly, a) a smoking room b) a cigar shop

dive (dīv) *vi.* dived, div'ing [OE. *dyfan*] 1. to plunge headfirst into water 2. to go under water; submerge, as a submarine 3. to plunge the hand or body suddenly into something [to *dive* into a foxhole] 4. to bring oneself zestfully into something [to *dive* into one's work] 5. to make a steep, sudden descent, as an aircraft —*vt.* to cause to dive; specif., to send (one's aircraft) into a dive —*n.* 1. a plunge into water 2. any sudden plunge 3. a sharp descent, as of an aircraft 4. [Colloq.] a cheap, disreputable bar, nightclub, etc. —**take a dive** [Slang] to lose a prizefight purposely by pretending to get knocked out

dive bomber an aircraft designed to release bombs while diving at a target —**dive'bomb'** *vt., vi.*

div·er (dīv'ər) *n.* one that dives; specif., a) one who works or explores under water b) any of several diving water birds, esp. the great northern diver

di·verge (dī vʉrj') *vi.* -verged', -verg'ing [ML. *divergere* < L. *dis-*, apart + *vergere*, to turn] 1. to branch off or go in different directions from a common point or from each other 2. to take on gradually a different form [customs *diverge*] 3. to depart from a given viewpoint, practice, etc.; differ —*vt.* to make diverge

di·ver·gence (-vʉr'jəns) *n.* 1. a diverging, or branching off 2. a becoming different in form or kind 3. departure from a particular viewpoint, practice, etc. 4. difference of opinion; disagreement Also **di·ver'gen·cy**, *pl.* -cies —**di·ver'gent** *adj.* —**di·ver'gent·ly** *adv.*

di·vers (dī'vərz) *adj.* [OFr.: see ff.] [Archaic] several; various

di·verse (dī vʉrs'; dī'vʉrs) *adj.* [OFr. < L. pp. of *divertere* < *dis-*, apart + *vertere*, to turn] 1. different; dissimilar 2. varied; diversified —**di·verse'ness** *n.*

di·ver·si·fy (də vʉr'sə fī') *vt.* -fied', -fy'ing [see prec. & -FY] 1. to make diverse; give variety to; vary 2. to divide up (investments, liabilities, etc.) among different companies, securities, etc. 3. to expand (a company, etc.) by varying products, operations, etc. —*vi.* to multiply business operations —**di·ver'si·fi·ca'tion** *n.*

di·ver·sion (də vʉr'zhən, dī-) *n.* 1. a diverting, or turning aside, esp. an official detour used by traffic when a main road is closed because of excess traffic, roadworks, etc. 2. distraction of attention 3. a pastime or amusement

di·ver·sion·ar·y (-ər ē) *adj.* serving to divert or distract [*diversionary* military tactics]

di·ver·si·ty (də vʉr'sə tē, dī-) *n., pl.* -ties 1. a being diverse; difference 2. variety

di·vert (-vʉrt') *vt.* [< OFr. < L. *divertere:* see DIVERSE] 1. to turn aside; deflect 2. to amuse; entertain 3. to distract the attention of —**di·vert'ing** *adj.* —**di·vert'ing·ly** *adv.*

di·ver·tic·u·li·tis (dī'vər tik'yoo līt'əs) *n.* [see -ITIS] inflammation of a diverticulum

di·ver·tic·u·lum (dī'vər tik'yoo ləm) *n., pl.* -la (-lə) [L. < *devertere* < *de-*, from + *vertere*, to turn] *Anat.* a normal or abnormal pouch or sac opening out from a tubular organ or main cavity

‡**di·ver·tisse·ment** (dē vər tēs män'; E. di vʉr'tis mənt) *n.* [Fr.] 1. a diversion; amusement 2. a short ballet, etc. as an entr'acte

Di·ves (dī'vēz) *n.* [ME. < use of L. *dives*, rich, in the parable in the Vulgate] any rich man: after the rich man in the parable in Luke's gospel: Luke 16: 19-31

di·vest (dī vest', də-) *vt.* [altered < earlier *devest*, ult. < L. *devestire* < *dis-*, from + *vestire*, to dress] 1. to strip (of clothing, etc.) 2. to deprive or dispossess (of rank, rights,

etc.) 3. to rid (*of* something) —**di·vest'i·ture** (-ə chər), **di·vest'ment, di·ves'ture** *n.*

di·vi (div'ē) [Colloq.] *clipped form of* DIVIDEND

di·vide (də vīd') *vt.* -vid'ed, -vid'ing [< L. *dividere*] 1. to separate into parts; split up 2. to separate into groups; classify 3. to make or keep separate as by a partition 4. to give out in shares; apportion 5. to cause to disagree; alienate 6. *Math.* to separate into equal parts by a divisor 7. *Mech.* to mark off the divisions of; graduate —*vi.* 1. to be or become separate; part 2. to disagree 3. to separate into groups in voting on a question 4. to share 5. *Math.* to do division —*n.* [Chiefly U.S.] a ridge that divides two drainage areas; watershed —**di·vid'a·ble** *adj.*

di·vid·ed (-id) *adj.* 1. a) separated into parts b) having indentations reaching to the base or midrib, as some leaves 2. disagreeing

div·i·dend (div'ə dend') *n.* [< L.] 1. the number or quantity to be divided 2. a) a sum of money to be divided among stockholders, creditors, etc. b) a single share of this 3. a bonus; benefit [his years of study paid *dividends*]

di·vid·er (də vīd'ər) *n.* a person or thing that divides; specif., a) [pl.] an instrument for dividing lines, etc.; compasses b) a set of shelves, etc. used to separate a room into distinct areas

div·i·na·tion (div'ə nā'shən) *n.* [< L. < pp. of *divinare:* see ff.] 1. the act or practice of trying to foretell the future or the unknown by occult means 2. a prophecy; augury 3. a successful or clever guess —**di·vin·a·to·ry** (də vin'ə tər ē) *adj.*

di·vine (də vīn') *adj.* [< OFr. < L. *divinus* < *divus*, a god] 1. of or like God or a god 2. given or inspired by God; holy; sacred 3. devoted to God; religious 4. supremely great, good, etc. 5. [Colloq.] very pleasing, attractive, etc. —*n.* 1. a clergyman 2. a theologian —*vt.* -vined', -vin'ing 1. to prophesy 2. to guess; conjecture 3. to find out by intuition —*vi.* 1. to engage in divination 2. to use a divining rod —**di·vine'ly** *adv.* —**di·vin'er** *n.*

Divine Office the prayers for the canonical hours

divine right of kings formerly, the concept that kings, etc. are chosen by God and hence are not answerable to their subjects for their actions

div·ing bell a large, hollow, air-filled apparatus in which divers can work under water

diving board a springboard projecting over a swimming pool, lake, etc., for use in diving

diving suit a heavy, waterproof garment worn by divers working under water: it has a detachable helmet into which air is pumped through a hose

divining rod a forked stick alleged to reveal hidden water or minerals by dipping downwards

di·vin·i·ty (də vin'ə tē) *n., pl.* -ties 1. the quality or condition of being divine 2. a god; deity 3. a divine power, virtue, etc. 4. the study of religion; theology —**the Divinity** God

di·vis·i·ble (də viz'ə b'l) *adj.* that can be divided, esp. without leaving a remainder —**di·vis'i·bil'i·ty** *n.*

di·vi·sion (də vizh'ən) *n.* 1. a dividing or being divided 2. a sharing or distribution 3. a difference of opinion; disagreement 4. a separation into groups in voting, esp. for a formal vote as in the House of Commons 5. anything that divides; partition; boundary 6. anything separated or distinguished from the larger unit of which it is a part; a section, group, rank, segment, etc. [*division* one of the Football League, Chancery *Division* of the Law Courts] 7. *Math.* the process of finding how many times a number (the *divisor*) is contained in another (the *dividend*): the answer is the *quotient* 8. *Mil.* a major tactical or administrative unit under one command; specif., an army unit larger than a regiment and smaller than a corps —**di·vi'sion·al** *adj.*

division bell the bell signifying that a vote is to be taken in parliament, etc.

division of labour the method of increasing efficiency of production by assigning different processes to different people

division sign the symbol (÷), indicating that the preceding number is to be divided by the following number (Ex.: 8 ÷ 4 = 2)

di·vi·sive (də vī'siv) *adj.* causing division; esp., causing disagreement or dissension —**di·vi'sive·ly** *adv.* —**di·vi'sive·ness** *n.*

di·vi·sor (də vī'zər) *n.* [L.] the number or quantity by which the dividend is divided to produce the quotient

di·vorce (də vôrs') *n.* [OFr. < L. *divortium* < *divertere:* see DIVERSE] 1. legal dissolution of a marriage 2. any complete separation or disunion —*vt.* -vorced', -vorc'ing 1. to dissolve legally a marriage between 2. to separate from (one's spouse) by divorce 3. to separate; disunite —*vi.* to get a divorce —**di·vorce'ment** *n.*

di·vor·cée (-vôr'sā', -sē') *n.* [Fr.] a divorced woman

div·ot (div'ət) *n.* [Scot. dial. < ?] *Golf* a lump of turf dislodged in making a stroke

di·vulge (də vulj', dī-) *vt.* -vulged', -vulg'ing [< L. *divulgare* < *dis-*, apart + *vulgare*, to make public < *vulgus*, the

common people] to make known; disclose; reveal
—**di·vul′gence** (-vul′jəns), **di·vulge′ment** *n.* —**di·vulg′er** *n.*
div·vy (div′ē) *vt., vi.* -**vied,** -**vy·ing** [clipped form of DIVIDE]
[Colloq.] to share; divide (*up*) —*n.* clipped form of
DIVIDEND, esp. one paid by a Cooperative Society
dix·ie (dik′sē) *n.* [< Hindi *degcī*, dim. of *degcā*, a pot,
kettle] a camp cooking-pot of large capacity
Dix·ie·land (-land′) *adj.* in, of, or like a style of jazz
modified by white New Orleans musicians, with a fast,
ragtime tempo —*n.* **1.** the southern states of the U.S.: also
Dixie Land 2. Dixieland jazz
DIY Do-It-Yourself
diz·en (diz′'n, dī′z'n) *vt.* [MDu. *disen*, to put flax on a
distaff < LowG. *diesse*, of flax] [Archaic or Pŏet.] same
as BEDIZEN
diz·zy (diz′ē) *adj.* -**zi·er,** -**zi·est** [OE. *dysig*, foolish] **1.**
feeling giddy or unsteady **2.** causing or likely to cause
giddiness [*dizzy* heights] **3.** confused; bewildered **4.**
[Colloq.] silly —*vt.* -**zied,** -**zy·ing** to make dizzy —**diz′zi·ly**
adv. —**diz′zi·ness** *n.*
D.J., DJ disc jockey
djel·la·ba (jə la′bə) *n.* same as JELLABA
djin·ni (ji nē′) *n.,* pl. **djinn** same as JINNI
D.L. Deputy Lieutenant
dl, dl. decilitre(s)
D layer the lowest layer of the ionosphere
D.Lit., D.Litt. [L. *Doctor Lit(t)erarum*] Doctor of Letters
DM, Dm deutsche mark
dm. decimetre(s)
D.Mus. Doctor of Music
DMZ demilitarized zone
DNA deoxyribonucleic acid
D.N.B. Dictionary of National Biography
D-no·tice [clipped form of *Defence Notice*] an official
notice sent to newspapers, etc. prohibiting publication of
certain material
do¹ (dōō) *vt.* **did, done, do′ing** [OE. *don*] **1.** *a*) to perform
(an action, etc.) [*do* great deeds] *b*) to carry out **2.** to
bring to completion; finish [*dinner* has been *done* for an
hour] **3.** to bring about; cause; produce [it *does* no harm]
4. to exert (efforts, etc.) [*do* your best] **5.** to deal with as is
required; attend to [*do* the ironing] **6.** to have as one's
occupation; work at **7.** to work out; solve [*do* a problem]
8. to produce (a play, etc.) [we *did* Hamlet] **9.** to play the
role of [she *did* Juliet] **10.** to write (a book), compose (a
musical score), etc. **11.** *a*) to cover (distance) [to *do* 30
miles to the gallon] *b*) to move along at a speed of [to *do*
60 miles an hour] **12.** to give; render [*do* honour to the
dead] **13.** to be convenient to; suit [this will *do* me very
well] **14.** [Colloq.] to provide; prepare; serve [this pub
does lunches] **15.** [Colloq.] to sightsee; visit [we *did* Rome
last year] **16.** [Colloq.] to cheat; swindle [you've been
done] **17.** [Colloq.] to serve (a jail term) —*vi.* **1.** to
behave [he *does* well when praised] **2.** to be active; work
[*do;* don't talk] **3.** to get along; fare [the patient is *doing*
well] **4.** to be adequate or suitable [that tie will *do*] **5.**
[Colloq.] to take place [anything *doing* tonight?] Auxiliary
uses of *do:* **1.** to give emphasis [please *do* stay] **2.** to ask
a question [*did* you write?] **3.** to help express negation [*do*
not go] **4.** to serve as a substitute verb [love me as I *do*
(love) you] **5.** to form inverted constructions after some
adverbs [little *did* he realize] —*n.,* pl. **do's** or **dos 1.**
[Colloq.] a party or social event **2.** something to be done
3. [*pl.*] share, esp. in **fair dos** —**do a** [Colloq.] act like —**do
away with 1.** to kill or destroy **2.** to throw away or
discard —**do by 1.** to act towards or for —**do for 1.** to act
as a housekeeper for; char **2.** to be sufficient **3.** [Colloq.]
to ruin; destroy —**do in** [Slang] **1.** to kill **2.** to exhaust
—**do over 1.** [Colloq.] to redecorate **2.** [Slang] to attack;
beat up —**dos and don'ts** rules of conduct —**do up 1.** to
wrap and tie up (a parcel, etc.) **2.** to redecorate; refurnish
3. to fasten (a dress, etc.) —**do with 1.** to make use of **2.**
[Colloq.] to appreciate having; find useful [I could *do* with a
new car] —**do without** to get along without —**have to do
with 1.** to be related to **2.** to deal with —**make do** to get
along with what is available
do² (dō) *n.* [It.: used instead of earlier *ut:* see GAMUT]
Music a syllable representing the first or last tone of the
diatonic scale
do. ditto
DOA, D.O.A. dead on arrival
do·a·ble (dōō′ə b'l) *adj.* that can be done
dob·bin (dob′in) *n.* [< *Dobbin,* nickname for *Robin*] a
horse, esp. a patient, plodding one
Do·ber·man pin·scher (dō′bər mən pin′shər) [< G.] a
breed of large dog, with smooth, dark hair and tan markings
doc (dok) *n.* [Slang] doctor
doch an dorris same as DEOCH AN DORIS
doc·ile (dō′sīl) *adj.* [Fr. < L. *docilis* < *docere,* to teach] **1.**
[Now Rare] easy to teach **2.** easy to manage or discipline;
tractable —**doc′ile·ly** *adv.* —**do·cil·i·ty** (dō sil′ə tē) *n.*
dock¹ (dok) *n.* [< MDu. *docke,* channel < ?] **1.** a large

excavated basin with floodgates, for receiving ships
between voyages **2.** [*pl.*] a dockyard **3.** *a*) a landing pier;
wharf *b*) the water between two piers **4.** [Chiefly U.S.] a
platform at which lorries or goods trains are loaded and
unloaded —*vt.* **1.** to pilot (a ship) to a dock **2.** to join
(vehicles) together in outer space —*vi.* **1.** to come into a
dock **2.** to connect with another vehicle in outer space —**in
dock** [Colloq.] **1.** in the garage for repair: said of a motor
vehicle **2.** in hospital: said of a person
dock² (dok) *n.* [< Fl. *dok,* cage] the place where the
accused stands or sits in court —**in the dock** on trial
dock³ (dok) *n.* [OE. *docce*] any of various coarse weeds
with large leaves and tap roots
dock⁴ (dok) *n.* [< OE. *-docca* or ON. *dockr*] **1.** the solid
part of an animal's tail **2.** an animal's bobbed tail —*vt.* **1.**
to cut off the end of (a tail); bob **2.** to bob the tail of **3.** to
deduct from (wages, etc.) **4.** to deduct from the wages of
5. to remove part of
dock·age¹ (dok′ij) *n.* **1.** docking accommodation **2.** the fee
for this **3.** the docking of ships
dock·age² (dok′ij) *n.* a docking, or cutting off
dock·er (dok′ər) *n.* **1.** one that docks **2.** a man employed
to load and unload ships
dock·et (dok′it) *n.* [earlier *doggette,* register] **1.** a
summary, as of legal decisions **2.** a list of cases to be tried
by a law court **3.** a customs certificate declaring that duty
has been paid **4.** a piece of paper accompanying or
referring to a package, etc., stating contents, delivery
instructions, etc. and often used as a receipt **5.** [Chiefly
U.S.] any list of things to be done; agenda —*vt.* **1.** to enter
in a docket **2.** to put a docket on; label
dock·side (dok′sīd′) *n.* the area beside a dock
dock·yard (-yärd′) *n.* a place with docks, machinery, etc.
for repairing or building ships
doc·tor (dok′tər) *n.* [< OFr. or < L. *doctor,* teacher < pp.
of *docere,* to teach] **1.** orig., a teacher or learned man **2.** a
person on whom a university or college has conferred any of
several high degrees [*Doctor* of Philosophy] **3.** a medical
practitioner **4.** [Colloq.] a person who carries out repairs
[a car *doctor,* tree *doctor*] —*vt.* [Colloq.] **1.** to try to
heal; apply medicine to **2.** to repair; mend **3.** to tamper
with **4.** to castrate; said esp. of dogs and cats —*vi.*
[Colloq.] **1.** to practise medicine —**doc′tor·al** (-əl) *adj.*
doc·tor·ate (-it) *n.* the degree or status of doctor conferred
by a university
doc·tri·naire (dok′trə ner′) *n.* [Fr.] a person who
dogmatically tries to apply theories regardless of the
practical problems involved —*adj.* adhering to a doctrine
or theory in an unyielding, dogmatic way —**doc′tri·nair′-
ism** *n.*
doc·trine (dok′trən) *n.* [< L. *doctrina* < *doctor:* see
DOCTOR] **1.** something taught; teachings **2.** something
taught as the principles of a religion, political party, etc.;
tenet or tenets; dogma **3.** a principle of law —**doc·tri·nal**
(dok trī′nal, dok′trə-) *adj.* —**doc′tri·nal·ly** *adv.*
doc·u·ment (dok′yoo mənt; *for v.* -ment′) *n.* [OFr. < L.
documentum, lesson, proof < *docere,* to teach] **1.** anything
printed, written, etc., relied upon to record or prove
something **2.** any proof —*vt.* **1.** to provide (a book, etc.)
with documents or supporting references **2.** to prove or
support by reference to documents —**doc′u·men′tal** *adj.*
doc·u·men·ta·ry (dok′yoo men′tər ē) *adj.* **1.** of, in,
supported by, or serving as a document or documents **2.**
dramatically showing or analysing news events, social
conditions, etc., with little or no fictionalization —*n.,* pl.
-**ries** a documentary film, television programme, etc.
doc·u·men·ta·tion (-mən tā′shən, -men-) *n.* **1.** the supplying
of documents or supporting references **2.** the documents or
references supplied **3.** the collecting, abstracting, and
coding of printed or written information for future reference
dod·der (dod′ər) *vi.* [ME. *daderen*] **1.** to shake or tremble,
as from old age **2.** to totter —**dod′der·er** *n.* —**dod′der·ing**
adj. —**dod′der·y** *adj.*
dod·dered (-ərd) *adj.* [prob. < ME. *dodden,* to cut off]
having lost its branches or top because of age, decay, etc.:
said of a tree
dod·dle (dod′'l) *n.* [< ?] [Colloq.] a simple task
do·dec·a- [< Gr. *dōdeka,* twelve] a prefix meaning twelve:
also, before a vowel, **do·dec-**
do·dec·a·gon (dō dek′ə gon′) *n.* [< Gr.: see DODECA- & -GON]
a plane figure with twelve angles and twelve sides
do·dec·a·he·dron (dō′dek ə hē′drən) *n.,* pl. -**drons, -dra**
(-drə) [< Gr.: see DODECA- & -HEDRON] a solid figure with
twelve plane faces —**do′dec·a·he′dral** *adj.*
dodge (doj) *vi.* **dodged, dodg′ing** [< ?] **1.** to move or twist
quickly aside, as to avoid a blow **2.** to use tricks or
evasions —*vt.* **1.** to avoid by moving quickly aside **2.** to
evade by trickery, cleverness, etc. **3.** to avoid meeting —*n.*
1. a dodging **2.** a trick used in evading or cheating
dodg·em (doj′əm) *n.* [DODG(E) + (TH)EM] an electrically
powered vehicle that moves erratically within an enclosure,
bumping other vehicles: found at fun-fairs, etc.

dodg·er (-ər) *n.* 1. a person who dodges 2. a shifty, dishonest person

dodg·y (doj′ē) *adj.* **dodg′i·er, dodg′i·est** [Colloq.] 1. risky; difficult; dangerous 2. uncertain; tricky

do·do (dō′dō) *n., pl.* **-dos, -does** [Port. *doudo,* lit., foolish, stupid] 1. a large bird, now extinct, that had rudimentary wings useless for flying: formerly found on Mauritius 2. an old-fashioned person; fogy

doe (dō) *n., pl.* **does, doe:** see PLURAL, II, D, 1 [OE. *da*] the female of the deer, or of the antelope, rabbit, or almost any other animal the male of which is called a buck

D.O.E. Department of the Environment

do·er (dōō′ər) *n.* 1. a person who does something 2. a person who gets things done

does (duz) *3rd pers. sing., pres. indic., of* DO¹

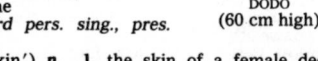

DODO
(60 cm high)

doe·skin (dō′skin′) *n.* 1. the skin of a female deer 2. leather made from this or, now usually, from lambskin 3. a fine, soft, smooth woollen cloth

does·n't (duz′′nt) does not

do·est (dōō′ist) *archaic 2nd pers. sing., pres. indic., of* DO¹: *used with thou*

do·eth (-th) *archaic 3rd pers sing., pres. indic., of* DO¹: *used with he*

doff (dof) *vt.* [ME. *doffen < don of:* see DO¹ & OFF] 1. to take off (clothes, etc.); esp., to remove or raise (one's hat) 2. to put aside or discard

dog (dog) *n., pl.* **dogs, dog:** see PLURAL, II, D, 1 [OE. *docga*] 1. any of a large group of domesticated animals belonging to the same family as the fox, wolf, jackal, etc. 2. the male of any of these 3. a mean, contemptible fellow 4. a prairie dog, dogfish, or other animal thought to resemble a dog 5. an andiron 6. [Colloq.] a boy or man [*lucky dog*] 7. [*pl.*] [Slang] feet 8. [*pl.*] [Colloq.] greyhound racing 9. [D-] *Astron.* either of the constellations Great Dog or Little Dog 10. *Mech.* a device for holding or grappling —*vt.* **dogged, dog′ging** 1. to follow or hunt like a dog 2. to trouble; plague; worry [he was *dogged* by misfortune] —*adv.* very; completely [*dog*-tired] —**a dog's age** [Colloq.] a long time —**a dog's life** a wretched existence —**dog eat dog** ruthless competition —**dog in the manger** a person who keeps others from using something which he cannot or will not use —**go to the dogs** [Colloq.] to deteriorate; degenerate —**like a dog's dinner** [Colloq.] flashily or stylishly: said esp. of someone's style of dressing

dog biscuit a hard biscuit containing ground bones, meat, etc., for feeding dogs

dog·cart (-kärt′) *n.* 1. a small, light cart drawn by dogs 2. a small, light, open carriage having two seats arranged back to back

dog collar 1. a collar for a dog 2. [Colloq.] the stiff, white collar worn by many clergymen

dog days the hot, humid days in July and August

doge (dōj) *n.* [It. < L. *dux,* leader] the chief magistrate of either of the former republics of Venice and Genoa

dog·ear (dog′ir′) *n.* a turned-down corner of the leaf of a book —*vt.* to turn down the corner or corners of (a leaf in a book) —**dog′eared** *adj.*

dog end [Slang] a cigarette end

dog·fight (-fīt′) *n.* a rough, violent fight, as between dogs; specif., *Mil.* combat as between fighter planes at close quarters

dog·fish (-fish′) *n., pl.* **-fish′, -fish′es:** see FISH 1. any of various small sharks 2. any of several other fishes, as the bowfin

dog·ged (dog′id) *adj.* [see DOG] not giving in readily; persistent; stubborn —**dog′ged·ly** *adv.* —**dog′ged·ness** *n.*

dog·ger·el (-ər əl) *n.* [prob. < It. *doga,* barrel stave] trivial, poorly constructed verse, usually of a comic sort; jingle —*adj.* designating or of such verse Also **dog′grel** (-rəl)

dog·gie bag (dog′ē) a bag supplied to a patron of a restaurant, in which he may place leftovers as to take to his dog: also **doggy bag**

dog·gish (-ish) *adj.* of or like a dog —**dog′gish·ly** *adv.* —**dog′gish·ness** *n.*

dog·go (-ō) *adv.* [< DOG] [Colloq.] out of sight: esp. in the phrase **lie doggo,** to lie low

dog·gone (dog′gon′) *interj.* [U.S.] damn! darn! —*vt.* **-goned′, -gon′ing** [U.S. Colloq.] to damn —*adj.* [U.S. Colloq.] damned: also **dog′goned′**

dog·gy, dog·gie (-ē) *n., pl.* **-gies** a little dog: a child's word —*adj.* **-gi·er, -gi·est** 1. of or like a dog 2. [Colloq.] fond of dogs

dog·house (-hous′) *n.* [U.S.] a kennel —**in the doghouse** [Colloq.] in disfavour

do·gie, do·gy (dō′gē) *n.* [< ?] in the western U.S., a stray or motherless calf

dog Latin spurious or incorrect Latin

dog·leg (dog′leg′) *n.* a sharp angle or bend like that formed by a dog's hind leg, as in a golf fairway

dog·ma (dog′mə) *n., pl.* **-mas, -ma·ta** (-mə tə) [L. < Gr. < *dokein,* to think] 1. a doctrine; tenet; belief 2. doctrines, tenets, or beliefs, collectively 3. a positive, arrogant assertion of opinion 4. *Theol.* a doctrine or body of doctrines formally and authoritatively affirmed

dog·mat·ic (dog·mat′ik) *adj.* 1. of or like dogma 2. asserted without proof 3. stating opinion in a positive or arrogant manner: also **dog·mat′i·cal** —**dog·mat′i·cal·ly** *adv.*

dog·ma·tism (dog′mə tiz′m) *n.* dogmatic assertion of opinion, usually without reference to evidence —**dog′-ma·tist** *n.*

dog·ma·tize (-tīz′) *vi.* **-tized′, -tiz′ing** to speak or write dogmatically —*vt.* to formulate or express as dogma —**dog′ma·tiz′er** *n.*

dog·nap (-nap′) *vt.* **-napped′, -nap′ping** [DOG + (KID)NAP] to steal (a dog) for ransom, etc. —**dog′nap′per** *n.*

do-good·er (dōō′good′ər) *n.* [Colloq.] a person who seeks to correct social ills in an idealistic, but usually impractical or superficial way —**do′-good′, do′-good′ing** *adj.* —**do′-goodism** *n.*

dog rose a European wild rose with single, pink flowers and hooked spines

dogs·bod·y (dogz′bod′ē) *n.* [Colloq.] a drudge

dog sledge a sledge drawn by dogs

Dog Star 1. the brightest star in the constellation Canis Major; Sirius 2. Procyon

dog-tired (-tīrd) *adj.* extremely tired; exhausted

dog·tooth (dog′tōōth) *n., pl.* **-teeth′** 1. a canine tooth 2. *Archit.* a moulding consisting of ornamental, pointed projections, used esp. in Norman and Early English architecture

dogtooth violet a European plant with a purple or rose flower: also **dog's-tooth violet**

dog·trot (-trot′) *n.* a slow, easy trot

dog·watch (-woch′) *n. Naut.* a duty period, either from 4 to 6 P.M. or from 6 to 8 P.M.

dog·wood (-wood′) *n.* 1. any of various trees esp. one found in Europe with greenish-white flowers and black berries 2. *a)* a similar American tree with small flowers surrounded by four large white or pink bracts *b)* its hard wood

doi·ly (doi′lē) *n., pl.* **-lies** [after name of a 17th-c. London draper] a small mat, as of lace or paper, used to protect or decorate a surface: also **doy′ley**

do·ings (dōō′iŋz) *n.pl.* 1. things done; actions, events, etc. 2. [Colloq.] a term for something whose name is not known, forgotten, etc.

do-it-your·self (dōō′it yoor self′) *n.* the practice of constructing, repairing, redecorating, etc. by oneself instead of hiring another to do it —*adj.* of, used for, or engaged in do-it-yourself

dol. *pl.* **dols.** dollar

‡**dol·ce vi·ta** (dōl′che vē′tä) [It., lit., (the) sweet life] a life of luxury and pleasure

dol·drums (dol′drəmz) *n.pl.* [< ? ME. *dul;* DULL] 1. low spirits; dull, listless feeling 2. sluggishness; stagnation 3. equatorial ocean regions noted for dead calms and light, fluctuating winds

dole¹ (dōl) *n.* [OE. *dal*] 1. a giving out of money or food to those in need 2. that which is thus given out 3. anything given out sparingly 4. a form of payment by a government to the unemployed —*vt.* **doled, dol′ing** to give sparingly or as dole (often with *out*) —**on the dole** receiving a dole (sense 4)

dole² (dōl) *n.* [see ff.] [Archaic] sorrow

dole·ful (dōl′fəl) *adj.* [< OFr. ult. < L. *dolere,* to suffer + *-ful,* -FUL] full of sorrow or sadness; mournful —**dole′ful·ly** *adv.* —**dole′ful·ness** *n.*

dol·i·cho·ce·phal·ic (dol′i kō′sə fal′ik) *adj.* [< Gr. *dolichos,* long + -CEPHALIC] having a relatively long head: also **dol′-i·cho·ceph′a·lous** (-sef′ələs): see CEPHALIC INDEX —**dol′-i·cho·ceph′a·ly** (-ə lē) *n.*

doll (dol) *n.* [< *Doll,* nickname for *Dorothy*] 1. a child's toy made to resemble a human being 2. a pretty but silly young woman 3. a pretty child 4. [Slang] *a)* any young woman *b)* any lovable person —*vt.,vi.* [Colloq.] to dress stylishly or showily (with *up*)

dol·lar (dol′ər) *n.* [< LowG. & Early ModDu. < G. *Thaler,* contr. < *Joachimsthaler,* coin made at *Joachimstal, Bohemia*] 1. the monetary unit of Canada, U.S., Australia, Ethiopia, etc.: see MONETARY UNITS, table 2. a coin or paper bill of the value of a dollar 3. [Colloq.] formerly, five shillings (25p)

dollar diplomacy the use of the economic power of a government to promote in other countries the business interests of its companies, etc.

dollar sign (or **mark**) a symbol, **$,** for dollar(s)

dol·lop (dol′əp) *n.* [< ?] 1. a soft mass, as of some food 2.

a measure or amount [a *dollop* of wit] —*vt.* to serve (*out*) in dollops

dol·ly (dol'ē) *n., pl.* **-lies** 1. a doll: child's word 2. any of several kinds of low, flat, wheeled frames or platforms for moving heavy objects —*vi.* **-lied, -ly·ing** to move a camera on a dolly (*in, out,* etc.) as in televising —*vt.* to move on a dolly —*adj.* [Colloq.] fashionable; attractive [a *dolly* bird]

dolly mixture a mixture of small, soft, coloured sweets

dol·man sleeve (dol'mən) [< Fr. < Turk. *dolama*, long robe] a kind of sleeve for a woman's coat or dress, tapering from a wide opening at the armhole to a narrow one at the wrist

dol·men (dol'mən) *n.* [Fr. < ? Bret. *taol*, a table + *men*, stone] a prehistoric monument formed by a large, flat stone laid across upright stones

do·lo·mite (do'lə mit') *n.* [after the Fr. geologist *Dolomieu* (1750-1801)] a common rock-forming mineral of calcium magnesium carbonate

do·lor·ous (do'lər əs) *adj.* 1. sorrowful or sad; mournful 2. painful —**do'lor·ous·ly** *adv.*

do·lour (do'lər) *n.* [< OFr. < L. < *dolere*, to suffer] [Poet.] sorrow; grief

dol·phin (dol'fən) *n.* [< OFr. < L. < Gr. *delphis* (gen. *delphinos*)] 1. any of several water-dwelling mammals, with numerous teeth and often a beaklike snout 2. either of two swift marine game fishes that change to bright colours out of water 3. a mooring buoy

dol·phin·ar·i·um (-er'ē əm) *n.* [< prec. + (AQU)ARIUM] an aquarium for dolphins, esp. one where the dolphins give public performances

dolt (dolt) *n.* [prob. < ME. pp. of *dullen*, to dull] a stupid, slow-witted person; blockhead —**dolt'ish** *adj.* —**dolt'ish·ly** *adv.* —**dolt'ish·ness** *n.*

-dom (dəm) [OE. *dom*, state] *a suffix meaning:* 1. the rank, position, or dominion of [*kingdom*] 2. fact or state of being [*martyrdom*] 3. a total of all who are [*officialdom*]

dom. 1. domestic 2. dominion

do·main (dō mān', də-) *n.* [< MFr. < L. < *dominus*, a lord] 1. territory under one government or ruler 2. land belonging to one person; estate 3. field or sphere of activity or influence [*domain* of discourse]

do·maine (dō mān') *n.* [Fr. < L. *dominus*, a lord] a vineyard

dome (dōm) *n.* [< Fr. < Pr. < LL. < Gr. *dōma*, housetop, house] 1. a hemispherical roof or one formed by a series of rounded arches or vaults on a round or many-sided base 2. any dome-shaped structure 3. [Slang] the head —*vt.* **domed, dom'ing** 1. to cover as with a dome 2. to form into a dome —*vi.* to swell out like a dome

Domes·day Book (doomz'dā') [said to be so named because it judged all men without bias, like the Last Judgment] the record of a land survey of England made under William the Conqueror

do·mes·tic (də mes'tik) *adj.* [< OFr. < L. *domesticus* < *domus*, house] 1. of the home or family [*domestic* joys] 2. of one's own country or the country referred to 3. made in the home country; native 4. domesticated; tame: said of animals 5. devoted to home and family life —*n.* a servant for the home, as a maid —**do·mes'ti·cal·ly** *adv.*

do·mes·ti·cate (də mes'tə kāt') *vt.* **-cat'ed, -cat'ing** 1. to accustom to home life; make domestic 2. *a)* to tame (wild animals) *b)* to adapt (wild plants) to home cultivation 3. to naturalize (a custom, word, etc.) from another country —*vi.* to become domestic —**do·mes'ti·ca'tion** *n.*

do·mes·tic·i·ty (dō'mes tis'ə tē) *n., pl.* **-ties** 1. home life; family life 2. devotion to home and family life 3. [*pl.*] household affairs

domestic science *same as* HOME ECONOMICS

dom·i·cile (dom'ə sil', -sil) *n.* [OFr. < L. < *domus*, house] a customary dwelling place; home; residence, esp. a person's permanent, legal residence —*vt.* **-ciled, -cil'ing** to establish (oneself or another) in a domicile —**dom'i·cil'i·ar·y** (-sil'ē ər ē) *adj.*

dom·i·cil·i·ate (dom'ə sil'ē āt') *vt.* **-at'ed, -at'ing** *same as* DOMICILE

dom·i·nance (dom'ə nəns) *n.* a dominating; being dominant; control; authority: also **dom'i·nan·cy**

dom·i·nant (-nənt) *adj.* 1. dominating; ruling; prevailing 2. *Genetics* designating or of that one of any pair of characters which, when both are present in the germ plasm, dominates the other and appears in the organism: opposed to RECESSIVE 3. *Music* of or based upon the fifth note of a diatonic scale —*n.* 1. *Ecology* the species of plant or animal that is most numerous or influential in a community 2. *Music* the fifth note of a diatonic scale —**dom'i·nant·ly** *adv.*

dom·i·nate (-nāt') *vt., vi.* **-nat'ed, -nat'ing** [< L. pp. of *dominari*, to rule < *dominus*, a master] 1. to rule or control by superior power or influence 2. to tower over; rise high above (the surroundings, etc.) —**dom'i·na'tion** *n.* —**dom'i·na·tive** (-nā tiv) *adj.* —**dom'i·na'tor** *n.*

dom·i·neer (dom'ə nir') *vi., vt.* [< Du. < Fr. < L.: see prec.] to rule (*over*) in a harsh or arrogant way; tyrannize; bully

dom·i·neer·ing (-iŋ) *adj.* overbearing; tyrannical —**dom'i·neer'ing·ly** *adv.*

Do·min·i·can (də min'i kən) *adj.* 1. of Saint Dominic or of a mendicant order founded by him 2. of the Dominican Republic —*n.* 1. a friar or nun of one of the Dominican orders 2. a native or inhabitant of the Dominican Republic

dom·i·nie (dom'ə nē) *n.* [< vocative case (*domine*) of L. *dominus*, a master] 1. in Scotland, a schoolmaster 2. [U.S. Colloq.] a clergyman

do·min·ion (də min'yən) *n.* [< ML. *dominio* < L. *dominus*, a lord] 1. rule or power to rule; sovereignty 2. a governed territory or country 3. [D-] formerly, any of certain self-governing member nations of the British Commonwealth of Nations

Dominion Day in Canada, July 1, a legal holiday, the anniversary of the proclamation in 1867 of the establishment of the Dominion of Canada

dom·i·no (dom'ə nō') *n., pl.* **-noes', -nos'** [Fr. & It. < dat. of L. *dominus*, a lord] 1. a loose cloak with wide sleeves, hood, and mask, worn at masquerades 2. a small mask for the eyes; half mask 3. one dressed in such a cloak or mask 4. a small, oblong piece of wood, etc. marked with dots 5. [*pl., with sing. v.*] a game played with such pieces

domino theory the theory that a certain result (**domino effect**) will follow a certain cause like a row of upright dominoes falling if only one is pushed; specif., the theory that if a nation becomes Communist, the nations nearby will also become Communist

DOMINOES

don¹ (don) *n.* [Sp. < L. *dominus*, master] 1. [D-] Sir; Mr.: a Spanish title of respect 2. a Spanish nobleman or gentleman 3. a distinguished man 4. a head, tutor, or fellow of any college of Oxford or Cambridge

don² (don) *vt.* **donned, don'ning** [contr. of *do on*] to put on (a garment, etc.)

‡**Do·ña** (dō'nyä) *n.* [Sp. < L. *domina*, mistress] 1. Lady; Madam: a Spanish title of respect 2. [d-] a Spanish lady

do·nate (dō nāt') *vt., vi.* **-nat'ed, -nat'ing** [prob. back-formation < DONATION] to give or contribute, as to some cause —**do'na·tor** *n.*

do·na·tion (dō nā'shən) *n.* [< L. < pp. of *donare* < *donum*, gift] 1. the act of donating 2. a gift or contribution

done (dun) *pp. of* DO¹ 1. completed 2. cooked 3. socially acceptable —**done (for)** [Colloq.] dead, ruined, finished, etc. —**done in** (or **up**) [Colloq.] exhausted; worn out

do·nee (dō nē') *n.* one who receives a donation

dong¹ (doŋ) *n.* [echoic] a sound of, or like that of, a large bell

dong² (doŋ) *n.* see MONETARY UNITS, table (Vietnam)

don·jon (dun'jən, don'-) *n.* [old sp. of DUNGEON] the heavily fortified inner tower of a castle

Don Juan (don'joo'ən; *Sp.* dôn Hwän') 1. *Sp. Legend* a dissolute nobleman and seducer of women 2. any man who seduces women; libertine

don·key (doŋ'kē) *n., pl.* **-keys** [< ? Duncan, a proper name, or < ? DUN¹] 1. a domesticated ass 2. a stupid or stubborn person 3. a small steam engine: in full, **donkey engine**

donkey jacket a jacket of thick woollen cloth worn chiefly by workmen

donkey's years [Colloq.] a very long time

‡**Don·na** (It. dôn'ä) *n.* [It. < L. *domina*, mistress] 1. Lady; Madam: an Italian title of respect 2. [d-] an Italian lady

don·nish (don'ish) *adj.* of or like a university don —**don'nish·ly** *adv.* —**don'nish·ness** *n.*

don·ny·brook (don'ē brook') *n.* [< a fair formerly held at *Donnybrook*, Ireland: scene of many fights] [Colloq.] a rough, rowdy fight or free-for-all

do·nor (dō'nər) *n.* [< Anglo-Fr. < L. *donator*] 1. one who donates; giver 2. one from whom blood for transfusion, tissue for grafting, etc. is taken

Don Qui·xo·te (don'kē hōt'ē, don'kwik'sət; *Sp.* dôn'-kē Hō'te) 1. a satirical romance by Cervantes 2. the chivalrous, unrealistic hero of this romance 3. an impractical idealist or defender of lost causes

don't (dōnt) 1. do not 2. does not: in this sense now generally considered substandard

don't-know (-nō) *n.* a person who has not yet reached a decision, esp. in answering a questionnaire

doo·dah (doo'dä') *n.* [fanciful extension of DO¹] [Colloq.]

BOTTLE-NOSED DOLPHIN (1.8-4 m long)

1. a trinket **2.** any small object or device whose name does not readily occur to one —**all of a doodah** agitated

doo·dle (dōōd'′l) *vi.* **-dled, -dling** [< ? Low G. *dudeltopf,* simpleton] to scribble or draw aimlessly, esp. when the attention is elsewhere —*n.* a mark, design, etc. made in doodling —**doo'dler** *n.*

doo·dle·bug (-bug′) *n.* [prec. + BUG] **1.** [Colloq.] a flying bomb, esp. one used by the Germans in World War II **2.** [U.S.] *same as* ANT LION (sense 1)

doo·hick·ey (dōō′hik′ē) *n.* [fanciful extension of DO[1]] [U.S. Colloq.] any small object or device whose name is not known or temporarily forgotten

doom (dōōm) *n.* [OE. *dom*] **1.** a judgment; esp., a sentence of condemnation **2.** destiny; fate **3.** tragic fate; ruin or death —*vt.* **1.** to pass judgment on; condemn **2.** to destine to a tragic fate **3.** to ordain as a penalty

dooms·day (dōōmz′dā′) *n.* **1.** *same as* JUDGMENT DAY **2.** any day of judgment

door (dôr) *n.* [OE. *dor, duru*] **1.** a movable structure for opening or closing an entrance, as to a building, room, cupboard, etc.: most doors turn on hinges, slide in grooves, or revolve on an axis **2.** the room or building to which a particular door belongs [two *doors* down the hall] **3.** *same as* DOORWAY —**lay at the door of** to blame (a person) for —**out of doors** outdoors —**show (someone) the door** to command (someone) to leave

door·bell (dôr′bel′) *n.* a bell rung by someone wishing to enter a building or room

door·jamb (-jam′) *n.* a vertical piece of wood, etc. forming the side of a doorway: also **door'post** (-pōst′)

door·keep·er (-kēp′ər) *n.* a person guarding the entrance of a house, hotel, etc.; porter

door·knob (-nob′) *n.* a small knob or lever on a door, usually for releasing the latch

door·man (-man′, -mən) *n., pl.* **-men** (-men′, -mən) a man whose work is opening the door of a building for those who enter or leave, hailing taxis, etc.

door·mat (-mat′) *n.* a mat to wipe the shoes on before entering a house, room, etc.

door·nail (-nāl′) *n.* a large-headed nail used in studding some doors —**dead as a doornail** dead beyond a doubt

door·plate (-plāt′) *n.* a plate on an entrance door, bearing the number, a name, etc.

door·sill (-sil′) *n.* a length of wood, masonry, etc. placed beneath a door; threshold

door·step (-step′) *n.* **1.** a step that leads from an outer door to a path, lawn, etc. **2.** [Colloq.] a thick slice of bread

door·stop (-stop′) *n.* any device for controlling or stopping the closing of a door

door-to-door (-tə dôr′) *adj., adv.* from one home to the next, calling on each in turn

door·way (-wā′) *n.* **1.** an opening in a wall that can be closed by a door **2.** any means of access

dop (dop) *n.* [Afrik.] a S. African brandy made from grape skins

dope (dōp) *n.* [Du. *doop,* sauce < *doopen,* to dip] **1.** any thick liquid or paste used as a lubricant or absorbent **2.** a varnish or filler, as for protecting the cloth covering of aeroplane wings **3.** any additive, as an antiknock compound **4.** [Slang] any drug or narcotic, or such drugs collectively **5.** [Slang] a slow-witted or stupid person **6.** [Slang] information, esp. as used for predicting —*vt.* **doped, dop'ing 1.** to give dope to **2.** to drug or stupefy **3.** to introduce an adulterant or additive into —*vi.* to administer a drug to oneself —**dope out** [U.S. Colloq.] to discover or work out —**dop'er** *n.*

dop·ey, dop·y (dō′pē) *adj.* **dop'i·er, dop'i·est** [Slang] **1.** under the influence of a narcotic **2.** lethargic or stupid —**dop'i·ness** *n.*

dop·pel·gäng·er (dop′'l gaŋ′ər) *n.* [G. < *Doppel,* double + *Gänger,* goer] the ghostly double or wraith of a living person

Dop·pler effect (dop′lər) [after Christian *Doppler* (1803–53), Austrian physicist] the apparent change in frequency of sound or light waves caused by relative motion between the source of radiation and the observer

do·ra·do (də rä′dō) *n.* [Sp., lit., gilded] *same as* DOLPHIN (sense 2)

Dor·ic (dor′ik) *adj.* [< L. < Gr. *Dōrikos,* of *Dōris,* an ancient region of Greece] designating or of the simplest of the classic orders of architecture, distinguished by fluted, heavy columns with simple capitals: cf. CORINTHIAN, IONIC —*n.* any rustic dialect of English with broad vowels, esp. that spoken in Scotland

dorm (dôrm) *n.* [Colloq.] *same as* DORMITORY

dor·mant (dôr′mənt) *adj.* [OFr. prp. of *dormir* < L. *dormire,* to sleep] **1.** sleeping **2.** as if asleep; quiet; still **3.** inactive, as some animals or plants in winter **4.** not in use; suspended —**dor'man·cy** (-mən sē) *n.*

DORIC
CAPITAL

dor·mer (dôr′mər) *n.* [< OFr. < L. *dormitorium:* see ff.] **1.** a window set upright in a sloping roof **2.** the roofed projection in which this window is set Also **dormer window**

dor·mi·to·ry (dôr′mə tər ē) *n., pl.* **-ries** [L. *dormitorium* < pp. of *dormire,* to sleep] **1.** a room with sleeping accommodation for a number of people **2.** a suburb of a large city where people live but do not work: in full **dormitory town 3.** a building with many rooms that provide sleeping and living accommodation for a number of people, as at a college

DORMER

Dor·mo·bile (dôr′mō bēl′) *a trademark for* a vanlike vehicle, often equipped with eating and sleeping facilities

dor·mouse (dôr′mous′) *n., pl.* **-mice** (-mīs′) [? altered by folk etym. (after *mous,* MOUSE) < OFr. *dormeuse,* sleepy < *dormir:* see DORMANT] a small rodent that resembles a squirrel, found in Europe and Asia

dorp (dôrp) *n.* [< Du. *dorp,* village] in S. Africa, a small town or village

dor·sal (dôr′s'l) *adj.* [< ML. < L. < *dorsum,* the back] of, on, or near the back —**dor'sal·ly** *adv.*

do·ry[1] (dôr′ē) *n.* [ME. *dorre* < MFr. *dorée,* lit., gilt] any of various spiny-finned food fishes, as the John Dory

do·ry[2] (dôr′ē) *n., pl.* **-ries** [AmInd. (Central America) *dori,* a dugout] [Chiefly U.S.] a small, flat-bottomed fishing boat with high sides

dos·age (dōs′ij) *n.* **1.** a dosing or being dosed **2.** the system to be followed in taking doses, as of medicine **3.** the amount used in a dose

dose (dōs) *n.* [OFr. < LL. < Gr. *dosis,* orig., a giving < *didonai,* to give] **1.** an amount of medicine to be taken at one time or at stated intervals **2.** amount of a punishment or other unpleasant experience undergone at one time **3.** the amount of ionizing radiation delivered to a specified area or body part —*vt.* **dosed, dos'ing** to give doses of medicine to —*vi.* to take a dose of medicine —**like a dose of salts** [Colloq.] very quickly

do·sim·e·ter (dō sim′ə tər) *n.* [see DOSE & -METER] a small device for measuring the radiation a person has absorbed

doss (dos) *n.* [< ?] [Slang] **1.** a bed, esp. in a cheap lodging house **2.** sleep —*vi.* to sleep, esp. in a doss house (often with *down*) —**dos'ser** *n.*

doss house [Slang] a place where a night's lodging can be had very cheaply

dos·si·er (dos′ē ā′) *n.* [Fr. < *dos,* the back: so named because labelled on the back] a collection of documents about some person or matter

dost (dust) *archaic 2nd pers. sing., pres. indic.,* of DO[1]: *used with* thou (chiefly as an auxiliary)

dot[1] (dot) *n.* [OE. *dott,* head of boil] **1.** a tiny spot, speck, or mark; point; as, *a)* the mark placed above an *i* or *j* *b)* *Math.* a decimal point *c) Music* a point after a note, increasing its time value by one half; also, a point above or below a note to show it is staccato **2.** any small, round spot **3.** a short sound or click in Morse code —*vt.* **dot'ted, dot'- ting 1.** to mark with a dot or dots **2.** to cover as with dots [trees *dotted* the landscape] **3.** [Slang] to hit —*vi.* to make a dot or dots —**dot one's i's and cross one's t's** to be minutely correct —**on the dot** [Colloq.] at the exact time —**dot'ter** *n.*

dot[2] (dot) *n.* [Fr. < L. *dos* (gen. *dotis*) < *dare,* to give] a woman's marriage dowry —**do·tal** (dōt′'l) *adj.*

dot·age (dōt′ij) *n.* [ME. < *doten,* DOTE] **1.** feeble and childish state due to old age; senility **2.** a doting; foolish or excessive affection

dot·ard (-ərd) *n.* [ME. < *doten,* DOTE] a foolish and doddering old person

dote (dōt) *vi.* **dot'ed, dot'ing** [ME. *doten*] **1.** to be foolish or weak-minded, esp. because of old age **2.** to be excessively or foolishly fond (with *on* or *upon*) —**dot'er** *n.* —**dot'ing** *adj.* —**dot'ing·ly** *adv.*

doth (duth) *archaic 3rd pers. sing., pres. indic.,* of DO[1] (chiefly in auxiliary uses)

dot·ter·el (dot′ər əl) *n., pl.* **-els, -el:** see PLURAL, II, D, 1 [< DOTE, because easy to catch] a European and Asian plover with a short bill

dot·tle (dot′'l) *n.* [< ME. var. of *dosel,* a plug] the tobacco plug left in the bowl of a pipe after it has been smoked

dot·ty (dot′ē) *adj.* **-ti·er, -ti·est 1.** covered with dots; dotted **2.** [Colloq.] feeble; unsteady **3.** [Colloq.] feeble-minded or crazy **4.** [Colloq.] extremely fond of —**dot'ti·ness** *n.*

Dou·ai Bible (dōō ä′) [< *Douai,* in France, where it was published in part (1609–10)] an English translation of the Bible from the Vulgate, for Roman Catholics: also **Douay Version, Douay Bible**

dou·ble (dub′'l) *adj.* [OFr. < L. *duplus,* lit., twofold] **1.** twofold; duplex **2.** having two layers; folded in two **3.**

having two of one kind; repeated [a *double* consonant, *double* glazing] **4.** being of two kinds; dual [a *double* standard] **5.** having two meanings; ambiguous **6.** twice as much, as many, as large, etc. **7.** of extra size, value, strength, etc. **8.** made for two [a *double* bed] **9.** two-faced; deceiving **10.** having a tone an octave lower [*double* bass] **11.** *Bot.* having more than one set of petals —*adv.* **1.** twofold **2.** two together; in pairs —*n.* **1.** anything twice as much, as many, or as large as normal **2.** a person or thing looking very much like another; duplicate; counterpart **3.** a stand-in, as in films **4.** a sharp shift of direction **5.** a trick; shift **6.** [*pl.*] a game of tennis, etc. with two players on each side **7.** [Colloq.] a double measure of whisky, brandy, etc. **8.** *Bridge* the doubling of an opponent's bid —*vt.* **-bled, -bling 1.** to make twice as much or many **2.** to fold **3.** to repeat or duplicate **4.** to be the double of **5.** *Bridge* to increase the point value or penalty of (an opponent's bid) **6.** *Naut.* to sail around [they *doubled* Cape Horn] —*vi.* **1.** to become double **2.** to turn sharply backwards [the animal *doubled* on its tracks] **3.** to serve as a double **4.** to serve an additional purpose or function —**double back 1.** to fold back **2.** to turn back in the direction from which one came —**double up 1.** to fold completely; clench (one's fist) **2.** to bend over, as in laughter or pain **3.** to share a room, etc. with someone —**at the double** [Colloq.] **1.** in double time **2.** quickly —**dou'bler** *n.*

double agent a spy who infiltrates an enemy espionage organization in order to betray it

dou·ble-bar·relled (-bar'əld) *adj.* **1.** having two barrels, as a kind of shotgun **2.** having a double purpose or meaning **3.** having two or more hyphenated parts: said of surnames

double bass (bās) the largest and deepest-toned instrument of the violin family (orig. of the viol family), with a range of approximately three octaves

double bassoon same as CONTRABASSOON

double boiler a utensil consisting of two pans, one of which fits over the other: food is cooked in the upper one by water boiling in the lower

dou·ble-breast·ed (-bres'tid) *adj.* overlapping across the breast and having a double row of buttons, as a coat

dou·ble-check (-chek') *vt., vi.* to check again; verify —*n.* the act of double-checking

double chin a fold of flesh beneath the chin

double concerto a concerto for two solo instruments

DOUBLE BASS

double cream cream with a high fat content

dou·ble-cross (-kros') *vt.* [Colloq.] to betray (a person) by doing the opposite of, or intentionally failing to do, what one has promised —**dou'ble-cross'er** *n.*

double cross [Colloq.] a double-crossing; treachery

double dagger a mark (‡) used in printing and writing to indicate a note or cross-reference

dou·ble-deal·ing (-dēl'iŋ) *n.* the act of doing the opposite of what one pretends to do; duplicity —*adj.* deceitful; treacherous —**dou'ble-deal'er** *n.*

dou·ble-deck·er (-dek'ər) *n.* **1.** any structure or vehicle with two levels, esp. a bus **2.** [Colloq.] a sandwich with two layers of filling

double dutch nonsense; gibberish

dou·ble-dyed (-dīd') *adj.* **1.** twice immersed in dye **2.** thoroughly infamous **3.** staunch [a *double-dyed* conservative]

dou·ble-edged (-ejd') *adj.* **1.** having two cutting edges **2.** applicable both ways, as an argument

dou·ble-en·ten·dre (do͞o'blän tän'drə, dub''l än-) *n.* [Fr. (now obs.), double meaning] a word or phrase with two meanings, esp. when one of them is risqué or indecorous

double entry a system of bookkeeping in which each transaction is entered as a debit and a credit

double exposure *Photog.* **1.** the making of two exposures on the same film or plate **2.** a photograph resulting from this

dou·ble-faced (dub''l fāst') *adj.* **1.** having two faces or aspects **2.** hypocritical; insincere

double feature two full-length films on the same cinema programme

double first 1. a person obtaining a first-class honours degree in two different subjects **2.** the two degrees earned

double helix the form of the DNA molecule consisting of two right-handed helical chains coiled around the same axis

dou·ble-joint·ed (-join'tid) *adj.* having joints that permit limbs, fingers, etc. to bend at other than the usual angles

dou·ble-knit (-nit') *adj.* knitted with a double stitch, which gives extra thickness to the fabric

dou·ble-park (-pärk') *vt., vi.* to park (a vehicle) parallel to another parked beside a kerb

double pneumonia pneumonia of both lungs

dou·ble-quick (-kwik') *adj.* very quick —*adv.* at this pace

dou·ble-reed (-rēd') *adj.* designating or of a group of woodwind instruments, as the oboe or bassoon, having two reeds separated by a narrow opening —*n.* a double-reed instrument

dou·ble-space (-spās') *vt., vi.* **-spaced', -spac'ing** to type (copy) so as to leave a full space between lines

double standard a system, code, etc. applied unequally; specif., one that is stricter for women than for men, esp. in matters of sex

dou·blet (dub'lit) *n.* [OFr. dim. of *double*, orig., something folded] **1.** a man's short, closefitting jacket of the 14th to the 16th cent. **2.** either of a pair of similar things **3.** a pair; couple **4.** either of two words that derive ultimately from the same source but have changed in form (e.g., *card, chart*)

double take a delayed reaction to some remark, situation, etc., in which there is first unthinking acceptance and then startled surprise or a second glance as the real meaning strikes one

double talk 1. ambiguous and deceptive talk **2.** deliberately confusing talk made up of a mixture of real words and meaningless syllables

double time a rate of payment twice as high as usual, as for overtime on Sundays

dou·ble-tree (dub''l trē') *n.* [DOUBLE + (SWINGLE) TREE] a crossbar on a wagon, plough, etc.

dou·bloon (du blo͞on') *n.* [< Fr. < Sp. < L. *duplus*, double] an obsolete Spanish gold coin

dou·bly (dub'lē) *adv.* **1.** twice **2.** two at a time

doubt (dout) *vi.* [< OFr. < L. *dubitare*] to be uncertain in opinion or belief; be undecided —*vt.* **1.** to be uncertain about; question **2.** to be inclined to disbelieve **3.** [Archaic] to be fearful of —*n.* **1.** *a)* a lack of conviction; uncertainty *b)* lack of trust **2.** a condition of uncertainty **3.** an unsettled point or matter; difficulty —**beyond (or without) doubt** certainly —**no doubt 1.** certainly **2.** probably **3.** admittedly —**doubt'a·ble** *adj.* —**doubt'er** *n.* —**doubt'ing·ly** *adv.*

doubt·ful (-fəl) *adj.* **1.** in doubt; not definite **2.** uncertain **3.** giving rise to doubt; questionable, as in reputation **4.** feeling doubt; unsettled —**doubt'ful·ly** *adv.* —**doubt'ful·ness** *n.*

doubt·ing Thomas (dout'iŋ) [after the apostle *Thomas*] a person who habitually doubts, as Thomas doubted the resurrection of Jesus

doubt·less (-lis) *adj.* [Rare] free from doubt —*adv.* **1.** without doubt; certainly **2.** probably —**doubt'less·ly** *adv.* —**doubt'less·ness** *n.*

douche (do͞osh) *n.* [Fr. < It. *doccia*, shower, orig., conduit, ult. < L. *ductus*, pp. of *ducere*, to lead] **1.** a jet of liquid applied externally or internally to some part of the body **2.** a bath or treatment of this kind **3.** a device for douching —*vt., vi.* douched, douch'ing to apply a douche (to)

dough (dō) *n.* [OE. *dag*] **1.** a mixture of flour, liquid, and other ingredients, worked into a soft, thick mass for baking into bread, etc. **2.** any pasty mass like this **3.** [Chiefly U.S. Slang] money

dough·boy (-boi') *n.* **1.** a dumpling that is boiled or steamed **2.** [Colloq.] a U.S. infantryman, esp. of World War I

dough·nut (-nut') *n.* a small, usually ring-shaped cake, fried in deep fat

dough·ty (dout'ē) *adj.* **-ti·er, -ti·est** [< OE. < *dugan*, to avail] valiant; brave: now used with a consciously archaic flavour —**dough'ti·ly** *adv.* —**dough'ti·ness** *n.*

dough·y (dō'ē) *adj.* **dough'i·er, dough'i·est** of or like dough; soft, pasty, etc. —**dough'i·ness** *n.*

Doug·las fir (or **spruce, pine, hemlock**) (dug'ləs) [after David *Douglas*, 19th-c. Brit. botanist] a tall evergreen tree of the pine family, native to W N. America and valued for its wood

dour (door, do͞or) *adj.* [< L. *durus*, hard] **1.** [Scot.] stern; severe **2.** [Scot.] obstinate **3.** sullen; gloomy —**dour'ly** *adv.* —**dour'ness** *n.*

douse¹ (dous) *vt.* doused, dous'ing [< ?] **1.** *Naut.* to lower (sails) quickly **2.** [Colloq.] to put out (a light or fire) quickly

douse² (dous) *vt.* doused, dous'ing [< ? prec.] **1.** to plunge or thrust suddenly into liquid **2.** to drench; pour liquid over —*vi.* to get immersed or drenched

douse³ (douz) *vi.* doused, dous'ing same as DOWSE²

dove (duv) *n.* [< ? ON. *dūfa*] **1.** a bird of the pigeon family, with a full-breasted body and short legs: a symbol of peace **2.** an advocate of the use of peaceful measures to solve international conflicts **3.** a person regarded as gentle or innocent —**dov'ish** *adj.*

dove·cote (duv'kōt') *n.* [DOVE + COTE] a small house or box with compartments for nesting pigeons: also **dove'-cot'** (-kot')

dove·tail (duv'tāl') *n.* **1.** a thing shaped like a dove's tail; specif., a projecting, wedge-shaped part that fits into a corresponding indentation to form a joint **2.** a joint thus formed —*vt.* **1.** to join together by means of dovetails **2.** to piece together (facts, etc.) —*vi.* to fit together closely or logically

dow·a·ger (dou'ə jər) *n.* [< OFr. < *douage*, dowry, ult. < L. *dos*: see DOT²] **1.** a widow with a title or property derived from her dead husband **2.** an elderly woman of wealth and dignity

dow·dy (dou'dē) *adj.* **-di·er, -di·est** [< ME. *doude*, unattractive woman] not neat or fashionable in dress; shabby —*n.*, *pl.* **-dies** a dowdy woman —**dow'di·ly** *adv.* —**dow'di·ness** *n.* —**dow'dy·ish** *adj.*

DOVETAIL

dow·el (dou'əl) *n.* [ME. *doule*] a peg or pin of wood, metal, etc., usually fitted into corresponding holes in two pieces to fasten them together —*vt.* **-elled, -el·ling** to fasten with dowels

dow·er (dou'ər) *n.* [< OFr. < ML. *dotarium* < L. *dos*: see DOT²] **1.** that part of a man's property which his widow inherits for life **2.** a dowry **3.** a natural talent, or endowment —*vt.* **1.** to give a dower to **2.** to endow (*with*)

dower house formerly, a house set apart for the use of a widow, esp. on her deceased husband's estate

DOWEL

Dow-Jones average [U.S.] a daily index of stock-exchange prices, based on the average price of a selected number of securities

down¹ (doun) *adv.* [< OE. *adune*, from the hill < *a-*, off + *dune*, hill] **1.** from a higher to a lower place **2.** in or on a lower position or level **3.** *a*) in or to a place thought of as lower; often, specif., southwards, or away from a capital or a university *b*) out of one's hands [put it *down*] **4.** below the horizon **5.** from an earlier to a later period or person **6.** into a low physical or emotional condition **7.** in an inferior position or condition **8.** to a lower amount or bulk **9.** into a tranquil or quiet state **10.** seriously; earnestly [get *down* to work] **11.** completely [loaded *down*] **12.** in cash [£5 *down*] **13.** in writing; on record [take *down* his name] —*adj.* **1.** directed towards a lower position **2.** in a lower place **3.** gone, brought, pulled, etc. down **4.** dejected; discouraged **5.** prostrate; ill **6.** completed [four *down*, six to go] **7.** in cash, as part of the purchase price [a *down* payment] **8.** *Sports* trailing an opponent by a specified number of points, strokes, etc. —*prep.* down towards, along, through, into, or upon —*vt.* **1.** *a*) to put, bring, get, throw, or knock down *b*) to defeat, as in a game **2.** to gulp or eat rapidly —*n.* a downward movement or depressed condition: see phr. UPS AND DOWNS at UP —**down and out 1.** *Boxing* knocked out **2.** penniless, friendless, ill, etc. —**down on** [Colloq.] hostile to; angry or annoyed with —**down tools** to cease work and go on strike —**down to the ground** thoroughly; completely —**down with!** do away with! —**have a down on** to have a grudge against someone

down² (doun) *n.* [< ON. *dūnn*] **1.** soft, fine feathers **2.** soft, fine hair or hairy growth

down³ (doun) *n.* [OE. *dun*, a hill] **1.** an expanse of open, high, grassy land: *usually used in pl.* **2.** [confused with *dune*] [Archaic] a sandy mound formed by the wind —**the Downs** either of two ranges of low, grassy hills in SE England

down·beat (-bēt') *n.* *Music* a downward stroke made by a conductor to show the first beat of each bar —*adj.* pessimistic or gloomy in outlook; depressing

down·cast (-kàst') *adj.* **1.** directed downwards **2.** very unhappy or discouraged; dejected

down·er (-ər) *n.* [Slang] any depressant or sedative, as a tranquillizer, barbiturate, etc.

down·fall (doun'fôl') *n.* **1.** *a*) a sudden fall, as from prosperity or power *b*) the cause of such a fall **2.** a sudden, heavy fall, as of rain

down·grade (-grād') *n.* [Chiefly U.S.] a downward slope, esp. in a road —*vt.* **-grad'ed, -grad'ing 1.** to demote to a less skilled job at lower pay **2.** to lower in importance, value, etc. **3.** to belittle —**on the downgrade** losing status, influence, health, etc.; declining

down·heart·ed (-här'tid) *adj.* discouraged; dejected —**down'heart'ed·ly** *adv.*

down·hill (-hil') *adv.* **1.** towards the bottom of a hill **2.** to a poorer condition, status, etc. —*adj.* **1.** sloping or going downwards **2.** of or having to do with skiing downhill —*n.* a skiing race downhill

Down·ing Street (doun'iŋ) [after Sir G. *Downing* (1623–84), who owned property there] **1.** street in the West End of London, location of some important government offices **2.** the British government

down payment the deposit paid on an item being bought on hire purchase, etc.

down·pipe (-pīp) *n.* a vertical pipe for carrying rain water from a roof gutter to ground level

down·pour (doun'pôr') *n.* a heavy rain

down·right (-rīt') *adv.* thoroughly; utterly —*adj.* **1.** absolute; thoroughgoing; utter **2.** straightforward; plain; frank —**down'right'ness** *n.*

Down's syndrome (dounz) [after J.L.H. *Down* (1828–96), Brit. physician] a congenital disease in which there is mental deficiency and a characteristic broad face, with slanting eyes, etc.; mongolism

down·stairs (doun'sterz') *adv.* **1.** down the stairs **2.** on or to a lower floor —*adj.* situated on a lower floor: also **downstair** —*n.* **1.** a lower floor or floors **2.** the servants of a household, collectively

down·stream (-strēm') *adv.*, *adj.* in the direction of the current of a stream

down·swing (-swiŋ') *n.* a downward trend, as in business: also **down'turn'** (-turn')

down-to-earth (-tə urth') *adj.* realistic or practical

down·town (-toun') *adj.*, *adv.* [Chiefly U.S.] of, in, like, to, or towards the lower part or main business section of a city or town —*n.* [Chiefly U.S.] the downtown section

down train a railway train leaving the chief terminus, esp. London

down·trod·den (-trod''n) *adj.* **1.** trampled on or down **2.** oppressed; tyrannized over

down under [Colloq.] Australia or New Zealand

down·ward (-wərd) *adv.*, *adj.* **1.** towards a lower place, state, etc. **2.** from an earlier to a later time Also **down'-wards** *adv.* —**down'ward·ly** *adv.*

down·wind (-wind') *adv.*, *adj.* in the direction in which the wind is blowing or usually blows

down·y (-ē) *adj.* **down'i·er, down'i·est 1.** of or covered with soft, fine feathers or hair **2.** soft and fluffy, like down **3.** [Slang] sharp; knowing —**down'i·ness** *n.*

dow·ry (dou'rē) *n.*, *pl.* **-ries** [see DOWER] **1.** the property that a woman brings to her husband at marriage **2.** a natural talent, gift, etc.

dowse¹ (dous) *vt.* **dowsed, dows'ing** *same as* DOUSE¹

dowse² (douz) *vi.* **dowsed, dows'ing** [< ?] to search for a source of water or minerals with a divining rod (**dowsing rod**) —**dows'er** *n.*

dox·ol·o·gy (dok sol'ə jē) *n.*, *pl.* **-gies** [ML. *doxologia* < Gr. < *doxa*, praise + *-logia*, -LOGY] a hymn of praise to God; specif., *a*) the **greater doxology**, which begins "Glory to God in the highest" *b*) the **lesser doxology**, which begins "Glory to the Father" *c*) a hymn beginning "Praise God from whom all blessings flow"

doy·en (doi'ən) *n.* [Fr.: see DEAN¹] the senior member of a group, profession, or society

doz. dozen; dozens

doze (dōz) *vi.* **dozed, doz'ing** [prob. < Scand.] to sleep lightly or fitfully; be half asleep —*vt.* to spend (time) in dozing —*n.* a light sleep; nap —**doze off** to fall into a light sleep —**doz'er** *n.*

doz·en (duz''n) *n.*, *pl.* **-ens** or, esp. after a number, **-en** [< OFr. < *douze*, twelve < L. < *duo*, two + *decem*, ten] a set of twelve —**doz'enth** *adj.*

doz·y (dō'zē) *adj.* **doz'i·er, doz'i·est 1.** sleepy; drowsy **2.** [Colloq.] stupid; dull —**doz'i·ly** *adv.* —**doz'i·ness** *n.*

DP, D.P. displaced person

D.Phil. Doctor of Philosophy

DPP, D.P.P. Director of Public Prosecutions

dpt. department

Dr. 1. Doctor **2.** Drive

dr. 1. debit **2.** debtor **3.** drachma(s) **4.** dram(s)

drab¹ (drab) *n.* [< Fr. *drap*, cloth < LL. *drappus*] a dull yellowish brown —*adj.* **drab'ber, drab'best 1.** of a dull yellowish-brown colour **2.** dull; monotonous —**drab'ly** *adv.* —**drab'ness** *n.*

drab² (drab) *n.* [< Celt. as in Ir. *drabog*, slattern] **1.** a slovenly woman **2.** a prostitute —*vi.* **drabbed, drab'bing** to fornicate with prostitutes

drachm (dram) *n.* *same as:* **1.** DRACHMA **2.** DRAM

drach·ma (drak'mə) *n.*, *pl.* **-mas, -mae** (-mē), **-mai** (-mī) [L. < Gr. *drachmē*, lit., a handful < *drassesthai*, to grasp] **1.** an ancient Greek silver coin **2.** the monetary unit of modern Greece: see MONETARY UNITS, table

Dra·co·ni·an (drā kō'nē ən) *adj.* [after *Draco*, 7th cent. B.C. Athenian statesman] **1.** of the very harsh laws attributed to Draco **2.** very severe or cruel

draft (dräft) *n.* [ME. *draught*, a drawing < OE. *dragan*, DRAW] **1.** a rough sketch of a piece of writing **2.** a plan or drawing of a work to be done **3.** a written order from one person, firm, etc. directing the payment of money to another; cheque **4.** a demand or drain made on something

5. [U.S.] *a)* the taking of persons for a special purpose, esp. compulsory military service *b)* those so taken —*vt.* **1.** [U.S.] to take, as for compulsory military service **2.** to draw off or away **3.** to make a preliminary sketch of or working plans for —*adj.* in a preliminary or rough form —**draft'a·ble** *adj.* —**draft'er** *n.*

draft·ee (dräf tē') *n.* [Chiefly U.S.] a person drafted, esp. for service in the armed forces

draft·y (dräf'tē) *adj.* **draft'i·er, draft'i·est** *U.S. sp. of* DRAUGHTY —**draft'i·ly** *adv.* —**draft'i·ness** *n.*

drag (drag) *vt.* **dragged, drag'ging** [< OE. *dragan* or ON. *draga*: see DRAW] **1.** to pull, draw, or move with effort, esp. along the ground; haul **2.** to force into some action, etc. **3.** to pull a grapnel, net, etc. over the bottom of (a river, etc.) in searching for something; dredge **4.** to draw a harrow over (land) **5.** to draw (something) out over a period of time —*vi.* **1.** to be dragged; trail **2.** to lag behind **3.** to move or pass too slowly **4.** to search a body of water with a grapnel, net, etc. **5.** [Slang] to draw (*on*) a cigarette, etc. **6.** [Slang] to participate in a drag race —*n.* **1.** something dragged along the ground; specif., *a)* a harrow *b)* a large, heavy coach **2.** a grapnel, dragnet, etc. **3.** anything that hinders **4.** a dragging **5.** [Slang] a puff of a cigarette, etc. **6.** [Slang] a dull or boring person, situation, etc. **7.** [Slang] clothing of the opposite sex, esp. woman's clothing worn by a man **8.** *Aeron.* a resisting force exerted on an aircraft, tending to retard its motion —**drag on** (or **out**) to prolong or be prolonged tediously —**drag one's feet** (or **heels**) to be uncooperative —**drag up 1.** to introduce unpleasantly [*drag up* old scandals] **2.** [Colloq.] to rear (children) carelessly —**drag'ger** *n.* —**drag'gy** *adj.* -**gi·er, -gi·est**

dra·gée (dra zhā') *n.* [Fr.] a sugar-coated sweet, nut, or pill

drag·gle (drag''l) *vt., vi.* -**gled, -gling** [freq. of DRAG] to make or become wet or dirty by dragging in mud or water

drag·net (-net') *n.* **1.** a net dragged along the bottom of a river, lake, etc. for catching fish **2.** a net for catching small game **3.** an organized system or network for catching criminals, etc.

drag·o·man (drag'ə mən) *n., pl.* -**mans, -men** [< OFr. < It. < MGr. *dragomanos* < Ar. *tarġumān*] in the Near East, an interpreter or guide

drag·on (drag'ən) *n.* [< OFr. < L. < Gr. *drakōn* < ? *derkesthai*, to see] **1.** a mythical monster, usually represented as a large reptile with wings and claws, breathing out fire and smoke **2.** a fierce person, esp. a strict chaperon

drag·on·fly (-flī') *n., pl.* -**flies'** a large, harmless insect having narrow, transparent, net-veined wings: it feeds mostly on flies, etc.

dragon's teeth an obstacle for tanks, etc., consisting of pointed spikes protruding from the ground

dra·goon (dra gōōn') *n.* [Fr. *dragon*: see DRAGON] a heavily armed cavalryman —*vt.* **1.** to harass or persecute by dragoons **2.** to force (*into* doing)

drag race a race between motor cars to test their rates of acceleration from a complete stop, specif., esp. in U.S. between hot-rod cars (**dragsters**) on a short, straight course (**drag strip**) —**drag'-race'** *vi.* -**raced', -rac'ing**

drain (drān) *vt.* [< OE. *dreahnian* < base of *dryge*, DRY] **1.** to draw off (liquid) gradually **2.** to draw liquid from gradually [to *drain* a swamp] **3.** to receive the waters of **4.** to drink all the liquid from (a cup, etc.) **5.** to exhaust (strength, emotions, or resources) gradually —*vi.* **1.** to flow off gradually **2.** to become dry by the drawing or flowing off of liquid **3.** to disappear gradually **4.** to discharge its waters [central Europe *drains* into the Danube] —*n.* **1.** a channel, pipe, tube, etc. for carrying off water, sewage, pus, etc. **2.** a draining **3.** that which gradually exhausts strength, etc. —**down the drain** lost in a wasteful, heedless way —**drain'er** *n.*

drain·age (-ij) *n.* **1.** the act, process, or method of draining **2.** a system of pipes, etc. for carrying off waste matter **3.** that which is drained off **4.** an area drained, as by a river

drainage basin the land drained by a river system

draining board a sloping board attached to a sink on which dishes, etc. are placed after being washed up

drain·pipe (-pīp') *n.* **1.** a large pipe used to carry off water, sewage, etc. **2.** [*pl.*] very narrow trousers, esp. as worn in the 1950's

drake (drāk) *n.* [< WGmc. hyp. *drako*, male] a male duck

dram (dram) *n.* [< OFr. < ML. < L. *drachma*: see DRACHMA] **1.** *Apothecaries' Weight* a unit equal to 1/8 ounce **2.** *Avoirdupois Weight* a unit equal to 1/16 ounce **3.** a small drink of spirits **4.** a small amount of anything

dra·ma (drä'mə) *n.* [LL. < Gr., a deed, drama < *draein*, to do] **1.** a literary composition that tells a story by means of dialogue and action, to be performed by actors; play **2.** the art or profession of writing, acting, or producing plays (often with *the*) **3.** plays collectively **4.** a series of events as interesting, vivid, etc. as a play **5.** the quality of being dramatic

Dram·a·mine (dram'ə mēn') *a trademark for* DIMENHYDRINATE —*n.* [**d-**] this substance

dra·mat·ic (drə mat'ik) *adj.* **1.** of or connected with drama **2.** *a)* like a play *b)* full of action; vivid, striking, exciting, etc. —**dra·mat'i·cal·ly** *adv.*

dra·mat·ics (-iks) *n.pl.* **1.** [*usually with sing. v.*] the art of performing or producing plays **2.** plays presented by amateurs **3.** histrionic or hysterical behaviour

dram·a·tis per·so·nae (dräm'ə tis pər sō'nē, dram'-) [ModL.] the characters in a play

dram·a·tist (dram'ə tist) *n.* a playwright

dram·a·tize (dram'ə tīz') *vt.* -**tized', -tiz'ing 1.** to make into a drama; adapt for performance on the stage, screen, etc. **2.** to regard or present in a dramatic manner —*vi.* **1.** to be capable of being dramatized **2.** to dramatize oneself —**dram'a·ti·za'tion** *n.* —**dram'a·tiz'er** *n.*

dram·a·tur·gy (-tur'jē) *n.* [< G. < Gr. *dramatourgia* < *drama*, DRAMA + *ergon*, work] the art of writing or producing plays —**dram'a·tur'gic, dram'a·tur'gi·cal** *adj.* —**dram'a·tur'gi·cal·ly** *adv.* —**dram'a·tur'gist, dram'-a·turge'** *n.*

drank (draŋk) *pt. of* DRINK

drape (drāp) *vt.* **draped, drap'ing** [< OFr. < *drap*, cloth: see DRAB[1]] **1.** to cover, hang, or decorate as with cloth or clothes in loose folds **2.** to arrange (a garment, cloth, etc.) artistically in folds or hangings —*vi.* to hang or fall in folds —*n.* **1.** the manner in which cloth hangs **2.** [Chiefly U.S.] cloth hanging in loose folds; esp., a drapery: *usually used in pl.*

drap·er (drā'pər) *n.* a dealer in fabrics, etc.

drap·er·y (drā'pər ē) *n., pl.* -**per·ies 1.** *a)* hangings, etc. arranged in loose folds *b)* an artistic arrangement of such hangings **2.** [Chiefly U.S.] [*pl.*] curtains of heavy material

dras·tic (dras'tik) *adj.* [Gr. *drastikos*, active < *dran*, to do] acting with force; having a violent effect; severe; harsh —**dras'ti·cal·ly** *adv.*

drat (drat) *interj.* [? < *God rot*] confound! bother!: a mild oath expressing annoyance —**drat'ted** *adj.*

draught (dräft) *n.* [ME. < OE. *dragan*, DRAW] **1.** *a)* drawing, as of a vehicle or load *b)* the thing, quantity, or load pulled **2.** *a)* a drawing in of a fish net *b)* the amount of fish caught in one draw **3.** *a)* drinking *b)* the amount taken at one drink **4.** *a)* a drink; specif. a dose of medicine *b)* [Colloq.] a portion of beer, ale, etc. drawn from a cask **5.** *a)* a drawing into the lungs, as of air *b)* the amount of air, etc. drawn in **6.** a current of air, as in a room **7.** a device regulating the current of air in a heating system **8.** *Naut.* the depth of water that a ship displaces, esp. when loaded —*adj.* **1.** used for pulling loads [*draught* animals] **2.** drawn from a cask on order [*draught* beer] —**feel the draught** to suffer financial losses

draught·board (-bôrd') *n.* a board with 64 squares of two alternating colours, used in draughts and chess

draught horse a strong horse capable of pulling heavy loads

draughts (dräfts) *n.pl.* [with sing. v.] a game played on a draughtboard by two players, each with twelve round, flat pieces to move

draughts·man (-mən) *n., pl.* -**men 1.** a person who draws plans of structures or machinery **2.** a person who draws up legal documents, speeches, etc. **3.** an artist skilful in drawing **4.** *Draughts* any of the round, flat pieces used in playing draughts —**draughts'man·ship'** *n.*

draught·y (dräf'tē) *adj.* **draught'i·er, draught'i·est** letting in, having, or exposed to a draught or draughts of air —**draught'i·ly** *adv.* —**draught'i·ness** *n.*

Dra·vid·i·an (drə vid'ē ən) *n.* **1.** any of a group of intermixed races chiefly in S India and N Ceylon **2.** the family of non-Indo-European languages spoken by these races, including Tamil, Malayalam, etc. —*adj.* of the Dravidians or their languages: also **Dra·vid'ic**

draw (drô) *vt.* **drew, drawn, draw'ing** [< OE. *dragan*] **1.** to make move towards one or along with one; pull; drag **2.** to pull up, down, in, across, back, etc. **3.** to need (a specified depth of water) to float in: said of a ship **4.** to attract; charm **5.** to breathe in; inhale **6.** to bring forth; elicit [his challenge *drew* no reply] **7.** to bring on; provoke [to *draw* enemy fire] **8.** to pull out; extract (a cork, sword, etc.) **9.** *a)* to remove (liquid) by sucking, draining, etc. *b)* to bring up, as water from a well *c)* to cause (liquid) to flow [to *draw* a bath, *draw* blood] **10.** to disembowel **11.** to get from some source [to *draw* a salary] **12.** to withdraw (money) held in an account **13.** to have accruing to it [savings *draw* interest] **14.** to write (a cheque or draft) **15.** to reach (a conclusion, etc.); deduce **16.** to bring (a game or contest) to a tie **17.** to stretch tautly or to full length **18.** to distort **19.** to flatten or shape (metal) by die stamping, hammering, etc. **20.** to make (metal) into wire by pulling it through holes **21.** to make (lines, pictures, etc.) as with a pencil, pen, brush, etc. **22.** to describe or formulate in words **23.** to cause (feet) to swell —*vi.* **1.** to draw something (in various senses of the *vt.*) **2.** to be drawn or have a drawing effect **3.** to come; move [to *draw* near] **4.** to shrink; contract **5.** to allow a draught, as of smoke, to move through [this fire *draws* well] **6.** to attract audiences **7.** to become stronger by infusion; said of tea —*n.* **1.** a drawing or being drawn (in various senses) **2.** the result of drawing **3.** a thing drawn **4.** the cards dealt as replacement in draw poker **5.** a tie; stalemate **6.** a thing that attracts interest, audiences, etc. —**draw away** to move away or ahead —**draw in 1.** to grow shorter: said esp. of days **2.** to entice; lure; entangle —**draw on** (or **nigh**) to approach —**draw out 1.** to extend **2.** to take out; extract **3.** to get (a person) to talk **4.** to leave a railway station: said of trains trains **5.** to grow longer: said esp. of days —**draw up 1.** to arrange in order **2.** to compose (a document) in proper form **3.** to stop

draw·back (-bak') *n.* anything that prevents or lessens full satisfaction; shortcoming

draw·bridge (-brij') *n.* a bridge that can be raised, lowered, or drawn aside

draw·ee (drô'ē') *n.* the party that the drawer directs, by a draft, etc., to pay money over to a third party (called *payee*)

draw·er (drô'ər; *for 4* drôr) *n.* **1.** a person or thing that draws **2.** one who draws an order for the payment of money **3.** a draughtsman **4.** a sliding box in a table, chest, bureau, etc., that can be drawn out and then pushed back into place

draw·ers (drôrz) *n.pl.* a form of undergarments with legs, worn chiefly by women

draw·ing (drô'iŋ) *n.* **1.** the act of one that draws; specif., the art of representing something by lines made on a surface with a pencil, pen, etc. **2.** a picture, design, etc. thus made **3.** a lottery

drawing pin a pin with a wide, flat head, that can be pressed into a board, etc. to support maps, notices, etc.

drawing room [< earlier *withdrawing room*, to which guests withdrew after dinner] **1.** a room where guests are received or entertained; sitting room **2.** a formal reception

draw·knife (drô'nīf') *n.*, *pl.* **-knives** (-nīvz') a knife with a handle at each end: the user draws it toward him in shaving a surface: also **drawing knife**

drawl (drôl) *vt., vi.* [prob. freq. of DRAW] to speak slowly, prolonging the vowels —*n.* a slow manner of speech in which vowels are prolonged —**drawl'er** *n.* —**drawl'ing·ly** *adv.*

drawn (drôn) *pp.* of DRAW —*adj.* **1.** pulled out of the sheath **2.** even; tied **3.** eviscerated **4.** tense; haggard

drawn·work (-wurk') *n.* ornamental work done on textiles by pulling out threads to produce a lacelike design

draw poker a form of poker in which each player is dealt five cards face down, and may be dealt replacements for unwanted cards (usually three or fewer)

draw sheet a sheet that can be removed from the bed while the bed is occupied

draw·string (drô'striŋ') *n.* a string that tightens or closes an opening, as of a bag, when drawn

dray (drā) *n.* [< OE. *dræge*, lit., something drawn < *dragan*, to draw] a low, sturdy cart with detachable sides, for carrying heavy loads —*vt.* to carry or haul on a dray —*vi.* to drive a dray

dray·age (-ij) *n.* **1.** the hauling of a load by dray **2.** the charge made for this

dray·man (-mən) *n.*, *pl.* **-men** the driver of a dray

dread (dred) *vt.* [OE. *drædan*] to anticipate with great fear, misgiving, or distaste —*n.* **1.** intense fear, esp. of something which may happen **2.** fear mixed with awe **3.** something dreaded —*adj.* **1.** dreaded or dreadful **2.** inspiring awe

dread·ful (-fəl) *adj.* **1.** inspiring dread; terrible or awesome **2.** [Colloq.] very bad, offensive, disagreeable, etc. —**dread'ful·ness** *n.*

dread·ful·ly (-fəl ē) *adv.* **1.** in a dreadful manner **2.** [Colloq.] very; extremely [*dreadfully* tired]

dread·nought (-nôt') *n.* a large, heavily armoured battleship with big guns

dream (drēm) *n.* [form < OE. *dream*, joy, music; sense < ON. *draumr*, a dream] **1.** a sequence of sensations, images, thoughts, etc. passing through a sleeping person's mind **2.** a fanciful vision of the conscious mind; daydream; reverie **3.** the state in which such a daydream occurs **4.** a fond hope or aspiration **5.** anything so lovely, transitory, etc. as to seem dreamlike —*vi.* **dreamed** (drēmd, dremt) or **dreamt** (dremt), **dream'ing 1.** to have dreams **2.** to have daydreams **3.** to think (*of*) as at all possible, fit, etc. —*vt.* **1.** *a)* to have (a dream or dreams) *b)* to have a dream of **2.** to spend in dreaming (with *away* or *out*) **3.** to imagine as possible —*adj.* ideal [her *dream* house] —**dream up** [Colloq.] to conceive of or devise —**like a dream** [Colloq.] effortlessly; easily —**dream'er** *n.* —**dream'ful** *adj.* —**dream'less** *adj.* —**dream'like** *adj.*

dream·boat (-bōt') *n.* [Slang] a person or thing that seems ideal to one or attracts one strongly

dream·y (drē'mē) *adj.* **dream'i·er, dream'i·est 1.** filled with

dreams **2.** visionary; impractical **3.** like something in a dream; misty, vague, etc. **4.** lulling; soothing [dreamy music] **5.** [Slang] delightful —**dream'i·ly** *adv.* —**dream'i·ness** *n.*

drear (drir) *adj.* [Poet.] dreary; melancholy

drear·y (-ē) *adj.* **drear'i·er, drear'i·est** [< OE. *dreorig*, sad, orig., bloody, gory] gloomy; cheerless; depressing; dismal; dull —**drear'i·ly** *adv.* —**drear'i·ness** *n.*

dredge¹ (drej) *n.* [prob. < MDu. *dregge*] **1.** a net attached to a frame, dragged along the bottom of a river, bay, etc. to gather shellfish, etc. **2.** an apparatus for scooping or sucking up mud, sand, etc., as in deepening or clearing channels, harbours, etc. **3.** a barge or other boat with a dredge on it —*vt.* **dredged, dredg'ing 1.** to gather (*up*) with or as with a dredge **2.** to enlarge or clean out (a river channel, harbour, etc.) with a dredge —*vi.* **1.** to use a dredge **2.** to search as with a dredge —**dredg'er** *n.*

dredge² (drej) *vt.* **dredged, dredg'ing** [< ME. *dragge*, sweetmeat, ult. < Gr. *tragēma*, dessert] **1.** to coat (food) with flour etc., as by sprinkling **2.** to sprinkle (flour, etc.) —**dredg'er** *n.*

dree (drē) *vt.* **dreed, dree'ing** [ME. < OE. *dreogan*, to suffer] [Scot. or Archaic] to endure; suffer —*adj.* [Scot. or Archaic] dreary; tedious

dregs (dregz) *n.pl.* [< ON. *dregg*] **1.** the particles that settle at the bottom of a liquid; lees **2.** the most worthless part [dregs of society] —**dreg'gi·ness** *n.* —**dreg'gy** *adj.* **-gi·er, -gi·est**

drench (drench) *vt.* [< OE. *drencan*, caus. of *drincan*, to drink] **1.** to make (a horse, cow, etc.) swallow a medicinal liquid **2.** to make wet all over; soak or saturate —*n.* **1.** a large liquid dose, esp. for a sick animal **2.** a drenching; soaking

Dres·den (drez'dən) *n.* [after *Dresden*, city in East Germany, where it is made] fine, elaborately decorated porcelain —*adj.* designating or of such porcelain

dress (dres) *vt.* **dressed, dress'ing** [< OFr. *drecier*, to arrange < L. *directus*: see DIRECT] **1.** to put clothes on; clothe **2.** to provide with clothing **3.** to decorate; trim; adorn **4.** to arrange a display in [to *dress* a shop window] **5.** to arrange or do up (the hair) **6.** to arrange (troops, etc.) in straight lines **7.** to apply medicines and bandages to (a wound, etc.) **8.** to treat in preparing for use, grooming, etc.; esp., *a)* to clean and draw (a fowl, etc.) *b)* to prepare for cooking, eating (crab, fish, etc.) *c)* to cultivate or fertilize (fields or plants) *d)* to smooth or finish (leather, stone, etc.) —*vi.* **1.** to put on or wear clothes **2.** to dress in formal clothes **3.** to get into a straight line —*n.* **1.** clothes; clothing; apparel **2.** a woman's one-piece garment with a skirt **3.** formal clothes **4.** external covering or appearance —*adj.* **1.** of or for dresses [dress material] **2.** worn on formal occasions [a *dress* suit] **3.** requiring formal clothes [a *dress* occasion] —**dress down** to scold severely; reprimand —**dress up 1.** to dress in formal clothes, or in clothes more elegant, showy, etc. than usual **2.** to improve the appearance or impression of [to *dress up* the facts]

dres·sage (drə säzh') *n.* [Fr., training] exhibition horsemanship in which the horse is controlled by very slight movements of the rider

dress circle a section of seats in a theatre or concert hall, usually the first gallery, where formal dress was orig. customary

dress·er¹ (dres'ər) *n.* **1.** a person who dresses people, as actors in their costumes, or things, as shop windows, leather, wounds, etc. **2.** one who dresses elegantly or in a certain way [a fashionable *dresser*] **3.** a person who assists a surgeon during operations

dress·er² (dres'ər) *n.* [< OFr. *dreceur*] **1.** formerly, a table on which food was prepared for serving **2.** a kitchen cupboard with shelves above **3.** [U.S.] a chest of drawers or dressing table

dress·ing (-iŋ) *n.* **1.** the act of one that dresses **2.** that which is used to dress something (as manure applied to soil, bandages applied to a wound, etc.) **3.** a sauce for salads, etc. **4.** a stuffing, as of bread and seasoning, for poultry, etc.

dress·ing-down (-doun') *n.* a sound scolding

dressing gown a loose robe for wear when one is undressed or lounging

dressing room a room for getting dressed in, esp. backstage in a theatre

dressing station a military first aid station near a combat area

dressing table a low table or chest of drawers with a mirror, for use while putting on cosmetics, grooming the hair, etc.

dress·mak·er (dres'māk'ər) *n.* one who makes women's dresses, suits, etc. to order —**dress'mak'ing** *n.*

dress parade a military parade in dress uniform

dress rehearsal a final rehearsal, as of a play, performed exactly as it is to take place

dress suit a man's formal suit for evening wear

dress·y (-ē) *adj.* **dress′i·er, dress′i·est** 1. showy in dress or appearance 2. stylish, elegant, etc. —**dress′i·ly** *adv.* —**dress′i·ness** *n.*

drew (drōō) *pt.* of DRAW

drey (drā) *n.* [< ?] a squirrel's nest

drib (drib) *vi., vt.* **dribbed, drib′bing** [< DRIP] [Obs.] to fall, or let fall, in driblets —**dribs and drabs** small amounts

drib·ble (-'l) *vi., vt.* **-bled, -bling** [freq. of DRIB] 1. to flow, or let flow, in drops or driblets; trickle 2. to come forth or let out a little at a time 3. to slaver; drool 4. in certain games, to move (the ball) along by rapid, repeated bounces, short kicks, or light taps —*n.* 1. a small drop, or a flowing in small drops 2. a very small amount 3. the act of dribbling a ball —**drib′bler** *n.* —**drib′bly** *adj.*

drib·let (-lit) *n.* [dim. of prec.] a small amount

dried (drīd) *pt. & pp.* of DRY

dri·er (drī′ər) *n.* 1. a substance added to paint, varnish, etc. to make it dry fast 2. *same as* DRYER —*adj. compar.* of DRY

dri·est (-ist) *adj. superl.* of DRY

drift (drift) *n.* [< OE. *drifan*, to drive] 1. a being driven or carried along, as by a current of air or water or by circumstances 2. the course on which something is directed 3. the deviation of a ship or aircraft from its course, caused by side currents or winds 4. *a*) a slow ocean current *b*) a gradual shifting *c*) a random course, variation, etc. 5. a tendency or trend 6. general meaning; tenor 7. *a*) something driven, as rain or snow before the wind *b*) a heap of snow, sand, etc. piled up by the wind, or floating matter washed ashore 8. a controlled four-wheel skid used for cornering at high speed 9. [S.Afr.] a ford 10. *Geol.* gravel, boulders, etc. moved and deposited by a glacier or water 11. *Mining* a horizontal passageway, as along the path of a vein —*vi.* 1. to be carried along as by a current 2. to go along aimlessly 3. to wander about from place to place, etc. 4. to pile up in heaps by force of wind or water 5. to move gradually away from a set position —*vt.* 1. to cause to drift 2. to cover with drifts

drift·age (-ij) *n.* 1. a drifting 2. deviation caused by drifting 3. that which has drifted

drift·er (-ər) *n.* 1. a thing or person that drifts 2. a small fishing vessel with a net that drifts with the tide

drift·wood (-wood′) *n.* wood drifting in the water, or that has been washed ashore

drill[1] (dril) *n.* [Du. *dril* < *drillen*, to bore] 1. a tool or apparatus for boring holes in wood, metal, etc. 2. a snail that bores into the shells of oysters and kills them 3. military or physical training, esp. of a group, as in marching, the manual of arms, or gymnastic exercises 4. the process of training or teaching by the repetition of an exercise 5. a single exercise in drilling 6. [Colloq.] the correct procedure for performing a task —*vt.* 1. to bore (a hole) in (something) with or as with a drill 2. to train in military or physical exercises 3. to teach by having do repeated exercises 4. to instil (ideas, etc. *into*) by repetition 5. [Slang] to penetrate with bullets —*vi.* 1. to bore a hole or holes 2. to engage in military, physical, or mental exercises —**drill′er** *n.*

DRILLS
(A, bow; B, hand; C, rotary oil)

drill[2] (dril) *n.* [< ? prec.] 1. a furrow in which seeds are planted 2. a row of planted seeds 3. a machine for making holes or furrows, dropping seeds into them, and covering them —*vt.* 1. to sow (seeds) in rows 2. to plant (a field) in drills

drill[3] (dril) *n.* [< earlier *drilling*, ult. < L. < *tri-*, TRI- + *licium*, a thread] a coarse linen or cotton twill, used for work clothes, linings, etc.

drill[4] (dril) *n.* [< ? native name] a bright-cheeked monkey native to W Africa

drill·mas·ter (-mäs′tər) *n.* 1. an instructor in military drill: also **drill sergeant** 2. one who teaches by drilling

drill press a machine tool for drilling holes

dri·ly (drī′lē) *adv. same as* DRYLY

drink (driŋk) *vt.* **drank, drunk, drink′ing** [OE. *drincan*] 1. to swallow (liquid) 2. to absorb (liquid or moisture) 3. to swallow the contents of 4. to join in (a toast) 5. to bring (oneself) into a specified condition by drinking 6. to use (*up*) or spend by drinking alcohol (often with *away*) —*vi.* 1. to swallow liquid 2. to absorb anything as if in drinking 3. to drink beer, wine, spirits to excess —*n.* 1. any liquid for drinking 2. alcoholic liquor 3. habitual or excessive use of alcohol —**drink in** to take in eagerly with the senses or with the mind —**drink to** to drink a toast to —**the drink**

[Colloq.] a body of water, esp. the sea —**drink′a·ble** *adj.* —**drink′er** *n.*

drinking fountain a device for providing a jet or flow of drinking water, esp. in a public place

drinking-up time the time allowed in a public house for finishing drinks bought just before closing time

drip (drip) *vi.* **dripped** or **dript, drip′ping** [OE. *dryppan*] 1. to fall in drops 2. to let drops of liquid fall —*vt.* to let fall in drops —*n.* 1. a falling in drops 2. liquid falling in drops, or the sound made by this 3. a projecting part of a sill, etc. that sheds rain water 4. [Slang] a person regarded as dull, insipid, etc.

drip-dry (-drī′) *adj.* designating or of fabrics or garments that dry quickly when hung soaking wet and require little or no ironing —*vi.* **-dried′, -dry′ing** to launder as a drip-dry fabric does

drip-feed (-fēd′) *vt.* to feed (something or someone) a liquid drop by drop, esp. intravenously —*n.* an apparatus for feeding in such a manner: also **drip**

drip·ping (drip′iŋ) *n.* the fat and juices that drip from roasting meat —*adv.* so as to drip; soaking

drip·py (-ē) *adj.* **-pi·er, -pi·est** 1. characterized by dripping water, rain, etc. 2. [Slang] excessively sentimental, stupid, etc.

drive (drīv) *vt.* **drove, driv′en, driv′ing** [OE. *drifan*] 1. to force to go; push forward 2. to force into or from a state or act [he *drove* her mad] 3. to force to work, usually to excess 4. *a*) to force as by a blow *b*) to hit or cast (a ball) hard and swiftly 5. to make penetrate 6. to produce by penetrating [to *drive* a hole through metal] 7. to control the movement of (a vehicle) 8. to transport in a vehicle 9. to cause to function 10. to push (a bargain, etc.) through 11. to chase (game) from cover —*vi.* 1. to advance violently; dash 2. to work or try hard 3. to drive a blow, ball, etc. 4. to be carried along; operate: said of a motor vehicle 5. to be conveyed in a vehicle 6. to operate a motor vehicle —*n.* 1. a driving 2. a journey in a vehicle 3. *a*) a road for motor vehicles *b*) a driveway 4. [U.S.] *a*) a rounding up of animals as for branding *b*) the animals rounded up 5. *a*) a hard, swift blow, thrust, etc. 6. an organized movement to achieve some purpose; campaign 7. aggressive vigour; energy; push 8. that which is urgent, as a basic biological impulse 9. *a*) the propelling mechanism of a motor vehicle, machine, etc. *b*) that arrangement in an automatic transmission of a motor vehicle allowing forward speeds 10. a systematic search for and chasing of game towards waiting guns —**drive at** 1. to aim at 2. to mean; intend —**let drive** to hit or aim

drive-in (-in′) *adj.* designating or of a restaurant, cinema, etc. that renders its services to persons who drive up and remain seated in their cars —*n.* such a restaurant, cinema, etc.

driv·el (driv′'l) *vi.* **-elled, -el·ling** [< OE. *dreflian*] 1. to let saliva flow from one's mouth; slobber 2. to speak in a silly or stupid manner —*vt.* to say in a silly, stupid, or nonsensical manner —*n.* silly, stupid talk; childish nonsense —**driv′el·ler** *n.*

driv·en (driv′'n) *pp.* of DRIVE —*adj.* moved along and piled up by the wind [*driven* snow]

driv·er (drī′vər) *n.* 1. a person who drives; specif., *a*) one who drives a motor car, etc. *b*) one who herds cattle *c*) one who makes his subordinates work hard 2. a thing that drives; specif., *a*) a mallet, hammer, etc. *b*) a wooden-headed golf club used in hitting the ball from the tee: also called **number 1 wood** *c*) any machine part that communicates motion —**the driver's seat** the position of control or dominance

drive·way (drīv′wā′) *n.* a path for cars, leading from a street to a garage, house, etc.

driving licence an official document authorizing a person to drive a motor vehicle

driz·zle (driz′'l) *vi., vt.* **-zled, -zling** [< OE. *drēosan*, to fall] to rain or let fall in fine, mistlike drops —*n.* a fine, mistlike rain —**driz′zly** *adj.*

drogue (drōg) *n.* [prob. < Scot. *drug*, DRAG] 1. *same as* SEA ANCHOR 2. a funnel-shaped device towed behind an aircraft for its drag effect (also **drogue parachute**), or as a target, etc.

droll (drōl) *adj.* [< Fr. < MDu. *drol*, short, stout fellow] amusing in an odd or wry way —**droll′ness** *n.* —**drol′ly** *adv.*

droll·er·y (-ər ē) *n., pl.* **-er·ies** 1. a droll act, remark, picture, story, etc. 2. the act of joking 3. quaint or wry humour

-drome (drōm) [< Gr. *dromos*, a running] a suffix meaning running, racecourse [*hippodrome*]

drom·e·dar·y (drom′ə dər ē) *n., pl.* **-dar·ies** [< OFr. < LL. < L. < Gr. < *dramein*, to run] the one-humped camel, found from N Africa to India and trained for fast riding

drone[1] (drōn) *n.* [< OE. *dran*] 1. a male honeybee, having only a reproductive function and no sting 2. an idle parasite or loafer 3. a pilotless aircraft directed by remote control —*vi.* **droned, dron′ing** to live in idleness; loaf

drone² (drōn) *vi.* **droned, dron'ing** [LME. *dronen* < prec.] 1. to make a continuous humming sound 2. to talk on and on in a monotonous way —*vt.* to utter in a dull, monotonous tone —*n.* 1. a continuous humming sound 2. any of the pipes of fixed tone in a bagpipe

dron·go¹ (droŋ'gō) *n., pl.* **-gos** [< Malagasy] any of various black songbirds found in Africa, India, and Australia

dron·go² (droŋ'gō) *n., pl.* **-gos** [< name of racehorse] [Aust. Slang] a slow-witted or foolish person

drool (drōōl) *vi.* [< DRIVEL] 1. to let saliva flow from one's mouth; drivel 2. to flow from the mouth, as saliva 3. [Slang] to speak in a silly or stupid way 4. [Slang] to be excessively enthusiastic, etc. —*vt.* to let drivel from the mouth —*n.* saliva running from the mouth

droop (drōōp) *vi.* [< ON. *drūpa*] 1. to sink, hang, or bend down 2. to lose vitality or strength 3. to become dejected —*vt.* to let sink or hang down —*n.* a drooping

droop·y (-ē) *adj.* **droop'i·er, droop'i·est** 1. tending to droop 2. [Colloq.] tired or dejected —**droop'i·ly** *adv.* —**droop'i·ness** *n.*

drop (drop) *n.* [OE. *dropa*] 1. a small quantity of liquid that is somewhat spherical, as when falling 2. a very small quantity of liquid 3. [*pl.*] liquid medicine taken in drops 4. a very small quantity of anything 5. a thing like a drop in shape, size, etc. 6. a dropping; sudden fall, descent, slump, etc. 7. *same as* AIRDROP 8. anything that drops or is used for dropping, as a drop curtain, a trapdoor, etc. 9. the distance between a higher and lower level —*vi.* **dropped, drop'ping** 1. to fall in drops 2. to fall; come down 3. to fall exhausted, wounded, or dead 4. to pass into a specified state [to *drop* off to sleep] 5. to come to an end [let the matter *drop*] 6. to become lower or less, as prices, etc. 7. to move down with a current of water or air —*vt.* 1. to let or make fall; release hold of 2. to give birth to: said of animals 3. to utter (a hint, etc.) casually 4. to send (a letter) 5. to cause to fall, as by wounding, killing, etc. 6. *a)* to stop or have done with *b)* to dismiss 7. to lower or lessen 8. to make (the voice) less loud 9. *same as* AIRDROP 10. to omit (a letter or sound) in a word 11. [Colloq.] to leave (a person or thing) at a specified place 12. [Slang] to lose (money or a game) —**at the drop of a hat** immediately —**drop back** 1. to move back; retreat 2. to be outdistanced: also **drop behind** —**drop in** (or **over, by,** etc.) to pay a casual or unexpected visit —**drop off** 1. to decline; decrease 2. [Colloq.] to fall asleep —**drop out** to stop being a member or participant

drop curtain a theatre curtain that is lowered and raised rather than drawn

drop-forge (-fôrj') *vt.* **-forged', -forg'ing** to pound (heated metal) between dies with a drop hammer or a press —**drop'-forg'er** *n.*

drop forging a product made by drop-forging

drop hammer 1. a machine for pounding metal into shape, with a heavy weight that is raised and then dropped on the metal 2. this weight

drop kick *Rugby* a kick in which the ball is dropped to the ground and kicked just as it rebounds —**drop'-kick'** *vt., vi.* —**drop'-kick'er** *n.*

drop leaf a hinged board attached to the end of a table as an extension of the surface —**drop'-leaf'** *adj.*

drop·let (-lit) *n.* a very small drop

drop-out (-out') *n.* 1. a person who withdraws esp. from university, college, society, etc. 2. *Rugby* a drop kick taken to restart the game, as after a touchdown

drop·per (-ər) *n.* 1. a person or thing that drops 2. a small tube of glass, plastic, etc. with a hollow rubber bulb at one end, used to release a liquid in drops

drop·pings (drop'iŋz) *n.pl.* dung of certain animals, as sheep, rabbits, and birds

drop press *same as* DROP HAMMER

drop scone a scone made by cooking spoonfuls of batter on a hot cooking surface

drop·sy (drop'sē) *n.* [< OFr. < L. < Gr. *hydrōps* < *hydōr,* water] *an earlier term for* OEDEMA —**drop'si·cal** (-si k'l), **drop'sied** *adj.* —**drop'si·cal·ly** *adv.*

drosh·ky (drosh'kē) *n., pl.* **-kies** [Russ. *drozhki*] a low, open, four-wheeled Russian carriage: also **dros'ky** (dros'-) *pl.* **-kies**

dro·soph·i·la (drə sof'ə lə, drō-) *n., pl.* **-lae'** (-lē') [ModL. < Gr. *drosos,* dew + fem. of *philos,* loving] a tiny fly used for laboratory experiments in heredity; fruit fly

dross (dros) *n.* [OE. *dros, dregs*] 1. a scum formed on the surface of molten metal 2. waste matter; rubbish —**dross'i·ness** *n.* —**dross'y** *adj.* **dross'i·er, dross'i·est**

drought (drout) *n.* [OE. *drugoth,* dryness < *drugian,* to dry up] 1. prolonged dry weather; lack of rain 2. a serious deficiency —**drought'y** *adj.* **drought'i·er, drought'i·est**

drouth (drouth) *n. same as* DROUGHT

drove¹ (drōv) *n.* [OE. *draf* < *drifan,* DRIVE] 1. a number of cattle, sheep, etc. driven or moving as a group; flock; herd 2. a moving crowd of people

drove² (drōv) *pt. of* DRIVE

drov·er (drō'vər) *n.* a person who herds droves of animals, esp. to market —**drov'ing** *n.*

drown (droun) *vi.* [prob. < var. of ON. *drukna*] to die by suffocation in water or other liquid —*vt.* 1. to kill by such suffocation 2. *a)* to cover with water; flood *b)* to overwhelm 3. to be so loud as to overcome (another sound): usually with *out* 4. to get rid of [to *drown* one's sorrow in drink]

drowse (drouz) *vi.* **drowsed, drows'ing** [< OE. *drusian,* to become sluggish] to sleep lightly; doze —*vt.* to spend (time) in drowsing —*n.* the act or an instance of drowsing; doze

drow·sy (drou'zē) *adj.* **-si·er, -si·est** 1. *a)* sleepy or half asleep *b)* making sleepy 2. brought on by sleepiness 3. peacefully quiet or inactive —**drow'si·ly** *adv.* —**drow'si·ness** *n.*

drub (drub) *vt.* **drubbed, drub'bing** [< ? Turk. *durb* < Ar. *darb,* a beating] 1. to beat as with a stick; cudgel 2. to defeat soundly in a fight, contest, etc. —*vi.* to drum or tap —*n.* a blow as with a club —**drub'ber** *n.*

drub·bing (drub'iŋ) *n.* a thorough beating or defeat

drudge (druj) *n.* [prob. < OE. *dreogan,* to suffer, undergo] a person who does hard, menial, or tedious work —*vi.* **drudged, drudg'ing** to do such work

drudg·er·y (druj'ər ē) *n., pl.* **-er·ies** work that is hard, menial, or tiresome

drug (drug) *n.* [< OFr. *drogue*] 1. any substance used as or in a medicine 2. a narcotic, hallucinogen, etc., esp. a habit-forming one —*vt.* **drugged, drug'ging** 1. to put a harmful drug in (a drink, etc.) 2. to administer a drug to 3. to stupefy as with a drug —*vi.* to take narcotics, hallucinogens, etc. —**drug on the market** something for which there is a plentiful supply but little demand

drug addict a habitual user of narcotics

drug·get (-it) *n.* [Fr. *drouguet,* dim. of *drogue,* trash] 1. formerly, a woollen or part-woollen material used for clothing 2. a coarse fabric used as a floor covering

drug·gist (-ist) *n.* 1. a dealer in drugs, medical equipment, etc. 2. [Chiefly U.S.] a pharmacist

drug·store (-stôr') *n.* [Chiefly U.S.] a shop where drugs and medical supplies are sold: most drugstores also sell a wide variety of goods

dru·id (drōō'id) *n.* [< Fr. < L. *druides,* pl. < Celt.] [often D-] 1. a member of a Celtic religious order in ancient Britain, Ireland, and France 2. officer of the Welsh Gorsedd, session of bards and druids concerned esp. with the eisteddfod —**dru·id'ic, dru·id'i·cal** *adj.* —**dru'id·ism** *n.*

drum (drum) *n.* [< Du. *trom*] 1. a percussion instrument consisting of a hollow cylinder or hemisphere with a membrane stretched tightly over the end or ends 2. the sound produced by beating a drum, or any sound like this 3. any drumlike cylindrical object; specif., *a)* a metal cylinder around which cable, etc. is wound in a machine *b)* a barrellike metal container for oil, etc. 4. any of various N. American fishes that make a drumming sound 5. *Anat. same as: a)* MIDDLE EAR *b)* EARDRUM —*vi.* **drummed, drum'ming** 1. to beat a drum 2. to beat or tap continually, as with the fingers —*vt.* 1. to beat out (a tune, etc.) as on a drum 2. to beat or tap continually 3. to assemble by beating a drum 4. to instil (ideas, facts, etc. *into*) by continued repetition —**beat the drum for** [Colloq.] to try to arouse enthusiasm for —**drum out of** to expel from in disgrace —**drum up** 1. to summon as by beating a drum 2. to get (business) by soliciting

drum·beat (-bēt') *n.* a sound made by beating a drum

drum·fish (-fish') *n., pl.* **-fish', -fish'es** see FISH *same as* DRUM (*n.* 4)

drum·head (-hed') *n.* the membrane stretched over the open end or ends of a drum

drum·lin (-lin) *n.* [< Ir. *druim,* a ridge + *-lin,* dim. suffix] a long ridge formed by glacial drift

drum major a person who leads or precedes a marching band, often twirling a baton —**drum majorette** *fem.*

drum·mer (-ər) *n.* 1. a drum player 2. an animal that makes a drumming sound 3. [see DRUM. phr. *drum up*] [Colloq.] a travelling salesman

drum·stick (-stik') *n.* 1. a stick for beating a drum 2. the lower half of the leg of a cooked fowl

drunk (druŋk) *pp. & archaic pt. of* DRINK —*adj.* [usually used in the predicate] 1. overcome by alcohol; intoxicated 2. overcome by any powerful emotion —*n.* [Slang] 1. a drunken person 2. a drinking spree

drunk·ard (druŋ'kərd) *n.* a person who often gets drunk; inebriate

drunk·en (-kən) *archaic pp. of* DRINK —*adj.* 1. intoxicated or habitually intoxicated 2. caused by or occurring during intoxication —**drunk'en·ly** *adv.* —**drunk'en·ness** *n.*

drupe (drōop) *n.* [< ModL. *drupa* < L. *drupa* (*oliva*), overripe (olive) < Gr. *dryppa*, olive] any fruit with a soft, fleshy part around an inner stone that contains the seed, as an apricot, cherry, plum, etc. —**dru·pa·ceous** (drōo pā′shəs) *adj.*

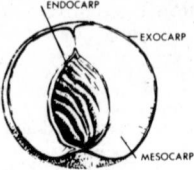

DRUPE (of peach)

drupe·let (-lit) *n.* a small drupe: a single blackberry consists of many drupelets
dry (drī) *adj.* **dri′er, dri′est** [OE. *dryge*] **1.** not under water [*dry land*] **2.** having no moisture; not wet or damp **3.** not shedding tears **4.** lacking rain [a *dry* summer] **5.** a) having lost water or moisture; arid, withered, dehydrated, etc. b) empty of water or other liquid **6.** thirsty **7.** not yielding milk [a *dry* cow] **8.** without butter, jam, etc. [*dry* toast] **9.** solid; not liquid **10.** not sweet [*dry* wine] **11.** having no mucous or watery discharge [a *dry* cough] **12.** prohibiting or opposed to the sale of wine, spirits, etc. [a *dry* area] **13.** plain or sober [*dry* facts] **14.** funny in a quiet but sharp way [*dry* wit] **15.** dull or boring —*vt.* **dried, dry′ing 1.** to make dry **2.** to preserve fruit, etc. by removing the moisture —*vi.* to become dry —**dry out 1.** to make or become thoroughly dry **2.** to withdraw from addiction to alcohol or drugs —**dry up 1.** to make or become thoroughly dry **2.** to make or become unproductive, uncreative, etc. **3.** to dry (plates, etc.) with a tea towel after they have been washed **4.** [Colloq.] to stop talking, esp. in public, as an actor, orator, etc. —**not dry behind the ears** [Colloq.] immature; inexperienced
dry·ad (drī′əd, -ad) *n., pl.* **-ads, -ad·es′** (-ə dēz′) [L. *dryas* (gen. *dryadis*) < Gr. < *drys*, an oak, tree] [*also* **D-**] *Gr. & Rom. Myth.* any nymph living in a tree; wood nymph
dry battery 1. an electric battery made up of several connected dry cells **2.** a dry cell
dry cell a voltaic cell containing an absorbent so that its contents cannot spill
dry-clean (drī′klēn′) *vt.* to clean (garments, etc.) with some solvent other than water, as naphtha, gasoline, etc. —**dry cleaner** —**dry cleaning**
dry-dock (drī dok′) *vt., vi.* to place or go into a dry dock
dry dock a dock from which the water can be emptied, used for building and repairing ships
dry·er (-ər) *n.* **1.** a person or thing that dries; specif., an apparatus for drying by heating or blowing air, esp. an appliance for drying hair **2.** *same as* DRIER
dry-eyed (-īd′) *adj.* shedding no tears
dry farming farming in an almost rainless region without irrigation: done by conserving the soil moisture and planting drought-resistant crops —**dry′-farm′** *vt., vi.* —**dry farmer**
dry fly *Angling* an artificial fly designed to float on top of the water
dry goods cloth, cloth products, thread, etc.
dry ice carbon dioxide solidified and compressed into snowlike cakes, used as a refrigerant
dry·ly (-lē) *adv.* in a dry manner; matter-of-factly
dry measure a system of measuring the volume of dry things, as grain, vegetables, etc., in the system in which 2 pints = 1 quart, 8 quarts = 1 peck, and 4 pecks = 1 bushel: see TABLE OF WEIGHTS AND MEASURES in Supplement
dry·ness (-nis) *n.* the quality or state of being dry
dry point 1. a needle for engraving lines on a copper plate without using acid **2.** a print from such a plate **3.** this way of engraving
dry rot 1. a fungous decay causing seasoned timber to crumble to powder **2.** a similar fungous disease of plants, fruits, etc. —**dry′-rot′** *vi., vt.* **-rot′ted, -rot′ting**
dry run 1. [Mil. Slang] practice in firing without using live ammunition **2.** [Slang] a rehearsal
dry-stone (-stōn′) *adj.* made without mortar: said of walls, etc.
dry wall a wall of rocks or stones with no mortar —**dry′-wall′** *adj.*
D.S., d.s. [It. *dal segno*] (repeat) from this sign
D.S., D.Sc. Doctor of Science
D.S.C., DSC Distinguished Service Cross
D.S.M., DSM Distinguished Service Medal
D.S.O., DSO Distinguished Service Order
D.S.T., DST Daylight Saving Time
D.T.'s, d.t.'s (dē′tēz′) [Colloq.] *same as* DELIRIUM TREMENS
Du. Dutch
du·al (dyōo′əl) *adj.* [L. *dualis* < *duo*, two] **1.** of two **2.** having or composed of two parts or kinds, like or unlike; double; twofold—*n. Linguis.* **1.** *same as* DUAL NUMBER **2.** a word having dual number —**du·al′i·ty** (-al′ə tē) *n.* —**du′al·ly** *adv.*
dual carriageway a road with a central reservation separating traffic travelling in opposite directions
du·al·ism (-iz′m) *n.* **1.** the state of being dual; duality **2.**

any theory or doctrine based on a twofold distinction, as the theory that the world is ultimately composed of mind and matter —**du′al·ist** *n.* —**du′al·is′tic** *adj.* —**du′al·is′ti·cal·ly** *adv.*
du·al·ize (-īz′) *vt.* **-ized′, -iz′ing** to make, or consider as, dual
dual number in some languages, a grammatical number indicating *two, a pair*: distinguished from *singular* and *plural*
dub[1] (dub) *vt.* **dubbed, dub′bing** [< OE. *dubbian*, to strike] **1.** to confer knighthood on by tapping on the shoulder with a sword **2.** to confer a title, name, or nickname upon **3.** to make smooth, as by hammering, scraping, or rubbing **4.** to dress (leather) by rubbing —**dub′ber** *n.*
dub[2] (dub) *vt.* **dubbed, dub′bing** [contr. < DOUBLE] **1.** to insert (dialogue, music, etc.) in a film or recording (often with *in*) **2.** to provide a film with a new soundtrack in a different language —*n.* dialogue, music, etc. so inserted —**dub′ber** *n.*
dub[3] (dub) *vi.* [< ?] [Colloq.] to pay (up); fork out
dub·bin (dub′'n) *n.* [< *dubbing*: see DUB[1] v. 4] a greasy preparation for softening and waterproofing leather: also **dub′bing**
du·bi·e·ty (dyōo bī′ə tē) *n.* [LL. *dubietas*] **1.** a being dubious **2.** *pl.* **-ties** a doubtful thing
du·bi·ous (dyōo′bē əs) *adj.* [< L. < *dubius*, uncertain] **1.** causing doubt; ambiguous **2.** feeling doubt; sceptical **3.** uncertain [*dubious* outcome] **4.** questionable [a *dubious* character] —**du′bi·ous·ly** *adv.* —**du′bi·ous·ness** *n.*
Dub·lin Bay prawn (dub′lən) a lobster-like sea crustacean whose flesh is eaten as scampi
du·cal (dyōo′k'l) *adj.* [see DUKE] of a duke or dukedom —**du′cal·ly** *adv.*
duc·at (duk′ət) *n.* [OFr. < It. *ducato*, coin with image of a duke < LL. *ducatus*: see DUCHY] **1.** any of several former European coins of gold or silver **2.** [pl.] money
du·ce (dōo′che) *n.* [It. < L. *dux*, leader] chief; leader: title (*Il Duce*) assumed by Benito Mussolini
duch·ess (duch′is) *n.* **1.** the wife or widow of a duke **2.** a woman who, like a duke, rules a duchy
duch·y (-ē) *n., pl.* **duch′ies** [< OFr. < LL. *ducatus*, military command < L. *dux*: see DUKE] the territory ruled by a duke or duchess; dukedom
duck[1] (duk) *n.* [< OE. *duce*, lit., diver < base of ff.] **1.** *pl.* **ducks, duck:** see PLURAL, II, D, 1 a swimming bird with a flat bill, short neck and legs, and webbed feet **2.** a female duck: opposed to DRAKE **3.** the flesh of a duck as food **4.** [Colloq.] dear or darling: used as a form of address **5.** *Cricket* a score of zero by a batsman —**like a (dying) duck in a thunderstorm** looking forlorn, helpless, or bedraggled —**like water off a duck's back** with no effect or reaction
duck[2] (duk) *vt., vi.* [ME. *douken* < hyp. OE. *ducan*, to dive] **1.** to plunge or dip under water for a moment **2.** to lower or move (the head, body, etc.) suddenly, as in avoiding a blow or in hiding **3.** [Colloq.] to avoid (a task, person, etc.) **4.** [Slang] to run (*in* or *out*) —*n.* a ducking
duck[3] (duk) *n.* [Du. *doek*] **1.** a cotton or linen cloth like canvas but finer and lighter in weight **2.** [pl.] [Colloq.] trousers made of this cloth
duck[4] (duk) *n.* [altered (after DUCK[1]) < DUKW, code name] [Slang] an amphibious motor vehicle
duck-bill (duk′bil′) *n.* *same as* PLATYPUS
ducking stool a chair at the end of a plank in which a culprit was tied and then ducked into water: a form of punishment formerly used in Europe and New England, U.S.
duck·ling (-liŋ) *n.* a young duck
ducks and drakes the game of throwing a small, flat stone so that it skims the surface of the water —**play ducks and drakes with** to deal with recklessly or squander
duck soup [U.S. Slang] something that is easy to do
duck·weed (-wēd′) *n.* a minute flowering plant that floats on ponds and sluggish streams
duck·y (-ē) *n.* [Colloq.] dear; darling: a term of endearment —*adj.* [Colloq.] **duck′i·er, duck′i·est** pleasing, delightful, etc.
duct (dukt) *n.* [< ML. < L. *ductus*, pp. of *ducere*, to lead] **1.** a tube or channel through which a fluid moves **2.** a tube in the body for the passage of excretions or secretions [a bile *duct*] **3.** a tubule in plant tissues, conducting resin, etc. **4.** a pipe or conduit enclosing wires **5.** a pipe through which air can flow, as in an air conditioning system —*vt.* to transport or convey through a duct: used chiefly in pp. —**duct′less** *adj.*
duc·tile (duk′til) *adj.* [see prec.] **1.** that can be stretched, drawn, or hammered thin without breaking: said of metals **2.** easily moulded; pliant **3.** easily led; tractable —**duc·til′i·ty** (-til′ə tē) *n.*
ductless gland an endocrine gland
dud (dud) *n.* [< ?] [Colloq.] **1.** a bomb or shell that fails to explode **2.** a person or thing that fails —*adj.* [Colloq.] worthless
dude (dyōod, dōod) *n.* [< ?] [Chiefly U.S.] **1.** a dandy; fop **2.** [Slang] a city fellow or tourist, esp. in the W U.S. —**dud′ish** *adj.* —**dud′ish·ly** *adv.*

dude ranch [Chiefly U.S.] a ranch or farm operated as a holiday resort, with horseback riding, etc.

dudg·eon (duj′ən) *n.* [prob. < Anglo-Fr. *en digeon,* at the dagger hilt] anger or resentment: now chiefly in **in high dudgeon,** very angry, offended, or resentful

duds (dudz) *n.pl.* [prob. < ON. < *dutha,* to wrap up, swathe] [Colloq.] **1.** clothes, esp. old clothes **2.** belongings

due (dyoo) *adj.* [< OFr. *deu,* pp. of *devoir,* to owe < L. *debere:* see DEBT] **1.** owed or owing as a debt, right, etc.; payable **2.** suitable; fitting; proper [*due* respect] **3.** enough; adequate [*due care*] **4.** expected or scheduled to arrive or be ready [the train is *due* now] —*adv.* exactly; directly [*due* west] —*n.* anything due; specif., *a)* deserved recognition *b)* [*pl.*] fees, tolls, or other charges [membership *dues*] —**become** (or **fall**) **due** to become payable as previously arranged —**due to 1.** caused by; resulting from [deaths *due to* cancer] **2.** [Colloq.] because of [*due to* his help, we won]

du·el (dyoo′əl) *n.* [< ML. < OL. *duellum* (L. *bellum*), war] **1.** a formal, prearranged fight between two persons armed with deadly weapons **2.** any contest suggesting such a fight [a verbal *duel*] —*vi., vt.* **-elled, -el·ling** to fight a duel (with) —**du′el·list, du′el·ler** *n.*

du·en·na (dyoo en′ə) *n.* [Sp. *dueña* < L. *domina,* mistress] **1.** an elderly woman who has charge of the young unmarried women of a Spanish or Portuguese family **2.** a chaperon or governess

due process (of law) the course of legal proceedings established to protect individual rights

du·et (dyoo et′) *n.* [< It. < L. *duo,* two] *Music* **1.** a composition for two voices or instruments **2.** the two performers of such a composition

duff[1] (duf) *n.* [dial. var. of DOUGH] a thick flour pudding boiled in a cloth bag

duff[2] (duf) *vt.* [? < DUFFER] **1.** to make old things look new; fake **2.** [Aust.] to steal (cattle) by altering the brand **3.** *Golf* to bungle a shot, esp. a drive **4.** [Colloq.] to beat (up) —*adj.* bad or useless [a *duff* car]

duf·fel, duf·fle (duf′'l) *n.* [Du. < *Duffel,* town in N Belgium] **1.** a coarse woollen cloth **2.** *same as* DUFFEL BAG

duffel (or **duffle**) **bag** a large, cylindrical cloth bag for carrying clothing and personal belongings

duffel (or **duffle**) **coat** a knee-length coat made of duffel or other wool cloth, usually with a hood

duf·fer (duf′ər) *n.* [< thieves' slang *duff,* to fake] [Slang] an incompetent or stupid person

dug[1] (dug) *pt. & pp. of* DIG

dug[2] (dug) *n.* [< same base as Dan. *dægge,* to suckle] a nipple, teat, or udder

du·gong (doo′gon) *n.* [Malay *dūyung*] a large, whalelike mammal of tropical seas

dug·out (dug′out′) *n.* **1.** a boat or canoe hollowed out of a log **2.** a shelter, as in warfare, dug in the ground or in a hillside

dui·ker (dīk′ər) *n., pl.* **-kers, -ker:** see PLURAL, II, D, 1 [Du. a diver] **1.** any of several small, African antelopes **2.** any of various S African cormorants

duke (dyook) *n.* [< OFr. < L. *dux,* leader < *ducere,* to lead] **1.** the ruler of an independent duchy **2.** a nobleman of the highest hereditary rank below that of a prince —**duke′-dom** *n.*

dukes (dyooks) *n.pl.* [< *duke,* short for *Duke of York,* used in 19th-c. rhyming slang for *fork,* fingers] [Slang] the fists or hands

dul·cet (dul′sit) *adj.* [< OFr. < L. *dulcis,* sweet] soothing or pleasant to hear; melodious

dul·ci·mer (dul′sə mər) *n.* [< OFr. < Sp. < L. < *dulce,* sweet + *melos* < ? Gr. *melos,* a song] **1.** a musical instrument with metal strings, which are struck with two small hammers by the player **2.** a violin-shaped stringed instrument of the southern Appalachians, U.S., plucked with a plectrum or a goose quill: also **dul′ci·more** ('-môr', -mər)

DULCIMER

dull (dul) *adj.* [OE. *dol,* stupid] **1.** mentally slow; stupid **2.** lacking sensitivity; unfeeling **3.** physically slow; sluggish **4.** lacking spirit; listless **5.** not active; slack **6.** causing boredom; tedious **7.** not sharp; blunt **8.** not felt keenly [a *dull* headache] **9.** not vivid **10.** not glossy **11.** not distinct [a *dull* thud] **12.** gloomy; cloudy —*vt., vi.* to make or become dull —**dull′-ish** *adj.* —**dull′ness, dul′ness** *n.* —**dul′ly** *adv.*

dull·ard (-ərd) *n.* a stupid person

dulse (duls) *n.* [Ir. & Gael. *duileasq*] any of several edible marine algae with large, red fronds

du·ly (dyoo′lē) *adv.* in due manner; specif., *a)* as due; rightfully *b)* when due; at the right time *c)* as required

Du·ma (doo′mä) *n.* [Russ. < Gmc., as in OE. *dom,* judgment] the parliament of czarist Russia (1905-17)

dumb (dum) *adj.* [OE.] **1.** lacking the power of speech; mute **2.** unwilling to talk; silent **3.** not accompanied by speech **4.** temporarily speechless, as from fear **5.** [G. *dumm*] [Colloq.] stupid; moronic —**dumb′ly** *adv.* —**dumb′ness** *n.*

dumb·bell (dum′bel′) *n.* **1.** a device usually used in pairs for muscular exercise: each pair has round weights joined by a short bar **2.** [Chiefly U.S. Slang] a dumb or stupid person

dumb blonde a blonde woman considered to be rather stupid

dumb cluck [Slang] a stupid person; fool

dumb·found, dum·found (dum′found′) *vt.* [DUMB + (CON)FOUND] to make speechless esp. by shocking

dumb show 1. formerly, a part of a play done in pantomime **2.** gestures without speech

dumb·wait·er (dum′wāt′ər) *n.* **1.** a small, portable stand for serving food **2.** [Chiefly U.S.] a small lift for sending food, rubbish, etc. from one floor to another

dum·dum (bullet) (dum′dum′) [< *Dumdum,* arsenal near Calcutta, India] a soft-nosed bullet that expands when it hits, inflicting a large wound

dum·my (dum′ē) *n., pl.* **-mies 1.** a person unable to talk **2.** a figure made in human form, as for displaying clothing, target practice, etc. **3.** an imitation or sham **4.** a person secretly acting for another while apparently representing his own interests **5.** a baby's rubber comforter or teat **6.** [Slang] a stupid person **7.** *Bridge,* etc. *a)* the declarer's partner, whose hand is exposed on the board and played by the declarer *b)* such a hand **8.** the skeleton copy, as of a book, containing blank pages and acting as a specimen of the finished product —*adj.* **1.** imitation; sham **2.** secretly acting as a front for another **3.** *Bridge,* etc. played with a dummy

dummy run a practice, rehearsal, or trial of some event

dump (dump) *vt.* [prob. < ON.] **1.** to empty out or unload as in a heap or mass **2.** *a)* to throw away (rubbish, etc.) esp. in or at a rubbish dump *b)* to get rid of abruptly or roughly **3.** to sell (a commodity) in a large quantity at a low price, esp. abroad —*vi.* **1.** to fall in a heap or mass **2.** to unload rubbish **3.** to dump commodities —*n.* **1.** a rubbish pile or a place for dumping **2.** *Mil.* a temporary storage centre, as for ammunition **3.** [Slang] a place that is unpleasant, ugly, etc. —**dump′er** *n.*

dump·ling (-liŋ) *n.* [< *dump,* lump + -LING[1]] **1.** a small piece of dough, steamed or boiled and served with meat or soup **2.** a crust of dough filled with fruit and steamed or baked **3.** [Colloq.] a short, plump person

dumps (dumps) *n.pl.* a state of depression, esp. in **down in the dumps**

dump truck [Chiefly U.S.] a tipper lorry

dump·y[1] (dum′pē) *adj.* **dump′i·er, dump′i·est** short and stout; squat —**dump′i·ly** *adv.* —**dump′i·ness** *n.*

dump·y[2] (dum′pē) *adj.* **dump′i·er, dump′i·est** [see DUMPS] melancholy; depressed

dun[1] (dun) *adj.* [OE.] dull greyish-brown —*n.* **1.** a dull greyish brown **2.** a dun horse

dun[2] (dun) *vt., vi.* **dunned, dun′ning** [? dial. var. of DIN] to ask (a debtor) repeatedly for payment —*n.* an insistent demand for payment of a debt

dunce (duns) *n.* [< *Dunsmen* or *Dunces,* followers of *Dun Scotus* (1265?-1308), Scot. philosopher] **1.** a dull, ignorant person **2.** a person slow at learning

dunce cap a cone-shaped hat which children slow at learning were formerly forced to wear in school

Dun·dee cake (dun dē′) a rich fruit cake decorated with almonds

dun·der·head (dun′dər hed′) *n.* [? < Du. *donder,* thunder] a stupid person; dunce

dune (dyoon) *n.* [Fr. < ODu. *duna*] a rounded hill or ridge of sand heaped up by the wind

dune buggy [from orig. use on sand dunes] a small, light motor car made from a standard, compact chassis and a prefabricated body

dung (duŋ) *n.* [OE.] **1.** animal excrement; manure **2.** filth —*vt.* to spread with dung, as in fertilizing —**dung′y** *adj.* —**dung′i·er, dung′i·est**

dun·ga·ree (duŋ′gə rē′) *n.* [Hindi *dungrī*] **1.** a coarse cotton cloth; specif., Indian calico or blue denim **2.** [*pl.*] work trousers or overalls of this cloth

dun·geon (dun′jən) *n.* [< OFr. *donjon*] **1.** *same as* DONJON **2.** a dark, underground cell or prison

dung·hill (duŋ′hil′) *n.* **1.** a heap of dung **2.** anything vile or filthy

dunk (duŋk) *vt.* [G. *tunken,* to dip < OHG. *dunchôn*] **1.** to dip (bread, cake, etc.) into coffee or other liquid before eating it **2.** to immerse in liquid for a short time

dun·lin (dun′lin) *n., pl.* **-lins, -lin:** see PLURAL, II, D, 1 [< DUN[1] + -LING[1]] a small sandpiper with a reddish back and a black patch on its belly

dun·nage (dun′ij) *n.* [< ML. *dennagium* < ?] **1.** a loose packing of any bulky material put round cargo for protection **2.** personal baggage or belongings

dun·no (du nō', də-) *vi., vt.* [Slang] *clipped form of* do not know

dun·nock (dun'ək) *n.* *same as* HEDGE SPARROW

dun·ny (dun'ē) *n.* [? < DUNG] 1. [Aust. & Dial.] a toilet 2. [Scot.] cellar or basement

du·o (dyōō'ō) *n., pl.* **du'os, du'i** (-ē) [It.] 1. *same as* DUET (esp. sense 2) 2. a pair; couple

du·o- [< L. *duo*, two] *a combining form meaning* two, double [*duologue*]

du·o·dec·i·mal (dyōō'ə des'ə m'l) *adj.* [< L. < *duo*, two + *decem*, ten + -AL] 1. relating to twelve or twelfths 2. consisting of or counting by twelves —*n.* 1. one twelfth 2. [*pl.*] *Math.* a system of numeration with twelve as its base

du·o·dec·i·mo (-mō') *n., pl.* **-mos** [< L. *in duodecimo*, in twelve] 1. a page size 1/12 of a printer's sheet 2. a book with pages of this size Also called *twelvemo*, and written *12mo* or *12* —*adj.* with pages of this size

du·o·de·num (dyōō'ə dē'nəm; dyōō'ō dē'nəm) *n., pl.* **-de'na** (-nə), **-de'nums** [< ML. < L. *duodeni*, twelve each: its length is about twelve fingers' breadth] the first section of the small intestine, between the stomach and the jejunum —**du'o·de'nal** *adj.*

du·o·logue (dyōō'ə log') *n.* [DUO- + (MONO)LOGUE] a conversation between two people

du·op·o·ly (dyōō op'ə lē) *n.* [DUO- + (MONO)POLY] control of a commodity or service by only two producers or suppliers

dup. duplicate

dupe (dyōōp) *n.* [Fr. < OFr. < L. *upupa*, hoopoe, stupid bird] a person easily tricked or fooled —*vt.* **duped, dup'ing** to deceive or cheat —**dup'a·ble** *adj.* —**dup'er** *n.* —**dup'er·y** *n., pl.* **-er·ies**

du·ple (dyōō'p'l) *adj.* [L. *duplus*: see DOUBLE] 1. double; twofold 2. *Music* having two (or a multiple of two) beats to the measure [*duple time*]

du·plex (dyōō'pleks) *adj.* [L. < *duo*, two + *-plex*, -fold, akin to *plaga*, area] 1. double; twofold 2. having two units operating in the same way or simultaneously —*n.* [U.S.] *same as* DUPLEX HOUSE —**du·plex'i·ty** *n.*

duplex house [U.S.] a semi detached house

du·pli·cate (dyōō'plə kit; *for v.* -kāt') *adj.* [< L. pp. of *duplicare*, to double: see DUPLEX] 1. double 2. having two similar parts 3. corresponding exactly 4. designating a game of bridge, etc. in which the same hands are played again by other players to compare scores —*n.* 1. an exact copy; replica; facsimile 2. a counterpart or double 3. a duplicate game of bridge, etc. —*vt.* **-cat'ed, -cat'ing** 1. to make double or twofold 2. to make an exact copy of 3. to make, do, or cause to happen again —**in duplicate** in two precisely similar forms —**du'pli·ca·ble, du'pli·cat'a·ble** *adj.* —**du'pli·ca'tion** *n.* —**du'pli·ca'tive** *adj.*

duplicating machine a machine for making exact copies of a letter, photograph, drawing, etc.: also **du'pli·ca'tor** *n.*

du·plic·i·ty (dyōō plis'ə tē) *n., pl.* **-ties** [< OFr. < LL. *duplicitas*: see DUPLEX] hypocritical cunning or deception; double-dealing

dur·a·ble (dyoor'ə b'l) *adj.* [OFr. < L. < *durare*, to last, harden < *durus*, hard] 1. lasting in spite of hard wear or frequent use 2. continuing to exist; stable —*n.* [*pl.*] *same as* DURABLE GOODS —**du'ra·bil'i·ty** *n.* —**du'ra·bly** *adv.*

durable goods goods usable for a relatively long time, as machinery, cars, or home appliances

du·ral·u·min (dyoo ral'yoo mən) *n.* [DUR(ABLE) + ALUMIN(IUM)] a strong, lightweight alloy of aluminium with copper, manganese, magnesium, and silicon

du·ra ma·ter (dyoor'ə māt'ər) [ML., lit., hard mother < an Ar. term] the outermost and toughest of the three membranes covering the brain and spinal cord: also **du'ra** *n.* —**du'ral** *adj.*

du·ra·men (dyoo rā'mən) *n.* [L. < *durare*: see DURABLE] *same as* HEARTWOOD

dur·ance (dyoor'əns) *n.* [< OFr. < L. *durans*, prp. of *durare*: see DURABLE] imprisonment: mainly in phrase **in durance vile**

du·ra·tion (dyoo rā'shən) *n.* [< ML. < pp. of L. *durare*: see DURABLE] 1. continuance in time 2. the time that a thing continues or lasts

dur·bar (dur'bär) *n.* [Hindi < Per. < *dar*, portal + *bār*, court] 1. formerly in India, a reception or audience held by a native prince or British governor 2. the place where this was held

du·ress (dyoo res') *n.* [< OFr. < L. *duritia*, hardness < *durus*, hard] 1. imprisonment 2. the use of force or threats [*signed under duress*]

dur·ing (dyoor'iŋ) *prep.* [ME. orig. prp. of *duren*, to last < OFr. < L.; see DURABLE] 1. throughout the entire time of 2. at some point in the entire time of; in the course of

dur·ra (door'ə) *n.* [Ar. *dhurah*] a kind of millet

durst (durst) *archaic pt. of* DARE

du·rum (wheat) (dyoor'əm) [L., neut. of *durus*, hard] a hard wheat that yields durum and semolina used in macaroni, spaghetti, etc.

dusk (dusk) *adj.* [< OE. *dox*, dark-coloured] [Poet.] dark in colour; dusky —*n.* 1. the dim part of twilight 2. gloom;

dusky quality —*vt., vi.* to make or become dusky or shadowy

dusk·y (dus'kē) *adj.* **dusk'i·er, dusk'i·est** 1. somewhat dark in colour; esp., swarthy 2. lacking light; dim 3. gloomy —**dusk'i·ly** *adv.* —**dusk'i·ness** *n.*

dust (dust) *n.* [OE.] 1. powdery earth or any finely powdered matter 2. a cloud of such matter 3. confusion; turmoil 4. *a*) earth *b*) disintegrated mortal remains 5. a humble or abject condition 6. anything worthless 7. *same as* GOLD DUST —*vt.* 1. to sprinkle with dust, powder, etc. 2. to sprinkle (powder, etc.) on 3. to rid of dust, as by brushing or wiping —*vi.* to remove dust, as from furniture —**bite the dust** to be killed, esp. in battle —**shake the dust off one's feet** to leave with disdain —**throw dust in (someone's) eyes** to mislead or decieve (someone) —**dust'less** *adj.*

dust·bin (-bin') *n.* a container for rubbish, esp. household rubbish

dust bowl a region where eroded topsoil is blown away by winds during droughts

dust cart a motor vehicle used for removing household and street rubbish

dust cover 1. *same as* DUST JACKET 2. a loose cover for furniture, as a sheet, etc.

dust·er (-ər) *n.* 1. a person or thing that dusts; specif., *a*) a brush or cloth for removing dust from furniture, etc. *b*) device for sprinkling on a powder, as on crops, etc.

dust jacket a detachable paper cover for protecting the binding of a book

dust·man (-mən) *n., pl.* **-men** a man whose work is removing rubbish, ashes, etc.

dust·pan (-pan') *n.* a shovellike receptacle into which dust or debris is swept from a floor

dust storm a windstorm that sweeps up clouds of dust when passing over an arid region

dust·up (-up') *n.* [Colloq.] a commotion or fight

dust·y (-ē) *adj.* **dust'i·er, dust'i·est** 1. covered with or full of dust 2. like dust; powdery 3. of the colour of dust —**not so dusty** [Colloq.] quite good —**dust'i·ly** *adv.* —**dust'i·ness** *n.*

Dutch (duch) *adj.* [< MDu. *Duutsch*, Dutch, German] 1. of the Netherlands, its people, language, or culture —*n.* the language of the Netherlands —**beat the Dutch** [U.S. Colloq.] to be very unusual —**go Dutch** [Colloq.] to have each pay his own expenses —**in Dutch** [Colloq.] in trouble or disfavour —**the Dutch** the people of the Netherlands

Dutch auction an auction at which the upset price is very high, and is gradually lowered till a purchaser is found

Dutch barn a farm building consisting of a roof and its supports: used for storing hay, etc.

Dutch door [U.S.] stable door

Dutch elm disease [from its first appearance in the Netherlands] a widespread fungous disease of elms that causes the tree to die

Dutch·man (-mən) *n., pl.* **-men** 1. a native or inhabitant of the Netherlands 2. a Dutch ship —**I'm a Dutchman** [Colloq.] a phrase used for emphasis to imply disbelief [*if that's your writing I'm a Dutchman*]

Dutch oven 1. a heavy metal pot with a high, arched lid, for cooking pot roasts, etc. 2. a metal container for roasting meats, etc., with an open side placed towards the fire

Dutch treat [Colloq.] any entertainment, etc. at which each participant pays his own expenses

Dutch uncle [Colloq.] a person who bluntly and sternly lectures or scolds someone else

du·te·ous (dyōōt'ē əs) *adj.* dutiful; obedient —**du'te·ous·ly** *adv.* —**du'te·ous·ness** *n.*

du·ti·a·ble (dyōōt'ē ə b'l) *adj.* necessitating payment of a duty or tax, as imported goods

du·ti·ful (dyōō'ti fəl) *adj.* 1. showing, or resulting from, a sense of duty 2. obedient —**du'ti·ful·ly** *adv.*

du·ty (dyōōt'ē) *n., pl.* **-ties** [< Anglo-Fr. *dueté*, what is due: see DUE & -TY[1]] 1. obedience or respect to parents, older people, etc. 2. conduct based on moral or legal obligation 3. any action required by one's occupation or position 4. a sense of obligation 5. service, esp. military service 6. a payment due to the government, esp. a tax imposed on imports, exports, etc. 7. service or use: see HEAVY-DUTY 8. *a*) the performance of a machine *b*) the amount of work a machine is meant to do —**on** (or **off**) **duty** at (or having time off from) one's work or duty

du·ty-bound (-bound) *adj.* obliged; beholden

duty-free shop a shop, usually at an airport, port, etc., where goods can be bought with no payment of a duty or tax

du·um·vir (dyōō um'vər) *n., pl.* **-virs, -vi·ri** (-və rī') [L. < *duo*, two + *vir*, a man] either of two magistrates in ancient Rome who held office jointly

du·um·vi·rate (-və rit) *n.* 1. governmental position held jointly by two men 2. two such men

du·vet (dōō'vā) *n.* [Fr.] a quilt filled with eiderdown or a mixture of terylene and eiderdown

du·ve·tyne, du·ve·tyn (dyōō'və tēn') *n.* [< Fr. < *duvet*, eiderdown] a soft, velvetlike textile, originally made of cotton and silk: also **duvetine**

dwale (dwāl) *n.* [? < Ice. *dvöl*, delay] *same as* BELLADONNA, sense 1

dwarf (dwôrf) *n., pl.* **dwarfs, dwarves** (dwôrvz) [OE. *dweorg*] **1.** a person, animal, or plant much smaller than usual for its species **2.** *Folklore* an ugly little being with supposed magic powers **3.** a star of relatively small mass and low luminosity: in full, **dwarf star** —*vt.* **1.** to stunt the growth of **2.** to make small or insignificant **3.** to make seem small by comparison —*vi.* to become stunted or dwarfed —*adj.* undersized; stunted —**dwarf′ish** *adj.* —**dwarf′ish·ness** *n.* —**dwarf′ism** *n.*

dwell (dwel) *vi.* **dwelt, dwell′ing** [OE. *dwellan*, to lead astray, hinder] to make one's home; reside —**dwell on** (or **upon**) to linger over in thought or speech —**dwell′er** *n.*

dwell·ing (-iŋ) *n.* a place to live in; residence; house; abode: also **dwelling place**

dwin·dle (dwin′d'l) *vi., vt.* **-dled, -dling** [freq. of ME. *dwinen* < OE. *dwinan*, to wither] to become or make smaller or less; diminish; shrink

dwt. [*d(enarius)* *w(eigh)t*] pennyweight(s)

DX, D.X. *Radio* **1.** distance **2.** distant

Dy *Chem.* dysprosium

dy·ad (dī′ad) *n.* [LL. < Gr. *dyo*, TWO] **1.** pair **2.** *Chem.* an atom, element, or radical with a valence of two —*adj.* consisting of two —**dy·ad′ic** *adj.*

Dy·ak (dī′ak) *n.* [Malay *dayak*, savage] a member of an aboriginal people of Borneo

dyb·buk (dib′ək) *n.* [Heb. *dibbūq* < *dābhaq*, to cleave] *Jewish Folklore* the spirit of a dead person that enters and possesses the body of a living person

dye (dī) *n.* [OE. *deag*] **1.** colour produced in fabric, hair, etc. by saturating it with a colouring agent; tint; hue **2.** any such colouring agent or a solution containing it —*vt.* **dyed, dye′ing** to colour as with a dye —*vi.* to take on colour in dyeing —**of** (the) **deepest dye** of the worst sort —**dy′er** *n.*

dyed-in-the-wool (dīd′'n thə wool′) *adj.* **1.** dyed before being woven **2.** thoroughgoing; unchanging

dye·ing (dī′iŋ) *n.* the process or work of colouring fabrics, hair, etc. with dyes

dye·stuff (dī′stuf′) *n.* any substance constituting or yielding a dye

dy·ing (dī′iŋ) *prp. of* DIE[1] —*adj.* **1.** about to die or end **2.** of or at the time of death —*n.* a ceasing to live or exist

dyke[1] (dīk) *n., vt. same as* DIKE

dyke[2] (dīk) *n.* [Slang] a lesbian

dy·nam·ic (dī nam′ik) *adj.* [< Fr. < Gr. < *dynamis*, power < *dynasthai*, tò be able] **1.** relating to energy or physical force in motion: opposed to STATIC **2.** relating to dynamics **3.** energetic; vigorous; forceful **4.** relating to change or productive activity Also **dy·nam′i·cal** —*n. same as* DYNAMICS (sense 2a) —**dy·nam′i·cal·ly** *adv.*

dy·nam·ics (-iks) *n.pl.* [*with sing. v. for 1, 2c, & 3*] **1.** the branch of mechanics dealing with the motions of material bodies under the action of given forces; kinetics **2.** a) the various forces, physical, moral, economic, etc., operating in any field b) the way such forces operate mutually c) the study of such forces **3.** the effect of varying degrees of loudness in musical performance

dy·na·mism (dī′nə miz'm) *n.* **1.** the theory that force or energy is the basic universal principle **2.** a dynamic quality —**dy′na·mis′tic** *adj.*

dy·na·mite (dī′nə mīt′) *n.* [coined (1866-67) by A. *Nobel* (1833-96), Swed. industrialist < Gr. *dynamis*: see DYNAMIC] **1.** a powerful explosive made of some absorbent soaked with nitroglycerin **2.** a person or thing that is potentially

dangerous —*vt.* **-mit′ed, -mit′ing** to blow up or destroy with dynamite —**dy′na·mit′er** *n.*

dy·na·mo (-mō′) *n., pl.* **-mos′** [< *dynamoelectric machine*] **1.** a machine that generates electricity: see GENERATOR **2.** a forceful, dynamic person

dy·na·mo- [< Gr. *dynamis*: see DYNAMIC] *a combining form meaning* power [*dynamoelectric*]

dy·na·mo·e·lec·tric (dī′nə mō i lek′trik) *adj.* having to do with the production of electrical energy from mechanical energy, or the reverse process: also **dy′na·mo·e·lec′tri·cal**

dy·na·mom·e·ter (-mom′ə tər) *n.* an apparatus for measuring force or power, esp. mechanical power —**dy′na·mo·met′ric** (-mō met′rik) *adj.* —**dy′na·mom′e·try** *n.*

dy·na·mo·tor (dī′nə mōt′ər) *n.* an electrical machine combining generator and motor, for transforming current from one voltage to another

dy·nast (dī′nast, -nəst; dī′-) *n.* [< L. < Gr. < *dynasthai*, to be strong] a ruler, esp. a hereditary ruler

dy·nas·ty (dī′nəs tē, dī′-) *n., pl.* **-ties** [see prec.] **1.** a succession of rulers who are members of the same family **2.** the period during which a certain family reigns —**dy·nas·tic** (dī nas′tik), **dy·nas′ti·cal** *adj.* —**dy·nas′ti·cal·ly** *adv.*

dyne (dīn) *n.* [Fr. < Gr. *dynamis*, power] the amount of force that imparts to a mass of one gramme an acceleration of one centimetre per second per second: equivalent to 10^{-5} newtons

Dy·nel (dī nel′) *a trademark for* a synthetic fibre —*n.* [**d-**] this fibre or a furlike fabric made from it

dys- [Gr.] *a prefix meaning* bad, ill, abnormal, impaired, difficult, etc. [*dysfunction*]

dys·en·ter·y (dis′'n tər ē, -trē) *n.* [< OFr. < L. < Gr. < *dys-*, bad + *entera*, bowels] a painful intestinal inflammation characterized by diarrhoea with bloody, mucous faeces —**dys′en·ter′ic** (-ter′ik) *adj.*

dys·func·tion (dis fuŋk′shən) *n.* abnormal, impaired, or incomplete functioning, as of a body organ or part —**dys·func′tion·al** *adj.*

dys·graph·i·a (dis graf′ē ə) *n.* [ModL. < DYS- + *graphos*, writing] the inability to write coherently

dys·lex·i·a (dis lek′sē ə) *n.* [ModL. < Gr. *dys-*, bad + *lexis*, speech < *legein*, to speak] impairment of the ability to read, often from brain injury or genetic defect—**dys·lex′ic** *adj.*

dys·men·or·rhoe·a (dis′men ə rē′ə) *n.* [ModL. < DYS- + Gr. *men*, month + *rhoia*, a flowing] painful or difficult menstruation

dys·pep·si·a (dis pep′shə, -sē ə) *n.* [L. < Gr. < *dys-*, bad + *pepsis*, cooking < *peptein*, to digest] impaired digestion; indigestion

dys·pep·tic (-tik) *adj.* **1.** of, causing, or having dyspepsia **2.** gloomy; grouchy —*n.* a person who has dyspepsia —**dys·pep′ti·cal·ly** *adv.*

dysp·ne·a (disp′nē ə, disp nē′ə) *n.* [< L. < Gr. < *dys-*, hard + *pnoē* < *pnein*, to breathe] difficult or painful breathing —**dysp·ne′al, dysp·ne′ic** *adj.*

dys·pro·si·um (dis prō′sē əm, -zē-, -shē-) *n.* [< Gr. *dysprositos*, difficult of access] a chemical element of the rare-earth group: symbol, Dy; at. wt., 162.50; at. no., 66: it is one of the most magnetic of all known substances

dys·tro·phy (dis′trə fē) *n.* [ModL. *dystrophia*: see DYS- & -TROPHY] **1.** faulty nutrition **2.** faulty development, or degeneration: cf. MUSCULAR DYSTROPHY —**dys·tro′phic** (-trof′ik) *adj.*

dz. dozen; dozens

dzo (zō) *n.* [< Tibetan *mdso*] a hybrid cross between a yak and a cow: also **dzho**

E

E, e (ē) *n., pl.* **E's, e's** **1.** the fifth letter of the English alphabet **2.** a sound of E or e

E (ē) *n.* *Music* a) the third tone in the ascending scale of C major b) the scale having this tone as the keynote

e **1.** *Physics* erg **2.** *Math.* the number used as the base of a system of logarithms, approximately 2.71828: written *e*

e- *a prefix meaning* out, from, etc.: see EX-

E, E., e, e. **1.** east **2.** eastern

E. **1.** Earl **2.** Easter **3.** English

E., e. **1.** earth **2.** engineer(ing)

ea. each

each (ēch) *adj., pron.* [< OE. *ælc*] every one of two or more considered separately —*adv.* apiece [ten pence *each*] —**each other** each one the other; one another: some use *each other* only of two and *one another* of more than two, but in common use no distinction is made [help *each other*] —**each way** in betting, to back a horse, etc. to either win or be placed

ea·ger (ē′gər) *adj.* [< OFr. *aigre* < L. *acer*, sharp, keen] feeling or showing keen desire; impatient or anxious to do or get —**ea′ger·ly** *adv.* —**ea′ger·ness** *n.*

eager beaver [Colloq.] a hardworking, conscientious person

ea·gle (ē′g'l) *n.* [< OFr. *aigle* < L. *aquila*] 1. a large, strong, flesh-eating bird of prey having sharp vision and powerful wings 2. a representation of the eagle as a symbol of a nation, etc.; esp., the national emblem of the U.S. 3. the standard of a Roman Legion, or French army 4. *Golf* a score of two below par on any hole

ea·gle-eyed (-īd′) *adj.* 1. having keen vision 2. [Colloq.] very alert and observant, esp. in a critical faultfinding way

ea·glet (ē′glit) *n.* a young eagle

-e·an (ē′ən) [< L. & Gr.] a suffix meaning of, belonging to, like [European]

ear[1] (ir) *n.* [OE. *eare*] 1. the part of the body that perceives sound; organ of hearing 2. the visible, external part of the ear 3. the sense of hearing 4. the ability to recognize slight differences in sound, esp. in musical tones 5. anything shaped or placed like an ear 6. attention; consideration; heed [lend an ear] —**be all ears** to listen attentively or eagerly —**fall on deaf ears** to be ignored or unheeded —**give one's ears** to be prepared to make any sacrifice —**have** (or **keep**) **an ear to the ground** to pay attention to the trends of public opinion —**lend an ear** to listen —**play by ear** to play (a musical instrument or piece) without the use of notation —**play it by ear** [Colloq.] to act as the situation demands —**turn a deaf ear** to be unwilling to listen or heed

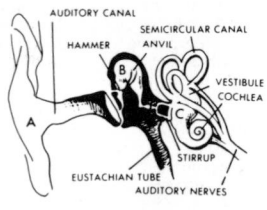

AUDITORY CANAL
SEMICIRCULAR CANAL
HAMMER ANVIL
VESTIBULE
COCHLEA
A
STIRRUP
EUSTACHIAN TUBE
AUDITORY NERVES

HUMAN EAR
(A, external ear;
B, middle ear;
C, inner ear)

ear[2] (ir) *n.* [< OE. *ær*] the grain-bearing spike of a cereal plant [an ear of corn] —*vi.* to sprout ears

ear·ache (ir′āk′) *n.* an ache or pain in the ear

ear·drum (-drum′) *n.* same as: 1. TYMPANIC MEMBRANE 2. MIDDLE EAR

ear·ful (-fool′) *n.* [Colloq.] 1. a quantity of something heard or overheard [get an earful of this] 2. a rebuke or scolding [to give someone an earful]

earl (url) *n.* [OE. *eorl*, warrior, nobleman] a British nobleman ranking above a viscount and below a marquess —**earl′dom** *n.*

ear·lap (ir′lap′) *n.* 1. the ear lobe 2. the external ear

Earl Marshal the marshal at certain state ceremonies and head of the Heralds' College

ear·ly (url′lē) *adv., adj.* -li·er, -li·est [< OE. < ær, before (see ERE) + -lice (see -LY[2])] 1. near the beginning of a given period of time or of a series, as of events 2. before the expected or usual time 3. in the far distant past 4. in the near future; before long —**ear′li·ness** *n.*

early bird [Colloq.] a person who arrives early or gets up early in the morning

early closing the custom followed by many shops of shutting for an afternoon one day a week

Early English a style of architecture used in England in the 12th and 13th cent. with lancet arches and plate tracery

Early Modern English English as spoken and written from about 1450 to about 1750

ear·mark (ir′märk′) *n.* 1. an identification mark put on the ear of an animal to show ownership 2. an identifying mark or feature; sign —*vt.* 1. to mark the ears of (livestock) for identification 2. to set a distinctive mark upon; identify 3. to reserve or set aside for a special purpose

ear·muffs (-mufs′) *n.pl.* cloth or fur coverings for the ears in cold weather

earn (urn) *vt.* [OE. *earnian*, to gain, lit., to harvest] 1. to receive (salary, wages, etc.) for one's labour or service 2. to get or deserve as a result of something done 3. to gain (interest, etc.) as profit —**earn′er** *n.*

ear·nest[1] (ur′nist) *adj.* [OE. *eornoste*] 1. serious and intense; not joking; zealous and sincere 2. not petty; important —**in earnest** 1. serious 2. in a determined manner —**ear′nest·ly** *adv.* —**ear′nest·ness** *n.*

ear·nest[2] (ur′nist) *n.* [< OFr. *erres* < L. *arrae*, pl. < Gr. *arrabōn* < Heb. *'ērābōn*] 1. money given as a part payment and pledge in binding a bargain: in full, **earnest money** 2. something given or done as an indication of what is to come; token

earn·ings (ur′niŋz) *n.pl.* 1. wages or other recompense 2. profits, interest, dividends, etc.

ear·phone (ir′fōn′) *n.* a receiver for radio, telephone, etc. held to or put into the ear

ear piercing the making of a hole in the ear lobes with a sterilized needle so that earrings may be worn

ear-pierc·ing (-pirs′iŋ) *adj.* shrill; deafening

ear·plug (-plug′) *n.* a plug inserted in the outer ear, as to keep out sound or water

ear·ring (-riŋ′) *n.* a ring or other small ornament for the lobe of the ear

ear·shot (-shot′) *n.* the distance within which a sound, esp. that of the unaided human voice, can be heard

earth (urth) *n.* [OE. *eorthe*] 1. the planet that we live on: it is the fifth largest planet of the solar system and the third in distance from the sun: diameter, 12 756 km. 2. this world, as distinguished from heaven and hell 3. all the people on the earth 4. land, as distinguished from sea or sky 5. soil; ground 6. [Poet.] a) the human body b) worldly matters 7. the hole of a burrowing animal 8. *Chem.* any of the metallic oxides which are reduced with difficulty, as alumina 9. *Elec.* the connection of an electrical conductor with the earth —*vt.* 1. to cover (up) with soil for protection, as seeds or plants 2. *Elec.* to connect a circuit, etc. with the earth —**come back** (or **down**) **to earth** to return to reality —**down to earth** practical; realistic —**on earth** of all things: an intensive [what on earth is that?] —**run to earth** 1. to hunt down 2. to find by search

earth·bound (-bound′) *adj.* 1. confined to or by the earth or earthly things 2. headed for the earth

earth closet a privy in which earth is applied to the excreta as a deodorant

earth·en (ur′thən) *adj.* 1. made of earth or of baked clay 2. earthly

earth·en·ware (-wer′) *n.* the coarser sort of containers, tableware, etc. made of baked clay

earth·ly (urth′lē) *adj.* 1. of the earth; specif., a) terrestrial b) worldly c) temporal or secular 2. conceivable; possible [no earthly reason for staying] —**not an earthly** [Colloq.] no chance whatever —**earth′li·ness** *n.*

earth·man (-man′) *n., pl.* -men′ (-men′) a person on or from the planet earth, as in science fiction: also **earth′ling**

earth·nut (-nut′) *n.* the root, tuber, or underground pod of various plants, as the peanut

earth·quake (-kwāk′) *n.* a shaking of the crust of the earth, caused by underground volcanic forces or by shifting of rock

earth sciences those sciences concerned with the structure, age, etc. of the earth, as geology, geography, etc.

earth·ward (-ward′) *adv., adj.* towards the earth: also **earth′wards** *adv.*

earth·work (-wurk′) *n.* 1. a defensive embankment made by piling up earth 2. *Engineering* the work of excavating or building embankments

earth·worm (-wurm′) *n.* a round, segmented worm that burrows in the soil

earth·y (ur′thē) *adj.* **earth′i·er, earth′i·est** 1. of or like earth or soil 2. a) coarse; unrefined b) simple and natural —**earth′i·ness** *n.*

ear trumpet a trumpet-shaped tube formerly used as a hearing aid by the partially deaf

ear·wax (ir′waks′) *n.* the yellowish, waxlike secretion in the canal of the outer ear; cerumen

ear·wig (-wig′) *n.* [< OE. < *eare*, EAR[1] + *wicga*, beetle, worm] any of an order of insects with short, horny forewings and a pair of forceps at the tail end

ease (ēz) *n.* [< OFr. *aise* < L. *adjacens*, lying nearby: see ADJACENT] 1. freedom from pain or trouble; comfort 2. natural, unstrained manner; poise 3. freedom from difficulty; facility 4. freedom from poverty; affluence 5. leisure; relaxation —*vt.* **eased, eas′ing** 1. to free from pain or trouble; comfort 2. to lessen (pain, anxiety, etc.) 3. to make easier; facilitate 4. to reduce the strain or pressure of 5. to move by careful shifting, etc. —*vi.* 1. to move or be moved by careful shifting, etc. 2. to lessen in tension, speed, pain, etc. —**at ease** 1. without pain, anxiety, etc. 2. *Mil.* relaxed, but keeping silent and staying in place —**ease oneself** to urinate or defecate —**take one's ease** to relax in comfort —**ease′ful** *adj.*

ea·sel (ē′z'l) *n.* [< Du. *ezel* (G. *Esel*), ass, ult. < L. *asinus*, ASS] an upright frame or tripod to hold an artist's canvas, a picture on display, etc.

ease·ment (ēz′mənt) *n.* 1. an easing or being eased 2. a comfort, relief, or convenience 3. *Law* a right that one may have in another's land, as a right of way

eas·i·ly (ē′zəl ē) *adv.* 1. in an easy way 2. by far [easily the best] 3. very likely [it may easily rain]

eas·i·ness (ē′zē nis) *n.* the quality or state of being easy to do or get, or of being at ease

east (ēst) *n.* [OE. *east*] 1. the direction to the right of a person facing north; direction in which sunrise occurs (90° on the compass, opposite west) 2. a region or district in or towards this direction 3. [E-] Asia and the nearby islands; the Orient —*adj.* 1. in, of, to, or towards the east 2. from the east **3.** [E-] designating the eastern part of a country, etc. —*adv.* in or towards the east

east·bound (-bound′) *adj.* going eastwards

East End a densely populated area of London containing industrial and dock areas

East·er (ēs′tər) *n.* [< OE. < *Eastre*, dawn goddess] **1.** an annual Christian festival celebrating the resurrection of Jesus, held on the first Sunday after the first full moon on or after March 21 **2.** this Sunday: also **Easter Sunday**

Easter egg a coloured egg or an egg-shaped sweet, esp. made of chocolate, used as an Easter gift

east·er·ly (ēs′tər lē) *adj., adv.* **1.** towards the east **2.** from the east

east·ern (-tərn) *adj.* **1.** in, of, or towards the east **2.** from the east **3.** [E-] of or characteristic of the East —**east′·ern·most** (-mōst′) *adj.*

Eastern Church 1. *a)* orig., the Christian Church in E Europe, W Asia, and Egypt *b)* those Churches descended from this Church and in union with Rome but having their own rite (**Eastern Rite**) **2.** *same as* ORTHODOX EASTERN CHURCH

east·ern·er (-ər) *n.* a native or inhabitant of the east

Eastern Hemisphere that half of the earth that includes Europe, Africa, Asia, and Australia

Eastern Orthodox Church *same as* ORTHODOX EASTERN CHURCH

East·er·tide (ēs′tər tīd′) *n.* the period after Easter, extending in various churches to Ascension Day, Whitsunday, or Trinity Sunday

east-north-east (ēst′nôrth′ēst′; *nautical* -nôr′-) *n.* the direction halfway between due east and northeast; 22°30′ north of due east —*adj., adv.* **1.** in or towards this direction **2.** from this direction

east-south-east (ēst′south′ēst′; *nautical* -sou′-) *n.* the direction halfway between due east and southeast; 22°30′ south of due east —*adj., adv.* **1.** in or towards this direction **2.** from this direction

east·ward (ēst′wərd) *adj., adv.* towards the east: also **east′wards** *adv.* —*n.* an eastward direction, point, or region

east·ward·ly (-lē) *adv., adj.* **1.** towards the east **2.** from the east

eas·y (ē′zē) *adj.* **eas′i·er, eas′i·est** [< OFr. *aisé* < *aise:* see EASE] **1.** that can be performed, obtained, etc. with ease; not difficult **2.** free from trouble, anxiety, pain, etc. **3.** providing comfort or rest **4.** not stiff or awkward **5.** not strict; lenient **6.** compliant or credulous **7.** *a)* unhurried *b)* gradual —*adv.* [Colloq.] **1.** easily [*easy* come, *easy* go] **2.** slowly and carefully —**easy does it** be careful —**easy on the eye** [Colloq.] pleasant to look at —**go easy on** (or **with**) [Colloq.] **1.** to use with restraint **2.** to treat leniently —**on easy street** [Colloq.] well-to-do —**take it easy** [Colloq.] **1.** to refrain from anger, haste, etc. **2.** to relax; rest

easy chair a stuffed or padded armchair

eas·y·go·ing (-gō′iŋ) *adj.* **1.** not hurried or agitated **2.** lenient or lackadaisical

eat (ēt) *vt.* **ate** (et, āt), **eat·en** (ēt′ən), **eat′ing** [OE. *etan*] **1.** to chew and swallow (food) **2.** to use up or destroy as by eating; consume or ravage (usually with *away* or *up*) **3.** to penetrate and destroy, as acid does; corrode **4.** to make by or as by eating [acid *ate* holes in the cloth] **5.** to bring (oneself) into a specified condition by eating **6.** [Slang] to worry or bother [what's *eating* him?] —*vi.* **1.** to eat food; have a meal or meals **2.** to destroy or use up something gradually (often with *into*) —**eat a person's salt** to be a guest or dependant of· someone —**eat one's words** to retract something said earlier —**eat out** to eat a meal at a restaurant —**eat′er** *n.*

eat·a·ble (-ə b′l) *adj.* fit to be eaten; edible —*n.* a thing fit to be eaten; food: *usually used in pl.*

eat·ing (-iŋ) *n.* **1.** the action of one that eats **2.** edible quality of food —*adj.* **1.** that eats **2.** good for eating uncooked [*eating* apples]

eats (ēts) *n.pl.* [Colloq.] food; meals

eau de Co·logne (ō′də kə lōn′) [Fr., lit. water of Cologne] a perfumed toilet water made of alcohol and aromatic oils: usually clipped to *cologne*

‡**eau de Nil** (ō′də nēl′) [Fr., lit. water of the Nile] pale green

‡**eau de vie** (ō′də vē′) [Fr., lit. water of life] brandy or other spirits

eaves (ēvz) *n.pl.,* *sing.* **eave** [orig. sing., OE. *efes*] the lower edge or edges of a roof, usually projecting beyond the sides of a building

eaves·drop (-drop′) *vi.* **-dropped′, -drop′ping** [prob. back-formation < *eavesdropper* < OE. *yfesdrype*, water from the eaves] to listen secretly to a private conversation —**eaves′drop′per** *n.*

ebb (eb) *n.* [OE. *ebba*] **1.** the flow of water back towards the sea, as the tide falls **2.** a weakening or lessening; decline —*vi.* **1.** to flow backwards; recede, as the tide **2.** to weaken or lessen; decline

ebb tide the outgoing or falling tide

eb·on (eb′ən) *adj., n.* [< L. *ebenus* < Gr. *ebenos* < Egypt. *hbnj* (Heb. *hobnim*)] [Poet.] *same as* EBONY

eb·on·ite (-īt′) *n.* *same as* VULCANITE

eb·on·ize (-īz′) *vt.* **-ized, -iz′ing** to give a finish to (wood, etc.) like that of ebony

eb·on·y (-ē) *n.,* *pl.* **-on·ies** [< LL. *ebenius* < *ebenus:* see EBON] **1.** the hard, heavy, dark, durable wood of certain tropical trees, used in decorative woodwork, etc. **2.** such a tree —*adj.* **1.** made of ebony **2.** like ebony, esp. in colour; dark; black

e·bul·lient (i bul′yənt) *adj.* [< L. prp. of *ebullire* < *e-*, out + *bullire*, to BOIL¹] **1.** bubbling; boiling **2.** overflowing with enthusiasm, etc.; exuberant —**e·bul′lience, e·bul′lien·cy** *n.* —**e·bul′lient·ly** *adv.*

e·bul·li·tion (eb′ə lish′ən) *n.* **1.** a boiling or bubbling up **2.** a sudden outburst, as of emotion

E.C. East Central

ec·cen·tric (ik sen′trik) *adj.* [< ML. < LL. < Gr. < *ek-*, out of + *kentron*, CENTRE] **1.** not having the same centre, as two circles: opposed to CONCENTRIC **2.** not having the axis exactly in the centre; off centre **3.** not exactly circular in shape or motion **4.** deviating from what is usual, as in conduct; odd; unconventional —*n.* **1.** a disc set off centre on a shaft in an apparatus for converting circular motion into back-and-forth motion **2.** an eccentric person —**ec·cen′tri·cal·ly** *adv.*

ec·cen·tric·i·ty (ek′sen tris′ə tē, -sən-) *n.,* *pl.* **-ties 1.** the state, quality, or amount of being eccentric **2.** deviation from what is usual, as usual, oddity

eccl., eccles. ecclesiastical

Eccles., Eccl. Ecclesiastes

ec·cle·si·as·tic (i klē′zē as′tik) *adj.* [< LL. < Gr. < *ekklēsia*, assembly, ult. < *ek-*, out + *kalein*, to call] *same as* ECCLESIASTICAL —*n.* a clergyman

ec·cle·si·as·ti·cal (-ti k′l) *adj.* of the church or the clergy —**ec·cle′si·as′ti·cal·ly** *adv.*

ec·cle·si·as·ti·cism (-tə siz′m) *n.* adherence to ecclesiastical principles, esp. the rituals and customs of a church, etc.

ec·cle·si·ol·o·gy (i klē′zē ol′ə jē) *n.* [< Gr. *ekklēsia*, assembly & -LOGY] the study of church architecture, art, etc.

ECG electrocardiogram

ech·e·lon (esh′ə lon′) *n.* [< Fr. < OFr. *eschelle* < L. *scala*, ladder] **1.** a steplike formation of ships, aircraft, or troops **2.** a functional or positional military subdivision **3.** *a)* an organizational level, as of responsibility *b)* persons at such a level —*vt., vi.* to assemble in echelon

e·chid·na (i kid′nə) *n.* [ModL. < L. < Gr. *echidna*, adder] a small, egg-laying, ant-eating Australasian mammal with a long snout and a spiny coat

e·chi·no·derm (i ki′nə durm′, ek′ə-) *n.* [< ModL. < Gr. *echinos*, sea urchin, hedgehog + *derma*, skin] any of a group of marine animals with a hard, spiny skeleton and radial body, as a starfish

e·chi·nus (i kī′nəs) *n.,* *pl.* **e·chi′ni** (-nī) [L. < Gr. *echinos:* see prec.] **1.** *same as* SEA URCHIN **2.** *Archit.* moulding under the abacus of the capital of a Doric column

ech·o (ek′ō) *n.,* *pl.* **-oes** [< L < Gr. *echo*] **1.** *a)* the repetition of a sound by reflection of sound waves from a surface *b)* a sound so made **2.** *a)* any repetition or imitation of words, ideas, etc. of another *b)* a person doing this **3.** sympathetic response **4.** a radar wave reflected from an object, appearing as a spot of light on a radarscope —*vi* **-oed, -o·ing** **1.** to resound with an echo **2.** to be repeated as an echo —*vt.* **1.** to repeat (the words, ideas, etc.) of (another) **2.** to repeat or reflect (sound) from a surface

echo chamber a room used in recording and broadcasting to increase resonance, produce echo effects, etc.

e·cho·ic (e kō′ik) *adj.* **1.** having the nature of an echo **2.** imitative in sound; onomatopoeic, as a word formed in approximate imitation of some sound (e.g., *clash*) —**ech′-o·ism** *n.*

ech·o·lo·ca·tion (ek′ō lō kā′shən) *n.* the determination, as by a bat, of an object's position by emission of soundwaves which are reflected back to the sender —**ech′o·lo′cate** *vt., vi.* **-cat·ed, -cat·ing**

echo sounding determination of water depth or of underwater distances by a device (**echo sounder**) that measures the time it takes for a sound wave to be reflected

é·clair (ā kler′, ē-, i-) *n.* [Fr., lit., lightning] a small, oblong pastry shell filled with whipped cream and covered with chocolate icing

ec·lamp·si·a (e klamp′sē ə) *n.* [ModL. < Gr. *eklampsis*, a shining forth] a disorder occurring in late pregnancy, characterised by convulsions and high blood pressure

é·clat (ā klä′, i-) *n.* [Fr. < *éclater*, to burst (out)] **1.** brilliant success **2.** dazzling display **3.** approval; acclaim **4.** fame; renown

ec·lec·tic (i klek′tik, e-) *adj.* [< Gr. < *ek-*, out + *legein*, to pick] **1.** selecting from various systems, doctrines, or sources **2.** composed of material selected thus —*n.* one who uses eclectic methods —**ec·lec′ti·cal·ly** *adv.* —**ec·lec′-ti·cism** (-siz′m) *n.*

e·clipse (i klips', ē-) *n.* [< OFr. < L. < Gr. *ekleipsis* < *ek-*, out + *leipein*, to leave] **1.** a partial or total obscuring of the sun when the moon comes between it and the earth (**solar eclipse**), or of the moon when the earth's shadow is cast upon it (**lunar eclipse**) **2.** a dimming or extinction, as of fame or glory —*vt.* **e·clipsed', e·clips'ing 1.** to cause an eclipse of **2.** to overshadow or surpass

e·clip·tic (i klip'tik, ē-) *n.* **1.** the apparent annual path of the sun on the celestial sphere **2.** a great circle on the celestial sphere formed by the intersection of an infinite plane through the earth's orbit with the celestial sphere —*adj.* of eclipses or the ecliptic

ECLIPSE
(of the sun)

ec·logue (ek'lôg) *n.* [< Fr. < L. < Gr. < *eklegein*: see ECLECTIC] a short pastoral poem, usually a dialogue between two shepherds

e·co- [< LL. < Gr. < *oikos*, house] *a combining form meaning* environment or habitat [*ecosystem*]

ecol. 1. ecological **2.** ecology

e·col·o·gy (ē kol'ə jē) *n.* [< G. < Gr. *oikos*, house + *-logia*, -LOGY] the interrelationship of organisms and their environment, or the study of this —**ec·o·log·i·cal** (ek'ə loj'- i k'l, ē'kə-), **ec'o·log'ic** *adj.* —**ec'o·log'i·cal·ly** *adv.* —**e·col'o·gist** *n.*

econ. 1. economic **2.** economics **3.** economy

e·con·o·met·rics (i kon'ə met'riks) *n.pl.* [*with sing. v.*] [< ECONOMY + METER² + -ICS] the use of mathematical and statistical methods to verify and develop economic theories —**e·con'o·met'ric** *adj.* —**e·con'o·me·tri'cian** (-mə trish'ən) *n.*

e·co·nom·ic (ē'kə nom'ik, ek'ə-) *adj.* **1.** of the management of the income, expenditures, etc. of a business, community, etc. **2.** of the production, distribution, and consumption of wealth **3.** of economics **4.** of the satisfaction of the material needs of people **5.** capable of being used, operated, etc. for profit; profitable **6.** inexpensive; economical

e·co·nom·i·cal (-i k'l) *adj.* **1.** not wasting money, time, material, etc.; thrifty or efficient **2.** expressed or done with economy **3.** of economics —**e'co·nom'i·cal·ly** *adv.*

e·co·nom·ics (-iks) *n.pl.* [*with sing. v.*] **1.** the science dealing with the production, distribution, and consumption of wealth and with the various related problems of labour, finance, taxation, etc. **2.** economic factors

e·con·o·mist (i kon'ə mist) *n.* a specialist in economics

e·con·o·mize (i kon'ə miz') *vi.* **-mized', -miz'ing** to avoid waste or reduce expenses —*vt.* to manage or use with thrift (often with *on*) —**e·con'o·mi·za'tion** *n.* —**e·con'o·miz'- er** *n.*

e·con·o·my (-mē) *n.,* *pl.* **-mies** [< L. < Gr. < *oikonomos*, manager < *oikos*, house + *nomos*, managing < *nemein*, to distribute] **1.** management of income, expenditures, etc. **2.** *a)* careful management of wealth, resources, etc.; thrift *b)* restrained or efficient use of one's materials, techniques, etc., as in the arts *c)* an instance of such management or use **3.** an orderly arrangement or management of parts **4.** an economic system of a specified kind, place, era, or condition

e·co·sphere (ē'kō sfir', ek'ō-) *n.* [ECO-+ -SPHERE] the parts of the universe, esp. on the earth, in which life can exist

e·co·sys·tem (ē'kō sis'təm, ek'ō-) *n.* [ECO- + SYSTEM] a given community of animals, plants, and bacteria and its interrelated physical and chemical environment

ec·ru (ek'rōō, ā'krōō) *adj., n.* [Fr. *écru*, unbleached < OFr. < *es-* (L. *ex-*), intens. + *cru*, raw < L. *crudus*] light tan; beige

ec·sta·sy (ek'stə sē) *n.,* *pl.* **-sies** [< OFr. < LL. < Gr. *ekstasis*, distraction < *ek-*, out + *histanai*, to place] **1.** an overpowering feeling of joy or delight; state of rapture **2.** a trance, as of a religious mystic

ec·stat·ic (ik stat'ik, ek-) *adj.* of, feeling, causing, or caused by ecstasy —**ec·stat'i·cal·ly** *adv.*

E.C.T. Electroconvulsive Therapy

ec·to- [ModL. < Gr. *ektos*, outside] *a combining form meaning* outside, external: also, before a vowel, **ect-**

ec·to·blast (ek'tə blast') *n.* [ECTO- + BLAST] **1.** the outer layer of a cell **2.** the outer primary layer of the embryo of a many-celled animal

ec·to·derm (ek'tə durm') *n.* [ECTO- + -DERM] the outer layer of cells of an embryo, from which the skin, hair, etc. develop —**ec'to·der'mal, ec'to·der'mic** *adj.*

ec·to·gen·e·sis (ek'tə jen'ə sis) *n.* [ECTO- + -GENESIS] origination outside the organism

ec·to·mor·phic (ek'tə môr'fik) *adj.* [ECTO- + -MORPHIC] designating or of the slender type of human body, in which the structures developed from the ectoderm predominate —**ec'to·morph'** *n.*

-ec·to·my (ek'tə mē) [< Gr. < *ek-*, out + *temnein*, to cut] *a combining form meaning* a surgical excision of [*appendicectomy*]

ec·to·plasm (ek'tə plaz'm) *n.* [ECTO- + -PLASM] **1.** the outer cytoplasm of a cell **2.** a vaporous, luminous substance believed by spiritualists to emanate from the medium in a trance —**ec'to·plas'mic** *adj.*

ec·u·men·i·cal (ek'yōō men'i k'l) *adj.* [< LL. < Gr. *oikoumenē* (*gē*), the inhabited (world) < *oikein*, to inhabit < *oikos*, house] **1.** general, or universal; esp., of the Christian church as a whole **2.** *a)* furthering the unity of Christian churches *b)* promoting better understanding among differing religious groups Also **ec'u·men'ic** —**ec'- u·men'i·cal·ism** *n.* —**ec'u·men'i·cal·ly** *adv.*

ec·u·men·i·cism (-i siz'm) *n.* *same as* ECUMENISM

ec·u·men·ism (ek'yōō mə niz'm, e kyōō'-) *n.* **1.** any ecumenical movement **2.** ecumenical principles or practice Also **ec'u·me·nic'i·ty** (-nis'ə tē) —**ec·u'men·ist** *n.*

ec·ze·ma (ek'sə mə) *n.* [ModL. < Gr. < *ek-*, out of + *zein*, to boil] a disorder of the skin in which it becomes inflamed, scaly, and very itchy —**ec·zem·a·tous** (ek sem'ə- təs) *adj.*

-ed (id, əd; d, t) [< OE.] **1.** *a suffix used:* *a)* to form the past tense and past participle of weak verbs [*wanted*] *b)* to form adjectives from nouns or verbs [*cultured*] or from adjectives ending in *-ate* [*serrated*] **2.** *a suffix added to nouns, meaning* having [*bearded*]

ed. 1. edited **2.** *pl.* **eds.** *a)* edition *b)* editor **3.** education

E·dam (cheese) (ē'dam) [orig. made in the Du. town of *Edam*] a round, mild, yellow cheese, usually coated with red paraffin

E.D.C. European Defence Community

Ed·da (ed'ə) [ON.] either of two early Icelandic literary works: *a)* the **Prose,** or **Younger, Edda** (c. 1230), a summary of Norse mythology *b)* the **Poetic,** or **Elder, Edda** (c. 1200), a collection of Old Norse poetry —**Ed·dic** (ed'ik), **Ed·da·ic** (i dā'ik) *adj.*

ed·dy (ed'ē) *n.,* *pl.* **-dies** [? < ON. *itha*] **1.** a current of air, water, etc. moving with a circular motion against the main current; little whirlpool or whirlwind **2.** a contrary movement or trend —*vi.* **-died, -dy·ing** to move in an eddy; whirl

eddy current *Physics* the electric current induced in an electromagnet, etc. by an alternating magnetic field

e·del·weiss (ā'd'l vis') *n.* [G. < *edel*, noble + *weiss*, white] a small, flowering plant of the composite family, native to the high mountains of Europe and C Asia, esp. the Alps, with white, woolly leaves and bracts

e·de·ma (i dē'mə) *n.,* *pl.* **-mas, -ma·ta** (-mə tə) *U.S. sp. of* OEDEMA

E·den (ē'd'n) *n.* [LL. < Heb. *'ēdhen*, lit., delight] any delightful place or state: after the garden where Adam and Eve first lived

e·den·tate (ē den'tāt) *adj.* [< L. pp. of *edentare*, to make toothless < *e-*, out + *dens*, tooth] **1.** without teeth **2.** of the edentates —*n.* any of an order of mammals with molars only or no teeth at all, as sloths and anteaters

edge (ej) *n.* [OE. *ecg*] **1.** the sharp, cutting part of a blade **2.** sharpness; keenness **3.** a projecting ledge, as of a cliff **4.** the line or part where something begins or ends; border; margin **5.** the line at which two surfaces of a solid meet **6.** the verge or brink, as of a condition **7.** [Colloq.] advantage [*you have the edge on me*] —*vt.* **edged, edg'ing 1.** *a)* to put an edge on *b)* to trim the edge of **2.** to make (one's way) sideways **3.** to move gradually or cautiously **4.** *Cricket* to hit (the ball) with the edge of the bat —*vi.* to move sideways or gradually or cautiously —**on edge 1.** nervously irritable or impatient **2.** almost involved; on the brink of —**set one's teeth on edge 1.** to give a sensation of tingling discomfort **2.** to irritate; provoke —**take the edge off** to dull the intensity or pleasure (of) —**edg'er** *n.*

edge·ways (-wāz') *adv.* with the edge foremost; on, by, or towards the edge: also [Chiefly U.S.] **edge'wise'** (-wiz') —**get a word in edgeways** to manage to say something in a conversation monopolized by others

edg·ing (ej'iŋ) *n.* something forming an edge

edg·y (-ē) *adj.* **edg'i·er, edg'i·est 1.** having an edge; sharp **2.** irritable; on edge —**edg'i·ly** *adv.* —**edg'i·ness** *n.*

ed·i·ble (ed'ə b'l) *adj.* [LL. *edibilis* < L. *edere*, to eat] fit to be eaten —*n.* anything fit to be eaten —**ed'i·bil'i·ty** (-bil'ə tē), **ed'i·ble·ness** *n.*

e·dict (ē'dikt) *n.* [< L. pp. of *edicere*, to proclaim < *e-*, out + *dicere*, to say] an official public proclamation issued by authority; decree

ed·i·fice (ed'ə fis) *n.* [< OFr. < L. *aedificium*, a building < *aedificare*: see ff.] **1.** a building, esp. a large, imposing one **2.** any complicated organization

ed·i·fy (ed'ə fi') *vt.* **-fied', -fy'ing** [< OFr. < L. *aedificare*, to build < *aedes*, a house + *-ficare* < *facere*, to make] to instruct so as to improve morally or spiritually —**ed'i·fi·ca'- tion** (-fi kā'shən) *n.* —**ed'i·fi'er** *n.*

ed·it (ed'it) *vt., vi.* [back-formation < EDITOR] **1.** to prepare (an author's works, a manuscript, etc.) for publication by

selecting, arranging, revising, etc. **2.** to govern the policy for (a newspaper or periodical) **3.** to prepare (a film, video tape, or recording) for presentation by cutting, rearranging, etc. **4.** to reword or alter written or recorded material, esp. for propaganda purposes —**edit out** to delete in editing
edit. 1. edited 2. edition 3. editor
e·di·tion (i dish'ən) *n.* [< L. *editio*, a publishing < *edere*: see ff.] **1.** a size, style, or form in which a book, etc. is published **2.** *a)* the total number of copies of a book, etc. published at about the same time *b)* one of these copies **3.** another version of something already existing, said, done, etc. [a younger *edition* of her mother]
ed·i·tor (ed'i tər) *n.* [< L. pp. of *edere*, to publish < *e-*, out + *dare*, to give] **1.** a person who edits **2.** a writer of editorials **3.** the head of a department of a newspaper, magazine, etc. **4.** a device used to edit (sense 3) —**ed'-i·tor·ship'n.**
ed·i·to·ri·al (ed'ə tôr'ē əl) *adj.* of, by, or characteristic of an editor or editors —*n.* a statement of opinion in a newspaper, etc. —**ed'i·to'ri·al·ly** *adv.*
ed·i·to·ri·al·ist (-ist) *n.* an editorial writer
ed·i·to·ri·al·ize (-īz') *vt., vi.* -**ized'**, -**iz'ing** **1.** to express editorial opinions about (something) **2.** to express editorial opinions in (an article, etc.) —**ed'i·to'ri·al·i·za'tion** *n.* —**ed'-i·to'ri·al·iz'er** *n.*
EDP electronic data processing
ed·u·ca·ble (ed'yoo kə b'l) *adj.* that can be educated or trained —**ed'u·ca·bil'i·ty** *n.*
ed·u·cate (ed'yoo kāt') *vt.* -**cat'ed**, -**cat'ing** [< L. pp. of *educare*, to train < *educere* < *e-*, out + *ducere*, to lead] **1.** to train, teach, instruct, or develop, esp. by formal schooling **2.** to pay for the schooling of (a person)
ed·u·cat·ed (-kāt'id) *adj.* **1.** having, or indicating, education **2.** based on knowledge or experience
ed·u·ca·tion (ed'yoo kā'shən) *n.* **1.** an educating or a being educated **2.** knowledge, ability, etc. thus developed **3.** a particular kind of instruction or training [a university *education*] **4.** study of the methods of teaching and learning —**ed'u·ca'tion·al, ed'u·ca'tive** *adj.* —**ed'u·ca'tion·al·ly** *adv.*
ed·u·ca·tion·ist (-ist) *n.* an educator; esp., an authority on educational theory: also **ed'u·ca'tion·al·ist**
ed·u·ca·tor (ed'yoo kāt'ər) *n.* **1.** a person whose work is to educate others; teacher **2.** a specialist in educational methods, theories, etc.
e·duce (i dyoos') *vt.* -**duced'**, -**duc'ing** [L. *educere*: see EDUCATE] **1.** to draw out; elicit **2.** to infer from data; deduce —**e·duc'i·ble** *adj.* —**e·duc'tion** (i duk'shən, ē-) *n.*
Ed·ward·i·an (ed wôr'dē ən) *adj.* designating or of the reign of any of the English kings named Edward, specif. of Edward VII
-ee (ē) [< OFr. *-é*, orig. masc. ending of pp. of verbs in *-er*] *a n.-forming suffix designating:* **1.** the recipient of a specified action or benefit [appointee, mortgagee] **2.** a person in a specified condition [absentee, employee]
E.E.C. European Economic Community
EEG electroencephalogram
eel (ēl) *n., pl.* **eels, eel:** see PLURAL, II, D, 1 [OE. *æl*] a snakelike fish with a long slippery body and no pelvic fins —**eel'like'**, **eel'y** *adj.*
eel·grass (-gras') *n.* an underwater flowering plant with long, grasslike leaves
eel·pout (-pout') *n., pl.* -**pout'**, -**pouts':** see PLURAL, II, D, 2 [OE. *ælepute*] **1.** a saltwater fish resembling the blenny **2.** *same as* BURBOT

EEL
(to 1.5 m long)

eel·worm (-wurm') *n.* any of various nematode worms, either free-living or parasitic on plants
e'en (ēn) *adv.* [Poet.] even —*n.* [Poet. or Dial.] even(ing)
-een (-ēn) [< Ir. *-ín*, dim. suffix] *a suffix used to form diminutives, esp. in Ireland* [colleen, poteen]
e'er (er) *adv.* [Poet.] ever
-eer (ir) [Fr. *-ier* < L. *-arius*] *a suffix used to form:* **1.** *nouns meaning* one that has to do with [mountaineer] or one that writes, makes, etc. [pamphleteer] **2.** *verbs meaning* to have to do with [electioneer]
ee·rie, ee·ry (ir'ē) *adj.* -**ri·er**, -**ri·est** [prob. ult. < OE. *earg*, timid] weird or uncanny, esp. in a frightening way —**ee'-ri·ly** *adv.* —**ee'ri·ness** *n.*
eff (ef) *interj.* [< F(UCK)] *a euphemism for* FUCK —*vi.* to swear —**effing and blinding** swearing profusely
ef·face (i fās', e-) *vt.* -**faced'**, -**fac'ing** [Fr. *effacer* < *e-* (L. *ex*, out) + *face*: see FACE] **1.** to rub out or wipe out; erase [to *efface* a memory] **2.** to make (oneself) inconspicuous —**ef·face'a·ble** *adj.* —**ef·face'ment** *n.* —**ef·fac'er** *n.*
ef·fect (ə fekt', i-) *n.* [< OFr. (& L.) < L. pp. of *efficere* < *ex-*, out + *facere*, to do] **1.** anything brought about by a cause or agent; result **2.** the power to produce results;

efficacy **3.** influence or action [a cathartic *effect*] **4.** general meaning; purport [he spoke to this *effect*] **5.** *a)* the impression produced, as by artistic design, a way of speaking, acting, etc. [done for *effect*] *b)* something that makes such an impression [cloud *effects*] **6.** the condition or fact of being in force [a law now in *effect*] **7.** [pl.] belongings; property [personal *effects*] —*vt.* to bring about; cause; accomplish —**in effect** **1.** in result; actually **2.** in essence; virtually —**take effect** to begin to produce results; become operative —**ef·fect'er** *n.*
ef·fec·tive (ə fek'tiv, i-) *adj.* **1.** having an effect **2.** producing a desired effect **3.** in effect; operative **4.** actual, not merely theoretical **5.** making a striking impression **6.** equipped and ready for combat —*n.* a combat-ready soldier, unit, etc. —**ef·fec'tive·ly** *adv.* —**ef·fec'tive·ness** *n.*
ef·fec·tu·al (ə fek'choo wəl, i-) *adj.* **1.** producing, or able to produce, the desired effect **2.** having legal force; valid —**ef·fec'tu·al'i·ty** (-wal'ə tē) *n.* —**ef·fec'tu·al·ly** *adv.*
ef·fec·tu·ate (-wāt') *vt.* -**at'ed**, -**at'ing** to bring about; effect —**ef·fec'tu·a'tion** *n.*
ef·fem·i·nate (i fem'ə nit) *adj.* [< L. pp. of *effeminare* < *ex-*, out + *femina*, woman] having or showing the appearance or qualities generally attributed to women; unmanly —**ef·fem'i·na·cy** (-nə sē) *n.* —**ef·fem'i·nate·ly** *adv.*
ef·fen·di (i fen'dē) *n., pl.* -**dis** [< Turk. < ModGr. < Gr. *authentēs*, a master] Sir; Master: former Turkish title of respect
ef·fer·ent (ef'ər ənt) *adj.* [< L. prp. of *efferre* < *ex-*, out + *ferre*, to bear] *Physiol.* carrying away from a central part; specif., designating nerves that carry impulses away from a nerve centre: opposed to AFFERENT
ef·fer·vesce (ef'ər ves') *vi.* -**vesced'**, -**vesc'ing** [< L. < *ex-*, out + *fervescere*, to begin to boil < *fervere*, to boil] **1.** to give off gas bubbles, as lemonade, soda, etc.; bubble **2.** to be lively —**ef'fer·ves'cence, ef'fer·ves'cen·cy** *n.* —**ef'-fer·ves'cent** *adj.* —**ef'fer·ves'cent·ly** *adv.*
ef·fete (e fēt', i-) *adj.* [L. *effetus*, exhausted by bearing < *ex-*, out + *fetus*, productive] **1.** no longer able to produce; spent and sterile **2.** decadent, soft, etc. —**ef·fete'ly** *adv.* —**ef·fete'ness** *n.*
ef·fi·ca·cious (ef'ə kā'shəs) *adj.* [L. *efficax* < *efficere* (see EFFECT) + -OUS] producing or capable of producing the desired effect; effective —**ef'fi·ca'cious·ly** *adv.* —**ef'fi·ca'-cious·ness** *n.*
ef·fi·ca·cy (ef'i kə sē) *n., pl.* -**cies** [see prec.] power to produce intended results; effectiveness
ef·fi·cien·cy (ə fish'ən sē, i-) *n., pl.* -**cies** **1.** ability to produce a desired effect with the least effort or waste; a being efficient **2.** the ratio of effective work to energy used in producing it: said of a machine, etc.
ef·fi·cient (-ənt) *adj.* [< L. prp. of *efficere*: see EFFECT] **1.** directly producing an effect or result; effective [the *efficient* cause] **2.** producing a desired effect with the least effort or waste —**ef·fi'cient·ly** *adv.*
ef·fi·gy (ef'ə jē) *n., pl.* -**gies** [< Fr. < L. *effigies* < *ex-*, out + *fingere*, to form] a statue or other likeness; often, a crude representation of a despised person —**burn (or hang) in effigy** to burn (or hang) a despised person's effigy in public protest
ef·flo·resce (ef'lô res', -lə-) *vi.* -**resced'**, -**resc'ing** [< L. < *ex-*, out + *florescere*, to blossom < *flos*, a flower] **1.** to blossom out; flower **2.** *Chem. a)* to change from crystals to a powder through loss of the water of crystallization *b)* to develop a powdery crust by evaporation or chemical change
ef·flo·res·cence (-res'əns) *n.* **1.** a flowering **2.** the time of flowering **3.** *Chem. a)* an efflorescing *b)* the resulting powder or crust **4.** *Med.* an eruption on the skin; rash —**ef'flo·res'cent** *adj.*
ef·flu·ence (ef'loo wəns) *n.* [< L. prp. of *effluere* < *ex-*, out + *fluere*, to flow] **1.** a flowing out or forth; emanation **2.** a thing that flows out or forth —**ef'flu·ent** *adj., n.*
ef·flu·vi·um (e floo'vē əm, i-) *n., pl.* -**vi·a** (-ə), -**vi·ums** [L., a flowing out: see prec.] **1.** a vaporous or invisible emanation; esp., a disagreeable or foul vapour or odour —**ef·flu'vi·al** *adj.*
ef·flux (ef'luks) *n.* [< L. pp. of *effluere*: see EFFLUENCE] **1.** the act of flowing out **2.** that which flows out in a stream
ef·fort (ef'ərt) *n.* [Fr. < OFr. < *esforcier*, to make an effort, ult. < L. *ex-*, intens. + *fortis*, strong] **1.** use of energy to do something; physical or mental exertion **2.** a try; attempt **3.** a result of working or trying; achievement —**ef'fort·less** *adj.* —**ef'fort·less·ly** *adv.* —**ef'fort·less·ness** *n.*
ef·fron·ter·y (e frun'tər ē, i-) *n., pl.* -**ter·ies** [< Fr. < L. *effrons*, shameless, barefaced < *ex-*, from +, *frons*, forehead] unashamed boldness; impudence
ef·ful·gence (e ful'jəns, i-) *n.* [< L. prp. of *effulgere* < *ex-*, forth + *fulgere*, to shine] great brightness; radiance —**ef·ful'gent** *adj.*
ef·fuse (e fyooz', i-) *vt., vi.* -**fused'**, -**fus'ing** [< L. pp. of *effundere* < *ex-*, out + *fundere*, to pour] to pour, or spread, out or forth
ef·fu·sion (e fyoo'zhən, i-) *n.* [see prec.] **1.** a pouring forth **2.** unrestrained expression in words

ef·fu·sive (-siv) *adj.* too demonstrative; gushing —**ef·fu'-sive·ly** *adv.* —**ef·fu'sive·ness** *n.*
EFTA European Free Trade Association
eft (eft) *n.* [OE. *efeta*] *same as* NEWT
eft·soon (eft sσon') *adv.* [OE. < *eft*, again + *sona*, soon] [Archaic] soon after: also **eft·soons'** (-sσonz')
Eg. 1. Egypt 2. Egyptian 3. Egyptology
e.g. [L. *exempli gratia*] for example
e·gad (i gad') *interj.* [prob. < *oh God*] a softened or euphemistic oath
e·gal·i·tar·i·an (i gal'ə ter'ē ən, ē-) *adj.* [< Fr. < *égalité*, equality + -IAN] of or for equal rights for all —*n.* an advocate of equal rights —**e·gal'i·tar'i·an·ism** *n.*
egg¹ (eg) *n.* [ON.] 1. an oval or round body laid by a female bird, fish, insect, etc. containing within a shell or membrane the germ of a new individual and food for its development 2. a female reproductive cell; ovum: also called **egg cell** 3. a hen's egg, raw or cooked 4. something egglike, esp. in shape 5. [Colloq.] a person [a bad *egg*] —**egg'y** *adj.*
egg² (eg) *vt.* [< ON. *eggja*, lit., to give edge to < *egg*, edge] to urge or incite (with *on*)

HEN'S EGG
(A, yolk; B, air space; C, white; D, outer shell membrane; E, inner shell membrane; F, chalaza-bearing membrane; G, chalaza; H, shell)

egg and spoon race a race in which competitors have to carry an egg in a spoon as they run: usually young children take part
eg·ger, eg·gar (eg'ər) *n.* [? < EGG¹ + -ER] a European moth with a reddish-brown body covered in scales
egg·head (-hed') *n.* [Slang] an intellectual
egg·nog (-nog') *n.* [EGG¹ + NOG] a drink of beaten eggs, milk, sugar, and nutmeg, often with rum, brandy, etc.
egg·plant (-plänt') *n.* 1. a plant of the nightshade family, with a large, ovoid, usually purple-skinned fruit eaten as a vegetable 2. the fruit: also called **aubergine**
egg·shell (-shel') *n.* the shell of an egg; esp., the hard, brittle covering of a bird's egg —*adj.* fragile and thin, like an eggshell
eggshell china a very thin, translucent porcelain
egg·whisk (-wisk') *n.* a kitchen utensil for beating eggs, etc.: also **eggbeater**
eg·lan·tine (eg'lən tēn') *n.* [< Fr. < OFr. *aiglent* < L. *aculeus*, a sting, dim. of *acus*, a point] a European rose with hooked spines, sweet-scented leaves, and usually pink flowers
e·go (ē'gō, eg'ō) *n., pl.* **e'gos** [L., I] 1. the self; the individual as aware of himself 2. egotism; conceit 3. *Psychoanalysis* the part of the psyche resolving conflicts between the impulses of the id, the demands of the environment, and the standards of the superego
e·go·cen·tric (eg'ō sen'trik, ē'gō-) *adj.* self-centred —*n.* an egocentric person —**e·go·cen'tri·cal·ly** *adv.* —**e'-go·cen·tric'i·ty** (-tris'ə tē) *n.* —**e'go·cen'trism** *n.*
e·go·ism (eg'ō iz'm, ē'gō-) *n.* 1. the tendency to be self-centered 2. self-conceit; egotism 3. the doctrine that self-interest is the proper goal of all human actions: opposed to ALTRUISM —**e'go·ist** *n.* —**e'go·is'tic, e'go·is'-ti·cal** *adj.* —**e'go·is'ti·cal·ly** *adv.*
e·go·ma·ni·a (ē'gō mā'nē ə, -mān'yə) *n.* abnormally excessive egotism —**e'go·ma'ni·ac'** (-ak') *n.* —**e'go·ma·ni'-a·cal** (-mə ni'ə k'l) *adj.*
e·go·tism (eg'ə tiz'm, ē'gə-) *n.* 1. constant, excessive reference to oneself in speaking or writing 2. self-conceit 3. selfishness *Egotism* is generally considered a more opprobrious term than *egoism* —**e'go·tist** *n.* —**e'go·tis'tic, e'go·tis'ti·cal** *adj.* —**e'go·tis'ti·cal·ly** *adv.*
ego trip [Colloq.] an act, project, etc. undertaken to boost one's own image or devoted entirely to one's own interests or feelings
e·gre·gious (i grē'jəs, -jē əs) *adj.* [L. *egregius*, apart from the herd, outstanding < *e-*, out + *grex*, a herd] remarkably bad; flagrant [an *egregious* error] —**e·gre'gious·ly** *adv.* —**e·gre'gious·ness** *n.*
e·gress (ē'gres) *n.* [< L. pp. of *egredi* < *e-*, out + *gradi*, step, go] 1. a going out; emergence: also **e·gres·sion** (i gresh'ən) 2. the right to go out 3. a way out; exit
e·gret (ē'grit, eg'rit) *n.* [< OFr. *aigrette* < Pr. < *aigron*, a heron < Frank.] 1. *pl.* -**grets, -gret:** see PLURAL, II, D, 1 a heronlike wading bird, usually with long, white plumes 2. aigrette (sense I)
E·gyp·tian (i jip'shən, ē-) *adj.* of Egypt, its people, etc. —*n.* 1. a native or inhabitant of Egypt 2. the language of the ancient Egyptians
E·gyp·tol·o·gy (ē'jip tol'ə jē) *n.* the study of ancient Egyptian culture, language, architecture, etc. —**E'gyp·tol'-o·gist** *n.*

eh (ā, e, en) *interj.* a sound expressing: 1. surprise 2. doubt or inquiry
EHF extremely high frequency
ei·der (i'dər) *n.* [ult. < ON. gen. of *æthr*] *pl.* -**ders, -der:** see PLURAL, II, D, 1 a large sea duck of northern regions: often **eider duck**
ei·der·down (-doun') *n.* 1. the soft, fine breast feathers, or down, of the eider duck, used to stuff quilts, pillows, etc. 2. a quilt so stuffed
ei·det·ic (ī det'ik) *adj.* [< Gr. < *eidos*, what is seen] designating or of unusually vivid or lifelike mental images —*n.* a person who experiences such mental images —**ei·det'i·cal·ly** *adv.*
eight (āt) *adj.* [OE. *eahta*] totalling one more than seven —*n.* 1. the cardinal number between seven and nine; 8; VIII 2. anything having eight units or members, or numbered eight, or shaped like 8; specif., the crew of a racing rowing boat; —**have one over the eight** to be intoxicated
eight ball [U.S.] a black ball with the number eight on it, used in playing pool —**behind the eight ball** [U.S. Slang] in a very unfavourable position
eight·een (ā'tēn') *adj.* [OE. *eahtatiene*] eight more than ten —*n.* the cardinal number between seventeen and nineteen; 18; XVIII
eight·eenth (ā'tēnth') *adj.* 1. preceded by seventeen others in a series; 18th 2. designating any of the eighteen equal parts of something —*n.* 1. the one following the seventeenth 2. any of the eighteen equal parts of something; 1/18
eight·fold (āt'fōld') *adj.* [see -FOLD] 1. having eight parts 2. having eight times as much or as many —*adv.* eight times as much or as many
eighth (ātth, āth) *adj.* 1. preceded by seven others in a series; 8th 2. designating any of the eight equal parts of something —*n.* 1. the one following the seventh 2. any of the eight equal parts of something; 1/8 3. *Music* the interval of an octave —**eighth·ly** *adv.*
eighth note *Music* U.S. name for QUAVER
eight·i·eth (āt'ē ith) *adj.* 1. preceded by seventy-nine others in a series; 80th 2. designating any of the eighty equal parts of something —*n.* 1. the one following the seventy-ninth 2. any of the eighty equal parts of something; 1/80
eight·some (-səm) *n.* a Scottish reel for eight dancers: also **eightsome reel**
eight·y (āt'ē) *adj.* [OE. (*hund*)*eahtatig*] eight times ten —*n., pl.* **eight'ies** the cardinal number between seventy-nine and eighty-one; 80; LXXX —**the eighties** the numbers or years, as of a century, from eighty to eighty-nine
ei·kon (ī'kon) *n.* *same as* ICON
ein·stein·i·um (īn stī'nē əm) *n.* [after Albert *Einstein* (1879–1955), German-born chemist] a radioactive chemical element produced by irradiating plutonium with neutrons: symbol, Fs; at. wt., 252 (?); at. no., 99
eis·tedd·fod (ī stedh'vod) *n., pl.* -**fods;** Welsh **eis·tedd·fod·au** (ī'stedh vo'di) [W., a sitting < *eistedd*, to sit] a yearly meeting in Wales of poets, musicians, etc., at which prizes are given for compositions and performances: 19th-cent. revival of an old Welsh custom
ei·ther (ī'thər) [OE. *æghwæther* < *a* (*æ*), always (see AYE¹) + *gehwæther*, each of two (cf. WHETHER)] 1. one or the other (of two) [use *either* hand] 2. each (of two) [doors open at *either* end of the room] —*pron.* one or the other (of two) —*conj.* a correlative used with *or*, implying a choice of alternatives [*either* go or stay] —*adv.* 1. any more than the other; also (after negatives) [if he won't, she won't *either*] 2. [Colloq.] an intensifier in a negative statement ["It's his. It isn't *either!*"]
e·jac·u·late (i jak'yə lāt') *vt., vi.* -**lat'ed, -lat'ing** [< L. pp. of *ejaculari* < *e-*, out + *jaculari*, to throw < *jaculum*, a dart < *jacere*, to throw] 1. to eject or discharge (esp. semen) 2. to utter suddenly and vehemently; exclaim —**e·jac'u·la'tion** *n.* —**e·jac'u·la'tor** *n.* —**e·jac'u·la·to·ry**
e·ject (i jekt', ē-) *vt.* [< L. pp. of *ejicere* < *e-*, out + *jacere*, to throw] 1. to throw out; expel; discharge 2. to drive out; evict —**e·ject'a·ble** *adj.* —**e·jec'tion** *n.* —**e·jec'tive** *adj.* —**e·jec'tor** *n.*
ejection seat a seat, esp. as fitted in military aircraft, that ejects the occupant in an emergency: also **ejector seat**
eke¹ (ēk) *vt.* **eked, ek'ing** [OE. *eacan* & *eacian*] [Archaic] to increase —**eke out** 1. to supplement [to *eke out* one's income with a second job] 2. to make (a living) with difficulty 3. to use (a supply) frugally
eke² (ēk) *adv., conj.* [OE. *eac*] [Archaic] also
EKG electrocardiogram
e·lab·o·rate (i lab'ər it; *for v.* -ə rāt') *adj.* [< L. pp. of *elaborare* < *e-*, out + *laborare* < *labor*, LABOUR] 1. developed in great detail 2. complicated 3. painstaking —*vt.* -**rat'ed, -rat'ing** 1. to produce by effort 2. to work out in careful detail 3. to change (food or substances in the body) into compounds that can be assimilated, etc. —*vi.* to state something in detail or add more details (usually with

on or upon) **—e·lab′o·rate·ly** *adv.* **—e·lab′o·rate·ness** *n.* **—e·lab′o·ra′tion** *n.* **—e·lab′o·ra·tive** *adj.* **—e·lab′o·ra′tor** *n.*

é·lan (ā län′; *Fr.* -län′) *n.* [Fr. < *élancer*, to dart] spirited self-assurance; verve; dash

e·land (ē′lənd) *n., pl.* **e′land, e′lands:** see PLURAL, II, D, 2 [Afrik. < Du., elk] either of two large, oxlike African antelopes with spirally twisted horns

e·lapse (i laps′) *vi.* **e·lapsed′, e·laps′ing** [< L. pp. of *elabi* < *e-*, out + *labi*, to glide] to slip by; pass: said of time

e·las·mo·branch (i laz′mə braŋk′, -las′-) *adj.* [< ModL. < Gr. *elasmos*, beaten metal + L. *branchia*, gills] of a class of fishes with cartilaginous skeletons, horny scales, and no air bladders **—n.** any fish of this class, as the shark, ray, etc.

e·las·tic (i las′tik) *adj.* [< ModL. < LGr. *elastikos* < Gr. *elaunein*, to drive] **1.** having the property of immediately returning to its original size, shape, or position after being stretched, squeezed, etc.; springy **2.** able to recover easily from dejection, fatigue, etc.; buoyant **3.** readily adaptable to circumstances **—n.** an elastic fabric loosely woven with strands of rubber, etc. running through it **—e·las′ti·cal·ly** *adv.* **—e·las·tic·i·ty** (i las′tis′ə tē, ē′las-) *n., pl.* **-ties**

e·las·ti·cate (i las′tə kāt′) *vt.* **-cat′ed, -cat′ing** to make (a fabric or part of a garment) elastic by inserting elastic sections or thread **—e·las′ti·ca′tion** *n.*

elastic band *same as* RUBBER BAND

e·las·ti·cize (i las′tə sīz′) *vt.* **-cized′, -ciz′ing** *same as* ELASTICATE

e·las·to·mer (i las′tə mər) *n.* [< ELAST(IC) + (POLY)MER] a rubberlike synthetic polymer, as silicone rubber **—e·las′-to·mer′ic** (-mer′ik) *adj.*

e·late (i lāt′, ē-) *vt.* **-lat′ed, -lat′ing** [< L. *elatus*, pp. of *efferre* < *ex-*, out + *ferre*, to bear] to raise the spirits of; make very proud, happy, joyful, etc. **—e·lat′ed·ly** *adv.* **—e·lat′ed·ness** *n.*

e·la·tion (i lā′shən, ē-) *n.* high spirits

E layer a layer of the ionosphere at an altitude of about 95 kilometres that can reflect radio waves

el·bow (el′bō) *n.* [OE. *elboga*] **1.** the joint between the upper and lower arm; esp., the outer part of the angle made by a bent arm **2.** anything bent like an elbow, as a pipe fitting **—vt., vi. 1.** to shove or jostle with the elbow **2.** to push (one's way) thus **—bend** (or **lift**) **one's elbow** to drink alcoholic liquor, esp. to excess **—out at (the) elbows** shabby or poor

elbow grease [Colloq.] vigorous physical effort

el·bow·room (- room′, -room′) *n.* room enough to move or work in; sufficient space or scope

ELBOW
(sense 2)

eld (eld) *n.* [< OE. < base of *ald,* OLD] [Archaic] **1.** old age **2.** ancient times; days of yore

eld·er¹ (el′dər) *adj.* [OE. *eldra,* compar. < base of *ald,* OLD] **1.** born or brought forth earlier than another or others; senior; older **2.** of superior rank, validity, etc. **3.** earlier; former **—n. 1.** an older person, esp. one with authority in a tribe or community **2.** an ancestor **3.** an officer in an early Christian church **4.** in some Protestant churches *a)* clergyman or pastor *b)* a member of the ruling body **—eld′-er·ship′** *n.*

el·der² (el′dər) *n.* [OE. *ellern*] a shrub or tree with flat-topped clusters of small white flowers and red or purple berries

el·der·ber·ry (-bər ē, -ber′ē) *n., pl.* **-ries 1.** *same as* ELDER² **2.** its berry, or drupe, used in wines, etc.

elder brother one of the governing members of Trinity House

elder hand in certain card games for two people, the player who plays first

eld·er·ly (-lē) *adj.* somewhat old; approaching old age **—eld′er·li·ness** *n.*

eld·est (el′dist) *adj.* [OE. superl. of *ald,* old] oldest; esp., first-born or oldest surviving

El Do·ra·do, El·do·ra·do (el′də rä′dō) *pl.* **-dos** [Sp., the gilded] **1.** a legendary country in S. America, supposed to be rich in gold and jewels **2.** any place that is, or is supposed to be, rich in gold, opportunity, etc.

el·dritch (el′drich) *adj.* [Early ModE. *elrich,* prob. < ME. *elf,* elf] eerie; unearthly

elec., elect. 1. electric **2.** electrical **3.** electricity

e·lect (i lekt′) *adj.* [< L. pp. of *eligere* < *e-*, out + *legere,* to choose] **1.** chosen; given preference **2.** elected but not yet installed in office [the mayor-*elect*] **3.** *Theol.* chosen by God for salvation and eternal life **—vt. 1.** to select for some office by voting **2.** to choose; select **—vi.** to make a choice; choose **—the elect 1.** persons belonging to a specially privileged group **2.** *Theol.* those who are elect

e·lec·tion (i lek′shən) *n.* **1.** a choosing or choice **2.** a choosing or being chosen for office by vote **3.** *Theol.* the selection by God of certain people for salvation and eternal life

e·lec·tion·eer (i lek′shə nir′) *vi.* to canvass votes for a candidate, party, etc. in an election **—e·lec′tion·eer′er** *n.* **—e·lec′tion·eer′ing** *n.*

e·lec·tive (i lek′tiv) *adj.* **1.** *a)* filled by election [an *elective* office] *b)* chosen by election **2.** of or based on election **3.** having the power to choose **4.** that may be chosen but is not required; optional **—e·lec′tive·ly** *adv.*

e·lec·tor (-tər) *n.* **1.** one who elects; specif., a qualified voter **2.** [U.S.] *a* a member of the electoral college **3.** [*usually* E-] any of the German princes of the Holy Roman Empire who took part in the election of the emperor **—e·lec′tor·al** *adj.*

electoral college [U.S.] an assembly elected by the voters to perform the formal duty of electing the president and the vicepresident of the United States

e·lec·tor·ate (-tər it) *n.* all those qualified to vote in an election

e·lec·tric (i lek′trik) *adj.* [ModL. *electricus,* orig., produced from amber by rubbing < ML. < L. *electrum,* amber < Gr. *ēlektron*] **1.** of, charged with, or conducting electricity [an *electric* wire] **2.** producing, or produced by, electricity [an *electric* generator] **3.** operated by electricity [an *electric* iron] **4.** very tense or exciting; electrifying **—n. 1.** a train, car, etc. operated by electricity **2.** [*pl.*] electrical equipment, esp. the electrical wiring of a house, office, etc.

e·lec·tri·cal (-tri k'l) *adj.* **1.** *same as* ·ELECTRIC **2.** connected with the science or use of electricity [an *electrical* engineer] **—e·lec′tri·cal·ly** *adv.*

electric blanket a blanket containing an element that is heated electrically

electric chair 1. a chair used in electrocuting persons sentenced to death **2.** the death sentence by electrocution

electric eel a large, eel-shaped fish of N S. America, with special organs that can give electric shocks

electric eye *same as* PHOTOELECTRIC CELL

electric fence a wire fence through which an electric current is run: used to control cattle, etc.

electric field a region at every point within which there is a force on an electric charge

electric fire a domestic appliance that supplies heat by means of an electrically operated metal coil

electric guitar a guitar whose tones are transmitted to an amplifier and loudspeaker through an electrical pickup attached to the instrument

e·lec·tri·cian (i lek′trish′ən, ē′lek-) *n.* a person whose work is the construction, repair, or installation of electric apparatus

e·lec·tric·i·ty (-tris′ə tē) *n.* **1.** a property of certain fundamental particles of all matter, as electrons (negative charges) and protons or positrons (positive charges) that have a force field associated with them and that can be separated by the expenditure of energy: electrical charge can be generated by friction, induction, or chemical change **2.** *a)* an electric current: see CURRENT (*n.* 3) *b)* an electric charge: see CHARGE (*n.* 2) **3.** the branch of physics dealing with electricity **4.** electric current used for lighting, heating, etc. **5.** strong emotional tension, excitement, etc.

electric needle a slender, pointed electrode used in surgery to cut and cauterize tissue, etc.

electric ray a cartilaginous fish with electric organs that can stun enemies or prey

e·lec·tri·fy (i lek′trə fī′) *vt.* **-fied′, -fy′ing 1.** to charge with electricity **2.** to give an electric shock to **3.** to give a shock of excitement to; thrill **4.** to equip for the use of electricity; provide with electric power **—e·lec′tri·fi′a·ble** *adj.* **—e·lec′-tri·fi·ca′tion** *n.* **—e·lec′tri·fi′er** *n.*

e·lec·tro (i lek′trō) *n., pl.* **-tros** *short for:* **1.** ELECTROTYPE **2.** ELECTROPLATE

e·lec·tro- a combining form meaning: **1.** electric [*electromagnet*] **2.** electrically [*electrocute*] **3.** electricity [*electrostatics*]

e·lec·tro·car·di·o·gram (i lek′trō kär′dē ə gram′) *n.* a tracing showing the changes in electric potential produced by contractions of the heart

e·lec·tro·car·di·o·graph (-kär′dē ə graf′) *n.* an instrument for making an electrocardiogram **—e·lec′tro·car′di·o·graph′-ic** *adj.* **—e·lec′tro·car′di·og′ra·phy** (-og′rə fē) *n.*

e·lec·tro·chem·is·try (-kem′is trē) *n.* the science dealing with the use of electrical energy to bring about a chemical reaction or with the generation of electrical energy by chemical action **—e·lec′tro·chem′i·cal** *adj.* **—e·lec′tro·chem′-i·cal·ly** *adv.*

e·lec·tro·con·vul·sive therapy (-kən vul′siv) *see* SHOCK THERAPY

e·lec·tro·cute (i lek′trə kyo͞ot′) *vt.* **-cut′ed, -cut′ing** [ELECTRO- + (EXE)CUTE] to kill with a charge of electricity; specif., to execute in the electric chair **—e·lec′tro·cu′tion** *n.*

e·lec·trode (i lek′trōd) *n.* [ELECTR(O-) + -ODE] any terminal that conducts an electric current into or away from various conducting substances in a circuit, as the anode or cathode in a battery, or that emits, collects, or controls the flow of electrons in an electron tube, as the cathode, plate, or grid

e·lec·tro·dy·nam·ics (i lek′trō dī nam′iks) *n.pl.* [*with sing.*

v.] the branch of physics dealing with the phenomena of electric currents and associated magnetic forces —**e·lec'-tro·dy·nam'ic** *adj.* —**e·lec'tro·dy·nam'i·cal·ly** *adv.*

e·lec·tro·en·ceph·a·lo·gram (-en sef'ə lə gram') *n.* a tracing showing the changes in electric potential produced by the brain

e·lec·tro·en·ceph·a·lo·graph (-en sef'ə lə graf') *n.* an instrument for making electroencephalograms —**e·lec'tro·en·ceph'a·lo·graph'ic** *adj.* —**e·lec'tro·en·ceph'a·log'ra·phy** (-ə log'rə fē) *n.*

e·lec·trol·y·sis (i lek'trol'ə sis) *n.* [ELECTRO- + -LYSIS] 1. the decomposition of an electrolyte by the action of an electric current passing through it 2. the removal of unwanted hair from the body by destroying the hair roots with an electrified needle

e·lec·tro·lyte (i lek'trə līt') *n.* [ELECTRO- + -LYTE] any substance which in solution can conduct an electric current by the movement of its dissociated positive and negative ions to the electrodes of opposite charge, where the ions are deposited as a coating, liberated as a gas, etc. —**e·lec'-tro·lyt'ic** (-lit'ik) *adj.* —**e·lec'tro·lyt'i·cal·ly** *adv.*

e·lec·tro·lyze (i lek'trə līz') *vt.* -lyzed', -lyz'ing to subject to electrolysis

e·lec·tro·mag·net (i lek'trō mag'nit) *n.* a soft iron core surrounded by a coil of wire, that temporarily becomes a magnet when an electric current flows through the wire

e·lec·tro·mag·net·ic (-mag net'ik) *adj.* of, produced by, or having to do with electromagnetism or an electromagnet —**e·lec'tro·mag·net'i·cal·ly** *adv.*

electromagnetic radiation the radiation formed by an electric and a magnetic field which can be conceived of as waves (**electromagnetic waves**) or particles (**photons**)

electromagnetic unit one of a former cgs system of measurements in which the magnetic constant is a unit

e·lec·tro·mag·net·ism (-mag'nə tiz'm) *n.* 1. magnetism produced by an electric current 2. the branch of physics dealing with the relations between electricity and magnetism

e·lec·trom·e·ter (i lek'trom'ə tər, ē'lek-) *n.* a device for detecting or measuring differences of potential by means of electrostatic or mechanical forces

e·lec·tro·mo·tive (i lek'trə mōt'iv) *adj.* 1. producing an electric current through differences in potential 2. relating to electromotive force

electromotive force the force that causes or tends to cause a current to flow in a circuit, equivalent to the potential difference between the terminals and commonly measured in volts

e·lec·tron (i lek'tron) *n.* [arbitrary coinage < ELECTR(IC) + -ON] any of the negatively charged particles that form a part of all atoms: the number of electrons circulating around a nucleus is equal to the number of positive charges on the nucleus

e·lec·tro·neg·a·tive (i lek'trō neg'ə tiv) *adj.* 1. having a negative electrical charge; tending to move to the positive electrode, or anode, in electrolysis 2. able to attract electrons, esp. in forming a chemical bond

e·lec·tron·ic (i lek'tron'ik, ē'lek-) *adj.* 1. of electrons 2. operating, produced, or done by the action of electrons or by devices dependent on such action —**e·lec'tron'i·cal·ly** *adv.*

electronic brain [Colloq.] an electronic computer

electronic data processing data processing by means of electronic equipment, esp. computers

electronic music music in which the sounds are originated or altered by electronic devices, and arranged and recorded on tape for presentation

electronic organ a musical instrument with a console like that of a pipe organ, but producing tones by means of electronic devices instead of pipes

e·lec·tron·ics (-iks) *n.pl.* [with sing. v.] the science that deals with the behaviour and control of electrons in vacuums and gases, and with the use of electron tubes, transistors, etc.

electron microscope an instrument for focusing a beam of electrons, using electric or magnetic fields, to form an enlarged image of an object on a fluorescent screen or photographic plate: it is much more powerful than any optical microscope

electron tube a sealed glass or metal tube completely evacuated or filled with gas at low pressure and having two or more electrodes, used to control the flow of electrons

e·lec·tron-volt (-vōlt') *n.* a unit of energy equal to that attained by an electron falling unimpeded through a potential difference of one volt

e·lec·tro·pho·re·sis (i lek'trō fə rē'sis) *n.* [ModL. < ELECTRO- + Gr. *phorēsis* < *pherein*, BEAR[1]] the migration of colloidal particles in an electric field —**e·lec'tro·pho·ret'ic** (-fə ret'ik) *adj.*

e·lec·troph·o·rus (i lek'trof'ər əs) *n.*, *pl.* -ri' (-ī') [ModL. < ELECTRO- + Gr. -*phoros* < *pherein*, BEAR[1]] an apparatus consisting of a resin disc and a metal plate, for generating static electricity by induction

e·lec·tro·plate (i lek'trə plāt') *vt.* -plat'ed, -plat'ing to

deposit a coating of metal on by electrolysis —*n.* anything so plated

e·lec·tro·pos·i·tive (i lek'trə poz'ə tiv) *adj.* 1. having a positive electrical charge; tending to move to the negative electrode, or cathode, in electrolysis 2. able to give up electrons, esp. in forming a chemical bond

e·lec·tro·scope (i lek'trə skōp') *n.* [ELECTRO- + -SCOPE] an instrument for detecting very small charges of electricity, as by the divergence of electrically charged strips of gold leaf —**e·lec'tro·scop'ic** (-skōp'ik) *adj.*

e·lec·tro·shock therapy (-shok') see SHOCK THERAPY

e·lec·tro·stat·ics (i lek'trə stat'iks) *n.pl.* [with sing. v.] the branch of physics dealing with the phenomena accompanying electric charges at rest, or static electricity —**e·lec'tro·stat'ic** *adj.* —**e·lec'tro·stat'i·cal·ly** *adv.*

ELECTROSCOPE

electrostatic unit one of a former cgs system of measurements in which the dieletric constant of a vacuum is a unit

e·lec·tro·ther·a·py (-thər'ə pē) *n.* the treatment of disease by means of electricity, as by diathermy —**e·lec'tro·ther'-a·pist** *n.*

e·lec·tro·type (i lek'trə tīp') *n.* Printing 1. a facsimile plate made by electroplating a wax or plastic impression of the surface to be reproduced 2. a print made from such a plate 3. same as ELECTROTYPY —*vt., vi.* -typed', -typ'ing to make an electrotype or electrotypes (of) —**e·lec'tro·typ'-er** *n.*

e·lec·tro·typ·y (-tīp'ē) *n.* the process of making electrotypes

e·lec·trum (i lek'trəm) *n.* [L. < Gr. *ēlektron*: see ELECTRIC] a light-yellow alloy of gold and silver

e·lec·tu·ar·y (i lek'tyōo wər ē) *n.*, *pl.* -ar·ies [< LL. < Gr. < *ek*-, out + *leichein*, to lick] a medicine mixed with honey or syrup to form a paste

el·ee·mos·y·nar·y (el'i mos'ə nər ē, el'ē ə-) *adj.* [< ML. < LL. < Gr. *eleēmosynē*, pity (in NT., alms) < *eleos*, mercy] 1. of or for charity; charitable 2. supported by or dependent on charity 3. given as charity; free

el·e·gance (el'ə gəns) *n.* 1. the quality of being elegant; specif., *a)* dignified richness and grace *b)* polished fastidiousness or refined grace 2. anything elegant Also, esp. for sense 2, **el'e·gan·cy**, *pl.* -cies

el·e·gant (-gənt) *adj.* [< Fr. < L. *elegans* < *e*-, out + hyp. *legare*, var. of *legere*, to choose] 1. characterized by dignified richness and grace, as of design, dress, style, etc.; tastefully luxurious 2. impressively fastidious or refined in manners and tastes 3. cleverly simple; ingenious 4. [Colloq.] excellent; fine —**el'e·gant·ly** *adv.*

el·e·gi·ac (el'ə jī'ak) *adj.* 1. Gr. & Rom. Prosody of or composed in dactylic hexameter couplets, the second line having only an accented syllable in the third and sixth feet: the form was used for elegies, etc. 2. of, like, or fit for an elegy 3. sad; mournful Also **el'e·gi'a·cal** —*n.* 1. an elegiac couplet 2. [pl.] a poem or poems written in such couplets

el·e·gize (el'ə jīz') *vi.* -gized', -giz'ing to write elegies —*vt.* to lament as in an elegy

el·e·gy (-jē) *n.*, *pl.* -gies [< Fr. < L. < Gr. *elegeia* < *elegos*, a lament] 1. a poem or song of lament and praise for the dead 2. any poem in elegiac verse 3. a poem, song, etc. in a mournfully contemplative tone —**el'e·gist** *n.*

elem. 1. element(s) 2. elementary

el·e·ment (el'ə mənt) *n.* [OFr. < L. *elementum*] 1. any of the four substances —earth, air, fire, water —formerly believed to constitute all physical matter 2. the natural or suitable environment, situation, etc. for a person or thing 3. *a)* a component part or quality, often one that is basic or essential *b)* a constituent group of a specified kind [the criminal *element*] 4. Chem. any substance that cannot be separated into different substances by ordinary chemical methods: all matter is composed of such substances 5. [pl.] Eccles. the bread and wine of Communion 6. Elec. the wire coil, etc. that becomes glowing hot, as in an electric oven —in one's element in the surroundings most pleasing and natural for one —the elements 1. the first or basic principles; rudiments 2. wind, rain, etc.; forces of the atmosphere See table of CHEMICAL ELEMENTS on next page

el·e·men·tal (el'ə men't'l) *adj.* 1. of the four elements (sense 1) 2. of or like the forces of nature 3. basic and powerful; primal [hunger is an *elemental* drive] 4. same as ELEMENTARY (sense 2 a) 5. being an essential part or parts 6. being a chemical element in uncombined form —*n.* a basic principle: usually used in pl. —**el'e·men'tal·ism** *n.* —**el'e·men'tal·ly** *adv.*

el·e·men·ta·ry (-tər ē, -trē) *adj.* 1. same as ELEMENTAL 2. *a)* of first principles or fundamentals; introductory; basic *b)* of or having to do with the formal instruction of children in

CHEMICAL ELEMENTS

With International Atomic Weights. Carbon at 12 is the standard.

	Symbol	Atomic Number	Atomic Weight		Symbol	Atomic Number	Atomic Weight
actinium	Ac	89	227(?)	mercury	Hg	80	200.59
aluminium	Al	13	26.9815	molybdenum	Mo	42	95.94
americium	Am	95	243.13	neodymium	Nd	60	144.24
antimony	Sb	51	121.75	neon	Ne	10	20.183
argon	Ar	18	39.948	neptunium	Np	93	237.00
arsenic	As	33	74.9216	nickel	Ni	28	58.71
astatine	At	85	210(?)	niobium	Nb	41	92.906
barium	Ba	56	137.34	nitrogen	N	7	14.0067
berkelium	Bk	97	248(?)	nobelium	No	102	255(?)
beryllium	Be	4	9.0122	osmium	Os	76	190.2
bismuth	Bi	83	208.980	oxygen	O	8	15.9994
boron	B	5	10.811	palladium	Pd	46	106.4
bromine	Br	35	79.909	phosphorus	P	15	30.9738
cadmium	Cd	48	112.40	platinum	Pt	78	195.09
calcium	Ca	20	40.08	plutonium	Pu	94	239.05
californium	Cf	98	251(?)	polonium	Po	84	210.05
carbon	C	6	12.01115	potassium	K	19	39.102
cerium	Ce	58	140.12	praseodymium	Pr	59	140.907
caesium	Cs	55	132.905	promethium	Pm	61	145(?)
chlorine	Cl	17	35.453	protactinium	Pa	91	231.10
chromium	Cr	24	51.996	radium	Ra	88	226.00
cobalt	Co	27	58.9332	radon	Rn	86	222.00
copper	Cu	29	63.546	rhenium	Re	75	186.2
curium	Cm	96	247(?)	rhodium	Rh	45	102.905
dysprosium	Dy	66	162.50	rubidium	Rb	37	85.47
einsteinium	Es	99	252(?)	ruthenium	Ru	44	101.07
erbium	Er	68	167.28	samarium	Sm	62	150.35
europium	Eu	63	151.96	scandium	Sc	21	44.956
fermium	Fm	100	257(?)	selenium	Se	34	78.96
fluorine	F	9	18.9984	silicon	Si	14	28.086
francium	Fr	87	223(?)	silver	Ag	47	107.868
gadolinium	Gd	64	157.25	sodium	Na	11	22.9898
gallium	Ga	31	69.72	strontium	Sr	38	87.62
germanium	Ge	32	72.59	sulphur	S	16	32.064
gold	Au	79	196.967	tantalum	Ta	73	180.948
hafnium	Hf	72	178.49	technetium	Tc	43	97(?)
helium	He	2	4.0026	tellurium	Te	52	127.60
holmium	Ho	67	164.930	terbium	Tb	65	158.924
hydrogen	H	1	1.00797	thallium	Tl	81	204.37
indium	In	49	114.82	thorium	Th	90	232.038
iodine	I	53	126.9044	thulium	Tm	69	168.934
iridium	Ir	77	192.2	tin	Sn	50	118.69
iron	Fe	26	55.847	titanium	Ti	22	47.90
krypton	Kr	36	83.80	tungsten	W	74	183.85
lanthanum	La	57	138.91	uranium	U	92	238.03
lawrencium	Lr	103	256(?)	vanadium	V	23	50.942
lead	Pb	82	207.19	xenon	Xe	54	131.30
lithium	Li	3	6.939	ytterbium	Yb	70	173.04
lutetium	Lu	71	174.97	yttrium	Y	39	88.905
magnesium	Mg	12	24.312	zinc	Zn	30	65.37
manganese	Mn	25	54.9380	zirconium	Zr	40	91.22
mendelevium	Md	101	258(?)				

basic subjects —el′e·men′ta·ri·ly **adv.** —el′e·men′-ta·ri·ness **n.**

elementary particle a subatomic particle that is capable of independent existence, as a neutron, proton, etc.

elementary school *same as* PRIMARY SCHOOL

el·e·phant (el′ə fənt) **n.**, *pl.* **-phants,** **-phant**: see PLURAL, II, D, 1 [< L. < Gr. *elephas* (gen. *elephantos*), elephant, ivory] a huge, thick-skinned mammal, the largest of extant four-footed animals, with a long, flexible snout (called a *trunk*) and, usually, two ivory tusks: the **African elephant** has a flatter head and larger ears than the **Asian** (or **Indian**) **elephant**

el·e·phan·ti·a·sis (el′ə fən tī′ə sis) **n.** a chronic disease of the skin characterized by the enlargement of the legs or other parts, and by the hardening of the skin: it is caused by obstruction of the lymphatic vessels, esp. by filarial worms

ELEPHANTS
(shoulder height:
African, 3-4 m;
Indian, 2.5 -3 m)

el·e·phan·tine (el′ə fan′tīn) **adj.** 1. of an elephant or elephants 2. like an elephant in size or gait; huge, heavy, slow, clumsy, etc.

elephant seal *same as* SEA ELEPHANT

El·eu·sin·i·an (el′yoo sin′ē ən) **adj.** [after *Eleusis*, ancient Gr. city near Athens, where celebrated] of the secret religious rites (**Eleusinian mysteries**) anciently celebrated in honour of Demeter and Persephone

elev. elevation

el·e·vate (el′ə vāt′) **vt.** **-vat′ed, -vat′ing** [< L. pp. of *elevare* < e-, out + *levare*, to lift < *levis*, light] 1. to lift up; raise 2. to raise in rank or position 3. to raise to a higher intellectual or moral level 4. to raise the spirits of; elate; exhilarate

el·e·vat·ed (-vāt′id) **adj.** 1. lifted up; raised; high 2. exalted; dignified; lofty 3. high-spirited; exhilarated 4. [Colloq.] slightly drunk

el·e·va·tion (el′ə vā′shən) **n.** 1. an elevating or being elevated 2. a high place or position 3. height above the surface of the earth 4. dignity; loftiness 5. a flat scale drawing of the front, rear, or side of a building, etc. 6. a ballet dancer's ability to leap high 7. *Astron.* altitude 8. *Geog.* height above sea level 9. *Mil.* the angle of a gun with the horizontal

el·e·va·tor (el′ə vāt′ər) **n.** 1. a person or thing that raises or lifts up 2. [U.S.] a lift (sense 10b) 3. a machine, usually consisting of buckets or scoops fastened to an endless belt, for hoisting grain etc. 4. [Chiefly U.S.] a warehouse for storing, hoisting, and discharging grain 5. a movable aerofoil like a horizontal rudder, for making an aircraft go up or down

e·lev·en (i lev′ən) **adj.** [OE. *endleofan*, lit., one left over (ten)] totalling one more than ten —**n.** 1. the cardinal number between ten and twelve; 11; XI 2. a football or cricket team

e·lev·en-plus (-plus′) **n.** an examination used, esp. formerly, to determine the form of secondary education: taken by children about eleven years old

e·lev·en·ses (-ən ziz) **n.pl.** [Colloq.] a light snack, usually with tea or coffee, taken in the middle of the morning

e·lev·enth (-ənth) **adj.** 1. preceded by ten others in a series; 11th 2. designating any of the eleven equal parts of something —**n.** 1. the one following the tenth 2. any of the eleven equal parts of something; 1/11 —**at the eleventh hour** at the last possible time

elf (elf) **n.**, *pl.* **elves** (elvz) [OE. *ælf*] 1. *Folklore* a tiny, often prankish fairy 2. a mischievous, small child or being —**elf′ish adj.** —**elf′ish·ly adv.** —**elf′ish·ness n.** —**elf′-like′ adj.**

elf·in (el′fin) **adj.** of, appropriate to, or like an elf; fairylike —**n.** an elf

elf·lock (elf′lok′) **n.** a tangled, matted lock of hair

e·lic·it (i lis′it) **vt.** [< L. pp. of *elicere* < e-, out + *lacere*, to entice] 1. to draw forth; evoke [to elicit a reply] 2. to cause to be revealed; draw out [to elicit facts] —**e·lic′i·ta′-tion n.** —**e·lic′i·tor n.**

e·lide (i līd′) **vt.** **e·lid′ed, e·lid′ing** [< L. *elidere* < e-, out + *laedere*, to strike] 1. to leave out; suppress; omit 2. to leave out or slur over (a vowel, syllable, etc.) in pronunciation —**e·lid′i·ble adj.**

el·i·gi·ble (el′i jə b'l) **adj.** [< ML. < L. *eligere*: see ELECT] 1. fit to be chosen; qualified 2. desirable, esp. for marriage —**n.** an eligible person —**el′i·gi·bil′i·ty n.** —**el′i·gi·bly adv.**

e·lim·i·nate (i lim′ə nāt′) **vt.** **-nat′ed, -nat′ing** [< L. pp. of

eliminare < e-, out + *limen*, threshold] 1. to take out; get rid of 2. to leave out of consideration; reject; omit 3. to drop (a person, team, etc. losing a round or match) from further competition 4. *Algebra* to get rid of (an unknown quantity) by combining equations 5. *Physiol.* to excrete —**e·lim′i·na′tion n.** —**e·lim′i·na′tive adj.** —**e·lim′i·na′tor n.** —**e·lim′i·na·to·ry adj.**

e·li·sion (i lizh′ən) **n.** 1. the eliding of a vowel, syllable, etc. in pronunciation (Ex.: it's, they'd, we've) 2. any leaving out of parts

é·lite (i lēt′, ā-) **n.** [< Fr., ult. < L. *eligere*: see ELECT] 1. [*also used with pl. v.*] the group or part of a group selected or regarded as the finest, best, most powerful, etc. 2. a size of type for typewriters, measuring 12 characters to the inch —**adj.** of, forming, or for an elite

é·lit·ism (-iz′m) **n.** government or control by an elite, or advocacy of such control —**e·lit′ist adj., n.**

e·lix·ir (i lik′sər) **n.** [< ML. < Ar. *al-iksīr*, prob. < Gr. *xērion*, powder for drying wounds < *xēros*, dry] 1. a hypothetical substance sought for by medieval alchemists to change base metals into gold or (in full, **elixir of life**) to prolong life indefinitely 2. [Rare] the quintessence 3. a cure-all 4. a medicine made of drugs in alcoholic solution, usually sweetened

Eliz. 1. Elizabeth 2. Elizabethan

E·liz·a·be·than (i liz′ə bē′thən, -beth′ən) **adj.** of or characteristic of the reign of Elizabeth I or Elizabeth II —**n.** an English person, esp. a writer, of the time of Queen Elizabeth I or Queen Elizabeth II

Elizabethan sonnet *same as* SHAKESPEAREAN SONNET

elk (elk) **n.**, *pl.* **elk, elks**: see PLURAL, II, D, 2 [OE. *eolh*] 1. a large, mooselike deer of N Europe and Asia, with broad antlers 2. [U.S.] *same as* WAPITI

ell (el) **n.** [OE. *eln*] a former English measure of length, mainly for cloth, equal to 115 cm.

el·lipse (i lips′, ə-) **n.**, *pl.* **-lip′ses** (-lip′siz) [< ModL. < Gr. < *elleipein*, to fall short (of a perfect circle)] *Geom.* the path of a point that moves so that the sum of its distances from two fixed points (called *foci*) is constant

el·lip·sis (i lip′sis, ə-) **n.**, *pl.* **-ses** (-sēz) [see prec.] 1. *Gram.* the omission of a word or words necessary for complete grammatical construction but understood in the context (Ex.: "if possible" for "if it is possible") 2. *Writing & Printing* a) a mark (. . . or formerly · · ·) indicating an intentional omission of words or letters, a lapse of time, etc. b) the use of such marks

ELLIPSE

el·lip·soid (-soid) **n.** *Geom.* a solid whose plane sections are all ellipses or circles —**adj.** shaped like an ellipsoid: also **el·lip′soi′dal**

el·lip·ti·cal (i lip′ti k'l, ə-) **adj.** 1. of, or having the form of, an ellipse 2. of or characterized by ellipsis; with a word or words omitted Also **el·lip′tic** —**el·lip′ti·cal·ly adv.**

elm (elm) **n.** [OE.] 1. a tall, hardy shade tree growing largely in the North Temperate Zone 2. the hard, heavy wood of this tree

el·o·cu·tion (el′ə kyoo′shən) **n.** [< L. < pp. of *eloqui*: see ELOQUENT] 1. style or manner of speaking or reading in public 2. the art of public speaking or declaiming —**el′o·cu′tion·ar·y adj.** —**el′o·cu′tion·ist n.**

E·lo·hist (e lō′hist) **n.** the unknown author of those parts of the Pentateuch which use the word Elohim for God

e·lon·gate (ē′lon gāt) **vt., vi.** **-gat·ed, -gat·ing** [< LL. pp. of *elongare*, to prolong < L. e-, out + *longus*, long] to make or become longer; stretch —**adj.** 1. lengthened; stretched 2. *Bot.* long and narrow —**e·lon·ga·tion** (ē lon′gā′shən, i′lon-) **n.**

e·lope (i lōp′, ə-) **vi.** **e·loped′, e·lop′ing** [Anglo-Fr. *aloper*, prob. < ME. < OE. < a-, away + *hleapan*, to run] 1. to run away secretly, esp. in order to get married 2. to run away; escape —**e·lope′ment n.** —**e·lop′er n.**

el·o·quence (el′ə kwəns) **n.** 1. speech or writing that is forceful, fluent, etc. 2. the art or manner of such speech or writing 3. persuasive power

el·o·quent (-kwənt) **adj.** [OFr. < L. prp. of *eloqui* < e-, out + *loqui*, to speak] 1. having, or characterized by, eloquence 2. vividly expressive —**el′o·quent·ly adv.**

El·san (el′san) a trademark for a type of chemical lavatory, used esp. at temporary campsites

else (els) **adj.** [OE. *elles*, adv. gen. of n. base *el-*, other] 1. different; other [somebody else] 2. in addition; more [is there anything else?] —**adv.** 1. in a different or additional time, place, or manner; otherwise [where else can I go?] 2. if not [study, (or) else you will fail]

else·where (-wer′, -hwer′) **adv.** in or to some other place; somewhere else

e·lu·ci·date (i loo′sə dāt′, ə-) **vt., vi.** **-dat′ed, -dat′ing** [< LL. pp. of *elucidare* < L. e-, out + *lucidus*, clear < *lux*, light] to make clear (esp. something abstruse); explain **—e·lu'-ci·da'tion** *n.* **—e·lu'ci·da'tive** *adj.* **—e·lu'ci·da'tor** *n.* **—e·lu'-ci·da·to·ry** *adj.*

e·lude (i lōōd') *vt.* **e·lud'ed, e·lud'ing** [< L. *eludere* < *e-*, out + *ludere*, to play] **1.** to avoid or escape from by quickness, cunning, etc.; evade **2.** to escape detection, notice, or understanding by **3.** to slip away from; escape [his name *eludes* me] **—e·lud'er** *n.* **—e·lu·sion** (i lōō'zhən, ə-) *n.*

e·lu·ent (i lōō'ənt) *n.* *Chem.* a fluid used for elution: also **e·lu'ant**

e·lu·sive (i lōō'siv) *adj.* **1.** tending to elude **2.** hard to grasp or retain mentally; baffling Also **e·lu'so·ry** (-sə rē) **—e·lu'-sive·ly** *adv.* **—e·lu'sive·ness** *n.*

e·lute (i lōōt') *vt.* **e·lut'ed, e·lut'ing** [< L. *elutus*, pp. of *eluere*, to wash out] *Chem.* to remove (absorbed material) by use of a solvent **—e·lu'tion** *n.*

el·ver (el'vər) *n.* [for *eelfare*, migration of eels] a young eel

elves (elvz) *n.* *pl. of* ELF

elv·ish (el'vish) *adj.* of or like an elf **—elv'ish·ly** *adv.*

E·ly·si·um (i liz'ē əm) *n.* [L < Gr.] any place or condition of ideal bliss or complete happiness: after the dwelling place of virtuous people after death in Greek mythology: also **Elysian Fields —E·ly·sian** (i liz'ē ən) *adj.*

em (em) *n.* **1.** the letter M, m **2.** *Printing* a square of any type body, used as a unit of measure, as of column width; esp., 12-point em, about 1/6 of an inch

'em (əm, 'm) *pron.* [Colloq.] them

e·ma·ci·ate (i mā'shē āt', -sē-) *vt.* **-at'ed, -at'ing** [< L. pp. of *emaciare* < *e-*, out + *macies*, leanness < *macer*, lean] to cause to become abnormally lean; cause to lose much flesh or weight, as by starvation or disease **—e·ma'ci·a'tion** *n.*

em·a·nate (em'ə nāt') *vi.* **-nat'ed, -nat'ing** [< L. pp. of *emanare* < *e-*, out + *manare*, to flow] to come forth; issue, as from a source **—vt.** [Rare] to send forth; emit

em·a·na·tion (em'ə nā'shən) *n.* **1.** an emanating **2.** something that comes forth from a source **3.** *Chem.* a) *same as* RADON b) a gas given off by several radioactive substances **—em'a·na'tive** *adj.*

e·man·ci·pate (i man'sə pāt') *vt.* **-pat'ed, -pat'ing** [< L. pp. of *emancipare* < *e-*, out + *mancipare*, to deliver up as property, ult. < *manus*, the hand + *capere*, to take] **1.** to set free (a slave, etc.); release from bondage or serfdom **2.** to free from restraint or influence **3.** to free from restriction, esp. to remove social or legal disadvantages from **—e·man'ci·pa'tion** *n.* **—e·man'ci·pa'tion·ist** *n.* **—e·man'ci·pa'tive, e·man'ci·pa·to·ry** (-pə tər ē) *adj.* **—e·man'ci·pa'tor** *n.*

e·man·ci·pist (-sə pist') *n.* *Aust. History* a transported convict who had completed his sentence

e·mas·cu·late (i mas'kyə lāt';for adj : lit) *vt.* **-lat'ed, -lat'ing** [< L. pp. of *emasculare* < *e-*, out + *masculus*, MASCULINE] **1.** to deprive (a male) of the power to reproduce, as by removing the testicles; castrate **2.** to destroy the strength or force of; weaken **—adj.** deprived of virility, strength, or vigour **—e·mas'cu·la'tive, e·mas'-cu·la·to·ry** (-lə tər ē) *adj.* **—e·mas'cu·la'tor** *n.*

em·balm (im bäm') *vt.* [< OFr. *embaumer*: see EN- & BALM] **1.** to treat (a dead body) with various chemicals to keep it from decaying rapidly **2.** to preserve in memory **3.** to make fragrant; perfume **—em·balm'er** *n.* **—em·balm'ment** *n.*

em·bank (im baŋk') *vt.* to protect, support, or enclose with a bank of earth, rubble, etc.

em·bank·ment (-mənt) *n.* **1.** the act or process of embanking **2.** a bank of earth, rubble, etc. used to keep back water, hold up a road, railway, etc.

em·bar·go (im bär'gō) *n., pl.* **-goes** [Sp., ult. < L. *in-*, in, on + ML. *barra*, BAR[1]] **1.** a government order prohibiting the entry or departure of commercial ships at its ports **2.** any restriction, restraint, or prohibition, esp. one imposed on commerce by law **—vt.** **-goed, -go·ing** to put an embargo on

em·bark (im bärk') *vt.* [<Fr. < Sp. or OPr. < *em-* (L. *in-*) + L. *barca*, BARK[3]] to put or take (passengers or goods) aboard a ship, aeroplane, etc. **—vi.** **1.** to go aboard a ship, aeroplane, etc. **2.** to begin a journey **3.** to get started in an enterprise **—em·bar·ka·tion** (em'bär kā'shən), **em·bark'-ment** *n.*

em·bar·rass (im bar'əs) *vt.* [< Fr. < Sp. < It. < *imbarrare*, to impede < *in-* (L. *in-*) + *barra*, BAR[1]] **1.** to cause to feel self-conscious; disconcert **2.** to cause difficulties to; hinder **3.** to cause to be in debt; cause financial difficulties to **4.** to complicate; perplex **—em·bar'rass·ing** *adj.* **—em·bar'-rass·ing·ly** *adv.* **—em·bar'rass·ment** *n.*

em·bas·sy (em'bə sē) *n., pl.* **-sies** [< MFr. < OIt. < Pr. < hyp. *ambaissa*: see AMBASSADOR] **1.** the position or functions of an ambassador **2.** the official residence or offices of an ambassador **3.** an ambassador and his staff **4.** a person or group sent on an official mission to a foreign government **5.** any important or official mission

em·bat·tle[1] (im bat''l) *vt.* **-tled, -tling** to provide with battlements; build battlements on

em·bat·tle[2] (im bat''l) *vt.* **-tled, -tling** to prepare or set in line for battle

em·bay (im bā') *vt.* to shut in; enclose or surround, as in a bay **—em·bay'ment** *n.*

em·bed (im bed') *vt.* **-bed'ded, -bed'ding** **1.** to set or fix firmly in a surrounding mass [to *embed* tiles in cement] **2.** to fix in the mind, memory, etc. **—em·bed'ment** *n.*

em·bel·lish (im bel'ish) *vt.* [< OFr. *embelir* < *em-* (L. *in*) + *bel* < L. *bellus*, beautiful] **1.** to decorate; ornament; adorn **2.** to improve (a story, etc.) by adding details, often of a fictitious kind; touch up **—em·bel'lish·ment** *n.*

em·ber[1] (em'bər) *n.* [< OE. *æmerge*] **1.** a glowing piece of coal, wood, etc. from a fire **2.** [pl.] the smouldering remains of a fire

em·ber[2] (em'bər) *adj.* [< OE. < *ymbryne* < *ymb*, round + *ryne*, a running] [often E-] designating or of three days (Wednesday, Friday, and Saturday) set aside for prayer and, sometimes, fasting in a specified week of each season of the year: observed in the Roman Catholic Church and certain other churches

em·bez·zle (im bez''l) *vt.* **-zled, -zling** [< Anglo-Fr. < OFr. < *en-* (see EN-) + *besillier*, to destroy] to steal (money, etc. entrusted to one's care); take by fraud for one's own use **—em·bez'zle·ment** *n.* **—em·bez'zler** *n.*

em·bit·ter (-bit'ər) *vt.* to cause to have bitter or more bitter feelings **—em·bit'ter·ment** *n.*

em·bla·zon (im blā'z'n) *vt.* [see BLAZON] **1.** to decorate (*with* coats of arms, etc.) **2.** to display brilliantly; decorate with bright colours **3.** to praise; celebrate **—em·bla'-zon·ment** *n.*

em·blem (em'bləm) *n.* [orig., inlaid work < L. < Gr. *emblēma*, insertion < *en-*, in + *ballein*, to throw] **1.** a visible symbol of a thing, idea, etc.; object that stands for or suggests something else [the cross is an *emblem* of Christianity] **2.** a sign, badge, or device

em·blem·at·ic (em'blə mat'ik) *adj.* of, containing, or serving as an emblem; symbolic: also **em'blem·at'i·cal** **—em'blem·at'i·cal·ly** *adv.*

em·bod·i·ment (im bod'ē mənt) *n.* **1.** an embodying or being embodied **2.** that in which some idea, quality, etc. is embodied [she is the *embodiment* of virtue]

em·bod·y (-bod'ē) *vt.* **-bod'ied, -bod'y·ing** **1.** to give bodily form to; incarnate **2.** to give definite or visible form to **3.** to bring together into, or make part of, an organized whole; incorporate [the latest findings *embodied* in the new book]

em·bold·en (-bōl'd'n) *vt.* to give courage to; cause to be bold or bolder

em·bo·lism (em'bə liz'm) *n.* *Med.* the obstruction of a blood vessel by an embolus

em·bo·lus (-ləs) *n., pl.* **-li'** (-lī') [ModL. < Gr. < *en-*, in + *ballein*, to throw] any foreign matter, as a blood clot or air bubble, carried in the bloodstream **—em·bol'ic** (-bol'ik) *adj.*

‡em·bon·point (än bōn pwan') *n.* [Fr. lit., in good condition] plumpness; corpulence

em·bos·om (im booz'em) *vt.* **1.** to embrace; cherish **2.** to enclose; surround; shelter

em·boss (-bos') *vt.* [< OFr.: see EN- & BOSS[2]] **1.** to decorate with designs, etc. raised above the surface **2.** to raise (a design, etc.) in relief **—em·boss'er** *n.* **—em·boss'ment** *n.*

em·bou·chure (om'boo shoor') *n.* [Fr. < *emboucher*, to put into the mouth < L. *in*, in + *bucca*, the cheek] **1.** the mouth of a river **2.** *Music* a) the mouthpiece of a wind instrument b) the method of applying the lips and tongue to the mouthpiece of a wind instrument

em·bow·er (im bou'ər) *vt.* to enclose or shelter in or as in a bower

em·brace (-brās') *vt.* **-braced', -brac'ing** [< OFr. < L. *im-*, in + *brachium*, an arm] **1.** to clasp in the arms lovingly or affectionately; hug **2.** to accept readily [to *embrace* an opportunity] **3.** to take up or adopt, esp. eagerly or seriously [to *embrace* a new profession] **4.** to encircle; surround **5.** to include; contain **6.** to perceive or understand quickly and accurately **—vi.** to clasp each other in the arms **—n.** an embracing; hug **—em·brace'a·ble** *adj.* **—em·brace'ment** *n.* **—em·brac'er** *n.*

em·bra·sure (im brā'zhər) *n.* [Fr. < obs. *embraser*, to widen an opening] **1.** an opening (for a door, window, etc.) with the sides slanted so that it is wider on the inside than on the outside **2.** an opening, as in a parapet, with the sides slanting outwards to increase the angle of fire of a gun

em·bro·cate (em'brō kāt', -brə-) *vt.* **-cat'ed, -cat'ing** [< LL. pp. of *embrocare*, to foment < L. < Gr. < *en-*, in + *brechein*, to wet] to moisten and rub (a part of the body) with an oil, liniment, etc. **—em'bro·ca'tion** *n.*

em·broi·der (im broi'dər) *vt.* [< OFr. < *en-*, in + *brosder*, to embroider] **1.** to ornament (fabric) with a design in needlework **2.** to make (a design, etc.) on fabric with needlework **3.** to embellish (a story, etc.); exaggerate **—vi.** **1.** to do embroidery **2.** to exaggerate **—em·broi'der·er** *n.*

em·broi·der·y (-ē) *n., pl.* **-der·ies** **1.** the art or work of ornamenting fabric with needlework **2.** embroidered work or fabric **3.** embellishment, as of a story **4.** an unnecessary but attractive addition

em·broil (im broil') *vt.* [< Fr.: see EN- & BROIL[2]] **1.** to confuse (affairs, etc.); mix up; muddle **2.** to draw into a conflict or fight; involve in trouble —**em·broil′ment** *n.*

em·bry·o (em′brē ō′) *n., pl.* **-os′** [ML. < Gr. *embryon* < *en-,* in + *bryein,* to swell] **1.** an animal in the earliest stages of its development in the uterus: the human organism up to the third month after conception is called an *embryo,* thereafter a *foetus.* **2.** *a)* an early or undeveloped stage of something *b)* anything in such a stage **3.** the rudimentary plant contained in a seed —*adj.* embryonic

em·bry·o- *a combining form meaning* embryo, embryonic [*embryology*]

em·bry·ol·o·gy (em′brē ol′ə jē) *n.* [EMBRYO- + -LOGY] the branch of biology dealing with the formation and development of embryos —**em′bry·o·log′ic** (-ə loj′ik), **em′·bry·o·log′i·cal** *adj.* —**em′bry·o·log′i·cal·ly** *adv.* —**em′bry·ol′·o·gist** *n.*

em·bry·on·ic (-on′ik) *adj.* **1.** of or like an embryo **2.** in an early stage; rudimentary

em·bus (em bus′) *vt., vi.* to put into or mount a bus: said esp. of troops

em·cee (em′sē′) *vt., vi.* **-ceed′, -cee′ing** [< M.C., sense 1] [Chiefly U.S. Colloq.] to act as master of ceremonies (for) —*n.* [Colloq.] a master of ceremonies

e·meer (ə mir′) *n. same as* EMIR —**e·meer′ate** *n.*

e·mend (i mend′) *vt.* [L. *emendare,* to correct < *e-,* out + *mendum,* a fault] to make scholarly corrections or improvements in (a text)

e·men·date (em′ən dāt′) *vt.* **-dat′ed, -dat′ing** *same as* EMEND —**e·men·da·tion** (ē′mən dā′shən, em′ən-) *n.* —**e′·men·da′tor** *n.* —**e·mend·a·to·ry** (i men′də tər ē) *adj.*

em·er·ald (em′ər əld, em′rəld) *n.* [< OFr. < VL. *smaraldus* < L. < Gr. *smaragdos*] **1.** a bright-green, transparent precious stone; green variety of beryl **2.** a similar variety of corundum **3.** bright green —*adj.* **1.** bright-green **2.** made of or with an emerald or emeralds **3.** designating or of a cut of gem in a rectangular style used esp. with emeralds

Emerald Isle [< its green landscape] Ireland

e·merge (i murj′) *vi.* **e·merged′, e·merg′ing** [L. *emergere* < *e-,* out + *mergere,* to dip] **1.** to rise as from a fluid **2.** *a)* to come forth into view; become visible *b)* to become apparent or known, esp. in a sudden or unexpected way **3.** to develop as something new, improved, etc. [a strong breed *emerged*] —**e·mer′gence** *n.* —**e·mer′gent** *adj.*

e·mer·gen·cy (i mur′jən sē) *n., pl.* **-cies** [orig. sense, an emerging] **1.** a sudden, generally unexpected occurrence or set of circumstances demanding immediate action **2.** a political condition that borders upon war —*adj.* for use in case of sudden necessity [an *emergency* exit]

emergent nation a country or state that has just recently become independent

e·mer·i·tus (i mer′ə təs) *adj.* [L., pp. of *emereri* < *e-,* out + *mereri,* to serve] retired from active service, usually for age, but retaining one's rank or title [professor *emeritus*]

e·mer·sion (ē mur′zhən, -shən) *n.* an emerging

em·er·y (em′ər ē, em′rē) *n.* [< Fr. < OFr. < It. < MGr. *smeri,* for Gr. *smyris,* emery] a dark, impure variety of corundum used in solid, crushed, or powdered form for grinding, polishing, etc.

emery board a strip of cardboard or wood with a rough surface of crushed emery used for filing the nails

e·met·ic (i met′ik) *adj.* [< L. < Gr. *emetikos* < *emein,* to vomit] causing vomiting —*n.* an emetic medicine or other substance

E.M.F., e.m.f., EMF, emf electromotive force

-e·mi·a (ēm′ē ə, ēm′yə) *U.S. var. of* -AEMIA

em·i·grant (em′ə grənt) *adj.* **1.** emigrating **2.** of emigrants or emigration —*n.* one who emigrates

em·i·grate (-grāt′) *vi.* **-grat′ed, -grat′ing** [< L. pp. of *emigrare* < *e-,* out + *migrare,* to move] to leave one country or region to settle in another —**em′i·gra′tion** *n.* —**em′i·gra·to·ry** (-tər ē) *adj.*

é·mi·gré, e·mi·gré (em′ə grā′) *n.* [Fr.] **1.** an emigrant **2.** a person forced to flee his country for political reasons

em·i·nence (em′ə nəns) *n.* [< OFr. < L. < prp. of *eminere,* to stand out] **1.** a high or lofty place, thing, etc., as a hill **2.** *a)* superiority in rank, position, etc.; greatness *b)* a person of eminence **3.** [E-] *R.C.Ch.* a title of honour used in speaking to or of a cardinal, preceded by *His* or *Your*

‡ém·i·nence grise (ā mē nä̃s grēz′) [Fr., lit., grey eminence: after the French monk who was Cardinal Richelieu's friend and adviser] a person who wields great power and influence unofficially and secretly

em·i·nent (em′ə nənt) *adj.* [< L.: see EMINENCE] **1.** rising high above others; high; lofty **2.** projecting; prominent **3.** standing high by comparison with others; exalted; distinguished **4.** outstanding; noteworthy —**em′i·nent·ly** *adv.*

eminent domain *Law* the right of a government to take private property for public use, just compensation usually being given to the owner

e·mir (i mir′) *n.* [Ar. *amir,* commander] **1.** in certain Moslem countries, a ruler, prince, or commander **2.** a title

given to Mohammed's descendants through his daughter Fatima —**e·mir′ate** (-it, -āt) *n.*

em·is·sar·y (em′ə ser ē) *n., pl.* **-sar·ies** [< L. < pp. of *emittere:* see EMIT] a person or agent, esp. a secret agent, sent on a specific mission —*adj.* of, or serving as, an emissary or emissaries

e·mis·sion (i mish′ən) *n.* **1.** an emitting; issuance **2.** something emitted; discharge —**e·mis′sive** *adj.*

e·mit (i mit′) *vt.* **e·mit′ted, e·mit′ting** [< L. *emittere* < *e-,* out + *mittere,* to send] **1.** to send out; give forth **2.** to utter (sounds, etc.) **3.** to transmit (a signal) as by radio waves **4.** to give off (electrons) under the influence of heat, etc. —**e·mit′ter** *n.*

Em·men·thal (em′ən täl′) *n.* [after the valley in Switzerland] a hard Swiss cheese full of holes

Em·my (em′ē) *n., pl.* **-mys** [altered < *Immy,* slang for a kind of TV camera] [U.S. Slang] any of the statuettes awarded annually in the U.S. for outstanding performances and productions in television

EmnE., EMnE. Early Modern English

e·mol·li·ent (i mol′yənt) *adj.* [< L. prp. of *emollire* < *e-,* out + *mollire,* to soften < *mollis,* soft] softening; soothing —*n.* an emollient preparation, esp. for the surface tissues of the body

e·mol·u·ment (i mol′yoo mənt) *n.* [< L. < *emolere* < *e-,* out + *molere,* to grind] gain from employment or position; salary, wages, fees, etc.

e·mote (i mōt′) *vi.* **e·mot′ed, e·mot′ing** [< ff., by analogy with DEVOTE] [Colloq.] to express emotion in a showy or theatrical manner

e·mo·tion (i mō′shən) *n.* [Fr. (prob. after *motion*) < L. *emovere* < *e-,* out + *movere,* to move] **1.** strong feeling; excitement **2.** any specific feeling, as love, hate, fear, anger, etc.

e·mo·tion·al (-′l) *adj.* **1.** of emotion or the emotions **2.** showing emotion, esp. strong emotion **3.** easily aroused to emotion **4.** appealing to or arousing the emotions —**e·mo′·tion·al·ly** *adv.*

e·mo·tion·al·ism (-′l iz′m) *n.* **1.** the tendency to be emotional **2.** display of emotion **3.** an appeal to emotion, esp. to sway an audience

e·mo·tion·al·ize (-′l īz′) *vt.* **-ized′, -iz′ing** to treat, present, or interpret in an emotional way —**e·mo′tion·al·i·za′tion** *n.*

e·mo·tive (i mōt′iv) *adj.* **1.** expressing or producing emotion **2.** relating to the emotions —**e·mo′tive·ly** *adv.*

Emp. **1.** Emperor **2.** Empire **3.** Empress

em·pan·el (im pan′′l) *vt.* **-elled, -el·ling** **1.** to enter the name or names of on a jury list **2.** to choose (a jury) from such a list

em·pa·thize (em′pə thīz′) *vi.* **-thized′, -thiz′ing** [< ff] to undergo or feel empathy (*with* another or others)

em·pa·thy (em′pə thē) *n.* [< Gr. < *en-,* in + *pathos,* feeling] intellectual or emotional identification with another —**em·path·ic** (im path′ik), **em·pa·thet·ic** (em′pə thet′ik) *adj.*

em·per·or (em′pər ər) *n.* [< OFr. < L. *imperator* < pp. of *imperare,* to command < *in-,* in + *parare,* to set in order] the supreme ruler of an empire

emperor penguin the largest penguin, growing to 1.3 m in height; found in Antarctica

em·pha·sis (em′fə sis) *n., pl.* **-ses′** (-sēz′) [L. < Gr. < *emphainein,* to indicate < *en-,* in + *phainein,* to show] **1.** force of expression, feeling, action, etc. **2.** special stress given to a syllable, word, phrase, etc. in speaking **3.** special attention given to something so as to make it stand out; importance; stress

em·pha·size (-sīz′) *vt.* **-sized′, -siz′ing** to give emphasis, or special force, to; stress

em·phat·ic (im fat′ik) *adj.* **1.** expressed, felt, or done with emphasis **2.** using emphasis in speaking, expressing, etc. **3.** very striking; forcible; definite [an *emphatic* defeat] **4.** *Gram.* designating or of a present tense or past tense in which a form of *do* is used as an auxiliary for emphasis (Ex.: I *do* care) —**em·phat′i·cal·ly** *adv.*

em·phy·se·ma (em′fə sē′mə) *n.* [Gr. < *en-,* in + *physaein,* to blow] abnormal distention of the alveoli, or air cells, of the lungs, accompanied by loss of elasticity in the tissues and impairment in breathing

em·pire (em′pir) *n.* [< OFr. < L. < *imperare:* see EMPEROR] **1.** supreme rule; absolute power or authority **2.** government by an emperor or empress **3.** *a)* a group of states or territories under the sovereignty of an emperor or empress *b)* a state uniting many territories and peoples under one ruler *c)* [usually E-] the British Empire **4.** an extensive social or economic organization under the control of a single person, family, or corporation —*adj.* [E-] of or characteristic of the first French Empire (1804–15) under Napoleon [*Empire* furniture]

empire builder a person who ruthlessly seeks to extend the scope and power of his authority

Empire Day *former name for* COMMONWEALTH DAY

em·pir·ic (em pir′ik) *n.* [< L. < Gr. < *empeiria,* experience < *en-,* in + *peira,* a trial] a person who relies solely on practical experience rather than on scientific principles —*adj.* empirical

em·pir·i·cal (-i k'l) *adj.* [see prec.] 1. relying or based solely on experiment and observation rather than theory [the empirical method] 2. relying or based on practical experience without reference to scientific principles [an empirical remedy] —**em·pir'i·cal·ly** *adv.*

em·pir·i·cism (-ə siz'm) *n.* 1. experimental method; search for knowledge by observation and experiment 2. *a)* a disregarding of scientific methods and relying solely on experience *b)* quackery 3. *Philos.* the theory that experience, esp. sense experience, is the only source of knowledge —**em·pir'i·cist** *n.*

em·place (im plās') *vt.* -placed', -plac'ing to place in position

em·place·ment (-mənt) *n.* 1. an emplacing; placement 2. the position in which something is placed; specif., *Mil.* the prepared position from which a heavy gun or guns are fired

em·plane (em plān') *vi.* -planed', -plan'ing same as ENPLANE

em·ploy (im ploi') *vt.* [< OFr. < L. implicare, to enfold: see IMPLY] 1. to make use of; use 2. to keep busy or occupied; devote 3. to provide work and pay for 4. to engage the services or labour of for pay; hire —*n.* the state of being employed; paid service; employment —**em·ploy'a·ble** *adj.*

em·ploy·ee (im ploi'ē, em'ploi ē') *n.* a person hired by another, or by a business firm, etc., to work for wages or salary

em·ploy·er (im ploi'ər) *n.* one who employs; esp., a person, business firm, etc. that hires one or more persons to work for wages or salary

em·ploy·ment (-mənt) *n.* 1. an employing or being employed 2. the thing at which one is employed; work; occupation; job 3. the number or percentage of persons gainfully employed

employment exchange same as LABOUR EXCHANGE

em·po·ri·um (em pôr'ē əm) *n.,* pl. -ri·ums, -ri·a (-ə) [L. < Gr. < emporos, traveller < en-, in + poros, way] 1. a place of commerce; trading centre; marketplace 2. a large store with a wide variety of things for sale

em·pow·er (im pou'ər) *vt.* 1. to give power to; authorize 2. to enable; permit —**em·pow'er·ment** *n.*

em·press (em'pris) *n.* 1. the wife of an emperor 2. a woman ruler of an empire

emp·ty (emp'tē) *adj.* -ti·er, -ti·est [< OE. æmettig, unoccupied < æmetta, leisure + -ig, -Y²] 1. containing nothing; having nothing in it 2. having no one in it; unoccupied [an empty house] 3. worthless; unsatisfying [empty pleasures] 4. meaningless; insincere; vain [empty promises] 5. [Colloq.] hungry —*vt.* -tied, -ty·ing 1. to make empty 2. to pour out or remove (the contents) of something 3. to unburden or discharge (oneself or itself) —*vi.* 1. to become empty 2. to pour out; discharge —*n.,* pl. -ties an empty container, esp. a bottle —**empty of** lacking; without; devoid of —**emp'ti·ly** *adv.* —**emp'ti·ness** *n.*

emp·ty-hand·ed (-han'did) *adj.* bringing or carrying away nothing

emp·ty-head·ed (-hed'id) *adj.* silly and ignorant

em·pur·ple (im pur'p'l) *vt., vi.* -pled, -pling to make or become purple

em·pyr·e·al (em pir'ē əl; em'pī rē'əl) *adj.* [< LL. < Gr. empyrios, fiery < en-, in + pyr, a fire] of the empyrean; heavenly; sublime

em·py·re·an (em'pī rē'ən; em pir'ē ən) *n.* [see prec. & -AN] 1. the highest heaven: among the ancients, the sphere of pure light or fire 2. the sky; the firmament —*adj.* same as EMPYREAL

e·mu (ē'myōō) *n.* [prob. < Port. ema, a crane] a large, nonflying Australian bird, similar to the ostrich but somewhat smaller

E.M.U., e.m.u., emu electromagnetic units

em·u·late (em'yə lāt') *vt.* -lat'ed, -lat'ing [< L. pp. of aemulari < aemulus, trying to equal] 1. to try to equal or surpass 2. to imitate (a person or thing admired) 3. to rival successfully —**em'u·la'tion** *n.* —**em'u·la'tive** *adj.* —**em'u·la'tor** *n.*

em·u·lous (em'yə ləs) *adj.* 1. desirous of equalling or surpassing 2. characterized or caused by emulation —**em'u·lous·ly** *adv.* —**em'u·lous·ness** *n.*

e·mul·si·fy (i mul'sə fī') *vt., vi.* -fied', -fy'ing to form into an emulsion —**e·mul'si·fi'a·ble** *adj.* —**e·mul'si·fi·ca'tion** *n.* —**e·mul'si·fi'er** *n.*

e·mul·sion (i mul'shən) *n.* [< ModL. < L. pp. of emulgere < e-, out + mulgere, to milk] a fluid, as milk, formed by the suspension of one liquid in another; specif., *a) Pharmacy* a preparation of an oily substance held in suspension in a watery liquid *b) Photog.* a suspension of a salt of silver in

gelatin or collodion, used to coat plates and film —**e·mul'sive** *adj.*

en (en) *n.* 1. the letter N, n 2. *Printing* a space half the width of an em

en- (in, en) [OFr. < L. in- < in, IN] 1. a prefix meaning: a) to put or get into or on [entrain] b) to cover with [enrobe] c) to make, cause to be [endanger, enfeeble] d) in or into [enclose] 2. a prefix used as an intensifier [enliven] It is assimilated to em- before p, b, m Many words with en- are also spelled in- (Ex.: enquire, inquire)

-en (ən, 'n) [< OE. suffixes -nian, -an, -en] any of several suffixes: 1. meaning: a) to become or cause to be [darken, weaken] b) to come to have, cause to have [strengthen] 2. meaning made of [woollen] 3. used to form the pp. of strong verbs [risen] 4. used to form plurals [children] 5. used to form diminutives [chicken]

en·a·ble (in ā'b'l) *vt.* -bled, -bling 1. to make able; provide with means, opportunity, power, or authority (to do something) 2. to make possible

enabling act a bill or act giving power to take action

en·act (in akt') *vt.* 1. to make (a bill, etc.) into a law; pass (a law); decree; ordain 2. to represent or perform in or as in a play; act out —**en·ac'tion** *n.* —**en·ac'tive** *adj.* —**en·ac'tor** *n.*

en·act·ment (-mənt) *n.* 1. an enacting or being enacted 2. something enacted, as a law

en·am·el (i nam''l) *n.* [see the v.] 1. a glassy, coloured, opaque substance fused to surfaces, as of metals, as an ornamental or protective coating 2. any smooth, hard, glossy coating like enamel 3. the hard, white, glossy coating of the crown of a tooth 4. anything enamelled 5. paint or varnish with a smooth, hard, glossy surface when it dries —*vt.* -elled, -el·ling [< Anglo-Fr. < en-(see EN-) + amyl < OFr. esmail, enamel] 1. to inlay or cover with enamel 2. to decorate in various colours, as if with enamel 3. to form an enamellike surface on —**en·am'el·ler, en·am'el·list** *n.*

en·am·our (in am'ər) *vt.* [< OFr. < en-, in + amour < L. amor, love] to fill with love and desire; charm; captivate: now mainly in the passive voice, with of [much enamoured of her]

en bloc (en blok'; Fr. än blôk') [Fr., lit., in a block] in one lump; as a whole; all together

†en brosse (än brôs') [Fr., lit., like a brush] cut short so as to stand up like brush bristles: said of hair

enc., encl. enclosure

en·camp (in kamp') *vi.* to set up a camp —*vt.* 1. to put in a camp 2. to form into a camp

en·camp·ment (-mənt) *n.* 1. an encamping or being encamped 2. a camp or campsite

en·cap·su·late (in kap'syoo lāt') *vt.* -lat'ed, -lat'ing 1. to enclose in or as if in a capsule 2. to condense; abridge Also **en·cap'sule** (-syool) -suled, -sul·ing —**en·cap'su·la'tion** *n.*

en·case (in kās') *vt.* -cased', -cas'ing 1. to cover completely; enclose 2. to put into a case or cases —**en·case'ment** *n.*

en·caus·tic (en kôs'tik) *adj.* [< L. < Gr. < en-, in + kaiein, to burn] done by a process of burning in or applying heat [encaustic tile] —*n.* a method of painting in which colours in wax are fused to a surface with hot irons —**en·caus'ti·cal·ly** *adv.*

-ence (əns, 'ns) [< OFr. -ence & L. -entia (see -ENT + -IA)] a suffix meaning act, fact, quality, state, result, or degree [conference, excellence]

†en·ceinte (än sant') *adj.* [Fr., ult. < L. in-, not + pp. of cingere, to gird] pregnant

en·ce·phal·ic (en'sə fal'ik) *adj.* [< Gr. enkephalos: see ENCEPHALO- & -IC] of or near the brain

en·ceph·a·li·tis (en sef'ə lit'is, en'sef-) *n.* [< ENCEPHALO- + -ITIS] inflammation of the brain —**en·ceph'a·lit'ic** (-lit'ik) *adj.*

encephalitis le·thar·gi·ca (li thär'ji kə) same as SLEEPING SICKNESS

en·ceph·a·lo- [< Gr. enkephalos, the brain] a combining form meaning of the brain: also **en·ceph'al·i**

en·ceph·a·lo·gram (en sef'ə lō gram') *n.* clipped form of: 1. ELECTROENCEPHALOGRAM 2. PNEUMOENCEPHALOGRAM

en·ceph·a·lon (-lon') *n.,* pl. -la (-lə) [ModL. < Gr. < en-, in + kephalē, the head] *Anat.* the brain —**en·ce·phal·ic** (en'sə fal'ik) *adj.*

en·chain (in chān') *vt.* 1. to bind with chains; fetter 2. to captivate —**en·chain'ment** *n.*

en·chant (in chänt') *vt.* [< OFr. < L. incantare, to bewitch: see INCANTATION] 1. to cast a spell over, as by magic; bewitch 2. to charm greatly; delight —**en·chant'er** *n.* —**en·chant'ress** *n.fem.*

en·chant·ing (-iŋ) *adj.* 1. charming; delightful 2. bewitching; fascinating —**en·chant'ing·ly** *adv.*

en·chant·ment (-mənt) *n.* 1. an enchanting or being enchanted 2. a magic spell or charm 3. something that charms greatly 4. great delight

en·chase (in chās') *vt.* -chased', -chas'ing [< OFr. enchasser: see CHASE³] 1. to put in a setting 2. to

EMU
(to 1.5 m high)

ornament by engraving, inlaying with gems, etc. **3.** to carve (designs, etc.)

en·chi·la·da (en′chə lä′də) *n.* [AmSp.] a tortilla usually rolled with meat inside and served with a chili-flavoured sauce

en·ci·pher (in sī′fər) *vt.* to convert (a message, etc.) from ordinary language into cipher or code

en·cir·cle (in sur′k'l) *vt.* **-cled, -cling 1.** to make a circle around; surround **2.** to move in a circle around —**en·cir′cle·ment** *n.*

en·clave (en′klāv) *n.* [Fr. < OFr. < L. *in*, in + *clavis*, a key] **1.** a territory surrounded by the territory of a foreign country **2.** a minority culture group that exists within a larger group

en·clit·ic (en klit′ik) *adj.* [< LL. < Gr. < *enklinein*, to lean towards] *Gram.* dependent for its stress on the preceding word, often one with which it has combined (Ex.: *man* in *layman*) —*n.* any such word or particle

en·close (in klōz′) *vt.* **-closed′, -clos′ing 1.** to shut in all around; fence in; surround **2.** to insert in an envelope, wrapper, etc., often together with something else **3.** to contain

en·clo·sure (-klō′zhər) *n.* **1.** an enclosing or being enclosed **2.** something that encloses **3.** something enclosed; specif., *a)* an enclosed place *b)* a document, money, etc. enclosed as with a letter

en·code (in kōd′) *vt.* **-cod′ed, -cod′ing** to put (information, etc.) into code —**en·cod′er** *n.*

en·co·mi·ast (en kō′mē ast′) *n.* [< Gr. < *enkōmiazein*, to praise] a person who speaks or writes encomiums; eulogist —**en·co′mi·as′tic** *adj.*

en·co·mi·um (en kō′mē əm) *n., pl.* **-mi·ums, -mi·a** (-ə) [L. < Gr. *enkōmion*, song of praise < *en-*, in + *kōmos*, a revel] a formal expression of high praise; eulogy; panegyric

en·com·pass (in kum′pəs) *vt.* **1.** to shut in all around; surround **2.** to contain; include **3.** to compass or achieve —**en·com′pass·ment** *n.*

en·core (oŋ′kôr, on kôr′) *interj.* [Fr., yet, again] again; once more —*n.* **1.** a demand by the audience, shown by applause, for further performance **2.** the performance or piece performed in answer to such a demand —*vt.* **-cored, -cor·ing** to demand further performance of or by

en·coun·ter (in koun′tər) *vt.* [< OFr. < L. *in*, in + *contra*, against] **1.** to meet unexpectedly; come upon **2.** to meet in conflict or battle **3.** to face (difficulties, trouble, etc.) —*vi.* to meet accidentally or in opposition —*n.* **1.** a direct meeting, as in conflict or battle **2.** an unexpected meeting

en·cour·age (in kur′ij) *vt.* **-aged, -ag·ing 1.** to give courage, hope, or confidence to; hearten **2.** to give support to; foster; help —**en·cour′ag·ing** *adj.* —**en·cour′ag·ing·ly** *adv.*

en·cour·age·ment (-mənt) *n.* **1.** an encouraging or being encouraged **2.** something that encourages

en·croach (in krōch′) *vi.* [< OFr. *encrochier*, to seize upon < *en-*, in + *croc*, a hook] **1.** to trespass or intrude (*on* or *upon* the rights, property, etc. of another), esp. stealthily **2.** to advance beyond the proper, original, or customary limits —**en·croach′ment** *n.*

en·crust (in krust′) *vt., vi.* same as INCRUST —**en′crus·ta′·tion** *n.*

en·cum·ber (in kum′bər) *vt.* [< OFr.: see EN- & CUMBER] **1.** to hold back the motion or action of, as with a burden; hinder **2.** to fill so as to obstruct; block up **3.** to load or weigh down; burden —**en·cum′ber·ment** *n.*

en·cum·brance (-brəns) *n.* **1.** something that encumbers; hindrance; burden **2.** *Law* same as INCUMBRANCE

-en·cy (ən sē, 'n sē) [L. *-entia*] a suffix meaning act, fact, quality, state, result, or degree [*dependency, emergency, efficiency*]

ency., encyc., encycl. encyclopedia

en·cyc·li·cal (in sik′li k'l) *adj.* [LL. *encyclicus* < Gr. < *en-*, in + *kyklos*, a circle] for general circulation: also **en·cyc′·lic** —*n.* R.C.Ch. a letter from the Pope to the bishops, usually dealing with doctrinal matters

en·cy·clo·pe·di·a, en·cy·clo·pae·di·a (in sī′klə pē′dē ə) *n.* [ModL. < Gr. *enkyklopaideia* < *enkyklios*, general + *paideia*, education] a book or set of books giving information on all or many branches of knowledge, or on one of these, generally in articles alphabetically arranged —**en·cy′clo·pe′dic, en·cy′clo·pae′dic** *adj.* —**en·cy′clo·pe′·di·cal·ly, en·cy′clo·pae′di·cal·ly** *adv.*

en·cy·clo·pe·dist, en·cy·clo·pae·dist (-pē′dist) *n.* **1.** a person who compiles or helps to compile an encyclopedia **2.** [E-] [*pl.*] the writers of the French Encyclopedia, edited by Diderot and d'Alembert

en·cyst (en sist′) *vt., vi.* to enclose or become enclosed in a cyst, capsule, or sac —**en·cyst′ment, en′cys·ta′tion** (-sis tā′shən) *n.*

end (end) *n.* [OE. *ende*] **1.** a limit or limiting part; boundary **2.** the last part of anything; final point; finish; conclusion **3.** a ceasing to exist; death or destruction **4.** the part at or near either extremity of anything; tip **5.** a purpose; intention; object **6.** an outcome; result; consequence **7.** a piece left over; remnant [odds and *ends*] **8.** the reason for being **9.** the limit of endurance, etc. [at his wits′ *end*] **10.** *Cricket* either of the two areas around each wicket —*vt.* **1.** to bring to an end; finish; stop **2.** to form the end of —*vi.* **1.** to come to an end; terminate: often with *up* **2.** to die —*adj.* at the end; final [*end product*] —**end it all** [Colloq.] to commit suicide —**ends of the earth** remote regions —**make an end of 1.** to finish; stop **2.** to do away with —**make (both) ends meet** to keep one's expenses within one's income —**no end** [Colloq.] extremely —**no end of** [Colloq.] a great many; a great deal —**on end 1.** in an upright position **2.** without interruption [for days *on end*] —**put an end to 1.** to stop **2.** to do away with —**the end** [Colloq.] the worst, esp. something beyond the limits of endurance

en·da·moe·ba (en′də mē′bə) *n.* [see ENDO- & AMOEBA] any of a genus of parasitic amoebas, including the species that causes amoebic dysentery in man: also U.S. sp. **en′da·me′·ba** —**en′da·moe′bic** *adj.*

en·dan·ger (in dān′jər) *vt.* to expose to danger, harm, or loss; imperil —**en·dan′ger·ment** *n.*

en·dear (in dir′) *vt.* to make dear or beloved

en·dear·ing (-iŋ) *adj.* **1.** that makes dear or well liked **2.** expressing affection [*endearing* tones]

en·dear·ment (-mənt) *n.* **1.** warm liking; affection **2.** a word or act expressing affection

en·deav·our (in dev′ər) *vi.* [< *en-* + OFr. *deveir*, duty < L. *debere*, to owe] to make an earnest attempt —*vt.* **1.** [Archaic] to try to achieve **2.** to try (*to do* something) —*n.* an earnest attempt or effort Also, U.S. sp., **en·deav′or**

en·dem·ic (en dem′ik) *adj.* [Fr. < Gr. < *en-*, in + *dēmos*, the people] **1.** native to a particular country, region, etc.: said of plants and animals **2.** restricted to and present in a particular country or locality: said of a disease: also **en·dem′i·cal** —*n.* **1.** an endemic plant or animal **2.** an endemic disease —**en·dem′i·cal·ly** *adv.* —**en·de·mic·i·ty** (en′-də mis′ə tē), **en·dem′ism** *n.*

en·der·mic (en dur′mik) *adj.* [< Gr. *en*, in + *derma*, the skin + -IC] acting by absorption through the skin

end game the final stage of a game of bridge, chess, etc.

end·ing (en′diŋ) *n.* **1.** *a)* the last part; finish *b)* death **2.** *Gram.* the final letter or letters added to a word base to make a derivative or an inflectional form [*-ed* is the *ending* in *wanted*]

en·dive (en′dīv) *n.* [OFr. < ML. < MGr. < L. *intibus* < Gr. *entybon*] **1.** a cultivated plant of the composite family, with curled, narrow leaves used in salads **2.** the young leaves of chicory (sense 1) blanched for salads

end·less (end′lis) *adj.* **1.** having no end; going on forever; eternal; infinite **2.** lasting too long [an *endless* speech] **3.** continual [*endless* interruptions] **4.** with the ends joined to form a closed unit that can move continuously over wheels, etc. [an *endless* belt] —**end′less·ly** *adv.* —**end′less·ness** *n.*

end·most (-mōst′) *adj.* at the end; farthest; last

en·do- [< Gr. *edon*, within] a combining form meaning within, inner [*endoderm*]: also, before a vowel, **end-**

en·do·blast (en′də blast′) *n.* same as ENDODERM

en·do·car·di·tis (en′dō kär dīt′is) *n.* [ModL. < ENDO- + Gr. *kardia*, heart + -ITIS] inflammation of the thin membrane lining the heart cavities

en·do·carp (en′də kärp′) *n.* the inner layer of the wall of a ripened ovary or fruit, as the stone round the seed of a plum

en·do·crine (en′də krin, -krīn′) *adj.* [ENDO- + Gr. *krinein*, to separate] **1.** designating or of any gland producing one or more internal secretions that, introduced into the bloodstream, are carried to other parts of the body whose functions they regulate **2.** designating or of such a secretion —*n.* any such gland or its secretion, as the thyroid, adrenal, and pituitary glands

en·do·cri·nol·o·gy (en′dō kri nol′ə jē, en krī-) *n.* the branch of medicine dealing with the endocrine glands and the internal secretions of the body —**en′do·cri′no·log′i·cal** (-nə loj′ə k'l) *adj.* —**en′do·cri·nol′o·gist** *n.*

en·do·derm (en′də durm′) *n.* the inner layer of cells of the embryo, from which is formed the lining of the digestive tract, of other internal organs, and of certain glands —**en′·do·der′mal, en′do·der′mic** *adj.*

en·dog·a·my (en dog′ə mē) *n.* [ENDO- + -GAMY] **1.** the custom of marrying only within one's own tribe, clan, etc.; inbreeding **2.** cross-pollination among flowers of the same plant —**en·dog′a·mous, en·do·gam·ic** (en′də gam′ik) *adj.*

en·dog·e·nous (en doj′ə nəs) *adj.* **1.** developing from within; originating internally **2.** *Biol.* growing or developing from or on the inside —**en·dog′e·nous·ly** *adv.*

en·do·mor·phic (en′də môr′fik) *adj.* [ENDO- + -MORPHIC] designating or of the fleshy or heavy type of human body, in which the structures developed from the endoderm predominate —**en′do·morph′** *n.*

en·do·plasm (en′də plaz′m) *n.* the inner part of the cytoplasm of a cell —**en′do·plas′mic** *adj.*

end organ any structure at the end of a nerve fibre that either receives a sensation or sends an impulse to a muscle

en·dorse (in dôrs′) *vt.* **-dorsed′, -dors′ing** [< OFr. < ML. < L. *in*, on + *dorsum*, the back] **1.** to write on the back of (a document); specif., to sign (one's name) as payee on the back of (a cheque, etc.) **2.** to give approval to; support; sanction **3.** to record an offence on a driving licence, publican's licence, etc. **—en·dors′a·ble** *adj.* **—en·dor·see** (in dôr′sē′, en′dôr sē′) *n.* **—en·dors′er** *n.*

en·dorse·ment (-mənt) *n.* **1.** an endorsing **2.** something written in endorsing; specif., *a)* the signature of a payee on the back of a cheque, etc. *b)* a statement endorsing a person, product, etc. *c)* a record of a motoring offence in a driving licence

en·do·skel·e·ton (en′də skel′ə t'n) *n.* the internal bony, supporting structure in vertebrates

en·do·sperm (en′də spurm′) *n.* [ENDO- + SPERM¹] a tissue which surrounds the developing embryo of a seed and provides food for its growth; albumen **—en′do·sper′mic** *adj.*

en·do·ther·mic (en′də thur′mik) *adj.* [ENDO- + THERMIC] designating or produced by a chemical reaction in which heat is absorbed

en·dow (in dou′) *vt.* [< Anglo-Fr. < OFr. < *en-*, in + *douer* < L. *dotare*, to endow] **1.** to provide with some talent, quality, etc. [*endowed* with courage] **2.** to think of as having some quality or characteristic [to *endow* gods with human traits] **3.** to give money or property so as to provide an income for the support of (a college, hospital, etc.)

en·dow·ment (-mənt) *n.* **1.** an endowing **2.** that with which something is endowed; bequest **3.** a gift of nature; talent, ability, etc.

endowment assurance an insurance policy by which a stated amount is paid to the assured after the period of time specified in the contract, or to the beneficiaries if the assured dies within the time specified: also **endowment insurance**

endowment policy an insurance policy by which a stated amount is paid to the insured after the period of time specified in the contract

end paper the stout paper used in book binding to cover the inner sides of the cover and provide fly leaves

end point **1.** the point at which anything is complete **2.** *Chem.* the point at which a titration is complete

end product the final result of any series of changes, processes, or chemical reactions

en·due (in dyōō′) *vt.* **-dued′, -du′ing** [< OFr. < L. *inducere*: see INDUCE] to provide (*with* something); specif., to endow (*with* qualities, talents, etc.)

en·dur·ance (in dyoor′əns) *n.* **1.** an enduring **2.** ability to last, continue, or remain **3.** ability to stand pain, distress, fatigue, etc.; fortitude **4.** duration

en·dure (in dyoor′) *vt.* **-dured′, -dur′ing** [< OFr. < LL. < L. < *in-*, in + *durare*, to harden < *durus*, hard] **1.** to hold up under (pain, fatigue, etc.); bear **2.** to put up with; tolerate **—vi.** **1.** to continue in existence; last; remain **2.** to bear pain, etc. without flinching; hold out **—en·dur′a·ble** *adj.* **—en·dur′a·bly** *adv.*

en·dur·ing (-iŋ) *adj.* lasting; permanent; durable **—en·dur′-ing·ly** *adv.* **—en·dur′ing·ness** *n.*

end·ways (end′wāz′) *adv.* **1.** on end; upright **2.** with the end foremost **3.** lengthways **4.** end to end Also [Chiefly U.S.] **end′wise′** (-wīz′)

-ene (ēn) [after L. *-enus*, Gr. *-ēnos*, adj. suffix] a suffix used: **1.** *Chem.* to form names for some hydrocarbons [*propylene, benzene*] **2.** to form some commercial names

ENE, E.N.E., e.n.e. east-northeast

en·e·ma (en′ə mə) *n.* [LL. < Gr. < *en-*, in + *hienai*, to send] **1.** a liquid injected into the colon through the anus, as a purgative, medicine, etc. **2.** such an injection

en·e·my (en′ə mē) *n.*, *pl.* **-mies** [< OFr. < L. *inimicus* < *in-*, not + *amicus*, friend] **1.** a person who hates another, and wishes or tries to injure him; foe **2.** *a)* a nation or force hostile to another *b)* troops, fleet, ship, member, etc. of a hostile nation **3.** a person hostile to an idea, cause, etc. **4.** anything injurious or harmful **—adj.** of an enemy

en·er·get·ic (en′ər jet′ik) *adj.* of, having, or showing energy; vigorous; forceful **—en′er·get′i·cal·ly** *adv.*

en·er·gize (en′ər jīz′) *vt.* **-gized′, -giz′ing** **1.** to give energy to; invigorate **2.** *Elec.* to apply a source of voltage or current to (a circuit, etc.) **—en′er·giz′er** *n.*

en·er·gy (en′ər jē) *n.*, *pl.* **-gies** [< LL. < Gr. *energeia* < *en-*, in + *ergon*, work] **1.** force of expression **2.** potential forces; capacity for action **3.** effective power **4.** *Physics* the capacity for doing work and overcoming resistance

en·er·vate (en′ər vāt′; *for adj.* i nur′vit) *vt.* **-vat′ed, -vat′ing** [< L. pp. of *enervare* < *e-*, out + *nervus*, a nerve, sinew] to deprive of strength, force, vigour etc.; debilitate **—adj.** enervated; weakened **—en′er·va′tion** *n.* **—en′er·va′tor** *n.*

‡**en fa·mille** (än fà mē′y′) [Fr.] **1.** with one's family; at home **2.** in an informal way

‡**en·fant ter·ri·ble** (än fän te rē′bl′) [Fr.] **1.** an unmanageable, mischievous child **2.** a person who causes trouble or embarrassment by his imprudent remarks or actions

en·fee·ble (in fē′b'l) *vt.* **-bled, -bling** to make feeble **—en·fee′ble·ment** *n.*

‡**en fête** (än fāt′) [Fr., lit., in festival] **1.** being decorated or attired for a holiday or festival **2.** keeping or enjoying a holiday or festival

en·fi·lade (en′fə lād′) *n.* [Fr. < *enfiler*, to thread < *en-* (L. *in*), in + *fil* (L. *filum*), a thread] **1.** gunfire directed from either flank along the length of a line of troops **2.** a placement of troops that makes them vulnerable to such fire **—vt.** **-lad′ed, -lad′ing** to direct such gunfire at (a column, etc.)

en·fold (in fōld′) *vt.* **1.** to wrap in folds; envelop **2.** to embrace **—en·fold′ment** *n.*

en·force (in fôrs′) *vt.* **-forced′, -forc′ing** **1.** to give force to [to *enforce* an argument by analogies] **2.** to bring about or impose by force [to *enforce* one's will on a child] **3.** to compel observance of (a law, etc.) **—en·force′a·ble** *adj.* **—en·force′ment** *n.* **—en·forc′er** *n.*

en·fran·chise (in fran′chīz) *vt.* **-chised, -chis·ing** **1.** to free from slavery, bondage, etc. **2.** to give a franchise to; specif., to admit to citizenship, esp. to the right to vote **3.** to give (a town or city) the right to be represented in parliament **—en·fran′chise·ment** (-chiz mənt) *n.* **—en·fran′chis·er** *n.*

Eng. **1.** England **2.** English

eng. **1.** engineer(ing) **2.** engraved **3.** engraving

en·gage (in gāj′) *vt.* **-gaged′, -gag′ing** [< OFr. *engagier*: see EN- & GAGE¹] **1.** to bind (oneself) by a promise; pledge; specif. (now only in the passive), to bind by a promise of marriage; betroth **2.** to hire; employ **3.** to arrange for the use of; reserve [to *engage* a hotel room] **4.** to draw into; involve, as in conversation **5.** to attract and hold (the attention, etc.) **6.** to keep busy; occupy **7.** to enter into conflict with (the enemy) **8.** to interlock with; mesh together [*engage* the gears] **—vi.** **1.** to pledge oneself; promise; undertake **2.** to involve oneself; be active [to *engage* in dramatics] **3.** to enter into conflict **4.** to interlock; mesh

en·gaged (-gājd′) *adj.* **1.** pledged; esp., pledged in marriage; betrothed **2.** occupied or busy **3.** involved in combat, as troops **4.** attached to or partly set into a wall, etc. [*engaged* columns] **5.** in gear; interlocked; meshed

en·gage·ment (-gāj′mənt) *n.* **1.** an engaging or being engaged; specif., *a)* a betrothal *b)* an appointment or commitment *c)* employment or period of employment, esp. in the performing arts *d)* a conflict; battle *e)* state of being in gear **2.** something that engages

engagement ring a ring usually given by a man to a woman when they become engaged to be married

en·gag·ing (-gāj′iŋ) *adj.* attractive; winning; charming **—en·gag′ing·ly** *adv.*

‡**en garde** (än gàrd′) [Fr.] *Fencing* on guard: the opening position in which the fencer is prepared either to attack or defend

en·gen·der (in jen′dər) *vt.* [< OFr. < L. < *in-*, in + *generare*, GENERATE] to bring into being; cause; produce [*militarism engenders* war]

engin. **1.** engineer **2.** engineering

en·gine (en′jən) *n.* [< OFr. < L. *ingenium*, genius < *in-*, in & base of *gignere*, to produce] **1.** any machine that uses energy to develop mechanical power; esp., a machine for starting motion in some other machine **2.** a railway locomotive **3.** any instrument or machine; apparatus [*engines* of torture] **4.** *same as* FIRE ENGINE

engine driver a man who drives a locomotive; a train driver

en·gi·neer (en′jə nir′) *n.* **1.** a person skilled in some branch of engineering [a mechanical *engineer*] **2.** *a)* an operator of engines or technical equipment [a radio *engineer*] *b)* a specialist in planning or directing operations in some technical field [an electrical *engineer*] **3.** a skilful or clever manager **4.** *Mil.* a member of that branch of the armed forces concerned with the construction and demolition of bridges, roads, etc. **—vt.** **1.** to plan, construct, or manage as an engineer **2.** to plan and direct skilfully [to *engineer* a business merger] **—vi.** to act as an engineer

en·gi·neer·ing (-iŋ) *n.* **1.** *a)* the science concerned with putting scientific knowledge to practical uses, divided into different branches, as civil, electrical, mechanical, or chemical engineering *b)* the planning, designing, construction, or management of machinery, roads, bridges, buildings, waterways, etc. **2.** a manoeuvring or managing

Eng·lish (iŋ′glish) *adj.* [OE. *Englisc*, lit., of the Angles] **1.** of England, its people, their culture, etc. **2.** of their language **—n.** **1.** the language of the people of England, the official language of the British Commonwealth, the U.S., Liberia, etc. **2.** the English language of a specific period: see OLD ENGLISH, MIDDLE ENGLISH, MODERN ENGLISH **3.** [*sometimes* e-] *Billiards*, [U.S.] side **—vt.** **1.** to translate into English **2.** to Anglicize (a foreign word) **—the English** the people of England

English horn *same as* COR ANGLAIS

Eng·lish·man (-mən) *n.*, *pl.* **-men** a native or inhabitant of England —**Eng′lish·wom′an** *n.fem.*, *pl.* **-wom′en**
English mustard mustard (sense 2) mixed with water
English setter any of a breed of setter with a white, long-haired coat with black, yellow, or orange spots
English sonnet [U.S.] *same as* SHAKESPEAREAN SONNET
en·gorge (in gôrj′) *vt.*, *vi.* **-gorged′**, **-gorg′ing** 1. to eat gluttonously; gorge; glut 2. *Med.* to congest with blood or other fluid —**en·gorge′ment** *n.*
engr. 1. engineer 2. engraved 3. engraver
en·graft (in grăft′) *vt.* 1. to graft (a shoot, etc.) from one plant onto another 2. to establish firmly; implant —**en·graft′ment** *n.*
en·grain (-grān′) *vt.* [ME. < OFr. *engrainer*, to dye scarlet] *same as* INGRAIN
en·grave (in grāv′) *vt.* **-graved′**, **-grav′ing** [< Fr. < *en-*, in + *graver*, to incise, ult. < Gr. *graphein*, to write] 1. to cut or etch (letters, designs, etc.) in or on (a surface) or into (a metal plate, wooden block, etc. for printing) 2. to print by means of such a plate, block, etc. 3. to impress deeply on the mind or memory —**en·grav′er** *n.*
en·grav·ing (-iŋ) *n.* 1. the act, process, or art of one who engraves 2. an engraved plate, design, etc. 3. a print made from an engraved surface
en·gross (in grōs′) *vt.* [< OFr.: see EN- & GROSS] 1. *a)* to write in the large letters once used for legal documents *b)* to make a final fair copy of (a document) 2. to express formally or in legal form 3. to take the entire attention of; occupy wholly; absorb —**en·gross′er** *n.* —**en·gross′ing** *adj.*, *n.* —**en·gross′ment** *n.*
en·gulf (in gulf′) *vt.* 1. to swallow up; overwhelm 2. to plunge, as into a gulf —**en·gulf′ment** *n.*
en·hance (-häns′) *vt.* **-hanced′**, **-hanc′ing** [< Anglo-Fr. < OFr. *enhaucier*, ult. < L. *in*, in + *altus*, high] to make greater, as in value, attractiveness, etc.; heighten —*vi.* to increase, as in value or price —**en·hance′ment** *n.* —**en·hanc′-er** *n.*
e·nig·ma (ə nig′mə) *n.*, *pl.* **-mas** [< L. < Gr. *ainigma* < *ainissesthai*, to speak in riddles < *ainos*, tale] 1. a perplexing, usually ambiguous, statement; riddle 2. a perplexing or baffling matter, person, etc. —**en·ig·mat·ic** (en′ig mat′ik), **e′nig·mat′i·cal** *adj.* —**e′nig·mat′i·cal·ly** *adv.*
en·join (in join′) *vt.* [< OFr. < L. < *in-*, in + *jungere*, to join] 1. to order; enforce [to enjoin silence] 2. to prohibit, esp. by legal injunction; forbid 3. to order (someone) to do something, esp. by legal injunction
en·joy (in joi′) *vt.* [< OFr. *enjoir* < *en-*, in + *joir* < L. *gaudere*, to be glad] 1. to have or experience with joy; get pleasure from; relish 2. to have the use or benefit of 3. to have as a condition; experience [to *enjoy* good health] —**enjoy oneself** to have a good time —**en·joy′a·ble** *adj.* —**en·joy′a·ble·ness** *n.* —**en·joy′a·bly** *adv.*
en·joy·ment (-mənt) *n.* 1. an enjoying 2. something enjoyed 3. pleasure; gratification; joy
en·kin·dle (en kin′d'l) *vt.* **-dled**, **-dling** 1. to set on fire; make blaze up 2. to stir up; arouse
enl. 1. enlarge 2. enlisted
en·lace (in lās′) *vt.* **-laced′**, **-lac′ing** 1. to wind about as with a lace; encircle; enfold 2. to entangle; interlace —**en·lace′ment** *n.*
en·large (in lärj′) *vt.* **-larged′**, **-larg′ing** 1. to make larger; increase in size, volume, extent, etc.; expand 2. *Photog.* to reproduce on a larger scale —*vi.* 1. to become larger; increase 2. to discuss at greater length or in greater detail (with *on* or *upon*) —**en·large′ment** *n.* —**en·larg′er** *n.*
en·light·en (in līt′'n) *vt.* 1. to give the light of knowledge to; free from ignorance, prejudice, or superstition 2. to give clarification to (a person) as to meanings, intentions, etc.; inform —**en·light′en·er** *n.*
en·light·en·ment (-mənt) *n.* an enlightening or being enlightened —**the Enlightenment** an 18th-cent. European philosophical and social movement characterized by rationalism
en·list (in list′) *vt.* 1. to enrol in some branch of the armed forces 2. to win the support of 3. to get (another's help, support, etc.) —*vi.* 1. to join some branch of the armed forces 2. to join or support a cause or movement (with *in*) —**en·list′ee′n**
enlisted man [U.S.] any man in the armed forces who is not a commissioned officer or warrant officer
en·list·ment (-mənt) *n.* 1. an enlisting or being enlisted 2. the period for which one enlists
en·liv·en (in lī′v'n) *vt.* to make active, vivacious, interesting, or cheerful; liven up or brighten —**en·liv′en·er** *n.* —**en·liv′en·ment** *n.*
en masse (on mas′; *Fr.* än mȧs′) [Fr., lit., in mass] in a group; as a whole; all together
en·mesh (en mesh′) *vt.* to catch in or as in the meshes of a net; entangle
en·mi·ty (en′mə tē) *n.*, *pl.* **-ties** [< OFr. < L. *inimicus*, ENEMY] the bitter attitude or feelings of an enemy or mutual enemies; hostility
en·no·ble (i nō′b'l) *vt.* **-bled**, **-bling** 1. to raise to the rank of

nobleman 2. to give a noble quality to; dignify —**en·no′-ble·ment** *n.* —**en·no′bler** *n.*
en·nui (on′wē; *Fr.* än nwē′) *n.* [Fr.: see ANNOY] weariness and dissatisfaction resulting from inactivity or lack of interest; boredom —**en·nuy·é** (on wē′yä) *adj.*
e·nor·mi·ty (i nôr′mə tē) *n.*, *pl.* **-ties** [< Fr. < L. < *enormis*, irregular, immense < *e-*, out + *norma*, rule] 1. great wickedness [the *enormity* of a crime] 2. a very wicked crime 3. enormous size or extent
e·nor·mous (i nôr′mas) *adj.* [see prec.] 1. very much exceeding the usual size, number, or degree; huge; vast 2. [Archaic] very wicked; outrageous —**e·nor′mous·ly** *adv.* —**e·nor′mous·ness** *n.*
e·no·sis (en′ō sis) *n.* [< ModGr. *henōsis*, union < Gr. *henoun*, to unite] the proposed union of Cyprus with Greece
e·nough (i nuf′) *adj.* [OE. *genoh*] as much or as many as necessary, desirable, or tolerable; sufficient —*n.* the amount or number needed, desired, or allowed —*adv.* 1. as much or as often as necessary; sufficiently 2. fully; quite [oddly *enough*] 3. just adequately; tolerably; fairly [he played well *enough*]
e·now (i nou′) *adj.*, *n.*, *adv.* [Archaic] enough
†**en pas·sant** (än pä sän′) [Fr.] in passing; by the way: used in chess, of the capture of a pawn, which has taken a first move of two squares, passing an opponent's pawn that dominates the first of those squares
en·plane (en plān′) *vi.* **-planed′**, **-plan′ing** to board an aeroplane
en·quire (in kwīr′) *vt.*, *vi.* **-quired′**, **-quir′ing** *same as* INQUIRE —**en·quir′y** *n.*, *pl.* **-quir′ies**
en·rage (in rāj′) *vt.* **-raged′**, **-rag′ing** to put into a rage; infuriate —**en·rage′ment** *n.*
†**en rap·port** (än rä pôr′) [Fr.] in harmony; in sympathy; in accord
en·rapt (in rapt′) *adj.* enraptured; rapt
en·rap·ture (-rap′chər) *vt.* **-tured**, **-tur·ing** to fill with great pleasure or delight: also **en·rav′ish**
en·rich (in rich′) *vt.* to make rich or richer; specif., *a)* to give more wealth to *b)* to give greater value or effectiveness to *c)* to decorate; adorn *d)* to fertilize (soil) *e)* to add vitamins, minerals, etc. to (bread, etc.) for more food value *f)* *Physics* to increase the concentration of an isotope in a mixture —**en·rich′ment** *n.*
en·rol (in rōl′) *vt.* **-rolled′**, **-roll′ing** 1. to record in a list 2. to enlist 3. to accept as a member —*vi.* to enrol oneself or become enrolled; register; become a member
en·rol·ment (-mənt) *n.* 1. an enrolling or being enrolled 2. a list of those enrolled 3. the number of those enrolled
en route (on rōōt′) [Fr.] on or along the way
Ens. Ensign
en·sconce (in skons′) *vt.* **-sconced′**, **-sconc′ing** [EN- + SCONCE²] 1. [Now Rare] to hide; conceal; shelter 2. to place or settle snugly
en·sem·ble (on som′b'l) *n.* [Fr. < OFr. < L. < *in-*, in + *simul*, at the same time] 1. all the parts considered as a whole; total effect 2. a whole costume, esp. of matching or complementary articles of dress 3. a company of actors, dancers, etc. 4. *Music a)* a small group of musicians performing together *b)* their instruments or voices *c)* the performance together of such a group, or of an orchestra, chorus, etc.
en·shrine (in shrīn′) *vt.* **-shrined′**, **-shrin′ing** 1. to enclose in or as in a shrine 2. to hold as sacred; cherish —**en·shrine′ment** *n.*
en·shroud (-shroud′) *vt.* to cover as if with a shroud; hide; veil; obscure
en·sign (en′sīn; *for 4 always*, -s'n) *n.* [< OFr. < L. < *insignia*: see INSIGNIA] 1. a badge, symbol, or token of office or authority 2. a flag or banner; specif., a national flag 3. *Brit. Army* formerly, a commissioned officer who served as standard-bearer 4. *U.S. Navy* a commissioned officer of the lowest rank —**en′sign·ship′**, **en′sign·cy** *n.*
en·si·lage (en′sil ij) *n.* [Fr.] 1. the preserving of green fodder by storage in a silo 2. green fodder so preserved; silage —*vt.* to store (green fodder) in a silo for preservation
en·slave (in slāv′) *vt.* **-slaved′**, **-slav′ing** 1. to put into slavery; make a slave of 2. to dominate; subjugate —**en·slave′ment** *n.* —**en·slav′er** *n.*
en·snare (-sner′) *vt.* **-snared′**, **-snar′ing** to catch in or as in a snare; trap —**en·snare′ment** *n.*
en·snarl (-snärl′) *vt.* to draw into a snarl or tangle
en·sue (in syōō′) *vi.* **-sued′**, **-su′ing** [< OFr., ult. < L. *insequi* < *in-*, in + *sequi*, to follow] 1. to come afterwards; follow immediately 2. to happen as a consequence; result
†**en suite** (än swēt′) [Fr., lit., in sequence] forming a set, or single unit [with bathroom *en suite*]
en·sure (in shoor′) *vt.* **-sured′**, **-sur′ing** [< Anglo-Fr. *enseurer*: see EN- & SURE] 1. to make sure; guarantee 2. to make safe; protect
E.N.T. *Med.* Ear, Nose and Throat
-ent (ənt, 'nt) [< OFr. *-ent*, L. *-ens* (gen. *entis*), stem ending of certain present participles] 1. *a suffix meaning that*

has, shows, or does [*insistent*] **2.** *a suffix meaning a person or thing that* [*superintendent, solvent*]

en·tab·la·ture (en tab′lə chər) *n.* [MFr. < It. *intavolatura* < *in-*, in + *tavola* < L. *tabula*, TABLE] *Archit.* **1.** a horizontal superstructure supported by columns and composed of architrave, frieze, and cornice **2.** any structure like this

ENTABLATURE — CORNICE, FRIEZE, ARCHITRAVE

en·ta·ble·ment (en tā′b′l mənt) *n.* [Fr. < OFr. < *entabler*] the platform of a pedestal, above the dado that supports a statue

en·tail (in tāl′) *vt.* [< ME. < *en-*, in + *taile*, an agreement < OFr. < *taillier*, to cut: see TAILOR] **1.** *Law* to limit the inheritance of (real property) to a specific line or class of heirs **2.** to cause or require as a necessary consequence; necessitate [*the plan entails work*] —*n.* **1.** an entailing or being entailed **2.** an entailed inheritance **3.** the order of descent for an entailed inheritance —**en·tail′ment** *n.*

en·tan·gle (in taŋ′g′l) *vt.* **-gled, -gling 1.** to involve in a tangle; ensnare **2.** to involve in difficulty **3.** to confuse; perplex **4.** to cause to be tangled; complicate —**en·tan′gle·ment** *n.*

en·ta·sis (en′tə sis) *n.,* pl. **-ses′** (-sēz′) [ModL. < Gr., lit., stretching] *Archit.* a slight, convex swelling in the shaft of a column: it corrects the illusion of concavity produced by a straight shaft

en·tente (on tänt′) *n.* [Fr. < OFr. < *entendre*, to understand] **1.** an understanding or agreement, as between nations **2.** the parties to this

en·tente cor·diale (än tänt′kôr dyäl′) [Fr., lit., cordial understanding] a treaty of friendship between nations

en·ter (en′tər) *vt.* [< OFr. *entrer* < L. *intrare* < *intra*, within] **1.** to come or go in or into **2.** to force a way into; penetrate **3.** to put into; insert **4.** to write down in a record, list, etc. [*to enter in the minutes*] **5.** to become a participant in (a contest) **6.** to join; become a member of (a school, club, etc.) **7.** to get (someone) admitted **8.** to start upon; begin (a career, etc.) **9.** to submit [*to enter a protest*] **10.** to register (a ship or cargo) at a customs house **11.** *Law* to place on record before a court —*vi.* **1.** to come or go into a place **2.** to pierce; penetrate —**enter into 1.** to engage in; take part in **2.** to form a part or component of **3.** to deal with; discuss —**enter on** (or **upon**) **1.** to begin; start **2.** to begin to possess or enjoy

en·ter·ic (en ter′ik) *adj.* [see ff.] intestinal: also **en·ter·al** (en′tər əl)

en·ter·o- [< Gr. *enteron*, intestine] *a combining form meaning* intestine: also **enter-**

en·ter·prise (en′tər prīz′) *n.* [< OFr. < *entreprendre*, to undertake < *entre-* (L. *inter*), in + *prendre* (L. *prehendere*), to take] **1.** an undertaking; project; specif., *a)* a bold, difficult, dangerous, or important undertaking *b)* a business venture or company **2.** willingness to undertake new or risky projects; energy and initiative **3.** active participation in projects —**en′ter·pris′er** *n.*

en·ter·pris·ing (-prī′ziŋ) *adj.* showing enterprise; full of energy and initiative; adventurous —**en′ter·pris′ing·ly** *adv.*

en·ter·tain (en′tər tān′) *vt.* [< OFr. *entre* < L. *inter*), between + *tenir* (L. *tenere*), to hold] **1.** to hold the interest of and give pleasure to; divert; amuse **2.** to give hospitality to; have as a guest **3.** to have in mind; consider, as an idea —*vi.* to have guests

en·ter·tain·er (-ər) *n.* a person who entertains; esp., popular singer, dancer, comedian, etc.

en·ter·tain·ing (-iŋ) *adj.* interesting and pleasurable; amusing —**en′ter·tain′ing·ly** *adv.*

en·ter·tain·ment (-mənt) *n.* **1.** an entertaining or being entertained **2.** something that entertains; interesting, diverting, or amusing thing; esp., a show or performance

en·thral (in thrôl′) *vt.* **-thralled′, -thrall′ing** [see EN- & THRALL] **1.** [Now Rare] to enslave **2.** to hold as if in a spell; captivate; fascinate — **en·thral′ment** *n.*

en·throne (-thrōn′) *vt.* **-throned′, -thron′ing 1.** to place on a throne; make a king, etc. of **2.** to accord the highest place to; exalt —**en·throne′ment** *n.*

en·thuse (-thyo͞oz′) *vi.* **-thused′, -thus′ing** [back-formation < ff.] [Colloq.] to express enthusiasm —*vt.* [Colloq.] to make enthusiastic

en·thu·si·asm (in thyo͞o′zē az′m) *n.* [< Gr. < *enthous*, possessed by a god, inspired < *en-*, in + *theos*, god] **1.** intense or eager interest; zeal; fervour **2.** something arousing this

en·thu·si·ast (-ast′) *n.* a person full of enthusiasm; an ardent admirer, a devotee, etc.

en·thu·si·as·tic (in thyo͞o′zē as′tik) *adj.* of, having, or showing enthusiasm; ardent —**en·thu′si·as′ti·cal·ly** *adv.*

en·tice (in tīs′) *vt.* **-ticed′, -tic′ing** [< OFr. *enticier*, to set afire, excite, prob. ult. < L. *in*, in + *titio*, a firebrand] to attract by offering hope of reward or pleasure; tempt —**en·tice′ment** *n.* —**en·tic′er** *n.* —**en·tic′ing·ly** *adv.*

en·tire (in tīr′) *adj.* [< OFr. *entier* < L. *integer*, untouched, whole] **1.** *a)* not lacking any of the parts; whole *b)* complete; absolute **2.** unbroken; intact **3.** being wholly of one piece **4.** not castrated **5.** *Bot.* having an unbroken margin, as some leaves —**en·tire′ly** *adv.* —**en·tire′ness** *n.*

en·tire·ty (in tīr′tē, -ə tē) *n.,* pl. **-ties 1.** the state or fact of being entire; wholeness; completeness **2.** an entire thing; whole —**in its entirety** as a whole

en·ti·tle (in tīt′′l) *vt.* **-tled, -tling 1.** to give a title or name to **2.** to honour or dignify by a title **3.** to give a right or legal title to —**en·ti′tle·ment** *n.*

en·ti·ty (en′tə tē) *n.,* pl. **-ties** [< Fr. or < ML. *entitas* < L. prp. of *esse*, to be] **1.** being; existence **2.** a thing that has definite, individual existence in reality or in the mind

en·to- [ModL. < Gr. *entos*, within] *a combining form meaning* within or inner

entom., entomol. entomology

en·tomb (in to͞om′) *vt.* to place in a tomb or grave; bury —**en·tomb′ment** *n.*

en·to·mo- [Fr. < Gr. *entoma* (*zōa*), lit., notched animals: cf. INSECT] *a combining form meaning* insect or insects

en·to·mol·o·gy (en′tə mol′ə jē) *n.* [see prec. & -LOGY] the branch of zoology that deals with insects —**en′to·mo·log′·i·cal** (-mə loj′i k′l), **en′to·mo·log′ic** *adj.* —**en′to·mo·log′·i·cal·ly** *adv.* —**en′to·mol′o·gist** *n.*

en·to·phyte (en′tə fīt′) *n.* [ENTO- + -PHYTE] a parasitic plant that lives inside other plants or inside animals

en·tou·rage (on′to͞o räzh′) *n.* [Fr. < *entourer*, to surround] a group of accompanying attendants, assistants, or associates; retinue

en·tr'acte (on trakt′) *n.* [Fr. < *entre-*, between + *acte*, an act] **1.** the interval between two acts of a play, opera, etc.; intermission **2.** music, a dance, etc. performed during this interval

en·trails (en′trālz) *n.pl.* [< OFr. < ML. *intralia* < L. < *interaneus*, internal < *inter*, between] **1.** the inner organs of men or animals; specif., the intestines; viscera; guts **2.** the inner parts of a thing

en·train (in trān′) *vt.* to put aboard a train, esp. troops —*vi.* to go aboard a train —**en·train′ment** *n.*

en·trance¹ (en′trəns) *n.* **1.** the act or point of entering **2.** a place for entering; door, gate, etc. **3.** permission or right to enter; admission

en·trance² (in träns′) *vt.* **-tranced′, -tranc′ing 1.** to put into a trance **2.** to enchant; charm; enrapture —**en·trance′ment** *n.* —**en·tranc′ing·ly** *adv.*

entrance fee the amount paid to enter an exhibition, club, etc.

en·trant (en′trənt) *n.* a person who enters

en·trap (in trap′) *vt.* **-trapped′, -trap′ping 1.** to catch as in a trap **2.** to trick into difficulty, as into incriminating oneself —**en·trap′ment** *n.*

en·treat (-trēt′) *vt.* [< Anglo-Fr. < OFr. < *en-*, in + *traiter*: see TREAT] to ask earnestly; beg; beseech; implore —*vi.* to make an earnest appeal; plead —**en·treat′ing·ly** *adv.* —**en·treat′ment** *n.*

en·treat·y (-ē) *n.,* pl. **-treat′ies** an earnest request; plea

en·tre·chat (ä′trə shä′) *n.* [Fr. < It. (*capriola*) *intrecciata*, intricate (leap)] *Ballet* a leap upwards during which the dancer repeatedly crosses his feet

en·tre·côte (än trə kōt′) *n.* [Fr.] a steak cut from between the ribs

en·tree, en·trée (on′trā) *n.* [< Fr. < OFr. *entrer*, ENTER] **1.** *a)* the act of entering *b)* the right or freedom to enter, participate, etc.; access **2.** *a)* [Chiefly U.S.] the main course of a meal *b)* formerly, and still in some countries, a dish served before the roast or between the main courses

en·trench (in trench′) *vt.* **1.** to surround or fortify with a trench or trenches **2.** to establish securely [*entrenched in office*] —*vi.* to encroach or infringe (*on* or *upon*) —**en·trench′ment** *n.*

en·tre·pre·neur (on′trə prə nur′) *n.* [Fr. < OFr. *entreprendre*: see ENTERPRISE] a person who organizes and manages a business undertaking, assuming the risk for the sake of profit

en·tro·py (en′trə pē) *n.* [G. *Entropie*, arbitrary use of Gr. *entropē*, a turning towards] a measure of the amount of energy unavailable for work in a thermodynamic system: entropy keeps increasing and available energy diminishing in a closed system, as the universe

en·trust (in trust′) *vt.* **1.** to charge with a trust or duty **2.** to assign the care of; turn over for safekeeping —**en·trust′·ment** *n.*

en·try (en′trē) *n.,* pl. **-tries** [< OFr. < *entrer*, ENTER] **1.** *a)* the act of entering; entrance *b)* the right or freedom to enter; entree **2.** a way or passage by which to enter; door, hall, etc. **3.** *a)* the recording of an item or note in a list, journal, etc. *b)* an item thus recorded **4.** the registration of a ship or cargo at a customs house **5.** one entered in a race, competition, etc. **6.** *Cards* a card with which a player or hand can win a trick and so gain the lead **7.** *Law* the taking possession of buildings, land, etc. by entering them

entry permit an authorization allowing entry into a country, usually not one's native country

en·twine (in twīn′) *vt., vi.* **-twined′, -twin′ing** to twine or twist together or around

e·nu·mer·ate (i nyōō′mə rāt′) *vt.* **-at′ed, -at′ing** [< L. pp. of *enumerare* < *e-*, out + *numerare*, to count < *numerus*, a number] **1.** to determine the number of; count **2.** to name one by one; specify, as in a list **—e·nu′mer·a·ble** *adj.* **—e·nu′mer·a′tion** *n.* **—e·nu′mer·a·tive** *adj.* **—e·nu′mer·a′tor** *n.*

e·nun·ci·a·ble (i nun′sē ə b'l) *adj.* ML. *enuntiabilis* capable of being enunciated **—e·nun′ci·a·bil′i·ty** *n.*

e·nun·ci·ate (i nun′sē āt′, -shē-) *vt.* **-at′ed, -at′ing** [< L. pp. of *enuntiare* < *e-*, out + *nuntiare*, ANNOUNCE] **1.** to state definitely **2.** to announce; proclaim **3.** to pronounce (words) **—vi.** to pronounce words, esp. clearly; articulate **—e·nun′ci·a′tion** *n.* **—e·nun′ci·a′tor** *n.*

en·u·re·sis (en′yōō rē′sis) *n.* [ModL. < Gr. *enourein*, to urinate in] inability to control urination; esp., bed-wetting **—en′u·ret′ic** (-ret′ik) *adj.*

en·vel·op (in vel′əp) *vt.* [< OFr. *envoluper*: see EN- & DEVELOP] **1.** to wrap up; cover completely **2.** to surround **3.** to conceal; hide **—en·vel′op·ment** *n.*

en·ve·lope (en′və lōp′, on′-) *n.* [< Fr. < OFr.: see prec.] **1.** a thing that envelops; wrapper; covering **2.** a folded paper container for letters, etc., usually with a gummed flap **3.** the bag that contains the gas in a dirigible or balloon **4.** *Biol.* any enclosing membrane, skin, etc. **5.** *Math.* a curve that is tangential to each one of a group of curves

en·ven·om (in ven′əm) *vt.* **1.** to put venom or poison on or into **2.** to fill with hate; embitter

en·vi·a·ble (en′vē ə b'l) *adj.* worthy to be envied or desired **—en′vi·a·ble·ness** *n.* **—en′vi·a·bly** *adv.*

en·vi·ous (-əs) *adj.* [< OFr. < L. < *invidia*, ENVY] feeling, showing, or resulting from envy **—en′vi·ous·ly** *adv.* **—en′vi·ous·ness** *n.*

en·vi·ron (in vī′rən) *vt.* [< OFr. < *environ*, about: see ENVIRONS] to surround; encircle

en·vi·ron·ment (in vī′rən mənt) *n.* [prec. + -MENT] **1.** surroundings **2.** all the conditions, circumstances, and influences surrounding, and affecting the development of, an organism or group of organisms **—en·vi′ron·men′tal** (-men′t'l) *adj.* **—en·vi′ron·men′tal·ly** *adv.*

en·vi·ron·men·tal·ist (in vī′rən men′t'l ist) *n.* a person working to solve environmental problems, such as air and water pollution, the careless use of natural resources, uncontrolled population growth, etc.

en·vi·rons (in vī′rəns, en′vər ənz) *n.pl.* [< OFr. < *en-*, in + *viron*, a circuit < *virer*, to turn] **1.** the districts surrounding a city; suburbs or outskirts **2.** surrounding area; vicinity

en·vis·age (en viz′ij) *vt.* **-aged, -ag·ing** [< Fr.: see EN- & VISAGE] to form an image of in the mind **—en·vis′age·ment** *n.*

en·vi·sion (en vizh′ən) *vt.* to imagine (something not yet in existence)

en·voy¹ (en′voi) *n.* [< Fr. < *envoyer*, to send < OFr. < *en-*(L. *in*), in + *voie* (L. *via*), way] **1.** a messenger; agent **2.** an agent sent by a government or ruler to transact diplomatic business: an **envoy extraordinary** ranks just below an ambassador

en·voy² (en′voi) *n.* [< OFr. *envoy*, lit., a sending: see prec.] a postscript to a poem, essay, or book, containing a dedication, explanation, etc.; also **en′voi**

en·vy (en′vē) *n.,* *pl.* **-vies** [< OFr. < L. *invidia* < *invidere*, to look askance at < *in-*, upon + *videre*, to look] **1.** a feeling of discontent and ill will because of another's advantages, possessions, etc. **2.** desire for some advantage, quality, etc. that another has **3.** an object of envious feeling **—vt. -vied, -vy·ing** to feel envy towards, at, or because of **—en′vi·er** *n.* **—en′vy·ing·ly** *adv.*

en·wrap (en rap′) *vt.* **-wrapped′, -wrap′ping** to wrap; envelop

en·wreathe (-rēth′) *vt.* **-wreathed′, -wreath′ing** to encircle with or as with a wreath

en·zo·ot·ic (en′zō ot′ik) *adj.* [< Gr. *en-*, in & *zōion*, animal] affecting animals in a certain area, climate, or season: said of diseases **—n.** an enzootic disease

en·zyme (en′zīm) *n.* [< G. < LGr. *enzymos*, leavened < Gr. *en-*, in + *zymē*, leaven] a proteinlike substance, formed in plant and animal cells, that acts as an organic catalyst in initiating or speeding up specific chemical reactions **—en′zy·mat′ic** (-zi mat′ik), **en·zy′mic** *adj.*

e·o- [< Gr. *ēōs*, dawn] a prefix meaning early, early part of a period [*Eocene*]

E·o·cene (ē′ə sēn′) *adj.* [EO- + Gr. *kainos*, new] designating or of the second and longest epoch of the Tertiary Period in the Cainozoic Era **—the Eocene** the Eocene Epoch or its rocks: see GEOLOGY, chart

e·o·hip·pus (ē′ō hip′əs) *n.* [ModL. < EO- + Gr. *hippos*, horse] any of a genus of extinct progenitors of the modern horse

E·o·li·an (ē ō′lē ən) *adj., n.* [U.S.] same as AEOLIAN

e·o·lith·ic (ē′ō lith′ik) *adj.* [EO- + -LITHIC] designating or of the early part of the Stone Age, during which crude stone tools were first used

e·on (ē′ən, ē′on) *n.* U.S. var. of AEON

e·o·sin (ē′ə sin) *n.* [< Gr. *ēōs*, dawn + -IN¹] a rosecoloured dye used as an industrial pigment and as a biological stain: also **e′o·sine** (-sin, -sēn′) **—e′o·sin′ic** *adj.*

-e·ous (ē əs) [< L. *-eus* + -OUS] a suffix meaning having the nature of, like [*beauteous*]

EP Extended Play

ep·arch (ep′ärk) *n.* [Gr. < *epi-*, over + *archos*, ruler] *Orthodox Eastern Church* a bishop or metropolitan **—ep′-arch·y** *n.*

ep·au·let, ep·au·lette (ep′ə let′) *n.* [< Fr. < OFr. < L. *spatula*: see SPATULA] a shoulder ornament, as on military uniforms

EPAULETTES

é·pée (e pā′, ā-) *n.* [Fr. < OFr. < L. < Gr. *spathē*, blade] a sword, esp. a thin, pointed sword without a cutting edge, used in fencing **—e·pee′ist, é·pée′ist** *n.*

ep·ei·ro·gen·e·sis (ep′ī rō jen′ə sis) *n.* [< Gr. *ēpeiros*, mainland + -GENESIS] the formation of continents by relatively slow movements of the earth's crust: also **ep′ei·rog′e·ny** (-roj′ə nē)

e·pergne (i purn′) *n.* [prob. < Fr. *épargne*, a saving] an ornamental centrepiece for a table, consisting of a stand with holders for sweets, fruit, flowers, etc.

ep·ex·e·ge·sis (ep ek′sə jē′sis) *n.* [< Gr. *epexēgēsis*, detailed account] additional explanation; further clarification, as by the addition of a word or words

Eph. Ephesians: also **Ephes.**

e·phah, e·pha (ē′fə) *n.* [< LL. < Heb. *'ēphāh*] an ancient Hebrew dry measure, estimated at from 1/3 bushel to a little over one bushel (33 litres)

e·phed·rine (i fed′rin) *n.* [< ModL. *Ephedra*, genus name of the plants < L. < Gr. *ephedra*, the horsetail] an alkaloid derived from certain Asiatic plants or synthesized, used to relieve nasal congestion and asthma

e·phem·er·a (i fem′ər ə) *n.,* *pl.* **-er·as, -er·ae′** (-ē′) [ModL. < Gr. *ephēmeros*, short-lived] **1.** same as MAYFLY **2.** an ephemeral thing

e·phem·er·al (i fem′ər əl) *adj.* [< Gr. < *epi-*, upon + *hēmera*, a day + -AL] **1.** lasting only one day **2.** short-lived; transitory **—n.** an ephemeral thing **—e·phem′er·al·ly** *adv.*

e·phem·er·id (-id) *n.* [see prec. & -ID] same as MAYFLY

e·phem·er·is (-is) *n.,* *pl.* **eph·e·mer·i·des** (ef′ə mer′ə dēz′) [see EPHEMERAL] a table giving the daily positions of a heavenly body for a given period

eph·od (ef′od, -əd) *n.* [< LL. < Heb. < *āphad*, to put on] an outer vestment formerly worn by Jewish priests

eph·or (ef′ôr) *n.,* *pl.* **-ors, -or·i** (-ə rī′) [< L. < Gr. < *epi-*, over + *horan*, to see] any of a body of five magistrates of ancient Sparta

ep·i- [< Gr. *epi*, at, on, upon, etc.] a prefix meaning on, upon, over, on the outside, anterior, beside [*epiglottis, epidemic, epidermis*]: also **ep-** (before a vowel) and **eph-** (in an aspirated word, as *ephemeral*)

ep·ic (ep′ik) *n.* [< L. < Gr. < *epos*, a word, song] **1.** a long narrative poem with a dignified style and certain formalities of structure, about the deeds of a traditional or historical hero or heroes, as the *Iliad* and *Odyssey* **2.** a prose narrative, play, etc. regarded as having the qualities of an epic **3.** a series of events regarded as a proper subject for an epic **—adj.** of, or having the nature of, an epic; heroic; grand; majestic: also **ep′i·cal** **—ep′i·cal·ly** *adv.*

ep·i·ca·lyx (ep′ə kā′liks, -kal′iks) *n.,* *pl.* **-lyx·es, -ly·ces′** (-lə sēz′) [EPI- +. CALYX] a ring of small leaves (called *bracts*) at the base of certain flowers, resembling an extra outer calyx

ep·i·can·thus (-kan′thəs) *n.* [EPI- + CANTHUS] a small fold of skin sometimes covering the inner corner of the eye **—ep′i·can′thic** *adj.*

ep·i·car·di·um (-kär′dē əm) *n.,* *pl.* **-di·a** (-ə) [ModL. < EPI- + Gr. *kardia*, heart] the innermost layer of the pericardium **—ep′i·car′di·al** *adj.*

ep·i·carp (ep′ə kärp′) *n.* [EPI- + -CARP] same as EXOCARP

ep·i·cene (ep′ə sēn′) *adj.* [< L. < Gr.< *epi-*, to + *koinos*, common] **1.** belonging to one sex but having characteristics of the other; hermaphroditic **2.** sexless **3.** effeminate, effete **—n.** an epicene person

ep·i·cen·tre (-sen′tər) *n.* **1.** the area of the earth's surface directly above the place of origin, or focus, of an earthquake **2.** a focal or central point **—ep′i·cen′tral** *adj.*

ep·i·cure (ep′i kyoor′) *n.* [< L. < Gr.: after *Epicurus* (341? -270 B.C.), Gr. philosopher] **1.** a person who enjoys and has a discriminating taste for fine foods and drinks **2.** [Archaic] a person who is especially fond of luxury and sensuous pleasure **—ep′i·cur·ism** *n.*

Ep·i·cu·re·an (ep′i kyoor′ē ən) *adj.* **1.** of Epicurus or his philosophy **2.** [e-] *a)* fond of luxury and sensuous pleasure, esp. that of eating and drinking *b)* suited to or characteristic of an epicure **—n. 1.** a follower of Epicurus or his philosophy **2.** [e-] an epicure **—Ep′i·cu·re′an·ism, ep′-i·cu·re′an·ism** *n.*

ep·i·cy·cle (ep′ə sī′k'l) *n.* [< LL. *epicyclus* < Gr. *epikyklos* < *epi-*, upon + *kyklos*, circle] a circle whose centre moves round in the circumference of a greater circle

ep·i·deic·tic (ep′ə dīk′tik) *adj.* [< Gr. < *epideiknynai*, to display] intended for display, esp. rhetorical display

ep·i·dem·ic (ep′ə dem′ik) *adj.* [< Fr. < *épidémie* < ML. < Gr. < *epi-*, among + *dēmos*, people] prevalent and spreading rapidly among many individuals in a community at the same time, as a contagious disease: also **ep′i·dem′-i·cal —n. 1.** an epidemic disease **2.** the epidemic spreading of a disease **3.** the rapid, widespread occurrence of a fad, fashion, etc. **—ep′i·dem′i·cal·ly** *adv.*

ep·i·der·mis (ep′ə dur′mis) *n.* [LL. < Gr. < *epi-*, upon + *derma*, the skin] **1.** the outermost layer of skin in vertebrates **2.** the outermost layer of cells covering seed plants and ferns **3.** any of various other integuments **—ep′-i·der′mal, ep′i·der′mic** *adj.*

ep·i·der·moid (-dur′moid) *adj.* like epidermis: also **ep′-i·der′moi′dal**

ep·i·di·a·scope (ep′ə dī′ə skōp′) *n.* [EPI- + DIA- + -SCOPE] an optical device for projecting on a screen a magnified image of an opaque or transparent object

ep·i·dur·al (ep′ə dyoo′əl) *adj.* [EPI- + DURA(MATER) + -AL] *Anat.* affecting or on the dura mater **—n.** an analgesia that gives relief from pain during a confinement without any loss of consciousness

ep·i·ge·al (ep′ə jē′əl) *adj.* [Gr. *epigeios*, on the earth] **1.** *Bot. a)* growing close to the ground *b)* directed above the ground after germination: said of cotyledons **2.** *Zool.* living on the surface of the earth

ep·i·glot·tis (ep′ə glot′is) *n.* [see EPI- & GLOTTIS] the thin, triangular, lidlike piece of cartilage that folds back over the opening of the windpipe during swallowing, thus preventing food, etc. from entering the lungs **—ep′-i·glot′tal, ep′i·glot′tic** *adj.*

ep·i·gram (ep′ə gram′) *n.* [< OFr. < L. < Gr. *epigramma* < *epi-*, upon + *graphein*, to write] **1.** a short poem with a witty or satirical point **2.** any terse, witty, pointed statement, often with a clever twist in thought (Ex.: "Experience is the name everyone gives to his mistakes") **—ep·i·gram·mat·ic** (ep′i grə mat′ik), **ep′i·gram·mat′i·cal** *adj.* **—ep′i·gram·mat′i·cal·ly** *adv.* **—ep′-i·gram′ma·tist** *n.*

ep·i·gram·ma·tize (ep′ə gram′ə tīz′) *vt., vi.* **-tized′, -tiz′ing** to express (something) epigrammatically; make epigrams (about)

ep·i·graph (ep′ə graf′, -gräf′) *n.* [Gr. *epigraphē*, inscription < *epigraphein*: see EPIGRAM] **1.** an inscription on a building, monument, etc. **2.** a motto or quotation at the beginning of a book, chapter, etc.

ep·i·graph·ic (ep′ə graf′ik) *adj.* of an epigraph or epigraphy: also **ep′i·graph′i·cal —ep′i·graph′i·cal·ly** *adv.*

e·pig·ra·phy (i pig′rə fē) *n.* [see EPIGRAPH] **1.** inscriptions collectively **2.** the study that deals with deciphering, interpreting, and classifying inscriptions **—e·pig′ra·phist, e·pig′ra·pher** *n.*

ep·i·lep·sy (ep′ə lep′sē) *n.* [< OFr. < LL. < Gr. *epilēpsia* < *epi-*, upon + *lambanein*, to seize] a chronic disease of the nervous system, characterized by convulsions and, often, unconsciousness

ep·i·lep·tic (ep′ə lep′tik) *adj.* of or having epilepsy **—n.** a person who has epilepsy

ep·i·logue (ep′ə log′) *n.* [< OFr. < L. < Gr. *epilogos*, conclusion < *epi-*, upon + *legein*, to say] **1.** a closing section of a novel, play, etc., providing further comment **2.** a short speech or poem spoken to the audience by one of the actors at the end of a play **3.** the actor speaking this **4.** the concluding daily programme on radio and television **e·pil·o·gist** (e pil′ə jist) *n.*

ep·i·neph·rine (ep′ə nef′rin, -rēn) *n.* U.S. name for ADRENALIN

E·piph·a·ny (i pif′ə nē) *n., pl.* **-nies** [< OFr. < LL. < Gr. *epiphaneia*, appearance < *epi-*, upon + *phainein*, to show] in many Christian churches, a yearly festival (January 6) commemorating the revealing of Jesus as the Christ to the Gentiles in the persons of the Magi

ep·i·phe·nom·e·non (ep′i fə nom′ə non′) *n., pl.* **-na** (-nə) [EPI- + PHENOMENON] **1.** a secondary or additional

phenomenon **2.** *Med.* an additional, usually unexpected occurrence in the course of a disease

ep·i·phyte (ep′ə fīt′) *n.* [EPI- + -PHYTE] a nonparasitic plant that grows on another plant, producing its own food by photosynthesis, as certain orchids, mosses, and lichens; air plant **—ep′i·phyt′ic** (-fit′ik) *adj.* **—ep′i·phyt′i·cal·ly** *adv.*

Epis. Epistle

Epis., Episc. **1.** Episcopal **2.** Episcopalian

e·pis·co·pa·cy (i pis′kə pə sē) *n., pl.* **-cies** [< LL. < *episcopus*, BISHOP] **1.** church government by bishops **2.** *same as* EPISCOPATE

e·pis·co·pal (-kə pəl) *adj.* [see prec.] **1.** of or governed by bishops **2.** [E-] designating or of any of various churches governed by bishops, as the Anglican Church **—e·pis′-co·pal·ly** *adv.*

E·pis·co·pa·li·an (i pis′kə pāl′yən, -pā′lē ən) *adj. same as* EPISCOPAL **—n.** [sometimes e-] a member of an episcopal church or a person believing in episcopal government **—E·pis′co·pa′li·an·ism** *n.*

e·pis·co·pate (i pis′kə pit, -pāt′) *n.* **1.** the position, rank, or term of office of a bishop **2.** a bishop's see **3.** bishops collectively

ep·i·sode (ep′ə sōd′) *n.* [< Gr. < *epeisodios*, following upon the entrance < *epi-*, upon + *eis-*, into + *hodos*, a way] **1.** any part of a novel, poem, musical composition, etc. that is complete in itself; incident **2.** any event or series of events complete in itself but forming part of a larger one **3.** any instalment of a serialized story or drama

ep·i·sod·ic (ep′ə sod′ik) *adj.* **1.** of the nature of an episode; incidental **2.** made up of episodes, often not well intergrated; sporadic Also **ep′i·sod′i·cal —ep′i·sod′i·cal·ly** *adv.*

ep·i·stax·is (ep′ə stak′sis) *n.* [ModL. < Gr. *epistazein*, to bleed at the nose] a nosebleed

e·pis·te·mol·o·gy (i pis′tə mol′ə jē) *n., pl.* **-gies** [< Gr. *epistēmē*, knowledge + -LOGY] the study or theory of the origin, nature, methods, and limits of knowledge **—e·pis′-te·mo·log′i·cal** (-mə loj′i k'l) *adj.* **—e·pis′te·mo·log′i·cal·ly** *adv.* **—e·pis′te·mol′o·gist** *n.*

e·pis·tle (i pis′'l) *n.* [< OFr. < L. < Gr. *epistolē* < *epi-*, to + *stellein*, to send] **1.** a letter, esp. a long, formal, instructive letter: now used humorously **2.** [E-] *a)* any of the letters of the Apostles in the New Testament *b)* a selection from these Epistles, read as part of Mass, Communion, etc. in various churches **—e·pis′tler** *n.*

e·pis·to·lar·y (-tə lər ē) *adj.* [see prec.] **1.** of or suitable to letters or letter writing **2.** contained in, conducted by, or made up of letters

ep·i·style (ep′ə stīl′) *n.* [L. < Gr. *epistylion* < *epi-*, on + *stylos*, column] *same as* ARCHITRAVE (sense 1)

ep·i·taph (ep′ə täf′) *n.* [< OFr. < L. *epitaphium*, eulogy < Gr. < *epi-*, upon + *taphos*, tomb] an inscription, as on a tomb, in memory of the person buried there **—ep′i·taph′ic, ep′i·taph′i·al** *adj.*

ep·i·the·li·um (ep′ə thē′lē əm) *n., pl.* **-li·ums, -li·a** (-ə) [ModL. < Gr. *epi-*, upon + *thēlē*, nipple] cellular tissue covering surfaces, forming glands, and lining most cavities of the body **—ep′i·the′li·al** *adj.*

ep·i·thet (ep′e thet′, -thət) *n.* [< L. < Gr. *epitheton* < *epi-*, on + *tithenai*, to put] **1.** a word or phrase used to characterize some person or thing, often specif. a disparaging one (Ex.: "egghead" for an intellectual) **2.** descriptive name or title (Ex.: Philip the Fair) **—ep′i·thet′-i·cal, ep′i·thet′ic** *adj.*

e·pit·o·me (i pit′ə mē) *n., pl.* **-mes** [L. < Gr. *epitomē*, abridgment < *epi-*, upon + *temnein*, to cut] **1.** a short statement of the main points of a book, report, etc.; abstract; summary **2.** a person or thing that is representative of the characteristics of a whole class

e·pit·o·mize (-mīz′) *vt.* **-mized′, -miz′ing** to make or be an epitome of **—e·pit′o·miz′er** *n.*

ep·i·zo·ot·ic (ep′ə zō ot′ik) *adj.* [< Fr. < Gr. *epi-*, upon + *zōion*, animal] epidemic among animals **—n.** an epizootic disease

EPNS Electroplated Nickel Silver

ep·och (ē′pok) *n.* [< ML. < Gr. *epochē*, a pause < *epi-*, upon + *echein*, to hold] **1.** the beginning of a new and important period in the history of anything [the first earth satellite marked a new *epoch* in man's study of the universe] **2.** a period of time considered in terms of noteworthy events, developments, persons, etc. [an *epoch* of social revolution] **3.** *Astron.* the time at which observations are made, as of the positions of planets or stars **4.** *Geol.* a subdivision of a geologic period [the Eocene *Epoch*] **—ep′och·al** *adj.* **—ep′och·al·ly** *adv.*

ep·ode (ep′ōd) *n.* [MFr. < L. < Gr. *epōidos*, aftersong < *epi-*, upon + *aeidein*, to sing] **1.** a form of lyric poem in which a short line follows a longer one **2.** final stanza in certain lyric odes, following the strophe and antistrophe

ep·o·nym (ep′ə nim′) *n.* [< Gr. < *epi-*, upon + *onyma*, a name] **1.** a real or mythical person from whose name the name of a nation, race, etc. is derived [William *Penn* is the *eponym* of *Penn*sylvania] **2.** a person whose name has become identified with some period, movement, theory, etc. —**e·pon·y·mous** (i pon'ə məs), **ep'o·nym'ic** (-nim'ik) *adj.*

ep·ox·y (e pok'sē) *adj.* [EP(I)- + OXY(GEN)] designating or of a compound in which an oxygen atom is joined to two carbon atoms in a chain to form a bridge; specif., designating a tough resin formed by polymerization, used in glues, etc. —*n., pl.* **-ox·ies** an epoxy resin

‡**ép·ris** (ā prē') *adj.* [Fr.] enamoured of; smitten

ep·si·lon (ep'sə lon', -lən) *n.* [Gr.] the fifth letter of the Greek alphabet (E, ε)

Ep·som salts (or **salt**) (ep'səm) [< *Epsom*, town in Surrey] a white, crystalline salt, magnesium sulphate, Mg $SO_4 \cdot 7H_2O$, used as a cathartic

eq. 1. equal 2. equation 3. equivalent

eq·ua·ble (ek'wə b'l) *adj.* [< L. < *aequare*, to make equal < *aequus*: see ff.] 1. not varying or fluctuating much; steady; uniform [an *equable* temperature] 2. even; serene [an *equable* temperament] —**eq'ua·bil'i·ty** *n.* —**eq'ua·bly** *adv.*

e·qual (ē'kwəl) *adj.* [< L. < *aequus*, plain, even, flat] 1. of the same quantity, size, number, value, degree, etc. 2. having the same rights, ability, rank, etc. 3. evenly proportioned; being balanced or uniform 4. having the necessary ability, power, courage, etc. (*to*) [equal to the challenge] 5. [Archaic] fair; just —*n.* any thing or person that is equal [to be the *equal* of another] —*vt.* **e'qualled, e'·qual·ling** 1. to be equal to; match in value 2. to do or make something equal to [to *equal* a record]

e·qual·i·tar·i·an (i kwol'ə ter'ē ən) *adj., n.* same as EGALITARIAN —**e·qual'i·tar'i·an·ism** *n.*

e·qual·i·ty (i kwol'ə tē) *n., pl.* **-ties** state or instance of being equal

e·qual·ize (ē'kwə līz') *vt.* **-ized', -iz'ing** 1. to make equal 2. to make uniform —*vi.* to become equal, esp., in football, to reach the same score as one's opponents —**e'qual·i·za'·tion** *n.* —**e'qual·iz'er** *n.*

e·qual·ly (ē'kwə lē) *adv.* in an equal manner; to an equal degree; uniformly, impartially, etc.

equal sign (or **mark**) the arithmetical sign (=), indicating equality (Ex.: 2 + 2 = 4)

e·qua·nim·i·ty (ek'wə nim'ə tē, ē'kwə-) *n.* [< L. < *aequus*, even + *animus*, the mind] calmness of mind; evenness of temper; composure

e·quate (i kwāt') *vt.* **e·quat'ed, e·quat'ing** [< L. pp. of *aequare*, to make equal < *aequus*, plain, even] 1. *a*) to make equal or equivalent *b*) to treat, regard, or express as equal, equivalent, or closely related 2. *Math.* to state the equality of; put in the form of an equation —**e·quat'a·ble** *adj.*

e·qua·tion (i kwā'zhən) *n.* 1. an equating or being equated 2. a complex whole 3. a statement of equality between two quantities, as shown by the equal sign (=) [a quadratic *equation*] 4. an expression in which symbols and formulas are used to represent a chemical reaction (Ex.: $H_2 SO_4$ + $2NaCl$ + $Na_2 SO_4$) —**e·qua'tion·al** *adj.*

e·qua·tor (i kwāt'ər) *n.* [< ML. < LL. *aequator* < L. *aequare*: see EQUATE] 1. an imaginary circle around the earth, equally distant from the North Pole and the South Pole: it divides the earth into the Northern Hemisphere and the Southern Hemisphere 2. any circle that divides a sphere, etc. into two equal parts 3. same as CELESTIAL EQUATOR

e·qua·to·ri·al (ē'kwə tôr'ē əl, ek'wə-) *adj.* 1. of or near the earth's equator 2. of any equator 3. like or characteristic of conditions near the earth's equator [*equatorial* heat]

eq·uer·ry (ek'wər ē; *also, esp. at court* i kwer') *n., pl.* **-ries** [altered (after L. *equus*, horse) < Fr. < OFr. *escuerie*, status of a squire] 1. formerly, an officer in charge of the horses of a royal or noble household 2. an officer who is a personal attendant on some member of a royal family

e·ques·tri·an (i kwes'trē ən) *adj.* [< L. *equestris* < *eques*, horseman < *equus*, a horse] 1. of horses, horsemen, or horsemanship 2. on horseback [an *equestrian* statue] —*n.* a rider on horseback, as in a circus —**e·ques'tri·an·ism** *n.* —**e·ques'tri·enne'** (-trē en') *n. fem.*

equi- [< L. *aequus*, equal] *a combining form meaning* equal, equally [*equidistant*]

e·qui·an·gu·lar (ē'kwə aŋ'gyə lər) *adj.* having all angles equal

e·qui·dis·tant (-dis'tənt) *adj.* equally distant —**e'qui·dis'·tance** *n.* —**e'qui·dis'tant·ly** *adv.*

e·qui·lat·er·al (-lat'ər əl) *adj.* [< LL. < L. *aequus*, equal + *latus*, side] having all sides equal [an *equilateral* triangle] —*n.* 1. a figure having equal sides 2. a side exactly equal to another

e·quil·i·brant (i kwil'ə brənt) *n.* [< Fr. < L. *aequilibrium*, EQUILIBRIUM] *Physics* a force or combination of forces that can balance another

e·quil·i·brate (i kwil'ə brāt', ē'kwə lī'brāt) *vt., vi.* **-brat'ed, -brat'ing** to bring into or be in equilibrium; balance or counterbalance —**equil'i·bra'tion** *n.* —**e·quil'i·bra'tor** *n.*

e·qui·li·brist (i kwil'ə brist) *n.* [Fr. *équilibriste*] a performer who does tricks of balancing, as a tightrope walker

e·qui·lib·ri·um (ē'kwə lib'rē əm) *n., pl.* **-ri·ums, -ri·a** (-ə) [L. *aequilibrium* < *aequus*, equal + *libra*, a balance] 1. a state

of balance or equality between opposing forces 2. a state of balance or adjustment of conflicting desires, interests, etc. 3. *a*) bodily stability or balance *b*) mental or emotional stability

e·quine (ē'kwīn, ek'wīn) *adj.* [< L. < *equus*, a horse] of, like, or characteristic of a horse —*n.* a horse

e·qui·noc·tial (ē'kwə nok'shəl) *adj.* 1. relating to either of the equinoxes 2. occurring at about the time of an equinox [an *equinoctial* storm] 3. equatorial —*n.* 1. same as CELESTIAL EQUATOR 2. an equinoctial storm

equinoctial circle (or **line**) same as CELESTIAL EQUATOR

e·qui·nox (ē'kwə noks') *n.* [< OFr. < ML. < L. < *aequus*, equal + *nox*, night] 1. the time when the sun crosses the equator, making night and day of equal length in all parts of the earth: the **vernal equinox** occurs about March 21, the **autumnal equinox** about September 22 2. either of the two points on the celestial equator where the sun crosses it on these dates: also **equinoctial point**

e·quip (i kwip') *vt.* **e·quipped', e·quip'ping** [< Fr. < OFr. *esquiper*, embark, prob. < OE. < *scip*, a ship; or < ? ON. *skipa*, to arrange] 1. to provide with what is needed; outfit 2. to prepare by training, instruction, etc. —**e·quip'per** *n.*

eq·ui·page (ek'wə pij) *n.* 1. the equipment of a ship, army, expedition, etc. 2. a carriage, esp. one with horses and liveried servants

e·quip·ment (i kwip'mənt) *n.* 1. an equipping or being equipped 2. whatever one is equipped with; supplies, furnishings, apparatus, etc. 3. one's abilities, knowledge, etc.

eq·ui·poise (ek'wə poiz', ē'kwə-) *n.* [EQUI- + $POISE^1$] 1. equal distribution of weight; state of balance 2. a weight or force that balances another

e·qui·pol·lent (ē'kwə pol'ənt) *adj.* [ME. < L. < *aequus*, equal + *pollens*, prp. of *pollere*, to be strong] 1. equal in force, weight, etc. 2. equivalent in meaning

eq·ui·se·tum (ek'wə sēt'əm) *n., pl.* **-tums, -ta** (-tə) [ModL. < L. < *equus*, horse + *saeta*, bristle] same as HORSETAIL (sense 2)

eq·ui·ta·ble (ek'wit ə b'l) *adj.* 1. characterized by equity; fair; just 2. *Law a*) having to do with equity, as distinguished from common or statute law *b*) valid in equity —**eq'ui·ta·ble·ness** *n.* —**eq'ui·ta·bly** *adv.*

eq·ui·ta·tion (ek'wə tā'shən) *n.* [< L. < pp. of *equitare*, to ride < *eques*, horseman] the art of riding on horseback; horsemanship

eq·ui·ty (ek'wət ē) *n., pl.* **-ties** [< OFr. < L. *aequitas*, equality < *aequus*, equal] 1. fairness; impartiality; justice 2. anything that is fair or equitable 3. the value of property beyond the total amount owed on it in mortages, etc. 4. [*pl.*] the ordinary shares of a limited company 5. [E-] the Actor's Trade Union 6. *Law a*) a system of rules and doctrines, as in Britain, supplementing common and statute law and superseding such law when it proves inadequate for just settlement *b*) a right or claim recognized in a court of equity

equiv. equivalent

e·quiv·a·lence (i kwiv'ə ləns) *n.* the condition of being equivalent; equality of quantity, value, meaning, etc.: also **e·quiv'a·len·cy**

e·quiv·a·lent (-lənt) *adj.* [< OFr. < LL. < L. *aequus*, equal + *valere*, to be strong] 1. equal in quantity, value, force, meaning, etc. 2. *Chem.* having the same valence 3. *Geom.* equal in area or volume but not of the same shape —*n.* 1. an equivalent thing 2. *Chem.* the quantity by weight (of a substance) that combines with one gramme of hydrogen or eight grammes of oxygen —**e·quiv'a·lent·ly** *adv.*

e·quiv·o·cal (i kwiv'ə k'l) *adj.* [< LL. *aequivocus* (see ff.) + -AL] 1. having two or more meanings; purposely vague or ambiguous [an *equivocal* reply] 2. uncertain; doubtful [an *equivocal* outcome] 3. suspicious; questionable [*equivocal* conduct] —**e·quiv'o·cal'i·ty** (-kal'ə tē), **e·quiv'o·cal·ness** *n.* —**e·quiv'o·cal·ly** *adv.*

e·quiv·o·cate (-kāt') *vi.* **-cat'ed, -cat'ing** [< LL. < *aequivocus*, of like sound < L. *aequus*, equal + *vox*, voice] to use equivocal terms in order to deceive, mislead, hedge, etc. —**e·quiv'o·ca'tion** *n.* —**e·quiv'o·ca'tor** *n.*

er (*variously* u, ə, ä, *etc.*) *interj.* a conventionalized representation of a sound often made by a speaker when hesitating briefly

-er (ər) *a suffix of various origins and meanings:* 1. [OE. *-ere*] *a*) a person having to do with [*hatter*]: see also -IER, -YER *b*) a person living in [*Londoner*] *c*) a thing or action connected with [*diner*] *d*) a person or thing that [*sprayer, roller*] 2. [OE. *-ra*] more: *added to many adjectives and adverbs to form the comparative degree* [*greater, later*] 3. [< Anglo-Fr. inf. suffix] *the action of* ....*ing: used in legal language* [*demurrer, waiver*] 4. [OE. *-rian*, freq. suffix] repeatedly [*flicker*]

Er *Chem.* erbium

E.R. 1. [L. *Edwardus Rex*] King Edward 2. [L. *Elizabetha Regina*] Queen Elizabeth

e·ra (ir'ə) *n.* [LL. *aera*, era, earlier sense, "counters" < pl. of L. *aes*, brass] 1. a system of reckoning time by numbering the years from some given date [the Christian *Era*] **2.** an event or date that marks the beginning of a new period in the history of something **3.** a period of time measured from some important occurrence or date **4.** a period of time considered in terms of noteworthy and characteristic events, men, etc. [an *era* of progress] **5.** any of the main divisions of geologic time [the Paleozoic *Era*]: see also EPOCH, PERIOD, AGE

e·ra·di·ate (ē rā′dē āt′) *vi.*, *vt.* **-at′ed**, **-at′ing** *same as* RADIATE —**e·ra′di·a′tion** *n.*

e·rad·i·cate (i rad′ə kāt′) *vt.* **-cat′ed**, **-cat′ing** [< L. pp. of *eradicare*, to root out < *e-*, out + *radix*, a root] **1.** to tear out by the roots; uproot **2.** to wipe out; destroy —**e·rad′-i·ca·ble** (-kə b'l) *adj.* —**e·rad′i·ca′tion** *n.* —**e·rad′i·ca′tive** *adj.* —**e·rad′i·ca′tor** *n.*

e·rase (i rās′) *vt.* **e·rased′**, **e·ras′ing** [< L. pp. of *eradere* < *e-*, out + *radere*, to scrape] **1.** to rub, scrape, or wipe out; efface **2.** to remove (something recorded) from (magnetic tape) **3.** to remove any sign of; obliterate, as from the mind —**e·ras′a·ble** *adj.*

e·ras·er (i rā′sər) *n.* a thing that erases; specif., a pad of felt or cloth for removing chalk marks from a blackboard

e·ra·sure (i rā′zhər) *n.* **1.** an erasing **2.** an erased word, mark, etc. **3.** the place where something has been erased

Er·a·to (er′ə tō′) *Gr. Myth.* the Muse of love poetry

er·bi·um (ur′bē əm) *n.* [ModL. < (*Ytt*)*erby*, Sw. town where first found] a metallic chemical element of the rare-earth group: symbol, Er; at. wt., 167.28; at. no., 68

ere (er) *prep.* [< OE. ær] [Archaic or Poet.] before (in time) —*conj.* [Archaic or Poet.] **1.** before **2.** sooner than; rather than

e·rect (i rekt′) *adj.* [< L. *erectus*, pp. of *erigere* < *e-*, up + *regere*, to make straight] **1.** upright; vertical **2.** sticking out or up; bristling; stiff —*vt.* **1.** to raise or construct (a building, etc.) • **2.** to set up; cause to arise [to *erect* social barriers] **3.** to set in an upright position; raise **4.** to put together; assemble **5.** [Archaic] to establish; found **6.** *Geom.* to construct or draw (a perpendicular, figure, etc.) upon a base line —**e·rec′tion** *n.* —**e·rect′ly** *adv.* —**e·rect′-ness** *n.* —**e·rec′tor** *n.*

e·rec·tile (i rek′til′) *adj.* that can become erect: used esp. of tissue that becomes swollen and rigid when filled with blood —**e·rec′til′i·ty** (-til′ə tē) *n.*

ere·long (er′lôŋ′) *adv.* [Archaic or Poet.] before long; soon

er·e·mite (er′ə mīt′) *n.* [< OFr. or LL.: see HERMIT] a religious recluse; hermit —**er′e·mit′ic** (-mit′ik), **er′e·mit′-i·cal** *adj.*

e·rep·sin (i rep′sin) *n.* [G. < L. pp. of *eripere* < *e-*, out + *rapere*, to snatch + G. *Pepsin*, PEPSIN] an enzyme mixture secreted by the intestine and involved in the breaking down of proteins into their component amino acids

erg¹ (urg) *n.* [< Gr. *ergon*, work] *Physics* the unit of work or energy in the cgs (metric) system, being the work done by one dyne acting through a distance of one centimetre: equivalent to 10^{-7} joules

erg² (urg) *n.* [Fr. < Ar. *'irj*] an area of shifting sand dunes, esp. in the Sahara

er·go (ur′gō, er′-) *conj.*, *adv.* [L.] therefore

er·go·nom·ics (ur′gə nom′iks) *n.pl.* [with *sing. v.*] [ERG¹ + (EC)ONOMICS] the study of the relationships between workers and their working environment

er·gos·ter·ol (ər gos′tə rōl′) *n.* [< ff. + STEROL] an alcohol, formerly prepared from ergot but now chiefly from yeast: when exposed to ultraviolet rays it produces a vitamin (D₂) used to prevent or cure rickets

er·got (ur′gət) *n.* [Fr. < OFr. *argot*, a cock's spur: from the shape of the growth] **1.** a fungous growth that invades the kernels of rye, or of other cereal plants **2.** the disease in which this occurs **3.** an extract of the dried rye fungus, used as a drug to contract blood vessels and smooth muscle tissue

e·rig·er·on (i rij′ə ron′) *n.* [L. < Gr. *ērigerōn* < *ēri*, early + *gerōn*, old man: from the hoary down on some varieties] any of a genus of plants of the composite family, as the fleabanes

Er·in (er′in) [Olr.] [Chiefly Poet.] Ireland

E·rin·y·es (i rin′ē ēz′) *n.pl.*, *sing.* **E·rin·ys** (i rin′is, -rī′nis) *Gr. Myth. same as* FURIES

erk (erk) *n.* [< ?] [Slang] an aircraftman in the R.A.F.

er·mine (ur′mən) *n.*, *pl.* **-mines**, **-mine**: see PLURAL, II, D, 1 [OFr.; prob. < MHG. < OHG. *harmo*, weasel] **1.** a weasel of northern regions whose fur is brown in summer but white with a black-tipped tail in winter **2.** the soft, white fur of this animal **3.** the position, rank, or functions of some peers, whose state robe is trimmed with ermine —**er′mined** *adj.*

ERMINE
(body 10-25 cm long; tail 2-15 cm long)

-ern (ərn) a suffix forming adjectives meaning from, concerning [*Southern, Northern*]

erne, ern (urn) *n.* [OE. *earn*] the European white-tailed eagle, which lives near the sea

Er·nie (ur′nē) *n.* [*e(lectronic) r(andom) n(umber) i(ndicator) e(quipment)*] the machine used to pick winning numbers of Premium Bonds

e·rode (i rōd′) *vt.* **e·rod′ed**, **e·rod′ing** [< Fr. < L. < *e-*, out, off + *rodere*, to gnaw] **1.** to eat into; wear away; disintegrate [acid *erodes* metal] **2.** to form by wearing away gradually [the stream *eroded* a gully] **3.** to cause to deteriorate, decay, or vanish —*vi.* to become eroded —**e·rod′i·ble** *adj.*

e·rog·e·nous (i roj′ə nəs) *adj.* [< Gr. *erōs*, love + -GENOUS] designating or of those areas of the body that are particularly sensitive to sexual stimulation

e·ro·sion (i rō′zhən) *n.* an eroding or being eroded —**e·ro′-sion·al** *adj.* —**e·ro′sive** *adj.*

e·rot·ic (i rot′ik) *adj.* [Gr. *erōtikos* < *erōs* (gen. *erōtos*), love] of, having, or arousing sexual feelings or desires; having to do with sexual love; amatory —**e·rot′i·cal·ly** *adv.*

e·rot·i·ca (-i kə) *n.pl.* [often with *sing. v.*] erotic books, pictures, etc.

e·rot·i·cism (-ə siz′m) *n.* **1.** erotic quality or character **2.** sexual excitement or behaviour **3.** preoccupation with sex Also, and for 2 now usually, **er·o·tism** (er′ə tiz′m)

e·ro·to·gen·ic (i rot′ə jen′ik; er′e tə-) *adj.* [*eroto-* (< Gr.), sexual desire + -GENIC] *same as* EROGENOUS

err (ur) *vi.* [< OFr. *errer* < L. *errare*, to wander] **1.** to be wrong or mistaken; fall into error **2.** to deviate from the established moral code; do wrong **3.** to act with bias, esp. favourable bias [to *err* on the side of justice]

er·rand (er′ənd) *n.* [OE. *ærende*] **1.** a short journey to do a definite thing, often for someone else **2.** the thing to be done on such a journey; purpose or object for which one goes or is sent

er·rant (er′ənt) *adj.* [OFr., prp. of *errer*, to travel, ult. < L. *iter*, a journey] **1.** roving or wandering, esp. in search of adventure [a knight-*errant*] **2.** *a)* [see ERR] erring or straying from what is right *b)* shifting about [an *errant* wind] —**er′rant·ly** *adv.* —**er′rant·ry** *n.*

er·rat·ic (i rat′ik) *adj.* [< OFr. < L. *erraticus* < pp. of *errare*, to wander] **1.** having no fixed course; irregular in action or behaviour **2.** eccentric; queer **3.** *Geol.* designating a boulder or rock formation transported some distance from its original source, as by a glacier —*n.* an erratic boulder —**er·rat′i·cal·ly** *adv.*

er·ra·tum (e rät′əm, -rāt′-) *n.*, *pl.* **-ta** (-ə) [L., neut. pp. of *errare*, to wander] an error in printing or writing

er·ro·ne·ous (ə rō′nē əs, e-) *adj.* containing or based on error; mistaken; wrong —**er·ro′ne·ous·ly** *adv.*

er·ror (er′ər) *n.* [< OFr. < L. *error* < *errare*, to wander] **1.** the state of believing what is untrue or incorrect **2.** a wrong belief; incorrect opinion **3.** something incorrect or wrong; inaccuracy; mistake **4.** transgression; wrongdoing; sin **5.** the amount by which something deviates from what is required or correct —**er′ror·less** *adj.*

er·satz (ur′zats, er′-) *n.*, *adj.* [G.] substitute or synthetic: the word usually suggests inferior quality

Erse (urs) *adj.*, *n.* [ME. *Erish*, var. of *Irisc*, Irish] *same as* GAELIC. *adj.* 2, n. 2

erst (urst) *adv.* [OE. *ærest*, superl. of *ær*, ere] [Archaic] formerly —*adj.* [Obs.] first

erst·while (-hwīl′) *adv.* [Archaic] some time ago; formerly —*adj.* former

e·ruct (i rukt′) *vt.*, *vi.* [< L. *eructare* < *e-*, out + *ructare*, to belch] to belch: also **e·ruc′tate** (-tāt) **-tat·ed**, **-tat·ing** —**e·ruc·ta·tion** (i ruk′tā shən; e′ruk-) *n.*

er·u·dite (er′oo dīt′, -yoo-) *adj.* [< L. pp. of *erudire*, to instruct < *e-*, out + *rudis*, RUDE] learned; scholarly —**er′-u·dite′ly** *adv.*

er·u·di·tion (er′oo dish′en, -yoo-) *n.* learning acquired by reading and study; scholarship

e·rupt (i rupt′) *vi.* [< L. *eruptus*, pp. of *erumpere* < *e-*, out + *rumpere*, to break] **1.** to burst forth or out, as from some restraint [the lava *erupted*, a riot *erupted*] **2.** to throw forth lava, water, steam, etc., as a volcano **3.** to break out in a rash **4.** to break through the gums, as a new tooth —*vt.* to cause to burst forth —**e·rupt′i·ble** *adj.*

e·rup·tion (i rup′shən) *n.* **1.** a bursting forth or out **2.** a throwing forth of lava, water, steam, etc. **3.** *Med. a)* a breaking out in a rash *b)* a rash —**e·rup′tive** *adj.* —**e·rup′-tive·ly** *adv.*

-er·y (ər ē) [< OFr. *-erie* < LL. *-aria*, or < OFr. *-ier* + *-ie* (L. *-ia*)] a suffix meaning: **1.** a place to [*tannery*] **2.** a place for [*nunnery*] **3.** the practice, act, or occupation of [*surgery*] **4.** the product or goods of [*pottery*] **5.** a collection of [*crockery*] **6.** the state or condition of [*drudgery*] **7.** the behaviour or qualities of [*tomfoolery*]

er·y·sip·e·las (er′ə sip′el əs, ir′-) *n.* [< L. < Gr. < *erythros*, red + *-pelas* (L. *pellis*), skin] an acute infectious disease of the skin or mucous membranes caused by a streptococcus and characterized by local inflammation and fever

e·ryth·ro- [< Gr. *erythros*, red] a combining form meaning: **1.** red [*erythrocyte*] **2.** erythrocyte

e·ryth·ro·cyte (i rith′rə sīt′) *n.* [prec. + -CYTE] a red blood corpuscle: it is a very small, circular disc and contains haemoglobin, which carries oxygen to the body tissues —**e·ryth′ro·cyt′ic** (-sit′ik) *adj.*

e·ryth·ro·my·cin (i rith′rə mī′sin) *n.* [ERYTHRO-+ Gr. *mykēs,* fungus + -IN¹] an antibiotic derived from a soil bacterium, used to treat various bacterial diseases

-es (iz, əz, z) [variously < OE. *-as, -s*] *a suffix used:* **1.** to form the plural of some nouns, as in *fishes:* see PLURAL **2.** to form the third person singular, present indicative, of verbs, as in (he) *kisses:* cf. **-s**

Es *Chem.* einsteinium

es·ca·drille (es′kə dril′; *Fr.* es kȧ drē′y′) *n.* [Fr. < Sp. < *escuadra,* squad] a squadron of aeroplanes, as in the French armed forces of World War I

es·ca·lade (es′kə lād′, es′kə lād′) *n.* [< Fr. < It. < *scalare,* to climb < L. *scala,* ladder] the act of climbing the walls of a fortified place by ladders —*vt.* **-lad′ed, -lad′ing** to climb (a wall, etc.) or enter (a fortified place) by ladders

es·ca·late (es′kə lāt′) *vi.* **-lat′ed, -lat′ing** [back-formation < ff.] **1.** to rise as on an escalator **2.** to expand, as from a limited conflict into a general war **3.** to increase rapidly, as prices —*vt.* to cause to escalate —**es′ca·la′tion** *n.*

es·ca·la·tor (-ər) *n.* [< ESCALA(DE) + *-tor,* as in (ELEVA)TOR] a moving stairway consisting of treads linked in an endless belt

escalator clause a clause in a contract by which wages, etc. are adjusted to cost of living, etc.

es·cal·lop (e skol′əp, -skal′-) *n., vt.* [< OFr.: see SCALLOP] *same as* SCALLOP

es·ca·lope (es′kə lop′) *n.* [< OFr. *escalope,* a shell] a thin slice of meat, usually veal, cut from the leg

es·ca·pade (es′kə pād′) *n.* [Fr., ult. < ff.] a reckless adventure or prank

es·cape (ə skāp′, e-) *vi.* **-caped′, -cap′ing** [< ONormFr. < L. *ex-,* out of + *cappa,* cloak (i.e., leave one's cloak] **1.** to get free; get away **2.** to avoid an illness, accident, pain, etc. **3.** to flow, drain, or leak away [gas *escaping* from a pipe] **4.** to slip away; disappear —*vt.* **1.** to get away from; flee from **2.** to manage to keep away from; avoid [to *escape* punishment] **3.** to come from involuntarily [a scream *escaped* her lips] **4.** to slip away from; be missed or forgotten [his name *escapes* me] —*n.* **1.** an escaping or the state of having escaped **2.** a means of escape **3.** an outward flow or leakage **4.** a temporary mental release from reality **5.** *Bot.* a garden plant growing wild —*adj.* **1.** giving temporary mental release from reality **2.** *a)* making escape possible [an *escape* hatch] *b)* giving a basis for evading a claim, responsibility, etc. [an *escape* clause] —**es·cap′a·ble** *adj.* —**es·cap′er** *n.*

es·cap·ee (ə skā′pē′, e-) *n.* a person who has escaped, esp. from confinement

es·cape·ment (ə skāp′mənt, e-) *n.* **1.** [Rare] a means of escape **2.** the part in a clock or watch that controls the speed and regularity of the balance wheel or pendulum, by means of a notched wheel (**escape wheel**), one tooth of which is allowed to escape from the detaining catch at a time **3.** a ratchet mechanism, esp. on a typewriter to regulate the horizontal movement of the carriage **4.** *Music* the mechanism in a piano which enables the hammer to "escape" after the string has been struck, so the string can vibrate

ESCAPEMENT

escape road a side road or track affording space for vehicles to stop, turn, etc., as on a hill

escape velocity the minimum speed required for a particle, space vehicle, etc. to escape permanently from the gravitational field of a planet, star, etc.

es·cap·ism (ə skāp′iz'm, e-) *n.* a tendency to escape from reality, the responsibilities of real life, etc., esp. by unrealistic imaginative activity —**es·cap′ist** *adj., n.*

es·ca·pol·o·gist (es′kə pol′ə jist) *n.* a performer who specializes in freeing himself from chains, ropes, boxes, etc. —**es′ca·pol′o·gy** *n.*

‡es·car·got (es kär gō′) *n.* [Fr.] a snail, esp. an edible variety

es·ca·role (es′kə rōl′) *n.* [Fr. < ML. < L. *esca,* food] *same as* ENDIVE (sense 1)

es·carp·ment (e skärp′mənt) *n.* [< Fr.: see SCARP] **1.** a steep slope or cliff formed by erosion or by faulting **2.** ground formed into a steep slope on the exterior of a fortification See also SCARP

-es·cence (es′'ns) *a n.-forming suffix corresponding to the adjective suffix* -ESCENT [*obsolescence*]

-es·cent (es′'nt) [< L. *escens, -escentis,* prp. ending] *an adj.-forming suffix meaning:* **1.** starting to be; being or becoming [*convalescent*] **2.** giving off or reflecting light, or exhibiting a play of colour [*phosphorescent*]

es·cha·tol·o·gy (es′kə tol′ə jē) *n.* [< Gr. *eschatos,* furthest + -LOGY] *Theol.* the doctrines, etc. dealing with the end and ultimate destiny of the present world —**es·cha·to·log·i·cal** (es′kə tə loj′i k'l) *n.*

es·cheat (es chēt′) *n.* [< OFr. < pp. of *escheoir,* to fall to one's share < VL. < L. *ex-,* out + *cadere,* to fall] *Law* **1.** the reverting of property to the lord of the manor, to the crown, or to the government when there are no legal heirs **2.** property so reverting —*vt., vi.* to confiscate or revert by escheat —**es·cheat′a·ble** *adj.*

es·chew (es chōō′) *vt.* [< Anglo-Fr. < OFr. < OHG. *sciuhan,* to fear] to keep away from (something harmful or disliked); shun —**es·chew′al** *n.*

es·cort (es′kôrt; *for v.* i skôrt′) *n.* [< Fr. < It. < *scorta* < *scorgere,* to lead < L. *ex-,* out + *corrigere,* to CORRECT] **1.** one or more persons (or cars, ships, aircraft, etc.) accompanying another or others to give protection or show honour **2.** a man or boy accompanying a woman or girl, as to a party **3.** accompaniment by an escort —*vt.* to go with as an escort

es·cri·toire (es′krə twär′) *n.* [< OFr. < LL. < pp. of L. *scribere,* to write] a writing desk or table; secretary

es·crow (es krō′) *n.* [OFr. *escroue,* scroll] *Law* a written agreement, as a bond or deed, put in the care of a third party until certain conditions are fulfilled —**in escrow** *Law* so put in the care of a third party

es·cu·do (es kōō′dō) *n., pl.* **-dos** [Sp., a shield < L. *scutum*] **1.** any of several obsolete coins of Spain and Portugal **2.** the monetary unit of Chile and Portugal: see MONETARY UNITS, table

es·cu·lent (es′kyoo lənt) *adj.* [< L. < *esca,* food] fit for food; eatable; edible —*n.* something fit for food, esp. a vegetable

es·cutch·eon (i skuch′ən) *n.* [ONormFr. < L. *scutum,* shield] a shield or shield-shaped surface on which a coat of arms is displayed —**a blot on one's escutcheon** a stain on one's honour

-ese (ēz, ēs) [< OFr. & It. < L. *-ensis*] *a suffix meaning:* **1.** (a native or inhabitant) of [*Javanese*] **2.** (in) the language or dialect of [*Cantonese*] **3.** (in) the style of [*journalese*]

ESE, E.S.E., e.s.e. east-southeast

es·ker, es·kar (es′kər) *n.* [Ir. *eiscir,* a ridge] a winding narrow ridge of sand or gravel, probably deposited by a stream flowing in or under glacial ice

Es·ki·mo (es′kə mō′) *n.* [< Fr. < Algonquian: lit., eater of raw flesh] **1.** *pl.* **-mos, -mo′** a member of a group of native N. American people living in Greenland, N Canada and Alaska, and the NE tip of Asia **2.** either of the two languages of the Eskimos —*adj.* of the Eskimos, their language, or their culture —**Es′ki·mo′an** *adj.*

Eskimo dog a strong breed of dog with greyish, shaggy fur, used by the Eskimos to pull sleds

E.S.N. Educationally Subnormal

e·soph·a·gus (i sof′ə gəs) *n., pl.* **-a·gi** (-jī′) *Chiefly U.S. sp. of* OESOPHAGUS

es·o·ter·ic (es′ə ter′ik) *adj.* [< Gr. < *esōteros,* inner, compar. of *esō,* within] **1.** *a)* understood by only a chosen few, as an inner group of disciples or initiates *b)* beyond the understanding or knowledge of most people; abstruse **2.** confidential; private —**es′o·ter′i·cal·ly** *adv.* —**es′o·ter′-i·cism** *n.*

ESP extrasensory perception

esp., espec. especially

es·pa·drille (es′pə dril′) *n.* [Fr. < Sp. *esparto,* ESPARTO] a shoe for casual wear, with a canvas upper and a sole of twisted rope or of rubber, etc.

es·pal·ier (es pal′yər) *n.* [Fr. < It. *spalliera,* support < *spalla,* the shoulder < L. *spatula:* see SPATULA] **1.** a lattice or trellis on which trees and shrubs are trained to grow flat **2.** a plant, tree, etc. so trained —*vt.* **1.** to train as or on an espalier **2.** to provide with an espalier

ESPALIER

es·par·to (es pär′tō) *n.* [Sp. < L. *spartum* < Gr. *sparton*] a long, coarse grass of Spain and N Africa, used to make paper, rope, shoes, etc.: also **esparto grass**

es·pe·cial (ə spesh′əl, es pesh′-) *adj.* special; particular; exceptional —**es·pe′-cial·ly** *adv.*

Es·pe·ran·to (es′pə ran′tō) *n.* [after pseudonym of Dr. L. L. Zamenhof (1859–1917), its inventor] an artificial language for international (chiefly European) use, based on word bases common to the main European languages

es·pi·al (ə spī′əl) *n.* **1.** an espying or being espied; observation **2.** discovery

es·pi·o·nage (es′pē ə näzh′, -nij′) *n.* [< Fr. < *espion,* a spy < It. *spione* < *spia,* a spy] **1.** the act of spying **2.** the use of spies by a government to learn the military secrets of other nations

es·pla·nade (es′plə nād′, -näd′) *n.* [Fr. < It. < *spianare* < L. *explanare,* to level: see EXPLAIN] a level, open space of ground; esp., *a)* a public walk or roadway, often along a shore; promenade *b)* an open level space in front of a fortified place, as a citadel, etc.

es·pous·al (i spou′z'l) *n.* 1. [*often pl.*] *a)* a betrothal ceremony *b)* a wedding 2. an espousing (of some cause, idea, etc.); advocacy

es·pouse (i spouz′) *vt.* -poused′, -pous′ing [< OFr. < LL. *sponsare* < L. *sponsus:* see SPOUSE] 1. to marry, esp. to take as a wife 2. to take up, support, or advocate (some cause, idea, etc.) —**es·pous′er** *n.*

es·pres·so (es pres′ō) *n.*, *pl.* **-sos** [It. *(caffè) espresso*, pressed-out (coffee)] coffee prepared in a special machine by forcing steam through finely ground coffee beans

es·prit (es prē′) *n.* [Fr.] 1. spirit 2. lively intelligence or wit

es·prit de corps (es prē′də kôr′) [Fr.] group spirit; sense of pride, honour, etc. shared by those in the same group or undertaking

es·py (ə spī′, es pī′) *vt.* -pied′, -py′ing [< OFr. *espier:* see SPY] to catch sight of; spy

Esq. Esquire

-esque (esk) [Fr. < It. *-esco*] *a suffix meaning:* 1. in the manner or style of [*Romanesque*] 2. having the quality of [*picturesque*]

Es·qui·mau (es′kə mō′) *n.*, *pl.* **-maux′** (-mō′, -mōz′), **-mau′** [Fr.] *same as* ESKIMO

es·quire (ə skwīr′, es′kwīr) *n.* [< OFr. < LL. *scutarius*, a shield-bearer < L. *scutum*, a shield] 1. formerly, candidate for knighthood, acting as attendant for a knight 2. a member of the gentry ranking just below a knight 3. [E-] a title of courtesy, usually abbrev. *Esq.*, placed after a man's surname

ESRO European Space Research Organization

ess (es) *n.*, *pl.* **ess′es** 1. the letter S, s 2. something shaped like an S

-ess (is, əs; *occas.* es) [< OFr. < LL. *-issa* < Gr.] *a suffix meaning* female [*lioness*]: as applied to persons (*poetess*, etc.), now often avoided as discriminating

es·say (e sā′; *for n.* 1 *usually, and for n.* 2 *always,* es′ā) *vt.* [< OFr. < LL. < L. *exagium*, a weighing < *ex-*, out of + *agere*, to do] to try; attempt —*n.* 1. an attempt; trial 2. a short, personal literary composition of an analytical or interpretive kind —**es·say′er** *n.*

es·say·ist (es′ā ist) *n.* a writer of essays

es·sence (es′'ns) *n.* [< OFr. & < L. *essentia* < *esse*, to be] 1. an entity 2. that which makes something what it is; fundamental nature or most important quality (of something) 3. *a)* a substance that keeps, in concentrated form, the flavour, fragrance, etc. of the plant, drug, food, etc. from which it is extracted *b)* a solution of such a substance in alcohol [vanilla *essence*] *c)* a perfume 4. *Philos. a)* inward nature; true substance *b)* indispensable conceptual characteristics and relations —**of the essence** essential; indispensable

Es·sene (es′ēn, ə sēn′) *n.* [< L. < Gr. *Essēnoi*] a member of a mystical Jewish sect, existing from the 2nd century B.C. to the 2nd century A.D.

es·sen·tial (ə sen′shəl) *adj.* 1. of or constituting the essence of something; basic; inherent 2. absolute; perfect 3. absolutely necessary; indispensable —*n.* [*sometimes pl.*] something necessary, fundamental, or indispensable —**es·sen·ti·al·i·ty** (i sen′shē al′ə tē) *n.* —**es·sen′tial·ly** *adv.* —**es·sen′tial·ness** *n.*

es·sen·tial·ism (-iz'm) *n.* *Philos.* a theory which stresses essence as opposed to existence

essential oil any volatile oil that gives distinctive odour, flavour, etc. to a plant, flower, or fruit

-est (ist, əst) [< OE. *-est, -ost, -ast*] *a suffix used to form:* 1. the superlative degree of adjectives and adverbs [*greatest, soonest*] 2. the archaic 2nd pers. sing., pres. indic., of verbs [*goest*]

est. 1. established 2. estimate 3. estimated

es·tab·lish (ə stab′lish) *vt.* [< OFr. *establir* < L. < *stabilis*, STABLE[1]] 1. to make stable; settle 2. to order, ordain, or enact (a law, statute, etc.) permanently 3. to set up (a nation, business, etc.); found 4. to cause to be; bring about [to *establish* good relations] 5. to settle in an office, or set up in business or a profession 6. to make a state institution of (a church) 7. to cause (a precedent, theory, etc.) to be accepted or recognized 8. to prove; demonstrate (a case at law) —**es·tab′lish·er** *n.*

established church the church given exclusive recognition and official support by a government; specif., [E-C-] the Church of England

es·tab·lish·ment (-mənt) *n.* 1. an establishing or being established 2. a thing established, as a business, military organization, household, etc. —**the Establishment** the ruling inner circle of any nation, institution, etc.

es·tate (ə stāt′) *n.* [< OFr. *estat*, STATE] 1. *a)* a condition or stage of life [to come to man's *estate*] *b)* status or rank 2. formerly, any of the three social classes having specific political powers: the clergy (**first estate**), the nobility (**second estate**), and the commons, or bourgeoisie (**third**

estate) 3. property; possessions 4. landed property; individually owned piece of land containing a residence 5. an area of ground, usually large, growing rubber, tea, grapes, etc. 6. a large area of new property development, esp. of houses or of industrial premises 7. *Law a)* the degree, nature, and extent of ownership that one has in land or other property *b)* all the property, real or personal, owned by one

estate agent 1. an agent responsible for the valuation, advertisement, and sale of property, esp. houses 2. the administrator of a landed estate; estate manager

estate car a motor car with folding or removable rear seats and rear door for loading and unloading luggage, equipment, etc.

estate duty *same as* DEATH DUTY

es·teem (ə stēm′) *vt.* [< OFr. < L. *aestimare*, to value, estimate] 1. to have great regard for; value highly; respect 2. to hold to be; consider —*n.* favourable opinion; high regard

es·ter (es′tər) *n.* [G., contr. < *Essig*, vinegar + *Äther*, ETHER] an organic compound, comparable to an inorganic salt, formed by the reaction of an acid and an alcohol, or a phenol: the organic radical of the alcohol or phenol replaces the acid hydrogen of the acid

es·thete (es′thēt′) *n.* [U.S.] *same as* AESTHETE —**es·thet′ic** (-that′ik) *adj.* —**es·thet′i·cal·ly** *adv.* —**es·thet′i·cism** (-ə siz′m) *n.*

es·thet·ics (es that′iks) *n.pl.* [U.S.] *same as* AESTHETICS

es·ti·ma·ble (es′tə mə b'l) *adj.* worthy of esteem —**es′·ti·ma·ble·ness** *n.* —**es′ti·ma·bly** *adv.*

es·ti·mate (es′tə māt′; *for n.* -mit) *vt.* **-mat′ed, -mat′ing** [< L. pp. of *aestimare:* see ESTEEM] 1. to form an opinion about 2. to determine generally but carefully (size, value, cost, etc.); calculate approximately —*vi.* to make an estimate —*n.* 1. a general calculation of size, value, etc.; esp., an approximate computation of the probable cost of a piece of work made by a person undertaking to do the work 2. an opinion or judgment —**es′ti·ma′tive** *adj.* —**es′ti·ma′tor** *n.*

es·ti·ma·tion (es′tə mā′shən) *n.* 1. an estimating 2. an opinion or judgment 3. esteem; regard

es·ti·val (es′tə v′l, es tī′-) *adj.* [U.S.] *same as* AESTIVAL

es·ti·vate (es′tə vāt′) *vi.* **-vat′ed, -vat′ing** [U.S.] *same as* AESTIVATE

es·top (e stop′) *vt.* **-topped′, -top′ping** [< Anglo-Fr. & OFr. < L. *stuppa*, tow] *Law* to stop or prevent by estoppel

es·top·pel (e stop′əl) *n.* [< OFr. *estoper:* see ESTOP] *Law* a rule of evidence where a person is precluded from denying the truth of a statement of facts he has previously asserted

es·to·vers (e stō′vərz) *n.* *pl.* [ME. < OFr. *estovoir*, to be necessary < L. *est opus* there is need] *Law* certain reasonable necessaries, as wood given to a tenant for fuel or repairs, alimony to a divorced wife, etc.

es·trange (ə strānj′) *vt.* **-tranged′, -trang′ing** [OFr. *estranger* < ML. < L. *extraneus*, STRANGE] 1. to remove; keep apart or away 2. to turn (a person) from an affectionate or friendly attitude to an indifferent, unfriendly, or hostile one; alienate the affections of —**es·trange′ment** *n.*

es·tro·gen (es′trə jən) *n.* [U.S.] *same as* OESTROGEN

estrous cycle [U.S.] *same as* OESTRUS CYCLE

es·trus (es′trəs, ēs′-) *n.* [U.S.] *same as* OESTRUS

es·tu·ar·y (es′choo wə rē, -tyoo-) *n.*, *pl.* **-ar′ies** [< L. < *aestus*, the tide] an inlet or arm of the sea; esp., the wide mouth of a river, where the tide meets the current —**es′·tu·ar′i·al, es′tu·ar·ine** (-in, -īn′) *adj.*

e.s.u., esu electrostatic unit(s)

-et (it, ət) [< OFr. *-et*, masc., *-ete* (Fr. *-ette*), fem.] *a suffix* added to nouns, meaning little [*islet*]

e·ta (ēt′ə) *n.* the seventh letter of the Greek alphabet (H, η): it is shown as ē in the etymologies of this dictionary

ETA, E.T.A. estimated time of arrival

‡é·ta·gère (ā tà zher′) *n.* [Fr.] a stand with open shelves like a whatnot, for displaying small art objects, ornaments, etc.

et al. 1. [L. *et alibi*] and elsewhere 2. [L. *et alii*] and others

etc. et cetera

et cet·er·a (et set′ər ə, set′rə) [L.] and others; and the like; and the rest, and so forth

et·cet·er·as (-əz, -rəz) *n.pl.* additional things or persons; customary extras

etch (ech) *vt.* [< Du. < G. < MHG. *etzen*, to cause to eat] 1. to make (a drawing, design, etc.) on metal, glass, etc. by the action of an acid, esp. by coating the surface with wax and letting the acid eat into lines and areas laid bare with a needle 2. to engrave (a metal plate, glass, etc.) in this way for use in printing such drawings, etc. 3. to depict or impress sharply and distinctly —*vi.* to make etchings —*n.* the process or act of etching —**etch′er** *n.*

etch·ant (ech′ənt) *n.* a substance, as an acid, used in etching

etch·ing (-iŋ) *n.* 1. an etched plate, drawing, or design 2. a print made from an etched plate **3.** the art of making such drawings, etc.

e·ter·nal (i tur'n'l) *adj.* [< OFr. < LL. *aeternalis* < L. < *aevum*, an age] **1.** without beginning or end; everlasting **2.** of eternity **3.** forever the same; unchanging [*eternal truths*] **4.** never stopping or ending; perpetual [*eternal rest*] **5.** [Colloq.] seeming never to stop; continual [*eternal bickering*] **6.** timeless —**the Eternal** God —**e·ter'nal·ly** *adv.* —**e·ter'nal·ness** *n.*

eternal triangle an emotional or sexual relationship involving three people, of which two are the same sex

e·ter·ni·ty (i tur'nə tē) *n., pl.* **-ties** **1.** the quality, state, or fact of being eternal; continuance without end **2.** infinite time; time without beginning or end **3.** a long period of time that seems endless **4.** the endless time after death

eternity ring a ring set all around with stones, symbolizing continuity: usually given by a husband to his wife

e·ter·nize (-nīz) *vt.* **-nized, -niz·ing** **1.** to make eternal **2.** to make famous forever; immortalize Also **e·ter'nal·ize'-ized', -iz'ing** —**e·ter'ni·za'tion** *n.*

-eth¹ (əth, ith) *same as* -TH² [*fortieth, sixtieth,* etc.]

-eth² (ith, əth) [< OE. -(a)*th*] archaic ending of the third person singular, present indicative, of verbs [*asketh, bringeth*]: see also -TH³

Eth. **1.** Ethiopia **2.** Ethiopian **3.** Ethiopic

eth·ane (eth'ān) *n.* [ETH(YL) + -ANE] an odourless, colourless, gaseous hydrocarbon, C_2H_6: it is found in natural gas and used as a fuel, etc.

eth·a·nol (eth'ə nol', ēth'-) *n.* [ETHAN(E) + -OL¹] *same as* ALCOHOL (sense 1)

eth·ene (eth'ēn) *n.* *same as* ETHYLENE

e·ther (ē'thər) *n.* [< L. < Gr. *aithēr* < *aithein,* to kindle, burn] **1.** the upper regions of space; clear sky **2.** *Chem.* a volatile, colourless, highly flammable liquid, $(C_2H_5)_2O$: it is used as an anaesthetic and a solvent for resins and fats **3.** *Physics* an invisible substance postulated (in older theory) as pervading space and serving as the medium for the transmission of radiant energy, as light waves

e·the·re·al (i thir'ē əl) *adj.* **1.** of or like the ether, or upper regions of space **2.** very light; airy; delicate **3.** heavenly —**e·the're·al'i·ty** (-al'ə tē), **e·the're·al·ness** *n.* —**e·the're·al·ly** *adv.*

e·the·re·al·ize (-ə līz') *vt.* **-ized, -iz'ing** to make, or treat as being, ethereal —**e·the're·al·i·za'tion** *n.*

e·ther·ize (ē'thə rīz') *vt.* **-ized, -iz'ing** to anaesthetize as by causing to inhale ether fumes —**e'ther·i·za'tion** *n.*

eth·ic (eth'ik) *n.* [see ff.] **1.** ethics or a system of ethics [the humanist *ethic*] **2.** any single element in a system of ethics —*adj.* *same as* ETHICAL

eth·i·cal (-i k'l) *adj.* [< L. < Gr. *ēthikos* < *ēthos,* character, custom + -AL] **1.** having to do with ethics or morality; or conforming to moral standards **2.** conforming to professional standards of conduct **3.** designating or of a drug available only on a doctor's prescription —**eth'i·cal'i·ty** (-kal'ə tē), **eth'i·cal·ness** *n.* —**eth'i·cal·ly** *adv.*

eth·ics (eth'iks) *n.pl.* [*with sing. v.* in 1 & 2, and occas. 3] [see prec.] **1.** the study of standards of conduct and moral judgment **2.** a treatise on this study **3.** the system or code of morals of a particular person, religion, group, profession, etc.

E·thi·o·pi·an (ē'thē ō'pē ən) *adj.* **1.** of, or relating to Ethiopia, its people, or its languages **2.** [Archaic] negro —*n.* **1.** a native of Ethiopia **2.** [Archaic] a negro

E·thi·op·ic (-op'ik, -ō'pik) *adj.* **1.** *same as* ETHIOPIAN **2.** of the Semitic languages of the Ethiopians —*n.* **1.** the classical Semitic language of Ethiopia, used in the liturgy of the Christian church in Ethiopia **2.** the group of languages spoken by Ethiopians, belonging to the Semitic branch of the Afro-Asiatic language family

eth·nic (eth'nik) *adj.* [< LL. < Gr. *ethnikos,* national < *ethnos,* nation] designating or of any of the basic groups or divisions of mankind or of a heterogeneous population, as distinguished by customs, characteristics, language, etc.; ethnological Also **eth'ni·cal** —**eth'ni·cal·ly** *adv.* —**eth'-nic·i·ty** *n.*

eth·no- [< Gr. *ethnos,* nation] a combining form meaning ethnic group or division; people or peoples [*ethnology*]: also, before a vowel, **ethn-**

eth·no·cen·trism (eth'nə sen'triz'm) *n.* the emotional attitude that one's own ethnic group, nation, or culture is superior to all others —**eth'no·cen'tric** *adj.* —**eth'no·cen'tri·cal·ly** *adv.* —**eth'no·cen·tric'i·ty** *n.*

eth·nog·ra·phy (eth nog'rə fē) *n.* the branch of anthropology that deals descriptively with specific cultures —**eth·nog'ra·pher** *n.* —**eth'no·graph'ic** (-nə graf'ik), **eth'-no·graph'i·cal** *adj.* —**eth'no·graph'i·cal·ly** *adv.*

eth·nol·o·gy (eth nol'ə jē) *n.* the branch of anthropology that deals with the comparative cultures of various peoples, including their distribution, characteristics, folklore, etc. —**eth·no·log'i·cal** (eth'nə loj'i k'l), **eth'no·log'ic** *adj.* —**eth'-no·log'i·cal·ly** *adv.* —**eth·nol'o·gist** *n.*

e·thol·o·gy (e thol'ə jē, ē-) *n.* [L. *ethologia,* character

portrayal < Gr.: see ETHOS & -LOGY] *Biol.* the scientific study of the characteristic behaviour patterns of animals —**e·tho·log·i·cal** (eth'ə loj'i k'l, ē'thə-) *adj.* —**e·thol'o·gist** *n.*

e·thos (ē'thos) *n.* [Gr. *ethos,* character] the characteristic attitudes, habits, beliefs, etc. of an individual or group

eth·yl (eth''l) *n.* [ETH(ER) + -YL] the monovalent hydrocarbon radical, C_2H_5, which forms the base of common alcohol, ether, and many other compounds

ethyl alcohol *same as* ALCOHOL (sense 1)

eth·yl·ene (eth'ə lēn') *n.* [ETHYL + -ENE] a colourless, flammable, gaseous hydrocarbon, C_2H_4, used as a fuel and anaesthetic, in hastening the ripening of fruits, and to form polyethylene

ethylene glycol a colourless, viscous alcohol used as an antifreeze, solvent, in resins, etc.

e·ti·o·late (ēt'ē ə lāt') *vt.* **-lat'ed, -lat'ing** [Fr. *étioler* < dial. var. of *éteule,* stubble, straw] **1.** to cause to be weak or unhealthy **2.** *Bot.* to blanch or bleach by depriving of sunlight: said esp. of leeks, etc. —**e'ti·o·la'tion** *n.*

e·ti·ol·o·gy (ēt'ē ol'ə jē) *n., pl.* **-gies** [U.S.] *same as* AETIOLOGY

et·i·quette (et'i kət, -ket') *n.* [Fr. *étiquette,* a ticket] **1.** the forms, manners, and ceremonies established by convention as acceptable or required in social relations **2.** conventional behaviour or practice in certain professions [medical *etiquette*]

Eton collar a broad, white linen collar worn with an Eton jacket, or a collar like this

Eton crop a very short, mannish hair style worn by women, esp. in the 1920's

Eton jacket a black waist-length jacket with broad lapels, left open in front, as that worn by students at Eton

E·trus·can (i trus'kən) *adj.* of Etruria, its people, their language, or culture —*n.* **1.** a native or inhabitant of Etruria **2.** the language of the ancient Etruscans Also **E·tru·ri·an** (i troor'ē ən)

et seq. **1.** [L. *et sequens*] and the following **2.** [L. *et sequentes* or *et sequentia*] and those that follow

-ette (et) [Fr.: see -ET] *a suffix meaning:* **1.** little [*statuette*] **2.** female [*usherette*] **3.** a substitute for [*leatherette*]

é·tude (ā'tyōōd; *Fr.* ā tüd') *n.* [Fr., STUDY] a musical composition for a solo instrument, designed to give practice in some special point of technique

ety., etym., etymol. **1.** etymological **2.** etymology

et·y·mol·o·gy (et'ə mol'ə jē) *n., pl.* **-gies** [< OFr. < L. < Gr. < *etymon,* literal sense of a word, neut. of *etymos,* true + -LOGY] the origin and development of a word, affix, phrase, etc.; the tracing of a word or words back as far as possible, or the branch of linguistics dealing with this —**et'-y·mo·log'i·cal** (-mə loj'ə k'l) *adj.* —**et'y·mo·log'i·cal·ly** *adv.* —**et'y·mol'o·gist** *n.* —**et'y·mol'o·gize'** (-jīz') *vt., vi.* **-gized', -giz'ing**

et·y·mon (et'ə mon') *n., pl.* **-mons', -ma** (-mə) [L. < Gr. *etymon,* literal sense of a word] **1.** the original form of a word **2.** a word or morpheme from which derivatives or compounds have developed

eu- [Fr. < Gr.] *a prefix meaning* good, well [*eulogy, eugenic*]: opposed to DYS-, CACO-

Eu *Chem.* europium

eu·ca·lyp·tus (yōō'kə lip'təs) *n., pl.* **-tus·es, -ti** (-tī) [ModL. < EU- + Gr. *kalyptos,* covered from the covering of the buds) < *kalyptein,* to cover] any of a genus of tall, chiefly Australian evergreen trees of the myrtle family, valued for their timber, gum, and oil: also **eu'ca·lypt'**

EUCALYPTUS
(tree and leaves)

eucalyptus oil an essential oil from eucalyptus leaves, used as an antiseptic and expectorant

Eu·cha·rist (yōō'kə rist) *n.* [< OFr. < LL. < Gr. *eucharistia,* gratitude < *eu-,* well + *charis,* favour] **1.** *same as* HOLY COMMUNION **2.** the consecrated bread and wine used in Holy Communion —**Eu'cha·ris'tic** *adj.*

eu·chre (yōō'kər) *n.* [earlier *yuker, uker* < ?] **1.** a card game for two, three, or four players, played with thirty-two cards **2.** a euchring or being euchred —*vt.* **-chred, -chring** **1.** to prevent (the trump-declaring opponent at euchre) from taking the required three tricks **2.** [Chiefly U.S. Colloq.] to outwit

Eu·clid·e·an, Eu·clid·i·an (yōō klid'ē ən) *adj.* of or relating to the postulates or axioms of Euclid, 5th cent. B.C. Greek philosopher [*Euclidean* geometry, *Euclidean* space]

eu·gen·ic (yoo jen'ik) *adj.* [< Gr.: see EU- & GENESIS] **1.** relating to the bearing of sound offspring **2.** of, relating to, or improved by eugenics Also **eu·gen'i·cal** —**eu·gen'i·cal·ly** *adv.*

eu·gen·i·cist (-ə sist) *n.* a specialist in or advocate of eugenics: also **eu·gen·ist** (yoo' jen'ist)

eu·gen·ics (yōo jen'iks) *n.pl.* [with *sing. v.*] the movement devoted to improving the human species by control of hereditary factors in mating

eu·lo·gis·tic (yōo'lə jis'tik) *adj.* of or expressing eulogy; praising highly —**eu'lo·gis'ti·cal·ly** *adv.*

eu·lo·gi·um (yōo lō'jē əm) *n.*, *pl.* **-gi·ums**, **-gi·a** (-ə) [ML.] *same as* EULOGY

eu·lo·gize (yōo'lə jīz') *vt.* **-gized'**, **-giz'ing** to praise as in a eulogy —**eu'lo·gist**, **eu'lo·giz'er** *n.*

eu·lo·gy (-jē) *n.*, *pl.* **-gies** [< ML. < Gr. < *eulegein*, to speak well of] **1.** speech or writing in praise of a person, event, or thing; esp., a funeral oration **2.** high praise

eu·nuch (yōo'nək) *n.* [< L. < Gr. *eunouchos*, bed guardian < *eunē*, bed + *echein*, to keep] a castrated man; esp., one in charge of a harem or employed as a chamberlain in an Oriental palace

eu·pep·si·a (yōo pep'shə, -sē ə) *n.* [ModL. < Gr. *eupepsia*, digestibility] good digestion —**eu·pep'tic** *adj.* —**eu·pep'·ti·cal·ly** *adv.*

eu·phe·mism (yōo'fə miz'm) *n.* [< Gr. < *eu-*, good + *phēmē*, voice < *phanai*, to speak] **1.** the use of a word or phrase that is less expressive or direct but considered less distasteful or offensive than another **2.** a word or phrase so substituted (Ex.: *remains* for *corpse*) —**eu'phe·mist** *n.* —**eu'·phe·mis'tic**, **eu'phe·mis'ti·cal** *adj.* —**eu'phe·mis'ti·cal·ly** *adv.*

eu·phe·mize (-mīz') *vt.*, *vi.* **-mized'**, **-miz'ing** to speak or write (of) euphemistically

eu·phon·ic (yōo fon'ik) *adj.* **1.** of euphony **2.** *same as* EUPHONIOUS Also **eu·phon'i·cal** —**eu·phon'i·cal·ly** *adv.*

eu·pho·ni·ous (yōo fō'nē əs) *adj.* characterized by euphony; having a pleasant sound; harmonious —**eu·pho'ni·ous·ly** *adv.* —**eu·pho'ni·ous·ness** *n.*

eu·pho·ni·um (-əm) *n.* a brass instrument like the baritone but having a more mellow tone

eu·pho·nize (yōo'fə nīz') *vt.* **-nized'**, **-niz'ing** to make euphonious

eu·pho·ny (yōo'fə nē) *n.*, *pl.* **-nies** [< LL. < Gr. < *eu-*, well + *phōnē*, voice] **1.** the quality of having a pleasing sound; pleasant combination of agreeable sounds in spoken words **2.** *Phonet.* the progressive change or mutation of speech sounds, as by assimilation, by which ease of pronunciation is attained

eu·phor·bi·a (yōo fôr'bē ə) *n.* [< L. < *Euphorbus*, physician of 1st cent. A.D.] *same as* SPURGE

eu·pho·ri·a (yōo fôr'ē ə) *n.* [ModL. < Gr. < *eu-*, well + *pherein*, to bear] a feeling of well-being or high spirits, specif. *Psychol.* one that seems exaggerated and without cause —**eu·phor'ic** *adj.*

eu·pho·ri·ant (-ənt) *n.* *Med.* a drug or other agent that produces euphoria

eu·pho·tic (yōo fōt'ik) *adj.* [< EU- + Gr. *phōs* (gen. *phōtos*), a light + -IC] *Ecol.* of or pertaining to the upper portion of a body of water receiving enough light for photosynthesis and plant growth

eu·phra·sy (yōo'frə sē) *n.*, *pl.* **-sies** [ME. < ML. < Gr. *euphrasia* < *euphrainein*, to cheer] *same as* EYE-BRIGHT

eu·phu·ism (yōo'fyoo wiz'm) *n.* [< *Euphues*, fictitious character in two works by J. Lyly < Gr. *euphyēs*, graceful < *eu-*; well + *phyē*, growth] **1.** an artificial, affected, high-flown style of speaking or writing, esp. such a style of the late 16th cent., characterized by alliteration, balanced sentences, far-fetched figures of speech, etc. **2.** an instance of this —**eu'phu·ist** *n.* —**eu'phu·is'tic**, **eu'phu·is'ti·cal** *adj.* —**eu'phu·is'ti·cal·ly** *adv.*

Eur. **1.** Europe **2.** European

Eur·a·sian (yōo rā'zhən, -shən) *adj.* **1.** of Eurasia **2.** of mixed European and Asian descent —*n.* a person with one European parent and one Asian parent, or of mixed European and Asian descent

Eur·a·tom (yoor'ə tom') European Atomic Energy Community, an agency of the European Economic Community

eu·re·ka (yōo rē'kə) *interj.* [Gr. *heurēka*] I have found (it): an exclamation of triumphant achievement

eu·rhyth·mics (yōo ri th'miks) *n.pl.* *same as* EURYTHMICS —**eu·rhyth'mic** *adj.* —**eu·rhyth'my** *n.*

Eu·ro- (yōor'ō) a combining form meaning: **1.** Europe, European [*Eurocrat*] **2.** Europe and, European and [*Euro-*American] Also, before a vowel, **Eur-** [*Eurasia*]

Eu·ro·dol·lars (-dol'ərz) *n.pl.* U.S. dollars used by banks, etc. outside the U.S. to finance short-term loans, esp. in international trade

Eu·ro·pe·an (yoor'ə pē'ən) *adj.* **1.** of or relating to Europe **2.** native to or derived from Europe **3.** concerned with, favouring, etc. the unity of Europe —*n.* **1.** a native or inhabitant of Europe **2.** loosely, any white person **3.** a person who regards Europe as an essential whole or supports the political unification of Europe —**Eu·ro·pe'·an·ism** *n.*

European Economic Community the European common market formed in 1958 by Belgium, France, West Germany,

Italy, Luxembourg, and the Netherlands and joined since by other European countries

Eu·ro·pe·an·ize (-īz') *vt.* **-ized'**, **-iz'ing** **1.** to make European in habits, dress, culture, etc. **2.** to integrate (the economy of a European nation) with that of other European nations, esp. in the European Economic Community —**Eu'·ro·pe·an·i·za'tion** *n.*

eu·ro·pi·um (yoo rō'pē əm) *n.* [ModL. < *Europe*] a chemical element of the rare-earth group: symbol, Eu; at wt., 151.96; at. no. 63

eu·ryth·mics (yoo ri th'miks) *n.pl.* [with *sing. v.*] [< L. < Gr. < *eu-*, well + *rhythmos*, RHYTHM] the art of performing various bodily movements in rhythm, usually to musical accompaniment —**eu·ryth'mic**, **eu·ryth'mi·cal** *adj.* —**eu·rhyth'my** *n.*

Eu·sta·chi·an tube (yoo stā'shən, -shē ən, -kē ən) [after B. Eustachio (1520–1574), It. anatomist] a slender tube between the middle ear and the pharynx, which serves to equalize air pressure on both sides of the eardrum

Eu·ter·pe (yoo tur'pē) *Gr. Myth.* the Muse of music and lyric poetry

eu·tha·na·si·a (yōo'thə nā'zhə, -zhē ə) *n.* [< Gr. < *eu-*, well + *thanatos*, death] **1.** an easy and painless death **2.** act or method of causing death painlessly to end suffering: advocated by some in cases of incurable, painful diseases

eu·then·ics (yoo than'iks) *n.pl.* [with *sing. v.*] [< Gr. *euthēnein*, to flourish + -ICS] the movement devoted to improving species and breeds, esp. the human species, by control of environmental factors

eu·troph·ic (-trof'ik, -trō'fik) *adj.* [< EU- + Gr. *trophikos* < *trophē*, food] designating or of a lake, pond, etc. rich in mineral and plant nutrients but often deficient in oxygen —**eu'troph·i·ca'tion** *n.*

ev, EV electron-volt

EVA extravehicular activity

e·vac·u·ate (i vak'yoo wāt') *vt.* **-at'ed, -at'ing** [< L. pp. of *evacuare* < *e-*, out + *vacuare*, to make empty < *vacuus*, empty] **1.** to make empty; remove the contents of; specif., to remove the air from **2.** to discharge (bodily waste, esp. faeces) **3.** to remove (inhabitants, troops, etc.) from (a place or area), as for protective purposes —*vi.* **1.** to withdraw, as from a danger area **2.** to discharge bodily waste —**e·vac'u·a'tion** *n.* —**e·vac'u·a'tive** *adj.* —**e·vac'u·a'·tor** *n.* —**e·vac'u·ee'** *n.*

e·vade (i vād') *vi.* **e·vad'ed, e·vad'ing** [< Fr. < L. < *e-*, out, from + *vadere*, to go] to be deceitful or clever in avoiding or escaping something —*vt.* **1.** to avoid or escape from by deceit or cleverness **2.** to avoid doing or answering directly [to *evade* income tax] —**e·vad'a·ble** *adj.* —**e·vad'er** *n.*

e·val·u·ate (i val'yoo wāt') *vt.* **-at'ed, -at'ing** [< Fr. < é-(L. *ex-*), out + *valuer*, to VALUE] **1.** to find the value or amount of **2.** to judge or determine the worth or quality of; appraise —**e·val'u·a'tion** *n.* —**e·val'u·a'tive** *adj.*

ev·a·nesce (ev'ə nes') *vi.* **-nesced'**, **-nesc'ing** [< L. < *e-*, out + *vanescere*, to vanish < *vanus*, empty] to fade from sight like mist or smoke; vanish

ev·a·nes·cent (-nes''nt) *adj.* tending to fade away; vanishing; fleeting —**ev'a·nes'cence** *n.* —**ev'a·nes'cent·ly** *adv.*

e·van·gel (i van'jəl) *n.* [< OFr. < LL. < L. < Gr. *euangelos*, bringing good news < *eu-*, well + *angelos*, messenger] [Archaic] **1.** the gospel **2.** [E-] any of the four Gospels **3.** an evangelist

e·van·gel·i·cal (ē'van jel'i k'l) *adj.* **1.** in, of, or according to the Gospels or the New Testament **2.** of those Protestant churches, as the Methodist and Baptist, that emphasize salvation by faith in the atonement of Jesus **3.** *same as* EVANGELISTIC Also **e'van·gel'ic** —*n.* a member of an evangelical church —**e'van·gel'i·cal·ism** *n.* —**e'van·gel'·i·cal·ly** *adv.*

e·van·gel·ism (i van'jə liz'm) *n.* **1.** a preaching of, or zealous effort to spread the gospel **2.** any zealous effort in propagandizing for a cause —**e·van'gel·is'tic** *adj.* —**e·van'·gel·is'ti·cal·ly** *adv.*

e·van·gel·ist (-list) *n.* **1.** [E-] any of the four writers of the Gospels; Matthew, Mark, Luke, or John **2.** anyone who evangelizes; esp., a travelling preacher

e·van·gel·ize (-līz') *vt.* **-ized'**, **-iz'ing** **1.** to preach the gospel to **2.** to convert to Christianity —*vi.* to preach the gospel —**e·van'gel·i·za'tion** *n.*

e·vap·o·rate (i vap'ə rāt') *vt.* **-rat'ed, -rat'ing** [< L. pp. of *evaporare* < *e-*, out + *vapor*, vapour] **1.** to change (a liquid or solid) into vapour **2.** to remove moisture from (milk, vegetables, etc.), as by heating, so as to get a concentrated product —*vi.* **1.** to become vapour **2.** to give off vapour **3.** to disappear; vanish —**e·vap'o·ra·bil'i·ty** *n.* —**e·vap'o·ra·ble** *adj.* —**e·vap'o·ra'tion** *n.* —**e·vap'o·ra·tive** *adj.* —**e·vap'o·ra'tor** *n.*

evaporated milk unsweetened milk thickened by evaporation to about half its weight, and then tinned: cf. CONDENSED MILK

e·va·sion (i vā'zhən) *n.* **1.** an evading; specif., an avoiding of a duty, question, etc. by deceit or cleverness **2.** a way of doing this; subterfuge

e·va·sive (-siv) *adj.* **1.** tending or seeking to evade; not straightforward *[evasive* action*]* **2.** hard to catch, grasp, etc.; elusive —**e·va'sive·ly** *adv.* —**e·va'sive·ness** *n.*

eve (ēv) *n.* [ME., var. of *even* < OE. *æfen*, EVENING] **1.** [Poet.] evening **2.** [*often* E-] the evening or day before a holiday *[Christmas Eve]* **3.** the period immediately before some event

e·ven¹ (ē'vən, -v'n) *adj.* [OE. *efne, efen*] **1.** flat; level; smooth *[even* surface*]* **2.** not varying; constant *[an even* tempo*]* **3.** calm; tranquil *[an even* disposition*]* **4.** in the same plane or line *[even* with the rim*]* **5.** equally balanced **6.** *a)* owing and being owed nothing *b)* with neither a profit nor a loss **7.** revenged for a wrong, insult, etc. **8.** just; fair *[an even* exchange*]* **9.** equal or identical in number, quantity, etc. **10.** exactly divisible by two: said of numbers **11.** exact *[an even* mile*]* —*adv.* **1.** moreover; however improbable; indeed; fully *[even* a fool could do it*]* **2.** exactly; just *[it happened even* as I expected*]* **3.** just as; while *[even* as he spoke, she entered*]* **4.** comparatively; still; yet *[an even* worse mistake*]* —*vt., vi.* to make, become, or be even; level (*off*) —**break even** [Colloq.] to finish as neither a winner nor a loser —**even if** despite the fact that; though —**even so** nevertheless; in any case —**even up** to make or become equal, esp. in respect of claims or debts: also **even out** —**e'ven·ly** *adv.* —**e'·ven·ness** *n.*

e·ven² (ē'vən) *n.* [see EVE] [Poet.] evening

e·ven·fall (-fôl') *n.* [Poet.] twilight; dusk

e·ven·hand·ed (-han'did) *adj.* impartial; fair —**e'·ven·hand'ed·ly** *adv.* —**e'ven·hand'ed·ness** *n.*

eve·ning (ēv'niŋ) *n.* [< OE. < *æfnian*, to become evening < *æfen*, evening] **1.** the last part of the day and early part of night **2.** the last period, as of life, a career, etc. —*adj.* in, for, or of the evening

evening dress clothes for wearing at a formal evening occasion, esp. a dinner jacket or long dress

evening primrose a plant having yellow flowers that open in the evening

eve·nings (-niŋz) *adv.* [Colloq.] during every evening or most evenings

evening star a bright planet, esp. Venus, seen in the western sky soon after sunset

even money equal stakes in betting, with no odds also **e·vens**

e·ven·song (ē'vən soŋ') *n.* **1.** *R.C.Ch.* vespers (see VESPER, sense 2a) **2.** *Anglican Ch.* the service assigned to the evening

e·vent (i vent') *n.* [OFr. < L. pp. of *evenire*, to happen < *e-*, out + *venire*, to come] **1.** a happening or occurrence, esp. when important **2.** a result; outcome **3.** a particular contest or item in a programme of sports —**in any event** no matter what happens; anyhow: also **at all events** —**in the event of** in case of —**in the event that** if it should happen that

e·ven-tem·pered (ē'vən tem'pərd) *adj.* not quickly angered or excited; placid; calm

e·vent·ful (i vent'fəl) *adj.* **1.** full of outstanding events **2.** having an important outcome —**e·vent'ful·ly** *adv.* —**e·vent'·ful·ness** *n.*

e·ven·tide (ē'vən tīd') *n.* [Archaic] evening

eventide home an old people's home, esp., formerly, one run by the Salvation Army

e·ven·tu·al (i ven'choo wəl) *adj.* **1.** [Archaic] depending on events; contingent **2.** happening in the end; ultimate —**e·ven'tu·al·ly** *adv.*

e·ven·tu·al·i·ty (i ven'choo wal'ə tē) *n., pl.* **-ties** a possible event, outcome, or condition; contingency

e·ven·tu·ate (i ven'choo wāt') *vi.* **-at'ed, -at'ing** to happen in the end; result (often with *in*)

ev·er (ev'ər) *adv.* [< OE. *æfre*] **1.** at all times; always *[lived happily ever* after*]* **2.** at any time *[have you ever* seen her?*]* **3.** at all; by any chance; in any way *[how can I ever* repay you?*]* —**did you ever?** [Colloq.] have you ever heard or seen such a thing? **4.** [U.S. Colloq.] truly; indeed *[was she ever* tired!*]* —**ever so** [Colloq.] very —**ever such** a [Slang] a very —**for ever and a day** always: also **for ever and ever**

ev·er·glade (ev'ər glād') *n.* [U.S.] swampland —**the Everglades** large tract of swampland in S & SE Florida, U.S.

ev·er·green (ev'ər grēn') *adj.* having green leaves throughout the year: opposed to DECIDUOUS —*n.* an evergreen plant or tree

ev·er·last·ing (ev'ər läs'tiŋ) *adj.* **1.** lasting forever; eternal **2.** going on for a long time **3.** going on too long; seeming never to stop —*n.* **1.** eternity **2.** *a)* any of various plants whose blossoms keep their colour and shape when dried; esp., an annual with pink, lilac, or white flowers *b)* the blossom of such a plant —**the Everlasting** God —**ev'·er·last'ing·ly** *adv.*

ev·er·more (-môr') *adv.* **1.** forever; constantly **2.** [Poet.] for all future time —**for evermore** forever

e·ver·sion (ē vur'zhən, -shən) *n.* an everting or being everted —**e·ver'si·ble** (-sə b'l) *adj.*

e·vert (ē vurt') *vt.* [L. *evertere* < *e-*, out + *vertere*, to turn] to turn outwards or inside out, as an eyelid

ev·er·y (ev'rē; *occas.* -ər ē) *adj.* [< OE. *æfre ælc*, lit., ever each] **1.** each, individually and separately *[every* man among you*]* **2.** the fullest possible; all that there could be *[he was given every* chance*]* **3.** each group or interval of (a specified number or time) *[a pill every* three hours*]* —**every last** [Slang] all, without exception —**every now and then** from time to time: also [Colloq.] **every so often** —**every other** each alternate, as the first, third, fifth, etc. —**every which way** [U.S. Colloq.] in complete disorder

ev·er·y·bod·y (-bod'ē) *pron.* every person; everyone

ev·er·y·day (-dā') *adj.* **1.** daily *[one's everyday* routine*]* **2.** suitable for ordinary days *[everyday* shoes*]* **3.** usual; common *[an everyday* occurrence*]*

Ev·er·y·man (-man) *n.* [after the 15th-c. morality play] [*often* e-] the ordinary person; the man in the street

ev·er·y·one (-wən, -wun') *pron.* everybody

every one every person or thing of those named *[remind every one* of the students*]*

ev·er·y·thing (-thiŋ) *pron.* **1.** every thing; all **2.** all things pertinent to a specified matter **3.** the most important thing *[money isn't everything]* —**have everything** [Colloq.] to possess all necessary attributes, possessions, etc.

ev·er·y·where (-wer', -hwer') *adv.* in or to every place

e·vict (i vikt') *vt.* [< L. *evictus*, pp. of *evincere*: see EVINCE] to remove (a tenant) from leased premises by legal procedure, as for failure to pay rent —**e·vic'tion** *n.*

ev·i·dence (ev'ə dəns) *n.* **1.** the condition of being evident **2.** something that makes another thing evident; indication; sign **3.** something that tends to prove **4.** *Law* something presented before a court, as a statement of a witness, an object, etc., which bears on or establishes the point in question —*vt.* **-denced, -denc·ing** **1.** to make evident; indicate; show **2.** to bear witness to; attest —**in evidence** plainly visible or perceptible

ev·i·dent (-dənt, -dent') *adj.* [< OFr. < L. *evidens*, clear < *e-*, from + prp. of *videre*, to see] easy to see or perceive; clear; obvious; plain —**ev'i·dent·ly** *adv.*

ev·i·den·tial (ev'ə den'shəl) *adj.* of, serving as, or providing evidence —**ev'i·den'tial·ly** *adv.*

e·vil (ē'v'l) *adj.* [OE. *yfel*] **1.** *a)* morally bad or wrong; wicked; depraved *b)* resulting from conduct regarded as immoral *[an evil* reputation*]* **2.** harmful; injurious **3.** offensive **4.** unlucky; disastrous —*n.* **1.** wickedness; depravity; sin **2.** anything that causes harm, pain, disaster, etc. —**the Evil One** the Devil —**e'vil·ly** *adv.* —**e'vil·ness** *n.*

e·vil·do·er (-dōo'ər) *n.* a person who does evil, esp. habitually —**e'vil·do'ing** *n.*

evil eye a look which, in superstitious belief, is able to harm or bewitch the one stared at; also, the supposed power to cast such a look: with **the**

e·vil-mind·ed (-mīn'did) *adj.* having an evil mind or disposition; specif., *a)* malicious or wicked *b)* inclined to view everything in an evil or obscene way —**e'vil-mind'·ed·ly** *adv.* —**e'vil-mind'ed·ness** *n.*

e·vince (i vins') *vt.* **e·vinced', e·vinc'ing** [< L. < *e-*, intens. + *vincere*, to conquer] to show plainly; make manifest; esp., to show that one has (a specified quality, feeling, etc.) —**e·vin'ci·ble** *adj.* —**e·vin'cive** *adj.*

e·vis·cer·ate (i vis'ə rāt') *vt.* **-at'ed, -at'ing** [< L. pp. of *eviscerare* < *e-*, out + *viscera*, VISCERA] **1.** to remove the entrails from **2.** to deprive of an essential part —**e·vis'·cer·a'tion** *n.*

ev·o·ca·ble (ev'ə kə b'l, i vō'kə b'l) *adj.* that can be evoked

ev·o·ca·tion (ev'ə kā'shən, ē'vō-) *n.* an evoking —**e·voc'a·tive** (i vok'ə tiv), —**e·voc'a·to·ry** (-tər ē) *adj.* —**e·voc'a·tive·ly** *adv.* —**e·voc'a·tive·ness** *n.* —**e'vo·ca'tor** *n.*

e·voke (i vōk') *vt.* **e·voked', e·vok'ing** [< Fr. < L. < *e-*, out + *vocare*, to call < *vox*, the voice] **1.** to conjure up (a spirit, etc.) **2.** to draw forth or elicit (a particular mental image, reaction, etc.) —**e·vok'er** *n.*

ev·o·lute¹ (ev'ə loot') *n.* [< L. *evolutus*: see EVOLUTION] *Math.* a curve that is the locus of the centre of curvature of another curve

ev·o·lute² (ev'ə loot') *vi., vt.* [< EVOLUTION] to evolve; develop by evolution

ev·o·lu·tion (ev'ə loo'shən) *n.* [< L. pp. of *evolvere*: see EVOLVE] **1.** an unfolding, opening out, or working out; process of development **2.** a result of this; thing evolved **3.** a movement that is part of a series or pattern **4.** a setting free or giving off, as of gas in a chemical reaction **5.** *Biol. a)* the development of a species, organism, or organ from its original to its present state *b)* a theory that all species of plants and animals developed from earlier forms: see DARWINIAN THEORY **6.** *Math.* the extracting of a root **7.** *Mil.* any of various manoeuvres by which troops, ships, etc. change formation —**ev′o·lu′tion·al** *adj.* —**ev′o·lu′-tion·al·ly** *adv.* —**ev′o·lu′tion·ar·y** *adj.*

ev·o·lu·tion·ist (-ist) *n.* a person who accepts the principles of evolution, esp. in biology —*adj.* 1. of the theory of evolution 2. of evolutionists —**ev′o·lu′tion·ism** *n.* —**ev′-o·lu′tion·is′tic** *adj.* —**ev′o·lu′tion·is′ti·cal·ly** *adv.*

e·volve (i volv′) *vt.* **e·volved′, e·volv′ing** [< L. < e-, out + volvere, to roll] 1. to develop by gradual changes; unfold 2. to set free or give off (gas, heat, etc.) 3. to produce or change by evolution —*vi.* 1. to develop gradually by a process of growth and change 2. to become disclosed; unfold —**e·volve′ment** *n.*

ewe (yōō; *dial.* yō) *n.* [OE. *eowu*] a female sheep

ew·er (yōō′ər) *n.* [< Anglo-Fr. < OFr. *evier*, ult. < L. *aquarius*: see AQUARIUM] a large water jug with a wide mouth

ex (eks) *prep.* [L.] without; exclusive of [ex interest] —*n., pl.* **ex′es** [Colloq.] one's divorced husband or wife

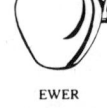

EWER

ex- [< OFr. or L., akin to Gr. *ex-, exŏ-*] 1. *a prefix meaning:* a) from, out [expel] b) beyond [excess] c) out of [expatriate] d) thoroughly [exterminate] e) upwards [exalt] It is assimilated to *ef-* before *f; e-* before *b, d, g, l, m, n, r,* and *v;* and, often, *ec-* before *c* or *s* 2. *a prefix meaning* former, previously [ex-convict]

Ex. Exodus

ex. 1. examined 2. example 3. except(ed) 4. express 5. extra

ex·ac·er·bate (ig zas′ər bāt′) *vt.* **-bat′ed, -bat′ing** [< L. pp. of *exacerbare* < ex-, intens. + acerbus, harsh, sour] 1. to make more intense or sharp; aggravate (disease, pain, feelings, etc.) 2. to irritate —**ex·ac′er·ba′tion** *n.*

ex·act (ig zakt′) *adj.* [< L. pp. of exigere, to measure < ex-, out + agere, to drive] 1. characterized by, requiring, or capable of accuracy of detail; methodical; correct 2. without variation; precise [an exact replica] 3. being the very (one specified or understood) 4. strict; severe; rigorous —*vt.* 1. to extort (with from or of) 2. to demand and get by authority or force (with from or of) 3. to make necessary; require —**ex·act′a·ble** *adj.* —**ex·act′ness** *n.* —**ex·ac′tor, ex·act′er** *n.*

ex·act·ing (-iŋ) *adj.* 1. making severe demands; not easily satisfied; strict 2. demanding great care, effort, etc.; arduous —**ex·act′ing·ly** *adv.* —**ex·act′ing·ness** *n.*

ex·ac·tion (ig zak′shən) *n.* 1. an exacting 2. an extortion 3. an exacted fee, tax, etc.

ex·ac·ti·tude (ig zak′tə tyōōd′) *n.* the quality of being exact; precision; accuracy

ex·act·ly (ig zakt′lē) *adv.* in an exact manner; accurately; precisely: also used as an affirmative reply, equivalent to "I agree," "quite true" —**not exactly** not at all; nowhere near: used ironically

ex·ag·ger·ate (ig zaj′ə rāt′) *vt.* **-at′ed, -at′ing** [< L. pp. of *exaggerare* < ex-, out + aggerare, to heap up < agger, a heap] 1. to think, speak, or write of as greater than is really so; overstate 2. to increase or enlarge to an abnormal degree —*vi.* to give an exaggerated account —**ex·ag′ger·at′ed·ly** *adv.* —**ex·ag′ger·a′tion** *n.* —**ex·ag′-ger·a′tive** *adj.* —**ex·ag′ger·a′tor** *n.*

ex·alt (ig zôlt′) *vt.* [< LL. *exaltare* < ex-, out, up + altus, high] to lift up; specif., a) to raise in status, dignity, power, wealth, etc. b) to praise; glorify; extol c) to fill with joy, pride, etc.; elate: used in the passive or in participial form d) to heighten or intensify the action or effect of —**ex·alt′ed·ly** *adv.* —**ex·alt′er** *n.*

ex·al·ta·tion (eg′zôl tā′shən) *n.* 1. an exalting or being exalted 2. elation; rapture

ex·am (ig zam′) *n.* [Colloq.] examination

ex·am·i·na·tion (ig zam′ə nā′shən) *n.* 1. an examining or being examined; investigation; inquiry 2. means or method of examining 3. a set of questions asked in testing; test —**ex·am′i·na′tion·al** *adj.* —**ex·am′i·na·to′ri·al** (-nə tôr′ē əl) *adj.*

examination paper 1. a written series of questions taken by an examination candidate 2. the written answers to such questions

ex·am·ine (ig zam′ən) *vt.* **-ined, -in·ing** [< OFr. < L. < *examen*, tongue of a balance, examination] 1. to look at or into critically or methodically to find out the facts, condition, etc. of; investigate; inspect 2. to test by questioning to find out the knowledge, skill, etc. of —**ex·am′i·na·ble** *adj.* —**ex·am′i·nee′** *n.* —**ex·am′in·er, ex·am′i·nant** *n.*

ex·am·ple (ig zäm′p'l) *n.* [< OFr. < L. *exemplum* < *eximere*, to take out < ex-, out + emere, to buy] 1. something selected to show the nature or character of the rest; sample 2. a case that serves as a warning or caution 3. a person or thing to be imitated; model 4. a problem, as in mathematics, that illustrates a principle or method —*vt.* **-pled, -pling** [Obs. except in the passive] to exemplify

—**set an example** to behave so as to be a pattern or model for others —**without example** having no precedent

ex·as·per·ate (ig zas′pə rāt′) *vt.* **-at′ed, -at′ing** [< L. pp. of *exasperare* < ex-, out + asperare, to roughen < asper, rough] to irritate or annoy very much; vex —**ex·as′per·at′-ing·ly** *adv.* —**ex·as′per·a′tion** *n.*

ex ca·the·dra (eks′kə thē′drə, kath′i drə) [ModL., lit., from the chair] with the authority that comes from one's rank or office: often used of certain authoritative papal pronouncements on faith or morals

ex·ca·vate (eks′kə vāt′) *vt.* **-vat′ed, -vat′ing** [< L. pp. of *excavare* < ex-, out + cavare, to make hollow < cavus, hollow] 1. to make a hole or cavity in, as by digging; hollow out 2. to form by hollowing out [to excavate a tunnel] 3. to uncover by digging; unearth 4. to dig out (earth, soil, etc.) —**ex′ca·va′tion** *n.* —**ex′ca·va′tor** *n.*

ex·ceed (ik sēd′) *vt.* [< OFr. < L. < ex-, out + cedere, to go] 1. to go or be beyond (a limit, measure, etc.) 2. to be more than or greater than; surpass —*vi.* to surpass others, as in quality or quantity

ex·ceed·ing (-iŋ) *adj.* surpassing; extraordinary; extreme —*adv.* [Archaic] extremely —**ex·ceed′ing·ly** *adv.*

ex·cel (ik sel′) *vi., vt.* **-celled′, -cel′ling** [< OFr. < L. < *excellere*, to rise] to be better or greater than (another or others)

ex·cel·lence (ek′səl əns) *n.* 1. the fact or condition of excelling; superiority 2. something in which a person or thing excels 3. [E-] *same as* EXCELLENCY

ex·cel·len·cy (-ən sē) *n., pl.* **-cies** 1. [E-] a title of honour applied to various persons of high position, as an ambassador, bishop, etc. 2. *same as* EXCELLENCE

ex·cel·lent (-ənt) *adj.* outstandingly good of its kind; of exceptional merit, virtue, etc. —**ex′cel·lent·ly** *adv.*

ex·cel·si·or (ek sel′sē ôr′; for n. ik sel′sē ər) *adj., interj.* [L., compar. of *exceisus*, high < excellere, EXCEL] higher; always upwards —*n.* long, thin wood shavings used for packing or as stuffing

ex·cept (ik sept′) *vt.* [< Fr. < L. < pp. of *excipere* < ex-, out + capere, to take] to leave out or take out; exclude; omit —*vi.* [Rare] to take exception; object —*prep.* leaving out; other than; but [to everyone except me] —*conj.* 1. [Archaic] unless 2. [Colloq.] were it not that [I'd quit except I need the money] —**except for** if it were not for

ex·cept·ing (-iŋ) *prep., conj.* *same as* EXCEPT

ex·cep·tion (ik sep′shən) *n.* 1. an excepting or being excepted; exclusion 2. anything that is excepted; specif., a) a case to which a rule, principle, etc. does not apply b) a person or thing different from others of the same class 3. an objection —**take exception** 1. to object 2. to resent; feel offended —**with the exception of** except —**ex·cep′-tion·less** *adj.*

ex·cep·tion·a·ble (-ə b'l) *adj.* liable or open to exception —**ex·cep′tion·a·bly** *adv.*

ex·cep·tion·al (-əl) *adj.* being an exception; not ordinary or average; esp., much above average in quality, ability, etc. —**ex·cep′tion·al·ly** *adv.*

ex·cerpt (ik surpt′; *also, and for n. always,* ek′surpt′) *vt.* [< L. pp. of *excerpere* < ex-, out + carpere, to pick] to select or quote (passages from a book, etc.); extract —*n.* a passage selected or quoted from a book, etc.; extract —**ex·cerp′tion** *n.*

ex·cess (ik ses′; *also, and for adj. usually,* ek′ses′) *n.* [< OFr. < L. pp. of *excedere:* see EXCEED] 1. action or conduct that goes beyond the usual, reasonable, or lawful limit 2. intemperance; overindulgence 3. an amount or quantity greater than is necessary, desirable, etc. 4. the amount or degree by which one thing exceeds another; surplus —*adj.* extra or surplus —**in excess of** more than —**to excess** too much

ex·ces·sive (ik ses′iv) *adj.* characterized by excess; being too much; immoderate —**ex·ces′sive·ly** *adv.* —**ex·ces′-sive·ness** *n.*

excess luggage luggage that is more than is allowed in weight, pieces, etc., esp. on an aeroplane: also **excess baggage**

ex·change (iks chānj′) *vt.* **-changed′, -chang′ing** [< OFr. < VL. hyp. *excambiare:* see EX- & CHANGE] 1. a) to give or transfer (for another thing in return) b) to receive or give another thing for (something returned) 2. to interchange (gifts, etc.) 3. to give up for a substitute or alternative [to exchange honour for wealth] —*vi.* 1. to make an exchange; barter 2. *Finance* to pass in exchange —*n.* 1. a giving or taking of one thing for another; barter 2. a giving to one another of similar things 3. the substituting of one thing for another 4. a thing given or received in exchange 5. a place for exchanging; esp., a place where trade is carried on by brokers, merchants, etc. [a stock exchange] 6. a central office in a telephone system, serving a certain area 7. a quarrel; argument 8. *Commerce, Finance* a) the payment of debts by negotiable drafts or bills of exchange b) a bill of exchange c) a fee paid for settling accounts or collecting a draft, bill of exchange, etc. d) an exchanging of a sum of money of one country for the equivalent in the money of another country e) the rate of exchange; value of one currency in terms of the other —*adj.* 1. exchanged 2. having to do with an exchange —**ex·change'a·bil'i·ty** *n.* —**ex·change'a·ble** *adj.* —**ex·chang'er** *n.*

exchange rate the ratio of the value of one currency in relation to the value of another, esp. in relation to the pound sterling [the *exchange rate* is &2.00 to the £]

ex·cheq·uer (iks chek'ər) *n.* [< OFr. *eschekier:* see CHEQUER] 1. [often E-] the British state department in charge of the national revenue 2. the funds in the British treasury 3. a treasury 4. money in one's possession; funds

ex·cis·a·ble (ik sī'zə b'l) *adj.* 1. subject to an excise tax 2. that can be cut out

ex·cise¹ (ek'sīz, -sīs; *for v.* ik sīz') *n.* [< MDu. < OFr. *assise:* see ASSIZE] 1. a tax on the manufacture, sale, or consumption of various commodities within a country, as wines, spirits, tobacco, etc.: also **excise tax** 2. the section of the government service responsible for the collection of excise —*vt.* -**cised', -cis'ing** to put an excise on

ex·cise² (ik sīz') *vt.* -**cised', -cis'ing** [< L. pp. of *excidere* < *ex-*, out + *caedere*, to cut] to remove (a tumour, etc.) by cutting out or away —**ex·ci'sion** (-sizh'ən) *n.*

ex·cise·man (ik sīz'mən) *n., pl.* -**men** (-mən) an official who collects excises

ex·cit·a·ble (ik sīt'ə b'l) *adj.* that is easily excited —**ex·cit'-a·bil'i·ty** *n.* —**ex·cit'a·bly** *adv.*

ex·ci·ta·tion (ek'sī tā'shən, -si-) *n.* an exciting or being excited (esp. in senses 4, 5, 6)

ex·cite (ik sīt') *vt.* -**cit'ed, -cit'ing** [< OFr. < L. *excitare* < *ex-*, out + pp. of *ciere*, to call] 1. to put into motion or activity; stir up 2. to arouse; provoke [to *excite* pity] 3. to arouse the feelings and passions of 4. *Elec.* to supply electric current to, as to produce a magnetic field 5. *Physics* to raise (a nucleus, atom, etc.) to a higher energy state 6. *Physiol.* to produce the response of (an organ, tissue, etc.) to a proper stimulus —**ex·cit'a·tive** (-ə tiv), **ex·cit'a·to·ry** (-ə tə rē) *adj.* —**ex·cit'er, ex·ci'tor** *n.*

ex·cit·ed (-id) *adj.* emotionally aroused; stirred up —**ex·cit'-ed·ly** *adv.*

ex·cite·ment (-mənt) *n.* 1. an exciting or being excited; agitation 2. something that excites

ex·cit·ing (-iŋ) *adj.* causing excitement; stirring, thrilling, etc. —**ex·cit'ing·ly** *adv.*

ex·claim (iks klām') *vi., vt.* [< Fr. < L. *exclamare* < *ex-*, out + *clamare*, to shout] to cry out; speak or say suddenly and excitedly, as in surprise, anger, etc.—**ex·claim'er** *n.*

ex·cla·ma·tion (eks'klə mā'shən) *n.* 1. the act of exclaiming 2. something exclaimed; interjection —**ex·clam·a·to·ry** (iks klam'ə tər ē) *adj.*

exclamation mark a mark (!) used after a word or sentence in writing or printing to express surprise, strong feeling, etc.

ex·clave (eks'klāv) *n.* [EX- + (EN)CLAVE] a territory (of a nearby specified country) surrounded by foreign territory, as formerly, East Prussia was a German exclave

ex·clo·sure (iks klō'zhər) *n.* [EX- + (EN)CLOSURE] an area protected against the entrance of animals, etc.

ex·clude (iks klōōd') *vt.* -**clud'ed, -clud'ing** [< L. *excludere* < *ex-*, out + *claudere*, CLOSE²] 1. to refuse to admit, consider, include, etc.; shut out; reject; bar 2. to put out; force out; expel —**ex·clud'a·ble** *adj.* —**ex·clud'er** *n.*

ex·clu·sion (-klōō'zhən) *n.* 1. an excluding or being excluded 2. a thing excluded —**to the exclusion of** so as to keep out, bar, etc. —**ex·clu'sion·a·ry** *adj.*

exclusion principle *same as* PAULI EXCLUSION PRINCIPLE

ex·clu·sive (-klōō'siv) *adj.* 1. excluding all others; shutting out other considerations, happenings, etc.[an *exclusive* interest] 2. excluding all but what is specified 3. not shared or divided; sole [an *exclusive* right] 4. a) excluding certain people or groups, as for social or economic reasons b) snobbish; undemocratic 5. dealing only in costly items [an *exclusive* shop] —*n.* something exclusive, specif., a story reported in only one newspaper —**exclusive of** not including or allowing for —**ex·clu'sive·ly** *adv.* —**ex·clu'-sive·ness** *n.*

ex·clu·siv·i·ty (eks'klōō siv'ə tē) *n.* the condition or practice of being exclusive; esp., clannishness or isolationism: also **ex·clu'siv·ism** —**ex·clu'siv·ist** *n., adj.* —**ex·clu'siv·is'tic** *adj.*

ex·com·mu·ni·cate (eks'kə myōō'nə kāt'; *for adj. and n., usually* -kit) *vt.* -**cat'ed, -cat'ing** to exclude, by ecclesiastical authority, from the sacraments, privileges, etc. of a church; censure by cutting off from communion with a church —*adj.* excommunicated —*n.* an excommunicated person —**ex'com·mu'ni·ca'tion** *n.* —**ex'com·mu'ni·ca'tive** *adj.* —**ex'com·mu'ni·ca'tor** *n.* —**ex'com·mu'ni·ca·to·ry** (-kə tər ē) *adj.*

ex·co·ri·ate (ik skôr'ē āt') *vt.* -**at'ed, -at'ing** [< L. pp. of *excoriare* < *ex-*, off + *corium*, the skin] 1. to strip, scratch, or rub off the skin of 2. to denounce harshly —**ex·co'ri·a'tion** *n.*

ex·cre·ment (eks'krə mənt) *n.* [< Fr. < L. < *excretus:* see EXCRETE] waste matter from the bowels; faeces —**ex'-cre·men'tal** (-men't'l) *adj.*

ex·cres·cence (iks kres'əns) *n.* [< OFr. < L. < *ex-*, out + *crescere*, to grow] 1. [Now Rare] a normal outgrowth, as a fingernail 2. an abnormal or disfiguring outgrowth, as a bunion —**ex·cres'cent** *adj.*

ex·cres·cen·cy (-ən sē) *n.* 1. the condition of being excrescent 2. *pl.* -**cies** *same as* EXCRESCENCE

ex·cre·ta (eks krēt'ə) *n.pl.* waste matter excreted from the body, esp. sweat, faeces, or urine —**ex·cre'tal** *adj.*

ex·crete (iks krēt') *vt., vi.* -**cret'ed, -cret'ing** [< L. *excretus,* pp. of *excernere* < *ex-*, out of + *cernere*, to sift] to separate (waste matter) from the blood or tissue and eliminate from the body —**ex·cre'tion** *n.* —**ex·cre'tive** *adj.*

ex·cre·to·ry (eks'krə tər ē) *adj.* of or for excreting —*n., pl.* -**ries** an excretory organ

ex·cru·ci·ate (iks krōō'shē āt') *vt.* -**at'ed, -at'ing** [< L. pp. of *excruciare* < *ex-*, intens. + *cruciare*, to crucify < *crux* (*gen. crucis*), a cross] 1. to cause intense bodily pain to; torture 2. to subject to mental anguish; torment —**ex·cru'-ci·a'tion** *n.*

ex·cru·ci·at·ing (-āt'iŋ) *adj.* 1. causing intense physical or mental pain 2. intense or extreme [*excruciating* care] 3. so bad as to be painful [an *excruciating* pun] —**ex·cru'ci·at'-ing·ly** *adv.*

ex·cul·pate (eks'kul pāt', ik skul'pāt) *vt.* -**pat'ed, -pat'ing** [< L. *ex,* out + pp. of *culpare,* to blame < *culpa,* fault] to free from blame; declare or prove guiltless —**ex·cul·pa·ble** (ik skul'pə b'l) *adj.* —**ex'cul·pa'tion** *n.* —**ex·cul'pa·to·ry** *adj.*

ex·cur·sion (ik skur'zhən) *n.* [< L. < pp. of *excurrere* < *ex-*, out + *currere*, to run] 1. a short trip or journey, as for pleasure 2. a round trip (on a train, bus, etc.) at special reduced rates 3. a group taking such a trip 4. a deviation or digression [an *excursion* into politics] 5. [Obs.] a military sortie; raid —*adj.* of or for an excursion —**ex·cur'-sion·a·ry** (-ə rē) *adj.* —**ex·cur'sion·ist** *n.*

excursion train a train that carries passengers at reduced rates, esp. for a day's outing

ex·cur·sive (-siv) *adj.* rambling; desultory; digressive —**ex·cur'sive·ly** *adv.* —**ex·cur'sive·ness** *n.*

ex·cuse (ik skyōōz'; *for n.* -skyōōs') *vt.* -**cused', -cus'ing** [< OFr. < L. *excusare* < *ex-*, from + *causa*, a charge] 1. to try to free (a person) of blame 2. to try to minimize (a fault); apologize or give reasons for 3. to disregard (an offence or fault); overlook [*excuse* my rudeness] 4. to release from an obligation, promise, etc. 5. to permit to leave 6. to serve as an explanation or justification for; justify; absolve —*n.* 1. a plea in defence of some action; apology 2. a release from obligation, duty, etc. 3. something that excuses; justifying factor 4. a pretended reason; pretext —**a poor** (or **bad,** etc.) **excuse for** a very inferior example of —**excuse oneself** 1. to apologize 2. to ask for permission to leave —**ex·cus'a·ble** *adj.* —**ex·cus'-a·bly** *adv.* —**ex·cus'er** *n.*

excuse-me-dance (-mē dāns') *n.* a dance in which a lady (**ladies' excuse-me**) may take another lady's partner or a gentleman (**gentlemen's excuse-me**) may take another gentleman's partner

ex·di·rec·to·ry (eks'də rek'tə rē) *adj.* not in a telephone directory, by request of the subscriber, and not disclosed to inquirers: said of a telephone number

ex·e·at (eks'ē at) *n.* [L., lit. let him go out] 1. a formal leave of absence granted to a student 2. permission from a bishop for a priest to move to another diocese

exec. 1. executive 2. executor

ex·e·cra·ble (ek'si krə b'l) *adj.* [L. *execrabilis*] abominable; detestable —**ex'e·cra·bly** *adv.*

ex·e·crate (-krāt') *vt.* -**crat'ed, -crat'ing** [< L. pp. of *execrare,* to curse < *ex-*, out + *sacrare*, to consecrate < *sacer,* sacred] 1. orig., to call down evil upon; curse 2. to denounce scathingly 3. to loathe; detest; abhor —*vi.* to curse —**ex'e·cra'tion** *n.* —**ex'e·cra'tive, ex'e·cra·to·ry** (-krə tər ē) *adj.* —**ex'e·cra'tor** *n.*

ex·e·cute (ek'sə kyōōt') *vt.* -**cut'ed, -cut'ing** [< OFr. < L. pp. of *ex(s)equi* < *ex-*, intens. + *sequi*, to follow] 1. to carry out; do; perform; fulfil 2. to carry into effect; administer (laws, etc.) 3. to put to death in accordance with a legally imposed sentence 4. to create in accordance with an idea, plan, etc. 5. to perform (a piece of music, etc.) 6. *Law* to make valid (a deed, contract, etc.) as by signing, sealing, and delivering —**ex'e·cut'a·ble** *adj.* —**ex'-e·cut'er** *n.*

ex·e·cu·tion (ek'sə kyōō'shən) *n.* 1. the act of executing; specif., a) a carrying out, doing, etc. b) a putting to death in accordance with a legally imposed sentence 2. the manner of doing or producing something, as of performing a piece of music 3. *Law* a writ, issued by a court, giving authority to put a judgment into effect —**ex'e·cu'tion·ar·y** *adj.*

ex·e·cu·tion·er (-ər) *n.* a person who carries out the death penalty

ex·ec·u·tive (ig zek'yə tiv) *adj.* 1. of, capable of, or concerned with, carrying out duties, functions, etc., as in a business **2.** empowered and required to administer (laws, government affairs, etc.); administrative: opposed to LEGISLATIVE (*adj.* 3) **3.** of managerial personnel or functions —*n.* **1.** a person, group, or branch of government empowered and required to administer the laws and affairs of a nation **2.** a person whose function is to administer or manage affairs, as of a company

executive officer *Mil.* an officer who is chief assistant to the commanding officer

ex·ec·u·tor (ig zek'yōōt'ər) *n.* **1.** a person who gets something done or produced **2.** a person appointed by a testator to carry out the provisions in his will —**ex·ec'u·to'·ri·al** (-tôr'ē əl), **ex·ec'u·to·ry** *adj.* —**ex·ec'u·trix** (-triks) *n.fem., pl.* **-trix·es, -tri'ces** (-tri'sēz)

ex·e·ge·sis (ek'sə jē'sis) *n., pl.* **-ge'ses** (-sēz) [< Gr. < *ex-*, out + *hēgeisthai*, to guide] analysis or interpretation of a word, literary passage, etc., esp. of the Bible —**ex'e·get'ic** (-jet'ik), **ex'e·get'i·cal** *adj.* —**ex'e·get'i·cal·ly** *adv.*

ex·e·gete (ek'sə jēt') *n.* an expert in exegesis

ex·em·plar (ig zem'plär, -plər) *n.* [< OFr. < LL. < L. *exemplum*, EXAMPLE] **1.** one that is considered worthy of imitation; model **2.** a typical specimen or example

ex·em·pla·ry (-plə rē) *adj.* **1.** serving as a model or example; worth imitating [*exemplary* behaviour] **2.** serving as a warning [*exemplary* punishment] **3.** serving as a sample; illustrative —**ex·em'pla·ri·ly** *adv.* —**ex·em'·pla·ri·ness** *n.*

exemplary damages *Law* damages beyond the actual loss, imposed as a punishment

ex·em·pli·fy (ig zem'plə fī') *vt.* **-fied', -fy'ing** [< OFr. < ML. < L. *exemplum*, an example + *facere*, to make] **1.** to show by example; serve as an example of **2.** to make a certified copy of (a document, etc.) under seal —**ex·em'·pli·fi·ca'tion** *n.*

ex·empt (ig zempt') *vt.* [< Anglo-Fr. < L. pp. of *eximere*: see EXAMPLE] to free from a rule or obligation which applies to others; excuse; release —*adj.* not subject to or bound by a rule, obligation, etc. applying to others —*n.* an exempted person —**ex·empt'i·ble** *adj.* —**ex·emp'tion** *n.*

ex·e·quies (ek'sə kwēz) *n.pl.* [ME. < OFr. < L. *exequiae* < *exequi* to follow up] funeral rites; obsequies

ex·er·cise (ek'sər sīz') *n.* [< OFr. < L. < pp. of *exercere*, to drive out (farm animals to work) < *ex-*, out + *arcere*, to enclose] **1.** active use or operation [the *exercise* of wit] **2.** performance (of duties, etc.) **3.** activity for training or developing the body or mind; esp., bodily exertion for the sake of health **4.** [*Sometimes pl.*] a series of movements to strengthen or develop some part of the body **5.** a problem or task to be worked out for developing some technical skill, as in mathematics or piano playing, etc. —*vt.* **-cised', -cis'-ing 1.** to use; employ [to *exercise* self-control] **2.** to put (the body, mind, etc.) into use so as to develop or train **3.** to drill (troops) **4.** to engage the attention and energy of, esp. so as to worry, perplex, or harass **5.** to exert or have (influence, control, etc.) **6.** to practise so as to develop [to *exercise* one's voice] —*vi.* to take exercise; do exercises —**ex'er·cis'a·ble** *adj.* —**ex'er·cis'er** *n.*

ex·ert (ig zurt') *vt.* [< L. < *exserere*, to stretch out < *ex-*, out + *serere*, to join] **1.** to put into action or use [*exert* your will] **2.** to apply (oneself) with great energy or effort —**ex·er'tive** *adj.*

ex·er·tion (ig zur'shən) *n.* **1.** the act, fact, or process of exerting **2.** energetic activity; effort

exes (eks'əs) *n.pl.* [Colloq.] expenses

ex·e·unt (ek'sē ənt, -oont, -unt) [L.] they (two or more characters) leave the stage: a stage direction

exeunt om·nes (om'nēz, -nās) [L.] all (of the characters who are on stage) leave: a stage direction

ex·fo·li·ate (eks fō'lē āt') *vt., vi.* **-at'ed, -at'ing** [< LL. pp. of *exfoliare*, to strip of leaves < *ex-*, out + *folium*, a leaf] to cast or come off in flakes, scales, or layers, as skin, bark, etc. —**ex·fo'li·a'tion** *n.* —**ex·fo'li·a·tive** *adj.*

ex gra·tia (grā'sha) [L. lit., out of kindness] given or granted as a favour, esp. where no legal obligation exists

ex·hale (eks hāl', ig zāl') *vi.* **-haled', -hal'ing** [< Fr. < L. *exhalare* < *ex-*, out + *halare*, to breathe] **1.** to breathe forth air **2.** to rise into the air as vapour; evaporate —*vt.* **1.** to breathe forth (air) **2.** to give off (vapour, fumes, etc.) —**ex·ha·la·tion** (eks'hə lā'shən, ek'sə-) *n.*

ex·haust (ig zôst') *vt.* [< L. pp. of *exhaurire* < *ex-*, out + *haurire*, to draw] **1.** to draw off or let out completely (air, gas, etc.), as from a container **2.** to use up; expend completely **3.** to empty completely; drain [to *exhaust* a well] **4.** to drain of power, resources, etc. **5.** to tire out; weaken **6.** to deal with or study completely and thoroughly [to *exhaust* a subject] —*vi.* to be let out, as gas or steam from an engine —*n.* **1.** the withdrawing of air, gas, etc. from a container or enclosure, as by means of a fan or pump **2.** *a)* the discharge of used steam, gas, etc. from the cylinders of an engine at the end of every working stroke of the pistons *b)* the pipe through which such steam, gas, etc. is released **3.** something given off, as fumes from a motor

vehicle engine —**ex·haust'i·bil'i·ty** *n.* —**ex·haust'i·ble** *adj.* —**ex·haust'less** *adj.*

ex·haus·tion (ig zôs'chən) *n.* **1.** an exhausting **2.** the state of being exhausted; esp., *a)* great fatigue or weariness *b)* complete consumption

ex·haus·tive (ig zôs'tiv) *adj.* **1.** exhausting or tending to exhaust **2.** leaving nothing out; covering every detail —**ex·haus'tive·ly** *adv.* —**ex·haus'tive·ness** *n.*

ex·hib·it (ig zib'it) *vt.* [< L. pp. of *exhibere* < *ex-*, out + *habere*, to hold, have] **1.** to show; display **2.** to present to public view **3.** *Law* to present (evidence, etc.) officially to a court —*vi.* to put pictures, wares, etc. on public display —*n.* **1.** a show; display **2.** an object or objects displayed publicly **3.** *Law* an object produced as evidence in a court —**ex·hib'i·tor, ex·hib'it·er** *n.*

ex·hi·bi·tion (ek'sə bish'ən) *n.* **1.** the act or fact of exhibiting **2.** the thing or things exhibited **3.** a public show or display, as of art **4.** an allowance or scholarship awarded to a student at some universities and schools

ex·hi·bi·tion·er (-ər) *n.* a pupil who has been awarded an exhibition (sense 4)

ex·hi·bi·tion·ism (-iz'm) *n.* **1.** a tendency to call attention to oneself or show off one's talents, skill,etc. **2.** *Psychol.* a tendency to expose parts of the body that are conventionally concealed —**ex'hi·bi'tion·ist** *n.* —**ex'hi·bi'·tion·is'tic** *adj.*

ex·hib·i·tive (ig zib'ə tiv) *adj.* serving or tending to exhibit (usually with *of*)

ex·hil·a·rate (ig zil'ə rāt') *vt.* **-rat'ed, -rat'ing** [< L. pp. of *exhilarare* < *ex-*, intens. + *hilarare*, to gladden < *hilaris*, glad] **1.** to make merry or lively **2.** to stimulate —**ex·hil'·a·ra'tive** *adj.* —**ex·hil'a·ra'tion** *n.*

ex·hort (ig zôrt') *vt., vi.* [< L. *exhortari* < *ex-*, out + *hortari*, to urge] to urge earnestly by advice, warning, etc.; entreat —**ex·hor·ta·tion** (eg'zôr tā'shən, ek'sər-) *n.* —**ex·hor'ta·to·ry** (-tə tə rē), **ex·hor'ta·tive** *adj.* —**ex·hort'-er** *n.*

ex·hume (ig zyōōm', iks hyōōm') *vt.* **-humed', -hum'ing** [< ML. *exhumare* < L. *ex*, out + *humus*, the ground] **1.** to dig out of the earth; disinter **2.** to reveal —**ex·hu·ma·tion** (eks'-hyoo mā'shən) *n.*

ex hy·poth·e·si (hī poth'ə sī) [L.] from the assumption; hypothetically

ex·i·gen·cy (ek'sə jən sē, ig sij'ən-) *n., pl.* **-cies** [see ff.] **1.** urgency **2.** a situation calling for immediate action or attention **3.** [*pl.*] pressing needs; demands [the *exigencies* of a situation] Also **ex'i·gence**

ex·i·gent (ek'sə jənt) *adj.* [< L. prp. of *exigere*: see EXACT] **1.** calling for immediate action or attention; urgent **2.** requiring more than is reasonable; demanding; exacting —**ex'i·gent·ly** *adv.*

ex·ig·u·ous (eg zig'yoo wəs) *adj.* [< L. < *exigere*: see EXACT] scanty; little; small; meagre —**ex·i·gu·i·ty** (ek'-sə gyōō'ə tē) *n.*

ex·ile (eg'zīl, ek'sīl) *n.* [< OFr. < L. *exilium* < *exul*, an exile] **1.** a prolonged, often enforced, living away from one's country, community, etc.; banishment, sometimes self-imposed **2.** a person in exile —*vt.* **-iled, -il·ing** to force (a person) to leave his country, community, etc.; banish —**ex·il·ic** (ig zil'ik, ik sil'ik) *adj.*

ex·ist (ig zist') *vi.* [< Fr. < L. *existere* < *ex-*, forth + *sistere*, to cause to stand] **1.** to have reality or actual being; be **2.** to occur or be present (*in*) **3.** to continue being; live —**ex·ist'ent** *adj.*

ex·ist·ence (-əns) *n.* **1.** the act of existing; state or fact of being **2.** continuance of being; life; living **3.** occurrence **4.** a manner of existing **5.** a being; entity; thing that exists

ex·is·ten·tial (eg'zis ten'shəl, ek'sis-) *adj.* **1.** of, based on, or expressing existence **2.** of, relating to, or as conceived of in, existentialism —**ex'is·ten'tial·ly** *adv.*

ex·is·ten·tial·ism (-shəl iz'm) *n.* a philosophical and literary movement which holds that man is totally free and responsible for his acts, and that this responsibility causes man's dread and anguish —**ex'is·ten'tial·ist** *n.*

ex·it (eg'zit, ek'sit) *n.* [L. *exitus*, orig. pp. of *exire* < *ex-*, out + *ire*, to go] **1.** an actor's departure from the stage **2.** a going out; departure **3.** a way out **4.** [L., 3rd pers. sing. pres. indic., of *exire*] he (or she) leaves: a stage direction —*vi.* to leave a place; depart

exit permit the authorization or permission to leave a certain country

‡**ex li·bris** (eks lē'bris, lī'-) [L.] **1.** from the library of: an inscription on bookplates **2.** a bookplate

ex·o- [< Gr. *exō*, without] a prefix meaning outside, outer, outer part

ex·o·bi·ol·o·gy (ek'sō bī ol'ə jē) *n.* [EXO- + BIOLOGY] the study of the possible existence of living organisms elsewhere in the universe than on earth —**ex'o·bi'o·log'i·cal** *adj.* —**ex'o·bi'ol'o·gist** *n.*

ex·o·carp (ek'sō kärp') *n.* [EXO- + -CARP] the outer layer of a ripened ovary or fruit; peel

ex·o·crine (ek'sə krin, -krīn', -krēn') *adj.* [EXO- + (ENDO)CRINE] designating or of a gland secreting externally, either directly or through a duct —*n.* any such gland, as a sweat gland, or its secretion

Exod. Exodus

ex·o·dus (ek'sə dəs) *n.* [< LL. < Gr. < *ex*-, out + *hodos*, way] a going out or forth, esp. in a large group —[E-] **1.** the departure of the Israelites from Egypt (with *the*) **2.** the second book of the Pentateuch, which describes this

ex of·fi·ci·o (eks'ə fish'ē ō') [L., lit., from office] by virtue of one's office, or position

ex·og·a·my (ek sog'ə mē) *n.* [EXO- + -GAMY] the custom of marrying only outside one's own tribe, clan, etc.; outbreeding—**ex·og'a·mous, ex·o·gam·ic** (ek'sə gam'ik) *adj.*

ex·og·e·nous (ek soj'ə nəs) *adj.* [EXO- + -GENOUS] **1.** developing from without; originating externally **2.** *Biol.* of or relating to external factors, as food, light, etc., that have an effect on an organism —**ex·og'e·nous·ly** *adv.*

ex·on (ek'son) *n.* [< Fr. pron. of *exempt*] one of the four officers of the yeoman of the guard

ex·on·er·ate (ig zon'ə rāt') *vt.* -at'ed, -at'ing [< L. pp. of *exonerare* < *ex*-, out + *onerare*, to load < *onus*, a burden] to free from a charge of guilt; declare or prove blameless —**ex·on'er·a'tion** *n.* —**ex·on'er·a'tive** *adj.* —**ex·on'er·a'tor** *n.*

ex·oph·thal·mos (ek'sof thal'məs) [< Gr. < *ex*-, out + *ophthalmos*, an eye] abnormal bulging out of the eyeball, caused by disease: also **ex'oph·thal'mus, ex'oph·thal'mi·a** (-mē ə) —**ex'oph·thal'mic** *adj.*

ex·or·bi·tant (ig zôr'bə tənt) *adj.* [< L. prp. of *exorbitare* < *ex*-, out + *orbita*, a track, ORBIT] going beyond what is reasonable, fair, usual, etc., as a price; excessive; extravagant —**ex·or'bi·tance, ex·or'bi·tan·cy** *n.* —**ex·or'bi·tant·ly** *adv.*

ex·or·cise, ex·or·cize (ek'sôr sīz') *vt.* -cised' or -cized', -cis'ing or -ciz'ing [< LL. < Gr. < *ex*-, out + *horkizein*, to make one swear < *horkos*, an oath] **1.** to drive (an evil spirit) out or away by ritual prayers, incantations, etc. **2.** to free from such a spirit —**ex'or·cis'er, ex'or·ciz'er** *n.*

ex·or·cism (-siz'm) *n.* **1.** the act of exorcising **2.** a formula or ritual used in exorcising —**ex'or·cist** *n.*

ex·or·di·um (ig zôr'dē əm) *n.,* pl. **-di·ums, -di·a** (-ə) [< L. < *ex*-, from + *ordiri*, to begin] **1.** a beginning **2.** the opening part of a speech, treatise, etc.

ex·o·skel·e·ton (ek'sō skel'ə t'n) *n.* *Zool.* any hard, external supporting structure, as the shell of crustaceans —**ex'o·skel'e·tal** *adj.*

ex·o·ther·mic (ek'sə thur'mik) *adj.* [EXO- + THERMIC] designating or produced by a chemical reaction in which heat is produced

ex·ot·ic (ig zot'ik) *adj.* [< L. < Gr. *exōtikos* < *exō*, outside] **1.** foreign; not native **2.** strangely beautiful, enticing, etc. —*n.* **1.** a foreign or imported thing **2.** a plant that is not native —**ex·ot'i·cal·ly** *adv.* —**ex·ot'i·cism** (-ə siz'm) *n.*

ex·ot·i·ca (-i kə) *n.pl.* [ModL. < L. neut. pl. of *exoticus*, exotic] foreign or unfamiliar things, as curious or rare art objects, strange customs, etc.

exotic dancer a belly dancer, striptease artist, or the like

exp. **1.** expenses **2.** export **3.** express

ex·pand (ik spand') *vt.* [< L. < *ex*-, out + *pandere*, to spread] **1.** to spread out; open out; stretch out; unfold **2.** to make greater in size, scope, etc.; enlarge; dilate **3.** to enlarge upon (a topic, idea, etc.); develop in detail or fully —*vi.* **1.** to spread out, unfold, enlarge **2.** to become increasingly relaxed, friendly, generous, or talkative —**ex·pand'a·ble** *adj.*

expanded metal sheet metal stretched out in latticelike strips, used as lath for plastering, etc.

ex·pand·er (ik spand'ər) *n.* **1.** a person or thing that expands **2.** *Electronics* a device for increasing the variations in signal amplitude in a transmission system according to a specified law

ex·panse (ik spans') *n.* a large, open area or unbroken surface; wide extent; great breadth

ex·pan·si·ble (ik span'sə b'l) *adj.* that can be expanded: also **ex·pand'a·ble** —**ex·pan'si·bil'i·ty** *n.*

ex·pan·sion (ik span'shən) *n.* **1.** an expanding or being expanded; enlargement **2.** an expanded thing or part **3.** the extent or degree of expansion **4.** a development or full treatment, as of a topic **5.** an increase, enlargement, etc. esp., in the activities of a company or the territory or economy of a country

ex·pan·sion·ar·y (-ər ē) *adj.* directed towards expansion

ex·pan·sion·ism (-iz'm) *n.* the policy of expanding a nation's territory or its sphere of influence, often at the expense of other nations —**ex·pan'sion·ist** *adj., n.* —**ex·pan'sion·is'tic** *adj.*

ex·pan·sive (ik span'siv) *adj.* **1.** tending or being able to expand **2.** of, or working by means of, expansion **3.** broad; extensive; comprehensive **4.** sympathetic;

demonstrative [an *expansive* person] —**ex·pan'sive·ly** *adv.* —**ex·pan'sive·ness** *n.*

ex·pa·ti·ate (ik spā'shē āt') *vi.* -at'ed, -at'ing [< L. pp. of *expatiari*, to wander < *ex*-, out + *spatiari*, to walk < *spatium*, space] to speak or write in great detail (*on* or *upon*) —**ex·pa'ti·a'tion** *n.* —**ex·pa'ti·a'to·ry** (-tə rē) *adj.*

ex·pa·tri·ate (eks pā'trē āt'; *for adj. & n., usually* -it) *vt.* -at'ed, -at'ing [< ML. pp. of *expatriare* < L. *ex*, out of + *patria*, fatherland < *pater*, father] **1.** to exile or banish **2.** to withdraw (oneself) from one's native land —*adj.* expatriated —*n.* an expatriated person —**ex·pa'tri·a'tion** *n.*

ex·pect (ik spekt') *vt.* [< L. < *ex*-, out + *spectare*, to look] **1.** to look for as likely to occur or appear; look forward to; anticipate **2.** to look for as due, proper, or necessary [to *expect* a reward] **3.** [Colloq.] to suppose; presume; guess —**be expecting** [Colloq.] to be pregnant —**ex·pect'a·ble** *adj.*

ex·pect·an·cy (ik spek'tən sē) *n.,* pl. **-cies** **1.** an expecting or being expected; expectation **2.** that which is expected, esp. on a statistical basis [life *expectancy*] Also **ex·pect'·ance**

ex·pect·ant (-tənt) *adj.* expecting; specif., *a*) having or showing expectation *b*) waiting, as for a position, the birth of a child, etc. —*n.* a person who expects something —**ex·pect'ant·ly** *adv.*

ex·pec·ta·tion (ek'spek tā'shən) *n.* **1.** a looking forward to; anticipation **2.** a looking for as due, proper, or necessary **3.** a thing looked forward to **4.** [*also pl.*] prospect of future success, prosperity, etc. —**in expectation** in the state of being looked for —**ex·pec·ta·tive** (ik spek'tə tiv) *adj.*

ex·pec·to·rant (ik spek'tər ənt) *adj.* causing or easing the bringing up of phlegm, mucus, etc. from the respiratory tract —*n.* an expectorant medicine

ex·pec·to·rate (-tə rāt') *vt., vi.* -rat'ed, -rat'ing [< L. pp. of *expectorare* < *ex*-, out + *pectus* (gen. *pectoris*), breast] **1.** to cough up and spit out (phlegm, mucus, etc.) **2.** to spit —**ex·pec'to·ra'tion** *n.*

ex·pe·di·en·cy (ik spē'dē ən sē) *n.,* pl. **-cies** **1.** the quality or state of being expedient; suitability for a given purpose **2.** the doing or consideration of what is of use or advantage rather than what is right or just; self-interest **3.** an expedient Also **ex·pe'di·ence**

ex·pe·di·ent (-ənt) *adj.* [< OFr. < L. prp. of *expedire*: see ff.] **1.** useful for effecting a desired result; suited to the circumstances; convenient **2.** based on what is of use or advantage rather than what is right or just; guided by self-interest —*n.* an expedient thing —**ex·pe'di·ent·ly** *adv.*

ex·pe·dite (ek'spə dīt') *vt.* -dit'ed, -dit'ing [< L. pp. of *expedire*, lit., to free one caught by the feet < *ex*-, out + *pes* (gen. *pedis*), foot] **1.** to speed up or make easy the progress or action of; facilitate **2.** to do quickly

ex·pe·di·tion (ek'spə dish'ən) *n.* [< OFr. < L. < pp. of *expedire*: see EXPEDITE] **1.** *a*) a journey, voyage, etc., as for exploration or battle *b*) the people, ships, etc. on such a journey **2.** efficient speed; dispatch —**ex'pe·di'tion·ar·y** *adj.*

ex·pe·di·tious (ek'spə dish'əs) *adj.* efficient and speedy; prompt —**ex'pe·di'tious·ly** *adv.*

ex·pel (ik spel') *vt.* -pelled', -pel'ling [< L. *expellere* < *ex*-, out + *pellere*, to thrust] **1.** to drive out by force; force out; eject **2.** to dismiss or send away by authority, as from a school, country, etc. —**ex·pel'la·ble** *adj.* —**ex·pel·lee** (ek'spel ē') *n.* —**ex·pel'ler** *n.*

ex·pel·lant, ex·pel·lent (-ənt) *adj.* [< L. *expellans*, prp. of *expellere*] expelling or tending to expel —*n.* an expellant medicine

ex·pend (ik spend') *vt.* [< L. *expendere*, to pay out < *ex*-, out + *pendere*, to weigh] **1.** to spend **2.** to consume by using; use up —**ex·pend'er** *n.*

ex·pend·a·ble (ik spen'də b'l) *adj.* **1.** that can be expended **2.** *Mil.* designating equipment (and hence, men) expected to be used up (or sacrificed) in service —*n.* a person or thing considered expendable —**ex·pend'a·bil'i·ty** *n.* —**ex·pend'·a·bly** *adv.*

ex·pend·i·ture (-də chər) *n.* **1.** an expending; a spending or using up of money, time, etc. **2.** the amount of money, time, etc. expended

ex·pense (ik spens') *n.* [< Anglo-Fr. < LL. *expensa* (*pecunia*), paid out (money) < L. pp. of *expendere*: see EXPEND] **1.** financial cost; fee **2.** any cost or sacrifice **3.** [*pl.*] *a*) charges met with in doing one's work, etc. *b*) money to pay for these charges **4.** a cause of spending —**at the expense of** with the payment, loss, etc. borne by

expense account **1.** an arrangement whereby certain expenses of an employee related to his work are paid for by his employer **2.** a record of these

ex·pen·sive (ik spen'siv) *adj.* requiring or involving much expense; high-priced; dear —**ex·pen'sive·ly** *adv.* —**ex·pen'sive·ness** *n.*

ex·pe·ri·ence (ik spir'ē əns) *n.* [< OFr. < L. < prp. of *experiri*, to try < *ex*-, out + base as in *peritus*, experienced] **1.** the act of living through an event or events **2.** anything or everything observed or lived through **3.** effect on one of anything or everything that has happened to him **4.** *a*) activity that includes training and personal participation *b)* the period of such activity *c)* knowledge, skill, or practice resulting from this —*vt.* **-enced, -enc·ing** to have experience of; undergo

ex·pe·ri·enced (-ənst) *adj.* **1.** having had much experience **2.** having learned from experience; made wise, competent, etc. by experience

ex·pe·ri·en·tial (ik spir′ē en′shəl) *adj.* of or based on experience —**ex·pe′ri·en′tial·ist** *n.* —**ex·pe′ri·en′tial·ly** *adv.*

ex·per·i·ment (ik sper′ə mənt, *for v.,* also -ment′) *n.* [< OFr. < L. *experimentum* < *experiri:* see EXPERIENCE] **1.** any action or process undertaken to discover something not yet known or to demonstrate or test something known **2.** the conducting of such tests or trials —*vi.* to make an experiment —**ex·per′i·ment′er** *n.*

ex·per·i·men·tal (ik sper′ə men′t'l) *adj.* **1.** of or based on experience rather than on theory or authority **2.** based on, tested by, or having the nature of, experiment **3.** of or used for experiments —**ex·per′i·men′tal·ism** *n.* —**ex·per′i·men′tal·ist** *n., adj.* —**ex·per′i·men′tal·ly** *adv.*

ex·per·i·men·ta·tion (ik sper′ə mən tā′shən, -men-) *n.* the conducting of experiments

ex·pert (ek′spərt; *also, for adj.,* ik spʉrt′) *adj.* [< OFr. < L. pp. of *experiri:* see EXPERIENCE] **1.** very skilful; having much training and knowledge in some special field **2.** of or from an expert [an *expert* opinion] —*n.* a person who is very skilful or highly trained and informed in some special field —**ex′pert·ly** *adv.* —**ex′pert·ness** *n.*

ex·pert·ise (ek′spər tēz′) *n.* [Fr.] the skill, knowledge, judgment, etc. of an expert

ex·pi·ate (ek′spē āt′) *vt.* **-at′ed, -at′ing** [< L. pp. of *expiare* < *ex-*, out + *piare*, to appease < *pius*, devout] **1.** to make amends for (wrongdoing or guilt); atone for **2.** to suffer for —**ex′pi·a·ble** (-ə b'l) *adj.* —**ex′pi·a′tion** *n.* —**ex′pi·a′tor** *n.*

ex·pi·a·to·ry (ek′spē ə tôr ē) *adj.* that expiates or is meant to expiate

ex·pi·ra·tion (ek′spə rā′shən) *n.* **1.** a breathing out, as of air from the lungs **2.** something breathed out **3.** a breathing one's last; dying **4.** a coming to an end; close —**ex·pir·a·to·ry** (ik spīr′ə tə rē) *adj.*

ex·pire (ik spīr′) *vt.* **-pired′, -pir′ing** [< L. *exspirare* < *ex-*, out + *spirare*, to breathe] to breathe out (air from the lungs) —*vi.* **1.** to breathe out air **2.** to breathe one's last breath; die **3.** to come to an end; terminate

ex·pi·ry (ik spīr′ē) *n., pl.* **-ries** [EXPIR(E) + -Y⁴] **1.** a coming to an end; termination [the *expiry* of the lease] **2.** [Archaic] death

ex·plain (ik splān′) *vt.* [< L. < *ex-*, out + *planare*, to make level < *planus*, level] **1.** to make plain or understandable **2.** to give the meaning or interpretation of; expound **3.** to account for; state reasons for —*vi.* to give an explanation —**explain away** to state reasons for so as to justify —**ex·plain oneself 1.** to make clear what one means **2.** to give reasons justifying one's conduct —**ex·plain′a·ble** *adj.* —**ex·plain′er** *n.*

ex·pla·na·tion (eks′plə nā′shən) *n.* **1.** an explaining **2.** something that explains **3.** the interpretation, meaning, etc. given in explaining

ex·plan·a·to·ry (ik splan′ə tə rē) *adj.* explaining or intended to explain: also **ex·plan′a·tive** (-ə tiv) —**ex·plan′a·to·ri·ly** *adv.*

ex·ple·tive (eks plē′tiv, eks′plə tiv) *n.* [< LL. < L. pp. of *explere* < *ex-*, out + *plere*, to fill] **1.** an oath or exclamation **2.** a word, phrase, etc. used merely to fill out a sentence or metrical line —*adj.* used to fill out a sentence, line, etc.: also **ex·ple′to·ry** (eks plē′tə rē, eks′plə-)

ex·pli·ca·ble (eks′pli kə b'l, iks plik′ə b'l) *adj.* that can be explained

ex·pli·cate (eks′pli kāt′) *vt.* **-cat′ed, -cat′ing** [< L. pp. of *explicare* < *ex-*, out + *plicare*, to fold] to make clear or explicit (something obscure or implied); explain fully —**ex′·pli·ca′tion** *n.* —**ex·pli·ca·tive** (-kāt′iv, ik splik′ə tiv), **ex′·pli·ca·to·ry** (-kə tə rē, ik splik′ə-) *adj.* —**ex′pli·ca′tor** *n.*

ex·plic·it (ik splis′it) *adj.* [< ML. < L. pp. of *explicare:* see prec.] **1.** clearly stated or expressed, with nothing implied; definite **2.** saying what is meant, without reservation; outspoken **3.** plain to see —**ex·plic′it·ly** *adv.* —**ex·plic′-it·ness** *n.*

ex·plode (ik splōd′) *vt.* **-plod′ed, -plod′ing** [orig., to drive off the stage by clapping and hooting < L. *explodere* < *ex-*, off + *plaudere*, to applaud] **1.** to expose as false; discredit [to *explode* a theory] **2.** to make burst with a loud noise **3.** to cause a rapid, violent change in by chemical reaction or by nuclear fission or fusion —*vi.* **1.** to burst noisily and violently **2.** to break forth noisily [to *explode* with anger] **3.** to increase very rapidly [an *exploding* population] —**ex·plod′a·ble** *adj.* —**ex·plod′er** *n.*

exploded view a photograph or drawing showing separately but in proper sequence and relationship the various parts of an assembly, as of a machine

ex·ploit (eks′ploit; *also, and for v. usually,* ik sploit′) *n.* [< OFr. < L. pp. of *explicare:* see EXPLICATE] an act remarkable for brilliance or daring; bold deed —*vt.* to

make use of; utilize productively **2.** to make use of or profit from the labour of (others) in an unethical way **3.** to use selfishly [to *exploit* friendship] —**ex·ploit′a·ble** *adj.* —**ex′-ploi·ta′tion** *n.* —**ex·ploit′a·tive, ex·ploi′tive** *adj.* —**ex·ploit′-er** *n.*

ex·plo·ra·tion (eks′plə rā′shən, -plô-) *n.* an exploring or being explored —**ex·plor·a·to·ry** (ik splor′ə tər ē), **ex·plor′-a·tive** (-tiv) *adj.*

ex·plore (ik splôr′) *vt.* **-plored′, -plor′ing** [L. *explorare*, to search out < *ex-*, out + *plorare*, to cry out] **1.** to look into closely; investigate **2.** to travel in (a region previously unknown or little known) for discovery **3.** *Med.* to examine (an organ, etc.) by operation, probing, etc., as in order to make a diagnosis —*vi.* to explore new regions, etc. —**ex·plor′er** *n.*

ex·plo·sion (ik splō′zhən) *n.* **1.** an exploding; esp., a blowing up; detonation **2.** the noise made by exploding **3.** a noisy outburst **4.** a sudden, rapid, and widespread increase

ex·plo·sive (-siv) *adj.* **1.** of, causing, or having the nature of, an explosion **2.** tending to explode; esp., tending to burst forth noisily **3.** *same as* PLOSIVE —*n.* **1.** a substance that can explode, as gunpowder **2.** *same as* PLOSIVE —**ex·plo′sive·ly** *adv.* —**ex·plo′sive·ness** *n.*

ex·po·nent (ik spō′nənt) *adj.* [< L. prp. of *exponere:* see EXPOUND] explaining, interpreting, or expounding —*n.* **1.** a person who expounds or promotes (principles, methods, etc.) **2.** a person or thing that is an example or symbol (*of* something) **3.** *Algebra* a small figure or symbol placed at the upper right of another figure or symbol to show how many times the latter is to be multiplied by itself (Ex.: b² = b x b) —**ex·po·nen·tial** (eks′pō nen′shəl) *adj.* —**ex′·po·nen′-tial·ly** *adv.*

exponential function *Math.* a quantity with a variable exponent

ex·port (ik spôrt′; *also, and for n. & adj. always,* eks′pôrt) *vt.* [< L. < *ex-*, out + *portare*, to carry] **1.** to carry or send (goods, etc.) to other countries, esp. for purposes of sale **2.** to carry or send (ideas, culture, etc.) from one place to another —*n.* **1.** something exported **2.** an exporting Also **ex′por·ta·tion** —*adj.* of or for exporting or exports —**ex·port′a·ble** *adj.* —**ex·port′er** *n.*

export reject an article falling below the standard for export that is sold in the country of manufacture, usually at a reduced price

ex·pose (ik spōz′) *vt.* **-posed′, -pos′ing** [< OFr. < L. pp. or *exponere:* see EXPOUND] **1.** *a)* to lay open (*to* danger, attack, ridicule, etc.); leave unprotected *b)* to make accessible or subject (*to* an influence or action) **2.** to leave out in the open, as to die **3.** to allow to be seen; reveal; display **4.** *a)* to make (a crime, fraud, etc.) known *b)* to make known the crimes, etc. of **5.** *Photog.* to subject (a sensitized film or plate) to radiation as of light rays —**expose oneself** to display one's sexual organs in public —**ex·pos′er** *n.*

ex·po·sé (eks′pō zā′) *n.* [Fr., pp. of *exposer*, to expose] a public disclosure of a scandal, crime, etc.

ex·posed (ik spōzd′) *adj.* **1.** not concealed; displayed for viewing **2.** left in the open; open to the weather **3.** vulnerable

ex·po·si·tion (eks′pə zish′ən) *n.* [< OFr. < L. pp. of *exponere:* see EXPOUND] **1.** a setting forth of facts, ideas, etc.; detailed explanation **2.** writing or speaking that sets forth or explains **3.** a large public exhibition or show **4.** the first section of certain musical forms, introducing the main theme or themes

ex·pos·i·tor (ik spoz′i tər) *n.* one that expounds or explains

ex·pos·i·to·ry (-ə tə rē) *adj.* of, like, or containing exposition; explanatory: also **ex·pos′i·tive** (-ə tiv)

ex post fac·to (eks′pōst fak′tō) [L., from (the thing) done afterwards] done or made afterwards, esp. when having retroactive effect

ex·pos·tu·late (ik spos′chə lāt′) *vi.* **-lat′ed, -lat′ing** [< L. pp. of *expostulare* < *ex-*, intens. + *postulare*, to demand] to reason with a person earnestly, objecting to his actions or intentions; remonstrate (*with*) —**ex·pos′tu·la′tion** *n.* —**ex·pos′tu·la′tor** *n.* —**ex·pos′tu·la·to·ry** (-lə tə rē) *adj.*

ex·po·sure (ik spō′zhər) *n.* **1.** an exposing or being exposed **2.** a location, as of a house, in relation to the sun, winds, etc. [an eastern *exposure*] **3.** the disclosure of shady or doubtful transactions; evil actions, etc. being unmasked **4.** a being exposed, when helpless, to the elements **5.** *Photog. a)* the subjection of a film or plate to light, etc. *b)* a film section for making one picture *c)* the time during which film is exposed

exposure meter *Photog.* an instrument for measuring the intensity of light on the subject and thus determining the correct exposure

ex·pound (ik spound′) *vt.* [< OFr. < L. < *ex-*, out + *ponere*, to put] **1.** to set forth; state in detail **2.** to explain or interpret —**ex·pound′er** *n.*

ex·press (ik spres′) *vt.* [< ML. < L. *expressus*, pp. of *exprimere* < *ex-*, out + *premere:* see PRESS¹] **1.** to press out or squeeze out (juice, etc.) **2.** to put into words; state **3.** to make known; show [his face *expressed* joy] **4.** to represent in art, music, etc. **5.** to show by a sign; symbolize —*adj.* **1.** *a)* expressed and not implied; explicit [an *express* wish] *b)* specific [his *express* reason for going] **2.** exact [the *express* image of her aunt] **3.** fast, direct, and making few stops [an *express* train] **4.** [Chiefly U.S.] having to do with express (*n.* 2) —*adv.* by express —*n.* **1.** an express train, bus, lift, etc. **2.** [Chiefly U.S.] *a)* a method or service for transporting goods rapidly: *b)* the things sent by express **3.** any method or means of swift transmission —**express oneself 1.** to state one's thoughts **2.** to give expression to one's feelings, imagination, talents, etc. —**ex·press'er** *n.* —**ex·press'i·ble** *adj.*

ex·press·age (-ij) *n.* [U.S.] **1.** the carrying of packages, etc. by express **2.** the charge for this

ex·pres·sion (ik spresh'ən) *n.* **1.** a pressing out or squeezing out, as of juice **2.** a putting into words **3.** a representing in art, music, etc. **4.** a manner of expressing; esp., eloquence in speaking, etc. **5.** a particular word or phrase [a trite *expression*] **6.** a showing of feeling, character, etc. [laughter is an *expression* of joy] **7.** a look, intonation, etc. that conveys meaning or feeling [a quizzical *expression*] **8.** a symbol or set of symbols expressing some mathematical fact **9.** a showing by a symbol, sign, figures, etc. —**ex·pres'sion·less** *adj.* —**ex·pres'sion·less·ly** *adv.*

ex·pres·sion·ism (-iz'm) *n.* an early 20th-cent. movement in art, drama, etc., characterized by distortion of reality and the use of symbols, stylization, etc. to give objective expression to inner experience —**ex·pres'sion·ist** *adj., n.* —**ex·pres'sion·is'tic** *adj.* —**ex·pres'sion·is·ti·cal·ly** *adv.*

expression mark one of a set of musical directions in the form of words, abbreviations or symbols, used to indicate details of performance, esp. volume

ex·pres·sive (ik spres'iv) *adj.* **1.** of or characterized by expression **2.** that expresses; indicative (*of*) [a song *expressive* of joy] **3.** full of meaning or feeling [an *expressive* nod] —**ex·pres'sive·ly** *adv.* —**ex·pres'sive·ness, ex·pres·siv'i·ty** *n.*

ex·press·ly (-lē) *adv.* **1.** plainly; definitely; explicitly **2.** especially; particularly

ex·pres·so (ek spres'ō) *n.* same as ESPRESSO

ex·press·way (ik spres'wā) *n.* [U.S.] a divided road for through traffic, with limited access and generally with overpasses or underpasses at intersections

ex·pro·pri·ate (eks prō'prē āt') *vt.* -at·ed, -at·ing [< ML. pp. of *expropriare* < L. *ex-*, out + *proprius*, one's own] to take (land, property, etc.) from its owner, esp. for public use —**ex·pro'pri·a'tion** *n.* —**ex·pro'pri·a'tor** *n.*

ex·pul·sion (ik spul'shən) *n.* an expelling, or forcing out, or the condition of being expelled —**ex·pul'sive** (-siv) *adj.*

ex·punge (ik spunj') *vt.* -punged', -pung'ing [L. *expungere* < *ex-*, out + *pungere*, to prick] to erase or remove completely; blot out or strike out; delete —**ex·punc'tion** (-spuŋk'shən) *n.*

ex·pur·gate (eks'pər gāt') *vt.* -gat·ed, -gat·ing [< L. pp. of *expurgare* < *ex-*, out + *purgare*, PURGE] to remove passages considered obscene or otherwise objectionable from (a book, etc.) —**ex'pur·ga'tion** *n.* —**ex'pur·ga'tor** *n.* —**ex·pur'ga·to·ry** *adj.*

ex·qui·site (eks'kwi zit, ik skwiz'it) *adj.* [< L. pp. of *exquirere*, to search out < *ex-*, out + *quaerere*, to ask] **1.** carefully done or elaborately made **2.** very beautiful, esp. in a delicate or carefully wrought way **3.** of highest quality; consummate **4.** highly sensitive; keenly discriminating [an *exquisite* ear for music] **5.** sharply intense; keen [*exquisite* pain] —*n.* one who makes a great show of being refined and fastidious in his tastes, etc. —**ex'qui·site·ly** *adv.* —**ex'qui·site·ness** *n.*

ex·serv·ice·man (eks'sur'vis mən) *n.* someone who has served in the Armed Forces, esp. during wartime —**ex·serv·ice·woman** (-woom'on) *n. fem.*

ext. 1. extension **2.** exterior **3.** external **4.** extinct **5.** extra **6.** extract

ex·tant (ik stant', ek'stənt) *adj.* [< L. prp. of *exstare* < *ex-*, out + *stare*, to stand] still existing

ex·tem·po·ra·ne·ous (ik stem'pə rā'nē əs) *adj.* [< LL.: see EXTEMPORE] **1.** made, done, or spoken without any preparation; offhand **2.** spoken with some preparation but not written out or memorized: cf. IMPROMPTU **3.** speaking without preparation **4.** improvised; makeshift —**ex·tem'po·ra'ne·ous·ly** *adv.*

ex·tem·po·rar·y (ik stem'pə rərē) *adj.* same as EXTEMPORANEOUS —**ex·tem'po·rar·i·ly** *adv.* —**ex·tem'po·rar·i·ness** *n.*

ex·tem·po·re (-pə rē) *adv., adj.* [L. < *ex*, out of + *tempore*, abl. of *tempus*, time] without preparation; offhand [to speak *extempore*]

ex·tem·po·rize (-rīz') *vi., vt.* -rized', -riz'ing **1.** to speak, perform, or compose extempore; improvise **2.** to contrive as a makeshift —**ex·tem'po·ri·za'tion** *n.* —**ex·tem'po·riz'er** *n.*

ex·tend (ik stend') *vt.* [L. *extendere* < *ex-*, out + *tendere*, to

stretch] **1.** *a)* to stretch out or draw out *b)* to draw out or lengthen in time or space; prolong **2.** to enlarge in area, scope, influence, etc.; expand; spread **3.** to stretch forth; hold out **4.** to offer; accord; grant **5.** to straighten out (a flexed limb of the body) **6.** to make (oneself) work or try hard —*vi.* **1.** to be extended **2.** to reach or stretch —**ex·tend'ed** *adj.* —**ex·tend'er** *n.* —**ex·tend'i·bil'i·ty** *n.*

extended family a social unit in which parents, grandparents, aunts and uncles, and children live in one household as a family unit: cf NUCLEAR FAMILY

extended player a record that is longer than average, usually containing three or four tracks instead of two: also **maxi single**

ex·ten·si·ble (ik sten'sə b'l) *adj.* that can be extended: also **ex·tend'i·ble** —**ex·ten'si·bil'i·ty** *n.*

ex·ten·sion (ik sten'shən) *n.* **1.** an extending or being extended **2.** range; extent **3.** a part that forms a continuation or addition **4.** an extra period of time allowed a debtor for making payment **5.** a service or system by which some of the facilities of an educational establishment, library, etc., are offered to those otherwise not able or eligible to use such facilities **6.** an extra telephone on the same line as the main telephone **7.** *Logic* the class of entities to which a given word correctly applies; denotation **8.** *Physics* that property of a body by which it occupies space —*adj.* designating a device that extends or can extend something else [*extension* ladder, *extension* cord] —**ex·ten'sion·al** *adj.*

ex·ten·sive (-siv) *adj.* **1.** of great extent, or area, amount, length, etc.; vast **2.** broad in scope, influence, etc.; far-reaching —**ex·ten'sive·ly** *adv.* —**ex·ten'sive·ness** *n.*

ex·ten·sor (-sər) *n.* a muscle that extends or straightens some part of the body, esp. a flexed arm or leg

ex·tent (ik stent') *n.* **1.** the space, amount, or degree to which a thing extends; size; length; breadth **2.** range or limits; scope; coverage **3.** an extended space; vast area

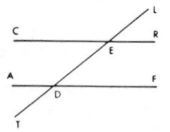

EXTENSOR

ex·ten·u·ate (ik sten'yoo wāt') *vt.* -at'ed, -at'ing [< L. pp. of *extenuare* < *ex-*, out + *tenuare*, to make thin < *tenuis*, thin] to lessen or seem to lessen the seriousness of (an offence, guilt, etc.) by giving excuses or serving as an excuse [*extenuating* circumstances] —**ex·ten'u·a'tion** *n.* —**ex·ten'u·a·to·ry, ex·ten'u·a'tive** *adj.*

ex·te·ri·or (ik stir'ē ər) *adj.* [L., compar. of *exter(us)*, on the outside: see EXTERNAL] **1.** *a)* on the outside; outer; outermost *b)* for use on the outside [*exterior* paint] **2.** acting or coming from without [*exterior* forces] —*n.* **1.** an outside or outside surface **2.** an outward appearance **3.** a picture, view, setting, etc. of an outdoor scene —**ex·te'ri·or·ly** *adv.*

exterior angle any of the four angles formed on the outside of two straight lines by a straight line cutting across them

ex·te·ri·or·i·ty (ik stir'ē ôr'atē) *n.* **1.** the state or quality of being exterior or exteriorized **2.** external aspect

ex·te·ri·or·ize (-ə rīz') *vt.* -ized', -iz'ing **1.** to give or attribute an external form or objective character to (states of mind, etc.) **2.** same as EXTERNALIZE —**ex·te'ri·or·i·za'tion** *n.*

EXTERIOR ANGLES
(CEL, LER, ADT, TDF)

ex·ter·mi·nate (ik stur'mə nāt') *vt.* -nat'ed, -nat'ing [< L. pp. of *exterminare*, to drive out, destroy < *ex-*, out + *terminus*, a boundary] to destroy or get rid of entirely, as by killing; wipe out; annihilate —**ex·ter'mi·na'tion** *n.* —**ex·ter'mi·na·to·ry, ex·ter'mi·na'tive** *adj.*

ex·ter·mi·na·tor (-nāt'ər) *n.* a person or thing that exterminates; specif., one whose work is exterminating rats, cockroaches, and other vermin

ex·ter·nal (ik stur'n'l) *adj.* [< L. *externus* < *exter(us)*, on the outside, compar. form < *ex*, out of (see EX-) + -AL] **1.** on the outside; outer; exterior **2.** on, or for use on, the outside of the body [a medicine for *external* use only] **3.** *a)* outwardly visible *b)* existing apart from the mind; material **4.** acting or coming from without **5.** *a)* for outward appearance or show; superficial *b)* not basic or essential **6.** having to do with foreign countries **7.** of an examination, degree, etc. taken by a student who is a member of but not resident at the university awarding the degree —*n.* **1.** an outside or outward surface or part **2.** [*pl.*] outward appearance or behaviour —**ex·ter·nal·i·ty** (eks'tər nal'ə tē) *n., pl.* -ties —**ex·ter'nal·ly** *adv.*

ex·ter·nal·ize (-īz') *vt.* -ized', -iz'ing **1.** to make external; embody **2.** same as EXTERIORIZE —**ex·ter'nal·i·za'tion** *n.*

ex·tinct (ik stiŋkt') *adj.* [< L. pp. of *exstinguere*: see

EXTINGUISH] **1.** having died down or burned out **2.** no longer active [an *extinct* volcano] **3.** no longer in existence [an *extinct* species]

ex·tinc·tion (ik stiŋk'shən) *n.* **1.** a putting out or being put out, as of a fire **2.** a destroying or being destroyed **3.** the fact or state of being or becoming extinct

ex·tin·guish (ik stiŋ'gwish) *vt.* [< L. *extinguere* < *ex-*, out + *stinguere*, to extinguish] **1.** to put out (a fire, etc.); quench **2.** to put an end to; destroy **3.** to eclipse; obscure —**ex·tin'guish·a·ble** *adj.* —**ex·tin'guish·er** *n.* —**ex·tin'guish·ment** *n.*

ex·tin·guish·er (-ər) *n.* a person or thing that extinguishes, esp. *same as* FIRE EXTINGUISHER

ex·tir·pate (ek'stər pāt',-stur-) *vt.* -pat'ed, -pat'ing [< L. pp. of *ex(s)tirpare* < *ex-*, out + *stirps*, root] **1.** to pull up by the roots **2.** to destroy completely; abolish —**ex'tir·pa'tion** *n.* —**ex'tir·pa'tive** *adj.* —**ex'tir·pa'tor** *n.*

ex·tol (ik stōl') *vt.* -tolled', -tol'ling [< L. *extollere* < *ex-*, up + *tollere*, to raise] to praise highly; laud —**ex·tol'ler** *n.* —**ex·tol'ment** *n.*

ex·tort (ik stôrt') *vt.* [< L. pp. of *extorquere* < *ex-*, out + *torquere*, to twist] to get (money, etc.) by violence, threats, misuse of authority, etc.; exact (*from*) —**ex·tort'er** *n.* —**ex·tor'tive** *adj.*

ex·tor·tion (ik stôr'shən) *n.* **1.** an extorting: sometimes applied to the exaction of too high a price **2.** *Law* the offence of an official who extorts **3.** something extorted —**ex·tor'tion·ate, ex·tor'tion·ar·y** *adj.*

ex·tor·tion·er (-ər) *n.* a person guilty of extortion: also **ex·tor'tion·ist**

ex·tra (eks'trə) *adj.* [contr. < EXTRAORDINARY; also < L. < *extra*, adv., more than outside: see ff.] **1.** more, larger, or better than is normal, expected, necessary, etc.; additional **2.** to be paid for by an added charge —*n.* an extra person or thing; specif., *a*) an additional charge *b*) formerly, a special newspaper edition for important news *c*) an extra benefit or feature *d*) a spare copy *e*) an extra worker *f*) *Cinema* an actor hired by the day to play a minor part *g*) *Cricket* a run that is not scored from the bat, as a bye, wide or no-ball —*adv.* more than usually [*extra* hot]

ex·tra- [L. < *exter(us)*: see EXTERNAL] *a prefix meaning* outside, outside the scope of, beyond, as in the following list:

extrafamilial extramarital
extragovernmental extraofficial
extrajudicial extraterrestrial

extra cover *Cricket* a fielding position between cover and mid-off

ex·tract (ik strakt'; *for n.* eks'trakt) *vt.* [< L. pp. of *extrahere* < *ex-*, out + *trahere*, to draw] **1.** to draw out by effort; pull out [to *extract* teeth, to *extract* a promise] **2.** to separate (metal) from ore **3.** to obtain by pressing, distilling, using a solvent, etc. [to *extract* juice from fruit] **4.** to deduce, derive, or elicit **5.** to copy out or quote (a passage from a book, etc.) **6.** *Math.* to compute (the root of a quantity) —*n.* something extracted; specif., *a*) a concentrated form of a food, flavouring, etc. [beef *extract*] *b*) quotation from a book, etc. —**ex·tract'a·ble, ex·tract'i·ble** *adj.* —**ex·trac'tive** *adj.* —**ex·trac'tor** *n.*

ex·trac·tion (ik strak'shən) *n.* **1.** an extracting; specif., the extracting of a tooth **2.** origin; lineage; descent **3.** a thing extracted; extract

ex·trac·tor fan (-tər) a device for extracting stale air and other gases from a room, building, etc.: also **ex·trac'tor** *n.*

ex·tra·cur·ric·u·lar (eks'trə kə rik'yə lər) *adj.* not part of the required curriculum but under the supervision of the school, as school plays, etc.

ex·tra·dite (eks'trə dīt') *vt.* -dit'ed, -dit'ing [backformation < ff.] **1.** to turn over (an alleged criminal, fugitive, etc.) to the jurisdiction of another country, state, etc. **2.** to obtain the extradition of —**ex'tra·dit'a·ble** *adj.*

ex·tra·di·tion (eks'trə dish'ən) *n.* [Fr. < L. *ex*, out + *traditio*, a surrender: see TRADITION] the turning over of an alleged criminal, fugitive, etc. by one country, state, etc. to another

ex·tra·dos (eks'trə dos') *n.* [Fr. < L. *extra*, beyond + Fr. *dos* < L. *dorsum*, back] *Archit.* the outside curved surface of an arch

ex·tra·ga·lac·tic (eks'trə gə lak'-tik) *adj.* outside or beyond the Galaxy, or Milky Way

ex·tra·le·gal (eks'trə lē'g'l) *adj.* outside legal control or authority —**ex'tra·le'gal·ly** *adv.*

ex·tra·mu·ral (-myoor'əl) *adj.* [EXTRA- + MURAL] outside the limits of a city, school, university, etc.

ex·tra·ne·ous (ik strā'nē əs) *adj.* [< L. *extraneus* < *extra*: see EXTRA-] **1.** coming from outside; foreign **2.** not essential **3.** not pertinent —**ex·tra'ne·ous·ly** *adv.* —**ex·tra'ne·ous·ness** *n.*

ex·traor·di·nar·y (ik strôr'd'n ər ē; eks'trə ôr'-) *adj.* [< L.

EXTRADOS

< *extra ordinem*, out of the usual order] **1.** not according to the usual custom or regular plan **2.** very unusual; exceptional; remarkable **3.** additional to the regular staff; sent on a special errand [an envoy *extraordinary*] —**ex·traor'di·nar·i·ly** *adv.* —**ex·traor'di·nar·i·ness** *n.*

ex·trap·o·late (ik strap'ə lāt') *vt., vi.* -lat'ed, -lat'ing [L. *extra* (see EXTRA-) + (INTER)POLATE] **1.** to estimate (a value, quantity, etc. beyond the known range) on the basis of certain known variables **2.** to arrive at (conclusions) by speculating on the basis of (known facts) —**ex·trap'o·la'tion** *n.* —**ex·trap'o·la'tive** *adj.* —**ex·trap'o·la'tor** *n.*

ex·tra·sen·so·ry (eks'trə sen'sər ē) *adj.* designating or of perception that seems to occur apart from the normal function of the senses

ex·tra·ter·ri·to·ri·al (-ter'ə tôr'ē əl) *adj.* **1.** outside the territorial limits or jurisdiction of the country, state etc. **2.** of extraterritoriality —**ex'tra·ter'ri·to'ri·al·ly** *adv.*

ex·tra·ter·ri·to·ri·al·i·ty (-tôr'ē al'ə tē) *n.* **1.** freedom from the jurisdiction of a country: a privilege of foreign diplomats, etc. **2.** jurisdiction of a country over its citizens in foreign lands

ex·trav·a·gance (ik strav'ə gəns) *n.* **1.** a going beyond reasonable or proper limits; excess **2.** a spending of more than is reasonable or necessary **3.** an instance of excess in spending, behaviour, or speech Also **ex·trav'a·gan·cy**, *pl.* -cies

ex·trav·a·gant (-gənt) *adj.* [< Anglo-Fr. < ML. prp. of *extravagari* < L. *extra*, beyond + *vagari*, to wander] **1.** going beyond reasonable limits; excessive or unrestrained **2.** too ornate or showy **3.** costing or spending too much —**ex·trav'a·gant·ly** *adv.*

ex·trav·a·gan·za (ik strav'ə gan'zə) *n.* [< It. *estravaganza*, extravagance] **1.** a literary, musical, or dramatic fantasy characterized by a loose structure and farce **2.** a spectacular, elaborate theatrical show, as some musicals

ex·trav·a·sate (ik strav'ə sāt') *vi., vt.* -sat'ed, -sat'ing [L. *extra* (see EXTRA-) + *vas*, a vessel + -ATE[1]] to escape or force to flow into surrounding tissue, as blood, lymph, lava, etc. —**ex·trav'a·sa'tion** *n.*

ex·tra·ve·hic·u·lar (eks'trə vē hik'yoo lər) *adj.* designating of activity by an astronaut outside a vehicle in space

ex·tra·ver·sion (eks'trə vur'zhən) *n.* *same as* EXTROVERSION —**ex'tra·vert'** (-vurt') *n.*

ex·treme (ik strēm') *adj.* [OFr. < L. *extremus*, superl. of *exterus*, outer: see EXTERNAL] **1.** at the end or outermost point; farthest away **2.** to the greatest or an excessive degree **3.** very unconventional **4.** deviating furthest from a central or moderate view; specif., furthest to the right or left in politics **5.** very severe; drastic —*n.* **1.** either of two things that are as different or as far as possible from each other **2.** an extreme degree **3.** an extreme act, expedient, etc. **4.** an extreme state **5.** *Math.* the first or last term of a proportion —**go to extremes** to be immoderate in speech or action —**in the extreme** to the utmost degree —**ex·treme'ly** *adv.* —**ex·treme'ness** *n.*

Extreme Unction *same as* ANOINTING OF THE SICK

ex·trem·ism (ik strēm'iz'm) *n.* a being extreme, esp. in politics —**ex·trem'ist** *adj., n.*

ex·trem·i·ty (ik strem'ə tē) *n.*, *pl.* -ties **1.** the outermost or utmost point or part; end **2.** the greatest degree **3.** a state of extreme necessity, danger, etc. **4.** the end of life; dying **5.** an extreme measure; strong action: *usually used in pl.* **6.** *a*) a body limb *b*) [pl.] the hands and feet

ex·tri·cate (eks'trə kāt') *vt.* -cat'ed, -cat'ing [< L. pp. of *extricare* < *ex-*, out + *tricae*, hindrances, vexations] to set free; disentangle (*from* a net, difficulty, embarrassment, etc.) —**ex'tri·ca·bil'i·ty** *n.* —**ex'tri·ca·ble** (-kə b'l) *adj.* —**ex'tri·ca'tion** *n.*

ex·trin·sic (eks strin'sik) *adj.* [< Fr. < L. *extrinsecus*, from without < *exter*, without + *secus*, following] **1.** not belonging to the real nature of a thing; not inherent **2.** being, coming, or acting from the outside; extraneous —**ex·trin'si·cal·ly** *adv.*

ex·tro·ver·sion (eks'trə vur'zhən, -shən) *n.* [< G. < L. *extra-* (see EXTRA-) + ML. *versio*, a turning: see VERSION] *Psychol.* an attitude in which a person directs his interest to things outside himself rather than to his own experiences and feelings: opposed to INTROVERSION

ex·tro·vert (eks'trə vurt') *n.* *Psychol.* a person characterized by extroversion; one who is active and expressive: opposed to INTROVERT —*adj.* characterized by extroversion: usually **ex'tro·vert'ed**

ex·trude (ik strōōd') *vt.* -trud'ed, -trud'ing [L. *extrudere* < *ex-*, out + *trudere*, to thrust] **1.** to push or force out **2.** to force (metal, plastic, etc.) through a die or very small holes to give it a certain shape —*vi.* to be extruded; esp., to protrude —**ex·trud'er** *n.* —**ex·tru'sion** (-strōō'zhən) *n.* —**ex·tru'sive** *adj.*

ex·u·ber·ance (ig zyōō'bər əns) *n.* [< Fr. < L. < prp. of *exuberare* < *ex-*, intens. + *uberare*, to bear abundantly < *uber*, udder] **1.** the state or quality of being exuberant; great abundance **2.** an instance of this; esp., action or speech showing high spirits Also **ex·u'ber·an·cy**, *pl.* -cies

ex·u·ber·ant (-ənt) *adj.* 1. growing profusely; luxuriant 2. full of life, vitality, or high spirits 3. excessively elaborate 4. very great; extreme —**ex·u'ber·ant·ly** *adv.*

ex·u·ber·ate (-bə rāt') *vi.* -**at'ed**, -**at'ing** [ME. < L. *exuberatus:* see EXUBERANCE] to be exuberant; feel or show exuberance, esp. in effusive or high-spirited behaviour

ex·ude (ig zyōōd') *vt.*, *vi.* -**ud'ed**, -**ud'ing** [< L. < *ex-*, out + *sudare*, to sweat < *sudor*, sweat] 1. to pass out in drops through pores, an incision, etc.; ooze 2. to diffuse or seem to radiate [to *exude* joy] —**ex·u·da·tion** (eks' yə dā'shən) *n.*

ex·ult (ig zult') *vi.* [< Fr. < L. *ex(s)ultare*, to leap for joy < *ex-*, intens. + *saltare*, freq. of *salire*, to leap] to rejoice greatly; be jubilant; glory

ex·ult·ant (-'nt) *adj.* exulting; triumphant; jubilant —**ex·ult'ant·ly** *adv.*

ex·ul·ta·tion (eg'zəl tā'shən, ek'səl-) *n.* [ME. < L. *exultatio:* see EXULT] the act of exulting; jubilation; triumph: also **ex·ult'ance** (ig zul'təns), **ex·ult'an·cy** (-tən sē)

ex·ur·bi·a (eks ur'bē ə) *n.* [EX- + (SUB)URBIA] [Chiefly U.S.] small, semirural communities beyond the suburbs —**ex·ur'ban** (-bən) *adj.* —**ex·ur'ban·ite'** (-bə nīt') *n.*, *adj.*

ex·u·vi·ate (ig zōō'vē āt') *vt.*, *vi.* -**at'ed**, -**at'ing** [< L. < *exuere*, to strip off + -ATE¹] to cast off (a skin, shell, etc.); moult —**ex·u'vi·a'tion** *n.*

-ey (ē, i) *same as* -Y²: used esp. after words ending in *y* [clayey]

ey·as (ī'əs) *n.* [ME. by faulty division of *a nyas* < Fr. *niais*, nestling] an unfledged bird; nestling; esp., a young hawk taken from its nest for training in falconry

eye (ī) *n.* [OE. *eage*] 1. the organ of sight in man and animals 2. a) the eyeball *b)* the iris 3. the area around the eye [a black *eye*] 4. [often pl.] sight; vision [weak *eyes*] 5. a look; glance 6. attention; observation 7. the power of judging, estimating, etc. by eyesight [a good *eye* for distances] 8. [often pl.] judgment; opinion [in the *eyes* of the law] 9. a thing like an eye in shape or function, as a bud of a potato, the hole of a needle, a loop of metal, any primitive, light-sensitive organ, etc. 10. [U.S. Slang] a detective: esp. in **private eye** 11. *Meteorol.* the calm, low-pressure centre (of a hurricane), around which the winds whirl —*vt.* **eyed**, **eye'ing** or **ey'ing** to look at; observe —**all eyes** extremely attentive —**all my eye** [Slang] nonsense; humbug: also **all my eye and Betty Martin** —**an eye for an eye** punishment or retaliation equivalent to the injury suffered —**catch one's eye** to attract one's attention —**easy on the eyes** [Slang] attractive —**feast one's eyes on** to look at with pleasure —**get one's eye in** to accustom oneself to one's surroundings: said esp. of batsmen beginning their innings in cricket —**have an eye for** to have a keen appreciation of —**have an eye to** to watch out for; attend to —**have eyes for** [Colloq.] to be interested in and want —**in the public eye** brought to public attention —**keep an eye on** to look after; watch —**keep an eye out for** to be watchful for —**keep one's eyes open** (or **peeled** or **skinned**) to be watchful —**lay** (or **set** or **clap**) **eyes on** to see; look at —**make sheep's eyes at** to look at flirtatiously; ogle —**my eye!** [Slang] an exclamation of contradiction, astonishment, etc. —**one in the eye** a rebuff; discomfiture —**open one's eyes** to make one aware of the facts —**run one's eye over** to glance over —**see eye to eye** to agree completely —**shut one's eyes to** to refuse to see or think about: also **turn a blind eye to** —**up to the eyes in** deeply engaged in —**with an eye to** regarding; with reference to; considering 2. with the intention or purpose of —**with one's eyes shut** 1. without noticing; unobservant 2. with great ease

eye·ball (-bôl') *n.* the ball-shaped part of the eye, enclosed by the socket and eyelids —**eyeball to eyeball** confronting closely; face to face [an *eyeball to eyeball* meeting]

eye·bath (-bäth) *n.* a small vessel used in applying medicine to the eyes or washing them

eye·black (-blak') *n.* another name for MASCARA

eye·bright (-brīt') *n.* any of various plants of the figwort family, esp. a small European plant with flowers marked with white, yellow, and purple: formerly used in treating eye disorders

eye·brow (-brou') *n.* 1. the bony arch over each eye 2. the arch of hair growing on this —**raise** (or **lift**) **an eyebrow** to appear sceptical, etc.

eye·catch·ing (-kach'iŋ) *adj.* tending to attract attention; striking

eyed (īd) *adj.* having eyes (of a specified kind) [blue-*eyed*]

eye·drop·per (ī'drop'ər) *n.* same as DROPPER (*n.* 2)

eye·ful (-fool') *n.* 1. a quantity of something in the eye 2. a full look at something 3. [Slang] a person or thing that looks striking or unusual —**get an eyeful of that** [Colloq.] to have a good look at (something)

eye·glass (-gläs') *n.* 1. a lens to help faulty vision; monocle 2. [Chiefly U.S.] [pl.] spectacles 3. same as EYEPIECE

eye·hole (-hōl') *n.* 1. the socket for the eyeball 2. a peephole 3. same as EYELET (sense 1)

eye·lash (-lash') *n.* 1. any of the hairs on the edge of the eyelid 2. a fringe of these hairs

eye·less (-lis) *adj.* without eyes; blind

eye·let (-lit) *n.* [< OFr. dim. of *oeil* < L. *oculus*, eye] 1. a small hole for receiving a cord, hook, etc. 2. a metal ring or short tube for lining such a hole 3. a small hole edged by stitching in embroidered work 4. a peephole or loophole —*vt.* to provide with eyelets

eye·lev·el (-lev''l) *adj.* on a level with the eyes looking straight ahead [an *eyelevel* grill]

eye·lid (-lid') *n.* either of the two folds of skin that cover and uncover the front of the eyeball

eye liner a cosmetic preparation applied in a thin line on the eyelid at the base of the eyelashes

eye·o·pen·er (-ō'p'n ər) *n.* 1. a surprising piece of news, sudden realization, etc. 2. [U.S. Colloq.] an alcoholic drink, esp. one taken early in the day

eye·piece (-pēs') *n.* in a telescope, microscope, etc., the lens or lenses nearest the viewer's eye

eye rhyme a partial rhyme in which the words are similar in spelling but pronounced differently (Ex.: lone, none)

eye shadow a coloured cosmetic preparation applied to the eyelids

eye·shot (-shot') *n.* range of vision

eye·sight (-sīt') *n.* 1. the power of seeing; sight; vision 2. the range of vision

eye·sore (-sôr') *n.* a thing that is unpleasant to look at

eye·spot (-spot') *n.* a small spot of pigment sensitive to light, found in many invertebrates

eye·strain (-strān') *n.* a tired or strained condition of the eye muscles, caused by too much use or an incorrect use of the eyes

eye·tie (ī'tī') *n.* [Slang] [often E-] an Italian: often a derogatory usage

eye·tooth (-tōōth') *n.*, *pl.* -**teeth'** a canine tooth of the upper jaw —**cut one's eyeteeth** to become experienced or sophisticated

eye·wash (-wosh') *n.* 1. a lotion for the eyes 2. [Slang] *a)* nonsense *b)* flattery *c)* something done only to impress an observer

eye·wit·ness (-wit'nis) *n.* 1. a person who sees something happen, as an accident, crime, etc. 2. a person who testifies to what he has seen

ey·rie, **ey·ry** (er'ē, ir'-) *n.*, *pl.* -**ries** [OFr. ML. *aeria*, area: sp. & meaning infl. by L. *aer*, air & ME. *ei*, egg] 1. the nest of an eagle or other bird of prey that builds in a high place 2. a house or stronghold on a high place

ey·rir (ā'rir) *n.*, *pl.* **au·rar** (ou'rär) [Ice. <ON., a coin, unit of weight <L. *aureus*, a gold coin, orig. adj., golden: see AUREATE] *see* MONETARY UNITS, table (Iceland)

F

F, f (ef) *n.*, *pl.* **F's**, **f's** 1. the sixth letter of the English alphabet 2. the sound of *F* or *f*

F (ef) *n.* *Music a)* the fourth tone in the ascending scale of C major *b)* the scale having this tone as the keynote

F *Physics* the symbol *for* farad

F 1. Fahrenheit 2. fathom 3. *Chem.* fluorine

F/, f/, f:, f. f-number

F- fighter (plane)

F. 1. Fahrenheit 2. Fellow 3. France 4. French 5. Friday

F., f. 1. farad 2. fathom 3. feminine 4. fluid 5. folio(s) 6. following 7. *Music* forte 8. franc(s)

fa (fä) *n.* [< ML. < *fa(muli)*: see GAMUT] *Music* a syllable representing the fourth tone of the diatonic scale

F.A. 1. Football Association 2. Fanny Adams

Fa·bi·an (fā'bē ən) *adj.* [< L. < *Fabius*, Roman general in 2nd Punic War] 1. using a cautious strategy of delay and avoidance of battle 2. designating or of an English socialist organization (**Fabian Society**) advocating gradual reforms —*n.* a member of the Fabian Society —**Fa'bi·an·ism** *n.*

fa·ble (fā′b'l) *n.* [< OFr. < L. *fabula,* a story < *fari,* to speak] **1.** a fictitious story meant to teach a moral lesson : the characters are usually talking animals **2.** a myth or legend **3.** a falsehood or fiction —*vi., vt.* **-bled, -bling** to write or tell (fables, legends, or falsehoods) —**fa′bler** *n.*

fa·bled (-b'ld) *adj.* **1.** legendary **2.** fictitious

fab·li·au (fab′lē ō′; *Fr.* fá blē ō′) *n., pl.* **-aux** (-ōz′; *Fr.* -ō′) [Fr. < OFr., dial. form of *fablel,* dim. of *fable,* FABLE] in medieval literature, esp. French, a short story in verse, often coarse, usually humorous, about ordinary life

fab·ric (fab′rik) *n.* [< MFr. < L. *fabrica,* a workshop < *faber,* a workman] **1.** *a)* anything made of parts put together *b)* the basic structure of anything **2.** the style or plan of construction **3.** any woven, knitted, or felted material

fab·ri·cate (fab′rə kāt′) *vt.* **-cat′ed, -cat′ing** [< L. pp. of *fabricari,* to build < *fabrica:* see prec.] **1.** to make, build, construct, etc., esp. by assembling parts; manufacture **2.** to make up (a story, lie, etc.) —**fab′ri·ca′tion** *n.* —**fab′ri·ca′tor** *n.*

fab·u·list (fab′yoo list) *n.* **1.** a person who writes or tells fables **2.** a liar

fab·u·lous (-ləs) *adj.* [< L. < *fabula:* see FABLE] **1.** of or like a fable; imaginary; fictitious; legendary **2.** incredible; astounding **3.** [Colloq.] wonderful —**fab′u·lous·ly** *adv.* —**fab′u·lous·ness** *n.*

fa·çade (fə säd′) *n.* [Fr. < It. < VL. *facia:* see ff.] **1.** the front of a building **2.** an imposing appearance concealing something shoddy

face (fās) *n.* [< OFr. < VL. *facia* < L. *facies,* the face] **1.** the front of the head; countenance **2.** the expression of the countenance **3.** a surface of a thing; esp., *a)* the main surface or side *b)* the front, upper, and outer surface *c)* any of the surfaces of a crystal *d)* Mining the exposed surface in a tunnel, etc., where work is being done **4.** the side or surface that is marked

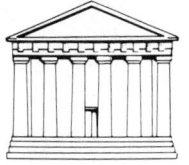

FAÇADE

or intended to be seen, as of a clock, playing card, etc. **5.** the appearance; outward aspect **6.** [< Chin. idiom] dignity; self-respect : in **lose** (or **save**) **face 7.** the topography (of an area) **8.** the functional or striking surface (of a tool, etc.) **9.** [Colloq.] effrontery; audacity **10.** *Typography a)* the printing surface of a letter or plate *b)* the design of type —*vt.* **faced, fac′ing 1.** to turn, or have the face turned, towards [the house *faces* the park] **2.** to meet face to face **3.** to confront with boldness, courage, etc. **4.** to put another material on the surface of **5.** to sew a facing to (a collar, etc.) **6.** to put a smooth surface on (a stone, tool, etc.) **7.** to turn (a card, etc.) with the face up —*vi.* **1.** to turn, or have the face turned, towards a specified thing or in a specified direction **2.** *Mil.* to pivot in a specified direction [right *face!*] —**face off** *Ice Hockey* to start play with a face-off —**face to face 1.** confronting one another **2.** in the presence of : followed by *with* —**face up to 1.** to confront and resist **2.** to realize and be ready to meet —**have a face as long as a fiddle** to look despondent —**in the face of 1.** in the presence of **2.** in spite of —**make a face** to distort the face; grimace —**on the face of it** apparently —**pull** (or **wear**) **a long face** to look sad, glum, disapproving, etc. —**set one's face against** to be determinedly against —**show one's face** to come and be seen —**to one's face** openly —**faced** *adj.* —**face′less** *adj.*

face card *same as* COURT CARD

face flannel *same as* FLANNEL (sense 2)

face fungus [Slang] a beard

face lifting 1. plastic surgery for removing wrinkles, sagging flesh, etc. from the face **2.** an altering, cleaning, etc., as of the exterior of a building Also **face lift** —**face′-lift′** *vt.*

face-off (-of′) *n. Ice Hockey* the starting of play by the referee's dropping the puck between two opposing players

face powder a cosmetic powder, as of flesh-coloured talc, applied to the face

fac·er (fā′sər) *n.* **1.** a person or thing that faces **2.** [Colloq.] *a)* a sudden blow in the face *b)* any sudden, unexpected difficulty or defeat

face-sav·ing (-sā′viŋ) *adj.* preserving or intended to preserve one's dignity or self-respect

fac·et (fas′it) *n.* [< Fr. dim. of *face:* see FACE] **1.** any of the small, polished plane surfaces of a cut gem **2.** any of the sides or aspects, as of a personality —*vt.* **-et·ed, -et·ing** to cut or make facets on

fa·ce·ti·ae (fə sē′shē ē′) *n.pl.* [L., pl of *facetia,* a jest] **1.** witty sayings **2.** ribald or coarsely witty writings

fa·ce·tious (fə sē′shəs) *adj.* [< Fr. < L. < *facetus,* witty] joking, trying to be, or intended to be, jocular, esp. at an inappropriate time —**fa·ce′tious·ly** *adv.* —**fa·ce′tious·ness** *n.*

face value 1. the value printed or written on a bank note,

bond, etc. **2.** the seeming value [to take a promise at *face value*]

face worker a person who works at a mine face

fa·ci·a (fā′shē ə, -shə) *n.* [var. of FASCIA] **1.** *a)* an instrument panel or dashboard, as of a motor car *b)* a board over a shop front with the proprietor's name **2.** *same as* FASCIA

fa·cial (fā′shəl) *adj.* of or for the face —*n.* a cosmetic treatment intended to improve facial appearance —**fa′cial·ly** *adv.*

-fa·cient (fā′shənt) [< L. prp. of *facere,* to make] *a suffix meaning* making or causing to become [*liquefacient*]

fa·ci·es (fā′shē ēz′) *n., pl* **fa′ci·es** [L., face] **1.** the general appearance of anything **2.** *Geol.* the characteristics of a rock body, part of a rock body, etc. that differentiate it from others **3.** *Med. a)* the appearance of the face *b)* a surface

fac·ile (fas′īl′) *adj.* [Fr. < L. *facilis* < *facere,* to make, do] **1.** not hard to do; easy **2.** acting, working, or done quickly and smoothly; fluent; ready **3.** not sincere or profound; superficial —**fac′ile·ly** *adv.* —**fac′ile·ness** *n.*

fa·cil·i·tate (fə sil′ə tāt′) *vt.* **-tat′ed, -tat′ing** [< Fr. < It. < L. *facilis* (see prec.) + -ATE¹] to make easy or easier —**fa·cil′i·ta′tion** *n.* —**fa·cil′i·ta′tive** *adj.*

fa·cil·i·ty (fə sil′ə tē) *n., pl* **-ties** [< OFr. < L. < *facilis,* FACILE] **1.** ease; absence of difficulty **2.** a ready ability; skill; fluency **3.** [*usually pl.*] the means by which something can be done **4.** a building, room, etc. for some activity

fac·ing (fās′iŋ) *n.* **1.** a lining, for decoration or reinforcement, sewn on a collar, cuff, etc. **2.** any material used for this **3.** a covering of contrasting material, as for decorating or protecting a building

fac·sim·i·le (fak sim′ə lē) *n.* [L. *fac,* imper. of *facere,* to make + *simile,* like] **1.** (an) exact reproduction or copy **2.** the transmission and reproduction of graphic matter by electrical means, as radio or wire —*adj.* of or like a facsimile —*vt.* **-led, -le·ing** to make a facsimile of

fact (fakt) *n.* [L. *factum,* deed < *facere,* to do] **1.** a deed; act : now esp. a criminal deed in **before** (or **after**) **the fact** [an accessory *after the fact*] **2.** a thing that has actually happened or is true **3.** the state of things as they are; reality; truth **4.** something said to have occurred or supposed to be true [check your *facts*] —**as a matter of fact** in reality; really : also **in fact, in point of fact** —**facts and figures** exact details; necessary information —**the facts of life 1.** basic information about life, esp. about sexual reproduction **2.** the harsh, unpleasant facts one must face in life

fac·tion (fak′shən) *n.* [< Fr. < L. *factio,* a making < pp. of *facere,* to do, act] **1.** a group of people in a political party, club, etc. working in a common cause against the main body; clique **2.** partisan conflict within an organization or country; dissension —**fac′tion·al** *adj.* —**fac′tion·al·ism** *n.* —**fac′tion·al·ist** *n., adj.* —**fac′tion·al·ly** *adv.*

fac·tious (fak′shəs) *adj.* **1.** producing or tending to produce faction, or dissension **2.** produced or characterized by faction —**fac′tious·ly** *adv.* —**fac′tious·ness** *n.*

fac·ti·tious (fak tish′əs) *adj.* [< L. < pp. of *facere,* to do] not genuine or spontaneous; forced or artificial —**fac·ti′·tious·ly** *adv.* —**fac·ti′tious·ness** *n.*

fac·ti·tive (fak′tə tiv) *adj.* [ModL., *factitivus,* irreg. < L. *factus* (see FACT)] *Gram.* of a verb taking a direct object and a complement (Ex.: *elect* him *mayor*)

fac·tor (fak′tər) *n.* [< OFr. < L. < pp. of *facere,* to do, make] **1.** a person who carries on business transactions for another **2.** any of the circumstances, conditions, etc. that bring about a result **3.** *Biol. same as* GENE **4.** *Math.* any of two or more quantities which form a product when multiplied together —*vt. Math.* to resolve into factors : also **fac′tor·ize** (-tə rīz′) **-ized, -iz′ing** —*vi.* to act as a factor (sense 1) —**fac′tor·a·ble** *adj.* —**fac′tor·i·za′tion** *n.* —**fac′-tor·ship′** *n.*

fac·tor·age (-ij) *n.* **1.** the business of a factor **2.** a factor's commission

fac·to·ri·al (fak tôr′ē əl) *n. Math.* the product of all the whole numbers from 1 up to and including a given number [the *factorial* of 4 is 1 x 2 x 3 x 4, or 24]

fac·to·ry (fak′tə rē, -trē) *n., pl.* **-ries** [see FACTOR] a building or buildings in which things are manufactured; manufacturing plant

factory farm a farm using industrial methods to promote maximum growth rate in animals

factory ship the vessel in a fishing fleet on which catch is processed

fac·to·tum (fak tōt′əm) *n.* [ModL. < L. *fac,* imper. of *facere,* to do + *totum,* all] a person hired to do all sorts of work; handyman

fac·tu·al (fak′choo wəl) *adj.* [FACT + (ACT)UAL] **1.** of or containing facts **2.** having the nature of fact; real; actual —**fac′tu·al′it·y** *n.* —**fac′tu·al·ly** *adv.*

fac·u·la (fak′yoo lə) *n., pl.* **-lae** (-lē) [L., dim. of *fax* (gen. *facis*), torch] bright areas visible on the surface of the sun, esp. near its edge

fac·ul·ta·tive (fak′'l tat′iv) *adj.* **1.** *a)* granting permission or authority *b)* optional **2.** contingent **3.** of a faculty or faculties **4.** *Biol.* capable of living under varying con-ditions

fac·ul·ty (fak'əl tē) *n., pl.* **-ties** [< OFr. < L. < *facilis*: see FACILE] **1.** formerly, the ability to perform an action **2.** any natural or specialized power of a living organism [the *faculty* of speech] **3.** special aptitude or skill; knack **4.** *a)* a university department *b)* the teaching staff of such a department **5.** [U.S.] all the teachers of a school, college, or university or of one of its divisions **6.** all the members of any profession **7.** an authorization **8.** *Psychol.* any of the powers formerly thought of as composing the mind, such as will, reason, etc.

fad (fad) *n.* [< Dial.] a custom, style, etc. that many people are interested in for a short time; craze —**fad'dish, fad'dy** *adj.* —**fad'dish·ly** *adv.* —**fad'dish·ness** *n.* —**fad'dism** *n.* —**fad'dist** *n.*

fade (fād) *vi.* **fad'ed, fad'ing** [< OFr. *fader* < *fade*, pale] **1.** to become less distinct; lose colour, brilliance, intensity, etc. **2.** to lose freshness or strength; wither; wane **3.** to disappear slowly; die out **4.** to lose braking power: said of brakes —*vt.* to cause to fade —**fade in** (or **out**) *Cinema, Radio & TV* to appear (or disappear) gradually or cause to do so; become or make more (or less) distinct —**fade'less** *adj.*

fade-in (-in') *n. Cinema, Radio & TV* a fading in of a scene or sound

fade-out (-out') *n. Cinema, Radio & TV* a fading out of a scene or sound

fae·ces (fē'sēz) *n.pl.* [L., lit., dregs] waste matter expelled from the bowels; excrement —**fae'cal** (-k'l) *adj.*

fa·er·ie, fa·er·y (fē'ē; *also, for l,* fâ'ər ē) *n.* [Archaic] **1.** fairyland **2.** *pl.* **-ies** a fairy —*adj.* [Archaic] fairy Also written **faërie, faëry**

Faer·o·ese (fer'ə wēz', fer'ō-) *adj.* of the Faeroe Islands, their people, lanuage, etc. —*n.* **1.** *pl.* **Faer'o·ese'** a native or inhabitant of the Faeroe Islands **2.** the language of the Faeroese Also sp. **Faroese**

faff (faf) *vi.* [< ?] [Colloq.] to dither; be flustered (usually with *about*)

fag[1] (fag) *vi.* **fagged, fag'ging** [< ?] **1.** to work hard and become very tired **2.** [Colloq.] to serve as a fag or servant —*vt.* to make tired by hard work —*n.* **1.** [Colloq.] *a)* drudgery *b)* a boy in an English public school who acts as a servant for another boy in a higher form, or class **2.** [U.S. Slang] a male homosexual: also **fag'got** (-ət)

fag[2] (fag) *n.* [< ff.] [Slang] a cigarette

fag end [< ME. *fagge*, broken thread] **1.** *a)* the last part or coarse end of a piece of cloth *b)* the frayed, untwisted end of a rope **2.** the last and worst part of anything, esp. of a cigarette

fag·got (fag'ət) *n.* [< OFr., ult. < Gr. *phakelos*, a bundle] **1.** a bundle of sticks or twigs, esp. for use as fuel **2.** a savoury roll made of liver, etc. **3.** *Metallurgy* a stack of iron or steel pieces to be welded into bars —*vt.* **1.** to form a faggot of **2.** to decorate with faggoting —**fag'got·y** *adj.*

fag·got·ing (-iŋ) *n.* **1.** a kind of drawnwork or hemstitch with wide spaces **2.** openwork decoration in which the thread is drawn in crisscross or barlike stitches across the open seam

Fah., Fahr. Fahrenheit

Fahr·en·heit (far'ən hīt') *adj.* [after G. D. *Fahrenheit,* 18th-c. G. physicist] designating or of a thermometer on which 32° is the freezing point and 212° the boiling point of water: abbrev. F

fa·ience (fī äns', fâ-) *n.* [Fr. < *Faenza,* Italy] earthenware having a colourful, opaque glaze

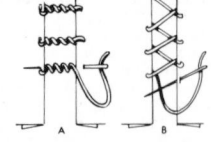

FAGGOTING (A, bar; B, crisscross)

fail (fāl) *vi.* [< OFr. < L. *fallere,* to deceive] **1.** to be lacking or insufficient; fall short; default **2.** to lose power or strength; weaken; die away **3.** to stop functioning **4.** to be unsuccessful in obtaining a desired end **5.** to become bankrupt **6.** *Educ.* to be unsuccessful in an examination —*vt.* **1.** to be of no help to; disappoint **2.** to leave; abandon [his courage *failed* him] **3.** to miss, neglect, or omit [to *fail* to go] **4.** *Educ. a)* to be unsuccessful in an examination —*n.* failure: esp. **in without fail,** without failing (to occur, do, etc.) —**fail of** to fail to achieve —**failed** *adj.*

fail·ing (-iŋ) *n.* **1.** a failure **2.** a slight fault or defect; weakness —*prep.* without; lacking

faille (fīl, fāl) *n.* [Fr.] a ribbed, soft fabric of silk or rayon, for dresses, etc.

fail-safe (fāl'sāf') *adj.* [FAIL, *v.* + SAFE, *adj.*] designating or of an intricate procedure designed to prevent malfunctioning or unintentional operation, as of nuclear-armed aircraft

fail·ure (fāl'yər) *n.* [see FAIL] **1.** the act or fact of failing, or falling short, losing strength, breaking down, going bankrupt, not doing or succeeding, etc. **2.** a person or thing that fails **3.** *Educ.* a failing to pass an examination, course, etc.

fain (fān) *adj.* [OE. *fægen,* glad] [Archaic] **1.** glad; ready **2.** reluctantly willing **3.** eager —*adv.* [Archaic] gladly or willingly [he would *fain* stay]

faint (fānt) *adj.* [< OFr., orig. pp. of *feindre*: see FEIGN] **1.** without strength; weak; feeble **2.** without courage; timid **3.** done without vigour or enthusiasm **4.** feeling weak and dizzy, as if about to swoon **5.** dim; indistinct **6.** slight [a *faint* hope] —*n.* a condition of temporary loss of consciousness —*vi.* to fall into a faint; swoon —**faint'ish** *adj.* —**faint'ly** *adv.* —**faint'ness** *n.*

faint·heart·ed (-här'tid) *adj.* cowardly; timid —**faint'-heart·ed·ly** *adv.* —**faint'heart'ed·ness** *n.*

fair[1] (fer) *adj.* [OE. *fæger*] **1.** beautiful [a *fair* maiden] **2.** unblemished; clean [a *fair* name] **3.** light in colour; blond [*fair* hair] **4.** clear and sunny **5.** easy to read; clear [a *fair* hand] **6.** just and honest; impartial; specif., free from discrimination based on race, religion, sex, etc. **7.** according to the rules [a *fair* blow] **8.** likely; promising [in a *fair* way to benefit] **9.** pleasant and courteous, often deceptively **10.** favourable; helpful [a *fair* wind] **11.** of moderately good size **12.** neither very bad nor very good; average —*adv.* **1.** in a fair manner [play *fair*] **2.** straight; squarely [struck *fair* in the face] **3.** [Dial. or Colloq.] extremely [I'm *fair* flummoxed] —*vt.* to give a smooth or streamlined surface to —**a fair treat** [Colloq.] a person or thing that is very pleasant —**fair and square** [Colloq.] with justice and honesty —**fair to middling** [Colloq.] moderately good; passable —**fair'ish** *adj.* —**fair'ness** *n.*

fair[2] (fer) *n.* [< OFr. < ML. < L. *feriae, pl.,* festivals] **1.** orig., a gathering of people at regular intervals for barter and sale of goods **2.** a collection, often mobile, of sideshows and amusements; funfair **3.** a large-scale exhibition to promote trade [a world *fair*] **4.** a regular assembly for the sale of goods, esp. livestock

fair cow [Aust. Slang] unpleasant situation

fair game **1.** game that may lawfully be hunted **2.** any legitimate object of attack or pursuit

fair·ground (fer'ground') *n.* an open space where fairs are held

fair-haired (-herd') *adj.* **1.** having blond hair **2.** [Colloq.] favourite [mother's *fair-haired* boy]

fair·ing[1] (-iŋ) *n.* [see FAIR[1], *vt.*] *Engineering* a part or structure added to an aircraft, etc., to smooth the outline and thus reduce drag

fair·ing[2] (-iŋ) *n.* [Obs.] a gift bought at a fair

Fair Isle [after the island in the Shetlands where it originated] a type of complex knitting pattern using coloured wools

fair·ly (-lē) *adv.* **1.** justly; equitably **2.** moderately; somewhat **3.** clearly; distinctly **4.** completely or really [his voice *fairly* rang]

fair-mind·ed (-mīn'did) *adj.* just; impartial —**fair'-mind'-ed·ly** *adv.* —**fair'-mind'ed·ness** *n.*

fair play an abiding by the rules or by decency and honour in sports, business, etc.

fair sex women collectively: used with *the*

fair-spo·ken (-spō'kən) *adj.* speaking or spoken civilly and pleasantly or smoothly and plausibly

fair·way (-wā') *n.* **1.** a navigable channel in a river, harbour, etc. **2.** the mowed part of a golf course between a tee and a green

fair-weath·er (-weth'ər) *adj.* **1.** suitable only for fair weather **2.** dependable only in easy circumstances [*fair-weather* friends]

fair·y (fer'ē) *n., pl.* **fair'ies** [< OFr. *faerie*] **1.** a tiny, graceful imaginary being in human form, supposed to have magic powers **2.** [Slang] a male homosexual —*adj.* **1.** of fairies **2.** like a fairy; graceful; delicate

fairy-cyc·le (-si'k'l) *n.* a child's bicycle

fairy godmother *n.* a benefactress

fair·y·land (-land') *n.* **1.** the imaginary land where the fairies live **2.** a lovely, enchanting place

fairy lights small, coloured, decorative lights used esp. outdoors and on Christmas trees

fairy ring a circle of dark grass, formerly attributed to fairies' dancing, caused by fungus

fairy tale **1.** a story about fairies, magic deeds, etc. **2.** an unbelievable or untrue story; lie: also **fairy story**

‡fait ac·com·pli (fe tà kōn plē') [Fr., lit., an accomplished fact] a thing already done, so that opposition or argument is useless

faith (fāth) *n.* [< OFr. < L. *fides* < *fidere,* to trust] **1.** unquestioning belief **2.** unquestioning belief in God, religious tenets, etc. **3.** a particular religion **4.** anything believed **5.** complete trust or confidence **6.** loyalty —*interj.* [Obs.] indeed —**bad faith** insincerity; duplicity —**good faith** sincerity; honesty —**in faith** indeed; really

faith·ful (-fəl) *adj.* **1.** keeping faith; loyal **2.** responsible; conscientious **3.** accurate; exact —**the faithful** the true believers or loyal followers —**faith'ful·ly** *adv.* —**faith'-ful·ness** *n.*

faith healing a method of treating illness by religious faith, praying, etc. also **faith curing** —**faith healer** *n.*
faith·less (-lis) *adj.* **1.** not keeping faith; dishonest; disloyal **2.** unreliable; undependable **3.** [Now Rare] without faith —**faith′less·ly** *adv.* —**faith′less·ness** *n.*
fake (fāk) *vt., vi.* **faked, fak′ing** [< ? G. *fegen*, to clean, sweep] to practise deception by giving a false indication or appearance of (something); feign —*n.* anything or anyone not genuine; fraud —*adj.* fraudulent; sham; false —**fak′er** *n.* —**fak′er·y** *n., pl.* **-er·ies**
fa·kir (fə kir′) *n.* [Ar. *faqīr,* lit., poor] **1.** a member of a Moslem holy sect who lives by begging **2.** a Hindu ascetic Also sp. **fa·keer′**
Fa·lange (fə′lanj) *n.* [Sp., lit., phalanx] a fascist organization that became the only official political party of Spain under Franco —**Fa·lang′ism** *n.* —**Fa·lang′ist** *n.*
fal·cate (fal′kāt) *adj.* [< L. < *falx* (gen. *falcis*), a sickle] sickle-shaped; curved; hooked: also **fal′ci·form** (fal′si fôrm)
fal·chion (fôl′chən, -shən) *n.* [< OFr. < L. *falx:* see prec.] **1.** a medieval sword with a short, broad, slightly curved blade **2.** [Poet.] any sword
fal·con (fôl′kən, fôl′-, fô′-) *n.* [< OFr. < LL. *falco* (gen. *falconis*), derived by folk etym. < L. *falx:* see FALCATE] **1.** any hawk trained to hunt and kill small game **2.** any hawklike bird with long, pointed wings and a short, curved, notched beak
fal·con·et (-et′) *n.* [dim. of FALCON] **1.** any small falcon **2.** [It. *falconetto* < Olt. *falcone,* FALCON] a light cannon
fal·con·ry (-rē) *n.* **1.** the art of training falcons to hunt game **2.** the sport of hunting with falcons —**fal′con·er** *n.*
fal·de·ral (fôl′də rôl′, fal′də ral′) *n.* [nonsense syllables] **1.** a showy but worthless trinket **2.** mere nonsense **3.** a refrain in some old songs
fald·stool (fôld′stōōl′) *n.* [M.E. *foldstol* < ML. *faldistolium,* folding stool] **1.** a portable stool or desk used in praying **2.** a bishop's backless chair **3.** *Anglican Ch.* a desk at which the litany is read
fall (fôl) *vi.* **fell, fall′en, fall′ing** [OE. *feallan*] **1.** to come down by the force of gravity, as when detached, pushed, dropped, etc. [apples *fall* from the tree] **2.** to come down suddenly from a standing or sitting position; tumble **3.** to be wounded or killed in battle **4.** to collapse **5.** to hang down [hair *falling* about her shoulders] **6.** to strike; hit [to *fall* wide of the mark] **7.** to take a downward direction [land *falling* away to the sea] **8.** to become lower in amount, degree, etc.; drop; abate [prices *fell*] **9.** to lose power [the government *fell*] **10.** to lose status, reputation, dignity, etc. **1.** *a)* to do wrong; sin *b)* to fail morally, esp. to become unchaste, as a prostitute **12.** to be captured or conquered **13.** to take on a dejected look [his face *fell*] **14.** to become lower in pitch or volume [her voice *fell*] **15.** to take place; occur [the meeting *fell* on a Friday] **16.** to come by lot, inheritance, etc. [the estate *falls* to the son] **17.** to pass into a specified condition; become [to *fall* ill] **18.** to come at a specified place [the accent *falls* on the third syllable] **19.** to be directed by chance [his eye *fell* on us] **20.** to be spoken involuntarily [an oath *fell* from his lips] **21.** to be divided (*into*) [to *fall* into two classes] **22.** *Cricket* used of wickets to mean the dismissing of a batsman [five wickets *fell* before lunch] —*n.* **1.** a dropping; descending **2.** a coming down suddenly from a standing or sitting position **3.** a downward direction or slope **4.** a becoming lower or less; reduction in value, price, etc. **5.** a capture; overthrow; ruin **6.** a loss of status, reputation, etc. **7.** something that has fallen [a *fall* of leaves] **8.** [U.S.] autumn **9.** the amount of what has fallen [a heavy *fall* of snow] **10.** the distance that something falls **11.** [usually *pl.*] water falling over a cliff, etc.; cascade **12.** *a)* the throwing of an opponent in wrestling on his back so that both shoulders touch the floor *b)* a division of a wrestling match —**fall about** [Colloq.] be helpless with laughter —**fall (all) over oneself** [Colloq.] to behave in too eager or zealous a manner —**fall away 1.** to take away friendship, support, etc.; desert **2.** to become less in size, strength, etc.; specif., to grow thin and weak —**fall back** to withdraw; give way; retreat —**fall back on** (or **upon**) to turn, or return, to for help —**fall behind 1.** to be outdistanced **2.** to be in arrears —**fall down on** [Colloq.] to fail in —**fall flat** to fail to have the desired effect —**fall for** [Colloq.] **1.** to fall in love with **2.** to be tricked by —**fall foul of 1.** to come into conflict with **2.** *Naut.* to come into collision with —**fall in 1.** to give way **2.** to run out: said of a lease **3.** *Mil.* to line up in proper formation —**fall in with 1.** to meet accidentally **2.** to agree to (a plan) —**fall off** to become smaller, less, worse, etc. —**fall on** (or **upon**) **1.** to attack **2.** to be the duty of —**fall out 1.** to quarrel **2.** to happen; result **3.** *Mil.* to leave one's place in a formation —**fall short 1.** to be lacking **2.** to fail to meet a standard or goal (with *of*) —**fall through** to come to nothing; fail —**fall to 1.** to begin; start **2.** to start attacking **3.** to start eating —**fall under 1.** to come under (an influence, etc.) **2.** to be classified as —**the Fall (of Man)**

Christian Theol. Adam's sin of yielding to temptation in eating the forbidden fruit
fal·la·cious (fə lā′shəs) *adj.* [see ff.] **1.** containing a fallacy **2.** misleading, deceptive, or delusive —**fal·la′cious·ly** *adv.* —**fal·la′cious·ness** *n.*
fal·la·cy (fal′ə sē) *n., pl.* **-cies** [< OFr. < L. < *fallax* (gen. *fallacis*) < *fallere,* to deceive] **1.** aptness to mislead **2.** a false or mistaken idea, opinion, etc.; error **3.** an error in reasoning; specif., *Logic* an argument based on incorrect demonstration, as a vicious circle
fall·en (fôl′ən) *adj.* **1.** having come down; dropped **2.** on the ground; prostrate **3.** degraded **4.** captured; over-thrown **5.** ruined **6.** dead
fallen arch a foot arch which has become flattened
fall guy [U.S. Slang] a person left to face the consequences, as of a scheme that has miscarried
fal·li·ble (fal′ə b'l) *adj.* [< ML. < L. *fallere,* to deceive] **1.** liable to be mistaken or deceived **2.** liable to be erroneous or inaccurate —**fal′li·bil′i·ty** *n.* —**fal′li·bly** *adv.*
falling sickness *former name for* EPILEPSY
falling star *same as* METEOR (sense 1)
fall-off (fôl′ôf′) *n.* the act or an instance of becoming less or worse; decline
Fal·lo·pi·an tube (fə lō′pē ən) [after G. *Fallopio,* It. anatomist (1523–62)] either of two slender tubes that carry ova from the ovaries to the uterus
fall·out (fôl′out′) *n.* **1.** the descent to earth of radioactive particles, as after a nuclear explosion **2.** these particles **3.** an incidental consequence
fal·low¹ (fal′ō) *n.* [< OE. *fealh*] **1.** land ploughed but not seeded for one or more seasons, to kill weeds, enrich the soil, etc. **2.** the ploughing of land to be left idle thus —*adj.* **1.** left uncultivated or unplanted **2.** untrained; inactive: said esp. of the mind —*vt.* to leave (land) unplanted after ploughing —**lie fallow** to remain uncultivated, unused, etc. for a time —**fal′low·ness** *n.*
fal·low² (fal′ō) *adj.* [< OE. *fealo*] pale-yellow.
fallow deer a small European deer having a yellowish coat spotted with white in summer
false (fôls) *adj.* **fals′er, fals′est** [< OFr. < L. pp. of *fallere,* to deceive] **1.** not true; in error; incorrect; wrong **2.** untruthful; lying **3.** disloyal; unfaithful **4.** deceiving; misleading [a *false* scent] **5.** not real; artificial; counterfeit [*false* teeth] **6.** not properly so named [*false* acacia] **7.** based on mistaken ideas [*false* pride] **8.** temporary, nonessential, or added on for protection, disguise, etc. [a *false* drawer] **9.** *Music* pitched inaccurately —*adv.* in a false manner —**play (a person) false** to deceive or betray (a person) —**false′ly** *adv.* —**false′ness** *n.*
false dawn a light similar to that of dawn which appears in the east just before sunrise
false-heart·ed (-här′tid) *adj.* disloyal; deceitful
false·hood (-hood′) *n.* **1.** lack of accuracy or truth; falsity **2.** the telling of lies; lying **3.** a false statement; lie **4.** a false belief, theory, idea, etc.
false imprisonment *Law* the unlawful arrest or detention of another person
false pretences misrepresentation of the facts to gain advantage
false quantity mispronunciation or misuse of a vowel giving it an incorrect length
false ribs the five lower ribs on each side of the body: so called because not directly attached to the breastbone
false step 1. a misstep **2.** a social blunder
fal·set·to (fôl set′ō) *n., pl.* **-tos** [It. dim. < L.: see FALSE] **1.** *a)* an artificial way of singing or speaking, in which the voice is placed in a register much higher than that of the natural voice *b)* this voice **2.** a person using falsetto: also **fal·set′tist** —*adj.* of or singing in falsetto —*adv.* in falsetto
fals·ies (fôl′sēz) *n.pl.* [Colloq.] pads worn with a brassiere to make the breasts look fuller
fal·si·fy (fôl′sə fī′) *vt.* **-fied′, -fy′ing** [< OFr. < ML. < L. *falsus,* FALSE + *facere,* to make] **1.** to make false; specif., *a)* to give an untrue account of *b)* to alter (a record, etc.) fraudulently **2.** to prove to be unfounded —*vi.* to tell falsehoods; lie —**fal′si·fi·ca′tion** *n.* —**fal′si·fi′er** *n.*
fal·si·ty (-tē) *n., pl.* **-ties 1.** the condition or quality of being false; specif., *a)* incorrectness *b)* dishonesty *c)* deceitfulness *d)* disloyalty **2.** something false; esp., a lie
Fal·staff·i·an (fôl stäf′ē ən) *adj.* [after *Falstaff,* a character in some of Shakespeare's plays] corpulent, jovial, and robustly comic
fal·ter (fôl′tər) *vi.* [ME. *faltren,* prob. < ON.] **1.** to move uncertainly or unsteadily; stumble **2.** to stumble in speech; stammer **3.** to act hesitantly; show uncertainty; waver **4.** to lose strength; weaken [the economy *faltered*] —*vt.* to say hesitatingly or timidly —*n.* **1.** a faltering **2.** a faltering sound —**fal′ter·er** *n.* —**fal′ter·ing·ly** *adv.*
fame (fām) *n.* [< OFr. < L. *fama,* fame, akin to *fari,* to speak] **1.** [Archaic] public report; rumour **2.** reputation, esp. for good **3.** the state of being well known or much

talked about; renown —*vt.* **famed, fam′ing** [Archaic] to tell about widely; make famous

famed (fāmd) *adj.* much talked about or widely known; famous; renowned (*for* something)

fa·mil·i·al (fə mil′ē əl, -yəl) *adj.* of, involving, or common to a family

fa·mil·i·ar (fə mil′ē ər, -yər) *adj.* [< OFr. < L. < familia, FAMILY] 1. friendly, informal, or intimate 2. too friendly; unduly intimate or bold 3. closely acquainted (*with*) [*familiar* with the Bible] 4. well-known; common [a *familiar* sight] —*n.* 1. a close friend 2. in superstitious belief, a spirit acting as servant to a witch: also **familiar spirit** —**fa·mil′i·ar·ly** *adv.*

fa·mil·i·ar·i·ty (fə mil′ē ar′ə tē) *n., pl.* **-ties** 1. intimacy 2. free and intimate behaviour 3. intimacy that is too bold or unwelcome 4. a highly intimate act, remark, etc.; specif., a caress 5. close acquaintance (*with* something)

fa·mil·iar·ize (fə mil′yə rīz′, -mil′ē ər-) *vt.* **-ized′, -iz′ing** 1. to make commonly known 2. to make (another or oneself) accustomed or fully acquainted —**fa·mil′iar·i·za′tion** *n.*

fam·i·ly (fam′ə lē, fam′lē) *n., pl.* **-lies** [L. familia, household < famulus, servant] 1. orig., all the people living in the same house; household 2. a) a social unit consisting of parents and their children b) the children of the same parents 3. a group of people related by ancestry or marriage; relatives 4. all those claiming descent from a common ancestor; tribe or clan; lineage 5. a group of things having a common source or similar features; specif., a) *Biol.* a taxonomic category, ranking above a genus and below an order b) *Linguis.* a group of languages having a common ancestral language c) *Math.* a set of curves, etc. with some shared property —*adj.* of or for a family —**in the** (or **a**) **family way** [Colloq.] pregnant

family allowance a sum of money paid regularly by the state or an employer to families with dependent children

family Bible a large Bible with pages for recording family births, deaths, and marriages

family man 1. a man who has a wife and children 2. a man devoted to his family and home

family name a surname

family planning *same as* BIRTH CONTROL

family tree 1. all the ancestors and descendants in a family 2. a chart showing their relationship

fam·ine (fam′ən) *n.* [< OFr., ult. < L. fames, hunger] 1. an acute and general shortage of food, or a period of this 2. any acute and general shortage 3. [Archaic] starvation; great hunger

fam·ish (-ish) *vt., vi.* [< OFr. < L. ad, to + fames, hunger] 1. to make or be very hungry; make or become weak from hunger 2. [Obs.] to starve to death —**to be famished** (or **famishing**) [Colloq.] to feel very hungry

fa·mous (fā′məs) *adj.* [< L. < fama, FAME] 1. having fame, or celebrity; renowned 2. [Colloq.] excellent; first-rate —**fa′mous·ly** *adv.*

fam·u·lus (fam′yoo ləs) *n., pl.* **-li′** (-lī′) [<L., a servant] an assistant, esp. of a medieval scholar

fan¹ (fan) *n.* [OE. fann < L. vannus, basket for winnowing grain] 1. orig., a device for winnowing grain 2. any device used to set up a current of air for ventilating or cooling; specif., a) any flat surface moved by hand b) a folding device of paper, cloth, etc. that opens as a sector of a circle c) a motor-driven device with revolving blades 3. anything in the shape of a fan (sense 2b) —*vt.* **fanned, fan′ning** 1. to move or agitate (air) as with a fan 2. to direct a current of air towards with or as with a fan; blow on 3. to stir up; excite 4. to blow or drive away with a fan 5. to spread out into the shape of a fan (*n.* 2b) 6. to separate (grain) from chaff —**fan out** to scatter or spread out like an open fan —**fan′like′** *adj.* —**fan′ner** *n.*

fan² (fan) *n.* [contr. < ff.] [Colloq.] a person enthusiastic about a specified sport, pastime, or performer; devotee [a football *fan*]

fa·nat·ic (fə nat′ik) *adj.* [< L. < fanum, a temple] unreasonably enthusiastic; excessively zealous: also **fa·nat′-i·cal** —*n.* a person whose extreme zeal, piety, etc. goes beyond what is reasonable; zealot —**fa·nat′i·cal·ly** *adv.*

fa·nat·i·cism (-ə siz′m) *n.* excessive and unreasonable zeal —**fa·nat′i·cize** (-sīz′) *vt., vi.* **-cized′, -ciz′ing**

fan belt *n.* in a motor vehicle, the belt driving the radiator cooling fan

fan·cied (fan′sid) *adj.* 1. imaginary; imagined 2. [Colloq.] expected to perform well

fan·ci·er (fan′sē ər) *n.* a person with a special interest in and knowledge of something, particularly plant or animal breeding [a dog *fancier*]

fan·ci·ful (fan′si fəl) *adj.* 1. full of fancy; having or showing a playful imagination [*fanciful* costumes] 2. not real, practical, etc.; imaginary [a *fanciful* tale] —**fan′ci·ful·ly** *adv.* —**fan′ci·ful·ness** *n.*

fan club a society of people who admire a particular celebrity

fan·cy (fan′sē) *n., pl.* **-cies** [contr. < FANTASY] 1. imagination, now esp. light, whimsical, or capricious

imagination 2. a mental image 3. an arbitrary idea; notion; caprice; whim 4. an inclination, liking, or fondness, often temporary [to take a *fancy* to someone] —*adj.* **-ci·er, -ci·est** 1. capricious; whimsical; fanciful 2. extravagant [a *fancy* price] 3. not plain; decorated, elaborate, ornamental, etc. [a *fancy* waistcoat] 4. of superior skill; intricate and difficult 5. bred for some special feature —*vt.* **-cied, -cy·ing** 1. to form an idea of; imagine 2. to have a liking for 3. to think or suppose 4. [Colloq.] to consider (a horse, etc.) a likely winner —**fancy (that)!** can you imagine (that)! —**fan′-ci·less** *adj.* —**fan′ci·ly** *adv.* —**fan′ci·ness** *n.*

fancy dress a costume representing a historical character, an animal, etc., worn at a dance, carnival, etc.

fan·cy-free (-frē′) *adj.* 1. free to fall in love; not married, engaged, etc. 2. carefree

fancy goods small, decorative articles; knickknacks

fan·cy man [Slang] 1. a woman's lover 2. a man supported by a woman; esp., a pimp

fan·cy woman [Slang] 1. a mistress 2. a prostitute

fan·cy·work (-wʉrk′) *n.* embroidery, crocheting, and other ornamental needlework

fan dance a dance in which a nude performer uses fans to attempt concealment and tantalize watchers

fan·dan·gle (fan daŋ′g'l) *n.* [?< FANDANGO] 1. elaborate or unnecessary ornament 2. nonsense

fan·dan·go (fan daŋ′gō) *n., pl.* **-gos** [Sp.] 1. a lively Spanish dance in rhythm varying from slow to quick 3/4 time 2. music for this

fane (fān) *n.* [L. fanum] [Archaic or Poet.] a temple or church

fan·fare (fan′fer′) *n.* [Fr., prob. < fanfaron, braggart] 1. a loud flourish of trumpets 2. noisy or showy display

fang (faŋ) *n.* [OE. < base of fon, to seize] 1. a) one of the long, pointed teeth with which meat-eating animals seize and tear their prey b) one of the long, hollow or grooved teeth through which poisonous snakes inject their venom 2. the pointed part of something —**fanged** (faŋd) *adj.* —**fang′less** *adj.*

FANGS

fan heater a heating device in which the heat produced by an electrically heated element is dispersed by an electric fan

fan·jet (-jet)′*n. same as* TURBOFAN (sense 1)

fan·light (fan′līt′) *n.* 1. a semicircular window, often with sash bars in a fanlike arrangement, over a door or larger window 2. a small rectangular window over a door, esp. one that opens

fan mail letters of praise or adulation from fans

fan·ny (fan′ē) *n.* [< ?] 1. [Slang] the female genitals: usually considered a vulgar term 2. [U.S. Slang] the buttocks

Fanny Adams [< name of a C19 murder victim] [Slang] 1. nothing at all: also **sweet Fanny Adams** 2. *Naut.* tinned meat

fan·tail (fan′tāl′) *n.* 1. a part, tail, or end spread out like an opened fan 2. *Naut.* the part of the main deck at the stern 3. *Zool.* a variety of domestic pigeon, a breed of goldfish, etc. with a fanlike tail

fan-tan (fan′tan′) *n.* [< Chin. fan, number of times + t'an, apportion] 1. a Chinese gambling game 2. a card game in which the players seek to discard all their cards in proper sequence Also **fan tan**

fan·ta·si·a (fan tā′zhə, -zē ə; fan′tə zē′ə) *n.* [It. < L.: see FANTASY] 1. a musical composition of no fixed form 2. a medley of familiar tunes

fan·ta·size (fan′tə sīz′) *vt., vi.* **-sized′, -siz′ing** [FANTAS(Y) + -IZE] to create or imagine (something) in a fantasy; have daydreams (about) —**fan′ta·sist** *n.*

fan·tas·tic (fan tas′tik) *adj.* [< OFr. < ML. < LL. < Gr. phantastikos, able to present to the mind < phainein, to show] 1. imaginary; unreal [*fantastic* terrors] 2. grotesque; odd; quaint [*fantastic* designs] 3. extravagant; capricious; eccentric [a *fantastic* plan] 4. [Colloq.] seemingly impossible; incredible [*fantastic* progress] Also **fan·tas′ti·cal** *adj.* —**fan·tas′ti·cal·ly** *adv.* —**fan·tas′ti·cal′i·ty,** —**fan·tas′ti·cal·ness** *n.*

fan·ta·sy (fan′tə sē, -zē) *n., pl.* **-sies** [< OFr. < L. < Gr. phantasia, appearance < phainein, to show] 1. imagination or fancy; esp., wild, visionary fancy 2. an unnatural or bizarre mental image 3. an odd notion; whim; caprice 4. a highly imaginative poem, play, etc. 5. *same as* FANTASIA 6. a daydream or daydreaming, esp. about an unfulfilled desire —*vt.* **-sied, -sy·ing** to form fantasies about —*vi.* to indulge in fantasies, as by daydreaming

fan vaulting *Archit.* vaulting having ribs that radiate, like those of a fan, from the top of a capital

FAO Food and Agriculture Organization (of the UN)

faq·uir (fə kir′) *n. same as* FAKIR

far (fär) *adj.* **far′ther, far′thest** [OE. feorr] 1. distant in space or time; not near 2. extending a long way [a *far* journey] 3. more distant [the *far* side of the room] 4.

very different in quality or nature [*far* from poor] —*adv.* **1.** very distant in space, time, or degree **2.** to or from a great distance in time or position **3.** very much [*far* better] **4.** to a certain distance or degree [how *far* did you go?] —*n.* a distant place [to come from *far*] —**a far cry from** very different from —**as far as 1.** to the distance, extent, or degree that **2.** [Colloq.] with reference to; as for —**by far** very much: also **far and away** —**far and near** (or **wide**) everywhere —**far be it from me** I would not presume or wish —**far gone** in an advanced state of deterioration —**far out** same as FAR-OUT (see below) —**few and far between** scarce; rare —**go far 1.** to cover much extent; last long **2.** to have a strong tendency **3.** to accomplish much —**go too far** to behave or speak in a manner exceeding reasonable limits —**in so far as** to the extent or degree that —**so far** up to this place, time, or degree —**so far as** to the extent or point that —**so far, so good** up to this point everything is all right —**far′ness** *n.*

far·ad (far′ad, -əd) *n.* [after M. *Faraday* (1791-1867), Brit. scientist] the SI unit of capacitance, equal to the amount that permits the storing of one coulomb of charge for each volt of applied potential

far·a·day (far′ə dā′) *n.* [after M. *Faraday*: see FARAD] the quantity of electricity required to liberate one gramme-equivalent of an ion

far·ad·ic (fə rad′ik) *adj.* [< FARAD] of or pertaining to induced electrical currents: also **far′a·da′ic** (-dā′ik)

far·an·dole (far′ən dōl′) *n.* [Fr. < Pr. *farandoulo*] **1.** a lively dance of S. France **2.** the music for this

far·a·way (far′ə wā′) *adj.* **1.** distant in time or place **2.** dreamy; abstracted [a *faraway* look]

farce (färs) *n.* [Fr. < L. *farcire*, to stuff: early farces were used to fill interludes between acts] **1.** an exaggerated comedy based on broadly humorous, highly unlikely situations **2.** broad humour of the kind found in such plays **3.** a ridiculous display, pretence, etc.

far·ci·cal (fär′si k'l) *adj.* of, or having the nature of, a farce; absurd, ridiculous, etc. —**far′ci·cal′i·ty** (-kal′ə tē) *n.* —**far′ci·cal·ly** *adv.*

far·del (fär′d'l) *n.* [OFr.] [Archaic] a burden

fare (fer) *vi.* **fared, far′ing** [OE. *faran*, to go, wander] **1.** [Poet.] to travel; go **2.** to happen; result [how did it *fare* with him?] **3.** to be in a specified condition; get on [he *fared* well on his trip] **4.** to eat or be given food —*n.* **1.** money paid for a trip in a train, taxi, plane, etc. **2.** a passenger who pays a fare **3.** *a)* food *b)* the usual diet

Far Eastern designating of or those countries east of India

fare stage 1. a section of a route, as a bus route, for which a set charge is imposed **2.** the stop marking the end of such a section

fare·well (fer′wel′; *for adj.* -wel′) *interj.* [FARE (imperative) + WELL[2]] goodbye —*n.* **1.** parting words; good wishes at parting **2.** a leaving or going away —*adj.* parting; last; final [a *farewell* gesture]

far-fetched (fär′fecht′) *adj.* resulting or introduced in a forced, or unnatural, way; strained

far-flung (-fluŋ′) *adj.* extending over a wide area

fa·ri·na (fə rē′nə) *n.* [L. < *far*, kind of grain] flour or meal made from cereal grains (esp. whole wheat), potatoes, nuts, etc.

far·i·na·ceous (far′ə nā′shəs) *adj.* [see prec.] **1.** containing, consisting of, or made from flour or meal **2.** like meal **3.** containing starch

farm (färm) *n.* [< OFr. < ML. *firma*, fixed payment < *firmare*, to lease < L. *firmus*, steadfast] **1.** the letting out, for a fixed amount, of the privilege to collect and keep taxes **2.** a piece of land (with house, barns, etc.) on which crops or animals are raised; orig., such land let out to tenants **3.** any place where certain things are raised [a tract of water for raising fish is a fish *farm*] —*vt.* **1.** *a)* to cultivate (land) *b)* to raise animals, etc. **2.** to collect (taxes, etc.) for a fixed amount **3.** to turn over to another for a fee —*vi.* to work on or operate a farm; raise crops or animals on a farm —**farm out 1.** to rent (land, a business, etc.) for a fixed payment **2.** to send (work) from a shop, office, etc. to workers on the outside

farm·er (fär′mər) *n.* **1.** a person who earns his living by farming; esp., one who manages or operates a farm **2.** a person who pays for a right, as, formerly, to collect and keep taxes **3.** a person who contracts to do something for a fixed price

farm·hand (fär′m′hand′) *n.* a hired farm labourer

farm·house (-hous′) *n.* a house on a farm; esp., the main dwelling house on a farm

farm·ing (fär′miŋ) *adj.* of or for agriculture —*n.* **1.** the business of operating a farm **2.** the letting out to farm of land, revenue, etc.

farm·stead (färm′sted′) *n.* the land and buildings of a farm

farm·yard (-yärd′) *n.* the yard surrounding or enclosed by the farm buildings

far·o (fer′ō) *n.* [Fr. *pharaon* < ? *Pharaoh*] a gambling game in which players bet on the cards to be turned up from the top of the dealer's pack

far-off (fär′of′) *adj.* distant; remote

fa·rouche (fə rōōsh′) *adj.* [Fr. < OFr., ult. < L. *foras*, out-of-doors] **1.** wild; savage **2.** lacking social grace

far-out (fär′out′) *adj.* [Colloq.] very advanced, experimental or nonconformist; esp., avant-garde

far·ra·go (fə rā′gō, -rä′-) *n.,* *pl.* **-goes** [L., mixed fodder, mixture < *far*: see FARINA] a confused mixture; jumble —**far·rag′i·nous** (-raj′ə nəs) *adj.*

far-reach·ing (fär′rēch′iŋ) *adj.* having a wide range, extent, influence, or effect

far·ri·er (far′ē ər) *n.* [< OFr. < ML. < L. *ferrum*, iron] a blacksmith who shoes horses; also, sometimes, one who treats their diseases —**far′ri·er·y** *n.,* *pl.* **-er·ies**

far·row (far′ō) *n.* [< OE. *fearh*, young pig] a litter of pigs —*vt., vi.* to give birth to (a litter of pigs)

far·see·ing (fär′sē′iŋ) *adj.* same as FARSIGHTED (senses 1 & 2)

far·sight·ed (-sīt′id) *adj.* **1.** capable of seeing far **2.** prudent in judgment and foresight **3.** having better vision for distant objects than for near ones —**far′sight′ed·ly** *adv.* —**far′sight′ed·ness** *n.*

fart (färt) *vi.* [< ME. *ferten* < OE. *feortan*] to pass wind from the anus —*n.* such a passing of wind Often a vulgar usage

far·ther (fär′thər) *adj.* *compar. of* FAR [ME. *ferther*, var. of *further*, FURTHER] **1.** more distant **2.** additional; further —*adv.* *compar. of* FAR **1.** at or to a greater distance or more remote point **2.** to a greater degree; further **3.** in addition; further In sense 2 of the *adj.* and senses 2 and 3 of the *adv.*, FURTHER is more commonly used

far·ther·most (-mōst′) *adj.* most distant; farthest

far·thest (fär′thist) *adj.* *superl. of* FAR [ME. *ferthest*: see FARTHER] most distant —*adv.* *superl. of* FAR **1.** at or to the greatest distance or most remote point **2.** to the greatest degree

far·thing (fär′thiŋ) *n.* [OE. *feorthing*, dim. of *feortha*, fourth] **1.** a former small British coin, equal to one quarter of an old penny **2.** a thing of little value; the least amount

far·thin·gale (fär′thiŋ gāl′) *n.* [OFr. *verdugale* < Sp. < *verdugo*, tree shoot, rod < *verde* < L. *viridis*, green] a hoop petticoat worn by women in the 16th and 17th centuries

fas·ces (fas′ēz) *n.pl.* [L., pl. of *fascis*, a bundle] a bundle of rods bound about an axe, carried before ancient Roman magistrates as a symbol of authority: later the symbol of Italian fascism

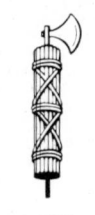

FASCES

fas·ci·a (fash′ē ə, fash′ə) *n.,* *pl.* **-ci·ae** (-ē′), **-ci·as** [L., a band] **1.** a flat strip; band **2.** *Anat.* a thin layer of connective tissue Cf. FACIA —**fas′ci·al** *adj.*

fas·ci·ate (fash′ē āt′) *adj.* [L. *fasciatus*, swathed] **1.** bound with a sash or bandage **2.** *Bot.* abnormally enlarged and flattened, as some plant stems **3.** *Zool.* marked by broad coloured bands Also **fas′ci·at′ed**

fas·ci·cle (fas′i k'l) *n.* [< OFr. < L. dim. of *fascis*: see FASCES] **1.** a single section of a book published as an instalments **2.** a small bundle or cluster, as of flowers, stems, etc. —**fas′ci·cled** *adj.*

fas·cic·u·late (fə sik′yoo lit, -lāt′) *adj.* [see prec.] formed of, or growing in, bundles or clusters: also **fas·cic′u·lat′ed** (-lāt′id), **fas·cic′u·lar**

fas·ci·nate (fas′ə nāt′) *vt.* **-nat′ed, -nat′ing** [< L. pp. of *fascinare*, to bewitch < *fascinum*, an enchanting] **1.** orig., to put under a spell **2.** to hold motionless, as by inspiring terror **3.** to hold the attention of by being very interesting or delightful; charm —**fas′ci·nat′ing·ly** *adv.*

fas·ci·na·tion (fas′ə nā′shən) *n.* **1.** a fascinating or being fascinated **2.** charm; allure

fas·ci·na·tor (fas′ə nāt′ər) *n.* **1.** a person who fascinates **2.** a woman's light scarf, knitted or crocheted: an old-fashioned term

fas·cine (fa sēn′) *n.* [Fr.< L. *fascis*: see FASCES] a bundle of sticks formerly used to strengthen trenches, fill ditches, etc., esp. in war

fas·cism (fash′iz'm) *n.* [It. *fascismo* < L. *fascis*: see FASCES] **1.** [F-] the doctrines, methods, or movement of the Fascisti **2.** a system of government characterized by dictatorship, belligerent nationalism, racism, militarism, etc.: first instituted in Italy in 1922 **3.** fascist behaviour

fas·cist (-ist) *n.* **1.** [F-] *a)* a member of the Fascisti *b)* a member of some similar party; Nazi, Falangist, etc. **2.** an adherent of fascism —*adj.* **1.** [F-] of Fascists or Fascism **2.** of, believing in, or practising fascism —**fa·scis′tic** (fə shis′tik) *adj.* —**fa·scis′ti·cal·ly** *adv.*

fash·ion (fash′ən) *n.* [< OFr. *faceon* < L. *factio*: see FACTION] **1.** the make, form, or shape of a thing **2.** [Now Rare] kind; sort **3.** way; manner **4.** the current style of dress, conduct, etc. **5.** something in the current style **6.** fashionable society [a man of *fashion*] —*vt.* **1.** to make or form in a certain way; shape **2.** to fit, accommodate (*to*) **3.** [Archaic] to contrive —**after** (or **in**) **a fashion** to some extent; in a kind of way (but not very well) —**fash′ion·er** *n.*

fash·ion·a·ble (-ə b'l) *adj.* **1.** in fashion; stylish **2.** of, characteristic of, or used by people who follow fashion —*n.* a fashionable person —**fash'ion·a·ble·ness** *n.* —**fash'ion·a·bly** *adv.*

fashion plate **1.** a picture showing a current style in dress **2.** a fashionably dressed person

fast¹ (fäst) *adj.* [OE. *fæst*] **1.** firm, fixed, or stuck **2.** firmly fastened or shut **3.** loyal; devoted **4.** that will not fade [*fast* colours] **5.** swift; quick; speedy **6.** permitting swift movement [a *fast* route] **7.** lasting a short time [a *fast* lunch] **8.** showing a time that is ahead of the correct time [his watch is *fast*] **9.** a) reckless; wild [a *fast* crowd] *b*) sexually promiscuous **10.** *Photog.* adapted to very short exposure time **11.** [Dial.] complete; sound [a *fast* sleep] —*adv.* **1.** firmly; fixedly **2.** thoroughly; soundly [*fast* asleep] **3.** rapidly; swiftly **4.** ahead of time **5.** in a reckless, dissipated way; wildly **6.** [Obs.] close; near [*fast* by the river] —**a fast one** [Slang] a deceptive act [to pull a *fast* one] —**make fast** **1.** *Naut.* to tie up **2.** to fix firmly —**play fast and loose** to behave with duplicity or insincerity

fast² (fäst) *vi.* [OE. *fæstan*] **1.** to abstain from all or certain foods, as in observing a holy day **2.** to eat very little or nothing —*n.* **1.** the act of fasting **2.** a period of fasting —**break one's fast** to eat food for the first time after fasting

fast·back (-bak') *n.* a motor car with an unbroken curve from windscreen to rear bumper

fast breeder reactor a breeder reactor that uses high energy neutrons to produce fissionable material

fast day a holy day, etc. observed by fasting

fas·ten (fäs'n) *vt.* [OE. *fæstnian* < base of *fæst*, FAST¹] **1.** to join (one thing *to* another); attach **2.** to make secure, as by locking, buttoning, etc. **3.** to hold or direct (the attention, etc.) steadily (*on*) **4.** to cause to be attributed; impute [to *fasten* a crime on someone] **5.** to force (oneself *on* or *upon* another) in an annoying way —*vi.* **1.** to become attached or joined **2.** to take a firm hold (*on* or *upon*); seize **3.** to concentrate (*on* or *upon*) **4.** to force (*on* or *upon* another) in an annoying way —**fas'ten·er** *n.*

fas·ten·ing (-iŋ) *n.* anything used to fasten; bolt, clasp, hook, lock, button, etc.

fas·tid·i·ous (fas tid'ē əs, fəs-) *adj.* [< L. < *fastidium*, a loathing < *fastus*, disdain + *taedium*: see TEDIUM] **1.** not easy to please; very critical **2.** daintily refined; easily disgusted —**fas·tid'i·ous·ly** *adv.* —**fas·tid'i·ous·ness** *n.*

fas·tig·i·ate (fas tij'ē it, -āt') *adj.* [< L. *fastigium*, a gable end] shaped like a cone; tapering

fast·ness (fäst'nis) *n.* **1.** the quality or condition of being fast **2.** a secure place; stronghold

fat (fat) *adj.* **fat'ter, fat'test** [OE. *fætt*, pp. of *fætan*, to fatten] **1.** containing or full of fat; oily; greasy **2.** a) fleshy; plump *b*) too plump; obese **3.** thick; broad **4.** fertile; productive [*fat* land] **5.** profitable; lucrative [a *fat* job] **6.** prosperous **7.** plentiful; ample **8.** stupid; dull **9.** [Slang] large or important [a *fat* role in a play] —*n.* **1.** any of various solid or semisolid oily or greasy materials found in animal tissue and in plant seeds **2.** fleshiness; corpulence **3.** the richest part of anything **4.** anything unnecessary that can be trimmed away **5.** *Chem.* a class of glyceryl esters of fatty acids, insoluble in water —*vt., vi.* **fat'ted, fat'ting** to make or become fat: now usually FATTEN —**a fat chance** [Slang] very little or no chance —**a fat lot** [Slang] very little or nothing —**chew the fat** [Slang] to talk together; chat —**kill the fatted calf for** to celebrate someone's return: see PRODIGAL SON —**the fat is in the fire** an action has been taken from which trouble is bound to result —**the fat of the land** the best obtainable; great luxury —**fat'ly** *adv.* —**fat'ness** *n.*

fa·tal (fāt'l) *adj.* [OFr. < L. *fatalis* < *fatum*, FATE] **1.** fateful; decisive [the *fatal* day arrived] **2.** resulting in death **3.** very destructive; most unfortunate —**fa'tal·ly** *adv.* —**fa'tal·ness** *n.*

fa·tal·ism (-iz'm) *n.* **1.** the belief that all events are determined by fate and are hence inevitable **2.** acceptance of every event as inevitable —**fa'tal·ist** *n.* —**fa'tal·is'tic** *adj.* —**fa'tal·is'ti·cal·ly** *adv.*

fa·tal·i·ty (fə tal'ə tē, fā-) *n., pl.* **-ties** **1.** fate or necessity; subjection to fate **2.** something caused by fate **3.** an inevitable liability to disaster **4.** a fatal quality; deadliness [the *fatality* of a disease] **5.** a death caused by a disaster, as in an accident, war, etc.

fate (fāt) *n.* [< L. *fatum*, oracle < neut. pp. of *fari*, to speak] **1.** the power or agency supposed to determine the outcome of events; destiny **2.** a) something supposedly determined by this power *b*) a person's lot or fortune **3.** final outcome **4.** death; destruction —*vt.* **fat'ed, fat'ing** to destine: now usually in the passive —**the Fates** *Gr. & Rom. Myth.* the three goddesses who control human destiny and life: see CLOTHO, LACHESIS, and ATROPOS

fat·ed (fāt'id) *adj.* **1.** destined **2.** doomed

fate·ful (-fəl) *adj.* **1.** prophetic **2.** having important consequences; decisive **3.** controlled as if by fate **4.**

bringing death or destruction —**fate'ful·ly** *adv.* —**fate'ful·ness** *n.*

fat·head (fat'hed') *n.* [Slang] a stupid person —**fat'head'·ed** *adj.*

fa·ther (fä'thər) *n.* [OE. *fæder*] **1.** a male parent; esp., a man as he is related to his child **2.** a) a stepfather *b*) father-in-law **3.** a guardian or protector **4.** [F-] God, or God as the first person of the Trinity **5.** a forefather; ancestor **6.** an originator; founder; inventor **7.** any of the leaders of a city, assembly, etc.: *usually used in pl.* **8.** [*often* F-] a) any of the important early Christian religious writers *b*) a Christian priest: used esp. as a title —*vt.* **1.** to be the father of; beget **2.** to care for as a father does; protect, rear, etc. **3.** to found, originate, or invent —**fa'ther·hood'** *n.* —**fa'ther·less** *adj.*

father confessor **1.** a priest who hears confessions **2.** a person in whom one habitually confides

father figure a person substituted in one's mind for one's father

fa·ther-in-law (-ən lô') *n., pl.* **fa'thers-in-law'** the father of one's wife or husband

fa·ther·land (-land') *n.* a person's native land or, sometimes, the land of his ancestors

fa·ther·ly (-lē) *adj.* of or like a father; kindly; protective —*adv.* [Archaic] in a fatherly manner —**fa'ther·li·ness** *n.*

Father of the House of Commons the M.P. with the longest unbroken service

Father's Day the third Sunday in June, a day set aside in honour of fathers

fath·om (fath'əm) *n.* [OE. *fæthm*, the two arms outstretched (to measure, etc.)] a nautical unit of depth or length, equal to 6 feet (1.8 m) —*vt.* **1.** to measure the depth of; sound **2.** to understand thoroughly —**fath'om·a·ble** *adj.* —**fath'om·less·ness** *n.*

fa·thom·e·ter (fath om'ə tər) a sonar device used to measure depth of oceans, etc.

fath·om·less (-las) *adj.* bottomless; of immeasureable depth

fa·tigue (fə tēg') *n.* [Fr. < L. *fatigare*, to weary] **1.** physical or mental exhaustion; weariness **2.** a) manual labour or menial duty, other than drill or instruction, assigned to soldiers: in full, **fatigue duty** *b*) [pl.] sturdy work clothing worn on fatigue duty: also **fatigue dress** **3.** the tendency of a metal or other material to crack under repeated stress —*vt., vi.* **-tigued', -tigu'ing** **1.** to make or become tired; weary **2.** to subject to or undergo fatigue —**fat'i·ga·ble** (fat'i gə b'l) *adj.* —**fat·i·ga·ble** (fat'i gə b'l) *n.*

fatigue party soldiers assigned to FATIGUE (sense 2*a*)

fat·stock (fat'stok') *n.* domestic animals fattened for sale as meat

fat·ten (fat'n) *vt., vi.* to make or become fat —**fat'ten·er** *n.*

fat·tish (-ish) *adj.* somewhat fat

fat·ty (-ē) *adj.* **-ti·er, -ti·est** **1.** of or containing fat **2.** very plump **3.** resembling fat; greasy; oily —*n.* [Colloq.] a fat person —**fat'ti·ness** *n.*

fatty acid **1.** any of a series of saturated organic acids having the general formula $C_nH_{2n+1}COOH$ **2.** any of a number of saturated or unsaturated organic acids usually having an even number of carbon atoms

fatty degeneration *Med.* a condition in which tissue, esp. that of the heart and liver, becomes infiltrated with droplets of fat

fa·tu·i·ty (fə tyoo'ə tē, fa-) *n., pl.* **-ties** **1.** complacent stupidity; smug foolishness **2.** a fatuous remark, act, etc. —**fa·tu'i·tous** *adj.*

fat·u·ous (fat'yoo wəs) *adj.* [L. *fatuus*, foolish] **1.** complacently stupid; foolish **2.** [Archaic] illusory —**fat'u·ous·ly** *adv.* —**fat'u·ous·ness** *n.*

‡**fau·bourg** (fō bōor'; E. fō'boorg) *n.* [Fr. for earlier *faux bourg*, lit., false town] a suburb

fau·ces (fô'sēz) *n.pl.* [L., throat] the passage leading from the back of the mouth into the pharynx —**fau'cal** (-kəl), **fau'cial** (-shəl) *adj.*

fau·cet (fô'sit) *n.* [< OFr., prob. < *faulser*, to breach, falsify < LL. < L. *falsus*, FALSE] **1.** a device with a valve for regulating the flow of liquid from a barrel **2.** [U.S.] a tap

fault (fôlt) *n.* [< OFr. *faulte*, ult. < L. *falsus*, FALSE] **1.** something that mars; flaw; defect **2.** a) a misdeed; offence *b*) an error; mistake **3.** responsibility for something wrong; blame [it's my *fault* that he's late] **4.** *Geol.* a fracture or zone of fractures in rock strata along with displacement of the strata **5.** *Tennis, Squash,* etc. an error in service —*vt.* **1.** to find fault with; blame **2.** *Geol.* to cause a fault in —*vi.* **1.** to commit a fault in tennis, etc. **2.** *Geol.* to develop a fault —**at fault** guilty of error; deserving blame —**find fault (with)** to seek and point out faults (of) —**to a fault** excessively

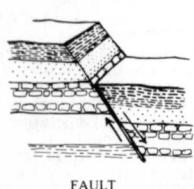

FAULT
(sense 4)

fault·find·ing (-fîn′diŋ) *n., adj.* finding fault; calling attention to defects —**fault′find′er** *n.*

fault·less (-lis) *adj.* without any fault; perfect —**fault′-less·ly** *adv.* —**fault′less·ness** *n.*

fault·y (-ē) *adj.* **fault′i·er, fault′i·est** having a fault or faults; imperfect —**fault′i·ly** *adv.* —**fault′i·ness** *n.*

faun (fôn) *n.* [< L. < *Faunus*, a Roman nature god] any of a class of minor Roman deities, usually represented as having the body of a man, but the horns, ears, tail, and hind legs of a goat

fau·na (fô′nə) *n.,* pl. **-nas, -nae** (-nē) [ModL. < LL. *Fauna,* Roman goddess] the animals of a specified region or time —**fau′nal** *adj.*

fau·vism (fō′viz′m) *n.* [< Fr. < *fauve*, wild beast] [often F-] a French form of expressionist painting characterized by bold distortions and strong, pure colour —**fauve** (fōv), **fau′-vist** *n., adj.*

faux pas (fō′pä′) *pl.* **faux pas** (fō′ päz′) [Fr., lit., false step] a social blunder; error in etiquette

fa·vor (fā′vər) *n., vt.* *U.S. sp. of* FAVOUR

fa·vour (fā′vər) *n.* [< OFr. < L. < *favere*, to favour] **1.** friendly regard; good will **2.** unfair partiality; favouritism **3.** a kind or obliging act **4.** a small gift, souvenir, or token —**vt.** **1.** to regard with favour; approve or like **2.** to be partial to; prefer unfairly **3.** to support; advocate **4.** to make easier; help [rain *favoured* his escape] **5.** to do a kindness for **6.** to look like; resemble [to *favour* one's mother] **7.** to use gently; spare [to *favour* an injured leg] —**find favour** to be pleasing —**in favour of 1.** approving; supporting **2.** to the advantage of **3.** payable to, as a cheque —**in one's favour** to one's advantage —**fa′vour·er** *n.*

fa·vour·a·ble (-ə b'l) *adj.* **1.** approving or commending **2.** helpful or advantageous **3.** pleasing or desirable [a *favourable* impression] —**fa′vour·a·ble·ness** *n.* —**fa′-vour·a·bly** *adv.*

fa·voured (fā′vərd) *adj.* **1.** treated with favour; specially privileged **2.** having (specified) features [ill-*favoured*]

fa·vour·ite (fā′vər it, fāv′rit) *n.* **1.** a person or thing regarded with special liking; specif., a person granted special privileges, as by a king, etc. **2.** a contestant regarded as most likely to win —*adj.* held in special regard; best liked; preferred

fa·vour·it·ism (-iz′m) *n.* **1.** the act of being unfairly partial **2.** the condition of being a favourite

fawn[1] (fôn) *vi.* [< OE. *fagnian* < *fagen*, var. of *fægen*, fain] **1.** to show friendliness by licking hands, wagging its tail, etc.: said of a dog **2.** to cringe and flatter (with *on* or *upon*) —**fawn′er** *n.* —**fawn′ing** *adj.* —**fawn′ing·ly** *adv.*

fawn[2] (fôn) *n.* [< OFr. *faon*, ult. < L. *fetus*, FOETUS] **1.** a young deer less than one year old **2.** a pale, yellowish brown —*adj.* of this colour —*vi., vt.* to bring forth (young): said of deer

fay (fā) *n.* [< OFr. < VL. < L. *fatum*, FATE] a fairy

faze (fāz) *vt.* **fazed, faz′ing** [< OE. *fesan*, to drive] [U.S. Colloq.] to disturb; disconcert

FBI, F.B.I. [U.S.] Federal Bureau of Investigation

F clef *same as* BASS CLEF

F.D. [L.; see FIDEI DEFENSOR] Defender of the Faith

Fe [L. *ferrum*] *Chem.* iron

fe·al·ty (fē′əl tē) *n., pl.* **-ties** [< OFr. *feauté* < L. *fidelitas,* FIDELITY] **1.** the loyalty owed by a vassal to his feudal lord **2.** [Archaic] loyalty

fear (fir) *n.* [OE. *fær,* danger] **1.** anxiety and agitation caused by the presence of danger, evil, pain, etc.; fright **2.** awe; reverence **3.** a feeling of uneasiness or apprehension; concern **4.** a cause for fear —*vt.* **1.** to be afraid of **2.** to feel reverence or awe for **3.** to expect with misgiving [I fear I am late] **4.** [Obs.] to frighten —*vi.* **1.** to feel fear **2.** to be uneasy or anxious —**for fear of** in order to avoid or prevent —**never fear** do not worry; there is no danger of that —**no fear** [Colloq.] by no means —**fear′less** *adj.* —**fear′less·ly** *adv.* —**fear′less·ness** *n.*

fear·ful (-fəl) *adj.* **1.** causing fear; dreadful **2.** feeling fear; afraid **3.** showing fear [a *fearful* look] **4.** [Colloq.] very bad, great, etc. [a *fearful* liar] —**fear′ful·ly** *adv.* —**fear′-ful·ness** *n.*

fear·some (-səm) *adj.* **1.** causing fear; frightful **2.** frightened; timid —**fear′some·ly** *adv.* —**fear′some·ness** *n.*

fea·si·ble (fē′zə b'l) *adj.* [< OFr. < *faire,* to make, do < L. *facere*] **1.** capable of being done or carried out; practicable; possible **2.** within reason; likely; probable **3.** capable of being used successfully; suitable —**fea′si·bil′i·ty** *pl.* **-ties, fea′si·ble·ness** *n.* —**fea′si·bly** *adv.*

feast (fēst) *n.* [< OFr. < VL. *festa* < pl. of L. *festum* < *festus, festal*] **1.** a festival; esp., a religious festival **2.** a rich and elaborate meal; banquet **3.** anything that gives pleasure by its abundance or richness —*vi.* **1.** to eat a rich, elaborate meal **2.** to have a special treat —*vt.* **1.** to entertain at a feast or banquet **2.** to delight or gratify [to *feast* one's eyes on a sight] —**feast′er** *n.*

feat (fēt) *n.* [< Anglo-Fr. < OFr. < L. *factum,* a deed < pp. of *facere*, to do] an act or deed showing unusual daring, skill, etc.

feath·er (feth′ər) *n.* [OE. *fether*] **1.** *Zool.* any of the growths covering the body of a bird and making up a large part of the wing surface **2.** anything like a feather in appearance, lightness, etc. **3.** [pl.] *a)* plumage *b)* attire **4.** class; kind [birds of a *feather*] —*vt.* **1.** to provide or adorn as with feathers **2.** to give a featheredge to **3.** to join by inserting a wedge-shaped part into a groove **4.** to turn the edge of (the blade of an oar or propeller) towards the line of movement —*vi.* **1.** to grow feathers **2.** to move, grow, or look like feathers **3.** to feather an oar or propeller —**feather in one's cap** an achievement worthy of pride —**feather one's (own) nest** to provide for one's own comfort or security —**in feather** feathered —**in fine feather** in very good humour, health, or form —**feath′ered** *adj.* —**feath′er·ing** *n.* —**feath′er·less** *adj.*

feath·er·bed (-bed′) *vt.* to pamper; spoil

feather bed a strong cloth container thickly filled with feathers or down, used as a mattress

feath·er·brain (-brān′) *n.* a silly, foolish, or frivolous person —**feath′er·brained′** *adj.*

feath·er·edge (-ej′) *n.* a very thin edge, easily broken or curled —*vt.* **-edged′, -edg′ing** to give such an edge to

feath·er·stitch (-stich′) *n.* an embroidery stitch forming a zigzag line —*vt., vi.* to embroider with such a stitch

feath·er·weight (-wāt′) *n.* **1.** any person or thing of light weight or small size **2.** *see* BOXING AND WRESTLING WEIGHTS, table —*adj.* **1.** of featherweights **2.** light or trivial

feath·er·y (-ē) *adj.* **1.** covered with or as with feathers **2.** resembling feathers; soft, light, etc. —**feath′er·i·ness** *n.*

fea·ture (fē′chər) *n.* [< OFr. < L. *factura,* a making < pp. of *facere*, to make] **1.** orig., the make, form, or appearance of a person or thing **2.** *a)* [pl.] the form or look of the face *b)* any of the parts of the face, as the eyes, nose, mouth, etc. **3.** a distinct or outstanding part or quality of something **4.** a prominently displayed or publicized attraction at an entertainment, sale, etc. **5.** a special story, article, etc. in a newspaper or magazine **6.** a full-length film, esp. as the main presentation —*vt.* **-tured, -tur·ing 1.** to give prominence to; make a feature of **2.** to sketch or show the features of **3.** to be a feature of —*vi.* to have a prominent part —**fea′ture·less** *adj.*

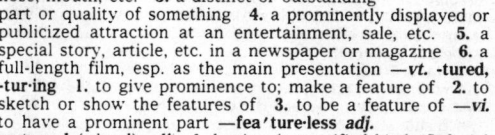

FEATHER-STITCH

fea·tured (-chərd) *adj.* **1.** having (a specified kind of) facial features [broad-*featured*] **2.** given special prominence as a main attraction

Feb. February

feb·ri- [< L. *febris*] *a combining form meaning fever* [febrifuge]

feb·ri·fuge (feb′rə fyōōj′) *n.* [< Fr.: see FEBRI- & -FUGE] any substance for reducing fever; antipyretic —*adj.* reducing fever

fe·brile (fē′brīl) *adj.* [< Fr. < L. *febris,* fever] of or characterized by fever; feverish —**fe·bril′i·ty** *n.*

Feb·ru·ar·y (feb′rə wer ē, feb′yoo wer′ē) *n.* [L. *Februarius* < *februa,* Roman festival of purification held on Feb. 15] the second month of the year, having 28 days (or 29 days in leap years): abbrev. **Feb., F.**

feck·less (fek′lis) *adj.* [Scot. < *feck* (< EFFECT) + -LESS] **1.** weak; ineffective **2.** careless; irresponsible —**feck′less·ly** *adv.* —**feck′less·ness** *n.*

fec·u·lent (fek′yoo lənt) *adj.* [< L. *faecula,* dim. < *faex,* dregs] of or like faeces; filthy; foul —**fec′u·lence** *n.*

fe·cund (fē′kənd, fek′ənd) *adj.* [< OFr. < L. *fecundus,* fruitful] fruitful or fertile; productive —**fe·cun·di·ty** (fi kun′-də tē) *n.*

fe·cun·date (fē′kən dāt′, fek′ən-) *vt.* **-dat′ed, -dat′ing** [< L. pp. of *fecundare* < *fecundus*: see prec.] **1.** to make fecund **2.** to fertilize; impregnate; pollinate —**fe′cun·da′tion** *n.*

fed (fed) *pt. & pp. of* FEED —**fed up** [Colloq.] having had enough to become disgusted, bored, etc.

Fed. 1. Federal **2.** Federated **3.** Federation

fed·a·yeen (fed′ä yēn′) *n.pl.* [Ar., lit., those who sacrifice themselves] Arab irregulars or guerrillas in the Middle East

fed·er·al (fed′ər əl, fed′rəl) *adj.* [< L. *foedus* (gen. *foederis*), a league] **1.** of or formed by a compact; specif., designating or of a union of states, groups, etc. in which each member subordinates its governmental power to a central authority in certain common affairs **2.** designating or of a central government in such a union **3.** [U.S.] [F-] of or supporting the northern states in the American Civil War; —*n.* a supporter of federal union —**fed′er·al·ism** *n.* —**fed′er·al·ist** *n.* —**fed′er·al·ly** *adv.*

fed·er·al·ize (fed′ər ə līz′, fed′rə-) *vt.* **-ized′, -iz′ing 1.** to unite (states, etc.) in a federal union **2.** to put under the authority of a federal government —**fed′er·al·i·za′tion** *n.*

Federal Reserve System [U.S.] a centralized banking system in the U.S. with supervisory powers over twelve Federal Reserve Banks, each a central bank for its district

fed·er·ate (fed′ər it; *for v.* -ə rāt′) *adj.* [< L. pp. of *foederare*

< *foedus:* see FEDERAL] united by common agreement under a central government or authority —*vt., vi.* -at´ed, -at´ing to unite in a federation

fed·er·a·tion (fed´ə rā´shən) *n.* 1. the act of uniting or of forming a union of states, groups, etc. by agreement of each member to subordinate its power to a central authority in common affairs 2. an organization formed thus; a federal union, as of states —**fed´er·a´tive** *adj.* —**fed´er·a´tive·ly** *adv.*

fe·do·ra (fə dôr´ə) *n.* [Fr. < *Fédora* (1882), play by V. Sardou, Fr. dramatist] a soft felt hat with the crown creased lengthwise and a curved brim

fee (fē) *n.* [< Anglo-Fr. *fee* & < OE. *feoh,* cattle, property] 1. orig., a fief 2. payment asked or given for professional services, admissions, licences, tuition, etc.; charge 3. *Law* an inheritance in land: an estate can be held with unrestricted rights of disposition (**fee simple**) or with restrictions as to a specified class of heirs (**fee tail**)

fee·ble (fē´b´l) *adj.* -bler, -blest [< OFr. < L. *flebilis,* to be wept over < *flere,* to weep] weak; not strong; specif., *a)* infirm [a *feeble* old man] *b)* without force or effectiveness [a *feeble* light] *c)* easily broken; frail [a *feeble* barrier] —**fee´ble·ness** *n.* —**fee´bly** *adv.*

fee·ble-mind·ed (-mīn´did) *adj.* mentally retarded: term no longer used in psychology —**fee´ble·mind´ed·ly** *adv.* —**fee´ble·mind´ed·ness** *n.*

feed (fēd) *vt.* fed, feed´ing [< OE. *fedan* < base of *foda,* food] 1. to give food to; provide food for 2. *a)* to provide as food [to *feed* oats to horses] *b)* to serve as food for 3. to provide something necessary for the growth or existence of; nourish [to *feed* one's anger] 4. to provide (material to be used up, processed, etc.) [to *feed* coal into a stove] 5. to provide with material [*feed* the stove] 6. to provide satisfaction for; gratify [to *feed* one's vanity] —*vi.* 1. to eat: said chiefly of animals 2. to flow steadily, as into a machine for use, processing, etc. —*n.* 1. *a)* food given to animals; fodder *b)* the amount of fodder given at one time 2. *a)* the material fed into a machine *b)* the part of the machine supplying this material *c)* the supplying of this material 3. [Colloq.] a meal —**feed on** (or **upon**) to be nourished or gratified by —**off one's feed** [Slang] lacking appetite; rather ill

feed·back (-bak´) *n.* 1. *Elec.* the transfer of part of the output back to the input: it may be an unwanted effect or one desired, as to reduce distortion 2. a process in which the result modifies the factors producing the result

feed·er (-ər) *n.* 1. a person or thing that feeds; specif., a device that feeds material into a machine 2. a child's bib 3. anything that supplies or leads into something else; a tributary 4. *Elec.* a cable supplying energy to a distribution centre

feeding bottle a bottle with a rubber teat from which infants suck liquid food

feel (fēl) *vt.* felt, feel´ing [OE. *felan*] 1. to touch; examine by touching or handling 2. to be aware of through physical sensation [to *feel* rain on the face] 3. *a)* to experience (an emotion or condition) *b)* to be emotionally moved by 4. to be aware of mentally 5. to think or believe, often for emotional reasons —*vi.* 1. to have physical sensation 2. to appear to be to the senses, esp. to the sense of touch [the water *feels* warm] 3. to have the indicated effect [it *feels* good to be home] 4. to search by touching; grope (*for*) 5. to be aware of being [to *feel* sad] 6. to be moved to sympathy, pity, etc. (*for*) —*n.* 1. the act of feeling 2. the sense of touch 3. the nature of a thing perceived through touch 4. an emotional sensation 5. instinctive ability or appreciation [a *feel* for design] —**feel like** [Colloq.] to have a desire for —**feel one's way** to move cautiously —**feel up to** [Colloq.] to feel capable of

feel·er (-ər) *n.* 1. a person or thing that feels 2. a specialized organ of touch in an animal or insect, as an antenna 3. a remark, question, offer, etc. made to sound out another

feel·ing (-iŋ) *adj.* sensitive and sympathetic —*n.* 1. the sense of touch, by which sensations of contact, pressure, temperature, and pain are transmitted through the skin 2. the ability to experience physical sensation 3. an awareness; sensation [a *feeling* of pain] 4. an emotion 5. [*pl.*] sensitivities; sensibilities [to hurt one's *feelings*] 6. sympathy or pity 7. *a)* an opinion or sentiment *b)* a premonition [a *feeling* of doom] 8. air; atmosphere [the lonely *feeling* of the city] 9. a natural ability or sensitive appreciation 10. the emotional quality in a work of art —**feel´ing·ly** *adv.*

feet (fēt) *n.* *pl. of* FOOT —**have feet of clay** to reveal weaknesses not previously known —**have one's feet on the ground** to be practical, realistic, etc. —**on one's feet** firmly established —**sit at the feet of** to be an admiring disciple or pupil of —**stand on one's own feet** to be independent —**sweep** (or **carry**) **off one's feet** 1. to fill with enthusiasm 2. to impress deeply

feign (fān) *vt.* [< OFr. *feindre* < L. *fingere,* to shape] 1. to make up (a story, excuse, etc.); fabricate 2. to make a false

show of; pretend —*vi.* to pretend; dissemble —**feigned** *adj.* —**feign´er** *n.* —**feign´ing·ly** *adv.*

feint[1] (fānt) *n.* [< Fr. pp. of *feindre:* see prec.] 1. a false show; sham 2. a pretended blow or attack intended to take the opponent off his guard, as in boxing or fencing —*vi., vt.* to deliver (such a blow or attack)

feint[2] (fānt)' *adj.* having lines ruled across the width of the page

feld·spar (feld´spär´, fel´-) *n.* [< G. < *Feld,* field + *Spat*(*h*), spar] any of several crystalline minerals made up of aluminium silicates with sodium, potassium, or calcium, usually glassy and moderately hard —**feld·spath´ic** (-spa´th ik), **feld·spa·th´ose** (-spath´ ōs) *adj.*

fe·lic·i·tate (fə lis´ə tāt´) *vt.* -tat´ed, -tat´ing [< L. pp. of *felicitare* < *felix,* happy] to wish happiness to —**fe·lic´i·ta´tion** *n.* —**fe·lic´i·ta´tor** *n.*

fe·lic·i·tous (-təs) *adj.* [< ff. + -OUS] 1. used or expressed in a way suitable to the occasion; appropriate 2. having the knack of appropriate and pleasing expression —**fe·lic´i·tous·ly** *adv.* —**fe·lic´i·tous·ness** *n.*

fe·lic·i·ty (-tē) *n.,* *pl.* -ties [< OFr. < L. < *felix* (gen. *felicis*), happy] 1. happiness; bliss 2. anything producing happiness 3. a quality of appropriate and pleasing expression in writing, speaking, etc. 4. an apt expression or thought

fe·line (fē´līn) *adj.* [< L. < *felis,* cat] 1. of a cat or the cat family 2. catlike; esp., *a)* sly, stealthy, etc. *b)* sleekly graceful —*n.* any animal of the cat family, including the cat, lion, panther, tiger, etc. —**fe´line·ly** *adv.* —**fe´line·ness, fe·lin·i·ty** (fi lin´ə tē) *n.*

fell[1] (fel) *pt. of* FALL

fell[2] (fel) *vt.* [OE. *fellan*] 1. to make fall; knock down 2. to cut down (a tree) 3. to turn over (the rough edge of a seam) and sew down flat on the underside —*n.* 1. the trees cut down in one season 2. a felled seam —**fell´a·ble** *adj.* —**fell´er** *n.*

fell[3] (fel) *adj.* [< OFr. < ML. *fello:* see FELON[1]] 1. fierce; terrible; cruel 2. [Archaic] causing death; deadly [a *fell* plague] —**at one fell swoop** with one hasty and destructive action —**fell´ness** *n.*

fell[4] (fel) *n.* [OE. *fel*] an animal's hide or skin

fell[5] (fel) *n.* [< Scand.] a moor; down

fel·lah (fel´ə) *n.,* *pl.* **fel´lahs;** Ar. **fel·la·heen, fel·la·hin** (fel´ə hēn´) [< Ar. < *falāha,* to plough] a peasant or farm labourer in Egypt or some other countries where Arabic is spoken

fel·la·ti·o (fe lāt´ē ō, -lāsh´-) *n.* [< L. *fellatus,* pp. of *fellare,* to suck] stimulation of the penis by the partner's mouth

fel·loe (fel´ō) *n.* same as FELLY

fel·low (fel´ō, -ə) *n.* [< Late OE. *feolaga,* partner < *feoh* (see FEE) + *laga,* a laying down] 1. a companion; associate 2. one of the same class or rank; equal 3. either of a pair of corresponding things; mate 4. a graduate student holding a fellowship in a university 5. a member of a learned society 6. at some British and U.S. universities, a member of the governing body 7. [Colloq.] *a)* a man or boy *b)* a person; one [a *fellow* must eat] 8. [Colloq.] a suitor; beau —*adj.* having the same ideas, position, work, etc.; associated [*fellow* workers]

fellow feeling 1. sympathy for others, usually arising from a common experience 2. a sense of common interest

fel·low·ship (-ship´) *n.* 1. companionship; friendly association 2. a mutual sharing, as of activity, etc. 3. a group of people with the same interests 4. an endowment, or a sum of money paid from it, for the support of a graduate student, scholar, etc., doing advanced study 5. the rank or position of a fellow in a university or college

fellow traveller a person who espouses the cause of a party without being a member

fel·ly (fel´ē) *n.,* *pl.* -lies [OE. *felg*] the rim of a spoked wheel, or a segment of the rim

fel·on[1] (fel´ən) *n.* [< OFr. < ML. *felo,* earlier *fello* < ?] *Law* a person guilty of a major crime; criminal —*adj.* [Poet.] wicked; base

fel·on[2] (fel´ən) *n.* [< ? same base as prec.] a painful, pus-producing infection at the end of a finger or toe, near the nail

fe·lo·ni·ous (fə lō´nē əs) *adj.* 1. [Poet.] wicked; base 2. *Law* of, like, or constituting a felony —**fe·lo´ni·ous·ly** *adv.* —**fe·lo´ni·ous·ness** *n.*

fel·o·ny (fel´ə nē) *n.,* *pl.* -nies [< OFr. < ML. < *felo,* FELON[1]] a major crime, as murder, arson, rape, etc.

fel·spar (fel´spär´) *n.* same as FELDSPAR

felt[1] (felt) *n.* [OE.] 1. a fabric of wool, often mixed with fur, cotton, rayon, etc., the fibres being worked together by pressure, heat, chemical action, etc.: also **felt´ing** 2. anything like felt, with a fuzzy, springy surface 3. anything made of felt —*adj.* made of felt —*vt.* 1. *a)* to make into felt *b)* to cover with felt 2. to mat (fibres) together —*vi.* to become matted together

felt[2] (felt) *pt. and pp. of* FEEL

fe·luc·ca (fə luk´ə, -lळ´kə) *n.* [< It. *feluca,* prob. < Ar.] a small, narrow ship propelled by oars or lateen sails, used esp. in the Mediterranean

fem. feminine

fe·male (fē'māl) *adj.* [< OFr. < L. dim. of *femina*, a woman] **1.** designating or of the sex that produces ova and bears offspring **2.** of, like, or suitable to members of this sex; feminine **3.** of women or girls **4.** having a hollow part shaped to receive a corresponding inserted part (called *male*): said of electric sockets, etc. **5.** *Bot.* having a pistil and no stamen —*n.* a female person, animal, or plant —**fe'-male·ness** *n.*

female impersonator a male entertainer who dresses as, and imitates, a woman

fem·i·nine (fem'ə nin) *adj.* [< OFr. < L. < *femina*, woman] **1.** of women or girls **2.** having qualities regarded as characteristic of women and girls **3.** suitable to or characteristic of a woman **4.** effeminate: said of a man **5.** *Gram.* designating or of the gender of words referring to females or things orig. regarded as female **6.** *Prosody* designating or of a rhyme of two or three syllables with only the first stressed (Ex.: danger, stranger) —*n.* *Gram.* **1.** the feminine gender **2.** a word or form in this gender —**fem'i·nine·ly** *adv.* —**fem'i·nin'i·ty, fem'i·nine·ness** *n.*

fem·i·nism (fem'ə niz'm) *n.* **1.** the principle that women should have political, economic, and social rights equal to those of men **2.** the movement to win these rights —**fem'-i·nist** *n., adj.* —**fem'i·nis'tic** *adj.*

fem·i·nize (fem'ə niz') *vt., vi.* -**nized'**, -**niz'ing** to make or become feminine or effeminate —**fem'i·ni·za'tion** *n.*

‡**femme fa·tale** (fäm fätäl') [Fr., lit., deadly woman] an alluring woman, esp. one who leads men to their ruin

fem·to- (fem'tō) [< Dan. *femten*, fifteen] a combining form meaning the factor 10^{-15} [*femtosecond*]

fe·mur (fē'mər) *n., pl.* **fe'murs, fem·o·ra** (fem'ər ə) [ModL. < L., thigh] same as THIGHBONE —**fem'o·ral** *adj.*

fen¹ (fen) *n.* [OE.] an area of low, flat, marshy land; swamp; bog —**The Fens** the flat, low-lying land around the Wash; formerly marsh, now fertile agricultural land —**fen'-ny** *adj.*

fen² (fen) *n.* see MONETARY UNITS, table (China)

fe·na·gle (fə nā'g'l) *vi., vt.* -**gled**, -**gling** same as FINAGLE —**fe·na'gler** *n.*

fence (fens) *n.* [ME. *fens*, short for *defens*, DEFENCE] **1.** a barrier of posts, wire, rails, etc., used as a boundary or means of protection or confinement **2.** the art of self-defence with foil, sabre, etc.; fencing **3.** *a)* one who buys and sells stolen goods *b)* a place for such dealings —*vt.* **fenced, fenc'ing 1.** to enclose, restrict, etc. with or as with a fence (with *in, off,* etc.) **2.** to keep (*out*) by or as by a fence —*vi.* **1.** to practise the art of fencing **2.** to avoid giving a direct reply; be evasive (with) **3.** to buy or sell stolen goods —**sit on the fence** to avoid taking sides; to be uncommitted —**fence'less** *adj.* —**fenc'er** *n.*

fen·ci·ble (fen'sə b'l) *n.* [ME. < defensible] [Obs.] a person who undertook military service in defence of his homeland only

fenc·ing (fen'siŋ) *n.* **1.** the art of fighting with a foil or other sword **2.** *a)* material for making fences *b)* a system of fences

fend (fend) *vt.* [ME. *fenden*, short for *defenden*, DEFEND] [Archaic] to defend —*vi.* to resist; parry —**fend for oneself** to get along without help from others —**fend off** to ward off; turn aside

fend·er (fen'dər) *n.* anything that fends off or protects something else; specif., *a)* a low metal divider placed in front of a fireplace to confine falling coal, etc. *b)* a cushion-like device, such as a tyre, hung over a ship's side when moored to protect against damage from a dock, etc.

fe·nes·tra (fi nes'trə) *n., pl.* -**trae** (-trē) [L., a window] **1.** a small opening, as in the inner wall of the middle ear **2.** a small, transparent spot, as in the wings of some insects **3.** any small opening in a membrane —**fe·nes'tral** *adj.*

fen·es·trat·ed (fen'ə strāt'id) *adj.* [< L. *fenestratus*, furnished with openings] **1.** having windows, openings, or perforations **2.** *Biol.* having fenestrae Also **fen·es'trate** (-trit, -trāt)

fen·es·tra·tion (fen'ə strā'shən) *n.* [ult. < L. *fenestra*, window] **1.** the arrangement of windows and doors in a building **2.** the surgical operation of making an opening into the inner ear in certain cases of otosclerosis

Fe·ni·an (fē'nē ən, fēn'yən) *n.* [< pl. of Ir. Gael. *Fiann*, the old militia of Ireland] a member of a secret Irish revolutionary group formed about 1858 to free Ireland from British rule —*adj.* of the Fenians —**Fe'ni·an·ism** *n.*

fen·nec (fen'ek) *n.* [Ar. *fanak*] a small, tawny African fox with very large pointed ears

fen·nel (fen''l) *n.* [< OE. < L. *feniculum*, dim. of *fenum*, hay] a tall herb of the parsley family, with yellow flowers: its aromatic seeds are used as a seasoning and in medicine

fen·u·greek (fen'yoo grēk) *n.* [< L. *faenum Graecum*, Greek hay] a plant of the legume family, native to SE Europe and W Asia

feoff (fef, fēf) *vt.* [< Anglo-Fr. < OFr. < *fieu, fief*] to give or sell a fief to —*n.* a fief —**feoff'ee** *n.* —**feoff'ment** *n.* —**feof'for, feoff'er** *n.*

-fer (fər) [< Fr. or L. < *ferre*, BEAR¹] a suffix meaning bearer, producer [*conifer*]

fe·ral (fir'əl) *adj.* [< L. < *ferus*, fierce + -AL] **1.** untamed; wild **2.** savage; brutal

fer-de-lance (fer'də läns') *n.* [Fr., iron tip of a lance] a large, poisonous snake, related to the rattlesnake, found in tropical America

fer·e·to·ry (fer'ə tər ē) *n.* [< L. *feretrum*, a bier] **1.** a shrine, usually portable, for a saint's relics **2.** a chapel in which this is kept

fe·ri·a (fir'ē ə) *n.* [LL. : see FAIR²] [Eccles.] a weekday, other than a Saturday, on which no feast occurs —**fe'ri·al** *adj.*

fer·ma·ta (fer mät'ə) *n.* [It. < *fermare*, to stop] *Music* **1.** the holding of a tone or rest beyond its written value, at the performer's discretion **2.** the sign (⌢) or (⌣) indicating this

fer·ment (fur'ment; *for v.* fər ment') *n.* [< OFr. < L. *fermentum* < *fervere*, to boil] **1.** a substance or organism causing fermentation, as yeast, bacteria, etc. **2.** same as FERMENTATION **3.** a state of excitement or agitation —*vt.* **1.** to cause fermentation in **2.** to excite; agitate —*vi.* **1.** to be in the process of fermentation **2.** to be excited or agitated —**fer·ment'a·ble** *adj.*

fer·men·ta·tion (fur'mən tā'shən, -men-) *n.* **1.** the breakdown of complex molecules in organic compounds, caused by a ferment [bacteria curdle milk by *fermentation*] **2.** excitement; agitation —**fer·ment·a·tive** (fər men'tə tiv) *adj.*

fer·mi (fur'mē, fer'-) *n.* [after E. *Fermi* (1901-54), It. nuclear physicist] a unit of length, equivalent to 10^{-13} cm, used in nuclear physics

fer·mi·on (fur'mē ən) *n.* [< *Fermi* (see prec.) + -ON] a subatomic particle, such as an electron, proton, or neutron, that obeys the PAULI EXCLUSION PRINCIPLE

fer·mi·um (fur'mē əm) *n.* [< *Fermi*, see FERMI] a radioactive chemical element: symbol, Fm; at. wt., 257(?); at. no., 100

fern (furn) *n.* [OE. *fearn*] any of a widespread class of nonflowering plants having roots, stems, and fronds, and reproducing by spores instead of by seeds —**fern'y** *adj.*

fern·er·y (fur'nər ē) *n., pl.* -**er·ies** a place where ferns are grown; collection of growing ferns

fern-tree (furn'trē) *n.* [Aust.] any of various very large, tree-like ferns

fe·ro·cious (fə rō'shəs) *adj.* [< L. *ferox* (gen. *ferocis*) < *ferus*, fierce + -OUS] **1.** fierce; savage; violently cruel **2.** [Colloq.] very great [a *ferocious* appetite] —**fe·ro'cious·ly** *adv.* —**fe·ro'cious·ness** *n.*

fe·roc·i·ty (fə ros'ə tē) *n., pl.* -**ties** wild force or cruelty; ferociousness

-fer·ous (fər əs) [L. *-fer* < *ferre*, BEAR¹ + -OUS] a suffix meaning bearing, producing [*coniferous*]

fer·rate (fer'āt) *n.* [< L. *ferrum*, iron] *Chem.* a salt formed by the union of ferric acid and a base

fer·ret (fer'it) *n.* [< OFr. < LL. dim. of *furo* < L. *fur*, thief] a small, weasellike animal, easily tamed and used for hunting rabbits, rats, etc. —*vt.* **1.** to force out of hiding as with a ferret **2.** to search for persistently and discover (facts, etc.); search (*out*) —*vi.* **1.** to hunt with ferrets **2.** to search around —**fer'ret·er** *n.* —**fer'ret·y** *adj.*

ferri- a combining form meaning containing ferric iron: see FERRO-

fer·ri·age (fer'ē ij) *n.* [< FERRY + -AGE] **1.** transportation by ferry **2.** the charge for this

fer·ric (fer'ik) *adj.* [FERR(O) + -IC] **1.** of, containing, or derived from iron **2.** *Chem.* designating or of iron with a valence of three, or compounds containing such iron

Fer·ris wheel (fer'is) [after G. *Ferris* (1859-1896), U.S. engineer who invented it] a large, upright wheel revolving on a fixed axle and having seats hanging from the frame: used in fairgrounds, etc.

fer·ro- [< L. *ferrum*, iron] a combining form meaning: **1.** iron [*ferromagnetic*] **2.** iron and [*ferromanganese*] **3.** containing ferrous iron

fer·ro·con·crete (fer'ō kon'krēt) *n.* same as REINFORCED CONCRETE

fer·ro·mag·net·ic (-mag net'ik) *adj.* designating a ma·terial, as iron, nickel, or cobalt, having a high magnetic permeability —**fer'ro·mag'net·ism** *n.*

fer·ro·man·ga·nese (-maŋ'gə nēs', -nēz') *n.* an alloy of iron and manganese, used for making hard steel

fer·rous (fer'əs) *adj.* [< L. *ferrum*, iron + -OUS] **1.** of, containing, or derived from iron **2.** *Chem.* designating or of iron with a valence of two, or compounds containing it

fer·ru·gi·nous (fə rōō'ji nəs) *adj.* [< L. < *ferrugo*, iron rust < *ferrum*, iron] **1.** of, containing, or having the nature of, iron **2.** having the colour of iron rust; reddish-brown

fer·rule (fer'əl, -ool) *n.* [< OFr. < L. *viriola*, dim. of *viriae*, bracelets] a metal ring or cap put around the end of a cane, tool handle, etc. to give added strength —*vt.* **-ruled, -rul·ing** to furnish with a ferrule Also **fer′rel**

fer·ry (fer′ē) *vt.* **-ried, -ry·ing** [OE. *ferian*, to carry] 1. to take across a river, etc. in a boat 2. to cross (a river, etc.) on a ferry 3. to deliver (aeroplanes) by flying to the destination —*vi.* to cross a river, etc. by ferry —*n., pl.* **-ries** 1. a system for carrying people, cars, etc. across a river, etc. by boat 2. a boat (**fer′ry·boat′**) used for this, or the place where it docks on either shore 3. the delivery of aeroplanes to their destination by flying them —**fer′ry·man** *n., pl.* **-men**

fer·tile (fur′tīl) *adj.* [< OFr. < L. *fertilis* < stem of *ferre*, BEAR[1]] 1. producing abundantly; rich in resources or invention; fruitful 2. able to produce young, seeds, fruit, etc. 3. capable of developing into a new individual; fertilized —**fer′tile·ly** *adv.* —**fer′tile·ness** *n.*

Fertile Crescent an area of fertile land in the Middle East, extending in a semicircle from Israel to the Persian Gulf, where early civilisations developed

fer·til·i·ty (fər til′ə tē) *n.* the quality, state, or degree of being fertile; fecundity

fertility drug a drug which induces the production of ova in women previously infertile

fer·til·ize (fur′til īz′) *vt.* **-ized′, -iz′ing** 1. to make fertile; make fruitful or productive 2. to spread fertilizer on 3. to make (the female reproductive cell or female individual) fruitful by introducing the male germ cell; impregnate —**fer′til·iz′a·ble** *adj.* —**fer′til·i·za′tion** *n.*

fer·til·iz·er (-ī′zər) *n.* one that fertilizes; specif., manure, chemicals, etc. put in soil to improve the quality or quantity of plant growth

fer·u·la (fer′yoo lə, -oo-) *n., pl.* **-lae** (-lē) [L., giant fennel] 1. any of a genus of umbelliferous plants 2. *same as* FERULE

fer·ule (fer′əl, -ool) *n.* [L. *ferula*, rod] a flat stick or ruler used for punishing children —*vt.* **-uled, -ul·ing** to strike with a ferule

fer·vent (fur′vənt) *adj.* [< L. prp. of *fervere*, to glow, boil] 1. hot; burning; glowing 2. having or showing great warmth of feeling; intensely earnest —**fer′ven·cy** (-vən sē) *n.* —**fer′vent·ly** *adv.*

fer·vid (fur′vəd) *adj.* [< L. < *fervere:* see prec.] 1. hot; glowing 2. impassioned; fervent; ardent —**fer′vid·ly** *adv.* —**fer′vid·ness** *n.*

fer·vour (fur′vər) *n.* [< OFr. < L. < *fervere:* see FERVENT] 1. intense heat 2. great warmth of emotion; ardour; zeal U.S. sp. **fer′vor**

fes·cue (fes′kyoo) *n.* [< OFr. < L. *festuca*, a straw] a tough grass used for pasture or lawns

fess, fesse (fes) *n.* [< OFr. < L. *fascia*, a band] *Heraldry* a horizontal band forming the middle third of an escutcheon

fes·tal (fes′t′l) *adj.* [< L. *festum*, feast] of or like a joyous celebration; festive —**fes′tal·ly** *adv.*

fes·ter (fes′tər) *vi.* [< OFr. < L. *fistula*, ulcer] 1. to form pus 2. to cause irritation; rankle 3. to decay —*vt.* 1. to cause pus to form in 2. to make rankle

fes·ti·val (fes′tə v′l) *n.* [< OFr. < ML. < L. *festivus:* see ff.] 1. a time or day of feasting or celebration 2. a celebration or series of performances of a certain kind [a Bach *festival*] 3. merrymaking; festivity —*adj.* of, for, or fit for a festival

fes·tive (fes′tiv) *adj.* [< L. *festivus* < *festum*, feast] of or for a feast or festival; merry; joyous —**fes′tive·ly** *adv.* —**fes′tive·ness** *n.*

fes·tiv·i·ty (fes tiv′ə tē) *n., pl.* **-ties** 1. merrymaking; gaiety 2. a) a festival b) [pl.] festive proceedings; things done in celebration

fes·toon (fes toon′) *n.* [< Fr. < It. *festone* < *festa*, feast] 1. a garland of flowers, leaves, etc. hanging in a loop or curve 2. any moulding or decoration like this —*vt.* to adorn with, form into, or join by festoons —**fes·toon′er·y** *n.*

fet·a (cheese) (fet′ə) [< ModGr. < It. *fetta*, a slice, ult. < L. *offa*, a piece] a white, soft cheese made in Greece from ewe's milk or goat's milk

fetch[1] (fech) *vt.* [OE. *feccan*] 1. to go after and come back with; bring; get 2. to cause to come; produce 3. to draw (a breath) or heave (a sigh, groan, etc.) 4. to bring as a price; sell for 5. [Colloq.] to deliver or deal (a blow, etc.) —*vi.* to go after things and bring them back —*n.* 1. a fetching 2. a trick; dodge —**fetch and carry** to perform minor or menial tasks —**fetch up** 1. [Colloq.] to reach; stop 2. [Colloq.] to vomit

fetch[2] (fech) *n.* [< ?] the double or apparition of a living person

fetch·ing (-iŋ) *adj.* attractive; charming —**fetch′ing·ly** *adv.*

fête (fāt) *n.* [Fr. < OFr.: see FEAST] a festival; entertainment, esp. one held outdoors, with stalls, etc., to raise money for charity —*vt.* **fêt′ed, fêt′ing** to celebrate or honour with a fête; entertain

fet·id (fet′id, fēt′-) *adj.* [< L. *f(o)etidus* < *f(o)etere*, to stink] having a bad smell, as of decay; stinking —**fet′id·ly** *adv.* —**fet′id·ness** *n.*

fet·ish (fet′ish, fēt′-) *n.* [< Fr. < Port. *feitiço*, a charm < L. *facticius*, FACTITIOUS] 1. any object believed by

superstitious people to have magical power 2. any thing or activity to which one is irrationally devoted 3. *Psychiatry* any nonsexual object that evokes fetishism Also sp. **fet′ich**

fet·ish·ism (-iz′m) *n.* 1. worship of or belief in fetishes 2. *Psychiatry* an abnormal condition in which erotic feelings are excited by a nonsexual object, as a foot, glove, etc. Also sp. **fet′ich·ism** —**fet′ish·ist** *n.* —**fet′ish·is′tic** *adj.*

fet·lock (fet′lok′) *n.* [ME. *fitlok* < MDu. or MLowG.] 1. a tuft of hair on the back of the leg of a horse, donkey, etc., just above the hoof 2. the joint or projection bearing this tuft

fe·tor (fēt′ər, fē′tòr) *n.* [L. *fetor, foetor* < *foetere:* see FETID] a strong, disagreeable smell; stench

fet·ter (fet′ər) *n.* [OE. *feter* < base of *fot*, foot] 1. a shackle or chain for the feet 2. anything that holds in check; restraint —*vt.* 1. to bind with fetters; shackle; chain 2. to hold in check; restrain

fet·tle (fet′′l) *vt.* **-tled, -tling** [ME. *fetlen*, to make ready, prob. < OE. *fetel*, belt] [Dial.] to tidy up —*n.* condition of body and mind [in fine *fettle*]

fe·tus (fēt′əs) *n.* *U.S. var. sp.* of FOETUS

feud[1] (fyood) *n.* [OFr. *faide* < Frank. *faida*] a bitter, long-continued, and deadly quarrel, esp. between clans or families—*vi.* to carry on a feud; quarrel —**feu′dal** *adj.* —**feud′ist** *n.*

feud[2] (fyood) *n.* [< ML. *feodum* < OHG. *feho*, cattle + *od*, wealth] land held from a feudal lord in return for service; fief

feu·dal (fyood′′l) *adj.* 1. of a feud (land) 2. of or like feudalism —**feu′dal·ly** *adv.*

feu·dal·ism (-iz′m) *n.* the economic, political, and social system (**feudal system**) in medieval Europe, in which land, worked by serfs who were bound to it, was held by vassals in exchange for military and other services given to overlords —**feu′dal·ist** *n.* —**feu′dal·is′tic** *adj.*

feu·dal·i·ty (fyoo dal′ə tē) *n.* [< Fr.] 1. the state of being feudal 2. a feudal holding; fief

feu·dal·ize (fyoo′də līz′) *vt.* **-ized′, -iz′ing** to make feudal; establish feudalism in —**feu′dal·i·za′tion** *n.*

feu·da·to·ry (fyoo′də tər ē) *n., pl.* **-ries** 1. a feudal vassal 2. a feudal estate; fief —*adj.* 1. of the feudal relationship between vassal and lord 2. owing feudal allegiance (*to*)

‡**feuil·le·ton** (fö yə tōn′) *n.* [Fr. < *feuillet*, a leaf] 1. that part of a French newspaper containing fiction, light reviews, etc. 2. any such writing

fe·ver (fē′vər) *n.* [< OE. *fefer* & OFr. *fievre*, both < L. *febris*] 1. a state of abnormally increased body temperature, often accompanied by a quickened pulse, delirium, etc. 2. any of various diseases characterized by a high fever 3. a condition of nervousness —*vt.* to cause fever in —**fe′vered** *adj.*

fe·ver·few (-fyoo′) *n.* [< OE., ult. < L. *febris*, fever + *fugia* < *fugare*, to drive away] a bushy plant of the composite family, with small, white heads of flowers

fe·ver·ish (-ish) *adj.* 1. having fever, esp. slight fever 2. of, like, or caused by fever 3. causing fever 4. greatly excited or agitated Also **fe′ver·ous** —**fe′ver·ish·ly** *adv.* —**fe′ver·ish·ness** *n.*

fever pitch a condition of intense excitement

fever therapy formerly, treatment of disease by an artificially induced fever

few (fyoo) *adj.* [OE. *feawe, pl.*] not many; a small number of —*pron., n.* not many; a small number —**a good few, quite a few** [Colloq.] a rather large number —**the few** a small select group —**few′ness** *n.*

fey (fā) *adj.* [OE. *fæge*, fated] 1. [Archaic or Scot.] a) fated to die b) highly excited 2. strange, as in being eccentric, puckish, visionary, etc. —**fey′ness** *n.*

fez (fez) *n., pl.* **fez′zes** [Fr. < Turk. < *Fez*, city in Morocco] a conical felt hat, usually red, with a black tassel hanging from its flat crown: formerly the Turkish national headdress of men

ff. 1. folios 2. following (pages, lines, entry, etc.) 3. fortissimo

fi·a·cre (fē à′kr) *n.* [Fr., after the Hotel St. *Fiacre* in Paris] a small carriage for hire

fi·an·cé (fē än′sā) *n.* [Fr., pp. of *fiancer* < OFr. *fiance*, a promise] the man to whom a woman is engaged to be married

fi·an·cée (fē än′sā) *n.* [Fr., fem. pp. of *fiancer:* see prec.] the woman to whom a man is engaged to be married

FEZ

fi·as·co (fē as′kō) *n., pl.* **-coes, -cos** [Fr. < It. (*far*) *fiasco*, to fail < *fiasco*, bottle] a complete failure; esp., an ambitious project that ends as a ridiculous failure

fi·at (fī′at, -ət) *n.* [L., let it be done] 1. an order issued by legal authority; decree 2. a sanction; authorization 3. any arbitrary order

fib (fib) *n.* [? ult. < *fable*] a lie about something unimportant —*vi.* **fibbed, fib′bing** to tell such a lie or lies —**fib′ber** *n.*

Fib·o·nac·ci sequence (fib ô nä′chi) [< Leonardo *Fibonacci*, fl. 1200, It. mathematician] the infinite series of numbers, 0, 1, 1, 2, 3, 5, 8, etc., in which each is the sum of the previous two

fi·bre (fī′bər) *n.* [< Fr. < L. *fibra*] 1. *a)* a slender, threadlike structure that combines with others to form animal or vegetable tissue *b)* the tissue so formed [muscle *fibre*] 2. *a)* any substance that can be separated into threadlike structures for weaving, etc. *b)* such a threadlike structure 3. a threadlike root 4. the texture of something 5. character or nature [a man of strong moral *fibre*] —**fi′bre·like′** *adj.*

fi·bre·board (-bôrd′) *n.* a flexible boardlike material made from pressed fibres of wood, etc., used in building

fi·bre·glass (-gläs′) *n.* a material made of finespun filaments of glass, and used for textiles, insulation, etc.

fibre optics the use of bundles of long, transparent, glass fibres in transmitting electromagnetic impulses, esp. optical images

fi·bril (fī′brəl) *n.* 1. a small fibre 2. a root hair —**fi′bril·lar** (-brəl ər), **fi′bril·lar·y** (-brə lər e) *adj.* —**fi′bril·lose** (-brə lōs′) *adj.*

fi·bril·la·tion (fib′rə lā′shən, fī′brə-)· *n.* [< FIBRIL + -ATION] a rapid series of contractions of the heart, causing weak and irregular heartbeats —**fi′bril·late** *vi.*

fi·brin (fī′brən) *n.* [FIBR(E) + -IN¹] an elastic, threadlike, insoluble protein formed in the clotting of blood —**fi′brin·ous** *adj.*

fi·brin·o·gen (fī brin′ə jən, -jen′) *n.* [< FIBRIN] a soluble protein occurring in blood plasma that is converted to fibrin when the blood clots

fi·bro- [< L. *fibra*, fibre] a *combining form* meaning of fibrous matter or structure: also, before a vowel, **fibr-**

fi·broid (fī′broid) *adj.* [FIBR(O)- + -OID] like, composed of, or forming fibrous tissue [*fibroid* tumours]

fi·bro·in (fī′brō in) *n.* [FIBRO- + -IN¹] a tough, elastic protein that is the main component of spiders' webs and raw silk

fi·bro·ma (fī brō′mə) *n., pl.* **-mas, -ma·ta** (-mə tə) [Mod L. FIBR(O)- + -OMA] a nonmalignant fibrous tumour —**fi·bro′·ma·tous** (-mə təs) *adj.*

fi·bro·sis (fī brō′sis) *n.* [FIBR(O)- + -OSIS] an abnormal increase in the amount of fibrous connective tissue in an organ or tissue —**fi·brot′ic** (-brot′ik) *adj.*

fi·bro·si·tis (fī′brə sīt′is) *n.* [Mod L. < *fibrosus*, FIBROUS + -ITIS] a rheumatic condition caused by the imflammation of the fibrous tissues

fi·brous (fī′brəs) *adj.* 1. containing or composed of fibres 2. like fibre

fib·u·la (fib′yoo lə) *n., pl.* **-lae′** (-lē′), **-las** [L., a clasp] 1. the long, thin, outer bone of the human leg below the knee 2. a similar bone in the hind leg of other animals —**fib′u·lar** *adj.*

-fic (fik) [< Fr. < -*fique* < L. -*ficus* < *facere*, to make] a *suffix* meaning making, creating [terrific]

-fi·ca·tion (fi kā′shən) [< Fr. & L., ult. < L. *facere*, to make] a *suffix* meaning a making, creating, causing [glorification]

fich·u (fish′oo) *n.* [Fr.] a three-cornered lace or muslin shawl for women, worn with the ends fastened or crossed in front

fick·le (fik′′l) *adj.* [OE. *ficol*] changeable or unstable in affection, interest, etc. —**fick′le·ness** *n.*

fic·tile (fik′til) *adj.* [L. *fictilis* < pp. of *fingere*, to form] 1. that can be moulded; malleable 2. formed of moulded clay 3. of pottery or ceramics

fic·tion (fik′shən) *n.* [< OFr. < L. *fictio*, a making < pp. of *fingere*, to form, mould] 1. anything made up or imagined, as a statement, story, etc. 2. *a)* any literary work portraying imaginary characters and events, as a novel, story, or play *b)* such works collectively 3. *Law* something accepted as fact for convenience, although not necessarily true —**fic′tion·al, fic′tive** *adj.* —**fic′tion·al·ly** *adv.*

fic·tion·al·ize (-′l īz′) *vt.* -**ized′**, -**iz′ing** to deal with (historical events, etc.) as fiction: also **fic′tion·ize′**—**fic′·tion·al·i·za′tion** *n.*

fic·ti·tious (fik tish′əs) *adj.* 1. of or like fiction; imaginary 2. not real; pretended 3. assumed for disguise or deception [a *fictitious* name] —**fic·ti′tious·ly** *adv.* —**fic·ti′tious·ness** *n.*

fid (fid) *n.* [< ?] 1. a hard, tapering pin for separating the strands of rope in splicing 2. a bar or pin for supporting something; specif., a square bar for supporting a topmast

-fid (fid) [< L. < *findere*, to cleave] a *combining form* meaning split or separated into parts

fid·dle (fid′′l) *n.* [OE. *fithele*] any stringed instrument played with a bow, esp. the violin —*vt.* -**dled**, -**dling** [Colloq.] to play (a tune) on a fiddle —*vi.* 1. [Colloq.] to play on a fiddle 2. to tamper or tinker (*with*), esp. in a nervous way —**fiddle around** [Colloq.] to pass time aimlessly —**fit as a fiddle** in excellent health —**play second fiddle** to take a subordinate position —**fid′dler** *n.*

fid·dle-fad·dle (fid′′l fad′′l) *n.* a triviality —*interj.* nonsense! —*vi.* to fuss; waste time

fiddler (crab) a small, burrowing crab, the male of which has one claw much larger than the other

fid·dle·stick (fid′′l stik′) *n.* 1. the bow for a fiddle 2. a trifle; mere nothing

fid·dle·sticks (-stiks′) *interj.* nonsense!

fid·dling (fid′liŋ) *adj.* trifling; futile

fid·dly (fid′lē) *adj.* troublesome and time consuming [a *fiddly* job]

FIDDLER CRAB
(width to 3.25 cm; length to 2.54 cm)

Fi·de·i De·fen·sor (fī dā′ē dā fen′-sôr, fi′dē ī di fen′sôr) [L., of the Faith] title given to Henry VIII by the pope: it appears on British coins issued before decimalization as *Fid.Def.*, and now as *F.D.*

fi·del·i·ty (fə del′ə tē) *n., pl.* -**ties** [< OFr. < L. < *fides*, FAITH] 1. faithful devotion to duty, obligations, or vows 2. accuracy of a description, translation, sound reproduction, etc.

fidg·et (fij′it) *n.* [< ? ON. *fikja*] 1. a being restless, nervous, or uneasy 2. a fidgety person —*vi.* to move about in a restless, nervous, or uneasy way —*vt.* to make restless or uneasy —**the fidgets** restless, uneasy feelings or movements —**fidg′et·i·ness** *n.* —**fidg′et·y** *adj.*

fi·du·ci·ar·y (fi dyoo′shē ər ē, -shə rē) *adj.* [< L. < *fiducia*, trust < *fidere*: see FAITH] 1. designating or of one who holds something in trust for another [a *fiduciary* guardian for a child] 2. held in trust [*fiduciary* property] 3. valuable only because of public confidence: said of certain paper money —*n., pl.* -**ar·ies** a trustee

fie (fī) *interj.* [< OFr., of echoic origin] for shame!: now often used in mock reproach

fief (fēf) *n.* [Fr.: see FEE] 1. under feudalism, heritable land held from a lord in return for service 2. the right to hold such land

field (fēld) *n.* [OE. *feld*] 1. a wide stretch of open land; plain 2. a piece of cleared land for raising crops or pasturing livestock 3. a piece of land for some particular purpose [a landing *field*] 4. an area of land producing some natural resource [a gold *field*] 5. any wide, unbroken expanse [a *field* of ice] 6. *a)* a battlefield *b)* a battle 7. an area of military operations 8. *a)* an area where practical work is done, away from the central office, laboratory, etc. *b)* a realm of knowledge or of special work [the *field* of electronics] 9. an area of observation, as in a microscope 10. the background, as on a flag or coin 11. an area where games and athletic events are held 12. all the entrants in a contest 13. *Cricket a)* a collective name for fielders *b)* the arrangement of the fielders [an attacking *field*] 14. *Physics* a space within which magnetic or electrical lines of force are active: in full, **field of force** —*adj.* 1. of, operating in, or held on the field or fields 2. living or growing in fields —*vt. Cricket,* etc. 1. to stop or catch or to catch and throw (a ball) in play 2. to put (a player) into a field position —*vi. Cricket,* etc. to play as a fielder —**play the field** to explore every opportunity —**take** (or **leave**) **the field** to begin (or withdraw from) activity in a game, military operation, etc.

field artillery movable artillery capable of accompanying an army into battle

field day 1. a day of military exercises and display, or of athletic events 2. a day of enjoyably exciting events or highly successful activity

field·er (-ər) *n. Cricket,* etc. a player who is fielding

field event *Athletics* any event, as the high jump, shot put, etc. that takes place on a field or similar area rather than a running track

field·fare (-fer) *n.* [< ?] a species of N European thrush, common in Britain in wintertime

field glass a small, portable, binocular telescope: *usually used in pl.* (**field glasses**)

field hospital a temporary military hospital near a battlefield

field magnet the magnet used to create and maintain the magnetic field in a motor or generator

field marshal *see* MILITARY RANKS, table

field mouse any of several kinds of mice that live in fields

field officer a colonel, lieutenant colonel, or major in the army

field·piece (fēld′pēs′) *n.* a mobile artillery piece

fields·man (fēldz′mən) *n., pl.* -**men** (-mən) a fielder in cricket

field·sports (-spôrts) *n.pl.* outdoor sports such as hunting, racing, etc.

field·work (-wurk′) *n.* 1. any temporary fortification made by troops in the field 2. the work of collecting scientific data in the field —**field′work′er** *n.*

fiend (fēnd) *n.* [OE. *feond*] 1. an evil spirit; devil 2. an inhumanly wicked or cruel person 3. [Colloq.] a person addicted to some activity, habit, etc. [a fresh-air *fiend*] —**the Fiend** the Devil —**fiend′like′** *adj.*

fiend·ish (-ish) *adj.* **1.** of or like a fiend; devilish; inhumanly wicked or cruel **2.** extremely vexatious or difficult —**fiend'ish·ly** *adv.* —**fiend'ish·ness** *n.*

fierce (firs) *adj.* **fierc'er, fierc'est** [< OFr. < L. *ferus*, wild] **1.** of a violently cruel nature; savage [a *fierce* dog] **2.** violent; uncontrolled [a *fierce* storm] **3.** intensely eager; ardent [a *fierce* effort] **4.** [Colloq.] very distasteful, bad, etc. —**fierce'ly** *adv.* —**fierce'ness** *n.*

fi·er·y (fī'ər ē) *adj.* **-er·i·er, -er·i·est** [ME. *firi*] **1.** containing or consisting of fire **2.** like fire; glaring, hot, etc. **3.** characterized by strong emotion; ardent **4.** easily stirred up; excitable [a *fiery* nature] **5.** inflamed [a *fiery* sore] —**fi'er·i·ly** *adv.* —**fi'er·i·ness** *n.*

fi·es·ta (fē es'tə) *n.* [Sp. < VL. *festa:* see FEAST] **1.** a religious festival; esp., a saint's day **2.** any gala celebration; holiday

F.I.F.A. Federation of International Football Associations

fife (fīf) *n.* [< G. < MHG. < OHG. *pfifa*] a small, shrill-toned musical instrument resembling a flute —*vt., vi.* **fifed, fif'ing** to play on a fife —**fif'er** *n.*

fif·teen (fif'tēn') *adj.* [OE. *fiftene*] five more than ten —*n.* the cardinal number between fourteen and sixteen; 15; XV —**The Fifteen** the Jacobite Rebellion of 1715

fif·teenth (-tēnth') *adj.* **1.** preceded by fourteen others in a series; 15th **2.** designating any of the fifteen equal parts of something —*n.* **1.** the one following the fourteenth **2.** any of the fifteen equal parts of something; 1/15

fifth (fifth) *adj.* [< OE. < *fif*, five] **1.** preceded by four others in a series; 5th **2.** designating any of the five equal parts of something —*n.* **1.** the one following the fourth **2.** any of the five equal parts of something; 1/5 **3.** *Music a)* the fifth tone of an ascending diatonic scale, or a tone four degrees above or below a given tone *b)* the interval between two such tones, or a combination of them —**fifth'ly** *adv.*

fifth column [orig. (1936) applied to Franco sympathizers inside Madrid, then besieged by four of his columns on the outside] a group of people who give aid and support to the enemy from within their own country —**fifth columnist**

fifth wheel any superfluous person or thing

fif·ti·eth (fif'tē ith) *adj.* **1.** preceded by forty-nine others in a series; 50th **2.** designating any of the fifty equal parts of something —*n.* **1.** the one following the forty-ninth **2.** any of fifty equal parts of something; 1/50

fif·ty (fif'tē) *adj.* [OE. *fiftig*] five times ten —*n., pl.* **-ties** the cardinal number between forty-nine and fifty-one; 50; L —**the fifties** the numbers or years, as of a century, from fifty to fifty-nine

fif·ty-fif·ty (fif'tē fif'tē) *adj.* [Colloq.] equal; even —*adv.* [Colloq.] equally

fig (fig) *n.* [< OFr., ult. < L. *ficus*] **1.** a small, hollow, pear-shaped fruit with sweet, seed-filled flesh **2.** a tree bearing this fruit **3.** a trifle [not worth a *fig*]

fig. **1.** figurative(ly) **2.** figure(s)

fight (fīt) *vi.* **fought, fight'ing** [OE. *feohtan*] **1.** to take part in a physical struggle or battle, specif. in a boxing match **2.** to struggle or work hard in trying to overcome; contend —*vt.* **1.** to oppose physically, as with fists in boxing or in battle with weapons, etc. **2.** to struggle against or contend with, as by argument **3.** to engage in or carry on (a war, conflict, etc.) **4.** to gain by struggle [he *fought* his way up] **5.** to cause to fight; manage (a boxer, etc.) —*n.* **1.** a physical struggle; battle; combat **2.** any struggle, contest, or quarrel **3.** power or readiness to fight —**fight it out** to fight until one side is defeated —**fight off** to struggle to avoid —**fight shy of** keep aloof from; avoid

fight·er (-ər) *n.* **1.** one that fights or is inclined to fight **2.** a boxer; prizefighter **3.** a small, fast, highly manoeuvrable aircraft for aerial combat

fight·er-bomb·er (-bom'ər) *n.* a high performance aircraft that combines the roles of interceptor and bomber

fighting chance a chance of success dependent on a struggle

fighting cock **1.** a gamecock **2.** a pugnacious person

fighting fish *same as* BETTA

fig leaf **1.** a leaf from a fig tree **2.** a representation of a fig leaf used in sculpture, etc. to cover the genitals of nude figures **3.** device intended to hide anything regarded as shameful

fig·ment (fig'mənt) *n.* [< L. *figmentum* < *fingere*, to make, devise] something merely imagined or made up in the mind

fig·u·rant (fig'yoo rənt'; *Fr.* fē gü ran') *n.* [Fr., prp. of *figurer*, to represent] **1.** a member of a corps de ballet **2.** a supernumerary on the stage —**fig'u·rante** (-rənt'; *Fr.* -ränt') *n. fem.*

fig·u·ra·tion (fig'yoo rā'shən) *n.* **1.** a forming; shaping **2.** form; appearance **3.** a representing by or ornamenting with figures —**fig'u·ra'tion·al** *adj.*

fig·u·ra·tive (fig'yoor ə tiv) *adj.* **1.** representing by means of a figure or symbol **2.** not in its usual, literal, or exact sense or reference; metaphorical **3.** containing or using figures of speech —**fig'u·ra·tive·ly** *adv.* —**fig'u·ra·tive·ness** *n.*

fig·ure (fig'ər) *n.* [< OFr. < L. *figura* < *fingere*, to form] **1.** the outline or shape of something; form **2.** the human form **3.** a person seen or thought of in a specified way [a great social *figure*] **4.** a likeness of a person or thing **5.** an illustration; diagram; picture **6.** an artistic design in fabrics, etc.; pattern **7.** *a)* the symbol for a number [the *figure* 5] *b)* [pl.] arithmetic **8.** a sum of money **9.** *Dancing & Skating* a series or pattern of steps or movements **10.** *Geom.* a surface or space bounded on all sides by lines or planes **11.** *Music* a series of consecutive tones or chords forming a distinct group **12.** *Rhetoric* *same as* FIGURE OF SPEECH —*vt.* **-ured, -ur·ing** **1.** to represent in definite form **2.** to represent mentally; imagine **3.** to ornament with a design **4.** to compute with figures —*vi.* **1.** to appear prominently; be conspicuous **2.** to do arithmetic **3.** [U.S. Colloq.] to be as expected —**figure in** to be included [his name *figures in* the article] —**figure out** **1.** to solve; compute **2.** [U.S. Colloq.] understand; reason out —**figure up** to add; total —**fig'ur·er** *n.*

fig·ured (-erd) *adj.* **1.** shaped; formed **2.** having a design or pattern **3.** *Music* with numbers to indicate accompanying chords: said of the bass

fig·ure·head (fig'ər hed') *n.* **1.** a carved figure on the bow of a ship **2.** a person holding a high position but having no real power or authority

figure of speech an expression, as a metaphor or simile, using words in a nonliteral or unusual sense to add vividness, etc. to what is said

figure skating ice skating in which the performer traces various elaborate figures on the ice

fig·u·rine (fig'ə rēn') *n.* [Fr. < It. *figurina*] a small sculptured or moulded figure; statuette

fig·wort (fig'wʉrt') *adj.* designating a large family of plants including the foxglove, snapdragon, etc. —*n.* any of a genus of plants of the figwort family, with square stems and small flowers

fil·a·gree (fil'ə grē') *n., adj., vt.* **-greed', -gree'ing** *same as* FILIGREE

fil·a·ment (fil'ə mənt) *n.* [Fr. < ML. < VL. < L. *filum*, a thread] **1.** a very slender thread or threadlike part; specif., *a)* the fine metal wire in a light bulb which is made incandescent by an electric current *b)* the wire cathode of a thermionic valve **2.** *Bot.* the stalk of a stamen bearing the anther —**fil'a·men·ta·ry** (-men'tər ē) *adj.* —**fil'a·men'ted, —fil'a·men'tous** *adj.*

fi·lar·i·a (fi ler'ē ə) *n., pl.* **fi·lar'i·ae** (-ē ē') [ModL. < L. *filum*, a thread] any of several kinds of threadlike parasitic worms that live in the blood and tissues of vertebrate animals —**fi·lar'i·al, fi·lar'i·an** *adj.*

fil·a·ri·a·sis (fil'ə rī'ə sis) *n.* [see prec.] a disease caused by filarial worms transmitted by mosquitoes: the worms cause swelling, esp. in the lower parts of the body

fil·bert (fil'bərt) *n.* [ult. < St. *Philibert*, whose feast came in the nutting season] **1.** the edible nut of a cultivated hazel tree **2.** a tree bearing this nut **3.** *same as* HAZELNUT

filch (filch) *vt.* [ME. *filchen*] to steal (esp. something small or petty); pilfer —**filch'er** *n.*

file[1] (fīl) *vt.* **filed, fil'ing** [Fr. < OFr. *filer*, to string papers on a thread < VL. *filare*, to spin < L. *filum*, a thread] **1.** to arrange (papers, etc.) in order for future reference **2.** to dispatch (a news story) to a newspaper office **3.** to register (an application, etc.) **4.** to put (a legal document) on public record **5.** to initiate (a legal action) —*vi.* to move in a line —*n.* **1.** a folder, etc. for keeping papers in order **2.** an orderly arrangement of papers, cards, etc., as for reference **3.** a line of persons or things, one behind another —**on file** kept as in a file for reference —**file'a·ble** *adj.* —**fil'er** *n.*

file[2] (fīl) *n.* [OE. *feol*] a steel tool with a rough, ridged surface for smoothing or grinding down something —*vt.* **filed, fil'ing** to smooth or grind down with a file —**fil'er** *n.*

file-fish (fīl'fish') *n., pl.* **-fish', -fish'es:** see FISH a fish with very small, rough scales

fi·let (fi lā', fil'ā) *n.* [see FILLET] **1.** a net or lace with a simple pattern on a square mesh background **2.** *same as* FILLET (*n.* 3) —*vt.* **-leted'** (-lād'), **-let'ing** (-lā'in) *same as* FILLET (*vt.* 2)

fi·let mi·gnon (fi lā'min yon'; *Fr.* fē lē mē nyōn') [Fr., lit., tiny fillet] a thick, round cut of lean beef grilled, usually with mushrooms and bacon

fil·i·al (fil'ē əl, fil'yəl) *adj.* [< LL. < L. *filius*, son, *filia*, daughter] **1.** of, suitable to, or due from a son or daughter [*filial* devotion] **2.** *Genetics* of the indicated generation (i.e., F₁, F₂, etc.) following the parental —**fil'i·al·ly** *adv.*

fil·i·bus·ter (fil'ə bus'tər) *n.* [< Sp. < MDu. *vrijbuiter*, freebooter] **1.** an adventurer who engages in unauthorized warfare against another country; freebooter **2.** [U.S.] a member of a legislative body who obstructs the passage of a bill by making long speeches, introducing irrelevant issues, etc.: also **fil'i·bus'ter·er** **3.** [U.S.] the use of such methods to obstruct a bill —*vi.* **1.** to engage in unauthorized warfare as a freebooter **2.** [U.S.] to engage in a filibuster —**vt.** [U.S.] to obstruct the passage of (a bill) by a filibuster

fil·i·gree (fil'ə grē') **n.** [< earlier *filigrain* < Fr. < L. *filum*, a thread + *granum*, grain] **1.** lacelike ornamental work of intertwined wire of gold, silver, etc. **2.** any delicate work or design like this —**adj.** like, made of, or made into filigree —**vt. -greed', -gree'ing** to ornament with filigree

fil·ing (fīl'iŋ) **n.** a small piece, as of metal, scraped off with a file: *usually used in pl.*

Fil·i·pine (fil'ə pēn') **adj.** same as PHILIPPINE

Fil·i·pi·no (fil'ə pē'nō) **n.** [Sp.] **1.** *pl.* **-nos** a native or citizen of the Philippines **2.** *see also* PILIPINO —**adj.** Philippine

fill (fil) **vt.** [OE. *fyllan* < base of *full*, FULL[1]] **1.** *a)* to put as much as possible into; make full *b)* to put a great amount of something into **2.** *a)* to take up or occupy all or nearly all the capacity or extent of [the crowd *filled* the room] *b)* to spread throughout **3.** *a)* to occupy (an office, position, etc.) *b)* to put a person into (an office, position, etc.) **4.** to satisfy (a need, requirement, etc.) **5.** to close or plug (holes, cracks, etc.) **6.** to satisfy the hunger or desire of —**vi.** to become full —**n. 1.** all that is needed to make full **2.** all that is needed to satisfy **3.** anything that fills; esp., earth, gravel, etc. used for filling holes, etc. —**fill in 1.** to fill with some substance **2.** to complete by supplying (something) **3.** to complete a (document, etc.) by inserting information **4.** to be a substitute —**fill one in on** [Colloq.] to provide one with additional details about —**fill out** to make or become rounder, shapelier, etc. —**fill up** to make or become completely full

fill·er (fil'ər) **n.** a person or thing that fills; specif., *a)* matter added to increase bulk, solidity, etc. *b)* a preparation used to fill in cracks, etc. *c)* the tobacco inside a cigar *d)* a short, space-filling item in a newspaper

fil·lér (fel'er) **n.,** *pl.* **-lér, -lérs** *see* MONETARY UNITS. table (Hungary)

fil·let (fil'it) **n.** [< OFr. dim. of *fil* < L. *filum*, a thread] **1.** a narrow band worn round the head as to hold the hair in place **2.** a thin strip or band **3.** a boneless, lean piece of meat or fish —**vt. 1.** to bind or decorate with a band, moulding, etc. **2.** to bone and slice (meat or fish)

fill·ing (fil'iŋ) **n. 1.** a thing used to fill something else; specif., *a)* the metal, plastic, etc. inserted by a dentist into a prepared cavity in a tooth *b)* the foodstuff used in a pastry shell, etc. **2.** the woof in a woven fabric

filling station *same as* SERVICE STATION

fil·lip (fil'əp) **n.** [echoic extension of FLIP[1]] **1.** the snap made by a finger held down by the thumb and then suddenly released **2.** a light tap given in this way **3.** anything that stimulates or livens up —**vt. 1.** to strike or snap with a fillip **2.** to stimulate or liven up —**vi.** to make a fillip

fil·ly (fil'ē) **n.,** *pl.* **-lies** [ON. *fylja*] **1.** a young female horse, specif. one under five years of age **2.** [Colloq.] a vivacious girl

FILLIP

film (film) **n.** [OE. *filmen*] **1.** a fine, thin skin or coating **2.** a flexible cellulose material covered with a substance sensitive to light and used in taking photographs or making cinema pictures **3.** a haze or blur, as over the eyes **4.** *a)* a sequence of photographs or drawings projected on a screen in such rapid succession as to create the optical illusion of moving persons and objects *b)* a play, story, etc. photographed as a film **5.** a gauzy web —**vt. 1.** to cover as with a film **2.** to take a photograph of **3.** to make a film of —**vi. 1.** to become covered with a film **2.** *a)* to make a film *b)* to be filmed or suitable for filming —**film'er n.**

film·ic (fil'mik) **adj.** of films or the art of making them

film·mog·ra·phy (fil mog'ra fē) **n. 1.** a list, book, etc., that deals with the films made by a particular director, actor, etc. **2.** any writing that deals with films

film·strip (film'strip') **n.** a length of film containing still photographs arranged in sequence for projection separately and used in teaching, etc.

film·y (fil'mē) **adj. film'i·er, film'i·est 1.** of or like a film; hazy, gauzy, etc. **2.** covered as with a film —**film'i·ly adv.** —**film'i·ness n.**

fils (fēls, fils) **n.,** *pl.* **fils** [< Ar. < LGr. *phollis*, a small coin] *see* MONETARY UNITS. table (Bahrain, Iraq, Jordan, Kuwait, Yemen)

fil·ter (fil'tər) **n.** [< OFr. < ML. *filtrum, feltrum*, felt (used for filters)] **1.** a device for passing a fluid through a porous substance so as to strain out solid particles, impurities, etc. **2.** any porous substance so used, as sand, charcoal, etc. **3.** *a)* a device that passes electric currents of certain frequencies only *b)* a device that absorbs certain light rays [a colour *filter* for a camera lens] —**vt. 1.** to pass (a fluid) through a filter **2.** to remove (solid particles, etc.) from a fluid with a filter **3.** to act as a filter for —**vi. 1.** to pass

through or as if through a filter **2.** to pass slowly [the news *filtered* through town]

fil·ter·a·ble (-ə b'l) **adj.** that can be filtered: also **fil'tra·ble** (-trə b'l) —**fil'ter·a·bil'i·ty n.**

filterable virus any virus: so called because most viruses can pass through fine filters that bacteria cannot pass through

filter bed a tank, covered trench, etc. with a sand or gravel bottom, used to filter water, sewage etc.

filter paper porous paper for filtering liquids

filter tip a mouthpiece attached to a cigarette to trap and absorb impurities

filth (filth) **n.** [OE. *fylthe* < base of *ful*, FOUL + -TH[1]] **1.** disgustingly offensive dirt, rubbish, etc. **2.** anything considered grossly indecent or obscene **3.** gross moral corruption

filth·y (fil'thē) **adj. filth'i·er, filth'i·est 1.** full of filth; disgustingly foul **2.** grossly obscene **3.** morally corrupt **4.** [Colloq.] very unpleasant [filthy weather] —**filth'i·ly adv.** —**filth'i·ness n.**

filthy lucre [Colloq.] money

fil·trate (fil'trāt) **vt. -trat·ed, -trat·ing** to filter —**n.** a filtered liquid —**fil·tra'tion n.**

fin (fin) **n.** [OE. *finn*] **1.** any of several winglike, membranous organs on the body of a fish, dolphin, etc., used in swimming and balancing **2.** anything like a fin in shape or use, as on an aircraft or boat —**finned adj.**

fin. 1. finance **2.** financial **3.** finis

fin·a·ble (fī'nə b'l) **adj.** liable to a fine

fi·na·gle (fə nā'g'l) **[It.]** to get or arrange by cleverness, persuasion, etc., or esp. by craftiness or trickery —**vi.** to use craftiness or trickery —**fi·na'gler n.**

fi·nal (fī'n'l) **adj.** [< OFr. < L. *finalis* < *finis*, end] **1.** of or coming at the end; last; concluding **2.** deciding; conclusive [a final decree] **3.** having to do with the ultimate purpose or end [a final cause] —**n. 1.** anything final **2.** [pl.] the last of a series of contests **3.** a final examination

fi·na·le (fə nä'lē) **n.**[It.] **1.** the concluding part of a musical composition or an entertainment **2.** the conclusion; end

fi·nal·ist (fī'nəl ist) **n.** a contestant who participates in the final, deciding contest of a series

fi·nal·i·ty (fī nal'ə tē) **n. 1.** the quality or condition of being final, settled, or complete; conclusiveness **2.** *pl.* **-ties** anything final

fi·nal·ize (fī'nəl īz') **vt. -ized', -iz'ing** [FINAL + -IZE] to make final —**fi'nal·i·za'tion n.**

fi·nal·ly (-ē) **adv. 1.** at the end; in conclusion **2.** decisively; conclusively

fi·nance (fə nans', fī'nans) **n.** [< OFr. < *finer*, to end, settle accounts < *fin* < L. *finis*, an end] **1.** [pl.] the money resources, income, etc. of a nation, organization, or person **2.** the managing or science of managing money matters —**vt. -nanced', -nanc'ing** to supply or obtain money or credit for

finance company a company which specializes in lending money for hire-purchase contracts; also **finance house**

fi·nan·cial (fə nan'shəl, fī-) **adj.** of finance, finances, or financiers —**fi·nan'cial·ly adv.**

financial year the twelve-month period between settlements of financial accounts: the British government financial year ends April 5

fin·an·ci·er (fi nan'sē ər, fī-) **n.** [Fr.] **1.** a person skilled in finance **2.** a person who engages in financial operations on a large scale —**vi.** to engage in financial operations, often specif. in a dishonest way

fin·back (fin'bak') **n.** a large whalebone whale of the eastern coast of the U.S., with a large dorsal fin

finch (finch) **n.** [OE. *finc*] any of a large group of small songbirds with short beaks, including the bunting, canary, and linnet

find (find) **vt. found, find'ing** [OE. *findan*] **1.** to happen on; discover by chance **2.** to get by searching **3.** to get sight or knowledge of; perceive; learn **4.** to experience or feel **5.** *a)* to recover (something lost) *b)* to get or recover the use of [we *found* our sealegs] **6.** to consider; think [he *finds* TV boring] **7.** to get to; reach [the arrow *found* its mark] **8.** to declare after deliberation [to *find* him guilty] **9.** to supply; furnish —**vi.** to announce a decision [the jury *found* for the accused] —**n. 1.** a finding **2.** something found, esp. something valuable —**find oneself 1.** to learn what one's real talents are and begin to apply them **2.** to become aware of being [to *find* oneself tired] —**find one's feet** to become capable or confident —**find out 1.** to discover; learn **2.** to learn the true character or identity of

find·er (fīn'dər) **n. 1.** a person or thing that finds **2.** a camera device that shows what will appear in the photograph **3.** a small telescope attached to, and used to locate objects for closer view with, a larger, more powerful one

‡**fin de siè·cle** (fan də sye'k'l') [Fr., end of the century] of or like the last years of the 19th century

find·ing (fīn′diŋ) *n.* **1.** the act of one who finds; discovery **2.** something found or discovered **3.** [*often pl.*] the conclusion reached after consideration of facts, as by a judge, scholar, etc.

fine[1] (fīn) *adj.* **fin′er, fin′est** [< OFr. < ML. *finus*, for L. *finis*, an end] **1.** orig., perfected **2.** superior in quality, character, ability, etc.; excellent **3.** *a)* good-looking good-looking [a *fine* young woman] *b)* elegant; refined [a *fine* gentleman] **4.** with no impurities; refined **5.** containing a specified proportion of pure metal: said of gold or silver **6.** clear and bright: said of the weather **7.** not heavy, gross, or coarse [*fine* sand] **8.** *a)* very thin [*fine* thread] *b)* very small [*fine* print] **9.** sharp; keen [a knife with a *fine* edge] **10.** discriminating; subtle [*fine* distinctions] **11.** having a delicate quality [*fine* china] **12.** involving precision [a *fine* adjustment] **13.** too elegant; affectedly refined [*fine* speeches] **14.** [Colloq.] terrible; disappointing [this is a *fine* mess] **15.** *Cricket* oblique to and behind the wicket [*fine* leg] —*adv.* **1.** *same as* FINELY **2.** [Colloq.] very well —*vt., vi.* **fined, fin′ing** to make or become fine or finer —**cut** (or **run**) **it fine 1.** to arrive at the last minute **2.** to leave only a very small reserve of something —**fine′ly** *adv.* —**fine′ness** *n.*

fine[2] (fīn) *n.* [< OFr. *fin* < L. *finis*, an end] a sum of money required to be paid as punishment for an offence —*vt.* **fined, fin′ing** to order to pay a fine —**in fine 1.** in conclusion **2.** in brief

fine art any of the art forms that include drawing, painting, sculpture, and ceramics, or, occasionally, architecture, literature, music, dramatic art, or dancing: *usually used in pl.*

fine-draw (-drô′) *vt.* **-drew′, -drawn′, -draw′ing** to sew together (torn edges) so carefully that the seam cannot be seen

fine-drawn (fīn′drôn′) *adj.* **1.** drawn out until very fine, as wire **2.** very subtle: said of reasoning, arguments, etc.

fine-grained (-grānd′) *adj.* having a fine, smooth grain, as some wood, leather, etc.

fin·er·y[1] (fīn′ər ē) *n., pl.* **-er·ies** showy, gay, elaborate decoration, esp. clothes, jewellery, etc.

fin·er·y[2] (fīn′ər ə) *n., pl.* **-er·ies** [Fr. *finerie* < *finer*, to refine] a refinery where malleable iron or steel is made

fines herbes (*Fr.*, fēn zerb) a mixture of fresh, finely-chopped herbs used to flavour omelettes, etc.

fine-spun (fīn′spun′) *adj.* **1.** delicate; fragile **2.** extremely or excessively subtle

fi·nesse (fi nes′) *n.* [Fr. < OFr. *fin*, FINE[1]] **1.** adroitness and delicacy of performance **2.** the ability to handle difficult situations diplomatically **3.** cunning; skill **4.** *Bridge* an attempt to take a trick with a lower card while holding a higher card not in sequence with it —*vt., vi.* **-nessed′, -ness′ing 1.** to manage by or use finesse **2.** *Bridge* to make a finesse with (a card)

fine-toothed comb (fīn′tŌŌtht′) a comb with fine, closely set teeth: also **fine-tooth comb** —**go over with a fine-toothed comb** to examine very thoroughly

fin·ger (fiŋ′gər) *n.* [OE.] **1.** any of the five parts at the end of the hand, esp. any of these other than the thumb **2.** the part of a glove covering a finger **3.** anything like a finger in shape or use **4.** an approximate measurement based on the breadth of a finger (about 2 cm) —*vt.* **1.** to touch or handle with the fingers **2.** to play (an instrument) by using the fingers on strings, keys, etc. —*vi.* to be fingered, as a violin —**get** (or **pull**) **one's finger out** [Colloq.] to begin or speed up activity, esp. after inital delay or slackness —**have a finger in the pie 1.** to participate **2.** to meddle —**put one's finger on** to indicate or ascertain exactly —**twist** (or **wrap**) **around one's little finger** to have easy and complete control or influence over

fin·ger·board (-bôrd′) *n.* a strip of hard wood in the neck of a violin, cello, etc., against which the strings are pressed with the fingers to produce the desired tones

finger bowl a small bowl to hold water for rinsing the fingers at table after a meal

fin·gered (fiŋ′gərd) *adj.* having fingers (of a specified kind or number) [thick-*fingered*]

fin·ger·ing (fiŋ′gər iŋ) *n.* **1.** a touching with the fingers **2.** *Music* a) technique of using the fingers on the strings, keys, etc. to produce tones *b)* directions on a score for using the fingers

fin·ger·ling (-liŋ) *n.* a small fish about the length of a finger

finger mark a mark or smudge left as by an unclean finger

fin·ger·nail (-nāl′) *n.* the horny substance on the upper part of the end joint of a finger

finger painting the process of painting by using the fingers or hand to spread paints made of starch, glycerin, and pigments (**finger paints**) on moistened paper —**fin′ger-paint′** (-pānt′) *vi., vt.*

finger plate an ornamental plate of metal, plastic, etc. fixed above a doorhandle to prevent soiling the woodwork with finger marks

finger post a signpost, often shaped like a pointing finger or hand

fin·ger·print (-print′) *n.* **1.** an impression of the lines and whorls on the inner surface of the end joint of the finger, used to identify a person **2.** a characteristic or identifying mark, trait, etc. —*vt.* to take the fingerprints of

fin·ger·stall (-stôl′) *n.* [ME. *finger stall*] a protective covering of rubber, leather, etc. for an injured finger

finger tip the tip of a finger —**have at one's finger tips 1.** to have available for instant use **2.** to be completely familiar with —**to one's** (or **the**) **finger tips** entirely; altogether

fin·i·al (fin′ē əl) *n.* [ME., orig. adj., FINAL] a decorative part at the tip of a spire, etc., or projecting upwards from the top of a cabinet, etc.

FINGERPRINT

fin·i·cal (fin′i k'l) *adj.* [< FINE[1]] *same as* FINICKY —**fin′i·cal·ly** *adv.*

fin·ick·y (fin′i kē) *adj.* [see prec.] too particular; excessively fastidious; fussy: also **fin′ick·ing, fin′nick·y** —**fin′ick·i·ness** *n.*

fi·nis (fin′is, fī′nis) *n., pl.* **-nis·es** [L.] the end, as of a book; conclusion

fin·ish (fin′ish) *vt.* [< OFr. < L. *finire* < *finis*, an end] **1.** *a)* to bring to an end; complete *b)* to come to the end of **2.** to use up; consume entirely **3.** to give final touches to **4.** to give (cloth, wood, etc.) a desired surface effect **5.** *a)* to cause the defeat, death, etc. of *b)* to render worthless, useless, etc. —*vi.* **1.** to come to an end **2.** to complete something being done —*n.* **1.** the last part; end **2.** anything used to give a desired surface effect, as varnish, wax, etc. **3.** completeness; perfection **4.** the manner or method of completion **5.** the way in which the surface, as of furniture, is finished **6.** refinement in manners, speech, etc. **7.** defeat, collapse, etc. or that which brings it about —**finish off 1.** to end or complete **2.** to kill or destroy —**finish up 1.** to end or complete **2.** to consume all of —**finish with 1.** to end or complete **2.** to end relations with —**fin′ished** *adj.* —**fin′ish·er** *n.*

finishing school a private school for girls that specializes in imparting social poise and polish

fi·nite (fī′nīt) *adj.* [< L. *finitus*, pp. of *finire*, FINISH] **1.** having definable limits; not infinite **2.** *Gram.* having limits of person, number, and tense: said of a verb —**fi′nite·ly** *adv.* —**fi′nite·ness** *n.*

fin·i·tude (fin′ə tyŌŌd′) *n.* the state or quality of being finite

fink (fiŋk) *n.* [< ?] [U.S. Slang] **1.** an informer or strikebreaker **2.** a person regarded as obnoxious

Finn. Finnish

fin·nan had·die (fin′ən had′ē) [prob. < *Findhorn* (Scot. fishing port) *haddock*] smoked haddock: also **finnan haddock**

Fin·nic (fin′ik) *adj.* **1.** Finnish **2.** of the group of languages to which Finnish belongs: see FINNO-UGRIK

Finn·ish (fin′ish) *adj.* **1.** of Finland **2.** of the Finns, their language, or culture —*n.* the Finno-Ugric language of the Finns

Fin·no- a combining form meaning Finn, Finnish

Fin·no-U·gric (fin′ō ŌŌ′grik, -yŌŌ′-) *adj.* designating or of a subfamily of the Uralic languages spoken in NE Europe, W Siberia, and Hungary: it includes Finnish, Estonian, Hungarian, etc. —*n.* this subfamily of languages Also **Fin′no-U′gri·an** (-grē ən)

fin·ny (fin′ē) *adj.* **1.** *a)* having fins *b)* like a fin **2.** of or being fish

fiord (fyôrd) *n.* [< Norw. < ON. *fjörthr*] a narrow inlet of the sea bordered by steep cliffs, esp. in Norway

fip·ple flute (fip′'l) [< ?] any of a class of vertical flutes, as the recorder, in which a plug (**fipple**) near the mouthpiece diverts the breath in producing the tones

fir (fur) *n.* [< OE. *fyrh*] **1.** a cone-bearing evergreen tree of the pine family **2.** its wood

FIORD

fire (fīr) *n.* [OE. *fyr*] **1.** the heat and light of combustion **2.** something burning, as fuel in a furnace **3.** a destructive burning [a forest *fire*] **4.** anything like fire in heat, brilliance, etc. **5.** torture by burning **6.** extreme distress; tribulation [go through *fire* and water] **7.** fever or inflammation **8.** strong feeling; fervour **9.** vivid imagination **10.** *a)* a discharge of firearms or artillery *b)* anything like this in speed and continuity [a *fire* of criticism] —*vt.* **fired, fir′ing 1.** to make burn; ignite **2.** to supply with fuel [to *fire* a furnace] **3.** to bake (bricks, pottery, etc.) in a kiln **4.** to dry by heat **5.** to animate, inspire, excite, etc. **6.** to shoot or discharge (a gun, bullet, etc.) **7.** to hurl or direct with force [to *fire* questions] **8.** to dismiss from a job; discharge —*vi.* **1.** to start burning;

flame **2.** to become excited or aroused **3.** to shoot a firearm **4.** to discharge a projectile —**between two fires** shot at, criticized, etc. from both sides —**catch (on) fire** to begin burning —**miss fire 1.** to fail to fire, as a gun **2.** to fail in an attempt —**on fire 1.** burning **2.** greatly excited —**open fire 1.** to begin to shoot **2.** to begin; start —**play with fire** to do something risky —**set fire to 1.** to make burn; ignite —**set the Thames on fire** to do something outstanding —**take fire 1.** to begin to burn **2.** to become excited —**under fire 1.** under attack, as by gunfire **2.** subjected to criticism, etc. —**fir′er** *n.*

fire alarm 1. a signal to announce the outbreak of a fire **2.** a bell, siren, etc. to give this signal

fire·arm (-ärm′) *n.* any weapon from which a shot is fired by explosive force; esp., such a weapon small enough to be carried, as a rifle

fire·back a reflector of metal or clay at the back of a grate, to send out the heat

fire·ball (-bôl) *n.* **1.** ball-shaped lightning **2.** a very bright ball of gas at the centre of a nuclear explosion **3.** a large, very bright meteor **4.** [Slang] an energetic person

fire blight a disease of plants causing them to appear as if scorched: also **fire blast**

fire·boat (-bôt′) *n.* a boat equipped with firefighting equipment, used along waterfronts

fire·bomb (-bom′) *n.* a bomb intended to start a fire; incendiary bomb —*vt.* to attack with a firebomb or firebombs

fire·box (-boks′) *n.* the place for the fire in a furnace, etc.

fire·brand (-brand′) *n.* **1.** a piece of burning wood **2.** a person who stirs up strife, etc.

fire·break (-brāk′) *n.* a strip of land cleared to stop the spread of fire, as in a forest

fire·brick (-brik′) *n.* a brick made to withstand great heat, used to line furnaces, etc.

fire brigade an organised body of firemen

fire·bug (-bug′) *n.* [U.S. Colloq.] a person who deliberately sets fire to buildings, etc.; pyromaniac

fire·clay (-klā′) *n.* a clay that can resist intense heat, used to make firebricks, furnace linings, etc.

fire company 1. a fire insurance company **2.** [U.S.] an organized body of firemen

fire control the process and procedures by which weapons are brought to bear on and engage a target

fire·crack·er (-krak′ər) *n.* [U.S.] a roll of paper that contains an explosive and an attached fuse, set off at celebrations, etc.

fire·crest (-krest) *n.* [FIRE + CREST] a small N European bird related to the goldcrest

fire·damp (-damp′) *n.* a gas, largely methane, formed in coal mines, which is explosive when mixed with a certain proportion of air

fire·dog (-dog′) *n.* *same as* ANDIRON

fire door a door of metal or other fire-resistant material designed to keep a fire from spreading

fire·eat·er (-ēt′ər) *n.* **1.** an entertainer who pretends to eat fire **2.** a belligerent person

fire engine a heavy road vehicle that carries firemen and firefighting equipment

fire escape a stairway, ladder, etc. down an outside wall, for escape from a burning building

fire extinguisher a portable device containing chemicals for spraying on a fire to put it out

fire·fight·er (-fīt′ər) *n.* *same as* FIREMAN (sense 1)

fire·fly (-flī′) *n.,* *pl.* **-flies′** a winged beetle whose abdomen glows with a luminescent light

fire guard (-gärd′) *n.* a meshed frame put before an open fire to protect against sparks, etc.

fire insurance insurance against loss or damage resulting from fire

fire irons the poker, shovel and tongs used for tending a fire

fire·light (-līt′) *n.* light from an open fire

fire·light·er (-līt′ər) *n.* a composition of highly combustible material for kindling a domestic fire

fire·lock (-lok) *n.* an old type of musket in which the priming mechanism was ignited by a spark

fire·man (-mən) *n.,* *pl.* **-men** (-mən) **1.** a man whose work is fighting fires; a member of a fire brigade **2.** a man who tends a furnace; stoker

fire opal an opal with flame-like sheen

fire·place (fīr′plās′) *n.* a place for a fire, esp. an open place built in a wall, at a chimney base

fire·plug (-plug′) *n.* [Chiefly U.S.] a street hydrant to which a hose can be attached for fighting fires

fire·pow·er (-pou′ər) *n.* *Mil.* **1.** the effectiveness of a weapon in terms of the accuracy and volume of its fire **2.** the capacity of a given unit to deliver fire

fire·proof (-prōof′) *adj.* that does not burn or is not easily destroyed by fire —*vt.* to make fireproof

fire·rais·ing (-rāz′iŋ) *n.* arson

fire screen 1. a decorative screen placed in the hearth when there is no fire **2.** formerly, a small screen used to protect the complexion from the direct heat of a fire

fire ship a ship filled with combustible materials, set on fire and floated among an enemy's ships to destroy them

fire·side (-sīd′) *n.* **1.** the part of a room near a fireplace; hearth **2.** home or home life

fire station the place where fire engines are kept and where firemen stay when on duty

fire stick a smouldering stick carried by Australian natives for lighting fires

fire·storm (-stôrm′) *n.* an intense fire over a large area, as one caused by an atomic explosion

fire·trap (-trap′) *n.* a building unsafe in case of fire, as because it lacks adequate exits

fire·wa·ter (-wôt′ər) *n.* [prob. transl. of AmInd. term] alcoholic spirits: now humorous

fire·weed (-wēd′) *n.* any of various plants that grow readily on cleared or burned-over land

fire·works (-wurks′) *n.pl.* **1.** devices in which combustible materials and explosives are ignited and produce coloured flames, sparks and smoke, sometimes with noise **2.** a display of fireworks **3.** [Colloq.] a burst of temper, heated argument, etc.

fir·ing (fīr′iŋ) *n.* **1.** the process of baking ceramics, etc. in a kiln **2.** the act of stoking a furnace, etc. **3.** the discharge of a firearm **4.** something used as fuel

firing line 1. the line from which gunfire is directed against the enemy **2.** the front position in any kind of activity

fir·kin (fur′kin) *n.* [< MDu. dim. of *vierdel,* a fourth] **1.** a small wooden tub for butter, lard, etc. **2.** a measure of capacity equal to 1/4 barrel

firm¹ (furm) *adj.* [< OFr. < L. *firmus*] **1.** not yielding easily under pressure; solid **2.** not moved or shaken easily; fixed; stable **3.** remaining the same; steady [a *firm* market] **4.** resolute; constant [a *firm* faith] **5.** showing determination, strength, etc. [a *firm* command] **6.** formally concluded; definite; final [a *firm* contract] —*vt., vi.* to make or become firm: sometimes with *up* —**firm′ly** *adv.* —**firm′ness** *n.*

firm² (furm) *n.* [It. *firma,* signature < L. < *firmus,* FIRM¹] a business company or partnership

fir·ma·ment (fur′mə mənt) *n.* [< OFr. < LL. < L. *firmare,* to strengthen < *firmus,* FIRM] the sky, viewed poetically as a solid arch or vault —**fir·ma·ment′al** *adj.*

fir·man (fur′mən, fər män′) *n.,* *pl.* **-mans** [Per. *fermān*] a decree or sanction given by an Oriental ruler

first (furst) *adj.* [< OE. *fyrst*] **1.** before any others; 1st: used as the ordinal of ONE **2.** happening or acting before all others; earliest **3.** foremost in rank, quality, importance, etc. **4.** *Music* playing or singing the part highest in pitch or the leading part —*adv.* **1.** *a)* before any other person or thing *b)* before doing anything else **2.** as the first point **3.** for the first time **4.** sooner; preferably —*n.* **1.** the first person, thing, class, place, etc. **2.** the first day of the month **3.** the beginning; start **4.** a first happening or thing of its kind **5.** [*pl.*] the best quality of merchandise **6.** the winning place, as in a race **7.** the first or lowest forward gear ratio of a motor vehicle

first aid emergency treatment for injury or sudden illness, before regular medical care is available —**first′-aid′** *adj.*

first·born (-bôrn′) *adj.* born first in a family; oldest —*n.* the firstborn child

first-class (-kläs′) *adj.* **1.** of the highest class, rank, quality, etc.; excellent **2.** designating or of the most expensive accommodation on a ship, seats on a train, etc. **3.** designating or of letters handled faster than second-class letters and carrying the highest postage rates —*adv.* by first-class post, means of transport, etc.

first cousin the son or daughter of one's aunt or uncle

first-day cover an envelope postmarked on the first day of the issue of its stamps

first finger the finger next to the thumb

first-foot (-foot′) [Chiefly Scot.] *n.* the first person to enter a household in the New Year: also **first-foot′er** —*vi.* to enter (a house) as first-foot—**first-foot′ing** *n.*

first fruits 1. the earliest produce of the season **2.** the first products, results, or profits of any activity

first-hand (-hand′) *adj., adv.* from the original producer or source; direct

first lady [U.S.] [often F- L-] the wife of the U.S. president

first·ling (-liŋ) *n.* **1.** the first of a kind **2.** the first fruit, produce, offspring, etc.

first·ly (-lē) *adv.* in the first place; first

first mate a merchant ship's officer next in rank below the master: also **first officer**

first mortgage a mortgage having priority over all other liens on the same property

first night the opening night of a play, opera, etc.

first-night·er (-nīt′ər) *n.* a person who regularly attends first nights

first offender a person convicted for the first time of an offence against the law

first person that form of a pronoun (as *I* or *we*) or verb (as *do*) which refers to the speaker or speakers

first-rate (-rāt′) *adj.* of the highest class, rank, or quality; excellent —*adv.* [Colloq.] very well

first water the best quality and purest lustre: said of gems, but also used figuratively

firth (furth) *n.* [< ON. *fjörthr*] a narrow arm of the sea; estuary

fis·cal (fis′kəl) *adj.* [Fr. < LL. < L. *fiscus*, money basket] 1. having to do with the public treasury or revenues 2. financial —*n.* in some countries, a public prosecutor —**fis′cal·ly** *adv.*

fiscal year *same as* FINANCIAL YEAR

fish (fish) *n., pl.* **fish;** in referring to different species, **fish′es:** see PLURAL, II. D. 2 [OE. *fisc*] 1. any of a large group of coldblooded animals living in water and having backbones, gills for breathing, fins, and, usually, scales 2. loosely, any animal living in water only, as a crab, oyster, etc. 3. the flesh of a fish used as food

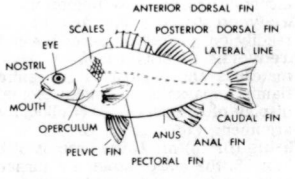

FISH

4. [Colloq.] a person thought of as like a fish in being easily lured, lacking emotion, etc. —[F-] the constellation Pisces —*vi.* 1. to catch or try to catch fish 2. to try to get something indirectly or by cunning (often with *for*) —*vt.* 1. to fish in (a stream, lake, etc.) 2. to grope for, find, and bring to view [he *fished* a coin out of his pocket] —*adj.* 1. of fish or fishing 2. selling fish —**drink like a fish** to drink heavily —**fish in troubled waters** to turn a disturbed situation to one's own advantage —**like a fish out of water** in surroundings not suited to one —**neither fish, flesh, nor fowl** (or **nor good red herring**) not anything definite or recognizable —**other fish to fry** other, more important things to attend to —**fish′a·ble** *adj.* —**fish′like** *adj.*

fish and chips fried fillets of fish served with chipped fried potatoes

fish cake a fried ball or cake of flaked fish and mashed potatoes

fish·er (fish′ər) *n.* 1. a fisherman 2. *pl.* **-ers, -er:** see PLURAL, II. D. 1 a flesh-eating animal of the marten family, like a weasel but larger: also called PEKAN

fish·er·man (-mən) *n., pl.* **-men** 1. a person who fishes for sport or for a living 2. a ship used in fishing

fish·er·y (-ē) *n., pl.* **-er·ies** 1. the business of catching fish 2. a place where fish are caught 3. the legal right to catch fish in certain waters or at certain times 4. a place where fish are bred

fish-eye lens (fish′ī′) a camera lens designed to record a 180-degree field of vision

fish finger a small, oblong-shaped portion of fish covered in breadcrumbs or batter

fish hawk *same as* OSPREY

fish·hook (-hook′) *n.* a hook, usually barbed, for catching fish

fish·ing (-iŋ) *n.* the catching of fish for sport or for a living

fishing rod a slender pole with an attached line, hook, and usually a reel, used in fishing

fish joint a joint, as of two railway lines, held together by fishplates along the sides

fish-ket·tle (ket′′l) *n.* a large oval pot in which fish are cooked whole

fish meal ground, dried fish, used as fertilizer or fodder

fish·mon·ger (-muŋ′gər) *n.* a dealer in fish

fish·plate (-plāt′) *n.* [prob. < Fr. *fiche*, means of fixing] either of a pair of steel plates bolting two rails together lengthwise, as on a railway

fish slice 1. a fish carver 2. a flat-bladed utensil for serving fish

fish·tail (-tāl′) *n.* 1. anything shaped like a fish's tail, specif., a nozzle with a narrow slot placed over a Bunsen burner to produce a fanlike flame 2. an aircraft manoeuvre in which the tail is swung from side to side to reduce speed —*vi.* to retard an aircraft's speed with a fishtail manoeuvre

fish·wife (-wif′) *n., pl.* **-wives′** (-wivz′) 1. a woman who sells fish 2. a coarse, scolding woman

fish·y (-ē) *adj.* **fish′i·er, fish′i·est** 1. of or full of fish 2. like a fish in odour, taste, etc. 3. dull or expressionless [a *fishy* stare] 4. [Colloq.] questionable; odd [a *fishy* story] —**fish′i·ly** *adv.* —**fish′i·ness** *n.*

fis·sile (fis′il) *adj.* [< L. < *fissus*, pp. of *findere*, to split] 1. that can be split 2. that can undergo fission; fissionable —**fis·sil·i·ty** (fi sil′ə tē) *n.*

fis·sion (fish′ən) *n.* [< L. < *fissus*: see prec.] 1. a splitting apart; division into parts 2. *same as* NUCLEAR FISSION 3. *Biol.* a form of asexual reproduction in which the parent organism divides into two or more parts, each becoming an independent individual —*vi., vt.* to undergo or cause to undergo nuclear fission —**fis′sion·a·ble** *adj.*

fis·sip·a·rous (fi sip′ər əs) *adj.* [< L. *fissus* (see FISSILE) + -PAROUS] *Biol.* reproducing by fission

fis·sure (fish′ər) *n.* [< OFr. < L. *fissura* < *fissus*: see FISSILE] 1. a long, narrow, deep cleft or crack 2. a dividing or breaking into parts —*vt., vi.* **-sured, -sur·ing** to crack or split apart

fist (fist) *n.* [< OE. *fyst*] 1. a hand with the fingers closed tightly into the palm 2. [Colloq.] *a)* a hand *b)* the grasp *c)* handwriting 3. *Printing* the sign ( ), used to direct special attention to something

fist·ic (fis′tik) *adj.* having to do with boxing; fought with the fists; pugilistic

fist·i·cuffs (fis′ti kufs′) *n.pl.* [< FIST + CUFF²] 1. a fight with the fists 2. the science of boxing

fis·tu·la (fis′tyōō lə) *n., pl.* **-las, -lae′** (-lē′) [< OFr. < L., a pipe, ulcer] an abnormal passage from an abscess, cavity, or hollow organ to the skin or to another abscess, cavity, or organ —**fis′tu·lous, fis′tu·lar** *adj.*

fit¹ (fit) *vt.* **fit′ted** or **fit, fit′ted, fit′ting** [ME. *fitten* < ? ON. *fitja*, to knit, tie] 1. to be suitable or adapted to 2. to be the proper size, shape, etc. for 3. *a)* to make or alter so as to fit *b)* to measure (a person) for something that must be fitted 4. to make suitable or qualified 5. *a)* to insert, as into a receptacle *b)* to make a place for (with *in* or *into*) 6. to equip; outfit (often with *out*) —*vi.* 1. to be suitable or proper 2. to be in accord or harmony (often with *in* or *into*) 3. to have the proper size or shape for a particular figure, space, etc. [his coat *fits* well] —*adj.* **fit′ter, fit′test** 1. adapted, qualified, or suited to some purpose, function, etc. 2. proper; right 3. in good physical condition; healthy —*n.* 1. a fitting or being fitted 2. the manner of fitting [a tight *fit*] 3. anything that fits —**fit′ly** *adv.* —**fit′ness** *n.*

fit² (fit) *n.* [OE. *fitt*, conflict] 1. any sudden, uncontrollable attack [a *fit* of coughing] 2. a sharp, brief display of feeling [a *fit* of anger] 3. a temporary burst of activity 4. *Med.* a seizure in which one loses consciousness or has convulsions or both —**by fits and starts** in an irregular way —**have** (or **throw**) **a fit** [Colloq.] to become very angry or upset

fitch (fich) *n.* [< OFr. < MDu. *vitsche*] *same as* POLECAT (sense 1): also **fitch′et** (-it), **fitch′ew** (-ōō)

fit·ful (fit′fəl) *adj.* characterized by intermittent activity, impulses, etc.; spasmodic —**fit′ful·ly** *adv.* —**fit′ful·ness** *n.*

fit·ment (-mənt) *n.* 1. an added part, as to a machine; accessory 2. [*often pl.*] any of the furnishings or equipment of a house, etc. attached to the building but not a structural part of it; fixture

fit·ted (fit′id) *adj.* designed to conform to the contours of that which it covers

fit·ter (-ər) *n.* 1. a person who alters or adjusts garments to fit 2. a person who installs or adjusts machinery, pipes, etc.

fit·ting (-iŋ) *adj.* suitable; proper; appropriate —*n.* 1. an adjustment or trying on of clothes, etc. for fit 2. a part used to join, adjust, or adapt other parts, as in a system of pipes 3. [*pl.*] the fixtures, furnishings, or decorations of a house, motor car, office, etc. —**fit′ting·ly** *adv.* —**fit′ting·ness** *n.*

Fitzgerald (-Lorentz) contraction a hypothesis, developed in the 1890's by L. G. Fitzgerald, Ir. physicist, and H. A. Lorentz, Du. physicist, and later shown to be a direct consequence of the theory of relativity, that a moving body contracts in length: significant only at speeds approaching those of light

five (fiv) *adj.* [< OE. *fif*] totalling one more than four —*n.* 1. the cardinal number between four and six; 5; V 2. anything having five units or members, or numbered five

five-cor·ners (-kôr′nərz) *n.* 1. an Australian flowering shrub 2. its fruit

five-finger exercise 1. an exercise for piano practice using all the fingers 2. any easy task

five·fold (-fōld′) *adj.* [see -FOLD] 1. having five parts 2. having five times as much or as many —*adv.* five times as much or as many

five o'clock shadow dark shade seen on a man's face, indicating a need to shave

fiv·er (fī′var) *n.* [Slang] a five-pound note

fives (fivz) *n.* [<?] a game of handball played against a wall

five-year plan a government plan, esp. in socialist economies, for intensive economic development over a five-year period

fix (fiks) *vt.* [< L. *fixus*, pp. of *figere*, to fasten] 1. *a)* to make firm, stable, or secure *b)* to fasten firmly 2. to set firmly in the mind 3. to direct steadily [to *fix* the eyes on a spot] 4. to make rigid 5. to make permanent or lasting 6. to establish definitely; set or determine 7. to set in order; adjust 8. to repair, mend, etc. 9. [Colloq.] to influence the result or action of (a race, election, etc) by bribery, trickery, etc. 10. [Colloq.] to revenge oneself on; punish 11. [Colloq.] to spay or castrate 12. *Chem. a)* to make solid or nonvolatile *b)* to combine (atmospheric nitrogen) in the form of useful compounds, as nitrates, ammonia, etc. 13. *Photog.* to make (a film, print, etc.) permanent by washing in a chemical solution —*vi.* to become fixed, firm, or stable

—*n.* 1. the position of a ship or aircraft determined as from the bearings of two or more known points 2. [Colloq.] a difficult or awkward situation; predicament 3. [Slang] an injection of a narcotic, as heroin —**fix on** (or **upon**) to choose —**fix up** [Colloq.] 1. to repair, mend, etc. 2. to set in order 3. to make arrangements for —**fix′a·ble** *adj.* —**fix′er** *n.*

fix·ate (fik sāt′) *vt., vi.* **-at′ed, -at′ing** 1. to make or become fixed 2. *Psychoanalysis* to subject to or undergo fixation

fix·a·tion (fik sā′shən) *n.* 1. a fixing or being fixed, as in chemistry, photography, etc. 2. popularly, an exaggerated preoccupation; obsession 3. *Psychoanalysis* attachment to objects of an earlier stage of psychosexual development [a father *fixation*]

fix·a·tive (fik′sə tiv) *adj.* that is able or tends to make permanent, prevent fading, etc. —*n.* a fixative substance, as a mordant

fixed (fikst) *adj.* 1. firmly placed or attached; not movable 2. established; set 3. steady; resolute 4. obsessive [a *fixed* idea] 5. [Colloq.] supplied with something, specif. money [comfortably *fixed* for life] 6. [Slang] with the outcome dishonestly prearranged 7. *Chem.* a) nonvolatile [*fixed* oils] b) incorporated into a stable compound from its free state, as atmospheric nitrogen —**fix·ed·ly** (fik′sid lē) *adv.* —**fix′ed·ness** *n.*

fixed star a star that appears to keep the same position in relation to other stars

fix·i·ty (-sə tē) *n.* 1. the quality or state of being fixed; steadiness or permanence 2. *pl.* **-ties** anything fixed

fixt (fikst) *poet. pt. and pp. of* FIX

fix·ture (fiks′chər) *n.* [< LL. *fixura* < L. *fixus* (see FIX): form infl. by MIXTURE] 1. anything firmly in place 2. any of the fittings or furnishings of a house, etc., attached to the building and considered legally a part of it [bathroom *fixtures*] 3. [Colloq.] a person or thing long-established in a place or job

fiz·gig (fiz′gig) *n.* [< ? ff.+ *gig,* girl] 1. a frivolous or flirtatious girl 2. a firework that fizzes as it moves

fizz (fiz) *n.* [echoic] 1. a hissing, sputtering sound, as of an effervescent drink 2. an effervescent drink —*vi.* 1. to make a hissing or bubbling sound 2. to give off gas bubbles; effervesce

fiz·zle (fiz′'l) *vi.* **-zled, -zling** [ME. *fesilen,* to break wind silently] 1. to make a hissing or sputtering sound 2. [Colloq.] to fail, esp. after a successful beginning (often with *out*) —*n.* 1. a hissing or sputtering sound 2. [Colloq.] a failure

fizz·y (fiz′ē) *adj.* **fizz′i·er, fizz′i·est** fizzing; effervescent

fjord (fyôrd) *n.* same as FIORD

Fl. 1. Flanders 2. Flemish

fl. 1. [L. *floruit*] (he or she) flourished 2. fluid

flab (flab) *n.* [back-formation < FLABBY] [Colloq.] soft, sagging flesh

flab·ber·gast (flab′ər gäst′) *vt.* [< ? ff. + AGHAST] to dumbfound; amaze

flab·by (flab′ē) *adj.* **-bi·er, -bi·est** [var. of *flappy* < FLAP] 1. lacking firmness; limp and soft [*flabby* muscles] 2. lacking force; weak —**flab′bi·ly** *adv.* —**flab′bi·ness** *n.*

flac·cid (flas′id) *adj.* [L. *flaccidus* < *flaccus,* flabby] 1. soft and limp; flabby 2. weak; feeble —**flac·cid′i·ty** *n.* —**flac′-cid·ly** *adv.*

fla·con (flå kōn′; *E.* flak′'n) *n.* [Fr.: see FLAGON] a small bottle with a stopper, as for perfume

flag¹ (flag) *n.* [< ? FLAG⁴, in obs. sense "to flutter"] 1. a piece of cloth with colours, patterns, or devices, used as a national or state symbol or as a signal; banner, standard 2. a small piece of cloth, paper, etc., like a flag, used as a signal or badge 3. the bushy tail of certain dogs, as setters —*vt.* **flagged, flag′ging** 1. to decorate or mark with flags 2. to signal with or as with a flag; esp., to signal to stop (often with *down*) —**flag′ger** *n.*

flag² (flag) *n.* [ON. *flaga,* slab of stone] same as FLAGSTONE —*vt.* **flagged, flag′ging** to pave with flagstones

flag³ (flag) *n.* [ME. *flagge,* akin ? to ff.] 1. any of various irises, with flowers of blue, purple, white, yellow, etc. 2. same as SWEET FLAG —**flag′gy** *adj.*

flag⁴ (flag) *vi.* **flagged, flag′ging** [< ? ON. *flakka,* to flutter] to lose strength; grow weak or tired

flag day a day on which miniature flags are given in return for donations to a charity fund

flag·el·lant (flaj′ə lənt) *n.* [see ff.] a person who whips; specif., one who whips himself or has himself whipped as for religious discipline —*adj.* engaging in flagellation

flag·el·late (flaj′ə lāt′) *vt.* **-lat′ed, -lat′ing** [< L. *flagellare,* to whip < *flagellum,* a whip] to whip; flog —*adj.* 1. having a flagellum or flagella: also **flag′el·lat′ed** 2. shaped like a flagellum —**flag′el·la′tion** *n.* —**flag′el·la′tor** *n.* —**flag′el·la′tor·y** *adj.*

fla·gel·lum (flə jel′əm) *n., pl.* **-la** (-ə), **-lums** [L.: see prec.] 1. *Biol.* a whiplike part serving as an organ of locomotion in certain cells, bacteria, protozoans, etc. 2. *Bot.* a threadlike shoot or runner

flag·eo·let¹ (flaj′ə let′, -lā′) *n.* [Fr., dim. of OFr. *flageol,* a

flag·eo·let² (flaj′ə let′, -lā′) *n.* [Fr.] a kind of kidney bean

flag·ging¹ (flag′iŋ) *adj.* [prp. of FLAG⁴] weakening or drooping —**flag′ging·ly** *adv.*

flag·ging² (flag′iŋ) *n.* flagstones or a pavement made of flagstones

fla·gi·tious (flə jish′əs) *adj.* [< L. < *flagitium,* shameful act < *flagitare,* to demand] shamefully wicked; vile and scandalous —**fla·gi′tious·ly** *adv.* —**fla·gi′tious·ness** *n.*

flag of convenience a foreign flag under which a company registers a ship to avoid the regulations, taxes, etc. of its own state

flag of truce a white flag shown to an enemy to indicate a desire to confer or parley

flag·on (flag′ən) *n.* [< OFr. *flacon* < LL. < *flasca,* flask] 1. a container for liquids, with a handle, a spout, and, often, a lid 2. the contents of a flagon

flag·pole (flag′pōl′) *n.* a pole on which a flag is flown: also **flag′staff** (-staf′)

fla·gran·cy (flā′grən sē) *n.* the quality or state of being flagrant: also **fla′grance**

fla·grant (flā′grənt) *adj.* [< L. prp. of *flagrare,* to blaze] glaringly bad; notorious; outrageous —**fla′grant·ly** *adv.*

‡**fla·gran·te de·lic·to** (flə gran′tē di lik′tō) [L.] same as IN FLAGRANTE DELICTO

flag·ship (flag′ship′) *n.* 1. the ship carrying the commander of a fleet or squadron and displaying his flag 2. the finest, largest, or newest ship of a steamship line

flag·stone (flag′stōn′) *n.* 1. any hard stone that splits into flat pieces used to pave walks, terraces, etc. 2. a piece of such stone

flag-wav·ing (flag′wā′viŋ) *n.* an emotional appeal calculated to arouse intense patriotic feelings —**flag′-wav′-er** *n.*

flail (flāl) *n.* [OFr. *flaiel* < L. *flagellum,* a whip] a farm tool having a free-swinging stick attached to a long handle, used to thresh grain by hand —*vt., vi.* 1. to thresh with a flail 2. to beat as with a flail 3. to move (one's arms) about like flails

FLAIL

flair (fler) *n.* [< OFr. < *flairer,* ult. < L. *fragare,* to smell] 1. keen, natural discernment 2. an aptitude; knack 3. [Colloq.] smartness in style; dash

flak (flak) *n.* [G. *Fl(ieger)-a(bwehr)k(anone),* antiaircraft gun] the fire of antiaircraft guns

flake¹ (flāk) *n.* [< Scand., as in Norw. *flak,* ice floe, ON. *flackna,* to flake off] 1. a small, thin mass [a *flake* of snow] 2. a thin piece or layer split or peeled off from anything; chip —*vt., vi.* **flaked, flak′ing** 1. to form into flakes 2. to chip or peel off in flakes 3. to make or become spotted with flakes —**flake out** [Slang] 1. to go to sleep 2. to faint —**flak′er** *n.*

flake² (flāk) *n.* [ME. *flake, fleke* < ON. *flaki, fleki,* hurdle] a rack for storing or drying food

flak·y (flāk′ē) *adj.* **flak′i·er, flak′i·est** 1. containing or made up of flakes 2. breaking easily into flakes —**flak′i·ly** *adv.* —**flak′i·ness** *n.*

‡**flam·bé** (flän bā′) *adj.* [Fr., lit., flaming] served with a flaming sauce containing brandy, rum, etc.

flam·beau (flam′bō) *n., pl.* **-beaux** (-bōz), **-beaus** [Fr., dim. of OFr. *flambe,* FLAME] a lighted torch

flam·boy·ant (flam boi′ənt) *adj.* [Fr. < OFr. < *flambe,* FLAME] 1. characterized by flamelike tracery of windows and florid decoration, as late French Gothic architecture 2. flamelike or brilliant 3. too showy or ornate —**flam·boy′-ance, flam·boy′an·cy** *n.* —**flam·boy′ant·ly** *adv.*

flame (flām) *n.* [< OFr. < L. < *flamma* < *flagrare,* to burn] 1. the burning gas of a fire, seen as a flickering light; blaze 2. a tongue of light rising from a fire 3. the state of burning with a blaze of light 4. a thing like a flame in heat, etc. 5. an intense emotion 6. a sweetheart: now usually humorous —*vi.* **flamed, flam′ing** 1. to burst into flame; blaze 2. to grow red or hot 3. to become very excited —*vt.* to treat with flame —**flame up** (or **out**) to burst out in or as in flame —**flam′y** *adj.*

flame-gun (flām′gun) *n.* a gun used to project flames onto weeds, etc., to destroy them

fla·men (flā′men) *n., pl.* **fla′mens, flam·i·nes** (flam′ə nēz′) [L.] in ancient Rome, a priest in the service of one particular god

fla·men·co (flə meŋ′kō) *n.* [Sp., Flemish < DuFl. *Flaming,* a Fleming] 1. the energetic, emotional style of dance or music of Spanish gypsies 2. *pl.* **-cos** a song or dance in this style

flame-out (flām'out') *n.* the ceasing of combustion in a jet engine, caused by an abnormal flight condition

flame thrower a military weapon for shooting a stream of flaming petrol, oil, etc.

flame tree 1. an Australian tree with maple-like leaves and brilliant scarlet flowers 2. any of various trees with brilliant red flowers

flam·ing (flā'miŋ) *adj.* 1. burning with flames; blazing 2. like a flame in brilliance or heat 3. ardent; passionate —**flam'ing·ly** *adv.*

fla·min·go (flə'miŋ'gō) *n., pl.* **-gos, -goes** [Port. < Sp. *flamenco,* lit., Flemish: infl. by *flama,* FLAME] a tropical wading bird with long legs, a long neck, and bright pink or red feathers

flam·ma·ble (flam'ə b'l) *adj.* easily set on fire: term now preferred to INFLAMMABLE in commerce, industry, etc. —**flam'ma·bil'i·ty** *n.*

flan (flan) *n.* [Fr. < OFr. *flaon* < ML. *flado* < OHG. *flado,* flat cake] 1. a piece of shaped metal ready to be made into a coin by the stamp of a die; blank 2. an open case made of pastry or sponge cake and filled with custard, fruit, cheese, etc.

flange (flanj) *n.* [< ? ME. *flaunch,* an outer edge of a coat of arms] a projecting rim or collar on a wheel, pipe, etc., to hold it in place, give it strength, or attach it to something else —*vt.* **flanged, flang'ing** to put a flange on

flank (flaŋk) *n.* [< OFr. *flanc*] 1. the fleshy side of a person or animal between the ribs and the hip 2. a cut of beef from this part 3. the side of anything 4. *Mil.* the right or left side of a formation or force —*adj.* of or having to do with the flank —*vt.* 1. to be at the side of 2. to place at the side, or on either side, of 3. *a)* to attack the side of (an enemy unit) *b)* to pass around the side of (an enemy unit) —*vi.* to be located at the side (with *on* or *upon*)

flank·er (-ər) *n.* a person or thing that flanks; specif., a projecting fortification used for protecting or attacking a flank

flan·nel (flan'l) *n.* [< W. *gwlanen* < *gwlan,* wool] 1. a soft, lightweight, loosely woven woollen cloth 2. a small cloth, usually of towelling, used in washing, esp. the face or body 3. [*pl.*] trousers, etc. made of light flannel 4. [Colloq.] evasive talk; flattery —*vt.* **-nelled, -nel·ling** 1. to wrap or clothe in flannel 2. to wash or clean with a flannel 3. [Colloq.] to flatter —**flan'nel·ly** *adj.*

flan·nel·ette (flan'ə let') *n.* a soft cotton cloth resembling flannel

flap (flap) *n.* [ME. *flappe* < v. *flappen*: prob. echoic] 1. anything flat and broad that is attached at one end and hangs loose or covers an opening 2. the motion or slapping sound of a swinging flap 3. a hinged section of an aeroplane wing, used in landing and taking off 4. [Colloq.] a commotion; fuss —*vt.* **flapped, flap'ping** 1. to slap with something flat and broad 2. to move back and forth or up and down [the bird *flapped* its wings] —*vi.* 1. to move back and forth or up and down, as in the wind; flutter 2. to fly or try to fly by flapping the wings 3. [Colloq.] to become excited or confused —**flap'less** *adj.* —**flap'py** *adj.*

flap·doo·dle (flap'dōod''l) *n.* [<?] [Colloq.] nonsense

flap·jack (flap'jak') *n.* a chewy biscuit made from rolled oats, sugar and butter

flap·per (flap'ər) *n.* 1. one that flaps 2. [Colloq.] in the 1920's, a young woman considered bold or unconventional in actions and dress

flare (fler) *vi.* **flared, flar'ing** [ME. *fleare* < ?] 1. to blaze up brightly or burn unsteadily 2. to burst out suddenly in anger, etc. (often with *up* or *out*) 3. to curve or spread outwards, as the bell of a trumpet —*vt.* to make flare —*n.* 1. a bright, brief, unsteady blaze of light 2. a very bright light used as a distress signal, etc. 3. a sudden, brief outburst, as of emotion or sound 4. *a)* a curving outwards, as of a skirt *b)* a part that curves or spreads outwards, 5. a short-lived outburst of brightness on the sun

flare-path (-päth) *n.* an area lit up to facilitate the landing or take-off of an aircraft

flare-up (-up') *n.* a sudden outburst of flame or of anger, trouble, etc.

flar·ing (fler'iŋ) *adj.* 1. blazing brightly for a little while 2. curving or spreading outward —**flar'ing·ly** *adv.*

flash (flash) *vi.* [ME. *flaschen,* to splash: echoic] 1. to send out a sudden, brief light, esp. at intervals 2. to sparkle or gleam 3. to speak abruptly, esp. in anger (usually with *out*) 4. to come or pass swiftly and suddenly —*vt.* 1. to send out (light, etc.) in sudden, brief spurts 2. to cause to flash 3. to signal with light 4. to send (news, etc.) swiftly or suddenly 5. [Colloq.] to show briefly or ostentatiously [to *flash* a roll of money] —*n.* 1. *a)* a sudden, brief light *b)* a sudden burst of flame or heat 2. a brief time; moment 3. a sudden, brief display [a *flash* of wit] 4. a brief item of news sent by telegraph or radio 5. *a)* a sudden rush of water down a river or watercourse *b)* a device, as a sluice, for producing such a rush 6. anything that flashes —*adj.* 1. happening swiftly or suddenly [a *flash* flood] 2. working with a flash of light [a *flash* camera] 3. sham; counterfeit

4. [Colloq.] *a)* ostentatious; showy *b)* of or relating to the criminal underworld —**flash in the pan** [orig. of priming in pan of a flintlock] 1. a sudden, apparently brilliant effort that fails 2. one that fails after such an effort —**flash'er** *n.* —**flash'ing·ly** *adv.*

flash·back (-bak') *n.* 1. an interruption in the continuity of a story, play, etc. by the presentation of some earlier episode 2. such an episode

flash·board (-bôrd') *n.* a board placed at the top of a dam to increase the depth or force of the stream

flash·bulb (-bulb') *n. Photog.* an electric light bulb giving a brief, dazzling light

flash burn injury or destruction of body tissue caused by exposure to a flash of intense radiant heat, esp. that of a nuclear explosion

flash·card (-kärd') *n.* any of a set of cards with words, numbers, etc. on them, flashed one by one before a class in a lesson

flash·cube (-kyōōb') *n.* a small, rotating cube containing a flashbulb in each of four sides

flash·gun (-gun') *Photog.* a synchronized device that simultaneously sets off a flashbulb and works the camera shutter

flash·ing (-iŋ) *n.* sheets of metal, etc. used to weatherproof joints, edges, etc., esp. of a roof

flash·light (-līt') *n.* 1. a brief, dazzling light for taking photographs at night or indoors 2. [U.S.] a torch

flash point the lowest temperature at which the vapour of a volatile oil will ignite with a flash

flash·y (-ē) *adj.* **flash'i·er, flash'i·est** 1. dazzling or bright for a little while 2. gaudy; showy —**flash'i·ly** *adv.* —**flash'i·ness** *n.*

flask (fläsk) *n.* [< ML. *flasco* & OE. *flasce* < LL. < *flasca*] 1. any small bottle with a narrow neck, used in laboratories, etc. 2. a small, flat pocket container for spirits, etc.

flat¹ (flat) *adj.* **flat'ter, flat'test** [< ON. *flatr*] 1. having a smooth, level surface 2. *a)* lying extended at full length *b)* spread out smooth and level 3. *a)* broad, even, and thin *b)* having a flat heel or no heel [*flat* shoes] 4. almost straight or level [a *flat* trajectory or flight] 5. absolute; positive [a *flat* denial] 6. not fluctuating [a *flat* rate] 7. having little or no sparkle or taste 8. monotonous; dull 9. not clear or full [a *flat* sound] 10. emptied of air [a *flat* tyre] 11. without gloss [*flat* paint] 12. *Art a)* lacking relief or perspective *b)* uniform in tint 13. *Music a)* below the true or proper pitch *b)* lower in pitch by a semitone [D-*flat*] 14. *Phonet.* designating the vowel *a* sounded with the tongue in a relatively level position, as in *can* —*adv.* 1. in a flat manner 2. in a flat position 3. *a)* exactly; precisely [ten seconds *flat*] *b)* bluntly; abruptly [she left him *flat*] 4. *Music* below the true or proper pitch —*n.* 1. a flat surface or part [the *flat* of the hand] 2. an expanse of level land 3. a low-lying marsh 4. a shallow; shoal 5. a piece of theatrical scenery on a flat frame 6. a deflated tyre 7. [*pl.*] flat-heeled shoes 8. *Music a)* a note or tone one semitone below another *b)* the symbol ( ) indicating such a note —*vt., vi.* **flat'ted, flat'ting** to make or become flat —**fall flat** to arouse no response —**flat'ly** *adv.* —**flat'ness** *n.* —**flat'tish** *adj.*

flat² (flat) *n.* [altered < Scot. dial. *flet* (OE. *flet*), a floor of a dwelling] living accommodation on one floor of a building

flat·boat (-bōt') *n.* a flat-bottomed boat for carrying cargo in shallow waters or on rivers

flat·fish (-fish') *n., pl.* **-fish', -fish'es**: see FISH a fish with a flat body and both eyes on the uppermost side, as the flounder, halibut, etc.

flat·foot (-foot') *n.* 1. a condition in which the instep arch of the foot has been flattened 2. [Slang] a policeman

flat·foot·ed (-foot'id) *adj.* 1. having flatfoot 2. [Colloq.] uninspired —**flat'-foot'ed·ly** *adv.* —**flat'-foot'ed·ness** *n.*

flat·i·ron (-ī'ərn) *n.* an iron for pressing clothes, usually triangular-shaped, and heated by being placed on a hot surface

flat·let (flat'lət) *n.* a small flat

flat race a horse race over a level course

flat spin 1. *Aero.* a spiral dive where an aircraft rotates in a plane more horizontal than vertical 2. [Colloq.] a state of confusion

flat·ten (-'n) *vt., vi.* 1. to make or become flat or flatter 2. to make or become prostrate —**flat'ten·er** *n.*

flat·ter (flat'ər) *vt.* [< OFr. *flater,* to smooth < Frank. *flat*] 1. to praise too much or insincerely, as to win favour 2. to try to please, or get the favour of, as by praise 3. to make seem more attractive than is so [his portrait *flatters* him] 4. to make feel pleased or honoured —*vi.* to use flattery —**flatter oneself** to be smug or deluded in thinking (that) —**flat'ter·er** *n.* —**flat'ter·ing·ly** *adv.*

flat·ter·y (flat'ər ē) *n., pl.* **-ter·ies** 1. a flattering 2. excessive or insincere praise

flat·u·lent (flat'yoo lənt) *adj.* [Fr. < ModL. < L. < *flare,* to blow] 1. of, having, or producing gas in the stomach or intestines 2. windy or empty in speech; pompous;

pretentious —**flat′u·lence, flat′u·len·cy** *n.* —**flat′u·lent·ly** *adv.*

flat·ware (flat′wer′) *n.* relatively flat tableware, as plates

flat·worm (-wʉrm′) *n.* same as PLATYHELMINTH

flaunt (flônt) *vi.* [prob. < *dial. flant*, to strut coquettishly] 1. to make a gaudy or impudent display 2. to flutter freely —*vt.* to show off proudly or impudently —**flaunt′ing·ly** *adv.*

flau·tist (flôt′ist) *n.* [It. *flautista* < *flauto*, flute] a flute player

flav·es·cent (flav es′ənt) *adj.* [< L. *flavescene*, to turn yellow] turning yellow; yellowish

fla·vin (flā′vin, flav′in) *n.* [< L. *flavus*, yellow + -IN¹] 1. a complex ketone, $C_{10}H_6N_4O_2$ 2. a natural or synthetic yellow pigment Also **fla′vine** (-vēn, -ēn)

fla·vone (flā′vōn, flav′ōn) *n.* [G. *flavon* < L. *flavus*, yellow] 1. colourless crystalline compound, used as a base for some yellow dyes 2. any derivative of this

fla·vo·pro·tein (flā vō prō′tēn, -prōt′ē in) *n.* any of a group of proteins linked chemically with flavins, that play a role in tissue respiration

fla·vor (flā′vər) *n.,vt.* U.S. sp. of FLAVOUR

fla·vour (flā′vər) *n.* [< OFr. *flaur* < L. *flatare*, freq. of *flare*, to blow] 1. a) the combined taste and smell of something b) taste in general 2. same as FLAVOURING 3. characteristic quality —*vt.* to give flavour to —**fla′vour·ful** *adj.* —**fla′vour·less** *adj.*

fla·vour·ing (-iŋ) *n.* an essence, extract, etc. added to a food or drink to give it a certain taste

flaw¹ (flô) *n.* [prob. < Scand.: see FLAKE] 1. a break, scratch, crack, etc. that spoils something; blemish 2. a defect; fault; error —*vt., vi.* to make or become faulty —**flaw′less** *adj.* —**flaw′less·ly** *adv.* —**flaw′less·ness** *n.*

flaw² (flô) *n.* [prob. < ON. *flaga*, sudden onset] a sudden, brief gust of wind; squall

flax (flaks) *n.* [OE. *fleax*] 1. any of a certain genus of plants; esp., a slender, erect annual with delicate blue flowers and narrow leaves: the seed (**flax′seed**′) yields linseed oil, and the fibres of the stem are spun into linen thread 2. these fibres

flax·en (-′n) *adj.* 1. of or made of flax 2. like flax in colour; pale-yellow: also **flax′y**

flax-lily (-li′lē) *n.* a New Zealand plant of the lily family which produces fibres

flay (flā) *vt.* [OE. *flean*] 1. to strip off the skin or hide of, as by whipping 2. to criticize or scold mercilessly 3. to rob; pillage —**flay′er** *n.*

F layer the highest regular layer of the ionosphere, reflecting high-frequency radio waves

flea (flē) *n.* [< OE. *fleah*] a small, wingless jumping insect that is parasitic and sucks blood —**a flea in one's ear** an annoying rebuff

flea-bane (-bān) *n.* [FLEA + BANE] any of several strong-smelling plants reputed to drive away fleas

flea-bite (bit′) *n.* 1. the bite of a flea 2. a slight annoyance or inconvenience

flea-bit·ten (-bit′'n) *adj.* 1. bitten by or infested with fleas 2. wretched; shabby

flea market an outdoor bazaar dealing mainly in cheap, secondhand goods

flea-pit (-pit) *n.* [Colloq.] a small, shabby and dirty cinema or theatre

flèche (flesh) *n.* [Fr., an arrow] a slender spire, esp. one over the intersection of the nave and the transepts in some Gothic churches

fleck (flek) *n.* [ON. *flekkr*] 1. a spot or small patch of colour, etc.; speck 2. a particle; flake —*vt.* to cover or sprinkle with flecks; speckle

fled (fled) *pt. & pp.* of FLEE

fledge (flej) *vi.* **fledged, fledg′ing** [< OE. (*un*)*flycge*, (un)fledged] to grow the feathers needed for flying —*vt.* 1. to rear (a young bird) until it can fly 2. to supply with feathers

fledg·ling (flej′liŋ) *n.* 1. a young bird just fledged 2. a young, inexperienced person Also **fledge′ling**

flee (flē) *vi.* **fled, flee′ing** [OE. *fleon*] 1. to run away or escape from danger, pursuit, etc. 2. to pass away swiftly; vanish 3. to go swiftly —*vt.* to run away from; shun —**fle′er** *n.*

fleece (flēs) *n.* [OE. *fleos*] 1. the wool covering a sheep or similar animal 2. the amount of wool cut from a sheep in one shearing 3. a covering like a sheep's 4. a fabric with a soft, warm pile —*vt.* **fleeced, fleec′ing** 1. to shear fleece from 2. to steal from by fraud; swindle —**fleec′er** *n.*

fleec·y (-ē) *adj.* **fleec′i·er, fleec′i·est** made of, covered with, or like fleece —**fleec′i·ly** *adv.* —**fleec′i·ness** *n.*

fleer (flir) *vi., vt.* [prob. < Scand.] to laugh derisively (at); sneer or jeer (at) —*n.* a derisive grimace, laugh, etc. —**fleer′ing·ly** *adv.*

fleet¹ (flēt) *n.* [OE. *fleot < fleotan*, to float] 1. a) a number of warships under one command b) an entire navy 2. any group of ships, trucks, buses, aircraft, etc. under one control

fleet² (flēt) *vi.* [OE. *fleotan*: see prec.] to move swiftly; fly —*adj.* swift; rapid —**fleet′ly** *adv.* —**fleet′ness** *n.*

fleet³ (flēt) *n.* [OE. *fleotan*: see FLEET¹] [Dial.] a small inlet; creek —**the Fleet** 1. a former small creek in London, now a covered sewer 2. a debtors' prison which stood near this creek: also **Fleet Prison**

Fleet Air Arm the flying service forming part of the Royal Navy

fleet chief petty officer see MILITARY RANKS, table

fleet·ing (flēt′iŋ) *adj.* passing swiftly; not lasting —**fleet′-ing·ly** *adv.* —**fleet′ing·ness** *n.*

Fleet Street [after the street in London where many newspaper offices are situated] British journalism or journalists collectively

Flem·ish (flem′ish) *adj.* of Flanders, the Flemings, or their language —*n.* the West Germanic language of the Flemings —**the Flemish** the people of Flanders

flense (flens) *vt.* **flensed, flens′ing** [< Du. *vlensen*, to cut blubber or skin from (a whale, seal, etc.): also **flench** (flench)

flesh (flesh) *n.* [OE. *flæsc*] 1. a) the soft substance of the body (of a person or animal); esp., the muscular tissue b) the skin of the body 2. meat; esp., meat other than fish or fowl 3. the pulpy or edible part of fruits and vegetables 4. the human body, as distinguished from the soul 5. human nature, esp. in its sensual aspect 6. all living beings, esp. all mankind 7. kindred: now mainly in **one's (own) flesh and blood**, one's close relatives 8. the typical colour of a white person's skin; yellowish pink —*vt.* 1. to incite to bloodshed, etc. by a foretaste 2. to fatten 3. to fill out by adding details, etc. (usually with *out*) —*vi.* to grow fat (usually with *out* or *up*) —**flesh and blood** the human body —**in the flesh** 1. alive 2. in person

flesh-col·oured (-kul′ərd) *adj.* yellowish-pink

flesh·er (-ər) *n.* [Scot.] a butcher

flesh·ings (-iŋz) *n.pl.* 1. flesh-coloured tights, worn by acrobats, etc. 2. pieces of flesh scraped from hides

flesh·ly (-lē) *adj.* **-li·er, -li·est** 1. of the body 2. sensual 3. same as FLESHY —**flesh′li·ness** *n.*

flesh·pot (-pot′) *n.* 1. a pot for cooking meat 2. [*pl.*] a) bodily comfort and pleasures; luxuries b) a place where such pleasures are provided

flesh wound a wound that does not reach the bones or vital organs

flesh·y (-ē) *adj.* **flesh′i·er, flesh′i·est** 1. having much flesh; plump 2. of or like flesh 3. having a firm pulp: said of some fruits —**flesh′i·ness** *n.*

fletch·er (flech′ər) *n.* [ME.< O FR. *flechier* < *fleche*, an arrow] [Obs.] a person who makes arrows

fleur-de-lis (flʉr′də lē′, -lēs′) *n., pl.* **fleurs-de-lis** (flʉr′-də lēs′) [< OFr. *flor de lis*, lit., flower of the lily] 1. same as IRIS (senses 3 & 4) 2. the coat of arms of the former French royal family 3. *Heraldry* a lilylike emblem Also sp. **fleur-de-lys**

fleur·et (flʉr′et) *n.* [< Fr. *fleurette*, a small flower] an ornament or motif resembling a flower

flew (flōō) *pt.* of FLY¹

flews (flōōz) *n.pl.* [< ?] the loose, hanging parts of the upper lip of a hound or other dog

FLEUR-DE-LIS

flex¹ (fleks) *vt., vi.* [< L. *flexus*, pp. of *flectere*, to bend] 1. to bend (an arm, knee, etc.) 2. to contract (a muscle)

flex² (fleks) *n.* [< FLEXIBLE] flexible, insulated electric wire

flex·i·ble (flek′sə b'l) *adj.* [< OFr. < L. < *flexus*: see FLEX¹] 1. able to bend without breaking 2. easily persuaded or influenced 3. adjustable to change —**flex′i·bil′i·ty** *n.* —**flex′i·bly** *adv.*

flex·ion (flek′shən) *n.* [< L. pp. of *flectare*, to bend] 1. a bending; flexing 2. a bent part 3. *Anat.* the bending of a joint or limb by means of the flexor muscles —**flex′ion·al** *adj.*

flex·or (-sər) *n.* [ModL. < L.: see FLEX¹] a muscle that bends a limb or other part of the body

flex·u·ous (-shoo wəs) *adj.* winding or wavering —**flex′-u·os′i·ty** (-wos′ə tē) *n., pl.* **-ties**

flex·ure (-shər) *n.* 1. a bending; curving; flexing 2. a bend; curve; fold —**flex′ur·al** *adj.*

flib·ber·ti·gib·bet (flib′ər tē jib′it) *n.* [< ?] an irresponsible, flighty person

flick¹ (flik) *n.* [echoic, but infl. by FLICKER¹] 1. a light, quick stroke, jerk, or snap 2. a light, snapping sound 3. a fleck; speck —*vt.* 1. to strike, remove, etc. with a light, quick stroke 2. to make such a stroke with (a whip, etc.) —*vi.* to flutter

flick² (flik) *n.* [< ff.] [Slang] a cinema film —**the flicks** [Slang] a cinema showing of an entire performance

flick·er¹ (flik′ər) *vi.* [OE. *flicorian*] 1. to move with a quick, light, wavering motion 2. to burn or shine unsteadily, as a candle flame —*vt.* to make flicker —*n.* 1.

a flickering **2.** a flame or light that flickers **3.** a quick, passing look or feeling —**flick′er·y** *adj.*

flick·er² (flik′ər) *n.* [echoic of its cry] any of several N. American woodpeckers, esp. one with wings of a golden colour on the underside

flick knife a knife with a retractable blade that springs out when a button on the handle is pressed

fli·er (flī′ər) *n. same as* FLYER

flight¹ (flīt) *n.* [OE. *flyht*] **1.** the act, manner, or power of flying or moving through space **2.** distance flown at one time, as by an aeroplane, bird, etc. **3.** a group of birds, arrows, etc. flying together **4.** *a)* a formation of military aircraft in flight *b)* a subdivision of a squadron in an air force **5.** an aeroplane scheduled to fly a certain trip **6.** *a* trip by aeroplane **7.** a soaring above the ordinary [a *flight* of fancy] **8.** a set of stairs, as between floors —**in the first** (or **top**) **flight** of the best quality

flight² (flīt) *n.* [< OE. < base of *fleon*, to flee] a fleeing, as from danger —**put to flight** to force to flee —**take** (**to**) **flight** to run away; flee

flight control 1. the control from the ground, as by radio, of aircraft in flight **2.** a station exercising such control

flight deck 1. the compartment in an airliner in which the pilots and crew sit **2.** the upper deck of an aircraft carrier where aircraft take off and land

flight·less (-lis) *adj.* not able to fly

flight lieutenant *see* MILITARY RANKS, table

flight path the course through the air taken or planned by an aircraft, rocket or projectile

flight recorder an electronic device fitted to an aircraft for collecting and storing information concerning its performance in flight, and often used to determine the cause of an accident: also called **black box**

flight sergeant *see* MILITARY RANKS, table

flight·y (-ē) *adj.* **flight′i·er, flight′i·est 1.** frivolous or irresponsible **2.** foolish; silly —**flight′i·ly** *adv.* —**flight′- i·ness** *n.*

flim·flam (flim′flam′) *n.* [< ?] **1.** nonsense **2.** a sly trick or deception —*vt.* **-flammed′, -flam′ming** [Colloq.] to trick —**flim′flam′mer·y** *n.*

flim·sy (flim′zē) *adj.* **-si·er, -si·est** [< ?] **1.** thin and easily broken or damaged; fragile **2.** weak or inadequate [a flimsy excuse] —*n.* **1.** a sheet of thin paper **2.** copy written on such paper, as by a reporter —**flim′si·ly** *adv.* —**flim′si·ness** *n.*

flinch (flinch) *vi.* [< OFr. *flenchir*] **1.** to draw back, as from a blow, difficulty, etc. **2.** to wince, as because of pain —*n.* a flinching

flin·ders (flin′dərz) *n.pl.* [< Scand., as in Norw. *flindra*, splinter] splinters or fragments

fling (flin) *vt.* **flung, fling′ing** [ME. *flingen*, to rush < ON. *flengja*, to whip] **1.** to throw, esp. with force; hurl **2.** to put abruptly or violently [to be *flung* into confusion] **3.** to move (one's limbs, head, etc.) suddenly or impulsively **4.** to throw (oneself) spiritedly (*into* a task, etc.) **5.** to cast aside —*vi.* to move suddenly and violently —*n.* **1.** a flinging **2.** a brief time of self-indulgence **3.** a spirited dance [the Highland *fling*] **4.** [Colloq.] a trial effort; try —**fling′er** *n.*

flint (flint) *n.* [OE.] **1.** a fine-grained, very hard, siliceous rock that makes sparks when struck with steel **2.** a piece of this stone, used to start a fire, for primitive tools, etc. **3.** anything like flint in hardness, use, etc. [a heart of *flint*, a lighter *flint* of iron-cerium alloy]

flint glass a hard, bright lead-oxide glass, used for lenses, crystal, etc.

flint·lock (-lok′) *n.* **1.** a gunlock using a flint in the hammer to strike sparks to ignite the powder **2.** an oldfashioned gun with such a lock

flint·y (flin′tē) *adj.* **flint′i·er, flint′i·est 1.** of or containing flint **2.** like flint; very hard or firm —**flint′i·ly** *adv.* —**flint′- i·ness** *n.*

flip¹ (flip) *vt.* **flipped, flip′ping** [echoic] **1.** to move with a quick jerk **2.** to snap (a coin) into the air with the thumb, as in betting on which side will land uppermost **3.** to turn (a card, etc.) over quickly —*vi.* **1.** to make a quick, light stroke or move; snap **2.** to flip a coin **3.** [Slang] to lose self-control from excitement, anger, etc.: also **flip one's lid** (or **wig**) —*n.* a flipping; snap, toss, etc.

flip² (flip) *n.* [prob. < prec.] a sweetened mixed drink of wine or spirits with egg, spices, etc.

flip³ (flip) *adj.* **flip′per, flip′pest** [contr. < FLIPPANT] [Colloq.] flippant; saucy; impertinent

flip-flop (flip′flop′) *n.* **1.** an acrobatic spring backwards from feet to hands to feet **2.** an abrupt change, as to the opposite opinion **3.** a flapping noise **4.** *Electronics* a circuit with two stable states, switching from one to the other on signal —*vi.* **-flopped′, -flop′ping** to do a flip-flop

flip·pan·cy (flip′ən sē) *n.* **1.** a being flippant **2.** *pl.* **-cies** a flippant act or remark

flip·pant (-ənt) *adj.* [Early ModE., nimble, prob. < FLIP¹] frivolous and disrespectful; saucy; impertinent —**flip′pant·ly** *adv.*

flip·per (-ər) *n.* [< FLIP¹] **1.** a broad, flat limb, as of a seal,

adapted for swimming **2.** a paddlelike rubber piece worn on each foot as a help in swimming **3.** [Slang] a hand

flip side [Colloq.] the reverse side (of a gramophone record), esp. the less important side

flirt (flurt) *vt.* [< ? OFr. *fleureter*, lit., move from flower to flower < *fleur*, FLOWER] to move quickly back and forth —*vi.* **1.** to move jerkily **2.** to woo someone lightly or frivolously **3.** to toy, as with an idea —*n.* **1.** a flirting movement **2.** a person who plays at love —**flirt′y** *adj.*

flir·ta·tion (flər tā′shən) *n.* a flirting, or playing at love

flir·ta·tious (-shəs) *adj.* flirting or inclined to flirt —**flir·ta′- tious·ly** *adv.* —**flir·ta′tious·ness** *n.*

flit (flit) *vi.* **flit′ted, flit′ting** [< ON. *flytja*] **1.** to pass or fly lightly and rapidly; dart; flutter **2.** [Scot. & North Eng.] to move house —*n.* a flitting —**flit′ter** *n.*

flitch (flich) *n.* [OE. *flicce*] the cured and salted side of a pig; side of bacon —*vt.* to cut into flitches

flit·ter (flit′ər) *vi., vt.* [freq. of FLIT] [Chiefly Dial.] same *as* FLUTTER

flit·ter·mouse (-mous) *n. same as* BAT²

float (flōt) *n.* [OE. *flota* < *fleotan*, to float] **1.** anything staying, or making something else stay, on or at a liquid's surface; specif., *a)* a fishing-line cork *b)* a floating, valve-controlling ball, etc. that regulates liquid level, as in a tank *c)* a buoyant device on an aircraft for landing on water **2.** a platform on wheels that carries a display or exhibit in a parade **3.** a sum of money used *a)* to provide change *b)* to cover small expenses —*vi.* **1.** to stay on or at a liquid's surface **2.** to drift gently on water, in air, etc. **3.** to move about vaguely and without purpose —*vt.* **1.** to make float **2.** to flood **3.** *a)* to put into circulation [*float* a bond issue] *b)* to establish or start (a business, etc.) **4.** to arrange for (a loan)

float·age (-ij) *n.* **1.** the act or power of floating **2.** anything that floats; esp. floating debris; flotsam: also sp. **flo′tage**

float·a·tion (flō tā′shən) *n. same as* FLOTATION

float·er (flōt′ər) *n.* **1.** one that floats **2.** *same as* FLOATING VOTER **3.** a person who changes his place of residence or work frequently

float·ing (-in) *adj.* **1.** that floats **2.** not fixed; moving about **3.** *Finance a)* designating an unfunded, short-time debt *b)* not permanently invested [*floating* capital] **4.** *Mech.* designating or of suspension that reduces vibration **5.** *Med.* displaced and more movable [a *floating* kidney]

floating anchor a sea anchor

floating light 1. a lightship **2.** a life-buoy with a lantern attached

floating ribs the eleventh and twelfth pairs of ribs, not attached to the breastbone or to other ribs but only to the vertebrae

floating voter a voter of no fixed political allegiance

floats (flōts) *n.pl. same as* FOOTLIGHTS

floc·cu·late (flok′yoo lāt′) *vt., vi.* **-lat′ed, -lat′ing** to collect (clouds, precipitates, etc.) into small, flocculent masses —**floc′cu·la′tion** *n.*

floc·cu·lent (-lənt) *adj.* [< L. *floccus*, flock of wool + -ULENT] woolly; fluffy —**floc′cu·lence** *n.*

floc·cu·lus (-yoo ləs) *n. pl.* **-li′** (-lē) [ModL., dim. < L. *floccus*: see FLOCCULENT] **1.** a small woolly or hairy tuft **2.** *Anat.* a small lobe on the underside of each half of the cerebellum **3.** *Astron.* a cloudy mark on the sun's surface, either light and composed of calcium, or dark and composed of hydrogen

flock¹ (flok) *n.* [OE. *flocc*, a troop] **1.** a group of certain animals, as goats or sheep, or of birds, living, feeding, etc. together **2.** any group, esp. a large one, as of church members —*vi.* to assemble or travel in a flock

flock² (flok) *n.* [< OFr. < L. *floccus*] **1.** a small tuft of wool, cotton, etc. **2.** wool or cotton waste used to stuff furniture, etc. **3.** tiny fibres put on wallpaper, etc. to form a velvety surface or design Also sp. **floc** —**flock′y** *adj.* **flock′- i·er, flock′i·est**

flock·ing (-in) *n.* **1.** *same as* FLOCK² (sense 3) **2.** a material or surface with flock on it

floe (flō) *n.* [prob. < Norw. *flo*, layer] *same as* ICE FLOE

flog (flog) *vt.* **flogged, flog′ging** [? cant abbrev. of L. *flagellare*, to whip] **1.** to beat with a stick, whip, etc. **2.** [Slang] to sell, esp. illegally —**flog a dead horse** to waste energy on something from which no results can come —**flog′ger** *n.*

flong (flon) *n.* [< Fr. *flan*, see FLAN] *Printing* prepared paper used for making moulds in stereotyping

flood (flud) *n.* [OE. *flod*] **1.** an overflowing of water on an area normally dry; deluge **2.** the flowing in of water from the sea as the tide rises **3.** a great flow or outpouring, as of words **4.** [Archaic] a large body of water —*vt.* **1.** to cover or fill with or as with a flood; inundate [rain *flooded* the earth, music *flooded* the room] **2.** to put much or too much liquid on or in —*vi.* **1.** to rise, flow, or gush out in or as in a flood **2.** to become flooded —**the Flood** *Bible* the great flood in Noah's time: Gen. 7

flood·gate (-gāt′) *n.* **1.** a gate in a stream or canal, to control water height and flow **2.** anything like this in controlling an outburst

flood·light (-līt´) *n.* **1.** a lamp that casts a broad beam of bright light **2.** such light —*vt.* **-light´ed** or **-lit´, -light´ing** to illuminate by a floodlight

flood tide the incoming or rising tide

floor (flôr) *n.* [OE. *flor*] **1.** the inside bottom surface of a room **2.** any bottom surface [the ocean *floor*] **3.** the platform of a bridge, pier, etc. **4.** a level or storey in a building **5.** *a)* the part of a legislative chamber, stock exchange, etc. occupied by members *b)* the members as a group **6.** the right to speak in an assembly **7.** a lower limit set on anything —*vt.* **1.** to cover or furnish with a floor **2.** to knock down **3.** [Colloq.] *a)* to defeat *b)* to make unable to act, as by shocking, amazing, confusing, etc. —**take the floor** **1.** to address a meeting **2.** to get up to dance

floor·age (-ij) *n.* the area of a floor: also **floor space**

floor·board (-bôrd´) *n.* a board in a floor

floor·ing (-iŋ) *n.* **1.** a floor **2.** floors collectively **3.** material for making a floor

floor plan a scale drawing of the layout of rooms, halls, etc. on one floor of a building

floor show a show presenting singers, dancers, etc. in a restaurant, nightclub, etc.

floo·zy, floo·zie (flōō´zē) *n., pl.* **-zies** [Slang] a loose, disreputable woman: also sp. **floo´sy, floo´sie**

flop (flop) *vt.* **flopped, flop´ping** [var. of FLAP] to flap or throw noisily and clumsily —*vi.* **1.** *a)* to move or flap around loosely or clumsily *b)* to fall or drop thus **2.** [Colloq.] to be a failure —*n.* **1.** the act or sound of flopping **2.** [Colloq.] a failure —*adv.* with a flop —**flop´per** *n.*

flop·py (-ē) *adj.* **-pi·er, -pi·est** [Colloq.] tending to flop —**flop´pi·ly** *adv.* —**flop´pi·ness** *n.*

flo·ral (flôr´əl) *adj.* of, made of, or like flowers

Flor·en·tine (flôr´ən tīn´) *adj.* of Florence, Italy, or its people, culture, or art —*n.* a native or inhabitant of Florence

flo·res·cence (flô res´ ʼns, flo-, flə-) *n.* [< L. prp. of *florescere* < *florere*, to bloom < *flos*, FLOWER] a blooming or flowering —**flo·res´cent** *adj.*

flo·ret (flôr´it) *n.* [< OFr. dim. of *flor* < L. *flos*, FLOWER] **1.** a small flower **2.** any of the small flowers making up the head of a composite plant

flo·ri·at·ed (flôr´ē āt´id) *adj.* having floral decorations —**flo´ri·a´tion** *n.*

flo·ri·bun·da (flôr´ə bun´də) *n.* [Mod.L., fem. of *floribundus*, flowering freely] any of a class of cultivated roses with clusters of small to medium-sized flowers produced in profusion

flo·ri·cul·ture (flôr´ə kul´chər, flo´rə-) *n.* the cultivation of flowers —**flo´ri·cul´tur·al** *adj.* —**flo´ri·cul´tur·ist** *n.*

flor·id (flôr´id) *adj.* [L. *floridus* < *flos*, FLOWER] **1.** flushed with red: said of the complexion **2.** showy; ornate —**flo·rid·i·ty** (flo rid´ə tē, flə-), **flor´id·ness** *n.* —**flor´id·ly** *adv.*

flo·rif·er·ous (flō rif´ər əs, flə-) *adj.* [L. *florifer* (< *flos*, a flower + *ferre*, BEAR¹) + -OUS] bearing flowers; blooming abundantly

flor·in (flor´in) *n.* [< OFr. < It. < L. *flos*, FLOWER: the figure of a lily was stamped on the original coins] **1.** a gold coin of medieval Florence **2.** any of various European or South African silver or gold coins **3.** a former British coin worth two shillings

flo·rist (flôr´ist) *n.* [< L. *flos*, FLOWER] a person who cultivates or sells flowers —**flo´ris·try** *n.*

flo·ris·tic (flo ris´tik) *adj.* of flowers or flora

floss (flos) *n.* [prob. < Fr. < L. *floccus*, FLOCK²] **1.** the rough silk covering a silkworm's cocoon **2.** short, downy waste fibres of silk **3.** a soft thread or yarn, as of silk (**floss silk**) or linen (**linen floss**), used in embroidery **4.** a soft, silky, flosslike substance **5.** *same as* DENTAL FLOSS

floss·y (-ē) *adj.* **floss´i·er, floss´i·est** of or like floss; downy; fluffy

flo·ta·tion (flō tā´shən) *n.* a floating; specif., the starting or financing of a business, etc., as by selling an entire issue of bonds

flo·til·la (flō til´ə, flə-) *n.* [Sp., dim. of *flota*, a fleet] a small fleet, or a fleet of small ships

flot·sam (flot´səm) *n.* [< OFr. < MDu. *vloten* (or OE. *flotian*), to float] the wreckage of a ship or its cargo floating at sea: chiefly in **flotsam and jetsam**, *a)* such wreckage or cargo either floating or washed ashore *b)* miscellaneous trifles *c)* transient, unemployed people

flounce¹ (flouns) *vi.* **flounced, flounc´ing** [prob. < Scand.] **1.** to move with quick, flinging motions of the body, as in anger **2.** to twist or turn abruptly; jerk —*n.* the act of flouncing

flounce² (flouns) *n.* [earlier *frounce* < OFr. < *froncir*, to wrinkle] a wide, ornamental ruffle, as on a skirt —*vt.* **flounced, flounc´ing** to trim with a flounce or flounces —**flounc´y** *adj.*

floun·der¹ (floun´dər) *vi.* [? var. of FOUNDER¹] **1.** to struggle or plunge about awkwardly, as in deep mud **2.** to speak or act in an awkward, confused way —*n.* a floundering

floun·der² (floun´dər) *n., pl.* **-ders, -der:** see PLURAL, II, D. 1 [< Scand.] any of a large group of flatfishes caught for food, as the halibut

flour (flour) *n.* [var. of FLOWER, after Fr. *fleur de farine*, lit., flower (i.e., best) of meal] **1.** a fine, powdery substance produced by grinding and sifting grain or certain roots, etc. **2.** any finely powdered substance —*vt.* to put flour on or in —**flour´y** *adj.*

flour·ish (flur´ish) *vi.* [< OFr. *florir*, to blossom, ult. < L. *flos*, FLOWER] **1.** to grow vigorously; thrive; prosper **2.** to be at the peak of development, activity, etc. **3.** to make showy, wavy motions **4.** [Now Rare] to perform a fanfare —*vt.* to brandish (a sword, hat, etc.) —*n.* **1.** anything done in a showy way **2.** a brandishing **3.** a decorative line or lines in writing **4.** a fanfare —**flour´ish·er** *n.* —**flour´-ish·ing** *adj.* —**flour´ish·ing·ly** *adv.*

flout (flout) *vt., vi.* [prob. < ME. *flouten*, to play the flute, hence, whistle (at)] to show scorn or contempt (for) —*n.* a flouting —**flout´er** *n.* —**flout´ing·ly** *adv.*

flow (flō) *vi.* [OE. *flowan*] **1.** to move as a liquid does **2.** to stream **3.** to move gently and smoothly; glide **4.** to pour out **5.** to be derived; proceed **6.** to hang loose or in waves [*flowing* hair] **7.** to rise, as the tide **8.** to be plentiful —*n.* **1.** a flowing, or the manner or rate of this **2.** anything that flows; stream or current **3.** a continuous production

flow chart a diagram showing the progress of work through a sequence of operations: also **flow sheet**

flow·er (flou´ər, flour) *n.* [< OFr. < L. *flos* (gen. *floris*), a flower] **1.** *a)* the structure of many plants that produces seeds, typically with brightly coloured petals and leaflike sepals; blossom; bloom *b)* the reproductive structure of any plant **2.** a plant cultivated for its blossoms **3.** the best or finest part or example **4.** the best period of a person or thing **5.** something decorative; esp., a figure of speech **6.** [*pl.*] *Chem.* a powder made from condensed vapours —*vi.* **1.** to produce flowers or blossoms; bloom **2.** to reach the best period —*vt.* to decorate with flowers or floral patterns —**in flower** in a state of flowering —**flow´er·less** *adj.* —**flow´-er·like´** *adj.*

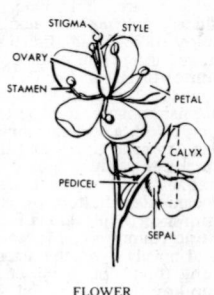

FLOWER

flow·ered (flou´ərd) *adj.* **1.** bearing or containing flowers **2.** having a floral design

flow·er·et (-ər it) *n.* **1.** *same as* FLORET **2.** [Poet.] a small flower

flower girl a girl or woman who sells flowers in the streets

flow·er·ing (-ər iŋ) *adj.* **1.** having flowers; in bloom **2.** bearing showy or profuse flowers

flower people [*often* F-P-] adherents, usually young people, of flower power, an anti-establishment cult of the late 1960's, which advocated peace and love

flow·er·pot (-pot´) *n.* a container, originally made of porous clay, in which to grow plants

flow·er·y (-ē) *adj.* **-er·i·er, -er·i·est** **1.** covered or decorated with flowers **2.** of or like flowers **3.** full of figurative and ornate expressions and fine words —**flow´er·i·ly** *adv.* —**flow´er·i·ness** *n.*

flow·ing (flō´iŋ) *adj.* **1.** moving; running **2.** fluent [a *flowing* style of writing] **3.** curving gracefully; falling in folds [*flowing* draperies] **4.** unrestrained [*flowing* tresses]

flown (flōn) *pp.* of FLY¹

fl. oz. fluid ounce; fluid ounces

flt. flight

flu (flōō) *n.* **1.** *a shortened form of* INFLUENZA **2.** popularly, any of various respiratory or intestinal infections caused by a virus

fluc·tu·ate (fluk´tyoo wāt´) *vi.* **-at´ed, -at´ing** [< L. pp. of *fluctuare* < *fluctus*, a wave] **1.** to move back and forth or up and down **2.** to vary irregularly —*vt.* to cause to fluctuate —**fluc´tu·ant** *adj.* —**fluc´tu·a´tion** *n.*

flue (flōō) *n.* [< ? OFr. *fluie*, a flowing] **1.** a tube or shaft for the passage of smoke, hot air, etc., as in a chimney **2.** *a)* *same as* FLUE PIPE *b)* the opening for air in a flue pipe

flu·ent (flōō´ənt) *adj.* [< L. prp. of *fluere*, to flow] **1.** flowing smoothly and easily **2.** able to write or speak easily, smoothly, and expressively —**flu´en·cy** *n.* —**flu´-ent·ly** *adv.*

flue pipe an organ pipe whose tone is produced by an air current striking a narrow side opening

fluff (fluf) *n.* [? blend of *flue*, downy mass + PUFF] **1.** soft, light down **2.** a loose, soft, downy mass, as of dust **3.** any light or trivial matter or talk **4.** *Theatre, Radio, TV* an error in speaking a line —*vt.* **1.** to shake or pat until loose, soft, and light **2.** *Theatre, Radio, TV* to make an error in speaking (one's lines, etc.) **3.** to botch; bungle —*vi.* **1.** to become fluffy **2.** to make an error —**bit of fluff** [Old Slang] an attractive girl

fluff·y (-ē) *adj.* **fluff′i·er, fluff′i·est 1.** soft and light like fluff; feathery **2.** covered with fluff —**fluff′i·ness** *n.*

flu·gel·horn (flōō′g'l hôrn) *n.* a type of valved brass musical instrument, consisting of a tube with a cup-shaped mouthpiece

flu·id (flōō′id) *adj.* [L. *fluidus* < *fluere*, to flow] **1.** that can flow; not solid **2.** of a fluid **3.** not settled or fixed *[fluid plans]* **4.** moving gracefully; flowing **5.** available for investment or as cash *[fluid assets]* —*n.* any substance that can flow; liquid or gas —**flu·id·ic** (flōō wid′ik) *adj.* —**flu·id′i·ty** *vt.* —**flu·id′i·ty, flu′id·ness** *n.* —**flu′id·ly** *adv.*

flu·id·ics (flōō wid′iks) *n.pl.* [*with sing.v.*] [FLUID + -ICS] the science or technology dealing with the control of a flow of air or fluid, used to perform functions of sensing, control, etc.

flu·id·ize (flōō′ə diz′) *vt.* **-ized, -iz′ing 1.** to make fluid **2.** to give fluid properties to (a solid), as by pulverizing

fluid ounce a liquid measure equal to 1/20 pint, or 28.4cm³: also **flu′id·ounce′** *n.*

fluke¹ (flōōk) *n.* [OE. *floc*] **1.** any of several flatfishes, esp. flounders **2.** a flatworm parasitic in internal organs of vertebrates

fluke² (flōōk) *n.* [prob. < prec.] **1.** the triangular, pointed end of an anchor arm, by which the anchor catches in the ground **2.** a barb or barbed head of an arrow, harpoon, etc. **3.** either of the two lobes of a whale's tail

fluke³ (flōōk) *n.* [< ?] **1.** [Old Slang] a lucky stroke in billiards, etc. **2.** [Colloq.] a lucky or unlucky outcome —*vt.* **fluked, fluk′ing** [Colloq.] to hit or get by a fluke

fluk·y (flōō′kē) *adj.* **fluk′i·er, fluk′i·est** [< prec.] [Colloq.] **1.** resulting from chance **2.** uncertain —**fluk′i·ness** *n.*

flume (flōōm) *n.* [< OFr. < L. *flumen*, river < *fluere*, to flow] **1.** an inclined chute or trough for carrying water to furnish power, transport logs, etc. **2.** [U.S.] a narrow gorge with a stream running through it —*vt.* **flumed, flum′ing** to send (logs, etc.) down a flume

flum·mer·y (flum′ər ē) *n., pl.* **-mer·ies** [W. *llymru*, soured oatmeal] **1.** any soft, light, fluffy or creamy pudding **2.** meaningless flattery or silly talk

flum·mox (flum′əks) *vt.* [< ?] [Slang] to confuse; perplex

flump (flump) *vt.,vi* [prob. echoic] to drop or move heavily and noisily —*n.* the act or sound of flumping

flung (flung) *pt. & pp.* of FLING

flun·key (flung′kē) *n., pl.* **-kies** [orig. Scot. < ? Fr. *flanquer*, to flank] **1.** one who obeys superiors in a servile way **2.** one having minor or menial tasks Also sp. **flun′ky** —**flun′key·ism** *n.*

flu·or (flōō′ər, -ôr) *n.* [ModL. < L. *flux* < *fluere*, to flow] *same as* FLUORITE

flu·o·resce (flōō′ə res′; floo res′, flô-) *vi.* **-resced′, -resc′ing** to show or undergo fluorescence

flu·o·res·cence (-'ns) *n.* [< FLUOR (SPAR) + -ESCENCE] **1.** the property of a substance, as fluorite, of producing light when acted upon by radiant energy, as ultraviolet rays or X-rays **2.** production of such light **3.** light so produced —**flu′o·res′cent** *adj.*

fluorescent lamp (or **tube**) a glass tube coated inside with a fluorescent substance giving off light (**fluorescent light**) when mercury vapour in the tube is acted upon by electrons from the cathode

fluor·i·date (floor′ə dāt′) *vt.* **-dat′ed, -dat′ing** to add fluorides to (a water supply) so as to reduce the incidence of tooth decay —**fluor′i·da′tion** *n.*

flu·o·ride (floor′īd) *n.* a compound of fluorine and another element or radical

fluor·i·nate (floor′ə nāt′) *vt.* **-nat′ed, -nat′ing 1.** to treat, or cause to combine, with fluorine **2.** *same as* FLUORIDATE —**fluor′i·na′tion** *n.*

flu·o·rine (floor′ēn) *n.* [< FLUOR + -INE⁴] a corrosive, poisonous, pale greenish-yellow, gaseous chemical element, the most reactive nonmetallic element known, forming fluorides with almost all elements: symbol, F; at. wt., 18.9984; at. no., 9

flu·o·rite (floor′īt) *n.* [< FLUOR(O)- + -ITE] calcium fluoride, a transparent, crystalline mineral of various colours: it is the principal source of fluorine and is used as a flux, in glassmaking, etc.

flu·o·ro- *a combining form meaning:* **1.** fluorine **2.** fluorescence Also before a vowel, **flu·or-**

flu·o·ro·car·bon (floor′ə kär′bən) *n.* any of a class of inert organic compounds containing carbon, fluorine, and sometimes hydrogen: used as lubricants, plastics, etc.

flu·o·rom·e·ter (floo rom′ə tər) *n.* an instrument for measuring the wavelength and intensity of fluorescence —**flu·o·ro·met·ric** (floor′ə met′rik) *adj.* —**flu·o·rom′e·try** *n.*

fluor·o·scope (floor′ə skōp′) *n.* [FLUORO-+ -SCOPE] a machine for examining internal structures by viewing the shadows cast on a fluorescent screen by objects through which X-rays are directed —*vt.* **-scoped′, -scop′ing** to

examine with a fluoroscope —**fluor′o·scop′ic** (-skop′ik) *adj.* —**fluor′o·scop′i·cal·ly** *adv.*

flu·o·ros·co·py (floo ros′kə pē) *n.* examination by fluoroscope —**flu·o·ros′co·pist** *n.*

flu·o·ro·sis (floo rō′sis) *n.* [Mod L.: see FLUORO- + -OSIS] a disorder resulting from the absorption of too much fluorine

fluor spar *same as* FLUORITE: also **flu′or·spar′** *n.*

flur·ry (flur′ē) *n., pl.* **-ries** [< ?] **1.** a sudden, brief rush of wind or fall of snow **2.** a sudden confusion or commotion **3.** a spurt of increased trading and price fluctuation in the stock market —*vt.* **-ried, -ry·ing** to confuse; agitate —*vi.* to move in a quick, flustered way

flush¹ (flush) *vi.* [blend of FLASH & ME. *flusschen*, to fly up suddenly] **1.** to flow and spread suddenly **2.** to blush or glow **3.** to become cleaned or emptied with a sudden flow of water, etc. **4.** to start up from cover: said of birds —*vt.* **1.** to make flow **2.** to clean or empty with a sudden flow of water, etc. **3.** to make blush or glow **4.** to excite; exhilarate *[flushed* with victory*]* **5.** to drive (game birds) from cover **6.** to make level or even —*n.* **1.** a sudden, rapid flow, as of water **2.** a sudden, vigorous growth *[the first flush* of youth*]* **3.** sudden excitement or exhilaration **4.** a blush or glow **5.** a sudden feeling of heat, as in a fever —*adj.* **1.** well supplied, esp. with money **2.** abundant **3.** *a)* making an even line or plane *b)* even with a margin or edge —*adv.* **1.** so as to be level or in alignment **2.** directly; squarely

flush² (flush) *n.* [Fr. *flux*: see FLUX] a hand of cards all in the same suit

flus·ter (flus′tər) *vt., vi.* [prob. < Scand.] to get confused or nervous —*n.* a flustered state

flute (flōōt) *n.* [< OFr. < Pr. *fläut* < ?] **1.** *a)* a high-pitched wind instrument consisting of a long, slender tube with finger holes and keys, played by blowing across a hole near one end *b)* any similar instrument, as the recorder **2.** an ornamental groove —*vt., vi.* **flut′ed, flut′ing 1.** to sing, speak, etc. in a flutelike tone **2.** to play on the flute **3.** to make ornamental grooves (in)

flut·ing (-ing) *n.* **1.** a series of ornamental grooves, as in a column **2.** the act of one that flutes

flut·ter (flut′ər) *vi.* [OE. *flotorian*, freq. of *flotian* < base of *fleotan*, to float] **1.** to flap the wings rapidly **2.** to wave or vibrate rapidly and irregularly *[a flag fluttering* in the wind*]* **3.** to move with quick vibrations, flaps, etc. **4.** to tremble; quiver **5.** to move about in a restless, fussy way —*vt.* **1.** to make flutter **2.** to excite or confuse —*n.* **1.** a fluttering **2.** a state of excitement or confusion **3.** [Colloq.] a modest bet or wager —**flut′ter·er** *n.* —**flut′ter·y** *adj*

flut·y (flōōt′ē) *adj.* **flut′i·er, flut′i·est** flutelike in tone; soft, clear, and high-pitched

flu·vi·al (flōō′vē əl) *adj.* [< L. < *fluvius*, a river < *fluere*, to flow] of, found in, or produced by a river: also **flu′vi·a·tile** (-ə til, -til)

flux (fluks) *n.* [< OFr. < L. *fluxus* < pp. of *fluere*, to flow] **1.** a flowing or flow **2.** a coming in of the tide **3.** continual change **4.** any abnormal discharge of fluid matter from the body **5.** *a)* a substance used to help fuse metals together, as in soldering *b)* a substance used, as in smelting, to fuse with undesired matter in forming a more fluid slag **6.** *Physics* the rate of flow of energy, fluids, etc. over a surface —*vt.* **1.** to make fluid **2.** to fuse (metals)

fly¹ (flī) *vi.* **flew, flown, fly′ing** [OE. *fleogan*] **1.** to move through the air by using wings, as a bird **2.** to travel through the air in an aircraft **3.** to be propelled through the air or through space, as a missile **4.** to operate an aircraft **5.** to wave or float in the air, as a flag or kite **6.** to move or go swiftly **7.** to flee —*vt.* **1.** *a)* to cause to float in the air *b)* to display (a flag) as from a pole **2.** to operate (an aircraft) **3.** to travel over in an aircraft **4.** to carry in an aircraft **5.** to flee from or avoid —*n., pl.* **flies 1.** a flap concealing the zipper, buttons, etc. in a garment **2.** a flap serving as a tent door **3.** the length of a flag from the staff outwards **4.** *same as: a)* FLYWHEEL *b)* FLYLEAF **5.** *[pl.] Theatre* the space behind and above the proscenium arch —**fly a kite 1.** to obtain money by accommodation bills **2.** to obtain an indication beforehand of the real state of affairs —**fly at** to attack by or as by springing towards —**fly high** [Colloq.] to be ambitious —**let fly** (**at**) **1.** to shoot or throw (at) **2.** to unleash a verbal attack (at)

fly² (flī) *n., pl.* **flies** [OE. *fleoge*] **1.** *a) same as* HOUSEFLY *b)* any of a large group of insects with two transparent wings, as the housefly and gnat *c)* any of several four-winged insects, as the mayfly **2.** a hooked lure for fishing, made to resemble an insect —**fly in amber** a relic of the past which is well-preserved —**fly in the ointment** a tiny flaw that destroys the value of a thing —**there are no flies on him** [Slang] he is very alert; not easily hoaxed

fly³ (flī) *adj.* [orig., thieves' slang < ?] [Slang] alert and knowing; sharp; quick

fly·a·ble (-ə b'l) *adj.* suitable or ready for flying *[flyable* weather, a *flyable* aeroplane*]*

fly agaric a poisonous mushroom

fly ash airborne bits of unburnable ash

fly·a·way (flī′ə wā′) *adj.* 1. streaming [*flyaway* hair] 2. capricious

fly·blown (-blōn′) *adj.* 1. full of flies' eggs or larvae 2. spoiled; tainted 3. [Colloq.] shabby; dingy

fly book a booklike case to hold artificial fishing flies

fly-by, fly-by (-bī′) *n., pl.* **-bies′** a flight past a given point by an aircraft or spacecraft, esp. the close approach of a spacecraft to a planet, etc., for observation

fly-by-night (-bī′nīt′) *adj.* not trustworthy, esp. financially —*n.* a fly-by-night person

fly·catch·er (-kach′ər) *n.* any of various small birds, esp. the pied flycatcher, that catch insects in flight

fly·er (-ər) *n.* 1. a thing that flies 2. an aviator 3. a bus, train, etc. on a fast timetable

fly-fish to fish by casting artificial flies

fly·ing (-iŋ) *adj.* 1. that flies or can fly 2. moving as if flying; fast 3. hasty and brief 4. of or for aircraft or aviators 5. organized to act quickly —*n.* the action of one that flies

flying bedstead an aircraft resembling a bedstead used in tests to develop vertical take-off jet aeroplanes

flying boat an aeroplane with a hull that permits it to land on and take off from water

flying bridge 1. a ferry boat which swings across stream, controlled partly by the current and partly by a rope attached to a buoy 2. *same as* PONTOON[2] (sense 2) 3. *Naut.* a small structure over the main bridge, from which a vessel may be conned

flying buttress a buttress connected to a wall by an arch, serving to resist outward pressure

flying colours 1. flags flying in the air 2. notable victory or success

flying doctor a doctor, esp. in Australia, who covers a wide area and visits his patients by aeroplane

flying fish any of a number of chiefly warm-water sea fishes with winglike pectoral fins that enable them to glide through the air

flying fox any of several fruit-eating bats with a foxlike head, living in Africa, Australia and S. Asia

flying gurnard a marine fish with winglike pectoral fins for gliding short distances in the air

flying jib a small, triangular sail in front of the jib

flying lemur a tree dwelling mammal of SE Asia, having a broad fold of skin on each side of the body between the forelimbs and the tail, that enables it to make long, gliding leaps

FLYING
BUTTRESS

flying machine early term for an aeroplane or other aircraft

flying officer *see* MILITARY RANKS, table

flying phalanger any of several small Australian marsupials with a thin membrane along the sides of the body, that enables them to make long, sailing leaps

flying saucer *same as* UFO

flying squirrel any of a number of squirrels with winglike folds of skin attached to the legs and body that enable them to make gliding leaps

flying start 1. the start of a race in which the contestants are already moving as they pass the starting line 2. any rapid beginning

flying wing an aircraft consisting mainly of one large wing and no fuselage

fly·leaf (flī′lēf′) *n., pl.* **-leaves′** (-lēvz′) a blank leaf at the beginning or end of a book

fly·o·ver (-ō′vər) *n.* 1. an intersection of two roads at which one is carried over the other by a bridge 2. [U.S.] *same as* FLY-PAST

fly·pa·per (-pā′pər) *n.* a sticky or poisonous paper set out to catch or kill flies

fly-past (-päst) *n.* a ceremonial flight of aircraft over a given area

fly·speck (-spek′) *n.* 1. a speck of fly excrement 2. any tiny spot —*vt.* to make flyspecks on

fly-spray (-sprā) *n.* a liquid squirted from an aerosol can to kill flies

fly·trap (-trap′) *n.* 1. any device for catching flies 2. a plant that catches insects

fly·way (-wā′) *n.* a flying route of migratory birds

fly·weight (-wāt′) *n. see* BOXING AND WRESTLING WEIGHTS, table —*adj.* of flyweights

fly·wheel (-hwēl′) *n.* a heavy wheel attached to a machine so as to regulate its speed and motion

Fm *Chem.* fermium

FM frequency modulation

F.M. Field Marshall

fm. 1. fathom 2. from

f-num·ber (ef′num′bər) *n. Photog.* the ratio of a lens diameter to its focal length: the lower the f-number, the shorter the exposure required

fo. folio

F.O. 1. Flying Officer 2. [obs.] Foreign Office

foal (fōl) *n.* [OE. *fola*] a young horse, mule, donkey, etc.; colt or filly —*vt., vi.* to give birth to (a foal)

foam (fōm) *n.* [OE. *fam*] 1. the whitish mass of bubbles formed on or in liquids by agitation, fermentation, etc. 2. something like foam, as frothy saliva 3. a rigid or spongy cellular mass made by gas bubbles dispersed in liquid rubber, plastic, etc. —*vi.* to produce foam; froth —*vt.* to cause to foam —**foam at the mouth** to be very angry; rage —**foam′less** *adj.*

foam rubber rubber treated to form a firm, spongy foam, used in seats, mattresses, etc.

foam·y (-ē) *adj.* **foam′i·er, foam′i·est** 1. foaming or covered with foam 2. of or like foam —**foam′i·ly** *adv.* —**foam′i·ness** *n.*

fob[1] (fob) *n.* [prob. < dial. G. *fuppe*, a pocket] 1. a watch pocket in the front of a man's trousers 2. a short ribbon or chain hanging from a watch in such a pocket, often with an ornament at the end 3. such an ornament

fob[2] (fob) *vt.* **fobbed, fob′bing** [< ME. *fobben*, to cheat] [Obs.] to cheat or deceive —**fob off** 1. to trick or put off (a person) with second-rate articles, lies, excuses, etc. 2. to get rid of (something worthless) by deceit or trickery

F.O.B., f.o.b. free on board

fo·cal (fō′k'l) *adj.* of or at a focus —**fo′cal·ly** *adv.*

fo·cal·ize (fō′kə līz′) *vt., vi.* **-ized′, -iz′ing** to adjust or come to a focus —**fo′cal·i·za′tion** *n.*

focal length the distance from the optical centre of a lens to the point where the light rays converge; length of the focus: also **focal distance**

focal plane the plane at right angles to the main axis of a lens

fo'c's'le (fōk′s'l) *n. phonetic spelling of* FORECASTLE

fo·cus (fō′kəs) *n., pl.* **fo′cus·es, fo′ci** (-sī) [ModL. < L., hearth] 1. the point where rays of light, heat, etc. or waves of sound come together, or from which they spread or seem to spread; specif., the point where rays of light reflected by a mirror or refracted by a lens meet 2. *same as* FOCAL LENGTH 3. adjustment of focal length to make a clear image 4. any centre of activity, attention, etc. 5. a part of the body where an infection is most active 6. *Math.* a) either of the two fixed points used in determining an ellipse b) any analogous point for a parabola or hyperbola —*vt.* **-cused** or **-cussed, -cus·ing** or **-cus·sing** 1. to bring into focus 2. to adjust the focal length of (the eye, a lens, etc.) so as to make a clear image 3. to concentrate [*focus* one's attention] —*vi.* to come to a focus —**in focus** clear; distinct —**out of focus** indistinct; blurred —**fo′cus·er** *n.*

fod·der (fod′ər) *n.* [OE. *fodor* < *foda*, food] coarse food for cattle, horses, etc., as hay and straw —*vt.* to feed with fodder

foe (fō) *n.* [OE. *fah*, hostile, (*ge*)*fah*, enemy] *same as* ENEMY (in all senses)

foehn (firn) *n.* [G. dial. *föhn*, ult. < L. *Favonius*, west wind] a warm, dry wind blowing down into the valleys of a mountain, esp. in the Alps

foe·man (fō′mən) *n., pl.* **-men** [Archaic] a foe

foe·tid (fet′id, fēt′-) *adj. same as* FETID

foe·tus (fēt′əs) *n., pl.* **-tus·es** [< L.*fetus*, a bringing forth] the unborn young of an animal while still in the uterus or egg, esp. in its later stages: cf. EMBRYO —**foe′tal** *adj.*

fog[1] (fog) *n.* [prob. < Scand.] 1. a large mass of water vapour condensed to fine particles, just above the earth's surface 2. a similar mass of smoke, dust, etc. obscuring the atmosphere 3. a vaporized liquid, as insecticide, widely dispersed 4. a state of mental confusion 5. a blur on a photograph or film —*vi.* **fogged, fog′ging** 1. to become covered by fog 2. to be or become blurred or dimmed —*vt.* 1. to cover with fog 2. to blur or dim 3. to confuse

fog[2] (fog) *n.* [ME. < ?] 1. a second growth of grass after the first mowing 2. grass left to grow long during the winter

fog bank a dense mass of fog

fog·bound (-bound′) *adj.* 1. surrounded or covered by fog 2. prevented from sailing, flying, etc. because of fog

fog·bow (-bō′) *n.* a phenomenon like a white or slightly tinted rainbow, sometimes seen in fog

fog·gy (-ē) *adj.* **-gi·er, -gi·est** 1. full of fog 2. dim; blurred 3. confused; perplexed —**fog′gi·ly** *adv.* —**fog′gi·ness** *n.*

fog·horn (-hôrn′) *n.* a horn blown to give warning to ships in a fog

fog-sig·nal (-sig′n'l) *n.* a small detonator placed on a railway track during fog, the explosion caused by a passing train acting as a signal to the driver

fo·gy (fō′gē) *n., pl.* **-gies** [< ?] a person who is oldfashioned or conservative: also **fo′gey,** *pl.* **-geys** —**fo′gy·ish** *adj.* —**fo′gy·ism** *n.*

foi·ble (foi′b'l) *n.* [obs. form of Fr. *faible*, FEEBLE] a small weakness in character; frailty

foil[1] (foil) *vt.* [< OFr. *fuler*, to trample on] 1. to keep from being successful; thwart; frustrate 2. *Hunting* to make (a scent, etc.) confused, as by recrossing

foil[2] (foil) *n.* [< OFr. < VL. < L. *folium*, a leaf] 1. a leaflike, rounded space or design, as in windows, etc. in

Gothic architecture **2.** a very thin sheet, leaf, or coating of metal **3.** a thin leaf of polished metal put under an inferior or artificial gem to give it brilliance **4.** one that sets off or enhances another by contrast **5.** [etym. unc.] *a)* a long, thin fencing sword with a button on the point to prevent injury *b)* [*pl.*] the art or sport of fencing with foils —*vt.* **1.** to cover or back with foil **2.** to decorate (windows, etc.) with foils

foist (foist) *vt.* [prob. < dial. Du. *vuisten*, to hide in the hand < *vuist*, a fist] **1.** to put in slyly or surreptitiously **2.** to impose by fraud; palm off

fol. folio

fold¹ (fōld) *vt.* [OE. *faldan*] **1.** to bend or press (something) so that one part is over another **2.** to draw together and intertwine [to *fold* the arms] **3.** to draw (wings) close to the body **4.** to clasp in the arms; embrace **5.** to wrap up; envelop —*vi.* **1.** to be or become folded **2.** [Colloq.] *a)* to fail; be forced to close, as a business *b)* to succumb, as to exhaustion —*n.* **1.** a folded part or layer **2.** a mark, hollow, or crease made by folding **3.** *Geol.* a rock layer folded by pressure —**fold in** *Cooking* to blend (an ingredient) into a mixture, using gentle, cutting strokes

fold² (fōld) *n.* [OE. *fald*] **1.** a pen in which to keep sheep **2.** a flock of sheep **3.** a group or organization with common aims, faith, etc., as a church —*vt.* to keep or confine in a pen

-fold (fōld) [OE. *-feald*] *a suffix meaning:* **1.** having (a specified number of) parts [tenfold] **2.** (a specified number of) times as many or as much

fold·a·way (fōld′ə wā′) *adj.* that can be folded for easy storage [a foldaway cot]

fold·er (fōl′dər) *n.* **1.** a person or thing that folds **2.** a sheet of heavy paper folded as a holder for papers **3.** an unstitched, folded booklet

fol·de·rol (fol′də rol′) *n.* same as FALDERAL

folding door a door with hinged leaves or accordion pleats that can be folded back

fo·li·a·ceous (fō′lē ā′shəs) *adj.* [< L. < *folium*, a leaf] **1.** of or like the leaf of a plant **2.** having leaves **3.** consisting of thin layers

fo·li·age (fō′lē ij) *n.* [< OFr. < VL. *folia* < L. *folium*, a leaf] **1.** leaves, as of a plant or tree **2.** a decoration consisting of a representation of leaves, branches, flowers, etc. —**fo′-li·aged** *adj.*

fo·li·ar (fō′lē ər) *adj.* [Mod L. *foliaris* < L. *folium*: see ff.] of or like a leaf

fo·li·ate (fō′lē āt′; *for adj., usually* -it) *vt.* -at′ed, -at′ing [L. *foliatus*, leafy < *folium*, a leaf] to divide into thin layers —*vi.* **1.** to separate into layers **2.** to send out leaves —*adj.* having or covered with leaves

fo·li·a·tion (fō′lē ā′shən) *n.* **1.** a growing of or developing into a leaf or leaves **2.** the state of being in leaf **3.** the way leaves are arranged in the bud **4.** the act of beating metal into layers **5.** a leaflike decoration

fo·lic acid (fō′lik) [< L. *folium*, a leaf + -IC] a crystalline substance of the vitamin B group, found in green leaves, etc. and used esp. in treating certain anaemias

fo·li·o (fō′lē ō′) *n., pl.* -li·os [L. abl. of *folium*, a leaf] **1.** a large sheet of paper folded once, so that it forms two leaves, or four pages, of a book, etc. **2.** a book (the largest regular size) made of sheets so folded **3.** a leaf of a book, etc. numbered on only one side **4.** the number of a page in a book, etc. —*adj.* of the size of a folio —**in folio** in the form of a folio

folk (fōk) *n., pl.* **folk, folks** [OE. *folc*] **1.** *a)* a people; nation; ethnic group *b)* the common people of such a group: with *the* **2.**[Colloq.] [*pl.*] people in general; persons [some folks don't agree] —*adj.* of or having to do with the common people —(one's) **folks** [Colloq.] (one's) family

folk dance **1.** a traditional dance of the common people of a country **2.** music for this

folk etymology the change that occurs in the form of a word over a period of prolonged usage so as to give it an apparent connection with some other word, as *Welsh rabbit* becomes *Welsh rarebit*

folk·lore (fōk′lôr′) *n.* **1.** the traditional beliefs, legends, sayings, etc. of a people **2.** the study of these —**folk′lor′ic** *adj.* —**folk′lor′ist** *n.*

folk medicine the treatment of disease, including the use of herbs, as practised by the common people over many years

folk music music made and handed down among the common people

folk-rock (-rok′) *n.* music with a rock-and-roll beat combined with words in a folk-song style

folk song **1.** a song made and handed down among the common people **2.** a song composed in imitation of such a song —**folk singer**

folk·sy (-sē) *adj.* -si·er, -si·est **1.** [Colloq.] friendly or sociable in a simple and direct manner **2.** affectedly simple —**folk′si·ly** *adv.* —**folk′si·ness** *n.*

folk tale (or **story**) a story, often legendary, made and handed down orally among the common people

folk·way (-wā′) *n.* any way of thinking, behaving, etc. characteristic of a certain social group

folk·weave (-wēv) *n.* a coarse fabric with a loose weave

fol·li·cle (fol′i k'l) *n.* [ModL. *folliculus* < L., a small bag, dim. of *follis*, bellows] **1.** *Anat.* any small sac, cavity, or gland for excretion or secretion [a hair *follicle*] **2.** *Bot.* a dry, one-celled seed capsule, opening along one side —**fol·li·cu·lar** (fə lik′yoo lər) *adj.* —**fol·lic′u·late** (-lit, -lāt′), **fol·lic′u·lat′ed** *adj.*

fol·low (fol′ō) *vt.* [< OE. *folgian*] **1.** to come or go after **2.** to chase; pursue **3.** to go along [follow the road] **4.** to come after in time, in a series, etc. **5.** to take the place of in rank, position, etc. **6.** to take up; engage in (a trade, etc.) **7.** to result from **8.** to take as a model; imitate **9.** to accept the authority of; obey **10.** to listen to, watch, or observe closely **11.** to understand the continuity or logic of —*vi.* **1.** to come, go, or happen after something else in place, sequence, or time **2.** to result —*n.* the act of following —**follow out** to carry out fully —**follow through** to continue and complete a stroke or action —**follow up** **1.** to pursue or investigate closely [to *follow up* a clue] **2.** to carry out fully **3.** to make more effective by doing something more

fol·low·er (fol′ō wər) *n.* one that follows; specif., *a)* a person who follows another's belief or teachings; disciple *b)* a servant or attendant *c)* [Obs.] a servant girl's admirer

fol·low·ing (-ō wiŋ) *adj.* that follows; next after —*n.* a group of followers or adherents —*prep.* after [following dinner he went home] —**the following** **1.** the one or ones to be mentioned immediately **2.** what follows

fol·low-on (-on′) *n.* *Cricket* an immediate second innings forced on a team scoring a prescribed number of runs fewer than its opponents in the first innings

fol·low-through (-thrōo′) *n.* **1.** the act or manner of continuing the swing or stroke of a club, racket, etc. after striking or releasing the ball, etc. **2.** the completing of an undertaking

fol·low-up (-up′) *adj.* following as a review, addition, etc. —*n.* **1.** a follow-up thing or event **2.** a following up, as with follow-up letters, visits, etc.

fol·ly (fol′ē) *n., pl.* -lies [< OFr. < *fol*: see FOOL] **1.** a lack of sense or rational conduct; foolishness **2.** any foolish action or belief **3.** any foolish but expensive undertaking, esp. a useless and needlessly extravagant structure

fo·ment (fō ment′) *vt.* [< OFr. < LL. *fomentare* < L. < *fovere*, to keep warm] **1.** to treat with warm water, medicated lotions, etc. **2.** to stir up; incite [to *foment* a riot] —**fo′men·ta′tion** *n.* —**fo′ment′er** *n.*

fond (fond) *adj.* [< ME. *fonned*, pp. of *fonnen*, to be foolish] **1.** [Now Rare] foolishly naive or hopeful **2.** tender and affectionate, sometimes in a foolish way **3.** foolishly credulous or trusting [fond hopes] —**fond of** having a liking for —**fond′ly** *adv.* —**fond′ness** *n.*

fon·dant (fon′dant) *n.* [Fr. < prp. of *fondre*, to melt] **1.** a soft, creamy paste made of sugar **2.** a sweet made of this

fon·dle (fon′d'l) *vt.* -dled, -dling [freq. of obs. *fond, v.*] to stroke lovingly; caress —**fon′dler** *n.*

fon·due, fon·du (fon′dyōō, -dōō) *n.* [Fr. < pp. of *fondre*, to melt] **1.** cheese melted in wine, used as a dip for cubes of bread, etc. **2.** any of various other dishes of hot, liquid ingredients, as hot oil into which cubes of meat are dipped for cooking

font (font) *n.* [OE. < L. *fons*, FOUNTAIN] **1.** a bowl to hold the water used in baptismal services **2.** a basin for holy water; stoup **3.** [Poet.] a fountain or spring **4.** any source; origin —**font′al** *adj.*

fon·ta·nelle (fon′tə nel′) *n.* [ME. *fontinel*, a hollow < OFr. dim. of *fontaine*, FOUNTAIN] any of the soft, boneless areas in the skull of a baby, later closed over when bone forms: also sp. **fon′ta·nel′**

FONTANELS

food (fōōd) *n.* [OE. *foda*] **1.** any substance taken into and assimilated by a plant or animal to keep it alive and enable it to grow; nourishment **2.** solid substances of this sort: distinguished from *drink* **3.** a specified kind of food **4.** anything that nourishes or stimulates [food for thought]

food chain *Ecol.* a sequence (as grass, rabbit, fox) in which each member feeds on the one below

food cycle *Ecol.* all the individual food chains in a community: also **food web**

food poisoning **1.** sickness from eating food contaminated by bacteria **2.** poisoning from naturally poisonous foods or from chemical contaminants in food

food·stuff (-stuf′) *n.* any material made into or used as food

fool¹ (fōōl) *n.* [< OFr. *fol* < LL. < L. *follis*, windbag] **1.** a silly person; simpleton **2.** a man formerly kept by a nobleman or king to entertain as a clown; jester **3.** a victim of a trick; dupe —*adj.* [U.S. Colloq.] foolish —*vi.* **1.** to act like a fool; be silly **2.** to joke —*vt.* to trick; deceive;

dupe —**be no** (or **nobody's**) **fool** to be shrewd and capable —**fool about** (or **around**) [Colloq.] 1. to behave irresponsibly or aimlessly 2. to meddle (*with*) —**fool away** [Colloq.] to squander —**play the fool** to clown

fool² (fōōl) *n.* [Early Mod E. < ? prec.] crushed stewed fruit mixed with cream

fool·er·y (-ər ē) *n., pl.* **-er·ies** (a) foolish action

fool·har·dy (-här′dē) *adj.* **-di·er, -di·est** foolishly daring; rash —**fool′har′di·ly** *adv.* —**fool′har′di·ness** *n.*

fool·ish (-ish) *adj.* 1. without good sense; silly; unwise 2. *a*) absurd *b*) abashed; embarrassed —**fool′ish·ly** *adv.* —**fool′-ish·ness** *n.*

fool·proof (-prōōf′) *adj.* so harmless, simple, or indestructible as not to be mishandled, damaged, misunderstood, etc.

fools·cap (fōōlz′kap′) *n.* 1. [from former watermark] a large size of writing paper 2. *same as* FOOL'S CAP

fool's cap a jester's cap with bells

fool's errand a fruitless errand

fool's gold iron pyrites or copper pyrites, resembling gold in colour

fool's paradise a state of illusory happiness

fool's-pars·ley (-pärs′lē) *n.* a poisonous, umbelliferous plant resembling parsley

foot (foot) *n., pl.* **feet:** see also sense 6 [OE. *fot*] 1. the end part of the leg, on which a person or animal stands or moves 2. the base or bottom [the *foot* of a page] 3. the last of a series 4. the end, as of a bed, towards which the feet are directed 5. the part of a stocking, etc. covering the foot 6. a measure of length, equal to 12 inches (c. 30 cm) (an average length of the human foot): symbol, ′ (e.g., 10′): abbrev. **ft.** (sing. & pl.): pl. often **foot** following a number [a six-*foot* man] 7. infantry 8. a group of syllables serving as a unit of metre in verse —*vi.* 1. to dance 2. to walk —*vt.* 1. to walk, dance, or run on, over, or through 2. to make the foot of (a stocking, etc.) 3. to add (a column of figures) and set down a total 4. [Colloq.] to pay (costs, etc.) [to *foot* the bill] —**foot it** [Colloq.] to dance, walk, or run —**have one foot in the grave** [Colloq.] to be near to death —**of foot** in walking or running [swift *of foot*] —**on foot** 1. walking or running 2. in process —**put one's best foot forward** [Colloq.] 1. to hurry 2. to do one's best 3. to try to appear at one's best —**put one's foot down** [Colloq.] to act decisively —**put one's foot in it** (or **in one's mouth**) [Colloq.] to make an embarrassing blunder —**under foot** 1. on the floor, etc. 2. in the way —**foot′less** *adj.*

foot·age (foot′ij) *n.* length expressed in feet

foot-and-mouth disease (foot′'n mouth′) an acute, contagious disease of cattle, deer, etc. characterized by fever and blisters in the mouth and around the hoofs

foot·ball (-bôl′) *n.* [ME. *foteballe*] 1. any of several field games played with an inflated leather ball by two teams, the object being to get the ball across the opponents' goal cf. SOCCER, RUGBY 2. the elliptical or round ball used in playing these games —**foot′ball·er** *n.*

foot·ball pools *same as* POOLS

foot·board (-bôrd′) *n.* 1. a board or small platform for supporting the feet or standing on 2. a vertical piece across the foot of a bed

foot·bridge (-brij′) *n.* a narrow bridge for pedestrians

foot-can·dle (-kan′d'l) *n.* formerly, a unit for measuring illumination: now replaced by the lumen

foot·ed (-id) *adj.* having a foot or feet, esp. of a specified number or kind [four-*footed*]

-foot·er (-ər) a combining form meaning a person or thing (a specified number of) feet tall, high, long, etc. [six-*footer*]

foot·fall (-fôl′) *n.* the sound of a footstep

foot·hill (-hil′) *n.* a low hill at or near the foot of a mountain or mountain range

foot·hold (-hōld′) *n.* 1. a place to put a foot down securely, as in climbing 2. a secure position

foot·ie (-ē) *n.* [Colloq.] football

foot·ing (-iŋ) *n.* 1. a secure placing of the feet 2. *a*) the condition of a surface for walking, running, etc. *b*) a secure place to put the feet 3. a secure position or basis 4. a basis for relationship [a friendly *footing*] 5. *a*) the adding of a column of figures *b*) the sum obtained 6. a projecting base under a column, wall, etc.: also **foot′er**

foot·le (foot′'l) *vi.* [< ?] [Colloq.] to act or talk foolishly or aimlessly —**foot′ling** *adj.*

foot·lights (-līts′) *n.pl.* a row of lights along the front of a stage at the actors' foot level —**the footlights** the theatre, or acting as a profession

foot·loose (-lōōs′) *adj.* free to go wherever one likes or do as one likes

foot·man (-mən) *n., pl.* **-men** a male servant who assists the butler in a household

foot·note (-nōt′) *n.* a note of comment or reference at the bottom of a page —*vt.* **-not′ed, -not′ing** to add such a note or notes to

foot·pad (-pad′) *n.* [see PAD³] formerly, a highway robber who travels on foot

foot·path (-päth′) *n.* a narrow path for pedestrians

foot·plate (-plāt′) *n.* the platform in a locomotive cab on which the crew stand to operate the controls

foot-pound (-pound′) *n.* a unit of energy, equal to the amount of energy required to raise a weight of one pound a distance of one foot

foot-pound-sec·ond (-pound′sek′ənd) *adj.* designating or of a system of measurement using the foot, pound, and second as the units of length, mass, and time, respectively

foot·print (-print′) *n.* a mark left by a foot

foot·race (-rās′) *n.* a race run on foot

foot·rest (-rest′) *n.* a support to rest the feet on

foot rot an inflammatory disease affecting sheep's feet

foot·sie, foot·sy (-sē) *n., pl.* **-sies** the foot: a child's term —**play footsie** (**with**) 1. to touch feet or legs (with) in a caressing way, as under the table 2. to flirt or have surreptitious dealings (with)

foot soldier a soldier on foot; infantryman

foot·sore (-sôr′) *adj.* having sore or tender feet, as from much walking

foot·step (-step′) *n.* 1. the distance covered in a step 2. the sound of a step; footfall 3. a footprint 4. a step in a stairway —**follow in** (**someone's**) **footsteps** to follow (someone's) example, vocation, etc.

foot·stool (-stōōl′) *n.* a low stool for supporting the feet of a seated person

foot·wear (-wer′) *n.* shoes, boots, slippers, etc.

foot·work (-wurk′) *n.* the act or manner of moving the feet, as in walking, boxing, dancing, etc.

foo·zle (fōō′z'l) *vt., vi.* **-zled, -zling** [< ? G. *fuseln*, to bungle] to make or do (something) awkwardly; esp., to bungle (a golf stroke) —*n.* the act or an instance of foozling —**foo′-zler** *n.*

fop (fop) *n.* [ME. *foppe*, a fool, prob. < MDu. or MLowG.] a vain, affected man who pays too much attention to his clothes, appearance, etc.; dandy —**fop′per·y** *n., pl.* **-per·ies** —**fop′pish** *adj.* —**fop′pish·ly** *adv.* —**fop′pish·ness** *n.*

for (fôr; *unstressed* fər) *prep.* [OE.] 1. in place of [to use coats for blankets] 2. in the interest of [his agent acted for him] 3. in defence of; in favour of 4. in honour of [to give a banquet for a notable] 5. with the aim or purpose of [to carry a gun for protection] 6. with the purpose of going to [to leave for home] 7. in order to be, become, get, have, keep, etc. [to walk for exercise] 8. in search of [looking for berries] 9. meant to be received by a specified person or thing, or to be used in a specified way [flowers for a girl, money for paying bills] 10. suitable to [a room for sleeping] 11. with regard to [need for improvement, an ear for music] 12. as being [to know for a fact] 13. considering the nature of [cool for July] 14. because of [to cry for pain] 15. in spite of [stupid for all her learning] 16. in proportion to [a pound tax for every four earned] 17. to the amount of [a bill for £50] 18. at the price of [sold for £10] 19. to the length, duration, etc. of; throughout [to work for an hour] 20. at (a specified time) [an appointment for two o'clock] —*conj.* because; seeing that [comfort him for he is sad] —**for** (one) to that (one) will, should, must, etc. [a book for you to read] —**O! for** I wish that I had

for- [OE., replacing *fer-*] an Old English and Middle English prefix meaning: 1. away, apart, off, etc. [*forbid*, *forget*, *forgo*] 2. very much [*forlorn*]

for·age (for′ij) *n.* [< OFr. < Frank. *fodr*, food] 1. food for domestic animals; fodder 2. a search for food or provisions —*vi.* **-aged, -ag·ing** 1. to search for food or provisions 2. to search for what one needs or wants —*vt.* 1. to get or take food or provisions from 2. to provide with forage; feed 3. to get by foraging —**for′ag·er** *n.*

forage cap a soldiers' undress cap

fo·ra·men (fo rā′mən, fə-) *n., pl.* **-ram′i·na** (-ram′ə nə), **-ra′-mens** [L. < *forare*, to bore] a small opening, esp. in a bone or in a plant ovule —**fo·ram′i·nal** (-ram′ə n'l), **fo·ram′i·nate** (-nit) *adj.*

for·a·min·i·fer (fôr′ə min′ə fər) *n., pl.* **fo·ram·i·nif·er·a** (fə ram′ə nif′ər ə) [< L. *foramen*: see prec. & -FER] any of a group of small, one-celled sea animals with calcareous shells full of tiny holes through which slender filaments project —**fo·ram′i·nif′er·al**, **fo·ram′i·nif′er·ous** *adj.*

for·as·much (fôr′əz much′) *conj.* inasmuch (*as*)

for·ay (for′ā) *vi., vi.* [< OFr. < *forrer*, to forage] to raid for spoils; plunder —*n.* a sudden attack or raid, as for spoils

for·bade, for·bad (fər bad′, fôr-) *pt. of* FORBID

for·bear¹ (fôr ber′, fär-) *vt.* **-bore′** or archaic **-bare′, -borne′, -bear′ing** [< OE.: see FOR- & BEAR¹] to refrain from; avoid (doing, saying, etc.) —*vi.* 1. to refrain or abstain 2. to control oneself —**for·bear′er** *n.* —**for·bear′-ing·ly** *adv.*

for·bear² (fôr′ber′) *n.* *same as* FOREBEAR

for·bear·ance (fôr ber′əns, fär-) *n.* 1. the act of forbearing 2. self-control; patient restraint

for·bid (fər bid′, fôr-) *vt.* **-bade′** or **-bad′, -bid′den** or archaic **-bid′, -bid′ding** [< OE.: see FOR- & BID] 1. to rule against; prohibit **2.** to command to stay away from; bar from **3.** to make impossible; prevent —**for·bid'dance** *n.* —**for·bid'den** *adj.*

forbidden fruit 1. *Bible* the fruit of the tree of knowledge of good and bad, forbidden to Adam and Eve: Gen. 2:17; 3:3 **2.** any sinful or forbidden pleasure

for·bid·ding (-iŋ) *adj.* looking dangerous, threatening, or disagreeable; repellent —**for·bid'ding·ly** *adv.*

for·bore (fôr bôr', fər-) *pt. of* FORBEAR[1]

for·borne (-bôrn') *pp. of* FORBEAR[1]

force[1] (fôrs) *n.* [OFr. < LL. < L. *fortis,* strong] **1.** strength; energy; power **2.** impetus [*the force* of a blow] **3.** physical power or coercion exerted against a person or thing **4.** *a)* the power to control, persuade, etc.; effectiveness *b)* a person or thing having influence, power, etc. [a *force* for good] **5.** *a)* military, naval, or air power *b)* [*pl.*] the collective armed strength, as of a nation *c)* any organized group of soldiers, sailors, police, etc. **6.** any group of people organized for some activity [a sales *force*] **7.** *Law* binding power; validity **8.** *Physics* the cause, or agent, that puts an object at rest into motion or alters the motion of a moving object —*vt.* **forced, forc'ing 1.** to cause to do something by force; compel **2.** to rape (a woman) **3.** *a)* to break open, into, or through by force *b)* to overpower or capture in this way **4.** to take by force; wrest; extort **5.** to drive as by force; push; impel **6.** to impose as by force (with *on* or *upon*) **7.** to effect or produce as by force [to *force* a smile] **8.** to strain [to *force* one's voice] **9.** to cause (plants, fruit, etc.) to develop faster by artificial means **10.** *Card Games* to cause (an opponent) to play (a particular card) or (one's partner) to make (a particular bid) —**in force 1.** in full strength **2.** in effect; valid —**force'a·ble** *adj.* —**force'less** *adj.* —**forc'er** *n.*

force[2] (fôrs) *n.* [< ON *fors*] [Dial.] a waterfall

forced (fôrst) *adj.* **1.** done or brought about by force; compulsory [*forced* labour] **2.** produced by unusual effort; strained [a *forced* smile] **3.** due to an emergency [a *forced* landing] **4.** at a pace faster than usual [a *forced* march] —**forc·ed·ly** (fôr'sid lē) *adv.*

force-feed (fôrs'fēd') *vt.* **-fed', -feed'ing** to feed as by a tube through the throat to the stomach

force·ful (-fəl) *adj.* full of force; powerful, vigorous, effective, etc. —**force'ful·ly** *adv.* —**force'ful·ness** *n.*

force·meat (-mēt') *n.* [< *farce meat* < *farce* (obs.), to stuff] meat chopped up and seasoned, usually for stuffing

for·ceps (fôr'səps) *n., pl.* **for'ceps** [L., orig., smith's tongs < *formus,* hot + *capere,* to take] small tongs or pincers for grasping, compressing, and pulling, used esp. by surgeons and dentists —**for'cip·ate** *adj.*

force pump a pump with a valveless plunger for forcing a liquid through a pipe under pressure

FORCEPS
(A, fine bent; B, scissors)

for·ci·ble (fôr'sə b'l) *adj.* **1.** done or effected by force **2.** having force: forceful —**for'ci·ble·ness** *n.* —**for'ci·bly** *adv.*

ford (fôrd) *n.* [OE.] a shallow place in a stream, river, etc. that can be crossed by wading, on horseback, in a car, etc. —*vt.* to cross (a stream) in this way —**ford'a·ble** *adj.*

for·done (fôr dun') *adj.* [Archaic] completely exhausted

fore (fôr) *adv.* [OE.] at, in, or towards the front: now only of a ship —*adj.* situated in front —*n.* the front thing or part —*interj. Golf* a shout warning those ahead that one is about to hit the ball —**to the fore 1.** to the front; into view **2.** available **3.** still active

'fore (fôr) *prep.* [Poet.] before

fore- [OE.: see FORE] a prefix meaning: **1.** before in time, place, order, or rank [*forenoon, foreman*] **2.** the front part of [*forearm*]

fore-and-aft (fôr'n aft') *adj. Naut.* from the bow to the stern; lengthwise or set lengthwise

fore and aft *Naut.* **1.** from the bow to the stern; lengthwise or set lengthwise **2.** at, in, or towards both the bow and the stern

fore·arm[1] (fôr'ärm') *n.* the part of the arm between the elbow and the wrist

fore·arm[2] (fôr ärm') *vt.* to arm in advance; prepare beforehand for any difficulty

fore·bear (fôr'ber') *n.* [< FORE + BE + -ER] an ancestor

fore·bode (fôr bōd') *vt., vi.* **-bod'ed, -bod'ing** [< OE.: see FORE- & BODE[1]] **1.** to be an omen or warning of (esp. something bad or harmful) **2.** to have a presentiment of (something bad or harmful) —**fore·bod'er** *n.* —**fore·bod'ing** *n., adj.* —**fore·bod'ing·ly** *adv.*

fore·brain (fôr'brān') *n.* the front part of the brain

fore·cast (fôr'käst'; *for v., also occas.* fôr käst') *vt.* **-cast'** or **-cast'ed, -cast'ing 1.** to estimate in advance; predict (weather, etc.) **2.** to serve as a prediction or

prophecy of —*vi.* to make a forecast —*n.* a prediction —**fore'cast'er** *n.*

fore·cas·tle (fōk's'l) *n.* [FORE + CASTLE] **1.** the upper deck of a ship in front of the foremast **2.** the front part of a merchant ship, where the sailors' quarters are located

fore·close (fôr klōz') *vt.* **-closed', -clos'ing** [< OFr. pp. of *forclore,* to exclude < *fors,* outside + *clore,* CLOSE[2]] **1.** to shut out; exclude; bar **2.** to take away the right to redeem (a mortgage, etc.) —*vi.* to foreclose a mortgage, etc. —**fore·clos'a·ble** *adj.* —**fore·clo'sure** (-klō'zhər) *n.*

fore·court (fôr'kôrt') *n.* **1.** a court at the front of a building, esp. a service station **2.** *Tennis,* etc. the part of the court nearest the net

fore·doom (fôr dōōm') *vt.* to doom in advance; condemn beforehand

fore·fa·ther (fôr'fä'thər) *n.* an ancestor

fore·fin·ger (-fiŋ'gər) *n.* the finger nearest the thumb; index finger; first finger

fore·foot (-foot') *n., pl.* **-feet'** either of the front feet of an animal with four or more feet

fore·front (-frunt') *n.* **1.** the extreme front **2.** the position of most activity, importance, etc.

fore·gath·er (fôr gath'ər) *vi. same as* FORGATHER

fore·go[1] (fôr gō') *vt., vi.* **-went', -gone', -go'ing** [OE. *foregan*] to go before in place, time, or degree

fore·go[2] (fôr gō') *vt. same as* FORGO

fore·go·ing (fôr'gō'iŋ) *adj.* previously said, written, etc. —**the foregoing 1.** the one or ones previously mentioned **2.** what has already been said or written

fore·gone (fôr gon') *adj.* **1.** that has gone before; previous **2.** *a)* previously determined *b)* inevitable or unavoidable: said of a conclusion

fore·ground (fôr'ground') *n.* **1.** the part of a scene, picture, etc. nearest the viewer **2.** the most noticeable or conspicuous position

fore·hand (-hand') *n.* a kind of stroke, as in tennis, made with the arm extended and the palm of the hand turned forwards —*adj.* **1.** foremost; front **2.** done or performed as or with a forehand: also **fore·hand'ed** —*adv.* with a forehand

fore·head (fôr'id, fôr'hed) *n.* the part of the face between the eyebrows and the hairline

for·eign (for'ən) *adj.* [< OFr. *forain* < LL. < L. *foras,* out-of-doors] **1.** situated outside one's own country, locality, etc. **2.** of, from, or characteristic of another country [a *foreign* language] **3.** concerning the relations of one country to another [*foreign* affairs] **4.** *a)* not characteristic *b)* not pertinent **5.** not organically belonging, as substances found in organisms where they do not naturally occur —**for'eign·ness** *n.*

Foreign and Commonwealth Office the department of the British government which deals with matters relating to other countries

for·eign·er (-ər) *n.* a person from another country, thought of as an outsider; alien

foreign minister in some countries, a member of a governmental cabinet in charge of foreign affairs

foreign office in some countries, the office of government in charge of foreign affairs

foreign secretary the minister in the British government in charge of foreign affairs

fore·know (fôr nō') *vt.* **-knew', -known', -know'ing** to know beforehand —**fore·know'a·ble** *adj.* —**fore·knowl·edge** (fôr'nol'ij) *n.*

fore·land (fôr'lənd) *n.* a headland; promontory

fore·leg (-leg') *n.* either of the front legs of an animal with four or more legs

fore·limb (-lim') *n.* a front limb, as an arm, foreleg, wing, or flipper

fore·lock (-lok') *n.* a lock of hair growing just above the forehead —**take time by the forelock** to seize a chance; to anticipate an issue

fore·man (-mən) *n., pl.* **-men** [orig., foremost man, leader] **1.** the chairman of a jury **2.** a man in charge of a department or group of workers in a factory, etc. —**fore'man·ship'** *n.*

fore·mast (fôr'mäst', -məst) *n.* the mast nearest the bow of a ship

fore·most (-mōst') *adj.* [< OE. superl. of *forma,* superl. of *fore,* fore] **1.** first in place or time **2.** first in rank or importance —*adv.* first

fore·named (-nāmd') *adj.* named or mentioned before

fore·noon (fôr'nōōn') *n.* the time from sunrise to noon; morning —*adj.* of or in the forenoon

fo·ren·sic (fə ren'sik) *adj.* [< L. *forensis,* public < *forum,* marketplace] of, characteristic of, or suitable for a law court, public debate, or formal argument —*n.* [*pl.*] debate or formal argument —**fo·ren'si·cal·ly** *adv.*

forensic medicine the application of medical knowledge to questions of law, as in determining cause of death, proper medical practice, etc.

fore·or·dain (fôr'ôr dān') *vt.* to ordain beforehand —**fore'·or·di·na'tion** (-dən ā'shən) *n.*

fore·paw (fôr′pô′) *n.* an animal's front paw

fore·quar·ter (-kwôr′tər) *n.* 1. the front half of a side of beef or the like 2. [*pl.*] the front quarters of a horse, etc., including the forelegs

fore·run (fôr run′) *vt.* **-ran′, -run′, -run′ning** [Rare] 1. to run before; precede 2. to be a sign of (a thing to follow) 3. to forestall

fore·run·ner (fôr′run′ər) *n.* 1. a messenger sent before or going before; herald 2. a sign that tells or warns of something to follow 3. *a)* a predecessor *b)* an ancestor

fore·sail (fôr′sāl′, -səl) *n.* 1. the lowest sail on the foremast of a square-rigged ship 2. the main triangular sail on the foremast of a fore-and-aft-rigged ship

fore·see (fôr sē′) *vt.* **-saw′, -seen′, -see′ing** to see or know beforehand **—fore·see′a·ble** *adj.* **—fore·se′er** *n.*

fore·shad·ow (-shad′ō) *vt.* to indicate or suggest beforehand; presage **—fore·shad′ow·er** *n.*

fore·shank (fôr′shaŋk′) *n.* 1. the upper part of the front legs of cattle 2. meat from this part

fore·sheet (-shēt′) *n.* 1. one of the ropes used to trim a foresail 2. [*pl.*] the space forward in an open boat

fore·shock (-shok′) *n.* a minor earthquake preceding a greater one at or near the same place

fore·shore (-shôr′) *n.* the part of a shore between highwater mark and low-water mark

fore·short·en (fôr shôr′t'n) *vt.* Drawing, Painting, etc. to represent some lines of (an object) as shorter than they actually are in order to give the illusion of proper relative size

fore·show (-shō′) *vt.* **-showed′, -shown′** or **-showed′, -show′ing** to show or indicate beforehand

fore·sight (fôr′sīt′) *n.* 1. *a)* a foreseeing *b)* the power to foresee 2. a looking forward 3. prudent regard or provision for the future **—fore′sight′ed** *adj.* **—fore′sight′ed·ly** *adv.* **—fore′sight′ed·ness** *n.*

fore·skin (-skin′) *n.* the fold of skin that covers the end of the penis; prepuce

for·est (fôr′ist) *n.* [OFr. < ML. (*silva*) *forestis*, (wood) unenclosed < L. *foris*, out-of-doors] 1. a thick growth of trees and underbrush covering an extensive tract of land; large woods 2. formerly, a tract of woodland or wasteland, usually the property of the sovereign, preserved for game 3. anything resembling a forest, esp. in density [a *forest* of telegraph poles] **—adj.** of or in a forest **—vt.** to cover with trees or woods **—for′est·ed** *adj.*

FORESHORTENED ARM

fore·stall (fôr stôl′) *vt.* [OE. *foresteall*, ambush: see FORE & STALL[2]] 1. to prevent by doing something ahead of time 2. to act in advance of; anticipate **—fore·stall′er** *n.* **—fore·stall′ment** *n.*

for·est·a·tion (fôr′is tā′shən) *n.* the planting or care of forests ·

fore·stay (fôr′stā′) *n.* a rope or cable reaching from the head of a ship's foremast to the bowsprit, for supporting the foremast

for·est·er (fôr′is tər) *n.* 1. a person trained in forestry or charged with the care of a forest 2. a person or animal that lives in a forest

for·est·ry (-trē) *n.* 1. [Rare] forest land 2. the science of planting and taking care of forests 3. systematic forest management for the production of timber, conservation, etc.

fore·taste (fôr′tāst′; *for v.* fôr tāst′) *n.* a taste or sample of what can be expected **—vt. -tast′ed, -tast′ing** [Rare] to taste beforehand

fore·tell (fôr tel′) *vt.* **-told′, -tell′ing** to tell or indicate beforehand; predict **—fore·tell′er** *n.*

fore·thought (fôr thôt′) *n.* 1. a thinking or planning beforehand 2. foresight; prudence **—fore′thought′ful** *adj.* **—fore′thought′ful·ly** *adv.*

fore·to·ken (fôr′tō′kən; *for v.* fôr tō′kən) *n.* a prophetic sign; omen **—vt.** to foreshadow

fore·top (fôr′top′, -təp) *n.* the platform at the top of a ship's foremast

fore·top·gal·lant (fôr′top gal′ənt, fôr′tə-) *adj.* designating or of the mast, sail, yard, etc. just above the foretopmast

fore·top·mast (fôr top′mäst′, məst) *n.* the section of mast extending above the foremast

fore·top·sail (-sāl′, -s'l) *n.* a sail set on the fore-topmast, above the foresail

for·ev·er (fər ev′ər, fôr-) *adv.* 1. for eternity; for always; endlessly 2. at all times; always Also **for·ev′er·more′** (-môr′)

fore·warn (fôr wôrn′) *vt.* to warn beforehand

fore·wing (fôr′wiŋ′) *n.* either of the front pair of wings in most insects

fore·wom·an (-woom′ən) *n.*, *pl.* **-wom′en** a woman serving as a foreman

fore·word (-wurd′, -wərd) *n.* an introductory remark, preface, or prefatory note

for·feit (fôr′fit) *n.* [< OFr. < forfaire, to transgress, ult. < L. *foris*, beyond + *facere*, to do] 1. something that one has to give up because of some crime, fault, or neglect; fine; penalty 2. the act of forfeiting **—adj.** lost or taken away as a forfeit **—vt.** to lose or be deprived of as a forfeit **—for′feit·a·ble** *adj.* **—for′feit·er** *n.*

for·fei·ture (fôr′fə chər) *n.* 1. a forfeiting 2. anything forfeited; penalty or fine

for·gath·er (fôr gath′ər) *vi.* 1. to come together 2. to meet by chance 3. to be friendly (with)

for·gave (fər gāv′, fôr-) *pt. of* FORGIVE

forge[1] (fôrj) *n.* [< OFr. < L. *fabrica*, workshop < *faber*, workman] 1. a furnace for heating metal to be wrought 2. a place where metal is heated and hammered or wrought into shape; smithy 3. a place where wrought iron is made, as from iron ore **—vt. forged, forg′ing** 1. to shape (metal) by blows or pressure, usually after heating 2. to form; shape; produce 3. to imitate for purposes of deception or fraud; esp., to counterfeit (a cheque, etc.) **—vi.** 1. to work at a forge 2. to commit forgery **—forg′er** *n.*

forge[2] (fôrj) *vt., vi.* **forged, forg′ing** [prob. altered < FORCE] 1. to move forward steadily, as if against difficulties 2. to move in a sudden spurt Often with *ahead*

for·ger·y (fôr′jər ē) *n., pl.* **-ger·ies** 1. the act or legal offence of forging documents, signatures, works of art, etc. to deceive 2. anything forged

for·get (fər get′, fôr-) *vt.* **-got′** or archaic **-gat′** (-gat′), **-got′ten** or archaic **-got′, -get′ting** [OE. *forgietan*] 1. to lose (facts, etc.) from the mind; be unable to remember 2. to overlook or neglect, either unintentionally or intentionally **—vi.** to forget things **—forget it** don't trouble to think about it **—forget oneself** 1. to think only of others 2. to behave in an improper or unseemly manner **—for·get′ta·ble** *adj.* **—for·get′ter** *n.*

for·get·ful (-f'l) *adj.* 1. apt to forget; having a poor memory 2. negligent 3. [Poet.] causing to forget **—for·get′ful·ly** *adv.* **—for·get′ful·ness** *n.*

for·get-me-not (-mē not′) *n.* a plant with small blue flowers, symbolic of friendship

for·give (fər giv′, fôr-) *vt.* **-gave′, -giv′en, -giv′ing** [OE. *forgiefan*] 1. to give up resentment against or the desire to punish; pardon 2. to overlook (an offence) 3. to cancel (a debt) **—vi.** to show forgiveness **—for·giv′a·ble** *adj.* **—for·giv′er** *n.*

for·give·ness (-nis) *n.* 1. a forgiving; pardon 2. inclination to forgive

for·giv·ing (-iŋ) *adj.* that forgives; inclined to forgive **—for·giv′ing·ly** *adv.* **—for·giv′ing·ness** *n.*

for·go (fôr gō′) *vt.* **-went′, -gone′, -go′ing** [OE. *forgan*] to do without; abstain from **—for·go′er** *n.*

for·got (fər got′, fôr-) *pt. & archaic pp. of* FORGET

for·got·ten (-'n) *pp. of* FORGET

for·int (fôr′int) *n.* see MONETARY UNITS, table (Hungary)

fork (fôrk) *n.* [OE. *forca* & Anglo-Fr. *forque*, both < L. *furca*, hayfork] 1. an instrument with a handle and two or more prongs, used as an eating utensil or, in much larger form, for pitching hay, etc. 2. something resembling a fork in shape: cf. TUNING FORK 3. a division into branches; bifurcation 4. the point where a river, road, etc. is divided into branches 5. any of these branches **—vi.** to divide into branches **—vt.** 1. to make into the form of a fork 2. to pick up, spear, or pitch with a fork **—fork over** (or **out, up**) [Colloq.] to pay out; hand over **—fork′ful′n.**, *pl.* **-fuls′**

forked (fôrkt) *adj.* 1. having a fork or forks; cleft [*forked* lightning] 2. having prongs [five-*forked*]

fork·lift (fôrk′lift′) *n.* a device, as on a vehicle, for lifting, stacking, etc. heavy objects: its projecting prongs are slid under the load and raised or lowered [*forklift* truck]

for·lorn (fər lôrn′, fôr-) *adj.* [< OE. pp. of *forleosan*, to lose utterly] 1. abandoned or deserted 2. wretched; miserable; pitiful 3. without hope; desperate 4. bereft (of) **—for·lorn′ly** *adv.* **—for·lorn′ness** *n.*

forlorn hope [< Du *verloren hoop*, lit., lost group] 1. [Obs.] a small group of soldiers sent on a very dangerous mission 2. an undertaking with very little chance of success 3. [through confusion with HOPE] a faint hope

form (fôrm) *n.* [< OFr. < L. *forma*] 1. the shape, outline, or configuration of anything; structure 2. *a)* the body or figure of a person or animal *b)* a model of a human figure used as a clothes dummy 3. anything used to give shape to something else; mould, as for poured concrete 4. the mode of existence a thing has or takes [water in the *form* of vapour] 5. arrangement; esp., orderly arrangement, often of a specified kind 6. a way of doing something [one's golf *form*] 7. a customary way of acting or behaving; ceremony; formality 8. a fixed order of words; formula 9. a printed document with blank spaces to be filled in 10. a particular kind, type, species, or variety 11. a condition of mind or body [a boxer in good *form*] 12. *a)* a chart giving information about horses in a race *b)* what can be expected, based on past performances [to react according to *form*] 13. a long, wooden bench, as formerly in a schoolroom 14. a class in school 15. *Gram.* any of the different appearances of a word in changes of inflection, spelling, etc.

["am" is a *form* of "be"] **16.** *Printing same as* FORME —*vt.* a frame for printing —*vt.* **1.** to shape; fashion; make, as in some particular way **2.** to train; instruct **3.** to develop (habits) **4.** to think of; conceive **5.** to organize into [to form a club] **6.** to make up; constitute —*vi.* **1.** to be formed **2.** to come into being; take form **3.** to take a specific form —**good** (or **bad**) **form** conduct in (or not in) accord with social custom

-form (fôrm) [< OFr. < L. *-formis* < *forma*, form] *a suffix meaning:* **1.** having the form of [*cuneiform*] **2.** having (a specified number of) forms [*multiform*]

for·mal (fôr'məl) *adj.* [L. *formalis*] **1.** of external form or structure, rather than nature or content **2.** according to fixed customs, rules, etc. **3.** *a*) appearing to be suitable, correct, etc. but not really so *b*) stiff in manner **4.** *a*) designed for wear at ceremonies, etc. [*formal dress*] *b*) requiring such clothes [a *formal dance*] **5.** done or made in orderly, regular fashion; methodical **6.** rigidly symmetrical [a *formal garden*] **7.** done or made according to the forms that make explicit, definite, etc. [a *formal contract*] **8.** designating education in schools, colleges, etc. **9.** designating or of that level of language usage characterized by expanded vocabulary, complete syntactical constructions, complex sentences, etc.: distinguished from COLLOQUIAL —**for'mal·ly** *adv.*

form·al·de·hyde (fôr mal'də hīd', fər-) *n.* [FORM(IC) + ALDEHYDE] a colourless, pungent gas, HCHO, used in solution as a disinfectant and preservative

for·ma·lin [FORMAL(DEHYDE) + -IN[1]] *n.* a solution of formaldehyde in water

for·mal·ism (fôr'məl iz'm) *n.* strict attention to outward forms and customs, as in art or religion —**for'mal·ist** *n., adj.* —**for'mal·is'tic** *adj.*

for·mal·i·ty (fôr mal'ə tē) *n., pl.* **-ties 1.** a being formal; specif., *a*) an observing of prescribed customs, rules, ceremonies, etc.; propriety *b*) careful or too careful attention to order, regularity, or convention; stiffness **2.** a formal or conventional act or requirement; ceremony or form

for·mal·ize (fôr'mə līz') *vt.* **-ized', -iz'ing 1.** to give definite form to **2.** to make formal **3.** to make official, valid, etc. —**for'mal·i·za'tion** *n.*

for·mant (fôr'mant) *n.* [G. < L. *formans*, prp. of *formane*, FORM] *Phonet.* any of the group of sound waves special to a particular vowel sound

for·mat (fôr'mat) *n.* [G. < L. pp. of *formare*, to form] **1.** the shape, size, and general makeup of a book, magazine, etc. **2.** general arrangement, as of a television programme

for·ma·tion (fôr mā'shən) *n.* **1.** a forming or being formed **2.** a thing formed **3.** the way in which something is formed or arranged; structure **4.** an arrangement or positioning, as of troops, ships, a football team, etc. **5.** *Geol.* a rock unit having some common character, as origin

form·a·tive (fôr'mə tiv) *adj.* **1.** helping to shape, develop, or mould [a *formative* influence] **2.** of formation or development [one's *formative* years] **3.** *Linguis.* serving to form words, as an affix —*n.* an affix

form class *Linguis.* a class made up of words having a distinctive position in constructions and certain formal features in common

form criticism a system of biblical analysis which categorizes passages of scripture into literary forms, as myth, proverb, etc., and relates them to their historical background

forme (fôrm) *n.* *Printing* the type, plates, etc. locked in a frame for printing

for·mer[1] (fôr'mər) *adj.* [ME. *formere*, compar. of *forme*, first < OE. *forma*: see FOREMOST] **1.** preceding in time; earlier; past **2.** first mentioned of two: opposed to LATTER: often a noun (with *the*)

form·er[2] (fôr'mər) *n.* a person or thing that forms

for·mer·ly (fôr'mər lē) *adv.* at or in a former or earlier time; in the past

for·mic (fôr'mik) *adj.* [< L. *formica*, an ant] **1.** of ants **2.** designating or of a colourless acid, HCOOH, found in ants, spiders, nettles, etc.

For·mi·ca (fôr mik'ə) [arbitrary coinage] *a trademark for a* laminated, heat-resistant plastic used for table tops, etc.

for·mi·da·ble (fôr'mə də b'l, fôr mid'-) *adj.* [OFr. < L. < *formidare*, to dread] **1.** causing fear or dread **2.** hard to handle or overcome **3.** awe-inspiring in size, excellence, etc. —**for'mi·da·bil'i·ty, for'mi·da·ble·ness** *n.* —**for'mi·da·bly** *adv.*

form·less (fôrm'lis) *adj.* having no regular form or plan —**form'less·ly** *adv.* —**form'less·ness** *n.*

form letter one of a number of duplicated letters, with the date, address, etc. filled in separately

for·mu·la (fôr'myoo lə) *n., pl.* **-las, -lae'** (-lē') [L., dim. of *forma*, form] **1.** a fixed form of words, esp. one that is used only as a conventional expression ["Very truly yours" is a *formula*] **2.** a rule or method for doing something, esp. when conventional and used or repeated without thought **3.** an exact statement of religious faith or doctrine **4.** a prescription for a medicine, a baby's food, etc. **5.** a set of

algebraic symbols expressing a mathematical fact, rule, etc. **6.** categorization of racing cars, usually according to engine capacity **7.** *Chem.* an expression of the composition, as of a compound, by a combination of symbols and figures

for·mu·lar·ize (-lə rīz') *vt.* **-ized', -iz'ing** *same as* FORMULATE (sense 1)

for·mu·lar·y (fôr'myoo lər ē) *n., pl.* **-lar·ies 1.** a collection of formulas or prescribed forms, as of prayers **2.** a formula **3.** *Pharmacy* a list of medicines with their formulas —*adj.* of formulas

for·mu·late (-lāt') *vt.* **-lat'ed, -lat'ing 1.** to express in or reduce to a formula **2.** to express (a theory, plan, etc.) in a systematic way —**for'mu·la'tion** *n.* —**for'mu·la'tor** *n.*

for·mu·lize (-līz') *vt.* **-lized', -liz'ing** *same as* FORMULATE (sense 1)

form·work (fôrm'wurk') *n.* a temporary arrangement of boards, etc. used to support concrete while it is setting: also **shut'ter·ing**

for·ni·cate (fôr'nə kāt') *vi.* **-cat'ed, -cat'ing** [< LL. pp. of *fornicari* < L. *fornix* (gen. *fornicis*), a brothel] to commit fornication —**for'ni·ca'tor** *n.*

for·ni·ca·tion (fôr'nə kā'shən) *n.* **1.** voluntary sexual intercourse between unmarried persons **2.** *Bible* any unlawful sexual intercourse

for·sake (fər sāk', fôr-) *vt.* **-sook'** (-sook'), **-sak'en, -sak'ing** [< OE. < *for-*, FOR- + *sacan*, to strive < *sacu*: see SAKE[1]] **1.** to give up; renounce (a habit, idea, etc.) **2.** to leave; abandon

for·sak·en (-sā'kən) *adj.* abandoned; desolate

for·sooth (fər sooth', fôr-) *adv.* [OE. *forsoth*] [Archaic] in truth; no doubt; indeed

for·swear (fôr swer') *vt.* **-swore'** (-swôr'), **-sworn', -swear'ing 1.** to swear or promise earnestly to give up **2.** to deny earnestly or on oath —*vi.* to swear falsely; commit perjury —**forswear oneself** to perjure oneself

for·syth·i·a (fər sith'ē ə, fôr-) *n.* [ModL., after W. *Forsyth*, 18th-c. Brit. botanist] a shrub of the olive family with yellow, bell-shaped flowers, which appear in early spring before the leaves

fort (fôrt) *n.* [OFr. < L. *fortis*, strong] **1.** a fortified place or building for military defence **2.** a permanent army post —**hold the fort** [Colloq.] to keep things in operation; remain on duty, etc.

forte[1] (fôrt, fôr'tā) *n.* [< OFr.: see FORT] that which one does particularly well; one's strong point

for·te[2] (fôr'tā, -tē) *adj., adv.* [It. < L. *fortis*, strong] *Music* loud: a direction to the performer —*n.* a forte note or passage

forth (fôrth) *adv.* [OE.] **1.** forwards; onwards **2.** out into view, as from hiding —**and so forth** and so on: equivalent to *etc.*

forth·com·ing (fôrth'kum'iŋ) *adj.* **1.** about to appear; approaching **2.** ready when needed [help was not *forthcoming*] —*n.* a coming forth; approach —**forth'com'ing·ness** *n.*

forth·right (-rīt') *adj.* straightforward; direct; frank —*adv.* straight forward; directly onward —**forth'right'ly** *adv.* —**forth'right'ness** *n.*

forth·with (fôrth'with', -with') *adv.* immediately

for·ti·eth (fôr'tē ith) *adj.* **1.** preceded by thirty-nine others in a series; 40th **2.** designating any of the forty equal parts of something —*n.* **1.** the one following the thirty-ninth **2.** any of the forty equal parts of something; 1/40

for·ti·fi·ca·tion (fôr'tə fi kā'shən) *n.* **1.** the act or science of fortifying **2.** a fort or defensive earthwork, wall, etc. **3.** a fortified place

for·ti·fy (fôr'tə fī') *vt.* **-fied', -fy'ing** [< OFr. < LL. *fortificare* < L. *fortis*, strong + *facere*, to make] **1.** to strengthen physically, emotionally, etc. **2.** to strengthen against attack, as by building forts, walls, etc. **3.** to support; corroborate (an argument, etc.) **4.** to strengthen (wine, etc.) by adding alcohol **5.** to add vitamins, minerals, etc. to (milk, etc.) so as to increase the food value —*vi.* to build military defences —**for'ti·fi'a·ble** *adj.* —**for'ti·fi'er** *n.*

for·tis·si·mo (fôr tis'ə mō') *adj., adv.* [It., superl. of *forte*, FORTE[2]] *Music* very loud: a direction to the performer —*n., pl.* **-mos', -mi'** (-mē') a fortissimo note or passage

for·ti·tude (fôr'tə tyood') *n.* [< L. < *fortis*, strong] patient endurance of misfortune, pain, etc.; firm courage —**for'ti·tu'di·nous** *adj.*

fort·night (fôrt'nīt') *n.* [< OE., lit., fourteen nights] two weeks

fort·night·ly (-lē) *adv., adj.* (happening or appearing) once every fortnight, or at two-week intervals —*n., pl.* **-lies** a periodical issued at two-week intervals

FOR·TRAN (fôr'tran) *n.* [*for(mula)* tran(*slation*)] a digital computer language similar to algebra

for·tress (fôr'trəs) *n.* [< OFr., ult. < L. *fortis*, strong] a fortified place; fort: often used figuratively —*vt.* to protect by a fortress

for·tu·i·tous (fôr tyoo'ə təs') *adj.* [< L. < *fors* (gen. *fortis*), luck] **1.** happening by chance; accidental **2.** bringing, or happening by, good luck; fortunate —**for·tu′i·tous·ly** *adv.* —**for·tu′i·tous·ness** *n.*

for·tu·i·ty (-tē) *n., pl.* **-ties** [< L. (see prec.) + -ITY] 1. a being fortuitous 2. chance or chance occurrence

for·tu·nate (fôr′chə nət) *adj.* [< L. pp. of *fortunare* < *fortuna,* FORTUNE] 1. having good luck; lucky 2. bringing, or coming by, good luck; favourable —**for′tu·nate·ly** *adv.* —**for′tu·nate·ness** *n.*

for·tune (fôr′chən) *n.* [OFr. < L. *fortuna* < *fors* (gen. *fortis*), luck] 1. the supposed power that brings good or bad to people; luck; chance; fate: often personified 2. what happens to one; one's lot, esp. future lot, good or bad [to call one's *fortune*] 3. good luck; success 4. wealth; riches —**for′tune·less** *adj.*

fortune hunter a person who tries to become rich, esp. by marrying a rich person

for·tune·tell·er (-tel′ər) *n.* a person who professes to foretell events in other people's lives —**for′tune·tell′ing** *n., adj.*

for·ty (fôr′tē) *adj.* [OE. *feowertig*] four times ten —*n., pl.* **-ties** the cardinal number between thirty-nine and forty-one; 40; XL —**the forties** the numbers or years, as of a century, from forty to forty-nine

Forty-Five (-fiv′) *n.* the Jacobite rebellion of 1745 (preceded by *the*)

for·ty-nin·er (fôr′tē nī′nər) *n.* [*also* F- N-] [U.S. Colloq.] a participant in the 1849 California gold rush

forty winks [Colloq.] a short sleep; nap

fo·rum (fôr′əm) *n., pl.* **-rums, -ra** (-ə) [L.] 1. the public square or marketplace of an ancient Roman city, where legal and political business was conducted 2. a law court; tribunal 3. *a*) an assembly or programme for the discussion of public matters *b*) an opportunity for open discussion —**the Forum** the forum of ancient Rome

for·ward (fôr′wərd) *adj.* [OE. *foreweard*] 1. at, towards, or of the front 2. advanced; specif., *a*) mentally advanced *b*) advanced socially, politically, etc. 3. onward; advancing 4. ready or eager; prompt 5. too bold; presumptuous 6. of or for the future [*forward* buying] —*adv.* 1. towards the front; ahead 2. towards the future [to look *forward*] 3. into view or prominence —*n.* *Football, Hockey,* etc. any of the players in a front position —*vt.* 1. to promote 2. to send; transmit 3. to send on to another address [to *forward* letters] —**for′ward·er** *n.* —**for′ward·ly** *adv.* —**for′ward·ness** *n.*

for·wards (-wərdz) *adv.* same as FORWARD

for·went (fôr went′) *pt. of* FORGO

fos·sa (fos′ə) *n., pl.* **-sae** (-ē) [ModL. < L., a ditch] *Anat.* a cavity, pit, or small hollow —**fos′sate** (-āt) *adj.*

fosse, foss (fos) *n.* [< OFr. < L. *fossa,* ditch] a ditch or moat, esp. in fortifications

fos·sick (fos′ik) *vi.* [dial., prob. ult. < FUSS] [Aust.] 1. to prospect or search, as for gold 2. to search about; rummage —*vt.* to search for

fos·sil (fos′'l) *n.* [< Fr. < L. *fossilis,* dug up < pp. of *fodere,* to dig up] 1. any hardened remains or traces of plant or animal life of some previous geological age, preserved in the earth's crust 2. anything like a fossil 3. a person who has outmoded, fixed ideas —*adj.* 1. of, like, or forming a fossil 2. dug from the earth [coal is a *fossil* fuel] 3. antiquated —**fos′sil·like′** *adj.*

fos·sil·if·er·ous (fos′ə lif′ər əs) *adj.* [< FOSSIL + -FEROUS] containing fossils

fos·sil·ize (fos′ə līz′) *vt.* **-ized′, -iz′ing** 1. to change into a fossil; petrify 2. to make out of date, rigid, or incapable of change —*vi.* to become fossilized —**fos′sil·i·za′tion** *n.*

fos·so·ri·al (fo sôr′ē əl) *adj.* [< LL. *fossorius* < L. *fossor,* digger] digging or adapted for digging; burrowing [*fossorial* claws]

fos·ter (fos′tər) *vt.* [OE. *fostrian,* to nourish < base of *foda,* food] 1. to bring up with care; rear 2. to help to develop; promote [to *foster* discontent] 3. to cherish [to *foster* a hope] —*adj.* 1. having the standing of a specified member of the family but not by birth or adoption [a *foster* child] 2. of or relating to the care of such a person [*foster* home] —**fos′ter·er** *n.*

fos·ter·age (-ij) *n.* 1. the rearing of a foster child 2. the state of being a foster child 3. a promoting, encouraging

fought (fôt) *pt. & pp. of* FIGHT

foul (faul) *adj.* [OE. *ful*] 1. stinking; loathsome [a *foul* odour] 2. extremely dirty; disgustingly filthy 3. full of dirt or foreign objects [a *foul* pipe] 4. rotten: said of food 5. not decent; obscene [*foul* language] 6. wicked; abominable 7. stormy; unfavourable [*foul* weather] 8. tangled; caught [a *foul* rope] 9. not according to the rules of a game; unfair 10. treacherous; dishonest 11. [Colloq.] unpleasant, disagreeable, etc. 12. *Printing* marked for errors or changes [*foul* copy] —*adv.* in a foul way —*n.* anything foul; specif., *a*) a collision of boats, contestants, etc. *b*) an infraction of rules, as of a game —*vt.* 1. to make foul; dirty; soil 2. to dishonour or disgrace 3. to obstruct; fill up [grease *fouls* sink drains] 4. to cover (a ship's bottom) with impeding growths 5. to entangle; catch [a rope *fouled*

in the shrouds] 6. to collide with 7. to make a foul against, as in a game —*vi.* 1. to be or become fouled (in various senses) 2. to break the rules of a game —**foul up** [Colloq.] to entangle or bungle —**run** (or **fall** or **go**) **foul of** 1. to collide with and become tangled in 2. to get into trouble with —**foul′ly** *adv.* —**foul′ness** *n.*

fou·lard (foo lärd′) *n.* [Fr.] 1. a lightweight material of silk, rayon, or sometimes cotton 2. a necktie, scarf, etc. of this material

foul play 1. unfair play; action that breaks the rules of the game 2. treacherous action or violence

found[1] (faund) *pt. & pp. of* FIND

found[2] (faund) *vt.* [< L. < *fundus,* bottom] 1. to set for support; base 2. to begin to build or organize; establish [to *found* a college] —*vi.* [Rare] to be based (*on* or *upon*)

found[3] (faund) *vt.* [< OFr. < L. *fundere,* to pour] 1. to melt and pour (metal) into a mould 2. to make by pouring molten metal into a mould; cast

foun·da·tion (faun dā′shən) *n.* 1. a founding or being founded; establishment 2. *a*) a fund or endowment to maintain a school, hospital, charity, research, etc. *b*) the organization administering such a fund 3. the base on which something rests; specif., the supporting part of a wall, house, etc. 4. basis 5. a woman's corset or girdle: also **foundation garment** —**foun·da′tion·al** *adj.*

found·er[1] (faun′dər) *vi.* [< OFr. < L. *fundus:* see FOUND[2]] 1. to stumble, fall, or go lame 2. to become stuck as in soft ground 3. to fill with water and sink: said of a ship 4. to break down; collapse; fail —*vt.* to cause to founder —*n.* [< the *vi.*, 1] an inflammation of a horse's foot

found·er[2] (faun′dər) *n.* a person who founds, or establishes

found·er[3] (faun′dər) *n.* a person who founds metals

found·ling (faund′liŋ) *n.* an infant of unknown parents that has been found abandoned

found·ry (faun′drē) *n., pl.* **-ries** 1. the act or work of founding metals; casting 2. metal castings 3. a place where metal is cast

fount[1] (faunt) *n.* [< OFr. < L. *fons,* FOUNTAIN] 1. [Poet.] a fountain or spring 2. a source

fount[2] (faunt) *n.* [Fr. *fonte* < OFr. *fondre:* see FOUND[3]] *Printing* a complete assortment of type in one size and style

foun·tain (faun′tən) *n.* [< OFr. < LL. *fontana* < L. < *fons* (gen. *fontis*), spring] 1. a natural spring of water 2. a source or origin of anything 3. *a*) an artificial spring, jet, or flow of water *b*) the basin, pipes, etc. where this flows *c*) same as DRINKING FOUNTAIN 4. a container or reservoir, as for ink, oil, etc. —**foun′tained** *adj.*

foun·tain·head (-hed′) *n.* 1. a spring that is the source of a stream 2. the original or main source of anything

fountain pen a pen which is fed ink from a supply in a reservoir or cartridge

four (fôr) *adj.* [OE. *feower*] totalling one more than three —*n.* 1. the cardinal number between three and five; 4; IV 2. anything having four units or members, or numbered four —**on all fours** 1. on all four feet 2. on hands and knees (or feet)

four-flush (fôr′flush′) *vi.* 1. *Stud Poker* to bluff when one holds four cards of the same suit (**four flush**) instead of the five in a true flush 2. [U.S. Colloq.] to bluff —**four′-flush′·er** *n.*

four·fold (-fōld′) *adj.* [see -FOLD] 1. having four parts 2. having four times as much or as many —*adv.* four times as much or as many

four-foot·ed (-foot′id) *adj.* having four feet

four-in-hand (-in hand′) *n.* 1. *a*) a team of four horses driven by one man *b*) a coach drawn by such a team 2. [U.S.] a necktie tied in a slipknot with the ends left hanging —*adj.* of a four-in-hand

four-leaf clover (-lēf′) a clover with four leaves, popularly supposed to bring good luck to the finder

four-letter word (-let′ər) any of several short words having to do with sex or excrement and generally regarded as offensive

four-o'clock (-ə klok′) *n.* any of several tropical American plants, esp. a garden plant with long-tubed blossoms that generally open late in the afternoon

four-post·er (-pōs′tər) *n.* a bedstead with tall corner posts often supporting a canopy or curtains

four·score (-skôr′) *adj., n.* four times twenty; eighty

four·some (-səm) *n.* 1. a group of four people 2. *Golf* a game involving four players

four·square (-skwer′) *adj.* 1. perfectly square 2. unyielding; firm 3. frank; forthright —*adv.* 1. in a square form 2. forthrightly

four-stroke (-strōk′) *adj.* firing once to every four strokes of the piston; said of an internal combustion engine

four·teen (-tēn′) *adj.* [OE. *feowertyne*] four more than ten —*n.* the cardinal number between thirteen and fifteen; 14; XIV

four·teenth (-tēnth′) *adj.* 1. preceded by thirteen others in a series; 14th 2. designating any of the fourteen equal parts of something —*n.* **1.** the one following the thirteenth **2.** any of the fourteen equal parts of something; 1/14

fourth (fôrth) *adj.* [< OE.] **1.** preceded by three others in a series; 4th **2.** designating any of the four equal parts of something —*n.* **1.** the one following the third **2.** any of the four equal parts of something; a quarter; 1/4 **3.** the fourth forward gear ratio of a motor vehicle **4.** *Music a)* the fourth tone of an ascending diatonic scale, or a tone three degrees above or below a given tone *b)* the interval between two such tones, or a combination of them —**fourth′ly** *adv.*

fourth dimension a dimension in addition to those of length, width, and depth: in the theory of relativity, time is regarded as this dimension —**fourth′-di·men′sion·al** *adj.*

fourth estate [cf. ESTATE (sense 2)] [often F- E-] journalism or journalists

fo·ve·a (fō′vē·ə) *n., pl.* **fo′ve·ae′**(-ē), **-ve·as** [L.] *Biol., etc.* a small pit or depression

fowl (foul) *n., pl.* **fowls, fowl:** see PLURAL, II, D, 1 [OE. *fugol*] **1.** any bird: used in combination [wild*fowl*] **2.** any of the larger domestic birds used as food, as the chicken, duck, turkey, etc. **3.** the flesh of any of these birds used for food —*vi.* to hunt wild birds for food or sport —**fowl′er** *n.* —**fowl′ing** *adj.*

fowling piece a shotgun for hunting wild fowl

fowl pest an acute and usually fatal viral disease of domestic fowl

fox (foks) *n., pl.* **fox′es, fox:** see PLURAL, II, D, 1 [OE.] **1.** a small, wild, flesh-eating mammal of the dog family, with a bushy tail: thought of as sly and crafty **2.** its fur, commonly reddish-brown or grey **3.** a sly, crafty person —*vt.* **1.** to stain (book leaves, prints, etc.) with brownish discolourations **2.** to trick by slyness or craftiness **3.** to bewilder or baffle —**foxed** *adj.*

FOX (average length 107 cm, including tail)

fox fire the luminescence of decaying wood and plant remains, caused by various fungi

fox·glove (foks′gluv′) *n.* [OE. *foxes glofa*] *same as* DIGITALIS (sense 1)

fox·hole (-hōl′) *n.* a hole dug in the ground as a temporary protection for one or two soldiers against enemy gunfire or tanks

fox·hound (-hound′) *n.* a strong, swift hound with a keen scent, bred and trained to hunt foxes

fox hunt a sport in which hunters on horses ride after hounds in pursuit of a fox —**fox′-hunt′** *vi.* —**fox hunter** —**fox hunting**

fox-shark (shärk) *n.* a type of large shark; the thresher

fox-tail (-tāl′) *n.* **1.** the tail of a fox **2.** a grass having cylindrical spikes bearing spikelets interspersed with stiff bristles

fox terrier a small, active terrier with a smooth or wire-haired coat, formerly trained to drive foxes out of hiding

fox trot 1. a horse gait that is a shuffling half-walk, half-trot **2.** *a)* a dance for couples in 4/4 time with a variety of steps, both fast and slow *b)* the music for such a dance —**fox′-trot′** *vi.* **-trot′ted, -trot′ting**

fox·y (fok′sē) *adj.* **fox′i·er, fox′i·est 1.** foxlike; crafty; sly **2.** covered with brownish stains —**fox′i·ly** *adv.* —**fox′-i·ness** *n.*

foy·er (foi′ā) *n.* [Fr. < ML. < L. *focus*, hearth] an entrance hall or a lobby, as in a theatre or hotel

F.P., f.p., fp foot-pound(s)

f.p., fp, fp. freezing point

F.P.A. Family Planning Association

fps, f.p.s. 1. feet per second **2.** foot-pound-second

Fr *Chem.* francium

Fr. 1. Father **2.** France **3.** French **4.** Friday

fr. franc; francs

Fra (frä) *n.* [It., abbrev. of *frate* < L. *frater*] brother: title given to an Italian friar or monk

fra·cas (frak′ä) *n., pl.* **fra·cas** (frak′äz) [Fr. < It. < *fracassare*, to smash] a noisy fight or loud quarrel; brawl

frac·tion (frak′shən) *n.* [< L. < pp. of *frangere*, to break] **1.** a small part, amount, etc.; portion; fragment **2.** *Chem.* a part separated, as by distillation, from a mixture, at its particular boiling point, etc. **3.** *Math. a)* an indicated quotient of two whole numbers, as 1/2, 13/4 *b)* any quantity expressed in terms of a numerator and denominator, as $2x/xy$ —**frac′tion·al** *adj.* —**frac′tion·al·ly** *adv.* —**frac′-tion·ar·y** *adj.* —**frac′tion·ize** *vt.*

fractional distillation *Chem.* a method of separating the various constituents of a liquid mixture by heating gradually and collecting each fraction as it passes over at its own boiling point

frac·tion·ate (-āt′) *vt.* **-at′ed, -at′ing 1.** to separate into fractions, or parts **2.** *Chem.* to separate into fractions by distillation, etc. —**frac′tion·a′tion** *n.*

frac·tious (frak′shəs) *adj.* [prob. < *fraction*, (obs.) discord + -OUS] **1.** unruly; rebellious; refractory **2.** peevish; irritable; cross —**frac′tious·ly** *adv.* —**frac′tious·ness** *n.*

frac·ture (frak′chər) *n.* [< OFr. < L. *fractura* < pp. of *frangere*, to break] **1.** a breaking or being broken **2.** a break, crack, or split **3.** a break in a bone or, occasionally, a tear in a cartilage **4.** the texture of the broken surface of a mineral as distinct from its cleavage —*vt., vi.* **-tured, -tur·ing 1.** to break, crack, or split **2.** to disrupt —**frac′-tur·al** *adj.*

frae (frā) *prep.* [Scot.] from

frae·num (frē′nəm) *n., pl.* **-nums, -na** (-nə) [L., lit., a bridle] a fold of skin or mucous membrane that checks the movements of an organ, as the fold under the tongue

frag·ile (fraj′īl) *adj.* [< OFr. < L. *fragilis* < *frangere*, to break] easily broken, damaged, or destroyed; frail; delicate —**fra·gil·i·ty** (frə jil′ə tē) *n.*

frag·ment (frag′mənt; *for v. also* frag ment′) *n.* [< L. < *frangere*, to break] **1.** a part broken away; broken piece **2.** a detached or incomplete part [a *fragment* of a song, novel, etc.] —*vt., vi.* to break into fragments —**frag·ment′-ed** *adj.*

frag·men·tar·y (frag′mən tər ē) *adj.* consisting of fragments or bits; not complete; disconnected: also **frag·men′tal** (-men′tal) —**frag′men·tar·i·ly** *adv.*

frag·men·tate (-tāt′) *vt., vi.* **-tat′ed, -tat′ing** to break into fragments —**frag′men·ta′tion** *n.*

fra·grance (frā′grəns) *n.* a fragrant smell; pleasant odour: also [Now Rare] **fra′gran·cy,** *pl.* **-cies**

fra·grant (frā′grənt) *adj.* [< L. prp. of *fragrare*, to emit a (sweet) smell] having a pleasant odour; sweet-smelling —**fra′grant·ly** *adv.*

frail[1] (frāl) *adj.* [< OFr. < L. *fragilis*, FRAGILE] **1.** easily broken, damaged, or destroyed; fragile; delicate **2.** slender and delicate; weak **3.** easily tempted; morally weak —**frail′ly** *adv.* —**frail′ness** *n.*

frail[2] (frāl) *n.* [ME. *fraiel* < OFr. *frael*, rush basket] **1.** a basket made of rushes, for packing figs, raisins, etc. **2.** the quantity of raisins, etc. packed in such a basket, varying from 23 to 34 kg

frail·ty (frāl′tē) *n.* **1.** the condition of being frail; weakness; esp., moral weakness **2.** *pl.* **-ties** any fault or failing arising from such weakness

frak·tur (fräk toor′) *n.* [G. < L. *fractura* (see FRACTURE): so named from its angular, broken lines] a kind of German black-letter type

fram·boe·si·a (fram bē′zē ə) *n.* [ModL. Fr. *framboise*, raspberry] *same as* YAWS

frame (frām) *vt.* **framed, fram′ing** [prob. < ON. *frami*, profit, benefit; some senses < OE. *framian*, to be helpful] **1.** to shape or form according to a pattern; design [to *frame* a constitution] **2.** to put together the parts of; construct **3.** to put into words; compose; devise **4.** to adjust; fit [a tax *framed* to benefit a few] **5.** to enclose (a picture, mirror, etc.) in a border **6.** [Colloq.] to falsify evidence, testimony, etc. beforehand so as to make (an innocent person) appear guilty —*n.* **1.** *a)* formerly, anything made of parts fitted together according to a design *b)* body structure in general; build **2.** skeletal or basic, supporting structure; framework, as of a house **3.** the framework supporting the chassis of a motor vehicle **4.** the structural case or border into which a window, door, etc. is set **5.** a border, often ornamental, surrounding a picture, etc. **6.** [pl.] the framework for a pair of spectacles **7.** any of certain machines built in or on a framework **8.** the way that anything is constructed or put together; form **9.** setting or background circumstances **10.** mood; temper [a bad *frame* of mind] **11.** an established order or system **12.** [Colloq.] the act of framing (sense 6) **13.** *Bowling, etc.* any of the divisions of a game **14.** *Cinematography* each of the small exposures composing a strip of film **15.** *Snooker, etc. a)* the wooden triangle used to set up the balls *b)* the balls when set up —*adj.* having a wooden framework, usually covered with boards [a *frame* house] —**fram′er** *n.*

frame of reference 1. *Math.* the fixed points, lines, or planes from which coordinates are measured **2.** the set of ideas, facts, or circumstances within which something exists

frame-up (-up′) *n.* [Colloq.] **1.** a falsifying of evidence, testimony, etc. to make an innocent person seem guilty **2.** a secret, deceitful arrangement or scheme made beforehand

frame·work (-wurk′) *n.* **1.** a structure to hold together or to support something built or stretched over or around it [the *framework* of a house] **2.** a basic structure, arrangement, or system **3.** *same as* FRAME OF REFERENCE

franc (fraŋk) *n.* [Fr. < L. *Francorum rex*, king of the French, device on the coin in 1360] **1.** the monetary unit and a coin of France, Belgium, Switzerland, and Luxembourg **2.** the monetary unit of various other countries

fran·chise (fran′chīz) *n.* [< OFr. < *franc*, free: see FRANK] **1.** *a)* any special right or privilege granted by a government, as to operate a public utility, etc. *b)* the jurisdiction over which this extends **2.** the right to vote; suffrage **3.** the right to market a product or provide a service in an area, as granted by a manufacturer or company —*vt.* **-chised, -chis·ing** to grant a franchise to

Fran·cis·can (fran sis′kən) *adj.* of Saint Francis of Assisi or the religious order founded by him in 1209 —*n.* any member of this order

fran·ci·um (fran′sē əm) *n.* [ModL. < *France*] a radioactive, metallic chemical element of the alkali group: symbol, Fr; at. wt., 223(?); at. no., 87

Fran·co- [ML. < LL. *Francus*, a Frank] *a combining form meaning:* 1. Frankish 2. of France or the French 3. France and; the French and [*Franco*-German]

fran·co·lin (fran′kə lin) *n.* [Fr. < It. *francolino*] any of several African and Asiatic partridges

fran·co·phone (fran′kə fōn) *adj.* French-speaking; used esp. of people in countries where French is a second language

fran·gi·ble (fran′jə b'l) *adj.* [< OFr. < ML. < L. *frangere*, to break] breakable; fragile —**fran′gi·bil′i·ty** *n.*

fran·gi·pan·i (fran′jə pän′ē) *n.*, *pl.* **-pan′i, -pan′is** [It. < Marquis *Frangipani* (16th-c. It. nobleman)] 1. any of several tropical American shrubs and trees with large, fragrant flowers 2. a perfume obtained from this flower 3. a pastry made with ground almonds Also **fran′-gi·pane′**(-pān′)

‡Fran·glais (frän glā′) *n.* [Fr., coined (1964) by René Etiemble, Fr. writer < *Fran* (çais), French + (*An*)*glais*, English] informal French containing a high proportion of words of English origin

frank (fraŋk) *adj.* [< OFr. *franc*, free < ML. < LL. *Francus*, a Frank, hence free man] 1. open and honest in expressing what one thinks or feels; candid 2. free from disguise or guile; clearly evident —*vt.* 1. formerly, *a)* to send letters, etc., free of postage, as by virtue of an official position *b)* to mark letters, etc., so that they can be sent free 2. to mark letters, etc., with an official stamp, other than a postage stamp, indicating payment of postage —*n.* 1. the privilege of sending letters, etc. free 2. a mark or signature on a letter, etc. indicating this privilege 3. any letter, etc. sent free in this way —**frank′ly** *adv.* —**frank′ness** *n.*

Frank. Frankish

Frank·en·stein (fraŋ′kən stīn′) 1. the title character in a novel (1818) by Mary Shelley: he is a young medical student who creates a monster that destroys him 2. popularly, the monster —*n.* anything that becomes dangerous to its creator

frank·furt·er, frank·fort·er (fraŋk′fər tər) *n.* [G., after *Frankfurt* (*am Main*)] a smoked sausage of beef or beef and pork, etc.

frank·in·cense (fraŋ′kən sens′) *n.* [< OFr.: see FRANK & INCENSE¹] a gum resin from various Arabian and NE African trees, burned as incense

franking machine a machine that prints marks on letters, etc., indicating that postage has been paid

Frank·ish (fraŋ′kish) *adj.* of the Franks, their language, or culture —*n.* the West Germanic language of the Franks

frank·lin (fraŋk′lin) *n.* [< Anglo-Fr. < ML. < *francus*: see FRANK] in England in the 14th and 15th cent., a landowner of free but not noble birth, ranking just below the gentry

fran·tic (fran′tik) *adj.* [see PHRENETIC] 1. wild with anger, pain, worry, etc.; frenzied 2. marked by frenzy [*frantic* efforts] —**fran′ti·cal·ly** or [Rare] **fran′tic·ly** *adv.*

frap·pé (fra pā′) *adj.* [Fr., pp. of *frapper*, to strike] partly frozen; iced; cooled —*n.* 1. a dessert made of partly frozen beverages, fruit juices, etc. 2. a drink made of some beverage poured over crushed ice

fra·ter (frā′tər) *n.* [ME. *freitour* < Anglo-Fr. *fraitur*, altered < OFr. *refreitor* < ML. *refectorium*] [Obs.] the eating room, or refectory, in a monastery

fra·ter·nal (frə tur′n'l) *adj.* [< ML. < L. *fraternus* < *frater*, a brother] 1. of or characteristic of brothers; brotherly 2. of or like a fraternal order or a fraternity 3. designating twins, of the same or different sex, developed from separately fertilized ova —**fra·ter′nal·ism** *n.* —**fra·ter′nal·ly** *adv.*

fra·ter·ni·ty (frə tur′nə tē) *n.*, *pl.* **-ties** 1. fraternal relationship or spirit; brotherliness 2. a group of people with the same beliefs, interests, work, etc. [the medical *fraternity*] 3. [U.S.] a male students' society, usually functioning as a social club and bearing a name composed of Greek letters

frat·er·nize (frat′ər nīz′) *vi.* **-nized′, -niz′ing** to associate in a brotherly manner; be friendly —**frat′er·ni·za′tion** *n.* —**frat′er·niz′er** *n.*

frat·ri·cide (frat′rə sīd′) *n.* [Fr. < LL. *fratricidium* < L. < *frater*, brother + *caedere*, to kill] 1. the act of killing one's own brother or sister 2. a person who kills his brother or sister —**frat′ri·ci′dal** (-sīd′'l) *adj.*

‡Frau (frou) *n.*, *pl.* **Frau′en** (-ən) [G.] a married woman; wife: used in Germany as a title corresponding to *Mrs.*

fraud (frôd) *n.* [< OFr. < L. *fraus* (gen. *fraudis*)] 1. deceit; trickery; cheating 2. an intentional deception or dishonesty; trick 3. a person who deceives or is not what he pretends to be

fraud·u·lent (frô′dyoo lənt) *adj.* 1. acting with fraud;

deceitful 2. based on or characterized by fraud 3. done or obtained by fraud —**fraud′u·lence, fraud′u·len·cy** *n.* —**fraud′u·lent·ly** *adv.*

fraught (frôt) *adj.* [< MDu. < *vracht*, a load] filled, charged, or loaded (*with*) [a life *fraught* with hardship]

‡Fräu·lein (froi′līn; *E.*froi′-, frou′-) *n.*, *pl.* **-lein**, *E.* **-leins** [G.] an unmarried woman: used in Germany as a title corresponding to *Miss*

Fraun·ho·fer lines (froun′hō′fər) [after Joseph von *Fraunhofer* (1787-1826), Bavarian optician, who first mapped them accurately] the dark lines visible in the spectrum of the sun or a star

frax·i·nel·la (frak′sə nel′ə) *n.* [ModL., dim of L. *fraxinus*, ash tree (the leaves resemble that of the ash)] a perennial plant of the rue family, with flowers that on hot nights give off a flammable gas

fray¹ (frā) *n.* [< AFFRAY] a noisy quarrel or fight; brawl

fray² (frā) *vt., vi.* [< OFr. < L. *fricare*, to rub] 1. to make or become worn, ragged, etc. by rubbing 2. to make or become weakened or strained —**fray its head** to rub off the velvet of new horns: said of deer

fra·zil (frā′z'l) *n.* [< Canad Fr. *frasil*, < Fr. *fraisil*, cinders, ult < L. *fax*, torch] spikes of ice that form in water moving turbulently enough to prevent the formation of a sheet of ice

fraz·zle (fraz′'l) *vt., vi.* **-zled,** [Dial. & U.S., prob. < dial. *fazle*] [Colloq.] 1. to wear to tatters; fray 2. to make or become physically or emotionally exhausted —*n.* [Colloq.] the state of being frazzled

freak (frēk) *n.* [< ? OE. *frician*, to dance] 1. *a)* a sudden fancy; odd notion; whim *b)* an unusual happening 2. any abnormal animal, person, or plant; monstrosity 3. [Slang] *a)* a user of a specified narcotic, hallucinogen, etc. [an acid *freak*] *b)* a devotee [a rock *freak*] *c)* same as HIPPIE —*adj.* oddly different from what is normal; queer —**freak out** [Slang] 1. to experience in an extreme way the mental reactions, hallucinations, etc. induced by a psychedelic drug 2. to make or become very excited, distressed, disorganized, etc. 3. to opt out of society and adopt an unconventional way of life; drop out —**freak′ish, freak′y** *adj.* —**freak′ish·ly** *adv.* —**freak′ish·ness** *n.*

freck·le (frek′'l) *n.* [< Scand.] a small, brownish spot on the skin, esp. as a result of exposure to the sun —*vt.* **-led, -ling** to cause freckles to appear on —*vi.* to become spotted with freckles —**freck′led, freck′ly** *adj.*

free (frē) *adj.* **fre′er, fre′est** [OE. *freo*] 1. *a)* not under the control or power of another; able to act or think without arbitrary restriction; having liberty; independent *b)* characterized by or resulting from liberty 2. having, or existing under, a government that does not impose arbitrary restrictions on the right to speak, assemble, petition, vote, etc. 3. able to move in any direction; not held; loose 4. not held or confined by a court, the police, etc. 5. not burdened by obligations, debts, discomforts, etc.; unhindered [*free* from pain] 6. at liberty; allowed [*free* to leave] 7. not confined to the usual rules or conventions [*free* verse] 8. not literal; not exact [a *free* translation] 9. not busy or in use 10. not constrained or stilted [a *free* gait] 11. *a)* generous; lavish [a *free* spender] *b)* profuse; copious 12. frank; straightforward 13. too frank or familiar in speech, action, etc.; forward 14. with no charge or cost [a *free* ticket] 15. exempt from certain impositions, as taxes or duties 16. clear of obstructions; open [*free* passage] 17. open to all [a *free* market] 18. not fastened [the *free* end of a rope] 19. not united; not combined [*free* oxygen] —*adv.* 1. without cost or payment 2. in a free manner —*vt.* **freed, free′ing** to make free; specif., *a)* to release from bondage or arbitrary power, obligation, etc. *b)* to clear of obstruction, etc.; disengage —**free and easy** informal; unceremonious —**free from** (or *of*) 1. lacking; without 2. beyond —**make free with** 1. to use freely 2. to take liberties with —**set free** to release; liberate —**with a free hand** with generosity; lavishly —**free′ly** *adv.* —**free′ness** *n.*

free·board (-bôrd′) *n.* the height of a ship's side from the main deck or gunwale to the waterline

free·boot·er (-bōōt′ər) *n.* [< Du. < *vrij*, free + *buit*, plunder] a pirate; buccaneer —**free′boot′** *vi.*

free·born (-bôrn′) *adj.* 1. born free, not in slavery 2. of or fit for a person so born

Free Church any Protestant church other than the Established Church: a nonconformist church

free city a city that is an autonomous state

freed·man (frēd′mən) *n.*, *pl.* **-men** a man legally freed from slavery or bondage

free·dom (frē′dəm) *n.* 1. the state or quality of being free; esp., *a)* exemption or liberation from the control of some other person or some arbitrary power; liberty; independence *b)* exemption from arbitrary restrictions on a specified civil right; civil or political liberty [*freedom* of speech] *c)* exemption or immunity from a specified obligation, discomfort, etc. [*freedom* from want] *d)* a being able to act, move, use, etc. without hindrance *e)* ease of movement or performance; facility *f)* a being free from the usual rules, conventions, etc. *g)* frankness or easiness of manner;

sometimes, an excessive frankness or familiarity 2. a right or privilege

free enterprise the economic doctrine of permitting private industry to operate under freely competitive conditions with a minimum of governmental control

free fall the unchecked fall of a body through the air; specif., the part of a parachutist's jump before the parachute is opened

free fight a confused fight in which a large number of people join; a melée

free flight the flight of a rocket after the fuel supply has been used up or shut off —**free'-flight' adj.**

free-for-all (frē'fər ôl') n. a disorganized, general fight; brawl —adj. open to anyone

free-form (-fôrm') adj. 1. having an irregular, usually curvilinear form or outline 2. unconventional, unrestrained, etc. in style, form, etc.

free-hand (-hand') adj. drawn by hand without the use of instruments, measurements, etc.

free-hand-ed (-han'did) adj. generous; liberal

free-hold (-hōld') n. 1. an estate in land held for life or with the right to pass it on through inheritance 2. the holding of an estate in this way —adj. of or held by freehold —**free'-hold'er n.**

free house a public house which is not owned by any brewery and therefore sells various brands of beer

free kick Soccer a kick allowed as compensation for an opponent's breach of the rules

free-lance (-läns') adj. of or acting as a free lance —vi. -lanced', -lanc'ing to work as a free lance

free lance 1. a medieval soldier who sold his services to any state or army 2. one who acts according to his principles and is not influenced by any group 3. a writer, artist, etc. not under contract, who sells his services to individual buyers: also **free'-lanc'er n.**

free-liv-ing (-liv'iŋ) adj. 1. freely indulging one's appetites, desires, etc. 2. Biol. not parasitic or symbiotic —**free liver**

free-load-er (-lō'dər) n. [U.S. Colloq.] a person who habitually imposes on others for free food, lodging, etc.

free love the principle or practice of sexual relations unrestricted by marriage or other legal obligations

free-man (-mən) n., pl. -men 1. a person not in slavery or bondage 2. a person who has full civil and political rights; citizen

free market any market where trade can be carried on without restrictions as to price, etc.

free-mar-tin (-mär'tin) n. [< ?] an imperfectly developed female calf, usually sterile, born as the twin of a male

Free-ma-son (frē'mās''n) n. a member of an international secret society having as its principles brotherliness, charity, and mutual aid; Mason

Free-ma-son-ry (-rē) n. 1. the principles, rituals, etc. of Freemasons 2. the Freemasons 3. [f-] a natural sympathy and understanding among persons with similar experiences

free on board delivered (by the seller) aboard the train, ship, etc. at the point of shipment, without charge

free-si-a (frē'zhē ə, -zhə, -zē ə) n. [ModL., after F. Freese, 19th-c. Ger. physician] a South African bulbous plant with fragrant, funnel-shaped flowers

free silver the free coinage of silver, esp. at a fixed ratio to the gold coined in the same period

free-spo-ken (-spō'k'n) adj. frank; outspoken

free-stand-ing (-stan'diŋ) adj. resting on its own support, without attachment

free-stone (-stōn') n. 1. a stone, esp. sandstone or limestone, that can be cut easily without splitting 2. a) a peach, plum, etc. in which the stone does not cling to the pulp of the ripened fruit b) such a stone —adj. having such a stone

free-style (-stīl') n. 1. Swimming a race in which competitors may choose any style 2. Wrestling a form of wrestling in which any type of hold or throw is allowed —adj. of or using freestyle

free-think-er (-thiŋ'kər) n. a person who forms his opinions about religion independently of tradition, authority, or established belief —**free'think'ing n., adj.** —**free thought**

free trade trade conducted without quotas on imports or exports, protective tariffs, etc.

free verse poetry not following regular metrical, rhyming, or stanzaic forms

free-way (-wā') n. [U.S.] 1. an expressway with interchanges for fully controlled access 2. a road without toll charges

free-wheel (-wēl',-hwēl') n. 1. in a bicycle, a device in the rear hub that permits the rear wheel to go on turning when the pedals are stopped 2. in some cars, a device that permits the drive shaft to go on turning when its speed exceeds that of the engine shaft, thus allowing coasting with the gears engaged —vi. to coast

free-will (-wil') adj. voluntary; spontaneous

free will 1. freedom of the will to choose a course of action without external coercion; freedom of choice 2. the doctrine that people have such freedom

Free World [sometimes f- w-] the non-Communist countries collectively, esp. those that are actively anti-Communist

freeze (frēz) vi. froze, fro'zen, freez'ing [OE. freosan] 1. to be formed into ice; be hardened by cold 2. to become covered or clogged with ice 3. to be or become very cold 4. to become attached by freezing 5. to die or be damaged by exposure to cold 6. to become motionless or fixed 7. to be made momentarily unable to move, act, or speak through fright, etc. 8. to become formal or unfriendly 9. Mech. to stick or become tight as a result of expansion of parts from overheating or inadequate lubrication —vt. 1. to cause to form into ice; harden or solidify by cold 2. to cover or clog with ice 3. to make very cold 4. to remove sensation from, as with a local anaesthetic 5. to preserve (food) by rapid refrigeration 6. to make fixed or attached by freezing 7. to kill or damage by exposure to cold 8. to make or keep motionless or stiff 9. to discourage as by cool behaviour 10. to make formal or unfriendly 11. a) to fix (prices, wages, an employee, etc.) at a given level or place by authoritative regulation b) to make (funds, assets, etc.) unavailable to the owners —n. 1. a freezing or being frozen 2. a period of cold, freezing weather —**freeze** [Colloq.] to hold fast to —**freeze out** 1. to die out through freezing, as plants 2. [Colloq.] to force out by a cold manner, competition, etc. —**freeze over** to become covered with ice —**freez'a-ble adj.**

freeze-dry (frēz'drī') vt. -dried', -dry'ing to subject (food, vaccines, etc.) to quick-freezing followed by drying under high vacuum at a low temperature —**freeze'-dry'er n.**

freez-er (-ər) n. 1. a refrigerator, compartment, or room for freezing and storing frozen foods 2. [Aust.] a sheep bred for export as frozen meat

freez-ing point the temperature at which a liquid freezes: for water, it is $32°F$ or $0°C$

freight (frāt) n. [< MDu. vracht, a load] 1. a method or service for transporting goods by water or air 2. the cost for such transportation 3. the goods transported; cargo 4. any load or burden —vt. 1. to load with freight 2. to load; burden

freight-age (-ij) n. 1. the charge for transporting goods 2. freight; cargo 3. the transportation of goods

freight-er (-ər) n. a ship or aircraft for carrying freight

freight liner a goods train carrying containers mounted on flat wagons

French (french) adj. of France, its people, their language, or culture —n. the Romance language of the French —**the French** the people of France —**French'man** (-mən) n., pl. -men —**French'wom'an n., pl. -wom'en**

French bread a long, slender loaf of crisp, white bread

French Canadian a Canadian of French ancestry

French chalk a very soft chalk used for marking lines on cloth or removing grease spots

French cuff a double cuff turned back on itself and fastened with a link

French doors U.S. name for FRENCH WINDOWS

French dressing a salad dressing made of vinegar, oil, and various seasonings

French fried potatoes U.S. name for potato chips: also **French fries**

French horn a brass wind instrument with a long, coiled tube ending in a wide, flaring bell

French·i·fy (-ə fī') vt., vi. -fied', -fy'-ing to make or become French or like the French in customs, ideas, manners, etc.

French leave an unauthorized or unceremonious departure; act of leaving secretly or in haste

French letter [Slang] a condom

French mustard mustard (sense 2) mixed with vinegar

French polish a preparation, usually shellac dissolved in alcohol, applied to furniture for a glossy finish

French seam a narrow seam sewed on both sides of the material to hide the raw edges of the cloth

FRENCH HORN

French toast 1. toast cooked on one side only 2. [U.S.] bread dipped in beaten egg and lightly fried

French windows two adjoining doors with glass panes from top to bottom, hinged at opposite sides of a doorway and opening in the middle

fre-net-ic (frə net'ik) adj. [see PHRENETIC] frantic; frenzied: also **fre-net'i-cal** —**fre-net'i-cal-ly adv.**

fre-num (frē'nəm) n., pl. -nums, -na (-nə) same as FRAENUM

fren-zy (fren'zē) n., pl. -zies [< OFr. < ML. < L. phrenesis, ult. < Gr. phrenitis, madness < phrēn, mind] wild outburst of feeling or action; brief delirium that is almost insanity —vt. -zied, -zy-ing to make frantic; drive mad —**fren'zied adj.** —**fren'zied-ly adv.**

freq. 1. frequent 2. frequentative

fre·quen·cy (frē′kwən sē) *n., pl.* **-cies** 1. frequent occurrence 2. the number of times any event, value, characteristic, etc. is repeated in a given period or group 3. *Physics* the number of periodic oscillations, vibrations, or waves per unit of time: now usually expressed in hertz

frequency modulation 1. the variation of the instantaneous frequency of a carrier wave in accordance with the signal to be transmitted 2. the system of radio broadcasting that uses this

fre·quent (frē′kwənt; *for v., usually* frē kwent′) *adj.* [< OFr. < L. *frequens,* crowded] 1. occurring often; happening repeatedly at brief intervals 2. constant; habitual —*vt.* to go to constantly; be at or in habitually —**fre′quen·ta′tion** *n.* —**fre·quent′er** *n.* —**fre′quent·ly** *adv.*

fre·quen·ta·tive (frē kwen′tə tiv) *adj. Gram.* expressing frequent and repeated action —*n. Gram.* a frequentative verb: *sparkle* is a frequentative of *spark*

fres·co (fres′kō) *n., pl.* **-coes, -cos** [It., fresh < OHG. *frisc*] 1. the art of painting with water colours on wet plaster 2. a painting or design so made —*vt.* to paint in fresco

fresh (fresh) *adj.* [< OE. *fersc,* altered after OFr. *fres, freshe*] 1. recently made, obtained, or grown [*fresh* coffee] 2. not salted, preserved, etc. 3. not spoiled or stale 4. not tired; vigorous; lively 5. not worn, soiled, etc.; bright; clean 6. youthful or healthy in appearance 7. not known before; new; recent 8. additional; further [a *fresh* start] 9. inexperienced; unaccustomed 10. having just arrived 11. original and stimulating [*fresh* ideas] 12. cool and refreshing [a *fresh* spring day] 13. brisk; strong: said of the wind 14. not salt: said of water 15. [Slang] saucy; impudent —*adv.* in a fresh manner; recently [*fresh*-painted] —**fresh′ly** *adv.* —**fresh′ness** *n.*

fresh·en (fresh′ən) *vt., vi.* to make or become fresh —**freshen up** to bath oneself, change into fresh clothes, etc. —**fresh′en·er** *n.*

fresh·er (-ər) *n. same as* FRESHMAN

fresh·et (-it) *n.* 1. a rush of fresh water flowing into the sea 2. a flooding of a stream because of melting snow or heavy rain

fresh·man (-mən) *n., pl.* **-men** 1. a first year student at university —*adj.* of or for first-year students

fresh·wa·ter (-wôt′ər) 1. of or living in water that is not salty 2. sailing only on inland waters, not on the sea 3. inland

freshwater sailor [Colloq.] a raw, incompetent sailor

fret¹ (fret) *vt.* **fret′ted, fret′ting** [OE. *fretan,* to eat up] 1. to wear away by gnawing, rubbing, corroding, etc. 2. to make by wearing away 3. to make rough; disturb 4. to irritate; vex; worry —*vi.* 1. to gnaw (*into, on,* or *upon*) 2. to become corroded, worn, etc. 3. to become rough or disturbed 4. to be irritated, vexed, etc.; worry —*n.* irritation; worry —**fret′ter** *n.*

fret² (fret) *n.* [prob. merging of OFr. *frete,* interlaced work & OE. *frætwa,* ornament] an ornamental pattern of straight bars joining one another at right angles to form a design —*vt.* **fret′ted, fret′ting** to ornament with a fret

fret³ (fret) *n.* [OFr. *frette,* a band] any of the lateral ridges across the fingerboard of a banjo, guitar, etc. to regulate the fingering —*vt.* **fret′ted, fret′ting** to furnish with frets

fret·ful (fret′fəl) *adj.* tending to fret; peevish —**fret′ful·ly** *adv.* —**fret′ful·ness** *n.*

fret saw a saw with a long, narrow, fine-toothed blade, for cutting curved patterns in thin boards or metal plates

FRETS

fret·work (fret′wurk′) *n.* decorative openwork

Freud·i·an (froi′dē ən) *adj.* of or according to Freud or his theories —*n.* a follower of Freud or his theories of psychoanalysis —**Freud′i·an·ism** *n.*

Freudian slip a mistake made in speaking by which, it is thought, the speaker inadvertently reveals his true motives, desires, etc.

Fri. Friday

fri·a·ble (frī′ə b'l) *adj.* [Fr. < L. *friabilis < friare,* to rub] easily crumbled into powder —**fri′a·bil′i·ty, fri′a·ble·ness** *n.*

fri·ar (frī′ər) *n.* [< OFr. *frere* < L. *frater,* brother] R.C.Ch. a member of any of several mendicant orders; esp., an Augustinian, Carmelite, Dominican, or Franciscan —**fri′ar·ly** *adj.*

fri·ar·bird (-burd′) *n.* any of a genus of honey eaters of the SW Pacific and Australia that have a naked, featherless head

friar's balsam tincture of benzoin used to heal wounds and as an inhalant

fri·ar·y (-ē) *n., pl.* **-ar·ies** 1. a monastery where friars live 2. a brotherhood of friars

fric·an·deau (frik′ən dō′) *n., pl.* **-deaux** (-dōz′) [Fr., irreg. < ? ff.] meat, esp veal, larded and braised

fric·as·see (frik′ə sē′, frik′ə sē′) *n.* [< Fr. < *fricasser,* to cut up and fry] meat cut into pieces, stewed or fried, and served in its own gravy —*vt.* **-seed′, -see′ing** to prepare as a fricassee

fric·a·tive (frik′ə tiv) *adj.* [< L. pp. of *fricare* (see FRICTION) + -IVE] pronounced by forcing the breath through a narrow slit formed at some point in the mouth, as *f, v, z* —*n.* a fricative consonant

fric·tion (frik′shən) *n.* [Fr. < L. < pp. of *fricare,* to rub] 1. a rubbing, esp. of one object against another 2. conflict because of differences of opinion, temperament, etc. 3. the resistance to motion of moving surfaces that touch —**fric′-tion·al** *adj.* —**fric′tion·al·ly** *adv.*

Fri·day (frī′dē, -dā) *n.* [OE. *frigedaeg,* lit., day of the goddess *Frigg,* in Norse Myth. the wife of Odin] 1. the sixth day of the week 2. [after the devoted servant of ROBINSON CRUSOE] a faithful follower or efficient helper: usually **man** (or **girl**) **Friday**

Fri·days (-dēz, -dāz) *adv.* [Colloq.] on or during every Friday

fridge (frij) *n.* [Colloq.] a refrigerator

fried (frīd) *pt. & pp. of* FRY¹

friend (frend) *n.* [OE. *freond*] 1. a person whom one knows well and is fond of; close acquaintance 2. a person on the same side in a struggle; ally 3. a supporter or sympathizer [a *friend* of the workers] 4. something thought of as like a friend 5. [F-] a member of the Society of Friends; Quaker —**friend at court** an influential acquaintance who can promote one's interests —**make** (or **be**) **friends with** to become (or be) a friend of —**friend′less** *adj.* —**friend′-less·ness** *n.*

friend·ly (-lē) *adj.* **-li·er, -li·est** 1. like, characteristic of, or suitable for a friend or friendship; kindly 2. not hostile; amicable 3. supporting; favourable [a *friendly* wind] 4. ready to be a friend —*adv.* in a friendly manner —**friend′-li·ly** *adv.* —**friend′li·ness** *n.*

friendly society an association of people who pay regular dues in return for life insurance, sickness benefits, etc.

friend·ship (-ship′) *n.* 1. the state of being friends 2. friendly feeling or attitude

fri·er (frī′ər) *n. same as* FRYER

frieze¹ (frēz) *n.* [< Fr. < ML. *frisium* < ? Frank.] 1. a decoration forming an ornamental band around a room, mantel, etc. 2. a horizontal band, often decorated with sculpture, between the architrave and cornice of a building

frieze² (frēz) *n.* [< OFr. < MDu.] a heavy wool cloth with a shaggy, uncut nap on one side

frig·ate (frig′it) *n.* [< Fr. < It. *fregata*] 1. a fast, medium-sized sailing warship of the 18th and early 19th cent. 2. a British warship larger than a corvette and smaller than a destroyer 3. a U.S. warship larger than a destroyer and smaller than a light cruiser

frigate bird a large, long-winged, tropical sea bird that robs other birds of their prey

fright (frīt) *n.* [OE. *fyrhto, fryhto*] 1. sudden fear or terror; alarm 2. an ugly, ridiculous, or startling person or thing —*vt.* [Rare] to frighten

fright·en (-'n) *vt.* 1. to cause to feel fright; make suddenly afraid; scare 2. to force (*away, out,* or *off*) or bring (*into* a specified condition) by frightening —**fright′en·ing·ly** *adv.*

fright·ful (-fəl) *adj.* 1. causing fright; alarming 2. shocking; terrible 3. [Colloq.] *a)* unpleasant; annoying *b)* great [in a *frightful* hurry] —**fright′ful·ly** *adv.* —**fright′-ful·ness** *n.*

frig·id (frij′id) *adj.* [< L. < *frigus,* coldness] 1. extremely cold 2. without warmth of feeling or manner; stiff and formal 3. habitually unaroused sexually: said of a woman —**fri·gid·i·ty** (frə jid′ə tē), **frig′id·ness** *n.* —**frig′id·ly** *adv.*

Frigid Zone either of two zones of the earth (**North Frigid Zone** & **South Frigid Zone**) between the polar circles and the poles

fri·jol (frē′hōl) *n., pl.* **fri·jo′les** (fri′hōlz, frē hō′lēz) [Sp. *frijol, frejol*] a bean, esp. the kidney bean, used for food in Mexico and the SW U.S.: also **fri·jo·le** (frē hō′lē)

frill (fril) *n.* [< ?] 1. a fringe of hair or feathers around the neck of a bird or animal 2. any unnecessary ornament; thing added only for show 3. a ruffle —*vt.* to decorate with a frill —**frill′ing** *n.* —**frill′y** *adj.* **frill′i·er, frill′i·est**

fringe (frinj) *n.* [< OFr. < L. *frimbria*] 1. a border or trimming of cords or threads, hanging loose or tied in bunches 2. anything like this [a *fringe* of hair] 3. an outer edge; border; margin 4. a part considered to be peripheral, extreme, or minor [the lunatic *fringe* of a political party] —*vt.* fringed, fring′ing 1. to decorate with or as with fringe 2. to be a fringe for; line [trees *fringed* the lawn] —*adj.* 1. at the outer edge [a *fringe* area] 2. additional [*fringe* benefits] 3. less important [*fringe* industries] —**fring′y** *adj.* **fring′i·er, fring′i·est**

fringe benefit an employee's benefit other than wages or salary, such as a pension or insurance

frip·per·y (frip′ər ē) *n., pl.* **-per·ies** [< Fr. < OFr. < *frepe,* a rag] 1. cheap, gaudy clothes 2. showy display in dress, manners, speech, etc.

Fris·bee (friz′bē) [< "Mother *Frisbie's*" cookie jar lids] [U.S.] *a trademark for* a plastic disc tossed back and forth in a game —*n.* [f-] such a disc

Fri·sian (frish′ən, frē′zhən) *adj.* of the Frisian Islands, N Netherlands, their people, or their language —*n.* 1. a native or inhabitant of the Frisian Islands or N Netherlands 2. the West Germanic language of the Frisians

frisk (frisk) *n.* [OFr. *frisque* < OHG. *frisc*] 1. a frolic; gambol 2. [Slang] the act of frisking a person —*vt.* [Slang] to search (a person) for concealed weapons, etc. by passing the hands quickly over his clothing —*vi.* to frolic; gambol

frisk·y (-ē) *adj.* **frisk′i·er, frisk′i·est** lively; frolicsome —**frisk′i·ly** *adv.* —**frisk′i·ness** *n.*

frit (frit) *n.* [Fr. *fritte*, ult. < L. *frigere*, FRY] 1. the partly fused mixture of sand and fluxes from which glass is made 2. a partly fused vitreous substance, ground and used as a basis for glazes and enamels —*vt., vi.* **frit′ted, frit′ting** to prepare (materials for glass) by heating; make into frit

frith (frith) *n.* *var. of* FIRTH

fri·til·lar·y (fri til′ər ē) *n., pl.* **-lar·ies** [ModL. < L. *fritillus*, dice box: from markings on the petals or wings] 1. a plant of the lily family, with nodding, bell-shaped flowers 2. any of a group of butterflies with spotted wings

frit·ter[1] (frit′ər) *n.* [< ? OFr. < L. *fractura*: see FRACTURE] [Rare] a small piece —*vt.* 1. [Rare] to break into small pieces 2. to waste (money, time, etc.) bit by bit on petty things (often with *away*) —**frit′ter·er** *n.*

frit·ter[2] (frit′ər) *n.* [< OFr., ult. < L. pp. of *frigere*, to fry] a small cake of fried batter, usually containing meat, fruit, etc.

fri·vol·i·ty (fri vol′ə tē) *n.* 1. a frivolous quality 2. *pl.* **-ties** a frivolous act or thing

friv·o·lous (friv′ə ləs) *adj.* [L. *frivolus*] 1. trifling; trivial 2. not properly serious or sensible; silly and light-minded —**friv′o·lous·ly** *adv.* —**friv′o·lous·ness** *n.*

frizz (friz) *vt., vi.* **frizzed, friz′zing** [Fr. *friser*] to form into small, tight curls —*n.* hair, etc. that is frizzed

friz·zle[1] (friz′'l) *vt., vi.* **-zled, -zling** [echoic alteration of FRY[1]] 1. to make or cause to make a sputtering, hissing noise, as in frying; sizzle 2. to make or become crisp by grilling or frying

friz·zle[2] (friz′'l) *vt., vi.* **-zled, -zling** [freq. of FRIZZ] to frizz; crimp —*n.* a small, tight curl

friz·zly (-lē) *adj.* **-zli·er, -zli·est** full of or covered with small, tight curls: also **friz′zy, -zi·er, -zi·est**

fro (frō) *adv.* [< ON. *frā*] backwards; back: now only in *to and fro:* see under TO —*prep.* [Scot.] from

frock (frok) *n.* [OFr. *froc* (or ML. *froccus*) < OFrank.] 1. a robe worn by friars, monks, etc. 2. a woman's dress 3. a loose garment, such as a peasant's smock —*vt.* 1. to clothe in a frock 2. to ordain as a priest —**frocked** *adj.*

frock coat a man's double-breasted dress coat with a full skirt reaching to the knees, worn chiefly in the 19th cent.

frog (frog) *n.* [OE. *frogga*] 1. a tailless, leaping, four-legged amphibian with a smooth skin and webbed feet: most species, when grown, can live either in water or on land 2. a horny pad in the sole of a horse's foot 3. a corded or braided loop used as a fastener or decoration on clothing 4. an attachment on a belt through which a scabbard is suspended 5. a device on railway lines for keeping trains on the proper rails at junctions 6. a device placed in a bowl, vase, etc. to hold the stems of flowers 7.[F-] [Slang] a Frenchman —**frog in the throat** a hoarseness due to throat irritation

METAMORPHOSIS OF FROG

frog·gy (-ē) *adj.* **-gi·er, -gi·est** 1. of or like a frog 2. full of frogs —*n.* [F-] [Slang] a Frenchman

frog·man (-man′) *n., pl.* **-men** (-mən) a person trained and equipped, as with scuba gear, for underwater demolition, exploration, etc.

frog·march (-märch) *n.* 1. a method of carrying a troublesome prisoner, face downwards, each limb being held 2. any method of making a resisting person move forward against his will —*vt.* 1. to carry in a frogmarch 2. to make someone move forward unwillingly

frog spit (or **spittle**) 1. *same as* CUCKOO SPIT 2. mats of filamentous algae floating on ponds

frol·ic (frol′ik) *adj.* [< Du. < MDu. *vrō*, merry] [Archaic] full of fun and pranks; merry —*n.* 1. a playful trick; prank 2. a lively party or game 3. merriment; fun —*vi.* **-icked, -ick·ing** 1. to make merry; have fun 2. to play or romp about in a happy, carefree way —**frol′ick·er** *n.*

frol·ic·some (-səm) *adj.* full of gaiety or high spirits; playful; merry: also **frol′ick·y**

from (from: unstressed frəm) *prep.* [OE. *from, fram*] 1. beginning at [to walk *from* the door] 2. starting with [*from* noon to midnight] 3. out of [he took a comb *from* his pocket] 4. with (a person or thing) as the maker, speaker, source, etc. [facts learned *from* reading] 5. at a place not near to [keep away *from* me] 6. out of the whole of or alliance with [take two *from* four] 7. out of the possibility or use of [kept *from* going] 8. out of the possession or control of [released *from* jail] 9. as not being like [to tell one *from* another] 10. by reason of; because of [to tremble *from* fear]

frond (frond) *n.* [L. *frons* (gen. *frondis*), leafy branch] 1. a leaf; specif., *a)* the leaf of a fern *b)* the leaf of a palm 2. the leaflike part, or shoot, of a lichen, seaweed, etc. —**fron′dage** *n.* —**frond′ed** *adj.*

front (frunt) *n.* [< OFr. < L. *frons* (gen. *frontis*), forehead] 1. outward, often assumed, attitude, behaviour, or appearance [to put on a bold *front*] 2. the part of something that faces forward; most important side 3. the first part; beginning 4. the place or position directly before a person or thing 5. a forward or leading position or situation 6. land along a seashore or large lake, esp. a promenade 7. the advanced area of contact between opposing sides in warfare 8. a specified area of activity [the home *front*] 9. a broad movement in which different groups are united for the achievement of common political or social aims 10. [U.S.] a person who serves as a public representative of a business, group, etc., as because of his prestige 11. a person or group used to cover the activity or objectives of another really in control 12. a stiff shirt bosom, worn with formal clothes 13. a face of a building; esp., the face with the principal entrance 14. *Meteorol.* the boundary between two masses of air that are different, as in density —*adj.* 1. at, to, in, on, or of the front 2. *Phonet.* articulated towards the front of the mouth, as *i* in *bid* or *e* in *met* —*vt.* 1. to face; be opposite to 2. to meet; confront 3. to defy; oppose 4. to supply or be a front to —*vi.* 1. to face in a certain direction 2. to be a front (senses 10 & 11) (with *for*) —**in front of** before; ahead of

front·age (-ij) *n.* 1. the front part of a building 2. the direction towards which this faces 3. the land between the front edge of a building and the street 4. *a)* the front boundary line of a building plot facing the street *b)* the length of this line 5. land bordering a street, river, lake, etc.

fron·tal[1] (-'l) *adj.* 1. of, in, on, at, or against the front 2. of or for the forehead —*n.* the bone forming the forehead: in full, **frontal bone** —**fron′tal·ly** *adv.*

fron·tal[2] (-'l) *n.* [ME. *frountel* ult. < L. *frontalia*, frontlet < *frons*: see FRONT & -AL] 1. an ornamental band or piece of armour worn on the forehead 2. an ornamental hanging for the front of an altar 3. a façade

front bench *n.* the leadership group of the government or opposition in the House of Commons —**front′bench′er**

fron·tier (frun tir′) *n.* [< OFr. < *front*: see FRONT] 1. the border between two countries 2. that part of a settled country which lies next to an unexplored region 3. any new or incompletely investigated field or area of learning, etc. [the *frontiers* of medicine] —*adj.* of, on, or near a frontier

fron·tiers·man (-tirz′mən) *n., pl.* **-men** a man who lives on the frontier

fron·tis·piece (frun′tis pēs′) *n.* [OFr. < LL. *frontispicium*, front view < L. *frons*, FRONT + *specere*, to look] 1. an illustration facing the first page or title page of a book or division of a book 2. *Archit.* a) the main façade b) a pediment over a door, window, etc.

front·let (frunt′lit) *n.* [< OFr., ult. < L. *frons*, FRONT] a band or phylactery worn on the forehead

front-page (frunt′pāj′) *adj.* fit to be printed on the front page of a newspaper; important

front-run·ner (-run′ər) *n.* one who is leading in a race or competition

frost (frost) *n.* [OE. < *freosan*, to freeze] 1. a freezing or being frozen 2. a temperature low enough to cause freezing 3. frozen dew or vapour; hoarfrost 4. coolness of action, feeling, manner, etc. —*vt.* 1. to cover with frost 2. to damage or kill by freezing 3. to give a frostlike surface to (glass)

frost·bite (-bīt′) *vt.* **-bit′, -bit′ten, -bit′ing** to injure the tissues of (a part of the body) by exposure to intense cold —*n.* tissue damage caused by such exposure

frost·ing (-iŋ) *n.* 1. a dull, frostlike finish on glass, metal, etc. 2. *U.S. name for* ICING (sense 1)

frost·y (-ē) *adj.* **frost′i·er, frost′i·est** 1. cold enough to produce frost; freezing 2. covered as with frost 3. cold in manner or feeling; unfriendly —**frost′i·ly** *adv.* —**frost′i·ness** *n.*

froth (froth) *n.* [ON. *frotha*] 1. foam 2. foaming saliva caused by disease or great excitement 3. light, trifling, or worthless talk, ideas, etc. —*vt.* 1. to cause to foam 2. to cover with foam 3. to spill forth as foam —*vi.* to foam

froth-blower (-blō'ər) *n.* [Colloq.] a beer-drinker
froth·y (-ē) *adj.* **froth'i·er, froth'i·est** **1.** foamy **2.** light; trifling; worthless —**froth'i·ly** *adv.* —**froth'i·ness** *n.*
frou-frou (fr$\overline{oo}$'fr$\overline{oo}$') *n.* [Fr.; echoic] a rustling or swishing, as of a skirt
fro·ward (frō'ərd, -wərd) *adj.* [ME., unruly: see FRO & -WARD] [Now Rare] not easily controlled; stubbornly wilful —**fro'ward·ly** *adv.* —**fro'ward·ness** *n.*
frown (froun) *vi.* [< OFr. < *froigne*, sullen face < Gaul.] **1.** to contract the brows, as in displeasure or concentrated thought **2.** to show displeasure or disapproval (with *on* or *upon*) —*vt.* to express (disapproval, etc.) by frowning —*n.* **1.** a contracting of the brows in sternness, thought, etc. **2.** any expression of displeasure or disapproval —**frown'er** *n.* —**frown'ing·ly** *adv.*
frowst (froust) *n.* [back formation < FROWSTY] stale, musty air —*vi.* to lounge about in a hot, stuffy room
frowst·y (-ē) *adj.* [prob. altered < ff.] musty of stuffy
frow·zy (frou'zē) *adj.* **-zi·er, -zi·est** [< ?] **1.** [Rare] bad-smelling **2.** dirty and untidy; slovenly Also sp. **frow'sy** —**frow'zi·ly** *adv.* —**frow'zi·ness** *n.*
froze (frōz) *pt.* of FREEZE
fro·zen (-'n) *pp.* of FREEZE —*adj.* **1.** turned into or covered with ice **2.** damaged or killed by freezing **3.** having heavy frosts and extreme cold [the *frozen* north] **4.** preserved by freezing, as food **5.** as if turned into ice [*frozen* with terror] **6.** without warmth or affection **7.** arbitrarily kept at a fixed level or in a fixed position **8.** not readily converted into cash [*frozen* assets]
F.R.S. Fellow of the Royal Society
fruc·ti·fy (fruk'tə fī') *vi., vt.* **-fied', -fy'ing** [< OFr. < L. *fructificare*: see FRUIT & -FY] to bear or cause to bear fruit —**fruc'ti·fer·ous** *adj.* —**fruc'ti·fi·ca'tion** *n.*
fruc·tose (fruk'tōs, frook'-) *n.* [< L. *fructus*, FRUIT + -OSE[1]] a crystalline sugar, $C_6H_{12}O_6$, found in sweet fruits and in honey; fruit sugar; levulose
fru·gal (fr$\overline{oo}$'g'l) *adj.* [L. *frugalis* < *frugi*, fit for food < *frux* (gen. *frugis*), fruits] **1.** not wasteful; thrifty **2.** not costly; inexpensive or meagre [a *frugal* meal] —**fru·gal'i·ty** (-gal'ə tē) *n., pl.* **-ties** —**fru'gal·ly** *adv.*
fru·giv·o·rous (fr$\overline{oo}$ jiv'ər əs) *adj.* [< L. *frux* (see FRUGAL)+ -VOROUS] fruit-eating
fruit (fr$\overline{oo}$t) *n.* see PLURAL, II, D, 3 [OFr. < L. *fructus* < pp. of *frui*, to enjoy] **1.** any plant product, as grain, flax, vegetables, etc.: *usually used in pl.* **2.** a sweet and edible plant structure, consisting of a fruit (sense 5), usually eaten raw or as a dessert **3.** the result or product of any action: *usually used in pl.* [the *fruits* of his labours] **4.** [Archaic] offspring **5.** *Bot.* the mature ovary of a flowering plant, with its contents, as the whole peach, pea pod, etc. —*vi., vt.* to bear or cause to bear fruit
fruit·age (-ij) *n.* **1.** the bearing of fruit **2.** a crop of fruit
fruit bat any of several fruit-eating bats, as the flying fox
fruit·cake (-kāk') *n.* a rich cake containing nuts, dried fruit, candied peel, spices, etc.
fruit·er·er (-ər ər) *n.* [ME. *fruterer*] a person who deals in fruit
fruit fly **1.** a small fly whose larvae feed on fruits and vegetables **2.** *same as* DROSOPHILA
fruit·ful (-fəl) *adj.* **1.** bearing much fruit **2.** producing much; productive; prolific **3.** producing results; profitable —**fruit'ful·ly** *adv.* —**fruit'ful·ness** *n.*
fru·i·tion (fr$\overline{oo}$ ish'ən) *n.* [OFr. < LL. < *frui*: see FRUIT] **1.** the pleasure of using or possessing **2.** the bearing of fruit **3.** fulfilment; realization
fruit·less (fr$\overline{oo}$t'lis) *adj.* **1.** without results; unsuccessful; vain **2.** bearing no fruit; sterile —**fruit'less·ly** *adv.* —**fruit'·less·ness** *n.*
fruit machine a slot machine that pays out when certain combinations of diagrams, often representing fruit, appear on a dial
fruit sugar *same as* FRUCTOSE
fruit tree a tree that bears edible fruit
fruit·wood (-wood') *n.* the wood of any of various fruit trees, used in furniture, panelling, etc.
fruit·y (fr$\overline{oo}$t'ē) *adj.* **fruit'i·er, fruit'i·est** **1.** like fruit in taste or smell **2.** rich or mellow in tone [a *fruity* voice] **3.** [Slang] full of coarse humour; salacious —**fruit'i·ly** *adv.* —**fruit'i·ness** *n.*
fru·men·ty (fr$\overline{oo}$'mən tē) *n.* [ME. < OF. < L. *frumentum*, grain] a kind of porridge made from hulled wheat boiled with milk, sweetened, and flavoured with spices: also **fur'·men·ty, fur'met·y, fur'mit·y**
frump (frump) *n.* [< Du. *frompelen* < *rompelen*, to rumple] a dowdy, unattractive woman —**frump'ish** *adj.* —**frump'y** *adj.* **frump'i·er, frump'i·est**
frus·trate (frus trāt', frus'trāt) *vt.* **-trat·ed, -trat·ing** [< L. pp. of *frustrare* < *frustra*, in vain] **1.** to cause to have no effect; nullify [to *frustrate* plans] **2.** to keep from an objective; foil [to *frustrate* a foe] **3.** *Psychol.* to keep from gratifying certain desires —*vi.* to become frustrated —**frus·tra'tion** *n.*

frus·tum (frus'təm) *n., pl.* **-tums, -ta** (-tə) [L., a piece, bit] the solid figure formed when the top of a cone or pyramid is cut off by a plane parallel to the base

FRUSTUM

fry[1] (frī) *vt., vi.* **fried, fry'ing** [< OFr. < L. *frigere*, to fry] to cook or be cooked, usually in hot fat or oil, over direct heat —*n., pl.* **fries** a fried food, esp. offal [pig's *fry*] —**fry'er** *n.*
fry[2] (frī) *n., pl.* **fry** [prob. a merging of ON. *frjo*, seed, with Anglo-Fr. *frei*, spawn] **1.** young fish **2.** small adult fish, esp. in large groups **3.** offspring —**small fry** **1.** children **2.** trivial people or things
frying pan a shallow pan with a handle, for frying food —**out of the frying pan into the fire** from a bad situation into a worse one
fry-up (-up) *n.* [Colloq.] a dish of several mixed, fried foods
f-stop (ef'stop') *n.* any of the settings for the f-number of a camera
ft. **1.** foot; feet **2.** fort
fth., fthm. fathom
fuch·sia (fyoo'shə) *n.* [ModL., after L. *Fuchs*, 16th-c. G. botanist] **1.** a shrubby plant with drooping pink, red, or purple flowers **2.** purplish red —*adj.* purplish-red
fuch·sin (fook'sin, fyook'-) *n.* [Fr. *fuchsine* < prec. + -ine, -IN[1]: from the colour] a purplish-red analine dye: also **fuch'sine** (-sin, -sēn)
fuck (fuk) *vi., vt.* [< ?] to have sexual intercourse —*n.* **1.** an act of sexual intercourse **2.** a partner in sexual intercourse Usually considered a vulgar term
fu·cus (fyoo'kəs) *n., pl.* **fu'ci** (-sī), **fu'cus·es** [L., rock lichen] any of various seaweeds with a flattened and forking plant body that bears swollen bladders
fud·dle (fud''l) *vt.* **-dled, -dling** [akin ? to G. dial. *fuddeln*, to swindle] to confuse or stupefy as with alcoholic liquor —*n.* a fuddled condition
fud·dy-dud·dy (fud'ē dud'ē) *n., pl.* **-dies** [prob. based on dial. *fud*, buttocks] [Slang] **1.** a fussy, critical person **2.** an old-fashioned person
fudge (fuj) *n.* [? echoic] **1.** empty talk; nonsense **2.** [< ?] a soft sweet made of butter, milk, sugar, flavouring, etc. **3.** *Printing* a short piece of last minute news, inserted directly in the plate of a newspaper page —*vt.* **fudged, fudg'ing** to make dishonestly or carelessly; fake —*vi.* **1.** to refuse to commit oneself **2.** to cheat
fu·el (fyoo'əl, fyool) *n.* [< OFr. *fouaille*, ult. < L. *focus*, fireplace] **1.** coal, oil, gas, wood, etc. burned to supply heat or power **2.** fissionable material, as in a nuclear reactor **3.** anything that maintains or intensifies strong feeling, etc. —*vt.* **-elled, -el·ling** to supply with fuel —*vi.* to get fuel **fu'el·ler** *n.*
fuel cell any of various devices that convert chemical energy directly into electrical energy
fuel oil any oil used for fuel
fug (fug) *n.* [altered < ? FOG[1]] the heavy air in a closed room, regarded as either oppressive and stuffy or warm and cosy —**fug'gy** *adj.*
-fuge (fyooj) [Fr. < L. *fugere*, to flee] a suffix meaning something that drives away [*vermifuge*]
fu·gi·tive (fyoo'jə tiv) *adj.* [< OFr. < L. pp. of *fugere*, to flee] **1.** fleeing or having fled, as from danger, justice, etc. **2.** passing quickly; fleeting; evanescent **3.** on matters of temporary interest [*fugitive* essays] **4.** roaming; shifting —*n.* **1.** a person who flees or has fled from danger, justice, etc. **2.** a fleeting or elusive thing —**fu'gi·tive·ly** *adv.*
fu·gle·man (fyoo'g'l mən) *n., pl.* **-men** (-mən) [altered < G. *Flugelmann*, file-leader] **1.** orig., a soldier, expert in drilling, who stood at the head of his unit as a model for others **2.** a leader or exemplar
fugue (fyoog) *n.* [Fr. < It. < L. < *fugere*, to flee] a musical composition in which a subject is announced by one voice and then developed contrapuntally by each of usually two or three other voices —**fu'gal** *adj.* —**fugu'ist** *n.*
‡**Füh·rer, Fueh·rer** (fü'rər, E. fyoor'ər) *n.* [G. < *führen*, to lead] leader: title used by A. Hitler
-ful (fəl, f'l; *for* 4, *usually* fool) [OE. < *full*, FULL[1]] a suffix meaning: **1.** full of, characterized by, having [*joyful*] **2.** having the qualities of [*masterful*] **3.** able or tending to [*helpful*] **4.** *pl.* **-fuls** the quantity that fills [*handful*]
ful·crum (fool'krəm, ful'-) *n., pl.* **-crums, -cra** (-krə) [L., akin to *fulcire*, to prop] **1.** the support or point of support on which a lever turns in raising or moving something **2.** a means of exerting influence, pressure, etc.

FULCRUM

ful·fil (fool fil') *vt.* **-filled', -fill'ing** [OE. *fullfyllan*] **1.** to carry out (something promised, predicted, etc.); cause to be or happen **2.** to do (something required); obey **3.** to satisfy (a condition) **4.** to bring to an end; complete

—fulfil oneself to realize completely one's ambitions, potentialities, etc. **—ful·fill'er** *n.* **— ful·fil'ment** *n.*

ful·gent (ful'jənt, fool'-) *adj.* [< L. prp. of *fulgere*, to flash] [Now Rare] very bright; radiant

ful·gu·rate (ful'gyoo rāt) *vi.* **-rat'ed, -rat'ing** [< L. *fulguratus*, pp. of *fulgurare*, to flash] to give off flashes of or like lightning **—vt.** 1. to give off in flashes 2. *Med.* to destroy (tissue) by electrical means **—ful'gu·ra'tion** *n.*

ful·gu·rite (-rīt') *n.* [L. *fulgur*, lightning + -ITE[1]] a glossy substance, usually tube-shaped, formed by fusion when sand, rock, etc. are struck by lightning

fu·lig·i·nous (fyoo lij'ə nəs) *adj.* [LL. *fuliginosus* < L. *fuligo*, soot] 1. sooty; smoky 2. dark; dusky

full[1] (fool) *adj.* [OE.] 1. having in it all there is space for; filled [a *full* jar] 2. having eaten all that one wants 3. occupying all of a given space [a *full* load] 4. well supplied or provided (with *of*) [a tank *full* of petrol] 5. filling the required number, measure, etc.; complete [a *full* dozen] 6. thorough; absolute [come to a *full* stop] 7. having reached the greatest development, size, etc. [a *full* moon] 8. having the same parents [*full* brothers] 9. having clearness, volume, and depth [a *full* tone] 10. of the highest rank [a *full* professor] 11. plump; round [a *full* face] 12. with loose, wide folds; ample [a *full* skirt] 13. deeply affected, engrossed, etc. **—n.** the greatest amount, extent, number, etc. **—adv.** 1. completely [a *full*-grown boy] 2. directly [struck *full* in the face] 3. very [*full* well] **—vt.** to make (a skirt, etc.) with loose folds **—vi.** to become full: said of the moon **—full time** as a full-time employee, student, etc. **—full up of** [Aust. slang] fed up with; tired of **—in full** 1. to, for, or with the full amount, value, etc. 2. not abbreviated or condensed

full[2] (fool) *vt., vi.* [< OFr., ult. < L. *fullo*, cloth fuller] to shrink and thicken (cloth, esp. of wool) with moisture, heat, and pressure

full·back (-bak') *n.* *Football*, etc. a defender in a team

full-blood·ed (-blud'id) *adj.* 1. of unmixed breed or race; purebred: also **full'-blood'** 2. vigorous; lusty 3. rich and full

full-blown (-blōn') *adj.* 1. in full bloom; open: said of flowers 2. fully developed; mature

full-bod·ied (-bod'ēd) *adj.* having much strength, flavour, substance, etc.

full dress formal clothes for important occasions; esp., formal evening clothes **—full'-dress'** *adj.*

full·er (fool'ər) *n.* one whose work is to full cloth

full·er's earth (fool'ərz) a highly absorbent clay used to remove grease from cloth in fulling, to clarify oils, etc.

full-fledged (-flejd') *adj.* completely developed or trained; of full rank or status

full house 1. a poker hand containing three of a kind and a pair, as three jacks and two fives 2. in bingo and similar games, the complete set of numbers needed to win 3. a theatre, etc., filled to capacity

full-length (-lenth') *adj.* 1. showing the whole length of an object or figure [a *full-length* portrait] 2. not shortened [a *full-length* novel]

full moon the phase of the moon when its entire illuminated hemisphere is seen as a full disc

full nelson *see* NELSON

full·ness, ful·ness (-nis) *n.* the quality or state of being full

full pitch *same as* FULL TOSS

full sail 1. with every sail set 2. with maximum speed and energy

full-scale (-skāl') *adj.* 1. according to the original or standard scale [a *full-scale* drawing] 2. to the utmost limit, degree, etc. [*full-scale* war]

full stop 1. the punctuation mark (.) used at the end of a sentence that is not a question or an exclamation 2. the dot (.) following many abbreviations

full-time (-tīm') *adj.* on a complete regular schedule

full time as a full-time employee, student, etc. [to work *full time*]

full toss *Cricket* a bowled ball that reaches the batsman without bouncing

full·y (-ē) *adv.* 1. to the full; completely; entirely 2. abundantly; amply 3. at least [*fully* two hours later]

fully fashioned shaped to conform to body contours, as stockings, knitwear, etc.

ful·mar (fool'mər) *n.* [ON. < *full*, foul. + *mår*, sea gull] a grey sea bird of the shearwater family, common in arctic regions: also **fulmar petrel**

ful·mi·nate (ful'mə nāt') *vi.* **-nat'ed, -nat'ing** [< L. pp. of *fulminare* < *fulmen*, lightning] 1. to explode with violence; detonate 2. to shout forth denunciations, decrees, etc. **—vt.** 1. to cause to explode 2. to shout forth (denunciations, etc.) **—n.** any of certain highly explosive compounds used in detonators and percussion caps **—ful'·mi·na'tion** *n.* **—ful'mi·na'tor** *n.* **—ful'mi·na·to·ry** *adj.*

ful·some (fool'səm) *adj.* [ME. < *ful*, FULL[1] + *-som*, -SOME[1], but perhaps infl. by *ful*, foul] disgusting or offensive, esp. because excessive or insincere [*fulsome* praise] **—ful'·some·ly** *adv.* **—ful'some·ness** *n.*

ful·vous (ful'vəs) *adj.* [< L. *fulvus*, tawny] dull, brownish-yellow; tawny

fu·ma·role (fyoo'mə rōl') *n.* [< Fr. *fumerolle* < LL. *fumarolium*, smoke hole] a vent in a volcanic area, from which smoke and gases arise **—fu'ma·rol'ic** (-rol'ik) *adj.*

fum·ble (fum'b'l) *vi., vt.* **-bled, -bling** [prob. < ON. *famla*, to grope] 1. to grope clumsily 2. to handle (a thing) clumsily; bungle 3. to lose one's grasp on (a football, etc.) while trying to catch or hold it 4. to make (one's way) as by groping **—n.** the act or fact of fumbling **—fum'bler** *n.* **—fum'bling·ly** *adv.*

fume (fyoom) *n.* [< OFr. < L. *fumus*] [often *pl.*] a gas, smoke, or vapour, esp. if offensive or suffocating **—vi.** 1. to give off fumes 2. to rise up or pass off in fumes 3. to show, or give way to, anger, annoyance, etc. **—vt.** 1. to expose to fumes 2. to give off as fumes

fumed, fum'ing 1. to give off fumes 2. to rise up or pass off in fumes 3. to show, or give way to, anger, annoyance, etc. **—vt.** 1. to expose to fumes 2. to give off as fumes

fu·mi·gant (fyoo'mə gənt) *n.* any substance used in fumigating

fu·mi·gate (-gāt') *vt.* **-gat'ed, -gat'ing** [< L. pp. of *fumigare* < *fumus*, smoke + *agere*, to make] to expose to the action of fumes, esp. in order to disinfect or kill the vermin in **—fu'mi·ga'tion** *n.* **—fu'mi·ga'tor** *n.*

fu·mi·to·ry (fyoo'mə tər ē) *n., pl.* **-ries** [ME. *fumeter*, ult. < ML. *fumus terrae*, lit., smoke of the earth] an annual plant, with rose-coloured flowers in spikes, and greyish foliage, formerly used in medicine

fum·y (fyoo'mē) *adj.* **fum'i·er, fum'i·est** full of or producing fumes; vaporous

fun (fun) *n.* [< ME. *fonne*, a fool, or *fonnen*, to be foolish < ?] 1. *a)* lively, gay play or playfulness; amusement, sport, recreation, etc. *b)* enjoyment or pleasure 2. a source of amusement; amusing person or thing **—adj.** [Colloq.] intended for pleasure and amusement [a *fun* gift] **—for** (or **in**) **fun** playfully; not seriously **—make fun of** to mock laughingly; ridicule

fu·nam·bu·list (fyoo nam'byoo list) *n.* [< L. *funambulus* < *funis*, a rope + *ambulare*, to walk] a tight-rope walker

func·tion (funk'shən) *n.* [OFr. < L. *functio* < pp. of *fungi*, to perform] 1. the normal or characteristic action of anything; esp., any of the specialized actions of an organ or part of an animal or plant 2. a specific duty or performance required for a particular activity [the *function* of an auditor] 3. a formal ceremony or social occasion 4. a thing that depends on and varies with something else 5. *Math.* a quantity whose value depends on that of another quantity or quantities **—vi.** 1. to act in a required manner; work 2. to have a function; be used (*as*)

func·tion·al (-əl) *adj.* 1. of a function or functions 2. *a)* performing a function *b)* designed with regard to usefulness rather than aesthetic appeal 3. *Med.* affecting a function of some organ without apparent structural or organic changes [a *functional* disease] **—func'tion·al·ly** *adv.*

func·tion·al·ism (-əl iz'm) *n.* emphasis on adapting the structure of anything to its function **—func'tion·al·ist** *n., adj.* **—func'tion·al·is'tic** *adj.*

func·tion·ar·y (-ər ē) *n., pl.* **-ar·ies** a person who performs a certain function; esp., an official

fund (fund) *n.* [L. *fundus*, bottom, land] 1. a supply that can be drawn on; stock; store [a *fund* of good humour] 2. *a)* a sum of money set aside for a particular purpose *b)* an organization to administer it *c)* [*pl.*] ready money **—vt.** 1. to provide money to pay the interest on (a debt) 2. to put or convert into a long-term debt that bears interest 3. to put in a fund; accumulate 4. to provide for with a fund **—the funds** British government securities representing national debt

fun·da·ment (fun'də mənt) *n.* [< OFr. < L. < *fundus*: see prec.] 1. the buttocks 2. the anus

fun·da·men·tal (fun'də men't'l) *adj.* [< ML. < L. *fundamentum* < *fundus*: see FUND] 1. of or forming a foundation or basis; basic; essential 2. primary; original 3. most important; chief 4. *Music a)* designating or of the lowest, or root, tone of a chord *b)* designating or of the prime or main tone of a harmonic series **—n.** 1. a principle, law, etc. serving as a basis; essential part 2. *Music* the fundamental tone of a chord or harmonic series **—fun'·da·men'tal·ly** *adv.*

fun·da·men·tal·ism (-iz'm) *n.* religious beliefs based on a literal interpretation of the Bible and regarded as fundamental to Christain faith **—fun'da·men'tal·ist** *n., adj.*

fundamental particle *same as* ELEMENTARY PARTICLE

fu·ner·al (fyoo'nər əl) *adj.* [< LL. < L. *funus* (gen. *funeris*), a funeral] of or for a funeral **—n.** 1. the ceremonies connected with burial or cremation of the dead 2. the procession accompanying the body to the place of burial or cremation 3. [Colloq.] concern; affair [that's your *funeral*] **—fu'ner·ar·y** *adj.*

funeral director *same as* UNDERTAKER

funeral home a place where bodies are prepared for burial or cremation; undertaker's establishment

fu·ne·re·al (fyoo nir'ē əl) *adj.* suitable for a funeral; sad and solemn; gloomy: also **fu·ne'bri·al** **—fu·ne're·al·ly** *adv.*

fun·fair (fun′fer) *n.* a collection of amusements and sideshows; amusement park

fun fur a coat, etc., for casual wear, made of synthetic and usually inexpensive fur

fun·gi·ble (fun′jə b′l) *adj.* [ML. *fungibilis* < L. *fungi*, to perform] *Law* designating movable goods, as grain, any unit or part of which can replace another unit, as in paying a debt

fun·gi·cide (fun′jə sīd′) *n.* [< FUNGUS & -CIDE] any substance that kills fungi —**fun′gi·ci′dal** *adj.*

fun·goid (fuŋ′goid) *adj.* like or characteristic of a fungus —*n.* a fungus

fun·gous (-gəs) *adj.* of, like, or caused by fungi

fun·gus (fuŋ′gəs) *n.,* pl. **fun·gi** (fun′jī, fuŋ′gī), **fun′gus·es** [L., prob. < Gr. *spongos*, a sponge] **1.** any of a group of thallophytes, including moulds, mildews, mushrooms, rusts, and smut, that lack chlorophyll and leaves and reproduce by means of spores **2.** something that grows rapidly like a fungus —*adj.* of, like, or caused by a fungus —**fun′gal** *adj.*

fu·nic·u·lar (fyoo nik′yoo lər) *adj.* [< L. *funiculus*, dim. of *funis*, a rope] of or worked by a rope or cable —*n.* a mountain railway on which counterbalanced cars ascend and descend by cables: also **funicular railway**

funk (fuŋk) *n.* [< ? Fl. *fonck*, dismay] [Colloq.] **1.** a cowering through fear; panic: also **blue funk 2.** a cowardly or fearful person —*vi.* [Colloq.] to be in a funk or panic —*vt.* [Colloq.] **1.** to be afraid of **2.** to shrink from in fear

fun·ky[1] (fuŋ′kē) *adj.* **-ki·er**, **-ki·est** in a funk, or panic

fun·ky[2] (fuŋ′kē) *adj.* **-ki·er**, **-ki·est** [orig. Negro argot, earthy < obs. *funk*, smell, smoke] *Jazz* having an earthy quality or style derived from early blues —**fun′ki·ness** *n.*

fun·nel (fun′'l) *n.* [< Pr. < L. (*in*)*fundibulum* < *in-*, in + *fundere*, to pour] **1.** a slender tube with a wide, cone-shaped mouth, for pouring liquids and powders into containers with small openings **2.** anything shaped like a funnel **3.** *a)* a cylindrical smokestack, as of a steamship *b)* a chimney or flue —*vi., vt.* **-nelled**, **-nel·ling 1.** to move or pour through a funnel **2.** to move into a central channel or place

fun·ny (fun′ē) *adj.* **-ni·er**, **-ni·est 1.** causing laughter; amusing; humorous **2.** [Colloq.] *a)* strange; queer *b)* deceptive; puzzling *c)* slightly ill; queasy —*n.,* pl. **-nies** [U.S. Colloq.] *same as* COMIC STRIP: *usually in pl.* —**fun′·ni·ly** *adv.* —**fun′ni·ness** *n.*

funny bone [prob. a pun on *humerus* (hence "humorous")] a place on the elbow where the ulnar nerve passes close to the surface: a sharp impact at this place causes a strange, tingling sensation in the arm

fur (fur) *n.* [< OFr. < *fuerre*, a sheath < Frank. *fodr*] **1.** the soft, thick hair covering the body of many mammals **2.** a skin bearing such hair, processed for making garments **3.** any garment made of such skins **4.** any furry deposit, specif., *a)* diseased matter on the tongue in illness *b)* the deposit on the inside of kettles, etc., left by water containing lime —*adj.* of fur —*vt.* **furred**, **fur′ring 1.** to line, cover, or trim with fur **2.** to coat with a furry deposit **3.** to make level with furring strips —*vi.* to become furred with a deposit —**make the fur fly** to cause dissension or fighting

fur. furlong

fur·be·low (fur′bə lō′) *n.* [var. of Fr. *falbala*] **1.** a flounce or ruffle **2.** [*usually pl.*] showy trimming —*vt.* to decorate as with furbelows

fur·bish (fur′bish) *vt.* [< OFr. *forbir* < WGmc.] **1.** to brighten by rubbing or scouring; burnish **2.** to make usable again; renovate (often with *up*) —**fur′bish·er** *n.*

fur·cate (fur′kāt; *for adj., also* -kit) *adj.* [< ML. < L. *furca*, a fork] forked —*vi.* **-cat·ed**, **-cat·ing** to branch; fork —**fur′cate·ly** *adv.* —**fur·ca′tion** *n.*

fur·fu·ra·ceous (fur′fyoo rā′shəs, -fə rā′-) *adj.* [LL. *furfuraceus* < *furfur*, bran] **1.** of or like bran **2.** covered with dandruff

Fu·ries (fyoor′ēz) *Gr. & Rom. Myth.* three female spirits who punished doers of unavenged crimes

fu·ri·ous (fyoor′ē əs) *adj.* [< OFr. < L. *furiosus*] **1.** full of fury or wild rage **2.** violently overpowering **3.** very great; intense [*furious* speed] —**fu′ri·ous·ly** *adv.* —**fu′ri·ous·ness** *n.*

furl (furl) *vt.* [< OFr. *ferlier* < *fermlier*, to tie up < *ferm*, FIRM[1] + *lier*, to tie] to roll up tightly and make secure, as a flag to a staff —*vi.* to become curled or rolled up —*n.* **1.** a roll or coil of something furled **2.** a furling or being furled

fur·long (fur′lôŋ) *n.* [< OE. < *furh*, a furrow + *lang*, LONG[1]] a measure of distance equal to 1/8 of a mile, or 220 yards (c. 20 m)

fur·lough (fur′lō) *n.* [< Du. *verlof*] a leave of absence; esp., a leave granted to military enlisted personnel —*vt.* [U.S.] to grant a furlough to

fur·nace (fur′nəs) *n.* [< OFr. < L. *fornax* < *fornus*, oven] **1.** an enclosed structure in which heat is produced for destroying refuse, reducing ores and metals, etc. **2.** any extremely hot place

fur·nish (fur′nish) *vt.* [< OFr. < *furnir* < OFrank.] **1.** to equip with whatever is necessary; esp., to put furniture into (a room, etc.) **2.** to supply; provide —**fur′nish·er** *n.*

fur·nish·ings (-iŋz) *n.pl.* the furniture, carpets, etc. for a room, etc.

fur·ni·ture (fur′ni chər) *n.* [Fr. *fourniture* < *fournir*, FURNISH] **1.** the movable things in a room, etc. which equip it for living, as chairs, beds, etc. **2.** the necessary equipment of a ship, trade, etc.

fu·ro·re (fyoo rôr′ē) *n.* [< OFr. *fureur* < L. *furor*] **1.** fury; rage **2.** *a)* widespread enthusiasm; craze *b)* a commotion or uproar Also, esp. U.S., **fu′ror** (fyoor′ôr)

fur·phy (fur′fē) *n.* [< *Furphy* foundry, which made carts for water, etc., used in World War I] [Aust. Slang] a rumour

furred (furd) *adj.* **1.** made, trimmed, or lined with fur **2.** having fur **3.** wearing fur **4.** having a furry coating, as the tongue **5.** made level with furring strips

fur·ri·er (fur′ē ər) *n.* **1.** a dealer in furs **2.** one who processes furs or makes and repairs fur garments —**fur′·ri·er·y** *n.,* pl. **-er·ies**

fur·ring (fur′iŋ) *n.* **1.** the act of trimming, lining, etc. with fur **2.** fur so used **3.** a furry coating, as on the tongue **4.** *a)* the levelling of a floor, wall, etc. with thin strips of wood or metal before adding boards or plaster *b)* the strips (in full, **furring strips**) so used

fur·row (fur′ō) *n.* [OE. *furh*] **1.** a narrow groove made in the ground by a plough **2.** anything like this, as a wrinkle on the face —*vt.* **1.** to make furrows in —*vi.* **1.** to make furrows **2.** to become wrinkled —**fur′row·y** *adj.*

fur·ry (fur′ē) *adj.* **-ri·er**, **-ri·est 1.** of, like, or made of fur **2.** covered with or wearing fur **3.** having a furlike coating —**fur′ri·ness** *n.*

fur·ther (fur′thər) *adj. alt. compar. of* FAR [OE. *furthra*] **1.** additional; more **2.** more distant; farther —*adv. alt. compar. of* FAR **1.** to a greater degree or extent **2.** in addition; moreover **3.** at or to a greater distance in space or time In sense 2 of the *adj.* and sense 3 of the *adv.,* FARTHER is more commonly used —*vt.* [< OE. *fyrthrian* < *furthra*] to give aid to; promote —**fur′ther·er** *n.*

fur·ther·ance (-əns) *n.* a furthering, or helping forward; advancement; promotion

further education education, usually full-time, for students above school age

fur·ther·more (-môr′) *adv.* besides; moreover; in addition

fur·ther·most (-mōst′) *adj.* most distant; furthest

fur·thest (fur′thist) *adj. alt. superl. of* FAR [ME., formed as superl. on analogy of *further*] most distant; farthest —*adv. alt. superl. of* FAR **1.** at or to the greatest distance in space or time **2.** to the greatest degree or extent; most

fur·tive (fur′tiv) *adj.* [< Fr. < L. *furtivus*, stolen < *fur*, thief] done or acting in a stealthy manner; surreptitious —**fur′tive·ly** *adv.* —**fur′tive·ness** *n.*

fu·ry (fyoor′ē) *n.,* pl. **-ries** [< OFr. < L. *furia* < *furere*, to rage] **1.** *a)* violent anger; wild rage *b)* a fit of this **2.** violence; vehemence; fierceness **3.** a violent, vengeful person **4.** [F-] any of the Furies —**like fury** [Colloq.] violently, swiftly, etc.

furze (furz) *n.* [OE. *fyrs*] a prickly evergreen shrub with yellow flowers, esp. on wastelands —**fur′zy** *adj.*

furze wren *same as* DARTFORD WARBLER

fus·cous (fus′kəs) *adj.* [< L. *fuscus*, dark; swarthy] dark grey or greyish brown in colour; dusky

fuse[1] (fyooz) *vt., vi.* **fused**, **fus′ing** [< L. pp. of *fundere*, to shed] **1.** to melt or to join by melting, as metals **2.** to unite or blend together

fuse[2] (fyooz) *n.* [< It. < L. *fusus*, hollow spindle] **1.** a tube or wick filled with combustible material for setting off an explosive charge **2.** any of various devices for detonating a bomb, projectile, etc. **3.** *Elec.* a strip of easily melted metal placed in a circuit as a safeguard: if the current becomes too strong, the metal melts, thus breaking the circuit —*vt.* **fused**, **fus′ing** to connect a fuse to —*vi.* to fail as the result of the blowing of a fuse —**blow a fuse 1.** to cause an electrical fuse to melt **2.** [Colloq.] to become very angry

fu·see (fyoo zē′) *n.* [Fr. *fusée*, rocket < ML. < L. *fusus*: see prec.] **1.** formerly, a friction match with a large head **2.** the spindle-shaped wheel in a clock or watch round which the chain is wound to equalize the power of the mainspring

fu·se·lage (fyoo′zə läzh′, -läj′, -lij) *n.* [Fr. < *fuselé*, tapering] the body of an aircraft, exclusive of the wings, tail, and engines

fu·sel oil (fyoo′z'l) [G. *Fusel*, inferior brandy, etc.] an oily, acrid, poisonous liquid occurring in insufficiently distilled alcoholic products

fu·si·ble (fyoo′zə b′l) *adj.* that can be fused or easily melted —**fu′si·bil′i·ty** *n.* —**fu′si·bly** *adv.*

fu·si·form (fyoo′zə fôrm′) *adj.* [< L. *fusus*, a spindle + -FORM] shaped like a spindle

fu·sil (fyoo′z'l) *n.* [Fr., orig., steel for striking sparks < ML. < L. *focus*, hearth] a light flintlock musket

fu·sil·ier (fyoo′zə lir′) *n.* formerly, a soldier armed with a fusil: the term *Fusiliers* is still applied to certain British regiments

fu·sil·lade (fyoo′zə lād′) *n.* [Fr. < *fusiller*, to shoot: see FUSIL] **1.** a simultaneous discharge of many firearms **2.**

something like this [a *fusillade* of questions] —*vt.* **-lad'ed,
-lad'ing** to shoot down or attack with a fusillade

fu·sion (fyōō'zhən) *n.* 1. a fusing or melting together 2. a blending; coalition [a *fusion* of political parties] 3. anything made by fusing 4. *same as* NUCLEAR FUSION

fuss (fus) *n.* [prob. echoic] 1. a flurry of nervous, excited activity; bustle 2. nervousness, agitation, etc. 3. [Colloq.] a quarrel 4. [Colloq.] a showy display of delight, etc. —*vi.* 1. to cause or make a fuss 2. to bustle about or worry over trifles —*vt.* [Colloq.] to bother unnecessarily

fuss·pot (-pot) *n.* [Colloq.] a fussy person

fuss·y (fus'ē) *adj.* **fuss'i·er, fuss'i·est** 1. bustling about or worrying over trifles 2. hard to please 3. showing or needing careful attention 4. full of unnecessary details —**fuss'i·ly** *adv.* —**fuss'i·ness** *n.*

fus·ta·nel·la (fus'tə nel'ə) *n.* [It., < Mod.Gr. *phoustani* < It. *fustagno,* fustian] a white, knee-length, pleated skirt worn by men in Greece and Albania

fus·ti·an (fus'tiən) *n.* [< OFr. < ML. < L. *fustis,* wooden stick] 1. formerly, a coarse cloth of cotton and linen 2. pompous, pretentious talk or writing —*adj.* 1. made of fustian 2. pompous; pretentious

fus·ty (fus'tē) *adj.* **fus'ti·er, fus'ti·est** [< *fust,* a musty smell < Early ModE., a cask < OFr., tree trunk] 1. smelling stale or stuffy; mouldy 2. old-fashioned —**fus'ti·ly** *adv.* —**fus'ti·ness** *n.*

fut. future

fu·thark (fōō'thärk) *n.* [< its first six letters: *f,u,th,a,r,k*] the runic alphabet: also sp. **futharc, futhorc, futhork**

fu·tile (fyōō'til) *adj.* [Fr. < L. *futilis,* lit., that easily pours out, hence worthless < *fundere,* to pour] 1. *a)* useless; vain; hopeless *b)* ineffective 2. trifling or unimportant —**fu'tile·ly** *adv.* —**fu·til·i·ty** (fyōō til'ə tē), *pl.* **-ties, fu'-tile·ness** *n.*

fut·tock (fut'ək) *n.* [< ? pronun. of *foot hook*] any of the curved timbers forming the ribs of a wooden ship

fu·ture (fyōō'chər) *adj.* [< OFr. < L. *futurus,* used as fut. part. of *esse,* to be] 1. that is to be or come 2. indicating time to come [the *future* tense of a verb] —*n.* 1. the time that is to come 2. what will happen; what is going to be 3. prospective condition; chance to be successful [he has a great *future* in law] 4. [*usually pl.*] a contract for a commodity bought or sold for delivery at a later date 5. *Gram. a)* the future tense *b)* a verb form in this tense —**fu'-ture·less** *adj.*

future perfect 1. a tense indicating an action or state as completed in relation to a specified time in the future 2. a verb form in this tense (Ex.: will have gone)

fu·tur·ism (-iz'm) *n.* a movement in the arts shortly before World War I which opposed traditionalism and stressed the dynamic movement and violence of the machine age —**fu'-tur·ist** *n., adj.*

fu·tur·is·tic (fyōō'chər is'tik) *adj.* of or having to do with the future or futurism —**fu'tur·is'ti·cal·ly** *adv.*

fu·tu·ri·ty (fyōō tyoor'ə tē *n., pl.* **-ties** 1. *a)* the future *b)* a future condition or event 2. the quality of being future

fu·tur·ol·o·gy (fyōō'chər ol'ə jē) *n.* [FUTUR(E) + -o- + -LOGY] a system of stating the probable form of future conditions by making assumptions based on known facts and observations —**fu'tur·ol'o·gist** *n.*

fuze (fyōōz) *n., vi., vt. U.S. sp.* of FUSE

fu·zee (fyōō zē') *n. same as* FUSEE

fuzz (fuz) *n.* [< ? Du. *voos,* or back-formation < FUZZY] very loose, light particles of down, wool, etc.; fine hairs or fibres [the *fuzz* on a peach] —*vi., vt.* 1. to cover or become covered with fuzz 2. to make or become fuzzy —**the fuzz** [< ? FUSSY (sense 2)] [Slang] a policeman or the police

fuzz·y (-ē) *adj.* **fuzz'i·er, fuzz'i·est** [prob. < LowG. *fussig,* spongy] 1. of, like, or covered with fuzz 2. not clear, distinct, or precise; blurred —**fuzz'i·ly** *adv.* —**fuzz'i·ness** *n.*

fwd. forward

-fy (fī) [< OFr. *-fier* < L. *-ficare* < *facere,* to make, do] a suffix meaning: 1. to make; cause to be [liquefy] 2. to cause to have; imbue with [glorify] 3. to become [putrefy]

fyl·fot (fil'fot) *n.* [< FILL + FOOT: so called because used to fill the foot of a stained glass window] a swastika

G

G, g (jē) *n., pl.* **G's, g's** 1. the seventh letter of the English alphabet 2. a sound of *G* or *g* 3. *Physics a)* gravity *b)* acceleration of gravity or a unit of acceleration equal to it, used to measure the force on a body undergoing acceleration

G (jē) *n. Music* 1. the fifth tone in the ascending scale of C major 2. the scale having this tone as the keynote

G. German

g gramme(s)

G., g. 1. *Elec.* conductance 2. gauge 3 guilder(s) 4. guinea(s) 5. gulf

Ga *Chem.* gallium

gab (gab) *vi.* **gabbed, gab'bing** [< ON. *gabba,* to mock] [Colloq.] to talk much or idly; chatter —*n.* [Colloq.] idle talk; chatter —**gift of the gab** [Colloq.] the ability to speak glibly —**gab'ber** *n.*

gab·ar·dine (gab'ər dēn', gab'ər dēn') *n.* [var. of GABERDINE] 1. a twilled cloth of wool, cotton, rayon, etc., with a fine, diagonal weave, used for suits, coats, dresses, etc. 2. a garment made of this cloth 3. *same as* GABERDINE

gab·ble (gab''l) *vi.* **-bled, -bling** [freq. of GAB] 1. to talk rapidly and incoherently; jabber 2. to utter rapid sounds, as a goose —*vt.* to utter rapidly and incoherently —*n.* rapid, incoherent talk or meaningless utterance —**gab'bler** *n.*

gab·bro (gab'rō) *n.* [It.< L. *glaber,* bare] any of a group of dark, heavy, igneous rocks, composed chiefly of pyroxene and feldspar

gab·by (-ē) *adj.* **-bi·er, -bi·est** [Colloq.] inclined to chatter; talkative —**gab'bi·ness** *n.*

gab·er·dine (gab'ər dēn', gab'ər dēn') *n.* [< OFr. *gaverdine,* kind of cloak < ? MHG. *walvart,* pilgrimage] 1. a loose coat of coarse cloth worn in the Middle Ages, esp. by Jews 2. *same as* GABARDINE

ga·bi·on (gā'bē ən) *n.* [Fr. < It. < *gabbia,* cage < L. *cavea:* see CAGE] 1. a cylinder of wicker filled with earth or stones, formerly used in building fortifications 2. a similar cylinder of metal, used in building dams, dikes, etc.

ga·ble (gā'b'l) *n.* [< OFr. < Gmc., as in ON. *gafl,* gable] 1. *a)* the triangular wall enclosed by the sloping ends of a ridged roof *b)* popularly, the whole section formed by these 2. an end wall having a gable at the top 3. a triangular decorative feature, as over a door or window —*vt.* **-bled, -bling** to put a gable or gables on

gable roof a roof forming a gable at each end

ga·by (gā'bē) *n.* [< Midland dial < ?] a simpleton

Gad (gad) *interj.* [euphemism for GOD] [*also* g-] a mild oath or expression of surprise, etc.

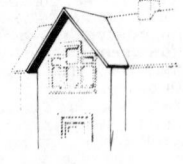

GABLE (sense 1)

gad¹ (gad) *vi.* **gad'ded, gad'ding** [? a back-formation < OE. *gædeling,* companion] to wander about in a restless way, as in seeking amusement —*n.* a gadding: chiefly in **on the gad** —**gad'der** *n.*

gad² (gad) *n.* [ON. *gaddr*] *same as* GOAD

gad·a·bout (gad'ə bout') *n.* [Colloq.] a person who gads about; restless seeker after fun, excitement, etc. —*adj.* fond of gadding

Gad·a·rene (gad'ə rēn') *adj.* [< the *Gadarene* swine (Luke 8:26-39) that ran into the sea after demons possessed them] moving rapidly and without control; headlong

gad·fly (-flī') *n., pl.* **-flies** [GAD² + FLY²] 1. a large fly that bites livestock, as the horsefly 2. a person who annoys or rouses others

gadg·et (gaj'it) *n.* [< ?] 1. any small mechanical contrivance 2. any small object

gadg·e·teer (gaj'ə tir') *n.* a person who contrives, or delights in, gadgets

gadg·et·ry (gaj'ə trē) *n.* 1. gadgets collectively 2. preoccupation with mere gadgets

ga·doid (gā'doid) *adj.* [< ModL. *gadus*, cod < Gr. *gados*, any kind of fish + -OID] of or like the cod family of fishes —*n.* any fish of this family

gad·o·lin·i·um (gad'ə lin'ē əm) *n.* [ModL., after J. *Gadolin* (1760-1852), Finn. chemist] a metallic chemical element of the rare-earth group: symbol, Gd; at. wt., 157.25; at. no., 64

ga·droon (gə drōōn') *n.* [Fr. *godron*] any of various oval-shaped beadings, flutings, or reedings used to decorate moulding, silverware, etc.

gad·wall (gad'wôl) *n., pl.* **-walls, -wall:** see PLURAL, II, D, 1 [< ?] a widely distributed greyish-brown wild duck

gad·zooks (gad'zōōks') *interj.* [< ? God's hooks] [Obs.] a mild oath

Gael (gāl) *n.* [contr. < Gael. *Gaidheal*] a Celt of Scotland, Ireland, or the Isle of Man; esp., a Celt of the Scottish Highlands —**Gael'dom** *n.*

Gael·ic (gāl'ik; gal'-) *adj.* 1. of the Gaels 2. of the Goidelic subbranch of the Celtic family of languages; of Scottish or Irish Gaelic —*n.* 1. the Goidelic subbranch of the Celtic family of languages 2. one of the Goidelic languages; esp., Scottish or Irish Gaelic; abbrev. **Gael.**

Gaelic coffee *same as* IRISH COFFEE

Gael·tacht (gāl'täkht) *n.* [< Ir. *Gael.*] that area of Ireland where Irish is the vernacular language

gaff[1] (gaf) *n.* [< OFr. < Pr. *gaf* or Sp. *gafa* < ?] 1. a large, strong hook on a pole, or a barbed 2. a sharp metal spur fastened to the leg of a gamecock 3. a spar or pole supporting a fore-and-aft sail —*vt.* to strike or land (a fish) with a gaff

gaff[2] (gaf) *n.* [prob. altered < earlier *gab*, mockery] [Slang] nonsense —**blow the gaff** to reveal a secret

gaffe (gaf) *n.* [Fr.] a blunder; faux pas

gaf·fer (gaf'ər) *n.* [altered < GODFATHER] 1. an old man: now usually humorous 2. [Colloq.] a foreman, as on a building site

gag (gag) *vt.* **gagged, gag'ging** [echoic] 1. to cause to retch or choke 2. to cover or stuff the mouth of, so as to keep from talking, crying out, etc. 3. to keep from speaking or expressing oneself freely, as by intimidation 4. to prevent or limit speech in —*vi.* to retch or choke —*n.* 1. something put into or over the mouth to prevent talking, etc. 2. any restraint of free speech 3. in parliament, a procedure by which debate may be halted and an immediate vote taken 4. a) a comical remark or act, as on the stage; joke *b*) a practical joke —**gag'ger** *n.*

ga·ga (gä'gä) *adj.* [Fr., orig., a fool: of echoic orig.] 1. senile; doting 2. crazy; insane

gage[1] (gāj) *n.* [< OFr., a pledge, pawn < Gmc.] 1. something pledged to insure that an obligation will be fulfilled; security 2. a pledge to appear and fight, as a glove thrown down by a challenging knight 3. a challenge —*vt.* **gaged, gag'ing** [Archaic] to offer as or bind by a pledge

gage[2] (gāj) *n., vt.* *same as* GAUGE

gage[3] (gāj) *n.* [Colloq.] a greengage

gag·gle (gag''l) *n.* [< ME. *gagelen*, to cackle] 1. a flock of geese 2. any group or cluster of persons or things —*vi.* to make a noise like a goose; to cackle

gag·man (-man') *n., pl.* **-men** (-men') a man who devises jokes, bits of comic business, etc., as for entertainers

gai·e·ty (gā'ə tē) *n., pl.* **-ties** 1. the state or quality of being gay; cheerfulness 2. merrymaking; festivity 3. finery; showy brightness

gail·lar·di·a (gā lär'dē ə) *n.* [ModL., after the 18th cent. Fr. botanist *Gaillard* de Marentonneau] any of several plants of the composite family, having large, showy flower heads with yellow or reddish petals and purple centres

gai·ly (gā'lē) *adv.* in a gay manner; specif., *a)* happily; merrily *b*) brightly; with bright display

gain (gān) *n.* [< OFr. < *gaaignier*, to earn] 1. an increase; addition; specif., *a*) [*often pl.*] an increase in wealth, earnings, etc.; profit *b*) an increase in advantage; improvement 2. the act of getting something; acquisition 3. *Electronics a)* an increase in signal strength *b*) the ratio of output to input —*vt.* 1. to get by labour; earn 2. to get by effort or merit; win 3. to attract [to *gain* one's interest] 4. to get as an addition, profit, or advantage 5. to make an increase in [to *gain* speed] 6. to go faster by [my watch *gained* two minutes] 7. to get to; reach —*vi.* 1. to make progress; improve or advance, as in health 2. to acquire profit 3. to become heavier 4. to be fast: said of a clock, etc. —**gain on** 1. to draw nearer to (an opponent in a race, etc.) 2. to make more progress than (a competitor)

gain·er (gā'nər) *n.* 1. a person or thing that gains 2. a dive in which the diver faces forward and does a backward somersault in the air

gain·ful (gān'f'l) *adj.* producing gain; profitable —**gain'-ful·ly** *adv.* —**gain'ful·ness** *n.*

gain·ly (gān'lē) *adj.* **-li·er, -li·est** [< ON. *gegn*, straight, fit] [Obs. or Dial.] shapely and graceful —**gain'li·ness** *n.*

gain·say (gān'sā') *vt.* **-said'** (-sed', -sād'), **-say'ing** [< OE. *gegn*, against + *seggan*, SAY] 1. to deny 2. to contradict 3. to speak or act against; oppose —*n.* a gainsaying —**gain'say'er** *n.*

'gainst, gainst (genst, gänst) *prep. poet. clip of* AGAINST

gait (gāt) *n.* [< ON. *gata*, path] 1. manner of walking or running 2. any of various foot movements of a horse, as a trot, canter, etc. —*vt.* to train (a horse) to certain gaits —**gait'ed** *adj.*

gai·ter (gāt'ər) *n.* [altered (after prec.) < Fr. *guêtre*] a cloth or leather covering for the instep and ankle and, sometimes, the calf of the leg; spat or legging —**gai'tered** *adj.*

gal (gal) *n.* [Colloq.] a girl

Gal. Galatians

gal. gallon; gallons

ga·la (gā'lə, gäl'ə) *n.* [It. < OFr. *gale*, enjoyment] 1. a festive occasion; festival; celebration 2. a competitive sporting occasion [a swimming *gala*] —*adj.* festive, or suitable for a festive occasion

ga·lac·tic (gə lak'tik) *adj.* [Gr. *galaktikos*, milky < *gala*, milk] 1. of or obtained from milk 2. *Astron.* of the Milky Way or some other galaxy

gal·a·go (gə lā'gō) *n.* [ModL.] any of a family of African mammals, allied to the lemur, and having large eyes and ears

ga·lah (gə lä') *n.* [< Abor.] a pink and grey Australian cockatoo

Gal·a·had (gal'ə had') [after the knight in Arthurian legend who through his purity won Holy Grail] a noble or chivalrous man

gal·an·tine (gal'ən tēn') *n.* [< OFr. < ML. *galatina*, jelly < L. pp. of *gelare*, CONGEAL] a mould of boned, seasoned, boiled white meat, as chicken or veal, chilled and served in its own jelly

gal·ax·y (gal'ək sē) [< LL. *galaxias* < Gr. < *gala*, milk] [*often* G-] *same as* MILKY WAY —*n., pl.* **-ax·ies** 1. any of innumerable vast groupings of stars 2. an assembly of illustrious people

gal·ba·num (gal'bə nəm) *n.* [ME. < L. < Gr. *chalbanē*] a bitter, odorous gum resin, obtained from various Asian plants

gale (gāl) *n.* [< ?] 1. a strong wind; specif., one of force 7 to 10 on the Beaufort scale (c. 45-90 km per hour) 2. an outburst [a *gale* of laughter]

ga·le·a (gā'lē ə) *n., pl.* **ga'le·ae** (-ē') [L., a helmet] *Biol.* a helmet-shaped part, esp. of a corolla or calyx —**ga'le·ate'**, —**ga'le·at'ed** *adj.*

ga·le·na (gə lē'nə) *n.* [L., lead ore] native lead sulphide, PbS, a lustrous, lead-grey mineral: it is the principal ore of lead: also **ga·le'nite** (-nīt)

Ga·len·ic (gə len'ik) *adj.* of or relating to the teachings of *Galen* (130?-200? A.D.), Gr. physician and writer on philosophy: also **Ga·len'i·cal**

Gal·i·le·an[1] (gal'ə lē'ən) *adj.* of Galilee or its people —*n.* a native or inhabitant of Galilee —**the Galilean** Jesus

Gal·i·le·an[2] (gal'ə lē'ən) *adj.* of *Galileo* (1564-1642), It. astronomer and physicist

gal·in·gale (gal'in gāl') *n.* [< OFr. *galingal*] 1. the aromatic root of various Indian plants of the ginger family, formerly used in cooking 2. a kind of English sedge Also **ga·lan·gal** (gə lan'gəl)

gal·i·ot (gal'ē ət) *n.* *same as* GALLIOT

gal·i·pot (gal'ə pot') *n.* [Fr., < ?] crude turpentine from a pine tree of S Europe

gall[1] (gôl) *n.* [OE. *galla*] 1. bile, the bitter, greenish fluid secreted by the liver and stored in the gallbladder 2. something bitter or distasteful 3. bitter feeling 4. [Colloq.] impudence; audacity

gall[2] (gôl) *n.* [OE. *gealla* < L. *galla*: see ff.] 1. a sore on the skin, esp. of a horse's back, caused by chafing 2. irritation or annoyance, or a cause of this —*vt.* 1. to make sore by rubbing; chafe 2. to irritate; annoy; vex

gall[3] (gôl) *n.* [< OFr. < L. *galla*, gallnut] a tumour on plant tissue caused by stimulation by fungi, insects, or bacteria: galls formed on oak trees have a high tannic acid content

gall. gallon

gal·lant (gal'ənt; *for adj.* 4 & *n., usually* gə lant'; *for v.,* *always* gə lant') *adj.* [< OFr. prp. of *galer*, to rejoice < *gale*: see GALA] 1. [Now Rare] showy and gay in dress or appearance 2. stately; imposing 3. brave and noble 4. polite and attentive to women —*n.* [Now Rare] 1. a high-spirited, stylish man 2. a man attentive and polite to women 3. a lover —*vt., vi.* [Now Rare] to court (a woman) —**gal'lant·ly** *adv.*

gal·lant·ry (gal'ən trē) *n., pl.* **-ries** 1. nobility of behaviour or spirit; heroic courage 2. the courtly manner of a gallant

3. an act or speech characteristic of a gallant **4.** amorous intrigue

gall·blad·der (gôl′blad′ər) *n.* a membranous sac attached to the liver, in which excess gall, or bile, is stored

gal·le·ass (gal′ē as′, -əs) *n.* [< Fr. < OFr. < It. < ML. *galea:* see GALLEY] a large, three-masted vessel having sails and oars and carrying heavy guns: used on the Mediterranean in the 16th and 17th cent.

gal·le·on (gal′ē ən) *n.* [Sp. *galeón* < ML. *galea:* see GALLEY] a large Spanish warship and trader of the 15th and 16th cent., with three or four decks at the stern

gal·ler·y (gal′ə rē) *n., pl.* **-ler·ies** [< Fr. < ML. *galeria*] **1.** a covered walk open at one side or having the roof supported by pillars **2.** a long, narrow balcony on the outside of a building **3.** a platform at the stern of an early sailing ship **4.** *a)* a platform or projecting upper floor in a church, theatre, etc.; esp., the highest of a series of such platforms in a theatre, with the cheapest seats *b)* the people occupying these seats *c)* a group of spectators, as at a sporting event **5.** a long, narrow corridor or room **6.** a room, building, or establishment for showing or selling art works **7.** a long, narrow place used for a specific purpose [a shooting *gallery*] **8.** an underground passage, as one used in mining **9.** a small, ornamental, raised rim surrounding a tray, tabletop, etc. —*vt.* **-ler·ied, -ler·y·ing** to furnish with a gallery —**play to the gallery** to try to win the approval of the public, esp. in a showy way

GALLEON

gal·ley (gal′ē) *n., pl.* **-leys** [< OFr. < ML. *galea,* < MGr. *galaia,* a kind of ship] **1.** a long, low, usually single-decked ship propelled by oars and sails, used in ancient and medieval times **2.** a ship's or aircraft's kitchen **3.** *Printing a)* a shallow, oblong tray for holding composed type to be put into a forme *b) same as* GALLEY PROOF

galley proof printer's proof taken from type in a galley to permit correction of errors before the type is made up in pages

galley slave **1.** a slave or convict sentenced or compelled to pull an oar on a galley **2.** a drudge

gall·fly (gôl′flī′) *n., pl.* **-flies′** a fly whose eggs cause galls when deposited in plant stems

gal·liard (gal′yərd) *n.* [ME. < OFr. *gaillard,* brave] **1.** a lively French dance popular in the 16th and 17th cent. **2.** music for this

Gal·lic (gal′ik) *adj.* **1.** of ancient Gaul or its people **2.** French

gal·lic acid (gal′ik) [< Fr. < *galle,* GALL³] an acid prepared from nutgalls, tannin, etc. and used in photography and the manufacture of inks, dyes, etc.

Gal·li·cism, gal·li·cism (gal′ə siz′m) *n.* a French idiom, expression, custom, trait, etc.

Gal·li·cize, gal·li·cize (-sīz′) *vt., vi.* **-cized′, -ciz′ing** to make or become French or like the French in thought, language, etc.

gal·li·gas·kins (gal′i gas′kinz) *n.pl.* [altered < Fr. *garguesque,* ult. < It. *Grechesca,* Grecian] loosely fitting breeches worn in the 16th and 17th cent.: later applied humorously to any loose breeches

gal·li·mau·fry (gal′ə mô′frē) *n., pl.* **-fries** [Fr. *galimafrée*] **1.** orig., a stew made of meat scraps **2.** a hotchpotch; jumble

gal·li·na·cean (gal′ə nā′shən) *adj. same as* GALLINACEOUS —*n.* any gallinaceous bird

gal·li·na·ceous (-shəs) *adj.* [< L. < *gallina,* hen < *gallus,* a cock] of, or having the nature of, an order of birds that nest on the ground, including poultry, pheasants, grouse, etc.

gall·ing (gôl′iŋ) *adj.* that galls; very annoying; vexing —**gall′ing·ly** *adv.*

gal·li·nule (gal′ə nyōōl′) *n.* [ModL. < L. dim. of *gallina:* see GALLINACEOUS] any of various marsh birds that both swim and wade

gal·li·ot (gal′ē ət) *n.* [< OFr. dim. of *galie* < ML. *galea,* GALLEY] **1.** a small, swift galley with sails and oars **2.** a light Dutch merchant ship with a single mast

gal·li·pot (gal′ə pot′) *n.* [see GALLEY & POT] a small pot or jar of glazed earthenware, esp. one used by chemists as a container for medicine

gal·li·um (gal′ē əm) *n.* [ModL. < L. *Gallia,* Gaul; also a pun on L. *gallus,* a cock, transl. of *Lecoq* (de Boisbaudran), its 19th-c. Fr. discoverer] a soft, bluish-white, metallic chemical element with a low melting point, used as a substitute for mercury: symbol, Ga; at. wt., 69.72; at. no., 31

gal·li·vant (gal′ə vant′) *vi.* [arbitrary elaboration of

GALLANT] **1.** orig., to gad about with members of the opposite sex **2.** to go about in search of amusement or excitement —**gal′li·vant′er** *n.*

gal·li·wasp (gal′ə wosp′) *n.* [< ?] a large, harmless, West Indian lizard

gall·nut (gôl′nut′) *n.* a nutlike gall, esp. on oaks

Gal·lo- (gal′ō) [L. < *Gallus,* a Gaul] a *combining form meaning:* **1.** French **2.** French and

gal·lon (gal′ən) *n.* [< ONormFr. *galon* < ML. *galo,* gallon, jug] **1.** a measure of capacity equal to 277·42 cubic inches (4·55 litres) **2.** [*pl.*] [Colloq.] a great amount

gal·lon·age (-ij) *n.* amount or capacity in gallons

gal·loon (gə lōōn′) *n.* [< Fr. < *galonner,* to braid] a braid, as of cotton, silk, or metal thread, used for trimming or binding

gal·lop (gal′əp) *vi.* [< OFr. *galoper* < Frank.] **1.** to go at a gallop **2.** to move or act very fast; hurry —*vt.* to cause to gallop —*n.* **1.** the fastest gait of a horse, etc., consisting of a succession of leaping strides with all the feet off the ground at one time **2.** a ride on a galloping animal **3.** any fast pace, speedy action, etc. —**gal′lop·er** *n.*

Gal·lo·way (gal′ə wā′) *n.* [< area in SW Scotland] **1.** any of a former Scottish breed of small, hardy horses **2.** any of a Scottish breed of black, hornless beef cattle

gal·lows (gal′ōz) *n., pl.* **-lows·es, -lows** [OE. *galga*] **1.** an upright frame with a crossbeam and a rope, for hanging condemned persons **2.** any structure like this **3.** the death sentence by hanging

gallows bird [Colloq.] a person who deserves hanging

gallows humour morbid or cynical humour

gallows tree a gallows

gall·stone (gôl′stōn′) *n.* a small, solid mass sometimes formed in the gallbladder or bile duct

Gal·lup poll (gal′əp) [after G. *Gallup* (1901-), U.S. statistician, its inventor] a method of assessing public opinion by putting questions to a cross-section of the population

gal·lus·es (gal′əs iz) *n.pl.* [< *gallus,* dial. var. of GALLOWS] [Dial. & U.S.] braces for trousers

gall wasp any of various small insects whose larvae produce galls in plants

ga·loot, gal·loot (gə lōōt′) *n.* [< ?] [Chiefly U.S. Slang] a clumsy or uncouth person

gal·op (gal′əp) *n.* [Fr.: see GALLOP] **1.** a lively round dance in 2/4 time **2.** music for this —*vi.* to dance a galop

ga·lore (gə lôr′) *adv.* [Ir. *go leór,* enough] in abundance; plentifully [to attract crowds *galore*]

ga·losh, ga·loshe (gə losh′) *n.* [< OFr. *galoche,* prob. < LL. *gallicula,* small shoe] an overshoe, esp. a high overshoe of rubber and fabric

ga·lumph (gə lumf′) *vi.* [coined by Lewis Carroll < GAL(LOP) + (TRI)UMPH] to march or bound along in a self-satisfied, triumphant manner

gal·van·ic (gal van′ik) *adj.* [< ff.] **1.** of, caused by, or producing an electric current, esp. from a battery **2.** stimulating or stimulated as if by electric shock; startling —**gal·van′i·cal·ly** *adv.*

gal·va·nism (gal′və niz′m) *n.* [< Fr. < It.: after L. *Galvani* (1737-98), It. physiologist and physicist] **1.** electricity produced by chemical action **2.** electrical current used in therapy

gal·va·nize (gal′və nīz′) *vt.* **-nized′, -niz′ing** **1.** to apply an electric current to **2.** to stimulate as if by electric shock; excite **3.** to plate (metal) with zinc —**gal′va·ni·za′tion** *n.*

gal·va·no- a *combining form meaning* galvanic, galvanism

gal·va·nom·e·ter (gal′və nom′ə tər) *n.* an instrument for detecting and measuring a small electric current —**gal′va·no·met′ric** (-nō met′rik) *adj.* —**gal′va·nom′e·try** (-trē) *n.*

gam (gam) *n.* [< dial. Fr. *gambe* < ML. *gamba* < Gr. *kampē,* a joint] [Slang] a leg

gam·bier, gam·bir (gam′bir) *n.* [Malay *gambir*] an astringent substance extracted from a Malayan plant of the madder family, and used in medicine, tanning and dyeing

gam·bit (gam′bit) *n.* [Fr. < OFr. < Sp. *gambito,* a tripping < It. < ML. *gamba,* a leg] **1.** *Chess* an opening in which a pawn or other piece is sacrificed to get an advantage in position **2.** a manoeuvre or action intended to gain an advantage

gam·ble (gam′b'l) *vi.* **-bled, -bling** [OE. *gamenian,* to play] **1.** to play games of chance for money, etc. **2.** to take a risk in order to gain some advantage —*vt.* to bet; wager —*n.* an act or undertaking involving risk of a loss —**gamble away** to squander or lose in gambling —**gam′bler** *n.*

gam·boge (gam bōzh′, -bōōzh′, -bōj′) *n.* [ModL. *gambogium* < *Cambodia*] a gum resin obtained from a tropical Asian tree, used as a yellow pigment and as a cathartic

gam·bol (gam′b'l) *n.* [< Fr. < Pr. < It. *gambata,* a kick < *gamba:* see GAM & GAMBIT] a jumping and skipping about in play; frolic —*vi.* **-bolled, -bol·ling** to jump and skip about in play; frolic

gam·brel (gam′brəl) *n.* [ONormFr. < OFr. *gambe:* see GAM]

1. the hock of a horse or similar animal 2. *same as* GAMBREL ROOF

gambrel roof a roof with two slopes on each side, the lower steeper than the upper, and a small gable at each end

game¹ (gām) *n.* [OE. < *gamen*] 1. any form of play; amusement; recreation; sport 2. *a*) any specific amusement or sport involving competition under specific rules *b*) a single contest in such a competition *c*) a subdivision of a contest, as in a set of tennis 3. the number of

GAMBREL ROOF

points required for winning 4. a victory; win 5. a set of equipment for a competitive amusement [to sell toys and games] 6. a way or quality of playing [to play a good game] 7. any test of skill, endurance, etc. 8. [Colloq.] *a*) a project; scheme *b*) trick; strategy [to see through another's game] 9. any activity undertaken in a lighthearted spirit 10. *a*) wild birds or animals hunted for sport or food *b*) their flesh used as food 11. any object of pursuit or attack: usually in **fair game** —*vi.* **gamed**, **gam'ing** to play cards, etc. for stakes; gamble —*adj.* 1. designating or of wild birds or animals hunted for sport or food 2. **gam'er**, **gam'est** *a*) plucky; courageous *b*) having enough spirit; ready (*for* something) —**a game that two can play** any play, behaviour, etc., that can be imitated to the disadvantage of its initiator —**give the game away** to reveal a secret or deception —**make game of** to make fun of; ridicule —**off one's game** performing poorly —**on the game** [Slang] engaged in prostitution —**play the game** [Colloq.] to follow the rules; behave as fairness or custom requires —**the game is up** failure is certain —**game'ly** *adv.* —**game'ness** *n.*

game² (gām) *adj.* [< ?] [Colloq.] lame or injured: said esp. of a leg

game-cock (gām'kok') *n.* a specially bred cock trained for cockfighting

game fish any fish regularly caught for sport

game-keep-er (-kēp'ər) *n.* a person employed to breed and take care of game birds and animals on estates

game laws laws regulating hunting and fishing in order to preserve game

game point *Tennis* etc. a point that would enable one player to win a game

games-man-ship (gāmz'mən ship') *n.* [< GAME¹ & (sport)smanship, see SPORTSMAN] skill in using ploys to gain a victory or advantage over another person

game-some (gām'səm) *adj.* playful; frolicsome —**game'some-ly** *adv.* —**game'some-ness** *n.*

game-ster (-stər) *n.* a gambler

gam-e-tan-gi-um (gam'ə tan'jē əm) *n.*, *pl.* **-gi-a** (-ə) [ModL. GAMET(O)- + Gr. *angeion*, a container] *Bot.* a plant structure in which gametes are produced

gam-ete (gam'ēt, ga mēt') *n.* [ModL. < Gr. *gametē*, a wife < *gamein*, to marry < *gamos*: see GAMO-] a reproductive cell that can unite with another gamete to form the cell (*zygote*) that develops into a new individual —**ga-met'ic** (gə met'ik) *adj.*

game theory a method of using mathematical analysis to select the best strategy so as to minimize one's maximum losses or maximize one's minimum winnings in a game, war, business competition, etc.

ga-me-to- a combining form meaning gamete

ga-me-to-phyte (gə mēt'ə fīt') *n.* in plants characterized by alternation of generations, the individual or generation that reproduces by eggs and sperms —**ga-me'to-phyt'ic** (-fit'ik) *adj.*

gam-in (gam'in) *n.* [Fr.] a neglected child left to roam the streets

gam-ine (gam'ēn') *n.* [Fr., fem. of prec.] a girl with a roguish, saucy charm

gam-ing (gā'min) *n.* the practice of gambling

gam-ma (gam'ə) *n.* [Gr.] 1. the third letter of the Greek alphabet (Γ, γ) 2. the third of a group or series

gamma globulin that fraction of blood serum which contains most antibodies: used in the temporary prevention of measles, hepatitis, etc.

gamma ray 1. an electromagnetic radiation emitted by the nucleus of a radioactive substance: similar to an X-ray, but shorter in wavelength 2. a stream of such radiation

gam-mer (gam'ər) *n.* [altered < GODMOTHER] an old woman: now usually contemptuous or humorous

gam-mon¹ (gam'ən) *n.* [< ONormFr. < *gambe*: see GAM] 1. the bottom end of a side of bacon 2. a smoked or cured ham or side of bacon

gam-mon² (gam'ən) *n.* [< ME. var. of *gamen*: see GAME¹] *Backgammon* a victory in which the winner gets rid of all his men before his opponent gets rid of any —*vt.* to defeat by scoring a gammon

gam-mon³ (gam'ən) *n., interj.* [< ?] [Colloq.] deceitful talk;

humbug —*vt., vi.* [Colloq.] 1. to talk humbug (to) 2. to deceive

gam-my (gam'ē) *adj.* [altered < ? GAME²] [Colloq.] *same as* GAME²

gam-o- [< Gr. *gamos*, marriage] a combining form meaning: 1. sexually united 2. joined or united

gam-o-pet-al-ous (gam'ə pet'l əs) *adj.* having the petals united so as to form a tubelike corolla

-ga-mous (gə məs) [< Gr. *gamos* (see GAMO-) + -OUS] a combining form meaning marrying, uniting sexually [*polygamous*]

gamp (gamp) *n.* [in allusion to the umbrella of Mrs. *Gamp* in Dickens' *Martin Chuzzlewit*] [Colloq.] a large umbrella; esp. one that is bulky or awkwardly wrapped

gam-ut (gam'ət) *n.* [ML. *gamma ut* < *gamma*, the lowest note of the medieval scale < Gr. *gamma*, GAMMA + *ut* < L. *ut*, that, in a medieval song whose phrases began on successive ascending major tones: *Ut* queant laxis *Re*sonare fibris, *Mi*ra gestorum *Fa*muli tuorum, *Sol*ve polluti *Labii* reatum, *Sancte Io*hannes] 1. *a*) the entire series of recognized notes in modern music *b*) any complete musical scale, esp. the major scale 2. the entire range or extent, as of emotions

gam-y (gā'mē) *adj.* **gam'i-er**, **gam'i-est** 1. having a strong flavour, like game kept uncooked until it is high 2. [Colloq.] spirited; plucky —**gam'i-ly** *adv.* —**gam'i-ness** *n.*

-ga-my (gə mē) [< Gr. *gamos*: see GAMO-] a combining form meaning marriage, sexual union [*polygamy*]

gan-der (gan'dər) *n.* [OE. *gan(d)ra*] 1. a male goose 2. a stupid or silly fellow 3. [Slang] a look: chiefly in the phrase **take a gander**

gang¹ (gan) *n.* [OE. < base of *gangan* (see ff.)] 1. a group of people associated together in some way; specif., *a*) a group of workers directed by a foreman *b*) an organized group of criminals *c*) a group of youths from one neighbourhood banded together; often, specif., a band of juvenile delinquents 2. a set of tools, machines, etc. designed to work together —*vi.* to form, or be associated in, a gang (with *up*) —*vt.* [Colloq.] to attack as a gang —**gang up on** [Colloq.] to attack as a group

gang² (gan) *vi.* [OE. *gangan*, to go] [Scot.] to go or walk

gang-bang (-ban') *n.* [Slang] an instance of sexual intercourse, sometimes forced, between one girl and several men in turn

gang-er (-ər) *n.* a foremen of a gang of workers

gang-gang (gan'gan') *n.* [Abor.] a grey Australian cockatoo; the male has a red head

gang-land (-land', -lənd) *n.* the sphere of criminal gangs

gan-gling (gan'glin) *adj.* [? < dial. *gangrel*, "lanky person"] tall, thin, and awkward; of loose, lanky build: also **gan'gly**

gan-gli-on (gan'glē ən) *n.*, *pl.* **-gli-a** (-ə), **-gli-ons** [LL. < Gr. *ganglion*, tumour] 1. a mass of nerve cells serving as a centre from which nerve impulses are transmitted 2. a centre of force, energy, etc. —**gan'gli-on'ic** (-on'ik) *adj.*

gang-plank (gan'plank') *n.* a narrow, movable platform by which to board or leave a ship

gan-grene (gan'grēn) *n.* [< Fr. < L. *gangraena* < Gr. < *gran*, to gnaw] decay of tissue in a part of the body when the blood supply is obstructed by injury, disease, etc. —**gan'gre-nous** (-grə nəs) *adj.*

gang-ster (gan'stər) *n.* a member of a gang of criminals —**gang'ster-ism** *n.*

gangue (gan) *n.* [Fr. < G. *Gang*, metallic vein, passage] the commercially worthless mineral matter found with ores in a deposit

gang-way (gan'wā') *n.* [OE. *gangweg*] 1. a passageway; specif., *a*) an opening in a ship's side for freight or passengers *b*) same as GANGPLANK 2. a passageway between rows of seats; specif., in the House of Commons, the aisle separating frontbenchers from backbenchers —*interj.* make room! clear the way!

gan-net (gan'it) *n.*, *pl.* **-nets**, **-net**: see PLURAL, II, D, 1 [OE. *ganot*] 1. any of several large sea birds; esp., a white, gooselike, web-footed bird that breeds on cliffs 2. a person who is greedy

gan-oid (gan'oid) *adj.* [< Fr. < Gr. *ganos*, brightness + -*eidēs*, -OID] of a group of fishes covered by rows of hard, glossy scales or plates, including the sturgeons and gars —*n.* a ganoid fish

gan-try (gan'trē) *n.*, *pl.* **-tries** [< OFr. < L. *canterius*, beast of burden < Gr. < *kanthōn*] 1. a frame for holding barrels horizontally 2. a framework that spans a distance, as one on wheels that carries a travelling crane 3. a wheeled framework with a crane, platforms at different levels, etc. used to position and service a rocket at its launching site

gaol (jāl) *n.* var. sp. of JAIL —**gaol'er** *n.*

gap (gap) *n.* [ON. < *gapa*, to yawn, GAPE] 1. a hole or opening made by breaking or parting; breach 2. a mountain pass or ravine 3. an interruption of continuity in space or time 4. a disparity between ideas, natures, etc. 5.

same as SPARK GAP —*vi.* **gapped, gap′ping** to come apart; open

gape (gāp) *vi.* **gaped, gap′ing** [< ON. *gapa*] 1. to open the mouth wide, as in yawning 2. to stare with the mouth open, as in wonder 3. to open wide, as a chasm —*n.* 1. an open-mouthed stare 2. a yawn 3. a wide opening 4. *Zool.* the measure of the widest possible opening of a mouth or beak —**the gapes** 1. a disease of poultry and birds, characterized by gaping 2. [Colloq.] a fit of yawning —**gap′er** *n.* —**gap′ing·ly** *adv.*

gar (gär) *n., pl.* **gar, gars:** see PLURAL, II, D, 2 [contr. < GARFISH] any of a group of freshwater ganoid fishes with elongated bodies, long beaklike snouts, and many sharp teeth

ga·rage (gar′äzh, -äj, -ij) *n.* [Fr. < *garer*, to protect] 1. a closed shelter for motor vehicles 2. an establishment where motor vehicles are repaired, serviced, bought and sold, and which usually also sells petrol, etc. —*vt.* **-raged, -rag·ing** to put or keep in a garage

garb (gärb) *n.* [< OFr. < It. *garbo*, elegance] 1. clothing; manner or style of dress 2. external form, covering, or appearance —*vt.* to clothe

gar·bage (gär′bij) *n.* [ME., entrails of fowls] worthless, useless or unwanted matter

gar·ble (gär′b'l) *vt.* **-bled, -bling** [< It. < *garbello*, a sieve < Ar. < *ghirbāl* < L. dim. *cribellum*, a small sieve] 1. to select, suppress, distort, etc. parts of (a story, etc.) in telling, so as to mislead or misrepresent 2. to confuse or mix up (a story, etc.) unintentionally —*n.* the act or result of garbling —**gar′bler** *n.*

gar·board (gär′bôrd′) *n.* [Du. *gaarbord* < *garen* (contr. of *gaderen*, to GATHER) + *board*, BOARD] *Shipbuilding* the planks or plates adjoining the keel: also **garboard strake**

‡**gar·çon** (gärson′) *n., pl.* **-çons′**(-son′) [Fr.] a waiter or male servant

gar·den (gär′d'n) *n.* [< ONormFr. *gardin* < Frank.] 1. a piece of ground, usually close to a house, for the growing of fruits, flowers, or vegetables 2. an area of fertile, well-cultivated land 3. [*often pl.*] a parklike place for public enjoyment, sometimes having special displays of animals or plants —*vi.* to work in or take care of a garden, lawn, etc. —*adj.* 1. of, for, or grown in a garden 2. ordinary; commonplace [*common* or *garden*] —**lead (someone) up the garden path** to mislead or deceive (someone) —**the Garden of England** Kent —**gar′den·er** *n.*

garden centre an establishment selling plants, equipment and furniture for the garden

garden city a planned town of limited size, surrounded by a rural belt, and designed to harmonize residential, industrial, and agricultual needs

gar·de·ni·a (gär dēn′yə, -dē′nē ə) *n.* [ModL., after A. *Garden*, 18th-c. Am. botanist] any of a genus of plants with glossy leaves and fragrant, white or yellow, waxy flowers

gar·fish (gär′fish′) *n., pl.* **-fish′, -fish es:** see FISH [< ME. *gare*, spear (OE. *gar*) + *fish*, fish] *same as* GAR

gar·ga·ney (gär′gə nē) *n.* [prob. < It. dial. *garganello*] a small, surface-feeding duck allied to the teal

gar·gan·tu·an (gär gan′tyoo wən) *adj.* [after a giant king in Rabelais' *Gargantua and Pantagruel*] huge; enormous

gar·gle (gär′g'l) *vt., vi.* **-gled, -gling** [< Fr. < *gargouille*, throat, spout] to rinse (the throat) with a liquid kept in motion by the slow expulsion of air from the lungs —*n.* 1. a liquid used for gargling 2. a gargling sound

gar·goyle (gär′goil) *n.* [< OFr. *gargouille*: see prec.] 1. a waterspout, usually in the form of a carved fantastic creature, projecting from the gutter of a building 2. a person with grotesque features

Gar·i·bal·di (biscuit) (gar ′ə bôl′dē) a kind of biscuit containing currants

gar·ish (ger′ish) *adj.* [prob. < ME. *gauren*, to stare] too bright or gaudy; showy —**gar′ish·ly** *adv.* —**gar′ish·ness** *n.*

GARGOYLE

gar·land (gär′lənd) *n.* [< OFr. *garlande*] a wreath of flowers, leaves, etc. —*vt.* to form into or decorate with a garland or garlands

gar·lic (gär′lik) *n.* [< OE. < *gar*, a spear + *leac*, a leek] 1. a bulbous plant of the lily family 2. its strong-smelling bulb, made up of small sections called cloves, used as a seasoning —**gar′lick·y** *adj.*

gar·ment (gär′mənt) *n.* [< OFr. *garnement* < *garnir*: see GARNISH] 1. any article of clothing 2. a covering —*vt.* to clothe

gar·ner (gär′nər) *n.* [< OFr. < L. *granarium* < *granum*, GRAIN] 1. a granary 2. a store of something —*vt.* 1. to gather up and store 2. to get or earn 3. to collect or gather

gar·net (gär′nit) *n.* [< OFr. < ML. *granatus* < *granum*, garnet, lit., POMEGRANATE] 1. any of a group of hard silicate minerals, chiefly crystalline: red varieties are used as gems 2. a deep red

gar·nish (gär′nish) *vt.* [< OFr. *garnir*, to furnish, protect < Gmc.] 1. to decorate; adorn; trim 2. to decorate (food) with something that adds colour or flavour 3. *Law* to bring garnishment proceedings against —*n.* 1. a decoration; ornament 2. something used to garnish food, as parsley —**gar′nish·er** *n.*

gar·nish·ee (gär′nə shē′) *n. Law* a person served with a garnishment —*vt.* **-eed′, -ee′ing** *Law* 1. to attach (a debtor's property, wages, etc.) by the authority of a court, so that it can be used to pay the debt 2. to serve with a garnishment

gar·nish·ing (gär′nish iŋ) *n. same as* GARNISHMENT (sense 1)

gar·nish·ment (gär′nish mənt) *n.* 1. a decoration; embellishment 2. *Law* a notice ordering a person not to dispose of a defendant's property or money in his possession pending settlement of the lawsuit

gar·ni·ture (gär′ni chər) *n.* garnish; decoration

gar·pike (gär′pīk′) *n. same as* GAR

gar·ret (gar′it) *n.* [ME. *garite*, a watchtower, loft < OFr. < *garir*, to watch < Frank.] the space or rooms just below the sloping roof of a house; attic

gar·ri·son (gar′ə s'n) *n.* [< OFr. < *garir* (see GARRET)] 1. troops stationed in a fort 2. a military post or station —*vt.* 1. to station troops in (a fortified place) for its defence 2. to place (troops) on duty in a garrison

gar·rotte (gə rot′) *n.* [Sp., orig., a stick used to wind a cord < OFr. < Frank.] 1. *a)* a method of execution, as formerly in Spain, by strangling with an iron collar *b)* the iron collar so used 2. *a)* a cord, length of wire, etc. for strangling a person in a surprise attack *b)* a disabling by strangling in this way —*vt.* **-rot′ted, -rot′ting** 1. to execute or attack with a garrote or by strangling 2. to disable by strangling, as in an attack for robbery Also *sp.* **ga·rotte′,** [U.S.] **gar·rote′** —**gar·rot′ter** *n.*

gar·ru·lous (gar′ə ləs) *adj.* [< L. < *garrire*, to chatter] talking much or too much, esp. about unimportant things; ʼloquacious —**gar·ru·li·ty** (gə rōō′lə tē), **gar′ru·lous·ness** *n.* —**gar′ru·lous·ly** *adv.*

gar·ter (gär′tər) *n.* [< ONormFr. *gartier* < OFr. *garet*, the back of the knee < Celt.] 1. an elastic band for holding a stocking or sock in position 2. [**G-**] *a)* the badge of the Order of the Garter, the highest order of British knighthood *b)* the order itself —*vt.* to fasten with a garter

garter snake any of various small, harmless, striped snakes common in N. America

garter stitch knitting in which all the rows are knitted in plain stitch

garth (gärth) *n.* [ME. < ON. *garthr*, akin to OE. *geard*, YARD²] [Archaic] an enclosed yard or garden

gas (gas) *n.* [ModL., coined by the Belgian chemist, Van Helmont (1577–1644), after Paracelsus' use of Gr. *chaos*, CHAOS, to mean "air"] 1. the fluid form of a substance in which it can expand indefinitely; form that is neither liquid nor solid; vapour 2. any mixture of flammable gases used for lighting, heating, or cooking 3. any gas used as an anaesthetic 4. any substance dispersed through the atmosphere, as in war, to act as a poison, irritant, or asphyxiant 5. gaseous matter formed in the stomach, bowels, etc. 6. [U.S. Colloq.] petrol 7. [Slang] *a)* idle or boastful talk *b)* [Chiefly U.S.] a person or thing that is very pleasing, exciting, etc. 8. *Mining* a mixture of firedamp with air that explodes if ignited —*vt.* **gassed, gas′-sing** 1. to supply with gas 2. to subject to the action of gas 3. to injure or kill by gas, as in war —*vi.* [Slang] to talk idly or boastfully —*adj.* of or using gas —**step on the gas** [Colloq.] to accelerate a motor vehicle

gas·bag (-bag′) *n.* 1. a bag to hold gas, as in a balloon 2. [Slang] a person who talks too much

gas chamber a room in which people are put to be killed with poison gas

Gas·con (gas′kən) *adj.* 1. of Gascony or its people, reputed to be boastful 2. [**g-**] boastful —*n.* 1. a native of Gascony 2. [**g-**] a boaster

gas·con·ade (gas′kə nād′) *n.* [see prec. & -ADE] boastful or blustering talk —*vi.* **-ad′ed, -ad′ing** to boast or bluster

gas·e·ous (gas′ē əs, gas′yəs) *adj.* 1. of, like, or in the form of gas 2. [Colloq.] *same as* GASSY (sense 1) —**gas′-e·ous·ness** *n.*

gas fitter a person whose work is installing and repairing gas pipes and fixtures

gas gangrene a gangrene in which bacilli multiply in dirty wounds, producing gas, muscle destruction and toxaemia

gash (gash) *vt.* [< OFr. *garser*, ult. < Gr. *charassein*, to sharpen, cut] to make a long, deep cut in; slash —*n.* a long, deep cut

gas·hold·er (gas′hōld ər) *n.* a large, usually cylindrical container for storing gas; gasometer

gas·i·fy (gas'ə fī') *vt., vi.* **-fied'**, **-fy'ing** to change into gas —**gas'i·fi·ca'tion** *n.*

gas jet **1.** a flame of illuminating gas **2.** a nozzle or burner at the end of a gas fixture

gas·ket (gas'kit) *n.* [prob. < OFr. *garcette,* small cord] **1.** a piece of metal, rubber, etc., sandwiched between the faces of a joint to seal it **2.** *Naut.* a rope or cord by which a furled sail is tied to the yard

gas·light (gas'līt) *n.* **1.** the light produced by burning illuminating gas **2.** a gas jet or burner —*adj.* of or characteristic of the period of gaslight illumination [*gaslight* melodrama]

gas·man (-man') *n.,* *pl.* **-men** (-men') a man employed to read household gas meters, supervise gas fittings, etc.

gas mantle a mantle (*n.* 3) for a gas burner

gas mask a filtering device worn over the face to protect against breathing in poisonous gases

gas meter an instrument for measuring the quantity of a gas, esp. of gas consumed as a fuel

gas·o·line, gas·o·lene (gas'ə lēn', gas'ə lēn') *n.* [GAS + -OL(E) + -INE⁴, -ENE] *U.S. name for* PETROL

gas·om·e·ter (gas om'ə tər) *n.* **1.** a container for holding and measuring gas **2.** *same as* GAS HOLDER

gasp (gäsp) *vi.* [< ON. *geispa,* to yawn] to inhale suddenly, as in surprise, or breathe with effort, as in choking —*vt.* to say with gasps —*n.* a gasping; catching of the breath with difficulty

gasp·er (-ər) *n.* [Slang] a cigarette, esp. a cheap one

gas ring a tubular metal ring, perforated to form a circle of gas jets and used for cooking

gas·sy (gas'ē) *adj.* **-si·er, -si·est** **1.** full of, containing, or producing gas; esp., flatulent **2.** like gas **3.** [Colloq.] full of talk —**gas'si·ness** *n.*

gas·tric (gas'trik) *adj.* [GASTR(O)- + -IC] of, in, or near the stomach

gastric juice the acid digestive fluid produced by glands in the mucous membrane lining the stomach: it contains enzymes and hydrochloric acid

gastric ulcer an ulcer of the stomach lining

gas·tri·tis (gas trīt'is) *n.* [GASTR(O)- + -ITIS] inflammation of the stomach, esp. of the stomach lining

gas·tro- [< Gr. *gastēr,* the stomach] *a combining form meaning* the stomach (and): also **gastr-**

gas·tro·en·ter·i·tis (gas'trō en'tə rīt'is) *n.* [< GASTRO- + ENTER(O)- + -ITIS] an inflammation of the stomach and the intestines

gas·tro·in·tes·ti·nal (-in tes'tə n'l) *adj.* of the stomach and the intestines

gas·tro·nome (gas'trə nōm') *n.* a person who enjoys and has a discriminating taste for foods: also **gas·tron'o·mer** (-tron'ə mər), **gas·tron'o·mist**

gas·tron·o·my (gas tron'ə mē) *n.* [< Fr. < Gr. < *gastēr,* the stomach + *nomos,* a rule] the art of good eating —**gas'·tro·nom'ic** (-trə nom'ik), **gas'tro·nom'i·cal** *adj.* —**gas'·tro·nom'i·cal·ly** *adv.*

gas·tro·pod (gas'trə pod') *n.* [< ModL. < GASTRO- + -POD] any of a large class of molluscs having a single, straight or spiral shell, as snails, limpets, etc., or no shell, as certain slugs: most gastropods move by means of a broad, muscular, ventral foot —**gas'tro·pod'ous** *adj.*

gas·tro·scope (gas'trə skōp) *n.* [GASTRO-+ -SCOPE] an instrument inserted through the mouth for visually inspecting the inside of the stomach

gas·tru·la (gas'trσo lə) *n.,* *pl.* **-lae'** (-lē'), **-las** [ModL. dim. < Gr. *gastēr,* the stomach] an embryo in an early stage of development, consisting of a sac with two layers, the ectoderm and endoderm

gas·works (gas'wurks) *n.pl.* [with sing. v.] a plant where gas, esp. coal gas, is made for distribution as a fuel

gat (gat) *archaic pt. of* GET

gate (gāt) *n.* [< OE. *geat*] **1.** a movable structure, esp. one that swings on hinges, controlling entrance or exit through an opening in a fence or wall **2.** an opening for passage through a fence or wall, with or without such a structure; gateway **3.** any means of entrance or exit **4.** a movable barrier, as at a level crossing **5.** a structure controlling the flow of water, as in a pipe, canal, etc. **6.** *a)* the total amount of admission money paid by spectators at a performance or exhibition *b)* the total number of such spectators **7.** the slatted metal frame that controls the positions of the gear lever in a motor vehicle **8.** *Electronics* a circuit that passes signals only when certain input conditions are satisfied —*vt.* to restrict (a student) to the school or college grounds as a punishment

gat·eau (gat'ō) *n.,* *pl.* **-eaux** (-ō, -ōz)[Fr., a cake] a rich, layered, elaborately-decorated cake

gate-crash·er (gāt'krash'ər) *n.* [Colloq.] a person who attends a social affair without an invitation or a performance, etc. without paying admission —**gate'-crash' vt., v.**

gate·fold (gāt'fōld') *n.* a page larger than the others in a magazine or book, ʰound so that it can be folded out

gate·house (-hous') *n.* a house beside or over a gateway, used as a porter's lodge, etc.

gate·keep·er (-kē'pər) *n.* a person in charge of a gate to control passage through it: also **gate'man,** *pl.* **-men**

gate·leg table (-leg') a table with drop leaves supported by gatelike legs that swing back to let the leaves drop: also **gate'legged'- table**

gate·post (-pōst') *n.* the post on which a gate is hung or to which it is fastened when closed

gate·way (-wā') *n.* **1.** an entrance in a fence, wall, etc. fitted with a gate **2.** a means of access

GATELEG TABLE

gath·er (ga*th*'ər) *vt.* [< OE. *gad(e)rian*] **1.** to bring together in one place or group **2.** to get gradually from various places, sources, etc.; accumulate **3.** to bring close **4.** to pick or collect by picking; harvest **5.** to infer; conclude **6.** to prepare (oneself, one's energies, etc.) to meet a situation **7.** to gain or acquire gradually [*to gather speed*] **8.** to draw (cloth) into fixed folds or pleats **9.** to wrinkle (one's brow) —*vi.* **1.** to come together; assemble **2.** to form pus; come to a head, as a boil **3.** to increase **4.** to become wrinkled: said of the brow —*n.* a pleat —**gath'er·er** *n.*

gath·er·ing (-iŋ) *n.* **1.** the act of one that gathers **2.** what is gathered; specif., *a)* a meeting; crowd *b)* a series of pleats **3.** a boil or abscess

Gat·ling gun (gat'liŋ) [after R. J. *Gatling,* 19th-c. U.S. inventor] an early kind of machine gun having a rotating cluster of barrels around an axis

G.A.T.T. General Agreement on Tariffs and Trade

gauche (gōsh) *adj.* [Fr. < MFr. *gauchir,* to become warped, ult. < Frank.] lacking social grace; awkward; tactless —**gauche'ly** *adv.* —**gauche'ness** *n.*

gau·che·rie (gō'shə rē') *n.* [see prec.] **1.** awkwardness; tactlessness **2.** a gauche act or expression

gau·cho (gou'chō) *n.,* *pl.* **-chos** [AmSp.] a cowboy of mixed Indian and Spanish ancestry, living on the S American pampas

gaud (gôd) *n.* [ME. *gaude,* a trinket, prob. ult. < L. *gaudium,* joy] a cheap, showy ornament

gaud·y¹ (gôd'ē) *adj.* **gaud'i·er, gaud'i·est** [prec. + -Y²] bright and showy, but in bad taste; cheaply ornate —**gaud'·i·ly** *adv.* —**gaud'i·ness** *n.*

gaud·y² (gôd'ē) *n.,* *pl.* **gaud'ies** [< L. *gaudium,* joy] a feast; esp., an annual dinner or reunion, at some universities

gauge (gāj) *n.* [< ONormFr. *gaugier,* to gauge] **1.** a standard measure or scale of measurement **2.** dimensions, capacity, thickness, etc. **3.** any device for measuring something, as the thickness of wire, steam pressure, etc. **4.** any means of estimating **5.** the distance between the rails of a railway: cf. STANDARD GAUGE, BROAD GAUGE, NARROW GAUGE **6.** the distance between parallel wheels at opposite ends of an axle **7.** the size of the bore of a shotgun expressed in terms of the number per pound of round lead balls of a diameter equal to that of the bore **8.** the thickness of sheet metal, diameter of wire, etc. **9.** the fineness of a knitted or woven fabric, usually expressed as the number of loops per centimetre **10.** *Naut.* the position of a vessel in relation·to the wind and to another vessel: also sp. **gage** —*vt.* **gauged,** **gaug'ing** **1.** to measure accurately by means of a gauge **2.** to measure the size, amount, or capacity of **3.** to estimate; judge **4.** to make conform with a standard —**gauge'a·ble** *adj.* —**gaug'er** *n.*

WIRE GAUGE

Gaul (gôl) *n.* **1.** any of the Celtic-speaking people of Gaul **2.** a Frenchman

‡Gau·lei·ter (gou'lī'tər) *n.* [G., < *Gau,* district + *Leiter,* leader] a regional chief in the Nazi movement, who acted as a provincial governor in Germany after Hitler came to power

Gaul·ish (gôl'ish) *adj.* of Gaul or the Gauls —*n.* the Celtic language spoken in ancient Gaul

gaunt (gônt) *adj.* [ME. *gawnte, gant* < ?] **1.** thin and bony; hollow-eyed and haggard, as from great hunger or age **2.** looking grim, forbidding, or desolate —**gaunt'ly** *adv.* —**gaunt'ness** *n.*

gaunt·let¹ (gônt'lit) *n.* [< OFr. dim. of *gant,* a glove < Frank.] **1.** a medieval glove, usually of leather covered with metal plates, worn to protect the hand in combat **2.** a long glove with a flaring cuff, or this cuff, covering the lower part of the arm —**take up the gauntlet** to accept a challenge —**throw down the gauntlet** to challenge, as to combat —**gaunt'let·ed** *adj.*

gaunt·let² (gônt'lit) *n.* [< Sw. *gatlopp,* a run down a lane < *gata,* lane + *lopp,* a run] **1.** a former military punishment in which the offender ran between two rows of men who struck him with clubs, etc. as he passed **2.** a series of troubles or difficulties —**run the gauntlet 1.** to be punished by means of the gauntlet **2.** to proceed while under attack from both sides, as by criticism or gossip

gaun·try (gôn′trē) *n.*, *pl.* **-tries** *same as* GANTRY

gauss (gous) *n.* [after K. *Gauss* (1777–1855), Ger. scientist] *Elec.* a cgs unit used in measuring magnetic induction or magnetic flux density, replaced in the SI units by the TESLA

gauze (gôz) *n.* [Fr. *gaze*] **1.** any very thin, transparent, loosely woven material, as of cotton or silk **2.** a thin mist

gauz·y (gôz′ē) *adj.* **gauz′i·er**, **gauz′i·est** thin, light, and transparent, like gauze; diaphanous —**gauz′i·ly** *adv.* —**gauz′i·ness** *n.*

gave (gāv) *pt.* of GIVE

gav·el (gav′'l) *n.* [? < Scot. *gable*, a tool < OE. *gafol*] a small mallet rapped on the table by a chairman, auctioneer, etc. to call for attention or silence

ga·vi·al (gā′vē əl) *n.* [Fr. < Hindi *ghariyāl*] a large crocodile of India, with a very long snout

ga·votte (gə vot′) *n.* [Fr. < Pr. *gavoto*, dance of the *Gavots*, an Alpine people] **1.** a 17th-cent. dance like the minuet, but livelier **2.** the music for this, in 4/4 time Also sp. **ga·vot′**

gawk (gôk) *n.* [prob. dial. var. of *gowk*, a simpleton] a clumsy, stupid fellow; simpleton —*vi.* to stare in a stupid way —**gawk′ish** *adj.*

gawk·y (gô′kē) *adj.* **gawk′i·er**, **gawk′i·est** [prob. < prec.] awkward; clumsy; ungainly —**gawk′i·ly** *adv.* —**gawk′i·ness** *n.*

gawp (gôp) *vi.* [dial., altered < ME. *galpen*, to yawn, gape] [Slang] to stare open-mouthed; gape

gay (gā) *adj.* [< OFr.] **1.** joyous and lively; merry **2.** bright; brilliant [*gay colours*] **3.** given to social pleasures [a *gay life*] **4.** wanton; licentious [a *gay dog*] **5.** [Colloq.] homosexual —**gay′ness** *n.*

gaze (gāz) *vi.* **gazed**, **gaz′ing** [< Scand.] to look intently and steadily; stare, as in wonder —*n.* a steady look —**gaz′er** *n.*

ga·ze·bo (gə zē′bō) *n.*, *pl.* **-bos**, **-boes** [< ?] a turret, balcony, or summerhouse with an extensive view

ga·zelle (gə zel′) *n.*, *pl.* **-zelles′**, **-zelle′**: see PLURAL, II, D, 1 [Fr. < Ar. *ghazāl*] any of various small, swift, graceful antelopes of Africa, the Near East, and Asia, with horns that twist back in a spiral and large, lustrous eyes

ga·zette (gə zet′) *n.* [Fr. < It. *gazzetta* < dial. *gazeta*, a small coin, price of a newspaper] **1.** a newspaper **2.** any of various official publications containing announcements and bulletins —*vt.* **-zet′ted**, **-zet′ting** to announce or list in a gazette

gaz·et·teer (gaz′ə tir′) *n.* **1.** [Obs.] a person who writes for a gazette **2.** a dictionary or index of geographical names

gaz·pa·cho (gäz pä′chō) *n.* [Sp.] a Spanish soup made with tomatoes, chopped cucumbers, onions, oil, vinegar, etc. and served cold

ga·zump (gə zump′) *vt.* [< ?] to raise the price of something, esp. a house, in the period between a verbal agreement to sell at a certain price and the signing of the contract

G.B. Great Britain

G.B.E. Grand Cross of the British Empire

G.C. George Cross

GCA *Aeron.* ground control approach

G.C.B. Grand Cross of the Bath

G.C.E. General Certificate of Education

G.C.I.E. Grand Commander of the Indian Empire

G clef *same as* TREBLE CLEF

G.C.M.G. Grand Cross of St. Michael and St. George

G.C.S.I. Grand Commander of the Star of India

G.C.V.O. Grand Cross of the Victorian Order

Gd *Chem.* gadolinium

Gdns. Gardens

Ge *Chem.* germanium

gear (gir) *n.* [prob. < ON. *gervi*, preparation] **1.** clothing; apparel, esp. up-to-date clothes and accessories **2.** apparatus or equipment for some particular task, as a workman's tools, a harness, etc. **3.** *a)* a toothed wheel, disc, etc. designed to mesh with another or with the thread of a worm *b)* [often *pl.*] a system of two or more gears meshed together so that the motion of one is passed on to the

GEARS

others *c)* a specific adjustment of such a system: in motor-vehicle transmissions, *high* or *top gear* provides greatest speed and *low*, *bottom*, or *first gear* greatest power *d)* any part of a mechanism performing a specific function [the steering *gear*] —*vt.* **1.** to furnish with gear; harness **2.** to adapt (one thing) so as to conform with another [to *gear* production to demand] **3.** *a)* to connect by gears *b)* to furnish with gears —*vi.* to be in, or come into, proper adjustment or working order —**in** (or **out of**) **gear 1.** (not) connected to the motor **2.** (not) in proper adjustment or

working order —**change gears 1.** to switch from one gear arrangement to another **2.** to alter one's method or approach

gear·box (-boks′) *n.* **1.** the unit consisting of the transmission gears in a transmission system **2.** a case enclosing gears to protect them from dirt

gear·ing (-iŋ) *n.* **1.** the act or manner of fitting a machine with gears **2.** a system of gears or other parts for transmitting motion **3.** *Accountancy* the ratio of a company's borrowing to its share capital

gear·lever (-lē′vər) *n.* a device for connecting or disconnecting any of a number of sets of transmission gears to a motor, etc.

gear·wheel (-wēl′, -hwēl′) *n.* a toothed wheel in a system of gears; cogwheel

geck·o (gek′ō) *n.*, *pl.* **-os**, **-oes** [Malay *gekok*, echoic of its cry] a soft-skinned, insect-eating, tropical lizard with suction pads on its feet

gee[1] (jē) *interj.*, *n.* [Early ModE. < ?] a word of command to a horse, ox, etc. meaning *a)* "turn to the right!" *b)* "go on!" or "go faster!" (with *up*) —*vt.*, *vi.* **geed**, **gee′ing** to turn to the right

gee[2] (jē) *interj.* [euphemistic contr. < JE(SUS)] [Chiefly U.S. Slang] an exclamation of surprise, wonder, etc.

gee·bung (jē′buŋ) *n.* [Abor.] **1.** any of various Australian shrubs bearing an edible fruit **2.** the fruit itself: also **gee′-bong**

geese (gēs) *n.* *pl.* of GOOSE

gee·zer (gē′zər) *n.* [< dial. *guiser*, a mummer < GUISE] [Slang] an eccentric old man

Gei·ger counter (gī′gər) [after H. *Geiger* (1882–1945), Ger. physicist] an instrument for detecting and counting ionizing particles: a refined version (**Geiger-Müller counter**) with an amplifying system is used for detecting and measuring radioactivity

gei·sha (gā′shə) *n.*, *pl.* **-sha**, **-shas** [Jap.] a Japanese girl trained in singing, dancing, etc., to serve as a hired companion to men

Geiss·ler tube (gīs′lər) [after H. *Geissler* (1814–79), its Ger. inventor] a glass tube having two electrodes and containing a gas which, when electrified, takes on a luminous glow of a colour characteristic of the gas

gel (jel) *n.* [< ff.] a jellylike substance formed by the coagulation of a colloidal solution into a solid phase —*vi.* **gelled**, **gel′ling** to form a gel

gel·a·tin (jel′ət in) *n.* [< Fr. < It. < *gelata*, jelly < pp. of *gelare*, to freeze] **1.** the tasteless, odourless, brittle substance extracted by boiling bones, hoofs, etc.; also, a similar vegetable substance: gelatin dissolves in hot water, forming a jellylike substance when cool, and is used in various foods, photographic film, etc. **2.** something, as a jelly, made with gelatin: also **gel′a·tine** (-tēn)

ge·lat·i·nize (jə lat′ən īz′, jel′ət ən īz′) *vt.* **-nized′**, **-niz′ing 1.** to change into gelatin or gelatinous matter **2.** *Photog.* to coat with gelatin —*vi.* to be changed into gelatin or gelatinous matter —**ge·lat′i·ni·za′tion** *n.*

ge·lat·i·nous (jə lat′ən əs) *adj.* **1.** of or containing gelatin **2.** like gelatin or jelly; viscous —**ge·lat′i·nous·ly** *adv.* —**ge·lat′i·nous·ness** *n.*

ge·la·tion[1] (je lā′shən) *n.* [L. *gelatio* < pp. of *gelare*, to freeze] solidification by cooling or freezing

ge·la·tion[2] (je lā′shən) *n.* [GEL + -ATION] coagulation to form a gel

geld (geld) *vt.* **geld′ed** or **gelt**, **geld′ing** [< ON. *gelda* < *geldr*, barren] **1.** to castrate (esp. a horse) **2.** to deprive of essential vigour; weaken

geld·ing (gel′diŋ) *n.* a gelded animal; esp., a castrated horse

gel·id (jel′id) *adj.* [L. *gelidus* < *gelu*, frost] extremely cold; icy —**ge·lid·i·ty** (jə lid′ə tē) *n.*

gel·ig·nite (jel′ig nīt′) *n.* [GE(LATIN) + L. *lign(um)*, wood + -ITE] a blasting explosive that is a mixture of nitroglycerin, nitrocellulose, ammonium nitrate, and some wood pulp

gem (jem) *n.* [< OFr. < L. *gemma*, a bud, gem] **1.** a precious or, occas., semi-precious stone, cut and polished for use as a jewel **2.** a highly valued person or thing —*vt.* **gemmed**, **gem′-ming** to adorn or set with or as with gems —**gem′my** *adj.*

Ge·ma·ra (ge mä′rə) *n.* [Aram. *gemārā*, completion] **1.** the second part of the Talmud, providing a commentary on the first part (the MISHNA) **2.** loosely, the Talmud

CUTS OF GEMS
(A, marquise; B, emerald; C, round; D, pear-shaped

gem·i·nate (jem′ə nāt′) *adj.* [< L. pp. of *geminare*, to double < *geminus*, a twin] growing or combined in pairs; coupled —*vt.* **-nat′ed**, **-nat′ing** to arrange in pairs; double —*vi.* to become doubled or paired —**gem′i·na′tion** *n.*

Gem·i·ni (jem'ə nī', -nē') [L., twins] 1. a N constellation containing the stars Castor and Pollux, represented as twins seated 2. the third sign of the zodiac: see ZODIAC, illus.

gem·ma (jem'ə) *n., pl.* **-mae** (-ē) [L.: cf. GEM] *Biol.* a budlike outgrowth which becomes detached and develops into a new organism

gem·mate (jem'āt) *adj.* [< L. pp. of *gemmare* < *gemma*, a bud] having, or reproducing by, gemmae —*vi.* **-mat·ed**, **-mat·ing** to have, or reproduce by, gemmae; bud —**gem·ma'tion** *n.*

gem·mip·a·rous (je mip'ər əs) *adj.* [< L. *gemma*, a bud + -PAROUS] *Biol.* of or reproducing by gemmation; budding

gem·mule (jem'yōōl) *n.* *Biol.* a small gemma

gem·ol·o·gy, gem·mol·o·gy (jem ol'ə jē) *n.* [< L. *gemma* (see GEM) + -O- + -LOGY: sp. infl. by GEM] the science or study of gems and gemstones

gems·bok (gemz'bok') *n., pl.* **-bok'**, **-boks'**: see PLURAL, II. D 2 [Afrik. < G. < *gemse* < VL. *camox*, CHAMOIS + *bock*, a buck] a large antelope of S Africa, with long, straight horns and a tufted tail

gem·stone (jem'stōn') *n.* any mineral that can be used as a gem when cut and polished

gen (jen) *n.* [*gen(eral)* information] [Colloq.] information —*vt., vi.* to make oneself fully informed about something (with *up*)

-gen (jən, jen) [< Fr. < Gr. < base of *gignesthai*, to be born] *a suffix meaning:* 1. something that produces [*oxygen, oestrogen*] 2. something produced (in a specified way) [*zymogen*]

Gen. 1. General 2. Genesis

gen. 1. gender 2. general 3. genitive 4. genus

gen·darme (zhän'därm; *Fr.* zhän därm') *n., pl.* **-darmes** (-därmz; *Fr.* -därm') [Fr., ult. < L. *gens*, a people + *de*, of + *arma*, arms] 1. in France, Belgium, etc., a soldier serving as an armed policeman 2. any policeman: a humorous usage

gen·dar·me·rie (zhän där'mə rē; *Fr.* zhän där mə rē') *n.* [Fr.] gendarmes collectively: also **gen·dar'mer·y**

gen·der (jen'dər) *n.* [< OFr. *gendre* < L. *genus*, origin, kind] 1. *Gram.* a) the classification by which nouns, pronouns, adjectives, etc. are variously grouped and inflected as masculine, feminine, or neuter: in English, only some nouns and the third person singular pronouns are distinguished according to gender b) any one of such groupings 2. [Colloq.] sex

gene (jēn) *n.* [< G. *Gen* < *pangen* (< Gr. *pan-*, PAN- + -gen, -GEN)] *Genetics* any of the units occurring at specific points on the chromosomes, by which hereditary characters are transmitted and determined: see DEOXYRIBONUCLEIC ACID (DNA)

ge·ne·al·o·gy (jē'nē ol'ə jē) *n., pl.* **-gies** [< OFr. < LL. < Gr. < *genea*, race, stock + -*logia*, -LOGY] 1. a chart or recorded history of the ancestry or descent of a person or family 2. the study of family descent 3. descent from an ancestor; pedigree; lineage —**ge'ne·a·log'i·cal** (-ə loj'i k'l, jen'ē-) *adj.* —**ge'ne·a·log'i·cal·ly** *adv.* —**ge'ne·al'o·gist** *n.*

gen·er·a (jen'ər ə) *n.* *pl. of* GENUS

gen·er·al (jen'ər əl, jen'rəl) *adj.* [< OFr. < L. *generalis* < *genus* (gen. *generis*), kind, class] 1. of, for, or from the whole or all; not particular, specialized or localized [a *general* anaesthetic] 2. of, for, or applying to a whole genus, kind, class, order, or race [the *general* classifications of matter] 3. existing or occurring extensively; widespread [a *general* unrest] 4. most common; usual [the *general* spelling of a word] 5. concerned with the main or overall features; lacking in details 6. not precise; vague [to speak in *general* terms] 7. highest in rank [*general* manager] —*n.* 1. the main or overall fact, idea, etc.: opposed to PARTICULAR 2. the head of a religious order 3. *see* MILITARY RANKS, table —**in general** 1. in the main; usually 2. without specific details —**gen'er·al·ness** *n.*

general assembly 1. [G- A-] the legislative assembly of the United Nations 2. in some U.S. states, the legislative assembly 3. the governing body of certain Protestant, esp. Presbyterian, churches

General Certificate of Education a public examination for which certificates are awarded at ordinary, advanced, or scholarship level, taken usually by pupils at secondary schools

general degree a degree awarded at some universities on completion of a nonspecialist course

general election an election in which every constituency chooses a representative

gen·er·al·is·si·mo (jen'ər ə lis'ə mō', jen'rə-) *n., pl.* **-mos'** [It., superl. of *generale*, GENERAL] in certain countries, 1. the commander in chief of all the armed forces 2. the commanding officer of several armies in the field

gen·er·al·i·ty (jen'ə ral'ə tē) *n., pl.* **-ties** 1. the condition or quality of being general 2. a general or nonspecific statement, expression, etc. 3. the bulk; main body

gen·er·al·i·za·tion (jen'ər ə lī zā'shən, jen'rəl ī-) *n.* 1. the

act or process of generalizing 2. a general idea, statement, etc. resulting from this

gen·er·al·ize (jen'ər ə līz', jen'rə-) *vt.* **-ized'**, **-iz'ing** to make general; esp., a) to state in terms of a general law b) to infer or derive (a general law or precept) from (particular instances) c) to emphasize the general character rather than specific details of d) to cause to be widely known or used —*vi.* 1. to formulate general principles from particulars 2. to talk in generalities 3. to become general or spread throughout an area

gen·er·al·ly (-lē) *adv.* 1. widely; popularly; extensively 2. in most instances; usually 3. in a general way; not specifically

general practitioner a practising doctor who does not specialize in any particular field of medicine

gen·er·al·pur·pose (-pur'pəs) *adj.* having a variety of uses; suitable for general use

gen·er·al·ship (-ship') *n.* 1. a) the rank, tenure, or authority of a general b) the military skill of a general 2. highly skilful leadership

general staff *Mil.* a group of officers who assist the commander in planning and supervising operations

general strike a strike by all, or most, of the workers of a country, province, etc.

gen·er·ate (jen'ə rāt') *vt.* **-at'ed**, **-at'ing** [< L. pp. of *generare* < *genus*, race, kind] 1. to produce (offspring); beget 2. to bring into being; cause to be 3. to originate or produce by a physical or chemical process 4. *Math.* to trace out or form (a line, plane, figure, or solid) by the motion of a point, line, or plane

gen·er·a·tion (jen'ə rā'shən) *n.* 1. the act or process of producing offspring 2. a bringing into being; production 3. a single stage in the succession of descent [father and son are two *generations*] 4. the average period (about thirty years) between the birth of successive generations 5. a) all the people born at about the same time b) a group of such people having something in common 6. *Math.* the generating of a line, figure, etc. —**gen'er·a'tion·al** *adj.*

generation gap the difference in outlook, resulting in lack of understanding or tolerance, between people of different generations

gen·er·a·tive (jen'ər ə tiv, -ə rāt'iv) *adj.* of, or having the power of, generation or production —**gen'er·a'tive·ly** *adv.* —**gen'er·a'tive·ness** *n.*

gen·er·a·tor (jen'ə rāt'ər) *n.* a person or thing that generates; specif., a) a machine for producing gas or steam b) a machine for changing mechanical energy into electrical energy; dynamo

gen·er·a·trix (jen'ə rā triks) *n., pl.* **-er·a'tri·ces'**(-ə rā'trə sēs') *Math.* a point, line, or plane whose motion generates a line, plane, figure, or solid

ge·ner·ic (jə ner'ik) *adj.* [< ML.: see GENUS & -IC] 1. of, applied to, or referring to a whole kind, class, or group; inclusive or general 2. that is not a trademark 3. *Biol.* of or characteristic of a genus —**gen·er'i·cal·ly** *adv.*

gen·er·os·i·ty (jen'ə ros'ə tē) *n.* 1. the quality of being generous; specif., a) magnanimity b) unselfishness 2. *pl.* **-ties** a generous act

gen·er·ous (jen'ər əs) *adj.* [L. *generosus*, of noble birth, excellent < *genus*: see GENUS] 1. noble-minded; gracious; magnanimous 2. willing to give or share; unselfish 3. large; ample [*generous* portions] 4. full-flavoured and strong: said of wine —**gen'er·ous·ly** *adv.* —**gen'er·ous·ness** *n.*

gen·e·sis (jen'ə sis) *n., pl.* **-ses** (-sēz') [< OE. & LL. < L. < Gr. < *gignesthai*, to be born] a beginning; origin —[G-] the book of the Bible, giving an account of the Creation

-gen·e·sis (jen'ə sis) *a combining form meaning* origination, creation, evolution (of something specified)

gen·et (jen'ət) *n.* *same as* JENNET

gen·et, gen·ette (jen'ət, jə net') *n.* [ME. < OFr. *genette* < Sp. *gineta* < Ar. *jarnayt*] 1. any of a genus of small, spotted African animals related to the civet 2. the fur of any of these

ge·net·ic (jə net'ik) *adj.* [< GENESIS] 1. of the genesis, or origin, of something 2. of genetics Also **ge·net'i·cal** —**ge·net'i·cal·ly** *adv.*

genetic code the order in which four chemical constituents are arranged in DNA molecules for transmitting genetic information to the cells

ge·net·ics (-iks) *n.pl.* [with sing. v.] [< GENETIC] the branch of biology that deals with heredity and variation in similar or related animals and plants —**ge·net'i·cist** (-ə sist) *n.*

Ge·ne·va bands (jə nē'və) [after the clerical garb of the Geneva Calvinists] two white linen strips hanging from the front of the collar, worn by some Protestant clergymen

Geneva Convention an international agreement signed at Geneva in 1864, establishing a code, later revised, for the care and protection in wartime of the sick, wounded, and prisoners of war

Geneva gown [cf. GENEVA BANDS] a long, loose,

wide-sleeved black gown, worn by many Protestant clergymen

ge·nial¹ (jēn'yəl, jē'nē əl) *adj.* [L. *genialis*, of birth < *genius*, GENIUS] 1. promoting life and growth; warm and mild [*a genial* climate] 2. cheerful, friendly, and sympathetic; amiable —**ge·ni·al·i·ty** (jē'nē al'ə tē) *n.* —**ge'nial·ly** *adv.*

ge·ni·al² (ji nī'əl) *adj.* [< Gr. *geneian*, a chin, + -AL] of the chin

gen·ic (jen'ik) *adj.* of, or relating to, genes; genetic

-gen·ic (jen'ik) *a combining form*: 1. *used to form adjectives corresponding to nouns ending in* -GEN *or* -GENY [*phylogenic*] 2. *meaning* suitable to [*photogenic*]

ge·nie (jē'nē) *n.* [Fr. *génie*] *same as* JINNI

gen·i·tal (jen'ə t'l) *adj.* [< OFr. < L. *genitalis* < pp. of *genere*, *gignere*, to beget] 1. of reproduction or the sexual organs 2. *Psychoanalysis* of an early stage of psychosexual development focusing on the genital organs

gen·i·tals (-t'lz) *n.pl.* [< prec.] the reproductive organs; esp., the external sex organs: also **gen'i·ta'li·a** (-tāl'yə, -tā'-lē ə)

gen·i·tive (jen'ə tiv) *adj.* [< OFr. < L. (*casus*) *genitivus*, lit., case of origin] designating, of, or in a case, as in Latin, shown by grammatical inflection or by analytical construction and typically expressing possession, source, etc. —*n.* 1. the genitive case 2. a word or construction in the genitive case —**gen'i·ti'val** (-tī'v'l) *adj.* —**gen'i·ti'val·ly** *adv.*

gen·i·to·u·ri·nar·y (jen'ə tō yoor'ənər ē) *adj.* designating or of the genital and urinary organs together

ge·ni·us (jē'nē əs, jēn'yəs) *n.*, *pl.* **ge'nius·es** for 3, 4, 5; **ge·ni·i** (jē'nē ī') for 1 & 2 [L., guardian spirit < base of *genere*, *gignere*, to produce] 1. a) [*often* G-] the guardian spirit of a person, place, etc. b) either of two spirits, one good and one evil, supposed to influence one's destiny c) a person considered as having strong influence over another 2. *same as* JINNI 3. particular character or spirit of a nation, place, age, etc. 4. a great natural ability or strong inclination (*for*) 5. a) great mental and inventive ability b) a person having this c) popularly, any person with a very high intelligence quotient

gen·o·cide (jen'ə sīd') *n.* [< Gr. *genos*, race, kind + -CIDE] the systematic killing of, or a programme of action intended to destroy, a whole national or ethnic group —**gen'o·ci'dal** (-sī'd'l) *adj.*

-gen·ous (jə nəs) [-GEN + -OUS] *a suffix meaning*: 1. producing, generating [*nitrogenous*] 2. produced by, generated in [*autogenous*]

gen·re (zhon'rə; Fr. zhän'r') *n.* [Fr. < L. *genus*: see GENUS] 1. a kind, or type, as of works of literature, art, etc. 2. *same as* GENRE PAINTING

genre painting painting in which subjects from everyday life are treated realistically

gens (jenz) *n.*, *pl.* **gen·tes** (jen'tēz) [L. < *gignere*, to beget] 1. in ancient Rome, a clan united by descent through the male line from a common ancestor 2. any tribe or clan

gent (jent) *n.* [Colloq.] a gentleman; man

gen·teel (jen tēl') *adj.* [< Fr. *gentil* < L. *gentilis*: see GENTLE] 1. formerly, elegant or fashionable 2. excessively or affectedly refined, polite, etc. —**gen·teel'ly** *adv.* —**gen·teel'ness** *n.*

gen·tian (jen'shən) *n.* [< OFr. < L. *gentiana*] 1. any of a large genus of plants with blue, white, red, or yellow flowers 2. the bitter root of the yellow gentian

gentian violet a violet dye used as an antiseptic and as a stain in microscopy

gen·tile (jen'tīl) *n.* [< Fr. *gentil* & L. *gentilis*, of the same gens, or clan] [*also* G-] 1. any person not a Jew; specif., a Christian 2. formerly, among Christians, a heathen or pagan 3. among Mormons, any person not a Mormon —*adj.* [*also* G-] 1. not Jewish 2. heathen; pagan 3. not Mormon

gen·til·i·ty (jen til'ə tē) *n.*, *pl.* **-ties** [< OFr. < L. < *gentilis*: see ff.] 1. the condition of belonging by birth to the upper classes 2. the quality of being genteel

gen·tle (jent''l) *adj.* **-tler**, **-tlest** [< OFr. < L. *gentilis*, of the same clan < *gens*, GENS] 1. of the upper classes or polite society 2. like or suitable to polite society; refined, courteous, etc. 3. [Archaic] noble; chivalrous [*a gentle* knight] 4. generous; kind 5. easily handled; tame [*a gentle* dog] 6. kindly; patient [*a gentle* disposition] 7. not violent or harsh [*a gentle* tap] 8. gradual [*a gentle* slope] —*n.* a maggot used for fishing bait —*vt.* **-tled**, **-tling** 1. to tame or train (a horse) 2. to calm as by stroking —**gen'-tle·ness** *n.* —**gen'tly** *adv.*

gen·tle·folk (-fōk') *n.pl.* people of high social standing: also **gen'tle·folks**

gen·tle·man (-mən) *n.*, *pl.* **-men** 1. a) orig., a man born into a family of high social standing b) any man of independent means who does not work for a living [*country gentleman*] 2. a courteous, gracious man 3. a valet: chiefly in **gentleman's gentleman** 4. any man: polite term, as (chiefly in pl.) of address

gen·tle·man-farm·er (-fär'mər) *n.*, *pl.* **gen'tle·men-farm'-ers** a wealthy man who owns and manages a farm as an avocation

gen·tle·man·ly (-lē) *adj.* of, characteristic of, or fit for a gentleman; well-mannered: also **gen'tle·man·like'** —**gen'-tle·man·li·ness** *n.*

gentlemen's (or gentleman's) agreement an unwritten agreement secured only by the parties' pledge of honour and not legally binding

gen·tle·wom·an (jent''l woom'ən) *n.*, *pl.* **-wom'en** 1. orig., a woman born into a family of high social standing; lady 2. [Now Rare] a courteous, gracious, considerate woman 3. formerly, a woman in attendance on a lady of rank

gen·try (jen'trē) *n.* [< OFr. *genterise*, ult. < L. *gentilis*: see GENTLE] 1. people of high social standing; esp., in Great Britain, the class of landowning people ranking just below the nobility 2. people of a particular class or group, esp. one considered to be inferior

gents (jentz) *n.pl.* [*with sing. v.*] [Colloq.] a men's lavatory

gen·u·flect (jen'yoo flekt') *vi.* [< ML. < L. *genu*, the knee + *flectere*, to bend] 1. to bend the knee, as in reverence or worship 2. to act submissively —**gen'u·flec'tion**, **gen'-u·flex'ion** (-flek'shən) *n.* —**gen'u·flec'tor** *n.* —**gen'u·flec'-to·ry** *adj.*

gen·u·ine (jen'yoo wən) *adj.* [L. *genuinus* < base of *gignere*, to be born] 1. of the original stock; purebred 2. really being what it is said to be; true; authentic 3. sincere and frank; honest —**gen'u·ine·ly** *adv.* —**gen'u·ine·ness** *n.*

ge·nus (jē'nəs) *n.*, *pl.* **gen·er·a** (jen'ər ə), **sometimes ge'-nus·es** [L., birth, origin, race, kind] 1. a class; kind; sort 2. *Biol.* a classification of plants or animals with common distinguishing characteristics: a genus is the main subdivision of a family and includes one or more species; the genus name is capitalized, the species name is not (Ex.: *Homo sapiens*, modern man) 3. *Logic* a class of things made up of subordinate classes, or species

-gen·y (jə nē) [< Gr.: see -GEN] *a suffix meaning* origin, production, development [*phylogeny*]

Geo. George

ge·o- [Gr. *geō-* < *gaia*, *gē*, the earth] *a combining form meaning*: 1. earth, of the earth [*geocentric*] 2. geographical [*geopolitics*]

ge·o·cen·tric (jē'ō sen'trik) *adj.* [prec. + -CENTRIC] 1. measured or viewed as from the centre of the earth 2. having or regarding the earth as a centre Also **ge'o·cen'-tri·cal** —**ge'o·cen'tri·cal·ly** *adv.*

ge·o·chro·nol·o·gy (-krə nol'ə jē) *n.* [GEO- + CHRONOLOGY] the branch of geology dealing with the age of the earth and its materials, the dating of evolutionary stages in plant and animal development, etc. —**ge'o·chron·o·log'i·cal** (-kron'ə loj'ik'l) *adj.*

ge·ode (jē'ōd) *n.* [Fr. *géode* < L. *geodes*, a precious stone < Gr. *geoeidēs*, earthlike] 1. a globular stone having a cavity lined with inward-growing crystals or layers of silica 2. a) such a cavity b) any formation like this —**ge·od'ic** (od'ik) *adj.*

ge·o·des·ic (jē'ə des'ik, -dē'sik) *adj.* 1. *same as* GEODETIC (sense 1) 2. designating the shortest line between two points on a surface, esp. a curved surface —*n.* a geodesic line

ge·od·e·sy (jē od'ə sē) *n.* [< Gr. < *gē*, the earth + *daiein*, to divide] the branch of applied mathematics concerned with measuring, or determining the shape, of the earth or a large part of its surface, or with locating exactly points on its surface —**ge·od'e·sist** *n.*

ge·o·det·ic (jē'ə det'ik) *adj.* 1. of or determined by geodesy 2. *same as* GEODESIC (sense 2) Also **ge'o·det'i·cal** —**ge'-o·det'i·cal·ly** *adv.*

geog. 1. geographic(al) 2. geography

ge·o·graph·i·cal (jē'ə graf'ik'l) *adj.* 1. of or according to geography 2. with reference to the geography of a particular region Also **ge'o·graph'ic** —**ge'o·graph'i·cal·ly** *adv.*

geographical mile *same as* NAUTICAL MILE

ge·og·ra·phy (jē og'rə fē) *n.*, *pl.* **-phies** [< L. < Gr. < *geō-*, GEO- + *graphein*, to write] 1. the science dealing with the surface of the earth, its division into continents and countries, and the climate, plants, animals, natural resources, people, and industries of the various divisions 2. the physical features of a region or place 3. a book about geography —**ge·og'ra·pher** *n.*

ge·oid (jē'oid) *n.* [G. *geoide* < Gr. *geoeidēs*, earthlike] the earth viewed as a hypothetical ellipsoid with the surface represented as a mean sea level

geol. 1. geologic(al) 2. geologist 3. geology

ge·o·log·ic (jē'ə loj'ik) *adj.* of or according to geology: also **ge'o·log'i·cal** —**ge'o·log'i·cal·ly** *adv.*

ge·ol·o·gy (jē ol'ə jē) *n.*, *pl.* **-gies** [< ML.: see GEO-& -LOGY] 1. the science dealing with the physical nature of the earth, including the structure and development of its crust and interior, types of rocks, fossil forms, etc. 2. the structure of

Geologic Time Chart

MAIN DIVISIONS OF GEOLOGIC TIME			PRINICIPAL PHYSICAL & BIOLOGICAL FEATURES
ERAS	PERIODS or SYSTEMS		
		Epochs or Series	
CAINOZOIC	QUATERNARY	Recent 12,000*	Glaciers restricted to Antartica and Greenland; development and spread of modern human culture.
		Pleistocene 600,000	Great glaciers covered much of Northern Hemisphere; appearance of modern man late in Pleistocene.
	TERTIARY	Pliocene 10,000,000	W North America uplifted; continued development of mammals; first possible apelike men appeared in Africa.
		Miocene 25,000,000	Renewed uplift of Alpine mountains: mammals began to acquire present-day characters; dogs, solid-hoofed horses, manlike apes appeared.
		Oligocene 35,000,000	Many older types of mammals became extinct; mastodons, first monkeys, and apes appeared.
		Eocene 55,000,000	Alpine mountain building (Himalayas, Alps, Andes, Rockies); expansion of early mammals; primitive horses appeared.
		Paleocene 65,000,000	Great development of primitive mammals.
MESOZOIC	CRETACEOUS 135,000,000		Chalk deposits laid down; dinosaurs reached maximum development & then became extinct; mammals small & very primitive.
	JURASSIC 180,000,000		Rocks of S and C Europe laid down; conifers & cycads dominant among plants; primitive birds appeared.
	TRIASSIC 230,000,000		Modern corals appeared & some insects of present-day types; great expansion of reptiles including earliest dinosaurs.
PALEOZOIC	PERMIAN 280,000,000		Trees of coal-forming forests declined; ferns abundant; conifers present; trilobites became extinct; reptiles surpassed amphibians.
	CARBONIFEROUS	UPPER CARBONIFEROUS 310,000,000	Hercynian mountain building (C Europe, E coast of North America); great coal-forming swamp forests flourished in N Hemisphere; seed-bearing terns abundant; cockroaches & first reptiles appeared.
		LOWER CARBONIFEROUS 345,000,000	Land plants became diversified; crinoids achieved greatest development; sharks of relatively modern types appeared; land animals little known.
	DEVONIAN 405,000,000		Land plants evolved rapidly, large trees appeared; brachiopods reached maximum development; many kinds of primitive fishes; first sharks, insects, & amphibians appeared.
	SILURIAN 425,000,000		Great mountains formed in NW Europe; first small land plants appeared; shelled cephalopods abundant; trilobites began decline; first jawed fish appeared.
	ORDOVICIAN 500,000,000		Caledonian mountain building; much limestone deposited in shallow seas; many marine invertebrates, first primitive jawless fish appeared.
	CAMBRIAN 600,000,000		Shallow seas covered parts of continents; abundant record of marine life, esp. trilobites & brachiopods; other fossils rare.
PRECAMBRIAN	LATE PRECAMBRIAN** 2,000,000,000		Metamorphosed sedimentary rocks and granite formed; first evidence of life, calcareous algae & invertebrates.
	EARLY PRECAMBRIAN** 4,500,000,000		Crust formed on molten earth; crystalline rocks much disturbed; history unknown.

* Figures indicate approximate number of years since the beginning of each division.　　　　** Regarded as separate eras.

the earth's crust in a given region or place **3.** a book about geology —**ge·ol'o·gist** *n.*

geom. 1. geometric(al) **2.** geometry

ge·o·mag·net·ic (jē'ō mag net'ik) *adj.* of or pertaining to the magnetic properties of the earth —**ge'o·mag'ne·tism** *n.*

ge·o·met·ric (jē'ə met'rik) *adj.* **1.** of or according to geometry **2.** characterized by straight lines, triangles, circles, etc., as a pattern Also **ge'o·met'ri·cal** —**ge'o·met'·ri·cal·ly** *adv.*

geometric progression a sequence of terms in which the ratio of each term to the preceding one is the same throughout (Ex.: 1, 2, 4, 8, etc.)

ge·om·e·trid (jē om'ə trid) *n.* [< ModL. < L. < Gr. < *geōmetrein:* see ff.] any of a family of moths whose larvae move by looping the body

ge·om·e·try (jē om'ə trē) *n., pl.* **-tries** [< OFr. < L. < Gr. *geōmetrein* < *gē*, earth + *metrein*, to measure] **1.** the branch of mathematics that deals with points, lines, surfaces, and solids, and examines their properties, measurement, and mutual relations in space **2.** a book about geometry —**ge·om'e·tri'cian** (-trish'ən), **ge·om'·e·ter** *n.*

ge·o·mor·phol·o·gy (-môr fol'ə jē) *n* [GEO- + MORPHOLOGY] the science dealing with the nature and origin of the earth's topographic features —**ge'o·mor·pho·log'ic** (-môr'fə loj'-ik), **ge'o·mor·pho·log'i·cal** *adj.*

ge·o·phys·ics (jē'ō fiz'iks) *n.pl.* [with sing. v.] the science that deals with weather, winds, tides, etc. and their effect on the earth —**ge'o·phys'i·cal** *adj.* —**ge'o·phys'i·cist** *n.*

ge·o·pol·i·tics (jē'ō pol'ə tiks) *n.pl.* [with sing. v.] [< G. *geopolitik*] **1.** the interrelationship of politics and geography, or the study of this **2.** any programme or policy, as for expansion, based on this —**ge'o·po·lit'i·cal** (-pə lit'i k'l) *adj.* —**ge'o·po·lit'i·cal·ly** *adv.* —**ge'o·pol'i·ti'·cian** *n.*

George Cross (jôrj) an award for bravery, esp. of civilians, instituted during World War II

geor·gette (jôr jet') *n.* [after *Georgette* de la Plante, Parisian modiste] a kind of thin crepe fabric, used for dresses, etc.: also **georgette crepe**

Geor·gian (jôr'jən; -jē ən) *adj.* **1.** *a)* of the reigns of George I, II, III, and IV of Britain (1714-1830) *b)* of the reigns of George V and VI of Britain (1910-52) **2.** of the Georgian S.S.R., its people, language, or culture **3.** of the state of Georgia, U.S. —*n.* **1.** *a)* a native or inhabitant of the Georgian S.S.R. *b)* the South Caucasian language of the Georgians **2.** a native or inhabitant of the state of Georgia, U.S.

ge·o·stat·ics (jē'ō stat'iks, jē'ə-) *n.pl.* [with sing. v.] [< GEO- + STATIC] the branch of physics dealing with the mechanics of the equilibrium of forces in rigid bodies

ge·o·sta·tion·ar·y (jē ō stā'shə nər ē) *adj.* [GEO- + STATIONARY] orbiting at such a speed that it appears to be stationary above the earth's surface: said of an artificial satellite

ge·o·stroph·ic (jē'ō strof'ik) *adj.* [< GEO- + Gr. *strophē*, a twist; turning + -IC] designating of or a force producing deflection as a result of the earth's rotation

ge·ot·ro·pism (jē ot'rə piz'm) *n.* [GEO- + -TROPISM] movement or growth in response to the force of gravity, either downwards, as of plant roots (**positive geotropism**), or upwards, as of stems (**negative geotropism**) —**ge·o·trop·ic** (jē'ə trop'ik) *adj.*

Ger. 1. German **2.** Germany

ger. 1. gerund **2.** gerundive

Ger·ald·ton waxflower (jer'ald tən) a W Australian cultivated shrub bearing pink, waxy flowers

ge·ra·ni·um (jə rā'nē əm, -rān'yəm) *n.* [L. < Gr. *geranion*, cranesbill: its seed capsule is beaked] **1.** a plant with showy pink or purple flowers and leaves with many lobes **2.** pop. name for a pelargonium **3.** an intense red colour

ger·bil, ger·bille (jʉr'b'l) *n.* [Fr. *gerbille* < ModL. *gerbillus* < *gerbo*, JERBOA] any of a subfamily of burrowing rodents related to the mouse, with long hind legs and tail, native to Africa and Asia

ger·fal·con (jʉr'fol'k'n, -fôl'-, -fô'-) *n.* same as GYRFALCON

ger·i·at·rics (jer'ē at'riks) *n.pl.* [with sing. v.] [< Gr. *gēras*, old age + -IATRICS] the branch of medicine that deals with the diseases and hygiene of old age —**ger'i·at'ric** *adj.* —**ger'i·a·tri'cian** (-ə trish'ən), **ger'i·at'rist** *n.*

germ (jʉrm) *n.* [< OFr. < L. *germen*, a sprout, bud] **1.** the rudimentary form from which a new organism is developed; seed, bud, etc. **2.** any microscopic organism, esp. one of the bacteria, that can cause disease **3.** that from which something can develop [the germ of an idea] —**germ'less** *adj.*

Ger·man (jʉr'mən) *adj.* [< L. *Germanus*, prob. < Celt.] of Germany, its people, language, or culture —*n.* **1.** a native or inhabitant of Germany **2.** the German language now spoken chiefly in Germany, Austria, and Switzerland, technically called New High German

ger·man (jʉr'mən) *adj.* [< OFr. < L. *germanus*, akin to

germen, GERM] closely related: now chiefly in compounds, meaning: *a)* having the same parents [a brother-*german*] *b)* being a first cousin [a cousin-*german*]

ger·man·der (jər man'dər) *n.* [< OFr. < ML. *germandra*, < Gr. < *chamai*, on the ground + *drys*, tree] any of a genus of plants with spikes of flowers that lack an upper lip

ger·mane (jər mān') *adj.* [var. of GERMAN] truly relevant; pertinent; to the point

Ger·man·ic (jər man'ik) *adj.* **1.** of Germany or the Germans; German **2.** designating of or the original language of the German peoples or the languages descended from it; Teutonic —*n.* **1.** the original language of the Germanic peoples: now called **Proto-Germanic** **2.** a principal branch of the Indo-European family of languages, comprising this language and the languages descended from it, including Norwegian, Icelandic, Swedish, Danish (all *North Germanic*), German, Dutch, Flemish, Frisian, English (all *West Germanic*), the extinct Gothic (*East Germanic*), etc. —**Ger·man'ic·ism** *n.*

ger·ma·ni·um (jər mā'nē əm) *n.* [ModL. < L. *Germania*, Germany] a rare, greyish-white, metallic chemical element that can be a semiconductor: symbol, Ge; at. wt., 72.59; at. no., 32

Ger·man·ize (jʉr'mə nīz') *vt., vi.* **-ized', -iz'ing** to make or become German in character, thought, language, etc. —**Ger'·man·i·za'tion** *n.*

German measles same as RUBELLA

Ger·man·o- a combining form meaning German, of Germany, or of the Germans

German shepherd dog same as ALSATIAN

German silver same as NICKEL SILVER

germ cell a cell from which a new organism can develop; egg or sperm cell

ger·mi·cide (jʉr'mə sīd') *n.* [< GERM + -CIDE] anything used to destroy germs —**ger'mi·ci'dal** *adj.*

ger·mi·nal (jʉr'mə n'l) *adj.* **1.** of, like, or characteristic of germs or germ cells **2.** in the first stage of growth or development —**ger'mi·nal·ly** *adv.*

ger·mi·nate (-nāt') *vi., vt.* **-nat'ed, -nat'ing** [< L. pp. of *germinare* < *germen*, GERM] **1.** to sprout or cause to sprout, as from a seed **2.** to start developing or growing —**ger'mi·na'tion** *n.* —**ger'mi·na'tive** *adj.* —**ger'mi·na'tor** *n.*

germ plasm the reproductive cells of an organism, particularly that part of the cells involved in heredity

germ warfare the deliberate contamination of enemy territory with disease germs in warfare

ger·on·tol·o·gy (jer'ən tol'ə jē) *n.* [< Gr. < *gerōn*, old man + -LOGY] the scientific study of the process of aging and of the problems of aged people —**ge·ron·to·log'i·cal** (jə ron'-tə loj'i k'l) *adj.* —**ger'on·tol'o·gist** *n.*

-ger·ous (jər əs) [L. -*ger* < *gerere*, to bear + -OUS] a suffix meaning producing or bearing

ger·ry·man·der (jer'i man'dər) *vt.* [< E. *Gerry*, governor of Massachusetts, U.S. when the method was employed (1812) + SALAMANDER (the shape of the redrawn electoral district)] **1.** to divide (a voting area) so as to give one political party a majority in as many electoral districts as possible **2.** to manipulate unfairly so as to gain advantage —*vi.* to engage in gerrymandering —*n.* the act or result of gerrymandering —**ger'ry·man'der·er** *n.*

ger·und (jer'ənd) *n.* [< LL. < L. *gerundus* < *gerere*, to do or carry out] *Gram.* a verbal noun ending in -*ing*, that is used like a noun but is able, like a verb, to take an object or an adverbial modifier (Ex.: *playing* in 'Playing golf is his only exercise") —**ge·run'di·al** (jə run'dē əl) *adj.*

ge·run·dive (jə run'div) *n.* [< LL. < prec.] **1.** a Latin verbal adjective with a typical gerund stem form, used as a future passive participle expressing duty, necessity, fitness, etc. **2.** a similar form in any language —**ge·run·di·val** (jer'ən dī'vəl) *adj.*

ges·so (jes'ō) *n.* [It., *gypsum*, chalk < L. *gypsum*, GYPSUM] plaster of Paris prepared for use in sculpture or bas-reliefs, or as a surface for painting

gest, geste (jest) *n.* [< OFr. < L. *gesta*, deeds, pl. pp. of *gerere*, to do, act] **1.** [Archaic] an adventure; exploit **2.** a romantic story of adventure, esp. a medieval tale in verse

ges·ta·gen (jest'ə jən) *n.* [< *gestation* (see GESTATE) + -GEN] *Med.* any substance which can induce hormonal changes resembling those of ovulation

Ge·stalt psychology (gə shtält', -stält', -stôlt') [G., lit., shape, form] a school of psychology, orig. German, based on the idea that the response of an individual in a given situation is a response to the whole situation, not to its components

Ge·sta·po (gə stä'pō; G. gə shtä'-) *n.* [< G. *Ge(heime) Sta(ats)po(lizei)*, secret state police] the secret police force of the German Nazi state

ges·tate (jes'tāt, jes tāt') *vt.* **-tat·ed, -tat·ing** [< L. pp. of *gestare*, freq. of *gerere*, to bear] to carry in the uterus during pregnancy —**ges·ta'tion** *n.*

ges·tic·u·late (jes tik'yə lāt') *vi.* **-lat·ed, -lat'ing** [< L. pp. of *gesticulari*, to gesture, ult. < pp. of *gerere*, to bear, do] to make or use gestures, esp. with the hands or arms, as in adding force to one's speech —*vt.* to express by gesticulating —**ges·tic′u·la′tive** *adj.* —**ges·tic′u·la′tor** *n.*

ges·tic·u·la·tion (jes tik′yə lā′shən) *n.* l. a gesticulating 2. a gesture, esp. an energetic one —**ges·tic′u·la·to·ry** (-lə tər ē) *adj.*

ges·ture (jes′chər) *n.* [< ML. < L. pp. of *gerere*, to bear, do] l. a movement of the body, or of part of the body, to express or emphasize ideas, emotions, etc. 2. anything said or done to convey a state of mind or intention, sometimes something said or done only for effect —*vi.* -tured, -tur·ing to with gestures —**ges′tur·al** *adj.* —**ges′tur·er** *n.*

get (get) *vt.* **got** or archaic **gat, got** or archaic and U.S. **got′-ten, get′ting** [< ON. *geta*] l. to come into the state of having; receive, win, gain, obtain, acquire, etc. 2. to reach; arrive at [to get home early] 3. to set up communication with, as by radio [to get Paris] 4. to go and bring [get your books] 5. to catch; capture; gain hold of 6. to learn; commit to memory 7. to persuade (a person) to do something [get him to leave] 8. to cause to act in a certain way [get the door to shut properly] 9. to cause to be or arrive [he got his hands dirty, he got it there on time] 10. to be sentenced to [he got ten years] 11. to prepare [to get lunch] 12. to give birth to; beget: usually said of animals 13. [Colloq.] to be obliged to; feel a necessity to (with *have* or *has*) [he's got to pass] 14. [Colloq.] to own; possess (with *have* or *has*) [he's got red hair] 15. [Colloq.] to be or become the master of; esp., *a*) to overpower [his illness finally got him] *b*) to puzzle; baffle [this problem gets me] *c*) to take into custody, wound, or kill 16. [Colloq.] to strike; hit [the blow got him in the eye] 17. [Colloq.] to catch the meaning or import of; understand 18. [Slang] to cause an emotional response in; irritate, please, thrill, etc. [her singing gets me] 19. [Slang] to notice [get the look on his face] —*vi.* l. to come or arrive [to get to work on time] 2. to come to be (doing something); come to be (in a situation, condition, etc.) [he got caught in the rain] 3. to contrive [to get to do something] 4. [Slang] to leave at once; used chiefly in the imperative *Get* is used as an informal auxiliary for emphasis in passive construction [we got beaten] —*n.* l. the young of an animal; offspring 2. [Now Rare] a begetting 3. [Slang] same as GIT —**get about** l. to move from place to place 2. to go to many social events, places, etc. 3. to circulate widely, as news —**get across** [Colloq.] l. to explain convincingly 2. to succeed, as in making oneself understood —**get around** to get about (in all senses) —**get at** l. to approach or reach 2. to apply oneself to [let's get at the work] 3. to imply 4. [Colloq.] to influence by bribery or intimidation 5. [Colloq.] to find fault; criticise, esp. in an indirect manner —**get away** l. to go away; leave 2. to escape 3. to start —**get away with** [Slang] to succeed in doing or taking without being discovered or punished —**get back** l. to return 2. to recover 3. [Slang] to get revenge (usually with *at*) —**get by** l. to be just acceptable 2. [Colloq.] to succeed without being discovered or punished 3. [Colloq.] to survive; manage —**get down to** to begin to consider or act on —**get in** l. to enter; join 2. to arrive 3. to put in —**get off** l. to come off, down, or out of 2. to leave; go away 3. to take off 4. to escape 5. to help to escape punishment 6. to start, as in a race —**get off with** [Colloq.] to establish a friendly or sexual relationship with —**get on** l. to go on or into 2. to put on 3. to proceed 4. to grow older 5. to succeed; make progress 6. to agree —**get out** l. to go out 2. to go away 3. to take out 4. to become no longer a secret 5. to publish —**get over** l. to recover from 2. to overcome —**get round** l. to circumvent 2. to gain favour with, or influence, by cajolery, flattery, etc. —**get round to** to get started on after a delay; find time for —**get somewhere** to succeed —**get through** l. to finish 2. to manage to survive 3. to push through 4. to make oneself clear (*to*) —**get together** l. to bring or come together; assemble 2. [Colloq.] to reach an agreement —**get up** l. to rise (from a chair, from sleep, etc.) 2. to contrive; organize 3. to dress elaborately 4. to intensify; develop [the wind got up] 5. [Colloq.] work at; learn [I must get up my maths for the exam] —**get′ta·ble, get′a·ble** *adj.* —**get′ter** *n.*

get·a·way (get′ə wā′) *n.* l. the act of starting, as in a race 2. the act of escaping, as from police

get-to·geth·er (get′tə geth′ər) *n.* an informal social gathering or meeting

get-up (get′up′) *n.* [Colloq.] l. general arrangement or composition 2. costume; outfit; dress

get-up-and-go (get′up′n gō′) *n.* [Colloq.] energy; drive; initiative

ge·um (jē′əm) *n.* [ModL. < L.] a genus of perennial plants of the rose type, including the herb-bennets or avens

gew·gaw (gyoo′gô, goo′-) *n.* [ME. *giuegoue, gugaw* < ?] something showy but useless; trinket

gey·ser (gī′zər, gā′-; *for 2, always* gē′-) *n.* [Ice. *Geysir*, a hot spring in Iceland, lit., gusher < ON. *gjosa*, to gush] l. a

spring from which columns of boiling water and steam gush into the air at intervals 2. a small, domestic, gas water heater

ghar·ry, ghar·ri (gar′ē) *n., pl.* **-ries** [Hindi *gāri*] in India, a horse-drawn or motorized cab for hire

ghast·ly (gäst′lē) *adj.* **-li·er, -li·est** [< OE. < *gast*, spirit, ghost] l. horrible; frightful 2. ghostlike; pale 3. [Colloq.] very unpleasant —*adv.* in a ghastly manner —**ghast′li·ness** *n.*

ghat, ghaut (gôt) *n.* [Hindi *ghāt*] in India, l. a mountain pass 2. a flight of steps leading down to a river landing for ritual bathers

gha·zi (gä′zē) *n.* [Ar. *ghāzi*, pp. of *ghazā*, to fight] a Moslem hero, esp. one who wars against the infidels

ghee (gē) *n.* [Hindi *ghī*] in India, a liquid butter specially made from cow's milk or buffalo milk

gher·a·o (gerä′ō, gerou′) *n., pl.* **-s** [< Hindi *gherna*, to encircle, besiege] a tactic practised in industrial disputes in India and Pakistan, by which employees detain their employers, etc., on their premises until their demands are met

gher·kin (gur′kin) *n.* [< Du. or LowG. *gurken*, ult. < Per. *angārah*] l. a tropical American cucumber bearing small, prickly fruit, used for pickles 2. the immature fruit of any cucumber when pickled

ghet·to (get′ō) *n., pl.* **-tos, -toes** [It., lit., foundry, ult. < L. *jactare*, to cast: the former Jewish quarter on a foundry site in Venice] l. in certain European cities, a section to which Jews were formerly restricted 2. any section of a city in which many members of some minority group live, or to which they are restricted by discrimination

ghil·lie (gil′ē) *n.* same as GILLIE

ghost (gōst) *n.* [OE. *gast*] l. orig., the spirit or soul: now only in **give up the ghost** (to die) and in HOLY GHOST 2. the supposed disembodied spirit of a dead person, conceived of as appearing to the living as a pale, shadowy apparition 3. a haunting memory 4. a faint semblance; slight trace [not a ghost of a chance] 5. [Colloq.] same as GHOSTWRITER 6. *Optics & TV* an unwanted secondary image or bright spot —*vi.* [Colloq.] to work as a ghostwriter —*vt.* l. to haunt 2. [Colloq.] to be the ghostwriter of —**ghost′hood′** *n.* —**ghost′like′** *adj.* —**ghost′li·ness** *n.* —**ghost′ly** *adj.* **-lier, -liest**

ghost town the remains of a town that has been permanently abandoned, esp. for economic reasons

ghost word [term invented by W.W. Skeat] a word created through a misprint or error in copying

ghost·writ·er (-rīt′ər) *n.* a person who writes speeches, articles, etc. for another who professes to be the author —**ghost′write′** *vt., vi.* **-wrote′, -writ′ten, -writ′ing**

ghoul (gool) *n.* [Ar. *ghūl*, demon < *ghāla*, to seize] l. *Oriental Folklore* an evil spirit that robs graves and feeds on the dead 2. a robber of graves 3. one who enjoys things that disgust or trouble most people —**ghoul′ish** *adj.* —**ghoul′ish·ly** *adv.* —**ghoul′ish·ness** *n.*

GHQ, G.H.Q. General Headquarters

ghyll (gil) *n.* var. of GILL[3]

GI (jē′ī′) *adj.* [Colloq.] of or characteristic of the U.S. armed forces —*n., pl.* **GI's, GIs** [Colloq.] any member of the U.S. armed forces

GI, G.I., g.i. gastrointestinal

gi. gill (unit of measure); gills

gi·ant (jī′ənt) *n.* [< ONormFr. < VL. < L. *gigas* < Gr.] l. any imaginary being of human form but of superhuman size and strength 2. a person or thing of great size, intellect, etc. —*adj.* of great size, strength, etc. —**gi′ant·ess** *n.fem.*

gi·ant·ism (-iz′m) *n.* abnormally great growth of the body, due to excessive production of growth hormone by the pituitary gland

giant panda a large, black-and-white, bearlike mammal of China and Tibet

giaour (jour) *n.* [< Turk. < Per. *gabr* < Ar. *kāfir*, infidel] in Moslem usage, a non-Moslem; esp., a Christian

gib (jib) *n.* [< ?] an adjustable piece of metal, etc., for keeping moving parts of a machine in place or for reducing friction —*vt.* **gibbed, gib′bing** to fasten or fit with a gib

Gib. [Colloq.] Gibraltar

gib·ber[1] (jib′ər) *vi., vt.* [echoic] to speak or utter rapidly and incoherently; chatter —*n.* unintelligible chatter; gibberish

GIANT PANDA
(1.2 m high at shoulder)

gib·ber[2] (gib′ər) *n.* [Abor.] [Aust.] a stone, rock

gib·ber·ish (jib′ər ish; gib′-) *n.* rapid and incoherent talk; unintelligible chatter; jargon

gib·bet (jib′it) *n.* [< OFr. dim. < Frank. *gibb*, forked stick] l. a gallows 2. a structure like a gallows, from which bodies of criminals already executed were hung and exposed to public scorn —*vt.* l. to execute by hanging 2. to hang on a gibbet 3. to expose to public scorn

gib·bon (gib′ən) *n.* [Fr.] a small, slender, long-armed ape of India, S China, and the East Indies, that lives in trees

gib·bous (gib′əs) *adj.* [< L. *gibbosus* < *gibba,* a hump] **1.** rounded and bulging **2.** designating the moon or a planet when more than half, but not all, of the disc is illuminated **3.** humpbacked —**gib·bos·i·ty** (gi bos′ə tē) *n.* —**gib′-bous·ly** *adv.*

gibe (jib) *vi., vt.* gibed, gib′ing [< ? OFr. *giber,* to handle roughly] to jeer, or taunt; scoff (at) —*n.* a jeer; taunt; scoff —**gib′er** *n.*

gib·let (jib′lit) *n.* [< OFr. *gibelet,* stew made of game] any of the parts of a fowl, as the heart, gizzard, neck, etc., usually cooked separately

gid·dy (gid′ē) *adj.* **-di·er, -di·est** [OE. *gydig,* insane, prob. < base of *god,* a god (i.e., "possessed by a god")] **1.** having a whirling, dazed sensation; dizzy **2.** causing such a sensation **3.** whirling **4.** *a)* inconstant; fickle *b)* frivolous; flighty —*vt., vi.* **-died, -dy·ing** to make or become giddy —**gid′-di·ly** *adv.* —**gid′di·ness** *n.*

gie (gē) *vt., vi.* gied or gae, gi·en (gē′ən), gie′ing [Scot. & Dial.] to give

gift (gift) *n.* [OE., wedding gift (< *giefan,* to give) & < ON. *gipt,* gift] **1.** something given to show friendship, affection, support etc.; present **2.** the act, power, or right of giving [in the *gift* of] **3.** a natural ability; talent —*vt.* to present with or as a gift —**look a gift horse in the mouth** to be critical of a gift or favour: from the practice of judging a horse's age by its teeth

gift coupon a voucher given on purchase of certain articles; a specified number may be collected and exchanged for a gift

gift·ed (-id) *adj.* **1.** having a natural ability; talented **2.** having superior intelligence

gift of tongues same as GLOSSOLALIA

gift token a voucher given as a present which the recipient can exchange for a gift of a certain value: also **gift voucher**

gift-wrap (-rap′) *vt.* -wrapped′, -wrap′ping to wrap as a gift, with decorative paper, ribbon, etc.

gig¹ (gig) *n.* [prob. < Scand.] **1.** a light, two-wheeled, open carriage drawn by one horse **2.** a long, light ship's boat —*vi.* gigged, gig′ging to travel in a gig

gig² (gig) *n.* [contr. < *fizgig* < Sp. *fisga,* kind of harpoon] a fish spear —*vt., vi.* gigged, gig′ging to spear or jab as with a gig

gig⁴ (gig) *n.* [< ?] [Slang] **1.** a job, esp. a single booking, to play or sing jazz, rock, etc. **2.** the performance itself

gi·ga- (jig′ə, gī-) [< Gr. *gigas,* giant] a combining form meaning one thousand million; 10⁹

gi·gan·tic (jī gan′tik) *adj.* [see GIANT] **1.** of, like, or fit for a giant **2.** huge; enormous; immense —**gi·gan′ti·cal·ly** *adv.*

gi·gan·tism (jī gan′tiz′m, jī′gan-) *n.* [see GIANT] **1.** the state of being gigantic **2.** same as GIANTISM

gig·gle (gig′l) *vi.* -gled, -gling [prob. < Du. *giggelen*] to laugh with uncontrollable, rapid, high-pitched sounds, suggestive of foolishness, nervousness, etc.; titter —*n.* such a laugh —**gig′gler** *n.* —**gig′gly** *adj.* -gli·er, -gli·est

gig·o·lo (zhig′ə lō, jig-) *n., pl.* -los [Fr.] a man paid by a woman to be her escort

gig·ot (jig′ət, zhē gō′) *n.* [Fr. < OFr., dim. < MHG. *giga,* fiddle] **1.** a leg of mutton, lamb, veal, etc. **2.** a leg-of-mutton sleeve

gigue (zhēg) *n.* [Fr.] a jig, esp. as a movement of a classical suite

Gi·la monster (hē′lə) [< the *Gila* River, Arizona] a stout, poisonous lizard covered with beadlike scales in alternating rings of black and orange: found in deserts of SW U.S.

gil·bert (gil′bərt) *n.* [after William G**il**bert (1540?-1603), Eng. physician] the cgs unit for magnetomotive force, equal to 0.7958 ampere-turn

gild¹ (gild) *vt.* gild′ed or gilt, gild′ing [OE. *gyldan* < base of *gold,* gold] **1.** *a)* to overlay with a thin layer of gold *b)* to coat with a gold colour **2.** to make appear bright and attractive **3.** to make (something) seem more attractive or valuable than it is —**gild′er** *n.*

gild² (gild) *n.* same as GUILD

gild·ing (gil′diŋ) *n.* **1.** the art or process of applying gold leaf or a substance like gold to a surface **2.** the substance so applied

gill¹ (gil) *n.* [prob. < Anglo-N.] **1.** the organ for breathing of most animals that live in water, as fish, lobsters, clams, etc. **2.** [pl.] *a)* the wattle of a fowl *b)* the jowl of a person **3.** a thin, leaflike, radiating plate on the undersurface of a mushroom —**gilled** *adj.*

gill² (jil) *n.* [< OFr. < LL. *gillo,* cooling vessel] a liquid measure, equal to 1/4 pint (0.142 litres)

GIBBON (46-63 cm long, head & body)

gill³ (gil) *n.* [ME. *gille* < ON. *gil*] **1.** a wooded ravine or glen **2.** a narrow stream; brook

gil·lie, gil·ly (gil′ē) *n., pl.* -lies [Scot. < Gael. *gille,* boy, page] **1.** in the Scottish Highlands, a sportsman's attendant **2.** a male servant

gil·li·flow·er (jil′ē flou′ər) *n.* [OFr. *gilofre* < LL. < Gr. < *karyon,* nut + *phyllon,* leaf] any of several plants with clove-scented flowers, as the clove pink: also sp. **gil·ly·flow′er**

gilt¹ (gilt) *alt. pt. & pp. of* GILD¹ —*adj.* overlaid with gilding —*n.* same as GILDING

gilt² (gilt) *n.* [ME. *gilte* < ON. *gyltr*] a young female pig; immature sow

gilt-edged (-ejd′) *adj.* **1.** having gilded edges **2.** of the highest quality, reliability or value [gilt-edged securities] Also **gilt′-edge′**

gim·bals (gim′b'lz, jim′-) *n.pl.* [with *sing. v.*] [< L. *gemellus,* dim. of *geminus,* twin] a pair of rings pivoted in axes at right angles to each other so that one is free to swing within the other: a ship's compass will keep a horizontal position when suspended in gimbals —**gim′balled** *adj.*

gim·crack (jim′krak′) *adj.* [altered < ME. *gibbecrak,* an ornament] showy but cheap and useless —*n.* a cheap, showy, useless thing; knickknack —**gim′crack′er·y** *n.*

gim·let (gim′lit) *n.* [< OFr. < MDu. dim. of *wimmel, wimble*] a small boring tool with a handle at right angles to a shaft with a spiral, pointed cutting edge —*vt.* to make a hole in as with a gimlet

gim·let-eyed (-īd′) *adj.* having a piercing glance

gim·mick (gim′ik) *n.* [< ?] **1.** any secret device, clever gadget, etc. **2.** any superficial feature designed to attract attention, interest or publicity —*vt.* to add gimmicks to —**gim′-mick·ry, gim′mick·er·y** *n.* —**gim′mick·y** *adj.*

gimp (gimp) *n.* [< ? Du.] a ribbonlike braided fabric, used to trim garments, furniture, etc.

GIMLET

gin¹ (jin) *n.* [< *geneva* < Du. *genever* < OFr. < L. *juniperus,* juniper] a strong alcoholic spirit distilled from grain and usually flavoured with juniper berries

gin² (jin) *n.* [< OFr., contr. < *engin,* ENGINE] **1.** a snare or trap, as for game **2.** a machine in which a vertical shaft is turned to drive a horizontal beam in a circle; used for lifting weights, etc. **3.** same as COTTON GIN —*vt.* ginned, gin′ning **1.** to catch in a trap **2.** to remove seeds from (cotton) with a gin —**gin′ner** *n.*

gin³ (jin) *vt., vi.* gan, gin′ning [ME. *ginnen* < OE. *beginnan,* to begin] [Archaic] to begin

gin⁴ (jin) *n.* same as GIN RUMMY —*vi.* ginned, gin′ning to win in gin rummy with no unmatched cards left in one's hand

gin⁵ (jin) *n.* [Abor.] [Aust.] an Aboriginal woman

gin·ger (jin′jər) *n.* [< OE. & OFr., both < ML. < L. *zingiber* < Gr. < Pali] **1.** an Asiatic plant grown for its aromatic rootstalk, used as a spice and in medicine **2.** the rootstalk, or the spice made from it **3.** a reddish-brown colour **4.** [Colloq.] vigour; spirit —**gin′ger·y** *adj.*

ginger ale a carbonated, sweet soft drink flavoured with ginger

ginger beer a drink like ginger ale but with a stronger flavour

gin·ger·bread (-bred′) *n.* [ME. *ginge bred* < *gingebras,* preserved ginger < OFr.] **1.** a cake flavoured with ginger and treacle **2.** showy ornamentation, as fancy carvings on gables, etc. —*adj.* cheap and showy: also **gin′ger·bread′y** —**take the gilt off the gingerbread** to destroy the illusion

ginger group a group within a party, association, etc., that enlivens or radicalizes its parent body

gin·ger·ly (-lē) *adv.* very carefully or cautiously —*adj.* very careful; cautious —**gin′ger·li·ness** *n.*

gin·ger·snap (-snap′) *n.* a crisp, spicy biscuit flavoured with ginger and treacle: also **ginger nut**

ging·ham (giŋ′əm) *n.* [< Du. or Fr., ult. < Malay *ginggang,* striped (cloth)] a cotton cloth, usually woven in stripes, checks, or plaids

gin·gi·li (jin′jə lē) *n.* [Hindi *jinjali*] **1.** same as SESAME **2.** the oil of sesame seed

gin·gi·val (jin′ji v'l) *adj.* of, or affecting, the gums

gin·gi·vi·tis (jin′jə vīt′əs) *n.* [ModL. < L. *gingiva,* the gum + -ITIS] inflammation of the gums

gin·gly·mus (jiŋ′gli məs, gin-) *n., pl.* -gly·mi (-mī) Anat. a joint like a hinge, as in the elbow and ankle

gink (giŋk) *n.* [? < dial. *gink,* a trick] [Slang] a man or boy, esp. one regarded as odd

gink·go (giŋ′kō) *n., pl.* gink′goes [Jap. *ginkyo* < Chin.] an Asiatic tree with fan-shaped leaves and yellow seeds enclosing an edible kernel: also **ging′ko,** *pl.* **ging′koes**

gin-palace (jin′pal′is) *n.* formerly, a public house, esp. a showily decorated one

gin rummy a variety of the card game rummy: a hand which totals no more than ten points in unmatched cards and has been exposed wins unless the opponent has fewer points or an equal number

gin·seng (jin´seŋ) *n.* [Chin. *jen shen*] **1.** a perennial plant with a thick, forked, aromatic root: some species are found in China and N. America **2.** the root of this plant, used medicinally

Gio·con·da (jō kon´də) *adj.* [after the portrait *La Gioconda* by Leonardo da Vinci] enigmatic; mysterious

gip (jip) *n., vt., vi.* *same as* GYP[1]

gip·sy (jip´sē) *n.* *same as* GYPSY

gi·raffe (jə raf´, -räf´) *n., pl.* **-raffes´, -raffe´:** see PLURAL, II, D, 1 [Fr. < It. *giraffa* < Ar. *zarāfa*] a large, cud-chewing animal of Africa, with a very long neck and legs: the tallest of existing animals

gir·an·dole (jir´ən dōl´) *n.* [Fr. < It. *girandola* ult. < Gr. *gyros*, a circle] **1.** a revolving cluster of fireworks **2** a revolving water jet **3.** a branched candleholder **4.** a pendant or earring with small stones grouped round a larger one

gir·a·sol (jir´ə sol´, -sōl) *n.* [Fr. < It. *girasole* < *girare*, to turn + *sole*, sun] *same as* FIRE OPAL: also **gir´a·sole** (-sōl´)

gird[1] (gurd) *vt.* **gird´ed** or **girt, gird´ing** [OE. *gyrdan*] **1.** to encircle or fasten with a belt or band **2.** to encircle; enclose **3.** to equip or endow **4.** to prepare (oneself) for action

gird[2] (gurd) *vi.* [ME. *girden*, to strike] to gibe; taunt (often with *at*) —*n.* a jibe; jeer

gird·er (gur´dər) *n.* [GIRD[1] + -ER] a large beam of timber or steel, for supporting the joists of a floor, a framework, etc.

gir·dle[1] (gur´d'l) *n.* [OE. *gyrdel*] **1.** a belt or sash for the waist **2.** anything that surrounds or encircles **3.** a woman's elasticized undergarment for supporting the waist and hips **4.** the rim of a cut gem **5.** a ring made by removing the bark around the trunk of a tree —*vt.* **-dled, -dling 1.** to surround or bind, as with a girdle **2.** to encircle **3.** to cut a ring of bark from (a tree) —**gir´dler** *n.*

gir·dle[2] (gur´d'l) *n.* *same as* GRIDDLE

girl (gurl) *n.* [ME. *girle, gurle*, youngster] **1.** a female child **2.** a young, unmarried woman **3.** a female servant **4.** [Colloq.] a woman of any age **5.** [Colloq.] a sweetheart —**girl´ish** *adj.* —**girl´ish·ly** *adv.* —**girl´ish·ness** *n.*

girl·friend (-frend´) *n.* [Colloq.] **1.** a sweetheart of a boy or man **2.** a girl who is one's friend

girl guide a member of the Girl Guides' Association, an organisation founded in 1910 to provide character-building activities for girls

girl·hood (-hood´) *n.* **1.** the state or time of being a girl **2.** girls collectively

girl·ie, girl·y (gur´lē) *n., pl.* **girl´ies** [Slang] a girl or woman —*adj.* [Slang] featuring nude or scantily dressed women [a *girlie* magazine]

gi·ro (jī´rō) *n., pl.* **-ros** [20th c., ult. < Gr. *gyros*, circuit] a banking system, operated by post offices and banks, which provides for the transfer of money between accounts or by giro cheque

girt[1] (gurt) *alt. pt. & pp. of* GIRD[1]

girt[2] (gurt) *vt.* [var. of GIRD[1]] **1.** to gird; girdle **2.** to fasten with a girth

girth (gurth) *n.* [< ON. *gjörth*] **1.** a band put around the belly of a horse, etc. to hold a saddle or pack **2.** the circumference, as of a tree trunk or person's waist —*vt.* **1.** to encircle **2.** to bind with a girth —*vi.* to measure in girth

gist (jist) *n.* [< OFr. *giste*, point at issue < *gesir*, to lie < L. *jacere*] the essence or main point, as of an article or argument

git (git) *n.* [20th c. < GET (*n.* 1)] [Slang] **1.** a contemptible person; a fool **2.** a bastard

git·tern (git´ərn) *n.* [< OFr. *guiterne*, altered < OSp. *guittarra*: see GUITAR] an obsolete, guitarlike musical instrument with wire strings

give (giv) *vt.* **gave, giv´en, giv´ing** [OE. *giefan*, infl. by ON. *gefa*] **1.** to turn over the control of without cost or exchange; make a gift of **2.** to hand or pass over to be cared for [he *gave* the porter his bag] **3.** to pay (a price) for goods, services, etc. **4.** to relay [*give* my regards] **5.** to cause to have; impart **6.** to confer (a title, position, etc.) **7.** to act as host of (a party, etc.) **8.** to produce; supply [cows *give* milk] **9.** a) to sacrifice [he *gave* his life for his country] b) to devote fully [he *gives* all his time to his work] **10.** to concede; yield **11.** to show; exhibit **12.** to offer; proffer **13.** to perform [to *give* a concert] **14.** to make (a gesture, movement, etc.) [to *give* a leap] **15.** to utter (words, etc.); state [*give* a reply] **16.** to inflict (punishment, etc.) —*vi.* **1.** to make gifts **2.** to bend, sink, move, etc. from force or pressure **3.** to be resilient **4.** to provide a view of or access to [the window *gives* on the park] **5.** [Colloq.] to happen: chiefly in **what gives?** —*n.* **1.** a bending, sinking, moving, etc. under pressure **2.** resiliency —**give and take** to exchange on an even basis —**give away 1.** to make a gift of **2.** to present (the bride) ritually to the bridegroom **3.** [Colloq.] to reveal; expose

—**give back** to return —**give forth** (or **off**) to send forth; emit —**give in 1.** to hand in **2.** to yield —**give it to** [Colloq.] to beat or scold —**give or take** plus or minus —**give out 1.** to emit **2.** to make public **3.** to distribute **4.** to become worn out or used up —**give over 1.** to transfer; hand over **2.** to assign to a particular purpose [the day was *given over* to pleasure] **3.** [Colloq.] to cease from doing; desist —**give to understand** (or **believe,** etc.) to cause to understand (or believe, etc.) —**give up 1.** to hand over; relinquish **2.** to stop; cease **3.** to admit failure and stop trying **4.** to lose hope for **5.** to devote wholly —**giv´er** *n.*

give-and-take (-'n tāk´) *n.* **1.** a mutual yielding and conceding **2.** a fair and equal exchange of remarks or retorts

give·a·way (-ə wā´) *n.* [Colloq.] **1.** an unintentional revelation or betrayal **2.** something that betrays or reveals; a clue —*adj.* very cheap [*giveaway* prices]

giv·en (giv´'n) *pp. of* GIVE —*adj.* **1.** bestowed; presented **2.** accustomed; inclined [*given* to lying] **3.** stated; specified **4.** assumed; granted **5.** issued; executed [*given* under his seal as mayor]

giz·zard (giz´ərd) *n.* [< OFr. *gisier* < L. *gigeria*, pl., cooked entrails of poultry] **1.** the second stomach of a bird: it has thick, muscular walls and a tough lining for grinding food **2.** [Colloq.] the stomach: humorous usage —**stick in one's gizzard** to be intolerable

Gk. Greek

gla·bel·la (glə bel´ə) *n., pl.* **-lae** (-ē) [ModL. < L. *glabellus*, dim. of *glaber*, bald] the smooth prominence on the forehead between the eyebrows, just above the nose —**gla·bel´lar** *adj.*

gla·brous (glā´brəs) *adj.* [< L. *glaber*, bald] without hair, down, or fuzz; bald —**gla´brous·ness** *n.*

gla·cé (gla sā´, -sē) *adj.* [Fr., pp. of *glacer*, to freeze < L. < *glacies*, ice] **1.** having a smooth, glossy surface **2.** candied or glazed, as fruits —*vt.* **-céed´, -cé´ing** to glaze (fruits, etc.)

gla·cial (glā´shəl, -sē əl) *adj.* [< L. < *glacies*, ice] **1.** of ice or glaciers **2.** of or produced by a glacial epoch **3.** freezing; frigid **4.** cold and unfriendly **5.** as slow as the movement of a glacier **6.** having an icelike appearance —**gla´cial·ly** *adv.*

glacial epoch any extent of geologic time when large parts of the earth were covered with glaciers; specif., the Pleistocene Epoch, when a large part of the Northern Hemisphere was intermittently covered with glaciers; ice age

gla·ci·ate (glā´sē āt´) *vt.* **-at´ed, -at´ing 1.** a) to cover with ice or a glacier b) to form into ice; freeze **2.** to expose to or change by glacial action —**gla´ci·a´ted** *adj.* —**gla´ci·a´tion** *n.*

glac·i·er (gla´sē ər, glā-) *n.* [Fr. < VL. < L. *glacies*, ice] a large mass of ice and snow that forms in areas where the rate of snowfall exceeds the melting rate: it moves slowly down a mountain, along a valley, etc.until it melts or breaks away

gla·ci·ol·o·gy (glā´sē ol´ə jē, gla-) *n.* [*glacio-* (< GLACIER) + -LOGY] **1.** the scientific study of the formation, movements, etc., of glaciers **2.** the glacial formations of a particular region —**gla´ci·o·log´i·cal** (-ə loj´i k'l) *adj.* —**gla´ci·ol´-o·gist** *n.*

gla·cis (glā´sis, glas´is, -sē) *n., pl.* **-cis** (-sēz), **-cis·es** (-sis əz) [Fr. < OFr. *glacier*, to slip < *glace*, ice] **1.** a gradual slope **2.** an embankment sloping down from a fortification

glad[1] (glad) *adj.* **glad´der, glad´dest** [OE. *glæd*] **1.** happy; pleased **2.** causing pleasure or joy; making happy **3.** very willing [I'm *glad* to help] **4.** bright or beautiful —*vt., vi.* **glad´ded, glad´ding** [Archaic] to gladden —**glad´ly** *adv.* —**glad´ness** *n.*

glad[2] (glad) *n.* [Colloq.] *same as* GLADIOLUS

glad·den (-'n) *vt., vi.* to make or become glad

glade (glād) *n.* [ME., prob. < *glad*, GLAD[1]] an open space in a wood or forest

glad eye [Slang] an inviting or flirtatious glance: usually in **give** (or **get**) **the glad eye**

glad·i·a·tor (glad´ē āt´ər) *n.* [L. < *gladius*, sword] in ancient Rome, a man who fought other men or animals in an arena as a public show: gladiators were slaves, captives, or paid performers —**glad´i·a·to´ri·al** (-ē ə tôr´ē əl) *adj.*

glad·i·o·lus (glad´ē ō´ləs, *occas.* glə di´ə ləs) *n., pl.* **-lus·es, -li** (-lī) [ModL. < L. dim. of *gladius*, sword] a plant with swordlike leaves and tall spikes of funnel-shaped flowers in various colours: also **glad´i·o´la** (-lə)

glad rags [Slang] fine or dressy clothes

glad·some (glad´səm) *adj.* joyful or cheerful —**glad´-some·ly** *adv.* —**glad´some·ness** *n.*

Glad·stone (bag) (glad´stən) [after W.E. *Gladstone*, Brit. prime minister] a travelling bag hinged so that it can open flat into two compartments of equal size

glair (gler) *n.* [< OFr. < L. *clarus*, clear] **1.** raw white of egg, used in sizing or glazing **2.** a size or glaze made from this **3.** any sticky matter resembling raw egg white —*vt.* to cover with glair —**glair´e·ous, —glair´y** *adj.*

glaive (glāv) *n*. [< OFr. < L. *gladius*, sword] [Archaic] a sword; esp., a broadsword

Glam. Glamorgan

glam·or (glam′ər) *n*. *alt. U.S. sp. of* GLAMOUR

glam·or·ize (glam′ə rīz′) *vt*. **-ized′**, **-iz′ing** to make glamorous —**glam′or·i·za′tion** *n*.

glam·or·ous (-ər əs) *adj*. full of glamour; fascinating; alluring —**glam′or·ous·ly** *adv*.

glam·our (glam′ər) *n*. [Scot. var. of *grammar* in sense of *gramarye*, magic] **1.** orig., a magic spell or charm **2.** seemingly mysterious and elusive fascination or allure, as of some person, scene, etc.; bewitching charm

glance¹ (gläns) *vi*. **glanced, glanc′ing** [prob. a blend < OFr. *glacier*, to slip + *guenchir*, to elude] **1.** to strike obliquely and go off at an angle **2.** to make an indirect or passing reference **3.** to flash or gleam **4.** to take a quick look —*vt*. to cause to strike (a surface) at an angle and be deflected —*n*. **1.** a glancing off **2.** a flash or gleam **3.** a quick look

glance² (gläns) *n*. [G. *Glanz*, lit., lustre] any of various ores with a metallic lustre

gland¹ (gland) *n*. [< Fr. < OFr. < L. *glandula*, tonsil, dim. of *glans* (gen. *glandis*), acorn] **1.** any organ that separates certain elements from the blood and secretes them in a form for the body to use (as an adrenal, a ductless gland, secretes epinephrine) or throw off (as a kidney, a gland with ducts, secretes urine) **2.** loosely, any structure like a gland in appearance, etc. [lymph *glands*]

gland² (gland) *n*. [< ?] *Mech*. a movable part that compresses the packing round a moving piece of machinery, as a piston rod, etc.

glan·ders (glan′dərz) *n.pl*. [with *sing. v.*] [OFr. *glandres*, lit., glands] a contagious disease of horses, mules, etc. characterized by fever, swelling of glands beneath the jaw, nasal inflammation, etc.

glan·du·lar (glan′dyə lər) *adj*. **1.** of, like, or having a gland or glands **2.** derived from or affected by glands —**glan′du·lar·ly** *adv*.

glandular fever *same as* INFECTIOUS MONONUCLEOSIS

glan·dule (glan′dyo͞ol) *n*. [Fr.] a small gland

glans (glanz) *n., pl*. **glan·des** (glan′dēz) [L., lit., acorn] **1.** the head, or end, of the penis: in full, **glans penis 2.** the corresponding part of the clitoris

glare (gler) *vi*. **glared, glar′ing** [ME. *glaren* < or akin to MDu. *glaren*, to gleam & OE. *glær*, amber] **1.** to shine with a steady, dazzling light **2.** to be too bright or showy **3.** to stare fiercely or angrily —*vt*. to express with a glare —*n*. **1.** a steady, dazzling light **2.** a too bright or dazzling display **3.** a fierce or angry stare

glar·ing (-iŋ) *adj*. **1.** dazzlingly bright **2.** too bright and showy **3.** staring fiercely **4.** flagrant [a *glaring* mistake] —**glar′ing·ly** *adv*.

glar·y (-ē) *adj*. **glar′i·er, glar′i·est** shining with a too bright light —**glar′i·ness** *n*.

glass (gläs) *n*. [OE. *glæs*] **1.** a hard, brittle substance, usually transparent, made by fusing silicates with soda or potash, lime, and, sometimes, metallic oxides **2.** *same as* GLASSWARE **3.** *a)* an article made of glass, as a drinking container, mirror, telescope, barometer, etc. *b)* [pl.] spectacles *c)* [pl.] binoculars **4.** the quantity contained in a drinking glass —*vt*. **1.** to mirror; reflect **2.** to equip with glass; glaze **3.** to make glassy —*vi*. to become glassy —*adj*. of, made of, or like glass —**glass in** to enclose with glass panes

glass blowing the art or process of shaping molten glass by blowing air into a mass of it at the end of a tube —**glass blower**

glass·ful (-fo͝ol) *n., pl*. **glass′fuls′** the amount that will fill a glass

glass·house (-hous′) *n*. **1.** *same as* GREENHOUSE **2.** [Slang] a military prison

glass·ine (glä sēn′) *n*. [GLASS + -INE¹] a thin, tough paper used for the windows on envelopes, etc.

glass·paper (gläs′pā′pər) *n*. paper coated with pulverized glass for polishing

glass snake a legless lizard found in the S U.S.: so called because its tail breaks off easily

glass·ware (gläs′wer′) *n*. articles made of glass

glass wool fine fibres of glass intertwined in a woolly mass, used in filters and as insulation

glass·wort (-wûrt′) *n*. a fleshy plant of the goosefoot family, found in saline coastal or desert areas: formerly used in glass-making

glass·y (-ē) *adj*. **glass′i·er, glass′i·est 1.** like glass, as in smoothness or transparency **2.** expressionless or lifeless [a *glassy* stare] —**glass′i·ly** *adv*. —**glass′i·ness** *n*.

Glau·ber's salt (or **salts**) (glou′bərz) [after J.R. *Glauber* (1604-68), Ger. chemist] sodium sulphate, a crystalline salt used as a cathartic, etc.

glau·co·ma (glô kō′mə) *n*. [L. < Gr. < *glaukos*: see ff. & -OMA] a disease of the eye marked by increased pressure in the eyeball: it leads to a gradual loss of sight —**glau·co′ma·tous** *adj*.

glau·cous (glô′kəs) *adj*. [< L. < Gr. *glaukos*, orig., gleaming] **1.** bluish-green or yellowish-green **2.** *Bot*. covered with a whitish bloom that can be rubbed off, as grapes, plums, etc.

glaze (glāz) *vt*. **glazed, glaz′ing** [ME. *glasen* < *glas*, GLASS] **1.** to fit (windows, etc.) with glass **2.** to give a hard, glossy finish or coating to; specif., *a)* to overlay (pottery, etc.) with a substance that gives a glassy finish when fused *b)* to cover (foods) with a coating of sugar syrup, etc. **3.** to cover with a thin layer of ice —*vi*. **1.** to become glassy or glossy **2.** to form a glaze —*n*. **1.** *a)* a glassy finish, as on pottery *b)* any substance used to form this **2.** a film or coating —**glaz′er** *n*.

gla·zi·er (glā′zē ər) *n*. a person whose work is fitting glass in windows, etc. —**gla′zier·y** *n*.

glaz·ing (-ziŋ) *n*. **1.** the work of a glazier **2.** a glass set or to be set in frames **3.** a glaze or the application of a glaze

G.L.C. Greater London Council

gleam (glēm) *n*. [OE. *glæm*] **1.** a flash or beam of light **2.** a faint light **3.** a reflected brightness, as from a polished surface **4.** a brief, faint manifestation, as of hope, etc. —*vi*. **1.** to shine with a gleam **2.** to be manifested briefly; appear suddenly —**gleam′y** *adj*.

glean (glēn) *vt., vi*. [< OFr. < VL. *glennare* < Celt.] **1.** to collect (grain left by reapers) from (a field) **2.** to collect (facts, etc.) bit by bit from (a source) —**glean′er** *n*.

glean·ings (-iŋz) *n.pl*. that which is gleaned

glebe (glēb) *n*. [< L. *gleba*, clod] **1.** church land forming part or all of a benefice **2.** [Poet.] soil; earth; land; field

glee (glē) *n*. [OE. *gleo*] **1.** lively joy; merriment **2.** a part song for three or more voices, usually unaccompanied

glee club a group formed to sing part songs

glee·ful (-fəl) *adj*. full of glee; merry: also **glee′some** —**glee′ful·ly** *adv*. —**glee′ful·ness** *n*.

glee·man (glē′mən) *n., pl*. **-men** (-mən) [ME. *gleman*] a medieval minstrel

glen (glen) *n*. [< ScotGael. hyp. *glenn* (now *gleann*)] a narrow, secluded valley

Glen·gar·ry (glen gar′ē) *n., pl*. **-ries** [< *Glengarry*, valley in Scotland] [*sometimes* g-] a Scottish cap for men, creased lengthwise across the top and often having short ribbons at the back: also **Glengarry bonnet** (or **cap**)

glib (glib) *adj*. **glib′ber, glib′best** [orig., slippery < or akin to Du. *glibberig*, slippery] **1.** done in a smooth, offhand way **2.** speaking or spoken in a smooth, fluent manner, often in a way too smooth and easy to be convincing —**glib′ly** *adv*. —**glib′ness** *n*.

glide (glīd) *vi*. **glid′ed, glid′ing** [OE. *glidan*] **1.** to flow or move smoothly and easily **2.** to pass gradually and unnoticed, as time **3.** *Aeron*. *a)* to fly in a glider *b)* to descend at a normal angle without engine power **4.** *Music, Phonet*. to make a glide —*vt*. to cause to glide —*n*. **1.** the act of gliding **2.** *a)* a smooth, gliding step *b)* any of various dances using such steps **3.** *Music* loosely, a slur **4.** *Phonet*. an intermediate sound made when the speech organs change from the position for one sound to another

glid·er (glīd′ər) *n*. **1.** a person or thing that glides **2.** an aircraft like an aeroplane except that it has no engine and is carried along by air currents

glim·mer (glim′ər) *vi*. [< base of OE. *glæm*, gleam] **1.** to give a faint, flickering light **2.** to appear or be seen faintly or dimly —*n*. **1.** a faint, flickering light **2.** a faint manifestation

glim·mer·ing (-iŋ) *n*. *same as* GLIMMER

glimpse (glimps) *vt*. **glimpsed, glimps′ing** [see GLIMMER] to catch a brief, quick view of, as in passing —*vi*. to look quickly; glance (at) —*n*. **1.** a flash **2.** a faint, fleeting appearance; slight trace **3.** a brief, quick view

glint (glint) *vi*. [prob. < Scand.] to gleam; flash —*n*. a gleam, flash, or glitter

glis·sade (gli säd′, -säd′) *n*. [Fr. < *glisser*, to slide] **1.** an intentional slide by a mountain climber down a steep, snow-covered slope **2.** *Ballet* a gliding step —*vi*. **-sad′ed, -sad′ing** to make a glissade

glis·san·do (gli san′dō, -sän′-) *n., pl*. **-di** (-dē), **-dos** [as if It. prp., equiv. to Fr. *glissant*, prp. of *glisser*, to slide] *Music* a sliding effect achieved by sounding a series of adjacent tones in rapid succession —*adj., adv*. (performed) with such an effect

glis·ten (glis′'n) *vi*. [OE. *glisnian*] to shine or sparkle with reflected light, as a wet or polished surface —*n*. a glistening

glis·ter (glis′tər) *vi., n*. archaic var. of GLISTEN

glit·ter (glit′ər) *vi*. [prob. < ON. *glitra*] **1.** to shine with a sparkling light **2.** to be brilliant, showy, or attractive —*n*. **1.** a bright, sparkling light **2.** showy brilliance or attractiveness **3.** bits of glittering decorative material —**glit′ter·y** *adj*.

gloam·ing (glō′miŋ) *n*. [OE. *glomung* < *glom*, twilight] evening dusk; twilight

gloat (glōt) *vi*. [prob. < ON. *glotta*, to grin scornfully] to gaze or think with malicious pleasure —*n*. the act of gloating —**gloat′er** *n*.

glob (glob) *n.* [prob. contr. < GLOBULE, after BLOB] a rounded mass or lump, as of a semisolid

glob·al (glō'b'l) *adj.* 1. globe-shaped 2. worldwide [*global war*] 3. complete —**glob'al·ly** *adv.*

glob·al·ism (-iz'm) *n.* a policy, outlook, etc. that is worldwide in scope —**glob'al·ist** *n., adj.*

globe (glōb) *n.* [< L. *globus*, a ball] 1. any round, ball-shaped thing; sphere; specif., a) the earth b) a spherical model of the earth 2. anything shaped like a globe, as a rounded glass cover for a lamp —*vt., vi.* **globed, glob'ing** to form or gather into a globe —**glo·bate** (glō'bāt) *adj.*

globe·fish (-fish') *n., pl.* **-fish'**, **-fish'es:** see FISH any of several tropical fishes that can puff themselves into a globular form

globe·flow·er (-flou'ər) *n.* 1. any of a genus of plants of the buttercup family with white, orange, or yellow globe-shaped flowers

globe-trot·ter (-trot'ər) *n.* a person who travels widely about the world, esp. for pleasure or sightseeing —**globe'-trot'ting** *n., adj.*

glo·big·er·i·na ooze (glō bij'ə ri'nə) [ModL. *Globigerina*, a genus of FORAMINIFERA] a fine, deep-sea sediment, formed mainly of fossilized shells and covering approximately one-third of the ocean floor

glo·boid (glō'boid) *adj.* shaped somewhat like a globe or ball —*n.* anything globoid

glo·bose (-bōs) *adj.* [L. *globosus*] *same as* GLOBOID: also **glo'bous** (-bəs) —**glo'bose·ly** *adv.*

glob·u·lar (glob'yə lər) *adj.* 1. shaped like a globe or ball; spherical 2. made up of globules —**glob'u·lar·ly** *adv.*

glob·ule (-yool) *n.* [Fr. < L. dim. of *globus*, a ball] a tiny ball or globe; esp., a drop of liquid

glob·u·lin (-yə lin) *n.* [GLOBUL(E) + -IN¹] any of a group of proteins in animal and vegetable tissue

glock·en·spiel (glok'ən spēl', -shpēl') *n.* [G. < *Glocke*, a bell + *Spiel*, play] a percussion instrument with flat metal bars set in a frame, that produce bell-like tones of the scale when struck with small hammers

glom·er·ate (glom'ər it) *adj.* [< L. pp. of *glomerare* < *glomus*, a ball] formed into a rounded mass; clustered —**glom'er·a'tion** *n.*

glom·er·ule (glom'ər ool') *n.* [< ModL. *glomerulus*, dim. < L. *glomus*, a ball] a compact cluster, as of a flower head

GLOCKENSPIEL

gloom (gloom) *vi.* [prob. < Scand.] 1. to be or look morose or dejected 2. to be or become dark, dim, or dismal —*vt.* to make dark, dismal, dejected, etc. —*n.* 1. darkness; dimness; obscurity 2. a dark place 3. deep sadness; dejection

gloom·y (-ē) *adj.* **gloom'i·er, gloom'i·est** 1. overspread with or enveloped in darkness or dimness 2. melancholy or sullen 3. causing gloom; depressing —**gloom'i·ly** *adv.* —**gloom'i·ness** *n.*

Glo·ri·a (glôr'ē ə) *n.* [L., glory] 1. either of the Latin hymns beginning *Gloria in Excelsis Deo* (glory be to God on high) or *Gloria Patri* (glory be to the Father) 2. the music for either 3. [g-] *same as* HALO (sense 2)

glo·ri·fy (glôr'ə fī') *vt.* **-fied', -fy'ing** [< OFr. < LL. < L. *gloria*, glory + *facere*, to make] 1. to make glorious; give glory to 2. to exalt in worship 3. to honour; extol 4. to make seem better, larger, finer, etc. —**glo'ri·fi·ca'tion** *n.* —**glo'ri·fi'er** *n.*

glo·ri·ole (glôr'ē ōl) *n.* [Fr. < L. *gloriola*, dim. of *gloria*, glory] a halo

glo·ri·ous (glôr'ē əs) *adj.* 1. full of glory; illustrious 2. giving glory 3. receiving or deserving glory 4. splendid; magnificent 5. [Colloq.] very delightful or enjoyable —**glo'ri·ous·ly** *adv.* —**glo'ri·ous·ness** *n.*

glo·ry (glôr'ē) *n., pl.* **-ries** [< OFr. < L. *gloria*] 1. a) great honour and admiration b) anything bringing this 2. worshipful adoration 3. the condition of highest achievement, prosperity, etc. 4. splendour; magnificence 5. heaven or the bliss of heaven 6. *same as* HALO (*n.* 1 & 2) —*vi.* **-ried, -ry·ing** to be very proud; exult (with *in*) —**gone to glory** dead —**in one's glory** at one's best, happiest, etc.

glory-hole (-hōl) *n.* [Colloq.] any room, cupboard, etc., used for storage, esp. one which is very untidy

Glos. Gloucestershire

gloss¹ (glos) *n.* [prob. < Scand.] 1. the lustre of a smooth, polished surface; sheen 2. a deceptively pleasant outward appearance, as in manners or speech —*vt.* 1. to make lustrous 2. to cover up (an error, fault, etc.) by minimizing (often with *over*) —*vi.* to become shiny —**gloss'er** *n.*

gloss² (glos) *n.* [< OFr. or < ML. < L. < Gr. *glōssa*, the tongue] 1. a translation inserted between the lines of a text 2. a note of comment or explanation, as in a footnote 3. a

glossary —*vt.* 1. to furnish (a text) with glosses 2. to interpret falsely —*vi.* to annotate —**gloss'er** *n.*

glos·sa·ry (glos'ə rē) *n., pl.* **-ries** [< L. < *glossa* < Gr. *glōssa*, the tongue] a list of difficult, technical, or foreign terms with definitions or translations, as for a particular author, subject, book, etc. —**glos·sar·i·al** (glo ser'ē əl) *adj.* —**glos'sar·ist** *n.*

glos·si·tis (glo sīt'is) *n.* [< Gr. *glossa*, tongue + -ITIS] *Med.* inflammation of the tongue

glos·so·la·li·a (glos'ə lā'lē ə) *n.* [ModL., ult. < Gr. *glōssa*, tongue + *lalein*, to speak] an ecstatic utterance of unintelligible speechlike sounds, regarded as caused by religious ecstasy

gloss·y (glos'ē) *adj.* **gloss'i·er, gloss'i·est** 1. having a smooth, shiny appearance or finish 2. specious —*n., pl.* **gloss'ies** 1. a photographic print with a glossy surface 2. [Colloq.] a magazine printed on glossy paper —**gloss'i·ly** *adv.* —**gloss'i·ness** *n.*

glot·tal (glot''l) *adj.* of or produced in or at the glottis: also **glot'tic**

glot·tis (glot'is) *n., pl.* **-tis·es, -ti·des'** (-ə dēz') [ModL. < Gr. < *glōtta*, var. of *glōssa*, the tongue] the opening between the vocal cords in the larynx

glove (gluv) *n.* [< OE. *glof* & ON. *glofi*] 1. a covering for the hand, with a separate sheath for each finger and the thumb 2. *Sports* a padded mitten worn by boxers: usually **boxing glove** —*vt.* **gloved, glov'ing** 1. to supply with gloves 2. to cover as with a glove —**put on the gloves** [Colloq.] to engage in boxing —**with the gloves off** with no restraint; ruthlessly: said of arguments, quarrels, etc.

glov·er (-ər) *n.* one who makes or sells gloves

glow (glō) *vi.* [OE. *glowan*] 1. to give off a bright light as a result of great heat; be incandescent or red-hot 2. to give out a steady, even light without flame 3. to be or feel hot 4. to radiate health 5. to be elated or enlivened by emotion 6. to be bright with colour —*n.* 1. a light given off as the result of great heat 2. steady, even light without flame or blaze 3. brilliance of colour 4. brightness of skin colour; flush 5. a sensation of warmth and well-being 6. warmth of emotion —**glow'ing** *adj.* —**glow'ing·ly** *adv.*

glow·er (glou'ər) *vi.* [prob. < ON.] to stare with sullen anger; scowl —*n.* a sullen, angry stare; scowl —**glow'er·ing** *adj.* —**glow'er·ing·ly** *adv.*

glow-worm (glō'wurm') *n.* a wingless insect or insect larva that gives off a luminescent light; esp., the wingless female or the larva of the firefly

glox·in·i·a (glok sin'ē ə, -zin'-) *n.* [ModL., after B. P. *Gloxin*, 18th-c. Ger. botanist] a cultivated tropical plant with bell-shaped flowers of various colours

gloze (glōz) *vt.* **glozed, gloz'ing** [< OFr. < *glose*: see GLOSS²] [Obs.] to explain away; gloss (often with *over*)

glu·cose (gloo'kōs) *n.* [Fr. < Gr. *gleukos*, sweet wine, sweetness] a crystalline sugar, $C_6H_{12}O_6$, occurring naturally in fruits, honey, etc.: the commercial form is prepared as a sweet syrup by hydrolysing starch in the presence of dilute acids

glu·co·side (gloo'kə sīd') *n.* [GLUCOS(E) + -IDE] any glycoside having glucose as its sugar constituent —**glu'·co·sid'ic** (-sid'ik) *adj.*

glue (gloo) *n.* [< OFr. *glu*, birdlime < LL. *glus*, glue] 1. a sticky, viscous substance made from animal skins, bones, hoofs, etc. by boiling, etc. and used to stick things together 2. any similar adhesive made from casein, resin, etc. —*vt.* **glued, glu'ing** to make stick as with glue —**glu'er** *n.*

glue·y (-ē) *adj.* **glu'i·er, glu'i·est** 1. like glue; sticky 2. covered with or full of glue

glum (glum) *adj.* **glum'mer, glum'mest** [prob. < ME. var. of *gloum(b)en*, to look morose] gloomy; sullen; morose —**glum'ly** *adv.* —**glum'ness** *n.*

glume (gloom) *n.* [ModL. *gluma* < L., husk] either of the two empty bracts at the base of a grass spikelet, etc. —**glu·ma'ceous, glu'mose** *adj.*

glut (glut) *vt.* **glut'ted, glut'ting** [< OFr. *gloter*, to swallow < L. *gluttire*] to eat like a glutton —*vt.* 1. to feed, fill, etc. to excess; surfeit 2. to flood (the market) with certain goods so that the supply is greater than the demand —*n.* 1. a glutting or being glutted 2. a supply of certain goods that is greater than the demand

glu·ten (gloot''n) *n.* [L., glue] a grey, sticky substance found in wheat and other grain, the protein part of flour and bread —**glu'ten·ous** *adj.*

glu·te·us (gloo tē'əs, gloot'ē-) *n., pl.* **-te'i** (-ī) [ModL. < Gr. *gloutos*, rump] any of the three muscles forming each of the buttocks —**glu·te'al** *adj.*

glu·ti·nous (gloot''n əs) *adj.* [< L. < *gluten*, glue] gluey; sticky —**glu'ti·nous·ly** *adv.*

glut·ton (glut''n) *n.* [< OFr. < L. *gluto* < *glutire*, to devour] 1. a person who greedily eats too much 2. a person with a great capacity for something 3. an animal of the weasel family: the WOLVERINE —**glut'ton·ize** *vt., vi.* **-ized', -iz'ing**

glut·ton·ous (-əs) *adj.* inclined to eat too much and greedily —**glut′ton·ous·ly** *adv.*

glut·ton·y (-ē) *n., pl.* **-ton·ies** the habit or act of eating too much

glyc·er·ide (glis′ər īd′) *n.* an ester of glycerol

glyc·er·in (glis′ər in) *n.* [< Fr. < Gr. *glykeros*, sweet] *popular and commercial term for* GLYCEROL: also sp. **glyc′er·ine** (-ēn)

glyc·er·ol (glis′ər ol′) *n.* [< prec. + -OL[1]] an odourless, colourless, syrupy liquid, $C_3H_8O_3$, prepared by the hydrolysis of fats and oils: used as a solvent, skin lotion, etc., and in explosives, etc.

gly·cine (glī′sēn) *n.* [< Gr. *glykys*, sweet + -INE[4]] a sweet, white crystalline aminoacid occurring in most proteins

gly·co- [< Gr. < *glykys*, sweet] *a combining form meaning* glycerol, sugar, glycogen: also, before a vowel, **glyc-**

gly·co·gen (glī′kə jən) *n.* [prec. + -GEN] a partially soluble, starchlike substance, $(C_6H_{10}O_5)_x$, produced in animal tissues, esp. in the liver and muscles, and changed into tissues, esp. sugar as the body needs it —**gly′co·gen′ic** (-jen′ik) *adj.*

gly·col (glī′kol) *n.* [GLYCOL(ERIN) + -OL[1]] **1.** *same as* ETHYLENE GLYCOL **2.** any of a group of alcohols of which ethylene glycol is the type

gly·col·y·sis (glī kol′ə sis) *n.* [GLYCO- + -LYSIS] the breakdown of sugars, glycogen, or other carbohydrates by enzymes into simpler compounds

gly·co·side (glī′kə sīd′) *n.* [Fr. < *glycose* (for GLUCOSE) + -ide, -IDE] any of a group of sugar derivatives, widely distributed in plants, which on hydrolysis yield a sugar and one or more other substances —**gly′co·sid′ic** (-sid′ik) *adj.*

glyph (glif) *n.* [Gr. *glyphē*, a carving] **1.** a carving or other symbolic character or sign, esp. when cut into a surface or carved in relief **2.** *Archit.* a vertical channel or groove

glyp·tic (glip′tik) *adj.* [< Fr. < Gr. *glyptos*, carved] having to do with carving or engraving, esp. on gems

glyp·to·dont (glip′tə dont) *n.* [ModL. < Gr. *glyptos*, carved + -ODONT: so called from its fluted front teeth] an extinct S. American mammal, related to the armadillo but much larger

glyp·to·graph (-graf′) *n.* [< Gr. *glyptos*, carved + -GRAPH] **1.** a design cut or engraved on a gem, seal, etc. **2.** a gem, seal, etc. so engraved —**glyp·tog·ra·phy** (glip tog′rə fē) *n.*

gm. gramme(s)

G.M. George Medal

G-man (jē′man′) *n., pl.* **G′-men′** (-men′) [associated with *g(overnment) man*, but prob. < *G* division of the Dublin Police] [U.S. Colloq.] an agent of the Federal Bureau of Investigation

Gmc. Germanic

G.M.T. Greenwich Mean Time

gnarl (närl) *n.* [back-formation < ff.] a knot on the trunk or branch of a tree —*vt., vi.* to make or become knotted or twisted

gnarled (närld) *adj.* [ult.< ME. *knur*, a knot] knotty and twisted [a *gnarled* tree, *gnarled* hands]: also **gnarl′y**

gnash (nash) *vt., vi.* [ME. *gnasten*, prob. < ON.] to grind or strike (the teeth) together, as in anger or pain —*n.* the act of gnashing

gnat (nat) *n.* [OE. *gnæt*] any of a number of small, two-winged insects some of which can bite or sting; a mosquito —**gnat′ty** *adj.*

gnath·ic (nath′ik) *adj.* [< Gr. *gnathos*, the jaw + -IC] of the jaw

gnaw (nô) *vt.* gnawed, gnawed or, rarely, gnawn, gnaw′ing [OE. *gnagen*] **1.** to bite and wear away bit by bit **2.** to make by gnawing **3.** to consume; corrode **4.** to torment, as by constant pain, fear, etc. —*vi.* **1.** to bite repeatedly (on, at, etc.) **2.** to have a gnawing effect

gnaw·ing (-iŋ) *n.* **1.** a sensation of dull, constant pain or suffering **2.** [*pl.*] pangs, as of hunger

gneiss (nīs) *n.* [< G. < OHG. *gneisto*, a spark] a coarse-grained, granitelike rock formed of layers of feldspar, quartz, mica, etc. —**gneiss′ic** *adj.*

gnoc·chi (no′kē; It. nyôk′kē) *n.pl.* [It., pl. of *gnocco*, dumpling] small, variously shaped dumplings of flour, and sometimes potato, served with a sauce

gnome (nōm) *n.* [Fr., ult. < Gr. *gnōmē*, thought] **1.** *Folklore* a dwarf supposed to dwell in the earth and guard its treasures **2.** [Colloq.] an international banker or financier [the *gnomes* of Zurich] —**gnom′ish** *adj.*

gno·mic (nō′mik) *adj.* [< Gr. *gnōmikos* < *gnōmē*, thought] wise and pithy; full of aphorisms —**gno′mi·cal·ly** *adv.*

gno·mon (nō′mon) *n.* [L. < Gr. < base of *gignōskein*, to know] a column, pin on a sundial, etc. that casts a shadow indicating the time of day —**gno·mon′ic** *adj.*

-gnomy [Gr. -*gnōmia* < *gnōmē*, thought] *a combining form meaning* art of judging or determining [*physiognomy*]

-gnosis [see ff.] *a combining form meaning* knowledge, recognition [*diagnosis*]

gnos·tic (nos′tik) *adj.* [< Gr. *gnōstikos* < *gnōsis*, knowledge] **1.** of or having knowledge **2.** [G-] of the Gnostics or Gnosticism —*n.* [G-] a believer in Gnosticism

Gnos·ti·cism (nos′tə siz′m) *n.* a system of belief combining ideas derived from Greek philosophy, Oriental mysticism, and, ultimately, Christianity

GNP gross national product

gnu (noo, nyoo) *n., pl.* **gnus, gnu**: see PLURAL, II, D, 1 [< the native (Bushman) name] a large African antelope with an oxlike head and horns and a horselike mane and tail; wildebeest

GNU (1-1.3 m high at shoulder)

go (gō) *vi.* **went, gone, go′ing** [OE. *gan*] **1.** to move along; travel; proceed **2.** to be in operation; work [the clock won't *go*] **3.** to gesture, act, or make sounds as specified or shown **4.** to take a particular course, line of action, etc.; proceed **5.** to result; turn out [the war *went* badly] **6.** to pass: said of time **7.** to pass from person to person, as a rumour **8.** to be in a certain state [he *goes* in rags] **9.** to become; turn [to *go* mad] **10.** to be expressed, sung, etc. [as the saying *goes*] **11.** to be in harmony; fit in **12.** to put oneself [to *go* to some trouble] **13.** to tend; help [facts that *go* to prove a case] **14.** to have force, acceptance, etc. [what he says *goes*] **15.** to leave; depart **16.** to pass away [the pain is *gone*] **17.** to die **18.** to be removed or eliminated **19.** to break away [the mast *went* in the storm] **20.** to fail; give way [his eyesight is *going*] **21.** to be given [the prize goes to you] **22.** to be sold [it *went* for £10] **23.** to extend to or along a specified place or time; reach **24.** to turn to, enter, or participate in a certain activity, occupation, etc. [to *go* to college] **25.** to pass (through), fit (into), etc. **26.** to be a divisor (into) **27.** to endure; last **28.** to continue (unpunished, unrewarded, etc.) **29.** to have a regular place [pencils *go* on the desk] —*vt.* **1.** to travel or proceed along [he's *going* my way] **2.** *a*) to bet *b*) to bid at cards **3.** [Colloq.] to furnish (bail) **4.** [Colloq.] to be willing to pay, bid, etc. (a specified sum) —*n., pl.* **goes 1.** the act of going **2.** a success **3.** [Colloq.] animation; energy **4.** [Colloq.] a state of affairs **5.** [Colloq.] an agreement, or bargain [is it a *go*?] **6.** [Colloq.] a try; attempt —*adj.* [Slang: orig. astronaut's jargon] functioning properly or ready to go —**as people** (or **things**) **go** in comparison with how other people (or things) are —**go about 1.** to be busy at; do **2.** to circulate **3.** *Naut.* to tack; change direction —**go after** [Colloq.] to try to catch or get —**go against** to be or act in opposition to —**go along with 1.** to agree **2.** to accompany —**go at** to attack or work at —**go back on** [Colloq.] **1.** to betray **2.** to break (a promise, etc.) —**go beyond** to exceed —**go by 1.** to pass **2.** to be guided by **3.** to be known or referred to by (the name of) —**go down 1.** to sink; set **2.** to suffer defeat **3.** to be perpetuated, as in history **4.** to leave university —**go down with** to start to be ill; catch (a disease) —**go for 1.** to behave as **2.** to try to get **3.** to support **3.** [Colloq.] to attack **4.** [Colloq.] to be attracted by —**go hard with** to cause trouble to —**go in for** [Colloq.] to engage or indulge in —**go into 1.** to inquire into **2.** to take up as a study or occupation —**go in with** to share obligations with; join —**go it** [Colloq.] to carry on; proceed [to *go* it alone] —**go off 1.** to leave, esp. suddenly **2.** to explode **3.** to deteriorate **4.** to happen **5.** to lessen in effect [the pain's *going off*] **6.** to harden: said of concrete, plaster, etc. **7.** [Colloq.] to develop a dislike of —**go on 1.** to continue **2.** to happen —**go out 1.** to be extinguished, become outdated, etc. **2.** to attend social affairs, the theatre, etc. **3.** to go on strike **4.** to be transmitted on radio, etc. —**go over 1.** to examine thoroughly **2.** to do again **3.** to review **4.** [Colloq.] to be successful —**go round 1.** to circulate **2.** to be sufficient [there was enough food to *go round*] **3.** to be long enough to surround —**go slow** to work slowly or deliberately curtail output as part of an industrial campaign —**go some** [Colloq.] to do or achieve quite a lot —**go through 1.** to perform thoroughly **2.** to endure; experience **3.** to search **4.** to get acceptance **5.** to spend —**go through with** to complete —**go together 1.** to harmonize **2.** [Colloq.] to be sweethearts —**go to the country** to hold a general election —**go under** to fail, as in business —**go up** to rise in price, etc.; increase —**go with** [Colloq.] to be a sweetheart of —**go without** to do without —**let go 1.** to let escape **2.** to release one's hold **3.** to give up; abandon —**let oneself go 1.** to be unrestrained in emotion, action, etc. **2.** to stop taking care of one's appearance —**no go** [Colloq.] not possible; no use —**on the go** [Colloq.] in constant motion or action —**to go** [Colloq.] left to complete, etc. [one finished, two *to go*]

goad (gōd) *n.* [OE. *gad*] **1.** a sharp-pointed stick for driving oxen **2.** any driving impulse; spur —*vt.* to drive as with a goad; prod into action

go·a·head (gō′ə hed′) *adj.* l. moving forward **2.** enterprising; pushing —*n.* permission or a signal to proceed: usually with *the*

goal (gōl) *n.* [ME. *gol,* boundary] **l.** the place where a race, trip, etc. is ended **2.** an end that one strives to attain; aim **3.** in certain games, *a*) the line, net, etc. over or into which the ball must go to score *b*) the act of so scoring *c*) the score made

goal·keep·er (-kēp′ər) *n.* in certain games, a player stationed at a goal to prevent the ball from crossing or entering it: also **goal′ie** (-ē)

goal kick *Soccer* a kick allowed to a defending player when an attacker has sent the ball over the goal line but not between the goal posts

goal line *Sport* the line marking each end of the pitch, on which the goals stand

go·an·na (gō′an′ə) *n.* [< IGUANA] [Aust. & N.Z.] any of various large lizards

goat (gōt) *n.* [OE. *gat*] **l.** *pl.* **goats, goat:** see PLURAL. II. D. l a cud-chewing mammal with hollow horns, related to the sheep **2.** a lecherous man **3.** [Colloq.] a stupid person —[G-] the constellation Capricorn —**get one's goat** [Colloq.] to annoy or anger one —**goat′ish** *adj.* —**goat′-ish·ly** *adv.* —**goat′ish·ness** *n.*

goat·ee (gō tē′) *n.* a pointed beard on a man's chin

goat·herd (gōt′hurd′) *n.* one who herds goats

goats·beard (gōts′bird′) *n.* a plant of the composite family, with large, yellow, rayed flowerheads; it opens fully only on sunny mornings: also called **Jack-go-to-bed-at-noon**

goat·skin (gōt′skin′) *n.* **l.** the skin of a goat **2.** leather made from this **3.** a container for wine, water, etc., made of this leather

goat·suck·er (-suk′ər) *n.* any of various large-mouthed, nocturnal birds that feed on insects, as the nightjar

gob¹ (gob) *n.* [< OFr. *gobe,* prob. < *gobet:* see GOBBET] **1.** a lump or mass, as of something soft **2.** [*pl.*] [Colloq.] a large quantity or amount **3.** [Slang] a globule of saliva —*vi.* [Slang] to spit

gob² (gob) *n.* [< ? Gaelic *gob,* beak, mouth] [Slang] the mouth

gob·bet (gob′it) *n.* [OFr. *gobet,* mouthful, prob. < Gaul.] [Archaic] **1.** a fragment or bit, esp. of raw flesh **2.** a lump; chunk **3.** a mouthful **4.** a literary extract

gob·ble¹ (gob′′l) *n.* [echoic, var. of GABBLE] the characteristic throaty sound made by a male turkey —*vi.* **-bled, -bling** to make this sound

gob·ble² (gob′′l) *vt., vi.* **-bled, -bling** [prob. < OFr. *gober,* to swallow < *gobe,* mouthful, GOB¹] **1.** to eat quickly and greedily **2.** to snatch (*up*)

gob·ble·dy·gook (gob′′l dē gook′) *n.* [Slang] pompous and wordy talk or writing, esp. of officialdom: also **gob′-ble·de·gook′**

gob·bler (gob′lər) *n.* a male turkey

Gob·e·lin (gob′ə lin, gō′bə-; *Fr.* gô blan′) *adj.* of or like a kind of tapestry made at the Gobelin works in Paris —*n.* Gobelin tapestry

go-be·tween (gō′bi twēn′) *n.* one who deals with each of two sides in making arrangements between them; intermediary

gob·let (gob′lit) *n.* [< OFr. < *gobel* < ? Bret. *gob*] **1.** orig., a cup without handles **2.** a drinking glass with a base and stem

gob·lin (gob′lin) *n.* [< OFr. < ML. *gobelinus,* ult. < ? Gr. *kobalos,* sprite] *Folklore* an evil or mischievous sprite, ugly or misshapen in form

go·by (gō′bē) *n., pl.* **-bies, -by:** see PLURAL. II. D. l [L. *gobio,* gudgeon < Gr. *kōbios*] any of a group of small, spiny-finned fishes: the ventral fins are sometimes modified into a suction disc

go-by (gō′bī′) *n.* [Colloq.] a passing by; esp., an intentional disregard or slight: chiefly in **give** (or **get**) **the go-by,** to slight (or be slighted)

go-cart (-kärt′) *n.* *same as* KART (sense 2)

god (god) *n.* [OE.] **1.** any of various beings conceived of as supernatural, immortal, and having power over people and nature; deity, esp. a male one **2.** an idol **3.** a person or thing deified or excessively honoured —[G-] in monotheistic religions, the creator and ruler of the universe, eternal, infinite, all-powerful, and all-knowing —**on the knees** (or **in the lap**) **of the gods** beyond human control or power

god·child (god′chīld′) *n., pl.* **-chil′dren** the person for whom a godparent is sponsor

god·daugh·ter (god′dôt′ər) *n.* a female godchild

god·dess (god′is) *n.* **1.** a female god **2.** a woman greatly admired, as for her beauty

go·de·tia (gō dē′shə, -shē ə) *n.* [after C.H. *Godet,* Swiss botanist] a plant of American origin, cultivated for its showy flowers

god·fa·ther (god′fä′thər) *n.* a male godparent

God-fear·ing (-fir′iŋ) *adj.* [*occas.* g-] **1.** fearing God **2.** devout; pious

God·for·sak·en (-fər sā′kən) *adj.* [*occas.* g-] **1.** depraved; wicked **2.** desolate; forlorn

God-giv·en (god′giv′ən) *adj.* [*occas.* g-] **1.** given by God **2.** very welcome; opportune

god·head (-hed′) *n.* **1.** godhood **2.** [G-] God

god·hood (-hood′) *n.* the state or quality of being a god; divinity

god·less (god′lis) *adj.* **1.** denying the existence of God or a god; irreligious **2.** impious; wicked —**god′less·ly** *adv.* —**god′less·ness** *n.*

god·like (-līk′) *adj.* like or suitable to God or a god; divine

god·ly (-lē) *adj.* **-li·er, -li·est** **1.** divine **2.** pious; devout; religious —**god′li·ness** *n.*

god·moth·er (-muth′ər) *n.* a female godparent

go·down (gō′doun′) *n.* [Anglo-Ind. < Malay *gedong*] in the Far East, a warehouse

god·par·ent (god′per′ənt) *n.* a person who sponsors a child, as at baptism, and assumes responsibility for its faith; godmother or godfather

God's acre a burial ground, esp. in a churchyard

god·send (god′send′) *n.* anything unexpected and needed or desired that comes at the opportune moment, as if sent by God

god·son (-sun′) *n.* a male godchild

God·speed (-spēd′) *n.* [contr. of *God speed you*] success; good fortune: a wish for the welfare a person starting on a journey or venture

god·wit (god′wit) *n.* [? echoic] a brownish wading bird, with a long bill that curves up at the tip

go·er (gō′ər) *n.* one that goes

gof·fer (gof′ər) *vt.* [Fr. *gaufrer,* to crimp < *gaufre,* honeycomb < Du. *wafel,* waffle, honeycomb] to pleat, crimp, or flute (cloth, paper, etc.) —*n.* **1.** an iron used to goffer cloth, etc. **2.** the act of pleating or fluting; also, a series of pleats, crimps or flutes: also **gof′fer·ing**

go-get·ter (gō′get′ər) *n.* [Colloq.] an enterprising and aggressive person

gog·gle (gog′′l) *vi.* **-gled, -gling** [ME. *gogelen*] **1.** *a*) to stare with bulging eyes *b*) to roll the eyes **2.** *a*) to bulge in a stare *b*) to roll: said of the eyes —*n.* **1.** a staring with bulging eyes **2.** [*pl.*] large spectacles, esp. those fitted with side guards to protect the eyes against dust, wind, water, etc. —*adj.* bulging or rolling: said of the eyes —**gog′-gle-eyed′** (-īd′) *adj.*

gog·gle·box (gog′′l boks) *n.* [Slang] a television set

go-go (gō′gō′) *adj.* [< Fr. à *gogo,* in plenty, ad lib.] **1.** of rock-and-roll dancing or cafés, etc. featuring it **2.** [Slang] lively, energetic, etc.

Goi·del·ic (goi del′ik) *adj.* [< OIr. *Góidel*] **1.** of the Gaels **2.** designating or of their languages —*n.* the subbranch of Celtic languages that includes Irish Gaelic, Scottish Gaelic, and Manx

go·ing (gō′iŋ) *n.* **1.** the act of one who goes **2.** a departure **3.** the condition of the ground or land as it affects travelling **4.** circumstances affecting progress —*adj.* **l.** moving; running; working **2.** operating successfully [a *going* concern] **3.** in existence or available [the best bet *going*] **4.** current [the *going* rate] —**be going to** to be intending to; will or shall —**get going** [Colloq.] to start —**get one going** [Slang] to make one excited, angry, etc. —**going on** [Colloq.] nearing or nearly (a specified age or time) —**going strong** continuing to function strongly, efficiently, successfully, etc.

go·ing-o·ver (-ō′vər) *n.* [Colloq.] **1.** an inspection, esp. a thorough one **2.** a severe scolding or beating

go·ings-on (gō′iŋz on′) *n.pl.* [Colloq.] actions or events, esp. when regarded with disapproval

goi·tre (goit′ər) *n.* [< Fr., ult. < L. *guttur,* throat] an enlarged thyroid gland, often visible as a swelling in the lower part of the front of the neck —**goi·tred** (goi′tərd), —**goi·trous** (goi′trəs) *adj.*

Gol·con·da (gol kon′də) *n.* [after an ancient city in S C India, noted for diamond cutting in the 16th cent.] a source of great wealth

gold (gōld) *n.* [OE.] **1.** a heavy, yellow, metallic chemical element that is highly ductile and malleable: it is a precious metal and is used in coins, jewellery, alloys, etc.: symbol, Au; at. wt., 196.967; at. no., 79 **2.** *a*) gold coin *b*) money; riches **3.** the bright yellow colour of gold **4.** a thing regarded as having the value, brilliance, etc. of gold **5.** an award given to mark the attainment of the highest standard, as in dancing, certain sports, etc. —*adj.* **1.** of, made of, or like gold **2.** having the colour of gold —**go off gold** leave the GOLD STANDARD

gold bloc the states which adhere to the GOLD STANDARD

gold·brick (-brik′) *n.* [U.S. Colloq.] anything worthless passed off as genuine or valuable

gold·crest (-krest') *n.* a small warbler with greenish plumage and a bright yellow-and-black crown

gold digger 1. a person who digs for gold 2. [Slang] a woman who tries to get money and gifts from her men friends

gold dust gold in very small bits or as a powder

gold·en (gōl'd'n) *adj.* 1. of, containing, or yielding gold 2. bright yellow, like gold 3. precious; excellent 4. prosperous and joyful 5. auspicious 6. richly mellow, as a voice 7. marking the 50th anniversary [a *golden* jubilee] —**gold'en·ly** *adv.* —**gold'en·ness** *n.*

Golden Age 1. *Gr. & Rom. Myth.* an early age in which people were ideally happy, innocent, etc. 2. [g- a-] a period of great progress, culture, etc.

golden eagle a large, strong eagle found in mountainous districts of the N Hemisphere, with brown feathers on the back of its head and neck

gold·en·eye (gōl'd'n ī') *n., pl.* **-eyes'**, **-eye'**: see PLURAL, II. D. 1 a swift, diving wild duck of Europe, Asia and N America, with yellow eyes and a dark-green back

Golden Fleece *Gr. Myth.* the fleece of gold guarded by a dragon until captured by Jason

golden hamster see HAMSTER

golden handshake [Colloq.] a sum of money given to an employee either on retirement or as compensation for loss of employment

golden mean the safe, prudent way between extremes; moderation

golden perch an Australian freshwater fish

golden retriever any of a breed of sporting dog with a thick, golden coat

gold·en·rod (-rod') *n.* a plant of the composite family, typically with long, branching stalks bearing clusters of small, yellow flower heads through late summer and autumn

golden rule the precept that one should behave towards others as one would want others to behave towards oneself: see Matt. 7:12; Luke 6:31

golden syrup a light golden-coloured treacle produced by the evaporation of cane sugar juice, and used to flavour puddings, cakes, etc.

golden wedding a 50th wedding anniversary

gold-filled (gōld'fild') *adj.* made of a base metal overlaid with gold

gold·finch (-finch') *n.* [OE. *goldfinc*] 1. a European songbird with yellow-streaked wings 2. any of several small American finches, esp. one the male of which has a yellow body and black markings on the wings

gold·fish (-fish') *n., pl.* **-fish'**, **-fish'es**: see FISH a small, golden-yellow or orange fish of the carp family, often kept in fishbowls

gold foil gold beaten into thin sheets slightly thicker than gold leaf —**gold'-foil'** *adj.*

gold leaf gold beaten into very thin sheets, used for gilding —**gold'-leaf'** *adj.*

gold medal a medal awarded to an entrant who is placed first in a competition

gold plate tableware made of gold

gold rush a rush of people to territory where gold has recently been discovered

gold·smith (-smith') *n.* a skilled worker who makes articles of gold

gold standard a monetary standard in which the basic currency unit is made equal to and redeemable by a specified quantity of gold

golf (golf) *n.* [< ?] an outdoor game played on a golf course with a small, hard ball and a set of clubs, the object being to hit the ball into each of 9 or 18 holes in turn, with the fewest possible strokes —*vi.* to play golf —**golf'er** *n.*

golf club 1. any of a set of clubs used in golf: each has a wooden or metal head and a long slender shaft 2. an organization operating a golf course, clubhouse, etc.

golf course (or **links**) a tract of land for playing golf, with tees, fairways, greens, etc.

Go·li·ath (gə li'əth) *n.* [after the Philistine giant killed by David: 1 Samuel 17] a giant

gol·li·wog (gol'ē wog') *n.* [< ? POLLIWOG: name first used in a series of U.S. children's books] a soft doll with a black face, usually made of cloth or rags

gol·lop (gol'əp) *vi., vt.* [< ? GULP] [Colloq.] to eat or drink quickly and greedily

gol·ly (gol'ē) *interj.* an exclamation of surprise, etc.: a euphemism for *God*

go·losh, **go·loshe** (gə losh') *n.* var. of GALOSH

G.O.M. Grand Old Man: originally W.E. Gladstone

-gon (gon, gən) [< Gr. < *gōnia*, an angle] a combining form meaning a figure having a (specified number of) angles [pentagon]

go·nad (gō'nad; *occas.* gon'ad) *n.* [< ModL. < Gr. *gonē*, a seed] an animal organ producing reproductive cells; ovary or testis —**go·nad'al** *adj.*

gon·do·la (gon'də lə) *n.* [It. (Venetian) < ?] 1. a long, narrow boat with a high, pointed prow and stern, propelled by a pole or one oar on the canals of Venice 2. the car of an airship or balloon 3. a car suspended from and moved along a cable, for holding passengers

GONDOLA

gon·do·lier (gon'də lir') *n.* a man who rows or poles a gondola

gone (gon) *pp.* of GO —*adj.* 1. moved away 2. ruined 3. lost 4. dead 5. faint; weak 6. used up; consumed 7. ago; past 8. [Colloq.] pregnant —**far gone** 1. deeply involved 2. very tired or ill —**gone on** [Colloq.] in love with; enraptured with

gon·er (gon'ər) *n.* [Colloq.] one beyond help or seemingly sure to die soon, be ruined, etc.

gon·fa·lon (gon'fə lən) *n.* [Fr. < OFr. < Frank. < *gund*, a battle + *fano*, banner] a flag hanging from a crosspiece instead of on an upright staff, usually ending in streamers —**gon'fa·lon·ier** *n.*

gong (gon) *n.* [Malay *gun*: echoic] 1. a slightly convex metallic disc that gives a loud, resonant tone when struck 2. a saucer-shaped bell with such a tone

go·ni·om·e·ter (gō'nē om'ə tər) *n.* [< Gr. *gōnia*, angle, + -METER] 1. an instrument for measuring angles, esp. of solid bodies 2. *Radio* an electric device used to determine the direction of signals from a transmitting station —**go·ni·o·met'ric** *adj.* —**go·ni·om'e·try** *n.*

-go·ni·um (gō'nē əm) [ModL. < Gr. *gonos*, seed] a combining form meaning a cell or structure in which reproductive cells are formed [sporogonium]

gonk (gonk) *n.* [20th c., < ?] a small, rounded, long-haired doll

gon·o·coc·cus (gon'ō kok'əs) *n., pl.* **-coc'ci** (-kok'sī) [ModL. < Gr. *gonos*, a seed + COCCUS] the microorganism that causes gonorrhoea

gon·or·rhoe·a (-rē'ə) *n.* [< LL. < Gr. < *gonos*, a seed, semen + *rhein*, to flow] a venereal disease marked by inflammation of the mucous membrane of the genitourinary tract and a discharge of mucus and pus —**gon'or·rhoe'al** *adj.*

-go·ny (gə nē) [< L. < Gr. < base of *gignesthai*, to be born] a combining form meaning something generated, produced, descended, etc. [cosmogony]

goo (gōō) *n.* [Slang] 1. anything sticky, as glue 2. anything sticky and sweet 3. sentimentality

good (good) *adj.* **bet'ter**, **best** [OE. *god*] 1. a) suitable to a purpose; efficient [a *good* lamp] b) beneficial [good exercise] 2. unspoiled [good eggs] 3. valid; genuine; real [good money] 4. healthy [good eyesight] 5. financially sound [a *good* investment] 6. honourable; worthy [one's *good* name] 7. enjoyable, happy, etc. [a *good* life] 8. dependable; reliable [good advice] 9. thorough [did a *good* job] 10. a) above average [a *good* novel] b) not for everyday use; best [her *good* china] 11. adequate; satisfying [a *good* meal] 12. morally sound or excellent; specif., a) virtuous b) pious c) kind, generous, etc. d) well-behaved; dutiful 13. proper; correct [good manners] 14. able; skilled [a *good* swimmer] 15. loyal or conforming [a *good* Methodist] 16. considerable [a *good* many] 17. full; complete [a *good* six hours] —*n.* something good; specif., a) worth; virtue; merit [the *good* in a man] b) benefit; advantage [for the *good* of all] c) something desirable or desired See also GOODS —*interj.* an exclamation of satisfaction, pleasure, etc. —**a good question** one which is difficult to answer readily —**as good as** virtually; nearly —**for good** (**and all**) for always; permanently —**good and** [Colloq.] very or altogether —**good for** 1. able to endure or be used for (a period of time) 2. worth 3. able to pay or give 4. sure to result in [good for a laugh] —**good on you** [Aust. & N.Z.] well-done; good for you —**make good** 1. to repay or replace 2. to fulfil 3. to succeed in doing; accomplish 4. to be successful 5. to prove —**no good** useless or worthless —**the good** 1. those who are good 2. what is morally good —**to the good** as a profit or advantage

Good Book the Bible (usually with *the*)

good-bye, **good-bye** (good'bī') *interj., n., pl.* **-byes'** [contr. of *God be with ye*] farewell: term used in parting

good day a salutation of greeting or farewell

good-for-nothing (good'fər nuth'iŋ) *adj.* useless or worthless —*n.* such a person

Good Friday the Friday before Easter Sunday, commemorating the crucifixion of Jesus

good-heart·ed (-här'tid) *adj.* kind and generous —**good'-heart'ed·ly** *adv.* —**good'-heart'ed·ness** *n.*

good humour a cheerful, agreeable, or pleasant mood —**good'-hu'moured** *adj.* —**good'-hu'moured·ly** *adv.*

good·ish (-ish) *adj.* fairly good or fairly large

good looks attractive appearance; esp., pleasing facial features —**good′·look′ing** *adj.*

good·ly (-lē) *adj.* **-li·er, -li·est** 1. of attractive appearance 2. of good quality; fine 3. rather large; ample —**good′li·ness** *n.*

good·man (-mən) *n., pl.* **-men** [Archaic] 1. a husband or master of a household 2. a title like *Mr.,* for a man ranking below a gentleman

good morning a salutation of greeting or farewell used in the morning

good nature a pleasant, agreeable, or kindly disposition —**good′·na′tured** *adj.* —**good′·na′tured·ly** *adv.*

good·ness (-nis) *n.* 1. the state or quality of being good; specif., *a)* virtue; excellence *b)* kindness; generosity 2. the best part —*interj.* an exclamation of surprise

good night a salutation of parting or farewell used at night

goods (goodz) *n.pl.* 1. movable personal property 2. merchandise; wares 3. merchandise when transported, esp. by rail —**deliver the goods** [Colloq.] to do or produce the thing required —**get** (or **have**) **the goods on** [Slang] to discover (or know) something incriminating about —**the goods** [Slang] what is required or genuine

good Samaritan one who pities and unselfishly helps another or others: Luke 10:30-37

Good Shepherd an epithet for JESUS: John 10:11

good-sized (good′sīzd′) *adj.* big or fairly big

good-tem·pered (-tem′pərd) *adj.* not easily angered or annoyed —**good′-tem′pered·ly** *adv.*

good turn a good deed; friendly, helpful act

good·wife (-wīf′) *n., pl.* **-wives′** (-wīvz′) [Archaic] 1. a wife or mistress of a household 2. a title like *Mrs.,* for a woman ranking below a lady

good will 1. a friendly or kindly attitude 2. cheerful consent; willingness 3. the value of a business in patronage, reputation, etc., over and beyond its tangible assets Also **good′·will′** *n.*

good·y¹ (-ē) *n., pl.* **good′ies** [Colloq.] 1. something good to eat, as a sweet 2. *same as* GOODY-GOODY —*adj.* [Colloq.] *same as* GOODY-GOODY —*interj.* a child's exclamation of delight

good·y² (-ē) *n., pl.* **good′ies** [< GOODWIFE] [Archaic] a woman, esp. an old woman or a housewife, of lowly social status: used as a title with the surname

good·y-good·y (good′ē good′ē) *adj.* [Colloq.] moral or pious in a smug, showy way —*n.* [Colloq.] a goody-goody person

goo·ey (gōō′ē) *adj.* **goo′i·er, goo′i·est** [Colloq.] 1. sticky 2. sticky and sweet 3. sentimental

goof (gōōf) *n.* [prob. ult. < It. *goffo,* clumsy] [Slang] 1. a stupid or silly person 2. a mistake; blunder —*vt.* [Slang] to bungle; botch —*vi.* [Slang] to fool around; mess about

goof·y (-ē) *adj.* **goof′i·er, goof′i·est** [Slang] like or characteristic of a goof; stupid or silly —**goof′i·ly** *adv.* —**goof′i·ness** *n.*

goog·ly (gōō′glē) *n.* [20th c., < ?] *Cricket* a ball which changes direction on the bounce in a way opposite from that which might be expected from the apparent action of the bowler's wrist and arm

goon (gōōn) *n.* [Slang] 1. [< ? GUN] a ruffian or thug 2. [after a comic-strip character of E.C. Segar, 20th-c. U.S. cartoonist] a person who is awkward, grotesque, stupid, etc.

goo·ney bird (gōō′nē) [< *gooney,* sailors' name for the albatross] an albatross of a black-footed species: also **goo′ny bird**

goop (gōōp) *n.* [20th cent., prob. altered < GOOF] [Slang] a fool

goos·an·der (gōō san′dər) *n.* [prob. < GOOSE. after *bergander,* shelduck] a large, fish-eating, diving duck with a long, slightly hooked and serrated red bill

goose (gōōs) *n., pl.* **geese;** for 4 & 5 **goos′es** [OE. *gos*] 1. a long-necked, web-footed, wild or domestic bird that is like a duck but larger, esp. the female 2. its flesh, used for food 3. a silly person 4. a tailor's pressing iron, with a long, curved handle 5. [U.S. Slang] a sudden, playful prod in the backside —*vt.* **goosed, goos′ing** [U.S. Slang] to prod suddenly and playfully in the backside so as to startle —**cook one's goose** [Colloq.] to spoil one's chances, hopes, etc. —**the goose that lays the golden eggs** the source of one's present and future benefits

goose·ber·ry (gooz′bər ē, -brē) *n., pl.* **-ries** 1. a small, round, sour berry used in preserves, etc. 2. the shrub it grows on —**play gooseberry** be an unwanted third person in relation to a couple

goose flesh a roughened condition of the skin in which the papillae are raised, caused by cold, fear, etc.: also **goose pimples** (or **skin**)

goose·foot (gōōs′foot′) *adj.* designating a family of plants including spinach and beets —*n., pl.* **-foots′** any of a genus of plants of this family, with small, green flowers and, often, fleshy foliage

goose·gog (gooz′gog) *n.* [< GOOSE(BERRY) + ? dial. *gog,* < *gob,* a lump] [Colloq.] a gooseberry

goose·grass (-gräs) *n. same as* CLEAVERS

goose·neck (gōōs′nek′) *n.* any of various mechanical devices shaped like a goose's neck, as a flexible rod for supporting a desk lamp

goose step a parade marching step in which the legs are raised high and kept rigidly unbent —**goose′-step′** *vi.* **-stepped′, -step′ping**

go·pher (gō′fər) *n.* [< ? Fr. *gaufre,* honeycomb: from its burrowing] 1. a burrowing rodent, about the size of a large rat, with wide cheek pouches: also **pocket gopher** 2. a striped ground squirrel of N American prairies, related to the chipmunk

Gor·di·an knot (gôr′dē ən) *Gr. Legend* a knot tied by King Gordius of Phrygia, to be undone only by the future master of Asia: Alexander the Great, failing to untie it, cut the knot with his sword —**cut the Gordian knot** to find a quick, bold solution for a problem

Gor·don setter (gôr′d'n) [after a Scot. dog fancier, the 4th Duke of *Gordon* (1745?-1827?)] a large gundog of a breed having a silky, black coat marked with brown

gore¹ (gôr) *n.* [OE. *gor,* dung, filth] blood shed from a wound; esp., clotted blood

gore² (gôr) *vt.* **gored, gor′ing** [< OE. *gar,* a spear] to pierce as with a horn or tusk

gore³ (gôr) *n.* [OE. *gara,* corner < base of *gar,* a spear] a tapering piece of cloth in a skirt, sail, etc. to give it fullness —*vt.* **gored, gor′ing** to make or insert a gore or gores in

gorge (gôrj) *n.* [< OFr., throat, ult. < L. *gurges,* whirlpool] 1. the throat or gullet 2. the maw or stomach, or food filling it 3. a deep, narrow pass between steep heights 4. [U.S.] a mass, as of ice, blocking a passage —*vi., vt.* **gorged, gorg′ing** to stuff (oneself) with food; glut —**make one's gorge rise** to make one disgusted, angry, etc.

gor·geous (gôr′jəs) *adj.* [< OFr. *gorgias,* beautiful] 1. brilliantly coloured; resplendent 2. [Slang] beautiful, wonderful, delightful, etc. —**gor′geous·ly** *adv.* —**gor′geous·ness** *n.*

gor·get (gôr′jit) *n.* [< OFr. < *gorge:* see GORGE] 1. a piece of armour to protect the throat 2. a collar 3. a patch of colour on a bird's throat

Gor·gi·o (gô′jē ō) *n.* [Romany] the gypsies' name for a person who is not a gypsy

gor·gon (gôr′gən) *n.* [from the three sisters in Gr. Myth., so horrible that the beholder was turned to stone] any ugly, terrifying or repulsive woman

gor·go·ni·an (gôr gō′nē ən) *n.* [ModL. *gorgonia* < L., coral] any of numerous corals having a horny or calcareous branching skeleton

Gor·gon·zo·la (gôr′gən zō′lə) *n.* [< *Gorgonzola,* town in Italy] a white Italian pressed cheese with veins of blue-green mould and a strong flavour

go·ril·la (gə ril′ə) *n.* [< Gr. *gorillai* < an W African name] 1. the largest and most powerful manlike ape, native to the jungles of equatorial Africa 2. [Slang] *a)* a person regarded as like a gorilla in appearance, strength, etc. *b)* a gangster; thug

gor·mand (gôr′mənd) *n. same as* GOURMAND

gor·mand·ize (gôr′mən dīz′) *vi., vt.* **-ized′, -iz′ing** [< Fr. *gourmandise,* gluttony] to eat or devour like a glutton —**gor′mand·iz′er** *n.*

gorm·less (gôrm′lis) *adj.* [altered < dial. *gaumless* < *gaum, gome,* care < ME. *gome*] [Colloq.] slowwitted; stupid

GORILLA
(1.2-1.7 m high)

gorse (gôrs) *n.* [OE. *gorst*] furze —**gors′y** *adj.*

gor·y (gôr′ē) *adj.* **gor′i·er, gor′i·est** 1. covered with gore; bloody 2. full of bloodshed or killing —**gor′i·ly** *adv.* —**gor′i·ness** *n.*

gosh (gosh) *interj.* an exclamation of surprise, wonder, etc.: a euphemism for *God*

gos·hawk (gos′hôk′) *n.* [< OE.: see GOOSE & HAWK¹] a large, swift hawk with short wings

gos·ling (goz′lin) *n.* [< ON.] a young goose

go-slow (gō′slō′) *n.* a deliberate slackening of the rate of production by organized labour as a tactic in industrial negotiations or conflict

gos·pel (gos′p'l) *n.* [OE. *gōdspel,* lit., good news] 1. [often G-] *a)* the teachings of Jesus and the Apostles *b)* the history of the life and teachings of Jesus 2. [G-] *a)* any of the first four books of the New Testament (*Matthew, Mark, Luke,* or *John*) *b)* an excerpt from any of these, read in a religious service 3. anything regarded as the absolute truth: also **gospel truth** 4. any doctrine or rule widely or ardently maintained 5. a style of folk singing originally associated with evangelistic revival meetings in the southern states of the U.S. —*adj.* of (the) gospel or evangelism

gos·sa·mer (gos′ə mər) *n.* [ME. *gosesomer,* lit., goose summer: the period in autumn when geese are in season]

1. a filmy cobweb in the air or on bushes or grass 2. a very thin, soft, filmy cloth 3. anything like gossamer —*adj.* light, thin, and filmy: also **gos′sa·mer·y** (-mər ē)

gos·sip (gos′əp) *n.* [< Late OE. *godsibbe*, godparent: see GOD & SIB] 1. [Obs. or Dial.] *a)* a godparent *b)* a close friend 2. one who chatters or repeats idle talk and rumours, esp. about others' private affairs 3. *a)* such talk or rumours *b)* chatter —*vi.* to indulge in idle talk or rumours about others —**gos′sip·er** *n.* —**gos′sip·y** *adj.*

gossip column a part of a newspaper which is devoted to gossip about well-known people

got (got) *pt. & pp. of* GET

Goth (goth) *n.* [< LL. < Gr. *Gothai*, pl.] an uncouth, uncivilized person: after the Germanic people that invaded the Roman Empire in the 3rd-5th cent. A.D.

Goth., goth. Gothic

Goth·ic (goth′ik) *adj.* 1. of the Goths or their language 2. designating or of a style of architecture developed in W Europe from the 12th to 16th cent., characterized by flying buttresses, pointed arches, etc. 3. [*sometimes* g-] *a)* medieval *b)* not classical *c)* barbarous 4. of a style of literature using a medieval or macabre setting, atmosphere, etc., to suggest horror and mystery —*n.* 1. the East Germanic language of the Goths 2. Gothic style, esp. in architecture 3. *Printing* [*often* g-] a plain type with straight lines of uniform width and no serifs —**Goth′i·cal·ly** *adv.* —**Goth′i·cism** *n.*

got·ten (got′'n) *Archaic and U.S. pp. of* GET

Göt·ter·däm·mer·ung (göt′ər dem′ər ŏoŋ) *n.* [G.] same as TWILIGHT OF THE GODS

gou·ache (gŏo äsh′) *n.* [Fr. < It. *guazzo*, water colour < L. < *aqua*, water] 1. a way of painting with opaque water colours mixed with gum 2. such a pigment 3. a painting made with such pigments

Gou·da (cheese) (gou′də) [< *Gouda*, city in Netherlands] a mild, semisoft to hard cheese, usually coated with red wax

gouge (gouj) *n.* [< OFr. < VL. *gubia*, for LL. *gulbia* < Celt.] 1. a chisel with a curved, hollowed blade, for cutting grooves or holes in wood 2. *a)* a gouging *b)* the groove or hole —*vt.* **gouged, goug′ing** 1. to make grooves or holes in as with a gouge 2. to scoop or dig out 3. in fighting, to push one's thumb into the eye of —**goug′er** *n.*

gou·lash (gŏo′lash, -läsh) *n.* [< G. < Hung. *gulyás*, herdsman, hence herdsman's food] a stew of beef or veal and vegetables, seasoned with paprika, etc.: also **Hungarian goulash**

gou·ra·mi (gŏor′ə mē, gŏo rä′mē) *n.*, *pl.* **-mis, -mi:** see PLURAL, II, D, 1 [Malay *gurami*] 1. a food fish of SE Asia, that builds a nest 2. any of a number of related fishes, mostly brightly coloured, that are often kept in aquariums

gourd (gŏord) *adj.* [< OFr. < L. *cucurbita*] designating a family of plants that includes the melon, pumpkin, etc. —*n.* 1. any trailing or climbing plant of this family 2. *a)* same as CALABASH (sense 2a) *b)* the ornamental, inedible fruit of certain related plants 3. the dried, hollowed-out shell of such a fruit, used as a drinking cup, dipper, etc.

gourde (gŏord) *n.* [Fr. < L. *gurdus*, heavy] see MONETARY UNITS, table (Haiti)

gour·mand (gŏor′mənd) *n.* [< OFr.] 1. a person who likes to indulge in good food and drink, sometimes to excess 2. same as GOURMET —**gour′mand′ism** *n.*

gour·man·dise (gŏor′mən dīz′) *n.* [Fr.] a love of and taste for good food

gour·met (gŏor′mā; *Fr.* gŏor me′) *n.* [Fr. < OFr. *gourmet*, wine taster] a person who likes and is an excellent judge of fine foods and drinks; epicure

gout (gout) *n.* [< OFr. < L. *gutta*, a drop] 1. a disease marked by deposits of uric acid salts in tissues and joints, esp. of the feet and hands, with swelling and great pain, esp. in the big toe 2. a spurt, splash, etc. —**gout′i·ly** *adv.* —**gout′i·ness** *n.* —**gout′y** *adj.* **gout′i·er, gout′i·est**

gouty-stem (gou′tē stem) *n.* the Australian baobab tree

gov., Gov. 1. government 2. governor

gov·ern (guv′ərn) *vt.* [< OFr. < L. *gubernare* < Gr. *kybernan*, to steer] 1. to exercise authority over; rule, control, manage, etc. 2. to influence the action or conduct of; guide 3. to hold in check; curb 4. to regulate the speed of 5. to be a rule or law for 6. *Gram. a)* to require (a word) to be in a particular case or mood *b)* to require (a particular case or mood) —*vi.* to govern someone or something; rule —**gov′ern·a·ble** *adj.*

gov·ern·ance (-ər nəns) *n.* control or rule

gov·ern·ess (-ər nəs) *n.* a woman employed in a private home to train and teach the children

gov·ern·ment (guv′ər mənt, -ərn mənt) *n.* 1. *a)* the exercise of authority over a state, district, group, etc.; control; rule *b)* the right, function, or power of governing 2. *a)* a system of ruling, controlling, etc. *b)* an established system of political administration by which a nation, state, etc. is governed *c)* the study of such systems 3. all the people that administer the affairs of a nation, state, institution, etc. 4. [*often* G-] the executive or administrative branch of government of a

particular nation 5. *Gram.* the influence of a word over the case or mood of another —**gov′ern·men′tal** *adj.* —**gov′ern·men′tal·ly** *adv.*

gov·er·nor (guv′ə nər, -ər nər) *n.* 1. a person who governs; esp., *a)* one appointed to govern a dependency, province, etc. *b)* the representative of the Crown in a British colony *c)* the elected head of any state of the U.S. *d)* one of the group directing an organization or institution 2. the administrator in charge of a prison 3. a device automatically controlling the speed of an engine or motor as by regulating fuel intake 4. [Colloq.] a person with authority; esp., one's father or employer —**gov′er·nor·ship′** *n.*

governor general *pl.* **governors general, governor generals** a governor with deputy governors under him, as in the British Commonwealth: also **gov′er·nor-gen′er·al** *n.*, *pl.* **gov′er·nors-gen′er·al**

govt., Govt. government

gowk (gouk) *n.* [< ON. *gaukr*, a cuckoo] [Scot. and N Eng. Dial.] a fool

gown (goun) *n.* [< OFr. < LL. *gunna*] 1. a woman's long, usually formal dress 2. a surgeon's smock 3. a long, flowing robe worn traditionally by certain officials, clergymen, professors, etc. 4. the members of a college, etc. collectively, as distinct from the other residents of the community [conflicts between town and *gown*] —*vt.* to dress in a gown

goy (goi) *n.*, *pl.* **goy′im** (-im), **goys** [Yid. < Heb. *gŏi*, tribe, nation] a Jewish name for a person who is not a Jew

G.P., g.p. general practitioner

Gp. Capt. Group Captain

GPO, G.P.O. General Post Office

Gr. 1. Grecian 2. Greece 3. Greek

gr. 1. grade 2. grain(s) 3. gramme(s) 4. great 5. gross 6. gunner

Graaf·i·an follicle (or **vesicle**) (gräf′ē ən) [after Regnier de Graaf (1641-73), Du. anatomist] any of the small, round, fluid-filled sacs in the ovary of higher mammals, each of which contains a maturing ovum

grab (grab) *vt.* **grabbed, grab′bing** [prob. < MDu., MLowG. *grabben*] 1. to seize or snatch suddenly 2. to get possession of by unscrupulous methods 3. [Slang] to impress (one) greatly —*vi.* to grab or try to grab something (often with *for*, *at*, etc.) —*n.* 1. a grabbing 2. something grabbed 3. a device for clutching something to be hoisted —**grab′ber** *n.*

grace (grās) *n.* [< OFr. < L. *gratia*, pleasing quality < *gratus*, pleasing] 1. beauty or charm of form, movement, or expression 2. an attractive quality, feature, manner, etc. 3. *a)* a sense of what is right and proper; decency *b)* thoughtfulness towards others 4. good will; favour 5. [Archaic] mercy 6. a delay granted beyond the date set for the performance or payment of an obligation 7. a short prayer of blessing or thanks for a meal 8. [G-] a title of respect in speaking to or of an archbishop, duke, or duchess 9. *Music* [*pl.*] ornamental notes or effects, collectively 10. *Theol. a)* the unmerited love and favour of God towards man *b)* divine influence acting in man to make him pure and good *c)* the condition of a person thus influenced *d)* a special virtue given to a person by God —*vt.* **graced, grac′ing** 1. to give or add grace or graces to 2. to honour; dignify 3. *Music* to add a grace note or notes to —**in the good** (or **bad**) **graces of** in favour (or disfavour) with —**with good** (or **bad**) **grace** in a willing (or unwilling) way

grace-and-fav·our (-ənd fā′vər) *adj.* granted rent-free by the sovereign of Britain [a *grace-and-favour* house]

grace·ful (-f'l) *adj.* having grace (sense 1) —**grace′ful·ly** *adv.* —**grace′ful·ness** *n.*

grace·less (-lis) *adj.* 1. lacking any sense of what is right or proper 2. clumsy or inelegant —**grace′less·ly** *adv.* —**grace′less·ness** *n.*

grace note *Music* a merely ornamental note

Grac·es (grā′siz) *Gr. Myth.* three sister goddesses who controlled pleasure, charm, elegance, and beauty in human life and in nature

gra·cious (grā′shəs) *adj.* 1. having or showing kindness, courtesy, charm, etc. 2. merciful; compassionate 3. polite to those held to be inferiors 4. marked by the taste, ease, etc. associated with prosperity, education, etc. [*gracious* living] —*interj.* an expression of surprise —**gra′cious·ly** *adv.* —**gra′cious·ness** *n.*

grack·le (grak′'l) *n.* [L. *graculus*, jackdaw] 1. any of several American blackbirds that are somewhat smaller than a crow 2. any of various Asian starlings

grad. 1. graduate 2. graduated

gra·date (grā dāt′) *vt., vi.* **-dat′ed, -dat′ing** [backformation < ff.] to change, etc. by gradation; shade into one another, as colours

gra·da·tion (grā dā′shən) *n.* [Fr. < L. *gradatio* < *gradus*: see ff.] 1. a forming or arranging in grades, stages, or steps 2. a gradual change by steps or stages 3. a shading of one tone or colour into another 4. a step, stage, or degree in a graded series **5.** *same as* ABLAUT —**gra·da'-tion·al** *adj.* —**gra·da'tion·al·ly** *adv.*

grade (grād) *n.* [Fr. < L. *gradus,* a step < *gradi,* to step] **1.** any of the stages in a systematic progression **2.** *a)* a degree in a scale of quality, rank, etc. *b)* an accepted standard or level *c)* a group of the same rank, merit, etc. **3.** a mark or rating on an examination, in a school course, etc. —*vt.* **grad'ed, grad'ing 1.** to classify by grades of quality, rank, etc.; sort **2.** to give a grade (sense 3) to **3.** to gradate —*vi.* **1.** to be of a certain grade **2.** to change by gradation —**make the grade** to overcome obstacles and succeed

-grade (grād) [< L. *gradi,* to walk] *a combining form meaning* walking or moving [*plantigrade*]

grade·ly (grād'lē) *adj.* [ME. *greithli,* ready, prompt < ON. *greidhligr* < *greidhr,* ready] [Dial.] fine; excellent

grad·er (grā'dər) *n.* a person or thing that grades

gra·di·ent (grā'dē ənt, -dyənt) *adj.* [< L. prp. of *gradi,* to step] ascending or descending with a uniform slope —*n.* **1.** *a)* a slope, as of a road *b)* the degree of such slope **2.** *Physics* the rate of change of temperature, pressure, etc.

grad·u·al (graj'oo wəl) *adj.* [< ML. < L. *gradus:* see GRADE] taking place little by little, not sharply or suddenly —*n.* *Eccles.* **1.** a set of verses, esp. from the Psalms, following the Epistle at Mass **2.** a book containing these and other sung parts of the Mass —**grad'u·al·ly** *adv.* —**grad'-u·al·ness** *n.*

grad·u·al·ism (-iz'm) *n.* the principle of seeking only gradual social or political change —**grad'u·al·ist** *n., adj.* —**grad'u·al·is'tic** *adj.*

grad·u·and (grad'yoo and) *n.* one about to receive an academic degree

grad·u·ate (grad'yoo wit; *for v., and occas. for n.,* -wāt') *n.* [< ML. pp. of *graduare,* to graduate < L. *gradus:* see GRADE] a person who has completed a course of study at a university or college and has received a degree or diploma —*vt.* —**at'ed, -at'ing 1.** to mark with degrees for measuring **2.** to grade by size, quality, etc. —*vi.* **1.** to become a graduate of a university, etc. **2.** to change, esp. advance, by degrees —*adj.* **1.** graduated from a university **2.** of or for studies leading to degrees above the bachelor's —**grad'u·a'tor** *n.*

grad·u·a·tion (gra'dyoo wā'shən) *n.* **1.** *a)* a graduating or being graduated from a university *b)* the ceremony connected with this **2.** *a)* a marking with degrees for measuring *b)* a degree or the degrees marked **3.** a grading by size, quality, etc.

Grae·cism (grē'siz'm) *n.* **1.** an idiom of the Greek language **2.** the spirit of Greek culture **3.** imitation of Greek style in the arts

Grae·cize (-sīz) *vt., vi.* **-cized, -cizing** to make Greek; give a Greek form to —*vi.* to imitate the Greeks in language, manner etc.

Grae·co- *a combining form meaning* **1.** Greek or Greeks **2.** Greek and or Greece and

Grae·co-Ro·man (grē'kō rō'mən) *adj.* of or influenced by both Greece and Rome

graf·fi·to (grə fēt'ō) *n., pl.* **-fi'ti** (-ē) [It., a scribbling] an inscription or drawing scratched or scribbled on a wall, etc. in a public place

graft (graft) *n.* [< OFr. *graffe* < L. < Gr. *grapheion,* stylus: from resemblance of the scion to a pointed pencil] **1.** *a)* a shoot or bud of a plant or tree inserted into the stem or trunk of another for continued growth as a permanent part *b)* the inserting of such a shoot, etc. or the place of insertion *c)* a tree or plant with such an insertion **2.** a joining of one thing to another as if by grafting **3.** *a)* a taking advantage of one's position to gain money, etc. dishonestly, as in politics *b)* anything so gained **4.** *Surgery a)* a piece of skin, bone, etc. transplanted from one body, or place on a body, to another, where it grows permanently *b)* such a transplanting **5.** [Slang] work; exertion —*vt.* **1.** *a)* to insert (a shoot or bud) as a graft *b)* to insert a graft of (one plant) in another *c)* to produce (a fruit, flower, etc.) by a graft **2.** to join as if by grafting **3.** *Surgery* to transplant as a graft —*vi.* **1.** to be grafted **2.** to make a graft **3.** to obtain money, etc. by graft —**graft'age** *n.* —**graft'er** *n.*

Grail (grāl) [< OFr. *graal* < ML. *gradalis,* cup < ?] *Medieval Legend* the cup or platter used by Jesus at the Last Supper and the receptacle of drops of blood from Jesus' body at the Crucifixion: also called **Holy Grail**

grain (grān) *n.* [< OFr. < L. *granum*] **1.** a small, hard seed or seedlike fruit, esp. of a cereal plant, as wheat, rice, etc. **2.** cereal seeds or cereal plants **3.** a tiny, solid particle, as of salt or sand **4.** a tiny bit [a *grain* of sense] **5.** the smallest unit in certain systems of weights; as the avoirdupois, equal to c. 0.0648 gramme **6.** *a)* the arrangement of fibres, layers, or particles of wood, leather, etc. *b)* the markings or texture due to this **7.** the side of leather from which the hair has been removed **8.** disposition; nature —*vt.* **1.** to form into grains; granulate **2.** to paint or finish in imitation of the grain of wood, marble, etc. **3.** *a)* to remove the grain from (leather) *b)* to

put a finish on the grain surface of (leather) —*vi.* to form grains —**against the** (or **one's**) **grain** contrary to one's feelings, nature, etc. —**grained** *adj.*

grain alcohol ethyl alcohol, esp. when made from grain

grain·y (-ē) *adj.* **grain'i·er, grain'i·est 1.** having a well-defined grain, as wood **2.** coarsely textured; granular —**grain'i·ness** *n.*

gral·la·to·ri·al (gral'ə tôr'ē əl) *adj.* [L. *grallator,* stilt-walker + -IAL] of or pertaining to wading birds characterized by long legs

gram (gram) *n.* [Port. *grão* < L. *granum,* a seed] any of certain plants of the legume family, used as fodder, esp. the chickpea

-gram (gram) [< Gr.: see GRAMME] *a combining form meaning:* something written or recorded [*telegram*]

gram. 1. grammar **2.** grammatical

gra·min·e·ous (grə min'ē əs) *adj.* [L. *gramineus* < *gramen,* grass] **1.** of the grass family **2.** of or like grass; grassy

gram·i·niv·o·rous (gram ə niv'ə əs) *adj.* [< L. *gramen,* grass + -VOROUS] feeding on grasses; grass-eating

gram·ma·logue (gram'ə log) *n.* [< Gr. *gramma,* letter and *logos,* word] *Shorthand* a sign or symbol representing one word

gram·mar (gram'ər) *n.* [< OFr. < L. < Gr. *grammatikē* (*technē*), (art) of grammar, learning < *grammata:* see GRAMME] **1.** language study dealing with word forms (*morphology*), word order in sentences (*syntax*), and now often language sounds (*phonology*) **2.** the system of word forms and word order of a given language at a given time **3.** a body of rules for speaking or writing a given language **4.** a book or treatise on grammar **5.** one's manner of speaking or writing as judged by how it conforms to the rules of grammar

gram·mar·i·an (grə mer'ē ən) *n.* a specialist or expert in grammar

grammar school 1. orig. an endowed secondary school teaching esp. Latin and Greek **2.** a state-maintained secondary school providing an education with a strong academic bias

gram·mat·i·cal (grə mat'i k'l) *adj.* **1.** of or according to grammar **2.** conforming to the rules of grammar —**gram·mat'i·cal·ly** *adv.* —**gram·mat'i·cal·ness** *n.*

gramme, gram (gram) *n.* [< Fr. < LL. < Gr. *gramma,* a small weight, lit., what is written < *graphein,* to write] the basic unit of weight in the metric system, equal to one thousandth of a kilogramme (about 1/28 oz.)

gram molecule *same as* MOLE[4]: also **gram-mo·lec·u·lar weight** (gram'mə lek'yoo lər)

gram·o·phone (gram'ə fōn') *n.* [arbitrary inversion of PHONOGRAM] an instrument for reproducing sound that has been transcribed in a special groove on a disc: a needle or stylus follows this groove —**gram'o·phon'ic** *adj.*

gram·pus (gram'pəs) *n., pl.* **-pus·es** [< OFr. *graspeis* < L. *crassus,* fat + *piscis,* fish] **1.** any of a genus of small, black, fierce whales related to the dolphins **2.** [Colloq.] a person who is breathing hard [puffing like a *grampus*]

gran (gran) *n.* [Colloq.] grandmother

gran·a·dil·la (gran'ə dil'ə) *n.* [Sp., dim of *granada,* pomegranate] the edible fruit of certain passionflowers

gran·a·ry (gran'ə rē) *n., pl.* **-ries** [< L. < *granum,* grain] **1.** a building for storing threshed grain **2.** a region producing much grain

grand (grand) *adj.* [OFr. < L. *grandis,* large] **1.** higher in rank or status than others with the same title **2.** most important; main [the *grand* ballroom] **3.** imposing in size, beauty, and extent **4.** marked by splendour and display **5.** distinguished; illustrious **6.** self-important; pretentious **7.** lofty and dignified, as in style **8.** overall [the *grand* total] **9.** [Colloq.] excellent, delightful, etc. —*n.* a grand piano —**grand'ly** *adv.* —**grand'ness** *n.*

grand- *a combining form meaning* of the generation older (or younger) than [*grandfather, grandson*]

gran·dam (gran'dam, -dəm) *n.* [< Anglo-Fr.: see GRAND & DAME] [Archaic] **1.** a grandmother **2.** an old woman Also sp. **gran'dame**

grand·aunt (grand'änt') *n.* *same as* GREAT-AUNT

grand·child (gran'chīld') *n., pl.* **-chil'dren** a child of one's son or daughter

grand·dad, grand·dad (gran'dad') *n.* [Colloq.] grandfather

grand·daugh·ter (-dôt'ər) *n.* a daughter of one's son or daughter

grand duchess 1. the wife or widow of a grand duke **2.** a woman who has the rank of a grand duke and rules a grand duchy **3.** in czarist Russia, a princess of the royal family

grand duchy the territory or a country ruled by a grand duke or a grand duchess

grand duke 1. the sovereign ruler of a grand duchy, ranking just below a king **2.** in czarist Russia, a prince of the royal family

grande dame (gränd däm) [Fr., great lady] a woman, esp. an older one, of great dignity or prestige

gran·dee (gran dē´) *n.* [Sp. & Port. *grande:* see GRAND] **1.** a Spanish or Portuguese nobleman of the highest rank **2.** a man of high rank

gran·deur (gran´dyoor) *n.* [Fr. < *grand:* see GRAND] **1.** splendour; magnificence **2.** moral and intellectual greatness; nobility

grand·fa·ther (gran´fä´thər, grand´-) *n.* **1.** the father of one's father or mother **2.** a forefather

grand·fa·ther·ly (-lē) *adj.* **1.** of a grandfather **2.** having the conventional characteristics of a grandfather; kindly, indulgent, etc.

‡**Grand Gui·gnol** (grän gē nyôl´) [the name of a former theatre in Paris noted for such drama] [occas. g- g-] any dramatic production designed to shock its audience with gruesome or macabre content

gran·dil·o·quent (gran dil´ə kwənt) *adj.* [< L. < *grandis,* grand + *loqui,* to speak] using high-flown, pompous, bombastic words and expressions —**gran·dil´o·quence** *n.* —**gran·dil´o·quent·ly** *adv.*

gran·di·ose (gran´dē ōs´) *adj.* [Fr. < It. < L. *grandis,* great] **1.** having grandeur; imposing; impressive **2.** pompous and showy —**gran´di·ose´ly** *adv.* —**gran´di·os´i·ty** (-os´ə tē) *n.*

grand jury *Law* in the U.S., and formerly in Britain, a jury that investigates accusations against persons charged with crime and indicts them for trial if there is sufficient evidence

grand·ma (gran´mä, gra´mä) *n.* [Colloq.] grandmother

grand mal (grän mäl´) [Fr., lit., great ailment] a type of epilepsy with convulsions and loss of consciousness: distinguished from PETIT MAL

grand·moth·er (gran´muth´ər, grand´-, gra´-) *n.* **1.** the mother of one's father or mother **2.** a female ancestor; ancestress

grand·moth·er·ly (-lē) *adj.* **1.** of a grandmother **2.** having the conventional characteristics of a grandmother; kindly, indulgent, etc.

Grand National an annual steeplechase run at Aintree, Liverpool

grand·neph·ew (gran´nef´yoo, -nev´yoo, -grand´-) *n.* the grandson of one's brother or sister

grand·niece (-nēs´) *n.* the granddaughter of one's brother or sister

grand opera opera, generally on a serious theme, in which the whole text is set to music

grand·pa (gran´pä, grand´-, gram´-) *n.* [Colloq.] grandfather

grand·par·ent (-per´ənt) *n.* a grandfather or grandmother

grand piano a large piano with strings set horizontally in a harp-shaped case

Grand Prix (grän prē´) [Fr., lit., great prize] any of various international formula motor races

grand·sire (gran´sīr´, grand´-) *n.* [Archaic] **1.** a grandfather **2.** a male ancestor **3.** an old man

grand slam 1. *Bridge* the winning of all the tricks in a deal **2.** *Sport* the winning of all major competitions in a sporting season, esp. in tennis and golf

grand·son (gran´sun´, grand´-) *n.* a son of one's son or daughter

grand·stand (-stand´) *n.* the main seating structure for spectators at a sporting event, etc.

grand tour a tour of continental Europe

grand·un·cle (grand´un´k'l) *n.* same as GREAT-UNCLE

grange (grānj) *n.* [< Anglo-Fr. < ML. *granica* < L. *granum,* grain] **1.** a farm with its dwelling house, barns, etc. **2.** [Archaic] a granary; barn

gran·ite (gran´it) *n.* [< It. *granito,* grained, ult. < L. *granum,* grain] a very hard, crystalline, plutonic rock consisting chiefly of feldspar and quartz —**gra·nit·ic** (grə nit´ik, gra-) *adj.*

gran·ite·ware (-wer´) *n.* a variety of ironware coated with a hard, grained enamel

gra·niv·o·rous (grə niv´ər əs) *adj.* [< L. *granum,* grain, + -VOROUS] feeding on grain and seeds

gran·ny, gran·nie (gran´ē) *n., pl.* **-nies** [Colloq.] **1.** a grandmother **2.** an old woman **3.** a fussy, exacting person **4.** same as GRANNY KNOT

granny knot a knot like a reef knot but with the ends crossed the wrong way, forming an awkward, insecure knot: also **granny's knot**

grant (gränt) *vt.* [< OFr. *craanter,* to promise, ult. < L. prp. of *credere,* to believe] **1.** to give (what is requested, as permission, etc.); assent to **2.** a) to give formally or according to legal procedure b) to transfer (property) by a deed **3.** to admit as true without proof; concede —*n.* **1.** a granting **2.** something granted, as property, a right, money, etc. —**take for granted** to accept as a matter of course —**grant´a·ble** *adj.* —**grant´er,** *Law* **grant´or** *n.*

grant·ee (gränt ē´) *n. Law* a person to whom a grant is made

Granth (grunt) *n.* [< Hindi < Sans. *grantha,* a knot, tying together, a book] the sacred scripture of the Sikhs

grant-in-aid (gränt´in ād´) *n., pl.* **grants´-in-aid´** a grant of funds, as by a foundation, to support a specific programme

gran·u·lar (gran´yoo lər) *adj.* **1.** containing or consisting of grains or granules **2.** like grains or granules **3.** having a grainy surface —**gran´u·lar´i·ty** (-lar´ə tē) *n.* —**gran´u·lar·ly** *adv.*

gran·u·late (-lāt´) *vt., vi.* **-lat´ed, -lat´ing 1.** to form into grains or granules **2.** to make or become rough on the surface by the development of granules —**gran´u·la´tion** *n.* —**gran´u·la´tive** *adj.* —**gran´u·la´tor, gran´u·lat´er** *n.*

gran·ule (gran´yool) *n.* [< LL. *granulum,* dim. of L. *granum,* a grain] **1.** a small grain **2.** a small, grainlike particle or spot

grape (grāp) *n.* [< OFr. *grape,* bunch of grapes < *graper,* to gather with a hook < Frank. *krappo,* hook] **1.** a small, round, smooth-skinned, juicy berry, growing in clusters on woody vines and eaten raw, used to make wine, etc. **2.** grapevine **3.** a dark purplish red **4.** same as GRAPESHOT

grape·fruit (-frōot´) *n.* **1.** a large, round, edible citrus fruit with a pale-yellow rind and a somewhat sour, juicy pulp **2.** the tree it grows on

grape hyacinth any of various small, bulbous plants of the lily family, with clusters of rounded blue flowers resembling tiny grapes

grape·shot (-shot´) *n.* a cluster of small iron balls formerly fired as a cannon charge

grape sugar same as DEXTROSE

grape·vine (-vīn´) *n.* **1.** a woody vine bearing grapes **2.** a secret means of spreading information: in full, **grapevine telegraph 3.** a rumour

graph[1] (graf, gräf) *n.* [short for *graphic formula*] **1.** a diagram, or a visual representation, as a broken line, that shows the relationship between certain sets of numbers **2.** *Math.* a) a picture showing the values taken on by a function b) a diagram consisting of nodes and links and representing logical relationships or sequences of events —*vt.* to represent by a graph

graph[2] (graf, gräf) *n.* [f. ff.] *Linguis.* a symbol used in a writing system that is not further subdivisible into other symbols

GRAPH

-graph (graf) [Gr. *-graphos* < *graphein,* to write] a combining form meaning: **1.** something that writes or records [*telegraph*] **2.** something written [*monograph*]

graph·eme (graf´ēm) *n.* [GRAPH[2] + -eme (as in PHONEME)] *Linguis.* a minimum unit of writing, such as a letter of an alphabet, that, although it may take different shapes, is regarded as a single representation of the same letter

-gra·pher (grə fər) a combining form meaning a person who writes, records, makes copies, etc. [*telegrapher, stenographer*]

graph·ic (graf´ik) *adj.* [< L. < Gr. *graphikos* < *graphein,* to write] **1.** described in realistic detail; vivid **2.** of the GRAPHIC ARTS **3.** a) of or expressed in handwriting b) written or inscribed **4.** shown by graphs or diagrams Also **graph´i·cal** —**graph´i·cal·ly** *adv.* —**graph´ic·ness** *n.*

-graph·ic (graf´ik) a combining form used to form adjectives corresponding to nouns ending in -GRAPH: also **-graph´i·cal**

graphic arts 1. any form of visual artistic representation, esp. painting, drawing, etc. **2.** those arts in which impressions are printed from various kinds of blocks, plates, etc., as etching, lithography, etc.

graph·ics (-iks) *n.pl.* [with sing. v.] [< GRAPHIC] **1.** the art of making drawings, as in architecture or engineering, in accordance with mathematical rules **2.** calculation of stresses, etc., from such drawings **3.** a) design as employed in the graphic arts b) same as GRAPHIC ARTS **4.** *Linguis.* the study of writing systems

graph·ite (graf´it) *n.* [G. *Graphit* < Gr. *graphein,* to write] a soft, black, lustrous form of carbon found in nature and used for lead in pencils, for lubricants, electrodes, etc. —**gra·phit·ic** (gra fit´ik) *adj.*

graph·ol·o·gy (gra fol´ə jē) *n.* [< Fr. < Gr. *graphein,* to write + -LOGY] the study of handwriting, esp. as a clue to character, aptitudes, etc. —**graph·ol´o·gi´cal** *adj.* —**graph·ol´o·gist** *n.*

graph paper paper with small ruled squares on which to make graphs, diagrams, etc.

-gra·phy (grə fē) [< L. < Gr. < *graphein,* to write] a combining form meaning: **1.** a process or method of writing, or graphically representing [*lithography*] **2.** a descriptive science [*geography*]

grap·nel (grap'n'l) *n*. [< OFr. *grapil* < Pr. < *grapa* < Frank. *krappo*: see GRAPE] **1.** a small anchor with several flukes **2.** an iron bar with claws at one end for grasping and holding things

‡grap·pa (grä'pä) *n*. [It.] an Italian brandy distilled from the lees left after pressing grapes to make wine

grap·ple (grap''l) *n*. [OFr. *grapil*: see prec.] **1.** *same as* GRAPNEL (sense 2) **2.** a device consisting of two or more hinged, movable iron prongs for grasping and moving heavy objects **3.** a coming to grips —*vt.* **grap'pled, grap'pling** to grip and hold; seize —*vi.* **1.** to use a grapple (sense 2) **2.** to struggle in hand-to-hand combat **3.** to struggle or try to cope (*with*) —**grap'pler** *n*.

grappling iron (or **hook**) *same as* GRAPNEL (sense 2): also **grap'pling** *n*.

grap·to·lite (grap'tə līt') *n*. [< Gr. *graptos*, written down + -LITE] any of various extinct marine animals, abundant in Paleozic times and common as fossils

grap·y (grā'pē) *adj*. of or like grapes

grasp (gräsp) *vt*. [ME. *graspen*, prob. < MLowG.] **1.** to take hold of firmly as with the hand; grip **2.** to take hold of eagerly; seize **3.** to understand; comprehend —*vi.* **1.** to try to seize (with *at*) **2.** to accept eagerly (with *at*) —*n.* **1.** the act of grasping **2.** control; possession **3.** the power to hold or seize **4.** comprehension —**grasp the nettle** tackle an unpleasant or difficult task —**grasp'a·ble** *adj*. —**grasp'er** *n*.

grasp·ing (-iŋ) *adj*. **1.** that grasps **2.** eager for gain; avaricious —**grasp'ing·ly** *adv*. —**grasp'ing·ness** *n*.

grass (gräs) *n*. [OE. *grærs, græs*] **1.** any of a family of plants with long, narrow leaves, jointed stems, and seedlike fruit, as wheat, rye, oats, etc. **2.** any of various green plants with long, narrow leaves that are eaten by grazing animals **3.** ground covered with grass; pasture land or lawn **4.** [Slang] marijuana —*vt.* **1.** to put (animals) out to pasture or graze **2.** to grow grass over **3.** to lay (textiles, etc.) on the grass for bleaching —*vi.* **1.** to become covered with grass **2.** [Slang] to inform on someone, esp. to the police (often with *on*) —**let the grass grow under one's feet** to waste one's time or neglect one's opportunities —**grass'-like'** *adj*.

grass·hop·per (-hop'ər) *n*. any of a group plant-eating insects with two pairs of wings and powerful hind legs adapted for jumping

grass·land (-land') *n*. **1.** land with grass growing on it, used for grazing; pasture land **2.** prairie

grass parrot any of several small, bright, Australian parrots, esp. the budgerigar

GRASSHOPPER
(c.3 cm long)

grass roots [Colloq.] **1.** the common people, thought of in relation to their attitudes on political issues **2.** the basic source or support, as of a movement —**grass'-roots'** *adj*.

grass tree an Australian tree which produces a tuft of grass-like leaves and one bulrush-shaped spike

grass widow a woman temporarily separated from her husband

grass·y (-ē) *adj*. **grass'i·er, grass'i·est** **1.** of or consisting of grass **2.** covered with grass **3.** green like growing grass —**grass'i·ness** *n*.

grate¹ (grāt) *vt*. **grat'ed, grat'ing** [< OFr. *grater* < Frank.] **1.** to grind into particles by scraping **2.** to rub against (an object) with a harsh, scraping sound **3.** to grind (the teeth) together with a rasping sound **4.** to irritate; annoy —*vi.* **1.** to grind or rub with a rasping sound **2.** to make a harsh or rasping sound **3.** to cause irritation or annoyance —**grat'er** *n*.

grate² (grāt) *n*. [< ML. < L. *cratis*, a hurdle] **1.** *same as* GRATING¹ **2.** a frame of metal bars for holding fuel in a fireplace, etc. **3.** a fireplace —*vt.* **grat'ed, grat'ing** to provide with a grate or grates

grate·ful (grāt'fəl) *adj*. [obs. *grate* (< L. *gratus*), pleasing + -FUL] **1.** feeling or expressing gratitude; thankful **2.** causing gratitude; welcome —**grate'ful·ly** *adv*. —**grate'ful·ness** *n*.

grat·i·cule (grat'i kyool) *n*. [< L. *craticula*, fine wickerwork] a grid of intersecting lines for indentification of points, as on a map, in a telescope, etc.

grat·i·fy (grat'ə fī') *vt*. **-fied', -fy'ing** [< Fr. < L. *gratificare* < *gratus*, pleasing + *-ficare*, -FY] **1.** to give pleasure or satisfaction to **2.** to indulge; humour —**grat'i·fi·ca'tion** *n*. —**grat'i·fi'er** *n*.

grat·ing¹ (grāt'iŋ) *n*. a framework of parallel or latticed bars set in a window, door, etc.

grat·ing² (grāt'iŋ) *adj*. **1.** harsh and rasping **2.** irritating or annoying —**grat'ing·ly** *adv*.

gra·tis (grat'is, grāt'-) *adv., adj*. [L. < *gratia*, a favour] without charge or payment; free

grat·i·tude (grat'ə tyood) *n*. [Fr. < ML. < L. *gratus*, thankful] a feeling of thankful appreciation for favours received; thankfulness

gra·tu·i·tous (grə tyoo'ə təs) *adj*. [< L. < *gratus*, pleasing] **1.** *a*) given or received without charge; free *b*) granted without obligation **2.** without cause or justification; uncalled-for —**gra·tu'i·tous·ly** *adv*. —**gra·tu'i·tous·ness** *n*.

gra·tu·i·ty (grə tyoo'ə tē) *n., pl.* **-ties** [see prec.] a gift of money, etc., esp. one given for a service rendered; tip

gra·va·men (grə vā'mən) *n., pl.* **-mens, gra·vam'i·na** (-vam'ə nə) [LL. < L. < *gravis*, heavy] **1.** a grievance **2.** *Law* the gist of an accusation

grave¹ (grāv) *adj*. [Fr. < L. *gravis*, heavy] **1.** important; weighty **2.** threatening; ominous [a *grave* illness] **3.** solemn or sedate **4.** sombre; dull **5.** low or deep in pitch —*n.* *same as* GRAVE ACCENT —**grave'ly** *adv*. —**grave'ness** *n*.

grave² (grāv) *n*. [OE. *græf* < *grafan*, to dig] **1.** *a*) a hole in the ground in which to bury a dead body *b*) any place of burial; tomb **2.** final end or death —*vt.* **graved, grav'en** or **graved, grav'ing** **1.** to carve out; sculpture **2.** [Archaic] to engrave; incise **3.** to impress or fix sharply and clearly —**make a person turn in his grave** to be or do something that would have shocked or distressed a person now dead —**grav'er** *n*.

grave accent a mark (`) used to indicate: **1.** in French, the quality of an open *e* (è), as in *chère* **2.** full pronunciation of a syllable normally elided, as in *lovèd* **3.** secondary stress, as in *týpewriter*

grave·clothes (grāv'klōthz') *n.pl.* the clothes in which a dead body is buried

grave·dig·ger (-dig'ər) *n.* a person whose work is digging graves

grav·el (grav''l) *n*. [< OFr. dim. of *grave*, coarse sand, beach] **1.** a loose mixture of pebbles and rock fragments coarser than sand **2.** *Med.* a deposit of small concretions in the kidneys, gallbladder, or urinary bladder —*vt.* **-elled, -el·ling** **1.** to cover (a walk, etc.) with gravel **2.** to perplex

grav·el·ly (-ē) *adj*. **1.** full of, like, or consisting of gravel **2.** sounding harsh [a *gravelly* voice]

grav·en (grāv'n) *alt. pp.* of GRAVE²

graven image an idol made from stone, wood, etc.

Graves (grāv) *n*. a light white or red wine from the region of Graves in SW France

grave·side (grāv'sīd') *n*. the area beside a grave —*adj.* being, or taking place beside a grave

grave·stone (-stōn') *n*. an engraved stone marking a grave; tombstone

grave·yard (-yärd') *n*. a burial ground; cemetery

graveyard shift [Colloq.] a work shift that starts during the night, usually at midnight

grav·id (grav'id) *adj*. [< L. *gravidus* < *gravis*, heavy] pregnant

gra·vim·e·ter (grə vim'ə tər) *n*. [Fr. *gravimètre* < L. *gravis*, heavy + Fr. *-mètre*, -METER] **1.** a device used to determine specific gravity, esp. of liquids **2.** an instrument used to measure the earth's gravitational pull at different places

grav·i·met·ric (grav'ə met'rik) *adj*. **1.** of, or using, measurement by weight **2.** relating to measurements of the pull of gravity

gra·vim·e·try (grə vim'ə trē) *n*. [< L. *gravis*, heavy + -METRY] the measurement of weight or density

grav·i·tate (grav'ə tāt') *vi*. **-tat'ed, -tat'ing** **1.** to move or tend to move in accordance with the force of gravity **2.** to be attracted or tend to move (*towards*) —**grav'i·ta'tive** *adj*.

grav·i·ta·tion (grav'ə tā'shən) *n*. **1.** the act, process, or fact of gravitating **2.** *Physics a*) the force by which every mass or particle of matter attracts and is attracted by every other mass or particle of matter *b*) the tendency of these masses or particles to move towards each other —**grav'i·ta'tion·al** *adj*. —**grav'i·ta'tion·al·ly** *adv*.

grav·i·ty (grav'ə tē) *n., pl.* **-ties** [< L. < *gravis*, heavy] **1.** the state or condition of being grave; esp., *a*) solemnity or sedateness; earnestness *b*) danger or threat *c*) seriousness **2.** weight; heaviness [*specific gravity*] **3.** lowness of musical pitch **4.** gravitation; esp., the force that tends to draw all bodies in the earth's sphere towards the centre of the earth

gra·vure (grə vyoor', grā'vyoor) *n*. [Fr. < *graver*, to carve < Frank.] **1.** *a*) any process that makes or uses intaglio printing plates *b*) a plate or print so made **2.** *clipped form of: a*) PHOTOGRAVURE *b*) ROTOGRAVURE

gra·vy (grā'vē) *n., pl.* **-vies** [? a misreading of OFr. *grané* < ? *grain*, cooking ingredients] **1.** the juice given off by meat in cooking **2.** a sauce made with this juice and flour, seasoning, etc. **3.** [Chiefly U.S. Slang] *a*) money easily obtained *b*) any extra benefit

gravy boat a boat-shaped dish for serving gravy

gray (grā) *adj*. *var., now chiefly U.S., sp.* of GREY

gray·ling (-liŋ) *n., pl.* **-ling, -lings:** see PLURAL, II, D, 2 [GRAY + -LING¹: from the colour] **1.** a freshwater game fish related to the salmon 2. any of several varieties of grey or brown butterfly

graze[1] (grāz) *vt.* **grazed, graz′ing** [OE. *grasian* < *græs*, grass] 1. to feed on (growing grass, herbage, etc.) 2. to put livestock to feed on (a pasture, etc.) 3. to cause (livestock) to graze 4. to be pasture for —*vi.* to feed on growing grass, etc. —**graz′er** *n.*

graze[2] (grāz) *vt.* **grazed, graz′ing** [prob. < prec. in sense "to come close to the grass"] 1. to touch or rub lightly in passing 2. to scrape or scratch in passing [the shot *grazed* him] —*vi.* to scrape, touch, or rub lightly against something in passing —*n.* a grazing, or a scratch or scrape caused by it

gra·zi·er (grā′zi ər) *n.* 1. a person who grazes beef cattle for sale 2. [Aust.] *a)* a cattle raiser *b)* a sheep farmer

graz·ing (grā′zin) *n.* land to graze on; pasture

Gr. Brit., Gr. Br. Great Britain

grease (grēs; *for v. also* grēz) *n.* [< OFr., ult. < L. *crassus*, fat] 1. melted animal fat 2. any thick, oily substance or lubricant —*vt.* **greased, greas′ing** 1. to smear or lubricate with grease 2. to bribe or tip: chiefly in **grease the palm** (or **hand**) of —**greas′er** *n.*

grease monkey [Colloq.] a mechanic, esp. one who works on cars or aircraft

grease-paint (-pānt′) *n.* a mixture of grease and colouring matter used by performers in making up

greas·y (grē′sē, -zē) *adj.* **greas′i·er, greas′i·est** 1. smeared or soiled with grease 2. containing grease, esp. much grease 3. like grease; oily; slippery 4. oily; unctuous: said of a person's manner —**greas′i·ly** *adv.* —**greas′i·ness** *n.*

great (grāt) *adj.* [OE. *great*] 1. of much more than ordinary size, extent, number, etc. [the *Great* Lakes, a *great* company] 2. much above the ordinary or average in some quality or degree; esp., *a)* existing in a high degree; intense [great pain] *b)* very much of a [a *great* reader] *c)* eminent; distinguished; superior [a *great* playwright] *d)* very impressive or imposing [great ceremony] *e)* having or showing nobility of mind, purpose, etc. [a *great* man] 3. of most importance; main; chief [the *great* seal] 4. designating a relationship one generation removed [*great*-grandmother] 5. [Colloq.] clever; skilful [great at tennis] 6. [Colloq.] excellent, splendid, fine, etc. —*n.* a great or distinguished person: *usually used in pl.* —**great′ly** *adv.* —**great′ness** *n.*

great-aunt (-änt′) *n.* a sister of any of one's grandparents; grandaunt

Great Bear the constellation URSA MAJOR

great blackback a large, heavy gull of Europe, Asia and N America: also **great black-backed gull**

great calorie *same as* CALORIE (sense 2)

great circle any circle described on the surface of the earth or other sphere by a plane which passes through the centre of the sphere: the shortest course between any two points on the earth's surface lies along a great circle passing through these points

great-coat (grāt′kōt′) *n.* a heavy overcoat

Great Dane any of a breed of large, powerful dog with short, smooth hair

great·en (grāt′'n) *vt., vi.* [Archaic] to make or become great or greater

great-grand·child (grāt′gran′child′) *n., pl.* **-chil′dren** a child of any of one's grandchildren —**great′-grand′daugh′-ter** *n.* —**great′-grand′son′** *n.*

great-grand·par·ent (-gran′per′ənt) *n.* a parent of any of one's grandparents —**great′-grand′fa′ther** *n.* —**great′-grand′moth′er** *n.*

great-great- a combining form used with nouns of relationship to indicate two degrees of removal [*great-great*-grandparent]

great gross twelve gross

great·heart·ed (-här′tid) *adj.* 1. brave; fearless; courageous 2. generous; unselfish

great-neph·ew (-nef′yōō-nev′-) *n.* a grandson of one's brother or sister; grandnephew —**great′-niece′** (-nēs′) *n.fem.*

Great Russian 1. a member of the chief East Slavonic people of Russia 2. their language

Greats (grāts) *n.pl.* 1. the B.A. course, esp. in classics and philosophy, at the University of Oxford 2. the final examination of this course

great seal the chief seal of a nation, state, etc., with which official papers are stamped

great-un·cle (-un′k'l) *n.* a brother of any of one's grandparents; granduncle

Great War World War I (1914-18)

greaves (grēvz) *n.pl.* [< OFr. pl. of *greve*, shin] armour for the legs from the ankle to the knee

grebe (grēb) *n., pl.* **grebes, grebe:** see PLURAL, II, D, 1 [Fr. *grèbe*] any of a family of diving and swimming birds related to the divers, with partially webbed feet, and legs set far back on the body

Gre·cian (grē′shən) *adj. same as* GREEK (sense 1) —*n.* a Greek

Grecian profile a profile in which the nose and forehead form an almost straight line

Gre·cism (grē′sizm′) *n. same as* GRAECISM

Gre·cize (grē′sīz) *vt., vi.* **-cized, -cizing** *same as* GRAECIZE

Gre·co- *same as* GRAECO-

greed (grēd) *n.* [back-formation < ff.] excessive desire; esp. for wealth or food

greed·y (-ē) *adj.* **greed′i·er, greed′i·est** [OE. *grædig*] 1. wanting or taking all that one can get; desiring more than one needs or deserves; avaricious 2. having too strong a desire for food and drink; gluttonous 3. intensely eager —**greed′i·ly** *adv.* —**greed′i·ness** *n.*

Greek (grēk) *n.* 1. a native or inhabitant of ancient or modern Greece 2. the branch of the Indo-European language family consisting of the dialects of Greece, ancient or modern —*adj.* 1. of ancient or modern Greece, its people, language, or culture 2. designating of, or using the rite of the Orthodox Eastern Church —**be Greek to one** to be incomprehensible to one

Greek cross a cross with four equal arms at right angles

Greek fire an incendiary material used in ancient warfare, described as able to burn in water

Greek (Orthodox) Church 1. the established church of Greece, an autonomous part of the Orthodox Eastern Church 2. *popular name for* ORTHODOX EASTERN CHURCH Also **Greek Church**

green (grēn) *adj.* [OE. *grene*] 1. of the colour that is characteristic of growing grass 2. overspread with green foliage [a *green* field] 3. keeping the green grass of summer; snowless [a *green* December] 4. sickly or bilious, as from illness, fear, etc. 5. not mature; unripe 6. not trained; inexperienced 7. easily led or deceived; naive 8. not dried, seasoned, or cured 9. fresh; new 10. flourishing; vigorous 11. [Colloq.] jealous —*n.* 1. the colour of growing grass; colour between blue and yellow in the spectrum 2. any green pigment or dye 3. anything coloured green, as clothing 4. [pl.] green leaves, branches, etc., 5. [pl.] green leafy plants or vegetables, as spinach, cabbage etc. 6. an area of smooth turf set aside for special purposes [a village *green*] 7. *Golf* a putting green —*vt., vi.* to make or become green —**the Green** Ireland's national colour —**green′ish** *adj.* —**green′ly** *adv.* —**green′-ness** *n.*

green·back (-bak′) *n.* [U.S. Colloq.] any piece of U.S. paper money printed in green ink on the back

green bean any of various bean plants, as the French bean, that have narrow, green, edible pods

green·belt (-belt′) *n.* an area round a city, preserved by official authority as open or agricultural land

Green Cross Code a code for children giving rules for road safety

green·er·y (grēn′ər ē) *n., pl.* **-er·ies** green vegetation, esp. when used for decoration; verdure

green-eyed (-īd′) *adj.* 1. having green eyes 2. very jealous

green·finch (-finch′) *n.* a finch with olive-green and yellow feathers, native to Europe

green fingers talent in growing plants

greenfly (-flī) *n.* a garden pest attacking rose bushes, fruit bushes, etc.; an aphid

green·gage (-gāj′) *n.* [after Sir William *Gage*, who introduced it into England, c. 1725] a large plum with golden-green skin and flesh

green·gro·cer (-grō′sər) *n.* a retail dealer in fresh vegetables and fruit —**green′gro′cer·y** *n.*

green·horn (-hôrn′) *n.* [orig. with reference to a young animal with immature horns] an inexperienced person; beginner; novice

green·house (-hous′) *n.* a building made mainly of glass, with heat and humidity regulated for growing plants; hothouse

green·ing (-in) *n.* any of various apples having greenish-yellow skins when ripe

green·keep·er (-kē′pər) *n.* a person in charge of maintaining a golf course

green-leek (grēn′lēk′) *n.* a small Australian parakeet

green light [after the green ("go") signal of a traffic light] [Colloq.] permission or authorization to proceed with some undertaking: usually in **give** (or **get**) **the green light**

green paper a report containing policy proposals to be discussed, esp. by parliament

green pepper the green, immature fruit of the sweet red pepper, eaten as a vegetable

green·room (-rōōm′, -room′) *n.* a waiting room in some theatres, for use by performers when they are offstage

green·shank (-shank′) *n.* a bird of the sandpiper family, with pale green legs

green-stick fracture (grēn′stik′) a partial fracture in which the bone is broken on only one side

green·sward (-swôrd′) *n.* green, grassy ground

green tea   tea prepared from leaves not fermented before drying

green turtle   a large, edible sea turtle with an olive-coloured shell

Green·wich (mean) time (grin′ij, gren′ich)   mean solar time of the prime meridian, which passes through Greenwich, a Greater London borough: used as the basis for standard time

green·wood (grēn′wood′) *n.*   a forest in leaf

greet[1] (grēt) *vt.* [OE. *gretan*]   **1.** to address with expressions of friendliness, respect, etc., as in meeting or by letter; hail; welcome   **2.** to meet, receive, or acknowledge (a person, event, etc.) in a specified way [he was *greeted* by a rifle shot]   **3.** to come or appear to; meet [a roaring sound *greeted* his ears] —**greet′er** *n.*

greet[2] (grēt) *vi.* [ME. *greten* < OE. *grætan*] [Scot] to weep; lament

greet·ing (grēt′iŋ) *n.*   **1.** the act or words of a person who greets; salutation; welcome   **2.** [*often pl.*] a message of regards from someone absent

greetings card   a decorated card bearing a greeting for some occasion, as a birthday

gre·gar·i·ous (grə ger′ē əs) *adj.* [< L. < *grex* (gen. *gregis*), a flock]   **1.** living in herds or flocks   **2.** fond of the company of others; sociable   **3.** having to do with a herd, flock, or crowd   **4.** *Bot.* growing in clusters —**gre·gar′i·ous·ly** *adv.* —**gre·gar′i·ous·ness** *n.*

Gregorian calendar   a corrected form of the Julian calendar, introduced by Pope Gregory XIII in 1582 and now used in most countries of the world

Gregorian chant   the ritual plainsong of the Roman Catholic Church, introduced under Pope Gregory I: it is unaccompanied and not divided into measures

greige (grāzh) *n.* [Fr. *grège*, raw (silk)] [Chiefly U.S.] a colour blending grey and beige —*adj.*   greyish-beige

grem·lin (grem′lən) *n.* [prob. < Dan. hyp. *græmling*, imp, dim. of obs. *gram*, a devil]   an imaginary small creature humorously blamed for the faulty operation of aircraft or other disruptions

gre·nade (grə nād′) *n.* [Fr. < OFr., pomegranate, ult. < L. *granatus*, having seeds < *granum*, a seed]   **1.** a small bomb detonated by a fuse and thrown by hand or fired from a rifle   **2.** a glass container thrown to break on impact and disperse the chemicals inside: used to spread smoke, tear gas, etc.

gren·a·dier (gren′ə dir′) *n.* [Fr. < *grenade*]   **1.** orig., an infantry soldier employed to carry and throw grenades   **2.** a member of a special regiment or corps, as the Grenadier Guards

gren·a·dine[1] (gren′ə dēn′, gren′ə dēn′) *n.* [Fr. < *grenade*, pomegranate]   a syrup made from pomegranate juice, used for flavouring drinks, etc.

gren·a·dine[2] (gren′ə dēn′, gren′ə dēn′) *n.* [Fr.]   a thin, loosely woven cloth, used for dresses, etc.

gres·so·ri·al (gre sôr′ē əl) *adj.* [< L. *gressus*, pp. of *gradi*, to walk]   adapted for walking

grew (grōō)   *pt.* of GROW

grey (grā) *adj.* [< OE. *græg*]   **1.** of the colour grey   **2.** *a)* darkish; dull *b)* dreary; dismal   **3.** *a)* having hair that is grey *b)* old   **4.** dressed in grey   **5.** designating a vague, intermediate area, as between morality and immorality —*n.*   **1.** a colour made by mixing black and white   **2.** a grey animal or thing —*vt., vi.* to make or become grey —**grey′·ly** *adv.* —**grey′ness** *n.*

grey·beard (grā′bird′) *n.*   an old man

Grey Friar   a Franciscan friar

grey·hound (grā′hound′) *n.* [OE. *grighund*]   any of a breed of tall, slender, swift hound with a narrow, pointed head and a smooth coat

grey·ish (-ish) *adj.*   somewhat grey

grey·lag (-lag′) *n.* [short for *grey lag goose:* from its colour and its late migration]   a wild grey goose of Europe and C Asia

grey matter   **1.** greyish nerve tissue of the brain and spinal cord, consisting of nerve cells and some nerve fibres   **2.** [Colloq] intelligence

GREYHOUND (70 cm high at shoulder)

grey squirrel   a large, grey squirrel with a bushy tail, native to E N. America; now common in Europe

grey·wacke (grā′wak′) *n.* [partial transl. of G. *Grauwacke*]   **1.** a nonporous, dark sandstone containing angular grains and fragments of other rocks   **2.** a fine-ground conglomerate resembling sandstone

grey wolf   a large, grey wolf that hunts in packs and was formerly common in the northern part of the Northern Hemisphere

grid (grid) *n.* [short for GRIDIRON]   **1.** a framework of parallel bars; gridiron; grating   **2.** a network of crossing parallel lines, as on graph paper   **3.** a metallic plate in a storage cell for conducting the electric current   **4.** an

electrode, usually a wire spiral or mesh, for controlling the passage of electrons or ions in an electron tube

grid·dle (grid′'l) *n.* [< Anglo-Fr. *gridil* < OFr. *graïl* < L. < *craticula*, gridiron < *cratis*, wickerwork]   a flat, metal plate or pan for cooking pancakes, etc. —*vt.* **-dled, -dling**   to cook on a griddle

grid·dle·cake (-kāk′) *n.*   a thin, flat batter cake cooked on a griddle

grid·i·ron (grid′ī′ərn) *n.* [ME. *gredirne*, folk etym. on *irne* (see IRON) < *gredire*, var. of *gredil*: see GRIDDLE]   **1.** a framework of metal bars or wires on which to cook meat or fish; grill   **2.** any framework resembling a gridiron   **3.** a framework above the stage in a theatre from which suspended scenery, lights, etc. are manipulated

grief (grēf) *n.* [< OFr. < *grever:* see GRIEVE]   **1.** intense emotional suffering caused by loss, disaster, etc.; acute sorrow; deep sadness   **2.** a cause or the subject of such suffering —**come to grief** to fail or be ruined

grief-strick·en (-strik′'n) *adj.*   stricken with grief; keenly distressed; sorrowful

griev·ance (grē′vəns) *n.*   **1.** a circumstance thought to be unjust or injurious and ground for complaint or resentment   **2.** complaint or resentment, or a statement expressing this, against a real or imagined wrong

grieve (grēv) *vt.* **grieved, griev′ing** [OFr. *grever* < L. *gravare*, to burden < *gravis*, heavy]   to cause to feel grief; afflict with deep sorrow or distress —*vi.* to feel deep sorrow or distress; mourn; lament —**griev′er** *n.*

griev·ous (grē′vəs) *adj.*   **1.** causing grief   **2.** showing or full of grief   **3.** causing suffering; severe   **4.** deplorable; atrocious [a *grievous* crime] —**griev′ous·ly** *adv.* —**griev′-ous·ness** *n.*

grif·fin (grif′ən) *n.* [< OFr. < OHG. or It. *grifo*, both < L. *gryphus* < Gr. < *grypos*, hooked]   a mythical animal, part eagle and part lion

grif·fon (grif′ən) *n.* [Fr., lit., a griffin]   **1.** *same as* GRIFFIN   **2.** any of various small, wire-haired breeds of dog, orig. from Belgium   **3.** any of various large vultures

grill[1] (gril) *n.* [Fr. *gril* < OFr. *graïl:* see GRIDDLE]   **1.** a gridiron (sense 1)   **2.** a device on a cooker to radiate heat downwards   **3.** grilled food   **4.** short for GRILLROOM —*vt.* **1.** to cook on a grill   **2.** to torture by applying heat   **3.** to question relentlessly —*vi.* to be subjected to grilling —**grilled** *adj.* —**grill′er** *n.*

grill[2] (gril) *n.*   *same as* GRILLE

gril·lage (-ij) *n.* [Fr., grating < *grille:* see ff.]   a system of beams laid crosswise to form a foundation for a building in soft soil

grille (gril) *n.* [Fr. < OFr. *graïlle:* see GRIDDLE]   an open grating of wrought iron, wood, etc., forming a screen to a door, window, or other opening, or used as a divider —**grilled** *adj.*

grill·room (gril′rōōm′) *n.*   a restaurant that makes a specialty of grilled foods

grill·work (-wurk′) *n.*   a grille, or something worked into the form of a grille

grilse (grils) *n., pl.* **grilse, grils′ es**: see PLURAL, II, D, 2 [< ?]   a young salmon on its first return from the sea to fresh water

grim (grim) *adj.* **grim′mer, grim′mest** [OE. *grimm*]   **1.** fierce; cruel; savage   **2.** hard and unyielding; relentless; stern   **3.** appearing stern, forbidding, harsh, etc.   **4.** repellent; uninviting; ghastly —**grim′ly** *adv.* —**grim′ness** *n.*

gri·mace (gri mās′, grim′əs) *n.* [Fr. < OFr. *grimuche*, prob. < Frank.]   a distortion of the face, as in expressing pain, contempt, etc., or a wry look —*vi.* **-maced′, -mac′ing** to make grimaces —**gri·mac′er** *n.*

gri·mal·kin (gri mal′kin, -môl′-) *n.* [earlier *gray malkin* (cat)]   **1.** a cat; esp., an old female cat   **2.** a malicious old woman

grime (grīm) *n.* [prob. < Fl. *grijm*]   sooty dirt rubbed into or covering a surface, as of the skin —*vt.* **grimed, grim′ing** to make very dirty or grimy

grim·y (grī′mē) *adj.* **grim′i·er, grim′i·est**   covered with grime; very dirty —**grim′i·ly** *adv.* —**grim′i·ness** *n.*

grin (grin) *vi.* **grinned, grin′ning** [OE. *grennian*]   **1.** to smile broadly   **2.** to draw back the lips and show the teeth in pain, scorn, etc. —*vt.* to express by grinning —*n.* the act or look of one who grins —**grin and bear it** to accept philosophically something painful or troublesome —**grin′-ner** *n.* —**grin′ning·ly** *adv.*

grind (grīnd) *vt.* **ground, grind′ing** [OE. *grindan*]   **1.** to crush into bits or fine particles between two hard surfaces; pulverize   **2.** to afflict with cruelty, hardship, etc.; oppress   **3.** to sharpen, shape, or smooth by friction   **4.** to press down or rub together harshly or gratingly [to *grind* one's teeth]   **5.** to operate by turning the crank of [to *grind* a coffee mill]   **6.** to produce as by grinding —*vi.* **1.** to perform the act of grinding something   **2.** to undergo grinding   **3.** to grate   **4.** [Colloq.] to study very hard and steadily —*n.* **1.** a grinding   **2.** the degree of fineness of something ground into particles   **3.** long, difficult work or study —**grind out** to produce by steady or laborious effort —**grind′ing·ly** adv.

grind·er (grīn′dər) n. 1. a person or thing that grinds; specif., a) any of various machines for crushing or sharpening b) a molar tooth c) [pl.] [Colloq.] the teeth

grind·stone (grīnd′stōn′) n. a revolving stone disc for sharpening tools or shaping and polishing things —**keep** (or **have** or **put**) **one's nose to the grindstone** to work hard and steadily

grin·go (griŋ′gō) n., pl. **-gos** [MexSp. < Sp., gibberish] in Latin America, a foreigner, esp. one who is British or N American

grip (grip) n. [< OE. gripa, handful < gripan, to seize] 1. a secure grasp; firm hold, as with the hand, teeth, etc. 2. any special manner of clasping hands, as between members of a secret society 3. the power of grasping firmly 4. mental grasp 5. firm control; mastery 6. a mechanical contrivance for clutching or grasping 7. the part by which something is grasped; handle 8.[Chiefly U.S.] a small travelling bag 9. Sports the manner of holding a bat, golf club, etc. —vt. **gripped grip′ping** 1. to take firmly and hold fast with the hand, teeth, etc. 2. to give a grip (n. 2) to 3. to fasten or join firmly (to) 4. a) to get and hold the attention of b) to have a strong emotional impact on —vi. to get a grip —**come to grips** to struggle or try to cope (with) —**grip′per** n.

gripe (grīp) vt. **griped, grip′ing** [OE. gripan, to seize] 1. formerly, a) to grasp; clutch b) to distress; afflict 2. to cause sudden, sharp pain in the bowels of 3. [Slang] to annoy; irritate —vi. 1. to feel sharp pains in the bowels 2. [Slang] to complain —n. 1. distress; affliction 2. a sudden, sharp pain in the bowels: usually used in pl. 3. [Slang] a complaint 4. [Archaic] a) a grasping b) control —**grip′er** n.

grippe (grip) n. [Fr., lit., a seizure < gripper < Frank.] earlier term for INFLUENZA

gri·saille (gri zī′, -zāl′; Fr. grē zä′y) n. [Fr. < gris, grey] a style of painting, esp. on glass, using only grey tints and giving the effect of sculpture in relief

gri·sette (gri zet′) n. [Fr., orig., grey woollen dress cloth < gris, grey] a French working girl

gris-gris (grē′grē) n., pl. **gris-gris** [Fr., of Afr. origin] an amulet, charm or spell: also sp. **gree-gree, gri-gri**

gris·ly (griz′lē) adj. **-li·er, -li·est** [OE. grislic] terrifying; ghastly —**gris′li·ness** n.

grist (grist) n. [OE.] grain that is to be or has been ground; esp., a batch of such grain —**grist to** (or **for**) **one's mill** anything one can use profitably

gris·tle (gris′'l) n. [OE.] cartilage, now esp. as found in meat —**gris′tli·ness** n. —**gris·tly** (gris′lē) adj.

grist·mill (grist′mil′) n. a mill for grinding grain, esp. for individual customers

grit (grit) n. [OE. greot] 1. rough, hard particles of sand, stone, etc. 2. a sandstone with sharp grains 3. stubborn courage; pluck —vt. **grit′ted, grit′ting** to grind (the teeth) in anger or determination —vi. to make a grating sound

grit·ty (grit′ē) adj. **-ti·er, -ti·est** 1. of, like, or containing grit; sandy 2. brave; plucky —**grit′ti·ly** adv. —**grit′ti·ness** n.

griz·zle¹ (griz′'l) n. [< OFr. < gris, grey] 1. [Archaic] grey hair 2. grey —vt., vi. **-zled, -zling** to make or become grey —adj. [Archaic] grey

griz·zle² (griz′'l) vi. [< ? GROUSE²] [Colloq.] to whine; whimper: used esp. of a child

griz·zled (griz′'ld) adj. 1. grey or streaked with grey 2. having grey hair

griz·zly (-lē) adj. **-zli·er, -zli·est** greyish; grizzled —n., pl. **-zlies** short for GRIZZLY BEAR

grizzly bear a large, ferocious bear of western N. America, with brown, grey, or yellow fur

groan (grōn) vi. [OE. granian] 1. to utter a deep sound expressing pain, distress, or disapproval 2. to make a creaking sound, as from great strain 3. to be so weighed down as to groan —vt. to utter with a groan or groans —n. a sound made in groaning —**groan′er** n. —**groan′ing·ly** adv.

groat (grōt) n. [< MDu. or < MLowG. grote] 1. an obsolete English silver coin worth four old pence 2. a trifling sum

groats (grōts) n.pl. [< OE. grotan, pl.] any grain that is hulled, or hulled and coarsely cracked

gro·cer (grō′sər) n. [< OFr. grossier < gros, GROSS] a shopkeeper who sells food and various household supplies

gro·cer·y (grō′sər ē) n., pl. **-cer·ies** 1. a grocer's shop 2. [pl.] the food and supplies sold by a grocer

grog (grog) n. [after Old Grog, nickname of E. Vernon (1684-1757), Brit. admiral] any alcoholic drink as rum, esp. when diluted with water

grog·gy (-ē) adj. **-gi·er, -gi·est** [< GROG + -Y²] 1. orig., drunk; intoxicated 2. shaky or dizzy —**grog′gi·ly** adv. —**grog′gi·ness** n.

grog·ram (grog′rəm) n. [< OFr. grosgrain, coarse grain (see GRAIN)] formerly, a coarse fabric of silk, or of silk, worsted, and mohair, often stiffened with gum

groin¹ (groin) n. [prob. < OE. grynde, abyss] 1. the hollow or fold where the abdomen joins either thigh 2. Archit. the sharp, curved edge at the junction of two intersecting vaults, or the rib covering it —vt. to build with a groin

GROIN

groin² (groin) n. var., esp. US., sp. of GROYNE

grom·met (grom′it, grum′-) n. [< obs. Fr. gromette, a curb] 1. a ring of rope or metal used to fasten the edge of a sail to its stay, hold an oar in place, etc. 2. an eyelet of metal, plastic, etc. Also **grum′met**

groom (grōōm, groom) n. [ME. grom, boy < ?] 1. a man or boy whose work is tending horses 2. any of various officials of the British royal household 3. same as BRIDEGROOM 4. [Archaic] a manservant —vt. 1. to clean and curry (a horse, dog, etc.) 2. to make neat and tidy 3. to train for a particular purpose [to groom a man for political office]

grooms·man (grōōmz′mən, groomz′-) n., pl. **-men** a man who attends a bridegroom at the wedding

groove (grōōv) n. [< ON. grof, a pit] 1. a long, narrow furrow cut in a surface with a tool 2. any channel or rut cut or worn in a surface 3. a habitual way of doing something; settled routine 4. [Slang] an exciting or stimulating person, place, experience, etc. —vt. **grooved, groov′ing** to make a groove or grooves in —vi. 1. [Slang] to have understanding, appreciation, enjoyment, etc. in a relaxed, unthinking way (usually with on or with) —**in the groove** [Slang] performing or performed with smooth, effortless skill: orig. of jazz

groov·y (grōō′vē) adj. **groov′i·er, groov′i·est** [< phrase in the groove: see prec.] [Slang] very pleasing

grope (grōp) vi. **groped, grop′ing** [OE. grapian, to seize] to feel or search about blindly or uncertainly —vt. to seek or find (one's way) by groping —n. a groping —**grop′er** n. —**grop′ing·ly** adv.

gros·beak (grōs′bēk′) n. [< Fr.: see GROSS & BEAK] any of various finchlike birds, with a thick, strong, conical bill

gro·schen (grō′shən) n., pl. **-schen** [G., ult. < ML. (denarius) grossus, lit., thick (denarius)] see MONETARY UNITS, table (Austria)

gros·grain (grō′grān′) n. [Fr. < OFr. gros, coarse + grain, GRAIN] a closely woven silk or rayon fabric with crosswise ribbing, used for ribbons, etc.

‡**gros point** (grō′pwän) n. [Fr., lit., large stitch] 1. a cross-stitch in embroidery 2. embroidery using this stitch

gross (grōs) adj. [< OFr. < LL. grossus, thick] 1. big or fat and coarse-looking; corpulent 2. flagrant; very bad 3. dense; thick 4. insensitive or unrefined 5. vulgar; obscene [gross language] 6. total; entire; with no deductions: opposed to NET² [gross income] —n. 1. pl. **gross′es** overall total, as of income, before deductions 2. pl. **gross** twelve dozen —vt., vi. [Colloq.] to earn (a specified total amount) before expenses are deducted —**in the gross** 1. in bulk; as a whole 2. wholesale: also **by the gross** —**gross′ly** adv. —**gross′ness** n.

gross national product the total value of a nation's annual output of goods and services

gross weight the total weight of a commodity, including the packaging or container

grosz (grôsh) n., pl. **grosz′y** (-ē) [Pol.] see MONETARY UNITS, table (Poland)

gro·tesque (grō tesk′) adj. [Fr. < It. < grotta, a grotto: from designs in Roman caves] 1. in or of a style of painting, sculpture, etc. in which forms of persons and animals are intermingled with foliage, etc. in a fantastic or bizarre design 2. characterized by distortions or incongruities in appearance, shape, etc.; bizarre 3. ludicrously eccentric; absurd —n. 1. a grotesque painting, sculpture, design, etc. 2. a grotesque thing or quality —**gro·tesque′ly** adv. —**gro·tesque′ness** n.

grot·to (grot′ō) n., pl. **-toes, -tos** [< It. < ML. grupta < VL. < L. crypta, crypt] 1. a cave 2. a cavelike summerhouse, shrine, etc. —**grot′toed** adj.

grot·ty (grot′ē) adj. [< GROTESQUE] [Slang] 1. ugly; unpleasant 2. unwell; miserable

grouch (grouch) vi. [< ME. grucchen: see GRUDGE] to grumble or complain in a sulky way —n. 1. a person who grouches continually 2. a grumbling or sulky mood 3. a complaint

grouch·y (-ē) adj. **grouch′i·er, grouch′i·est** in a grouch; grumbling; sulky —**grouch′i·ly** adv. —**grouch′i·ness** n.

ground¹ (ground) n. [OE. grund, bottom] 1. a) orig., the lowest part or bottom of anything b) the bottom of a body of water 2. the solid surface of the earth 3. the soil of the earth; earth; land 4. a) a particular piece of land [a burial ground] b) [pl.] land surrounding or attached to a building; esp., the lawns, gardens, etc. of an estate 5. any particular area of reference, discussion, etc.; subject [arguments covering the same *ground*] **6.** [*often pl.*] basis; foundation **7.** [*often pl.*] the logical basis of a conclusion, action, etc.; valid reason or cause **8.** the underlying, often primed, surface of a painting, coloured pattern, etc. **9.** [*pl.*] the particles that settle to the bottom of a liquid; dregs [coffee *grounds*] **10.** *Elec. U.S.* name for EARTH (sense 9) —*adj.* **1.** of, on, or near the ground **2.** growing or living in or on the ground —*vt.* **1.** to set on, or cause to touch, the ground **2.** to cause (a ship, etc.) to run aground **3.** to found on a firm basis; establish **4.** to base (a claim, argument, etc.) on something specified **5.** to instruct (a person) in the elements or first principles of **6.** to keep (an aircraft or pilot) from flying —*vi.* to strike the bottom or run ashore: said of a ship —**break ground 1.** to dig; excavate **2.** to plough **3.** to start any undertaking —**break new ground 1.** to do something that has not been done before; pioneer —**cover ground 1.** to move or traverse a certain distance **2.** to make a certain amount of progress —**cut the ground from under one** (or **one's feet**) to deprive one of effective defence or argument —**from the ground up** completely; thoroughly —**gain ground 1.** to move or forwards **2.** to make progress **3.** to gain in strength, popularity, etc. —**get off the ground** to get (something) started; begin to make progress —**give ground** to withdraw under attack; yield —**hold** (or **stand**) **one's ground** to keep one's position against opposition —**lose ground 1.** to drop back; fall behind **2.** to lose in strength, popularity, etc. —**run into the ground** [Colloq.] to overdo (a thing) —**shift one's ground** to change one's argument or defence —**suit down to the ground** [Colloq.] to suit completely

ground² (ground) *pt. & pp.* of GRIND

ground·age (groun'dij) *n.* [GROUND¹ + -AGE] a fee charged for permitting a ship to remain in a port

ground bass *Music* a short phrase played repeatedly in the bass against the harmonies of the upper parts

ground control personnel, electronic equipment, etc. on the ground for guiding aircraft or spacecraft in takeoff, flight, and landing operations

ground cover any of various dense, low-growing plants used instead of grass for covering the ground

ground crew a group of people in charge of the maintenance and repair of aircraft: also **ground staff**

ground floor that floor of a building which is on or near the ground level —**in on the ground floor** [Colloq.] in at the beginning of an enterprise and thus in an advantageous position

ground glass 1. glass whose surface has been ground so that it diffuses light and is not transparent **2.** glass ground into fine particles

ground·hog (ground'hog) *n.* [prob. transl. of Du. *aardvark*, AARDVARK] same as WOODCHUCK

ground·ing (ground'iŋ) *n.* [< GROUND¹] basic general knowledge of a subject

ground ivy a creeping plant with round, toothed leaves and blue flowers

ground·less (-lis) *adj.* without reason or cause —**ground'-less·ly** *adv.* —**ground'less·ness** *n.*

ground·ling (-liŋ) *n.* **1.** *a)* a fish that lives close to the bottom of the water *b)* an animal that lives on or in the ground *c)* a plant that grows close to the ground **2.** [orig. of spectators in a theatre pit] a person lacking critical taste

ground·nut (-nut') *n.* **1.** any of various N. American plants with edible tubers or tuberlike parts, as the peanut **2.** the edible tuber or tuberlike part

ground plan 1. same as FLOOR PLAN **2.** a first or basic plan

ground·sel (ground's'l, groun'-) *n.* [< OE., ? < *gund*, pus + *swelgan*, to swallow: from use in poultices] any of a group of plants of the composite family, with usually yellow, rayed flower heads

ground·sheet (ground'shēt) *n.* a waterproof cover placed on the ground, as in a tent

ground·sill (ground'sil) *n.* the bottom horizontal timber in a framework: also **ground'sel** (-s'l)

grounds·man (groundz'mən) *n.* a person who tends the grounds of a playing field, estate, cemetery, etc.

ground squirrel any of various small, burrowing animals related to tree squirrels and chipmunks

ground·swell (ground'swel') *n.* **1.** a violent swelling or rolling of the ocean, caused by a distant storm or earthquake **2.** a rapidly growing wave of public opinion, etc. Also **ground swell**

ground water water found underground in porous rock strata and soils, as in a spring

ground·work (-wurk') *n.* a foundation; basis

ground zero the surface area directly below or above the point of detonation of a nuclear bomb

group (groop) *n.* [< Fr. < It. *gruppo*] **1.** a number of persons or things gathered together and forming a unit; cluster; band **2.** a collection of objects or figures forming a design, as in a work of art **3.** a number of persons or things classified together because of common characteristics,

interests, etc. **4.** *Chem.* same as RADICAL **5.** *Mil.* a unit made up of two or more battalions or squadrons —*vt., vi.* to form into a group or groups —*adj.* of or involving a group —**group'ing** *n.*

group captain see MILITARY RANKS, table

group·er (groop'ər) *n., pl.* **-ers, -er:** see PLURAL, II, D, 1 [Port. *garoupa*] any of several large fishes found in warm seas

group·ie (groop'ē) *n.* [Colloq.] a girl fan of rock groups or other popular personalities, who follows them about, often in the hope of achieving sexual intimacy

grouse¹ (grous) *n., pl.* **grouse** [Early ModE. < ?] any of a number of game birds with a round, plump body, as the black grouse

grouse² (grous) *vi.* **groused, grous'ing** [orig. Brit. army slang < ?] [Colloq.] to complain; grumble —*n.* [Colloq.] a complaint —**grous'er** *n.*

grout (grout) *n.* [OE. *grut*] **1.** a thin mortar used to fill chinks, as between tiles **2.** a fine plaster for finishing surfaces **3.** [usually *pl.*] sediment; dregs —*vt.* to fill or finish with grout —**grout'er** *n.*

grove (grōv) *n.* [< OE. *graf*] **1.** a small wood or group of trees without undergrowth **2.** a group of trees planted to bear fruit, nuts, etc.; orchard

grov·el (grov'l) *vi.* **-elled, -el·ling** [< earlier *grovelling*, *adv.*, face downwards < ON.] **1.** to lie prone or crawl in a prostrate position, esp. abjectly **2.** to behave humbly or abjectly **3.** to wallow in what is low or contemptible —**grov'el·ler** *n.*

grow (grō) *vi.* **grew, grown, grow'ing** [OE. *growan*] **1.** to come into being or be produced naturally; spring up **2.** to exist as living vegetation; thrive [cactus *grows* in sand] **3.** to increase in size and develop towards maturity **4.** to increase in size, quantity, or degree **5.** to come to be; become [to *grow* weary] **6.** to become attached or united by growth —*vt.* **1.** to cause to grow; raise; cultivate **2.** to cover with a growth: used in the passive **3.** to allow to grow [to *grow* a beard] **4.** to cause to be or to exist; develop —**grow into** to grow or develop so as to be or to fit [a boy *grows into* a man; he *grew into* his job] —**grow on** to become gradually more acceptable, likable, etc. —**grow out of 1.** to develop from **2.** to outgrow —**grow up** to reach maturity; become adult —**grow'er** *n.*

growing pains 1. recurrent pains in the joints and muscles, esp. of the legs, of growing children **2.** difficulties experienced in the early development of any enterprise

growl (groul) *vi.* [< ? OFr. < MDu. *grollen*, to be noisy] **1.** to make a low, rumbling, menacing sound in the throat, as a dog does **2.** to complain angrily —*vt.* to express by growling —*n.* the act or sound of growling —**growl'er** *n.* —**growl'ing·ly** *adv.*

grown (grōn) *pp.* of GROW —*adj.* **1.** having completed its growth; mature **2.** covered with a growth **3.** cultivated as specified [home-*grown*]

grown-up (grōn'up') *adj.* **1.** adult **2.** of or for adults —*n.* an adult: also **grown'up'**

growth (grōth) *n.* **1.** a growing or developing **2.** degree or extent of increase in size, weight, power, etc. **3.** something that grows or has grown [a thick *growth* of grass] **4.** an outgrowth or offshoot **5.** a tumour or other abnormal mass of tissue in or on the body

groyne (groin) *n.* [< ? OFr. *groign*, snout < LL. *grunium*, snout: or var. of GROIN¹] a wall or jetty built out from a riverbank or seashore to control erosion; a breakwater

grub (grub) *vi.* **grubbed, grub'bing** [ME. *grubben*] **1.** to dig in the ground **2.** to work hard, esp. at menial or tedious jobs; drudge —*vt.* **1.** [U.S. and Aust.] to clear (ground) of roots and stumps by digging them up **2.** to dig up as by the roots; uproot (often with *up*) —*n.* **1.** the short, fat, wormlike larva of an insect, esp. of a beetle **2.** a drudge **3.** [Slang] food —**grub'ber** *n.*

grub·by (-ē) *adj.* **-bi·er, -bi·est 1.** infested with grubs **2.** dirty; messy; untidy **3.** inferior, mean, etc. —**grub'bi·ly** *adv.* —**grub'bi·ness** *n.*

grub·stake (-stāk') *n.* [GRUB, *n.* 3 + STAKE] [U.S. Colloq.] **1.** money or supplies advanced to a prospector in return for a share in his findings **2.** money advanced for any enterprise —*vt.* [U.S. Colloq.] **-staked', -stak'ing** to provide with a grubstake —**grub'stak'er** *n.*

Grub-street (grub'strēt) *n.* [< earlier name of a London street where many literary hacks lived] literary hacks —*adj.* [also g-] of or like literary hacks

grudge (gruj) *vt.* **grudged, grudg'ing** [OFr. *grouchier*] **1.** to envy (someone) because of his possession or enjoyment of (something) **2.** to give with reluctance —*n.* a strong feeling of hostility or ill will against someone over a grievance —**grudg'er** *n.* —**grudg'ing** *adj.* —**grudg'ing·ly** *adv.*

gru·el (groo'əl, grool) *n.* [OFr., coarse meal] thin, easily digested porridge made by cooking meal in water or milk

gru·el·ling (-iŋ) *adj.* [prp. of obs. v. *gruel*, to punish] extremely trying; exhausting

grue·some (groo'səm) *adj.* [< dial. *grue*, to shudder +

-SOME[1]] causing horror or loathing; grisly —**grue'some·ly** *adv.* —**grue'some·ness** *n.*

gruff (gruf) *adj.* [< Early ModDu. *grof*] **1.** rough or surly in manner or speech; rude **2.** harsh and throaty; hoarse —**gruff'ly** *adv.* —**gruff'ness** *n.*

grum·ble (grum'b'l) *vi.* **-bled, -bling** [prob. < Du. *grommelen*] **1.** to make low, unintelligible sounds in the throat **2.** to mutter or complain in a surly way **3.** to rumble —*vt.* to express by grumbling —*n.* a grumbling, esp. in complaint —**grum'bler** *n.* —**grum'bling·ly** *adv.* —**grum'bly** *adj.*

grum·met (grum'ət) *n. same as* GROMMET

grump (grump) *n.* [prob. echoic] **1.** [*often pl.*] a fit of bad humour **2.** a grumpy person —*vi.* to complain and grumble

grump·y (grum'pē) *adj.* **grump'i·er, grump'i·est** [prec. + -Y[2]] grouchy; peevish; bad-tempered: also **grump'ish** —**grump'i·ly** *adv.* —**grump'i·ness** *n.*

Grun·dy, Mrs. (grun'dē) [a prudish busybody referred to in an 18th-c. play] a personification of conventional social disapproval, prudishness, narrow-mindedness, etc. —**Grun'dy·ism** *n.*

grun·ion (grun'yən) *n., pl.* **-ion, -ions:** see PLURAL, II, D, 2 [prob. < Sp.] a sardine-shaped fish of the California coast

grunt (grunt) *vi.* [OE. *grunnettan*, freq. of *grunian*, to grunt] **1.** to make the short, deep, hoarse sound of a pig **2.** to make a sound like this, as in annoyance —*vt.* to express by grunting —*n.* **1.** the sound of grunting **2.** a saltwater fish that grunts when removed from water —**grunt'er** *n.*

Gru·yère (cheese) (grōo yer') [< *Gruyère*, Switzerland] a light-yellow Swiss cheese, rich in butterfat

gr. wt. gross weight

gryph·on (grif'ən) *n. same as* GRIFFIN

grys·bok (grĭs'bok) *n.* [Du., < Du. *grys*, grey + *bok*, BUCK[1]] a small S. African antelope

G.S., g.s. **1.** general secretary **2.** general staff **3.** ground speed

G-string (jē'striŋ') *n.* **1.** a narrow loincloth **2.** a similar band, worn by striptease dancers

G-suit (-sōot',-syōot') *n.* [*G* for *gravity*] a garment for pilots or astronauts, pressurized to counteract the effects of rapid acceleration or deceleration

gt. 1. [L. *gutta*] *pl.* **gtt.** *Pharmacy* a drop **2.** great

G.T. [It. *gran turismo*] *Motoring* sports tourer capable of high speeds

gtd. guaranteed

GU, g.u. genitourinary

guai·a·cum (gwī'ə kəm) *n.* [ModL. < genus name] **1.** *a)* any of several tropical American trees with purplish flowers and hard, durable wood *b)* this wood **2.** a greenish-brown resin from certain of these trees, used in medicine, in varnishes, etc.

gua·na·co (gwə nä'kō) *n., pl.* **-cos, -co:** see PLURAL, II, D, 1 [Sp. < Quechua *huanacu*] a woolly, reddish-brown, wild animal of the Andes, related to the camel and llama

gua·nine (gwä'nēn) *n.* [< ff. + -INE[4]] an organic base, that is in deoxyribonucleic acid and is found in all plant and animal tissues

gua·no (gwä'nō) *n., pl.* **-nos** [Sp. < Quechua *huanu*, dung] **1.** the manure of sea birds, found especially on islands off the coast of Peru: it is used as a fertilizer **2.** any fertilizer resembling this

guar. guaranteed

GUANACO
(1.2m high
at shoulder)

Gua·ra·ní (gwä'rə nē') *n.* [*Guaraní*, lit., warrior] **1.** *pl.* **-nís', -ní'** a member of a tribe of S. American Indians who lived east of the Paraguay River **2.** their language **3.** [g-] *pl.* **-nís'** *see* MONETARY UNITS, table (Paraguay)

guar·an·tee (gar'ən tē') *n.* [altered < GUARANTY] **1.** *same as* GUARANTY (*n.* 1 & 3) **2.** *a)* a pledge that something will be replaced if it is not as represented *b)* a positive assurance that something will be done in the manner specified **3.** a guarantor **4.** one who receives a guaranty **5.** something that promises the happening of some event [the dark clouds were a *guarantee* of rain] —*vt.* **-teed', -tee'ing 1.** to give a guarantee or guaranty for **2.** to promise [I *guarantee* to be there]

guar·an·tor (gar ən tôr', gar'ən tôr') *n.* one who makes or gives a guaranty or guarantee

guar·an·ty (gar ən tē') *n., pl.* **-ties** [< OFr. < *garant*, a warrant < Frank.] **1.** a pledge by which a person promises to pay another's debt or fulfil another's obligation if the other fails to do so **2.** an agreement that secures the existence or maintenance of something **3.** something given or held as security **4.** a guarantor —*vt.* **-tied, -ty·ing** *same as* GUARANTEE

guard (gärd) *vt.* [< the *n.*] **1.** to watch over and protect; defend; shield **2.** *a)* to keep from escape or trouble *b)* to

hold in check; control; restrain *c) Sports* to keep (an opponent) from making a gain or scoring; also, to cover (a goal or area) in defensive play —*vi.* **1.** to keep watch (*against*) **2.** to act as a guard —*n.* [< OFr. < *garder*, to protect < Gmc.] **1.** the act or duty of guarding; defence; protection **2.** a posture of defence, as in boxing, fencing, etc. **3.** any device that protects against injury or loss **4.** a person or group that guards; specif., *a)* a sentinel or sentry *b)* the official in general charge of a railway train *c)* [*pl.*] [*often* G-] a special unit of troops assigned to the British royal household *d)* a military unit with a ceremonial function [a colour *guard*] —**mount guard** to go on sentry duty —**off (one's) guard** not alert for defence —**on (one's) guard** alert for defence —**stand guard** to do sentry duty —**guard'er** *n.*

guard·ed (-id) *adj.* **1.** kept safe; watched over and protected; defended **2.** held in check; supervised **3.** cautious; noncommittal —**guard'ed·ly** *adv.* —**guard'ed·ness** *n.*

guard·house (-hous') *n. Mil.* **1.** a building used by the members of a guard when not on duty: also **guard room 2.** a building where personnel are confined for minor offences or while awaiting court-martial

guard·i·an (-ē ən) *n.* **1.** a person who guards or takes care of another person, property, etc. **2.** a person legally placed in charge of the affairs of a minor or of someone incapable of managing his own affairs —*adj.* protecting —**guard'i·an·ship'** *n.*

guards·man (gärdz'mən) *n., pl.* **-men** a member of The Guards or of any military guard

gua·va (gwä'və) *n.* [Sp. *guayaba* < native name in Brazil] **1.** any of several tropical American plants, esp. a tree bearing a yellowish, edible fruit **2.** the fruit

gua·yu·le (gwə yōo'lē) *n.* [AmSp. < Nahuatl *quauhitl*, plant + *olli*, gum] **1.** a small shrub of N Mexico, Texas, etc. **2.** rubber (**guayule rubber**) obtained from it

gu·ber·na·to·ri·al (gōo'bər nə tôr'ē əl) *adj.* [L. < *gubernator*, governor < *gubernare*, to steer] [Chiefly U.S.] of a governor or his office

gudg·eon[1] (guj'ən) *n.* [< OFr. < L. *gobio* < Gr. *kōbios*] **1.** a small, European freshwater fish, easily caught, and used for bait **2.** a goby or killifish **3.** a person easily cheated or tricked; dupe —*vt.* [Slang] to cheat; trick; dupe

gudg·eon[2] (guj'ən) *n.* [ME. *gogoun* < OFr. *gojon*, pivot] **1.** a metal pin or shaft at the end of an axle, on which a wheel turns **2.** the socket of a hinge, into which the pin is fitted **3.** the part of a shaft that revolves in a bearing

guel·der-rose (gel'dər rōz') *n.* [after *Gelderland*, a province of the Netherlands] a European shrub bearing clusters of white flowers: also called **snowball tree**

gue·non (gen'ən; *Fr.* gə nôn) *n.* [Fr.] any of a number of long-tailed African monkeys

guer·don (gur'd'n) *n., vt.* [< OFr., ult. < OHG. *widar*, back + *lōn*, reward] [Archaic] reward

Guern·sey (gurn'zē) *n., pl.* **-seys** [after one of the Channel Islands, where the breed originated] any of a breed of dairy cattle, usually fawn-coloured with white markings

guer·ril·la, gue·ril·la (gə ril'ə) *n.* [Sp. dim. of *guerra*, war < OHG.] any member of a small defensive force of irregular soldiers, usually volunteers, making surprise raids, esp. behind the lines of an invading enemy army —*adj.* of or by guerrillas

guess (ges) *vt., vi.* [prob. < MDu. *gessen*] **1.** to form a judgment or estimate of (something) without actual knowledge or enough facts for certainty; conjecture; surmise **2.** to judge correctly by doing this **3.** [U.S.] to think or suppose [I *guess* I can do it] —*n.* **1.** a guessing **2.** something guessed; conjecture; surmise —**guess'er** *n.*

guess·work (-wurk') *n.* **1.** the act of guessing **2.** a judgment, result, etc. arrived at by guessing

guest (gest) *n.* [ON. *gestr*] **1.** *a)* a person entertained at the home of another; visitor *b)* a person entertained by another acting as host at a restaurant, theatre, etc. **2.** any paying customer of a hotel, restaurant, etc. **3.** a person receiving the hospitality of a club, institution, etc. of which he is not a member **4.** a person who appears on a programme by special invitation **5.** an organism, as an insect, that lives on or in the abode of another —*adj.* **1.** for guests **2.** performing by special invitation [a *guest* artist] —*vi.* to be, or perform as, a guest

guest house an establishment offering accommodation; boarding house

guest rope 1. a rope in addition to the tow rope, used to steady a vessel being towed **2.** a rope fastened along a ship's side for attaching boats coming alongside

guff (guf) *n.* [echoic] [Slang] **1.** foolish talk; nonsense **2.** brash or insolent talk

guf·faw (gə fô') *n.* [echoic] a loud, coarse burst of laughter —*vi.* to laugh in this way

guid·ance (gīd'əns) *n.* **1.** the act of guiding; direction; leadership **2.** something that guides **3.** advice or assistance **4.** the process of directing the course of a spacecraft, missile, etc.

guide (gīd) *vt.* **guid′ed, guid′ing** [OFr. *guider*, var. of *guier* < Frank.] **1.** to point out the way for; conduct; lead **2.** to direct the course of (a vehicle, implement, etc.) **3.** to direct in (policies, actions, work, etc.); manage; regulate —*vi.* to act as a guide —*n.* a person or thing that guides; specif., a) one who leads others on a trip or tour b) one who directs, or serves as the model for, another in his conduct, career, etc. c) a part that controls the motion of other parts d) a guidebook e) a book giving instruction in the elements of some subject; handbook [a *guide* to mathematics] f) same as GIRL GUIDE —**guid′a·ble** *adj.*

guide·book (-book′) *n.* a book containing directions and information for tourists

guided missile a military missile whose course is controlled by radio signals, radar devices, etc.

guide dog a dog trained to lead a blind person

guide·line (-līn′) *n.* a standard or principle by which to determine a policy or action: also **guide line**

guide·post (-pōst′) *n.* **1.** a post, as at a roadside, with a sign and directions for travellers **2.** anything that serves as a guide, standard, etc.

guid·er (gīd′ər) *n.* the adult leader of a company of girl guides

gui·don (gīd′'n) *n.* [Fr. < It. *guidone*] **1.** the identification flag of a military unit **2.** the soldier carrying it

guild (gild) *n.* [< OE. *gyld* and ON. *gildi*, both < base seen in OE. *gieldan*, to pay] **1.** in medieval times, a union of men in the same craft or trade to uphold standards and protect the members **2.** any association for mutual aid and the promotion of common interests

guil·der (gil′dər) *n.* [< ME. < MDu.: see GULDEN] **1.** the monetary unit and a coin of the Netherlands: see MONETARY UNITS, table **2.** a former coin of the Netherlands, Germany, or Austria

guild·hall (gild′hôl′) *n.* **1.** a hall where a guild meets **2.** a town hall

guilds·man (gildz′mən) *n., pl.* **-men** (-mən) a member of a guild

guile (gīl) *n.* [OFr. *guile*, prob. < Frank. *wigila*, guile] slyness and cunning in dealing with others; craftiness —**guile′less** *adj.* —**guile′less·ly** *adv.* —**guile′less·ness** *n.* —**guile·ful** (-fəl) *adj.* full of guile; deceitful —**guile′ful·ly** *adv.* —**guile′ful·ness** *n.*

guil·le·mot (gil′ə mot′) *n.* [Fr., dim. of *Guillaume*, William] any of various narrow-billed, northern diving birds

guil·loche (gi losh′) *n.* [Fr. < *guillocher*, to ornament with lines] a decorative design in which curved lines are interwoven, forming a series of spaces between them

guil·lo·tine (gil′ə tēn′; *for v.* gil′ə tēn′) *n.* [Fr., after J. I. Guillotin (1738–1814), who advocated its use] **1.** an instrument for beheading by means of a heavy blade dropped between two grooved uprights **2.** a device with long, rigid, blade for cutting or trimming sheet material, as paper, metal, etc. **3.** a surgical instrument for removing tonsils, growths, etc. **4.** in Parliament, a form of closure under which a bill is divided into compartments, certain groups of which must be dealt with each day —*vt.* **-tined′, -tin′ing 1.** to behead with a guillotine **2.** to cut or trim (paper, etc.) with a guillotine **3.** in Parliament, to limit debate by means of a guillotine

GUILLOTINE

guilt (gilt) *n.* [OE. *gylt*, a sin] **1.** a) the act or state of having done a wrong or committed an offence b) a feeling of self-reproach resulting from a belief that one has done something wrong or immoral **2.** conduct involving guilt; crime; sin

guilt·less (-lis) *adj.* **1.** free from guilt; innocent **2.** having no knowledge or experience (with *of*) —**guilt′less·ly** *adv.* —**guilt′less·ness** *n.*

guilt·y (gil′tē) *adj.* **guilt′i·er, guilt′i·est 1.** having guilt; deserving blame or punishment **2.** having one's guilt proved; legally judged an offender **3.** showing or conscious of guilt [a *guilty* look] **4.** of, or involving, guilt or a sense of guilt [a *guilty* conscience] —**guilt′i·ly** *adv.* —**guilt′i·ness** *n.*

guin·ea (gin′ē) *n.* **1.** [first coined of gold from *Guinea*] a former British gold coin, last minted in 1813, equal to 21 shillings **2.** formerly, the sum of 21 shillings **3.** same as GUINEA FOWL

guinea fowl [orig. imported from *Guinea*] a domestic fowl with a featherless head, rounded body, and dark feathers spotted with white

guinea hen 1. a female guinea fowl **2.** any guinea fowl

guinea pig [prob. orig. brought to England by ships plying between England, *Guinea*, and S. America] **1.** a small, fat mammal of the rat family, with short ears and no external

tail, kept as a pet or used in biological experiments **2.** any person or thing used in an experiment or test

gui·pure (gē pyoor′) *n.* [Fr. < *guiper*, to cover with silk] **1.** lace without any ground mesh, having the patterns held together by connecting threads **2.** a kind of gimp (fabric)

guise (gīz) *n.* [OFr. < OHG. *wisa*, manner] **1.** manner of dress; garb **2.** outward aspect; semblance **3.** a false appearance; pretence [under the *guise* of friendship]

guis·er (gīz′ər) *n.* [< prec. + -ER] [Scot. and N Eng.] a mummer

gui·tar (gi tär′) *n.* [< Fr. < Sp. *guitarra* < Ar. < Gr. *kithara*, lyre] a musical instrument related to the lute but having a flat back and usually six strings that are plucked or strummed with the fingers or a plectrum —**gui·tar′ist** *n.*

Gu·lag (goo′lag) *n.* [Russ.] the central administrative department of the Soviet security service, responsible for prisons, labour camps, etc.

gulch (gulch) *n.* [prob. < dial. *gulch*, to swallow greedily] a steep-walled valley cut by a swift stream; deep, narrow ravine

gul·den (gool′dən) *n., pl.* **-dens, -den** [MDu. *gulden (florijn)*, golden (florin)] same as GUILDER

gules (gyoolz) *n.* [ME. *goules* < OFr. *goules*, gules, red-dyed ermine] red, esp. as a colour in heraldry

gulf (gulf) *n.* [< OFr. < It. *golfo*: ult. < Gr. *kolpos*, bosom] **1.** a large area of ocean, larger than a bay, reaching into land **2.** a wide, deep chasm or abyss **3.** a wide or impassable gap or separation —*vt.* to swallow up; engulf

Gulf States 1. states on the Gulf of Mexico; Alabama, Florida, Louisiana, Mississippi and Texas **2.** the oil-producing states around the Persian Gulf: Iran, Iraq, Kuwait, Saudi Arabia, Bahrein, Qatar, the United Arab Emirates, and Oman

Gulf Stream warm ocean current flowing from the Gulf of Mexico across the Atlantic and flowing around the British Isles, producing a milder climate than usual at the latitude

gulf·weed (-wēd′) *n.* a greenish-brown seaweed found in the Gulf Stream and the Sargasso Sea: also **Sargasso, sargasso weed**

gull¹ (gul) *n., pl.* **gulls, gull:** see PLURAL, II, D, 1 [< Celt.] a water bird with large wings, webbed feet, and white and grey feathers

gull² (gul) *n.* [prob. < ME. *golle*, silly fellow, lit., unfledged bird < ?] [Archaic] a person easily tricked; dupe —*vt.* to cheat; trick

Gul·lah (gul′ə) *n.* [< ? *Gola* (*Gula*) or < ? *Ngola*, tribal groups in Africa] **1.** any of a group of Negroes living in coastal S. Carolina and Georgia, U.S., and esp. on the nearby sea islands **2.** their English dialect

gul·let (gul′ət) *n.* [OFr. *goulet* < L. *gula*, throat] **1.** the tube leading from the mouth to the stomach; oesophagus **2.** the throat or neck

gul·li·ble (gul′ə b'l) *adj.* easily tricked; credulous —**gul′·li·bil′i·ty** *n.* —**gul′li·bly** *adv.*

gul·ly (gul′ē) *n., pl.* **-lies** [altered < ME. *golet*, water channel, orig., gullet: see GULLET] **1.** a channel worn by running water; small, narrow ravine **2.** *Cricket* a) a close fielding position on the off side behind the wicket b) a fielder playing in this position —*vt.* **-lied, -ly·ing** to make a gully in

gulp (gulp) *vt.* [prob. < Du. *gulpen*, to gulp] **1.** to swallow hastily, greedily, or in large amounts **2.** to choke back as if swallowing —*vi.* to catch the breath as in swallowing —*n.* **1.** the act of gulping **2.** the amount swallowed at one time —**gulp′er** *n.* —**gulp′ing·ly** *adv.*

gum¹ (gum) *n.* [< OFr. < L. *gumma* < Egypt. *kemai*] **1.** a sticky, colloidal carbohydrate found in certain trees and plants, which dries into a brittle mass that dissolves or swells in water **2.** any similar plant secretion, as resin **3.** any plant gum processed for use in industry, art, etc. **4.** a) an adhesive, as on the back of a postage stamp b) any of various sticky substances or deposits **5.** same as GUM TREE **6.** same as CHEWING GUM —*vt.* **gummed, gum′ming** to coat, unite, or stiffen with gum —*vi.* **1.** to secrete or form gum **2.** to become sticky or clogged —**gum up** [Colloq.] to put out of working order

gum² (gum) *n.* [OE. *goma*] [often *pl.*] the firm flesh surrounding the base of the teeth —*vt.* **gummed, gum′ming** to chew with toothless gums

gum ammoniac same as AMMONIAC

gum arabic a gum obtained from several African acacias, used in medicine and sweets, for stabilizing emulsions, etc.

gum·bo (gum′bō) *n.* [< Bantu name for okra] **1.** same as OKRA **2.** a soup thickened with unripe okra pods **3.** a fine, silty soil esp. in the W U.S., which becomes sticky and nonporous when wet: also **gumbo soil**

gum·boil (gum′boil′) *n.* an abscess on the gum

gum boot same as WELLINGTON BOOT

gum·drop (-drop′) *n.* a small, firm jellylike sweet, made of sweetened gum arabic or gelatin, usually coloured and flavoured

gum·my¹ (gum′ē) *adj.* **-mi·er, -mi·est 1.** having the nature of gum; sticky **2.** covered with or containing gum **3.** yielding gum —**gum′mi·ness** *n.*

gum·my² (gum′ē) *adj.* toothless

gump (gump) *n.* [Colloq.] gumption

gump·tion (gump′shən) *n.* [< Scot. dial.] [Colloq.] **1.** orig., common sense **2.** courage and initiative; enterprise and boldness

gum resin a mixture of gum and resin, given off by certain trees and plants

gum tree any of various trees that yield gum, as the eucalyptus —**up a gum tree** [Colloq.] to be in a quandary; in difficulties

gum·wood (-wood′) *n.* the wood of a gum tree

gun (gun) *n.* [< ME. *gunne, gonne* ? ON. *Gunnhildr,* fem. name (< *gunnr,* war + *hildr,* battle)] **1.** a weapon consisting of a metal tube from which a projectile is discharged by the force of an explosive; specif., *a)* technically, a heavy weapon, as a cannon, etc. *b)* a rifle *c)* popularly, a pistol or revolver **2.** any similar device not discharged by an explosive [an air *gun*] **3.** a discharge of a gun in signalling or saluting **4.** anything like a gun in shape or use **5.** a member of, or a place in, a shooting party or syndicate —*vi.* **gunned, gun′ning** to shoot or hunt with a gun —*vt.* **1.** [Colloq.] to shoot (a person) (often with *down*) **2.** [Slang] to advance the throttle of (an engine) so as to increase the speed —**give it the gun** [Slang] to cause something to start or gain speed —**go great guns** [Slang] to act with speed and efficiency —**gun for 1.** to hunt for with a gun **2.** [Slang] to seek —**jump the gun** [Slang] to begin before the signal to start, or before the proper time —**stick to one's guns** to be firm under attack

gun·boat (-bōt′) *n.* a small armed ship of shallow draught, used to patrol rivers, etc.

gunboat diplomacy diplomacy reinforced with the threat of military action

gun·cot·ton (-kot′'n) *n.* nitrocellulose in a highly nitrated form, used as an explosive

gun dog a dog, as a pointer, setter, etc., trained to find or retrieve game

gun·fight (-fīt′) *n.* a fight between persons using pistols or revolvers —**gun′fight′er** *n.*

gun·fire (-fīr′) *n.* the firing of a gun or guns

gunk (guŋk) *n.* [< ? G(OO) + (J)UNK¹] [Slang] any oily or thick, messy substance —**gunk′y** *adj.*

gun·lock (gun′lok′) *n.* in some guns, the mechanism by which the charge is set off

gun·man (-mən) *n., pl.* **-men 1.** a man armed with a gun, esp. an armed gangster or hired killer **2.** a man skilled in the use of a gun

gun·met·al (-met′'l) *n.* **1.** a kind of bronze formerly used for making cannons; also, any metal or alloy treated to resemble this **2.** the dark grey colour (**gunmetal grey**) of tarnished gunmetal —*adj.* dark grey

gun·nel¹ (gun′'l) *n.* [< ?] a small, slimy fish found in the N Atlantic

gun·nel² (gun′'l) *n. same as* GUNWALE

gun·ner (gun′ər) *n.* **1.** a soldier, sailor, etc. who helps fire artillery **2.** an artilleryman, esp. a private **3.** a naval warrant officer in charge of a ship's guns **4.** a hunter with a gun

gun·ner·y (-ē) *n.* **1.** heavy guns **2.** the science of making and using heavy guns and projectiles

gun·ny (gun′ē) *n., pl.* **-nies** [< Hindi < Sans. *gōni,* a sack] **1.** a coarse, heavy fabric of jute or hemp, used for sacks **2.** *same as* GUNNYSACK

gun·ny·sack (-sak′) *n.* a sack made of gunny

gun·play (gun′plā′) *n.* an exchange of gunshots, as between gunmen and police

gun·point (-point′) *n.* the muzzle of a gun —**at gunpoint** under threat of being shot with a gun

gun·pow·der (-pou′dər) *n.* an explosive powder, esp. a mixture of sulphur, saltpetre, and charcoal, used in cartridges, shells, etc., for blasting, etc.

gun·run·ning (-run′iŋ) *n.* the smuggling of guns and ammunition into a country —**gun′run′ner** *n.*

gun·shot (-shot′) *n.* **1.** shot fired from a gun **2.** the range of a gun —*adj.* caused by a shot from a gun

gun·sling·er (gun′sliŋ′ər) *n.* [Slang] a gunman

gun·smith (-smith′) *n.* a person who makes or repairs small guns

gun·stock (-stok′) *n.* the wooden handle or butt to which the barrel of a gun is attached

Gun·ter's chain (gun′tərz) [after Edmund *Gunter* (1581-1626), Eng. mathematician] a surveyor's chain 66 feet (c. 20m) in length

gun·wale (gun′'l) *n.* [first applied to bulwarks supporting a ship's guns] the upper edge of the side of a ship or boat

gun·yah (gun′yə) *n.* [Abor.] [Aust] an aboriginal name for a hut

gup·py (gup′ē) *n., pl.* **-pies** [after R. *Guppy,* of Trinidad] a tiny, brightly coloured tropical fish

gur·gle (gur′g'l) *vi.* **-gled, -gling** [prob. echoic] **1.** to flow with a bubbling or rippling sound **2.** to make such a sound

in the throat —*vt.* to utter with a gurgle —*n.* the act or sound of gurgling

gur·nard (gur′nərd) *n., pl.* **-nards, -nard:** see PLURAL, II, D, 1 [< OFr. < *grogner,* to grunt] *same as* FLYING GURNARD

gu·ru (goor′ōō) *n.* [Hindi < Sans. *guru-h,* venerable] **1.** in Hinduism, one's spiritual adviser **2.** a leader with devoted followers

gush (gush) *vi.* [prob. akin to ON. *gjosa,* to gush] **1.** to flow out suddenly and plentifully **2.** to have a sudden, plentiful flow of blood, tears, etc. **3.** to express exaggerated enthusiasm or feeling —*vt.* to cause to flow out suddenly and plentifully —*n.* **1.** a sudden, plentiful outflow **2.** gushing talk or writing —**gush′ing** *adj.* —**gush′ing·ly** *adv.*

gush·er (-ər) *n.* **1.** a person who gushes **2.** an oil well from which oil spouts without being pumped

gush·y (-ē) *adj.* **gush′i·er** characterized by gush (*n. 2*) —**gush′i·ly** *adv.* —**gush′i·ness** *n.*

gus·set (gus′it) *n.* [< OFr. *gousset*] **1.** a triangular or diamond-shaped piece inserted in a garment, glove, etc., to make it stronger or roomier **2.** a triangular metal brace for reinforcing a corner or angle —*vt.* to furnish with a gusset —**gus′-set·ed** *adj.*

GUSSET

gust (gust) *n.* [< ON. *gustr* < *gjosa,* to gush] **1.** a sudden, strong rush of air or wind **2.** a sudden outburst of rain, laughter, rage, etc. —*vi.* to blow in gusts

gus·ta·to·ry (gus′tə tər ē) *adj.* of or having to do with tasting or the sense of taste: also **gus′ta·tive**

gus·to (gus′tō) *n.* [It. & Sp. < L. *gustus,* taste] **1.** [Obs.] taste; liking **2.** zest; relish **3.** great vigour

gust·y (gus′tē) *adj.* **gust′i·er, gust′-i·est** characterized by gusts of air or wind, or by sudden outbursts —**gust′i·ly** *adv.* —**gust′i·ness** *n.*

gut (gut) *n.* [OE. *guttas,* pl. < base of *geotan,* to pour] **1.** *a)* [*pl.*] the bowels; entrails *b)* the stomach or belly Regarded as an indelicate usage **2.** all or part of the alimentary canal, esp. the intestine **3.** tough cord made from animal intestines, used for violin strings, surgical sutures, etc. **4.** a narrow passage or gully **5.** [*pl.*] [Colloq.] the basic or inner parts **6.** [*pl.*] [Colloq.] *a)* daring, courage, etc. *b)* forcefulness; tenacity —*vt.* **gut′ted, gut′ting 1.** to remove the intestines from; eviscerate **2.** to destroy the interior of, as by fire —*adj.* [Colloq.] urgent and basic [*gut* issues in politics]

gut·less (gut′lis) *adj.* [Slang] lacking courage

guts·y (gut′sē) *adj.* **guts′i·er, guts′i·est** [Slang] **1.** full of guts; courageous, forceful, etc. **2.** greedy —**guts′i·ness** *n.*

gut·ta-per·cha (gut′ə pur′chə) *n.* [< Malay < *gētah,* gum < *pērchah,* tree from which it is obtained] a rubberlike gum produced from the latex of various SE Asian trees, used in insulation, dentistry, etc.

gut·tate (gut′āt) *adj.* [L. *guttatus* < *gutta,* a drop] **1.** in the form of drops **2.** spotted, as with drops

gut·ter (gut′ər) *n.* [< OFr. < L. *gutta,* a drop] **1.** a trough along or under the eaves of a roof, to carry off rain water **2.** any narrow channel, as along the side of a road or street to carry off water **3.** a place or way of living characterized by squalor, poverty, etc. (with *the*) **4.** the adjoining inner margins of two facing pages in a book, etc. —*vt.* to furnish with gutters —*vi.* **1.** to flow in a stream **2.** to melt rapidly so that the wax runs down in channels: said of a candle

gutter press journalism that seeks sensationalism in its coverage

gut·ter·snipe (-snīp′) *n.* a child living in the slums, for the most part in the streets: contemptuous term

gut·tur·al (gut′ər əl) *adj.* [< L. *guttur,* throat] **1.** of the throat **2.** loosely, produced in the throat; harsh, rasping, etc.: said of sounds **3.** formed with the back of the tongue close to or against the soft palate, as the *k* in *keen* —*n.* a guttural sound —**gut′tur·al·ly** *adv.* —**gut′tur·al·ness** *n.*

guy¹ (gī) *n.* [< OFr. < *guier,* to GUIDE] a rope, chain, etc. attached to something to steady or guide it —*vt.* to guide or steady with a guy

guy² (gī) *n.* [after *Guy Fawkes*] **1.** a person who looks odd **2.** [Slang] *a)* a man or boy; fellow *b)* any person —*vt.* to make fun of; ridicule

guz·zle (guz′'l) *vi., vt.* **-zled, -zling** [< ? OFr. < *gosier,* throat] to drink or eat greedily or immoderately —**guz′-zler** *n.*

gybe (jīb) *n., vi., vt.* **gybed, gyb′ing** *same as* JIBE¹

gym (jim) *n.* [Colloq.] *same as:* **1.** GYMNASIUM **2.** PHYSICAL EDUCATION

gym·kha·na (jim kä′nə) *n.* [Anglo-Ind., prob. altered (after GYMNASIUM) < Hindi & Urdu *gend-khāna,* racket court] **1.** a place where athletic contests or games are held **2.** any of

various contests or games are held **2.** any of various contests involving skill, now used esp. of equestrian events

gym·na·si·um (jim nā′zē əm) *n., pl.* **-si·ums, -si·a** (-ə) [L. < Gr. *gymnasion*, ult. < *gymnos*, naked] **1.** a room or building equipped for physical training and athletic sports **2.** [G-] (gim nä′zē ŏom) in Germany and some other European countries, a secondary school for students preparing to enter a university —**gym·na′si·al** *adj.*

gym·nast (jim′nast) *n.* an expert in gymnastics

gym·nas·tic (jim nas′tik) *adj.* [< L. < Gr.: see GYMNASIUM] of or having to do with gymnastics: also **gym·nas′ti·cal** —**gym·nas′ti·cal·ly** *adv.*

gym·nas·tics (-tiks) *n.pl.* exercises that develop and train the body and the muscles

gymno- [< Gr. *gymnos*, naked] *a combining form meaning* naked, stripped, bare: also **gymn-**

gym·no·sperm (jim′nə spurm′) *n.* [< ModL. < Gr.: see prec. & -SPERM] any of a large class of seed plants having the ovules borne on open scales, usually in cones, as pines and cedars —**gym′no·sper′mous** (-spur′məs) *adj.* —**gym′·no·sper′my** (-spur′mē) *n.*

gymp (gimp) *n.* *same as* GIMP

gym shoe a plimsoll

gym·slip (jim′slip′) *n.* a tunic or pinafore dress worn, esp. formerly, by schoolgirls, often as part of school uniform

gynaeco- [< Gr. < *gynē*, a woman] *a combining form meaning* woman, female: also **gynaec-**

gyn·ae·col·o·gy (gī′nə kol′ə jē) *n.* [prec. + -LOGY] the branch of medicine dealing with the specific functions, diseases, etc. of women —**gyn′ae·co·log′ic** (-kə loj′ik), **gyn′ae·co·log′i·cal** *adj.* —**gyn′ae·col′o·gist** *n.*

gyn·an·dro·morph (jī nan′drə môrf′) *n.* [< Gr. *gynandros*, of doubtful sex + -MORPH] an abnormal organism, such as an insect, that has both male and female characteristics

gyn·an·drous (jī nan′drəs) *adj.* [< Gr. *gynandros*: see prec.] *Bot.* having the stamen, or male organ, and pistil, or female organ, united in one column, as in the orchids

gy·noe·ci·um (jī nē′sē əm, jī-, gī-) *n., pl.* **-ci·a** (-ə) [ModL. < L., ult. < Gr. *gynē*, a woman + *oikos*, house] the female organ or organs of a flower; pistil or pistils: also sp. **gyn·ae·ce·um** (jī′nə sē′əm) *pl.* **-ce′a** (-ə) or [esp. U.S.] **gy·ne′ci·um,** *pl.* **-ci·a** (-ə)

gyn·o·phore (jin′ə fôr′, ji′nə-, gī′nə-) *n.* [< Gr. *gynē*, woman + -PHORE] a stalk bearing the gynoecium above the petals and stamens

-gyn·ous (ji nəs) [< ModL. < Gr. < *gynē*, a woman] *a combining form meaning:* **1.** woman or female [polygynous] **2.** having female organs or pistils as specified [androgynous]

-gyn·y (ji nē) *a combining form used to form nouns from adjectives ending in* -GYNOUS

gyp¹ (jip) *n.* [prob. < GYPSY] [Colloq.] **1.** an act of cheating; swindle **2.** a swindler: also **gyp′per, gyp′ster** —*vt., vi.* **gypped, gyp′ping** [Colloq.] to swindle; cheat

gyp² (jip) *n.* [< ?GYPSY] a male servant at a college, esp. at Cambridge

gyp³ (jip) *n.* [< ? *gee up*: see GEE; hence *to give gyp*, to beat] [Slang] severe pain [his arthritis gave him *gyp*]

gyp·soph·i·la (jip sof′ə lə) *n.* [ModL.: see GYPSUM & -PHIL(E)] any of a genus of plants of the pink family, bearing clusters of small white or pink flowers with a delicate fragrance, as baby's breath

gyp·sum (jip′səm) *n.* [L. < Gr. *gypsos*, chalk < Sem.] a hydrated sulphate of calcium, $CaSO_4.2H_2O$, occurring naturally in sedimentary rocks and used for making plaster of Paris, in treating soil, etc. —**gyp′se·ous** *adj.*

Gyp·sy (jip′sē) *n., pl.* **-sies** [earlier *gypcien* < *Egipcien*, Egyptian: orig. thought to have come from Egypt] **1.** [also **g-**] a member of a wandering Caucasoid people with dark skin and black hair, believed to have originated in India: they are known throughout the world as musicians, fortunetellers, etc. **2.** *same as* ROMANY (sense 2) **3.** [g-] a person whose appearance or habits are like those of a Gypsy —*adj.* of or like a Gypsy or Gypsies

gypsy moth a brownish or white European moth: its larvae feed on leaves, damaging trees and plants

gy·rate (jī′rāt′; *for adj.* jī′rāt) *vi.* **-rat′ed, -rat′ing** [< L. pp. of *gyrare*, to turn, ult. < Gr. *gyros*, a circle] to move in a circular or spiral path; rotate or revolve on an axis; whirl —*adj.* spiral, coiled, or circular —**gy·ra′tion** *n.* —**gy′ra′tor** *n.* —**gy·ra·to·ry** (jī′rə tər ē, jī rā′tər ē) *adj.*

gyre (jīr) *n.* [< L. < Gr. *gyros*, a circle] [Chiefly Poet.] **1.** a circular or spiral motion; whirl **2.** a circular or spiral form; ring or vortex —*vi., vt.* **gyred, gyr′ing** [Chiefly Poet.] to whirl

gyr·fal·con (jur′fol′kən, -fôl′-, -fô′-) *n.* [< OFr. *girfaucon* < Frank.] a large, fierce, strong falcon of N Europe, Asia and N. America

gy·ro (jī′rō) *n., pl.* **-ros** short for: **1.** GYROSCOPE **2.** GYROCOMPASS

gyro- [< Gr. *gyros*, a circle] *a combining form meaning:* **1.** gyrating [gyroscope] **2.** gyroscope [gyrocompass] Also, before a vowel, **gyr-**

gy·ro·com·pass (-kum′pəs) *n.* a compass consisting of a motor-operated gyroscope whose rotating axis points to the geographic north pole instead of to the magnetic pole

gy·ro·pi·lot (jī′rō pī′lət) *n.* *same as* AUTOMATIC PILOT

gy·ro·scope (-skōp′) *n.* [GYRO- + -SCOPE] a wheel mounted in a ring so that its axis is free to turn in any direction: when the wheel is spun rapidly, it will keep its original plane of rotation no matter which way the ring is turned —**gy′ro·scop′ic** (-skop′ik) *adj.* —**gy′ro·scop′i·cal·ly** *adv.*

gy·ro·sta·bi·liz·er (jī′rō stā′bə lī′zər) *n.* a device consisting of a gyroscope spinning in a vertical plane, used to stabilize the side-to-side rolling of a ship

gyve (jīv) *n., vt.* **gyved, gyv′ing** [< Anglo-Fr. *gyves*, pl.] [Archaic or Poet.] fetter; shackle

GYROSCOPE

H

H, h (āch) *n., pl.* **H's, h's** **1.** the eighth letter of the English alphabet **2.** the sound of *H* or *h*

H (āch) *n.* something shaped like an *H* —*adj.* shaped like *H*

H **1.** *Chem.* hydrogen **2.** *Physics* the symbol for henry

h hour

H., h. **1.** harbour **2.** hard(ness) **3.** height **4.** high **5.** hour(s) **6.** husband

ha (hä) *interj.* [echoic] an exclamation variously expressing surprise, anger, triumph, etc. —*n.* the sound of this exclamation or of a laugh

ha hectare(s)

haar (här) *n.* [< ? ON. *harr*, hoary] a cold mist off the North Sea

ha·ba·ne·ra (hä′bə ner′ə; *Sp.* ä′bä nä′rä) *n.* [Sp., lit., of *Habana*, Havana] **1.** a slow Cuban dance **2.** the music for this

ha·be·as cor·pus (hā′bē əs kôr′pəs) [L., (that) you have the body] *Law* a writ requiring that a detained person be brought before a court to decide the legality of his detention or imprisonment

hab·er·dash·er (hab′ər dash′ər) *n.* [prob. < Anglo-Fr. *hapertas*, kind of cloth] **1.** a dealer in various small

articles, such as ribbons, thread, etc. **2.** [U.S.] a men's outfitters

hab·er·dash·er·y (-ē) *n., pl.* **-er·ies** **1.** things sold by a haberdasher **2.** a haberdasher's shop

hab·er·geon (hab′ər jən) *n.* [OFr. *haubergeon*, dim. of *hauberc*, hauberk] **1.** a short, high-necked jacket of mail **2.** *same as* HAUBERK

ha·bil·i·ment (hə bil′ə mənt) *n.* [< MFr. < *habiller*, to clothe] **1.** [*usually pl.*] clothing; dress **2.** [*pl.*] [Archaic] furnishings or equipment; trappings

ha·bil·i·tate (-tāt′) *vt.* **-tat′ed, -tat′ing** [< ML. pp. of *habilitare*, to make suitable] **1.** [Archaic] to clothe; equip; outfit **2.** to qualify for a post, esp. as a lecturer in a German university —**ha·bil′i·ta′tion** *n.* —**ha·bil′i·ta′tive** *adj.*

hab·it (hab′it) *n.* [OFr. < L. *habitus* < pp. of *habere*, to have] **1.** a distinctive religious costume **2.** a costume for certain occasions [a riding *habit*] **3.** characteristic or usual way of being, doing, growing, etc.; character, tendency, disposition, etc. **4.** *a)* a thing done often and, hence, easily; practice; custom *b)* an acquired pattern of action that is automatic and thus difficult to break **5.** an addiction, esp. to narcotics —*vt.* to dress

hab·it·a·ble (-ə b'l) *adj.* fit to be lived in —**hab'it·a·bil'i·ty** , **hab'it·a·ble·ness** *n.* —**hab'it·a·bly** *adv.*

hab·it·ant (-ənt) *n.* [Fr. < L. prp. of *habitare*, to inhabit] an inhabitant; resident

hab·i·tat (hab'ə tat') *n.* [L., it inhabits] 1. native environment 2. the place where a person or thing is ordinarily found

hab·i·ta·tion (hab'ə tā'shən) *n.* 1. an inhabiting; occupancy 2. a place in which to live; dwelling; home 3. a colony or settlement

hab·it-form·ing (hab'it fôr'miŋ) *adj.* resulting in the formation of a habit or in addiction

ha·bit·u·al (hə bit'yoo wəl) *adj.* 1. done by habit or fixed as a habit; customary 2. being or doing a certain thing by habit; steady [a *habitual* smoker] 3. much seen, done, or used; usual; frequent —**ha·bit'u·al·ly** *adv.*—**ha·bit'u·al·ness** *n.*

ha·bit·u·ate (-yoo wāt') *vt.* -**at'ed**, -**at'ing** [< LL., ult. < L. *habitus*: see HABIT] to make used (*to*); accustom; familiarize —**ha·bit'u·a'tion** *n.*

hab·i·tude (hab'ə tyood') *n.* 1. habitual condition of mind or body; disposition 2. custom

ha·bit·u·é (hə bit'yoo wā') *n.* [Fr.] a person who frequents a certain place or places

H.A.C. Honourable Artillery Company

ha·chure (hə shoor'; *also, for n.,* hash'oor) *n.* [Fr. < OFr. *hacher*, to chop] any of a series of short parallel lines used, esp. in map making, to represent a sloping or elevated surface —*vt.* -**chured'**, -**chur'ing** to shade with hachures

ha·ci·en·da (hä'sē en'də) *n.* [Sp. < L. *facienda*, things to be done < *facere*, to do] in Latin America, 1. a large estate, ranch, etc. 2. the main dwelling on such an estate

hack¹ (hak) *vt.* [OE. *haccian*] 1. *a)* to chop or cut roughly or irregularly *b)* to shape, trim, etc. thus *c)* in some sports, esp. Rugby, to foul by kicking an opponent's shin 2. to break up (land) with a hoe, etc. —*vi.* 1. to make rough or irregular cuts 2. to give harsh, dry coughs —*n.* 1. a tool for hacking; axe, etc. 2. a slash, gash or notch 3. a kick on the shin, esp. in Rugby football 4. a harsh, dry cough —**hack'er** *n.*

hack² (hak) *n.* [contr. < HACKNEY] 1. a horse for hire 2. a saddle horse 3. an old, worn-out horse 4. a person hired to do routine writing 5. [U.S.] a devoted, unquestioning worker for a political party —*vt.* 1. to employ as a hack 2. to hire out (a horse, etc.) 3. to wear out by constant use —*vi.* to ride a horse slowly, at a gentle pace —*adj.* 1. employed as a hack 2. done by a hack 3. stale; trite

hack³ (hak) *n.* [orig., board on which falcon's nest was put, var. of HATCH²] 1. a rack for drying cheese, holding cattle food, etc. 2. a row of unbaked bricks set out to dry

hack·a·more (hak'ə môr') *n.* [altered < Sp. *jaquima*, halter < Ar. *shakīma*] [U.S.] a rope or rawhide halter, used in breaking horses

hack·ber·ry (hak'bər ē) *n., pl.* -**ries** [< Scand.] 1. an American tree with small fruit resembling a cherry 2. its fruit or its wood

hack·er·y (hak'ər ē) *n.* [< Hindi *chhakra*, a cart] an Indian two-wheeled bullock cart

hack·le¹ (hak'l) *n.* [ME. *hechele*, prob. infl. by dial. *hackle*, bird's plumage < OE. *hacele*] 1. a comb for separating the fibres of flax, hemp, etc. 2. any of the long, slender feathers at the neck of a rooster, pigeon, etc. 3. *Fishing a)* a tuft of feathers from a rooster's neck, used in making artificial flies *b)* such a fly 4. [*pl.*] the bristling hairs on a dog's neck and back —*vt.* -**led**, -**ling** to separate the fibres of (flax, hemp, etc.) with a hackle —**get one's hackles up** to become tense with anger; bristle

hack·le² (hak'l) *vt., vi.* -**led**, -**ling** [freq. of HACK¹] to cut roughly; hack; mangle —**hack'ly** *adj.*

hack·ma·tack (hak'mə tak') *n.* [AmInd. (Algonquian)] same as TAMARACK

hack·ney (hak'nē) *n., pl.* -**neys** [< ME. ? < *Hackeney* (now *Hackney*), the village where horses were formerly raised] 1. a horse for ordinary driving or riding 2. a carriage for hire

hack·neyed (-nēd') *adj.* made trite and commonplace by overuse

hack·saw (hak'sô') *n.* a saw for cutting metal, consisting of a narrow, fine-toothed blade held in a frame: also **hack saw**

HACKSAW

had (had; *unstressed* həd, əd) *pt. & pp.* of HAVE: also used to indicate preference or necessity, with certain words and phrases, such as *rather, better, as well* (Ex.: I *had* better leave)

had·dock (had'ək) *n., pl.* -**dock**, -**docks**: see PLURAL, II, D, 2 [< ? OFr. *hadot*] a food fish related to the cod, found off the coasts of Europe and N. America

hade (hād) *n.* [< dial. *hade*, to slope, < ?] *Geol.* the angle between the plane of a fault or vein and the vertical plane —*vi.* —**had'ed**, **had'ing** *Geol.* to incline from the vertical plane

Ha·des (hā'dēz) 1. *Gr. Myth. a)* the home of the dead, beneath the earth *b)* the ruler of the underworld 2. the resting place of the dead: used in some New Testament translations —*n.* [*often* **h-**] [Colloq.] hell: a euphemism

Had·ith (had'ith; hä dēth') *n.* [Ar.] the body of tradition about Mohammed that supplements the Koran

hadj (haj) *n.* same as HAJJ

hadj·i (-ē) *n.* same as HAJJI

had·n't (had''nt) had not

had·ron (had'ron) *n.* [20th c. < Gr. *hadros*, thick] an elementary particle capable of taking part in a strong nuclear interaction

hadst (hadst) *archaic 2nd pers. sing., past indic., of* HAVE: used *with* thou

haem (hēm) *n.* [contr. < HAEMATIN] the nonprotein, iron-containing pigment forming part of the haemoglobin molecule

hae·mal (hē'məl) *adj.* [HAEM + -AL] 1. of the blood or blood vessels: also **hae'ma·tal** 2. of the side of the body in which the heart and main blood vessels are located

hae·mat- same as HAEMATO-

hae·mat·ic (hi mat'ik) *adj.* [Gr. *haimatikos*] of, filled with, or coloured like blood

haem·a·tin (hem'ə tin, hē'mə-) *n.* [HAEMAT- + -IN¹] a dark brown or blackish substance obtained by the decomposition of haemoglobin

haem·a·tite (hem'ə tīt', hē'mə-) *n.* [L. < Gr. *haimatitēs*, bloodlike < *haima*, blood] ferric oxide, an important iron ore, brownish red or black —**haem'a·tit'ic** (-tit'ik) *adj.*

hae·ma·to- [< Gr. *haima* (gen. *haimatos*), blood] a *combining form meaning* blood: also (before a vowel) **haemat-**

haem·a·to·crit (hi mat'ə krit') *n.* [< HAEMATO- + Gr. *kritēs*, a judge] 1. a centrifuge for measuring the relative volumes of blood cells and fluid in blood 2. the proportion of blood cells to a volume of blood so measured: also **haematocrit reading**

haema·tol·o·gy (hē'mə tol'ə jē, hem'ə-) *n.* the study of blood and its diseases —**hae'ma·to·log'ic** (-tə loj'ik), **hae'ma·to·log'i·cal** *adj.* —**hae'ma·tol'o·gist** *n.*

hae·ma·to·ma (hē'mə tō'mə) *n., pl.* -**mas**, -**ma·ta** (-tə) [ModL.: see HAEMAT(O)- & -OMA] a local swelling or tumour filled with bloody fluid

hae·ma·tu·ri·a (hē'mə tyoor'ē ə; hem'ə-) *n.* [HAEMAT- + -URIA] the presence of red blood cells in the urine

-hae·mi·a (hē'mēə) same as -AEMIA

hae·mo- [< Gr. < *haima*, blood] a *combining form meaning* blood [*haemoglobin*]: also **hemo-**

hae·mo·cy·a·nin (-sī'ə nin) *n.* [HAEMO-+ Gr. *kyanos*, blue + -IN¹] a blue, oxygen-carrying blood pigment containing copper, found in many crustaceans and molluscs

hae·mo·cy·tom·e·ter (hē'mō sī tom'ə tər, hem'ō-) *n.* [HAEMO- + CYTO- + -METER] a device for counting the number of cells in a sample of blood

hae·mo·glo·bin (hē'mə glō'bin, hem-; hē'mə glō'bin) *n.* [contr. < *haematoglobulin*: see HAEMATO + GLOBULIN] the red colouring matter of the red blood corpuscles: it carries oxygen from the lungs to the tissues, and carbon dioxide from the tissues to the lungs

hae·mol·y·sis (hi mol'ə sis) *n.* [HAEMO- + -LYSIS] the destruction of red corpuscles with liberation of haemoglobin into the surrounding fluid —**hae·mo·lyt·ic** (hē'mə lit'ik, hem'ə-) *adj.*

hae·mo·phil·i·a (hē'mə fil'ē ə, hem'ə-) *n.* [ModL.: see HAEMO-, -PHILE, & -IA] a hereditary condition in which one of the normal blood-clotting factors is absent, causing prolonged bleeding from even minor cuts —**hae'mo·phil'i·ac** (-fil'ē ak) *n.* —**hae'mo·phil'ic** *adj.*

haem·or·rhage (hem'ər ij) *n.* [< Fr. < L. < Gr. < *haima*, blood + *rhēgnynai*, to break] the escape of large quantities of blood from a blood vessel; heavy bleeding —*vi.* -**rhaged**, -**rhag·ing** to have a haemorrhage —**haem'or·rhag'ic** (-ə raj'-ik) *adj.*

haem·or·rhoid (hem'ə roid') *n.* [< L. < Gr. < *haima*, blood + *rhein*, to flow] a painful swelling of a vein in the region of the anus, often with bleeding: *usually used in pl.* —**haem'-or·rhoid'al** *adj.*

hae·mo·sta·sis (hi mō stā'sis, hē-) *n.* [ModL. < Gr. *haimostasis*: see HAEMO- & STASIS] the stoppage of bleeding

hae·mo·stat (hē'mə stat', hem'o-) *n.* [HAEMO- + -STAT] anything used to stop bleeding; specif., a clamplike instrument used in surgery

haer·e·mai (hīr'i mī) *interj.* [Maori, lit., come hither] [N.Z.] welcome

ha·fiz (häf'iz) *n.* [Ar. *hafiz*, a person who remembers] title for a Moslem who has memorized the Koran

haf·ni·um (haf'nē əm) *n.* [ModL. < L. *Hafnia*, Roman name of Copenhagen] a metallic chemical element found with zirconium and somewhat resembling it: symbol Hf; at. wt., 178.49; at. no., 72

haft (haft) *n.* [OE. *hæft*] a handle or hilt of a knife, axe, etc. —*vt.* to fit with a haft

hag (hag) *n.* [< OE. *hægtes* < *haga*, a hedge] 1. a witch 2. an ugly, often vicious old woman —**hag′gish** *adj.*

Hag. Haggai

hag·fish (hag′fish′) *n.*, *pl.* **-fish′**, **-fish′es**: see FISH [HAG + FISH] a small, eellike saltwater fish with a round, sucking mouth and horny teeth, with which it bores into other fish and devours them

Hag·ga·da, Hag·ga·dah (hə gä′də) *n.*, *pl.* **-ga·dot′** (-dōt′) [Heb. *haggādāh* < *higgid*, to tell] 1. *a*) [*often* h-] in the *Talmud*, an anecdote that explains some point of law *b*) the part of the Talmud devoted to such narratives 2. the narrative of the Exodus read at the Seder during Passover —**hag·gad·ic** (hə gad′ik, -gä′dik) *adj.*

hag·gard (hag′ərd) *adj.* [MFr. *hagard*, untamed] 1. having a wild, wasted, worn look, as from grief or illness 2. *Falconry* designating a hawk captured after reaching maturity —**hag′gard·ly** *adv.* —**hag′gard·ness** *n.*

hag·gis (hag′is) *n.* [?ME. *hagas*, kind of pudding] a Scottish dish made of the lungs, heart, etc. of a sheep or calf, mixed with suet, seasoning, and oatmeal and boiled in the animal's stomach

hag·gle (hag′'l) *vt.* **-gled**, **-gling** [freq. of Scot. *hag*, to chop, cut] [Now Rare] to hack; mangle —*vi.* to argue about terms, price, etc.; wrangle —*n.* a haggling —**hag′gler** *n.*

hag·i·o- [< Gr. *hagios*, holy] a prefix meaning saintly, sacred: also, before a vowel, **hag·i-**

Hag·i·og·ra·pha (hag′ē og′rə fə) *n.pl.* [LL. < Gr. *hagiographa*: see HAGIO- & -GRAPH] the third and final part of the Jewish Scriptures

hag·i·og·ra·pher (hag′ē og′rə fər) *n.* 1. any of the authors of the Hagiographa 2. an author of lives of the saints

hag·i·o·graph·ic (hag′ē ə graf′ik) *adj.* 1. of hagiography or the Hagiographa 2. idealizing its subject: said of a biography Also **hag′i·o·graph′i·cal**

hag·i·og·ra·phy (hag′ē og′rə fē) *n.*, *pl.* **-phies** [HAGIO- + -GRAPHY] 1. the writing or study of lives of the saints 2. a book of such lives

hag·i·ol·a·try (hag′ē ol′ə trē) *n.* [HAGIO- + -LATRY] worship of the saints

hag·i·ol·o·gy (hag′ē ol′ə jē, hä′jē-) *n.*, *pl.* **-gies** [prec. + -LOGY] 1. literature about saints' lives and legends, sacred writings, etc. 2. a list of saints —**hag′i·o·log′ic** (-ə loj′ik), **hag′i·o·log′i·cal** *adj.* —**hag′i·ol′o·gist** *n.*

hag·rid·den (hag′rid′'n) *adj.* obsessed or harassed, as by fears

hah (hä) *interj.*, *n.* *same as* HA

ha-ha (hä′hä′) *n.* [Fr. *haha* < ?] a fence, wall etc. set in a ditch round a garden or park so as not to hide the view from within: also sp. **ha′ha′**

haik (hīk, häk) *n.* [Ar.] a sheetlike woollen or cotton cloth worn by Arabs as an outer garment

hai·ku (hī′kōō) *n.* [Jap.] 1. a Japanese verse form of three unrhymed lines of 5, 7, and 5 syllables respectively, usually on some subject in nature 2. *pl.* **-ku** a poem in this form

hail¹ (hāl) *vt.* [< ON. < *heill*, whole, sound] 1. to welcome, greet, etc. as with cheers; acclaim 2. to salute as [they *hailed* him their leader] 3. to call out to, as in summoning [to *hail* a taxi] —*vi.* *Naut.* to call out or signal to a ship —*n.* 1. a hailing or greeting 2. the distance that a shout will carry [within *hail*] —*interj.* an exclamation of tribute, greeting, etc. —**hail fellow well met** very friendly to everyone: also **hail fellow, hail-fellow** —**hail from** to come from (one's birthplace, etc.) —**hail′er** *n.*

hail² (hāl) *n.* [OE. *hægel*] 1. small, rounded pieces of ice that sometimes fall during thunderstorms; hailstones 2. a falling, showering, etc. of or like hail [a *hail* of bullets] —*vi.* to pour down hail [it is *hailing*] —*vt.* to shower, hurl, etc. violently like hail (often with *on* or *upon*) [to *hail* curses on someone]

Hail Mary *pl.* **Hail Marys** same as AVE MARIA (sense 2)

hail·stone (hāl′stōn′) *n.* a pellet of hail

hail·storm (-stôrm′) *n.* a storm with hail

hair (her) *n.* [OE. *hær*] 1. any of the fine, threadlike outgrowths from the skin of an animal or human being 2. a growth of these; esp., the growth covering the human head or the skin of most mammals 3. an extremely small space, degree, etc. 4. a threadlike growth on a plant —*adj.* 1. made of or with hair 2. for the care of the hair [*hair* tonic] —**get in one's hair** [Colloq.] to annoy one —**keep one's hair on** [Colloq.] to stay calm —**let one's hair down** [Colloq.] be very informal, relaxed, etc. —**make one's hair stand on end** to horrify one —**not turn a hair** to show no fear, surprise, etc. —**split hairs** to make petty distinctions; quibble —**to a hair** exactly; perfectly —**hair′less** *adj.* —**hair′less·ness** *n.* —**hair′like′** *adj.*

hair·breadth (-bredth′) *n.* an extremely small space or amount —*adj.* very narrow; close Also **hairs′breadth′, hair's′-breadth′**

hair·cloth (-klôth′) *n.* cloth woven from horsehair, camel's hair, etc.: used esp. for upholstery

hair·cut (-kut′) *n.* 1. a cutting of the hair of the head 2. the style in which the hair is cut —**hair′cut′ter** *n.*

hair·do (-dōō′) *n.*, *pl.* **-dos′** the style in which (a woman's) hair is arranged; coiffure

hair·dress·er (-dres′ər) *n.* a person whose work is dressing (women's) hair —**hair′dress′ing** *n.*, *adj.*

hair·grip (-grip′) *n.* a small metal clip for holding hair in place

hair·line (-līn′) *n.* 1. a very thin line or stripe 2. the outline of the hair on the head, esp. above the forehead

hair·net (-net′) *n.* a net or fine-meshed cap for keeping the hair in place

hair·piece (-pēs′) *n.* 1. a toupee or wig 2. a section of extra hair attached to a woman's real hair to give greater body or length

hair·pin (-pin′) *n.* a small, usually U-shaped, piece of wire, etc., for keeping the hair in place —*adj.* U-shaped [a *hairpin* bend]

hair·rais·ing (-rā′ziŋ) *adj.* [Colloq.] causing the hair to stand on end; terrifying —**hair′-rais′er** *n.*

hair shirt a shirt or girdle of haircloth, worn for self-punishment by religious ascetics

hair-slide (-slīd′) *n.* an ornamental hinged clasp for holding hair in place

hair·split·ting (-split′iŋ) *adj.*, *n.* making petty distinctions; quibbling —**hair′split′ter** *n.*

hair·spring (-spriŋ′) *n.* a very slender, hairlike coil that controls the regular movement of the balance wheel in a watch or clock

hair·streak (-strēk) *n.* any of a number of small butterflies with narrow white streaks on the wings

hair trigger a trigger so delicately adjusted that slight pressure on it discharges the firearm

hair·y (-ē) *adj.* **hair′i·er**, **hair′i·est** 1. covered with hair 2. of or like hair 3. [Slang] difficult, distressing, etc. —**hair′i·ness** *n.*

hajj (haj) *n.* [Ar. *ḥajj* < *ḥajji*, to go on a pilgrimage] the pilgrimage to Mecca that every Moslem is expected to take at least once

haj·ji, haj·i (haj′ē) *n.* [< Ar., pilgrim: see prec.] a Moslem who has made a pilgrimage to Mecca

hake (hāk) *n.*, *pl.* **hake, hakes:** see PLURAL, II, D, 2 [prob. < ON. *haki*, a hook (from shape of the jaw)] any of various marine food fishes related to the cod

hak·e·a (hä′kē ə) *n.* [after Baron *Hake* of Hanover, Ger. botanist] any of various Australian shrubs or small trees

ha·kim¹ (hä kēm′) *n.* [Ar. *ḥakīm*, wise, learned] in Moslem regions, a doctor; physician

ha·kim² (hä′kēm, -kim) *n.* [Ar. *ḥākim*, governor] in Moslem regions, a ruler, judge, or governor

Ha·la·kha, Ha·la·cha (hä′lä khä′, hə lä′khə) *n.*, *pl.* **-la·khot′, -la·chot′** (-khōt) [Heb.] that part of traditional Jewish literature, esp. of the Talmud, concerned with the law

ha·la·tion (hä lä′shən, ha-) *n.* [HAL(O) + -ATION] *Photog.* an undesirable spreading or reflection of light on a negative, appearing like a halo around highlights

hal·berd (hal′bərd) *n.* [ult. < MHG. *helmbarte* < *helm*, handle + *barte*, an axe] a combination spear and battle-axe used in the 15th and 16th cent.: also **hal′bert** (-bərt) —**hal′berd·ier′** (-bər dir′) *n.*

hal·cy·on (hal′sē ən) *n.* [< L. < Gr. *alkyōn*, kingfisher] a legendary bird, identified with the kingfisher, supposed to have a peaceful, calming influence on the sea at the time of the winter solstice —*adj.* 1. of the halcyon 2. tranquil, happy, idyllic, etc.: esp. in phrase **halcyon days**

hale¹ (hāl) *adj.* **hal′er**, **hal′est** [OE. *hal*] sound in body; vigorous and healthy —**hale′ness** *n.*

hale² (hāl) *vt.* **haled**, **hal′ing** [< OFr. *haler*, prob. < ODu. *halen*: see HAUL] to force (one) to go [*haled* him into court]

hal·er (hä′lər) *n.*, *pl.* **-er·u′** (-ə rōō′), **-ers** [Czech, ult. < MHG. *Haller* (*pfenninc*), (penny of) Hall, a Ger. coin made at Hall, Swabia] see MONETARY UNITS, table (Czechoslovakia)

half (häf) *n.*, *pl.* **halves** [OE. *healf*] 1. either of the two equal, or almost equal, parts of something 2. a half hour [*half* past one] 3. *Basketball, Football,* etc. either of the two equal periods of the game, between which the players rest 4. [Colloq.] half a pint, esp. of beer —*adj.* 1. *a*) being either of the two equal parts *b*) being about a half of the amount, length, etc. 2. incomplete; partial —*adv.* 1. to an extent approximately or exactly fifty percent of the whole 2. [Colloq.] to some extent [to be *half* convinced] 3. [Colloq.] by any means; at all: used with *not* [not *half* bad] —**by half** considerably; too much [he's too busy by *half*] —**in half** into halves —**not the half of** only a small part of **half-and-half** (häf′'n häf′) *n.* something that is half one thing and half another; esp., a mixture of equal parts of porter and ale, beer and stout, etc. —*adj.* combining two things equally —*adv.* in two equal parts

half·back (-bak′) *n.* *Football, Hockey,* etc. a player positioned behind the forwards

half-baked (-bākt′) *adj.* 1. only partly baked 2. not completely planned or thought out 3. having or showing little intelligence and experience

half·beak (-bēk') *n.* any of several small long-bodied tropical sea fishes with a greatly extended lower jaw

half binding a style of book binding in which leather etc., is used to surround the spine and cover the corners

half-blood (-blud') *n.* 1. a person related to another through one parent only 2. *same as* HALF-BREED —*adj. same as* HALF-BLOODED

half blood 1. kinship through one parent only [sisters of the *half blood*] 2. *same as* HALF-BLOODED

half-blood·ed (-blud'id) *adj.* 1. related through one parent only 2. born of parents of different races

half boot a boot reaching halfway up the lower leg

half-breed (-brēd') *n.* a person whose parents are of different races —*adj. same as* HALF-BLOODED Sometimes regarded as a contemptuous term

half brother a brother through one parent only

half-caste (-kāst') *n.* a half-breed; esp., an offspring of one European parent and one Asiatic parent —*adj.* of a half-caste

half cock the halfway position of the hammer of a firearm, when the trigger is locked —**go off half-cocked** 1. to go off too soon: said of a firearm 2. to fail because of inadequate preparation or premature starting: also **go off at half cock** —**half'-cocked'** *adj.*

half crown a former Brit. coin worth two shillings and sixpence (12·5 new pence): also **half a crown**

half gainer a dive in which the diver, facing forward, does a backward somersault in the air so as to enter the water headfirst, facing the board

half-heart·ed (-här'tid) *adj.* with little enthusiasm, determination, interest, etc. —**half'heart'ed·ly** *adv.* —**half'-heart'ed·ness** *n.*

half hitch a knot made by passing the end of the rope around the rope and then through the loop thus made: it is the simplest kind of hitch

half-hour (-our') *n.* 1. half of an hour; thirty minutes 2. the point thirty minutes after any given hour —*adj.* 1. lasting for thirty minutes 2. occurring every thirty minutes —**half'-hour'ly** *adj., adv.*

half-hunter (-hun'tər) *n.* a watch with a hinged metal lid in which a small opening allows the time to be read while still protecting the glass

half-inch (-inch') *vt., vi.* [rhyming slang for *to pinch*] [Slang] to steal

half landing a landing halfway up a flight of stairs

half-life (-līf') *n.* the period required for the disintegration of half of the atoms in a sample of some radioactive substance: also **half life**

half-mast (-mäst') *n.* the position of a flag lowered about halfway down its staff, as in public mourning —*vt.* to hang (a flag) at half-mast

half measure *n.* an inadequate measure or action, esp. a compromise: *usually used in pl.*

half-moon (-mōōn') *n.* 1. the moon when only half its disc is clearly seen 2. anything shaped like a half-moon or crescent

half nelson *see* NELSON

half note *U.S. name for* MINIM (*sense* 3)

half·pen·ny (hā'pə nē, hāp'nē) *n., pl.* **-pence** (-pens), **-pen·nies** a coin worth half of one penny —*adj.* worth a halfpenny, or very little

half pint 1. a liquid or dry measure equal to 1/4 quart 2. [Slang] a small person

half-seas-over (-sēz ō'vər) *adj.* [Slang] partly drunk

half sister a sister through one parent only

half size any of a series of sizes in clothing that is halfway between two sizes

half-sole (haf'sōl') *vt.* **-soled'**, **-sol'ing** to repair (shoes or boots) by attaching new half soles

half sole a sole (of a shoe or boot) from the arch to the toe

half sovereign a former Brit. coin worth ten shillings (50 new pence)

half step [U.S.] *Music same as* SEMITONE

half term a short holiday midway through an academic term

half-tim·bered (-tim'bərd) *adj. Archit.* made of a wooden framework having the spaces filled with plaster, brick, etc.

half time the rest period between halves of a football match, basketball game, etc.

half title 1. the title of a book, often abbreviated, appearing on the odd-numbered page preceding (or sometimes following) the main title page 2. the title of a subdivision of a book appearing on the odd-numbered page immediately preceding that division

half·tone (-tōn') *n.* 1. *Art* a tone or shading between light and dark 2. [U.S.] *Music same as* SEMITONE 3. *Photoengraving* a) a technique of shadings by dots produced by photographing the object from behind a fine screen b) a photoengraving so made

half-track (-trak') *n.* an army truck, armoured vehicle, etc. with tractor treads instead of rear wheels, but with a pair of wheels in front

half-truth (-trōōth') *n.* a statement or account containing only some of the facts, the rest being left out often with the intention of deceiving

half·way (-wā') *adj.* 1. equally distant between two points, states, etc. 2. incomplete; partial —*adv.* 1. half the distance; to the midway point 2. incompletely; partially —**meet halfway** to be willing to compromise with

halfway house 1. a place to rest midway on a journey 2. the halfway point in any progression 3. a place where persons are aided in readjusting to society following imprisonment, etc.

half-wit (-wit') *n.* a stupid, silly, or imbecilic person; fool; dolt —**half'-wit'ted** *adj.*

hal·i·but (hal'ə bət) *n., pl.* **-but, -buts:** see PLURAL, II, D, 2 [< ME. < *hali,* holy + *butt,* because eaten on holidays] a large, edible flatfish found in northern seas, esp. the **Atlantic halibut**

hal·ide (hal'īd, hā'līd) *n.* [HAL(OGEN) + -IDE] *Chem.* a compound of a halogen with another element or a radical —*adj. same as* HALOID

hal·i·eu·tic (hal i ōō'tik) *adj.* [< Gr. *halieutikos*] pertaining to fishing

hal·ite (hal'īt, hā'līt) *n.* [< Gr. *hals,* salt + -ITE] native sodium chloride; rock salt

hal·i·to·sis (hal'ə tō'sis) *n.* [ModL. < L. *halitus,* breath + -OSIS] bad-smelling breath

hall (hôl) *n.* [OE. *heall* < base of *helan,* to cover] 1. the dwelling of a baron, squire, etc. 2. the large, main living-room in a castle or manor house 3. [sometimes H-] the headquarters of a guild, etc. 4. a large public or semipublic room or auditorium for gatherings, entertainments, etc. 5. [sometimes H-] a residential building in a university 6. *a)* in some colleges, a dining-room *b)* a dinner eaten there 7. a passageway or room between the entrance and the interior of a building 8. a passageway or corridor onto which rooms open

hal·le·lu·jah, hal·le·lu·iah (hal'ə lōō'yə) *interj.* [< LL. < Gr. < Heb. < *hallelū,* praise + *yāh,* Jehovah] praise (ye) the Lord! —*n.* an exclamation, hymn, or song of praise to God

hal·liard (hal'yərd) *n. same as* HALYARD

hall·mark (hôl'märk') *n.* 1. an official mark stamped on British gold and silver articles orig. at Goldsmiths' Hall in London, as a guarantee of genuineness 2. any mark or symbol of genuineness or high quality —*vt.* to put a hallmark on

hal·lo (ha lō', hə lō') *interj.* [var. of HALLOO] an exclamation *a)* of greeting or of response, as in telephoning *b)* to attract attention *c)* of surprise —*n., pl.* **-los** a saying of 'hallo' —*vi., vt.* **-loed'**, **-lo'ing** to say 'hallo' (to)

hal·loo (hə lōō') *vi., vt.* **-looed'**, **-loo'ing** 1. to call out in order to attract the attention of (a person) 2. to urge on (hounds) by shouting 3. to shout —*interj., n.* a shout or call; also **hal·lo, hal·loa**

hal·low (hal'ō) *vt.* [OE. *halgian* < *halig,* holy] 1. to make holy or sacred; consecrate 2. to regard as holy; honour as sacred

hal·lowed (hal'ōd; *in poetry or liturgy, often* hal'ə wid) *adj.* 1. made holy or sacred 2. honoured as holy —**hal'-lowed·ness** *n.*

Hal·low·een, Hal·low·e'en (hal'ō wēn') *n.* [contr. < *all hallow even*] the evening of October 31st, which is followed by All Saints' Day

Hall·statt (hôl'stat', hal'shtat) *adj.* [from archaeological remains at *Hallstatt,* near Salzburg, Austria] designating an Iron Age culture (*c.* 700-400 B.C.) in C. Europe

hal·lu·ci·nate (hə lōō'sə nāt') *vi., vt.* **-nat'ed, -nat'ing** [< L. pp. of *hallucinari,* to wander mentally] to have or cause to have hallucinations —**hal·lu'ci·nant** *adj., n.*

hal·lu·ci·na·tion (hə lōō'sə nā'shən) *n.* 1. the apparent perception of sights, sounds, etc. that are not actually present 2. the imaginary thing apparently seen, heard, etc. —**hal·lu'ci·na·tive, hal·lu'ci·na·to·ry** (-nə tər ē) *adj.*

hal·lu·ci·no·gen (hə lōō'sə nə jen) *n.* a drug or other substance that produces hallucinations —**hal·lu'ci·no·gen'ic** *adj.*

hal·lux (hal'əks) *n., pl.* **-lu·ces** (-yōō sēz) [ModL., altered < L. *hallex, allex,* big toe] the first toe on either side of the hind legs of a terrestrial vertebrate; in man, the big toe

hall·way (hôl'wā') *n.* 1. a passageway or room between the entrance and the interior of a building 2. a passageway; corridor; hall

halm (hôm) *n. same as* HAULM

hal·ma (hal'mə) *n.* [Gr., lit., a leap] a board game in which players move their pieces in turn by single squares or by hopping over other pieces to reach their opponent's base

ha·lo (hā'lō) *n., pl.* **-los, -loes** [< L. < Gr. *halōs,* circular threshing floor, halo around the sun < *halein,* to grind] 1. a ring of light that seems to encircle the sun, moon, etc. 2. a symbolic ring or disc of light shown around the head of a saint, etc. 3. the glory with which a famed, revered, or idealized person or thing is invested —*vt.* **-loed, -lo·ing** to encircle with a halo

hal·o·gen (hal'ə jən) *n.* [< Gr. *hals* (gen. *halos*), salt + -GEN] any of the five very active, nonmetallic chemical elements, fluorine, chlorine, bromine, astatine, and iodine —**ha·log·e·nous** (ha loj′ə nəs) *adj.*

hal·o·gen·ate (-jə nāt′) *vt.* **-at′ed, -at′ing** to treat or combine with a halogen —**hal′o·gen·a′tion** *n.*

hal·oid (hal′oid, hā′loid) *adj.* [< Gr. *hals,* salt + -OID] of or like a halide —*n.* same as HALIDE

halt¹ (hôlt) *n.* [< Fr. < G. < *halten,* to hold] a stop, esp. a temporary one, as in marching —*vi., vt.* to come or bring to a halt —**call a halt** to order a stop

halt² (hôlt) *vi.* [< OE. *healtian* < *healt,* adj.] **1.** [Archaic] to limp **2.** to be uncertain; hesitate [to *halt* in one's speech] **3.** to have defects in flow, as of rhythm or logic —*adj.* [Archaic] limping; lame —*n.* [Archaic] a lameness —**the halt** those who are lame —**halt′ing·ly** *adv.*

hal·ter¹ (hôl′tər) *n.* [OE. *hælftre*] **1.** a rope, strap, etc. for tying or leading an animal **2.** a rope for hanging a person; noose **3.** a style of woman's garment for covering the breast, held up by a loop around the neck —*vt.* to put a halter on (an animal)

hal·ter² (hôl′tər, hal′-) *n., pl.* **hal·ter·es** (-tir′ēz) [ModL. < Gr. *halter,* weight held (to give impetus) in leaping] either of a pair of knobbed, threadlike, modified second wings serving as balancing organs in dipteran insects: also **hal′·tere** (-tir)

hal·vah, hal·va (häl vä′) *n.* [< Turk. < Ar. *halwa*] an Eastern confection made of ground sesame seeds and nuts mixed with honey, etc.

halve (hav) *vt.* **halved, halv′ing 1.** to divide into two equal parts **2.** to share equally (*with* someone) **3.** to reduce to half **4.** *Golf* to play (a hole, match, etc.) in the same number of strokes as one's opponent

halves (havz) *n. pl. of* HALF —**by halves 1.** incompletely; imperfectly **2.** halfheartedly —**go halves** to share expenses, etc. equally

hal·yard (hal′yərd) *n.* [< ME. *halier* < *halien* (see HALE²)] a rope or tackle for raising or lowering a flag, sail, etc.

ham (ham) *n.* [OE. *hamm*] **1.** the part of the leg behind the knee **2.** *a)* the back of the thigh *b)* the thigh and the buttock together **3.** the hock or hind leg of a four-legged animal **4.** the upper part of a pig's hind leg, salted, smoked, etc. **5.** [Colloq.] an amateur radio operator **6.** [Slang] an incompetent actor or performer, esp. one who overacts —*vi.* **hammed, ham′ming** to overact

ham·a·dry·ad (ham′ə drī′ad, -ad) *n.* [< L. < Gr. *Hamadryas*] **1.** [*also* H-] *Gr. Myth.* a dryad; wood nymph whose life was bound up with that of the tree in which she lived **2.** same as KING COBRA **3.** a baboon of Arabia and N Africa

ham·burg·er (ham′bur gər) *n.* [earlier *Hamburg steak,* after *Hamburg* in West Germany] a fried or baked cake of minced meat, often eaten as a sandwich in a round bun

hame (hām) *n.* [< MDu., horse collar] either of the two rigid pieces along the sides of a horse's collar, to which the traces are attached

ham-fisted (-fist′id) *adj.* [Colloq.] clumsy: also **ham-handed**

Ham·it·ic (ha mit′ik, hə-) *adj.* **1.** of Ham or the Hamites **2.** designating or of a group of African languages, including ancient Egyptian, Berber, and Cushitic

ham·let (ham′lit) *n.* [< OFr. dim. of *hamel,* itself dim. of LowG. *hamm,* enclosed area] a very small village

ham·mam (ham′am, -am′) *n.* [Ar.] a Turkish bath

ham·mer (ham′ər) *n.* [OE. *hamor*] **1.** a tool for pounding, usually consisting of a metal head and a handle **2.** a thing like this tool in shape or use; specif., *a)* the mechanism that strikes the firing pin or cap in a firearm *b)* any of the felted mallets that strike against the strings of a piano *c)* a power tool for pounding **3.** the malleus, one of the bones of the middle ear **4.** an auctioneer's gavel **5.** *Sports* a heavy metal ball attached to a wire and thrown for distance in a field event (**hammer throw**) —*vt.*

CLAW HAMMER

BALL PEEN HAMMER

TYPES OF HAMMER

1. to strike repeatedly as with a hammer **2.** to make or fasten with a hammer **3.** to drive, force, or shape as with hammer blows —*vi.* to strike repeated blows as with a hammer —**come** (or **go**) **under the hammer** be offered for sale by an auctioneer —**hammer and tongs** with all one's might; vigorously —**hammer** (**away**) **at 1.** to work energetically at **2.** to keep emphasizing —**hammer out 1.** to shape or flatten by hammering **2.** to take out by hammering **3.** to develop or work out by careful thought or repeated effort —**ham′mer·er** *n.* —**ham′mer·like′** *adj.*

hammer and sickle the emblem on the flag of the U.S.S.R.,

the hammer representing the industrial workers and the sickle, the peasants

hammer beam either of a pair of short, horizontal beams that project from opposite walls to support arched braces and struts

ham·mer·head (-hed′) *n.* a medium-sized shark that has a mallet-shaped head

ham·mer·lock (-lok′) *n.* a wrestling hold in which one arm of the opponent is twisted upwards behind his back

ham·mer·toe (-tō′) *n.* **1.** a condition in which the first joint of a toe is permanently bent downwards, resulting in a clawlike deformity **2.** such a toe

ham·mock (ham′ək) *n.* [Sp. *hamaca* < native WInd. name] a length of netting, canvas, etc. swung from ropes at both ends and used as a bed or couch

ham·my (ham′ē) *adj.* **-mi·er, -mi·est** [Slang] like or characteristic of a ham (actor); overacting

ham·per¹ (ham′pər) *vt.* [ME. *hampren*] to hinder; impede; encumber

ham·per² (ham′pər) *n.* [< OFr. < *hanap,* a cup < Frank.] **1.** a large basket, usually with a cover **2.** such a basket with its contents, usually food

ham·ster (ham′stər) *n.* [G.] a ratlike animal with large cheek pouches: it is often used in scientific experiments or kept as a pet

ham·string (ham′striŋ′) *n.* **1.** one of the tendons at the back of the human knee **2.** the great tendon at the back of the hock in a four-legged animal —*vt.* **-strung′, -string′ing 1.** to disable by cutting a hamstring **2.** to make powerless

ham·u·lus (ham′yoo ləs) *n., pl.* **-u·li** (-lī) [ModL. < L., dim. of *hamus,* a hook] a small hook or hook-shaped part, as at the end of barbicels of feathers, or at the end of some bones, etc.

hand (hand) *n.* [OE.] **1.** the part of the human arm below the wrist, used for grasping **2.** the corresponding part in apes, monkeys, etc. **3.** a side, direction, or position indicated by a hand [at one's right *hand*] **4.** *a)* possession or care [the papers are in my *hands*] *b)* power; authority **5.** control; power [to strengthen one's *hand*] **6.** an active part; share [take a *hand* in this work] **7.** *a)* a handshake, as a pledge *b)* a promise to marry **8.** skill; ability [a master's *hand*] **9.** *a)* handwriting *b)* a signature **10.** a clapping of hands; applause [they gave the singer a *hand*] **11.** assistance; help [to lend a *hand*] **12.** a person whose chief work is with his hands, as a sailor, farm labourer, etc. **13.** a person regarded as having some special skill [quite a *hand* at sewing] **14.** a person (or, sometimes, thing) from or through which something comes; source [to get a story at second *hand*] **15.** anything like a hand, as the pointer on a clock **16.** the breadth of a hand, about 10 centimetres **17.** *Card Games a)* the cards held by a player at one time *b)* a player *c)* a round of play —*adj.* of, for, made by, or controlled by the hand —*vt.* **1.** to give as with the hand; transfer **2.** to help, conduct, steady, etc. with the hand [to *hand* a lady into her car] —(at) **first hand** from the original source —**at hand 1.** near; close by **2.** immediately available **3.** imminent —(at) **second hand 1.** not from the original source **2.** previously used —**at the hand** (or **hands**) **of** through the action of —**by hand** not by machines but with the hands —**change hands** to pass from one owner to another —**from hand to mouth** with just enough for immediate needs —**hand down 1.** to bequeath **2.** to announce (a verdict, etc.) —**hand in** to give; submit —**hand in** (or **and**) **glove** in intimate association —**hand in hand 1.** holding one another's hand **2.** together —**hand it to** [Colloq.] to give deserved credit to —**hand off** *Rugby* to ward off (an opponent) using a hand-off —**hand on** to pass along; transmit —**hand out** to distribute —**hand over** to give up; deliver —**hand over fist** [Colloq.] easily and in large amounts —**hands down** without effort; easily —**hands off!** don't touch! don't interfere! —**hand to hand** at close quarters: said of fighting —**have one's hands full** to be extremely busy —**in hand 1.** in order or control **2.** in possession **3.** in process —**keep one's hand in** to keep in practice in order to retain one's skill —**lay hands on 1.** to attack physically **2.** to seize; take **3.** to touch with the hands in blessing, etc. —**off one's hands** no longer in one's care —**on every hand** on all sides; also **on all hands** —**on hand 1.** near **2.** available **3.** present —**on one's hands** in one's care —**on the one hand** from one point of view —**on the other hand** from the opposed point of view —**out of hand 1.** out of control **2.** immediately; without reservation or close examination [to condemn *out of hand*] —**show one's hand** to disclose one's intentions —**take in hand 1.** to take control of **2.** to handle; treat **3.** to try; attempt —**to hand 1.** near; accessible **2.** in one's possession —**turn** (or **put**) **one's hand to** to undertake; work at —**wash one's hands of** to refuse to go on with or take responsibility for —**with a high hand** with arrogance —**with clean hands** without guilt —**hand′less** *adj.*

hand- *a combining form meaning* of, with, by, or for a hand or hands [handclasp, handcuff]

hand·bag (hand′bag′) *n.* **1.** a small container for money, toilet articles, keys, etc., carried by women **2.** a small suitcase

hand·ball (-bôl′) *n.* **1.** a game played on an outdoor pitch or an indoor court, in which a ball is thrown by hand from player to player **2.** the round, inflated leather ball used in this game

hand·bar·row (-bar′ō) *n.* a frame carried by two people, each holding a pair of handles attached at either end

hand·bill (-bil′) *n.* a small printed notice, advertisement, etc. to be passed out by hand

hand·book (-book′) *n.* **1.** a compact reference book on some subject; manual **2.** a guidebook

hand·breadth (-bredth′, -bretth′) *n.* the breadth of the human palm, about 10 centimetres

h.&c. hot and cold

hand·cart (-kärt′) *n.* a small cart, often with only two wheels, pulled or pushed by hand

hand·clasp (-kläsp′) *n.* a clasping of each other's hand in greeting, farewell, etc.

hand·craft (-kräft′) *n.* *same as* HANDICRAFT —*vt.* to make by hand with skill —**hand′craft′ed** *adj.*

hand·cuff (-kuf′) *n.* either of a pair of connected metal rings that can be locked about the wrists, as in fastening a prisoner to a policeman: *usually used in pl.* —*vt.* to put handcuffs on; manacle

hand·ed (han′did) *adj.* **1.** having, or for use by one having, a specified handedness [right-*handed*] **2.** having or using a specified number of hands [two-*handed*] **3.** involving (a specified number of) players [a three-*handed* game of cards]

hand·ed·ness (-nis) *n.* ability in using one hand more skilfully than the other

hand·ful (hand′fool′) *n.*, *pl.* **-fuls′** **1.** as much or as many as the hand will hold **2.** a relatively small number or amount **3.** [Colloq.] someone or something hard to manage

hand·gun (-gun′) *n.* any firearm that is held and fired with one hand, as a pistol

hand·i·cap (han′dē kap′) *n.* [orig. a game in which forfeits were drawn from a cap < *hand in cap*] **1.** *a)* a race or other competition in which difficulties are imposed on the superior contestants, or advantages given to the inferior, to make their chances of winning equal *b)* such a difficulty or advantage **2.** something that hampers one; disadvantage **3.** *Golf* the average no. of strokes above par which a player takes to complete a course —*vt.* **-capped′, -cap′ping** **1.** to give a handicap to **2.** to cause to be at a disadvantage; hinder —**the handicapped** those who are physically disabled or mentally retarded —**hand′i·cap′per** *n.*

hand·i·craft (han′dē kräft′) *n.* [OE. *handcræft*] **1.** expertness with the hands **2.** an occupation or art calling for skilful use of the hands, as weaving —**hand′i·crafts′man** *n.*, *pl.* **-men**

hand·i·work (-wurk′) *n.* **1.** *same as* HANDWORK **2.** anything made or done by a particular person

hand·ker·chief (haŋ′kər chif, -chēf′) *n.*, *pl.* **-chiefs, -chieves** (-chifs, -chēfs′, -chivz, -chēvz′) **1.** a small, square piece of cloth for wiping the nose, eyes, or face, or worn for ornament **2.** a kerchief

han·dle (han′d'l) *n.* [OE., < *hand*, HAND] **1.** that part of a utensil, tool, etc. which is to be held, turned, etc. with the hand **2.** a thing like a handle **3.** [Colloq.] a person's title [a *handle* to one's name] **4.** an opportunity or excuse for doing something [his failure served as a *handle* to his enemies] **5.** the quality, as of textiles, perceived by feeling or touching; feel —*vt.* **-dled, -dling** **1.** to touch, lift, etc. with the hand or hands **2.** to operate or use with the hands [he *handles* the reins well] **3.** to manage, control, etc. **4.** to deal with [to *handle* a problem tactfully] **5.** to sell or deal in **6.** to behave toward; treat —*vi.* to respond to control [the car *handles* well] —**fly off the handle** [Colloq.] to become violently angry or excited —**han′dle·less** *adj.*

han·dle·bar (-bär′) *n.* **1.** [often *pl.*] a curved metal bar with handles on the ends, for steering a bicycle, etc. **2.** [Colloq.] a moustache with long curved ends: in full, **handlebar moustache**

han·dler (han′dlər) *n.* a person or thing that handles; specif., *a)* a boxer's trainer and second *b)* a person who trains and manages an animal

hand·made (hand′mād′) *adj.* made by hand, not by machine

hand·maid·en (-mād′'n) *n.* **1.** [Archaic] a woman or girl servant **2.** that which accompanies in a useful but subordinate capacity Also **hand′maid′**

hand-me-down (-mē doun′) *n.* [Colloq.] a used article of clothing, etc. which is passed along to someone else —*adj.* [Colloq.] **1.** used; secondhand **2.** ready-made and cheap

hand-off (-ôf) *n.* *Rugby* the act of warding or thrusting off an opposing player with the open hand

hand organ a barrel organ played by turning a crank by hand

hand·out (hand′out′) *n.* **1.** clothing, food or money given to a needy or destitute person **2.** a leaflet, statement, etc. handed out as for publicity

hand·pick (-pik′) *vt.* **1.** to pick (fruit or vegetables) by hand **2.** to choose with care or for a special purpose —**hand′picked′** *adj.*

hand·rail (-rāl′) *n.* a rail serving as a guard or hand support, as along a stairway

hand·saw (-sô′) *n.* a saw used with one hand

hand's-breadth (handz′bredth′, -bretth′) *n.* *same as* HANDBREADTH

hand·sel (han′s'l, hant′-) *n.* [< ON. *handsal*, sealing of a bargain by a handclasp] a present for good luck, as at the new year or on the launching of a new business —*vt.* **-selled, -sel·ling** to give a handsel to

hand·set (hand′set′) *n.* a telephone mouthpiece and receiver in a single unit, held in one hand

hand·shake (-shāk′) *n.* a gripping of each other's hand in greeting, agreement, etc.

HANDSET

hand·some (han′səm) *adj.* [orig., easily handled < ME.: see HAND & -SOME[1]] **1.** large; considerable [a *handsome* sum] **2.** generous; gracious [a *handsome* gesture] **3.** good-looking; of pleasing appearance, esp. in a manly or dignified way —**handsome is that** (or as) **handsome does** people are judged by their deeds, not by their looks —**hand′some·ly** *adv.* —**hand′some·ness** *n.*

hand·spring (hand′spriŋ′) *n.* a gymnastic feat in which the performer turns over in midair with one both hands touching the ground

hand·stand (-stand′) *n.* a gymnastic feat of supporting oneself upright on the hands with the arms outstretched

hand-to-hand (han′tə hand′) *adj.* in close contact; at close quarters: said of fighting

hand-to-mouth (-mouth′) *adj.* barely subsisting

hand·work (hand′wurk′) *n.* work done or made by hand, not by machine —**hand′worked′** *adj.*

hand·writ·ing (-rīt′iŋ) *n.* **1.** writing done by hand, with pen, pencil, etc. **2.** a style or form of such writing —**hand′writ′ten** (-rit′'n) *adj.*

hand·y (han′dē) *adj.* **hand′i·er, hand′i·est** **1.** close at hand; easily reached **2.** easily used or managed **3.** useful [the extra money will come in *handy*] **4.** clever with the hands; deft —**hand′i·ly** *adv.* —**hand′i·ness** *n.*

han·dy·man (-man′) *n.*, *pl.* **-men′** a man who does odd jobs

hang (haŋ) *vt.* **hung, hang′ing**; for vt. 3 & vi. 4 **hanged** is preferred pt. & pp. [OE. *hangian*] **1.** to attach to something above with no support from below; suspend **2.** to attach so as to permit free motion [to *hang* a door on its hinges] **3.** to put to death by suspending from a rope about the neck **4.** to fasten (pictures, etc.) to a wall **5.** to ornament or cover [to *hang* a room with pictures] **6.** to paste (wallpaper) to walls **7.** [Chiefly U.S.] to deadlock (a jury) by one's vote **8.** to suspend (game) till it becomes slightly decomposed and therefore more tasty **9.** to fix (something) *on* a person or thing —*vi.* **1.** to be suspended **2.** to swing, as on a hinge **3.** to fall in folds as cloth, a coat, etc. **4.** to die by hanging **5.** to droop; bend **6.** to be doubtful or unresolved [hang in the balance] **7.** to have one's pictures exhibited at a museum, etc. —*n.* the way that a thing hangs —**get** (or **have**) **the hang of** [Colloq.] **1.** to learn (or have) the knack of **2.** to understand the significance or idea of —**hang around** (or **about**) [Colloq.] to loiter around —**hang back** (or **off**) to be reluctant to advance —**hang fire** to be unsettled or undecided —**hang heavily** (or **heavy**) pass slowly (of time) —**hang on** **1.** to keep hold **2.** to persevere **3.** to depend on **4.** to listen attentively to **5.** [Colloq.] to wait [hang on a minute] —**hang out** **1.** to lean out **2.** to display, as by suspending **3.** [Slang] to frequent —**hang over** to project, hover, or loom over —**hang together** **1.** to stick together **2.** to make sense, as a story —**hang up** **1.** to put on a hanger, hook, etc. **2.** to end a telephone conversation by replacing the receiver **3.** to delay or suspend the progress of —**not care** (or **give**) **a hang about** [Colloq.] to not care the least bit about —**hang′a·ble** *adj.*

hang·ar (haŋ′ər) *n.* [Fr., a shed] a repair shed or shelter for aircraft

hang·dog (haŋ′dog′) *n.* a contemptible, sneaking person —*adj.* **1.** contemptible, sneaking, or abject **2.** ashamed and cringing [a *hangdog* expression]

hang·er (haŋ′ər) *n.* **1.** a person who hangs things [a *paperhanger*] **2.** a thing that hangs **3.** a thing on which objects, as garments, are hung **4.** a wood on a hillside

hang·er-on (-on′) *n.*, *pl.* **hang′ers-on′** a follower or dependent; specif., *a)* one who attaches himself to another, to some group, etc. although not wanted *b)* a sychophant; parasite

hang gliding the sport of gliding through the air while hanging suspended by a harness from a large type of kite (**hang glider**)

hang·ing (haŋ'iŋ) *adj.* 1. suspended 2. leaning over 3. located on a steep slope 4. deserving or imposing the death penalty 5. designating indentation in which the first line of a paragraph touches the left margin; the other lines being indented beneath it —*n.* 1. a suspending or being suspended 2. a putting to death by hanging 3. something hung, as a tapestry

hanging valley a tributary valley entering a main valley at a much higher level because of over-deepening of the main valley, esp. by glacial erosion

hang·man (-mən) *n., pl.* **-men** an executioner who hangs convicted criminals

hang·nail (-nāl') *n.* [altered < ME. *angnail* < OE. *angnægl*, a corn] a bit of torn skin hanging at the side or base of a fingernail

hang·out (-out') *n.* [Slang] a place frequented by some person or group

hang·o·ver (-ō'vər) *n.* 1. something remaining from a previous time or state; a survival 2. headache, nausea, etc. occurring as an aftereffect of drinking much alcohol

hang-up (-up') *n.* [Slang] an emotional problem that cannot easily be resolved

hank (haŋk) *n.* [prob. < Scand.] 1. a loop or coil of something flexible 2. a standard length of coiled thread or yarn

hank·er (haŋ'kər) *vi.* [prob. < Du. or LowG.] to crave or long (followed by *after, for,* or an infinitive) —**hank'er·er** *n.* —**hank'er·ing** *n.*

han·kie, han·ky (haŋ'kē) *n., pl.* **-kies** [Colloq.] a handkerchief

han·ky-pan·ky (haŋ'kē paŋ'kē) *n.* [altered < HOCUS-POCUS] [Colloq.] trickery or deception

Han·sard (han'sərd, -sārd) *n.* [after Luke *Hansard* (1752-1828) and descendants, by whom reports were compiled and printed till 1839] the official record of proceedings in the Brit. parliament

hanse (hans) *n.* [ult. < OHG. *hansa,* band of men] a medieval guild of merchants: also **han·sa** (han'sə) —**the Hanse** a medieval league of free towns in N Germany and adjoining countries, for economic advancement and protection: also **Hanseatic League**

Han·se·at·ic (han'sē at'ik) *adj.* of the Hanse

han·sel (han'sl) *n.* *same as* HANDSEL

Han·sen's disease (han's'nz, hän'-) [after A. *Hansen* (1841-1912), Norw. physician] *same as* LEPROSY

han·som (cab) (han'səm) [after J. A. *Hansom* (1803-1882), Brit. inventor] a two-wheeled covered carriage for two passengers, pulled by one horse: the driver's seat is above and behind the cab

Hants. Hampshire

Ha·nu·ka (khä'noo kä', -kə; hä'-) *n.* [Heb. *ḥanŭkkāh,* dedication] a Jewish festival in early winter commemorating the rededication of the Temple by the Maccabees in 165 B.C.: also **Ha'nuk·kah', Ha'nuk·ka'**

han·u·man (hun'ŏŏ män, han'-) *n.* [Hindi] a small, long-tailed monkey of SE Asia —[H-] *Hindu Myth.* a demigod in the form of a monkey

hap (hap) *n.* [< ON. *happ*] [Archaic] chance; luck —*vi.* **happed, hap'ping** to occur by chance; happen

hap·haz·ard (hap'haz'ərd) *n.* [prec. + HAZARD] mere chance; accident —*adj.* 1. not planned; casual 2. careless —*adv.* by chance; casually —**hap'haz'ard·ly** *adv.* —**hap'-haz'ard·ness** *n.*

hap·less (hap'lis) *adj.* unfortunate; unlucky —**hap'less·ly** *adv.* —**hap'less·ness** *n.*

hap·lo·gra·phy (hap log'rə fē) *n.* [< Gr. *haplous,* single + -GRAPHY] the accidental omission of a letter or syllable in writing (Ex. *eidontics* for *eidodontics*)

hap·loid (hap'loid) *adj.* [< Gr. *haploos,* single + -OID] *Biol.* having the full number of chromosomes normally occurring in the mature germ cell: see DIPLOID —**hap'loi'dy** (-loi'dē) *n.*

hap·lol·o·gy (hap lol'ə jē) *n.* [< Gr. *haplous* see prec., + -LOGY] the dropping of one of two similar or identical successive syllables or sounds in speaking (Ex. : *lib'ry* for *library*)

hap·ly (hap'lē) *adv.* [Archaic] by chance

hap·pen (hap''n) *vi.* [ME. *happenen:* see HAP & -EN] 1. to take place; occur 2. to be or occur by chance 3. to have the luck or occasion; chance [I *happened* to see it] 4. to come by chance (*along, by, in,* etc.) —*adv.* [Dial.] perhaps —**happen on** (or **upon**) to meet or find by chance —**happen to** to be done to or be the fate of; befall

hap·pen·ing (-iŋ) *n.* 1. something that happens; occurrence; incident; event 2. an entertainment, performance, etc., which is spontaneous or improvised, and which usually involves its spectators

hap·py (hap'ē) *adj.* **-pi·er, -pi·est** [ME. *happi* < HAP] 1. favoured by circumstances; lucky; fortunate 2. having, showing, or causing a feeling of pleasure, joy, etc. 3.

suitable and clever; apt; felicitous [a *happy* suggestion] —**hap'pi·ly** *adv.* —**hap'pi·ness** *n.*

happy event [Colloq.] the birth of a baby

hap·py-go-luck·y (-gō luk'ē) *adj.* easygoing; trusting to luck —*adv.* haphazardly; by chance

haptic (hap'tik) *adj.* [< Gr. *haptein,* to touch + -IC] having to do with the sense of touch; tactile

ha·ra-ki·ri (hä'rə kir'ē, har'ə-) *n.* [Jap. *hara,* belly + *kiri,* a cutting] ritual suicide by disembowelment: it was practised by high-ranking Japanese to avoid facing disgrace

ha·rangue (hə raŋ') *n.* [< OFr. *arenge* < OIt. < *aringo,* site for public assemblies < Goth.] a long, blustering or scolding speech; tirade —*vi., vt.* **-rangued', -rangu'ing** to speak or address in a harangue —**ha·rangu'er** *n.*

har·ass (hə ras', har'əs) *vt.* [Fr. *harasser* < OFr. *harer,* to set a dog on < Frank.] 1. to trouble, worry, or torment, as with cares, debts, etc. 2. to trouble by repeated raids or attacks, etc.; harry —**har·ass'er** *n.* —**har·ass'ment** *n.*

har·bin·ger (här'bin jər) *n.* [OFr. *herbergeor,* provider of lodging < *herberge,* a shelter < Frank] a person or thing that comes before to announce or indicate what follows; herald —*vt.* to serve as a harbinger of

har·bor (här'bər) *n., vt., vi.* U.S. sp. of HARBOUR

har·bour (här'bər) *n.* [< OE. < *here,* army + *beorg,* a shelter] 1. a place of refuge, safety, etc.; shelter 2. a protected inlet of a sea, lake, etc., for anchoring ships; port —*vt.* 1. to serve as, or provide, a place of protection to; shelter or house 2. to hold in the mind; cling to [to *harbour* a grudge] —*vi.* to take shelter, as in a harbour —**har'-bour·er** *n.* —**har'bour·less** *adj.*

har·bour·age (-ij) *n.* 1. a shelter for ships 2. shelter or lodgings

harbour master the official in charge of enforcing the regulations governing the use of a harbour

hard (härd) *adj.* [OE. *heard*] 1. not easily pierced or crushed; firm to the touch; solid and compact 2. having firm muscles; vigorous and robust 3. powerful; violent [a *hard* blow] 4. demanding great effort or labour; difficult; specif., *a*) difficult to do [*hard* work] *b*) difficult to understand or explain [a *hard* question] *c*) firmly fastened or tied [a *hard* knot] 5. not easily moved; unfeeling [a *hard* heart] 6. practical and shrewd [a *hard* customer] 7. *a*) firm or definite, esp. in an aggressive way [a *hard* line in foreign policy] *b*) undeniable or actual [*hard* facts] 8. causing pain or discomfort; specif., *a*) difficult to endure [a *hard* life] *b*) harsh; severe; stern [a *hard* master] 9. sharp or too sharp [*hard* outlines, a *hard* red] 10. having in solution mineral salts that interfere with the lathering of soap: said of water 11. energetic and persistent [a *hard* worker] 12. strongly alcoholic [*hard* liquor] 13. [Colloq.] designating any drug, as heroin, that is addictive and potentially very damaging to the body or mind 14. popularly, designating the letter *c* sounded as in *can* or the letter *g* sounded as in *gun* 15. *Commerce* high and stable: said of a market, prices, etc. —*adv.* 1. energetically and persistently [work *hard*] 2. with strength, violence, or severity [hit *hard*] 3. with difficulty [*hard*-earned] 4. so as to withstand much wear, use, etc. [*hard*-wearing clothes] 5. firmly; tightly [secure *hard* and fast] 6. close; near [we live *hard* by] 7. so as to be or make firm or solid [to freeze *hard*] 8. with vigour and to the fullest extent [turn *hard* right] —**be hard on** 1. to treat severely 2. to be difficult or unpleasant for —**hard and fast** invariable; strict —**hard-of-hearing** partially deaf —**hard put** to it having considerable difficulty —**hard up** [Colloq.] in great need of something, esp. money —**hard'ness** *n.*

hard·back (-bak') *n.* a hard-cover book

hard-bit·ten (-bit''n) *adj.* stubborn; tough; enduring; dogged [*hard*-bitten soldiers]

hard·board (-bôrd') *n.* a boardlike material made in sheets by subjecting fibres from wood chips to pressure and heat

hard-boiled (-boild') *adj.* 1. cooked in boiling water until both the white and the yolk solidify: said of an egg 2. [Colloq.] not affected by sentiment, pity, etc.; tough; callous

hard case 1. [Colloq.] a person who is difficult to deal with, or impossible to reform 2. [Aust. Slang] a person who is amusing

hard coal *same as* ANTHRACITE

hard copy computer output that can be read by the aided or unaided eye, as contrasted with output that is machine-readable only

hard-core (-kôr') *adj.* 1. constituting or of a hard core 2. absolute; complete; thorough

hard core the firm, unyielding, or unchanging central part or group

hard-cov·er (-kuv'ər) *adj.* designating any book bound in a relatively stiff cover: also **hard'-bound'** (-bound') See also PAPERBACK

hard·en (här'd'n) *vt., vi.* to make or become hard (in various senses) —**hard'en·er** *n.*

hard·ened (-d'nd) *adj.* 1. made hard or harder 2. confirmed or inveterate in a callous way

hard·fist·ed (härd'fis'tid) *adj.* stingy; miserly

hard hat 1. a protective helmet worn by construction workers, etc. 2. [U.S. Slang] such a worker

hard·head·ed (-hed'id) *adj.* 1. shrewd and unsentimental; practical 2. stubborn —**hard'head'ed·ly** *adv.* —**hard'head'ed·ness** *n.*

hard·heart·ed (-här'tid) *adj.* unfeeling; pitiless —**hard'-heart'ed·ly** *adv.* —**hard'heart'ed·ness** *n.*

har·di·hood (här'dē hood') *n.* boldness, daring, fortitude, vigour, etc.

hard labour formerly, compulsory physical labour imposed, with imprisonment, as a punishment for some crimes

hard landing a landing, as of a rocket on the moon, made at such a high speed as to destroy the equipment

hard-line (härd'līn') *adj.* characterized by an aggressive, unyielding position in politics, foreign policy, etc.

hard·ly (härd'lē) *adv.* 1. with difficulty 2. severely; harshly 3. only just; scarcely: often used ironically to mean "not at all" [*hardly* the person to ask] 4. probably not; not likely

hard-nosed (-nōzd') *adj.* [U.S. Slang] 1. tough; stubborn 2. shrewd and practical —**hard'nose'** *n.*

hard of hearing [Colloq.] slightly deaf

hard pad a disease in dogs, similar to distemper, and often fatal

hard palate the bony part of the roof of the mouth

hard·pan (-pan') *n.* 1. a layer of hard, clayey soil 2. solid, unploughed ground 3. the hard, underlying part of anything; solid foundation

hard paste a porcelain made with kaolin and petuntse, of Chinese origin and made in Europe from the early 18th cent.: cf. SOFT PASTE

hard-pressed (-prest') *adj.* in difficulties; burdened; harassed

hard sell high-pressure salesmanship —**hard'-sell'** *adj.*

hard-shell (-shel') *adj.* 1. having a hard shell: also **hard'-shelled'** 2. [Chiefly U.S. Colloq.] strict; strait-laced; uncompromising, esp. in religious matters

hard·ship (-ship') *n.* 1. hard circumstances of life 2. a thing hard to bear

hard shoulder a surfaced verge along a motorway for emergency stops

hard·tack (-tak') *n.* [HARD + *tack* (food)] unleavened bread made in very hard, large biscuits: traditionally a part of army and navy rations

hard·top (-top') *n.* a motor car like a convertible in having no post between the front and rear windows, but with a metal top that cannot fold back

hard·ware (-wer') *n.* 1. articles made of metal, as tools, nails, fittings, utensils, etc. 2. heavy military equipment or its parts 3. *a*) apparatus used for controlling spacecraft, etc. *b*) the mechanical, magnetic, and electronic design, structure, and devices of a computer: cf. SOFTWARE

hard·wood (-wood') *n.* 1. any tough, heavy timber with a compact texture 2. *Forestry* wood other than that from a needle-bearing conifer 3. a tree yielding hardwood

har·dy¹ (här'dē) *adj.* **-di·er, -di·est** [< OFr. pp. of *hardir*, to make bold < Frank.] 1. bold and resolute; daring 2. too bold; rash 3. able to withstand fatigue, privation, etc.; vigorous 4. able to survive the winter without special care: said of plants —**har'di·ly** *adv.* —**har'di·ness** *n.*

har·dy² (här'dē) *n.* [prob. HARD + -y²] a chisel with a square shank, used by blacksmiths; it fits into a square hole (**hardy hole**) in the anvil

hare (her) *n., pl.* **hares, hare:** see PLURAL, II, D, 1 [OE. *hara*] a swift mammal related to the rabbit, with long ears, soft fur, a cleft upper lip, a short tail, and long, powerful hind legs; specif., one that does not burrow and whose young are furry at birth —**run** (or **hold**) **with the hare and hunt** (or **run**) **with the hounds** to play a double game; to try to maintain friendly relations with both sides

hare and hounds a game in which some players, called 'hounds', chase others, called 'hares', who have left a trail of paper scraps along their route

hare·bell (-bel') *n.* a slender, delicate perennial, with clusters of blue, bell-shaped flowers

hare·brained (-brānd') *adj.* having or showing little sense; reckless, flighty, giddy, rash, etc.

hare·lip (-lip') *n.* 1. a congenital deformity consisting of a harelike cleft of the lip 2. a lip with such a deformity —**hare'lipped'** *adj.*

ha·rem (hä rēm', her'əm) *n.* [Ar. *harīm*, lit., prohibited (place)] 1. that part of a Moslem's household in which the women live 2. the wives, concubines, women servants, etc. in a harem 3. a number of female animals, as of fur seals, who mate and lodge with one male Also **ha·reem** (hä rēm')

hare's foot (-foot) *n.* an annual plant with downy heads of pink or white flowers: also **hare's-foot clover**

hare-wal·la·by (-wol'ə bē) *n.* the smallest of the wallabies, resembling a hare

har·i·cot (har'ə kō') *n.* [Fr., ult. < ? Nahuatl *ayecotli*, bean] 1. *same as* KIDNEY BEAN 2. the pod or seed of other edible beans

ha·ri·jan (hu'rij ən, ha'-) *n.* [Hindi, lit., man of God] a member of certain classes in India, formerly considered untouchable

ha·ri-ka·ri (hä'rē kä'rē) *n.* *same as* HARA-KIRI

hark (härk) *vi.* [< ? OE. *heorcnian*, to hearken] to listen carefully: usually in the imperative —**hark back** to go back; revert

hark·en (här'k'n) *vi., vt.* *same as* HEARKEN

harl (härl) *n.* [ME. *herle*] 1. the barb of a feather, with which an artificial fishing fly is trimmed 2. a fly trimmed with this

Har·le·quin (här'lə kwin, -kin) [< Fr. < OFr. *hierlekin*, demon] a traditional comic character in pantomime, who wears a mask and gay, spangled, diamond patterned tights of many colours —*n.* [h-] a clown; buffoon —*adj.* [h-] 1. comic; ludicrous 2. of many colours; colourful

har·le·quin·ade (här'lə kwi nād') *n.* [Fr. *arlequinade*] 1. that part of a pantomime in which the Harlequin and the clown play leading parts 2. comic pranks; buffoonery

Harley Street (här'lē) 1. a street in C London famous for its large number of medical specialists' consulting rooms 2. medical specialists collectively

har·lot (här'lət) *n.* [OFr., rogue] a prostitute

HARLEQUIN

har·lot·ry (-rē) *n.* 1. prostitution 2. prostitutes, collectively

harm (härm) *n.* [OE. *hearm*] 1. hurt; injury; damage 2. moral wrong; evil —*vt.* to do harm to; hurt, damage, etc. —**harm'er** *n.*

har·mat·tan (här'mə tan', här'ma'tən) *n.* [Sp.] a dry, dusty wind that blows from the interior of Africa towards the Atlantic, esp. from November to March

harm·ful (-fəl) *adj.* causing or able to cause harm; hurtful —**harm'ful·ly** *adv.* —**harm'ful·ness** *n.*

harm·less (-lis) *adj.* causing no harm; inoffensive —**harm'-less·ly** *adv.* —**harm'less·ness** *n.*

har·mon·ic (här mon'ik) *adj.* 1. harmonious in feeling or effect; agreeing 2. *Music a*) of or in harmony *b*) pertaining to an overtone —*n.* 1. *same as* OVERTONE (sense 1) 2. *Elec.* an alternating-current voltage or current or a component of this, whose frequency is some integral multiple of a fundamental frequency —**har·mon'i·cal·ly** *adv.*

har·mon·i·ca (-i kə) *n.* [L.: see HARMONY] a small wind instrument played with the mouth; mouth organ: it has a series of graduated metal reeds that vibrate and produce tones when air is blown or sucked across them

harmonic motion a periodic motion, or vibration, along a straight line in which the restoring force is proportional to the displacement

har·mon·ics (-iks) *n.pl.* [*with sing. v.*] the physical science dealing with musical sounds

har·mo·ni·ous (här mō'nē əs) *adj.* [< Fr.: see HARMONY] 1. having parts combined in a proportionate, orderly, or pleasing arrangement 2. having similar feelings, ideas, interests, etc. 3. having musical tones combined to give a pleasing effect —**har·mo'ni·ous·ly** *adv.* —**har·mo'-ni·ous·ness** *n.*

har·mo·nist (här'mə nist) *n.* a musician expert in harmony —**har'mo·nist'ic** *adj.*

har·mo·ni·um (här mō'nē əm) *n.* [< Fr.: see HARMONY] a small kind of reed organ

har·mo·nize (här'mə nīz') *vi.* **-nized', -niz'ing** 1. to be in harmony; accord; agree 2. to sing in harmony —*vt.* 1. to make harmonious; bring into agreement 2. to add chords to (a melody) so as to form a harmony —**har'mo·ni·za'tion** *n.* —**har'mo·niz'er** *n.*

har·mo·ny (här'mə nē) *n., pl.* **-nies** [< OFr. < L. < Gr. *harmonia* < *harmos*, a fitting] 1. a combination of parts into a pleasing or orderly whole 2. agreement in feeling, action, ideas, etc.; peaceable or friendly relations 3. a state of agreement or proportionate arrangement of colour size, shape, etc. 4. agreeable sounds; music 5. *Music a*) the simultaneous sounding of two or more tones, esp. when satisfying to the ear *b*) structure in terms of the arrangement, modulation, etc. of chords *c*) the study of this structure

har·ness (här'nis) *n.* [< OFr. *harneis*, armour < ON.] 1. orig., armour for a man or horse 2. the leather straps and metal pieces by which a horse, etc. is fastened to a vehicle, plough, or load 3. any trappings or gear similar to this —*vt.* 1. to put harness on (a horse, etc.) 2. to control so as to use the power of [to *harness* one's energy] —**in harness** in or at one's routine work

harness race a horse race between either trotters or pacers, each pulling a sulky and driver

harp (härp) *n.* [OE. *hearpe*] 1. a musical instrument with strings stretched across an open, triangular frame, held upright and played by plucking with the fingers 2. a harp-shaped object or implement —*vi.* **1.** to play a harp **2.** to persist in talking or writing tediously or continuously (*on* or *upon* something) —**harp'er** *n.*

harp·ist (här'pist) *n.* a harp player

har·poon (här poon') *n.* [< MDu. < MFr. < *harper*, to claw ? < ON. *harpa*, to squeeze] a barbed missile attached to a cord and hurled or fired from a gun when hunting whales, etc. —*vt.* to strike or kill with a harpoon —**har·poon'er** *n.*

harp seal a brownish-grey seal of the N Atlantic and Arctic Oceans

harp·si·chord (härp'si kôrd') *n.* [< obs. Fr. or < It.: see HARP & CORD] a stringed musical instrument with a keyboard, predecessor of the piano: the strings are plucked by leather or quill points by pressing the keys —**harp'-si·chord'ist** *n.*

har·py (här'pē) *n.,* *pl.* **-pies** [< MFr. < L. < Gr. < *harpazein*, to seize] a greedy or grasping person: after the hideous, winged monsters in Greek mythology, which were half bird and half woman

har·que·bus (här'kwi bəs) *n.* [< Fr., ult. < Du. *haak*, hook + *bus*, a gun] an early type of portable gun —**har·que·bu·sier** (-bōō'zē ə) *n.*

har·ri·dan (har'i d'n) *n.* [prob. < Fr. *haridelle*, worn-out horse] a disreputable, shrewish old woman

har·ri·er[1] (har'ē ər) *n.* [< HARE + -IER] **1.** a dog like the foxhound, used for hunting hares and rabbits **2.** a cross-country runner

har·ri·er[2] (har'ē ər) *n.* **1.** one who harries **2.** a hawk that preys on small mammals, reptiles, etc.

Harris tweed (har'is) [< *Harris,* a district in the Outer Hebrides] *a trademark for* a soft, all-wool tweed, handwoven on the islands of the Outer Hebrides

har·row (har'ō) *n.* [prob. < ON. *harfr*] a heavy frame with spikes or sharp-edged discs, drawn by a horse or tractor and used for breaking up and levelling ploughed ground, covering seeds, etc. —*vt.* **1.** to draw a harrow over (land) **2.** to cause mental distress to; torment; vex —*vi.* to take harrowing [ground that *harrows* well] —**har'row·er** *n.* —**har'row·ing** *adj.* —**har'row·ing·ly** *adv.*

har·rumph (hə rumpf': *conventionalized pronun.*) *vi.* [echoic] **1.** to clear one's throat, esp. in a studied, pompous way **2.** to protest in a pompous or self-righteous way —*n.* a harrumphing

har·ry (har'ē) *vt.* **-ried, -ry·ing** [< OE. *hergian* < base of *here,* army] **1.** to raid and ravage or rob; plunder **2.** to torment; harass **3.** to force along

harsh (härsh) *adj.* [ME. *harsk*] **1.** unpleasantly sharp or rough to the ear, eye, taste, or touch; grating, glaring, bitter, coarse, etc. **2.** unpleasantly crude or abrupt **3.** rough, crude, or forbidding in appearance **4.** excessively severe; cruel or unfeeling —**harsh'en** *vt., vi.* —**harsh'ly** *adv.* —**harsh'ness** *n.*

hart (härt) *n., pl.* **harts, hart:** see PLURAL, II, D, 1 [OE. *heorot*] a male of the European red deer, esp. after its fifth year; stag

har·tal (här'tal, här'təl, här täl') *n.* [Hindi] in India, a suspension of work, esp. as an expression of political protest

har·te·beest (här'tə bēst', härt'bēst') *n., pl.* **-beests', -beest'**: see PLURAL, II, D, 1 [obs. Afrik. < *harte,* hart + *beest,* beast] a large, swift South African antelope having long horns curved backwards at the tips

harts·horn (härts'hôrn') *n.* **1.** a hart's horn **2.** [Now Rare] ammonium carbonate, used in smelling salts: orig. obtained from deer's antlers

harts'-tongue, harts-tongue (-tuŋ') *n.* a fern with narrow, simple fronds

har·um-scar·um (her'əm sker'əm) *adj.* [< ? HARE + SCARE + 'EM] acting or done in a reckless or rash way —*adv.* in a harum-scarum manner —*n.* a harum-scarum person or action

ha·rus·pex (hə rus'peks, har'əs peks) *n., pl.* **-rus'pi·ces**'(-pə sēz') [L.] a soothsayer in ancient Rome who professed to foretell the future by interpreting the entrails of sacrificial animals —**ha·rus'pi·cal** (-pi k'l) *adj.*

har·vest (här'vist) *n.* [OE. *hærfest*] **1.** the time of the year when grain, fruit, vegetables, etc. are reaped and gathered in **2.** a season's yield of grain, fruit, etc.; crop **3.** the gathering in of a crop **4.** the outcome of any effort —*vt., vi.* **1.** to gather in (a crop, etc.) **2.** to gather the crop from (a field) **3.** to get (something) as the result of an action or effort —**har'vest·a·ble** *adj.*

har·vest·er (-ər) *n.* **1.** a person who gathers in a crop of grain, fruit, etc. **2.** any of various farm machines for harvesting crops

harvest festival a religious thanksgiving service in autumn

harvest home **1.** the bringing home of the last harvest load; end of harvest **2.** a festival celebrating this **3.** a song sung by harvesters bringing home the last load

har·vest·man (-mən) *n., pl.* **-men** **1.** a man who harvests **2.** a spiderlike animal with long, thin legs and a short, broad, segmented abdomen

harvest moon the full moon at or about the time of the autumnal equinox, September 22nd or 23rd

harvest mouse a very small mouse inhabiting cornfields, hedgerows, etc.

has (haz; *unstressed* həz, əz) *3rd pers. sing., pres. indic.,* of HAVE

has-been (haz'bin') *n.* [Colloq.] a person or thing whose popularity or effectiveness is past

hash[1] (hash) *vt.* [Fr. *hacher,* to chop] **1.** a dish of diced, cooked meat, often with vegetables, reheated in a sauce **2.** something mixed up; a jumble **3.** a reuse of old material —**make a hash of** [Colloq.] to mess up; bungle —**settle one's hash** [Colloq.] to overcome or subdue one

hash[2] (hash) *n.* [Slang] hashish

hash·ish (hash'ēsh, -ish) *n.* [Ar. *hashīsh,* dried hemp] a drug formed from the resin contained in the flowering tops of Indian hemp, chewed or smoked for its intoxicating or euphoric effects: also **hash'eesh** (-ēsh)

Has·i·dim (has'ə dim; *Heb.* khä sē'dim) *n.pl., sing.* **Has·id** (has'id; *Heb.* khä'sid) [< Heb. *hāsid,* a pious person] a sect of Jewish mystics, orig. in 18th-cent. Poland, that emphasizes joyful worship —**Ha·sid·ic** (ha sid'ik) *adj.*

has·let (has'lit, hāz'-) *n.* [ME. *hastelet* < OFr. < *haste,* meat cooked on a spit] a dish made from heart, liver, etc., fried together and usually made into a loaf to be eaten cold

has·n't (haz'nt) has not

hasp (hasp) *n.* [OE. *hæpse*] a hinged metal fastening for a door, window, lid, etc.: esp., a metal piece fitted over a staple and fastened by a bolt or padlock —*vt.* [Rare] to fasten with a hasp

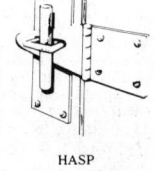

HASP

has·sle (has''l) *n.* [< ?] [Colloq.] **1.** a heated argument; squabble **2.** a troublesome situation —*vi.* **-sled, -sling** [Colloq.] to have a heated argument —*vt.* [Chiefly U.S. Colloq.] to cause trouble or difficulty for; harass

has·sock (has'ək) *n.* [OE. *hassuc*] **1.** [Now Rare] a thick clump or tuft of grass **2.** a firmly stuffed cushion used as a footstool, for kneeling on, etc., esp. in a church

hast (hast; *unstressed* həst) *archaic 2nd pers. sing., pres. indic.,* of HAVE: *used with* thou

has·tate (has'tāt) *adj.* [< L. < *hasta,* a spear] having a triangular shape, as some leaves

haste (hāst) *n.* [OFr. *haste* < Frank.] **1.** quickness of motion; hurrying **2.** careless or reckless hurrying [*haste* makes waste] **3.** necessity for hurrying; urgency —*vt., vi.* **hast'ed, hast'ing** [Rare] *same as* HASTEN —**in haste** **1.** in a hurry **2.** in too great a hurry —**make haste** to hasten

has·ten (hās''n) *vt.* to cause to be or come faster; speed up —*vi.* to move swiftly; hurry

hast·y (hās'tē) *adj.* **hast'i·er, hast'i·est** **1.** done or made with haste; hurried **2.** done or made too quickly and with too little thought; rash [a *hasty* decision] **3.** short tempered or impetuous **4.** showing irritation or impatience [*hasty* words] —**hast'i·ly** *adv.* —**hast'i·ness** *n.*

hat (hat) *n.* [OE. *hætt*] a covering for the head, usually with a brim and crown —*vt.* **hat'ted, hat'ting** to cover or provide with a hat —**pass the hat** to take up a collection —**take one's hat off to** to salute or congratulate —**talk through one's hat** [Colloq.] to talk nonsense —**under one's hat** [Colloq.] secret —**hat'less** *adj.*

hat·band (-band') *n.* a band of cloth around the crown of a hat, just above the brim

hat·box (-boks') *n.* a box or case for carrying or storing a hat or hats

hatch[1] (hach) *vt.* [ME. *hacchen*] **1.** *a)* to bring forth (young) from an egg or eggs by applying warmth *b)* to bring forth young from (an egg or eggs) **2.** to bring (a plan, idea, etc.) into existence; esp., to plot —*vi.* **1.** to bring forth young: said of eggs **2.** to come forth from the egg —*n.* **1.** the process of hatching **2.** the brood hatched —**hatch'er** *n.* —**hatch'ling** *n.*

hatch[2] (hach) *n.* [OE. *hæcc,* a grating] **1.** an opening in a wall, as between a kitchen and a dining room, for serving food **2.** *same as* HATCHWAY **3.** a covering for a ship's hatchway, or a lid or trapdoor for a hatchway in a building

hatch[3] (hach) *vt.* [< OFr. < *hache,* an axe] to mark or engrave with fine, crossed or parallel lines so as to indicate shading —*n.* any of these lines

hatch·back (-bak') *n.* [HATCH[2] + BACK] a car body with a rear that swings up, providing a wide opening and large storage area

hatch·el (hach'əl) *n., vt.* **-elled, -el·ling** *same as* HACKLE[1]

hatch·er·y (hach'ər ē) *n., pl.* **-er·ies** a place for hatching eggs, esp. those of fish or poultry

hatch·et (hach'it) *n.* [< OFr. dim. of *hache,* an axe] **1.** a small axe with a short handle, for use with one hand **2.** *same as* TOMAHAWK —**bury the hatchet** to stop fighting; make peace

hatchet man [Colloq.] **1.** [U.S.] a man hired to commit murder **2.** any person assigned by another to carry out disagreeable or unscrupulous tasks

hatch·ing (hach'iŋ) *n.* [HATCH[3] + -ING] **1.** the drawing or engraving of fine, parallel or crossed lines to show shading **2.** such lines

hatch·ment (hach′mənt) *n.* [for earlier *atcheament*, altered < ACHIEVEMENT] *Heraldry* a panel, usually diamond-shaped, bearing the coat of arms of someone who has died

hatch·way (-wā′) *n.* **1.** a covered opening in a ship's deck **2.** a similar opening in the floor or roof of a building

hate (hāt) *vt.* **hat′ed, hat′ing** [OE. *hatian*] **1.** to have strong dislike or ill will for; despise **2.** to dislike or wish to avoid; shrink from [to *hate* arguments] —*vi.* to feel hatred —*n.* **1.** a strong feeling of dislike or ill will; hatred **2.** a person or thing hated —**hate′a·ble, hat′a·ble** *adj.* —**hat′er** *n.*

hate·ful (-fəl) *adj.* **1.** [Now Rare] feeling or showing hate; malevolent **2.** causing or deserving hate; odious —**hate′-ful·ly** *adv.* —**hate′ful·ness** *n.*

hath (hath) *archaic* 3rd pers. sing., pres. indic., of HAVE

hat·rack (hat′rak′) *n.* a rack, set of pegs or hooks, etc. to hold hats

ha·tred (hā′trid) *n.* [ME. < *hate*, hate + *-red* < OE. *ræden*, state] strong dislike or ill will

hat·ter (hat′ər) *n.* one who makes or sells hats

hat trick 1. in cricket, the taking of three wickets by one bowler with three successive balls **2.** any achievement of three successive points, goals, in other games

hau·ber·geon (hô′bər jən) *n. obs. var. of* HABERGEON

hau·berk (hô′bərk) *n.* [< OFr., ult. < Frank. *hals*, the neck + *bergan*, to protect] a medieval coat of armour, usually of chain mail

haugh·ty (hôt′ē) *adj.* **-ti·er, -ti·est** [< OFr. *haut*, high < L. *altus* + -y²] **1.** having or showing great pride in oneself and contempt or scorn for others **2.** [Archaic] lofty; noble —**haugh′ti·ly** *adv.* —**haugh′ti·ness** *n.*

haul (hôl) *vt.* [< OFr. *haler*, to draw < ODu. *halen*, to fetch] **1.** to move by pulling or drawing; tug; drag **2.** to transport by wagon, truck, etc. [to *haul* coal] **3.** *same as* HALE² **4.** *Naut.* to change the course of (a ship) by setting the sails —*vi.* **1.** to pull; tug **2.** to shift direction: said of the wind **3.** *Naut.* to change the course of a ship by trimming sail —*n.* **1.** the act of hauling; pull; tug **2.** *a)* the amount of fish taken in a single pull of a net *b)* [Colloq.] the amount gained, won, earned, etc. at one time **3.** the distance or route covered in transporting or travelling **4.** a load transported —**haul up 1.** to sail nearer the direction of the wind **2.** [Colloq.] to call to account —**in** (or **over**) **the long haul** over a long period of time —**haul′er** *n.*

haul·age (-ij) *n.* **1.** the act or process of hauling **2.** the charge made for hauling, as by a railway

haul·ier (hôl′yər) *n.* **1.** a mine worker who hauls coal to the foot of the shaft **2.** a person or organization that transports goods by road

haulm (hôm) *n.* [ME. *halm* < OE. *healm, halm,* straw] the stalks or stems of beans, peas, etc., esp. after the crop has been gathered

haunch (hônch) *n.* [< OFr. *hanche* < Gmc.] **1.** the part of the body including the hip, buttock, and thickest part of the thigh **2.** an animal's loin and leg together

haunt (hônt) *vt.* [< OFr. *hanter,* to frequent] **1.** to visit (a place) often or continually **2.** to seek the company or companionship of; run after **3.** to recur repeatedly to [memories *haunted* her] **4.** to fill the atmosphere of; pervade [a house *haunted* by sorrow] —*n.* a place often visited or frequented [to make the library one's *haunt*]

haunt·ed (-id) *adj.* supposedly frequented by ghosts

haunt·ing (-iŋ) *adj.* often recurring to the mind [a *haunting* melody] —**haunt′ing·ly** *adv.*

Hau·sa (hou′sə, -sä) *n.* **1.** *pl.* **-sas, -sa** any member of an Islamic people of W Africa living mainly in N Nigeria **2.** their language

haus·frau (hous′frou′) *n.* [Ger., < *Haus,* house and *Frau,* woman] a German housewife, esp. one exclusively preoccupied with domestic affairs

haut·boy (hō′boi′, ō′-) *n.* [< Fr. < *haut,* high + *bois,* wood] **1.** *earlier name for* OBOE **2.** a species of strawberry

‡**haute cou·ture** (ōt kōō tür′) [Fr., lit., high sewing] the leading designers and creators of new fashions in women's clothing, or their creations

haute cuisine (ōt kwē zēn′) [Fr., lit., high kitchen] the preparation of fine food by highly skilled chefs, or the food so prepared

hau·teur (ō tür′; Fr. ō tër′) *n.* [Fr. < *haut,* high, proud] disdainful pride; haughtiness; snobbery

‡**haut monde** (ō mōnd′) [Fr.] high society

Ha·van·a (hə van′ə) *n.* [after *Havana,* capital of Cuba] **1.** a cigar made in Cuba or of Cuban tobacco **2.** Cuban

have (hav; hav, əv; *before* 'to' haf) *vt.* **had, hav′ing** [OE. *habban*] **1.** to hold; own; possess [to have wealth] **2.** to possess as a part, characteristic, etc. [the week *has* seven days] **3.** to be afflicted with [to *have* a cold] **4.** to experience; undergo [*have* a good time] **5.** to understand or know [to *have* a little Spanish] **6.** to hold or keep in the mind [to *have* an idea] **7.** to declare or state [so gossip *has* it] **8.** *a)* to get, take, or obtain [*have* a look at it] *b)* to

eat or drink [*have* some tea] **9.** to bear or beget (offspring) **10.** to perform; engage in [to *have* an argument] **11.** *a)* to cause to [*have* him sing] *b)* to cause to be [*have* it mended] **12.** to be in a certain relation to [to *have* a wife] **13.** to feel and show [*have* pity on her] **14.** to permit; tolerate [I won't *have* this noise] **15.** [Colloq.] *a)* to hold at a disadvantage [I *had* my opponent there] *b)* to deceive; cheat [they were *had* in that business deal] *c)* to engage in sexual intercourse with *Have* is used as an auxiliary to form phrases expressing completed action, as in the perfect tenses (Ex.: I *had* left), and with infinitives to express obligation or necessity (Ex.: we *have* to go) *Have got* often replaces *have Have* is conjugated in the present indicative: (I) *have,* (he, she, it) *has,* (we, you, they) *have;* in the past indicative (I, he, she, it, we, you, they) *had* Archaic forms are: (thou) *hast, hadst,* (he, she, it) *hath* —*n.* a person or nation with relatively much wealth or rich resources —**have at** [Archaic] to attack; strike —**have done** to stop; finish —**have had it** [Colloq.] to be defeated, disgusted, etc. or no longer popular, useful, etc.—**have it both ways** to adopt either of contradictory alternatives to suit different moods or occasions —**have it good** [Colloq.] to be well-off —**have it out** to settle a disagreement by fighting or discussion —**have on 1.** to be wearing **2.** to have an engagement **3.** to deceive or mislead playfully; trick —**have to be** [Colloq.] to be unquestionably

have·lock (hav′lok) *n.* [after Sir Henry *Havelock* (1795-1857), Brit. general in India] a light cloth covering for a military cap, falling over the back of the neck for protection against the sun

ha·ven (hā′vən) *n.* [OE. *hæfen*] **1.** a port; harbour **2.** any sheltered, safe place; refuge —*vt.* to provide a haven for

have-not (hav′not′) *n.* a person or nation with little or no wealth or resources [the haves and *have-nots*]

have·n't (hav′nt) have not

ha·ver (hā′vər) *vi.* [< ?] to talk foolishly or waste time in foolish talk

hav·er·sack (hav′ər sak′) *n.* [< Fr. < G. Dial. *habersack,* lit., sack of oats] a canvas bag for rations, worn on the back or over one shoulder, as by soldiers and hikers

hav·il·dar (hav′il där′) *n.* [Hindi, < Per. *hawaldar,* one holding charge] an Indian sergeant in the British Indian army

hav·oc (hav′ək) *n.* [< Anglo-Fr. < OFr. *havot,* plunder] great destruction and devastation —**cry havoc 1.** orig., to give (an army) the signal for pillaging **2.** to warn of great danger —**play havoc with** to devastate; destroy; ruin

haw¹ (hô) *n.* [OE. *haga*] **1.** the berry of the hawthorn **2.** *same as* HAWTHORN

haw² (hô) *n.* [< ?] the nictitating membrane of an animal

haw³ (hô) *vi.* [echoic] to hesitate in speaking; falter: usually in HEM AND HAW (see HEM²) —*n.* a sound made by a speaker when hesitating briefly

Ha·wai·ian (hə wī′yən) *adj.* of Hawaii, its people, language, etc. —*n.* **1.** a native or inhabitant of Hawaii; specif., a native of Polynesian descent **2.** the Polynesian language of the Hawaiians

haw·finch (hô′finch′) *n.* [HAW¹ + FINCH] a small, brown bird with brightly-coloured wings, widely distributed in the N hemisphere

hawk¹ (hôk) *n.* [OE. *hafoc*] **1.** any of a group of birds of prey characterized by short, rounded wings, a long tail and legs, and a hooked beak and claws **2.** an advocate of all-out war or of the provocation of open hostilities —*vi.* to hunt birds with the help of hawks —*vt.* to prey on as a hawk does —**hawk′er** *n.* —**hawk′ing** *n.* —**hawk′ish** *adj.* —**hawk′-like′** *adj.*

hawk² (hôk) *vt., vi.* [< HAWKER] to advertise or peddle (goods) in the street by shouting

hawk³ (hôk) *vi.* [echoic] to clear the throat audibly —*vt.* to bring up (phlegm) by coughing —*n.* an audible clearing of the throat

hawk (hôk) *n.* [< ?] a small, square board with a handle underneath for holding mortar or plaster

hawk·er (hôk′ər) *n.* [ult. < MLowG. *hoken,* to peddle] a person who hawks goods in the street

hawk-eyed (-īd′) *adj.* keen-sighted like a hawk

hawk·moth (-moth′) *n.* a moth with a thick, tapering body, slender wings, and a long feeding tube used for sucking the nectar of flowers

hawks·bill (turtle) (hôks′bil′) a medium-sized turtle of warm seas, having a hawklike beak and a shell from which tortoise shell is obtained

hawk·weed (hôk′wēd′) *n.* a plant of the composite family, with yellow or scarlet ray flowers

hawse (hôz) *n.* [< ON. *hals,* the neck] **1.** that part of the bow of a ship containing the hawseholes **2.** *same as* HAWSEHOLE **3.** the space between the bow of a ship and the anchors **4.** the arrangement of port and starboard anchor ropes when a vessel is riding on both anchors

hawse·hole (-hōl′) *n.* any of the holes in a ship's bow through which a hawser or cable is passed

haw·ser (hô′zər) *n.* [< Anglo-Fr. < OFr. *haucier,* ult. < L.

altus, high] a large rope or small cable, by which a ship is anchored, moored, or towed

haw·thorn (hô′thôrn′) *n.* [< OE. < *haga*, hedge + *thorn*] a thorny shrub or small tree of the rose family, with flowers of white, pink, or red, and small, red fruits (*haws*) resembling miniature apples

hay (hā) *n.* [OE. *hieg*] grass, alfalfa, clover, etc. cut and dried for use as fodder —*vi.* to mow grass, alfalfa, etc. and spread it out to dry —**make hay** [Slang] to go to bed to sleep —**make hay of** to turn into confusion —**make hay while the sun shines** to make the most of an opportunity

hay·box (hā′boks) *n.* a cooking apparatus consisting of a box filled with hay in which heated food is left to continue cooking

hay·cock (-kok′) *n.* a small, conical heap of hay drying in a field

hay fever an acute inflammation of the eyes and upper respiratory tract: it is an allergic reaction, caused by the pollen of some grasses and trees

hay·field (hā′fēld′) *n.* a field of grass, alfalfa, etc. to be made into hay

hay·loft (-loft′) *n.* a loft, or upper storey, in a barn or stable, for storing hay

hay·mak·er (-mā′kər) *n.* 1. a person who cuts hay and spreads it out to dry 2. a machine used to accelerate drying of hay 3. [Slang] a powerful blow with the fist

hay·mow (-mou′) *n.* 1. a pile of hay in a barn 2. *same as* HAYLOFT

hay·ride (-rīd′) *n.* a pleasure ride taken by a group in a wagon partly filled with hay

hay·seed (-sēd′) *n.* 1. grass seed shaken from mown hay 2. [U.S. Old Slang] a rustic; yokel

hay·stack (-stak′) *n.* a large heap of hay piled up outdoors: also **hay′rick′** (-rik′)

hay·wire (hā′wīr′) *n.* wire for tying up bales of hay —*adj.* [Colloq.] 1. out of order; confused 2. crazy: usually in go **haywire**, to become crazy

haz·ard (haz′ərd) *n.* [OFr. *hasard*, game of dice < Ar. *az-zahr*] 1. an early game of chance played with dice 2. chance 3. risk; peril; danger 4. an obstacle on a golf course —*vt.* to risk or venture

haz·ard·ous (-əs) *adj.* risky; dangerous —**haz′ard·ous·ly** *adv.* —**haz′ard·ous·ness** *n.*

haze[1] (hāz) *n.* [prob. < HAZY] 1. a thin vapour of fog, smoke, dust, etc. in the air 2. slight confusion or vagueness of mind —*vi., vt.* **hazed, haz′ing** to make or become hazy (often with *over*)

haze[2] (hāz) *vt.* **hazed, haz′ing** [< ? OFr. *haser*, to irritate] 1. [Naut. Slang] to annoy or punish by overwork, unnecessary orders, etc. 2. [U.S.] to initiate or discipline (fellow students) by forcing to do humiliating or painful things

ha·zel (hā′z′l) *n.* [OE. *hæsel*] 1. a shrub or tree related to the birch, bearing edible nuts 2. *same as* HAZELNUT 3. a light brown —*adj.* 1. of the hazel tree 2. light-brown: hazel eyes are usually flecked with green or grey —**ha′zel·ly** *adj.*

ha·zel·nut (-nut′) *n.* the small, edible, roundish nut of the hazel; filbert

ha·zy (hā′zē) *adj.* **-zi·er, -zi·est** [prob. < OE. *hasu*, dusky] 1. characterized by haze; somewhat foggy or smoky 2. vague, obscure, or indefinite [*hazy* thinking] —**ha′zi·ly** *adv.* —**ha′zi·ness** *n.*

Hb *the symbol for* haemoglobin

HB hard black (of pencil lead)

H.B.M. His (or Her) Britannic Majesty

H-bomb (āch′bom′) *n.* *same as* HYDROGEN BOMB

H.C. 1. Holy Communion 2. House of Commons

H.C.F. Honorary Chaplain to the Forces

H.C.F., h.c.f. highest common factor

hdqrs. headquarters

he (hē; *unstressed* hi, ē, i) *pron.* *for pl. see* THEY [OE.] 1. the man, boy, or male animal previously mentioned 2. the person; the one; anyone [*he* who laughs last laughs best] *He* is the nominative case form of the masculine third personal pronoun —*n., pl.* **hes** a man, boy, or male animal *adj.* male

He *Chem.* helium

H.E. 1. high explosive 2. His Eminence 3. His (or Her) Excellency

head (hed) *n.* [OE. *heafod*] 1. the top part of the body in man, the apes, etc., or the front part in most other animals: in higher animals it is a bony structure containing the brain, and including the eyes, ears, nose, and mouth 2. *a)* the head as the seat of reason, memory, and imagination; mind; intelligence [to use one's *head*] *b)* aptitude; ability [to have a *head* for figures] *c)* [Colloq.] a headache 3. a person [dinner at five pounds a *head*] 4. *pl.* **head** the head as a unit of counting [fifty *head* of cattle] 5. the obverse of a coin, usually showing a head: often **heads** 6. the highest or uppermost part or thing; top; specif., *a)* the top of a page, column, etc. *b)* a title of a section, chapter, etc. *c)* a chief point of discussion *d)* a headline *e)* froth floating on newly poured effervescent beverages *f)* that end of a cask or barrel which is uppermost 7. the foremost part of a thing; front; specif., *a)* a part associated with the human head [the *head* of a bed] *b)* the front part of a ship; bow *c)* *Naut.* a toilet, or lavatory *d)* the front position, as of a column of marching men *e)* either end of something 8. the projecting part of something; specif., *a)* the part designed for holding, striking, etc. [the *head* of a pin] *b)* a headland *c)* a projecting place, as in a boil, where pus is about to break through *d)* the part of a tape recorder that records or plays back the magnetic signals on the tape 9. the membrane stretched across the end of a drum, tambourine, etc. 10. the source of a river, stream, etc. 11. a source of water kept at some height to supply a mill, etc. 12. the pressure in an enclosed fluid, as steam 13. a position of leadership or honour [the *head* of the class] 14. the person in charge; leader, ruler, director, etc. 15. a headmaster 16. *Bot.* *a)* a dense, flattened cluster of flowers, as in the dandelion *b)* a large, compact bud [a *head* of cabbage] 17. *Mining* a road driven into a coalface for proving or working a mine 18. *Music* the rounded part of a note, at the end of the stem 19. [Slang] a habitual user of marijuana, LSD, etc. —*adj.* 1. of or having to do with the head 2. most important; principal; first 3. to be found at the top or front 4. striking against the front [*head* current] —*vt.* 1. to be chief of or in charge of 2. to lead; precede 3. to supply (a pin, etc.) with a head 4. [Rare] to behead 5. to trim the higher part from (a tree or plant); poll 6. to cause to go in a specified direction 7. *Soccer* to hit (the ball) with one's head —*vi.* 1. to grow or come to a head 2. to set out; travel [to *head* eastwards] —**by a head** by a small margin —**come to a head** 1. to be about to suppurate, as a boil 2. to culminate —**give someone his head** to let someone do as he likes —**go to one's head** 1. to confuse or intoxicate one 2. to make one vain —**hang** (or **hide**) **one's head** to lower one's head or conceal one's face as in shame —**head off** 1. to get ahead of and intercept 2. to prevent; forestall [to *head* off trouble] —**head over heels** 1. deeply; completely 2. hurriedly; recklessly —**keep** (or **lose**) **one's head** to keep (or lose) one's poise, self-control, etc. —**keep one's head above water** 1. to remain afloat 2. to keep oneself alive, out of debt, etc. —**make head or tail of** to understand: usually in the negative —**off the top of one's head** [Colloq.] at random; extempore —**on** (or **upon**) **one's head** as one's responsibility or misfortune —**off one's head** [Colloq.] crazy —**over one's head** 1. too difficult to understand 2. to a higher authority —**put** (or **lay**) **heads together** to consult or scheme together —**take it into one's head** to conceive the notion, plan, etc. —**turn one's head** 1. to make one dizzy 2. to make one vain

-head (hed) *same as* -HOOD [godhead]

head·ache (hed′āk′) *n.* 1. a continuous pain in the head 2. [Colloq.] a cause of worry, trouble, etc.

head·board (-bôrd′) *n.* a board or frame that forms the head of a bed, etc.

head·dress (-dres′) *n.* 1. a covering or decoration for the head 2. [Obs.] a style of arranging the hair

head·ed (-id) *adj.* 1. formed into a head, as cabbage 2. having a heading

-head·ed (-id) *a combining form meaning:* 1. having a (specified kind of) head [clearheaded] 2. having (a specified number of) heads [two-headed]

head·er (-ər) *n.* 1. a person or device that puts heads on pins, nails, rivets, etc. 2. a machine that takes off the heads of grain and loads them into a truck 3. [Colloq.] a headlong fall or dive 4. a wooden beam placed between two long beams with the ends of short beams resting against it 5. a brick or stone laid against the thickness of a wall with the short end exposed in the wall face 6. *Soccer* the act of heading the ball

head·first (-furst′) *adv.* 1. with the head in front; headlong 2. in a reckless way; rashly; impetuously Also **head′fore′most** (-fôr′mōst)

head·gear (-gir′) *n.* 1. a covering for the head; hat, cap, headdress, etc. 2. the harness for the head of a horse, etc. 3. the hoisting mechanism at the pithead of a mine

head·hunt·er (-hun′tər) *n.* a member of any of certain primitive tribes who remove the heads of slain enemies and preserve them as trophies —**head′hunt′ing** *n.*

head·ing (-iŋ) *n.* 1. something forming or used to form the head, top, edge, or front; specif., an inscription at the top of a chapter, page, etc., giving the title, topic, etc. 2. a topic or category 3. the direction in which a ship, plane, etc. is moving: usually expressed as a compass reading 4. *Mining* *a)* a horizontal tunnel; drift *b)* the end of such a tunnel

head·land (-land) *n.* a point of land reaching out into the water; esp., a promontory

head·light (-līt′) *n.* a light with a reflector and lens, at the front of a car, locomotive, etc.: also **head′lamp′** (-lamp′)

head·line (-līn′) *n.* 1. a line at the top of a page, giving the running title, page number, etc. 2. a line or lines at the top of a newspaper article, giving its topic 3. an important news item —*vt.* **-lined′, -lin′ing** 1. to provide with a headline 2. to give featured billing to

head·long (-lôŋ′) *adv.* [< ME. *hedelinge(s)* < *hede*, head + -*linge*, adv. suffix] 1. with the head first; headfirst 2. with uncontrolled speed and force 3. recklessly; rashly; impetuously —*adj.* 1. having the head first 2. moving with uncontrolled speed and force 3. reckless; impetuous

head·man (hed′mən, -man′) *n., pl.* **-men** (-mən, -men′) a leader, chief, or overseer

head·mas·ter (-mäs′tər) *n.* the man who is principal of a school —**head′mas′ter·ship′** *n.* —**head′mis′tress** (-mis′tris) *n. fem.*

Headmasters′ Conference a professional body of headmasters of independent schools

head·most (-mōst′) *adj.* in the lead; foremost

head·on (-on′) *adj., adv.* 1. with the head or front foremost [a *head-on* collision] 2. directly or in direct opposition [meet problems *head-on*]

head·phone (-fōn′) *n.* a telephone or radio receiver held to the ear by a band over the head

head·piece (-pēs′) *n.* 1. a protective covering for the head, as a helmet 2. the mind; intellect

head·pin (-pin′) *n. Tenpin Bowling* the pin at the front of a triangle of bowling pins

head·quar·ters (-kwôr′tərz) *n.pl.* [often with *sing. v.*] 1. the main office, or centre of operations, of one in command, as in an army or police force 2. the main office in any organization —**head′quar′ter** *vt.*

head·race (-rās′) *n.* the channel or race furnishing water as to a mill wheel

head·rest (-rest′) *n.* a support for the head, as on a dentist's chair

head·room (-rōōm′) *n.* space or clearance overhead, as in a doorway or tunnel

head·set (-set′) *n.* an earphone or earphones, often with a mouthpiece transmitter attached

head·ship (-ship′) *n.* 1. the position or authority of a chief or leader; leadership; command 2. the position of headmaster or headmistress of a school

head·shrink·er (-shriŋ′kər) *n.* 1. a headhunter who shrinks his victims' heads 2. [Slang] a psychiatrist

heads·man (hedz′mən) *n., pl.* **-men** an executioner who beheads those condemned to die

head square (-skwer′) *n.* a head scarf

head·stall (hed′stôl′) *n.* the part of a bridle or halter that fits over a horse's head

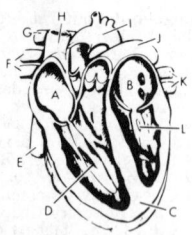

HEADSET

head start an early start or other advantage given to or taken by a contestant or competitor

head·stock (-stok′) *n.* the support for a revolving or moving part of a machine; specif., the part of a lathe supporting the spindle

head·stone (-stōn′) *n.* 1. [Rare] a cornerstone 2. a stone marker placed at the head of a grave

head·stream (-strēm′) *n.* a stream forming the source of another and larger stream

head·strong (-stroŋ′) *adj.* 1. determined not to follow orders, advice, etc. but to do as one pleases; self-willed 2. showing such determination [*headstrong* desire] —**head′-strong′ness** *n.*

head-up display a projection of aircraft instrument readings onto the windscreen to enable the pilot to see them without moving his eyes

head voice 1. the high register of the human voice 2. falsetto

head·wait·er (-wāt′ər) *n.* a supervisor of waiters, often in charge of table reservations

head·wa·ters (-wôt′ərz,) *n.pl.* the small streams that are the sources of a river

head·way (-wā) *n.* 1. forward motion 2. progress in work, etc. 3. *same as* HEADROOM 4. the difference in time or distance between two trains, ships, etc. travelling the same route

head wind a wind blowing in the direction directly against the course of a ship, aircraft, etc.

head·word (-wurd′) *n.* a key word at the beginning of a line, paragraph, etc., as the word defined in a dictionary entry

head·work (hed′wurk′) *n.* mental effort; thought

head·y (-ē) *adj.* **head′i·er, head′i·est** 1. impetuous; rash; wilful 2. tending to affect the senses; intoxicating —**head′-i·ly** *adv.* —**head′i·ness** *n.*

heal[1] (hēl) *vt.* [OE. *hælan* < *hal*, sound, healthy] 1. to make well or healthy again 2. *a)* to cure (a disease) *b)* to cause (a wound, sore, etc.) to become closed or scarred 3. to free from grief, troubles, evil, etc. 4. to remedy (grief, troubles, etc.) —*vi.* 1. to become well or healthy again; be cured 2. to become closed or scarred: said of a wound —**heal′er** *n.*

heal[2] (hēl) *vt. same as* HELE

health (helth) *n.* [OE. *hælth* < *hal*, sound, healthy + -TH] 1. physical and mental well-being; freedom from disease, etc. 2. condition of body or mind [good *health*] 3. a wish for a person's health and happiness, as in drinking a toast 4. soundness or vitality, as of a society or culture —*adj.* 1. relating to health [*health* service] 2. relating to foods, etc. that are, or are reputed to be, beneficial to the health

health centre headquarters for administration of medical welfare in a district

health·ful (-fəl) *adj.* 1. helping to produce or maintain health; wholesome 2. [Rare] *same as* HEALTHY —**health′-ful·ly** *adv.* —**health′ful·ness** *n.*

Health Service *same as* NATIONAL HEALTH SERVICE

health visitor a nurse, appointed by a local authority or attached to a doctor's practice, who visits people's homes chiefly in connection with the health of babies and children

health·y (hel′thē) *adj.* **health′i·er, health′i·est** 1. having good health 2. showing or resulting from good health [a *healthy* appetite] 3. *same as* HEALTHFUL. 4. [Colloq.] large, vigorous, etc. [a *healthy* yell] —**health′i·ly** *adv.* —**health′i·ness** *n.*

heap (hēp) *n.* [OE. *heap*, a troop, band] 1. a pile or mass of things jumbled together 2. [Colloq.] a large amount 3. [Slang] an old car —*vt.* 1. to make a heap of 2. to give in large amounts [to *heap* gifts on one] 3. to fill (a plate, etc.) full or to overflowing —*vi.* to accumulate or rise in a heap or pile

hear (hir) *vt.* **heard** (hurd), **hear′ing** [OE. *hieran*] 1. to perceive or sense (sounds) by the ear 2. to listen to and consider; specif., *a)* to pay attention to or listen to carefully or officially [to *hear* a child's lesson] *b)* to conduct a hearing of (a law case, etc.); try *c)* to consent to; grant [hear my plea] 3. to be informed of; be told —*vi.* 1. to be able to hear sounds 2. to listen 3. to be told (*of* or *about*) —**hear from** to get a letter, telegram, etc. from —**hear! hear!** well said! —**hear out** to listen till the end, without interrupting —**not hear of** to forbid or refuse to consider —**hear′er** *n.*

hear·ing (-iŋ) *n.* 1. the act or process of perceiving sounds 2. the sense by which sounds are perceived 3. opportunity to speak, sing, etc.; audience 4. a court appearance before a judge, other than a trial 5. a formal meeting of an official body for hearing and gathering testimony, etc. 6. the distance a sound will carry [within *hearing*]

hearing aid a small, battery-powered electronic device worn to compensate for hearing loss

heark·en (här′kən) *vi.* [OE. *heorcnean* < *hieran*, to hear] [Archaic] to pay careful attention; listen carefully —*vt.* [Archaic] to hear; heed

hear·say (hir′sā′) *n.* something one has heard but does not know to be true; rumour; gossip —*adj.* based on hearsay

hearse (hurs) *n.* [< OFr. < L. *hirpex*, a harrow] 1. a vehicle used in a funeral for carrying the corpse 2. [Archaic] a bier or coffin

heart (härt) *n.* [OE. *heorte*] 1. the hollow, muscular organ that circulates the blood by alternate dilation and contraction 2. any place or part centrally located like the heart [*hearts* of celery, the *heart* of the city] 3. the central, vital, or main part; essence; core 4. the human heart considered as the centre of emotions, personality attributes, etc.; specif., *a)* inmost thought and feeling [to know in one's *heart*] *b)* one's emotional nature; disposition [to have a kind *heart*] *c)* any of various humane feelings; love, sympathy, etc. *d)* mood; feeling [to have a heavy *heart*] *e)* spirit or courage [to lose *heart*] 5. a loved one 6. *a)* a conventionalized design of a heart, shaped like this: ♥ *a)* any of a suit of playing cards marked with such symbols in red *b)* [*pl.*] this suit of cards *c)* [*pl.*] a card game in which the object is to avoid getting hearts in the tricks taken 8. a fertile condition in land [a field in good *heart*] —*vi.* to develop a heart (said of vegetables) —**after one's own heart** that pleases one perfectly —**at heart** in one's innermost nature —**break one's heart** to overwhelm one with grief or disappointment —**by heart** by or from memorization —**change of heart** a change of mind, affections, etc. —**eat one's heart out** to brood over some frustration or in regret —**have one's heart in one's mouth (or boots)** to be full of fear or nervous anticipation —**have one's heart in the right place** to be well-meaning —**heart**

HUMAN HEART
(A, right atrium; B, left atrium; C, myocardium; D, right ventricle; E, inferior vena cava; F, pulmonary veins; G, pulmonary artery; H, superior vena cava; I, aorta; J, pulmonary artery; K, pulmonary veins; L, left ventricle)

and soul with all one's effort, enthusiasm, etc. —**lose one's heart (to)** to fall in love (with) —**set one's heart on** to have a fixed desire for —**take heart** to cheer up —**take to heart** 1. to consider seriously 2. to be troubled by —**to one's heart's content** as much as one desires —**wear one's heart on one's sleeve** to show one's feelings plainly —**with all one's heart** with complete sincerity, devotion, etc.

heart·ache (-āk′) *n.* sorrow or grief

heart attack any sudden instance of heart failure, esp., a CORONARY THROMBOSIS

heart·beat (-bēt′) *n.* one pulsation, or full contraction and dilation, of the heart

heart block defective transmission of impulses regulating the heartbeat

heart·break (-brāk′) *n.* overwhelming sorrow, grief, or disappointment —**heart′break′ing** *adj.* —**heart′bro′ken** *adj.*

heart·burn (-burn′) *n.* a burning sensation beneath the breastbone resulting from a spastic backflow of acid stomach contents into the oesophagus

heart·ed (-id) *adj.* having a (specified kind of) heart: used in compounds [*stouthearted*]

heart·en (-'n) *vt.* to cheer up; encourage

heart failure the inability of the heart to pump enough blood through the body

heart·felt (-felt′) *adj.* with or expressive of deep feeling; sincere

hearth (härth) *n.* [OE. *heorth*] 1. the stone or brick floor of a fireplace 2. a) the fireside b) the home 3. the lowest part of a blast furnace, where the molten metal settles, or the floor of a furnace on which the ore or metal rests for exposure to the flame

hearth·stone (-stōn′) *n.* 1. the stone forming a hearth 2. a soft stone used for whitening a hearth, doorsteps, etc.

heart·i·ly (härt′il ē) *adv.* 1. in a sincere, cordial way 2. with enthusiasm or vigour 3. with zestful appetite 4. completely; fully; very

heart·i·ness (-ē nis) *n.* a being hearty

heart·less (-lis) *adj.* 1. [Now Rare] lacking spirit or courage 2. lacking kindness; hard and pitiless —**heart′-less·ly** *adv.* —**heart′less·ness** *n.*

heart·rend·ing (-ren′diŋ) *adj.* causing much grief or mental anguish —**heart′-rend′ing·ly** *adv.*

heart-search·ing (-surch′iŋ) *n.* honest and thorough investigation of one's own feelings

hearts·ease, heart's-ease (härts′ēz′) *n.* 1. peace of mind 2. *same as* WILD PANSY

heart·sick (härt′sik′) *adj.* sick at heart; extremely unhappy or despondent: also **heart′sore′** (-sôr′)

heart-strick·en (-strik′'n) *adj.* deeply grieved or greatly dismayed: also **heart′-struck′** (-struk′)

heart·strings (-striŋz′) *n.pl.* [orig. tendons or nerves formerly believed to brace and sustain the heart] deepest feelings or affections

heart-throb (-throb′) *n.* 1. *same as* HEARTBEAT 2. [Old Slang] a) one's sweetheart b) the object of one's romantic admiration, as a film star

heart-to-heart (-tə härt′) *adj.* intimate and candid —*n.* an intimate, confidential talk

heart·warm·ing (-wôr′miŋ) *adj.* such as to kindle a warm glow of genial feelings

heart·wood (-wood′) *n.* the hard wood at the core of a tree trunk: cf. SAPWOOD

heart·y (-ē) *adj.* **heart′i·er, heart′i·est** [see HEART & -Y²] 1. extremely warm and friendly; most cordial 2. enthusiastic; wholehearted [*hearty* support] 3. strongly felt or expressed [a *hearty* dislike] 4. strong and healthy 5. a) nourishing and plentiful [a *hearty* meal] b) liking plenty of food [a *hearty* eater] —*n., pl.* **heart′ies** [Archaic] a friend; comrade; esp., a fellow sailor (usually preceded by *my*)

heat (hēt) *n.* [OE. *hætu*] 1. the quality of being hot; hotness: in physics, heat is considered a form of energy whose effect is produced by the accelerated vibration of molecules 2. a) much hotness; great warmth b) *same as* FEVER 3. degree of hotness or warmth 4. a feeling of hotness or warmth 5. hot weather or climate 6. the warming of a room, house, etc., as by a boiler: al[s]o **heating** 7. appearance as an indication of hotness [blue *heat* in metals] 8. a) strong feeling; excitement, ardour, anger, etc. b) the period or condition of such feeling [in the *heat* of battle] 9. a single effort, bout, or trial; esp., a preliminary round of a race, etc. 10. a) sexual excitement b) the period of this in animals; esp., the oestrus of females [on *heat*] 11. *Metallurgy* a single heating, as of metal, in a furnace or forge 12. [Slang] a) coercion b) great pressure, as in criminal investigation —*vt., vi.* 1. to make or become warm or hot 2. to make or become excited

heat barrier *same as* THERMAL BARRIER

heat capacity the amount of heat required to raise the temperature of a substance or system one degree

heat·ed (hēt′id) *adj.* 1. hot 2. vehement, impassioned, or angry —**heat′ed·ly** *adv.*

heat·er (-ər) *n.* a stove, radiator, etc. for heating a room, car, water, etc.

heat exchanger any device for transferring heat to a cooler medium from a warmer one

heat exhaustion a mild form of heatstroke, characterized by faintness, dizziness, heavy sweating, etc.

heath (hēth) *n.* [OE. *hæth*] 1. a tract of open wasteland, covered with heather, low shrubs, etc. 2. any of various shrubs and plants that grow on heaths, as heather —*adj.* designating a family of woody plants, including the rhododendron, azalea, etc. —**heath′y** *adj.*

heath·bird (-burd′) *n.* *same as* BLACK GROUSE

hea·then (hē′thən) *n., pl.* **-thens, -then** [OE. *hæthen*] 1. orig., a member of any people not worshipping the God of Israel 2. anyone not a Jew, Christian, or Moslem 3. a person regarded as uncivilized, irreligious, etc. —*adj.* 1. of heathens; pagan 2. irreligious, uncivilized, etc. —**hea′-then·dom** *n.* —**hea′then·ish** *adj.* —**hea′then·ism** *n.*

hea·then·ize (-īz′) *vt., vi.* **-ized′, -iz′ing** to make or become heathen

heath·er (heth′ər) *n.* [altered (after HEATH) < ME. *haddyr*] a low-growing plant of the heath family with stalks of small, bell-shaped, purplish-pink flowers —*adj.* like heather in colour or appearance —**heath′er·y** *adj.*

heather mixture a fabric, usually tweed, of intermingled colours resembling those of heather

Heath Robinson [after William *Heath Robinson* (d. 1944), Brit. cartoonist] of such fantastically impracticable design that it is unlikely to work

heat lightning lightning without thunder, seen near the horizon, esp. on hot summer evenings

heat prostration *same as* HEAT EXHAUSTION

heat rash *same as* PRICKLY HEAT

heat sink a point of a system designed to be at a lower temperature than its surroundings, used to dissipate heat from that system

HEATHER

heat·stroke (hēt′strōk′) *n.* a condition resulting from excessive exposure to intense heat, characterized by high fever and collapse

heat wave 1. unusually hot weather, resulting from a slowly moving air mass of relatively high temperature 2. a period of such weather

heaume (hōm) *n.* [Fr. < OFr. *helme*: see HELMET] a heavy helmet worn in the Middle Ages

heave (hēv) *vt.* **heaved** or (esp. *Naut.*) **hove, heav′ing** [< OE. *hebban*] 1. to raise or lift, esp. with effort 2. to lift in this way and throw 3. to make rise or swell 4. to utter (a sigh, etc.) with great effort 5. *Naut.* a) to raise, haul, etc. by pulling with a rope or cable b) to move (a ship) in a specified manner or direction —*vi.* 1. to swell up; bulge out 2. to rise and fall rhythmically 3. a) to retch or vomit b) to pant; breathe hard; gasp 4. *Naut.* a) to tug or haul (on or at a cable, rope, etc.) b) to proceed; move [a ship *hove* into sight] —*n.* the act or effort of heaving —**heave ho!** pull hard! —**heave to** 1. *Naut.* to stop forward movement 2. to stop —**heav′er** *n.*

heav·en (hev′'n) *n.* [OE. *heofon*] 1. [usually pl.] the space surrounding the earth; firmament 2. *Theol.* a) [often H-] the place where God and his angels are and where the blessed go after death b) [H-] God; Providence 3. a) any place of great beauty and pleasure b) a state of great happiness —**move heaven and earth** to do all that can be done

heav·en·ly (-lē) *adj.* 1. of or in the heavens [the sun is a *heavenly* body] 2. a) causing or marked by great happiness, beauty, etc. b) [Colloq.] very pleasing, attractive, etc. 3. *Theol.* of or in heaven; holy; divine —**heav′-en·li·ness** *n.*

heav·en·ward (-wərd) *adv., adj.* towards heaven: also **heav′en·wards** *adv.*

heaves (hēvz) *n.pl.* [with *sing. v.*] a respiratory disease of horses, marked by forced breathing, coughing, heaving of the flanks, etc.

Heav·i·side layer (hev′ē sīd′) [after O. *Heaviside* (1850-1925), Brit. physicist] *same as* E LAYER

heav·y (hev′ē) *adj.* **heav′i·er, heav′i·est** [OE. *hefig* < base of *hebban*, to heave + -*ig*, -Y²] 1. hard to lift or move because of great weight; weighty 2. of concentrated weight for the size 3. above the usual or a defined weight 4. larger, greater, rougher, more intense, etc. than usual [a *heavy* blow, a *heavy* vote, a *heavy* sea, *heavy* thunder, *heavy* features] 5. being such to an unusual extent [a *heavy* drinker] 6. serious; grave [a *heavy* responsibility] 7. hard to endure [*heavy* demands] 8. hard to do or manage [*heavy* work] 9. hard to bear [*heavy* sorrow] 10. sorrowful [a *heavy* heart] 11. burdened with sleep or fatigue [*heavy* eyelids] 12. hard to digest [a *heavy* meal] 13. not leavened properly [a *heavy* cake] 14. clinging; penetrating [a *heavy* odour] 15. cloudy; gloomy [a *heavy* sky] 16. tedious; dull 17. clumsy; awkward [a *heavy* gait] 18. designating any large, basic industry that uses massive machinery 19. heavily armed 20. *Chem.* designating an isotope of greater atomic weight than the normal or most abundant isotope 21. *Theatre* serious, tragic, or villainous —*adv.* heavily [*heavy*-laden] —*n., pl.* **heav′ies** 1. something heavy 2. *Theatre a*) a serious, tragic, or villainous role *b*) an actor who plays such roles —**hang heavy** to pass tediously; drag —**heavy with child** pregnant —**heav′i·ly** *adv.* —**heav′i·ness** *n.*

heav·y-du·ty (-dyōōt′ē) *adj.* made to withstand great strain, bad weather, etc.

heav·y-hand·ed (-han′did) *adj.* 1. clumsy or tactless 2. cruel; tyrannical —**heav′y-hand′ed·ly** *adv.* —**heav′y-hand′ed·ness** *n.*

heav·y-heart·ed (-här′tid) *adj.* sad; depressed —**heav′y-heart′ed·ly** *adv.* —**heav′y-heart′ed·ness** *n.*

heavy hydrogen *same as* DEUTERIUM

heav·y·set (-set′) *adj.* [U.S.] stout or stocky in build

heavy spar *same as* BARITE

heavy water water composed of isotopes of hydrogen of atomic weight greater than one or of oxygen greater than 16, or of both; esp., deuterium oxide

heav·y·weight (-wāt′) *n.* 1. a person or animal weighing much more than average 2. *see* BOXING AND WRESTLING WEIGHTS, table 3. [Colloq.] a very intelligent or important person

Heb. 1. Hebrew 2. Hebrews

heb·dom·a·dal (heb dom′ə dəl) *adj.* [< L. < Gr. *hebdomas*, seven (days) < *hepta*, seven] weekly —**heb·dom′a·dal·ly** *adv.*

heb·e·tate (heb′ə tāt) *vt., vi.* -tat′ed, -tat′ing [< L. *hebetatus*, pp. of *hebetare*, to make dull or blunt] to make or become dull or stupid —*adj. Biol.* having a blunt point, as certain leaves —**heb′e·tude** *n.*

He·bra·ic (hi brā′ik) *adj.* of or characteristic of the Hebrews, their language, culture, etc.; Hebrew —**He·bra′i·cal·ly** *adv.* —**He′bra·ize** *vt., vi.*

He·bra·ism (hē′brā iz′m) *n.* 1. a Hebrew idiom, custom, etc. 2. the characteristic ethical system, moral attitude, etc. of the Hebrews —**He′bra·ist** *n.* —**He′bra·is′tic** *adj.*

He·brew (hē′brōō) *n.* [< OFr., ult. < Heb. *'ibhri*, lit., one from across (the river)] 1. any member of a group of Semitic peoples tracing descent from Abraham, Isaac, and Jacob; specif., an Israelite: in modern, but not recent, usage interchangeable with *Jew* 2. *a*) the ancient Semitic language of the Israelites, in which most of the Old Testament was written *b*) its modern form, the official language of Israel —*adj.* 1. of Hebrew or the Hebrews 2. *same as* JEWISH

hec·a·tomb (hek′ə tōm, -tōōm′) *n.* [< L. < Gr. < *hekaton*, a hundred + *bous*, ox] 1. in ancient Greece, the mass slaughter of 100 cattle as an offering to the gods 2. any large-scale slaughter

heck (hek) *interj., n.* [Colloq.] *a euphemism for* HELL

heck·le (hek′'l) *vt.* -led, -ling [ME. < *hechele*: see HACKLE¹] to annoy or harass (a speaker, etc.) by interrupting with questions or taunts —**heck′ler** *n.*

hec·tare (hek′ter) *n.* [Fr.: see HECTO- & ARE²] a metric measure of surface, equal to 10000 square metres (100 ares or 2.471 acres)

hec·tic (hek′tik) *adj.* [< OFr. < LL. < Gr. *hektikos*, habitual] 1. of or characteristic of a wasting disease, as tuberculosis, or the fever accompanying this 2. feverish or flushed 3. full of confusion, rush, excitement, etc. —**hec′ti·cal·ly** *adv.*

hec·to- [Fr. < Gr. *hekaton*, a hundred] *a combining form meaning* a hundred

hec·to·gramme, hec·to·gram (hek′tə gram′) *n.* [< Fr.: see prec. & GRAMME] a metric measure of weight, equal to 100 grammes (3.527 ounces)

hec·to·graph (-graf′) *n.* [< G. < *hekto-*, HECTO- + -*graph*, -GRAPH] a duplicating device by which written or typed matter is transferred to a sheet of gelatin, from which many copies can be taken —*vt.* to duplicate by means of a hectograph

hec·tor (hek′tər) *n.* [< *Hector*, a Trojan hero] a swaggering fellow; bully —*vt., vi.* to browbeat; bully

he'd (hēd) 1. he had 2. he would

hed·dle (hed′'l) *n.* [prob. altered < ME. *helde* < OE. *hefeld*, weaving thread] any of a series of parallel wires or cords in the harness of a loom, used to separate and guide the warp threads

hedge (hej) *n.* [OE. *hecg*] 1. a row of closely planted shrubs, bushes, etc. forming a boundary or fence 2. any fence or barrier 3. the act of hedging 4. anything which serves as a shield or protection [a *hedge* against inflation] —*adj.* 1. of, in, or near a hedge 2. low, disreputable, etc. —*vt.* **hedged, hedg′ing** 1. to place a hedge around or along 2. to hinder or guard as with a barrier; hem in 3. to try to

avoid loss in (a bet, risk, etc.) by making counterbalancing bets, etc. —*vi.* to refuse to commit oneself; avoid direct answers —**hedg′er** *n.*

hedge·hog (hej′hog′) *n.* 1. a small, insect-eating mammal, with sharp spines on the back, which bristle and form a defence when the animal curls up 2. the American porcupine

hedge·hop (-hop′) *vi.* -hopped′, -hop′ping [Colloq.] to fly an aircraft very close to the ground, as for spraying insecticide —**hedge′hop′per** *n.*

hedge·row (-rō′) *n.* a row of shrubs, bushes, etc., forming a hedge

hedge sparrow a small European bird with a brown back and wings and a grey breast: also called **dunnock**

he·don·ic (hē don′ik) *adj.* [Gr. *hedonikos* < *hēdonē*, pleasure] 1. having to do with pleasure 2. *Psychol.* dealing with pleasurable and unpleasurable feelings

he·do·nism (hēd′ən iz′m) *n.* [< Gr. *hēdonē*, pleasure] 1. the doctrine that pleasure or happiness is the principal good and the proper aim of action 2. pleasure-seeking as a way of life —**he′do·nist** *n.* —**he′do·nis′tic** *adj.* —**he′do·nis′ti·cal·ly** *adv.*

-he·dral (hē′drəl) *a combining form used to form adjectives from nouns ending in* -HEDRON

-he·dron (hē′drən) [< Gr. < *hedra*, a side, base] *a combining form meaning* a geometric figure or crystal with (a specified number of) surfaces

hee·bie-jee·bies (hē′bē jē′bēz) *n. pl.* [coined by W. B. De Beck (1890-1942), U.S. cartoonist] [Slang] a state of nervousness; jitters (with *the*)

heed (hēd) *vt., vi.* [OE. *hedan*] to pay close attention (to); take careful notice (of) —*n.* close attention; careful notice —**heed′ful** *adj.* —**heed′ful·ly** *adv.*

heed·less (-lis) *adj.* not taking heed; careless; unmindful —**heed′less·ly** *adv.* —**heed′less·ness** *n.*

hee-haw (hē′hô′) *n., vi.* [echoic] *same as* BRAY

heel¹ (hēl) *n.* [OE. *hela*] 1. the back part of the human foot, under the ankle 2. the corresponding part of the hind foot of an animal 3. that part of a stocking, etc. which covers the heel 4. the built-up part of a shoe, supporting the heel 5. anything like the human heel in location, shape, or function, as the end of a loaf of bread 6. [Colloq.] a despicable person; cad —*vt.* 1. to furnish with a heel 2. to follow closely at the rear of 3. to touch or move as with the heel 4. [Colloq.] to provide (a person) with money: usually used in the passive [*well-heeled*] —*vi.* 1. to follow at the heels of someone [the dog won't *heel*] —**at heel** just behind —**cool one's heels** [Colloq.] to be kept waiting for some time —**down at heel** 1. with the heels of one's shoes worn down 2. shabby; seedy —**kick up one's heels** to have fun —**on** (or **upon**) **the heels of** close behind —**out at the heel(s)** 1. having holes in the heels of one's shoes or socks 2. shabby; seedy —**take to one's heels** to run away: also **show a clean pair of heels** —**to heel** 1. just behind 2. under control —**turn on one's heel** to turn around abruptly —**heel′er** *n.* —**heel′less** *adj.*

heel² (hēl) *vi.* [OE. *hieldan*] to lean to one side; list: said esp. of a ship —*vt.* to make (a ship) list —*n.* the act or extent of heeling

heel³ (hēl) *vt. same as* HELE

heel·ball (-bôl) *n.* [orig. used by shoemakers in polishing the edges of heels and soles] a ball or stick of beeswax mixed with lampblack and used in making rubbings of brasses, etc.

heeled (hēld) *adj.* 1. provided with a heel 2. [Colloq.] having money 3. [Colloq.] armed, esp. with a gun

heel·tap (hēl′tap′) *n.* 1. a layer of leather, etc. serving as a lift in the heel of a shoe 2. small amount of alcoholic drink left in a glass after drinking

heft (heft) *n.* [< base of HEAVE] [U.S. Colloq.] 1. weight 2. importance —*vt.* [U.S. Colloq.] 1. to lift or heave 2. to estimate the weight of by lifting —*vi.* [U.S. Colloq.] to weigh

heft·y (hef′tē) *adj.* **heft′i·er, heft′i·est** [Colloq.] 1. weighty; heavy 2. large and powerful 3. big or fairly big —**heft′i·ly** *adv.* —**heft′i·ness** *n.*

he·gem·o·ny (hi gem′ə nē; hi jem′-) *n., pl.* -**nies** [< Gr. < *hēgemōn*, leader] leadership or dominance, esp. of one nation over others —**heg·e·mon·ic** (hej′ə mon′ik, hē′jə-) *adj.*

he·gi·ra (hi jī′rə, hej′ər ə) *n.* [ML. < Ar. *hijrah*, lit., flight] 1. [often H-] the forced journey of Mohammed from Mecca to Medina in 622 A.D.: the Moslem era dates from this event 2. any journey for safety or as an escape; flight

heif·er (hef′ər) *n.* [OE. *heahfore*] a young cow that has not borne a calf

heigh (hī, hā) *interj.* an exclamation to attract notice, show pleasure, express surprise, etc.

heigh-ho (-hō′) *interj.* an exclamation of mild surprise, boredom, fatigue, etc.

height (hīt) *n.* [OE. *heihthu* < *heah*, high] 1. the topmost point of anything 2. the highest limit or degree; extreme [the *height* of absurdity] 3. the distance from the bottom to the top 4. elevation or distance above a given level, as above the surface of the earth or sea; altitude 5. a relatively great distance above a given level or from bottom to top **6.** [*often pl.*] a high place; eminence

height·en (hīt′'n) *vt., vi.* **1.** to bring or come to a higher position **2.** to make or become larger, greater, etc.; increase —**height′en·er** *n.*

hei·nous (hā′nəs, hē′-) *adj.* [< OFr. < *haine*, hatred < Frank.] outrageously evil or wicked; abominable —**hei′- nous·ly** *adv.* —**hei′nous·ness** *n.*

heir (er) *n.* [< OFr. < L. *heres*] **1.** a person who inherits or is entitled to inherit another's property or title upon the other's death **2.** a person who appears to get some trait from a predecessor or to carry on in his tradition —**heir′- dom, heir′ship′n.**

heir apparent *pl.* **heirs apparent** the heir whose right to a certain property or title cannot be denied if he outlives the ancestor

heir·ess (-is) *n.* a woman or girl who is an heir, esp. to great wealth

heir·loom (-lo͞om′) *n.* [HEIR + LOOM¹] **1.** a piece of personal property that goes to an heir **2.** any treasured possession handed down from generation to generation

heir presumptive *pl.* **heirs presumptive** an heir whose right to a certain property or title will be lost if someone more closely related is born before the ancestor dies

hei·ti·ki (hā tī′ki) *n.* [Maori < *hei*, to hang, & *tiki*, creator] [N.Z.] a greenstone neck ornament, representing an ancestor, worn by Maoris

he·ji·ra (hi jī′rə, hej′ər ə) *n.* *same as* HEGIRA

held (held) *pt. & pp. of* HOLD¹

hele (hēl) *vt.* [OE. *helian* < *hellan*, to hide] to insert (cuttings, etc.) into the soil to keep them moist before planting them permanently (with *in*)

he·li·a·cal (hi lī′ə kəl) *adj.* [LL. *Heliacus* Gr. *heliakos* < *helios*, the sun + -AL] of or near the sun; solar

hel·i·cal (hel′i kəl, hē′lə-) *adj.* of, or having the form of, a helix; spiral —**hel′i·cal·ly** *adv.*

hel·i·ces (hel′ə sēz′, hē′lə-) *n.* *alt. pl. of* HELIX

he·li·chry·sum (he li krī′səm) *n.* [L., lit., the marigold] a plant with shining white, yellow or reddish heads which keep their colour when dried: popularly called an *everlasting*

hel·i·coid (hel′ə koid′, hē′lə-) *adj.* [< *helix*, a spiral + *eidos*, form] shaped like a spiral; coiled: also **hel′i·coi′dal** —*n.* Geom. a spiral or screw-shaped surface

hel·i·con (hel′ə kon, -kən) *n.* [prob. < Gr. *helix*, a spiral: from the shape] a brass wind instrument, similar to a bass tuba

Hel·i·con·i·an (hel ə kŏn′ē ən) *adj.* of Helicon, a mountain group in SC Greece: in Greek mythology, the home of the Muses

hel·i·cop·ter (hel′ə kop′tər) *n.* [< Fr. < Gr. *helix*, a spiral + *pteron*, wing] a kind of aircraft moved in any direction, or kept hovering, by large, rotary blades (*rotors*) mounted horizontally —*vi., vt.* to travel or convey by helicopter

he·li·o- [L. < Gr. < *hēlios*, the sun] *a combining form meaning* the sun, bright, radiant: also **heli-**

he·li·o·cen·tric (hē′lē ō sen′trik) *adj.* [HELIO- + -CENTRIC] **1.** calculated from, or viewed as from, the centre of the sun **2.** having or regarding the sun as the centre

he·li·o·graph (hē′lē ə graf′) *n.* [HELIO- + -GRAPH] a device for sending a message (**heliogram**) or signalling by flashing the sun's rays from a mirror —*vt., vi.* to signal or communicate by heliograph —**he′li·og′ra·pher** (-og′rə fər) *n.* —**he′li·o·graph′ic** *adj.* —**he′li·og′ra·phy** *n.*

he·li·om·e·ter (-om′ə tər) *n.* [Fr. *héliomètre*; see HELIO- & -METER: so called because orig. used in measuring the sun's diameter] an instrument formerly used for measuring the angular distance between two stars

he·li·o·scope (-os kōp) *n.* [< Gr. *helios*, the sun & *skopein*, to look] a form of telescope adapted for viewing the sun without damaging the eyes

he·li·o·sis (hē li ō′sis) *n.* [see HELI(O)- + -OSIS] sunstroke

he·li·o·stat (he′lē ə stat′) *n.* [Mod L. *heliostata*: see HELIO-+ -STAT] a device consisting of a mirror slowly revolved by clockwork so as to reflect the sun's rays in a fixed direction

he·li·o·trope (hē′lē ə trōp′, hēl′yə-) *n.* [< Fr. < L. < Gr. < *hēlios*, the sun + *trepein*, to turn] **1.** formerly, a sunflower **2.** a plant with fragrant clusters of small, white or reddish-purple flowers **3.** reddish purple **4.** *same as* BLOODSTONE —*adj.* reddish-purple

he·li·ot·ro·pism (hē′lē ot′rə piz′m) *n.* the tendency of certain plants or other organisms to turn toward or from light, esp. sunlight —**he′li·o·trop′ic** (-ə trop′ik) *adj.* —**he′- li·o·trop′i·cal·ly** *adv.*

hel·i·port (hel′ə pôrt′) *n.* [HELI(COPTER) + (AIR)PORT] a flat place where helicopters land and take off

he·li·um (hē′lē əm) *n.* [ModL. < Gr. *hēlios*, the sun] one of the chemical elements, a very light, inert, colourless gas: it is used for inflating balloons, etc.: symbol, He; at. wt., 4.0026; at. no., 2

he·lix (hē′liks) *n., pl.* **-lix·es, -li·ces′** (hel′ə sēz′, hē′lə-) [L. < Gr., a spiral < *helissein*, to turn around] **1.** any spiral, either lying in a single plane or, esp., moving around a cone, cylinder, etc. as a screw thread does **2.** the folded rim of

cartilage around the outer ear **3.** *Archit.* an ornamental spiral

hell (hel) *n.* [OE. *hel* < base of *helan*, to hide] **1.** *Bible* the place where the spirits of the dead are **2.** [*often* H-] *a*) *Christianity* the place to which sinners and unbelievers go after death for punishment *b*) those in hell *c*) the powers of evil or darkness **3.** any place or condition of evil, pain, cruelty, etc. **4.** [Colloq.] any very disagreeable experience —*interj.* an exclamation of irritation, anger, emphasis, etc.: regarded as profanity —**catch** (or get) **hell** [Slang] to receive a severe scolding, punishment, etc. —**come hell or high water** no matter what difficulties may arise —**for the hell of it** [Slang] for no serious reason —**hell for leather** at full speed

he'll (hēl; *unstressed* hil, il) **1.** he will **2.** he shall

Hel·lad·ic (he lad′ik) *adj.* relating to the preclassical culture of the Greek mainland

hell·bent (helbent′) *adj.* [Slang] firmly or recklessly determined (with *on*)

hell·cat (hel′kat′) *n.* **1.** a witch **2.** an evil, spiteful, bad-tempered woman

hel·le·bore (hel′ə bôr′) *n.* [< OFr. < L. < Gr. *helleboros*, orig. prob. "plant eaten by fawns"] **1.** any of a group of winter-blooming plants of the buttercup family, with flowers shaped like buttercups but of various colours **2.** any of a group of plants of the lily family **3.** the poisonous rhizomes of certain of these plants that have been used in medicine

Hel·lene (hel′ēn) *n.* [< Gr.] a Greek

Hel·len·ic (hə len′ik, he-; hel en′-) *adj.* **1.** of the Hellenes; Greek **2.** of the history, language, or culture of the ancient Greeks from the late 8th century B.C. to the death of Alexander the Great (323 B.C.) —*n.* the language of ancient Greece

Hel·len·ism (hel′ən iz′m) *n.* **1.** a Greek phrase, idiom, or custom **2.** the character, thought, culture, or ethics of ancient Greece **3.** adoption of the Greek language, customs, etc. —**Hel′len·ist** *n.*

Hel·len·is·tic (hel′ə nis′tik) *adj.* **1.** of or characteristic of Hellenism **2.** of Greek history, culture, etc. after the death of Alexander the Great (323 B.C.) —**Hel′len·is′ti·cal·ly** *adv.*

Hel·len·ize (hel′ə nīz′) *vt.*, *vi.* **-ized′, -iz′ing** to make or become Greek, as in customs, ideals, etc. —**Hel′len·i·za′tion** *n.* —**Hel′len·iz′er** *n.*

hell·fire (hel′fīr′) *n.* the fire or torment of hell

hell·ion (hel′yən) *n.* [U.S. Colloq.] a person fond of devilry; mischievous troublemaker

hell·ish (hel′ish) *adj.* **1.** of, from, or like hell **2.** devilish; fiendish **3.** [Colloq.] very unpleasant; detestable —**hell′- ish·ly** *adv.* —**hell′ish·ness** *n.*

hel·lo (he lō′, hə lō′, hel′ō) *interj.* *var. sp. of* HALLO

hell's angel a member of a motorcycling gang of violent youths

helm¹ (helm) *n., vt.* [OE.] *archaic var. of* HELMET

helm² (helm) *n.* [OE. *helma*] **1.** the wheel or tiller or, with the rudder, etc., all the gear by which a ship is steered **2.** the control or leadership, as of an organization —*vt.* to guide; steer

hel·met (hel′mət) *n.* [OFr., dim. of *helme*, helmet < Frank.] **1.** a hard, protective head covering, variously designed for use in combat, certain sports, diving, etc. **2.** something like such a head covering in appearance or function —*vt.* to equip with a helmet —**hel′met·ed** *adj.*

hel·minth (hel′minth) *n.* [Gr. *helmins* (gen. *helminthos*)] a worm or wormlike animal; esp., a parasite of the intestine, as the tapeworm, hookworm, or roundworm —**hel·min·thic** (hel-min′thik) *adj.*

helms·man (helmz′mən) *n., pl.* **-men** the man at the helm; person who steers a ship

Hel·ot (hel′ət) *n.* [< L. < Gr. *Heilōtes*, serfs] **1.** a member of the lowest class of serfs in ancient Sparta **2.** [h-] any serf or slave —**hel′ot·ism** *n.* —**hel′- ot·ry** *n.*

help (help) *vt.* [OE. *helpan*] **1.** to make things easier or better for (a person); aid; assist; specif., *a*) to give (one in need) relief, money, etc. *b*) to share the labour of [*help* us lift this] *c*) to aid in getting (*up, down, in, to, into, out of,* etc.) **2.** to make it easier for (something) to exist, happen, improve, etc.; promote **3.** to remedy; relieve [this will *help* your cough] **4.** *a*) to keep from; avoid [she can't *help* crying] *b*) to stop, prevent, change, etc. [faults that can't be *helped*] **5.** to serve or wait on (a customer, etc.) —*vi.* **1.** to give assistance; be useful or beneficial **2.** to act as a waiter, clerk, etc. —*n.* **1.** a helping; aid; assistance **2.** relief; remedy **3.** *a*) a hired helper, as a servant, farm-hand, etc. *b*) hired helpers; employees —**cannot help but** to be compelled or obliged to —**cannot help oneself** to be the

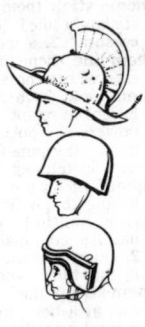

HELMETS

victim of circumstances, a habit, etc. —**help oneself to** 1. to serve oneself with (food, etc.) 2. to steal —**help out** to help in getting or doing something —**so help me (God)** as God is my witness: used in oaths —**help′er** *n.*

help·ful (-fəl) *adj.* giving help; useful —**help′ful·ly** *adv.* —**help′ful·ness** *n.*

help·ing (-iŋ) *n.* 1. a giving of aid; assisting 2. a portion of food served to one person

help·less (-lis) *adj.* 1. not able to help oneself; weak 2. lacking help or protection 3. incompetent; ineffective —**help′less·ly** *adv.* —**help′less·ness** *n.*

help·mate (-māt′) *n.* [altered < ff.] a helpful companion; specif., a wife or husband

help·meet (-mēt′) *n.* [misreading of "an *help meet* for him" (Gen. 2:18)] *same as* HELPMATE

hel·ter-skel·ter (hel′tər skel′tər) *adv.* [arbitrary formation] in haste and confusion; in a disorderly, hurried manner —*adj.* hurried and confused; disorderly —*n.* 1. anything helter-skelter 2. a high, spiral slide, as at a fairground

helve (helv) *n.* [OE. *helfe*] the handle of a tool, esp. of an axe or hatchet —*vt.* **helved, helv′ing** to put a helve on

Hel·ve·tian (hel vē′shən) *adj.* [< *Helvetia*, L. name of Switzerland] Swiss

hem[1] (hem) *n.* [OE.] 1. the border on a garment or piece of cloth, usually made by folding the edge and sewing it down 2. any border or edge —*vt.* **hemmed, hem′ming** to fold back the edge of and sew down —**hem in** (or **around**) or **about**) 1. to encircle; surround 2. to confine or restrain —**hem′mer** *n.*

hem[2] (hem; *conventionalized pronun.*) *interj.*, *n.* the sound made in clearing the throat —*vi.* **hemmed, hem′ming** 1. to make this sound, as to get attention or show doubt 2. to grope about in speech, seeking the right words: usually in **hem and haw**

he-man (hē′man′) *n.* [Colloq.] a strong, virile man

hemat-, hemato-, hemo-, *U.S. sp. of* HAEMAT-, HAEMATO-, HAEMO-

hem·er·a·lo·pi·a (hem′ər ə lō′pē ə) *n.* [ModL. < Gr. < *hēmera*, day + *alaos*, blind + *ōps*, eye + -IA] an eye defect in which vision is reduced in bright light —**hem′er·a·lop′ic** (-lop′ik) *adj.*

hem·i- [Gr. *hēmi-*] a prefix meaning half

hem·i·dem·i·sem·i·qua·ver (hem′ē dem′ē sem′ē kwä′vər) *n. Music* a note having one sixty-fourth the duration of a whole note: see NOTE, *illus.*

hem·i·ple·gi·a (hem i plē′jē ə, -jə) *n.* [ModL. < MGr. *hēmiplēgia*, paralysis: see HEMI- & -PLEGIA] paralysis of one side of the body —**hem′i·ple′gic** (-jik) *adj.*, *n.*

he·mip·ter·an (hi mip′tər ən) *n.* [< ModL.: see HEMI- & PTERO-] any of a group of insects, including bedbugs, lice, aphids, etc., with piercing and sucking mouthparts —**he·mip′ter·ous** *adj.*

hem·i·sphere (hem′ə sfir′) *n.* [< L. < Gr.: see HEMI- & SPHERE] 1. half of a sphere or globe 2. *a)* any of the halves of the earth: the Northern, Southern, Eastern, or Western Hemisphere *b)* a model or map of any of these halves —**hem′i·spher′i·cal** (-sfer′i kəl), **hem′i·spher′ic** *adj.* —**hem′i·spher′i·cal·ly** *adv.*

hem·i·stich (hem′i stik′) *n.* [< L. < Gr. < *hēmi-*, half + *stichos*, a line] 1. half a line of verse, esp. as divided by the caesura 2. a metrically short line of verse

hem·line (hem′līn′) *n.* the bottom edge of a dress, coat, etc., where the edge meets the leg

hem·lock (hem′lok′) *n.* [OE. *hymlic*] 1. *a)* a poisonous European plant of the parsley family, with small white flowers *b)* a poison made from this plant 2. *a)* an evergreen tree of the pine family, with short, flat needles: the bark is used in tanning *b)* the wood of this tree

hemp (hemp) *n.* [OE. *hænep*] 1. *a)* a tall Asiatic plant having tough fibre in its stem *b)* the fibre used to make rope, sailcloth, etc. *c)* a substance, such as marijuana, hashish, etc., made from the leaves and flowers of this plant 2. *a)* any of various plants yielding a hemplike fibre, as sisal *b)* this fibre —**hemp′en** *adj.*

hem·stitch (hem′stich′) *n.* 1. an ornamental stitch, used esp. at a hem, made by pulling out several parallel threads and tying the cross threads into small bunches 2. decorative needlework done with this stitch —*vt.* to put hemstitches on —**hem′stitch′er** *n.* —**hem′stitch′ing** *n.*

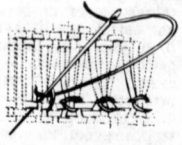

HEMSTITCH

hen (hen) *n.* [< OE. *henn*, fem. of *hana*, rooster] 1. the female of the chicken (the domestic fowl) 2. the female of various other birds

hen·bane (-bān′) *n.* a coarse, hairy, foul-smelling, poisonous plant of the nightshade family, used in medicine

hence (hens) *adv.* [< OE. *heonan*, from here + -(e)s, adv. gen. suffix] 1. from this place; away [go *hence*] 2. *a)* from this time [a year *hence*] *b)* thereafter; subsequently

3. from this life 4. for this reason; therefore —*interj.* [Archaic] go away! —**hence with** [Archaic] away with!

hence·forth (-fôrth′) *adv.* from this time on: also **hence′-for′ward**

hench·man (hench′mən) *n.*, *pl.* **-men** [OE. *hengest*, male horse + -*man*: orig. sense prob. "groom"] 1. a trusted helper or follower 2. a political underling who seeks to advance himself 3. any of the followers of a criminal gang leader

hen·dec·a- (hen′dek ə, hen dek′ə) [< Gr. *hendeka*, eleven] a combining form meaning eleven

hen·di·a·dys (hen dī′ə dis) *n.* [ML. < Gr. phrase *hen dia dyoin* one (thing) by means of two] a figure of speech in which two nouns joined by *and* are used instead of a noun and a modifier (Ex.: *fear and haste* for *fearful haste*)

hen·e·quen (hen′ə kin) *n.* [< Sp. < native Yucatan name] 1. a tropical American agave, cultivated for the hard fibre of the leaves 2. the fibre, similar to the related sisal, used for rope, twine, mats, etc.

henge (henj) *n.* [back-formation from *Stonehenge*] a circular monument of stone or wood, usually with an outer bank or ditch

hen harrier the common harrier, of moors and marshes

hen·house (hen′hous′) *n.* a shelter for poultry

hen·na (hen′ə) *n.* [Ar. *hinnā′*] 1. *a)* plant with white or red flowers *b)* a dye extracted from its leaves, often used to tint the hair auburn 2. reddish brown —*adj.* reddish-brown —*vt.* **-naed, -na·ing** to tint with henna

hen·ner·y (hen′ər ē) *n.*, *pl.* **-ner·ies** a place where poultry is kept or raised

hen·o·the·ism (hen′ə thē iz′m) *n.* [19th c., < Gr. *hen*, one & *theos*, god] belief in one god without denying the existence of others —**hen′o·the·ist** *n.* —**hen′o·the·is′tic** *adj.*

hen party [Colloq.] a social gathering for women only

hen·peck (hen′pek′) *vt.* to nag and domineer over (one's husband) —**hen′pecked′** *adj.*

hen·ry (hen′rē) *n.*, *pl.* **-rys, -ries** [after J. *Henry* (1797-1878), U.S. physicist] *Elec.* the SI unit of inductance, equal to the inductance of a circuit in which the variation of current at the rate of one ampere per second induces an electromotive force of one volt

hep (hep) *adj.* [< ?] [Slang] *earlier form of* HIP[3]

he·pat·ic (hi pat′ik) *adj.* [< L. < Gr. < *hēpar*, the liver] 1. of or affecting the liver 2. like the liver in colour or shape

he·pat·i·ca (-i kə) *n.* [ModL. (see prec.): it has liver-shaped leaves] a small plant of the buttercup family, with spring flowers of white, pink, blue, or purple

hep·a·ti·tis (hep′ə tīt′is) *n.* [ModL. < Gr. *hēpar* (gen. *hepatos*), liver + -ITIS] inflammation of the liver

Hep·ple·white (hep′'l hwīt′) *adj.* [after G. *Hepplewhite* (?-1786), Brit. cabinetmaker] designating or of a style of furniture with graceful curves

hep·ta- [< Gr. *hepta*, seven] a combining form meaning seven: also, before a vowel, **hept-**

hep·ta·chlor (hep′tə klôr′) *n.* an insecticide similar to chlordane

hep·tad (hep′tad) *n.* [< Gr. *hepta*, seven] a series or group of seven

hep·ta·gon (hep′tə gon′) *n.* [< Gr.: see HEPTA- & -GON] a plane figure with seven angles and seven sides —**hep·tag′-o·nal** (-tag′ə n′l) *adj.*

hep·ta·he·dron (hep′tə hē′dron) *n.*, *pl.* **-drons, -dra** (drə) [ModL.: see HEPTA- & -HEDRON] a solid figure with seven plane surfaces —**hep′ta·he′dral** *adj.*

hep·tam·e·ter (hep tam′ə tər) *n.* [HEPTA- + -METER] a line of verse with seven metrical feet

hep·tane (hep′tān) *n.* [HEPT(A)- + -ANE] a flammable, colourless liquid hydrocarbon used as a standard in octane rating, etc.

hep·tar·chy (hep′tär kē) *n.*, *pl.* **-chies** 1. government by seven rulers 2. a group of seven allied kingdoms, specif. [the **H-**] in Anglo-Saxon England before the 9th century—**hep′tar·chic, hep′tar·chic·al** *adj.*

her (hur; *unstressed* ər) *pron.* [OE. *hire*] 1. *objective case of* SHE: also used colloquially as a predicate complement with a linking verb (Ex.: that's *her*) —*possessive pronominal adj.* of, belonging to, made, or done by her

her. heraldry

her·ald (her′əld) *n.* [< OFr. *heralt* < Frank.] 1. formerly, an official who made proclamations, carried state messages, took charge of tournaments, etc. 2. in Britain, an official in charge of genealogies, heraldic arms, etc. 3. a person who announces significant news 4. a person or thing that presages what is to follow; forerunner; harbinger —*vt.* 1. to announce, foretell, etc. 2. to publicize

he·ral·dic (hə ral′dik) *adj.* of heraldry or heralds

her·ald·ry (her′əl drē) *n.*, *pl.* **-ries** 1. the art or science having to do with coats of arms, genealogies, etc. 2. heraldic devices 3. heraldic ceremony or pomp

herb (hurb) *n.* [< OFr. < L. *herba*] 1. any seed plant whose stem withers away annually, as distinguished from a tree or shrub whose woody stem lives from year to year 2. any plant used as a medicine, seasoning, or flavouring, as mint, thyme, basil, or sage —**her·bif′er·ous,** —**herb′like′** adj. —**herb′y** adj.

her·ba·ceous (hər bā′shəs) adj. 1. of or like an herb 2. like a green leaf in texture, colour, etc.

herbaceous border a flower bed that contains primarily perennials rather than annuals, esp. one forming a border to a path or lawn

herb·age (hur′bij) n. 1. herbs collectively, esp. those used as pasturage; grass 2. the green foliage and juicy stems of herbs

herb·al (hur′b'l) adj. of herbs —n. formerly, a book about herbs or plants

herb·al·ist (-ist) n. 1. orig., a botanist 2. a person who grows, collects, or deals in herbs

her·bar·i·um (hər ber′ē əm) n., pl. -i·ums, -i·a (-ə) [LL. < L. herba, herb] 1. a collection of dried plants used for botanical study 2. a room, building, etc. for keeping such a collection

her·bi·cide (hur′bə sīd′) n. [< L. herba, herb + -CIDE] any chemical substance used to destroy plants, esp. weeds —**her′bi·ci′dal** adj.

her·bi·vore (-vôr′) n. [Fr.] a herbivorous animal

her·biv·o·rous (hər biv′ər əs) adj. [< L. herba, herb + -VOROUS] feeding chiefly on grass or other plants

Her·cu·le·an (hur′kyə lē′ən, hər kyōō′lē ən) adj. 1. of Hercules 2. [usually h-] a) having the great size and strength of Hercules b) calling for great strength, size, or courage, as a task

herd[1] (hurd) n. [OE. heord] 1. a number of cattle or other large animals feeding, living, or being driven together 2. a crowd 3. the common people; masses: contemptuous term —vt., vi. to form into or move as a herd, group, crowd, etc.

herd[2] (hurd) n. [OE. hierde] a herdsman: now chiefly in combination [cowherd] —vt. to tend or drive as a herdsman —**herd′er** n.

herd instinct the tendency of humans and some animals to live in groups and to be uneasy when apart from the group

herds·man (hurdz′mən) n., pl. -men a person who keeps or tends a herd

here (hir) adv. [OE. her] 1. at or in this place: often used as an intensive [John here is a good player] 2. towards, to, or into this place [come here] 3. at this point in action, speech, etc.; now 4. in earthly life —interj. an exclamation used to call attention, answer a roll call, etc. —n. this place or point —**here and there** in, at, or to various places —**here goes!** an exclamation used when the speaker is about to do something daring, disagreeable, etc. —**neither here nor there** beside the point; irrelevant

here·a·bout (hir′ə bout′) adv. in this general vicinity: about or near here: also **here′a·bouts′**

here·af·ter (hir äf′tər) adv. 1. from now on; in the future 2. following this, as in a writing 3. in the state or life after death —n. 1. the future 2. the state or life after death

here·at (hir at′) adv. [Archaic] 1. at this time; when this occurred 2. at this; for this reason

here·by (hir′bī′) adv. by this means

he·red·i·ta·ble (hə red′i tə b'l) adj. same as HERITABLE —**he·red′i·ta·bil′i·ty** n.

her·e·dit·a·ment (her′ə dit′ə mənt) n. [ML. heredit-amentum] any property that can be inherited

he·red·i·tar·y (hə red′ə tər ē) adj. [< L. < hereditas: see ff.] 1. a) of, or passed down by, inheritance from an ancestor b) having title, etc. by inheritance 2. of, or passed down by, heredity 3. being such because of attitudes, beliefs, etc. passed down through generations —**he·red′i·tar·i·ly** adv. —**he·red′i·tar·i·ness** n.

he·red·i·ty (hə red′ə tē) n., pl. -ties [< Fr. < L. hereditas, heirship < heres, heir] 1. the transmission of characteristics from parents to offspring by means of genes in the chromosomes 2. all the characteristics that one inherits genetically

Her·e·ford (her′ə fərd) n. [orig. bred in Herefordshire, former county of England] any of a breed of beef cattle having a white face and a red body with white markings

here·in (hir in′) adv. [Archaic] 1. in here 2. in this writing 3. in this matter, detail, etc.

here·in·a·bove (hir′in ə buv′) adv. [Archaic] in the preceding part (of this document, speech, etc.): also **here′-in·be·fore′**

here·in·af·ter (-äf′tər) adv. [Archaic] in the following part (of this document, speech, etc.): also **here′in·be·low′**

here·in·to (hir in′tōō) adv. [Archaic] 1. into this place 2. into this matter, condition, etc.

here·of (-ov′) adv. [Archaic] 1. of this 2. concerning this

here·on (-on′) adv. same as HEREUPON

here's (hirz) here is

he·re·si·arch (hə rē′zē ärk′, -sē-; -rez′ē-) n. [LL. (Eccles) < Gr. hairesiarchēs, leader of a school] the founder or head of a heresy or heretical sect

here's to! here's a toast to! I wish joy, etc. to!

her·e·sy (her′ə sē) n., pl. -sies [< OFr. < L. < Gr. hairesis, a selection, sect < hairein, to take] 1. a) a religious belief opposed to the orthodox doctrines of a church; esp., such a

belief denounced by the church b) rejection of a belief that is part of church dogma 2. any opinion opposed to established views or doctrines 3. the holding of any such belief or opinion

her·e·tic (her′ə tik) n. a person who professes a heresy; esp., a church member who holds beliefs opposed to church dogma —adj. same as HERETICAL

he·ret·i·cal (hə ret′i k'l) adj. 1. of heresy or heretics 2. characterized by, or having the nature of, heresy —**he·ret′-i·cal·ly** adv.

here·to (hir tōō′) adv. [Archaic] to this (document, etc.) [attached hereto]: also **here·un′to**

here·to·fore (hir′tə fôr′, hir′tə fôr′) adv. [Archaic] up to now; until the present; before this

here·un·der (hir un′dər) adv. [Archaic] 1. under or below this (in a document, etc.) 2. under the terms stated here

here·up·on (hir′ə pon′, hir′ə pon′) adv. 1. immediately following this 2. concerning this

here·with (hir with′, -with′) adv. 1. along with this 2. by this method or means

her·i·ot (her′ē ət) n. [ME. heriet] a payment in chattels or money made to a feudal lord from the possessions of a tenant who had died

her·it·a·ble (her′it ə b'l) adj. 1. that can be inherited 2. that can inherit —**her′it·a·bil′i·ty** n.

her·it·age (her′ət ij) n. [OFr. < LL. < L. hereditas: see HEREDITY] 1. property that is or can be inherited 2. a) something handed down from one's ancestors or the past, as a characteristic, a culture, tradition, etc. b) birthright

her·maph·ro·dite (hər maf′rə dīt′) n. [< L. < Gr. < Hermaphroditos, son of Hermes and Aphrodite, united in a single body with a nymph] 1. a person or animal with the sexual organs of both the male and the female 2. a plant having stamens and pistils in the same flower 3. short for HERMAPHRODITE BRIG —adj. having the characteristics of a hermaphrodite —**her·maph′ro·dit′ism, her·maph′ro·dism** n.

hermaphrodite brig a ship with a square-rigged foremast and a fore-and-aft-rigged mainmast

her·maph·ro·dit·ic (-dit′ik) adj. of or like a hermaphrodite; also **her·maph′ro·dit′i·cal** —**her·maph′ro·dit′i·cal·ly** adv.

her·me·neu·tic (hur′mə nyōōt′ik) adj. [Gr. hermeneutikos < hermēneuein, to interpret] relating to interpretation, esp. of Biblical texts —**her·me·neu′tics** n. pl. [with sing. v.]

her·met·ic (hər met′ik) adj. [< ModL. < L. < Gr. Hermēs (reputed founder of alchemy)] airtight: also **her·met′i·cal** —**her·met′i·cal·ly** adv.

her·mit (hur′mit) n. [< OFr. < LL. < LGr. < Gr. erēmitēs < erēmos, solitary] a person who lives by himself in a secluded spot, often from religious motives; recluse —**her·mit′ic, her·mit′i·cal** adj. —**her·mit′i·cal·ly** adv. —**her′-mit·like′** adj.

her·mit·age (-ij) n. 1. the place where a hermit lives 2. a place where a person can live away from other people; secluded retreat

hermit crab any of various soft-bellied crabs that live in the empty shells of certain molluscs, as snails

her·ni·a (hur′nē ə) n., pl. -ni·as, -ni·ae′ (-ē′) [L.] the protrusion of all or part of an organ, esp. a part of the intestine, through a tear in the wall of the surrounding structure; rupture —**her′ni·al, her′ni·ar·y** adj.

he·ro (hir′ō) n., pl. -roes [< L. < Gr. hērōs] 1. Myth. & Legend a man of great strength and courage, favoured by the gods and in part descended from them 2. any man admired for his courage, nobility, or exploits 3. any man regarded as an ideal or model 4. the central, usually sympathetic, male character in a novel, play, poem, etc. 5. a central figure who played an admirable role in any important event or period

he·ro·ic (hi rō′ik) adj. 1. like or characteristic of a hero or his deeds [heroic poem] 2. of, about, or characterized by heroes and their deeds; epic [a heroic poem] 3. exalted; eloquent [heroic words] 4. exceptionally daring and risky [heroic measures] 5. Art somewhat larger than life-size [a heroic statue] Also **he·ro′i·cal** —n. 1. a) a heroic poem b) [pl.] same as HEROIC VERSE 2. [pl.] extravagant or melodramatic talk or action, meant to seem heroic —**he·ro′-i·cal·ly** adv.

heroic age the period in ancient times when the legendary heroes or demigods of a culture are said to have lived

heroic couplet a pair of rhymed lines in iambic pentameter

heroic verse the verse form in which epic poetry is traditionally written, as iambic pentameter

her·o·in (her′ə win) n. [G., orig. a trademark] a very powerful, habit-forming narcotic, a derivative of morphine

her·o·ine (her′ə win) n. a girl or woman hero in life or literature

her·o·ism (-wiz′m) n. the qualities and actions of a hero or heroine; great bravery, nobility, etc.

her·on (her′ən) n., pl. -ons, -on: see PLURAL, II, D, 1 [< OFr. hairon < Frank.] any of a group of wading birds with a long neck, long legs, and a long, tapered bill

her·on·ry (-rē) n., pl. -ries a place where many herons gather to breed

hero worship great or exaggerated admiration for heroes —he′ro-wor′ship *vt.* —he′ro-wor′ship·per *n.*

her·pes (hur′pēz) *n.* [L. < Gr. < *herpein*, to creep] a virus disease characterized by the eruption of small blisters on the skin and mucous membranes —**her·pet·ic** (har pet′ik) *adj.*

herpes simplex a form of herpes principally involving the mouth, lips, and face

herpes zos·ter (zos′tar) [Gr. *zōstēr*, a girdle] a viral infection of certain sensory nerves, causing pain and an eruption of blisters along the course of the affected nerve; shingles

her·pe·tol·o·gy (hur′pə tol′ə jē) *n.* [< Gr. *herpeton*, reptile + -LOGY] the branch of zoology having to do with the study of reptiles and amphibians —**her′pe·to·log′ic** (-tə loj′ik), **her′pe·to·log′i·cal** *adj.* —**her′pe·tol′o·gist** *n.*

‡**Herr** (her) *n.*, *pl.* **Her′ren** (-ən) in Germany, a man; gentleman: also used as a title corresponding to *Mr.* or *Sir*

her·ring (her′iŋ) *n.*, *pl.* **-rings, -ring**: see PLURAL, II, D, 1 [OE. *hæring*] 1. a small food fish of the N Atlantic: eaten cooked, dried, salted, or smoked: the young are tinned as sardines 2. loosely, the sprat, pilchard, etc.

her·ring·bone (-bōn′) *n.* 1. the spine of a herring, with the ribs extending from opposite sides in rows of parallel, slanting lines 2. a pattern with such a design or anything having such a pattern —*adj.* having the pattern of a herringbone —*vi., vt.* **-boned′, -bon′ing** to stitch, weave, arrange, etc. in a herringbone pattern

herring gull a common gull that has white plumage with black-tipped wings and pink legs

hers (hurz) *pron.* that or those belonging to her: used without a following noun [that book is *hers, hers* are better]: also used after *of* to indicate possession [a friend of *hers*]

her·self (hər self′) *pron.* a form of the 3rd pers. sing., fem. pronoun, used: a) as an intensive [she went *herself*] b) as a reflexive [she hurt *herself*] c) as a quasi-noun meaning "her real or true self" [she is not *herself* today]

Herts. Hertfordshire

hertz (hurts) *n.*, *pl.* **hertz** [see ff.] the SI unit of frequency, equal to one cycle per second

Hertz·i·an waves (hurt′sē ən, hert′-) [after H. R. *Hertz* (1857–1894), Ger. physicist] [*sometimes* h-] radio waves or other electromagnetic radiation resulting from the oscillations of electricity in a conductor

he′s (hēz) 1. he is 2. he has

hes·i·tan·cy (hez′ə tən sē) *n.*, *pl.* **-cies** hesitation or indecision; doubt: also **hes′i·tance**

hes·i·tant (-tənt) *adj.* hesitating or undecided; doubtful —**hes′i·tant·ly** *adv.*

hes·i·tate (-tāt′) *vi.* **-tat′ed, -tat′ing** [< L. pp. of *haesitare*, intens. of *haerere*, to stick] 1. to stop in indecision; pause or delay in acting or deciding 2. to pause; stop momentarily 3. to be reluctant [I *hesitate* to ask] 4. to pause continually in speaking; stammer —**hes′i·tat′er, hes′i·ta′tor** *n.* —**hes′i·tat′ing·ly** *adv.*

hes·i·ta·tion (hez′ə tā′shən) *n.* a hesitating; specif., a) indecision b) reluctance c) halting speech d) a pausing —**hes′i·ta′tive** *adj.* —**hes′i·ta′tive·ly** *adv.*

Hes·pe·ri·an (hes pir′ē ən) *adj.* [< L. *Hesperius* < Gr. *Hesperia*, western, evening] 1. of the Hesperides 2. [Poet.] western

hes·per·i·di·um (hes′pə rid′ē əm) *n.*, *pl.* **-di·a** (-ə) [< Mod L. *hesperidium*, orange] the fruit of a citrus plant, as an orange

Hes·per·us (hes′pər əs) *n.* [L.] the evening star, esp. Venus: also **Hes′per**

Hes·sian (hes′ē ən, hesh′ən) *adj.* of Hesse or its people —*n.* 1. a native or inhabitant of Hesse 2. a mercenary, esp. one who fought for the British in the War of American Independence 3. [h-] a coarse cloth of jute or hemp

Hessian fly a small, two-winged American fly whose larvae destroy wheat crops

hest (hest) *n.* [< OE. *hæs*, command < *hatan*, to call] [Archaic] behest; order

he·tae·ra (hi tir′ə) *n.*, *pl.* **-rae** (-ē), **-ras** [< Gr. < *hetairos*, companion] in ancient Greece, a courtesan: also **he·tai′ra** (-tī′rə), *pl.* **-rai** (-rī)

he·tae·rism (-iz′m) *n.* [see prec.] 1. cohabitation without legal marriage; concubinage 2. a system of communal marriage supposed to have been practised among some early peoples Also **he·tai′·rism** (-tī′riz′m)

het·er·o- [< Gr. < *heteros*, the other (of two)] a combining form meaning other, another, different [*heterosexual*]: opposed to HOMO-: also **heter-**

het·er·o·clite (het′ər ə klīt′) *adj.* [HETERO- + Gr. *klinein*, to bend] departing from the standard; irregular —*n.* an irregularly formed word

het·er·o·cy·clic (het′ər ō sī′klik, -sik′lik) *adj.* designating or of a cyclic molecular arrangement of atoms of carbon and other elements

het·er·o·dox (het′ər ə doks′) *adj.* [< Gr. < *hetero-*, HETERO-

+ *doxa*, opinion] departing from or opposed to the usual beliefs or established doctrines, esp. in religion; unorthodox

het·er·o·dox·y (-dok′sē) *n.*, *pl.* **-dox′ies** 1. the quality or fact of being heterodox 2. a heterodox belief or doctrine

het·er·o·dyne (-dīn′) *adj.* [HETERO- + DYNE] designating or of the combination of two different radio frequencies to produce beats with new frequencies —*vi.* **-dyned′, -dyn′ing** to combine two different frequencies so as to produce such beats

het·er·o·ga·mete (het′ər ō gam′ēt) *n.* a gamete of different size and form from the one with which it unites

het·er·og·a·mous (het′ər og′ə məs) *adj.* 1. characterized by the uniting of heterogametes 2. characterized by reproduction in which sexual and asexual generations alternate 3. bearing flowers that are sexually different —**het′er·og′a·my** (-mē) *n.*

het·er·o·ge·ne·ous (het′ər ə jē′nē əs, -jēn′yəs) *adj.* [< ML. < Gr. < *hetero-*, HETERO- + *genos*, a kind] 1. differing or opposite in structure, quality, etc.; dissimilar 2. composed of unrelated or unlike elements or parts; varied —**het′er·o·ge·ne′i·ty** (-jə nē′ə tē) *n.*, *pl.* **-ties** —**het′er·o·ge′ne·ous·ly** *adv.* —**het′er·o·ge′ne·ous·ness** *n.*

het·er·ol·o·gous (het′ər ol′ə gəs) *adj.* [< HETERO- + Gr. *logos*, relation] 1. consisting of different elements 2. *Med.* a) derived from different species b) not normal in structure, etc.

het·er·om·er·ous (-om′ər əs) *adj.* [HETERO- + -MEROUS] *Bot.* having different numbers of parts in different whorls

het·er·o·mor·phic (-môr′fik) *adj.* [HETERO- + -MORPHIC] 1. differing from the standard type 2. having different forms at various stages of development Also **het′er·o·mor′phous** —**het′er·o·mor′phism** *n.*

het·er·on·o·mous (het′ər on′ə məs) *adj.* [HETERO- + Gr. *nomos*, law + -OUS] 1. subject to another's law 2. subject to different laws of growth —**het′er·on′o·my** (-mē) *n.*

het·er·o·nym (het′ər ə nim′) *n.* [< Gr. < *hetero-*, HETERO- + *onyma*, name] a word with the same spelling as another but with a different meaning and pronunciation (Ex.: *tear*, a drop from the eye, *tear*, to rip) —**het′er·on′y·mous** (-on′ə məs) *adj.*

het·er·o·phyl·lous (het′ər ə fil′əs) *adj.* [HETERO- + -PHYLLOUS] growing leaves of different forms on the same stem or plant —**het′er·o·phyl′ly** *n.*

het·er·o·sex·u·al (het′ər ə sek′shoo wəl) *adj.* 1. of or characterized by sexual desire for those of the opposite sex 2. *Biol.* of different sexes —*n.* a heterosexual individual —**het′er·o·sex′u·al′i·ty** (-wal′ə tē) *n.*

het·er·o·tax·is (het′ər ə tak′sis) *n.* [HETERO- + Gr. *taxis*, arrangement] an abnormal arrangement, as of bodily organs, rock strata, etc.: also **het′er·o·tax′i·a** (-sē ə), **het′er·o·tax′y**

het·er·o·troph·ic (-trof′ik) *adj.* [HETERO- + -TROPHIC] obtaining food from organic matter only

het·er·o·zy·gote (-zī′gōt) *n.* [HETERO- + -ZYGOTE] a plant or animal having different alleles at a single locus on a chromosome, and hence not breeding true to type; hybrid

het·man (het′mən) *n.*, *pl.* **-mans** [Pol. < G. < *Haupt*, head + *Mann*, man] a Cossack chief

het up (het) [*het*, dial. pt. & pp. of *heat*] [Colloq.] excited or angry

heu·ris·tic (hyoo ris′tik) *adj.* [< Gr. *heuriskein*, to discover] helping to discover or learn

hew (hyoo) *vt.* **hewed, hewed** or **hewn, hew′ing** [OE. *heawan*] 1. to chop or cut with an axe, knife, etc. 2. to make or shape by or as by cutting or chopping with an axe, etc. 3. to chop *down* (a tree) with an axe —*vi.* 1. to make cutting or chopping blows with an axe, knife, etc. 2. [U.S.] to adhere (*to* a line, principle, etc.) —**hew′er** *n.*

hexa- [< Gr. *hex*, six] a combining form meaning six [*hexagram*]: also, before a vowel, **hex-**

hex·a·chlo·ro·phene (hek′sə klôr′ə fēn′) *n.* [< HEXA- + CHLORO- + PHENOL] a white powder used, esp. formerly, in deodorants, soaps, etc. to kill bacteria

hex·ad (hek′sad) *n.* [< Gr. *hexas*, six] a series or group of six

hex·a·gon (hek′sə gon′) *n.* [< L. < Gr. < *hex*, six + *gōnia*, a corner, angle] a plane figure with six angles and six sides —**hex·ag′o·nal** (-sag′ə n'l) *adj.* —**hex·ag′o·nal·ly** *adv.*

hex·a·gram (hek′sə gram′) *n.* [HEXA- + -GRAM] a six-pointed star formed by extending all sides of a regular hexagon to points of intersection

hex·a·he·dron (hek′sə hē′drən) *n.*, *pl.* **-drons, -dra** (-drə) [see HEXA- & -HEDRON] a solid figure with six plane surfaces —**hex′a·he′dral** *adj.*

hex·am·e·ter (hek sam′ə tər) *n.* [< L. < Gr.: see HEXA- & -METER] 1. a line of verse containing six metrical feet 2. verse consisting of hexameters —*adj.* having six metrical feet

hex·ane (hek′sān) *n.* [HEX(A)- + -ANE] any of the five colourless, volatile, liquid hydrocarbons, C_6H_{14}, of the paraffin series

hex·a·pod (hek′sə pod′) *n.* [see HEXA- & -POD] an insect (sense 1) —*adj.* having six legs, as a true insect: also **hex·ap·o·dous** (hek sap′ə dəs)

hex·ose (hek′sōs) *n.* [HEX(A)- + -OSE] any of a group of simple sugars containing six carbon atoms in each molecule, as dextrose

hey (hā) *interj.* [ME. *hei,* echoic formation] an exclamation used to attract attention, express surprise, etc., or in asking a question

hey·day (hā′dā′) *n.* the time of greatest health, vigour, success, prosperity, etc.; prime

hey presto a conjuror's phrase announcing the surprise moment in a trick

Hf *Chem.* hafnium

HF, H.F., hf, h.f. high frequency

hf. half

Hg [L. *hydrargyrum*] *Chem.* mercury

HG., H.G. High German

H.G. His (or Her) Grace

hg hectogramme; hectogrammes

hgt. height

H.G.V. heavy goods vehicle

HH double hard (of pencil lead)

H.H. 1. His (or Her) Highness 2. His Holiness

hhd. hogshead

hi (hī) *interj.* [ME. *hy,* var. of *hei,* HEY] [Chiefly U.S.] an exclamation of greeting

hi·a·tus (hī āt′əs) *n., pl.* **-tus·es, -tus** [L., pp. of *hiare,* to gape] 1. a break or gap where a part is missing or lost 2. any gap 3. a slight pause in pronunciation between two successive vowel sounds, as between the *e*'s in *reentry*

hi·ba·chi (hi bä′chē) *n., pl.* **-chis** [Jap. < *hi,* fire + *bachi,* bowl] a charcoal-burning brazier and grill of Japanese design

hi·ber·nal (hī bʉr′nəl) *adj.* [< L. < *hibernus:* see ff.] of winter; wintry

hi·ber·nate (hī′bər nāt′) *vi.* **-nat·ed, -nat·ing** [< L. pp. of *hibernare* < *hibernus,* wintry] to spend the winter in a dormant state —**hi′ber·na′tion** *n.* —**hi′ber·na′tor** *n.*

Hi·ber·ni·a (hī bʉr′nē ə) [L.] *poet. name of* Ireland —**Hi·ber′ni·an** *adj., n.*

Hi·ber·ni·cism (hī bʉr′nə siz′m) *n.* [< prec.] an Irish characteristic, custom, idiom, etc.

hi·bis·cus (hi bis′kəs) *n.* [< L. *hibiscus*] a plant, shrub, or small tree related to the mallow, with large, colourful flowers

hic·cup (hik′əp) *n.* [altered < Early ModE. *hikop, hicket,* of echoic orig.: sp. infl. by association with COUGH] 1. sudden, involuntary contraction of the diaphragm that closes the glottis at the moment of breathing, making a sharp, quick sound 2. [*pl.*] a condition of repeated contractions of this kind —*vi.* **-cuped -cup·ing** to make a hiccup —*vt.* to utter with a hiccup Also **hic·cough** (hik′əp)

‡**hic ja·cet** (hik′jā′sit, hēc yä′ket) [L.] 1. here lies: inscribed on tombstones 2. an epitaph

hick (hik) *n.* [altered < *Richard,* a masculine name] [Chiefly U.S. Colloq.] an awkward, unsophisticated person regarded as typical of rural areas: somewhat contemptuous term —*adj.* [Colloq.] of or like a hick

hick·o·ry (hik′ər ē, hik′rē) *n., pl.* **-ries** [< AmInd. *pawcohiccora,* product made from the nuts] 1. a N. American tree related to the walnut, with smooth-shelled, edible nuts 2. any of various Australian trees with hard wood 3. the hard wood of the hickory 4. its nut: also **hickory nut**

hi·dal·go (hi dal′gō) *n., pl.* **-gos** [Sp., contr. of *hijo de algo,* son of something] a Spanish nobleman of secondary rank, below that of a grandee

hid·den (hid′'n) *alt. pp.* of HIDE[1] —*adj.* concealed; secret

hide[1] (hīd) *vt.* **hid, hid′den** or **hid, hid′ing** [OE. *hydan*] 1. to put or keep out of sight; secrete; conceal 2. to keep secret 3. to keep from being seen by covering up, obscuring, etc. 4. to turn away [to *hide* one's head in shame] —*vi.* 1. to be concealed 2. to conceal oneself —*n.* a place of concealment, as for a bird watcher, hunter, etc. —**hid′er** *n.*

hide[2] (hīd) *n.* [OE. *hid*] 1. an animal skin or pelt, either raw or tanned 2. [Colloq.] the skin of a person —*vt.* **hid′ed, hid′ing** [Colloq.] to beat; flog —**neither hide nor hair** nothing whatsoever

hide[3] (hīd) *n.* [ME. < OE. *higid* < base of *hiwan,* household] an obsolete Brit. land measure, varying from about 60 to 120 acres

hide-and-seek (hīd′'n sēk′) *n.* a children's game in which one player tries to find the other players, who have hidden

hide·a·way (hīd′ə wā′) *n.* [Colloq.] a place where one can hide, be secluded, etc.

hide·bound (-bound′) *adj.* 1. having the hide tight over the body structure, as an emaciated cow 2. obstinately conservative and narrow-minded

hid·e·ous (hid′ē əs) *adj.* [< Anglo-Fr. < OFr. < *hide,* fright] horrible; very ugly or revolting; dreadful —**hid′e·ous·ly** *adv.* —**hid′e·ous·ness** *n.*

hide-out (hīd′out′) *n.* [Colloq.] a hiding place

hid·ing[1] (hīd′iŋ) *n.* 1. *a)* the act of one that hides *b)* the condition of being hidden: usually in the phrase **in hiding** 2. [Now Rare] a place to hide

hid·ing[2] (hīd′iŋ) *n.* [Colloq.] a severe beating

hi·dro·sis (hi drō′sis, hī-) *n.* [ModL., ult. < Gr. *hidrōs,* sweat] perspiration —**hi drot′ik** *adj.*

hie (hī) *vi., vt.* **hied, hie′ing** or **hy′ing** [OE. *higian*] [Archaic or Poet.] to hurry or hasten: usually reflexive

hi·er·arch (hī′ə rärk, hī′rärk) *n.* [< ML. < Gr. < *hieros,* sacred + *archos,* ruler] a chief priest

hi·er·ar·chy (-rär′kē) *n., pl.* **-chies** [< OFr. < ML.: see prec.] 1. a system of church government by priests or other clergy in graded ranks 2. the group of officials in such a system 3. a group of persons or things arranged in order of rank, grade, etc. —**hi′er·ar′chi·cal, hi′er·ar′chic, hi′er·ar′chal** *adj.* —**hi′er·ar′chi·cal·ly** *adv.*

hi·er·at·ic (hī′ə rat′ik) *adj.* [< L. < Gr. *hieratikos* < *hieros,* sacred] 1. of or used by priests; priestly 2. designating or of the abridged form of cursive hieroglyphic writing once used by Egyptian priests Also **hi′er·at′i·cal** —**hi′er·at′i·cal·ly** *adv.*

hi·er·o·glyph (hī′ər ə glif′, hī′rə-) *n.* same as HIEROGLYPHIC

hi·er·o·glyph·ic (hī′ər ə glif′ik, hī′rə-) *adj.* [< Fr. < LL. < Gr. < *hieros,* sacred + *glyphein,* to carve] 1. of, like, or written in hieroglyphics 2. hard to read or understand Also **hi′er·o·glyph′i·cal** —*n.* 1. a picture or symbol representing a word, syllable, or sound, used by the ancient Egyptians and others 2. [*usually pl.*] a method of writing using hieroglyphics 3. a symbol, sign, etc. hard to understand 4. [*pl.*] writing hard to decipher —**hi′er·o·glyph′i·cal·ly** *adv.*

hi·er·o·phant (hī′ər ə fant′, hī′rə-) *n.* [LL. *hierophanta* < Gr. *hieros,* holy, + *phainein,* to show] 1. a priest who presided at sacred mysteries 2. an interpreter of sacred mysteries

hi-fi (hī′fī′) *n.* 1. same as HIGH FIDELITY 2. a radio, etc. having high fidelity —*adj.* of or having high fidelity of sound reproduction

hig·gle (hig′'l) *vi.* **-gled, -gling** same as HAGGLE —**hig′gler** *n.*

hig·gle·dy-pig·gle·dy (hig′'l dē pig′'l dē) *adv.* [redupl., prob. after PIG] in disorder; in jumbled confusion —*adj.* disorderly; jumbled; confused

high (hī) *adj.* [OE. *heah*] 1. of more than normal height; lofty; tall: not used of persons 2. extending upwards a (specified) distance 3. situated far above the ground or other level 4. reaching to or done from a height [a *high* jump, a *high* dive] 5. above others in rank, position, quality, character, etc.; superior 6. grave; very serious [*high* treason] 7. greatly developed; complex: usually in the comparative [*higher* mathematics] 8. main; principal; chief [a *high* priest] 9. greater in size, amount, degree, power, etc. than usual [*high* prices] 10. advanced to its acme or fullness [*high* noon] 11. expensive; costly 12. luxurious and extravagant [*high* living] 13. haughty; overbearing 14. raised or acute in pitch; sharp; shrill 15. slightly tainted; strong-smelling: said of meat, esp. game 16. extremely formal in matters of ceremony, doctrine, etc. 17. excited; elated [*high* spirits] 18. far from the equator [a *high* latitude] 19. designating or of that gear ratio of a motor vehicle transmission which produces the highest speed 20. [Slang] *a)* drunk; intoxicated *b)* under the influence of a drug 21. *Phonet.* produced with the tongue held in a relatively elevated position: said of a vowel, as (ē) —*adv.* 1. in a high manner 2. in or to a high level, degree, rank, etc. —*n.* 1. a high level, place, etc. 2. an area of high barometric pressure 3. [Slang] a condition of euphoria induced as by drugs —**high and dry** stranded —**high and low** everywhere —**on high** 1. high above 2. in heaven —**high and mighty** [Colloq.] arrogant; haughty —**on high** 1. high above 2. in heaven

high·ball (-bôl′) *n.* [U.S.] an alcoholic drink, usually whisky, served with water, soda water, ginger ale, etc. and ice in a tall glass

high-born (-bôrn′) *adj.* of noble birth

high·boy (-boi′) *n.* [U.S.] a high chest of drawers mounted on legs: cf. TALLBOY

high-bred (-bred′) *adj.* showing good breeding; cultivated

high-brow (-brou′) *n.* [Colloq.] a person who is or tries to be intellectual —*adj.* [Colloq.] of or for a highbrow

high·chair (-cher′) *n.* a baby's chair with an attached tray, mounted on long legs

High Church that party of the Anglican Church which emphasizes the importance of the priesthood and of traditional rituals and doctrines —**High′-Church′** *adj.* —**High′-Church′man** *n., pl.* **-men**

high comedy 1. comedy reflecting the life of the upper social classes, characterized by a witty, sardonic treatment 2. a situation or instance of extreme humour

high commissioner 1. the chief representative of the

HICKORY
(leaf, nut & tree)

British government to one of the Commonwealth countries or from one of these countries to the British government **2.** the chief officer of a commission

higher education education beyond secondary school, usually at colleges and universities

high·er-up (hī'ər up') *n.* [Colloq.] a person of higher rank or position

high explosive any explosive in which the combustion of the particles is very rapid, producing great shattering effect: used esp. in shells, bombs, etc.

high·fa·lu·tin, high·fa·lu·ting (hī'fə lo͞ot'ʼn) *adj.* [Colloq.] ridiculously pretentious or pompous

high fidelity in radio, sound recording, etc., a nearly exact reproduction of a wide range of sound frequencies, from about 20 to 20000 hertz

high·fli·er, high·fly·er (-flī'ər) *n.* **1.** a person or thing that flies high **2.** *a)* a person who acts or talks in an extravagant manner *b)* an ambitious person *c)* a person who achieves, or is capable of achieving, success —**high'fly'ing** *adj.*

high-flown (-flōn') *adj.* **1.** extravagantly ambitious **2.** high-sounding but meaningless; bombastic

high frequency any radio frequency between 3 and 30 megahertz

High German 1. the West Germanic dialects spoken in C and S Germany: distinguished from Low German **2.** the official and literary form of the German language, technically called *New High German:* see also Old High German, Middle High German

high-grade (-grād') *adj.* of superior quality

high·hand·ed (-han'did) *adj.* acting or done in an overbearing or arbitrary manner —**high'hand'ed·ly** *adv.* —**high'hand'ed·ness** *n.*

high-hat (-hat') *adj.* [Chiefly U.S. Slang] snobbish and aloof —*n.* [Chiefly U.S. Slang] a snob —*vt.* -**hat'ted, -hat'·ting** [Chiefly U.S. Slang] to treat snobbishly; snub

high·jack (-jak') *vt.* [Colloq.] *same as* HIJACK

high jump 1. an athletic event in which the contestants jump for height over a horizontal bar **2.** [Colloq.] severe punishment [he's for the *high jump*]

high·land (-lənd) *n.* a region higher than adjacent land and containing many hills or mountains —*adj.* of, in, or from such a region —**the Highlands** mountainous region occupying nearly all of N Scotland —**high'land·er, High'·land·er** *n.*

Highland cattle a breed of cattle with shaggy hair, usually reddish-brown, and long horns

Highland fling a lively dance of the Highlands

high life 1. the luxurious way of life of fashionable society **2.** a W. African dance

high·light (-līt') *n.* **1.** *a)* a part on which light is brightest *b)* a part of a painting, etc. on which light is represented as brightest *c)* the representation or effect of such light in a painting, etc. Also **high light 2.** the most important or interesting part, scene, etc. —*vt.* **1.** to give a highlight or highlights to **2.** to give prominence to **3.** to be the most outstanding in

high·ly (-lē) *adv.* **1.** in a high office or rank **2.** very much; extremely **3.** favourably **4.** at a high wage, salary, etc.

highly strung nervous and tense; highly sensitive

High Mass *R.C.Ch.* a sung Mass, usually celebrated with the complete ritual, at which the celebrant is assisted by a deacon and subdeacon: also **Solemn High Mass, Solemn Mass**

high-mind·ed (-mīn'did) *adj.* **1.** [Obs.] haughty **2.** having or showing high ideals, principles, etc. —**high'-mind'ed·ly** *adv.* —**high'-mind'ed·ness** *n.*

high·ness (-nis) *n.* **1.** the quality or state of being high; height **2.** [H-] a title used in speaking to or of a member of a royal family (with *His, Her,* or *Your*)

high-pitched (-picht') *adj.* **1.** high in pitch; shrill **2.** exalted **3.** agitated **4.** steep in slope: said of roofs

high-pow·ered (-pou'ərd) *adj.* **1.** very powerful **2.** of a high intellectual standard [a *high-powered* lecturer] **3.** forceful; dynamic [*high-powered* management]

high-pres·sure (-presh'ər) *adj.* **1.** *a)* having, using, or withstanding relatively high pressure *b)* having a high barometric pressure **2.** using forcefully persuasive or insistent methods or arguments —*vt.* -**sured, -sur·ing** [Colloq.] to urge with such methods or arguments

high priest a chief priest; specif., the chief priest of the ancient Jewish priesthood

high-proof (-pro͞of') *adj.* high in alcohol content

high-rise (-rīz') *adj.* designating or of a tall block of flats, office building, etc. of many storeys —*n.* a high-rise building

high-road (-rōd') *n.* **1.** a main road; highway **2.** an easy or direct way

high school a secondary school, esp. a grammar school

high seas open ocean waters outside the territorial limits of any single nation

high season the busiest time at a holiday resort, etc.

high-sound·ing (-soun'diŋ) *adj.* sounding pretentious or impressive

high-spir·it·ed (-spir'i tid) *adj.* **1.** having or showing a courageous or noble spirit **2.** spirited; fiery **3.** gay; lively —**high'-spir'it·ed·ly** *adv.*

high street the main street of a town, usually containing the principal shops (often preceded by *the*)

high table the table in a college dining hall, at a public function, etc., at which the most important guests, members of staff, etc., sit

high tea an evening meal consisting of a main dish, usually cooked, followed by cakes, etc., with tea to drink

high-ten·sion (hī'ten'shən) *adj.* having, carrying, or operating under a high voltage

high tide 1. the highest level to which the tide rises **2.** the time when the tide is at this level **3.** any culminating point or time

high time 1. none too soon **2.** [Colloq.] a gay, exciting time: also **high old time**

high-toned (-tōnd') *adj.* **1.** [Now Rare] high in tone or pitch **2.** characterized by dignity, high principles, etc. **3.** [U.S. Colloq.] of or imitating the manners, attitudes, etc. of the upper classes

high treason treason against the ruler or government

high water 1. *same as* HIGH TIDE **2.** the highest level reached by a body of water

high-wa·ter mark (hī'wôt'ər) **1.** the highest level reached by a body of water **2.** the mark left after high water has receded **3.** a culminating point; highest point

high·way (-wā') *n.* **1.** a public road **2.** a main road; thoroughfare Now chiefly a legal and U.S. usage

Highway Code a booklet of rules and advice compiled by the Ministry of the Environment for the guidance of users of public roads

high·way·man (-wā mən) *n., pl.* -**men** formerly, a man who robbed travellers on a highway

H.I.H. His (or Her) Imperial Highness

hi·jack (hī'jak') *vt.* [prob. *hi* (for HIGH) + JACK, *v.*] [Colloq.] **1.** to steal (goods in transit, a truck and its contents, etc.) from (a person) by force **2.** to swindle, as by the use of force **3.** to force the driver, etc. (of a vehicle) to go to a nonscheduled destination —*n.* the act of hijacking —**hi'jack'er** *n.*

hike (hīk) *vi.* **hiked, hik'ing** [< dial. *heik*] to take a long, vigorous walk; tramp or march —*vt.* [Colloq.] to pull up; hoist (with *up*) —*n.* a long, vigorous walk —**hik'er** *n.*

hi·lar·i·ous (hi ler'ē əs) *adj.* [< L. < Gr. *hilaros,* cheerful] **1.** noisily merry; boisterous and gay **2.** provoking laughter; funny —**hi·lar'i·ous·ly** *adv.* —**hi·lar'i·ous·ness** *n.*

hi·lar·i·ty (hi lar'ə tē) *n.* the state or quality of being hilarious; noisy merriment

Hil·a·ry (hil'ər ē) [after St. *Hilary* of Poitiers, whose festival is January 13th] the spring session or term in law and at certain British universities

hill (hil) *n.* [OE. *hyll*] **1.** a natural raised part of the earth's surface, often rounded, smaller than a mountain **2.** a small pile, heap, or mound [an *anthill*] —*vt.* to shape into or like a hill —**over the hill** [Colloq.] **1.** absent without permission; AWOL **2.** in one's decline —**hill'er** *n.*

hill-bil·ly (hil'bil'ē) *n., pl.* -**lies** [HILL + *Billy,* dim. of *William,* a masculine name] [U.S. Colloq.] a person who lives in or comes from the mountains or backwoods: somewhat contemptuous term —*adj.* **1.** [U.S. Colloq.] of or characteristic of hillbillies **2.** designating folk music originating chiefly from certain mountainous regions of the U.S.

hill·ock (hil'ək) *n.* a small hill; mound —**hill'ock·y** *adj.*

hill·side (hil'sīd') *n.* the side or slope of a hill

hill·top (-top') *n.* the top of a hill

hill·y (-ē) *adj.* **hill'i·er, hill'i·est 1.** full of hills **2.** like a hill; steep —**hill'i·ness** *n.*

hilt (hilt) *n.* [OE.] the handle of a sword, dagger, tool, etc. **(up) to the hilt** thoroughly; entirely

hi·lum (hī'ləm) *n., pl.* **hi'la** (-lə) [ModL. < L., little thing] *Bot.* a scar on a seed, marking the place where it was attached to the seed stalk

him (him; *unstressed* im, əm) *pron.* [OE.] *objective case of* HE: also used colloquially as a predicate complement with a linking verb (Ex.: that's *him*)

H.I.M. His (or Her) Imperial Majesty

hi·mat·i·on (hi mat'ē on', -ən) *n., pl.* -**mat'i·a** (-ə) [Gr.] an ancient Greek outer garment consisting of a long rectangle of cloth draped over the left shoulder and wound round the body

HILUM

him·self (him self') *pron.* a form of the 3rd pers. sing., masc. pronoun, used: *a)* as an intensive [he went *himself*] *b)* as a reflexive [he hurt *himself*] *c)* as a quasi-noun meaning "his real or true self" [he is not *himself* today] *d)* [Irish] as a subject [*himself* will have his tea now]

Hi·na·ya·na (hē'nə yä'nə) *same as* THERAVADA

hind[1] (hīnd) *adj.* **hind′er, hind′most** or **hind′er·most**[prob. < HINDER[2]] back; rear; posterior

hind[2] (hīnd) *n.*, *pl.* **hinds, hind:** see PLURAL, II, D, 1 [OE.] the female of the red deer, in and after its third year

hind[3] (hīnd) *n.* [OE. *hina, higna*] **1.** in N England and Scotland, a skilled farm worker or servant **2.** [Archaic] a simple peasant; rustic

hind·brain (-brān′) *n.* the hindmost of the three primary divisions of the vertebrate brain

hin·der[1] (hin′dər) *vt.* [OE. *hindrian*] **1.** to keep back; restrain; prevent; stop **2.** to make difficult for; thwart; frustrate —*vi.* to be a hindrance

hind·er[2] (hīn′dər) *adj.* [OE. *hinder*, *adv.*, behind: now felt as compar. of HIND[1]] hind; rear; posterior

Hin·di (hin′dē) *adj.* [Hindi *hindī* < *Hind*: see HINDU] of or associated with northern India —*n.* an Indo-Iranian language, the main, now official, language of India

hind·most (hīnd′mōst′) *adj. superl.* of HIND[1]; farthest back; last: also **hind′er·most′**

Hin·doo (hin′dōō, hin dōō′) *adj.*, *n.*, *pl.* **-doos** same as HINDU

hind·quar·ter (hīnd′kwôr′tər) *n.* **1.** a hind leg and loin of a carcass of veal, beef, lamb, etc. **2.** [*pl.*] the hind part of a four-legged animal

hin·drance (hin′drəns) *n.* **1.** the act of hindering **2.** any person or thing that hinders; obstacle

hind·sight (hīnd′sīt′) *n.* an understanding, after the event, of what should have been done

Hin·du (hin′dōō, hin dōō′) *n.* [< Per. < *Hind*, India, ult. < Sans. *sindhu*, river, the Indus] **1.** any of the peoples of India that speak an Indic language **2.** a follower of Hinduism **3.** popularly, any native of India —*adj.* **1.** of the Hindus, their language, etc. **2.** of Hinduism

Hin·du·ism (hin′dōō wiz′m) *n.* the religion and social system of the Hindus

Hin·du·sta·ni (-stan′ē, -stä′nē) *n.* the most important dialect of Western Hindi, used as a trade language in N India —*adj.* **1.** of Hindustan or its people **2.** of Hindustani

hinge (hinj) *n.* [< ME. *hengen*, to hang] **1.** a joint, etc. on which a door, gate, lid, etc. swings **2.** a natural joint, as of the bivalve shell of a clam or oyster **3.** anything on which matters turn or depend —*vt.* **hinged, hing′ing** to equip with or attach by a hinge —*vi.* to be contingent; depend (*on*)

hin·ny[1] (hin′ē) *n.*, *pl.* **-nies** [L. *hinnus* < Gr. *innos*] the offspring of a male horse and a female donkey: cf. MULE[1]

hin·ny[2] (hin′ē) *n.* [var of HONEY] [Dial.] a term of endearment, esp. for a woman or child

hint (hint) *n.* [< OE. *henten*, to seize] **1.** a slight indication of a fact, wish, etc.; indirect suggestion or reference **2.** a very small amount or degree; trace —*vt.*, *vi.* to give a hint (*of*) —**hint at** to suggest indirectly; intimate —**take a hint** to perceive and act on a hint —**hint′er** *n.*

hin·ter·land (hin′tər land′) *n.* [G. < *hinter*, back + *Land* *land*] **1.** the land or district behind that bordering on a coast or river **2.** an area far from big cities and towns; remote country **3.** an area located near and dependent on a large city, esp. a port

hip[1] (hip) *n.* [OE. *hype*] **1.** *a)* the part of the body surrounding and including the joint formed by each thighbone and pelvis *b)* same as HIP JOINT **2.** the angle formed by the meeting of two sloping sides of a roof —*vt.* **hipped, hip′ping** to make (a roof) with such an angle

hip[2] (hip) *n.* [OE. *heope*] the fleshy fruit of the rose: it is rich in vitamin C

hip[3] (hip) *adj.* **hip′per, hip′pest** [< ? *hep*] [Slang] **1.** *a)* sophisticated; knowing; aware *b)* fashionable; stylish **2.** of or associated with hipsters or hippies —**get** (or **be**) **hip to** [Slang] to become (or be) informed or knowledgeable about —**hip′ness** *n.*

hip[4] (hip) *interj.* an exclamation used in cheers [*hip, hip, hurray!*]

hip-bath (-bäth) *n.* a portable bath for sitting in immersed to the hips

hip·bone (hip′bōn′) *n.* **1.** same as: *a)* INNOMINATE BONE *b)* ILIUM **2.** the neck of the femur

hip joint the junction between the thighbone and its socket in the pelvis

hipped[1] (hipt) *adj.* **1.** having hips of a specified kind [*broad-hipped*] **2.** *Archit.* having a hip or hips [a *hipped roof*]

hipped[2] (hipt) *adj.* [< HYP(OCHONDRIA)] [Slang] having a great interest; obsessed (*with on*)

hip·pie (hip′ē) *n.* [< HIP[3] + -IE] [Slang] a young person alienated from conventional society, who has turned to mysticism, drugs, communal living, etc.

hip·po (hip′ō) *n.*, *pl.* **-pos** [Colloq.] a hippopotamus

hip·po·cam·pus (hip′ə kam′pəs) *n.*, *pl.* **-cam′pi** (-pī) [L. < Gr. < *hippos*, horse + *kampos*, sea monster] **1.** Gr. & Rom. Myth. a sea monster with a horse's head and a dolphin's tail **2.** any of various small fish with a horse-like head and neck; sea-horse **3.** a ridge along each lateral ventricle of the brain —**hip′po·cam′pal** *adj.*

hip·po·cras (hip′ə kras′) *n.* [ME. *ypocras* < OFr.] a former cordial of spiced wine

Hippocratic oath [after *Hippocrates* (460?-370? B.C.), Gr. physician: called the *Father of medicine*] the oath generally taken by medical graduates: it sets forth an ethical code for the medical profession

hip·po·drome (hip′ə drōm) *n.* [< Fr. < L. < Gr. < *hippos*, a horse + *dromos*, a course] **1.** in ancient Greece and Rome, an oval course for horse races and chariot races, surrounded by tiers of seats **2.** an arena or building for a circus, etc.

hip·po·griff, hip·po·gryph (-grif′) *n.* [< Fr., ult. < Gr. *hippos*, horse, + LL. *gryphus*, GRIFFIN] a mythical monster with a horse's hindquarters and a griffin's head and wings

hip·po·pot·a·mus (hip′ə pot′ə məs) *n.*, *pl.* **-mus·es, -mi** (-mī′), **-mus:** see PLURAL, II, D, 1 [L. < Gr. < *hippos*, horse + *potamos*, river] a large, plant-eating mammal with a heavy, thick-skinned, almost hairless body and short legs: it lives chiefly in or near rivers in Africa

hip·py[1] (hip′ē) *n.*, *pl.* **-pies** [Slang] same as HIPPIE

hip·py[2] (hip′ē) *adj.* [Colloq.] having large hips [she has a tendency to be *hippy*]

hip roof a roof with sloping ends and sides

hip·ster[1] (hip′stər) *n.* [Slang] **1.** a hip person **2.** a beatnik: term of the 1950's and early 1960's

hip·ster[2] (hip′stər) *adj.* designating trousers, etc., cut with a low waist so that the top encircles the hips —*n.* [*pl.*] trousers etc., designed in this way

hi·ra·ga·na (hi′rə gä′nə) *n.* [Jap.] a widely used system of Japanese syllabic writing

hir·cine (hur′sīn, -sin) *adj.* [< L. < *hircus*, goat] of or like a goat, esp. in odour

hire (hīr) *n.* [OE. *hyr*] **1.** the amount paid for the services of a person or the use of a thing **2.** a hiring or being hired —*vt.* **hired, hir′ing 1.** to get the services of (a person) or the use of (a thing) in return for payment; employ or engage **2.** to give the use of (a thing) or the services of (oneself or another) for payment (often with *out*) —**for hire** available for work or use, for payment: also **on hire** —**hire out** to work for payment —**hir′a·ble, hire′a·ble** *adj.* —**hir′er** *n.*

hire·ling (-liŋ) *n.* [see HIRE & -LING[1]] a person who will follow anyone's orders for pay; mercenary

hire-purchase (-pur′chəs) *n.* a system by which a hired article becomes the property of the hirer after a stipulated number of payments: also **hire-purchase system**

hir·sute (hur′sōōt, hər syōōt′) *adj.* [L. *hirsutus*] hairy; shaggy; bristly —**hir′sute·ness** *n.*

hir·sut·ism (hur′sət iz′m) *n.* a heavy, esp. abnormal, growth of hair

his (hiz) *pron.* [OE.] that or those belonging to him: used without a following noun [that book is *his*, *his* are better] : also used after *of* to indicate possession [a friend of *his*] —*possessive pronominal adj.* of, belonging to, or done by him

His·pan·ic (his pan′ik) *adj.* Spanish or Spanish and Portuguese —**His·pan′i·cism** (-ə siz′m) *n.*

his·pid (his′pid) *adj.* [L. *hispidus*] covered with rough bristles or small spines

hiss (his) *vi.* [echoic] **1.** to make a sound like that of a prolonged *s*, as of a goose, snake, escaping steam, etc. **2.** to show dislike or disapproval by hissing —*vt.* **1.** to say or indicate by hissing **2.** to condemn, force, or drive by hissing —*n.* the act or sound of hissing —**hiss′er** *n.*

hist (st; hist) *interj.* be quiet! listen!

hist. 1. historian **2.** historical **3.** history

his·ta·mine (his′tə mēn′, -mən) *n.* [see HISTO- & AMINE] an amine released by the tissues in allergic reactions: it dilates blood vessels, stimulates gastric secretion, etc. —**his′- ta·min′ic** (-min′ik) *adj.*

his·to- [< Gr. *histos*, a loom, web] a combining form meaning tissue [*histology*]: also **hist-**

his·to·gen·e·sis (his′tə jen′ə sis) *n.* [HISTO- + -GENESIS] *Biol.* the process of tissue development and differentiation —**his′- to·ge·net′ic** (-jə net′ik) *adj.*

his·to·gram (his′tə gram′) *n.* [HISTO(RY) + -GRAM] a graph using vertical columns to illustrate frequency distribution

his·tol·o·gy (his tol′ə jē) *n.* [prec. + -LOGY] the branch of biology concerned with the microscopic study of the structure of tissues —**his·to·log·ic** (his′tə loj′ik), **his′to·log′- i·cal** *adj.* —**his′to·log′i·cal·ly** *adv.* —**his·tol′o·gist** *n.*

his·tol·y·sis (-ə sis) *n.* [HISTO- + -LYSIS] *Biol.* the breaking down and dissolution of organic tissues —**his·to·lyt·ic** (his′- tə lit′ik) *adj.*

his·to·ri·an (his tôr′ē ən) *n.* **1.** a writer of history **2.** an authority on or specialist in history

his·tor·ic (his tor′ik) *adj.* historical; esp., famous in history

his·tor·i·cal (-i k'l) *adj.* **1.** of or concerned with history as a science [the *historical* method] **2.** providing evidence for a fact of history [a *historical* document] **3.** based on people or events of the past [a *historical* novel] **4.** established by history; factual **5.** in chronological order **6.** famous in

history: now usually HISTORIC —**his·tor'i·cal·ly** *adv.* —**his·tor'i·cal·ness** *n.*

historical present the present tense used in telling about past events: also **historic present**

his·tor·i·cism (his tor'i siz''m) *n.* a theory of history holding that the course of events is determined by unchangeable laws or cyclic patterns

his·to·ric·i·ty (his'tə ris'ə tē) *n.* the condition of having actually occurred in history

his·to·ri·og·ra·pher (his tor'ē og'rə fər) *n.* [< LL. < Gr. *historia,* history + *graphein,* to write] a historian; esp., one appointed to write the history of some institution, country, etc. —**his·to'ri·o·graph'ic** (-ə graf'ik), **his·to'ri·o·graph'i·cal** *adj.* —**his·to'ri·o·graph'i·cal·ly** *adv.* —**his·to'ri·og'ra·phy** *n.*

his·to·ry (his'tə rē, his'trē) *n., pl.* **-ries** [< L. < Gr. *historia* < *histōr,* learned] 1. an account of what has happened; narrative 2. *a)* what has happened in the life of a people, country, institution, etc. *b)* a systematic account of this 3. all recorded events of the past 4. the branch of knowledge that deals systematically with the recording, analysing, and correlating of past events 5. a known or recorded past [this coat has a *history*] —**make history** to be or do something important enough to be recorded

his·tri·on·ic (his'trē on'ik) *adj.* [< LL. < L. *histrio,* actor] 1. of, or having the nature of, acting or actors 2. overacted or overacting; theatrical; artificial —**his'tri·on'i·cal·ly** *adv.*

his·tri·on·ics (-iks) *n.pl.* [*sometimes with sing. v.*] 1. theatricals; dramatics 2. an artificial or affected manner, display of emotion, etc.

hit (hit) *vt.* **hit, hit'ting** [OE. *hittan* < ON. *hitta,* to meet with] 1. to come against, usually with force; strike [the car *hit* the tree] 2. to give a blow to; strike 3. to strike by throwing or shooting a missile [to *hit* the target] 4. to cause to bump or strike, as in falling, moving, etc. 5. to affect strongly or adversely [a town *hit* hard by floods] 6. to come upon by accident or after search [to *hit* the right answer] 7. to reach; attain [stocks *hit* a new high] 8. *same as* STRIKE, *vt.* 9, 10, 11 9. [Slang] to apply oneself to steadily or frequently [to *hit* the bottle] —*vi.* 1. to give a blow or blows; strike 2. to attack suddenly 3. to knock, bump, or strike 4. to come by accident or after search (with *on* or *upon*) 5. [Chiefly U.S.] to ignite the combustible mixture in its cylinders: said of an internal-combustion engine —*n.* 1. a blow that strikes its mark 2. a collision 3. an effectively witty or sarcastic remark 4. a stroke of good fortune 5. a successful and popular song, book, play, etc. —**hit it off** to get along well together; be congenial —**hit or miss** in a haphazard or aimless way —**hit the (right) nail on the head** 1. to guess correctly 2. to express a point exactly —**hit the road** [Slang] to leave; go away —**make a hit** to be a success —**hit'ter** *n.*

hit-and-run (-'n run') *adj.* hitting and then fleeing [a *hit-and-run* driver]

hitch (hich) *vi.* [ME. *hicchen,* to move jerkily < ?] 1. to move jerkily; 2. to become fastened or caught 3. [Colloq.] to hitchhike —*vt.* 1. to move, pull, or shift with jerks 2. to raise or pull up with jerks (with *up*) 3. to fasten with a hook, knot etc. 4. [Colloq.] to marry: usually in the passive 5. [Colloq.] to hitchhike —*n.* 1. a short, sudden movement or pull; tug; jerk 2. a hobble; limp 3. a hindrance; obstacle 4. a catching or fastening; catch 5. [Colloq.] a ride obtained by hitchhiking 6. *Naut.* a kind of knot that can be easily undone —**without a hitch** smoothly and successfully —**hitch'er** *n.*

hitch·hike (-hīk') *vi.* **-hiked', -hik'ing** to travel by asking for rides from motorists along the way —*vt.* to get (a ride) or make (one's way) by hitchhiking —**hitch'hik'er** *n.*

hith·er (hith'ər) *adv.* [OE. *hider*] to this place; here —*adj.* on or towards this side; nearer

hith·er·most (-mōst') *adj.* nearest

hith·er·to (-tōō', hith'ər tōō') *adv.* until this time; to now

Hit·ler·ism (hit'lər-iz'm) *n.* the fascist programme, ideas, and methods of Hitler and the Nazis —**Hit'ler·ite'** (-īt') *n., adj.*

hit parade the list of currently most popular records

Hit·tite (hit'īt) *n.* 1. any of an ancient people of Asia Minor and Syria (fl. 1700-700 B.C.) 2. the language of the Hittites —*adj.* of the Hittites, their language, or culture

hive (hīv) *n.* [OE. *hyf*] 1. a box or other shelter for a colony of domestic bees; beehive 2. a colony of bees living in a hive 3. a crowd of busy, active people 4. a place with many busy people —*vt.* **hived, hiv'ing** 1. to gather (bees) into a hive 2. to store up (honey) in a hive —*vi.* 1. to enter a hive 2. to live together as in a hive —**hive off** 1. to withdraw in a group, as bees 2. to assign work to a subsidiary department, etc. 3. to transfer (assets etc.) of a company to another group —**hive'less** *adj.* —**hive'like' adj.*

hives (hīvz) *n.* [orig. Scot. dial.] an allergic skin condition characterized by the appearance of intensely itching wheals

hl hectolitre

H.L. House of Lords

hm hectometre

H.M. 1. Her Majesty 2. His Majesty

H.M.A.S. His (or Her) Majesty's Australian Ship

H.M.C.S. His (or Her) Majesty's Canadian Ship

H.M.I. His (or Her) Majesty's Inspector (of Schools)

H.M.N.Z.S. His (or Her) Majesty's New Zealand Ship

H.M.S. 1. His (or Her) Majesty's Service 2. His (or Her) Majesty's Ship or Steamer

H.M.S.O. His (or Her) Majesty's Stationery Office

H.N.C. Higher National Certificate

H.N.D. Higher National Diploma

ho (hō) *interj.* an exclamation of surprise, derision, etc.: also used to get attention [land *ho!*]

Ho *Chem.* holmium

ho. house

hoar (hôr) *adj.* [OE. *har*] *same as* HOARY

hoard (hôrd) *n.* [OE. *hord*] a supply stored up and hidden or kept in reserve —*vi.* to store away money, goods, etc. —*vt.* to accumulate and store away —**hoard'er** *n.* —**hoard'ing** *n.*

hoard·ing (hôr'din) *n.* [< OFr. < Frank. *hurda,* a pen, fold] 1. a temporary wooden fence around a site of building construction or repair 2. a large board for displaying advertisements

hoar·frost (hôr'frost') *n.* white, frozen dew on the ground, leaves, etc.; rime

hoar·hound (-hound') *n.* *same as* HOREHOUND

hoarse (hôrs) *adj.* **hoars'er, hoars'est** [OE. *has*] 1. sounding harsh and grating, rough and husky, etc. 2. having a rough, husky voice —**hoarse'ly** *adv.* —**hoarse'ness** *n.*

hoars·en (-'n) *vt., vi.* to make or become hoarse

hoar·y (hôr'ē) *adj.* **hoar'i·er, hoar'i·est** 1. white, grey, or greyish-white 2. having white or grey hair because very old 3. very old; ancient —**hoar'i·ly** *adv.* —**hoar'i·ness** *n.*

hoax (hōks) *n.* [< ? HOCUS] a trick or fraud, esp. one meant as a practical joke —*vt.* to deceive with a hoax —**hoax'-er** *n.*

hob¹ (hob) *n.* [? var. of HUB] 1. a projecting ledge at the back or side of a fireplace, for keeping a kettle, pan, etc. warm 2. a peg used as a target in quoits, etc.

hob² (hob) *n.* [old form of *Rob,* for *Robin* Goodfellow, elf of English folklore] an elf; goblin

hob·ble (hob''l) *vi.* **-bled, -bling** [ME. *hobelen* < base of *hoppen,* HOP¹ + freq. suffix] 1. to go unsteadily, haltingly, etc. 2. to walk lamely; limp —*vt.* 1. to cause to limp 2. to hamper the movement of (a horse, etc.) by tying two legs together 3. to hinder —*n.* 1. a halting walk; limp 2. a rope, strap, etc. used to hobble a horse —**hob'bler** *n.*

hob·ble·de·hoy (hob''l dē hoi') *n.* [< ?] an awkward, gawky, adolescent youth

hob·by¹ (hob'ē) *n., pl.* **-bies** [ME. *hoby* < ? Du. *hobben,* to move back and forth] 1. a hobbyhorse 2. something that a person likes to work at, collect, etc. in his spare time —**hob'by·ist** *n.*

hob·by² (hob'ē) *n., pl.* **-bies** [< ME. < OFr. *hobet,* dim. of *hobe,* a hawk] a small falcon

hob·by·horse (-hôrs') *n.* 1. a toy consisting of a horse's head on a stick that one pretends to ride 2. *same as* ROCKING HORSE 3. a favourite topic or fixed idea [on one's *hobby-horse*]

hob·gob·lin (hob'gob'lin) *n.* [HOB² + GOBLIN] 1. an elf; goblin 2. a bogy; bugbear

hob·nail (-nāl') *n.* [HOB¹, sense 2 + NAIL] a short nail with a broad head, put on the soles of heavy shoes to prevent wear or slipping —*vt.* to put hobnails on —**hob'nailed' adj.**

hob·nob (nob') *vi.* **-nobbed', -nob'bing** [< ME. *habben,* to have + *nabben,* not to have, esp. with reference to alternation in drinking] to be on close terms (*with*); associate in a familiar way

ho·bo (hō'bō) *n., pl.* **-bos, -boes** [U.S.] 1. esp. formerly, a migratory worker 2. a vagrant; tramp

Hob·son's choice (hob'sənz) [after T. *Hobson* (1544?-1631), Eng. liveryman, who let horses in strict order according to their position near the door] a choice of taking what is offered or nothing

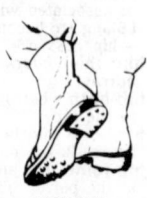

HOBNAILS

hock¹ (hok) *n.* [OE. *hoh,* the heel] the joint bending backward in the hind leg of a horse, ox, etc., but corresponding to the human ankle —*vt.* to disable by cutting the tendons of the hock

hock² (hok) *n.* [< *Hochheimer* < *Hochheim,* Germany] a white Rhine wine

hock³ (hok) *vt., n.* [< Du. *hok,* prison, (slang) debt] [U.S. Slang] *same as* PAWN¹

hock·ey (hok'ē) *n.* [prob. < OFr. *hoquet,* bent stick] 1. a team game played on a field, in which the players, using curved sticks (**hockey sticks**), try to hit a ball into their opponents' goal **2.** [U.S.] *same as* ICE HOCKEY

ho·cus (hō′kəs) *vt.* **-cussed, cus·sing** [contr. < ff.] **1.** to play a trick on; dupe **2.** to drug **3.** to put drugs in (a drink)

ho·cus-po·cus (-pō′kəs) *n.* [imitation L.] **1.** meaningless words used as a formula by conjurers **2.** sleight of hand; legerdemain **3.** trickery; deception —*vt.*, *vi.* **-cussed, -cus·sing** [Colloq.] to trick; dupe

hod (hod) *n.* [prob. < MDu. *hodde*] **1.** a long-handled wooden trough, used for carrying bricks, mortar, etc. on the shoulder **2.** a coal scuttle

Hodge (hoj) *n.* [var. of *Roger*, a masculine name] a countryman; a rustic

hodge-podge (hoj′poj′) *n.* [< OFr. *hochepot*, stew < *hocher*, to shake + *pot*, POT] *same as* HOTCHPOTCH

Hodg·kin's disease (hoj′kinz) [after Dr. T. *Hodgkin* (1798–1866)] a disease characterized by progressive enlargement of the lymph nodes

ho·di·er·nal (hō′di ur′nəl) *adj.* [< L. *hodie*, today] relating to the present day

ho·dom·e·ter (hō dom′i tər) *n.* same as ODOMETER

hoe (hō) *n.* [< OFr. *houe* < OHG. < *houwan*, to hew] a tool with a thin, flat blade set across the end of a long handle, used for weeding, loosening soil, etc. —*vt.*, *vi.* **hoed, hoe′ing** to dig, cultivate, weed, etc. with a hoe —**ho′er** *n.*

hoe·down (-doun) *n.* [infl. by BREAKDOWN, sense 2] [U.S.] **1.** a lively dance, often a square dance **2.** music for this **3.** a party at which hoedowns are danced

hog[1] (hog) *n.*, *pl.* **hogs, hog:** see PLURAL, II, D, 1 [OE. *hogg*] **1.** a pig; esp., a full-grown pig of more than 54kg (120 pounds) raised for its meat **2.** [Colloq.] a selfish, greedy, or filthy person —*vt.* **hogged, hog′ging** [Colloq.] to take all of or an unfair share of —**go the whole hog** [Colloq.] to go all the way

hog[2] (hog) *n.* [OE. *hogg*] a young sheep not yet shorn Also **hogg**

ho·gan (hō′gon) *n.* [Navaho *qoghan*, house] the typical dwelling of the Navaho Indians, built of earth walls supported by timbers

hog·back (hog′bak′) *n.* a ridge with a sharp crest and abruptly sloping sides: also **hog's back**

hog·fish (-fish′) *n.* a fish with bristles on its head

hog·get (hog′it) *n.* [HOG[2] + -ET] a yearling sheep

hog·gish (hog′ish) *adj.* like a hog; very selfish, greedy, coarse, or filthy —**hog′gish·ly** *adv.* —**hog′gish·ness** *n.*

hog·ma·nay (hog′mə nā′) *n.* [< ?] [Scot.] New Year's Eve

hog·nose snake (hog′nōz′) any of several small, harmless N. American snakes with a flat snout: also **hog′nosed′ snake**

hogs·head (hogz′hed′) *n.* [ME. *hoggeshede*, lit., hog's head] **1.** a large barrel or cask of varying capacity **2.** any of various liquid measures, esp. one equal to 63 gallons (286 litres)

hog·wash (-wosh′) *n.* **1.** refuse fed to pigs; swill **2.** useless or insincere talk, writing, etc.

hoick (hoik) *vt.* [< ?] [Slang] to raise abruptly and sharply

hoi pol·loi (hoi′pə loi′) [Gr., the many] the common people; the masses: usually patronizing

hoist (hoist) *vt.* [< earlier *hyce* < Du. *hijschen* & LowG. *hissen*] to raise aloft; lift, esp. by means of a pulley, crane, etc. —*n.* **1.** a hoisting **2.** an apparatus for raising heavy things —**hoist with one's own petard** caught in one's own trap

hoi·ty-toi·ty (hoit′ē toit′ē) *adj.* [< obs. *hoit*, to be noisily mirthful] haughty or petulant

hok·ku (ho′kōō) *n.* *same as* HAIKU

ho·kum (hōk′əm) *n.* [altered < HOCUS(-POCUS)] [Slang] **1.** crudely comic or mawkishly sentimental elements in a play, story, etc., used to gain an immediate emotional response **2.** nonsense; humbug

hold[1] (hōld) *vt.* **held, hold′ing;** archaic pp. **hold′en** [OE. *haldan*] **1.** to take and keep with the hands, arms, or other means; grasp; clutch **2.** to keep from going away; not let escape [to hold a prisoner] **3.** to keep in a certain position or condition [hold your head up] **4.** to restrain or control; specif., a) to keep from falling; support b) to keep from acting [hold your tongue] c) to get and keep control of [to hold our attention] d) to maintain [to hold a course] e) to keep (a room, etc.) for use later **5.** to have and keep as one's own; own; occupy [he holds the office of mayor] **6.** to have or conduct together; specif., to carry on (a meeting, conversation, etc.) **7.** to have room for; contain [this can holds a litre] **8.** to have or keep in the mind **9.** to regard; consider [to hold a statement to be untrue] **10.** to keep a telephone line open by not replacing the receiver **11** Law

a) to decide; decree b) to possess by legal title [to hold a mortgage] **12.** *Music* to prolong (a tone or rest) —*vi.* **1.** to retain a hold, firm contact, etc. [hold tight] **2.** to go on being firm, loyal, etc. [he held to his resolve] **3.** to remain unbroken or unyielding [the rope held] **4.** to be true or valid [a rule which still holds] **5.** to stop; continue [the wind held steady] **6.** to halt: usually in the imperative —*n.* **1.** a grasping or seizing; grip; specif., a way of gripping an opponent in wrestling **2.** a thing to hold on by **3.** a controlling force; restraining authority [to have a hold over someone] **4.** an order to make a temporary halt or delay **5.** an order reserving something **6.** [Archaic] a stronghold **7.** *Music* same as FERMATA —**catch hold of** to seize; grasp —**get hold of 1.** to seize; grasp **2.** to acquire **3.** [Colloq.] to make contact with (a person) —**hold back 1.** to restrain **2.** to refrain **3.** to retain —**hold down 1.** to restrain **2.** [Colloq.] to have and keep (a job) —**hold forth 1.** to preach; lecture **2.** to offer —**hold hard** stop; wait a minute —**hold in 1.** to keep in or back **2.** to control oneself —**hold off 1.** to keep at a distance **2.** to keep from attacking or doing something —**hold on 1.** to retain one's hold **2.** to persist **3.** [Colloq.] stop! wait! **4.** [Colloq.] to wait, esp. during a telephone call until a person, information, etc. is found —**hold one's own** to persist in spite of obstacles —**hold out 1.** to last; endure **2.** to stand firm **3.** to offer —**hold out for** [Colloq.] to stand firm in demanding —**hold out on** [Colloq.] to keep something from someone —**hold over 1.** to postpone consideration of or action on **2.** to keep or stay for an additional period —**hold up 1.** to prop up **2.** to show **3.** to last; endure **4.** to stop; delay **5.** to stop forcibly and rob —**hold with 1.** to agree with **2.** to approve of —**lay (or take) hold of 1.** to seize; grasp **2.** to get control of —**with no holds barred** [Colloq.] with no set rules or limits

hold[2] (hōld) *n.* [altered < HOLE or < MDu. < *hol*] an area below the decks, as in a ship, for carrying cargo

hold·all (hōld′ôl′) *n.* a large travelling bag or case

hold·er (hōld′ər) *n.* **1.** a person who holds; specif., one who is legally entitled to payment of a bill, note, or cheque **2.** a device for holding something

hold·fast (-fäst′) *n.* a specialized organ or part by which certain animals and plants attach themselves to an object

hold·ing (-iŋ) *n.* **1.** land, esp. a farm, rented from another **2.** [*usually pl.*] property owned, esp. stocks or bonds

holding company a corporation organized to hold bonds or stocks of other corporations, which it usually controls

hold·up (-up′) *n.* **1.** a stoppage; delay **2.** the act of stopping forcibly and robbing

hole (hōl) *n.* [OE. *hol*] **1.** a hollow place; cavity [a hole in the ground] **2.** an animal's burrow or lair; den **3.** a small, dingy, squalid place **4.** a) an opening in or through anything; gap b) a tear or rent, as in a garment **5.** a flaw; fault; defect [holes in an argument] **6.** [Colloq.] an embarrassing situation; predicament **7.** *Golf* a) a cylindrical cup sunk into a green, into which the ball is to be hit b) any of the sections of a course, including the tee, fairway, and green **8.** *Physics* an energy state in which particle is missing, esp. when the energy levels above and below are occupied —*vt.* **holed, hol′ing** to put or drive into a hole —**hole in one** *Golf* the act of getting the ball into the hole on the shot from the tee —**hole up** [U.S. Colloq.] **1.** to hibernate, usually in a hole **2.** to shut oneself in —**pick holes in** to pick out errors or flaws in —**hole′y** *adj.*

hole-and-corner (-′nd kôr′nər) *adj.* [Colloq.] furtive or secretive; shady

hol·i·day (hol′ə dā) *n.* [< ME. *holidei* < OE. *haligdag:* see HOLY + DAY] **1.** a religious festival: see HOLY DAY **2.** [*often pl.*] a period in which a break is taken from work or studies for rest or recreation **3.** a day on which work is suspended by law or custom **4.** a rest or respite from something —*adj.* of or suited to a holiday; joyous —*vi.* to spend one's holidays [they holidayed at Margate]

holiday camp a site providing accommodation and recreational facilities, for people to spend a holiday

hol·i·day-mak·er (-mā′kər) *n.* a person on holiday

ho·li·er-than-thou (hō′lē ər than thou) *adj.* annoyingly sanctimonious or self-righteous

ho·li·ly (hō′lə lē) *adv.* in a holy manner

ho·li·ness (-lē nis) *n.* **1.** a being holy **2.** [H-] a title of the Pope (with *His* or *Your*)

ho·lism (hō liz′m) *n.* [HOL(O)- + -ISM] the view that an organic whole has a reality greater than, and independent of, the sum of its parts

hol·land (hol′ənd) *n.* [< *Holland*, where first made] a linen or cotton cloth used for clothing, window blinds, etc.

hol·lan·daise sauce (hol′ən dāz′) [Fr., of Holland] a creamy sauce, as for vegetables, made of butter, egg yolks, lemon juice, etc.

Hol·lands (hol′əndz) *n.* [Du. *hollandsch* (*genever*), Dutch (gin)] gin made in the Netherlands

hol·ler (hol′ər) *vi.*, *vt.*, *n.* [altered < HOLLO] [Colloq.] shout or yell

---

TYPES OF HOE
(A, wire; B, Dutch; C, swan-necked draw; D, plain draw

hol·lo (hol'ō, hə lō') *interj., n., pl.* **-los** 1. a shout or call, as to attract a person's attention or to urge on hounds in hunting 2. a shout of greeting or surprise —*vi., vt.* **-loed, -lo·ing** 1. to shout (at) so as to attract attention 2. to urge on (hounds) by calling out "hollo" 3. to shout, in greeting or surprise

hol·low (hol'ō) *adj.* [OE. *holh*] 1. having a cavity within it; not solid 2. shaped like a cup or bowl; concave 3. deeply set; sunken [*hollow* cheeks] 4. empty or worthless [*hollow* praise] 5. hungry 6. deep-toned and muffled, as though resounding from something hollow —*adv.* in a hollow manner —*n.* 1. a hollow place; cavity; hole 2. a valley —*vt., vi.* to make or become hollow —**beat (someone) hollow** [Colloq.] to outdo or surpass by far —**hollow out** to make by hollowing —**hol'low·ly** *adv.* —**hol'low·ness** *n.*

hollow-ware (hol'ō wer') *n.* metal articles, such as kettles, pots etc., that are hollow

hol·ly (hol'ē) *n., pl.* **-lies** [OE. *holegn*] 1. a small tree or shrub with glossy, sharp-pointed leaves and bright-red berries 2. the leaves and berries, used as Christmas ornaments

hol·ly·hock (hol'ē hok') *n.* [< OE. *halig*, holy + *hoc*, mallow] 1. a tall, biennial plant of the mallow family, with a hairy stem and large, showy flowers of various colours 2. its flower

Hol·ly·wood (hol'ē wood') *n.* [after *Hollywood*, a section of Los Angeles, once the site of many U.S. film studios] the U.S. film industry or its way of life, etc.

holm[1] (hōm) *n.* same as HOLM OAK
holm[2] (hōm) *n.* [ME. < OE., sea: sense infl. by cognate ON. *holmr*, island] 1. an islet in a river or lake 2. low, flat land by a river

hol·mi·um (hōl'mē əm) *n.* [ModL. < *Holmia*, Latinized form of *Stockholm*] a metallic chemical element of the rare-earth group: symbol, Ho; at. wt., 164.930; at. no., 67

HOLLYHOCK

holm oak [< OE. *holegn*, holly] 1. a south European evergreen oak with hollylike leaves 2. its wood

hol·o- [Fr. < L. < Gr. *holos*, whole] *a combining form meaning* whole, entire [*holography*]

hol·o·caust (hol'ə kôst', hō'lə-) *n.* [< OFr. < LL. < Gr. < *holos*, whole + *kaustos*, burnt: see CAUSTIC] great destruction of life, esp. by fire

Hol·o·cene (hol'ə sēn') *adj.* [HOLO- + Gr. *kainos*, recent] designating the Recent Epoch of geological time

hol·o·gram (hol'ə gram', hō'lə-) *n.* a photographic plate containing the record of the interference pattern produced by means of holography

hol·o·graph (-graf') *adj.* [< Fr. < LL. < LGr. < Gr. *holos*, whole + *graphein*, to write] written entirely in the handwriting of the person under whose name it appears —*n.* a holograph document, letter, etc. —**hol'o·graph'ic** *adj.*

ho·log·ra·phy (hə log'rə fē) *n.* [HOLO- + -GRAPHY] a method used to produce three-dimensional images by laser light and to record on a photographic plate the interference patterns from which an image can be reconstructed

hol·o·phote (hol'ə fōt) *n.* [HOLO- + Gr. *phos* (gen. *photos*), light] an apparatus in a light-house to reflect all the light in the required direction

Hol·o·thu·ri·a (hol'ə thyoor'ē ə) *n. pl.* [L.] a genus of sea-slugs; the sea cucumbers

holp (hōlp) *archaic pt. & obs. pp. of* HELP
hol·pen (hōl'p'n) *archaic pp. of* HELP
hols (holz) *n. pl.* [Colloq.] holidays

Hol·stein (hōl'stēn, -stīn) *n.* [after *Schleswig-Holstein*, where orig. bred] *U.S. name for* FRIESIAN

hol·ster (hōl'stər) *n.* [Du.] a pistol case, usually of leather and attached to a belt or saddle

holt[1] (hōlt) *n.* [ME. < OE.] [Archaic] 1. a small wood 2. a wooded hill

holt[2] (hōlt) *n.* [< HOLD[1]] an otter's den

ho·ly (hō'lē) *adj.* **-li·er, -li·est** [OE. *halig* < base of *hal*, sound, whole] [*often* H-] 1. dedicated to religious use; consecrated; sacred 2. spiritually pure; sinless; saintly 3. regarded with or deserving deep respect or reverence 4. [Slang] very much of a [a *holy* terror] —*n., pl.* **-lies** a holy thing or place

Holy Communion any of various Christian rites in which bread and wine are consecrated and received as the body and blood of Jesus or as symbols of them; sacrament of the Eucharist

holy day a day consecrated to religious observances or to a religious festival

Holy Father a title of the Pope
Holy Ghost the third person of the Trinity
Holy Grail see GRAIL

Holy Land Palestine

holy of holies 1. the innermost part of the Jewish tabernacle and Temple, where the ark of the covenant was kept 2. any most sacred place

holy orders 1. the sacrament or rite of ordination 2. the position of being an ordained Christian minister or priest 3. ranks or grades of the Christian ministry; specif., a) *R.C.Ch. same as* MAJOR ORDERS or, sometimes, MINOR ORDERS b) *Anglican Ch.* bishops, priests, and deacons

Holy Roman Empire empire of WC Europe, comprising the German-speaking peoples & N Italy: begun in 800 A.D. or, in another view, in 962, it lasted until Francis II resigned as emperor in 1806

Holy Scripture (or **Scriptures**) *see* BIBLE

Holy See the position, authority, or court of the Pope; Apostolic See

Holy Spirit the spirit of God; specif., the third person of the Trinity

ho·ly·stone (hō'lē stōn') *n.* [<] a flat piece of sandstone for scouring a ship's wooden decks —*vt.* **-stoned'**, **-ston'ing** to scour with a holystone

Holy Synod the administrative council of any branch of the Orthodox Eastern Church

Holy Week the week before Easter
Holy Writ the Bible

hom·age (hom'ij) *n.* [< OFr. < ML. *hominaticum* < L. *homo*, a man] 1. orig., a) a public avowal of allegiance by a vassal to his lord b) an act done or thing given to show the relationship between lord and vassal 2. anything given or done to show reverence, honour, etc.: usually with *do* or *pay* [to pay *homage* to a hero]

hom·burg (hom'bərg) *n.* [< *Homburg*, Prussia] a man's felt hat with a crown dented front to back and a stiff, slightly curved brim

home (hōm) *n.* [OE. *ham*] 1. the place where a person (or family) lives; one's dwelling place 2. the city, region, or country where one was born or reared 3. a place where one likes to be; restful or congenial place 4. the members of a family as a unit; a household and its affairs 5. an institution for the care of orphans, the aged, etc. 6. the natural environment of an animal, plant, etc. 7. the place of origin, development, etc. [Paris is the *home* of fashion] 8. in many games, the base or goal; —*adj.* 1. of one's home or country; domestic 2. of or at the centre of operations 3. played in the city, at the school, etc. where the team originates —*adv.* 1. at, to, or in the direction of home 2. to the point aimed at 3. to the heart of a matter; closely —*vi.* **homed, hom'ing** 1. to go to one's home 2. to have a home —**at home** 1. in one's own house, city, or country 2. as if in one's own home; comfortable; at ease 3. willing to receive visitors —**bring (something) home to** to impress upon or make clear to —**home and dry** [Colloq.] safe; successful —**home (in) on** to be directed as by radar to (a destination) —**home'less** *adj.* —**home'like'** *adj.*

home·bod·y (-bod'ē) *n., pl.* **-bod'ies** a person whose interests and activities focus on the home

home-brew (-broo') *n.* an alcoholic beverage, esp. beer, made at home

Home Counties the counties surrounding London

home·com·ing (-kum'iŋ) *n.* arrival at home

home economics the science and art of managing a home, including nutrition, budgeting, etc.

home farm a farm near or attached to the house of a landed proprietor who has other farms on his estate

Home Guard a volunteer, part-time force recruited for the defence of the United Kingdom in World War 2

home help a woman employed to do housework

home·land (-land') *n.* the country in which one was born or makes one's home

home·ly (-lē) *adj.* **-li·er, -li·est** 1. characteristic of or suitable for home or home life; plain or simple [*homely* virtues] 2. not elegant; crude 3. [U.S.] not good-looking; plain or unattractive —**home'li·ness** *n.*

home-made (-mād') *adj.* 1. made at home 2. as if made at home; esp., plain, simple, or crude

ho·me·o-, hom·oe·o [Gr. *homoio-* < *homos*, same] *a combining form meaning* like, the same, similar

Home Office the department of the Brit. government responsible for law and order, immigration control, and other internal affairs

ho·me·op·a·thy, ho·moe·op·a·thy (hō'mē op'ə thē) *n.* [< G.: see HOMEO- & -PATHY] a system of medical treatment based on the theory that certain diseases can be cured with small doses of drugs which in a healthy person and in large doses would produce symptoms like those of the disease: opposed to ALLOPATHY —**ho'me·o·path'**, **ho'moe·o·path** (-ə path'), **ho·me·op'a·thist**, **ho·moe·op'a·thist** *n.* —**ho'me·o·path'ic**, **ho'moe·o·path'ic** (-ə path'ik) *adj.*

ho·me·o·sta·sis, ho·moe·o·sta·sis (hō'mē ō stā'sis) *n.* [ModL.: see HOMEO- & STASIS] the tendency to maintain, or the maintenance of, stability or equilibrium within an organism, social group, etc. —**ho'me·o·stat'ic, ho'-moe·o·stat'ic** (-stat'ik) *adj.*

home·own·er (hōm'ō'nər) *n.* a person who owns the house he lives in

hom·er (hō'mər) *n.* *same as* HOMING PIGEON

Ho·mer·ic (hō mer'ik) *adj.* of, like, or characteristic of the poet Homer, his poems, or the Greek civilization that they describe (c. 1200–800 B.C.)

home rule the administration of the affairs of a country, colony, city, etc. granted to the citizens who live in it by a superior governing authority

Home Secretary in Britain, the Secretary of State for Home Affairs; the head of the Home Office

home·sick (-sik') *adj.* longing for home —**home'sick'-ness** *n.*

home·spun (-spun') *n.* 1. cloth made of yarn spun at home 2. coarse, loosely woven cloth like this —*adj.* 1. spun at home 2. made of homespun 3. plain; homely [*homespun virtues*]

home·stead (-sted') *n.* 1. a place where a family makes its home, including the land, house, and outbuildings 2. [U.S.] tract of public land granted by the U.S. government to a settler to develop as a farm —**home'stead'er** *n.*

home·stretch (-strech') *n.* 1. the part of a race track between the last turn and the finish line 2. the final part of any undertaking

home·ward (hōm'wərd) *adv., adj.* towards home: also **home'wards** *adv.*

home·work (-wurk') *n.* 1. work done at home 2. schoolwork to be done outside the classroom 3. preparatory or introductory work or study

home·y (-ē) *adj.* **hom'i·er, hom'i·est** *same as* HOMY —**hom'-y·ness** *n.*

hom·i·cide (hom'ə sīd') *n.* [< OFr. < LL. < L. < *homo,* a man + *caedere,* to cut, kill] 1. any killing of one human being by another 2. a person who kills another —**hom'i·ci'-dal** *adj.*

hom·i·let·ics (hom'ə let'iks) *n.pl.* [*with sing.* v.] [< LL. < Gr. < *homilein,* to converse < *homilos:* see ff.] the art of writing and preaching sermons —**hom'i·let'ic, hom'i·let'-i·cal** *adj.*

hom·i·ly (hom'ə lē) *n.,* *pl.* **-lies** [< OFr. < LL. *homilia* < Gr. < *homilos,* assembly, prob. < *homou,* together + *ilē,* crowd] 1. a sermon, esp. one about something in the Bible 2. a solemn, moralizing talk or writing —**hom'i·list** *n.*

hom·ing (hō'miŋ) *adj.* 1. homeward bound 2. having to do with guidance to a goal, target, etc.

homing pigeon a pigeon trained to find its way home from distant places

hom·i·nid (hom'ə nid) *n.* [< ModL. *Hominidae* (family name)] any form of man, extinct or living

hom·i·noid (-noid') *n.* [< ModL. *Hominoidea* (superfamily name)] any form of man or the great apes, extinct or living —*adj.* manlike

ho·mo¹ (hō'mō) *n.,* *pl.* **hom·in·es** (hom'ə nēz') [L., a man] any of a genus of primates including modern man (*Homo sapiens*) and extinct species of man

homo² (hō'mō) *n.,* *pl.* **-mos** [Colloq.] a homosexual person —*adj.* [Colloq.] homosexual

ho·mo- [< Gr. < *homos,* same] *a combining form meaning* same, equal, like

ho·mo·ge·ne·ous (hō'mə jē'nē əs, hom'ə-) *adj.* [< ML. < Gr. < *homos,* same + *genos,* a race, kind] 1. the same in structure, quality, etc.; similar or identical 2. composed of similar or identical parts; uniform —**ho'mo·ge·ne'i·ty** (-jə nē'ə tē) *n.* —**ho'mo·ge·ne·ous·ly** *adv.* —**ho'mo·ge'-ne·ous·ness** *n.*

ho·mog·e·nize (hə moj'ə nīz') *vt.* **-nized', -niz'ing** 1. to make homogeneous 2. to make more uniform throughout; specif., to process (milk) so that the fat particles are so finely divided and emulsified that the cream does not separate on standing Also **ho·mog'e·nise** —**ho·mog'e·ni·za'-tion** *n.* —**ho·mog'e·niz·er** *n.*

ho·mog·e·nous (-ə nəs) *adj.* [HOMO- + -GENOUS] having similarity in structure because of common descent —**ho·mog'e·ny** (-nē) *n.*

hom·o·graph (hom'ə graf', hō'mə-) *n.* [HOMO- + -GRAPH] a word with the same spelling as another but with a different meaning and origin (Ex.: *bow,* the front part of a ship, *bow,* to bend) —**hom'o·graph'ic** *adj.*

ho·moi·o·ther·mal (hō moi'ō thur'məl) *n.* [< Gr. *homoios,* similar + THERMAL] *Zool.* warmblooded: also **ho·moi'-o·ther'mic**

ho·mol·o·gize (hō mol'ə gīz', hə-) *vt.* **-gized', -giz'ing** 1. to make homologous 2. to demonstrate homology in —*vi.* to be homologous

ho·mol·o·gous (-ə gəs) *adj.* [< Gr. < *homos,* same + *legein,* to say] 1. matching in structure, position, character, etc. 2. *Biol.* corresponding in structure and deriving from a common origin, as the wing of a bat and the foreleg of a mouse —**hom·o·logue** *n.*

ho·mol·o·gy (hō mol'ə jē, hə-) *n.,* *pl.* **-gies** 1. the quality or

state of being homologous 2. a homologous correspondence or relationship —**ho·mo·log'·i·cal** *adj.*

ho·mol·o·sine projection (hə mol'ə sin, hō-; -sīn') [< Gr. *homalos,* even, level + SINE] a map of the earth's surface with the land areas shown in their proper relative size and form, with a minimum of distortion

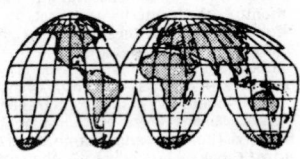
HOMOLOSINE PROJECTION

ho·mo·mor·phism (hō'mə môr'fiz'm) *n.* [HOMO- + -MORPH + -ISM] 1. similarity in form 2. *Biol.* resemblance or correspondence without actual relationship, in structure or origin 3. *Math.* a structure-preserving function Also **ho'mo·mor'phy** —**ho'-mo·mor'phic, ho'mo·mor'phous** *adj.*

hom·o·nym (hom'ə nim, hō'mə-) *n.* [< Fr. < L. < Gr. < *homos,* same + *onyma,* name] a word with the same pronunciation as another but with a different meaning, origin, and, usually, spelling (Ex.: *bore* and *boar*) —**ho·mon·y·mous** (hō mon'ə məs), **hom'o·nym'ic** *adj.*

hom·o·phone (hom'ə fōn') *n.* [< Gr. < *homos,* same + *phōnē,* a sound] 1. any of two or more letters or groups of letters having the same pronunciation (Ex.: *c* in *civil* and *s* in *song*) 2. *same as* HOMONYM

hom·o·phon·ic (hom'ə fon'ik, hō'mə-) *adj.* [< Gr.: see prec.] 1. *Music* having a single part, or voice, carrying the melody 2. of, or having the nature of, a homonym —**ho·moph·o·ny** (hō mof'ə nē) *n.,* *pl.* **-nies**

ho·mop·ter·ous (hō mop'tər əs) *adj.* [HOMO- + -PTEROUS] belonging to an order of insects with sucking mouthparts and two pairs of membranous wings of uniform thickness throughout, as aphids, cicadas, etc.

Ho·mo sa·pi·ens (hō'mō sā'pē enz', hō'mō sap'ē ənz) [ModL.: see HOMO & SAPIENT] modern man; mankind; human being: the only living species of the genus *Homo*

ho·mo·sex·u·al (hō'mə sek'shoo wəl) *adj.* of or having sexual desire for those of the same sex as oneself —*n.* a homosexual person —**ho'mo·sex'u·al'i·ty** (-wal'ə tē) *n.* —**ho'mo·sex'u·al·ly** *adv.*

ho·mo·zy·gote (hō'mō zī'gōt) *n.* [HOMO- + ZYGOTE] a plant or animal having two identical alleles at a single locus on a chromosome, and hence breeding true to type; purebred

ho·mun·cu·lus (hō mun'kyoo ləs) *n.,* *pl.* **-li** (-lī) [L., dim. of *homo,* man] a little man; dwarf

hom·y (hō'mē) *adj.* **hom'i·er, hom'i·est** having qualities usually associated with home; comfortable, familiar, etc. —**hom'i·ness** *n.*

Hon., hon. 1. honourable 2. honorary

hone (hōn) *n.* [< OE. *han,* a stone] a whetstone used to sharpen cutting tools, esp. razors —*vt.* **honed, hon'ing** to sharpen as with a hone

hon·est (on'əst) *adj.* [< OFr. < L. *honestus < honor, honour*] 1. that will not lie, cheat, or steal; trustworthy; truthful 2. *a)* showing fairness and sincerity [*an honest effort*] *b)* gained by fair methods [*an honest living*] 3. being what it seems; genuine [*to give honest measure*] 4. frank and open [*an honest face*] 5. [Archaic] chaste —*adv.* [Colloq.] honestly; truly: an intensive

hon·est·ly (-lē) *adv.* 1. in an honest manner 2. truly; really: an intensive [*honestly,* it is so]

hon·es·ty (on'əs tē) *n.* 1. the state or quality of being honest; specif., *a)* being truthful, trustworthy, or upright *b)* sincerity; straightforwardness 2. a plant with purple flowers and semi-transparent, silvery seedpods

hon·ey (hun'ē) *n.,* *pl.* **-eys** [OE. *hunig*] 1. a thick, sweet, syrupy substance that bees make as food from the nectar of flowers 2. sweet quality; sweetness 3. sweet one; darling 4. [U.S. Colloq.] something pleasing or excellent of its kind —*adj.* 1. of or like honey 2. sweet; dear —*vt.* **-eyed** or **-ied, -ey'ing** 1. to make sweet or pleasant as with honey 2. to flatter

hon·ey·bee (-bē') *n.* a bee that makes honey

hon·ey·comb (-kōm') *n.* 1. the structure of six-sided wax cells made by bees to hold their honey, eggs, etc. 2. any thing like this —*vt.* 1. to fill with holes like a honeycomb; riddle 2. to permeate or undermine [*honeycombed* with intrigue] —*adj.* of, like, or patterned after a honeycomb: also **hon'ey·combed'**

hon·ey·dew (-dyoo') *n.* 1. a sweet fluid exuded from various plants 2. a sweet substance secreted by some juice-sucking plant insects 3. *short for* HONEYDEW MELON

honeydew melon a variety of melon with a smooth, whitish rind and sweet, greenish flesh

honey eater any of a large family of Australasian birds with a long tongue adapted for catching insects or sucking nectar from flowers

hon·eyed (hun'ēd) *adj.* 1. sweetened, covered, or filled with honey **2.** sweet as honey; flattering or affectionate [*honeyed* words]

hon·ey·moon (hun'ē moon') *n.* [as if < HONEY + MOON (? in reference to the waning of the affection of newlyweds), but ? folk-etym. for ON. *hjūnōttsmānathr*, lit., wedding-night month] **1.** formerly, the first month of marriage **2.** the holiday spent together by a newly married couple **3.** a brief period of apparent agreement —*vi.* to have or spend a honeymoon —**hon'ey·moon'er** *n.*

hon·ey·suck·le (-suk''l) *n.* **1.** any of a genus of largely woody plants with small, fragrant flowers of red, yellow, or white **2.** any of several similar plants

hon·ied (hun'ēd) *adj.* same as HONEYED

honk (hoŋk) *n.* [echoic] **1.** the call of a wild goose **2.** any similar sound, as of a car horn —*vi., vt.* to make or cause to make such a sound —**honk'er** *n.*

hon·ky-tonk (hoŋ'kē toŋk') *n.* [< ?] **1.** [Slang] a cheap, disreputable cabaret or nightclub **2.** a style of ragtime piano-playing

hon·or (on'ǝr) *n. U.S. sp. of* HONOUR

hon·o·ra·ri·um (on'ǝ rer'ē ǝm) *n., pl.* **-ri·ums, -ri·a** (-ǝ) [L. *honorarium (donum)*, honorary (gift)] a payment as to a professional person for services which no fee is set

hon·or·ar·y (on'ǝ rǝ rē) *adj.* [L. *honorarius*, of or conferring honour] **1.** given as an honour only [an *honorary* degree] **2.** *a)* designating an office held as an honour only, without service or pay *b)* holding such an office —**hon'or·ar'i·ly** *adv.*

hon·or·if·ic (on'ǝ rif'ik) *adj.* [< L. < *honor* + *facere*, to make] conferring honour; showing respect [an *honorific* title] —**hon'or·if'i·cal·ly** *adv.*

hon·our (on'ǝr) *n.* [< OFr. < L. *honor, honos*] **1.** high regard or great respect given or received; esp. *a)* glory; fame; renown *b)* good reputation; credit **2.** a keen sense of right and wrong; adherence to principles considered right [to behave with *honour*] **3.** chastity; purity **4.** high rank or position; distinction [the great *honour* of the presidency] **5.** [H-] a title given to judges (preceded by *His, Her,* or *Your*) **6.** something done or given as a token of respect; specif., *a)* a social courtesy [may I have the *honour* of this dance?] *b)* [*pl.*] public ceremonies of respect [funeral *honours*] *c)* [*pl.*] special distinction given to students for high academic achievement *d)* [*pl.*] a specialized degree course **7.** one that brings respect and fame to a school, country, etc. **8.** Bridge *a)* any of the five highest cards in a suit *b)* [*pl.*] the four or five highest cards of the trump suit *c)* [*pl.*] in a no-trump hand, the aces **9.** *Golf* the privilege of driving first from the tee —*vt.* **1.** to respect greatly; regard highly **2.** to treat with deference and courtesy **3.** to worship (a deity) **4.** to do something in honour of **5.** to accept and pay when due [to *honour* a cheque] —**do honour to 1.** to show great respect for **2.** to bring honour to —**do the honours** to act as host or hostess, esp. by making introductions, serving at table, etc. —**on** (or **upon**) **one's honour** staking one's good name on one's truthfulness or reliability

hon·our·a·ble (-ǝ b'l) *adj.* **1.** worthy of being honoured; specif., *a)* [H-] of high rank: used as a title of courtesy for certain officials and for the children of certain British peers *b)* noble; illustrious *c)* of good reputation; respectable **2.** having or showing a sense of right and wrong; upright **3.** bringing honour [*honourable* mention] **4.** accompanied with marks of respect [an *honourable* burial] —**hon'our·a·bly** *adv.*

honourable mention a citation of honour esp. to one who was not a winner, as in a competition

honours of war special privileges granted to a defeated enemy, as that of continuing to bear arms

honour system in some schools, prisons, etc., a system whereby individuals are trusted to obey rules, do their work, take tests, etc. without direct supervision

hooch (hooch) *n.* [< Alaskan Ind. *hoochinoo*, crude alcoholic liquor] [Slang] alcoholic liquor, esp. when made or obtained surreptitiously

hood[1] (hood) *n.* [OE. *hod*] **1.** a covering for the head and neck, worn separately or as part of a robe or cloak **2.** anything like a hood in shape or use; specif., *a)* the folding roof of a convertible car *b)* the folding waterproof canopy of a baby's pram *c)* *Falconry* the covering for a falcon's head when it is not chasing game —*vt.* to cover as with a hood —**hood'ed** *adj.* —**hood'less** *adj.*

hood[2] (hood, hood) *n.* [Slang] short for HOODLUM

-hood (hood) [< OE. *had*, order, condition, rank] a suffix meaning: **1.** state, quality, condition [*childhood*] **2.** the whole group of (a specified class, profession, etc.) [*priesthood*]

Hood, Robin see ROBIN HOOD

hooded crow a common crow of Europe and Asia, with a grey body and black head, wings and tail: also called **hood·ie-crow** (hood'ē)

hood·lum (hood'lǝm) *n.* [prob. < G. dial. *hudilump*, wretch] a wild, lawless person, often a member of a gang of criminals —**hood'lum·ism** *n.*

hood·man-blind (hood'mǝn blind') *n.* [Archaic] same as BLINDMAN'S BUFF

hoo·doo (hoo'doo) *n., pl.* **-doos** [var. of VOODOO] [Chiefly U.S.] **1.** same as VOODOO **2.** [Colloq.] *a)* a person or thing that causes bad luck *b)* bad luck —*vt.* [Colloq.] to bring bad luck to

hood·wink (hood'wiŋk') *vt.* [HOOD[1] + WINK] **1.** orig., to blindfold **2.** to deceive; trick; dupe

hoo·ey (hoo'ē) *interj., n.* [echoic] [Slang] nonsense; humbug

hoof (hoof, hoof) *n., pl.* **hoofs, hooves** (hoovz, hoovz) [OE. *hof*] the horny covering on the feet of cattle, deer, horses, etc., or the entire foot —*vt., vi.* [Colloq.] to walk (often with *it*) —**on the hoof** not butchered; alive —**hoofed** *adj.* —**hoof'less** *adj.*

hoof·beat (-bēt') *n.* the sound made by the hoof of an animal when it runs, walks, etc.

hoof·er (hoof'ǝr, hoof'-) *n.* [Slang] a professional dancer, esp. a tap dancer, soft-shoe dancer, etc.

hoo·ha (hoo'hä') *n.* [echoic] [Colloq.] a noisy fuss or commotion

hook (hook) *n.* [< OE. *hoc*] **1.** a curved or bent piece of metal, wood, etc. used to catch, hold, or pull something; specif., *a)* a curved piece of wire with a barbed end, for catching fish *b)* a curved piece used to hang things on, etc. [a coat *hook*] *c)* a small metal catch inserted in a loop, or eye, to fasten clothes together **2.** a curved metal implement for cutting grain, etc. **3.** something shaped like a hook, as a curving headland or cape **4.** *Boxing* a short blow delivered with the arm bent at the elbow **5.** *Music* any of the lines extending from the stem of a note, indicating its value —*vt.* **1.** to fasten as with a hook **2.** to take hold of or catch as with a hook **3.** to shape into a hook **4.** to make (a rug) by drawing strips of cloth or yarn through a canvas or burlap backing with a hook **5.** [Colloq.] to steal; snatch **6.** *Boxing* to hit with a hook —*vi.* **1.** to curve as a hook does **2.** to be fastened with a hook or hooks **3.** to be caught by a hook —**by hook or by crook** by any means, honest or dishonest —**hook, line and sinker** completely —**hook up** to arrange and connect the parts of (a radio, etc.) —**off the hook** [Colloq.] out of trouble, freed from an obligation, etc. —**on one's own hook** [Colloq.] by oneself, without help from others —**sling one's hook** [Slang] to depart

hook·ah, hook·a (hook'ǝ) *n.* [Ar. *huqqah*] an Oriental tobacco pipe with a long, flexible tube by means of which the smoke is drawn through water in a vase or bowl and cooled

HOOKAH

hooked (hookt) *adj.* **1.** curved like a hook **2.** having a hook or hooks **3.** made with a hook [a *hooked* rug] **4.** [Slang] addicted as to the use of a drug (often with *on*) **5.** [Slang] married

hook·er[1] (hook'ǝr) *n.* **1.** one that hooks **2.** [U.S. Slang] a prostitute **3.** *Rugby* the centre forward in the front row of a scrum

hook·er[2] (hook'ǝr) *n.* [Du. *hoeker*] **1.** a small Dutch sailing ship **2.** a fishing smack

Hooke's law (hooks) [after Robert Hooke (1635-1703), Eng. physicist, chemist and inventor] the principle that the stress imposed on an elastic body is directly proportional to the strain produced

hook·up (-up') *n.* **1.** the arrangement and connection of parts, circuits, etc., as in (a) radio **2.** [Colloq.] a connection or alliance

hook·worm (-wurm') *n.* any of a number of small, parasitic roundworms with hooks around the mouth, infesting the small intestine and causing a disorder (**hookworm disease**) characterized by anaemia, weakness, and abdominal pain

hoo·li·gan (hoo'li gǝn) *n.* [< ? *Hooligan* (or *Houlihan*), an Irish family in London] [Slang] a hoodlum, esp. a young one —**hoo'li·gan·ism** *n.*

hoop[1] (hoop) *n.* [OE. *hop*] **1.** a circular band or ring for holding together the staves of a barrel, cask, etc. **2.** anything like a hoop; specif., *a)* any of the rings forming the framework of a hoop skirt *b)* a large ring, often with paper stretched over it, used for circus performers or animals to jump through *c)* a child's toy shaped like a hoop and rolled along the ground *d)* *Basketball* the metal rim of the basket *e)* *Croquet* any of the iron arches through which the ball is driven —*vt.* to bind or fasten as with a hoop; encircle —**go (or be put) through the hoop** to suffer difficulties; undergo an ordeal

hoop[2] (hoop) *n.* same as WHOOP

hoop·la (hoop'lä) *n.* **1.** a game in which rings are thrown to encircle, and so win, prizes **2.** [U.S. Colloq.] *a)* great excitement *b)* showy publicity

hoo·poe (hoo'poo) *n.* [< Fr. *huppe* < L. *upupa*, prob.

echoic] a bird of Africa, C Asia, and Europe with a long, curved bill and an erectile crest

hoop skirt a skirt worn over a framework of hoops, or rings, to make it spread out

hoo·ray (hoo rā', hə-, hoo-) *interj., n., vi., vt.* *same as* HURRAH

hoose·gow, hoos·gow (hoos'gou) *n.* [< Sp. *juzgado,* court of justice, ult. < L. *judex,* JUDGE] [U.S. Slang] a jail

hoot[1] (hoot) *vi.* [orig. eehoic] **1.** to utter its characteristic hollow sound: said of an owl **2.** to utter a sound like this **3.** to shout, esp. in scorn or disapproval **4.** to sound a horn; honk **5.** [Colloq.] to laugh loudly —*vt.* **1.** to express (scorn, disapproval, etc.) by hooting **2.** to express scorn or disapproval by hooting **3.** to chase away by hooting [to *hoot* an actor off the stage] —*n.* **1.** the sound that an owl makes **2.** any sound like this **3.** a shout of scorn or disapproval **4.** the least bit; whit [not worth a *hoot*] **5.** [Colloq.] an amusing or ridiculous person or thing

hoot[2] (hoot) *n.* [< Maori *utu*] [N.Z. slang] money

hoot·en·an·ny (hoot'n an'ē) *n., pl.* **-nies** [a fanciful coinage] [U.S.] a meeting of folk singers, as for public entertainment

hoot·er (hoot'ər) *n.* **1.** a person or thing that hoots, specif., *a)* a car horn *b)* a factory siren **2.** [Colloq.] a nose

hoots (hoots) *interj.* [? var. of HOOT[1]] [Scot.] an exclamation of objection, irritation or impatience

Hoo·ver (hoo'vər) *a trademark for* a type of vacuum cleaner —*n.* [h-] popularly, any vacuum cleaner —*vt.* [h-] to clean with a vacuum cleaner

hooves (hoovz, hoovz) *n.* *alt. pl. of* HOOF

hop[1] (hop) *vi.* **hopped, hop'ping** [OE. *hoppian*] **1.** to make a short leap or leaps on one foot **2.** to move by leaping or springing on both (or all) feet at once, as a bird, frog, etc. **3.** [Colloq.] *a)* to go or move briskly *b)* to take a short, quick trip (with *up, down,* or *over*) —*vt.* to jump over [to *hop* a fence] —*n.* **1.** a hopping **2.** [Colloq.] a dance, esp. an informal one **3.** [Colloq.] a short flight in an aircraft —**hop it** [Slang] go away —**on the hop** [Colloq.] **1.** active; busy **2.** unawares; unprepared [caught *on the hop*]

hop[2] (hop) *n.* [< MDu. *hoppe*] **1.** a climbing plant with the female flowers borne in small cones **2.** [*pl.*] the dried ripe cones, used for flavouring beer, ale, etc. —*vt.* **hopped, hop'-ping** to flavour with hops

hop-bind (-bīnd) *n.* the stalk on which hops grow: also **hop-bine** (-bīn)

hope (hōp) *n.* [OE. *hopa*] **1.** a feeling that what is wanted will happen **2.** the thing that one has a hope for **3.** a reason for hope **4.** a person or thing on which one may base some hope **5.** [Archaic] trust; reliance —*vt.* **hoped, hop'ing 1.** to want and expect **2.** to want very much —*vi.* **1.** to have hope (*for*) **2.** [Archaic] to trust or rely —**hope against hope** to continue having hope though it seems baseless —**hop'er** *n.*

hope chest U.S. name for BOTTOM DRAWER

hope·ful (-fəl) *adj.* **1.** feeling or showing hope **2.** inspiring or giving hope —*n.* a person who hopes, or seems likely, to succeed —**hope'ful·ness** *n.*

hope·ful·ly (-ē) *adv.* **1.** in a hopeful manner **2.** [Colloq.] it is to be hoped (that) [*hopefully* we will win]: regarded by some as a loose usage

hope·less (-lis) *adj.* **1.** without hope **2.** allowing no hope [a *hopeless* situation] **3.** impossible to solve, deal with, etc. —**hope'less·ly** *adv.* —**hope'less·ness** *n.*

hop·lite (hop'līt) *n.* [< Gr. < *hoplon,* a tool] a heavily armed foot soldier of ancient Greece

hop·per (hop'ər) *n.* **1.** a person or thing that hops **2.** any hopping insect **3.** a container from which the contents can be emptied slowly and evenly [the *hopper* of an automatic coal stoker]

hop·sack·ing (hop'sak'iŋ) *n.* [lit., sacking for hops] **1.** a coarse material for bags **2.** a fabric somewhat simulating this, used for suits, etc. Also **hop'sack'**

hop·scotch (hop'skoch') *n.* [HOP[1] + SCOTCH] a children's game in which each player hops from one compartment to another of a figure drawn on the ground

ho·ra·ry (hô'rə rē) *adj.* [ML. *horarius* < L. *hora,* hour] **1.** of or indicating an hour or hours **2.** occurring once every hour

horde (hôrd) *n.* [< Fr. < G. < Pol. *horda* < Turk. *ordū*] **1.** a nomadic tribe or clan of Mongols **2.** a large, moving crowd; swarm —*vi.* **hord'ed, hord'ing** to form or gather in a horde

hore·hound (hôr'hound') *n.* [< OE. < *har,* white + *hune,* horehound] **1.** a bitter labiate plant with white, downy leaves **2.** a bitter juice extracted from its leaves **3.** a cough medicine or lozenge made with this juice

ho·ri·zon (hə rī'z'n) *n.* [< OFr. < L. < Gr. *horizōn* (*kyklos*), the bounding (circle)] **1.** the line where the sky seems to meet the earth: called **visible** or **apparent horizon 2.** [*usually pl.*] the limit of one's experience, interest, knowledge, etc.

hor·i·zon·tal (hor'ə zon't'l) *adj.* **1.** *a)* parallel to the plane of the horizon; not vertical *b)* placed or acting in a

horizontal direction **2.** flat and even; level **3.** at, or made up of elements at, the same level or status [a *horizontal* amalgamation] —*n.* a horizontal line, plane, etc. —**hor'·i·zon·tal'i·ty** (-tal'ə tē) *n.* —**hor'i·zon'tal·ly** *adv.*

hor·mone (hôr'mōn) *n.* [< Gr. < *horman,* to excite < *hormē,* impulse] **1.** a substance formed in some organ of the body, as the adrenal glands, pituitary, etc., and carried to another organ or tissue, where it has a specific effect: often prepared synthetically **2.** a similar substance in plants —**hor·mo'nai** (-mō'n'l), **hor·mon·ic** (-mon'ik) *adj.*

horn (hôrn) *n.* [OE.] **1.** *a)* a hard, permanent projection of bone or keratin, that grows on the head of cattle, sheep, etc. *b)* the antler of a deer, shed annually **2.** anything that protrudes from the head of an animal, as a tentacle of a snail **3.** the substance that horns are made of **4.** a container made by hollowing out a horn **5.** a cornucopia **6.** anything shaped like a horn; specif., *a)* a peninsula or cape *b)* either end of a crescent *c)* a projection above the pommel of a cowboy's saddle **7.** *a)* an instrument made of horn and sounded by blowing *b)* any brass instrument; specif., the French horn; also, *Jazz* any wind instrument *c)* a device sounded to give a warning [a *foghorn*] *d)* a horn-shaped loudspeaker —*vt.* **1.** to strike or gore with the horns **2.** to furnish with horns —*adj.* made of horn —**horn in (on)** [Colloq.] to meddle (in) —**pull (or draw or haul) in one's horns 1.** to hold oneself back **2.** to withdraw; recant **3.** to economize —**horned** *adj.* —**horn'-less** *adj.* —**horn'like** *adj.*

horn·beam (-bēm) *n.* **1.** any of various small, hardy trees of the birch family **2.** the very hard, white wood of this tree

horn·bill (-bil') *n.* any of a family of large, tropical, birds of Asia and Africa with a huge, curved bill

horn·blende (-blend') *n.* [G.: see HORN & BLENDE] a black, rock-forming mineral, a type of amphibole common in some granitic rocks

horn·book (-book') *n.* a parchment sheet with the alphabet, numbers, etc. on it, mounted on a small board under a thin, clear plate of horn: formerly a child's primer

horned toad any of several small, scaly American lizards that eat insects and have short tails and hornlike spines

horned viper a poisonous N African snake with a hornlike spine above each eye

hor·net (hôr'nit) *n.* [OE. *hyrnet*] any of several large, yellow-and-black social wasps —**hornets' nest** an unpleasant situation; trouble [stir up a *hornets' nest*]

horn of plenty same as CORNUCOPIA

horn·pipe (hôrn'pīp') *n.* **1.** an obsolete wind instrument with a bell and mouthpiece made of horn **2.** a lively dance formerly popular with sailors **3.** music for this

horn·swog·gle (-swog''l) *vt.* **-gled, -gling** [< ?] [Chiefly U.S. Slang] to swindle; trick

horn·y (hôr'nē) *adj.* **horn'i·er, horn'i·est 1.** of, like, or made of horn **2.** having horns **3.** toughened and calloused **4.** [Slang] lustful —**horn'i·ness** *n.*

ho·ro·loge (hor'ə lōj') *n.* [< OFr. < L. < Gr. < *hōra,* hour + *legein,* to tell] [Now Rare] a timepiece; clock, hourglass, sundial, etc.

ho·rol·o·gist (ho rol'ə jist) *n.* an expert in horology; maker of or dealer in timepieces: also **ho·rol'o·ger**

ho·rol·o·gy (ho rol'ə jē) *n.* [< Gr. *hōra,* hour + -LOGY] the science or art of measuring time or making timepieces —**hor·o·log·ic** (hor'ə loj'ik), **hor'o·log'i·cal** *adj.*

hor·o·scope (hor'ə skōp') *n.* [Fr. < L. < Gr. < *hōra,* hour + *skopos,* watcher] **1.** the position of the planets and stars with relation to one another at a given time, esp. at a person's birth, regarded in astrology as determining his destiny **2.** a chart of the zodiacal signs and the positions of the planets, etc. by which astrologers profess to tell a person's future —**hor'o·scop'ic** (-skop'ik) *adj.* —**ho·ros·co·py** (ho ros'kə pē) *n.*

hor·ren·dous (ho ren'dəs) *adj.* [L. *horrendus* < prp. of *horrere,* to bristle] horrible; frightful —**hor·ren'dous·ly** *adv.*

hor·ri·ble (hor'ə b'l) *adj.* [< OFr. < L. < *horrere:* see prec.] **1.** causing a feeling of horror; terrible; dreadful **2.** [Colloq.] very bad, ugly, unpleasant, etc. —**hor'ri·ble·ness** *n.* —**hor'-ri·bly** *adv.*

hor·rid (hor'id) *adj.* **1.** causing a feeling of horror; terrible; revolting **2.** very bad, ugly, unpleasant, etc. —**hor'rid·ly** *adv.* —**hor'rid·ness** *n.*

hor·rif·ic (ho rif'ik, hə-) *adj.* horrifying

hor·ri·fy (hor'ə fī') *vt.* **-fied', -fy'ing 1.** to cause to feel horror **2.** [Colloq.] to shock or disgust —**hor'ri·fi·ca'tion** *n.*

hor·rip·i·la·tion (ho rip'ə lā'shən) *n.* [LL. *horripilatio* < *horripilare,* to bristle with hairs] the erection of hair, as from fear, disease, or cold; goose flesh

hor·ror (hor'ər) *n.* [< OFr. < L. *horror* < *horrere,* to bristle, be afraid] **1.** the strong feeling caused by something frightful or shocking; terror and repugnance **2.** strong dislike or aversion **3.** the quality of causing horror **4.** something that causes horror **5.** [Colloq.] something very bad, ugly, disagreeable, etc. —*adj.* intended to cause

horror [*horror* films] —**the horrors** [Colloq.] a fit of extreme nervousness, panic, etc.

‡**hors de com·bat** (ôr′də kŏn bà′) [Fr., out of combat] put out of action; disabled

hors d'oeu·vre (ôr′dʉrv′; *Fr.* ôr dö′vr′) *pl.* **hors′-d'oeuvres** (dʉrvz′); *Fr.* **hors d'oeu′vre** [Fr., lit., outside the work] an appetizer, as olives, anchovies, canapés, etc., served usually at the beginning of a meal

horse (hôrs) *n.,* *pl.* **hors′es, horse:** see PLURAL, II, D, 1 [OE. *hors*] **1.** a large, strong animal with four legs, solid hoofs, and flowing mane and tail, long ago domesticated for drawing loads, carrying riders, etc. **2.** the full-grown male of the horse **3.** a frame on legs to support something [a *sawhorse*] **4.** *slang for:* a) HORSEPOWER b) HEROIN **5.** *Gym.* a padded block on legs, used for jumping or vaulting **6.** *Mil.* [with *pl. v.*] mounted troops; cavalry —*vt.* **horsed, hors′ing** to supply with a horse or horses; put on horseback —*vi.* to mount or go on horseback —*adj.* **1.** of a horse or horses **2.** mounted on horses **3.** large, strong, or coarse of its kind [*horseradish*] —**from the horse's mouth** [Colloq.] from the original or authoritative source of information —**hold one's horses** [Colloq.] to curb one's impatience —**horse around** [Colloq.] to engage in horseplay —**horse of another** (or **a different**) **colour** an entirely different matter —**on one's high horse** [Colloq.] acting in an arrogant or disdainful manner —**to horse!** mount your horse!

HORSE (sense 5)

horse·back (-bak′) *n.* the back of a horse —*adv.* on horseback

horse block a block of stone or wood used when mounting, or dismounting from, a horse

horse-box (-boks′) *n.* a van or trailer for transporting horses

horse brass a brass ornament, usually circular, originally attached to a horse's harness

horse chestnut 1. a) a tree with large, palmately compound leaves, clusters of pink or white flowers, and glossy brown seeds b) its seed **2.** any of various related shrubs or trees —**horse′-chest′nut** *adj.*

horse·flesh (-flesh′) *n.* **1.** the flesh of the horse, esp. as food **2.** horses collectively

horse·fly (-flī′) *n.,* *pl.* **-flies′** any of various large flies, the female of which sucks the blood of horses, cattle, etc.

horse·hair (-her′) *n.* **1.** hair from the mane or tail of a horse **2.** a stiff fabric made from this hair; haircloth —*adj.* **1.** of horsehair **2.** covered or stuffed with horsehair

horse·hide (-hīd′) *n.* **1.** the hide of a horse **2.** leather made from this

horse latitudes either of two belts of calms, light winds, and high barometric pressure, at c. 30°–35° N. and S. latitude

horse·laugh (-läf′) *n.* a loud, boisterous, usually derisive laugh; guffaw

horse·leech (-lēch′) *n.* **1.** a large, freshwater leech **2.** [Archaic] a veterinary surgeon

horse·less (-lis) *adj.* **1.** without a horse **2.** self-propelled [a *horseless* carriage]

horse·man (-mən) *n.,* *pl.* **-men 1.** a man who rides on horseback **2.** a man skilled in the riding or care of horses —**horse′man·ship′** *n.*

horse opera [U.S. Slang] *same as* WESTERN (*n.*)

horse pistol a large pistol formerly carried by horsemen

horse·play (-plā′) *n.* rough, boisterous fun

horse·pow·er (-pou′ər) *n.* a unit for measuring the power of motors or engines, equal to 746 watts or to a rate of 33 000 foot-pounds per minute

horse·rad·ish (-rad′ish) *n.* **1.** a plant of the cabbage family, grown for its pungent, white root **2.** a relish made by grating this root

horse sense [Colloq.] ordinary common sense

horse·shoe (hôr′shōō′, hôrs′-) *n.* **1.** a flat, U-shaped, protective metal plate nailed to a horse's hoof **2.** anything shaped like this —*vt.* **-shoed′, -shoe′ing** to fit with a horseshoe or horseshoes —**horse′sho′er** *n.*

horseshoe bat any of several species of bat with leaf-shaped appendages on the snout

horseshoe crab a sea arthropod shaped like the base of a horse's foot and having a long, spinelike tail: also **king crab**

horse·tail (hôrs′tāl′) *n.* **1.** a horse's tail **2.** a rushlike plant with hollow, jointed stems and scalelike leaves

horse trade [U.S.] any bargaining marked by shrewd calculation —**horse′-trade′** *vi.* **-trad′ed, -trad′ing** —**horse′-trad′er** *n.*

horse·whip (-hwip′, -wip′) *n.* a whip for driving or

managing horses —*vt.* **-whipped′, -whip′ping** to lash with a horsewhip

horse·wom·an (-wōom′ən) *n.,* *pl.* **-wom′en 1.** a woman who rides on horseback **2.** a woman skilled in the riding or care of horses

horst (horst) *n.* [G.] *Geol.* a raised, usually elongated, rock mass between two faults

hors·y (hôr′sē) *adj.* **hors′i·er, hors′i·est 1.** of, like, or suggesting a horse; esp., having large features and a big body that looks strong but awkward **2.** of, like, or characteristic of people who are fond of horses, fox hunting, or horse racing Also **hors′ey** —**hors′i·ly** *adv.* —**hors′i·ness** *n.*

hort. 1. horticultural **2.** horticulture

hor·ta·to·ry (hôr′tə tər ē) *adj.* [< LL. < L. pp. of *hortari,* freq. of *horiri,* to urge] **1.** encouraging or urging to good deeds **2.** exhorting; giving advice Also **hor′ta·tive** —**hor′ta′tion** *n.*

hor·ti·cul·ture (hôr′tə kul′chər) *n.* [< L. *hortus,* a garden + *cultura,* culture] the art or science of growing flowers, fruits, vegetables, etc. —**hor′ti·cul′tur·al** *adj.* —**hor′ti·cul′tur·ist** *n.*

Hos. Hosea

ho·san·na (hō zan′ə) *n., interj.* [< OE. < LL. < Gr. *hōsanna* < Heb. *hōshī′āh nnā,* lit., save, we pray] an exclamation of praise to God

hose (hōz) *n.,* *pl.* **hose** or, for 3, usually **hos′es** [OE. *hosa*] **1.** orig., a man's tightfitting outer garment covering the hips, legs, and feet **2.** [*pl.*] a) stockings b) socks **3.** [prob. infl. by Du. *hoos,* water pipe] a flexible pipe or tube, used to convey fluids, esp. water from a hydrant —*vt.* **hosed, hos′ing** to water with a hose

ho·sen (hō′z'n) *n. archaic pl.* of HOSE (*n.* 1 & 2)

ho·sier (hō′zyər) *n.* a person who makes or sells hosiery

ho·sier·y (-ē) *n.* **1.** hose; stockings and socks **2.** similar knitted or woven goods

hos·pice (hos′pis) *n.* [Fr. < L. < *hospes,* host, guest] a place of shelter for travellers, esp. such a shelter maintained by monks

hos·pi·ta·ble (hos′pi tə b'l, hos pit′ə-) *adj.* [MFr. < ML. < *hospes:* see prec.] **1.** showing or characterized by friendliness, kindness, and solicitude toward guests **2.** favouring health, growth, etc. [a *hospitable* climate] **3.** receptive or open, as to new ideas —**hos′pi·ta·bly** *adv.*

hos·pi·tal (hos′pi t'l) *n.* [< OFr. < LL. *hospitale,* inn < L. < *hospes:* see HOSPICE] **1.** [Archaic] a charitable institution [a *foundling hospital*] **2.** an institution where the ill or injured may receive medical or surgical treatment, nursing care, lodging, etc.

hos·pi·tal·i·ty (hos′pə tal′ə tē) *n.,* *pl.* **-ties** the act, practice, or quality of being hospitable

hos·pi·tal·ize (hos′pi t'l īz′) *vt.* **-ized′, -iz′ing** to send to, put in, or admit to a hospital —**hos′pi·tal·i·za′tion** *n.*

hos·pi·tal·ler (hos′pi tal ər) *n.* a person, esp. a member of certain religious orders, dedicated to the care of the sick or poor in hospitals

host[1] (hōst) *n.* [< OFr. < ML. < L. *hostia,* animal sacrificed] a wafer of the Eucharist; esp., [H-] a consecrated wafer

host[2] (hōst) *n.* [< OFr. < L. *hospes:* see HOSPICE] **1.** a man who entertains guests in his own home or at his own expense **2.** a man who keeps an inn or hotel **3.** any organism on or in which another (called a *parasite*) lives —*vi., vt.* to act as host or hostess (to)

host[3] (hōst) *n.* [< OFr. < ML. < L. *hostis,* army] **1.** an army **2.** a multitude; great number

hos·tage (hos′tij) *n.* [< OFr. < *hoste:* see HOST[2]] a person given as a pledge, or taken prisoner as by an enemy, until certain conditions are met

hos·tel (hos′t'l) *n.* [see HOSPITAL] **1.** [Archaic] an inn; hostelry **2.** *same as* YOUTH HOSTEL **3.** a residential establishment for nurses, students, etc.

hos·tel·ler (-ər) *n.* **1.** [Archaic] an innkeeper **2.** a traveller who stops at youth hostels

hos·tel·ry (-rē) *n., pl.* **-ries** [Archaic] an inn; hotel

host·ess (hōs′tis, hōs tes′) *n.* **1.** a woman who entertains guests in her own home or at her own expense; often, the wife of a host **2.** a) a stewardess, as on an aeroplane b) a woman employed in a club, restaurant, etc. to receive and serve patrons c) a woman who serves as paid partner at a public dance hall

hos·tile (hos′til) *adj.* [< L. < *hostis,* enemy] **1.** of or characteristic of an enemy **2.** unfriendly; antagonistic **3.** not hospitable; adverse —**hos′tile·ly** *adv.*

hos·til·i·ty (hos til′ə tē) *n., pl.* **-ties 1.** a feeling of enmity, ill will, unfriendliness, etc. **2.** a) an expression of enmity and ill will; hostile act b) [*pl.*] acts of war; warfare

hos·tler (os′lər) *n.* [contr. of HOSTELLER] *same as* OSTLER

hot (hot) *adj.* **hot′ter, hot′test** [OE. *hat*] **1.** a) having a high temperature, esp. one that is higher than that of the human body b) having a relatively or abnormally high temperature

2. producing a burning sensation [*hot* pepper] **3.** full of or characterized by any intense feeling or activity, as *a)* impetuous; excitable [a *hot* temper] *b)* violent; angry [*hot* words] *c)* full of enthusiasm; eagerly intent *d)* lustful *e)* very controversial **4.** following closely [*hot* pursuit] **5.** as if heated by friction; specif., *a)* electrically charged [a *hot* wire] *b)* [Colloq.] highly radioactive **6.** designating or of a colour that suggests heat, as intense red **7.** [Colloq.] that has not yet lost heat, freshness, etc.; specif., *a)* recent; new [*hot* news] *b)* clear; strong [a *hot* scent] *c)* recent and from an inside source [a *hot* tip] **8.** [Slang] *a)* recently stolen *b)* sought by the police **9.** [Slang] excellent, good, etc. **10.** *Jazz* designating or of music or playing having exciting rhythmic and tonal effects, improvisation, etc. —*adv.* in a hot manner —**hot under the collar** [Colloq.] embarrassed; annoyed —**hot up** [Colloq.] to heat or warm up —**make it hot for** [Colloq.] to make things uncomfortable for —**sell** (or **go**) **like hot cakes** [Colloq.] to be sold or disappear rapidly —**hot′ly** *adv.* —**hot′ness** *n.*

hot air [Slang] empty or pretentious talk

hot-bed (-bed′) *n.* **1.** a bed of earth covered with glass and heated by manure, for forcing plants **2.** any place that fosters rapid growth

hot-blood-ed (-blud′id) *adj.* easily excited; excitable, ardent, passionate, reckless, etc.

hot-box (-boks′) *n.* an overheated bearing on an axle or shaft

hot cell a shielded enclosure used in handling radioactive materials by remote control

hotch-potch (hoch′poch′) *n.* [ME. *hochepot* < OFr., stew] **1.** a thick stew of various meats and vegetables **2.** any jumbled mixture; mess

hot cross bun a bun marked with a cross, eaten esp. on Good Friday

hot dog [Colloq.] a sausage, esp. a frankfurter, served in a soft roll

ho-tel (hō tel′, ōt-) *n.* [< Fr. < OFr. *hostel*, HOSTEL] an establishment providing lodging, and often meals, for travellers, semipermanent guests, etc.

ho-tel-ier (hō′tel yā′, -tel′ē ǝ) *n.* [Fr.] an owner or manager of a hotel

hot-foot (hot′foot′) *adv.* [Colloq.] in great haste

hot-head (-hed′) *n.* a hotheaded person

hot-head-ed (-hed′id) *adj.* **1.** quick-tempered; easily made angry **2.** hasty; impetuous —**hot′head′ed-ly** *adv.* —**hot′-head′ed-ness** *n.*

hot-house (-hous′) *n.* a heated building for growing plants; greenhouse —*adj.* **1.** grown in a hothouse **2.** needing careful treatment; delicate

hot line a telephone or telegraph line for direct, instant communication in an emergency or crisis, esp. between heads of state

hot money capital transferred from one commercial centre to another to take advantage of the highest interest rates

hot pepper any of various pungent peppers

hot-plate (-plāt′) *n.* **1.** an electrically heated plate on a cooker **2.** a portable device, heated electrically or by spirit lamps, etc., on which food can be kept warm

hot-pot (-pot′) *n.* meat and vegetables cooked together in a tightly covered pot

hot potato a matter that is difficult to handle, as because it is very controversial, risky, etc.

hot-press (-pres′) *vt.* to exert heat and pressure on, as in glossing paper or cloth —*n.* a machine for doing this

hot rod [Slang] **1.** [Chiefly U.S.] an old car adjusted or rebuilt for quick acceleration and high speed **2.** [Chiefly U.S.] a driver of hot rods: also **hot rodder**

hot seat [Slang] **1.** any position of embarrassment, difficulty, etc., **2.** [U.S.] *same as* ELECTRIC CHAIR

hot-spur (-spur′) *n.* [nickname of *Sir Henry Percy*: cf. Shakespeare's *Henry IV*] a rash, hotheaded person

hot stuff [Colloq.] any person or thing considered important, exciting, sexually attractive, etc.

hot-tem-pered (-tem′pǝrd) *adj.* having a fiery temper; easily made angry

Hot-ten-tot (hot′'n tot′) *n.* [Afrik.: echoic origin] **1.** a member of a nomadic pastoral people of SW Africa **2.** their language —*adj.* of the Hottentots or their language

hot war actual warfare: opposed to COLD WAR

hot water [Colloq.] trouble: preceded by *in* or *into*

hot-water bottle (hot′wôt′ǝr) a container, usually made of rubber, filled with hot water and used to provide warmth

hound (hound) *n.* [OE. *hund*, a dog] **1.** any of several breeds of hunting dogs with long, drooping ears and short hair **2.** any dog **3.** a contemptible person **4.** *a)* [Chiefly U.S. Slang] a devotee or fan *b)* a keen pursuer [a *newshound*] —*vt.* **1.** to hunt or chase with or as with hounds [to *hound* a debtor] **2.** to urge on; incite to pursuit —**follow the** (or **ride to**) **hounds** to hunt (a fox, etc.) on horseback with hounds

hounds-tooth check (houndz′tōōth′) a pattern of irregular broken checks, used in woven material

hour (our) *n.* [< OFr. < L. < Gr. *hōra*, hour, time] **1.** a division of time, one of the twenty-four parts of a day; sixty minutes **2.** a point or period of time; specif., *a)* a fixed point or period of time for a particular activity, etc. [the dinner *hour*] *b)* [pl.] a period fixed for work, etc. [office *hours*] *c)* [pl.] the usual times for getting up or going to bed [to keep late *hours*] *d)* an indefinite period of a specified kind [his finest *hour*] **3.** the time of day as indicated by a timepiece **4.** a measure of distance set by the time it takes to travel it **5.** *Astron.* 1/24 of a SIDEREAL DAY **6.** *Eccles. a) same as* CANONICAL HOUR *b)* the prayers said at a canonical hour —**after hours** after the regular hours for business, school, etc. —**of the hour** prominent at this time —**the small** (or **wee**) **hours** the hours just after midnight

hour circle *Astron.* a great circle on the celestial sphere passing through the celestial poles and a specified point, such as a star

hour-glass (-gläs′) *n.* an instrument for measuring time by the trickling of sand, mercury, etc. from one glass bulb to another below it: the shift of contents is measured in hours —*adj.* of or like an hourglass in shape: said esp. of a female figure with a narrow waist

hou-ri (hoor′ē, hou′rē) *n., pl.* **-ris** [Fr. < Per. *hūri* < Ar., ult. < *hawira*, to be dark-eyed] a beautiful nymph of the Moslem Paradise

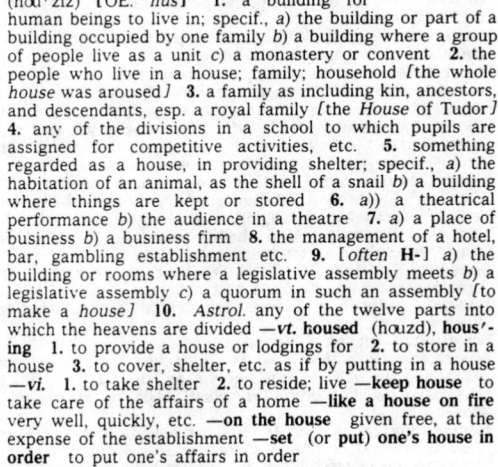

HOURGLASS

hour-ly (our′lē) *adj.* **1.** done or happening every hour or during an hour **2.** reckoned by the hour [*hourly* wage] **3.** continual —*adv.* **1.** at or during every hour **2.** at any hour **3.** continually

house (hous; *for v.* houz) *n., pl.* **hous-es** (hou′ziz) [OE. *hus*] **1.** a building for human beings to live in; specif., *a)* the building or part of a building occupied by one family *b)* a building where a group of people live as a unit *c)* a monastery or convent **2.** the people who live in a house; family; household [the whole *house* was aroused] **3.** a family as including kin, ancestors, and descendants, esp. a royal family [the *House* of Tudor] **4.** any of the divisions in a school to which pupils are assigned for competitive activities, etc. **5.** something regarded as a house, in providing shelter; specif., *a)* the habitation of an animal, as the shell of a snail *b)* a building where things are kept or stored **6.** a)) a theatrical performance *b)* the audience in a theatre **7.** *a)* a place of business *b)* a business firm **8.** the management of a hotel, bar, gambling establishment etc. **9.** [often **H-**] *a)* the building or rooms where a legislative assembly meets *b)* a legislative assembly *c)* a quorum in such an assembly [to make a *house*] **10.** *Astrol.* any of the twelve parts into which the heavens are divided —*vt.* **housed** (houzd), **hous′-ing 1.** to provide a house or lodgings for **2.** to store in a house **3.** to cover, shelter, etc. as if by putting in a house —*vi.* **1.** to take shelter **2.** to reside; live —**keep house** to take care of the affairs of a home —**like a house on fire** very well, quickly, etc. —**on the house** given free, at the expense of the establishment —**set** (or **put**) **one's house in order** to put one's affairs in order

house agent *same as* ESTATE AGENT (sense 1)

house arrest detention of an arrested person in his own house, often under guard

house-boat (-bōt′) *n.* a large, flat-bottomed boat designed for use as a dwelling place

house-break-ing (-brāk′in) *n.* the act of breaking into another's house to commit theft or some other felony —**house′break′er** *n.*

house-coat (-kōt′) *n.* a woman's long, loose garment for casual wear at home

house-craft (-kräft′) *n.* the art of managing a home

house-fly (-flī′) *n., pl.* **-flies′** a two-winged fly found in and around houses: it feeds on rubbish, manure, and food

house-ful (-fool′) *n.* as much as a house will hold or provide room for [a *houseful* of guests]

house-hold (-hōld′) *n.* **1.** all those living in one house; family, or family and servants **2.** the home and its affairs —*adj.* **1.** of a household **2.** ordinary

house-hold-er (-hōl′dǝr) *n.* **1.** one who owns or maintains a house **2.** the head of a household

household word a very familiar word or saying

house-keep-er (-kēp′ǝr) *n.* a woman who manages a home, esp. one hired to do so

house-keep-ing (-in) *n.* **1.** the management of a house and domestic affairs **2.** the amount of money available per week or month for buying food, etc.

house-lights (-līts′) *n.pl.* lights that illuminate the part of a theatre where the audience sits

house·maid (-măd') *n.* a girl or woman servant who does housework

housemaid's knee an inflammation of the saclike cavity covering the kneecap

house·man (-mən) *n.* a recently qualified doctor who holds a resident post in a hospital

house martin a bird of the swallow family that builds its nest under the eaves of a house

house·moth·er (-muth'ər) *n.* a woman in charge of a children's home, etc.

house mouse a small, grey, or brownish-grey, mouse commonly found in houses

house of cards any flimsy structure, plan, etc.

House of Commons the lower branch of the legislature of Great Britain or Canada

house of correction [U.S.] a place of short-term confinement for persons convicted of minor offences

House of Keys (kēz) the elective branch of the legislative of the Isle of Man

House of Lords the upper house of the British Parliament, consisting of the Lords temporal and spiritual

House of Representatives the lower branch of the legislature of the U.S., of the Australian federal parliament, and of certain other law-making bodies

house organ a periodical published by a business firm for its employees, affiliates, etc.

house party the entertainment of guests overnight or over a period of a few days, usually in a country house

house-proud (-praüd) *adj.* concerned, sometimes excessively, to keep one's home clean, tidy and attractive

house·room (-rōōm', -rōom') *n.* available space; accommodation

house sparrow a small, brownish bird, the common street sparrow of built-up areas

house·top (-top') *n.* the top of a house; roof —**from the housetops** publicly and widely

house-trained (-trānd) *adj.* trained to live in a house (i.e., to void outdoors or in a special place): said of a dog, cat, etc. —**house'-train** vt.

house·warm·ing (-wôr'miŋ) *n.* a party given by or for someone moving into a new home

house·wife (-wīf'; *for 2, usually* huz'if) *n., pl.* **-wives'** (-wīvz'; *for 2, usually* huz'ivz) 1. a woman, esp. a married woman, who manages a household 2. a small sewing kit —**house'wife'ly** *adj., adv.* —**house'wif'er·y** *n.*

house·work (-wurk') *n.* the work involved in housekeeping, such as cleaning, cooking, etc.

hous·ey-hous·ey (hou'zē hou'zē) *n.* same as LOTTO

hous·ing¹ (haü'ziŋ) *n.* 1. the act of providing shelter or lodging 2. shelter or lodging, as in houses, flats, etc. 3. houses collectively 4. a shelter; covering 5. *Mech.* a frame, box, etc. for containing some part

hous·ing² (haü'ziŋ) *n.* [< OFr. *houce* < Frank.] an ornamental covering draped over a horse

housing estate a planned residential area, including houses, shops, etc.

hove (hōv) *alt. pt. & pp. of* HEAVE

hov·el (hov'l) *n.* [ME. < ?] 1. a low, open shed for sheltering animals, storing equipment, etc. 2. any small, miserable dwelling; hut —*vt.* **-elled, -el·ling** to shelter in a hovel

hov·er (hov'ər) *vi.* [< ME. freq. of *hoven*, to stay] 1. to stay suspended or flutter in the air near one place 2. to linger or wait close by, esp. in a protective way 3. to be in an uncertain condition; waver —*n.* a hovering —**hov'-er·er** *n.*

hov·er·craft (-kräft') *n.* [HOVER + (AIR)CRAFT] a vehicle which travels across land or water supported by a cushion of air and driven forwards by propellers

hov·er·train (-trān) *n.* a train that moves over a concrete track and is supported by a cushion of air supplied by fans on its underside

how (haü) *adv.* [OE. *hu*] 1. in what manner or way 2. in what state or condition 3. for what reason; why 4. by what name 5. with what meaning 6. to what extent, degree, amount, etc. 7. at what price *How* is also used in exclamations and as an intensive —**and how!** [Slang] very much so; completely [he ran *and how!*] —**how about** what is your thought concerning? —**how now?** what is the meaning of this? —**how so?** how is it so?

how·be·it (haü bē'it) *adv.* [Archaic] however it may be; nevertheless

how·dah (haü'də) *n.* [Anglo-Ind. < Hindi < Ar. *haudaj*] a canopied seat for riding on the back of an elephant or camel

how do you do? how is your health? A conventionalized expression of greeting upon being introduced to, or meeting someone

how·dy (haü'dē) *interj.* [contr. < how do you (do)?] [U.S. Dial. or Colloq.] an expression of greeting

how·ev·er (haü ev'ər) *adv.* 1. no matter how; in whatever manner 2. to whatever degree or extent 3. by what

means: intensive of HOW 4. nevertheless; yet: often used as a conjunctive adverb Also [Poet.] **how·e'er'** (-er')

how·itz·er (haü'it sər) *n.* [< Du. < Early ModG. < Czech *haufnice*, orig., a sling] a short cannon, firing shells in a relatively high trajectory

howl (haül) *vi.* [ME. *houlen* < echoic base] 1. to utter the long, wailing cry of wolves, dogs, etc. 2. to utter a similar cry of pain, anger, etc. 3. to make a sound like this [the wind *howls*] 4. to shout or laugh in scorn, mirth, etc. —*vt.* 1. to utter with a howl 2. to drive or effect by howling —*n.* 1. the long, wailing cry of a wolf, dog, etc. 2. any similar sound 3. [Colloq.] something hilarious —**howl down** to drown out with shouts of scorn, etc.

howl·er (haül'ər) *n.* 1. a person or thing that howls 2. [Colloq.] a ludicrous blunder

howl·ing (-iŋ) *adj.* 1. that howls 2. mournful; dreary [howling wilderness] 3. [Colloq.] great [a howling success] —**howl'ing·ly** *adv.*

how·so·ev·er (haü'sō ev'ər) *adv.* 1. to whatever degree or extent 2. by whatever means

how's that? 1. What do you think of that? 2. *Cricket* a phrase used in appealing to the umpire to declare a batsman out: also **how·zat?** (haü zat')

hoy¹ (hoi) *n.* [ME. *hoye* < MDu. *hoei*] 1. a former type of small vessel resembling a sloop 2. a heavy barge

hoy² (hoi) *interj.* [ME.] an exclamation to attract attention, drive animals, etc.

hoy·den (hoid''n) *n.* [< ? Du. *heiden*, heathen] a bold, boisterous girl; tomboy —*adj.* bold and boisterous; tomboyish —*vi.* to behave like a hoyden —**hoy'den·ish** *adj.*

Hoyle (hoil) *n.* a book of rules and instructions for card games, orig. compiled by Edmond Hoyle (1672-1769) —**according to Hoyle** according to the rules and regulations; in a fair way

H.P. Houses of Parliament

HP, H.P., hp, h.p. 1. high pressure 2. hire purchase 3. horsepower

HQ, H.Q., hq, h.q. headquarters

hr. *pl.* **hrs.** hour; hours

HR Home Rule

H.R.H. His (or Her) Royal Highness

H.S. high school

H.S.H. His (or Her) Serene Highness

HT high tension

ht. 1. heat 2. *pl.* **hts.** height

hub (hub) *n.* [? akin to HOB¹] 1. the centre part of a wheel, etc. 2. a centre of interest, importance, or activity

hub·ble-bub·ble (hub''l bub''l) *n.* [echoic] 1. a tobacco pipe in which the smoke is drawn through water, causing a bubbling sound 2. a bubbling sound 3. hubbub; uproar

hub·bub (hub'ub') *n.* [prob. < Celt.] a confused sound of many voices; uproar; tumult

hub·by (hub'ē) *n., pl.* **-bies** [Colloq.] a husband

hub·cap (hub'kap') *n.* a tightfitting metal cap for the hub of a wheel, esp. of a car

hu·bris (hyōō'bris) *n.* [Gr. *hybris*] wanton insolence or arrogance resulting from excessive pride or from passion—**hu·bris'tic** *adj.*

huck·a·back (huk'ə bak') *n.* [< ?] a coarse linen or cotton cloth with a rough surface, used for towelling: also **huck**

huck·le·ber·ry (huk''l bər ē) *n., pl.* **-ries** [prob. altered < *hurtleberry*, WHORTLEBERRY] 1. a shrub of the heath family, common in the U.S., having dark-blue berries with ten large seeds 2. the fruit of this shrub

huck·ster (huk'stər) *n.* [< MDu. *hoekster* < *hoeken*, to peddle] 1. a peddler, esp. of fruits, vegetables, etc. 2. an aggressive or haggling merchant 3. [U.S. Colloq.] a person engaged in advertising or promotion —*vt.* 1. to sell; peddle 2. to haggle 3. [Chiefly U.S.] to sell or advertise, esp. in an aggressive way —**huck'ster·ism** *n.*

hud·dle (hud''l) *vi.* **-dled, -dling** [? var. of ME. *hoderen*, to cover up] 1. to crowd close together, as cows do in a storm 2. to draw or hunch oneself up, as from cold —*vt.* 1. to crowd close together 2. to hunch or draw (oneself) up 3. to do, put, or make hastily and carelessly 4. to push in a hurried manner —*n.* 1. a confused crowd or heap 2. confusion; jumble 3. [Colloq.] a private, informal conference

hue¹ (hyōō) *n.* [OE. *heow*] 1. colour; esp., the distinctive characteristics of a given colour 2. a particular shade or tint of a given colour —**hued** *adj.*

hue² (hyōō) *n.* [< OFr. *hu*, a warning cry] a shouting; outcry: now only in **hue and cry**, meaning: *a)* orig., a loud shout or cry by those pursuing a felon *b)* any loud outcry or clamour

huff¹ (huf) *vt.* [prob. echoic] to make angry; offend —*vi.* 1. to blow; puff 2. to become angry —*n.* a condition of smouldering anger or resentment

huff² (huf) *vt.* *Draughts* to remove (an opponent's man) from the board as a penalty for not effecting a capture —*n.* an act of huffing

huff·y (-ē) *adj.* **huff′i·er, huff′i·est** 1. easily offended; touchy 2. angered or offended —**huff′i·ly** *adv.* —**huff′i·ness** *n.*

hug (hug) *vt.* **hugged, hug′ging** [prob. < ON. *hugga*, to comfort] 1. to put the arms around and hold closely, esp. affectionately 2. to squeeze tightly with the forelegs, as a bear does 3. to cling to (a belief, opinion, etc.) 4. to keep close to [the bus *hugged* the kerb] —*vi.* to embrace one another closely —*n.* 1. a close, fond embrace 2. a tight hold with the arms, as in wrestling 3. a bear's squeeze —**hug′ga·ble** *adj.*

huge (hyōōj) *adj.* [OFr. *ahuge*] very large; gigantic; immense —**huge′ly** *adv.* —**huge′ness** *n.*

hug·ger-mug·ger (hug′ər mug′ər) *n.* [prob. based on ME. *mokeren*, to conceal] 1. a confusion; muddle; jumble 2.[Archaic] secrecy —*adj.* confused; muddled —*adv.* 1. in a confused or jumbled manner 2. [Archaic] secret

Hugh·ie (hyōō′ē) [Aust. Colloq.] *a jocular term for* fate or the deity, esp. with reference to rain [send her down, *Hughie!*]

Hu·gue·not (hyōō′gə nō) *n.* [MFr. < G. *Eidgenosse*, confederate] any French Protestant of the 16th or 17th century

huh (hu, huh) *interj.* an exclamation used to express contempt, surprise, etc., or to ask a question

hu·la (hōō′lə) *n.* [Haw.] a native Hawaiian dance marked by flowing gestures: also **hu′la-hu′la**

Hula-hoop (-hōōp′) [< prec. + HOOP] *a trademark for* a light hoop twirled round the body in play or exercise by rotating the hips

hulk (hulk) *n.* [OE. *hulc*] 1. a big, unwieldy ship 2. a) the body of a ship, esp. if old and dismantled b) [usually pl.] a dismantled ship used as a storehouse or prison 3. a deserted wreck or ruins 4. a big, clumsy person or thing —*vi.* to loom bulkily

hulk·ing (hul′kiŋ) *adj.* large, heavy, and often unwieldy or clumsy: also **hulk′y** (-kē)

hull¹ (hul) *n.* [OE. *hulu*] 1. the outer covering of a seed or fruit, as the husk of grain, shell of nuts, etc. 2. the calyx of some fruits, as the strawberry 3. any outer covering —*vt.* to take the hull or hulls off —**hull′er** *n.*

hull² (hul) *n.* [special use of prec., prob. infl. by Du. *hol*, ship's hold] 1. the frame or body of a ship, excluding the masts, sails, rigging, superstructure, etc. 2. a) the main body of an airship b) the frame or main body of a flying boat, amphibian, hydrofoil, etc. —*vt.* to pierce the hull of (a ship) with a torpedo, etc.

hul·la·ba·loo (hul′ə bə lōō′) *n.* [echoic, based on ff.] a clamour or hubbub

hul·lo (hə lō′) *interj., n., vt., vi.* same as: 1. HOLLO 2. HALLO

hum¹ (hum) *vi.* **hummed, hum′ming** [echoic] 1. to make the low, murmuring sound of a bee, a motor, etc. 2. to sing with the lips closed, not producing words 3. to give forth a confused, droning sound [the room *hummed* with voices] 4. [Colloq.] to be full of activity 5. [Colloq.] to stink —*vt.* 1. to sing (a tune, etc.) with the lips closed 2. to produce an effect on by humming [to *hum* a child to sleep] —*n.* the act or sound of humming —**hum′mer** *n.*

hum² (həm: *conventionalized pronun.*) *interj., n.* same as: 1. HEM² 2. HUMPH —*vi.* **hummed, hum′ming** same as HEM²

hu·man (hyōō′mən) *adj.* [< OFr. < L. *humanus*] 1. of, belonging to, or typical of mankind [the *human* race] 2. consisting of or produced by men [*human* society] 3. having or showing qualities characteristic of people [*human* values] —*n.* a person: the phrase **human being** is still preferred by some —**hu′man·ness** *n.*

hu·mane (hyōō mān′, hyoo-) *adj.* [earlier var. of prec.] 1. kind, tender, merciful, sympathetic, etc. 2. civilizing; humanizing [*humane* learning] —**hu·mane′ly** *adv.* —**hu·mane′ness** *n.*

hu·man·ism (hyōō′mə niz'm) *n.* 1. the quality of being human; human nature 2. any system of thought or action based on the nature, dignity, and ideals of man; specif., a rationalist movement that holds that man can be ethical, find self-fulfilment, etc. without recourse to supernaturalism 3. the study of the humanities 4. [H-] the intellectual and cultural secular movement that stemmed from the study of classical Greek and Roman culture in the Middle Ages and helped give rise to the Renaissance —**hu′man·ist** *n., adj.* —**hu′man·is′tic** *adj.* —**hu′man·is′ti·cal·ly** *adv.*

hu·man·i·tar·i·an (hyōō man′ə ter′ē ən, hyoo-) *n.* a person devoted to promoting the welfare of humanity; philanthropist —*adj.* helping humanity —**hu·man′i·tar′i·an·ism** *n.*

hu·man·i·ty (hyōō man′ə tē, hyoo-) *n., pl.* **-ties** 1. the fact or quality of being human; human nature 2. the human race; mankind; people 3. the fact or quality of being humane; kindness, mercy, sympathy, etc. —**the humanities** 1. languages and literature, esp. classical Greek and Latin 2. the branches of learning concerned with human thought

and relations; esp., literature, philosophy, the fine arts, history, etc.

hu·man·ize (hyōō′mə nīz′) *vt., vi.* **-ized′, -iz′ing** 1. to make or become human 2. to make or become humane —**hu′man·i·za′tion** *n.* —**hu′man·iz′er** *n.*

hu·man·kind (hyōō′mən kīnd′) *n.* the human race; mankind; people

hu·man·ly (-lē) *adv.* 1. in a human manner 2. by human means 3. from a human viewpoint

hu·man·oid (-oid′) *adj.* nearly human —*n.* a nearly human creature; specif., a) any of the earliest ancestors of modern man b) in science fiction, a reasoning, human-like creature of another planet

hum·ble (hum′b'l) *adj.* **-bler, -blest** [OFr. < L. *humilis*, low, akin to *humus*, earth] 1. having or showing a consciousness of one's defects or shortcomings; not proud 2. low in condition or rank; lowly; unpretentious —*vt.* **-bled, -bling** 1. to lower in condition or rank; abase 2. to make modest or humble in mind —**hum′ble·ness** *n.* —**hum′bler** *n.* —**hum′bly** *adv.*

hum·ble·bee (-bē′) *n.* [ME. *humbylbee* < *humblen*, to hum] *same as* BUMBLEBEE

humble pie [< *umbles*, entrails of a deer < OFr. *nombles* < L. < *lumbus*, loin] formerly, a pie made of the offal of a deer, served to the servants after a hunt —**eat humble pie** to undergo humiliation, as by admitting one's error

hum·bug (hum′bug′) *n.* [< ?] 1. a) a fraud; sham b) misleading or empty talk 2. a person who is not what he claims to be 3. a spirit of trickery, deception, etc. 4. a peppermint boiled sweet, usually striped —*vt.* **-bugged′, -bug′ging** to dupe; deceive; hoax —*interj.* nonsense! —**hum′bug′ger** *n.* —**hum′bug′ger·y** *n.*

hum·ding·er (hum′diŋ′ər) *n.* [Slang] a person or thing considered excellent of its kind

hum·drum (hum′drum′) *adj.* lacking variety; dull; monotonous —*n.* humdrum talk, routine, etc.

hu·mec·tant (hyōō mek′tənt) *n.* [< L. prp. of *humectare*, ult. < *umere*, to be moist] a substance, as glycerol, added or applied to another to help it retain moisture

hu·mer·us (hyōō′mər əs) *n., pl.* **-mer·i** (-ī′) [L. *humerus, umerus*, the upper arm] the bone of the upper arm or forelimb, extending from the shoulder to the elbow —**hu′mer·al** *adj.*

hu·mid (hyōō′mid) *adj.* [< Fr. < L. *humidus*, ult. < *umere*, to be moist] full of water vapour; damp; moist —**hu′mid·ly** *adv.*

hu·mid·i·fy (hyōō mid′ə fī′) *vt.* **-fied′, -fy′ing** to make humid; moisten; dampen —**hu·mid′i·fi·ca′tion** *n.* —**hu·mid′i·fi′er** *n.*

hu·mid·i·ty (-tē) *n., pl.* **-ties** 1. moistness; dampness 2. the amount of moisture in the air —**relative humidity** the ratio of the amount of moisture in the air to the maximum amount that the air could contain at the same temperature, stated as a percentage

hu·mi·dor (hyōō′mə dôr′) *n.* a jar, case, etc. with a device for keeping tobacco, etc. moist

hu·mil·i·ate (hyōō mil′ē āt′, hyoo-) *vt.* **-at′ed, -at′ing** [< L. pp. of *humiliare* < L. *humilis*, HUMBLE] to hurt the pride or dignity of by causing to seem foolish, etc.; mortify —**hu·mil′i·a′tion** *n.*

hu·mil·i·ty (hyōō mil′ə tē) *n.* [< OFr. < L. *humilitas*] the state or quality of being humble; absence of pride or self-assertion

hum·ming·bird (hum′iŋ bʉrd′) *n.* any of a family of very small, brightly coloured birds with a long, slender bill and narrow wings that vibrate rapidly, with a humming sound

hum·mock (hum′ək) *n.* [orig. naut. < ?] 1. a low, rounded hill; knoll 2. a ridge or rise in an ice field 3. [U.S.] a tract of wooded land, higher than a surrounding marshy area —**hum′mock·y** *adj.*

hu·mor (hyōō′mər) *n., vt. U.S. sp. of* HUMOUR

hu·mor·al (hyōō′mər əl) *adj.* [ModL. *humoralis* < L. *humor*] relating to the humours of the body

hu·mor·esque (hyōō′mə resk′) *n.* [G. *Humoreske*] a light, fanciful, or playful musical composition

hu·mor·ist (hyōō′mər ist) *n.* 1. a person with a good sense of humour 2. a professional writer or teller of amusing stories, jokes, etc.

hu·mor·ous (-əs) *adj.* having or expressing humour; funny; amusing; comical —**hu′mor·ous·ly** *adv.* —**hu′mor·ous·ness** *n.*

hu·mour (hyōō′mər) *n.* [< OFr. < L. *humor, umor*, moisture, fluid] 1. formerly, any of the four fluids (**cardinal humours**) considered responsible for one's health and disposition: blood, phlegm, choler (yellow bile), or melancholy (black bile) 2. a) a person's temperament b) a mood; state of mind 3. whim; fancy; caprice 4. comic or amusing quality 5. a) the ability to appreciate or express what is funny, amusing, or ludicrous b) the expression of this in speech, writing, or action 6. any fluid or fluidlike substance of the body [the aqueous *humour*] —*vt.* 1. to comply with the mood or whim of (another); indulge 2. to adapt oneself to —**out of humour** cross; disagreeable —**hu'-mour·less** *adj.*

hump (hump) *n.* [< or akin to LowG. *humpe*, thick piece] 1. a rounded, protruding lump, as the fleshy mass on the back of a camel: in man, a hump is caused by a deformity of the spine 2. a hummock; mound 3. [Colloq.] a fit of depression or sulks [he's got the *hump*] —*vt.* 1. to hunch; arch [the cat *humped* its back] 2. [Colloq.] to carry, esp. heavy objects; heave —*vi.* 1. to exert oneself 2. to hurry —**over the hump** [Colloq.] over the worst part —**humped** *adj.* —**hump'y** *adj.* **-i·er, -i·est**

hump·back (-bak') *n.* 1. a humped, deformed back 2. a person having a humped back; hunchback 3. a large whale having long flippers and a dorsal fin resembling a humpback—**hump'backed'** *adj.*

humph (humf: *conventionalized pronun.*) *interj., n.* a snorting or grunting sound expressing doubt, surprise, disdain, disgust, etc.

Hump·ty Dump·ty (hump'tē dump'tē) the personification of an egg in an old nursery rhyme

hump·y (hum'pē) *n.* [< Abor. *oompi*] [Aust.] a native hut

hu·mus (hyōo'məs) *n.* [L., earth] the brown or black organic part of the soil, resulting from the partial decay of plant and animal matter

Hun (hun) *n.* [after the *Huns*, a warlike asiatic people who invaded Europe in the 4th and 5th centuries A.D.] 1. [often h-] any savage or destructive person; vandal 2. [Slang] a German —**Hun'nish** *adj.*

hunch (hunch) *vt.* [< ?] to draw (one's body, etc.) up so as to form a hump —*vi.* to push oneself forwards jerkily —*n.* 1. a hump 2. a chunk; hunk 3. [Colloq.] a premonition or suspicion

hunch·back (-bak') *n.* *same as* HUMPBACK (senses 1, 2) —**hunch'backed'** *adj.*

hun·dred (hun'drəd) *n.* [OE.] 1. the cardinal number next above ninety-nine; ten times ten; 100; C 2. [Obs.] a division of an English county —*adj.* ten times ten

hun·dred·fold (-fōld') *adj.* [see -FOLD] having a hundred times as much or as many —*adv.* a hundred times as much or as many

hundreds and thousands tiny beads of coloured sugar used in decorating cakes, etc.

hun·dredth (hun'drədth) *adj.* 1. preceded by ninety-nine others in a series; 100th 2. designating any of the hundred equal parts of something —*n.* 1. the one following the ninety-ninth 2. any of the hundred equal parts of something; 1/100

hun·dred·weight (hun'drəd wāt) *n.* 1. [Brit.] formerly a unit of weight equal to 112 pounds (c. 50kg) 2. [U.S.] a unit of weight equal to 100 pounds (c. 45kg) 3. a metric unit of weight equal to 50kg

hung (hung) *pt. & pp. of* HANG —**hung up (on)** [Slang] 1. emotionally disturbed (by) 2. baffled, frustrated, etc. (by) 3. addicted (to); obsessed (by)

Hung. 1. Hungarian 2. Hungary

Hun·gar·i·an (hung ger'ē ən) *adj.* of Hungary, its people, their language, or culture —*n.* 1. a native or inhabitant of Hungary 2. the Finno-Ugric language of the Hungarians; Magyar

hun·ger (hun'gər) *n.* [OE. *hungor*] 1. *a)* the discomfort, pain, or weakness caused by a need for food *b)* famine; starvation 2. a need or appetite for food 3. any strong desire; craving —*vi.* 1. to be hungry 2. to crave; long (with *for* or *after*)

hunger march a protest march by the unemployed, etc., to publicize their condition

hunger strike a refusal, as of a prisoner, to eat until certain demands are granted

hun·gry (hun'grē) *adj.* **-gri·er, -gri·est** 1. feeling or showing hunger; specif., *a)* wanting or needing food *b)* craving; eager [hungry for praise] 2. not fertile; barren: said of soil —**hun'gri·ly** *adv.* —**hun'gri·ness** *n.*

Hungry Forties the period 1840-49 in Brit. history, a time of widespread poverty

hunk (hunk) *n.* [Fl. *hunke*, hunk] [Colloq.] a large piece, lump, or slice of bread, meat, etc.

hun·ker (hun'kər) *vi.* [prob. < or akin to ON. *hokra*, to creep] to settle down on one's haunches; squat or crouch —*n.* [*pl.*] haunches

hun·ky-do·ry (hun'kē dôr'ē) *adj.* [Chiefly U.S. Colloq.] all right; satisfactory; fine

hunt (hunt) *vt.* [OE. *huntian*] 1. to go out to kill or catch (game) for food or sport 2. to search carefully for; try to find 3. *a)* to chase; drive *b)* to hound; harry 4. *a)* to go through (a wood, etc.) in pursuit of game *b)* to search (a place) carefully 5. to use (dogs or horses) in chasing game —*vi.* 1. to go out after game 2. to search; seek —*n.* 1. a hunting 2. a group of people who hunt together 3. a district covered in hunting 4. a search

hunt·er (-ər) *n.* 1. a person who hunts 2. a horse trained

for hunting 3. a watch with a hinged case to protect the glass

hunter's moon the full moon following the harvest moon

hunt·ing (-in) *n.* the act of a person or animal that hunts —*adj.* of or for hunting

hunting-box (boks') *n.* a small lodge used during the hunting season

hunt·ress (hun'tris) *n.* a woman who hunts

hunts·man (hunts'mən) *n., pl.* **-men** 1. a hunter 2. a person who trains and looks after hounds

hur·dle (hur'd'l) *n.* [OE. *hyrdel*] 1. a portable frame of interlaced twigs, etc., used as a temporary fence 2. any of a series of framelike barriers over which horses or runners must leap in a race (the **hurdles**) 3. a difficulty to be overcome; obstacle —*vt.* **-dled, -dling** 1. to fence off with hurdles 2. to jump over (a barrier), as in a race 3. to overcome (an obstacle) —**hur'-dler** *n.*

HURDLES

hur·dy-gur·dy (hur'dē gur'dē) *n., pl.* **-gur'dies** [prob. echoic] 1. an early, lutelike instrument played by turning a crank 2. *same as* BARREL ORGAN

hurl (hurl) *vt.* [prob. < ON.] 1. to throw with force or violence 2. to cast down; overthrow 3. to utter vehemently —*vi.* to move with speed and force; to rush —*n.* a violent throw —**hurl'er** *n.*

hurl·ing (-in) *n.* [< prec.] an Irish game resembling hockey: also **hur·ley**

hurl·y-burl·y (hur'lē bur'lē) *n., pl.* **-burl'ies** a turmoil; uproar —*adj.* disorderly and confused

hur·rah (hə rä', -rä') *interj.* [ult. echoic] a shout of joy, approval, etc. —*n.* 1. a shouting of "hurrah" 2. excitement, commotion, etc. —*vi., vt.* to cheer; shout "hurrah" (for) Also **hur·ray'** (-rā')

hur·ri·cane (hur'ə kān', -kən) *n.* [< Sp. < WInd. *huracan*] a violent tropical cyclone with winds of more than force 12 (118 km/h) on the Beaufort scale, often with torrential rains

hurricane deck the upper deck of a passenger ship

hurricane lamp an oil lamp or candlestick with a tall glass chimney to keep the flame from being blown out

hur·ried (hur'ēd) *adj.* in a hurry; rushed or rushing —**hur'-ried·ly** *adv.* —**hur'ried·ness** *n.*

hur·ry (hur'ē) *vt.* **-ried, -ry·ing** [prob. akin to HURL] 1. to move, send, or carry with haste 2. to cause to occur or be done more rapidly or too rapidly 3. to urge or cause to act soon or too soon —*vi.* to move or act with haste —*n.* 1. a rush; urgency 2. eagerness to do, act, go, etc. quickly —**hur'ri·er** *n.*

hur·ry-scur·ry, hur·ry-skur·ry (-skur'ē) *n.* a disorderly confusion —*vi.* **-ried, -ry·ing** to hurry and scurry about —*adj.* hurried and confused —*adv.* in a hurried, confused manner

hurst (hurst) *n.* [ME. < OE. *hyrst*, hillock] 1. a hillock 2. a grove or wooded hillock

hurt (hurt) *vt.* **hurt, hurt'ing** [OFr. *hurter*, to push, hit, prob. < Frank.] 1. to cause pain or injury to; wound 2. to harm or damage in any way 3. to offend or distress —*vi.* 1. to cause injury, damage, or pain 2. to give or have the sensation of pain; be sore —*n.* 1. a pain or injury 2. harm or damage 3. something that wounds the feelings —*adj.* damaged; injured —**hurt'er** *n.*

hurt·ful (-fəl) *adj.* causing hurt; harmful —**hurt'ful·ly** *adv.* —**hurt'ful·ness** *n.*

hur·tle (hurt''l) *vi.* **-tled, -tling** [< freq. of ME. *hurten*, HURT] 1. orig., to crash; collide 2. to move swiftly and with great force —*vt.* to throw, shoot, or fling with great force; hurl

hus·band (huz'bənd) *n.* [Late OE. *husbonda* < ON. < *hūs*, house + *bondi*, freeholder] a married man —*vt.* to manage economically; conserve

hus·band·man (-mən) *n., pl.* **-men** [Archaic] a farmer

hus·band·ry (huz'bən drē) *n.* 1. orig., management of domestic affairs, resources, etc. 2. careful, thrifty management 3. farming

hush (hush) *vt.* [< ME. < *huscht*, quiet] 1. to make quiet or silent 2. to soothe; lull —*vi.* to be or become quiet or silent —*n.* quiet; silence —*interj.* an exclamation calling for silence —**hush up** to keep secret; suppress

hush-hush (hush'hush') *adj.* [Colloq.] very secret; most confidential

hush money money paid to a person to keep him from telling something

husk (husk) *n.* [prob. < MDu. *huuskijn*, dim. of *huus*, a house] 1. the dry outer covering of various fruits or seeds, as of an ear of corn 2. the dry, rough, or useless outside covering of anything —*vt.* to remove the husk from —**husk'er** *n.*

hus·ky[1] (hus′kē) *n.,* *pl.* **-kies** [altered < ? Eskimo] [*sometimes* H-] a hardy dog used for pulling sledges in the Arctic

husk·y[2] (hus′kē) *adj.* **husk′i·er, husk′i·est** 1. *a)* full of or consisting of husks *b)* like a husk 2. sounding deep and hoarse; rough 3. big and strong; robust —*n., pl.* **husk′ies** a husky person —**husk′i·ly** *adv.* —**husk′i·ness** *n.*

hus·sar (hŏ zär′, hə-) *n.* [< Hung. < Serb. *husar* < L. *cursus:* see CORSAIR] a member of any European regiment of light-armed cavalry, usually with brilliant dress uniforms

Huss·ite (hus′īt) *n.* a follower of John Huss (1369?-1415), Bohemian religious reformer and martyr —*adj.* of Huss or his teachings

hus·sy (huz′ē, hus′-) *n., pl.* **-sies** [contr. < ME. *huswife, housewife*] 1. a woman, esp. one of low morals 2. a bold, saucy girl; minx

hus·tings (hus′tiŋz) *n.pl.* [*usually with sing.* v.] [OE. < ON. < *hûs,* a house + *thing,* assembly] 1. [Obs.] the temporary platform where candidates for parliament stood for nomination and delivered speeches 2. the proceedings at an election 3. [U.S.] the route followed by a campaigner for political office

hus·tle (hus′'l) *vt.* **-tled, -tling** [Du. *hutseln,* to shake up] 1. to push about; jostle in a rude, rough manner 2. to force in a rough, hurried manner [he *hustled* them into the bus] 3. [Colloq.] to hurry (a person, a job, etc.) 4. [Slang] to get, victimize, etc. by aggressive tactics —*vi.* 1. to move hurriedly 2. [Colloq.] to work or act rapidly or energetically 3. *a)* [Slang] to obtain money by aggressive or dishonest means *b)* [U.S. Slang] to work as a prostitute —*n.* 1. a hustling 2. [Colloq.] energetic action; drive —**hus′tler** *n.*

hut (hut) *n.* [< Fr. < MHG. < OHG. *hutta*] 1. a little house or shed of the plainest or crudest kind 2. a temporary structure, as at a school, army camp, etc. —*vt., vi.* **hut′ted, hut′ting** to shelter or be sheltered in or as in a hut

hutch (huch) *n.* [OFr. *huche,* bin < ML. *hutica,* a chest] 1. a bin, chest, or box for storage 2. a pen or coop for small animals 3. a hut; a small house

hut·ment (hut′mənt) *n.* [< HUT + -MENT] a group of huts, as in an army camp

huz·zah, huz·za (hə zä′) *interj., n., vi., vt.* [echoic] *former var. of* HURRAH

H.V., HV, h.v., hv high voltage

H.W.(M.) high water (mark)

hy·a·cinth (hī′ə sinth) *n.* [< L. < Gr. *hyakinthos*] 1. *a)* among the ancients, a blue gem *b)* a reddish-orange or brownish gem 2. a plant of the lily family, with spikes of fragrant, bell-shaped flowers 3. a bluish purple —**hy′a·cin′thine** (-sin′thin, -thin) *adj.*

Hy·a·des (hī′ə dēz) *n. pl.* [L. < Gr.] 1. *Gr. Myth.* the daughters of Atlas, placed in the sky by Zeus 2. an open cluster of more than 200 stars in the constellation Taurus

hy·ae·na (hī ē′nə) *n.* *same as* HYENA

hy·a·line (hī′ə lin, -līn′) *adj.* [< LL. < Gr. < *hyalos,* glass] transparent as glass; glassy: also **hy′a·loid′** (-loid′) —*n.* anything transparent or glassy

hy·a·lite (hī′ə līt′) *n.* [< Gr. < *hyalos,* glass + -ITE] a colourless variety of opal

hyaloid membrane a delicate membrane containing the vitreous humour of the eye

hy·brid (hī′brid) *n.* [L. *hybrida,* offspring of mixed parentage] 1. the offspring of two animals or plants of different species, etc. 2. anything of mixed origin, unlike parts, etc. 3. *Linguis.* a word made up of elements from different languages —*adj.* of, or having the nature of, a hybrid —**hy′brid·ism, hy·brid′i·ty** *n.*

hy·brid·ize (hī′brə dīz′) *vi., vt.* **-ized′, -iz′ing** to produce or cause to produce hybrids; crossbreed —**hy′brid·i·za′tion** *n.* —**hy′brid·iz′er** *n.*

hy·da·tid (hī′də tid) *n.* [Gr. *hydatis,* watery vesicle] a cyst containing watery fluid and the larvae of certain tapeworms —*adj.* of or like such a cyst

hydr- *same as* HYDRO-: used before vowels

hy·dra (hī′drə) *n., pl.* **-dras, -drae** (-drē) [Gr. *hydra,* water serpent, esp. the nine-headed serpent of Gr. myth.] 1. any persistent or ever-increasing evil: in the myth each head grew back double when cut off 2. a small freshwater polyp with a soft, tubelike body and a mouth surrounded with tentacles

hy·dran·ge·a (hī drān′jə, -jē ə) *n.* [ModL. < HYDR- + Gr. *angeion,* vessel] a shrubby plant, with opposite leaves and large, showy clusters of white, blue, or pink flowers

hy·drant (hī′drənt) *n.* [< Gr. *hydôr,* water] an outlet from a water main, usually an upright pipe with a valve attached, from which water can be drawn for fighting fires, etc.

hy·drate (hī′drāt) *n.* [HYDR- + -ATE] a compound formed by the chemical combination of water and some other substance [plaster of Paris, $2CaSO_4 \cdot H_2O$, is a *hydrate*] —*vi., vt.* **-drat·ed, -drat·ing** 1. to become or cause to become a hydrate 2. to combine with water —**hy·dra′tion** *n.* —**hy′-dra·tor** *n.*

hy·drau·lic (hī drô′lik, -drô′-) *adj.* [< Fr. < L. < Gr. *hydraulikos;* ult. < *hydôr,* water + *aulos,* tube] 1. of hydraulics 2. operated by the movement and pressure of liquid, esp. of a liquid forced through an aperture, etc. [*hydraulic* brakes] 3. setting or hardening under water [*hydraulic* cement] —**hy·drau′li·cal·ly** *adv.*

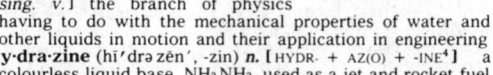

HYDRAULIC PRESS

hydraulic ram a device to move a flowing liquid up by using the momentum of the flowing liquid

hy·drau·lics (-liks) *n.pl.* [*with sing.* v.] the branch of physics having to do with the mechanical properties of water and other liquids in motion and their application in engineering

hy·dra·zine (hī′drə zēn′, -zin) *n.* [HYDR- + AZ(O) + -INE[4]] a colourless liquid base, NH_2NH_2, used as a jet and rocket fuel

hy·dric (hī′drik) *adj.* [HYDR- + -IC] of or containing hydrogen

hy·dride (hī′drīd) *n.* [HYDR- + -IDE] a compound of hydrogen with another element or a radical

hy·dri·od·ic acid (hī′drē od′ik) [HYDR- + IODIC] a strong acid, HI, that is a solution of the gas hydrogen iodide in water

hy·dro (hī′drō) *n., pl.* **-dros** a hotel, resort, etc., where people go to get hydropathic treatment

hy·dro- [< Gr. *hydôr,* water] a combining form meaning: 1. water [*hydrometer*] 2. containing hydrogen [*hydrocyanic*]

hy·dro·car·bon (hī′drə kär′bən) *n.* any compound, as benzene, containing only hydrogen and carbon

hy·dro·ceph·a·lus (hī′drə sef′ə ləs) *n.* [ModL. < Gr. < *hydôr,* water + *kephalê,* head] a condition characterized by an abnormal amount of fluid in the cranium, causing enlargement of the head: also **hy′dro·ceph′a·ly** (-lē) —**hy′-dro·ce·phal′ic** (-sə fal′ik) *adj., n.* —**hy′dro·ceph′a·lous** *adj.*

hy·dro·chlo·ric acid (hī′drə klor′ik) [HYDRO- + CHLORIC] a strong, corrosive acid, HCl, that is a solution of the gas hydrogen chloride in water

hy·dro·chlo·ride (-klôr′īd) *n.* a compound of hydrochloric acid and an organic base

hy·dro·cy·an·ic acid (hī′drō sī an′ik) [HYDRO- + CYANIC] a weak, highly poisonous acid, HCN, a colourless liquid with the odour of bitter almonds

hy·dro·dy·nam·ics (-dī nam′iks) *n.pl.* [*with sing.* v.] the branch of physics dealing with the motion and action of water and other liquids —**hy′dro·dy·nam′ic** *adj.* —**hy′-dro·dy·nam′i·cal·ly** *adv.*

hy·dro·e·lec·tric (-i lek′trik) *adj.* producing, or relating to the production of, electricity by water power —**hy′-dro·e·lec′tric′i·ty** *n.*

hy·dro·flu·or·ic acid (hī′drə flôr′ik, -floor′, -floō or-) [HYDRO- + FLUOR(INE) + -IC] an acid, HF, existing as a colourless, fuming, corrosive liquid: it is used in etching glass

hy·dro·foil (hī′drə foil′) *n.* [HYDRO- + (AERO)FOIL] 1. a winglike structure on the hull of some watercraft: at high speeds the craft skims along on the hydrofoils 2. a craft with hydrofoils

hy·dro·gen (hī′drə jən) *n.* [< Fr.: see HYDRO- + -GEN] a flammable, colourless, odourless, gaseous chemical element, the lightest of all known substances: symbol, H; at. wt., 1.00797; at. no., 1 —**hy·drog·e·nous** (hī droj′ə nəs) *adj.*

hy·dro·gen·ate (hī′drə jə nāt′, hī droj′ə-) *vt.* **-at′ed, -at′ing** to combine or treat with hydrogen, as in making a solid fat of oil —**hy′dro·gen·a′tion** *n.*

hydrogen bomb a highly destructive nuclear bomb, in which the atoms of heavy hydrogen are fused by explosion of a nuclear-fission unit in the bomb

hydrogen ion the positively charged ion in all acids: symbol, H[+]

hy·dro·gen·ize (hīd′rə jə nīz′, hī droj′ə-) *vt.* **-ized -izing** *same as* HYDROGENATE

hydrogen peroxide an unstable liquid, H_2O_2, often used, diluted, as a bleach or disinfectant, and in more concentrated form as a rocket fuel

hydrogen sulphide a gaseous compound, H_2S, with the characteristic odour of rotten eggs

hy·drog·ra·phy (hī drog′rə fē) *n.* [< Fr.: see HYDRO- & -GRAPHY] the study, description, and mapping of oceans, lakes, and rivers —**hy·drog′ra·pher** *n.* —**hy·dro·graph·ic** (hī′-drə graf′ik), **hy′dro·graph′i·cal** *adj.*

hy·droid (hī′droid) *adj.* [HYDR(A) + -OID] 1. like a hydra or polyp 2. of or related to the group of hydrozoans of which the hydra is a member —*n.* any member of a group of hydrozoans, mostly marine, typically consisting of polyps

hy·drol·o·gy (hī drol′ə jē) *n.* [ModL. *hydrologia:* see HYDRO- & -LOGY] the study of the distribution, circulation, conservation, use, etc., of the water of the earth and its atmosphere

hy·drol·y·sis (hī drol′ə sis) *n., pl.* **-ses**′ (-sēz′) [HYDRO- + -LYSIS] the breaking up of a substance, often in the presence of a catalyst, into other substances by reaction with water, as a starch into glucose, natural fats into glycerol and fatty acids, etc. —**hy'dro·lyse** *vt., vi.* —**hy·dro·lyt·ic** (hī'drə lit'ik) *adj.*

hy·dro·lyte (hī'drə lit') *n.* any substance undergoing hydrolysis

hy·dro·lyze (-līz') *vt., vi.* -**lyzed'**, -**lyz'ing** U.S. *sp.* of HYDROLYSE

hy·dro·mel (hī'drə mel') *n.* [ME. *ydromel*, ult. < Gr. *hydōr*, water + *meli*, honey] a mixture of honey and water that becomes mead when fermented

hy·drom·e·ter (hī drom'ə tər) *n.* [HYDRO- + -METER] an instrument consisting of a graduated, weighted tube, usedfor measuring the specific gravity of liquids —**hy·dro·met·ric** (hī'drə met'rik), **hy'dro·met'ri·cal** *adj.* —**hy·drom'e·try** *n.*

hy·dro·naut (hī'drō nôt') *n.* [HYDRO + Gr. *nautēs*, sailor] a crew member of a deep sea vehicle, other than a submarine

hy·drop·a·thy (hī drop'ə thə) *n.* [HYDRO- + -PATHY] a system of treating all diseases by the external or internal use of water —**hy·dro·path·ic** (hī'drə path'ik) *adj.* —**hy·drop'a·thist** *n.*

hy·dro·phil·ic (hī'drə fil'ik) *adj.* [HYDRO- + -PHIL(IA) +-IC] capable of uniting with or taking up water

hy·dro·pho·bi·a (hī'drə fō'bē ə) *n.* [LL. < Gr.: see HYDRO- & -PHOBIA] 1. an abnormal fear of water 2. [from the symptomatic inability to swallow liquids] *same as* RABIES —**hy'dro·pho'bic** *adj.*

hy·dro·phone (hī'drə fōn') *n.* [HYDRO- + -PHONE] an instrument for detecting and registering the distance and direction of sound transmitted through water

hy·dro·phyte (hī'drə fīt') *n.* [HYDRO- + -PHYTE] any plant growing only in water or very wet earth —**hy'dro·phyt'ic** (-fit'ik) *adj.*

hy·dro·plane (-plān') *n.* [HYDRO- + PLANE[4]] 1. a small, light motorboat with hydrofoils or with a flat bottom that can skim along the water at high speeds 2. *same as* SEAPLANE 3. a horizontal vane on the hull of a submarine for controlling its vertical motion —*vi.* -**planed'**, -**plan'ing** 1. to drive or ride in a hydroplane 2. to skim along like a hydroplane

hy·dro·pon·ics (hī'drə pon'iks) *n.pl.* [*with sing.* v.] [< HYDRO- + Gr. *ponos*, labour + -ICS] the cultivation of plants in solutions, or moist inert material, containing minerals, instead of in soil —**hy'dro·pon'ic** *adj.* —**hy'·dro·pon'i·cal·ly** *adv.*

hy·dro·pow·er (hī'drə pou'ər) *n.* hydroelectric power

hy·dro·sphere (-sfir') *n.* [HYDRO- + -SPHERE] 1. all the water on the surface of the earth 2. the moisture in the atmosphere surrounding the earth

hy·dro·stat·ics (hī'drə stat'iks) *n.pl.* [*with sing.* v.] [< Fr.: see HYDRO- & STATIC] the branch of physics having to do with the pressure and equilibrium of water and other liquids —**hy'dro·stat'ic**, **hy'dro·stat'i·cal** *adj.* —**hy'dro·stat'i·cal·ly** *adv.*

hy·dro·ther·a·peu·tics (hī'drō thər ə pyōōt'iks) *n.pl.* [*with sing.* v.] *same as* HYDROTHERAPY —**hy'dro·ther·a·peu'tic** *adj.*

hy·dro·ther·a·py (-ther'ə pē) *n.* [HYDRO-+ THERAPY] the treatment of disease, esp. in physical therapy, by the use of baths, compresses, etc.

hy·dro·ther·mal (-thur'məl) *adj.* [HYDRO- + THERMAL] relating to the action of water at high temperature, esp. in forming rocks and minerals

hy·drot·ro·pism (hī drot'rə piz'm) *n.* [HYDRO- + -TROPISM] movement or growth, as of a plant root, in response to the stimulus of moisture —**hy·dro·trop·ic** (hī'drə trop'ik) *adj.*

hy·drous (hī'drəs) *adj.* [HYDR- + -OUS] containing water, as certain chemical compounds

hy·drox·ide (hī drok'sīd) *n.* [HYDR- + OXIDE] a compound consisting of an element or radical combined with the hydroxyl radical (OH)

hy·drox·yl (-sil) *n.* the monovalent radical OH, present in all hydroxides

hy·dro·zo·an (hī'drə zō'ən) *adj.* [< HYDRA + ZO(O)- + -AN] of a class of coelenterate animals having a saclike body and a mouth that opens directly into the body cavity —*n.* any animal of this class, as a hydra, hydroid, etc.

hy·e·na (hī ē'nə) *n.* [< L. < Gr. *hyaina* < *hys*, a pig] a wolflike animal of Africa and Asia, with a characteristic shrill cry: hyenas feed on carrion and are thought of as cowardly

hy·giene (hī'jēn) *n.* [< Fr. < Gr. *hygieinē* < *hygiēs*, healthy] 1. the science of health and its maintenance; system of principles for preserving health and preventing disease 2. hygienic practices

hy·gien·ic (hī jē'nik) *adj.* 1. of hygiene or health 2. promoting health; sanitary —**hy'gi·en'i·cal·ly** *adv.*

hy·gien·ics (-iks) *n.pl.* [*with sing.* v.] the science of health; hygiene

hy·gien·ist (hī'jē nist ; hī jē'-) *n.* an expert in hygiene

hy·gro- [< Gr. *hygros*, wet] *a combining form meaning* wet, moisture: also, before a vowel, **hygr-**

hy·grom·e·ter (hī grom'ə tər) *n.* [< Fr.: see prec. & -METER] any of various instruments for measuring moisture in the air

—**hy·gro·met·ric** (hī'grə met'rik) *adj.* —**hy·grom'e·try** (-trē) *n.*

hy·gro·scope (hī'grə skōp') *n.* [HYGRO- + -SCOPE] an instrument that indicates, without actually measuring, changes in atmospheric humidity

hy·gro·scop·ic (hī'grə skop'ik) *adj.* 1. *a)* absorbing moisture from the air *b)* changed by the absorption of moisture 2. of or according to a hygroscope —**hy'·gro·scop'i·cal·ly** *adv.*

hy·ing (hī'iŋ) *alt. prp. of* HIE

hy·la (hī'lə) *n.* [< Gr. *hylē*, wood] *same as* TREE FROG

hy·lo·zo·ism (hī'lə zō'iz'm) *n.* [< Gr. *hylo*, matter + *zōē*, life] the doctrine that all matter has life, or that life is inseparable from matter

hy·men[1] (hī'mən) *n.* [Gr. *hymēn*, membrane] the thin membrane that usually closes part of the opening of the vagina in a virgin —**hy'men·al** *adj.*

hy·men[2] (hī'mən) *n.* [after Hymen, in Gr. myth. the god of marriage] [Poet.] 1. marriage 2. a wedding song

hy·me·ne·al (hī'mə nē'əl) *adj.* [see HYMEN[2]] of marriage —*n.* [Poet.] a wedding song

hy·me·nop·ter·an (hī'mə nop'tər ən) *n.* [< Gr. < *hymēn*, membrane + *pteron*, a wing + -AN] any of a large order of insects, including wasps, bees, ants, etc., which have a sucking mouth and four membranous wings —**hy'me·nop'·ter·ous** *adj.*

hymn (him) *n.* [< OE. & OFr. < LL. < Gr. *hymnos*] 1. a song in praise or honour of God, a god, or gods 2. any song of praise —*vt.* to praise in a hymn —*vi.* to sing a hymn —**hym'nic** *adj.* —**hym'nist** (-nist) *n.*

hym·nal (him'nəl) *n.* a collection of religious hymns: also **hymn'book'**, **hym'na·ry** (-nā'rē) *adj.* of hymns

hym·no·dy (-nə dē) *n.* [< ML. < Gr.: see HYMN & ODE] 1. the singing of hymns 2. hymns collectively 3. *same as* HYMNOLOGY —**hym'no·dist** *n.*

hym·nol·o·gy (him nol'ə jē) *n.* [< ML. < Gr.: see HYMN & -LOGY] 1. the study of hymns, their history, use, etc. 2. the composition of hymns 3. *same as* HYMNODY (sense 2) —**hym·nol'o·gist** *n.*

hy·oid (hī'oid) *adj.* [< Fr. < ModL. < Gr. *hyoeidēs*, shaped like the letter *υ* (upsilon) < *hy*, upsilon + *eidos*, form] designating or of a U-shaped bone at the base of the tongue —*n.* a hyoid bone

hy·o·scine (hī'ə sēn', -sin) *n.* [< ff.] *same as* SCOPOLAMINE

hy·os·cy·a·mine (hī'ə sī'ə mēn', -min) *n.* [< L. *hyoscyamus*, henbane Gr. *hyoskyamos*] a colourless, poisonous alkaloid obtained from henbane and other plants of the nightshade family, and used in medicine

hyp. 1. hypotenuse 2. hypothesis 3. hypothetical

hy·pae·thral (hi pē'thrəl) *adj.* [< L < Gr. *hypaithros* < HYPO- + *aither*, air + -AL] open to the sky; roofless: said of classical buildings

hy·pal·la·ge (hī pal'ə jē) *n.* [< Gr. *hypo*, HYPO- + *allagē*, change] a figure of speech in which the syntactical relations between two terms are reversed; transferred epithet (Ex.: *the duke's dead fortunes* for *the dead duke's fortunes*)

hype (hīp) *vt.* **hyped**, **hyp'ing** [< HYPODERMIC] [Slang] to stimulate, excite, etc. artificially by or as by the injection of a drug: usually with *up*

hy·per- [Gr. < *hyper*, over, above] *a prefix meaning* over, above, more than normal, excessive [*hypercritical*]

hy·per·a·cid·i·ty (hī'pər ə sid'ə tē) *n.* excessive acidity, as of the gastric juice —**hy'per·ac'id** (-as'id) *adj.*

hy·per·ac·tive (-ak'tiv) *adj.* extremely or abnormally active —**hy'per·ac·tiv'i·ty** (-tiv'ə tē) *n.*

hy·per·ae·mi·a (hī'pər ē'mē ə) *n.* [ModL.: see HYPER- + -AEMIA] increased blood flow or congestion of blood in the body

hy·per·aes·the·sia (-es thē'zhə) *n.* [ModL. < Gr. *hyper*, HYPER- + *aisthēsis*, perception] an abnormal sensitivity of the skin or some other organ

hy·per·ba·ton (hī pur'bə tən) *n.* [Gr. *hyper*, HYPER- + *baineen*, to go] inversion of the natural order of words for the sake of emphasis (Ex.: *that I don't believe* for *I don't believe that*)

hy·per·bo·la (hī pur'bə lə) *n.*, *pl.* -**las**, occas. -**lae'** (-lē') [ModL. < Gr. *hyperbolē* < *hyper-*, over + *ballein*, to throw] a curve formed by the section of a cone cut by a plane more steeply inclined to the base than to the side of the cone

hy·per·bo·le (-bə lē) *n.* [L. < Gr.: see prec.] exaggeration for effect, not meant to be taken literally (Ex.: He's as strong as an ox)

hy·per·bol·ic (hī'pər bol'ik) *adj.* 1. of, having the nature of, or using hyperbole; exaggerated or exaggerating 2. of, or having the form of, a hyperbola Also **hy'per·bol'i·cal** —**hy'per·bol'i·cal·ly** *adv.*

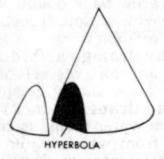

HYPERBOLA

hy·per·bo·lize (hī pur'bə līz') *vt., vi.* -**lized'**, -**liz'ing** to express with or use hyperbole

hy·per·bo·loid (-bə loid) *n.* a quadric surface of which the plane sections are hyperbolas for some orientations and ellipses for others

hy·per·bo·re·an (hī′pər bôr′ē ən, -bə rē′ən) *adj.* [< LL. < L. < Gr. *hyperboreos*, beyond the north wind] 1. of the far north 2. very cold —*n.* [H-] *Gr. Myth.* an inhabitant of a region of sunshine and eternal spring, beyond the north wind

hy·per·crit·i·cal (-krit′i k'l) *adj.* too critical —hy′**per·crit′·i·cal·ly** *adv.* —hy′**per·crit′i·cism** *n.*

hy·per·gly·cae·mi·a (-glī sē′mē ə) *n.* [ModL. < HYPER- + Gr. *glykys*, sweet + -AEMIA] an abnormally high concentration of sugar in the blood

hy·per·gol·ic (hī′pər gol′ik) *adj.* [< G. *Hypergol*, a hypergolic liquid fuel] igniting spontaneously when mixed together, as rocket fuel and oxidizer combinations

hy·per·mar·ket (hī′pər mä′kit) *n.* a huge store, larger than a supermarket, usually on the outskirts of a town

hy·per·me·tro·pi·a (hī′pər mi trō′pē ə) *n.* [ModL. < Gr. *hypermetros*, excessive + -ōpia, -OPIA] farsightedness; abnormal vision in which distant objects are seen more clearly than near ones —hy′**per·me·trop′ic** (-trop′ik) *adj.*

hy·per·on (hī′pər on′) *n.* [HYPER- + (BARY)ON] any of a class of baryons which are heavier than the nucleons

hy·per·o·pi·a (-ō′pē ə) *n.* *same as* HYPERMETROPIA —hy′**per·op′ic** (-op′ik) *adj.*

hy·per·sen·si·tive (-sen′sə tiv) *adj.* abnormally or excessively sensitive —hy′**per·sen′si·tiv′i·ty** *n.*

hy·per·son·ic (-son′ik) *adj.* designating, of, or moving at a speed equal to about five times the speed of sound or greater: see SONIC —hy′**per·son′ic·al·ly** *adv.*

hy·per·sthene (hī′pər sthēn′) *n.* [< Fr. < HYPER- + Gr. *sthēnos*, strength] a lustrous, greenish-black or dark-brown mineral of the pyroxene group

hy·per·ten·sion (-ten′shən) *n.* abnormally high blood pressure, or a disease of which this is the chief sign—hy′**per·ten′sive** *adj.*, *n.*

hy·per·ther·mi·a (hī′pər thur′mē ə) *n.* [< HYPER- + Gr. *thermē*, heat + -IA] an abnormally high body temperature

hy·per·thy·roid·ism (-thī′roid iz'm) *n.* 1. excessive activity of the thyroid gland 2. the disorder caused by this, characterized by nervousness, a rapid pulse,etc. —hy′**per·thy′roid** *adj.*, *n.*

hy·per·tro·phy (hī′pur′trə fē) *n.* [ModL.: see HYPER- & -TROPHY] an abnormal increase in the size of an organ or tissue —*vi., vt.* **-phied, -phy·ing** to undergo or cause to undergo hypertrophy —hy′**per·troph·ic** (hī′pər trof′ik) *adj.*

hy·per·ven·ti·la·tion (hī′pər ven′ti lā′shən) *n.* very rapid or deep breathing that overoxygenates the blood, causing dizziness, fainting, etc. —hy′**per·ven′ti·late′** *vi., vt.* **-lat′ed, -lat′ing**

hy·pha (hī′fə) *n., pl.* **-phae** (-fē) [ModL. < Gr. *hyphē*, a web] any of the threadlike parts making up the mycelium of a fungus —hy′**phal** *adj.*

hy·phen (hī′f'n) *n.* [LL. < Gr. < *hypo-*, under + *hen*, neut. acc. of *heis*, one] a mark (-) used between the parts of a compound word or the syllables of a divided word, as at the end of a line —*vt.* *same as* HYPHENATE

hy·phen·ate (-āt′) *vt.* **-at′ed, -at′ing** 1. to connect by a hyphen 2. to write or print with a hyphen —*adj.* hyphenated —hy′**phen·a′tion** *n.*

hyp·no- [< Gr. *hypnos*, sleep] *a combining form meaning:* 1. sleep 2. hypnotism

hyp·noid (hip′noid) *adj.* resembling sleep or hypnosis: also **hyp′noid′al**

hyp·nol·o·gy (hip nol′ə jē) *n.* [HYPNO- + -LOGY] the science dealing with sleep and hypnotism

hyp·no·pae·di·a, hyp·no·pe·di·a (hip nə pē′dē ə) *n.* [HYPNO- + Gr. *paideia*, instruction] learning, or being conditioned by, facts reiterated while one is asleep

hyp·no·sis (hip nō′sis) *n., pl.* **-ses** (-sēz) [ModL.: see HYPNO-& -OSIS] 1. a sleeplike condition psychically induced, usually by another person, in which the subject is in a state of altered consciousness and responds, with certain limitations, to the suggestions of the hypnotist 2. *same as* HYPNOTISM

hyp·no·ther·a·py (hip′nō ther′ə pē) *n.* [HYPNO-THERAPY] the treatment of disease by hypnotism

hyp·not·ic (hip not′ik) *adj.* [< Fr. < LL. < Gr. *hypnōtikos*, tending to sleep < *hypnos*, sleep] 1. causing sleep; soporific 2. of, like, or inducing hypnosis 3. easily hypnotized —*n.* 1. any agent causing sleep 2. a hypnotized person or one easily hypnotized —hyp·not′·i·cal·ly *adv.*

hyp·no·tism (hip′nə tiz'm) *n.* 1. the act or practice of inducing hypnosis 2. the science of hypnosis —hyp′**no·tist** *n.*

hyp·no·tize (-tīz′) *vt.* **-tized′, -tiz′ing** 1. to induce hypnosis in 2. to spellbind by or as if by hypnotism —hyp′**no·tiz′·a·ble** *adj.*

hy·po¹ (hī′pō) *n., pl.* **-pos** (-pōz) *short for* HYPODERMIC

hy·po² (hī′pō) *n.* [contr. < HYPOSULPHITE] *same as* SODIUM THIOSULPHATE

hy·po- [Gr. < *hypo*, less than] *a prefix meaning:* 1.

under, beneath [*hypodermic*] 2. less than, deficient in [*hypothyroid*] 3. *Chem.* having·a lower state of oxidation

hy·po·blast (hī′pə blast′) *n.* [HYPO- + -BLAST] *same as* ENDODERM

hy·po·caust (hī′pə kôst′) *n.* [< L. < Gr. *hypokauston* < *hypokaiein*, to heat from below] a space below the floor in some ancient Roman buildings, into which hot air was piped to warm the rooms

hy·po·chlo·rite (hī′pə klôr′īt) *n.* any salt of hypochlorous acid

hy·po·chlo·rous acid (-klôr′əs) [HYPO- + CHLOROUS] an unstable acid, HClO, known only in solution and used as a bleach and oxidizer

hy·po·chon·dri·a (hī′pə kon′drē ə) *n.* [ModL. < LL., pl., abdomen (supposed seat of this condition) < Gr. < *hypo-*, under + *chondros*, cartilage of the sternum] abnormal anxiety over one's health, often with imaginary illnesses and severe melancholy

hy·po·chon·dri·ac (-ak′) *adj.* of or having hypochondria: also **hy′po·chon·dri′a·cal** (-kən drī′ə k'l) —*n.* a person who has hypochondria —hy′**po·chon·dri·a·cal·ly** *adv.*

hy·po·chon·dri·a·sis (-kən drī′ə sis) *n.* *same as* HYPOCHONDRIA

hy·po·co·ris·tic (hī′pə ko ris′tik, hip′ə) *adj.* [< Gr. *hypokorizesthai*, to call by a pet name] of or being a pet name, diminutive, or term of endearment

hy·po·cot·yl (hī′pə kot′'l) *n.* [HYPO- + COTYL(EDON)] the part of the axis, or′ stem, below the cotyledons in the embryo of a plant—hy′**po·cot′y·lous** *adj.*

hy·poc·ri·sy (hi pok′rə sē) *n., pl.* **-ries** [< OFr. < L. < G. *hypokrisis*, acting a part, ult. < *hypo-*, under + *krinesthai*, to dispute] a pretending to be what one is not, or to feel what one does not feel; esp., a pretence of virtue, piety, etc.

hypo·crite (hip′ə krit) *n.* [< OFr. < L. *hypocrita*, an actor: see prec.] a person who pretends to be better than he really is, or to be pious, virtuous, etc. without really being so —hyp′**o·crit′i·cal** (-krit′i k'l) —hyp′**o·crit′i·cal·ly** *adv.*

hy·po·cy·cloid (hī′pə sī′kloid) *n.* [HYPO- + CYCLOID] *Geom.* the curve traced by a point on the circumference of a circle that rolls round the inner cicumference of another circle

hy·po·der·mic (hī′pə dur′mik) *adj.* [HYPO- + DERM(A)¹ + -IC] 1. of the parts under the skin 2. injected under the skin —*n.* *same as:* 1. HYPODERMIC INJECTION 2. HYPODERMIC SYRINGE —hy′**po·der′mi·cal·ly** *adv.*

hypodermic injection the injection of a medicine or drug under the skin

hypodermic syringe a piston syringe as of glass, attached to a hollow metal needle (**hypodermic needle**), used for giving hypodermic injections

hy·po·der·mis (-mis) *n.* [ModL.: see HYPO- & DERMIS] 1. *Bot.* a specialized layer of cells, as for support or water storage, just beneath the epidermis of a plant 2. *Zool.* an epidermis secreting an overlying cuticle, as in arthropods and annelids

hy·po·gas·tri·um (hī′pə gas′trē əm) *n., pl.* **-tri·a** (-ə) [ModL. < Gr. *hypogastrion*, lower belly] the lower, middle part of the abdomen

hy·po·ge·al (-jē′əl) *adj.* [< LL. *hypogeus*, underground (< Gr. *hypogaias* < *hypo-*, under + *gē*, earth) + -AL] occurring, growing, living, etc., underground

hy·po·gene (hī′pə jēn′, hip′ə-) *adj.* [HYPO- + Gr. *-genēs* see -GEN] formed, taking place, or originating under the earth

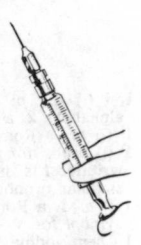

HYPODERMIC SYRINGE

hy·po·nas·ty (hī′pə nas′tē) *n.* [HYPO- + Gr. *nastos*, pressed + -Y] *Bot.* the condition in which an organ, such as a leaf, turns upwards because of the more rapid growth of the cells of the under-surface

hy·po·phos·phate (hī′pə fos′fāt) *n.* a salt or ester of hypophosphoric acid

hy·po·phos·phite (-fos′fīt) *n.* a salt or ester of hypophosphorous acid

hy·po·phos·phor·ic acid (-fos for′ik) an acid, H₄P₂O₆, obtained when phosphorus is slowly oxidized in moist air

hy·po·phos·pho·rous acid (-fos′fər əs) a monobasic acid of phosphorus, H₃PO₂: it is a strong reducing agent

hy·poph·y·sis (hī pof′ə sis) *n., pl.* **-ses′** (-sēz′) [Gr., undergrowth] *same as* PITUITARY GLAND

hy·po·sta·sis (hī pos′tə sis) *n., pl.* **-ses′** (sēz) [Gr. *hypostasis*, a foundation] 1. the essence or essential nature of anything 2. the substance of each of the three divisions of the Godhead 3. *Med.* excess of blood in an organ

hy·po·style (hī′pə stil′, hip′ə-) *adj.* [< Gr. *hypostylos*, resting on pillars] having a roof supported by pillars

hy·po·sul·phite (hī′pə sul′fīt) *n.* 1. any salt of hyposulphurous acid 2. *a popular but erroneous var. of* SODIUM THIOSULPHATE

hy·po·sul·phu·rous acid (-səl fyoor′əs) an unstable acid, H₂S₂O₄, which has strong reducing properties

hy·po·tax·is (-tak′sis) *n.* [ModL. < Gr. *hypotaxis*,

submission] *Gram.* the dependent relation of a clause or construction on another —**hy′po·tac′tic** (-tak′tik) *adj.*

hy·po·ten·sion (-ten′shən) *n.* abnormally low blood pressure —**hy′po·ten′sive** *adj.*

hy·pot·e·nuse (hī pot′ən yōōs′) *n.* [< L. < Gr. *hypoteinousa,* lit., subtending < *hypo-,* under + *teinein,* to stretch] the side of a right-angled triangle opposite the right angle: also **hy·poth′e·nuse** (hī poth′-)

hy·po·thal·a·mus (hī′pə thal′ə məs) *pl.* **-mi′** (-mī′) [ModL.: see HYPO- & THALAMUS] the part of the brain that forms the floor of the third ventricle and regulates many body functions, as temperature —**hy′po·tha·lam′ic** (-thə lam′ik) *adj.*

hy·poth·ec (hī poth′ik, hi-) *n.* [< Fr. < LL. < Gr. *hypothēkē,* pledge] *Law* security given to a creditor over a debtor's property without transfer of possession or title

hy·poth·e·cate (hī poth′ə kāt′) *vt.* **-cat′ed, -cat′ing** [< ML. pp. of *hypothecare,* ult. < Gr. *hypotithenai,* to pledge] to pledge (property) to another as security; mortgage —**hy·poth′e·ca′tion** *n.* —**hy·poth′e·ca′tor** *n.*

hy·po·ther·mi·a (hīp ə thur′mē ə) *n.* [ModL. < HYPO- + Gr. *thermē,* heat] a subnormal body temperature

hy·poth·e·sis (hī poth′ə sis) *n.,* *pl.* **-ses′** (-sēz′) [Gr. < *hypo-,* under + *tithenai,* to place] an unproved theory, proposition, etc. tentatively accepted to explain certain facts or (**working hypothesis**) to provide a basis for further investigation, argument, etc.

hy·poth·e·size (-sīz′) *vi.* **-sized′, -siz′ing** to make a hypothesis —*vt.* to assume; suppose

hy·po·thet·i·cal (hī′pə thet′i k'l) *adj.* **1.** based on or involving a hypothesis; assumed; supposed **2.** given to the use of hypotheses [a *hypothetical* mind] **3.** *Logic* conditional [a *hypothetical* proposition] Also **hy′po·thet′ic** —**hy′po·thet′i·cal·ly** *adv.*

hy·po·thy·roid·ism (hī′pō thī′roid iz′m) *n.* **1.** deficient activity of the thyroid gland **2.** the disorder resulting from this, characterized by a retarded rate of metabolism, sluggishness, puffiness, etc. —**hy′po·thy′roid** *adj., n.*

hyp·sog·ra·phy (hip sog′rə fē) *n.* [< Gr. *hypsos,* height + -GRAPHY] **1.** the scientific study, surveying and mapping of the earth's topography **2.** *a)* topography or relief *b)* a map showing this **3.** *same as* HYPSOMETRY

hyp·som·e·try (-som′ə trē) *n.* [< Gr. *hypsos,* height + -METRY] the measurement of surface elevations above a given point, esp. sea level

hy·rax (hī′raks) *n.,* *pl.* **-rax·es, -ra·ces′** (-rə sēz′) [Gr., shrew mouse] a small, hoofed mammal of Africa and SW Asia, that feeds on plants

hys·sop (his′əp) *n.* [< OFr. < L. < Gr. *hyssōpos* < Heb. *ēzōbh*] **1.** a fragrant, blue-flowered labiate plant, used in folk medicine as a tonic, stimulant, etc. **2.** *Bible* a plant whose twigs were used for sprinkling in certain ancient Jewish rites

hys·ter·ec·to·my (his′tə rek′tə mē) *n.,* *pl.* **-mies** [< Gr. *hystera,* uterus + -ECTOMY] surgical removal of all or part of the uterus

hys·ter·e·sis (his′tə rē′sis) *n.* [Gr., a deficiency] *Physics* a lag of effect, as in magnetization, when the forces acting on a body are changed

hys·te·ri·a (his tir′ē ə) *n.* [ModL. < ff. + -IA] **1.** a psychiatric condition characterized by excitability, sensory and motor disturbances, or the unconscious simulation of organic disorders **2.** any outbreak of wild, uncontrolled excitement, such as fits of laughing and crying

hys·ter·ic (his ter′ik) *adj.* [< L. < Gr. *hysterikos,* suffering in the womb < *hystera,* uterus: the ancients thought of hysteria as a woman's disorder caused by disturbances of the uterus] *same as* HYSTERICAL —*n.* **1.** [*usually pl., occas.* with *sing. v.*] a hysterical fit **2.** a person subject to hysteria

hys·ter·i·cal (-i k'l) *adj.* [prec. + -AL] **1.** of, like, or characteristic of hysteria **2.** [Colloq.] extremely comical **3.** having or subject to hysteria —**hys·ter′i·cal·ly** *adv.*

hys·ter·on pro·te·ron (his′tər on′pro′tər on) [LL. < Gr. *husteron proteron,* latter (placed as) former] **1.** a figure of speech in which the natural order of ideas is reversed (Ex.: *bred and born*) **2.** *Logic* the fallacy of assuming as true what is to be proved

Hz *Physics the symbol for* hertz

I

I, i (ī) *n.,* *pl.* **I's, i's** **1.** the ninth letter of the English alphabet **2.** a sound of *I* or *i*

I¹ (ī) *n.* a Roman numeral for 1 —*adj.* shaped like *I*

I² (ī) *pron.* for pl. see WE [OE. *ic*] the person speaking or writing: *I* is the nominative case form of the first personal singular pronoun —*n.,* *pl.* **I's** the ego

i (ī) *n.* **1.** a Roman numeral for 1 [page *iii*] **2.** *Math.* the symbol for √−1, the square root of −1

I *Chem.* iodine

I., i. **1.** island(s) **2.** isle(s)

-i·a (ē ə, yə) [L. & Gr.] *a suffix used in:* **1.** names of certain diseases [*pneumonia*] **2.** names of some plants and animals [*zinnia*]

I.A.E.A. International Atomic Energy Agency

-i·al (ē əl, yəl, əl) [L. *-ialis, -iale*] *same as* -AL (senses 1, 2) [*racial, centennial*]

i·amb (ī′amb, -am) *n.* [< Fr. < L. < Gr. *iambos*] a metrical foot of two syllables, the first unaccented and the other accented, as in English verse (Ex.: "Tŏ bé, ŏr nŏt tŏ bé")

i·am·bic (ī am′bik) *adj.* of or made up of iambs —*n.* **1.** an iamb **2.** an iambic verse

i·am·bus (-bəs) *n.,* *pl.* **-bus·es, -bi** (-bī) [L.] *same as* IAMB

-i·an (ē ən, yən, ən) [< L. *-ianus*] *same as* -AN [*Indian, reptilian, Grecian*]

-i·an·a (ē an′ə) *same as* -ANA

-i·a·sis (ī′ə sis) [< Gr. *-iasis*] *a combining form meaning* diseased condition [*psoriasis*]

I.A.T.A. International Air Transport Association

-i·at·rics (ē at′riks) [< Gr. < *iatros,* physician] *a combining form meaning* treatment of disease [*paediatrics*]

i·at·ro·gen·ic (ī at′rə jen′ik) *adj.* [< Gr. *iatros,* physician + -GENIC] caused by a physician's words or actions: said esp. of imagined symptoms

-i·a·try (ī′ə trē) [< Gr. *iatreia,* healing] *a combining form meaning* medical treatment [*psychiatry*]

I.B.A. Independent Broadcasting Authority

i·bex (ī′beks) *n.,* *pl.* **i′bex·es, i·bi·ces** (ib′ə sēz′, ī′bə-),

i′bex: see PLURAL, II, D, 1 [L.] any of certain wild goats of Europe, Asia, or Africa: the male has large, backward-curved horns

ibid. [L. *ibidem*] in the same place: used in citing again the book, page, etc. cited just before

-i·bil·i·ty (ə bil′ə tē) *pl.* **-ties** [< L. *-ibilitas*] *a suffix used to* form nouns from adjectives ending in -IBLE [*sensibility*]

i·bis (ī′bis) *n.,* *pl.* **i′bis·es, i′bis:** see PLURAL, II, D, 1 [L. < Gr. < Egypt. *hib*] a large wading bird related to the herons, with long legs and a long, curved bill, as the sacred ibis of the Nile

-i·ble (i b'l, ə b'l) [L. *-ibilis*] *same as* -ABLE [*legible*]

I·bo (ē′bō) *n.* [< the native name] **1.** *pl.* **I′bos, I′bo** any member of an African people of SE Nigeria **2.** their Kwa language

I.B.R.D. International Bank for Reconstruction and Development

-ic (ik) [< Fr. *-ique* or L. *-icus* or Gr. *-ikos*] **1.** a suffix forming adjectives, meaning: *a)* of, having to do with [*volcanic*] *b)* like, having the nature of [*angelic*] *c)* produced by, caused by [*photographic*] *d)* producing, causing [*psychedelic*] *e)* consisting of, containing [*dactylic*] *f)* having, affected by [*lethargic*] *g)* *Chem.* of or derived from [*citric*]; also, of a higher valence than the compound ending in *-ous* [*nitric*] **2.** a suffix forming nouns, meaning a person or thing having the nature of, affected by, belonging to, producing, etc. [*paraplegic, cynic, hypnotic*]

i/c **1.** in charge **2.** internal combustion

I.C.A. Institute of Chartered Accountants in England and Wales

-i·cal (i k'l, ə k'l) [< LL. < *-icus,* -IC + *-alis,* -AL] *same as* -IC: adjectives formed with *-ical* sometimes have differentiated meanings (e.g., *historical, economical*) beyond those of the corresponding *-ic* forms

I.C.A.O. International Civil Aviation Organization

ICBM intercontinental ballistic missile

ice (īs) *n.* [OE. *is*] **1.** water frozen solid by cold **2.** a piece, layer, or sheet of this **3.** anything like frozen water in appearance, etc. **4.** coldness in manner or attitude **5.** a helping of *a*) water ice *b*) ice cream **6.** icing **7.** [U.S. Slang] diamonds —*vt.* **iced, ic′ing 1.** to change into ice; freeze **2.** to cover with ice **3.** to cool by putting ice on, in, or around **4.** to cover with icing —*vi.* to freeze (often with *up* or *over*) —**break the ice 1.** to make a start by getting over initial difficulties **2.** to make a start towards getting better acquainted —**cut no ice** [Colloq.] to have no effect —**on ice** [Slang] **1.** in readiness or reserve **2.** in abeyance **3.** with success assured —**on thin ice** [Colloq.] in a risky situation

-ice (is, əs) [< OFr. *-ice* < L. *-itius*] *a suffix meaning* condition or quality of [*justice*]

Ice. 1. Iceland **2.** Icelandic

I.C.E. 1. Institution of Civil Engineers **2.** internal-combustion engine

ice age *same as* GLACIAL EPOCH

ice bag a bag, as of rubber, for holding ice, applied to the body to reduce a swelling, ease pain, etc.

ice·berg (īs′bʉrg′) *n.* [prob. via Du. *ijsberg*, lit., ice mountain < Scand.] a great mass of ice broken off from a glacier and floating in the sea

ice·blink (-bliŋk′) *n.* [after Du. *ijsblink* or Da. *isblink*] a brightness in the sky caused by the reflection of light from an expanse of ice

ice·boat (-bōt′) *n.* **1.** a light, boatlike frame, often triangular, equipped with runners and driven over ice by a sail, propeller, or jet engine **2.** *same as* ICEBREAKER (sense 1)

ice·bound (-bound′) *adj.* **1.** held fast by ice, as a boat **2.** made inaccessible by ice, as a port

ice·box (-boks′) *n.* **1.** a cabinet with ice in it for keeping foods, etc. cold **2.** the ice-making compartment of a refrigerator **3.** [U.S.] a refrigerator

ice·break·er (-brā′kər) *n.* **1.** a sturdy ship for breaking a channel through ice **2.** anything lessening formality

ice·cap (-kap′) *n.* a mass of glacial ice that spreads slowly out from a centre

ice-cold (īs′kōld′) *adj.* very cold

ice cream [orig., *iced cream*] a sweet, creamy frozen food made from variously flavoured cream and milk products and often containing gelatin, eggs, fruits, etc. —**ice′-cream′** *adj.*

ice·fall (-fôl) *n.* a steep part of a glacier, with deep crevasses, resembling a frozen waterfall

ice field 1. *same as* ICECAP **2.** an extensive area of floating sea ice

ice floe 1. *same as* ICE FIELD (sense 2) **2.** a single piece, large or small, of floating sea ice

ice hockey a team game played on ice, in which the players, using curved sticks and wearing skates, try to drive a rubber disc (*puck*) into their opponents' goal

ice·house (-hous′) *n.* a storeroom for ice, often underground

Ice·lan·dic (īs lan′dik) *adj.* of Iceland, its people, their language, or culture —*n.* the N. Germanic language of the Icelanders

ice lolly frozen ice cream or water ice on a stick

ice·man (īs′man′, -mən) *n., pl.* **-men** (-men′, -mən) **1.** [Chiefly U.S.] a person who sells or delivers ice **2.** a person skilled in travelling on ice

ice pack 1. a large, floating expanse of ice masses frozen together **2.** an ice bag, folded cloth, etc. filled with crushed ice and applied to the body, as to reduce a swelling or ease pain

ice pick a sharply pointed metal tool used to chop ice into small pieces

ice plant a succulent plant with thick leaves covered with glistening cells which resemble ice crystals

ice sheet a thick layer of ice covering an extensive area for a long period, as in the ice age

ice shelf a thick mass of glacial ice along a polar shore, often protruding out to sea for many miles

ice skate a skate for skating on ice: see SKATE[1] (sense 1) —**ice′-skate′** *vi.* **-skat′ed, -skat′ing** —**ice skater**

I.Chem.E. Institution of Chemical Engineers

ich·neu·mon (ik nyoo′mən) *n.* [< Gr. *ichneumon*, lit., tracker < *ichnos*, a track] **1.** the Egyptian species of mongoose **2.** *same as* ICHNEUMON FLY

ichneumon fly a hymenopteran insect whose larvae live as parasites in or on other insect larvae: also **ichneumon wasp**

ich·nog·ra·phy (ik nog′rə fē) *n.* [< Fr. or L. < Gr. *ichnographia*, a ground plan] **1.** a scale drawing of a ground plan of a building **2.** the art of drawing such plans

i·chor (ī′kôr, -kər) *n.* [Gr. *ichōr*] **1.** *Gr. Myth.* the fluid flowing instead of blood in the veins of the gods **2.** a watery discharge from a wound or sore —**i′chor·ous** (-kər əs) *adj.*

ichthy·o- [< Gr. < *ichthys*, a fish] *a combining form meaning* fish, like a fish: also **ichthy-i**

ich·thy·oid (ik′thē oid′) *adj.* [< prec. + -OID] like a fish —*n.* a fishlike vertebrate

ich·thy·ol·o·gy (ik′thē ol′ə jē) *n.* [< ModL.: see ICHTHYO- & -LOGY] the branch of zoology dealing with fishes —**ich′-**

thy·o·log′i·cal (-ə loj′i k'l), **ich′thy·o·log′ic** *adj.* —**ich′-thy·ol′o·gist** *n.*

ich·thy·o·saur (ik′thē ə sôr′) *n.* [< ModL. < ICHTHYO- + Gr. *sauros*, lizard] a prehistoric marine reptile, now extinct, which had a fishlike body, four paddle-shaped flippers, and a dolphinlike head —**ich′thy·o·sau′ri·an** (-sôr′ē ən) *adj.*

I.C.I. Imperial Chemical Industries

-i·cian (ish′ən) [< Fr.: see -IC & -IAN] *a suffix meaning* a person engaged in, practising, or specializing in [*physician*]

i·ci·cle (ī′si k'l) *n.* [< OE. < *is*, ice + *gicel*, piece of ice] a hanging piece of ice, formed by the freezing· of dripping water —**i′ci·cled** *adj.*

ic·ing (ī′siŋ) *n.* **1.** a mixture, as of sugar, butter, flavouring, etc., for covering a cake or pastries **2.** the formation of ice on an object, as on a ship or an aircraft

icing sugar granulated sugar ground to a powder

I.C.M.A. Institute of Cost and Management Accountants

i·con (ī′kon) *n.* [L. < Gr. *eikōn*, an image] **1.** an image **2.** *Orthodox Eastern Ch.* an image or picture of Jesus, Mary, a saint, etc., venerated as sacred —**i·con·ic** (ī kon′ik) *adj.*

i·con·o- [< Gr. *eikōn*, an image] *a combining form meaning* image, figure: also **icon-**

i·con·o·clast (ī kon′ə klast′) *n.* [< ML. < MGr. < Gr. *eikōn*, an image + *klaein*, to break] **1.** *a*) anyone opposed to the religious use of images *b*) anyone who deliberately destroys religious images, as the Roundheads in the Civil War **2.** a person who attacks or ridicules traditional or venerated institutions or ideas —**i·con′o·clasm** *n.* —**i·con′o·clas′tic** *adj.* —**i·con′o·clas′ti·cal·ly** *adv.*

i·co·nog·ra·phy (ī′kə nog′rə fē) *n.* [< Gr. *eikonographia*, a sketch] **1.** the art of illustrating by pictures, figures, etc. **2.** the study of pictures, images, etc., esp. of portraits of a specific person **3.** *same as* ICONOLOGY

i·co·nol·a·try (ī′kə nol′ə trē) *n.* [ICONO- + -LATRY] the worship of images —**i′co·nol′a·ter** *n.*

i·co·nol·o·gy (-ə jē) *n.* [ICONO- + -LOGY] **1.** the study of icons, etc. **2.** icons collectively **3.** symbolism

i·con·o·scope (ī kon′ə skōp′) *n.* [ICONO-+ -SCOPE] an early form of television camera tube

i·co·sa·he·dron (ī′kō sə hē′drən, ī′ko-, ī′kə-) *n., pl.* **-he′dra** (-drə), **-drons** [< Gr. *eikosi*, twenty + -HEDRON] a solid figure with twenty plane surfaces

-ics (iks) [-IC + -S (*pl.*)] *a pl. suffix meaning*: **1.** [usually with *sing. v.*] *a*) art, science, study [*economics*] *b*) arrangement, system [*statistics*] **2.** [usually with *pl. v.*] *a*) activities, practices [*histrionics*] *b*) qualities, properties [*atmospherics*]

ic·tus (ik′təs) *n., pl.* **-tus·es, -tus** [< L. < pp. of *icere*, to hit] **1.** rhythmical or metrical stress, or accent **2.** *Med.* a stroke or sudden attack

i·cy (ī′sē) *adj.* **i′ci·er, i′ci·est 1.** having much ice; full of or covered with ice **2.** of ice **3.** like ice; slippery or very cold **4.** cold in manner; unfriendly —**i′ci·ly** *adv.* —**i′ci·ness** *n.*

id (id) *n.* [ModL. < L., it] *Psychoanalysis* that part of the psyche which is the reservoir of the instinctual drives, dominated by the pleasure principle and irrational wishing

-id (id, əd) [ult. < L. or Gr.] *a suffix meaning*: **1.** a thing belonging to or connected with [*Aeneid, arachnid*] **2.** *Chem. same as* -IDE

ID, I.D. [U.S.] identification

id. [L. *idem*] the same

I'd (īd) **1.** I had **2.** I would **3.** I should

I.D.A. International Development Association

-i·dae (i dē′) [ModL.] *a suffix used to form the name of* a zoological family [*Canidae* (the dog family)]

-ide (īd; *occas.* id) [< (OX)IDE] *a suffix added to part of the* name of the nonmetallic or electronegative element or radical in a binary compound [*sodium chloride*] *or used in* forming the name of a class of compounds [*glycoside*]

i·de·a (ī dē′ə) *n.* [L. < Gr. *idea*, appearance of a thing] **1.** a thought; mental conception or image; notion **2.** an opinion or belief **3.** a plan; scheme; intention **4.** a hazy perception; vague impression; inkling **5.** meaning or significance **6.** *Philos.* according to Plato, a model or archetype of which all real things are but imperfect imitations

i·de·al (ī dē′əl; *also, esp. for adj.* 2 & 4 *and for n.,* ī dēl′) *adj.* [< Fr. < LL. < L. *idea*: see prec.] **1.** existing as an idea; being a model or archetype **2.** thought of as perfect; exactly as one would wish **3.** identifying or illustrating an idea or conception **4.** existing only in the mind as an image or concept; imaginary **5.** *Philos.* of idealism —*n.* **1.** a conception of something in its most excellent form **2.** a perfect model or standard **3.** a goal or principle

i·de·al·ism (ī dē′əl iz′m) *n.* **1.** behaviour or thought based on a conception of things as one thinks they should be **2.** the representation of idealized persons or things in art or literature **3.** a striving to achieve one's ideals **4.** *Philos.* any theory which holds that things exist only as ideas in the mind or that things are really imperfect imitations of unchanging models or forms having independent existence apart from the material world: cf. MATERIALISM

i·de·al·ist (-ist) *n.* **1.** *a*) a person whose behaviour or thought is based on ideals *b*) a visionary or impractical

dreamer 2. an adherent or practitioner of idealism in art, literature, or philosophy—*adj.* *same as* IDEALISTIC
i·de·al·is·tic (ī′dē ə lis′tik) *adj.* 1. of or characteristic of an idealist 2. of, characterized by, or based on idealism —**i′de·al·is′ti·cal·ly** *adv.*
i·de·al·ize (ī dē′ə līz′) *vt.* **-ized′, -iz′ing** to make ideal; regard or show as perfect or more nearly perfect than is true —*vi.* 1. to form an ideal 2. to represent things in the manner of an idealist —**i·de′al·i·za′tion** *n.* —**i·de′al·iz′er** *n.*
i·de·al·ly (ī dē′əl ē) *adv.* 1. in an ideal manner; perfectly 2. in theory
i·de·ate (ī′dē āt′, ī dē′āt) *vt., vi.* **-at′ed, -at′ing** to form an idea (of) —**i′de·a′tion** *n.* —**i′de·a′tion·al** *adj.* —**i′de·a′tion·al·ly** *adv.*
‡**i·dée fixe** (ē dā fēks′) [Fr.] a fixed idea; obsession
‡**i·dem** (ī′dem, ē′-) *pron.* [L.] the same as that previously mentioned
i·den·tic (ī den′tik) *adj.* [see IDENTITY] *Diplomacy* using the same language or following the same course in international relations as another power
i·den·ti·cal (ī den′ti k'l) *adj.* [< ML. < LL. *identitas* (see IDENTITY) + -AL] 1. the very same 2. exactly alike 3. designating twins, always of the same sex, developed from a single fertilized ovum and very much alike in appearance —**i·den′ti·cal·ly** *adv.*
i·den·ti·fi·ca·tion (ī den′tə fi kā′shən) *n.* 1. an identifying or being identified 2. anything by which a person or thing can be identified 3. *Psychoanalysis* a mainly unconscious process by which a person thinks, feels, and acts in a way which resembles his image of another person important to him
identification parade a line of people, similar in appearance, from which a suspected criminal is to be recognized
i·den·ti·fy (ī den′tə fī′) *vt.* **-fied′, -fy′ing** 1. to make identical; treat as the same 2. to show to be the very person or thing known, described, or claimed 3. to connect or associate closely 4. *Psychoanalysis* to make identification of (oneself) with someone else —*vi.* to understand and share another's feelings; sympathize (*with*) —**i·den′ti·fi′a·ble** *adj.* —**i·den′ti·fi′er** *n.*
I·den·ti·kit (ī den′tə kit) [IDENTI(FICATION) + KIT] *a trademark for* a composite picture, formed from descriptions given, of a person of whom no actual photograph or picture is available —*adj.* resembling, or assembled like, an Identikit
i·den·ti·ty (-tē) *n., pl.* **-ties** [< Fr. < LL. *identitas* < L. *idem,* the same] 1. the condition or fact of being the same or exactly alike; sameness 2. *a)* the condition or fact of being a specific person or thing; individuality *b)* the condition of being the same as a person or thing described or claimed
id·e·o- [< Fr. *ideo-* or < Gr. *idea*] *a combining form meaning* idea [*ideology*]
id·e·o·gram (id′ē ə gram′, ī′dē-) *n.* [prec. + -GRAM] 1. a graphic symbol representing an object or idea without expressing the sounds that form its name 2. a symbol representing an idea rather than a word (Ex.: 5, +, ÷) Also **id′e·o·graph** —**id′e·o′graph·y** *n.*
id·e·o·graph·ic (id′ē ə graf′ik) *adj.* of, or having the nature of, an ideogram: also **id′e·o·graph′i·cal** —**id′e·o·graph′i·cal·ly** *adv.*
i·de·o·log·i·cal (ī′dē ə loj′i k'l, id′ē ə-) *adj.* of or concerned with ideology: also **i′de·o·log′ic** —**i′de·o·log′i·cal·ly** *adv.*
i·de·ol·o·gy (ī′dē ol′ə jē, id′ē-) *n., pl.* **-gies** [< Fr.: see IDEO- & -LOGY] 1. the study of ideas, their nature and source 2. thinking of an idealistic, abstract, or impractical nature 3. the doctrines, opinions, or way of thinking of an individual, class, etc.; specif., the ideas on which a political, economic, or social system is based —**i′de·ol′o·gist** *n.*
ides (īdz) *n.pl.* [*often with sing. v.*] [Fr. < L. *idus*] in the ancient Roman calendar, the 15th day of March, May, July, or October, or the 13th of the other months
‡**id est** (id est) [L.] that is (to say)
id·i·o·cy (id′ē ə sē) *n., pl.* **-cies** 1. the state of being an idiot 2. great foolishness or stupidity
id·i·om (id′ē əm) *n.* [< Fr. & LL. < Gr. < *idios,* one's own] 1. the language or dialect of a people, region, etc. 2. the usual way in which the words of a particular language are joined together to express thought 3. an accepted phrase or expression having a meaning different from the literal 4. the style of expression characteristic of an individual 5. a characteristic style, as in art or music
id·i·o·mat·ic (id′ē ō mat′ik, id′ē ə-) *adj.* 1. characteristic of a particular language 2. using or having many idioms 3. of, or having the nature of, an idiom or idioms —**id′i·o·mat′i·cal·ly** *adv.*
id·i·o·syn·cra·sy (id′ē ə siŋ′krə sē, -sin′-) *n., pl.* **-sies** [< Gr. < *idio-,* one's own + *synkrasis,* mixture < *syn-,* together + *kerannynai,* to mix] 1. the temperament peculiar to a person or group 2. any personal peculiarity, mannerism, reaction, etc. —**id′i·o·syn·crat′ic** (-sin krat′ik) *adj.* —**id′·i·o·syn·crat′i·cal·ly** *adv.*

id·i·ot (id′ē ət) *n.* [OFr. < L. < Gr. *idiōtēs,* ignorant person < *idios,* one's own] 1. a person having severe mental retardation: an obsolescent term: see MENTAL RETARDATION 2. a very foolish or stupid person
id·i·ot·ic (id′ē ot′ik) *adj.* of or like an idiot; very foolish or stupid —**id′i·ot′i·cal·ly** *adv.*
i·dle (ī′d'l) *adj.* **i′dler, i′dlest** [OE. *idel,* empty] 1. *a)* worthless; useless [*idle* talk] *b)* futile; pointless [an *idle* wish] 2. baseless; unfounded [*idle* rumours] 3. *a)* unemployed *b)* not in use [*idle* machines] 4. lazy —*vi.* **i′dled, i′dling** 1. to move slowly or aimlessly 2. to be unemployed or inactive 3. to operate without transmitting any power, esp. with disengaged gears —*vt.* 1. to waste; squander [*idling* away one's youth] 2. to make (a motor, etc.) idle 3. to make inactive or unemployed —**i′dle·ness** *n.* —**i′dly** *adv.*
i·dler (īd′lər) *n.* 1. one who loafs 2. *a)* a gearwheel placed between two others to transfer motion from one to the other without changing their direction or speed: also **idler gear** (or **wheel**), **idle wheel** *b)* a pulley guiding a belt or taking up slack: also **idler pulley**
i·dol (ī′d'l) *n.* [< OFr. < L. < Gr. *eidōlon,* an image < *eidos,* form] 1. an image of a god, used as an object of worship 2. an object of excessive devotion or admiration, as a pop star, etc.

IDLE WHEEL

i·dol·a·ter (ī dol′ə tər) *n.* [< OFr. < LL. < LGr. < *eidōlon* (see prec.) + *latris,* servant] 1. a worshipper of idols 2. a devoted admirer; adorer —**i·dol′a·tress** (-tris) *n.fem.*
i·dol·a·trize (-trīz′) *vt., vi.* **-trized′, -triz′ing** to worship as an idolater
i·dol·a·trous (-trəs) *adj.* 1. of, or having the nature of, idolatry 2. worshipping idols 3. having or showing excessive admiration or devotion —**i·dol′a·trous·ly** *adv.* —**i·dol′a·trous·ness** *n.*
i·dol·a·try (-trē) *n., pl.* **-tries** 1. worship of idols 2. excessive devotion or reverence
i·dol·ize (ī′dəl īz′) *vt.* **-ized′, -iz′ing** 1. to make an idol of 2. to love or admire excessively —*vi.* to worship idols —**i′dol·i·za′tion** *n.* —**i′dol·iz′er** *n.*
i·dyll, i·dyl (īd′'l, ī′d'l) *n.* [< L. < Gr. dim. of *eidos,* a form, image] 1. a short poem or prose work describing a simple, pleasant scene of rural or pastoral life 2. a scene or incident suitable for such a work 3. any seemingly perfect or innocent incident or period —**i·dyl′lic** *adj.* —**i·dyl′li·cal·ly** *adv.* —**i′dyll·ist** *n.*
-ie (ē) [earlier form of -Y¹] *a suffix meaning:* 1. small, little [*doggie*]: often used to express affection 2. one that is as specified [*softie*]
IE, I.E. Indo-European
i.e. [L. *id est*] that is (to say)
I.E.E. Institution of Electrical Engineers
-i·er (ir, ər, ē′ər, yər) [< OFr. < L. *-arius*] *a suffix meaning* a person concerned with (a specified action or thing) [*bombardier, furrier*]
if (if) *conj.* [OE. *gif*] 1. on condition that; in case that [if I come, I'll see him] 2. granting that [if he was there, I didn't see him] 3. whether [ask him *if* he knows her] *If* is also used in exclamations expressing: *a)* a wish [if I had only known!] *b)* surprise, annoyance, etc. [*if* that isn't the limit!] —*n.* 1. a supposition 2. a condition [too many *ifs* and buts] —**as if** as the situation would be if; as though
I.F. intermediate frequency
I.F.C. International Finance Corporation
iff *Logic* if and only if
if·fy (if′ē) *adj.* [Colloq.] full of uncertainty
ig·loo (ig′lōō) *n., pl.* **-loos** [Esk. *igdlu,* snow house] an Eskimo house or hut, usually dome-shaped and built of blocks of packed snow
ig·ne·ous (ig′nē əs) *adj.* [< L. < *ignis,* a fire] 1. of, like, or containing fire 2. formed by volcanic action or intense heat [*igneous* rock]
ig·nis fat·u·us (ig′nis fat′yoo wəs) *pl.* **ig·nes fat·u·i** (ig′nēz fat′yoo wī′) [ML. < L. *ignis,* a fire + *fatuus,* foolish] 1. a light seen at night moving over swamps, etc., probably caused by a combustion of marsh gas: popularly called *will-o'-the-wisp, jack-o'-lantern* 2. a deceptive hope, goal, or influence; delusion
ig·nite (ig nīt′) *vt., vi.* **-nit′ed, -nit′ing** [< L. pp. of *ignire* < *ignis,* a fire] 1. to set burning 2. to get excited —**ig·nit′a·ble, ig·nit′i·ble** *adj.* —**ig·nit′er, ig·ni′tor** *n.*
ig·ni·tion (ig nish′ən) *n.* 1. an igniting or means of igniting 2. in an internal-combustion engine, *a)* the igniting of the explosive mixture in the cylinder *b)* the device or system for doing this
ignition key key used to activate the engine of a vehicle powered by internal combustion
ig·ni·tron (ig nī′tron, ig′nə tron′) *n.* [IGNI(TE) + (ELEC)TRON] a type of mercury-arc rectifier with a mercury-pool cathode and a single anode

ig·no·ble (ig nō′b'l) *adj.* [MFr. < L. < *in-*, not + *nobilis*, known] not noble in character or quality; dishonourable; base; mean —**ig·no′ble·ness** *n.* —**ig·no′bly** *adv.*

ig·no·min·i·ous (ig′nə min′ē əs) *adj.* 1. shameful; disgraceful 2. despicable 3. degrading —**ig′no·min′·i·ous·ly** *adv.* —**ig′no·min′i·ous·ness** *n.*

ig·no·min·y (ig′nə min′ē) *n., pl.* -**min′ies** [< Fr. < L. *ignominia* < *in-*, without + *nomen*, name] 1. loss of one's reputation; shame and dishonour 2. disgraceful or shameful quality or action

ig·no·ra·mus (ig′nə rā′məs) *n., pl.* -**mus·es** [< the name of a lawyer in a 17th-c. play; L., lit., we ignore (a legal term)] an ignorant person

ig·no·rance (ig′nər əns) *n.* the condition or quality of being ignorant; lack of knowledge

ig·no·rant (-ənt) *adj.* [< OFr. < L. prp. of *ignorare*: see ff.] 1. lacking knowledge, education, or experience 2. caused by or showing lack of these 3. unaware (*of*) —**ig′no·rant·ly** *adv.*

ig·nore (ig nôr′) *vt.* -**nored**′, -**nor′ing** [< Fr. < L. *ignorare* < *in-*, not + base of *gnarus*, knowing] to disregard deliberately; pay no attention to; refuse to consider —**ig·nor′er** *n.*

i·gua·na (i gwä′nə) *n.* [Sp. < S. AmInd. *iuana*] a large, harmless, tropical American lizard with spines from neck to tail

i·guan·o·don (i gwän′ə don) *n.* [Mod.L. < prec. + -ODON(T)] a large, vegetarian dinosaur

LAND IGUANA
(to 1.5 m long)

IHP, I.H.P., ihp., i.h.p. indicated horsepower

IHS a contraction misread from the Greek word IHΣOYΣ, Jesus, used as a symbol or monogram

i·ke·ba·na (ē′ke bä′nä) *n.* [Jap.] the Japanese art of arranging flowers in rhythmic, decorative designs

i·kon (ī′kon) *n. var. of* ICON

il- *see* IN-.[1], IN.[2]

-ile (il) [< Fr. *-il, -ile* < L. *-ilis*] a suffix meaning of, having to do with, that can be, like, suitable for [*docile, missile*]: sometimes -**il** [*civil*]

il·e·i·tis (il′ē īt′is) *n.* inflammation of the ileum

il·e·um (il′ē əm) *n., pl.* **il′e·a** (-ə) [ModL. < L., flank, groin (var. of *ilium*)] the lowest part of the small intestine —**il′·e·ac′** (-ak′), **il′e·al** (-əl) *adj.*

i·lex (ī′leks) *n.* [L.] *same as:* 1. HOLLY 2. HOLM OAK

-il·i·ty (il′ə tē) *pl.* -**ties** a suffix used in nouns formed from adjectives ending in -ILE, -IL [*imbecility, civility*]

il·i·um (il′ē əm) *n., pl.* **il′i·a** (-ə) [ModL.: see ILEUM] the flat, uppermost section of the innominate bone —**il′·iac′** (-ak′) *adj.*

ilk (ilk) *adj.* [Scot. dial. < OE. *ilca*, same] [Obs.] same; like —*n.* kind; sort: only in **of that** (or **his, her,** etc.) **ilk:** a misunderstanding of the orig. Scottish phrase meaning "of the same name"

ill (il) *adj.* **worse, worst** [< ON. *illr*] 1. *a*) morally bad [*ill repute*] *b*) adverse [*ill fortune*] *c*) not kind or friendly [*ill will*] *d*) unfavourable [an *ill* omen] 2. not healthy, normal, or well; sick 3. faulty; improper [with an *ill* grace] —*n.* anything causing harm, trouble, pain, etc.; evil —*adv.* **worse, worst** 1. in, an ill way; specif., *a*) badly *b*) unkindly 2. with difficulty; scarcely [he can *ill* afford it] —**ill at ease** uneasy; uncomfortable

I'll (īl) 1. I shall 2. I will

ill. 1. illustrated 2. illustration

ill-ad·vised (il′əd vīzd′) *adj.* showing or resulting from a lack of sound advice or proper consideration; unwise —**ill′·ad·vis′ed·ly** (-vī′zid lē) *adv.*

ill-bred (-bred′) *adj.* badly brought up; rude

ill-con·sid·ered (-kən sid′ərd) *adj.* not properly considered; not suitable or wise

ill-dis·posed (-dis pōzd′) *adj.* 1. having a bad disposition; malicious or malevolent 2. unfriendly or unfavourable (*towards*)

il·le·gal (i lē′gəl) *adj.* not lawful; against the law or against the rules —**il·le·gal′i·ty** (il′ē gal′ə tē) *n., pl.* -**ties** —**il·le′·gal·ly** *adv.*

il·leg·i·ble (i lej′ə b'l) *adj.* difficult or impossible to read because badly written or printed, faded, etc. —**il·leg′i·bil′i·ty** *n.* —**il·leg′i·bly** *adv.*

il·le·git·i·mate (il′ə jit′ə mit) *adj.* 1. born of parents not married to each other 2. incorrectly deduced 3. not lawful 4. unsanctioned —**il′le·git′i·ma·cy** (-mə sē) *n., pl.* -**cies** —**il′le·git′i·mate·ly** *adv.*

ill fame bad reputation —**house of ill fame** a brothel

ill-fat·ed (il′ fāt′id) *adj.* 1. having or sure to have an evil fate or unlucky end 2. unlucky

ill-fa·voured (-fā′vərd) *adj.* 1. unpleasant or ugly in appearance 2. offensive

ill-found·ed (-foun′did) *adj.* not supported by facts or sound reasons

ill-got·ten (-got′'n) *adj.* obtained by evil, unlawful, or dishonest means [ill-gotten gains]

ill humour a disagreeable, cross, or sullen mood or state of mind —**ill′-hu′moured** *adj.* —**ill′-hu′moured·ly** *adv.*

il·lib·er·al (i lib′ər əl) *adj.* 1. [Archaic] without culture; unrefined 2. intolerant; narrow-minded 3. miserly; stingy —**il·lib′er·al′i·ty** (-ə ral′ə tē) *n.* —**il·lib′er·al·ly** *adv.*

il·lic·it (i lis′it) *adj.* not allowed by law, custom, etc.; unlawful —**il·lic′it·ly** *adv.* —**il·lic′it·ness** *n.*

il·lim·it·a·ble (i lim′it ə b'l) *adj.* without limit or bounds —**il·lim′it·a·bil′i·ty, il·lim′it·a·ble·ness** *n.* —**il·lim′it·a·bly** *adv.*

il·lit·er·a·cy (i lit′ər ə sē) *n.* 1. the state of being illiterate 2. *pl.* -**cies** a mistake (in writing or speaking) suggesting poor education

il·lit·er·ate (-it) *adj.* [L. *illiteratus*, unlettered] 1. ignorant; uneducated; esp., not knowing how to read or write 2. having or showing limited knowledge, experience, or culture 3. violating accepted usage in language —*n.* an illiterate person —**il·lit′er·ate·ly** *adv.*

ill-man·nered (il′man′ərd) *adj.* rude; impolite

ill nature an unpleasant, disagreeable disposition —**ill′-na′·tured** *adj.* —**ill′-na′tured·ly** *adv.*

ill·ness (-nis) *n.* the condition of being ill; sickness; disease

il·log·ic (i loj′ik) *n.* lack of logic

il·log·i·cal (-i k'l) *adj.* not logical; using or based on faulty reasoning —**il·log′i·cal′i·ty** (-i kal′ə tē), **il·log′i·cal·ness** *n.* —**il·log′i·cal·ly** *adv.*

ill-spent (il′spent′) *adj.* misspent; wasted

ill-starred (-stärd′) *adj.* unlucky; doomed

ill-tem·pered (-tem′pərd) *adj.* bad-tempered

ill-timed (-tīmd′) *adj.* coming or done at the wrong time; inopportune

ill-treat (il′trēt′) *vt.* to treat unkindly, cruelly, or unfairly; abuse —**ill′-treat′ment** *n.*

il·lu·mi·nance (i lōō′mə nəns) *n.* *same as* ILLUMINATION (sense 2)

il·lu·mi·nant (-nənt) *adj.* giving light; illuminating —*n.* something that gives light

il·lu·mi·nate (-nāt′) *vt.* -**nat′ed, -nat′ing** [< L. pp. of *illuminare* < *in-*, in + *luminare*, to light < *lumen*, a light] 1. *a*) to give light to; light up *b*) to brighten; animate 2. *a*) to make clear; explain *b*) to inform; enlighten 3. to make famous 4. to decorate with lights 5. to decorate (an initial letter, a page border, etc.) with designs of gold, bright colours, etc. —**il·lu′mi·na·ble** *adj.* —**il·lu′mi·na′tive** *adj.* —**il·lu′mi·na′tor** *n.*

il·lu·mi·na·ti (i lōō′mə nät′ē) *n.pl., sing.* -**to** (-ō) [< L., pl. of *illuminatus*, enlightened] 1. people who have, or profess to have, special intellectual or spiritual enlightenment 2. [I-] any of various societies, usually secret, composed of such people

il·lu·mi·na·tion (i lōō′mə nā′shən) *n.* 1. an illuminating or being illuminated 2. the intensity of light per unit of area 3. the designs used in illuminating manuscripts 4. [*pl.*] lights, esp. coloured ones, used as decorations, as at a seaside resort

il·lu·mine (i lōō′min) *vt.* -**mined, -min·ing** *same as* ILLUMINATE —**il·lu′mi·na·ble** *adj.*

illus., illust. 1. illustrated 2. illustration

ill-us·age (il′yōō′sij, -zij) *n.* unfair, unkind, or cruel treatment; abuse: also **ill usage**

ill-use (-yōōz′; *for n.* -yōōs′) *vt.* -**used**′, -**us′ing** to subject to ill-usage —*n. same as* ILL-USAGE

il·lu·sion (i lōō′zhən) *n.* [< OFr. < L. < pp. of *illudere*, to mock] 1. a false idea or conception 2. an unreal or misleading appearance or image 3. a false perception or interpretation of what one sees 4. a hallucination —**il·lu′·sion·al, il·lu′sion·ar·y** *adj.*

il·lu·sion·ist (-ist) *n.* an entertainer who performs sleight-of-hand tricks

il·lu·sive (i lōō′siv) *adj.* illusory; unreal —**il·lu′sive·ly** *adv.* —**il·lu′sive·ness** *n.*

il·lu·so·ry (-sər ē) *adj.* producing, based on, or having the nature of, illusion; deceptive; unreal —**il·lu′so·ri·ly** *adv.* —**il·lu′so·ri·ness** *n.*

il·lus·trate (il′ə strāt′) *vt.* -**trat′ed, -trat′ing** [< L. pp. of *illustrare* < *in-*, in + *lustrare*, to illuminate] 1. to make clear or explain, as by examples or comparisons 2. *a*) to furnish (books, etc.) with explanatory or decorative drawings, pictures, etc. *b*) to explain or decorate: said of pictures, etc. —*vi.* to illustrate something —**il′lus·tra′tor** *n.*

il·lus·tra·tion (il′ə strā′shən) *n.* 1. an illustrating or being illustrated 2. an explanatory example, story, etc. 3. an explanatory or decorative picture, diagram, etc. —**il′lus·tra′·tion·al** *adj.*

il·lus·tra·tive (il′ə strāt′iv, i lus′trə tiv) *adj.* serving to illustrate —**il·lus′tra·tive·ly** *adv.*

il·lus·tri·ous (i lus′trē əs) *adj.* [< L. *illustris*, bright] very distinguished; famous; eminent —**il·lus′tri·ous·ly** *adv.* —**il·lus′tri·ous·ness** *n.*

ill will unfriendly feeling; hostility; hate

ILO, I.L.O. International Labour Organization

I.L.P. Independent Labour Party

ILS instrument landing system

I'm (īm) I am

im- see IN-[1], IN-[2]

im·age (im'ij) *n.* [OFr. < L. < *imago* < base of *imitari*, to imitate] **1.** a representation of a person or thing, drawn, painted, etc.; esp., a statue **2.** the visual impression of something produced by a mirror, lens, etc. **3.** a copy; counterpart; likeness **4.** *a)* a mental picture of something; conception *b)* the public conception of a person, product, etc., often created by publicity **5.** a type; embodiment [the *image* of laziness] **6.** a figure of speech, esp. a metaphor or simile —*vt.* **-aged, -aging 1.** to portray; delineate **2.** to reflect; mirror **3.** to picture in the mind **4.** to typify **5.** to describe vividly

im·age·ry (im'ij rē, -ər ē) *n., pl.* **-ries 1.** mental images **2.** descriptions and figures of speech

i·mag·i·na·ble (i maj'ə nə b'l) *adj.* that can be imagined —**i·mag'i·na·bly** *adv.*

i·mag·i·nar·y (i maj'ə nər ē) *adj.* **1.** existing only in the imagination; unreal **2.** *Math.* designating or of the square root of a negative quantity —**i·mag'i·nar·i·ly** *adv.* —**i·mag'-i·nar·i·ness** *n.*

i·mag·i·na·tion (i maj'ə nā'shən) *n.* **1.** *a)* the act or power of forming mental images of what is not actually present *b)* the act or power of creating mental images of what has never been actually experienced, or of creating new images or ideas by combining previous experiences **2.** anything imagined **3.** a foolish notion **4.** responsiveness to the imaginative creations of others **5.** resourcefulness in dealing with new or unusual experiences

i·mag·i·na·tive (i maj'ə nə tiv, -nāt'iv) *adj.* **1.** having, using, or showing imagination **2.** given to imagining **3.** of or resulting from imagination —**i·mag'i·na·tive·ly** *adv.* —**i·mag'i·na·tive·ness** *n.*

i·mag·ine (i maj'in) *vt., vi.* **-ined, -in·ing** [< OFr. < L. *imaginari* < *imago*, an IMAGE] **1.** to make a mental image (of); conceive in the mind **2.** to suppose; guess; think —*interj.* an exclamation of surprise

im·ag·ism (im'ə jiz'm) *n.* a movement in modern poetry (c. 1909-1917) using precise, concrete images, free verse, and suggestion —**im'ag·ist** *n., adj.* —**im'ag·is'tic** *adj.*

i·ma·go (i mā'gō) *n., pl.* **-goes, -gos, i·mag·i·nes** (i maj'ə nēz') [ModL. < L., an IMAGE] an insect in its final, adult, reproductive stage

i·mam (i mäm') *n.* [Ar. *imām*] **1.** the prayer leader in a Moslem mosque **2.** [often I-] title for a Moslem ruler

i·mam·ate (-āt) *n.* **1.** the territory ruled by an imam **2.** the office or function of an imam

im·bal·ance (im bal'əns) *n.* lack of balance

im·be·cile (im'bə sēl, -sil) *n.* [< Fr. < L. *imbecilis*, feeble] **1.** a person having moderate mental retardation: obsolescent term: see MENTAL RETARDATION **2.** a very foolish or stupid person —*adj.* very foolish or stupid: also **im'be·cil'ic** (-sil'ik)

im·be·cil·i·ty (im'bə sil'ə tē) *n., pl.* **-ties 1.** the state of being an imbecile **2.** great foolishness or stupidity **3.** an imbecile act or remark

im·bed (im bed') *vt. same as* EMBED

im·bibe (im bīb') *vt.* **-bibed', -bib'ing** [< L. *imbibere* < *in-*, in + *bibere*, to drink] **1.** *a)* to drink (esp. alcoholic liquor) *b)* to take in with the senses or mind; drink in **2.** to absorb (moisture) —*vi.* to drink, esp. alcoholic liquor —**im·bib'-er** *n.*

im·bri·cate (im'brə kit; *also, and for v. always,* -kāt') *adj.* [< LL. pp. of *imbricare*, to cover with tiles < L. gutter tile < *imber*, rain] **1.** overlapping evenly, as tiles or fish scales **2.** ornamented as with overlapping scales —*vt., vi.* **-cat'ed, -cat'ing** to make or be imbricate —**im'bri·cate·ly** *adv.* —**im'bri·ca'tion** *n.*

im·bro·glio (im brōl'yō) *n., pl.* **-glios** [It. < *imbrogliare*, to embroil] **1.** an involved and confusing situation **2.** a confused misunderstanding or disagreement

im·brue (im brōo') *vt.* **-brued', -bru'ing** [< OFr., ult. < L. *imbibere*: see IMBIBE] to wet, soak, or stain, esp. with blood —**im·brue'ment** *n.*

im·bue (im byōo') *vt.* **-bued', -bu'ing** [< L. *imbuere*] **1.** [Rare] to saturate **2.** to fill with colour; dye **3.** to permeate or inspire (*with* principles, ideas, emotions, etc.)

IMCO Intergovernmental Maritime Consultative Organization

I.Mech.E. Institution of Mechanical Engineers

I.M.F. International Monetary Fund

imit. 1. imitation **2.** imitative

im·i·tate (im'ə tāt') *vt.* **-tat'ed, -tat'ing** [< L. pp. of *imitari*, to imitate] **1.** to follow the example of **2.** to act the same as; mimic **3.** to copy the form, colour, etc. of **4.** to be like in appearance; resemble —**im'i·ta·ble** (-tə b'l) *adj.* —**im'-i·ta'tor** *n.*

im·i·ta·tion (im'ə tā'shən) *n.* **1.** an imitating **2.** the result or product of imitating —*adj.* made to resemble something that is usually superior or genuine [*imitation* leather]

im·i·ta·tive (im'ə tāt'iv, im'i tat'iv) *adj.* **1.** formed from a model **2.** given to imitating **3.** not genuine **4.** sounding

like the thing signified, as the word *clang* —**im'i·ta'tive·ly** *adv.* —**im'i·ta'tive·ness** *n.*

I.M.M. Institution of Mining and Metallurgy

im·mac·u·late (i mak'yə lit) *adj.* [< L. < *in-*, not + pp. of *maculare*, to soil < *macula*, a spot] **1.** perfectly clean; spotless **2.** without flaw **3.** pure; innocent; sinless **4.** [Colloq.] perfect; faultless [his serve was *immaculate*] —**im·mac'u·late·ly** *adv.* —**im·mac'u·late·ness, im·mac'-u·la·cy** (-lə sē) *n.*

im·ma·nent (im'ə nənt) *adj.* [< LL. prp. of *immanere* < *in-*, in + *manere*, to remain] **1.** living, remaining, or operating within; inherent **2.** present throughout the universe: said of God —**im'ma·nence, im'ma·nen·cy** *n.* —**im'ma·nent·ly** *adv.*

im·ma·te·ri·al (im'ə tir'ē əl) *adj.* **1.** not consisting of matter; spiritual **2.** that does not matter; not pertinent; unimportant —**im'ma·te'ri·al'i·ty** (-al'ə tē) *n., pl.* **-ties** —**im'ma·te'ri·al·ly** *adv.*

im·ma·te·ri·al·ism (-iz'm) *n.* the theory that material things exist only as mental perceptions or ideas —**im'ma·te'-ri·al·ist** *n.*

im·ma·ture (im'ə tyoor', -choor') *adj.* **1.** not mature or ripe; not completely grown or developed **2.** not finished or perfected —**im'ma·ture'ly** *adv.* —**im'ma·tu'ri·ty, im'-ma·ture'ness** *n.*

im·meas·ur·a·ble (i mezh'ər ə b'l) *adj.* not measurable; boundless —**im·meas'ur·a·bil'i·ty, im·meas'ur·a·ble·ness** *n.* —**im·meas'ur·a·bly** *adv.*

im·me·di·a·cy (i mē'dē ə sē) *n.* the quality or condition of being immediate

im·me·di·ate (i mē'dē it) *adj.* [< LL.: see IN-[2] & MEDIATE] having nothing coming between; with no intermediary; specif., *a)* not separated in space; in direct contact; closest; also, close by *b)* not separated in time; without delay *c)* of the present *d)* next in order, succession, etc.; also, directly or closely related *e)* directly affecting; direct *f)* understood directly or intuitively [an *immediate* inference]

im·me·di·ate·ly (-lē) *adv.* in an immediate manner; specif., *a)* without intervening agency or cause *b)* without delay; at once —*conj.* as soon as [go *immediately* he comes]

im·me·mo·ri·al (im'ə môr'ē əl) *adj.* extending back beyond memory or record —**im'me·mo'ri·al·ly** *adv.*

im·mense (i mens') *adj.* [Fr. < L. < *in-*, not + pp. of *metiri*, to measure] **1.** very large; vast; huge **2.** [Slang] very good; excellent —**im·mense'ly** *adv.* —**im·mense'ness** *n.*

im·men·si·ty (i men'sə tē) *n., pl.* **-ties 1.** great size or extent **2.** infinite space or being

im·merge (i murj') *vi.* **-merged', -merg'ing** [see ff.] to plunge, as into a liquid

im·merse (i murs') *vt.* **-mersed', -mers'ing** [< L. pp. of *immergere*, to plunge: see IN-[1] & MERGE] **1.** to plunge or dip into or as if into a liquid **2.** to baptize by dipping under water **3.** to absorb deeply; engross [*immersed* in study] —**im·mers'i·ble** *adj.* —**im·mer'sion** *n.*

immersion heater an electric coil or rod that heats water while directly immersed in it

im·mi·grant (im'ə grənt) *n.* one that immigrates —*adj.* immigrating

im·mi·grate (-grāt') *vi.* **-grat'ed, -grat'ing** [< L. pp. of *immigrare*: see IN-[1] & MIGRATE] to come into a new country or region, esp. in order to settle there: opposed to EMIGRATE —**im'mi·gra'tion** *n.* —**im'mi·gra'to·ry** *adj.*

im·mi·nence (im'ə nəns) *n.* **1.** a being imminent: also **im'-mi·nen·cy 2.** something imminent

im·mi·nent (-nənt) *adj.* [< L. prp. of *imminere* < *in-*, in + *minere*, to project] likely to happen soon: said of danger, evil, etc. —**im'mi·nent·ly** *adv.*

im·mis·ci·ble (i mis'ə b'l) *adj.* [< IN-[2] + MISCIBLE] that cannot be mixed, as oil and water —**im·mis'ci·bil'i·ty** *n.* —**im·mis'ci·bly** *adv.*

im·mit·i·ga·ble (i mit'i gə b'l) *adj.* [LL. *immitigabilis*: see IN-[2] & MITIGATE] that cannot be mitigated

im·mo·bile (i mo'bīl, -bēl) *adj.* not movable or moving; stable; motionless —**im'mo·bil'i·ty** *n.*

im·mo·bi·lize (i mō'bə līz') *vt.* **-lized', -liz'ing 1.** to make immobile **2.** to prevent the movement of (a limb or joint) with splints or a cast —**im·mo'bi·li·za'tion** *n.*

im·mod·er·ate (i mod'ər it) *adj.* not moderate; without restraint; excessive —**im·mod'er·ate·ly** *adv.* —**im·mod'er·a'-tion, im·mod'er·ate·ness, im·mod'er·a·cy** (-ə sē) *n.*

im·mod·est (i mod'ist) *adj.* not modest; specif., *a)* indecent; improper *b)* bold; forward —**im·mod'est·ly** *adv.* —**im·mod'-es·ty** *n.*

im·mo·late (im'ə lāt') *vt.* **-lat'ed, -lat'ing** [< L. pp. of *immolare*, to sprinkle with sacrificial meal < *in-*, on + *mola*, meal] to sacrifice; esp., to kill as a sacrifice —**im'-mo·la'tion** *n.* —**im'mo·la'tor** *n.*

im·mor·al (i mor'əl) *adj.* not in conformity with accepted principles of right behaviour; wicked; sometimes, specif., unchaste; lewd —**im·mor'al·ly** *adv.*

im·mo·ral·i·ty (im'ə ral'ə tē, im'ə-) *n.* **1.** the state or quality of being immoral **2.** immoral behaviour **3.** *pl.* **-ties** an immoral act or practice

im·mor·tal (i môr't'l) *adj.* **1.** not mortal; living or lasting forever **2.** of immortal beings or immortality **3.** lasting a long time; enduring **4.** having lasting fame —*n.* an immortal being; specif., *a*) [*pl.*] the ancient Greek or Roman gods *b*) a person of lasting fame —**im·mor·tal·i·ty** (-tal′ə tē) *n.* —**im·mor′tal·ly** *adv.*

im·mor·tal·ize (i môr′tə līz′) *vt.* **-ized′, -iz′ing** to make immortal; esp., to give lasting fame to —**im·mor′tal·i·za′tion** *n.* —**im·mor′tal·iz′er** *n.*

im·mor·telle (im′ôr tel′) *n.* [Fr. fem. of *immortel,* undying] same as EVERLASTING (*n.* 2)

im·mov·a·ble (i moov′ə b'l) *adj.* **1.** that cannot be moved; firmly fixed **2.** motionless; stationary **3.** unyielding; steadfast **4.** unemotional; impassive —*n.* [*pl.*] *Law* immovable objects or property, as land, buildings, etc. —**im·mov′a·bil′i·ty, im·mov′a·ble·ness** *n.* —**im·mov′a·bly** *adv.*

im·mune (i myoon′) *adj.* [< L. *immunis,* exempt < *in-,* without + *munia,* duties] **1.** having immunity; specif., *a*) exempt from or protected against something disagreeable or harmful *b*) not susceptible to a specified disease because having the specific antibodies **2.** relating to immunity

immune body same as ANTIBODY

im·mu·ni·ty (i myoon′ə tē) *n.,* pl. **-ties 1.** exemption or freedom from something burdensome or otherwise unpleasant **2.** resistance to or protection against a specified disease

im·mu·nize (im′yoo nīz′) *vt.* **-nized′, -niz′ing** to give immunity to —**im′mu·ni·za′tion** *n.*

im·mu·no- (i myoo′nō, im′yoo nō′) *a combining form* meaning immune, immunity [*immunology*]

im·mu·no·gen·ic (im′yoo nō jen′ik) *adj.* producing immunity —**im′mu·no·gen′i·cal·ly** *adv.*

im·mu·nol·o·gy (im′yoo nol′ə jē) *n.* the branch of medicine dealing with immunity to disease or with allergic reactions, etc. —**im′mu·no·log′i·cal** (-nə loj′i k'l), **im′mu·no·log′ic** *adj.* —**im′mu·no·log′i·cal·ly** *adv.* —**im′mu·nol′o·gist** *n.*

im·mure (i myoor′) *vt.* **-mured′, -mur′ing** [< OFr. < ML. *immurare* < L. *im-,* in + *murus,* a wall] to shut up as within walls —**im·mure′ment** *n.*

im·mu·ta·ble (i myoot′ə b'l) *adj.* never changing or varying; unchangeable —**im·mu′ta·bil′i·ty, im·mu′ta·ble·ness** *n.* —**im·mu′ta·bly** *adv.*

imp (imp) *n.* [< OE., ult. < Gr. *emphyta,* scion < *em-,* in + *phyton,* a plant] **1.** a young demon **2.** a mischievous child —*vt.* to repair (the wing or tail of a falcon) by grafting on (feathers)

imp. 1. imperative **2.** imperfect **3.** imperial **4.** impersonal **5.** import **6.** importer **7.** imprimatur

im·pact (im pakt′; *for n.* im′pakt) *vt.* [< L. pp. of *impingere,* to press firmly together] to force tightly together; wedge —*n.* **1.** a striking together; collision **2.** the force of a collision; shock **3.** the power of an event, idea, etc. to produce changes, move feelings, etc.—**im·pac′-tion** *n.*

im·pact·ed (im pak′tid) *adj.* **1.** firmly lodged in the jaw: said of a tooth unable to erupt **2.** [U.S.] densely populated

im·pair (im per′) *vt.* [< OFr., ult. < L. *in-,* intens. + *pejor,* worse] to make worse, less, weaker, etc.; damage; reduce —**im·pair′ment** *n.*

im·pa·la (im pä′lə, -pä′lä) *n.,* pl. **-la, -las:** see PLURAL, II, D, 2 [Zulu] a medium-sized, reddish antelope of C and S Africa

im·pale (im pāl′) *vt.* **-paled′, -pal′ing** [< Fr. < ML. *impalare* < L. *in-,* on + *palus,* a pole] **1.** to pierce through with, or fix on, something pointed **2.** to torture by fixing on a stake **3.** to make helpless, as if fixed on a stake [*impaled by her glance*] —**im·pale′ment** *n.*

IMPACTED TOOTH

im·pal·pa·ble (im pal′pə b'l) *adj.* **1.** not perceptible to the touch **2.** too slight or subtle to be grasped easily by the mind —**im·pal′pa·bil′i·ty** *n.* —**im·pal′pa·bly** *adv.*

im·pan·el (im pan′'l) *vt.* **-elled, -el·ling** same as EMPANEL

im·part (im pärt′) *vt.* [< OFr. < L. *impartire:* see IN-[1] & PART] **1.** to give a share or portion of; give **2.** to tell; reveal —**im·part′a·ble** *adj.* —**im′par·ta′tion** *n.* —**im·part′-er** *n.*

im·par·tial (im pär′shəl) *adj.* favouring no one side or party more than another; fair —**im·par′ti·al′i·ty** (-shē al′ə tē) *n.* —**im·par′tial·ly** *adv.*

im·part·i·ble (im pär′tə b'l) *adj.* [see IN-[2] & PARTIBLE] that cannot be partitioned or divided: said of an estate

im·pass·a·ble (im päs′ə b'l) *adj.* that cannot be passed, crossed, or travelled over —**im·pass′a·bil′i·ty** *n.* —**im·pass′-a·bly** *adv.*

im·passe (im′päs, im päs′, am päs′) *n.* [Fr.] **1.** a passage open only at one end; blind alley **2.** a situation offering no escape; deadlock

im·pas·si·ble (im pas′ə b'l) *adj.* [< OFr. < LL. < L. *im-,* not + *passibilis* < *pati,* to suffer] **1.** that cannot feel pain **2.**

that cannot be injured **3.** that cannot be moved emotionally —**im·pas′si·bil′i·ty** *n.* —**im·pas′si·bly** *adv.*

im·pas·sion (im pash′ən) *vt.* [It. *impassionare*] to fill with passion; arouse emotionally

im·pas·sioned (im pash′ənd) *adj.* filled with passion; passionate; fiery; ardent —**im·pas′sioned·ly** *adv.*

im·pas·sive (im pas′iv) *adj.* **1.** not feeling pain; insensible **2.** not feeling or showing emotion; placid; calm —**im·pas′-sive·ly** *adv.* —**im·pas′sive·ness, im·pas·siv·i·ty** (im′-pə siv′ə tē) *n.*

im·pas·to (im päs′tō) *n.* [< It. *impastare,* to paste over] painting with the paint laid on thickly

im·pa·tience (im pā′shəns) *n.* lack of patience; specif., *a*) annoyance because of delay, opposition, etc. *b*) restless eagerness to do something, etc.

im·pa·ti·ens (im pā′shē enz′, -shənz) *n.* [ModL. < L.: see ff.] a plant with spurred flowers and pods that burst and scatter their seeds when ripe

im·pa·tient (im pā′shənt) *adj.* feeling or showing impatience —**im·pa′tient·ly** *adv.*

im·peach (im pēch′) *vt.* [< OFr. < LL. *impedicare,* to entangle < L. *in-,* in + *pedica,* a fetter < *pes,* foot] **1.** to challenge or discredit (a person's honour, etc.) **2.** to challenge the practices or honesty of; esp., to bring (a public official) before the proper tribunal on a charge of wrongdoing —**im·peach′a·bil′i·ty** *n.* —**im·peach′a·ble** *adj.* —**im·peach′ment** *n.*

im·pec·ca·ble (im pek′ə b'l) *adj.* [< L. < *in-,* not + *peccare,* to sin] **1.** not liable to sin or wrongdoing **2.** without defect or error; flawless —**im·pec′ca·bil′i·ty** *n.* —**im·pec′ca·bly** *adv.*

im·pe·cu·ni·ous (im′pi kyoo′nē əs) *adj.* [< IN-[2] + obs. *pecunious,* wealthy < OFr. < L. < *pecunia,* money] having no money; penniless —**im′pe·cu′ni·os′i·ty** (-os′ə tē), **im′pe·cu′ni·ous·ness** *n.* —**im′pe·cu′ni·ous·ly** *adv.*

im·ped·ance (im pēd′əns) *n.* [IMPED(E) + -ANCE] the total opposition (a combination of resistance and reactance) offered by an electric circuit to the flow of an alternating current of a single frequency: it is measured in ohms

im·pede (im pēd′) *vt.* **-ped′ed, -ped′ing** [< L. *impedire* < *in-,* in + *pes* (gen. *pedis*), foot] to bar or hinder the progress of; obstruct or delay —**im·ped′er** *n.*

im·ped·i·ment (im ped′ə mənt) *n.* [< L. *impedimentum,* hindrance] anything that impedes; specif., a speech defect; lisp, stammer, etc. —**im·ped·i·men′tal** *adj.*

im·ped·i·men·ta (im ped′ə men′tə) *n.pl.* [L., pl.: see prec.] things hindering progress, as on a trip; esp., baggage, supplies, etc., as those carried with an army

im·pel (im pel′) *vt.* **-pelled′, -pel′ling** [L. *impellere* < *in-,* on + *pellere,* to drive] **1.** to push, drive, or move forwards; propel **2.** to force, compel, or urge —**im·pel′lent** *adj., n.*

im·pend (im pend′) *vi.* [L. *impendere* < *in-,* in + *pendere,* to hang] to be about to happen; threaten —**im·pend′ing** *adj.*

im·pen·e·tra·ble (im pen′i trə b'l) *adj.* **1.** that cannot be penetrated or passed through **2.** that cannot be solved or understood; unfathomable **3.** unreceptive to ideas, influences, etc. **4.** *Physics* having that property of matter by which two bodies are prevented from occupying the same space at the same time —**im·pen′e·tra·bil′i·ty** *n.* —**im·pen′e·tra·bly** *adv.*

im·pen·i·tent (im pen′ə tənt) *adj.* without regret, shame, or remorse; unrepentant —*n.* an impenitent person —**im·pen′-i·tence, im·pen′i·ten·cy** *n.* —**im·pen′i·tent·ly** *adv.*

imper. imperative

im·per·a·tive (im per′ə tiv) *adj.* [< LL. < pp. of L. *imperare,* to order] **1.** of or indicating power or authority; commanding [*an imperative gesture*] **2.** absolutely necessary; urgent **3.** *Gram.* designating or of a verb mood expressing a command, request, etc. —*n.* **1.** a compelling rule, duty, etc. **2.** a command **3.** *Gram. a*) the imperative mood *b*) a verb in this mood —**im·per′a·tive·ly** *adv.* —**im·per′a·tive·ness** *n.*

im·pe·ra·tor (im′pe rät′ôr, -rät′-; -ər) *n.* [L. < pp. of *imperare,* to command] in ancient Rome, a title of honour for generals and, later, emperors —**im·per·a·to·ri·al** (im pir′ə tôr′ē əl) *adj.*

im·per·cep·ti·ble (im′pər sep′tə b'l) *adj.* not easily perceived by the senses or mind; very slight, gradual, subtle, etc. —**im′per·cep′ti·bil′i·ty** *n.* —**im′per·cep′ti·bly** *adv.*

im·per·cep·tive (-tiv) *adj.* not perceiving; lacking perception —**im′per·cep′tive·ness** *n.*

im·per·cip·i·ent (-sip′ē ənt) *adj.* same as IMPERCEPTIVE —**im′per·cip′i·ence** *n.*

imperf. 1. imperfect **2.** imperforate

im·per·fect (im pur′fikt) *adj.* **1.** not finished or complete; lacking in something **2.** not perfect; having a defect or error **3.** in the grammar of certain inflected languages, designating or of a verb tense indicating an incomplete or continuous past action or state: in English, "was writing" is a form like the imperfect tense —*n. Gram.* **1.** the imperfect tense **2.** a verb in this tense —**im·per′fect·ly** *adv.* —**im·per′fect·ness** *n.*

im·per·fec·tion (im′pər fek′shən) *n.* **1.** a being imperfect **2.** a shortcoming; defect; blemish

im·per·fo·rate (im pur'fər it, -fə rāt') *adj.* 1. having no holes or openings 2. having a straight edge without perforations: said of a postage stamp Also **im·per'fo·rat'-ed —n.** an imperforate stamp **—im·per'fo·ra'tion** *n.*

im·pe·ri·al (im pir'ē əl) *adj.* [< OFr. < L. < *imperium*, empire] 1. of an empire 2. of a country having control over other countries or colonies 3. of, or having the rank of, an emperor or empress 4. having supreme authority 5. majestic; august 6. of great size or superior quality 7. *a)* formerly, of the British Empire, now the Commonwealth *b)* of a system of weights and measures, formerly official in Britain *—n.* 1. formerly, a size of writing paper (22 x 31 inches, c. 56 x 76 cm) 2. a pointed tuft of beard on the lower lip and chin **—im·pe'ri·al·ly** *adv.*

im·pe·ri·al·ism (-iz'm) *n.* 1. imperial state, authority, or government 2. the policy and practice of forming and maintaining an empire by conquest, colonization, economic or political domination, etc. **—im·pe'ri·al·ist** *n., adj.* **—im·pe'ri·al·is'tic** *adj.* **—im·pe'ri·al·is'ti·cal·ly** *adv.*

im·per·il (im per'əl) *vt.* **-illed, -il·ling** to put in peril **—im·per'il·ment** *n.*

im·pe·ri·ous (im pir'ē əs) *adj.* [< L. < *imperium*, empire] 1. arrogant; domineering 2. urgent **—im·pe'ri·ous·ly** *adv.* **—im·pe'ri·ous·ness** *n.*

im·per·ish·a·ble (im per'ish ə b'l) *adj.* that will not die or decay; indestructible; immortal **—im·per'ish·a·bil'i·ty** *n.* **—im·per'ish·a·bly** *adv.*

im·per·ma·nent (im pur'mə nənt) *adj.* not permanent; not lasting; temporary **—im·per'ma·nence, im·per'ma·nen·cy** *n.* **—im·per'ma·nent·ly** *adv.*

im·per·me·a·ble (im pur'mē ə b'l) *adj.* not permeable; not permitting passage, esp. of fluids **—im·per'me·a·bil'i·ty** *n.* **—im·per'me·a·bly** *adv.*

im·per·mis·si·ble (im'pər mis'ə b'l) *adj.* not permissible; not allowed

im·per·son·al (im pur's'n əl) *adj.* 1. not personal; specif., *a)* without reference to any particular person [an *impersonal* comment] *b)* not existing as a person [an *impersonal* force] *c)* without human warmth or sympathy [an *impersonal* manner] 2. *Gram. a)* designating or of a verb occurring only in the third person singular (Ex.: "it is snowing") *b)* indefinite: said of a pronoun *—n.* an impersonal verb or pronoun **—im·per'son·al'i·ty** (-al'ə tē) *n.* **—im·per'son·al·ly** *adv.*

im·per·son·al·ize (-ə līz') *vt.* **-ized', -iz'ing** to make impersonal

im·per·son·ate (im pur'sə nāt') *vt.* **-at'ed, -at'ing** 1. [Now Rare] to personify; embody 2. to act the part of 3. *a)* to mimic (a person) for purposes of entertainment *b)* to pretend to be (an officer, etc.) with fraudulent intent **—im·per'son·a'tion** *n.* **—im·per'son·a'tor** *n.*

im·per·ti·nence (im pur'tin əns) *n.* 1. the quality or fact of being impertinent; specif., *a)* irrelevance *b)* insolence 2. an impertinent act, remark, etc. Also **im·per'ti·nen·cy,** *pl.* **-cies**

im·per·ti·nent (-ənt) *adj.* [ME. < OFr. < L. *impertinens*] 1. not pertinent; irrelevant 2. insolent **—im·per'ti·nent·ly** *adv.*

im·per·turb·a·ble (im'pər tur'bə b'l) *adj.* that cannot be perturbed or excited; impassive **—im'per·turb'a·bil'i·ty** *n.* **im'per·turb'a·ble·ness** *n.* **—im'per·turb'a·bly** *adv.*

im·per·vi·ous (im per'vē əs) *adj.* 1. not pervious; impermeable 2. not affected by (with *to*) **—im·per'vi·ous·ly** *adv.* **—im·per'vi·ous·ness** *n.*

im·pe·ti·go (im'pə tī'gō) *n.* [L. < *impetere:* see IMPETUS] a skin disease with eruption of pustules; esp., a contagious disease of this kind

im·pet·u·os·i·ty (im pet'yoo wos'ə tē) *n.* 1. the quality of being impetuous 2. *pl.* **-ties** an impetuous action or feeling

im·pet·u·ous (im pet'yoo wəs) *adj.* [< OFr. < LL. < L. *impetus:* see ff.] 1. moving with great force or violence; rushing 2. acting or done suddenly with little thought; rash; impulsive **—im·pet'u·ous·ly** *adv.* **—im·pet'u·ous·ness** *n.*

im·pe·tus (im'pə təs) *n., pl.* **-tus·es** [L. < *impetere,* to attack < *in-,* in + *petere,* to rush at] 1. the force with which a body moves against resistance, resulting from its mass and initial velocity 2. a stimulus to action; incentive

im·pi (im'pi) *n., pl.* **-pi, pies** [< Zulu] a group of Bantu warriors

im·pi·e·ty (im pī'ə tē) *n.* 1. lack of piety, esp. towards God 2. *pl.* **-ties** an impious act or remark

im·pinge (im pinj') *vi.* **-pinged', -ping'ing** [L. *impingere* < *in-,* in + *pangere,* to strike] 1. *a)* to strike or hit (*on, upon,* or *against*) *b)* to touch (*on* or *upon*) 2. to make inroads or encroach (*on* or *upon*) **—im·pinge'ment** *n.* **—im·ping'er** *n.*

im·pi·ous (im'pē əs) *adj.* not pious; specif., lacking reverence for God **—im'pi·ous·ly** *adv.* **—im'pi·ous·ness** *n.*

imp·ish (imp'ish) *adj.* of or like an imp; mischievous **—imp'ish·ly** *adv.* **—imp'ish·ness** *n.*

im·plac·a·ble (im plak'ə b'l, -plā'kə-) *adj.* not placable; that cannot be appeased or pacified **—im·plac'a·bil'i·ty** *n.* **—im·plac'a·bly** *adv.*

im·plant (im plänt'; *for n.* im'plänt') *vt.* 1. to plant firmly; embed 2. to fix firmly in the mind; instil 3. *Med.* to insert

(an organ, tissue, etc.) within the body *—n. Med.* an implanted organ, etc. **—im'plan·ta'tion** (-plän tā'shən) *n.*

im·plau·si·ble (im plô'zə b'l) *adj.* not plausible **—im·plau'-si·bil'i·ty** *n.,* adj. **—im·plau'si·bly** *adv.*

im·ple·ment (im'plə mənt; *for v.* -ment') *n.* [< LL. *implementum,* a filling up < L. *implere* < *in-,* in + *plere,* to fill] 1. any tool, instrument, utensil, etc. used or needed in a given activity 2. a means to an end *—vt.* 1. to carry into effect 2. to provide the means for accomplishing 3. to provide with implements **—im'ple·men'tal** *adj.* **—im'-ple·men·ta'tion** (-mən tā'shən) *n.*

im·pli·cate (im'plə kāt') *vt.* **-cat'ed, -cat'ing** [< L. pp. of *implicare:* see IMPLY] 1. to cause to be involved in or associated with a crime, fault, etc. 2. to imply **—im'pli·ca'-tion** *n.* **—im'pli·ca'tive** *adj.* **—im'pli·ca'tive·ly** *adv.*

im·plic·it (im plis'it) *adj.* [< L. pp. of *implicare:* see IMPLY] 1. suggested or to be understood though not plainly expressed; implied: distinguished from EXPLICIT 2. necessarily or naturally involved though not plainly apparent or expressed; inherent 3. without reservation or doubt; absolute **—im·plic'it·ly** *adv.* **—im·plic'it·ness** *n.*

im·plied (im plīd') *adj.* involved, suggested, or understood without being directly expressed

im·plode (im plōd') *vt., vi.* **-plod'ed, -plod'ing** [< IN.¹ + (EX)PLODE] to burst inwards **—im·plo'sion** (-plō'zhən) *n.* **—im·plo'sive** *adj.*

im·plore (im plôr') *vt.* **-plored', -plor'ing** [< L. *implorare* < *in-,* intens. + *plorare,* to cry out] 1. to ask earnestly for; beseech 2. to beg (a person) to do something **—im·plor'-ing·ly** *adv.*

im·plu·vi·um (im plōō'vi əm) *n.* [L.] a rectangular basin in the court of a Roman house to receive the rainwater

im·ply (im plī') *vt.* **-plied', -ply'ing** [< OFr. < L. *implicare,* to involve < *in-,* in + *plicare,* to fold] 1. to have as a necessary part, condition, or effect [war *implies* killing] 2. to indicate indirectly; hint; suggest [he *implied* that we cheat]

im·pol·der (im pōl'dər) *vt.* to make a polder of; reclaim land from the sea

im·po·lite (im'pə līt') *adj.* not polite; discourteous; rude **—im'po·lite'ly** *adv.* **—im'po·lite'ness** *n.*

im·pol·i·tic (im pol'ə tik) *adj.* not politic; unwise; injudicious **—im·pol'i·tic·ly** *adv.*

im·pon·der·a·ble (im pon'dər ə b'l) *adj.* [< LL.: see IN.² & PONDER] 1. that cannot be weighed or measured 2. that cannot be conclusively determined or explained *—n.* anything imponderable **—im·pon'der·a·bil'i·ty** *n.* **—im·pon'-der·a·bly** *adv.*

im·port (im pôrt'; *also, and for n.* always, im'pôrt) *vt.* [< L. *importare* < *in-,* in + *portare,* to carry] 1. *a)* to bring in from the outside *b)* to bring (goods) from another country, esp. for selling 2. to mean; signify *—vi.* to be of importance; matter *—n.* 1. the importing of goods 2. [often *pl.*] something imported 3. meaning 4. importance **—im·port'a·ble** *adj.* **—im·port'er** *n.*

im·por·tance (im pôr'təns) *n.* the state or quality of being important; significance; consequence

im·por·tant (-tənt) *adj.* [Fr. < OIt. < ML. prp. of *importare:* see IMPORT] 1. meaning a great deal; having much significance or consequence 2. having, or acting as if having, power, authority, high position, etc. **—im·por'tant·ly** *adv.*

im·por·ta·tion (im'pôr tā'shən) *n.* 1. an importing or being imported 2. something imported

im·por·tu·nate (im pôr'tyoo nit) *adj.* urgent or annoyingly persistent in asking or demanding **—im·por'tu·nate·ly** *adv.* **—im·por'tu·nate·ness** *n.*

im·por·tune (im'pôr tyoon, im pôr'chən) *vt.* **-tuned', -tun'-ing** [< Fr. < OFr. < L. *importunus,* troublesome < *in-,* not + (*op*)*portunus:* see OPPORTUNE] to trouble with requests or demands; entreat persistently *—vi.* to be importunate **—im'por·tune'ly** *adv.* **—im'por·tun'er** *n.*

im·por·tu·ni·ty (-tyoon'ə tē) *n., pl.* **-ties** an importuning or being importunate

im·pose (im pōz') *vt.* **-posed', -pos'ing** [< Fr. < L. *imponere* < *in-,* on + *ponere,* to place] 1. to place (a burden, tax, etc. *on* or *upon*) 2. to force (oneself) on another 3. to pass off by deception; foist 4. to arrange (pages of type) in a frame for printing **—impose on** (or *upon*) 1. to put to some trouble or use unfairly for one's own benefit 2. to cheat or defraud **—im·pos'er** *n.*

im·pos·ing (im pō'zin) *adj.* impressive in size, dignity, etc. **—im·pos'ing·ly** *adv.*

im·po·si·tion (im'pə zish'ən) *n.* 1. an imposing or imposing on; specif., *a)* a taking advantage of friendship, etc. *b)* the laying on of hands, as at ordination, etc. 2. something imposed; specif., *a)* a tax, fine, etc. *b)* an unjust burden or requirement *c)* a deception; fraud *d)* an essay, etc. set as a punishment at school

im·pos·si·bil·i·ty (im pos'ə bil'ə tē) *n.* 1. the fact or quality of being impossible 2. *pl.* **-ties** something that is impossible

im·pos·si·ble (im pos'ə b'l) *adj.* not possible; specif., *a)* not capable of being, being done, or happening b) not capable of being endured, used, agreed to, etc. because disagreeable or unsuitable —**im·pos'si·bly** adv.

im·post[1] (im'pōst) n. [OFr. < ML. < L. impositus, pp. of imponere: see IMPOSE] 1. a tax; esp., a duty on imported goods 2. the weight assigned to a horse in a handicap race

im·post[2] (im'pōst) n. [ult. < L.: see prec.] the top part of a pillar, pier, etc. supporting an arch

im·pos·tor (im pos'tər) n. [see IMPOSE] a person who deceives or cheats others, esp. by pretending to be someone or something that he is not

im·pos·ture (-chər) n. the act or practice of an impostor; fraud; deception

im·po·tence (im'pə təns) n. the quality or condition of being impotent: also **im'po·ten·cy**

im·po·tent (-tənt) adj. [see IN-[2] & POTENT] 1. lacking physical strength 2. ineffective, powerless, or helpless 3. unable to engage in sexual intercourse, esp. because of an inability to have an erection: said of male animals —**im'-po·tent·ly** adv.

im·pound (im pound') vt. 1. to shut up (an animal) in a pound 2. to take and hold (evidence, etc.) in legal custody 3. to gather and enclose (water) for irrigation, etc. —**im·pound'ment** n.

im·pov·er·ish (im pov'ər ish, -pov'rish) vt. [< OFr. < em-(< L. in-, in) + povre (< L. pauper, poor)] 1. to make poor 2. to deprive of strength, resources, etc. —**im·pov'-er·ish·ment** n.

im·prac·ti·ca·ble (im prak'ti kə b'l) adj. 1. not capable of being carried out in practice [an impracticable plan] 2. not capable of being used [an impracticable road] —**im·prac'-ti·ca·bil'i·ty, im·prac'ti·ca·ble·ness** n. —**im·prac'ti·ca·bly** adv.

im·prac·ti·cal (im prak'tə k'l) adj. not practical; specif., a) not functional or useful b) not handling practical matters well c) idealistic —**im·prac'ti·cal'i·ty, im·prac'ti·cal·ness** n.

im·pre·cate (im'prə kāt') vt. -cat'ed, -cat'ing [< L. pp. of imprecari < in-, on + precari, to PRAY] to pray for or invoke (evil, a curse, etc.) —**im'pre·ca'tion** n. —**im'pre·ca'-tor** n. —**im'pre·ca·to·ry** adj.

im·pre·cise (im'pri sīs') adj. not precise or definite —**im'-pre·cise'ly** adv. —**im'pre·ci'sion** n.

im·preg·na·ble[1] (im preg'nə b'l) adj. [< OFr.: see IN-[2] & PREGNABLE] 1. not capable of being captured or entered by force 2. unshakable; firm —**im·preg'na·bil'i·ty** n. —**im·preg'na·bly** adv.

im·preg·na·ble[2] (im preg'nə b'l) adj. [IMPREGN(ATE) + -ABLE] that can be impregnated

im·preg·nate (im preg'nāt; for adj. -nit) vt. -nat·ed, -nat·ing [< LL. pp. of impraegnare, to make pregnant < L. in-, in + praegnans, PREGNANT] 1. to fertilize 2. to make pregnant 3. to fill or saturate 4. to imbue (with ideas, feelings, etc.) —adj. impregnated —**im'preg·na'tion** n. —**im·preg'-na·tor** n.

im·pre·sa·ri·o (im'prə sär'ē ō) n., pl. -ri·os [It. < impresa, enterprise, ult. < L. in-, in + prehendere, to take, grasp] the organizer or manager of an opera company, concert series, etc.

im·pre·scrip·ti·ble (im'pri skrip'tə b'l) adj. that cannot rightfully be taken away or revoked; inviolable —**im'-pre·scrip'ti·bly** adv.

im·press[1] (im pres') vt. [< IN-[1] + PRESS[2]] 1. to force (men) into public service, esp. into a navy 2. to levy or seize for public use —**im·press'ment** n.

im·press[2] (im pres'; for n. im'pres) vt. [< L. pp. of imprimere: see IN-[1] & PRESS[1]] 1. to use pressure on so as to leave a mark 2. to mark by using pressure; stamp; imprint 3. a) to affect strongly the mind or emotions of b) to arouse the interest or approval of 4. to fix in the memory —n. 1. an impressing 2. any mark, imprint, etc.; stamp 3. a quality or effect produced by some strong influence —**im·press'i·bil'i·ty** n. —**im·press'i·ble** adj. —**im·press'i·bly** adv.

im·pres·sion (im presh'ən) n. 1. an impressing 2. a) a mark, imprint, etc. made by physical pressure b) an effect produced on the mind or senses c) the effect produced by any effort or activity [cleaning made no impression on the stain] 3. a vague notion 4. an amusing impersonation 5. Printing a) a printed copy b) all the copies printed at one time from a set of type or plates —**im·pres'sion·al** adj.

im·pres·sion·a·ble (-ə b'l) adj. easily affected by impressions; capable of being influenced; sensitive —**im·pres'sion·a·bil'i·ty** n. —**im·pres'sion·a·bly** adv.

im·pres·sion·ism (-iz'm) n. a theory and school of art whose chief aim is to capture an impression of a subject, esp. to reproduce the play of light on surfaces: the term has been extended to literature and music which seeks to convey moods and impressions —**im·pres'sion·ist** n., adj. —**im·pres'sion·is'tic** adj. —**im·pres'sion·is'ti·cal·ly** adv.

im·pres·sive (im pres'iv) adj. impressing or tending to impress the mind or emotions; striking, imposing, etc. —**im·pres'sive·ly** adv. —**im·pres'sive·ness** n.

im·prest (im'prest) n. [It. impresto, a loan, ult. < L. praestare, to become surety for] a loan, as from government funds —adj. Accounting designating a fund, as of petty cash, replenished at the end of a certain period in proportion to what has been spent

im·pri·ma·tur (im'pri mät'ər, -māt'-) n. [ModL., let it be printed (see ff.)] 1. licence or permission to publish or print a book, article, etc.; specif., R.C.Ch. such permission granted by an ecclesiastical censor 2. any sanction or approval

im·print (im print'; for n. im'print) vt. [< OFr. < L. imprimere < in-, on + premere, to PRESS[1]] 1. to mark by pressing or stamping; impress 2. to press [to imprint a kiss on the cheek] 3. to fix in the memory —n. 1. a mark made by imprinting 2. a lasting effect or characteristic result 3. a publisher's or printer's note, as on the title page of a book, giving his name, the place of publication, etc

im·print·ing (im print'in) n. Psychol. a learning mechanism of very young animals by which an initial stimulus establishes an irreversible behaviour pattern with reference to the same stimulus in the future

im·pris·on (im priz''n) vt. 1. to put or keep in prison; jail 2. to restrict, limit, or confine in any way —**im·pris'-on·ment** n.

im·prob·a·ble (im prob'ə b'l) adj. not probable; unlikely to happen or be true —**im'prob·a·bil'i·ty** n., pl. -ties —**im·prob'a·bly** adv.

im·promp·tu (im promp'tyōō) adj., adv. [Fr. < L. in promptu, in readiness: see PROMPT] without preparation or advance thought; offhand —n. an impromptu speech, performance, etc.

im·prop·er (im prop'ər) adj. 1. not proper or suitable; poorly adapted; unfit 2. not in accordance with the truth, fact, etc.; incorrect 3. not in good taste; indecent; indecorous 4. not normal or regular —**im·prop'er·ly** adv. —**im·prop'er·ness** n.

improper fraction a fraction in which the denominator is less than the numerator (Ex.: 5/3)

im·pro·pri·ate (im prō'prē āt'; for adj. usually -it) vt. -at'ed, -at'ing [< ML. impropriatus, pp. of impropriare, to take as one's own] to transfer (church income or property) to private individuals or corporations —adj. impropriated —**im·pro'pri·a'tion** n. —**im·pro'pri·a'tor** n.

im·pro·pri·e·ty (im'prə prī'ə tē) n., pl. -ties 1. the quality of being improper 2. improper action or behaviour 3. an improper use of a word (Ex.: "borrow" for "lend")

im·prove (im prōōv') vt. -proved', -prov'ing [< Anglo-Fr. < en-, in + prou, gain < LL. < L. prodesse, to be of advantage] 1. to use (time, etc.) profitably 2. to make better 3. to make (land or structures) more valuable by cultivation, construction, etc. —vi. to become better —**improve on** (or **upon**) to do or make better than —**im·prov'a·bil'i·ty** n. —**im·prov'a·ble** adj. —**im·prov'er** n.

im·prove·ment (-mənt) n. 1. an improving or being improved; esp., a) betterment b) an increase in value c) profitable use 2. a) an addition or change that improves something or adds to its value b) a person or thing representing a higher degree of excellence

im·prov·i·dent (im prov'ə dənt) adj. failing to provide for the future; lacking foresight or thrift —**im·prov'i·dence** n. —**im·prov'i·dent·ly** adv.

im·pro·vise (im'prə vīz') vt., vi. -vised', -vis'ing [< Fr. < It. < improvisso, unprepared < L. < in-, not + pp. of providere, to foresee, PROVIDE] 1. to compose and simultaneously perform without any preparation; extemporize 2. to make, provide, or do with whatever is at hand —**im·prov·i·sa·tion** (im prov'ə zā'shən, im'prə vi-, im'-prə vi-) n. —**im·prov'i·sa'tion·al** adj. —**im'pro·vis'er, im'-pro·vi'sor, im·prov'i·sa'tor** n.

im·pru·dent (im prōōd'ənt) adj. not prudent; without thought of the consequences; rash; indiscreet —**im·pru'-dence** n. —**im·pru'dent·ly** adv.

im·pu·dence (im'pyōō dəns) n. 1. the quality of being impudent 2. impudent speech or behaviour: also **im'-pu·den·cy**, pl. -cies

im·pu·dent (-dənt) adj. [< Fr. < L. < in-, not + prp. of pudere, to feel shame] 1. orig., immodest; shameless 2. shamelessly bold; disrespectful; insolent —**im'pu·dent·ly** adv.

im·pugn (im pyōōn') vt. [< OFr. < L. < in-, against + pugnare, to fight] to attack by argument or criticism; oppose or challenge as false or questionable —**im·pugn'a·ble** adj. —**im·pug·na·tion** (im'pəg nā'shən) n. —**im·pugn'er** n.

im·pulse (im'puls) n. [< L. pp. of impellere, IMPEL] 1. a) an impelling, or driving forwards with sudden force b) an impelling force; push; impetus c) the motion or effect caused by such a force 2. a) incitement to action arising from a state of mind or an external stimulus b) a sudden inclination to act, without conscious thought 3. Elec. a momentary surge in one direction of voltage or current; a pulse 4. Physiol. a stimulus transmitted in a muscle or nerve, which causes or inhibits activity

impulse buying unpremeditated buying, without consideration of the necessity or otherwise of the purchase

impulsion 380 inbreed

im·pul·sion (im pul′shən) *n.* 1. an impelling or being impelled 2. an impelling force; impetus

im·pul·sive (-siv) *adj.* 1. impelling; driving forwards 2. *a)* acting or likely to act on impulse *b)* resulting from impulse [an *impulsive* remark] —**im·pul′sive·ly** *adv.* —**im·pul′siveness** *n.*

im·pu·ni·ty (im pyōō′nə tē) *n.* [< Fr. < L. < *impunis* < *in-*, without + *poena*, punishment] exemption from punishment, penalty, or harm

im·pure (im pyoor′) *adj.* not pure; specif., *a)* unclean; dirty *b)* unclean according to religious ritual *c)* immoral; obscene *d)* mixed with foreign matter; adulterated *e)* mixed so as to lack purity in colour, style, etc. *f)* not idiomatic or grammatical —**im·pure′ly** *adv.* —**im·pure′ness** *n.*

im·pu·ri·ty (-pyoor′ə tē) *n.* 1. a being impure 2. *pl.* **-ties** an impure thing or element

im·pute (im pyōōt′) *vt.* **-put′ed, -put′ing** [< OFr. < L. < *in-*, to + *putare*, to estimate, think] to attribute (esp. a fault or misconduct) to another; charge with; ascribe —**im·put′a·bil′i·ty** *n.* —**im·put′a·ble** *adj.* —**im′pu·ta′tion** *n.* —**im·put′a·tive** *adj.*

I.Mun.E. Institution of Municipal Engineers

in (in, ən, 'n) *prep.* [OE.] 1. contained or enclosed by; inside [in the room] 2. wearing [a lady *in* red] 3. during the course of [done *in* a day] 4. at or near the end of [return *in* an hour] 5. perceptible to (one of the senses) [in sight] 6. out of a group of [one *in* ten] 7. amidst; surrounded by [in a storm] 8. affected by; having [in trouble] 9. employed at or occupied by [in business, *in* a search for truth] 10. with regard to; as concerns [weak in faith, *in* my opinion] 11. with; by; using [to paint *in* oil, speak *in* French] 12. made of [done *in* wood] 13. because of; for [to cry *in* pain] 14. by way of [in recompense] 15. belonging to [not *in* his nature] 16. into [come *in* the house] 17. (of some animals) pregnant with [in foal] *In* expresses inclusion with relation to space, place, time, state, circumstances, manner, quality, a class, etc. —*adv.* 1. from a point outside to one inside [to invite visitors *in*] 2. *a)* so as to be contained by a certain space, condition, or position *b)* so as to be in office or power 3. so as to be agreeing or involved [he fell *in* with our plans] 4. so as to form a part [mix in the cream] 5. in some games, so as to take a turn at something [the last batsman went *in* after tea] 6. at, inside one's home, etc. [he stayed in all day] 7. alight [to keep the fire *in*] —*adj.* 1. that is successful or in power [the *in* group] 2. inner; inside 3. ingoing [the *in* door] 4. gathered, counted, etc. [the harvest is *in*] 5. [Colloq.] *a)* currently smart, popular, etc. [an *in* joke] *b)* belonging to a particular group [the *in* place to be] —*n.* 1. a person, group, etc. in power, office, etc.: *usually used in pl.* 2. [Colloq.] special influence, favour etc. —**have it in for** [Colloq.] to hold a grudge against —**have it in one** to be capable of —**in for** certain to have or get (usually an unpleasant experience) —**in on** having a share or part of —**ins and outs** all the parts, details, and intricacies —**in that** because; since —**in with** associated with as a friend, partner, etc.

in-[1] [< the prep. IN; also < OE. & MFr. *in-* or OFr. *en-* < L. *in-* < *in*] a prefix meaning in, into, within, on, towards [*inbreed, induct*]: also used as an intensive in some words of Latin origin [*inflame*] and assimilated to *il-* before *l* [*illuminate*], *ir-* before *r* [*irrigate*], and *im-* before *m. p,* and *b*

in-[2] [< OFr. & ML. < L. *in-*] a prefix meaning no, not, without, non- [*inhumane*]: assimilated to *il-* before *l* [*illegal*], *ir-* before *r* [*irregular*], and *im-* before *m, p,* and *b*

-in[1] (in) [see -INE[4]] a suffix used in forming the names of various compounds [*albumin, streptomycin*]

-in[2] (in) a combining form used in terms formed by analogy with SIT-IN [*teach-in*]

In *Chem.* indium

in. inch; inches

-i·na (ē′nə) [L.] a suffix used to form feminine names, titles, etc. [*Christina, czarina*]

in·a·bil·i·ty (in′ə bil′ə tē) *n.* a being unable; lack of ability, capacity, means, or power

in ab·sen·ti·a (in ab sen′ti ə, əb sen′shə, ab sen′shē ə) [L., lit., in absence] although not present

in·ac·ces·si·ble (in′ək ses′ə b'l) *adj.* not accessible; specif., *a)* impossible to reach or enter *b)* that cannot be seen, talked to, etc. *c)* not obtainable —**in′ac·ces′si·bil′i·ty** *n.* —**in′ac·ces′si·bly** *adv.*

in·ac·cu·ra·cy (in ak′yər ə sē) *n.* 1. lack of accuracy 2. *pl.* **-cies** an error; mistake

in·ac·cu·rate (-yər it) *adj.* not accurate; not correct; not exact; in error —**in·ac′cu·rate·ly** *adv.*

in·ac·tion (in ak′shən) *n.* absence of action or motion; inertness or idleness

in·ac·ti·vate (-tə vāt′) *vt.* **-vat′ed, -vat′ing** 1. to make inactive 2. *Chem.* to destroy the activity of (a substance), as by heat —**in·ac′ti·va′tion** *n.*

in·ac·tive (-tiv) *adj.* 1. not active; inert 2. idle;

sluggish 3. not functioning 4. [U.S.] not in active service in the armed forces —**in·ac′tive·ly** *adv.* —**in′ac·tiv′i·ty** *n.*

in·ad·e·quate (in ad′ə kwət) *adj.* not adequate; not sufficient —**in·ad′e·qua·cy** *pl.* **-cies, in·ad′e·quate·ness** *n.* —**in·ad′e·quate·ly** *adv.*

in·ad·mis·si·ble (in′əd mis′ə b'l) *adj.* not admissible; not to be allowed, granted, etc. —**in′ad·mis′si·bil′i·ty** *n.* —**in′ad·mis′si·bly** *adv.*

in·ad·vert·ence (in′əd vur′təns) *n.* 1. a being inadvertent 2. an instance of this; oversight; mistake Also **in′ad·vert′en·cy,** *pl.* **-cies**

in·ad·vert·ent (-tənt) *adj.* 1. not attentive or observant 2. due to oversight; unintentional —**in′ad·vert′ent·ly** *adv.*

in·ad·vis·a·ble (in′əd vī′zə b'l) *adj.* not advisable; not wise or prudent —**in′ad·vis′a·bil′i·ty** *n.*

in·al·ien·a·ble (in āl′yən ə b'l) *adj.* that may not be taken away or transferred [*inalienable* rights] —**in·al′ien·a·bil′i·ty** *n.* —**in·al′ien·a·bly** *adv.*

in·am·o·ra·ta (in am′ ə rät′ə, in′am-) *n.* [It. < *innamorare,* to fall in love] a woman in relation to the man who is her lover; sweetheart or mistress

in·ane (in ān′) *adj.* [L. *inanis*] 1. empty 2. lacking sense; silly; foolish —**in·ane′ly** *adv.*

in·an·ga (in′aŋ ə) *n.* [Maori] the New Zealand whitebait

in·an·i·mate (in an′ə mit) *adj.* 1. not animate; without (animal) life 2. not animated; dull —**in·an′i·mate·ly** *adv.* —**in·an′i·mate·ness** *n.*

in·a·ni·tion (in′ə nish′ən) *n.* [< ME. < OFr. < L. *inanitus,* empty] emptiness; weakness, esp. exhaustion from lack of food

in·an·i·ty (in an′ə tē) *n.* 1. a being inane; specif., *a)* emptiness *b)* silliness 2. *pl.* **-ties** something inane; senseless or silly act, remark, etc.

in·ap·pe·tence (in ap′ə təns) *n.* lack of appetite or desire: also **in·ap′pe·ten·cy** —**in·ap′pe·tent** *adj.*

in·ap·pli·ca·ble (in ap′li kə b'l, in ap li′-) *adj.* not applicable; not suitable; inappropriate —**in′ap·pli·ca·bil′i·ty** *n.* —**in·ap′pli·ca·bly** *adv.*

in·ap·po·site (in ap′ə zit) *adj.* not apposite; irrelevant —**in·ap′po·site·ly** *adv.* —**in·ap′po·site·ness** *n.*

in·ap·pre·ci·a·ble (in′ə prē′shə b'l, -shē ə-) *adj.* too small to be observed or have any value; negligible —**in′ap·pre′ci·a·bly** *adv.*

in·ap·pre·ci·a·tive (-shə tiv, -shē ə-, -shē āt′iv) *adj.* not feeling or showing appreciation —**in·ap·pre·ci·a′tion, in′ap·pre′ci·a·tive·ness** *n.*

in·ap·pro·pri·ate (in′ə prō′prē it) *adj.* not appropriate; not suitable, fitting, or proper —**in′ap·pro′pri·ate·ly** *adv.* —**in′ap·pro′pri·ate·ness** *n.*

in·apt (in apt′) *adj.* 1. not apt; inappropriate 2. lacking skill or aptitude; inept —**in·apt′i·tude′** (-ap′tə tyōōd′) *n.* —**in·apt′ly** *adv.* —**in·apt′ness** *n.*

in·arch (in ärch′) *vt.* [IN-[1] + ARCH[1]] to graft (a plant) by uniting a shoot to another plant while both are growing on their own roots

in·ar·tic·u·late (in′är tik′yə lit) *adj.* 1. produced without the articulation of normal speech [an *inarticulate* cry] 2. *a)* unable to speak, as because of strong emotion; mute *b)* not able to speak coherently or effectively 3. *Zool.* without joints, hinges, etc. —**in′ar·tic′u·late·ly** *adv.* —**in′ar·tic′u·late·ness** *n.*

in·ar·tis·tic (in′är tis′tik) *adj.* not artistic; lacking artistic taste —**in′ar·tis′ti·cal·ly** *adv.*

in·as·much as (in′əz much′əz) 1. seeing that; since; because 2. to the extent that

in·at·ten·tion (in′ə ten′shən) *n.* failure to pay attention; heedlessness; negligence

in·at·ten·tive (-tiv) *adj.* not attentive; heedless —**in′at·ten′tive·ly** *adv.* —**in′at·ten′tive·ness** *n.*

in·au·di·ble (in ô′də b'l) *adj.* not audible; that cannot be heard —**in·au·di·bil′i·ty** *n.* —**in·au′di·bly** *adv.*

in·au·gu·ral (in ô′gyə rəl, -gə ral) *adj.* [Fr.] 1. of an inauguration, or ceremonial induction into office 2. that begins a series —*n.* an inaugural ceremony or address

in·au·gu·rate (-rāt′) *vt.* **-rat′ed, -rat′ing** [< L. pp. of *inaugurare,* to practice augury] 1. to induct into office with a formal ceremony 2. to make a formal beginning of 3. to celebrate formally the first public use of —**in·au′gu·ra′tion** *n.* —**in·au′gu·ra′tor** *n.*

in·aus·pi·cious (in′ô spish′əs) *adj.* not auspicious; unfavourable; unlucky; ill-omened —**in′aus·pi′cious·ly** *adv.* —**in′aus·pi′cious·ness** *n.*

in·board (in′bôrd′) *adv., adj.* [< in board: see BOARD] 1. inside the hull or bulwarks of a ship or boat 2. close or closer to the fuselage or hull of an aircraft —*n.* 1. a marine motor mounted inboard 2. a boat with such a motor

in·born (in′bôrn′, -bôrn′) *adj.* present in the organism at birth; innate; natural

in·bred (in′bred′) *adj.* 1. innate or deeply instilled 2. resulting from inbreeding

in·breed (in′brēd′) *vt.* **-bred′, -breed′ing** to breed by continual mating of individuals of the same or closely related stocks —*vi.* to engage in such breeding

inc. 1. including 2. inclusive 3. incorporated 4. increase

in·cal·cu·la·ble (in kal'kyə lə b'l) *adj.* 1. that cannot be calculated; too great or too many to be counted 2. unpredictable; uncertain —**in·cal'cu·la·bil'i·ty** *n.* —**in·cal'·cu·la·bly** *adv.*

in·can·desce (in'kən des') *vi., vt.* **-desced', -desc'ing** to become or make incandescent

in·can·des·cent (-des'ənt) *adj.* [< L.: see IN.[1] & CANDESCENT] 1. glowing with intense heat; red-hot or, esp., white-hot 2. very bright; shining brilliantly —**in'can·des'·cence** *n.* —**in'can·des'cent·ly** *adv.*

incandescent lamp a lamp in which the light is produced by a filament contained in a vacuum and heated to incandescence by an electric current

in·can·ta·tion (in'kan tā'shən) *n.* [OFr. < LL. < L. pp. of *incantare*, enchant < *in-*, IN.[1] + *cantare*, to chant] 1. the chanting of special words or a formula in magic spells or rites 2. words or a formula so chanted —**in'can·ta'tion·al** *adj.* —**in·can'·ta·to·ry** (-kan'tə tar ē) *adj.*

in·ca·pa·ble (in kā'pə b'l) *adj.* not capable; lacking the necessary ability, competence, qualifications, etc. —**incapable of** 1. not allowing or admitting; not able to accept or experience *[incapable of change]* 2. lacking the ability or fitness for 3. not legally qualified for —**in·ca·pa·bil'i·ty, in·ca'pa·ble·ness** *n.* —**in·ca'pa·bly** *adv.*

in·ca·pac·i·tate (in'kə pas'ə tāt') *vt.* **-tat'·ed, -tat'ing** 1. to make unable or unfit; esp., to make incapable of normal activity; disable 2. *Law* to disqualify —**in'ca·pac'·i·ta'tion** *n.*

in·ca·pac·i·ty (in'kə pas'ə tē) *n., pl.* **-ties** 1. lack of capacity, power, or fitness; disability 2. legal ineligibility

in·car·cer·ate (in kär'sə rāt') *vt.* **-at'ed, -at'ing** [< ML. pp. of *incarcerare* < L. *in*, in + *carcer*, prison] 1. to imprison; jail 2. to confine —**in·car'cer·a'tion** *n.* —**in·car'cer·a'tor** *n.*

in·car·na·dine (in kär'nə din', -din) *adj.* [< Fr. < It. *incarnatino* < LL. *incarnatus:* see ff.] 1. flesh-coloured; pink 2. red; esp., blood-red —*n.* the colour of either flesh or blood —*vt.* **-dined', -din'ing** to make incarnadine

in·car·nate (in kär'nit; *also, and for v. always,* -nāt) *adj.* [< LL. *incarnatus,* pp. of *incarnari,* to become flesh < L. *in-,* in + *caro,* flesh] endowed with a human body; personified *[evil incarnate]* —*vt.* **-nat·ed, -nat·ing** 1. to give bodily form to; embody 2. to give actual form to; make real 3. to be the type or embodiment of

in·car·na·tion (in'kär nā'shən) *n.* [see prec.] 1. endowment with a human body 2. [I-] the taking on of human form and nature by Jesus as the Son of God 3. any person or animal serving as the embodiment of a god or spirit 4. any person or thing serving as the embodiment of a quality or concept

in·case (in kās') *vt.* **-cased', -cas'ing** *same as* ENCASE —**in·case'ment** *n.*

in·cau·tion (in kô'shən) *n.* lack of caution

in·cau·tious (-shəs) *adj.* not cautious; not careful or prudent; reckless; rash —**in·cau'tious·ly** *adv.* —**in·cau'·tious·ness** *n.*

in·cen·di·ar·y (in sen'dē er'ē) *adj.* [< L. < *incendium,* a fire < *incendere:* see ff.] 1. relating to the wilful destruction of property by fire 2. designed to cause fires, as certain bombs 3. wilfully stirring up strife, riot, etc. —*n., pl.* **-ar·ies** 1. a person who wilfully destroys property by fire 2. a person who wilfully stirs up strife, riot, etc. 3. an incendiary bomb, substance, etc. —**in·cen'di·a·rism** (-ə riz'm) *n.*

in·cense[1] (in'sens) *n.* [< OFr. < LL. < L. pp. of *incendere,* to inflame < *in-,* in + *candere,* to burn] 1. a) any substance burned for its pleasant odour b) the odour or smoke so produced 2. any pleasant odour 3. pleasing attention or praise —*vt.* **-censed, -cens·ing** 1. to make fragrant with incense 2. to burn or offer incense to —*vi.* to burn incense

in·cense[2] (in sens') *vt.* **-censed', -cens'ing** [< OFr. < L. pp. of *incendere:* see prec.] to make very angry; enrage —**in·cense'ment** *n.*

in·cen·so·ry (in sens'ər ē) *n. same as* CENSER

in·cen·tive (in sen'tiv) *adj.* [< LL. *incentivum* < L. < *in-,* on + *canere,* to sing] stimulating to action; encouraging; motivating —*n.* a stimulus; motive

in·cept (in sept') *vt.* [< L. *inceptare,* to begin] to take in; ingest —*vi.* formerly, to receive a master's or doctor's degree at Cambridge University

in·cep·tion (in sep'shən) *n.* [< L. < pp. of *incipere:* see INCIPIENT] a beginning; start

in·cep·tive (-tiv) *adj.* [< OFr. < LL. < pp. of *incipere:* see INCIPIENT] 1. beginning; introductory 2. *Gram.*

expressing the beginning of an action —*n.* an inceptive verb —**in·cep'tive·ly** *adv.*

in·cer·ti·tude (in sur'tə tyōod') *n.* [Fr. < ML.: see IN.[2] + CERTITUDE] 1. an uncertain state of mind; doubt 2. insecurity

in·ces·sant (in ses'ənt) *adj.* [< LL. < L. *in-,* not + prp. of *cessare,* to CEASE] never ceasing; continuing or repeated endlessly; constant —**in·ces'san·cy** *n.* —**in·ces'sant·ly** *adv.*

in·cest (in'sest) *n.* [< L. < *in-,* not + *castus,* chaste] sexual intercourse between persons too closely related to marry legally

in·ces·tu·ous (in ses'tyoo wəs) *adj.* 1. guilty of incest 2. of, or having the nature of, incest —**in·ces'tu·ous·ly** *adv.* —**in·ces'tu·ous·ness** *n.*

inch[1] (inch) *n.* [OE. *ynce* < L. *uncia,* a twelfth, OUNCE[1]] 1. a measure of length equal to 1/12 foot (2.54 cm): symbol, *"* (e.g., 10″): abbrev. **in.** (*sing. & pl.*) 2. a fall (of rain, snow, etc.) that would cover a surface to the depth of one inch 3. a very small amount, degree, or distance —*vt., vi.* to move by degrees; move very slowly —**every inch** in all respects; thoroughly —**inch by inch** gradually; slowly: also **by inches** —**within an inch of** very close to; almost to —**within an inch of one's life** almost to one's death

inch[2] (inch) *n.* [ME. < Gael. *innis,* island] in Scotland and Ireland, a small island

inch·meal (inch'mēl') *adv.* [INCH[1] + ME. *mele,* a measure] gradually; inch by inch: also **by inchmeal**

in·cho·ate (in kō'it) *adj.* [< L. pp. of *inchoare, incohare,* to begin, orig. "hitch up" < *in-,* in + *cohum,* a strap from plough to yoke] 1. just begun; in the early stages 2. not yet clearly formed; disordered —**in·cho'ate·ly** *adv.* —**in·cho'·ate·ness** *n.* —**in'cho·a'tion** (-ā'shən) *n.*

in·cho·a·tive (-ə tiv) *adj., n. Gram. same as* INCEPTIVE

inch·worm (inch'wurm') *n. same as* MEASURING WORM

in·ci·dence (in'si dəns) *n.* 1. the act, fact, or manner of falling upon or influencing 2. the degree or range of occurrence or effect; extent of influence See also ANGLE OF INCIDENCE

in·ci·dent (-dənt) *adj.* [< OFr. < ML. < prp. of L. *incidere* < *in-,* on + *cadere,* to fall] 1. likely to happen in connection with; incidental (*to*) *[the cares incident to parenthood]* 2. falling upon or affecting *[incident rays]* —*n.* 1. something that happens; occurrence 2. a minor event or episode, esp. one in a novel, play, etc. 3. an apparently minor incident, etc. that may have serious results

in·ci·den·tal (in'si den't'l) *adj.* 1. happening or likely to happen in connection with something more important; casual 2. secondary or minor —*n.* 1. something incidental 2. [*pl.*] miscellaneous items

in·ci·den·tal·ly (-dent'l ē, den't'l ē) *adv.* 1. in an incidental manner 2. by the way

incidental music music included in the presentation of a play, film, etc. to heighten mood or effect on the audience

in·cin·er·ate (in sin'ə rāt') *vt., vi.* **-at'ed, -at'ing** [< ML. pp. of *incinerare* < L. *in,* to + *cinis,* ashes] to burn to ashes; burn up —**in·cin'er·a'tion** *n.*

in·cin·er·a·tor (-rāt'ər) *n.* a furnace or other device for incinerating rubbish

in·cip·i·ent (in sip'ē ənt) *adj.* [< L. prp. of *incipere,* to begin < *in-,* on + *capere,* to take] just beginning to exist or to come to notice *[an incipient illness]* —**in·cip'i·ence, in·cip'·i·en·cy** *n.* —**in·cip'i·ent·ly** *adv.*

in·cise (in siz') *vt.* **-cised', -cis'ing** [< Fr. < L. pp. of *incidere* < *in-,* into + *caedere,* to cut] to cut into with a sharp tool; specif., to engrave or carve —**in·cised'** *adj.*

in·ci·sion (-sizh'ən) *n.* 1. the act or result of incising; cut 2. incisive quality 3. *Surgery* a cut made into a tissue or organ

in·ci·sive (in sī'siv) *adj.* 1. cutting into 2. sharp; keen; penetrating; acute *[an incisive mind]* —**in·ci'sive·ly** *adv.* —**in·ci'sive·ness** *n.*

in·ci·sor (in sī'zər) *n.* any of the front cutting teeth between the canines in either jaw

in·cite (in sit') *vt.* **-cit'ed, -cit'ing** [< OFr. < L. < *in-,* in, on + *citare,* to arouse] to urge to action; stir up; rouse —**in·cite'ment, in·ci·ta·tion** (in'sī tā'shən, -si-) *n.* —**in·cit'·er** *n.*

in·ci·vil·i·ty (in'sə vil'ə tē) *n.* [see IN.[2] & CIVIL] 1. a lack of courtesy or politeness; rudeness 2. *pl.* **-ties** a rude or discourteous act

incl. 1. inclosure 2. including 3. inclusive

in·clem·ent (in klem'ənt) *adj.* [< L.: see IN.[2] & CLEMENT] 1. rough; severe; stormy 2. lacking mercy or leniency; harsh —**in·clem'en·cy** *n., pl.* **-cies** —**in·clem'ent·ly** *adv.*

in·cli·na·tion (in'klə nā'shən) *n.* 1. an inclining, leaning, bowing, etc. 2. a slope; slant 3. the extent or degree of incline from the horizontal or vertical 4. the angle made by two lines or planes 5. a) a particular bent of mind; tendency b) a liking or preference —**in'cli·na'tion·al** *adj.*

in·cline (in klin'; *for n., usually* in'klin) *vi.* **-clined', -clin'ing** [< OFr. < L. < *in-,* on + *clinare,* to lean] 1. to lean; slope; slant 2. to bow the body or head 3. to have a tendency 4. to have a preference or liking —*vt.* 1. to

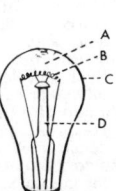

INCANDESCENT LAMP
(A, inert gas filling; B, coiled tungsten wire filament; C, glass envelope; D, glass support; E, metal base)

cause to lean, slope, etc. **2.** to bend or bow (the body or head) **3.** to make willing; influence —*n.* an inclined plane or surface; slope; grade —**incline one's ear** to listen willingly —**in·clin′a·ble** *adj.* —**in·clined′** *adj.* —**in·clin′er** *n.*

inclined plane a plane surface set at any angle other than a right angle against a horizontal surface

in·cli·nom·e·ter (in′klənom′-ətər) *n.* [< INCLINE + -METER] **1.** same as CLINOMETER **2.** an instrument that measures the inclination of an axis of an aircraft or ship in relation to the horizontal

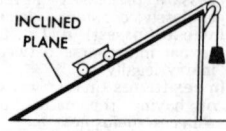

INCLINED PLANE

in·close (in klōz′) *vt.* **-closed′, -clos′ing** *same as* ENCLOSE —**in·clo′sure** (-klō′zhər) *n.*

in·clude (in klōōd′) *vt.* **-clud′ed, -clud′ing** [< L. < *in-*, in + *claudere*, to close] **1.** to shut up or in; enclose **2.** to have as part of a whole; contain; comprise **3.** to take into account; put in a total, category, etc. —**include out** [Colloq.] to exclude definitely [*include* me *out* of it] —**in·clud′a·ble, in·clud′i·ble** *adj.*

in·clu·sion (in klōō′zhən) *n.* **1.** an including or being included **2.** something included

in·clu·sive (in klōō′siv) *adj.* **1.** including or tending to include; esp., taking everything into account **2.** including the terms, limits, or extremes mentioned [the first to the tenth *inclusive*] —**inclusive of** including —**in·clu′sive·ly** *adv.* —**in·clu′sive·ness** *n.*

incog. incognito

in·cog·ni·to (in′kog nēt′ō, in kog′ni tō) *adv., adj.* [It. < L. < *in-*, not + pp. of *cognoscere*, to know] with true identity unrevealed or disguised; under an assumed name, rank, etc. —*n., pl.* **-tos 1.** a person who is incognito **2.** *a)* the state of being incognito *b)* the disguise assumed —**in′cog·ni′ta** (-ə, -tə) *adj., n.fem., pl.* **-tas**

in·cog·ni·zant (in kog′nə zənt; *occas.* -kon′ə-) *adj.* unaware of —**in·cog′ni·zance** *n.*

in·co·her·ence (in′kō hir′əns) *n.* **1.** a being incoherent **2.** incoherent speech, thought, etc. Also **in′co·her′en·cy,** *pl.* **-cies**

in·co·her·ent (-ənt) *adj.* not coherent; specif., *a)* lacking cohesion; not sticking together *b)* not logically connected; disjointed *c)* characterized by incoherent speech, thought, etc. —**in′co·her′ent·ly** *adv.*

in·com·bus·ti·ble (in′kəm bus′tə b'l) *adj.* not combustible; that cannot be burned —*n.* an incombustible substance —**in′com·bus′ti·bil′i·ty** *n.*

in·come (in′kum′) *n.* the money or other gain received, esp. in a given period, by an individual, company, etc. for labour or services, or from property, investments, etc.

income tax a tax on net income or on that part of income which exceeds a certain amount

in·com·ing (in′kum′iŋ) *adj.* coming in or about to come in —*n.* a coming in

in·com·men·su·ra·ble (in′kə men′shər ə b'l, -sər-) *adj.* **1.** that cannot be measured or compared by the same standard or measure **2.** not worthy of comparison **3.** having no common divisor —*n.* an incommensurable thing, quantity, etc. —**in′com·men′su·ra·bil′i·ty** *n.* —**in′com·men′su·ra·bly** *adv.*

in·com·men·su·rate (-it) *adj.* not commensurate; specif., *a)* not proportionate; not adequate *b)* same as INCOMMENSURABLE (sense 1) —**in′com·men′su·rate·ly** *adv.*

in·com·mode (in′kə mōd′) *vt.* **-mod′ed, -mod′ing** [< Fr. < L. < *in-*, not + *commodus*, convenient] to inconvenience; put to some trouble; bother

in·com·mo·di·ous (-mō′dē əs) *adj.* **1.** causing inconvenience; uncomfortable **2.** inconveniently small, narrow, etc. —**in′com·mo′di·ous·ly** *adv.* —**in′com·mo′di·ous·ness** *n.*

in·com·mu·ni·ca·ble (in′kə myōō′ni kə b'l) *adj.* that cannot be communicated or told —**in′com·mu′ni·ca·bil′i·ty** *n.* —**in′com·mu′ni·ca·bly** *adv.*

in·com·mu·ni·ca·do (in′kə myōō′nə kä′dō) *adj.* [Sp.] unable or not allowed to communicate, as when in solitary confinement

in·com·mu·ni·ca·tive (in′kə myōō′nə kə tiv) *adj.* same as UNCOMMUNICATIVE

in·com·pa·ra·ble (in kom′pər ə b'l; *occas.* in′kəm par′ə b'l) *adj.* that cannot be compared; specif., *a)* having no basis of comparison; incommensurable *b)* beyond comparison; unequalled; matchless [*incomparable* skill] —**in′com′pa·ra·bil′i·ty** *n.* —**in′com′pa·ra·bly** *adv.*

in·com·pat·i·ble (in′kəm pat′ə b'l) *adj.* **1.** not compatible; not able to exist in harmony; not going, or getting along, well together **2.** logically contradictory **3.** not suitable for being used together: said of certain drugs or medicines —*n.* an incompatible person or thing —**in′com·pat′i·bil′i·ty** *n., pl.* **-ties** —**in′com·pat′i·bly** *adv.*

in·com·pe·tent (in kom′pə tənt) *adj.* **1.** without adequate ability, knowledge, fitness, etc. **2.** not legally qualified —*n.*

an incompetent person —**in·com′pe·tence, in·com′pe·ten·cy** *n.* —**in·com′pe·tent·ly** *adv.*

in·com·plete (in′kəm plēt′) *adj.* **1.** lacking a part or parts **2.** unfinished; not concluded **3.** not perfect; not thorough —**in′com·plete′ly** *adv.* —**in′com·plete′ness, in′com·ple′tion** *n.*

in·com·pre·hen·si·ble (in′kom pri hen′sə b'l, in kom′-) *adj.* not comprehensible; that cannot be understood —**in′com·pre·hen′si·bil′i·ty** *n.* —**in′com·pre·hen′si·bly** *adv.*

in·com·pre·hen·sion (-shən) *n.* lack of comprehension; inability to understand

in·com·press·i·ble (in′kəm pres′ə b'l) *adj.* that cannot be compressed —**in′com·press′i·bil′i·ty** *n.*

in·con·ceiv·a·ble (in′kən sē′və b'l) *adj.* that cannot be conceived; that cannot be thought of, imagined, etc. —**in′con·ceiv′a·bil′i·ty, in′con·ceiv′a·ble·ness** *n.* —**in′con·ceiv′a·bly** *adv.*

in·con·clu·sive (in′kən klōō′siv) *adj.* not conclusive or final; not leading to a definite result —**in′con·clu′sive·ly** *adv.* —**in′con·clu′sive·ness** *n.*

in·con·dite (in kon′dit, -dīt) *adj.* [L. *inconditus* < *in-*, not + *conditus*, pp. of *condere*, to put together] poorly constructed; lacking finish; crude: said of literary works

in·con·gru·i·ty (in′kən grōō′ə tē, in′kon-) *n.* **1.** a being incongruous; specif., *a)* lack of harmony or agreement *b)* lack of fitness or appropriateness **2.** *pl.* **-ties** something incongruous

in·con·gru·ous (in kon′groo wəs) *adj.* not congruous; specif., *a)* lacking harmony or agreement *b)* having inharmonious parts, elements, etc. *c)* unsuitable; inappropriate —**in·con′gru·ous·ly** *adv.* —**in·con′gru·ous·ness** *n.*

in·con·se·quent (in kon′sə kwent′, -kwənt) *adj.* not consequent; specif., *a)* not following as a result *b)* not following as a logical inference; irrelevant *c)* not proceeding in logical sequence —**in·con′se·quence′** *n.* —**in·con′se·quent′ly** *adv.*

in·con·se·quen·tial (in kon′sə kwen′shəl) *adj.* **1.** inconsequent; illogical **2.** of no consequence; unimportant —*n.* something inconsequential —**in′con·se·quen′ti·al′i·ty** (-shē al′ə tē) *n.* —**in′con·se·quen′tial·ly** *adv.*

in·con·sid·er·a·ble (in′kən sid′ər ə b'l) *adj.* not worth consideration; trivial; small —**in′con·sid′er·a·ble·ness** *n.* —**in′con·sid′er·a·bly** *adv.*

in·con·sid·er·ate (-it) *adj.* without thought or consideration for others; thoughtless —**in′con·sid′er·ate·ly** *adv.* —**in′con·sid′er·a′tion, in′con·sid′er·a′tion** (-ə rā′shən) *n.*

in·con·sis·ten·cy (in′kən sis′tən sē) *n.* **1.** a being inconsistent **2.** *pl.* **-cies** an inconsistent act, remark, etc. Also **in′con·sis′tence**

in·con·sis·tent (-tənt) *adj.* not consistent; specif., *a)* not in agreement or harmony; incompatible *b)* not uniform; self-contradictory [*inconsistent* testimony] *c)* not holding to the same principles or practice; changeable —**in′con·sis′tent·ly** *adv.*

in·con·sol·a·ble (in′kən sōl′ə b'l) *adj.* that cannot be consoled —**in′con·sol′a·bil′i·ty, in′con·sol′a·ble·ness** *n.* —**in′con·sol′a·bly** *adv.*

in·con·so·nant (in kon′sə nənt) *adj.* not consonant; not in harmony or agreement —**in·con′so·nance** *n.* —**in·con′so·nant·ly** *adv.*

in·con·spic·u·ous (in′kən spik′yoo wəs) *adj.* not conspicuous; attracting little attention —**in′con·spic′u·ous·ly** *adv.* —**in′con·spic′u·ous·ness** *n.*

in·con·stant (in kon′stənt) *adj.* not constant; changeable; specif., *a)* not remaining firm in mind or purpose *b)* fickle *c)* not uniform; irregular —**in·con′stan·cy** *n.* —**in·con′stant·ly** *adv.*

in·con·test·a·ble (in′kən tes′tə b'l) *adj.* not to be contested; unquestionable —**in′con·test′a·bil′i·ty** *n.* —**in′con·test′a·bly** *adv.*

in·con·ti·nent¹ (in kont′in ənt) *adj.* [< OFr. < L.: see IN.² & CONTINENT] **1.** *a)* without self-restraint, esp. in regard to sexual activity *b)* unrestrained **2.** incapable of containing, holding, etc. **3.** unable to restrain a natural discharge, as of urine —**in·con′ti·nence** *n.* —**in·con′ti·nent·ly** *adv.*

in·con·ti·nent² (in kon′tə nənt) *adv.* [ME. < OFr. < L. *in continenti* (*tempore*), in continuous (time)] [Archaic] immediately

in·con·tro·vert·i·ble (in′kon trə vur′tə b'l, in kon′-) *adj.* that cannot be controverted; not disputable or debatable; undeniable —**in′con·tro·vert′i·bil′i·ty** *n.* —**in′con·tro·vert′i·bly** *adv.*

in·con·ven·ience (in′kən vēn′yəns, -ē əns) *n.* **1.** a being inconvenient; lack of comfort, ease, etc. **2.** anything inconvenient Also **in′con·ven′ien·cy,** *pl.* **-cies** —*vt.* **-ienced, -ienc·ing** to cause inconvenience to; trouble; bother

in·con·ven·ient (-yənt, -ē ənt) *adj.* not convenient; not favourable to one's comfort; causing trouble, bother, etc. —**in′con·ven′ient·ly** *adv.*

in·con·vert·i·ble (in′kən vur′tə b'l) *adj.* that cannot be converted; that cannot be changed or exchanged —**in′con·vert′i·bil′i·ty** *n.*

in·co·or·di·na·tion (in′kō ôr′də nā′shən) *n.* lack of coordination; esp., inability to adjust the muscles in producing complex movements

in·cor·po·rate (in kôr′pər it; *for v.* -pə rāt′) *adj.* [< LL.: see IN-[1] & CORPORATE] combined, merged, or incorporated —*vt.* -rat·ed, -rat·ing 1. to combine with something already formed; embody 2. to bring together into a single whole; merge 3. to admit into association as a member 4. to form into a corporation 5. to give material form to —*vi.* 1. to unite or combine into a single whole 2. [Chiefly U.S.] to form a corporation —**in·cor′po·ra′tion** *n.* —**in·cor′po·ra′tive** *adj.* —**in·cor′po·ra′tor** *n.*

in·cor·po·re·al (in′kôr pôr′ē əl) *adj.* not corporeal; without material body or substance —**in·cor·po·re·al′i·ty** *n.* —**in′-cor·po′re·al·ly** *adv.*

in·cor·rect (in′kə rekt′) *adj.* not correct; specif., a) improper b) untrue; inaccurate; wrong; faulty —**in′cor·rect′-ly** *adv.* —**in′cor·rect′ness** *n.*

in·cor·ri·gi·ble (in kor′i jə b'l) *adj.* not corrigible; that cannot be corrected, improved, or reformed, esp. because firmly set, as a habit, or because set in bad habits, as a child —*n.* an incorrigible person —**in·cor′ri·gi·bil′i·ty, in·cor′-ri·gi·ble·ness** *n.* —**in·cor′ri·gi·bly** *adv.*

in·cor·rupt (in′kə rupt′) *adj.* not corrupt; sound, pure, upright, honest, etc. —**in′cor·rupt′ly** *adv.* —**in′cor·rupt′-ness** *n.*

in·cor·rupt·i·ble (-rup′tə b'l) *adj.* that cannot be corrupted, esp. morally —**in′cor·rupt′i·bil′i·ty** *n.* —**in′cor·rupt′i·bly** *adv.*

incr. 1. increase 2. increased 3. increasing

in·cras·sate (in kras′āt) *adj.* [< L. *incrassatus*, pp. of *incrassare*, to make thick] *Biol.* thickened; swollen

in·crease (in krēs′; *also, and for n. always,* in′krēs) *vi.* -creased′, -creas′ing [< OFr. < L. < *in-*, in + *crescere*, to grow] 1. to become greater in size, amount, etc.; grow 2. to become greater in numbers by producing offspring; multiply —*vt.* to cause to become greater in size, amount, etc. —*n.* 1. an increasing or becoming increased 2. the result or amount of an increasing —**on the increase** increasing —**in·creas′a·ble** *adj.* —**in·creas′er** *n.*

in·creas·ing·ly (in krēs′iŋ lē) *adv.* more and more; to an ever-increasing degree

in·cred·i·ble (in kred′ə b'l) *adj.* 1. not credible; unbelievable 2. so great, unusual, etc. as to seem impossible —**in·cred′-i·bil′i·ty** *n.* —**in·cred′i·bly** *adv.*

in·cre·du·li·ty (in′krə dyoo′lə tē) *n.* unwillingness or inability to believe; doubt

in·cred·u·lous (in krej′oo ləs) *adj.* 1. unwilling or unable to believe; doubting 2. showing doubt or disbelief —**in·cred′-u·lous·ly** *adv.*

in·cre·ment (in′krə mənt, iŋ′-) *n.* [ME. < L. *incrementum* < *increscere*, increase] 1. a becoming greater or larger; increase; gain 2. amount of increase [an annual *increment* of £100 in salary] —**in′cre·men′tal** (-men′t'l) *adj.*

in·crim·i·nate (in krim′ə nāt′) *vt.* -nat·ed, -nat·ing [< ML.: see IN-[1] & CRIMINATE] 1. to charge with a crime; accuse 2. to involve in, or make appear guilty of, a crime or fault —**in·crim′i·na′tion** *n.* —**in·crim′i·na·to·ry** *adj.*

in·crust (in krust′) *vt.* 1. to cover as with a crust 2. to decorate, as with gems —*vi.* to form a crust —**in′crus·ta′-tion** *n.*

in·cu·bate (iŋ′kyoo bāt′, in-) *vt.* -bat·ed, -bat·ing [< L. pp. of *incubare* < *in-*, on + *cubare*, to lie] 1. to sit on and hatch (eggs) 2. to keep (eggs, embryos, etc.) in a favourable environment for hatching or developing 3. to develop, as by thought or planning —*vi.* to undergo incubation

in·cu·ba·tion (iŋ′kyoo bā′shən, in′-) *n.* 1. an incubating or being incubated 2. the phase in the development of a disease between the infection and the first appearance of symptoms —**in′cu·ba′tion·al** *adj.* —**in′cu·ba′tive, in′cu-ba·to·ry** *adj.*

in·cu·ba·tor (iŋ′kyoo bāt′ər, in′-) *n.* a person or thing that incubates; specif., a) an artificially heated container for hatching eggs b) a similar apparatus in which premature babies are kept for a period c) an apparatus for developing bacterial cultures

in·cu·bus (iŋ′kyoo bəs, in′-) *n., pl.* -bus·es, -bi (-bī′) [< LL., nightmare (in ML., a demon) < L. *incubare*: see INCUBATE] 1. a spirit or demon thought in medieval times to have sexual intercourse with sleeping women 2. a nightmare 3. an oppressive burden

in·cul·cate (in kul′kāt, in′kul kāt′) *vt.* -cat·ed, -cat·ing [< L. pp. of *inculcare* < *in-*, in + *calcare*, to trample underfoot *calx*, a heel] to impress upon the mind by repetition or persistent urging —**in′cul·ca′tion** *n.* —**in·cul′ca·tor** *n.*

in·cul·pate (in kul′pāt, in′kul pāt′) *vt.* -pat·ed, -pat·ing [< ML. pp. of *inculpare* < L. *in*, on + *culpa*, a fault, blame] *same as* INCRIMINATE —**in′cul·pa′tion** *n.* —**in·cul′pa·to·ry** *adj.*

in·cum·ben·cy (in kum′bən sē) *n., pl.* -cies 1. a duty or obligation 2. a) the holding and administering of a position b) tenure of office

in·cum·bent (-bənt) *adj.* [< L. prp. of *incumbere* < *in-*, on + *cubare*, to lie down] 1. lying, resting, or pressing with its weight on something else 2. currently in office —*n.* the holder of an office or benefice —**incumbent on** (or **upon**) resting upon as a duty or obligation

in·cum·ber (in kum′bər) *vt. same as* ENCUMBER

in·cum·brance (-brəns) *n.* 1. *Law* a lien, claim, mortgage, etc. on property 2. *same as* ENCUMBRANCE

in·cu·nab·u·la (in′kyoo nab′yə lə) *n.pl., sing.* -u·lum (-ləm) [< L. < *in-*, in + *cunabula*, neut. pl., a cradle] 1. the very first stages of anything; beginnings 2. early printed books; esp., books printed before 1500 —**in′cu·nab′u·lar** *adj.*

in·cur (in kur′) *vt.* -curred′, -cur′ring [< L. < *in-*, in + *currere*, to run (to something undesirable) [to *incur* a debt] 2. to bring upon oneself through one's own actions —**in·cur′ra·ble** *adj.*

in·cur·a·ble (in kyoor′ə b'l) *adj.* not curable; that cannot be remedied or corrected [an *incurable* romantic] —*n.* a person having an incurable disease —**in·cur′a·bil′i·ty** *n.* —**in·cur′a·bly** *adv.*

in·cu·ri·ous (in kyoor′ē əs) *adj.* not curious; uninterested; indifferent —**in·cu·ri·os·i·ty** (in′kyoor ē os′ə tē), **in·cu′-ri·ous·ness** *n.* —**in·cu′ri·ous·ly** *adv.*

in·cur·sion (in kur′shən) *n.* [< L. *incursio* < *incurrere*: see INCUR] 1. a running in; inroad 2. a sudden, brief invasion or raid —**in·cur′sive** *adj.*

in·curve (in kurv′) *vt., vi.* -curved′, -curv′ing to curve inwards —**in·cur·va′tion** *n.*

in·cus (iŋ′kəs) *n., pl.* **in·cu·des** (in kyoo′dēz) [ModL. < L., anvil] the central one of the three small bones in the middle ear: also called *anvil*

in·cuse (in kyooz′) *adj.* [L. *incusus*, pp. of *incudere*, to forge] hammered or stamped in: said of the design on a coin, etc. —*n.* such a design —*vt.* to impress (a coin, etc.) with a design

Ind. 1. India 2. Indian 3. Indies

ind. 1. independent 2. index 3. industrial 4. indicative

in·da·ba (in dä′bä) *n.* [Zulu *in-daba*, subject] in South Africa, a council, esp. a tribal council

in·debt·ed (in det′id) *adj.* 1. in debt 2. obliged; owing gratitude

in·debt·ed·ness (-nis) *n.* 1. a being indebted 2. the amount owed; all one's debts

in·de·cen·cy (in dē′sən sē) *n.* 1. a being indecent 2. *pl.* -cies an indecent act, statement, etc.

in·de·cent (-sənt) *adj.* not decent; specif., a) not proper and fitting; unseemly b) morally offensive; obscene —**in·de′-cent·ly** *adv.*

in·de·ci·pher·a·ble (in′di sī′fər ə b'l) *adj.* that cannot be deciphered; illegible —**in′de·ci′pher·a·bil′i·ty** *n.*

in·de·ci·sion (in′di sizh′ən) *n.* inability to decide or a tendency to change the mind frequently

in·de·ci·sive (-sī′siv) *adj.* 1. not decisive 2. showing indecision; hesitating or vacillating —**in′de·ci′sive·ly** *adv.* —**in′de·ci′sive·ness** *n.*

in·de·clin·a·ble (in′di klin′ə b'l) *adj. Gram.* having no case inflections; not declinable

in·dec·o·rous (in dek′ər əs; *occas.* in′di kôr′əs) *adj.* lacking decorum, good taste, etc. —**in·dec′o·rous·ly** *adv.* —**in·dec′o·rous·ness** *n.*

in·de·co·rum (in′di kôr′əm) *n.* 1. lack of decorum 2. indecorous conduct, speech, etc.

in·deed (in dēd′) *adv.* [see IN, *prep.* & DEED] certainly; truly; admittedly —*interj.* an exclamation of surprise, doubt, sarcasm, etc.

indef. indefinite

in·de·fat·i·ga·ble (in′di fat′i gə b'l) *adj.* [< MFr. < L. < *in-*, not + *defatigare*, to tire out: see DE- & FATIGUE] that cannot be tired out; untiring —**in′de·fat′i·ga·bil′i·ty** *n.* —**in′-de·fat′i·ga·bly** *adv.*

in·de·fea·si·ble (in′di fē′zə b'l) *adj.* that cannot be undone or made void —**in′de·fea′si·bil′i·ty** *n.* —**in′de·fea′si·bly** *adv.*

in·de·fect·i·ble (in′di fek′tə b'l) *adj.* [IN-[2] + DEFECT + -IBLE] 1. not likely to fail, decay, etc. 2. without a fault; perfect

in·de·fen·si·ble (in′di fen′sə b'l) *adj.* 1. that cannot be defended 2. that cannot be justified —**in′de·fen′si·bil′i·ty** *n.* —**in′de·fen′si·bly** *adv.*

in·de·fin·a·ble (-fin′ə b'l) *adj.* that cannot be defined —**in′-de·fin′a·bil′i·ty** *n.* —**in′de·fin′a·bly** *adv.*

in·def·i·nite (in def′ə nit) *adj.* not definite; specif., a) having no exact limits b) not precise in meaning; vague c) not clear in outline; blurred d) not sure; uncertain e) *Gram.* not limiting or specifying [a and an are *indefinite* articles, *any* is an *indefinite* pronoun] —**in·def′i·nite·ly** *adv.* —**in·def′-i·nite·ness** *n.*

in·de·his·cent (in′di his′ənt) *adj.* not dehiscent; not opening at maturity to discharge its seeds —**in′de·his′-cence** *n.*

in·del·i·ble (in del′ə b'l) *adj.* [< L., ult. < *in-*, not + *delere*, to destroy] 1. that cannot be erased, blotted out, eliminated, etc.; permanent 2. leaving an indelible mark [indelible ink] —**in·del′i·bil′i·ty** *n.* —**in·del′i·bly** *adv.*

in·del·i·ca·cy (in del′i kə sē) *n.* 1. a being indelicate 2. *pl.* -cies something indelicate

in·del·i·cate (-kit) *adj.* not delicate; coarse; esp., lacking propriety or modesty —**in·del′i·cate·ly** *adv.* —**in·del′·i·cate·ness** *n.*

in·dem·ni·fy (in dem′nə fī′) *vt.* **-fied′, -fy′ing** [< L. *indemnis,* unhurt < *in-,* not + *damnum,* hurt + -FY] 1. to protect against loss, damage, etc.; insure 2. *a)* to repay for loss or damage *b)* to make good (a loss) —**in·dem′ni·fi·ca′·tion** *n.* —**in·dem′ni·fi′er** *n.*

in·dem·ni·ty (-tē) *n., pl.* **-ties** 1. protection or insurance against loss, damage, etc. 2. legal exemption from penalties incurred by one's actions 3. repayment for loss, damage, etc.

in·de·mon·stra·ble (in′di mon′strə b'l, in dem′ən-) *adj.* [LL. *indemonstrabilis*] not demonstrable; that cannot be proved

in·dent¹ (in dent′; *for n., usually* in′dent) *vt.* [< OFr. < ML. < L. *in,* in + *dens,* tooth] 1. *a)* to cut toothlike points into (an edge or border); notch; also, to join by mating notches *b)* to make jagged in outline 2. to bind (a servant or apprentice) by indenture 3. to space (the first line of a paragraph, etc.) in from the usual margin 4. to write out (a contract, etc.) in duplicate 5. to order by an indent —*vi.* 1. to form or be marked by notches, points, or a jagged border 2. to space in from the margin 3. to draw up an order or requisition in duplicate or triplicate —*n.* 1. a notch or cut in an edge 2. an indenture 3. an indented line, paragraph, etc. 4. an official order or requisition for goods 5. an order form, esp. one used in foreign trade

in·dent² (in dent′; *for n., usually* in′dent) *vt.* [IN-¹ + DENT] 1. to make a dent in 2. to press (a mark, etc.) in —*n.* a dent, or slight hollow

in·den·ta·tion (in′den tā′shən) *n.* 1. an indenting or being indented 2. a notch, cut, or inlet on a coastline, etc. 3. a dent, or slight hollow 4. an indention; space in from a margin

in·den·tion (in den′shən) *n.* 1. a spacing in from the margin 2. an empty or blank space left by this 3. *a)* a dent *b)* the making of a dent

in·den·ture (in den′chər) *n.* [< INDENT¹: orig., duplicates of a contract had correspondingly jagged edges for identification] 1. a written contract or agreement 2. [*often pl.*] a contract binding a person to work for another, as an apprentice to a master —*vt.* **-tured, -tur·ing** to bind by indenture

in·de·pend·ence (in′di pen′dəns) *n.* a being independent; freedom from the control of another

in·de·pend·en·cy (-dən sē) *n., pl.* **-cies** 1. *same as* INDEPENDENCE 2. an independent nation, etc.

in·de·pend·ent (-dənt) *adj.* 1. free from the influence or control of others; specif., *a)* free from the rule of another; self-governing *b)* free from persuasion or bias; objective [an *independent* observer] *c)* self-confident; self-reliant *d)* not adhering to any political party [an *independent* candidate] *e)* not connected with others; separate 2. *a)* not depending on another, esp. for financial support *b)* designating, of, or having an income large enough to enable one to live without working 3. [I-] of or having to do with Independents —*n.* a person who is independent in thinking, action, etc.; specif., [*often* I-] a member of Parliament not adhering to any political party —**independent of** apart from; regardless of —**in′de·pend′ent·ly** *adv.*

independent clause *Gram. same as* MAIN CLAUSE

independent school a school which does not receive financial support from the government or local authorities

independent variable *Math.* a quantity whose value may be determined freely without reference to other variables

in-depth (in′depth′) *adj.* carefully worked out, detailed, thorough, etc. [an *in-depth* study]

in·de·scrib·a·ble (in′di skri′bə b'l) *adj.* that cannot be described; beyond the power of description —**in′de·scrib′·a·bil′i·ty** *n.* —**in′de·scrib′a·bly** *adv.*

in·de·struct·i·ble (in′di struk′tə b'l) *adj.* that cannot be destroyed —**in′de·struct′i·bil′i·ty** *n.* —**in′de·struct′i·bly** *adv.*

in·de·ter·mi·na·ble (in′di tur′mi nə b'l) *adj.* not determinable; specif., *a)* that cannot be decided *b)* that cannot be ascertained —**in′de·ter′mi·na·ble·ness** *n.* —**in′·de·ter′mi·na·bly** *adv.*

in·de·ter·mi·nate (-nit) *adj.* not determinate; specif., *a)* inexact in its limits, nature, etc.; indefinite; vague *b)* not yet settled; inconclusive —**in′de·ter′mi·na·cy,** **in′de·ter′·mi·nate·ness** *n.* —**in′de·ter′mi·nate·ly** *adv.*

in·de·ter·mi·na·tion (in′di tur′mə nā′shən) *n.* 1. lack of determination 2. the state or quality of being indeterminate

in·dex (in′deks) *n., pl.* **-dex·es, -di·ces′** (-də sēz′) [L. < *indicare,* INDICATE] 1. *short for* INDEX FINGER 2. a pointer, as the needle on a dial 3. an indication or sign [performance is an *index* of ability] 4. *a)* an alphabetical list of names, subjects, etc. together with the page numbers where they appear in the text, usually placed at the end of a publication *b) short for* THUMB INDEX *c)* a catalogue [a library *index*] 5. *a)* the relation or ratio of one amount or dimension to another, or the formula expressing this relation *b)* a number used to measure changes in prices, wages, etc.: it shows percentage variation from an arbitrary

standard: in full, **index number** 6. [I-] *R.C.Ch.* formerly, a list of books forbidden to be read 7. *Math. a)* an exponent (sense 3) *b)* a number or symbol placed above and to the left of a radical (Ex.: $\sqrt[3]{8}$, $\sqrt[n]{x}$) 8. *Printing* a sign (☞) calling special attention to certain information —*vt.* 1. *a)* to make an index of or for *b)* to include in an index *c)* to supply with a thumb index 2. to indicate —**in′dex·er** *n.* —**in·dex′i·cal** *adj.*

index finger the finger next to the thumb

In·di·a·man (in′diə mən) *n., pl.* **-men** formerly, a large merchant ship engaged in trade with India or the East Indies

In·di·an (in′dē ən) *adj.* 1. of India or the East Indies, their people, or culture 2. of any of the aboriginal peoples (**American Indians**) of N. America, S. America, or the West Indies, or of their cultures 3. of a type used or made by Indians —*n.* 1. a native of India or the East Indies 2. a member of any of the aboriginal peoples of N. America, S. America, or the West Indies 3. popularly, any of the languages spoken by American Indians

Indian club a club of wood, metal, etc. shaped like a tenpin and swung in the hand for exercise

Indian corn *same as* MAIZE (sense 2)

Indian file *same as* SINGLE FILE

Indian ink 1. a black pigment of lampblack mixed with a gelatinous substance and dried into cakes or sticks 2. a liquid ink made from this

Indian meal meal made from maize; cornmeal

Indian rope-trick the climbing of a rope which, apparently, is not attached to anything

Indian summer a period of mild, warm, hazy weather following the first frosts of late autumn

Indian tobacco a poisonous annual plant, common in the E U.S., with light blue flowers in spikes

INDIAN CLUB

India paper 1. an absorbent paper made in China and Japan from vegetable fibre, used in taking proofs from engraved plates 2. a thin, strong, opaque printing paper, used for some Bibles, dictionaries, etc.

India (or india) rubber 1. crude, natural rubber obtained from latex 2. *same as* RUBBER¹ (sense 3) —**In′di·a-rub′ber** *adj.*

In·dic (in′dik) *adj.* 1. of India 2. designating or of a subgroup of the Indo-Iranian branch of the Indo-European language family, including many of the languages of India, Pakistan, etc.

indic. indicative

in·di·cate (in′də kāt′) *vt.* **-cat′ed, -cat′ing** [< L. pp. of *indicare* < *in-,* in + *dicare,* to declare] 1. to direct attention to; point out 2. to be or give a sign of; signify [fever *indicates* illness] 3. to show the need for; call for; make necessary [a material for which dry cleaning is *indicated*] 4. to show or point out as a cause, treatment, or outcome: said of a disease, etc. 5. to state briefly; suggest [he *indicated* guidelines for action]

in·di·ca·tion (in′də kā′shən) *n.* 1. an indicating 2. something that indicates, or shows; sign 3. something that is indicated as necessary 4. the amount or degree registered by an indicator

in·dic·a·tive (in dik′ə tiv) *adj.* 1. giving an indication or intimation; signifying: also **in·dic·a·to·ry** (in dik′ə tər ē, in′·dik-) 2. designating or of that mood of a verb used to express an act, state, or occurrence as actual, or to ask a question of fact —*n.* 1. the indicative mood 2. a verb in this mood —**in·dic′a·tive·ly** *adv.*

in·di·ca·tor (in′də kāt′ər) *n.* 1. a person or thing that indicates; specif., any device, as a gauge, dial, register, or pointer, that measures something 2. any substance used to indicate the acidity or alkalinity of a solution, the beginning or end of a chemical reaction, etc., by changes in colour 3. a device, usually a flashing light, for showing that a motor vehicle is about to turn left or right

in·di·ces (in′də sēz′) *n.* alt. pl. of INDEX

in·di·ci·a (in dish′ē ə, -dish′ə) *n.pl.* [L., ult. < *index: see* INDEX] 1. marks or tokens 2. [U.S.] printed markings on letters etc. in place of stamps or cancellations

in·dict (in dit′) *vt.* [< Anglo-L. *indictare,* ult. < L. *in,* against + *dictare: see* DICTATE] to charge with the commission of a crime; esp., to make formal accusation against on the basis of positive legal evidence —**in·dict′a·ble** *adj.* —**in·dict′er, in·dict′or** *n.*

in·dict·ment (in dīt′mənt) *n.* 1. an indicting or being indicted 2. a charge; specif., a formal accusation charging someone with a crime, (formerly, and still in U.S., presented by a grand jury to the court)

in·dif·fer·ence (in dif′ər əns, -dif′rəns) *n.* a being indifferent; specif., *a)* lack of concern or interest *b)* lack of importance or meaning

in·dif·fer·ent (-ənt, -rənt) *adj.* 1. having or showing no preference; neutral 2. having or showing no interest, concern, etc.; uninterested or unmoved 3. of no importance 4. not particularly good or bad, large or small, etc.; average 5. not really good 6. neutral in quality, as a chemical or

magnet; inactive **7.** not very good; poor: said esp. of health
—**in·dif′fer·ent·ly** *adv.*

in·dif·fer·ent·ism (-iz′m) *n.* the state of being indifferent;
esp., *a*) indifference to religion *b*) the belief that all religions
have equal validity

in·di·gence (in′di jəns) *n.* the condition of being indigent:
also **in′di·gen·cy**

in·dig·e·nous (in dij′ə nəs) *adj.* [< LL. < L. *indigena* < OL.
indu, in + *gignere*, to be born] **1.** existing, growing, or
produced naturally in a region or country; native (*to*) **2.**
innate; inborn —**in·dig′e·nous·ly** *adv.* —**in·dig′e·nous·ness** *n.*

in·di·gent (in′di jənt) *adj.* [OFr. < L. prp. of *indigere*, to be
in need < OL. *indu*, in + *egere*, to need] poor; needy —*n.*
an indigent person —**in′di·gent·ly** *adv.*

in·di·gest·i·ble (in′di jəs′tə b'l, -di-) *adj.* not digestible; not
easily digested —**in′di·gest′i·bil′i·ty** *n.*

in·di·ges·tion (in′di jes′chən, -jesh′-) *n.* **1.** inability to
digest, or difficulty in digesting, food **2.** the discomfort
caused by this

in·dig·nant (in dig′nənt) *adj.* [< L. prp. of *indignari*, to
consider unworthy, ult. < *in-*, not + *dignus*, worthy]
feeling or expressing indignation —**in·dig′nant·ly** *adv.*

in·dig·na·tion (in′dig nā′shən) *n.* anger or scorn that is a
reaction to injustice or meanness

in·dig·ni·ty (in dig′nə tē) *n.*, *pl.* **-ties** something that
humiliates, insults, or injures the dignity or self-respect;
affront

in·di·go (in′di gō′) *n.*, *pl.* **-gos′, -goes′** [Sp. < L. *indicum* <
Gr. < *Indikos*, Indian < *India*, India] **1.** a blue dye
obtained from certain plants or made synthetically **2.** a
plant of the legume family that yields indigo **3.** a deep
violet blue: also **indigo blue** —*adj.* of a deep violet-blue:
also **in′di·go′-blue′**

in·di·rect (in′di rekt′, -dī-) *adj.* not direct; specif., *a*) not
straight; roundabout *b*) not straight to the point or object
[an indirect reply] *c*) not straightforward; dishonest
[indirect dealing] *d*) not immediate; secondary [an
indirect result] —**in′di·rect′ly** *adv.* —**in′di·rect′ness** *n.*

in·di·rec·tion (-rek′shən) *n.* **1.** roundabout act, procedure,
or means **2.** deceit; dishonesty

indirect lighting lighting reflected, as from a ceiling, or
diffused so as to avoid glare

indirect object *Gram.* the person or thing indirectly
affected by the action of the verb, i.e., the one to which
something is given or for which something is done (Ex.: *him*
in "do *him* a favour")

indirect speech *same as* REPORTED SPEECH

indirect tax a tax on manufactured goods, imports, etc.
paid indirectly when included in the price

in·dis·cern·i·ble (in′di sur′nə b'l, -zur′-) *adj.* that cannot be
discerned; imperceptible —**in′dis·cern′i·bly** *adv.*

in·dis·ci·pline (in dis′ə plin) *n.* lack of discipline

in·dis·creet (in′dis krēt′) *adj.* not discreet; lacking
prudence; unwise —**in′dis·creet′ly** *adv.* —**in′dis·creet′-
ness** *n.*

in·dis·crete (in′dis krēt′) *adj.* [L. *indiscretus*, unseparated]
not separated into distinct parts

in·dis·cre·tion (in′dis kresh′ən) *n.* **1.** lack of discretion **2.**
an indiscreet act or remark

in·dis·crim·i·nate (in′dis krim′ə nit) *adj.* **1.** not based on
careful selection; random or promiscuous **2.** not
discriminating; not making careful choices or distinctions
—**in′dis·crim′i·nate·ly** *adv.* —**in′dis·crim′i·nate·ness, in′-
dis·crim′i·na′tion** *n.*

in·dis·pen·sa·ble (in′dis pen′sə b'l) *adj.* **1.** that cannot be
dispensed with or neglected **2.** absolutely necessary or
required —*n.* an indispensable person or thing —**in′-
dis·pen′sa·bil′i·ty** *n.* —**in′dis·pen′sa·bly** *adv.*

in·dis·pose (in′dis pōz′) *vt.* **-posed′, -pos′ing** **1.** to make
unfit or unable **2.** to make unwilling or disinclined **3.** to
make slightly ill

in·dis·posed (-pōzd′) *adj.* **1.** slightly ill **2.** unwilling;
disinclined

in·dis·po·si·tion (in′dis pə zish′ən) *n.* **1.** a slight illness **2.**
unwillingness; disinclination

in·dis·pu·ta·ble (in′dis pyōō′tə b'l, in dis′pyōō tə-) *adj.* that
cannot be disputed; unquestionable —**in′dis·pu′ta·bil′i·ty** *n.*
—**in′dis·pu′ta·bly** *adv.*

in·dis·sol·u·ble (in′di sol′yōō b'l) *adj.* that cannot be
dissolved, decomposed, or destroyed; firm; lasting —**in′-
dis·sol′u·bil′i·ty** *n.* —**in′dis·sol′u·bly** *adv.*

in·dis·tinct (in′dis tiŋkt′) *adj.* not distinct; specif., *a*) not
seen, heard, or perceived clearly; obscure *b*) not separate or
separable; not plainly defined —**in′dis·tinct′ly** *adv.* —**in′-
dis·tinct′ness** *n.*

in·dis·tin·guish·a·ble (-tiŋ′gwish ə b'l) *adj.* that cannot be
distinguished or recognized as different or separate —**in′-
dis·tin′guish·a·bly** *adv.*

in·dite (in dīt′) *vt.* **-dit′ed, -dit′ing** [< OFr., ult. < L.: see
INDICT] to put in writing; compose and write —**in·dite′-
ment** *n.* —**in·dit′er** *n.*

in·di·um (in′dē əm) *n.* [ModL. < L. *indicum*, indigo: from its

spectrum] a rare metallic chemical element, soft, ductile,
and silver-white: symbol, In; at. wt., 114.82; at. no., 49

in·di·vid·u·al (in′di vid′yōō wəl) *adj.* [< ML. < L.
individuus, not divisible] **1.** existing as a separate thing or
being; single; particular **2.** of, for, or by a single person or
thing **3.** of or characteristic of a single person or thing **4.**
unique or striking [an individual style] —*n.* **1.** a single
thing, being, or organism, esp. as a member of a class, etc.
2. [Colloq.] a person

in·di·vid·u·al·ism (-iz′m) *n.* **1.** individual character;
individuality **2.** the doctrine of unrestricted individual
freedom in economic enterprise **3.** the doctrine that the
state exists to serve the individual **4.** the doctrine that
self-interest is the proper goal of all human actions; egoism
5. *a*) action based on any such doctrine *b*) the leading of
one's life in one's own way without conforming to
conventions —**in′di·vid′u·al·ist** *n., adj.* —**in′di·vid′u·al·is′tic**
adj.

in·di·vid·u·al·i·ty (in′di vid′yōō wal′ə tē) *n.*, *pl.* **-ties** **1.** *a*)
the sum of the characteristics that set one person or thing
apart; individual character *b*) personal identity; personality
2. separate existence

in·di·vid·u·al·ize (-vid′yōō wə līz, -vij′ōō līz′) *vt.* **-ized′, -iz′-
ing** **1.** to make individual; mark as different from others **2.**
to make suitable for a particular individual **3.** to consider
individually; specify —**in′di·vid′u·al·i·za′tion** *n.*

in·di·vid·u·al·ly (-vid′yōō wəl ē, -vij′əl ē) *adv.* **1.** one at a
time; separately **2.** as an individual; personally **3.** in a way
showing individual characteristics; distinctively

in·di·vid·u·ate (-vid′yōō wāt′) *vt.* **-at′ed, -at′ing** [< ML. <
L. *individuus*: see INDIVIDUAL] **1.** to differentiate from
others of the same species; individualize **2.** to form into an
individual

in·di·vis·i·ble (in′di viz′ə b'l) *adj.* **1.** that cannot be divided
2. *Math.* that cannot be divided without leaving a
remainder —*n.* anything indivisible —**in′di·vis′i·bil′i·ty** *n.*
—**in′di·vis′i·bly** *adv.*

In·do- (in′dō) *a combining form meaning* **1.** Indian **2.**
India and; Indian and [Indo-European]

in·doc·tri·nate (in dok′trə nāt′) *vt.* **-nat′ed, -nat′ing** [prob.
< OFr. *endoctriner*: see IN-¹ & DOCTRINE] **1.** to instruct in
doctrines, theories, or beliefs, as of a sect **2.** to instruct;
teach —**in·doc′tri·na′tion** *n.* —**in·doc′tri·na′tor** *n.*

In·do-Eu·ro·pe·an (in′dō yoor′ə pē′ən) *adj.* designating or
of a family of languages that includes most of those spoken
in Europe and many of those spoken in southwestern Asia
and India —*n.* **1.** this family of languages, including the
Indo-Iranian, Greek, Italic, Germanic, and Slavic languages
2. the hypothetical language from which these languages are
thought to have descended

In·do-I·ra·ni·an (-i rä′nē ən) *adj.* designating or of a
subfamily of the Indo-European language family that
includes Indic and Iranian

in·dole (in′dōl) *n.* [< INDIGO + PHENOL] a white, crystalline
compound obtained from indigo and used in perfumery, etc.

in·do·lent (in′də lənt) *adj.* [< LL. < L. *in-*, not + prp. of
dolere, to feel pain] **1.** disliking or avoiding work; idle; lazy
2. *Med. a*) causing little pain *b*) slow to heal —**in′do·lence** *n.*
—**in′do·lent·ly** *adv.*

in·dom·i·ta·ble (in dom′it ə b'l) *adj.* [< LL. < L. < *in-*, not
+ pp. of *domitare*, intens. < *domare*, to tame] not easily
discouraged or defeated; unyielding —**in·dom′i·ta·bil′i·ty,
in·dom′i·ta·ble·ness** *n.* —**in·dom′i·ta·bly** *adv.*

In·do·ne·sian (in′də nē′zhən, -shən) *adj.* **1.** of Indonesia, its
people, etc. **2.** designating or of a large group of
Malayo-Polynesian languages spoken in Indonesia, the
Philippines, Java, etc. —*n.* **1.** a member of a race of people
of Indonesia, the Philippines, Java, etc. **2.** an inhabitant of
Indonesia **3.** the Indonesian languages **4.** the official
Malay language of Indonesia

in·door (in′dôr′) *adj.* **1.** of the inside of a house or building
2. living, belonging, or carried on within a house or building

in·doors (in′dôrz′) *adv.* in or into a house or other building

in·dorse (in dôrs′) *vt.* **-dorsed′, -dors′ing** *same as* ENDORSE

in·drawn (in′drôn′) *adj.* **1.** drawn in **2.** [Chiefly U.S.]
introspective

in·dri (in′drē) *n.* [Fr. < Malagasy *indry*, behold!:
erroneously taken for the name of the animal] a black and
white, tailless lemur of Madagascar

in·du·bi·ta·ble (in dyōō′bi tə b'l) *adj.* that cannot be
doubted; unquestionable —**in·du′bi·ta·bly** *adv.*

in·duce (in dyōōs′) *vt.* **-duced′, -duc′ing** [< L. *inducere* <
in-, in + *ducere*, to lead] **1.** to lead on to some action,
condition, etc.; persuade **2.** *a*) to bring on; cause [to induce
vomiting with an emetic] *b*) to cause labour to begin, as
with the use of drugs, etc. [the birth was induced] **3.** to
draw (a general rule or conclusion) from particular facts **4.**
Physics to bring about (an electric or magnetic effect) in a
body by exposing it to the influence of a field of force
—**in·duc′er** *n.* —**in·duc′i·ble** *adj.*

in·duce·ment (-mənt) *n.* **1.** an inducing or being induced **2.**
anything that induces; motive

in·duct (in dukt′) *vt.* [< L. pp. of *inducere*: see INDUCE] **1.**

formerly, to bring or lead in **2.** to place formally in a benefice or an official position **3.** to initiate **4.** [U.S.] to enrol for military service, esp. if compulsory

in·duct·ance (-duk'təns) *n.* the property of an electric circuit by which a varying current in it induces voltages in the same circuit or in one nearby

in·duc·tile (in duk'til) *adj.* not ductile, malleable, or pliant —**in'duc·til'i·ty** (-til'ə tē) *n.*

in·duc·tion (in duk'shən) *n.* **1.** an inducting or being inducted; installation **2.** a bringing forward of separate facts or instances, esp. so as to prove a general statement **3.** the transference of the mixed air and fuel from the carburettor to the cylinder of an internal combustion engine **4.** *Logic* reasoning from particular facts to a general conclusion; also, a conclusion so reached: opposed to DEDUCTION **5.** *Math.* a method of proving a theorem by showing that, if it holds true for all the numbers preceding a given number, it must hold true for the next following number **6.** *Physics* the act or process by which an electric or magnetic effect is produced in an electrical conductor or magnetizable body when it is exposed to the influence of a field of force

induction coil an apparatus made up of two magnetically coupled coils in a circuit in which interruptions of the direct-current supply to one coil produce an alternating current of high potential in the other

induction heating the heating of a conducting material by means of electric current induced by an alternating magnetic field

in·duc·tive (in duk'tiv) *adj.* **1.** of or using logical induction [*inductive* reasoning] **2.** produced by induction **3.** of inductance or electrical or magnetic induction —**in·duc'-tive·ly** *adv.* —**in·duc'tive·ness** *n.*

in·duc·tor (-tər) *n.* a person or thing that inducts; specif., a device designed to introduce inductance into an electric circuit

in·due (in dyo͞o') *vt.* -**dued'**, -**du'ing** same as ENDUE

in·dulge (in dulj') *vt.* -**dulged'**, -**dulg'ing** [L. *indulgere*, to be kind to] **1.** to yield to or satisfy (a desire); give oneself up to [to *indulge* a craving for sweets] **2.** to gratify the wishes of; humour —*vi.* to give way to one's own desires; indulge oneself (*in* something) —**in·dulg'er** *n.*

in·dul·gence (in dul'jəns) *n.* **1.** an indulging or being indulgent **2.** a thing indulged in **3.** a giving way to one's desires **4.** a favour or privilege **5.** *R.C.Ch.* a remission of temporal or purgatorial punishment still due for a sin after the guilt has been forgiven

in·dul·gent (-jənt) *adj.* indulging or inclined to indulge; kind or lenient, often to excess —**in·dul'gent·ly** *adv.*

in·du·na (in do͞o'nə) *n.* [< Zulu *nduna*, an official] in South Africa, a native councillor or leader

in·du·rate (in'dyoo rāt') *vt.* -**rat'ed**, -**rat'ing** [< L. pp. of *indurare* < *in*-, in + *durare*, to harden] **1.** to make hard; harden **2.** to make callous or unfeeling **3.** to cause to be firmly established —*vi.* to become indurated —*adj.* **1.** hardened **2.** callous or unfeeling —**in'du·ra'tion** *n.* —**in'du·ra'tive** *adj.*

in·du·si·um (in dyo͞o' zē əm, -zhē-) *n.*, *pl.* -**si·a** (-ə) [ModL. < L., undergarment, tunic] **1.** *Anat. & Zool.* a) a covering membrane b) a case enclosing an insect larva **2.** *Bot.* a membranous outgrowth on the undersides of the leaves of some ferns to protect the spores —**in·du'si·al** *adj.*

in·dus·tri·al (in dus'trē əl) *adj.* **1.** having the nature of or characterized by industries **2.** of, connected with, or resulting from industries **3.** working in industries **4.** of or concerned with people working in industries **5.** for use by industries: said of products —**in·dus'tri·al·ly** *adv.*

industrial action any action, such as a strike or go-slow, taken by employees to prevent or hinder production as a protest against working conditions

industrial arts [U.S.] the mechanical and technical skills used in industry, esp. as taught in schools

industrial estate an area set aside for industrial and business use, usually on the outskirts of a city

in·dus·tri·al·ism (in dus'trē əl iz'm) *n.* social and economic organization characterized by large industries, machine production, concentration of workers in cities, etc.

in·dus·tri·al·ist (-ə list) *n.* a person who owns or manages an industrial enterprise

in·dus·tri·al·ize (-ə līz') *vt.* -**ized'**, -**iz'ing** **1.** to develop industrialism in **2.** to organize as an industry —*vi.* to become industrial —**in·dus'tri·al·i·za'tion** *n.*

industrial relations relations between industrial employers and their employees

in·dus·tri·ous (in dus'trē əs) *adj.* characterized by earnest, steady effort; hard-working —**in·dus'tri·ous·ly** *adv.* —**in·dus'tri·ous·ness** *n.*

in·dus·try (in'dəs trē) *n.*, *pl.* -**tries** [< MFr. < L. *industria* < *industrius*, active] **1.** earnest, steady effort; diligence in work **2.** systematic work **3.** a) any particular branch of productive, esp. manufacturing, enterprise [the paper *industry*]: also, all such enterprises collectively b) any

large-scale business activity [the TV *industry*] **4.** the owners and managers of industry

in·dwell (in dwel') *vi.*, *vt.* -**dwelt'**, -**dwell'ing** to dwell (in); reside (within) —**in·dwell'er** *n.*

-ine¹ (īn, in, ēn, ən) [< Fr. < L. *-inus*] a suffix meaning of, having the nature of, like [*divine*, *marine*, *crystalline*]

-ine² (in, ən, īn, ēn) [< L. < Gr. *-inē*] a suffix used to form feminine nouns [*heroine*]

-ine³ (in, ən) [Fr. < L. *-ina*] a suffix used to form certain abstract nouns [*medicine*, *doctrine*]

-ine⁴ (ēn, in, īn, ən) [arbitrary use of L. *-inus*] a suffix used to form certain commercial names [*Vaseline*] or the chemical names of a) halogens [*iodine*] b) alkaloids or nitrogen bases [*morphine*]

in·e·bri·ate (in ē'brē āt'; for adj. & n., usually -it) *vt.* -**at'ed**, -**at'ing** [< L. pp. of *inebriare*, ult. < *in*-, intens. + *ebrius*, drunk] **1.** to make drunk; intoxicate **2.** to excite; exhilarate —*adj.* drunk; intoxicated —*n.* a drunken person, esp. a drunkard —**in·e'bri·at'ed** *adj.* —**in·e'bri·a'-tion, in·e·bri·e·ty** (in'ē brī'ə tē) *n.*

in·ed·i·ble (in ed'ə b'l) *adj.* not edible; not fit to be eaten —**in'ed·i·bil'i·ty** *n.*

in·ed·it·ed (in ed'it id) *adj.* **1.** unpublished **2.** not edited

in·ed·u·ca·ble (in ej'ə kə b'l) *adj.* thought to be incapable of being educated —**in·ed'u·ca·bil'i·ty** *n.*

in·ef·fa·ble (in ef'ə b'l) *adj.* [< MFr. < L. < *in*-, not + *effabilis*, utterable < *ex*-, out + *fari*, to speak] **1.** too overwhelming to be expressed in words **2.** too sacred to be spoken —**in'ef·fa·bil'i·ty, in·ef'fa·ble·ness** *n.* —**in·ef'fa·bly** *adv.*

in·ef·face·a·ble (in'i fās'ə b'l) *adj.* that cannot be effaced; impossible to wipe out —**in·ef'face·a·bil'i·ty** *n.* —**in·ef'face'-a·bly** *adv.*

in·ef·fec·tive (in'i fek'tiv) *adj.* **1.** not effective; not producing the desired effect **2.** not capable of performing satisfactorily; incompetent; inefficient —**in'ef·fec'tive·ly** *adv.* —**in'ef·fec'tive·ness** *n.*

in·ef·fec·tu·al (-tyoo wol) *adj.* not effectual; not producing or not able to produce the desired effect —**in'ef·fec'tu·al'-i·ty** (-wal'ə tē), **in'ef·fec'tu·al·ness** *n.* —**in'ef·fec'tu·al·ly** *adv.*

in·ef·fi·ca·cious (in'ef ə kā'shəs) *adj.* not efficacious; unable to produce the desired effect [an *inefficacious* medicine] —**in'ef·fi·ca'cious·ly** *adv.* —**in'ef·fi·ca'-cious·ness** *n.*

in·ef·fi·ca·cy (in ef'i kə sē) *n.* lack of efficacy; inability to produce the desired effect

in·ef·fi·cient (in'ə fish'ənt) *adj.* not efficient; specif., a) not producing the desired effect with a minimum use of energy, time, etc. b) lacking the necessary ability; incapable —**in'-ef·fi'cien·cy** *n.* —**in'ef·fi'cient·ly** *adv.*

in·e·las·tic (in'i las'tik) *adj.* not elastic; inflexible, rigid, unyielding, unadaptable, etc. —**in'e·las'tic·al·ly** *adv.* —**in'-e·las·tic'i·ty** (-las tis'ə tē) *n.*

in·el·e·gance (in el'ə gəns) *n.* **1.** lack of elegance **2.** something inelegant Also **in·el'e·gan·cy**, *pl.* **-cies**

in·el·e·gant (-gənt) *adj.* not elegant; lacking refinement, good taste, grace, etc.; coarse; crude —**in·el'e·gant·ly** *adv.*

in·el·i·gi·ble (in el'i jəb'l) *adj.* not eligible; not qualified under the rules —*n.* an ineligible person —**in·el'i·gi·bil'i·ty** *n.* —**in·el'i·gi·bly** *adv.*

in·e·luc·ta·ble (in'i luk'tə b'l) *adj.* [< L. < *in*-, not + *eluctabilis*, resistible < *eluctari*, to struggle] not to be avoided or escaped; inevitable —**in'e·luc'ta·bil'i·ty** *n.* —**in'-e·luc'ta·bly** *adv.*

in·ept (in ept') *adj.* [< Fr. < L. < *in*-, not + *aptus*, fit] **1.** unsuitable; unfit **2.** wrong in a foolish and awkward way [*inept* praise] **3.** clumsy or bungling; inefficient —**in·ept'ly** *adv.* —**in·ept'ness** *n.*

in·ept·i·tude (in ep'tə yo͞od') *n.* **1.** the quality or condition of being inept **2.** an inept act, remark, etc.

in·e·qua·ble (in ek'wə b'l) *adj.* [IN.² + EQUABLE] **1.** changeable **2.** not uniform **3.** unfairly distributed

in·e·qual·i·ty (in'i kwol'ə tē) *n.*, *pl.* -**ties** **1.** a being unequal; lack of equality **2.** an instance of this; specif., a) a difference in size, amount, quality, rank, etc. b) an unevenness in surface c) a lack of proper proportion; unequal distribution **3.** *Math.* a) the relation between two unequal quantities b) an expression of this

in·eq·ui·ta·ble (in ek'wit əb'l) *adj.* not equitable; unfair; unjust —**in·eq'ui·ta·bly** *adv.*

in·eq·ui·ty (in ek'wət ē) *n.* **1.** lack of justice; unfairness **2.** *pl.* -**ties** an instance of this

in·e·rad·i·ca·ble (in'i rad'ə kə b'l) *adj.* that cannot be eradicated —**in'e·rad'i·ca·bly** *adv.*

in·ert (in urt') *adj.* [< L. < *in*-, not + *ars*, ART¹] **1.** without power to move or act **2.** inactive; dull; slow **3.** having few or no active properties [an *inert* gas] —**in·ert'ly** *adv.* —**in·ert'ness** *n.*

in·er·tia (in ur'shə) *n.* [see prec.] **1.** *Physics* the tendency of matter to remain at rest (or to keep moving in the same direction) unless affected by an outside force **2.** a tendency to remain fixed, inactive, unchanging, etc.; disinclination to move or act —**in·er'tial** *adj.*

inertial guidance (or **navigation**) the guidance (or navigation) of an aircraft, spacecraft, etc. along a preassigned course by means of self-contained, automatic instruments that utilize the laws of inertia

inertia reel a reel holding a seat belt and enabling it to adjust itself automatically

inertia selling the sending of unrequested goods to householders, relying on their paying for the goods rather than taking the trouble to return them

in·es·cap·a·ble (in'ə skăp'ə b'l) *adj.* that cannot be escaped or avoided; inevitable —**in'es·cap'a·bly** *adv.*

in·es·sen·tial (in'ə sen'shəl) *adj.* not essential; unnecessary; unimportant —*n.* something inessential

in·es·ti·ma·ble (in es'tə mə b'l) *adj.* too great or valuable to be properly measured or estimated —**in·es'ti·ma·bly** *adv.*

in·ev·i·ta·ble (in ev'ə tə b'l) *adj.* [< L. < *in-*, not + *evitabilis*, avoidable] that cannot be avoided; certain to happen —**in·ev'i·ta·bil'i·ty** *n.* —**in·ev'i·ta·bly** *adv.*

in·ex·act (in'ig zakt') *adj.* not exact; not accurate —**in'·ex·act'ly** *adv.* —**in'ex·act'i·tude**, **in'ex·act'ness** *n.*

in·ex·cus·a·ble (in'ik skyo͞o'zə b'l) *adj.* that cannot or should not be excused; unjustifiable —**in'ex·cus'a·bil'i·ty** *n.* —**in'ex·cus'a·bly** *adv.*

in·ex·haust·i·ble (in'ig zôs'tə b'l) *adj.* that cannot be exhausted; specif., *a*) that cannot be used up or emptied *b*) tireless —**in'ex·haust'i·bil'i·ty** *n.* —**in'ex·haust'i·bly** *adv.*

in·ex·o·ra·ble (in ek'sər ə b'l) *adj.* [< L. < *in-*, not + *exorare*, to move by entreaty] 1. that cannot be influenced by entreaty; unrelenting 2. that cannot be altered, checked, etc. [*inexorable* fate] —**in·ex'o·ra·bil'i·ty** *n.* —**in·ex'o·ra·bly** *adv.*

in·ex·pe·di·ent (in'ik spē'dē ənt) *adj.* not expedient; not suitable or practicable; unwise —**in'ex·pe'di·en·cy**, **in'·ex·pe'di·ence** *n.* —**in'ex·pe'di·ent·ly** *adv.*

in·ex·pen·sive (in'ik spen'siv) *adj.* not expensive; costing relatively little; cheap —**in'ex·pen'sive·ly** *adv.* —**in'ex·pen'·sive·ness** *n.*

in·ex·pe·ri·ence (in'ik spir'ē əns) *n.* lack of experience or of the knowledge or skill resulting from experience —**in'·ex·pe'ri·enced** *adj.*

in·ex·pert (in ek'spərt) *adj.* not expert; unskilful; amateurish —**in·ex'pert·ly** *adv.* —**in·ex'pert·ness** *n.*

in·ex·pi·a·ble (in ek'spē ə b'l) *adj.* that cannot be expiated or atoned for [an *inexpiable* sin]

in·ex·pli·ca·ble (in eks'pli kə b'l, in'iks plik'ə b'l) *adj.* not explicable; that cannot be explained or understood —**in·ex'·pli·ca·bil'i·ty** *n.* —**in·ex'pli·ca·bly** *adv.*

in·ex·plic·it (in'ik splis'it) *adj.* vague; indefinite; not clearly stated —**in'ex·plic'it·ly** *adv.* —**in'ex·plic'it·ness** *n.*

in·ex·press·i·ble (in'ik spres'ə b'l) *adj.* that cannot be expressed; indescribable or unutterable —*n.* [*pl.*] [Obs. Colloq.] trousers —**in'ex·press'i·bil'i·ty** *n.* —**in'ex·press'·i·bly** *adv.*

in·ex·pres·sive (in'ik spres'iv) *adj.* not expressive; lacking meaning or expression —**in'ex·pres'sive·ly** *adv.* —**in'·ex·press'ive·ness** *n.*

‡**in ex·ten·so** (in ik sten'sō) [L.] at full length

in·ex·tin·guish·a·ble (in'ik stiŋ'gwish ə b'l) *adj.* not extinguishable; that cannot be put out or stopped —**in'·ex·tin'guish·a·bly** *adv.*

‡**in ex·tre·mis** (in'ik strē'mis) [L., in extremity] at the point of death

in·ex·tri·ca·ble (in eks'tri kə b'l, in'ik strik'ə b'l) *adj.* 1. that one cannot extricate oneself from 2. that cannot be disentangled or untied 3. insolvable —**in·ex'tri·ca·bil'i·ty** *n.* —**in·ex'tri·ca·bly** *adv.*

inf. 1. [L. *infra*] below 2. infantry: also **Inf.** 3. infinitive 4. information

in·fal·li·ble (in fal'ə b'l) *adj.* [< ML.: see IN.² & FALLIBLE] 1. incapable of error; never wrong 2. not liable to fail, go wrong, etc.; reliable 3. *R.C.Ch.* incapable of error in setting forth doctrine on faith and morals: said esp. of the Pope speaking in an official capacity —**in·fal'li·bil'i·ty** *n.* —**in·fal'li·bly** *adv.*

in·fa·mous (in'fə məs) *adj.* 1. having a very bad reputation; notorious 2. causing or deserving a bad reputation —**in'·fa·mous·ly** *adv.*

in·fa·my (-mē) *n.*, *pl.* **-mies** [< OFr. < L.: see IN.² & FAMOUS] 1. very bad reputation; disgrace; dishonour 2. the quality of being infamous; great wickedness 3. an infamous act

in·fan·cy (in'fən sē) *n.*, *pl.* **-cies** 1. the state or period of being an infant; babyhood 2. the beginning or earliest stage of anything 3. *Law* the state of being a minor; period before the age of legal majority

in·fant (in'fənt) *n.* [< OFr. < L., ult. < *in-*, not + prp. of *fari*, to speak] 1. a very young child; baby 2. *Law* a minor —*adj.* 1. of or for infants or infancy 2. in a very early stage

in·fan·ta (in fan'tə) *n.* [Sp. & Port., fem. of *infante*: see ff.] 1. any daughter of a king of Spain or Portugal 2. the wife of an infante

in·fan·te (-tā) *n.* [Sp. & Port. < L.: see INFANT] any son of a king of Spain or Portugal, except the heir to the throne

in·fan·ti·cide (in fan'tə sid') *n.* [Fr. < LL.: see INFANT & -CIDE] 1. the murder of a baby 2. a person guilty of this

in·fan·tile (in'fən til') *adj.* 1. of infants or infancy 2. like or characteristic of an infant; babyish 3. in the earliest stage of development

infantile paralysis same as POLIOMYELITIS

in·fan·ti·lism (in'fən til iz'm, in fan'-) *n.* immature or childish behaviour; specif., *Psychol.* an abnormal state in which such behaviour persists into adult life

in·fan·tine (in'fən tin') *adj.* infantile

in·fan·try (in'fən trē) *n.*, *pl.* **-tries** [< Fr. < It. < *infante*, child, knight's page, foot soldier] 1. foot soldiers collectively; esp., that branch of an army consisting of soldiers trained and equipped to fight chiefly on foot 2. [I-] a (designated) infantry regiment

in·fan·try·man (-mən) *n.*, *pl.* **-men** (-mən) a soldier in the infantry

infant school a school for children aged between four or five and seven

in·farct (in färkt') *n.* [ML. *infarctus* < L. *infarcire*, to stuff] an area of dead or dying tissue resulting from obstruction of the blood vessels normally supplying the part —**in·farc'·tion** *n.*

in·fat·u·ate (in fat'yo͞o wāt') *vt.* **-at'ed**, **-at'ing** [< L. pp. of *infatuare* < *in-*, intens. + *fatuus*, foolish] 1. to make foolish 2. to inspire with foolish or shallow love —*adj.* infatuated —*n.* a person who is infatuated —**in·fat'u·a'·tion** *n.*

in·fat·u·at·ed (-id) *adj.* 1. foolish 2. completely carried away by foolish or shallow love

in·fau·na (in'fô nə) *n.* [IN.¹ + FAUNA] creatures which live in the sea bed

in·fect (in fekt') *vt.* [< MFr. < L. pp. of *inficere*, to stain < *in-*, in + *facere*, to make] 1. to contaminate with a disease-producing organism 2. to cause to become diseased by bringing into contact with such an organism 3. to invade (an individual, organ, tissue, etc.) 4. to imbue with one's feelings or beliefs —**in·fec'tor** *n.*

in·fec·tion (in fek'shən) *n.* 1. an infecting; specif., *a*) a causing to become diseased *b*) an affecting with one's feelings or beliefs 2. a being infected, esp. by bacteria, viruses, etc. 3. something that results from infecting or being infected; specif., a disease resulting from infection (sense 2) 4. anything that infects

in·fec·tious (-shəs) *adj.* 1. likely to cause infection 2. designating a disease that can be communicated by infection (sense 2) 3. tending to spread to others [an *infectious* laugh] —**in·fec'tious·ly** *adv.* —**in·fec'tious·ness** *n.*

infectious hepatitis a viral disease causing inflammation of the liver

infectious mononucleosis an acute disease, esp. of young people, characterized by fever, swollen lymph nodes, etc.: also called **glandular fever**

in·fec·tive (in fek'tiv) *adj.* likely to cause infection —**in·fec'tive·ness**, **in'fec·tiv'i·ty** *n.*

in·fe·lic·i·tous (in'fə lis'ə təs) *adj.* not felicitous; unfortunate or unsuitable —**in'fe·lic'i·tous·ly** *adv.*

in·fe·lic·i·ty (-tē) *n.* 1. a being infelicitous 2. *pl.* **-ties** something infelicitous; unsuitable or inapt remark, action, etc.

in·fer (in fur') *vt.* **-ferred'**, **-fer'ring** [< L. *inferre* < *in-*, in + *ferre*, to bring] 1. to conclude by reasoning from something known or assumed 2. *a*) to lead to as a conclusion; indicate *b*) [Colloq.] to indicate indirectly; imply: a loose usage —*vi.* to draw inferences —**in·fer'·a·ble**, **in·ferr'a·ble** *adj.* —**in·fer'a·bly** *adv.* —**in·fer'rer** *n.*

in·fer·ence (in'fər əns) *n.* 1. an inferring; specif., the deriving of a conclusion by induction or deduction 2. something inferred; conclusion

in·fer·en·tial (in'fə ren'shəl) *adj.* of or based on inference —**in'fer·en'tial·ly** *adv.*

in·fe·ri·or (in fir'ē ər) *adj.* [L., compar. of *inferus*, low] 1. lower in space; placed lower down 2. lower in order, status, rank, etc. 3. lower in quality or value than (with *to*) 4. poor in quality; below average —*n.* an inferior person or thing —**in·fe'ri·or'i·ty** (-or'ə tē) *n.*

inferiority complex 1. *Psychol.* a neurotic condition resulting from various feelings of inferiority or inadequacy, often manifested through overcompensation in excessive aggressiveness, etc. 2. popularly, any feeling of inferiority, inadequacy, etc.

in·fer·nal (in fur'n'l) *adj.* [< OFr. < LL. *infernalis*, ult. < L. *inferus*: see INFERIOR] 1. *a*) of the ancient mythological world of the dead *b*) of hell 2. hellish; fiendish 3. [Colloq.] hateful; outrageous —**in·fer'nal·ly** *adv.*

infernal machine earlier name for a booby trap or time bomb

in·fer·no (in fur'nō) *n.*, *pl.* **-nos** [It. < L.: see INFERNAL] hell or any place suggesting hell

in·fer·tile (in fur'til) *adj.* not fertile; barren; sterile —**in·fer·til·i·ty** (in'fər til'ə tē) *n.*

in·fest (in fest′) *vt.* [< Fr. < L. < *infestus*, hostile] **1.** to overrun or swarm about in large numbers, usually so as to be harmful or troublesome **2.** to be parasitic in or on —**in′·fes·ta′tion** *n.*

in·feu·da·tion (in′fyoo dā′shən) *n.* [ML. *infeudatio* < pp. of *infeudare*, to enfeoff] in feudal society: *a)* the granting of an estate in fee *b)* the granting of tithes to laymen

in·fi·del (in′fə d'l) *n.* [< MFr. < L. < *in-*, not + *fidelis*, faithful] **1.** a person who does not believe in a particular, esp. the prevailing, religion **2.** a person who holds no religious belief **3.** historically, the Moslems, esp. at the time of the Crusades —*adj.* **1.** that is an infidel; unbelieving **2.** of infidels

in·fi·del·i·ty (in′fə del′ə tē) *n., pl.* **-ties 1.** the fact or state of being an infidel **2.** unfaithfulness or disloyalty to another; esp., sexual unfaithfulness of a husband or wife; adultery **3.** an unfaithful or disloyal act

in·field (in′fēld′) *n.* **1.** the farmland near to a farmhouse **2.** *Cricket a)* the area of ground near the wicket *b)* the fieldsmen stationed there

in·fight·ing (in′fīt′iŋ) *n.* **1.** fighting, esp. boxing, at close range **2.** intense competition or conflict, often personal, as between political opponents or within an organization —**in′·fight′er** *n.*

in·fil·trate (in fil′trāt, in′fil trāt′) *vi., vt.* **-trat·ed, -trat·ing 1.** to pass into or through (a substance), as in filtering **2.** to pass, or cause (individual troops) to pass, through weak places in the enemy's lines **3.** to penetrate, or cause to penetrate (a region or group) gradually or stealthily, so as to gain influence or control —*n.* something that infiltrates —**in′fil·tra′tion** *n.* —**in′fil·tra′tive** *adj.* —**in′fil·tra′tor** *n.*

infin. infinitive

in·fi·nite (in′fə nit) *adj.* [< L.: see IN-² & FINITE] **1.** lacking limits or bounds; extending beyond measure or comprehension; endless **2.** very great; vast; immense **3.** *Math.* indefinitely large; greater than any finite number —*n.* something infinite —**the Infinite (Being)** God —**in′·fi·nite·ly** *adv.* —**in′fi·nite·ness** *n.*

in·fin·i·tes·i·mal (in′fin ə tes′ə mal, in fin′-) *adj.* [< ModL. < L. *infinitus*, infinite (patterned after *centesimus*, hundredth)] **1.** too small to be measured; infinitely small **2.** *Math.* of an infinitesimal —*n.* **1.** an infinitesimal quantity **2.** *Math.* a variable non-zero number which is understood to be smaller in absolute value than any preassigned non-zero number —**in′fin·i·tes′i·mal·ly** *adv.*

in·fin·i·tive (in fin′ə tiv) *adj.* [< LL. < L. *infinitus* (*modus*), lit., unlimited (mood)] *Gram.* of or connected with an infinitive —*n.* *Gram.* the form of the verb which expresses existence or action without reference to person, number, or tense: usually following the marker *to* (*to go*) or another verb form (*let him try*) —**in·fin′i·ti′val** (-tī′val) *adj.*

in·fin·i·tude (-tyo͞od′) *n.* **1.** a being infinite **2.** an infinite quantity or extent

in·fin·i·ty (-tē) *n., pl.* **-ties 1.** the quality of being infinite **2.** endless or unlimited space, time, distance, amount, etc. **3.** an indefinitely large number or amount

in·firm (in furm′) *adj.* **1.** not firm or strong physically; weak; feeble **2.** not firm in mind or purpose; vacillating **3.** not stable; frail; shaky, as a structure **4.** not secure or valid —**in·firm′ly** *adv.* —**in·firm′ness** *n.*

in·fir·ma·ri·an (in fər mer′ē ən) *n.* a person responsible for running an infirmary, esp. in a monastery

in·fir·ma·ry (in fur′mə rē) *n., pl.* **-ries** a place for the care of the sick, injured, or infirm; esp., a building or room, as in a monastery, school, etc., that serves as a hospital or dispensary

in·fir·mi·ty (-mə tē) *n.* **1.** a being infirm; feebleness; weakness **2.** *pl.* **-ties** *a)* a physical weakness or defect *b)* a moral weakness

in·fix (in fiks′; *also, and for n.* always, in′fiks′) *vt.* **1.** to fasten or set firmly in or on **2.** to fix firmly in the mind; instil **3.** to place (an infix) within the body of a word —*n.* *Linguis.* an element inserted into the middle of a word rather than at the end or the beginning

‡in fla·gran·te de·lic·to (in flə gran′tē di lik′tō) [L.] in the very act of committing the offence

in·flame (in flām′) *vt.* **-flamed′, -flam′ing** [< OFr. < L.: see IN-¹ & FLAME] **1.** to set on fire **2.** to arouse passion, desire, or violence in; excite intensely **3.** to increase the intensity of (passion, desire, etc.) **4.** to cause inflammation in (some organ or tissue) —*vi.* **1.** to become roused, excited, etc. **2.** to catch fire **3.** to become hot, feverish, sore, etc. —**in·flam′er** *n.*

in·flam·ma·ble (in flam′ə b'l) *adj.* **1.** *same as* FLAMMABLE **2.** easily excited —*n.* anything flammable —**in·flam′·ma·bil′i·ty** *n.* —**in·flam′ma·bly** *adv.*

in·flam·ma·tion (in′flə mā′shən) *n.* **1.** an inflaming or being inflamed **2.** a condition of some part of the body in reaction to injury, infection, etc., characterized by redness, pain, heat, and swelling

in·flam·ma·to·ry (in flam′ə tər ē) *adj.* **1.** rousing or likely to rouse excitement, anger, violence, etc. **2.** *Med.* of or characterized by inflammation

in·flat·a·ble (in flāt′ə b'l) *adj.* capable of being inflated —*n.* any structure or object made of strong, inflatable plastic

in·flate (in flāt′) *vt.* **-flat′ed, -flat′ing** [< L. pp. of *inflare* < *in-*, in + *flare*, to blow] **1.** to blow full or swell out as with air or gas **2.** to raise in spirits; make proud **3.** to increase or raise beyond what is normal; specif., to cause inflation of (money, credit, etc.) —*vi.* to become inflated —**in·flat′er, in·fla′tor** *n.*

in·fla·tion (in flā′shən) *n.* **1.** an inflating or being inflated **2.** an increase in the amount of money in circulation, resulting in a fall in its value and a rise in prices —**in·fla′·tion·ar·y** *adj.*

in·fla·tion·ism (-iz′m) *n.* advocacy or promotion of monetary inflation —**in·fla′tion·ist** *adj., n.*

in·flect (in flekt′) *vt.* [< L. *inflectere* < *in-*, in + *flectere*, to bend] **1.** to turn, bend, or curve **2.** to vary the tone or pitch of (the voice) **3.** *Gram.* to change the form of (a word) by inflection, as in conjugating or declining —*vi.* to be changed by inflection —**in·flec′tive** *adj.*

in·flec·tion, in·flex·ion (in flek′shən) *n.* **1.** a turn, bend, or curve **2.** a change in tone or pitch of the voice **3.** *Gram. a)* the change of form by which some words indicate certain grammatical relationships, as number, case, gender, tense, etc. *b)* an inflected form *c)* an inflectional element

in·flec·tion·al, in·flex·ion·al (-'l) *adj.* of, having, or showing grammatical inflection —**in·flec′tion·al·ly, in·flex′·ion·al·ly** *adv.*

in·flex·i·ble (in flek′sə b'l) *adj.* not flexible; specif., *a)* that cannot be bent or curved; rigid *b)* firm in mind or purpose; stubborn *c)* that cannot be changed; unalterable —**in·flex′·i·bil′i·ty, in·flex′i·ble·ness** *n.* —**in·flex′i·bly** *adv.*

in·flict (in flikt′) *vt.* [< L. pp. of *infligere* < *in-*, against + *fligere*, to strike] **1.** to cause (pain, wounds, etc.) as by striking **2.** to impose (a punishment, disagreeable task, etc. on or upon) —**in·flict′er, in·flic′tor** *n.* —**in·flic′tive** *adj.*

in·flic·tion (in flik′shən) *n.* **1.** an inflicting **2.** something inflicted, as punishment

in·flight (in′flīt′) *adj.* done, occurring, shown, etc. while an aircraft is in flight

in·flo·res·cence (in′flô res′əns, -flə-) *n.* [< ModL. < LL.: see IN-¹ & FLORES-CENCE] *Bot.* **1.** the producing of blossoms; flowering **2.** the arrangement of flowers on a stem or axis **3.** a single flower cluster **4.** flowers collectively —**in′·flo·res′cent** *adj.*

in·flow (in′flō′) *n.* **1.** a flowing in or into **2.** anything that flows in

in·flu·ence (in′-floo wəns) *n.* [< OFr. < ML. prp. of *influere* < *in-*, in + *fluere*, to flow] **1.** *a)* the power of persons or things to affect others *b)* the effect of such power **2.** the ability to produce effects indirectly by means of power based on wealth, high position, etc. **3.** one that has influence —*vt.* **-enced, -encing** to have influence on; affect the nature, behaviour, or thought of —**under the influence** [Colloq.] drunk

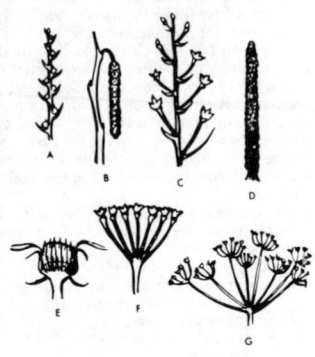

TYPES OF INFLORESCENCE
(A, spike; B, catkin; C, raceme; D, spadix; E, head with
disc flowers and ray flowers;
F, umbel; G, compound umbel)

in·flu·ent (in′floo ənt) *adj.* [L. *influens*, flowing in] flowing in —*n.* **1.** something following in, as a tributary **2.** *Ecol.* an organism that has an important effect within an ecological community but is not a dominant

in·flu·en·tial (in′floo wen′shəl) *adj.* having or exerting influence, esp. great influence; powerful —**in′flu·en′tial·ly** *adv.*

in·flu·en·za (in′floo wen′zə) *n.* [It., lit., an influence (because attributed to astrological influences)] an acute, contagious, infectious disease, caused by a virus and characterized by inflammation of the respiratory tract, fever, and muscular pain —**in′flu·en′zal** *adj.*

in·flux (in′fluks′) *n.* [Fr. < LL. pp. of *influere*: see INFLUENCE] **1.** a flowing in or continual coming in; inflow **2.** the point where a river joins another body of water

in·fo (in′fō) *n.* [Colloq.] information

in·fold (in fōld′) *vt.* *same as* ENFOLD

in·form (in fôrm′) *vt.* [< OFr. < L.: see IN-¹ & FORM] **1.** *a)* to give character to *b)* to inspire; animate **2.** to give knowledge of something to; tell —*vi.* **1.** to give information

2. to give information laying blame or accusation upon another, esp. to the police (with *on* or *against*)

in·for·mal (in fôr′məl) *adj.* not formal; specif., *a)* not according to fixed customs, rules, etc. *b)* casual, easy, or relaxed *c)* for everyday use or casual wear *d)* not requiring formal dress *e) same as* COLLOQUIAL —**in·for′mal·ly** *adv.*

in·for·mal·i·ty (in′fôr mal′ə tē) *n.* **1.** a being informal **2.** *pl.* **-ties** an informal act

informal vote [Aust. & N.Z.] **1.** a spoilt ballot paper **2.** an invalid vote

in·form·ant (in fôr′mənt) *n.* a person who gives, or serves as a source of, information

in·for·ma·tion (in′fər mā′shən) *n.* **1.** an informing or being informed; esp., a telling or being told **2.** news; word **3.** knowledge acquired in any manner; facts; data **4.** a person or agency answering questions as a service to others **5.** any data stored in a computer **6.** *Law* a charge made before a magistrate or court as a method of initiating legal proceedings —**in′for·ma′tion·al** *adj.*

information theory the study of processes of communication and the transmission of messages

in·form·a·tive (in fôr′mə tiv) *adj.* giving information; instructive —**in·form′a·tive·ly** *adv.*

in·formed (in fôrmd′) *adj.* having much information, knowledge, or education

in·form·er (in fôr′mər) *n.* a person who informs; esp., one who secretly accuses, or gives evidence against, another, often for a reward

in·fra- (in′frə-) [< L. *infra*, below] *a prefix meaning* below, beneath [*infrared*]

in·frac·tion (in frak′shən) *n.* [< L. < pp. of *infringere*: see INFRINGE] a violation of a law, pact, etc.

in·fra dig (in′frə dig′) [< L. *infra dig(nitatem)*] [Colloq.] beneath one's dignity

in·fran·gi·ble (in fran′jə b'l) *adj.* **1.** that cannot be broken or separated **2.** that cannot be violated or infringed —**in·fran′gi·bil′i·ty, in·fran′gi·ble·ness** *n.* —**in·fran′gi·bly** *adv.*

in·fra·red (in′frə red′) *adj.* designating or of those invisible rays just beyond the red of the visible spectrum: their waves are longer than those of the spectrum colours and give off penetrating heat

in·fra·son·ic (-son′ik) *adj.* designating or of a frequency of sound below the range audible to the human ear —**in′fra·son′ic·al·ly** *adv.*

in·fra·struc·ture (in′frə struk′chər) *n.* **1.** the basic requirements of a developed economy, as roads, power, education, etc. **2.** the network of services, bases, etc. required as the basis of a military operation —**in′fra·struc′tur·al** *adj.*

in·fre·quent (in frē′kwənt) *adj.* not frequent; happening seldom; rare —**in·fre′quen·cy, in·fre′quence** *n.* —**in·fre′quent·ly** *adv.*

in·fringe (in frinj′) *vt.* **-fringed′, -fring′ing** [L. *infringere* < *in-*, in + *frangere*, to break] to break (a law or agreement); violate —**infringe on** (or **upon**) to break in on; encroach on (the rights, etc. of others) —**in·fringe′ment** *n.* —**in·fring′er** *n.*

in·fun·dib·u·lar (in fun dib′yoo lər) *adj.* [< L. *infundibulum*, funnel] funnel-shaped

in·fu·ri·ate (in fyoor′ē āt′) *vt.* **-at′ed, -at′ing** [< ML. pp. of *infuriare* < L. *in-*, in + *furia*, rage] to cause to become very angry; enrage —**in·fu′ri·at′ing·ly** *adv.* —**in·fu′ri·a′tion** *n.*

in·fuse (in fyooz′) *vt.* **-fused′, -fus′ing** [< L. pp. of *infundere* < *in-*, in + *fundere*, to pour] **1.** to instil or impart (qualities, etc.) **2.** to imbue or inspire (*with* a quality, feeling, etc.) **3.** to steep or soak (tea leaves, etc.) so as to extract flavour or other qualities —*vi.* to undergo infusion —**in·fus′er** *n.*

in·fu·si·ble (in fyoo′zə b'l) *adj.* that cannot be fused or melted —**in·fu′si·bil′i·ty, in·fu′si·ble·ness** *n.*

in·fu·sion (in fyoo′zhən) *n.* **1.** an infusing **2.** something infused **3.** the liquid extract that results from steeping a substance in water

in·fu·so·ri·an (in′fyoo sôr′ē ən) *n.* [< ModL.: from their occurrence in infusions] any of certain protozoans having cilia that permit free movement —*adj.* of these protozoans: also **in′fu·so′ri·al**

-ing (in) **1.** [< OE. *-ende*] *a suffix used to form the present participle* [*hearing*] **2.** [< OE. *-ung*] *a suffix used to form verbal nouns meaning:* a) the act or an instance of [*talking*] b) something produced by the action of [*painting*] c) something that does the action of [a head covering] d) material used for [*carpeting*] **3.** [< OE.] *a suffix, sometimes with diminutive force, meaning* one of a specified kind [*farthing*]

in·gem·i·nate (in jem′ə nāt′) *vt.* **-nat′ed, -nat′ing** [< L. *ingeminatus*, pp. of *ingeminare*, to repeat] [Now Rare] to stress; to repeat

in·gen·ious (in jēn′yəs, -ē əs) *adj.* [< MFr. < L. < *ingenium*, ability < *in-*, in + *gignere*, to produce] **1.** clever, resourceful, and inventive **2.** cleverly or originally made or done —**in·gen′ious·ly** *adv.* —**in·gen′ious·ness** *n.*

in·gé·nue (an′zhə noo′, -jə-; *Fr.* an zhā nü′) *n., pl.* **-nues′** (-nooz′; *Fr.* -nü′) [< Fr. < L. *ingenuus*, INGENUOUS] **1.** an innocent, inexperienced young woman **2.** *Theatre a)* the role of such a character *b)* an actress playing such a role

in·ge·nu·i·ty (in′jə nyoo′ə tē) *n.* [< L. < *ingenuus* (see ff.): associated with INGENIOUS] a being ingenious; cleverness, originality, etc.

in·gen·u·ous (in jen′yoo wəs) *adj.* [< L. *ingenuus* < *in-*, in + *gignere*, to produce] **1.** frank; open; candid **2.** simple; artless; naive —**in·gen′u·ous·ly** *adv.* —**in·gen′u·ous·ness** *n.*

in·gest (in jest′) *vt.* [< L. pp. of *ingerere* < *in-*, into + *gerere*, to carry] to take (food, drugs, etc.) into the body, as by swallowing or absorbing —**in·ges′tion** *n.* —**in·ges′tive** *adj.*

in·gle (in′g'l) *n.* [Scot. < Gael. *aingeal*, fire] [Dial.] **1.** a fire or blaze **2.** a fireplace

in·gle·nook (-nook′) *n.* a corner by a fireplace: also **ingle nook**

in·glo·ri·ous (in glôr′ē əs) *adj.* **1.** not giving or deserving glory; shameful; disgraceful **2.** [Now Rare] without glory; not famous —**in·glo′ri·ous·ly** *adv.* —**in·glo′ri·ous·ness** *n.*

in·go·ing (in′gō′in) *adj.* going in; entering

in·got (in′gət) *n.* [? < MFr. *lingot* (with faulty separation of *l-*)] a mass of metal cast into a bar or other convenient shape

in·graft (in gräft′) *vt. same as* ENGRAFT

in·grain (in′grān) *adj.* [< ME. < OFr. *engrainer*, to dye scarlet] **1.** dyed in the fibre, before manufacture [*ingrain carpet*] **2.** deeply infused

in·grained (in grānd′, in′grānd) *adj.* **1.** worked into the fibre; firmly fixed or established **2.** inveterate; thoroughgoing [an ingrained law]

in·grate (in′grāt) *n.* [< OFr. < L. < *in-*, not + *gratus*, grateful] [Now Rare] an ungrateful person

in·gra·ti·ate (in grā′shē āt′) *vt.* **-at′ed, -at′ing** [< L. < *in*, in + *gratia*, favour] to bring (oneself) into another's favour or good graces —**in·gra′ti·at′ing·ly** *adv.* —**in·gra′ti·a′tion** *n.*

in·grat·i·tude (in grat′ə tyood′) *n.* lack of gratitude; ungratefulness

in·gre·di·ent (in grē′dē ənt) *n.* [< L. prp. of *ingredi*: see INGRESS] **1.** any of the things that a mixture is made of **2.** a component part of anything

in·gress (in′gres) *n.* [< L. pp. of *ingredi*, to enter < *in-*, into + *gradi*, to go] **1.** the act of entering: also **in·gres′sion** (-gresh′ən) **2.** the right to enter **3.** an entrance —**in·gres′sive** *adj.*

in·grow·ing (in′grō′in) *adj.* growing within, inwards, or into; esp., growing into the flesh —**in′growth** *n.*

in·grown (-grōn′) *adj.* grown within, inwards, or into; esp., grown into the flesh, as a toenail

in·gui·nal (in′gwə n'l) *adj.* [< L. < *inguen*, the groin] of or near the groin

in·gulf (in gulf′) *vt. same as* ENGULF

in·gur·gi·tate (in gur′jə tāt′) *vt.* **-tat′ed, -tat′ing** [< L. *ingurgitatus*, pp. of *ingurgitare*, to flood in] to swallow greedily; guzzle —**in·gur′gi·ta′tion** *n.*

in·hab·it (in hab′it) *vt.* [< OFr. < L. *inhabitare* < *in-*, in + *habitare*, to dwell] to live in (a region, house, etc.); occupy —**in·hab′it·a·bil′i·ty** *n.* —**in·hab′it·a·ble** *adj.* —**in·hab′i·ta′tion** *n.* —**in·hab′it·er** *n.*

in·hab·it·ant (-i tənt) *n.* a person or animal that inhabits some specified region, house, etc.

in·hal·ant (in hāl′ənt) *adj.* used in inhalation —*n.* a medicine to be inhaled as a vapour

in·hale (in hāl′) *vt., vi.* **-haled′, -hal′ing** [L. *inhalare* < *in-*, in + *halare*, to breathe] to breathe in; draw (air, vapour, smoke, etc.) into the lungs —**in·ha·la·tion** (in′hə lā′shən) *n.*

in·hal·er (-ər) *n.* **1.** a person who inhales **2.** *same as* RESPIRATOR (sense 1) **3.** an apparatus for administering medicinal vapours in inhalation

in·har·mon·ic (in′här mon′ik) *adj.* not harmonic; discordant

in·har·mo·ni·ous (-mō′nē əs) *adj.* not harmonious; discordant, in conflict, etc. —**in′har·mo′ni·ous·ly** *adv.* —**in′·har·mo′ni·ous·ness** *n.*

in·here (in hir′) *vi.* **-hered′, -her′ing** [< L. < *in-*, in + *haerere*, to stick] to be inherent; exist as a quality, characteristic, or right (*in*)

in·her·ent (in hir′ənt, in her′-) *adj.* [see prec.] existing in someone or something as a natural and inseparable quality or right; inborn —**in·her′ence, in·her′en·cy** *n., pl.* **-cies** —**in·her′ent·ly** *adv.*

in·her·it (in her′it) *vt.* [< OFr. < LL., ult. < L. *in*, in + *heres*, heir] **1.** to receive (property, etc.) by or as if by inheritance or bequest from a predecessor **2.** to have (certain characteristics) by heredity —*vi.* to receive an inheritance —**in·her′i·tor** *n.* —**in·her′i·tress** (-i tris), **in·her′i·trix** (-i triks) *n.fem.*

in·her·it·a·ble (-ə b'l) *adj.* **1.** capable of inheriting; having the rights of an heir **2.** that can be inherited —**in·her′it·a·bil′i·ty, in·her′it·a·ble·ness** *n.*

in·her·it·ance (-əns) *n.* **1.** the action of inheriting **2.** something inherited or to be inherited; legacy; bequest **3.** right

to inherit 4. anything received as if by inheritance **5.** any characteristic passed on by heredity

in·hib·it (in hib′it) *vt.* [< L. pp. of *inhibere*, to curb < *in-*, in + *habere*, to hold] to hold back or keep from some action, feeling, etc. —**in·hib′i·tive, in·hib′i·to·ry** (-i tər ē) *adj.* —**in·hib′i·tor, in·hib′it·er** *n.*

in·hi·bi·tion (in′hi bish′ən, in′ə-) *n.* **1.** an inhibiting or being inhibited **2.** a mental or psychological process that restrains an action, emotion, or thought

in·hos·pi·ta·ble (in hos′pi tə b'l, in′hos pit′ə b'l) *adj.* **1.** not hospitable **2.** not offering protection, shelter, etc.; barren; forbidding —**in·hos′pi·ta·ble·ness** *n.* —**in·hos′pi·ta·bly** *adv.*

in·hos·pi·tal·i·ty (in′hos pi tal′ə tē, in hos′-) *n.* lack of hospitality; inhospitable treatment

in·hu·man (in hyo͞o′mən, -yo͞o′-) *adj.* not human; esp., not having normal human characteristics; unfeeling, cruel, etc. —**in·hu′man·ly** *adv.*

in·hu·mane (in′hyo͞o mān′) *adj.* not humane; unmoved by the suffering of others; cruel, brutal, unkind, etc. —**in′·hu·mane′ly** *adv.*

in·hu·man·i·ty (-man′ə tē) *n.* **1.** a being inhuman or inhumane **2.** *pl.* **-ties** an inhuman or inhumane act or remark

in·hume (in hyo͞om′) *vt.* **-humed, -hum′ing** [< Fr. < L. *inhumare*, to bury] to bury (a dead body) —**in′hu·ma′tion** *n.*

in·im·i·cal (in im′i k'l) *adj.* [< LL. < L. *inimicus*, ENEMY] **1.** hostile; unfriendly **2.** in opposition; adverse —**in·im′i·cal·ly** *adv.*

in·im·i·ta·ble (in im′ə tə b'l) *adj.* that cannot be imitated or matched; too good to be equalled or copied —**in·im′i·ta·bil′·i·ty, in·im′i·ta·ble·ness** *n.* —**in·im′i·ta·bly** *adv.*

in·iq·ui·tous (in ik′wə təs) *adj.* showing iniquity; wicked; unjust —**in·iq′ui·tous·ly** *adv.* —**in·iq′ui·tous·ness** *n.*

in·iq·ui·ty (-wə tē) *n.* [< OFr. < L. < *iniquus*, unequal < *in-*, not + *aequus*, equal] **1.** lack of righteousness or justice; wickedness **2.** *pl.* **-ties** a wicked, unjust, or unrighteous act

in·i·tial (i nish′əl) *adj.* [< Fr. < L. *initialis*, ult. < *in-*, in + *ire*, to go] having to do with or occurring at the beginning —*n.* a capital, or upper-case, letter; specif., the first letter of a name —*vt.* **-tialled, -tial·ling** to mark or sign with an initial or initials

in·i·tial·ly (-ē) *adv.* at the beginning; first

Initial Teaching Alphabet an alphabet of 44 characters, with a single sound for each character, for teaching beginners to read English

in·i·ti·ate (i nish′ē āt′; *for adj. & n., usually* -it) *vt.* **-at′ed, -at′ing** [< L. pp. of *initiare*: see INITIAL] **1.** to bring into practice or use **2.** to teach the fundamentals of some subject to **3.** to admit as a member into a society, etc., esp. with a special or secret ceremony —*adj.* initiated —*n.* a person who has recently been, or is about to be, initiated —**in·i′ti·a′tor** *n.*

in·i·ti·a·tion (i nish′ē ā′shən) *n.* **1.** an initiating or being initiated **2.** the ceremony by which one is initiated into a society, etc.

in·i·ti·a·tive (i nish′ē ə tiv, -nish′ə-) *adj.* of, or having the nature of, initiation —*n.* **1.** the action of taking the first step or move **2.** the characteristic of originating new ideas or methods; ability to think or act without being urged; enterprise **3.** *a)* the right of a group of citizens to introduce a matter for legislation to the legislature or directly to the voters, as in Switzerland and some U.S. states *b)* the procedure for this

in·i·ti·a·to·ry (-tər ē) *adj.* **1.** beginning; introductory **2.** of or used in an initiation

in·ject (in jekt′) *vt.* [< L. pp. of *injicere* < *in-*, in + *jacere*, to throw] **1.** to force or drive (a fluid) into some passage or cavity or into some part of the body by means of a syringe, etc. **2.** to fill by injection **3.** to introduce (a missing quality, etc.) **4.** [Now Rare] to interject (a remark, etc.) —**in·ject′a·ble** *adj.* —**in·jec′tion** *n.* —**in·jec′tor** *n.*

in·ju·di·cious (in′jo͞o dish′əs) *adj.* not judicious; showing poor judgment; not discreet or wise —**in′ju·di′cious·ly** *adv.* —**in′ju·di′cious·ness** *n.*

in·junc·tion (in junk′shən) *n.* [< LL. < pp. of *injungere*, ENJOIN] **1.** an enjoining; command **2.** an order **3.** a writ or order from a court prohibiting a person or group from carrying out a given action, or ordering a given action to be done —**in·junct′** *vt.* —**in·junc′tive** *adj.*

in·jure (in′jər) *vt.* **-jured, -jur·ing** [see INJURY] **1.** to do physical harm to; hurt **2.** to offend (one's feelings, etc.) **3.** to weaken (a reputation, etc.) **4.** to be unjust to —**in′·jur·er** *n.*

in·jured (in′jərd) *adj.* **1.** hurt; wronged **2.** feeling or displaying a sense of injury [with an *injured* expression]

in·ju·ri·ous (in joor′ē əs) *adj.* **1.** injuring or likely to injure; harmful **2.** offensive or abusive —**in·ju′ri·ous·ly** *adv.* —**in·ju′ri·ous·ness** *n.*

in·ju·ry (in′jər ē) *n., pl.* **-ries** [< L. *injuria*, ult. < *in-*, not + *jus* (gen. *juris*), right] **1.** physical harm to a person, etc. **2.**

an injurious act; injustice, as in injuring a person's feelings or rights, a reputation, etc.

injury time *Football* extra time allowed at the end of a match to compensate for time lost through a player's injury

in·jus·tice (in jus′tis) *n.* **1.** the quality of being unjust or unfair **2.** an unjust act; injury

ink (ink) *n.* [OFr. *enque* < LL. < Gr. *enkauston*, red ink < *enkaiein*, to burn in] **1.** a coloured liquid used for writing, etc. **2.** a sticky, coloured paste used in printing **3.** a dark, liquid secretion squirted out by cuttlefish, etc. for protection **4.** [Aust. Slang] cheap wine —*vt.* **1.** to cover with ink **2.** to mark or colour with ink (often with *in*) —**ink′er** *n.* —**ink′-like′** *adj.*

inkblot test *same as* RORSCHACH TEST

inked (inkt) *adj.* [Aust. Slang] drunk

ink·horn (-hôrn′) *n.* a small container made of horn, etc., formerly used to hold ink

ink·ling (ink′lin) *n.* **1.** an indirect suggestion; hint **2.** a vague idea or notion

ink·stand (ink′stand′) *n.* a small stand holding an inkwell, pens, etc.

ink·well (ink′wel) *n.* a container for holding ink, usually set in a desk, inkstand, etc.

ink·y (in′kē) *adj.* **ink′i·er, ink′i·est 1.** like ink in colour; dark; black **2.** coloured, marked, or covered with ink —**ink′i·ness** *n.*

in·laid (in′lād′, in lād′) *adj.* **1.** set in pieces into a surface of another material so as to form a smooth surface **2.** decorated with such a surface

in·land (in′lənd; *for n. & adv., usually* -land′) *adj* **1.** of, located in, or confined to the interior of a country or region; away from the coast or border **2.** within a country; domestic —*n.* inland areas —*adv.* into or towards the interior

Inland Revenue a department of the British government that administers and collects major direct taxes, such as income tax

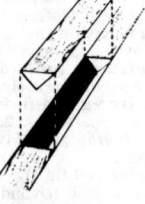

INLAID WOOD

in-law (in′lô′) *n.* [< (MOTHER-)IN-LAW, etc.] [Colloq.] a relative by marriage

in·lay (in′lā′; *for v., also* in lā′) *vt.* **-laid′, -lay′ing 1.** *a)* to set (pieces of wood, metal, etc.) into, and level with, a surface to make a design *b)* to decorate thus **2.** to add extra silverplating to —*n., pl.* **-lays′ 1.** inlaid decoration or material **2.** a filling for a tooth made from a mould and cemented into the cavity —**in′lay′er** *n.*

in·let (in′let, -lit) *n.* **1.** *a)* a narrow strip of water extending into a body of land from a river, lake, ocean, etc. *b)* a narrow strip of water between islands **2.** an entrance, as to a culvert

in·li·er (in′lī′ər) *n.* [IN.¹ + LIE¹ + -ER] an outcrop area of older rocks entirely surrounded by younger rocks

‡**in lo·co pa·ren·tis** (in lō′kō pə ren′tis) [L.] in the place of a parent

in·ly (in′lē) *adv.* [Poet.] **1.** inwardly **2.** intimately

in·mate (in′māt′) *n.* [IN-¹ + MATE¹] a person living with others in the same building, now esp. one confined with others in a prison, etc.

‡**in me·di·as res** (in mā′dē äs rās′) [L., lit., into the midst of things] in the middle of the action

‡**in me·mo·ri·am** (in mə môr′ē əm) [L.] in memory (of)

in·most (in′mōst′) *adj.* **1.** located farthest within **2.** most intimate or secret [*inmost* thoughts]

inn (in) *n.* [OE.] **1.** an establishment providing food and lodging for travellers; hotel **2.** a restaurant or tavern Now chiefly in the names of such places

in·nards (in′ərdz) *n.pl.* [< INWARD] [Dial. or Colloq.] **1.** the internal organs of the viscera **2.** the inner part of anything, esp. an engine or machine

in·nate (i nāt′, in′āt) *adj.* [< L. pp. of *innasci* < *in-*, in + *nasci*, to be born] **1.** existing naturally rather than acquired [*innate* talent] **2.** existing as an inherent attribute [the *innate* humour of a situation] —**in·nate′ly** *adv.* —**in·nate′ness** *n.*

in·ner (in′ər) *adj.* **1.** located farther within; interior **2.** of the mind or spirit **3.** more intimate or secret [the inner emotions] —*n. a)* the part of a target next to the bull's-eye or centre *b)* a shot which hits this

inner city the sections of a large city in or near its centre, esp. when crowded or blighted

inner man 1. one's mind or soul **2.** humorously, one's stomach

in·ner·most (in′ər mōst′) *adj.* **1.** located farthest within **2.** most intimate or secret

inner tube an inflatable rubber tube that fits inside a pneumatic tyre casing

in·ner·vate (in′ər vāt′) *vt.* **-vat·ed, -vat·ing** [< IN.¹ + NERVE + -ATE¹] **1.** to supply (a part of the body) with nerves **2.** to stimulate (a muscle, etc.) to action

in·nings (in′iŋz) *n.pl.* [with sing. *v.*] [OE. *inning*, a getting in] 1. *Cricket*, etc. a) the period of play in which a team has a turn at batting b) a numbered round of play in which both teams have a turn at batting 2. the period of, or opportunity for, action; exercise of authority, etc. 3. [sing.] [U.S.] an innings in baseball

inn·keep·er (in′kē′pər) *n.* the proprietor of an inn

in·no·cence (in′ə səns) *n.* a being innocent; specif., a) freedom from sin or guilt b) guilelessness; simplicity c) naiveté d) harmlessness e) ignorance: also **in′no·cen·cy**

in·no·cent (in′ə sənt) *adj.* [< OFr. < L. < *in-*, not + prp. of *nocere*, to do wrong to] 1. free from sin, evil, or guilt; specif., a) doing or thinking nothing morally wrong; pure b) not guilty of a specific crime or offence c) free from harmful effect or cause 2. a) knowing no evil b) without guile or cunning; artless c) naive d) ignorant 3. totally lacking (with *of*) —*n.* 1. a person knowing no evil or sin, as a child 2. a very naive person —**in′no·cent·ly** *adv.*

in·noc·u·ous (i nok′yoo wəs) *adj.* [< L. < *in-*, not + *nocuus*, harmful < *nocere*, to harm] 1. that does not injure or harm; harmless 2. not controversial or offensive; dull and uninspiring —**in·noc′u·ous·ly** *adv.* —**in·noc′u·ous·ness** *n.*

in·nom·i·nate bone (i nom′ə nit) [< LL. *innominatus*, unnamed + BONE] either of two large, irregular bones of the pelvis, each formed of the ilium, ischium, and pubis; hipbone

in·no·vate (in′ə vāt′) *vi.* -**vat′ed**, -**vat′ing** [< L. pp. of *innovare* < *in-*, in + *novare*, to alter < *novus*, new] to introduce new methods, devices, etc. —*vt.* [Now Rare] to bring in as an innovation —**in′no·va′tive** *adj.* —**in′no·va′tor** *n.*

in·no·va·tion (in′ə vā′shən) *n.* 1. an innovating 2. something newly introduced; new method, practice, device, etc. —**in′no·va′tion·al** *adj.*

in·nu·en·do (in′yoo wen′dō) *n.*, *pl.* -**does**, -**dos** [L., abl. of gerund of *innuere*, to nod to, hint] an indirect remark, gesture, or reference, usually implying something derogatory; insinuation

in·nu·mer·a·ble (i nyoo′mər ə b'l) *adj.* too numerous to be counted; countless —**in·nu′mer·a·bil′i·ty**, **in·nu′mer·a·ble·ness** *n.* —**in·nu′mer·a·bly** *adv.*

in·nu·mer·ate (-it) *adj.* not numerate; lacking the knowledge needed to deal with scientific, esp. mathematical, concepts —**in·nu′mer·a·cy** *n.*

in·oc·u·late (i nok′yoo lāt′) *vt.* -**lat′ed**, -**lat′ing** [< L. pp. of *inoculare*, to engraft a bud < *in-*, in + *oculus*, an eye, bud] 1. to inject a serum, vaccine, etc. into (a living organism), esp. in order to create immunity 2. to implant microorganisms into (soil, a culture medium, etc.) to develop a culture, stimulate growth, etc. 3. to imbue with ideas, etc. —**in·oc′u·la·bil′i·ty** *n.* —**in·oc′u·la·ble** *adj.* —**in·oc′u·la′tion** *n.* —**in·oc′u·la′tive** *adj.* —**in·oc′u·la′tor** *n.*

in·oc·u·lum (i nok′yoo ləm) *n.* [ModL.] material used in an innoculation, as bacteria: also **in·oc′u·lant**

in·of·fen·sive (in′ə fen′siv) *adj.* not offensive; unobjectionable; causing no harm or annoyance —**in′of·fen′sive·ly** *adv.* —**in′of·fen′sive·ness** *n.*

in·of·fi·cious (in′ə fish′əs) *adj.* [L. *inofficiosus*, undutiful] *Law* showing neglect of moral duty: said esp. of a will that unreasonably deprives an heir of his just inheritance

in·op·er·a·ble (in op′ər ə b'l) *adj.* not operable; specif., that will not practicably allow of surgical operation

in·op·er·a·tive (-ər ə tiv, -ə rāt′iv) *adj.* not operative; without effect —**in·op′er·a·tive·ness** *n.*

in·op·por·tune (in op′ər tyoon′) *adj.* not opportune; coming or happening at a poor time; not appropriate —**in·op′por·tune′ly** *adv.* —**in·op′por·tune′ness** *n.*

in·or·di·nate (in ôr′din it) *adj.* [< L.: see IN-² & ORDINATE] 1. disordered; not regulated 2. lacking restraint or moderation; excessive —**in·or′di·nate·ly** *adv.* —**in·or′di·nate·ness** *n.*

in·or·gan·ic (in′ôr gan′ik) *adj.* not organic; specif., a) designating or composed of matter that is not animal or vegetable; not living b) not like an organism in structure c) designating or of any chemical compound not organic d) designating or of the branch of chemistry dealing with these compounds —**in′or·gan′i·cal·ly** *adv.*

in·os·cu·late (in os′kyoo lāt′) *vt., vi.* -**lat′ed**, -**lat′ing** [IN-¹ + OSCULATE] 1. a) join by openings at the ends: said of arteries, etc. b) to intertwine: said of climbing plants, etc. 2. to unit closely

in·o·si·tol (i nō′sə tol′) *n.* [< Gr. *is* (gen. *inos*), muscle + -IT(E) + -OL¹] a sweet crystalline alcohol, esp. the form found in the vitamin B complex that apparently promotes growth: also **in·o·site** (in′ə sit′)

in patient a patient who lives in hospital while receiving treatment

‡**in per·pe·tu·um** (in′pər pech′oo wəm) [L.] forever

in·put (in′poot) *n.* what is put in; specif., a) the amount of money, material, effort, etc. put into a project or process b) electric current or power put into a circuit, machine, etc. c) information fed into a computer, etc. —*vt.* to feed data into a computer —*adj.* relating to input [input area]

in·quest (in′kwest) *n.* [< OFr. < VL. pp. of hyp. *inquaerere*: see INQUIRE] 1. a judicial inquiry, as a coroner's investigation of a death 2. the jury or group holding such an inquiry 3. the verdict of such an inquiry 4. [Colloq.] a detailed investigation of a fault, mistake, etc.

in·qui·e·tude (in kwī′ə tyood′) *n.* restlessness; uneasiness

in·qui·line (in′kwə lin′, -lin) *n.* [L. *inquilinus*, inhabitant] an animal, usually an insect, that lives in the home of another

in·quire (in kwir′) *vi.* -**quired′**, -**quir′ing** [< OFr. < LL. hyp. *inquaerere*, for L. *inquirere* < *in*, into + *quaerere*, to seek] 1. to ask a question or questions 2. to carry out an examination or investigation (usually with *into*) —*vt.* to seek information about [to *inquire* the way] —**inquire after** to pay respects by asking about the health of —**in·quir′er** *n.* —**in·quir′ing·ly** *adv.*

in·quir·y (in kwir′ē) *n., pl.* -**quir·ies** 1. the act of inquiring 2. an investigation or examination 3. a question; query

in·qui·si·tion (in′kwə zish′ən) *n.* [ME. < OFr. < L. *inquisitio*] 1. an inquiring; investigation 2. [I-] R.C.Ch. a) formerly, the general tribunal established to discover and suppress heresy and heretics b) the activities of this tribunal 3. a) any harsh or arbitrary suppression of dissent or nonconformity b) any relentless questioning 4. *Law* an inquest or any judicial inquiry —**in′qui·si′tion·al** *adj.*

in·quis·i·tive (in kwiz′ə tiv) *adj.* [< ME., ult. < L. *inquirere*: see INQUIRE] 1. inclined to ask many questions or seek information 2. unnecessarily curious; meddlesome; prying —**in·quis′i·tive·ly** *adv.* —**in·quis′i·tive·ness** *n.*

in·quis·i·tor (-tər) *n.* 1. an official whose work is making an inquisition 2. any harsh or prying questioner 3. [I-] an official of the Inquisition

in·quis·i·to·ri·al (in kwiz′ə tôr′ē əl) *adj.* 1. of, or having the nature of, an inquisitor or an inquisition 2. inquisitive —**in·quis′i·to′ri·al·ly** *adv.*

in re (in rē, rā) [L.] in the matter (of); concerning

I.N.R.I. [L. *Iesus Nazarenus, Rex Iudaeorum*] Jesus of Nazareth, King of the Jews

in·road (in′rōd′) *n.* 1. a sudden invasion or raid 2. [usually *pl.*] any injurious, inconvenient or troublesome encroachment

in·rush (-rush′) *n.* a rushing in; inflow; influx

ins. 1. inches 2. insulated 3. insurance

in·sa·lu·bri·ous (in′sə loo′brē əs) *adj.* [< L. *insalubris* + -OUS] unhealthy; unwholesome —**in′sa·lu′bri·ty** (-brə tē) *n.*

in·sane (in sān′) *adj.* 1. not sane; mentally ill or deranged; mad: cf. INSANITY 2. of or for insane people [an *insane* asylum] 3. very foolish; senseless —**in·sane′ly** *adv.*

in·san·i·tar·y (in san′ə tər ē) *adj.* not sanitary; unhealthful

in·san·i·ty (in san′ə tē) *n., pl.* -**ties** 1. the state of being insane; mental illness or derangement: a term used formally in law but not in psychiatry 2. great folly; extreme senselessness

in·sa·ti·a·ble (in sā′shə b'l, -shē ə-) *adj.* constantly wanting more; that cannot be satisfied; very greedy —**in·sa′ti·a·bil′i·ty** *n.* —**in·sa′ti·a·bly** *adv.*

in·sa·ti·ate (-shē it) *adj.* not satiated; insatiable —**in·sa′ti·ate·ly** *adv.* —**in·sa′ti·ate·ness** *n.*

in·scribe (in skrib′) *vt.* -**scribed′**, -**scrib′ing** [< L.: see IN-¹ & SCRIBE] 1. a) to mark or engrave (words, symbols, etc.) on some surface b) to write on, mark, or engrave (a surface) 2. to add the name of (someone) to a list; enrol 3. a) to dedicate (a book, etc.) informally b) to write a short, signed message in (a book, etc. one is presenting as a gift) 4. to fix or impress deeply in the mind, memory, etc. 5. to register the names of stockholders in a record book, instead of issuing them with certificates [inscribed stock] 6. *Geom.* to draw (a figure) inside another figure so that their boundaries touch at as many points as possible —**in·scrib′a·ble** *adj.* —**in·scrib′er** *n.*

in·scrip·tion (in skrip′shən) *n.* 1. an inscribing 2. something inscribed or engraved, as on a coin or monument 3. a) an informal dedication in a book, etc. b) a short, signed message written in a book, etc. one is presenting as a gift —**in·scrip′tive**, **in·scrip′tion·al** *adj.*

in·scru·ta·ble (in skroot′ə b'l) *adj.* [< LL. < L. *in-*, not + *scrutari*, to examine] that cannot be easily understood; completely obscure or mysterious; enigmatic —**in·scru′ta·bil′i·ty**, **in·scru′ta·ble·ness** *n.* —**in·scru′ta·bly** *adv.*

in·sect (in′sekt) *n.* [< L. *insectum (animale)*, lit., notched (animal): from the segmented bodies] 1. any of a large class of small arthropod animals, including beetles, bees, flies, wasps, etc., having, in the adult state, a head, thorax, and abdomen, three pairs of legs, and, usually, two pairs of membranous wings 2. popularly, any of a group of small animals, usually wingless, including spiders, centipedes, ticks, mites, etc.

in·sec·tar·i·um (in sek ter′ē əm) *n., pl.* -**i·a** (-ə) [ModL.] a place where insects are raised, esp. for study: also **in·sec·tar·y** (in′sek ter′ē, in sek′ tər ē)

in·sec·ti·cide (in sek′tə sid′) *n.* any substance used to kill insects —**in·sec′ti·ci′dal** *adj.*

in·sec·ti·vore (in sek′tə vôr′) *n.* [< ModL.: see INSECT & -VOROUS] 1. any of an order of insect-eating mammals, including moles, shrews, hedgehogs, etc. **2.** any animal or plant that feeds on insects —**in·sec·tiv·o·rous** (in'sek tiv'ər əs) *adj.*

in·se·cure (in'si kyoor') *adj.* not secure; specif., *a)* not safe from danger *b)* not confident; filled with anxieties *c)* not firm or dependable —**in'se·cure'ly** *adv.* —**in'se·cu'ri·ty** *n., pl.* **-ties**

in·sem·i·nate (in sem'ə nāt') *vt.* **-nat'ed, -nat'ing** [< L. pp. of *inseminare* < *in-,* in + *seminare,* to sow < *semen,* seed] **1.** to sow seeds in; esp., to impregnate with semen **2.** to implant (ideas, etc.) in (the mind, etc.) —**in·sem'i·na'tion** *n.*

in·sen·sate (in sen'sāt, -sit) *adj.* **1.** lacking sensation; inanimate **2.** without sense or reason; stupid **3.** without feeling for others; insensitive —**in·sen'sate·ly** *adv.*

in·sen·si·ble (in sen'sə b'l) *adj.* **1.** lacking sensation; unable to perceive with the senses **2.** having lost sensation; unconscious **3.** not recognizing or realizing; unaware; indifferent **4.** so small or slight as to be virtually imperceptible —**in·sen'si·bil'i·ty** *n.* —**in·sen'si·bly** *adv.*

in·sen·si·tive (-tiv) *adj.* not sensitive; having little or no reaction (*to*) —**in·sen'si·tive·ly** *adv.* —**in·sen'si·tiv'i·ty,** **in·sen'si·tive·ness** *n.*

in·sen·ti·ent (in sen'shē ənt, -shənt) *adj.* not sentient; without life, consciousness, or perception —**in·sen'ti·ence** *n.*

in·sep·a·ra·ble (in sep'ər ə b'l) *adj.* that cannot be separated or parted —*n.* [*pl.*] inseparable persons or things —**in·sep'·a·ra·bil'i·ty, in·sep'a·ra·ble·ness** *n.* —**in·sep'a·ra·bly** *adv.*

in·sert (in surt'; *for n.* in'sərt) *vt.* [< L. pp. of *inserere* < *in-,* in + *serere,* to join] to put or fit (something) into something else; set in —*n.* anything inserted or for insertion; esp., an extra leaf or section inserted in a newspaper, etc. —**in·sert'er** *n.*

in·ser·tion (in sur'shən) *n.* **1.** an inserting or being inserted **2.** something inserted; specif., *a)* a piece of lace or embroidery that can be set into a piece of cloth for ornamentation *b)* a single placement of an advertisement, as in a newspaper **3.** *Anat.* the point of attachment of a muscle to the part that it moves

in·ser·vice (in'sur'vis) *adj.* designating or of training given to employees in connection with their work to help them develop skills, etc.

in·set (in set'; *also, and for n.* always, in'set) *vt.* **-set', -set'·ting** to set into something; insert —*n.* something set in; insert; specif., *a)* a smaller map, etc. set within the border of a larger one *b)* a piece of material set into a garment

in·shal·lah (in shä'lä) *interj.* [Ar.] God willing

in·shore (in'shôr', in shôr') *adv., adj.* **1.** in towards the shore **2.** near the shore —**inshore of** nearer than (something else) to the shore

in·side (in'sīd', -sīd'; *for prep. & adv., usually* in'sīd') *n.* **1.** the part within; inner side, surface, or part **2.** the part closest to something implied, as the part of a pavement closest to the buildings **3.** [*pl.*] [Colloq.] the internal organs of the body; viscera —*adj.* **1.** on or in the inside; internal **2.** working or used indoors **3.** known only to insiders; secret or private [the *inside* story] **4.** in some games, designating a forward who plays in the midfield area [*inside* right] —*adv.* **1.** on or to the inside; within **2.** indoors —*prep.* in; within; into; in less than [finish *inside* a week] —**inside out** **1.** with the inside where the outside should be; reversed **2.** [Colloq.] thoroughly; completely —**on the inside** **1.** in a position of confidence, special advantage or favour, etc. **2.** in one's inner thoughts or feelings

inside job [Colloq.] a crime committed by, or with the aid of, a person employed or trusted by the victim

in·sid·er (in sī'dər) *n.* **1.** a person inside a given place or group **2.** a person having or likely to have secret or confidential information

in·sid·i·ous (in sid'ē əs) *adj.* [< L. < *insidiae,* an ambush < *in-,* in + *sedere,* to sit] **1.** characterized by treachery or slyness; crafty **2.** more dangerous than seems evident [an *insidious* disease] —**in·sid'i·ous·ly** *adv.* —**in·sid'i·ous·ness** *n.*

in·sight (in'sīt') *n.* **1.** the ability to see and understand clearly the inner nature of things, esp. by intuition **2.** a clear understanding of the inner nature of some specific thing —**in'sight'ful** *adj.*

in·sig·ni·a (in sig'nē ə) *n.pl.* (in sense 1), *n.sing.* (in sense 2) [< L., pl. of *insigne,* ult. < *in-,* in + *signum,* a mark] **1.** *sing.* **in·sig'ne** (-nē) badges, emblems, etc., as of rank or membership **2.** *pl.* **in·sig'ni·as** such a badge, emblem, etc.

in·sig·nif·i·cant (in'sig nif'ə kənt) *adj.* **1.** having little or no meaning **2.** having little or no importance; trivial **3.** small; unimposing **4.** low in position, character, etc. —**in'sig·nif'·i·cance, in'sig·nif'i·can·cy** *n.* —**in'sig·nif'i·cant·ly** *adv.*

in·sin·cere (in'sin sir') *adj.* not sincere; deceptive or hypocritical —**in'sin·cere'ly** *adv.*

in·sin·cer·i·ty (-ser'ə tē) *n.* **1.** a being insincere **2.** *pl.* **-ties** an insincere act, remark, etc.

in·sin·u·ate (in sin'yoo wāt') *vt.* **-at'ed, -at'ing** [< L. pp. of *insinuare* < *in-,* in + *sinus,* curved surface] **1.** to introduce or work into gradually, indirectly, and artfully **2.** to hint

indirectly; imply —*vi.* to make insinuations —**in·sin'u·at'·ing·ly** *adv.* —**in·sin'u·a'tive** *adj.* —**in·sin'u·a'tor** *n.*

in·sin·u·a·tion (in sin'yoo wā'shən) *n.* **1.** an insinuating **2.** something insinuated; specif., *a)* a sly hint *b)* an act or remark intended to win favour

in·sip·id (in sip'id) *adj.* [< Fr. < LL. < L. *in-,* not + *sapidus,* savoury < *sapere,* to taste] **1.** without flavour; tasteless **2.** not exciting; dull; lifeless —**in'si·pid'i·ty, in·sip'id·ness** *n.* —**in·sip'id·ly** *adv.*

in·sist (in sist') *vi.* [< MFr. < L. *insistere* < *in-,* in + *sistere,* to stand] to take and maintain a stand or make a firm demand (often with *on* or *upon*) —*vt.* **1.** to demand strongly **2.** to declare firmly —**in·sist'er** *n.* —**in·sist'ing·ly** *adv.*

in·sist·ent (in sis'tənt) *adj.* **1.** insisting or demanding; persistent in demands or assertions **2.** compelling the attention [an *insistent* rhythm] —**in·sist'ence, in·sist'en·cy** *n.* —**in·sist'ent·ly** *adv.*

‡**in si·tu** (in sī'too) [L.] in position

in·snare (in sner') *vt.* **-snared', -snar'ing** *same as* ENSNARE

in·so·bri·e·ty (in'sə brī'ə tē, -sō-) *n.* lack of sobriety; intemperance, esp. in drinking

in·so·far (in'sə fär', -sō-) *adv.* to such a degree or extent (usually with *as*)

in·so·la·tion (in'sō lā'shən) *n.* [L. *insolatio*] **1.** exposure to the sun's rays for *a)* drying, bleaching, etc. *b)* treatment of disease **2.** same as SUNSTROKE **3.** *a)* the radiation received from the sun *b)* the rate of such radiation per unit of surface

in·sole (in'sōl') *n.* **1.** the inside sole of a shoe **2.** an extra, removable inside sole for comfort

in·so·lent (in'sə lənt) *adj.* [< L. < *in-,* not + prp. of *solere,* to be accustomed] **1.** boldly disrespectful in speech or behaviour; impertinent; impudent **2.** [Now Rare] over-bearing —**in'so·lence** *n.* —**in'·so·lent·ly** *adv.*

INSOLE

in·sol·u·ble (in sol'yoo b'l) *adj.* **1.** that cannot be solved; unsolvable **2.** that cannot be dissolved; not soluble —**in·sol'u·bil'i·ty, in·sol'u·ble·ness** *n.* —**in·sol'u·bly** *adv.*

in·solv·a·ble (in sol'və b'l) *adj.* not solvable

in·sol·vent (in sol'vənt) *adj.* **1.** not solvent; unable to pay debts; bankrupt **2.** not enough to pay all debts [an *insolvent* inheritance] **3.** of insolvents —*n.* an insolvent person —**in·sol'ven·cy** *n., pl.* **-cies**

in·som·ni·a (in som'nē ə) *n.* [< L. < *in-,* without + *somnus,* sleep] abnormally prolonged inability to sleep, esp. when chronic —**in·som'ni·ac'** (-ak') *n., adj.*

in·so·much (in'sō much', -sə-) *adv.* **1.** to such a degree or extent; so (with *that*) **2.** inasmuch (as)

in·sou·ci·ant (in soo'sē ənt) *adj.* [Fr.] calm and untroubled; carefree; indifferent —**in·sou'ci·ance** (-əns) *n.* —**in·sou'·ci·ant·ly** *adv.*

in·span (in span') *vt., vi.* **-spanned', -span'ning** [Afrik. < Du. *inspannen*] in South Africa, to harness or yoke (animals) to a wagon, etc.

in·spect (in spekt') *vt.* [< L. pp. of *inspicere* < *in-,* at + *specere,* to look] **1.** to look at carefully; examine critically **2.** to examine or review (troops, etc.) officially —**in·spec'·tive** *adj.*

in·spec·tion (in spek'shən) *n.* **1.** careful examination **2.** official examination, as of troops

in·spec·tor (in spek'tər) *n.* **1.** one who inspects; official examiner **2.** an officer in a police force, ranking next below a superintendent —**in·spec'to·ral, in'spec·to'ri·al** (-tôr'ē əl) *adj.* —**in·spec'tor·ship'** *n.*

in·spec·tor·ate (-it, -āt') *n.* **1.** the position or duties of an inspector **2.** inspectors collectively **3.** the district supervised by an inspector

in·spi·ra·tion (in'spə rā'shən) *n.* **1.** a breathing in; inhaling **2.** an inspiring or being inspired mentally or emotionally **3.** *a)* any stimulus to creative thought or action *b)* an inspired idea, action, etc. **4.** a prompting of something written or said **5.** *Theol.* a divine influence upon human beings —**in'·spi·ra'tion·al** *adj.* —**in'spi·ra'tion·al·ly** *adv.*

in·spi·ra·tor (in'spi rā tər) *n.* an appliance for drawing in vapour, etc.

in·spire (in spīr') *vt.* **-spired', -spir'ing** [< OFr. < L. *inspirare* < *in-,* in + *spirare,* to breathe] **1.** to draw (air) into the lungs; inhale **2.** to influence, stimulate, or impel, as to some creative or effective effort **3.** to guide or motivate by divine influence **4.** to arouse (a thought or feeling) [kindness *inspires* love] **5.** to affect with a specified feeling [praise *inspires* us with confidence] **6.** to cause to be written or said —*vi.* **1.** to inhale **2.** to give inspiration —**in·spir'a·ble** *adj.* —**in·spir'er** *n.* —**in·spir'ing·ly** *adv.*

in·spired (in spīrd') *adj.* **1.** actuated by divine influence **2.** prompted, but not openly acknowledged, by a superior authority **3.** prompted by intuition [an *inspired* guess]

in·spir·it (in spir'it) *vt.* to put spirit into; cheer; hearten —**in·spir'it·ing** *adj.*

in·spis·sate (in spis'āt, in'spə sāt') *vt., vi.* **-sat·ed, -sat·ing**

[< LL., ult. < L. *in-*, in + *spissus*, thick] to thicken by evaporation; condense **—in′spis·sa′tion** *n*. **—in′spis·sa′- tor** *n*.

Inst. 1. Institute **2.** Institution

inst. 1. instant (*adj.* 2) **2.** instrumental

in·sta·bil·i·ty (in′stə bil′ə tē) *n*. unstable condition; lack of firmness, steadiness, etc.

in·sta·ble (in stā′b′l) *adj*. *same as* UNSTABLE

in·stall (in stôl′) *vt*. **-stalled′, -stall′ing** [< ML. < *in-*, in + *stallum* < OHG. *stal*, a place] **1.** to place in an office, rank, etc. with formality **2.** to establish in a place or condition [to *install* oneself in a seat] **3.** to fix in position for use [to *install* new fixtures] **—in·stall′er** *n*.

in·stal·la·tion (in′stə lā′shən) *n*. **1.** an installing or being installed **2.** apparatus, etc. installed [a heating *installation*] **3.** any military post, camp, base, etc.

installment plan *U.S. name for* HIRE PURCHASE

in·stal·ment[1] (in stôl′mənt) *n*. [< earlier *estall*, to arrange payments for < OFr. < OHG. *stal*: see INSTALL] **1.** any of the parts of a debt or other sum of money to be paid at regular times over a specified period **2.** any of several parts, as of a serial story, appearing at intervals

in·stal·ment[2] (in stôl′mənt) *n*. an installing or being installed; installation

in·stance (in′stəns) *n*. [OFr. < L. *instantia*, a being present < *instans*: see ff.] **1.** an example; case; illustration **2.** a step in proceeding; occasion [in the first *instance*] **—vt. -stanced, -stanc·ing 1.** to exemplify **2.** to use as an example; cite **—at the instance of** at the suggestion of **—for instance** as an example

in·stant (in′stənt) *adj*. [< MFr. < L. *instans*, prp. of *instare* < *in-*, upon + *stare*, to stand] **1.** urgent; pressing **2.** of the current month [your letter of the 13th *instant*] **3.** soon to happen; imminent **4.** without delay; immediate **5.** designating a food or beverage in readily soluble, concentrated, or precooked form, that can be prepared quickly **—adv.** [Poet.] at once **—n. 1.** a moment **2.** a particular moment **—the instant** as soon as

in·stan·ta·ne·ous (in′stən tā′nē əs, -tān′yəs) *adj*. **1.** done, made, or happening in an instant **2.** done or made without delay; immediate **—in′stan·ta′ne·ous·ly** *adv*. **—in′stan·ta′- ne·ous·ness** *n*.

in·stan·ter (in stan′tər) *adv*. [L., pressingly] immediately

in·stant·ly (in′stənt lē) *adv*. **1.** in an instant; without delay; immediately **2.** [Archaic] urgently; pressingly **—conj.** as soon as; the instant that

in·star (in′stär′) *n*. [L., lit., a shape] any of the various stages of an insect or other arthropod between moults

in·state (in stāt′) *vt*. **-stat′ed, -stat′ing** to put in a particular status, position, or rank; install **—in·state′ment** *n*.

in·stead (in sted′) *adv*. [IN + STEAD] in place of the person or thing mentioned [to feel like crying and laugh *instead*] **—instead of** in place of

in·step (in′step′) *n*. **1.** the upper part of the arch of the foot, between the ankle and the toes **2.** the part of a shoe or stocking covering this

in·sti·gate (in′stə gāt′) *vt*. **-gat′ed, -gat′- ing** [< L. pp. of *instigare*, to incite] **1.** to urge on or incite to some action **2.** to cause by inciting; foment [to *instigate* a rebellion] **—in′sti·ga′tion** *n*. **—in′sti·ga′tive** *adj*. **—in′sti·ga′tor** *n*.

in·stil (in stil′) *vt*. **-stilled′, -still′ing** [< MFr. < L. *instillare*, ult. < *in-*, in + *stilla*, a drop] **1.** to put in drop by drop **2.** to put (an idea, principle, feeling, etc.) in or *into* gradually **—in′stil·la′tion** *n*. **—in·still′er** *n*. **—in·still′ment, in·stil′- ment** *n*. Also [Chiefly U.S.] **instill**

in·stinct (in′stiŋkt; *for adj.* in stiŋkt′) *n*. [< L. pp. of *instinguere*, to impel] **1.** (an) inborn tendency to behave in a way characteristic of a species; natural, unacquired response to stimuli [suckling is an *instinct* in mammals] **2.** a natural or acquired tendency or talent; knack; gift [an *instinct* for doing the right thing] **—adj.** filled or charged (*with*) [a look *instinct* with pity] **—in·stinc·tu·al** (in stiŋk′choo wəl) *adj*.

in·stinc·tive (in stiŋk′tiv) *adj*. **1.** of, or having the nature of, instinct **2.** prompted or done by instinct **—in·stinc′tive·ly** *adv*.

in·sti·tute (in′stə tyoot′) *vt*. **-tut′ed, -tut′ing** [< L. pp. of *instituere* < *in-*, in + *statuere*, to set up] **1.** to set up; establish; found **2.** to start; initiate [to *institute* a search] **3.** to install in office **—n.** something instituted; specif., *a*) an established principle, law, or custom *b*) an organization for the promotion or teaching of art, science, research, etc. *c*) a building used by such an organization *d*) a school specializing in art, music, technical subjects, etc. *e*) *same as* INSTITUTION (sense 3) **—in′sti·tut′er, in′sti·tu′tor** *n*.

in·sti·tu·tion (in′stə tyoo′shən) *n*. **1.** an instituting or being instituted; establishment **2.** an established law, custom, practice, etc. **3.** *a*) an organization having a social, educational, or religious purpose, as a school, church, etc. *b*)

the building housing such an organization **4.** [Colloq.] a well-established person or thing

in·sti·tu·tion·al (-′l) *adj*. **1.** of, or having the nature of, an institution **2.** of or to institutions, rather than individuals **3.** dull; routine [*institutional* meals] **4.** [U.S.] of advertising intended primarily to gain prestige rather than immediate sales **—in′sti·tu′tion·al·ism** *n*. **—in′sti·tu′- tion·al·ly** *adv*.

in·sti·tu·tion·al·ize (in′stə tyoo′shən ə līz) *vt*. **-ized′, -iz′ing 1.** to make into an institution **2.** to make institutional **3.** to place in an institution, as for treatment **—in′sti·tu′- tion·al·i·za′tion** *n*.

instr. 1. instructor **2.** instrument

in·struct (in strukt′) *vt*. [< L. pp. of *instruere*, to erect < *in-*, in + *struere*, to pile up] **1.** to communicate knowledge to; teach **2.** to inform or guide [the judge *instructs* the jury] **3.** to order or direct

in·struc·tion (in struk′shən) *n*. **1.** an instructing; education **2.** *a*) knowledge, information, etc. given or taught *b*) a lesson or rule **3.** *a*) a command or order *b*) [*pl*.] directions **—in·struc′tion·al** *adj*.

in·struc·tive (-tiv) *adj*. serving to instruct; giving knowledge or information **—in·struc′tive·ly** *adv*. **—in·struc′- tive·ness** *n*.

in·struc·tor (-tər) *n*. **1.** a teacher **2.** [U.S.] a college teacher ranking below an assistant professor **—in·struc′- tor·ship′** *n*. **—in·struc′tress** *n.fem.*

in·stru·ment (in′strə mənt) *n*. [< OFr. < L. *instrumentum* < *instruere*: see INSTRUCT] **1.** *a*) a thing by means of which something is done; means *b*) a person used by another to bring something about **2.** a tool or implement **3.** a device for indicating or measuring conditions, performance, etc., or, sometimes, for controlling operations, esp. in aircraft **4.** any of various devices producing musical sound **5.** *Law* a document, as a deed, contract, etc. **—vt.** to provide with instruments

in·stru·men·tal (in′strə men′t′l) *adj*. **1.** serving as a means; helpful (*in* bringing something about) **2.** of or performed with an instrument or tool **3.** of, performed on, or written for a musical instrument or instruments **—in′stru·men′tal·ly** *adv*.

in·stru·men·tal·ist (-men′t′l ist) *n*. a person who performs on a musical instrument

in·stru·men·tal·i·ty (-men tal′ə tē) *n., pl.* **-ties 1.** a being instrumental **2.** a means or agency

in·stru·men·ta·tion (-tā′shən) *n*. **1.** the arrangement of music for instruments **2.** a using or equipping with instruments, esp. scientific instruments **3.** the instruments used **4.** *same as* INSTRUMENTALITY

instrument panel (or **board**) a panel or board with instruments, gauges, etc. mounted on it, as in a car or aircraft

in·sub·or·di·nate (in′sə bôr′din it) *adj*. not submitting to authority; disobedient **—n.** an insubordinate person **—in′- sub·or′di·nate·ly** *adv*. **—in′sub·or′di·na′tion** *n*.

in·sub·stan·tial (in′səb stan′shəl) *adj*. not substantial; specif., *a*) not real; imaginary *b*) not solid or firm **—in′- sub·stan′ti·al′i·ty** (-shē al′ə tē) *n*.

in·suf·fer·a·ble (in suf′ər ə b′l) *adj*. not sufferable; intolerable; unbearable **—in·suf′fer·a·bly** *adv*.

in·suf·fi·cien·cy (in′sə fish′ən sē) *n., pl.* **-cies 1.** lack of sufficiency; deficiency; inadequacy **2.** inability of an organ, etc. to function normally

in·suf·fi·cient (-ənt) *adj*. not sufficient; inadequate **—in′- suf·fi′cient·ly** *adv*.

in·suf·flate (in′sə flāt, in suf′lāt) *vt*. **-flat·ed, -flat·ing** [< L. *insufflatus*, pp. of *insufflare*, to breathe into] **1.** to blow or breathe into or on **2.** *Eccles.* to breathe on (baptismal waters, etc.) as a ritual act **3.** *Med.* to blow (powder, air, etc.) into a cavity of the body **—in′suf·fla′tion** *n*.

in·suf·fla·tor (in′sə flāt′ər) *n*. a device used for making latent fingerprints visible by blowing a fine dust over them

in·su·lar (in′syoo lər) *adj*. [< L. < *insula*, island] **1.** of, or in the form of, an island **2.** living or situated on an island **3.** like an island **4.** of or like islanders, esp. when regarded as narrow-minded, illiberal, etc. **—in′su·lar′i·ty** (-lar′ə tē), **in′su·lar·ism** *n*. **—in′su·lar·ly** *adv*.

in·su·late (-lāt′) *vt*. **-lat′ed, -lat′ing** [< L. *insulatus*, made like an island < *insula*, island] **1.** to set apart; detach from the rest; isolate **2.** to separate or cover with a nonconducting material in order to prevent the passage or leakage of electricity, heat, sound, etc.

in·su·la·tion (in′syoo lā′shən) *n*. **1.** an insulating or being insulated **2.** any material used to insulate

in·su·la·tor (in′syoo lāt′ər) *n*. anything that insulates; esp., a device of glass or porcelain for insulating electric wires

in·su·lin (in′syoo lin) *n*. [< L. *insula*, island + -IN[1]: referring to islands of special tissue in the pancreas] **1.** a secretion of the pancreas, which helps the body use sugar and other carbohydrates **2.** an extract from the pancreas of sheep, oxen, etc., used hypodermically in the treatment of diabetes mellitus

in·sult (in sult′; *for n.* in′sult) *vt*. [< MFr. < L. *insultare* <

in-, in, on + *saltare*, freq. of *salire*, to leap] to treat or speak to with scorn, insolence, or disrespect —*n.* 1. an insulting act, remark, etc. 2. *Med.* injury to tissues or organs —**in·sult′er** *n.* —**in·sult′ing** *adj.* —**in·sult′ing·ly** *adv.*

in·su·per·a·ble (in sōō′pər ə b'l, -syōō′-) *adj.* not superable; that cannot be overcome or passed over; insurmountable —**in·su′per·a·bil′i·ty** *n.* —**in·su′per·a·bly** *adv.*

in·sup·port·a·ble (in′sə pôrt′ə b'l) *adj.* not supportable; specif., *a*) intolerable *b*) incapable of being upheld —**in′·support′a·bly** *adv.*

in·sur·ance (in shoor′əns) *n.* 1. an insuring or being insured against loss by fire, accident, death, etc. 2. *a*) a contract (**insurance policy**) whereby the insurer guarantees the insured that a certain sum will be paid for a specified loss *b*) the premium specified for such a contract 3. the amount for which life, property, etc. is insured 4. the business of insuring against loss

in·sure (in shoor′) *vt.* -**sured′**, -**sur′ing** [see ENSURE] 1. to take out or issue insurance on (something or someone) 2. *same as* ENSURE —*vi.* to give or take out insurance —**in·sur′a·bil′i·ty** *n.* —**in·sur′a·ble** *adj.*

in·sured (in shoord′) *n.* a person whose life, property, etc. is insured against loss

in·sur·er (in shoor′ər) *n.* a person or company that insures others against loss or damage

in·sur·gence (in sur′jəns) *n.* a rising in revolt; insurrection : also **in·sur′gen·cy**

in·sur·gent (-jənt) *adj.* [< L. prp. of *insurgere* < *in*-, upon + *surgere*, to rise : see SURGE] rising up against established authority —*n.* one engaged in insurgent activity —**in·sur′gent·ly** *adv.*

in·sur·mount·a·ble (in′sər moun′tə b'l) *adj.* not surmountable; that cannot be overcome —**in′sur·mount′a·bil′·i·ty** *n.* —**in′sur·mount′a·bly** *adv.*

in·sur·rec·tion (in′sə rek′shən) *n.* [< MFr. < LL. < pp. of L. *insurgere*: see INSURGENT] a rising up against established authority; rebellion; revolt —**in′sur·rec′tion·al** *adj.* —**in′sur·rec′tion·ar·y** *adj., n., pl.* -**ar·ies** —**in′sur·rec′·tion·ist** *n.*

in·sus·cep·ti·ble (in′sə sep′tə b'l) *adj.* not susceptible (*to* or *of*); not easily affected or influenced —**in′sus·cep′ti·bil′i·ty** *n.* —**in′sus·cep′ti·bly** *adv.*

in·swing·er (in′swiŋ ər) *n.* *Cricket* a ball which swings in from the off-side towards the wicket

int. 1. interest 2. interior 3. internal 4. international

in·tact (in takt′) *adj.* [< L. < *in*-, not + *tactus*, pp. of *tangere*, to touch] with nothing missing or injured; kept or left whole —**in·tact′ness** *n.*

in·tagl·io (in tal′yō, -täl′-) *n., pl.* -**ios** [It. < *in*-, in + *tagliare*, to cut < LL. *taliare*: see TAILOR] 1. a design or figure carved or engraved below the surface 2. a gem or stone ornamented in this way 3. the art of making such designs or figures —*vt.* -**ioed**, -**io·ing** to carve, etc. in intaglio —**in·tagl′i·at′ed** *adj.*

in·take (in′tāk′) *n.* 1. a taking in 2. the amount, thing, or body of people, taken in 3. the place at which a fluid is taken into a pipe, channel, etc.

in·tan·gi·ble (in tan′jə b'l) *adj.* not tangible; specif., *a*) that cannot be touched *b*) representing value that is neither intrinsic nor material [good will as an *intangible* asset] *c*) hard to define or grasp —*n.* something intangible —**in·tan′·gi·bil′i·ty** *n., pl.* -**ties** —**in·tan′gi·bly** *adv.*

in·tar·si·a (in tär′sē ə) *n.* [It. *intarsio*] a type of mosaic inlay, esp. of the Italian Renaissance

in·te·ger (in′tə jər) *n.* [L., untouched, whole] 1. anything complete in itself; whole 2. any whole number or zero: distinguished from FRACTION

in·te·gral (in′tə grəl; *also, exc. for adj.* 4, in teg′rəl) *adj.* [< prec.] 1. necessary for completeness; essential 2. whole or complete 3. made up of parts forming a whole 4. *Math.* of or having to do with integers; not fractional —*n.* a whole —**in′te·gral′i·ty** (-gral′ə tē) *n.* —**in′te·gral·ly** *adv.*

integral calculus the branch of higher mathematics dealing with the process (*integration*) of finding the quantity or function of which a given quantity or function is the differential

in·te·grand (in′tə grand′) *n.* [< L. *integrandus*, gerundive of *integrare*, to make whole] *Math.* the function or expression to be integrated

in·te·grant (-grənt) *adj.* [L. *integrans*, prp. of *integrare*: see prec.] integral —*n.* an integral part; constituent

in·te·grate (-grāt′) *vt.* -**grat′ed**, -**grat′ing** [< L. pp. of *integrare* < *integer*, whole] 1. to make whole or complete 2. to bring (parts) together into a whole; unify 3. to indicate the sum or total of 4. to remove legal and social barriers imposing segregation upon (racial groups) or in (communities) —*vi.* to become integrated —**in′te·gra′tion** *n.* —**in′te·gra′tive** *adj.* —**in′te·gra′tor** *n.*

integrated circuit an electronic circuit containing interconnected amplifying devices formed on a single body, or chip, of semiconductor material

in·te·gra·tion·ist (-grā′shən ist) *n.* one who advocates

integration, esp. of racial groups —*adj.* believing in or advocating integration

in·teg·ri·ty (in teg′rə tē) *n.* [see INTEGER] 1. a being complete; wholeness 2. unimpaired condition; soundness 3. uprightness, honesty, and sincerity

in·teg·u·ment (in teg′yoo mənt) *n.* [< L. < *in*-, upon + *tegere*, to cover] an outer covering, as of the body or of a plant; skin, shell, hide, etc. —**in·teg·u·ment′al**, **in·teg′u·men′·ta·ry** *adj.*

in·tel·lect (in′təl ekt′) *n.* [< L. < pp. of *intellegere*, to understand < *inter*-, between + *legere*, to choose] 1. the ability to reason or understand 2. great mental ability; high intelligence 3. *a*) a mind or intelligence *b*) a person of high intelligence

in·tel·lec·tion (in′təl ek′shən) *n.* [ME. < ML. *intellectio*] 1. the process of using the intellect; thinking 2. a thought or perception

in·tel·lec·tu·al (in′təl ek′tyoo wəl, -choo-) *adj.* 1. of, pertaining to, or appealing to the intellect 2. *a*) requiring or involving the intellect *b*) inclined towards intellectual activities 3. showing high intelligence —*n.* a person having intellectual tastes or work —**in′tel·lec′tu·al′i·ty** (-tyoo wal′ə tē, -choo-) *n.* —**in′tel·lec′tu·al·ly** *adv.*

in·tel·lec·tu·al·ism (-iz′m) *n.* a being intellectual; devotion to intellectual pursuits —**in′tel·lec′tu·al·ist** *n.* —**in′tel·lec′·tu·al·is′tic** *adj.*

in·tel·li·gence (in tel′ə jəns) *n.* [< OFr. < L. *intelligentia* < prp. of *intelligere*: see INTELLECT] 1. *a*) the ability to learn or understand from experience; mental ability *b*) the ability to respond successfully to a new situation *c*) any degree of cleverness, shrewdness, etc. 2. news or information 3. *a*) the gathering of secret information, as for military purposes *b*) the persons or agency employed at this 4. an intelligent being

intelligence quotient a number indicating a person's level of intelligence : it is the mental age (as shown by intelligence tests) multiplied by 100 and divided by the chronological age

intelligence test a series of problems intended to test the intelligence of an individual

in·tel·li·gent (-jənt) *adj.* 1. having or using intelligence 2. having or showing high intelligence; bright, clever, wise, etc. 3. [Archaic] aware (*of* something) —**in·tel′li·gent·ly** *adv.*

in·tel·li·gent·si·a (in tel′ə jent′sē ə, -gent′-) *n.pl.* [*also with sing.* v.] [< Russ. < L.: see INTELLIGENCE] the people regarded as, or regarding themselves as, the educated class; intellectuals collectively

in·tel·li·gi·ble (in tel′i jə b'l) *adj.* [< L. < *intelligere*: see INTELLECT] that can be understood; clear; comprehensible —**in·tel′li·gi·bil′i·ty** *n.* —**in·tel′li·gi·bly** *adv.*

in·tem·per·ance (in tem′pər əns) *n.* 1. a lack of temperance or restraint; immoderation 2. excessive drinking of alcoholic liquor

in·tem·per·ate (-it) *adj.* 1. not temperate; specif., *a*) not moderate; excessive *b*) severe or violent [an *intemperate* wind] 2. drinking too much alcoholic liquor —**in·tem′·per·ate·ly** *adv.*

in·tend (in tend′) *vt.* [< OFr. < L. *intendere*, to aim at < *in*-, at + *tendere*, to stretch] 1. to have in mind as a purpose; plan; purpose 2. to mean (something) to be or be used (*for*); design; destine 3. to mean or signify —*vi.* to have a purpose or intention —**in·tend′er** *n.*

in·tend·an·cy (in ten′dən sē) *n., pl.* -**cies** 1. the position or duties of an intendant 2. intendants collectively

in·tend·ant (-dənt) *n.* [Fr. < L. prp. of *intendere*: see INTEND] a director, manager of a public business, superintendent, etc.

in·tend·ed (-did) *adj.* 1. meant; planned; purposed 2. prospective; future —*n.* [Colloq.] the person whom one has agreed to marry

in·tense (in tens′) *adj.* [< MFr. < L. pp. of *intendere*: see INTEND] 1. occurring or existing in a high degree; very strong [an *intense* light] 2. strained to the utmost; earnest [intense thought] 3. having or showing strong emotion, great seriousness, etc. 4. characterized by much action, emotion, etc. —**in·tense′ly** *adv.* —**in·tense′ness** *n.*

in·ten·si·fy (in ten′sə fī′) *vt.* -**fied′**, -**fy′ing** 1. to make intense or more intense; strengthen 2. *Photog.* to increase the density or contrast of a film or plate —*vi.* to become intense or more intense; increase —**in·ten′si·fi·ca′tion** *n.* —**in·ten′si·fi′er** *n.*

in·ten·si·ty (in ten′sə tē) *n., pl.* -**ties** 1. a being intense; specif., *a*) extreme degree of anything *b*) great energy or vehemence, as of emotion 2. relative strength, magnitude, etc. 3. the degree of purity of colour; saturation 4. *Physics* the amount of force or energy of heat, light, sound, etc. per unit area, volume, etc.

in·ten·sive (-siv) *adj.* 1. increasing in degree or amount 2. of or characterized by intensity; thorough; exhaustive 3. designating very attentive hospital care given to patients, as after surgery 4. *Agric.* designating a system of farming which aims at the increase of crop yield per unit area 5. *Gram.* giving force or emphasis (Ex.: "very" in "the very same man") —*n.* 1. anything that intensifies 2. an

intensive word, prefix, etc. —**in·ten'sive·ly** *adv.* —**in·ten'-**
sive·ness *n.*
in·tent (in tent') *adj.* [< L. pp. of *intendere*: see INTEND] 1.
firmly directed; earnest 2. *a)* having the attention firmly
fixed; engrossed *b)* strongly resolved [intent on going] —*n.*
1. an intending 2. something intended; specif., *a)* a
purpose; aim *b)* meaning or import 3. *Law* one's mental
attitude at the time of doing an act —**to all intents and**
purposes in almost every respect; practically —**in·tent'ly**
adv. —**in·tent'ness** *n.*
in·ten·tion (in ten'shən) *n.* 1. an intending; determination to
do a specified thing or act in a specified way 2. *a)* anything
intended; aim or purpose *b)* [pl.] purpose in regard to
marriage
in·ten·tion·al (-shən 'l) *adj.* 1. having to do with intention
2. done purposely; intended —**in·ten'tion·al·ly** *adv.*
in·ter (in tur') *vt.* **-terred', -ter'ring** [< OFr. < L. *in*, in +
terra, earth] to put (a dead body) into a grave or tomb;
bury
in·ter- [L. < *inter*, *prep.*] *a combining form meaning:* 1.
between or among [interdepartmental] 2. with or on each
other (or one another), together, mutual, reciprocal,
mutually, or reciprocally [interact]
in·ter·act (in'tər akt') *vi.* to act on one another —**in'-**
ter·ac'tion *n.* —**in'ter·ac'tive** *adj.*
‡**in·ter a·li·a** (in'tər ā'lē ə) [L.] among other things
in·ter·breed (in'tər brēd') *vt., vi.* **-bred', -breed'ing** *same*
as HYBRIDIZE
in·ter·ca·lar·y (in tur'kə lər ē) *adj.* [< L.: see ff.] added to
the calendar: said of an extra day, month, etc. inserted in a
calendar year to make it correspond to the solar year
in·ter·ca·late (-lāt') *vt.* **-lat'ed, -lat'ing** [< L. pp. of
intercalare, to insert < *inter-*, between + *calare*, to call] 1.
to insert (a day, month, etc.) in the calendar 2. to
interpolate or insert —**in·ter'ca·la'tion** *n.*
in·ter·cede (in'tər sēd') *vi.* **-ced'ed, -ced'ing** [< L. < *inter-*,
between + *cedere*, to go] 1. to plead or make a request on
behalf of another or others 2. to intervene for the purpose
of producing agreement; mediate —**in'ter·ced'er** *n.*
in·ter·cel·lu·lar (-sel'yoo lər) *adj.* located between or
among cells
in·ter·cept (in'tər sept'; *for n.* in'tər sept') *vt.* [< L. pp. of
intercipere < *inter-*, between + *capere*, to take] 1. to
seize, stop, or interrupt on the way; cut off [to intercept a
message] 2. *Math.* to mark off between two points, lines,
or planes —*n.* 1. *Math.* the part of a line, plane, etc.
intercepted 2. *Mil.* the intercepting of enemy aircraft,
missiles, etc. —**in'ter·cep'tion** *n.* —**in'ter·cep'tive** *adj.*
in·ter·cep·tor, in·ter·cept·er (-ər) *n.* 1. a person or thing
that intercepts 2. a fast, highly manoeuvrable aircraft used
to intercept enemy aircraft
in·ter·ces·sion (in'tər sesh'ən) *n.* an interceding;
mediation, pleading, or prayer on behalf of another or
others —**in'ter·ces'sion·al** *adj.*
in·ter·ces·sor (in'tər ses'ər, in'tər ses 'ər) *n.* a person who
intercedes —**in'ter·ces'so·ry** *adj.*
in·ter·change (in'tər chānj'; *for n.* in'tər chānj') *vt.*
-changed', -chang'ing 1. to give and take mutually;
exchange [to interchange ideas] 2. to put (each of two
things) in the other's place 3. to alternate [to interchange
work with play] —*vi.* to change places with each other
—*n.* 1. an interchanging 2. a motorway junction with
interconnecting roads and bridges designed to prevent
vehicles crossing on the same level
in·ter·change·a·ble (in'tər chān'jə b'l) *adj.* that can be
interchanged, esp. in position or use —**in'ter·change'a·bil'-**
i·ty *n.* —**in'ter·change'a·bly** *adv.*
in·ter·cit·y (-sit'ē) *adj.* between cities [inter-city rail
services]
in·ter·col·le·gi·ate (-kə lē'jət, -jē ət) *adj.* between or among
colleges
in·ter·com (in'tər kom') *n.* a radio or telephone
intercommunication system, within a building, aircraft, etc.
in·ter·com·mu·ni·cate (in'tər kə myoo'nə kāt') *vt., vi.* **-cat'-**
ed, -cat'ing to communicate with or to each other or one
another —**in'ter·com·mu'ni·ca'tion** *n.*
in·ter·com·mun·ion (-kə myoo n'yən) *n.* mutual
communion, as among religious groups
in·ter·com·mu·ni·ty (-kə myoo'nə tē) *n.* 1. mutual
possession; holding in common 2. state of being common
to various groups, etc.
in·ter·con·nect (-kə nekt') *vt., vi.* to connect with one
another —**in'ter·con·nec'tion** *n.*
in·ter·cos·tal (-kos't'l) *adj.* [see INTER- & COSTAL] between
the ribs —**in'ter·cos'tal·ly** *adv.*
in·ter·course (in'tər kôrs') *n.* [< OFr. < L.: see INTER- &
COURSE] 1. communication or dealings between or among
people, countries, etc.; interchange of products, services,
ideas, etc. 2. the sexual joining of two individuals;
copulation: in full, **sexual intercourse**
in·ter·cur·rent (-kur'ənt) *adj.* [L. *intercurrens*, running
between] 1. intervening 2. occurring during another
disease and modifying it

in·ter·de·nom·i·na·tion·al (in'tər di nom'ə nā'shən 'l) *adj.*
between, among, shared by, or involving different religious
denominations
in·ter·de·part·men·tal (-di pärt'men't'l) *adj.* between or
among departments
in·ter·de·pend·ence (-di pen'dəns) *n.* dependence on each
other; mutual dependence: also **in'ter·de·pend'en·cy** —**in'-**
ter·de·pend'ent *adj.* —**in'ter·de·pend'ent·ly** *adv.*
in·ter·dict (in'tər dikt'; *for n.* in'tər dikt') *vt.* [< OFr. < L.
pp. of *interdicere*, to forbid < *inter-*, between + *dicere*, to
speak] 1. to prohibit (an action); forbid with authority 2.
to restrain from doing or using something 3. to hinder (the
enemy) or isolate (an area, etc.) by bombing, etc. 4.
R.C.Ch. to exclude (a person, parish, etc.) from certain acts
or privileges —*n.* an official prohibition or restraint;
specif., *R.C.Ch.* an interdicting of a person, parish, etc. —**in'-**
ter·dic'tion *n.* —**in'ter·dic'to·ry, in'ter·dic'tive** *adj.*
in·ter·dig·i·tate (-dij'ə tāt') *vi.* **-tat'ed, -tat'ing** to interlock
like the fingers of folded hands
in·ter·dis·ci·pli·nar·y (-dis'ə pli nər ē) *adj.* involving two or
more disciplines, or branches of learning
in·ter·est (in'trist, in'tər ist; *for v. also* -tə rest') *n.* [< ML.
interesse, compensation < L. < *inter-*, between + *esse*, to
be: altered after OFr. *interest* < L., it interests] 1. a right
or claim to something 2. *a)* a share or participation in
something *b)* anything in which one participates or has a
share 3. [often pl.] advantage; welfare; benefit 4. [usually
pl.] a group of people having a common concern or
dominant power in some industry, occupation, cause, etc.
[the steel *interests*] 5. *a)* a feeling of intentness, concern,
or curiosity about something *b)* the power of causing this
feeling *c)* something causing this feeling 6. importance;
consequence [a matter of little *interest*] 7. *a)* money paid
for the use of money *b)* the rate of such payment, expressed
as a percentage per unit of time 8. an increase over what is
owed [to repay kindness with *interest*] —*vt.* 1. to involve
the interest of 2. to cause to have an interest in or take
part in 3. to excite the attention or curiosity of —**in the**
interest (or **interests**) **of** for the sake of; in order to
promote
in·ter·est·ed (-id) *adj.* 1. having an interest or share 2.
influenced by personal interest; prejudiced 3. feeling or
showing interest, or curiosity —**in'ter·est·ed·ly** *adv.* —**in'-**
ter·est·ed·ness *n.*
in·ter·est·ing (-iŋ) *adj.* exciting interest, curiosity, or
attention —**in an interesting condition** [Obs. Colloq.]
pregnant —**in'ter·est·ing·ly** *adv.*
in·ter·face (in'tər fās') *n.* 1. a plane forming the common
boundary between two parts of matter or space 2. a point
or means of communication between two systems,
disciplines, groups, etc. —*vt., vi.* **-faced', -fac'ing** to
interconnect with another system, discipline, group, etc.
in·ter·fac·ing (-fās'iŋ) *n.* a piece of fabric sewn between the
facing and the garment, as at the neck, to give shape and
firmness
in·ter·fere (in'tər fir') *vi.* **-fered', -fer'ing** [< OFr. < *entre-*,
INTER- + *férir* < L. *ferire*, to strike] 1. to come into
collision or opposition; clash; conflict 2. to come between
for some purpose; intervene; meddle 3. *Physics* to affect
each other by interference: said of vibrating waves
—**interfere with** 1. to hinder; prevent 2. to molest, esp.
sexually —**in'ter·fer'er** *n.* —**in'ter·fer'ing·ly** *adv.*
in·ter·fer·ence (-fir'əns) *n.* 1. an interfering 2. something
that interferes 3. *Physics* the mutual action of two waves
of vibration, as of sound, light, etc., in reinforcing or
neutralizing each other 4. *Radio & TV* static, unwanted
signals, etc., producing a distortion of sounds or images
in·ter·fer·om·e·ter (in'tər fi rom'ə tər) *n.* [< INTERFERE +
-METER] an instrument for measuring wavelengths of light,
etc. by means of interference phenomena —**in'ter·fer·o·met'-**
ric (-fir'ə met'rik) *adj.* —**in'ter·fer·om'e·try** *n.*
in·ter·fer·on (-fir'on) *n.* [INTERFER(E) + -on, arbitrary suffix]
a cellular protein produced by the body to inhibit growth of
an infecting virus
in·ter·fold (-fōld') *vt., vi.* to fold together or inside one
another
in·ter·fuse (-fyooz') *vt.* **-fused', -fus'ing** 1. to combine by
mixing, blending, or fusing together 2. to spread itself
through; pervade —*vi.* to fuse; blend —**in'ter·fu'sion** *n.*
in·ter·ga·lac·tic (-gə lak'tik) *adj.* existing or occurring
between or among galaxies
in·ter·group (in'tər groop') *adj.* between or involving
different social, ethnic, or racial groups
in·ter·im (in'tər im) *n.* [L., meanwhile < *inter*, between]
the period of time between; meantime —*adj.* temporary;
provisional [an interim council]
in·te·ri·or (in tir'ē ər) *adj.* [< MFr. < L., compar. of *inter*,
between] 1. situated within; inner 2. away from the coast,
border, etc.; inland 3. of the domestic affairs of a country
4. private —*n.* 1. the interior part of anything; specif., *a)*
the inside of a room or building *b)* the inland part of a
country or region *c)* the inner nature of a person or thing *d)*
a picture of the inside of a room 2. the domestic affairs of a

country [the Minister of the *Interior*] —in·te'ri·or'i·ty (-or'ə tē) *n.* —in·te'ri·or·ly *adv.*

interior angle any of the four angles formed on the inside of two straight lines by a straight line cutting across them: cf. EXTERIOR ANGLE

interior decoration the decorating and furnishing of the interior of a room, house, etc.

in·te·ri·or·ize (-īz') *vt.* -ized', -iz'ing to make (a concept, value, etc.) part of one's inner nature

interj. interjection

in·ter·ject (in'tər jekt') *vt.* [< L. pp. of *interjicere* < *inter*-, between + *jacere*, to throw] to throw in between; insert; interpose —in'ter·jec'tor *n.*

in·ter·jec·tion (-jek'shən) *n.* 1. an interjecting 2. something interjected, as a word or phrase 3. *Gram.* an exclamatory word or phrase (Ex.: ah! well!) —in'ter·jec'tion·al, in'ter·jec'to·ry *adj.*

in·ter·lace (-lās') *vt., vi.* -laced', -lac'ing [< OFr.: see INTER- & LACE] 1. to unite by passing over and under each other; weave together 2. to connect intricately —in'ter·lace'ment *n.*

in·ter·lard (-lärd') *vt.* [< Fr.: see INTER- & LARD] 1. to intersperse; diversify [to *interlard* a lecture with quotations] 2. to be intermixed in

in·ter·lay (-lā') *vt.* -laid' (-lād'), -lay'ing to lay or put between or among —in'ter·lay'er *n.*

in·ter·leaf (in'tər lēf') *n.*, *pl.* -leaves' (-lēvz') a leaf, usually blank, bound between the other leaves of a book, for notes, etc. —in'ter·leave' (-lēv') *vt.* -leaved', -leav'ing

in·ter·line[1] (in'tər līn') *vt.* -lined', -lin'ing to write or print (something) between the lines of (a text, document, etc.) —in'ter·lin'e·a'tion (-lin'ē ā'shən) *n.*

in·ter·line[2] (in'tər līn') *vt.* -lined', -lin'ing to put a lining between the outer material and the ordinary lining of (a garment)

in·ter·lin·e·ar (in'tər lin'ē ər) *adj.* 1. written or printed between the lines 2. having the same text in different languages printed in alternate lines Also in'ter·lin'e·al

in·ter·lin·ing (in'tər lī'niŋ) *n.* a lining between the outer cloth and the ordinary lining

in·ter·link (in'tər liŋk') *vt.* to link together

in·ter·lock (-lok') *vt., vi.* to lock together; join with one another —*n.* a being interlocked —*adj.* closely knitted [an *interlock* vest]

interlocking directorates boards of directors having some members in common, so that their corporations are more or less under the same control

in·ter·loc·u·tor (-lok'yə tər; *for 2, often* -lok'ə tər) *n.* [< L. pp. < *inter*, between + *loqui*, to talk] 1. a person taking part in a conversation 2. the master of ceremonies in a minstrel show

in·ter·loc·u·to·ry (-lok'yə tər ē) *adj.* 1. of, having the nature of, or occurring in dialogue; conversational 2. *Law* pronounced during the course of a suit, pending final decision

in·ter·lop·er (in'tər lō'pər) *n.* [prob. < INTER- + LOPE] a person who meddles in others' affairs

in·ter·lude (in'tər lōōd') *n.* [< OFr. < ML. < L. *inter*, between + *ludus*, play] 1. a short, humorous play formerly presented between the parts of a miracle play or morality play 2. any performance between the acts of a play 3. music played between the parts of a song, play, etc. 4. a) a period of different activity between two events b) intervening time or, rarely, space

in·ter·mar·ry (in'tər mar'ē) *vi.* -ried, -ry·ing to become connected by marriage: said of persons of different races, religions, etc. —in'ter·mar'riage *n.*

in·ter·med·dle (-med''l) *vi.* -dled, -dling to meddle in the affairs of others —in'ter·med'dler *n.*

in·ter·me·di·ar·y (-mē'dē ar ē) *adj.* 1. acting between two persons; acting as a mediator 2. intermediate —*n.*, *pl.* -ar·ies a go-between; mediator

in·ter·me·di·ate (-mē'dē it; *for v.* -āt') *adj.* [< ML. < L. < *inter*-, between + *medius*, middle] being or happening between; in the middle —*n.* 1. anything intermediate 2. *same as* INTERMEDIARY —*vi.* -at'ed, -at'ing to act as an intermediary; mediate —in'ter·me'di·ate·ly *adv.* —in'·ter·me'di·ate·ness, in'ter·me'di·a·cy (-ə sē) *n.* —in'ter·me'·di·a'tion *n.* —in'ter·me'di·a'tor *n.*

in·ter·ment (in tur'mənt) *n.* an interring; burial

in·ter·mez·zo (in'tər met'sō, -med'zō) *n.*, *pl.* -zos, -zi (-sē, -zē) [It.] 1. a short, light musical entertainment between the acts of a play or opera 2. *Music a)* a short movement connecting the main parts of a composition *b)* any of certain short works similar to this

in·ter·mi·na·ble (in tur'mi nə b'l) *adj.* not terminable; lasting, or seeming to last, forever; endless —in'ter'·mi·na·ble·ness *n.* —in·ter'mi·na·bly *adv.*

in·ter·min·gle (in'tər miŋ'g'l) *vt., vi.* -gled, -gling to mix together; mingle; blend

in·ter·mis·sion (-mish'ən) *n.* 1. an intermitting or being intermitted; interruption 2. an interval of time between periods of activity; pause, as between acts of a play

in·ter·mit (-mit') *vt., vi.* -mit'ted, -mit'ting [< L. < *inter*-, between + *mittere*, to send] to stop for a time; cease at intervals

in·ter·mit·tent (-mit'ənt) *adj.* stopping and starting again at intervals; periodic —in'ter·mit'tence *n.* —in'ter·mit'·tent·ly *adv.*

in·ter·mix (-miks') *vt., vi.* to mix together; blend —in'·ter·mix'ture *n.*

in·tern (in'tərn; *for vt. usually* in turn') *n.* [< Fr. < L. *internus*, internal] [U.S.] 1. a doctor serving as an assistant resident in a hospital, generally just after graduation from medical school 2. an apprentice teacher, journalist, etc. —*vi.* [U.S.] to serve as an intern Also in'·terne —*vt.* to detain and confine within a country or a definite area [to *intern* aliens in time of war] —in·tern'·ment *n.*

in·ter·nal (in tur'n'l) *adj.* [< ML. < L. *internus*] 1. of or on the inside; inner 2. to be taken inside the body [internal remedies] 3. of or belonging to the inner nature of a thing; intrinsic [internal evidence] 4. of or belonging to a person's inner nature or mind; subjective 5. domestic; nonforeign —in'ter·nal'i·ty (-nal'ə tē) *n.* —in·ter'nal·ly *adv.*

in·ter·nal-com·bus·tion engine (-kəm bus'chən) an engine, as in a car, in which the power is produced by the combustion of a fuel-and-air mixture within the cylinders

in·ter·nal·ize (in tur'n'l īz') *vt.* -ized', -iz'ing to make internal; specif., to make (others' ideas, values, etc.) a part of one's own patterns of thinking —in'ter·nal·i·za'tion *n.*

internal medicine the branch of medicine dealing with the diagnosis and nonsurgical treatment of diseases

in·ter·na·tion·al (in'tər nash'ən 'l) *adj.* 1. between or among nations [an *international* treaty] 2. concerned with the relations between nations [an *international* court] 3. for the use of all nations [international waters] 4. of, for, or by people in various nations —*n.* an international organization; esp., [I-] any of several international socialist organizations in existence variously from 1864 —in'ter·na'·tion·al'i·ty *n.* —in'ter·na'tion·al·ly *adv.*

international date line *same as* DATE LINE

in·ter·na·tion·al·ism (in'tər nash'ən 'l iz'm) *n.* the principle of international cooperation for the common good —in'·ter·na'tion·al·ist *n.*

in·ter·na·tion·al·ize (-īz') *vt.* -ized', -iz'ing to make international; bring under international control —in'ter·na'·tion·al·i·za'tion *n.*

International Phonetic Alphabet a set of phonetic symbols for international use: each symbol represents a single sound, whether the sound occurs in only one language or in more than one

in·ter·ne·cine (in'tər nē'sīn) *adj.* [< L. < *inter*-, between + *necare*, to kill] mutually destructive or harmful [internecine warfare]

in·tern·ee (in'tər nē') *n.* a person interned as a prisoner of war, enemy alien, political dissident, etc.

in·ter·nist (in'tər nist, in tur'nist) *n.* a doctor who specializes in internal medicine

in·ter·of·fice (in'tər of'is) *adj.* between or among the offices within an organization

in·ter·pel·late (in'tər pel'āt, in tur'pə lāt') *vt.* -lat·ed, -lat·ing [< L. pp. of *interpellare*, to interrupt < *inter*-, between + *pellere*, to drive] to ask (a cabinet minister, etc.) formally for an explanation of his action or policy: a form of political challenge in some national legislatures —in'ter·pel'lant *adj.*, *n.* —in'ter·pel·la'tion *n.*

in·ter·pen·e·trate (-pen'ə trāt') *vt.* -trat'ed, -trat'ing to penetrate thoroughly; permeate —*vi.* to penetrate mutually —in'ter·pen'e·tra'tion *n.*

in·ter·per·son·al (-pur'sə n'l) *adj.* 1. between persons 2. of or involving relations between persons —in'ter·per'son·al·ly *adv.*

in·ter·phone (in'tər fōn') *n.* an intercom telephone system, as between office departments

in·ter·plan·e·tar·y (in'tər plan'ə tər ē) *adj.* 1. between planets 2. within the solar system but outside the atmosphere of any planet or the sun

in·ter·play (in'tər plā') *n.* action, effect, or influence on each other or one another; interaction

in·ter·plead·er (in'tər plēd'ər) *n.* [Anglo-Fr. *entrepleder*, to interplead] a legal proceeding by which a person sued by two or more persons having the same claim against him may compel them to go to trial with each other to arrive at a settlement —in'ter·plead' *vi.* to initiate an interpleader

In·ter·pol (in'tər pol) *n.* [inter(national) pol(ice)] an international police organisation which coordinates the police activities of member nations against international criminals: full name, *International Criminal Police Organisation*

in·ter·po·late (in tur'pə lāt') *vt.* -lat'ed, -lat'ing [< L. < *inter*-, between + *polire*, to polish] 1. to change (a book, text, etc.) by putting in new words, subject matter, etc. 2. to insert between or among others [to *interpolate* a remark] 3. *Math.* to estimate a missing value by taking an average of known values at neighbouring points —*vi.* to make interpolations —**in·ter′po·lat′er, in·ter′po·la′tor** *n.* —**in·ter′po·la′tion** *n.* —**in·ter′po·la′tive** *adj.*

in·ter·pose (in′tər pōz′) *vt.* -**posed′**, -**pos′ing** [Fr. *interposer*, altered < L. *interpositus*, pp. of *interponere*, to set between] **1.** to place between; insert **2.** to introduce by way of intervention **3.** to put in as an interruption —*vi.* **1.** to be or come between **2.** to intervene **3.** to interrupt —**in′ter·pos′al** *n.* —**in′ter·pos′er** *n.* —**in′ter·po·si′tion** (-pə zish′ən) *n.*

in·ter·pret (in tur′prit) *vt.* [< MFr. < L. *interpretari* < *interpres*, negotiator] **1.** to explain the meaning of; clarify **2.** to translate (oral remarks) **3.** to have one's own understanding of; construe [to *interpret* a laugh as derisive] **4.** to bring out the meaning of; esp., to give one's own conception of, as in performing a play —*vi.* to act as an interpreter; translate —**in·ter′pret·a·ble** *adj.* —**in·ter′pre·tive, in·ter′pre·ta′tive** *adj.*

in·ter·pre·ta·tion (in tur′prə tā′shən) *n.* **1.** the act or result of interpreting; explanation, translation, etc. **2.** the expression of a person's conception of a work of art, subject, etc. through acting, writing, etc. —**in·ter′pre·ta′tion·al** *adj.*

in·ter·pret·er (in tur′prə tər) *n.* a person who interprets; specif., a person whose work is translating a foreign language orally

in·ter·ra·cial (in′tər rā′shəl) *adj.* between, among, or for persons of different races

in·ter·reg·num (-reg′nəm) *n., pl.* -**reg′nums**, -**reg′na** (-nə) [L. < *inter*-, between + *regnum*, a REIGN] **1.** an interval between two successive reigns, when the country has no sovereign **2.** any period without the usual ruler, governor, etc. **3.** any break in a series or in a continuity

in·ter·re·late (-ri lāt′) *vt., vi.* -**lat′ed, -lat′ing** to make, be, or become mutually related —**in′terre·la′tion** *n.* —**in′ter·re·la′tion·ship′** *n.*

in·ter·ro·gate (in ter′ə gāt′) *vt.* -**gat′ed, -gat′ing** [< L. pp. of *interrogare* < *inter*-, between + *rogare*, to ask] to ask questions of formally in examining [to *interrogate* a witness] —*vi.* to ask questions —**in·ter′ro·ga′tor** *n.*

in·ter·ro·ga·tion (in ter′ə gā′shən) *n.* **1.** an interrogating or being interrogated; examination **2.** a question **3.** *Telecommunications* the transmission of triggering pulses to a transponder —**in·ter′ro·ga′tion·al** *adj.*

interrogation mark (or **point**) *same as* QUESTION MARK

in·ter·rog·a·tive (in′tə rog′ə tiv) *adj.* asking, or having the form of, a question —*n.* an interrogative word, element, etc. (Ex.: what? where?) —**in′ter·rog′a·tive·ly** *adv.*

in·ter·rog·a·to·ry (-ə tər ē) *adj.* expressing a question —*n., pl.* -**ries** a formal set of questions —**in′ter·rog′a·to·ri·ly** *adv.*

in·ter·rupt (in′tə rupt′) *vt.* [< L. pp. of *interrumpere* < *inter*-, between + *rumpere*, to break] **1.** *a*) to break into (a discussion, etc.) *b*) to break in upon (a person) while he is speaking, working, etc. **2.** to make a break in the continuity of; obstruct —*vi.* to make an interruption —**in′ter·rupt′er** *n.* —**in′ter·rup′tive** *adj.*

in·ter·rupt·er, in·ter·rupt·or (-ər) *n.* **1.** a person or thing that interrupts **2.** *Elec.* a mechanism used to interrupt, or intermittently open and close, a circuit

in·ter·rup·tion (in′tə rup′shən) *n.* **1.** an interrupting or being interrupted **2.** anything that interrupts **3.** an intermission

in·ter·scho·las·tic (in′tər skə las′tik) *adj.* between or among schools [an *interscholastic* debate]

in·ter·sect (in′tər sekt′) *vt.* [< L. pp. of *intersecare* < *inter*-, between + *secare*, to cut] to divide into two parts by passing through or across —*vi.* to cross each other

in·ter·sec·tion (-sek′shən) *n.* **1.** an intersecting **2.** a place of intersecting; specif., *a*) the point or line where two lines or surfaces meet or cross *b*) the place where two streets cross

in·ter·sec·tion·al (-′l) *adj.* **1.** of or forming an intersection **2.** between sections or regions

in·ter·sex (in′tər seks′) *n.* *Biol.* an abnormal individual having characteristics intermediate between those of male and female

in·ter·sex·u·al (in′tər sek′shoo wəl) *adj.* **1.** between the sexes [*intersexual* rivalry] **2.** of or like an intersex

in·ter·space (in′tər spās′; *for v.* in′tər spās′) *n.* a space between —*vt.* -**spaced′, -spac′ing** **1.** to make spaces between **2.** to fill spaces between

in·ter·sperse (in′tər spurs′) *vt.* -**spersed′, -spers′ing** [< L. pp. of *interspergere* < *inter*-, among + *spargere*, to scatter] **1.** to scatter among other things; put here and there **2.** to decorate or diversify with things scattered here and there —**in′ter·sper′sion** (-spur′zhən, -shən) *n.*

in·ter·state (in′tər stāt′) *adj.* between states of a federal government, esp. in the U.S. [*interstate* commerce]

in·ter·stel·lar (in′tər stel′ər) *adj.* [INTER- + STELLAR] between or among the stars

in·ter·stice (in tur′stis) *n., pl.* -**stic·es** (-stis iz, -stə sēz′) [Fr. < LL. < *inter*-, between + *sistere*, to set < *stare*, to

---

stand] a small space between things or parts; crevice; crack —**in·ter·sti·tial** (in′tər stish′əl) *adj.* —**in′ter·sti′tial·ly** *adv.*

in·ter·twine (in′tər twīn′) *vt., vi.* -**twined′, -twin′ing** to twine together; intertwist

in·ter·twist (-twist′) *vt., vi.* to twist together

in·ter·ur·ban (-ur′bən) *adj.* [INTER- + URBAN] [Chiefly U.S.] between cities or towns

in·ter·val (in′tər v'l) *n.* [< OFr. < L. < *inter*-, between + *vallum*, a WALL] **1.** a space between two things **2.** a period of time between two events **3.** a short period between parts of a play, concert, etc. **4.** the extent of difference between two qualities, conditions, etc. **5.** *Music* the difference in pitch between two tones —**at intervals 1.** now and then **2.** here and there —**in′ter·val′lic** (-val′ik) *adj.*

in·ter·vene (in′tər vēn′) *vi.* -**vened′, -ven′ing** [< L. < *inter*-, between + *venire*, to come] **1.** to come or be between **2.** to occur between two events, etc. **3.** to come or be in between as something irrelevant **4.** to come between as an influencing force **5.** *Law* to come in as a third party to a suit, for the protection of one's own interests —**in′ter·ven′er**, *Law* **in′ter·ve′nor** *n.* —**in′ter·ven′ient** (-yənt) *adj.*

in·ter·ven·tion (in′tər ven′shən) *n.* **1.** an intervening **2.** any interference in the affairs of others, esp. of one state in the affairs of another —**in′ter·ven′tion·ist** *n., adj.*

in·ter·view (in′tər vyōō′) *n.* [< Fr.: see INTER- & VIEW] **1.** a meeting of people face to face, as for evaluating a job applicant **2.** *a*) a meeting in which a person is asked about his views, activities, etc., as by a reporter *b*) a published account of this —*vt.* to have an interview with —*vi.* to acquit oneself at an interview [he *interviews* badly] —**in′ter·view·ee′** *n.* —**in′ter·view′er** *n.*

in·ter·weave (in′tər wēv′) *vt., vi.* -**wove′, -wo′ven, -weav′ing** **1.** to weave together; interlace **2.** to connect closely; intermingle

in·tes·tate (in tes′tāt, -tit) *adj.* [< L. < *in*-, not + pp. of *testari*, to make a will] **1.** having made no will **2.** not disposed of by a will —*n.* a person who has died intestate —**in·tes′ta·cy** (-tə sē) *n.*

in·tes·tin·al (in tes′ti n'l) *adj.* of or in the intestines —**in·tes′tin·al·ly** *adv.*

in·tes·tine (in tes′tin) *adj.* [< L. *intestinus* < *intus*, within] internal, with regard to a country or community; domestic —*n.* [*usually pl.*] the lower part of the alimentary canal, extending from the stomach to the anus and consisting of a convoluted upper part (**small intestine**) and a lower part of greater diameter (**large intestine**); bowel(s)

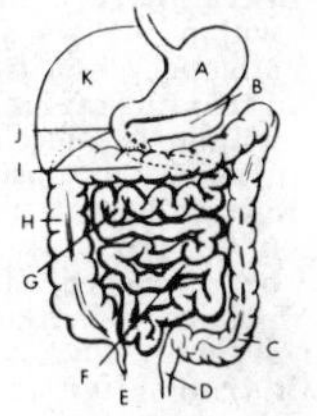

in·thral (in thrôl′) *vt.* -**thralled′, -thrall′ing** *same as* ENTHRAL

in·ti·ma·cy (in′tə mə sē) *n., pl.* -**cies** **1.** a being intimate; familiarity **2.** an intimate act; esp., [*usually pl.*] illicit sexual intercourse

in·ti·mate (in′tə mit; *for v.* -māt′) *adj.* [< L. *intimus*, superl. of *intus*, within] **1.** fundamental; essential [the *intimate* structure of the atom] **2.** most private or personal [one's *intimate* feelings] **3.** closely associated; very familiar [an *intimate* friend] **4.** suggesting privacy, romance, etc. [an *intimate* nightclub] **5.** *a*) resulting from careful study *b*) very close [*intimate* kinship] **6.** having illicit sexual relations —*n.* an intimate friend or companion —*vt.* -**mat′ed, -mat′ing** [< L. pp. of *intimare*, to announce < *intimus*] to hint or imply —**in′ti·mate·ly** *adv.* —**in′ti·mate·ness** *n.*

in·ti·ma·tion (in′tə mā′shən) *n.* **1.** the act of intimating **2.** a formal announcement: now chiefly in law **3.** a hint; suggestion

in·tim·i·date (in tim′ə dāt′) *vt.* -**dat′ed, -dat′ing** [< ML. pp. of *intimidare* < L. *in*-, in + *timidus*, afraid] **1.** to make timid; make afraid **2.** to force or deter with threats; cow —**in·tim′i·da′tion** *n.* —**in·tim′i·da′tor** *n.*

in·tinc·tion (in tiŋk′shən) *n.* [LL. *intinctio* < L. *intingere*, to dip in] the act of dipping the Eucharistic bread into the consecrated wine, so that the communicant receives both together

in·tit·ule (in tit′yool) *vt.* -**uled, -ul·ing** [ME. < OFr. < LL. *intitulare*, to entitle] to entitle (an act of parliament, etc.)

intl. international

in·to (in′tōō, -too, -tə) *prep.* [OE.] **1.** to the inside of; towards and within [into a house] **2.** advancing to the midst of (a period of time) [dancing far *into* the night] **3.** to the form, substance, etc. of [divided *into* parts] **4.** so as to strike [to bump *into* a door] **5.** to the work, activity, etc.

[INTESTINES diagram with labels: K, A, B, J, H, I, G, F, E, D, C]

INTESTINES
(A, stomach; B, pancreas; C, descending colon; D, rectum; E, appendix; F, ileum; G, jejunum; H, ascending colon; I, transverse colon; J, duodenum; K, liver)

of [to go *into* teaching] **6.** *Math.* used to indicate division [3 *into* 21 is 7]

in·tol·er·a·ble (in tol′ər ə b'l) *adj.* not tolerable; unbearable; too severe, painful, etc. to be endured —**in·tol′er·a·bil′i·ty, in·tol′er·a·ble·ness** *n.* —**in·tol′er·a·bly** *adv.*

in·tol·er·ance (in tol′ər əns) *n.* **1.** lack of tolerance, esp. of others' opinions, beliefs, etc.; bigotry **2.** a sensitivity to some food, medicine, etc.

in·tol·er·ant (-ənt) *adj.* not tolerant; unwilling to tolerate others' opinions, beliefs, etc. or persons of other races, background, etc.; bigoted —**intolerant of** not able or willing to tolerate —**in·tol′er·ant·ly** *adv.* —**in·tol′er·ant·ness** *n.*

in·to·na·tion (in′tə nā′shən) *n.* **1.** an intoning **2.** the manner of singing or playing tones with regard to accuracy of pitch **3.** variations in pitch in speaking that affect the meaning **4.** the manner of applying pitch to a spoken sentence or phrase [a question ending with a rising intonation] —**in′to·na′tion·al** *adj.*

in·tone (in tōn′) *vt.* **-toned′, -ton′ing** [< OFr. < ML.: see IN·[1] & TONE] **1.** to utter or recite in a singing tone or in prolonged monotones; chant **2.** to give a particular intonation to —*vi.* to speak or recite in a singing tone or in prolonged monotones; chant Also **in·ton·ate** —**in·ton′er** *n.*

in to·to (in tō′tō) [L.] as a whole; entirely

in·tox·i·cant (in tok′sə kənt) *n.* something that intoxicates; esp., alcoholic liquor —*adj.* intoxicating

in·tox·i·cate (-kāt′) *vt.* **-cat′ed, -cat′ing** [< ML. pp. of *intoxicare*, to poison, ult. < L. *in-*, in + *toxicum*, a poison: see TOXIC] **1.** to make drunk **2.** to excite to a point beyond self-control **3.** *Med.* to poison

in·tox·i·ca·tion (in tok′sə kā′shən) *n.* **1.** a making or becoming drunk **2.** a feeling of wild excitement; frenzy **3.** *Med.* a poisoning or becoming poisoned

intr. intransitive

in·tra- [L. < *intra*, within] a combining form meaning within, inside [intramural]

in·trac·ta·ble (in trak′tə b'l) *adj.* not tractable; specif., *a)* hard to manage; unruly or stubborn *b)* hard to work, cure, etc. —**in·trac′ta·bil′i·ty, in·trac′ta·ble·ness** *n.* —**in·trac′ta·bly** *adv.*

in·tra·dos (in trā′dōs, -dos) *n.* [Fr. < L. *intra*, within + Fr. *dos* < L. *dorsum*, the back] the inside curve or surface of an arch or vault

in·tra·mu·ral (in′trə myoor′əl) *adj.* [INTRA- + MURAL] within the walls or limits of a college, etc. [intramural athletics] —**in′tra·mu′ral·ly** *adv.*

in·tra·mus·cu·lar (-mus′kyə lər) *adj.* located or injected within the muscle —**in′tra·mus′cu·lar·ly** *adv.*

intrans. intransitive

in·tran·si·gent (in tran′sə jənt) *adj.* [< Fr. < Sp. < L. *in-*, IN·[2] + prp. of *transigere*, to settle] refusing to compromise, be reconciled, etc. —*n.* one who is intransigent, esp. in politics —**in·tran′si·gence, in·tran′si·gen·cy** *n.* —**in·tran′si·gent·ly** *adv.*

in·tran·si·tive (in tran′sə tiv) *adj.* not transitive; designating a verb that does not require a direct object to complete its meaning —*n.* an intransitive verb —**in·tran′si·tive·ly** *adv.*

in·tra·state (in′trə stāt′) *adj.* [Chiefly U.S.] within a state

in·tra·u·ter·ine (-yoot′ər in, -yoo′tə rin′) *adj.* within the uterus

intrauterine (contraceptive) device any of various devices, as a coil or loop of plastic, inserted in the uterus as a contraceptive

in·tra·ve·nous (-vē′nəs) *adj.* [INTRA- + VENOUS] in, or directly into, a vein or veins [an intravenous injection] —**in′tra·ve′nous·ly** *adv.*

in·tray (-trā′) *n.* a tray or receptacle for incoming papers, letters etc.

in·trench (in trench′) *vt., vi.* same as ENTRENCH

in·trep·id (in trep′id) *adj.* [< L. < *in-*, not + *trepidus*, alarmed] unafraid; bold; fearless; very brave —**in·tre·pid′i·ty** (-trə pid′ə tē), **in·trep′id·ness** *n.* —**in·trep′id·ly** *adv.*

in·tri·ca·cy (in′tri kə sē) *n.* **1.** an intricate quality or state; complexity **2.** *pl.* **-cies** something intricate; involved matter, etc.

in·tri·cate (in′tri kit) *adj.* [< L. pp. of *intricare*, to entangle < *in-*, in + *tricae*, perplexities] **1.** hard to follow or understand because full of puzzling parts, details, or relationships [an intricate problem] **2.** full of elaborate detail —**in′tri·cate·ly** *adv.* —**in′tri·cate·ness** *n.*

in·trigue (in trēg′; for *n.*, also in′trēg) *vi.* **-trigued′, -trigu′ing** [< Fr. < It. < L. *intricare*: see prec.] **1.** to carry on a secret love affair **2.** to plot or scheme secretly or underhandedly —*vt.* **1.** to get by secret or underhand plotting **2.** to excite the interest or curiosity of [caves intrigue her] —*n.* **1.** secret or underhanded plotting **2.** a secret or underhanded plot or scheme **3.** a secret love affair —**in·trig·ant, in·trigu′er** *n.* —**in·trigu′ing·ly** *adv.*

in·trin·sic (in trin′sik, -zik) *adj.* [< MFr. < LL. *intrinsecus*, inward < *intra*, within + *secus*, close] belonging to

the real nature of a thing; essential; inherent: also **in·trin′si·cal** —**in·trin′si·cal·ly** *adv.* —**in·trin′si·cal·ness** *n.*

in·tro (in′trō) *n.* [Colloq.] introduction

in·tro- [L. < *intro*, on the inside] a combining form meaning into, within, inwards [introvert]

introd., intro. **1.** introduction **2.** introductory

in·tro·duce (in′trə dyoos′) *vt.* **-duced′, -duc′ing** [< L. *intro-*, within + *ducere*, to lead] **1.** to lead or bring in **2.** to put in; insert [to introduce a drain into a wound] **3.** to add as a new feature [introduce some humour into the play] **4.** to bring into use, knowledge, or fashion [space science has introduced many new words] **5.** *a)* to make acquainted; present *(to)* [introduce me to her] *b)* to present (a person) to society *c)* to give knowledge or experience of [they introduced him to music] **6.** to bring forward [introduce a bill in parliament] **7.** to start; begin [to introduce a talk with a joke] —**in′tro·duc′er** *n.* —**in′tro·duc′i·ble** *adj.*

in·tro·duc·tion (-duk′shən) *n.* **1.** an introducing or being introduced **2.** anything brought into use, knowledge, or fashion **3.** anything that introduces; specif., *a)* the preliminary section of a book, speech, etc. *b)* a preliminary guide or text *c)* an opening section of music **4.** the formal presentation of one person to another, to society, etc.

in·tro·duc·to·ry (-duk′tər ē) *adj.* used as an introduction; preliminary: also **in′tro·duc′tive** —**in′tro·duc′to·ri·ly** *adv.*

in·tro·it (in trō′it; in′trō it, -troit) *n.* [< MFr. < L. *introitus*, an entrance, ult. < *intro-*, within + *ire*, to go] **1.** a psalm or hymn at the opening of a Christian worship service **2.** [I-] *R.C.Ch.* the first variable part of the Mass, consisting of a few psalm verses followed by the *Gloria Patri* and then repeated

in·tro·mit (in′trə mit′) *vt.* **-mit′ted, -mit′ting** [L. *intromittere*, to send into] **1.** to put in; insert **2.** to allow to enter; let in —**in′tro·mis′sion** (-mish′ən) *n.* —**in′tro·mit′tent** *adj.*

in·tro·spec·tion (in′trə spek′shən) *n.* [< L. < pp. of *introspicere*, ult. < *intro-*, within + *specere*, to look] a looking into one's own mind, feelings, etc. —**in′tro·spec′tive** *adj.* —**in′tro·spec′tive·ly** *adv.*

in·tro·ver·sion (-vur′shən) *n.* [see ff.] *Psychol.* an attitude in which a person directs his interest to his own experiences and feelings rather than upon external objects or other persons: opposed to EXTROVERSION —**in′tro·ver′sive** *adj.*

in·tro·vert (in′trə vurt′; for *v.*, also in′trə vurt′) *vt.* [< L. *intro-*, within + *vertere*, to turn] **1.** to direct (one's interest, mind, etc.) upon oneself **2.** to bend (something) inwards —*vi.* to become introverted —*n.* *Psychol.* a person characterized by introversion: opposed to EXTROVERT —*adj.* characterized by introversion: usually **in′tro·vert′ed**

in·trude (in trood′) *vt.* **-trud′ed, -trud′ing** [< L. < *in-*, in + *trudere*, to thrust] **1.** to push or force (something *in* or *upon*) **2.** to force (oneself) upon others without being asked or welcomed **3.** *Geol.* to force (liquid magma, etc.) into or between solid rocks —*vi.* to intrude oneself —**in·trud′er** *n.*

in·tru·sion (in troo′zhən) *n.* **1.** an intruding **2.** *Geol. a)* the invasion of liquid magma, etc. into or between solid rock *b)* intrusive rock **3.** *Law* the act of unlawfully occupying a vacant estate, etc.

in·tru·sive (-siv) *adj.* **1.** intruding **2.** *Geol.* formed by intruding —**in·tru′sive·ly** *adv.* —**in·tru′sive·ness** *n.*

in·trust (in trust′) *vt.* same as ENTRUST

in·tu·bate (in′tyoo bāt′) *vt.* **-bat′ed, -bat′ing** [IN·[1] + TUB(E) + -ATE[1]] to insert a tube into (an orifice, as the larynx) to administer gas or admit air —**in′tu·ba′tion** *n.*

in·tu·it (in tyoo′it) *vt., vi.* to know intuitively or learn by intuition —**in·tu′it·a·ble** *adj.*

in·tu·i·tion (in′tyoo wish′ən) *n.* [LL. < L. pp. of *intueri* < *in-*, in + *tueri*, to look at] **1.** *a)* the direct knowing or learning of something without conscious reasoning *b)* the ability to do this **2.** something known or learned in this way —**in′tu·i′tion·al** *adj.* —**in′tu·i′tion·al·ly** *adv.*

in·tu·i·tive (in tyoo′i tiv) *adj.* **1.** having to do with, having, or perceiving by intuition **2.** perceived by intuition [an intuitive truth] —**in·tu′i·tive·ly** *adv.* —**in·tu′i·tive·ness** *n.*

in·tu·mesce (in′tyoo mes′) *vi.* [L. *intumescere*, to begin to swell] to swell; enlarge —**in′tu·mes′cence** *n.* —**in′tu·mes′cent** *adj.*

in·tus·sus·cep·tion (in′tə sə sep′shən) *n.* [< L. < *intus*, within + *susceptio*, < *suscipere*, to take up] **1.** the telescoping of one section of the intestines into another **2.** *Biol.* the process of taking in food and converting it into tissue

in·unc·tion (in ungk′shən) *n.* [L. *inunctio*: see UNCTION] **1.** the rubbing of ointment, etc. into the skin **2.** an ointment

in·un·date (in′ən dāt′) *vt.* **-dat′ed, -dat′ing** [< L. pp. of *inundare* < *in-*, in + *undare*, to flood < *unda*, a wave] **1.** to cover completely with water; flood; deluge **2.** to overwhelm [inundated by requests] —**in·un·dant** (in un′dənt) *adj.* —**in′un·da′tion** *n.* —**in·un·da′tor** *n.* —**in·un′da·to·ry** (-də tər ē) *adj.*

in·ure (in yoor′) *vt.* **-ured′, -ur′ing** [< ME. *in*, in + *ure*, practice, work < OFr. *ovre* < L. *opera*, a work] to make accustomed to something difficult, painful, etc. —*vi.* to come into use or take effect; chiefly a legal use —**in·ure′·ment** *n.*

in·u·tile (in y$\overline{oo}$t′il) *adj.* [ME. < MFr. <L. *inutilis*, useless] useless; unprofitable —**in·u·til′·i·ty** *n.*

inv. 1. invented 2. inventor 3. invoice

‡**in va·cu·o** (in vak′y$\overline{oo}$ ō′) [L.] in a vacuum

in·vade (in vād′) *vt.* -**vad′ed**, -**vad′ing** [< L. < *in-*, in + *vadere*, to go] 1. to enter forcibly, as to conquer 2. to crowd into; throng [tourists *invading* the beaches] 3. to intrude upon; violate [he *invaded* my privacy] 4. to spread through with harmful effects [disease *invades* tissue] —*vi.* to make an invasion —**in·vad′er** *n.*

in·va·lid¹ (in′və lid) *adj.* [< L.: see IN.² + VALID] 1. not well; weak and sickly 2. of or for invalids [an *invalid* home] —*n.* a weak, sickly person; esp., one who is chronically ill or disabled —*vt.* 1. to disable or weaken 2. to remove (a soldier, sailor, etc.) from active duty because of injury or illness —**in′va·lid·ism** *n.*

in·val·id² (in val′id) *adj.* not valid; having no force; null or void —**in·va·lid′i·ty** (in′və lid′ə tē) *n.* —**in·val′id·ly** *adv.*

in·val·i·date (in val′ə dāt′) *vt.* -**dat′ed**, -**dat′ing** to make invalid; deprive of legal force —**in·val′i·da′tion** *n.* —**in·val′-i·da′tor** *n.*

in·val·u·a·ble (in val′yoo wə b'l, -yə b'l) *adj.* too valuable to be measured; priceless —**in·val′u·a·ble·ness** *n.* —**in·val′-u·a·bly** *adv.*

In·var (in vär′) [contr. < INVARIABLE] a trademark for a steel alloy containing approximately 36% nickel, used for making precision instruments

in·var·i·a·ble (in ver′ē ə b'l) *adj.* not variable; unchanging; constant; uniform —**in·var′i·a·bil′i·ty**, **in·var′i·a·ble·ness** *n.* —**in·var′i·a·bly** *adv.*

in·var·i·ant (-ənt) *adj.* not varying; constant —*n.* *Math.* an entity that is unchanged by a given transformation —**in·var′-i·ance** *n.*

in·va·sion (in vā′zhən) *n.* an invading; specif., *a)* an entering or being entered by an attacking military force *b)* an intruding upon others *c)* the onset, as of a disease —**in·va′sive** *adj.*

in·vec·tive (in vek′tiv) *adj.* [< MFr. < LL. < L. pp. of *invehere*: see ff.] inveighing; vituperative —*n.* 1. a violent verbal attack; insults, curses, etc. 2. an abusive term; insult, curse, etc. —**in·vec′tive·ly** *adv.* —**in·vec′tive·ness** *n.*

in·veigh (in vā′) *vi.* [< L. *invehi*, to attack < *invehere* < *in-*, in + *vehere*, to carry] to make a violent verbal attack; talk or write bitterly (*against*); rail —**in·veigh′er** *n.*

in·vei·gle (in vē′g'l, -vā′-) *vt.* -**gled**, -**gling** [< MFr. *aveugler*, to blind < L. *ab*, from + *oculus*, an eye] to lead on with deception; entice or trick into doing something, etc. —**in·vei′gle·ment** *n.* —**in·vei′gler** *n.*

in·vent (in vent′) *vt.* [< L. pp. of *invenire* < *in-*, on + *venire*, to come] 1. to think up; devise in the mind [to *invent* excuses] 2. to think out or produce (a new device, etc.); devise for the first time

in·ven·tion (in ven′shən) *n.* 1. an inventing or being invented 2. the power of inventing; ingenuity 3. something invented; specif., *a)* something thought up; esp., a falsehood *b)* a new device or contrivance 4. *Music* a short composition developing a motif in counterpoint

in·ven·tive (-tiv) *adj.* 1. of or characterized by invention 2. skilled in inventing; creative —**in·ven′tive·ly** *adv.* —**in·ven′-tive·ness** *n.*

in·ven·tor (-tər) *n.* a person who invents; esp., one who devises a new contrivance, method, etc.

in·ven·to·ry (in′vən trē, -tər ē) *n.*, *pl.* -**ries** [< ML. < LL. < L. pp. of *invenire*: see INVENT] 1. a detailed list of articles, goods, etc., as the effects of a house 2. [U.S.] *a)* a dealer's stock *b)* stocktaking —*vt.* -**ried**, -**ry·ing** 1. to make an inventory 2. to appear on an inventory —**in′ven·to′ri·al** (-vən tôr′ē əl) *adj.* —**in′ven·to′ri·al·ly** *adj.*

In·ver·ness (in′vər nes′) *n.* [after the former county of Scotland] [often i-] 1. an overcoat with a long, removable cape 2. the cape: also **Inverness cape**

in·verse (in vurs′, in′vurs′) *adj.* inverted; reversed in order or relation; directly opposite [an *inverse* ratio] —*n.* any inverse thing; direct opposite —**in·verse′ly** *adv.*

in·ver·sion (in vur′zhən, -shən) *n.* 1. an inverting or being inverted 2. something inverted; reversal 3. *Chem.* a) a chemical change in which an optically active substance becomes optically inactive or rotates polarized light in the opposite direction *b)* the conversion of an isomeric compound to its opposite 4. *Gram. & Rhetoric* a reversal of the normal order of words in a sentence (Ex.: "said he" for "he said") 5. *Math.* a) the process of using an opposite rule or method *b)* an interchange of the terms of a ratio 6. *Meteorol.* an atmospheric condition in which a layer of warm air traps cooler air near the surface of the earth, preventing the normal rising of surface air 7. *Music* the reversal of the position of the tones in an interval or chord, as by raising the lower tone by an octave —**in·ver′sive** *adj.*

in·vert (in vurt′; *for n.* in′vurt′) *vt.* [< L. < *in-*, to +

vertere, to turn] 1. to turn upside down 2. to change to the direct opposite; reverse the order, position, direction, etc. of 3. to subject to inversion —*n.* 1. anything inverted 2. a homosexual 3. *a)* the lower, inner surface of a drain, etc. *b)* an inverted arch —**in·vert′i·ble** *adj.*

in·ver·te·brate (in vur′tə brit, -brāt′) *adj.* 1. not vertebrate; having no backbone, or spinal column 2. of invertebrates —*n.* any animal without a backbone; any animal other than a fish, amphibian, reptile, bird, or mammal

inverted comma *same as* QUOTATION MARK

in·vert·er (in vur′tər) *n.* *Elec.* a device for changing direct current into alternating current

invert sugar a mixture of dextrose and levulose, found in fruits and produced artificially by the hydrolysis of sucrose

in·vest (in vest′) *vt.* [< L. < *in-*, in + *vestire*, to clothe < *vestis*, clothing] 1. to clothe; array 2. *a)* to cover or surround as with a garment [fog *invests* the city] *b)* to endow with qualities, attributes, etc. 3. to install in office with ceremony 4. to furnish with power, privilege, or authority 5. to put (money) into business, shares, bonds, etc. for the purpose of obtaining a profit 6. to spend (time, effort, etc.) with the expectation of some satisfaction 7. *Mil.* to besiege (a town, port, etc.) —*vi.* 1. to invest money 2. [Colloq.] to buy [to *invest* in some new shoes] —**in·ves′-tor** *n.*

in·ves·ti·gate (in ves′tə gāt′) *vt.* -**gat′ed**, -**gat′ing** [< L. pp. of *investigare*, to trace out, ult. < *vestigium*, a track] to search into; inquire into systematically —*vi.* to make an investigation —**in·ves′ti·ga·ble** (-gə b'l) *adj.* —**in·ves′ti·ga′-tive**, **in·ves′ti·ga·to·ry** (-gə tər ē) *adj.* —**in·ves′ti·ga′tor** *n.*

in·ves·ti·ga·tion (in ves′tə gā′shən) *n.* 1. an investigating or being investigated 2. a careful examination or inquiry —**in·ves′ti·ga′tion·al** *adj.*

in·ves·ti·ture (in ves′tə chər) *n.* a formal investing with an office, power, authority, etc.

in·vest·ment (in vest′mənt) *n.* 1. an investing or being invested 2. an outer covering 3. *same as* INVESTITURE 4. *a)* the investing of money *b)* the amount of money invested *c)* anything in which money is or may be invested

investment trust an organisation that invests its members' capital in a wide range of securities to provide profit and reduce the risk of depreciation

in·vet·er·ate (in vet′ər it) *adj.* [< L. pp. of *inveterare*, to age < *in-*, in + *vetus*, old] 1. firmly established over a long period; deep-rooted 2. settled in a habit, practice, prejudice, etc.; habitual —**in·vet′er·a·cy** *n.* —**in·vet′er·ate·ly** *adv.*

in·vid·i·ous (in vid′ē əs) *adj.* [< L. < *invidia*, ENVY] 1. such as to excite ill will or envy; giving offence 2. giving offence by discriminating unfairly [invidious comparisons] —**in·vid′i·ous·ly** *adv.* —**in·vid′i·ous·ness** *n.*

in·vig·i·late (in vij′ə lāt′) *vi.* -**lat′ed**, -**lat′ing** [< L. *invigilatus*, pp. of *invigilare*, to watch over] to supervise, esp. candidates during an examination

in·vig·or·ate (in vig′ə rāt′) *vt.* -**at′ed**, -**at′ing** [IN.¹ + VIGOUR + -ATE¹] to give vigour to; fill with energy; enliven —**in·vig′or·a′tion** *n.* —**in·vig′or·a′tive** *adj.* —**in·vig′or·a′-tor** *n.*

in·vin·ci·ble (in vin′sə b'l) *adj.* [< MFr. < L.: see IN.² & VINCIBLE] that cannot be overcome; unconquerable —**in·vin′ci·bil′i·ty**, **in·vin′ci·ble·ness** *n.* —**in·vin′ci·bly** *adv.*

in·vi·o·la·ble (in vī′ə lə b'l) *adj.* 1. not to be violated; not to be profaned or injured; sacred [an *inviolable* promise] 2. that cannot be violated; indestructible —**in·vi′o·la·bil′i·ty** *n.* —**in·vi′o·la·bly** *adv.*

in·vi·o·late (in vī′ə lit, -lāt′) *adj.* not violated; kept sacred or unbroken —**in·vi′o·la·cy** (-lə sē), **in·vi′o·late·ness** *n.* —**in·vi′o·late·ly** *adv.*

in·vis·i·ble (in viz′ə b'l) *adj.* 1. not visible; that cannot be seen 2. out of sight 3. imperceptible 4. kept hidden 5. *Econ.* relating to services, as banking; insurance, etc., rather than goods —*n.* an invisible thing or being —**the Invisible** 1. God 2. the unseen world —**in·vis′i·bil′i·ty**, **in·vis′-i·ble·ness** *n.* —**in·vis′i·bly** *adv.*

in·vi·ta·tion (in′və tā′shən) *n.* 1. an inviting to come somewhere or do something 2. the message or note used in inviting

in·vite (in vīt′; *for n.* in′vīt) *vt.* -**vit′ed**, -**vit′ing** [< Fr. < L. *invitare*] 1. to ask courteously to come somewhere or do something 2. to make a request for [to *invite* questions] 3. to give occasion for [action that *invites* scandal] 4. to tempt; entice —*n.* [Colloq.] an invitation

in·vit·ing (-vīt′in) *adj.* tempting; enticing

in·vo·ca·tion (in′və kā′shən) *n.* 1. an invoking of God, the Muses, etc. for blessing, help, etc. 2. a formal prayer used in invoking, as at the beginning of a church service 3. *a)* a conjuring of evil spirits *b)* an incantation —**in′vo·ca′tion·al** *adj.* —**in·voc′a·to·ry** (-vok′ə tər ē) *adj.*

in·voice (in′vois) *n.* [prob. orig. pl. of ME. *envoie*, a message: see ENVOY¹] 1. an itemized list of goods sent or shipped to a buyer, stating quantities, prices, transport charges, etc. **2.** [Rare] a shipment of invoiced goods —*vt.* **-voiced, -voic·ing** to present an invoice for or to

in·voke (in vōk′) *vt.* **-voked′, -vok′ing** [< MFr. < L. < *in-*, on + *vocare*, to call] **1.** to call on (God, the Muses, etc.) for blessing, help, etc. **2.** to put into use (a law, penalty, etc.) as pertinent **3.** to call forth; cause **4.** to summon (evil spirits) by incantation; conjure **5.** to ask solemnly for; implore —**in·vok′er** *n.*

in·vo·lu·cre (in′və lōō′kər) *n.* [Fr. < L. *involucrum*, wrapper < *involvere*, INVOLVE] **1.** *Anat.* a membraneous covering or envelope **2.** *Bot.* a ring of bracts at the base of a flower, flower cluster, or fruit —**in′vo·lu′cral** (-krəl) *adj.*

in·vol·un·tar·y (in vol′ən tər ē) *adj.* not voluntary; specif., *a*) not done of one's own free will *b*) unintentional; accidental *c*) not consciously controlled [sneezing is *involuntary*] —**in·vol′un·tar·i·ly** *adv.* —**in·vol′un·tar·i·ness** *n.*

in·vo·lute (in′və lōōt′) *adj.* [L. *involutus*, pp. of *involvere*, INVOLVE] **1.** intricate; involved **2.** rolled up or curled in a spiral; having the whorls wound closely [*involute* shells] **3.** *Bot.* rolled inwards at the edges [*involute* leaves] —*n. Math. a*) the curve traced by any point of a taut string when it is wound upon or unwound from a fixed curve on the same plane with it *b*) the locus of any fixed point on a moving tangent which rolls, but does not slide, on a curve —*vi.* **-lut′ed, -lut′ing** to become involute or undergo involution

in·vo·lu·tion (in′və lōō′shən) *n.* **1.** an involving or being involved; entanglement **2.** something involved; complication; intricacy **3.** *Math.* the raising of a quantity to any given power **4.** *Med.* reduction or shrinking in size of an organ —**in′vo·lu′tion·al** *adj.* —**in′vo·lu′tion·ar·y** *adj.*

in·volve (in volv′) *vt.* **-volved′, -volv′ing** [< L. < *in-*, in + *volvere*, to roll] **1.** orig., to enfold or envelop **2.** to make intricate or complicated **3.** to entangle in difficulty, danger, etc.; implicate **4.** to draw or hold within itself; include [a riot *involving* thousands] **5.** to include by necessity; entail; require [saving money *involves* thrift] **6.** to relate to or affect [his honour is *involved*] **7.** to make busy; occupy [*involved* in research] —**in·volve′ment** *n.*

in·vul·ner·a·ble (in vul′nər ə b'l) *adj.* **1.** that cannot be wounded or injured **2.** proof against attack —**in·vul′·ner·a·bil′i·ty** *n.* —**in·vul′ner·a·bly** *adv.*

in·ward (in′wərd) *adj.* **1.** situated within; internal **2.** mental or spiritual **3.** directed towards the inside [the *inward* pull of a centrifuge] —*n.* **1.** the inside **2.** [*pl.*] the entrails —*adv.* **1.** towards the inside or centre **2.** into the mind or spirit Also **in′wards** *adv.*

in·ward·ly (-lē) *adv.* **1.** in or on the inside; internally **2.** in the mind or spirit **3.** towards the inside or centre

in·ward·ness (-nis) *n.* **1.** the inner nature or meaning **2.** spirituality **3.** introspection

in·weave (in wēv′) *vt.* **-wove, -wo′ven** or **-wove, -weav′-ing** to weave in

in·wrap (in rap′) *vt.* **-wrapped′, -wrap′ping** *same as* ENWRAP

in·wrought (in rôt′) *adj.* **1.** worked or woven into a fabric: said of a pattern, etc. **2.** closely blended with other things

in·ya·la (in yä′lə) *n.* [< Zulu] a South African antelope

Io *Chem.* ionium

i·od·ic (ī od′ik) *adj.* of or containing iodine; esp. with a valence of five

i·o·dide (ī′ə dīd′) *n.* a compound of iodine with another element or with a radical

i·o·di·nate (ī′ə di nāt′) *vt.* **-nat′ed, -nat′ing** to treat or cause to combine with iodine —**i′o·di·na′tion** *n.*

i·o·dine (ī′ə dēn′) *n.* [Fr. *iode* (< Gr. *iōdēs*, violetlike < *ion*, a violet + *eidos*, a form) + -INE⁴] **1.** a nonmetallic chemical element of the halogen family, consisting of greyish-black crystals that volatilize into a violet-coloured vapour: used as an antiseptic, in photography, etc.: symbol, I; at. wt., 126.9044; at. no., 53: a radioactive isotope (**iodine 131**) is used in medical diagnosis and therapy **2.** tincture of iodine, used as an antiseptic

i·o·dize (ī′ə dīz′) *vt.* **-dized′, -diz′ing** to treat with iodine or an iodide

i·o·do·form (ī ō′də fôrm′) *n.* [*iodo-* (< Fr. *iode*, IODINE) + FORM(IC)] a yellowish, crystalline compound of iodine, CHI₃, used as an antiseptic in surgical dressings

I.O.M. Isle of Man

i·on (ī′ən, -on) *n.* [< Gr. *ion*, prp. of *ienai*, to go] an electrically charged atom or group of atoms, the electrical charge of which results from a neutral atom or group of atoms losing or gaining one or more electrons: such loss (resulting in a CATION), or gain (resulting in an ANION), occurs during electrolysis, by the action of certain forms of radiant energy, etc. —**i·on·ic** (ī on′ik) *adj.*

-ion [< Fr. < L. *-io* (gen. *-ionis*)] *a suffix meaning* the act, condition, or result of [*translation, correction*]

ion exchange a chemical process whereby ions are reversibly transferred between an insoluble solid and a fluid mixture: used in water softening; etc.

I·on·ic (ī on′ik) *adj.* designating or of that one of the three orders of Greek architecture distinguished by ornamental scrolls on the capitals: cf. CORINTHIAN, DORIC

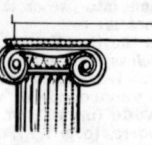
IONIC CAPITAL

i·o·ni·um (ī ō′nē əm) *n.* [ION + ModL. ending *-ium*] a radioactive isotope of thorium

i·on·ize (ī′ə nīz′) *vt., vi.* **-ized′, -iz′-ing** to change or be changed into ions; dissociate into ions, as a salt dissolved in water, or become electrically charged, as a gas under radiation —**i′on·i·za′·tion** *n.* —**i′on·iz′er** *n.*

i·on·o·sphere (ī on′ə sfir′) *n.* the outer part of the earth's atmosphere, consisting of changing layers characterized by an appreciable electron and ion content —**i·on·o·spher′ic** *adj.*

i·o·ta (ī ōt′ə) *n.* **1.** the ninth letter of the Greek alphabet (I, ι) **2.** a very small quantity; jot

IOU, I.O.U. (ī′ō′yōō′) **1.** I owe you **2.** a signed note bearing these letters, acknowledging a debt

-ious (ē əs, yəs, əs) [see -OUS] *a suffix used to form adjectives corresponding to nouns that end in* -ION [*rebellious*] *or meaning* having, characterized by [*furious*]

I.O.W. Isle of Wight

IPA International Phonetic Alphabet

ip·e·cac (ip′ə kak′) *n.* [< Port. < Tupi] **1.** a tropical S. American plant of the madder family **2.** the dried roots of this plant **3.** a preparation from the dried roots, used to induce vomiting Also **ip·e·cac·u·an·ha** (ip′ə kak′yōō wan′ə)

ip·o·moe·a (ip′ə mē′ə, ī pə mē′ə) *n.* [Mod L. < Gr. *ips* (ger. *ipos*), a worm + *homoios*, like] any of various twining plants of the morning-glory family, with funnel-shaped flowers

‡ip·se dix·it (ip′sē dik′sit) [L., he himself has said (it)] a dogmatic statement

ip·so fac·to (ip′sō fak′tō) [L.] by that very fact

IQ, I.Q. intelligence quotient

ir- *see* IN-¹ & IN-²

Ir *Chem.* iridium

IR, ir, i-r infrared

Ir. 1. Ireland **2.** Irish

I.R.A. Irish Republican Army

i·ra·de (i rä′dē) *n.* [Turk. < Ar. *iradah*, will] formerly, a written decree of a Moslem ruler

I·ra·ni·an (i rä′nē ən, ī-) *adj.* of Iran, its people, their language, or culture —*n.* **1.** one of the people of Iran; Persian **2.** a subbranch of the Indo-European family of languages, including Persian

i·ras·ci·ble (i ras′ə b'l, ī-) *adj.* [< MFr. < LL. < L. *irasci*: see ff.] easily angered; quick-tempered —**i·ras′ci·bil′i·ty, i·ras′ci·ble·ness** *n.* —**i·ras′ci·bly** *adv.*

i·rate (ī rāt′) *adj.* [L. *iratus* < *irasci*, to be angry < *ira*, ire] angry; wrathful; incensed —**i·rate′ly** *adv.* —**i·rate′ness** *n.*

IRBM intermediate range ballistic missile

ire (īr) *n.* [< OFr. < L. *ira*] anger; wrath —**ire′ful** *adj.* —**ire′ful·ly** *adv.* —**ire′ful·ness** *n.*

i·ren·ic (ī ren′ik, ī rē′nik) *adj.* [Gr. *eirenikos* < *eiréné*, peace] promoting peace; pacific: also **i·ren′i·cal** —**i·ren′·i·cal·ly** *adv.*

ir·i·da·ceous (ir′ə dā′shəs, īr′-) *adj.* [Mod L. *iridaceus*] belonging to the iris family

ir·i·des·cent (ir′ə des′ənt) *adj.* [< L. *iris* (< Gr. *iris*), rainbow + -ESCENT] having or showing shifting changes in colour or an interplay of rainbowlike colours —**ir′i·des′·cence** *n.* —**ir′i·des′cent·ly** *adv.*

i·rid·i·um (i rid′ē əm, ī-) *n.* [ModL. < L. *iris* (< Gr. *iris*), rainbow: from the changing colour of some of its salts] a white, heavy, brittle, metallic chemical element found in platinum ores: alloys of iridium are used for pen points and bearings of watches: symbol, Ir; at. wt., 192.2; at. no., 77

i·ris (ī′ris) *n., pl.* **i′ris·es, ir·i·des** (ir′ə dēz′, ī′rə-) [L. < Gr. *iris*, rainbow] **1.** a rainbow **2.** the round, pigmented membrane surrounding the pupil of the eye **3.** a plant with sword-shaped leaves and showy flowers composed of three petals and three drooping sepals **4.** the flower of this plant

iris diaphragm a device consisting of thin, overlapping metal plates that can be adjusted to form an aperture of varying size for camera lenses, etc.

I·rish (ī′rish) *adj.* of Ireland, its people, their language, or culture —*n.* **1.** *same as* IRISH GAELIC **2.** the English dialect of Ireland —**the Irish** the people of Ireland —**I′rish·man** *n., pl.* **-men** —**I′rish·wom′an** *n.fem., pl.* **-wom′en**

Irish bridge a shallow stream or open drain crossing a road

IRIS

Irish bull *same as* BULL³
Irish coffee coffee made with Irish whiskey and cream
Irish Gaelic the Celtic language of Ireland
Irish setter any of a breed of setter with a coat of long, silky, reddish-brown hair
Irish stew a stew of mutton, potatoes, and onions
Irish terrier any of a breed of small, lean dog with a wiry, reddish coat
Irish wolfhound any of a breed of very large, heavy, powerful dog with a rough coat
i·ri·tis (ī rīt′is) *n.* [IR(IS) + -ITIS] inflammation of the iris of the eye
irk (urk) *vt.* [ME. *irken,* to be weary of] to annoy, disgust, irritate, tire out, etc.
irk·some (-səm) *adj.* that tends to irk; tiresome or annoying —**irk′some·ly** *adv.* —**irk′some·ness** *n.*
IRN, I.R.N. Independent Radio News
I.R.O. 1. Inland Revenue Office 2. International Refugee Organisation
i·ron (ī′ərn) *n.* see PLURAL, II, D, 3 [< OE. *iren, isern, isen* < Gmc.] 1. a white, malleable, ductile, metallic chemical element: it is the most common and important of all metals: symbol, Fe; at. wt., 55.847; at. no., 26 2. any tool, device, etc. made, or formerly made, of iron, as *a)* a device with a handle and flat undersurface, used, when heated, for pressing clothes or cloth *b)* a rodlike device with a brand at one end, heated for branding cattle: in full, **branding iron** 3. [*pl.*] *a)* iron shackles or chains *b)* stirrups 4. firm strength; power 5. *Golf* any of a set of numbered clubs with metal heads 6. a medicine containing iron 7. a leg-support for a malformed or paralysed limb —*adj.* 1. of or consisting of iron 2. like iron, as *a)* firm [an iron will] *b)* strong 3. cruel; merciless —*vt.* 1. to furnish or cover with iron 2. to press (clothes or cloth) with a hot iron —*vi.* to iron clothes or cloth —**have many** (or **several,** etc.) **irons in the fire** to be engaged in many (or several, etc.) activities —**iron out** to smooth out; eliminate —**strike while the iron is hot** to act at the opportune time
i·ron·bark (-bärk′) *n.* 1. any of several Australian eucalyptus trees with hard wood and hard, grey bark 2. the wood of any of these trees
i·ron·bound (-bound′) *adj.* 1. bound with iron 2. hard; rigid; unyielding; inflexible 3. edged with rocks or cliffs, as a coast
i·ron·clad (-klad′) *adj.* 1. covered or protected with iron 2. difficult to change or break [an *ironclad* agreement] —*n.* formerly, a warship armoured with thick iron plates
iron curtain 1. a barrier of secrecy and censorship regarded as isolating the Soviet Union and other countries in its sphere 2. any similar barrier
iron hand firm, rigorous, severe control —**i′ron·hand′ed** *adj.*
iron horse [Old Colloq.] a railway engine
i·ron·i·cal (ī ron′i k'l) *adj.* [< L. < Gr. < *eirōneia* (see IRONY) + -AL] 1. meaning the contrary of what is expressed 2. using or tending to use irony 3. directly opposite to what might be expected Also **i·ron′ic** —**i·ron′i·cal·ly** *adv.*
ironing board (or **table**) a cloth-covered board or stand on which clothes are ironed
i·ron·ist (ī′rə nist) *n.* a writer or speaker noted for his frequent use of irony
iron lung a large metal respirator enclosing all the body but the head, used for maintaining artificial respiration
Iron Maiden a former instrument of torture consisting of a case in the form of a woman, with spikes inside
i·ron·mas·ter (ī′ərnmäs′tər) *n.* a manufacturer of iron
i·ron·mon·ger (ī′ərn muŋ′gər) *n.* a dealer in hardware —**i′ron·mon′ger·y** *n.*
iron pyrites *same as* PYRITE
iron rations emergency food supplies, esp. for soldiers, etc. in action
i·ron·sides (-sīdz′) *n.pl.* [with *sing.* v.] *same as* IRONCLAD
i·ron·stone (-stōn′) *n.* 1. any rock rich in iron 2. a hard variety of white ceramic ware
i·ron·ware (-wer′) *n.* things made of iron
i·ron·weed (-wēd′) *n.* a plant of the composite family, with clusters of tubular, purple flowers
i·ron·wood (-wood′) *n.* 1. any of various trees with extremely hard wood 2. the wood
i·ron·work (-wurk′) *n.* articles or parts made of iron —**i′ron·work′er** *n.*
i·ron·works (-wurks′) *n.pl.* [often with *sing.* v.] a place where iron is smelted or heavy iron goods are made
i·ro·ny¹ (ī′rən ē) *n., pl.* **-nies** [< Fr. < L. < Gr. *eirōneia* < *eirōn,* dissembler in speech < *eirein,* to speak] 1. expression in which the intended meaning of the words is the direct opposite of their usual sense [the *irony* of calling a stupid plan "clever"] 2. a set of circumstances or a result that is the opposite of what might be expected [an *irony* that the fire station burned]
i·ron·y² (ī′ər nē) *adj.* of, like, or containing iron
ir·ra·di·ate (i rā′dē āt′; *for adj., usually* -it) *vt.* **-at′ed, -at′ing** [< L. pp. of *irradiare:* see IN-¹ & RADIATE] 1. to shine upon;

light up; make bright 2. to enlighten 3. to radiate; diffuse 4. to expose to or treat by exposing to X-rays, ultraviolet rays, etc. —*vi.* to emit rays; shine —*adj.* irradiated —**ir·ra′di·ance, ir·ra′di·an·cy** *n.* —**ir·ra′di·ant** *adj.* —**ir·ra′di·a′tion** *n.* —**ir·ra′di·a′tive** *adj.* —**ir·ra′di·a′tor** *n.*
ir·ra·tion·al (i rash′ən 'l) *adj.* 1. lacking the power to reason 2. senseless; unreasonable; absurd 3. *Math.* designating a real number not expressible as an integer or a quotient of two integers —**ir·ra′tion·al′i·ty** (-ə nal′ə tē) *n., pl.* **-ties** —**ir·ra′tion·al·ly** *adv.*
ir·re·claim·a·ble (ir′i klā′mə b'l) *adj.* that cannot be reclaimed —**ir′re·claim′a·bil′i·ty** *n.* —**ir′re·claim′a·bly** *adv.*
ir·rec·on·cil·a·ble (i rek′ən sīl′ə b'l, i rek′ən sīl′-) *adj.* that cannot be reconciled; that cannot be brought into agreement; incompatible —*n.* one who is irreconcilable and refuses to compromise —**ir·rec′on·cil′a·bil′i·ty** *n.* —**ir·rec′on·cil′a·bly** *adv.*
ir·re·cov·er·a·ble (ir′i kuv′ər ə b'l) *adj.* that cannot be recovered, rectified, or remedied; irretrievable —**ir′re·cov′·er·a·bly** *adv.*
ir·re·cu·sa·ble (ir′i kyōō′zə b'l) *adj.* [< Fr. or LL. < L. *in,* not + *recusare,* to refuse] that cannot be refused or rejected
ir·re·deem·a·ble (ir′i dēm′ə b'l) *adj.* 1. that cannot be bought back 2. that cannot be converted into coin, as certain kinds of paper money 3. that cannot be changed or reformed —**ir′re·deem′a·bly** *adv.*
ir·re·den·tist (ir′i den′tist) *n.* [< It. < (*Italia*) *irredenta,* unredeemed (Italy)] a person who advocates a policy of recovering territory formerly a part of his country; specif., [*usually* I-] a member of an Italian political party, after 1878, with such a policy —**ir′re·den′tism** *n.*
ir·re·duc·i·ble (ir′i dyōōs′ə b'l) *adj.* that cannot be reduced —**ir′re·duc′i·bil′i·ty** *n.* —**ir′re·duc′i·bly** *adv.*
ir·ref·ra·ga·ble (i ref′rə gə b'l) *adj.* [< LL. < L. *in-,* IN-² + *refragari,* to oppose] that cannot be refuted; indisputable —**ir·ref′ra·ga·bil′i·ty** *n.* —**ir·ref′ra·ga·bly** *adv.*
ir·re·fran·gi·ble (ir′i fran′jə b'l) *adj.* [IR- + REFRANGIBLE] 1. that cannot be broken or violated 2. that cannot be refracted
ir·ref·u·ta·ble (i ref′yoo tə b'l, ir′i fyōot′ə b'l) *adj.* that cannot be refuted or disproved —**ir·ref′u·ta·bil′i·ty** *n.* —**ir·ref′u·ta·bly** *adv.*
irreg. 1. irregular 2. irregularly
ir·reg·u·lar (i reg′yə lər) *adj.* 1. not conforming to established rule, method, usage, standard, etc.; out of the ordinary 2. immoral; lawless; disorderly 3. not straight or even; not symmetrical; not uniform in shape, design, etc. 4. uneven in occurrence; variable 5. *Gram.* not inflected in the usual way [*go* is an *irregular* verb] 6. *Mil.* not belonging to the regularly established army —*n.* a person or thing that is irregular —**ir·reg′u·lar′i·ty** *n., pl.* **-ties** —**ir·reg′u·lar·ly** *adv.*
ir·rel·e·vant (i rel′ə vənt) *adj.* not relevant; not pertinent; not to the point —**ir′rel′e·vance, ir·rel′e·van·cy** *n., pl.* **-cies** —**ir·rel′e·vant·ly** *adv.*
ir·re·li·gious (ir′i lij′əs) *adj.* 1. not religious 2. indifferent or hostile to religion 3. profane; impious —**ir′re·li′gion** *n.* —**ir′re·li′gion·ist** *n.* —**ir′re·li′gious·ly** *adv.*
ir·re·me·di·a·ble (ir′i mē′dē ə b'l) *adj.* that cannot be remedied; incurable —**ir′re·me′di·a·ble·ness** *n.* —**ir′re·me′·di·a·bly** *adv.*
ir·re·mis·si·ble (-mis′ə b'l) *adj.* not remissible; specif., *a)* that cannot be excused or pardoned *b)* that cannot be shirked —**ir′re·mis′si·bly** *adv.*
ir·re·mov·a·ble (-mōō′və b'l) *adj.* not removable —**ir′-re·mov′a·bil′i·ty** *n.* —**ir′re·mov′a·bly** *adv.*
ir·rep·a·ra·ble (i rep′ər ə b'l) *adj.* not reparable; that cannot be repaired, mended, remedied, etc. —**ir·rep′a·ra·bil′i·ty** *n.* —**ir·rep′a·ra·bly** *adv.*
ir·re·place·a·ble (ir′i plās′ə b'l) *adj.* not replaceable
ir·re·press·i·ble (-pres′ə b'l) *adj.* that cannot be repressed or restrained —**ir′re·press′i·bil′i·ty** *n.* —**ir′re·press′i·bly** *adv.*
ir·re·proach·a·ble (-prō′chə b'l) *adj.* blameless; faultless —**ir′re·proach′a·bil′i·ty, ir′re·proach′a·ble·ness** *n.* —**ir′-re·proach′a·bly** *adv.*
ir·re·sist·i·ble (-zis′tə b'l) *adj.* that cannot be resisted; too strong, fascinating, etc. to be withstood —**ir′re·sist′i·bil′i·ty, ir′re·sist′i·ble·ness** *n.* —**ir′re·sist′i·bly** *adv.*
ir·res·o·lute (i rez′ə lōōt′) *adj.* not resolute; wavering in decision or purpose —**ir·res′o·lute′ly** *adv.* —**ir·res′o·lute′-ness** *n.* —**ir·res′o·lu′tion** *n.*
ir·re·spec·tive (ir′i spek′tiv) *adj.* [Rare] showing disregard for persons or consequences —**irrespective of** regardless of —**ir′re·spec′tive·ly** *adv.*
ir·re·spon·si·ble (ir′i spon′sə b'l) *adj.* not responsible; specif., *a)* not accountable for actions *b)* showing the lack of a sense of responsibility —**ir′re·spon′si·bil′i·ty, ir′re·spon′-si·ble·ness** *n.* —**ir′re·spon′si·bly** *adv.*
ir·re·spon·sive (-siv) *adj.* not responsive —**ir′re·spon′-sive·ness** *n.*
ir·re·triev·a·ble (-trēv′ə b'l) *adj.* that cannot be retrieved,

recovered, restored, or recalled —**ir·re·triev′a·bil′i·ty** *n.* —**ir′re·triev′a·bly** *adv.*

ir·rev·er·ence (i rev′ər əns) *n.* 1. lack of reverence 2. an act or statement showing this —**ir·rev′er·ent** *adj.* —**ir·rev′er·ent·ly** *adv.*

ir·re·vers·i·ble (ir′i vur′sə b′l) *adj.* not reversible; specif., *a)* that cannot be repealed or annulled *b)* that cannot be run backwards, etc. —**ir′re·vers′i·bil′i·ty** *n.* —**ir′re·vers′i·bly** *adv.*

ir·rev·o·ca·ble (i rev′ə kə b′l) *adj.* that cannot be revoked or undone —**ir·rev′o·ca·bil′i·ty, ir·rev′o·ca·ble·ness** *n.* —**ir·rev′o·ca·bly** *adv.*

ir·ri·ga·ble (ir′i gə b′l) *adj.* that can be irrigated

ir·ri·gate (ir′ə gāt′) *vt.* -**gat′ed, -gat′ing** [< L. pp. of *irrigare* < *in-,* in + *rigare,* to water] 1. to supply (land) with water by means of artificial ditches, etc. 2. *Med.* to wash out (a cavity, wound, etc.) with water or other fluid —**ir′ri·ga′tion** *n.* —**ir′ri·ga′tive** *adj.* —**ir′ri·ga′tor** *n.*

ir·ri·ta·ble (ir′i tə b′l) *adj.* 1. easily annoyed or provoked; impatient 2. *Med.* excessively or pathologically sensitive to a stimulus 3. *Physiol.* able to respond to a stimulus —**ir′ri·ta·bil′i·ty, ir′ri·ta·ble·ness** *n.* —**ir′ri·ta·bly** *adv.*

ir·ri·tant (-tənt) *adj.* causing irritation —*n.* something causing irritation —**ir′ri·tan·cy** *n.*

ir·ri·tate (-tāt′) *vt.* -**tat′ed, -tat′ing** [< L. pp. of *irritare,* to excite] 1. to provoke to impatience or anger; annoy 2. to make (a part of the body) inflamed or sore 3. *Physiol.* to excite (an organ, muscle, etc.) to a characteristic action by a stimulus —**ir′ri·ta′tive** *adj.*

ir·ri·ta·tion (ir′ə tā′shən) *n.* 1. an irritating or being irritated 2. something that irritates 3. *Med.* an excessive response to stimulation in an organ or part; specif., a sore or inflamed condition

ir·rupt (i rupt′) *vi.* [< L. pp. of *irrumpere* < *in-,* in + *rumpere,* to break] 1. to burst violently (*into*) 2. *Ecol.* to increase abruptly in size of population —**ir·rup′tion** *n.* —**ir·rup′tive** *adj.*

is (iz) [OE.] *3rd pers. sing., pres. indic., of* BE

is. 1. island(s) 2. isle(s)

Isa., Is. Isaiah

i·sa·go·ge (ī′sə gō′jē) *n.* [L. < Gr., ult. < *eis-,* into + *agein,* to lead] an introduction, as to a branch of study —**i′sa·gog′ic** (-goj′ik) *adj.*

i·sa·tin (ī′sə tən, -tin) *n.* [< L. < Gr. *isatis, woad*] a reddish-orange, crystalline compound produced by the oxidation of indigo and used in making dyes

I.S.B.N. International Standard Book Number

is·chae·mi·a (is kē′mē ə) *n.* [ModL. < Gr. < *ischein,* to hold + *haima,* blood] a lack of blood supply in an organ or tissue —**is·chae′mic** *adj.*

is·chi·um (is′kē əm) *n., pl.* -**chi·a** (-ə) [L. < Gr. *ischion,* hip] the lowermost of the three sections of the hipbone

-ise (īz) *var. of* -IZE

is·en·trop·ic (īs′en trop′ik) *adj.* [ISO- + ENTROPY) + -IC] having or occurring at constant entropy

-ish (ish) 1. [OE. *-isc*] *a suffix meaning:* a) of or belonging to (a specified people) [*Spanish*] b) like or characteristic of [*devilish*] c) tending to, verging on [*bookish, knavish*] d) somewhat, rather [*tallish*] e) [Colloq.] approximately, about [*thirtyish*] 2. [< OFr.] *a suffix found in verbs of French origin* [*finish*]

i·sin·glass (ī′z′n glas′, -ziŋ-) *n.* [prob. < MDu. < *huizen,* sturgeon + *blas,* bladder] 1. a form of gelatin prepared from fish bladders, used as a clarifying agent and adhesive 2. mica, esp. in thin sheets

isl. *pl.* **isls.** 1. island 2. isle

Is·lam (is′läm, iz′-; -ləm, -lam; is läm′) *n.* [Ar. *islām,* lit., submission (to God's will)] 1. the Moslem religion, a monotheistic religion in which the supreme deity is Allah and the founder and chief prophet is Mohammed 2. Moslems collectively 3. all the lands in which the Moslem religion predominates —**Is·lam′ic** (-lam′-,-läm′-), **Is′·lam·it′ic** (-lə mit′ik) *adj.* —**Is′lam·ism** *n.* —**Is′·lam·ite′** (-lə mīt′) *n.*

Is·lam·ize (is′lə mīz′, iz′-) *vt., vi.* -**ized′, -iz′ing** to subject or adapt to Islam —**Is′lam·i·za′tion** *n.*

is·land (ī′lənd) *n.* [< ME. *iland* (respelled after unrelated ISLE) < OE. *igland,* lit., island land & *ealand,* lit., water land] 1. a land mass not as large as a continent, surrounded by water 2. anything like an island in position or isolation 3. *Anat.* a cluster of cells differing from surrounding tissue in formation, etc. —*vt.* 1. to make into or like an island 2. to intersperse as with islands

island authority a local government administrative area of Scotland

is·land·er (-ər) *n.* a native or inhabitant of an island

isle (īl) *n.* [< OFr. < ML. < L. *insula*] an island, esp. a small one —*vt.* **isled, isl′ing** *same as* ISLAND —*vi.* to live on an isle

is·let (ī′lit) *n.* a very small island

islets (or **islands**) **of Lang·er·hans** (läŋ′ər häns′, laŋ′ər hans′) [after P. *Langerhans* (1847–88), G.

histologist] irregular groups of endocrine cells in the pancreas: they produce insulin

ism (iz′m) *n.* a doctrine, theory, system, etc., esp. one whose name ends in *-ism*

-ism (iz′m; iz əm) [< OFr. & < L. *-isma* (< Gr. *-isma*) & *-ismus* (< Gr. *-ismos*)] *a suffix meaning:* 1. the act, practice, or result of [*terrorism*] 2. the condition of being [*pauperism*] 3. conduct or qualities characteristic of [*patriotism*] 4. the doctrine, school, or theory of [*socialism*] 5. devotion to [*nationalism*] 6. an instance, example, or peculiarity of [*witticism*] 7. an abnormal condition caused by [*alcoholism*]

is·n't (iz′′nt) is not

I.S.O. 1. Imperial Service Order 2. International Organization for Standardization

i·so- [< Gr. *isos,* equal] *a combining form meaning* equal, similar, alike, identical: also **is-**

i·so·bar (ī′sə bär′) *n.* [< prec. + Gr. *baros,* weight] 1. a line on a map connecting points on the earth's surface having equal barometric pressure 2. any of two or more forms of an atom having the same atomic weight but different atomic numbers —**i′so·bar′ic** (-bar′-ik) *adj.*

i·so·cheim (ī′sə-kim′) *n.* [< ISO- + Gr. *cheima,* winter] a line on a map connecting points on the earth's surface that have the same mean winter temperature

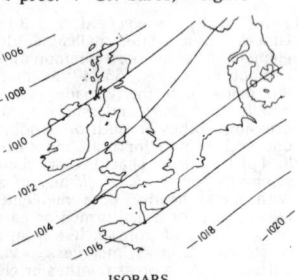

ISOBARS

i·soch·ro·nal (ī sok′rə n′l) *adj.* [< ModL. < Gr. < *isos,* equal + *chronos,* time + -AL] 1. equal in length of time 2. occurring at equal intervals of time Also **i·soch′ro·nous** —**i·soch′ro·nism** *n.*

i·so·cline (ī′sə klīn′) *n.* [< ISO- + Gr. *klinein,* to slope] an anticline or syncline so compressed that the strata on both sides of the axis dip equally in the same direction —**i′so·cli′nal, i′so·clin′ic** (-klin′ik) *adj.* —**i′so·cli′nal·ly** *adv.*

i·so·cy·clic (ī′sō sī′klik, -sik′lik) *adj.* [ISO- + CYCLIC] consisting of or being a ring of atoms of the same element

i·so·dy·nam·ic (ī′sō dī nam′ik) *adj.* [ISO- + DYNAMIC] 1. having equal force 2. connecting or showing points on the earth's surface having equal magnetic intensity

i·so·ge·o·therm (ī′sō jē′ə thurm′) *n.* [< ISO + GEO- + Gr. *thermē,* heat] an imaginary line connecting points beneath the earth's surface that have the same average temperature

i·so·gloss (ī′sə glos) *n.* [< ISO- + Gr. *glossa,* tongue] a line drawn round an area within which a common linguistic feature is found

i·so·gon·ic (ī′sə gon′ik) *adj.* [ISO- + -GON + -IC] 1. of or having equal angles 2. connecting or showing points on the earth's surface having the same magnetic declination —*n.* an isogonic line

i·so·hel (ī′sə hel′) *n.* [< ISO- + Gr. *helios,* the sun] a line on a map connecting points having equal hours of sunshine in a standard period

i·so·hy·et (ī′sō hī′ət) *n.* [< ISO- + Gr. *hyetos,* rain] a line on a map connecting points having equal amounts of rainfall

i·so·late (ī′sə lāt′, is′ə-; *for n., usually* -lit) *vt.* -**lat′ed, -lat′ing** [back-formation < *isolated* < It. < *isola* (< L. *insula*), island] 1. to set apart from others; place alone 2. *Chem.* to separate (an element or compound) in pure form from another compound or mixture 3. *Med.* to place (a patient with a contagious disease) apart from others to prevent the spread of infection —**i′so·la·ble** (-lə b′l) *adj.* —**i′so·la′tion** *n.* —**i′so·la′tor** *n.*

i·so·la·tion·ist (ī′sə lā′shən ist, is′ə-) *n.* a person who advocates isolation; specif., one who opposes the involvement of his country in international agreements, etc. —*adj.* of isolationists or their policy —**i′so·la′tion·ism** *n.*

i·so·mer (ī′sə mər) *n.* [< Gr. < *isos,* equal + *meros,* a part] 1. any of two or more chemical compounds having the same elements in the same proportion by weight but differing in properties because of differences in the structure of their molecules 2. *Physics* any of two or more nuclei possessing the same number of neutrons and protons, but having different radioactive properties —**i′so·mer′ic** (-mer′ik) *adj.* —**i·som′er·ism** (ī säm′ər iz′m) *n.*

i·som·er·ous (ī säm′ər əs) *adj.* [see ISOMER] *Bot.* having the same number of parts in each whorl

i·so·met·ric (ī′sə met′rik) *adj.* [< Gr. < *isos,* equal + *metron,* a measure + -IC] 1. of or having equality of measure: also **i′so·met′ri·cal** 2. of isometrics —*n.* [*pl.*] a method of physical exercise in which one set of muscles is briefly tensed in opposition to another set of muscles or to an immovable object —**i′so·met′ri·cal·ly** *adv.*

i·so·mor·phic (-môr′fik) *adj.* [ISO- + -MORPHIC] having similar or identical structure or form: also **i′so·mor′phous** (-fəs)

i·so·mor·phism (ī′sə môr′fiz'm) *n.* [ISO- + -MORPH + -ISM] 1. *Biol.* a similarity in structure of organisms belonging to different species 2. *Chem.* an identity or similarity in the crystalline form of substances of different elements but similar composition 3. *Math.* a one-to-one correspondence between groups —**i′so·morph′** *n.*

i·so·pleth (ī′sə pleth′) *n.* [< Gr. *isoplēthēs*, equal in number] the line connecting points on a graph or map that have equal or corresponding values with regard to certain variables

i·so·pod (-päd′) *n.* [ISO- + -POD] any of an order of crustaceans with a flat, oval body and seven pairs of similar legs

i·so·prene (ī′sə prēn′) *n.* [< ISO- + PR(OPYL) + -ENE] a colourless, volatile liquid, used in making synthetic rubber, resins, etc.

i·sos·ce·les (ī sos′ə lēz′) *adj.* [LL. < Gr. *isoskelēs* < *isos*, equal + *skelos*, a leg] designating a triangle with two equal sides

i·so·seis·mal (ī′sə sīz′m'l, -sīs-′) *adj.* [< ISO- + Gr. *seismos*, earthquake + -AL] 1. of equal intensity of earthquake shock 2. connecting or showing points of such equal intensity on the earth's surface

i·sos·ta·sy (ī sos′tə sē) *n.* [< ISO-+ Gr. *stasis*, a standing still] 1. a condition of equal pressure on every side 2. *Geol.* approximate equilibrium in large, equal areas of the earth's crust, preserved by the action of gravity upon the different substances in the crust in proportion to their densities

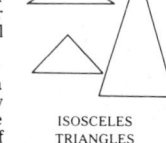

ISOSCELES TRIANGLES

i·so·there (ī′sə thir′) *n.* [ISO- + Gr. *theros*, summer] a line on a map connecting points that have the same mean summer temperature

i·so·therm (ī′sə thʉrm′) *n.* [< Fr. < *iso-*, ISO- + Gr. *thermē*, heat] a line on a map connecting points on the earth's surface having the same mean temperature or the same temperature at a given time

i·so·ther·mal (ī′sə thʉrm′l) *adj.* 1. of or indicating equality or constancy of temperature 2. of isotherms —*n.* same as ISOTHERM —**i′so·ther′mal·ly** *adv.*

i·so·ton·ic (-ton′ik) *adj.* [< Gr. < *isos*, equal + *tonos*, a stretching + -IC] 1. having equal tension 2. designating or of a salt solution having the same osmotic pressure as another with which it is compared —**i′so·ton′i·cal·ly** *adv.* —**i′so·to·nic′i·ty** (-tō nis′ə tē) *n.*

i·so·tope (ī′sə tōp′) *n.* [< ISO- + Gr. *topos*, place] any of two or more forms of an element having the same or very closely related chemical properties and the same atomic number but different atomic weights [uranium *isotopes* U 235, U 238, U 239] —**i′so·top′ic** (-top′ik, -tō′pik) *adj.* —**i·sot′ro·py** (-pē)

i·so·trop·ic (ī′sə trop′ik, -trō′pik) *adj.* [ISO- + -TROPIC] having physical properties, as conductivity, elasticity, etc., that are the same regardless of the direction of measurement: also **i·sot·ro·pous** (ī sot′rə pəs) —**i·sot′ro·py** (-pē)

I spy a children's guessing game —**I spy strangers** a demand for all but members and officials of the House of Commons to leave

Is·ra·el (iz′rē əl, -rä-) *n.* [< OFr. < LL. < Gr. < Heb. *yisrā′ēl*, lit. contender with God: from the name given to Jacob after he wrestled with an angel: Gen. 32:28] 1. the Jewish people, as descendants of Jacob 2. their ancient land 3. the modern Jewish state

Is·ra·el·ite (iz′rē ə līt′, -rä-; iz′rə līt′) *n.* any of the people of ancient Israel or their descendants; Jew; Hebrew —*adj.* of ancient Israel or the Israelites; Jewish: also **Is′ra·el·it′ish** (-līt′ish), **Is′ra·el·it′ic** (-līt′ik)

is·su·ance (ish′ōō wəns) *n.* an issuing; issue

is·sue (ish′ōō, is′yōō) *n.* [< OFr. pp. of *isser*, to go out < L. *exire* < *ex-*, out + *ire*, to go] 1. an outgoing; outflow 2. a place or means of going out; exit; outlet 3. a result; consequence 4. offspring; a child or children 5. profits, as from property; proceeds 6. a point or matter under dispute 7. a sending or giving out 8. all that is put forth and circulated at one time [the May *issue* of a magazine, an *issue* of bonds] 9. *Med.* a discharge of blood, pus, etc. —*vi.* -**sued**, -**su·ing** 1. to go, pass, or flow out; emerge 2. to be descended; be born 3. to be derived or result (*from* a cause) 4. to end or result (*in* an effect) 5. to come as revenue 6. to be published; be put forth and circulated —*vt.* 1. to let out; discharge 2. to give or deal out [to *issue* supplies] 3. to publish; put forth publicly or officially [to *issue* bonds, periodicals, an edict, etc.] —**at** (or **in**) **issue** in dispute; still to be decided —**join issue** to meet in conflict, argument, etc. —**take issue** to disagree —**is′-su·a·ble** *adj.* —**is′su·er** *n.*

-ist (ist, əst) [< OFr. < L. < Gr. *-istēs*] a suffix meaning: 1. a person who does, makes, or practises [*moralist, satirist*] 2. a person skilled in or occupied with [*chemist, violinist*] 3. an adherent of [*anarchist*]

isth·mi·an (is′mē ən) *adj.* of an isthmus —*n.* a native or inhabitant of an isthmus

isth·mus (is′məs, is′thməs) *n., pl.* -**mus·es**, -**mi** (-mī) [L. < Gr. *isthmos*, a neck] a narrow strip of land having water at each side and connecting two larger bodies of land

-is·tic (is′tik) [< MFr. < L. < Gr. *-istikos*, or in Eng. < -IST + -IC] a suffix used to form adjectives from nouns ending in -ISM and -IST [*realistic, artistic*]: also **-is′ti·cal**

is·tle (ist′lē) *n.* [< AmSp. < Nahuatl *ichtli*] a fibre obtained from certain tropical American plants, used for baskets, etc.

it¹ (it) *pron.* *for pl.* *see* THEY [OE. *hit*] the animal or thing under discussion *It* is used as: a) the subject of an impersonal verb [*it* is snowing] b) the grammatical subject of a clause of which the actual subject is a following clause, etc. [*it* is settled that he will go] c) an object of indefinite sense [to lord *it* over someone] d) the antecedent to a relative pronoun from which it is separated by a predicate [*it* is your car that I want] e) a reference to something indefinite but understood [*it's* all right, no harm was done] f) [Colloq.] an emphatic predicate pronoun referring to the person, thing, situation, etc. which is considered ultimate, final, or perfect [zero hour is here; this is *it*] —*n.* the player, as in the game of tag, who must do some specific thing 2. [Colloq.] charm; sex appeal —**that's it** [Colloq.] that is: a) the difficulty b) the end [that's *it* for today] c) exactly what is required —**with it** [Slang] alert, informed, or hip

it² (it) *n.* [contr. < *Italian*] [Colloq.] Italian vermouth [gin and *it*]

It., Ital. 1. Italian 2. Italic 3. Italy

I.T.A. Independent Television Authority

i.t.a. initial teaching alphabet

ital. italic (type)

I·tal·ian (i tal′yən) *adj.* of Italy, its people, their language, etc. —*n.* 1. a native or inhabitant of Italy 2. the Romance language of the Italians

I·tal·ian·ate (-it, -āt) *adj.* of Italian form, appearance, or character

I·tal·ic (i tal′ik) *adj.* 1. of ancient Italy, its people, etc. 2. designating or of the subfamily of the Indo-European languages that includes Latin and the Romance languages —*n.* the Italic languages collectively

i·tal·ic (i tal′ik, ī-) *adj.* [< its first use in an *Italian* edition of Virgil] designating or of a type in which the characters slant upward to the right, used variously, as to emphasize words [*this is italic type*] —*n.* [usually pl., sometimes with sing. v.] italic type or print

i·tal·i·cize (i tal′ə sīz′) *vt.* -**cized**′, -**ciz′ing** 1. to print in italics 2. to underscore (copy) to indicate it is to be printed in italics —**i·tal′i·ci·za′tion** *n.*

itch (ich) *vi.* [OE. *giccan*] 1. to feel an irritating sensation on the skin, with the desire to scratch 2. to have a restless desire —*n.* 1. an itching on the skin 2. a restless desire; hankering [an *itch* to travel] —**itching palm** greediness for money —**the itch** any of various skin disorders accompanied by severe irritation of the skin; specif., SCABIES

itch·y (-ē) *adj.* **itch′i·er**, **itch′i·est** like, feeling, or causing an itch —**itch′i·ly** *adv.* —**itch′i·ness** *n.*

-ite (it) [< OFr. or L. < Gr. *-itēs*] a suffix meaning: 1. a native or inhabitant of [*suburbanite*] 2. a descendant from [*Israelite*] 3. an adherent or member of [*Ludite*] 4. a commercially manufactured product [*dynamite*] 5. a fossil [*trilobite*] 6. a salt or ester of an acid whose name ends in -ous [*nitrite*] 7. a (specified) mineral or rock [*anthracite*]

i·tem (it′əm) *adv.* [< L. < *ita*, so, thus] also: used before each article in a series being enumerated —*n.* 1. an article; unit; separate thing 2. a bit of news or information

i·tem·ize (-īz′) *vt.* -**ized**′, -**iz′ing** to specify the items of; set down by items [*itemize* the bill] —**i′tem·i·za′tion** *n.*

it·er·ate (it′ə rāt′) *vt.* -**at′ed**, -**at′ing** [< L. pp. of *iterare* < *iterum*, again] to utter or do again or repeatedly —**it′-er·ant** (-ər ənt) *adj.* —**it′er·a′tion** *n.* —**it′er·a′tive** *adj.*

i·tin·er·an·cy (ī tin′ər ən sē, i-) *n.* 1. an itinerating or being itinerant 2. official work requiring constant travel from place to place or frequent change of residence Also **i·tin′-er·a·cy** (-ə sē)

i·tin·er·ant (-ənt) *adj.* [< LL. prp. of *itinerari*, to travel < L. *iter*, a walk] travelling from place to place or on a circuit —*n.* a person who travels from place to place —**i·tin′-er·ant·ly** *adv.*

i·tin·er·ar·y (ī tin′ə rər ē, i-) *adj.* [see prec.] of travelling, journeys, routes, or roads —*n., pl.* -**ar·ies** 1. a route 2. a record of a journey 3. a guidebook for travellers 4. a detailed plan or outline for a proposed journey

i·tin·er·ate (-rāt′) *vi.* -**at′ed**, -**at′ing** [< LL. pp. of *itinerari*: see ITINERANT] to travel from place to place or on a circuit —**i·tin′er·a′tion** *n.*

-i·tion (ish′ən) [< Fr. *-ition* or L. *-itio* (gen. *-itionis*)] *var.* of -ATION [*nutrition*]

-i·tious (ish′əs) [L. *-icius, -itius*] *a suffix that is used to form adjectives from nouns ending in* -ITION *and that means* of, having the nature of, characterized by [*nutritious*]

-i·tis (īt′əs, -is) [ModL. < L. < Gr. *-itis*] *a suffix meaning* inflammatory disease or inflammation of (a specified part or organ) [*sinusitis*]

it'll (it′'l) **1.** it will **2.** it shall

I.T.O. International Trade Organization

its (its) *pron.* that or those belonging to it —*possessive pronominal adj.* of, belonging to, or done by it

it's (its) **1.** it is **2.** it has

it·self (it self′) *pron.* a form of the 3rd pers. sing., neuter pronoun, used: *a)* as an intensive [*the work itself* is easy] *b)* as a reflexive [the dog bit *itself*] *c)* as a quasi-noun meaning "its real, true, or actual self" [the bird is not *itself* today]

it·ty-bit·ty (it′ē bit′ē) *adj.* [alteration < *little bit*] [Colloq.] very small; tiny Also **it·sy-bit·sy** (it′sē bit′sē)

I.T.U. International Telecommunications Union

ITV independent television

-i·ty (ə tē, i-) [< OFr. *-ité* < L. *-itas*] *a suffix meaning* state, condition [*chastity, possibility*]

IU, I.U. international unit(s)

IUD intrauterine (contraceptive) device: also **IUCD**

i.v. 1. initial velocity **2.** intravenous(ly)

I've (īv) I have

-ive (iv) [< Fr. *-if*, fem. *-ive* < L. *-ivus*] *a suffix meaning:* **1.** of, relating to, having the nature of [*substantive*] **2.** tending to [*creative*]

i·vied (ī′vēd) *adj.* covered or overgrown with ivy

i·vo·ry (ī′vər ē, īv′rē) *n., pl.* **-ries** [< OFr. < L. < *ebur* < Egypt. *āb, ābu*, elephant] **1.** the hard, white substance forming the tusks of elephants, walruses, etc. **2.** any substance like ivory **3.** the colour of ivory; creamy white **4.** a tusk of an elephant, etc. **5.** [*pl.*] things made of or suggesting ivory; specif., [Slang] *a)* piano keys *b)* teeth *c)* dice —*adj.* **1.** of or like ivory **2.** creamy-white

ivory nut *same as* VEGETABLE IVORY

ivory tower 1. a place of retreat from the world **2.** figuratively, a place of mental withdrawal from reality and action

i·vy (ī′vē) *n., pl.* **i′vies** [OE. *ifig*] **1.** a climbing plant with a woody stem and evergreen leaves **2.** any of various similar plants, as ground ivy, poison ivy, etc.

I.W.W., IWW Industrial Workers of the World

ix·i·a (ik′sē ə) *n.* [Mod. L. < Gr. *ixas*, birdlime: from the viscid nature of some of the species] any of a genus of South African plants of the iris family

ix·tle (iks′tlē, is′-) *n. same as* ISTLE

iz·ard (ī′zəd) *n.* [< Fr. *isard*] a brilliantly coloured variety of chamois, found in the Pyrenees

-i·za·tion (ə zā′shən, ī-) *a suffix used to form nouns from verbs ending in* -IZE [*realization*]

-ize (īz) [< OFr. < LL. < Gr. *-izein*] *a suffix meaning:* **1.** to cause to be or become; make [*democratize*] **2.** to become or become like [*crystallize*] **3.** to treat or combine with [*oxidize*] **4.** to engage in; act in a specified way [*soliloquize, theorize*]

iz·zard (iz′ərd) *n.* [var. of ZED] [Archaic or Dial.] the letter Z

J

J, j (jā) *n., pl.* **J's, j's 1.** the tenth letter of the English alphabet **2.** the sound of J or j

J *Physics* the symbol for joule

J. 1. Journal **2.** Judge **3.** Justice

jab (jab) *vt., vi.* **jabbed, jab′bing** [< ME. *jobben*, to peck] **1.** to poke or thrust, as with a sharp instrument **2.** to punch with short, straight blows —*n.* **1.** a quick thrust, blow, or punch **2.** [Colloq.] an injection with a hypodermic syringe

jab·ber (jab′ər) *vi., vt.* [prob. echoic] to speak or say quickly, incoherently, or nonsensically; chatter —*n.* fast, incoherent, nonsensical talk —**jab′ber·er** *n.*

jab·ber·wock·y (jab′ər wok′ē) *n.* [< *Jabberwocky*, a nonsense poem by Lewis Carroll] meaningless syllables that seem to make sense; gibberish

jab·i·ru (jab′ə rōō) *n.* [Port. < Tupi *jabirú*] **1.** a large, wading stork of tropical America **2.** a similar bird found in Africa

ja·bot (zha bō′, ja-) *n.* [Fr., bird's crop] a trimming or frill, as of lace, attached to the neck or front of a blouse, bodice, or shirt

jaç·a·na, ja·ca·na (zhä′sə nä′) *n.* [Port. < Tupi] any of several tropical and subtropical birds with long toes that enable them to walk on the floating leaves of water plants

jac·a·ran·da (jak′ə ran′də) *n.* [ModL. < Port. < Tupi] a tropical American tree with finely divided foliage and large clusters of lavender flowers

ja·cinth (jā′sinth, jas′inth) *n.* [< OFr. < L. *hyacinthus*: see HYACINTH] **1.** *same as* HYACINTH (sense 1 *b*) **2.** a reddish-orange colour

jack (jak) *n., pl.* for 4,5 **jacks, jack:** see PLURAL, II, D, 1 [< OFr. < LL. *Jacobus*, Jacob: a masculine name] **1.** [often J-] *a)* a man or boy; fellow *b)* a sailor **2.** *same as* BOOTJACK **3.** *a)* any of various devices used to lift or hoist something heavy a short distance [hydraulic *jack*, car *jack*] *b)* a device for turning a spit in roasting **4.** a male donkey **5.** any of various fishes, as the pickerel, pike, etc. **6.** a wooden bar attached to each key of a harpsichord, etc. that raises the plectrum when the key is depressed **7.** *Elec.* a plug-in receptacle used to make electric contact **8.** *Games a)* a playing card with a page boy's picture on it; knave *b)* any of the small pebbles or six-pronged metal pieces used in playing jacks: see JACKS *c)* in the game of bowls, the target ball **9.**

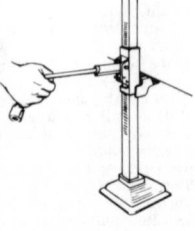

JACK (sense 3*a*)

Naut. a small flag flown on a ship's bow as a signal or to show nationality —*vt.* to raise by means of a jack —*adj. male:* of some animals —**before you can** (or **could**) **say Jack Robinson** suddenly; very quickly —**every man jack** everyone —**jack in** [Colloq.] to give up or abandon (an activity) —**jack up 1.** to raise by means of a jack **2.** [Colloq.] to raise (prices, salaries, etc.)

jack- [see prec.] *a combining form meaning:* **1.** male [*jackass*] **2.** large or strong [*jackboot*] **3.** boy; fellow: used in hyphenated compounds [*jack*-in-the-box]

jack·al (jak′ôl) *n., pl.* **-als, -al:** see PLURAL, II, D, 1 [< Turk. < Per. *shagāl* < Sans.] **1.** a yellowish-grey, meat-eating wild dog of Asia and N Africa, smaller than the wolf **2.** one who does dishonest or humiliating tasks for another

jack·a·napes (jak′ə nāps′) *n.* [< nickname of a 15th-c. Duke of Suffolk] **1.** formerly, a monkey **2.** a conceited, insolent fellow; saucy rascal

jack·a·roo, jack·e·roo (jak′ə rōō) *n., pl.* **-roos** [JACK-(KANG)AROO] [Aust.] a novice on a ranch or sheep station

jack·ass (jak′as′) *n.* [JACK- + ASS] **1.** a male donkey **2.** a stupid or foolish person; nitwit

jack·boot (-bōōt′) *n.* [JACK- + BOOT¹] **1.** a heavy, sturdy military boot that reaches above the knee **2.** oppressive, overbearing behaviour

jack·daw (-dô′) *n.* [JACK- + DAW] **1.** a European black bird related to the crow, but smaller **2.** *same as* GRACKLE (sense 1)

jack·et (jak′it) *n.* [< OFr. dim. of *jaque* < proper name *Jacques*] **1.** a short coat **2.** an outer covering; specif., *a) same as* DUST JACKET *b)* the insulating casing on a boiler, etc. *c)* the skin of a potato, etc. [potatoes cooked in their *jackets*] —*vt.* **1.** to put a jacket, or coat, on **2.** to cover with a casing, wrapper, etc.

Jack Frost frost or cold weather personified

jack-in-of·fice (jak′in of′is) *n., pl.* **jacks-**[see JACK-, 3] an official with a high opinion of his own importance

jack-in-the-box (jak′in *th*ə boks′) *pl.* **-box′es** a toy consisting of a box from which a little figure on a spring jumps up when the lid is lifted: also **jack′-in-a-box′**

Jack Ketch (kech) an official hangman

jack·knife (jak′nif′) *n., pl.* **-knives′** (-nīvz′) [JACK- + KNIFE] **1.** a large pocketknife **2.** a dive in which the diver keeps his knees unbent, touches his feet with his hands, and then straightens out just before plunging into the water —*vi.* **-knifed′, -knif′ing 1.** to bend at the middle as in jackknife dive **2.** to turn on the coupling so as to form a sharp angle with each of a said ofa vehicle and its trailer

jack-of-all-trades (jak′əv ôl′trādz′) *n., pl.* **jacks′-** [see

JACK-, 3] [*often* J-] a person who can do many kinds of work acceptably; handyman

jack-o'-lan·tern (jak'ə lan'tərn) *n.*, *pl.* **-terns** 1. a shifting, elusive light seen over marshes at night; will-o'-the-wisp 2. a hollow pumpkin, real or artificial, cut to look like a face and used as a lantern

jack plane a carpenter's tool, used for rough-planing timber

jack·pot (jak'pot') *n.* [JACK, *n.* 8 a + POT] 1. cumulative stakes in a poker game, played for only when some player has a pair of jacks or better to open 2. any cumulative stakes, as in a slot machine **—hit the jackpot** [Slang] 1. to win the jackpot 2. to attain the highest success

jack rabbit [JACK(ASS) + RABBIT: from its long ears] a large hare of W N. America, with long ears and strong hind legs

jacks (jaks) *n.pl.* [< JACKSTONE] [with *sing. v.*] a children's game in which pebbles or small, six-pronged metal pieces are tossed and picked up in various ways, esp. while bouncing a small ball

jack staff the staff from which the jack flies on a ship

jack·stone (jak'stōn') *n.* [for dial. *checkstone* < *check*, pebble] 1. *same as* JACK (*n.* 8 b) 2. [*pl.*, with *sing. v.*] *same as* JACKS

jack-straws (-strôz') *n.* [JACK- + STRAW] *same as* SPILLIKINS

jack-tar (-tär) *n.* [JACK + TAR²] [*often* J-] a sailor

Jac·o·be·an (jak'ə bē'ən) *adj.* [< *Jacobus*, Latinized form of *James*] 1. of James I of England 2. of the period in England when he was king (1603-1625) **—*n.*** a poet, diplomat, etc. of this period

Jac·o·bin (jak'ə bin) *n.* [< the Church of St. *Jacques* in Paris, the society's meeting place] 1. any member of a society of radical democrats in France during the Revolution of 1789 2. a political radical **—*adj.*** of the Jacobins: also **Jac'o·bin'ic**, **Jac'o·bin'i·cal** **—Jac'o·bin·ism** *n.* **—Jac'·o·bin·ize** *vt.*

Jac·o·bite (jak'ə bīt') *n.* [cf. JACOBEAN] a supporter of James II of England after his abdication, or of his descendants' claims to the throne **—Jac'o·bit'ic** (-bit'ik), **Jac'o·bit'i·cal** *adj.* **—Jac'o·bit·ism** *n.*

Ja·cob's ladder (jā'kəbz) 1. *Bible* the ladder to heaven that Jacob saw in a dream: Gen. 28:12 2. a ladder made of rope, wire, etc., used on ships 3. a plant with blue, bell-shaped flowers, and leaves with a ladder-like arrangement

Jacob's staff a surveyor's rod used to support a compass

Jac·quard (ja kärd') *n.* [after the Fr. inventor, J. M. *Jacquard* (1752-1834)] a loom (**Jacquard loom**) having an endless belt of cards punched with holes arranged to produce a figured weave (**Jacquard weave**)

jac·ta·tion (jak tā'shən) *n.* [L. *jactatio*, a throwing, boasting < *jactare*: see JET¹] 1. the act of bragging 2. *Med. same as* JACTITATION

jac·ti·ta·tion (jak'ti tā'shən) *n.* [ML. *jactitatio* < L. *jactitare*, to utter, tell in public < *jactare*, to throw: see JET¹] 1. the act of bragging 2. a false boast or claim that tends to harm another person 3. *Med.* restless tossing or jerking of body in severe illness

jade¹ (jād) *n.* [Fr. < Sp. < *piedra de ijada*, stone of the side: from the notion that it cured pains in the side] 1. a hard stone, usually green, used in jewellery, carvings, etc. 2. a green colour of medium hue **—*adj.*** 1. made of jade 2. green like jade

jade² (jād) *n.* [< ON. *jalda*, a mare < Finn.] 1. a horse, esp. a worn-out, worthless one 2. a loose or disreputable woman 3. [Now Rare] a saucy young woman **—*vt., vi.*** 1. to make or become tired, weary, or worn-out **—jad'ish** *adj.*

jad·ed (jā'did) *adj.* 1. tired; worn-out; wearied 2. satiated **—jad'ed·ly** *adv.* **—jad'ed·ness** *n.*

jade·ite (jā'dīt) *n.* [JAD(E)¹ + -ITE] a hard, translucent, complex silicate; a variety of jade

‡**j'a·doube** (zhä doōb') *interj.* [Fr., I adjust] *Chess* a player's warning to an opponent that he is about to adjust a piece, but not to move it

Jaf·fa (jaf'ə) *n.* [after *Jaffa*, seaport in Israel] a kind of large orange or grapefruit with a thick skin, grown in Israel

jag¹ (jag) *n.* [ME. *jagge*] 1. a sharp, toothlike projection 2. [Archaic] a notch or pointed tear, as in cloth **—*vt.*** **jagged**, **jag'ging** 1. to notch or pink (cloth, etc.) 2. to tear raggedly

jag² (jag) *n.* [< ?] [Slang] 1. an intoxicated condition due to alcohol or drugs 2. a drunken spree 3. a period of uncontrolled activity [a crying *jag*]

jag·ged (jag'id) *adj.* having sharp projecting points or notches **—jag'ged·ly** *adv.* **—jag'ged·ness** *n.*

jag·ger·y (jag'ər ē) *n.* [Anglo-Ind. < Hind. *jāgri* < Sans. *śarkarā*, sugar] a dark, crude sugar from the sap of certain species of palm trees

jag·uar (jag'yoo wər, -wär) *n.*, *pl.* **-uars, -uar**: see PLURAL, II, D, 1 [Port. < Tupi] a large cat, yellowish with black spots, found from SW U.S. to Argentina: it is similar to the leopard, but larger

jai a·lai (hī'lī', hī'ə lī') [Sp. < Basque *jai*, celebration + *alai*, merry] a Latin American game like handball, played

with a curved basket fastened to the arm, for catching and hurling the ball

jail (jāl) *n.* [< OFr. *gaole* < LL. *caveola*, dim. of L. *cavea*, a cage] 1. a building for confining those awaiting trial or convicted of offences 2. imprisonment **—*vt.*** to put or keep in jail

jail·bird (-bʉrd') *n.* [Colloq.] 1. a prisoner in a jail 2. a person often put in jail

jail·break (-brāk') *n.* a breaking out of jail

jail·er, jail·or (-ər) *n.* a person in charge of a jail or of prisoners

jail fever typhus, formerly common in jails

Jain (jīn) *n.* [< Hindi < Sans. *jina*, saint] a believer in Jainism **—*adj.*** of the Jains or their religion Also **Jai·na** (jī'-nə), **Jain'ist**

Jain·ism (jīn'iz'm) *n.* a Hindu religion founded in the 6th cent. B.C.: it emphasizes asceticism and reverence for all living things

jake (jāk) *adj.* [< ?] [Aust. Slang] satisfactory; ready; all right **—she's jake** everything is all right

jal·ap (jal'əp) *n.* [Fr. < Sp. < *Jalapa*, city in Mexico] 1. the dried root of a Mexican plant, formerly used as a purgative 2. the plant

ja·lop·y (jə lop'ē) *n.*, *pl.* **-lop'ies** [< ?] [Slang] an old, ramshackle motor car

jal·ou·sie (jal'ə sē') *n.* [Fr. < OFr. *gelosie*, jealousy (see JEALOUS)] a window, blind, or door formed of adjustable, horizontal slats of wood, metal, or glass, etc. for regulating the air or light entering

jam¹ (jam) *vt.* **jammed**, **jam'ming** [< ?] 1. to squeeze into or through a confined space 2. to bruise or crush 3. to push or crowd 4. to pack full or tight 5. to fill or block (a passageway, etc.) by crowding in 6. to wedge or make stick so that it cannot move or work 7. to make (radio or radar signals) unintelligible, as by sending out others on the same wavelength **—*vi.*** 1. to become wedged or stuck fast, esp. so as to become unworkable 2. to push against one another in a confined space 3. [Slang] *Jazz* to improvise **—*n.*** 1. a jamming or being jammed 2. a group of persons or things blocking a passageway, etc. [a traffic *jam*] 3. [Colloq.] a difficult situation 4. *same as* JAM SESSION **—jam on** to apply or activate suddenly [to *jam* on the brakes]

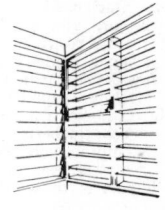

JALOUSIES

jam² (jam) *n.* [< ? prec.] a food made by boiling fruit with sugar to a thick mixture **—jam tomorrow** a promise of some pleasant future event that often does not occur

jamb (jam) *n.* [< OFr. *jambe* < LL. *gamba*, a leg] a side post of an opening for a door, window, etc.

jam·ba·lay·a (jum'bə lī'ə) *n.* [Am.Fr. < ModPr. *jambalaia*] a Creole stew made of rice and shrimp, oysters, crabs, ham, chicken, etc.

jam·bo·ree (jam'bə rē') *n.* [< ?] 1. [Colloq.] *a)* a boisterous party or revel *b)* a gathering with planned entertainment 2. a national or international assembly of boy scouts

jam·my (jam'ē) *adj.* 1. of, like, or smeared with jam 2. [Slang] lucky; excellent [*jammy* beggar]

jam·packed (jam'pakt') *adj.* tightly packed

jam session an informal gathering of jazz musicians to play improvisations

Jan. January

jan·gle (jaŋ'g'l) *vi.* **-gled**, **-gling** [< OFr. *jangler*] 1. to make a harsh, inharmonious sound, as of a bell out of tune 2. to quarrel noisily **—*vt.*** 1. to utter in a harsh, inharmonious manner 2. to cause to make a harsh sound 3. to irritate very much [to *jangle* one's nerves] **—*n.*** 1. noisy talk or arguing 2. a harsh sound **—jan'gler** *n.*

jan·i·tor (jan'i tər) *n.* [L., doorkeeper < *janua*, door] the caretaker of a building, who does routine maintenance **—jan'i·to'ri·al** (-ə tôr'ē əl) *adj.*

jan·i·zar·y (jan'ə zər ē) *n.*, *pl.* **-zar·ies** [< Fr. < It. < Turk. < *yeni*, new + *cheri*, soldiery] [*often* J-] 1. a Turkish soldier, orig. one in the former sultan's guard 2. any very loyal supporter Also **jan'is·sar·y** (-sər ē)

Jan·sen·ism (jan's'n iz'm) *n.* [after Cornelis *Jansen* (1585-1638), Du. R.C. theologian] the rigorous doctrines of Cornelis Jansen, who believed in predestination, denied free will, and held that man, though depraved in nature, is unable to resist God's grace **—Jan'sen·ist** *n., adj.* **—Jan'·sen·is'tic** *adj.*

Jan·u·ar·y (jan'yoo wər ē) *n.*, *pl.* **-ar·ies** [< L. *Januarius* (*mensis*), (the month) of Janus] the first month of the year, having 31 days: abbrev. **Jan.**

ja·pan (jə pan') *n.* [orig. from Japan] 1. a varnish giving a hard, glossy finish 2. objects decorated and varnished in the Japanese style **—*vt.*** **-panned'**, **-pan'ning** to varnish with japan

Jap·a·nese (jap'ə nēz') *adj.* of Japan, its people, language, culture, etc. —*n.* **1.** *pl.* **-nese**′ a native of Japan **2.** the language of Japan

Japanese cherry a flowering cherry tree with pink or white flowers

Japanese quince a spiny plant of the rose family, with pink or red flowers and green fruit

Japanese stranglehold a wrestling hold in which an opponent's arms are used to exert pressure on his windpipe

jape (jāp) *vi.* **japed, jap′ing** [ME. *japen*] **1.** to joke; jest **2.** to play tricks —*vt.* [Now Rare] to make fun of —*n.* **1.** a joke or jest **2.** a trick —**jap′er·y** *n., pl.* **-er·ies**

ja·pon·i·ca (jə pon′i kə) *n.* [ModL., fem. of *Japonicus*, of Japan < *Japonia*, Japan < Fr. *Japon*] *a popular name for* JAPANESE QUINCE, CAMELLIA, etc.

jar¹ (jär) *vi.* **jarred, jar′ring** [ult. echoic] **1.** to make a harsh sound; grate **2.** to have a harsh, irritating effect (*on* one) **3.** to vibrate from a sudden impact **4.** to clash, disagree, or quarrel —*vt.* **1.** to make vibrate by sudden impact **2.** to cause to give a harsh or discordant sound **3.** to jolt or shock —*n.* **1.** a harsh, grating sound **2.** a vibration due to a sudden impact **3.** a jolt or shock **4.** a sharp clash or quarrel

jar² (jär) *n.* [Fr. *jarre* < OPr. or Sp. < Ar. *jarrah*, earthen water container] **1.** a container made of glass, stone, or earthenware, with a large opening and no spout **2.** as much as a jar will hold: also **jar′ful′ 3.** [Colloq.] a glass or drink of beer, etc.

jar³ (jär) *n.* [see AJAR¹] [Archaic] a turn: now only in **on the jar,** ajar; partly open

jar·di·nière (jär′dən ir′; *Fr.* zhàr dē nyer′) *n.* [< Fr. < *jardin,* a garden] **1.** an ornamental bowl, pot, or stand for flowers or plants **2.** a garnish for meats, of several vegetables cooked separately

jar·gon (jär′gən) *n.* [MFr., a chattering] **1.** incoherent speech; gibberish **2.** a language or dialect that seems incomprehensible or outlandish to one **3.** a hybrid language or dialect; esp., pidgin **4.** the specialized vocabulary and idioms of those in the same work, profession, etc., as of sports writers: see SLANG —**jar′gon·is′tic** *adj.*

jarl (yärl) *n.* [ON., a man of noble birth] *Medieval History* a Scandinavian chieftain or great noble —**jarl′dom** *n.*

jar·rah (ja′rə) *n.* [< Abor.] **1.** a eucalyptus tree native to Australia **2.** the hard, durable wood of this tree

jas·mine, jas·min (jaz′min, jas′-) *n.* [< Fr. < Ar. < Per. *yāsamīn*] **1.** a tropical and subtropical plant of the olive family, with fragrant flowers of yellow, red, or white **2.** any of several other similar plants with fragrant flowers

jas·pé (jas′pā) *adj.* [Fr., p.p. of *jasper,* marble] like jasper; mottled —*n.* a cotton cloth of shaded effect used for bedcovers, curtains, etc.

jas·per (jas′pər) *n.* [< MFr. < L. < Gr. *iaspis*] **1.** an opaque variety of coloured quartz, usually reddish, yellow, or brown **2.** *Bible* a precious stone, probably an opaque green quartz

ja·to, JA·TO (jā′tō) *n.* [*j*(et)-*a*(ssisted) *t*(ake)o(ff)] an aeroplane takeoff assisted by small, solid-propellant rockets

jaun·dice (jôn′dis) *n.* [< OFr. *jaunisse,* ult. < L. *galbinus,* greenish yellow < *galbus,* yellow] **1.** *a)* a condition in which the eyeballs, skin, and urine become abnormally yellow as a result of bile pigments in the blood *b)* popularly, a disease causing this, as hepatitis **2.** bitterness or prejudice caused by jealousy, envy, etc. —*vt.* **-diced, -dic·ing 1.** to cause to have jaundice **2.** to make bitter or prejudiced through jealousy, envy, etc.

jaunt (jônt) *vi.* [< ?] to take a short trip for pleasure —*n.* such a trip; excursion

jaunting car a light, two-wheeled cart used in Ireland, with seats on both sides

jaun·ty (-ē) *adj.* **-ti·er, -ti·est** [< Fr. *gentil,* genteel] **1.** dapper; chic **2.** gay and carefree; sprightly; perky —**jaun′-ti·ly** *adv.* —**jaun′ti·ness** *n.*

Ja·va man (jä′və) a type of primitive man (*Homo erectus*) known from fossil remains found in Java

Jav·a·nese (jäv′ə nēz′) *adj.* of Java, its people, etc. —*n.* **1.** *pl.* **-nese**′ a native or inhabitant of Java **2.** the Indonesian language of Java

jav·e·lin (jav′lin, jav′ə lin) *n.* [MFr. *javeline,* fem. dim. < *javelot,* a spear] **1.** a light spear for throwing **2.** a pointed wooden or metal shaft, about 260 cm long, thrown for distance as a field event (**javelin throw**) in athletics

jaw (jô) *n.* [< ? OFr. *joue,* cheek] **1.** either of the two bony parts that hold the teeth and frame the mouth **2.** either of two parts that open and close to grip or crush something, as in a monkey wrench or vice **3.** [*pl.*] *a)* the mouth *b)* the entrance of a canyon, valley, etc. **4.** [*pl.*] something grasping or imminent [the *jaws* of death] **5.** [Slang] talk; esp., abusive or boring talk —*vi.* [Slang] to talk, esp. in a boring or abusive way —*vt.* [Slang] to scold or reprove

jaw·bone (-bōn′) *n.* a bone of a jaw, esp. of the lower jaw

jaw·break·er (-brā′kər) *n.* **1.** a hard, usually round sweet **2.** [Slang] a word that is hard to pronounce

jay (jā) *n.* [< OFr. *gai* < LL. *gaius,* a jay] **1.** any of several

birds of the crow family **2.** [Chiefly U.S.] *same as* BLUE JAY **3.** [Colloq.] a stupid or foolish person

jay·walk (jā′wôk′) *vi.* [JAY, 3 + WALK] [Colloq.] to walk in or across a street carelessly without obeying traffic rules and signals —**jay′walk′er** *n.* —**jay′walk′ing** *n.*

jazz (jaz) *n.* [< ? Creole patois *jass,* sexual term] **1.** a kind of music characterized by syncopation, rubato, melodic variations, and unusual tonal effects on the saxophone, clarinet, trumpet, trombone, etc. **2.** loosely, any popular dance music **3.** [Slang] remarks, acts, etc. regarded as hypocritical, tiresome, etc. —*adj.* of, in, or like jazz —*vt.* **1.** to play or arrange as jazz **2.** [Slang] to enliven or embellish (usually with *up*) —**jazz′i·ly** *adv.* —**jazz′i·ness** *n.* —**jazz′y** *adj.* **-i·er, -i·est**

jazz·band (-band′) *n.* a group of jazz musicians playing together, esp. a group containing players of wind and brass instruments

jazz·man (jaz′man′) *n., pl.* **-men** (-men′) a jazz musician

jeal·ous (jel′əs) *adj.* [< OFr. *gelos* < ML. *zelosus*: see ZEAL] **1.** very watchful or careful in guarding or keeping [*jealous* of one's rights] **2.** *a)* resentfully suspicious, as of a rival [a husband *jealous* of other men] *b)* resentfully envious *c)* resulting from such feelings [a *jealous* rage] **3.** [Now Rare] requiring exclusive loyalty [a *jealous* God] —**jeal′-ous·ly** *adv.* —**jeal′ous·ness** *n.*

jeal·ous·y (-ē) *n., pl.* **-ous·ies 1.** the quality or condition of being jealous **2.** an instance of this; jealous feeling

jean (jēn) *n.* [< OFr. *Janne* < ML. < L. *Genua,* Genoa] **1.** a durable, twilled cotton cloth, used for work clothes and casual wear **2.** [*pl.*] trousers of this material, often blue, or of denim

jeep (jēp) *n.* [after a creature in a comic strip by E. C. Segar (1894-1938)] a small, rugged, military automotive vehicle with a 1/4-ton capacity and a four-wheel drive —[J-] a *trademark for* a similar vehicle for civilian use

jee·pers (jē′pərz) *interj.* [altered < *Jesus*] a mild exclamation of surprise, etc.

jeer (jir) *vt., vi.* [< ? CHEER] to make fun of (a person or thing) in a rude, sarcastic manner; mock; scoff (at) —*n.* a jeering remark; sarcastic or derisive comment —**jeer′er** *n.* —**jeer′ing·ly** *adv.*

je·had (ji had′) *n. same as* JIHAD

Je·ho·vah (ji hō′və) [transliteration of Heb. sacred name for God] God; (the) Lord

Jehovah's Witnesses a proselytizing Christian sect founded by Charles T. Russell (1852-1916)

je·hu (jē′hyōō) *n.* [< *Jehu* in the Bible: II Kings 9] [Colloq.] a fast, reckless driver: a humorous usage

je·june (ji jōōn′) *adj.* [L. *jejunus,* empty] **1.** not nourishing **2.** not interesting or satisfying; dull **3.** not mature; childish —**je·june′ly** *adv.* —**je·june′ness** *n.*

je·ju·num (ji jōō′nəm) *n., pl.* **-na** (-nə) [< L.: see JEJUNE] the middle part of the small intestine, between the duodenum and the ileum —**je·ju′nal** *adj.*

Jek·yll and Hyde (jek′l'n hid′) [< *The Strange Case of Dr. Jekyll and Mr. Hyde,* novel by R. L. Stevenson] a person with two distinct personalities, esp. one good and one evil

jell (jel) *vi., vt.* [back-formation < JELLY¹] **1.** to become or make into jelly **2.** [Colloq.] to take or give definite form; crystallize [the plans didn't *jell*]

jel·la·ba (jə la′bə) *n.* [Ar. *jallabah*] a long, loose, outer garment worn by many Arab men

jel·li·fy (jel′ə fī′) *vt., vi.* **-fied′, -fy′ing** to change into jelly —**jel′li·fi·ca′tion** *n.*

jel·ly¹ (jel′ē) *n., pl.* **-lies** [< OFr. pp. of *geler* < L. *gelare,* to freeze] **1.** a soft, partially transparent, gelatinous food resulting from the cooling of fruit juice boiled with sugar, or of meat juice cooked down **2.** any substance like this —*vt.* **-lied, -ly·ing 1.** to make into jelly **2.** to coat, fill, or serve with jelly —*vi.* to become jelly —**jel′ly·like′** *adj.*

jel·ly² (jel′ē) *n.* [Slang] *short for* GELIGNITE

jel·ly·ba·by (jel′ē bā′bē) *n., pl.* **-bies** a small, baby-shaped gelatinous sweet

jelly bomb a bomb made from gelignite

jel·ly·fish (-fish′) *n., pl.* **-fish′, -fish′es:** see FISH **1.** an invertebrate sea animal with a body made up largely of jellylike substance and shaped like an umbrella: it has long, hanging tentacles with stinging cells on them **2.** [Colloq.] a weak-willed person

jem·my (jem′ē) *n., pl.* **-mies** [< dim. of *James,* a masculine name] a short crowbar, used by burglars to pry open windows, etc. —*vt.* **-mied, -my·ing** to pry open with a jemmy or similar tool

jen·net (jen′it) *n.* [< MFr. < Sp. *jinete,* horseman < Ar. *Zenāta,* a tribe of Barbary] any of a breed of small Spanish horses

jen·ny (jen′ē) *n., pl.* **-nies** [< *Jenny,* a feminine name] **1.** *short for*

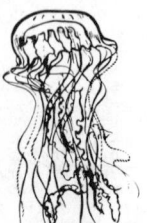

JELLYFISH
(to 40 cm long)

SPINNING JENNY **2.** *a)* the female of some birds [a *jenny wren*] *b)* a female donkey

jeop·ard·ize (jep′ər dīz′) *vt.* **-ized′, -iz′ing** to put in jeopardy; risk loss, failure, etc. of; endanger

jeop·ard·y (-dē) *n., pl.* **-ard·ies** [< OFr. *jeu parti*, lit., a game with even chances, ult. < L. *jocus*, a game + pp. of *partire*, to divide] **1.** great danger; peril **2.** *Law* the situation of an accused person on trial for a crime

je·quir·i·ty (ji kwir′ə tē) *n., pl.* **-ties** [Fr. *jéquirity* < Tupi-Guarani] an Indian shrub with poisonous red and black seeds used for ornaments and in medicine

Jer. Jeremiah

jer·bil (jur′b'l) *n.* same as GERBIL

jer·bo·a (jər bō′ə) *n.* [Ar. *yarbū*] any of various small, nocturnal, leaping rodents of N Africa and Asia, with very long hind legs

jer·e·mi·ad (jer′ə mī′əd) *n.* a lamentation or tale of woe: in allusion to the *Lamentations of Jeremiah*

jerk¹ (jurk) *vt.* [< ?] to pull, twist, push, or throw with a sudden, sharp movement —*vi.* **1.** to move with a jerk or in jerks **2.** to twitch —*n.* **1.** a sharp, abrupt pull, twist, push, etc. **2.** a sudden muscular contraction caused by a reflex action **3.** [Chiefly U.S. Slang] a person regarded as stupid, foolish, etc.

jerk² (jurk) *vt.* [altered (after prec.) < Sp. *charqui* < Quechua] to preserve (meat) by slicing into strips and drying in the sun

jer·kin (jur′kin) *n.* [< ?] **1.** a closefitting, sleeveless jacket of a kind worn in the 16th and 17th cent. **2.** a sleeveless jacket or waistcoat

jerk·y (-ē) *adj.* **jerk′i·er, jerk′i·est 1.** characterized by jerks; making sudden starts and stops; spasmodic **2.** [U.S. Slang] stupid, dull, foolish, etc. —**jerk′i·ly** *adv.* —**jerk′i·ness** *n.*

jer·o·bo·am (jer′ə bō′əm) *n.* [< *Jeroboam* in the Bible: 1 Kings 11:26-14:20] a large wine bottle, esp. for champagne

Jer·ry (jer′ē) *n.* [< GERMAN] [Slang] **1.** a German, esp. a German soldier **2.** the Germans collectively

jer·ry (jer′ē) *n.* [< *Jeremiah*] [Slang] a chamber pot

jer·ry-built (jer′ē bilt′) *adj.* [prob. < name *Jerry*, infl. by JURY²] built poorly, of cheap materials

jer·ry·man·der (jer′i man′dər) *vt.* see GERRYMANDER

Jer·sey (jur′zē) *n., pl.* **-seys** [after *Jersey*, in the Channel Islands] **1.** any of a breed of small, reddish-brown dairy cattle, originally from Jersey **2.** [**j-**] *a)* a soft, elastic, knitted cloth *b)* any closefitting, knitted upper garment

Je·ru·sa·lem artichoke (jə rōō′sə ləm) [altered (after *Jerusalem*) < It. *girasole*, sunflower] **1.** a tall N. American sunflower with edible potatolike tubers **2.** such a tuber

jess (jes) *n.* [< OFr. *gets*, pl. < L. *jactus*, a casting] a strap for a falcon's leg, with a ring for attaching a leash —*vt.* to fasten jesses on

jes·sa·mine (jes′ə min) *n.* same as JASMINE

Jes·se window (jes′ē) a stained glass window representing the descent of Christ from Jesse

jest (jest) *n.* [OFr. *geste*, an exploit < L. pp. of *gerere*, to perform] **1.** a mocking remark; gibe; taunt **2.** a joke or humorous remark **3.** mere fun; joking [said in *jest*] **4.** something to be laughed at or joked about —*vi.* **1.** to jeer; mock **2.** to be playful in speech and actions; joke

jest·er (-ər) *n.* one who jests; esp., a professional fool employed by a medieval ruler to amuse him

Jes·u·it (jezh′ōō wit, jez′-; -yōō-) *n.* **1.** a member of the Society of Jesus, a Roman Catholic religious order for men founded by Ignatius Loyola in 1534 **2.** a dissembler or equivocator —**Jes′u·it′i·cal** *adj.*

Je·sus (jē′zəs) [LL. *Iesus* < Gr. *Iēsous* < Heb. *yēshū′a*, contr. of *yehōshu′a*, help of Jehovah] c. 8-4 B.C.-29? A.D. (see CHRISTIAN ERA): founder of the Christian religion: also called **Jesus Christ, Jesus of Nazareth**: see also CHRIST

jet¹ (jet) *vt., vi.* **jet′ted, jet′ting** [< MFr. *jeter*, ult. < L. *jactare*, freq. of *jacere*, to throw] **1.** to spout, gush, or shoot out in a stream **2.** to travel or convey by jet aircraft —*n.* **1.** a stream of liquid or gas emitted or forced out, as from a spout **2.** a spout or nozzle for emitting a jet **3.** a jet-propelled aeroplane: in full, **jet (aero)plane** —*adj.* **1.** jet-propelled **2.** of jet propulsion or jet-propelled aircraft [the *jet* age]

jet² (jet) *n.* [< OFr. < L. < Gr. *gagatēs*, jet < *Gagas*, town in Asia Minor] **1.** a hard, black variety of lignite: sometimes used in jewellery **2.** a deep, lustrous black —*adj.* **1.** made of jet **2.** black like jet

jet belt a belt equipped with a small jet engine and flying gear, that can be used by one person: also **jet flying belt**

jet-black (-blak′) *adj.* glossy black, like jet

je·té (zhə tā′) *n.* [Fr., pp. of *jeter*, to throw] *Ballet* a spring from one foot to the other, made with a kicking movement of the leg

jet engine an engine, esp. fitted to aircraft, that uses the principles of jet propulsion

jet lag a disruption of circadian rhythms, associated with high-speed travel by jet aircraft

jet-pro·pelled (-prə peld′) *adj.* driven by jet propulsion

jet propulsion a method of propelling aircraft, boats, etc. by the reaction caused when gases are emitted under pressure through a rear vent or vents

jet·sam (jet′səm) *n.* [var. of JETTISON] **1.** that part of the cargo thrown overboard to lighten a ship in danger: cf. FLOTSAM **2.** such discarded cargo washed ashore **3.** discarded things

jet set a social set of rich, fashionable people who travel widely in pursuit of pleasure

jet stream 1. any of several bands of high-velocity winds moving from west to east around the earth at altitudes of from 13 to 16 km **2.** the stream of exhaust from a rocket engine

jet·ti·son (jet′ə s'n, -z'n) *n.* [< Anglo-Fr. < OFr. *getaison* < L. < *jactare*, to throw] **1.** a throwing overboard of goods to lighten a ship, aircraft, etc. in an emergency **2.** same as JETSAM —*vt.* **1.** to throw (goods) overboard **2.** to discard (something)

jet·ton (jet′ən) *n.* [Fr. < MFr. < *jeter*, to calculate, lit., to throw] a counter or token, esp. a chip used to represent money in gambling games: also **jet′on**

jet·ty (jet′ē) *n., pl.* **-ties** [< OFr. *jetée*, orig. pp. of *jeter*: see JET¹] **1.** a kind of wall built out into the water to restrain currents, protect a harbour, etc. **2.** a landing pier **3.** a projecting part of a building

Jew (jōō) *n.* [< OFr. < L. *Judaeus* < Gr. < Heb. *yehūdī*, member of the tribe of Judah] **1.** a person descended, or regarded as descended, from the ancient Hebrews **2.** a person whose religion is Judaism

jew·el (jōō′əl) *n.* [< OFr. *joel* < *jeu*, a trifle < L. *jocus*, a joke] **1.** a valuable ring, necklace, etc., esp. one set with gems **2.** a precious stone; gem **3.** any person or thing that is very precious or valuable **4.** a small gem or gemlike bit used as one of the bearings in a watch —*vt.* **-elled, -el·ling** to decorate or set with jewels

jew·el·ler (-ər) *n.* a person who makes, deals in, or repairs jewellery, watches, etc.

jeweller's rouge a finely powdered rouge used as a metal polish

jew·el·ler·y (jōō′əl rē) *n.* jewels collectively: U.S. sp. **jew′-el·ry**

Jew·ess (jōō′is) *n.* a Jewish woman or girl

jew·fish (-fish′) *n., pl.* **-fish′, -fish′es:** see FISH any of several large fish found in warm seas, as one found off Western Australia

Jew·ish (-ish) *adj.* of or having to do with Jews or Judaism —*n.* [Colloq.] same as YIDDISH —**Jew′ish·ness** *n.*

Jew·ry (jōō′rē) *n., pl.* **-ries 1.** formerly, a district inhabited by Jews; ghetto **2.** Jewish people collectively

jew's-ear (jōōz′ir′) *n.* an edible, saucer-shaped fungus that occurs on living or dead wood

jew's-harp, jews'-harp (jōōz′härp′) *n.* a small musical instrument consisting of a lyre-shaped metal frame held between the teeth and played by plucking a projecting bent piece with the finger

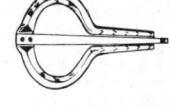

JEW'S HARP

Jez·e·bel (jez′ə bel′, -b'l) *n.* [after *Jezebel*, the wicked woman who married Ahab, king of Israel] [also **j-**] a shameless, wicked woman

jib¹ (jib) *n.* [prob. < GIBBET] **1.** the projecting arm of a crane **2.** the boom of a derrick

jib² (jib) *vi., vt.* **jibbed, jib′bing** [< Dan. *gibbe*, to jibe] *Naut.* to jibe; shift —*n.* a triangular sail projecting ahead of the foremast —**cut of one's jib** [Colloq.] one's appearance

jib³ (jib) *vi.* **jibbed, jib′bing** [prob. < prec.] **1.** to stop and refuse to go forward; balk **2.** to start or shy (at something) **3.** to be reluctant, or obstinately refuse, to do something (usually with *at*) —*n.* an animal that jibs, as a horse —**jib′-ber** *n.*

jib·ba (jib′ə) *n.* [< Ar. *jubbah*] a long loose coat worn by Muslim men: also **jib′bah, jub′bah**

jib boom a spar fixed to and extending beyond the bowsprit of a ship: the jib is attached to it

jibe¹ (jīb) *vi.* **jibed, jib′ing** [< Du. *gijpen*] **1.** to shift from one side of a ship to the other, as a fore-and-aft sail when the course is changed in a following wind **2.** to change the course of a ship so that the sails shift thus **3.** [U.S. Colloq.] to be in harmony, agreement, or accord —*vt. Naut.* to cause to jibe —*n.* a shift of sail or boom from one side of a ship to another

jibe² (jīb) *vi., vt., n.* same as GIBE —**jib′er** *n.*

jif·fy (jif′ē) *n., pl.* **-fies** [< ?] [Colloq.] a very short time; instant [done in a *jiffy*]: also **jiff**

jig (jig) *n.* [prob. < MFr. *giguer*, to dance < *gigue*, a fiddle] **1.** *a)* a fast, gay, springy dance, usually in triple time *b)* the music for such a dance **2.** any of various fishing lures that are jiggled up and down in the water **3.** any of several mechanical devices operated in a jerky manner, as a sieve for separating ores, a drill, etc. **4.** a device used as a guide for a tool or as a template —*vi., vt.* **jigged, jig′ging 1.** to dance (a jig) **2.** to move jerkily up and down or to and fro

—the jig is up [Slang] all chances for success are gone: said of a risky or improper activity

jig·ger[1] (jig′ər) *n.* [prob. < Afr. origin] *same as* CHIGOE

jig·ger[2] (jig′ər) *n.* **1.** one who jigs **2.** [U.S.] *a*) a small glass used to measure whisky, gin, etc. *b*) the quantity of whisky, etc. in a jigger **3.** *same as* JIG (*n.* 2) **4.** *Billiards same as* BRIDGE[1] (*n.* 6) **5.** *Mech.* any of several devices that operate with a jerky, up-and-down motion **6.** *Naut. a*) a small tackle *b*) a small sail *c*) *same as* JIGGER MAST

jig·gered (jig′ərd) *adj.* [< ?] [Colloq.] amazed; confounded: often used instead of damned [I'll be *jiggered*]

jigger mast a mast in the stern of a ship

jig·ger·y-pok·er·y (jig′ər ē pō′kər ē) *n.* [alt. < Scot. *joukery-paukery* < *jouk*, a trick] [Colloq.] trickery or deception; hanky-panky

jig·gle (jig′'l) *vt., vi.* **-gled, -gling** [freq. of *jig, v.*] to move in a succession of quick, slight jerks; rock lightly —*n.* a jiggling movement

jig·gly (jig′lē) *adj.* moving or tending to move with a jiggle; unsteady

jig·saw (jig′sô) *n.* a saw with a narrow blade set in a frame, that moves with an up-and-down motion for cutting along curved or irregular lines, as in scrollwork: also **jig saw** —*vt.* to cut or form with a jigsaw

jigsaw puzzle a puzzle made by cutting up a picture into pieces of irregular shape, which must be put together again to re-form the picture

JIGSAW

ji·had (ji had′) *n.* [Ar., a contest, war] **1.** a holy war fought by Moslems against the foes of Islam **2.** a vigorous crusade in support of a cause

Jill (jil) *n.* [< *Jill,* dim. of *Gillian:* a feminine name] [often j-] [Now Rare] a girl or woman; esp., a sweetheart

jilt (jilt) *n.* [< *jillet,* dim. of prec.] a person, esp. a woman, who rejects a lover or suitor after accepting or encouraging him —*vt.* to reject or cast off (a previously accepted lover or sweetheart)

Jim Crow [name of an early Negro minstrel song] [*also* j-c-] [U.S. Colloq.] discrimination against or segregation of Negroes —**Jim′-Crow′** *vt., adj.* —**Jim Crow′ism**

jim·jams (jim′jamz′) *n.pl.* [arbitrary echoic formation] [Slang] **1.** delirium tremens **2.** a nervous feeling; jitters (usually with *the*)

jim·my (jim′ē) *n., vt.* *U.S. sp. of* JEMMY

jin·gle (jiŋ′g'l) *vi.* **-gled, -gling** [ME. *gingelen*, prob. echoic] **1.** to make light, ringing sounds, as small bells or bits of metal striking together; tinkle **2.** to have obvious, easy rhythm, simple repetitions of sound, etc., as some poetry and music —*vt.* to cause to jingle —*n.* **1.** a jingling sound **2.** a verse that jingles [advertising *jingles*] —**jin′gly** (-glē) *adj.*

jin·go (jiŋ′gō) *n., pl.* **-goes** [< phr. *by jingo* in a patriotic Brit. music-hall song (1878)] one who boasts of his patriotism and favours an aggressive, warlike foreign policy; chauvinist —*adj.* of jingoes —**jin′go·ism** *n.* —**jin′go·ist** *n.* —**jin′go·is′tic** *adj.* —**jin′go·is′ti·cal·ly** *adv.*

jink (jiŋk) *vi.* [< ?] to move swiftly or with sudden turns, as in dodging a pursuer, esp. in Rugby football —*n.* **1.** an eluding, as by a quick sudden turn **2.** [*pl.*] lively pranks: in full, usually, **high jinks**

jinn (jin) *n., pl. of* JINNI: popularly regarded as a singular, with the pl. **jinns**

jin·ni (ji nē′, jin′ē) *n., pl.* **jinn** [< Ar.] *Moslem Legend* a supernatural being that can take human or animal form and influence human affairs

jin·rik·i·sha (jin rik′shô, -shə) *n.* [< Jap. < *jin,* a man + *riki,* power + *sha,* carriage] a small, two-wheeled carriage with a hood, pulled by one or two men, esp. formerly in the Orient: also sp. **jin·rick′sha, jin·rik′sha**

jinx (jiŋks) *n.* [< L. *iynx* < Gr. *iynx*, the wryneck (bird used in black magic)] [Colloq.] **1.** a person or thing supposed to bring bad luck **2.** a spell of bad luck —*vt.* [Colloq.] to bring bad luck to

jit·ney·ing (jit′nē iŋ) *n.* [< ?] [Aust. Slang] the multiple hiring of a taxi by different clients at the same time

jit·ter (jit′ər) *vi.* [? echoic] [Colloq.] to be nervous; have the jitters; fidget —**the jitters** [Colloq.] a very uneasy, nervous feeling; the fidgets —**jit′ter·y** *adj.*

jit·ter·bug (-bug′) *n.* [prec. + BUG] **1.** a dance for couples, esp. in the early 1940's, involving fast, acrobatic movements to swing music **2.** a dancer of the jitterbug —*vi.* **-bugged′, -bug′ging** to dance the jitterbug

jiu·jit·su, jiu·jut·su (jōō jit′sōō) *n. var. of* JUJITSU

jive (jīv) *vi.* **jived, jiv′ing** [< ?] to play, or dance to, jive music —*n.* former slang (c. 1930-45) for JAZZ or SWING

jo (jō) *n., pl.* **joes** [var. of JOY] [Scot.] a sweetheart

job (job) *n.* [< ?] **1.** a specific piece of work, as in one's trade, or done by agreement for pay **2.** a task; chore; duty **3.** the thing or material being worked on or the resulting product **4.** a position of employment; work **5.** [Colloq.] a criminal act or deed, as a theft, etc. **6.** [Colloq.] any happening, affair, matter, object, etc. [bad *job*] —*adj.* hired or done by the job —*vi.* **jobbed, job′bing** **1.** to do odd jobs **2.** to act as a jobber or broker **3.** to engage in jobbery —*vt.* **1.** to buy and sell (goods) as a wholesaler; handle as middleman **2.** to let or sublet (work, contracts, etc.) —**jobs for the boys** [Colloq.] jobs given to or created for one's supporters —**just the job** [Colloq.] exactly what is needed —**odd jobs** miscellaneous pieces of work —**on the job 1.** while working at one's job **2.** [Slang] attentive to one's task or duty —**job′less** *adj.*

job·ber (job′ər) *n.* **1.** a wholesaler; middleman, esp. dealing in stocks **2.** a person who works by the job or who does piecework

job·ber·y (-ər ē) *n.* the carrying on of public business dishonestly for private gain

job·bing (-iŋ) *adj.* not regularly employed; working by the piece [*jobbing* gardener, *jobbing* printer]

job lot 1. an assortment of goods for sale as one quantity **2.** any random assortment

Job's comforter (jōbz) a person who aggravates one's misery while attempting or pretending to comfort: see Job 16: 1-5

Jock (jok) *n.* [Scot. form of *Jack,* a masculine name] [Slang] a Scot, esp. a Scottish soldier

jock (jok) *n.* clipped form of: **1.** JOCKEY **2.** JOCKSTRAP

jock·ey (jok′ē) *n., pl.* **-eys** [< Scot. dim. of *Jack,* a masculine name] **1.** a person whose work is riding horses in races **2.** [Slang] the operator of a specified vehicle, machine, etc. —*vt., vi.* **-eyed, -ey·ing** **1.** to ride (a horse) in a race **2.** to cheat; swindle **3.** to manoeuvre for position or advantage

jock·strap (jok′strap′) *n.* [*jock,* penis + STRAP] an elastic belt with a pouch to support the genitals, worn by men

jo·cose (jō kōs′, jə-) *adj.* [< L. < *jocus,* a joke] joking or playful; humorous —**jo·cose′ly** *adv.* —**jo·cos′i·ty** (-kos′ə tē) *pl.* **-ties, jo·cose′ness** *n.*

joc·u·lar (jok′yə lar) *adj.* [< L. dim. of *jocus,* a joke] **1.** joking; full of fun **2.** said as a joke —**joc′u·lar′i·ty** (-lar′ə tē) *n., pl.* **-ties** —**joc′u·lar·ly** *adv.*

joc·und (jok′ənd) *adj.* [< OFr. < LL. < L. *jucundus,* pleasant < *juvare,* to help] cheerful; genial; gay —**jo·cun·di·ty** (jō kun′də tē) *n., pl.* **-ties** —**joc′und·ly** *adv.*

jodh·pur (jod′pər) *n.* [after *Jodhpur,* former state in India] **1.** [*pl.*] riding breeches made loose and full above the knees and tight from knees to ankles **2.** an ankle-high boot, usually with a side strap

jo·ey (jō′ē) *n.* [Abor. *joë*] [Aust.] **1.** a young kangaroo **2.** any young animal

jog (jog) *vt.* **jogged, jog′ging** [ME. *joggen,* to spur] **1.** *a*) to give a little shake or jerk to *b*) to nudge **2.** to shake up or revive (a person's memory) **3.** to cause to jog —*vi.* to move along at a slow, steady, jolting pace or trot —*n.* **1.** a little shake or nudge **2.** a slow, steady, jolting motion or trot —**jog′ger** *n.*

jog·ging (-iŋ) *n.* a slow jolting run or trot, esp. as a keep-fit exercise

jog·gle[1] (jog′'l) *vt., vi.* **-gled, -gling** [freq. of JOG] to shake or jolt slightly —*n.* a slight jolt

jog·gle[2] (jog′'l) *n.* [?< JAG[1]] **1.** a joint made by putting a notch in one surface and a projection in the other to fit into it **2.** the notch or projection —*vt.* **-gled, -gling** to join by joggles

jog·trot 1. a slow, steady trot **2.** a leisurely way of doing something

john (jon) *n.* [Chiefly U.S. Slang] a toilet

John Barleycorn malt liquor, etc., personified

John Bull [title character in John Arbuthnot's *History of John Bull* (1712)] a personification of England or an Englishman

John Doe *see* DOE

John·ny, John·nie (jon′ē) *n., pl.* **-nies** [< *Johnny,* nickname for *John,* a masculine name] [Colloq.] any man or boy

john·ny·cake (jon′ē kāk′) *n.* [< Eng. dial. *jannock,* bread of oatmeal] [Aust.] wheatmeal bread baked on a griddle

John·ny-come-late·ly (-kum′lāt′lē) *n.* [Colloq.] a recent arrival at a certain place or position, or someone who has only recently taken a certain stand

Johnny Raw a novice; new recruit

John·so·ni·an (jon sō′nē ən) *adj.* [after Samuel *Johnson* (1709-84), Brit. lexicographer & writer] **1.** of, like, or characteristic of Samuel Johnson or his style **2.** written in a formal or pompous style, full of Latinate constructions —*n.* an imitator, admirer, or student of Johnson and his work

‡**joie de vi·vre** (zhwàd vē′vr′) [Fr.] joy of living

join (join) *vt.* [< OFr. *joindre* < L. *jungere*] **1.** to bring together; connect; combine **2.** to make into one; unite [*join* forces, *joined* in wedlock*]* **3.** to become a part or member of (a club, etc.) **4.** to go to and combine with *[*the path *joins* the road*]* **5.** to enter into the company of; accompany *[join* us soon*]* **6.** [Colloq.] to adjoin —*vi.* **1.** to come together; meet **2.** to enter into association or become a member: often with *up* **3.** to participate (*in* a conversation, singing, etc.) —*n.* a place of joining, as a seam in a coat —**join battle** to start fighting

join·er (-ər) *n.* **1.** a person or thing that joins **2.** a workman who finishes interior woodwork, as doors, moulding, stairs, etc. **3.** [Colloq.] a person given to joining various organizations

join·er·y (-ər ē) *n.* **1.** the work or skill of a joiner **2.** any of various joints made in woodworking

joint (joint) *n.* [< OFr. < L. pp. of *jungere*, to join] **1.** a place where, or way in which, two things or parts are joined **2.** one of the parts of a jointed whole **3.** a large cut of meat, often with the bones still in it, as for a roast **4.** [Slang] *a)* a cheap bar, restaurant, etc. *b)* any building, etc. **5.** [Slang] a marijuana cigarette **6.** *Anat.* a place or part where two bones, etc. are joined, usually so that they can move **7.** *Bot.* a point where a branch or leaf grows out of the stem —*adj.* **1.** common to two or more as to ownership or action *[joint* property*]* **2.** sharing with someone else *[*a *joint* owner*]* —*vt.* **1.** to fasten together by a joint or joints **2.** to give a joint or joints to **3.** to cut (meat) into joints —**out of joint 1.** not in place at the joint; dislocated **2.** disordered —**joint'ed** *adj.* —**joint'er** *n.*

joint account a bank account registered in the name of two or more persons, any of whom may make deposits and withdrawals

joint·ly (-lē) *adv.* in common; together

joint return a single income tax return filed by a married couple, combining their incomes

joint stock stock or capital held in a common fund

joint-stock company (-stok') a business firm owned by the stockholders in shares which each may sell or transfer independently

join·ture (join'chər) *n.* [< OFr. < L. < *jungere*, to join] *Law* **1.** an arrangement by which a husband settles property on his wife for her use after his death **2.** the property thus settled

joist (joist) *n.* [< OFr. *giste*, a bed; ult. < L. *jacere*, to lie] any of the parallel beams that hold up the planks of a floor or the laths of a ceiling —*vt.* to provide with joists

joke (jōk) *n.* [L. *jocus*] **1.** anything said or done to arouse laughter; a funny anecdote or amusing trick **2.** a thing done or said merely in fun **3.** a person or thing to be laughed at —*vi.* joked, jok'-ing **1.** to tell or play jokes **2.** to say or do something as a joke; jest —*vt.* to bring to a specified condition by joking —**jok'ing·ly** *adv.*

jok·er (jō'kər) *n.* **1.** a person who jokes **2.** any hidden, unsuspected difficulty **3.** an extra playing card used in some games

JOISTS

jol·li·fy (jol'ə fī') *vt., vi.* -fied', -fy'ing [Colloq.] to make or be jolly or merry —**jol'li·fi·ca'tion** *n.*

jol·li·ty (-ə tē) *n.* a being jolly; fun; gaiety

jol·ly (jol'ē) *adj.* -li·er, -li·est [< OFr. *joli*, joyful; prob. < ON. *jol*, YULE] **1.** full of high spirits and good humour **2.** [Colloq.] enjoyable; pleasant —*adv.* [Colloq.] very; altogether —*vt., vi.* -lied, -ly·ing [Colloq.] **1.** to try to make (a person) feel good or agreeable by coaxing, flattering, etc. (often with *along*) **2.** to make fun of (someone) —*n., pl.* -lies [Colloq.] a British marine —**jol'li·ly** *adv.* —**jol'li·ness** *n.*

jolly (boat) [< MDu. *jolle*, yawl] a ship's small boat

Jolly Roger a black flag of pirates, with white skull and crossbones

jolt (jōlt) *vt.* [earlier *jot*, to jog, orig. echoic: prob. infl. by *jowl*, to strike] **1.** to shake up or jar, as with a bumpy ride or sharp blow **2.** to shock or surprise —*vi.* to move along in a bumpy, jerky manner —*n.* **1.** a sudden jerk, bump, etc., as from a blow **2.** a shock or surprise —**jolt'er** *n.* —**jolt'ing·ly** *adv.* —**jolt'y** *adj.*

Jo·nah (jō'nə) *n.* [after *Jonah*, the Hebrew prophet thrown overboard in a storm] any person said to bring bad luck by his presence

jon·gleur (joŋ'glər) *n.* [Fr. < OFr. *jogleor*, juggler: see JUGGLE] a wandering minstrel in medieval France and Britain

jon·quil (joŋ'kwəl) *n.* [< Fr. < Sp. dim. *junquillo* < L. *juncus*, a rush] **1.** a species of narcissus having relatively small yellow flowers and long, slender leaves **2.** its bulb or flower

Jor·dan almond (jôr'dən) [prob. < OFr. *jardin*, garden] a variety of large Spanish almond used in sweets

josh (josh) *vt., vi.* [< ?] [U.S. Colloq.] to ridicule in a good humoured way; tease jokingly; banter —**josh'er** *n.* —**josh'-ing·ly** *adv.*

joss (jos) *n.* [PidE. < Port. *deos* < L. *deus*, a god] a figure of a Chinese god

joss house a Chinese temple

joss stick a thin stick of dried, fragrant wood dust, burned by the Chinese as incense

jos·tle (jos''l) *vt., vi.* -tled, -tling [earlier *justle*, freq.: see JOUST] **1.** to bump or push, as in a crowd; shove roughly **2.** to contend (*with* someone *for* something) —*n.* a jostling —**jos'tler** *n.*

jot (jot) *n.* [< L. < Gr. *iōta*, the letter *i*, the smallest letter] a trifling amount; the smallest bit —*vt.* jot'ted, jot'ting to make a brief note of (usually with *down*)

jo·ta (hō'tä) *n.* [Sp. < OSp. < *sotar*, to dance] a Spanish dance in 3/4 time performed by a man and woman to the rhythm of castanets

jot·ter (jot'ər) *n.* **1.** a person who jots down notes **2.** a small notebook for rough notes

jot·ting (jot'iŋ) *n.* a short note jotted down

joule (jool) *n.* [after J. P. *Joule*, 19th.-c. Brit. physicist] *Physics* the SI unit of energy, work, and quantity of heat; equivalent to one newton per metre

jounce (jouns) *n.* [< ?] a jolt or bounce —*vt., vi.* jounced, jounc'ing to jolt or bounce —**jounc'y** *adj.*

jour·nal (jur'n'l) *n.* [< OFr., lit., daily < L. *diurnalis* < *dies*, day] **1.** a daily record of happenings, as a diary **2.** a record of the transactions of a legislature, club, etc. **3.** a ship's logbook **4.** a newspaper, magazine, etc. **5.** *Bookkeeping* a book of original entry for recording every transaction with an indication of its proper account **6.** *Mech.* the part of a rotatory axle or shaft that turns in a bearing

journal box *Mech.* a housing for a journal

jour·nal·ese (jur'n'l ēz') *n.* a style of writing characteristic of many newspapers, magazines, etc.; superficial style, with many clichés

jour·nal·ism (jur'n'l iz'm) *n.* **1.** the work of gathering, writing, and publishing or disseminating news, as through newspapers, etc. or by radio and TV **2.** newspapers and magazines collectively

jour·nal·ist (-ist) *n.* a person whose occupation is journalism; reporter, news editor, etc. —**jour'nal·is'tic** *adj.* —**jour'nal·is'ti·cal·ly** *adv.*

jour·nal·ize (jur'nə līz') *vt., vi.* -ized', -iz'ing to record (transactions, daily events, etc.) in a journal

jour·ney (jur'nē) *n., pl.* -neys [< OFr. *journee* < LL. < L. *diurnus*, daily: see JOURNAL] a travelling from one place to another; trip —*vi.* -neyed, -ney·ing to go on a trip; travel

jour·ney·man (-mən) *n., pl.* -men [ME. < *journee*, day's work + *man*] **1.** formerly, a worker qualified to work at his trade, after serving his apprenticeship **2.** now, a worker who has learned his trade **3.** an experienced craftsman of average ability

joust (joust, joost) *n.* [< OFr. < *juster* < L. *juxta*, beside] **1.** a combat with lances between two knights on horseback **2.** [*pl.*] a tournament —*vi.* to engage in a joust —**joust'-er** *n.*

Jove (jōv) *same as* JUPITER —**by Jove!** an exclamation of astonishment, emphasis, etc. —**Jo·vi·an** (jō'vē ən) *adj.*

jo·vi·al (jō'vē əl, -vyəl) *adj.* [Fr. < LL. *Jovialis*, of Jupiter < L. *Jovis*: see prec.] full of hearty, playful good humour; genial —**jo'vi·al'i·ty** (-al'ə tē) *n.* —**jo'vi·al·ly** *adv.*

jowl[1] (joul) *n.* [< OE. *ceafl*, jaw] **1.** a jaw; esp., the lower jaw with the chin and cheeks **2.** the cheek

jowl[2] (joul) *n.* [< OE. *ceole*, throat] [often *pl.*] the fleshy, hanging part under the lower jaw —**jowl'y** *adj.*

joy (joi) *n.* [< OFr. *joie* < LL. < L. *gaudium*, joy] **1.** a very glad feeling; happiness; delight **2.** anything causing such feeling **3.** the expression of such feeling **4.** [Colloq.] success or luck *[*to get no *joy]* —*vi.* to be full of joy; rejoice

joy·ful (joi'fəl) *adj.* feeling, expressing, or causing joy; glad; happy —**joy'ful·ly** *adv.* —**joy'ful·ness** *n.*

joy·less (-lis) *adj.* without joy; unhappy; sad —**joy'less·ly** *adv.* —**joy'less·ness** *n.*

joy·ous (-əs) *adj.* full of joy; happy; gay; glad —**joy'ous·ly** *adv.* —**joy'ous·ness** *n.*

joy ride [Colloq.] a motor car ride merely for pleasure, often with reckless speed and, sometimes, in a stolen car —**joy rider** —**joy riding**

joy stick [Slang] the control stick of an aircraft

J.P. justice of the peace

Jpn. **1.** Japan **2.** Japanese

Jr., jr. junior

jub·bah (jub'ə) *n. same as* JIBBA

ju·bi·lant (jōō'bəl ənt) *adj.* [L. *jubilans*, prp. of *jubilare*: see ff.] joyful and triumphant; elated —**ju'bi·lance** *n.* —**ju'-bi·lant·ly** *adv.*

ju·bi·late (jōō'bə lāt') *vi.* -lat'ed, -lat'ing [< L. pp. of *jubilare*, to shout for joy < *jubilum*, wild shout] to rejoice, as in triumph; exult

ju·bi·la·tion (jōō'bə lā'shən) *n.* **1.** a jubilating **2.** a happy celebration, as of victory

ju·bi·lee (jōō'bə lē') *n.* [< OFr. < LL. < Gr. < Heb. *yōbēl*, a horn (trumpet): infl. by L. *jubilum*, wild shout] **1.** *Jewish*

History a celebration held every fifty years in which all bondmen were freed, mortgaged lands restored to the owners, etc.: Lev. 25:8-17 **2.** a 50th or 25th anniversary **3.** a time or occasion of rejoicing **4.** jubilation; rejoicing **5.** R.C.Ch. a year proclaimed as a solemn time for gaining a plenary indulgence

Jud. Judges

Ju·da·ic (jōō dā′ik) *adj.* of the Jews or Judaism; Jewish —**Ju·da′i·cal·ly** *adv.*

Ju·da·ism (jōō′də iz′m, -dā-) *n.* **1.** the Jewish religion, a monotheistic religion based on the laws and teachings of the Holy Scripture and the Talmud **2.** observance of Jewish morality, traditions, etc. —**Ju′da·ist** *n.* —**Ju′da·is′tic** *adj.*

Ju·da·ize (-īz′) *vi., vt.* **-ized′, -iz′ing** to conform to, or make conform to, Judaism —**Ju′da·i·za′tion** *n.*

Ju·das (jōō′dəs) *n.* [after *Judas* Iscariot, the disciple who betrayed Jesus] a traitor or betrayer

Judas tree a tree of the legume family, with clusters of rose-pink flowers

jud·der (jud′ər) *n.* [altered < ? SHUDDER] vibration or shaking motion —*vi.* to shake, wobble, or vibrate

Judg. Judges

judge (juj) *n.* [< OFr. < L. *judex* < *jus*, law + *dicere*, to say] **1.** a public official with authority to hear and decide cases in a court of law **2.** a person designated to determine the winner, settle a controversy, etc. **3.** a person qualified to decide on the relative worth of anything [a good *judge* of music] **4.** any of the governing leaders of the ancient Israelites before the time of the kings —*vt., vi.* **judged, judg′ing 1.** to hear and pass judgment (*on*) in a court of law **2.** to determine the winner of (a contest) or settle (a controversy) **3.** to form an opinion about **4.** to criticize or censure **5.** to think or suppose **6.** *Jewish History* to govern —**judg′er** *n.* —**judge′ship** *n.*

judge advocate *pl.* **judge advocates** a military legal officer; esp., an officer designated to act as prosecutor at a court-martial

judg·ment (juj′mənt) *n.* **1.** a judging; deciding **2.** a legal decision; order or sentence given by a judge or law court **3.** a debt resulting from a court order **4.** an opinion or estimate **5.** criticism or censure **6.** power of comparing and deciding; understanding **7.** [J-] *short for* LAST JUDGMENT Also *sp.* **judge′ment** —**judg·men′tal** (-men′t'l) *adj.*

Judgment Day *Theol.* the time of God's final judgment of all people; end of the world

ju·di·ca·to·ry (jōō′di kə tər ē, jōō di′-) *adj.* [< LL. < L. pp. of *judicare*, to judge < *judex*, a JUDGE] having to do with administering justice; judging —*n., pl.* **-ries 1.** a court of law; tribunal **2.** law courts collectively

ju·di·ca·ture (-chər) *n.* **1.** the administering of justice **2.** the position, functions, or legal power of a judge **3.** the extent of legal power of a judge or court of law **4.** a court of law **5.** judges or courts of law collectively

ju·di·cial (jōō dish′əl) *adj.* [< OFr. < L. *judicialis* < *judex*, a JUDGE] **1.** of judges, law courts, or their functions **2.** allowed, enforced, or set by order of a judge or law court **3.** like or befitting a judge **4.** fair; unbiased —**ju·di′cial·ly** *adv.*

ju·di·ci·ar·y (jōō dish′ē er′ē, -dish′ər ē) *adj.* of judges, law courts, or their functions —*n., pl.* **-ar′ies 1.** the part of government that administers justice **2.** a system of law courts **3.** judges collectively

ju·di·cious (-dish′əs) *adj.* [< Fr. < L. *judicium*, judgment < *judex*, a JUDGE] having, applying, or showing sound judgment; wise and careful —**ju·di′cious·ly** *adv.* —**ju·di′·cious·ness** *n.*

ju·do (jōō′dō) *n.* [Jap. < *jū*, soft + *dō*, art] a form of jujitsu, esp. as a means of self-defence

ju·dy (jōō′dē) *n.* [< *Judith*, a feminine name] [Colloq.] a girl; young woman

jug (jug) *n.* [a pet form of *Judith* or *Joan*, feminine names] **1.** a) a container, usually with a handle and lip, for holding and pouring liquids b) the contents of a jug **2.** [Slang] a jail —*vt.* **jugged, jug′ging 1.** to put into a jug **2.** to stew in a covered earthenware container **3.** [Slang] to jail —**jug′ful** (-fool′) *n.*

ju·gate (jōō′gāt, -git) *adj.* [< L. pp. of *jugare*, to yoke < *jugum*, a yoke] *Biol.* paired or connected

jug·ger·naut (jug′ər nôt′) *n.* [after Hindi *Jagannath*, an incarnation of the Hindu god Vishnu] **1.** a) anything that exacts blind devotion b) any terrible, irresistible force c) a large, heavy lorry

jug·gins (jug′inz) *n.* [?< surname *Juggins*] [Slang] a simpleton; a dupe

jug·gle (jug′'l) *vt.* **-gled, -gling** [< OFr. *jogler* < L. *joculari*, to joke < *jocus*, a joke] **1.** to perform skilful tricks of sleight of hand with (balls, knives, etc.) **2.** to make awkward attempts to catch or hold (a ball, etc.) **3.** to use trickery so as to deceive or cheat [to *juggle* figures to show a profit] —*vi.* to toss up a number of balls, knives, etc. and keep them continuously in the air —*n.* **1.** a juggling **2.** a clever trick or deception —**jug′gler** (jug′lər) *n.* —**jug′gler·y** *n., pl.* **-gler·ies**

jug·u·lar (jug′yoo lər) *adj.* [< LL. < L. *jugulum*, collarbone < *jugum*, a yoke] **1.** of the neck or throat **2.** of a jugular vein —*n.* **1.** either of two large veins in the neck carrying blood back from the head to the heart: in full, **jugular vein 2.** an individual's most vulnerable point —**have an instinct for the jugular** to be prone to attack people's weak points

juice (jōōs) *n.* [< OFr. < L. *jus*] **1.** the liquid part of a plant, fruit, or vegetable **2.** a liquid in or from animal tissue [gastric *juice*] **3.** [Colloq.] energy; vitality **4.** [Slang] a) electricity b) petrol, oil, or any liquid fuel **5.** [Slang] alcoholic liquor —*vt.* **juiced, juic′ing** to extract juice from —**juice up** [Chiefly U.S.] to add power, vigour, excitement, etc. to —**juice′less** *adj.* —**juic′er** *n.*

juic·y (jōō′sē) *adj.* **juic′i·er, juic′i·est 1.** full of juice; succulent **2.** [Colloq.] full of interest; piquant; spicy **3.** [Colloq.] highly profitable —**juic′i·ly** *adv.* —**juic′i·ness** *n.*

ju·jit·su (jōō jit′sōō) *n.* [< Jap. < *jū*, soft + *jutsu*, art] a Japanese system of wrestling in which the strength and weight of an opponent are used against him: also **ju·jut·su** (-jit′sōō, -jut′-)

ju·ju (jōō′jōō) *n.* [Hausa, an evil spirit, fetish] **1.** a magic charm or fetish used by some West African tribes **2.** its magic

ju·jube (jōō′jōōb) *n.* [Fr. < ML. < L. *zizyphum* < Gr. *zizyphon*] **1.** the edible, datelike fruit of a tree or shrub growing in warm climates **2.** this tree or shrub **3.** a gelatinous, fruit-flavoured lozenge

juke·box (jōōk′boks′) *n.* [Gullah *juke*, wicked (as in *juke-house*, house of prostitution), WAfr. orig.] a coin-operated electric gramophone: a record is chosen by pushing a button: also **juke box**

ju·lep (jōō′ləp) *n.* [< MFr. < Ar. < Per. < *gul*, rose + *āb*, water] *same as* MINT JULEP

Ju·li·an calendar (jōō′lē ən) the calendar introduced by Julius Caesar in 46 B.C., in which the ordinary year had 365 days and every fourth year (leap year) had 366 days: replaced by the Gregorian calendar

ju·li·enne (jōō′lē en′; *Fr.* zhü lyen′) *n.* [Fr., origin obscure] a clear soup containing vegetables cut into strips or bits —*adj.* *Cooking* cut into strips: said of vegetables

Ju·ly (joo lī′, jōō-) *n., pl.* **-lies′** [< Anglo-Fr. < L. < *mensis Julius*, the month of Julius (Caesar)] the seventh month of the year, having 31 days: abbrev. **Jul.**

jum·ble (jum′b'l) *vt.* **-bled, -bling** [< ?] **1.** to mix in a confused, disorderly heap **2.** to confuse mentally —*vi.* to be jumbled —*n.* **1.** a confused mixture or heap **2.** a muddle **3.** items or goods for a jumble sale —**jum′bly** *adj.*

jumble sale a sale of second-hand goods, often in aid of a charity or other worthy cause

jum·bo (jum′bō) *n., pl.* **-bos** [< Gullah *jamba*, elephant; infl. by P. T. Barnum's use of it for his elephant, *Jumbo*] a very large person, animal, or thing —*adj.* very large

jumbo jet a large, jet-propelled passenger aircraft

jum·buck, jum·buk (jum′buk) *n.* [< Abor.] [Aust.] a sheep

jump (jump) *vi.* [< ?] **1.** to move oneself suddenly from the ground, etc. by using the leg muscles; leap; spring **2.** to jerk; bob; bounce **3.** to leap from an aircraft using a parachute **4.** to act or react eagerly (often with *at*) **5.** to pass suddenly as from one topic to another **6.** to rise suddenly, as prices **7.** to form, arrive at prematurely, as a conclusion, etc. **8.** [Slang] to be lively and animated **9.** *Bridge* to make an unnecessarily high bid (**jump bid**) to increase the previous bid **10.** *Draughts* to move a piece over an opponent's piece, thus capturing it —*vt.* **1.** a) to leap over b) to skip over **2.** to cause to leap [to *jump* a horse over a fence] **3.** to advance (a person) by bypassing others **4.** to leap upon; spring aboard **5.** to cause (prices, etc.) to rise suddenly **6.** [Chiefly U.S.Colloq.] to attack suddenly **7.** [Colloq.] to react to prematurely, in anticipation **8.** [Slang] to leave suddenly [to *jump* town] **9.** *Draughts* to capture (an opponent's piece) —*n.* **1.** a jumping; leap **2.** a distance jumped **3.** a descent from an aircraft by parachute **4.** a thing to be jumped over **5.** a sudden transition **6.** a sudden rise, as in prices **7.** a sudden, nervous start or jerk; twitch **8.** *Athletics* a contest in jumping **9.** *Draughts* a move by which an opponent's piece is captured —**get** (or **have**) **the jump on** [Slang] to get (or have) an advantage over —**jump a claim** to seize land claimed by someone else —**jump bail** to forfeit one's bail by running away —**jump down someone's throat** [Slang] to address someone sharply; to scold —**jump on** (or **all over**) [Slang] to scold; censure —**jump the queue** to move ahead of others waiting for transport, jobs, etc. —**jump the track** to go suddenly off the rails —**one jump ahead** one step ahead of a rival —**on the jump** [Colloq.] very busy

jumped-up (jumpt′-up′) *adj.* upstart

jump·er¹ (jum′pər) *n.* **1.** a person, animal, or thing that jumps **2.** a short wire used to make an electrical connection

jump·er² (jum′pər) *n.* [< dial. *jump*, short coat, prob. < Fr. *jupe* < Sp. < Ar. *jubbah*, undergarment] **1.** a loose jacket or blouse, worn as to protect clothing or as part of a sailor's outfit   **2.** a sweater or pullover

jumping bean   the seed of a Mexican plant, which is made to jump or roll about by the movements of a moth larva inside it

jumping jack   a child's toy consisting of a little jointed figure made to jump about by pulling a string

jump jet   a fixed-wing jet aircraft that can land and take off vertically

jump leads   heavy electric cables with crocodile clips at each end: used to start a motor vehicle with a flat battery

jump-off (-of) in showjumping, an extra round that decides the winner of the competition

jump suit   **1.** an overall worn by paratroops, etc.   **2.** any one-piece garment like this

jump·y (jum′pē) *adj.* **jump′i·er, jump′i·est**   **1.** moving in jumps, jerks, etc.   **2.** easily startled; apprehensive —**jump′**-i·ly *adv.* —**jump′i·ness** *n.*

Jun., jun.   junior

jun·co (juŋ′kō) *n.,* pl. **-cos** [< ModL. < Sp. < L. *juncus,* a rush]   a sparrowlike bird of North and Central America, with a grey or black head

junc·tion (juŋk′shən) *n.* [< L. < *jungere,* to join]   **1.** a joining or being joined   **2.** a place or point of joining or crossing, as of roads or railways   **3.** the region separating two kinds of semiconductor material —**junc′tion·al** *adj.*

junc·ture (-chər) *n.* [< L.: see prec.]   **1.** a joining or being joined   **2.** a point or line of joining or connection; joint   **3.** a point of time, esp. a crisis   **4.** a state of affairs   **5.** *Linguis.* the transition marking the boundary between one speech sound and the next

June (jōōn) *n.* [< OFr. < L. < *mensis Junius,* the month of *Juno*]   the sixth month of the year, having 30 days: abbrev. **Jun.**

jun·gle (juŋ′g'l) *n.* [< Hindi < Sans. *jangala,* desert]   **1.** land with a dense growth of trees, vines, etc., as in the tropics, usually inhabited by predatory animals   **2.** any tangled growth   **3.** [Slang] a place where people compete ruthlessly —**jun′gly** *adj.*

jungle fever   any of several diseases of tropical regions; esp. a severe malarial fever of the East Indies

jun·ior (jōōn′yər) *adj.* [L. compar. of *juvenis,* young]   **1.** the younger: written *Jr.* after the name of a son who bears the same name as his father   **2.** of more recent position or lower status [a *junior* partner]   **3.** of later date   **4.** made up of younger members —*n.* **1.** a younger person   **2.** person of lower standing or rank   **3.** [U.S.] a student in the next-to-last year of a high school or college —**one's junior** a person younger than oneself

junior lightweight   *see* BOXING AND WRESTLING WEIGHTS, table

junior marine   *see* MILITARY RANKS, table

junior middleweight   *see* BOXING AND WRESTLING WEIGHTS, table

junior school   a school for children aged between 7 and 12: *see* INFANT SCHOOL

junior seaman   *see* MILITARY RANKS, table

junior technician   *see* MILITARY RANKS, table

junior welterweight   *see* BOXING AND WRESTLING WEIGHTS, table

ju·ni·per (jōō′nə pər) *n.* [L. *juniperus*]   a small evergreen shrub or tree with scalelike foliage and berrylike cones

junk¹ (juŋk) *n.* [< ? Port. *junco,* a reed < L. *juncus*]   **1.** orig., old rope used for making oakum, mats, etc.   **2.** old metal, paper, rags, etc.   **3.** [Colloq.] useless stuff; rubbish   **4.** [Slang] a narcotic drug; esp., heroin —*vt.* [U.S. Colloq.] to throw away or sell as junk; discard —**junk′y** *adj.*

junk² (juŋk) *n.* [Sp. & Port. *junco* < Jav. *joñ*]   a Chinese flat-bottomed ship

Jun·ker (yooŋ′kər) *n.* [G. < MHG. < OHG. *jung,* young + *herro,* lord]   a German of the militaristic, landowning class; Prussian aristocrat

jun·ket (juŋ′kit) *n.* [ult. < L. *juncus,* a rush: orig. sold in reed baskets]   **1.** formerly, curds with cream   **2.** milk sweetened, flavoured, and thickened into curd with rennet   **3.** a feast or picnic   **4.** an excursion for pleasure   **5.** an excursion by an official, paid for out of public funds —*vi.* to go on a junket —*vt.* to entertain at a feast —**jun′**-ket·eer′** (-kə tir′), **jun′ket·er** *n.* —**jun′ket·ing** *n.*

JUNK

junk·ie, junk·y (juŋ′kē) *n.,* pl. **junk′ies**   [Slang] a drug addict, esp. one addicted to heroin

junk·man (juŋk′man′) *n.,* pl. **-men** (-men′)   [U.S.] a rag-and-bone man

jun·ta (jun′tə) *n.* [Sp. < L. pp. of *jungere,* to join]   **1.** a Spanish or Latin American legislature or council   **2.** a group of political intriguers; also, a group of military men in power after a coup d'état: also **jun·to** (jun′tō), pl. **-tos**

Ju·pi·ter (jōō′pə tər) [L.]   **1.** the chief Roman god: identified

with the Greek god Zeus   **2.** the largest planet of the solar system and the fifth in distance from the sun: diameter, c.141 600 km

Ju·ras·sic (jōō ras′ik) *adj.* [Fr. *jurassique* < *Jura* (Mountains)]   designating or of the second period of the Mesozoic Era, immediately following the Triassic —**the Jurassic** the Jurassic Period or its rocks: see GEOLOGY, chart

ju·rat (joor′at) *n.* [Fr. < ML. *juratus,* lit., one sworn < L. *jurare,* to swear]   **1.** a municipal officer of the Cinque Ports, similar to an alderman   **2.** a magistrate in certain French towns and the Channel Islands   **3.** *Law* a record kept of the time, place, etc. of an affidavit

ju·rid·i·cal (joo rid′i'l) *adj.* [< L. < *jus,* law + *dicere,* to declare + -AL]   of judicial proceedings, or of law: also **ju·rid′ic** —**ju·rid′i·cal·ly** *adv.*

ju·ris·dic·tion (joor′is dik′shən) *n.* [< OFr. < L. < *jus,* law + *dictio* < *dicere,* to declare]   **1.** the administering of justice; authority to hear and decide cases   **2.** authority or power in general   **3.** the range of authority —**ju′ris·dic′**-tion·al** *adj.* —**ju′ris·dic′tion·al·ly** *adv.*

ju·ris·pru·dence (-prōō′dəns) *n.* [< L. < *jus,* law + *prudentia,* a foreseeing]   **1.** the science or philosophy of law   **2.** a part or division of law —**ju′ris·pru·den′tial** (-den′shəl) *adj.* —**ju′ris·pru·den′tial·ly** *adv.*

ju·rist (joor′ist) *n.* [< MFr. < ML. < L. *jus,* law]   an expert in law; writer on law

ju·ris·tic (joo ris′tik) *adj.*   of jurists or jurisprudence; relating to law —**ju·ris′ti·cal·ly** *adv.*

ju·ror (joor′ər) *n.*   **1.** a member of a jury; juryman   **2.** a person taking an oath, as of allegiance

ju·ry¹ (joor′ē) *n.,* pl. **-ries** [< OFr. < ML. < L. *jurare,* to swear < *jus,* law]   **1.** a group of people sworn to hear evidence in a law case and to give a decision in accordance with their findings   **2.** a group selected to decide the winners in a contest

ju·ry² (joor′ē) *adj.* [< ?]   *Naut.* for temporary use; makeshift [a jury mast]

ju·ry·man (-mən) *n.,* pl. **-men**   *same as* JUROR (sense 1)

ju·ry-rigged (-rigd′) *adj.* [see JURY²]   *Naut.* rigged for temporary use

just¹ (just) *adj.* [< OFr. < L. *justus,* lawful < *jus,* law]   **1.** right or fair [a just decision]   **2.** righteous; upright [a just man]   **3.** deserved; merited [just praise]   **4.** lawful   **5.** proper, fitting, etc.   **6.** well-founded [a just suspicion]   **7.** correct or true   **8.** accurate; exact —*adv.* **1.** precisely; exactly [just one o'clock]   **2.** almost at the point of [just leaving]   **3.** only [just a taste]   **4.** barely [just missed the train]   **5.** a very short time ago [just left the room]   **6.** immediately [just to my right]   **7.** [Colloq.] quite; really [looks just right] —**just now** a moment ago —**just the same** [Colloq.] nevertheless —**just′ness** *n.*

just² (just) *n., vi.*   *same as* JOUST

jus·tice (jus′tis) *n.* [ME. < OFr. < L. < *justus:* see JUST]   **1.** a being righteous   **2.** fairness   **3.** a being correct   **4.** sound reason; rightfulness   **5.** reward or penalty as deserved   **6.** the use of authority to uphold what is right, just, or lawful   **7.** the administration of law   **8.** *same as:* a) JUDGE b) JUSTICE OF THE PEACE —**bring to justice** to cause (a wrongdoer) to be tried in court and duly punished —**do justice to**   **1.** to treat fitly or fairly   **2.** to enjoy properly —**do oneself justice** to do something in a manner worthy of one's abilities —**jus′tice·ship′** *n.*

justice of the peace   a local magistrate, authorized to decide minor cases, etc.

jus·ti·ci·ar·y (jus ti′shə rē) *n.,* pl. **-ar·ies** [ME. < ML. *justitiarius* < L. *justitia:* see JUSTICE]   **1.** the chief political and judicial officer under the Norman and early Plantagenet kings   **2.** an officer of justice —*adj.* relating to the administration of justice or the office of a judge —**the Justiciary** judges collectively

jus·ti·fi·a·ble (jus′tə fī′ə b'l, jus′tə fī′ə b'l) *adj.*   that can be justified or defended as correct —**jus′ti·fi′a·bil′i·ty** *n.* —**jus′**-ti·fi′a·bly** *adv.*

jus·ti·fi·ca·tion (jus′tə fi kā′shən) *n.*   **1.** a justifying or being justified   **2.** a fact that justifies

justification by faith   *Theol.* the act by which a sinner is freed through faith from the penalty of his sin and is accepted by God as righteous

jus·ti·fy (jus′tə fī) *vt.* **-fied′, -fy′ing** [< OFr. < LL., ult. < L. *justus,* just + *facere,* to make]   **1.** to show to be just, right, or reasonable   **2.** *Theol.* to free from blame   **3.** to supply good grounds for   **4.** to space (type) to make the lines correct in length —*vi.* *Law* to show an adequate reason for something done —**jus′ti·fi′er** *n.*

jus·tle (jus′'l) *vt., vi., n.*   *same as* JOSTLE

just·ly (just′lē) *adv.*   **1.** in a just manner   **2.** rightly   **3.** deservedly

jut (jut) *vi., vt.* **jut′ted, jut′ting** [prob. var. of JET¹]   to stick out; project —*n.* a part that juts

jute (jōōt) *n.* [Hindi *jhuto* < Sans. *jūta,* matted hair]   **1.** a strong fibre used for making burlap, sacks, rope, etc.   **2.** either of two East Indian plants yielding this fibre

ju·ve·nile (jōō′və nil) *adj.* [< L. < *juvenis,* young]   **1.** a) young; youthful b) immature; childish **2.** of, characteristic of, or suitable for children or young persons —n. **1.** a young person; child or youth **2.** an actor who plays youthful roles **3.** a book for children **4.** Biol. an immature animal or plant —ju'venil'i·ty (-nil'ə tē) n.

juvenile court a law court for cases involving children under a specified age

juvenile delinquency antisocial or unlawful behaviour by minors of not more than a specified age —**juvenile delinquent**

ju·ve·nil·ia (jōō'və nil'ē ə, -nil'yə) n. pl. [L., neut. pl. of juvenilis, JUVENILE] **1.** writings, paintings, etc. done in childhood or youth

jux·ta·pose (juk'stə pōz') vt. -posed', -pos'ing [< Fr. < juxta- (< L. juxta, near) + poser, POSE¹] to put side by side or close together —**jux'ta·po·si'tion** n.

K

K, k (kā) n., pl. **K's, k's 1.** the eleventh letter of the English alphabet **2.** the sound of K or k

K 1. Physics the symbol for kelvin **2.** Chess king **3.** knit 4. [ModL. kalium] potassium

k kilo

K., k. 1. Elec. capacity **2.** Music Köchel (in numbering Mozart's works)

Kaa·ba (kä'bə, kä'ə bə) [Ar. ka'bah, lit., square building < ka'b, a cube] the sacred Moslem shrine at Mecca, towards which believers turn when praying: it contains a black stone supposedly given to Abraham by the angel Gabriel

kab·a·la, kab·ba·la (kab'ə lə, kə bä'lə) n. same as CABALA

ka·bob (kə bob') n. same as KEBAB

Ka·bu·ki (kə bōō'kē) n. [Jap. < kabu, music and dancing + ki, spirit] [also k-] a form of Japanese drama with formalized pantomime, dance, and song, and with male actors in all roles

Ka·byle (kə bīl') n. [Fr. < Ar. qabā'il, pl. of qabīlah, tribe] **1.** a member of the Algerian or Tunisian Berber tribes **2.** the Berber language of the Kabyles

ka·di (kä'dē, kä'-) n. same as CADI

Kaf·fir (kaf'ər) n. [Ar. kāfir, infidel < prp. of kafara, to be sceptical] **1.** a member of any of several Bantu-speaking tribes in South Africa **2.** [k-] same as KAFIR

kaf·fi·yeh (kə fē'yə) n. [< Ar.] a headdress of draped cotton cloth worn by Arabs

kaf·ir (kaf'ər) n. [Ar. kāfir: see KAFFIR] **1.** a grain sorghum grown in dry regions for grain and fodder: also **kafir corn 2.** [K-] same as KAFFIR

kaf·ka·esque (kaf'kə esk') adj. [< Franz Kafka, Austrian writer + -ESQUE] of or designating a situation whose outcome is predetermined by faceless people

kaf·tan (kaf'tən) n. same as CAFTAN

ka·goul (kə gōōl') n. same as CAGOULE

kai·ak (kī'ak) n. same as KAYAK

kai·ser (kī'zər) n. [Gmc. borrowing < L. Caesar] emperor: the title [K-] of the rulers of the Holy Roman Empire (962–1806), of Austria (1804–1918), and of Germany (1871–1918)

ka·ka (kä'kə) n. [Maori: echoic of the bird's cry] a New Zealand parrot with an olive-brown body

ka·ke·mo·no (kak'i mōn'ō) n., pl. -nos [< Jap. < kake, hanging + mono, thing] a Japanese paper or silk wall hanging, usually long and narrow, with a picture or inscription in it and a roller at the bottom

ka·la a·zar (kä'lə ə zär') n. [Hindi. kala-azar, lit. black disease] an infectious disease of S Asia and Mediterranean countries caused by a protozoan parasite

kale (kāl) n. [Scot. var. of COLE] a hardy, nonheading cabbage with loose, spreading, curled leaves

ka·lei·do·scope (kə lī'də skōp') n. [< Gr. kalos, beautiful + eidos, form + -SCOPE] **1.** a small tube containing loose bits of coloured glass, plastic, etc. reflected by mirrors so that various symmetrical patterns appear when the tube is rotated **2.** anything that constantly changes —**ka·lei'·do·scop'ic** (-skop'ik) adj. —**ka·lei'do·scop'i·cal·ly** adv.

kal·ends (kal'əndz) n.pl. same as CALENDS

Ka·le·va·la (kä'lə vä'lä) [Finn., lit., land of heroes] a Finnish epic poem

kale·yard (kāl'yärd') n. [Scot.] a kitchen garden: applied to the fiction of J. M. Barrie and others (the **kaleyard school**) dealing with Scottish life and using Scottish dialect: also **kail'yard**

Kal·muck, Kal·muk (kal'muk) n. **1.** a member of a group of Mongol peoples living chiefly in the NE Caucacus and N Sinkiang **2.** their Altaic, western Mongolic language Also **Kal'myk** (-mik)

ka·long (kä'loŋ) n. [Javanese kalori] a large, fruit-eating bat of the Malay Archipelago

kal·so·mine (kal'sə mīn', -min) n., vt. -mined', -min'ing same as CALCIMINE

Ka·ma·su·tra (kä'mə sōō'trə) [Sans. < kāma, love + sūtra, manual] a Hindu love manual written in the 8th cent.: also **Kama Sutra**

kame (kām) n. [North Brit. var. of COOMB] a hill or short, steep ridge of stratified sand or gravel deposited in contact with glacial ice

ka·mi·ka·ze (ka'mi kä'zē) n. [Jap., lit., divine wind < kami, divine + kaze, the wind] **1.** a suicide attack by a Japanese aircraft pilot in World War II **2.** the aircraft or pilot in such an attack

kam·pong (kam'pôŋ) n. [Malay] a small Malay village or cluster of native huts

Ka·nak·a (kə nak'ə, kan'ə kə) n. [Haw., man] **1.** a Hawaiian **2.** a native of the South Sea Islands, esp. one used formerly as slave labour in Australia

Ka·na·rese (ka'nə rēz') n. **1.** pl. -rese' any of a group of people living in south-western India **2.** the Dravidian language of the Kanarese

kan·ga·roo (kaŋ'gə rōō') n., pl. -roos', -roo': see PLURAL, II, D, 1 [said (by James Cook) to be native name] a leaping, plant-eating mammal native to Australia and neighbouring islands, with short forelegs, strong, large hind legs, and a long, thick tail: the female has a pouch in front, in which she carries her young

kangaroo closure the confinement of discussion esp. in Parliament to selected amendments

kangaroo court [Colloq.] a mock court illegally passing and executing judgment, as among factory workers or prison inmates

kangaroo rat a small, kangaroo-like marsupial found in Australia

kan·ji (kan'jē) n., pl. -ji, -jis [Jap.] a Japanese writing system derived from Chinese characters

KANU Kenya African National Union

ka·o·lin (kā'ə lin) n. [Fr. < Chin. kao-ling, name of hill where found] a fine white clay used in making porcelain

ka·on (kä'on) n. [ka (the letter K) + (MES)ON] any of four mesons having a mass approximately 970 times that of an electron

ka·pok (kā'pok) n. [Malay kapoq] the silky fibres around the seeds of a tropical tree: used for stuffing mattresses, sleeping bags, etc.

kap·pa (kap'ə) n. [Gr.] the tenth letter of the Greek alphabet (Κ, κ)

ka·put (kə pōōt', -poot') adj. [G. kaputt, lost, ruined, broken] [Slang] ruined, destroyed, defeated, etc.

kar·a·bi·ner (kar'ə bē'nər) n. [< G. Karabinerhaken, a snap-hook] Mountaineering a special chain link fitted with a spring clip

kar·a·kul (kar'ə kəl) n. [< Kara Kul, lake in SC U.S.S.R.] **1.** a broad-tailed sheep of C Asia **2.** same as BROADTAIL (sense 2)

kar·at (kar'ət) n. U.S. sp. of CARAT (n 2)

ka·ra·te (kə rät'ē) n. [Jap. < kara, empty + te, hand] a Japanese system of self-defence in which blows are struck with the side of the open hand

kar·ma (kär'mə) n. [Sans., a deed, fate] Buddhism & Hinduism a person's actions in one reincarnation thought of as determining his fate in the next

ka·ross (kə ros') n. [Afrik. karos] in South Africa, a cape, blanket, or rug made of animal skins

kar·ri (kar'ē) n. [< Abor.] a species of Australian eucalyptus tree, that grows to a great size

kar·roo, ka·roo (kə rōō', ka-) n., pl. -roos' [Hottentot karo] in South Africa, a dry tableland

karst (kärst) n. [G. < Karst, name of the hinterland of Trieste, altered < Slovenian Kras] a region made up of porous limestone containing deep fissures and characterized by underground caves and streams

kart (kärt) n. [altered < CART] **1.** any of various small vehicles **2.** a small, flat, 4-wheeled, motorized vehicle for one person, used in racing (**karting**): also **go-kart, go-cart**

kar·y·o- [ModL. < Gr. karyon, a nut, kernel] a combining form meaning: **1.** nut, kernel **2.** Biol. the nucleus of a cell

kas·bah (kaz'bä) n. same as CASBAH

kat·a- same as CATA-: also, before a vowel, **kat-**

kat·y·did (kāt'ē did') n. [echoic of shrill sound made by the males] a large, green, American tree insect resembling the grasshopper

kau·ri (kou'rē) *n.* [Maori] **1.** a tall pine tree of New Zealand **2.** its wood **3.** a resin (**kauri resin, kauri gum**) from this tree, used in varnishes, etc.

ka·wa-ka·wa (kä'wə kä'wə) *n.* [< Maori] a decorative New Zealand shrub with fragrant leaves

kay·ak (kī'ak) *n.* [Esk.] an Eskimo canoe made of skins completely covering a wooden frame except for an opening for the paddler

kay·o (kā'ō') *vt.* **-oed'**, **-o'ing** [< KO] [Slang] *Boxing* to knock out —*n.* [Slang] *Boxing* a knockout

ka·zoo (kə zōō') *n.* [echoic] a toy musical instrument consisting of a small, open tube with a top hole covered by a membrane that vibrates to give a buzzing quality to tones hummed through the tube

K.B. 1. King's Bench **2.** Knight Bachelor

K.B.E. Knight Commander of the British Empire

kc, kc. kilocycle; kilocycles

K.C. King's Counsel

kcal. kilocalorie; kilocalories

K.C.B. Knight Commander of the Bath

K.C.M.G., KCMG Knight Commander of St. Michael and St. George

ke·a (kā'ə, kē'ə) *n.* [Maori] a large, green parrot of New Zealand that sometimes kills sheep by tearing at their backs to eat the kidney fat

ke·bab (kə bäb') *n.* [Ar. *kabāb*] **1.** [*often pl.*] a dish consisting of small pieces of marinated meat grilled or roasted on a skewer, often with alternating pieces of onion, tomato, etc. **2.** a piece of such meat

Kech·ua (kech'wä) *n.* *same as* QUECHUA —**Kech'uan** *adj., n.*

kedge (kej) *vt., vi.* **kedged, kedg'ing** [ME. *caggen*, to fasten < ?] to move (a ship) by hauling on a rope fastened to an anchor dropped at some distance —*n.* a light anchor, esp. for such use: also **kedge anchor**

ked·ger·ee (kej'ə rē) *n.* [Hindi *khicarī*] **1.** an Indian dish of rice boiled with onions, pulse, and butter **2.** a British breakfast dish of fish, boiled rice, and eggs

keek (kēk) *n., vi.* [prob. < MDu. *kiken*, to look] [Scot.] *same as* PEEP²

keel¹ (kēl) *n.* [ME. *kele* < MDu. *kiel*, boat < Gmc. *keula*] **1.** a flat-bottomed barge or vessel used on the Tyne **2.** a measure of coal equivalent to about 21 tons (21.3 tonnes)

keel² (kēl) *n.* [< ON. *kjolr*] **1.** the chief timber or steel piece along the entire length of the bottom of a ship or boat **2.** anything like a ship's keel in position, appearance, etc. **3.** the ridged breastbone of flying birds —*vt., vi.* to turn over on its side so as to turn up the keel —**keel over 1.** to turn over; upset **2.** to fall in a faint, etc. —**on an even keel** upright and level, steady, stable, etc.

keel·haul (-hôl') *vt.* **1.** to haul (a person) under the keel of a ship as a punishment **2.** to scold or rebuke harshly

keel·son (kel's'n, kēl'-) *n.* [prob. via Du. *kolsem* < Dan. < *kjøl*, KEEL + *sville*, sill] a beam or set of timbers or metal plates fastened inside a ship's hull along the keel for added strength

keen¹ (kēn) *adj.* [OE. *cene*, wise] **1.** having a sharp edge or point **2.** sharp in force; piercing [a *keen* wind] **3.** sharp and quick in seeing, hearing, thinking, etc.; acute **4.** eager; enthusiastic **5.** strong or intense, as a desire **6.** [Colloq.] extremely competitive —**keen on** fond of; devoted to —**keen'ly** *adv.* —**keen'ness** *n.*

keen² (kēn) *n.* [< Ir. < *caoinim*, I wail] [Irish] a wailing for the dead; dirge —*vt., vi.* [Irish] to lament or wail for (the dead)

keen·er (-ər) *n.* a professional wailer at an Irish funeral

keep (kēp) *vt.* **kept, keep'ing** [< OE. *cepan*, to behold, lay hold of] **1.** to observe with due ceremony; celebrate [*keep* the Sabbath] **2.** to fulfil (a promise, etc.) **3.** to follow (a routine, diet, etc.) **4.** to go on maintaining [*keep* pace] **5.** to protect; guard; defend **6.** to watch over; take care of; tend **7.** to raise (livestock) **8.** to maintain in good order or condition; preserve **9.** to provide for; support **10.** to supply with food or lodging for pay [to *keep* boarders] **11.** to have in one's service or for one's use [to *keep* servants] **12.** to make regular entries in, detailing transactions, happenings, etc. [to *keep* books, a diary, etc.] **13.** to carry on; conduct; manage **14.** to make stay in a specified condition, position, etc. [to *keep* an engine running] **15.** to hold for future use or a long time **16.** to have regularly in stock for sale **17.** to hold in custody **18.** to detain **19.** to restrain from action **20.** to withhold **21.** to conceal (a secret) **22.** to continue to have or hold; not lose or give up **23.** to stay in or at (a path, course, or place) —*vi.* **1.** to stay in a specified condition, position, etc. **2.** to continue; go on; persevere (often with *on*) **3.** to hold oneself back; refrain

[to *keep* from telling someone] **4.** to stay fresh; not spoil; last **5.** to require no immediate attention [a task that will *keep*] —*n.* **1.** orig., care, charge, or custody **2.** *a*) a donjon *b*) a fort; castle **3.** food and shelter; support; livelihood —**for keeps** [Colloq.] **1.** with the winner keeping what he wins **2.** forever —**keep at** to continue doing; persist in —**keep back 1.** to refuse to reveal **2.** to stay a distance —**keep to 1.** to persevere in **2.** to adhere to **3.** to remain in —**keep to oneself 1.** to avoid others **2.** to refrain from telling —**keep track of** [Colloq.] to continue to be informed about —**keep up 1.** to maintain in good condition **2.** to continue **3.** to maintain the pace **4.** to remain informed about (with *on* or *with*)—**keep up with the Joneses** to try to obtain the same material goods as one's neighbours

keep·er (-ər) *n.* a person or thing that keeps; specif., *a*) a guard, as of prisoners, animals, etc. *b*) a guardian or protector *c*) a caretaker

keep·ing (-iŋ) *n.* **1.** observance (of a rule, holiday, etc.) **2.** care; charge **3.** maintenance or means of this; keep **4.** reservation for future use; preservation —**in keeping with** in conformity or accord with

keep·sake (-sāk') *n.* something kept, or to be kept, in memory of the giver; memento

kef (kef) *n.* [Ar., colloq. form of *kaif*, well-being] **1.** a dreamy condition produced by smoking a narcotic **2.** marijuana or other narcotic smoked to produce such a condition

kef·fi·yah (ke'fē'yə) *n.* *same as* KAFFIYEH

keg (keg) *n.* [< or akin to ON. *kaggi*, keg] a small barrel, usually of less than ten gallons (45.5 litres)

ke·loid (kē'loid) *n.* [< Fr. < Gr. *chēlē*, claw + *-oeidēs*, -OID] an excessive growth of scar tissue on the skin —**ke·loi'dal** *adj.*

kelp (kelp) *n.* [ME. *culp*] **1.** any of various large, coarse, brown seaweeds **2.** ashes of seaweed, from which iodine is obtained

kel·pie¹, kel·py¹ (kel'pē) *n.,* *pl.* **-pies** [Scot. < ? Gael. *calpa*, colt] *Gaelic Folklore* a water spirit, supposed to take the form of a horse and drown people

kel·pie², kel·py² (kel'pē) *n.,* *pl.* **-ies** [< ?] a breed of Australian sheepdog

kel·son (kel's'n) *n.* *same as* KEELSON

Kelt (kelt) *n.* *same as* CELT —**Kelt'ic** *adj., n.*

kelt (kelt) *n.* [Scot.] a salmon that has spawned

kel·ter (kel'tər) *n.* [Colloq.] *same as* KILTER

kel·vin (kel'vin) *n.* the SI unit of thermodynamic temperature defined as the fraction 1/273.16 of the thermodynamic temperature of the triple point of water

Kelvin scale [after 1st Baron *Kelvin*, 19th-c. Brit. physicist] *Physics* a scale of temperature measured in degrees Celsius from absolute zero (−273.15° C)

kempt (kempt) *adj.* [ME., combed: in mod. use, back-formation < UNKEMPT] [Colloq.] neat; tidy; well-groomed: a humorous usage

ken (ken) *vt., vi.* **kenned, ken'ning** [OE. *cennan*, lit., to cause to know] [Scot.] to know (*of* or *about*) —*n.* range of knowledge; understanding

ken·do (ken'dō) *n.* [Jap.] stylized swordplay, with bamboo swords: a Japanese sport

ken·nel (ken'¹) *n.* [< OFr. *chenil* < L. *canis*, a dog] **1.** a house or shelter for dogs **2.** [*often pl.*] a place where dogs are bred or kept **3.** a pack of dogs —*vt.* **-nelled, -nel·ling** to place or keep in a kennel —*vi.* to live or take shelter in a kennel

kep·i (kep'ē, kā'pē) *n.,* *pl.* **kep'is** [Fr. *kèpi* < G. dial. *käppi*, dim. of *kappe*, a CAP] a visored cap with a flat, round top, worn by French soldiers

kept (kept) *pt. & pp.* of KEEP —*adj.* maintained as a mistress [a *kept* woman]

ker·a·tin (ker'ə tin) *n.* [< Gr. *keras* (gen. *keratos*), horn + -IN¹] a tough, fibrous, insoluble protein, the principal matter of hair, nails, horn, etc.

ker·a·tose (ker'ə tōs') *adj.* [< Gr. *keras* (gen. *keratos*), horn + -OSE¹] (esp. of certain sponges) having a skeleton composed of a horny substance

kerb (kurb) *n.* [var. of CURB] the stone or concrete edging forming a gutter along a street

kerb·stone (-stōn) *n.* any of the stones, or a row of stones, making up a kerb

ker·chief (kur'chif) *n.* [< OFr. *covrechef* < *covrir*, to cover + *chef*, the head] **1.** a piece of cloth worn over the head or around the neck **2.** a handkerchief —**ker'chiefed** (-chift) *adj.*

kerf (kurf) *n.* [OE. *cyrf* < *ceorfan*, to CARVE] the cut made by a saw —*vt.* to make a kerf in

ker·fuf·fle (kər fuf'l) *n.* [< ?] [Colloq.] a commotion; disorder; agitation

ker·mes (kur'mēz) *n.* [< Fr. < Ar. & Per. *qirmiz*, crimson] **1.** the dried bodies of certain Mediterranean insects, used to make a purple-red dye **2.** the insect

ker·mis, ker·mess (kur'mis) *n.* [< Du. < *kerk*, a church + *mis*, MASS] **1.** in the Netherlands, Belgium, etc., an outdoor fair or carnival **2.** [U.S.] any similar fair or entertainment, usually for charity

kern¹ (kurn) *n.* [Fr. *carne,* a hinge < OFr. < L. *cardo*] that part of the face of a letter of type which projects beyond the body

kern², kerne (kurn) *n.* [ME. < OIr. *ceitern,* band of soldiers, soldier] **1.** formerly, a light-armed foot soldier of Ireland or the Scottish highlands **2.** [Archaic] a boor

ker·nel (kur'n'l) *n.* [OE. *cyrnel,* dim. of *corn,* seed] **1.** a grain or seed, as of corn, wheat, etc. **2.** the inner, softer part of a nut, fruit stone, etc. **3.** the central, most important part of something; essence —*vt.* **-nelled, -nel·ling** to enclose as a kernel

ker·o·sene' (ker'ə sēn', ker'ə sēn') *n.* [Gr. *kēros,* wax + -ENE] a thin oil distilled from petroleum or shale oil, used as a fuel, solvent, etc.: also, esp. in science and industry, sp. **kerosine**

ker·sey (kur'zē) *n., pl.* **-seys** [< *Kersey,* village in England] a coarse, lightweight woollen cloth, usually ribbed and with a cotton warp

ker·sey·mere (kur'zē mir') *n.* [altered (after prec.) < CASSIMERE] *same as* CASSIMERE

kes·trel (kes'trəl) *n.* [OFr. *cresserelle:* origin echoic] a small, brown and grey European falcon that can hover in the air against the wind

ketch (kech) *n.* [< ME. *cacchen,* to catch: orig. used of fishing vessels] a fore-and-aft rigged sailing vessel with a mainmast towards the bow and a relatively tall mizzenmast, forward of the rudderpost, towards the stern: distinguished from YAWL

ketch·up (kech'əp) *n.* [Malay *kēchap,* a fish sauce < Chin. *ke-tsiap*] a sauce for meat, fish, etc.; esp., a thick sauce **(tomato ketchup)** made of tomatoes flavoured with onion, salt, sugar, and spice

ke·tone (kē'tōn) *n.* [G. *Keton,* var. of Fr. *acétone: see* ACETONE] an organic chemical compound containing the bivalent radical CO in combination with two hydrocarbon radicals

ket·tle (ket''l) *n.* [ON. *ketill* < L. dim. of *catinus,* bowl] **1.** a metal container for boiling or cooking things, specif., one with a handle and a spout, either enclosed or with a lid, used for boiling water **2.** a kettledrum

ket·tle·drum (-drum') *n.* a percussion instrument consisting of a hollow hemisphere and a top made of parchment, etc. that can be tightened or loosened to change the pitch; timpano

kettle of fish a difficult situation

kev, Kev (kev) *n., pl.* **kev, Kev** [*k(ilo-) e(lectron-) v(olts)*] a unit of energy equal to one thousand (10³) electron-volts

key¹ (kē) *n., pl.* **keys** [OE. *cæge*] **1.** an instrument, usually of metal, for moving the bolt of a lock and thus locking or unlocking something **2.** anything like this; specif., *a)* a device to turn a bolt, etc. [a skate *key*] *b)* a pin, bolt, etc. put into a hole or space to hold parts together *c)* any of the levers, or the discs, etc. connected to them, pressed down to operate a piano, clarinet, typewriter, etc. *d)* a device for opening or closing an electric circuit *e)* an implement for winding up a clock **3.** a place so located as to give control of a region **4.** a thing that explains or solves, as a book of answers **5.** a controlling or essential person or thing **6.** tone of voice; pitch **7.** tone of thought or expression [in a cheerful *key*] **8.** a dry, winged fruit of various trees, as the ash **9.** *Music* a system of notes forming a given scale; tonality —*adj.* controlling; essential; important —*vt.* **keyed, key'ing 1.** to fasten or lock with a key **2.** to furnish with a key **3.** to set the tone or pitch of **4.** to bring into harmony **5.** *same as* KEYBOARD **6.** to roughen a surface, as for plastering, etc. —**key up** to make tense or excited

key² (kē) *n., pl.* **keys** [Sp. *cayo*] a reef or low island

key·board (kē'bôrd') *n.* the row(s) of keys of a piano, typewriter, linotype, etc.—*vt.* to set (a text) in type using a composing machine having a keyboard

keyed (kēd) *adj.* **1.** having keys, as some musical instruments **2.** pitched in a specified key **3.** roughened, as for plastering, etc.

key·hole (kē'hōl') *n.* an opening (in a lock) into which a key is inserted

key industry an industry upon which other industries depend or which is vital for a country's survival

key money a sum of money demanded from a new tenant as a condition of granting a lease: now illegal in the U.K.

key·note (kē'nōt') *n.* **1.** the lowest, basic note or tone of a musical scale **2.** the basic idea or ruling principle, as of a speech, policy, etc. —*vt.* **-not'ed, -not'ing 1.** to give the keynote of —**key'not'er** *n.*

keynote speech (or **address**) a speech, as at a conference, setting forth the main line of policy

key punch a keyboard machine that records data by punching holes in cards, later fed into machines for sorting, etc. —*vt.* to keyboard in this way

key ring a metal ring for holding keys

key signature *Music* the presence or absence of one or more sharps or flats after the clef on the staff, showing the key

key·stone (-stōn') *n.* **1.** the central, topmost stone of an arch **2.** a main or supporting part or principle

Kg kilogramme(s)

K.G. Knight of (the Order of) the Garter

KGB, K.G.B. [Russ. *K(omitet) G(osudarstvennoye) B(ezopasnosti),* Committee of State Security] the security police, or intelligence agency, of the Soviet Union

KEYSTONE

kha·di (kä'dē) *n.* [Hindi *khādī*] homespun cotton cloth made in India: also **khad·dar** (kä'dər)

kha·ki (kä'kē) *adj.* [< Hindi < Per. *khāk,* dust] **1.** dull yellowish-brown **2.** made of khaki (cloth) —*n., pl.* **-kis 1.** a dull yellowish brown **2.** strong, twilled cloth of this colour **3.** [*often pl.*] a khaki uniform or trousers

kha·lif (kāl'if') *n. same as* CALIPH

khan¹ (kän, kan) *n.* [< Turki *khān,* lord] **1.** a title of Turkish, Tatar, and Mongol rulers in the Middle Ages **2.** a title of honour in Iran, Afghanistan, etc. —**khan'ate** (-āt) *n.*

khan² (kän) *n.* [Ar. *khān*] in Turkey and other Eastern countries, an inn or caravanserai

khe·dive (kə dēv') *n.* [< Fr. < Turk. < Per. *khidīw,* prince] the title of the Turkish viceroys of Egypt, from 1867 to 1914 —**khe·di'val** *adj.*

Khmer (k'mer) *n.* [native name] **1.** one of a native people of SW Asia **2.** their Mon-Khmer language

kHz kilohertz

kib·ble¹ (kib''l) *vt.* **-bled, -bling** [< ?] to grind into coarse bits —*n.* kibbled food for dogs, etc.

kib·ble² (kib''l) *n.* [< G. *Kübel*] a large riveted steel bucket used in mining for raising ore to the surface

kib·butz (ki boots', -boots') *n., pl.* **kib·but·zim** (kē'-boo tsēm') [ModHeb.] an Israeli collective settlement, esp. a collective farm

kib·lah (kib'lä) *n.* [Ar. *qiblah,* something placed opposite < *qabala,* to be opposite] the point towards which Moslems turn when praying, the location of the black stone at Mecca: see KAABA

ki·bosh (ki'bosh) *n.* [< ? Yid.] [Slang] orig., nonsense —**put the kibosh on** to put an end to; veto

kick (kik) *vi.* [ME. *kiken* < ?] **1.** to strike out with the foot or feet **2.** to spring back suddenly, as a gun when fired; recoil **3.** [Colloq.] to object; complain **4.** *Football* to kick the ball —*vt.* **1.** to strike suddenly with the foot or feet **2.** to drive (a ball, etc.) in this way **3.** to make (one's way) by kicking **4.** to score (a goal in football) by kicking **5.** [Slang] to get rid of (a habit) —*n.* **1.** a blow with the foot **2.** a kicking **3.** a sudden thrust, as the recoil of a gun when fired **4.** [Colloq.] a stimulating effect, as of alcoholic liquor **5.** [Colloq.] [*often pl.*] pleasure; thrill **6.** *Football a)* a kicking of the ball *b)* the kicked ball —**kick around** (or **about**) [Colloq.] **1.** to treat roughly **2.** to move from place to place **3.** to lie about unnoticed **4.** to think about or discuss —**kick back** [Colloq.] to recoil suddenly and unexpectedly **2.** [Chiefly U.S. Slang] to give back (part of one's pay, etc.) —**kick off 1.** to put a football into play with a kick **2.** to start (a campaign, etc.) —**kick on** [Colloq.] **1.** to turn on (a switch, etc.) **2.** to begin operating —**kick out** [Colloq.] to get rid of; expel —**kick up** [Colloq.] to cause (trouble, etc.) —**kick upstairs** [Colloq.] to promote to an effectively powerless position

kick·back (-bak') *n.* **1.** [Colloq.] a sharp reaction **2.** [Chiefly U.S. Slang] *a)* a giving back of part of one's pay, etc. *b)* the money returned

kick·er (-ər) *n.* **1.** one that kicks **2.** [U.S. Slang] *a)* a surprise ending *b)* a hidden difficulty

kick·ing (-iŋ) *adj.* still alive, esp. in **alive and kicking**

kick·off (-of') *n.* **1.** the act of kicking off in football **2.** the start of a campaign, etc.

kick·shaw (kik'shô') *n.* [< Fr. *quelque chose,* something] **1.** a fancy food or dish; delicacy **2.** a trinket; trifle; gewgaw Also **kick'shaws'** (-shôz')

kick·stand (kik'stand') *n.* a short metal bar fastened to a bicycle or motorcycle: when kicked down it holds the stationary cycle upright

kick starter a foot-operated lever used for starting motorcycle engines

kid (kid) *n.* [prob. < Anglo-N.] **1.** a young goat **2.** its flesh, used as food **3.** leather from the skin of young goats, used for gloves, shoes, etc. **4.** [Colloq.] a child —*adj.* **1.** made of kidskin **2.** [Chiefly U.S. Colloq.] younger [my *kid* sister] —*vt., vi.* **kid'ded, kid'ding 1.** to give birth to (a

KETTLEDRUMS

or kids): said of goats or antelopes **2.** [Colloq.] to deceive, fool, or tease playfully —**kid′der** n. —**kid′like′, kid′dish** adj.
Kid·der·min·ster (kid′ər min′stər) n. a kind of ingrain or reversible carpet, orig. made at Kidderminster
kid·dy, kid·die (kid′ē) n., pl. **-dies** [dim. of KID] [Colloq.] a child
kid gloves soft, smooth gloves made of kidskin —**handle with kid gloves** [Colloq.] to treat with care, tact, etc.
kid·nap (-nap′) vt. **-napped′, -nap′ping** [KID + dial. nap, NAB] **1.** to steal (a child) **2.** to seize and hold (a person) against his will, by force or fraud, often for ransom —**kid′-nap′per** n.
kid·ney (kid′nē) n., pl. **-neys** [ME. kidenei < ?] **1.** either of a pair of glandular organs in vertebrates, which separate waste products from the blood and excrete them as urine **2.** an animal kidney, used as food **3.** a) temperament b) kind; sort
kidney bean the kidney-shaped seed of the common garden bean of the legume family
kidney machine a machine which takes over the function of damaged human kidneys
kidney stone a hard mineral deposit formed in the kidney from phosphates, urates, etc.
kid·skin (kid′skin′) n. leather from the skin of young goats, used for gloves, shoes, etc.

KIDNEYS
(A, right kidney; B, left kidney; C, vena cava; D, aorta; E, ureter; F, renal vein; G, renal artery; left kidney shown in cross section)

kid's stuff [Slang] anything which is extremely straightforward
kie·kie (kē′kē) n. [Maori] a New Zealand climbing shrub
kike (kīk) n. [< ?] [U.S. Slang] a Jew: a derogatory term
kil. kilometre; kilometres
kil·der·kin (kil′dər kin) n. [< MDu. kindekijn < kintal, hundredweight] an obsolete unit of capacity equal to about 18 gallons
kill (kil) vt. [ME. killen < ? OE. cwellan] **1.** to cause the death of; make die **2.** a) to destroy the vital or active qualities of b) to destroy; put an end to **3.** to defeat or veto (legislation) **4.** to spend (time) on trivial matters **5.** to stop (an engine, etc.), turn off (a light, etc.), or muffle (sound) **6.** to prevent publication of (a newspaper story) **7.** to spoil the effect of: said of colours, etc. **8.** [Colloq.] to overcome with laughter, chagrin, surprise, etc. [dressed to kill] **9.** [Colloq.] to make feel great pain or exhaustion **10.** [Slang] to drink the last, or all, of (a bottle of whisky, etc.) —vi. **1.** to destroy life **2.** to die off —n. **1.** an act of killing **2.** an animal or animals killed **3.** an enemy plane, ship, etc. destroyed—**in at the kill** present at the end of some action, particularly a hunt—**kill time** to waste time while waiting for an event, appointment, etc.
kill·er (kil′ər) n. **1.** a person, animal, or thing that kills, esp. habitually **2.** same as KILLER WHALE
killer whale any of several fierce, greyish to black, small whales that hunt in large packs and prey on large fish, seals, and other whales
kil·lick (kil′ik) n. [< ?] Naut. any small anchor, esp. one, used formerly, made of a heavy stone
kil·li·fish (kil′ē fish′) n., pl. **-fish′, -fish′es**: see FISH [< KILL² + -IE + FISH] any of several minnowlike freshwater fishes used in mosquito control and as bait: also **kil′lie** pl. **-lies**
kill·ing (kil′in) adj. **1.** causing death; deadly **2.** exhausting **3.** [Colloq.] very comical —n. **1.** slaughter; murder **2.** [Colloq.] a sudden, great profit or success —**kill′ing·ly** adv.
kill-joy (-joi′) n. a person who destroys or lessens other people's enjoyment: also **kill′joy′**
kiln (kiln, kil) n. [< OE. cylne < L. culina, kitchen] a furnace or oven for drying, burning, or baking something, as bricks, pottery, or grain —vt. to dry, burn, or bake in a kiln
kiln-dry (-drī′) vt. **-dried′, -dry′ing** to dry in a kiln
ki·lo (kē′lō, kil′ō) n., pl. **-los** [Fr.] short for: **1.** KILOGRAMME **2.** KILOMETRE
kilo- [Fr. < Gr. chilioi, thousand] a combining form meaning a thousand [kilogramme]
kilo. **1.** kilogramme **2.** kilometre
kil·o·bar (kil′ə bär′) n. [see KILO- & BAR²] a metric unit of pressure equal to 1000 bars
kil·o·cal·o·rie (kil′ə kal′ər ē) n. 1000 calories; great calorie
kil·o·cy·cle (-sī′k'l) n. former name for KILOHERTZ
kil·o·gramme, kil·o·gram (-gram′) n. the SI unit of mass, defined in terms of the international standard kilogramme at Sèvres
kil·o·hertz (-hurts′) n., pl. **-hertz′** 1000 hertz
kil·o·li·tre (-lēt′ər) n. a unit of capacity equal to 1000 litres, or one cubic metre: also U.S. **kil′o·li′ter**
ki·lo·me·tre (ki lom′ə tər, kil′ə mēt′ər) n. a unit of length or distance, equal to 1000 metres: also U.S. **ki·lo′me·ter** —**kil·o·met·ric** (kil′ə met′rik) adj.
kil·o·ton (kil′ə tun′) n. the explosive force of 1000 tons of TNT
kil·o·volt (-vōlt′) n. 1000 volts
kil·o·watt (-wot′) n. a unit of electrical power, equal to 1000 watts
kil·o·watt-hour (-our′) n. a unit of electrical energy or work, equal to that done by one kilowatt acting for one hour
kilt (kilt) vt. [ME. kilten, prob. < Scand.] **1.** [Scot.] to tuck up (a skirt, etc.) **2.** to pleat **3.** to provide a kilt for —n. a pleated skirt reaching to the knees; esp., the tartan skirt worn sometimes by men of the Scottish Highlands—**kilt′ed** adj.
kil·ter (kil′tər) n. [< ?] [Colloq.] good condition; proper order: now chiefly in **out of kilter**: also **kel′ter**
kim·ber·lite (kim′bər līt′) n. [< Kimber(ley), town in S. Africa + -LITE] a kind of peridotite which sometimes contains diamonds

KILT

ki·mo·no (kə mō′nō) n., pl. **-nos** [Jap.] **1.** a loose outer garment with short, wide sleeves and a sash, a traditional costume of Japanese men and women **2.** a woman's dressing gown like this
kin (kin) n. [< OE. cynn] relatives; family; kindred —adj. related, as by blood —**(near) of kin** (closely) related
-kin (kin) [< MDu. -ken, -kijn, dim. suffix] a suffix meaning little [lambkin]
kin·aes·the·si·a (kin′is thē′zhə, -zhē ə) n. same as KINESTHESIA
kin·cob (kin′kob) n. [< Urdu kimkhāb] a rich Indian textile of silk or muslin, usually embroidered with gold or silver
kind (kīnd) n. [< OE. cynd] **1.** [Archaic] a) origin b) nature c) manner **2.** a natural group or division [the rodent kind] **3.** essential character **4.** sort; class —adj. **1.** sympathetic, friendly, gentle, generous, etc. **2.** cordial [kind regards] —**in kind** **1.** in goods or produce instead of money **2.** with something like that received —**kind of** somewhat; rather —**of a kind** **1.** of the same kind; alike **2.** mediocre or inferior
kin·der·gar·ten (kin′dər gär′t'n) n. [G., lit., garden of children] a school or class of children, usually under five years old, in which teaching is by means of games, music, simple handicrafts, etc.
kind·heart·ed (kīnd′här′tid) adj. having or resulting from a kind heart; sympathetic; kindly —**kind′heart′ed·ly** adv. —**kind′heart′ed·ness** n.
kin·dle (kin′d'l) vt. **-dled, -dling** [ME. kindlen, freq. < ON. kynda] **1.** to set on fire; ignite **2.** to start (a fire) **3.** to excite (interest, feelings, etc.) **4.** to make bright —vi. **1.** to catch fire **2.** to become excited **3.** to become bright —**kin′-dler** n.
kin·dling (kin′dlin) n. bits of dry wood or other easily lighted material for starting a fire
kind·ly (kīnd′lē) adj. **-li·er, -li·est** **1.** kind; gracious; benign **2.** agreeable; pleasant [a kindly climate] —adv. **1.** in a kind, gracious way **2.** agreeably **3.** please [kindly reply] —**take kindly to** **1.** to be naturally attracted to **2.** to accept willingly —**kind′li·ness** n.
kind·ness (-nis) n. **1.** the state, quality, or habit of being kind **2.** kind act or treatment
kin·dred (kin′drid) n. [< OE. cynn, kin + ræden, condition] **1.** formerly, family relationship **2.** relatives or family; kin —adj. of like nature [kindred spirits]
kine (kīn) n.pl. [ME. kin < cou (< OE. cy, pl. of cu, COW¹) + -(e)n] [Archaic] cows; cattle
kin·e·mat·ics (kin′ə mat′iks) n.pl. [with sing. v.] [< Fr. < Gr. kinēma, motion < kinein, to move + -ICS] the branch of mechanics dealing with abstract motion, without reference to force or mass —**kin′e·mat′ic, kin′e·mat′i·cal** adj.
kin·e·scope (kin′ə skōp′) n. [< Gr. < kinein, to move + -SCOPE] **1.** a cathode-ray tube used in television receivers, etc. for picture display **2.** a film record of such display
ki·ne·sics (ki nē′siks, kī-) n.pl. [with sing. v.] [< Gr. kinēsis, motion + -ICS] the study of bodily movements, facial expressions, etc. as ways of communication —**ki·ne′-sic** adj.
kin·es·the·si·a (kin′is thē′zhə, -zhē ə) n. [ModL. < Gr. kinein, to move + aisthēsis, perception] the sensation of position, movement, etc. of bodily parts, perceived through nerve end organs in muscles, tendons, and joints: also **kin′-es·the′sis** (-sis) —**kin′es·thet′ic** (-thet′ik) adj.
ki·net·ic (ki net′ik) adj. [Gr. kinētikos < kinein, to move] **1.** of or resulting from motion **2.** energetic or dynamic
kinetic art sculpture or assemblage involving the use of moving parts, sounds, shifting lights, etc.
ki·net·ics (-iks) n.pl. [with sing. v.] same as DYNAMICS (sense 1)

kin·folk (kin'fōk') *n.pl.* [chiefly U.S.] family; relatives; kin; kindred

king (kiŋ) *n.* [OE. *cyning*] 1. the male ruler of a monarchy; male monarch, limited or absolute 2. *a)* a man who is supreme in some field [an oil *king*] *b)* something supreme in its class 3. a playing card with a picture of a king on it 4. *Chess* the chief piece, movable one square in any direction: see CHECKMATE 5. *Draughts* a piece crowned upon reaching the opponent's base and hence movable backwards and forwards —*adj.* chief (in size, importance, etc.)

king·bolt (-bōlt') *n.* a vertical bolt connecting the front axle of a wagon, etc., or the bogies with a railway carriage, to allow pivoting

King Charles Spaniel a toy breed of spaniel with very long ears and a wavy coat made fashionable by Charles II of England

king cobra a large, hooded, very poisonous snake native to India

king crab *same as* HORSESHOE CRAB

king·cup (-kup') *n.* 1. *same as* BUTTERCUP 2. the marsh marigold

king·dom (-dəm) *n.* [OE. *cyningdom*: see KING & -DOM] 1. a government or country headed by a king or queen; monarchy 2. a realm; domain [the *kingdom* of poetry] 3. any of the three great divisions of things in nature (the animal, vegetable, and mineral kingdoms)

king·fish (-fish') *n.* *pl.* -**fish'**, -**fish'es**: see FISH any of various large food fishes of the Atlantic or Pacific coast of the U.S.

king·fish·er (-fish'ər) *n.* a brightly-coloured bird with a large, crested head, a large, strong beak, and a short tail

King James Version [chiefly U.S.] *same as* AUTHORIZED VERSION

king·let (kiŋ'lit) *n.* [see -LET] 1. a petty, unimportant king 2. any of several small songbirds, as the goldcrest

king·ly (kiŋ'lē) *adj.* -**li·er**, -**li·est** of, like, or fit for a king; royal; regal; noble —*adv.* [Archaic] in the manner of a king —**king'li·ness** *n.*

king·mak·er (-mā'kər) *n.* a politically powerful person who manages to place people in positions of authority

king-of-arms (-əv ärmz') *n.* in Great Britain, any of the chief officers who decide questions of heraldry

king of beasts an epithet for a lion

king of birds an epithet for an eagle

King of the Castle a children's game in which each attempts to dislodge the other from a mound or hillock

king penguin a species of penguin with a greyish-blue back and black plumage on the head

king·pin (-pin') *n.* 1. *same as* KINGBOLT 2. [Colloq.] the main or essential person or thing

king post *Carpentry* a vertical supporting post between the apex of a triangular truss and the base, or tie beam

King's (or **Queen's**) **Bench** [so called because the sovereign used to sit there on a raised bench] *Law* formerly, the supreme court of common law; now, one of the three divisions of the High Court of Justice

KING POST

king's (or **queen's**) **English, the** standard (esp. British) English

king's (or **queen's**) **evidence** *Law* evidence given for the Crown by a person against his former associates in crime: used esp. in the phrase **turn king's** (or **queen's**) **evidence**

king's evil a former name for SCROFULA: so called from the belief that the king's touch would heal it

king·ship (kiŋ'ship') *n.* 1. the position, rank, or dignity of a king 2. the rule of a king

king-size (-sīz') *adj.* [Colloq.] bigger than normal [a *king-size* bed]: also **king'-sized'**

King's (or **Queen's**) **Messenger** an official who carries government despatches, at home or abroad

kink (kiŋk) *n.* [< Scand.] 1. a short twist, curl, or bend in a rope, hair, etc. 2. a painful cramp, as in the neck 3. an eccentricity; quirk 4. a difficulty or defect, as in a plan —*vi., vt.* to form or cause to form a kink

kin·ka·jou (kiŋ'kə jōō') *n.* [Fr., *quincajou*, a misapplication of AmInd. name, whence CARCAJOU] a nocturnal, tree-dwelling, raccoonlike mammal of Central and South America, with yellowish-brown fur, large eyes, and a long, prehensile tail

kink·y (kiŋ'kē) *adj.* **kink'i·er**, **kink'i·est** 1. full of kinks; tightly curled [kinky hair] 2. [Slang] weird, bizarre, etc.; specif., sexually abnormal —**kink'i·ness** *n.*

ki·no (kē'nō) *n.* [< WAfr. (Mandingo) native name] an astringent drug obtained from the gum of a tree found in W Africa and S India

kins·folk (kinz'fōk') *n.pl.* var. of KINFOLK

kin·ship (kin'ship') *n.* 1. family relationship 2. relationship; close connection

kins·man (kinz'mən) *n.*, *pl.* -**men** a relative; esp., a male relative —**kins'wom'an** (-wōm'ən) *n.fem.*, *pl.* -**wom'en** (-wim'ən)

ki·osk (kē'osk) *n.* [< Fr. < Turk. < Per. *kūshk*, palace] 1. in Turkey and Persia, an open summerhouse or pavilion 2. a somewhat similar small structure open at one or more sides, used as a newsstand, bandstand, etc. 3. a telephone box

kip[1] (kip) *n.* [prob. < Du.] the untanned hide of a calf, lamb, or other young or small animal

kip[2] (kip) *n.*, *pl.* **kips**, **kip** [Thai] *see* MONETARY UNITS, table (Laos)

kip[3] (kip) *n.* [KI(LO) + P(OUND)[1]] a unit of weight equal to 1000 pounds

kip[4] (kip) *n.* [< Dan. *kippe*, low alehouse] [Slang] 1. sleep 2. a bed —*vi.* **kipped, kip'ping** [Slang] to sleep

kip·per (kip'ər) *vt.* [< ? the *n.*] to cure (herring, salmon, etc.) by cleaning, salting, and drying or smoking —*n.* [OE. *cypera*] 1. a male salmon or sea trout during or shortly after the spawning season 2. a kippered herring, salmon, etc.

kirk (kurk; *Scot.* kirk) *n.* [ME. *kirke* < OE. *cirice*, CHURCH] [Scot. & North Eng.] a church

kir·mess (kur'mis) *n.* var. of KERMIS

kirsch·was·ser (kirsh'väs'ər) *n.* [G. < *Kirsche*, cherry, + *Wasser*, water] a colourless alcoholic drink distilled from the fermented juice of black cherries: often **kirsch**

kir·tle (kur't'l) *n.* [OE. *cyrtel*, ult. < ? L. *curtus*, short + -*el*, dim. suffix] [Archaic] 1. a man's tunic or coat 2. a woman's dress or skirt

kis·met (kiz'met, kis'-) *n.* [< Turk. < Ar. *qismah*, a portion, fate] fate; destiny

kiss (kis) *vt.* [OE. *cyssan*] 1. to touch or caress with the lips in affection, greeting, etc. 2. to touch lightly —*vi.* to kiss each other —*n.* a kissing —**kiss goodbye** 1. to kiss in leaving 2. [Colloq.] to give up all hope of gaining or regaining —**kiss'a·ble** *adj.*

kiss curl a circular curl on the forehead or cheek

kiss·er (-ər) *n.* 1. a person who kisses 2. [Slang] *a)* the mouth or lips *b)* the face

kissing gate a U- or V-shaped enclosure allowing only one person through at a time

kiss of life artificial resuscitation whereby air is blown into the victim's lung through his mouth by the rescuer: also called **mouth-to-mouth resuscitation**

kit (kit) *n.* [prob. < MDu. *kitte*, a wooden tub] 1. personal equipment, esp. as packed for travel 2. a set of tools, articles for special use, parts to be assembled, etc. 3. a container for such equipment, tools, etc. 4. [Colloq.] lot; collection: now chiefly in **the whole kit and caboodle**, everybody or everything—*vt., vi.* **kit'ted, kit'ting** to fit out or be fitted out with kit

kit·bag (-bag) *n.* a bag, usually canvas, that holds kit

kitch·en (kich'ən) *n.* [< OE. *cycene* < LL. *coquina* < L. *coquere*, to cook] 1. a room or place for preparing and cooking food 2. a staff that cooks and serves food

kitch·en·ette (kich'ə net') *n.* a small, compact kitchen

kitchen garden a garden in which vegetables, and sometimes fruit, are grown, usually for home use

kitchen midden [transl. of Dan. *kökkenmödding*] a mound of shells, animal bones, etc. marking the site of a prehistoric settlement

kitchen sink an emphasis on the more mundane, and often unpleasant aspects of life in art, drama, etc., esp. since the mid 1950's

kitch·en·ware (kich'ən wer') *n.* kitchen utensils

kite (kīt) *n.* [OE. *cyta*] 1. a bird of the hawk family, with long, pointed wings and, usually, a forked tail 2. a light wooden frame covered with paper or cloth, to be flown in the wind at the end of a string 3. [*pl.*] the highest sails of a ship 4. a bad cheque or the like used to raise money or maintain credit temporarily —*vi.* **kit'ed, kit'ing** 1. [Colloq.] to fly like a kite 2. to get money or credit by using bad cheques, etc. —*vt.* to issue (a bad cheque, etc.) as a kite

kite-mark (kīt'märk) the kite-shaped mark on goods signifying that they are approved by the British Standards Institution

kith (kith) *n.* [OE. *cyth* < base of *cuth*, known: see UNCOUTH] friends, acquaintances, or neighbours: now only in **kith and kin**, friends, acquaintances, and relatives; also, often, relatives, or kin

kitsch (kich) *n.* [G., gaudy trash < dial. *kitschen*, to smear] pretentious but shallow art, writing, etc., designed for popular appeal —**kitsch'y** *adj.*

kit·ten (kit''n) *n.* [< OFr. var. of *chaton*, dim. of *chat*, cat] a young cat —*vi.* **to have kittens** to react with disapproval, anxiety, shock, etc.

kit·ten·ish (-ish) *adj.* like a kitten; playful; frisky; often, playfully coy —**kit'ten·ish·ly** *adv.* —**kit'ten·ish·ness** *n.*

kit·ti·wake (kit'i wāk') *n.*, *pl.* -**wakes'**, -**wake'**: see PLURAL, II, D, 1 [echoic of its cry] any of several sea gulls of the Arctic and North Atlantic

kit·ty[1] (kit′ē) *n., pl.* **-ties** 1. a kitten 2. *a pet name for* a cat of any age

kit·ty[2] (kit′ē) *n., pl.* **-ties** [prob. < KIT] 1. in poker, etc., *a)* the stakes or pot *b)* a pool from the winnings, to pay for refreshments, etc. 2. any money pooled for some special use

ki·wi (kē′wē) *n., pl.* **-wis** [Maori: echoic of its cry] 1. a tailless New Zealand bird with undeveloped wings, hairlike feathers, and a long, slender bill 2. [Colloq.] a New Zealander

K.K.K., KKK Ku Klux Klan

kl, kl. kilolitre; kilolitres

Klan (klan) *n.* short for KU KLUX KLAN —**Klans′man** *n., pl.* -**men**

Klax·on (klak′s'n) *a trademark for* a kind of electric horn with a loud, shrill sound —*n.* [k-] such a horn

Klee·nex (klē′neks) *a trademark for* soft tissue paper used as a handkerchief, etc. —*n.* [occas. k-] a piece of such paper

klep·to·ma·ni·a (klep′tə mā′nē ə) *n.* [ModL. < Gr. *kleptēs*, thief + -MANIA] an abnormal, persistent impulse to steal —**klep′to·ma′ni·ac′** (-ak′) *n.*

klieg light (klēg) [after A. & J. *Kliegl*, 20th-c. U.S. inventors] a very bright, hot arc light used to light film sets: also sp. **kleig**

klip·das (klip′das) *n.* [Afrik.,< *klip,* rock + *das,* badger] S African name for the hyrax of Cape Colony

klip·spring·er (klip′spriŋ′ər) *n., pl.* **-ers, -er** [Afrik. < *klip,* a rock + *springer,* springer] a small, agile mountain antelope of S and E Africa

kloof (kloof) *n.* [Afrik. < Du. *klooven,* to cleave] in South Africa, a deep, narrow valley; gorge

klys·tron (klīs′tron) *n.* [< Gr. < *klyzein,* to wash + (ELEC)TRON] an electron tube used as an oscillator, amplifier, etc. in ultrahigh frequency circuits to modify the velocity of an electron stream

km, km. kilometre; kilometres

knack (nak) *n.* [ME. *knak,* sharp blow: prob. echoic] 1. *a)* a trick; device *b)* a clever way of doing something 2. ability to do something easily

knack·er (nak′ər) *n.* [Early ModE., harness maker < ?] 1. a person who buys and slaughters worn-out horses and sells their flesh as dog's meat, etc. 2. a person who buys and wrecks old houses, etc. and sells their materials 3. [usually *pl.*] [Slang] testicles —*vt.* [Slang] to exhaust; tire [he was *knackered*]

knag (nag) *n.* [ME. *knagge*] 1. a knot in wood 2. a peg

knap (nap) *vt., vi.* **knapped, knap′ping** [LME. *knappon,* akin to Du. *knappen,* to snap, eat] 1. to rap or snap 2. to split flints for walling

knap·sack (nap′sak′) *n.* [Du. *knapzak < knappen,* to eat + *zak,* a sack] a leather or canvas bag or case worn on the back, as by soldiers or hikers, for carrying equipment or supplies

knap·weed (nap′wēd′) *n.* [earlier *knopweed:* see KNOP & WEED] a plant of the composite family; esp., a hardy perennial with heads of rose-purple flowers

knar (när) *n.* [ME. *knarre*] a knot in a tree or in timber

knave (nāv) *n.* [OE. *cnafa,* boy] 1. [Archaic] *a)* a male servant *b)* a man of humble status 2. a deceitful rascal; rogue 3. a jack (the playing card)

knav·er·y (nāv′ər ē) *n., pl.* **-er·ies** behaviour or an act characteristic of a knave; rascality

knav·ish (-ish) *adj.* like a knave; esp., dishonest; deceitful —**knav′ish·ly** *adv.* —**knav′ish·ness** *n.*

knead (nēd) *vt.* [OE. *cnedan*] 1. to work (dough, clay, etc.) into a pliable mass by pressing and squeezing, usually with the hands 2. to massage with similar movements 3. to make or form as by kneading —**knead′er** *n.*

knee (nē) *n.* [OE. *cneow*] 1. the joint between the thigh and the lower part of the human leg 2. any similar or corresponding joint, as in an animal's forelimb 3. anything like a knee, esp. like a bent knee 4. the part of a stocking, trouser leg, etc. covering the knee —*vt.* **kneed, knee′ing** 1. to hit or touch with the knee 2. [Colloq.] to make trousers baggy at the knee—**bring to one's knees** to force to submit or give in

knee breeches *same as* BREECHES (sense 1)

knee·cap (-kap′) *n.* a movable bone at the front of the human knee; patella: also **knee′pan′** (-pan′) —*vt.* to shoot through the kneecap as a punishment

knee-deep (-dēp′) *adj.* 1. sunk to the knees, as in water 2. so deep as to reach the knees

knee-high (-hī′) *adj.* so high or tall as to reach to the knees —**knee-high to a grasshopper** [Canad. Colloq.] very young

knee·hole (-hōl′) *n.* a space for the knees, as under a desk top

kneel (nēl) *vi.* **knelt, kneel′ing** [OE. *cneowlian < cneow,* knee] to bend or rest on a knee or the knees —**kneel′er** *n.*

knee·pad (nē′pad′) *n.* a pad worn to protect the knee, esp. by sportsmen

knell (nel) *vi.* [OE. *cnyllan*] 1. to ring in a slow, solemn way; toll 2. to sound ominously or mournfully —*vt.* to call or announce as by a knell —*n.* 1. the sound of a tolling bell 2. an omen of death, failure, etc.

knelt (nelt) *pt. and pp. of* KNEEL

knew (nyoo) *pt. of* KNOW

knick·er·bock·ers (nik′ər bok′ərz) *n.pl.* [< Diedrich Knickerbocker, fictitious author of Washington Irving's *History of New York*] short, loose trousers gathered in at or just below the knees

knick·ers (nik′ərz) *n.pl.* [contr. < prec.] a woman's undergarment covering the lower trunk and often with elasticated legs

knick·knack (nik′nak′) *n.* [redupl. of KNACK] a small ornamental article or contrivance

knife (nīf) *n., pl.* **knives** [OE. *cnif*] 1. a cutting or stabbing instrument with a sharp blade, single-edged or double-edged, set in a handle 2. a cutting blade, as in a machine —*vt.* **knifed, knif′ing** 1. to cut or stab with a knife 2. [Colloq.] to hurt, defeat, etc. by treachery —*vi.* to pass into or through something quickly, like a sharp knife —**have one's knife into someone** to have a grudge against or victimize someone —**under the knife** [Colloq.] under surgery —**knife′like** *adj.*

knife-edge (-ej′) *n.* a metal wedge whose fine edge serves as the fulcrum for a scale beam, pendulum, etc.

knight (nīt) *n.* [OE. *cniht,* boy] 1. in the Middle Ages, *a)* a military attendant of the king or other feudal superior, typically holding land in fief *b)* later, a man of high birth who after serving as page and squire was formally raised to honourable military rank and pledged to chivalrous conduct 2. in Great Britain, a man who for some achievement is given honorary nonhereditary rank next below a baronet, entitling him to use *Sir* before his Christian name 3. [usually K-] a member of any society that officially calls its members *knights* 4. [Poet.] a lady's devoted champion or attendant 5. *Chess* a piece typically shaped like a horse's head —*vt.* to make (a man) a knight

knight-er·rant (-er′ənt) *n., pl.* **knights′-er′rant** 1. a medieval knight wandering in search of adventure 2. a chivalrous or quixotic person —**knight′-er′rant·ry** (-er′ən trē) *n., pl.* **-ries**

knight·hood (-hood′) *n.* 1. the rank or vocation of a knight 2. knightly conduct 3. knights

knight·ly (-lē) *adj.* 1. of or like a knight; chivalrous, brave, etc. 2. consisting of knights —**knight′li·ness** *n.*

knight of the road 1. a tramp 2. a commercial traveller

Knight Templar *pl.* **Knights Templars,** a member of a military and religious order established among the Crusaders c. 1118

knit (nit) *vt., vi.* **knit′ted** *or* **knit, knit′ting** [OE. *cnyttan* < base of *cnotta,* a knot] 1. to make (cloth or clothing) by looping yarn or thread together with special needles 2. to form into cloth in this way 3. to join closely and firmly 4. to draw (the brows) together —*n.* cloth or a garment made by knitting —**knit′ter** *n.*

knit·ting (-iŋ) *n.* 1. the action of a person or thing that knits 2. knitted work

knitting machine a machine (usually electric) used for knitting

knitting needle an eyeless, long needle used in pairs, etc. in knitting by hand

knit·wear (-wer′) *n.* knitted clothing

knives (nīvz) *n. pl. of* KNIFE

knob (nob) *n.* [< or akin to MLowG. *knobbe,* a knot, bud, etc.] 1. a rounded lump or protuberance 2. a handle, usually round, of a door, drawer, etc. 3. a rounded hill or mountain —**with knobs on** [Slang] that, and more: usually ironic —**knobbed** *adj.*

knob·by (nob′ē) *adj.* **-bi·er, -bi·est** 1. covered with knobs 2. like a knob —**knob′bi·ness** *n.*

knob·ker·rie (-ker ē) *n.* [Afrik. *knopkirie* < Du. *knobbe,* knob + Hottentot *kirri,* a club] a short club with a knobbed end, used as a weapon by some South African tribes and as a truncheon by the native police

knock (nok) *vi.* [OE. *cnocian*] 1. to strike a blow, as with the fist; esp., to rap on a door 2. to bump; collide 3. to make a thumping or rattling noise, as an engine 4. [Colloq.] to find fault —*vt.* 1. to hit; strike 2. to make by hitting or striking [to knock a hole in the wall] 3. [Colloq.] to find fault with —*n.* 1. a knocking 2. a sharp blow; rap, as on a door 3. a thumping or rattling noise, as in an engine 4. [Colloq.] a misfortune or trouble —**knock about** (or **around**) [Colloq.] 1. to wander about; roam 2. to treat roughly —**knock back** [Slang] to drink or eat —**knock down** 1. to strike down 2. to take apart 3. to indicate the sale of at an auction —**knock it off!** [Slang] quit it! specif., stop talking! —**knock off** 1. [Colloq.] to stop working 2. [Colloq.] to deduct 3. [Colloq.] to make or do hastily or easily 4. [Slang] to kill 5. [Slang] to steal —**knock on** *Rugby* to play the ball forward with the hand or arm —**knock (oneself) out** to exert oneself as to point of exhaustion —**knock out** 1. *Boxing* to score a knockout over 2. to make unconscious or exhausted 3. to defeat, destroy, etc. 4. [Colloq.] to do; make; specif., to compose, write, etc., esp. casually or hastily —**knock sideways** [Colloq.] to disconcert sharply; discomfit —**knock together** to make or compose hastily or crudely —**knock up** 1. [Colloq.] a) to exhaust b) to wake (someone) as by knocking at the door 2. [U.S. Slang] to make pregnant

knock·a·bout (-ə baut′) n. 1. a small, one-masted yacht with a mainsail, jib, and centreboard or keel, but no bowsprit 2. something for knockabout use —adj. 1. rough; noisy; boisterous 2. made or suitable for rough use

knock·down (-daun′) adj. 1. that knocks down; overwhelming 2. made so as to be easily taken apart [a knockdown table] 3. reduced as low as possible: said of prices —n. 1. a knocking down; felling 2. blow that knocks down

knock·er (-ər) n. 1. one that knocks; specif., a small metal ring, knob, etc. on a door, for knocking 2. (usually pl.) [Slang] a female breast

knock·er-up (-up′) n. formerly, a person employed to wake workmen in the early morning

knock·ing-shop (-iŋ shop) n. [Slang] a brothel

knock-knee (-nē′) n. 1. a condition in which the legs bend inward at the knees 2. [pl.] such knees —**knock′-kneed′** adj.

knock·out (-aut′) adj. that knocks out, as a blow —n. 1. a knocking out or being knocked out 2. a) a blow that knocks out b) Boxing a victory won when the opponent is knocked down and cannot rise before an official count of ten 3. [Slang] a very attractive or striking person or thing

knockout drops [Slang] a drug put into a drink to cause the drinker to become unconscious

knoll (nōl) n. [OE. cnoll] a hillock; mound

knot[1] (not) n. [OE. cnotta] 1. a lump or knob in a thread, cord, etc., as formed by a tangle drawn tight 2. a fastening made by intertwining or tying together pieces of string, rope, etc. 3. an ornamental bow of ribbon or twist of braid 4. a small group or cluster 5. something that ties closely or intricately; esp., the bond of marriage 6. a problem; difficulty 7. a knotlike part, as in a tense muscle; specif., a) a hard lump on a tree where a branch grows out b) a cross section of such a lump, appearing cross-grained in a board c) a joint on a plant stem where leaves grow out 8. Naut. a unit of speed of one nautical mile (1852 m) an hour [a speed of 10 knots] —vt. knot′ted, knot′ting 1. to tie or intertwine in or with a knot 2. to tie closely or intricately; entangle —vi. 1. to form a knot or knots 2. to make knots for fringe —**get knotted** [Slang] an expression of disapproval or rejection —**tie the knot** [Colloq.] to get married —**knot′ted** adj. —**knot′ter** n.

knot[2] (not) n. [rare ME. knotte < ?] a small sandpiper that breeds in arctic regions

knot·grass (not′gräs′) n. a common weed with slender stems and narrow leaves: also **knot′weed′** (-wēd′)

knot·hole (-hōl′) n. a hole in a board, etc. where a knot has fallen out

knot·ty (-ē) adj. -ti·er, -ti·est 1. full of knots [a knotty board] 2. hard to solve; puzzling [a knotty problem] —**knot′ti·ness** n.

knout (naut) n. [Russ. knut < Sw., a knot] a leather whip formerly used in Russia to flog criminals —vt. to flog with a knout

know (nō) vt. knew, known, know′ing [OE. cnawan] 1. to be well informed about [to know the facts] 2. to be aware of; have perceived or learned [to know that one is loved] 3. to have securely in the memory [the actor knows his lines] 4. to be acquainted or familiar with 5. to have understanding of or skill in as a result of study or experience [to know music] 6. to recognize [I'd know that face anywhere] 7. to recognize as distinct; distinguish [to know right from wrong] 8. [Archaic] to have sexual intercourse with —vi. 1. to have knowledge 2. to be sure, informed, or aware —**in the know** [Colloq.] having confidential information —**know better** to be aware that one could or should act better or think more correctly —**know what's what** to be very shrewd and wide-awake —**know′a·ble** adj. —**know′er** n.

know-all (-ôl′) n. [Colloq.] a conceited person who thinks he knows everything

know-how (-hau′) n. [Colloq.] knowledge of how to do something well; technical skill

know·ing (-iŋ) adj. 1. having knowledge or information 2. shrewd; clever 3. implying shrewd understanding or secret knowledge [a knowing look] 4. deliberate —**know′ing·ly** adv. —**know′ing·ness** n.

knowl·edge (nol′ij) n. 1. the act, fact, or state of knowing 2. acquaintance with facts; range of information, awareness, or understanding 3. what is known; learning; enlightenment 4. the body of facts, principles, etc. accumulated by mankind —**to (the best of) one's knowledge** as far as one knows; within the range of one's information

knowl·edge·a·ble (-ə b'l) adj. having or showing knowledge

or intelligence —**knowl′edge·a·bil′i·ty, knowl′edge·a·ble·ness** n. —**knowl′edge·a·bly** adv.

known (nōn) pp. of KNOW

know-noth·ing (nō′nuth′iŋ) n. an ignoramus

knuck·le (nuk′'l) n. [< or akin to MDu. & MLowG. knokel, little bone] 1. a joint of the finger; esp., the joint connecting a finger to the rest of the hand 2. the knee or hock joint of a pig or other animal, used as food 3. [pl.] same as BRASS KNUCKLES —vt. -led, -ling to strike, press, or touch with the knuckles —**knuckle down** 1. to rest the knuckles on the ground in shooting a marble 2. to work energetically or seriously —**knuckle under** to yield; give in —**near the knuckle** [Colloq.] (of a joke) almost indecent

knuck·le-dust·er (-dus′tər) n. linked metal rings or a metal bar with finger holes, worn for rough fighting

knuck·le·head (-hed′) n. [Colloq.] a stupid person

knurl (nurl) n. [prob. blend of ME. knur, a knot + GNARL] 1. a knot, knob, nodule, etc. 2. any of a series of small beads or ridges, as along the edge of a coin —vt. to make knurls on —**knurled** adj.

knurl·y (-ē) adj. knurl′i·er, knurl′i·est full of knurls, as wood; gnarled

KO (kā′ō′) vt. KO′d, KO′ing [Slang] Boxing to knock out —n., pl. KO's [Slang] Boxing a knockout Also K.O., k.o.

ko·a·la (kō ä′lə) n. [< Abor.] an Australian, tree-dwelling marsupial animal with thick, grey fur: it feeds on eucalyptus leaves and buds

ko·bold (kō′bold) n. [G.] Ger. Folklore 1. a helpful or mischievous sprite in households; brownie 2. a gnome in mines, etc.

ko·di·ak bear (kō′dē ak′) a very large, brown bear found on Kodiak Island and in adjacent areas of Alaska

ko·el (kō′əl) n. [Hindi < Sans. kokila: origin echoic] any of various cuckoos of India, the East Indies, and Australia

KOALA
(70-90 cm long)

kohl (kōl) n. [Ar. kuḥl] a cosmetic preparation used, esp. in Eastern countries, for eye makeup

kohl·ra·bi (kōl′rä′bē) n., pl. -bies [G. < It., pl. of cavolo rapa, cole rape: cf. COLE & RAPE[2]] a garden vegetable related to the cabbage, with an edible bulbous stem

koi·ne (koi′nā, -nē) n. [Gr. koinē (dialektos) common (dialect)] [also K-] 1. the language used throughout the Greek world during the Hellenistic and Roman periods 2. a regional dialect or language that has become the common language of a larger area

ko·la (kō′lə) n. same as COLA

kola nut the seed of the cola

ko·lin·sky (kə lin′skē, kō-) n., pl. -skies [< Russ. < Kola, Russian district] 1. any of several weasels of Asia 2. the golden-brown fur of such a weasel

kol·khoz (kol khôz′) n. [Russ. < kol(lektivnoe), collective + knoz(aĭstvo), household, farm] a collective farm in the Soviet Union

Kol Nid·re (kōl nē′drä, nid′rə) n. [Aram. kōl nidhrē, lit., all our vows] 1. the prayer of atonement recited in synagogues at the opening of Yom Kippur eve services 2. the music for this

koo·doo (kōō′dōō) n., pl. -doos, -doo: see PLURAL, II, D, 1 same as KUDU

kook (kook) n. [< ? cuckoo] [Chiefly U.S. Slang] a person regarded as silly, eccentric, crazy, etc. —**kook′y, kook′ie** adj. kook′i·er, kook′i·est

kook·a·bur·ra (kook′ə bur′ə, -bur′) n. [< Abor.] an Australian kingfisher with an abrupt, harsh cry suggestive of loud laughter: also **laughing jackass**

ko·peck, ko·pek (kō′pek) n. [< Russ. < kopye, a lance] a monetary unit, and a coin, equal to 1/100 of a ruble: see MONETARY UNITS, table (U.S.S.R.)

kop·je (kop′ē) n. [Afrik. dim. of kop, head] in South Africa, a small hill; hillock

Ko·ran (kô rän′; kə-) n. [Ar. qur'ān, lit., book, reading < qara'a, to read] the sacred book of the Moslems: its contents are reported revelations made to Mohammed by Allah —**Ko·ran′ic** adj.

Ko·re·an (kə rē′ən) adj. of Korea, its people, etc. —n. 1. a native of Korea 2. the language of the Koreans

ko·ru·na (kō rōō′nä) n., pl. ko·ru·ny, ko·run′ [Czech < L. corona, a crown] see MONETARY UNITS, table (Czechoslovakia)

ko·sher (kō′shər; for v., usually kosh′ər) adj. [Heb. kāshēr, fit, proper] 1. Judaism a) clean or fit to eat according to the dietary laws: Lev. 11 b) dealing in such food 2. [Slang] all right, proper, etc. —n. kosher food —vt. to make kosher

kow·hai (kō′hī) n. [Maori] a New Zealand shrub or tree with golden flowers

kow·tow (kou′tou′, kō′-) n. [Chin. k'o-t'ou, lit., knock head] the act of kneeling and touching the ground with the forehead to show great deference, submissive respect, homage, etc. —*vi.* 1. to make a kowtow 2. to show submissive respect (*to*)

Kr *Chem.* krypton

kraal (kräl) *n.* [Afrik. < Port. *curral*, pen for cattle] 1. a village of South African natives, usually surrounded by a stockade 2. a fenced enclosure for cattle or sheep in South Africa

krait (krīt) *n.* [Hindi *karait*] a very poisonous, yellow-banded snake, found in SC and SE Asia

kra·ken (krä'k'n) *n.* [Norw.] a legendary sea monster of northern seas

krantz (kränts) *n.* [Afrik. < Du. *Krans*, a wreath] in S. Africa 1. a crown of rocks on the top of a mountain 2. a precipice

krem·lin (krem'lin) *n.* [Fr. < Russ. *kreml'*] in Russia, the citadel of a city —**the Kremlin** 1. the citadel of Moscow, formerly housing government offices of the Soviet Union 2. the government of the Soviet Union

Krem·lin·ol·o·gy (krem'lin ol'ə jē) *n.* [prec. & -LOGY] [Colloq.] the study of the government, foreign policy, etc. of the Soviet Union —**Krem'lin·ol'o·gist** *n.*

krill (kril) *n., pl.* **krill** [Norw. *kril*, young fry (of fish)] a small, shrimplike crustacean, the main food of baleen whales

krim·mer (krim'ər) *n.* [G. < *Krim*, Crimea] a greyish, tightly curled fur made from the pelts of Crimean lambs

kris (krēs) *n.* [Malay *kerīs*] a Malay dagger with a wavy blade; creese

kro·na (krō'nə; *Sw.* krōō'nə) *n., pl.* **-nor** (-nôr) [Sw. < L. *corona*, crown] *see* MONETARY UNITS, table (Sweden)

kró·na (krō'nə) *n., pl.* **-nur** (-nər) [Ice. < ML. *corona*, a crown] *see* MONETARY UNITS, table (Iceland)

kro·ne (krō'nə) *n., pl.* **-ner** (-nər) [Dan. < L. *corona*, crown] *see* MONETARY UNITS, table (Denmark, Norway)

krul·ler (krul'ər) *n.* *same as* CRULLER

kryp·ton (krip'ton) *n.* [< Gr. neut. of *kryptos*, hidden < *kryptein*, to hide] a rare, inert, gaseous chemical element present in very small quantities in air: symbol, Kr; at. wt., 83.80; at. no., 36

Kshat·ri·ya (kshat'rē ə) *n.* [Sans. *kṣatriya* < *kṣatra*, rule] among the Hindus, a member of the military caste, next below the Brahmans

Kt *Chess* knight

kt. 1. karat 2. kiloton(s)

ku·dos (kyōō'dos) *n.* [Gr. *kydos*, glory] praise for an achievement; glory; fame

ku·du (kōō'dōō) *n., pl.* **-dus, -du:** see PLURAL, II, D, 1 [Hottentot] a large, greyish-brown African antelope with long, twisted horns

Ku Klux Klan (kyōō'kluks'klan) [< Gr. *kyklos*, a circle + *klan*, arbitrary sp. for CLAN] [U.S.] 1. a secret society of white men founded in the S States after the Civil War to reestablish and maintain white supremacy 2. a U.S. secret, terrorist society organized in 1915: it is anti-Negro, anti-Semitic, anti-Catholic, etc.

kuk·ri (koo'kri) *n.* [Hindi, *kukri*] a short, curved knife with a broad blade, used by the Gurkhas

ku·lak (kōō läk') *n.* [Russ., lit., fist < Estonian] a well-to-do farmer in Russia who profited from the labour of poorer peasants and who opposed the Soviet collectivization of the land

ku·miss (kōō'mis) *n.* [G. < Russ. < Tatar *kumiz*] mare's or camel's milk fermented and used as a drink by Tatar nomads of Asia

küm·mel (kim''l; *G.* küm'əl) *n.* [G., caraway < OHG. *kumil* < L. *cuminum:* see CUMIN] a colourless liqueur flavoured with caraway seeds, anise, cumin, etc.

kum·quat (kum'kwot) *n.* [< Chin. *chin-chü*, golden orange] 1. a small, orange-coloured, oval fruit, with a sour pulp and a sweet rind, used in preserves 2. a tree that bears this fruit

kung fu (koon'fōō', goon') [< Chin.] a Chinese system of self-defence, like karate but emphasizing circular rather than linear movements

Kurd (kurd) *n.* [Turk. & Ar.] any of a nomadic Moslem people living chiefly in Kurdistan —**Kurd'ish** *adj., n.*

kur·ra·jong (kur'ə jong') *n.* [< Abor.] any of several Australian trees yielding fibres used for weaving mats, ropes etc.

kur·to·sis (kər tō'sis) *n.* [< Gr. *kyrtōsis*, a bulging < *kyrtos*, curved] the degree of sharpness of peak of the graph of a statistical distribution indicative of the concentration round the mean

Kush·it·ic (kush it'ik) *adj., n.* *same as* CUSHITIC

kvass, kvas (kväs) *n.* [Russ. *kvas*] a Russian fermented drink made from rye, barley, rye bread, etc.

kW. kilowatt; kilowatts

kwa·cha (kwä'chä) *n., pl.* **-cha** [native term, lit., dawn] *see* MONETARY UNITS, table (Malawi, Zambia)

kwa·shi·or·kor (kwa'shē ôr'kôr) *n.* [< name in Ghana] a severe disease of young children, caused by chronic deficiency of protein and calories and characterized by stunted growth, oedema, etc.

kwh, K.W.H., kw.-hr., kw-hr kilowatt-hour

ky·ak (kī'ak) *n.* *same as* KAYAK

ky·an·ize (kī'ə nīz') *vt.* **-ized', -iz'ing** [after J.H. *Kyan* (1774-1850), Ir. inventor of the process] to make (wood) resistant to decay by treatment with a solution of corrosive sublimate

kyat (kyät) *n.* [Burmese] *see* MONETARY UNITS, table (Burma)

kyle (kīl) *n.* [Gael. *caol*, a strait] a narrow strait or channel [*Kyle* of Lochalsh]

ky·loe (kī'lō) *n.* [< ?] any of a breed of small, long-horned cattle in the Scottish Hebrides and Highlands

Kym·ric (kim'rik) *adj., n.* *same as* CYMRIC

Kym·ry, Kym·ri (-rē) *n.pl.* *same as* CYMRY

ky·mo·graph (kī'mə gräf') *n.* [< Gr. *kyma*, a wave + -GRAPH] an apparatus consisting of a rotating drum and stylus for recording wavelike motions, variations, or modulations, such as muscular contractions, the pulse, etc.

L

L, l (el) *n., pl.* **L's, l's** 1. the twelfth letter of the English alphabet 2. the sound of *L* or *l*

L (el) *n., pl.* **L's** 1. an object shaped like **L**; esp., an extension of a building that gives the whole a shape resembling **L** 2. a Roman numeral for 50 —*adj.* shaped like **L**

L 1. Latin 2. Learner (driver) 3. Licentiate

L., l. 1. lake 2. latitude 3. law 4. leaf 5. league 6. left 7. length 8. *pl.* **LL., ll.** line 9. link 10. lira; lire 11. litre 12. low 13. [L. *libra*, pl. *librae*] pound(s)

£ pounds

la¹ (lä, lô) *interj.* [Dial. or Archaic] an exclamation of surprise or emphasis

la² (lä) *n.* [see GAMUT] *Music* a syllable representing the sixth tone of the diatonic scale

La *Chem.* lanthanum

lab (lab) *n.* [Colloq.] a laboratory

Lab. 1. Labour 2. Labrador

la·bel (lä'b'l) *n.* [OFr., a rag, strip < Gmc.] 1. a card, strip of paper, etc. marked and attached to an object to indicate its nature, contents, ownership, destination, etc. 2. a descriptive word or phrase applied to a person, group, etc. as a convenient generalized classification 3. an identifying brand of a company —*vt.* **-belled, -bel'ling** 1. to attach a label to 2. to classify as; call; describe — **la'bel·ler** *n.*

la·bi·a (lä'bē ə) *n.* *pl. of* LABIUM

la·bi·al (-əl) *adj.* [< ML. < L. *labium*, a lip] 1. of the labia, or lips 2. *Phonet.* formed mainly with the lips: said esp. of *b, m,* and *p* —*n.* a labial sound —**la'bi·al·ly** *adv.*

la·bi·ate (lä'bē āt', -it) *adj.* [< L. *labium*, a lip] 1. formed or functioning like a lip 2. having a lip or lips 3. *Bot.* having the calyx or corolla so divided that one part overlaps the other like a lip

la·bile (lä'b'l, -īl) *adj.* [< L. < *labi*, to slip] liable to change; unstable —**la·bil'i·ty** *n.*

la·bi·o·den·tal (lä'bē ō den't'l) *adj.* [< L. *labium*, a lip + DENTAL] *Phonet.* formed with the lower lip against the upper teeth, as the sounds of *f* and *v* —*n.* a labiodental sound

la·bi·um (lä'bē əm) *n., pl.* **-bi·a** (-ə) [L., a lip] *Anat., Bot.,* etc. a lip or liplike organ; specif., [*pl.*] the outer folds of skin (**labia majora**) or the inner folds of mucous membrane (**labia minora**) of the vulva

lab·o·ra·to·ry (la bor'ə tər ē, lab'ər ə-) *n., pl.* **-ries** [< ML. < L.: see LABOUR, *vi.*] 1. a room or building for scientific experimentation or research 2. a place for preparing chemicals, drugs, etc. 3. a place where theories, methods, etc., as in education, are tested, demonstrated, etc. —*adj.* of or performed in, or as in, a laboratory

la·bo·ri·ous (lə bôr′ē əs) *adj.* 1. involving or calling for much hard work; difficult 2. industrious; hard-working —**la·bo′ri·ous·ly** *adv.* —**la·bo′ri·ous·ness** *n.*

la·bour (lā′bər) *n.* [< OFr. < L. *labor*] 1. physical or mental exertion; work; toil 2. a specific task 3. *a)* all wage-earning workers as a group: distinguished from CAPITAL[1] or MANAGEMENT *b)* all manual workers whose work is characterized largely by physical exertion 4. trade unions collectively 5. [L-] *same as* LABOUR PARTY 6. the work accomplished by workers collectively 7. *Med.* the process of giving birth to a child —*vi.* [< OFr. < L. *laborare* < the *n.*] 1. to work; toil 2. to work hard 3. to move slowly and with difficulty [the car *laboured up the hill*] 4. to be burdened (with *under*) [to *labour* under a delusion] 5. to undergo, and suffer the pains of, childbirth —*vt.* to develop in too great detail [to *labour* a point]

Labour Day 1. in many countries, the first of May, a legal holiday in honour of labour 2. a similar holiday in the U.S. & Canada on the first Monday in September

la·boured (lā′bərd) *adj.* made or done with great effort; not easy and natural; strained

la·bour·er (lā′bər ər) *n.* one who labours; esp., a wage-earning worker whose work is characterized largely by physical exertion

Labour Exchange formerly, a government office set up locally to help the unemployed find work: also **employment exchange**

la·bour-in·ten·sive (-in ten′siv) *adj.* requiring manual rather than mechanical labour to produce goods, increase productivity, or secure higher earnings [restaurants are *labour-intensive* concerns]

La·bour·ite (lā′bə rīt′) *n.* a member or supporter of the British Labour Party

labour party 1. a political party organized to protect and further the rights of workers, or one dominated by organized labour 2. [L- P-] such a party in Great Britain:

la·bour-sav·ing (lā′bər sā′viŋ) *adj.* eliminating or lessening physical labour [*labour-saving* appliances]

Lab·ra·dor retriever (lab′rə dôr′) any of a breed of medium-sized dog used in retrieving game, having a black or yellow coat of short, thick hair

la·bret (lā′bret) *n.* [dim. of L. *labrum*, LIP] an ornament of wood, bone, etc. worn in a hole pierced through the lip

la·bur·num (lə bʉr′nəm) *n.* [L.] a small, poisonous tree or shrub of the legume family, with drooping racemes of yellow flowers

lab·y·rinth (lab′ə rinth′) *n.* [< L. < Gr. *labyrinthos*] 1. a structure containing an intricate network of winding passages hard to follow without losing one's way; maze 2. a complicated, perplexing arrangment, condition, etc. 3. *Anat.* the inner ear

lab·y·rin·thine (lab′ə rin′thīn) *adj.* of, constituting, or like a labyrinth; intricate: also **lab′·y·rin′thi·an** (-thē ən), **lab′y·rin′·thic**

lac (lak) *n.* [< Hindi < Sans. *lākṣā*] 1. a resinous substance secreted on various trees in S Asia by certain scale insects: when melted, strained, and rehardened, it forms shellac 2. *same as* LAKH

LABYRINTH

lac·co·lith (lak′ə lith) *n.* [< Gr. *lakkos*, cistern, pit + -LITH] *Geol.* a flat-based dome of igneous rock situated between two layers of older, sedimentary rock

lace (lās) *n.* [OFr. *laz* < L. *laqueus*, a noose] 1. a string, ribbon, etc. used to draw together and fasten the parts of a shoe, corset, etc. 2. braid of gold or silver, as for trimming uniforms 3. a fine netting or openwork fabric of linen, silk, etc., woven in ornamental designs —*vt.* **laced**, **lac′ing** 1. to draw the ends of (a garment, shoe, etc.) together and fasten with a lace 2. to compress the waist of by lacing a corset, etc. 3. to pass (a cord, etc.) in and out *through* eyelets, fabric, etc. 4. to weave together; intertwine 5. to ornament with lace 6. to streak, as with colour; intersperse 7. to thrash; beat 8. to add a dash of brandy, whisky, etc. to (a beverage) —*vi.* 1. to be fastened with a lace [these shoes *lace*] 2. [Colloq.] to attack physically or verbally (with *into*)

lac·er·ate (las′ə rāt′; *also for adj.* -ər it) *vt.* **-at′ed**, **-at′ing** [< L. pp. of *lacerare* < *lacer*, mangled] 1. to tear jaggedly; mangle 2. to hurt (one's feelings, etc.) deeply —*adj.* 1. torn; mangled 2. *Bot.* having jagged edges

lac·er·a·tion (las′ə rā′shən) *n.* 1. a lacerating 2. the result of lacerating; jagged tear or wound

lace-up *n.* a shoe fastened with laces: also **lace-up shoe**

lace·wing (lās′wiŋ′) *n.* any of a large group of insects with four delicate, gauzy wings

lace·work (-wʉrk′) *n.* lace, or any openwork decoration like lace

lach·es (lach′iz) *n.* [OFr. *laschesse*, ult. < L. *laxus*, lax] *Law* failure to do the required thing at the proper time; inexcusable delay

Lach·e·sis (lak′ə sis) *Gr. & Rom. Myth.* that one of the three Fates who determines the span of life

lach·ry·mal (lak′rə məl) *adj.* [< ML. < L. *lacrima*, TEAR[2]] 1. of, characterized by, or producing tears 2. *same as* LACRIMAL (sense 1)

lach·ry·ma·tion (-mā′shən) *n. same as* LACRIMATION

lach·ry·ma·to·ry (lak′rəmə tər ē) *adj.* of, causing, or producing tears

lach·ry·mose (-mōs′) *adj.* [< L. < *lacrima*, TEAR[2]] 1. inclined to shed many tears; tearful 2. causing tears; sad —**lach′ry·mose′ly** *adv.*

lac·ing (lās′iŋ) *n.* 1. the act of a person who laces 2. a thrashing; beating 3. a cord or lace, as a shoelace 4. gold or silver braid used to trim a uniform, etc.

la·cin·i·ate (lə sin′ē āt, -it) *adj.* [< L. *lacinia*, flap, edge of a garment] *Biol.* cut deeply into narrow, uneven segments; jagged

lack (lak) *n.* [< or akin to MLowG., MDu. *lak*] 1. the fact or condition of not having enough; shortage; deficiency 2. the fact or condition of not having any; complete absence 3. the thing that is lacking or needed —*vi.* 1. to be wanting or missing 2. *a)* to be short (with *in* or *for*) *b)* to be in need —*vt.* 1. to be deficient in or entirely without 2. to fall short by [*lacking* one gramme of being a kilogramme]

lack·a·dai·si·cal (lak′ə dā′zi k'l) *adj.* [ult. < *alack the day*] showing lack of interest or spirit; listless; languid —**lack′·a·dai′si·cal·ly** *adv.*

lack·ey (lak′ē) *n., pl.* **-eys** [< Fr. < Sp. *lacayo*] 1. a male servant of low rank; footman 2. a servile follower; toady —*vt., vi.* **-eyed**, **-ey·ing** to serve as a lackey

lack·lus·tre (lak′lus′tər) *adj.* lacking brightness; dull [*lacklustre* eyes] —*n.* [Rare] dullness Also, U.S. sp., **lack′lus′ter**

la·con·ic (lə kon′ik) *adj.* [< L. < Gr. *Lakōn*, a Laconian, Spartan] brief or terse in speech or expression; using few words —**la·con′i·cal·ly** *adv.*

lac·o·nism (lak′ə niz′m) *n.* [Gr. *lakōnizein*, to imitate the Laconians] 1. economy of expression 2. a terse phrase or saying

lac·quer (lak′ər) *n.* [< Fr. < Port. < *laca*, gum lac] 1. a coating substance of natural or synthetic resins, nitrocellulose, etc. dissolved in a solvent that evaporates rapidly leaving a tough, adherent film: pigments are often added to form **lacquer enamels** 2. a natural resin varnish obtained from certain trees in China and Japan, or woodenware (in full, **lac′quer·ware′**, **lac′quer·work′**) coated with it —*vt.* to coat with or as with lacquer —**lac′quer·er** *n.*

lac·ri·mal (lak′rə məl) *adj.* 1. *Anat.* designating, of, or near the glands that secrete tears 2. *same as* LACHRYMAL (sense 1)

lac·ri·ma·tion (lak′rə mā′shən) *n.* [< L. < pp. of *lacrimare*, to weep < *lacrima*, TEAR[2]] normal or excessive secretion or shedding of tears

la·crosse (lə kros′) *n.* [CanadFr. < Fr. *la*, the + *crosse*, a crutch] a ball game in which two teams of ten men each, using long-handled, pouched rackets, try to advance a small rubber ball across the field into the opponents' goal

LACROSSE

lac·tate (lak′tāt) *vi.* **-tat·ed**, **-tat·ing** [< L. pp. of *lactare* < *lac* (see LACTO-)] to secrete milk —*n.* any salt or ester of lactic acid

lac·ta·tion (lak tā′shən) *n.* 1. the secretion of milk by a mammary gland 2. the period during which milk is secreted 3. the suckling of young

lac·te·al (lak′tē əl) *adj.* [< L. *lacteus* < *lac* (see LACTO-) + -AL] 1. of or like milk; milky 2. containing or carrying chyle, the milky fluid that is a product of digestion —*n.* any of the lymphatic vessels that carry chyle from the small intestine to the blood

lac·tic (lak′tik) *adj.* [< Fr.: see LACTO- & -IC] of or obtained from milk

lactic acid a yellowish or clear, syrupy organic acid produced by the fermentation of lactose when milk sours

lac·to- [< L. *lac* (gen. *lactis*), milk] a combining form meaning: 1. milk 2. *Chem.* lactic acid or lactate Also, before a vowel, **lact-**

lac·tose (lak′tōs) *n.* [LACT(O)- + -OSE[1]] a white, crystalline sugar, $C_{12}H_{22}O_{11}$, found in milk and used in baby foods, medicine, etc.

la·cu·na (lə kyōō′nə) *n., pl.* **-nas**, **-nae** (-nē) [L., a ditch < *lacus*, lake] 1. a space where something has been omitted or has come out; missing part; gap; hiatus 2. *Anat., Biol.* any of the very small cavities in bone that are filled with bone cells —**la·cu′nar** (-nər), **la·cu′nal** *adj.*

lac·y (lā′sē) *adj.* **lac′i·er**, **lac′i·est** 1. of lace 2. like lace; having a delicate open pattern —**lac′i·ly** *adv.* —**lac′i·ness** *n.*

lad (lad) *n.* [ME. *ladde*] **1.** a boy or youth **2.** [Colloq.] any man; fellow: familiar term **3.** a boy or man who works in a stable: also **stable lad**

lad·a·num (lad'ə nəm) *n.* [L. *ladanum* < Gr. *ladanon*] a dark resin obtained from various rock roses, used in perfumery

lad·der (lad'ər) *n.* [OE. *hlæder*] **1.** a framework of two parallel sidepieces connected by rungs or crosspieces on which a person steps in climbing up or down **2.** anything by means of which a person climbs or rises [the *ladder* of success] **3.** a vertical break in a woven fabric, esp. in a stocking —*vt., vi.* to have or cause to have a ladder (*n.* 3)

ladder back a type of chair in which the back is constructed of horizontal slats between two uprights

lad·die (lad'ē) *n.* [Chiefly Scot.] a young lad

lade (lād) *vt., vi.* lad'ed, lad'ed or lad'en, lad'ing [OE. *hladan*] **1.** to load **2.** to dip (water, etc.) with a ladle; bail; ladle

lad·en (lād''n) *alt. pp. of* LADE —*adj.* **1.** loaded **2.** burdened; afflicted [*laden* with sorrow]

la·di·da, la·de·da (lä'dē dä') *adj.* [Colloq.] affected in speech, manners, etc.; pretentiously refined

La·dies (lā'dēz) *n.pl.* [with *sing. v.*] a women's public toilet

Ladies' Gallery a section of the public gallery of the House of Commons reserved for women

lad·ing (lā'diŋ) *n.* **1.** the act of one that lades **2.** a load; cargo; freight

la·dle (lā'd'l) *n.* [OE. *hlædel* < *hladan*, to draw water] a long-handled, cuplike spoon for dipping out liquids —*vt.* -dled, -dling **1.** to dip out with or as with a ladle **2.** to carry in a ladle —**ladle out** to distribute lavishly —**la'-dle·ful'** *n., pl.* -fuls' —**la'dler** *n.*

la·dy (lā'dē) *n., pl.* -dies [OE. *hlæfdige* < *hlaf*, loaf + base of *dæge*, kneader] **1.** a woman with the rights, rule, or authority of a lord **2.** *a)* a woman of high social position *b)* a woman who is polite, refined,and well-mannered **3.** any woman **4.** [L-] the Virgin Mary (usually with *Our*) **5.** [L-] in Great Britain, the title given to women of certain ranks —*adj.* female [a *lady* barber]

la·dy·bird (-burd') *n.* a small, roundish beetle with a spotted back, that feeds chiefly on insect pests and their eggs

Lady Bountiful [after a character in Farquhar's comedy *The Beaux Stratagem* (1707)] a charitable woman, esp. one who gives ostentatiously

Lady Day *same as* ANNUNCIATION (sense 2 *b*)

la·dy-in-wait·ing (-in wāt'iŋ) *n., pl.* la'dies-in-wait'ing a woman attending, or waiting upon, a queen or princess

la·dy-kill·er (-kil'ər) *n.* a man who behaves towards women as if he were irresistible to them

la·dy·like (-līk') *adj.* like or suitable for a lady; refined; well-bred

la·dy·love (-luv') *n.* a sweetheart

lady of the bedchamber *n., pl.* **ladies of the bedchamber** *same as* LADY-IN-WAITING

lady's finger **1.** *another name for* BHINDI **2.** [S Afr.] a species of small banana

la·dy·ship (-ship') *n.* the rank or position of a lady: used in speaking to or of a woman having the title of *Lady*, always preceded by *your* or *her*

la·dy-slip·per (-slip'ər) *n.* any of certain wild orchids whose flowers somewhat resemble a slipper: also **la'dy's-slip'per**

lae·vo- (lē'vō, -və) [< L. *laevus*, left] a combining form meaning: **1.** towards or on the left-hand side **2.** *Chem.* laevorotatory

lae·vo·ro·ta·to·ry (-rōt'ə tər ē) *adj.* [LAEVO- & ROTATION] **1.** turning to the left, in an anticlockwise direction **2.** *Chem.* that turns the plane of polarized light anticlockwise

lag¹ (lag) *vi.* lagged, lag'ging [? akin to MDan. *lakke*, to go slowly] **1.** *a)* to fall, move, or stay behind; loiter *b)* to be retarded in motion, development, etc. **2.** to wane; flag —*n.* **1.** a falling behind or being retarded in motion, development, etc. **2.** the amount of such falling behind —**lag'ger** *n.*

LADY SLIPPER

lag² (lag) *vt.* lagged, lag'ging [prob. < Scand. as in Sw. *lagg*, barrel stave] to cover a boiler, cylinder, etc., with insulating material —*n.* **1.** a barrel stave **2.** a narrow strip of insulating material

lag³ (lag) *n.* [< ?] [Colloq.] **1.** a convict or ex-convict [an old *lag*] **2.** a term of imprisonment —*vt.* lagged, lag'-ging to arrest or put in prison

lag bolt *same as* LAG SCREW

la·ger (beer) (lä'gər) [G. *Lagerbier*, lit., storehouse beer] a beer which is stored for several months for aging after it has been brewed

lag·gard (lag'ərd) *n.* [< LAG¹ + -ARD] a slow person, esp. one who is always falling behind —*adj.* slow or late in

doing things; falling behind —**lag'gard·ly** *adv., adj.* —**lag'-gard·ness** *n.*

lag·ging (lag'iŋ) *n.* [< LAG² + -ING] **1.** insulating material wrapped around pipes, boilers, etc., to prevent loss of heat **2.** the act of applying this insulating material

la·goon (lə gōōn') *n.* [< Fr. *lagune* & It. *laguna* < L. *lacuna*, lake] **1.** a shallow lake or pond, esp. one connected with a larger body of water **2.** the water enclosed by a circular coral reef **3.** shallow salt water separated from the sea by dunes

lag screw a wood screw with a boltlike head

lah-di-dah, lah-de-dah (lä'dē dä') *adj.* *same as* LA-DI-DA

la·ic (lā'ik) *adj.* [< LL. *laicus* < Gr. < *laos*, the people] of the laity; secular; lay: also **la'i·cal** —*n.* a layman —**la'-i·cal·ly** *adv.*

la·i·cize (lā'ə sīz') *vt.* -cized', -ciz'ing [LAIC + -IZE] to turn over to laymen; secularize

laid (lād) *pt. & pp. of* LAY¹

laid paper paper having evenly spaced parallel lines water-marked in it

lain (lān) *pp. of* LIE¹

lair¹ (ler) *n.* [OE. *leger*] the resting place of a wild animal; den

lair² (ler) *n.* [? alt. < *leery*] [Aust.] a flashily-dressed man

laird (lerd; *Scot.* lärd) *n.* [Scot. form of LORD] in Scotland, a landowner, esp. a wealthy one

lair·i·ness (ler'i nis) *n.* [Aust.] crude or ostentatious behaviour

lair·y (ler'ē) *adj.* [Aust.] overdressed

lais·sez faire (les'ā fer', lez'-) [Fr., let (people) do (as they please)] noninterference; specif., the policy of letting the owners of industry and business operate without governmental regulation or control: also sp. **lais'ser faire**—**lais'-sez-faire'** *adj.*

la·i·ty (lā'ət ē) *n., pl.* -ties [< LAY³] **1.** all the people not included among the clergy; laymen collectively **2.** all the people not belonging to any given profession

lake¹ (lāk) *n.* [OE. *lacu* & OFr. *lac*, both < L. *lacus*, lake] **1.** a large, inland body of water, usually fresh water **2.** a pool of oil or other liquid

lake² (lāk) *n.* [see LAC] **1.** *a)* a dark-red pigment prepared from cochineal *b)* its colour **2.** an insoluble colouring compound precipitated from a solution of a dye by adding a metallic salt

Lake District (or **Country**) lake & mountain region in NW England: home of Wordsworth, Coleridge, & Southey (the **Lake poets**): also called the **Lakes, Lake'land'**

lake dwelling a dwelling built on wooden piles rising above the surface of a lake, esp. in prehistoric times —**lake dweller**

Lakeland terrier any of a breed of wired-haired terriers, originally from the Lake District

lake trout a large, grey game fish of deep, cold lakes of the N U.S. and Canada

lakh (lak) *n.* [< Hindi (see LAC): prob. in reference to the abundance of the insects] in India and Pakistan, **1.** the sum of 100000: said specifically of rupees **2.** any indefinitely large number

Lal·lans (lal'ənz) *n.* [Scot. var. of LOWLANDS] a dialect of the Lowlands of Scotland, esp. as developed by modern Scottish writers

lam¹ (lam) *vt., vi.* lammed, lam'ming [< Scand., as in ON. *lemja*] [Slang] to beat; thrash; flog

lam² (lam) *n.* [< ? prec.] [U.S. Slang] headlong flight, usually to escape arrest or punishment: used in phrase **on the lam**

Lam. Lamentations

la·ma (lä'mə) *n.* [Tibetan *blama*] a Buddhist priest or monk in Lamaism: cf. DALAI LAMA

La·ma·ism (lä'mə iz'm) *n.* a form of Buddhism found in C Asia, characterized by elaborate ritual and a strong hierarchal organization —**La'ma·ist** *adj., n.* —**La'ma·is'tic** *adj.*

la·ma·ser·y (lä'mə sər ē) *n., pl.* -ser·ies [< Fr.] a monastery of lamas

lamb (lam) *n.* [OE.] **1.** a young sheep **2.** its flesh used as food **3.** lambskin **4.** a gentle or innocent person, esp. a child **5.** a dear **6.** a person easily tricked or outwitted —*vi.* to give birth: said of a ewe —**the Lamb** Jesus —**lamb'like'** *adj.*

lam·baste (lam bāst') *vt.* -bast'ed, -bast'ing [LAM¹ + BASTE³] **1.** to beat soundly; thrash **2.** to scold or criticize severely Also sp. **lam·bast'**

lamb·da (lam'də) *n.* the eleventh letter of the Greek alphabet (Λ, λ)

lam·bent (lam'bənt) *adj.* [< L. prp. of *lambere*, to lick] **1.** playing lightly over a surface; flickering **2.** softly glowing **3.** light and graceful [*lambent* wit] —**lam'ben·cy** *n.* —**lam'-bent·ly** *adv.*

lamb·kin (lam'kin) *n.* **1.** a little lamb **2.** a child or young person: a term of affection

lam·bre·quin (lam'bər kin, -brə-) *n.* [Fr. < Du. *lamperkin* < *lamper*, a veil + -*kin*, dim. suffix] **1.** a fabric covering for a knight's helmet **2.** drapery hanging from a door, window, mantelpiece, etc.

lamb·skin (lam′skin′) *n.* **1.** the skin of a lamb, esp. with the fleece left on it **2.** leather or parchment made from the skin of a lamb

lamb's lettuce a plant with lilac flowers found in cornfields and used in salads: also called **corn salad**

lamb's tail *another name for* CATKIN

lamb's wool **1.** soft, fine wool **2.** a fabric made from such wool

lame (lām) *adj.* [OE. *lama*] **1.** crippled; esp., having an injured leg or foot that makes one limp **2.** stiff and very painful [a *lame* back] **3.** poor, weak, ineffectual, etc. [a *lame* excuse] —*vt.* **lamed, lam′ing** to make lame —**lame′·ly** *adv.* —**lame′ness** *n.* —**lam′ish** *adj.*

la·mé (lä′mā) *n.* [Fr., laminated < *lame*, metal plate] a cloth interwoven with metallic threads

lame duck **1.** a disabled, ineffectual, or helpless person or thing **2.** [U.S.] an elected official whose term extends beyond the time of the election at which he was not reelected

la·mel·la (lə mel′ə) *n.*, *pl.* **-lae** (-ē), **-las** [L., dim. of LAMINA] *Biol.* a thin, platelike part, layer, organ, or structure —**la·mel′lar, lam·el·late** (lam′ə lāt′, lə mel′āt) *adj.* —**la·mel′lar·ly** *adv.*

la·mel·li·branch (lə mel′i braŋk′) *n.* [see prec. & BRANCHIAE] any of a class of molluscs, including the clams, oysters, etc., having platelike gills and bivalve shells

la·ment (lə ment′) *vi.* [< Fr. < L. < *lamentum*, a wailing] to feel or express deep sorrow; mourn; grieve —*vt.* **1.** to mourn or grieve for **2.** to regret deeply —*n.* **1.** a lamentation; wail **2.** a song, poem, etc. mourning a loss, death, etc.; elegy or dirge —**la·ment′er** *n.* —**la·ment′ing·ly** *adv.*

lam·en·ta·ble (lam′ən tə b′l) *adj.* to be lamented; regrettable; distressing —**lam′en·ta·bly** *adv.*

lam·en·ta·tion (lam′ən tā′shən) *n.* a lamenting

la·ment·ed (lə men′tid) *adj.* mourned for: usually said of someone dead —**la·ment′ed·ly** *adv.*

lam·i·na (lam′ə nə) *n.*, *pl.* **-nae** (-nē′), **-nas** [L.] **1.** a thin flake, scale, or layer **2.** the flat, expanded part of a leaf —**lam′i·nar** (-nər), **lam′i·nal** *adj.*

lam·i·nate (lam′ə nāt′; *for adj.* & *n. usually* -nit) *vt.* **-nat′ed, -nat′ing** **1.** to form or press into a thin sheet or layer **2.** to separate into thin layers **3.** to cover with or bond to thin layers, as of clear plastic **4.** to make by building up in layers —*vi.* to split into thin layers —*adj.* same as LAMINATED —*n.* something made by laminating, as a plastic surface for work tops —**lam′i·na·ble** (-nə b′l) *adj.* —**lam′i·na′tion** *n.* —**lam′i·na′tor** *n.*

lam·i·nat·ed (-nāt′id) *adj.* composed of or built in thin sheets or layers, as of fabric, wood, plastic, etc., that have been bonded or pressed together

Lam·mas (lam′əs) *n.* [ME. *lammasse* < OE. *hlammæsse, hlamæsse, hlafmaesse*, lit., loaf mass, bread feast] **1.** a harvest festival formerly held on August 1, when bread baked from the first crop of wheat was consecrated **2.** this day (**Lammas Day**) or this time (**Lam′mas·tide′**) of the year

lam·mer·gei·er, lam·mer·gey·er (lam′ər gī ə) *n.* [G. *Lämmergeier* < *Lämmer*, lambs + *Geier*, vulture] a large, rare vulture of S Europe, Africa, and Asia

lamp (lamp) *n.* [< OFr. < LL. *lampada*, ult. < Gr. *lampein*, to shine] **1.** a container with a wick for burning oil, alcohol, etc. to produce light or heat **2.** any device for producing light or therapeutic rays, as a gas jet with a mantle, an electric light bulb, or an ultraviolet bulb **3.** a holder, stand, or base for such a device

lamp·black (-blak′) *n.* fine soot produced by the incomplete combustion of oils and other forms of carbon: used as a pigment in paint, ink, etc.

lam·per eel (lam′pər) same as LAMPREY

lamp·light (lamp′līt′) *n.* light given off by a lamp

lamp·light·er (-ər) *n.* **1.** formerly, a person who lit and extinguished gas street lamps **2.** [U.S.] something, as an electrical device, used to light lamps

lam·poon (lam pōōn′) *n.* [< Fr. < *lampons*, let us drink (refrain in a drinking song)] a piece of strongly satirical writing, usually attacking or ridiculing someone —*vt.* to attack or ridicule in a lampoon —**lam·poon′er, lam·poon′ist** *n.* —**lam·poon′er·y** *n.*

lamp·post (lam′pōst′, lamp′-) *n.* a post supporting a street lamp

lam·prey (lam′prē) *n.*, *pl.* **-preys** [< OFr. < ML. *lampreda*] an eellike parasitic fish with a funnel-shaped, jawless, sucking mouth: it preys on other fish

lamp·shade (lamp′shād′) *n.* an ornamental covering, partial or complete, for an electric, gas, or oil lamp, made of glass, porcelain, fabric, etc.

la·nai (lä nī′, la-) *n.* [Haw.] a veranda or open-sided living room of a kind found in Hawaii

Lan·cas·tri·an (laŋ kas′trē ən) *adj.* of Lancashire or Lancaster —*n.* a supporter of the house of Lancaster during the Wars of the Roses

lance (läns) *n.* [OFr. < L. *lancea*] **1.** a thrusting weapon consisting of a long wooden shaft with a sharp metal head **2.** a lancer **3.** any sharp instrument like a lance, as a fish spear **4.** a surgical lancet —*vt.* **lanced, lanc′ing** **1.** to attack or pierce with a lance **2.** to cut open as with a lancet

lance corporal see MILITARY RANKS, table

lance·let (läns′lit) *n.* [LANCE + -LET] a small, invertebrate, fishlike sea animal closely related to the vertebrates; amphioxus

lan·ce·o·late (lan′sē ə lāt′, -lit) *adj.* [< LL. < *lanceola*, little lance] narrow and tapering like the head of a lance, as certain leaves

lanc·er (län′sər) *n.* a cavalry soldier armed with a lance or a member of a cavalry regiment originally armed with lances

lanc·ers (-sərz) *n.pl.* [with *sing.* v.] [< prec.] **1.** a 19th-cent. quadrille **2.** music for this

lan·cet (län′sit) *n.* [< OFr. dim. of *lance*, LANCE] **1.** a small, pointed surgical knife, usually two-edged, used for making small incisions, skin punctures, etc. **2.** same as: a) LANCET ARCH b) LANCET WINDOW

lancet arch a narrow, sharply pointed arch

lancet window a narrow, sharply pointed window without tracery, set in a lancet arch

lance·wood (läns′wood′) *n.* **1.** a tough, elastic wood used for fishing rods, billiard cues, etc. **2.** a tropical tree yielding such wood

Lancs. Lancashire

land (land) *n.* [OE.] **1.** the solid part of the earth's surface not covered by water **2.** a) a country, region, etc. b) a country's people **3.** ground or soil [rich *land*, high *land*] **4.** ground considered as property [to invest in *land*] **5.** rural regions [to return to the *land*] **6.** *Econ.* natural resources —*vt.* **1.** to put or set on shore from a ship **2.** to bring into or end up in a particular place or condition [a fight *landed* him in jail] **3.** to set (an aircraft) down on land or water **4.** to catch [to *land* a fish] **5.** [Colloq.] to get or win [to *land* a job] **6.** [Colloq.] to deliver (a blow) —*vi.* **1.** to leave a ship and go on shore **2.** to come to a port or to shore: said of a ship **3.** to arrive at a specified place or condition: often with *up* [to *land up* broke] **4.** to alight or come to rest, as after a flight, jump, or fall —**land on one's feet** to be lucky

land agent a person employed by an estate-owner to collect rents, let farms, etc.

lan·dau (lan′dô) *n.* [< *Landau*, German town where orig. made] a four-wheeled carriage with the top in two sections, either of which can be lowered independently

lan·dau·let (lan′də let′) *n.* [LANDAU + -LET] **1.** a small landau **2.** a motor car with a hood that folds back over part of the body

land·drost (land′drôst′) *n.* [Afrik. < *land*, land + *drost*, bailiff] a South African district magistrate

land·ed (lan′did) *adj.* **1.** owning land [*landed* gentry] **2.** consisting of land or real estate [a *landed* estate]

land·fall (land′fôl′) *n.* **1.** a sighting of land from a ship at sea **2.** the land sighted **3.** a landing by ship or aircraft

land·girl (land′gurl′) *n.* a member of the Women's Land Army recruited to replace agricultural workers called up for military service in World Wars 1 and 11

land·grave (-grāv′) *n.* [< G. < *Land*, land + *Graf*, a count] **1.** in medieval Germany, a count having jurisdiction over a specified territory **2.** later, the title of certain German princes

land·hold·er (-hōl′dər) *n.* an owner or occupant of land —**land′hold′ing** *adj., n.*

land·ing (lan′diŋ) *n.* **1.** the act of coming to shore or putting ashore **2.** the place where a ship is unloaded or loaded **3.** a platform at the end of a flight of stairs **4.** the act of alighting, as after a flight, jump, or fall

landing craft naval craft designed to bring troops and equipment close to shore

landing field a field with a smooth surface to enable aircraft to land and take off easily

landing gear the undercarriage of an aircraft, including wheels, pontoons, etc.

landing net a baglike net attached to a long handle, for taking a hooked fish from the water

landing strip same as AIRSTRIP

land·la·dy (land′lā′dē) *n.*, *pl.* **-dies** a woman landlord

länd·ler (lend′lər) *n.* [G., < Dial. *Landl*, Upper Austria, where it originated] **1.** a gliding country dance in 3/4 time from Austria **2.** the music for it

land·less (-lis) *adj.* not owning land

land·locked (-lokt′) *adj.* **1.** entirely or almost entirely surrounded by land, as a bay or a country **2.** cut off from the sea and confined to fresh water [*landlocked* salmon]

land·lord (-lôrd′) *n.* **1.** a person, esp. a man, who rents or leases land, houses, etc. to others **2.** a man who keeps a boarding house, inn, etc.

land·lub·ber (-lub′ər) *n.* a person who has had little experience at sea, and is therefore awkward aboard a ship: a sailor's term of contempt

land·mark (-märk′) *n.* **1.** any fixed object used to mark the boundary of a piece of land **2.** any prominent feature of the landscape, as a tree, identifying a particular locality **3.** an event, discovery, etc. considered as a high point or turning point in the development of something

land·mass (-mas′) *n.* a very large area of land; esp., a continent

land mine an explosive charge hidden under the surface of the ground and detonated by pressure upon it

land·own·er (land′ō′nər) *n.* one who owns land —**land′-own′er·ship′** *n.* —**land′own′ing** *adj., n.*

land reform the redistribution of agricultural land by breaking up large landholdings and apportioning shares to small farmers, peasants, etc.

land·scape (-skāp′) *n.* [< Du. < *land*, land + *-schap*, -SHIP] **1.** a picture representing natural, inland scenery **2.** an expanse of natural scenery seen in one view —*vt.* **-scaped′**, **-scap′ing** to change the natural features of (a plot of ground) so as to make it more attractive, as by adding lawns, bushes, trees, etc. —**land′scap′er** *n.*

landscape architecture the art or profession of planning or changing the natural scenery of a place for a desired effect —**landscape architect**

landscape gardening the art or work of arranging lawns, trees, etc. on a plot of ground to make it more attractive —**landscape gardener**

land·scap·ist (-skăp′ist) *n.* a painter of landscapes

land·slide (-slīd′) *n.* **1.** the sliding of a mass of rocks or earth down a hillside or slope **2.** the mass sliding down **3.** an overwhelming majority of votes for a candidate, party, etc. in an election

land·slip (-slip′) *n.* same as LANDSLIDE (senses 1 & 2)

lands·man (landz′mən) *n., pl.* **-men** a person who lives on land: distinguished from SEAMAN

land·ward (land′wərd) *adv.* towards the land: also **land′-wards** —*adj.* situated or facing towards the land

lane (lān) *n.* [OE. *lanu*] **1.** a narrow way between hedges, walls, etc.; narrow country road or city street **2.** any narrow way, as an opening in a crowd **3.** *same as: a)* AIR LANE *b)* SEA LANE **4.** a marked strip of road wide enough for a single line of cars, etc. **5.** any of the parallel courses marked off for contestants in a race **6.** *Bowling* a long, narrow strip of highly polished wood, along which the balls are rolled; alley

lang. language

lang·syne (laŋ′sīn′, -zīn′) *adv.* [Scot. < *lang*, LONG¹ + *syne*, since] [Scot.] long ago —*n.* [Scot.] the long ago; bygone days Also **lang syne**

lan·guage (laŋ′gwij) *n.* [< OFr. < *langue*, tongue < L. *lingua*] **1.** *a)* human speech *b)* the ability to communicate by human speech *c)* the vocal sounds used in speech, or the written symbols for them **2.** *a)* any means of communicating, as gestures, animal sounds, etc. [the *language* of flowers] *b)* a special set of symbols, rules, etc. used for transmitting information, as in a computer **3.** all the vocal sounds, words, and ways of combining them common to a particular nation, tribe, etc. **4.** the special words, phrases, and style of expression of a particular group, writer, etc. [the *language* of teen-agers] **5.** the study of language or languages; linguistics

language laboratory a room equipped with tape recorders, earphones, and audiovisual devices, where language skills are developed

lan·guid (laŋ′gwid) *adj.* [< Fr. < L. < *languere*, to be faint] **1.** without vigour or vitality; drooping; weak **2.** without interest or spirit; listless **3.** sluggish; slow —**lan′guid·ly** *adv.* —**lan′guid·ness** *n.*

lan·guish (-gwish) *vi.* [< OFr. < L. < *languere*: see prec.] **1.** to lose vigour or vitality; become weak; droop **2.** to live under distressing conditions [to *languish* in poverty] **3.** to become slack or dull [his interest *languished*] **4.** to suffer with longing; pine **5.** to put on a sentimental or wistful air —**lan′guish·er** *n.* —**lan′guish·ing** *adj.* —**lan′guish·ing·ly** *adv.* —**lan′guish·ment** *n.*

lan·guor (laŋ′gər) *n.* [< OFr. < L. < *languere*: see LANGUID] **1.** a lack of vigour or vitality; weakness **2.** a lack of interest or spirit; listlessness **3.** tenderness of mood or feeling **4.** the condition of being still, sluggish, or dull —*vi.* **lan′guored, lan′guor·ing** to grow weak; become listless —**lan′guor·ous** *adj.* —**lan′guor·ous·ly** *adv.* —**lan′-guor·ous·ness** *n.*

lan·gur (luŋ′goor′) *n.* [< Hindi < Sans. *lāṅgūlin*, lit., having a tail] any of certain monkeys of SE Asia, with a long tail and a chin tuft

lan·iard (lan′yərd) *n.* same as LANYARD

la·ni·ar·y (lan′ē ər ē) *adj.* [<L. *lanius*, butcher < *laniare*, to tear] adapted for tearing: used esp. of canine teeth —*n.* a tooth adapted for tearing

la·nif·er·ous (lə nif′ər əs) *adj.* [< L. *lanifer*, wool-bearing < *lana*, wool] *Biol.* bearing wool or fleecy hairs resembling wool

lank (laŋk) *adj.* [OE. *hlanc*] **1.** long and slender; lean **2.** straight and limp; not curly: said of hair —**lank′ly** *adv.* —**lank′ness** *n.*

lank·y (laŋ′kē) *adj.* **lank′i·er, lank′i·est** awkwardly tall and lean or long and slender —**lank′i·ly** *adv.* —**lank′i·ness** *n.*

lan·o·lin (lan′ə lin) *n.* [< L. *lana*, wool + *oleum*, oil + -IN¹] a fatty substance obtained from sheep wool and used in ointments, cosmetics, etc.: also **lan′o·line** (-lin, -lēn)

lan·tern (lan′tərn) *n.* [< OFr. < L. *lanterna* < Gr. *lamptēr* < *lampein*, to shine] **1.** a transparent case for holding a light and protecting it from wind and weather **2.** the room containing the lamp at the top of a lighthouse **3.** an open or windowed structure on the roof of a building, in a tower, etc. to admit light and air

lantern jaw **1.** a projecting lower jaw **2.** [pl.] long, thin jaws, with sunken cheeks, that give the face a gaunt look —**lan′tern-jawed′** *adj.*

lantern slide a photographic slide for projection, as, originally, by a magic lantern

lan·tha·nide series (lan′thə nīd′) [< ff.] the rare-earth group of chemical elements from element 57 (lanthanum) to element 71 (lutetium)

lan·tha·num (-nəm) *n.* [ModL. < Gr. *lanthanein*, to be concealed] a silvery, metallic chemical element of the rare-earth group: symbol, La; at. wt., 138.91; at. no., 57

lant·horn (lan′tərn) *n.* [altered by folk etym. < LANTERN, after HORN, material once used for the sides] *archaic var. of* LANTERN

la·nu·go (lə nyōō′gō) *n.* [L., down < *lana*, WOOL] a soft, downy growth, esp. that covering a new-born child

lan·yard (lan′yərd) *n.* [< MFr. *laniere* < OFr. < *lasne*, noose: altered after YARD¹] **1.** a short rope used on board ship for holding or fastening something **2.** a cord used by sailors, etc. to hang a knife, whistle, etc. around the neck **3.** a cord for firing certain types of cannon

la·od·i·ce·an (lā′od ə sē′ən) *adj.* [after *Laodicea* in Asia Minor: see Rev. 3: 14-16] lukewarm; indifferent, esp. in one's attitude to religious matters —*n.* a person having such an attitude, esp. to religious matters

lap¹ (lap) *n.* [OE. *læppa*] **1.** [Now Rare] the loose lower part of a garment, which may be folded over **2.** *a)* the front part from the waist to the knees of a person in a sitting position *b)* the part of the clothing covering this **3.** that in which one is cared for, sheltered, etc. **4.** *a)* an overlapping part *b)* such overlapping *c)* amount or place of this **5.** one complete circuit around a race track **6.** a lapping **7.** a revolving disc for cutting and polishing glass, gems, etc. —*vt.* **lapped, lap′ping** **1.** to fold (over or on) **2.** to wrap; enfold **3.** to hold as in the lap; envelop **4.** to place partly upon something else [to *lap* one board over another] **5.** to lie partly upon; overlap [one board *laps* the other] **6.** to get a lap ahead of (an opponent) in a race —*vi.* **1.** to lie partly on something or on one another; overlap **2.** to extend beyond something in space or time (with *over*) —**drop** (or **dump**, etc.) **into someone's lap** to cause to be someone's responsibility

lap² (lap) *vi., vt.* **lapped, lap′ping** [OE. *lapian*] **1.** to drink (a liquid) by dipping it up with the tongue as a dog does **2.** to move or strike gently with a light splash: said of waves, etc. —*n.* **1.** a lapping **2.** the sound of lapping —**lap up** **1.** to take up (liquid) by lapping **2.** [Colloq.] to take in eagerly —**lap′per** *n.*

lap dissolve *Cinema & TV* a dissolving view in which a new scene is blended in with a scene being faded out, as by lapping two exposures on one film

lap dog a pet dog small enough to hold in the lap

la·pel (lə pel′) *n.* [dim. of LAP¹] either of the front parts of a coat folded back and forming a continuation of the collar —**la·pelled′** *adj.*

lap·ful (lap′fool′) *n., pl.* **-fuls′** as much as a lap can hold

lap·i·dar·y (lap′ə dər ē) *n., pl.* **-dar·ies** [< LL. *lapidarius* < L. < *lapis*, a stone] a workman who cuts, polishes, and engraves precious stones —*adj.* **1.** of or connected with the art of cutting and engraving precious stones **2.** like an inscription on a monument; short, precise, and elegant

la·pil·lus (lə pil′əs) *n., pl.* **-pil′li** (ī) [L., dim. of *lapis*, stone] a small fragment of igneous rock ejected from a volcano

lap·is laz·u·li (lap′is laz′yoo lī′, lazh′-; -lē′) [ModL. < L. *lapis*, a stone + ML. gen. of *lazulus*, < Ar.: see AZURE] **1.** an azure-blue, opaque, stone **2.** a blue pigment obtained from it **3.** its colour

lap joint a joint made by overlapping parts: also **lapped joint** —**lap′-joint′** *vt.*

lap of honour a circuit of the field or track by the winner(s) in a race or football game, etc.

Lapp (lap) *n.* **1.** a member of a Mongoloid people living in Lapland: also **Lap′land′er** **2.** their Finno-Ugric language: also **Lap′pish**

lap·pet (lap′it) *n.* [dim. of LAP¹] a small fold or flap, as of a garment or as of flesh

LAP JOINT

lapse (laps) *n.* [L. *lapsus*, a fall < pp. of *labi*, to slip] **1.** a slip or small error [a *lapse* of memory] **2.** *a)* a falling away from a moral standard; moral slip *b*) a falling or slipping into a lower or worse condition, esp. for a short time **3.** a passing away, as of time **4.** *Law* the termination of a right or privilege through disuse, failure of some contingency, or failure to meet stated obligations —*vi.* **lapsed, laps′ing 1.** to slip into a specified state [to *lapse* into a coma] **2.** to slip or deviate from a higher standard or fall into former erroneous ways; backslide **3.** to pass away: said of time **4.** to come to an end; stop [his subscription *lapsed*] **5.** to become forfeit or void because of failure to pay the premium at the stipulated time: said of an insurance policy —**laps′-a·ble, laps′i·ble** *adj.*

lapse rate the rate of decrease of an atmospheric variable, usually temperature, with increase of altitude

lap·wing (lap′wiŋ) *n.* [altered by folk etym. < OE. *hleapewince* < *hleapan*, to leap + *wince* < *wincian*, WINK] a crested plover noted for its irregular, wavering flight: also called **peewit**

lar·board (lär′bərd, -bôrd′) *n.* [< OE. *hladan*, to lade + *bord*, side] the left-hand side of a ship as one faces forward; port —*adj.* on or of this side Now replaced by PORT⁴

lar·ce·ny (lär′sə nē) *n., pl.* **-nies** [< Anglo-Fr. < OFr. < L. < *latrocinari*, to rob < *latro*, robber] *Law* the unlawful taking away of another's property with the intention of depriving him of it; theft: sometimes differentiated before 1827 as **grand larceny** (more than 12 d) and **petty larceny** (less than this amount) —**lar′ce·nist** *n.* —**lar′ce·nous** *adj.*

larch (lärch) *n.* [< G. < L. *larix*] **1.** a tree of the pine family, found throughout the N Hemisphere, bearing cones and needlelike leaves that are shed annually **2.** the tough wood of this tree

lard (lärd) *n.* [< OFr. < L. *lardum*] the fat of pigs, melted down and clarified —*vt.* **1.** to smear with lard or other fat; grease **2.** to put strips of fat pork, bacon, etc. on (meat or poultry) before cooking **3.** to add to; embellish [a talk *larded* with jokes] —**lard′y** *adj.* **-i·er, -i·est**

lard·er (lär′dər) *n.* [< OFr. *lardier* < ML. < L. *lardum*, lard] **1.** a place where the food supplies of a household are kept; pantry **2.** a supply of food

larding needle an instrument for inserting lardons in meat prior to cooking

lar·don (lär′dən) *n.* [ME. < MFr. < *lard*, LARD] a strip of bacon or fat used to lard meat: also **lar·doon′** (-d o͞o n′)

lard·y cake (lär′dē) a rich, sweet cake made of bread dough, lard, sugar, and dried fruit

lar·es (lar′ēz, lā′rēz) *n.pl., sing.* **lar** (lär) [L.] in ancient Rome, guardian ancestral spirits

lares and penates 1. the household gods of the ancient Romans **2.** the treasured belongings of a family or household

large (lärj) *adj.* **larg′er, larg′est** [OFr. < L. *largus*] **1.** big; great; specif., *a*) taking up much space; bulky *b*) enclosing much space; spacious [a *large* office] *c*) of great extent or amount [a *large* sum] **2.** big as compared with others of its kind **3.** operating on a big scale [a *large* manufacturer] —*adv.* in a large way —**at large 1.** free; not confined **2.** fully; in complete detail **3.** in general; taken altogether —**large′ness** *n.*

large·ly (-lē) *adv.* **1.** much; in great amounts **2.** for the most part; mainly

larger-than-life *adj.* legendary or eminent [Churchill was a *larger-than-life* figure]

large-scale (-skāl′) *adj.* **1.** drawn to a large scale **2.** of wide scope; extensive [*large-scale* business operations]

lar·gess, lar·gesse (lär jes′, lär′jis) *n.* [OFr. < *large*, LARGE] **1.** generous giving **2.** a gift or gifts generously given

lar·ghet·to (lär get′ō) *adj., adv.* [It. < *largo*: see LARGO] *Music* relatively slow, but faster than largo —*n., pl.* **-tos** a larghetto movement or passage

larg·ish (lär′jish) *adj.* rather large

lar·go (lär′gō) *adj., adv.* [It., large, slow < L. *largus*, large] *Music* slow and stately —*n., pl.* **-gos** a largo movement or passage

lar·i·at (lar′ē it) *n.* [Sp. *la reata*, the rope] **1.** a rope used for tethering grazing horses, etc. **2.** same as LASSO

lark¹ (lärk) *n.* [OE. *læwerce*] **1.** any of a large family of songbirds; esp., the skylark **2.** any of various similar American birds, as the meadowlark

lark² (lärk) *vi.* [? altered after prec. < dial. *lake* < ME. *laike*, to play] to play or frolic —*n.* a frolic or spree —**lark′ish, lark′y** *adj.*

lark·spur (lärk′spur′) *n.* a common garden plant with spurred flowers, related to the delphinium

larn (lärn) *vt.* [Dial.] **1.** same as LEARN **2.** to teach [that'll *larn* him]

lar·ri·kin (lar′ə kin) *n.* [? < dial. *larack*, to frolic or romp] a rough; a disorderly person —*adj.* rowdy

lar·rup (lar′əp) *vt.* [akin to or < Du. *larpen*] [Colloq.] to whip; flog; beat

lar·va (lär′və) *n., pl.* **-vae** (-vē), **-vas** [L., ghost] the early, free-living, immature form of any animal that changes

structurally when it becomes an adult [the caterpillar is the *larva* of the butterfly] —**lar′val** *adj.*

la·ryn·ge·al (lə rin′jē əl) *adj.* **1.** of, in, or near the larynx **2.** used for treating the larynx

lar·yn·gi·tis (lar′ən jīt′əs) *n.* [ff. + -ITIS] inflammation of the larynx, often with a temporary loss of voice —**lar′-yn·git′ic** (-jit′ik) *adj.*

la·ryn·go- [< Gr.] *a combining form meaning:* **1.** the larynx **2.** laryngeal and Also **laryng-**

la·ryn·go·scope (lə riŋ′gə skōp′) *n.* [prec. + -SCOPE] an instrument for examining the larynx —**lar·yn·gos·co·py** (lar′iŋ gos′kə pē) *n.*

lar·ynx (lar′iŋks) *n., pl.* **lar′ynx·es, la·ryn·ges** (lə rin′jēz) [< Gr. *larynx*] **1.** the structure of muscle and cartilage at the upper end of the human trachea, containing the vocal cords and serving as the organ of voice: see EPIGLOTTIS, illus. **2.** a similar structure in other animals

la·sa·gna (lə zän′yə) *n.* [It., the noodle < L. *lasanum* (< Gr. *lasanon*), a pot] a dish of wide, flat noodles baked in layers with cheese, tomato sauce, minced meat, etc.

las·car (las′kər) *n.* [< Hindi < Per. *lashkar* < Ar. *al-'askar*, army] an Oriental sailor, esp. one who is a native of India

las·civ·i·ous (lə siv′ē əs) *adj.* [< ML. < L. < *lascivus*, wanton] **1.** characterized by or expressing lust or lewdness; wanton **2.** tending to excite lust —**las·civ′i·ous·ly** *adv.* —**las·civ′i·ous·ness** *n.*

lase (lāz) *vi.* **lased, las′ing** to emit laser light

la·ser (lā′zər) *n.* [*l(ight) a(mplification by) s(timulated) e(mission of) r(adiation)*] a device that amplifies focused coherent light waves and concentrates them in a narrow, very intense beam

lash¹ (lash) *n.* [ME. *lassche* < ?] **1.** a whip, esp. the flexible striking part **2.** a stroke as with a whip **3.** an eyelash —*vt.* **1.** to strike or drive as with a lash; flog **2.** to swing quickly or angrily; switch [the cat *lashed* her tail] **3.** to strike with great force [waves *lashed* the cliffs] **4.** to attack violently in words; censure or rebuke **5.** to incite by appealing to the emotions —*vi.* **1.** to move quickly or violently; switch **2.** to make strokes as with a whip —**lash out 1.** to strike out violently **2.** to speak angrily —**lash′-er** *n.*

lash² (lash) *vt.* [< OFr. *lachier*: see LACE] to fasten or tie with a rope, etc.

lash·ing¹ (-iŋ) *n.* **1.** a whipping **2.** a strong rebuke

lash·ing² (-iŋ) *n.* **1.** the act of fastening or tying with a rope, etc. **2.** a rope, etc. so used

lash·ings (lash′iŋz) *n.pl.* [Colloq.] large amounts; lots (often with *of*)

lash-up (lash′up′) *n.* [Colloq.] a temporary or improvised contrivance

lass (las) *n.* [ME. *lasse*, prob. < ON.] **1.** a young woman; girl **2.** a sweetheart

Las·sa fever (las′ə) [after *Lassa*, village in E Nigeria, where first detected] an acute virus disease endemic to western Africa, characterized by high fever and inflammation of various body organs

las·sie (las′ē) *n.* [dim. of LASS] [Scot.] **1.** a young girl **2.** a sweetheart

las·si·tude (las′ə tyo͞od′) *n.* [Fr. < L. < *lassus*, faint] a state or feeling of being tired and listless; weariness; languor

las·so (las′o͞o, lə so͞o′) *n., pl.* **-sos, -soes** [Sp. *lazo* < L. *laqueus*, noose] a long rope with a sliding noose at one end, used to catch cattle or horses —*vt.* **-soed, -so·ing** to catch with a lasso —**las′so·er** *n.*

last¹ (last) *adj. alt. superl. of* LATE [< OE. *latost*, superl. of *læt*: see LATE] **1.** being or coming after all others in place or time; furthest from the first; final **2.** only remaining **3.** most recent [*last* month] **4.** least likely [the *last* person to suspect] **5.** utmost; greatest **6.** lowest in rank, as a prize **7.** newest [the *last* thing in hats] **8.** conclusive [he always wants the *last* word] **9.** individual: a redundant intensive [eat every *last* bite] —*adv.* **1.** after all others; at the end **2.** most recently **3.** finally —*n.* **1.** someone or something which comes last [the *last* of the kings] **2.** end [friends to the *last*] —**at (long) last** finally —**see the last of** to see for the last time

last² (last) *vi.* [< OE. *læstan*] **1.** to remain in existence or operation; continue; endure **2.** to remain in good condition **3.** to continue unconsumed, unspent, etc.; be enough (for) [food to *last* (for) a month] —*vt.* to continue or endure throughout: often with *out* [doubtful whether he can *last* (out) the year] —**last′er** *n.*

last³ (last) *n.* [OE. *læste < last*, footstep] a form shaped like a foot, on which shoes are made or repaired —*vt.* to form with a last —**stick to one's last 1.** to keep to one's own work **2.** to mind one's own business —**last′er** *n.*

last-ditch (-dich′) *adj.* made, done, etc. in a final, often desperate effort to resist or oppose

last·ing (läs′tiŋ) *adj.* that lasts a long time; enduring; durable [a *lasting* peace] —**last′ing·ly** *adv.* —**last′ing·ness** *n.*

Last Judgment *Theol.* the final judgment of mankind at the end of the world

last·ly (läst′lē) *adv.* in conclusion; finally

last name a surname or family name

last rites 1. final rites for a dead person 2. sacraments administered to a dying person

last straw [from the last straw that broke the camel's back in the fable] the last of a sequence of troubles or annoyances that results in a breakdown, loss of patience, etc.

Last Supper the last supper eaten by Jesus with his disciples before the Crucifixion

last trump the trumpet supposed to waken the dead for the Last Judgement

last word 1. a) the final word or speech, regarded as settling the argument b) final authority 2. something regarded as perfect 3. [Colloq.] the very latest style

Lat. Latin

lat. latitude

La·ta·ki·a (lat'ə kē'ə) n. [< *Latakia*, a seaport in Syria] a fine grade of Turkish smoking tobacco

latch (lach) n. [OE. *læccan*, to catch] 1. a fastening for a door or gate consisting of a bar that falls into a notch on the doorjamb or gatepost: now often used of a spring lock on a door 2. a fastening for a window, etc. —*vt., vi.* to fasten with a latch —**latch onto** [Colloq.] 1. to attach (oneself) to 2. to understand —**on the latch** fastened by the latch but not bolted

latch·key (-kē') n. a key for drawing back or unfastening the latch of a door

latchkey child a child who regularly arrives home to an empty house because his parents have not returned from work

latch·string (-striŋ') n. a cord fastened to a latch so that it can be raised from the outside

late (lāt) adj. *lat·er* or *lat'ter, lat'est* or *last* [OE. *læt*] 1. happening, coming, etc. after the usual or expected time; tardy 2. a) happening, continuing, etc. far on in the day, night, year, etc. [a *late* party] b) far advanced in a period, development, etc. [the *late* Middle Ages] 3. recent [of *late* years] 4. having been so recently but not now 5. having recently died —*adv.* *lat'er, lat'est* or *last* 1. after the usual or expected time 2. at or until an advanced time of the day, night, year, etc. 3. towards the end of a period, development, etc. 4. recently [as *late* as yesterday] —**late in the day** [Colloq.] at some late point in the proceedings, etc., usually when it is too late to make any changes —**of late** lately —**late'ness** n.

la·teen (la tēn', lə-) adj. [< Fr. < (*voile*) *latine*, Latin (sail)] 1. designating or of a triangular sail attached to a long yard suspended from a short mast: used chiefly on Mediterranean vessels 2. having such a sail —*n.* a vessel with such a sail: also **la·teen'er**

Late Greek the Greek language of the period after classical Greek, seen chiefly in writings from c.200 to c.600 A.D.

Late Latin the Latin language of the period after classical Latin, seen chiefly in writings from c.200 to c.600 A.D.

LATEEN SAIL

late·ly (lāt'lē) adv. recently; a short while ago

La Tène (lá ten') [name of the site of such a find on Lake of Neuchâtel] designating an Iron Age, Celtic culture of C and W Europe, characterized by the use of decorations on weapons, utensils, etc.

la·tent (lāt''nt) adj. [< L. prp. of *latere*, to lurk] lying hidden and undeveloped within a person or thing; concealed, dormant, etc. [a *latent* talent] —**la'ten·cy** n. —**la'tent·ly** adv.

lat·er (lāt'ər) adj. *alt. compar.* of LATE —*adv. compar.* of LATE at a later time; subsequently —**later on** subsequently

lat·er·al (lat'ər əl) adj. [< L. < *latus* (gen. *lateris*), a side] of, at, from, or towards the side; sideways [*lateral* movement] —*n.* 1. any lateral part, growth, etc. —**lat'er·al·ly** adv.

lateral thinking [arbitrary coinage] a way of solving problems by finding unorthodox solutions

lat·er·ite (lat'ə rīt') n. [L. *later*, brick, tile + ITE] Geol. 1. a brick-coloured rock found in India 2. a red, ferruginous clay often dried in the sun and used for building

lat·est (lāt'ist) *alt. superl.* of LATE —**at the latest** no later than (the time specified) —**the latest** the most recent thing, development, etc.

la·tex (lā'teks) n., pl. **lat·i·ces** (lat'ə sēz'), **la'tex·es** [L., a fluid] 1. a milky liquid in certain plants and trees, as the rubber tree, milkweed, etc.: used esp. as the basis of rubber 2. an emulsion in water of particles of synthetic rubber or plastic: used in rubber goods, adhesives, paints, etc.

lath (lāth) n., pl. **laths** (lāthz, lāths) [OE. *lætt*] 1. any of the thin, narrow strips of wood used in building lattices or nailed to studs, rafters, etc. as a groundwork for plastering, tiling,

etc. 2. any framework for plaster, as wire screening or expanded metal 3. laths collectively —*vt.* to cover with laths

lathe (lāth) n. [prob. < MDu. *lade*] a machine for shaping an article of· wood, metal, etc. by holding and turning it rapidly against the edge of a cutting tool —*vt.* lathed, **lath'**-ing to shape on a lathe

lath·er (lath'ər, lä'thər) n. [OE. *leathor*, washing soda or soap] 1. the foam formed by soap or other detergent in water 2. foamy sweat, as on a race horse 3. [Slang] an agitated state —*vt.* to cover with lather —*vi.* to form, or become covered with, lather —**lath'er·y** adj.

la·thi (lä'tē) n. [Hindi] in India, a heavy stick of bamboo and iron, used as a club by police, soldiers, etc.

lath·ing (lāth'iŋ) n. 1. laths collectively, esp. when used as a base for plaster 2. the putting up of laths on walls, etc. Also **lath'work'** (-wurk')

Lat·in (lat'in) adj. 1. of ancient Latium or its people 2. of ancient Rome or its people 3. of or in the language of ancient Latium and ancient Rome 4. designating or of the languages derived from Latin, the peoples who speak them, their countries, etc. —*n.* 1. a native or inhabitant of ancient Latium or ancient Rome 2. the Italic language of ancient Latium and ancient Rome 3. a person, as a Spaniard or Italian, whose language is derived from Latin

Lat·in·ate (-āt') adj. of, derived from, or similar to Latin: also **La·tin·ic** (la tin'ik)

Lat·in·ism (-iz'm) n. a Latin idiom or expression, used in another language

Lat·in·ist (-ist) n. a scholar in Latin

Lat·in·ize (-īz') *vt.* -ized', -iz'ing 1. to translate into Latin 2. to give Latin form or characteristics to —*vi.* to use Latin expressions, forms, etc. —**Lat'in·i·za'tion** n. —**Lat'in·iz'er** n.

Latin Rite the Latin liturgy formerly used in the Roman Catholic Church

lat·ish (lāt'ish) adj., adv. somewhat late

lat·i·tude (lat'ə tyōōd') n. [OFr. < L. *latitudo* < *latus*, wide] 1. extent; scope; range of applicability 2. freedom from narrow restrictions 3. *Geog.* a) angular distance, measured in degrees, north or south from the equator b) a place or region in relation to its latitude —**lat'i·tu'di·nal** adj. —**lat'i·tu'di·nal·ly** adv.

lat·i·tu·di·nar·i·an (lat'ə tyōō'də ner'ē ən) adj. [see prec. & -ARIAN] liberal in one's views; permitting free thought, esp. in religious matters —*n.* one who is very liberal in his views and, in religion, cares little about particular creeds and forms —**lat'i·tu·di·nar'i·an·ism** n.

la·trine (lə trēn') n. [Fr. < L. *latrina* < *lavare*, to wash] a toilet, privy, etc. for the use of a large number of people, as in an army camp

-la·try (lə trē) [< Gr. < *latreia*, service] a combining form meaning worship of or excessive devotion to [*idolatry*]

lat·ter (lat'ər) adj. *alt. compar.* of LATE [OE. *lættra*, compar. of *læt*, late] 1. a) later; more recent b) nearer the end or close [the *latter* part of May] 2. last mentioned of two: opposed to FORMER[1]: often a noun (with *the*)

lat·ter-day (-dā') adj. of recent or present time

Lat·ter-day Saint see MORMON

lat·ter·ly (lat'ər lē) adv. lately; recently

lat·tice (lat'is) n. [OFr. *lattis* < MHG. *latte*, a lath] 1. an openwork structure of crossed strips of wood, metal, etc. used as a screen, support, etc. 2. a door, shutter, trellis, etc. formed of such a structure 3. *Physics* a three-dimensional pattern of points in space, as of atoms in a solid or crystal —*vt.* -ticed, -tic·ing 1. to arrange like a lattice 2. to furnish with a lattice

lattice window a window of small, diamond-shaped glass panes set in a lattice of strips of lead

lat·tice·work (-wurk') n. 1. a lattice 2. lattices collectively Also **lat'tic·ing**

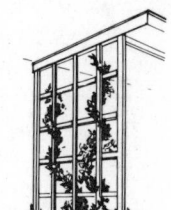
LATTICE

laud (lôd) n. [< OFr. < ML. *laudes*, pl. < L. *laus*, praise] 1. praise 2. any song of praise 3. [pl.] *Eccles.* [often L-] the service of dawn which constitutes the second (or, together with matins, the first) of the canonical hours and includes psalms of praise to God —*vt.* to praise; extol

laud·a·ble (-ə b'l) adj. worthy of being lauded; praiseworthy —**laud'a·bil'i·ty, laud'a·ble·ness** n. —**laud'a·bly** adv.

laud·a·num (lôd''n əm) n. [ModL., altered use of ML. var. of L. *ladanum*, mastic] 1. formerly, any of various opium preparations 2. a solution of opium in alcohol

lau·da·tion (lô dā'shən) n. a lauding or being lauded; praise; commendation

laud·a·to·ry (lôd'ə tər ē) adj. expressing praise; eulogistic: also **laud'a·tive**

laugh (läf) *vi.* [OE. *hleahhan*] 1. to make the vocal sounds and facial movements that express mirth, amusement, ridicule, etc. 2. to feel or suggest joyousness —*vt.* 1. to express with laughter 2. to cause to be by means of laughter [to *laugh* oneself hoarse] —*n.* 1. the act or sound of laughing 2. anything that provokes or is fit to provoke laughter 3. [pl.] [Colloq.] mere diversion or pleasure —**have the last laugh** to win after apparent defeat —**laugh at** 1. to be amused by 2. to make fun of 3. to be indifferent to or contemptuous of —**laugh in** (or **up**) **one's sleeve** to laugh secretly or inwardly —**laugh off** to scorn, avoid, or reject by laughter or ridicule —**laugh out of** (or **on**) **the other** (or **wrong**) **side of the mouth** to change from joy to sorrow, from amusement to annoyance, etc. —**no laughing matter** a serious matter —**laugh'er** n.

laugh·a·ble (-əb'l) adj. of such a nature as to cause laughter; amusing or ridiculous —**laugh'a·ble·ness** n. —**laugh'a·bly** adv.

laugh·ing (-iŋ) adj. 1. that laughs or seems to laugh [a laughing brook] 2. uttered with laughter —n. laughter —**laugh'ing·ly** adv.

laughing gas nitrous oxide used as an anaesthetic: it may cause laughter and exhilaration

laugh·ing·stock (läf'iŋ stok') n. a person or thing made the object of ridicule

laugh·ter (läf'tər) n. 1. the action or sound of laughing 2. an indication of amusement [with laughter in her eyes]

launch[1] (lônch) vt. [< OFr. lanchier < LL. < L. lancea, LANCE] 1. to hurl, discharge, or send off (a weapon, blow, rocket, etc.) 2. to cause (a newly built vessel) to slide into the water; set afloat 3. to set in operation; start [to launch an attack] 4. to start (a person) on some course —vi. 1. to put to sea (often with out or forth) 2. to start on some new course or enterprise (often with out or forth) 3. to throw oneself (into) with vigour; plunge [to launch into a tirade] —n. the act or process of launching a ship, spacecraft, etc. —adj. designating or of facilities, sites, etc. used in launching spacecraft or missiles —**launch'er** n.

launch[2] (lônch) n. [Sp. or Port. lancha < ?] 1. formerly, the largest boat carried by a warship 2. an open, or partly enclosed, motorboat

launching pad the platform from which a rocket, guided missile, etc. is launched: also **launch pad**

launch window the period during which conditions are favourable for launching a spacecraft on a particular mission

laun·der (lôn'dər) vt. [< OFr. < ML. < LL. lavandaria, things to be washed < L. < lavare, to wash] to wash, or wash and iron, (clothes, etc.) —vi. 1. to withstand washing [this fabric launders well] 2. to do laundry —**laun'der·er** n.

Laun·der·ette (lôn'də ret'lôn'dret') a service mark for a self-service laundry —n. [l-] such a laundry: also **Laun·drette**

laun·dress (lôn'dris) n. a woman whose work is washing clothes, ironing, etc.

Laun·dro·mat (lôn'drə mat') [< a trademark for an automatic washing machine] a service mark for a self-service laundry —n. [l-] such a laundry

laun·dry (lôn'drē) n., pl. **-dries** 1. a laundering 2. a place where laundering is done 3. clothes, etc. laundered or to be laundered

laun·dry·man (-mən) n., pl. **-men** a man who works for a laundry, esp. one who collects and delivers laundry

laun·dry·wom·an (-woom'ən) n., pl. **-wom'en** same as LAUNDRESS

lau·re·ate (lôr'ē it) adj. [< L. < laurea (corona), laurel (wreath) < laurus, laurel] 1. crowned with a laurel wreath as a mark of honour 2. honoured —n. 1. one on whom honour is conferred 2. same as POET LAUREATE —**lau'·re·ate·ship'** n.

lau·rel (lor'əl) n. [< OFr. < L. laurus] 1. an evergreen tree or shrub, native to S Europe, with large, glossy, aromatic leaves; bay 2. the foliage of this tree, esp. as woven into wreaths such as those used by the ancient Greeks to crown victors in contests 3. [pl.] a) fame; honour b) victory 4. a tree or shrub resembling the true laurel, as the mountain laurel —vt. **-relled, -rel·ling** 1. to crown with laurel 2. to honour —**look to one's laurels** to beware of having one's achievements surpassed —**rest on one's laurels** to be satisfied with what one has already achieved

lau·res·ti·nus, lau·rus·ti·nus (lô'rə stī'nəs) n. [ModL.< L. laurus, laurel & tinus, wild laurel] a tall evergreen shrub grown around the Mediterranean

lav (lav) [Colloq.] lavatory

la·va (lä'və) n. [It. < dial. lave < L. labes, a fall < labi, to slide] 1. melted rock issuing from a volcano 2. such rock when cool and solid

lav·age (lav'ij) n. [Fr.< L. lavare, to wash] Med. the washing out of an organ, as the stomach, intestinal tract, or sinuses

lav·a·liere, lav·a·lier (lav'ə lir') n. [Fr. lavallière, kind of tie] 1. an ornament hanging from a chain, worn round the neck 2. a small microphone, worn round the neck

lav·a·to·ry (lav'ə tər ē) n., pl. **-ries** [LL. lavatorium < L. lavare, to wash] 1. a washbowl 2. a room equipped with a washbowl, flush toilet, etc.

lavatory paper see TOILET PAPER

lave (lāv) vt., vi. **laved, lav'ing** [< OE. lafian & OFr. laver, both < L. lavare, to wash] [Poet.] to wash or bathe

lav·en·der (lav'ən dər) n. [< Anglo-Fr. < ML. lavandria < ?] 1. a fragrant European plant having spikes of pale-purplish flowers and yielding an aromatic oil (**oil of lavender**) 2. the dried flowers, leaves, and stalks of this plant, used to perfume clothes, linens, etc. 3. a pale purple —adj. pale-purple

lavender water a perfume or toilet water made from flowers of the lavender plant

la·ver (lä'vər) n. [< OFr. < L. < lavare, to wash] [Archaic] a large basin to wash in

lav·ish (lav'ish) adj. [< MFr. < OFr. lavasse, torrent of rain, prob. < laver < L. lavare, to wash] 1. very generous or liberal in giving or spending, often extravagantly so 2. more than enough; very abundant [lavish entertainment] —vt. to give or spend liberally —**lav'ish·ly** adv. —**lav'ish·ness** n.

law (lô) n. [OE. lagu < Anglo-N.] 1. a) all the rules of conduct established and enforced by the authority, legislation, or custom of a given community or other group b) any one of such rules 2. the condition existing when obedience to such rules is general [to establish law and order] 3. the branch of knowledge dealing with such rules; jurisprudence 4. the system of courts in which such rules are referred to in securing justice [to resort to law] 5. all such rules dealing with a particular activity [business law] 6. common law, as distinguished from equity 7. the profession of lawyers, judges, etc. (often with the) 8. a) a sequence of events in nature or in human activities occurring with unvarying uniformity under the same conditions: often **law of nature** b) the formulation in words of such a sequence 9. any rule or principle expected to be observed [the laws of health] 10. Eccles. a divine commandment 11. Math., Logic, etc. a general principle to which all applicable cases must conform [the laws of exponents] —**go to law** to take a dispute to a law court for settlement —**in** (or **at**) **law** according to the laws —**lay down the law** 1. to give orders in an authoritative manner 2. to give a scolding (to) —**read law** to study to become a lawyer —**the Law** 1. the Mosaic law, or the part of the Hebrew Scriptures containing it; specif., the Pentateuch 2. [l-] [Colloq.] a policeman or the police

law-a·bid·ing (lô'ə bīd'iŋ) adj. obeying the law

law agent in Scotland, a solicitor

law-and-order (lô'n ôr'dər) adj. in favour of strict law enforcement to suppress crime and violence he was a law-and-order candidate for office —**law and order**

law-break·er (-brā'kər) n. a person who violates the law —**law'break'ing** adj., n.

law court a court for administering justice under the law

law courts 1. courts in which law cases are heard and judged 2. [L- C-] the buildings in London where many major trials are held

law·ful (-fəl) adj. 1. in conformity with the law; permitted by law [a lawful act] 2. recognized by law; just [lawful debts] —**law'ful·ly** adv. —**law'ful·ness** n.

law·giv·er (-giv'ər) n. one who draws up or enacts a code of laws for a nation or people; lawmaker; legislator —**law'·giv'ing** n., adj.

lawks (lôks) interj. an exclamation of surprise, etc.: a euphemism for Lord

law·less (-lis) adj. 1. without law; not regulated by the authority of law [a lawless city] 2. not in conformity with law; illegal [lawless practices] 3. not obeying the law; unruly —**law'less·ly** adv. —**law'less·ness** n.

Law Lord a member of the House of Lords qualified by his judicial experience to participate in the legal work of the House

law·mak·er (-mā'kər) n. one who makes or helps to make laws; esp., a legislator —**law'mak'ing** adj., n.

lawn[1] (lôn) n. [< OFr. < Bret. lann, country] land covered with grass kept closely mown, esp. around a house —**lawn'·y** adj.

lawn[2] (lôn) n. [< Laon, city in France, where made] a fine, sheer cloth of linen or cotton, used for blouses, curtains, etc. —**lawn'y** adj.

lawn mower a hand-propelled or power-driven machine for cutting the grass of a lawn

lawn tennis see TENNIS

law of the Medes and Persians a law that cannot be revoked: Dan.6:8

law·ren·ci·um (lo ren'sē əm) n. [after E. O. Lawrence, 20th-c. U.S. physicist] a radioactive chemical element produced by nuclear bombardment of californium: symbol, Lr; at. wt., 256 (?); at. no., 103

Law·ren·tian (lo ren'shē ən) adj. relating to, or characteristic of, D. H. Lawrence —n. a student or devotee of D. H. Lawrence

law·suit (lô'soot') n. a suit at law between two parties; case before a civil court

law term 1. a word or phrase peculiar to legal documents, etc. 2. a period in the year when the law courts sit

law·yer (lô'yər) n. a person whose profession is advising others in matters of law or representing them in lawsuits

lax (laks) *adj.* [L. *laxus*] 1. loose; slack; not rigid or tight 2. not strict or exact; careless [*lax* morals] —**lax′ly** *adv.* —**lax′ness** *n.*

lax·a·tive (lak′sə tiv) *adj.* [< OFr. < ML. *laxativus* < LL. < pp. of L. *laxare* < *laxus*, loose] tending to make lax; specif., making the bowels loose and relieving constipation —*n.* any laxative medicine

lax·i·ty (lak′sə tē) *n.* lax quality or condition

lay¹ (lā) *vt.* **laid, lay′ing** [OE. *lecgan* < pt. base of OE. *licgan*, to LIE¹] 1. to cause to fall with force; knock down [one punch *laid* him low] 2. to place or put so as to rest, lie, etc.; deposit (with *on, in*, etc.) [*lay* the pen on the desk] 3. *a*) to put down (bricks, carpeting, etc.) in the correct way for a specific purpose *b*) to situate in a particular place [the scene is *laid* in France] 4. to place; put; set [to *lay* emphasis on accuracy] 5. to produce and deposit (an egg or eggs) 6. *a*) to cause to settle [to *lay* the dust] *b*) to allay, overcome, or appease [to *lay* one's fears] 7. to smooth down [to *lay* the nap of cloth] 8. to stake as a bet; wager 9. to impose (a tax, penalty, etc. *on* or *upon*) 10. to work out; devise [to *lay* plans] 11. to set (a table) with silverware, plates, etc. 12. to present or assert [to *lay* claim to property] 13. to attribute; charge; impute [to *lay* the blame on Tom] —*vi.* 1. to lay an egg or eggs 2. to lie; recline: a dialectal or substandard usage 3. *Naut.* to go; proceed [all hands *lay* aft] —*n.* the way in which something is situated or arranged [the *lay* of the land] —**lay aside** to set aside for the future; save: also **lay by** —**lay bare** to disclose —**lay down** 1. to sacrifice (one's life) 2. to declare emphatically 3. to store away, as wine in a cellar —**lay in** to get and store away —**lay into** [Slang] to attack with blows or words —**lay it on (thick)** [Colloq.] 1. to exaggerate 2. to flatter effusively —**lay off** 1. to discharge (an employee), esp. temporarily 2. to mark off the boundaries of 3. [Slang] to cease —**lay on** 1. to spread on 2. to attack with force —**lay oneself open** to expose oneself to attack, blame, etc. —**lay open** 1. to cut open 2. to expose —**lay out** 1. to spend 2. to arrange according to a plan 3. to spread out (clothes, equipment, etc.) 4. to make (a dead body) ready for burial —**lay up** 1. to store for future use 2. to disable; confine to bed or the sickroom —**lay up in lavender** to preserve for future use —**lay waste** to devastate or pillage

lay² (lā) *pt. of* LIE¹

lay³ (lā) *adj.* [< OFr. < LL. *laicus* < Gr. < *lāos*, the people] 1. of the laity, or ordinary people, as distinguished from the clergy 2. not belonging to or connected with a given profession [a legal handbook for *lay* readers]

lay⁴ (lā) *n.* [OFr. *lai*] 1. a short poem, esp. a narrative poem, for singing 2. [Archaic or Poet.] a song or melody

lay·a·bout (lā′ə bout′) *n.* [Colloq.] a lazy idler or loafer

lay analyst a psychoanalyst who is not a medical doctor

lay brother a member of a monastery who has taken vows of poverty, chastity, and obedience but is not ordained: also **lay sister**

lay-by (-bī′) *n.* 1. a widened section of a stream, canal, etc. for vessels to pass or stop 2. a widened section along a road allowing vehicles to park

lay·er (lā′ər) *n.* 1. a person or thing that lays 2. a single thickness, coat, fold, or stratum 3. a shoot (of a living plant) bent down and partly covered with earth so that it may take root —*vt., vi.* to grow (a plant) by means of a layer —**lay′er·ed** *adj.*

lay·ette (lā et′) *n.* [Fr., dim. of *laie*, drawer < Fl. < MDu. *lade*, a chest] a complete outfit for a newborn baby, including clothes, bedding, etc.

lay figure [earlier *layman* < Du. < MDu. *led*, limb + *man*, man] 1. an artist's jointed model of the human form, on which drapery is arranged 2. a person who is a mere puppet or a nonentity

Lay Lord a member of the House of Lords other than a Law Lord

lay·man (lā′mən) *n., pl.* **-men** [LAY³ + MAN] 1. a member of the laity; person not a clergyman 2. a person not belonging to or skilled in a given profession

lay·off (lā′ôf′) *n.* the act of laying off; esp., temporary unemployment, or the period of this

lay of the land 1. the arrangement of the natural features of an area 2. the existing state of affairs Also **lie of the land**

lay·out (lā′out′) *n.* 1. the act of laying something out 2. the manner in which anything is laid out; arrangement; specif., the plan or makeup of a newspaper, page, advertisement, etc. 3. the thing laid out 4. an outfit or set

lay·o·ver (-ō′vər) *n.* [Chiefly U.S.] a stopping for a while in some place during a journey

lay reader a church member licensed to take some services, though not ordained

lay·stall (lā′stôl) *n.* a rubbish dump; place for putting refuse, dung, etc.

la·zar (laz′ər, lā′zər) *n.* [< ML. *lazarus*, leper, ult. < *Lazarus*, the brother of Mary and Martha, raised from the dead by Jesus: John II] [Rare] a poor, diseased, esp. leprous person

laz·a·ret·to (laz′ə ret′ō) *n., pl.* **-tos** [It. < Santa Madonna di *Nazaret*, Venetian church used as a plague hospital; initial after *lazzaro*, leper] formerly, a public hospital for poor people having contagious diseases, esp. for lepers: also **laz′-a·ret′, laz′a·rette′** (-ret′)

laze (lāz) *vi.* **lazed, laz′ing** to be lazy or idle —*vt.* to spend (time, etc.) in idleness —*n.* an act or instance of lazing

la·zy (lā′zē) *adj.* **-zi·er, -zi·est** [prob. < MLowG. or MDu.] 1. not eager or willing to work or exert oneself; slothful 2. slow and heavy; sluggish [a *lazy* river] —*vi., vt.* **-zied, -zy·ing** same as LAZE —**la′zi·ly** *adv.* —**la′zi·ness** *n.*

la·zy·bones (-bōnz′) *n.* [Colloq.] a lazy person

Lazy Susan [U.S.] a revolving tray with sections

lb. [L. *libra*, pl. *librae*] pound; pounds

lbs. pounds

l.b.w. *Cricket* leg before wicket

L/C, l/c letter of credit

l.c. 1. [L. *loco citato*] in the place cited 2. *Printing* lower case

L.C.C. (formerly) London County Council

L.C.D., l.c.d. least (or lowest) common denominator

L.C.J. Lord Chief Justice

L.C.M., l.c.m. least (or lowest) common multiple

L/Cpl. lance corporal

L.D.S. 1. Latter-day Saints 2. Licentiate in Dental Surgery

lea (lē) *n.* [OE. *leah*] [Chiefly Poet.] a meadow, grassy field, or pasture; grassland

L.E.A. Local Education Authority

leach (lēch) *vt.* [prob. < OE. *leccan*, to water] 1. to cause (a liquid) to filter down through some material 2. to wash (wood ashes, etc.) with a filtering liquid 3. to extract (a soluble substance) from some material [lye is *leached* from wood ashes] —*vi.* 1. to lose soluble matter through a filtering liquid 2. to dissolve and be washed away —*n.* 1. a leaching 2. a sievelike container used in leaching —**leach′a·ble** *adj.* —**leach′er** *n.*

lead¹ (lēd) *vt.* **led, lead′ing** [OE. *lædan*] 1. *a*) to direct the course of by going before or along with; conduct; guide *b*) to mark the way for [lights to *lead* you there] 2. to guide by physical contact, pulling a rope, etc. [to *lead* a horse] 3. to conduct (water, steam, rope, etc.) in a certain direction, channel, etc. 4. to direct by influence, etc. to a course of action or thought; cause; prompt 5. to be the head or leader of (an expedition, orchestra, etc.) 6. *a*) to be at the head of [to *lead* one's class] *b*) to be ahead of by a specified margin 7. to live; spend [to *lead* a hard life] 8. *Card Games* to begin the play with (a card or suit) —*vi.* 1. to show the way by going before or along; act as guide 2. to submit to being led: said esp. of a horse 3. to be or form a way (*to, from, under*, etc.); go 4. to come, or bring one, as a result (with *to*) [one thing *led* to another] 5. to be or go first 6. *Boxing* to aim a first blow 7. *Card Games* to play the first card —*n.* 1. leadership 2. example [follow his *lead*] 3. *a*) first or front place; precedence *b*) the amount or distance ahead [to hold a safe *lead*] 4. the strap or string by which a dog is held in check 5. anything that leads, as a clue 6. *Boxing* a blow used in leading 7. *Card Games* the right of playing first, or the card or suit played 8. *Elec.* a wire carrying current from one point to another in a circuit 9. *Journalism* same as LEAD STORY 10. *Mining* a stratum of ore 11. *Music* the main melody in a harmonic composition 12. *Theatre a*) a main role *b*) an actor or actress playing such a role —*adj.* acting as leader [the *lead* horse] —**lead a person a dog's life** to torment someone constantly —**lead a woman to the altar** to marry her —**lead off** to begin —**lead on** 1. to conduct further 2. to lure —**lead up to** to prepare the way for

lead² (led) *n.* [OE.] 1. a heavy, soft, malleable, bluish-grey metallic chemical element used for piping and in numerous alloys: symbol, Pb; at. wt., 207.19; at. no., 82 2. anything made of this metal; specif., *a*) a weight for sounding depths at sea, etc. *b*) *Printing* a thin strip of type metal inserted to increase the space between lines of type 3. bullets 4. a thin stick of graphite, used in pencils —*adj.* made of or containing lead —*vt.* 1. to cover, line, or weight with lead 2. *Printing* to increase the space between (lines of type) by inserting leads

lead·en (led′'n) *adj.* 1. made of lead 2. having the heaviness of lead; hard to move 3. sluggish; dull 4. depressed; gloomy 5. of a dull grey —**lead′en·ly** *adv.* —**lead′en·ness** *n.*

lead·er (lē′dər) *n.* 1. a person or thing that leads; guiding head [*Leader* of the House of Commons] 2. a horse harnessed before all others or in the foremost span 3. a pipe for carrying fluid 4. a tendon 5. a section of blank film or recording tape at the beginning of a reel 6. *Bot.* the central stem of a plant 7. *Fishing* a short piece of plastic, etc. attaching the hook, lure, etc. to the line 8. *Journalism* the editorial in a newspaper 9. *Music a*) the main performer, as in a vocal section *b*) the leader of the first violins, often an assistant to the conductor: in full, **leader of the orchestra** 10. [*pl.*] *Printing* dots, dashes, etc. in a line, used to direct the eye across the page —**lead′er·less** *adj.* —**lead′er·ship′** *n.*

lead glass (led)   glass that contains lead oxide

lead-in (lĕd'in') *n.*   1. the wire leading from an aerial or antenna to a receiver or transmitter   2. an introduction —*adj.* that is a lead-in

lead·ing[1] (led'iŋ) *n.*   1. a covering or being covered with lead   2. strips or sheets of lead   3. *Printing* the strips of lead inserted between the lines of type to provide white space

lead·ing[2] (lē'diŋ) *n.*   guidance; direction —*adj.* 1. that leads; guiding   2. principal; chief   3. playing the lead in a play, film, etc. [*leading* lady]

lead·ing aircraftman (lē'diŋ)   see MILITARY RANKS, table

lead·ing edge (lē'diŋ)   *Aeron.* the front edge of a propeller blade or aerofoil

lead·ing light (lē'diŋ)   an important or influential member of a club, community, etc.

lead·ing note (lē'diŋ)   *Music* 1. the note a semitone below the keynote   2. any note that tends most naturally to resolve to the note lying one semitone above it

lead·ing question (lē'diŋ)   a question put in such a way as to suggest the answer sought

lead·ing rating (lē'diŋ)   see MILITARY RANKS, TABLE

lead·ing rein (lē'diŋ)   1. a rein used to lead a horse, used esp. with someone learning to ride   [*usually pl.*] straps or a harness used to assist and control a child who is learning to walk   3. excessive restraint or guidance

lead·ing strings (lē'diŋ)   *same as* LEADING REIN (sense 2 & 3)

lead-off (lĕd'of') *n.*   the first in a series of actions, moves, etc.

lead pencil (led)   a pencil consisting of a slender stick of graphite encased in wood, etc.

lead poisoning (led)   an acute or chronic poisoning caused by the absorption of lead into the body

lead screw (lĕd)   a screw running alongside the bed of a lathe and moving the lathe's carriage

lead story (lĕd)   the major news story in a newspaper

lead tetraethyl   *same as* TETRAETHYL LEAD

lead time (lĕd)   the period of time from the decision to make a product to its actual production

leaf (lēf) *n.,*   *pl.* **leaves** [OE. *leaf*] 1. any of the flat, thin, expanded organs, usually green, growing from the stem of a plant   2. popularly, *a)* the blade of a leaf *b)* a petal   3. leaves collectively [*choice tobacco leaf*]   4. a sheet of paper with a page on each side   5. *a)* a thin sheet of metal *b)* such sheets collectively [*gold leaf*]   6. *a)* a hinged section of a table top *b)* a board inserted into a table top to increase its surface   7. a flat, hinged or movable part of a folding door, shutter, etc. —*vi.* 1. to bear leaves (often with *out*)   2. to turn the pages of a book, etc. (with *through*) —*vt.* to turn the pages of —**in leaf** with foliage —**take a leaf from someone's book** to follow someone's example —**turn over a new leaf** to make a new start —**leaf'less** *adj.* —**leaf'-like'** *adj.*

leaf·age (-ij) *n.*   leaves collectively; foliage

leaf bud   a bud from which only stems and leaves develop

leaf·let (-lit) *n.*   1. one of the divisions of a compound leaf   2. a small or young leaf   3. a separate sheet of printed matter, often folded but not stitched

leaf mould   1. a rich soil consisting largely of decayed leaves   2. a mould that forms on leaves

leaf·stalk (-stôk') *n.*   the slender, usually cylindrical portion of a leaf, which supports the blade and is attached to the stem

leaf·y (lē'fē) *adj.* **leaf'i·er, leaf'i·est** 1. of, consisting of, or like a leaf or leaves   2. having many leaves   3. having broad leaves, as spinach —**leaf'i·ness** *n.*

league[1] (lēg) *n.* [< OFr. < It. *liga* < *legare* < L. *ligare*, to bind]   1. a covenant made by nations, groups, or individuals for promoting common interests, etc.   2. an association or alliance formed by such a covenant   3. *Sports* a group of teams organized to compete against one another   4. [Colloq.] a division according to grade or quality —*vt., vi.* **leagued, leagu'ing** to form into a league —**in league** allied —**leagu'er** *n.*

league[2] (lēg) *n.* [< OFr. < LL. *leuga*, Gallic mile < Celt.]   a measure of distance varying in different times and countries: in English-speaking countries it is usually about 5 kilometres

league table   a list of sports clubs ranked in order [the football *league table*]

leak (lēk) *vi.* [< ON. *leka*, to drip]   1. to let a fluid substance out or in accidentally [the boat *leaks*]   2. to enter or escape in this way, as a fluid (often with *in* or *out*)   3. to become known little by little [the truth *leaked* out] —*vt.* 1. to allow to leak   2. to allow to become known —*n.* 1. an accidental hole or crack that lets something out or in   2. any means of escape for something that ought not to be let out, lost, etc.   3. leakage   4. a disclosure, supposedly accidental but actually intentional: in full, **news leak**   5. *a)* a loss of electrical charge through faulty insulation *b)* the point where this occurs

leak·age (-ij) *n.*   1. an act or instance of leaking; leak   2. something that leaks in or out   3. the amount that leaks in or out

leak·y (lē'kē) *adj.* **leak'i·er, leak'i·est** having a leak or leaks —**leak'i·ness** *n.*

leal (lēl) *adj.* [< OFr. < L. *legalis*: see LEGAL] [Archaic or Scot.] loyal; true —**leal'ly** *adv.*

lean[1] (lēn) *vi.* **leaned** or **leant, lean'ing** [OE. *hlinian*] 1. to bend or deviate from an upright position; stand at a slant; incline   2. to bend the body so as to rest part of one's weight upon something [he *leaned* on the desk]   3. to depend for aid, etc.; rely (*on* or *upon*)   4. to have a particular mental inclination; tend (*towards* or *to*) —*vt.* to cause to lean —*n.* an inclination; slant —**lean'er** *n.*

lean[2] (lēn) *adj.* [OE. *hlæne*] 1. with little flesh or fat; thin; spare   2. containing little or no fat: said of meat   3. lacking in richness, profit, etc.; meagre —*n.* meat containing little or no fat —**lean'ly** *adv.* —**lean'ness** *n.*

lean·ing (lē'niŋ) *n.*   1. the act of a person or thing that leans   2. tendency; inclination

leant (lent)   *alt. pt. & pp. of* LEAN[1]

lean-to (lēn'tōo') *n., pl.* **lean'-tos'** 1. a shed with a sloping roof resting against trees, etc.   2. a structure, as the wing of a building, whose sloping roof abuts a wall or building

leap (lēp) *vi.* **leaped** (lept, lēpt) or **leapt** (lept), **leap'ing** [OE. *hleapan*] 1. to jump; spring   2. to move suddenly or swiftly, as if by jumping; bound   3. to accept eagerly something offered (with *at*) —*vt.* 1. to pass over by a jump   2. to cause to leap [to *leap* a horse over a wall] —*n.* 1. a jump; spring   2. the distance covered in a jump   3. a place that is, or is to be, leaped over or from —**by leaps and bounds** very rapidly —**leap in the dark** a risky act whose consequences cannot be foreseen —**leap'er** *n.*

leap·frog (-frog') *n.*   a game in which each player in turn jumps over the bent back of each of the other players —*vi.* **-frogged', -frog'ging** 1. to skip (*over*)   2. to progress in jumps or stages —*vt.* to jump or skip over

leap year   a year of 366 days, occurring every fourth year: the additional day is February 29: a leap year is a year whose number is exactly divisible by four, or, in the case of century years, by 400

learn (lurn) *vt.* **learned** or **learnt** (lurnt), **learn'ing** [OE. *leornian*] 1. to get knowledge of (a subject) or skill in (an art, trade, etc.) by study, experience, etc.   2. to come to know [to *learn* what happened]   3. to come to know how [to *learn* to swim]   4. to memorize   5. to acquire as a habit or attitude   6. [Dial.] to teach —*vi.* 1. to gain knowledge or skill   2. to be informed; hear (*of* or *about*) —**learn'a·ble** *adj.* —**learn'er** *n.*

learn·ed (lur'nid; *for 3* lurnd) *adj.*   1. having or showing much learning; erudite   2. of or characterized by study and learning   3. acquired by study, experience, etc. [a *learned* response] —**learn'ed·ly** *adv.* —**learn'ed·ness** *n.*

learner driver   someone who is learning to drive a motor vehicle but who has not yet passed a driving test

learn·ing (lur'niŋ) *n.*   1. the acquiring of knowledge or skill   2. acquired knowledge or skill

lease (lēs) *n.* [< Anglo-Fr. *les* < OFr. < L. *laxare*, to loosen < *laxus*, loose]   a contract by which a landlord gives to a tenant the use of lands, buildings, etc. for a specified time and for fixed payments; also, the period of time specified —*vt.* **leased, leas'ing** 1. to give by a lease; let   2. to get by a lease —**leas'a·ble** *adj.* —**leas'er** *n.*

leash (lēsh) *n.* [< OFr. < L. *laxa*, fem. of *laxus*, loose]   a cord, strap, etc. by which a dog or other animal is held in check; lead —*vt.* 1. to put a leash on   2. to control as by a leash —**hold in leash** to control —**strain at the leash** to be impatient to be free

least (lēst) *adj. alt. superl. of* LITTLE [< OE. *læsest, læst,* superl. of *læssa,* LESS]   smallest in size, degree, importance, etc. —*adv.* in the smallest degree —*n.* the smallest in size, amount, importance, etc. —**at (the) least** 1. with no less   2. at any rate —**not in the least** not at all

least common denominator   the least common multiple of the denominators of two or more fractions

least common multiple   the smallest positive whole number that is exactly divisible by two or more given whole numbers [the *least common multiple* of 4, 5, and 10 is 20]

least·ways (-wāz') *adv.*   [Colloq.] at least; anyway

leat (lēt) *n.* [OE. *gelæt,* a junction] a channel conveying water to a mill

leath·er (leth'ər) *n.* [OE. *lether*] 1. animal skin prepared for use by removing the hair and tanning   2. any article made of this —*adj.* 1. of or made of leather —*vt.* [Colloq.] to whip, as with a leather strap

leath·er·ing (-iŋ) *n.*   [Colloq.] a beating; thrashing

leath·er·jack·et (-jak'it) *n.*   1. any of various tropical fishes   2. the tough-skinned larva of certain craneflies

leath·ern (leth'ərn) *adj.*   1. made of leather   2. like leather

leath·er·neck (leth'ər nek') *n.*   [from the leather-lined collar, formerly part of the Marine uniform] [U.S. Slang] a U.S. Marine

leath·er·y (-ē) *adj.* like leather; tough and flexible —**leath'·er·i·ness** *n.*

leave¹ (lēv) *vt.* **left, leav'ing** [OE. *læfan*, lit., to let remain] **1.** to allow to remain [*leave* some cake for me] **2.** to make, place, etc., and cause to remain behind one [to *leave* footprints] **3.** to have remaining after one [the deceased *leaves* a widow] **4.** to bequeath **5.** to entrust (with *to* or *up to*) [to *leave* a decision to another] **6.** to give as a remainder [ten minus two *leaves* eight] **7.** to go away from **8.** to cause to be in a certain condition [the flood *left* them homeless] **9.** to abandon; forsake **10.** to stop living in, working for, or belonging to **11.** [Dial.] to let or allow [*leave* us go now] —*vi.* to go away or set out —**leave off** **1.** to stop; cease **2.** to stop doing or using —**leave out** **1.** to omit **2.** to fail to consider —**leave** (**someone**) **alone** to refrain from bothering (someone) —**leav'er** *n.*

leave² (lēv) *n.* [OE. *leaf*] **1.** permission **2.** *a)* permission to be absent from duty or work *b)* the period for which this is granted —**by your leave** with your permission —**on leave** absent from duty with permission —**take leave of** to say goodbye to —**take one's leave** to depart

leave³ (lēv) *vi.* **leaved, leav'ing** [see LEAF] to put forth, or bear, leaves; leaf

leaved (lēvd) *adj.* having leaves [narrow-*leaved*]

leav·en (lev''n) *n.* [< OFr. < L. *levamen*, alleviation < *levare*, to raise] **1.** a small piece of fermenting dough used for producing fermentation in a fresh batch of dough **2.** *same as* LEAVENING —*vt.* **1.** to make (batter or dough) rise with a leavening agent **2.** to spread through, causing a gradual change

leav·en·ing (-iŋ) *n.* **1.** a substance, such as yeast, used to make batter or dough rise by the formation of gas **2.** any influence working on something to bring about a gradual change

leave of absence a leave from work or duty, esp. for a long time; also, the period of time

leaves (lēvz) *n.* *pl.* of LEAF

leave-tak·ing (lēv'tāk'iŋ) *n.* the act of taking leave, or saying goodbye

leav·ings (-iŋz) *n.pl.* things left over; leftovers, remnants, refuse, etc.

le·bens·raum (lā'bəns roum') *n.* [G., living space] territory for political and economic expansion: term originating in Nazi imperialism

lech (lech) *vi.* [Slang] to behave like a lecher; lust (*for, after,* etc.) —*n.* [Slang] **1.** a lecherous desire **2.** a lecherous person

lech·er (lech'ər) *n.* [< OFr. < *lechier,* to be a debauchee, lit., lick] a lewd, grossly sensual man

lech·er·ous (-əs) *adj.* lustful; lewd —**lech'er·ous·ly** *adv.* —**lech'er·ous·ness** *n.*

lech·er·y (-ē) *n., pl.* **-er·ies** gross sensuality

lec·i·thin (les'ə·thin) *n.* [< Gr. *lekithos,* yolk of an egg + -IN¹] a fatty compound found in nerve tissue, blood, egg yolk, and some vegetables: used in medicines, foods, etc.

lec·tern (lek'tərn) *n.* [< OFr. < ML. *lectrum* < L. pp. of *legere,* to read] **1.** a reading desk in a church; esp., such a desk from which a part of the Scriptures is read during the service **2.** a stand for holding the notes, speech, etc., as of a lecturer

lec·tor (lek'tər) *n.* [LME < L., reader] **1.** the person who reads the lessons in a church service **2.** *R.C.Ch.* a member of the second of four minor orders **3.** a lecturer in certain universities

lec·ture (lek'chər) *n.* [< ML. *lectura* < pp. of *legere,* to read] **1.** an informative talk given before an audience, class, etc., and usually prepared beforehand **2.** a lengthy scolding —*vi.* **-tured, -tur·ing** to give a lecture —*vt.* to give a lecture to —**lec'tur·er** *n.* —**lec'ture·ship'** *n.*

LECTERN

led (led) *pt. & pp.* of LEAD¹

le·der·ho·sen (lā'dər hō'zən) *n.* [G. < MHG. *lederhose* < *leder,* LEATHER + *hose,* TROUSERS] short leather trousers worn with braces by men and boys in the Alps

ledge (lej) *n.* [prob. < ME. *leggen:* see ff.] **1.** a shelf or shelflike projection **2.** a projecting ridge of rocks **3.** *Mining* a vein —**ledg'ed, ledg'y** *adj.*

ledg·er (lej'ər) *n.* [prob. < ME. *leggen,* to lay, or *liggen,* to lie] **1.** *Bookkeeping* the book of final entry, in which a record of debits, credits, and all money transactions is kept **2.** *Angling* a wire trace or similar arrangement that allows the weight to rest on the bottom and the bait to float freely [*ledger* bait] —*vi.* *Angling* to fish using a ledger

ledger line *same as* LEGER LINE

lee (lē) *n.* [OE. *hleo,* shelter] **1.** shelter; protection **2.** a sheltered place, esp. one on the side away from the wind **3.** *Naut.* the side or part away from the wind —*adj.* of or on the side away from the wind

leech¹ (lēch) *n.* [OE. *læce*] **1.** formerly, a physician **2.** any of a number of annelid worms with suckers, living in water or wet earth: one bloodsucking species was formerly used to bleed patients **3.** a person who is a parasite —*vt.* **1.** to bleed with leeches **2.** to drain dry —*vi.* to act as a parasite

leech² (lēch) *n.* [LME. *lyche*] the free or outside edge of a sail

Lee En·field (lē'en'fēld) (after J. P. *Lee* (? - 1904), U.S. engineer & *Enfield* where form of rifle designed) a type of rifle used esp. formerly by the British Army

LEECH
(to 8 cm long)

leek (lēk) *n.* [OE. *leac*] an onionlike vegetable having a bulb with a cylindrical stem, and broad leaves: a Welsh national emblem

leer (lir) *n.* [OE. *hleor*] a sly, sidelong look showing salaciousness, malicious triumph, etc. —*vi.* to look with a leer —**leer'ing·ly** *adv.*

leer·y (lir'ē) *adj.* **leer'i·er, leer'i·est** wary; suspicious

lees (lēz) *n.pl.* [< OFr. < ML. *lia*] dregs or sediment, as of wine

lee shore the shore on the lee side of a ship; shore towards which the wind is blowing and driving a ship

lee·ward (lē'wərd; *naut.* lōo'ərd) *adj.* in the direction towards which the wind blows; of the lee side: opposed to WINDWARD —*n.* the lee part or side —*adv.* towards the lee

lee·way (lē'wā') *n.* **1.** the leeward drift of a ship or aircraft from the true course **2.** [Colloq.] *a)* margin of time, money, etc. *b)* room for freedom of action

left¹ (left) *adj.* [OE. *lyft,* weak] **1.** *a)* designating or of that side of one's body which is towards the west when one faces north, the side of the less-used hand in most people *b)* designating or of the corresponding side of anything *c)* closer to the left side of a person directly facing the thing mentioned **2.** of the bank of a river on the left of a person facing downstream **3.** of the political left; radical or liberal —*n.* **1.** *a)* all or part of the left side *b)* a direction or location on the left side **2.** *Boxing a)* the left hand *b)* a blow delivered with the left hand **3.** [*often* L-] *Politics* a radical or liberal position, party, etc. (often with *the*): from the location of their seats in some European legislatures —*adv.* on or towards the left hand or left side —**have two left feet** to be very clumsy

left² (left) *pt. & pp.* of LEAVE¹

left-hand (left'hand') *adj.* **1.** on or directed towards the left **2.** of, for, or with the left hand

left-hand·ed (-han'did) *adj.* **1.** using the left hand more skilfully than the right **2.** done with the left hand **3.** clumsy; awkward **4.** designating an insincere or ambiguous compliment **5.** made for use with the left hand **6.** turning from right to left —*adv.* with the left hand [to write *left-handed*] —**left'-hand'ed·ly** *adv.* —**left'-hand'ed·ness** *n.* —**left'-hand'er** *n.*

left·ist (-ist) *n.* a person whose political position is radical or liberal; member of the left —*adj.* radical or liberal —**left'ism** *n.*

left-luggage office a place at a railway station, etc. where luggage, etc. may be left for a small charge

left·o·ver (-ō'vər) *n.* something left over, as from a meal —*adj.* remaining unused, etc.

left·ward (-wərd) *adv., adj.* on or towards the left: also **left'wards** *adv.*

left wing the more radical or liberal section of a political party, group, etc. —**left'-wing'** *adj.* —**left'-wing'er** *n.*

left·y (lef'tē) *n., pl.* **left'ies** [Slang] **1.** a left-handed person: often used as a nickname **2.** a left-winger in politics

leg (leg) *n.* [< ON. *leggr*] **1.** one of the parts of the body by means of which animals stand and walk: in human beings, either of the two lower limbs **2.** a cut of meat consisting of the leg **3.** the part of a garment covering the leg **4.** anything resembling a leg in shape or use, as one of the supports of a piece of furniture **5.** any of the stages of a course or journey **6.** *Cricket* that part of the field to the left of, and behind, the batsman **7.** *Math.* either of the sides of a triangle other than its base or, in a right-angled triangle, its hypotenuse —*vi.* **legged, leg'ging** [Colloq.] to walk or run: used chiefly in the phr. **leg it** —**not have a leg to stand on** [Colloq.] to have absolutely no defence, excuse, etc. —**on one's** (or **its**) **last legs** [Colloq.] not far from death, breakdown, etc. —**pull someone's leg** [Colloq.] to make fun of or fool someone —**shake a leg** [Slang] to hurry —**stretch one's legs** to walk, esp. after sitting a long time —**leg'less** *adj.*

leg. **1.** legal **2.** legislative **3.** legislature

leg·a·cy (leg'ə sē) *n., pl.* **-cies** [< OFr. *legacie* < ML. < L. *legatus:* see LEGATE] **1.** money or property left to someone by a will **2.** anything handed down from, or as from, an ancestor

le·gal (lē'gəl) *adj.* [< MFr. < L. *legalis* < *lex* (gen. *legis*), law] 1. of, based on, or authorized by law 2. permitted by law [a *legal* act] 3. that can be enforced in a court of law 4. of or applicable to lawyers [*legal* ethics] 5. in terms of the law [a *legal* offence] —**le′gal·ly** *adv.*

legal aid financial assistance available to people unable to meet their legal costs

le·gal·ese (lē′gə lēz′) *n.* the special vocabulary of legal forms, documents, etc., often thought of by the layman as incomprehensible

le·gal·ism (lē′gəl iz'm) *n.* strict, often too strict and literal adherence to law —**le′gal·ist** *n.* —**le′gal·is′tic** *adj.*

le·gal·i·ty (li gal′ə tē) *n., pl.* **-ties** quality, condition, or instance of being legal or lawful

le·gal·ize (lē′gə līz′) *vt.* **-ized′, -iz′ing** to make legal or lawful —**le′gal·i·za′tion** *n.*

legal tender money that may be legally offered in payment of an obligation and that a creditor must accept

leg·ate (leg′it) *n.* [< OFr. < L. pp. of *legare,* to send as ambassador < *lex,* law] an envoy or ambassador, esp. one officially representing the Pope —**leg′ate·ship′ n.**

leg·a·tee (leg′ə tē′) *n.* one to whom a legacy is bequeathed

le·ga·tion (li gā′shən) *n.* 1. a diplomatic minister and his staff, representing their government in a foreign country and ranking just below an embassy 2. their headquarters

le·ga·to (li gät′ō) *adj., adv.* [It., pp. of *legare* < L. *ligare,* to tie] *Music* in a smooth, even style, with no noticeable interruption between the notes

leg before wicket *Cricket* a dismissal because the ball, if it had not hit part of the batsman's body (except his hand) would, in the umpire's opinion, have hit the wicket

leg break *Cricket* a bowled ball that spins from leg to off on pitching

leg·end (lej′ənd) *n.* [< OFr. < ML. *legenda,* things to be read < L. pl. gerundive of *legere,* to read] 1. *a)* a story handed down for generations and popularly believed to have a historical basis: cf. MYTH *b)* all such stories belonging to a particular group of people 2. *a)* a notable person much talked about in his own time *b)* the stories of his exploits 3. an inscription on a coin, medal, etc. 4. a descriptive title, key, etc., as under an illustration

leg·end·ar·y (lej′ən dər ē) *adj.* 1. of, based on, or presented in legends; traditional 2. worthy of being considered in legend [his generosity was *legendary*]

leg·end·ry (-drē) *n.* legends collectively

leg·er·de·main (lej′ər di mān′) *n.* [< MFr. *leger de main,* lit., light of hand] 1. sleight of hand; tricks of a stage magician 2. trickery; deceit

leg·er line (lej′ər) [altered < *ledger line*] *Music* a short line written above or below the staff, for notes beyond the range of the staff

leg·ged (leg′id, legd) *adj.* having (a specified number or kind of) legs [long-*legged*]

leg·ging (leg′iŋ) *n.* [often *pl.*] a covering of canvas, leather, etc. for protecting the leg below the knee

leg·gy (leg′ē) *adj.* **-gi·er, -gi·est** 1. having long and awkward legs [a *leggy* colt] 2. [Colloq.] having long, well-shaped legs —**leg′gi·ness** *n.*

leg·horn (leg′hôrn, li gôrn′) *n.* [after *Leghorn,* city in Italy] 1. [sometimes L-] any of a breed of small chicken, orig. developed in the Mediterranean region 2. *a)* a plaiting made of Italian wheat straw *b)* a broad-brimmed hat of this straw

leg·i·ble (lej′ə b'l) *adj.* [< LL. *legibilis* < *legere,* to read] 1. that can be read or deciphered 2. that can be read easily —**leg′i·bil′i·ty** *n.* —**leg′i·bly** *adv.*

le·gion (lē′jən) *n.* [< OFr. < L. *legio* < *legere,* to select] 1. *Rom. History* a military division varying at times from 3000 to 6000 foot soldiers, with additional cavalrymen 2. a large group of soldiers; army [the French Foreign *Legion*] 3. a large number; multitude

le·gion·ar·y (-ər ē) *adj.* of or constituting a legion —*n., pl.* **-ar·ies** a member of a legion

le·gion·naire (lē′jə ner′) *n.* [< Fr. < L.] a member of a legion

Legionnaire's disease [after the outbreak at a meeting of the American Legion in Philadelphia in 1976] a serious disease caused by viruses and having symptoms similar to those of pneumonia

leg·is·late (lej′is lāt′) *vi.* **-lat′ed, -lat′ing** [< LEGISLATOR] to make or pass a law or laws —*vt.* to cause to be, become, go, etc. by making laws

leg·is·la·tion (lej′is lā′shən) *n.* [< LL. < L. *lex* (gen. *legis*), law + *latio,* a proposing < pp. of *ferre,* to BEAR[1]] 1. the making of a law or laws 2. the law or laws made

leg·is·la·tive (lej′is lāt′iv) *adj.* 1. of legislation 2. of a legislature or its members 3. having the power to make laws [a *legislative* assembly] 4. enforced by legislation —**leg′is·la′tive·ly** *adv.*

leg·is·la·tor (-lāt′ər) *n.* [< L.: see LEGISLATION] a member of a legislative assembly; lawmaker

leg·is·la·ture (-lā′chər) *n.* a body of persons given the responsibility and power to make laws for a country, state, etc.

le·git (lə jit′) *n.* [Slang] the legitimate theatre, drama, etc. —*adj.* [Slang] legitimate

le·git·i·ma·cy (lə jit′ə mə sē) *n.* a being legitimate

le·git·i·mate (-mit; *for v.* -māt′) *adj.* [< ML. pp. of *legitimare,* to make lawful, ult. < L. *lex,* law] 1. born of parents legally married to each other 2. *a)* lawful *b)* conforming to the law 3. ruling by the rights of heredity [a *legitimate* king] 4. *a)* logically correct [a *legitimate* inference] *b)* justifiable or justified 5. conforming to established rules, standards, etc. 6. *Theatre* designating or of stage plays, as distinguished from films, pictures, vaudeville, etc. —*vt.* **-mat′ed, -mat′ing** same as LEGITIMIZE —**le·git′i·mate·ly** *adv.* —**le·git′i·ma′tion** *n.*

le·git·i·ma·tize (lə jit′ə mə tīz′) *vt.* **-tized′, -tiz′ing** same as LEGITIMIZE

le·git·i·mist (-mist) *n.* a supporter of legitimate authority or, esp., of claims to monarchy based on the rights of heredity —**le·git′i·mism** *n.*

le·git·i·mize (-mīz′) *vt.* **-mized′, -miz′ing** 1. to make or declare legitimate 2. to make seem just, right, or reasonable —**le·git′i·mi·za′tion** *n.*

leg·man (leg′man′) *n., pl.* **-men′** 1. a newspaperman who gathers information at the scene of events or at various sources 2. a person employed in a business to run errands, collect information etc.

leg-of-mut·ton (leg′ə mut′'n, -əv-) *adj.* shaped like a leg of mutton: said of a sleeve that puffs out towards the shoulder, etc.

leg-pull (-pool′) *n.* a practical joke or mild humorous deception

leg·room (leg′rōōm′) *n.* adequate space for the legs while seated, as in a car

leg·ume (leg′yōōm, li gyōōm′) *n.* [< Fr. < L. *legumen* < *legere,* to gather] 1. any of a large family of plants, including the peas, beans, clovers, etc., with fruit that is a pod splitting along two sutures: many legumes are nitrogen-fixing 2. the pod or seed of some members of this family, used for food

le·gu·mi·nous (li gyōō′min əs) *adj.* 1. of, having the nature of, or bearing legumes 2. of the family of plants to which peas and beans belong

leg·work (leg′wurk′) *n.* [Colloq.] travel away from the centre of work as a routine part of a job, as of a legman

lei (lā, lā′ē) *n., pl.* **leis** [Haw.] in Hawaii, a wreath of flowers and leaves

Leib·nitz·i·an (līb nits′ē ən) *adj.* [after Baron G. W. von Leibnitz (1646-1716), G. philosopher and mathematician] of, like, or characteristic of the philosophy propounded by Leibnitz in which matter was conceived as existing in the form of atoms (or monads) in mutual harmony, each with an individual force emanating from God —*n.* a follower of Leibnitz or his work.

Leics. Leicestershire

leis·ter (lēs′tər) *n.* [< Scand.] a kind of fish spear, usually with three prongs —*vt.* to spear (fish) with a leister

lei·sure (lezh′ər) *n.* [< OFr. < L. *licere,* to be permitted] free, unoccupied time that can be used for rest, recreation, etc. —*adj.* 1. free and unoccupied; spare [*leisure* time] 2. having much leisure [the *leisure* class] —**at leisure** 1. having free time 2. with no hurry 3. not occupied or engaged —**at one's leisure** when one has the time or opportunity —**lei′sured** *adj.*

lei·sure·ly (-lē) *adj.* without haste; slow —*adv.* in an unhurried manner —**lei′sure·li·ness** *n.*

leit·mo·tif, leit·mo·tiv (līt′mō tēf′) *n.* [< G. < *leiten,* to lead + *Motiv,* MOTIVE] 1. a short musical phrase representing and recurring with a given character, situation, etc. as in Wagner's operas 2. a dominant theme or underlying pattern

lek (lek) *n.* see MONETARY UNITS, table (Albania)

LEM (lem) Lunar Excursion Module

lem·an (lem′ən, lē′mən) *n.* [ME. *lemman* < *lef,* dear (see LIEF) + *man*] [Archaic] a sweetheart or lover (man or woman); esp., a mistress

lem·ma (lem′ə) *n., pl.* **-mas, -ma·ta** (-ə tə) [L. < Gr. *lēmma,* something taken for granted] 1. the subject of a gloss, annotation, etc. that is used for a heading 2. *Logic* a premise taken for granted 3. *Math.* a subsidiary proposition

lem·me (lem′mē′) *vt.* [Colloq.] let me

lem·ming (lem′iŋ) *n., pl.* **-mings, -ming:** see PLURAL, II, D, 1 [Dan. < ON.] a small arctic rodent resembling the mouse but having a short tail and fur-covered feet

lem·on (lem′ən) *n.* [< MFr. < Ar. *laimūn* < Per. *līmūn*] 1. a small, edible citrus fruit with a pale-yellow rind and a juicy, sour pulp 2. the small, spiny, semitropical tree bearing this fruit 3. pale yellow 4. [Slang] *a)* something that is defective *b)* an inadequate person —*adj.* 1.

pale-yellow 2. made with or flavoured like lemon —**lem′-on·y** *adj.*

lem·on·ade (lem′ə nād′) *n.* a drink made of lemon juice and water, usually sweetened, often effervescent

lemon balm an aromatic herb used in flavouring food, liqueurs, and medicines

lemon curd a paste made from lemons, eggs, and butter, used as a spread or a filling: also **lemon cheese**

lemon grass a perennial grass with a large, loose flower spike: it is cultivated in tropical regions as the source of an aromatic oil used in perfumery

lemon sole a flat fish, like the sole, valued as food

lemon squash 1. a drink made from a sweetened lemon concentrate and water 2. the lemon concentrate

lem·pi·ra (lem pir′ə) *n., pl.* **-ras** [AmSp., after *Lempira*, native chief] *see* MONETARY UNITS, table (Honduras)

le·mur (lē′mər) *n.* [< L. *lemures*, ghosts] a small primate related to the monkey, with large eyes and soft, woolly fur: found mainly in Madagascar and active mostly at night

lend (lend) *vt.* **lent, lend′ing** [OE. *lænan* < *læn*, a loan] 1. to let another use or have (a thing) temporarily 2. to let out (money) at interest 3. to give; impart [to *lend* an air of mystery] —*vi.* to make a loan or loans —**lend an ear** (or **ears**) to listen —**lend itself** (or **oneself**) **to** to be useful for or open to —**lend′er** *n.*

lending library a library from which books may be borrowed, sometimes for a fee

lend-lease (-lēs′) *n.* in World War II, material aid in the form of munitions, tools, food, etc. granted to Britain and her allies by the U.S., in return for the use of Allied military bases —**lend′-lease′** *vt.* **-leased′**, **-leas′ing**

length (length, lengkth) *n.* [OE. *lengthu* < base of *lang*, long + -TH[1]] 1. the measure of how long a thing is from end to end; the greatest dimension of anything 2. extent in space or time 3. a long stretch or extent 4. the state or fact of being long 5. a piece of a certain length [a *length* of pipe] 6. a unit of measure consisting of the length of an object or animal in a race [the boat won by two *lengths*] —**at full length** completely extended —**at length** 1. finally 2. in full —**go to any length** (or **great lengths**) to do whatever is necessary

length·en (-'n) *vt., vi.* to make or become longer —**length′en·er** *n.*

length·man (-man′) *n., pl.* **-men** (-men′) a man employed to maintain a particular section of a railway, road, etc.

length·ways (-wāz′) *adv., adj.* in the direction of the length: also [U.S.] **length′wise′** (-wīz′)

length·y (-ē) *adj.* **length′i·er**, **length′i·est** long; esp., too long —**length′i·ly** *adv.* —**length′i·ness** *n.*

le·ni·ent (lē′ni ənt, lēn′yənt) *adj.* [< L. prp. of *lenire*, to soften < *lenis*, soft] not harsh or severe in disciplining, judging, etc.; mild; merciful —**le′ni·en·cy**, *pl.* **-cies, le′-ni·ence** *n.* —**le′ni·ent·ly** *adv.*

Len·in·ism (len′in iz'm) *n.* the communist theories and policies of Lenin, including his theory of the dictatorship of the proletariat —**Len′in·ist** *n., adj.*

len·i·tive (len′ə tiv) *adj.* [< ML. < L. pp. of *lenire*, to soften] soothing or assuaging; lessening pain —*n.* a lenitive medicine, etc.

len·i·ty (-tē) *n.* [< OFr. < L. < *lenis*, mild: see LENIENT] 1. a being lenient; mildness; gentleness 2. *pl.* **-ties** a lenient act

le·no (lē′nō) *n.* [Fr. *linon* < *lin*, flax] a thin, linen cloth resembling muslin

lens (lenz) *n.* [L., lentil: a double-convex lens is shaped like the seed] 1. *a)* a piece of glass, or other transparent substance, with two curved surfaces, or one plane and one curved, bringing together or spreading rays of light passing through it: lenses are used in optical instruments *b)* a combination of two or more lenses 2. a transparent biconvex body of the eye: it focuses upon the retina light rays entering the pupil

LENS
(A, plano-convex; B, double-convex; C, divergent meniscus; D, double-concave; E, plano-concave)

Lent (lent) *n.* [OE. *lengten*, the spring < *lang*, long: because the spring days lengthen] the period of forty weekdays from Ash Wednesday to Easter, observed variously in Christian churches by fasting and penitence

lent (lent) *pt. & pp.* of LEND

-lent (lənt) [L. *-lentus*, *-ful*] a *suffix* meaning full of, characterized by [*virulent, fraudulent*]

Lent·en (lent′'n) *adj.* [*also* l-] 1. of connected with, or suitable for Lent 2. meagre; cheerless [*lenten fare*]

len·tic·u·lar (len tik′yoo lər) *adj.* [L. *lenticularis* < *lenticula*, dim. of *lens*] 1. shaped like a lentil or biconvex lens 2. of the lens of an eye

len·til (lent′il, -'l) *n.* [< OFr. < L. *lenticula*, dim. of *lens*, lentil] 1. a Mediterranean leguminous plant with small, edible seeds shaped like double-convex lenses 2. the seed of this plant

len·to (len′tō) *adv., adj.* [It. < L. *lentus*, slow] *Music* slow —*n., pl.* **-tos** a lento passage or movement

lent term that part of a University session between Christmas and Easter

Le·o (lē′ō) [L.: see LION] 1. a N constellation between Cancer and Virgo 2. the fifth sign of the zodiac: see ZODIAC, illus.

le·one (lē ōn′) *n.* *see* MONETARY UNITS, table (Sierra Leone)

Le·o·nine (lē′ə nīn′) *adj.* [< ?] of, or characteristic of a kind of Latin elegiac verse of hexameters and pentameters, the last word of the line rhyming with the middle word

le·o·nine (lē′ə nīn′) *adj.* [< OFr. < L. < *leo*, LION] of, characteristic of, or like a lion: said esp. of thick, tawny hair

leop·ard (lep′ərd) *n., pl.* **-ards, -ard**: see PLURAL, II, D, 1 [< OFr. < LL. < Gr. *leopardos* < *leōn*, lion + *pardos*, panther] 1. a large, ferocious animal of the cat family, with a black-spotted tawny coat, found in Africa and Asia 2. [U.S.] same as JAGUAR —**leop′ard·ess** *n.fem.*

le·o·tard (lē′ə tärd′) *n.* [after J. *Léotard*, 19th-c. Fr. aerialist] a one-piece, tightfitting garment for the torso, worn by acrobats, dancers, etc.

lep·er (lep′ər) *n.* [< OFr. < L. < Gr. < *lepros*, rough, scaly < *lepein*, to peel] 1. a person having leprosy 2. a person to be shunned

lep·i·dop·ter·an (lep′ə dop′tər ən) *n.* [< ModL. < Gr. *lepis*, a scale + -PTER(OUS) + -AN] any of a large order of insects, including the butterflies and moths, characterized by two pairs of broad, membranous wings covered with very fine scales —**lep′i·dop′ter·ous** *adj.*

lep·i·dop·ter·ist (-ist) a person who studies or collects moths and butterflies

lep·re·chaun (lep′rə kôn′) *n.* [Ir. *lupracān* < OIr. < *lu*, little + dim. of *corp* (< L. *corpus*), body] *Irish Folklore* a fairy in the form of a little old man who can reveal a buried crock of gold to anyone who catches him

lep·ro·sy (lep′rə sē) *n.* [see LEPER] a chronic, infectious disease caused by a bacterium that attacks the skin, flesh, nerves, etc.: it is characterized by ulcers, white scaly scabs, deformities, and wasting of body parts

lep·rous (-rəs) *adj.* 1. of or like leprosy 2. having leprosy

-lep·sy (lep′sē) [< Gr. *-lēpsia* < *lēpsis*, an attack] a *combining form* meaning a fit, attack, seizure [*catalepsy*] : also **-lep′si·a**

lep·ton[1] (lep′ton) *n., pl.* **-ta** (-tə) [Gr. < *leptos*, thin, small < *lepein*, to peel] *see* MONETARY UNITS, table (Greece)

lep·ton[2] (lep′ton) *n., pl.* **-ta** [Gr. < *leptos*, thin, fine + -ON] *Physics* one of a group of primary particles of small mass which do not interact strongly with other particles, including electrons, neutrinos, etc.

les·bi·an (lez′bē ən) *adj.* [in allusion to Sappho and her followers, in Lesbos] [*sometimes* L-] of homosexuality between women —*n.* [*sometimes* L-] a homosexual woman —**les′bi·an·ism** *n.*

lese maj·es·ty (lēz′maj′is tē) [< Fr. < L. fem. of *laesus*, pp. of *laedere*, to hurt + *majestas*, majesty] 1. a crime against the sovereign; treason 2. any insolence towards one to whom deference is due

le·sion (lē′zhən) *n.* [< MFr. < L. *laesio* < pp. of *laedere*, to harm] 1. an injury; hurt 2. an injury, sore, etc. in an organ or tissue of the body resulting in impairment or loss of function

less (les) *adj.* *alt. compar.* of LITTLE [OE. *læs, læssa*] not so much, so many, so great, etc.; smaller; fewer —*adv. compar.* of LITTLE not so much; to a smaller extent —*n.* a smaller amount —*prep.* minus [a year *less* five days] —**less and less** decreasingly —**no less a person than** a person of no lower importance, rank, etc. than

-less (lis, ləs) [OE. *-leas* < *leas*, free] a *suffix meaning*: 1. without, lacking [*valueless*] 2. that does not [*tireless*] 3. that cannot be [*dauntless*]

les·see (les ē′) *n.* [see LEASE] a person to whom property is leased; tenant

less·en (les′'n) *vt.* 1. to make less; decrease 2. [Archaic] to disparage —*vi.* to become less

less·er (les′ər) *adj.* *alt. compar.* of LITTLE [LESS + -ER] smaller, less, or less important —*adv.* less

lesser panda a reddish, raccoonlike mammal of the Himalayan region

les·son (les′'n) *n.* [< OFr. *leçon* < L. < pp. of *legere*, to read] 1. something to be learned; specif., a) an exercise that a student is to prepare or learn b) a unit of instruction; teaching session c) something from which useful knowledge or salutary principles can be learned; example d) [pl.] course of instruction [music *lessons*] 2. a selection from the Bible, read as part of a church service [the first (or second) *lesson*] 3. a rebuke; reproof

les·sor (les′ôr, les ôr′) *n.* [Anglo-Fr. < *lesser:* see LEASE] one who gives a lease; landlord

lest (lest) *conj.* [< OE. < *thy læs the,* lit., by the less that] **1.** for fear that; in case [speak low *lest* you be overheard] **2.** that: used after expressions denoting fear [afraid *lest* he should fall]

let¹ (let) *vt.* **let** or obs. **let′ted, let′ting** [OE. *lætan,* to leave behind] **1.** to leave; abandon: now only in **let alone** (or **let be**), to refrain from bothering, etc. **2.** *a)* to rent; hire out *b)* to assign (a contract) **3.** to allow or cause to escape [to *let* blood] **4.** to allow to pass, come, or go [*let* me in] **5.** to allow; permit [*let* me help] **6.** to cause to: usually with *know* or *hear* [*let* me hear from you] **7.** to suppose; assume When used in commands, suggestions, or dares, *let* serves as an auxiliary [*let* us go] —*vi.* to be rented or leased [house to *let*] **1.** to lower **2.** to slow up **3.** to disappoint —**let drop** (or **fall**) drop, accidentally or on purpose a word or hint [she *let drop* her parents were out] —**let go** to release or relax —**let off 1.** to give forth (steam, etc.) **2.** to deal leniently with —**let on** [Colloq.] **1.** to indicate one's awareness of a fact **2.** to pretend —**let out 1.** to release **2.** to rent out **3.** to reveal (a secret, etc.) **4.** to make a garment larger by reducing (the hem, etc.) **5.** to dismiss, as school —**let up 1.** to relax **2.** to cease

let² (let) *vt.* **let′ted** or **let, let′ting** [OE. *lettan,* lit., to make late] [Archaic] to hinder; obstruct —*n.* **1.** an obstacle or impediment: used in **without let or hindrance 2.** in tennis, etc., an interference with the course of the ball in some specific way, making it necessary to play the point over again

-let (lit, lət) [< MFr. *-el* (< L. *-ellus*) + *-et,* both dim. suffixes] *a suffix meaning:* **1.** small [ringlet] **2.** a small object worn as a band on [anklet]

let·down (let′doun′) *n.* **1.** a slowing up or feeling of dejection, as after great excitement, effort, etc. **2.** a disappointment or disillusionment

le·thal (lē′thəl) *adj.* [L. *let(h)alis* < *letum,* death] **1.** causing or capable of causing death; fatal or deadly **2.** of or suggestive of death —**le·thal′i·ty** (-thal′ə tē) *n.* —**le′thal·ly** *adv.*

le·thar·gic (li thär′jik) *adj.* **1.** of or producing lethargy **2.** abnormally drowsy or dull, sluggish, etc. —**le·thar′gi·cal·ly** *adv.*

leth·ar·gy (leth′ər jē) *n.,* *pl.* **-gies** [< OFr. < LL. < Gr. < *lēthargos,* forgetful < *lēthē* (see ff.) + *argos,* idle < *a-,* not + *ergon,* work] **1.** a condition of abnormal drowsiness or torpor **2.** a great lack of energy; sluggishness, apathy, etc.

Le·the (lē′thē) [L. < Gr. *lēthē,* oblivion] *Gr. & Rom. Myth.* the river of forgetfulness, in Hades, whose water produced loss of memory in those who drank of it —*n.* oblivion; forgetfulness —**Le·the′an** (lē thē′ən) *adj.*

let's (lets) let us

Lett (let) *n.* **1.** a member of a people living in Latvia and adjacent Baltic regions **2.** *same as* LETTISH

let·ter (let′ər) *n.* [< OFr. < L. *littera*] **1.** any of the characters of the alphabet, theoretically representing a speech sound **2.** a written or printed message, usually sent by post **3.** [*usually pl.*] an official document authorizing someone or something **4.** [*pl.*] *a)* literature generally *b)* learning; knowledge **5.** literal meaning; exact wording —*vt.* **1.** to mark with letters [to *letter* a poster] **2.** to set down in hand-printed letters —*vi.* to make hand-printed letters —**to the letter** just as written or directed —**let′ter·er** *n.*

letter bomb a thin explosive device in an envelope which detonates when the envelope is opened

letter box 1. a box for receiving letters, as on the inside of a house door **2.** *same as* PILLAR BOX

let·tered (let′ərd) *adj.* **1.** able to read and write **2.** very well educated **3.** inscribed with letters

let·ter·head (let′ər hed′) *n.* **1.** the name, address, etc. of a person or firm printed as a heading on sheets of letter paper **2.** such a sheet

let·ter·ing (-iŋ) *n.* **1.** the process of putting letters on something by inscribing, printing, etc. **2.** the letters so made

letter of credit a letter from a bank asking that the holder of the letter be allowed to draw specified sums of money from other banks or agencies

let·ter-per·fect (-pur′fikt) *adj.* **1.** correct in every respect **2.** knowing one's lesson, theatrical role, etc. perfectly

let·ter·press (-pres′) *n.* **1.** *a)* the method of printing from raised surfaces, as set type *b)* matter printed by this method **2.** reading matter, as distinguished from illustrations

letters (or letter) of marque formerly, a government document authorizing an individual to arm a ship and capture enemy merchant ships: also **letters (or letter) of marque and reprisal**

letters patent a document granting a patent

letter writer 1. one who writes letters **2.** a letter press or other machine for making copies of letters

Let·tish (let′ish) *adj.* of the Letts or their language —*n.* the Baltic language of the Letts; Latvian

‡**let·tre de ca·chet** (let r′ də ká shä′) *pl.* **let·tres de ca·chet′** (letr′) [Fr.] a sealed letter; esp., in France before the Revolution, a letter containing a royal warrant for the imprisonment without trial of a specified person

let·tuce (let′is) *n.* [< OFr. < L. *lactuca* < *lac,* milk: from its milky juice] **1.** a hardy, annual composite plant, grown for its crisp, succulent, green leaves **2.** the leaves, much used for salads **3.** various plants that resemble lettuce, e.g. lamb's lettuce

let-up (let′up′) *n.* [< phr. *let up*] [Colloq.] **1.** a slackening or lessening **2.** a stop or pause

le·u (le′oo) *n.,* *pl.* **lei** (lā) [Rumanian < L. *leo,* lion] *see* MONETARY UNITS, table (Rumania)

leu·co- [< Gr. *leukos,* white] *a combining form meaning* white or colourless: also, before a vowel, **leuc-**

leu·co·cyte (lyoo′kə sit′) *n.* [see prec. & -CYTE] any of the small, colourless cells in the blood, lymph, and tissues, which are important in the body's defences against infection; white blood corpuscle —**leu′co·cyt′ic** (-sit′ik) *adj.*

leu·co·ma (lyoo kō′mə) *n.* [Mod L. < Gr. *leukōma,* < *leukos,* white] a dense white opacity of the cornea, caused by injury or inflammation

leu·kae·mi·a (lyoo kē′mē ə) *n.* [ModL. < Gr. *leukos,* white + -AEMIA] any of a group of diseases of the blood-forming organs, resulting in an abnormal increase in the production of leucocytes: also sp. **leu·ke·mi·a** —**leu·kae′mic** (-mik) *adj.* —**leu·ke′mold** (-mold) *adj.*

lev (lef) *n.,* *pl.* **le·va** (le′və) [Bulg., ult. < Gr. *leōn,* lion] *see* MONETARY UNITS, table (Bulgaria)

Lev. Leviticus

Le·vant (lə vant′) [< Fr. < It. *levante* (< L. prp. of *levare,* to raise), applied to the East, where the sun "rises"] region on the E Mediterranean, including all countries bordering the sea between Greece & Egypt —*n.* [l-] *same as* LEVANT MOROCCO —**Lev·an·tine** (lev′ən tin′, -tēn′; lə van′tin) *adj., n.*

le·vant·er (lə van′tər) *n.* [< LEVANT] **1.** a strong wind that blows over the Mediterranean area from the east **2.** an inhabitant of the Levant

Levant morocco a fine morocco leather with a large, irregular grain, used esp. in bookbinding

le·va·tor (lə vāt′ər) *n.,* *pl.* **lev·a·to·res** (lev′ə tər ēz), **le·va′tors** [ModL. < pp. of L. *levare,* to raise] a muscle that raises a limb or other part of the body

lev·ee¹ (lev′ē) *n.* [< Fr. pp. of *lever,* to raise < L. *levare*] [U.S.] **1.** an embankment built alongside a river to prevent high water from flooding bordering land **2.** a quay **3.** a low ridge of earth around a field to be irrigated —*vt.* **lev′-eed,** **lev′ee·ing** to build a levee along

lev·ee² (lev′ē; lə vē′, -vā′) *n.* [< Fr. < *se lever,* to rise: see prec.] formerly, a morning reception held by a sovereign or person of high rank upon arising

lev·el (lev′'l) *n.* [< OFr. < L. *libella,* dim. of *libra,* a balance] **1.** an instrument for determining whether a surface is evenly horizontal **2.** *a)* a horizontal plane or line; esp., such a plane as a basis for measuring elevation [sea *level*] *b)* the height of such a plane **3.** *a)* a horizontal area **4.** the same horizontal plane [the seats are on a *level*] **5.** normal position or proper place [water seeks its *level*] **6.** position, rank, degree of concentration, etc. in a scale of values [*levels* of income] —*adj.* **1.** perfectly flat and even **2.** not sloping **3.** even in height (**with**) **4.** even with the top of the container [a *level* teaspoonful] **5.** *a)* equal in importance, rank, degree, etc. *b)* conforming to a specified level [high-*level* talks] *c)* equally advanced in development *d)* uniform in tone, colour, pitch, volume, rate, etc. **6.** *a)* well-balanced; equable *b)* calm or steady **7.** [Slang] honest —*vt.* **-elled, -el·ling 1.** to make level, even, flat, equal (as in rank), etc. **2.** to knock to the ground; demolish **3.** to raise (a gun, etc.) for firing **4.** to aim or direct —*vi.* **1.** to aim a gun, etc. (**at**) **2.** to bring people or things to an equal rank, condition, etc. (usually with *down* or *up*) **3.** [U.S. Slang] to be frank (**with** someone) —**level off 1.** to give a flat, horizontal surface to **2.** *Aeron.* to come or bring to a horizontal line of flight: also **level out 3.** to become stable or constant —**one's level best** [Colloq.] the best one can do —**on the level** [Slang] honest(ly) and fair(ly) —**lev′-el·ler** *n.* —**lev′el·ly** *adv.* —**lev′el·ness** *n.*

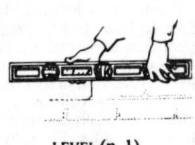

LEVEL (n. 1)

level crossing the place where one railway intersects another railway or a road on the same level

lev·el·head·ed (-hed′id) *adj.* having or showing an even temper and sound judgment —**lev′el·head′ed·ly** *adv.* —**lev′el·head′ed·ness** *n.*

level pegging [Colloq.] the absence of any difference between two contestants [it was *level pegging* at the top of the first division]

lev·er (lē′vər) *n.* [< OFr. < *lever*, to raise < L. *levare* < *levis*, LIGHT²] 1. a bar used to open by force, as a crowbar 2. a means to an end 3. *Mech.* a device consisting of a bar turning about a fixed point, the fulcrum, using power or force applied at a second point to lift or sustain a weight at a third point; hence, any handle, etc. used to operate something —*vt.* to move, lift, etc. with a lever —*vi.* to use a lever

lev·er·age (-ij) *n.* 1. the action of a lever 2. the mechanical power resulting from this 3. increased means of accomplishing some purpose

LEVERS

lev·er·et (lev′ər it) *n.* [< MFr. dim. of *levre* < L. *lepus*, hare] a hare during its first year

lev·i·a·ble (lev′ē ə b'l) *adj.* 1. that can be levied upon; taxable; assessable 2. that can be levied

le·vi·a·than (lə vī′ə thən) *n.* [LL. < Heb. *liwyāthān*] 1. *Bible* a sea monster, thought of as a reptile or a whale 2. anything huge or very powerful

lev·i·er (lev′ē ər) *n.* one who levies taxes, etc.

Le·vi's (lē′vīz) [after *Levi* Strauss, the U.S. maker] *a trademark for* closefitting trousers of heavy denim, reinforced at the seams, etc. with small copper rivets —*n.pl.* such trousers: usually written **le′vis**

lev·i·tate (lev′ə tāt′) *vt.* -tat′ed, -tat′ing [< L. *levis*, LIGHT² by analogy with GRAVITATE] to cause to rise and float in the air —*vi.* to rise and float in the air —**lev′i·ta′tor** *n.*

lev·i·ta·tion (lev′ə tā′shən) *n.* 1. a levitating or being levitated 2. the illusion of raising and keeping a heavy body in the air with little or no support

lev·i·ty (lev′ə tē) *n.,* *pl.* -ties [< OFr. < L. *levitas* < *levis*, LIGHT²] 1. [Rare] buoyancy 2. lightness of disposition, conduct, etc.; easy, improper gaiety; frivolity 3. fickleness

lev·u·lose (lev′yoo lōs′) *n.* same as FRUCTOSE

lev·y (lev′ē) *n.,* *pl.* lev′ies [< MFr. fem. pp. of *lever*: see LEVER] 1. an imposing and collecting of a tax, fine, etc. 2. the amount levied 3. *a)* the enlistment, usually compulsory, of personnel, as for military service *b)* a group so enlisted —*vt.* lev′ied, lev′y·ing 1. to impose or collect (a tax, fine, etc.) 2. to enlist (troops) for military service, usually by force 3. to wage (war) —*vi.* 1. to make a levy 2. *Law* to seize property to satisfy a judgment (often with *on*)

lewd (lood, lyood) *adj.* [OE. *læwede*, lay, unlearned] showing, or intended to excite, lust or sexual desire, esp. in an offensive way —**lewd′ly** *adv.* —**lewd′ness** *n.*

lew·is·ite (loo′ə sīt′) *n.* [after W. L. *Lewis* (1878-1943), U.S. chemist] a pale-yellow, odourless, arsenical compound used as a blistering poison gas

Lew·is (machine) gun (loo′is) [after its U.S. inventor Col. I. N. *Lewis* (1858-1931)] a light, aircooled, gas-operated machine gun used in World War I

‡lex (leks) *n.,* *pl.* le·ges (lē′jēz, lā′gās) [L.] law

lex·i·cal (lek′si k'l) *adj.* [ModL. *lexicalis* < Gr. *lexikon*, lexicon] 1. of, or relating to, items of vocabulary in a language 2. of, or relating to, a lexicon

lex·i·cog·ra·pher (lek′sə kog′rə fər) *n.* [< LGr. < Gr. *lexikon*, LEXICON + *graphein*, to write] a person who writes or compiles a dictionary

lex·i·cog·ra·phy (-fē) *n.* [see prec.] the act, art, or work of writing or compiling a dictionary —**lex·i·co·graph·ic** (lek′si kə graf′ik), **lex′i·co·graph′i·cal** *adj.*

lex·i·con (lek′si kən, -kon′) *n.* [Gr. *lexikon* < *lexis*, a word < *legein*, to say] 1. a dictionary, esp. of an ancient language 2. the special vocabulary of a particular author, field of study, etc.

lex·ig·ra·phy (lex ig′rə fē) *n.* [Gr. *lexis*, speech + *graphein*, to write] a system of writing in which each symbol represents a word

ley (lā) *n.* [< LEA] farmland temporarily under grass

Ley·den jar (or **vial**) (līd′'n) [< *Leiden*, city in the Netherlands, where invented] a condenser for static electricity, consisting of a glass jar with a coat of tinfoil outside and inside and a metallic rod connecting with the inner lining and passing through the lid

LF, L.F., lf, l.f. low frequency

lf., lf lightface

LG., L.G. Low German

LGr., L.Gr. Late Greek

l.h., L.H., LH left hand

Li *Chem.* lithium

li·a·bil·i·ty (lī′ə bil′ə tē) *n.,* *pl.* -ties 1. the state of being liable 2. anything for which a person is liable 3. [*pl.*] *Accounting* all the entries on a balance sheet showing the debts of a person or business, as accounts and notes payable 4. something that works to one's disadvantage

li·a·ble (lī′ə b'l) *adj.* [prob. via Anglo-Fr. < OFr. *lier* < L. *ligare*, to bind] 1. legally bound, as to make good a loss; responsible 2. likely to have, suffer from, etc.; subject to [*liable* to heart attacks] 3. likely (*to* do, have, get, etc.

something unpleasant or unwanted) [*liable* to cause hard feelings]

li·aise (lē āz′) *vi.* -aised′, -ais′ing [back-formation < ff.] to establish liaison (usually with *with*)

li·ai·son (lē ā′zon; *for 3, Fr.* lye zōn′) *n.* [Fr. < OFr. < L. < *ligare*, to bind] 1. a connecting of the parts of a whole, as of military units, in order to bring about proper coordination of activities 2. an illicit love affair 3. in spoken French, the linking of words by pronouncing the final consonant of one word as though it were the initial consonant of the following word, as in the phrase *chez elle* (pronounced shā zel′)

li·a·na (lē än′ə, -an′ə) *n.* [NormFr. *liane*, ult. < L. *viburnum*, wayfaring tree] any luxuriantly growing, woody, tropical vine that roots in the ground and climbs, as around tree trunks: also **li·ane′** (-än′, -an′)

li·ar (lī′ər) *n.* a person who tells lies

Li·as (lī′əs) *n.* [ME. *lyas* < OFr. *liois*, kind of limestone] a series of rocks, the oldest or lowest part of the Jurassic system, noted for its fossils

lib (lib) *n.* *clipped form of* liberation (see LIBERATE)

Lib. 1. Liberal 2. Liberia

lib. 1. [L. *liber*] book 2. librarian 3. library

li·ba·tion (lī bā′shən) *n.* [< L. *libatio* < *libare*, to pour out] 1. the ritual of pouring out wine or oil upon the ground as a sacrifice to a god 2. the liquid so poured out 3. an alcoholic drink: used humorously —**li·ba′tion·al** *adj.*

li·bel (lī′b'l) *n.* [OFr. < L. *libellus*, dim. of *liber*, a book] 1. any false and malicious written or printed statement, or any sign, picture, etc., tending to injure a person's reputation unjustly 2. the act of publishing such a thing 3. anything that gives an unflattering or damaging picture of the subject it is dealing with —*vt.* -belled, -bel·ling 1. to publish or make a libel against 2. to give an unflattering or damaging picture of — **li′bel·ler** *n.*

li·bel·lous (-əs) *adj.* 1. of or involving a libel 2. given to writing and publishing libels; defamatory —**li′bel·lous·ly** *adv.*

lib·er·al (lib′ər əl, lib′rəl) *adj.* [< L. *liberalis* < *liber*, free] 1. orig., suitable for a freeman; not restricted: now only in LIBERAL ARTS, etc. 2. giving freely; generous 3. ample; abundant [a *liberal* reward] 4. not restricted to the literal meaning [a *liberal* interpretation of the Bible] 5. broad-minded 6. favouring reform or progress, as in religion, education, etc.; specif., favouring political reforms tending towards democracy 7. [L-] designating or of a political party upholding liberal principles, as in Great Britain or Canada —*n.* 1. a person favouring liberalism 2. [L-] a member of a liberal political party —**lib′er·al·ly** *adv.* —**lib′er·al·ness** *n.*

liberal arts 1. the seven branches of medieval education 2. the subjects of an academic university course, esp. in the U.S., including literature, philosophy, languages, history, etc., as distinguished from professional or technical subjects

lib·er·al·ism (-iz′m) *n.* the quality or state of being liberal, esp. in politics or religion

lib·er·al·i·ty (lib′ə ral′ə tē) *n.,* *pl.* -ties the quality or state of being liberal; specif., *a)* generosity *b)* tolerance; broad-mindedness

lib·er·al·ize (lib′ər ə līz′, lib′rə-) *vt., vi.* -ized′, -iz′ing to make or become liberal —**lib′er·al·i·za′tion** *n.* —**lib′er·al·iz′-er** *n.*

lib·er·ate (lib′ə rāt′) *vt.* -at′ed, -at′ing [< L. pp. of *liberare*, to free < *liber*, free] 1. to release from slavery, enemy occupation, etc. 2. [Slang] to steal or loot, esp. from a defeated enemy in wartime 3. *Chem.* to free from combination in a compound —**lib′er·a′tion** *n.* —**lib′er·a′-tor** *n.*

lib·er·tar·i·an (lib′ər ter′ē ən) *n.* a person who advocates full civil liberties —*adj.* of or upholding such liberties —**lib′er·tar′i·an·ism** *n.*

li·ber·ti·cide (li bur′tə sīd′) *n.* [Fr. *liberticide*, killing liberty] a destroyer of liberty —*adj.* destroying liberty

lib·er·tine (lib′ər tēn′, -tin) *n.* [< L. < *libertus*, freedman < *liber*, free] a man who leads an unrestrained, sexually immoral life; rake —*adj.* licentious —**lib′er·tin·ism, lib′-er·tin·age** *n.*

lib·er·ty (lib′ər tē) *n.,* *pl.* -ties [< OFr. < L. *libertas* < *liber*, free] 1. freedom from slavery, captivity, or any other form of arbitrary control 2. the sum of rights possessed in common by the people of a community, state, etc.: see also CIVIL LIBERTIES 3. a particular right, franchise, freedom, etc. 4. a too free, too familiar, or impertinent action or attitude 5. the limits within which a certain amount of freedom may be exercised [to have the *liberty* of the third floor] 6. *Philos.* freedom to choose —**at liberty** 1. not confined; free 2. allowed (to do or say something) 3. not busy or in use —**take liberties** 1. to be too familiar or impertinent in action or speech 2. to deal (*with* facts, etc.) in a distorting way

liberty boat a boat carrying sailors with leave to go ashore

li·bid·i·nous (li bid′ə nəs) *adj.* [see ff.] full of or characterized by lust; lewd; lascivious —**li·bid′i·nous·ly** *adv.* —**li·bid′i·nous·ness** *n.*

li·bi·do (li bē′dō, -bī′-) *n.* [L., desire, wantonness < *libet*, it pleases] 1. the sexual urge or instinct 2. *Psychoanalysis* energy of the psyche associated with the positive, loving instincts —**li·bid′i·nal** (-bid′′n al) *adj.* —**li·bid′i·nal·ly** *adv.*

Li·bra (li′brə, lē′-) [L., a balance] 1. a S constellation between Virgo and Scorpio 2. the seventh sign of the zodiac: see ZODIAC, illus.

li·bra (li′brə) *n., pl.* **-brae** (-brē) [L.] pound

li·brar·i·an (li brer′ē ən) *n.* 1. a person in charge of a library 2. a qualified library worker —**li·brar′i·an·ship**′ *n.*

li·brar·y (li′brə rē) *n., pl.* **-brar·ies** [< OFr. < *libraire*, copyist < L. < *liber*, a book] 1. a room or building where a collection of books, periodicals, etc. is kept for reading or reference 2. a public or private institution in charge of the care and circulation of such a collection 3. a collection of books, periodicals, etc.

li·bra·tion (li brā′shən) *n.* [< L. *libratio*, < *libra*, a balance] *Astron.* an apparent, or real, oscillation of the moon enabling approximately nine per cent of the surface facing away from earth to be seen

li·bret·tist (li bret′ist) *n.* a writer of librettos

li·bret·to (li bret′ō) *n., pl.* **-tos, -ti** (-ē) [It., dim. of *libro*, a book < L. *liber*] 1. the words, or text, of an opera, oratorio, etc. 2. a book containing these words

lice (lis) *n. pl. of* LOUSE

li·cence (lis′′ns) *n.* [< OFr. < L. *licentia* < prp. of *licere*, to be permitted] 1. formal or legal permission to do something specified [*licence* to marry, hunt, etc.] 2. a document, tag, etc. indicating that such permission has been granted 3. *a)* freedom to deviate from strict conduct, rule, or practice [poetic *licence*] *b)* an instance of this 4. excessive, undisciplined freedom, constituting an abuse of liberty Also, U.S. sp., **license**

li·cense (lis′′ns) *vt.* **-censed, cens·ing** [< prec.] to give licence or a licence to or for; permit formally —**li′cens·a·ble** *adj.*

li·cen·see (lis′′n sē′) *n.* a person to whom a licence is granted

li·cens·er (lis′′n sər) *n.* a person with authority to grant licences: also sp., *Law,* **li′cen·sor**

li·cen·ti·ate (li sen′shē it, -āt′) *n.* 1. a person licensed to practise a specified profession 2. in certain European and Canadian universities, an academic degree between that of bachelor and that of doctor —**li·cen′ti·ate·ship**′ *n.*

li·cen·tious (li sen′shəs) *adj.* [< L. < *licentia*: see LICENCE] 1. [Rare] disregarding accepted rules and standards 2. morally unrestrained, esp. in sexual activity; lascivious —**li·cen′tious·ly** *adv.* —**li·cen′tious·ness** *n.*

li·chee (lē′chē′) *n.* same as LITCHI

li·chen (li′kən, lich′ən) *n.* [L. < Gr., prob. < *leichein*, to lick] any of a large group of small plants composed of a fungus and an alga growing in close association to form a dual plant, commonly adhering in coloured patches to rock, wood, soil, etc. —**li′chen·ous, li′chen·ose**′ (-ōs′) *adj.*

lich gate (lich) [ME. < OE. *lic,* akin to G. *Leiche,* corpse + GATE] a roofed gate at the entrance to a churchyard, where a coffin can be set down to await the arrival of the clergyman

licht (likht) *adj., adv., n., vi., vt.* *Scot. var. of* LIGHT[1]

lic·it (lis′it) *adj.* [< L. pp. of *licere,* to be permitted] permitted; lawful —**lic′it·ly** *adv.* —**lic′it·ness** *n.*

lick (lik) *vt.* [OE. *liccian*] 1. to pass the tongue over [to *lick* one's lips] 2. to bring into a certain condition by passing the tongue over [to *lick* one's fingers clean] 3. to pass lightly over like a tongue [flames *licking* the logs] 4. [Colloq.] *a)* to whip; thrash *b)* to vanquish —*vi.* to move lightly and quickly, as a flame —*n.* 1. the act of licking with the tongue 2. a small quantity; bit 3. *short for* SALT LICK 4. [Colloq.] *a)* a sharp blow *b)* a short, rapid burst of activity *c)* a fast pace; clip —**lick and a promise** a hasty, superficial effort in cleaning, etc. —**lick into shape** [Colloq.] to bring into proper condition —**lick one's chops** to anticipate eagerly —**lick one's wounds** to remain retired after a severe defeat —**lick up** to consume as by licking

lick·er·ish (lik′ər ish) *adj.* [< Anglo-Fr. form of OFr. *lecheros*] [Archaic] 1. lecherous; lustful; lewd 2. greedy or eager, esp. to eat or taste

lick·e·ty-split (lik′ə tē split′) *adv.* [fanciful formation based on LICK, *n.* 4 *c*] [Colloq.] at great speed

lick-spit·tle (lik′spit′′l) *n.* a servile flatterer; toady: also **lick′spit**′

lic·o·rice (lik′ər ish, -is; lik′rish) *n.* same as LIQUORICE

lic·tor (lik′tər) *n.* [L.] a minor Roman official who carried the fasces and cleared the way for the chief magistrates

lid (lid) *n.* [OE. *hlid*] 1. a movable cover, as for a box, pot, etc. 2. *short for* EYELID 3. [Colloq.] a curb or restraint [to put a *lid* on gambling] 4. [Slang] a cap, hat, etc. —**lid′-ded** *adj.* —**lid′less** *adj.*

li·do (lē′dō) *n.* [< *Lido*, island in NE Italy] 1. a pleasure resort 2. a public swimming pool

lie[1] (li) *vi.* **lay, lain, ly′ing** [OE. *licgan*] 1. to be or put oneself in a reclining position along a relatively horizontal surface (often with *down*) 2. to rest on a support in a more or less horizontal position: said of inanimate things 3. to be or remain in a specified condition [motives that *lie* hidden] 4. to be situated [Scotland *lies* to the north of England] 5. to extend [the road that *lies* before us] 6. to be; exist [the love that *lies* in her eyes] 7. to be buried or entombed 8. [Archaic] to stay overnight or for a short while 9. [Archaic] to have sexual intercourse (*with*) —*n.* 1. the way in which something is situated or arranged; lay [the *lie* of the land] 2. an animal's lair —**lie down on the job** [Colloq.] to put forth less than one's best efforts —**lie in** 1. to be in confinement for childbirth 2. to stay in bed in the morning —**lie off** *Naut.* to stay at a distance from shore or another ship —**lie over** to stay and wait until some future time —**lie to** *Naut.* to lie stationary with the head to the wind: said of a ship —**take lying down** to submit to (punishment, a wrong, etc.) without protest —**li′er** *n.*

lie[2] (li) *vi.* **lied, ly′ing** [OE. *leogan*] 1. to make a statement or statements that one knows to be false, esp. with intent to deceive 2. to give a false impression —*n.* 1. a thing said or done in lying; falsehood 2. anything that gives or is meant to give a false impression —**give the lie to** 1. to charge with telling a lie 2. to prove to be false

lie-a-bed (li′ə bed′) *n.* [LIE + ABED] someone who does not get out of bed early in the morning

†**Lieb·frau·milch** (lēb′frou milk′; G. lēp′frou milkh) *n.* [G. < *Liebfrau,* Virgin Mary + *Milch,* milk (after *Liebfrauenstift,* convent in Worms where first made)] a white table wine from the Rhine vineyards

lied (lēd; *G.* lēt) *n., pl.* **lied′er** (lē′dər; *G.*-dər) [G.] a German song, esp. one of a lyrical, often popular, character

lie detector a polygraph used on persons suspected of lying to record the physiological changes assumed to occur when the subject lies in answering questions

lief (lēf) *adj.* [OE. *leof*] [Archaic or Obs.] 1. dear; beloved 2. willing —*adv.* willingly; gladly: only in **would** (or **had**) **as lief,** etc.

liege (lēj) *adj.* [< OFr., prob. < Frank. base but infl. by L. *ligare,* to bind] 1. *Feudal Law a)* entitled to the service and allegiance of his vassals [a *liege* lord] *b)* bound to give service and allegiance to the lord [*liege* subjects] 2. loyal; faithful —*n.* *Feudal Law* 1. a lord or sovereign 2. a subject or vassal

liege·man (-mən) *n., pl.* **-men** 1. a vassal 2. a loyal follower Also **liege man**

li·en (lēn, lē′ən) *n.* [Fr. < L. *ligamen,* a band < *ligare,* to bind] *Law* a claim on the property of another as security for the payment of a debt

li·erne (lē urn′) *n.* [Fr. < MF. *lier,* to bind] *Archit.* a short rib used in Gothic vaulting to correct the trusses and intersections of the main ribs

lieu (lyōō) *n.* [OFr. < L. *locus,* place] place: now chiefly in **in lieu of,** in place of; instead of

lieu·ten·ant (lef ten′ənt) *n.* [< MFr. < *lieu,* place + *tenant,* holding < L. *tenere,* to hold] 1. one who acts for a superior, as during the latter's absence 2. *see* MILITARY RANKS, table Abbrev. **Lieut., Lt.** —**lieu·ten′an·cy** (-ən sē) *n., pl.* **-cies**

lieutenant colonel *see* MILITARY RANKS, table

lieutenant commander *see* MILITARY RANKS, table

lieutenant general *see* MILITARY RANKS, table

lieutenant governor the official head of government of a Canadian province, appointed by the governor general: also **lieu·ten′ant-gov′er·nor** *n.*

life (lif) *n., pl.* **lives** [OE. *lif*] 1. that property of plants and animals (ending at death and distinguishing them from inorganic matter) which makes it possible for them to take in food, get energy from it, grow, etc. 2. the state of possessing this property [brought back to *life*] 3. a living being, esp. a human being [the *lives* lost in wars] 4. living things collectively [plant *life*] 5. the time a person or thing is alive, or a specific portion of such time [his early *life*] 6. a sentence of imprisonment for the rest of one's life 7. one's manner of living [a *life* of ease] 8. the people and activities of a given time, or in a given setting or class [military *life,* low *life*] 9. human existence and activity [to learn from *life*] 10. *a)* an individual's lifetime experiences *b)* an account of this 11. the existence of the soul [eternal *life*] 12. something essential to the continued existence of something else [freedom of speech is the *life* of democracy] 13. the source of vigour or liveliness [the *life* of the party] 14. vigour; liveliness 15. the period of flourishing, usefulness, functioning, etc. [fads have a short *life*] 16. representation in art from living models [a class in *life*] 17. [Colloq.] another chance [to get a *life*] —*adj.* of, in, or for life —**a matter of life and death** a matter of extreme importance or urgency —**as large** (or **big**) **as life** 1. life-size 2. in actual fact —**for dear life** with a desperate intensity —**for life** 1. for the duration of one's life 2. in order to save one's life —**from life** from a living model —**not on your life** by no means; certainly not —**see life** to have a wide variety of experiences —**take life** to kill

—**take one's (own) life** to commit suicide —**to the life** like the living original; exactly —**true to life** true to reality

life belt a life buoy in the form of a belt

life-blood (-blud´) *n.* **1.** the blood necessary to life **2.** a vital element or animating influence

life-boat (-bōt´) *n.* any of the small boats carried by a ship for use if the ship must be abandoned

life buoy a buoyant device for saving a person from drowning by keeping his body afloat, as a ring or sleeveless jacket of canvas-covered cork

life cycle the changes undergone during the lifetime of one generation of an organism to the appearance of the same initial form in the next

life expectancy the number of years that an individual of a given age may expect on the average to live, as projected in statistical tables

life-giv-ing (-giv´iŋ) *adj.* **1.** that gives or can give life **2.** refreshing —**life´-giv´er** *n.*

life-guard (-gärd´) *n.* an expert swimmer employed at a beach, a pool, etc. to prevent drownings

life insurance insurance in which a stipulated sum is paid to the beneficiary or beneficiaries at the death of the insured, or to the insured when he reaches a specified age

life jacket (or vest) a life buoy in the form of a sleeveless jacket

life-less (-lis) *adj.* **1.** without life; specif., *a)* inanimate *b)* dead **2.** dull; listless —**life´less-ly** *adv.* —**life´less-ness** *n.*

life-like (-līk´) *adj.* **1.** resembling actual life **2.** closely resembling a real person or thing

life-line (-līn´) *n.* **1.** a rope for saving life, as one thrown to a person in the water **2.** the rope used to raise or lower a diver **3.** a commercial route or transport line of vital importance

LIFE JACKET

life-long (-lôŋ´) *adj.* lasting or not changing during one's whole life [a *lifelong* love]

life peer a peer whose title lapses at his death

life preserver **1.** a club or bludgeon, esp. one kept for self-defence **2.** [U.S.] a life belt or life jacket

lif-er (līf´ər) *n.* [Slang] a person sentenced to imprisonment for life

life raft a small, inflatable raft or boat

life-sav-er (-sā´vər) *n.* **1.** a person or thing that saves people from drowning, as a lifeguard **2.** [Colloq.] a person or thing that is of great timely help —**life´sav´ing** *adj., n.*

life sciences the branches of science concerned with the structure and behaviour of living organisms, as biology, botany, biochemistry, etc.

life-size (-sīz´) *adj.* of the same size as the person or thing represented: said of a picture, sculpture, etc.: also **life´-sized´**

life span **1.** *same as* LIFETIME **2.** the longest period of time that a typical individual can be expected to live

life style one's way of life as typified by one's activities, attitudes, possessions, etc.

life-time (-tīm´) *n.* the length of time that someone lives, or that something lasts, functions, etc. —*adj.* lasting for such a period [a *lifetime* job]

life-work (-wurk´) *n.* the work or task to which a person devotes his life; chief work in life: also **life's work**

lift (lift) *vt.* [< ON. *lypta*, air] **1.** to bring up to a higher position; raise **2.** to pick up and move or set [*lift* the box down from the shelf] **3.** to hold up **4.** to raise in rank, condition, spirits, etc.; elevate; exalt **5.** to end (a blockade, siege, etc.) by withdrawing forces **6.** to revoke or rescind (a ban or order) **7.** to subject to FACE LIFTING **8.** [Colloq.] to plagiarize [to *lift* a passage from another writer] —*vi.* **1.** to exert strength in raising or trying to raise something **2.** to rise and vanish; be dispelled [the fog *lifted*] **3.** to become raised; go up —*n.* **1.** a lifting, raising, or rising **2.** the amount lifted **3.** the distance through which something is lifted **4.** lifting force, power, or influence **5.** elevation of spirits or mood **6.** elevated position or carriage, as of the neck, head, etc. **7.** a ride in a car or bus in the direction one is going **8.** help of any kind **9.** a rise in the ground **10.** the means by which something is lifted; specif., *a)* any layer of leather in the heel of a shoe *b)* a cage or car for hoisting or lowering people or things attached by cables to a machine that moves it in a shaft *c)* a device used to transport people up or down a slope [ski *lift*] —**lift´er** *n.*

lift-off (-ôf´) *n.* the vertical thrust and rise of a spacecraft, missile, etc. as it is launched

lig-a-ment (lig´ə mənt) *n.* [< L. < *ligare*, to bind] **1.** a bond or tie **2.** *Anat.* a band of tough tissue connecting bones or holding organs in place

li-gate (lī´gāt) *vt.* -**gat-ed**, -**gat-ing** to tie with a ligature, as a bleeding artery —**li-ga´tion** *n.*

lig-a-ture (lig´ə chər) *n.* [< MFr. < LL. < pp. of L. *ligare*, to bind] **1.** a tying or binding together **2.** a thing used for this; tie, bond, etc. **3.** a written or printed character

containing two or more letters united, as **ff, fl, th 4.** *Music a)* a curved line indicating a slur *b)* the notes slurred **5.** *Surgery* a thread or wire used to tie up an artery, etc. —*vt.* -**tured,** -**tur-ing** to tie or bind together with a ligature

li-ger (lī´gər) *n.* [LI(ON) + (TI)GER] the offspring of a male lion and a female tiger

light[1] (līt) *n.* [OE. *leoht*] **1.** *a)* the form of electromagnetic radiation that acts upon the retina of the eye, optic nerve, etc., making sight possible: the speed of light is 299 300 km per second *b)* a similar form of radiant energy not acting on the normal retina, as ultraviolet and infrared radiation **2.** the sensation that light stimulates in the organs of sight **3.** brightness; illumination, often of a specified kind **4.** a source of light, as the sun, a lamp, etc. **5.** *same as* TRAFFIC LIGHT **6.** the light from the sun; daylight or dawn **7.** a thing by means of which something can be started burning [a *light* for a cigar] **8.** the means by which light is let in; window **9.** knowledge or information; enlightenment [to shed *light* on the past] **10.** spiritual inspiration **11.** public knowledge or view **12.** the way in which something is seen; aspect [presented in a favourable *light*] **13.** facial expression [a *light* of recognition in his eyes] **14.** an outstanding figure [one of the shining *lights* of the school] —*adj.* **1.** having light; bright **2.** pale in colour; whitish; fair —*adv.* palely [a *light* blue colour] —*vt.* **light´ed** or **lit, light´ing 1.** to set on fire; ignite [to *light* a bonfire] **2.** to cause to give off light [to *light* a lamp] **3.** to furnish with light [lamps *light* the streets] **4.** to brighten; animate **5.** to show the way to by giving light —*vi.* **1.** to catch fire **2.** to be lighted; brighten (usually with *up*) —**according to one's lights** as one's opinions, information, or standards may direct —**in the light of** considering —**see the light (of day) 1.** to come into existence **2.** to come into public view **3.** to understand —**strike a light 1.** to make a flame, as with a match **2.** [Colloq.] an exclamation of surprise

light[2] (līt) *adj.* [OE. *leoht*] **1.** having little weight; not heavy **2.** having little weight for its size **3.** below the usual or defined weight [a *light* coin] **4.** less than usual or normal in amount, extent, force, intensity, etc.; specif., *a)* striking with little force [a *light* blow] *b)* of less than the usual quantity or density [a *light* rain] *c)* not coarse, massive, etc.; graceful [*light* tracery] *d)* soft, muted, or muffled [a *light* sound] *e)* not prolonged or intense [*light* applause] **5.** of little importance; not serious [*light* conversation] **6.** easy to bear; not burdensome [a *light* duty] **7.** easy to do; not difficult [*light* work] **8.** gay; happy; buoyant [*light* spirits] **9.** flighty; frivolous; capricious **10.** loose in morals; wanton **11.** dizzy; giddy **12.** of an amusing or nonserious nature [*light* reading] **13.** containing little alcohol [*light* wine] **14.** *a)* not as full as usual [a *light* meal] *b)* easy to digest **15.** well leavened; soft and spongy [a *light* cake] **16.** loose in consistency; porous [*light* sand] **17.** moving with ease and nimbleness [*light* on one's feet] **18.** carrying little weight **19.** unstressed or slightly stressed: said of syllables **20.** designating or of industry equipped with relatively light machinery and producing small products **21.** designating, of, or equipped with light weapons, armour, etc. —*adv.* lightly —*vi.* **light´-ed** or **lit, light´ing 1.** [Now Dial.] to dismount; alight **2.** to come to rest after travelling through the air [ducks *lighting* on the pond] **3.** to come or happen (*on* or *upon*) by chance **4.** to strike suddenly, as a blow —**light in the head 1.** dizzy **2.** simple; foolish —**light into** [Colloq.] **1.** to attack **2.** to scold —**light out** [Colloq.] to depart suddenly —**make light of** to treat as unimportant —**light´-ish** *adj.*

light air a wind speed of 1 on the Beaufort scale (c. 1-5 km/h)

light breeze a wind speed of 2 on the Beaufort scale (c. 6-11 km/h)

light-en[1] (-'n) *vt.* **1.** to make light; illuminate **2.** to make light or pale —*vi.* **1.** to become light; grow brighter **2.** to shine brightly; flash **3.** to give off flashes of lightning —**light´en-er** *n.*

light-en[2] (-'n) *vt.* **1.** *a)* to make lighter in weight *b)* to reduce the load of **2.** to make less severe, harsh, etc. **3.** to make more cheerful —*vi.* **1.** to become lighter in weight **2.** to become more cheerful —**light´en-er** *n.*

light-er[1] (-ər) *n.* a person or thing that lights something or starts it burning; esp., a small device for lighting a cigarette, etc.

light-er[2] (-ər) *n.* [< MDu. < *lichten*, to make light < *licht*, LIGHT[2]] a large open barge used chiefly in loading or unloading larger ships lying offshore —*vt., vi.* to transport (goods) in a lighter

light-er-age (-ər ij) *n.* **1.** the loading or unloading of a ship, or transportation of goods, by means of a lighter **2.** the charge for this

light-face (līt´fās´) *n.* *Printing* type having thin, light lines —*adj.* having thin, light lines: also **light´faced´**

light-fin-gered (-fiŋ´gərd) *adj.* **1.** having a light touch **2.** skilful at stealing, esp. by picking pockets

light flyweight *see* BOXING AND WRESTLING WEIGHTS, table

light-foot·ed (-foot′id) *adj.* stepping lightly and gracefully: also [Poet.] **light′-foot′**—**light′-foot′ed·ly** *adv.*

light-hand·ed (-han′did) *adj.* 1. having a light, delicate touch 2. having little to carry

light-head·ed (-hed′id) *adj.* 1. mentally confused or feeling giddy; dizzy 2. flighty; frivolous —**light′head′ed·ly** *adv.* —**light′head′ed·ness** *n.*

light-heart·ed (-här′tid) *adj.* free from care; gay —**light′-heart′ed·ly** *adv.* —**light′heart′ed·ness** *n.*

light heavyweight *see* BOXING AND WRESTLING WEIGHTS, table

light·house (-hous′) *n.* a tower located at some place important or dangerous to navigation: it has a very bright light at the top, and often foghorns, sirens, etc., by which ships are guided and warned

light industry an industry producing small or light articles, such as electronic components, textiles, etc.

light·ing (-iŋ) *n.* 1. a giving light or being lighted; illumination; ignition 2. the distribution of light and shade, as in a painting 3. the art or manner of arranging stage lights

lighting-up time the time after which vehicles on the road must show lights: usually half an hour after sunset

light·ly (-lē) *adv.* 1. with little weight or pressure; gently 2. to a small degree or amount 3. nimbly; deftly 4. cheerfully; merrily 5. with indifference or neglect 6. with little or no reason 7. with little or no punishment [to let someone off *lightly*]

light middleweight *see* BOXING AND WRESTLING WEIGHTS, table

light-mind·ed (-mīn′did) *adj.* not serious; frivolous —**light′-mind′ed·ly** *adv.* —**light′-mind′ed·ness** *n.*

light·ness¹ (-nis) *n.* 1. the quality or intensity of lighting; brightness 2. a) paleness b) the relative amount of light reflected by an object

light·ness² (-nis) *n.* 1. the state of being light, not heavy 2. mildness, nimbleness, delicacy, cheerfulness, lack of seriousness, etc.

light·ning (-niŋ) *n.* [< ME. *lightnen*, to LIGHTEN¹] 1. a flash of light in the sky caused by the discharge of atmospheric electricity from one cloud to another or between a cloud and the earth 2. such a discharge of electricity —*vi.* to give off such a discharge —*adj.* like lightning —**like (greased) lightning** like a flash; very quickly

lightning conductor a pointed metal rod placed high on a building, etc. and earthed to divert lightning from the structure

light opera a short, amusing musical play

lights¹ (līts) *n.pl.* [from their light weight] the lungs of animals, used as food

lights² (līts) *n.pl.* *same as* TRAFFIC LIGHT

light·ship (līt′ship′) *n.* a ship moored in a place dangerous to navigation and bearing lights, foghorns, sirens, etc. to warn or guide pilots

light·some (-səm) *adj.* 1. nimble, graceful, or lively 2. lighthearted; gay 3. frivolous

lights out 1. a signal, as in a military camp or boarding school, etc., to extinguish lights at bedtime 2. bedtime

light·weight (-wāt′) *n.* 1. one below normal weight 2. *see* BOXING AND WRESTLING WEIGHTS, table 3. a person of limited influence, intelligence, etc. —*adj.* 1. light in weight 2. not serious

light welterweight *see* BOXING AND WRESTLING WEIGHTS, table

light-year (-yir′) *n.* *Astron.* a unit of distance equal to the distance that light travels in a vacuum in one year, approximately 10^{16} metres

lig·ne·ous (lig′nē əs) *adj.* [< L. *ligneus* < *lignum*, wood] of, or having the nature of, wood; woody

lig·nin (lig′nin) *n.* [L. *lignum*, wood + -IN¹] an organic substance found in wood and certain plants that adds stiffness and strength to the cell walls

lig·nite (lig′nīt) *n.* [< Fr.: see LIGNEOUS & -ITE] a soft, brownish-black coal in which the texture of the original wood can still be seen —**lig·nit′ic** (-nit′ik) *adj.*

lig·num vi·tae (lig′nəm vīt′ē) [ModL. < L., wood of life] 1. *same as* GUAIACUM (sense 1) 2. *commercial name for* the very hard wood of the guaiacum

lig·ro·in (lig′rō in) *n.* [arbitrary coinage] *chemists'* term *for* BENZINE

lik·a·ble (līk′ə b'l) *adj.* having qualities that inspire liking; attractive, genial, etc. —**lik′a·ble·ness, lik′a·bil′i·ty** *n.*

like¹ (līk) *adj.* [OE. *gelic*] 1. having almost or exactly the same characteristics; similar; equal [on this and the *like* subjects] 2. [Dial.] likely —*adv.* [Colloq.] likely [*like* as not, he is already there] —*prep.* 1. similar to; resembling [she is *like* a bird] 2. similarly to [she sings *like* a bird, *like* father, *like* son] 3. characteristic of [not *like* her to cry] 4. in the mood for; desirous of [to feel *like* sleeping] 5. indicative of [it looks *like* a clear day tomorrow] 6. [Colloq.] as for example [fruit, *like* pears, for dessert] —*conj.* [Colloq.] 1. as [it was just *like* you said] 2. [Chiefly U.S.] as if [it looks *like* he is late] —*n.* a person or thing regarded as the equal or counterpart of another or of the person or thing being discussed [did you ever see the *like* of it?] —*vt.* **liked, lik′ing** [Obs.] to liken —**and the like** and others of the same kind —**like anything** [Colloq.] very much —**like blazes** (or **crazy, the devil, mad,** etc.) [Colloq.] with furious energy, speed, etc. —**nothing like** not at all like —**something like** 1. almost like; about 2. [Colloq.] exactly what is desired or needed; perfect —**the like** (or **likes**) **of** [Colloq.] any person or thing like

like² (līk) *vi.* **liked, lik′ing** [OE. *lician*] to be so inclined; choose [leave whenever you *like*] —*vt.* 1. to be pleased with; have a preference for; enjoy 2. to want or wish [I would *like* to go] —*n.* [*pl.*] preferences or tastes —**lik′er** *n.*

-like (līk) [see LIKE¹] *a suffix meaning* like, characteristic of, suitable for [doglike, homelike]

like·a·ble (līk′ə b'l) *adj.* *same as* LIKABLE

like·li·hood (līk′lē hood′) *n.* (a) probability

like·ly (līk′lē) *adj.* **-li·er, -li·est** [prob. < OE. *geliclic* or < cognate ON. *likligr*] 1. credible; probable [a *likely* cause] 2. reasonably to be expected [it is *likely* to rain] 3. suitable [a *likely* man for the job] 4. promising [a *likely* lad] —*adv.* probably [he will very *likely* go] —**not likely** [Colloq.] there is no chance

like-mind·ed (līk′mīn′did) *adj.* having the same ideas, tastes, etc.; agreeing mentally —**like′-mind′ed·ly** *adv.* —**like′-mind′ed·ness** *n.*

lik·en (-'n) *vt.* to represent or describe as being like, or similar; compare

like·ness (-nis) *n.* 1. the state or quality of being like; similarity 2. (the same) form or shape [Zeus took on the *likeness* of a bull] 3. something that is like; copy, facsimile, portrait, etc. [to take someone's *likeness*]

like·wise (-wīz′) *adv.* [short for *in like wise*] 1. in the same manner 2. also; too; moreover

lik·ing (līk′iŋ) *n.* 1. fondness; affection 2. preference; taste; pleasure [not to my *liking*]

li·ku·ta (lē kyōō′tä) *n.,* *pl.* **ma·ku′ta** (mä-) *see* MONETARY UNITS, table (Zaire)

li·lac (lī′lək) *n.* [Fr. < Ar. < Per. *nīlak*, bluish < *nīl*, indigo] 1. a shrub or tree of the olive family, with large clusters of tiny, fragrant flowers ranging in colour from white to lavender 2. the flower cluster of this plant 3. a pale-purple colour —*adj.* pale-purple

Lil·li·pu·tian (lil′ə pyōō′shən) *adj.* [after *Lilliput*, the land inhabited by tiny people in Swift's *Gulliver's Travels*] 1. of Lilliput or its people 2. very small; tiny 3. narrow-minded —*n.* 1. an inhabitant of Lilliput 2. a very small person 3. a narrow-minded person

lilt (lilt) *vt., vi.* [ME. *lilten*] to sing, speak, or play with a light, graceful rhythm —*n.* 1. a gay song or tune with a swingy rhythm 2. a light, swingy, and graceful rhythm or movement —**lilt′ing** *adj.* —**lilt′ing·ly** *adv.*

lil·y (lil′ē) *n.,* *pl.* **lil′ies** [< OE. < L. *lilium*] 1. any of a large genus of plants of the lily family, grown from a bulb and having typically trumpet-shaped flowers, white or coloured 2. the flower or the bulb of any of these 3. any of several similar plants, as the waterlily 4. the fleur-de-lis, as in the royal arms of France —*adj.* 1. designating a family of plants including the lilies, tulips, onions, etc. 2. like a lily, as in whiteness, delicacy, purity, etc. —**gild the lily** to attempt vain improvements on something that is already excellent or perfect

lil·y-liv·ered (lil′ē liv′ərd) *adj.* cowardly; timid

lily of the valley *pl.* **lilies of the valley** a plant of the lily family which has a single pair of oblong leaves and a single raceme of very fragrant, small, white, bell-shaped flowers

LILY OF THE VALLEY

lil·y-white (-wīt′, -hwīt′) *adj.* 1. white as a lily 2. innocent and pure: often used sarcastically

li·ma bean (lī′mə) [after *Lima*, Peru] [*also* L- b-] 1. a bean plant with creamy flowers and broad pods 2. its broad, flat, nutritious seed

limb¹ (lim) *n.* [OE. *lim*] 1. an arm, leg, or wing 2. a large branch of a tree 3. a part that projects like an arm or leg 4. a person or thing regarded as a part or agent 5. [Colloq.] a naughty child —**out on a limb** [Colloq.] 1. in a precarious position or situation 2. isolated, esp. because of unpopular opinions —**limb′less** *adj.*

limb² (lim) *n.* [< Fr. < ML. < L. *limbus*, edge] a border or edge; specif., *Astron.* the apparent outer edge of a heavenly body

limbed (limd) *adj.* having (a specified number or kind of) limbs [four-*limbed*]

lim·ber¹ (lim′bər) *adj.* [< ? LIMB¹] 1. easily bent; flexible 2. able to bend the body easily; lithe —*vt.* to make limber —*vi.* to make oneself limber, as by exercises (usually with up) —**lim′ber·ness** *n.*

lim·ber² (lim′bər) *n.* [< ?] the two-wheeled, detachable front part of a gun carriage —*vt., vi.* to attach the limber to (a gun carriage)

lim·bo (lim′bō) *n.,* pl. **-bos** [< L. (in) limbo, (in or on) the border] 1. [*often* L-] in some Christian theologies, a region bordering on hell, the abode after death of unbaptized children and righteous people who lived before Jesus 2. a place or condition of oblivion or neglect 3. an indeterminate state midway between two others

lim·bo² (lim′bō) *n.,* pl. **-bos** [20th c., < ?] a West Indian dance in which the dancers pass, while leaning backwards, under a bar which is gradually lowered

Lim·bur·ger (cheese) (lim′bər gər) [< *Limburg*, a Belgian province] a semisoft cheese of whole milk, with a strong odour: also **Lim′burg (cheese)**

lime¹ (līm) *n.* [OE. *lim*] 1. *short for* BIRDLIME 2. a white substance, calcium oxide, CaO, obtained by the action of heat on limestone, shells, etc. and used in making mortar and cement and in neutralizing acid soil —*vt.* **limed, lim′ing** 1. to cement 2. to smear with birdlime 3. to catch with birdlime 4. to treat with lime

lime² (līm) *n.* [Fr. < Pr. < Ar. *līma*: cf. LEMON] 1. a small, lemon-shaped, greenish-yellow citrus fruit with a juicy, sour pulp 2. the small, semitropical tree that it grows on —*adj.* 1. made with or of limes 2. having a flavour like that of limes

lime³ (līm) *n.* [< earlier *line* < ME. *lind*: see LINDEN] a tree with dense, heart-shaped leaves

lime·ade (līm′ād′) *n.* a drink of lime juice and water, usually sweetened

lime green a yellowish-green colour

lime·kiln (līm′kiln′) *n.* a furnace in which limestone, shells, etc. are burned to make lime

lime·light (-līt′) *n.* 1. a brilliant light created by the incandescence of lime, formerly used in theatres to throw an intense beam of light upon a particular part of the stage, an actor, etc. 2. a prominent position before the public

lim·er·ick (lim′ər ik, lim′rik) *n.* [prob. < Ir. refrain containing the name *Limerick*, a county of Ireland] a rhymed, nonsense poem of five anapaestic lines

lime·stone (līm′stōn′) *n.* rock consisting mainly of calcium carbonate, from which building stones, lime, etc. are made: cf. MARBLE

lime-wash (-wosh) *n.* a slaked solution of lime and water for whitewashing walls

lime-wa·ter (-wôt′ər) *n.* a solution of calcium hydroxide in water, used to neutralize acids

lim·ey (lī′mē) *n.* [from the LIME² juice formerly served to British sailors to prevent scurvy] [U.S. Slang] 1. a British sailor or, sometimes, soldier 2. any Briton —*adj.* [U.S. Slang] British

lim·it (lim′it) *n.* [< OFr. < L. *limes* (gen. *limitis*)] 1. the point, line, or edge where something ends or must end; boundary 2. [*pl.*] bounds 3. the greatest amount allowed [a catch of ten trout is the *limit*, a ten-pence *limit* on raising a bet in poker] —*vt.* to set a limit to; restrict; curb —**the limit** [Colloq.] any person or thing regarded as quite unbearable, remarkable, etc. —**lim′it·a·ble** *adj.* —**lim′it·er** *n.*

lim·i·tar·y (lim′ə tər ē) *adj.* [L. *limitaris*] serving as a limit or boundary; restrictive

lim·i·ta·tion (lim′ə tā′shən) *n.* 1. a limiting or being limited 2. qualification; restriction 3. *Law* a period of time, fixed by statute, during which legal action can be brought, as for settling a claim —**lim′i·ta′tive** *adj.*

lim·it·ed (lim′it id) *adj.* 1. a) confined within bounds; restricted b) narrow in scope 2. exercising governmental powers under constitutional restrictions [a *limited* monarch] 3. restricting the liability of each partner or shareholder to the amount of his actual investment [a *limited* company] —**lim′it·ed·ly** *adv.* —**lim′it·ed·ness** *n.*

limited liability of a joint stock company in which the liability of the shareholder is in proportion to the amount of his stock

lim·it·less (-lis) *adj.* without limits; unbounded; vast —**lim′·it·less·ly** *adv.* —**lim′it·less·ness** *n.*

limn (lim) *vt.* **limned, limn·ing** (lim′iŋ, -niŋ) [< OFr. *enluminer* < L. *illuminare*, to make light] [Obs.] 1. to paint or draw 2. to portray in words; describe —**limn·er** (lim′ər, -nər) *n.*

lim·nol·o·gy (lim nol′ə jē) *n.* [< Gr. *limnē*, marsh + -LOGY] the study of the features and properties of fresh water, esp. lakes and ponds —**lim′no·log′i·cal** (-nə loj′i k′l) *adj.* —**lim′nol′o·gist** *n.*

Li·moges (lē mozh′; Fr. lē mōzh′) *n.* [after *Limoges*, city in WC France where it is made] a fine porcelain: also **Limoges ware**

lim·ou·sine (lim′ə zēn′, lim′ə zēn′) *n.* [Fr., lit., a hood] 1. any large, luxurious motor car, esp. one driven by a chauffeur 2. [Chiefly U.S.] a buslike motor car used to carry passengers to or from an airport, etc.

limp¹ (limp) *vi.* [< OE. *lemphealt*, lame] 1. to walk with or as with a lame leg 2. to move jerkily, laboriously, etc. —*n.* a halt or lameness in walking —**limp′er** *n.* —**limp′ing·ly** *adv.*

limp² (limp) *adj.* [?< base of prec.] 1. lacking stiffness;

drooping, wilted, etc. 2. lacking firmness or vigour —**limp′-ly** *adv.* —**limp′ness** *n.*

limp·et (lim′pit) *n.* [< OE. < ML. *lempreda*] a mollusc which clings to rocks, timbers, etc. by means of a thick, fleshy foot

limpet mine a small underwater suction mine attached to the hull of a ship

lim·pid (lim′pid) *adj.* [< Fr. < L. *limpidus* < OL. *limpa*, water] 1. perfectly clear; transparent [*limpid* waters] 2. clear and simple [*limpid* prose] —**lim·pid′i·ty, lim′pid·ness** *n.* —**lim′pid·ly** *adv.*

lim·y (lī′mē) *adj.* **lim′i·er, lim′i·est** 1. covered with, consisting of, or like birdlime; sticky 2. of, like, or containing lime —**lim′i·ness** *n.*

lin·age (lī′nij) *n.* 1. the number of written or printed lines on a page 2. payment based on the number of lines produced by a writer

linch·pin (linch′pin′) *n.* [< OE. *lynis*, linchpin] 1. a pin that goes through the end of an axle outside the wheel to keep the wheel from coming off 2. a person or thing on which the success of a project, organization, etc. depends

Lincoln green a bright-green cloth orig. made in Lincoln: associated esp. with Sherwood Forest

Lincs. Lincolnshire

linc·tus (liŋk′təs) *n.* [< L. *linctum*, to lick] a soothing, syrupy cough mixture

lin·den (lin′dən) *n.* [ME., *adj.* < OE. *lind*, linden] *same as* LIME³

line¹ (līn) *n.* [merging of OE. *line*, a cord, with OFr. *ligne* (both < L. *linea*, lit., linen thread < *linum*, flax)] 1. *a*) a cord, rope, wire, or string *b*) a fine, strong cord with a hook, used in fishing *c*) a cord, steel tape, etc. used in measuring or levelling 2. a wire or system of wires connecting stations in a telephone or telegraph system 3. any wire, pipe, etc., or system of these, for conducting gas, water, electricity, etc. 4. a very thin, threadlike mark; specif., *a*) a long, thin mark made by a pencil, pen, chalk, knife, etc. *b*) a thin crease in the palm or on the face 5. a limit; demarcation 6. outline; contour 7. [*usually pl.*] a plan of making or doing 8. a row or series of persons or things; specif., a row of written or printed characters across a page or column 9. *same as* LINEAGE¹ 10. the descendants of a common ancestor or of a particular breed 11. *a*) a transport system consisting of regular trips by buses, ships, etc. between points *b*) a company operating such a system *c*) one branch of such a system *d*) a single track of a railway 12. the course or direction anything moving takes [the *line* of fire] 13. course of conduct, action, explanation, etc. 14. a person's trade or occupation, or the things he deals in [what's his *line?*] 15. a stock of goods of a particular quality, variety, variety, etc. 16. *a*) the field of one's special knowledge or interest *b*) a source or piece of information [a *line* on a bargain] 17. a short letter, note, or card [drop me a *line*] 18. a verse of poetry 19. [*pl.*] all the speeches of any one character in a play 20. [*pl.*] a marriage certificate: in full **marriage lines** 21. [*pl.*] in some schools, a punishment consisting of copying out some passage of literature, etc. [Jones was given 100 *lines* for talking] 22. [L-] the regular regiments of the army 23. [Colloq.] flattering talk that is insincere 24. *Geog.* an imaginary circle of the earth or of the celestial sphere, as the equator 25. *Math.* a) the path of a moving point b) such a path when considered perfectly straight 26. *Mil.* a) a formation of ships, troops, etc. abreast of each other b) the area or position in closest contact with the enemy during combat c) the troops in this area d) the combatant branches of the army as distinguished from the supporting branches and the staff 27. *Music* any of the long parallel marks forming the staff 28. *T.V.* any of a number of narrow horizontal bands forming a television picture —*vt.* **lined, lin′ing** 1. to mark with lines 2. to trace with or as with lines 3. to bring into alignment (often with *up*) 4. to form a line along 5. to place objects along the edge of —*vi.* to form a line (usually with *up*) —**all along the line** 1. everywhere 2. at every turn of events —**bring** (or **come, get**) **into line** to bring (or come) into alignment —**down the line** completely; entirely —**draw the** (or **a**) **line** to set a limit —**get a line on** [Colloq.] to find out about —**hard lines** [Colloq.] misfortune; bad luck —**hold the line** to stand firm —**in** (or **out of**) **line** in (or not in) alignment, agreement, or conformity —**in line for** being considered for —**lay** (or **put**) **it on the line** 1. to pay up 2. to speak frankly and in detail —**line up** to bring into or take a specified position —**on a line** in the same plane; level —**read between the lines** to discover a hidden meaning or purpose in something written, said, or done —**lin′a·ble, line′a·ble** *adj.*

line² (līn) *vt.* **lined, lin′ing** [< OE. *lin*, ult. < or akin to L. *linum*, flax] 1. to put a layer or lining of a different material on the inside of 2. to be used as a lining in 3. to fill; stuff: now chiefly in **line one's pockets**, to make money, esp. greedily or unethically

lin·e·age¹ (lin′ē ij) *n.* [< OFr. *lignage* < *ligne*: see LINE¹] 1.

direct descent from an ancestor **2.** ancestry; family; stock **3.** *same as* LINE[1] (*n.* 10)

line·age[2] (li′nij) *n.* *same as* LINAGE

lin·e·al (lin′ē əl) *adj.* **1.** in the direct line of descent from an ancestor **2.** hereditary **3.** of or composed of lines; linear —**lin′e·al·ly** *adv.*

lin·e·a·ment (lin′ē ə mənt) *n.* [< L. *lineamentum* < *linea*, LINE[1]] **1.** any of the features of the body, usually of the face, esp. with regard to its outline **2.** a distinctive feature *Usually used in pl.*

lin·e·ar (lin′ē ər) *adj.* **1.** of or relating to a line or lines **2.** made of or using lines **3.** extended in a line **4.** designating or of a style of art in which line is emphasized **5.** having an effect directly proportional to its cause **6.** *Algebra* of the first degree —**lin′e·ar′i·ty** (-ē ar′ə tē) *n.* —**lin′e·ar·ly** *adv.*

linear accelerator *Physics* a device by which charged particles are accelerated along a straight line

linear B a pictographic script on clay tablets found in Crete and discovered to be an archaic form of Greek: **Linear A,** a similar script, remains undeciphered

linear measure **1.** measurement of length **2.** a system of measuring length, esp. the system in which 100 centimetres = 1 metre or that in which 12 inches = 1 foot: see TABLE OF WEIGHTS AND MEASURES in Supplement

linear motor a form of induction motor in which the fixed and moving parts are linear and parallel: used esp. to propel a vehicle along a track

lin·e·a·tion (lin′ē ā′shən) *n.* [ME. *lyneacion* < L. *lineatio*] **1.** marking with lines **2.** a system or series of lines

line drawing a drawing done entirely in lines, from which a cut (**line cut**) can be photoengraved for printing

line·man (lin′mən) *n.,* *pl.* -**men** **1.** a man who carries a surveying line, tape, etc. **2.** a man whose work is setting up and repairing telephone, telegraph, or electric power lines

linemen's climber a device with sharp spikes, fastened to the shoe or strapped to the leg to aid in climbing telephone poles, etc.

lin·en (lin′ən) *n.* see PLURAL, II, D, 3 [OE. < *lin,* flax] **1.** thread or cloth made of flax **2.** [*often pl.*] things made of linen, or of cotton, etc., as tablecloths, sheets, etc. —*adj.* **1.** spun from flax [*linen thread*] **2.** made of linen

linen draper a retail merchant who deals in linen, cloth, etc.

lin·en·fold (-fōld) *adj.* carved or moulded to resemble folds of fabric [*linenfold panelling*]

line of battle troops or ships drawn up to fight

line of fire **1.** the course of a bullet, shell, etc. **2.** a position open to attack of any kind

line of force a line in a field of electrical or magnetic force that indicates the direction taken by the force at any point

line-out (-out) *n.* *Rugby* a movement in which the ball is thrown in from touch towards parallel lines of opposing forwards

lin·er[1] (li′nər) *n.* **1.** a person or thing that traces lines **2.** a steamship, passenger aircraft, etc. in regular service on a specific route **3.** a cosmetic applied in a fine line, as along the eyelid

lin·er[2] (li′nər) *n.* **1.** a person who makes or attaches linings **2.** a lining

lines·man (linz′mən) *n.,* *pl.* -**men** **1.** *same as* LINEMAN **2.** *Football, Tennis* an official who reports whether the ball is inside or outside the lines he is assigned to watch

line·up (lin′up′) *n.* an arrangement of persons or things in or as in a line; specif., *a)* a group including a suspected criminal lined up by the police for identification *b)* *Football, Rugby,* etc. the list of a team's players arranged according to playing position etc.

ling[1] (lin) *n.,* *pl.* **ling, lings:** see PLURAL, II, D, 2 [akin to MDu. *lange,* ON. *langa*] an edible fish related to the cod, found in the North Atlantic

ling[2] (lin) *n.* [ON. *lyng*] *same as* HEATHER

-ling[1] (lin) [OE.] a suffix added to nouns, meaning: **1.** small [*duckling*] **2.** having a connection, esp. of an unimportant or contemptible kind, with the specified thing [*hireling*]

-ling[2] (lin) [OE.] [Archaic or Dial.] a suffix meaning extent or condition [*darkling*]

ling. linguistics

lin·gam (lin′gəm) *n.* [Sans. *lingam,* lit., token, symbol] the phallic symbol used in the worship of the Hindu god Siva: also **lin′ga**

lin·ger (lin′gər) *vi.* [< North ME. freq. of *lengen,* to delay < OE. < base of *lang,* LONG[1]] **1.** to continue to stay, esp. through reluctance to leave **2.** to continue to live although very close to death **3.** to be unnecessarily slow in doing something; loiter —**lin′ger·er** *n.* —**lin′ger·ing** *adj.* —**lin′ger·ing·ly** *adv.*

lin·ge·rie (lan′zhə rē′) *n.* [Fr.] women's underwear and night clothes of silk, nylon, lace, etc.

lin·go (lin′gō) *n.,* *pl.* -**goes** [Pr. < L. *lingua,* tongue] language; esp., a dialect, jargon, or special vocabulary that one is not familiar with: a humorous or disparaging term

lin·gua fran·ca (lin′gwə fran′kə) *pl.* **lin′gua fran′cas,**

lin·guae fran·cae (lin′gwē fran′sē) [It., lit., Frankish language] **1.** a hybrid language of Italian, Spanish, French, Greek, Arabic, and Turkish elements, spoken in certain Mediterranean ports **2.** any hybrid language used for communication between different peoples, as pidgin English

lin·gual (lin′gwəl) *adj.* [< ML. < L. *lingua,* the tongue] **1.** of the tongue **2.** of language or languages **3.** articulated with the tongue —*n.* *Phonet.* a lingual sound, as *l* or *t* —**lin′gual·ly** *adv.*

lin·gui·form (lin′gwə fôrm′) *adj.* [< L. *lingua,* the tongue + -FORM] shaped like a tongue

lin·guist (lin′gwist) *n.* [< L. *lingua,* the tongue + -IST] **1.** a specialist in linguistics **2.** *same as* POLYGLOT (sense 1)

lin·guis·tic (lin gwis′tik) *adj.* **1.** of language **2.** of linguistics —**lin·guis′ti·cal·ly** *adv.*

linguistic atlas an atlas charting the geographical distribution of linguistic forms and usages

lin·guis·tics (lin gwis′tiks) *n.pl.* [*with sing. v.*] **1.** the science of language, including phonology, morphology, syntax, and semantics: often **general linguistics 2.** the study of the structure, development, etc. of a particular language

lin·i·ment (lin′ə mənt) *n.* [< LL. < L. *linere,* to smear] a medicated liquid to be rubbed on the skin to soothe sore, sprained, or inflamed areas

lin·ing (li′nin) *n.* [see LINE[2]] the material covering an inner surface

link[1] (link) *n.* [< Scand.] **1.** any of the series of rings or loops making up a chain **2.** *a)* a section of something resembling a chain [*a link of sausage*] *b)* an element in a series of circumstances [*a weak link in the evidence*] **3.** anything serving to connect or tie [*a link with the past*] **4.** one division (1/100) of a surveyor's chain, equal to c. 20 cm **5.** *Chem. same as* BOND[1] —*vt., vi.* to join together with a link or links —**link′er** *n.*

link[2] (link) *n.* [prob. < ML. < L. *lychnus,* a light] a torch made of tow and pitch

link·age (lin′kij) *n.* **1.** a linking or being linked **2.** a series or system of links

linking verb a verb that functions chiefly as a connection between a subject and a predicate complement (Ex.: *be, seem, become,* etc.); copula

linkman (-mən) *n.,* *pl.* **men** **1.** formerly, someone who carried a torch for pedestrians in dark streets: also **linkboy 2.** someone who links various parts of T.V. and radio broadcasts

links (links) *n.pl.* [OE. *hlinc,* a slope] *same as* GOLF COURSE

link-up (link′up′) *n.* a joining together of two objects, factions, interests, etc.

Lin·nae·an, Lin·ne·an (li nē′ən) *adj.* [after C. Linnaeus, 18th-c. Swed. botanist] designating or of a system of classifying plants and animals by using a double name, the first word naming the genus, and the second the species

lin·net (lin′it) *n.* [OFr. *linette* < *lin* (< L. *linum*), flax: the bird likes to feed on flaxseed] a small finch found in Europe, Asia, and Africa

li·no (li′nō) *n.,* *pl.* -**nos** linoleum

li·no·cut (li′nō kut′) *n.* [< ff. + CUT] **1.** a design cut into the surface of a linoleum block **2.** a print made from this

li·no·le·um (li nō′lē əm) *n.* [coined < L. *linum,* flax + *oleum,* oil] a hard, washable floor covering made of a mixture of ground cork, ground wood, and oxidized linseed oil with a canvas backing

Lin·o·type (lin′ō tip′) [< *line of type*] a trademark for a typesetting machine that casts an entire line of type in one bar, or slug —*n.* [*often* l-] **1.** a machine of this kind **2.** matter set in this way —*vt., vi.* [l-] -**typed′,** -**typ′ing** to set (matter) with this machine —**lin′o·typ′ist, lin′o·typ′er** *n.*

lin·seed (lin′sēd′) *n.* [OE. *linsæd*] the seed of flax

linseed cake compressed mass of husks of linseed, after the oil has been pressed out, used for feeding cattle

linseed oil a yellowish oil extracted from flaxseed, used in oil paints, etc.

lin·sey-wool·sey (lin′zē wōōl′zē) *n.,* *pl.* -**wool′seys** [ME. < *lin,* flax + *wolle,* wool] a coarse cloth made of linen (or cotton) and wool: also **lin′sey**

lint (lint) *n.* [prob. < *lin,* linen] **1.** scraped and softened linen formerly used as a dressing for wounds **2.** bits of thread, unravellings, or fluff from cloth or yarn —*vi.* to give off lint —**lint′less** *adj.* —**lint′y** *adj.* **lint′i·er, lint′i·est**

lin·tel (lin′t'l) *n.* [OFr., ult. < L. *limen,* threshold] the horizontal crosspiece over a door, window, etc., carrying the weight of the structure above it

lin·ters (lin′tərz) *n.pl.* [U.S.] the short, fuzzy fibres clinging to cotton seeds after ginning, used in making cotton wool, etc.

lin·y (li′nē) *adj.* **lin′i·er, lin′i·est 1.** like a line; thin **2.** marked with lines

li·on (li′ən) *n.,* *pl.* **li′ons, li′on:** see PLURAL, II, D, 1 [OFr. < L. *leo* (gen. *leonis*) < Gr. *leōn*] **1.** a large, powerful mammal of the cat family, found in Africa and SW Asia, with a tawny coat, a tufted tail, and, in the adult male, a shaggy mane **2.** a person of great courage or strength **3.** a celebrity —**li′on·ess** *n.fem.*

lion and unicorn 1. the heraldic beasts supporting the British royal coat of arms **2.** the protagonists in a nursery rhyme

li·on·heart·ed (lī′ən härt′id) *adj.* very brave

li·on·ize (lī′ə nīz′) *vt.* **-ized′, -iz′ing** to treat as a celebrity —**li′on·i·za′tion** *n.* —**li′on·iz′er** *n.*

lion's mouth grave danger

lion's share the biggest and best portion

lip (lip) *n.* [OE. *lippa*] **1.** either of the two fleshy folds forming the edges of the mouth **2.** anything like a lip, as in structure or in being an edge or rim; specif., *a)* the projecting rim of a jug, cup, etc. *b)* the mouthpiece of a wind instrument *c) same as* LABIUM **3.** [Slang] insolent talk —*vt.* **lipped, lip′ping 1.** to touch with the lips; specif., to place the lips in the proper position for playing (a wind instrument) **2.** to utter softly —*adj.* **1.** formed with a lip or the lips; labial **2.** from the lips only; spoken, but insincere —**bite one's lips** to keep back one's anger, annoyance, etc. —**curl one's lip** to display one's scorn —**hang on the lips of** to listen to with close attention —**keep a stiff upper lip** [Colloq.] to avoid becoming frightened or discouraged —**lip′less** *adj.*

li·pase (lī′pās, lip′ās) *n.* [< ff. + -ASE] an enzyme that aids in digestion by hydrolizing fats into fatty acids and glycerol

lip·o- [< Gr. *lipos*, fat] *a combining form meaning* of or like fat, fatty: also, before a vowel, **lip-**

li·pog·ra·phy (li pog′rə fē) *n.* [< Gr. *leipein*, omit + -GRAPHY] the accidental omission of words or letters in writing

li·poid (lip′oid, lī′poid) *adj.* [LIP(O)- + -OID] *Biochem., Chem.* resembling fat: also **li·poi′dal**

lipped (lipt) *adj.* having a lip or lips: often in compounds [tight-*lipped*]

Lip·pi·zan·er (lip′ət sän′ər) *n.* [after *Lippiza*, the imperial Austrian stud farm, near Trieste] any of a breed of grey to white horses used esp. in dressage exhibitions: also sp. **Lip′-iz·zan′er**

lip-read (lip′rēd′) *vt., vi.* **-read′** (-red′), **-read′ing** to recognize (a speaker's words) by lip reading —**lip reader**

lip reading the act or skill of recognizing a speaker's words by watching the movement of his lips: it is taught esp. to the deaf

lip service insincere expression of respect, loyalty, support, etc.

lip·stick (-stik′) *n.* a small stick of cosmetic paste, set in a case, for colouring the lips

liq. 1. liquid **2.** liquor

liq·ue·fa·cient (lik′wə fā′shənt) *n.* [< L.: see LIQUEFY] something that causes liquefaction

liq·ue·fac·tion (-fak′shən) *n.* a liquefying or being liquefied

liq·ue·fy (lik′wə fī′) *vt., vi.* **-fied′, -fy′ing** [< Fr. < L. < *liquere*, to be liquid + *facere*, to make] to change into a liquid —**liq′ue·fi′a·ble** *adj.* —**liq′ue·fi′er** *n.*

li·ques·cent (li kwes′'nt) *adj.* [< L. prp. of *liquescere* < *liquere*, to be liquid] becoming liquid; melting —**li·ques′-cence** *n.*

li·queur (li kyŏŏ′ər) *n.* [Fr.] any of certain sweet, syrupy alcoholic liquors, variously flavoured

liq·uid (lik′wid) *adj.* [< OFr. < L. *liquidus* < *liquere*, to be liquid] **1.** readily flowing; fluid; specif., that can move freely, unlike a solid, but does not expand indefinitely like a gas **2.** clear; limpid [*liquid* eyes] **3.** flowing smoothly and gracefully [*liquid* verse] **4.** readily convertible into cash [*liquid* assets] **5.** without friction and like a vowel, as the consonants *l* and *r* —*n.* a liquid substance —**liq·uid′i·ty, liq′uid·ness** *n.* —**liq′uid·ly** *adv.*

liquid air air brought to a liquid state by being subjected to great pressure and then cooled by its own expansion

liq·ui·date (lik′wə dāt′) *vt.* **-dat′ed, -dat′ing** [< ML. pp. of *liquidare*, to make clear < L. *liquidus*, liquid] **1.** to settle the amount of (indebtedness, damages, etc.) **2.** to settle the accounts of (a bankrupt business, etc.) by apportioning assets and debts **3.** to pay or settle (a debt) **4.** to convert (holdings or assets) into cash **5.** to dispose of or get rid of, as by killing —*vi.* to liquidate debts, accounts, etc. —**liq′-ui·da′tor** *n.*

liq·ui·da·tion (lik′wə dā′shən) *n.* a liquidating or being liquidated —**go into liquidation** to close one's business by collecting assets and settling all debts

liq·uid·ize (lik′wə dīz′) *vt.* **-ized′, -iz′ing** to cause to have a liquid quality

liq·ui·diz·er (lik′wə dīz′ər) *n.* a kitchen appliance used to make purées, etc.

liquid measure 1. the measurement of liquids **2.** a system of measuring liquids; esp., the system in which 100 millilitres = 1 litre or 2 pints = 1 quart, etc.: see TABLE OF WEIGHTS AND MEASURES in Supplement

liquid oxygen a light-bluish liquid boiling at −183°C, produced by fractionation of liquid air

liquid paraffin refined paraffin, used medicinally as a lubricant

liq·uor (lik′ər) *n.* [< OFr. *licor* < L. *liquor*] **1.** any liquid or juice **2.** an alcoholic drink, esp. one made by distillation, as whisky or rum

liq·uo·rice (lik′ər ish, -is; lik′rish) *n.* [< OFr. < LL. *liquiritia*, ult. < Gr. *glykys*, sweet + *rhiza*, root] **1.** a European plant of the legume family **2.** its dried root or the black flavouring extract made from this **3.** a sweet flavoured with, or as with, this extract

li·ra (lir′ə) *n., pl.* **-re** (-ā), for 2 **-ras** [It. < L. *libra*, a balance] the monetary unit of **1.** Italy **2.** Turkey See MONETARY UNITS, table

lisle (līl) *n.* [< *Lisle*, earlier sp. of *Lille*, city in France] **1.** a fine, hard, extra-strong cotton thread: in full **lisle thread 2.** a fabric, or stockings, gloves, etc., knitted or woven of lisle —*adj.* made of lisle

lisp (lisp) *vi.* [< OE. < *wlisp*, a lisping] **1.** to substitute the sounds (th) and (*th*) for the sounds of *s* and *z* **2.** to speak imperfectly or like a child —*vt.* to utter with a lisp —*n.* **1.** the act or speech defect of lisping **2.** the sound of lisping —**lisp′er** *n.* —**lisp′ing·ly** *adv.*

lis·some, lis·som (lis′əm) *adj.* [altered < *lithesome*] moving gracefully or with ease and lightness; lithe, limber, agile, etc. —**lis′some·ly, lis′som·ly** *adv.* —**lis′some·ness, lis′-som·ness** *n.*

list¹ (list) *n.* [merging of OE. *liste* & Anglo-Fr. *liste* < OFr. < Gmc.] **1.** formerly, a narrow strip or border; specif., *a)* a strip of cloth *b)* a stripe of colour *c)* a boundary **2.** the selvage of cloth **3.** a series of names, words, numbers, etc. set forth in order; catalogue, roll, etc. **4.** *same as* LIST PRICE See also LISTS —*vt.* **1.** formerly, to edge with, or arrange in, stripes or bands **2.** *a)* to set forth (a series of names, items, etc.) in order *b)* to enter in a list, directory, catalogue, etc. —*vi.* to be listed for sale, as in a catalogue (at the price specified) —**list′er** *n.* —**list′ing** *n.*

list² (list) *vt.* [OE. *lystan* < base of *lust*, desire] [Archaic] to be pleasing to; suit —*vi.* [Archaic] to wish; like; choose

list³ (list) *vt., vi.* [prob. specialized use of prec.] to tilt to one side, as a ship —*n.* a tilting or inclining to one side

list⁴ (list) *vt., vi.* [OE. *hlystan* < base of *hlyst*, hearing] [Archaic] to listen (to)

listed building a building listed as being of historical or architectural importance, thus preserving it from demolition, etc.

lis·ten (lis′'n) *vi.* [OE. *hlysnan*: for base see LIST⁴] **1.** to make a conscious effort to hear; attend closely, so as to hear **2.** to give heed; take advice —*n.* the act of listening —**listen in 1.** to listen to others' conversation; esp., to eavesdrop **2.** to listen to a broadcast —**lis′ten·er** *n.*

listening post *Mil.* a forward position set up to obtain early warning of enemy movement

list·er (lis′tər) *n.* [< LIST¹ + -ER] a plough with a double mouldboard which heaps the earth on both sides of the furrow

list·less (list′lis) *adj.* [LIST² + -LESS] having or showing no interest in what is going on, as because of illness, weariness, dejection, etc.; spiritless; languid —**list′less·ly** *adv.* —**list′-less·ness** *n.*

list price retail price as given in a list or catalogue, discounted in sales to dealers, etc.

lists (lists) *n.pl.* [ME. *listes*, specialized use of *liste*, strip, border] **1.** *a)* the high fence enclosing an area where knights held tournaments *b)* this area itself or the tournament held there **2.** any place or realm of combat, conflict, etc. —**enter the lists** to enter a contest or struggle

lit (lit) *alt. pt. & pp. of* LIGHT¹

lit. 1. literal **2.** literally **3.** literary **4.** literature

lit·a·ny (lit′ən ē) *n., pl.* **-nies** [< OFr. < LL. < Gr. *litaneia* < *litē*, a request] **1.** a form of prayer in which the clergy and the congregation take part alternately, with recitation of supplications and fixed responses **2.** any dreary recital

li·tchi (lī′chē′) *n.* [Chin. *li-chih*] **1.** a Chinese evergreen tree **2.** the dried or preserved fruit of this tree (**litchi nut**), with a single seed, a sweet, edible pulp, and a rough, papery shell

-lite (līt) [Fr., for *-lithe:* see -LITH] *a combining form meaning* stone: used in the names of minerals, rocks, and fossils [*chrysolite*]

li·ter (lēt′ər) *n.* *U.S.* sp. of LITRE

lit·er·a·cy (lit′ər ə sē) *n.* the state or quality of being literate; ability to read and write

lit·er·al (lit′ər əl) *adj.* [< MFr. < LL. *litteralis* < L. *littera*, a letter] **1.** following the exact words of the original [a *literal* translation] **2.** based on the actual words in their ordinary meaning; in a basic or strict sense [the *literal* meaning of a passage] **3.** habitually interpreting statements or words according to their actual denotation; matter-of-fact [a *literal* mind] **4.** real; not going beyond the actual facts [the *literal* truth] —**lit′er·al·i·ty** (-ə ral′ə tē) *n., pl.* **-ties** —**lit′er·al·ly** *adv.* —**lit′er·al·ness** *n.*

lit·er·al·ism (-iz′m) *n.* **1.** the tendency to take words, statements, etc. in their literal sense **2.** thoroughgoing realism in art —**lit′er·al·ist** *n.* —**lit′er·al·is′tic** *adj.*

lit·er·al·ize (-ə līz′) *vt.* **-ized′, -iz′ing** to interpret literally —**lit′er·al·i·za′tion** *n.*

lit·er·ar·y (lit′ə rə rē) *adj.* **1.** *a)* of or dealing with literature *b)* of or having to do with books [*literary* agents] **2.** of the relatively formal language of literature **3.** *a)* versed in literature *b)* making literature a profession —**lit′-er·ar·i·ness** *n.*

literary executor a person to whom the copyright of published and unpublished works is assigned in a will

lit·er·ate (lit′ər it) *adj.* [< L. < *littera*, a letter] **1.** able to read and write **2.** having or showing extensive learning or culture —*n.* a literate person —**lit′er·ate·ly** *adv.*

lit·e·ra·ti (lit′ə rät′ē) *n.pl.* [It. < L.] men of letters; scholarly or learned people

‡**lit·e·ra·tim** (-rät′im, -rät′-) *adv.* [ML. < L. *littera*, a letter] letter for letter; literally

lit·er·a·ture (lit′ər ə chər, lit′rə choor′) *n.* [< OFr. < L. *litteratura* < *littera*, a letter] **1.** the profession of an author **2.** *a)* all the writings of a particular time, country, etc., esp. those of an imaginative or critical character valued for excellence of form and expression [French *literature*] *b)* all the writings on a particular subject **3.** [Colloq.] printed matter of any kind

-lith (lith) [Fr. *-lithe* < Gr. *lithos*, stone] a combining form meaning stone [monolith]

Lith. **1.** Lithuania **2.** Lithuanian

lith., litho., lithog. **1.** lithograph **2.** lithography

lith·arge (lith′ärj, li thärj′) *n.* [< OFr. < L. < Gr. *lithargyros* < *lithos*, a stone + *argyros*, silver] an oxide of lead, PbO, used in storage batteries, paints, etc.

lithe (lῑth) *adj.* **lith′er, lith′est** [OE. *lithe*, soft, mild] bending easily; supple; limber: also **lithe′some** (-səm) —**lithe′ly** *adv.* —**lithe′ness** *n.*

lith·i·a (lith′ē ə) *n.* [ModL. < Gr. *lithos*, stone] lithium oxide, Li₂O, a white, crystalline compound

-lith·ic (lith′ik) a combining form meaning of a (specified) stage in the use of stone [neolithic]

lith·i·um (lith′ē əm) *n.* [ModL. < LITHIA] a soft, silver-white, metallic chemical element, the lightest known metal: symbol, Li; at. wt., 6.939; at. no., 3

lith·o (lith′ō) *n., pl.* **-os;** *vt., vi.* **-oed, -o·ing** clipped form of LITHOGRAPH

lith·o- [< Gr. *lithos*, a stone] a combining form meaning stone, rock: also, before a vowel, **lith-**

lith·o·graph (lith′ə graf′) *n.* a print made by lithography —*vi.,* *vt.* to make (prints or copies) by lithography —**li·thog·ra·pher** (li thog′rə fər) *n.*

li·thog·ra·phy (li thog′rə fē) *n.* [LITHO-+ -GRAPHY] the art or process of printing from a flat stone or metal plate: the design is put on the surface with a greasy material, and then water and printing ink are successively applied; the greasy parts, which repel water, absorb the ink, but the wet parts do not —**lith·o·graph·ic** (lith′ə graf′ik) *adj.* —**lith′o·graph′-i·cal·ly** *adv.*

li·thol·o·gy (li thol′ə jē) *n.* [< Gr. *lithos*, stone + -LOGY] the scientific study of the structure and composition of rocks, usually with the unaided eye

lith·o·sphere (lith′ə sfir′) *n.* [LITHO-+ SPHERE] the solid, rocky part of the earth; earth's crust

li·thot·o·my (li thot′ə mē) *n., pl.* **-mies** [< LL. < Gr.: LITHO- & -TOMY] the surgical removal of a stone from the bladder

lit·i·ga·ble (lit′i gə b'l) *adj.* that gives cause for litigation, or a lawsuit; actionable

lit·i·gant (lit′ə gənt) *n.* a party to a lawsuit

lit·i·gate (-gāt′) *vt.* **-gat′ed, -gat′ing** [< L. pp. of *litigare* < *lis* (gen. *litis*), dispute + *agere*, to do] to contest in a lawsuit —*vi.* to carry on a lawsuit —**lit′i·ga′tor** *n.*

lit·i·ga·tion (lit′ə gā′shən) *n.* **1.** the carrying on of a lawsuit **2.** a lawsuit

li·ti·gious (li tij′əs) *adj.* **1.** *a)* given to carrying on litigations *b)* quarrelsome **2.** disputable at law **3.** of lawsuits —**li·ti′-gious·ly** *adv.* —**li·ti′gious·ness** *n.*

lit·mus (lit′məs) *n.* [ON. *litmose*, lichen used in dyeing < *litr*, colour + *mosi*, moss] a purple colouring matter obtained from various lichens: it turns blue in bases and red in acids

litmus paper absorbent paper treated with litmus and used as an acid-base indicator

li·tre (lēt′ər) *n.* [Fr. < ML < Gr. *litra*, a pound] a unit of capacity in the metric system, now defined as equal to 1000 cubic centimetres

Litt.D. [L. *Lit(t)erarum Doctor*] Doctor of Letters; Doctor of Literature

lit·ter (lit′ər) *n.* [< OFr. *litiere* < ML. < *lectus*, a couch] **1.** a framework having long horizontal shafts near the bottom and enclosing a couch on which a person can be carried **2.** a stretcher for carrying the sick or wounded **3.** straw, hay, etc. used as bedding for animals, as a covering for plants, etc. **4.** the young borne at one time by a dog, cat, etc. **5.** things lying about in disorder; esp., bits of

scattered rubbish **6.** untidiness; disorder —*vt.* **1.** to bring forth (a number of young) at one time: said of certain animals **2.** to make messy with things scattered about **3.** to scatter about carelessly —*vi.* to bear a litter of young

lit·té·ra·teur (lit′ər ə tur′) *n.* [Fr.] a literary man; man of letters

litter bin a receptacle for waste paper, etc.

lit·ter·lout (lit′ər lout) *n.* a person who litters a public place with rubbish, bits of paper, etc.

lit·tle (lit′'l) *adj.* **less** or **less′er, least** [OE. *lytel*] **1.** small in size; not big, large, or great **2.** small in amount, number, or degree **3.** short in duration or distance; brief **4.** small in importance or power [the rights of the *little* man] **5.** small in force, intensity, etc.; weak **6.** trivial; trifling **7.** lacking in breadth of view; narrow-minded [a *little* mind] **8.** young: said of children or animals *Little* is sometimes used to express endearment [bless your *little* heart] —*adv.* **less, least 1.** in a small degree; only slightly; not much **2.** not in the least [he *little* suspects the plot] —*n.* **1.** *a)* a small amount, degree, etc. *b)* not much [*little* was done] **2.** a short time or distance —**little by little** by slow degrees or small amounts; gradually —**make little of** to treat as unimportant —**not a little** very much; very —**lit′tle·ness** *n.*

Little Bear the constellation URSA MINOR

Little League [U.S.] a league of baseball teams for children —**Little Leaguer**

little people the fairies

little slam *Bridge* the winning of all but one trick

little theatre [Chiefly U.S.] **1.** a small theatre, as of a college, art group, etc., usually noncommercial and amateur **2.** drama produced by such theatres

little woman [Colloq.] one's wife

lit·to·ral (lit′ər əl) *adj.* [L. *litoralis* < *litus* (gen. *litoris*), seashore] of, on, or along the shore —*n.* the region along the shore

li·tur·gi·cal (li tur′jə k'l) *adj.* **1.** of or constituting a liturgy **2.** used in or using a liturgy —**li·tur′gi·cal·ly** *adv.*

lit·ur·gy (lit′ər jē) *n., pl.* **-gies** [< Fr. < ML. < Gr. *leitourgia*, public service, ult. < *leōs*, people + *ergon*, work] **1.** prescribed forms or ritual for public worship in any of various religions or churches **2.** the Eucharistic service

liv·a·ble (liv′ə b'l) *adj.* **1.** fit or pleasant to live in, as a house **2.** that can be lived through; endurable **3.** agreeable to live with Also sp. **liveable** —**liv′a·bil′i·ty, liv′a·ble·ness** *n.*

live¹ (liv) *vi.* **lived, liv′ing** [OE. *libban*] **1.** to be alive; have life **2.** *a)* to remain alive *b)* to endure **3.** *a)* to pass one's life in a specified manner [to *live* happily] *b)* to conduct one's life [to *live* by a strict moral code] **4.** to enjoy a full and varied life **5.** *a)* to maintain life [to *live* on a pension] *b)* to be dependent for a living (with *off*) **6.** to feed; subsist [to *live* on fruits and nuts] **7.** to make one's dwelling; reside —*vt.* **1.** to carry out in one's life [to *live* one's faith] **2.** to spend; pass [to *live* a useful life] —**live and let live** to be tolerant —**live down** to live in such a way as to wipe out the shame of (some fault, misdeed, etc.) —**live in** to sleep at the place where one is in domestic service —**live it up** [Colloq.] to indulge in pleasures, extravagances, etc. that one usually forgoes —**live on air** to appear to take little or no food —**live together 1.** to share a house, etc. **2.** to have a permanent sexual relationship outside marriage: also **live in sin** —**live up to** to act in accordance with (ideals, promises, etc.) —**live well** to live in luxury —**live with** to tolerate; endure

live² (līv) *adj.* [< ALIVE] **1.** having life; not dead **2.** of the living state or living beings **3.** having positive qualities, as of warmth, vigour, vitality, brilliance, etc. [a *live* organization] **4.** of immediate or present interest [a *live* issue] **5.** *a)* still burning or glowing [a *live* spark] *b)* not extinct [a *live* volcano] **6.** unexploded [a *live* shell] **7.** unused; unexpended [*live* steam] **8.** carrying electrical current [a *live* wire] **9.** *a)* involving a performance in person, not one on film, tape, etc.; transmitted during the actual performance *b)* recorded at a public performance **10.** *Mech.* imparting motion or power

live birth the birth of a live baby as opposed to one that is stillborn

-lived (līvd) [see LIFE & -ED] a combining form meaning having (a specified kind or duration of) life [short-lived]

live·li·hood (līv′lē hood′) *n.* [OE. *liflad* < *lif*, life + *-lad*, course] means of supporting life; subsistence

live·long (liv′lon′) *adj.* [ME. *lefe longe*, lit., lief long (cf. LIEF), in which *lief* is merely intens.] long or tediously long in passing; whole; entire [the *livelong* day]

live·ly (līv′lē) *adj.* **-li·er, -li·est** [OE. *liflic*] **1.** full of life; active; vigorous **2.** full of spirit; exciting; animated [a *lively* debate] **3.** gay; cheerful **4.** moving quickly and lightly, as a dance **5.** vivid; keen [*lively* colours] **6.** bounding back with great resilience [a *lively* ball] —*adv.* in a lively manner —**live′li·ness** *n.*

liv·en (lī′vən) *vt., vi.* to make or become lively or gay; cheer (*up*) —**liv′en·er** *n.*

live oak 1. an evergreen oak of the U.S. **2.** the hard wood of these trees

liv·er[1] (liv'ər) *n.* [OE. *lifer*] **1.** the largest glandular organ in vertebrate animals: it secretes bile and has an important function in metabolism **2.** the liver of cattle, fowl, etc. used as food

liv·er[2] (liv'ər) *n.* a person who lives (in a specified way or place) [a clean *liver*]

liv·er·ied (liv'ər ēd, liv'rēd) *adj.* wearing a livery

liv·er·ish (liv'ər ish) *adj.* [Colloq.] **1.** bilious **2.** peevish; cross —**liv'er·ish·ness** *n.*

liv·er·sausage (-sô'sij) *n.* a sausage containing minced liver

liver spot a brownish spot on the skin, formerly attributed to faulty functioning of the liver

liv·er·wort (liv'ər wurt') *n.* any of a class of plants, often forming dense, green mosslike mats on rocks, soil, etc. in moist places

LIVER
(A, liver; B, stomach; C, small intestine; D, large intestine)

liv·er·y (liv'ər ē, liv'rē) *n.*, *pl.* -er·ies [< OFr. *livree*, gift of clothes to a servant < *livrer*, to deliver < L. *liberare*, to free] **1.** an identifying uniform such as is worn by servants or those in some particular group, trade, etc. **2.** the people wearing such uniforms **3.** characteristic dress or appearance **4.** *a)* the keeping and feeding of horses for a fixed charge *b)* the keeping of horses, vehicles, or both, for hire *c)* a stable providing these services: also **livery stable**

liv·er·y·man (-mən) *n.*, *pl.* -men a person who owns or works in a livery stable

lives (līvz) *n.* *pl. of* LIFE

live·stock (līv'stok') *n.* domestic animals kept for use on a farm or raised for sale and profit

live wire 1. a wire carrying an electric current **2.** [Colloq.] an energetic and enterprising person

liv·id (liv'id) *adj.* [< Fr. < L. *lividus*] **1.** discoloured by a bruise; black-and-blue **2.** greyish-blue; lead-coloured [*livid* with rage]: sometimes taken to mean pale, white, or red **3.** [Colloq.] enraged; furious —**li·vid·i·ty** (li vid'ə tē), **liv'id·ness** *n.*

liv·ing (liv'iŋ) *adj.* **1.** alive; having life **2.** in active operation or use [a *living* institution] **3.** of persons alive [within *living* memory] **4.** in its natural state or place, or having its natural force, etc. [hewn from the *living* rock] **5.** still spoken and undergoing changes [a *living* language] **6.** true to reality; lifelike [the *living* image] **7.** of life or the sustaining of life [*living* conditions] **8.** suited for social and recreational activities in a house [the *living* area] **9.** presented in person before a live audience [*living* theatre] **10.** very [the *living* daylights] —*n.* **1.** the state of being alive **2.** the means of sustaining life; livelihood **3.** manner of existence [the standard of *living*] **4.** a church benefice —**the living** those that are still alive

living death a life of unrelieved misery

living room a room in a home, with sofas, chairs, etc., used for socializing, entertaining, etc.

living wage a wage sufficient to maintain a person and his family in reasonable comfort

liz·ard (liz'ərd) *n.* [< OFr. *lesard* < L. *lacerta*] **1.** any of a group of reptiles with a long slender body and tail, a scaly skin, and four legs (sometimes vestigial), as the gecko, slow worm, chameleon, and iguana **2.** loosely, any of various similar animals, as alligators or salamanders

L.J. Lord Justice

'll *contraction of* will or shall [I'll go]

LL., L.L. Late Latin

ll., ll lines

L.L. Lord Lieutenant

lla·ma (lä'ma) *n.*, *pl.* -mas, -ma: see PLURAL, II, D, 1 [Sp. < Quechua] a S. American animal related to the camel but smaller and without humps: it is used as a beast of burden and for its wool, flesh, and milk

lla·no (lä'nō; *Sp.* lyä'nō) *n.*, *pl.* -nos (-nōz; *Sp.* -nôs) [Sp. < L. *planus*, plain] a grassy plain in the southwest U.S. and in Spanish America

LL.B. [L. *Legum Baccalaureus*] Bachelor of Laws

LL.D. [L. *Legum Doctor*] Doctor of Laws

LL.M. [L. *Legum Magister*] Master of Laws

Lloyd's (loidz) *n.* [< *Lloyd's* coffeehouse, meeting place of the original associates] an association formed in the early 18th cent. by underwriters dealing with marine insurance and shipping news: it now handles many kinds of insurance and publishes an annual list (**Lloyd's Register**) of the seagoing vessels of all countries

lm *Physics* the symbol for lumen

lo (lō) *interj.* [OE. *la*] look! see!

loach (lōch) *n.* [< OFr. *loche*] a small freshwater fish with barbels around the mouth, found in Europe & Asia

load (lōd) *n.* [OE. *lad*, a course, way] **1.** something carried or to be carried at one time; burden **2.** the amount that can be carried: a measure of weight or quantity varying with the type of conveyance [a *cartload* of coal] **3.** something

carried with difficulty; specif., *a)* a heavy burden or weight *b)* a great mental burden [a *load* off one's mind] **4.** the weight that a structure bears or the stresses that are put upon it **5.** a single charge, as of powder and bullets, for a firearm **6.** [*often pl.*] [Colloq.] a great amount or number [*loads* of friends] **7.** *Elec.* the amount of power delivered by a generator, motor, etc. or carried by a circuit **8.** *Mech.* the external resistance offered to an engine by the machine that it is operating —*vt.* **1.** to put something to be carried into or upon; fill with a load [to *load* a wagon] **2.** to put into or upon a carrier [to *load* coal] **3.** to burden; oppress **4.** to supply in abundance [to *load* one with honours, *loaded* with money] **5.** to put ammunition into (a gun or firearm), film into (a camera), etc. **6.** to weight (dice) unevenly for fraudulent use **7.** to add extra costs, a filler, etc. to **8.** to phrase (a question, etc.) so as to elicit a desired response —*vi.* **1.** to put in or receive a charge, cartridge, etc. **2.** to put on or take on passengers, goods, etc. —**get a load of** [Slang] **1.** to listen to or hear **2.** to look at or see —**have a load on** [Chiefly U.S. Slang] to be intoxicated —**load'er** *n.* —**load'ing** *n.*

load·ed (-id) *adj.* [Slang] **1.** intoxicated **2.** rich; well-endowed

load·star (lōd'stär') *n.* *same as* LODESTAR

load·stone (lōd'stōn') *n.* *same as* LODESTONE

loaf[1] (lōf) *n.*, *pl.* **loaves** (lōvz) [OE. *hlaf*] **1.** a portion of bread baked in one piece, commonly of oblong shape **2.** any mass of food shaped somewhat like a loaf of bread and baked [a meat *loaf*]

loaf[2] (lōf) *vi.* [prob. < ff.] to loiter or lounge about; idle, dawdle, etc. —*vt.* to spend (time) idly (often with *away*)

loaf·er (-ər) *n.* [prob. < G. *Landläufer*, a vagabond] a person who loafs

loam (lōm) *n.* [OE. *lam*] **1.** a rich soil of clay, sand, and organic matter **2.** popularly, any rich, dark soil —*vt.* to fill or top with loam —**loam'y** *adj.*

loan (lōn) *n.* [< ON. *lān*] **1.** the act of lending **2.** something lent; esp., a sum of money lent, often at interest —*vt.*, *vi.* to lend —**on loan** lent for temporary use or service

loan·er (-ər) *n.* one who loans

loan shark [U.S. Colloq.] a person who lends money at exorbitant or illegal rates of interest

loan·word (-wurd') *n.* [after G. *Lehnwort*] a word of one language taken into another and naturalized (Ex.: KINDERGARTEN < G.)

loath (lōth) *adj.* [OE. *lath*, hostile] unwilling; reluctant [to be *loath* to depart] —**nothing loath** willing(ly)

loathe (lōth) *vt.* **loathed, loath'ing** [OE. *lathian*, to be hateful] to feel intense dislike or disgust for; abhor; detest —**loath'er** *n.*

loath·ing (lōth'iŋ) *n.* intense dislike, disgust, or hatred; abhorrence

loath·ly[1] (lōth'lē) *adv.* [Rare] unwillingly

loath·ly[2] (lōth'lē) *adj.* rare var. *of* LOATHSOME

loath·some (lōth'sam, lōth'-) *adj.* causing loathing; disgusting —**loath'some·ly** *adv.* —**loath'some·ness** *n.*

loaves (lōvz) *n.* *pl. of* LOAF[1]

lob (lob) *n.* [ME. *lobbe*, lit., heavy, thick] *Tennis* a stroke in which the ball is sent high into the air, dropping into the back of the opponent's court —*vt.* **lobbed, lob'bing** to send (a ball) in a lob —*vi.* **1.** to move heavily and clumsily **2.** to lob a ball —**lob'ber** *n.*

lo·bar (lō'bər) *adj.* of a lobe or lobes

lo·bate (-bāt) *adj.* having or formed into a lobe or lobes —**lo'bate·ly** *adv.*

lo·ba·tion (lō bā'shən) *n.* **1.** the condition of having lobes **2.** the process of forming lobes **3.** a lobe

lob·by (lob'ē) *n.*, *pl.* -bies [LL. *lobia*: see LODGE] **1.** a hall or large anteroom, as a waiting room of a hotel, theatre, etc. **2.** a group of people who try to influence M.P.s, officials, etc. in the passage of legislation or the formation of policy on behalf of a particular interest **3.** the corridor in the House of Commons to which members retire to vote on a division: also called **division lobby** —*vi.* -bied, -by·ing to frequent the lobby, as of the House of Commons, to influence members or collect parliamentary news —*vt.* **1.** to get or try to get legislators to vote for or against (a measure) by lobbying **2.** to bring about (the passage of a bill, etc.) by lobbying

lobby correspondent a reporter who frequents the lobby (n. 3) to gain parliamentary news

lob·by·ist (-ist) *n.* [Chiefly U.S.] a person, acting for a special interest group, who tries to influence the voting on legislation —**lob'by·ism** *n.*

lobe (lōb) *n.* [Fr. < LL. < Gr. *lobos*] a rounded projecting part; specif., *a)* the fleshy lower end of the human ear *b)* any of the main divisions of an organ [a *lobe* of the brain, lung, or liver] *c)* any of the rounded divisions of the leaves of certain trees —**lobed** *adj.*

lo·bec·to·my (lō bek'tə mē) *n.* *pl.* -mies [LOBE + -ECTOMY] the surgical removal of a lobe of an organ or gland, as the lung or brain

lo·be·li·a (lō bēl′yə, -bē′lē ə) *n.* [ModL., after Matthias de *L'Obel* (1538-1616), Fl. botanist] any of a genus of plants with white, blue, or red flowers of very irregular shape

lob·lol·ly (lob′lol′ē) *n., pl.* **-lies** [prob. < dial. *lob*, to boil + dial. *lolly*, broth] **1.** a common pine of the SE U.S. **2.** the wood of this tree: also **loblolly pine**

lo·bot·o·my (lō bot′ə mē) *n., pl.* **-mies** [< LOBE + -TOMY] a surgical operation in which a lobe of the brain is cut into or across

lob·scouse (lob′skous′) *n.* [*lob* (as in LOBLOLLY) + *scouse* < ?] a sailor's stew of meat, vegetables, and hardtack

lob·ster (lob′stər) *n., pl.* **-sters, -ster:** see PLURAL, II, D, 1 [OE. *lopustre* < *loppe*, spider (from external resemblance) + -*estre*: see -STER] **1.** a large, edible sea crustacean with compound eyes, long antennae, and five pairs of legs, the first pair of which are modified into large pincers **2.** any similar crustacean, as the spiny lobster **3.** the flesh of these animals used as food

lobster pot a wickerwork trap for catching lobsters

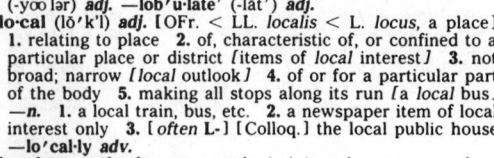

LOBSTER
(to 60 cm long)

lob·ule (lob′yōōl) *n.* **1.** a small lobe **2.** a subdivision of a lobe —**lob′u·lar** (-yoo lər) *adj.* —**lob′u·late′** (-lāt′) *adj.*

lo·cal (lō′k'l) *adj.* [OFr. < LL. *localis* < L. *locus*, a place] **1.** relating to place **2.** of, characteristic of, or confined to a particular place or district [*items of local interest*] **3.** not broad; narrow [*local outlook*] **4.** of or for a particular part of the body **5.** making all stops along its run [*a local bus*] —*n.* **1.** a local train, bus, etc. **2.** a newspaper item of local interest only **3.** [*often* L-] [Colloq.] the local public house —**lo′cal·ly** *adv.*

local anaesthetic an anaesthetic injected so as to produce insensibility in one part of the body only

local authority the governing body of a county, district, or other locality

local call a telephone call to a place within a certain radius, charged at a low rate

local colour behaviour, speech, etc. characteristic of a certain region or time, introduced into a novel, play, etc. to supply realism

lo·cale (lō kal′) *n.* [Fr. *local*] a place or locality, esp. with reference to events, etc. connected with it, often as a setting for a story, etc.

lo·cal·ism (lō′kə liz′m) *n.* **1.** a local custom **2.** a word, meaning, expression, pronunciation, etc. peculiar to one locality **3.** provincialism

lo·cal·i·ty (lō kal′ə tē) *n., pl.* **-ties** **1.** position with regard to surrounding objects, landmarks, etc. **2.** a place; district

lo·cal·ize (lō′kə līz′) *vt.* **-ized′, -iz′ing** to make local; limit, confine, or trace to a particular place, area, or locality —**lo′·cal·iz′a·ble** *adj.* —**lo′cal·i·za′tion** *n.*

local option the right to decide by a vote of the residents whether something, esp. the sale of alcoholic liquor, shall be permitted in their locality

lo·cate (lō kāt′) *vt.* **-cat′ed, -cat′ing** [< L. pp. of *locare* < *locus*, a place] **1.** to designate the site of (a mining claim, etc.) **2.** to establish in a certain place [*the offices were located* in the Town Hall] **3.** to discover the position of after a search [*to locate* a lost object] **4.** to show the position of [*to locate* Guam on a map] **5.** to assign to a particular place, etc. —**lo·cat′er, lo·ca′tor** *n.*

lo·ca·tion (lō kā′shən) *n.* **1.** a locating or being located **2.** position; place; situation **3.** an area marked off for a specific purpose **4.** *Cinema* an outdoor set or setting, away from the studio, where scenes are photographed: chiefly in **on location** —**lo·ca′tion·al** *adj.*

loc·a·tive (lok′ə tiv) *adj.* [< L. pp. of *locare*: see LOCATE] *Linguis.* expressing place at which or in which —*n.* **1.** the locative case (in Latin, Greek, etc.) **2.** a word in this case

loc. cit. [L. *loco citato*] in the place cited

loch (lokh, lok) *n.* [< Gael. & OIr.] [Scot.] **1.** a lake **2.** an arm of the sea, esp. when narrow and nearly surrounded by land

lo·ci (lō′sī) *n.* *pl. of* LOCUS

lock[1] (lok) *n.* [OE. *loc*, a bolt, enclosure] **1.** a mechanical device for fastening a door, strongbox, etc. by means of a key or combination **2.** anything that fastens something else and prevents it from operating **3.** a locking together; jam **4.** an enclosed part of a canal, waterway, etc. equipped with gates so that the level of the water can be changed to raise or lower boats from one level to another **5.** the mechanism of a firearm used to explode the ammunition charge **6.** the extent to which a vehicle's front wheels will turn [on full *lock* the car was able to make a U-turn] **7.** *same as* AIR LOCK **8.** *Rugby* a player in the second row of the scrum: also **lock forward 9.** *Wrestling* a hold in which a part of the opponent's body is firmly gripped —*vt.* **1.** to fasten (a door, case, etc.) by means of a lock **2.** to shut (*up, in, out*); confine [*locked* in jail] **3.** to fit closely; link [we

locked arms] **4.** to embrace tightly **5.** to jam together so as to make immovable [*locked* gears] **6.** to put in a fixed position **7.** to move (a ship) through a lock —*vi.* **1.** to become locked **2.** to intertwine or interlock —**lock out** to keep (workers) from a place of employment in seeking to force terms upon them —**lock, stock, and barrel** [Colloq.] completely

lock[2] (lok) *n.* [OE. *loc*] **1.** a curl, tress, or ringlet of hair **2.** [*pl.*] [Poet.] the hair of the head **3.** a tuft of wool, cotton, etc.

lock·er (lok′ər) *n.* **1.** a person or thing that locks **2.** a chest, cupboard, drawer, etc. which can be locked, esp. one for individual use

locker room a room equipped with lockers

lock·et (lok′it) *n.* [< OFr. *locquet*, dim. of *loc*, a latch < Frank.] a small, hinged ornamental case of gold, silver, etc., for holding a picture, lock of hair, etc.: it is usually worn on a necklace

lock·jaw (lok′jô′) *n.* [short for earlier *locked jaw*] *same as* TETANUS

lock keeper one in charge of a canal lock

lock·out (-out′) *n.* the locking out of workers by an employer

lock·smith (-smith′) *n.* a person whose work is making or repairing locks and keys

lock step a way of marching in very close file

lock·up (-up′) *n.* **1.** a jail **2.** a shop or private garage that is separate from living accommodation

lo·co[1] (lō′kō) *n.* [Colloq.] a locomotive

lo·co[2] (lō′kō) *n.* [MexSp. < Sp., mad < L. *ulucus*, owl] [U.S.] *same as:* **1.** LOCOWEED **2.** LOCO DISEASE —*vt.* **-coed, -co·ing** to poison with locoweed —*adj.* [U.S. Slang] crazy; demented

lo·co- [< L. *locus*, a place] a combining form meaning from place to place [*locomotion*]

‡lo·co ci·ta·to (lō′kō sī tāt′ō) [L.] in the place cited or quoted

loco disease a nervous disease of horses, sheep, and cattle, caused by locoweed poisoning: also **lo′co·ism** *n.*

lo·co·mo·tion (lō′kə mō′shən) *n.* [LOCO- + MOTION] motion, or the power of moving, from one place to another

lo·co·mo·tive (-mōt′iv) *adj.* **1.** of locomotion **2.** moving or capable of moving from one place to another **3.** designating or of engines that move under their own power [*locomotive* design] —*n.* an engine that can move about by its own power; esp., an electric, steam, or diesel engine on wheels, designed to push or pull a railway train

lo·co·mo·tor (lō′kə mōt′ər) *n.* a person or thing with power of locomotion —*adj.* of locomotion

locomotor ataxia *same as* TABES DORSALIS

lo·co·weed (lō′kō wēd′) *n.* any of several plants of the legume family, which are common in western N America and cause loco disease

lo·cum te·nens (lō′kəm tē′nənz) [ML. < L. *locum*, place + *tenens*, holding] a person taking another's place for the time being; temporary substitute as for a doctor or clergyman: also **locum**

lo·cus (lō′kəs) *n., pl.* **lo·ci** (-sī) [L.] **1.** a place **2.** *Math.* a line, plane, etc. every point of which satisfies a given condition

lo·cust (lō′kəst) *n.* [< L. *locusta*] any of various large grasshoppers; specif., a migratory grasshopper often travelling in great swarms destroying vegetation

locust tree 1. *a)* a spiny tree of the legume family, found in the U.S. and having racemes of fragrant white flowers *b)* the yellowish, hard wood of this tree **2.** the carob

LOCUST
(to 5 cm long)

lo·cu·tion (lō kyōo′shən) *n.* [< L. *locutio* < pp. of *loqui*, to speak] **1.** a word, phrase, or expression **2.** a particular style of speech

lode (lōd) *n.* [var. of LOAD (< OE. *lad*, course)] *Mining* **1.** a vein containing metallic ore and filling a fissure in rock **2.** any deposit of ore separated from the adjoining rock **3.** any rich source

lo·den (lō′d'n) *adj.* [G. < MHG. < OHG. *lodo*, coarse cloth] **1.** designating or of a fulled, waterproof wool cloth, used for coats **2.** of a dark, olive green often used for this cloth

lode·star (lōd′stär′) *n.* [see LODE & STAR] **1.** a star by which a person directs his course; esp., the North Star **2.** a guiding principle or ideal

lode·stone (-stōn′) *n.* **1.** a strongly magnetic variety of the mineral magnetite **2.** something that attracts as with magnetic force

lodge (loj) *n.* [< OFr. *loge*, arbour < LL. *lobia* < Gmc.] **1.** a small house for special or seasonal use [a hunting *lodge*] **2.** *a)* the meeting place of a local chapter, as of freemasons, etc. *b)* such a local chapter **3.** the den of certain animals, esp. beavers **4.** *a)* the hut or tent of an American Indian *b)* those who live in it **5.** a small house at the entrance to the grounds of a country mansion **6.** a room, usually at the main gate, used by porters, etc. at a university —*vt.* **lodged, lodg′ing 1.** to house, esp. temporarily **2.** to rent rooms to **3.** to deposit for safekeeping **4.** to place or land by shooting, thrusting, etc. (with *in*) **5.** to bring (a complaint, etc.) before legal authorities **6.** to confer (powers) upon (with *in*) —*vi.* **1.** to live in a certain place for a time **2.** to live (*with* another or *in* his home) as a paying guest **3.** to come to rest and remain firmly fixed (*in*)

lodg·er (loj′ər) *n.* a person or thing that lodges; esp., one who rents a room in another's home

lodg·ing (-iŋ) *n.* **1.** a place to live in, esp. temporarily **2.** [*pl.*] a room or rooms rented in a private home

lodging house a house with furnished rooms for rent

lodg·ment (-mənt) *n.* **1.** a lodging or being lodged **2.** a lodging place **3.** an accumulation of deposited material Also sp. **lodge′ment**

lo·ess (lō′es) *n.* [G. *Löss* < *lösch*, loose] a fine-grained, yellowish-brown, extremely fertile loam deposited by the wind —**lo·ess′i·al** *adj.*

loft (loft) *n.* [OE. < ON. *lopt*, upper room, sky] **1.** *a)* an attic or atticlike space just below the roof of a house, barn, etc. *b)* [U.S.] an upper storey of a warehouse or factory **2.** a gallery [the choir *loft* in a church] **3.** *a)* the slope given to the face of a golf club to aid in hitting the ball in a high curve *b)* the height of a ball hit in a high curve —*vt.* **1.** to store in a loft **2.** to hit or throw (a golf ball, etc.) into the air in a high curve —*vi.* to loft a ball —**loft′er** *n.*

loft·y (lof′tē) *adj.* **loft′i·er, loft′i·est 1.** very high [a *lofty* mountain] **2.** elevated; noble; grand **3.** haughty; too proud; arrogant —**loft′i·ly** *adv.* —**loft′i·ness** *n.*

log¹ (log) *n.* [ME. *logge*, prob. < or akin to ON. *lāg*, felled tree] **1.** a section of the trunk or of a large branch of a felled tree **2.** a device (orig. a quadrant of wood) for measuring the speed of a ship: see also LOG CHIP **3.** a daily record of a ship's speed, progress, etc. and of the events in its voyage; logbook **4.** *a)* a similar record of an aircraft's flight *b)* a record of a pilot's flying time, experience, etc. **5.** any record of progress or occurrences —*adj.* made of a log or logs —*vt.* **logged, log′ging 1.** to saw (trees) into logs **2.** to cut down the trees of (a region) **3.** to enter or record in a log **4.** to sail or fly (a specified distance) —*vi.* to cut down trees and transport the logs to a sawmill —**like a log** inert, heavy [she slept *like a log*]

log² (log) *n.* clipped form of LOGARITHM

lo·gan (log′ən) *n.* [? < Cornish dial. *log*, to rock + STONE] a rocking stone, esp. a large boulder poised on top of another: also **logan stone**

lo·gan·ber·ry (lō′gən bər ē) *n.*, *pl.* **-ries** [after J. H. *Logan* (1841–1928), U.S. horticulturist] **1.** a hybrid bramble developed from the blackberry and the red raspberry **2.** its purplish-red fruit

log·a·rithm (log′ə rith′m) *n.* [ModL. < Gr. *logos*, a ratio + *arithmos*, number] *Math.* the exponent of the power to which a fixed number (the *base*) must be raised in order to produce a given number (the *antilogarithm*): logarithms are normally computed to the base of 10 and are used for shortening mathematical calculations —**log′a·rith′mic** *adj.* —**log′a·rith′mi·cal·ly** *adv.*

log·book (log′book′) *n.* **1.** *same as* LOG¹ (senses 3, 4, & 5) **2.** a book showing the registration details of a motor vehicle

log chip a flat piece of wood attached to a line (**log line**) and reel (**log reel**) and thrown into the water to measure a ship's speed

loge (lōzh) *n.* [Fr.: see LODGE] a box in a theatre

log·ger (log′ər) *n.* [U.S.] a person whose work is logging; lumberjack

log·ger·head (log′ər hed′) *n.* [dial. *logger*, block of wood (< LOG¹) + HEAD] **1.** a sea turtle of the Atlantic with a large head: also **loggerhead turtle 2.** [Dial.] a stupid fellow —**at loggerheads** in disagreement; quarrelling

log·gi·a (lo′jē ə, lo′jə; *It.* lôd′jä) *n.*, *pl.* **-gi·as**; *It.* **log′gie** (-jē) [It.: see LODGE] an arcaded or roofed gallery built into or projecting from the side of a building, often one overlooking an open court

log·ging (log′iŋ) *n.* the occupation of cutting down trees, cutting them into logs, and transporting them to the sawmill

LOGGIA

log·ic (loj′ik) *n.* [< OFr. < L. < Gr. *logikē* (*technē*), logical (art) < *logos*, word, speech, thought] **1.** the science of correct reasoning, dealing with relationships among propositions **2.** a book on this science **3.** correct reasoning; valid induction or deduction **4.** way of reasoning [poor *logic*] **5.** necessary connection or outcome, as of events **6.** the systematized interconnections in an electronic digital computer

log·i·cal (loj′i k'l) *adj.* **1.** of or used in the science of logic **2.** according to the principles of logic, or correct reasoning **3.** necessary or expected because of what has gone before

4. using correct reasoning —**log′i·cal′i·ty** (-kal′ə tē), **log′-i·cal·ness** *n.* —**log′i·cal·ly** *adv.*

-log·i·cal (loj′i k'l) a suffix used to form adjectives from nouns ending in -LOGY [*biological*]: also **-log·ic**

lo·gi·cian (lō jish′ən) *n.* an expert in logic

-logist (lə jist′) a combining form meaning one who is skilled in a subject [*psychologist, biologist*]

lo·gis·tics (lō jis′tiks) *n.pl.* [with sing. v.] [< Fr. < *logis*, lodgings < *loger*, to quarter] the branch of military science having to do with procuring, maintaining, and transporting materiel, personnel, and facilities —**lo·gis′tic, lo·gis′ti·cal** *adj.* —**lo·gis′ti·cal·ly** *adv.*

log·jam (log′jam′) *n.* **1.** logs jammed together in a stream **2.** an accumulation of many items to deal with

log·o·gram log′ə gram′) *n.* [< Gr. *logos*, word + -GRAM] a letter, character, or symbol used to represent an entire word (Ex: £ for *pound*)

log·or·rhoe·a (log′ə rē′ə) *n.* [ModL. < Gr. *logos*, word + *rhein*, to flow] excessive talkativeness, esp. when incoherent and uncontrollable

log-roll (log′rōl′) *vi.* to take part in logrolling —*vt.* to get passage of (a bill) by logrolling —**log′roll′er** *n.*

log-roll·ing (-rōl′iŋ) *n.* **1.** the act of rolling logs away, as by a group clearing land **2.** mutual aid, esp. among politicians, as by voting for each other's bills **3.** *same as* BIRLING

-logue (log) [Fr. < L. < Gr. < *logos*: see LOGIC] a combining form meaning: **1.** a (specified kind of) speaking or writing [*monologue*] **2.** a student or scholar [*sinalogue*]

log·wood (log′wood′) *n.* [so named from being imported in logs] **1.** the hard, brownish-red wood of a Central American and West Indian tree: it yields a dye used as a stain **2.** this tree or dye

-lo·gy (lə jē) [ult. < Gr. < *logos*: see LOGIC] a combining form meaning: **1.** a (specified kind of) speaking [*eulogy*] **2.** science, doctrine, or theory of [*biology, theology*]

loin (loin) *n.* [< OFr. *loigne*, ult. < L. *lumbus*] **1.** [usually *pl.*] the lower part of the back on either side of the backbone between the hipbones and the ribs **2.** the front part of the hindquarters of beef, lamb, veal, etc. with the flank removed **3.** [*pl.*] the hips and the lower abdomen regarded as a part of the body to be clothed or as the region of strength and procreative power —**gird (up) one's loins** to prepare to do something difficult

loin·cloth (-kloth′) *n.* a cloth worn about the loins, as by some tribes in warm climates

loi·ter (loit′ər) *vi.* [< MDu. *loteren*] **1.** to spend time idly (often with *about*); linger **2.** to move slowly and lazily, with frequent pauses —*vt.* to spend (time) idly —**loi′ter·er** *n.*

loll (lol) *vi.* [< MDu. *lollen*] **1.** to lean or lounge about in a lazy manner **2.** to hang in a relaxed manner; droop —*vt.* to let droop —**loll′er** *n.*

Lol·lard (lol′ərd) *n.* [< MDu. *lollaerd*, lit., a mutterer (of prayers)] any of the followers of John Wycliffe in 14th-and 15th-cent. England

lol·li·pop, lol·ly·pop (lol′ē pop′) *n.* [prob. < dial. *lolly*, the tongue + *pop*] a boiled sweet fixed to the end of a small stick **2.** *short for* ICE LOLLY

lollipop man [Colloq.] someone, usually carrying a pole with a circular sign on top, employed to stop traffic so children may cross the road —**lollipop lady** *fem.*

lol·lop (lol′əp) *vi.* [extended < LOLL, prob. after GALLOP] **1.** to lounge about; loll **2.** to move in a clumsy or relaxed, bobbing way

lol·ly (lol′ē) *n.*, *pl.* **-lies** [contr. < *lollypop*: see LOLLIPOP] **1.** money **2.** [Colloq.] *same as* LOLLIPOP **3.** [Aust.] any sweet

Lom·bard (lom′bərd, -bärd) *n.* **1.** a native or inhabitant of Lombardy **2.** one of a Germanic tribe that settled in the Po Valley —*adj.* of Lombardy or the Lombards: also **Lom·bar′dic**

Lombard Street [after the *Lombard* merchants & bankers who settled there in the 12th. cent.] street in London where many banks & financial houses are located

Lom·bar·dy poplar (lom′bər dē) a tall, slender poplar with upward curving branches

Lon·don pride (lun′dən) a kind of saxifrage, with pink flowers, common in cottage gardens

lone (lōn) *adj.* [< ALONE] **1.** by oneself; solitary **2.** lonely **3.** unmarried or widowed **4.** *a)* isolated *b)* unfrequented —**lone′ness** *n.*

lone·ly (-lē) *adj.* **-li·er, -li·est 1.** alone; solitary **2.** *a)* isolated *b)* unfrequented **3.** unhappy at being alone; longing for friends, etc. **4.** causing such a feeling —**lone′li·ly** *adv.* —**lone′li·ness** *n.*

lon·er (lō′nər) *n.* [Colloq.] one who avoids the company of others

lone·some (lōn′səm) *adj.* **1.** having or causing a lonely feeling **2.** unfrequented; desolate —*n.* [Colloq.] self [all by my *lonesome*] —**lone′some·ly** *adv.* —**lone′some·ness** *n.*

long¹ (loŋ) *adj.* [OE. *long, lang*] **1.** measuring much from one end or point to the other in space or time **2.** of a specified extent in length [a metre *long*] **3.** of greater than usual or standard length, quantity, etc. [a *long* list] **4.**

overextended in length   5. tedious; slow   6. extending to what is distant in space or time; far-reaching [a *long* view of the matter]   7. large; big [*long* odds, a *long* chance]   8. well supplied [*long* on excuses]   9. holding a supply of a commodity or security in anticipation of a rise in price   10. requiring a relatively long time to pronounce: said of a speech sound —*adv.*   1. for a long time   2. for the duration of [all day *long*]   3. at a much earlier or a much later time [to stay *long* after midnight] —*n.*   1. a signal, syllable, etc. of long duration   2. a long time [it won't take *long*] —**as** (or **so**) **long as**   1. during the time that   2. seeing that; since   3. provided that —**before long**   soon —**in the long run**   eventually; finally —**the long and (the) short of**   the whole story of in a few words

long[2] (loŋ) *vi.* [OE. *langian*]   to feel a strong yearning; wish earnestly [to *long* to go home]

long. longitude

lon·ga·nim·i·ty (loŋ'gə nim'ə tē) *n.* [< L. *longus*, long + *animus*, mind]   patient endurance of injuries; forbearance

long·boat (loŋ'bōt') *n.*   the largest boat carried on a merchant sailing ship

long·bow (-bō') *n.*   a large bow drawn by hand and shooting a long, feathered arrow: cf. CROSSBOW

long·cloth (-klôth') *n.*   a soft cotton fabric of fine quality

long·dis·tance (-dis'təns) *adj.*   1. covering long distances [a *long-distance* lorry driver]   2. connecting points that are far apart [a *long-distance* telephone call]

long division   the process of dividing one number by another and putting the steps down in full

long·drawn (-drôn') *adj.*   continuing for a long time; prolonged: also **long'-drawn'-out'**

lon·gev·i·ty (lon jev'ə tē) *n.* [< L. < *longus*, long + *aevum*, age]   1. *a)* great span of life *b)* length of life   2. length of service

long face   a glum, disconsolate look —**long'-faced'** *adj.*

long·hair (loŋ'her') *adj.* [Colloq.] designating or of intellectuals or their tastes; specif., preferring classical music to jazz or popular tunes: also **long'haired'** —*n.* [Colloq.]   1. an intellectual; specif., a longhair musician   2. *same as* HIPPIE

long·hand (-hand') *n.*   ordinary handwriting, with the words written out in full

long haul   1. transport of goods or people over long distances   2. any effort made over a long distance or for a long time

long·head·ed, long·head·ed (-hed'id) *adj.*   1. having a long head   2. having much foresight; shrewd —**long'-head'ed·ly** *adv.* —**long'-head'ed·ness** *n.*

long·horn (-hôrn') *n.*   any of a breed of long-horned cattle found esp. in Britain or in SW U.S.

long·ing (-iŋ) *n.*   strong desire; yearning —*adj.*   feeling or showing a yearning —**long'ing·ly** *adv.*

long·ish (-ish) *adj.*   somewhat long

lon·gi·tude (lon'jə tyōōd', lon'gə-) *n.* [< L. *longitudo* < *longus*, LONG[1]]   1. length   2. distance east or west on the earth's surface, measured as an arc of the equator (in degrees up to 180° or by the difference in time) between the meridian passing through a particular place and a standard or prime meridian, usually the one passing through Greenwich

lon·gi·tu·di·nal (lon'jə tyōōd''n əl, lon'gə-) *adj.*   1. of or in length   2. running or placed lengthways [sound is a *longitudinal* wave]   3. of longitude —**lon'gi·tu'di·nal·ly** *adv.*

long johns   [Colloq.] long underwear

long jump   an athletic event that is a jump for distance rather than height

long leg   *Cricket*   a fielding position near the boundary behind and on the left of the batsman

long·lived (loŋ'livd', -livd') *adj.*   having or tending to have a long life span or existence

long·play·ing (loŋ'plā'iŋ) *adj.*   designating or of a gramophone record with microgrooves, for playing at 33 1/3 revolutions per minute

long·range (-rānj') *adj.*   1. having a range of great distance   2. taking the future into consideration [*long-range* plans]

long·shore (-shôr') *adj.* [contr. < ALONGSHORE]   existing, occurring, employed, or working along the shore or waterfront —*adv.*   along the shore

long shot   [Colloq.] a betting choice that has little chance of winning and, hence, carries great odds —**not by a long shot**   [Colloq.] not at all

long·sight·ed (-sīt'id) *adj.*   *same as* FARSIGHTED —**long'-sight'ed·ly** *adv.* —**long'sight'ed·ness** *n.*

long·stand·ing (-stan'diŋ) *adj.*   having continued for a long time

long·suf·fer·ing (-suf'ər iŋ) *adj.*   bearing injuries, insults, trouble, etc. patiently for a long time —*n.*   long and patient endurance of trials —**long'-suf'fer·ing·ly** *adv.*

long suit   1. the suit in which a card player holds the most cards   2. something at which one excels

long·term (-turm') *adj.*   1. for or extending over a long time   2. designating or of a capital gain, loan, etc. that involves a relatively long period

long·time (-tīm') *adj.*   over a long period of time

long trousers   trousers reaching to the ankles, as opposed to shorts

‡**lon·gueur** (lôn gër'; *E.* loŋ gur') *n.* [Fr.]   a long, boring section, as in a novel, musical work, etc.

long vacation   the long period of holiday in the summer during which universities, law courts, etc., are closed

long·waist·ed (loŋ'wās'tid) *adj.*   with a low waistline

long·ways (-wāz') *adv.*   *same as* LENGTHWAYS: also **long'-wise'** (-wīz')

long·wind·ed (-win'did) *adj.*   1. not easily winded by exertion   2. *a)* speaking or writing at great length *b)* tiresomely long —**long'-wind'ed·ly** *adv.* —**long'-wind'ed·ness** *n.*

loo[1] (lōō) *n.* [< Fr. *lanturelu*]   a card game played for a pool made up of stakes and forfeits

loo[2] (lōō) *n.* [< ? Fr. *l'eau*, water]   [Colloq.] a toilet

loo·fah (lōō'fə) *n.* [Ar. *lūfah*]   the fibrous interior of a plant of the gourd type, used as a bath sponge

look (look) *vi.* [OE. *locian*]   1. to see   2. *a)* to direct one's eyes in order to see *b)* to direct one's attention mentally upon something   3. to search   4. to appear; seem   5. to be facing in a specified direction   6. to expect (followed by an infinitive) —*vt.*   1. to direct one's eyes on [*look* him in the face]   2. to express by one's looks [to *look* one's disgust]   3. to appear as having attained (some age) [he *looks* his years] —*n.*   1. the act of looking; glance   2. outward aspect [the *look* of a beggar]   3. [Colloq.] *a)* [*usually pl.*] appearance [from the *looks* of things]   *b)* [*pl.*] personal appearance, esp. of a pleasing nature [to have *looks* and youth] —*interj.*   1. see!   2. pay attention! —**look after**   to take care of —**look alive** (or **sharp**)! be alert! —**look down on** (or **upon**)   to regard with contempt —**look for**   1. to search for   2. to expect —**look forward to**   to anticipate, esp. eagerly —**look in** (**on**)   to pay a brief visit (to) —**look on**   1. to be an observer or spectator   2. to consider; regard —**look** (**like**) **oneself**   to seem in normal health, spirits, etc. —**look out**   1. to be on the watch; be careful   2. to look for or select by inspection —**look out for**   1. to be wary about   2. to take care of —**look over**   to examine; inspect —**look to**   1. to take care of   2. to rely upon   3. to expect —**look up**   1. to search for in a reference book, etc.   2. [Colloq.] to pay a visit to   3. [Colloq.] to improve —**look up to**   to admire —**look'er** *n.*

look·er-on (look'ər on') *n.*, *pl.* **look'ers-on'**   an observer or spectator; onlooker

looking glass   a (glass) mirror

look·ing-glass (-gläs') *adj.*   topsy-turvy; inverted [spies live in a *looking-glass* world]

look·out (look'out') *n.*   1. a careful watching for someone or something   2. a place for keeping watch, esp. a high place   3. a person detailed to watch   4. outlook, chances or view; prospect   5. [Colloq.] concern; business [that's your *lookout*]

look-see (-sē') *n.* [? < PidE. < LOOK + SEE]   [Slang] a quick look or inspection

loom[1] (lōōm) *n.* [OE. (ge)*loma*, tool, utensil]   a machine for weaving thread or yarn into cloth

loom[2] (lōōm) *vi.* [< ?]   to appear, take shape, or come in sight indistinctly, esp. in a large or threatening form [the peak *loomed* up before us, disaster *loomed* ahead]

loon[1] (lōōn) *n.* [earlier *loom* < ON. *lomr*]   a name given to several fish-eating diving birds, esp. the great northern diver

loon[2] (lōōn) *n.* [Scot. *loun* < ?]   1. a clumsy, stupid person   2. a crazy person

loon·y (lōō'nē) *adj.* **loon'i·er, loon'i·est** [< LUNATIC]   [Slang] crazy; demented —*n.*, *pl.* **loon'ies** [Slang] a loony person Also **loon'ey**

loony bin   [Slang] a mental hospital

loop (lōōp) *n.* [< Anglo-N. forms corresponding to ON. *hlaup*, a leap, *hlaupa*, to run]   1. the figure formed by a line, thread, wire, etc. that curves back to cross itself   2. anything having or forming this figure, as a written *h*   3. sharp bend, as in a mountain road   4. a ring-shaped fastening or ornament   5. a plastic intrauterine contraceptive device (usually with *the*)   6. *Aeron.* a manoeuvre in which an aeroplane describes a closed curve or circle in the vertical plane —*vt.*   1. to make a loop or loops in or of   2. to wrap around one or more times [*loop* the wire around the post]   3. to fasten with a loop or loops —*vi.*   1. to form a loop or loops   2. *Aeron.* to perform a loop or loops —**loop the loop**   to make a vertical loop in the air, as in an aeroplane —**loop'er** *n.*

loop·hole (-hōl') *n.* [prob. < MDu. *lupen*, to peer + HOLE]   1. a hole or narrow slit in the wall of a fort, etc. for looking or shooting through   2. a means of evading an obligation, a law, etc.

loop·y (lōōp'ē) *adj.* **loop'i·er, loop'i·est** [Slang] crazy; foolish

loose (lōōs) *adj.* [< ON. *lauss*]   1. not confined or restrained; free   2. not put up in a package [*loose* salt]   3. readily available [*loose* change]   4. not firmly fastened down or in [a *loose* wheel]   5. not taut; slack   6. not tight [*loose* clothing] 7. not compact or compactly constructed [*loose* soil, a *loose* frame] 8. not restrained [*loose* talk] 9. not precise; inexact [a *loose* translation] 10. sexually immoral; lewd 11. a) not strained [a *loose* cough] b) moving freely or excessively [*loose* bowels] 12. [Colloq.] relaxed; easy —*adv.* loosely; in a loose manner —*vt.* **loosed, loos'ing** 1. to make loose; specif., a) to set free; unbind b) to make less tight c) to make less compact d) to free from restraint; relax 2. to let fly; release [he *loosed* the arrow] —*vi.* 1. to become loose 2. to let fly: shoot (with *off*) —**break loose** to free oneself; escape —**cast loose** to untie or unfasten —**let loose (with)** to release; let go —**on the loose** 1. not confined or bound; free 2. [Colloq.] having fun in a free, unrestrained manner —**set (or turn) loose** to make free; release —**loose'ly** *adv.* —**loose'ness** *n.*

loose cover a removable, fitted cloth cover for an armchair, sofa, etc.

loose ends minor bits of unfinished work, etc. —**at a loose end** unsettled, unoccupied, unemployed, etc.

loose-joint·ed (-join'tid) *adj.* 1. having loose joints 2. moving freely; limber —**loose'-joint'ed·ly** *adv.* —**loose'-joint'ed·ness** *n.*

loose-leaf (-lēf') *adj.* having leaves, or sheets, that can easily be removed or replaced

loos·en (lōōs''n) *vt., vi.* to make or become loose or looser —**loosen up** [Colloq.] 1. to talk freely 2. to give money generously 3. to relax —**loos'en·er** *n.*

loose·strife (-strīf') *n.* [transl. of L. *lysimachia* < Gr. < *lyein*, to slacken + *machē*, battle] 1. a plant with leafy stems and purple spikes of white, rose, or yellow flowers 2. a plant (**purple loosestrife**) with spikes of purple flowers

loot (lōōt) *n.* [Hindi *lūt* < Sans. *lunt*, to rob] 1. goods stolen or taken by force; plunder; spoils 2. [Slang] money, gifts, etc. —*vt., vi.* to plunder —**loot'er** *n.*

lop¹ (lop) *vt.* **lopped, lop'ping** [OE. *loppian*, prob. < Scand.] 1. to trim (a tree, etc.) by cutting off branches or twigs 2. to remove by or as by cutting off —*n.* something lopped off —**lop'per** *n.*

lop² (lop) *vi.* **lopped, lop'ping** [prob. akin to LOB] 1. to hang down loosely 2. to move in a halting way —*adj.* hanging down loosely

lope (lōp) *vi.* **loped, lop'ing** [< ON. *hlaupa*, to leap] to move with a long, swinging stride or in an easy canter —*vt.* to cause to lope —*n.* a long, easy, swinging stride

lop-eared (lop'ird') *adj.* having ears that droop or hang down

lop-sid·ed (-sid'id) *adj.* 1. noticeably heavier, bigger, or lower on one side 2. not balanced; uneven —**lop'sid'ed·ly** *adv.* —**lop'sid'ed·ness** *n.*

lo·qua·cious (lō kwā'shəs) *adj.* [< L. *loquax* < *loqui*, to speak] very talkative; fond of talking —**lo·qua'cious·ly** *adv.* —**lo·qua'cious·ness** *n.*

lo·quac·i·ty (-kwas'ə tē) *n.* talkativeness, esp. when excessive

lo·quat (lō'kwot, -kwət) *n.* [< Chin. (Cantonese) *lō kwat*, lit., rush orange] 1. a small evergreen tree native to China and Japan 2. the small, yellow, edible, plumlike fruit of this tree

lor (lôr) *interj.* [contr. < LORD] an expression of surprise

Lor·an (lôr'an) *n.* [< *Lo(ng) Ra(nge) N(avigation)*] [also l-] a system by which a ship or aircraft can determine its position by the difference in time between radio signals sent from two or more known stations

lord (lôrd) *n.* [OE. *hlaford* < *hlaf*, loaf + *weard*, keeper] 1. a person having great power and authority; ruler; master 2. the head of a feudal estate 3. [L-] a) God b) Jesus Christ [in the year of our *Lord* 1565] 4. a) a nobleman holding the rank of baron, viscount, earl, or marquess; member of the House of Lords b) a man who by courtesy or because of his office is given the title of Lord 5. [L-] [pl.] the House of Lords in the British Parliament (usually with *the*) 6. [L-] in Great Britain, the title of a lord, variously used —*interj.* [often L-] an exclamation of surprise or irritation —**lord it (over)** to domineer (over)

Lord Chief Justice the president of one division of the High Court of Justice, second only to the Lord Chancellor

Lord (High) Chancellor the highest officer of state of Great Britain, keeper of the Great Seal, privy councillor, presiding officer of the House of Lords, etc.

Lord High Steward of England 1. formerly the highest officer of state, ranking next to the sovereign 2. the official who presides at coronations

Lord Lieutenant 1. the representative of the Crown in a county 2. formerly, the British viceroy in Ireland

lord·ly (-lē) *adj.* **-li·er, -li·est** of, like, characteristic of, or suitable to a lord; specif., a) noble; grand b) haughty; overbearing —*adv.* in the manner of a lord —**lord'li·ness** *n.*

Lord Mayor the title of the mayor of London and of the mayor of several other British cities

Lord Mayor's Show a procession of decorated vehicles, bands, etc. on the day the Lord Mayor of London assumes office

Lord of Misrule formerly, a person who presided over revels and games at Christmas, usually in a nobleman's house

Lord President chief presiding judge of the Court of Session

Lord President of the Council the cabinet minister who presides over meetings of the Privy Council

Lord Privy Seal 1. formerly, the cabinet minister in charge of the privy seal 2. a senior cabinet minister who has no official duties

Lord Provost the chief magistrate in one of five Scottish burghs, including Edinburgh and Glasgow

Lord's (lôrdz) *n.* [< Thomas *Lord*, founder] Lord's cricket ground, now headquarters of the M.C.C.

Lord's day Sunday

lord·ship (lôrd'ship) *n.* 1. the rank or authority of a lord 2. rule; dominion 3. [also L-] a title used in speaking of or to a lord: with *his* or *your*

Lord's Prayer the prayer beginning *Our Father*, which Jesus taught his disciples: Matt. 6:9-13

lords spiritual the archbishops and bishops who are members of the House of Lords

Lord's Supper 1. *same as* LAST SUPPER 2. Holy Communion; Eucharist

lords temporal those members of the House of Lords who are not clergymen

lore (lôr) *n.* [OE. *lar*] knowledge or learning; specif., all the knowledge concerning a particular subject, esp. that of a traditional nature

lor·gnette (lôr nyet') *n.* [Fr. < *lorgner*, to spy, peep < OFr. *lorgne*, squinting] a pair of glasses, or an opera glass, attached to a handle

LORGNETTE

lorn (lôrn) *adj.* [ME., pp. of *losen*, to lose] 1. [Obs.] lost; ruined 2. [Archaic] forsaken, forlorn, bereft, or desolate

lor·ry (lor'ē) *n., pl.* **-ries** [prob. < dial. *lurry, lorry*, to tug] 1. a low, flat wagon without sides 2. a motor vehicle used to transport heavy loads along motorways, roads, etc.

lo·ry (lôr'ē) *n., pl.* **-ries** [Malay *lūrī*] a small, brightly coloured parrot native to Australia and nearby islands

lose (lōōz) *vt.* **lost, los'ing** [< OE. *losian*, to be lost + *leosan*, to lose] 1. to bring to ruin or destruction 2. to become unable to find; mislay [I *lost* my key] 3. to have taken from one by accident, death, removal, etc.; suffer the loss of 4. to get rid of [dieting to *lose* weight] 5. to fail to keep or maintain [to *lose* one's temper, to *lose* one's job] 6. a) to fail to see, hear, or understand b) to fail to keep in sight, mind, etc. 7. to fail to have, get, take, etc.; miss 8. to fail to win [to *lose* a game] 9. to cause the loss of [it *lost* him his job] 10. to wander from and not be able to find (one's way, etc.) 11. to confuse, bewilder, or alienate 12. to waste; squander [to *lose* time] 13. to outdistance 14. to engross or preoccupy [to be *lost* in reverie] 15. to go slower by [my watch *lost* a minute] —*vi.* 1. to suffer loss 2. to be defeated in a contest, etc. 3. to be slow: said of a timepiece —**lose oneself** 1. to go astray; become bewildered 2. to become engrossed —**lose one's seat** to be defeated in a parliamentary election: said of a sitting member —**lose out** [Colloq.] to fail —**lose out on** [Colloq.] to fail to take advantage of or gain —**los'a·ble** *adj.*

los·er (lōō'zər) *n.* 1. one that loses; esp., [Colloq.] one that seems doomed to lose 2. a person who reacts to loss as specified [a poor *loser*]

los·ing (-zin) *n.* [pl.] losses by gambling —*adj.* 1. that loses [a *losing* team] 2. resulting in loss [a *losing* proposition]

loss (los) *n.* [< ? OE. *los*, ruin] 1. a losing or being lost 2. the damage, disadvantage, etc. caused by losing something 3. the person, thing, or amount lost 4. Insurance a) death, damage, etc. that is the basis for a valid claim b) the amount paid by the insurer 5. Mil. a) the losing of military personnel in combat by death, injury, or capture b) [pl.] those lost in this way c) [pl.] ships, aircraft, etc. lost in battle —**at a loss (to)** puzzled or uncertain (how to)

loss leader any article that a shop sells cheaply or below cost to attract customers

lost (lost) *pt. & pp. of* LOSE —*adj.* 1. destroyed; ruined 2. not to be found; missing 3. no longer held, possessed, seen, heard, or known 4. not gained or won 5. having wandered from the way 6. bewildered; ill at ease 7. wasted; squandered —**lost in** engrossed in —**lost on** without effect on —**lost to** 1. no longer in the possession of 2. no longer available to 3. insensible to

Lost Generation [sometimes l- g-] 1. the number of talented young men killed in World War I 2. the authors, esp. U.S. authors, who were active in the period after World War I

lot (lot) *n.* [OE. *hlot*] 1. any of a number of counters, etc.

drawn from at random to decide a matter by chance **2.** the use of such a method [to choose men by *lot*] **3.** the decision arrived at by this means **4.** what one receives as the result of such a decision; share **5.** one's portion in life; fortune [her unhappy *lot*] **6.** a plot of ground **7.** *a)* a number of persons or things regarded as a group, as items to be sold at an auction *b)* a quantity of material processed at the same time **8.** [*often pl.*] [Colloq.] a great number or amount **9.** [Colloq.] sort (of person) [he's a bad *lot*] **10.** [U.S.] a film studio —*adv.* very much [a *lot* richer]: also **lots** —*vt.* **lot′ted, lot′ting** to divide into lots —*vi.* to draw or cast lots —**cast** (or **throw**) **in one's lot with** to share the fortunes of —**draw** (or **cast**) **lots** to decide an issue by using lots —**the lot** [Colloq.] the entire amount or number

loth (lōth) *adj. alt. sp. of* LOATH

Lo·thar·i·o (lō·thär′ē·ō′; -ther′-) *n., pl.* **-i·os′** [after the young rake in a play by Nicholas Rowe (1674-1718)] [*often l-*] a lighthearted seducer of women

lo·tion (lō′shən) *n.* [< L. < pp. of *lavare*, to wash] a liquid preparation used, as on the skin, for washing, soothing, healing, etc.

lot·ter·y (lot′ər ē) *n., pl.* **-ter·ies** [< MFr. < MDu. < *lot*, lot] **1.** a game of chance in which people buy numbered chances on prizes, the winning numbers being drawn by lot **2.** any undertaking involving chance selection, as by the drawing of lots

lot·to (lot′ō) *n.* [It. < Fr. < MDu. *lot*, lot] a game of chance played with cards having squares numbered in rows: counters are placed on those numbers corresponding to numbered discs drawn by lot

lo·tus, lo·tos (lōt′əs) *n.* [L. < Gr. *lōtos* < Heb. *lōt*] **1.** *Gr. Legend* a plant whose fruit was supposed to induce a dreamy languor and forgetfulness **2.** any of several tropical African and Asiatic waterlilies, as the white lotus of Egypt **3.** a plant of the legume family, with yellow, purple, or white flowers

lo·tus-eat·er (-ēt′ər) *n.* in the *Odyssey*, one of a people who ate the fruit of the lotus and became indolent, dreamy, and forgetful of duty

lotus position in yoga, a sitting position in which each foot is placed on the opposite thigh

loud (loud) *adj.* [OE. *hlud*] **1.** strongly audible: said of sound **2.** sounding with great intensity [a *loud* bell] **3.** noisy **4.** clamorous; emphatic [*loud* denials] **5.** [Colloq.] too vivid; flashy [a *loud* pattern] **6.** [Colloq.] unrefined; vulgar —*adv.* in a loud manner —**loud′ish** *adj.* —**loud′ly** *adv.* —**loud′ness** *n.*

loud-hail·er (-hāl′ər) *n.* a portable electronic voice amplifier

loud-mouthed (-moutht′, -mouthd′) *adj.* talking in a loud, irritating voice —**loud′mouth′** *n.*

loud·speak·er (-spē′kər) *n.* a device for converting electric current into sound waves and for amplifying this sound

lough (lokh) *n.* [ME., prob. < Gaelic & OIr. *loch*, LOCH] [Ir.] **1.** a lake **2.** an arm of the sea

lou·is d'or (loo′ē dôr′) [Fr., gold louis] **1.** an old French gold coin of varying value **2.** a later French gold coin worth 20 francs

lounge (lounj) *vi.* **lounged, loung′ing** [Scot. dial. < ? *lungis*, laggard] **1.** to stand, move, sit, etc. in a relaxed or lazy way **2.** to spend time in idleness —*vt.* to spend (time) by lounging —*n.* **1.** an act or time of lounging **2.** a room, as in a hotel or theatre, with comfortable furniture **3.** a couch or sofa **4.** a living room in a private house **5.** a bar in a public house or hotel —**loung′er** *n.*

lounge suit a man's suit of matching jacket and trousers for daytime wear

loupe (loop) *n.* [Fr., ult. prob. < OHG. *luppa*, shapeless mass] a small, high-powered magnifying lens held close to the eye, used by jewellers, etc.

lour (lour) *vi., n. same as* LOWER²

louse (lous; *also, for v.,* louz) *n., pl.* **lice** [OE. *lus* (pl. *lys*)] **1.** *a)* a small, wingless, parasitic insect that infests the hair or skin of man and some other mammals *b)* any of various arthropods that suck blood or juice from other animals or plants **2.** any similar insect, arachnid, etc., as the wood louse **3.** *pl.* **lous′es** [Slang] a person regarded as mean, contemptible, etc. —*vt.* **loused, lous′ing** [Rare] to delouse —**louse up** [Slang] to botch; spoil; ruin

lous·y (lou′zē) *adj.* **lous′i·er, lous′i·est 1.** infested with lice **2.** [Slang] dirty, disgusting, or contemptible **3.** [Slang] poor; inferior: a generalized epithet of disapproval **4.** [Slang] oversupplied (*with*) —**lous′i·ly** *adv.* —**lous′i·ness** *n.*

lout (lout) *n.* [prob. < ME. *lutien*, to lurk < OE. *lutian*] a clumsy, stupid fellow; boor —**lout′ish** *adj.* —**lout′ish·ly** *adv.* —**lout′ish·ness** *n.*

lou·ver (loo′vər) *n.* [MFr. *lover* < ?] **1.** an opening fitted with sloping slats so as to admit light and air but shed rain **2.** any of these slats: also **louver board 3.** any set of slats or fins used to control ventilation, etc. Also **lou′vre** —**lou′-vered** *adj.*

lov·a·ble (luv′ə b'l) *adj.* inspiring love; easily loved; endearing: also sp. **love′a·ble** —**lov′a·bil′i·ty, lov′a·ble·ness** *n.* —**lov′a·bly** *adv.*

lov·age (luv′ij) *n.* [ME. *loveache*, < OFr. *levesche* < L. *ligusticum*, the plant of Liguria] a European umbelliferous plant, sometimes used as flavouring and also as a home medicine

love (luv) *n.* [OE. *lufu*] **1.** a deep affection for or attachment or devotion to someone, or the expression of this **2.** good will towards others **3.** *a)* a strong liking for or interest in something [a *love* of music] *b)* the object of such liking **4.** *a)* a strong, usually passionate, affection of one person for another *b)* the object of this; sweetheart **5.** sexual passion or intercourse **6.** [*L-*] *a)* Cupid *b)* [Rare] Venus **7.** *Tennis* a score of zero —*vt.* **loved, lov′ing 1.** to feel love for **2.** to show love for by fondling, kissing, etc. **3.** to take great pleasure in [to *love* books] **4.** to benefit from [plants *love* light] —*vi.* to feel the emotion of love —**fall in love** (**with**) to begin to feel love (for) —**for the love of** for the sake of —**in love** feeling love —**make love 1.** to woo or embrace, kiss, etc. **2.** to have sexual intercourse —**not for love or money** not under any conditions

love affair an amorous relationship between two people not married to each other

love apple [Archaic] the tomato

love·bird (-burd′) *n.* any of various small parrots, often kept as cage birds: the mates appear to be greatly attached to each other

love child a euphemism for an illegitimate child; bastard

love·less (-lis) *adj.* without love; specif., *a)* feeling no love *b)* unloved —**love′less·ly** *adv.* —**love′less·ness** *n.*

love-lies-bleed·ing (-liz′blēd′iŋ) *n.* a cultivated amaranth with spikes of small, red flowers

love·lorn (-lôrn′) *adj.* deserted by one's sweetheart; pining from love

love·ly (-lē) *adj.* **-li·er, -li·est** having qualities that inspire love, admiration, etc.; specif., *a)* beautiful *b)* morally or spiritually attractive *c)* [Colloq.] highly enjoyable [a *lovely* party] —*n., pl.* **-lies** [Colloq.] a beautiful young woman —**love′li·ly** *adv.* —**love′li·ness** *n.*

love potion a magic drink supposed to arouse in the drinker love for a certain person

lov·er (-ər) *n.* a person who loves; specif., *a)* a sweetheart *b)* [pl.] a couple in love with each other *c)* a partner, esp. the male partner, in a love affair *d)* a person who greatly enjoys some (specified) thing [a *lover* of jazz] —**lov′er·ly** *adj., adv.*

love seat a small sofa seating two persons

love·sick (-sik′) *adj.* **1.** so much in love as to be unable to act normally **2.** expressive of such a condition —**love′sick′-ness** *n.*

lov·ey-dov·ey (luv′ē duv′ē) *adj.* [LOVE + -Y² + DOVE + Y²] [Slang] very or excessively affectionate, amorous, or sentimental

lov·ing (-iŋ) *adj.* feeling or expressing love —**lov′ing·ly** *adv.* —**lov′ing·ness** *n.*

loving cup a large drinking cup with two handles, formerly passed among guests at banquets: now often given as a trophy in sports, etc.

lov·ing-kind·ness (-kīnd′nis) *n.* kindness resulting from or expressing love

low¹ (lō) *adj.* [ME. *lah* < ON. *lagr*] **1.** *a)* not high or tall *b)* not far above the ground **2.** depressed below the surrounding surface [*low* land] **3.** of little height; shallow **4.** of little quantity, degree, value, etc. **5.** of less than normal height, depth, degree, etc. **6.** below others in order, position, etc. **7.** near the horizon [the sun is *low*] **8.** near the equator [*low* latitudes] **9.** exposing the neck and shoulders [a dress with a *low* neckline] **10.** in hiding **11.** deep [a *low* bow] **12.** lacking energy; weak **13.** depressed; melancholy **14.** not of high rank; humble **15.** vulgar; coarse **16.** mean; contemptible [a *low* trick] **17.** unfavourable [to have a *low* opinion of someone] **18.** having less than a normal amount of some usual element [*low* in calories] **19.** not advanced in evolution, development, etc. [a *low* form of plant life] **20.** relatively recent [a manuscript of *low* date] **21.** designating or of the gear ratio of a motor vehicle transmission which produces the lowest speed and greatest power **22.** *a)* not well supplied with [*low* on fuel] *b)* [Colloq.] short of ready cash **23.** *a)* not loud *b)* deep in pitch **24.** very informal in matters of ceremony, doctrine, etc. **25.** *Phonet.* produced with the tongue held low in the mouth: said of some vowels, as (ä) —*adv.* **1.** in, to, or toward a low position, level, etc. **2.** in a low manner **3.** quietly; softly **4.** with a deep pitch —*n.* something low; specif., *a)* a low level, point, degree, etc. *b)* *Meteorol.* an area of low barometric pressure —**lay low 1.** to cause to fall by hitting **2.** to overcome or kill —**lie low 1.** to keep oneself hidden **2.** to wait patiently —**low′ness** *n.*

low² (lō) *vi.* [OE. *hlowan*] to make the characteristic sound of a cow; moo —*vt.* to express by lowing —*n.* the characteristic sound of a cow

low-born (-bôrn′) *adj.* of humble birth

low-bred (-bred′) *adj.* ill-mannered; vulgar

low·brow (-brou´) *n.* [Colloq.] a person lacking or regarded as lacking intellectual tastes —*adj.* [Colloq.] of or for a lowbrow

Low Church that party of the Anglican Church which attaches little importance to the priesthood or to traditional rituals, doctrines, etc. —**Low´-Church´** *adj.*

low comedy comedy that gets its effect mainly from action and situation, as burlesque, farce, etc.

low·down (lō´doun´; *for adj.* -doun´) *n.* [Slang] the pertinent facts (with *the*) —*adj.* [Colloq.] mean; contemptible

low·er¹ (lō´ər) *adj. compar. of* LOW¹ **1.** below or farther down in place, rank, dignity, etc. **2.** less in quantity, value, intensity, etc. **3.** farther south, closer to the mouth of a river, etc. **4.** [L-] *Geol.* earlier: used of a division of a period —*vt.* **1.** to let or put down [*lower* the window] **2.** to reduce in height, amount, value, etc. [to *lower* prices] **3.** to weaken or lessen [to *lower* one's resistance] **4.** to demean; degrade **5.** to reduce (a sound) in volume or in pitch —*vi.* to become lower; sink; fall

low·er² (lou´ər) *vi.* [ME. *louren*] **1.** to scowl or frown **2.** to appear dark and threatening —*n.* a frowning or threatening look

Lower Carboniferous see GEOLOGY, chart

lower case small-letter type used in printing, as distinguished from capital letters (*upper case*) —**low´-er-case´** *adj.* —**low´er-case´** *vt.* -cased´, -cas´ing

lower class the social class below the middle class; working class, or proletariat

lower deck **1.** the deck directly above the hold **2.** the crew of a ship other than the officers

Lower House [*often* l- h-] the larger and more representative branch of a legislature having two branches, as the House of Commons

low·er·ing (lou´ər iŋ) *adj.* **1.** scowling; frowning darkly **2.** dark, as if about to rain or snow —**low´er·ing·ly** *adv.*

low·er·most (lō´ər mōst´) *adj.* lowest

lower world **1.** *same as* NETHER WORLD **2.** the earth

low frequency any radio frequency between 30 and 300 kilohertz

Low German **1.** *same as* PLATTDEUTSCH **2.** the West Germanic languages, other than High German, including Plattdeutsch, English, Dutch, Frisian, etc.

low-grade (lō´grād´) *adj.* of inferior quality

low-key (-kē´) *adj.* of low intensity, tone, etc.; subdued or restrained: also **low´-keyed´**

low·land (lō´land; *also, for n.,* -land´) *n.* land that is below the level of the surrounding land —*adj.* of, in, or from such a region —**the Lowlands** lowland region in SC Scotland —**low´land·er, Low´land·er** *n.*

Low Latin nonclassical, esp. medieval, Latin

low·ly (-lē) *adj.* -li·er, -li·est **1.** of or suited to a low position or rank **2.** humble; meek **3.** ordinary —*adv.* **1.** humbly; meekly **2.** in a low manner, position, etc. **3.** softly; gently —**low´li·ness** *n.*

Low Mass a Mass said, not sung, less ceremonial than High Mass, and offered by one priest

low-mind·ed (-mīn´did) *adj.* having or showing a coarse, vulgar mind —**low´-mind´ed·ly** *adv.* —**low´-mind´ed·ness** *n.*

low-pitched (-picht´) *adj.* **1.** low in pitch **2.** having little slope, as a roof **3.** of low intensity; restrained

low-pres·sure (-presh´ər) *adj.* **1.** *a)* having or using a relatively low pressure *b)* having a low barometric pressure **2.** not energetic or forceful

low profile an unobtrusive presence, or concealed activity

low-rise (-rīz´) *adj.* [Chiefly U.S.] designating or of a building, esp. a block of flats, having only a few storeys

low-spir·it·ed (-spir´it id) *adj.* in low spirits; sad; depressed —**low´-spir´it·ed·ly** *adv.*

low tide **1.** the lowest level reached by the ebbing tide **2.** the time when the tide is at this level **3.** the lowest point reached by anything

low water **1.** *same as* LOW TIDE **2.** water at its lowest level, as in a stream

low-wa·ter mark (-wôt´ər) **1.** a mark showing low water **2.** the lowest point reached

lox¹ (loks) *n.* [via Yid. < G. *Lachs*, salmon] a variety of salty smoked salmon

lox² (loks) *n.* [*l(iquid)* *ox(ygen)*] oxygen in a liquid state, used in a fuel mixture for rockets

loy·al (loi´əl) *adj.* [Fr. < OFr. < L. *legalis*: see LEGAL] **1.** faithful to one's country **2.** faithful to those persons, ideals, etc. that one is under obligation to defend or support **3.** relating to or indicating loyalty —**loy´al·ly** *adv.*

loy·al·ist (-ist) *n.* **1.** a person who supports the established government of his country during times of revolt **2.** a supporter of the Stuart cause in the 17th cent. **3.** [*often* L-] in the War of American Independence, a colonist who was loyal to the British government **4.** [L-] in the Spanish Civil War, one who remained loyal to the Republic, opposing Franco **5.** in Northern Ireland, a protestant opposing the unification of Ireland —**loy´al·ism** *n.*

loyal toast the toast drunk in pledging allegiance to the Sovereign, usually after a meal

loy·al·ty (-tē) *n., pl.* -ties quality, state, or instance of being loyal; faithful adherence, etc.

loz·enge (loz´ənj) *n.* [OFr. *losenge*, prob. < Gaul.] **1.** a plane figure with four equal sides and two obtuse angles; diamond **2.** a cough drop, sweet, etc., orig. in this shape

LP [*L(ong)* *P(laying)*] *a trademark for* a long-playing record —*n.* a long-playing record

LPG liquefied petroleum gas: also **LP-gas**

L-plate a sign attached to the front and back of a motor vehicle, consisting of the letter L, serving to indicate that the driver is a learner

Lr *Chem.* lawrencium

LSD [*l(y)s(ergic acid)* *d(iethylamide)*] a psychedelic drug that produces behaviour and symptoms, as hallucinations, delusions, etc., like those of certain psychoses

L.S.D., £.s.d., l.s.d. [L. *librae, solidi, denarii*] pounds, shillings, pence

L.S.E. London School of Economics

Lt. Lieutenant

Ltd., ltd. limited

Lu *Chem.* lutetium

lu·au (lōō ou´, lōō´ou´) *n.* [Haw.] a Hawaiian feast, usually with entertainment

lub·ber (lub´ər) *n.* [< ME. < *lobbe-* (see LOB)] **1.** a big, slow, clumsy person **2.** a landlubber —**lub´ber·li·ness** *n.* —**lub´ber·ly** *adj., adv.*

lube (lōōb) *n.* **1.** a lubricating oil: also **lube oil** **2.** [Colloq.] a lubrication

lu·bra (lōō´brə) *n.* [Abor.] [Aust.] a black woman; a female aborigine

lu·bri·cant (lōō´brə kənt) *adj.* reducing friction by providing a smooth film as a covering over parts that move against each other —*n.* a substance for reducing friction in this way, as oil or grease

lu·bri·cate (-kāt´) *vt.* -cat´ed, -cat´ing [< L. pp. of *lubricare* < *lubricus*, smooth] **1.** to make slippery or smooth **2.** to apply a lubricant to —*vi.* to serve as a lubricant —**lu´-bri·ca´tion** *n.* —**lu´bri·ca´tive** *adj.* —**lu´bri·ca´tor** *n.*

lu·bric·i·ty (lōō bris´ə tē) *n., pl.* -ties [< Fr. < LL. *lubricitas*] **1.** slipperiness; smoothness **2.** shiftiness **3.** lewdness —**lu·bri´cious** (-brish´əs), **lu·bri·cous** (-bri kəs) *adj.*

lu·cent (lōō´s´nt) *adj.* [< L. prp. of *lucere*, to shine] **1.** giving off light; shining **2.** translucent or clear —**lu´cen·cy** *n.* —**lu´cent·ly** *adv.*

lu·cerne, lu·cern (lōō surn´) *n.* [< Fr. < ModPr., ult. < L. *lucerna*, a lamp < *lucere*, to shine] *same as* ALFALFA

lu·cid (lōō´sid) *adj.* [< L. < *lucere*, to shine] **1.** [Poet.] bright; shining **2.** transparent **3.** designating an interval of sanity in a mental disorder **4.** readily understood **5.** rational —**lu·cid´i·ty, lu´cid·ness** *n.* —**lu´cid·ly** *adv.*

Lu·ci·fer (lōō´sə fər) [OE. < L. < *lux* (gen. *lucis*), LIGHT¹ + *ferre*, to BEAR¹] **1.** [Poet.] the planet Venus when it is the morning star **2.** *Theol.* Satan, esp. as leader of the revolt of the angels before his fall —*n.* [l-] an early type of friction match

luck (luk) *n.* [prob. < MDu. *luk*, contr. < *gelucke*] **1.** the seemingly chance happening of events which affect one; fortune; fate **2.** good fortune, success, etc. —**push one's luck** [Colloq.] to take superfluous risks —**down on one's luck** in misfortune; unlucky —**in luck** lucky —**out of luck** unlucky —**try one's luck** to try to do something without being sure of the outcome —**worse luck** unfortunately

luck·less (-lis) *adj.* having no good luck; unlucky —**luck´-less·ly** *adv.* —**luck´less·ness** *n.*

luck·y (luk´ē) *adj.* **luck´i·er, luck´i·est** **1.** having good luck; fortunate **2.** resulting fortunately **3.** believed to bring good luck —**luck´i·ly** *adv.* —**luck´i·ness** *n.*

lucky dip **1.** a receptacle from which one chooses from among a number of unseen articles **2.** any assortment of alternative plans, solutions, etc. from which choice is made by chance rather than design

lu·cra·tive (lōō´krə tiv) *adj.* [< L. pp. of *lucrari*, to gain < *lucrum*: see ff.] producing wealth or profit; profitable —**lu´cra·tive·ly** *adv.* —**lu´cra·tive·ness** *n.*

lu·cre (lōō´kər) *n.* [< L. *lucrum*, gain, riches] riches; money: chiefly derogatory, as in **filthy lucre**

lu·cu·brate (lōō´kyoo brāt´) *vi.* -brat´ed, -brat´ing [< L. pp. of *lucubrare*, to work by candlelight < *lux*, light] **1.** to work, study, or write laboriously, esp. late at night **2.** to write in a scholarly manner —**lu´cu·bra´tor** *n.*

lu·cu·bra·tion (lōō´kyoo brā´shən) *n.* **1.** a lucubrating **2.** a learned or carefully elaborated work **3.** [*often pl.*] any literary composition: humorous usage suggesting pedantry

lud a form of lord, as in addressing a judge in a law court

Lud·dite (lud´īt) *n.* [< ? Ned *Ludd*, an 18th cent. workman who destroyed industrial machinery] **1.** any of the textile workers who organized machine breaking (1811-1816) in the belief that mechanization had produced unemployment in the textile industries **2.** any opponent of industrial change or innovation

lu·di·crous (lo͞o′di krəs) *adj.* [L. *ludicrus* < *ludus*, a game] causing laughter because absurd or ridiculous —**lu′-di·crous·ly** *adv.* —**lu′di·crous·ness** *n.*

lu·do (lo͞o′dō) *n.* [L. lit., I play] a children's game played with counters, a special board and dice

luff (luf) *n.* [< ODu. *loef*, weather side (of a ship)] 1. a sailing close to the wind 2. the forward edge of a fore-and-aft sail —*vi.* to turn the bow of a ship towards the wind

lug[1] (lug) *vt.* **lugged, lug′ging** [ME. *luggen*, prob. < Scand.] to carry or drag with effort —*n.* 1. an earlike projection by which a thing is held or supported 2. a heavy nut used with a bolt to secure a wheel to an axle 3. a shallow box in which fruit is shipped 4. [Colloq.] an ear

lug[2] (lug) *n. clipped form of* LUGSAIL

lug[3] (lug) *n. clipped form of* LUGWORM

luge (lo͞ozh) *n.* [Fr.] a racing toboggan for one or two persons —*vi.* **luged, luge′ing** to race with luges

Lu·ger (lo͞o′gər) [G.] *a trademark for* a German semiautomatic pistol —*n.* [*often* l-] this pistol

lug·gage (lug′ij) *n.* [LUG[1] + -AGE] suitcases, bags, trunks, etc.

luggage van a special van on a passenger train for heavy luggage

lug·ger (lug′ər) *n.* a small vessel equipped with a lugsail or lugsails

lug·sail (lug′s'l, -sāl′) *n.* [< ? LUG[1]] a four-sided sail attached to an upper yard that hangs obliquely on the mast

lu·gu·bri·ous (loo goo′brē əs) *adj.* [L. *lugubris* < *lugere*, to mourn + -OUS] very sad or mournful, esp. in a way that seems exaggerated or ridiculous —**lu·gu′bri·ous·ly** *adv.* —**lu·gu′bri·ous·ness** *n.*

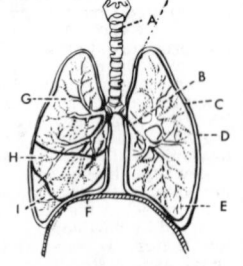
LUGSAIL

lug·worm (lug′wurm′) *n.* [< ? + WORM] a bristly, segmented worm that burrows in muddy sand along the shore and is used for bait

luke·warm (lo͞ok′wôrm′) *adj.* [ME. *luke*, tepid + *warm*, warm] 1. barely or moderately warm: said of liquids 2. not very eager or enthusiastic —**luke′warm′ly** *adv.* —**luke′-warm′ness** *n.*

lull (lul) *vt.* [ME. *lullen*, origin echoic] 1. to calm by gentle sound or motion: chiefly in **lull to sleep** 2. to bring into a specified condition by soothing and reassuring 3. to quiet; allay [to lull one's fears] —*vi.* to become calm —*n.* a short period of quiet or of comparative calm

lull·a·by (lul′ə bī′) *n., pl.* **-bies** a song for lulling a baby to sleep —*vt.* **-bied′, -by′ing** to lull as with a lullaby

lum·ba·go (lum bā′gō) *n.* [< L. *lumbus*, loin] backache, esp. in the lower back

lum·bar (lum′bər) *adj.* [< L. *lumbus*, loin] of or near the loins; specif., designating or of the vertebrae, nerves, etc. in the part of the body just below the thoracic part

lum·ber[1] (lum′bər) *n.* [< ? LOMBARD: orig., pawnshop, hence pawned or stored articles] 1. discarded household articles, furniture, etc. stored away or taking up room 2. [Chiefly Canad.] timber sawn into beams, boards, etc. of convenient sizes —*vt.* 1. to clutter with useless articles or rubbish 2. to remove (timber) from (an area) —*vi.* to cut down timber and saw it into lumber —**lum′ber·er** *n.* —**lum′ber·ing** *n.*

lum·ber[2] (lum′bər) *vi.* [ME. *lomeren* < ? Scand.] 1. to move heavily, clumsily, and, often, noisily 2. to rumble —**lum′ber·ing** *adj.* —**lum′ber·ing·ly** *adv.*

lum·ber·jack (lum′bər jak′) *n. same as* LOGGER

lum·ber·yard (-yärd′) *n.* [U.S.] a place where timber is kept for sale

lu·men (lo͞o′mən) *n., pl.* **-mi·na** (-mi nə), **-mens** [ModL. < L., light] 1. the SI unit of luminous flux; the amount of light falling per second on a unit area at a unit distance from a uniform point source of one candela 2. the bore of a hollow needle, catheter, etc. 3. *Anat.* the passage within a tubular organ

lu·mi·nance (lo͞o′mə nəns) *n.* [< L. *lumen* (see LUMEN) + -ANCE] 1. a being luminous 2. luminous intensity

lu·mi·nar·y (lo͞o′mə nər ē) *n., pl.* **-nar·ies** [< OFr. < LL. < L. *luminare* < *lumen*, light] 1. a body that gives off light, such as the sun or moon 2. *a)* a famous intellectual *b)* any notable person

lu·mi·nesce (lo͞o′mə nes′) *vi.* **-nesced′, -nesc′ing** [back-formation < ff.] to be or become luminescent

lu·mi·nes·cence (-əns) *n.* [< L. *lumen*, a light + -ESCENCE] any giving off of light caused by the absorption of radiant energy, etc. and not by incandescence; any cold light —**lu′-mi·nes′cent** *adj.*

lu·mi·nif·er·ous (-nif′ər əs) *adj.* [< L. *lumen*, a light + -FEROUS] giving off or transmitting light

lu·mi·nous (lo͞o′mə nəs) *adj.* [L. *luminosus* < *lumen*, a light] 1. giving off light; bright 2. illuminated 3. glowing in the dark, as paint with a phosphor in it 4. enlightened or

enlightening —**lu′mi·nos′i·ty** (-nos′ə tē), *pl.* **-ties, lu′mi-nous·ness** *n.* —**lu′mi·nous·ly** *adv.*

lumme (lum′ē) *interj.* [contr. < *Lord love me*] an expression of surprise

lum·mox (lum′əks) *n.* [< ?] [Dial. & U.S. Colloq.] a clumsy, stupid person

lump[1] (lump) *n.* [ME. *lumpe*] 1. a solid mass of no special shape; hunk 2. a small cube, or oblong piece, etc., specif. of sugar 3. a swelling; bulge 4. a large amount; mass 5. a clodlike person 6. [*usually* L-] a system of employment, esp. in the building industry, under which workers are paid as sub-contractors rather than employees —*adj.* in lumps [lump sugar] —*vt.* 1. to put together in a lump or lumps 2. to treat or deal with in a mass, or collectively 3. to make lumps in —*vi.* to become lumpy —**in the lump** all together —**lump in one's throat** a tight feeling in the throat, as from restrained emotion

lump[2] (lump) *vt.* [< ?] [Colloq.] to put up with (something disagreeable) [if you don't like it, you can *lump* it]

lump·ish (lump′ish) *adj.* 1. like a lump 2. clumsy, dull, etc. —**lump′ish·ly** *adv.* —**lump′ish·ness** *n.*

lump sum a gross, or total, sum paid at one time

lump·y (lum′pē) *adj.* **lump′i·er, lump′i·est** 1. full of lumps [lumpy custard] 2. covered with lumps 3. rough: said of water 4. like a lump; heavy; clumsy —**lump′i·ly** *adv.* —**lump′i·ness** *n.*

Lu·na (lo͞o′nə) [L., moon] 1. *Rom. Myth.* the goddess of the moon 2. the moon personified

lu·na·cy (lo͞o′nə sē) *n., pl.* **-cies** [LUNA(TIC) + -CY] 1. insanity 2. utter foolishness

luna moth a large N American moth with crescent-marked wings, the hind pair of which end in elongated tails

lu·nar (lo͞o′nər) *adj.* [< L. < *luna*, the moon] of, on, or like the moon

lunar eclipse *see* ECLIPSE (sense 1)

lunar (excursion) module the module used to go between the spacecraft orbiting the moon and the moon's surface

lunar month *see* MONTH (sense 3)

lunar year a period of twelve lunar months

lu·nate (lo͞o′nāt) *adj.* [< L. < *luna*, the moon] crescent-shaped: also **lu′nat·ed** —**lu′nate·ly** *adv.*

lu·na·tic (lo͞o′nə tik) *adj.* [< OFr. < LL. *lunaticus*, moon-struck, crazy < L. *luna*, moon] 1. [Rare] *a)* insane *b)* of lunacy *c)* of or for insane persons 2. utterly foolish —*n.* an insane person

lunatic asylum [Rare] a mental hospital

lunatic fringe the minority considered fanatical in any political, social, or other movement

lunch (lunch) *n.* [< ?] any light meal; esp., the midday meal between breakfast and dinner —*vi.* to eat lunch —*vt.* to provide lunch for —**lunch′er** *n.*

lunch·eon (lun′chən) *n.* [< prec., prob. after dial. *nuncheon*, a snack] a lunch; esp., a formal lunch with others

luncheon voucher a voucher or ticket issued to employees and redeemable at a restaurant for food: also **L.V.**

lunch·room (lunch′ro͞om′) *n.* a restaurant where light quick meals, as lunches, are served

lung (lung) *n.* [OE. *lungen*] either of the two spongelike respiratory organs in the thorax of vertebrates, that oxygenate the blood and remove carbon dioxide from it —**at the top of one's lungs** in one's loudest voice

lunge[1] (lunj) *n.* [< Fr. < *allonger*, to lengthen < *a-* (< L. *ad*), to + *long* (< L. *longus*), long] 1. a sudden thrust, as with a sword 2. a sudden plunge forward —*vi., vt.* **lunged, lung′ing** to move, or cause to move, with a lunge —**lung′er** *n.*

lunge[2] (lunj) *n.* [Fr., back-formation < *allonge*, extension] 1. a long rope fastened to a horse's head and held by the trainer, who causes the horse to move in a circle 2. the use of the lunge in training horses —*vt.* **lunged, lung′ing** to put a horse through his paces using a lunge Also **longe**

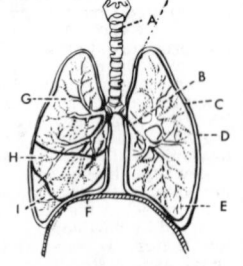
LUNGS
(A, trachea; B, bronchus; C, visceral pleura; D, parietal pleura; E, bron-chiole; F, diaphragm; G, upper lobe; H, middle lobe; I, lower lobe)

lung·fish (lung′fish′) *n., pl.* **-fish′, -fish′es:** see FISH any of various fishes having lungs as well as gills

lung·wort (-wurt′) *n.* [OE. *lungenwyrt*] a plant with large, spotted leaves and clusters of blue or purple flowers

Lu·per·ca·li·a (lo͞o′pər kā′lē ə, -kāl′yə) *n.pl.* an ancient Roman fertility festival, held in February: also **Lu′-per·cal′**(-kal′) *n.sing.* —**Lu′per·ca′li·an** *adj.*

lu·pin (lo͞o′pin) *n.* [< L. < *lupus*, a wolf] 1. a plant of the legume family, with racemes of white, rose, yellow, or blue flowers and pods containing beanlike seeds **2.** the seed of this plant, used in some parts of Europe as food

lu·pine (loo′pīn) *adj.* [< L.< *lupus*, a wolf] **1.** of a wolf or wolves **2.** wolflike; fierce

lu·pus (loo′pəs) *n.* [ModL. < L., a wolf] any of various diseases with skin lesions, esp. tuberculosis of the skin

lurch[1] (lurch) *vi.* [< ?] **1.** to roll, pitch, or sway suddenly forward or to one side **2.** to stagger —*n.* a lurching movement

lurch[2] (lurch) *vi.* [var. of LURK] [Obs.] to lurk —*vt.* [Archaic] to cheat; steal; rob

lurch[3] (lurch) *n.* [Fr. *lourche*, name of a 16th-c. game, prob. < OFr. *lourche*, duped] a situation in certain card games, in which the loser has less than half the score of the winner —**leave in the lurch** to leave in a difficult situation

lurch·er (lur′chər) *n.* **1.** *a)* a person that lurches or lurks *b)* a thief; poacher **2.** a crossbred dog trained to hunt silently, used by poachers

lure (loor) *n.* [< MFr. < OFr. *loirre*, prob. < Gmc.] **1.** a feathered device on the end of a long cord, used in falconry to recall the hawk **2.** *a)* the power of attracting or enticing *b)* anything having this power **3.** a bait used in fishing —*vt.* **lured, lur′ing** to attract; entice —**lur′er** *n.*

lu·rid (loor′id) *adj.* [L. *luridus*, pale yellow, ghastly] **1.** [Rare] deathly pale **2.** glowing through a haze, as flames enveloped by smoke **3.** *a)* startling; sensational *b)* characterized by violent passion or crime —**lu′rid·ly** *adv.* —**lu′rid·ness** *n.*

lurk (lurk) *vi.* [ME. *lurken*, akin to *louren*, LOWER[2]] **1.** to stay hidden, ready to attack, etc. **2.** to exist unobserved, be present as a latent threat, etc. **3.** to move furtively —**lurk′-er** *n.*

lus·cious (lush′əs) *adj.* [ME. *lucius*, prob. var. of *licious*, DELICIOUS, infl. by ff.] **1.** very pleasing to taste or smell; delicious **2.** *a)* delighting any of the senses *b)* voluptuous —**lus′cious·ly** *adv.* —**lus′cious·ness** *n.*

lush[1] (lush) *adj.* [< OFr. *lasche*, lax, loose, ult. < L. *laxus*] **1.** tender and full of juice **2.** of or characterized by rich growth [*lush* vegetation, *lush* fields] **3.** characterized by richness, abundance, or extravagance —**lush′ly** *adv.* —**lush′ness** *n.*

lush[2] (lush) *n.* [< ?] [Slang] **1.** formerly, alcoholic liquor **2.** [Chiefly U.S.] an alcoholic —*vi., vt.* [Slang] to drink (alcoholic liquor)

lust (lust) *n.* [OE., pleasure, appetite] **1.** a desire to satisfy one's sexual needs; esp., strong sexual desire **2.** *a)* excessive desire [a *lust* for power] *b)* great zest —*vi.* to feel an intense desire, esp. sexual desire —**lust′ful** *adj.* —**lust′ful·ly** *adv.* —**lust′ful·ness** *n.*

lus·ter (lus′tər) *n., vt., vi.* -tred, -tring *U.S. sp. of* LUSTRE

lus·tral (lus′trəl) *adj.* [L. *lustralio* < LUSTRUM] of, used in, or connected with ceremonial purification

lus·trate (lus′trāt) *vt.* -trat·ed, -trat·ing [< L. pp. of *lustrare*: see LUSTRUM] to purify by means of certain ceremonies —**lus·tra′tion** *n.*

lus·tre (lus′tər) *n.* [< Fr. < It. < L. *lustrare*, to illumine] **1.** gloss; sheen **2.** brightness; radiance **3.** *a)* radiant beauty *b)* fame; glory **4.** a glossy fabric of cotton and wool **5.** the reflecting quality and brilliance of the surface of a mineral **6.** the metallic, sometimes irridescent appearance of glazed pottery —*vt.* **1.** to give a lustrous finish to **2.** to add glory to —*vi.* to be or become lustrous

lus·tre·ware (-wer′) *n.* highly glazed earthenware decorated by the application of metallic oxides to the glaze: also, chiefly U.S. sp., **lusterware**

lus·trous (-trəs) *adj.* having lustre; shining; bright —**lus′-trous·ly** *adv.* —**lus′trous·ness** *n.*

lus·trum (lus′trəm) *n., pl.* -trums, -tra (-trə) [L., orig., prob. illumination] **1.** in ancient Rome, a purification of all the people by means of ceremonies held every five years **2.** a five-year period

lust·y (lus′tē) *adj.* lust′i·er, lust′i·est full of vigour; strong, robust, hearty, etc. —**lust′i·ly** *adv.* —**lust′i·ness** *n.*

lu·ta·nist, lu·te·nist (loot′ən ist) *n.* a lute player

lute[1] (loot) *n.* [< MFr. < OFr. < Ar. *al′ūd*, lit., the wood] an early stringed instrument with a rounded back and a long, fretted neck often bent in a sharp angle

lute[2] (loot) *n.* [< OFr. < L. *lutum*, mud, clay] a clayey cement used as a sealing agent for the joints of pipes, etc. —*vt.* **lut′ed, lut′ing** to seal with lute

lu·te·in·iz·ing hormone (loot′ē in īz′-iŋ) [ult. < (CORPUS) LUTEUM] a hormone of the pituitary that esp. stimulates ovulation and the development of the corpus luteum

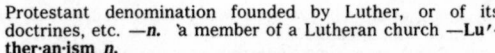

LUTE

lu·te·ti·um (loo tē′shē əm) *n.* [ModL. < L. *Lutetia*, ancient Rom. name of Paris] a metallic chemical element of the rare-earth group: symbol, Lu; at. wt., 174.97; at. no., 71

Lu·ther·an (loo′thər ən) *adj.* **1.** of Martin Luther **2.** of the Protestant denomination founded by Luther, or of its doctrines, etc. —*n.* 'a member of a Lutheran church —**Lu′-ther·an·ism** *n.*

Lu·tine Bell (loo′tēn) a bell, taken from the ship *Lutine*, kept at Lloyd's in London and rung before important announcements, esp. the loss of a vessel

lut·ist (loot′ist) *n.* a lute player

lux (luks) *n., pl.* **lux, lux′es** [< L. *lux*, LIGHT[1]] the SI unit of illuminance; equivalent to one lumen per square metre

luxe (looks, luks) *n.* [Fr. < L. *luxus*, luxury] richness, elegance, luxury, etc.: see also DELUXE

lux·u·ri·ant (lug zhoor′ē ənt, luk shoor′-) *adj.* [< L. prp. of *luxuriare*: see ff.] **1.** growing with vigour and in abundance; lush; teeming **2.** richly or extravagantly full, varied, elaborate, etc. **3.** *same as* LUXURIOUS —**lux·u′-ri·ance, lux·u′ri·an·cy** *n.* —**lux·u′ri·ant·ly** *adv.*

lux·u·ri·ate (-āt′) *vi.* -at′ed, -at′ing [< L. pp. of *luxuriare*, to be too fruitful < *luxuria*, LUXURY] **1.** to grow with vigour and in great abundance **2.** to live in great luxury **3.** to revel (*in*) —**lux·u′ri·a′tion** *n.*

lux·u·ri·ous (-əs) *adj.* **1.** fond of or indulging in luxury **2.** filled with or providing luxury; splendid, rich, comfortable, etc. —**lux·u′ri·ous·ly** *adv.* —**lux·u′ri·ous·ness** *n.*

lux·u·ry (luk′shə rē, lug′zhə-) *n., pl.* -ries [< OFr. < L. *luxuria* < *luxus*, luxury] **1.** the enjoyment of the best and most costly things that offer the greatest comfort and satisfaction **2.** anything giving such enjoyment, usually something considered unnecessary to life and health **3.** any unusual pleasure or comfort —*adj.* characterized by luxury

L.V. Luncheon Voucher

lx *Physics the symbol for* lux

LXX Septuagint

-ly[1] (lē) [OE. *-lic*] a suffix used to form adjectives and meaning: **1.** like, characteristic of, suitable to [*manly*] **2.** happening (once) every (specified period of time) [*monthly*]

-ly[2] (lē) [OE. *-lice* < *-lic*] a suffix used to form adverbs and meaning: **1.** in a (specified) manner, to a (specified) extent or direction, in or at a (specified) time or place [*harshly*, *outwardly*, *hourly*] **2.** in the (specified) order of sequence [*secondly*]

ly·can·thro·py (lī kan′thrə pē) *n.* [ModL. *lycanthropia* < Gr. *lykos*, wolf + *anthrōpos*, a man] **1.** a form of mental disorder in which the patient imagines himself to be a wolf **2.** Folklore the magical power to transform oneself or another into a wolf —**ly·can·throp·ic** (lī′kən throp′ik) *adj.*

‡ly·cée (lē′sā′) *n.* [Fr. < L.: see ff.] in France, a state secondary school

ly·ce·um (lī sē′əm) *n.* [L. < Gr. *Lykeion*, the Lyceum, the grove at Athens where Aristotle taught] [Chiefly U.S.] **1.** a lecture hall **2.** an organization presenting public lectures, concerts, etc.

ly·chee (lī′chē) *n. same as* LITCHI

lych gate *see* LICH GATE

lye (lī) *n.* [OE. *leag*] **1.** orig., a strong alkaline solution obtained by leaching wood ashes **2.** any strongly alkaline substance: Lye is used in cleaning and in making soap

ly·ing[1] (lī′iŋ) *prp. of* LIE[1]

ly·ing[2] (lī′iŋ) *prp. of* LIE[2] —*adj.* false; not truthful —*n.* the telling of a lie or lies

ly·ing-in (-in′) *n.* confinement in childbirth —*adj.* of or for childbirth [a *lying-in* hospital]

lymph (limf) *n.* [L. *lympha*, spring water (infl. by Gr. *nymphē*, NYMPH)] a clear, yellowish fluid resembling blood plasma, found in the lymphatic vessels of vertebrates

lym·phat·ic (lim fat′ik) *adj.* **1.** of, containing, or conveying lymph **2.** sluggish; without energy —*n.* a lymphatic vessel

lymph node any of many small, compact structures lying in groups along the course of the lymphatic vessels and producing lymphocytes: also, esp. formerly, **lymph gland**

lym·pho- a combining form meaning of lymph or the lymphatics: also, before a vowel, **lymph-**

lym·pho·cyte (lim′fə sīt′) *n.* [pref. + -CYTE] a variety of leucocyte formed in lymphatic tissue —**lym′pho·cyt′ic** (-sit′-ik) *adj.*

lymph·oid (lim′foid) *adj.* of or like lymph or the tissue of the lymph nodes

lynch (linch) *vt.* [< LYNCH LAW] to murder (an accused person) by mob action and without lawful trial, as by hanging —**lynch′er** *n.* —**lynch′ing** *n.*

lynch law [after Capt. William *Lynch* (1742–1820), member of a vigilance committee in Pittsylvania, Virginia, U.S., in 1780] the practice of killing by lynching

lynch·pin (linch′pin′) *n. same as* LINCHPIN

lynx (liŋks) *n., pl.* **lynx′es, lynx:** see PLURAL, II, D, 1 [L. < Gr. *lynx*] any of a group of wildcats found throughout the Northern Hemisphere and characterized by a short tail, long, tufted ears, and keen vision

lynx-eyed (-īd′) *adj.* having very keen sight

Lyon King of Arms (lī′ən) the chief herald of Scotland, presiding over **Lyon Court**, which deals with questions of heraldry

ly·on·naise (lī′ə nāz′; Fr. lyô nez′) *adj.* [Fr., fem. of

Lyonnais, of Lyon] prepared with finely sliced onions, as potatoes with fried onions

Ly·ra (lī′rə) a N constellation: it contains Vega

ly·rate (lī′rāt) *adj.* shaped like a lyre

lyre (līr) *n.* [< L. < Gr. *lyra*] a small stringed instrument of the harp family, played by the ancient Greeks

lyre·bird (-burd′) *n.* an Australian songbird: the long tail feathers of the male resemble a lyre when spread

lyr·ic (lir′ik) *adj.* [< Fr. or L.: both < Gr. *lyrikos*] 1. suitable for singing, as to the accompaniment of a lyre; songlike; specif., designating poetry expressing the poet's emotions and thoughts: sonnets, odes, etc. are lyric poems 2. writing lyric poetry 3. *same as* LYRICAL 4. having a relatively high voice with a light, flexible quality [a lyric tenor] —*n.* 1. a lyric poem 2. [*usually pl.*] the words of a song

LYRE

lyr·i·cal (-i k′l) *adj.* 1. *same as* LYRIC 2. expressing rapture or great enthusiasm —**lyr′i·cal·ly** *adv.*

lyr·i·cism (lir′ə siz′m) *n.* lyric quality, style, expression, etc.

lyr·i·cist (-sist) *n.* a writer of lyrics, esp. lyrics for popular songs

-lyse (līz) *a combining form used to form verbs corresponding to nouns ending in* -LYSIS [*electrolyze*]

ly·sin (lī′s'n) *n.* [< Gr. *lysis* (see ff.) + -IN¹] any antibody capable of dissolving bacteria, blood corpuscles, etc.

ly·sis (lī′sis) *n.* [ModL. < Gr. *lysis*, a loosening < *lyein*, to loose] 1. cell destruction by lysins 2. the gradual ending of disease symptoms

-ly·sis (lə sis) [see prec.] *a combining form meaning* a loosing, dissolution, dissolving, destruction [*catalysis, paralysis*]

-lyte (līt) [< Gr. *lytos* < *lyein*: see LYSIS] *a combining form meaning* a substance subjected to a process of decomposition [*hydrolyte*]

-lyt·ic (lit′ik) 1. *a combining form used to form adjectives corresponding to nouns ending in* -LYSIS [*catalytic*] 2. *Biochem.* a combining form meaning hydrolysis by enzymes

M

M, m (em) *n., pl.* **M's, m's** 1. the thirteenth letter of the English alphabet 2. the sound of *M* or *m*

M (em) *n.* the Roman numeral for 1000

M. 1. Medieval 2. *Music* mezzo 3. Monday 4. *pl.* **MM.** Monsieur 5. Motorway

M., m. 1. majesty 2. male 3. married 4. masculine 5. *Physics* mass 6. meridian 7. mile(s) 8. minim 9. minute(s) 10. month 11. [L. *meridies*] noon [*A.M., P.M.*]

m metre; metres

ma (mä) *n.* [Colloq.] mamma; mother

M.A. [L. *Magister Artium*] Master of Arts

ma'am (mam, mäm; *unstressed* məm, 'm) *n.* [Colloq.] madam: used in direct address

Mac (mak) *n.* [< MAC-, MC-] [Colloq.] a Scotsman

mac (mak) *n. see* MACK

Mac- (mak, mək, mə) [< Ir. & Gael. *mac*, son] *a prefix meaning* son of: used in Scottish and Irish family names: also **Mc-, Mᶜ-, M'-**

ma·ca·bre (mə käb′rə, -kä′bər) *adj.* [Fr. < OFr. (*danse*) *Macabré*, (dance) of death] gruesome; grim and horrible

mac·ad·am (mə kad′əm) *n.* [after J. L. *McAdam* (1756-1836), Brit. engineer] small broken stones used in making roads, usually combined with tar or asphalt

mac·a·dam·i·a nut (mak′ə dā′mē ə) [after J. *Macadam* (d. 1865), Brit. chemist in Australia] a spherical, hard-shelled, edible nut from an Australian tree, also cultivated in Hawaii, etc.

mac·ad·am·ize (mə kad′ə mīz′) *vt.* -ized′, -iz′ing to make, repair, or cover (a road) by rolling successive layers of macadam on it

ma·caque (mə käk′) *n.* [Fr. < Port. *macaco*] any of a group of monkeys of Asia, Africa, and the East Indies, with a nonprehensile tail

mac·a·ro·ni (mak′ə rō′nē) *n.* [It. *maccaroni*, pl. < LowGr. *makaria*, broth barley] 1. pasta in the form of tubes, etc., often baked with cheese, minced beef, etc. 2. *pl.* -nies an 18th-cent. British dandy

mac·a·roon (mak′ə rōōn′) *n.* [< Fr. < It. *maccaroni*, MACARONI] a small biscuit made chiefly of egg white, crushed almonds or coconut, and sugar

ma·caw¹ (mə kô′) *n.* [Port. *macao*, prob. < Braz. (Tupi) native name] a large, bright-coloured, harsh-voiced parrot of Central and South America

ma·caw² (mə kô′) *n.* [< ?] a kind of palm-tree found in S. America and the Caribbean

Macc. Maccabees

mace¹ (mās) *n.* [< OFr. *masse*] 1. a heavy, spiked, armour-breaking club, used in the Middle Ages 2. *a*) a staff used as a symbol of authority by certain officials, esp. as carried before the Speaker of the House of Commons *b*) a person who carries a mace: also **mace′bear′er**

mace² (mās) *n.* [< OFr. *macis* < ML. < L. *makir*, a fragrant resin] a spice, usually ground, made from the dried outer covering of the nutmeg

ma·cé·doine (mas′i dwän′; *Fr.* må så dwän′) *n.* [Fr. lit., Macedonia:? referring to mixture of diverse races there] 1.

a mixture of diced vegetables or fruits served in jelly 2. a medley

mac·er·ate (mas′ə rāt′) *vt.* -at′ed, -at′ing [< L. pp. of *macerare*, to soften] 1. to soften and break down the parts of by soaking in liquid for some time 2. loosely, to break, tear, chop, etc. into bits 3. to cause to waste away or grow thin —*vi.* to waste away; grow thin —**mac′er·a′tion** *n.* —**mac′er·a′tor** *n.*

Mach (mak) *n.* *clipped form of* MACH NUMBER

mach. 1. machine 2. machinery 3. machinist

ma·che·te (mə shet′ē, -chet′ē) *n.* [Sp., dim. of *macho*, ult. < L. *marcus*, a hammer] a large, heavy-bladed knife used for cutting down sugar cane or undergrowth in the West Indies, Central, and South America

Mach·i·a·vel·li·an (mak′ē ə vel′ē ən, -vel′-yən) *adj.* of or like Machiavelli, the 15th cent. Florentine statesman, or the political principles of craftiness and duplicity advocated by him—*n.* a follower of such principles —**Mach′i·a·vel′li·an·ism** *n.*

MACHETE

ma·chic·o·late (mə chik′ə lāt′) *vt.* -lat′ed, -lat′ing [< ML. pp. of *machicolare* < MFr., prob. < L. *masticare*, MASTICATE + *col*, the neck: from use of machicolations to drop stones, etc.] to put machicolations in (a parapet, etc.)

ma·chic·o·la·tion (mə chik′ə lā′shən) *n.* an opening, as in the floor of a gallery or parapet, through which hot liquids, rocks, etc. could be dropped by the defenders of a fortress

mach·i·nate (mak′ə nāt′) *vi., vt.* -nat′ed, -nat′ing [< L. pp. of *machinari*, to plot < *machina*, MACHINE] to devise, plan, or plot artfully, esp. to do evil —**mach′i·na′tor** *n.*

mach·i·na·tion (mak′ə nā′shən) *n.* an artful or secret plot or scheme, esp. an evil one: *usually used in pl.*

ma·chine (mə shēn′) *n.* [Fr. < L. *machina* < Gr. *mēchos*, contrivance] 1. a vehicle, as a motor car: old-fashioned term 2. a structure consisting of a framework and various fixed and moving parts, for doing some kind of work; mechanism [a sewing machine] 3. a person or organization regarded as acting like a machine; esp., the smoothly functioning complex organization 4. the members of a political party who control policy and confer patronage 5. *Mech.* a device, as a lever or pulley, that transmits, or changes the application of, energy —*adj.* 1. of a machine or machines 2. made or done by machinery 3. standardized; stereotyped —*vt.* -chined′, -chin′ing to make, shape, etc. by machinery —**ma·chin′a·ble** *adj.*

machine age a time, such as the present, when many mechanical devices are in use at work or home

machine gun an automatic gun, usually with a cooling apparatus, firing a rapid stream of bullets fed into it by a belt —**ma·chine′-gun′** (-gun′) *vt.* -gunned′, -gun′ning

ma·chin·er·y (mə shēn′ər ē) *n., pl.* -er·ies 1. machines collectively 2. the working parts of a machine 3. any means by which something is kept in action or a desired result is obtained [the *machinery* of government]

machine shop a factory for making or repairing machines or machine parts

machine tool a power-driven tool, as an electric lathe or drill —**ma·chine′-tool′** *adj., vt.*

ma·chin·ist (-ist) *n.* 1. a person who makes or repairs machinery 2. a worker skilled in using machine tools or one who operates a machine

‡**ma·chis·mo** (ma chiz′mō) *n.* [< Sp. *macho*, masculine, ult. < L.] strong or aggressive masculinity; virility

Mach number (mak) [after Ernst *Mach* (1838–1916), Austrian physicist] [*also* m-] a number representing the ratio of the speed of an object to the speed of sound through the same medium, as air

-machy (mə kē) [< Gr. *mache*, a battle] a combining form meaning struggle, contest of

mack (mak) *n.* clipped form of MACKINTOSH

mack·er·el (mak′ər əl, mak′rəl) *n., pl.* **-el, -els**: see PLURAL, II, D, 2 [< OFr. *makerel* < ?] an edible fish of the North Atlantic, with a greenish, blue-striped back and a silvery belly

mackerel sky a sky with rows of small, fleecy clouds, like the streaks on a mackerel's back

mack·in·tosh, mac·in·tosh (mak′in tosh′) *n.* [after C. *Macintosh* (1766–1843), the Brit. inventor] a waterproof raincoat, or the fabric for it

mac·ra·mé (mə krä′mē, mak′rə mā′) *n.* [Fr. < It. < Turk. *makrama*, napkin < Ar. *miqramah*, a veil] 1. a coarse fringe or lace of thread or cord knotted in designs 2. the craft of making these fringes

mac·ro- [< Gr. *makros*, long] a combining form meaning long (in extent or duration), large, enlarged, or elongated: also, before a vowel, **macr-**

mac·ro·bi·ot·ics (mak′rō bī ot′iks) *n.pl.* [with sing. v.] [< prec. + Gr. *biōtikos* < *bios*, life] the art of prolonging life, as by a special diet —**mac′ro·bi·ot′ic** *adj.*

mac·ro·ceph·a·ly (mak′rə sef′ə lē) *n.* [MACRO- + CEPHAL(O)- + -Y[3]] a condition in which the head or cranial capacity is abnormally large —**mac′ro·ceph′a·lous, mac′-ro·ce·phal′ic** (-si fal′ik) *adj.*

mac·ro·cosm (mak′rə koz′m) *n.* [< Fr. < ML.: see MACRO-& COSMOS[1]] 1. the universe 2. any large, complex entity —**mac′ro·cos′mic** *adj.*

mac·ro·e·co·nom·ics (mak′rō ē′kə nom′iks, -ek′ə-) *n.* a branch of economics dealing with the large units and forces in the economy of a country or group of countries

mac·ro·mol·e·cule (mak′rə mol′ə kyool′) *n.* a very large molecule, as a polymer molecule, composed of hundreds or thousands of atoms

ma·cron (ma′kron) *n.* [< Gr. neut. of *makros*, long] a short, straight mark (‾) placed horizontally over a vowel to indicate that it is long or is to be pronounced in a certain way

mac·ro·scop·ic (mak′rə skop′ik) *adj.* [MACRO- + -SCOP(E) + -IC] 1. visible to the naked eye 2. having to do with large groups or units Also **mac′ro·scop′i·cal**

mac·u·la (mak′yoo lə) *n., pl.* **-lae** (-lē′), **-las** [L.] a spot, blotch, etc.; esp., a) a discoloured spot on the skin b) a sunspot —**mac′u·lar** *adj.*

macula lu·te·a (loot′ē ə) [ModL., lit., yellowish spot] a small yellowish area of especially keen vision on the retina

mad (mad) *adj.* **mad′der, mad′dest** [< OE. pp. of (ge)mædan, to drive mad] 1. mentally ill; insane 2. frenzied; frantic [*mad* with fear] 3. foolish and rash; unwise 4. foolishly enthusiastic or fond [*mad* about clothes] 5. wildly amusing; hilarious 6. having rabies [a *mad* dog] 7. a) angry (often with at) b) showing anger 8. [S. Afr. Colloq.] excellent —**mad as a hatter** (or **March hare**) completely crazy

mad·am (mad′əm) *n., pl.* **mad′ams**; for 1, usually **mes·dames** (mā dam′) [< Fr., orig. ma dame < L. mea domina, my lady] 1. a woman; lady: a polite term of address 2. the mistress of a household 3. a woman in charge of a brothel 4. [Slang] a precocious, pompous or pert girl or young woman

mad·ame (mad′əm; *Fr.* mà dàm′) *n., pl.* **mes·dames** (mā dam′; *Fr.* mā dàm′) [Fr.: see prec.] a married woman: French title equivalent to *Mrs.*: abbrev. **Mme.**

mad·cap (mad′kap′) *n.* [MAD + CAP, fig. for head] a reckless, impulsive person, esp. a girl —*adj.* reckless and impulsive

mad·den (mad′'n) *vt., vi.* to make or become mad; make or become insane, angry, or wildly excited —**mad′den·ing** *adj.* —**mad′den·ing·ly** *adv.*

mad·der (mad′ər) *n.* [OE. mædere] 1. any of various plants of the madder family; esp., a perennial vine with small, yellow flowers 2. a) the red root of this vine b) a red dye made from this 3. crimson —*adj.* designating a family of chiefly tropical herbs, shrubs, and trees, including bedstraw, coffee, etc.

mad·ding (-iŋ) *adj.* [Rare] 1. raving; frenzied [“the madding crowd”] 2. making mad

made (mād) *pt. & pp.* of MAKE —*adj.* 1. constructed; formed 2. produced artificially [*made* flowers] 3. invented; contrived [a *made* word] 4. prepared from various ingredients [a *made* dish] 5. sure of success [a *made* man] —**be made for** to be well-matched or ideally suited —**have (got) it made** [Slang] to be assured of success

Ma·deir·a (mə dir′ə) *n.* [after *Madeira*, the island off NW Africa] [also m-] a fortified wine

mad·e·leine (mad′əl in) *n.* [Fr., after *Madeleine* Paulnier, 19th-c. Fr. cook] a small, rich cake

ma·de·moi·selle (mad′ə mə zel′, mam zel′; *Fr.* màd-mwa zel′) *n.,* *Fr.* *pl.* **mesde·moi·selles** (mād mwà zel′) [Fr. < ma, my + *demoiselle*, young lady] an unmarried woman or girl: French title equivalent to *Miss*: abbrev. **Mlle.**

made-to-or·der (mād′tə ôr′dər) *adj.* made to conform to the customer's specifications; custom-made 2. [Colloq.] very suitable, just right Also **made-to-measure**

made-up (-up′) *adj.* 1. put together; arranged [a *made-up* page of type] 2. invented; false [a *made-up* story] 3. with cosmetics applied

mad·house (mad′hous′) *n.* 1. [Archaic] a place of confinement for the mentally ill 2. any place of turmoil, noise, and confusion

mad·ly (mad′lē) *adv.* 1. insanely 2. wildly; furiously 3. foolishly 4. extremely

mad·man (mad′man′, -mən) *n., pl.* **-men′** (-men′, -mən) an insane person; lunatic; maniac —**mad′wom′an** *n.fem., pl.* **-wom′en**

mad·ness (-nis) *n.* 1. insanity 2. great anger 3. great folly 4. wild excitement 5. rabies

Ma·don·na (mə don′ə) *n.* [It. < ma, my (< L. mea) + donna, lady (< L. domina)] 1. Mary, mother of Jesus 2. a picture or statue of Mary

ma·dras (mə dras′, -dräs′) *n.* [< *Madras*, city in India] a fine, firm cotton cloth, usually striped or checked, used for shirts, dresses, etc.

‡**ma·dre** (ma′dre) *n.* [Sp.] mother

mad·re·pore (mad′rə pôr′) *n.* [< Fr. < It. < *madre*, mother + poro, a pore] any of various branching corals that form reefs and islands in tropical seas —**mad′re·por′ic, mad′-re·por′i·an** *adj.*

mad·ri·gal (mad′ri gəl) *n.* [< It. *madrigale* < ?] 1. a short poem, usually of love, that can be set to music 2. a contrapuntal part song, without accompaniment, popular in the 15th to 17th cent. 3. loosely, any song —**mad′-ri·gal·ist** *n.*

Mae·ce·nas (mi sē′nəs) *n.* [after *Maecenas* (70?-8 B.C.), Rom. statesman] any wealthy, generous patron

mael·strom (māl′strəm) *n.* [Early ModDu. < malen, to grind + stroom, a stream] 1. any large or violent whirlpool: after the whirlpool off the W coast of Norway 2. a violently agitated state of mind, conditions, affairs, etc.

mae·nad (mē′nad) *n.* [< L. < Gr. < mainesthai, to rave] 1. [often M-] a female worshipper of Dionysus; bacchante 2. a frenzied woman —**mae·nad′ic** (mi nad′ik) *adj.*

ma·es·to·so (mīs tō′sō; It. mä′e stō′sō) *adj., adv.* [It.] *Music* with majesty or dignity

ma·es·tro (mīs′trō) *n., pl.* **-tros, -tri** (-trē) [It. < L. magister, a MASTER] a master in any art; esp., a great composer, conductor, or teacher of music

Mae West (mā′ west′) [after *Mae West* (1892-), shapely U.S. actress] an inflated life-jacket

Ma·fi·a, Maf·fi·a (ma′fē ə) *n.* [It. maffia, hostility to law] an alleged secret society of criminals in the U.S. and other countries

Ma·fi·o·si (ma′fē ō′sē) *n.pl., sing.* **-so′** (-sō′) [It.] members of the Mafia

mag. 1. magazine 2. magnetism 3. magnitude

mag·a·zine (mag′ə zēn′, mag′ə zēn′) *n.* [< Fr. < OFr. < It. < Ar. < makhzan, a granary < khazana, to store up] 1. a warehouse or military supply depot 2. a space in which explosives are stored, as in a fort or warship 3. a supply chamber, as the space in a rifle from which the cartridges are fed, the space in a camera from which the film is fed, etc. 4. things kept in a magazine, as munitions or supplies 5. a publication that appears at regular intervals and contains stories, articles, etc. and, usually, advertisements

mag·da·lene (mag′də lēn, -lin) *n.* [LL. < Gr. < *Magdala*, town in Galilee] a reformed and repentant prostitute: after Mary Magdalene in the Bible who was identified with the woman in Luke 7:37 ff.

Mag·da·le·ni·an (mag′də lē′nē ən) *adj.* [Fr. magdalénien after La Madeleine, rock shelter in SW France where many of the artifacts were found] of a culture or late period of the Old Stone Age, characterized by cave art and tools of bone and stone

Ma·gel·lan·ic cloud (maj′ə lan′ik) [after Ferdinand *Magellan* (1480?-1521), Port. navigator] *Astron.* either of two cloudlike, irregular galaxies visible in the southern heavens, that are the nearest of the eternal galaxies to the Milky Way

ma·gen·ta (mə jen'tə) *n.* [< *Magenta*, town in Italy] purplish red —*adj.* purplish-red

mag·got (mag'ət) *n.* [ME. *magotte*] 1. a wormlike insect larva, as the legless larva of the housefly 2. an odd notion; whim —**mag'got·y** *adj.*

Ma·gi (mā'jī) *n.pl., sing.* **Ma'gus** (-gəs) [L., pl. of *magus* < Gr. < OPer. *magush*] 1. the priestly caste in ancient Media and Persia 2. *Douai Bible* the wise men from the East who brought gifts to the infant Jesus: Matt. 2:1–13 —**Ma'gi·an** (-jē ən) *adj., n.*

mag·ic (maj'ik) *n.* [< OFr. < L. < Gr. < *magikos*, of the MAGI] 1. the use of charms, spells, etc. in seeking or pretending to control events or forces 2. any power or influence that seems mysterious or hard to explain [the *magic* of love] 3. the art of producing illusions by sleight of hand, etc. —*adj.* 1. of, produced by, or using magic 2. producing extraordinary results, as if by magic —**magic away** to bring about the disappearance of someone or something, as if by magic —**mag'i·cal** *adj.* —**mag'i·cal·ly** *adv.*

ma·gi·cian (mə jish'ən) *n.* [< OFr. *magicien*] an expert in magic; specif., *a*) a sorcerer; wizard *b*) a performer skilled in magic (sense 3)

magic lantern *old-fashioned term for* a slide projector for showing still pictures from slides

Ma·gi·not Line (mazh'ə nō') [after André *Maginot* (1877-1932), Fr. minister of war] any line of defence which is regarded as impregnable: after the system of defences built by France in the 1930's on the E frontier

mag·is·te·ri·al (maj'is tir'ē əl) *adj.* [< ML. < LL. < L. *magister*, a MASTER] 1. of or suitable for a magistrate or master 2. authoritative 3. domineering; pompous —**mag'is·te'ri·al·ly** *adv.*

mag·is·tra·cy (maj'is trə sē) *n., pl.* **-cies** 1. the position, office, or jurisdiction of a magistrate 2. magistrates collectively: also **mag'is·tra·ture**

mag·is·trate (-trāt', -trit) *n.* [< L. < *magister*, MASTER] 1. a civil officer empowered to administer the law 2. a minor official with limited judicial powers, as a justice of the peace

magistrate's court a court dealing with minor crimes, certain civil actions and licensing matters

mag·ma (mag'mə) *n.* [L. < Gr. < *massein*, to knead] molten rock deep in the earth, from which igneous rock is formed

Mag·na Char·ta (or **Car·ta**) (mag'nə kär'tə) [ML., lit., great charter] 1. the charter that King John was forced by the English barons to grant at Runnymede, June 15, 1215, interpreted as guaranteeing certain civil and political liberties 2. any constitution guaranteeing certain liberties

mag·na·nim·i·ty (mag'nə nim'ə tē) *n.* 1. a magnanimous quality or state 2. *pl.* **-ties** a magnanimous act

mag·nan·i·mous (mag nan'ə məs) *adj.* [< L. < *magnus*, great + *animus*, soul] generous in overlooking injury or insult; rising above pettiness or meanness —**mag·nan'i·mous·ly** *adv.*

mag·nate (mag'nāt) *n.* [< LL. < L. *magnus*, great] a very influential person, esp. in business

mag·ne·sia (mag nē'zhə, -shə) *n.* [ModL., ult. < Gr. *Magnēsia*, area in Thessaly] magnesium oxide, MgO, a white, tasteless powder used as a mild laxative and antacid, and as an insulating substance —**mag·ne'sian, mag·ne'sic** (-sik) *adj.*

mag·ne·si·um (mag nē'zē əm) *n.* [ModL. < prec.] a light, silver-white, malleable metallic chemical element: it burns with a hot, white light, and is used in photographic flashbulbs, etc.: symbol, Mg; at. wt., 24.312; at. no., 12

mag·net (mag'nit) *n.* [< OFr. < L. *magnes* < Gr. *Magnētis* (*lithos*), (stone) of Magnesia: see MAGNESIA] 1. any piece of iron, steel, or lodestone that has the property of attracting iron, steel, etc. 2. a person or thing that attracts

mag·net·ic (mag net'ik) *adj.* 1. having the properties of a magnet 2. of, producing, or caused by magnetism 3. of the earth's magnetism 4. that can be magnetized 5. powerfully attractive [a *magnetic* personality] —**mag·net'i·cal·ly** *adv.*

magnetic bottle *Physics* a geometrical configuration whose extent is outlined by magnetic lines of force that will confine a hot plasma

magnetic field a region of space in which there is an appreciable magnetic force

magnetic flux the sum of all the lines of force in a magnetic field

magnetic force the attracting or repelling force between a magnet and a ferromagnetic material, between a magnet and a current-carrying conductor, etc.

magnetic mine a naval mine exploded when the metal hull of a ship passing near it deflects a magnetic needle, thus detonating the charge

magnetic needle a slender bar of magnetized steel which,

when swinging freely on a pivot, as in a compass, points towards the magnetic poles

magnetic north the direction towards which a magnetic needle points, usually not true north

magnetic pickup a gramophone pickup in which a part of the stylus assembly vibrates in a magnetic field between two coils so as to induce a current

magnetic pole 1. either pole of a magnet 2. either point on the earth's surface towards which a magnetic needle points: the north and south magnetic poles do not precisely coincide with the geographical poles

magnetic recording the recording of electrical signals by means of changes in areas of magnetization on a tape (**magnetic tape**) or disc

magnetic storm a worldwide disturbance of the earth's magnetic field, believed to be caused by sunspot activity

magnetic tape a thin plastic ribbon coated with iron oxide particles, used as a storage medium for magnetic recording

mag·net·ism (mag'nə tiz'm) *n.* 1. the property or quality of being magnetic 2. the force to which this is due 3. the branch of physics dealing with magnetic phenomena 4. personal charm

mag·net·ite (-tīt') *n.* a black iron oxide, an important iron ore: called *lodestone* when magnetic

mag·net·ize (mag'nə tīz') *vt.* **-ized', -iz'ing** 1. to give magnetic properties to (steel, iron, etc.) 2. to attract or charm (a person) —*vi.* to become magnetic —**mag'net·iz'a·ble** *adj.* —**mag'net·i·za'tion** *n.* —**mag'net·iz'er** *n.*

mag·ne·to (mag nēt'ō) *n., pl.* **-tos** a dynamo in which one or more permanent magnets produce the magnetic field; esp., a small machine of this sort connected with an internal-combustion engine to generate the current providing a spark for the ignition

mag·ne·to- [see MAGNET] a combining form meaning: 1. magnetism, magnetic force 2. magnetoelectric

mag·ne·to·e·lec·tric (-i lek'trik) *adj.* designating or of electricity produced by changing magnetic fields in the vicinity of electric conductors —**mag·ne'to·e·lec'tric'i·ty** (-tris'ə tē) *n.*

mag·ne·tom·e·ter (mag'nə tom'ə tər) *n.* an instrument for measuring magnetic forces

mag·ne·to·mo·tive (mag nēt'ō mōt'iv) *adj.* designating or of a force that causes magnetic flux

mag·ne·to·sphere (mag nēt'ə sfir') *n.* [MAGNETO- + -SPHERE] that region surrounding a planet in which the planetary magnetic field is stronger than the interplanetary field

mag·ne·tron (mag'nə tron') *n.* [MAGNE(T) + (ELEC)TRON] an electron tube in which the flow of electrons is acted upon by an externally applied magnetic field to produce microwave frequencies

mag·ni- [< L. *magnus*, great] a combining form meaning great, big, large [magnificent]

Mag·nif·i·cat (mag nif'i kat') *n.* [L.] 1. the hymn of the Virgin Mary in Luke 1:46-55 2. any musical setting for this

mag·ni·fi·ca·tion (mag'nə fi kā'shən) *n.* 1. a magnifying or being magnified 2. the power of magnifying 3. a magnified image or model

mag·nif·i·cence (mag nif'ə səns) *n.* [OFr. < L. < *magnificus*, noble < *magnus*, great + *facere*, to do] richness and splendour, as of furnishings, colour, dress, etc.; stately or imposing beauty; grandeur

mag·nif·i·cent (-sənt) *adj.* [OFr. < LL. *magnificens*: see prec.] 1. beautiful and grand or stately; rich or sumptuous, as in construction, decoration, etc. 2. exalted: said of ideas, etc. 3. [Colloq.] very good; excellent —**mag·nif'i·cent·ly** *adv.*

mag·nif·i·co (-kō') *n., pl.* **-coes', -cos'** [It. < L. *magnificus*: see MAGNIFICENCE] a person of high rank or great importance

mag·ni·fy (mag'nə fī') *vt.* **-fied', -fy'ing** [< OFr. < L. *magnificare*: see MAGNIFICENCE] 1. [Rare] to make greater 2. to exaggerate [to *magnify* one's sufferings] 3. to increase the apparent size of, esp. by means of a lens 4. [Archaic] to praise; extol —*vi.* to have the power of increasing the apparent size of an object —**mag'ni·fi'er** *n.*

magnifying glass a lens that increases the apparent size of an object seen through it

mag·nil·o·quent (mag nil'ə kwənt) *adj.* [< L. < *magnus*, great + prp. of *loqui*, to speak] 1. pompous or grandiose in speech or style of expression 2. boastful or bombastic —**mag·nil'o·quence** *n.* —**mag·nil'o·quent·ly** *adv.*

mag·ni·tude (mag'nə tyōōd') *n.* [< L. < *magnus*, great] 1. greatness; specif., *a*) of size *b*) of extent *c*) of influence 2. *a*) size *b*) loudness (of sound) *c*) importance 3. *Astron.* the degree of brightness of a fixed star: the brightest stars are of the first magnitude 4. *Math.* a number given to a quantity for purposes of comparison with other quantities of the same class —**of the first magnitude** of the greatest importance

mag·no·li·a (mag nō'lē ə, -nōl'yə) *n.* [ModL., after P. *Magnol*

(1638-1715), Fr. botanist]   1. any of a group of trees or shrubs with large, fragrant flowers of white, pink, or purple   2. the flower

mag·num (mag'nəm) *n.* [L., neut. sing. of *magnus*, great] a wine bottle holding twice as much as the usual bottle, or about 2 quarts or 2.3 litres

‡**mag·num o·pus** (mag'nəm ō'pəs) [L.]   1. a great work, esp. of art or literature; masterpiece   2. a person's greatest work or undertaking

mag·pie (mag'pī') *n.* [< *Mag*, dim. of *Margaret*, a feminine name + PIE³]   1. a noisy bird related to the crows and jays, with black-and-white colouring and a long, tapering tail   2. a person who chatters   3. a person who collects odds and ends

mag·uey (mag'wā) *n.* [Sp.]   1. a fleshy-leaved, fibre-yielding agave of the SW U.S., Mexico, and Central America; esp., the century plant   2. the fibre from this plant

Mag·yar (mag'yär; *Hung.* môd'yär) *n.* [Hung.]   1. a member of the people constituting the main ethnic group in Hungary   2. their language; Hungarian —*adj.* of the Magyars, their language, etc.

Ma·ha·bha·ra·ta (mə hä'bä'rə tə) [Sans.] one of the two great epics of India, written in Sanskrit about 200 B.C.: also **Ma·ha·bha'ra·tam** (-təm)

ma·ha·ra·jah, ma·ha·ra·ja (mä'hə rä'jə) *n.* [< Sans. < *mahā*, great + *rājā*, king] formerly in India, a prince; specif., the sovereign prince of a native state

ma·ha·ra·ni, ma·ha·ra·nee (-nē) *n.* [< Hindi < *mahā*, great + *rānī*, queen] in India, the wife of a maharajah

ma·ha·ri·shi (mä'hä rish'ē, mə-) *n.* [Hindi *mahārishi* < *mahā*, great + *rshi*, sage] a Hindu teacher of mysticism and transcendental meditation

ma·hat·ma (mə hat'mə, -hät'-) *n.* [< Sans. < *mahā*, great + *ātman*, soul] *Theosophy & Buddhism* any of a class of wise and holy persons held in special regard or reverence

Ma·ha·ya·na (mä'hə yä'nə) *n.* [Sans. *mahāyāna*, lit., greater vehicle] a branch of Buddhism that stresses idealism, disinterested love, etc.; it developed mainly in China, Korea, and Japan

Mah·di (mä'dē) *n.* [Ar. *mahdīy*, one guided aright < *hadā* to lead aright] a leader and prophet expected by Moslems to appear on earth before the world

mah-jongg, mah-jong (mä'joŋ') *n.* [< Chin. *ma-ch'iao*, lit., house sparrow (a figure on one of the tiles)] a game of Chinese origin, played with 136 or 144 small tiles

ma·hog·a·ny (mə hog'ə nē) *n., pl.* -**nies** [< ?]   1. any of various tropical trees, esp. one of tropical America, with hard, reddish-brown wood valued for furniture   2. the wood of any of these trees   3. reddish brown —*adj.*   1. made of mahogany   2. reddish-brown

ma·hout (mə hout') *n.* [< Hindi < Sans. *mahāmātra*, lit., great in measure] in India and the East Indies, an elephant driver or elephant keeper

maid (mād) *n.* [< ME. contr. < *maiden*]   1. *a)* a girl or young unmarried woman *b)* a virgin   2. a girl or woman servant

maid·en (mād'n) *n.* [OE. *mægden*]   1. *a)* a girl or young unmarried woman *b)* a virgin   2. a race horse that has never won a race —*adj.*   1. of, characteristic of, for, or suitable for a maiden or maidens   2. *a)* unmarried *b)* virgin   3. untried; unused; new; fresh   4. first or earliest [a *maiden* voyage]

maid·en·hair (-her') *n.* any of various ferns with delicate brown to black fronds and slender stalks: also **maidenhair fern**

maidenhair tree *same as* GINKGO

maid·en·head (-hed') *n.*   1. [Archaic] maidenhood; virginity   2. the hymen

maid·en·hood (-hood') *n.* the state or time of being a maiden: also **maid'hood'**

maid·en·ly (-lē) *adj.*   1. of a maiden   2. like or suitable for a maiden; modest, gentle, etc. —*adv.* [Archaic] in a maidenly manner —**maid'en·li·ness** *n.*

maiden name the surname that a woman had when not yet married

maiden over *Cricket* an over in which no runs are scored

maid of all work   1. a woman employed for doing general housework   2. someone doing a variety of work

maid of honour   1. an unmarried woman, usually of noble birth, attending a queen or princess   2. a tartlet, esp. with a curd cheese filling

maid·ser·vant (-sur'vənt) *n.* a girl or woman servant

mail¹ (māl) *n.* [OFr. *male*, ult. < OHG. *malaha*, wallet]   1. letters, papers, packages, etc. transported and delivered by the post office   2. a train, ship, or aircraft that carries mail —*adj.* of mail [mail boat] —*vt.* [U.S.] to send by mail, as by putting into a letter box —**mail'a·bil'i·ty** *n.* —**mail'-a·ble** *adj.* —**mail'er** *n.*

mail² (māl) *n.* [OFr. *maille* < L. *macula*, a mesh of a net]   1. a flexible body armour made of small metal rings, loops of chain, or scales   2. the hard protective covering of some animals, as turtles —*vt.* to cover or protect as with mail —**mailed** *adj.*

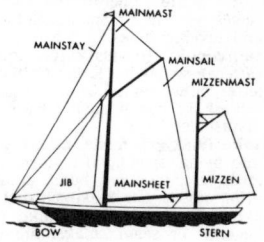

MAIL

mail·bag (māl'bag') *n.*   1. a bag, as of leather, in which a postman carries the mail he delivers   2. a heavy canvas bag in which mail is transported: also **mail sack**

mail·box (-boks') *n.* [U.S.] letter box

mail·ing list (māl'iŋ) a special list of names and addresses used by an organization, business, etc. in mailing out its literature, advertising matter, etc.

mail·lot (ma yō') *n.* [Fr., dim. < *maille*, knitted material, lit., mail]   1. a swimming suit; esp. a one-piece swimming suit for women   2. a garment like this, worn by gymnasts, etc.

mail·man (māl'man', -mən) *n., pl.* -**men** (-men', -mən) [U.S.] a postman

mail order an order for goods to be sent by post —**mail'-or'der** *adj.*

mail-order firm a business establishment that takes mail orders and sends goods by post

maim (mām) *vt.* [OFr. *mahaigner*] to deprive of the use of some necessary part of the body; cripple; mutilate; disable

main¹ (mān) *n.* [OE. *mægen*]   1. physical strength; force: now only in **with might and main**, with all one's strength   2. the principal part or point: usually in **in the main**, mostly, chiefly   3. a principal pipe or line in a distributing system for water, gas, etc.   4. [Poet.] the ocean   5. [Archaic] the mainland   6. [Obs.] any broad expanse —*adj.*   1. orig., strong; powerful   2. chief in size, importance, etc.; principal —**by main force** (or **strength**) by sheer force (or strength)

main² (mān) *n.* [prob. < prec.]   1. a series of matches in cockfighting   2. a throw of the dice in dice games   3. a match in various sports, such as archery, boxing, and bowling

main chance self-interest: usually in **have an eye to the main chance**

main clause in a complex sentence, a clause that can function syntactically as a complete sentence by itself; independent clause

main·land (mān'land', -lənd) *n.* the main land mass of a continent, as distinguished from nearby islands, etc. —**main'land'er** *n.*

main·line (-līn') *n.* the major railway line between two points, usually joined along the way by branch lines—*adj.* designating a railway station on a mainline —*vt.* -**lined'**, -**lin'ing** [Slang] to inject (a narcotic drug) directly into a large vein —**main'lin'er** *n.*

main·ly (-lē) *adv.* chiefly; principally; in the main

main·mast (-məst, -mäst') *n.* the principal mast of a vessel

main·sail (-s'l, -sāl') *n.*   1. in a square-rigged vessel, the sail set from the main yard: also **main course**   2. in a fore-and-aft-rigged vessel, the large sail set from the mainmast

main·sheet (-shēt') *n.* the line controlling the angle at which a mainsail is set

main·spring (-spriŋ') *n.*   1. the principal, or driving, spring in a clock, watch, etc.   2. the chief motive, incentive, or impelling cause

main·stay (-stā') *n.*   1. the supporting line run forward from the mainmast   2. a chief support

main·stream (-strēm') *n.* the main current or prevailing trend of thought, action, etc.

main·tain (mān tān') *vt.* [< OFr. *maintenir*, ult. < L. *manu tenere*, to hold in the hand]   1. to keep or keep up; carry on   2. *a)* to keep in continuance [food *maintains* life]   *b)* to keep in a certain condition, as of repair [to *maintain* roads]   3. to hold (a place, etc.) against attack   4. *a)* to uphold or defend, as by argument *b)* to declare positively; assert   5. to support by aid, influence, etc.   6. to provide the means of existence for [to *maintain* a family] —**main·tain'a·ble** *adj.* —**main·tain'er** *n.*

main·te·nance (mān'tən əns) *n.*   1. a maintaining or being maintained; upkeep, continuance, support, defence, etc.   2. means of support or sustenance; livelihood

main·top (mān'top') *n.* a platform at the head of the lower section of the mainmast

main·top·mast (mān'top'məst) *n.* the section of the mainmast above the maintop

[Figure: rigging diagram with labels MAINMAST, MAINSTAY, MAINSAIL, MIZZENMAST, JIB, MAINSHEET, MIZZEN, BOW, STERN]

main·top·sail (-s'l, -sāl) *n.* the sail above the mainsail on the mainmast

main yard the lower yard on the mainmast

mai·son·ette, mai·son·nette (mā'zə nət') *n.* [Fr., dim. of *maison*, house] 1. a small house 2. a flat usually on more than one floor

‡**maî·tre d'hô·tel** (me'tr' dô tel') [Fr., lit., master of the house] 1. a butler or steward 2. a headwaiter

maize (māz) *n.* [Sp. *maíz* < WInd. *mahiz*] 1. a cultivated cereal plant, with the grain borne on cobs enclosed in husks, mostly used as cattle feed; Indian corn 2. the colour of ripe maize; yellow —*adj.* yellow

Maj. Major

ma·jes·tic (mə jes'tik) *adj.* having majesty; grand, stately, dignified, etc.: also **ma·jes'ti·cal** —**ma·jes'ti·cal·ly** *adv.*

maj·es·ty (maj'is tē) *n., pl.* **-ties** [< OFr. < L. *majestas* < base of *major*, compar. of *magnus*, great] 1. sovereign power or dignity 2. [M-] a title used in speaking to or of a sovereign, preceded by *His, Her,* or *Your* 3. grandeur or stateliness

ma·jol·i·ca (mə jol'i kə, -yol'-) *n.* [It. *maiolica* < *Maiolica, Majorca*] a variety of Italian pottery, enamelled, glazed, and richly decorated

ma·jor (mā'jər) *adj.* [L., compar. of *magnus*, great] 1. *a)* greater in size, amount, or extent *b)* greater in importance or rank *c)* most significant 2. of full legal age 3. constituting the majority 4. *Music a)* designating an interval greater than the corresponding minor by a semitone *b)* characterized by major intervals, scales, etc. [the *major* key] *c)* based on the scale pattern of the major mode: see MAJOR SCALE —*vi.* [U.S.] *Educ.* to specialize in a subject [to *major* in physics] —*n.* 1. a superior in some class or group 2. *see* MILITARY RANKS, table 3. [U.S.] *Educ. a)* major field of study *b)* a student specializing in a (specified) subject 4. *Law* a person of full legal age 5. *Music* a major interval, key, etc.

ma·jor-do·mo (mā'jər dō'mō) *n., pl.* **-mos** [< Sp. or It. < LL. < L. *major*, greater, an elder + gen. of *domus*, house] 1. a man in charge of a great or royal household; chief steward 2. any steward or butler: humorous usage

major general *pl.* **major generals** *see* MILITARY RANKS, table

ma·jor·i·ty (mə jor'ə tē) *n., pl.* **-ties** [< Fr. < ML. < L. *major:* see MAJOR] 1. the greater part or larger number; more than half 2. the excess of the larger number of votes cast for one candidate, bill, etc. over the rest of the votes 3. the group or party with the majority of votes 4. the state or time of being legally an adult 5. *Mil.* the rank or position of a major —**in the majority** being a member of a majority party or casting a vote as part of a majority

major league [U.S.] a principal league in a professional sport; specif., [M- L-] [*pl.*] the two main leagues of professional baseball clubs —**ma'jor-league'** *adj.* —**ma'-jor-leagu'er** *n.*

major order *R.C.Ch.* the order of priest, deacon, or subdeacon

major scale one of the two standard diatonic musical scales, with half steps instead of whole steps after the third and seventh tones

ma·jus·cule (mə jus'kyool, maj'əs-) *n.* [Fr. *majuscula* (*littera*), somewhat larger (letter), dim. < *major*] 1. a large letter, either capital or uncial, used in printing or writing 2. writing in which such letters are used —*adj.* written in majuscules

make (māk) *vt.* **made, mak'ing** [OE. *macian*] 1. to bring into being; specif., *a)* to form by shaping or putting parts, ideas, etc. together; build, create, devise, etc. *b)* to cause; bring about [to *make* corrections] *c)* to cause to be available; provide [to *make* room] 2. to cause to be, become, or seem [*make* him chairman]: sometimes used reflexively [*make* yourself comfortable] 3. to prepare for use [*make* the beds] 4. to amount to [1000 grammes *make* a kilo] 5. to have, or prove to have, the qualities of or for [to *make* a fine leader] 6. to set up; establish [to *make* rules] 7. *a)* to acquire, as by one's behaviour [to *make* friends] *b)* to get by earning, investing, etc. [to *make* a fortune] 8. to cause the success of [that venture *made* him] 9. to understand [what do you *make* of that?] 10. to estimate to be [I *make* the distance about 500 miles] 11. *a)* to do, execute, accomplish, etc. [to *make* a quick turn] *b)* to engage in [to *make* war] 12. to deliver (a speech) or utter (remarks, etc.) 13. to cause or force [*make* him behave] 14. to arrive at; reach [the ship *made* port] 15. to go or travel; traverse [to *make* 500 miles the first day] 16. [Colloq.] to succeed in getting a position on, etc. [to *make* the team] 17. *Elec.* to close (a circuit); effect (a contact) —*vi.* 1. to start (to do something) [she *made* to go] 2. to tend, extend, or point (*to, towards,* etc.) 3. to behave in a specified manner [*make* bold, *make* merry] 4. to cause something to be in a specified condition [*make* ready] —*n.* 1. the act or process of making 2. the amount made; output 3. the way in which something is made; style; build 4. type, sort, or character; nature [a

man of this *make*] 6. *Elec.* the closing of a circuit —**make a bag** to shoot a number of game —**make a book** to collect bets on an event or series of events —**make after** to chase or follow —**make a meal of** 1. to eat, as a meal 2. to do something laboriously or fussily —**make a move** to take even the slightest action; do anything [don't *make a move*] —**make away with** 1. to steal 2. to get rid of 3. to kill —**make believe** to pretend —**make do** to use something as a substitute for proper equipment; to manage with whatever means available —**make for** 1. to head for 2. to attack 3. to help effect —**make it** [Colloq.] to do or achieve a certain thing —**make off with** to steal —**make or break** to cause the success or failure of —**make out** 1. to see with some difficulty 2. to understand 3. to write out 4. to fill in (a blank form, etc.) 5. to (try to) show or prove to be 6. to succeed; get along —**make over** 1. to change; renovate 2. to transfer the ownership of —**make up** 1. to put together; compose 2. to form; constitute 3. to invent 4. to complete by providing what is lacking 5. to compensate (*for*) 6. to become friendly again after a quarrel 7. to put cosmetics on 8. to decide (one's mind) 9. to select and arrange type, illustrations, etc. for (a book, page, etc.) —**make up to** to try to ingratiate oneself with —**on the make** [Colloq.] trying to succeed financially, socially, etc., esp. in an aggressive way

make-be·lieve (māk'bə lēv') *n.* 1. pretence; feigning 2. a pretender —*adj.* pretended; feigned

mak·er (-ər) *n.* 1. a person or thing that makes 2. [M-] God 3. *Law* the signer of a promissory note —**meet one's Maker** to die

make·shift (-shift') *n.* a thing that will do for a while as a substitute; temporary expedient —*adj.* that will do for a while as a substitute

make·up, make-up (-up') *n.* 1. the way in which something is put together; composition 2. nature; disposition 3. the cosmetics, wigs, costumes, etc. put on for theatrical roles 4. cosmetics generally 5. the arrangement of type, illustrations, etc. in a book, newspaper, etc. —*adj.* of or for making-up

make·weight (-wāt') *n.* 1. anything added to a scale to complete the required weight 2. an unimportant person or thing added to make up some lack

mak·ing (mā'kiŋ) *n.* 1. the act of one that makes or the process of being made 2. the cause of success or advancement [an experience that will be the *making* of him] 3. *a)* something made *b)* the quantity made at a single time

mak·ings (mā'kiŋz) *n.pl.* 1. the material or potential needed [to have the *makings* or a good doctor] 2. [Slang] the materials used for rolling a cigarette, consisting of loose tobacco and cigarette paper

ma·ku·ta (mä koo'tä) *n. pl.* of LIKUTA

mal- [Fr. < L. < *male*, badly < *malus*, bad] a prefix meaning bad or badly, wrong, ill [*maladjustment*]

Mal. 1. Malachi 2. Malay 3. Malayan

mal·a·chite (mal'ə kīt') *n.* [< L. < Gr. *malachē*, mallow: from its colour] native basic copper carbonate, a green mineral used for table tops, vases, etc.

mal·ad·just·ed (mal'ə jus'tid) *adj.* poorly adjusted, esp. to the circumstances of one's life —**mal'ad·just'ment** *n.*

mal·ad·min·is·ter (-əd min'ə stər) *vt.* to administer badly or corruptly —**mal'ad·min'is·tra'tion** *n.*

mal·a·droit (mal'ə droit') *adj.* [Fr.: see MAL- & ADROIT] awkward; clumsy; bungling —**mal'a·droit'ly** *adv.* —**mal'-a·droit'ness** *n.*

mal·a·dy (mal'ə dē) *n., pl.* **-dies** [< OFr. *malade*, sick < LL. *male habitus*, out of condition: see MAL- & HABIT] a disease; illness; sickness

Mal·a·ga (mal'ə gə) *n.* 1. a large, white, oval grape 2. a white, sweet wine, orig. from Málaga

ma·laise (ma lāz') *n.* [Fr. < *mal*, bad (see MAL-) + *aise*, EASE] 1. a vague feeling of physical discomfort or uneasiness, as early in an illness 2. a vague feeling of moral or social decline

mal·a·mute (mal'ə myoot') *n.* [< *Malemute*, name of an Eskimo tribe] a strong dog with a thick coat and a bushy tail: it was developed as a sled dog by the Alaskan Eskimo: in full, **Alaskan malamute:** also sp. **malemute, malemiut**

mal·a·prop (mal'ə prop') *adj.* [< ff.] using or characterized by malapropisms: also **mal'a·prop'i·an** (-ē ən) —*n.* same as MALAPROPISM

mal·a·prop·ism (mal'ə prop iz'm) *n.* [after Mrs. *Malaprop*, a character in Sheridan's *The Rivals*] 1. ludicrous misuse of words, esp. of words that sound somewhat alike 2. an instance of this

mal·ap·ro·pos (mal'ap rə pō', mal ap'-) *adj., adv.* [Fr.: see MAL- & APROPOS] inappropriate(ly); inopportune(ly)

ma·lar·i·a (mə ler'ē ə) *n.* [It., contr. of *mala aria*, bad air] an infectious disease, generally recurrent, caused by protozoans transmitted to man by the bite of an infected mosquito, esp. the anopheles: it is characterized by severe chills and fever —**ma·lar'i·al, ma·lar'i·an, ma·lar'i·ous** *adj.*

ma·lar·key, ma·lar·ky (mə lär′kē) *n.* [< ? Irish surname] [Slang] insincere talk; nonsense

mal·a·thi·on (mal′ə thī′on) *n.* an organic phosphate, used as an insecticide

Ma·lay (mā′lā, mə lā′) *n.* 1. a member of a large group of brown-skinned peoples living in the Malay Peninsula, the Malay Archipelago, and nearby islands 2. their Indonesian language —*adj.* of the Malays, their country, language, culture, etc.

Ma·lay·an (mə lā′ən) *adj. same as* INDONESIAN (sense 2) —*n.* 1. *same as* MALAY (sense 1) 2. *same as* INDONESIAN (sense 3)

Ma·lay·o-Pol·y·ne·sian (mə lā′ō pol′ə nē′zhən, -shən) *adj.* designating or of a family of languages spoken over a large area in the C & W Pacific, including Polynesian, Indonesian, etc. —*n.* these languages

mal·con·tent (mal′kən tent′) *adj.* [OFr.: see MAL- & CONTENT[1]] dissatisfied or rebellious —*n.* a dissatisfied or rebellious person

‡**mal de mer** (mȧl də mer′) [Fr.] seasickness

male (māl) *adj.* [< OFr. < L. *masculus,* dim. of *mas,* a male] 1. designating or of the sex that fertilizes the ovum of the female and begets offspring 2. of, like, or suitable for members of this sex; masculine 3. consisting of men or boys 4. designating or having a part shaped to fit into a corresponding hollow part 5. *Bot.* designating or of fertilizing bodies, organs, etc. —*n.* 1. a male person; man or boy 2. a male animal or plant —**male′ness** *n.*

mal·e·dic·tion (mal′ə dik′shən) *n.* [OFr. < LL. *maledictio* < L., abuse: see MAL- & DICTION] a calling down of evil on someone; curse

mal·e·fac·tion (-fak′shən) *n.* wrongdoing; crime

mal·e·fac·tor (mal′ə fak′tər) *n.* [L. < pp. of *malefacere* < *male,* evil + *facere,* to do] an evildoer or criminal

ma·lef·ic (mə lef′ik) *adj.* [L. *maleficus* < *malefacere,* evildoing] causing disaster; harmful; evil

ma·lef·i·cent (mə lef′ə sənt) *adj.* [see prec.] harmful; hurtful; evil —**ma·lef′i·cence** *n.*

ma·lev·o·lent (mə lev′ə lənt) *adj.* [< OFr. < L. < *male,* evil + prp. of *velle,* to wish] wishing evil or harm to others; spiteful; malicious —**ma·lev′o·lence** *n.* —**ma·lev′o·lent·ly** *adv.*

mal·fea·sance (mal fē′zəns) *n.* [obs. Fr. *malfaisance* < *mal,* evil + prp. of *faire,* to do] wrongdoing or misconduct, esp. by a public official: distinguished from MISFEASANCE, NONFEASANCE —**mal·fea′sant** *adj.*

mal·for·ma·tion (mal′fôr mā′shən) *n.* faulty, irregular, or abnormal formation of a body or part —**mal·formed′** (-fôrmd′) *adj.*

mal·func·tion (mal funk′shən) *vi.* to fail to function as it should —*n.* the act or an instance of malfunctioning

mal·ic acid (mal′ik, mā′lik) [< Fr. < L. < Gr. *mēlon,* apple] a colourless, organic acid, occurring in apples and other fruits

mal·ice (mal′is) *n.* [OFr. < L. < *malus,* bad] 1. active ill will; desire to harm another; spite 2. *Law* evil intent —**malice aforethought** a deliberate intention and plan to do something unlawful

ma·li·cious (mə lish′əs) *adj.* having, showing, or caused by malice; spiteful —**ma·li′cious·ly** *adv.* —**ma·li′cious·ness** *n.*

ma·lign (mə līn′) *vt.* [< OFr. < LL. < L. *malignus,* wicked < *male,* ill + base of *genus,* born] to speak evil of; slander —*adj.* 1. showing ill will; malicious 2. evil; sinister 3. very harmful; malignant —**ma·lign′er** *n.*

ma·lig·nan·cy (mə lig′nən sē) *n.* 1. a being malignant: also **ma·lig′nance** 2. *pl.* **-cies** a malignant tumour

ma·lig·nant (-nənt) *adj.* [< LL. < L. *malignus:* see MALIGN] 1. having an evil influence; malign 2. wishing evil; malevolent 3. very harmful 4. very virulent; causing or likely to cause death [a cancer is a *malignant* growth] —**ma·lig′nant·ly** *adv.*

ma·lig·ni·ty (-nə tē) *n.* 1. intense ill will or desire to harm others; great malice 2. the quality of being very harmful or dangerous 3. *pl.* **-ties** a malignant act, event, or feeling

ma·lines (mə lēn′; *Fr.* mȧ lēn′) *n.* [< *Malines,* Belgian city] a thin, somewhat stiff, silk net: also **ma·line′**

ma·lin·ger (mə lin′gər) *vi.* [< Fr. *malingre,* sickly] to pretend to be ill in order to escape duty or work; shirk —**ma·lin′ger·er** *n.*

mall (môl, mal) *n.* [var. of MAUL] 1. a shaded walk or public promenade 2. a street for pedestrians only, with shops on each of the sides

mal·lard (mal′ərd) *n., pl.* **-lards, -lard:** see PLURAL, II, D, 1 [OFr. *malart*] the common wild duck, from which the domestic duck is descended: the male has a green head and a band of white around the neck

mal·le·a·ble (mal′ē ə b'l) *adj.* [< ML. < L. *malleare,* to hammer < *malleus,* a hammer] 1. that can be hammered, pounded, or pressed into various shapes without breaking 2. pliable; adaptable —**mal′le·a·bil′i·ty, mal′le·a·ble·ness** *n.*

mal·lee (mal′ē) *n.* [Abor.] 1. any of several shrubby species of Australian eucalyptus 2. in Australia, a dense thicket, formed by such plants

mal·let (mal′it) *n.* [< MFr. dim. of *mail* < OFr. *maile:* see MAUL] 1. a kind of hammer, usually with a wooden head and a short handle, for driving a chisel, etc. 2. *a*) a long-handled hammer used in playing croquet *b*) a similar instrument used in playing polo 3. a small, light hammer used for playing a vibraphone, xylophone, etc.

mal·le·us (mal′ē əs) *n., pl.* **mal′le·i** (-ī′) [L., a hammer] the outermost of the three small bones in the middle ear of mammals, shaped somewhat like a hammer

mal·low (mal′ō) *n.* [OE. *mealuwe* < L. *malva*] 1. any of a group of plants, with dissected or lobed leaves and large, showy flowers 2. any of various other related plants, as the marsh mallow

malm (mäm) *n.* [ME. *malme* < OE. *mealm-,* sand] 1. *a*) a soft, crumbly, greyish-white limestone *b*) a soft, chalky loam formed from this 2. clay and chalk mixed for use in making bricks

malm·sey (mäm′zē) *n.* [< ML. < Gr. *Monembasia,* Greek town] 1. a strong, full-flavoured, sweet white wine 2. the grape from which this is made

mal·nour·ished (mal nur′isht) *adj.* improperly nourished

mal·nu·tri·tion (mal′nyoo trish′ən) *n.* faulty or inadequate nutrition; poor nourishment

mal·o·dor·ous (mal ō′dər əs) *adj.* having a bad odour; stinking —**mal·o′dour** —**mal·o′dor·ous·ly** *adv.*

mal·prac·tice (mal prak′tis) *n.* 1. injurious or unprofessional treatment of a patient by a physician or surgeon 2. misconduct or improper practice in any professional or official position —**mal′prac·ti′tion·er** (-tish′ən ər) *n.*

malt (môlt) *n.* [OE. *mealt*] 1. barley or other grain softened by soaking, germination and then kiln-dried: used for brewing and distilling certain alcoholic liquors 2. such liquor, esp. beer, ale, etc. —*adj.* made with malt —*vt.* 1. to change (barley, etc.) into malt —*vi.* 1. to be changed into malt 2. to change barley, etc. into malt —**malt′y** *adj.* **malt′i·er, malt′i·est**

malted milk a drink made by mixing a powdered preparation of dried milk and malted cereals with milk

Mal·tese (môl tēz′) *adj.* of Malta, its inhabitants, etc. —*n.* 1. *pl.* **-tese′** a native or inhabitant of Malta 2. the Arabic language of Malta 3. a variety of domestic cat with bluish-grey fur: in full, **Maltese cat**

Maltese cross a cross whose arms look like arrowheads pointing inward

malt extract a sticky, sugary substance obtained from malt soaked in water

malt house a place where malt is made and stored

Mal·thu·sian (mal thoo′zhən, -zē ən) *adj.* [after R. *Malthus* (1766-1834), Brit. economist] designating or of a theory that the increasing population of the world is naturally restricted by war, famine, and disease —*n.* a supporter of this theory

malt liquor beer, ale, etc. made from malt by fermentation

malt·ose (môl′tōs) *n.* a white, crystalline sugar obtained by the action of the diastase of malt on starch: also called **malt sugar**

mal·treat (mal trēt′) *vt.* [< Fr.: see MAL- & TREAT] to treat roughly, unkindly, or brutally; abuse —**mal·treat′ment** *n.*

malt·ster (môlt′stər) *n.* one who makes malt

mal·ver·sa·tion (mal′vər sā′shən) *n.* [Fr. < *malverser,* to commit malpractices < L. *male,* badly + *versari,* to turn, occupy oneself] corrupt conduct or fraudulent practices in public office or other position of trust

mam (mam) *n.* [Colloq.] mother

mam·ba (mäm′bə) *n.* [Zulu *imamba*] any of several extremely poisonous, African tree snakes; esp. a long South African snake coloured green and black

mam·bo (mäm′bō) *n.* [AmSp.] a rhythmic ballroom dance to music of Cuban Negro origin in 1/4 time with a heavy accent on the second and fourth beats —*vi.* to dance the mambo

Mam·e·luke (mam′ə look′) *n.* [obs. Fr. *mameluk* < Ar. *mamlick,* slave] 1. a member of a military caste, orig. made up of slaves, that dominated Egypt from 1250-1811 2. [m-] in Moslem countries, a slave

mam·il·la (ma mil′ə, mə-) *n., pl.* **-lae** (-ē) [L. *mam(m)illa,* dim. of *mamma:* see MAMMA[2]] 1. a nipple 2. any nipple-shaped or breast-shaped protuberance —**mam′il·lar′-y** *adj.*

mam·ma[1] (ma′mə; *occas.* məmä′) *n.* [like L. *mamma,* mother, Sans. *mā,* Gr. *mammē* < baby talk] mother: a child's word: also **ma′ma**

mam·ma[2] (mam′ə) *n., pl.* **-mae** (-ē) [L., breast] a gland for secreting milk, present in the female of all mammals; mammary gland

mam·mal (-əl) *n.* [< ModL. < LL. < L. *mamma:* see prec.] any of a large class of warmblooded vertebrates whose offspring are fed with milk secreted by the female mammary glands —**mam·ma·li·an** (mə mā′lē ən, ma-) *adj., n.*

mam·ma·ry (mam′ər ē) *adj.* designating or of the milk-secreting glands; of the mammae

mam·mon (mam′ən) *n.* [< LL. < Gr. < Aram. *māmōnā,*

riches] [often **M-**] riches regarded as an object of worship and greedy pursuit —**mam′mon·ism** n.

mam·moth (mam′əth) n. [Russ. mamont] an extinct elephant with a hairy skin and long tusks curving upwards —adj. very big; huge; enormous

mam·my (mam′ē) n., pl. -**mies** [dial. var. of MAMMA¹] 1. mamma; mother: a child's word 2. [Chiefly U.S.] a Negro woman who takes care of white children

HAIRY MAMMOTH
(to 4 m high
at shoulder)

man (man) n., pl. **men** (men) [OE. mann] 1. a human being; person; specif., one of that species (see HOMO SAPIENS) of primates having the most highly developed brain and articulate speech 2. the human race; mankind: used without the or a 3. an adult male human being 4. a) an adult male servant, follower, subordinate, etc. b) a male employee c) [Archaic] a vassal 5. a husband or a lover 6. a person with qualities conventionally regarded as manly 7. any of the pieces used in chess, draughts, etc. 8. [Colloq.] fellow; chap [my good man] —vt. **manned, man′ning** 1. to furnish with men for work, defence etc. [to man a ship] 2. to take assigned places in, on, or at [man the guns!] 3. to strengthen; brace [to man oneself for an ordeal] —**interj.** [Slang] an exclamation of emphasis: often used neutrally to preface or resume one's remarks —adj. male —**as a** (or **one**) **man** in unison; unanimously —**be one's own man** 1. to be free and independent 2. to be in full control of oneself —**he is your man** he can accommodate you —**man and boy** first as a boy and then as a man —**man in the moon** the apparent resemblance in the moon's face to a man —**the Man** [U.S. Slang] 1. the person having authority over one, as a policeman 2. a white man, as opposed to a black one —**to a man** with no one as an exception

-man (mən, man) a combining form meaning man or person of a specified kind, in a specified activity, etc. [Frenchman, sportsman]

Man. 1. Manila (paper) 2. Manitoba

ma·na¹ (mä′nə) n. [< Polynesian] the supernatural force to which certain primitive peoples attribute good fortune, magical powers, etc.

ma·na² (mä′nə) n. [Maori] power, prestige, right, or authority

man about town a worldly man who spends much time in fashionable restaurants, clubs, etc.

man·a·cle (man′ə k'l) n. [< OFr. < L. manicula, dim. of manus, hand] 1. a handcuff; fetter or shackle for the hand 2. any restraint Usually used in pl. —vt. -**cled, -cling** 1. to put handcuffs on; fetter 2. to restrain; hamper

man·age (man′ij) vt. -**aged, -ag·ing** [It. maneggiare < mano, hand < L. manus] 1. orig., to train (a horse) in his paces 2. to control the movement or behaviour of 3. to have charge of; direct [to manage a household] 4. [Rare] to handle or use carefully 5. to get (a person) to do what one wishes, esp. by tact, flattery, etc. 6. to succeed in accomplishing; contrive —vi. 1. to carry on business 2. to contrive to get along

man·age·a·ble (man′ij ə b'l) adj. that can be managed; controllable —**man′age·a·bil′i·ty, man′age·a·ble·ness** n. —**man′age·a·bly** adv.

managed currency a currency regulated through procedures that alter the amount of money in circulation so as to control credit prices, etc. rather than being tied to a precious metal, such as gold: see also GOLD STANDARD

man·age·ment (man′ij mənt) n. 1. the act, art, or manner of managing, controlling, etc. 2. skilful managing 3. executive ability 4. the persons managing a business, institution, etc.

man·ag·er (-ij ər) n. a person who manages the affairs of a business, institution, client, team, etc. —**man′ag·er·ship′** n.

man·a·ge·ri·al (man′ə jir′ē əl) adj. of a manager or management —**man′a·ge′ri·al·ism** n. —**man′a·ge′ri·al·ly** adv.

man·ag·ing (man′ə jiŋ) adj. 1. interfering, meddlesome 2. being in command; controlling [managing director of ICI]

‡ma·ña·na (mä nyä′nə) n. [Sp.] tomorrow —adv. 1. tomorrow 2. at some indefinite future time

man-at-arms (man′ət ärmz′) n., pl. **men′-at-arms′** (men′-) formerly, a soldier, esp., a heavily armed medieval soldier on horseback

man·a·tee (man′ə te , man ə tē′) n. [Sp. manatí < native (Carib) name] a large, plant-eating aquatic mammal living in shallow tropical waters, having flippers and a broad, flat, rounded tail; sea cow

Manchester School a group of political economists, headed by Cobden and Bright, who advocated free trade and laissez-faire

Man·chu (man chōō′, man′chōō) n. 1. pl. -**chus, -chu′** a member of a Mongolian people of Manchuria: the Manchus conquered China in 1643-44 and ruled until 1912 2. the language of the Manchus —adj. of Manchuria, the Manchus, their language, etc.

Man·cu·ni·an (man kyōō′nē ən, -kyōōn′yən) adj. [< ML. Mancunium, Manchester] of Manchester —n. a native or inhabitant of Manchester

-man·cy (man′sē) [< OFr. < LL. < Gr. manteia, divination] a combining form meaning divination [chiromancy]

man·da·la (mun′də lə) n. [Sans. mandala] a circular design of concentric geometric forms symbolizing the universe or wholeness in Hinduism and Buddhism

man·da·mus (man dā′məs) n. [L., we command] Law a writ commanding that a specified thing be done, issued by a higher court to a lower one, or to a corporation, agency, official, etc.

man·da·rin (man′də rin) n. [< Port. < Hindi mantrī, minister of state < Sans. < mantra, counsel] 1. a high official of China under the Empire 2. a member of any elite group 3. [**M-**] the official or main dialect of Chinese 4. a small, sweet orange with a loose rind: in full, **mandarin orange** —adj. 1. of a Chinese style of dress, esp. a narrow, closefitting, stand-up collar parted in the front 2. elegant or overrefined, as in literary style —**man′da·rin·ism** n.

man·date (man′dāt) n. [< L. neut. pp. of mandare, to command < manus, a hand + pp. of dare, to give] 1. an authoritative order or command 2. a) formerly, a commission from the League of Nations to a country to administer some region, colony, etc. b) the area that is so administered 3. the wishes of constituents expressed to a representative, etc. and regarded as an order 4. Law an order from a higher court or official to a lower one —vt. -**dat·ed, -dat·ing** to assign (a region, etc.) as a mandate —**man′da′tor** n.

man·da·to·ry (man′də tər ē) adj. 1. of, like, or containing a mandate 2. authoritatively commanded or required; obligatory 3. holding a mandate (sense 2) —**man′da·to·ri·ly** adv.

man·di·ble (man′də b'l) n. [OFr. < LL. < mandibulum < L. mandere, to chew] the jaw; specif., a) the lower jaw of a vertebrate b) either of the most forward pair of biting jaws of an insect or other arthropod c) either jaw of a beaked animal —**man·dib′u·lar** (-dib′yōō lər) adj.

man·do·lin (man′d'l in′, man′də lin′) n. [< Fr. < It. dim. of mandola < LL. < LGr. pandoura, kind of lute] a musical instrument with four or five pairs of strings and a deep, rounded sound box: it is played with a plectrum —**man′do·lin′ist** n.

man·drake (man′drāk) n. [by folk etym. < OE. mandragora < LL. < L. < Gr. mandragoras] 1. a) a poisonous plant of the nightshade family, with a short stem and a thick root b) the root, formerly used in medicine as a narcotic Also **man·drag·o·ra** (man drag′ər ə) 2. same as MAY APPLE

MANDOLIN

man·drel, man·dril (man′drəl) n. [prob. < Fr. mandrin] 1. a spindle or bar inserted into something to hold it while it is being machined 2. a metal bar used as a core around which metal, glass, etc. is cast, moulded or shaped

man·drill (man′dril) n. [MAN + DRILL⁴] a large, fierce, strong baboon of W Africa

mane (mān) n. [OE. manu] the long hair growing from the top or sides of the neck of certain animals, as the horse, lion, etc. —**maned** adj. —**mane′less** adj.

ma·nège, ma·nege (ma nezh′, -näzh′) n. [Fr. < It. maneggio: see MANAGE] 1. the art of riding and training horses 2. a school teaching this art 3. the paces of a trained horse

ma·nes (mä′nēz) n.pl. [L.] [often **M-**] Ancient Rom. Religion the deified souls of the dead, esp. of dead ancestors

ma·neu·ver (mə nōō′vər) n., vi., vt. -**vered, -vering** chiefly U.S. sp. of MANOEUVRE

man Friday see FRIDAY

man·ful (man′fəl) adj. manly; brave, resolute, strong, etc. —**man′ful·ly** adv. —**man′ful·ness** n.

man·ga·nese (maŋ′gə nēs′, -nēz′) n. [< Fr. < It., by metathesis < ML. magnesia: see MAGNESIA] a greyish-white, metallic chemical element, usually hard and brittle, which rusts like iron but is not magnetic: used in various alloys: symbol, Mn; at. wt., 54.9380; at. no., 25

mange (mānj) n. [< OFr. mangeue, an itch, ult. < L. manducare: see MANGER] a skin disease of mammals caused by parasitic mites and characterized by itching, loss of hair, etc.

man·gel-wur·zel (maŋ′g'l wur′z'l, -wurt′-) n. [G., ult. < Mangold, beet + Wurzel, a root] a variety of large beet, used as food for cattle, esp. in Europe: also **mangel**

man·ger (mān′jər) n. [OFr. mangeure, ult. < L. manducare, to eat < mandere, to chew] a box or trough to hold hay, etc. for horses or cattle to eat

man·gle¹ (maŋ′g'l) vt. -**gled, -gling** [Anglo-Fr. mangler < OFr. mehaigner, to maim] 1. to mutilate by repeatedly and roughly cutting, hacking, etc. **2.** to spoil; botch; mar —**man'gler** *n.*

man·gle[2] (maŋ'g'l) *n.* [Du. *mangel* < G. < MHG. < L. < Gr. *manganon*, war machine] a machine for pressing and smoothing cloth, esp. sheets and other flat pieces, between heavy rollers —*vt.* **-gled, -gling** to press in a mangle —**man'gler** *n.*

man·go (maŋ'gō) *n.,* *pl.* **-goes, -gos** [Port. *manga* < Malay < Tamil *măn-kăy*] **1.** a yellow-red, somewhat acid tropical fruit with a thick rind and juicy pulp **2.** the tree on which it grows

man·grove (maŋ'grōv) *n.* [altered (after GROVE) < Port. *mangue* < Sp. *mangle* < ?] a tropical tree with branches that spread and send down roots, thus forming more trunks

man·gy (măn'jē) *adj.* **-gi·er, -gi·est** **1.** having or caused by the mange **2.** shabby and filthy; squalid **3.** mean and low; despicable —**man'gi·ly** *adv.* —**man'gi·ness** *n.*

man·han·dle (man'han'd'l) *vt.* **-dled, -dling** **1.** [Rare] to move or do by human strength only, without mechanical aids **2.** to handle roughly

Man·hat·tan (man hat''n) *n.* [after the island on which most of New York City is built] [*often* m-] a cocktail made of whisky and vermouth, usually with a dash of bitters

man·hole (man'hōl') *n.* a hole through which a man can get into a sewer, conduit, ship's tank, etc. for repair work or inspection

man·hood (man'hood') *n.* **1.** the state or time of being a man **2.** manly qualities; virility, courage, resolution, etc. **3.** men collectively

man-hour (-our') *n.* an industrial time unit equal to one hour of work done by one person

man·hunt (-hunt') *n.* a hunt for a man, esp. for a fugitive: also **man hunt**

ma·ni·a (mā'nē ə) *n.* [LL. < Gr. *mania* < *mainesthai*, to rage] **1.** wild or violent mental disorder; specif., the manic phase of manic-depressive psychosis, characterized generally by abnormal excitability, excessive activity, etc. **2.** an excessive, persistent enthusiasm; obsession; craze

-ma·ni·a (mā'nē ə) [see prec.] *a combining form meaning:* **1.** a (specified) type of mental disorder [*kleptomania*] **2.** a continuing, intense enthusiasm or craving for [*bibliomania*]

ma·ni·ac (mā'nē ak') *adj.* wildly insane; raving —*n.* **1.** violently insane person; lunatic **2.** [Colloq.] an enthusiast [a car *maniac*] —**ma·ni·a·cal** (mə nī'ə k'l) *adj.* —**ma·ni'·a·cal·ly** *adv.*

man·ic (man'ik; mā'nik) *adj.* having, characterized by, or like mania

man·ic-de·pres·sive (-di pres'iv) *adj.* designating, of, or having a psychosis characterized by alternating periods of mania and mental depression —*n.* a person who has this psychosis

Man·i·chae·ism, Man·i·che·ism (man'ə kē'iz'm) *n.* [after *Manichaeus*, 3rd-cent. Persian prophet] a religious philosophy of the 3rd to 7th cent. A.D. emphasizing a universal conflict between good and evil: also **Man'i·chae'-an·ism** —**Man'i·chae'an** *n., adj.*

man·i·cure (man'ə kyoor') *n.* [Fr. < L. *manus,* a hand + *cura,* care] the care of the hands; esp., a trimming, polishing, etc. of the fingernails —*vt.* **-cured', -cur'ing** **1.** to trim, polish, etc. (the fingernails) **2.** to give a manicure to

man·i·fest (man'ə fest') *adj.* [< OFr. < L. *manifestus,* lit., struck by the hand, palpable] apparent to the senses, esp. to sight, or to the mind; evident; obvious —*vt.* **1.** to make clear or evident; reveal **2.** to prove; be evidence of —*vi.* to appear to the senses —*n.* **1.** an itemized list of a ship's cargo, to be shown to customs officials **2.** a list of passengers and cargo on aircraft —**man'i·fest'a·ble** *adj.* —**man'i·fest'ly** *adv.*

man·i·fes·ta·tion (man'ə fes tā'shən, -fəs-) *n.* **1.** a manifesting or being manifested **2.** something that manifests [his smile was a *manifestation* of joy] **3.** any of the forms in which a being is thought to manifest itself **4.** a public demonstration

man·i·fes·to (man'ə fes'tō) *n.,* *pl.* **-toes** [It. < *manifestare,* to MANIFEST] a public declaration of motives and intentions by a government or by an important person or group

man·i·fold (man'ə fōld') *adj.* [OE. *manigfeald:* see MANY & -FOLD] **1.** having many and various forms, parts, etc. **2.** of many sorts [*manifold duties*] **3.** being such in many ways [a *manifold* villain] **4.** made up of or operating several units or parts of one kind —*n.* **1.** something that is manifold **2.** a pipe with one inlet and several outlets or with one outlet and several inlets, for connecting with other pipes, as the cylinder exhaust system in a motor car —*vt.* **1.** to make manifold **2.** to make a number of copies of [to *manifold* a letter with carbon paper] —**man'i·fold'er** *n.* —**man'i·fold'ly** *adv.* —**man'i·fold'ness** *n.*

MANIFOLD
(A, manifold;
B, cylinder)

man·i·kin (man'ə kin) *n.* [Du. *manneken* < *man,* man + dim. suffix *-ken*] **1.** a little man; dwarf **2.** *same as* MANNEQUIN

Ma·nil·a (mə nil'ə) *n.* [after the city in the Philippines] [*often* m-] *same as:* **1.** MANILA HEMP **2.** MANILA PAPER Also **Ma·nil'la**

Manila hemp [*often* m-] a strong, tough fibre from the leafstalks of the abacá, used in making rope, paper, etc.

Manila paper [*often* m-] strong, buff or brownish paper orig. made of Manila hemp, now of various fibres

ma·nil·la (mə nil'ə) *n.* [Sp. *manilla,* dim. of *mano,* hand < L. *manus,* hand] an early form of currency in W Africa in the pattern of a small bracelet

man in the street the average person

man·i·oc (man'ē ak') *n.* [Fr. < Tupi *manioca*] *same as* CASSAVA

ma·nip·u·late (mə nip'yə lāt') *vt.* **-lat'ed, -lat'ing** [ult. < Fr. < L. *manipulus,* handful < *manus,* a hand + base of *plere,* to fill] **1.** to work, operate, or treat with or as with the hands, esp. with skill **2.** to manage or control artfully, often in an unfair or fraudulent way **3.** to change or falsify (figures, accounts, etc.) for one's own purposes —**ma·nip'·u·la·ble, ma·nip'u·lat'a·ble** *adj.* —**ma·nip'u·la'tion** *n.* —**ma·nip'u·la'tive** *adj.* —**ma·nip'u·la'tor** *n.*

man·i·tou (man'ə too') *n.* [< Algonquian name] any of various nature spirits believed in by Algonquian Indians: also **man'i·tu, man'i·to'** (-tō')

man·kind (man'kīnd'; *also,* & *for 2 always,* man'kīnd') *n.* **1.** all human beings; the human race **2.** all human males ; the male sex

man·like (man'līk') *adj.* **1.** like or characteristic of a man or men **2.** fit for a man; masculine

man·ly (-lē) *adj.* **-li·er, -li·est** **1.** having qualities generally regarded as befitting a man; strong, brave, etc. **2.** fit for a man [*manly* sports] —*adv.* in a manly way —**man'·li·ness** *n.*

man-made (-mād') *adj.* made by man; synthetic

man·na (man'ə) *n.* [OE. < LL. < Gr. < Aram. *mannā* < Heb. *mān*] **1.** *Bible* food miraculously provided for the Israelites in the wilderness: Ex. 16:14-36 **2.** anything badly needed that comes unexpectedly

manned (mand) *pp.* of MAN —*adj.* having a human crew, or carrying humans [the Apollo was a *manned* spacecraft]

man·ne·quin (man'ə kin) *n.* [Fr. < Du.: see MANIKIN] **1.** a model of the human body, used by window dressers, artists, etc. **2.** a woman whose work is modelling clothes in stores, etc.

man·ner (man'ər) *n.* [< OFr., ult. < L. *manuarius,* of the hand < *manus,* a hand] **1.** a way or method in which something is done or happens **2.** a way of acting; personal, esp. customary, behaviour or bearing **3.** [*pl.*] *a)* ways of social life [a comedy of *manners*] *b)* ways of social behaviour; deportment [good *manners*] *c)* polite ways of social behaviour [the child lacks *manners*] **4.** characteristic style or method in art, etc. **5.** *a)* kind; sort [what *manner* of man is he?] *b)* [with *pl. v.*] kinds; sorts [all *manner* of things] —**by all manner of means** of course; surely —**by any manner of means** in any way; at all —**by no manner of means** in no way; definitely not —**in a manner of speaking** in a certain sense or way —**to the manner born** as if accustomed from birth to the way or usage spoken of —**man'ner·less** *n.*

man·nered (-ərd) *adj.* **1.** having manners or a manner of a specified sort [ill-*mannered,* soberly *mannered*] **2.** artificial, stylized, or affected

man·ner·ism (man'ər iz'm) *n.* **1.** excessive use of some distinctive manner in art, literature, speech, or behaviour **2.** a peculiarity of manner in behaviour, speech, etc. that has become a habit—**man'ner·ist** *n.* —**man'ner·is'tic** *adj.*

man·ner·ly (-lē) *adj.* showing good manners; polite —*adv.* politely —**man'ner·li·ness** *n.*

man·ni·kin (man'ə kin) *n.* *alt. sp.* of MANIKIN

man·nish (man'ish) *adj.* of, like, or fit for a man [she walks with a *mannish* stride] —**man'nish·ly** *adv.* —**man'·nish·ness** *n.*

ma·noeu·vre (mə noo'vər) *n.* [Fr. *manoeuvre* < ML. < L. *manu operare,* to work by hand] **1.** a planned and controlled movement of troops, warships, aircraft, etc. **2.** [*pl.*] practice movements of troops, warships, aircraft, etc. **3.** any skilful change of movement or direction in driving a vehicle, controlling an aircraft, etc. **4.** a stratagem; scheme —*vi., vt.* **1.** to or cause to perform manoeuvres **2.** to manage or plan skilfully; scheme **3.** to move, get, put, make, etc. by some stratagem —**ma·noeu'vra·bil'i·ty** *n.* —**ma·noeu'vra·ble** *adj.*

man of God **1.** a holy man; saint, hermit, etc. **2.** a clergyman; minister, priest, rabbi, etc.

man of letters a writer, scholar, etc., esp. one whose work is in the field of literature

man of the world a man familiar with and tolerant of various sorts of people and their ways

man-of-war (man′əv wôr′, -ə wôr′) *n.*, *pl.* **men′-of-war′** an armed naval vessel; warship

man-of-war bird *same as* FRIGATE BIRD

ma·nom·e·ter (mə nom′ə tər) *n.* [< Fr. < Gr. *manos*, rare (in sense "thin, sparse") + Fr. *-mètre*, -METER] an instrument for measuring the pressure of gases or liquids —**man·o·met·ric** (man′ə met′rik), **man′o·met′ri·cal** *adj.*

man·or (man′ər) *n.* [< OFr. < *manoir*, to dwell < L. *manere*, to remain] **1.** in England, a landed estate, orig. of a feudal lord and subject to the jurisdiction of his court **2.** a mansion, as on an estate: also **manor house 3.** [Colloq.] a police district —**ma·no·ri·al** (mə nôr′ē əl) *adj.*

manor house the house of the lord of a manor

man·pow·er (man′pou′ər) *n.* **1.** power furnished by human physical strength **2.** the collective strength or availability for work of the people in given area, nation, etc. Also **man power**

‡**man·qué** (mon kā′) *adj.* [Fr. < pp. of *manquer*, to fail, be lacking] **1.** unsuccessful or defective **2.** would-be Placed after the noun it modifies [a scholar *manqué*] —**man·quée** (-kā′) *adj.fem*

man·sard (roof) (man′särd) [after F. *Mansard*, 17th-c. Fr. architect] a roof with two slopes on each of the four sides, the lower steeper than the upper

manse (mans) *n.* [< ML. < pp. of L. *manere*, to dwell] **1.** a parsonage, esp. in Scotland **2.** [Archaic] a mansion

man·ser·vant (man′sur′vant) *n.*, *pl.* **men·ser·vants** (men′sur′vants) a male servant: also **man servant**

-man·ship (mən ship) [< (GAMES)-MANSHIP] *a combining form meaning* talent or skill (esp. in gaining advantage) in connection with: freely used in coinages [oneupmanship, quotemanship]

MANSARD ROOF

man·sion (man′shən) *n.* [OFr. < L. *mansio*, a dwelling < pp. of *manere*, to dwell] a large, imposing house; stately residence

Mansion House official residence of the Lord Mayor of London

man-sized (man′sīzd′) *adj.* [Colloq.] of a size fit for a man; large; big: also **man′-size′**

man·slaugh·ter (-slôt′ər) *n.* the killing of a human being by another, esp. such killing when unlawful but without malice aforethought

man·ta (ray) (man′tə) [Sp. < LL. *mantum*, a cloak] *same as* DEVILFISH (sense 1)

man·tel (man′t'l) *n.* [see MANTLE] **1.** the facing of stone, marble, etc. about a fireplace, including a shelf or slab above it **2.** the shelf or slab

man·tel·et (man′t'l it, mant′lit) *n.* [OFr., dim. of prec.] **1.** a short mantle or cape **2.** a protective shelter or screen: also **mant′let**

man·tel·piece (man′t'l pēs′) *n.* a mantel shelf, or this shelf and the side elements framing the fireplace in front

man·tic (man′tik) *adj.* [Gr. *mantikos* < *mantis*, seer, soothsayer] of, or having powers of, divination; prophetic

man·til·la (man til′ə, -tē′ə) *n.* [Sp. < LL. < L. *mantellum*, a mantle] a woman's scarf, as of lace, worn over the hair and shoulders, as in Spain or Mexico

man·tis (man′tis) *n.*, *pl.* **-tis·es, -tes** (-tēz) [ModL. < Gr. *mantis*, prophet, seer] a long, slender insect that feeds on other insects and grasps its prey with stout, spiny forelegs often held up together as if praying

man·tis·sa (man tis′ə) *n.* [L., (useless) addition] the decimal part of a logarithm

man·tle (man′t'l) *n.* [< OE. & OFr. < L. *mantellum*] **1.** a loose, sleeveless cloak or cape **2.** anything that clokes or envelops **3.** a small, mesh hood which becomes white-hot over a flame and gives off light **4.** *same as* MANTEL **5.** *Geol.* a) the layer of the earth's interior between the crust and the core b) *same as* MANTLEROCK **6.** *Zool.* the glandular flap or folds of the body wall of a mollusc, etc., typically secreting a shell-forming fluid —*vt.* **-tled, -tling** to cover with or as with a mantle; cloak —*vi.* **1.** to be or become covered, as a surface with froth **2.** to blush or flush

man·tle·rock (-rok′) *n.* the loose, unconsolidated material on the solid rock of the earth's crust

man·tra (mun′trə, man′-) *n.* [Sans., akin to *mantar*, thinker] *Hinduism* a hymn or text, esp. from the Veda, chanted as an incantation or prayer

man·u·al (man′yŏŏ wəl, -el, -əl) *adj.* [< OFr. < L. < *manus*, a hand] **1.** of a hand or the hands **2.** made, done, worked, or used by the hands **3.** involving or doing hard physical work requiring use of the hands —*n.* **1.** a handy book of instructions, etc. for use as a guide **2.** a keyboard of an organ console or harpsichord **3.** prescribed drill in the handling of a rifle: also **manual of arms** —**man′u·al·ly** *adv.*

manual alphabet the finger alphabet used by the deaf and dumb

manual training training in practical arts and crafts, as metalworking, etc.

man·u·fac·to·ry (man′yə fak′tər ē, -yŏŏ-) *n.*, *pl.* **-ries** same as FACTORY

man·u·fac·ture (man′yə fak′chər, -yŏŏ-) *n.* [Fr. < ML. < L. < *manus*, a hand + *factura*, a making < *facere*, to make] **1.** the making of goods by hand or, esp., by machinery, often on a large scale and with division of labour **2.** anything so made **3.** the making of something in a way regarded as mechanical —*vt.* **-tured, -tur·ing 1.** to make by hand or, esp., by machinery, often on a large scale, etc. **2.** to work (wool, steel, etc.) into usable form **3.** to produce (something) in a way regarded as mechanical **4.** to make up (excuses, evidence, etc.)

man·u·fac·tur·er (-chər ər) *n.* a person or company in the business of manufacturing; esp., a factory owner

man·u·ka (mä′nŏŏ kə, mä nŏŏ′kə) *n.* [Maori] a tea-tree, found in Australia and New Zealand, bearing masses of snowy-white blossoms; the natives use the leaves to brew tea

man·u·mis·sion (man′yə mish′ən, -yŏŏ-) *n.* [see ff.] a freeing or being freed from slavery; emancipation

man·u·mit (-mit′) *vt.* **-mit′ted, -mit′ting** [< OFr. < L. < *manus*, a hand + *mittere*, to send] to free from slavery —**man′u·mit′ter** *n.*

ma·nure (mə nyŏŏr′) *vt.* **-nured′, -nur′ing** [< Anglo-Fr. < OFr. *manouvrer*, to work with the hands, cultivate] to put manure on or into (soil) —*n.* animal excrement or other substance used to fertilize soil —**ma·nur′er** *n.*

man·u·script (man′yə skript′, -yŏŏ-) *adj.* [< L. < *manus*, a hand + pp. of *scribere*, to write] written by hand or with a typewriter —*n.* **1.** a written or typewritten book, article, etc.; esp., an author's copy of his work, as submitted to a publisher or printer **2.** writing as distinguished from print

Manx (maŋks) *adj.* of the Isle of Man, its people, etc. —*n.* their Goidelic language, now nearly extinct —**the Manx** the people of the Isle of Man

Manx cat [also m-] any of a breed of domestic cat that has no tail

Manx·man (-mən) *n.*, *pl.* **-men** a native or inhabitant of the Isle of Man —**Manx′wom′an** *n.fem.*, *pl.* **-wom′en**

man·y (men′ē) *adj.* **more, most** [OE. *manig*] **1.** consisting of some large, indefinite number; numerous **2.** relatively numerous (preceded by *as, too,* etc.) —*n.* a large number (of persons or things) —*pron.* many persons or things **Many a** (or **an, another**) with a singular noun or pronoun is equivalent to many with the plural (e.g., *many a man*) —**a good many** [with *pl. v.*] a relatively large number —**a great many** [with *pl. v.*] an extremely large number —**many's the time** often —**the many 1.** the majority of people **2.** the people; the masses

man·y·plies (men′ē plīz′) *n.* [prec. + pl. of PLY¹; *n.*] *same as* OMASUM

man·y·sid·ed (-sīd′id) *adj.* **1.** having many sides or aspects **2.** having many possibilities, qualities, interests, or accomplishments —**man′y·sid′ed·ness** *n.*

mao (mou) *adj.* [after Mao Tse-tung] of a style worn in China, like clothing worn by Mao Tse-tung [mao jacket]

Mao·ism (mou′iz'm) *n.* the communist theories and policies of Mao Tse-tung —**Mao′ist** *adj.*, *n.*

Ma·o·ri (mou′rē, mä′ə rē) *n.* **1.** *pl.* **-ris, -ri** any of a brown-skinned people native to New Zealand, of Polynesian origin **2.** their Polynesian language —*adj.* of the Maoris, their language, etc.

Ma·o·ri·land (mou′rē land) a Maori name for New Zealand

map (map) *n.* [< ML. *mappa* (*mundi*), map (of the world) < L. *mappa*, napkin] **1.** a representation, usually flat, of all or part of the earth's surface, ordinarily showing countries, bodies of water, cities, etc. **2.** a similar representation of the sky, showing stars, planets, etc. **3.** any maplike representation **4.** [Slang] the face —*vt.* **mapped, map′ping 1.** to make a map of; represent on a map **2.** to plan in detail [to map out a project] **3.** to survey for making a map **4.** *Math.* to link the elements of one set with the elements of another set —**put on the map** to make well known —**wipe off the map** to put out of existence —**map′per** *n.*

ma·ple (mā′p'l) *n.* [OE. *mapel(treo)*] **1.** any of a large group of trees with opposite leaves and two-winged fruits, grown for wood, sap, or shade **2.** the hard, fine-grained, light-coloured wood **3.** the flavour of maple syrup or of maple sugar —*adj.* **1.** of maple **2.** flavoured with maple

maple leaf the leaf of the maple tree, used as an emblem for Canada

maple sugar sugar from boiled-down maple syrup

maple syrup syrup made by boiling down the sap of the sugar maple

ma·quis (mä kē′; Fr. mȧ kē′) *n.* [Fr. < It. *macchia*, a thicket] **1.** a zone of shrubby, evergreen plants in the Mediterranean area, used as a hiding place by guerrilla fighters, etc. **2.** [often M-] a) *pl.* **-quis′**(-kēz′; Fr.-kē′) a member of the French underground fighting against the Nazis in World War II b) this organization

mar (mär) *vt.* **marred, mar′ring** [OE. *mierran*, to hinder] to hurt or spoil the looks, value, perfection, etc. of; impair, damage

Mar. March

mar. 1. marine 2. maritime 3. married

mar·a·bou (mar′ə bōō′) *n.* [Fr. < Port. < Ar. *murābit*, hermit] 1. any of certain large storks; esp., a) a dark-green African species b) the Indian adjutant 2. soft feathers from the wings and tail of the marabou Also **mar′a·bout** (-bōōt′)

ma·ra·ca (mə ra′kə) *n.* [Port. *maracá* < the Braz. native name] a percussion instrument consisting of a dried gourd or a gourd-shaped rattle with loose pebbles in it, shaken to beat out a rhythm

mar·a·schi·no (mar′ə skē′nō, -shē′-) *n.* [It. < *marasca*, kind of cherry < *amaro*, bitter] a strong, sweet liqueur or cordial made from the fermented juice of a kind of black wild cherry

maraschino cherries cherries in a syrup flavoured with maraschino

ma·ras·mus (mə raz′məs) *n.* [ML. < Gr. *marasmos*, a wasting away] a condition of progressive emaciation, esp. in infants, as from inability to assimilate food **—ma·ras′mic** *adj.*

mar·a·thon (mar′ə thon′) *n.* 1. a footrace of 26 miles, 385 yards (42.2 km): so called in allusion to the Greek runner who carried word of the victory at Marathon to Athens 2. any long-distance or endurance contest

ma·raud (mə rôd′) *vi.* [< Fr. < *maraud*, vagabond, prob. < dial. *maraud*, tomcat, echoic of cry] to rove in search of plunder; make raids **—vt.** to raid; plunder **—ma·raud′er** *n.*

mar·ble (mär′b'l) *n.* [< OFr. < L. < Gr. *marmaros*, white glistening stone] 1. a hard, metamorphic limestone, white or coloured and sometimes streaked or mottled, which can take a high polish 2. a) a piece or slab of this stone, used as a monument, etc. b) a sculpture in marble 3. anything like marble in hardness, coldness, etc. 4. a) a little ball of stone, glass, or clay, used in games b) [pl., with sing. v.] a children's game in which a marble is propelled with the thumb at other marbles in a marked circle 5. [pl.] [Slang] brains; good sense [to lose one's *marbles*] **—adj.** of or like marble **—vt.** **-bled, -bling** to stain (book edges) to look mottled or streaked like marble

mar·bled (mär′bəld) *adj.* [< prec.] with fat evenly distributed in streaks throughout: said of meat

mar·ble·ize (-īz′) *vt.* **-ized′, -iz′ing** to make, colour, grain, or or streak in imitation of marble

marc (märk) *n.* [Fr. < *marcher*, to trample] 1. refuse of grapes, seeds, fruits, etc. after pressing 2. a brandy distilled from this

mar·ca·site (mär′kə sīt′) *n.* [< Fr. < ML. < Ar. *marqashītā*] 1. a pale, distinctively crystallized pyrite (**white iron pyrite**) 2. this mineral or polished steel cut and used like brilliants

mar·cel (mär sel′) *n.* [after *Marcel* Grateau, early 20th-c. Fr. hairdresser] a series of even waves put in the hair with a curling iron: also **marcel wave** **—vt.** **-celled′, -cel′ling** to put such waves in (hair)

March (märch) *n.* [< OFr. < L. *Martius* (*mensis*), (month) of Mars] the third month of the year, having 31 days: abbrev. **Mar.**

march¹ (märch) *vi.* [Fr. *marcher* < OFr., prob. < Frank.] 1. to walk with regular, steady steps, as in a military formation 2. to walk in a grave, stately way 3. to advance or progress steadily **—vt.** to make march or go **—n.** 1. a marching 2. a steady advance; progress 3. a regular, steady step or pace 4. the distance covered in marching [a day's *march*] 5. a long, tiring walk 6. a piece of music for marching 7. an organized walk by people demonstrating on a public issue [a peace *march*] **—on the march** marching **—steal a march on** to get an advantage over secretly **—march′er** *n.*

march² (märch) *n.* [OFr. *marche* < Frank. hyp. *marka*, boundary] a boundary, border, or frontier **—vi.** [Rare] to have a common border (*with*); border **—the Marches** borderlands between England and Scotland and between England and Wales

March hare a hare in breeding time, proverbially regarded as an example of madness

marching orders orders to march, go, or leave

mar·chion·ess (mär′shə nis, mär′shə nes′) *n.* [< ML. fem. of *marchio*, prefect of the marches, or borderlands] 1. the wife or widow of a marquis or marquess 2. a lady whose own rank equals that of a marquis or marquess

march·pane (märch′pān′) *n.* same as MARZIPAN

march-past (märch′päst′) *n.* [MARCH¹ + PAST] a review of troops as they march past a saluting point

Mar·di gras (mär′di grä′) [Fr., lit., fat Tuesday] Shrove Tuesday, the last day before Lent: a day of carnival, as in Paris and New Orleans

mare¹ (mer) *n.* [OE. *mere*, fem. of *mearh*, horse] a fully mature female horse, mule, donkey, etc.

ma·re² (mär′ē) *n., pl.* **-ri·a** (-ē ə) [L., sea] 1. a sea 2. a large, dark area on the surface of the moon or of Mars

mare's-nest (merz′nest′) *n.* 1. a hoax; delusion 2. a disorderly or confused condition; mess

mare's-tail (-tāl′) *n.* long, narrow formations of cirrus cloud, shaped somewhat like a horse's tail

mar·ga·rine (mär′jə rēn′) *n.* [Fr.] a spread or cooking fat made of refined vegetable oils processed to the consistency of butter: also **mar′ga·rin′**

marge¹ (märj) *n.* [Fr. < L. *margo*, margin] [Archaic or Poet.] a border; edge; margin

marge² (märj) *n.* [Colloq.] clipped form of MARGARINE

mar·gin (mär′jən, jin) *n.* [L. *margo* (gen. *marginis*)] 1. a border, edge, or brink 2. the blank border of a printed or written page 3. a limit to what is desirable or possible 4. a) an amount of money, supplies, etc. beyond what is needed b) provision for increase, addition, or advance 5. the amount by which something is higher or lower 6. *Business, Finance* a) the difference between the cost and selling price of goods b) money or collateral deposited with a broker, etc., either to meet legal requirements or to insure him against loss on contracts which he undertakes for a buyer or seller of stocks, etc. 7. *Econ.* the minimum return of profit needed to continue activities **—vt.** 1. to provide with a margin 2. *Business* to deposit a margin upon

mar·gin·al (-'l) *adj.* 1. written or printed in the margin 2. of a margin 3. at, on, or close to the margin 4. slight **—mar′gin·al′i·ty** (-al′ə tē) *n.* **—mar′gin·al·ly** *adv.*

marginal seat *Politics* a constituency in which a political party cannot be sure of retaining a majority: cf. SAFE SEAT

mar·gin·ate (mär′jə nāt′; *also for adj.* -nit) *vt.* **-at′ed, -at′ing** to provide with a margin **—adj.** having a distinct margin: also **mar′gin·at′ed** **—mar′gin·a′tion** *n.*

mar·grave (mär′grāv) *n.* [< MDu. < MHG. < OHG. < *marc*, a border + *graf*, a count] 1. orig., a military governor of a border province in Germany 2. the title of certain princes of Germany

mar·gra·vine (mär′grə vēn′) *n.* a margrave's wife

mar·gue·rite (mär′gə rēt′) *n.* [Fr., a pearl] 1. same as DAISY (sense 1) 2. a cultivated chrysanthemum with a single flower 3. any of various daisylike plants of the composite family

ma·ri·a (mär′ē ə) *n. pl. of* MARE²

ma·ri·a·chi (mär′ē ä′chē) *n., pl.* **-chis** [MexSp. < ?] 1. one of a strolling band of musicians in Mexico 2. such a band 3. their music

mar·i·gold (mar′ə gōld′) *n.* [< *Marie* (prob. the Virgin *Mary*) + *gold*, GOLD] 1. a plant of the composite family, with red, yellow, or orange flowers 2. its flower 3. any of several unrelated plants

ma·ri·jua·na, ma·ri·hua·na (mar′ə wä′nə, -hwä′-) *n.* [AmSp. < ? native word] 1. same as HEMP (sense 1 a) 2. its dried leaves and flowers, smoked for the psychological effects

ma·rim·ba (mə rim′bə) *n.* [< Afr. (Bantu), a kind of percussive instrument] a kind of xylophone, usually with resonators under the wooden bars

ma·ri·na (mə rē′nə) *n.* [It. & Sp., seacoast < L. *marinus*: see MARINE] a small harbour with dockage, supplies, and services for small pleasure craft

mar·i·nade (mar′ə nād′) *n.* [Fr. < Sp. < *marinar*, to pickle, ult. < L. *marinus*: see MARINE] 1. a spiced pickling solution, esp. with oil and wine or vinegar, in which meat, fish, or salad is steeped 2. meat, etc. so steeped **—vt.** **-nad′-ed, -nad′ing** same as MARINATE

mar·i·nate (mar′ə nāt′) *vt.* **-nat′ed, -nat′ing** [< It. < *marinare*, to pickle: see prec.] to steep (meat, etc.) in a marinade **—mar′i·na′tion** *n.*

ma·rine (mə rēn′) *adj.* [< L. *marinus* < *mare*, the sea] 1. of, found in, or formed by the sea or ocean 2. a) of navigation on, or shipping by, the sea; nautical; maritime b) naval 3. used, or to be used, at sea 4. a) trained for service at sea, etc., as certain troops b) of such troops **—n.** 1. a) see MILITARY RANKS, table b) a member of the Royal Marines 2. naval or merchant ships collectively [the merchant *marine*] 3. in some countries, the governmental department of naval affairs 4. a picture of a ship or sea scene

mar·i·ner (mar′ə nər) *n.* [< Anglo-Fr. < ML. < L. *marinus*, MARINE] a sailor; seaman

Mar·i·ol·a·try (mer′ē ol′ə trē, mar′-) *n.* [Gr. *Maria*, Mary + -LATRY] veneration of the Virgin Mary, when regarded as carried to an idolatrous extreme

mar·i·o·nette (mar′ē ə net′) *n.* [Fr., dim. of *Marion*, a feminine name] a puppet or little jointed doll moved by strings or wires from above, often on a little stage

Mar·ist (mar′ist, mer′-) *adj.* [Fr. *Mariste* < *Marie*, Mary] R.C.Ch. 1. of or dedicated to the Virgin Mary 2. of the Society of Mary (**Marist Fathers**) founded in 1816 **—n.** a member of this group

mar·i·tal (mar′ə t'l) *adj.* [< L. < *maritus*, a husband] of marriage **—mar′i·tal·ly** *adv.*

mar·i·time (mar′ə tīm′) *adj.* [L. *maritimus* < *mare*, the sea] 1. on, near, or living near the sea 2. of sea navigation, shipping, etc. 3. nautical

mar·jo·ram (mär′jər əm) *n.* [< OFr. < ML., prob. < L. *amaracus* < Gr. *amarakos*] any of various perennial plants of the labiate family; esp., **sweet marjoram**, having aromatic leaves used in cooking

mark¹ (märk) *n.* [OE. *mearc*, orig., boundary] 1. a line, spot, stain, scratch, mar, etc. on a surface 2. a sign, symbol, or indication; specif., *a*) a printed or written sign or stroke [punctuation *marks*] *b*) a brand, label, etc. put on an article to show the owner, maker, etc. *c*) a sign of some quality, character, etc. [courtesy is the *mark* of a gentleman] *d*) a numerical assessment of proficiency, as in an examination *e*) a cross, etc. made by a person unable to write his signature 3. a standard of quality, etc. [up to the *mark*] 4. importance; distinction [a man of *mark*] 5. impression; influence [left his *mark* in history] 6. a visible object of known position, serving as a guide 7. a line, dot, etc. used to indicate position, as on a graduated scale 8. an object aimed at; target; end; goal 9. the butt of an attack, criticism, etc. 10. a taking notice; heed 11. *Sports* the starting line of a race 12. *Rugby* the place from which a penalty or free kick is taken —*vt.* 1. to put or make a mark or marks on 2. to identify as by a mark 3. to draw, write, record, etc. 4. to show by a mark 5. to show plainly; manifest [a smile *marking* joy] 6. to distinguish; characterize 7. to take notice of; heed 8. to grade; rate 9. to put price labels on 10. to keep (score, etc.); record 11. *Football* to follow closely the movements of a player in the opposing team, so as to hinder his play —*vi.* 1. to make a mark or marks 2. to observe; take note 3. *Games* to keep score —**hit the mark** 1. to achieve one's aim 2. to be right —**make one's mark** to achieve fame —**mark down** 1. to write down; record 2. to mark for sale at a reduced price —**mark off** (or **out**) to mark the limits of —**mark time** 1. to keep time while at a halt by lifting the feet as if marching 2. to suspend progress for a time —**mark up** 1. to cover with marks 2. to mark for sale at an increased price —**miss the mark** 1. to fail in achieving one's aim 2. to be inaccurate —**wide of** (or **beside**) **the mark** 1. not striking the point aimed at 2. irrelevant —**mark′er** *n.*

mark² (märk) *n.* [< OE. < ON. *mork*, a half pound of silver] 1. a unit of the old German Empire, superseded by the reichsmark, and of East Germany: see MONETARY UNITS, table 2. *same as* DEUTSCHE MARK

mark·down (märk′doun′) *n.* 1. a marking for sale at a reduced price 2. the amount of reduction

marked (märkt) *adj.* 1. having a mark or marks 2. singled out as an object of hostility, etc. [a *marked* man] 3. noticeable; distinct [a *marked* change] —**mark′ed·ly** (mär′kid lē) *adv.* —**mark′ed·ness** *n.*

mar·ket (mär′kit) *n.* [< ONormFr. < L. *mercatus*, trade < pp. of *mercari*, to trade < *merx*, merchandise] 1. *a*) a gathering of people for buying and selling things *b*) the people gathered 2. an open space or a building with goods for sale from stalls, etc.: also **mar′ket·place′** 3. a shop selling a particular item [an antique *market*] 4. a region where goods can be bought and sold [the European *market*] 5. *a*) trade in goods, stocks, etc. [an active *market*] *b*) trade in a specified commodity [the wheat *market*] *c*) the people associated in such trade 6. *short for* STOCK MARKET 7. demand (for goods or services) [a good *market* for new products] 8. supply (of goods or services) [reduced labour *market*] —*vt.* 1. to send or take to market 2. to offer for sale 3. to sell —*vi.* 1. to buy or sell 2. to buy provisions —**be in the market for** to be seeking to buy —**be on the market** to be offered for sale —**buyer's market** a state of trade favourable to the buyer (relatively heavy supply and low prices) —**put on the market** to offer for sale —**seller's market** a state of trade favourable to the seller (relatively heavy demand and high prices) —**mar′ket·a·bil′i·ty** *n.* —**mar′ket·a·ble** *adj.* —**mar′ket·er, mar′ket·eer′** (-kə tir′) *n.*

market cross a town cross marking the site of markets in medieval towns

market garden an establishment where fruit and vegetables are grown and sold —**market gardener** *n.*

mar·ket·ing (-iŋ) *n.* 1. the act of buying or selling in a market 2. the business of moving goods from the producer to the consumer, involving packaging, advertising, etc.

market price the prevailing price of a commodity

market research the study of the demands or needs of consumers in relation to particular goods or services

market town a town that holds a public market, esp. an agricultural centre in a rural area

market value the price that a commodity can be expected to bring in a given market

mark·ing (mär′kiŋ) *n.* 1. the act of making a mark or marks 2. a mark or marks 3. the characteristic arrangement of marks, as on fur or feathers

mark·ka (märk′kä) *n., pl.* **-kaa** (-kä) [Finn. < Sw. *mark*: see MARK²] *see* MONETARY UNITS, table (Finland)

marks·man (märks′mən) *n., pl.* **-men** a person who shoots, esp. with skill —**marks′man·ship′** *n.*

mark·up (märk′up′) *n.* 1. a marking for sale at an increased price 2. the amount of increase, esp. to allow for dealer's profit

marl (märl) *n.* [< OFr. < ML. dim. of L. *marga*, marl < Gaul.] a crumbly mixture of clay, sand, and limestone, usually with shell fragments—*vt.* to cover or fertilize with marl —**marl′y** *adj.*

mar·lin (mär′lin) *n., pl.* **-lin, -lins**: see PLURAL, II, D, 2 [< MARLINSPIKE] any of several large, slender deep-sea fishes related to the sailfish, esp. the **blue marlin** of the Atlantic

mar·line (mär′lin) *n.* [Du. *marlijn*, altered (after *lijn*, LINE¹) a small cord of two loose strands for winding around the ends of ropes to prevent fraying: also **mar′lin, mar′lin** (-liŋ)

mar·line·spike, mar·lin·spike (-spīk′) *n.* a pointed iron instrument for separating rope strands, as in splicing: also **mar′ling·spike′** (-liŋ-)

mar·ma·lade (mär′mə lād′) *n.* [< OFr. < Port. < *marmelo*, quince < L. *melimelum* < Gr. < *meli*, honey + *mēlon*, apple] a jam made of oranges or some other fruits and sugar

Mar·mite (mär′mīt) *a trademark for* a yeast and vegetable extract used to flavour stews, soups, etc. —*n.* [m-] this substance

mar·mite (mär′mīt) *n.* [Fr. *marmite*, pot] a large cooking pot, usually made of earthenware

mar·mo·re·al (mär môr′ē əl) *adj.* [< L. < *marmor*, marble + -AL] of or like marble: also **mar·mo′re·an** —**mar·mo′re·al·ly** *adv.*

mar·mo·set (mär′mə zet′, -set′) *n.* [< OFr. *marmouset*, grotesque figure] a very small monkey of South and Central America, with thick, soft fur

mar·mot (mär′mət) *n.* [< Fr. < earlier *marmottaine*, prob. < L. *mus montanus*, mountain mouse] any of a group of thick-bodied, gnawing and burrowing rodents with coarse fur and a short, bushy tail

ma·roon¹ (mə rōōn′) *n., adj.* [Fr. *marron*, chestnut < It. *marrone*] dark brownish red

ma·roon² (mə rōōn′) *n.* [< Fr. < AmSp. *cimarrón*, wild < OSp. *cimarra*, thicket] in the West Indies and Surinam, 1. orig., a fugitive Negro slave 2. a descendant of such slaves —*vt.* 1. to put (a person) ashore in some desolate place and abandon him there 2. to leave abandoned, helpless, etc.

mar·plot (mär′plot′) *n.* a person or, sometimes, a thing spoiling a plan by officious interference

Marq. 1. Marquess 2. Marquis

marque¹ (märk) *n.* [MFr. < Pr. *marca*] reprisal: obsolete except in LETTERS OF MARQUE

marque² (märk) *n.* [Fr., ult. < OIt. *marca*, a mark] an identifying nameplate or emblem on a motor car

mar·quee (mär kē′) *n.* [< Fr. *marquise* (misunderstood as pl.), orig. a canopy over an officer's tent] 1. a large tent, as for an outdoor entertainment 2. [U.S.] a rooflike projection or awning over an entrance, as to a theatre

mar·quess (mär′kwis) *n. same as* MARQUIS

mar·que·try, mar·que·terie (mär′kə trē) *n.* [< Fr. < *marque*, a mark] decorative inlaid work of wood, ivory, etc., as in furniture or flooring

mar·quis (mär′kwis; *Fr.* mär kē′) *n., pl.* **-quis·es; *Fr.* -quis′** (-kē′) [< OFr. < ML. *marchisus*, prefect of a frontier town < *marca*, borderland] 1. a British nobleman ranking above an earl and below a duke 2. in European countries a nobleman ranking above an earl or count and below a duke —**mar′quis·ate** (-kwə zit) *n.*

mar·quise (mär kēz′; *Fr.* már kēz′) *n.* 1. the wife or widow of a marquis 2. a lady whose rank in her own right equals that of a marquis 3. a gem cut as a pointed oval

mar·qui·sette (mär′ki zet′, -kwi-) *n.* [dim. of Fr. *marquise*, awning: see MARQUEE] a thin, meshlike fabric used for curtains, dresses, etc.

mar·riage (mar′ij) *n.* [OFr. < *marier*: see MARRY¹] 1. the state of being married; relation between husband and wife; wedlock 2. the act or rite of marrying; wedding 3. any close union

mar·riage·a·ble (mar′ij ə b'l) *adj.* old enough or suitable for marriage; likely to marry —**mar′riage·a·bil′i·ty** *n.*

marriage bureau a business concern set up to introduce people, wishing to get married, to one another

marriage certificate an official document giving the place and date of the wedding ceremony and the names of the couple taking part

marriage guidance advice given, usually by a marriage

MARMOSET
(body to 38 cm long; tail to 45 cm long)

guidance counsellor, to couples who experience difficulties in their marriages

marriage lines *same as* MARRIAGE CERTIFICATE

marriage portion *same as* DOWRY

mar·ried (mar′ēd) *adj.* **1.** living together as husband and wife **2.** having a husband or wife **3.** of marriage or married people **4.** closely joined —*n.* a married person: chiefly in **young marrieds**

‡**mar·ron gla·cés** (ma rôn′gla sā′) [Fr.] chestnuts cooked in syrup and glazed

mar·row (mar′ō) *n.* [OE. *mearg*] **1.** the soft, vascular, fatty tissue that fills the cavities of most bones **2.** the innermost, essential, or choicest part; pith **3.** *same as* VEGETABLE MARROW —**mar′row·y** *adj.*

mar·row·bone (-bōn′) *n.* a bone having marrow

mar·row·fat (-fat′) *n.* a variety of large, rich pea: also **marrowfat pea, marrow pea**

mar·ry[1] (mar′ē) *vt.* **-ried, -ry·ing** [< OFr. *marier* < L. < *maritus*, a husband] **1.** *a)* to join as husband and wife *b)* to join (a man) to a woman as her husband, or (a woman) to a man as his wife **2.** to take as husband or wife **3.** to join closely —*vi.* **1.** to get married **2.** to enter into a close relationship —**marry off** to give in marriage: said of a parent or guardian —**mar′ri·er** *n.*

mar·ry[2] (mar′ē) *interj.* [euphemistic respelling of (the Virgin) *Mary*] [Archaic or Dial.] an exclamation of surprise, anger, etc.

Mars (märz) **1.** *Rom. Myth.* the god of war: identified with the Greek god Ares **2.** *a personification of* war **3.** a planet of the solar system, fourth in distance from the sun: diameter, c. 6758 km

Mar·sa·la (mär sä′lə) *n.* [< *Marsala*, seaport in W Sicily] a light, fortified, sweet white wine

Mar·seil·laise (mär′sə lāz′; *Fr.* már sä yäz′) [Fr., lit., of Marseille] the French national anthem, composed (1792) during the French Revolution

Mar·seilles (mär sālz′) *n.* [after *Marseille*, seaport in S France] a thick, strong cotton cloth with a raised weave

marsh (märsh) *n.* [OE. *merisc*] a tract of low, wet, soft land; swamp; bog; morass

mar·shal (mär′shəl) *n.* [< OFr. *mareschal* < OHG. *marah*, horse + *scalh*, servant] **1.** *a)* a high official of a medieval royal household *b)* a high state official [*Earl Marshal*] **2.** a military commander; specif., *a)* *same as* FIELD MARSHAL *b)* in various foreign armies, a general officer of the highest rank **3.** an official in charge of ceremonies, processions, etc. **4.** [U.S.] a Federal officer appointed to a judicial district to perform functions like those of a sheriff —*vt.* **-shalled, -shal·ling** **1.** to arrange (troops, things, ideas, etc.) in order; dispose **2.** *a)* to direct as a marshal; manage *b)* to lead or guide ceremoniously —**mar′shal·cy, mar′-shal·ship′** *n.*

marshalling yard a railway depot for goods trains

Marshal of the Royal Air Force *see* MILITARY RANKS, table

marsh fever *another name for* MALARIA

marsh gas a gaseous product, chiefly methane, formed from decomposing vegetable matter

marsh·mal·low (märsh′mel′ō, -mal′ō) *n.* **1.** orig., a confection made from the root of the marsh mallow **2.** a soft, spongy confection of sugar, starch, flavouring, and gelatin

marsh mallow a pink-flowered, perennial, European plant with a root sometimes used in medicine

marsh marigold a marsh plant of the buttercup family, with bright-yellow flowers

marsh tit a greyish-brown European tit that lives in woods, hedges, etc.

marsh·y (mär′shē) *adj.* **marsh′i·er, marsh′i·est** **1.** of, like, or containing a marsh or marshes; swampy **2.** growing in marshes —**marsh′i·ness** *n.*

mar·su·pi·al (mär sōō′pē əl) *adj.* **1.** of or like a marsupium **2.** of an order of mammals whose young are carried by the female for several months after birth in an external pouch of the abdomen —*n.* an animal of this kind, as a kangaroo, opossum, etc.

mar·su·pi·um (-əm) *n.*, *pl.* **-pi·a** (-ə) [ModL. < L. < Gr. dim. of *marsypos*, a pouch] the pouch on the abdomen of a female marsupial

mart (märt) *n.* [MDu., var. of *markt*] a market

mar·tel·lo tower (mär tel′ō) [It. *martello*, a hammer, folk-etym. substitution for *mortella*, a tower < *Mortello*, in Corsica, where such a tower was attacked by Brit. fleet in 1794] [*occas.* M-] a circular fort of masonry, formerly built on coasts to protect against invaders: also **mar·tel′lo** *n.*

mar·ten (mär′tən) *n.*, *pl.* **-tens, -ten:** *see* PLURAL, II, D, 1 [< OFr. < *martre*] **1.** a small, flesh-eating mammal like a weasel but larger, with soft, thick, valuable fur **2.** the fur

mar·tial (mär′shəl) *adj.* [< L. *martialis*, of Mars] **1.** of or connected with war, soldiers, etc.; military [*martial music*] **2.** warlike; militaristic [*martial spirit*] —**mar′tial·ism** *n.* —**mar′tial·ist** *n.* —**mar′tial·ly** *adv.*

martial law temporary rule by the military authorities over the civilians, as in time of war

Mar·tian (mär′shən) *adj.* of Mars (god or planet) —*n.* an imagined inhabitant of the planet Mars

mar·tin (mär′tin) *n.* [Fr.] **1.** a stout-billed bird of the swallow family, as the house martin **2.** any of various swallowlike birds

mar·ti·net (mär′t′n et′) *n.* [after Gen. J. *Martinet*, 17th-c. Fr. drillmaster] a very strict disciplinarian or stickler for rigid regulations

mar·tin·gale (mär′tin gāl′) *n.* [Fr., prob. < Sp. *almártaga*, check, rein < Ar.] **1.** the strap of a horse's harness passing from the noseband to the girth between the forelegs, to keep the horse from rearing or throwing back its head **2.** a lower stay for the jib boom of a sailing vessel Also **mar′-tin·gal′** (-gal′)

mar·ti·ni (mär tē′nē) *n.*, *pl.* **-nis** [altered < earlier *Martinez*: reason for name unc.] **1.** [*also* M-] a cocktail of gin and dry vermouth **2.** a *trademark for* Italian vermouth

Mar·tin·mas (mär′tin məs) *n.* [see -MAS] Saint Martin's Day, a church festival held on November 11

mar·tyr (mär′tər) *n.* [OE. < LL. < Gr. *martyr*, a witness] **1.** a person tortured or killed because of his faith or beliefs **2.** a person suffering great pain or misery for a long time [he was a *martyr* to bronchial catarrh] —*vt.* to make a martyr of —**mar′tyr·dom** *n.*

mar·tyr·ize (mär′tə rīz′) *vt.* **-ized, -iz′ing** to make a martyr of —*vi.* to be or become a martyr —**mar′tyr·i·za′-tion** *n.*

mar·tyr·ol·o·gy (mär′tə rol′ə jē) *n.*, *pl.* **-gies** **1.** *a)* a list of martyrs *b)* R.C.Ch. a list of Saints **2.** a historical account of religious martyrs **3.** such accounts collectively —**mar′-tyr·ol′o·gist** *n.*

mar·vel (mär′v′l) *n.* [< OFr. *merveille* < VL. < L. neut. pl. of *mirabilis*, wonderful < *mirari*, to admire] a wonderful or astonishing thing; prodigy or miracle —*vi.* **-velled, -vel·ling** to be amazed; wonder —*vt.* to wonder at or about (followed by a clause)

mar·vel·lous (mär′v′l əs) *adj.* **1.** causing wonder; astonishing, extraordinary, incredible, etc. **2.** [Colloq.] fine; splendid —**mar′vel·lous·ly** *adv.* —**mar′vel·lous·ness** *n.*

Marx·ism (märk′siz′m) *n.* the system of thought developed by Karl Marx, his co-worker Friedrich Engels, and their followers: also **Marx′i·an·ism** —**Marx′ist, Marx′i·an** *adj.*, *n.*

Marx·ism-Len·in·ism (märk′siz′m-len′in iz′m) *n.* the modification of Marxism by Lenin analysing imperialism as capitalism and advocating that revolutionary class struggle should be promoted in underdeveloped countries —**Marx′-ist-Len′in·ist** *n.*, *adj.*

mar·zi·pan (mär′zi pan′) *n.* [G. < It. *marzapane*, confection < ML. < Ar.] a confection of various shapes and colours made of a paste of ground almonds, sugar, and egg white

-mas (məs) a *combining form for* MASS meaning a (specified) church festival [*Martinmas*]

Ma·sai (mä sī′) *n.* **1.** *pl.* **-sai′, -sais′** any member of a pastoral people of Kenya and Tanzania **2.** their language

masc., mas. masculine

mas·ca·ra (mas kar′ə) *n.* [< Sp. < It. *maschera*: see MASK] a cosmetic for colouring the eyelashes —*vt.* **-ca′raed, -ca′-ra·ing** to put mascara on

mas·cot (mas′kot, -kət) *n.* [< Fr. < Pr. dim. of *masco*, sorcerer] any person, animal, or thing supposed to bring good luck by being present

mas·cu·line (mas′kyə lin) *adj.* [< OFr. < L. < *masculus*, male < *mas*, male] **1.** male; of men or boys **2.** having qualities generally regarded as characteristic of men and boys, as strength, vigour, etc. **3.** suitable for or typical of a man **4.** mannish **5.** *Gram.* designating or of the gender of words referring to males or things conventionally regarded as male **6.** *Prosody* designating or of a rhyme of stressed final syllables (Ex.: enjoy, destroy) —*n.* *Gram.* **1.** the masculine gender **2.** a word or form in this gender —**mas′-cu·line·ly** *adv.* —**mas′cu·lin′i·ty** *n.*

mas·cu·lin·ize (-li nīz′) *vt.* **-ized′, -iz′ing** to make masculine; esp., to produce male characteristics in (a female) —**mas′cu·lin′i·za′tion** *n.*

ma·ser (mā′zər) *n.* [*m*(*icrowave*) *a*(*mplification by*) *s*(*timulated*) *e*(*mission of*) *r*(*adiation*)] a device, operating at microwave, infrared, etc. frequencies, in which atoms in crystal or gas are concentrated, raised to a higher energy level, then emitted in a very narrow beam

mash (mash) *n.* [< OE. *masc-*, in *mascwyrt*, infused malt] **1.** crushed or ground malt or meal soaked in hot water for making wort, used in brewing beer **2.** a mixture of bran, meal, etc. in warm water for feeding horses, etc. **3.** any soft mixture or mass **4.** [Colloq.] mashed potatoes —*vt.* **1.** to mix (crushed malt, etc.) in hot water for making wort **2.** to change into a soft mass by beating, crushing, etc. **3.** to crush and injure or damage **4.** [Dial.] to brew (tea)

mash·er (-ər) *n.* one that mashes; specif., a device for mashing vegetables, etc.

mash·ie (mash′ē) *n.* [< ? Fr. *massue*, a club] a golf club with a metal head used for lofting and medium-length shots: also called **number 5 iron**

mask (mäsk) *n.* [Fr. *masque* < It. *maschera*, prob. < Ar. *maskhara*, buffoon] **1.** a covering to conceal or disguise all or part of the face **2.** anything that conceals or disguises **3.** a masque or masquerade **4.** a person wearing a mask **5.** *a*) a sculptured or moulded likeness of the face *b*) a grotesque or comic representation of a face, worn to amuse or frighten **6.** a protective covering for the face or head [a gas *mask*] **7.** a covering for the mouth and nose, as for administering an anaesthetic, preventing infection, etc. **8.** the face or head of a dog, fox, etc. —*vt.* to conceal, cover, disguise, etc. with or as with a mask —*vi.* **1.** to put on a mask **2.** to hide or disguise one's true motives, character, etc. —**masked** *adj.* —**mask′er** *n.*

MASKS

masked ball a ball at which masks and fancy costumes are worn

mask·ing tape (mäs′kiŋ) an adhesive tape for covering borders, etc., as during painting

mas·och·ism (mas′ə kiz′m, maz′-) *n.* [after L. von Sacher-*Masoch* (1835–1895), Austrian writer] the getting of pleasure, specif. sexual pleasure, from being dominated or hurt physically or psychologically —**mas′och·ist** *n.* —**mas′-och·is′tic** *adj.* —**mas′och·is′ti·cal·ly** *adv.*

ma·son (mā′s'n) *n.* [< OFr. < ML. *matio*] **1.** a person whose work is building with stone, brick, etc. **2.** [M-] same as FREEMASON

Ma·son-Dix·on line (mā′s'n dik′s'n) [after C. *Mason* & J. *Dixon*, who surveyed it, 1763–67] boundary line between Pennsylvania & Maryland, regarded as separating the Northern States from the Southern States of U.S.: also **Mason and Dixon's line**

Ma·son·ic (mə son′ik) *adj.* [also **m-**] of Masons (Freemasons) or Masonry (Freemasonry)

ma·son·ry (mā′s'n rē) *n.,* *pl.* **-ries** **1.** the trade or art of a mason **2.** something built by a mason or masons; brickwork or stonework **3.** [usually **M-**] same as FREEMASONRY

masque (mask, mäsk) *n.* [see MASK] **1.** a masquerade; masked ball **2.** a former kind of dramatic entertainment with a mythical or allegorical theme and lavish costumes, music, etc. —**masqu′er** *n.*

mas·quer·ade (mas′kə rād′, mäs′-) *n.* [< Fr. < It. dial. var. of *mascherata* (< *maschera*): see MASK] **1.** a ball or party at which masks and fancy costumes are worn **2.** a costume for such a ball, etc. **3.** *a*) a disguise; pretence *b*) a living or acting under false pretences —*vi.* **-ad′ed, -ad′ing** **1.** to take part in a masquerade **2.** to live or act under false pretences —**mas′quer·ad′er** *n.*

Mass (mas) *n.* [OE. *mæsse* < LL. < *missa* in L. *ite, missa est* (*contio*), go, (the meeting) is dismissed] [also **m-**] **1.** the service of the Eucharist in the Roman Catholic Church and some other churches, consisting of a series of prayers and ceremonies **2.** a musical setting for certain parts of this service

mass (mas) *n.* [OFr. *masse* < L. < Gr. *maza*, barley cake] **1.** a piece or amount of indefinite shape or size [a *mass* of clay, a *mass* of cold air] **2.** a large quantity or number [a *mass* of bruises] **3.** bulk; size **4.** the main part; majority **5.** *Physics* the quantity of matter in a body as measured in its relation to inertia —*adj.* **1.** *a*) of a large number of things [*mass* production] *b*) of a large number of persons [a *mass* meeting] **2.** of, like, or for the masses [*mass* education] —*vt., vi.* to gather or form into a mass —**in the mass** collectively —**the masses** the great mass of common people; specif., the working people

mas·sa·cre (mas′ə kər) *n.* [Fr. < OFr. *maçacre*, shambles] **1.** the indiscriminate, merciless killing of human beings **2.** a large-scale slaughter of animals —*vt.* **-cred, -cring** **1.** to kill indiscriminately and mercilessly and in large numbers **2.** to handle roughly [to *massacre* Beethoven] —**mas′sa·crer** (-krər) *n.*

mas·sage (mə säzh′) *n.* [Fr. < *masser*, to massage < Ar. *massa*, to touch] a rubbing, kneading, etc. of part of the body, as to stimulate circulation and make muscles or joints supple —*vt.* **-saged′, -sag′ing** to give a massage to —**mas·sag′er** *n.*

mas·sé (**shot**) (ma sā′) [Fr. < *masse*, billiard cue] a stroke in billiards made by hitting the cue ball off centre with the cue held vertically so as to make the ball move in a curve

mas·seur (ma sʉr′, mə-; *Fr.* mà sɛr′) *n.* [Fr.] a man whose work is giving massages —**mas·seuse** (sʉrz′; *Fr.* -söz′) *n.fem.*

mass grave a grave containing the bodies of many people, all buried at the same time

mass hysteria the irrational behaviour evidenced in large crowds by people who would not normally be affected by hysteria

mas·sif (ma sēf′, mas′ēf) *n.* [Fr., lit., solid] *Geol.* a distinctive, compact group of mountains

mas·sive (mas′iv) *adj.* **1.** *a*) forming or consisting of a large mass; big and solid; bulky *b*) larger or greater than normal [a *massive* dose of drugs] **2.** large and imposing or impressive **3.** large-scale; extensive —**mas′sive·ly** *adv.* —**mas′sive·ness** *n.*

mass media those means of communication that reach and influence large numbers of people, esp. newspapers, magazines, radio, and television

mass meeting a large public meeting to discuss public affairs, demonstrate public approval or disapproval, etc.

mass number *Physics, Chem.* the number of neutrons and protons in the nucleus of an atom

mass observation the study of the social and economic problems of the masses

mass production quantity production of goods, esp. by machinery and division of labour —**mass′-pro·duce′** *vt.* **-duced′, -duc′ing**

mass spectrometer an instrument which, by passing ionized particles through electric and magnetic fields, separates and counts isotopes according to their mass

mast[1] (mäst) *n.* [OE. *mæst*] **1.** a tall spar or hollow metal structure rising vertically from the keel or deck of a vessel and used to support the sails, yards, radar and radio equipment, etc. **2.** any vertical pole, as in a crane —*vt.* to put masts on —**before the mast** [Now Rare] as a common sailor

mast[2] (mäst) *n.* [OE. *mæst*] beechnuts, acorns, chestnuts, etc., esp. as food for pigs

mas·ta·ba, mas·ta·bah (mas′tə bə) *n.* [< Ar.] an oblong structure with a flat roof and sloping sides, built over the opening of a mummy chamber or burial pit in ancient Egypt and used as a tomb

mas·tec·to·my (mas tek′tə mē) *n.,* *pl.* **-mies** [MAST(O) -ECTOMY] the surgical removal of a breast

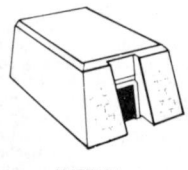

MASTABA

mas·ter (mäs′tər) *n.* [< OE. *mægester* & OFr. *maistre*; both < L. *magister* < base of L. *magnus*, great] **1.** a man who rules others or has control, authority, or power over something; specif., *a*) a man who is head of a household or institution *b*) an employer *c*) an owner of an animal or slave *d*) the captain of a merchant ship *e*) a victor *f*) a male schoolteacher *g*) a person whose teachings in religion, philosophy, etc. one follows *h*) [M-] Jesus Christ (with *our,* etc.) **2.** a person very skilled in some work, profession, etc.; expert; specif., *a*) a highly skilled workman qualified to follow his trade independently *b*) an artist regarded as great **3.** [M-] a title variously applied to *a*) any man or youth: now superseded by the variant *Mister,* usually written *Mr. b*) a boy regarded as too young to be addressed as *Mr. c*) a man who heads some institution, group, etc. *d*) in Scotland, the heir apparent of a viscount or baron *e*) a person who is a MASTER OF ARTS (or SCIENCE, etc.) **4.** *Law* any of several court officers appointed to assist the judge **5.** an original copy, matrix, stencil etc., from which duplicates are made **6.** *Chess* a player who has played and won a specified number of tournament games —*adj.* **1.** being a master **2.** of a master **3.** chief; main; controlling; specif., designating a mechanism or contrivance that controls others, sets a standard or norm, etc. [a *master* switch] —*vt.* **1.** to become master of; control, conquer, etc. **2.** to become an expert in (an art, science, etc.)

master-at-arms (-ət ärmz′) *n.,* *pl.* **mas′ters-at-arms′** a naval petty officer who acts as a police officer on board a warship or merchant ship

master builder **1.** a person skilled in building; esp., formerly, an architect **2.** a building contractor

mas·ter·ful (-fəl) *adj.* **1.** fond of acting the part of a master; imperious **2.** having or showing the ability of a master; expert; skilful —**mas′ter·ful·ly** *adv.* —**mas′ter·ful·ness** *n.*

Master in Chancery the chief clerk of the Chancery Division of the Law Courts

master key a key that will open every one of a set of locks

mas·ter·ly (-lē) *adj.* showing the ability or skill of a master; expert —*adv.* in a masterly manner —**mas′ter·li·ness** *n.*

master mason **1.** a highly skilled mason **2.** [often M-M-] a Freemason of the third degree

master mechanic a skilled mechanic, esp. one serving as foreman

mas·ter·mind (-mīnd′) *n.* **1.** a very intelligent person, esp. one with the ability to plan or direct a group project **2.** [M-] a trademark for a game played on a special board, requiring logical thinking —*vt.* to be the mastermind of (a project)

Master of Arts (or **Science,** etc.) **1.** a degree given by a college or university to a person who has usually completed

a prescribed course of post graduate study in the humanities (or in science, etc.) **2.** a person who has this degree
master of ceremonies 1. a person who supervises a ceremony **2.** a person who presides over an entertainment, introducing the participants, filling in the intervals with jokes, etc.
Master of the Rolls the Court of Appeal judge who acts as keeper of the records and as head of the Public Record Office
mas·ter·piece (-pēs') *n.* **1.** a thing made or done with masterly skill **2.** the greatest work made or done by a person or group: also **mas'ter·work**'
mas·ter·ship (mäs'tər ship') *n.* **1.** the state of being a master; rule; control **2.** the position, duties, or term of office of a master **3.** masterly ability
mas·ter·stroke (-strōk') *n.* a masterly action, move, or achievement
master touch the brilliant handling of anything by an expert
mas·ter·y (mäs'tər ē, -trē) *n., pl.* **-ter·ies 1.** mastership **2.** ascendancy or victory; the upper hand **3.** expert skill or knowledge [*his mastery of chess*]
mast·head (mäst'hed') *n.* **1.** the top part of a ship's mast **2.** that part of a newspaper or magazine stating its address, publishers, editors, etc. —*vt.* to display at the masthead
mas·tic (mas'tik) *n.* [OFr. < LL. < L. < Gr. *mastichē*] **1.** a yellowish resin obtained from a Mediterranean evergreen tree, used as an astringent and in making varnish, adhesives, etc. **2.** the tree: in full, **mastic tree**
mas·ti·cate (mas'tə kāt') *vt.* **-cat'ed, -cat'ing** [< LL. pp. of *masticare* < Gr. *mastichan*, to gnash < *mastax*, a mouth] **1.** to chew up (food, etc.) **2.** to grind, cut, or knead (rubber, etc.) to a pulp —**mas'ti·ca'tion** *n.* —**mas'ti·ca'tor** *n.*
mas·ti·ca·to·ry (mas'tə kā'tər ē) *adj.* of or for mastication; specif., adapted for chewing —*n., pl.* **-ries** any substance chewed but not swallowed, to increase saliva flow
mas·tiff (mas'tif) *n.* [< OFr. *mastin*, ult. < L. *mansuetus*, tame] a large, powerful, smooth-coated dog with hanging lips and drooping ears
mas·ti·tis (mas tīt'is) *n.* [MAST(O)- + -ITIS] inflammation of the breast or udder
mas·to- [< Gr. *mastos*, the breast] *a combining form meaning* of or like a breast: also **mast-**
mas·to·don (mas'tə don') *n.* [ModL. < Fr. < Gr. *mastos*, a breast + *odous*, a tooth: from the nipplelike processes on its molars] a large, extinct animal resembling the elephant but larger
mas·toid (mas'toid) *adj.* [< Gr. < *mastos*, a breast + *eidos*, form] **1.** shaped like a breast or nipple **2.** designating, of, or near a projection of the temporal bone behind the ear —*n.* **1.** the mastoid projection **2.** [Colloq.] *same as* MASTOIDITIS
mas·toid·i·tis (mas'toi dīt'is) *n.* inflammation of the mastoid
mas·tur·bate (mas'tər bāt') *vi., vt.* **-bat'ed, -bat'ing** [< L. pp. of *masturbari*, ult. < *manus*, hand + *stuprum*, defilement] to manipulate one's own genitals, or the genitals of (another), for sexual gratification —**mas'tur·ba'tion** *n.* —**mas'tur·ba'tor** *n.* —**mas'tur·ba'to·ry** (-bā'tər ē) *adj.*
mat¹ (mat) *n.* [< OE. *meatt* < LL. *matta* < ?] **1.** a flat, coarse fabric of woven or plaited hemp, straw, etc. **2.** a piece of this or of corrugated rubber, etc., used as a doormat, etc. **3.** a flat piece of cloth, woven straw, etc. put under a vase, dish, etc. **4.** a thickly padded floor covering, as in a gymnasium for wrestling, etc. **5.** anything growing or interwoven in a thick tangle [*a mat of hair*] —*vt.* **mat'-ted, mat'ting 1.** to cover as with a mat **2.** to form into a thick tangle —*vi.* to become felted or thickly tangled —**on the mat** [Colloq.] in trouble because of some misdemeanour
mat² (mat) *adj.* [Fr. < OFr. *mat*, defeated, prob. < L. *mattus*, drunk < *madere*, to be drunk] *same as* MATTE —*n.* **1.** *same as* MATTE **2.** a border, as of cardboard or cloth, put around a picture, usually between the picture and the frame —*vt.* **mat'ted, mat'ting 1.** to produce a dull surface or finish on **2.** to frame (a picture) with a mat
mat³ (mat) *n.* [Colloq.] a matrix; printing mould
mat·a·dor (mat'ə dôr') *n.* [Sp. < *matar*, to kill < *mate*, checkmate] the bullfighter who kills the bull with a sword after performing a series of actions with a cape to anger and tire the animal
match¹ (mach) *n.* [< OFr. *mesche*, prob. < L. *myxa*, lamp wick < Gr.] **1.** orig., a wick or cord prepared to burn at a uniform rate, used for firing guns or explosives **2.** a slender piece of wood, cardboard, etc. tipped with a composition that catches fire by friction, sometimes only on a specially prepared surface
match² (mach) *n.* [OE. *(ge)mæcca*, a mate] **1.** any person or thing equal or similar to another in some way; specif., *a)* a person, group, or thing able to cope with another as an equal *b)* a counterpart or facsimile **2.** two or more persons or things that go together in appearance, size, etc. [*meet*

one's *match*] **3.** a contest or game; competition **4.** a marriage or mating **5.** a person regarded as a suitable mate —*vt.* **1.** to join in marriage; mate **2.** to compete with successfully **3.** to put in opposition (*with*); pit (*against*) **4.** to be equal, similar, or suitable to **5.** to make, show, or get a competitor, counterpart, or equivalent to [*match this cloth*] **6.** to suit or fit (one thing) to another **7.** to fit (things) together —*vi.* to be equal, similar, suitable, etc. in some way —**match'a·ble** *adj.* —**match'er** *n.*
match·box (-boks') *n.* a small box for holding matches
match·less (mach'lis) *adj.* having no equal; peerless —**match'less·ly** *adv.* —**match'less·ness** *n.*
match·lock (-lok') *n.* **1.** an old type of gunlock in which the charge of powder was ignited by a slow-burning match (wick or cord) **2.** a musket with such a gunlock
match·mak·ing¹ (-mā'kin) *n.* the work or business of making matches (for burning) —**match'mak'er** *n.*
match·mak·ing² (-mā'kin) *n.* **1.** the arranging of marriages for others **2.** the arranging of wrestling or boxing matches, etc. —**match'mak'er** *n.*
match play *Golf* a form of play in which the score is calculated by counting holes won rather than strokes taken: cf. MEDAL PLAY
match·stick (mach'stik) *n.* *same as* MATCH¹ (sense 2)
match·wood (-wood') *n.* **1.** wood for making matches **2.** very small pieces: splinters
mate¹ (māt) *n.* [MDu. < *gemate* < Gmc.] **1.** a companion or fellow worker, esp. as a familiar term of address **2.** one of a matched pair **3.** *a)* a husband or wife *b)* the male or female of paired animals **4.** *Naut. a)* an officer of a merchant ship, ranking below the captain *b)* an assistant [*a carpenter's mate*] —*vt., vi.* **mat'ed, mat'ing 1.** to join as a pair **2.** to couple in marriage or sexual union
mate² (māt) *n., interj., vt.* **mat'ed, mat'ing** *same as* CHECKMATE
ma·té (mä'tā, mat'ā) *n.* [AmSp. < Quechua *mati*, calabash (used to steep the brew)] **1.** a beverage made from the dried leaves of a S American tree **2.** this tree or its leaves Also sp. **mate**
mat·e·lot (mat'lō) *n.* [< Fr. *matelot*, sailor] [Colloq.] a sailor: also **matlow, matlo**
ma·ter (māt'ər) *n.* [L.] [Colloq.] mother: often preceded by *the*
ma·te·ri·al (mə tir'ē əl) *adj.* [< LL. < L. *materia*, matter] **1.** of matter; relating to or consisting of what occupies space; physical [*a material object*] **2.** *a)* of the body or bodily needs, etc. [*material pleasures*] *b)* of or fond of comfort, wealth, etc.; worldly [*material success*] **3.** important, essential, etc. (*to the matter under discussion*) —*n.* **1.** what a thing is, or may be, made of; elements or parts **2.** ideas, notes, etc. that may be developed; data **3.** cloth or other fabric **4.** [*pl.*] tools, articles, etc. for a specified use [*writing* materials] —**ma·te'ri·al'i·ty** (-al'ə tē) *n.*
ma·te·ri·al·ism (-iz'm) *n.* **1.** the philosophical doctrine that everything in the world, including thought, will, and feeling, can be explained only in terms of matter **2.** the tendency to be more concerned with material than with spiritual values —**ma·te'ri·al·ist** *adj., n.* —**ma·te'ri·al·is'tic** *adj.* —**ma·te'-ri·al·is'ti·cal·ly** *adv.*
ma·te·ri·al·ize (mə tir'ē ə līz') *vt.* **-ized', -iz'ing 1.** to represent in material form **2.** to make (a spirit, etc.) appear in bodily form —*vi.* **1.** to become fact; be realized [*a plan that never materialized*] **2.** to take on, or appear in, bodily form: said of spirits, etc. **3.** to appear suddenly or unexpectedly —**ma·te'ri·al·i·za'tion** *n.*
ma·te·ri·al·ly (-lē) *adv.* **1.** with regard to the matter, content, etc. and not the form **2.** physically **3.** to a great extent; considerably
ma·te·ri·a med·i·ca (mə tir'ē ə med'i kə) [ML. < L. *materia*, matter + fem. of *medicus*, medical] **1.** the drugs and other remedial substances used in medicine **2.** the branch of medical science that deals with such substances, their uses, etc.
ma·te·ri·el, ma·té·ri·el (mə tir'ē el') *n.* [Fr.: see MATERIAL] the necessary materials and tools; specif., weapons, supplies, etc. of armed forces
ma·ter·nal (mə tur'n'l) *adj.* [< MFr. < L. < *mater*, a mother] **1.** of or like a mother; motherly **2.** derived or inherited from a mother **3.** related through the mother's side of the family [*maternal* grandparents] —**ma·ter'nal·ly** *adv.*
ma·ter·ni·ty (mə tur'nə tē) *n.* **1.** the state of being a mother; motherhood **2.** the qualities of a mother; motherliness —*adj.* **1.** for pregnant women [*a maternity* dress] **2.** for the care of women giving birth and of newborn babies [*a maternity* ward]
maternity home a hospital where women stay during childbirth: also **maternity hospital**
mate·y (māt'ē) *adj.* [MATE¹ + -Y²] [Colloq.] friendly or intimate —*n.* [Colloq.] a friend —**mate'y·ness, mat'-i·ness** *n.*
math. 1. mathematical **2.** mathematician

math·e·mat·i·cal (math'ə mat'i k'l) *adj.* [< ML. < L. < Gr. < *mathēma*, what is learned < *manthanein*, to learn] 1. of, like, or concerned with mathematics 2. rigorously precise, accurate, etc. —**math·e·mat'i·cal·ly** *adv.*

math·e·ma·ti·cian (math'ə mə tish'ən, math'mə-) *n.* an expert or specialist in mathematics

math·e·mat·ics (math'ə mat'iks) *n.pl.* [with *sing. v.*] [see MATHEMATICAL & -ICS] the group of sciences (arithmetic, geometry, algebra, calculus, etc.) dealing with quantities, magnitudes, and forms, and their relationships, attributes, etc., by the use of numbers and symbols

maths (maths) *n. clipped form of* MATHEMATICS

mat·il·da (mə til'də) *n.* [Aust.] a bushman's swag, or bundle [*walking* or *waltzing matilda*]

mat·in (mat'n) *n.* [OFr. < L. *matutinus*, of the morning < *Matuta*, goddess of dawn] 1. [*pl.*] [*often* M-] a) R.C.Ch. the first of the seven canonical hours b) Anglican Ch. the service of public morning prayer 2. [Poet.] a morning song —*adj.* 1. of matins 2. of morning —**mat'in·al** *adj.*

mat·i·nee, mat·i·née (mat'ə nā') *n.* [< Fr.: see prec.] a daytime reception, esp.; esp., a performance, as of a play, in the afternoon

matinée coat a baby's short coat, usually knitted of wool

ma·tri- [< L. *mater* (gen. *matris*), a mother] *a combining form meaning* mother [*matriarch*]

ma·tri·arch (mā'trē ärk') *n.* [prec. + -ARCH] a mother who rules her family or tribe; specif., a woman who is head of a matriarchy —**ma'tri·ar'chal** (-är'k'l) *adj.*

ma·tri·ar·chy (-trē är'kē) *n., pl.* -**chies** 1. a form of social organization in which the mother is head of the family or tribe, descent being traced through the female line 2. rule or domination by women —**ma'tri·ar'chic** *adj.*

matric (mə trik') *a clipped form of* MATRICULATION

mat·ri·cide (mat'rə sid', mā'trə-) *n.* [< L. < *mater*, mother + *caedere*, to kill] 1. the act of killing one's mother 2. a person who kills his mother —**mat'ri·ci'dal** *adj.*

ma·tric·u·late (mə trik'yoo lāt'; *also, for n.*, -lit) *vt., vi.* -**lat'ed**, -**lat'ing** [< ML. pp. of *matriculare*, to register < LL. dim. of *matrix*, MATRIX] to enrol, esp. as a student in a college or university —*n.* a person so enrolled —**ma·tric'u·lant** *n.* —**ma·tric'u·la'tion** *n.*

mat·ri·mo·ny (mat'rə mō'nē, -mə nē) *n., pl.* -**nies** [< OFr. < L. *matrimonium* < *mater*, a mother] 1. the act or rite of marriage 2. the state of being husband and wife 3. married life —**mat'ri·mo'ni·al** *adj.* —**mat'ri·mo'ni·al·ly** *adv.*

ma·trix (mā'triks) *n., pl.* -**tri·ces'** (mā'trə sēz', mat'rə-), -**trix·es** [LL., womb, ult. < L. *mater* (gen. *matris*), mother] 1. orig., the womb; uterus 2. that within which something originates, takes form, etc.; specif., a die or mould for casting or shaping 3. *Printing* a) a metal mould for casting the face of type b) an impression, as of papier-mâché, from which a plate can be made

ma·tron (mā'trən) *n.* [< OFr. < L. *matrona* < *mater*, a mother] 1. a wife or widow, esp. one with a mature manner 2. a) a woman manager of the domestic arrangements of a school or other institution b) a woman in charge of the nursing staff of a hospital 3. [U.S.] a woman guard, as in a jail —**ma'tron·al** *adj.* —**ma'tron·li·ness** *n.* —**ma'tron·ly** *adj.*

matron of honour a married woman acting as principal attendant to the bride at a wedding

Matt. Matthew

matte (mat) *n.* [var. of MAT²] a dull surface or finish, often roughened —*adj.* not shiny or glossy; dull Also sp. **matt** —**mat'ted** *adj.*

mat·ted (mat'id) *adj.* 1. closely tangled together in a dense mass 2. covered with matting or mats

mat·ter (mat'ər) *n.* [< OFr. < L. *materia*, material] 1. what a thing is made of; constituent material 2. whatever occupies space and is perceptible to the senses in some way: in modern physics, matter and energy are regarded as mutually convertible equivalents 3. any specified sort of substance [*colouring matter*] 4. material or content of thought or expression, as distinguished from style or form 5. an amount or quantity [*a matter of a few days*] 6. a) a thing or affair [*business matters*] b) cause or occasion [*no laughing matter*] 7. importance; significance [*it's of no matter*] 8. trouble; difficulty (with *the*) [*what's the matter?*] 9. pus 10. *Printing* a) copy b) type set up —*vi.* 1. to be of importance; have significance 2. to form and discharge pus; suppurate —**as a matter of fact** in fact; really —**for that matter** 1. as far as that is concerned: 2. indeed on consideration —**no matter** 1. it is of no importance 2. regardless of [*no matter what you say*]

mat·ter-of-course (mat'ər əv kôrs') *adj.* 1. coming naturally in the course of events; routine 2. reacting to events in a calm and natural way

matter of course a thing to be expected as a natural or logical occurrence

mat·ter-of-fact (-əv fakt', -ə fakt') *adj.* sticking strictly to facts; literal, unimaginative, etc. —**mat'ter-of-fact'ly** *adv.* —**mat'ter-of-fact'ness** *n.*

mat·ting¹ (mat'iŋ) *n.* 1. a fabric of fibre, as straw or hemp, for mats, floor covering, wrapping, etc. 2. mats collectively 3. the making of mats

mat·ting² (mat'iŋ) *n.* [see MATTE] 1. the production of a dull surface or finish 2. such a surface or finish 3. a mat, or border

mat·tins (mat'inz) *n.pl. var. of* MATINS (see MATIN, *n.*)

mat·tock (mat'ək) *n.* [OE. *mattuc*] a tool like a pickaxe but with at least one flat blade, for loosening the soil, digging up roots, etc.

mat·tress (mat'ris) *n.* [< OFr. < It. *materasso* < Ar. *matrah*, cushion] 1. a casing of strong cloth filled with cotton, hair, foam rubber, etc., and usually coiled springs, and used on or as a bed 2. an inflatable pad used in the same way: in full, **air mattress**

MATTOCK

mat·u·rate (mat'yoo rāt') *vi.* -**rat'ed**, -**rat'ing** [< L. pp. of *maturare*, to MATURE] 1. to suppurate; discharge pus 2. to ripen; mature —**ma·tur·a·tive** (mə tyoor'ə tiv, mach'oo rāt'iv, mat'yoo-) *adj.* —**mat'u·ra'tion** *n.*

ma·ture (mə tyoor', -choor') *adj.* [< L. *maturus*, ripe] 1. a) full-grown, as plants or animals b) ripe, as fruits c) fully developed, as a person 2. fully developed, perfected, etc. [*a mature scheme*] 3. of a state of full development [*of mature age*] 4. due: said of a note, bond, etc. —*vt.* -**tured'**, -**tur'ing** 1. to bring to full growth, or to ripeness 2. to develop fully —*vi.* 1. to become fully grown or ripe 2. to become due: said of a note, etc. —**ma·ture'ly** *adv.* —**ma·ture'ness** *n.*

ma·tu·ri·ty (-ə tē) *n.* 1. a) a being full-grown, ripe, or fully developed b) a being perfect, complete, or ready 2. a) a becoming due b) the time at which a note, etc. becomes due

ma·tu·ti·nal (mə tyoot'ə n'l, ma tyoo tī'n'l) *adj.* [< L. < *matutinus*: see MATIN] of or in the morning; early —**ma·tu'ti·nal·ly** *adv.*

mat·zo (mat'sə, -sô) *n., pl.* **mat'zot**, **mat'zoth** (-sōt), **mat'zos** [< Heb. *matstsäh*, unleavened] flat, thin unleavened bread eaten by Jews during the Passover, or a piece of this; also **mat'sah**

maud·lin (môd'lin) *adj.* [< ME. *Maudeleyne*, (Mary) Magdalene (often represented as weeping)] 1. foolishly and tearfully or weakly sentimental 2. tearfully sentimental as when drunk

mau·gre, mau·ger (mô'gər) *prep.* [< OFr. *maugré*, lit., with displeasure] [Archaic] in spite of

maul (môl) *n.* [< OFr. < L. *malleus*, a hammer] 1. a very heavy hammer or mallet for driving stakes, etc. 2. *Rugby* a scrimmage —*vt.* 1. to bruise or lacerate 2. to handle roughly or clumsily —**maul'er** *n.*

maun·der (môn'dər) *vi.* [prob. freq. of obs. *maund*, to beg] 1. to move or act in a vague, aimless way 2. to talk in an incoherent, rambling way —**maun'der·er** *n.*

Maundy money specially minted coins given by the British sovereign to poor people at a Maundy Thursday ceremony

Maun·dy Thursday (môn'dē) [OFr. *mandé* < LL. *mandatum*, commandment of God < L.: from use in a prayer on that day] the Thursday before Easter

mau·so·le·um (mô'sə lē'əm, -zə-) *n., pl.* -**le'ums**, -**le'a** (-lē'ə) [after the tomb of Mausolus, king of an ancient land in Asia Minor] a large, imposing tomb —**mau'so·le'an** (-ən) *adj.*

mauve (mōv, môv) *n.* [Fr., mallow < L. *malva*, mallow] any of several shades of delicate purple —*adj.* of such a colour

mav·er·ick (mav'ər ik, mav'rik) *n.* [after S. *Maverick*, 19th-c. Texas rancher who did not brand his cattle] [U.S.] 1. an unbranded animal, esp. a stray calf, formerly the property of the first one who branded it 2. [Colloq.] a person who acts independently of his political party or group

ma·vis (mā'vis) *n.* [< OFr.] *same as* SONG THRUSH

maw (mô) *n.* [OE. *maga*] 1. orig., the stomach 2. the throat, gullet, jaws, etc. of a voracious animal 3. anything thought of as devouring without end

mawk·ish (mô'kish) *adj.* [lit., maggoty < ON. *mathkr*, maggot] 1. insipid or nauseating 2. sentimental in a weak, insipid way, so as to be sickening —**mawk'ish·ly** *adv.* —**mawk'ish·ness** *n.*

max. maximum

max·i (mak'sē) *n.* [< MAXI(MUM)] [Colloq.] a maxicoat or maxiskirt, etc.

max·i- [< MAXI(MUM)] *a combining form meaning* maximum, very large, very long [*maxicoat*]

max·il·la (mak sil'ə) *n., pl.* -**lae** (-ē) [L.] 1. in vertebrates the upper jaw, or a major bone or cartilage of it 2. in insects, crabs, etc., one of the first or second pair of jaws or head appendages situated just behind the mandibles

max·il·lar·y (mak sil'ə rē) *adj.* designating, of, or near the jaw or jawbone —*n., pl.* -**lar·ies** *same as* MAXILLA

max·im (mak'sim) *n.* [< MFr. < ML. < LL. *maxima*

(*propositio*), the greatest (premise): see MAXIMUM] a concisely expressed rule of conduct; precept

max·i·ma (mak′sə mə) *n.* *alt. pl. of* MAXIMUM

max·i·mal (-m′l) *adj.* highest or greatest possible; of or constituting a maximum —**max′i·mal·ly** *adv.*

max·i·mize (mak′sə mīz′) *vt.* -**mized**′, -**miz′ing** to increase to the maximum —**max′i·mi·za′tion** *n.* —**max′i·miz′er** *n.*

max·i·mum (-məm) *n., pl.* -**mums, -ma** (-mə) [L., neut. of *maximus*, superl. of *magnus*, great] 1. the greatest quantity, number, etc. possible or permissible 2. the highest degree or point reached or recorded —*adj.* 1. greatest possible, permissible, or reached 2. of marking or setting a maximum

max·well (maks′wel) *n.* [after James Clark *Maxwell* (1831-79), Brit. physicist] a unit of magnetic flux, equal to the flux through one square centimetre at a right angle to a magnetic field with an intensity of one gauss: equivalent to 10^{-8} webers

May (mā) *n.* [OFr. < L. < *Maia*, goddess of increase] 1. the fifth month of the year, having 31 days 2. the springtime of life; youth

may (mā) *v.aux.* *pt.* **might** [OE. *mæg*] an auxiliary preceding an infinitive (without *to*) and expressing: 1. orig., ability or power: now generally replaced by *can* [*may* I help you?] 2. possibility or likelihood [it *may* rain] 3. permission [*you may go*] 4. contingency, as in clauses of purpose, result, concession, or condition [they died that we *may* be free] 5. wish, hope, or prayer [*may* he rest in peace]

Ma·ya (mä′yə) *n.* 1. *pl.* **Ma′yas, Ma′ya** a member of a tribe of Indians in SE Mexico and Central America, who had a highly developed civilization 2. their language —*adj.* of the Mayas —**Ma′yan** *adj., n.*

May apple 1. a woodland plant with shield-shaped leaves and a single large, white flower, found in the E U.S. 2. its edible, yellow, oval fruit

may·be (mā′bē) *adv.* [ME. (for *it may be*)] perhaps

May bug *same as* COCKCHAFER

May·day (mā′dā′) *n.* [< Fr. (*venez*) *m'aider*, (come) help me] the international radiotelephone signal for help, used by ships and aircraft in distress

May Day May 1: as a traditional spring festival, often celebrated by dancing, crowning a May queen, etc.; as an international labour holiday, observed in many countries by parades, demonstrations, etc.

may·est (mā′ist) *archaic 2nd pers. sing., pres. indic., of* MAY: *used with* thou

may·flow·er (-flou′ər) *n.* a plant that flowers in early spring; esp., the cowslip, marsh marigold, etc. —[M-] the ship on which the Pilgrims sailed to America (1620)

may·fly (-flī′) *n., pl.* -**flies**′ a slender insect with gauzy wings held vertically when at rest: the adult lives only a few hours or a few days

may·hap (mā′hap′, mā′hap′) *adv.* [< *it may hap(pen)*] [Archaic] perhaps; maybe: also **may′hap′pen**

may·hem (mā′hem, mā′əm) *n.* [see MAIM] 1. *Law* the offence of maiming a person; specif., *a*) orig., injury inflicted on another so as to cause loss of a part or function necessary for self-defence *b*) any intentional mutilation of another's body 2. loosely, any deliberate destruction or violence

MAYFLY
(body to 2.5 cm)

May·ing (mā′iŋ) *n.* [*also* m-] the celebration of May Day, as by gathering flowers, dancing, etc.

may·n't (mā′nt, mānt) may not

may·on·naise (mā′ə nāz′) *n.* [Fr., prob. ult. < *Mahón*, Minorca] a creamy salad dressing made by beating together egg yolks, oil, lemon juice or vinegar, and seasoning

may·or (mā′ər, mer) *n.* [< OFr. *maire* < L. *major*, greater] the chief administrative official of a city, town, or other municipality —**may′or·al** *adj.* — **may′or·ess** *n. fem.*

may·or·al·ty (-əl tē) *n., pl.* -**ties** the office or term of office of a mayor

May·pole (mā′pōl′) *n.* a high pole decorated with ribbons, around which merrymakers dance on May Day

May queen a girl chosen to be queen of the merrymakers on May Day

mayst (māst) *archaic 2nd pers. sing., pres. indic., of* MAY: *used with* thou

May·time (mā′tīm′) *n.* the month of May: also **May′tide′**(-tīd′)

may tree the hawthorn

maze (māz) *n.* [< OE. *amasian*, to amaze & pp. *amasod*, puzzled] 1. a confusing, intricate network of winding pathways; labyrinth 2. a state of confusion or bewilderment —**ma′zy** *adj.* -**zi·er, -zi·est** —**ma′zi·ly** *adv.* —**ma′zi·ness** *n.*

ma·zur·ka, ma·zour·ka (mə zur′kə, -zoor′-) *n.* [Pol.

mazurka, woman from Mazovia, region of C Poland] 1. a lively Polish dance like the polka 2. music for this, generally in 3/4 or 3/8 time

M.B. [L. *Medicinae Baccalaureus*] Bachelor of Medicine

M.B.A. Master of Business Administration

M.B.E. Member of the Order of the British Empire

M.C. 1. Master of Ceremonies 2. Military Cross

M.C.C. Marylebone Cricket Club

Mc·Car·thy·ism (mə kär′thē iz′m) *n.* [after J. *McCarthy*, U.S. senator (1946-57)] the use of indiscriminate, often unfounded, accusations, inquisitorial investigative methods, sensationalism, etc., ostensibly in the suppression of communism

Mc·Coy (mə koi′), **the (real)** [Slang] the real person or thing, not a substitute

M.Ch(ir). [L. *Magister Chirurgiae*] Master of Surgery

Md *Chem.* mendelevium

M.D. [L. *Medicinae Doctor*] Doctor of Medicine

Mdm. *pl.* **Mdms.** Madam

MDu. Middle Dutch

me (mē) *pron.* [OE.] *objective case of* I: also used colloquially as a predicate complement with a linking verb (Ex.: that's *me*)

ME. Middle English

M.E. 1. Mechanical Engineer 2. Methodist Episcopal 3. Mining Engineer

‡me·a cul·pa (mē′ə kul′pə, mä′ä kool′pä) [L.] (by) my fault; I am to blame

mead[1] (mēd) *n.* [OE. *meodu*] an alcoholic drink made of fermented honey and water, often with spices, fruit, malt, etc. added

mead[2] (mēd) *n.* [OE. *mæd*] [Poet.] a meadow

mead·ow (med′ō) *n.* [< OE. *mædwe*, oblique case of *mæd*] 1. a piece of grassland, esp. one whose grass is grown for use as hay 2. low, level grassland near a stream, etc. —**mead′ow·y** *adj.*

mead·ow·lark (-lärk′) *n., pl.* -**larks**′, -**lark**′: see PLURAL, II, D. 1 either of two N. American songbirds having brown-and-black upper parts and a yellow breast

mead·ow·sweet (-swēt′) a very fragrant plant with creamy, feathery flowers

mea·gre (mē′gər) *adj.* [< OFr. < L. *macer*, lean] 1. thin; lean; emaciated 2. of poor quality or small amount; inadequate Also, U.S., **mea′ger** —**mea′gre·ly** *adv.* —**mea′-gre·ness** *n.*

meal[1] (mēl) *n.* [OE. *mæl*] 1. any of the times for eating; breakfast, lunch, dinner, etc. 2. the food served or eaten at such a time

meal[2] (mēl) *n.* [OE. *melu*] 1. any edible grain, coarsely ground and unbolted [*oatmeal*] 2. any substance similarly ground or powdered

meal·ie (mēl′ē) *n.* [Afrik. *milje* < Port. *milho*, millet] in South Africa, 1. [*pl.*] *same as* MAIZE 2. an ear of maize

meals-on-wheels (mēlz′on wēlz′, -hwēlz′) *n.* a service taking hot meals to the infirm and elderly, run as a branch of the social services

meal ticket 1. [U.S.] a luncheon voucher 2. a person, job, skill, etc. depended on as one's means of support

meal·time (mēl′tīm′) *n.* the usual time for serving or eating a meal

meal·y (mēl′ē) *adj.* **meal′i·er, meal′i·est** 1. like meal; powdery, dry, soft, etc. 2. of or containing meal 3. covered with meal 4. floury in colour; pale 5. mealy-mouthed —**meal′i·ness** *n.*

meal·y-mouthed (-mouthd′, -moutht′) *adj.* evasive, euphemistic, insincere, etc. in what one says

mean[1] (mēn) *vt.* **meant** (ment), **mean′ing** [OE. *mænan*] 1. to have in mind; intend; purpose [he *means* to go] 2. *a*) to intend for a certain person or purpose [a gift *meant* for you] *b*) to destine [he was *meant* to be a doctor] 3. to intend to express or imply [to say what one *means*] 4. to signify; denote [the German word "ja" *means* "yes"] —*vi.* 1. to have a purpose in mind: chiefly in **mean well**, to have good intentions 2. to have a (specified) degree of importance, effect, etc. [she *means* little to him] —**mean well by** to have good intentions toward

mean[2] (mēn) *adj.* [OE. (ge)mæne] 1. low in quality, value, or importance; poor [paid no mean sum] 2. poor in appearance; shabby [a *mean* dwelling] 3. ignoble; base; petty 4. stingy; miserly 5. [U.S.] bad-tempered; unmanageable: said of a horse, etc. 6. contemptibly bad-tempered, selfish, etc. 7. humiliated 8. [Slang] hard to cope with; difficult —**mean′ly** *adv.* —**mean′ness** *n.*

mean[3] (mēn) *adj.* [< OFr. < L. *medianus* < *medius*, middle] 1. halfway between extremes; intermediate as to quantity, quality, etc. 2. average; middling —*n.* 1. what is between extremes; intermediate state, quality, course, etc. 2. moderation 3. *Math. a*) a number between the smallest and largest values of a set of quantities, obtained by some prescribed method: unless otherwise qualified, *same as* ARITHMETIC MEAN *b*) the second or third term of a four-term proportion See also MEANS

me·an·der (mē an′dər) *n.* [< L. < Gr. *maiandros* < the name of a winding river in Asia Minor] 1. [*pl.*] windings or convolutions, as of a stream 2. an aimless wandering —*vi.* 1. to take a winding course: said of a stream 2. to wander aimlessly or idly —**mean′drous** (-drəs) *adj.*

mean·ie, mean·y (mē′nē) *n., pl.* **mean′ies** [Colloq.] a person who is mean, selfish, cruel, etc.

mean·ing (mē′niŋ) *n.* 1. what is meant; what is intended to be, or in fact is, signified, indicated, etc.; import, sense, or significance [the *meaning* of a word] 2. [Archaic] intention —*adj.* 1. that has meaning; significant 2. intending

mean·ing·ful (-fəl) *adj.* full of meaning; having significance or purpose —**mean′ing·ful·ly** *adv.* —**mean′ing·ful·ness** *n.*

mean·ing·less (-lis) *adj.* having no meaning; without significance or purpose —**mean′ing·less·ly** *adv.* —**mean′ing·less·ness** *n.*

means (mēnz) *n.pl.* [< MEAN³, *n.*] 1. [*with sing. or pl. v.*] that by which something is done or obtained; agency [a fast *means* of travel] 2. resources or wealth [a person of *means*] —**by all means** 1. without fail 2. certainly —**by any means** in any way possible; somehow —**by means of** by using; with the aid of —**by no (manner of) means** not at all; certainly not —**means to an end** a method of getting what one wants

mean (solar) time time having exactly equal divisions

means test a financial investigation of a person's eligibility for financial or social help

meant (ment) *pt. & pp. of* MEAN¹

mean·time (mēn′tīm′) *adv.* 1. in or during the intervening time 2. at the same time —*n.* the intervening time Also, and for adv. now usually, **mean′while′** (-wīl′, -hwīl′)

mea·sles (mē′z′lz) *n.pl.* [*with sing. v.*] [ME. *maseles,* ? infl. by ME. *mesel,* leper < OFr. < L. *misellus,* wretch] 1. an acute, infectious, communicable virus disease, characterized by small red spots on the skin, high fever, nasal discharge, etc., and occurring most frequently in childhood 2. any of various similar but milder diseases; esp., rubella (called *German measles*)

mea·sly (mēz′lē) *adj.* **-sli·er, -sli·est** 1. infected with measles 2. [Colloq.] contemptibly slight, worthless, or skimpy

meas·ur·a·ble (mezh′ər ə b′l) *adj.* that can be measured —**meas′ur·a·bil′i·ty, meas′ur·a·ble·ness** *n.* —**meas′ur·a·bly** *adv.*

meas·ure (mezh′ər) *n.* [< OFr. *mesure* < L. *mensura* < pp. of *metiri,* to measure] 1. the extent, dimensions, capacity, etc. of anything, esp. as determined by a standard 2. a determining of extent, dimensions, etc.; measurement 3. a) unit of measurement, as a centimetre, metre, or litre b) any standard of valuation; criterion 4. a system of measurement [dry *measure*] 5. an instrument or container for measuring [a litre *measure*] 6. a definite quantity measured out 7. an extent or degree not to be exceeded [remain within *measure*] 8. proportion, quantity, or degree [in large *measure*] 9. course of action; step [reform *measures*] 10. a statute; law 11. a) rhythm in verse; metre b) a metrical unit; foot of verse 12. a dance or dance movement 13. [*pl.*] *Geol.* strata: now chiefly in —**coal measures** 14. *Music* a) a bar b) musical time —*vt.* **-ured, -ur·ing** 1. to find out or estimate the extent, dimensions, etc. of, esp. by a standard 2. to set apart or mark off by measuring (often with *off* or *out*) 3. to make a judgment of by comparing [to *measure* one's foe] 4. to bring into comparison or rivalry (*against*) 5. to be a device for measuring [a clock *measures* time] —*vi.* 1. to get or take measurements 2. to be of specified measurements 3. to allow of measurement —**a measure of** some degree of —**beyond (or above) measure** exceedingly; extremely —**for good measure** as a bonus or something extra —**in a measure** to some extent; somewhat —**made to measure** custom-made: said of clothes —**measure up** to prove to be qualified —**measure up to** to meet (expectations, a standard, etc.) —**take measures** to do things to accomplish a purpose —**take someone's measure** to estimate someone's ability, character, etc. —**meas′ur·er** *n.*

meas·ured (-ərd) *adj.* 1. determined by a standard 2. regular or uniform 3. a) rhythmical b) metrical 4. calculated, deliberate, etc., as speech —**meas′ured·ly** *adv.*

meas·ure·less (mezh′ər lis) *adj.* too large to be measurable; vast; immense —**meas′ure·less·ly** *adv.* —**meas′ure·less·ness** *n.*

meas·ure·ment (-mənt) *n.* 1. a measuring or being measured 2. extent or quantity determined by measuring 3. a system of measuring

measuring jug a graduated jug used to measure ingredients for cookery

measuring worm the caterpillar larva of any geometrid moth

meat (mēt) *n.* [OE. *mete*] 1. food: now dialectal except in **meat and drink** 2. the flesh of animals used as food; esp., the flesh of mammals and, sometimes, of fowl 3. the substance or essence [the *meat* of a story] 4. [Archaic] a meal —**meat′less** *adj.*

meat·ball (-bôl′) *n.* a small ball of minced meat, seasoned and cooked, often with sauce, etc.

meat safe a cupboard of perforated zinc or gauze-covered wooden frame for storing meat, esp. in hot weather

me·a·tus (mē āt′əs) *n., pl.* **-tus·es, -tus** [LL. < L., a passage, pp. of *meare,* to pass] a natural passage or duct in the body, or its opening

meat·y (mēt′ē) *adj.* **meat′i·er, meat′i·est** 1. of, like, or having the flavour of, meat 2. full of meat 3. full of substance; thought-provoking; pithy —**meat′i·ness** *n.*

Mec·ca (mek′ə) *n.* [after the holy city of Islam in Saudi Arabia] [often **m-**] any place that many people feel drawn to —**Mec′can** *adj., n.*

mec·ca·no (mi kä′nō) *a trademark for* small-scale fitments used to make engineering models

mech. 1. mechanical 2. mechanics

me·chan·ic (mə kan′ik) *adj.* [< L. < Gr. < *mēchanē,* a machine] *rare or archaic var. of* MECHANICAL —*n.* a worker skilled in using tools or in making, operating, and repairing machines

me·chan·i·cal (-i k′l) *adj.* 1. having to do with, or having skill in the use of, machinery or tools 2. produced or operated by machinery 3. of, or in accordance with, the science of mechanics 4. automatic, as if from force of habit; machinelike [her acting is *mechanical*] —**me·chan′-i·cal·ly** *adv.*

mechanical advantage the rates of the output force of a mechanism to the input force

mechanical drawing drawing done, as by a draughtsman, with T squares, scales, compasses, etc.

mechanical equivalent of heat *Physics* a factor used for converting units of energy, considered as units of work, into heat units

mech·a·ni·cian (mek′ə nish′ən) *n.* a person skilled in the design, operation, care, etc. of machinery

me·chan·ics (mə kan′iks) *n.pl.* [*with sing. v.*] 1. the branch of physics that deals with the motion of material bodies and the action of forces on bodies: cf. STATICS, DYNAMICS, KINEMATICS 2. knowledge of machinery 3. the mechanical aspect; technical part [the *mechanics* of writing]

mech·a·nism (mek′ə niz′m) *n.* [< ModL. < Gr. *mēchanē,* a machine] 1. the working parts of a machine; works [the *mechanism* of a clock] 2. a) a system whose parts work together as in a machine [the *mechanism* of the universe] b) any physical or mental process by which some result is produced c) a mechanical part of a device [timing *mechanism*] 3. the mechanical aspect; technical part 4. the theory that all phenomena can ultimately be explained in terms of physics and chemistry —**mech′a·nist** *n.* —**mech′-a·nis′tic** *adj.* —**mech′a·nis′ti·cal·ly** *adv.*

mech·a·nize (mek′ə nīz′) *vt.* **-nized′, -niz′ing** 1. to make mechanical 2. to do or operate by machinery, not by hand 3. to bring about the use of machinery in (an industry, etc.) 4. to equip (an army, etc.) with motor vehicles, tanks, etc. —**mech′a·ni·za′tion** *n.* —**mech′a·niz′er** *n.*

mech·an·o·ther·a·py (mek′ə nō thər′ə pē) *n.* [< Gr. *mēchanē,* a machine + THERAPY] the treatment of disease by mechanical means, such as massage —**mech′an·o·ther′-a·pist** *n.*

Mech·lin (mek′lin) *n.* [< E. name of *Mechelen,* in Belgium] a fine lace, with the design clearly outlined by a thread: also **Mechlin lace**

Med *a clipped form of* MEDITERRANEAN

med. 1. medical 2. medicine 3. medieval 4. medium

M.Ed. Master of Education

med·al (med′′l) *n.* [< Fr. < It. *medaglia,* ult. < LL. *medialis,* MEDIAL] 1. a small, flat piece of metal with a design or inscription on it, made to commemorate some event, or awarded for some distinguished action, merit, etc. 2. a disc bearing a religious symbol, blessed as by a priest and worn as a religious token

me·dal·lion (mə dal′yən) *n.* [< Fr. < It.: see MEDAL] 1. a large medal 2. any of various designs, carvings, etc. like a medal in shape, used decoratively, as in architecture

med·al·list (-′l ist, -list) *n.* 1. a person who designs or makes medals 2. a person who has been awarded a medal 3. *Golf* the low scorer in a qualifying round of medal play preliminary to a tournament Also U.S. sp. **med′al·ist**

medal play *Golf* a form of competitive play in which the score is calculated by counting the total number of strokes taken to play the designated number of holes: cf. MATCH PLAY

med·dle (med′′l) *vi.* **-dled, -dling** [< OFr. *medler* < VL. < L. *miscere,* to mix] 1. to concern oneself with other people's affairs without being asked or needed; interfere (*in* or *with*) 2. to tamper (*with*) —**med′dler** *n.*

med·dle·some (-səm) *adj.* meddling or inclined to meddle —**med′dle·some·ness** *n.*

Mede (mēd) *n.* a native or inhabitant of Media

me·di·a (mē′dē ə) *n. alt. pl. of* MEDIUM: see MEDIUM (*n.* 3)

me·di·ae·val (mē′dē ē′v′l, med′ē-) *adj. same as* MEDIEVAL —**me′di·ae′val·ism** *n.*

me·di·al (mē′dē əl) *adj.* [< LL. < L. *medius,* middle] 1. of or in the middle; median **2.** average; mean —**me′di·al·ly** *adv.*

me·di·an (-ən) *adj.* [< L. < *medius*, middle] **1.** middle; intermediate **2.** *a)* designating a line from a vertex of a triangle to the middle of the opposite side *b)* designating a line joining the midpoints of the nonparallel sides of a trapezoid **3.** *Statistics* designating the middle number in a series arranged in order of size, or, if there is no middle value, the average of the two middle numbers —*n.* a median number, point, or line —**me′di·an·ly** *adv.*

me·di·ate (mē′dē āt′; *for adj.* -it) *vi.* **-at′ed, -at′ing** [< LL. pp. of *mediare* < L. *medius*, middle] **1.** to be in an intermediate position **2.** to be an intermediary between persons or sides —*vt.* **1.** to settle by mediation **2.** to be the medium for bringing about (a result) —*adj.* dependent on, acting by, or connected through some intervening agency —**me′di·ate·ly** *adv.* —**me′di·a′tor** *n.*

me·di·a·tion (mē′dē ā′shən) *n.* a mediating; intervention for settling differences between persons, nations, etc. —**me′di·a′tive** *adj.* —**me′di·a·to·ry** (-ə tər ē) *adj.* —**me′di·a·tor′ial** *adj.*

med·ic¹ (med′ik) *n.* [Colloq.] **1.** a physician or surgeon **2.** a medical student or intern

med·ic² (med′ik) *n.* [< L. < Gr. *mēdikē* (*poa*), (grass) of Media] any of various leguminous plants, as alfalfa: also sp. **med′ick**

med·i·ca·ble (med′i kə b'l) *adj.* that can be cured, healed, or relieved by medical treatment

med·i·cal (med′i k'l) *adj.* [< Fr. < LL. < L. *medicus*, physician] of or connected with the practice or study of medicine —**med′i·cal·ly** *adv.*

medical certificate a certificate issued by a doctor to a worker who is unfit, in order that he may claim sick leave

medical jurisprudence *see* FORENSIC MEDICINE

medical officer someone employed by the local authority to be in charge of the health services for that area

med·i·ca·ment (med′i kə mənt, mə dik′ə-) *n.* same as MEDICATION (sense 2)

med·i·cate (med′ə kāt′) *vt.* **-cat′ed, -cat′ing** [< L. pp. of *medicari*, to heal] **1.** to treat with medicine **2.** to add a medicinal substance to —**med′i·ca′tive** *adj.*

med·i·ca·tion (med′ə kā′shən) *n.* **1.** a medicating or being medicated **2.** a medicine; substance for curing or healing, or for relieving pain

me·dic·i·nal (mə dis′'n 'l) *adj.* of, or having the properties of, medicine; curing, healing, or relieving —**me·dic′i·nal·ly** *adv.*

med·i·cine (med′ə s'n; med′sin) *n.* [< OFr. < L. < *medicus*, physician] **1.** the science and art of diagnosing, treating, and preventing disease **2.** the branch of this science that makes use of drugs, diet, etc., as distinguished esp. from surgery **3.** any substance, as a drug, used in treating disease, healing, relieving pain, etc. **4.** among primitive peoples *a)* any object, rite, etc. supposed, to have supernatural powers as a remedy, preventive, etc. *b)* magical power —**take one's medicine** to endure just punishment, etc.

medicine ball a large, heavy, leather-covered ball, tossed from one person to another for exercise

medicine man among primitive peoples, esp. North American Indians, a man supposed to have supernatural powers of curing disease and controlling spirits; shaman

med·i·co (med′i kō′) *n.,* pl. **-cos′** [It.] [Colloq.] **1.** a doctor **2.** a medical student

me·di·e·val (mē′dē ē′v'l, med′ē-) *adj.* [< L. *medius*, middle + *aevum*, age] of, like, characteristic of, or suggestive of the Middle Ages —**me′di·e′val·ly** *adv.*

Medieval Greek the Greek language as it was used in the Middle Ages, from c.600–c.1500 A.D.

me·di·e·val·ism (-iz'm) *n.* **1.** medieval spirit, beliefs, customs, etc. **2.** devotion to these **3.** a belief, custom, etc. of the Middle Ages

me·di·e·val·ist (-ist) *n.* **1.** a specialist in medieval history, literature, art, etc. **2.** a person devoted to medieval customs, beliefs, etc.

Medieval Latin the Latin language used in Europe in the Middle Ages, from c.600–c.1500 A.D.

me·di·o·cre (mē′dē ō′kər) *adj.* [< Fr. < L. *mediocris* < *medius*, middle + *ocris*, a peak] **1.** neither very good nor very bad; ordinary; average **2.** not good enough; inferior

me·di·oc·ri·ty (mē′dē ok′rə tē) *n.,* pl. **-ties** **1.** a being mediocre **2.** mediocre ability or attainment **3.** a person of mediocre abilities, etc.

Medit. Mediterranean

med·i·tate (med′ə tāt′) *vt.* **-tat′ed, -tat′ing** [< L. pp. of *meditari*] **1.** [Rare] to study; ponder **2.** to plan or intend —*vi.* to think deeply and continuously; reflect —**med′i·ta′tive** *adj.* —**med′i·ta′tive·ly** *adv.* —**med′i·ta′tor** *n.*

med·i·ta·tion (med′ə tā′shən) *n.* **1.** act of meditating; deep reflection, esp. on sacred matters as a devotional act **2.** [*often pl.*] oral or written material, as a sermon, based on meditation

Med·i·ter·ra·ne·an (med′i tə rā′nē ən) *adj.* [< L. < *medius,*

middle + *terra*, land] of the Mediterranean Sea or nearby regions —*n.* a person who lives near the Mediterranean Sea

me·di·um (mē′dē əm) *n.,* pl. **-di·ums;** also (except sense 7), and for sense 3 usually, **-di·a** (-ə) [L., neut. of *medius*, middle] **1.** *a)* something intermediate *b)* a middle state or degree; mean **2.** an intervening thing through which a force acts **3.** any means, agency, etc.; specif., a means of communication that reaches the general public **4.** any surrounding substance in which bodies exist **5.** environment **6.** a nutritive substance, as agar, for cultivating bacteria, etc. **7.** a person through whom communications are supposedly sent from the spirits of the dead **8.** any material or technique as used in art **9.** a liquid mixed with pigments to give fluency —*adj.* **1.** intermediate in quality, amount, degree, size, etc. **2.** neither rare nor well-done: said of meat

medium bowler *Cricket* a bowler who is neither a fast nor a slow bowler: also called **medium pace bowler**

medium wave any radio frequency between 200 kilohertz and 2 megahertz (100 to 2000 metres) Also, **medium frequency**

med·lar (med′lər) *n.* [< OFr. < L. < Gr. *mespilon*] **1.** a small tree of the rose family, growing in Europe and Asia **2.** its small, brown, applelike fruit, eaten when partly decayed

med·ley (med′lē) *n.,* pl. **-leys** [< OFr. < pp. of *medler*: see MEDDLE] **1.** a mixture of things not usually placed together **2.** a musical piece made up of tunes or passages from various works

medley race **1.** a relay race in which each contestant must cover a different distance: also **medley relay** **2.** a swimming race in which a different stroke must be used for each length of the pool

me·dul·la (mi dul′ə) *n.,* pl. **-dul′las, -dul′lae** (-ē) [L., the marrow] **1.** *Anat. a)* same as MEDULLA OBLONGATA *b)* the inner substance of an organ *c)* bone marrow **2.** *Bot.* same as PITH (*n.* 1) —**med·ul·lar·y** (med′ə lər ē, mej′-; mĭ dul′ər ē) *adj.*

medulla ob·lon·ga·ta (ob′loŋ gät′ə) [ModL., oblong medulla] the widening continuation of the spinal cord forming the lowest part of the brain: it controls breathing, circulation, etc.

me·du·sa (mə dyσσ′sə, -zə) *n.,* pl. **-sas, -sae** (-sē, -zē) [after *Medusa*, one of the three Gorgons, slain by Perseus, in Greek Mythology] *Zool.* same as JELLYFISH

meed (mēd) *n.* [OE. *med*] [Archaic] a merited recompense or reward

meek (mēk) *adj.* [< ON. *miukr*, gentle] **1.** patient and mild; not inclined to anger or resentment **2.** too submissive; spineless; spiritless —**meek′ly** *adv.* —**meek′ness** *n.*

meer·schaum (mir′shəm, -shôm) *n.* [G. < *Meer*, sea + *Schaum*, foam] **1.** a soft, white, claylike mineral used for tobacco pipes, etc. because heat-resistant **2.** a pipe made of this

meet¹ (mēt) *vt.* **met, meet′ing** [OE. *metan*] **1.** to come upon; esp., to come face to face with **2.** to be present at the arrival of [to *meet* a bus] **3.** to come into contact, connection, etc. with [the ball *met* the bat] **4.** *a)* to come into the presence of *b)* to be introduced to; get acquainted with *c)* to keep an appointment with **5.** *a)* to contend with *b)* to face [to *meet* angry words with a laugh] *c)* to deal with effectively [to *meet* an objection] **6.** to experience [to *meet* disaster] **7.** to come within the perception of (the eye, ear, etc.) **8.** *a)* to comply with; satisfy (a demand, etc.) *b)* to pay (a bill, etc.) —*vi.* **1.** to come together, as from different directions **2.** to come into contact, connection, etc. **3.** to become acquainted; be introduced **4.** to be opposed in or as in battle; fight **5.** to be united **6.** to assemble **7.** to come together for discussion, etc. (*with*) —*n.* **1.** a meeting, gathering, etc. [an athletic *meet*] **2.** the people who meet or the place of meeting —**meet a person half-way** to be willing to compromise —**meet a person's eye** to exchange glances with someone —**meet with** **1.** to experience **2.** to receive **3.** to encounter: also **meet up with**

meet² (mēt) *adj.* [< OE. (ge)*mæte*, fitting] [Now Rare] suitable; proper; fit —**meet′ly** *adv.*

meet·ing (mēt′iŋ) *n.* **1.** a coming together of persons or things **2.** an assembly; gathering of people **3.** an assembly or place of assembly for worship **4.** a series of horse or dog races **5.** a point of contact; junction

meet·ing·house (-hous′) *n.* a building used for public meetings, esp. for public worship

meg·a- [Gr. < *megas*, great] a combining form meaning: **1.** large, great, powerful [*megaphone*] **2.** a million (of) [*megaton*] Also, before a vowel, **meg-**

meg·a·death (meg′ə deth′) *n.* [see MEGA-] one million dead persons, as from a hypothetical nuclear explosion

meg·a·hertz (-hurts′) *n.,* pl. **-hertz** [see MEGA-] one million hertz: formerly **meg′a·cy′cle** (-sī′k'l)

meg·a·lith (-lith′) *n.* [MEGA- + -LITH] a huge stone, esp. one used in prehistoric monuments —**meg′a·lith′ic** *adj.*

meg·a·lo- [ModL. < Gr. < *megas*, large] a combining form *meaning:* 1. large, great, powerful [*megalomania*] 2. abnormal enlargement

meg·a·lo·ma·ni·a (meg'ə lō mā'nē ə, -mān'yə) *n.* [ModL.: see prec. & MANIA] a mental disorder characterized by delusions of grandeur, wealth, power, etc. —**meg'a·lo·ma'ni·ac'** (-ak') *adj., n.* —**meg'a·lo·ma·ni'a·cal** (-mə nī'ə k'l) *adj.* —**meg'a·lo·man'ic** (-man'ik) *adj.*

meg·a·lop·o·lis (meg'ə lop'ə ləs) *n.* [Gr., great city] a vast, heavily populated urban area, including many cities —**meg'·a·lo·pol'i·tan** (-lə pol'ət'n) *adj., n.*

meg·a·phone (meg'ə fōn') *n.* [see MEGA-] a large, funnel-shaped device for increasing the volume of the voice and directing it —*vt., vi.* **-phoned'**, **-phon'ing** to magnify or direct (the voice) with a megaphone —**meg'a·phon'ic** (-fon'·ik) *adj.*

meg·a·pode (-pōd') *n.* [MEGA- + -POD] any of a family of large-footed, mound-building birds of Australia and the East Indies

meg·a·ton (-tun') *n.* [see MEGA-] the explosive force of a million tons of TNT —**meg'a·ton'nage** *n.*

meg·ger (meg'gər) *a trademark for* an apparatus that measures insulation resistance

meg·ohm (meg'ōm) *n.* one million ohms

me·grim (mē'grəm) *n.* [< OFr.: see MIGRAINE] 1. [Archaic] a whim; fancy 2. [*pl.*] [Rare] low spirits

mei·o·sis (mī ō'sis) *n.* [ModL. < Gr. < *meioun*, to make smaller] the process of nuclear division in the formation of germ cells that halves the number of chromosomes present in the somatic cells of an animal or plant —**mei·ot'ic** (-ot'·ik) *adj.*

Meis·ter·sing·er (mīs'tər siŋ'ər, -ziŋ'ər) *n., pl.* **-sing'er** [G., lit., master singer] a member of one of the German guilds organized in the 14th-16th cent. for cultivating music and poetry

mel·a·mine (mel'ə mēn') *n.* [G. *Melamin*] a white, crystalline compound used in making synthetic resins

mel·an·cho·li·a (mel'ən kō'lē ə, -kōl'yə) *n.* [ModL. < LL.: see ff.] a mental disorder characterized by extreme depression, brooding, etc. —**mel'an·cho'li·ac'** (-kō'lē ak') *adj., n.*

mel·an·chol·y (mel'ən kol'ē) *n., pl.* **-chol'ies** [< OFr. < LL. < Gr. *melancholia* < *melas*, black + *cholē*, bile: orig., referring to black bile as the humour causing this] 1. *a)* sadness and depression of spirits *b)* a tendency to be sad or depressed 2. pensiveness —*adj.* 1. sad and depressed; gloomy 2. causing sadness or depression 3. pensive —**mel'an·chol'ic** *adj.* —**mel'an·chol'i·cal·ly** *adv.*

Mel·a·ne·sian (-zhən, -shən) *adj.* of Melanesia, its people, or their languages —*n.* 1. a member of the dark-skinned native people of Melanesia 2. the branch of Malayo-Polynesian languages of Melanesia

mé·lange (mā länzh', -länj') *n.* [Fr. < *mêler*, to mix] a mixture or medley; hodgepodge

mel·a·nin (mel'ə nin) *n.* [< Gr. *melas*, black + -IN[1]] a brownish-black pigment found in skin, hair, etc.

Mel·ba toast (mel'bə) [after Nellie *Melba* (1861–1931), Australian soprano] slightly stale bread sliced thin and toasted until brown and crisp

meld (meld) *vt., vi.* [G. *melden*, to announce] *Card Games* to declare (a combination of cards in one's hand), esp. by putting them face up on the table —*n.* 1. a melding 2. the cards melded

me·lee, mê·lée (me'lā, me lā', mā'lā) *n.* [Fr. *mêlée* < OFr.: see MEDLEY] a noisy, confused, hand-to-hand fight among a number of people

mel·io·rate (mēl'yə rāt') *vt., vi.* **-rat'ed**, **-rat'ing** [< LL. pp. of *meliorare* < L. *melior*, better] to make or become better; improve —**mel'io·ra·ble** (-yər ə b'l) *adj.* —**mel'io·ra'·tion** *n.* —**mel'io·ra'tive** *adj.* —**mel'io·ra'tor** *n.*

me·lis·ma (mə liz'mə) *n., pl.* **-ma·ta** (-mə tə), **-mas** [Gr. *melisma*, song] a succession of different notes sung upon one syllable as in plainsong and eastern music

mel·lif·er·ous (mə lif'ər əs) *adj.* [L. *mellifer* < *mel*, honey + -*fer* + -OUS] producing honey

mel·lif·lu·ous (mə lif'loo wəs) *adj.* [< L. < *mel*, honey + *fluere*, to flow] sounding sweet and smooth; honeyed [*mellifluous tones*]: also **mel·lif'lu·ent** (-wənt) —**mel·lif'·lu·ous·ly** *adv.* —**mel·lif'lu·ous·ness** *n.*

mel·low (mel'ō) *adj.* [prob. < OE. *melu*, MEAL[2]] 1. soft, sweet, and juicy because ripe: said of fruit 2. full-flavoured; matured: said of wine, etc. 3. full, rich, soft, and pure: said of sound, light, etc. 4. moist and rich: said of soil 5. made soft, gentle, and understanding by experience 6. slightly intoxicated —*vt., vi.* to make or become mellow —**mel'low·ly** *adv.* —**mel'low·ness** *n.*

me·lo·de·on (mə lō'dē ən) *n.* [G. *Melodion* < *Melodie*, melody] a small keyboard organ in which air is drawn through metal reeds by means of a bellows

me·lod·ic (mə lod'ik) *adj.* 1. of or like melody 2. same as MELODIOUS —**me·lod'i·cal·ly** *adv.*

me·lo·di·ous (mə lō'dē əs) *adj.* 1. containing or producing melody 2. pleasing to hear; tuneful —**me·lo'di·ous·ly** *adv.* —**me·lo'di·ous·ness** *n.*

mel·o·dist (mel'ə dist) *n.* a singer or composer of melodies

mel·o·dize (mel'ə dīz') *vt.* **-dized'**, **-diz'ing** [ML. *melodizare*] 1. to make melodious 2. to set to melody —*vi.* to compose melodies —**mel'o·diz'er** *n.*

mel·o·dra·ma (mel'ə drä'mə) *n.* [< Fr., ult. < Gr. *melos*, song + *drama*, drama] 1. orig., a sensational or romantic stage play with interspersed songs 2. now, a drama with exaggerated conflicts and emotions, stereotyped characters, etc. 3. any sensational, highly emotional action, utterance, etc. —**mel'o·dram·a·tist** (-dram'ə tist) *n.*

mel·o·dra·mat·ic (mel'ə drə mat'ik) *adj.* of or like melodrama; sensational, violent, and extravagantly emotional —**mel'o·dra·mat'i·cal·ly** *adv.* —**mel'o·dra·mat'ics** *n.pl.*

mel·o·dy (mel'ə dē) *n., pl.* **-dies** [< OFr. < LL. < Gr. *melōidia* < *melos*, song + *aeidein*, to sing] 1. pleasing sounds or arrangement of sounds in sequence 2. *Music a)* a sequence of single tones to produce a rhythmic whole; often, a tune, song, etc. *b)* the leading part in a harmonic composition

mel·on (mel'ən) *n.* [< OFr. < LL. *melo* for L. *melopepo* < Gr. < *mēlon*, apple + *pepōn*, melon] the large, juicy, many-seeded fruit of certain trailing plants of the gourd family, as the watermelon, cantaloupe, etc.

Mel·pom·e·ne (mel pom'ə nē') *Gr. Myth.* the Muse of tragedy

melt (melt) *vt., vi.* **melt'ed**, **melt'ing**, archaic pp. **molt'en** [OE. *meltan*, *vi.*, *mieltan*, *vt.*] 1. to change from a solid to a liquid state, generally by heat 2. to dissolve; disintegrate 3. to disappear or cause to disappear gradually (often with *away*) 4. to merge gradually; blend [the sea *melts* into the sky] 5. to soften [a story to *melt* our hearts] —*n.* a melting or being melted —**melt down** to melt (previously formed metal) so that it can be cast or moulded again —**melt in one's mouth** 1. to require little chewing 2. to taste especially delicious —**melt'a·bil'i·ty** *n.* —**melt'a·ble** *adj.* —**melt'er** *n.* —**melt'ing·ly** *adv.*

melting point the temperature at which a specified solid becomes liquid: abbrev. **melt. pt.**

melting pot a country, etc. in which people of various nationalities and races are assimilated

mel·ton (mel't'n) *n.* [< *Melton* Mowbray, England] a heavy woollen cloth with a short nap

Melton Mowbray pie a veal and ham pie first made at Melton Mowbray

melt·wa·ter (melt'wô'tər) *n.* water produced by the melting of snow or ice

mem. 1. member 2. memorandum

mem·ber (mem'bər) *n.* [< OE. < L. *membrum*] 1. a limb or other part or organ of a person, animal, or plant 2. a distinct part of a whole, as of a series, an equation, a structure, etc. 3. a person belonging to an organization or group

member of parliament a member of the House of Commons or similar legislative body, as in many Commonwealth countries

mem·ber·ship (-ship') *n.* 1. the state of being a member 2. all the members of a group 3. the number of members

mem·brane (mem'brān) *n.* [L. *membrana* < *membrum*, member] a thin, soft, pliable layer of animal or plant tissue that covers or lines an organ or part —**mem'braned** *adj.* —**mem'bra·nous** (-brə nəs) *adj.* —**mem'bra·nous·ly** *adv.*

me·men·to (mi men'tō, mə-) *n., pl.* **-tos**, **-toes** [L., imperative of *meminisse*, to remember] anything serving as a reminder; esp., a souvenir

‡**me·men·to mo·ri** (mi men'tō mō'rī, -rē) [L., remember you must die] any reminder of death

mem·o (mem'ō) *n., pl.* **-os** *clipped form of* MEMORANDUM

mem·oir (mem'wär) *n.* [< Fr. *mémoire* < L. *memoria*, MEMORY] 1. a biography 2. [*pl.*] an autobiography 3. [*pl.*] a record of events based on the writer's personal observation or knowledge 4. a report of a scientific study, etc.

mem·o·ra·bil·i·a (mem'ər ə bil'ē ə, -bil'yə) *n.pl., sing.* **mem'·o·rab'i·le** (-ə rä'bə lē) [L.] things worth remembering or recording and collecting

mem·o·ra·ble (mem'ər ə b'l, mem'rə-) *adj.* worth remembering; notable —**mem'o·ra·bil'i·ty** *n.* —**mem'·o·ra·bly** *adv.*

mem·o·ran·dum (mem'ə ran'dəm) *n., pl.* **-dums**, **-da** (-də) [L.] 1. *a)* a short note written to help one remember something *b)* a record, as of events, for future use 2. an informal written communication, as in a business office 3. a short written statement of the terms of an agreement, contract, or transaction

me·mo·ri·al (mə môr'ē əl) *adj.* [see MEMORY] serving to help people remember some person or event —*n.* 1. anything meant to help people remember some person or event, as a statue, holiday, etc. 2. a statement of facts, often with a petition for action, sent to a government, official, etc.

me·mo·ri·al·ize (-īz') *vt.* **-ized'**, **-iz'ing** 1. to commemorate 2. to present a petition to

mem·o·rize (mem'ə rīz') *vt.* **-rized', -riz'ing** to commit to memory —**mem'o·ri·za'tion** *n.*

mem·o·ry (mem'ər ē, mem'rē) *n.,* *pl.* **-ries** [< OFr. < L. *memoria* < *memor*, mindful] **1.** the power, act, or process of recalling to mind facts or experiences **2.** the total of what one remembers **3.** a person, thing, etc. remembered **4.** the period over which remembering extends [within the *memory* of living men] **5.** commemoration or remembrance [in *memory* of his son] **6.** reputation after death **7.** the components of a computer, etc. that retain information

mem·sa·hib (mem sä'ib, -säb') *n.* [Anglo-Ind.: *mem* for MA'AM + Hindi *sāhib*, SAHIB] in India formerly, a term of address for a European married woman as used by servants, etc.

men (men) *n.* *alt. pl. of* MAN

men·ace (men'is) *n.* [< OFr. < L. *minacia* < *minax*, threatening < *minari*, to threaten] **1.** a threat or threatening **2.** anything threatening harm or evil **3.** [Colloq.] an annoying person —*vt., vi.* **-aced, -ac·ing** to threaten —**men'ac·ing·ly** *adv.*

me·nad (mē'nad) *n.* *alt. sp. of* MAENAD

mé·nage, me·nage (mā näzh', mə-) *n.* [< Fr. < OFr. *manage* < *manoir* (see MANOR)] **1.** a household **2.** the management of a household

‡ménage à trois (mā näzh'à trwä) [Fr. lit., household of three] an arrangement by which a married couple and the lover of one of them live together

me·nag·er·ie (mə naj'ər ē, -näzh'-) *n.* [< Fr. < *ménage:* see MENAGE] **1.** a collection of wild animals kept in cages for exhibition **2.** a place where such animals are kept

mend (mend) *vt.* [ME. *menden*, shortened from *amenden*, AMEND] **1.** to repair; restore to good condition **2.** to make better; improve; reform [*mend* your manners] **3.** to atone for: now only in **least said, soonest mended** —*vi.* **1.** to improve, esp. in health **2.** to grow together or heal, as a fracture —*n.* **1.** a mending; improvement **2.** a mended place —**on the mend** improving, esp. in health —**mend'-a·ble** *adj.* —**mend'er** *n.*

men·da·cious (men dā'shəs) *adj.* [< L. *mendax* (gen. *mendacis*)] not truthful; lying; false —**men·da'cious·ly** *adv.* —**men·da'cious·ness** *n.* —**men·dac'i·ty** (-das'ə tē) *n., pl.* **-ties**

men·de·le·vi·um (men'də lē'vē əm) *n.* [ModL., after D.I. *Mendeleev* (1834-1907), Russ. chemist] a radioactive chemical element of the actinide series: symbol, Md; at. wt., 258(?); at. no., 101

Men·dels laws (men'd'lz) the principles of hereditary phenomena discovered and formulated by Gregor Mendel (1822-84), holding that characteristics as height, colour, etc., are inherited in definite, predictable combinations

men·di·cant (men'di kənt) *adj.* [< L. prp. of *mendicare*, to beg] asking for alms; begging [*mendicant* friars] —*n.* **1.** a beggar **2.** a mendicant friar —**men'di·can·cy, men·dic·i·ty** (mən dis'ə tē) *n.*

men·folk (men'fōk') *n.pl.* men

men·ha·den (men hād''n) *n., pl.* **-den, -dens:** see PLURAL, II, D, 2 [< Algonquian name] a sea fish related to the herring, common along the Atlantic coast of N. America: used for making oil and fertilizer

men·hir (men'hir) *n.* [Fr. < Bret. *men*, stone + *hir*, long] a tall, upright stone erected probably as a monument in prehistoric times

me·ni·al (mē'nē əl, mēn'yəl) *adj.* [< Anglo-Fr. < OFr. *meisniee*, household < L. *mansio:* see MANSION] **1.** of or fit for servants **2.** servile; low; mean —*n.* **1.** a domestic servant **2.** a servile, low person —**me'ni·al·ly** *adv.*

me·nin·ges (mə nin'jēz) *n.pl., sing.* **me·ninx** (mē'ninks) [ModL., pl. of *meninx* < Gr. *mēninx*, a membrane] the three membranes that envelop the brain and spinal cord —**me·nin'ge·al** (-jē əl) *adj.*

men·in·gi·tis (men'in jīt'is) *n.* inflammation of the meninges, esp. as the result of infection —**men'in·git'ic** (-jit'ik) *adj.*

me·nis·cus (mi nis'kəs) *n., pl.* **-nis'cus·es, -nis'ci** (-nis'ī, -kī) [ModL. < Gr. *mēniskos*, dim. of *mēnē*, the moon] **1.** a crescent-shaped thing **2.** a lens convex on one side and concave on the other **3.** the curved upper surface of a column of liquid

Men·non·ite (men'ə nīt') *adj.* [after *Menno* Simons (1496?-1561?), a leader] a member of an evangelical Christian sect: Mennonites oppose the taking of oaths and military service, and favour plain dress

MENISCUS (left, mercury; right, water)

‡me·no (me'nō) *adv.* [It.] *Music* less

men·o·pause (men'ə pôz') *n.* [< Gr. *mēn*, month + *pauein*, to make cease] the permanent cessation of menstruation; change of life —**men'o·paus'al** *adj.*

men·o·rah (mə nôr'ə) *n.* [Heb., lamp stand] a candelabrum

with seven branches, a symbol of Judaism, or with nine branches, used during Hanuka

men·ses (men'sēz) *n.pl.* [L., pl. of *mensis*, month] the periodic flow of blood from the uterus: normally every four weeks, from puberty to menopause

Men·she·vik (men'shə vik') *n., pl.* **-viks, -vik'i** (-vē'kē) [Russ. < *menshe*, the smaller] [*also* m-] a member of the minority faction of the Social Democratic Party of Russia, which opposed the Bolsheviks from 1903 —**Men'she·vism** *n.* —**Men'she·vist** *n., adj.*

men·stru·ate (men'stroo wāt', -strāt) *vi.* **-at'ed, -at'ing** [< L. pp. of *menstruare* < *mensis*, month] to have a discharge of the menses —**men'stru·al** *adj.* —**men'stru·a'tion** *n.* —**men'stru·ous** *adj.*

men·stru·um (-stroo wəm) *n., pl.* **-stru·ums, -stru·a** (-wə) [ML., < neut. of L. *menstruus:* from an alchemistic notion of the power of the menses as a solvent] a liquid that dissolves a solid; solvent

men·sur·a·ble (men'shər ə b'l, -sər-) *adj.* that can be measured; measurable —**men'sur·a·bil'i·ty** *n.*

men·su·ral (-əl) *adj.* [LL. *mensuralis*] **1.** of measure **2.** *Music* having a definite rhythm and notes with strictly determined values

men·su·ra·tion (men'shə rā'shən, -sə-) *n.* [< LL. < pp. of *mensurare* < L. *mensura*, MEASURE] **1.** a measuring **2.** the branch of mathematics dealing with the determination of length, area, or volume —**men'su·ra·tive** (-rāt'iv) *adj.*

-ment (mənt, mint) [< OFr. < L. *-mentum*] a suffix meaning: **1.** a result or product [*improvement*] **2.** a means or instrument [*adornment*] **3.** the act, process, or art [*movement*] **4.** the state, fact, or degree [*disappointment*]

men·tal (men't'l) *adj.* [< MFr. < LL. < L. *mens* (gen. *mentis*), the mind] **1.** of or for the mind [*mental* aids] **2.** done by or in the mind [*mental* arithmetic] **3.** mentally ill [a *mental* patient] **4.** for the mentally ill [a *mental* hospital] **5.** having to do with telepathy, etc. —**men'tal·ly** *adv.*

mental healing the treatment of diseases by mental concentration or hypnotic suggestion

men·tal·i·ty (men tal'ə tē) *n., pl.* **-ties** mental capacity, power, or activity; mind

mental reservation a qualification (of a statement) that one thinks but does not express

mental retardation congenital subnormality of intelligence: it ranges from *mild* to *moderate* and *severe:* these terms have replaced *moron, imbecile,* and *idiot:* formerly called **mental deficiency**

men·thol (men'thol) *n.* [G. < L. *mentha*, MINT[2] + *-ol*, -OL[1]] a white, waxy, crystalline alcohol obtained from oil of peppermint and used in medicine, cosmetics, etc.

men·tho·lat·ed (men'thə lāt'id) *adj.* containing or impregnated with menthol

men·tion (men'shən) *n.* [OFr. < L. *mentio* < stem of *mens*, the mind] **1.** a brief reference or statement **2.** a citing for honour —*vt.* **1.** to refer to or speak about briefly or incidentally **2.** to cite for honour —**don't mention it** a phrase used to accept apology or thanks gracefully —**make mention of** to mention —**not to mention** without even mentioning —**men'tion·a·ble** *adj.*

men·tor (men'tər) *n.* [after *Mentor* the adviser of Odysseus, in Greek Mythology] **1.** a wise, loyal adviser **2.** a teacher or coach

men·u (men'yōō) *n., pl.* **men'us** [Fr., small, detailed < L. *minutus:* see MINUTE[2]] **1.** a detailed list of the foods served at a meal or available at a restaurant **2.** the foods served

me·ow, me·ou (mē ou', myou) *n.* [echoic] the characteristic vocal sound made by a cat —*vi.* to make such a sound

me·per·i·dine (mə per'ə dēn') *n.* a synthetic narcotic used as a sedative and analgesic

Meph·i·stoph·e·les (mef'ə stof'ə lēz') *n.* [after the devil to whom Faust sold his soul] a crafty, powerful, sardonic person: also **Me·phis·to** (mə fis'tō) —**Me·phis·to·phe·le·an, Me·phis·to·phe·li·an** (mef'is tə fē'lē ən, mə fis'-) *adj.*

me·phit·ic (mə fit'ik) *adj.* [< L. *mephitis*, a stench] **1.** bad-smelling **2.** poisonous; noxious

me·pro·ba·mate (mə prō'bə māt') *n.* a bitter, white powder used as a tranquillizer

mer·can·tile (mur'kən tīl) *adj.* [Fr. < It. < *mercante*, a merchant < L. prp. of *mercari:* see MERCHANT] **1.** of or characteristic of merchants or trade; commercial **2.** of mercantilism

mer·can·til·ism (-iz'm) *n.* the earlier doctrine that the economic interests of a nation could be strengthened by the government through protective tariffs, by a balance of exports over imports, etc. —**mer'can·til·ist** *n., adj.*

Mer·ca·tor projection (mər kāt'ər) [after G. *Mercator* (1512-94), Fl. cartographer] a method of making maps on which the meridians are equally spaced parallel straight lines and the parallels of latitude are parallel straight lines spaced farther apart as they get farther from the equator: areas are increasingly distorted toward the poles

mer·ce·nar·y (mur′sə nər ē) *adj.* [< L. < *merces*, wages] 1. working or done for payment only; venal; greedy 2. designating a soldier serving for pay in a foreign army —*n.*, *pl.* -*nar·ies* 1. a mercenary soldier 2. a hireling —**mer′ce·nar·i·ly** *adv.* —**mer′ce·nar·i·ness** *n.*

mer·cer (mur′sər) *n.* [< OFr. < *merz*, goods < L. *merx*] a dealer in textiles

mer·cer·ize (mur′sə rīz′) *vt.* -**ized′**, -**iz′ing** [after J. Mercer (1791-1866), Brit. calico dealer] to treat (cotton thread or fabric) with a caustic soda solution in order to strengthen it, give it a silky lustre, and make it more receptive to dyes

mer·chan·dise (mur′chən dīz′; *for n., also* -dīs′) *n.* [< OFr. < *marchant:* see ff.] things bought and sold; goods; wares —*vt.*, *vi.* -**dised′**, -**dis′ing** 1. to buy and sell; carry on trade in (some kind of goods) 2. to promote and organize the sale of (a product) —**mer′chan·dis′er** *n.*

mer·chant (mur′chənt) *n.* [OFr. *marchant*, ult. < L. *mercari*, to trade < *merx*, wares] 1. a person whose business is buying and selling goods for profit 2. [Scot.] a person who sells goods at retail; storekeeper 3. [Colloq.] someone who specializes in or is well-known for something [a speed *merchant*] —*adj.* 1. of or used in trade 2. of the merchant navy —*vt.* to deal in; trade

mer·chant·a·ble (-ə b′l) *adj.* that can be sold; marketable

merchant bank a financial institution dealing in commercial investment and long-term credit for manufacturers, etc. —**merchant banking** *n.* —**merchant banker** *n.*

mer·chant·man (-mən) *n.*, *pl.* -**men** a ship used in commerce

merchant navy 1. all the ships of a nation that are used in commerce 2. their personnel

‡**mer·ci** (mer sē′) *interj.* [Fr.] thank you

Mer·cian (-shən) *adj.* of Mercia, its people, etc. —*n.* 1. a native or inhabitant of Mercia 2. the Old English dialect of the Mercians

mer·ci·ful (mur′si fəl) *adj.* full of mercy; having, feeling, or showing mercy; lenient; clement —**mer′ci·ful·ly** *adv.* —**mer′ci·ful·ness** *n.*

mer·ci·less (-lis) *adj.* without mercy; having, feeling, or showing no mercy; pitiless; cruel —**mer′ci·less·ly** *adv.* —**mer′ci·less·ness** *n.*

mer·cu·ri·al (mər kyoor′ē əl) *adj.* 1. [M-] of Mercury (the god or planet) 2. of or containing mercury 3. caused by the use of mercury 4. having qualities suggestive of mercury; quick, quick-witted, changeable, fickle, etc. —*n.* a drug or preparation containing mercury —**mer·cu′ri·al·ly** *adv.* —**mer·cu′ri·al·ness** *n.*

mer·cu·ric (mər kyoor′ik) *adj.* of or containing mercury, esp. with a valence of two

mercuric chloride a very poisonous, white, crystalline compound, $HgCl_2$, used as an antiseptic, etc.

Mer·cu·ro·chrome (mər kyoor′ə krōm′) [see MERCURY, *n.* & -CHROME] *a trademark for* a compound used as an antiseptic in the form of a red solution —*n.* [m-] this solution

mer·cu·rous (mər kyoor′əs, mur′kyoo rəs) *adj.* of or containing mercury, esp. with a valence of one

Mer·cu·ry (mur′kyoo rē) [L. *Mercurius*] 1. *Rom. Myth.* the messenger of the gods, god of commerce, manual skill, eloquence, and cleverness: identified with the Greek god Hermes 2. the smallest planet in the solar system and the one nearest to the sun: diameter, c. 4,830 km —*n.* [< ML. < L., Mercury] [m-] 1. a heavy, silver-white metallic chemical element, liquid at ordinary temperatures; quicksilver: it is used in thermometers, dentistry, etc.: symbol, Hg; at. wt., 200.59; at. no., 80 2. the mercury column in a thermometer or barometer [the *mercury* is rising]

mer·cu·ry-va·pour lamp (-vā′pər) a discharge tube containing mercury vapour

mer·cy (mur′sē) *n.*, *pl.* -**cies** [< OFr. < L. *merces*, payment, reward] 1. a refraining from harming or punishing offenders, enemies, etc.; kindness in excess of what may be expected 2. imprisonment rather than death for those found guilty of capital crimes 3. a disposition to forgive or be kind 4. the power to forgive or be kind; clemency 5. kind or compassionate treatment 6. a fortunate thing; blessing —*interj.* [U.S.] a mild exclamation of surprise, annoyance, etc. —**at the mercy of** completely in the power of

mercy flight an aircraft flight to bring a seriously ill or injured person to hospital from an isolated community

mercy killing *same as* EUTHANASIA

mere¹ (mir) *adj.* *superl.* **mer′est** [< L. *merus*, unmixed, pure] nothing more or other than; only (as said to be) [a *mere* boy]

mere² (mir) *n.* [OE.] 1. [Poet.] a lake or pond 2. [Obs.] the sea or an arm of the sea

me·re³ (mā′rā) *n.* [Maori] 1. a stone war-club carried by a Maori chief 2. a miniature club in greenstone worn as an ornament

-mere (mir) [< Gr. *meros*, a part] *a combining form meaning* part

mere·ly (mir′lē) *adv.* 1. no more than; and nothing else; only 2. [Obs.] absolutely

mer·e·tri·cious (mer′ə trish′əs) *adj.* [< L. < *meretrix*, a prostitute < *mereri*, to serve for hire] 1. alluring by false, showy charms; flashy; tawdry 2. superficially plausible; specious —**mer′e·tri′cious·ly** *adv.* —**mer′e·tri′cious·ness** *n.*

mer·gan·ser (mər gan′sər) *n.*, *pl.* -**sers**, -**ser:** see PLURAL, II, D, 1 [ModL. < L. *mergus*, diver + *anser*, goose] *same as* GOOSANDER

merge (murj) *vi.*, *vt.* **merged, merg′ing** [L. *mergere*, to dip] 1. to lose or cause to lose identity by being absorbed, swallowed up, or combined 2. to unite; combine

merg·er (mur′jər) *n.* a merging; specif., the combination of several companies, etc. in one

me·rid·i·an (mə rid′ē ən) *adj.* [< OFr. < L. < *meridies*, noon, ult. < *medius*, middle + *dies*, day] 1. of or at noon 2. of or passing through the highest point in the daily course of any heavenly body 3. of or at the highest point, as of power 4. of or along a meridian —*n.* 1. orig., the highest point reached by a heavenly body in its course 2. the highest point of power, prosperity, etc.; zenith 3. a great circle of the celestial sphere passing through the poles of the heavens and the zenith and nadir of any given point 4. a) a great circle of the earth passing through the geographical poles and any given point on the earth's surface b) the half of such a circle between the poles c) any of the lines of longitude on a globe or map, representing such a half circle

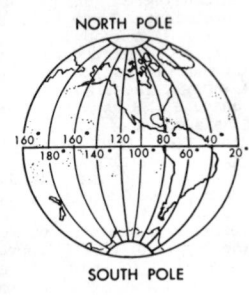

NORTH POLE

SOUTH POLE

MERIDIANS

me·rid·i·o·nal (mə rid′ē ən əl) *adj.* [ME. < OFr. < LL. *meridionalis*, southern] 1. southern 2. of the people living in the south, esp. of France 3. of a meridian —*n.* [often M-] an inhabitant of the south, esp. of France

me·ringue (mə rang′) *n.* [Fr. < ?] 1. egg whites beaten stiff and mixed with sugar, often browned in the oven and used as a covering for pies, cakes, etc. 2. a baked cake or shell made of this

me·ri·no (mə rē′nō) *n.*, *pl.* -**nos** [Sp., prob. < (Beni) *Merin*, name of a nomadic Berber tribe] 1. one of a hardy breed of sheep with long, fine wool 2. the wool 3. a fine, soft yarn made from this wool 4. a soft, thin cloth made of this yarn —*adj.* designating or of this sheep, wool, etc.

mer·it (mer′it) *n.* [< OFr. < L. *meritum* < pp. of *mereri*, to earn] 1. [*sometimes pl.*] the state, fact, or quality of deserving well or ill; desert 2. worth; value; excellence 3. something deserving reward, praise, etc. 4. a mark, badge, etc. awarded for excellence 5. [*pl.*] essential rightness or wrongness [to decide a case on its *merits*] —*vt.* to deserve —**mer′it·less** *adj.*

mer·i·toc·ra·cy (mer′ə tok′rə sē) *n.* an intellectual elite, based on academic achievement —**mer′it·o·crat′** *n.* —**mer′it·o·crat′ic** *adj.*

mer·i·to·ri·ous (mer′ə tôr′ē əs) *adj.* having merit; deserving reward, praise, etc. —**mer′i·to·ri·ous·ly** *adv.* —**mer′i·to′ri·ous·ness** *n.*

merl, merle (murl) *n.* [< OFr. < L. *merula*] [Archaic or Poet.] the European blackbird

mer·lin (mur′lin) *n.* [ME. < OFr. *esmerillon*, dim. of *esmeril*, merlin] a small, black and white European falcon

mer·maid (mur′mād′) *n.* [see MERE² & MAID] an imaginary sea creature with the body of a beautiful woman and the tail of a fish —**mer′man′** *n.masc.*, *pl.* -**men′**

-mer·ous (mər əs) [< Gr. *meros*, a part] *a suffix meaning* having (a specified number of) parts

Mer·o·vin·gi·an (mer′ō vin′jē ən, -jən) *adj.* designating or of the Frankish line of kings who reigned in Gaul (ancient France) from c. 500 to 751 A.D. —*n.* a king of this line

mer·ri·ment (mer′i mənt) *n.* merrymaking; gaiety and fun; mirth; hilarity

mer·ry (mer′ē) *adj.* -**ri·er**, -**ri·est** [OE. *myrge*] 1. full of fun and laughter; gay; mirthful 2. festive [the *merry* month of May] 3. [Colloq.] slightly drunk; tipsy —**make merry** to have fun —**mer′ri·ly** *adv.* —**mer′ri·ness** *n.*

mer·ry-an·drew (mer′ē an′droo) *n.* [MERRY + *Andrew*, a masculine name: orig. unc.] a buffoon; clown

mer·ry-go-round (-gō round′) *n.* 1. *same as* ROUNDABOUT, *n.* 3 2. a whirl or busy round, as of pleasure

merry hell [Colloq.] a great commotion; pandemonium

mer·ry·mak·ing (-mā′kiŋ) *n.* 1. a making merry and having fun; festivity 2. a merry festival or entertainment —*adj.* taking part in merrymaking; gay and festive —**mer′ry·mak′er** *n.*

me·sa (mā′sə) *n.* [Sp. < L. *mensa*, a table] a small, high plateau or flat tableland with steep sides, esp. in the SW U.S.

mé·sal·li·ance (mā zal′ē əns) *n.* [Fr.] a marriage with a person of a lower social status

mes·cal (mes kal′) *n.* [Sp. *mezcal* < Nahuatl *mexcalli*] 1. a colourless, alcoholic, Mexican spirit made from the fermented juice of various agaves 2. any plant from which this spirit is made 3. a small cactus whose buttonlike tops (**mescal buttons**) when chewed cause hallucinations

mes·ca·line (mes′kə lēn′, -lin) *n.* [prec. + -INE⁴] a white, crystalline alkaloid, a psychedelic drug obtained from mescal buttons

mes·dames (mā dam′; *Fr.* mā dàm′) *n. pl. of* MADAME, MADAM (sense 1), or MRS.: abbrev. **Mmes.**

mes·de·moi·selles (mā′də mə zel′; *Fr.* mād mwà zel′) *n. pl. of* MADEMOISELLE: abbrev. **Mlles.**

me·seems (mē sēmz′) *v.impersonal pt.* **me·seemed′** [Archaic] (it) seems to me: also **me·seem′eth**

mes·en·ter·y (mez′′n tər ē, mes′-) *n., pl.* **-ter·ies** [< ML. < Gr. < *mesos*, middle + *enteron*, intestine] a supporting membrane or membranes enfolding some internal organ and attaching it to the body wall or to another organ —**mes′-en·ter′ic** *adj.*

mesh (mesh) *n.* [prob. < MDu. *maesche*] 1. any of the open spaces of a net, screen, sieve, etc. 2. [*pl.*] the threads, cords, etc. forming these openings 3. a net or network 4. a netlike, woven material, as that used for stockings 5. a structure of interlocking metal links 6. anything that entangles or snares —*vt., vi.* 1. to entangle or become entangled 2. to engage or become engaged: said of gears or gear teeth 3. to interlock 4. to coordinate or harmonize effectively (*with*) —**in mesh** in gear; interlocked —**mesh′y** *adj.*

mesh·work (mesh′wurk′) *n.* meshes; network

me·si·al (mē′zē əl) *adj.* [< Gr. *mesos*, mid + -IAL] of, in, towards, or along the middle; median

mes·mer·ism (mez′mər iz′m, mes′-) *n.* [after F. A. *Mesmer* (1734-1815), G. physician] 1. hypnotism 2. irresistible attraction —**mes·mer′ic** (-mer′ik) *adj.* —**mes·mer′i·cal·ly** *adv.* —**mes′mer·ist** *n.*

mes·mer·ize (-īz′) *vt.* **-ized′, -iz′ing** to hypnotize; esp., to spellbind, or fascinate —**mes′mer·i·za′tion** *n.* —**mes′mer·iz′-er** *n.*

mesne (mēn) *adj.* [Legal Fr. form of Anglo-Fr. *meen* < OFr. *meien*, in the middle] *Law* middle; intermediate; intervening

mes·o- [< Gr. *mesos*, middle] *a combining form meaning* in the middle, intermediate: also **mes-**

mes·o·blast (mes′ō blast′, mez′-) *n.* [MESO- + -BLAST] *same as* MESODERM —**mes′o·blas′tic** *adj.*

mes·o·carp (-kärp′) *n.* [MESO- + -CARP] the middle layer of the wall of a ripened ovary or fruit, as the flesh of a plum —**mes′o·car′pic** *adj.*

mes·o·derm (-durm′) *n.* [MESO- + -DERM] the middle layer of cells of an embryo, from which the skeleton, muscles, etc. develop —**mes′o·der′mal, mes′o·der′mic** *adj.*

mes·o·lith·ic (mes′ō lith′ik, mez′-) *adj.* [MESO- + -LITHIC] designating or of a cultural period between the paleolithic and neolithic, during which certain animals and plants were domesticated

mes·o·mor·phic (-môr′fik) *adj.* [MESO- + -MORPHIC] designating or of the muscular type of human body, in which the structures developed from the mesoderm predominate —**mes′o·morph′n.**

mes·on (mē′son, -zon) *n.* [MES(O)- + (ELECTR)ON] an unstable particle between the electron and proton in mass, first observed in cosmic rays —**me·son·ic** (mē son′-ik, -zon′-) *adj.*

mes·o·sphere (mes′ə sfir′) *n.* [MESO- + SPHERE] an atmospheric zone above the stratosphere, extending between 25 and 80 kilometres above the earth's surface

Mes·o·zo·ic (mes′ō zō′ik, mez′-) *adj.* [MESO- + ZO- + -IC] designating or of a geologic era after the Paleozoic and before the Cainozoic —**the Mesozoic** the Mesozoic Era or its rocks: see GEOLOGY, chart

mes·quite, mes·quit (mes kēt′, mes′kēt) *n.* [Sp. *mezquite* < Nahuatl *mizquitl*] a thorny tree or shrub common in the SW U.S. and in Mexico: its sugary, beanlike pods are used as fodder

mess (mes) *n.* [< OFr. < L. *missus*, a course (at a meal)] 1. a quantity of food for a meal or dish 2. a portion of soft food, as porridge 3. unappetizing food 4. a) a group of people who regularly have their meals together, as in the army b) the meal eaten by such a group c) the place where such a group eats 5. a jumble; hotchpotch 6. a) a state of trouble or difficulty b) a state of being untidy or dirty c) [Colloq.] a person in either of these states —*vt.* 1. to supply meals to 2. to make dirty or untidy; also, to bungle; botch: often with *up* —*vi.* 1. to eat as one of a mess (sense 4a) 2. to make a mess 3. to putter or meddle —**mess around** (or **about**) 1. to putter around 2. to play the fool 3. [U.S. Colloq.] to get involved (*with*)

mes·sage (mes′ij) *n.* [OFr. < ML. < pp. of L. *mittere*, to send] 1. a report, request, etc. sent between persons 2. an official or formal communiqué 3. the chief idea that an artist, writer, etc. seeks to communicate in a work —*vt., vi.* **-saged, -sag·ing** to send (as) a message —**get the message** [Colloq.] to get the implications of a hint, etc.

mes·sag·es (-iz) *n.pl.* [Dial.] errands to buy groceries, etc.; shopping

mes·sen·ger (mes′′n jər) *n.* [< OFr. *messagier*: see MESSAGE] 1. a person who carries a message or is sent on an errand 2. [Archaic] a harbinger

mess hall a room or building where a group, as of soldiers, regularly have their meals

Mes·si·ah (mə sī′ə) [< LL. < Gr. *Messias* < Aram. < Heb. *māshīah*, lit., anointed] 1. *Judaism* the promised and expected deliverer of the Jews 2. *Christianity* Jesus Also **Mes·si′as** (-əs) —*n.* [m-] any expected saviour —**Mes·si·an·ic** (mes′ē an′ik) *adj.*

mes·sieurs (mes′ərz; *Fr.* mā syö′) *n. pl. of* MONSIEUR: abbrev. **MM.**: see also MESSRS.

mess jacket a man's short, closefitting jacket, as that worn by officers in the mess for formal dinners

mess kit the compactly arranged metal or plastic plates and eating utensils carried by a soldier or camper for use in the field: also **mess gear**

mess·mate (mes′māt′) *n.* a person with whom one regularly has meals, as in the navy

Messrs. (mes′ərz) Messieurs: now used chiefly as the pl. of MR.

mess tin a soldier's cooking-vessel, the lid of which can be used as a plate and the lower part as a cup or bowl

mess·y (mes′ē) *adj.* **mess′i·er, mess′i·est** in or like a mess; untidy, disordered, dirty, etc. —**mess′i·ly** *adv.* —**mess′-i·ness** *n.*

mes·ti·zo (mes tē′zō) *n., pl.* **-zos, -zoes** [Sp. < LL. *misticius*, of mixed race < L. pp. of *miscere*, to mix] a person of mixed parentage; esp., the offspring of a Spaniard or Portuguese and an American Indian —**mes·ti′za** (-zə) *n.fem.*

Met (met) *n.* [Colloq.] *clipped form of* METEOROLOGICAL [the *Met* office weather report]

met (met) *pt. & pp. of* MEET¹

met. metropolitan

met·a- [< Gr. *meta*, along with, after, between] *a prefix meaning*: 1. changed, transposed [*metamorphosis, metathesis*] 2. after, beyond, higher [*metaphysics*] Also, before a vowel, **met-**

me·tab·o·lism (mə tab′ə liz′m) *n.* [< Gr. *metabolē*, change < *meta*, beyond + *ballein*, to throw] the continuous processes in living organisms and cells, comprising those by which food is built up into protoplasm and those by which protoplasm is broken down into simpler substances or waste matter, with the release of energy for all vital functions —**met·a·bol·ic** (met′ə bol′ik) *adj.*

me·tab·o·lize (-līz′) *vt., vi.* **-lized′, -liz′ing** to change by or subject to metabolism —**me·tab′o·liz′a·ble** *adj.*

me·tab·o·lous (-ləs) *adj.* [< Gr. *metabolos*, changeable + -OUS] of or undergoing metamorphosis

met·a·car·pus (met′ə kär′pəs) *n., pl.* **-pi** (-pī) [ModL. < Gr. < *meta*, beyond + *karpos*, the wrist] 1. the part of the hand consisting of the five bones between the wrist and the fingers 2. the part of a land vertebrate's forelimb between the carpus and the phalanges —**met′a·car′pal** *adj., n.*

met·age (mēt′ij) *n.* [METE¹ + -AGE] 1. official measurement of contents or weight of coal, grain, etc. 2. the charge for this

met·al (met′′l) *n.* [OFr. < L. *metallum* < Gr. *metallon*, mine] 1. *a*) any of a class of chemical elements, as iron, gold, aluminium, etc., generally characterized by ductility, lustre, conductivity of heat and electricity, and the ability to replace the hydrogen of an acid to form a salt *b*) an alloy of such elements, as brass, bronze, etc. 2. any substance consisting of metal 3. material; substance 4. molten material for making glassware 5. broken stones, cinders, etc. used as in making roads —*adj.* made of metal —*vt.* **-alled, -al·ling** to cover or supply with metal

metal., metall. 1. metallurgical 2. metallurgy

met·a·lan·guage (met′ə laŋ′gwij) *n.* [Gr. *meta*, beyond + language] a language used to talk about other languages, usually including the languages being discussed within the vocabulary of the metalanguage

metal lath lath of expanded metal or metal mesh

me·tal·lic (mə tal′ik) *adj.* 1. of, or having the nature of, metal 2. containing, yielding, or producing metal 3. like or suggestive of metal [a *metallic* sound] —**me·tal′li·cal·ly** *adv.*

met·al·lif·er·ous (met′′l if′ər əs) *adj.* [< L. < *metallum*, metal + *ferre*, to BEAR¹ + -OUS] containing, yielding, or producing metal or ore

met·al·lize (-īz′) *vt.* **-ized′, -iz′ing** 1. to treat, cover or impregnate with metal 2. to make metallic

met·al·log·ra·phy (met′′l log′rə fē) *n.* [Fr. *métallographie*: see METAL & -GRAPHY] the study of the structure and physical properties of metals, esp. by the use of the microscope and X-rays —**met·al·lo·graph·ic** (mə tal′ə graf′-ik) *adj.*

met·al·loid (met′'loid′) *n.* an element having some of, but not all, the properties of metals, as arsenic or silicon
met·al·lur·gy (met′'lur′jē; me tal′-) *n.* [ModL. < Gr. < *metallon*, metal, mine + *ergon*, work] the science of separating metals from their ores and preparing them for use, by smelting, refining, etc. —**met′al·lur′gi·cal, met′-al·lur′gic** *adj.* —**met′al·lur′gi·cal·ly** *adv.* —**met′al·lur′gist** *n.*
met·al·work (-wurk′) *n.* 1. things made of metal 2. the making of such things: also **met′al·work′ing** —**met′-al·work′er** *n.*
met·a·mor·phic (met′ə môr′fik) *adj.* of, characterized by, causing, or formed by metamorphism or metamorphosis
met·a·mor·phism (-môr′fiz′m) *n.* 1. *same as* METAMORPHOSIS 2. change in the structure of rocks under pressure, heat, etc. which turns limestone into marble, granite into gneiss, etc.
met·a·mor·phose (-fōz, -fōs) *vt., vi.* **-phosed, -phos·ing** to change in form or nature; transform
met·a·mor·pho·sis (-môr′fə sis) *n., pl.* **-ses** (-sēz) [L. < Gr. < *metamorphoun*, to transform < *meta*, over + *morphē*, form] 1. *a)* change of form or structure, as, in myths, by magic *b)* the form resulting from this 2. a marked change of character, appearance, etc. 3. *Biol.* a change in form or function as a result of development; specif., the physical transformation undergone by various animals after the embryonic state, as of the tadpole to the frog
met·a·phor (met′ə fôr′, -fər) *n.* [< Fr. < L. < Gr., ult. < *meta*, over + *pherein*, to carry] a figure of speech that suggests a likeness by speaking of one thing as if it were another, different thing (Ex.: the curtain of night, "all the world's a stage"): cf. SIMILE —**mix metaphors** to use two or more inconsistent metaphors in a single expression (Ex.: the storm of protest was nipped in the bud) —**met′a·phor′i·cal, met′a·phor′ic** *adj.* —**met′a·phor′i·cal·ly** *adv.*
met·a·phys·i·cal (met′ə fiz′i k'l) *adj.* 1. of, or having the nature of, metaphysics 2. so subtle as to be hard to understand 3. supernatural 4. designating or of the school of early 17th-cent. English poets, including John Donne, whose verse is characterized by subtle and fanciful images —**met′a·phys′i·cal·ly** *adv.*
met·a·phys·ics (met′ə fiz′iks) *n.pl.* [with sing. v.] [< ML. < Gr. *(ta) meta (ta) physika*, lit., (that) after (the) *Physics* (in Aristotle's works)] 1. the branch of philosophy that deals with first principles and seeks to explain the nature of being and of the origin and structure of the world 2. speculative philosophy in general —**met′a·phy·si′cian** (-fə zish′ən) *n.*
met·a·sta·ble (-stā′b'l) *adj.* having a state of apparent equilibrium although capable of changing to a more stable state
me·tas·ta·sis (mə tas′tə sis) *n., pl.* **-ses** (-sēz) [ModL. < LL. < Gr. < *meta*, after + *histanai*, to place] the spread of disease from one part of the body to another unrelated to it, as of cancer cells by way of the bloodstream —**met·a·stat·ic** (met′ə stat′ik) *adj.* —**met′a·stat′i·cal·ly** *adv.*
me·tas·ta·size (-sīz′) *vi.* **-sized′, -siz′ing** to spread to other parts of the body by metastasis
met·a·tar·sus (met′ə tär′səs) *n., pl.* **-tar·si** (-sī) [ModL. < Gr. *meta-*, after + *tarsus*, sole of the foot] 1. the part of the human foot consisting of the five bones between the ankle and toes 2. the part of a land vertebrate's hind limb, between the tarsus and phalanges —**met′a·tar′sal** *adj., n.*
me·tath·e·sis (mə tath′ə sis) *n., pl.* **-ses** (-sēz) [LL. < Gr. < *meta*, over + *tithenai*, to place] transposition or interchange; specif., the transposition of letters or sounds in a word, as in *clasp* (from Middle English *clapse*) —**met·a·thet·ic** (met′ə thət′ik), **met′a·thet′i·cal** *adj.* —**met′-a·thet′i·cal·ly** *adv.*
met·a·zo·an (met′ə zō′ən) *n.* [ModL. *metazoa* see META- & -ZOA) + -AN] any of the very large zoological division made up of all animals whose bodies are composed of many cells arranged into definite organs —*adj.* of the metazoans
mete[1] (mēt) *vt.* **met′ed, met′ing** [OE. *metan*] 1. to allot; distribute; apportion (usually with *out*) 2. [Archaic] to measure
mete[2] (mēt) *n.* [OFr. < L. *meta*] a boundary
me·tem·psy·cho·sis (mi temp′si kō′sis, -tem′-; met′əm sī-) *n., pl.* **-ses** (-sēz) [LL. < Gr. < *meta*, over + *empsychoun*, to put a soul into < *en*, in + *psyche*, soul] the supposed passing of the soul at death into another body; transmigration
me·te·or (mēt′ē ər) *n.* [< ML. < Gr. < *meteōra*, things in the air < *meta*, beyond + *eōra*, a hovering in the air] 1. the flash and streak of light, the ionized trail, etc. occurring when a meteoroid is heated by its entry into the earth's atmosphere: popularly called *shooting* (or *falling*) *star* 2. loosely, a meteoroid or meteorite
me·te·or·ic (mēt′ē ôr′ik) *adj.* 1. atmospheric or meteorological 2. of a meteor or meteors 3. like a meteor; momentarily brilliant, flashing, or swift —**me′te·or′i·cal·ly** *adv.*
me·te·or·ite (mēt′ē ə rīt′) *n.* that part of a relatively large meteoroid that passes through the atmosphere and falls to earth as a mass of metal or stone —**me′te·or·it′ic** (-rit′ik) *adj.*
me·te·or·oid (mēt′ē ə roid′) *n.* any of the many small, solid bodies travelling through outer space, which are seen as meteors when they enter the earth's atmosphere —**me′-te·or·oi′dal** *adj.*
me·te·or·o·log·i·cal (mēt′ē ər ə loj′i k'l) *adj.* 1. of weather or climate 2. of meteorology: also **me′te·or·o·log′ic** —**me′-te·or·o·log′i·cal·ly** *adv.*
Meteorological Office a department of the Civil Service responsible for collecting meteorological data from all over the world, and for providing weather forecasts
me·te·or·ol·o·gy (mēt′ē ə rol′ə jē) *n.* [< Gr.: see METEOR & -LOGY] the science of the atmosphere and its phenomena; study of weather and climate —**me′te·or·ol′o·gist** *n.*
meteor shower the effect produced by a group of meteoroids entering the earth's atmosphere in parallel paths
me·ter[1] (mē′tər) *n.* chiefly *U.S. sp.* of METRE
me·ter[2] (mēt′ər) *n.* 1. [< METE[1] + -ER] a person who measures 2. [< ff.] *a)* an instrument or apparatus for measuring and recording the quantity or rate of flow of gas, electricity, water, etc. passing through it *b) same as* PARKING METER —*vt.* to measure or record with a meter
-me·ter (mēt′ər, mi tər) [Fr. *-mètre* or ModL. *-metrum*, both < Gr. *metron*, a measure] a suffix meaning: 1. a device for measuring [*barometer*] 2. having (a specified number of) metrical feet [*pentameter*]
me·ter·age (mēt′ər ij) *n.* measurement as by a meter, or the charge for this
meter maid [Colloq.] a female traffic warden responsible for reporting parking violations
Meth. Methodist
meth·a·done (meth′ə dōn′) *n.* [an acronym of the chemical name] a synthetic narcotic drug sometimes used in the treatment of hard-drug addicts
meth·ane (meth′ān) *n.* [METH(YL) + -ANE] a colourless, odourless, flammable gas, CH_4, present in marsh gas, firedamp, and natural gas: it is used as a fuel, etc.
methane series a series of saturated hydrocarbons having the general formula C_nH_{2n+2}: methane is the first member
meth·a·nol (meth′ə nol′) *n.* [METHAN(E) + -OL[1]] a colourless, flammable, poisonous liquid, CH_3OH, obtained by the destructive distillation of wood and used as a fuel, solvent, and antifreeze, and in the making of paints, etc.
me·thinks (mi thiŋks′) *v.impersonal* *pt.* **me·thought′** [< OE. < *me*, to me + *thyncth*, it seems < *thyncan*, to seem] [Archaic] it seems to me
meth·od (meth′əd) *n.* [< Fr. < L. < Gr. *methodos*, pursuit < *meta*, after + *hodos*, a way] 1. a way of doing anything; mode; process; esp., a regular, orderly procedure or way of teaching, investigating, etc. 2. a system in doing things or handling ideas 3. regular, orderly arrangement
me·thod·i·cal (mə thod′i k'l) *adj.* characterized by method; orderly; systematic: also **me·thod′ic** —**me·thod′i·cal·ly** *adv.* —**me·thod′i·cal·ness** *n.*
Meth·od·ism (meth′ə diz′m) *n.* 1. the doctrines, organization, etc. of the Methodists 2. [m-] excessive adherence to systematic procedure
Meth·od·ist (-dist) *n.* a member of a Protestant Christian denomination that developed from the evangelistic teachings of John and Charles Wesley —*adj.* of or characteristic of the Methodists or Methodism: also **Meth′-od·is′tic**
meth·od·ize (-dīz′) *vt.* **-ized′, -iz′ing** to make methodical; systematize —**meth′od·iz′er** *n.*
meth·od·ol·o·gy (meth′ə dol′ə jē) *n., pl.* **-gies** [ModL.: see METHOD & -LOGY] 1. the science of method, or orderly arrangement 2. a system of methods, as in any particular science —**meth′od·o·log′i·cal** (-də loj′i k'l) *adj.* —**meth′-od·o·log′i·cal·ly** *adv.* —**meth′od·ol′o·gist** *n.*
me·thought (mi thôt′) *pt.* of METHINKS
meths (meths) *n.* [Colloq.] *clipped form of* METHYLATED SPIRITS
meth·yl (meth′əl) *n.* [< Fr., ult. < Gr. *methy*, wine + *hylē*, wood] the monovalent hydrocarbon radical CH_3, normally existing only in combination
methyl alcohol *same as* METHANOL
meth·yl·ate (meth′ə lāt′) *vt.* **-at′ed, -at′ing** to mix with methanol, often in order to make the resulting mixture undrinkable
methylated spirits ethyl alcohol made unfit to drink by the addition of methanol
methyl chloride a gas, CH_3Cl, which when compressed becomes a sweet, transparent liquid: it is used as a refrigerant and local anaesthetic
meth·yl·ene (meth′ə lēn′) *n.* [Fr. *méthylène*, < Gr. *methy*, wine + *hylē*, wood] the bivalent hydrocarbon radical CH_2, normally existing only in combination
me·tic·u·lous (mə tik′yoo ləs) *adj.* [L. *meticulosus*, fearful < *metus*, fear] extremely or excessively careful about details; scrupulous or finicky —**me·tic′u·lous·ly** *adv.* —**me·tic′-u·lous·ness, me·tic′u·los′i·ty** (-los′ə tē) *n.*

mé·tier (mā tyā′) *n.* [Fr. < OFr. *mestier* < L.: see MINISTRY] a trade, profession, or occupation

Me·ton·ic cycle (mə ton′ik) [after *Meton*, Athenian astronomer (5th cent. B.C.)] a cycle of almost 19 years after which time the phases of the moon recur on the same day of the month

me·ton·y·my (mə ton′ə mē) *n.,* *pl.* **-mies** [< LL. < Gr. < *meta*, change + *onyma*, name] use of the name of one thing for that of another associated with it (Ex.: "the press" for "journalists") —**met·o·nym·ic** (met′ə nim′ik), **met′·o·nym′i·cal** *adj.*

me·tre (mē′tər) *n.* [< OFr. < L. < Gr. *metron*, measure] 1. *a)* rhythm in verse; measured, patterned arrangement of syllables, primarily according to stress and length *b)* the specific rhythmic pattern of a stanza 2. rhythm in music 3. the SI unit of length, defined as 1 650 763·73 wavelengths in-vacuo of the orange-red radiation of Krypton-86

-me·tre (mēt′ər, mi tər) [Fr. *-mètre* see -METER] 1. (a specified number of) metres [*kilometre*] 2. (a specified fraction of) a metre [*centimetre*]

me·tre-kil·o·gramme-sec·ond (-kil′ə gram sek′ənd) *adj.* designating or of a system of measurement in which the metre, kilogramme, and second are used as the units of length, mass, and time, respectively

met·ric (met′rik) *adj.* 1. *same as* METRICAL 2. *a)* of the metre (unit of length) *b)* designating or of the system of measurement based on the metre: see METRIC SYSTEM —**go metric** [Colloq.] to change to the metric system of measurement

met·ri·cal (-ri k'l) *adj.* 1. of or composed in metre or verse 2. of, involving, or used in measurement; metric —**met′·ri·cal·ly** *adv.*

met·ri·ca·tion (met′rə kā′shən) *n.* the process of changing over to the metric system of weights and measures —**met′·ri·cate′** *vt.* **-cat′ed, -cat′ing** *adj.*

met·ri·cize (met′rə sīz′) *vt.* **-cized′, -ciz′ing** to change into the metric system of weights and measures

metric system a decimal system of weights and measures in which the gramme (.0022046 pound), the metre (39.37 inches), and the litre (61.025 cubic inches) are the basic units of weight, length, and capacity, respectively

metric ton *same as* TONNE

met·ro·nome (met′rə nōm′) *n.* [< Gr. *metron*, measure + *nomos*, law] a clockwork device with an inverted pendulum that beats time, as in setting a musical tempo, at a rate determined by the position of a sliding weight on the pendulum —**met′ro·nom′ic** (-nom′ik) *adj.*

me·trop·o·lis (mə trop′əl is) *n.,* *pl.* **-lis·es** [L. < Gr. < *mētēr*, a mother + *polis*, a city] 1. the main city, often the capital, of a country, state, etc., esp. [M-] London 2. any large city or centre of population, culture, etc. 3. the main diocese of an ecclesiastical province

METRONOME

met·ro·pol·i·tan (met′rə pol′ə t'n) *adj.* 1. of or constituting a metropolis (senses 1 & 2) 2. designating or of a metropolitan (sense 2) or metropolis (sense 3) 3. designating or of a population area consisting of a central city and smaller surrounding communities —*n.* 1. a person who lives in and is wise in the ways of a metropolis (senses 1 & 2) 2. *a)* an archbishop having authority over the bishops of a church province *b)* a bishop just below a Patriarch in the Orthodox Eastern Church

metropolitan magistrate a London magistrate, who receives a salary and is a qualified barrister

-me·try (mə trē) [< Gr. < *metron*, measure] *a terminal combining form meaning* the process, art, or science of measuring [*geometry*]

met·tle (met′'l) *n.* [var. of METAL, used figuratively] quality of character; spirit; courage; ardour —**on one's mettle** prepared to do one's best

met·tle·some (met′'l səm) *adj.* full of mettle; spirited; ardent, brave, etc.: also **met′tled**

mev, MeV (mev) *n.,* *pl.* **mev, MeV** [M(ILLION) E (ELECTRON)V(OLTS)] a unit of energy equal to one million (10⁶) electron-volts

mew¹ (myōō) *n.* [< OFr. < *muer* < L. *mutare*, to change] a cage, as for hawks while moulting See also MEWS —*vt.* to confine in or as in a cage

mew² (myōō) *n.* [echoic] the characteristic vocal sound made by a cat —*vi.* to make this sound

mew³ (myōō) *n.* [OE. mæw] a sea gull

mewl (myōōl) *vi.* [freq. of MEW²] to cry weakly, like a baby; whimper or whine —**mewl′er** *n.*

mews (myōōz) *n.pl.* [*usually with sing. v.*] [< MEW¹] 1. stables or carriage houses, now often converted into dwellings, as along an alley 2. such an alley

Mex. 1. Mexican 2. Mexico

Mex·i·can (mek′si kən) *adj.* of Mexico, its people, their dialect of Spanish, or their culture —*n.* 1. a native or inhabitant of Mexico 2. Nahuatl

me·zu·za (mə zoo′zə) *n.,* *pl.* **-zot** (-zōt), **-zas** [Heb. *mēzūzāh*, doorpost] *Judaism* a small scroll inscribed with Biblical verses (Deuteronomy 6:4-9 & 11:13-21) and attached in a case to the doorpost of the home: also sp. **me·zu′zah**

mez·za·nine (mez′ə nēn′, mez′ə nēn′) *n.* [Fr. < It. < *mezzano*, middle, ult. < L. *medius*] a low-ceilinged storey between two main storeys in a building, usually in the form of a balcony projecting partly over the main floor: also **mezzanine floor**

mez·zo (met′sō, med′zō, mez′ō) *adj.* [It. < L. *medius*, middle] *Music* medium; moderate; half —*adv.* *Music* moderately; somewhat [*mezzo forte, mezzo piano*] —*n.,* *pl.* **-zos** *clipped form of*: 1. MEZZO-SOPRANO 2. MEZZOTINT

mez·zo-so·pra·no (-sə prä′nō) *n.,* *pl.* **-nos, -ni** (-nē) [It.] 1. a woman's voice or part between soprano and contralto 2. a singer with such a voice —*adj.* of or for a mezzo-soprano

mez·zo·tint (-tint′) *n.* [< It.: see MEZZO & TINT] 1. a method of engraving on a copper or steel plate by scraping or polishing parts of a roughened surface to produce impressions of light and shade 2. an engraving so produced —*vt.* to engrave by this method

MF, M.F., mf, m.f. medium frequency

mf *Music* mezzo forte

mfd. manufactured

mfg. manufacturing

M.F.H. Master of Foxhounds

MFr. Middle French

mfr. *pl.* **mfrs.** manufacturer

Mg *Chem.* magnesium

mg, mg. milligramme; milligrammes

MGr. Medieval (or Middle) Greek

Mgr. 1. Manager 2. Monseigneur 3. Monsignor

MHG. Middle High German

mho (mō) *n.* [OHM spelt backwards] [Obs.] *same as* SIEMENS

MHz, Mhz megahertz

mi (mē) *n.* [ML.: see GAMUT] *Music* a syllable representing the third tone of the diatonic scale

M.I. Military Intelligence

mi. mile(s)

M.I.5 Military Intelligence, section 5, dealing with counterintelligence

M.I.6 Military Intelligence, section 6, dealing with intelligence and espionage

mi·aow, mi·aou (mē ou′, myou) *n., vi.* *same as* MEOW

mi·as·ma (mī az′mə) *n.,* *pl.* **-mas, -ma·ta** (-mə tə) [ModL. < Gr. < *miainein*, to pollute] 1. a vapour rising as from marshes or decomposing organic matter, formerly supposed to poison the air 2. an unwholesome atmosphere, influence, etc. —**mi·as′mal, mi′as·mat′ic** (-mat′ik), **mi·as′mic** *adj.*

Mic. Micah

mi·ca (mī′kə) *n.* [ModL. < L., a crumb, infl. by *micare*, to shine] any of a group of minerals that crystallize in thin, somewhat flexible, easily separated layers, resistant to heat and electricity: a transparent form is often called ISINGLASS —**mi·ca·ceous** (mī kā′shəs) *adj.*

mice (mīs) *n.* *pl. of* MOUSE

M.I.C.E. Member of the Institution of Civil Engineers

Mich. Michaelmas

Mich·ael·mas (mik′'l məs) *n.* [see -MAS] the feast of the archangel Michael, celebrated on September 29: also **Michaelmas Day**

Michaelmas daisy any of various asters, wild or cultivated, that bloom in the autumn

Michaelmas term 1. the autumn term at Oxford and Cambridge Universities and some other educational establishments 2. the law term of the High Court beginning just after Michaelmas

M.I.Ch.E. Member of the Institution of Chemical Engineers

mick·ey (mik′ē) *n.* [prob < *Mickey*, nickname for masculine name *Michael*, taken as typical Irish name] 1. [Slang] an Irishman: also **mick** 2. [Slang] spirit; pride: chiefly in the following phrases —**take the mickey** to make fun; mock —**take the mickey out of** to deflate (a person)

Mick·ey Finn (mik′ē fin′) [*also* m- f-] [Slang] an alcoholic drink to which a powerful narcotic or purgative has been secretly added: often shortened to **Mick′ey, mick′-ey** *n.,* *pl.* **-eys**

mick·le (mik′'l) *adj., adv., n.* [OE. *micel*] [Archaic or Scot.] much

mi·cra (mī′krə) *n.* *alt. pl. of* MICRON

mi·cro- [< Gr. < *mikros*, small] *a combining form meaning:* 1. little; small; minute [*microfilm*] 2. enlarging or amplifying [*microscope, microphone*] 3. microscopic [*microchemistry*] 4. one millionth part of (a specified unit) [*microgramme*]

mi·crobe (mī′krōb) *n.* [Fr. < Gr. *mikros*, small + *bios*, life] a microscopic organism; esp., any of the bacteria that cause disease; germ —**mi·cro′bic, mi·cro′bi·al, mi·cro′bi·an** *adj.*

mi·cro·bi·ol·o·gy (mī′krō bī ol′ə jē) *n.* the branch of biology that deals with microorganisms —**mi′cro·bi·o·log′-i·cal** (-ə loj′ə k′l), **mi′cro·bi′o·log′ic** *adj.* —**mi′cro·bi·ol′-o·gist** *n.*

mi·cro·ceph·a·ly (mī′krə sef′′l ē) *n.* [MICRO- + CEPHAL(O)- + -Yᶟ] a condition in which the head or cranial capacity is abnormally small —**mi′cro·ceph′a·lous, mi′cro·ce·phal′ic** (-sə fal′ik) *adj.*

mi·cro·chem·is·try (-kem′is trē) *n.* the chemistry of microscopic or submicroscopic quantities or objects

mi·cro·cop·y (mī′krə kop′ē) *n., pl.* **-cop′ies** a copy of printed matter, etc. produced in very greatly reduced size, as by microfilming

mi·cro·cosm (mī′krə koz′m) *n.* a little world; miniature universe; specif., man, a community, etc. regarded as a miniature of the world —**mi′cro·cos′mic** *adj.* —**mi′cro·cos′-mi·cal·ly** *adv.*

mi·cro·dot (-dot′) *n.* [MICRO- + DOT¹] a copy, as of written or printed matter, reduced by microphotography to the size of a pinhead, used in espionage, etc.

mi·cro·e·lec·tron·ics (mī′krō i′lek tron′iks) *n.pl.* (with *sing. v.*) [MICRO- + ELECTRONICS] the science dealing with the theory, design, and applications of small circuits (**microcircuits**) used in computers, etc.

mi·cro·fiche (mī′krə fēsh′) *n.* [Fr. < *micro-*, MICRO- + *fiche*, a small card] a small sheet of microfilm, containing a number of pages of microcopy

mi·cro·film (-film′) *n.* film on which documents, printed pages, etc. are photographed in a reduced size for convenience in storage and use —*vt., vi.* to photograph on microfilm

mi·cro·gramme (-gram′) *n.* one millionth of a gramme

mi·cro·groove (-grōōv′) *n.* a very narrow needle groove, as for a long-playing gramophone record

mi·crom·e·ter (mī krom′ə tər) *n.* [< Fr.: see MICRO- & -METER] 1. an instrument for measuring very small distances, angles, etc., used on a telescope or microscope 2. same as MICROMETER CALIPER

micrometer caliper (or **calipers**) calipers with a micrometer screw, for extremely accurate measurement

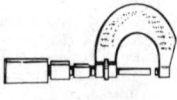

MICROMETER

micrometer screw a finely threaded screw of definite pitch, with a head graduated to show how much the screw has been moved in or out

mi·crom·e·try (-trē) *n.* measurement with micrometers

mi·cro·min·i·a·tur·ize (-chə rīz′) *vt.* **-ized′, -iz′ing** to provide with electronic equipment of extremely small size —**mi′cro·min′i·a·tur·za′tion** *n.*

mi·cron (mī′kron) *n., pl.* **-crons, -cra** (-krə) [ModL. < Gr. *mikros*, small] one millionth of a metre, or one thousandth of a millimetre

Mi·cro·ne·sian (mī′krə nē′zhən, -shən) *adj.* of Micronesia, its people, their language, etc. —*n.* 1. a native of Micronesia 2. any of the Malayo-Polynesian languages of Micronesia

mi·cro·or·gan·ism (mī′krō ôr′gə niz′m) *n.* any microscopic or ultramicroscopic animal or vegetable organism; esp., any of the bacteria, viruses, etc.

mi·cro·phone (mī′krə fōn′) *n.* [MICRO- + -PHONE] an instrument containing a device that converts the mechanical energy of sound waves into an electric signal, as for radio —**mi′cro·phon′ic** (-fon′ik) *adj.*

mi·cro·print (-print′) *n.* a photographic copy so greatly reduced that it can be read only through a magnifying device

mi·cro·scope (mī′krə skōp′) *n.* [< ModL.: see MICRO- & -SCOPE] an instrument consisting essentially of a lens or combination of lenses, for making very small objects, as microorganisms, look larger

mi·cro·scop·ic (mī′krə skop′ik) *adj.* 1. so small as to be invisible or obscure except through a microscope; minute 2. of or with a microscope 3. like or suggestive of a microscope Also **mi′cro·scop′i·cal** —**mi′cro·scop′i·cal·ly** *adv.*

mi·cros·co·py (mī kros′kə pē) *n.* the use of a microscope; investigation by means of a microscope —**mi·cros′co·pist** *n.*

mi·cro·struc·ture (mī′krō struk′chər) *n.* the structure as of a metal or alloy, seen under a microscope

mi·cro·wave (mī′krə wāv′) *adj.* designating or of the electromagnetic spectrum lying between the far infrared and some lower frequency limit, usually between 300 000 and 300 megahertz —*n.* any electromagnetic wave of such frequency

microwave oven an oven which cooks food very rapidly by use of microwaves

mic·tu·rate (mik′tyoo rāt′) *vi.* **-rat′ed, -rat′ing** [< L. pp. of *micturire* < *mingere*, to urinate] to urinate —**mic′tu·ri′-tion** (-rish′ən) *n.*

mid¹ (mid) *adj.* [OE. *midd*] 1. same as MIDDLE 2. *Phonet.* produced with the tongue in a position midway between high and low: said of some vowels, as (e) —*n.* [Archaic] the middle

mid² (mid) *prep.* [Poet.] amid: also **'mid**

mid- a combining form meaning middle or middle part of [*midbrain, midday*]

mid·air (-er′) *n.* any point in space, not in contact with the ground or other surface —*adj.* of a point not in contact with the earth [a *midair* collision of aircraft]

mid·brain (mid′brān′) *n.* the middle part of the brain

mid·day (mid′dā′) *n.* [OE. *middæg*] the middle part of the day; noon —*adj.* of midday

mid·den (mid′′n) *n.* [prob. < Scand.] 1. a dunghill or refuse heap 2. short for KITCHEN MIDDEN

mid·dle (mid′′l) *adj.* [OE. *middel*] 1. halfway between two given points, times, limits, etc.; also, equally distant from the ends, etc.; in the centre 2. in between; intermediate 3. [M-] *Geol.* designating a division, as of a period, between *Upper* and *Lower* 4. [M-] *Linguis.* designating a stage in language development intermediate between *Old* and *Modern* [*Middle* English] —*n.* 1. a point or part halfway between extremes; middle point, time, etc. 2. something intermediate 3. the middle part of the body; waist —*vt., vi.* **-dled, -dling** to put in the middle

middle age the time of life between youth and old age: now usually the years from about 40 to about 65 —**mid′-dle-aged′** *adj.*

Middle Ages the period of European history between ancient and modern times, 476 A.D.–c.1450 A.D.

middle-age spread a plumpness that often appears around the waist, usually during middle age

Middle America 1. Mexico, Central America, and, sometimes, the West Indies 2. the American middle class, esp. of the Middle West

mid·dle·brow (mid′′l brou′) *n.* [Colloq.] a person regarded as having conventional tastes and limited intellectual appreciation, esp. in art or music —*adj.* [Colloq.] of or for a middlebrow

middle C the musical note of the first leger line below the treble staff and the first above the bass staff

middle class the social class between the aristocracy or very wealthy and the lower working class —**mid′-dle-class′** *adj.*

middle course a course steered between two extremes; a mean

middle ear the eardrum and the adjacent cavity containing the hammer, the anvil, and the stirrup

Middle East 1. area from Afghanistan to Egypt, including Arabia, Cyprus, & Asiatic Turkey 2. sometimes, the Near East, excluding the Balkans —**Middle Eastern**

Middle English the English language as written and spoken between c.1100 and c.1500

Middle French the French language as written and spoken between c. 1300 and c. 1500

middle game *Chess* the portion of the game played after the opening and before the endgame

Middle Greek same as MEDIEVAL GREEK

Middle High German the High German language as written and spoken between c.1100 and c.1500

Middle Irish the Irish language as written and spoken between c. 1000 and c. 1400

Middle Latin same as MEDIEVAL LATIN

Middle Low German the Low German language as written and spoken between c.1100 and c.1500

mid·dle·man (mid′′l man′) *n., pl.* **-men′** (-men′) 1. a trader who buys commodities from the producer and sells them to the retailer or, sometimes, directly to the consumer 2. a go-between

mid·dle·most (-mōst′) *adj.* same as MIDMOST

middle name 1. the name between a christian name and a surname 2. the characteristic, peculiarity, or character of a person [modesty was his *middle name*]

mid·dle-of-the-road (-əv thə rōd′) *adj.* avoiding extremes, esp. of the political left or right

middle passage the passage from West Africa to the West Indies or America that was the route of the former slave trade

middle school a school between primary school and high school for children between 10 and 14

mid·dle·weight (-wāt′) *see* BOXING AND WRESTLING WEIGHTS, table

Middle West region of the NC U.S. between the Rocky Mountains & the E border of Ohio, north of the Ohio River & the S borders of Kansas & Missouri —**Middle Western**

mid·dling (mid′liŋ) *adj.* of middle size, quality, grade, state, etc.; medium —*adv.* [Colloq.] moderately; somewhat —*n.* 1. [*pl.*] products of medium quality, size, or price 2. [*pl.*] particles of coarsely ground grain, often mixed with bran —**fair to middling** [Colloq.] moderately good or well

Middx. Middlesex

mid·dy (mid′ē) *n., pl.* **-dies** 1. [Colloq.] a midshipman 2. [Aust. Colloq.] a half-pint glass of beer

mid·field (mid′fēld) *n. Soccer* the area of the pitch between the penalty areas —*adj.* of the midfield [he was a *midfield* player]

midge (mij) *n.* [OE. *mycg*] 1. a small, two-winged, gnatlike insect 2. a very small person

midg·et (mij′it) *n.* 1. a very small person 2. anything very small of its kind —*adj.* very small of its kind; miniature

mid heavyweight *see* BOXING AND WRESTLING WEIGHTS, table

mid·i (mid′ē) *n.* [< MID, after MINI-] [Colloq.] a midiskirt or midicoat —*adj.* of clothing reaching to below the knee or midcalf

mid·i·ron (mid′ī′ərn) *n.* a golf club with a metal head, used for fairway shots of medium distance: now usually called *number 2 iron*

mid·land (mid′lənd) *n.* 1. the middle region of a country; interior 2. [M-] an English dialect of the Midlands —*adj.* 1. of or in the midland; inland 2. [M-] of the Midlands —**the Midlands** region in WC England, around Birmingham

mid·most (mid′mōst′) *adj.* exactly in the middle, or nearest the middle —*adv.* in the middle or midst —*prep.* in the middle or midst of —*n.* the middle part

mid·night (-nīt′) *n.* the middle of the night; twelve o'clock at night —*adj.* 1. of or at midnight 2. like midnight; very dark —**burn the midnight oil** to study or work very late at night

midnight sun the sun visible at midnight in the arctic or antarctic regions during the summer

mid-off *n.* Cricket the fielding position close to and on the bowler's left, when the batsman is right-handed

mid-on *n.* Cricket the fielding position close to and on the bowler's right, when the batsman is right-handed

mid·point (-point′) *n.* a point at or close to the middle or centre, or equally distant from the ends

mid·rib (-rib′) *n.* the central vein of a leaf

mid·riff (-rif) *n.* [< OE. < *midd*, MID¹ + *hrif*, belly] 1. *same as* DIAPHRAGM (sense 1) 2. the middle part of the torso, between the abdomen and the chest —*adj.* designating or of a garment that bares this part

mid·ship (-ship′) *adj.* of the middle of a ship

mid·ship·man (-ship′mən) *n.*, *pl.* **-men** *see* MILITARY RANKS, table

mid·ships (-ships′) *adv.* *same as* AMIDSHIPS

midst¹ (midst, mitst) *n.* the middle; central part: now mainly in phrases as below —**in our** (or **your, their**) **midst** among us (or you, them) —**in the midst of** 1. in the middle of 2. during

midst² (midst, mitst) *prep.* [Poet.] in the midst of; amidst; amid: also **'midst**

mid·stream (mid′strēm′) *n.* the middle of a stream

mid·sum·mer (-sum′ər) *n.* 1. the middle of summer 2. popularly, the time of the summer solstice, about June 21 —*adj.* of, in, or like midsummer

Midsummer's Day June 24, feast of St. John the Baptist

mid·term (-tʉrm′) *adj.* occurring in the middle of the term

mid-Vic·to·ri·an (mid′vik tôr′ē ən) *adj.* 1. of or characteristic of the middle part of Queen Victoria's reign in Great Britain (c.1850–1890) 2. old-fashioned, prudish, morally strict, etc. —*n.* 1. a person who lived during this period 2. a person of mid-Victorian ideas, manners, etc.

mid·way (mid′wā′; *also, for adj. & adv.*,-wā′) *n.* orig., a middle way or course —*adj., adv.* in the middle

mid·week (-wēk′) *n., adj.* (in) the middle of the week —**mid′week′ly** *adj., adv.*

mid·wick·et (-wik′it) *n.* Cricket the fielding position opposite the middle of the wicket and usually near the boundary

mid·wife (mid′wīf′) *n., pl.* **-wives′** (-wīvz′) [OE. *mid*, with + *wif*, woman] a woman whose work is helping women in childbirth

mid·wif·er·y (mid′wif′ə rē) *n.* the work of a midwife

mid·win·ter (-win′tər) *n.* 1. the middle of the winter 2. popularly, the time of the winter solstice, about December 22 —*adj.* of, in, or like midwinter

mid·year (-yir′) *adj.* occurring in the middle of the (calendar or academic) year

M.I.E.E. Member of the Institution of Electrical Engineers

mien (mēn) *n.* [< DEMEAN², but altered after Fr. *mine*, look, air] 1. a way of carrying and conducting oneself; manner 2. a way of looking; appearance

miff (mif) *n.* [prob. echoic of a sound of disgust] [Colloq.] a trivial quarrel or fit of the sulks; tiff or huff —*vt., vi.* [Colloq.] to offend or take offence

might¹ (mīt) *v.* [OE. *mihte*] 1. *pt. of* MAY 2. an auxiliary with present or future sense, generally equivalent to *may* [*it might rain*]

might² (mīt) *n.* [OE. *miht*] 1. great or superior strength, power, force, or vigour 2. strength or power of any degree

might-have-been (mīt′hav′bēn) *n.* a past possibility, esp. a person who might have achieved more in his field or profession

might·y (-ē) *adj.* [OE. *mihtig*] **might′i·er, might′i·est** 1. having might; powerful; strong 2. remarkably large, extensive, etc.; great —*adv.* [Colloq.] very; extremely —**might′i·ly** *adv.* —**might′i·ness** *n.*

mi·gnon (min′yon; Fr. mē nyōn′) *adj.* [Fr.] small, delicately formed, and pretty —**mi·gnonne** (min′yən; Fr. mē nyōn′) *adj.fem.*

mi·gnon·ette (min′yə net′) *n.* [< Fr. dim. of *mignon*: see prec.] a plant bearing spikes of small greenish, whitish, or reddish flowers

mi·graine (mī′grān, mē′-) *n.* [Fr. < OFr. < LL. *hemicrania* < Gr. < *hēmi-*, half + *kranion*, skull] a type of intense, periodically returning headache, usually limited to one side of the head —**mi·grain′ous** *adj.*

mi·grant (mī′grənt) *adj.* migrating; migratory —*n.* a person, bird, or animal that migrates; specif., a farm labourer who moves from place to place to harvest seasonal crops

mi·grate (mī grāt′) *vi.* **-grat′ed, -grat′ing** [< L. pp. of *migrare*, to migrate] 1. to move from one place to another, esp. to another country 2. to move from one region to another with the change in seasons, as many birds 3. to move from place to place to harvest seasonal crops —**mi·gra′tor** *n.*

mi·gra·tion (mī grā′shən) *n.* 1. a migrating 2. a group of people or birds, fishes, etc. migrating together 3. Chem. a) the shifting of position of one or more atoms within a molecule b) the movement of ions toward an electrode —**mi·gra′tion·al** *adj.*

mi·gra·to·ry (mī′grə tər ē, mī grā′tər ē) *adj.* 1. migrating; characterized by migration 2. of migration 3. roving; wandering

mih·rab (mē′rab) *n.* [Ar. *michrab*] a niche in that wall of a mosque which faces towards Mecca

mi·ka·do (mi kä′dō) *n., pl.* **-dos** [Jap. < *mi*, exalted + *kado*, gate] [*often* M-] the emperor of Japan: title no longer used

mike¹ (mīk) *n.* [Colloq.] a microphone

mike² (mīk) *vi.* [< OFr. *muchier*, to skulk] to shirk hard work; to malinger —*n.* idling

mike³ (mīk) *n.* a var. for MICKEY

mil (mil) *n.* [< L. *mille*, thousand] 1. a unit of length, equal to 1/1000 inch, used in measuring the diameter of wire 2. a unit of angle measurement for artillery fire, missile launching, etc., equal to 1/6400 of the circumference of a circle 3. *see* MONETARY UNITS, table (Cyprus)

mil. 1. military 2. militia

mi·la·dy, mi·la·di (mi lā′dē) *n.* [Fr. < E. *my lady*] an English noblewoman or gentlewoman

mil·age (mīl′ij) *n.* alt. sp. of MILEAGE

milch (milch) *adj.* [OE. *-milce*] giving milk; kept for milking [*milch cows*]

mild (mīld) *adj.* [OE. *milde*] 1. a) gentle or kind in disposition, action, or effect; not severe, harsh, etc. b) not extreme; moderate [a *mild* winter] 2. having a soft, pleasant flavour; not strong, bitter, etc.: said of tobacco, cheese, etc. —*n.* mild ale —**mild′ly** *adv.* —**mild′ness** *n.*

mild and bitter a mixture of mild ale and bitter ale, usually half-and-half

mil·dew (mil′dyo͞o′) *n.* [OE. *meledeaw*, lit., honeydew] 1. a fungus that attacks various plants or appears on damp cloth, paper, etc. as a furry, whitish coating 2. any such coating or discolouration —*vt., vi.* to affect or become affected with mildew —**mil′dew′y** *adj.*

mild steel malleable steel with a low carbon content

mile (mīl) *n., pl.* **miles**, dial. **mile** [< OE. < L. *milia* (*passuum*), thousand (paces)] a unit of linear measure, equal to 1 760 yards (1 609.35 metres), used in English-speaking countries: in full, **statute mile**: *see* NAUTICAL MILE

mile·age (-ij) *n.* 1. an allowance for travelling expenses at a specified amount per mile 2. total number of miles travelled, etc. 3. rate per mile 4. the amount of use one can get from something

mile·post (-pōst′) *n.* a signpost showing the distance in miles from a specified place

mil·er (mīl′ər) *n.* one who competes in mile races

mile·stone (mīl′stōn′) *n.* 1. a stone or pillar set up to show the distance in miles from a specified place 2. a significant event in history, in one's career, etc.

mil·foil (mil′foil′) *n.* [ME. < OFr. < L. *millefolium*, thousand-leaved] *same as* YARROW

mi·lieu (mēl yoo′; Fr. mē lyơ′) *n., pl.* **-lieus′**; Fr. **-lieux′** (-lyơ′) [Fr. < OFr. < *mi*, middle + *lieu*, a place] environment; esp., social setting

mil·i·tant (mil′i tənt) *adj.* [< L. prp. of *militare*, to serve as a soldier < *miles* (gen. *militis*), a soldier] 1. fighting 2. ready and willing to fight; esp., vigorous in support of a cause —*n.* a militant person —**mil′i·tan·cy** *n.* —**mil′i·tant·ly** *adv.*

mil·i·ta·rism (mil′ə tər iz′m) *n.* 1. military spirit or its dominance in a nation 2. the policy of maintaining a strong military organization in aggressive preparedness for war —**mil′i·ta·rist** *n.* —**mil′i·ta·ris′tic** *adj.* —**mil′i·ta·ris′ti·cal·ly** *adv.*

mil·i·ta·rize (mil′i tə rīz′) *vt.* **-rized′, -riz′ing** 1. to equip and prepare for war 2. to fill with warlike spirit —**mil′i·ta·ri·za′tion** *n.*

MILITARY RANKS

NAVY	ARMY	MARINES	AIR FORCE

Commissioned

NAVY	ARMY	MARINES	AIR FORCE
			Marshal of the Royal Air Force
Admiral of the Fleet	Field Marshal		Air Chief Marshal
Admiral	General	General	Air Marshal
Vice-Admiral	Lieutenant-General	Lieutenant-General	Air Vice-Marshal
Rear-Admiral	Major-General	Major-General	Air Commodore
Commodore	Brigadier		Group Captain
Captain	Colonel	Colonel	Wing Commander
Commander	Lieutenant-Colonel	Lieutenant-Colonel	Squadron Leader
Lieutenant-Commander	Major	Major	Flight Lieutenant
Lieutenant	Captain	Captain	Flying Officer
Sub-Lieutenant ⎱	Lieutenant	Lieutenant ⎱	
Acting Sub-Lieutenant ⎰		Acting-Lieutenant ⎰	
Midshipman[1]		Second-Lieutenant	Pilot Officer[1]
	Second-Lieutenant		

Non-commissioned

NAVY	ARMY	MARINES	AIR FORCE
Fleet Chief Petty Officer	Warrant Officer	Regimental Sergeant Major	Warrant Officer
Chief Petty Officer	Staff-Sergeant	Colour Sergeant	Flight Sergeant ⎱ Chief Technician ⎰
Petty Officer	Sergeant	Sergeant (called Band Sergeant)	Sergeant
Leading Rating[2]	Corporal		Corporal
	Lance-Corporal	Corporal	
Able Rating ⎱	Private		Junior Technician
Ordinary Rating ⎰		Marine	Senior Aircraftman/woman ⎱ Leading Aircraftman/woman ⎰ Aircraftman
Junior Seaman (boys service)		Junior Marine (boys service)	

[1]Junior to Army Second Lieutenant
[2]Junior to Army Corporal

mil·i·tar·y (mil′ə tər ē) *adj.* [< Fr. < L. *militaris* < *miles*: see MILITANT] 1. of, characteristic of, for, fit for, or done by soldiers or the armed forces 2. of, for, or fit for war 3. of the army —**the military** the army or the armed forces; esp., army officers as an influential force —**mil′i·tar·i·ly** *adv.*

military attaché an army officer attached to his nation's embassy or legation in a foreign country

military band a band with brass, woodwind and percussion that is capable of marching while performing

military police soldiers assigned to carry on police duties for the army

mil·i·tate (mil′ə tāt′) *vi.* -**tat′ed**, -**tat′ing** [< L. pp. of *militare*: see MILITANT] to be directed (*against*); operate or work (*against* or, rarely, *for*): said of facts, actions, etc.

mi·li·tia (mə lish′ə) *n.* [L., soldiery < *miles*: see MILITANT] any army composed of civilians rather than professional soldiers, called up in time of emergency —**mi·li′tia·man** (-mən) *n., pl.* -**men**

milk (milk) *n.* [OE. *meolc*] 1. a white liquid secreted by the mammary glands of female mammals for suckling their young 2. cow's milk, etc. drunk by humans as a food or used to make butter, cheese, etc. 3. any liquid or juice like this [coconut *milk, milk* of magnesia] —*vt.* 1. to draw milk from the mammary glands of (a cow, etc.) 2. to extract (something) as if by milking [to *milk* venom from a snake] 3. to extract something from as if by milking [to *milk* a rich uncle for his money] —*vi.* 1. to give milk 2. to draw milk —**milk′er** *n.* —**milk′ing** *n.*

milk and honey being prosperous; easy circumstances

milk-and-wa·ter (-ən wôt′ər) *adj.* insipid; weak; wishy-washy; namby-pamby

milk chocolate eating chocolate that has been made with milk, having a creamy taste

milk float a shallow cart, usually powered by batteries and used for delivering milk

milk leg *a former term for* a painful swelling of the leg, caused by clotting in the femoral veins, as in childbirth

milk·maid (-mād′) *n.* a girl or woman who milks cows or works in a dairy; dairymaid

milk·man (-man′) *n., pl.* -**men′** (-men′) a man who sells or delivers milk

milk of magnesia a milky-white fluid, a suspension of magnesium hydroxide, Mg(OH)$_2$, in water, used as a laxative and antacid

milk pudding a hot or cold pudding made by boiling milk with rice, tapioca, sago, etc.

milk run [Slang] a routine mission, as of a bomber aircraft, not expected to be dangerous

milk·shake (-shāk′) *n.* a drink made of milk, flavouring, and, usually, ice cream, mixed until frothy

milk·sop (-sop′) *n.* an unmanly man or boy; sissy

milk sugar *same as* LACTOSE

milk tooth any of the temporary, first set of teeth in a child or the young of other mammals

milk·weed (-wēd′) *n.* any of a group of plants with a milky juice and pods which when ripe burst to release plumed seeds

milk·wort (-wurt′) *n.* [formerly supposed to increase milk in nursing mothers] any of various plants with showy flowers of various colours

milk·y (mil′kē) *adj.* **milk′i·er, milk′i·est** 1. like milk; esp., white as milk 2. of or containing milk 3. timid, meek, etc. —**milk′i·ness** *n.*

Milky Way a broad, faint band of light seen as an arch across the sky at night, created by billions of distant stars and masses of gas

mill (mil) *n.* [OE. *mylen*, ult. < LL. *molina* < L. *mola*, millstone] 1. *a)* a building with machinery for grinding corn into flour or meal *b)* a machine for grinding corn 2. a machine for grinding or crushing any solid material [a coffee *mill*] 3. *a)* any of various machines for cutting, stamping, shaping, etc. *b)* [Colloq.] a place where things are done, produced, issued, etc. in a rapid, mechanical way 4. a factory [a textile *mill*] 5. a raised edge, ridged surface, etc. made by milling 6. *Boxing* a match —*vt.* 1. to grind, work, form, etc. by, in, or as in a mill 2. to raise and ridge the edge of (a coin) 3. [Slang] to fight, esp. with the fists —*vi.* to move slowly in a circle, as cattle, or aimlessly, as a confused crowd (often with *around* or *about*) —**through the mill** [Colloq.] through a hard, painful, instructive experience —**milled** *adj.*

mill·dam (mil′dam′) *n.* a dam built across a stream to raise its level enough to provide water power for turning a mill wheel

mil·len·ni·um (mi len′ē əm) *n., pl.* -**ni·ums, -ni·a** (-ə) [ModL. < L. *mille*, thousand + *annus*, year] 1. a period of 1,000 years 2. [also M-] *Theol.* the period of a thousand years during which some believe Christ will reign on earth (with *the*): Rev. 20:1-5 3. a period of peace and happiness for everyone —**mil·len′ni·al** *adj.* —**mil·len′ni·al·ism** *n.*

mil·le·pede (mil′ə pēd′) *n.* *same as* MILLIPEDE

mil·le·pore (-pôr′) *n.* [< Fr. < *mille*, thousand + *pore* < L. *porus*, PORE^2] any of a genus of hydrozoans that form leaflike, porous masses of coral

mill·er (mil′ər) *n.* 1. a person who owns or operates a mill, esp. a corn mill 2. a tool used for milling

mill·er's-thumb (mil′ərz thum′) *n.* any of several small freshwater fishes with spiny fins and a broad, flat head

mil·les·i·mal (mi les′ə m'l) *adj.* [L. *millesimal*, thousandth] 1. thousandth 2. of or consisting of thousandths —*n.* a thousandth

mil·let (mil′it) *n.* see PLURAL, II, D, 3 [< MFr., dim. of *mil* < L. *milium*, millet] 1. a cereal grass whose small grain is used for food in Europe and Asia 2. the grain

MILKWEED PODS

mill hand a person employed in a factory or mill

mil·li- [< L. *mille*, thousand] *a combining form meaning* a 1000th part of [*millimetre*]

mil·li·am·me·ter (mil'ə am'mēt'ər) *n.* [MILLI- + AM(PERE) + -METER] an ammeter used to measure the current in milliamperes

mil·li·am·pere (mil'ē am'pir) *n.* one thousandth of an ampere

mil·liard (mil'yərd, -yärd') *n.* [Fr. < *million* (see MILLION) -*ard* (see -ARD), orig. "large million"] 1 000 millions

mil·lieme (mēl yem', mē-) *n.* [< Fr. < MFr. < *mille*, a thousand < L.] *see* MONETARY UNITS, table (Libya)

mil·li·gramme (mil'ə gram') *n.* one thousandth of a gramme

mil·li·li·tre (-lēt'ər) *n.* one thousandth of a litre

mil·lime (mil'ēm, -im) *n.* [Fr.: see MILLIEME] *see* MONETARY UNITS, table (Tunisia)

mil·li·me·tre (mil'ə mēt'ər) *n.* one thousandth of a metre

mil·li·mi·cron (mil'ə mī'kron) *n.,* *pl.* **-crons, -cra** one thousandth of a micron, or ten angstroms: a unit of length for measuring waves of light, etc.

mil·li·ner (mil'ə nər) *n.* [< *Milaner*, importer of dress wares from Milan] a person who designs, makes, trims, or sells women's hats

mil·li·ner·y (mil'ə nər ē) *n.* 1. women's hats, headdresses, etc. 2. the work or business of a milliner

mill·ing (mil'iŋ) *prp. of* MILL —*n.* 1. the process or business of grinding corn into flour or meal 2. the grinding, cutting, or processing of metal, cloth, etc. in a mill

milling machine a machine with a table on which material rests as it is fed against a rotating cutter (**milling cutter**) for cutting, grinding, shaping, etc.

mil·lion (mil'yən) *n.* [OFr. < It. *milione* < *mille*, thousand < L.] a thousand thousands; 1 000 000 —*adj.* 1. amounting to one million in number 2. very many —**mil'lionth** *adj., n.*

mil·lion·aire (mil'yə ner') *n.* [< Fr.] a person worth at least a million pounds, francs, dollars etc.

mil·li·pede (mil'ə pēd') *n.* [< L. < *mille*, thousand + *pes* (gen. *pedis*), a foot] a many-legged arthropod with two pairs of legs on most of its segments

mill·pond (mil'pond') *n.* a pond from which water flows for driving a mill wheel

mill·race (-rās') *n.* 1. the current of water that drives a mill wheel 2. the channel in which it runs

Mills bomb a type of high-explosive hand grenade

mill·stone (-stōn') *n.* 1. either of a pair of large, flat, round stones between which grain, etc. is ground 2. a heavy burden 3. something that grinds, pulverizes, or crushes

mill·stream (-strēm') *n.* water flowing in a millrace

mill wheel the wheel, usually a water wheel, that drives the machinery in a mill

mill·work (-wurk') *n.* work done in a mill —**mill'work'er** *n.*

mill·wright (-rīt') *n.* 1. one who designs, builds, or installs mills or their machinery 2. a worker who installs or repairs the machinery in a plant

milo·me·ter (mil'om'ə tər) *n.* an instrument used to determine how many miles a vehicle has travelled

mi·lord (mi lôrd') *n.* [Fr. < E. *my lord*] an English nobleman: used as a term of address

milt (milt) *n.* [prob. < Scand.] 1. the reproductive glands of male fishes, esp. when filled with germ cells and the milky fluid containing them 2. fish sperm —*adj.* breeding: said of male fishes —*vt.* to fertilize (fish roe) with milt —**milt'er** *n.*

mime (mīm) *n.* [< L. < Gr. *mimos*] 1. an ancient Greek or Roman farce, in which people and events were mimicked and burlesqued 2. the representation of an action, character, mood, etc. by means of gestures rather than words 3. an actor who performs in mimes —*vt.* mimed, **mim'ing** to mimic or act out as a mime —*vi.* to act as a mime, usually without speaking —**mim'er** *n.*

M.I.Mech.E. Member of the Institution of Mechanical Engineers

mim·e·o·graph (mim'ē ə gräf', mim'yə-) *n.* [a former trademark < Gr. *mimeomai*, I imitate + -GRAPH] a machine for making copies of written, drawn, or typewritten matter by means of a stencil —*vt.* 1. to make copies of on such a machine 2. to make (copies) on such a machine

mi·me·sis (mi mē'sis, mī-) *adj.* [Mod L. < Gr. *mimesis*, imitation] imitation; specif., a) *Art & Literature* representation as of human speech or behaviour b) *Biol.* same as MIMICRY

mi·met·ic (mi met'ik) *adj.* [< Gr. < *mimeisthai*, to imitate] 1. of or characterized by imitation; imitative 2. of or characterized by mimicry —**mi·met'i·cal·ly** *adv.*

mim·ic (mim'ik) *adj.* [< L. < Gr. < *mimos*, a mime] 1. imitative 2. of, or having the nature of, mimicry or imitation 3. make-believe; mock —*n.* a person or thing that imitates; esp., an actor skilled in mimicry —*vt.* **mim'icked, mim'ick·ing** 1. to imitate in speech or action, as in ridicule 2. to copy closely 3. to take on the appearance of —**mim'ick·er** *n.*

mim·ic·ry (-rē) *n.,* *pl.* **-ries** 1. the practice, art, instance, or way of mimicking 2. close resemblance, in colour, form, or behaviour, of one organism to another or to some object in its environment

M.I.Min.E. Member of the Institution of Mining Engineers

mi·mo·sa (mi mō'sə, -zə) *n.* [ModL. < L. *mimus*, mime] a tree, shrub, or herb of the legume family, growing in warm regions, with heads or spikes of small white, yellow, or pink flowers

Min. 1. Ministry 2. Minister

min. 1. mineralogy 2. minim(s) 3. minimum 4. mining 5. minor 6. minute(s)

mi·na (mī'nə) *n.* same as MYNA: also sp. **mi'nah**

min·a·ret (min'ə ret', min'ə ret') *n.* [Fr. < Turk. < Ar. *manārah*, lighthouse] a high, slender tower attached to a Moslem mosque, with balconies from which a muezzin calls the people to prayer

MINARET

min·a·to·ry (min'ə tar ē) *adj.* [< OFr. LL. < pp. of L. *minari*, to threaten] menacing; threatening

mince (mins) *vt.* **minced, minc'ing** [OFr. *mincier*, ult. < L. *minutus*, small] 1. to cut up (meat, etc.) into very small pieces 2. to express or do with affected elegance or daintiness 3. to lessen the force of; weaken [to *mince* no words] —*vi.* 1. to speak or act with affected elegance or daintiness 2. to walk with short steps or in an affected, dainty manner —*n.* minced meat —**not mince matters** to speak frankly —**minc'er** *n.*

mince·meat (-mēt') *n.* a mixture of chopped apples, spices, suet, raisins, etc. used as a pie filling —**make mincemeat of** to defeat or refute completely

mince pie a pie with a filling of mincemeat

minc·ing (min'siŋ) *adj.* 1. affectedly elegant or dainty 2. with short steps or affected daintiness [a *mincing* walk] —**minc'ing·ly** *adv.*

mind (mīnd) *n.* [OE. (ge)*mynd*] 1. memory or remembrance [to bring to *mind* a story] 2. what one thinks; opinion [speak your *mind*] 3. a) that which thinks, perceives, feels, etc.; the seat of consciousness b) the intellect c) attention d) the psyche (sense 2) 4. reason; sanity [to lose one's *mind*] 5. a person having intelligence [the great *minds* of today] 6. way, state, or direction of thinking and feeling [the reactionary *mind*] —*vt.* 1. to direct one's mind to; specif., a) to pay attention to; heed b) [Chiefly U.S.] to obey c) to take care of; look after [*mind* the baby] d) to be careful about [*mind* those rickety stairs] 2. a) to care about; feel concern about b) to object to; dislike [to *mind* the cold] 3. [Dial.] to remember 4. [Dial. or Archaic] to remind —*vi.* 1. to pay attention; give heed 2. to be obedient 3. to be careful 4. a) to care; feel concern b) to object —**bear (or keep) in mind** to remember —**be in one's right mind** to be sane —**be in two minds** to be undecided or irresolute —**blow one's mind** [Slang] 1. to be hallucinated as by drugs 2. to be amazed, confused, etc. —**call to mind** 1. to remember 2. to be a reminder of —**change one's mind** to change one's opinion or one's intention —**come to mind** 1. to occur to 2. to be remembered —**do you mind?** 1. do you object? 2. [Colloq.] please desist from doing that; stop that —**give (someone) a piece of one's mind** to criticize or rebuke sharply —**have a (good or great) mind to** to feel (strongly) inclined to —**have half a mind to** to be somewhat inclined to —**have in mind** 1. to remember 2. to think of 3. to intend; purpose —**know one's own mind** to know one's own real thoughts, desires, etc. —**make up one's mind** to form a definite opinion or decision —**meeting of (the) minds** an agreement —**mind out** 1. to be careful 2. to pay attention —**mind your backs** give way —**never mind** don't be concerned; it doesn't matter —**on one's mind** 1. occupying one's thoughts 2. worrying one —**out of one's mind** 1. insane 2. frantic (with worry, grief, etc.) —**put in mind** to remind —**set one's mind on** to be determinedly desirous of —**take one's mind off** to turn one's thoughts or attention from —**to one's mind** in one's opinion —**mind'er** *n.*

mind·ed (mīn'did) *adj.* 1. having a (specified kind of) mind [high-*minded*] 2. inclined; disposed

mind·ful (mīnd'fəl) *adj.* having in mind; aware or careful (*of*) [to be *mindful* of the danger] —**mind'ful·ly** *adv.* —**mind'ful·ness** *n.*

mind·less (-lis) *adj.* 1. showing little or no intelligence; thoughtless 2. taking no thought; heedless (*of*) —**mind'less·ly** *adv.* —**mind'less·ness** *n.*

mind reader one who professes to be able to perceive another's thoughts —**mind reading**

mind's eye the imagination

mine¹ (mīn) *pron.* [OE. *min*] that or those belonging to me: used without a following noun [this is *mine*, *mine* are better]: also used after *of* to indicate possession [a friend of

mine] —*possessive pronominal adj.* [Mainly Archaic] my: formerly used before a vowel or *h* [*mine* eyes, *mine* honour] now used after a noun in direct address [daughter *mine*]

mine² (mīn) *n.* [< MFr. < ? Celt.] **1.** a) a large excavation made in the earth, from which to extract metallic ores, coal, etc. b) a deposit of ore, coal, etc. **2.** any great source of supply [a *mine* of information] **3.** *Mil.* a) a tunnel dug under an enemy's trench, fort, etc., in which an explosive is placed to destroy the enemy fortifications b) an explosive charge in a container, buried in the ground for destroying enemy troops on land, or placed in the sea for destroying enemy ships —*vi.* **mined, min'ing** to dig a mine; specif., a) to dig ores, coal, etc. from the earth b) to dig or lay military mines —*vt.* **1.** a) to dig in (the earth) for ores, coal, etc. b) to dig (ores, coal, etc.) from the earth **2.** to take from (a source) **3.** to place explosive mines in or under **4.** to undermine slowly by secret methods

mine detector an electromagnetic device for locating the position of hidden explosive mines

mine field an area on land or in water where explosive mines have been set

mine·lay·er (mīn'lā'ər) *n.* a ship especially equipped to lay explosive mines in the water

min·er (-ər) *n.* a person whose work is digging coal, ore, etc. in a mine

min·er·al (min'ər əl, min'rəl) *n.* [OFr. < ML. neut. of *mineralis* < *minera*, a mine] **1.** an inorganic substance occurring naturally in the earth and having distinctive physical properties and a composition expressible by a chemical formula: sometimes applied to organic substances in the earth, such as coal **2.** an ore **3.** any substance that is neither vegetable nor animal **4.** any of certain elements, as iron, vital to animals and plants —*adj.* of, like, or containing a mineral or minerals

mineral. **1.** mineralogical **2.** mineralogy

min·er·al·ize (min'ər ə līz', min'rə-) *vt.* **-ized', -iz'ing** **1.** to convert (organic matter) into a mineral **2.** to impregnate (water, etc.) with minerals **3.** to convert (a metal) into an ore —**min'er·al·i·za'tion** *n.* —**min'er·al·iz'er** *n.*

min·er·al·o·gy (min'ə ral'ə jē) *n.* **1.** the scientific study of minerals **2.** *pl.* **-gies** a book about minerals —**min'·er·a·log'i·cal** (-ər ə loj'i k'l) *adj.* —**min'er·a·log'i·cal·ly** *adv.* —**min'er·al'o·gist** *n.*

mineral oil **1.** any oil found in the rock strata of the earth; specif., petroleum **2.** a colourless, tasteless oil derived from petroleum and used as a laxative

mineral water water naturally or artificially impregnated with mineral salts or gases

mineral wool a fibrous material made from rock and melted slag and used to insulate buildings

mi·ne·stro·ne (min'ə strō'nē) *n.* [It., ult. < L. *ministrare*, to serve] a thick vegetable soup containing vermicelli, barley, etc. in a meat broth

mine sweeper a ship for destroying enemy mines

mine worker a miner

Ming (miŋ) Chin. dynasty (1368–1644): period noted for scholarly achievements and artistic works, esp. porcelain

min·gle (miŋ'g'l) *vt.* **-gled, -gling** [< OE. *mengan*, to mix] to mix together; combine; blend —*vi.* **1.** to be or become mixed, blended, etc. **2.** to join or unite with others —**min'·gler** *n.*

min·gy (min'jē) *adj.* **-gi·er, -gi·est** [< MEAN² & STINGY¹] [Colloq.] mean and stingy; miserly

min·i- [< MINI(ATURE)] a combining form meaning: **1.** miniature, very small, very short [*miniskirt*] **2.** of less scope, extent, etc. than usual [*mini-crisis*]

min·i·a·ture (min'i chər) *n.* [< It. *miniatura* < ML. < L. *miniare*, to paint red < *minium*, red lead] **1.** a) a very small painting, esp. a portrait b) the art of making these **2.** a copy or model on a very small scale —*adj.* on or done on a very small scale; minute —**in miniature** on a small scale; greatly reduced —**min'i·a·tur·ist** *n.*

min·i·a·tur·ize (-īz') *vt.* **-ized', -iz'ing** to make in a small and compact form —**min'i·a·tur·i·za'tion** *n.*

min·im (min'im) *n.* [< L. *minimus*: see MINIMUM] **1.** the smallest liquid measure, 1/60 fluid dram, or about a drop **2.** a tiny portion **3.** *Music* a note having one half the duration of a semibreve: see NOTE, illus. —*adj.* smallest; tiniest

min·i·mize (min'ə mīz') *vt.* **-mized', -miz'ing** to reduce to or estimate at a minimum, or the least possible amount, degree, etc. —**min'i·mi·za'tion** *n.* —**min'i·miz'er** *n.*

min·i·mum (-məm) *n., pl.* **-mums, -ma** (-mə) [L., neut. of *minimus*, least < *minor*, minor] **1.** the smallest quantity, number, or degree possible or permissible **2.** the lowest degree or point reached or recorded —*adj.* **1.** smallest possible, permissible, or reached **2.** of, marking, or setting a minimum or minimums —**min'i·mal** *adj.* —**min'i·mal·ly** *adv.*

minimum wage a wage established by contract or by law as the lowest that may be paid to employees doing a specified type of work

min·ing (mī'niŋ) *n.* the act, process, or work of removing ores, coal, etc. from a mine

min·ion (min'yən) *n.* [Fr. *mignon*, darling] **1.** a favourite, esp. one who is a servile follower: term of contempt **2.** a subordinate official **3.** *Printing* a size of type, 7 point —*adj.* [Rare] dainty

minion of the law same as POLICEMAN

min·i·skirt (min'ē skurt') *n.* [MINI- + SKIRT] a very short skirt ending well above the knee

min·is·ter (min'is tər) *n.* [< OFr. < L. *minister*, a servant < *minor*, lesser] **1.** a person appointed to take charge of some governmental department **2.** a diplomatic officer sent to a foreign nation to represent his government **3.** anyone authorized to carry out the spiritual functions of a church, conduct worship, preach, etc.; **4.** any person or thing thought of as serving as the agent of some power, force, etc. [a *minister* of evil] —*vt.* [Archaic] to administer —*vi.* **1.** to serve as a clergyman in a church **2.** to give help (to)

min·is·te·ri·al (min'is tir'ē əl) *adj.* **1.** of a minister or (the) ministry **2.** subordinate or instrumental **3.** administrative; executive —**min'is·te'ri·al·ly** *adv.*

Minister of State **1.** a government minister other than a cabinet minister **2.** any government minister

Minister of the Crown a cabinet minister

minister plenipotentiary *pl.* **ministers plenipotentiary** a diplomatic representative with full authority to negotiate

min·is·trant (min'is trənt) *adj.* serving as a minister; ministering —*n.* a person who ministers, or serves

min·is·tra·tion (min'is trā'shən) *n.* **1.** the act of serving as a minister or clergyman **2.** help or care —**min'is·tra·tive** *adj.*

min·is·try (min'is trē) *n., pl.* **-tries** **1.** the act of ministering, or serving **2.** a) the office or function of a minister of religion b) such ministers collectively; clergy **3.** a) the department under a minister of government b) his term of office c) his headquarters d) such ministers collectively

min·i·ver (min'ə vər) *n.* [< OFr. < *menu*, small + *vair*, kind of fur < *varius*, variegated] a white fur used for trimming garments, esp. ceremonial robes, as of royalty

mink (miŋk) *n., pl.* **minks, mink:** see PLURAL, II, D, 1 [< Scand.] **1.** a slim, carnivorous mammal with partly webbed feet; esp., a dark-brown weasel living in water part of the time **2.** its valuable fur, soft, thick, and white to brown in colour

MINK
(43-70 cm long, including tail)

min·ne·sing·er (min'i siŋ'ər) *n.* [G. < MHG. *minne*, love + *senger*, singer] any of a number of German lyric poets and singers of the 12th to 14th cent.

min·now (min'ō) *n., pl.* **-nows, -now:** see PLURAL, II, D, 1 [< or akin to OE. *myne*] **1.** any of a large number of usually small freshwater fishes, used commonly as bait **2.** any very small fish

Mi·no·an (mi nō'ən) *adj.* [after *Minos* a king of Crete, in Greek Mythology] designating or of an advanced prehistoric culture that flourished in Crete from c. 2800-c. 1100 B.C.

mi·nor (mī'nər) *adj.* [L.] **1.** a) lesser in size, amount, or extent b) lesser in importance or rank **2.** under full legal age **3.** constituting the minority **4.** sad; melancholy **5.** *Music* a) designating an interval smaller than the corresponding major by a semitone b) characterized by minor intervals, scales, etc. c) based on the scale pattern of the minor mode: see MINOR SCALE —*vi.* [U.S.] *Educ.* to pursue a secondary specialization [to *minor* in French] —*n.* **1.** a person under full legal age **2.** [U.S.] *Educ.* a minor field of study **3.** *Music* a minor interval, key, etc.

minor axis the shorter or shortest axis of an ellipse or ellipsoid

mi·nor·i·ty (mə nor'ə tē, mī-) *n., pl.* **-ties** **1.** the lesser part or smaller number; less than half **2.** a racial, religious, or political group smaller than and differing from the larger, controlling group **3.** the period or condition of being under full legal age

minor league [U.S.] any league in a professional sport, as baseball, other than the major leagues —**mi'nor-league'** *adj.* —**mi'nor-leagu'er** *n.*

minor order R.C.Ch. any of the four lower orders below that of subdeacon, requisite for aspirants to major orders

minor piece Chess a bishop or knight

minor scale one of the two standard diatonic scales, with half steps instead of whole steps, in ascending, after the second and seventh tones (**melodic minor scale**) or after the second, fifth, and seventh tones (**harmonic minor scale**)

minor suit Bridge diamonds or clubs

min·ster (min'stər) *n.* [OE. *mynster* < LL. *monasterium*, MONASTERY] **1.** the church of a monastery **2.** any of various large churches or cathedrals

min·strel (min'strəl) *n.* [< OFr., servant, orig., official <

LL. < L. *ministerium*, ministry] **1.** any of a class of lyric poets and singers of the Middle Ages, who travelled from place to place singing and reciting **2.** [Poet.] a poet, singer, or musician **3.** a performer in a minstrel show

minstrel show a comic variety show presented by a company of performers with blackened faces, who sing, tell jokes, etc.

min·strel·sy (-sē) *n., pl.* **-sies 1.** the art or occupation of a minstrel **2.** a group of minstrels **3.** a collection of minstrels' ballads or songs

mint[1] (mint) *n.* [OE. *mynet*, coin < L. < *Moneta*, epithet of Juno, in whose temple money was coined] **1.** a place where money is coined by the government **2.** a large amount [a *mint* of ideas] **3.** a source of manufacture or invention —*adj.* new, as if freshly minted [a postage stamp in *mint* condition] —*vt.* **1.** to coin (money) **2.** to invent or create; fabricate —**mint'er** *n.*

mint[2] (mint) *n.* [OE. *minte*] **1.** a plant of the labiate family with leaves used for flavouring and in medicine **2.** a sweet flavoured with mint —*adj.* designating a family of plants, as the spearmint, peppermint, and applemint, with aromatic leaves, volatile oil, and square stems

mint·age (min'tij) *n.* **1.** the act or process of minting money **2.** money so produced **3.** the cost of minting money **4.** the impression made on a coin

mint sauce a sauce flavoured with mint leaves, served esp. with lamb

mint julep [U.S.] a frosted drink consisting of whisky or brandy, sugar, and mint leaves

min·u·end (min'yoo wend') *n.* [< L. gerundive of *minuere*: see MINUTE[2]] *Arith.* the number or quantity from which another is to be subtracted

min·u·et (min'yoo wet') *n.* [Fr. *menuet* (see MENU), orig., very small: from the small steps taken] **1.** a slow, stately dance of the 17th and 18th cent., for groups of couples **2.** the music for this, in 3/4 time

mi·nus (mī'nəs) *prep.* [L., neut. sing. of *minor*, less] **1.** reduced by the subtraction of; less [four *minus* two] **2.** [Colloq.] without [*minus* a toe] —*adj.* **1.** indicating subtraction [a *minus* sign] **2.** negative [a *minus* quantity] **3.** somewhat less than [a mark of A *minus*] **4.** *Elec.* same as NEGATIVE [the *minus* terminal] —*n.* **1.** a minus sign **2.** a negative quantity

mi·nus·cule (mi nus'kyool, min'ə skyool') *adj.* [Fr. < L. *minusculus*, rather small] very small

minus sign *Math.* a sign (-), indicating subtraction or negative quantity

min·ute[1] (min'it) *n.* [< OFr. < ML. *minuta* < L. (*pars*) *minuta* (*prima*), (first) small (part): see ff.] **1.** the sixtieth part of any of certain units; specif., *a)* 1/60 of an hour; sixty seconds *b)* 1/60 of a degree of an arc **2.** a moment; instant **3.** a specific point in time **4.** a measure of the distance usually covered in a minute [ten *minutes* from the city centre] **5.** a note or memorandum; specif., [*pl.*] an official record of what was said and done at a meeting, etc. —*vt.* **-ut·ed, -ut·ing** to make minutes of; record —**the minute (that)** as soon as —**up to the minute** in the latest style, fashion, etc.

min·ute[2] (mī nyoot') *adj.* [< L. pp. of *minuere*, to lessen < *minor*, less] **1.** very small; tiny **2.** of little importance; trifling **3.** of or attentive to tiny details; exact; precise —**mi·nute'ly** *adv.* —**mi·nute'ness** *n.*

minute book (min'it) a book in which the minutes of a meeting are recorded

minute gun (min'it) a cannon firing at intervals of a minute, as a sign of distress or mourning

minute hand (min'it) the longer hand of a clock or watch, which indicates the minutes and moves round the dial once every hour

min·ute·man (min'it man') *n., pl.* **-men'** (-men') [U.S.] [*also* M-] a member of the American civilian army during the American War of Independence who volunteered to be ready for military service at a minute's notice

min·ute steak (min'it) a small, thin steak that can be cooked quickly

mi·nu·ti·ae (mi nyoo'shi ē') *n.pl.*, *sing.* **-ti·a** (-shē ə, -shə) [L. < *minutus*, MINUTE[2]] small or relatively unimportant details

minx (minks) *n.* [< ?] a pert, saucy young woman

Mi·o·cene (mī'ə sēn') *adj.* [< Gr. *meiōn*, less + *kainos*, recent] designating or of the fourth epoch of the Tertiary Period in the Cainozoic Era —**the Miocene** the Miocene Epoch or its rocks: see GEOLOGY, chart

mi·o·sis (mī ō'sis) *n., pl.* **-ses** (sēz) [ModL. < Gr. *myein*, to close + -OSIS] abnormal contraction of the pupil of the eye —**mi·ot'ic** (-ot'ik) *adj., n.* Also **myosis**

mir·a·belle (mir'ə bel', mir'ə bel') *n.* [Fr.] **1.** a European variety of plum tree **2.** its sweet, small golden fruit **3.** a brandy distilled from these fruits

mir·a·cle (mir'ə k'l) *n.* [OFr. < L. *miraculum* < *mirari*, to wonder at < *mirus*, wonderful] **1.** an event or action that apparently contradicts known scientific laws [the *miracles* in the Bible] **2.** a remarkable thing; marvel **3.** a wonderful example [a *miracle* of tact] **4.** *same as* MIRACLE PLAY

miracle play any of a class of medieval religious dramas dealing with events in the lives of the saints: cf. MYSTERY PLAY

mi·rac·u·lous (mi rak'yoo ləs) *adj.* **1.** having the nature of a miracle; supernatural **2.** like a miracle; marvellous **3.** able to work miracles —**mi·rac'u·lous·ly** *adv.* —**mi·rac'u·lous·ness** *n.*

mi·rage (mi räzh') *n.* [Fr. < (*se*) *mirer*, to be reflected < L. *mirari*, to wonder at: see MIRACLE] **1.** an optical illusion in which the image of a distant object, as an oasis, is made to appear nearby: it is caused by the refraction of light rays from the object through layers of air of different temperatures and densities **2.** something that falsely appears to be real

mire (mīr) *n.* [< ON. *myrr*] **1.** an area of wet, soggy ground; bog **2.** deep mud or slush —*vt.* **mired, mir'ing 1.** to cause to get stuck in or as in mire **2.** to soil with mud or dirt —*vi.* to sink or stick in mud —**in the mire** in difficulties

mirk (murk) *n. alt. sp. of* MURK —**mirk'y** *adj.* **mirk'i·er, mirk'i·est**

mir·ror (mir'ər) *n.* [< OFr. < L. *mirari*, to wonder at] **1.** a smooth surface that reflects images; esp., a looking glass **2.** anything that truly pictures or describes [a play that is a *mirror* of life] —*vt.* to reflect as in a mirror

mirror image an image as seen in a mirror, i.e., with the right side as though it were the left, and vice versa

mirror writing writing reversed, as if it were seen in a mirror

mirth (murth) *n.* [OE. *myrgth* < base of *myrig*, pleasant] joyfulness, gaiety, or merriment, esp. when characterized by laughter

mirth·ful (-fəl) *adj.* full of, expressing, or causing mirth; merry —**mirth'ful·ly** *adv.* —**mirth'ful·ness** *n.*

mirth·less (-lis) *adj.* without mirth or joy —**mirth'less·ly** *adv.* —**mirth'less·ness** *n.*

mir·y (mīr'ē) *adj.* **mir'i·er, mir'i·est 1.** boggy; swampy **2.** muddy; dirty —**mir'i·ness** *n.*

mis- [OE. *mis-* or OFr. *mes-*] *a prefix meaning:* **1.** wrong or wrongly, bad or badly [*misplace, misrule*] **2.** no, not [*mistrust, misfire*]

mis·ad·ven·ture (mis'ad ven'chər) *n.* an unlucky accident; bad luck; mishap

mis·ad·vise (-əd vīz') *vt.* **-vised', -vis'ing** to advise badly —**mis·ad'vice'** (-vīs') *n.*

mis·al·li·ance (-ə lī'əns) *n.* an improper alliance; esp., an unsuitable marriage

mis·al·ly (-ə lī') *vt.* **-lied', -ly'ing** to ally unsuitably or inappropriately

mis·an·thrope (mis'ən thrōp', miz'-) *n.* [< Gr. < *misein*, to hate + *anthrōpos*, man] one who hates or distrusts all people: also **mis·an·thro·pist** (mis an'thrə pist) —**mis·an·throp'ic** (-throp'ik), **mis·an·throp'i·cal** *adj.* —**mis·an·throp'i·cal·ly** *adv.*

mis·an·thro·py (mis an'thrə pē, miz'-) *n.* hatred or distrust of all people

mis·ap·ply (mis'ə plī') *vt.* **-plied', -ply'ing** to apply or use badly or improperly [to *misapply* one's energies, a trust fund, etc.] —**mis'ap·pli·ca'tion** *n.*

mis·ap·pre·hend (-ap rə hend') *vt.* to misunderstand —**mis'ap·pre·hen'sion** (-hen'shən) *n.*

mis·ap·pro·pri·ate (mis'ə prō'prē āt') *vt.* **-at'ed, -at'ing** to appropriate to a bad, incorrect, or dishonest use —**mis'ap·pro'pri·a'tion** *n.*

mis·be·come (-bi kum') *vt.* **-came', -come', -com'ing** to be unbecoming to; be unsuitable for

mis·be·got·ten (-bi got''n) *adj.* wrongly or unlawfully begotten; specif., born out of wedlock: also **mis'be·got'**

mis·be·have (-bi hāv') *vt.* **-haved', -hav'ing** to behave wrongly —*vt.* to conduct (oneself) improperly —**mis'be·hav'er** *n.* —**mis'be·hav'iour** (-yər) *n.*

mis·be·lief (-bə lēf') *n.* wrong, false, or unorthodox belief

misc. 1. miscellaneous **2.** miscellany

mis·cal·cu·late (mis kal'kyoo lāt') *vt., vi.* **-lat'ed, -lat'ing** to calculate incorrectly; miscount or misjudge —**mis'·cal·cu·la'tion** *n.*

mis·call (-kôl') *vt.* to call by a wrong name

mis·car·riage (-kar'ij) *n.* **1.** failure to carry out what was intended [a *miscarriage* of justice] **2.** failure of post, etc. to reach its destination **3.** the expulsion of a foetus from the womb before it is sufficiently developed to survive: see ABORTION

mis·car·ry (-kar'ē) *vi.* **-ried, -ry·ing 1.** *a)* to go wrong; fail: said of a plan, project, etc. *b)* to go astray; fail to arrive: said of post, etc. **2.** to suffer a miscarriage of a foetus

mis·cast (-käst') *vt.* **-cast', -cast'ing** to cast (an actor or a play) unsuitably

mis·ce·ge·na·tion (mis'i jə nā'shən, mi sej'ə-) *n.* [coined (c.1863) < L. *miscere*, to mix + *genus*, race + -ATION] marriage or sexual relations between a man and woman of different races, esp. between a white and a black

mis·cel·la·ne·ous (mis'ə lā'nē əs, -yəs) *adj.* [< L. < *miscellus*, mixed < *miscere*, to mix] **1.** consisting of various kinds; varied; mixed 2. having various qualities, etc.; many-sided —**mis′cel·la′ne·ous·ly** *adv.* —**mis′cel·la′ne·ous·ness** *n.*

mis·cel·la·ny (mis′ə lā′nē; mi sel′ə nē) *n., pl.* **-nies** [see prec.] 1. a miscellaneous collection, esp. of literary works 2. [*often pl.*] such a collection of writings, as in a book

mis·chance (mis chäns′) *n.* bad luck; misadventure

mis·chief (mis′chif) *n.* [< OFr. < *meschever*, to come to grief < *mes-*, mis- + *chief*, end] 1. harm or damage, esp. that done by a person 2. *a*) action that causes harm or trouble *b*) a person causing damage or annoyance 3. a tendency to annoy with playful tricks 4. *a*) a prank; playful, annoying trick *b*) playful, harmless teasing —**do (someone) a mischief** to injure, wound or kill

mis·chief-mak·er (-mā′kər) *n.* a person who causes mischief; esp., one who creates trouble by gossiping —**mis′chief-mak′ing** *n., adj.*

mis·chie·vous (mis′chi vəs) *adj.* 1. causing mischief; specif., *a*) injurious; harmful *b*) prankish; teasing 2. inclined to annoy with playful tricks; naughty —**mis′chie·vous·ly** *adv.* —**mis′chie·vous·ness** *n.*

mis·ci·ble (mis′ə b'l) *adj.* [< ML. < L. *miscere*, to mix] that can be mixed —**mis′ci·bil′i·ty** *n.*

mis·con·ceive (mis′kən sēv′) *vt., vi.* **-ceived′, -ceiv′ing** to conceive or interpret wrongly; misunderstand —**mis′con·cep′tion** (-sep′shən) *n.*

mis·con·duct (-kən dukt′; *for n.* mis kon′dukt) *vt.* 1. to manage badly or dishonestly 2. to conduct (oneself) improperly —*n.* 1. bad or dishonest management 2. wilfully improper behaviour

mis·con·strue (-kən strōō′) *vt.* **-strued′, -stru′ing** to construe wrongly; misinterpret —**mis′con·struc′tion** (-struk′shən) *n.*

mis·count (mis kount′; *for n. usually* mis′kount) *vt., vi.* to count incorrectly —*n.* an incorrect count

mis·cre·ant (mis′krē ənt) *adj.* [OFr. *mescreant*, unbelieving < *mes-*, mis- + prp. of *croire*, to believe] 1. villainous; evil 2. [Archaic] unbelieving —*n.* 1. a criminal; villain 2. [Archaic] an unbeliever —**mis′cre·an·cy** *n.*

mis·cue (mis kyōō′) *n.* 1. *Billiards* a shot spoiled by the cue's slipping off the ball 2. [Colloq.] a mistake; error —*vi.* **-cued′, -cu′ing** 1. to make a miscue 2. *Theatre* to miss one's cue

mis·date (-dāt′) *vt.* **-dat′ed, -dat′ing** to date (a letter, etc.) incorrectly —*n.* a wrong date

mis·deal (-dēl′) *vt., vi.* **-dealt′, -deal′ing** to deal (playing cards) wrongly —*n.* a wrong deal —**mis′deal′er** *n.*

mis·deed (mis dēd′) *n.* a wrong or wicked act; crime, sin, etc.

mis·de·mean (mis′di mēn′) *vt., vi.* [Rare] to conduct (oneself) badly; misbehave

mis·de·mean·our (-ər) *n.* 1. [Rare] a misbehaving 2. *Law* any minor offence for which, formerly, statute provided a lesser punishment than for a felony Also U.S. sp. **mis′de·mean′or**

mis·di·rect (mis′də rekt′, -dī-) *vt.* to direct wrongly or badly —**mis′di·rec′tion** *n.*

mis·do (mis dōō′) *vt.* **-did′, -done′, -do′ing** to do wrongly —**mis·do′er** *n.* —**mis·do′ing** *n.*

mis·doubt (-dout′) *vt.* [Archaic] 1. to distrust 2. to fear —*vi.* [Archaic] to have doubts —*n.* [Archaic] suspicion; doubt

‡**mise en scène** (mē zän sen′) [Fr.] 1. the staging of a play, film, etc. including the setting, arrangement of the actors, etc. 2. surroundings; environment

mis·em·ploy (mis′em ploi′) *vt.* to employ wrongly or badly; misuse —**mis′em·ploy′ment** *n.*

mi·ser (mī′zər) *n.* [L., wretched] a greedy, stingy person who hoards money for its own sake, even at the expense of his own comfort

mis·er·a·ble (miz′ər ə b'l, miz′rə-) *adj.* [< Fr. < L. *miserabilis* < *miser*, wretched] 1. in a condition of misery; wretched 2. causing misery, discomfort, etc. [*miserable weather*] 3. bad; inferior; inadequate [*a miserable performance*] 4. pitiable 5. shameful —**mis′er·a·ble·ness** *n.* —**mis′er·a·bly** *adv.*

Mis·e·re·re (miz′ə rer′ē, -rir′-) *n.* [LL., have mercy: first word of the psalm in the Vulgate] 1. the 51st Psalm (50th in the Douai Version) 2. a musical setting for this

mis·er·i·cord, mis·er·i·corde (miz′ər i kôrd′, miz er′ə kôrd′) *n.* [ME. < OFr. < L. *misere*, pity + *cor*, heart] 1. formerly *a*) a relaxation of monastic rules *b*) the room where such relaxations were permitted 2. a narrow ledge on the underside of a hinged seat in a choir stall offering support to the occupant when standing 3. a dagger used to give the death stroke to a knight wounded in a medieval tournament

mi·ser·ly (mī′zər lē) *adj.* like or characteristic of a miser; greedy and stingy —**mi′ser·li·ness** *n.*

mis·er·y (miz′ər ē) *n., pl.* **-er·ies** [< OFr. < L. < *miser*, wretched] 1. a condition of great wretchedness or suffering, because of pain, sorrow, poverty, etc.; distress 2. a cause of such suffering; pain, sorrow, poverty, squalor, etc.

mis·fea·sance (mis fē′zəns) *n.* [< OFr. < *mes-*, mis- + *faire* (< L. *facere*), to do] *Law* wrongdoing; specif., the doing of a lawful act in an unlawful or improper manner infringing on the rights of others: distinguished from MALFEASANCE, NONFEASANCE —**mis·fea′sor** (-zər) *n.*

mis·file (-fīl′) *vt.* **-filed′, -fil′ing** to file (papers, etc.) in the wrong place or order

mis·fire (-fīr′) *vi.* **-fired′, -fir′ing** 1. to fail to ignite properly: said of an internal-combustion engine 2. to fail to be discharged: said of a firearm, missile, etc. 3. to fail to achieve the desired effect —*n.* an act or instance of misfiring

mis·fit (mis fit′; *for n. also, & for 3 always,* mis′fit′) *vt., vi.* **-fit′ted, -fit′ting** to fit badly —*n.* 1. a misfitting 2. a garment, etc. that misfits 3. a person not suited to his position, associates, etc.

mis·for·tune (mis fôr′chən) *n.* 1. bad luck; ill fortune; trouble; adversity 2. an instance of this; unlucky accident; mishap

mis·give (-giv′) *vt.* **-gave′, -giv′en, -giv′ing** to cause fear, doubt, or suspicion in [*his heart misgave him*] —*vi.* to feel fear, doubt, etc.

mis·giv·ing (-giv′iŋ) *n.* [*often pl.*] a disturbed feeling of fear, doubt, apprehension, etc.

mis·gov·ern (-guv′ərn) *vt.* to govern or administer badly —**mis·gov′ern·ment** *n.*

mis·guide (-gīd′) *vt.* **-guid′ed, -guid′ing** to guide wrongly; lead into error or misconduct; mislead —**mis·guid′ance** *n.* —**mis·guid′ed·ly** *adv.* —**mis·guid′ed·ness** *n.* —**mis·guid′er** *n.*

mis·han·dle (mis han′d'l) *vt.* **-dled, -dling** to handle badly or roughly; abuse, mismanage, etc.

mis·hap (mis′hap′) *n.* an unlucky accident

mis·hit (mis′hit) *n. Sport* a faulty shot or stroke —*vt.* **-hit·ting, -hit** to hit a ball with a faulty stroke

mish·mash (mish′mash′) *n.* a hotchpotch; jumble

Mish·na, Mish·nah (mish nä′, mish′nə) *n., pl.* **Mish·na·yot** (mish′nä yōt′) [< ModHeb. < Heb. *shānāh*, to repeat, learn] the first part of the Talmud, containing interpretations of scriptural ordinances, compiled by the rabbis about 200 A.D.

mis·in·form (mis′in fôrm′) *vt.* to supply with false or misleading information —**mis′in·form′ant, mis′in·form′er** *n.* —**mis′in·for·ma′tion** *n.*

mis·in·ter·pret (-in tur′prit) *vt.* to interpret wrongly; understand or explain incorrectly —**mis′in·ter′pre·ta′tion** *n.* —**mis′in·ter′pret·er** *n.*

mis·judge (mis juj′) *vt., vi.* **-judged′, -judg′ing** to judge wrongly or unfairly —**mis·judg′ment, mis·judge′ment** *n.*

mis·la·bel (-lā′b'l) *vt., vi.* **-belled, -bel·ling** to label incorrectly

mis·lay (-lā′) *vt.* **-laid′, -lay′ing** 1. to put in a place afterwards forgotten 2. to put down or install improperly [*to mislay floor tiles*]

mis·lead (-lēd′) *vt.* **-led′, -lead′ing** 1. to lead in a wrong direction; lead astray 2. to deceive or delude 3. to lead into wrongdoing —**mis·lead′ing** *adj.* —**mis·lead′ing·ly** *adv.*

mis·man·age (-man′ij) *vt., vi.* **-aged, -ag·ing** to manage or administer badly —**mis·man′age·ment** *n.*

mis·match (-mach′) *vt.* to match badly or unsuitably —*n.* a bad or unsuitable match

mis·mate (mis māt′) *vt., vi.* **-mat′ed, -mat′ing** to mate badly or unsuitably

mis·name (-nām′) *vt.* **-named′, -nam′ing** to give or apply a wrong name to

mis·no·mer (mis nō′mər) *n.* [< OFr. < *mes-*, mis- + *nomer*, to name < L. *nominare*: see NOMINATE] 1. the use of a wrong name or epithet for some person or thing 2. a name or epithet wrongly used

mis·o- [< Gr. < *misein*, to hate] *a combining form meaning* hatred or hating [*misogyny*]: also **mis-**

mi·sog·a·my (mi sog′ə mē) *n.* [prec. + -GAMY] hatred of marriage —**mi·sog′a·mist** *n.*

mi·sog·y·ny (mi sog′ə nē) *n.* [< Gr.: see MISO- & -GYNY] hatred of women —**mi·sog′y·nist** *n.* —**mi·sog′y·nous, mi·sog′y·nic** *adj.*

mis·place (mis plās′) *vt.* **-placed′, -plac′ing** 1. to put in a wrong place 2. to bestow (one's trust, affection, etc.) unwisely 3. *same as* MISLAY (sense 1) —**mis·place′ment** *n.*

mis·play (-plā′) *vt., vi.* to play wrongly or badly, as in a game

mis·print (mis print′; *for n. usually* mis′print′) —*vt.* to print incorrectly —*n.* an error in printing

mis·pri·sion (mis prizh′ən) *n.* [< OFr. < pp. of *mesprendre*, to take wrongly < *mes-*, mis- + *prendre* < L. *prehendere*, to take] *Law* 1. misconduct or neglect of duty, esp. by a public official 2. act of contempt against a government or court

misprision of felony (or **treason**) *Law* the offence of concealing knowledge of another's felony (or treason)

mis·prize (mis prīz′) *vt.* **-prized′, -priz′ing** [< OFr. < *mes-*, mis- + LL. *pretiare*, to value < L. *pretium*, a price] to despise or undervalue

mis·pro·nounce (mis′prə nouns′) *vt., vi.* **-nounced′, -nounc′-**

ing to give (a word) a pronunciation different from any of the accepted standard pronunciations —**mis′pro·nun′ci·a′·tion** (-nun′sē ā′shən) *n.*

mis·quote (mis kwōt′) *vt., vi.* **-quot′ed, -quot′ing** to quote incorrectly —**mis′quo·ta′tion** *n.*

mis·read (-rēd′) *vt., vi.* **-read′** (-red′), **-read′ing** (-rēd′iŋ) to read wrongly, esp. so as to misinterpret or misunderstand

mis·rep·re·sent (mis′rep ri zent′) *vt.* 1. to represent falsely; give an untrue idea of 2. to be a bad representative of —**mis′rep·re·sen·ta′tion** *n.*

mis·rule (mis rōōl′) *vt.* **-ruled′, -rul′ing** to rule badly or unjustly; misgovern —*n.* 1. misgovernment 2. disorder or riot —**mis·rul′er** *n.*

miss[1] (mis) *vt.* [OE. *missan*] 1. to fail to hit, meet, catch, do, see, hear, etc. 2. to let (an opportunity, etc.) go by 3. to escape; avoid [he *missed* being hit] 4. to fail or forget to do, keep, attend, etc. [he *missed* his appointment] 5. to notice, feel, or regret the absence or loss of —*vi.* 1. to fail to hit something aimed at 2. to fail to be successful 3. to misfire, as an engine —*n.* a failure to hit, obtain, etc. —**give (something) a miss** to avoid (something) —**miss the boat** [Colloq.] to fail to seize an opportunity

miss[2] (mis) *n., pl.* **miss′es** [contr. of MISTRESS] 1. [M-] a title used in speaking to or of an unmarried woman or girl, placed before the name [*Miss* Smith, the *Misses* Smith] 2. a young unmarried woman or girl 3. a size in clothing for young women

miss. 1. mission 2. missionary

mis·sal (mis′'l) *n.* [< ML. < LL. *missa,* MASS] *R.C.Ch.* a book containing all the prayers, rites, etc. for the Mass throughout the year

mis·shape (mis shāp′) *vt.* **-shaped′, -shaped′** or archaic **-shap′en, -shap′ing** to shape badly; deform

mis·shap·en (-′n) *adj.* badly shaped; deformed —**mis·shap′·en·ly** *adv.* —**mis·shap′en·ness** *n.*

mis·sile (mis′il) *adj.* [L. *missilis* < pp. of *mittere,* to send] that can be, or is, thrown or shot —*n.* a weapon or other object, as a spear, bullet, rocket, etc., designed to be thrown or launched towards a target; often, specif., a guided missile

mis·sile·ry (-rē) *n.* 1. the science of building and launching guided missiles 2. guided missiles collectively

miss·ing (mis′iŋ) *adj.* absent; lost; lacking; specif., absent after combat, but not definitely known to be dead or taken prisoner

missing link something necessary for completing a series; specif. the hypothetical animal supposed to bridge the gap between anthropoid apes and man in evolution

mis·sion (mish′ən) *n.* [L. *missio* < pp. of *mittere,* to send] 1. a sending out or being sent out with authority to perform a special duty, as by a church, government, etc. 2. *a)* group of persons sent by a church to spread its religion, esp. in a foreign land *b)* its headquarters *c)* [*pl.*] organized missionary work 3. a group of technicians, etc. sent to a foreign country 4. the special duty or function for which someone is sent 5. the special task for which a person is apparently destined in life; calling 6. any charitable or religious organization for doing welfare work for the needy 7. *Mil.* an assigned combat operation; esp., a single combat flight by an aeroplane or group of aircraft —*adj.* of a mission or missions —*vt.* to send on a mission

mis·sion·ar·y (-ər ē) *adj.* of or characteristic of religious missions or missionaries —*n., pl.* **-ar·ies** a person sent on a mission; specif., a person sent out by his church to preach, teach, and proselytize, as in a foreign country considered heathen: also **mis′sion·er**

mis·sis (mis′əz) *n.* [altered < MISTRESS] [Colloq.] one's wife: also used with *the:* also **mis′sus**

Mis·sis·sip·pi·an (mis′ə sip′ē ən) *adj.* 1. of the Mississippi River 2. of the state of Mississippi, U.S. 3. designating or of the first coal-forming period of the Palaeozoic Era in N. America, corresponding to the Lower Carboniferous period in Europe —*n.* a native or inhabitant of Mississippi —**the Mississippian** Period or its rocks

mis·sive (mis′iv) *n.* [Fr. < ML. < L. pp. of *mittere,* to send] a letter or written message

mis·speak (mis spēk′) *vt., vi.* **-spoke′, -spok′en, -speak′ing** to speak or say incorrectly

mis·spell (-spel′) *vt., vi.* **-spelled′** or **-spelt′, -spell′ing** to spell incorrectly

mis·spell·ing (-spel′iŋ) *n.* (an) incorrect spelling

mis·spend (-spend′) *vt.* **-spent′, -spend′ing** to spend improperly or wastefully

mis·state (-stāt′) *vt.* **-stat′ed, -stat′ing** to state incorrectly or falsely —**mis·state′ment** *n.*

mis·step (mis step′) *n.* 1. a wrong or awkward step 2. a mistake in conduct; faux pas

mist (mist) *n.* [OE.] 1. a large mass of water vapour like a light fog 2. a cloud of dust, gas, etc. 3. a fine spray, as of perfume 4. a film before the eyes, blurring the vision [through a *mist* of tears] 5. anything that obscures the understanding, memory, etc. —*vt., vi.* to obscure with or as with a mist

mis·take (mi stāk′) *vt.* **-took′, -tak′en** or obs. **-took′, -tak′-**

ing [ON. *mistaka,* to take wrongly] 1. to understand or perceive wrongly 2. to take to be another [he *mistook* me for another] —*vi.* to make a mistake —*n.* 1. a fault in understanding, interpretation, etc. 2. a blunder; error —**and no mistake** [Colloq.] certainly —**mis·tak′a·ble** *adj.*

mis·tak·en (-stāk′'n) *adj.* 1. wrong; having an incorrect understanding, perception, etc.: said of persons 2. incorrect; misunderstood: said of ideas, etc. —**mis·tak′en·ly** *adv.*

mis·ter (mis′tər) *n.* [weakened form of MASTER] 1. [M-] a title used in speaking to or of a man, placed before his name or office and usually written *Mr.* 2. [Colloq.] sir: in direct address, not followed by a name

mis·time (mis tīm′) *vt.* **-timed′, -tim′ing** 1. to do at an inappropriate time 2. to judge incorrectly the time of

mistle thrush the largest of the European thrushes, supposed to be partial to mistletoe berries: also **missel thrush**

mis·tle·toe (mis′'l tō′) *n.* [< OE. < *mistel,* mistletoe + *tan,* a twig] 1. an evergreen plant with yellowish-green leaves and waxy white, poisonous berries, parasitic on trees 2. a sprig of this, hung as a Christmas decoration

mis·took (mi stook′) *pt. & obs. pp.* of MISTAKE

mis·tral (mis′trəl, mi sträl′) *n.* [Fr. < Pr., lit., master-wind < L. < *magister,* MASTER] a cold, dry, north wind that blows over the Mediterranean coast of France and nearby regions

mis·treat (mis trēt′) *vt.* to treat wrongly or badly —**mis·treat′ment** *n.*

mis·tress (mis′tris) *n.* [< OFr. fem. of *maistre,* MASTER] 1. a woman who rules others or controls something; specif., *a)* a woman head of a household or institution *b)* a woman schoolteacher 2. [*sometimes* M-] something regarded as feminine that has control, power, etc. [England was *Mistress* of the seas] 3. a woman who has sexual relations with, and may be supported by, a man to whom she is not married 4. [Archaic] a sweetheart 5. [M-] formerly, a title prefixed to the name of a woman: now replaced by the abbreviations *Mrs.* or *Miss*

mistress of the robes the title of the lady in charge of the Queen's wardrobe

mis·tri·al (mis trī′əl) *n. Law* a trial made void because of an error in the proceedings

mis·trust (-trust′) *n.* lack of trust or confidence; suspicion —*vt., vi.* to have no trust or confidence in; doubt —**mis·trust′ful** *adj.* —**mis·trust′ful·ly** *adv.* —**mis·trust′·ful·ness** *n.*

mist·y (mis′tē) *adj.* **mist′i·er, mist′i·est** 1. of or like mist 2. characterized by or covered with mist 3. *a)* blurred or dimmed, as by mist *b)* obscure or vague —**mist′i·ly** *adv.* —**mist′i·ness** *n.*

mis·un·der·stand (mis′un dər stand′, mis un′-) *vt.* **-stood′, -stand′ing** to fail to understand correctly; miscomprehend or misinterpret

mis·un·der·stand·ing (-stan′diŋ) *n.* 1. a failure to understand correctly 2. a quarrel; disagreement

mis·un·der·stood (-stood′) *adj.* 1. not properly understood 2. not properly appreciated

mis·us·age (mis yōō′sij, -zij) *n.* 1. incorrect usage, as of words 2. bad or harsh treatment

mis·use (mis yōōz′; *for n.* -yōōs′) *vt.* **-used′, -us′ing** 1. to use improperly; misapply 2. to treat badly or harshly; abuse —*n.* incorrect or improper use —**mis·us′er** *n.*

mis·val·ue (-val′yōō) *vt.* **-ued, -u·ing** to fail to value properly or adequately

mis·word (-wurd′) *vt.* to word incorrectly

mis·write (-rīt′) *vt.* **-wrote′, -writ′ten, -writ′ing** to write incorrectly

mite[1] (mīt) *n.* [OE.] any of a large number of tiny arachnids, often parasitic upon animals, insects, or plants, or infesting prepared foods

mite[2] (mīt) *n.* [< MDu., ult. same as prec.] 1. *a)* a very small sum of money *b)* formerly, a coin of very small value 2. a bit; a little [a *mite* slow] 3. a very small creature

mi·ter (mīt′ər) *n., vt.* **-tered, -ter·ing** *U.S. sp.* of MITRE

Mith·ra·ism (mith′rə iz′m, -rā-) *n.* the ancient Persian religion based on worship of Mithras —**Mith′ra·ist** *n., adj.* —**Mith′ra·is′tic** *adj.*

mith·ri·da·tism (mith′rə dāt′iz′m) *n.* [< L. *mithridatium* < *Mithridates* VI of Pontus, said to have such immunity to poisons] immunity to large doses of poisons by prior conditioning of the body with periodic and gradually increased doses —**mith′ri·dat′ic** (-dat′ik) *adj.* —**mith′·ri·dat·ize** *vt.*

mit·i·gate (mit′ə gāt′) *vt., vi.* **-gat′ed, -gat′ing** [< L. pp. of *mitigare,* to make mild < *mitis,* mild + *agere,* to drive] to make or become milder, less severe, or less painful —**mit′·i·ga·ble** (-i gə b′l) *adj.* —**mit′i·ga′tion** *n.* —**mit′i·ga′tive** *adj.* —**mit′i·ga′tor** —**mit′i·ga·to·ry** (-gə tə rē) *adj.*

mi·to·sis (mī tō′sis, mi-) *n., pl.* **-ses** (-sēz) [ModL. < Gr. *mitos,* thread + -OSIS] *Biol.* the indirect method of nuclear division of cells: the nuclear chromatin first appears as long threads which in turn break into chromosomes that are split lengthwise —**mi·tot′ic** (-tot′ik) *adj.* —**mi·tot′i·cal·ly** *adv.*

mi·tral (mī′trəl) *adj.* of or like a mitre

mitral valve the valve between the left atrium and left ventricle of the heart

mi·tre[1] (mīt′ər) *n.* [< OFr. < L. < Gr. *mitra*, a headband] 1. a tall, ornamented cap with peaks in front and behind, worn by bishops and abbots as a mark of office 2. the office or rank of a bishop —*vt.* to invest with the office of bishop

mi·tre[2] (mīt′ər) *n.* [prob. < prec.] *Carpentry* 1. a kind of joint formed by fitting together two pieces, bevelled to form a corner (usually a right angle): also **mitre joint** 2. either of the facing surfaces of such a joint —*vt.* 1. to fit together in a mitre 2. to bevel the edges of to form a mitre

MITRE

mitt (mit) *n.* [contr. < MITTEN] 1. a woman's glove covering part of the arm, the hand, and sometimes part of the fingers 2. *same as* MITTEN 3. [Slang] a hand 4. *a)* [U.S.] *Baseball* a padded glove worn for protection [catcher's *mitt*] *b)* a boxing glove

mit·ten (mit′'n) *n.* [< OFr. *mitaine*] 1. a glove with a thumb but no separately divided fingers 2. *earlier var.* of MITT (sense 1)

MITRE JOINT

mit·ti·mus (mit′i məs) *n.* [L. we send < *mittere*: see MISSION] 1. *Law* a warrant or writ for putting into prison a person convicted of crime 2. dismissal, as from office

mix (miks) *vt.* **mixed, mix′ing** [prob. < *mixt*, mixed < Fr. < L. pp. of *miscere*, to mix] 1. to blend together in a single mass or compound 2. to make by blending ingredients [to *mix* a cake] 3. to join; combine [to *mix* work and play] 4. to cause to associate [to *mix* boys with girls in a school] —*vi.* 1. to be mixed; be blended; mingle 2. to associate or get along —*n.* 1. a mixing or being mixed 2. a state of confusion 3. a mixture, as of ingredients for making something —**mix it** to cause mischief or trouble —**mix up** 1. to mix thoroughly 2. to confuse —**mix′a·ble** *adj.*

mixed (mikst) *adj.* 1. joined or blended in a single mass or compound 2. made up of different parts, elements, races, etc. 3. consisting of or involving both sexes [*mixed* company] 4. confused; muddled

mixed bag a random assortment or mixture, esp. of diverse elements, types of people, etc.

mixed blessing an event or situation that has advantages and disadvantages

mixed doubles *Sport* a doubles game in which each pair is composed of one man and one woman

mixed farming combined arable and livestock farming

mixed grill a dish of several kinds of grilled meats, esp. sausages, bacon, etc.

mixed marriage marriage between persons of different religions or races

mixed media 1. the use of more than two media for an effect, as by combining acting, flashing lights, tape recordings, etc. 2. *Painting* the use of different media, as oil and crayon, in the same composition

mixed number a number consisting of a whole number and a fraction, as $3^2/3$

mixed-up (-up′) *adj.* in a state of mental confusion; bewildered

mix·er (mik′sər) *n.* one that mixes; specif., *a)* a person with reference to his sociability *b)* a machine or an electric appliance for mixing 2. *Electronics* a device in which two or more input signals, often of different frequencies, are combined to give a single output signal

mix·ture (miks′chər) *n.* 1. a mixing or being mixed 2. something mixed 3. *Chem.* a substance containing two or more ingredients: distinguished from COMPOUND[1] in that the constituents are not in fixed proportions, retain their individual characteristics, and are physically separable —**the mixture as before** a repeat of various elements [the film was *the mixture as before*]

mix-up (miks′up′) *n.* a condition or instance of confusion

miz·zen, miz·en (miz′'n) *adj.* [< or akin to MFr. *misaine* < It. < L. *medianus*: see MEDIAN] of the mizzenmast —*n.* 1. a fore-and-aft sail set on the mizzenmast 2. *clipped form of* MIZZENMAST

miz·zen·mast (-məst, -mäst′) *n.* the mast nearest the stern in a ship with two or three masts

miz·zle[1] (miz′'l) *vt., vi.* **-zled, -zling** [LME. *misellen* < prob. LowG. *miseln*, to drizzle] to rain in a fine mist; drizzle —*n.* a misty rain; drizzle —**miz′zly** *adv.*

miz·zle[2] (miz′'l) *vi.* **-zled, -zling** [< ?] [Slang] to decamp; to run off

mk. *pl.* **mks.** 1. mark (monetary unit) 2. markka

mks, m.k.s., M.K.S. metre-kilogramme-second

mkt. market

ML. Medieval (or Middle) Latin

ml. 1. mile 2. millilitre(s): also **ml**

M.Litt. [L. *Magister Litterarum*] Master of Letters

Mlle. *pl.* **Mlles.** Mademoiselle

MLowG. Middle Low German

mm millimetre(s)

MM. Messieurs

M.M. Military Medal

Mme. Madame

Mmes. Mesdames

M.Mus. Master of Music

Mn *Chem.* manganese

M'Nagh·ten rules (mək nôrt′ən) *Law* the rules used to decide if an insane person is responsible for his actions; first formulated in the 19th cent. trial of M'Naghten

mne·mon·ic (nē mon′ik) *adj.* [< Gr. < *mnēmōn*, mindful < *mnasthai*, to remember] 1. helping, or meant to help, the memory 2. of mnemonics or memory —**mne·mon′i·cal·ly** *adv.*

mne·mon·ics (-iks) *n.pl.* 1. [*with sing. v.*] a technique for improving memory by the use of certain formulas 2. such formulas

mo (mō) *n.* [Colloq.] *clipped form of* MOMENT (sense 1)

-mo (mō) [< L. abl. ending] a suffix meaning having (a specified number of) leaves as a result of folding a sheet of paper [*twelvemo*]

Mo *Chem.* molybdenum

mo., m.o. money order

M.O., MO 1. Medical Officer 2. money order

mo·a (mō′ə) *n.* [< Maori] any of an extinct group of very large, flightless birds of New Zealand, resembling the ostrich

moan (mōn) *n.* [prob. < base of OE. *mænan*, to complain] 1. formerly, a lamentation 2. a low, mournful sound of sorrow or pain 3. any similar sound, as of the wind 4. a complaint [she had a *moan* about it] —*vi.* 1. to make a moan 2. to complain, lament, etc. —*vt.* 1. to say with a moan 2. to bewail [to *moan* one's fate]

moat (mōt) *n.* [OFr. *mote*] a deep, broad ditch dug around a fortress or castle, and often filled with water, for protection against invasion —*vt.* to surround with or as with a moat

mob (mob) *n.* [< L. *mobile* (*vulgus*), excitable (crowd)] 1. a disorderly and lawless crowd; rabble 2. any crowd 3. the common people: contemptuous term 4. [Slang] a gang of criminals 5. [Aust.] a large number [a *mob* of sheep] —*vt.* **mobbed, mob′bing** 1. to crowd around and attack, jostle, annoy, etc. 2. to throng —**mob′bish** *adj.*

mob·cap (mob′kap′) *n.* [< MDu. *mop*, woman's cap + CAP] formerly, a woman's cap, worn indoors, with a high, puffy crown, often tied under the chin

mo·bile (mō′bil) *adj.* [OFr. < L. *mobilis* < *movere*, to move] 1. *a)* moving, or able to move, from place to place *b)* movable by means of a motor vehicle [a *mobile* shop] 2. that can change rapidly or easily, as to suit moods or needs; flexible, adaptable, fluid, etc. 3. designating or of a society in which one may move freely or advance from one class to another —*n.* an abstract sculpture with parts that can move, as a suspended arrangement of thin forms, rings, etc. —**mo·bil·i·ty** (mō bil′ə tē) *n.*

mobile home a large caravan equipped as a home, to be parked somewhere more or less permanently

mo·bi·lize (mō′bə līz′) *vt.* **-lized′, -liz′ing** 1. *a)* to make movable *b)* to put into motion, circulation, or use 2. to make ready for immediate active service in war 3. to organize (people, resources, etc.) for any active service or use —*vi.* to become mobilized, as for war —**mo′bi·liz′a·ble** *adj.* —**mo′bi·li·za′tion** *n.* —**mo′bi·liz′er** *n.*

Mö·bi·us strip (mur′bē əs) [after A. *Möbius* (1790–1868), G. mathematician] a surface with only one side, formed from a narrow strip of paper given a half twist and then pasted together

mob·oc·ra·cy (mob ok′rə sē) *n.,* *pl.* **-cies** [MOB + (DEM)OCRACY] 1. rule by a mob 2. the mob as ruler

mob·ster (mob′stər) *n.* [Slang] a gangster

moc·ca·sin (mok′ə sin) *n.* [< Algonquian] 1. a heelless shoe of soft, flexible leather, worn orig. by N American Indians 2. a similar shoe, but with a hard sole and heel

moccasin flower *same as* LADY-SLIPPER

mo·cha (mok′ə, mō′kə) *n.* [after *Mocha*, seaport in Yemen] 1. a choice grade of coffee grown orig. in Arabia 2. a flavouring made from coffee or coffee and chocolate 3. a type of soft, velvety leather —*adj.* 1. flavoured with coffee or coffee and chocolate 2. reddish-brown

MOCCASINS

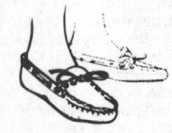

mock (mok) *vt.* [OFr. *mocquer*, to mock] 1. to hold up to scorn or contempt; ridicule **2.** to mimic, as in fun or derision **3.** to lead on and disappoint; deceive **4.** to defy and make futile —*vi.* to express scorn, ridicule, etc. —*n.* **1.** a mocking **2.** an object of ridicule **3.** an imitation —*adj.* **1.** sham; imitation **2.** practice [*mock* 'O' levels were held at Christmas] —**mock′ing·ly** *adv.*

mock·er (-ər) *n.* one who mocks —**put the mocker(s) on** [Colloq.] to frustrate or bring bad luck to (someone or something)

mock·er·y (-ər ē) *n., pl.* **-er·ies** **1.** a mocking **2.** an object of ridicule **3.** a false, derisive, or impertinent imitation **4.** vain effort; futility

mock-he·ro·ic (-hi rō′ik) *adj.* mocking, or burlesquing, heroic manner, action, or character —**mock′-he·ro′i·cal·ly** *adv.*

mock·ing·bird (mok′iŋ burd′) *n.* an American songbird able to imitate many birdcalls

mock orange any of a genus of shrubs with fragrant white flowers like those of the orange: also called **syringa**

mock turtle soup a soup made from calf's head, veal, etc., spiced to taste like green turtle soup

mock-up (mok′up′) *n.* **1.** a scale model or replica of a structure or apparatus, used for instructional or experimental purposes **2.** a layout of printed matter

mod¹ (mod) *n.* [< MOD(ERN)] [*also* M-] [Colloq.] a member of a youth cult in the mid-60's

mod² (mod) *n.* [Gael.] a festival to encourage the study and practice of Gaelic songs and poetry

mod. **1.** moderate **2.** modern

mod·al (mōd′'l) *adj.* of or indicating a mode or mood; specif., *Gram.* of or expressing mood —**mo·dal·i·ty** (mō dal′ə tē) *n., pl.* **-ties** —**mod′al·ly** *adv.*

modal auxiliary an auxiliary verb used with another to indicate its mood: *can, may, might, must, should,* and *would* are *modal auxiliaries*

mod cons a *clipped form of* modern conveniences

mode (mōd) *n.* [L. *modus,* measure, manner] **1.** a manner or way of acting, doing, or being **2.** [Fr. < L. *modus*] customary usage, or current fashion or style **3.** *Music* the arrangement, or any specific arrangement, of tones and semitones in a scale **4.** *Statistics* the value, number, etc. most frequent in a given series

mod·el (mod′'l) *n.* [< Fr. < It. *modello,* dim. of *modo* < L. *modus,* MODE] **1.** *a)* a small copy or representation of an existing or planned object, as a ship, building, etc. *b)* same as ARCHETYPE (sense 1) *c)* a representation of the supposed structure of something *d)* a piece of sculpture in wax or clay from which a finished work in bronze, marble, etc. is to be made **2.** a person or thing considered as a standard of excellence to be imitated **3.** a style or design [a 1972 *model*] **4.** *a)* a person who poses for an artist or photographer *b)* any person or thing serving as a subject for an artist *c)* a person employed to display clothes by wearing them —*adj.* **1.** serving as a model, or standard of excellence **2.** representative; typical —*vt.* **-elled, -el·ling** **1.** *a)* to make a model of *b)* to plan or form after a model **2.** to shape or form in or as in clay, wax, etc. **3.** to display (a dress, etc.) by wearing —*vi.* **1.** to make a model or models **2.** to serve as a model (sense 4) —**mod′el·ler** *n.*

mod·er·ate (mod′ər it; *for v.* -ə rāt′) *adj.* [< L. pp. of *moderare,* to restrain] **1.** within reasonable limits; avoiding extremes; temperate **2.** mild; not violent [*moderate* weather] **3.** of average or medium quality, range, etc. [*moderate* skills] —*n.* a person holding moderate views, as in politics or religion —*vt., vi.* **-at′ed, -at′ing** **1.** to make or become moderate **2.** to preside over (a meeting, etc.) —**mod′er·ate·ly** *adv.* —**mod′er·ate·ness** *n.*

mod·er·a·tion (mod′ə rā′shən) *n.* **1.** a moderating, or bringing within bounds **2.** avoidance of extremes **3.** absence of violence; calmness —**in moderation** to a moderate degree; without excess

mod·e·ra·to (-rät′ō) *adj., adv.* [It.] *Music* with moderation in tempo

mod·er·a·tor (mod′ə rāt′ər) *n.* **1.** a person or thing that moderates; specif., a person who presides at a meeting, debate, etc. [the *Moderator* of the Church of Scotland] **2.** a substance, as graphite or heavy water, used to slow down high-energy neutrons in a nuclear reactor —**mod′er·a′tor·ship′** *n.*

mod·ern (mod′ərn) *adj.* [< Fr. < LL. *modernus* < L. *modo,* just now, orig. abl. of *modus,* measure] **1.** of the present or recent times; specif., *a)* of the latest styles, methods, ideas, etc.; up-to-date *b)* designating or of certain contemporary trends in art, music, literature, dance, etc. **2.** of the period of history from c.1450 A.D. to now **3.** [*often* M-] designating the most recent stage of a language [*Modern* English] —*n.* **1.** a person living in modern times **2.** a person with modern ideas, standards, etc. —**mo·der′ni·ty** (mo dur′nə tē, mə-) *n., pl.* **-ties** —**mod′ern·ly** *adv.* —**mod′ern·ness** *n.*

Modern English the English language since about the mid-15th cent.: cf. EARLY MODERN ENGLISH

Modern Hebrew Hebrew in post-Biblical times, esp. as the language of modern Israel

mod·ern·ism (-iz′m) *n.* **1.** *a)* modern practices, ideas, etc., or sympathy with these *b)* a modern idiom, practice, or usage **2.** [M-] *Christianity* any movement redefining doctrine in the light of modern science, etc. —**mod′ern·ist** *n., adj.* —**mod′ern·is′tic** *adj.* —**mod′ern·is·ti·cal·ly** *adv.*

mod·ern·ize (mod′ər nīz′) *vt., vi.* **-ized′, -iz′ing** to make or become modern in style, design, methods, etc. —**mod′ern·i·za′tion** *n.* —**mod′ern·iz′er** *n.*

modern languages the current European languages as a subject of study

Modern Latin the Latin used since c.1500, chiefly in scientific literature

mod·est (mod′ist) *adj.* [< Fr. < L. *modestus* < *modus,* measure] **1.** having or showing a moderate opinion of one's own value, abilities, etc.; not vain **2.** not forward; shy or reserved [*modest* behaviour] **3.** behaving, dressing, etc. decorously or decently **4.** moderate or reasonable; not extreme [a *modest* request] **5.** quiet and humble in appearance, style, etc. [a *modest* home] —**mod′est·ly** *adv.*

mod·es·ty (mod′is tē) *n.* the quality or state of being modest; specif., *a)* unassuming or humble behaviour *b)* moderation *c)* decency; decorum

ModGr. Modern Greek

ModHeb. Modern Hebrew

mod·i·cum (mod′i kəm) *n.* [L., neut. of *modicus,* moderate] a small amount; bit

mod·i·fi·ca·tion (mod′ə fi kā′shən) *n.* a modifying or being modified; specif., *a)* a partial or slight change in form *b)* a product of this *c)* a slight reduction *d)* a qualification or limitation of meaning

mod·i·fi·er (mod′ə fī′ər) *n.* a person or thing that modifies; esp., a word, phrase, or clause that limits the meaning of another word or phrase [adjectives and adverbs are *modifiers*]

mod·i·fy (mod′ə fī′) *vt.* **-fied′, -fy′ing** [< MFr. < L. *modificare,* to limit < *modus,* measure + *facere,* to make] **1.** to change or alter, esp. slightly or partially **2.** to limit or lessen slightly; moderate [to *modify* a penalty] **3.** *Gram.* to limit the meaning of; qualify ["old" *modifies* "man" in *old man*] **4.** *Linguis.* to change (a vowel) by umlaut —*vi.* to be modified —**mod′i·fi′a·ble** *adj.*

mod·ish (mōd′ish) *adj.* in the latest style; fashionable —**mod′ish·ly** *adv.* —**mod′ish·ness** *n.*

mo·diste (mō dēst′) *n.* [Fr. < *mode:* see MODE] a woman who makes or deals in fashionable clothes, hats, etc. for women: somewhat old-fashioned term

ModL. Modern Latin

mod·u·lar (mod′yoo lər) *adj.* **1.** of a module or modulus **2.** designating or of units of standardized size, design, etc. that can be arranged or fitted together in various ways

mod·u·late (-lāt′) *vt.* **-lat′ed, -lat′ing** [< L. pp. of *modulari* < dim. of *modus,* measure] **1.** to regulate, adjust, or adapt **2.** to vary the pitch, intensity, etc. of (the voice) **3.** *Radio* to vary the amplitude, frequency, or phase of (an oscillation, as a carrier wave) in accordance with some signal —*vi.* to shift from one key to another within a musical composition —**mod′u·la′tion** *n.* —**mod′u·la·to·ry** *adj.*

mod·ule (mod′yool) *n.* [Fr. < L. dim. of *modus,* measure] **1.** a standard or unit of measurement, as in architecture **2.** *a)* any of a set of units, as cabinets, designed to be arranged or joined in various ways *b)* a detachable section, compartment, or unit with a specific function, as in a spacecraft *c)* *Electronics* a compact assembly functioning as a component of a larger unit

mod·u·lus (mod′yoo ləs) *n., pl.* **-u·li′** (-lī′) [ModL. < L.: see prec.] *Physics* a constant expressing the measure of some property, as elasticity

‡**mo·dus o·pe·ran·di** (mō′dəs op′ə ran′dī, -dē) [L.] mode of operation; method

‡**modus vi·ven·di** (vi ven′dī, -dē) [L.] **1.** mode of living **2.** a temporary compromise in a dispute

mog (mog) *n.* [< ?] [Slang] a cat: also **mog′gie** (-gē)

Mo·gul (mō′gul, -g'l; mō gul′) *n.* [Per. *Mughul*] **1.** a Mongol, or Mongolian; esp., any of the Mongolian conquerors of India or their descendants **2.** [m-] a powerful or important person

M.O.H. Medical Officer of Health

mo·hair (mō′her) *n.* [< OIt. < Ar. *mukhayyar*] **1.** the hair of the Angora goat **2.** yarn or a fabric made from this hair —*adj.* of mohair

Moham. Mohammedan

Mo·ham·med·an (mō ham′i d'n) *adj.* of Mohammed or the Moslem religion —*n.* same as MOSLEM: term used mainly by non-Moslems

Mo·ham·med·an·ism (-iz′m) *n.* same as ISLAM: term used mainly by non-Moslems

moi·e·ty (moi′ə tē) *n., pl.* **-ties** [< OFr. < L. < *medius,* middle] **1.** a half **2.** an indefinite part

moil (moil) *vi.* [< OFr. *moillier,* to moisten < L. *mollis,* soft] to toil —*vt.* [Archaic] to moisten or soil —*n.* 1. toil 2. turmoil —**moil'er** *n.*

moire (mwär, môr) *n.* [Fr., watered silk < E. MOHAIR] a fabric, as silk or rayon, having a watered, or wavy, pattern

moi·ré (mwä rā′, mô-; môr′ā) *adj.* [Fr.] having a watered, or wavy, pattern —*n.* 1. a watered pattern pressed into cloth, etc. with engraved rollers 2. *same as* MOIRE

moist (moist) *adj.* [OFr. *moiste* < L. *mucidus*, mouldy < *mucus*, mucus] 1. slightly wet; damp 2. tearful —**moist'ly** *adv.* —**moist'ness** *n.*

mois·ten (mois′'n) *vt., vi.* to make or become moist —**mois'ten·er** *n.*

mois·ture (-chər) *n.* water, etc. causing a slight wetness or dampness —**mois'ture·less** *adj.*

mois·tur·ize (-īz′) *vt., vi.* -**ized**′, -**iz'ing** to add or restore moisture to (the skin, air, etc.) —**mois'tur·iz'er** *n.*

moke (mōk) *n.* [< ?] 1. [Slang] a donkey 2. [Aust.] an inferior horse; nag

mo·ko (mō′kō) *n., pl.* -**s** [Maori] tattooing as practised by the Maoris

mo·ksa (mō′ksə) *n.* [< Sans. *moksa*] [Hindu] the liberation of the spirit from the cycle of temporal existence: also **muk·ti** (mook′tē)

mol *Physics* the symbol for mole

mol. 1. molecular 2. molecule

mo·lar[1] (mō′lər) *adj.* [< L. < *mola*, millstone] 1. used for or capable of grinding 2. designating or of a tooth or teeth adapted for grinding —*n.* a molar tooth: in man there are twelve molars

mo·lar[2] (mō′lər) *adj.* [MOL(E)[4] + -AR] 1. *Chem.* relating to the mole or gramme-molecular weight; specif., designating a solution containing one mole of solute per litre of solution 2. [< L. *moles*, mass (see MOLE[3]) + -AR] *Physics* of a body (of matter) as a whole

mo·las·ses (mə las′iz) *n.* [< Port. *melaco* < LL. *mellaceum*, must < L. < *mel*, honey] [Chiefly U.S.] treacle

mold (mōld) *n. U.S. sp. of* MOULD —**mold'y** *adj.* **mold'i·er, mold'i·est**

mold·board (mōld′bôrd′) *n. U.S. sp. of* MOULDBOARD

mold·er (mōl′dər) *vi., vt. U.S. sp. of* MOULDER

mold·ing (mōl′diŋ) *n. U.S. sp. of* MOULDING

mold·y (mōl′dē) *adj. U.S. sp. of* MOULDY

mole[1] (mōl) *n.* [OE. *mal*] a small, congenital spot on the human skin, usually dark-coloured and slightly raised, often hairy

mole[2] (mōl) *n.* [< or akin to MDu. *mol*] a small, burrowing, insect-eating mammal with small eyes and ears, shovellike forefeet, and soft fur: moles live mainly underground

mole[3] (mōl) *n.* [< Fr. < LGr. < L. *moles*, a mass] 1. a breakwater 2. a harbour formed by a breakwater

mole[4] (mōl) *n.* [< G. *Mol*] the SI unit of substance, defined as the amount of substance which contains as many elementary units (specified as atoms, molecules, ions, etc.) as there are atoms in 0.012 kg of carbon-12; thus, the quantity of a substance having a weight in grammes numerically equal to its molecular weight

Mo·lech (mō′lek) *n.* [from the ancient god of the Phoenicians, etc., to whom children were sacrificed by burning] anything demanding terrible sacrifice: also **Moloch**

mo·lec·u·lar (mə lek′yə lər) *adj.* of, produced by, or existing between molecules —**mo·lec′u·lar′i·ty** (-lar′ə tē) *n.* —**mo·lec′u·lar·ly** *adv.*

molecular biology the branch of biology dealing with the chemical and physical structure and activities of the molecules in living matter

molecular weight the sum of the atomic weights of all atoms in a given molecule

mol·e·cule (mol′ə kyo̅o̅l′) *n.* [< Fr. < ModL. *molecula*, dim. of L. *moles*, a mass] 1. the smallest particle of an element or compound that can exist in the free state and still retain the characteristics of the element or compound 2. a small particle

mole·hill (mōl′hil′) *n.* a small ridge or mound of earth, formed by a burrowing mole

mole·skin (-skin′) *n.* 1. the soft, dark-grey skin of the mole, used as fur 2. *a)* a strong cotton fabric with a soft nap, used for work clothes, etc. *b)* [*pl.*] trousers of this

mo·lest (mə lest′, mō-) *vt.* [< OFr. < L. < *molestus*, troublesome < *moles*, a burden] 1. to annoy or meddle with so as to trouble or harm 2. to make improper sexual advances to (esp. a child) —**mo·les·ta·tion** (mō′les tā′shən, mol′əs-) *n.* —**mo·lest'er** *n.*

moll (mol) *n.* [< var. of name *Molly*] [Slang] 1. a gangster's mistress 2. a prostitute

mol·lah (mōl′ə) *n. same as* MULLAH

mol·li·fy (mol′ə fī′) *vt.* -**fied**′, -**fy'ing** [< MFr. < LL. < L. *mollis*, soft + *facere*, to make] 1. to soothe, pacify, or appease 2. to make less severe or violent —**mol'li·fi·ca'-tion** *n.* —**mol'li·fi'er** *n.*

mol·lusc (mol′əsk) *n.* [< Fr. < ModL. *molluscus*, soft

< *mollis*, soft] any of a large group of invertebrate animals, including clams, oysters, snails, squids, etc., having a soft, usually unsegmented body often enclosed in a hard shell and usually having gills and a foot —**mol·lus·can** (mə lus′kən) *adj., n.*

mol·ly (mol′ē) *n., pl.* -**lies** [< ModL. < F. N. *Mollien* (1758–1850), Fr. statesman] any of certain brightly coloured tropical and subtropical American fishes often kept in aquariums: also **mol'lie**

mol·ly·cod·dle (mol′ē kod′'l) *n.* [< *Molly*, personal name + CODDLE] a man or boy used to being coddled, or protected, pampered, etc. —*vt.* -**dled, -dling** to pamper; coddle —**mol'ly·cod'dler** *n.*

Mo·lo·tov cocktail (mô′lə tof) [after V. M. *Molotov* (1890–), Russ. statesman] [Slang] a bottle filled with an inflammable liquid, plugged with a rag, ignited, and hurled as a grenade against vehicles, etc.

molt (mōlt) *n., vt., vi. chiefly U.S. sp. of* MOULT

mol·ten (mōl′t'n) *archaic pp. of* MELT —*adj.* 1. melted or liquefied by heat 2. made by being melted and cast in a mould

mol·to (mōl′tō) *adv.* [It.] *Music* very; much

mol. wt. molecular weight

mo·ly (mō′lē) *n.* [L. < Gr. *moly*] 1. *Classical Myth* a herb with magic powers given to Odysseus to protect him from Circe's incantation 2. a type of wild garlic found in S Europe

mo·lyb·de·nite (mə lib′də nīt′) *n.* a scaly or foliated, lead-grey ore of molybdenum, MoS_2

mo·lyb·de·num (-nəm) *n.* [ModL. < L. *molybdaena* < Gr. < *molybdos*, lead] a soft, lustrous, silver-white metallic chemical element, used in alloys, etc.: symbol, Mo; at. wt., 95.94; at. no., 42

mo·ment (mō′mənt) *n.* [< L. *momentum*, movement < *movere*, to move] 1. an indefinitely brief period of time; instant [he'll be here in just a *moment*] 2. a definite point in time 3. a brief time of being important or outstanding 4. importance; consequence [news of great *moment*] 5. *Mech. a)* the tendency to cause rotation about a point or axis *b)* a measure of this —**the moment** the present time

mo·men·tar·i·ly (mō′mən tər ə lē, mō′mən ter′ə lē) *adv.* 1. for a moment or short time 2. in an instant 3. from moment to moment

mo·men·tar·y (mō′mən tər ē, -trē) *adj.* 1. lasting for only a moment; passing 2. [Now Rare] recurring every moment 3. [U.S.] likely to occur at any moment —**mo'-men·tar·i·ness** *n.*

mo·ment·ly (mō′mənt lē) *adv.* 1. every moment 2. at any moment 3. for a single moment

moment of truth 1. the point in a bullfight when the matador faces the bull for the kill 2. a critical or crucial moment

mo·men·tous (mō men′təs) *adj.* of great moment; very important [a *momentous* decision] —**mo·men'tous·ly** *adv.* —**mo·men'tous·ness** *n.*

mo·men·tum (mō men′təm) *n., pl.* -**tums, -ta** (-tə) [ModL. < L.: see MOMENT] 1. the impetus of or as of a moving object 2. *Physics & Mech.* the quantity of motion of a moving body, equal to the product of its mass and its velocity

mon- *same as* MONO-: used before a vowel

Mon. 1. Monastery 2. Monday 3. Monsignor

mon. 1. monastery 2. monetary

mo·nad (mō′nad, mon′əd) *n.* [LL. *monas* (gen. *monadis*) < Gr. < *monos*, alone] 1. a unit; something simple and indivisible 2. *Biol.* any simple, single-celled organism 3. *Chem.* an atom, element, or radical with a valence of one —*adj.* of a monad or monads —**mo·nad'ic, mo·nad'i·cal** *adj.*

mo·nan·drous (mə nan′drəs) *adj.* [Gr. *monandros*, having one husband] 1. having only one husband at a time 2. characterized by monandry 3. having only one stamen, as some flowers —**mo·nan'dry** *n.*

mon·arch (mon′ərk, -ärk) *n.* [< LL. < Gr. < *monos*, alone + *archein*, to rule] 1. the hereditary head of a state; king, queen, etc. 2. a person or thing surpassing others of the same kind 3. a large, migrating butterfly of N America

mo·nar·chal (mə när′k'l) *adj.* of a monarch: also **mo·nar'-chi·al** (-kē əl) —**mo·nar'chal·ly** *adv.*

mo·nar·chi·cal (-ki k'l) *adj.* 1. of or like a monarch or monarchy 2. favouring a monarchy Also **mo·nar'chic** —**mo·nar'chi·cal·ly** *adv.*

mon·ar·chism (mon′ər kiz'm, -är-) *n.* monarchical principles or the advocacy of these —**mon'ar·chist** *n., adj.* —**mon'ar·chis'tic** *adj.*

mon·ar·chy (-kē) *n., pl.* -**ar·chies** a government or state headed by a monarch

mon·as·ter·y (mon′ə star ē) *n., pl.* -**ter·ies** [< LL. < LGr. *monastērion* < *monazein*, to be alone < *monos*, alone] the residence of a group of people, esp. monks, retired from the world under religious vows —**mon'as·te'ri·al** (-stir′ē əl) *adj.*

mo·nas·tic (mə nas′tik) *adj.* 1. of or characteristic of monasteries **2.** of or characteristic of monks or nuns; ascetic; self-denying Also **mo·nas'ti·cal** —*n.* a monastic person —**mo·nas'ti·cal·ly** *adv.*

mo·nas·ti·cism (-tə siz'm) *n.* the monastic system, state, or way of life —**mon'as·ti·cize** *vt.* -izing, -ized

mon·au·ral (mon ôr'l) *adj.* [MON(O)-+ AURAL] designating or of sound reproduction that uses only one source of sound, giving a monophonic effect —**mon·au'ral·ly** *adv.*

mon·a·zite (mon'ə zīt') *n.* [G. *Monazit* < Gr. *monazein*, to be alone] a native phosphate of the rare-earth metals, a major source of cerium, lanthanum, etc. and thorium

Mon·day (mun'dē, -dā) *n.* [OE. *monandæg*, moon's day] the second day of the week

Mon·days (-dēz, -dāz) *adv.* [Colloq.] on or during every Monday

‡**monde** (mônd) *n.* [Fr.] the world; society

‡**mon Dieu** (môn dyö') [Fr.] my God

mo·ne·cious (mə nē'shəs, mō-) *adj.* *same as* MONOECIOUS

Mo·nel metal (mō nel') [after A. *Monell* (d. 1921), U.S. manufacturer] *a trademark for* an alloy mainly of nickel and copper, very resistant to corrosion

mon·e·tar·y (mun'ə tər ē) *adj.* [< LL. < L. *moneta*, a MINT[1]] **1.** of the coinage or currency of a country: see table of MONETARY UNITS on next page **2.** of money; pecuniary —**mon'e·tar·i·ly** *adv.*

mon·e·tize (-tīz') *vt.* -tized', -tiz'ing [< L. *moneta*, a MINT[1] + -IZE] **1.** to coin into money **2.** to legalize as money —**mon'e·ti·za'tion** *n.*

mon·ey (mun'ē) *n., pl.* **-eys, -ies** [< OFr. < L. *moneta*, a MINT[1]] **1.** *a)* pieces of gold, silver, copper, etc., stamped by government authority and used as a medium of exchange; coin or coins: also called **hard money** *b)* any paper note authorized to be so used; bank notes; bills: see PAPER MONEY **2.** anything used as a medium of exchange **3.** any sum of money **4.** wealth **5.** *same as* MONEY OF ACCOUNT —**for one's money** [Colloq.] in one's opinion —**in the money** [Slang] wealthy —**make money** to gain profits —**money for jam** money, esp. profit, obtained with very little trouble —**one's money's worth** full value or benefit —**place** (or **put**) **money on** to bet on —**put money into** to invest money in —**put one's money where one's mouth is** [Slang] be prepared to back up one's opinions by action —**mon'-ey·less** *adj.*

mon·ey·bag (-bag') *n.* **1.** a bag for money **2.** [*pl.*, *with sing. v.*] [Colloq.] a rich person

money-box (-boks) *n.* a closed box with a slit for holding one's small savings

mon·ey-chang·ing (-chān'jiŋ) *n.* the exchanging of currency, usually of different countries, esp. at an established or official rate —**mon'ey-chang'er** *n.*

mon·ey·eyed (mun'ēd) *adj.* **1.** wealthy; rich **2.** of, from, or representing money [*moneyed* interests]

mon·ey-grub·ber (-grub'ər) *n.* a person who is greedily intent on accumulating money —**mon'ey-grub'bing** *adj., n.*

mon·ey·lend·er (-len'dər) *n.* a person whose business is lending money at interest

mon·ey·mak·er (-mā'kər) *n.* a person or thing that makes money or a profit —**mon'ey-mak'ing** *adj., n.*

money of account a monetary denomination used in keeping accounts, etc., esp. one not issued in coin or in paper money, as, formerly in Britain, the guinea

mon·ey-spin·ner (-spin'ər) *n.* **1.** an idea, person or thing that is a source of wealth **2.** a small spider supposed to bring good luck: also **money spider**

Mong. **1.** Mongolia **2.** Mongolian

mon·ger (muŋ'gər) *n.* [OE. *mangere* < L. *mango*, dealer] a dealer or trader: usually in compounds [*fishmonger*]: some·times used figuratively [*scandalmonger*]

mon·go (moŋ'gō) *n., pl.* **-gos** *see* MONETARY UNITS, table (Mongolia)

Mon·gol (moŋ'g'l, -gol) *adj.* *same as* MONGOLIAN —*n.* **1.** a native of Mongolia or of an adjacent region in E Siberia **2.** *same as* MONGOLOID **3.** any Mongolic language, esp. that of the Mongolian People's Republic

Mongol. Mongolian

Mon·go·li·an (moŋ gō'lē ən, -yən) *adj.* **1.** of Mongolia, its people, or their culture **2.** *same as* MONGOLOID **3.** *same as* MONGOLIC (*adj.* 1) —*n.* **1.** a native of Mongolia **2.** *same as* MONGOLOID **3.** any Mongolic language

Mon·gol·ic (moŋ gol'ik, mon-) *adj.* **1.** designating or of a subfamily of Altaic languages spoken by the Mongols and including Kalmuck **2.** *same as:* a) MONGOLIAN (*adj.* 1) b) MONGOLOID (*adj.* 1 & 2) —*n.* any Mongolic language

Mon·gol·ism (moŋ'gə liz'm) *n.* [*often* m-] *earlier term for* DOWN'S SYNDROME

Mon·gol·oid (-loid') *adj.* **1.** of or characteristic of the natives of Mongolia **2.** designating or of one of the major groups of mankind: it includes most of the peoples of Asia, the Eskimos, the N. American Indians, etc. **3.** [*often* m-] of or having Down's syndrome —*n.* **1.** a member of the Mongoloid group **2.** a person having Down's syndrome

mon·goose (moŋ'gōos) *n., pl.* **-goos·es** [< native name] a ferretlike, flesh-eating mammal found in Africa and Asia, esp. India, noted for its ability to kill rodents, snakes, etc.

mon·grel (muŋ'grəl) *n.* [< base of OE. *mengan*, to mix] **1.** an animal or plant produced by crossing breeds or varieties; esp., a dog of this kind **2.** anything produced by indiscriminate mixture —*adj.* of mixed breed, race, origin, or character Often a derogatory usage —**mon'grel·i·za'-tion** *n.* —**mon'grel·ize'** *vt.* -ized', -iz'ing

MONGOOSE
(body 22-65 cm long; tail 22-50 cm long)

'mongst, mongst (muŋst) *prep.* archaic var. of AMONGST

mon·ied (mun'ēd) *adj.* *same as* MONEYED

mon·ies (mun'ēz) *n.* alt. pl. of MONEY

mon·i·ker, mon·ick·er (mon'i kər) *n.* [< ?] [Slang] a person's name or nickname

mo·nism (mō'niz'm, mon'iz'm) *n.* [ModL. *monismus* < Gr. *monos*, single] *Philos.* the doctrine that there is only one ultimate substance or principle, whether mind (*idealism*), matter (*materialism*), or something that is the basis of both —**mo'nist** *n.* —**mo·nis'tic, mo·nis'ti·cal** *adj.* —**mo·nis'-ti·cal·ly** *adv.*

mo·ni·tion (mō nish'ən) *n.* [OFr. < L. < pp. of *monere*, to warn] **1.** admonition; warning; caution **2.** an official or legal notice

mon·i·tor (mon'ə tər) *n.* [L. < pp. of *monere*, to warn] **1.** [Rare] one who advises or warns **2.** in some schools, a student chosen to help keep order, record attendance, etc. **3.** a large, flesh-eating lizard of Africa, S Asia, and Australia **4.** formerly, an armoured warship with a low, flat deck and heavy guns in revolving turrets **5.** a person who monitors **6.** a device or instrument used for monitoring **7.** *Radio & TV* a receiver or speaker, as in a control room, for checking the quality of transmission —*vt., vi.* **1.** to watch or check on (a person or thing) for some reason **2.** to check on or regulate the performance of (a machine, aircraft, etc.) **3.** to test for radioactive contamination with a monitor **4.** to listen to (a broadcast, another's telephone conversation, etc.) to gather some specified type of information **5.** *Radio & TV* to check with a monitor —**mon'i·tress** *n.fem.* —**mon'-i·to'ri·al** (-tôr'ē əl) *adj.* —**mon'i·tor·ship'** *n.*

mon·i·to·ry (mon'ə tər ē) *adj.* giving monition; admonishing —*n., pl.* **-ries** a monitory letter

monk (muŋk) *n.* [OE. *munuc* < LL. < Gr. *monos*, alone] **1.** orig., a man living in solitary self-denial for religious reasons **2.** a member of certain male religious orders, generally under vows, as of poverty, obedience, and chastity —**monk'ish** *adj.* —**monk'ish·ly** *adv.*

mon·key (muŋ'kē) *n., pl.* **-keys** [prob. < or akin to MLowG. *Moneke*, the son of Martin the Ape in the medieval beast epic *Reynard the Fox*] **1.** any of the primates except man and the lemurs; specif., any of the smaller, long-tailed primates **2.** a person regarded as like a monkey, as a mischievous child **3.** [Slang] £500 —*vi.* [Colloq.] to play, trifle, or meddle —**a monkey on one's back** [Slang] **1.** addiction to a drug **2.** any burdensome obsession, problem, etc.

monkey business [Colloq.] foolish, mischievous, or deceitful tricks or behaviour

monkey nut *another name for* PEANUT

monkey puzzle a tall, coniferous tree, originally from S. America, widely grown as an ornamental tree

mon·key·trick (-trik') *n.* [Colloq.] a mischievous trick or prank: *usually used in pl.*

monkey wrench a wrench with one movable jaw, adjusted by a screw to fit various sizes of nut, etc.

monk's cloth a heavy cloth, as of cotton, with a basket weave, used for curtains, etc.

monks·hood (muŋks'hood') *n.* *same as* ACONITE (sense 1)

mon·o (mon'ō) *adj.* clipped form of MONOPHONIC

mon·o- [Gr. < *monos*, single] a prefix meaning one, alone, single [*monograph*]

mon·o·bas·ic (mon'ə bā'sik) *adj.* *Chem.* designating an acid whose molecule contains one hydrogen atom replaceable by a metal or positive radical

mon·o·chro·mat·ic (-krō mat'ik) *adj.* [< L. < Gr.: see ff. & -IC] of or having one colour: also **mon'o·chro'ic** (-krō'ik) —**mon'o·chro·mat'i·cal·ly** *adv.*

mon·o·chrome (mon'ə krōm') *n.* [< ML. < Gr. < *monos*, single + *chrōma*, colour] a painting, drawing, or photograph in one colour or shades of one colour —**mon'-o·chro'mic** *adj.* —**mon'o·chro'mist** *n.*

mon·o·cle (mon'ə k'l) *n.* [Fr. < LL. *monoculus*, one-eyed < Gr. *monos*, single + L. *oculus*, eye] an eyeglass for one eye only —**mon'o·cled** *adj.*

mon·o·cli·nal (mon'ə klī'n'l) *adj.* *Geol.* designating or of strata dipping in one direction —*n.* *same as* MONOCLINE

Monetary Units of All Nations

Country	Basic Unit	Chief Fractional Unit	Country	Basic Unit	Chief Fractional Unit
Afganistan	afghani	pul	Kuwait	dinar	fils
Albania	lek	quintar	Laos	kip	at
Algeria	dinar	centime	Lebanon	pound	piastre
Andorra	franc	centime	Lesotho	rand	cent
	peseta	centimo	Liberia	dollar	cent
Angola	escudo	centavo	Libya	dinar	millieme
Argentina	peso	centavo	Liechtenstein	franc	rappen
Australia	dollar	cent	Luxembourg	franc	centime
Austria	schilling	groschen	Malagasy	franc	centime
Bahamas	dollar	cent	Malawi	kwacha	tambala
Bahrain	dinar	fils	Malaysia	dollar	cent
Bangladesh	taka	paisa	Maldive Is.	rupee	cent
Barbados	dollar	cent	Mali	franc	centime
Belgium	franc	centime	Malta	pound	cent
Belize	dollar	cent	Mauritania	ouguiya	khoum
Benin	franc	centime	Mauritius	rupee	cent
Bermuda	dollar	cent	Mexico	peso	centavo
Bhutan	ngultrum	tikchung	Monaco	franc	centime
Bolivia	peso boliviano	centavo	Mongolia	tugrik	mongo
Botswana	pula		Morocco	dirham	centime
Brazil	cruzeiro	centavo	Mozambique	escudo	centavo
Brunei	dollar	cent	Nauru	dollar	cent
Bulgaria	lev	stotinka	Nepal	rupee	pice
Burma	kyat	pya	Netherlands	guilder	cent
Burundi	franc	centime	New Zealand	dollar	cent
Cambodia	riel	sen	Nicaragua	córdoba	centavo
Cameroun	franc	centime	Niger	franc	centime
Canada	dollar	cent	Nigeria	naira	kobo
Cape Verde Is.	escudo	centavo	Norway	krone	øre
Central African Republic	franc	centime	Oman	rial	baisa
			Pakistan	rupee	paisa
Chad	franc	centime	Panama	balboa	centesimo
Chile	peso	escudo	Paraguay	guaraní	centimo
China	yuan	fen	Peru	sol	centavo
China (Taiwan)	dollar	cent	Philippines	peso	centavo
			Poland	zloty	grosz
Colombia	peso	centavo	Portugal	escudo	centavo
Congo	franc	centime	Qatar	riyal	dirham
Costa Rica	colón	centimo	Rhodesia	dollar	cent
Cuba	peso	centavo	Rumania	leu	ban
Cyprus	pound	mil	Rwanda	franc	centime
Czechoslovakia	koruna	haler	San Marino	lira	centesimo
Denmark	krone	øre	Saudi Arabia	riyal	qursh
Dominican Republic	peso	centavo	Senegal	franc	centime
			Sierra Leone	leone	cent
Ecuador	sucre	centavo	Singapore	dollar	cent
Egypt	pound	piastre	Somalia	shilling	cent
El Salvador	colon	centavo	South Africa	rand	cent
Equatorial Guinea	ekpwele	centimo	Spain	peseta	céntimo
Ethiopia	dollar	cent	Sri Lanka	rupee	cent
Fiji	dollar	cent	Sudan	pound	piastre
Finland	markka	penni	Surinam	guilder	cent
France	franc	centime	Swaziland	emalangeni	cent
Gabon	franc	centime	Sweden	krona	öre
Gambia	dalasi	butut	Switzerland	franc	centime
Germany, East	mark	pfennig	Syria	pound	piastre
Germany, West	deutsche mark	pfennig	Tanzania	shilling	cent
Ghana	cedi	pesewa	Thailand	baht	satang
Greece	drachma	lepton	Togo	franc	centime
Grenada	dollar	cent	Tonga	pa'anga	seniti
Guatemala	quetzal	centavo	Trinadad & Tobago	dollar	cent
Guinea	franc	centime			
Guinea-Bissau	peso		Tunisia	dinar	millime
Guyana	dollar	cent	Turkey	lira	piastre
Haiti	gourde	centime	Uganda	shilling	cent
Honduras	lempira	centavo	United Arab Emirates	dirham	fils
Hungary	forint	fillér			
Iceland	króna	eyrir	United Kingdom	pound	penny
India	rupee	paisa	United States	dollar	cent
Indonesia	rupiah	sen	Upper Volta	franc	centime
Iran	rial	dinar	Uruguay	peso	centesimo
Iraq	dinar	fils	U.S.S.R.	ruble	kopeck
Ireland	pound	penny	Vatican City	lira	centesimo
Israel	pound	agora	Venezuela	bolívar	céntimo
Italy	lira	centesimo	Vietnam	dong	hào
Ivory Coast	franc	centime	Western Samoa	dollar	cent
Jamaica	dollar	cent	Yemen, People's Democratic Rep. of	dinar	fils
Japan	yen	sen			
Jordan	dinar	fils	Yemen Arab Rep.	riyal	bugshah
Kenya	shilling	cent	Yugoslavia	dinar	para
Korea, North	won	jun	Zaire	zaire	likuta
Korea, South	won	jun	Zambia	kwacha	ngwee

mon·o·cline (mon′ə klīn′) *n.* [< MONO- + Gr. *klinein*, to incline] a monoclinal rock fold or structure

mon·o·clin·ic (mon′ə klin′ik) *adj.* [see prec. & -IC] designating a crystalline form that has three unequal axes, two of which intersect at right angles while the third is oblique to one of the others

mon·o·cli·nous (mon′ə klī′nəs) *adj.* [< ModL. < MONO- + Gr. *klinē*, a bed] *Bot.* having stamens and pistils in the same flower

mon·o·cot·y·le·don (mon′ə kot′il ē′dən) *n.* a flowering plant with one seed leaf (cotyledon) —**mon′o·cot′y·le′don·ous** *adj.*

mo·noc·ra·cy (mə nok′rə sē) *n., pl.* -cies [MONO- + -CRACY] government by one person —**mon′o·crat′ic** *adj.*

mo·noc·u·lar (mə nok′yə lər) *adj.* [< LL. *monoculus* (see MONOCLE) + -AR] 1. having only one eye 2. of, or for use by, only one eye —*n.* a field glass or telescope with only one eyepiece

mon·o·cy·cle (-sī′k'l) *n.* same as UNICYCLE

mon·o·dy (mon′ə dē) *n., pl.* -dies [< LL. < Gr. *monōidia* < *monos*, alone + *aeidein*, to sing] 1. a solo lament or dirge, as in ancient Greek tragedy 2. a poem mourning someone's death 3. *Music* a) a style of composition in which the melody is carried by one part, or voice b) a composition in this style —**mo·nod·ic** (mə nod′ik), **mo·nod′i·cal** *adj.* —**mo·nod′i·cal·ly** *adv.*

mo·noe·cious (mə nē′shəs, mō-) *adj.* [< MON(O)- + Gr. *oikos*, a house] *Bot.* having separate male flowers and female flowers on the same plant, as in maize —**mo·noe′cism** (-siz'm) *n.*

mo·nog·a·my (mə nog′ə mē) *n.* [< Fr. < LL. < Gr.: see MONO- & -GAMY] 1. the practice or state of being married to only one person at a time 2. *Zool.* the practice of having only one mate —**mo·nog′a·mist** *n.* —**mo·nog′a·mous, mon·o·gam·ic** (mon′ə gam′ik) *adj.*

mon·o·gram (mon′ə gram′) *n.* [< LL. < Gr. *mono-*, MONO- + *gramma*, letter] the initials of a name, combined in a single design —*vt.* -grammed′, -gram′ming to put a monogram on —**mon′o·gram·mat′ic** (-grə mat′ik) *adj.*

mon·o·graph (mon′ə gräf′) *n.* [MONO- + -GRAPH] a writing, esp. a scholarly one, on a single subject or aspect of a subject —**mon′o·graph′ic** (-graf′ik) *adj.* —**mo·nog′ra·pher, mo·nog′ra·phist** *n.*

mo·nog·y·nous (mə noj′ə nəs) *adj.* 1. characterized by monogyny 2. *Bot.* having one style or pistil

mo·nog·y·ny (-nē) *n.* [MONO- + -GYNY] the practice of being married to only one woman at a time

mon·o·hull (mon′ō hul′) *n.* a sailing vessel with a single hul: cf. CATAMARAN

mon·o·lith (mon′ə lith′) *n.* [< Fr. < L. < Gr. < *monos*, single + *lithos*, stone] 1. a single large block or piece of stone 2. something made of this, as an obelisk 3. something like a monolith in size, unity of structure or purpose, etc. —**mon′o·lith′ic** *adj.* —**mon′o·lith′ism** *n.*

mon·o·logue (mon′ə log′) *n.* [Fr. < Gr. < *monos*, alone + *legein*, to speak] 1. a long speech, esp. one monopolizing a conversation 2. a poem, etc. in the form of a soliloquy 3. a part of a play in which one character speaks alone; soliloquy 4. a play, skit, or recitation for one actor only —**mon′o·logu′ist, mo·nol·o·gist** (mə nol′ə jist) *n.* —**mon·o·log′i·cal** *adj.* —**mo·nol′o·gize** *vt.*

mon·o·ma·ni·a (mon′ə mā′nē ə) *n.* 1. an excessive interest in or enthusiasm for some one thing; craze 2. a mental disorder characterized by irrational preoccupation with one subject —**mon′o·ma′ni·ac** (-mā′nē ak′) *n.* —**mon′o·ma·ni′a·cal** (-mə nī′ə k'l) *adj.*

mo·no·mark (mon′ō mark′) *n.* [MONO- + MARK¹] a registered combination of letters and numbers serving to identify a product

mon·o·mer (mon′ə mər) *n.* [MONO- + Gr. *meros*, a part] a simple molecule that can form polymers by combining with identical or similar molecules —**mon′o·mer′ic** (-mer′ik) *adj.*

mon·o·met·al·lism (mon′ə met′əl iz'm) *n.* the use of only one metal, usually gold or silver, as the monetary standard —**mon′o·me·tal′lic** (-mə tal′ik) *adj.* —**mon′o·met′al·list** *n.*

mo·no·mi·al (mo nō′mē əl) *adj.* [MO(NO)- + (BI)NOMIAL] consisting of only one term, esp. in algebra —*n.* a monomial expression, quantity, etc.

mon·o·nu·cle·o·sis (mon′ə nyoo′klē ō′sis) *n.* [MO(NO)- + NUCLE(US) + -OSIS] 1. same as INFECTIOUS MONONUCLEOSIS 2. presence in the blood of too many cells with a single nucleus

mon·o·phon·ic (-fon′ik) *adj.* designating or of sound reproduction using a single channel

mon·oph·thong (mon′əf thôn′) *n.* [< Gr. *monophthongos* < *monos*, single + *phthongos*, sound] a simple or pure vowel

Mo·noph·y·site (mə nof′ə sīt′) *n.* [< L. < Gr. *monos*, single + *physis*, nature] *Theol.* one who believes that Christ had only one nature, part human and part divine, a tenet held by members of the Coptic Church —**Mo·noph′y·sit′ic** (-sit′ik, mon′ə fə-) *adj.*

mon·o·plane (mon′ə plān′) *n.* an aircraft with only one pair of wings

mo·nop·o·list (mə nop′ə list) *n.* 1. a person who has a monopoly 2. a person who favours monopoly —**mo·nop′·o·lis′tic** *adj.* —**mo·nop′o·lis′ti·cal·ly** *adv.*

mo·nop·o·lize (-līz′) *vt.* -lized′, -liz′ing 1. to get, have, or exploit a monopoly of 2. to dominate or occupy completely —**mo·nop′o·li·za′tion** *n.* —**mo·nop′o·liz′er** *n.*

mo·nop·o·ly (-lē) *n., pl.* -lies [< L. < Gr. < *monopōlia*, exclusive sale < *monos*, single + *pōlein*, to sell] 1. exclusive control of a commodity or service in a given market, or control that makes possible the fixing of prices 2. such control granted by a government 3. any exclusive possession or control 4. something held or controlled as a monopoly 5. a company, etc. that has a monopoly

mon·o·rail (mon′ə rāl′) *n.* 1. a single rail serving as a track for cars suspended from it or balanced on it 2. a railway with such a track

mon·o·so·di·um glu·ta·mate (mon′ə sō′dē əm gloo′tə māt′) a white, crystalline powder used in foods to enhance flavour

mon·o·syl·lab·ic (mon′ə si lab′ik) *adj.* 1. having only one syllable 2. consisting of, using, or speaking in monosyllables —**mon′o·syl·lab′i·cal·ly** *adv.*

mon·o·syl·la·ble (mon′ə sil′ə b'l) *n.* a word of one syllable

mon·o·the·ism (mon′ə thē iz'm) *n.* [MONO- + THEISM] the doctrine or belief that there is only one God —**mon′o·the·ist** *n.* —**mon′o·the·is′tic, mon′o·the·is′ti·cal** *adj.* —**mon′o·the·is′ti·cal·ly** *adv.*

mon·o·tint (mon′ə tint′) *n.* same as MONOCHROME

mon·o·tone (-tōn′) *n.* 1. utterance of successive words without change of pitch or key 2. monotony of tone, style, colour, etc. 3. a single, unchanging musical tone 4. recitation, singing, etc. in such a tone 5. a person who sings in such a tone —**mon′o·ton′ic** (-ton′ik) *adj.*

mo·not·o·nous (mə not′ən əs) *adj.* [< LL. < Gr.: see MONO-& TONE] 1. going on in the same tone without variation 2. having little or no variety 3. tiresome because unvarying —**mo·not′o·nous·ly** *adv.* —**mo·not′o·nous·ness** *n.*

mo·not·o·ny (-ē) *n.* 1. sameness of tone or pitch 2. lack of variety 3. tiresome sameness

mon·o·treme (mon′ə trēm′) *n.* [< ModL. < Gr. *monos*, single + *trēma*, hole] any of the lowest order of mammals (platypuses and echidnas), which lay eggs and have a single opening for the excretory and genital organs —**mon′o·trem′a·tous** (-trem′ə təs, -trē′mə-) *adj.*

mon·o·type (-tīp′) *n.* [MONO- + -TYPE] 1. *Biol.* the only type of its group 2. *Printing* type produced by Monotype —[M-] a trademark for either of a pair of machines for casting and setting up type in separate characters: one, a casting machine, is controlled by a paper tape perforated on the other, a keyboard machine

mon·o·va·lent (mon′ə vā′lənt) *adj.* *Chem.* same as UNIVALENT —**mon′o·va′lence, mon′o·va′len·cy** *n.*

mon·ox·ide (mə nok′sīd, mon ok′-) *n.* an oxide with one atom of oxygen in each molecule

Mon·sei·gneur (mon′sen yur′; *Fr.* môn se nyēr′) *n., pl.* **Mes·sei·gneurs** (mes′en yurz′; *Fr.* mā se nyēr′) [Fr., lit., my lord] 1. a French title of honour given to persons of high birth or rank, as princes, bishops, etc. 2. [often m-] a person with this title

mon·sieur (mə syur′; *Fr.* mə syö′) *n., pl.* **mes·sieurs** (mes′ərz; *Fr.* mā syö′) [Fr., lit., my lord] a man; gentleman: French title [M-], equivalent to *Mr.* or *Sir*: abbrev. **M., Mons.**

Monsig. 1. Monseigneur 2. Monsignor

Mon·si·gnor (mon sēn′yər; *It.* môn′sē nyôr′) *n., pl.* **-gnors** (-yərz) *It.* **-gno′ri** (-nyô′rē) [It., lit., my lord] 1. a title of certain Roman Catholic prelates 2. [often m-] a person with this title

mon·soon (mon soon′) *n.* [< MDu. < Port. < Ar. *mausim*, a season] 1. a seasonal wind of the Indian Ocean and S Asia, blowing from the southwest from April to October, and from the northeast the rest of the year 2. the rainy season, when this wind blows from the southwest —**mon·soon′al** *adj.*

mon·ster (mon′stər) *n.* [< OFr. < L. *monstrum*, divine portent < *monere*, to warn] 1. any plant or animal greatly malformed, lacking parts, etc. 2. any imaginary creature with striking incongruities in form, as a centaur or unicorn 3. something monstrous 4. any very cruel or wicked person 5. any huge animal or thing —*adj.* huge; enormous; monstrous

mon·strance (mon′strəns) *n.* [OFr. < ML. < L. *monstrare*, to show] *R.C.Ch.* a receptacle in which the consecrated Host is exposed for adoration

mon·stros·i·ty (mon stros′ə tē) *n.* 1. the state or quality of being monstrous 2. *pl.* -ties a monstrous thing or creature

mon·strous (mon′strəs) *adj.* 1. abnormally large; enormous 2. very unnatural in shape, type, or character 3. having the character or appearance of a monster 4.

horrible; hideous **5.** hideously wrong or evil —*adv.* [Archaic] very; extremely —**mon'strous·ly** *adv.* —**mon'-strous·ness** *n.*

mon·tage (mon täzh', môn-) *n.* [Fr. < *monter*, MOUNT²] **1.** *a)* the art or process of making a composite picture from a number of different pictures *b)* a picture so made **2.** *Cinema & T.V. a)* the art or process of producing a sequence of abruptly alternating or superimposed scenes or images *b)* such a sequence **3.** any technique, as in literature, with a similar sequence of elements —*vt.* **-taged', -tag'ing** to incorporate in a montage

mon·te (mon'tē) *n.* [Sp., lit., mountain, hence heap of cards] a game in which players bet on the colour of cards to be turned up

Mon·tes·so·ri method (or **system**) (mon'tə sôr'ē) [after Maria *Montessori* (1870–1952), It. educator who devised it] a system of teaching young children which emphasizes training of the senses and guidance intended to encourage self-education

month (munth) *n.* [OE. *monath*] **1.** any of the twelve parts into which the calendar year is divided: also **calendar month 2.** *a)* the time from any day of one month to the corresponding day of the next *b)* a period of four weeks or 30 days **3.** the period of a complete revolution of the moon (in full, **lunar month**) **4.** one twelfth of the solar year (in full, **solar month**) —**month after month** every month —**month by month** each month —**month in, month out** every month

month·ly (munth'lē) *adj.* **1.** continuing or lasting for a month **2.** done, happening, payable, etc. every month —*n., pl.* **-lies** a periodical published once a month —*adv.* once a month; every month

mon·u·ment (mon'yə mənt) *n.* [OFr. < L. *monumentum* < *monere*, to remind] **1.** something set up to keep alive the memory of a person or event, as a tablet, statue, building, etc., esp. [M-] a column in London in memory of the fire of London, 1666 **2.** a writing, etc. serving as a memorial **3.** *a)* a work of enduring significance [*monuments* of learning] *b)* an outstanding example [a *monument* of bigotry] **4.** a stone boundary marker **5.** [Obs.] a tomb

mon·u·men·tal (mon'yə men't'l) *adj.* **1.** of, suitable for, or serving as a monument **2.** like a monument; massive, enduring, etc. **3.** of lasting importance **4.** very great; colossal [*monumental* pride] —**mon'u·men'tal·ly** *adv.*

mon·u·men·tal·ize (-īz') *vt.* **-ized', -iz'ing** to memorialize as by a monument; make monumental

monumental mason a maker and engraver of tombstones

-mo·ny (mō'nē, mə-) [L. *-monia, -monium*] a suffix meaning a resulting thing or state [patrimony]

moo (mōō) *n., pl.* **moos** [echoic] the vocal sound made by a cow; lowing sound —*vi.* **mooed, moo'ing** to make this sound; low

mooch (mōōch) *vi., vt.* [ult. < OFr. *muchier*, to hide] **1.** to loaf, loiter or walk aimlessly or idly **2.** to lurk; skulk —**mooch'er** *n.*

moo cow a child's name for a COW¹

mood¹ (mōōd) *n.* [OE. *mod*, mind] **1.** a particular state of mind or feeling; humour, or temper **2.** a prevailing feeling, spirit, or tone **3.** [*pl.*] fits of morose, sullen, or uncertain temper —**in the mood** in a favourable state of mind

mood² (mōōd) *n.* [< MODE, altered after prec.] *Gram.* that aspect of verbs which indicates whether the action or state expressed is regarded as a fact (*indicative mood*), as a matter of supposition, desire, etc. (*subjunctive mood*), or as a command (*imperative mood*)

mood·y (mōō'dē) *adj.* **mood'i·er, mood'i·est 1.** subject to or characterized by gloomy, sullen, or changing moods **2.** resulting from or indicating such a mood —**mood'i·ly** *adv.* —**mood'i·ness** *n.*

Moog Synthesizer (mōōg) [after Robert *Moog* (1935-), U.S. engineer] a *trademark for* an electronic instrument capable of producing a wide range of musical sounds

mool·vie (mool'vi) *n.* [Hindi] an expert in Moslem law; a teacher

moon (mōōn) *n.* [OE. *mona*] **1.** the satellite of the earth, that revolves around it once in 29½ days and shines at night by reflecting the sun's light **2.** this body as it appears at a particular time of the month: see NEW MOON, HALF-MOON, FULL MOON, OLD

PHASES OF THE MOON

MOON **3.** a month; esp., a lunar month **4.** *same as* MOONLIGHT **5.** anything shaped like the moon (i.e., an orb or crescent) **6.** any satellite of a planet —*vi.* to behave in an idle, dreamy, or abstracted way —*vt.* to pass (time) in mooning —**over the moon** elated; very excited

moon·beam (-bēm') *n.* a ray of moonlight

moon·calf (-käf') *n.* **1.** an idiot or fool **2.** a youth who spends time mooning about

moon-faced (-fāst') *adj.* round-faced

moon·fish (-fish') *n., pl.* **-fish', -fish'es:** see FISH an oval-shaped sea fish found in the warmer coastal waters of North and South America

moon·let (-lit) *n.* a small moon or artificial satellite

moon·light (-līt') *n.* the light of the moon —*adj.* **1.** of moonlight **2.** lighted by the moon **3.** done or occurring by moonlight, or at night

moonlight flit a hurried departure by night to escape one's creditors

moon·light·ing (-līt'iŋ) *n.* [from the usual night hours of such jobs] the practice of holding a second regular job in addition to one's main job

moon·lit (-lit') *adj.* lighted by the moon

moon·quake (-kwāk') *n.* a trembling of the surface of the moon, thought to be caused by internal rock slippage or, possibly, meteorite impact

moon·scape (-skāp') *n.* [MOON + (LAND)SCAPE] the surface of the moon or a representation of it

moon·shee (mōōn'shē) *n.* [Urdu *munshī* < Ar. *munshīh*, writer] in India a secretary or teacher of languages

moon·shine (-shīn') *n.* **1.** the light of the moon **2.** foolish or empty talk, ideas, etc. **3.** [U.S. Colloq.] whisky unlawfully made or smuggled

moon·shin·er (-shī'nər) *n.* [U.S. Colloq.] a person who makes and sells alcoholic liquor unlawfully

moon·shot (-shot') *n.* the launching of a rocket to the moon

moon·stone (-stōn') *n.* a translucent feldspar with a pearly lustre, used as a gem

moon·struck (-struk') *adj.* **1.** crazed; lunatic **2.** romantically dreamy **3.** dazed or distracted Also **moon'-strick'en** (-strik''n)

moon·y (-ē) *adj.* **moon'i·er, moon'i·est** mooning; listless; dreamy

Moor (moor) *n.* [< OFr. < L. < Gr. *Mauros*] **1.** a member of a Moslem people of mixed Arab and Berber descent living in NW Africa **2.** a member of a group of this people that invaded and occupied Spain in the 8th cent. A.D. —**Moor'-ish** *adj.*

moor¹ (moor) *n.* [OE. *mor*] a tract of open, rolling wasteland, usually covered with heather and often marshy; heath

moor² (moor) *vt.* [< or akin to MDu. *maren*, LowG. *moren*, to tie] **1.** to hold (a ship, etc.) in place by cables or chains as to a pier or buoy **2.** to secure —*vi.* **1.** to moor a ship, etc. **2.** to be secured as by cables —**moor'age** (-ij) *n.*

moor·hen (moor'hen') *n.* a common aquatic bird of the rail family, inhabiting ponds, lakes, etc.

moor·ing (-iŋ) *n.* **1.** [*often pl.*] the lines, cables, etc. by which a ship, etc. is moored **2.** [*pl.*] a place where a ship, etc. is moored **3.** [*often pl.*] beliefs, habits, ties, etc. that make one feel secure

moor·land (-land') *n.* *same as* MOOR¹

moose (mōōs) *n., pl.* **moose** [< Algonquian] **1.** the largest animal of the deer family, native to the N U.S. and Canada: the male has huge antlers **2.** *same as* ELK (sense 1)

MOOSE
(1.4–1.8 m high at shoulder)

moot (mōōt) *n.* [OE. *mot, gemot*, a meeting] **1.** an early English assembly of freemen to administer justice, etc. **2.** a discussion or argument, esp. of a case in a moot court: see FISH —*adj.* **1.** debatable **2.** so hypothetical as to be meaningless —*vt.* **1.** to debate or discuss **2.** to propose for discussion or debate

moot court a mock court in which hypothetical cases are tried as an exercise for law students

mop (mop) *n.* [ult. < ? L. *mappa*, napkin] **1.** a bundle of rags or yarn, or a sponge, etc., fastened to the end of a stick, as for washing floors **2.** anything suggestive of this, as a thick head of hair —*vt.* **mopped, mop'ping** to wash, wipe, or remove with or as with a mop —**mop up** [Colloq.] to finish —**mop'per** *n.*

mope (mōp) *vi.* **moped, mop'ing** [akin to MDu. *mopen*] to be gloomy and apathetic —*n.* **1.** a person who mopes **2.** [*pl.*] low spirits —**mop'er** *n.* —**mop'ey, mop'y, mop'ish** *adj.* —**mop'ish·ly** *adv.*

mo·ped (mō'ped') *n.* [< MO(TOR) + PED(AL)] a bicycle propelled by a small motor

mo·poke (mō'pōk) *n.* [< imitation of bird's note] **1.** a small spotted owl, found in New Zealand and Australia **2.** [Aust.] a bird related to the nightjar Also **more'pork** (môr'pôrk)

Mopp, Mrs *see* MRS MOPP

mop·pet (mop′it) *n.* [< ?] [Colloq.] a little child: a term of affection

Mor. Morocco

mor·a (môr′ə) *n.* [It.] a guessing game played with the fingers, popular in many countries, including China and Italy: also **mor·ra**

mo·raine (mə rān′, mo-) *n.* [Fr. < *morre*, a muzzle] a mass of rocks, gravel, sand, etc. deposited by a glacier, along its side (**lateral moraine**), at its lower end (**terminal moraine**), or beneath the ice (**ground moraine**) —**mo·rain′al, mo·rain′ic** *adj.*

mor·al (môr′əl) *adj.* [< L. < *mos*, pl. *mores*, manners, morals] **1.** relating to, dealing with, or capable of distinguishing between, right and wrong in conduct **2.** of, teaching, or in accordance with, the principles of right and wrong **3.** good or right in conduct or character; sometimes, specif., sexually virtuous **4.** designating support, etc. that involves sympathy without action **5.** being virtually such because of its effect on thoughts, attitudes, etc. [a *moral* victory] **6.** based on strong probability [a *moral* certainty] —*n.* **1.** a moral lesson taught by a fable, event, etc. **2.** [*pl.*] principles, standards, or habits with respect to right or wrong in conduct; ethics; sometimes, specif., standards of sexual behaviour —**mor′al·ly** *adv.*

mo·rale (mə rāl′, mo-) *n.* [Fr., fem. of *moral*: see prec.] moral or mental condition with respect to courage, discipline, confidence, enthusiasm, etc. [the *morale* of the troops was low]

mor·al·ist (môr′əl ist) *n.* **1.** a person who moralizes **2.** a person who adheres to a system of moral teaching **3.** a person who seeks to impose his morals on others —**mor′al·is′tic** *adj.* —**mor′al·is′ti·cal·ly** *adv.*

mo·ral·i·ty (mə ral′ə tē, mo-) *n.*, *pl.* **-ties** **1.** moral quality or character; rightness or wrongness, as of an action **2.** a being in accord with the principles or standards of right conduct; virtue **3.** principles of right and wrong in conduct; ethics **4.** moral instruction or lesson **5.** a narrative with a moral lesson **6.** *same as* MORALITY PLAY

morality play any of a class of allegorical dramas of the 15th and 16th cent., whose characters were personifications, as Everyman, Vice, etc.

mor·al·ize (môr′ə līz′) *vi.* **-ized′, -iz′ing** to consider or discuss matters of right and wrong, often in a self-righteous way —*vt.* **1.** *a*) to explain in terms of right and wrong *b*) to draw a moral from **2.** to improve the morals of —**mor′·al·i·za′tion** *n.* —**mor′al·iz′er** *n.*

moral philosophy *same as* ETHICS

Moral Rearmament a worldwide movement for moral and spiritual renewal founded (1938) by Frank Buchman at Oxford: also called **Buchmanism** and the **Oxford Group**

mo·rass (mə ras′, mo-) *n.* [< Du. < OFr. < Frank. *marisk*, a swamp] a tract of low, soft, watery ground; bog; swamp: often used figuratively of a difficult or troublesome state of affairs

mor·a·to·ri·um (môr′ə tôr′ē əm) *n.*, *pl.* **-ri·ums, -ri·a** (-ə) [ModL. < LL. < L. < *mora*, a delay] **1.** a legal authorization, usually by an emergency law, to delay payment of money due **2.** the effective period of such an authorization **3.** any authorized delay or stopping of some specified activity

Mo·ra·vi·an (mo rā′vē ən, mə-) *adj.* **1.** of Moravia, its people, etc. **2.** of the religious sect of Moravians —*n.* **1.** a native or inhabitant of Moravia **2.** the Czech dialect of Moravia **3.** a member of a Protestant sect founded by people from Moravia (c.1722)

mo·ray (mor′ā; mo rā′, mə-) *n.* [< Port. < L. *muraena*, kind of fish < Gr. *myraina*] a voracious, brilliantly coloured eel, found esp. among coral reefs: in full, **moray eel**

mor·bid (môr′bid) *adj.* [L. *morbidus*, sickly < *morbus*, disease] **1.** of, having, or caused by disease; diseased **2.** having or showing an interest in gruesome or gloomy matters **3.** gruesome; horrible [*morbid* details of a crime] —**mor·bid′i·ty, mor′bid·ness** *n.* —**mor′bid·ly** *adv.*

mor·bif·ic (môr bif′ik) *adj.* [Fr. *morbifique*, < L. *morbus*, disease + *facere*, to make] causing or leading to disease: also **mor·bif′i·cal**

mor·dant (môr′d′nt) *adj.* [< OFr. prp. of *mordre* < L. *mordere*, to bite] **1.** biting, caustic, or sarcastic [*mordant* wit] **2.** corrosive **3.** acting as a mordant —*n.* **1.** a substance used in dyeing to fix the colours **2.** an acid, etc. used in etching to bite lines, areas, etc. into the surface—**mor′dan·cy** *n.* —**mor′dant·ly** *adv.*

more (môr) *adj.* *superl.* MOST [OE. *mara*] **1.** greater in amount, quantity, or degree: used as the comparative of MUCH **2.** greater in number: used as the comparative of MANY **3.** additional; further [take *more* tea] —*n.* **1.** a greater amount, quantity, or degree **2.** [*with pl. v.*] a greater number (*of*) [*more* of us are going] **3.** something additional or further [*more* can be said] —*adv.* *superl.* MOST **1.** in or to a greater degree or extent: used with many adjectives and adverbs (regularly with those of three or more syllables) to form comparatives **2.** in addition; further —**more and more 1.** increasingly **2.** a constantly increasing amount, quantity, etc. —**more or less 1.** somewhat **2.** approximately —**more than 1.** extremely [she was *more than* pleased] **2.** in addition to

more·ish (môr′ish) *adj.* [< MORE + -ISH] [Colloq.] appetizing, tempting, esp. making one want more

mo·rel (mə rel′, mo-) *n.* [< Fr. < MDu. < OHG. *morhila*, dim. of *morha*, carrot] an edible mushroom that looks like a sponge on a stalk

mo·rel·lo (mə rel′ō) *n.*, *pl.* **-los** [It. *morello*, dark-skinned < L. *amarus*, bitter] a variety of small sour cherry with dark-red skin and juice

more·o·ver (môr ō′vər) *adv.* in addition to what has been said; besides; further; also

mo·res (môr′āz) *n.pl.* [L., pl. of *mos*, custom] folkways that, through general observance, develop the force of law

mor·ga·nat·ic (môr′gə nat′ik) *adj.* [< ML. < *morganaticum*, altered < OHG. *morgengeba*, morning gift given to one's bride (in lieu of any share of a husband's property)] designating or of a form of marriage in which a man of royalty or nobility marries a woman of inferior social status with the provision that neither she nor their offspring may lay claim to his rank or property —**mor′ga·nat′i·cal·ly** *adv.*

MOREL

mor·gen (môr′gən) *n.*, *pl.* **-gen, -gens** [Du. & G., lit., MORNING: hence area ploughed in one morning] **1.** a land measure formerly used in the Netherlands and still used in South Africa, equal to about 2 acres, or 0.8 hectare **2.** a land measure formerly used in Prussia and Scandinavia, equal to about 2/3 acre or 0.26 hectares

morgue (môrg) *n.* [Fr.] **1.** a place where the bodies of unknown dead persons or those dead of unknown causes are kept to be examined, identified, etc. **2.** a newspaper office's reference library of back numbers, clippings, etc.

mor·i·bund (môr′ə bund) *adj.* [< L. *moribundus* < *mori*, to die] **1.** dying **2.** coming to an end **3.** having little or no vitality left —**mor′i·bund′i·ty** *n.*

mo·ri·on (môr′ē on′) *n.* [Fr. < Sp. < *morra*, crown of the head] a crested, visorless helmet of the 16th and 17th cent., with a curved brim coming to a peak in front and behind

Mo·ris·co (mə ris′kō, mo-) *adj.* [Sp. < *Moro*, Moor] Moorish —*n.*, *pl.* **-cos, -coes** a Moor; esp., one of the Moors of Spain

mor·ish (môr′ish) *adj.* *var. of* MOREISH

Mor·mon (môr′mən) *n.* a member of the Church of Jesus Christ of Latter-day Saints (commonly called the *Mormon Church*), founded in the U.S. in 1830 by Joseph Smith —*adj.* of the Mormons or their religion —**Mor′mon·ism** *n.*

morn (môrn) *n.* [OE. *morne*] [Poet.] morning

mor·nay (môr′nā′) *adj.* [? < Phillipe de *Mornay* (1549-1623)] denoting a white sauce to which cheese is added

morn·ing (môr′niŋ) *n.* [ME. *morweninge* (by analogy with EVENING) < OE. *morgen*] **1.** the first or early part of the day, from midnight, or esp. dawn, to noon **2.** the first or early part [the *morning* of life] **3.** dawn; daybreak —*adj.* of, suited to, or occurring, appearing, etc. in the morning

morning after [Colloq.] a hangover, or painful awakening

morning dress formal daytime dress for men, including a cutaway frock coat (**morning coat**)

morning glory a twining annual plant with heart-shaped leaves and trumpet-shaped flowers of lavender, blue, pink, or white

morning paper a newspaper produced in the early hours of the morning, usually to be read at breakfast

morning room a room used esp. in the morning, for breakfast, etc.

morn·ings (-niŋz) *adv.* [Colloq.] during every morning or most mornings

morning sickness nausea and vomiting occurring in the morning during the first months of pregnancy

morning star a planet, esp. Venus, visible in the eastern sky before sunrise

Mo·ro (môr′ō) *n.* [Sp., a Moor] **1.** *pl.* **-ros, -ro** a member of a group of Moslem Malay tribes living in the S Philippines **2.** their language

mo·roc·co (mə ro′kō) *n.* [after Morocco in NW Africa] a fine, soft leather made, orig. in Morocco, from goatskins: also **morocco leather**

mo·ron (môr′on) *n.* [arbitrary use of Gr. neut. of *mōros*, foolish] **1.** a person having mild mental retardation **2.** [Colloq.] a very stupid person —**mo·ron′ic** *adj.* —**mo·ron′i·cal·ly** *adv.* —**mo·ron′i·ty, mo′ron·ism** *n.*

mo·rose (mə rōs′) *adj.* [L. *morosus*, fretful < *mos* (gen.

moris), manner] **1.** ill-tempered; gloomy, sullen, etc. **2.** characterized by gloom —**mo·rose′ly** *adv.* —**mo·rose′ness** *n.*

-morph (môrf) [< Gr. *morphē,* form] *a combining form meaning* one having a (specified) form

mor·pheme (môr′fēm) *n.* [< Fr. < Gr. *morphē,* form] the smallest meaningful unit or form in a language: it may be an affix (*re-* in *refill*), a base (*do* in *undo*), or an inflectional form (*-s* in *girls*) —**mor·phe′mic** *adj.* —**mor·phe′mi·cal·ly** *adv.*

-mor·phic (môr′fik) [< Gr. *morphē,* form + -IC] *a combining form meaning* having a (specified) form or shape [*anthropomorphic*]

mor·phine (môr′fēn) *n.* [< G. or Fr. < ModL. *morphium* < L. *Morpheus,* Roman god of sleep and dreams] a bitter, white or colourless, crystalline alkaloid derived from opium and used in medicine to relieve pain: also **mor′phi·a** (-fē ə)

mor·phol·o·gy (môr fol′ə jē) *n.* [< G. < Gr. *morphē,* form + -LOGY] **1.** the branch of biology dealing with the form and structure of animals and plants **2.** the branch of linguistics dealing with the internal structure and forms of words —**mor′pho·log′i·cal** (-fə loj′i k′l), **mor′pho·log′ic** *adj.* —**mor′pho·log′i·cal·ly** *adv.* —**mor·phol′o·gist** *n.*

-mor·phous (môr′fəs) [< Gr. < *morphē,* form] *same as* -MORPHIC

mor·ris (mor′is) *adj.* [< ME. *morys,* MOORISH] of an old folk dance performed esp. on May Day, in which fancy costumes are worn, often those associated with characters in the Robin Hood legends —*n.* this dance

Morris chair [after William *Morris* (1834-96), Brit. poet & artist] an armchair with an adjustable back

morris man a dancer in a morris dance: also **morris dancer**

mor·ro (mor′ō) *n., pl.* -ros [Sp.] a rounded hill or point of land

mor·row (mor′ō) *n.* [< OE. *morgen,* morning] [Poet.] **1.** morning **2.** the next day **3.** the time just after some particular event

Morse (mors) *adj.* [after Samuel *Morse* (1791-1872), U.S. inventor] [often **m-**] designating or of a code, or alphabet, consisting of a system of dots and dashes, or short and long sounds, used in telgraphy, etc. —*n.* the Morse code

mor·sel (môr′s′l) *n.* [< OFr. dim. of *mors* < L. *morsum,* a bite < pp. of *mordere,* to bite] **1.** a small bite or portion of food **2.** a small amount; bit

mor·tal (môr′t′l) *adj.* [< OFr. < L. *mortalis* < *mors* (gen. *mortis*), death] **1.** that must eventually die **2.** of man as a being who must eventually die **3.** of this world **4.** of death **5.** causing death; fatal **6.** to the death [*mortal* combat] **7.** not to be pacified [a *mortal* enemy] **8.** very intense; grievous [*mortal* terror] **9.** [Colloq.] a) extreme; very great b) very long and tedious c) possible [of no *mortal* good to anyone] **10.** R.C.Ch. causing spiritual death: said of sins regarded as serious —*n.* a being who must eventually die; esp., a human being —*adv.* [Dial.] extremely —**mor′tal·ly** *adv.*

mor·tal·i·ty (môr tal′ə tē) *n.* **1.** the mortal nature of man **2.** death on a large scale, as from disease or war **3.** the proportion of deaths to the population of a region, nation, etc.; death rate **4.** the proportion that fail **5.** human beings collectively

mor·tar (môr′tər) *n.* [< OE. & OFr. < L. *mortarium*] **1.** a very hard bowl in which substances are ground or pounded to a powder with a pestle **2.** a short-barrelled cannon with a low muzzle velocity, which hurls shells in a high trajectory **3.** a mixture of cement or lime with sand and water, used between bricks, etc., or as plaster —*vt.* **1.** to plaster together with mortar **2.** to attack with mortar shells

mor·tar·board (-bôrd′) *n.* **1.** a square board with a handle beneath, on which mortar is carried **2.** an academic cap with a square, flat top,

mort·gage (môr′gij) *n.* [< OFr. < *mort,* dead + *gage,* GAGE¹] *Law* **1.** the pledging of property to a creditor as security for the payment of a debt **2.** the deed by which this pledge is made —*vt.* -gaged, -gag·ing **1.** *Law* to pledge (property) by a mortgage **2.** to put an advance claim or liability on [he *mortgaged* his future]

mort·ga·gee (môr′gə jē′) *n.* a person to whom property is mortgaged

mort·ga·gor, mort·gag·er (môr′gi jər) *n.* a person who mortgages property

mor·tice (môr′tis) *n., vt. alt. sp.* of MORTISE

mor·ti·cian (môr tish′ən) *n.* [< L. *mors,* death + -ICIAN] [U.S.] *same as* UNDERTAKER

mor·ti·fi·ca·tion (môr′tə fi kā′shən) *n.* **1.** a mortifying or being mortified; specif., a) the control of physical desires by self-denial, fasting, etc. b) shame, humiliation, etc. **2.** something causing shame, humiliation, etc. **3.** old term for GANGRENE

mor·ti·fy (môr′tə fī′) *vt.* -fied′, -fy′ing [< OFr. < LL. *mortificare,* to kill < L. *mors,* death (see MORTAL) + *facere,* to make] **1.** to punish (one's body) or control (one's physical desires) by self-denial, fasting, etc. **2.** to shame, humiliate, etc. **3.** [Now Rare] to make gangrenous —*vi.* [Now Rare] to become gangrenous —**mor′ti·fi′er** *n.*

mor·tise (môr′tis) *n.* [MFr. *mortaise* < Ar. *murtazza,* joined] a notch or hole cut, as in a piece of wood, to receive a projecting part (*tenon*) shaped to fit —*vt.* -tised, -tis·ing **1.** to join or fasten securely, esp. with a mortise and tenon **2.** to cut a mortise in

mortise chisel a specially strong chisel, designed for making mortises

mortise lock a lock set into a mortise in a door so that the mechanism of the lock is enclosed by the door

mort·main (môrt′mān′) *n.* [< OFr. < ML. < L. pp. of *mori,* to die + *manus,* hand] *Law* a transfer of lands or houses to a corporate body, as a church, for perpetual ownership

mor·tu·ar·y (môr′tyoo wər ē) *n., pl.* -ar′ies [< LL. < L. *mortuus,* dead] a place where dead bodies are kept before burial or cremation, as a morgue or funeral parlour —*adj.* **1.** of or having to do with the burial of the dead **2.** of death

Mo·sa·ic (mō zā′ik) *adj.* of Moses or the writings, principles, etc. attributed to him

mo·sa·ic (mō zā′ik) *n.* [< OFr. < ML. *musaicum* < LL. < L. *musa,* MUSE] **1.** the process of making pictures or designs by inlaying small bits of coloured stone, glass, etc. in mortar **2.** a picture or design so made **3.** anything resembling this **4.** the photosensitive plate in a television camera tube —*adj.* of or resembling mosaic or a mosaic —*vt.* -icked, -ick·ing to make by or as by mosaic —**mo·sa′i·cal·ly** *adv.* —**mo·sa′i·cist** (-ə sist) *n.*

Mosaic law the ancient Hebrew law, ascribed to Moses and contained mainly in the Pentateuch

mo·sey (mō′zē) *vi.* [< *vamose,* var. of VAMOOSE] [Chiefly U.S. Slang] **1.** to amble along **2.** to go away

Mos·lem (moz′ləm, muz′-, mos′-) *n.* [Ar. *muslim,* true believer < *aslama,* to resign oneself (to God)] an adherent of Islam —*adj.* of Islam or the Moslems: also **Mos·lem′ic** (-lem′ik) —**Mos′lem·ism** *n.*

mosque (mosk) *n.* [< MFr. < It. < Ar. *masjid* < *sajada,* to pray] a Moslem temple or place of worship

mos·qui·to (mə skēt′ō) *n., pl.* -toes, -tos [Sp. & Port., dim. of *mosca* < L. *musca,* a fly] a two-winged insect, the female of which has skin-piercing, bloodsucking mouthparts: some varieties transmit diseases, as malaria and yellow fever —**mos·qui′to·ey** (-ē) *adj.*

mosquito craft a light, manoeuvrable naval vessel

mosquito net (or **netting**) a fine mesh curtain for keeping out mosquitoes

moss (mos) *n.* [OE. *mos,* a swamp] **1.** a very small, green plant growing in velvety clusters on rocks, trees, moist ground, etc. **2.** any of various similar plants, as some lichens, algae, etc. **3.** [Chiefly Scot.] a peat bog or swamp —*vt.* to cover with a growth of moss —**moss′like′** *adj.*

moss agate agate with mosslike markings

moss hag a portion of a peat moor from which the peat has been cut

mos·so (môs′sō) *adv.* [It. pp. *muovere,* to move] *Music* with movement; rapidly

moss rose 1. *same as* PORTULACA **2.** a variety of the cabbage rose with a roughened, mossy flower stalk and calyx

moss stitch *Knitting* rows alternating plain and purl stitches yielding a knobbly pattern

moss·troop·er (-troo′pər) *n.* [< Scot. *moss,* a swamp] **1.** any of the raiders who infested the swampy borderland between England and Scotland in the 17th cent. **2.** a raider; marauder

moss·y (-ē) *adj.* **moss′i·er, moss′i·est 1.** full of or covered with moss or a mosslike growth **2.** like moss —**moss′i·ness** *n.*

most (mōst) *adj. compar.* MORE [OE *mast*] **1.** greatest in amount, quantity, or degree: used as the superlative of MUCH **2.** greatest in number: used as the superlative of MANY **3.** in the greatest number of instances [*most* fame is fleeting] —*n.* **1.** the greatest amount, quantity, or degree **2.** [with pl. v.] the greatest number (of) —*adv.* **1.** *compar.* MORE in or to the greatest degree or extent: used with many adjectives and adverbs (regularly with those of three or more syllables) to form superlatives **2.** very [a *most* beautiful morning] —**at (the) most** at the very limit; not more than —**make the most of** to take the fullest advantage of

-most (mōst) [OE. *-mest*] *a suffix used in forming superlatives* [foremost, hindmost]

most·ly (mōst′lē) *adv.* **1.** for the most part **2.** chiefly; principally **3.** usually; generally

Most Reverend the form of address used for archbishops or Irish Roman Catholic bishops

mot (mō) *n.* [Fr., a word < L. *muttum,* a grunt] a witticism or pithy remark

M.O.T. Ministy of Transport

mote (mōt) *n.* [OE. *mot*] a speck, as of dust

mo·tel (mō tel') *n.* [MO(TORIST) + (HO)TEL] a hotel for those travelling by car, with accessible parking

mo·tet (mō tet') *n.* [OFr. dim. of *mot*, a word] a contrapuntal, polyphonic song of a sacred nature

moth (moth) *n., pl.* **moths** (mothz, moths) [OE. *moththe*] a four-winged, chiefly night-flying insect related to the butterfly but generally smaller and less brightly coloured; specif., a small moth (**clothes moth**) whose larvae eat holes in woollens, furs, etc. **2.** the holes in clothing caused by such larvae: often preceded by *the*

moth·ball (-bôl') *n.* a small ball of naphthalene, the fumes of which repel moths, as from woollens, furs, etc. —*vt.* to store with protective covering —**in** (or **out of**) **mothballs** put into (or taken from) storage

moth·eat·en (-ēt''n) *adj.* **1.** gnawed away in patches by moths, as cloth **2.** worn-out **3.** outdated

moth·er[1] (muth'ər) *n.* [OE. *modor*] **1.** a woman who has borne a child; esp., a woman as she is related to her child **2.** *a)* a stepmother *b)* a mother-in-law **3.** the female parent of a plant or animal **4.** that which is the origin, source, or nurturer of something **5.** *a)* a woman having the responsibility and authority of a mother *b)* a woman who is the head (**mother superior**) of a religious establishment **6.** [Rare] an elderly woman: used as a title of affectionate respect —*adj.* **1.** of, like, or like that of a mother **2.** native [*mother* tongue] —*vt.* **1.** to be the mother of **2.** to care for as a mother does —**moth'er·less** *adj.*

moth·er[2] (muth'ər) *n.* [altered (after prec.) < MDu. *moeder*] *same as* MOTHER OF VINEGAR

Mother Car·ey's chicken (ker'ēz) [< ?] any of various oceanic petrels; esp., *same as* STORMY PETREL (sense 1)

mother country **1.** *same as* MOTHERLAND **2.** the original country of emigrants

mother earth **1.** the earth as a mother, particularly in its fertility **2.** soil; ground

Mother Goose the imaginary creator of a collection of English nursery rhymes

moth·er·hood (muth'ər hood') *n.* **1.** the state of being a mother **2.** the qualities or character of a mother **3.** mothers collectively

mother image (or **figure**) a person substituted in one's mind for one's mother

moth·er·in·law (-ən lô') *n., pl.* **moth'ers·in·law'** the mother of one's husband or wife

moth·er·land (-land') *n.* a person's native land

mother lode the main vein of ore in a region

moth·er·ly (-lē) *adj.* of, like, or befitting a mother; maternal —*adv.* [Archaic] in a motherly manner —**moth'er·li·ness** *n.*

moth·er·na·ked (-nā'kid) *adj.* as naked as when one was born; completely naked

moth·er·of·pearl (-əv purl') *n.* the hard, pearly internal layer of certain marine shells, as of the pearl oyster, used for making pearl buttons, etc.; nacre —*adj.* mother-of-pearl

mother of vinegar [see MOTHER[2]] a stringy, gummy, slimy substance formed by bacteria in vinegar or on the surface of fermenting liquids

Mother's Day a Sunday in Lent set aside in honour of mothers: also **Mothering Sunday**

mother ship a large ship in charge of smaller vessels, esp. a warship serving as a focal point for submarines

mother's meeting **1.** a parish meeting of mothers **2.** any meeting where gossip is exchanged

mother tongue **1.** one's native language **2.** a language from which another derives

mother wit native intelligence; common sense

moth·proof (moth'proof') *adj.* treated chemically so as to repel moths —*vt.* to make mothproof

moth·y (moth'ē) *adj.* **moth'i·er, moth'i·est** **1.** infested with moths **2.** moth-eaten

mo·tif (mō tēf') *n.* [Fr.: see MOTIVE] **1.** a main element, idea, etc.; specif., a theme or subject that is repeated with various changes, as in a piece of music, a book, etc. **2.** a repeated figure in a design

mo·tile (mōt'īl) *adj.* [< L. pp. of *movere*, to move + -ILE] *Biol.* capable of or exhibiting spontaneous motion —**mo·til·i·ty** (mō til'ə tē) *n.*

mo·tion (mō'shən) *n.* [< L. *motio* < pp. of *movere*, to move] **1.** a moving from one place to another; movement **2.** a moving of the body or any of its parts **3.** a meaningful movement of the hand, eyes, etc.; gesture **4.** a suggestion; esp., a proposal formally made in an assembly or meeting **5.** *a)* the evacuation of the bowels *b)* [often *pl.*] faeces —*vi.* to make a meaningful movement of the hand, head, etc. —*vt.* to direct or command by a meaningful gesture —**go through the motions** to do something in a mechanical or merely formal way —**in motion** moving or in operation —**mo'tion·less** *adj.* —**mo'tion·less·ly** *adv.*

motion picture [U.S.] a film (sense 4)

mo·ti·vate (mōt'ə vāt') *vt.* **-vat'ed, -vat'ing** to provide with, or affect as, a motive or motives; incite —**mo'ti·va'tion** *n.* —**mo'ti·va'tion·al** *adj.* —**mo'ti·va'tive** *adj.* —**mo'ti·va'tor** *n.*

mo·tive (mōt'iv) *n.* [< OFr. *motif* < ML. < L. pp. of *movere*, to move] **1.** some inner drive, impulse, etc. that causes one to act in a certain way; incentive; goal **2.** *same as* MOTIF —*adj.* of, causing, or tending to cause motion —*vt.* **-tived, -tiv·ing** *same as* MOTIVATE —**mo'tive·less** *adj.*

-mo·tive (mōt'iv) [< prec. (adj.)] a suffix meaning moving, of motion [*locomotive*]

motive power **1.** any power, as steam, electricity, etc., used to impart motion **2.** an impelling force

‡**mot juste** (mō zhüst') *pl.* **mots justes** (mō zhüst') [Fr.] the right word; exact, appropriate word or phrase

mot·ley (mot'lē) *adj.* [< ?] **1.** of many colours **2.** wearing many-coloured garments [a *motley* fool] **3.** of many different elements [a *motley* group] —*n.* **1.** cloth of mixed colours **2.** a garment of various colours, worn by a jester **3.** a combination of diverse elements

mo·to·cross (mō'tō kros') *n.* [MOTO(R) + CROSS(-COUNTRY)] a cross-country race for lightweight motorcycles

mo·tor (mōt'ər) *n.* [L., a mover < pp. of *movere*, to move] **1.** anything that produces or imparts motion **2.** an engine; esp., an internal-combustion engine for propelling a vehicle **3.** clipped form of MOTOR CAR **4.** *Elec.* a machine for converting electrical energy into mechanical energy —*adj.* **1.** producing motion **2.** of or powered by a motor [a *motor* bicycle] **3.** of, by, or for motor vehicles **4.** for motorists [*motor* spares] **5.** designating or of a nerve carrying impulses from the central nervous system to a muscle producing motion **6.** of, manifested by, or involving muscular movements [*motor* skills] —*vi.* to travel by motor car

motor bicycle a bicycle driven by a motor; a moped

mo·tor·bike (-bīk') *n.* [Colloq.] a motorcycle

mo·tor·boat (-bōt') *n.* a boat propelled by a motor

mo·tor·bus (-bus') *n.* a passenger bus propelled by a motor: also **motor coach**

mo·tor·cade (-kād') *n.* [MOTOR + (CAVAL)CADE] [U.S.] a procession of motor cars

motor car **1.** a passenger car propelled by an engine, esp. an internal-combustion engine, and used for travelling on streets or roads **2.** a small, open car propelled by a motor and used on a railway by workmen Also **motorcar**

mo·tor·cy·cle (-sī'k'l) *n.* a two-wheeled vehicle, like a bicycle, propelled by an internal-combustion engine —*vi.* **-cled, -cling** to ride a motorcycle —**mo'tor·cy'clist** *n.*

mo·tor·ist (mōt'ər ist) *n.* a person who drives a motor car or travels by motor car

mo·tor·ize (mōt'ə rīz') *vt.* **-ized', -iz'ing** **1.** to equip with motor-driven vehicles **2.** to make mobile by mounting on a motor vehicle **3.** to equip (a vehicle, etc.) with a motor —**mo'tor·i·za'tion** *n.*

mo·tor·man (mōt'ər mən) *n., pl.* **-men** **1.** a person who drives an electric locomotive **2.** a person who operates a motor

motor nerve a nerve which controls muscular movement

motor pool a group of motor vehicles kept for use as needed, as by military personnel

motor vehicle a vehicle on wheels having its own motor and not running on rails, for use on roads, as a motor car or bus

mo·tor·way (mōt'ər wā) *n.* [MOTOR + WAY] a main road for fast moving traffic with separate carriageways for vehicles travelling in opposite directions

M.O.T. test a compulsory annual test of the roadworthiness of motor vehicles over a certain age

mot·tle (mot''l) *vt.* **-tled, -tling** [back-formation < *mottled* < MOTLEY + -ED] to mark with blotches or streaks of different colours —*n.* a mottled pattern, as of marble —**mot'tled** *adj.*

mot·to (mot'ō) *n., pl.* **-toes, -tos** [It., a word: see MOT] **1.** a word, phrase, or sentence chosen as expressive of the goals or ideals of a nation, group, etc. and inscribed on something **2.** a maxim adopted as a principle of behaviour

‡**moue** (moo) *n., pl.* **moues** (moo) [Fr. < OFr. *moue*, a grimace] a pouting grimace

mouil·lé (moo yā') *adj.* [Fr. pp. of *mouiller*, to moisten] *Phonetics* palatalized, as Spanish ñ in *cañon* or French *ll* in *fille*

mou·jik (moo zhēk', moo'zhik) *n. same as* MUZHIK

mould[1] (mōld) *n.* [OFr. *molle* < L. *modulus*: see MODULE] **1.** a hollow form for shaping something plastic or molten **2.** a frame, shaped core, etc. on or around which something is modelled **3.** a pattern or model for something **4.** something formed in or on, or as if in or on, a mould, as aspic etc. **5.** form or shape, esp. that given by a mould **6.** distinctive character or nature —*vt.* **1.** to make or shape in or on, or as if in or on, a mould **2.** to influence (opinion, etc.) strongly **3.** to fit closely to the contours of **4.** to ornament by or with moulding **5.** to make a mould of for a casting —**mould'a·ble** *adj.* —**mould'er** *n.*

mould[2] (mōld) *n.* [ME. *moul*: sp. prob. infl. by ff.] **1.** a downy or furry fungous growth on organic matter, esp. in the presence of dampness or decay **2.** any fungus producing such a growth —*vt., vi.* to make or become mouldy

mould⁴ (mōld) *n.* [OE. *molde*, earth] loose, soft soil, esp. when rich with decayed organic matter

mould·board (-bôrd′) *n.* **1.** a curved iron plate on a ploughshare, for turning over the soil **2.** a large plate like this at the front of a bulldozer or snowplough, angled to push material aside **3.** one of the boards used to form a mould for concrete

mould·er (mōl′dər) *vt. vi.* [see MOULD³ + -ER] to crumble into dust; decay

mould·ing (mōl′diŋ) *n.* **1.** the act of one that moulds **2.** something moulded **3.** *a)* the ornamental contour of a cornice, jamb, etc. *b)* a cornice or similar projecting or sunk ornamentation *c)* a shaped strip of wood, etc., for finishing or decorating walls (esp. near the ceiling), furniture, etc.

mould·y (mōl′dē) *adj.* **mould′i·er, mould′i·est** **1.** covered with a growth of mould **2.** musty or stale, as from age or decay **3.** [Colloq.] miserable, dull, etc. —**mould′i·ness** *n.*

moult (mōlt) *vi.* [OE. *(be)mutian*, to exchange < L. *mutare*, to change] to shed skin, feathers, etc. prior to replacement by a new growth: said of reptiles, birds, etc. —*vt.* to shed thus —*n.* **1.** a moulting **2.** the parts shed —**moult·er** *n.*

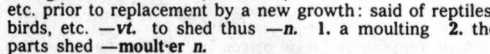

MOULDINGS

mound (maund) *n.* [< ? MDu. *mond*, protection, infl. by MOUNT¹] a heap or bank of earth, sand, etc., whether built or natural; small hill —*vt.* to heap up in a mound

mound builder **1.** *same as* MEGAPODE **2.** [*often* M- B-] the early American Indian peoples who built the burial mounds and earthworks found in the Middle West and South East of the U.S.

mount¹ (maunt) *n.* [< OE. *munt* & OFr. *mont*, both < L. *mons*] a mountain or hill: now poetic or [M-] before a proper name [*Mount* Everest]

mount² (maunt) *vi.* [< OFr. *munter*, ult. < L. *mons*: see prec.] **1.** to climb; ascend (often with *up*) **2.** to climb up on something; esp., to get on a horse or bicycle, etc. for riding **3.** to increase in amount [profits are *mounting*] —*vt.* **1.** to go up; ascend; climb [to *mount* stairs] **2.** *a)* to get up on (a horse, bicycle, etc.) for riding *b)* to set on or provide with a horse *c)* to get up on (a platform, stool, etc.) **3.** to place on something raised (with *on*) [*mount* the statue on a pedestal] **4.** to place or fix on or in the proper support, backing, etc., as a gem in a setting, a specimen on a microscope slide, etc. **5.** to arrange (a skeleton, dead animal, etc.) for exhibition **6.** to furnish the costumes, settings, etc. for producing (a play) **7.** to prepare for and undertake (an expedition, campaign, etc.) **8.** *Mil.* *a)* to place (a gun) in position for use *b)* to be armed with (cannon) [this ship *mounts* six cannon] *c)* to post (a guard) on sentry duty *d)* to go on (guard) as a sentry —*n.* **1.** the act or manner of mounting (a horse, etc.) **2.** a horse, bicycle, etc. for riding **3.** the support, setting, etc. on or in which something is mounted —**mount′a·ble** *adj.* —**mount′er** *n.*

moun·tain (maun′tin) *n.* [< OFr. *montaigne*, ult. < L. *mons*, MOUNT¹] **1.** a natural raised part of the earth's surface, larger than a hill **2.** [*pl.*] a chain or group of such elevations: also **mountain chain, mountain range** **3.** a large pile, heap, or mound **4.** a very large amount —*adj.* **1.** of mountains **2.** situated, living, or used in the mountains **3.** like a mountain

mountain ash a small tree with clusters of white flowers and red berries: also **rowan**

mountain cat any of various animals as the puma, bob cat, etc.

mountain dew [Colloq.] **1.** orig., Scotch whisky **2.** any whisky esp. when illegally distilled, as by someone living in the mountains

moun·tain·eer (maun′tin ir′) *n.* **1.** a person who lives in a mountainous region **2.** a mountain climber —*vi.* to climb mountains, as for sport

mountain goat *same as* ROCKY MOUNTAIN GOAT

mountain laurel an evergreen shrub of E N America, with pink and white flowers and shiny leaves

mountain lion *same as* PUMA

moun·tain·ous (maun′tin əs) *adj.* **1.** full of mountains **2.** like a mountain; esp., very large

mountain sickness a feeling of weakness, nausea, etc. brought on at high altitudes by the rarefied air

moun·tain·top (-top′) *n.* the top of a mountain

mountain trout a small minnow found in the colder fresh waters of Australia and S America

moun·te·bank (maun′tə baŋk) *n.* [< It. < *montare*, to mount + *in*, on + *banco*, a bench] **1.** orig., a person who

sold quack medicines in a public place, attracting an audience by tricks, stories, etc. **2.** any charlatan, or quack —*vi.* to act as a mountebank —**moun′te·bank·er·y** *n.*

mount·ed (maun′tid) *adj.* provided with a mount, or horse, vehicle, support, etc. [*mounted* police]

Mount·ie, Mount·y (maun′tē) *n., pl.* **-ies** [Colloq.] a member of the Royal Canadian Mounted Police

mount·ing (maun′tiŋ) *n.* something serving as a backing, support, setting, etc.

mounting block a slab of stone or wooden block used to facilitate mounting of a horse

mourn (môrn) *vi., vt.* [OE. *murnan*] **1.** to feel or express sorrow for (something regrettable) **2.** to grieve for (someone who has died) —**mourn′er** *n.*

mourn·ful (-fəl) *adj.* **1.** of mourning; feeling or expressing grief or sorrow **2.** causing sorrow; melancholy —**mourn′-ful·ly** *adv.* —**mourn′ful·ness** *n.*

mourn·ing (môr′niŋ) *n.* **1.** a sorrowing; specif., the expression of grief at someone's death, or the period of this **2.** black clothes, drapery, etc., worn or displayed as a sign of grief —*adj.* of or expressing mourning —**mourn′ing·ly** *adv.*

mourning band a strip of black cloth or crêpe worn, usually around the arm, to show mourning

mourning dove a grey, wild dove of the U.S.: so called because of its cooing, regarded as mournful

mou·sa·ka (mōō sä′kə) *n.* [ModGr.] *var. of* MOUSSAKA

mouse (maus; *for v., usually* mauz) *n., pl.* **mice** [OE. *mus*] **1.** any of numerous small rodents found throughout the world; esp., the **house mouse**, which infests human dwellings **2.** a timid or spiritless person **3.** [Slang] a dark, swollen bruise under the eye —*vi.* **moused, mous′ing** **1.** to hunt for mice **2.** to search for something busily and stealthily

mouse-coloured (-kul′ərd) *adj.* being the colour of a mouse; an indeterminate greyish-brown

mous·er (mau′zər, -sər) *n.* a cat, dog, etc. with reference to its ability to catch mice

mouse-trap (-trap′) *n.* **1.** a trap for catching mice **2.** [Colloq.] cheese of an inferior quality

mous·ey (mau′sē, -zē) *adj.* *same as* MOUSY

mous·sa·ka (mōō sä′kə) *n.* [ModGr.] a dish originating in the Near East, consisting of meat, esp. mutton, aubergines, and tomatoes, topped with a cheese sauce

mousse (mōōs) *n.* [Fr., foam, prob. < L. *mulsa*, kind of mead] **1.** a light chilled or frozen dessert made with egg white, gelatin, whipped cream, fruit, or flavouring **2.** a similar preparation made from fish, ham, etc.

‡mousse·line (mōōs lēn′) *n.* [Fr.] **1.** a fine stiff fabric made of rayon or silk **2.** fine glass with a lacelike pattern

‡mousse·line de laine (də len′) [Fr. lit., muslin of wool] a lightweight woollen cloth used for dresses

‡mousse·line de soie (də swä′) [Fr. lit., muslin of silk] a gauzelike silk or rayon cloth used for wedding gowns, etc.

mous·tache (mə stäsh′) *n.* [< Fr. < It. *mostacchio* < MGr. < Gr. *mystax*, upper lip] **1.** the hair on the upper lip of men **2.** the hair or bristles growing about an animal's mouth

moustache cup a drinking cup partly covered on top, to keep the moustache dry

mous·y (mau′sē, -zē) *adj.* **mous′i·er, mous′i·est** **1.** of, characteristic of, or like a mouse; quiet, timid, etc. **2.** same as MOUSE-COLOURED **3.** infested with mice —**mous′i·ness** *n.*

mouth (mauth; *for v.* mauth) *n., pl.* **mouths** (mauthz) [OE. *muth*] **1.** the opening through which an animal takes in food; specif., the cavity in the head which contains the teeth and tongue and through which sounds are uttered **2.** the mouth regarded as the organ of eating and speaking **3.** a grimace **4.** any opening regarded as like the mouth [the *mouth* of a river, of a jar, of a cavern, etc.] **5.** [Colloq.] boastful or rude talk [he is all *mouth*] —*vt.* **1.** to say, esp. in an affected or pompous manner **2.** to form (a word) with the mouth soundlessly **3.** to rub with the mouth or lips —*vi.* to speak in a pompous manner; declaim —**down in (or at) the mouth** [Colloq.] depressed; unhappy —**mouth′-er** (mauth′ər) *n.* —**mouth′like** *adj.*

-mouthed (mauthd) *a combining form meaning* having a (specified kind of) mouth, voice, etc.[loudmouthed]

mouth·ful (mauth′fool′) *n., pl.* **-fuls′** **1.** as much as the mouth can hold **2.** the usual amount taken into the mouth **3.** a small amount

mouth organ *same as* HARMONICA

mouth·part (-pärt′) *n.* any of various structures or organs around the mouth in arthropods, used for biting, grasping, etc.: *usually used in pl.*

mouth·piece (-pēs′) *n.* **1.** a part placed at, or forming, a mouth **2.** the part of a musical instrument, telephone, etc., held in or to the mouth **3.** a person, periodical, etc. used by others to express their views, ideas, etc. **4.** [Slang] a criminal's lawyer

mouth·wash (-wosh′) *n.* a flavoured liquid used for rinsing the mouth or gargling

mouth·y (mau′thē, -thē) *adj.* **mouth′i·er, mouth′i·est**

excessively talkative, esp. in a bombastic or rude way —**mouth′i·ly** *adv.* —**mouth′i·ness** *n.*

mou·ton (m$\overline{oo}$′ton) *n.* [Fr., sheep: see MUTTON] lambskin, processed to resemble beaver, seal, etc.

mov·a·ble (m$\overline{oo}$′və b'l) *adj.* 1. that can be moved from one place to another 2. changing in date from one year to the next [*movable* holidays] —*n.* 1. something movable 2. *Law* personal property, as furniture: *usually used in pl.* Also **move′a·ble** —**mov′a·bil′i·ty** *n.* —**mov′a·bly** *adv.*

move (m$\overline{oo}$v) *vt.* **moved, mov′ing** [< Anglo-Fr. < OFr. < L. *movere*] 1. to change the place or position of 2. to set or keep in motion; impel, stir, etc. 3. to cause (*to act, do, say,* etc.); prompt 4. to arouse the emotions, passions, etc. of 5. to propose; esp., to propose formally, as in a meeting 6. to cause (the bowels) to evacuate 7. *Commerce* to dispose of (goods) by selling —*vi.* 1. to change place or position 2. to change one's residence 3. to be active [to *move* in artistic circles] 4. to make progress; advance 5. to take action 6. to be, or be set, in motion; turn, revolve, etc. 7. to make a formal application (*for*) [*move* for a new trial] 8. to evacuate: said of the bowels 9. [Colloq.] to depart [time to be *moving* on] 10. *Chess, Draughts,* etc. to change the position of a piece 11. *Commerce* to be disposed of by sale: said of goods —*n.* 1. act of moving; movement 2. one of a series of actions towards some goal 3. a change of residence 4. *Chess, Draughts,* etc. the act of moving or one's turn to move —**get a move on** [Slang] 1. to start moving 2. to hurry —**move along** go elsewhere, esp. in response to a policeman's request —**move house** to change one's residence —**move in on** [Slang] to draw near to and try to gain control of —**move over** to move to another place or position, esp. an adjacent one —**move up** to promote or be promoted —**not move a muscle** to be completely still; motionless —**on the move** [Colloq.] moving about from place to place

move·ment (-mənt) *n.* 1. the act, process, or manner of moving; specif., *a*) an action of a person or group *b*) a shift in position *c*) an evacuation (of the bowels) *d*) *Mil.* a change in the location of troops, ships, etc., as part of a manoeuvre 2. *a*) organized action by people working together towards some goal *b*) those active in this way 3. a tendency; trend 4. the progress of events in a literary work; action 5. the effect of motion in painting, sculpture, etc. 6. *Mech.* the moving parts of a mechanism [the *movement* of a clock] 7. *Music a*) any of the principal divisions of a symphony or other extended composition *b*) *same as* TEMPO OR RHYTHM 8. *Prosody* rhythmic flow

mov·er (-ər) *n.* a person or thing that moves; specif., 1. a proposer or instigator [the prime *mover*] 2. [U.S.] a removal man or firm

mov·ie (m$\overline{oo}$′vē) *n.* [contr. < *moving picture*] [Chiefly U.S.] a film —**the movies** [Chiefly U.S.] 1. the cinema industry 2. a showing of a film

mov·ie·go·er (-gō′ər) *n.* [Chiefly U.S.] a person who goes to the cinema, esp. often or regularly

mov·ing (m$\overline{oo}$′viŋ) *adj.* that moves; specif., *a*) changing, or causing to change, place or position *b*) causing motion or action *c*) stirring the emotions —**mov′ing·ly** *adv.*

moving pavement a moving surface formed by an endless belt extending along a level stretch, for conveying pedestrians who step onto it

moving staircase (or **stairway**) *same as* ESCALATOR

mow (mō) *vt., vi.* **mowed, mowed** or **mown, mow′ing** [OE. *mawan*] 1. to cut down (standing grass or grain) with a sickle, lawn mower, etc. 2. to cut grass or grain from (a lawn, field, etc.) —**mow down** 1. to cause to fall like grass or grain being cut 2. to kill or destroy —**mow′er** *n.*

mown (mōn) *alt. pp. of* MOW

MP, M.P. Military Police

mp [It. *mezzo piano*] *Music* moderately soft

M.P. 1. Member of Parliament 2. Mounted Police

M.P., m.p. melting point

mpg, m.p.g. miles per gallon

mph, m.p.h. miles per hour

M.Phil. Master of Philosophy

Mr. (mis′tər) *pl.* **Messrs.** (mes′ərz) mister: used before the name or title of a man

M.R. Master of the Rolls

M.R.C. Medical Research Council

Mrs. (mis′iz) *pl.* **Mmes.** (mā dam′) mistress: now used as a title before the name of a married woman

Mrs. Mopp a charwoman

MS 1. Mississippi 2. multiple sclerosis

MS., ms., ms *pl.* **MSS., mss., mss** manuscript

Ms. (miz) a title used for both married and unmarried women; the feminine of Mr.

M.S., M.Sc. Master of Science

MScand Middle Scandinavian

MSG monosodium glutamate

m′sieur (mə syʉr′; *Fr.* mə syö′) *n.* monsieur

Mt., mt. *pl.* **mts.** 1. mount 2. mountain

M.Tech. Master of Technology

mtg. 1. meeting 2. mortgage: also **mtge.**

mtn. mountain

mu (my$\overline{oo}$) *n.* [< Gr.] the twelfth letter of the Greek alphabet (M, μ)

much (much) *adj.* **more, most** [OE. *mycel*] great in quantity, amount, degree, etc. —*adv.* 1. to a great degree or extent [*much* happier] 2. just about; nearly [*much* the same, *much* of a size] 3. at frequent intervals; often [do you dine out *much*?] —*n.* 1. a great amount or quantity [*much* to be done] 2. something great, outstanding, etc. [not *much* to look at] —**a bit much** [Colloq.] somewhat extreme; intemperate —**as much as** 1. to the degree that 2. practically; virtually —**make much of** to treat or consider as of great importance —**much as** 1. almost as 2. though

much·ness (much′nis) *n.* magnitude, as of quantity, degree, etc. —**much of a muchness** very much alike; very similar

mu·ci·lage (my$\overline{oo}$′s'l ij) *n.* [< MFr. < LL. *mucilago,* musty juice < L. *mucere,* to be mouldy] 1. any of various thick, sticky substances produced in certain plants 2. any watery solution of gum, glue, etc. used as an adhesive

mu·ci·lag·i·nous (my$\overline{oo}$′sə laj′ə nəs) *adj.* 1. of or like mucilage; sticky 2. producing mucilage

muck (muk) *n.* [< or akin to ON. *myki,* dung] 1. moist manure 2. black earth containing decaying matter, used as a fertilizer 3. anything unclean or degrading; dirt; filth —*vt.* 1. to fertilize with muck 2. [Colloq.] to dirty as with muck 3. [Slang] to make a mess of; bungle (often with *up*) —**muck about** (or **around**) [Slang] 1. to waste time; potter 2. to interfere (with); annoy —**muck in** to join in or share something, such as duties, work, etc. —**muck′y** *adj.* **muck′i·er, muck′i·est**

muck·er (-ər) *n.* 1. *Mining* a person who shifts broken rock or waste 2. a heavy fall, as from a horse 3. [Colloq.] a friend, mate, pal

muck·rake (-rāk′) *vi.* **-raked′, -rak′ing** [coined c.1906: see MUCK & RAKE¹] to search for· and publicize corruption by public officials, businessmen, etc. —**muck′rak′er** *n.*

muck·sweat (-swet′) *n.* a profuse or copious sweat

mu·cous (my$\overline{oo}$′kəs) *adj.* 1. of, containing, or secreting mucus 2. like mucus or covered with or as with mucus; slimy —**mu·cos′i·ty** (-kos′ə tē) *n.*

mucous membrane a mucus-secreting membrane lining body cavities and canals, as the mouth, etc., connecting with the external air

mu·cus (my$\overline{oo}$′kəs) *n.* [L.] the slimy secretion that moistens and protects the mucous membranes

mud (mud) *n.* [prob. < a LowG. source] wet, soft, sticky earth —*vt.* **mud′ded, mud′ding** to cover or soil with or as with mud —**here's mud in your eye** [Colloq.] a humorous drinking toast —**throw** (or **sling**) **mud at** [Colloq.] to slander or defame; vilify

mud-bath (-bäth′) *n.* 1. a bath of mud impregnated with mineral salts used for the treatment of rheumatism, etc. 2. any game, esp. soccer or rugby, taking place in muddy conditions

mud·dle (mud′'l) *vt.* **-dled, -dling** [< MUD] 1. to mix up; jumble; bungle 2. to confuse; befuddle, as with strong drink —*vi.* to act or think in a confused way —*n.* mess, confusion, etc. —**muddle through** to succeed in spite of confusion

mud·dle-head·ed (-hed′id) *adj.* stupid; blundering; confused —**mud·dle-head′ed·ness** *n.*

mud·dy (-ē) *adj.* **-di·er, -di·est** 1. full of or spattered with mud 2. not clear; cloudy [*muddy* coffee] 3. confused, obscure, etc. [*muddy* thinking] —*vt., vi.* **-died, -dy·ing** to make or become muddy —**mud′di·ly** *adv.* —**mud′di·ness** *n.*

mud·fish (-fish′) *n., pl.* **-fish′, -fish′es:** see FISH any of various fishes that live in mud or muddy water

mud·guard (-gärd′) *n.* a metal frame over the wheels of a motor car or bicycle, etc., to protect against splashing mud, etc.

mud hen any of various birds that live in marshes, as the coot, rail, etc.

mud·lark (-lärk′) *n.* 1. any of various birds that frequent muddy areas 2. formerly, one who made a living by picking up odds and ends in the mud of tidal rivers 3. [Colloq.] a street urchin

mud·pack (-pak′) *n.* a paste made up of fuller's earth, astringents, etc., used as a facial

mud puppy a N American salamander that lives in mud under water

mud·sling·ing (-sliŋ′iŋ) *n.* unscrupulous attacks against an opponent, as in a political campaign —**mud′sling′er** *n.*

mud turtle a small turtle of North and Central America that lives in muddy ponds, streams, etc.

muesli (my$\overline{oo}$′zlē) *n.* [SwissG.] a mixture of uncooked cereals, esp. rolled oats, usually mixed with nuts, fruits, etc. and eaten with milk or cream

mu·ez·zin (m$\overline{oo}$ ez′in) *n.* [< Ar. *mu'adhdhin* < *adhana,* to proclaim] a Moslem crier who calls the people to prayer at the proper hours

muff (muf) *n.* [Du. *mof* < Walloon < Fr. *moufle*, a mitten] 1. a cylindrical covering of fur, etc. into which the hands are placed from either end for warmth 2. any bungling action —*vt., vi.* to do (something) badly or awkwardly; specif., to bungle (a catch), as in cricket

muf·fin (muf'in) *n.* [< ?] a thick, plain, yeast roll, usually served hot and buttered

muffin man a man who used to sell muffins in the street

muf·fle (muf''l) *vt.* -fled, -fling [prob. akin to OFr. *enmouflé*, muffled < *moufle*, a mitten] 1. to wrap in a shawl, blanket, etc. so as to hide, keep warm, etc. 2. to wrap or cover in order to deaden or prevent sound 3. to deaden (a sound) 4. to stifle —*n.* a covering, etc. used for muffling

muf·fler (-lər) *n.* 1. a scarf worn around the throat, as for warmth 2. [U.S.] a silencer (sense 3)

muf·ti (muf'tē) *n., pl.* -tis [Ar. < *āftā*, to judge] 1. in Moslem countries, an interpreter of religious law 2. ordinary clothes, esp. when worn by one who usually wears a uniform

mug (mug) *n.* [prob. < Scand.] 1. a heavy drinking cup of earthenware or metal with a handle 2. as much as a mug will hold 3. [Slang] *a)* the face *b)* the mouth 4. [Colloq.] a stupid or gullible person —*vt.* **mugged, mug'ging** 1. to assault, esp. from behind and usually with intent to rob 2. [Colloq.] to learn by studying (often with *up*) —*vi.* 1. to mug, or assault, someone 2. [Slang] to grimace, esp. in overacting 3. to study very hard —**a mug's game** something only a gullible or simple person would do —**mug'ger** *n.*

mug·gins (mug'inz) *n.* [< personal name *Muggins*, associated with slang *mug*, cardsharper's dupe] 1. any of various simple card games 2. [Slang] a dupe; fool

mug·gy (mug'ē) *adj.* -gi·er, -gi·est [prob. < or akin to ON. *mugga*, a drizzle] hot, damp, and close [*muggy* weather] —**mug'gi·ness** *n.*

muk·luk (muk'luk') *n.* [Esk. *muklok*, a large seal] an Eskimo boot made of sealskin or reindeer skin

mu·lat·to (mə lat'ō, myoo-) *n., pl.* -toes [Sp. & Port. *mulato*, of mixed breed < *mulo*, mule < L. *mulus*] 1. a person who has one Negro parent and one white parent 2. popularly, any person with mixed Negro and Caucasoid ancestry

mul·ber·ry (mul'ber'ē, -bər'ē) *n., pl.* -ries [OE. *morberie* < L. *morum*, mulberry + OE. *berie*, a berry] 1. any of several trees that bear edible fruits resembling the raspberry 2. this fruit 3. purplish red —*adj.* designating a family of plants including the mulberry, fig, and breadfruit

mulch (mulch) *n.* [ME. *molsh*, soft] leaves, straw, peat moss, etc., spread on the ground around plants to prevent evaporation of water from the soil, freezing of roots, etc. —*vt.* to apply mulch to

mulct (mulkt) *vt.* [L. *mulctare* < *multa*, a fine] 1. to punish by a fine or by depriving of something 2. to extract (money) from (someone), as by fraud —*n.* a fine or similar penalty

mule[1] (myool) *n.* [< OFr. < L. *mulus*] 1. the (usually sterile) offspring of a donkey and a horse, esp. of a jackass and a mare 2. a machine that draws and spins cotton fibres into yarn and winds the yarn 3. [Colloq.] a stubborn person

mule[2] (myool) *n.* [Fr., ult. < L. *mulleus*, red shoe] a slipper that does not cover the heel

mule skinner [U.S. Colloq.] a driver of mules

mu·le·ta (myoo lāt'ə, -let'ə) *n.* [Sp.] a red flannel cloth draped over a stick and manipulated by the matador in a bullfight

mu·le·teer (myoo'lə tir') *n.* [< OFr.] a driver of mules

mul·ga (mul'gə) *n.* [Abor.] 1. in Australia, one of several species of acacia 2. scrub comprising a dense growth of acacia 3. the outback; bush

mu·li·eb·ri·ty (myoo'lē eb'rə tē) *n.* [LL. *muliebritas* < L. *muliebris*, womanly] 1. the condition of being a woman 2. the qualities characteristic of a woman

mul·ish (myool'ish) *adj.* like a mule; stubborn; obstinate —**mul'ish·ly** *adv.* —**mul'ish·ness** *n.*

mull[1] (mul) *vt., vi.* [< ?] [Colloq.] to cogitate or ponder (usually with *over*)

mull[2] (mul) *vt.* [< ?] to heat, sweeten, and flavour with spices (ale, cider, wine, etc.)

mull[3] (mul) *n.* [contr. < *mulmul* < Hindi & Per. *malmal*] a thin, soft muslin

mull[4] (mul) *n.* [ON. *muli*, a snout] [Scot.] a headland or promontory [*Mull* of Galloway]

mul·lah, mul·la (mul'ə, mool'-) *n.* [Turk., Per., & Hindi *mulla* < Ar. *mawlā*] a Moslem teacher or interpreter of the religious law: used as a general title of respect for a learned man

mul·lein (mul'in) *n.* [OFr. *moleine*, ult. < L. *mollis*, soft] a tall plant of the figwort family, with spikes of yellow, lavender, or white flowers

mul·let (mul'it) *n., pl.* -lets, -let: see PLURAL, II, D, 1 [OFr. *mulet*, dim. < L. *mullus*, red mullet] any of a group of edible, spiny-rayed fishes found in fresh and salt waters; specif., the **striped** (or **grey**) **mullet**

mul·li·ga·taw·ny (mul'i gə tô'nē) *n.* [Tamil *milagutannir*, pepper water] an East Indian soup of meat, etc., flavoured with curry

mul·lion (mul'yən, -ēən) *n.* [prob. < OFr. *moienel* < L. *medianus*, middle] a slender, vertical dividing bar between the lights of windows, panels, etc.—*vt.* to furnish with mullions —**mul'lioned** *adj.*

mul·lock (mul'ək) *n.* [ME. *mulloc* < *mal*, dust + -*oc*, -OCK] in Australia, the refuse earth or rock left over in mining

MULLIONS

mul·lo·way (mul'ə wā) *n.* [< ?] a large food fish found off the coast of E Australia

mul·tan·gu·lar (mul taŋ'gyoo lər) *adj.* having many angles: also **mul'ti·an'gu·lar** (mul'tē aŋ'-)

mul·ti- [L. < *multus*, much, many] *a combining form meaning:* 1. having many [*multicoloured*] 2. more than two [*multilateral*] 3. many times more than [*multimillionaire*] Also, before a vowel, **mult-** The meanings of the following words can be determined by combining the meanings of their component elements:

multicellular	multilingual	multispeed
multicoloured	multilobate	multispiral
multidimensional	multinucleate	multistorey
multidirectional	multiphase	multivalve
multifold	multipinnate	multivitamin
multifoliate	multipolar	multivocal
multilevel	multipurpose	multivoiced
multilinear	multiracial	multivolume

mul·ti·far·i·ous (mul'tə fer'ē əs) *adj.* [L. *multifarius* < *multus*, many] having many kinds of parts or elements; of great variety —**mul'ti·far'i·ous·ly** *adv.* —**mul'ti·far'i·ous·ness** *n.*

mul·ti·flo·ra rose (-flôr'ə) a rose with thick clusters of small flowers, grown esp. for hedges

mul·ti·form (mul'tə fôrm') *adj.* having many forms, shapes, etc. —**mul'ti·for'mi·ty** *n.*

mul·ti·lat·er·al (mul'ti lat'ər əl) *adj.* 1. many-sided 2. involving more than two nations, etc. [a *multilateral* treaty] —**mul'ti·lat'er·al·ly** *adv.*

mul·ti·me·di·a (-mē'dē ə) *n.* same as MIXED MEDIA

mul·ti·mil·lion·aire (-mil'yə ner') *n.* a person whose wealth amounts to many millions of pounds, dollars, francs, etc.

mul·ti·na·tion·al (-nash'ə n'l) *adj.* 1. of or involving a number of nations 2. designating or of a company with branches in a number of countries 3. comprising persons of many nationalities —*n.* a multinational company

mul·tip·a·rous (mul tip'ər əs) *adj.* [< ModL.: see MULTI- & -PAROUS] *Zool.* normally bearing more than one offspring at a delivery

mul·ti·par·tite (mul'ti pär'tīt) *adj.* 1. divided into many parts 2. same as MULTILATERAL (sense 2)

mul·ti·ple (mul'tə p'l) *adj.* [Fr. < L. *multiplex* < *multus*, many + -*plex*, -fold: see DUPLEX] 1. having or consisting of many parts, elements, etc.; manifold 2. *Elec.* designating or of a circuit with two or more conductors in parallel —*n.* a number that is a product of some specified number and another number [10 is a *multiple* of 5]

mul·ti·ple-choice (-chois') *adj.* designating a question for which one of several proposed answers is to be selected, or a test made up of such questions

multiple sclerosis a disease in which there is damage to the central nervous system: it is marked by speech defects, lack of coordination, etc.

multiple shop a retail business with branches in different parts of the town or country: see also CHAIN STORE

mul·ti·plex (-pleks') *adj.* [L. *multiplex*, MULTIPLE] 1. multiple 2. designating or of a system for transmitting or receiving simultaneously two or more messages or signals over a common circuit, carrier wave, etc. —*vt.* to send (messages or signals) by a multiplex system

mul·ti·pli·a·ble (mul'tə pli'əb'l) *adj.* that can be multiplied: also **mul'ti·plic'a·ble** (-plik'ə b'l)

mul·ti·pli·cand (mul'tə pli kand') *n.* [< L. *multiplicandus*, to be multiplied] *Math.* the number that is, or is to be, multiplied by another (the *multiplier*)

mul·ti·pli·ca·tion (-pli kā'shən) *n.* a multiplying or being multiplied; specif., *Math.* a method used to find the result of adding a specified quantity repeated a specified number of times: indicated in arithmetic by the symbol ×

multiplication table a table for memorization showing the results of multiplying each number of a series, usually 1 to 12, by each of the numbers in succession

mul·ti·plic·i·ty (-plis'ə tē) *n.* [< LL. < L. *multiplex*,

MULTIPLE] **1.** a being manifold or various **2.** a great number

mul·ti·pli·er (mul'tə plī'ər) *n.* **1.** a person or thing that multiplies or increases **2.** *Math.* the number by which another number (the *multiplicand*) is, or is to be, multiplied

mul·ti·ply¹ (mul'tə plī') *vt.* -plied', -ply'ing [< OFr. < L. *multiplicare* < *multiplex*, MULTIPLE] **1.** to cause to increase in number, amount, degree, etc. **2.** *Math.* to find the product of by multiplication —*vi.* **1.** to increase in number, amount, etc., esp. by procreation **2.** *Math.* to do multiplication

mul·ti·ply² (mul'tə plē) *adv.* in multiple ways

mul·ti·stage (mul'ti stāj') *adj.* having several propulsion systems, used and discarded in sequence: said of a rocket or missile

mul·ti·tude (mul'tə tyōōd') *n.* [OFr. < L. *multitudo* < *multus*, many] **1.** a large number of persons or things; host, myriad, etc. **2.** the masses (preceded by *the*)

mul·ti·tu·di·nous (mul'tə tyōōd'in əs) *adj.* **1.** very numerous, many **2.** consisting of many parts, elements, etc. —**mul'ti·tu'di·nous·ly** *adv.*

mul·ti·va·lent (mul'ti vā'lənt, mul tiv'ə lənt) *adj.* *Chem.* same as POLYVALENT (sense 2) —**mul'ti·va'lence** *n.*

mul·ti·ver·si·ty (mul'tə vur'sə tē) *n.*, *pl.* -ties [Chiefly U.S.] the modern large and complex university with its many colleges, extensions, etc., regarded as being impersonal, bureaucratic, etc.

mul·ture (mul'chər) *n.* [ME. *multer* < L. *molere*, to grind] formerly, a fee paid to the owner of a mill for the privilege of having one's grain ground there, usually a percentage of the grain or of the ground flour

mum¹ (mum) *vi.* mummed, mum'ming [< OFr. *momer* < *momo*, echoic for grimace] to wear a mask or costume in fun; specif., to act as a mummer at Christmas time

mum² (mum) *n.* [Colloq.] mother

mum³ (mum) *adj.* [ME. *momme*, echoic of sound made with closed lips] silent; not speaking —*interj.* do not speak! —**mum's the word** say nothing

mum·ble (mum'b'l) *vt., vi.* -bled, -bling [ME. *momelen*] **1.** to speak or say indistinctly, as with the mouth partly closed **2.** [Rare] to chew gently and ineffectively —*n.* a mumbled utterance —**mum'bler** *n.* —**mum'bling·ly** *adv.*

mum·bo jum·bo (mum'bō jum'bō) [of Afr. orig.: < ?] **1.** [M- J-] among certain West African tribes, an idol or god supposed to protect the people from evil **2.** any idol or fetish **3.** meaningless ritual, gibberish, etc.

mum·mer (mum'ər) *n.* [see MUM¹] **1.** one who wears a mask or disguise for fun; specif., any of the masked and costumed persons who travel from house to house acting folk plays at Christmas time **2.** any actor

mum·mer·y (-ē) *n.*, *pl.* -mer·ies **1.** performance by mummers **2.** any show or ceremony regarded as pretentious or hypocritical

mum·mi·fy (mum'ə fī') *vt.* -fied', -fy'ing to make into or like a mummy —*vi.* to shrivel or dry up —**mum'mi·fi·ca'tion** *n.*

mum·my¹ (mum'ē) *n.*, *pl.* -mies [< Fr. < ML. < Ar. *mūmiyā* < Per. *mum*, wax] **1.** a dead body preserved by embalming, as by the ancient Egyptians **2.** any well-preserved dead body

mum·my² (mum'ē) *n.*, *pl.* -mies [< MUM²] [Colloq.] mother

mumps (mumps) *n.pl.* [with sing. v.] [pl. of obs. *mump*, a grimace] **1.** an acute communicable disease, caused by virus and characterized by swelling of the salivary glands **2.** sulks —**mump'ish** *adj.*

mun. municipal

munch (munch) *vt., vi.* [ME. *monchen*, echoic] to chew steadily, often with a crunching sound

mun·dane (mun dān', mun'dān) *adj.* [< OFr. < L. < *mundus*, world] **1.** of the world; esp., worldly, as distinguished from heavenly, etc. **2.** commonplace; everyday

mun·ga (muŋ'gə) *n.* [? < Fr. *manger*, to eat] [Aust. & N.Z. Slang] food; a meal

mu·nic·i·pal (myōō nis'ə p'l) *adj.* [< L. < *municeps*, citizen of a free town < *munia*, official duties + *capere*, to take] **1.** of or having to do with a city, town, etc. or its local government **2.** having local self-government —**mu·nic'·i·pal·ly** *adv.*

mu·nic·i·pal·i·ty (myōō nis'ə pal'ə tē) *n.*, *pl.* -ties [see prec.] a city, town, etc. having its own government

mu·nic·i·pal·ize (myōō nis'ə pə līz') *vt.* -ized', -iz'ing **1.** to bring under the control or ownership of a municipality **2.** to make a municipality of —**mu·nic'i·pal·i·za'tion** *n.*

mu·nif·i·cent (myōō nif'ə sənt) *adj.* [< L. < *munificus*, bountiful < *munus*, a gift + *facere*, to make] **1.** very generous in giving **2.** given with great generosity —**mu·nif'·i·cence** *n.* —**mu·nif'i·cent·ly** *adv.*

mu·ni·tion (myōō nish'ən) *vt.* to provide with munitions

mu·ni·tions (-ənz) *n.pl.* [< MFr. < L. < *munire*, to fortify] war supplies; esp., weapons and ammunition

mu·on (myōō'on) *n.* [MU + (MES)ON] a positively or negatively charged subatomic particle with a mass 207 times that of an electron

mu·ral (myoor'əl) *adj.* [Fr. < (MES)ON] *muralis* < *murus*, a wall] **1.** of, on, in, or for a wall **2.** like a wall —*n.* a picture or photograph, esp. a large one, painted or applied directly on a wall —**mu'ral·ist** *n.*

mur·der (mur'dər) *n.* [OE. *morthor* & OFr. *mordre*] the unlawful and malicious or premeditated killing of one human being by another —*vt.* **1.** to kill unlawfully and with malice **2.** to spoil or botch, as in performance [she murdered that song] —*vi.* to commit murder —**cry (or scream) blue murder** to make a scene —**get away with murder** [Colloq.] to escape detection or punishment for a blameworthy act —**mur'der·er** *n.* —**mur'der·ess** *n.fem.*

mur·der·ous (-əs) *adj.* **1.** of, having the nature of, or characteristic of murder; brutal **2.** capable or guilty of, or intending, murder **3.** [Colloq.] very dangerous, trying, etc. —**mur'der·ous·ly** *adv.* —**mur'der·ous·ness** *n.*

mu·ri·at·ic acid (myoor'ē at'ik) [< Fr. < L. < *muria*, brine] hydrochloric acid: a commercial term

murk (murk) *n.* [< ON. *myrkr*, dark] darkness; gloom —*adj.* [Archaic] dark or dim

murk·y (mur'kē) *adj.* murk'i·er, murk'i·est **1.** dark or gloomy **2.** heavy and obscure with smoke, mist, etc. —**murk'i·ly** *adv.* —**murk'i·ness** *n.*

mur·mur (mur'mər) *n.* [< OFr. < L.: echoic word] **1.** a low, indistinct, continuous sound, as of a stream, far-off voices, etc. **2.** a mumbled complaint **3.** *Med.* any abnormal sound heard, esp. in the region of the heart —*vi.* **1.** to make a murmur **2.** to mumble a complaint —*vt.* to say in a murmur —**mur'mur·er** *n.* —**mur'mur·ing** *adj.* —**mur'mur·ous** *adj.*

mur·phy (mur'fē) *n.*, *pl.* -phies [< *Murphy*, Ir. surname] [Slang] a potato

mur·rain (mur'in) *n.* [< OFr. *morine* < L. *mori*, to die] **1.** any of various infectious diseases of cattle **2.** [Archaic] a pestilence; plague

mur·ther (mur'thər) *n., vt., vi.* dial. var. of MURDER

mus. **1.** museum **2.** music **3.** musical

Mus.B., Mus. Bac. [L. *Musicae Baccalaureus*] Bachelor of Music

mus·ca·dine (mus'kə din, -dīn') *n.* [altered < MUSCATEL] a variety of grape grown in the SE U.S.

mus·cat (mus'kət, -kat) *n.* [Fr. . < Pr. < It. *moscato*, musk, wine < LL. *muscus*, musk] **1.** a variety of sweet grape from which muscatel and raisins are made **2.** same as MUSCATEL (sense 1)

mus·ca·tel (mus'kə tel') *n.* [OFr. *muscadel*, ult. < It. *moscato*, MUSCAT] **1.** a rich, sweet wine made from the muscat **2.** same as MUSCAT (sense 1) Also **mus'·ca·del'** (-del')

mus·cle (mus''l) *n.* [Fr. < L. *musculus*, dim. of *mus*, a mouse] **1.** any of the body organs consisting of bundles of fibres that can be contracted and expanded to produce bodily movements **2.** the tissue making up such an organ **3.** muscular strength; brawn **4.** [Colloq.] power based on force —*vi.* -cled, -cling [U.S. Colloq.] to make one's way by sheer force (usually with *in*)

mus·cle-bound (-bound') *adj.* having some of the muscles enlarged and less elastic, as from too much exercise

mus·cle·man (-man) *n.*, *pl.* -men **1.** a man with highly developed muscles **2.** a henchman employed by a gangster to intimidate victims or opponents

Mus·co·vite (mus'kə vīt') *n.* a Russian, esp. of Moscow —*adj.* of Russia or of Moscow

Muscovy duck [altered < *musk duck*] a common domesticated duck with a large crest

mus·cu·lar (mus'kyə lər) *adj.* **1.** of, consisting of, or accomplished by a muscle or muscles **2.** having well-developed muscles; strong; brawny —**mus'cu·lar'i·ty** (-lar'ə tē) *n.* —**mus'cu·lar·ly** *adv.*

muscular dystrophy a chronic disease characterized by a progressive wasting of the muscles

mus·cu·la·ture (mus'kyə lə chər) *n.* [Fr.] the arrangement of the muscles of a body or of some part of the body; muscular system

Mus.D., Mus.Doc., Mus.Dr. [L. *Musicae Doctor*] Doctor of Music

Muse (myōōz) *n.* [< OFr. < L. < Gr. *mousa*] **1.** *Gr. Myth.* any of the nine goddesses who presided over literature and the arts and sciences **2.** [m-] the spirit regarded as inspiring a poet or artist

muse (myōōz) *vi.* mused, mus'ing [< OFr. *muser*, to loiter] to think deeply; meditate —*vt.* to think or say meditatively —*n.* deep meditation

mu·sette (myōō zet') *n.* [ME. < OFr. < *muser*, to play music] **1.** a small French bagpipe of the 17th and 18th cent. **2.** a soft pastoral melody, in imitation of the tunes played on this

mu·se·um (myōō zē'əm) *n.* [L. < Gr. *mouseion*, place for the

Muses < *mousa*, a Muse] a building, room, etc. for preserving and exhibiting artistic, historical, or scientific objects

museum piece 1. an object of sufficient age or interest to be kept in a museum 2. [Colloq.] a person or thing regarded as antiquated or decrepit

mush[1] (mush) *n.* [prob. var. of MASH] 1. any thick, soft mass 2. [Colloq.] maudlin sentimentality

mush[2] (mush) *interj.* [prob. < *mush on*, altered < Fr. *marchons*, let's go] in Canada and Alaska, a shout commanding sledge dogs to start or to go faster —*vi.* to travel on foot over snow, usually with a dog sledge —*n.* a journey by mushing

mush-room (mush'rōōm', -room') *n.* [OFr. *moisseron* < LL. *mussirio*] 1. any of various rapid-growing, fleshy fungi having a stalk with an umbrellalike top; popularly, any edible variety, as distinguished from the poisonous ones (*toadstools*) 2. anything like a mushroom in shape or rapid growth —*adj.* 1. of or made with mushrooms 2. like a mushroom in shape or rapid growth —*vi.* 1. to grow or spread rapidly 2. to flatten out at the end so as to resemble a mushroom

mushroom cloud the large mushroom-shaped cloud of smoke, debris, etc. produced by a nuclear explosion

mush·y (mush'ē) *adj.* **mush'i·er, mush'i·est** 1. like mush; thick and soft 2. [Colloq.] maudlin and sentimental —**mush'i·ly** *adv.* —**mush'i·ness** *n.*

mu·sic (myōō'zik) *n.* [< OFr. < L. < Gr. *mousikē* (*technē*), musical (art) < *mousa*, a Muse] 1. the art and science of combining tones in varying melody, harmony, etc., esp. so as to form complete and expressive compositions 2. the tones so arranged, or their arrangement 3. any rhythmic sequence of pleasing sounds, as of birds, etc. 4. a musical composition or compositions; esp., the written or printed score 5. ability to respond to or take pleasure in music —**face the music** [Colloq.] to accept the consequences, however unpleasant —**set to music** to compose music for (a poem, etc.)

mu·si·cal (-zi k'l) *adj.* 1. of or for the creation or performance of music 2. melodious or harmonious 3. fond of or skilled in music 4. set to music —*n.* a theatrical or film production with dialogue and a musical score with popular songs and dances: in full, **musical comedy** (or **play**, or **drama**) —**mu'si·cal'i·ty** (-kal'ə tē) *n.* —**mu'si·cal·ly** *adv.*

musical box a mechanical musical instrument containing a bar with tuned steel teeth that are struck by pins so arranged on a revolving cylinder as to produce a certain tune or tunes

musical chairs a game in which the players march to music around empty chairs (one fewer than the number of players) and rush to sit down each time the music stops: the player with no seat drops out

music hall 1. a variety entertainment consisting of songs, comic tunes, etc., esp. such an entertainment in the style of the Edwardian period 2. the theatre where such entertainments are staged

mu·si·cian (myōō zish'ən) *n.* a person skilled in music; esp., a professional performer of music —**mu·si'cian·ly** *adj.* —**mu·si'cian·ship'** *n.*

mu·si·col·o·gy (myōō'zi kol'ə jē) *n.* [< It.: see MUSIC & -LOGY] the systematized study of the science, history, and methods of music —**mu'si·co·log'i·cal** (-kə loj'i k'l) *adj.* —**mu'si·col'o·gist** *n.*

music paper paper specially ruled for writing musical scores

music-stool (-stōōl') *n.* 1. an adjustable stool for a pianist 2. a stool with a hinged top and a recess for storing sheet music

mus·ing (myōō'ziŋ) *adj.* that muses; meditative —*n.* meditation; reflection —**mus'ing·ly** *adv.*

musk (musk) *n.* [< OFr. < LL. < Gr. < Per. *mušk*, musk < Sans. *muska*, testicle] 1. a substance with a strong, penetrating odour; obtained from a small sac (**musk bag**) under the skin of the abdomen in the male musk deer: used as the basis of numerous perfumes 2. the odour of this substance, now often created synthetically —**musk'like' *adj.***

musk deer a small, hornless deer of the uplands of C Asia: the male secretes musk

mus·kel·lunge (mus'kə lunj') *n.*, *pl.* -**lunge**'[< Ojibway *maskinoje*] [U.S.] a large pike of the Great Lakes and upper Mississippi: also called **mus'kie** (-kē)

mus·ket (mus'kit) *n.* [< MFr. < It. *moschetto*, orig. fledged arrow < L. *musca*, a fly] a smooth-bore, long-barrelled firearm, used, as by infantry soldiers, before the invention of the rifle

mus·ket·eer (mus'kə tir') *n.* a soldier armed with a musket

mus·ket·ry (mus'kə trē) *n.* 1. the skill of firing muskets or other small arms 2. muskets or musketeers, collectively

musk·mel·on (musk'mel'ən) *n.* [MUSK + MELON] any of several roundish fruits growing on a plant of the gourd family, as the cantaloupe: they have a thick rind and sweet, juicy flesh

musk ox a hardy ox of arctic America and Greenland, with a long, coarse, hairy coat, large, curved horns, and a musklike odour

musk·rat (musk'rat') *n.*, *pl.* -**rats**', -**rat**': see PLURAL, II, D, 1 1. a N American rodent living in water and having glossy brown fur and a musklike odour 2. its fur

musk rose a Mediterranean rose with fragrant, usually white, flowers

musk·y (mus'kē) *adj.* **musk'i·er, musk'i·est** of, like, or smelling of musk —**musk'i·ness** *n.*

Mus·lim (muz'ləm, mooz'-) *n.*, *adj.* same as MOSLEM

mus·lin (muz'lin) *n.* [< Fr. < It. *mussolino* < *Mussolo*, Mosul, city in Iraq] a plain-weave cotton fabric, usually a fine fabric, used for wrapping food, etc.

MUSKRAT
(body 20-33 cm long; tail 15-30 cm

mus·quash (mus'kwosh) *n.*, *pl.* -**quash·es**, -**quash**: see PLURAL II, D, 1 [< AmInd.(Algonquian)] another name for MUSKRAT, esp. the fur

mus·sel (mus'l) *n.* [< OE., ult. < L. *musculus*, mussel, MUSCLE] any of various bivalve molluscs; specif., a) an edible saltwater variety b) a large freshwater variety with a pearly shell formerly made into buttons

Mus·sul·man (mus''l mən) *n.*, *pl.* -**mans** [< Per. < Ar. *muslim*] [Now Rare] a Moslem

must[1] (must; *unstressed* məst) *v.aux.* *pt.* **must** [< OE. *moste*, pt. of *motan*, may] an auxiliary used with the infinitive of various verbs (without *to*) to express: 1. compulsion, obligation, or necessity [I must pay her, I must say] 2. probability [you *must* be my cousin] 3. certainty [all men *must* die] *Must* is sometimes used with the verb understood [shoot if you *must*] —*n.* [Colloq.] something that must be done, had, read, seen, etc. [this book is a *must*] —**must be** 1. certainly is 2. surely are

must[2] (must) *n.* [OE. < L. *mustum*, new wine < *mustus*, fresh] the juice pressed from grapes or other fruit before it has fermented

must[3] (must) *n.* a musty quality or state

mus·tache (mə stash', mus'tash) *n.* *U.S.* var. of MOUSTACHE

mus·ta·chio (məs tä'shō, -shē ō') *n.*, *pl.* -**chios** [< Sp. or It.] a moustache, esp. a large, bushy one —**mus·ta'chioed** *adj.*

mus·tang (mus'taŋ) *n.* [< AmSp. < Sp. *mesteño*, belonging to the graziers, wild] a small wild or half-wild horse of the SW plains of the U.S.

mus·tard (mus'tərd) *n.* [< OFr. *moustarde* < L. *mustum*, MUST[2] (orig. added to the condiment)] 1. any of several plants with yellow flowers and slender pods 2. the ground or powdered seeds from these pods, often prepared as a paste, used as a pungent seasoning 3. a dark yellow

mustard and cress a salad made of mustard and cress leaves

mustard gas [from its mustardlike odour] a volatile liquid used as a poison gas in war

mustard plaster a plaster made with powdered mustard, applied to the skin as a counterirritant

mus·ter (mus'tər) *vt.* [< OFr. < ML. < L. *monstrare*, to show < *monere*, to warn] 1. to assemble (troops, etc.) 2. to gather up; collect; summon (often with *up*) [to *muster* up strength] 3. to total in number —*vi.* to assemble as for inspection or roll call —*n.* 1. an assembling, as of troops for inspection 2. a) the persons or things assembled b) the total of these 3. the list of persons in a military or naval unit: also **muster roll** —**pass muster** to measure up to the required standards

mus·n't (mus''nt) must not

mus·ty (mus'tē) *adj.* -**ti·er, -ti·est** [ult. < ? MOIST] 1. having a stale, mouldy smell or taste 2. stale, trite, or antiquated [*musty* ideas] —**mus'ti·ly** *adv.* —**mus'ti·ness** *n.*

mu·ta·ble (myōō'tə b'l) *adj.* [< L. < *mutare*, to change] 1. that can be changed 2. given to changing; inconstant 3. subject to mutation —**mu'ta·bil'i·ty, mu'ta·ble·ness** *n.* —**mu'ta·bly** *adv.*

mu·ta·gen (myōō'tə jən) *n.* [MUTA(TION) + -GEN] *Biol.* any substance or agent, as X-rays, mustard gas, etc., capable of increasing the frequency of mutation

mu·tant (myōō't'nt) *adj.* [< L. prp. of *mutare*, to change] undergoing mutation —*n.* an animal or plant with inheritable characters that differ from those of the parents

mu·tate (myōō tāt') *vi., vt.* -**tat·ed, -tat'ing** [< L. pp. of *mutare*, to change] to change; specif., to undergo or cause to undergo mutation

mu·ta·tion (myōō tā'shən) *n.* 1. a changing or being changed 2. a change, as in form, nature, etc. 3. *Biol.* a) a sudden variation in some inheritable character of an animal or plant b) an individual resulting from such variation; mutant —**mu·ta'tion·al** *adj.* —**mu·ta'tion·al·ly** *adv.*

mute (my̅o̅ot) *adj.* [< OFr. < L. *mutus*] 1. not speaking; voluntarily silent 2. unable to speak 3. not spoken [a *mute* appeal] 4. not pronounced; silent, as the *e* in *mouse* 5. *Law* refusing to plead when arraigned —*n.* 1. a person who does not speak; specif., one who cannot speak because deaf; deaf-mute 2. a letter that is not pronounced 3. *Law* a defendant who refuses to plead when arraigned 4. *Music* a device used to soften the tone of an instrument —*vt.* **mut′ed, mut′ing** 1. to soften the sound of, as with a mute 2. to tone down (a colour) —**mute′ly** *adv.* —**mute′ness** *n.*

MUTES
(A, violin mute; B, on violin bridge; C, trumpet mute; D, in bell of trumpet)

mute swan a common swan of Europe and Asia with pure white plumage and an orange-red beak

mu·ti·late (my̅o̅ot′ə lāt′) *vt.* **-lat′ed, -lat′ing** [< L. pp. of *mutilare* < *mutilus*, maimed] 1. to cut off or damage a limb, etc. of (a person or animal) 2. to damage or otherwise make imperfect, esp. by removing an essential part or parts —**mu′ti·la′tion** *n.* —**mu′ti·la′tive** *adj.* —**mu′ti·la′tor** *n.*

mu·ti·neer (my̅o̅ot′ə nir′) *n.* one guilty of mutiny

mu·ti·nous (my̅o̅ot′ə nəs) *adj.* 1. taking part or likely to take part in a mutiny 2. of or having to do with mutiny —**mu′ti·nous·ly** *adv.* —**mu′ti·nous·ness** *n.*

mu·ti·ny (my̅o̅ot′ə nē) *n., pl.* **-nies** [< Fr. < OFr. *mutin*, riotous < *meute*, a revolt, ult. < L. *movere*, to move] forcible revolt against constituted authority; esp., rebellion of soldiers or sailors against their officers —*vi.* **-nied, -ny·ing** to take part in a mutiny; revolt

Mutiny Act a former ordinance, passed annually by Parliament, dealing with discipline in the army and navy

mutt (mut) *n.* [prob. < *muttonhead*, a dolt] [Slang] 1. a stupid person; blockhead 2. a mongrel dog; cur

mut·ter (mut′ər) *vi., vt.* [ME. *moteren*] to speak or say in low tones with the lips almost closed, often in a complaining way; grumble —*n.* 1. a muttering 2. something muttered —**mut′ter·er** *n.*

mut·ton (mut′'n) *n.* [OFr. *moton*, a ram < ML. *multo*, sheep] the flesh of sheep, esp. a grown sheep, used as food —**mutton dressed up as lamb** an older person, thing, or idea dressed up or presented so as to look young or new —**mut′ton·y** *adj.*

mutton chop 1. a piece cut from the rib of a sheep for grilling or frying 2. [*pl.*] side whiskers shaped like mutton chops

mut·ton·head (-hed′) *n.* [Slang] a stupid person

mu·tu·al (my̅o̅o′choo wəl) *adj.* [< MFr. < L. *mutuus*, reciprocal < *mutare*, to change] 1. *a*) done, felt, etc. by each of two or more for or towards the other or others; reciprocal [*mutual* admiration] *b*) of each other [*mutual* enemies] 2. [Colloq.] shared in common; joint [our *mutual* friend] —**mu′tu·al′i·ty** (-wal′ə tē) *n., pl.* **-ties** —**mu′·tu·al·ly** *adv.*

mutual admiration society a family or group of people who continually overpraise one another

mutual insurance company a company in which policyholders share in the profits

muu·muu (m̅o̅o′m̅o̅o) *n.* [< Haw., lit., cut off] a full, long, loose garment for women, usually in a bright print as orig. worn in Hawaii

Mu·zak (my̅o̅o′zak) *a trademark for* a system of transmitting recorded music to restaurants, factories, etc. —*n.* the music transmitted

‡**mu·zhik, mu·zjik** (m̅o̅o zhēk′, m̅o̅o′zhik) *n.* [Russ.] in czarist Russia, a peasant

muz·zle (muz′'l) *n.* [< OFr. *musel*, snout < ML. *musum* < ?] 1. the part of the head of a dog, horse, etc. including the mouth, nose, and jaws 2. a device, as of straps, fastened over the mouth of an animal to prevent its biting or eating 3. anything that prevents free speech 4. the front end of the barrel of a firearm —*vt.* **-zled, -zling** 1. to put a muzzle on (an animal) 2. to prevent from talking or expressing an opinion —**muz′zler** *n.*

muz·zle-load·er (-lōd′ər) *n.* any firearm loaded through the muzzle —**muz′zle-load′ing** *n.*

muzzle velocity the velocity of a projectile as it leaves the muzzle of a firearm

muz·zy (muz′ē) *adj.* **-zi·er, -zi·est** [prob. < MU(DDY) + (FU)ZZY] [Colloq.] 1. confused, befuddled 2. blurred —**muz′zi·ly** *adv.* —**muz′zi·ness** *n.*

M.V.O. Member of the Royal Victorian Order

MW megawatt; megawatts

mW milliwatt; milliwatts

Mx 1. maxwell 2. Middlesex

my (mī; *unstressed, often* mə) *possessive pronominal adj.*

[OE. *min*] of, belonging to, made, or done by me —*interj.* an exclamation of surprise, dismay, etc.

my·al·ism (mī′ə liz′m) *n.* [prob. < native name] W Indian witchcraft

my·all (mī′ôl) *n.* [< Abor.] an Australian acacia with hard, sweet-smelling wood used to make tobacco pipes

my·ce·li·um (mī sē′lē əm) *n., pl.* **-li·a** (-ə) [ModL. < Gr. *mykēs*, a mushroom] the thallus, or vegetative part, of a fungus, made of a mass of threadlike tubes —**my·ce′li·al** *adj.*

My·ce·nae·an (mī′sə nē′ən) *adj.* 1. of Mycenae 2. designating or of a civilization that existed in Greece, Asia Minor, etc. from 1500 to 1100 B.C.

-my·cete (mī′sēt, mī sēt′) [< ModL. < Gr. < *mykēs*, a mushroom] *a combining form meaning* one of a specified class of fungi

my·co- [< Gr. *mykēs*, fungus] *a combining form meaning* fungus: also, before a vowel, **myc-**

my·col·o·gy (mī kol′ə jē) *n.* [< ModL.: see prec. & -LOGY] the branch of botany dealing with fungi —**my·co·log·ic** (mī′kə loj′ik), **my′co·log′i·cal** *adj.* —**my·col′o·gist** *n.*

my·co·sis (mī kō′sis) *n., pl.* **-ses** (-sēz) [ModL.: see MYC(O)-& -OSIS] 1. the growth of parasitic fungi in any part of the body 2. a disease caused by such fungi —**my·cot′ic** (-kot′-ik) *adj.*

my·e·li·tis (mī′ə līt′is) *n.* [ModL. < Gr. *myelos*, marrow MYC(O)-& -ITIS] inflammation of the spinal cord or the bone marrow

my·e·lo·gram (mī′ə lō gram′) *n.* [< Gr. *myelos*, marrow + -GRAM] an X-ray of the spinal cord, taken after the injection of a contrast substance —**my′e·log′ra·phy** (-log′rə fē) *n.*

my·na, my·nah (mī′nə) *n.* [Hindi *mainā*] any of a group of tropical birds of SE Asia related to the starling: some species can mimic speech

.Myn·heer (mīn her′, -hir′) *n.* [Du. *mijn heer*, lit., my lord] Sir; Mr.: a Dutch title of address

my·o- [< Gr. *mys* (gen. *myos*), a muscle] *a combining form meaning* muscle: also, before a vowel, **my-**

my·o·car·di·um (mī′ə kär′dē əm) *n.* [ModL.: see prec. + CARDIO-] the muscular substance of the heart —**my′o·car′-di·al** *adj.*

my·ope (mī′ōp) *n.* [Fr. < Gr. *myōps*, short-sighted] a person having myopia

my·o·pi·a (mī ō′pē ə) *n.* [ModL. < Gr. < *myein*, to close + *ōps*, an eye] abnormal vision in which light rays from distant objects focus in front of the retina instead of on it, so that the objects are not seen distinctly; shortsightedness —**my·op′ic** (-op′ik) *adj.* —**my·op′i·cal·ly** *adv.*

my·o·so·tis (mī′ə sōt′is) *n.* [ModL. < Gr. *myosōtis*, mouse ear] any of the borage family of plants, including the forget-me-not, having light-green leaves and white, blue, or pink flowers

myr·i·ad (mir′ē əd) *n.* [< Gr. *myrias* (gen. *myriados*), ten thousand < *myrios*, countless] 1. orig., ten thousand 2. any indefinitely large number 3. a great number of persons or things —*adj.* 1. countless; innumerable 2. of a highly varied nature

myr·i·a·pod (mir′ē ə pod′) *adj.* [see prec. & -POD] having many legs; specif., of a large group of arthropods having a long body of many segments, each with one or more pairs of jointed legs, as the centipedes —*n.* any animal of this group

myr·mi·don (mur′mə don′, -dən) *n., pl.* **-dons** [after the tribe of Thessalian warriors who fought under Achilles in the Trojan war] an unquestioning follower or subordinate

myrrh (mur) *n.* [< OE. & OFr. < L. < Gr. *myrrha* < Ar. *murr*] 1. a fragrant, bitter-tasting gum resin exuded from any of several plants of Arabia and E Africa, used in making incense, perfume, etc. 2. any of these plants

myr·tle (mur′t'l) *n.* [< OFr. < ML. dim. of L. *myrtus* < Gr. *myrtos*] 1. a shrub with evergreen leaves, white or pink flowers, and dark berries 2. any of various other evergreen plants —*adj.* designating a family of evergreen trees and shrubs, including myrtle, eucalyptus, guava, clove, and blue gum

my·self (mī self′, mə-) *pron.* a form of the 1st pers. sing. pronoun, used: *a*) as an intensive [I went *myself*] *b*) as a reflexive [I hurt *myself*] *c*) as a quasi-noun meaning "my real or true self" [I am not *myself* today]

mys·te·ri·ous (mis tir′ē əs) *adj.* of, containing, implying, or characterized by mystery —**mys·te′ri·ous·ly** *adv.* —**mys·te′ri·ous·ness** *n.*

mys·ter·y¹ (mis′tə rē, -trē) *n., pl.* **-ter·ies** [< L. < Gr. *mystērion*, ult. < *myein*, to initiate into the mysteries, orig., to close (eyes or mouth)] 1. something unexplained, unknown, or kept secret 2. *a*) anything that remains so secret or obscure as to excite curiosity *b*) a novel, play, etc. involving an event of this kind, esp. one about a crime and its solution 3. obscurity or secrecy 4. [*pl.*] secret rites or doctrines known only to the initiated [the Eleusinian *mysteries*] 5. *same as* MYSTERY PLAY 6. *Theol.* any religious truth divinely revealed and to be accepted on faith

mys·ter·y² (mis′tə rē) *n., pl.* **-ter·ies** [< ML. *misterium*, altered < L. *ministerium*, office, by confusion with *mysterium*, a secret rite] [Archaic] a craft or craft guild

mystery play any of a class of medieval dramatic representations of Biblical events

mystery tour a bus tour, the itinerary of which is not known beforehand by the passengers

mys·tic (mis'tik) *adj.* [< L. < Gr. *mystikos* < *mystēs*, one initiated] **1.** *same as* MYSTICAL **2.** mysterious, secret, occult, awe-inspiring, etc. [*mystic* rites, *mystic* powers] —*n.* one who professes to undergo mystical experiences by which he learns truths beyond human understanding

mys·ti·cal (-ti k'l) *adj.* **1.** of mystics or mysticism; esp., based on intuition, meditation, etc. of a spiritual nature **2.** spiritually symbolic **3.** *same as* MYSTIC (sense 2) —**mys'·ti·cal·ly** *adv.*

mys·ti·cism (-tə siz'm) *n.* **1.** the beliefs or practices of mystics **2.** the doctrine that knowledge of spiritual truths can be acquired by intuition and meditation **3.** vague or obscure thinking or belief

mys·ti·fy (mis'tə fī') *vt.* **-fied'**, **-fy'ing** [< Fr. < *mystère*, mystery + *-fier*, -FY] **1.** a) to puzzle or perplex b) to bewilder deliberately **2.** to involve in mystery; make obscure —**mys'ti·fi·ca'tion** *n.*

mys·tique (mis tēk') *n.* [Fr., mystic] the quasi-mystical attitudes and feelings surrounding some person, institution, activity, etc.

myth (mith) *n.* [< LL. < Gr. *mythos*, a word, legend] **1.** a traditional story of unknown authorship, serving usually to explain some phenomenon of nature, the origin of man, or the customs, religious rites, etc. of a people: cf. LEGEND **2.** such stories collectively; mythology **3.** any fictitious story **4.** any imaginary person or thing

myth. mythology

myth·i·cal (-i k'l) *adj.* **1.** of, or having the nature of, a myth or myths **2.** existing only in myth **3.** imaginary or fictitious; not based on fact Also **myth'ic** —**myth'i·cal·ly** *adv.*

myth·i·cize (-ə sīz') *vt.* **-cized'**, **-ciz'ing** to make into, or explain as, a myth —**myth'i·ciz'er** *n.*

my·thol·o·gize (mi thol'ə jīz') *vi.* **-gized'**, **-giz'ing** to relate, compile, or explain myths —*vt.* to make into a myth: also **myth·i·cize** (mith'ə sīz') **-cized'**, **-ciz'ing** —**my·thol'o·giz'er** *n.*

my·thol·o·gy (mi thol'ə jē) *n.*, *pl.* **-gies** [< LL. < Gr. *mythos*, myth + *-logia*, -LOGY] **1.** the study of myths **2.** myths collectively; esp., all the myths of a specific people or about a specific being —**myth·o·log·i·cal** (mith'ə loj'i k'l), **myth'o·log'ic** *adj.* —**myth'o·log'i·cal·ly** *adv.* —**my·thol'o·gist** *n.*

myth·o·ma·ni·a (mith'ə mā'nē ə, -mān'yə) *n.* [ModL.: see MYTH & -MANIA] *Psychiatry* an abnormal tendency to lie —**myth'o·ma'ni·ac'** *adj., n.*

myth·os (mīth'os) *n.* **1.** a myth or body of myths **2.** the attitudes, beliefs, etc. most characteristic of a particular group or society

myx·oe·de·ma (mik'sə dē'mə) *n.* [ModL. < Gr. *myxa*, mucus & OEDEMA] a disease caused by failure of the thyroid gland and characterized by a slowing down of mental and physical activity

myx·o·ma (mik sō'mə) *n.*, *pl.* **-mas**, **-ma·ta** (-mə tə) [< Gr. *myxa*, mucus + -OMA] a tumour of connective tissue cells containing a mucuslike material

myx·o·ma·to·sis (mik'sə mə tō'sis) *n.* [see prec. & -OSIS] **1.** the presence of many myxomas **2.** an infectious virus disease in rabbits, characterized by tumorous growths

N

N, n (en) *n.*, *pl.* **N's, n's 1.** the fourteenth letter of the English alphabet **2.** the sound of N or *n*

n (en) *n.* **1.** *Math.* the symbol for an indefinite number **2.** *Physics* the symbol for neutron

N 1. *Chem.* nitrogen **2.** *Physics* the symbol for newton

N, N., n, n. 1. north **2.** northern **3.** *Chess* knight

n. 1. net **2.** neuter **3.** noon **4.** noun **5.** number

Na [L. *natrium*] *Chem.* sodium

N.A. North America

N.A.A.F.I. 1. Navy, Army and Air Force Institutes **2.** a shop or canteen run by this organization for servicemen

nab (nab) *vt.* **nabbed, nab'bing** [prob. var. of dial. *nap*, to snatch < Scand.] [Colloq.] **1.** to seize suddenly; snatch **2.** to arrest or catch (a felon or wrongdoer) —**nab'ber** *n.*

na·bob (nā'bob) *n.* [< Hindi < Ar. *nuwwāb*, pl. of *nā'ib*, deputy] **1.** a native provincial deputy or governor of the old Mogul Empire in India **2.** a very rich man, esp. one who obtained his fortune in India

na·celle (nə sel') *n.* [Fr. < LL. *navicella*, dim. of L. *navis*, a ship] a streamlined enclosure on an aircraft, esp. that which houses an engine

na·cre (nā'kər) *n.* [Fr. < It. < Ar. *naqqārah*, drum] *same as* MOTHER-OF-PEARL

na·cre·ous (-krē əs) *adj.* **1.** of or like nacre **2.** yielding nacre **3.** iridescent; lustrous Also **na'crous**

na·dir (nā'dər, -dir) *n.* [< MFr. < ML. < Ar. *nazīr* (*as-samt*), opposite (the zenith)] **1.** that point of the celestial sphere directly opposite to the zenith and directly below the observer **2.** the lowest point

nae (nā) *adv.* [Scot.] no; not —*adj.* no

nae·vus (nē'vəs) *n.*, *pl.* **nae'vi** (-vī) [ModL. < L. *naevus*] a coloured spot on the skin, usually congenital; birthmark or mole —**nae'void** (-void) *adj.*

naf·fy (na'fē) *n.* [Colloq.] *same as* N.A.A.F.I.

nag[1] (nag) *vt.* **nagged, nag'ging** [< Scand.] **1.** to annoy by continual scolding, faultfinding, urging, etc. **2.** to keep troubling, worrying, etc. —*vi.* **1.** to urge, scold, etc. constantly **2.** to cause continual discomfort, pain, etc. —*n.* a person, esp. a woman, who nags: also **nag'ger** —**nag'ging·ly** *adv.* —**nag'gy** *adj.* **-gi·er, -gi·est**

nag[2] (nag) *n.* [ME. *nagge* < ?] **1.** a horse that is worn-out, old, etc. **2.** a small riding horse

na·ga·na (nə gä'nə) *n.* [<Zulu *u(lu)-nakane*] an infectious disease affecting horses and cattle in tropical Africa, transmitted by tsetse flies

Na·hua·tl (nä'wät 'l) *n.* [Nahuatl] **1.** *pl.* **Na'hua·tls, Na'·hua·tl** a member of any of a number of Indian tribes of Mexico **2.** their Uto-Aztecan language **3.** a branch of the Uto-Aztecan language family, spoken in Mexico and C America

nai·ad (nā'ad, nī'-; -əd) *n.*, *pl.* **-ads, -a·des'** (-ə dēz') [< Fr. < L. < Gr. *Naïas* < *naein*, to flow] **1.** [*also* N-] *Gr. & Rom. Myth.* any of the nymphs living in and giving life to springs, fountains, rivers, etc. **2.** *Zool.* the aquatic nymph of certain insects

na·if, na·ïf (nä ēf') *adj.* [Fr.] *same as* NAIVE

nail (nāl) *n.* [OE. *nægl*] **1.** a) the thin, horny substance growing out at the ends of the fingers and toes b) a claw **2.** a tapered piece of metal, commonly pointed and with a head, driven with a hammer to hold pieces of wood together, serve as a peg, etc. —*vt.* **1.** to attach, fasten together, or fasten shut with nails **2.** to fix (the eyes, attention, etc.) steadily on an object **3.** to discover or expose (a lie, etc.) **4.** [Colloq.] to catch, capture, etc. **5.** [Colloq.] to hit squarely —**hit the nail on the head** to do or say whatever is exactly right —**nail down** to settle definitely; make sure —**on the nail** at once, immediately, esp. where payment is concerned

NAILS
(A, common wire; B, flooring; C, finishing; D, oval; E, screw)

nail·brush (-brush') *n.* a small, stiff brush for cleaning the fingernails

nail·er (nāl'ər) *n.* one who makes nails —**nail'er·y** *n.*

nail file a small, flat file for trimming the fingernails

nail polish a kind of lacquer, usually coloured, applied to the fingernails or toenails as a cosmetic: also **nail varnish**

nail scissors a pair of small scissors, often curved, for trimming finger and toe nails

nail set a tool for sinking a nail so that it is below the surface of the wood Also **nail punch**

nain·sook (nān'sook) *n.* [< Hindi < *nain*, the eye + *sukh*, pleasure] a thin, lightweight cotton fabric

nai·ra (nī'rə) *n.*, *pl.* **nai'ra** [dim. of *Nigeria*] the monetary unit of Nigeria: see MONETARY UNITS, table

na·ive, na·ïve (nä ēv', nī-) *adj.* [Fr., fem. of *naïf* < L. *nativus*, natural] **1.** unaffectedly or foolishly simple; artless; unsophisticated **2.** not suspicious; credulous —**na·ive'ly, na·ïve'ly** *adv.*

na·ive·té, na·ïve·té (nä ēv'tā, nī-) *n.* [Fr.] **1.** a being naive **2.** a naive action or remark Also **na·ive'ness, na·ïve'ness, na·ive'ty** (-tē), **na·ïve'ty**

na·ked (nā′kid) *adj.* [OE. *nacod*] 1. *a*) completely unclothed; nude *b*) uncovered; exposed: said of parts of the body 2. destitute 3. without protection or defence 4. without its usual covering; specif., *a*) out of its sheath [a *naked* sword] *b*) without decoration, etc. [a *naked* wall] 5. without additions, etc.; plain [the *naked* truth] 6. not aided by a microscope, telescope, etc. [the *naked* eye] —**na′ked·ly** *adv.* —**na′ked·ness** *n.*

naked ape a human being

N.A.L.G.O. National and Local Government Officers' Association

nam·by-pam·by (nam′bē pam′bē) *adj.* [orig. satirical nickname of *Ambrose Philips*, 18th-c. Eng. poet] weakly sentimental; insipidly pretty or nice —*n.*, *pl.* **-bies** 1. namby-pamby talk or writing 2. a namby-pamby person

name (nām) *n.* [OE. *nama*] 1. a word or phrase by which a person, thing, or class of things is known; title 2. a word or phrase expressing some quality considered descriptive; epithet 3. *a*) reputation *b*) good reputation 4. a family or clan 5. appearance only, not reality [chief in *name* only] 6. a famous person —*adj.* carrying a name [a *name* tag] —*vt.* **named, nam′ing** 1. to give a name or title to 2. to designate or refer to by name 3. to identify by the right name [*name* the oceans] 4. to nominate or appoint to a post, honour, or office 5. to set or specify (a day, price, etc.) 6. to speak about; mention —**call names** to swear at —**in the name of** 1. in appeal to 2. by the authority of 3. as belonging to —**keep one's name on the books** to remain a member of a club, college, organisation —**name names** to identify specific persons, esp. as doing wrong —**name the day** to decide on a date, esp. for a wedding —**to one's name** belonging to one —**you name it** anything whatever —**name′a·ble** *adj.* —**nam′er** *n.*

name-call·ing (-kôl′iŋ) *n.* the use of abusive names in attacking another —**name′-call′er** *n.*

name day 1. the feast day of the saint after whom one is named 2. *another name for* TICKET DAY

name-drop·per (-drop′ər) *n.* a person who tries to impress others by often mentioning famous persons in a familiar way —**name′-drop′ping** *n.*

name·less (-lis) *adj.* 1. without a name 2. left unnamed 3. not well known 4. indescribable 5. too horrid to specify [*nameless* crimes] —**name′less·ly** *adv.* —**name′less·ness** *n.*

name·ly (-lē) *adv.* that is to say; to wit

name·plate (-plāt′) *n.* a piece of metal, etc. on which a name is inscribed

name·sake (-sāk′) *n.* a person with the same name as another, esp. if named after the other

name tape a tape with a person's name embroidered or woven on it, used to identify a garment

nan·keen, nan·kin (nan kēn′) *n.* [< *Nanking*, city in China] 1. a buff-coloured, durable cotton cloth, orig. from China 2. [*pl.*] trousers made of this

Nankeen hawk an Australian bird, brightly coloured: also **Nankeen kestrel**

nan·ny (nan′ē) *n.* *pl.* **-nies** [< *Nan*, dim of Ann(a), a feminine name] 1. a child's nurse 2. [Colloq.] grandmother

nanny goat [see prec.] a female goat

na·no- [< Gr. *nanos*, dwarf] *a combining form meaning* one thousand-millionth part of

na·no·sec·ond (nan′ō sek′ənd) *n.* one thousand-millionth of a second

nap¹ (nap) *vi.* **napped, nap′ping** [OE. *hnappian*] 1. to sleep lightly for a short time 2. to be careless or unprepared [he was caught *napping*] —*n.* a brief, light sleep

nap² (nap) *n.* [< or akin to MDu. & MLowG. *noppe*] 1. the downy or hairy surface of cloth formed by short hairs or fibres, raised by brushing, etc. 2. any similar surface, as of the flesh side of leather —*vt.* **napped, nap′ping** to raise a nap on by brushing, etc. —**nap′less** *adj.* —**napped** *adj.*

nap³ (nap) *n.* [clipped form of NAPOLEON] 1. a card game for two or more players, similar to whist 2. *Horse Racing* a tip, supposed to be a certainty to win —*vt* **napped, nap′ping** to name a horse as a winner —**go nap** 1. a bid in the game of nap to win all the tricks 2. to risk all on one chance

na·palm (nā′päm) *n.* [*na*(*phthene*) + *palm*(*itate*)], salt of palmitic acid] 1. a jellylike substance with petrol or oil in it, used in flamethrowers and bombs 2. the chemical used to produce this substance —*vt.* to attack or burn with napalm

nape (nāp) *n.* [ME.] the back of the neck

na·per·y (nā′pər ē) *n.* [< MFr. < OFr. *nappe*: see NAPKIN] [Archaic or Scot.] household linen; esp., table linen

naph·tha (naf′thə, nap′-) *n.* [L. < Gr. < Per. *neft*, pitch] a flammable, volatile liquid made by distilling petroleum, coal tar, wood, etc. and used as a fuel, solvent, etc.

naph·tha·lene (-lēn′) *n.* [prec. + -*l*- + -ENE] a white, crystalline, aromatic hydrocarbon, C₁₀H₈, made by distilling coal tar and used in moth repellents and in certain dyes, etc.: also **naph′tha·lin′**—**naph′tha·len′ic** (-lē′nik, -len′ik) *adj.*

naph·thol (naf thol, nap′-) *n.* [NAPHTH(ALENE) + -OL¹] either

of two white, crystalline compounds, C₁₀H₇OH, derived from naphthalene and used as antiseptics and in dyes, etc.

Na·pi·er's bones (nā′pē ərz) a set of graduated rods formerly used for multiplication and division, based on a method invented by John Napier

nap·kin (nap′kin) *n.* [< OFr. *nappe* < L. *mappa*, cloth] 1. a small cloth or paper used while eating for protecting the clothes and wiping the fingers or lips 2. any small cloth, towel, etc. 3. *same as* NAPPY²

napkin ring a ring, often ornate, for holding a table napkin

na·po·le·on (nə pō′lē ən, -pōl′yən) *n.* [after *Napoleon I*, Emperor of France (1804-15)] 1. a former gold coin of France, equivalent to 20 francs 2. *original name of* NAP³

nap·py¹ (nap′ē) *adj.* **-pi·er, -pi·est** [? <NAP² + -Y²] foaming; heady; strong: said of ale —*n.* ale

nap·py² (nap′ē) *n.*, *pl.* **-pies** [< NAP(KIN) + -Y¹] a soft, absorbent cloth folded and arranged between the legs and around the waist of a baby: also called **napkin**

nap·py³ (nap′ē) *adj.* **-pi·er, -pi·est** covered with nap; downy, shaggy, etc. —**nap′pi·ness** *n.*

nar·cis·sism (när sis′iz′m) *n.* [after *Narcissus*, a youth in Gr. mythology who pined away for love of his own reflection in a spring, & -ISM] 1. self-love 2. *Psychoanalysis* the first stage of libidinal development, in which the self is an erotic object Also **nar′cism** —**nar·cis′sist** *n.*, *adj.* —**nar·cis′sis′tic** *adj.*

nar·cis·sus (när sis′əs) *n.*, *pl.* **-cis′sus, -cis′sus·es, -cis′si** (-ī) [ModL. < L. < Gr. *narkissos*, ? akin to *narkē* (see NARCOTIC): in reference to the narcotic properties] any of a genus of bulb plants with smooth leaves and white, yellow, or orange flowers, including the daffodils and jonquils

nar·co- [< Gr. *narkē*, stupor] *a combining form meaning* narcosis, sleep, stupor: also, before a vowel, **narc-**

nar·co·lep·sy (när′kə lep′sē) *n.* [NARCO- + LEPSY] a condition marked by short attacks of irresistible drowsiness —**nar′co·lep′tic** *adj.*, *n.*

nar·co·sis (när kō′sis) *n.* a condition of deep stupor which passes into unconsciousness, caused by a narcotic or certain chemicals

nar·co·syn·the·sis (när′kō sin′thə sis) *n.* [NARCO- + SYNTHESIS] a method of treating an acute traumatic neurosis by working with a patient while he is under the influence of a hypnotic drug

nar·cot·ic (när kot′ik) *n.* [< OFr. < ML. < Gr. *narkoun*, to benumb < *narkē*, numbness] 1. a drug, as opium, used to relieve pain and induce sleep: narcotics are often addictive and in excessive doses can cause stupor, coma, or death 2. anything with a soothing, lulling, or dulling effect —*adj.* 1. of, like, or producing narcosis 2. of, by, or for narcotic addicts

nar·co·tism (när′kə tiz′m) *n.* 1. *same as* NARCOSIS 2. addiction to narcotics

nar·co·tize (när′kə tīz′) *vt.* **-tized′, -tiz′ing** 1. to subject to a narcotic; stupefy 2. to lull or dull the senses of —**nar′-co·ti·za′tion** *n.*

nard (närd) *n.* [< OFr. < L. < Gr. *nardos*, ult. < Sans.] *same as* SPIKENARD (sense 2)

nar·es (ner′ēz) *n.pl.*, *sing.* **nar′is** (-is) [L.] the nasal passages; esp., the nostrils —**nar′i·al** (-ē əl), **nar′ine** (-in, -īn) *adj.*

nar·ghi·le (när′gə lē′, -lā′) *n.* [< Turk. & Per. < Per. *nargīl*, coconut tree: orig. made of coconut shell] *same as* HOOKAH: also sp. **nar′gi·le, nar′gi·leh′**

nark (närk) *n.* [<Romany *nak*, a nose] [Slang] 1. an informer or spy 2. [Aust.] an annoying person —*vt.*, *vi.* [Slang] 1. to inform on (a person) 2. to make, be, or become annoyed, angry, etc. —**nark it** [Slang] stop it; keep quiet —**nark′y** *adj.*

nar·rate (na rāt′) *vt.*, *vi.* **-rat·ed, -rat·ing** [< L. pp. of *narrare*, to relate] 1. to tell (a story) 2. to give an account of (events)

nar·ra·tion (nə rā′shən) *n.* 1. a narrating 2. *same as* NARRATIVE 3. writing or speaking that narrates, as fiction —**nar·ra′tion·al** *adj.*

nar·ra·tive (nar′ə tiv) *adj.* 1. in story form 2. concerned with narration —*n.* 1. a story; account; tale 2. the art or practice of relating stories or accounts —**nar′ra·tive·ly** *adv.*

nar·ra·tor (nə rāt′ər) *n.* 1. a person who relates a story, etc. 2. a person who reads narrative passages, as between scenes of a play

nar·row (nar′ō) *adj.* [OE. *nearu*] 1. small in width; not wide 2. limited in meaning, size, amount, or extent [a *narrow* majority] 3. limited in outlook; not liberal; prejudiced 4. close; careful [a *narrow* inspection] 5. with barely enough space, time, etc. [a *narrow* escape] 6. limited in means [*narrow* circumstances] 7. *Phonetics* tense: said of the tongue —*vi.*, *vt.* to decrease or limit in width, extent, or scope —*n.* 1. a narrow part or place, esp. in a valley, road, etc. 2. [*usually pl.*] a narrow passage; strait —**nar′row·ly** *adv.* —**nar′row·ness** *n.*

narrow boat a long, narrow canal boat, esp. with a beam of 2.1 m (7 feet)

narrow gauge 1. a width (between railway lines) less than standard (56¹/₂ in., 143.5 cm) **2.** a narrow-gauge railway or carriage —**nar'row-gauge'**, **nar'row-gauged'** *adj.*

nar·row-mind·ed (-mīn'did) *adj.* limited in outlook; not liberal; prejudiced —**nar'row-mind'ed·ly** *adv.* —**nar'-row-mind'ed·ness** *n.*

narrow seas the seas separating Britain from the continent of Europe

nar·thex (när'thəks) *n.* [LGr., exterior portico] **1.** in early Christian churches, a porch or portico **2.** a church vestibule leading to the nave

nar·whal (när'wəl, -hwəl) *n.* [< Scand., as in Norw. & Dan. *narhval*] an arctic cetacean valued for its oil and ivory: the male has a long, spiral tusk extending from the upper jaw: also **nar'wal** (-wəl), **nar'-whale'** (-hwāl')

nar·y (ner'ē) *adj.* [< *ne'er a*, never a] [U.S. & Dial.] not any; no (with *a* or *an*) [*nary* a doubt]

NARWHAL
(body 3-5 m long; tusk to 3 m long)

N.A.S. National Association of Schoolmasters

NASA (nas'ə) [U.S.] National Aeronautics and Space Administration

na·sal (nā'z'l) *adj.* [< ModL. < L. *nasus*, a nose] **1.** of the nose **2.** produced by making breath go through the nose, as the sounds of *m, n, ng* (ŋ) **3.** characterized by such sounds [a *nasal* voice] —*n.* a nasal sound —**na·sal·i·ty** (nā zal'ə tē) *n.* —**na'sal·ly** *adv.*

na·sal·ize (nā'zə līz') *vt., vi.* -**ized'**, -**iz'ing** to pronounce or speak with a nasal sound or sounds —**na'sal·i·za'tion** *n.*

nas·cent (nas''nt, nā's'nt) *adj.* [< L. prp. of *nasci*, to be born] **1.** coming into being; being born **2.** beginning to form, grow, or develop: said of ideas, cultures, etc. —**nas'-cence, nas'cen·cy** *n.*

na·so- [< L. *nasus*, nose] *a combining form meaning:* **1.** nose, nasal **2.** nasal and

na·stur·tium (nə stur'shəm, na-) *n.* [L. < *nasus*, nose + pp. of *torquere*, to twist: from its pungent odour] **1.** a plant with shield-shaped leaves and red, yellow, or orange flowers **2.** the flower

nas·ty (näs'tē) *adj.* -**ti·er**, -**ti·est** [< ? or akin to Du. *nestig*, dirty] **1.** very dirty; filthy **2.** nauseating **3.** morally offensive; indecent **4.** very unpleasant, mean, or harmful —**a nasty piece of work** [Colloq.] an unpleasant person —**nas'ti·ly** *adv.* —**nas'ti·ness** *n.*

nat. **1.** national **2.** native **3.** natural

na·tal (nāt''l) *adj.* [< L. *natalis* < pp. of *nasci*, to be born] **1.** of or connected with one's birth **2.** dating from birth **3.** native: said of a place

na·tant (nāt''nt) *adj.* [< L. prp. of *natare*, to swim] swimming or floating

na·ta·to·ri·al (nāt'ə tôr'ē əl) *adj.* [< LL. < L. *natator*, swimmer (see prec.) + -AL] of, characterized by, or adapted for swimming: also **na'ta·to·ry**

natch (nach) *adv.* [Slang] naturally; of course

na·tes (nā'tēz) *n.pl.* [L.] the buttocks

nathe·less (nāth'lis, nath'-) *adv.* [< OE. < *na*, never + *the*, the + *læs*, less] [Archaic] nevertheless —*prep.* [Archaic] notwithstanding Also **nath'less** (nath'-)

na·tion (nā'shən) *n.* [< OFr. < L. *natio* < pp. of *nasci*, to be born] **1.** a community of people with a territory, history, economic life, culture, and language in common **2.** the people of a territory united under a single government; country **3.** a people or tribe —**na'tion·hood'** (-hood') *n.*

na·tion·al (nash'ə n'l) *adj.* **1.** of a nation or the nation **2.** affecting a (or the) nation as a whole —*n.* **1.** a citizen of a nation **2.** [N-] *same as* GRAND NATIONAL —**na'tion·al·ly** *adv.*

national anthem a patriotic hymn or song commonly sung by people of a nation at public gatherings

National Assistance a former name for the supplementary benefits available under the National Insurance scheme

National Debt the total debt of central government, including government stocks, Treasury bills, savings certificates, etc.

national grid **1.** the system connecting electric power stations by a network of high-voltage power lines **2.** the metric coordinate system used in Ordnance Survey maps of the British Isles

National Guard [U.S.] a state military force that can be called into federal service by the president

National Health Service a system introduced in Britain in 1948 by which medical services are funded mainly by taxation rather than by payments by individuals

National Insurance an insurance scheme operated by the British government, based on contributions from employers and employees and providing State aid for the sick, jobless, retired, etc.

na·tion·al·ism (-iz'm) *n.* **1.** *a)* patriotism *b)* narrow, jingoist patriotism **2.** the putting of national interests and security

above international considerations **3.** the desire for or advocacy of national independence —**na'tion·al·ist** (-ist) *n., adj.* —**na'tion·al·is'tic** *adj.* —**na'tion·al·is'ti·cal·ly** *adv.*

na·tion·al·i·ty (nash'ə nal'ə tē) *n., pl.* -**ties** **1.** national quality or character **2.** the status of belonging to a particular nation by birth or naturalization **3.** the condition or fact of being a nation **4.** a national group, esp. of immigrants from some other country: in full, **nationality group**

na·tion·al·ize (nash'ə nə līz') *vt.* -**ized'**, -**iz'ing** **1.** to make national **2.** to transfer ownership or control of (land, industries, etc.) to the nation —**na'tion·al·i·za'tion** *n.* —**na'-tion·al·iz'er** *n.*

National Savings Bank a savings bank run by the government, through the Post Office

national service compulsory military service, usually for a fixed period of time; conscription

National Trust a society founded in Britain in 1895 for the purpose of preserving and administering places of historic interest or natural beauty

na·tion·wide (nā'shən wīd') *adj.* by or throughout the whole nation; national

na·tive (nāt'iv) *adj.* [< MFr. < L. *nativus* < pp. of *nasci*, to be born] **1.** inborn; innate; natural **2.** belonging to a locality or country by birth, production, or growth; indigenous [a *native* Australian, *native* plants] **3.** *a)* being the place of one's birth [one's *native* land] *b)* belonging to one because of the place of one's birth [one's *native* language] **4.** as found in nature; unaltered by man **5.** occurring in a pure state in nature [*native* gold] **6.** of or characteristic of the people born in a certain place —*n.* **1.** a person born in the region indicated, esp. one whose ancestors were also born there or as distinguished from an invader, colonist, etc. **2.** a plant or animal indigenous to a place and growing or living there naturally **3.** a permanent resident, not a mere visitor —**go native** to adopt the simpler way of life found in the country one is visiting etc.: usually a derogatory term —**na'tive·ly** *adv.* —**na'-tive·ness** *n.*

na·tive-born (-bôrn') *adj.* born in a specified place or country

na·tiv·i·ty (nə tiv'ə tē) *n., pl.* -**ties** [see NATIVE] **1.** birth **2.** *Astrol.* the horoscope for one's birth —**the Nativity** **1.** the birth of Jesus **2.** Christmas Day

natl. national

NATO (nā'tō) North Atlantic Treaty Organization

NATSOPA (nat sō'pə) National Society of Operative Printers, Graphical & Media Personnel

nat·ter (nat'ər) *vi.* [var. of dial. *gnatter*, to grumble] [Colloq.] **1.** to chatter idly; talk on at length **2.** find fault, grumble —*n.* [Colloq.] chat or talk

nat·ter·jack toad (nat'ər jak') [< ? echoic] a small toad with a yellow stripe along the centre of its back

nat·ty (nat'ē) *adj.* -**ti·er**, -**ti·est** [< ? NEAT¹] trim and smart in appearance or dress [a *natty* suit] —**nat'ti·ly** *adv.* —**nat'-ti·ness** *n.*

nat·u·ral (nach'ər əl, nach'rəl) *adj.* [< OFr. < L. *naturalis*, by birth] **1.** of or arising from nature **2.** produced or existing in nature; not artificial **3.** dealing with nature [a *natural* science] **4.** as found in nature; unaltered by man **5.** real or physical, rather than spiritual, intellectual, or imaginary **6.** *a)* innate; inborn [*natural* abilities] *b)* having certain qualities innately [a *natural* comedian] **7.** based on instinctive moral feeling [*natural* rights] **8.** true to nature; lifelike [a *natural* likeness] **9.** normal or usual [a *natural* outcome] **10.** customarily expected [a *natural* courtesy] **11.** free from affectation **12.** *a)* illegitimate [a *natural* child] *b)* not adoptive [*natural* parents] **13.** *Music a)* without flats or sharps *b)* neither sharpened nor flattened —*n.* **1.** an idiot **2.** [Colloq.] a person who is naturally expert **3.** [Colloq.] a sure success **4.** a yellowish-grey colour **5.** *Cards* a hand totalling 21 when dealt, in vingt-et-un **6.** *Music a)* the sign (♮) cancelling a preceding sharp or flat: in full, **natural sign** *b)* the note affected: in full, **natural note** *c)* a white key on the piano —**nat'u·ral·ness** *n.*

natural childbirth a method of childbirth in which the mother is taught to relax so that a normal delivery will require little or no anaesthesia

natural gas a mixture of gaseous hydrocarbons, chiefly methane, occurring naturally in the earth and conveyed through pipes to be used as a fuel

natural history the study of the animal, vegetable, and mineral world, esp. in a popular way

nat·u·ral·ism (-iz'm) *n.* **1.** action or thought based on natural desires or instincts **2.** *Literature, Art,* etc. faithful adherence to nature; realism: specif. applied to the realism of a group of 19th-cent. French writers **3.** *Philos.* the belief that the natural world is all that exists

nat·u·ral·ist (-ist) *n.* **1.** a person who studies animals and plants **2.** a person who believes in or practises naturalism —*adj.* *same as* NATURALISTIC

nat·u·ral·is·tic (nach'rə lis'tik) *adj.* **1.** of natural history or naturalists **2.** of or characterized by naturalism **3.** in accordance with, or in imitation of, nature —**nat′u·ral·is′·ti·cal·ly** *adv.*

nat·u·ral·ize (nach′rə līz′) *vt.* -**ized**′, -**iz**′**ing 1.** to confer citizenship upon (someone of foreign birth) **2.** to adopt and make common (a custom, word, etc.) from another place **3.** to adapt (a plant or animal) to a new environment —*vi.* to become naturalized —**nat′u·ral·i·za′tion** *n.*

natural language a language that has evolved naturally as the means of communication among people as opposed to an artificial language or code

nat·u·ral·ly (nach′rə lē) *adv.* **1.** in a natural manner **2.** by nature; innately **3.** as one might expect; of course

natural number any positive integer, as 1, 2, etc.

natural philosophy *earlier name for* NATURAL SCIENCE (specif., physics)

natural resources the forms of wealth supplied by nature, as coal, oil, water power, etc.

natural science the systematized knowledge of nature, including biology, chemistry, physics, etc.

natural selection the process in evolution by which those individuals (of a species) with characters that help them to become adapted to their specific environment tend to transmit their characters, while those less able to become adapted tend to die out

natural wastage loss of personnel in the normal course of events, as because of death, retirement, etc.

na·ture (nā′chər) *n.* [< OFr. < L. *natura* < pp. of *nasci*, to be born] **1.** the quality or qualities that make something what it is; essence **2.** inborn character, disposition, or tendencies **3.** kind; sort **4.** the basic biological functions, instincts, drives, etc. **5.** normal or acceptable behaviour **6.** the sum total of all things in the physical universe **7.** [*sometimes* N-] the power, force, etc. that seems to regulate this **8.** the primitive state of man **9.** a simple way of life close to or in the outdoors **10.** natural scenery, and the plants and animals in it —**by nature** naturally; inherently —**call of nature** [Colloq.] the desire, or need to urinate or defecate —**in a state of nature 1.** completely naked **2.** not cultivated or tame **3.** uncivilized —**of** (or **in**) **the nature of** having the essential character of; like

-**na·tured** (nā′chərd) *a combining form meaning* having or showing a (specified kind of) nature, disposition, or temperament [good-*natured*]

nature study the study of plant or animal life by direct observation, esp. in an elementary, non-technical manner

nature trail a path set out in woods, etc., so as to facilitate the study of nature by its users

naught (nôt) *n.* [< OE. < *na*, no + *wiht*, a person] **1.** nothing **2.** *Arith.* the figure zero (0) —*adj.* [Archaic or Obs.] **1.** worthless **2.** evil *Also* **nought** —**set at naught** to defy; scorn

naugh·ty (nôt′ē) *adj.* -**ti·er**, -**ti·est** [< obs. *naught*, wicked] **1.** not behaving properly; disobedient: used esp. of children **2.** improper or obscene —**naugh′ti·ly** *adv.* —**naugh′ti·ness** *n.*

nau·se·a (nô′sē ə, -zē ə, -zhə) *n.* [L. < Gr. *nausia*, sea-sickness < *naus*, a ship] **1.** a feeling of sickness at the stomach, with an urge to vomit **2.** disgust —**nau′se·ant** *adj., n.*

nau·se·ate (-sē āt′, -shē-, -zē-, -zhē-) *vt.*, *vi.* -**at**′**ed**, -**at**′**ing** to feel or cause to feel nausea —**nau′se·at′ing·ly** *adv.* —**nau′se·a′tion** *n.*

nau·seous (nô′shəs, -zē əs, -sē-) *adj.* causing nausea; sickening —**nau′seous·ly** *adv.* —**nau′seous·ness** *n.*

naut. nautical

nautch (nôch) *n.* [< Hindi < Prakrit < Sans. *nṛtya*, dancing < *nṛt*, to dance] in India, a performance by professional dancing girls (**nautch girls**)

nau·ti·cal (nôt′i k'l) *adj.* [< Fr. < L. < Gr. < *nautēs*, sailor < *naus*, a ship] of or relating to sailors, ships, or navigation —**nau′ti·cal·ly** *adv.*

nautical almanac an almanac published annually giving information specially useful to navigators and astronomers

nautical mile an international unit of distance for sea and air navigation, equal to 6 076.11549 feet (1 852 metres)

nau·ti·lus (nôt′əl əs) *n.*, *pl.* -**lus·es**, -**li**′ (-ī′) [ModL. < L. < Gr. *nautilos*, sailor < *naus*, a ship] **1.** any of a genus of tropical, cephalopod molluscs with a many-chambered, spiral shell having a pearly interior **2.** *same as* PAPER NAUTILUS

nav. 1. naval **2.** navigation **3.** navigator

na·val (nā′v'l) *adj.* [< Fr. < L. *navalis* < *navis*, a ship] of, having, characteristic of, or for a navy, its ships, personnel, etc.

naval officer one who holds any command on board a warship

nave[1] (nāv) *n.* [ML. *navis* < L., a ship] the main part of a church,

NAUTILUS
(shown in
cross section)

extending between side aisles from the chancel to the principal entrance

nave[2] (nāv) *n.* [OE. *nafu*] the hub of a wheel

na·vel (nā′v'l) *n.* [OE. *nafela*] the small scar or depression in the middle of the abdomen, where the umbilical cord was attached to the foetus

navel orange a seedless orange having a navellike depression containing a small, secondary fruit

na·vel·wort (nā′vəl wurt′) *n.* another name for PENNYWORT

na·vic·u·lar (nə vik′yoo lər) *adj.* [LL. *navicularis* < L. *navicula*, dim. of *navis*, a ship] shaped like a boat: said esp. of certain bones —*n.* any of various boat-shaped bones; esp. *a)* a bone in the wrist *b)* a bone on the inner side of the human foot, in front of the anklebone

navig. 1. navigation **2.** navigator

nav·i·ga·ble (nav′i gə b'l) *adj.* [see ff.] **1.** wide or deep enough, or free enough from obstructions, for ships, etc. to go through **2.** that can be steered or directed [a *navigable* balloon] —**nav′i·ga·bil′i·ty** *n.* —**nav′i·ga·bly** *adv.*

nav·i·gate (nav′ə gāt′) *vi.* -**gat**′**ed**, -**gat**′**ing** [< L. pp. of *navigare* < *navis*, a ship + *agere*, to lead] **1.** to steer, or direct, a ship or aircraft **2.** [Colloq.] to make one's way; walk **3.** (as a passenger) to direct a motor car by informing the driver of the route —*vt.* **1.** to travel through or over (water, air, or land) in a ship or aircraft **2.** to steer, or direct the course of (a ship or aircraft) **3.** [Colloq.] to make one's way on or through

nav·i·ga·tion (nav′ə gā′shən) *n.* the act or practice of navigating; esp., the science of locating the position and plotting the course of ships and aircraft —**nav′i·ga′tion·al** *adj.* —**nav′i·ga′tion·al·ly** *adv.*

navigation lights lights designed to show approximately which way a ship or aircraft is travelling

nav·i·ga·tor (nav′ə gāt′ər) *n.* **1.** a person who navigates; esp., one skilled in the navigation of a ship or aircraft **2.** an explorer by ship

nav·vy (nav′ē) *n.*, *pl.* -**vies** [abbrev. of prec.] an unskilled labourer, as on canals, roads, etc.

na·vy (nā′vē) *n.*, *pl.* -**vies** [< OFr. *navie*, ult. < L. *navis*, a ship] **1.** [Archaic] a fleet of ships **2.** all warships of a nation **3.** [*often* N-] *a)* the entire sea force of a nation, including vessels, personnel, stores, yards, etc. *b)* the governmental department in charge of this **4.** *same as* NAVY BLUE

navy blue [from the colour of naval uniform] very dark, purplish blue

Navy List the official list of officers & ships of the British Navy

navy yard [Chiefly U.S.] a dockyard for building and repairing naval ships, storing naval supplies, etc.

na·wab (nə wäb′, -wôb′) *n.* [Hindi *navāb*] *same as* NABOB

nay (nā) *adv.* [< ON. < *ne*, not + *ei*, ever] **1.** no: now seldom used except in an oral vote **2.** not that only, but also [he is well-off, *nay*, rich] —*n.* **1.** a refusal or denial **2.** a negative vote or voter **3.** a negative answer

Naz·a·rene (naz′ə rēn′, naz′ə rēn′) *adj.* of Nazareth or the Nazarenes —*n.* **1.** a native or inhabitant of Nazareth **2.** a member of an early sect of Jewish Christians —**the Nazarene** Jesus

Naz·a·rite, Naz·i·rite (naz′ə rīt′) *n.* [< LL. < Gr. < Heb. *nāzar*, to consecrate] among the ancient Hebrews, a person adhering to certain strict religious vows

Na·zi (nät′sē, nat′-) *adj.* [G., contr. of *nationalsozialistische* in party name] designating or of the German fascist political party (*National Socialist German Workers' Party*), that ruled Germany under Hitler (1933-45) —*n.* **1.** a member of this party **2.** [*often* n-] a supporter of this party or its ideology; fascist —**Na′zi·fi·ca′tion** *n.* —**Na′zi·fy′, na′·zi·fy′** *vt.* -**fied**′, -**fy**′**ing** —**Na′zism** (-siz′m), **Na′zi·ism** (-sē iz′m) *n.*

Nb *Chem.* niobium

N.B. New Brunswick

N.B., n.b. [L. *nota bene*] note well

N.C.B. National Coal Board

NCO, N.C.O. noncommissioned officer

Nd *Chem.* neodymium

N.D., n.d. no date

ne- *same as* NEO-: used before a vowel

Ne *Chem.* neon

NE, N.E., n.e. 1. northeast **2.** northeastern

né (nā) *adj.* [Fr. pp. of *naître* < L. *nasci*, to be born] born: used to indicate the name a man was born with [Lord Beaverbrook, *né* William Aitken]: see also NÉE

Ne·an·der·thal (nē an′dər täl′) *adj.* [name of German valley where remains were found] designating or of a form of primitive man of the paleolithic period

neap (nēp) *adj.* [OE. *nep*- in *nepflod*, neap tide] designating either of the two lowest monthly tides, occurring just after the first and third quarters of the lunar month —*n.* neap tide

Ne·a·pol·i·tan (nē′ə pol′ə t'n) *adj.* of Naples —*n.* a native or inhabitant of Naples

near (nir) *adv.* [OE. *near*, nearer, compar. of *neah*, nigh] **1.**

at a short distance in space or time 2. [Colloq.] almost; nearly *[I was near stifled]* —*adj.* 1. close in distance or time; not far 2. close in relationship; akin 3. close in friendship; intimate 4. *a)* close in degree; narrow *[a near escape] b)* almost happening *[a near accident]* 5. on the left side, facing forward: said of an animal in double harness, a motor car wheel, etc.: opposed to OFF 6. short or direct *[the near way]* 7. stingy 8. somewhat resembling; approximating —*prep.* close to in space, time, degree, etc. —*vt., vi.* to draw near (to); approach —**near at hand** very close in time or space —**near'ness** *n.*

near·by (nir′bī′) *adj., adv.* near; close at hand

Near Eastern of or designating those countries near the E end of the Mediterranean

near·ly (-lē) *adv.* almost; not quite *[nearly finished]* —**not nearly** not at all; far from

near miss 1. a bomb, etc. that does not score a direct hit on the target but comes close enough to cause some damage 2. any result that is nearly but not quite successful

near·sight·ed (-sīt′id) *adj.* same as SHORT SIGHTED (sense 1) —**near'sight'ed·ly** *adv.* —**near'sight'ed·ness** *n.*

near thing [Colloq.] an event, etc. whose outcome only just falls short of failure, success, etc. *[he caught the train, but it was a near thing]*

neat[1] (nēt) *adj.* *[< Fr. < L. nitidus, shining, trim < nitere, to shine]* 1. *a)* clean and orderly; trim; tidy *b)* tidy, skilful, and precise *[a neat worker]* *c)* free of superfluities; simple 2. unmixed; straight *[to drink whisky neat]* 3. well-proportioned 4. cleverly phrased or done; adroit —**neat'ly** *adv.* —**neat'ness** *n.*

neat[2] (nēt) *n., pl.* **neat** [OE. *neat*] [Now Rare] a bovine animal; ox, cow, etc.

neat·en (nēt′'n) *vt.* to make neat

'neath, neath (nēth) *prep.* [Poet.] beneath

neat·herd (nēt′hurd′) *n.* [Now Rare] a cowherd

neat's-foot oil (nēts′foot′) a light-yellow oil obtained by boiling the feet and shinbones of cattle, used mainly as a dressing for leather

neb (neb) *n.* [OE. *nebb*] [Now Chiefly Dial.] 1. a beak, nose, or snout 2. a nib

N.E.B. 1. National Enterprise Board 2. New English Bible

neb·u·la (neb′yə lə) *n., pl.* **-lae** (-lē′), **-las** [ModL. < L., fog] any of several vast cloudlike patches seen in the night sky, consisting of very distant groups of stars or of gaseous masses or of galaxies —**neb'u·lar** *adj.*

nebular hypothesis the theory that the solar system was formed by the condensation of a gaseous mass

neb·u·los·i·ty (neb′yə los′ə tē) *n.* 1. a nebulous quality or condition 2. *pl.* **-ties** a nebula

neb·u·lous (neb′yə ləs) *adj.* 1. of or like a nebula 2. unclear; vague; indefinite Also **neb'u·lose'** (-lōs′) —**neb'-u·lous·ly** *adv.* —**neb'u·lous·ness** *n.*

nec·es·sar·i·ly (nes′ə ser′ə lē, nes′ə sər-) *adv.* 1. because of necessity 2. as a necessary result

nec·es·sar·y (nes′ə sər ē) *adj.* *[< L. < necesse, unavoidable < ne-, not + cedere, to give way]* 1. that cannot be done without; essential; indispensable 2. that must happen; inevitable 3. that must be done; required 4. that follows logically; undeniable —*n., pl.* **-sar·ies** a thing necessary to life, to some purpose, etc.: often used in pl.

ne·ces·si·tar·i·an·ism (nə ses′ə ter′ē ən iz′m) *n.* the theory that there is no free will, but that human behaviour is causally determined by previous actions —**ne·ces'si·tar'i·an** *n., adj.*

ne·ces·si·tate (nə ses′ə tāt′) *vt.* **-tat'ed, -tat'ing** 1. to make (something) necessary or unavoidable 2. [Now Rare] to compel —**ne·ces'si·ta'tion** *n.*

ne·ces·si·tous (-təs) *adj.* 1. needy 2. necessary 3. urgent —**ne·ces'si·tous·ly** *adv.*

ne·ces·si·ty (-tē) *n., pl.* **-ties** *[< OFr. < L. < necesse:* see NECESSARY] 1. natural causation; fate 2. anything inevitable, unavoidable, etc. 3. *a)* the compulsion of circumstances, custom, law, etc. *b)* what is required by this 4. great need 5. something that cannot be done without; necessary thing: often used in pl. 6. the state or quality of being necessary —**of necessity** necessarily

neck (nek) *n.* [OE. *hnecca*] 1. that part of man or animal joining the head to the body 2. a narrow part between the head, or end, and the body, or base, of any object, as of a violin 3. that part of a garment which covers or is nearest the neck 4. a narrow, necklike part; specif., *a)* a narrow strip of land *b)* the narrowest part of a bottle, vase, etc. or of an organ of the body *c)* a strait—*vt., vi.* [Slang] to hug, kiss, and caress in making love —**get it in the neck** [Slang] to be severely reprimanded or punished; be hard hit —**neck and neck** very close or even, as in a race —**neck of the woods** [U.S.] a region or locality —**neck or nothing** risking all; reckless —**risk one's neck** to put one's life, career, etc. in danger —**stick one's neck out** to expose oneself to possible failure, ridicule, etc. —**neck'er** *n.* —**neck'ing** *n.*

neck·band (-band′) *n.* 1. a band worn around the neck 2.

the part of a garment that encircles the neck; esp., the part fastened to the collar

neck·cloth (-kloth′) *n.* [Archaic] same as CRAVAT

neck·er·chief (nek′ər chif, -chēf′) *n.* a kerchief worn around the neck

neck·lace (nek′lis) *n.* [NECK + LACE] a string of beads, jewels, etc. or a fine chain of gold, silver, etc. worn as an ornament around the neck

neck·line (-līn′) *n.* the line formed by the edge of a garment around or nearest the neck

neck·piece (-pēs′) *n.* 1. a decorative scarf, esp. of fur 2. a piece of armour for the neck

neck·tie (-tī′) *n.* a decorative band for the neck, tied in front in a slipknot or bow

neck·wear (-wer′) *n.* articles worn about the neck, as neckties, scarfs, etc.

necro- [< Gr. *nekros*, dead body] *a combining form meaning* death, corpse: also **necr-**

ne·crol·o·gy (ne krol′ə jē) *n., pl.* **-gies** [see prec. & -LOGY] 1. a list of people who have died 2. an obituary —**nec·ro·log·i·cal** (nek′rə loj′i k'l) *adj.* —**nec'ro·log'i·cal·ly** *adv.* —**ne·crol'o·gist** *n.*

nec·ro·man·cy (nek′rə man′sē) *n.* [< OFr. < ML. *nigromantia* < L. < Gr. *nekros*, corpse + *manteia*, divination] 1. divination by alleged communication with the dead 2. sorcery —**nec'ro·man'cer** *n.* —**nec'ro·man'tic** *adj.*

nec·ro·phil·i·a (nek′rə fil′ē ə) *n.* [< NECRO- + -PHILIA] an abnormal fascination with death and the dead; esp., an erotic attraction for corpses: also **ne·croph·i·lism** (ne krof′ə liz′m) —**nec'ro·phile'** (-fīl′) *n.* —**nec'ro·phil'i·ac, ne·croph'i·lous** *adj.*

ne·crop·o·lis (nə krop′ə lis) *n., pl.* **-lis·es** [< Gr. < *nekros*, dead body + *polis*, city] a cemetery, esp. one belonging to an ancient city

ne·cro·sis (ne krō′sis) *n., pl.* **-ses** (-sēz) [ModL. < LL. < Gr. < *nekroun*, to make dead < *nekros*, dead body] the death or decay of tissue in a part of a living body or plant, as from disease —**ne·crose** (ne krōs′, nek′rōs) *vt., vi.* **-crosed', -cros'ing** —**ne·crot'ic** (-krot′ik) *adj.*

nec·tar (nek′tər) *n.* [L. < Gr. *nektar*, lit., that overcomes death] 1. *Gr. Myth.* the drink of the gods 2. any very delicious beverage 3. *Bot.* the sweetish liquid in many flowers, made into honey by bees —**nec'tar·ous** *adj.*

nec·tar·ine (nek′tə rēn′, nek′tə rēn′) *n.* [orig. adj. of *nectar*] a variety of peach having a smooth skin without down

nec·ta·ry (nek′tər ē) *n., pl.* **-ries** a nectar-secreting flower part —**nec·tar'i·al** (-ter′ē əl) *adj.*

N.E.D.C. National Economic Development Council

ned·dy[1] (ne′dē) *n., pl.* **-dies** [< Edward] a child's word for donkey

ned·dy[2] (ne′dē) *n.* [< N.E.D.C.] [Colloq.] the National Economic Development Council

née (nā) *adj.* [Fr., fem. pp. of *naître* < L. *nasci*, to be born] born: used to indicate the maiden name of a married woman *[Mrs. Helen Jones, née Smith]*

need (nēd) *n.* [OE. *nied*] 1. necessity or obligation 2. lack of something required or desired 3. something required or desired *[one's daily needs]* 4. *a)* a condition of deficiency, or one requiring relief or supply *[a friend in need]* *b)* poverty; extreme want —*vt.* to have need of; lack; require *Need* is often used as an auxiliary followed by an infinitive with or without *to*, meaning "to be obliged, must" *[he need not come, he needs to be careful]* —*vi.* 1. [Archaic] to be necessary *[it needs not]* 2. to be in need See also NEEDS —**have need to** to be compelled to; must —**if need be** if it is required —**need'er** *n.*

need-fire (-fir′) *n.* [NEED + FIRE] 1. a beacon 2. a fire, produced by friction, thought to act as a charm against disease

need·ful (-fəl) *adj.* 1. necessary 2. [Archaic] needy —*n.* [Colloq.] money, esp. ready money —**need'ful·ly** *adv.* —**need'ful·ness** *n.*

nee·dle (nēd′'l) *n.* [OE. *nædl*] 1. a small, slender, sharp-pointed piece of steel with a hole for thread, used for sewing 2. *a)* a slender, hooked rod of steel, bone, etc., for crocheting *b)* a similar but hookless rod, for knitting 3. a short, pointed piece of metal, etc. that moves in gramophone record grooves to transmit vibrations 4. a pointed instrument for etching or engraving 5. the pointer of a compass, gauge, meter, etc. 6. the thin, short, pointed leaf of the

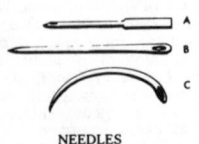

NEEDLES
(A, sewing machine; B, straight; C, surgical)

pine, spruce, etc. 7. a thin rod that opens or closes a passage in a valve (**needle valve**) 8. the sharp, very slender metal tube at the end of a hypodermic syringe 9. *same as* ELECTRIC NEEDLE 10. a needlelike structure or part 11. [Colloq.] a spur or goad 12. [Slang] an attack of nerves —*vt.* **-dled, -dling** 1. to sew, puncture, etc. with a needle

2. [Colloq.] a) to goad b) to tease or heckle —**look for a needle in a haystack** to search for something that is almost impossible to find —**nee′dle·like′** adj. —**nee′dler** n.

nee·dle·book (-book′) n. strips of cloth arranged like the leaves of a book, to hold needles

nee·dle·bush (-boosh′) n. one of two Australian trees, both with fine sharp spines

needle game a game which is fiercely contested and in which there is an element of personal antagonism between the players: also **needle match**

nee·dle·point (-point′) n. **1.** an embroidery of woollen threads on canvas, as in tapestry **2.** lace made on a paper pattern, with a needle instead of a bobbin: in full, **needlepoint lace**

need·less (nēd′lis) adj. not needed; unnecessary —**need′less·ly** adv. —**need′less·ness** n.

needle time Radio the amount of programme time during which recorded music is played

nee·dle·wom·an (nēd′′l woom′ən) n., pl. -wom′en a woman who does needlework; esp., a seamstress

nee·dle·work (-wurk′) n. work done with a needle; sewing or embroidery —**nee′dle·work′er** n.

need·n't (nēd′′nt) need not

needs (nēdz) adv. [OE. nedes] [Now Rare] of necessity; necessarily (with must) [he must needs obey]

need·y (nēd′ē) adj. need′i·er, need′i·est in need; very poor; destitute —**need′i·ness** n.

ne′er (ner) adv. [Poet.] never

ne′er-do-well (-doo wel′) n. a shiftless, irresponsible person —adj. lazy, worthless, etc.

ne·far·i·ous (ni fer′ē əs) adj. [< L. < nefas, crime < ne-, not + fas, lawful] very wicked; iniquitous —**ne·far′i·ous·ly** adv. —**ne·far′i·ous·ness** n.

neg. **1.** negative **2.** negatively

ne·gate (ni gāt′) vt. -gat′ed, -gat′ing [see ff.] **1.** to deny the existence or truth of **2.** to make ineffective —**ne·ga′tor, ne·gat′er** n.

ne·ga·tion (ni gā′shən) n. [< Fr. < L. < pp. of negare, to deny] **1.** a denying; denial **2.** the lack or opposite of something positive

neg·a·tive (neg′ə tiv) adj. [see prec.] **1.** expressing denial or refusal; saying "no" **2.** opposite to or lacking what is positive [a negative personality]; specif., a) Biol. directed away from the source of a stimulus [negative tropism] b) Math. less than zero; minus c) Med. not indicating the presence of symptoms, bacteria, etc. d) Photog. reversing the relation of light and shade of the original subject **3.** Elec. a) of, generating, or charged with NEGATIVE ELECTRICITY b) having an excess of electrons —n. **1.** a word, phrase, statement, etc. expressing denial, rejection, or refusal **2.** the point of view opposing the positive or affirmative **3.** an impression of a sculpture, etc. that shows it in reverse **4.** the plate in a voltaic battery where the lower potential is **5.** Math. a negative quantity **6.** Photog. an exposed and developed negative film or plate, from which positive prints are made —vt. -tived, -tiv·ing **1.** a) to refuse; reject b) to veto **2.** to deny; contradict **3.** to disprove **4.** to neutralize —**in the negative 1.** in refusal or denial of a plan, etc. **2.** with a negative answer —**neg′a·tive·ly** adv. —**neg′·a·tive·ness, neg′a·tiv′i·ty** n.

negative electricity the kind of electricity in a body of resin rubbed with wool: it represents an excess of electrons

neg·a·tiv·ism (neg′ə tiv iz′m) n. Psychol. an attitude characterized by ignoring or resisting suggestions or orders from others —**neg′a·tiv·ist** n., adj. —**neg′a·tiv·is′tic** adj.

ne·glect (ni glekt′) vt. [< L. pp. of neglegere < neg-, not + legere, to gather] **1.** to ignore or disregard **2.** to fail to attend to properly **3.** to leave undone —n. **1.** a neglecting or being neglected **2.** lack of proper care —**neg·lect′er, neg·lec′tor** n.

ne·glect·ful (-fəl) adj. negligent (often with of) —**neg·lect′·ful·ly** adv. —**neg·lect′ful·ness** n.

nég·li·gé, neg·li·gee (neg′lə zhā′) n. [< Fr., fem. pp. of négliger, to neglect] **1.** a woman's loosely fitting dressing gown **2.** any informal or careless attire —adj. carelessly or incompletely dressed

neg·li·gence (neg′li jəns) n. **1.** the quality or condition of being negligent **2.** an instance of this

neg·li·gent (-jənt) adj. [< OFr. < L. prp. of negligere: see NEGLECT] **1.** habitually failing to do the required thing **2.** careless, lax, inattentive, etc. —**neg′li·gent·ly** adv.

neg·li·gi·ble (neg′li jə b′l) adj. that can be neglected or disregarded because small, unimportant, etc. —**neg′li·gi·bil′·i·ty** n. —**neg′li·gi·bly** adv.

ne·go·ti·a·ble (ni gō′shē ə b′l, -shə b′l) adj. that can be negotiated; specif., a) legally transferable, as a promissory note b) that can be passed, crossed, etc. —**ne·go′ti·a·bil′·i·ty** n.

ne·go·ti·ate (-shē āt′) vi. -at′ed, -at′ing [< L. pp. of negotiari < negotium, business < nec-, not + otium, ease] to confer or discuss with a view to reaching agreement —vt. **1.** to settle or conclude (a transaction, treaty, etc.) **2.** to transfer or sell (negotiable paper) **3.** to succeed in crossing, moving through, etc. —**ne·go′ti·a′tor** n.

ne·go·ti·a·tion (ni gō′shē ā′shən) n. a negotiating; specif., [often pl.] a conferring or bargaining to reach agreement —**ne·go′ti·a·to·ry** (-ə tər ē) adj.

Ne·gress (nē′gris) n. a Negro woman or girl

Ne·gril·lo (nə gril′ō) n., pl. -los, -loes [Sp. dim. of negro, NEGRO[1]] an African Pygmy

Ne·gri·to (nə grēt′ō) n., pl. -tos, -toes [Sp., dim. of negro, NEGRO] a member of any of various groups of dwarfish Negroid peoples of the East Indies, the Philippines, and Africa —**Ne·grit′ic** (-grit′ik) adj.

ne·gri·tude (neg′rə tyood′, nē′grə-) n. [Fr. négritude, coined < nègre, black + -i- + -tude, a n. forming suffix] [also N-] the affirmation by Negroes of their distinctive cultural heritage, esp. in Africa

Ne·gro (nē′grō) n., pl. -groes [Sp. & Port. negro < L. niger, black] **1.** a member of the Negroid peoples of Africa, living chiefly south of the Sahara **2.** same as NEGROID **3.** any person with Negro ancestors See BLACK (n. 3) —adj. of Negroes

Ne·groid (nē′groid) adj. designating or of a major group of mankind that includes the dark-skinned peoples of Africa and of Melanesia, New Guinea, etc. —n. a Negroid person

Ne·gus (nē′gəs) n. [Amharic něgūš, king] the title of the former rulers of Ethiopia

ne·gus (nē′gəs) n. [after Col. Francis Negus (d. 1732), who first made it] a beverage of hot water, wine, and lemon juice, sweetened and spiced

neigh (nā) vi. [OE. hnægan] to utter the characteristic cry of a horse; whinny —n. this cry

neigh·bour (nā′bər) n. [< OE. < neah (see NIGH) + gebur, farmer] **1.** a person who lives near another **2.** a person or thing situated near another **3.** a fellow man —adj. nearby; adjacent —vt., vi. to live or be situated near or nearby Also, U.S. sp., **neighbor**

neigh·bour·hood (-hood′) n. **1.** a being neighbours **2.** a district or area, esp. with regard to some characteristic **3.** people living near one another; community —**in the neighbourhood of 1.** near (a place) **2.** [Colloq.] approximately

neigh·bour·ly (nā′bər lē) adj. like or appropriate to neighbours; friendly —**neigh′bour·li·ness** n.

nei·nei (nē′nē′) n. [Maori] an ornamental New Zealand shrub

nei·ther (nē′ther, nī′-) adj., pron. [OE. na-hwæther, lit., not whether] not either [neither boy went, neither of them sings] —conj. **1.** not either: in the pair of correlatives neither . . . nor [can neither laugh nor cry] **2.** nor [he doesn't smoke, neither does he drink] —adv. [Colloq.] either (after negative expressions) [I don't care, neither]: a loose usage

nel·ly (nel′ē) n. [< Nelly Duff, rhyming slang for puff, tailors' slang] life; existence: only in **not on your nelly**

nel·son (nel′s'n) n. [< personal name Nelson] a wrestling hold; specif., a hold (half nelson) in which one arm is placed under the opponent's arm from behind with the hand pressing the back of his neck, or a hold (full nelson) in which both arms are so placed under the opponent's arms

nem·a·tode (nem′ə tōd′) n. [< ModL. < Gr. nēma (gen. nēmatos), thread + -ODE] any of a phylum of long, cylindrical worms, as the hookworm

Nem·bu·tal (nem′byə tôl′, -tal′) [N(A)+ E(THYL) + M(ETHYL) + BU(TYL) + (BARBI)TAL] a trademark for an odourless, white, crystalline powder used in medicine as a sedative and analgesic

Nem·e·sis (nem′ə sis) n., pl. -ses (-sēz′) [L. < Gr. < nemein, to deal out] **1.** a) just punishment b) retributive punishment c) one who imposes this punishment d) the act of suffering this punishment **2.** anyone or anything that it seems will surely defeat or thwart one After the goddess of retribution or vengeance in Greek myth

neo- [< Gr. neos, new] a combining form meaning: **1.** [often N-] new, recent [neolithic] **2.** in a new or different way [neocolonialism]

ne·o·clas·sic (nē′ō klas′ik) adj. designating or of a revival of classic style in art, literature, etc.: also **ne′o·clas′si·cal** —**ne′o·clas′si·cism** n. —**ne′o·clas′si·cist** n.

ne·o·co·lo·ni·al·ism (-kə lō′nē əl iz′m) n. the survival or revival of colonialism, as by the exploitation of a supposedly independent region by a foreign power —**ne′o·co·lo′ni·al** adj. —**ne′o·co·lo′ni·al·ist** n., adj.

ne·o·dym·i·um (nē′ə dim′ē əm) n. [< NEO- + (DI)DYMIUM] a metallic chemical element of the rare-earth group: symbol, Nd; at. wt., 144.24; at. no., 60

ne·o·lith·ic (nē′ə lith′ik) adj. [NEO-+ -LITHIC] designating or of the later part of the Stone Age, during which polished stone tools and metal tools were first used

ne·ol·o·gism (nē ol′ə jiz′m) n. [< Fr.: see NEO-, -LOGY, & -ISM] **1.** a new word or a new meaning for an established word **2.** the use of these Also **ne·ol′o·gy,** pl. -gies —**ne·o·log′i·cal** (nē′ə loj′ik'l) adv. —**ne′o·log′i·cal·ly** adv. —**ne·ol′o·gis′tic, ne·ol′o·gis′ti·cal** adj.

ne·ol·o·gize (-jīz') *vi.* -gized', -giz'ing to invent or use neologisms —**ne·ol'o·gist** *n.*

ne·o·my·cin (nē'ə mī'sin) *n.* [< NEO- + Gr. *mykēs*, fungus + -IN¹] a broad-spectrum antibiotic used esp. in treating infections of the skin and eye

ne·on (nē'on) *n.* [ModL. < Gr. *neon*, neut. of *neos*, new] a rare, colourless, and inert gaseous chemical element: symbol, Ne; at. wt., 20.183; at. no., 10

neon lamp a tube containing neon, which glows red when an electric current is sent through it

ne·on·tol·o·gy (nē'on tol'ə jē) *n.* [NEO- + ONTOLOGY] *Biol.* the study of living species of animals: cf. PALEONTOLOGY —**ne'on·tol'og·ist** *n.*

ne·o·phyte (nē'ə fīt') *n.* [< LL. < Gr. < *neos*, new + *phytos* < *phyein*, to produce] 1. a new convert 2. any beginner; novice

ne·o·plasm (-plaz'm) *n.* [NEO- + -PLASM] an abnormal growth of tissue, as a tumour —**ne'o·plas'tic** *adj.*

Ne·o·pla·to·nism (nē'ō plāt''n iz'm) *n.* any of various schools of philosophy based on a modified Platonism; esp., a 3rd cent. Alexandrian school, stressing the possibility of a mystical union with the One by ecstasy, etc.

ne·o·prene (nē'ə prēn') *n.* [NEO- + (chloro)prene] an acetylene derivative] a synthetic rubber highly resistant to oil, heat, light, and oxidation

ne·o·ter·ic (nē'ə ter'ik) *adj.* [LL. < Gr. *neōterikos* < *neōteros*, compar. of *neos*, NEW] recent; new —*n.* a modern person; one accepting new ideas and practices —**ne·o·ter'i·cal·ly** *adv.*

Ne·pal·i (ni pôl'ē, -päl'-) *n.* 1. the Indic language of Nepal 2. an inhabitant of Nepal

ne·pen·the (ni pen'thē) *n.* [L. < Gr. < *nē-*, not + *penthos*, sorrow] 1. a drug supposed by the ancient Greeks to cause forgetfulness of sorrow 2. the plant from which the drug was obtained 3. anything causing forgetfulness of sorrow Also **ne·pen'thes** (-thēz) —**ne·pen'the·an** (-thē ən) *adj.*

neph·ew (nef'yōō; nev'-) *n.* [< OFr. < L. *nepos*] 1. the son of one's brother or sister 2. the son of one's brother-in-law or sister-in-law

ne·phol·o·gy (ni fol'ə jē) *n.* [< Gr. *nephos*, cloud + -LOGY] the branch of meteorology dealing with clouds —**neph·o·log·i·cal** (nef'ə loj'ik'l) *adj.* —**ne·phol'o·gist** *n.*

ne·phrid·i·um (ne frid'ē əm) *n.,* pl. **-i·a** (-ə) [ModL. < Gr. dim. of *nephros*, kidney] 1. an excretory tubule of many invertebrates, as worms, molluscs, etc. 2. any of the excretory tubules of a vertebrate embryo —**ne·phrid'i·al** *adj.*

ne·phrit·ic (nə frit'ik) *adj.* [< LL. < Gr. *nephros*, kidney] 1. of a kidney or the kidneys; renal 2. of or having nephritis

ne·phri·tis (nə frīt'əs) *n.* [see ff. & -ITIS] disease of the kidneys, characterized by inflammation, fibrosis, etc.

neph·ro- [< Gr. *nephros*, kidney] a combining form meaning kidney: also, before a vowel, **nephr-**

ne plus ul·tra (nē plus ul'trə) [L., no more beyond] the highest point of perfection

nep·o·tism (nep'ə tiz'm) *n.* [< Fr. < It. < L. *nepos* (gen. *nepotis*), nephew] favouritism shown to relatives, esp. in appointment to desirable positions —**nep'o·tist** *n.* —**nep'·o·tis'tic** *adj.*

Nep·tune (nep'tyōōn) [1. *Rom. Myth.* the god of the sea: identified with the Greek god Poseidon 2. a planet of the solar system, eighth in distance from the sun: diameter, c.47 470 000 km

nep·tu·ni·um (nep tyōō'nē əm) *n.* [ModL.: named after the planet Neptune] a radioactive chemical element produced by irradiating uranium atoms with neutrons: symbol, Np; at. wt., 237.00; at. no., 93

N.E.R.C. National Environment Research Council

ne·rine (nē rī'ne) *n.* [<?] a genus of S African bulbous plants, including the Guernsey lily, with pink or red flowers

ner·o·li (ner'ə lē) *n.* [< Princess of *Nerole* (17th cent.) said to have discovered it] an oil distilled from orange flowers and used in perfumery: in full **neroli oil**

nerv·ate (nur'vāt) *adj.* *Bot.* having nerves, or veins

ner·va·tion (nar vā'shən) *n.* same as VENATION

nerve (nurv) *n.* [< OFr. < L. *nervus*] 1. a tendon: now chiefly in **strain every nerve,** to try as hard as possible 2. any of the cordlike fibres carrying impulses between the body organs and the central nervous system 3. emotional control; courage [a man of *nerve*] 4. strength; vigour 5. [pl.] the nervous system regarded as indicating health, emotional stability, etc. 6. [pl.] nervousness 7. [Colloq.] impudent boldness; audacity 8. *Biol.* a vein in a leaf or insect's wing —*vt.* **nerved, nerv'ing** 1. to give strength or courage to 2. to brace (oneself) —**bundle of nerves** a very nervous or unstable person —**get on one's nerves** [Colloq.] to make one irritable —**nerves of steel** unshakeable; not easily frightened

nerve block a method of local anaesthesia by stopping the impulses through a particular nerve

nerve cell 1. same as NEURON 2. occasionally, a nerve cell body without its processes

nerve centre 1. any group of nerve cells that function

together in controlling some specific sense or bodily activity, as breathing 2. a control centre; headquarters

nerve gas any of several liquids whose vapours can paralyse the respiratory and central nervous systems when absorbed through the eyes, lungs, or skin

nerve impulse an electrical wave transmitted along a nerve that has been stimulated

nerve·less (nurv'lis) *adj.* 1. without strength, force, courage, etc.; weak; unnerved 2. not nervous; controlled 3. *Biol.* without nerves —**nerve'less·ly** *adv.* —**nerve'·less·ness** *n.*

nerve-rack·ing, nerve-wrack·ing (-rak'iŋ) *adj.* very trying to one's patience or equanimity

nerv·ous (nur'vəs) *adj.* 1. orig., strong; sinewy 2. vigorous in expression; animated 3. of the nerves 4. made up of or containing nerves 5. characterized by or having a disordered state of the nerves 6. emotionally tense, restless, agitated, etc. 7. fearful; apprehensive —**nerv'·ous·ly** *adv.* —**nerv'ous·ness, ner·vos'i·ty** (-vos'ə tē) *n.*

nervous breakdown a psychotic or neurotic disorder that impairs the ability to function normally: a popular, nontechnical term

nervous system all the nerve cells and nervous tissues in an organism, including, in the vertebrates, the brain, spinal cord, nerves, etc.

ner·vure (nur'vyoor) *n.* [Fr.: see NERVE & -URE] *Zool.* same as VEIN (*n.* 2)

nerv·y (nur'vē) *adj.* **nerv'i·er, nerv'i·est** 1. nervous; excitable 2. full of courage; bold —**nerv'i·ly** *adv.* —**nerv'·i·ness** *n.*

nes·ci·ent (nesh'ənt, -ē ənt) *adj.* [< L. prp. of *nescire* < *ne-*, not + *scire*, to know] 1. ignorant 2. same as AGNOSTIC —**nes'ci·ence** *n.*

ness (nes) *n.* [ME. *nesse* < OE. *næs*, akin to OE. *nosu*, NOSE] a promontory; headland: now chiefly in place names [*Inverness*]

-ness (nis, nəs) [OE. *-nes(s)*] a suffix meaning state, quality, or instance of being [*greatness, sadness, weakness*]

nest (nest) *n.* [OE.] 1. the structure made or the place chosen by birds for laying their eggs and sheltering their young 2. the place used by hornets, fish, etc. for spawning or breeding 3. a cosy place to live; retreat 4. a resort, haunt, or den or its frequenters [a *nest* of thieves] 5. a swarm or colony of birds, insects, etc. 6. a set of similar things, each fitting within the one next larger [a *nest* of tables] —*vi.* 1. to build or live in a nest 2. to fit one into another —*vt.* 1. to make a nest for 2. to place in or as in a nest 3. to fit (an object) closely within another —**nest'a·ble** *adj.* —**nest'er** *n.*

‡**n'est-ce pas?** (nes pä') [Fr.] isn't that so?

nest egg 1. an artificial or real egg left in a nest to induce a hen to lay more eggs there 2. money, etc. put aside as a reserve or to set up a fund

nes·tle (nes'l) *vi.* **-tled, -tling** [OE. *nestlian*] 1. to settle down comfortably and snugly 2. to press close for comfort or in affection 3. to lie sheltered or partly hidden, as a house among trees —*vt.* 1. to rest or press in a snug, affectionate manner 2. to house as in a nest; shelter —**nes'·tler** *n.*

nest·ling (nest'liŋ, nes'-) *n.* 1. a young bird not yet ready to leave the nest 2. a young child

net¹ (net) *n.* [OE. *nett*] 1. a fabric of string, cord, etc., loosely knotted in an openwork pattern and used to snare birds, fish, etc. 2. a trap; snare 3. a meshed fabric used to hold, protect, or mark off something [a hairnet, tennis *net*] 4. a fine, meshed, lacelike cloth 5. same as NETWORK (sense 2) —*vt.* **net'ted, net'ting** 1. to make into a net 2. to snare or acquire, as with a net 3. to shelter or enclose as with a net —*vi.* to make nets or network —**net'like** *adj.*

net² (net) *adj.* [Fr.: see NEAT¹] 1. remaining after certain deductions or allowances have been made, as for expenses, weight of containers, etc. 2. final [net result] —*n.* a net amount, profit, weight, price, etc. —*vt.* **net'ted, net'ting** to gain as profit, etc.

net·ball (net'bôl') *n.* a team game played mainly by women, in which a ball is thrown through a netted ring attached to a post —**net'ball·er** *n.*

neth·er (neth'ər) *adj.* [OE. *neothera*] lower or under [the *nether* world]

nether garments [Archaic] same as TROUSERS

neth·er·most (neth'ər mōst') *adj.* lowest

nether world *Theol. & Myth.* the world of the dead or of punishment after death; hell: also **nether regions**

net profit the profit remaining after all operating expenses have been deducted from the gross or total profit

nett (net) *n.* var. sp. of NET²

net·ting (net'iŋ) *n.* 1. the act or process of making nets or fishing with them 2. netted material

net·tle (net''l) *n.* [OE. *netele*] any of a number of related weeds with stinging hairs —*vt.* **-tled, -tling** 1. to sting with or as with nettles 2. to irritate; annoy; vex —**net'tler** *n.*

nettle rash same as HIVES

net·tle-tree (-trē′) *n.* a large Australian shrub or tree, with rigid stinging hairs

net·work (net′wurk′) *n.* 1. any arrangement or fabric of parallel wires, threads, etc. crossed at regular intervals by others so as to leave open spaces 2. a thing resembling this; specif., *a)* a system of connecting roads, canals, etc. *b) Radio & TV* a chain of transmitting stations *c)* a system, etc. of cooperating individuals

neu·ral (nyoor′əl) *adj.* [NEUR(O) + -AL] of a nerve, nerves, or the nervous system

neu·ral·gia (nyoo ral′jə) *n.* [ModL.: see NEURO- & -ALGIA] severe pain along the course of a nerve —**neu·ral′gic** (-jik) *adj.*

neu·ras·the·ni·a (nyoor′əs thē′nē ə) *n.* [ModL. < NEUR(O)- + Gr. *astheneia*, weakness] a type of neurosis, usually the result of emotional conflicts, characterized by irritability, fatigue, anxiety, etc. —**neu′ras·then′ic** (-then′ik) *adj., n.*

neu·ri·tis (nyoo rīt′əs) *n.* [ModL.: see ff. & -ITIS] inflammation of a nerve or nerves, accompanied by pain —**neu·rit′ic** (-rit′ik) *adj.*

neu·ro- [< Gr. *neuron*, nerve] *a combining form meaning* of a nerve, nerves, or the nervous system [*neuropathy*]: also, before a vowel, **neur-**

neu·rol·o·gy (nyoo rol′ə jē) *n.* [ModL.: see prec. & -LOGY] the branch of medicine dealing with the nervous system and its diseases —**neu·ro·log′i·cal** (nyoor′ə loj′i k'l) *adj.* —**neu·rol′o·gist** *n.*

neu·ron (nyoor′on) *n.* [ModL. < Gr. *neuron*, nerve] the structural and functional unit of the nervous system, consisting of the nerve cell body and all its processes: also **neu′rone** (-ōn) —**neu′ro·nal** (-ə nəl), **neu·ron·ic** (nyoo ron′ik) *adj.*

neu·ro·pa·thol·o·gy (nyoor′ō pə thol′ə jē) *n.* the branch of pathology dealing with diseases of the nervous system —**neu′ro·pa·thol′o·gist** *n.*

neu·rop·a·thy (nyoo rop′ə thē) *n.* [NEURO- + -PATHY] any disease of the nervous system —**neu·ro·path·ic** (nyoor′ə path′ik) *adj.*

neu·ro·psy·chi·a·try (nyoor′ō sə kī′ə trē) *n.* a branch of medicine combining neurology and psychiatry

neu·rop·ter·an (nyoo rop′tər ən) *n.* [< ModL. < NEURO- + Gr. *pteron*, wing + -AN] any of an order of insects with four membranous wings and biting mouthparts —**neu·rop′ter·ous** *adj.*

neu·ro·sis (nyoo rō′sis) *n., pl.* **-ses** (-sēz) [ModL.: see NEURO- & -OSIS] a functional mental disorder characterized by combinations of anxiety, compulsions and obsessions, phobias, depression, etc.

neu·ro·sur·ger·y (nyoor′ō sur′jər ē) *n.* the branch of surgery involving some part of the nervous system, including the brain and spinal cord

neu·rot·ic (nyoo rot′ik) *adj.* of or having a neurosis —*n.* a neurotic person —**neu·rot′i·cal·ly** *adv.* —**neu·rot′i·cism** (-ə siz′m) *n.*

neut. neuter

neu·ter (nyoot′ər) *adj.* [< MFr. < L. < *ne-*, not + *uter*, either] 1. [Archaic] neutral 2. *Biol. a)* having no sexual organs; asexual *b)* having undeveloped or imperfect sexual organs in the adult, as the worker bee 3. *Gram.* designating or of the gender that refers to things regarded as neither masculine nor feminine —*n.* 1. a castrated or spayed animal 2. *Biol.* a neuter plant or animal 3. *Gram. a)* the neuter gender *b)* a neuter word —*vt.* to castrate or spay (an animal)

neu·tral (nyoo′trəl) *adj.* [Fr. < ML. < L. < *neuter*: see prec.] 1. not taking part in either side of a quarrel or war 2. of or characteristic of a nation not taking part in a war or not taking sides in a power struggle 3. not one thing or the other; indifferent 4. having little or no decided colour 5. *Biol.* same as NEUTER 6. *Chem.* neither acid nor alkaline 7. *Elec.* neither negative nor positive 8. *Phonet.* pronounced as the vowel is in most unstressed syllables, which tends to become (ə) —*n.* 1. a nation not taking part in a war 2. a neutral person 3. a neutral colour 4. *Mech.* a disengaged position of gears, when they do not transmit power from the engine: also called **neutral gear** —**neu′-tral·ly** *adv.*

neu·tral·ism (-iz′m) *n.* a policy, or the advocacy of a policy, of remaining neutral, esp. in international power conflicts —**neu′tral·ist** *adj., n.* —**neu′tral·is′tic** *adj.*

neu·tral·i·ty (nyoo tral′ə tē) *n.* 1. the quality, state, or character of being neutral 2. the status or policy of a nation not participating in a war between other nations

neu·tral·ize (nyoo′trə līz′) *vt.* **-ized′, -iz′ing** 1. to declare (a nation, etc.) neutral in war 2. to destroy or counteract the effectiveness, force, etc. of 3. *Chem.* to destroy the active properties of [an alkali *neutralizes* an acid] 4. *Elec.* to

make electrically neutral —**neu′tral·i·za′tion** *n.* —**neu′-tral·iz′er** *n.*

neu·tri·no (nyoo trē′nō) *n., pl.* **-nos** [It., coined by E. Fermi < *neutrone* (< NEUTRON) + dim. suffix *-ino*] *Physics* a neutral particle having a mass approaching zero

neu·tron (nyoo′tron) *n.* [NEUTR(AL) + (ELECTR)ON] a fundamental particle in the nucleus of an atom: neutrons are uncharged and have about the same mass as protons

neutron star a heavenly object thought to be a collapsed star consisting of many densely packed neutrons

né·vé (ne′vā′) *n.* [Fr. (< Swiss dial.), glacier, ult, < L. *nix* (gen. *nivis*), snow] a mass of snow-ice, not yet converted into a glacier

nev·er (nev′ər) *adv.* [OE. *næfre* < *ne*, not + *æfre*, ever] 1. not ever; at no time 2. not at all; in no case; under no conditions 3. [Colloq.] surely not —**never so** to any extent or degree

nev·er·more (nev′ər môr′) *adv.* never again

never-never (nev′ər nev′ər) *n.* [Colloq.] the hire purchase system of buying —*adj.* imaginary, unrealistic, etc.

never-never land [after the fairyland in J. M. Barrie's *Peter Pan*] an unreal or unrealistic place or situation

nev·er·the·less (nev′ər thə les′) *adv.* in spite of that; nonetheless; however

new (nyoo) *adj.* [OE. *niwe*] 1. appearing, thought of, developed, discovered, made, etc. for the first time 2. *a)* different [a *new* hairdo] *b)* strange; unfamiliar 3. not yet familiar or accustomed [*new* to the job] 4. designating the more or most recent of two or more things of the same class [the *new* library] 5. recently grown; fresh [*new* potatoes] 6. not previously used or worn 7. modern; recent; fashionable 8. more; additional 9. starting as a repetition of a cycle, series, etc. [the *new* year] 10. having just reached a position, rank, place, etc. [a *new* arrival] 11. refreshed in spirits, health, etc. [a *new* man] 12. [N-] same as MODERN (sense 3) —*n.* something new (with *the*) —*adv.* 1. again 2. newly; recently —**new wine in old bottles** new ideas, institutions, etc. added to an established order —**new′ish** *adj.* —**new′ness** *n.*

new blood new people, regarded as a potential source of fresh ideas, renewed vigour, etc.

new·born (nyoo′bôrn′) *adj.* 1. recently born; just born 2. reborn

New·burg (-bərg) *adj.* served in a rich, creamy sauce made with butter, egg yolks, and wine

new candle see CANDLE (*n.* 3)

new·com·er (nyoo′kum′ər) *n.* a person who has come recently; recent arrival

new·el (nyoo′əl) *n.* [< OFr. < LL. *nucalis*, like a nut < L. *nux*, nut] 1. the upright pillar around which the steps of a winding staircase turn 2. the post at the top or bottom of a flight of stairs, supporting the handrail: also **newel post**

new·fan·gled (nyoo′faŋ′g'ld) *adj.* [< ME. < *newe*, new + *-fangel* < base of OE. *fon*, to take] new; novel: a humorously derogatory term

new foundation a religious institution, such as a cathedral, founded after the Reformation

New·found·land dog (nyoo′fənd land′, -lənd; nyoo found′-land′) any of a North American breed of large, powerful, shaggy-haired dogs

New High German see GERMAN, HIGH GERMAN

New Jerusalem *Bible* heaven: Rev. 21:2

new-laid (nyoo′lād′) *adj.* freshly laid or produced: said of eggs

new look 1. having a fashionable appearance 2. [often N-L-] a fashion, introduced by Dior in 1947, in which women's dresses had long, full skirts and narrow waists

new·ly (nyoo′lē) *adv.* 1. recently; lately 2. anew; afresh 3. in a new way or style

new·ly·wed (-wed′) *n.* a recently married person

new maths a system for teaching basic mathematics based on the use of sets

new moon the moon when it is between the earth and the sun, with its dark side towards the earth: it emerges as a crescent curving to the right

new-mown (nyoo′mōn′) *adj.* freshly mown or cut: said of hay or grass

news (nyooz) *n.pl.* [with *sing. v.*] [after OFr. *noveles* or ML. *nova*, pl. of *novum*, what is new] 1. new information about anything; information previously unknown 2. reports of recent happenings, esp. those broadcast, printed in a newspaper, etc. 3. any person or thing featured in such reports —**in the news** much talked about —**make news** to do something reported as news

news·a·gent (-ā′jənt) *n.* a person who sells newspapers, magazines, etc., esp. as a retailer

news bulletin the latest news, esp. as broadcast by radio and television

news·cast (-kāst′) *n.* [NEWS + (BROAD)CAST] a programme of news broadcast over radio or TV —**news′-cast′er** *n.* —**news′cast′ing** *n.*

news conference same as PRESS CONFERENCE

news·flash (-flash) *n.* a brief item of urgent or important news, esp. one that interrupts a radio or TV programme

news·let·ter (-let'ər) *n.* a news bulletin issued at regular intervals to a special group

news·mon·ger (-muŋ'gər) *n.* a gossip

news·pa·per (-pā'pər) *n.* a regular publication, usually a daily or weekly, containing news, opinions, advertisements, etc. —**news'pa'per·man** *n.*, *pl.* -**men'** —**news'pa'per·wom'-an** *n.fem.*, *pl.* -**wom'en**

New·speak (nyōō'spēk') *n.* [coined by G. *Orwell*] the use of ambiguous and deceptive talk, as by government officials seeking to mould public opinion; language used in this way

news·print (nyōōz'print') *n.* a cheap paper, made mainly from wood pulp, for newspapers, etc.

news reader a broadcaster mainly responsible for reading the news on the radio or television: also called **news'cast'er**

news·reel (-rēl') *n.* a short film of news events

news room 1. the room in a reference library where newspapers can be consulted 2. the room where newscasts and newspapers are prepared

news·stand (-stand') *n.* a stand at which newspapers, magazines, etc. are sold

new star *same as* NOVA

New Style the method of reckoning time in accordance with the Gregorian calendar

news·wor·thy (nyōōz'wur'thē) *adj.* timely and important or interesting

news·y (-ē) *adj.* **news'i·er**, **news'i·est** [Colloq.] containing much news

newt (nyōōt) *n.* [by syllabic merging of ME. *an eute* < OE. *efeta*, eft] any of various small amphibians

New Testament the part of the Bible containing the life and teachings of Jesus and his followers

new·ton (nyōōt'n) *n.* [after Sir Isaac *Newton* (1642-1727), Eng. mathematician] the SI unit of force: the force which imparts to a mass of 1 kilogramme an acceleration of 1 metre per second per second

NEWT
(7-10 cm long)

Newton's laws of Motion the three propositions about the relation between the forces acting on and the motion of a body, first formulated by Isaac Newton

New Town 1. any of a number of planned communities built in Great Britain since World War II 2. [often n- t-] any housing development like this

New World the Western Hemisphere; the Americas —**new'-world' adj.**

new year [*also* N- Y-] 1. the year just about to begin or just begun (usually with *the*) 2. the first day or days of the new year

New Year's Day January 1, the first day of a calendar year, usually a legal holiday

New Year's Eve the evening before New Year's Day

next (nekst) *adj.* *older superl.* of NIGH [OE. *neahst*, superl. of *neah*, nigh] nearest; immediately preceding or following —*adv.* 1. in the time, place, degree, or rank immediately preceding or following 2. on the first subsequent occasion [when next we meet] —*prep.* beside; nearest to [sit *next* the tree] —*n.* the one immediately following —**next door** (to) 1. in or at the house adjacent to (to) 2. almost

next-door (neks'dôr') *adj.* in or at the next house, building, etc.

next of kin one's relative(s) most nearly related

nex·us (nek'səs) *n.*, *pl.* -**us·es**, **nex'us** (-ōōs) [L. < pp. of *nectere*, to bind] 1. a connection, tie, or link between individuals of a group, members of a series, etc. 2. the group or series connected

N.F., Nfld., Nfd. Newfoundland

N.F.U. National Farmers' Union

N.G. New Guinea

N.G., n.g. [Slang] no good

N.G.A. National Graphical Association

ngai·o (nī'ō) *n.*, *pl.* -**os** [Maori] a New Zealand tree with light, white wood.

ngwee ('n gwē') *n.*, *pl.* **ngwee** [native term, lit., bright] *see* MONETARY UNITS, table (Zambia)

N.H.S. National Health Service

Ni *Chem.* nickel

N.I. 1. Northern Ireland 2. National Insurance

ni·a·cin (nī'ə sin) *n.* [NI(COTINIC) AC(ID) + -IN¹] a white, odourless substance, C₆H₅O₂N, found in protein foods: it is a member of the vitamin B complex, used in treating pellagra

nib (nib) *n.* [var. of NEB] 1. the bill or beak of a bird 2. the point of a pen 3. the projecting end of anything; point; sharp prong

nib·ble (nib''l) *vt., vi.* -**bled**, -**bling** [prob. akin to MLowG. *nibbelen*] 1. to eat (food) with quick, small bites, as a mouse does 2. to bite at with small, gentle bites —*n.* 1. a small bite or morsel 2. a nibbling —**nib'bler** *n.*

nib·lick (nib'lik) *n.* [< ?] *Golf* a club, a number 9 iron, giving a great deal of lift

nibs (nibz) *n.* [< ?] [Colloq.] an important, or esp. selfimportant, person (with *his*)

nice (nīs) *adj.* **nic'er**, **nic'est** [OFr., stupid < L. *nescius*, ignorant < *ne-*, not + *scire*, to know] 1. difficult to please; fastidious 2. delicate; precise; discriminative; subtle [a *nice* distinction] 3. calling for accuracy, care, tact, etc. [a *nice* problem] 4. a) finely discriminating b) minutely accurate 5. morally scrupulous 6. a) agreeable; pleasant b) attractive; pretty c) kind; considerate d) respectable e) good; excellent —**nice and** [Colloq.] altogether; very [my tea is *nice and* hot] —**nice work** a phrase used to signify approval of a task, etc. performed well —**nice'ly adv.** —**nice'ness n.**

ni·ce·ty (nī'sə tē) *n.*, *pl.* -**ties** 1. a being nice; specif., a) scrupulosity b) precision; accuracy, as of discrimination or perception c) fastidiousness; refinement 2. the quality of calling for delicacy or precision in handling 3. a subtle or minute detail, distinction, etc. 4. something choice or dainty —**to a nicety** exactly

niche (nich) *n.* [Fr. < OFr., ult. < L. *nidus*, a nest] 1. a recess in a wall for a statue, bust, or vase 2. a place or position particularly suitable to the person or thing in it 3. *Ecol.* the particular role of an organism in its total environment —*vt.* **niched, nich'ing** to place in a niche

STATUE IN NICHE

Ni·chrome (nī'krōm') a *trademark for* a nickel-chromium alloy with a high electrical resistance, used in electric heating elements, etc.

nick (nik) *n.* [prob. akin to *nocke*, notch] 1. small cut, chip, etc. made on the edge or surface of wood, metal, china, etc.; notch 2. [Slang] prison —*vt.* 1. to make a nick or nicks in 2. a) to wound slightly b) to strike glancingly 3. to hit or catch at the right time 4. [Slang] to steal —**in good nick** [Colloq.] in good condition or repair —**in the nick of time** just before it is too late

nick·el (nik''l) *n.* [Sw. < G. *Kupfernickel*, copper demon: so called because the copperlike ore contains no copper] 1. a hard, silver-white, malleable metallic chemical element, used in alloys and for plating: symbol, Ni; at. wt., 58.71; at. no., 28 2. a U.S. or Canadian coin made of an alloy of nickel and copper and equal to five cents —*vt.* -**elled, -el·ling** to plate with nickel

nick·el·o·de·on (nik'ə lō'dē ən) *n.* [< NICKEL + MELODEON] [U.S.] a player piano or early type of jukebox operated by putting a nickel in a slot

nickel plate a thin layer of nickel deposited by electrolysis on metallic objects to prevent rust —**nick'el-plate' vt. -plat'-ed, -plat'ing**

nickel silver a hard, tough, ductile, malleable alloy composed essentially of nickel, copper, and zinc

nick·er¹ (nik'ər) *vi.* [prob. < freq. of NEIGH] to utter a low, whinnying sound: said of a horse —*n.* this sound

nick·er² (nik'ər) *n.* [< ?] [Colloq.] a pound sterling

nick·nack (nik'nak') *n.* *same as* KNICKKNACK

nick·name (nik'nām') *n.* [by syllabic merging of ME. *an ekename*, a surname] 1. a substitute, often descriptive name given to a person or thing, as in fun, affection, etc., as "Doc," "Shorty," etc. 2. a familiar form of a name, as "Dick" for "Richard" —*vt.* -**named', -nam'ing** to give a nickname to

nic·o·tine (nik'ə tēn', -tin) *n.* [Fr. < ModL., after J. *Nicot*, 16th-c. Fr. diplomat who introduced tobacco into France] a poisonous alkaloid, found in tobacco leaves and used as an insecticide —**nic'o·tin'ic** (-tin'ik, -tē'nik) *adj.*

nicotinic acid *same as* NIACIN

nic·tate (nik'tāt) *vi.* -**tat·ed, -tat·ing** *same as* NICTITATE —**nic·ta'tion n.**

nic·ti·tate (nik'tə tāt') *vi.* -**tat'ed, -tat'ing** [< ML. pp. of *nictitare*, freq. < L. *nictare*, to wink] to wink or blink rapidly, as birds and animals with a nictitating membrane —**nic'ti·ta'tion n.**

nictitating membrane a transparent third eyelid hinged at the inner side or lower lid of the eye of various animals

nid·i·fy (nid'ə fī') *n.* -**fied'**, -**fy'ing** [< *nidificare* < *nidus*, NEST + *facere*, to make] to build a nest —**nid'i·fi·ca'tion n.**

niece (nēs) *n.* [< OFr. < LL. < L. *neptis*] 1. the daughter of one's brother or sister 2. the daughter of one's brother-in-law or sister-in-law

niff (nif') *vi.* [? < dial *niffy*, smelly] to smell, usually unpleasantly —*n.* an odour, usually unpleasant

nif·ty (nif'tē) *adj.* -**ti·er**, -**ti·est** [prob. < MAGNIFICENT] [Slang] attractive, smart, stylish, enjoyable, etc.: a generalized term of approval

nig·gard (nig'ərd) *n.* [prob. < Scand.] a stingy person; miser —*adj.* stingy; miserly

nig·gard·ly (-lē) *adj.* 1. stingy; miserly 2. small, few, or scanty [a *niggardly* sum] —*adv.* stingily —**nig′gard-li·ness** *n.*

nig·ger (nig′ər) *n.* [< Fr. *nègre*, black] 1. a derogatory term for a negro 2. a derogatory term for any dark-skinned person —**nigger in the woodpile** a hidden snag or hindrance

nigger brown a very dark, chocolate brown

nig·gle (nig′'l) *vi.* **-gled, -gling** [prob. akin to Norw. dial. *nigla*] to work fussily; be finicky —*vt.* to annoy, irritate —**nig′gler** *n.* —**nig′gling** *adj., n.*

nigh (nī) *adv.* [OE. *neah*] [Chiefly Archaic or Dial.] 1. near in time, place, etc. 2. almost —*adj.* **nigh′er, nigh′est** or, older, **next** [Chiefly Archaic or Dial.] 1. near; close 2. direct or short —*prep.* [Chiefly Archaic or Dial.] near —*vi., vt.* [Archaic] to approach

night (nīt) *n.* [OE. *niht*] 1. the period of darkness between sunset and sunrise 2. the evening at the end of a specified day [Christmas *night*] 3. the darkness of night 4. any period or condition of darkness or gloom; specif., *a)* a period of intellectual or moral degeneration *b)* a time of grief *c)* death —*adj.* 1. of, for, or at night 2. active or working at night —**make a night of it** to celebrate all night —**night and day** continuously or continually

night-bell (-bel′) *n.* a bell in a doctor's house, telephone exchange, etc. used for emergency calls

night bird a person who works at night or otherwise stays up late

night blindness imperfect vision in the dark or in dim light: a symptom of vitamin A deficiency

night-bloom·ing cereus (-blōō′min) any of various cactuses that bloom at night

night boat a boat, usually a passenger ferry, that crosses at night [the *night boat* for Dublin]

night·cap (-kap′) *n.* 1. a cap worn in bed, esp. formerly, to protect the head from cold 2. [Colloq.] an alcoholic drink taken at bedtime

night clothes clothes to be worn in bed, as pyjamas

night·club (-klub′) *n.* a place of entertainment open at night for eating, drinking, dancing, etc.

night·dress (-dres′) *n.* a loose dress worn in bed by women

night·fall (-fôl′) *n.* the close of day; dusk

night·gown (-goun′) *n.* 1. *same as* NIGHTDRESS 2. *same as* NIGHTSHIRT

night·hawk (-hôk′) *n.* 1. any of a group of American night birds related to the goatsuckers 2. *same as:* a) NIGHTJAR b) NIGHT OWL

night·ie (nīt′ē) *n.* *colloq. dim. of* NIGHTDRESS

night·in·gale (nīt′'n gāl′, -iŋ-) *n.* [< OE. < *niht*, night + base of *galan*, to sing] a small European thrush with a russet back and buff underparts, known for the melodious singing of the male, esp. at night

night·jar (nīt′jär′) *n.* [NIGHT + JAR¹] any of a large group of nocturnal insect-eating birds, esp. a common European bird with a sustained trilling callnote

night latch a door latch with a bolt opened from the outside by a key and from the inside by a knob

night light a small, dim light kept on all night, as in a hallway, bathroom, sickroom, etc.

night·long (-lôŋ′) *adj.* lasting the entire night —*adv.* during the entire night

night·ly (-lē) *adj.* 1. of or like the night 2. done or occurring every night —*adv.* 1. at night 2. every night

night·mare (-mer′) *n.* [< ME. < *niht*, night + *mare*, demon] 1. a frightening dream, often accompanied by a feeling of oppression and helplessness 2. any frightening experience —**night′mar′ish** *adj.*

night out 1. a gay, festive evening 2. formerly, the evening of the week when a resident servant could go out

night owl 1. an owl active chiefly at night 2. *same as* NIGHT BIRD

nights (nīts) *adv.* on every night or most nights

night safe a safety-deposit box set in the wall of a bank to receive money, etc. after the bank closes

night school a school held in the evening, as for adults unable to attend by day

night·shade (nīt′shād′) *n.* [OE. *nihtscada*] 1. any of a large genus of flowering plants of the nightshade family, including BLACK NIGHTSHADE 2. *same as* BELLADONNA (sense 1) —*adj.* designating a large family of poisonous and nonpoisonous plants, including the tobacco, tomato, potato, petunia, and eggplant

night·shirt (-shurt′) *n.* a long, loose, shirtlike garment, worn in bed, esp. formerly, by men or boys

night·spot (-spot′) *n.* *colloq. var. of* NIGHTCLUB

night stand a small table at the bedside

night·time (-tīm′) *n.* the period of darkness from sunset to sunrise

night watch 1. a watching or guarding during the night 2. the period of time the watch is kept 3. any of the periods into which the night was formerly divided for such guarding: *usually used in pl.* 4. the person or persons doing such guarding

night watchman 1. a watchman hired for duty at night 2.

Cricket a batsman sent in to play out time when a wicket has fallen near the end of a day's play

night·wear (-wer′) *n.* *same as* NIGHT CLOTHES

night·y (-ē) *n., pl.* **night′ies** *alt. sp. of* NIGHTIE

ni·gres·cent (nī gres′'nt) *adj.* [L. *nigrescens*, prp of *nigrescere*, to grow black < *niger*, black] becoming or tending to become black —**ni·gres′cence** *n.*

ni·hil·ism (nī′ə liz'm, nē′-, ni′hi-) *n.* [< L. *nihil*, nothing + -ISM] 1. *Philos. a)* the denial of the existence of any basis for knowledge *b)* the general rejection of customary beliefs in morality, religion, etc. 2. the belief that there is no meaning or purpose in existence 3. *a)* [N-] a revolutionary movement in Russia (c.1860–1917) which advocated the destruction of existing social, political, and economic institutions *b)* loosely, any terroristic revolutionary movement —**ni′hil·ist** *n.* —**ni′hil·is′tic** *adj.*

nil (nil) *n.* [L., contr. of *nihil*] nothing

nil·gai (nil′gī) *n., pl.* **-gais, -gai:** see PLURAL, II, D, 1 [Per. *nīlgāw*, blue cow] a large, grey Indian antelope: also **nil′-gau** (-gô)

nim·ble (nim′b'l) *adj.* **-bler, -blest** [< OE. *numol* < *niman*, to take] 1. quick-witted; alert [a *nimble* mind] 2. showing mental quickness [a *nimble* reply] 3. moving quickly and lightly —**nim′ble·ness** *n.* —**nim′bly** *adv.*

nim·bo·stra·tus (nim′bō strāt′əs, -strāt′əs) *n.* [ModL.: see ff. & STRATUS] an extensive, dark, low-level cloud, commonly bringing rain or snow

nim·bus (nim′bəs) *n., pl.* **-bi** (-bī), **-bus·es** [L., rain cloud] 1. orig., any rain-producing cloud 2. a bright cloud supposedly surrounding gods or goddesses appearing on earth 3. an aura of splendour about any person or thing 4. a halo surrounding the heads of saints, etc., as in pictures

nim·rod (nim′rod) *n.* [after *Nimrod*, the mighty hunter: Gen. 10:8-9] [*sometimes* N-] a hunter

nin·com·poop (nin′kəm pōōp′, niŋ′-) *n.* [< ?] a stupid, silly person; fool; simpleton

nine (nīn) *adj.* [OE. *nigon*] totalling one more than eight —*n.* 1. the cardinal number between eight and ten; 9; IX 2. anything having nine units or members, or numbered nine —**999** the telephone number for emergency services in Britain —**the Nine** the nine Muses —**to the nines** 1. to perfection 2. in the most elaborate manner [dressed *to the nines*] —**to have nine lives** to have a remarkable ability to survive dangers (originally said of cats)

nine days' wonder anything that arouses great excitement or interest, but only for a short time

nine·fold (-fōld′) *adj.* [see -FOLD] 1. having nine parts 2. having nine times as much or as many —*adv.* nine times as much or as many

nine·pins (-pinz′) *n.* 1. [pl. *with sing. v.*] another name for skittles, (see SKITTLE *n.* 1) 2. any of the pins used in this game

nine·teen (-tēn′) *adj.* [OE. *nigontyne*] nine more than ten —*n.* the cardinal number between eighteen and twenty; 19; XIX —**talk** (or **chatter,** etc.) **nineteen to the dozen** to talk or chatter very animatedly

nine·teenth (-tēnth′) *adj.* 1. preceded by eighteen others in a series; 19th 2. designating any of the nineteen equal parts of something —*n.* 1. the one following the eighteenth 2. any of the nineteen equal parts of something; 1/19

nineteenth hole [Colloq.] in golf, the bar of the clubhouse

nine·ti·eth (nīn′tē ith) *adj.* 1. preceded by eighty-nine others in a series; 90th 2. designating any of the ninety equal parts of something —*n.* 1. the one following the eighty-ninth 2. any of the ninety equal parts of something; 1/90

nine·ty (nīn′tē) *adj.* [OE. *nigontig*] nine times ten —*n., pl.* **-ties** the cardinal number between eighty-nine and ninety-one; 90; XC (or LXXXX) —**the nineties** the numbers or years, as of a century, from ninety to ninety-nine

ning nong (niŋ′noŋ′) [Aust. Slang] a stupid person: also **nong**

nin·ny (nin′ē) *n., pl.* **-nies** [prob. by syllabic merging and contr. of *an innocent*] a fool; dolt

ninth (nīnth) *adj.* [OE. *nigonthe*] 1. preceded by eight others in a series; 9th 2. designating any of the nine equal parts of something —*n.* 1. the one following the eighth 2. any of the nine equal parts of something; 1/9 —**ninth′ly** *adv.*

ni·o·bi·um (nī ō′bē əm) *n.* [ModL. < L. *Niobe*, the Queen of Thebes in Gr. myth. who was the daughter of Tantalus: from association with tantalum: see TANTALUM] a grey or white metallic chemical element used in chromium steels, in jet engines and rockets, etc.: symbol, Nb; at. wt., 92.906; at. no., 41

nip¹ (nip) *vt.* **nipped, nip′ping** [prob. < MLowG. *nippen* or ON. *hnippa*] 1. to pinch or squeeze, as between two surfaces; bite 2. to sever (shoots, etc.) as by pinching or clipping 3. to check the growth of [to *nip* in the bud] 4. to have a painful or injurious effect on because of cold [frost *nipped* the plants] —*vi.* 1. to give a nip or nips 2. to move quickly (with *along*) —*n.* 1. a nipping; pinch; bite 2. a piece nipped off 3. a stinging quality, as in cold air 4. stinging cold; frost

nip² (nip) *n.* [prob. < Du. < base of *nippen*, to sip] a small drink of liquor; dram; sip —*vt., vi.* to drink (liquor) in nips

nip·per (nip′ər) *n.* 1. anything that nips, or pinches 2. [*pl.*] any of various tools for grasping or severing, as pliers, pincers, or forceps 3. the pincerlike claw of a crab, lobster, etc. 4. [Colloq.] a small boy

nip·ple (nip′′l) *n.* [prob. < dim. of NEB] 1. the part of a breast or udder through which a baby or young animal sucks milk from its mother; teat 2. a teatlike part, as of rubber, for a baby's bottle 3. any projection or thing resembling a nipple in shape or function

nip·py (nip′ē) *adj.* -pi·er, -pi·est 1. tending to nip 2. cold in a stinging way 3. [Colloq.] quick; nimble; active —**nip′-pi·ness** *n.*

nir·va·na (nir vä′nə, nər-; -van′ə) *n.* < Sans.] [*also* N-] *Buddhism* the state of perfect blessedness achieved by the extinction of the self and all desires or passions

Nis·sen hut (nis′′n) [after P.N. *Nissen* (1871-1930), engineer in the Canadian army] a military shelter made of corrugated steel, having a semicircular cross section; first used by the British Army in World War I

nit¹ (nit) *n.* [OE. *hnitu*] 1. the egg of a louse or similar insect 2. a young louse, etc.

nit² (nit) *n.* [Colloq.] *short for* NITWIT

nit³ (nit) *n.* [< L. *nitor*, brightness] a unit of luminance: one candela per square metre

nit-pick·ing (nit′pik′iŋ) *adj., n.* paying too much attention to petty details, esp. with the intention of finding fault —**nit′-pick′er** *n.*

ni·trate (nī′trāt; *for v.*, nī trāt′) *n.* [Fr. < *nitre*, NITRE] 1. a salt or ester of nitric acid 2. potassium nitrate or sodium nitrate, used as a fertilizer —*vt.* -trat′ed, -trat′ing to treat or combine with nitric acid or a nitrate; esp., to make into a nitrate —**ni·tra′tion** *n.*

ni·tre (nīt′ər) *n.* [< MFr. < L. < Gr. *nitron*] *same as:* 1. POTASSIUM NITRATE 2. SODIUM NITRATE Also, chiefly U.S., **ni′ter**

ni·tric (nī′trik) *adj.* 1. of or containing nitrogen 2. designating or of compounds in which nitrogen has a higher valence than in the corresponding nitrous compounds

nitric acid a colourless, corrosive acid, HNO_3

ni·tride (nī′trīd) *n.* [NITR(O)- + -IDE] a compound of nitrogen with a more electropositive element

ni·tri·fy (nī′trə fī′) *vt.* -fied′, -fy′ing [< Fr.: see NITRE & -FY] 1. to impregnate (soil, etc.) with nitrates 2. to cause the oxidation of (ammonium salts, atmospheric nitrogen, etc.) to nitrites and nitrates, as by the action of soil bacteria, etc. —**ni′tri·fi·ca′tion** *n.* —**ni′tri·fi′er** *n.*

ni·trite (nī′trīt) *n.* a salt or ester of nitrous acid

ni·tro- [see NITRE] a *combining form used to indicate:* 1. the presence of nitrogen compounds made as by the action of nitric or nitrous acid [*nitrocellulose*] 2. the presence of the NO_2 radical [*nitrobenzene*] Also, before a vowel, **nitr-**

ni·tro·ben·zene (nī′trō ben′zēn) *n.* a poisonous yellow liquid, $C_6H_5NO_2$, prepared by treating benzene with nitric acid, used in dyes, etc.

ni·tro·cel·lu·lose (-sel′yōō lōs′) *n.* a substance produced by the action of nitric acid upon wood, cotton, etc.: used in making explosives, plastics, etc. —**ni′tro·cel′lu·los′ic** *adj.*

ni·tro·gen (nī′trə jən) *n.* [< Fr.: see NITRO- & -GEN] a colourless, tasteless, odourless gaseous chemical element forming nearly four fifths of the atmosphere: it is a component of all living things: symbol N; at. wt., 14.0067; at. no., 7 —**ni·trog·e·nous** (nī troj′ə nəs) *adj.*

nitrogen cycle the cycle of natural processes through which atmospheric nitrogen is converted by nitrogen fixation into compounds used by plants and animals in the formation of proteins and is eventually returned by decay to its original state

nitrogen dioxide a poisonous, reddish-brown gas, NO_2, used in making nitric acid, as a rocket-fuel oxidizer, etc.

nitrogen fixation 1. the conversion of atmospheric nitrogen into nitrates by soil bacteria (**nitrogen fixers**) in the nodules of legumes 2. the conversion of free nitrogen into useful nitrogenous compounds by various industrial processes —**ni′tro·gen-fix′ing** *adj.*

ni·trog·e·nize (nī troj′ə nīz′, nī′trə jə-) *vt.* -nized′, -niz′ing to combine with nitrogen or its compounds

nitrogen mustard any of a class of compounds similar to mustard gas, used in cancer research and treatment

ni·tro·glyc·er·in, ni·tro·glyc·er·ine (nī′trə glis′ər in, -trō-) *n.* a thick, explosive oil, $C_3H_5(ONO_2)_3$, prepared by treating glycerin with a mixture of nitric and sulphuric acids: used in medicine and in making dynamites and propellants

ni·trous (nī′trəs) *adj.* 1. of, like, or containing nitre 2. designating or of compounds in which nitrogen has a lower valence than in the corresponding nitric compounds

nitrous acid an acid, HNO_2, known only in solution or in the form of its salts (*nitrites*)

nitrous oxide a colourless, nonflammable gas, N_2O, used as an anaesthetic and in aerosols

nit·ty (nit′ē) *adj.* -ti·er, -ti·est full of nits

nit·ty-grit·ty (-grit′ē) *n.* [rhyming extension of GRITTY] [Slang] the actual, basic facts, elements, issues, etc.

nit·wit (nit′wit′) *n.* [*nit* (< G. dial. for G. *nicht*, not) or ? NIT + WIT¹] a stupid person

nix (niks) *n., pl.* **nix′es**, G. **nix′e** (nik′sə) [G.] *Germanic Myth.* a water sprite —**nix·ie** (nik′sē) *n.fem.*

NNE, N.N.E., n.n.e. north-northeast

NNW, N.N.W., n.n.w. north-northwest

no¹ (nō) *adv.* [OE. *na* < *ne a*, lit., not ever] 1. [Scot. or Rare] not [*whether or no*] 2. not in any degree [*no worse*] 3. nay; not so: the opposite of YES, used to deny, refuse, or disagree —*adj.* not any; not a [*no errors*] —*n., pl.* **noes, nos** 1. refusal or denial 2. a negative vote or voter

no² (nō) *n., pl.* **no** [Jap. *nō*] [*often* N-] a classic form of Japanese drama with music and dancing: also **noh**

No *Chem.* nobelium

No. 1. north 2. northern 3. number: also **no.**

n.o. *Cricket* not out

No·ah's Ark (nō′əz) [after the ark built by *Noah*: Gen. 5:28-10:32] a child's toy in the shape of an ark containing wooden figures of animals and men

nob¹ (nob) *n.* [later form of KNOB] 1. [Slang] the head 2. in cribbage the jack of the same suit as the card cut from the pack [one for his *nob*]

nob² (nob) *n.* [< ? prec.] [Slang] a person of wealth and high social status

no-ball (nō′bôl) *n.* *Cricket* an improperly bowled ball for which one run is scored by the batting side —*interj.* a call by the umpire indicating this

nob·ble (nob′′l) *vt.* -bled, -bling [? freq. of NAB] [Slang] 1. to disable (a horse) as by drugging to prevent it winning a race 2. to win over by bribery or other underhand methods 3. to cheat or swindle 4. to get hold of; grab 5. to kidnap —**nob′bler** *n.*

nob·bler (nob′lər) *n.* [< NOBBLE] [Aust. Slang] a glass of spirits

nob·by (nob′ē) *adj.* -bi·er, -bi·est [< ? NOB²] [Slang] stylish

no·bel·i·um (nō bel′ē əm) *n.* [after *Nobel* Institute in Stockholm, where discovered] a radioactive chemical element produced by the nuclear bombardment of curium: symbol, No; at. wt., 255(?); at. no., 102

no·bil·i·ty (nō bil′ə tē) *n., pl.* -ties 1. a being noble 2. high station or rank in society 3. the class of people of noble rank: in Great Britain, the peerage (with *the*)

no·ble (nō′b′l) *adj.* -bler, -blest [OFr. < L. *nobilis*, lit., well-known] 1. famous or renowned 2. having or showing high moral qualities 3. having excellent qualities 4. grand; stately [a *noble* view] 5. of high rank or title; aristocratic —*n.* a person having hereditary rank or title; nobleman; peer —**no′ble·ness** *n.* —**no′bly** *adv.*

no·ble·man (-mən) *n., pl.* -men a member of the nobility; peer —**no′ble·wom′an** *n.fem., pl.* -wom′en

noble savage primitive man as idealized by the 18th cent. Romantics, esp. Rousseau

no·blesse o·blige (nō bles′ō blēzh′) [Fr., lit., nobility obliges] the obligation of people of high rank or social position to be kind and generous

no·bod·y (nō′bod′ē, -bəd ē) *pron.* not anybody; no one —*n., pl.* -bod′ies a person of no importance

nock (nok) *n.* [< Scand.] 1. a notch for holding the string at either end of a bow 2. the notch in the end of an arrow, for the bowstring

no-claim bonus a refund of part of the premium paid to the holder of an insurance policy, esp. one covering a motor car, if no claims are made within a specified period: also **no-claims bonus**

noc·tam·bu·lism (nok tam′byōō liz′m) *n.* [Fr. < L. *nox*, NIGHT + *ambulare*, to walk] walking in one's sleep: also **noc·tam′bu·la′tion** —**noc·tam′bu·lant** *n.* —**noc·tam′bu·list** *n.*

noc·tu·id (nok′tyōō wid) *n.* [< ModL. < L. *noctua*, night owl < *nox*, night] any of a large family of moths which fly at night, including many of those flying into lighted houses

noc·tur·nal (nok tur′n′l) *adj.* [LL. *nocturnalis* < L. < *nox*, night] 1. of, done, or happening in the night 2. active during the night —**noc·tur′nal·ly** *adv.*

noc·turne (nok′tərn) *n.* [Fr.] 1. a painting of a night scene 2. a romantic, dreamy musical composition, appropriate to night

nod (nod) *vi.* nod′ded, nod′ding [ME. *nodden*] 1. to bend the head forward quickly, as in agreement, greeting, command, etc. 2. to let the head fall forward involuntarily because of drowsiness 3. to be careless; make a slip 4. to sway back and forth or up and down, as plumes —*vt.* 1. to bend (the head) forward quickly 2. to signify (assent, approval, etc.) by doing this —*n.* 1. a nodding 2. [N-] the imaginary realm of sleep and dreams: usually **land of Nod** —**nod′der** *n.* —**nod off** to fall asleep

nodding acquaintance a slight, not intimate, acquaintance with a person or thing

nod·dle (nod′′l) *n.* [ME. *nodle* < ?] [Colloq.] the head or brains —*vt., vi.* -dled, -dling to nod the head, as through drowsiness

nod·dy (nod′ē) *n.*, *pl.* **-dies** [< ? NOD] 1. a fool; simpleton 2. a tropical sea bird with dark feathers and a short tail

node (nōd) *n.* [L. *nodus*, knot] 1. a knot; knob; swelling 2. a central point 3. *Astron.* either of the two diametrically opposite points at which the orbit of a heavenly body intersects a fundamental plane 4. *Bot.* that part of a stem from which a leaf starts to grow 5. *Physics* the point, line, or surface of a vibrating object where there is comparatively no vibration —**nod′al** *adj.*

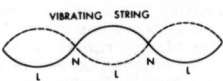

VIBRATING STRING

NODES
(N, nodes formed when vibrating string is stopped at intervals along its length; L, loops between nodes)

nod·ule (noj′ool) *n.* [L. *nodulus*, dim of *nodus*, a knot] 1. a small knot or rounded lump 2. *Bot.* a small knot or joint on a stem or root, esp. one containing nitrogen-fixing bacteria —**nod′u·lar, nod′·u·lose, nod′u·lous** *adj.*

no·el, no·ël (nō el′) *n.* [Fr. *noël* < OFr. < L. *natalis*, NATAL] 1. a Christmas carol 2. [N-] *same as* CHRISTMAS

no entry a sign prohibiting entry to a street, door, etc.: also **no entry sign**

nog, nogg (nog) *n.* [< East Anglian dial.] 1. a strong ale 2. *same as* EGGNOG

nog·gin (nog′in) *n.* [prob. < prec.] 1. a small cup or mug 2. one fourth of a pint: a measure for ale or liquor 3. [Colloq.] the head

no-go (nō′gō′) *adj.* [Slang] 1. not functioning properly 2. hopeless

no-go area a district in a town separated by barricades, usually erected by a paramilitary organization, esp. in Northern Ireland

no-hop·er (-hōp′ər) *n.* [Aust. Slang] a person or horse thought to have little chance of success

noise (noiz) *n.* [OFr. < L. *nausea*: see NAUSEA] 1. *a)* loud shouting; clamour *b)* any loud, disagreeable sound 2. sound [the *noise* of rain] 3. any unwanted electrical signal within a communication system —*vt.* **noised, nois′ing** to spread (a report, rumour, etc.)

noise·less (-lis) *adj.* with little or no noise; silent —**noise′·less·ly** *adv.* —**noise′less·ness** *n.*

noi·some (noi′səm) *adj.* [see ANNOY & -SOME¹] 1. injurious to health; harmful 2. foul-smelling; offensive —**noi′some·ly** *adv.* —**noi′some·ness** *n.*

nois·y (noi′zē) *adj.* **nois′i·er, nois′i·est** 1. making noise 2. making more sound than is expected or customary 3. full of noise; clamorous —**nois′i·ly** *adv.* —**nois′i·ness** *n.*

‡no·lens vo·lens (nō′lenz vō′lenz) [L.] unwilling (or) willing; whether or not one wishes it

nol·le pros·e·qui (nol′ē pros′ə kwi′) [L., to be unwilling to prosecute] *Law* formal notice that prosecution in a criminal case or civil suit will be partly or entirely ended

nom. nominative

no·mad (nō′mad) *n.* [< L. < Gr. < *nemein*, to pasture] 1. a member of a tribe or people having no permanent home, but moving about constantly in search of food, pasture, etc. 2. a wanderer —*adj.* wandering: also **no·mad′ic** —**no·mad′·i·cal·ly** *adv.* —**no′mad·ism** *n.*

no man's land 1. a piece of land to which no one has a recognized title 2. the area on a battlefield separating the combatants 3. an indefinite area of operation, involvement, etc.

nom de guerre (nom′də ger′) *pl.* **noms′de guerre′** [Fr., lit., a war name] a pseudonym

nom de plume (nom′də ploom′) *pl.* **noms′de plume′** [Fr.] a pen name; pseudonym

no·men·cla·ture (nō men′klə chər, nō′mən klā′chər) *n.* [< L. < *nomen*, name + pp. of *calare*, to call] 1. the system of names used in a branch of learning, or for the parts of a mechanism 2. a system of naming

nom·i·nal (nom′i n'l) *adj.* [< L. < *nomen*, a name] 1. of, or having the nature of, a name 2. of or having to do with a noun 3. in name only, not in fact [the *nominal* leader] 4. relatively very small [a *nominal* fee] —*n.* a noun; also, any word or phrase, as an adjective, used like a noun —**nom′·i·nal·ly** *adv.*

nom·i·nal·ism (-iz'm) *n.* [Fr. *nominalisme*: see prec. & -ISM] the philosophical doctrine that general or universal nouns such as "triangle" do not stand for an object but are merely names —**nom′i·nal·is′tic** *adj.* —**nom′i·nal·ist** *n.*, *adj.*

nominal value *same as* PAR VALUE

nom·i·nate (nom′ə nāt′) *vt.* **-nat′ed, -nat′ing** [< L. < pp. of *nominare* < *nomen*, a name] 1. to name or appoint to an office or position 2. *a)* to name as a candidate for election or appointment *b)* to propose as a candidate for an award or honour —**nom′i·na′tion** *n.* —**nom′i·na′tor** *n.*

nom·i·na·tive (nom′ə nə tiv; *for adj* 1, *also* -nāt′iv) *adj.* 1. named or appointed to a position or office 2. *Gram.* designating or of the case of the subject of a finite verb and the words (appositives, predicate adjectives, etc.) that agree with it; active case —*n.* 1. the nominative case 2. a word in this case

nom·i·nee (nom′ə nē′) *n.* [NOMIN(ATE) + -EE] a person who is nominated, esp. a candidate for election

-no·my [< Gr. < *nomos*, law] a combining form meaning the systematized knowledge of [astronomy]

non- [< L. *non*, not] a prefix meaning not: used to give a negative force, esp. to nouns, adjectives, and adverbs: *non-* is less emphatic than *in-* and *un-*, which often give a word an opposite meaning (Ex.: *nonhuman, inhuman*) The list below includes the more common compounds formed with *non-* that do not have special meanings; they will be understood if *not* is used before the meaning of the base word

non·age (non′ij, nō′nij) *n.* [< Anglo-Fr. < OFr.: see NON- & AGE] 1. *Law* the state of being under full legal age 2. the period of immaturity

non·a·ge·nar·i·an (non′ə ji ner′ē ən, nō′nə-) *adj.* [< L. < *nonaginta*, ninety] ninety years old, or between the ages of ninety and one hundred —*n.* a person of this age

non·ag·gres·sion pact (non′ə gresh′ən) an agreement between two nations not to attack each other, usually for a specified period of years

non·a·gon (non′ə gon′) *n.* [< L. *nonus*, ninth + -GON] a polygon with nine angles and nine sides

non·a·ligned (non′ə lind′) *adj.* not aligned with either side in a conflict —**non′a·lign′ment** *n.*

nonce (nons) *n.* [ME. (for the) *nones*, formed by syllabic merging < (for then) *ones*, lit., for the once] the present use, occasion, or time; time being: chiefly in **for the nonce**

nonce word a word coined and used for a single or particular occasion

non·cha·lant (non′shə lənt) *adj.* [Fr. < *non*, not + *chaloir*, to care for < L. *calere*, to be warm] 1. without warmth or enthusiasm 2. showing cool lack of concern; casually indifferent —**non′cha·lance′** *n.* —**non′cha·lant′ly** *adv.*

non-com (non′kom′) *n.* *colloq.* *clipped form of* NONCOMMISSIONED OFFICER

non·com·bat·ant (non kom′bə tənt) *n.* 1. a member of the armed forces whose activities do not include actual combat, as a chaplain 2. any civilian in wartime —*adj.* of noncombatants

nonabrasive	nonalphabetic	nonassimilation	noncarnivorous
nonabsorbent	nonamendable	nonathletic	noncategorical
nonacademic	non-American	nonatmospheric	non-Catholic
nonacceptance	nonanalytic	nonattendance	non-Caucasoid
nonacid	non-Anglican	nonattributive	noncellular
nonactinic	nonantagonistic	nonautomatic	noncertified
nonactive	nonapologetic	nonbacterial	nonchargeable
nonaddictive	nonapostolic	nonbasic	nonchemical
nonadjectival	nonappearance	nonbeliever	non-Christian
nonadjustable	nonappearing	nonbelieving	noncitizen
nonadministrative	nonapplicable	nonbelligerent	noncivilized
nonadvantageous	nonaquatic	non-Biblical	nonclassical
nonadverbial	non-Arab	nonbreakable	nonclassifiable
nonaesthetic	non-Arabic	non-British	nonclerical
nonaffiliated	nonaristocratic	non-Buddhist	nonclinical
non-African	nonarithmetical	nonbudding	noncoalescing
nonaggression	nonartistic	nonburnable	noncoercive
nonaggressive	non-Aryan	nonbusiness	noncohesive
nonagreement	non-Asiatic	noncaloric	noncollapsible
nonagricultural	nonassertive	noncancerous	noncollectable
nonalcoholic	nonassessable	noncanonical	noncollectible
nonalgebraic	nonassignable	noncapitalistic	noncollegiate
nonallergic	nonassimilable	noncarbonated	noncombat

non·com·mis·sioned officer (non'kə mish'ənd) an enlisted person of any of various ranks in the armed forces from corporal to sergeant major: see MILITARY RANKS, table

non·com·mit·tal (-kə mit''l) *adj.* not committing one to any point of view or course of action —**non'com·mit'tal·ly** *adv.*

non·com·pli·ance (-kəm plī'əns) *n.* failure or refusal to comply —**non'com·pli'ant** *adj.*

non com·pos men·tis (non'kom'pəs men'tis) [L.] *Law* not of sound mind; mentally incapable of handling one's own affairs: often **non compos**

non·con·duc·tor (non'kən duk'tər) *n.* a substance that does not readily transmit certain forms of energy, as electricity, sound, heat, etc.

non·con·form·ist (-kən fôr'mist) *adj.* not following established customs, beliefs, etc. —*n.* a person who is nonconformist; esp. [N-], a Protestant who is not a member of the Anglican Church —**non'con·form'ism, non'con·form'i·ty** *n.*

non·co·op·er·a·tion (-kō op'ə rā'shən) *n.* 1. failure to work together or act jointly 2. refusal to cooperate with a government, as by nonpayment of taxes: used as a form of protest, as by Mohandas Gandhi against the former British government in India —**non'co·op'er·a'tion·ist** *n.* —**non'-co·op'er·a·tive** *adj.* —**non'co·op'er·a'tor** *n.*

non·de·script (non'di skript') *adj.* [< L. *non*, not + pp. of *describere*, DESCRIBE] 1. belonging to no definite class or type; hard to classify or describe 2. having no outstanding features —*n.* a nondescript person or thing

non·du·ra·ble goods (-dyoor'ə b'l) goods usable for a relatively short time, as food, apparel, or fabrics: also **nondurables** *n.pl.*

none¹ (nun) *pron.* [OE. *nan* < *ne*, not + *an*, one] 1. no one; not anyone [*none* but Jack can do it] 2. [*usually with pl. v.*] no persons or things; not any [there are *none* on the

table] —*n.* no part; nothing [I want *none* of it] —*adv.* in no way; not at all [*none* the worse for wear]

none² (nōn) *n.* [OE. *non*: see NOON] *Eccles.* [often N-] the fifth of the canonical hours

non·en·ti·ty (non en'tə tē) *n., pl.* **-ties** 1. the state of not existing 2. something that exists only in the mind 3. a person of no importance

nones (nōnz) *n.pl.* [< L. < *nonus*, ninth < *novem*, nine] 1. in the ancient Roman calendar, the ninth day before the ides of a month 2. *same as* NONE²

none-so-pretty (nun'sō prit'ē) *n.* a common Brit. plant: also called **London pride, Nancy pretty**

non·es·sen·tial (non'i sen'shəl) *adj.* not essential; of relatively no importance; unnecessary —*n.* a nonessential person or thing

none·such (nun'such') *n.* a person or thing unrivalled or unequalled; nonpareil

none·the·less (nun'thə les') *adv.* in spite of that; nevertheless: also **none the less**

non-Eu·clid·e·an (non'yōo klid'ē ən) *adj.* designating or of a geometry that rejects any of Euclid's postulates

non·e·vent (-i vent') *n.* an event that fails to attract attention or otherwise take on significance

non·fea·sance (non fē'z'ns) *n.* *Law* failure to do what duty requires to be done

non·fer·rous (-fer'əs) *adj.* 1. not made of or containing iron 2. designating or of metals other than iron

non·he·ro (non'hir'ō) *n.* *same as* ANTIHERO

no·nil·lion (nō nil'yən) *n.* [Fr. < L. *nonus*, ninth + Fr. *million*] 1. in Great Britain and Germany, the number represented by 1 followed by 54 zeros 2. in the U.S. and France, the number represented by 1 followed by 30 zeros —*adj.* amounting to one nonillion in number

non·in·ter·ven·tion (non'in tər ven'shən) *n.* the state or

noncombining	noncrucial	nonedible	nonflowing
noncombustible	noncrystalline	noneditorial	nonfluctuating
noncommunicable	nonculpable	noneducable	nonflying
noncommunicant	noncumulative	noneducational	nonfocal
noncommunicating	noncurrent	noneffective	nonforfeiture
non-Communist	nondamageable	nonefficient	nonformal
noncompensating	nondecaying	nonelastic	nonfreezing
noncompetent	nondeceptive	nonelective	non-French
noncompeting	nondeciduous	nonelectric	nonfulfilment
noncompetitive	nondeductible	nonelectrolyte	nonfunctional
noncompletion	nondefensive	nonemotional	nonfundamental
noncompressible	nondefilement	nonendemic	nongaseous
noncompression	nondefining	nonenforceable	nongenetic
noncompulsory	nondehiscent	non-English	non-Germanic
nonconclusive	nondelivery	nonentailed	nongovernmental
nonconcurrence	nondemocratic	nonepiscopal	nongranular
noncondensing	nondenominational	nonequal	non-Greek
nonconducive	nondepartmental	nonequivalent	nongregarious
nonconducting	nondeparture	nonerotic	nonhabitable
nonconductive	nondependence	noneternal	nonhabitual
nonconferrable	nondepositor	nonethical	nonhabituating
nonconfidential	nonderivative	noneugenic	nonhazardous
nonconflicting	nonderogatory	non-European	non-Hellenic
nonconformance	nondestructive	nonevangelical	nonhereditary
nonconforming	nondetachable	nonevolutionary	nonheritable
noncongealing	nondetonating	nonexchangeable	nonhistoric
noncongenital	nondevelopment	nonexclusive	nonhuman
nonconnective	nondevotional	nonexcusable	nonhumorous
nonconscious	nondialectal	nonexecutive	nonidentical
nonconsecutive	nondictatorial	nonexempt	nonimaginary
nonconsent	nondifferentiation	nonexistence	nonimitative
nonconservative	nondiffractive	nonexistent	nonimmune
nonconstitutional	nondiffusible	nonexpansive	nonimmunized
nonconstructive	nondiffusing	nonexpendable	nonimportation
nonconsultative	nondiplomatic	nonexperienced	nonimpregnated
noncontagious	nondirectional	nonexperimental	noninclusive
noncontemporary	nondisappearing	nonexpert	nonindependent
noncontentious	nondischarging	nonexplosive	non-Indian
noncontiguous	nondisciplinary	nonextensive	nonindictable
noncontinental	nondiscrimination	nonextraditable	nonindividualistic
noncontinuance	nondiscriminatory	nonfactual	nonindustrial
noncontinuous	nondisparaging	nonfading	noninfected
noncontraband	nondisposal	nonfat	noninfectious
noncontradictory	nondistinctive	nonfatal	noninflammable
noncontributory	nondivergent	nonfattening	noninflammatory
noncontrolled	nondivisible	nonfederal	noninflationary
noncontroversial	nondoctrinal	nonfederated	noninflectional
nonconventional	nondocumentary	nonfertile	noninformative
nonconvergent	nondogmatic	nonfestive	noninheritable
nonconvertible	nondramatic	nonfiction	noninjurious
nonconviction	nondrinker	nonfictional	noninstructional
noncoordinating	nondriver	nonfigurative	nonintegrated
noncorresponding	nondrying	nonfilterable	nonintellectual
noncorrodible	nondutiable	nonfinancial	nonintelligent
noncorroding	nondynastic	nonfireproof	nonintercourse
noncreative	nonearning	nonfissionable	noninterference
noncriminal	nonecclesiastical	nonflammable	noninternational
noncritical	noneconomic	nonflowering	nonintersecting

fact of not intervening; esp., a refraining by one nation from interference in the affairs of another —**non′in·ter·ven′-tion·ist** *adj., n.*

non·i·ron (-ī′ərn) *adj.* not requiring ironing: said of fabrics, etc.

non·ju·ror (non joor′ər) *n.* a person who refuses to take an oath of allegiance, as to his ruler or government —**non·ju′-ring** *adj.*

non·met·al (-met′'l) *n.* an element lacking the characteristics of a metal; specif., any of the elements (e.g., oxygen, carbon, nitrogen, fluorine) whose oxides form acids —**non′me·tal′lic** *adj.*

non·mor·al (-mor′əl) *adj.* not connected in any way with morality; not moral and not immoral

non·nu·cle·ar (-nyōō′klē ər) *adj.* not nuclear; specif., not operated by or using nuclear energy

non·ob·jec·tive (non′əb jek′tiv) *adj.* same as NONREPRESENTATIONAL —**non′ob·jec′tiv·ism** *n.* —**non′ob·jec′-tiv·ist** *n.*

non·pa·reil (non′pə rel′) *adj.* [Fr. < *non,* not + *pareil,* equal, ult. < L. *par,* equal] unequalled; peerless —*n.* **1.** someone or something unequalled or unrivalled **2.** *Printing* formerly a size of type about 6 point

non·par·ti·san (non pär′tə z'n) *adj.* not partisan; esp., not controlled by or supporting, any single political party: also **non′par′ti·zan** —**non·par′ti·san·ship′** *n.*

non·plus (non plus′, non′plus′) *n.* [L. *non,* not + *plus,* more] a condition of perplexity in which one is unable to go, speak, or act further [at a *nonplus*] —*vt.* **-plussed′, -plus′sing** to put in a nonplus; bewilder

non·pro·duc·tive (non′prə duk′tiv) *adj.* **1.** not productive **2.** not directly related to the production of goods, as clerks, salesmen, etc. —**non′pro·duc′tive·ly** *adv.* —**non′pro·duc′-tive·ness** *n.*

non·prof·it (non prof′it) *adj.* not intending or intended to earn a profit

non·pro·lif·er·a·tion (non′prō lif′ə rā′shən) *n.* the limitation of production and distribution, esp. of nuclear weapons as the result of a treaty

non-pros (-pros′) *vt.* **-prossed′, -pros′sing** to enter a judgment of non prosequitur against (a plaintiff or his suit)

non pro·se·qui·tur (non′prō sek′wi tər) [L., he does not prosecute] *Law* a judgment entered against a plaintiff who fails to appear at the court proceedings of his suit

non·rep·re·sen·ta·tion·al (non′rep ri zən tā′shən 'l) *adj.* designating or of art that does not attempt to represent in recognizable form any object in nature; abstract —**non′-rep·re·sen·ta′tion·al·ism** *n.*

non·res·i·dent (non rez′ə dənt) *adj.* not residing in a specified place; esp., not residing in the locality where one works, attends school, etc. —*n.* a nonresident person —**non·res′i·dence, non·res′i·den·cy** *n.* —**non′res·i·den′tial** *adj.*

non·re·sist·ant (non′ri zis′tənt) *adj.* not resistant; submitting to force or arbitrary authority —*n.* a person who believes that force and violence should not be used to oppose arbitrary authority, however unjust —**non′re·sist′-ance** *n.*

non·re·stric·tive (-ri strik′tiv) *adj.* *Gram.* designating a clause, phrase, or word felt as not essential to the sense, or purely descriptive, and hence usually set off by commas (Ex.: John, *who is six feet tall,* is younger than Bill)

non·sched·uled (non shed′yoold) *adj.* designating or of an airline, aircraft, etc. making commercial flights on demand, not on a regular schedule

non·sec·tar·i·an (non′sek ter′ē ən) *adj.* not sectarian; not confined to any specific religion

non·sense (non′sens, -səns) *n.* [NON- + SENSE] **1.** words or actions that convey an absurd meaning or no meaning at all **2.** things of relatively no importance or value **3.** impudent or foolish behaviour —*adj.* designating or of syllables or words constructed so as to have no meaning —*interj.* how foolish! how absurd!

nonsense verse light verse which is senseless or absurd but which has the sound of poetry, esp. as written by Lewis Carroll and Edward Lear

non·sen·si·cal (non sen′si k'l) *adj.* unintelligible, foolish, absurd, etc. —**non·sen′si·cal·ly** *adv.* —**non·sen′si·cal·ness, non·sen′si·cal′i·ty** (-kal′ə tē) *n.*

nonintoxicant	nonmuscular	nonphysiological	nonreigning
nonintoxicating	nonmystical	nonpoetic	nonrelative
nonintuitive	nonmythical	nonpoisonous	nonreligious
noninvolvement	nonnarcotic	nonpolitical	nonremovable
noniodized	nonnational	nonporous	nonrenewable
nonionized	nonnative	nonpossession	nonrepayable
nonirradiated	nonnatural	nonpredatory	nonrepentance
nonirritant	nonnavigable	nonpredictable	nonrepresentative
nonirritating	nonnegotiable	nonpreferential	nonreproductive
non-Islamic	non-Negro	nonprejudicial	nonresidual
non-Jewish	nonneutral	nonprescriptive	nonresonant
nonjudicial	nonnucleated	nonproducer	nonrestricted
non-Latin	nonnutritious	nonprofessional	nonretentive
nonlegal	nonnutritive	nonprofessorial	nonretiring
nonlethal	nonobedience	nonprofitable	nonretractile
nonlicensed	nonobservance	nonprogressive	nonreturnable
nonlinear	nonobservant	nonprohibitive	nonreversible
nonliquefying	nonobstructive	nonprolific	nonrevertible
nonliquid	nonoccupational	nonprophetic	nonrevolving
nonliquidating	nonoccurence	nonproportional	nonrhetorical
nonliterary	nonodorous	nonproprietary	nonrhyming
nonliterate	nonofficial	nonproscriptive	nonrhythmic
nonliving	nonoperating	nonprotective	nonrigid
nonlocal	nonoperational	nonprotein	nonritualistic
nonmagnetic	nonoperative	non-Protestant	nonrival
nonmailable	non-Oriental	nonpsychic	non-Roman
nonmaintenance	nonoxidizing	nonpublic	nonromantic
nonmalignant	nonoxygenated	nonpuncturable	nonrotating
nonmalleable	nonpalatal	nonpunishable	nonroyal
nonmarital	nonpapal	nonracial	nonrural
nonmaritime	nonparallel	nonradiating	nonsacred
nonmarrying	nonparasitic	nonradical	nonsacrificial
nonmartial	nonparental	nonradioactive	nonsalable
nonmaterial	nonparishioner	nonratable	nonsalaried
nonmaterialistic	nonparliamentary	nonrational	nonsalutary
nonmaternal	nonparochial	nonreader	nonsaturated
nonmathematical	nonpaying	nonrealistic	non-Scandinavian
nonmechanical	nonpayment	nonreality	nonscholastic
nonmedicinal	nonperceptual	nonreciprocal	nonscientific
nonmelodious	nonperforated	nonreciprocating	nonscoring
nonmember	nonperformance	nonrecognition	nonseasonal
nonmercantile	nonperiodical	nonrecoverable	nonsecret
nonmetaphysical	nonperishable	nonrecurrent	nonsecretory
nonmetropolitan	nonpermanent	nonrecurring	nonsectional
nonmigratory	nonpermeable	nonredeemable	nonsecular
nonmilitant	nonpermissible	nonrefillable	nonsedentary
nonmilitary	nonperpendicular	nonregenerating	nonseditious
nonmineral	nonpersecution	nonregimented	nonsegregated
nonmortal	nonpersistent	nonregistered	nonsegregation
non-Moslem	nonphilosophical	nonregistrable	nonselective
nonmunicipal	nonphysical	nonregulation	non-Semitic

non·se·qui·tur (non′sek′wi tər) [L., lit., it does not follow] **1.** a conclusion or inference that does not follow from the premises **2.** a remark having no bearing on what has just been said

non·skid (non′skid′) *adj.* so constructed as to reduce skidding: said of a tyre tread, etc.

non·stand·ard (non stan′dərd) *adj.* not standard; specif., designating or of locutions, pronunciations, etc. not considered to be standard speech, as slang usages, obscenities, etc.

non·start·er (-stärt′ər) *n.* **1.** a competitor who fails to run in a race for which he has entered **2.** a person, idea, etc. with little or no chance of success

non·stick (-stik) *adj.* coated with a substance that prevents food adhering: said of saucepans, etc.

non·stop (-stop′) *adj., adv.* without a stop

non·such (nun′such′) *n. same as* NONESUCH

non·suit (non′sŌŌt′) *n.* [< Anglo-Fr.: see NON-& SUIT] *Law* a judgment against a plaintiff due to his failure to proceed to trial or to establish a valid case or adequate evidence —*vt.* to bring a nonsuit against (a plaintiff or his case)

non trop·po (non tro′pō) [It.] *Music* not too much; moderately

non-U (non′yŌŌ′) [Colloq.] not characteristic of the upper classes: said esp. of language, table manners, etc.

non·un·ion (non yŌŌn′yən) *n.* failure to mend or unite: said of a broken bone —*adj.* **1.** not belonging to a trade union **2.** not made or serviced under conditions required by a trade union **3.** refusing to recognize a trade union —**non·un′·ion·ism** *n.* —**non·un′ion·ist** *n.*

non·vi·o·lence (-vī′ə ləns) *n.* an abstaining from violence or physical force, as in opposing government policy —**non·vi′·o·lent** *adj.*

non·vot·er (non vōt′ər) *n.* a person who does not vote or is not permitted to vote —**non·vot′ing** *adj.*

noo·dle¹ (nŌŌ′d′l) *n.* [prob. < earlier *noddle*, the head] a simpleton; fool

noo·dle² (nŌŌ′d′l) *n.* [G. *Nudel*] a flat, narrow strip of dry dough, usually made with egg and served in soup, etc.

nook (nook) *n.* [ME. *nok*] **1.** a corner, esp. of a room **2.** a small recess or secluded spot

noon (nŌŌn) *n.* [OE. *non* < L. *nona* (*hora*), ninth (hour): cf. NONES, now recited at midday] **1.** twelve o'clock in the daytime; midday **2.** the highest point or culmination —*adj.* of or occurring at noon (midday)

noon·day (-dā′) *n., adj.* noon (midday)

no one no person; not anybody; nobody

noon·time (-tīm′) *n., adj.* noon (midday): also **noon′tide′**

noose (nŌŌs) *n.* [prob. via Pr. < L. *nodus*] **1.** a loop formed in a rope, cord, etc. by means of a slipknot so that the loop tightens as the rope is pulled **2.** anything that restricts one's freedom; tie, bond, etc. —*vt.* **noosed, noos′ing** **1.** to catch or hold as in a noose **2.** to form a noose in (a rope, etc.) —**the noose** death by hanging

no-par (nō′pär′) *adj.* having no stated par value [a *no-par* certificate of stock]

nor (nôr; *unstressed* nər) *conj.* [ME., contr. of *nother*, neither] and not; and not either: used as the second of the correlatives *neither.* ... *nor* or after some other negative [I can *neither* go *nor* stay; not for sale, *nor* for rent]

nor′, nor (nôr) north: used especially in compounds [*nor′western*]

Nor. North

Nor·dic (nôr′dik) *adj.* [< ModL. < Fr. < *nord*, north < OE. *north*] designating or of a physical type of the Caucasoid peoples exemplified by the long-headed, tall, blond people of Scandinavia

nor·ep·i·neph·rine (nôr′ep′ə nef′rin, -rēn) *n.* [< NOR(MAL) + EPINEPHRINE] a hormone of the adrenal medulla, that constricts blood vessels, helps transmit nerve impulses, etc.

Nor·folk jacket (or **coat**) (nôr′fək) a loose-fitting, single-breasted, belted jacket with box pleats

no·ri·a (nôr′ē ə) *n.* [Sp. < Ar. *nā'ūrah*] in Spain and the Orient, a water wheel with buckets at its circumference to raise and discharge water

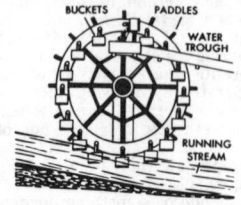

NORIA

norm (nôrm) *n.* [< L. *norma*, carpenter's square] a standard, model, or pattern; esp., *a*) a standard of achievement as represented by the average achievement of a large group *b*) an ideal standard of conduct or one typical of a certain group

Norm. Norman

nor·mal (nôr′m′l) *adj.* [< L. < *norma*, a rule] **1.** conforming with or constituting an accepted standard or norm; esp., corresponding to the average of a large group; natural; usual; regular **2.** naturally occurring [*normal* immunity] **3.** *Chem. a*) designating or of a salt formed by replacing all the replaceable hydrogen of an acid *b*) designating a solution of an acid or base containing 1.00797 grammes of hydrogen ions per litre **4.** *Math. perpendicular*; at right angles **5.** *Med., Psychol. a*) free from disease, disorder, etc.; esp., average in intelligence or development *b*) mentally sound —*n.* **1.** anything normal **2.** the usual state, amount, degree, etc. **3.** *Math.* a perpendicular —**nor′mal·cy, nor·mal′i·ty** (-mal′ə tē) *n.*

nor·mal·ize (nôr′mə līz′) *vt., vi.* **-ized′, -iz′ing** **1.** to bring or come to the normal, or usual, state **2.** to bring or come into conformity with a standard —**nor′mal·i·za′tion** *n.* —**nor′mal·iz′er** *n.*

nor·mal·ly (-lē) *adv.* **1.** in a normal manner **2.** under normal circumstances; ordinarily

Nor·man (nôr′mən) *n.* [< OFr. *Normant* or ML. *Normannus*, both < Frank.] **1.** any of the Scandinavians who occupied Normandy in the 10th cent. A.D. **2.** a descendant of the Normans and French who conquered England in 1066 **3.** same as NORMAN FRENCH **4.** a native or inhabitant of Normandy —*adj.* of Normandy, the Normans, their language, or culture —**Nor′·man·esque′** (-esk′) *adj.*

Norman French the French spoken in England by the Norman conquerors; Anglo-French —**Nor′man-French′** *adj.*

Norman style a style of Romanesque architecture used in Britain in the 11th and 12th cent.; characterized by rounded arches and massive masonry walls

norm·a·tive (nôr′mə tiv) *adj.* of or establishing a norm, or standard —**norm′a·tive·ly** *adv.*

norn (nôrn) *n.* [ON. *norn*] *Norse Myth.* any of three goddesses, representing the past, present, and future, who determine the destiny of gods and men

Norse (nôrs) *adj.* [prob. < Du. *Noorsch*, a Norwegian <

nonsensitive	nonspiritual	nonsynchronous	nonunderstandable
nonsensitized	nonspirituous	nonsyntactic	nonuniform
nonsensory	nonspottable	nonsynthesized	nonuniversal
nonsensuous	nonstaining	nonsystematic	nonusable
nonserious	nonstandardized	nontarnishable	nonuse
nonservile	nonstarting	nontaxable	nonuser
nonsexual	nonstatic	nonteachable	nonutilitarian
non-Shakespearean	nonstationary	nontechnical	nonutilized
nonsharing	nonstatistical	nonterrestrial	nonvegetative
nonshattering	nonstatutory	nonterritorial	nonvenereal
nonshrinkable	nonstrategic	nontestamentary	nonvenomous
nonsinkable	nonstretchable	nontheatrical	nonverbal
nonslaveholding	nonstriated	nontheological	nonvernacular
non-Slavic	nonstriker	nontherapeutic	nonvertical
nonsmoker	nonstriking	nonthinking	nonviable
nonsocial	nonstructural	nontoxic	nonviolation
nonsocialist	nonsubmissive	nontraditional	nonvirulent
nonsolid	nonsubscriber	nontragic	nonviscous
nonsolvent	nonsuccessful	nontransferable	nonvisual
non-Spanish	nonsuccessive	nontransitional	nonvitreous
nonsparing	nonsupporting	nontransparent	nonvocal
nonspeaking	nonsuppurative	nonreasonable	nonvocational
nonspecialist	nonsustaining	nontributary	nonvolatile
nonspecialized	nonsymbolic	nontropical	nonvolcanic
nonspecializing	nonsymmetrical	nontuberculous	nonwhite
nonspecific	nonsympathizer	nontypical	nonworker
nonspeculative	nonsymphonic	nontyrannical	nonwoven
nonspherical	nonsymptomatic	nonulcerous	nonyielding

noord, north] Scandinavian, esp. West Scandinavian —*n.* 1. the Scandinavian, esp. the West Scandinavian, group of languages 2. *same as* NORWEGIAN —**the Norse** 1. the Scandinavians 2. the West Scandinavians

Norse·man (-mən) *n., pl.* **-men** a member of the ancient Scandinavian people; Northman

north (nôrth) *n.* [OE.] 1. the direction to the right of a person facing the sunset (0˚ or 360˚ on the compass, opposite south) 2. a region or district in or towards this direction 3. [*often* N-] the northern part of the earth, esp. the arctic regions —*adj.* 1. in, of, to, or towards the north 2. from the north [*north* wind] 3. [N-] designating the northern part of a country, etc. —*adv.* in or towards the north —**the North** 1. that part of England north of the Humber 2. that part of the U.S. north of the Mason-Dixon line

north·bound (-bound′) *adj.* going northwards

North Briton *another name for* SCOT (sense 2)

north country the northern part of England or Britain, esp. Yorkshire, Northumbria & Cumbria —**north-coun′try·man**

Northd. Northumberland

north·east (nôrth′ēst′; *nautical,* nôr-) *n.* 1. the direction halfway between north and east; 45˚ east of due north 2. a region or district in or towards this direction —*adj.* 1. in, of, to, or towards the northeast 2. from the northeast, as a wind —*adv.* in, towards, or from the northeast —**the Northeast** the northeastern part of England, esp. Northumberland and Durham

north·east·er (nôrth′ēs′tər; *nautical,* nôr-) *n.* a storm or strong wind from the northeast

north·east·er·ly (-tər lē) *adj., adv.* 1. in or towards the northeast 2. from the northeast

north·east·ern (-tərn) *adj.* 1. in, of, or towards the northeast 2. from the northeast 3. [N-] of or characteristic of the Northeast

north·east·ward (nôrth′ēst′wərd; *nautical,* nôr-) *adv., adj.* towards the northeast: also **north′east′wards** *adv.* —*n.* a northeastward direction, point, or region

north·east·ward·ly (-lē) *adj., adv.* 1. towards the northeast 2. from the northeast, as a wind

north·er (nôr′thər) *n.* [Chiefly Southern U.S.] a storm or strong wind from the north

north·er·ly (-lē) *adj., adv.* 1. towards the north 2. from the north

north·ern (nôr′thərn) *adj.* 1. in, of or towards the north 2. from the north 3. [N-] of or characteristic of the North —**north′ern·most′** *adj.*

north·ern·er (nôr′thər nər, -thə nər) *n.* a native or inhabitant of the north, specif. [N-] of the North of England or the northern part of the U.S.

Northern Hemisphere that half of the earth north of the equator

northern lights *same as* AURORA BOREALIS

north·land (nôrth′land′, -lənd) *n.* [*also* N-] the northern region of a country —**north′land′er** *n.*

north light light coming through a north-facing window, esp. prized by painters

North·man (-mən) *n., pl.* **-men** *same as* NORSEMAN

north-north·east (nôrth′nôrth′ēst′; *nautical,* nôr′nôr-) *n.* the direction halfway between due north and northeast; 22˚30′east of due north —*adj., adv.* 1. in or towards this direction 2. from this direction

north-north·west (-west′) *n.* the direction halfway between due north and northwest; 22˚30′west of due north —*adj., adv.* 1. in or towards this direction 2. from this direction

North Pole the northern end of the earth's axis

North-Sea gas natural gas obtained from deposits beneath the North Sea

North Star Polaris, the bright star almost directly above the North Pole; polestar

Northum. Northumbria

north·ward (nôrth′wərd; *nautical,* nôr′thərd) *adv., adj.* towards the north: also **north′wards** *adv.* —*n.* a northwards direction, point, etc.

north·ward·ly (-lē) *adj., adv.* 1. towards the north 2. from the north

north·west (nôrth′west′; *nautical,* nôr-) *n.* 1. the direction halfway between north and west; 45˚ west of due north 2. a district or region in or towards this direction —*adj.* 1. in, of, or towards the northwest 2. from the northwest —*adv.* in, towards, or from the northwest —**the Northwest** the northwestern part of England, esp. Lancashire and the Lake District

north·west·er (nôrth′wes′tər; *nautical,* nôr-) *n.* a storm or strong wind from the northwest: also **nor′west′er**

north·west·er·ly (-tər lē) *adj., adv.* 1. in or towards the northwest 2. from the northwest

north·west·ern (-tərn) *adj.* 1. in, of, or towards the northwest 2. from the northwest 3. [N-] of or characteristic of the Northwest

north·west·ward (nôrth′west′wərd; *nautical,* nôr-) *adv.,*

adj. towards the northwest: also **north′west′wards** *adv.* —*n.* a northwestward direction, point, or region

north·west·ward·ly (-lē) *adj., adv.* 1. towards the northwest 2. from the northwest, as a wind

Norw. 1. Norway 2. Norwegian

Nor·we·gian (nôr wē′jən) *adj.* of Norway, its people, their language, etc. —*n.* 1. a native or inhabitant of Norway 2. the North Germanic language of the Norwegians

Nos., nos. numbers

nose (nōz) *n.* [OE. *nosu*] 1. the part of the human face between the eyes and the mouth, having two openings for breathing and smelling 2. the corresponding part in animals; snout, muzzle, etc. 3. the sense of smell 4. power to track or perceive as by scent [a *nose* for news] 5. anything noselike in shape or position; projecting part, as a prow, front of an aircraft, etc. 6. the smell or bouquet of wine, tea, etc. 7. [Slang] a police informer —*vt.* **nosed, nos′ing** 1. to discover or perceive as by smell 2. to rub with the nose 3. to push with the nose (with *aside,* etc.) 4. to push (a way, etc.) with the front forward [the ship *nosed* its way into the harbour] —*vi.* 1. to smell; sniff 2. to pry inquisitively 3. to advance; move forwards —**by a nose** 1. by the length of the animal's nose in horse racing, etc. 2. by a very small margin —**lead by the nose** to dominate completely —**look down one's nose at** [Colloq.] to be disdainful of —**nose out** 1. to defeat by a very small margin 2. to discover, as by smelling —**nose over** to turn over on its nose: said of an aircraft moving on the ground —**on the nose** [Slang] that (a specified horse, etc.) will finish first in a race —**pay through the nose** to pay an unreasonable price —**turn up one's nose at** to sneer at; scorn —**under one's (very) nose** in plain view

nose bag a bag filled with grain, fastened over a horse's muzzle for feeding

nose·band (nōz′band′) *n.* that part of a bridle or halter which passes over the animal's nose

nose·bleed (-blēd′) *n.* a bleeding from the nose

nose cone the cone-shaped foremost part of a rocket or missile, resistant to intense heat

nose dive 1. a swift, downward plunge of an aircraft, nose first 2. any sudden, sharp drop —**nose′-dive′** *vi.* **-dived′, -div′ing**

nose drops medication administered through the nose with a dropper

nose flute a flute blown with the nostrils, esp. in Thailand, Fiji, etc.

nose·gay (nōz′gā′) *n.* [NOSE + GAY (in obs. sense of "gay object")] a small bouquet

nose·piece (-pēs′) *n.* 1. that part of a helmet which protects the nose 2. *same as* NOSEBAND 3. anything noselike in form or position, as the nozzle of a hose or lower end of a microscope 4. the bridge of a pair of spectacles

nose rag [Slang] a handkerchief

nose ring 1. a metal ring passed through the nose of an animal for leading it about 2. a ring of bone or metal worn in the nose as an ornament

nose wheel a wheel fitted to the forward end of a vehicle, esp. the landing wheel under the nose of an aircraft

nos·ey (nō′zē) *adj.* **nos′i·er, nos′i·est** *same as* NOSY

nosh (nosh) *vt., vi.* [< Yid. < G. *naschen,* to nibble] [Slang] to eat (a snack) —*n.* [Slang] food —**nosh′er** *n.*

nosh-up (nosh-up) *n.* [Slang] a meal, esp. a large and satisfying one

no-side (nō sīd′) *n. Rugby* the end of the match, signalled by the referee's whistle

nos·tal·gia (nos tal′jə, nəs-, nôs-; -jē ə) *n.* [ModL. < Gr. *nostos,* a return + -ALGIA] 1. a longing for home; homesickness 2. a longing for something far away or of former times —**nos·tal′gic** (-jik) *adj.* —**nos·tal′gi·cal·ly** *adv.*

nos·tril (nos′trəl) *n.* [OE. *nosthyrl* < *nosu,* nose + *thyrel,* hole] either of the openings into the nose

no-strings (nō′strins′) *adj.* free of conditions or limitations [a *no-strings* wages agreement]

nos·trum (nos′trəm) *n.* [L., ours] 1. *a)* a medicine made by the person selling it *b)* a quack medicine 2. a pet scheme for solving some problem

nos·y (nō′zē) *adj.* **nos′i·er, nos′i·est** [Colloq.] prying; inquisitive —**nos′i·ly** *adv.* —**nos′i·ness** *n.*

Nosy Par·ker (pär′kər) [NOSY + proper name *Parker*] [*also* **n- p-,** **N- P-**] [Colloq.] a nosy person

not (not) *adv.* [ME., unstressed form of *nought*] in no manner; to no degree: a term of negation —**not half** very, very much —**not quite** 1. nearly 2. obviously not [*not* quite proper] 3. [Colloq.] socially undesirable

‡**no·ta be·ne** (nō′tä bē′nē, nō′tä be′nā) [L.] note well; take particular notice

no·ta·bil·i·ty (nōt′ə bil′ə tē) *n.* 1. *pl.* **-ties** a notable person 2. the quality of being notable

no·ta·ble (nōt′ə b'l) *adj.* [OFr. < L. *notabilis* < *notare,* to note] worthy of notice; remarkable —*n.* a famous or well-known person —**no′ta·bly** *adv.*

no·tar·i·al (nō ter′ē əl) *adj.* of or done by a notary —**no·tar′-i·al·ly** *adv.*

no·ta·rize (nōt′ə rīz′) *vt.* **-rized′, -riz′ing** [U.S.] to certify or attest (a document) as a notary —**no′ta·ri·za′tion** *n.*

no·ta·ry (nōt′ər ē) *n., pl.* **-ries** [< OFr. < L. < *notare,* to note] someone, usually a solicitor, who attests deeds and writings esp. for use in legal proceedings abroad: also **notary public**

no·ta·tion (nō tā′shən) *n.* [< L. < *notare,* to NOTE] **1.** the use of a system of signs or symbols for words, quantities, etc. **2.** any such system used in algebra, music, etc. **3.** a brief note jotted down **4.** [Rare] the noting of something in writing —**no·ta′tion·al** *adj.*

notch (noch) *n.* [by syllabic merging of ME. *an oche* < OFr. *oche,* a notch] **1.** a V-shaped cut in an edge or surface **2.** [Colloq.] a step; degree [a *notch* below average] —*vt.* **1.** to cut a notch or notches in **2.** to record or tally, as by notches —**notched** *adj.* —**notch′er** *n.*

note (nōt) *n.* [OFr. < L. *nota,* a mark, sign < pp. of *noscere,* to know] **1.** a distinguishing feature [a *note* of joy] **2.** importance or distinction [a man of *note*] **3.** *a)* a brief, written statement of a fact, etc., as to aid memory *b)* [*pl.*] a record of experiences, etc. **4.** a comment or explanation, as at the foot of a page **5.** notice; heed [worthy of *note*] **6.** *a)* a short, informal letter *b)* a formal diplomatic or other official communication **7.** *a)* any of certain commercial papers relating to debts or payment of money [a promissory *note*] *b)* a piece of paper currency **8.** a cry or call, as of a bird **9.** a signal or intimation [a *note* of warning] **10.** [Archaic] a tune or song **11.** *Music a)* a tone of definite pitch *b)* a symbol for a tone, indicating pitch and duration *c)* a key of a piano, etc. —*vt.* **not′ed, not′ing 1.** to heed; observe **2.** to put in writing; make a note of **3.** to mention specially **4.** to signify or indicate —**compare notes** to exchange views —**strike** (or **hit**) **the right note** to behave in a manner appropriate to the occasion —**take notes** to write down notes, as during a lecture —**note′less** *adj.*

NOTES
(A, semibreve; B, minim;
C, crotchet; D, quaver;
E, semiquaver;
F, demisemiquaver;
G, hemidemisemiquaver)

note·book (-book′) *n.* a book for memorandums

note·case (-kās′) *n. same as* WALLET

not·ed (nōt′id) *adj.* distinguished; renowned; eminent —**not′ed·ly** *adv.* —**not′ed·ness** *n.*

note paper paper for writing notes, or letters

note·wor·thy (-wur′*thē*) *adj.* worthy of note; outstanding; remarkable —**note′wor′thi·ly** *adv.* —**note′wor′thi·ness** *n.*

noth·ing (nuth′iŋ) *n.* [OE. *na thing*] **1.** *a)* no thing; not anything *b)* no part, trace, etc. **2.** nothingness **3.** a thing that does not exist **4.** *a)* something of little or no value, importance, etc. *b)* a person considered of no value or importance **5.** a nought; zero —*adv.* not at all —**for nothing 1.** at no cost; free **2.** in vain **3.** without reason —**have nothing on 1.** to be naked **2.** to have no appointments [he has *nothing on* tonight] **3.** not to be a match for (someone) **4.** to possess no incriminating evidence against —**in nothing flat** [Colloq.] in almost no time at all —**make nothing of 1.** to treat as of little importance **2.** to fail to understand —**nothing but** nothing other than —**nothing doing** [Colloq.] **1.** no: used in refusal **2.** no result, accomplishment, etc. —**nothing less than** no less than: also **nothing short of** —**think nothing of 1.** to attach no importance to **2.** to regard as easy to do

noth·ing·ness (-nis) *n.* **1.** nonexistence **2.** lack of value, meaning, etc. **3.** unconsciousness or death **4.** anything nonexistent, useless, etc.

no·tice (nōt′is) *n.* [MFr. < L. *notitia* < *notus:* see NOTE] **1.** announcement or warning **2.** a brief mention or review of a book, play, etc. **3.** a written or printed sign giving some public information, warning, or rule **4.** *a)* attention; regard; heed *b)* courteous attention **5.** a formal warning of intention to end an agreement or contract at a certain time [to give a tenant *notice*] **6.** dismissal from employment —*vt.* **-ticed, -tic·ing 1.** *a)* to refer to or comment on *b)* to review briefly **2.** *a)* to observe; pay attention to *b)* to be courteous or responsive to —**at short notice** with little warning —**serve notice** to give formal warning, as of intentions; announce —**take notice** to pay attention; observe

no·tice·a·ble (-ə b′l) *adj.* **1.** readily noticed; conspicuous **2.** significant —**no′tice·a·bly** *adv.*

notice board a board or wall area on which bulletins, notices or displays are put up

no·ti·fi·a·ble (nōt′ə fī′əb′l) *adj.* that must be reported to the health authorities [*notifiable* diseases]

no·ti·fi·ca·tion (nōt′ə fi kā′shən) *n.* **1.** a notifying or being notified **2.** the notice given or received **3.** the letter, form, etc. notifying

no·ti·fy (nōt′ə fī′) *vt.* **-fied′, -fy′ing** [< MFr. < L. < *notus*

(see NOTE) + *facere,* to make] **1.** to give notice to; inform **2.** to give notice of; announce —**no′ti·fi′er** *n.*

no·tion (nō′shən) *n.* [Fr. < L. < *notus:* see NOTE] **1.** *a)* a mental image *b)* a vague thought **2.** a belief; opinion; view **3.** an inclination; whim **4.** an intention **5.** [*pl.*] [U.S.] small, useful articles, as needles, thread, etc., sold in a shop

no·tion·al (-′l) *adj.* **1.** of or expressing notions, or concepts **2.** imaginary; not actual **3.** having visionary ideas; fanciful **4.** *Gram.* having full lexical, as distinguished from relational, meaning —**no′tion·al·ly** *adv.*

no·to·ri·e·ty (nōt′ə rī′ə tē) *n.* the quality or state of being notorious

no·to·ri·ous (nō tôr′ē əs) *adj.* [ML. *notorius* < LL. < L. *notus:* see NOTE] **1.** well-known **2.** widely but unfavourably known or talked about —**no·to′ri·ous·ly** *adv.* —**no·to′ri·ous·ness** *n.*

not proven (prō′vən) *Scots Law* a verdict given when the evidence is insufficient to warrant a conviction

no-trump (nō′trump′) *adj. Bridge* with no suit being trumps —*n. Bridge* a no-trump bid or hand

not sufficient a banker's phrase written on a cheque signifying that insufficient funds are in the account to pay it: also **N/S.**

Notts. Nottinghamshire

not·with·stand·ing (not′with stan′diŋ, -with-) *prep.* in spite of [he flew on, *notwithstanding* the storm] —*adv.* all the same; nevertheless [he will go, *notwithstanding*] —*conj.* although

nou·gat (noo′gä, nug′ət) *n.* [Fr. < Pr. < *noga* < L. *nux,* nut] a confection of sugar paste with nuts

nought (nôt) *n.* [OE. *nowiht* < *ne,* not + *awiht,* aught] **1.** nothing **2.** *Arith.* the figure zero (0) —*adj.* [Archaic or Obs.] **1.** worthless **2.** evil —*adv.* [Archaic] in no way; not at all —**set at nought** to defy; scorn Also **naught**

noughts and crosses a game in which two players take turns marking either X's or O's in an open block of nine squares, the object being to complete a line of three of one's mark first

noun (noun) *n.* [< OFr. < L. *nomen,* a name] *Gram.* **1.** any of a class of words naming or denoting a person, thing, action, quality, etc. [Ex.: *boy, water,* and *truth* are nouns] **2.** any word, phrase, or clause so used —**noun′al** *adj.*

nour·ish (nur′ish) *vt.* [< OFr. *norrir* < L. *nutrire*] **1.** to feed or sustain with substances necessary to life and growth **2.** to foster; develop; promote (a feeling, attitude, habit, etc.) —**nour′ish·er** *n.* —**nour′ish·ing** *adj.* —**nour′ish·ing·ly** *adv.*

nour·ish·ment (-mənt) *n.* **1.** a nourishing or being nourished **2.** something that nourishes

nous (noos, nous) *n.* [Gr. *nous, noos*] **1.** [Colloq.] common sense **2.** *Philos.* mind; understanding; reason; intellect

nou·veau riche (noo′vō rēsh′) *pl.* **nou·veaux riches** (noo′-vō rēsh′) [Fr., newly rich] a newly rich person: often connoting lack of culture

‡**nou·velle vague** (noo′vel väg′) [Fr., new wave] *Cinema* a movement in the French cinema esp. by directors Truffaut & Godard

Nov. November

no·va (nō′və) *n., pl.* **-vae** (-vē), **-vas** [ModL. < L. *nova* (*stella*), new (star)] *Astron.* a star that suddenly becomes vastly brighter and then loses brightness through months or years

nov·el (nov′′l) *adj.* [< OFr. < L. *novellus,* dim. of *novus,* new] new and unusual —*n.* [< It. < L. *novella,* new things < *novellus*] **1.** a relatively long fictional prose narrative with a more or less complex plot **2.** the literary form including all such narratives (with *the*) —**nov′el·is′tic** *adj.*

nov·el·ette (nov′ə let′) *n.* a short novel, esp. one regarded as trivial or sentimental

nov·el·ist (nov′′l ist) *n.* a person who writes novels

nov·el·ize (nov′ə līz′) *vt.* **-ized′, -iz′ing** to make into or like a novel —**nov′el·i·za′tion** *n.*

no·vel·la (nō vel′ə; *It.* nō vel′lä) *n., pl.* **-las, -le** (-ē; *It.* -le) [It.] **1.** a short prose narrative, often satiric, as a tale by Boccaccio **2.** a short novel; novelette

nov·el·ty (nov′′l tē) *n., pl.* **-ties 1.** the quality of being novel **2.** something novel; innovation **3.** a small, often cheap, cleverly made article, as a toy or ornament: *usually used in pl.*

No·vem·ber (nō vem′bər) *n.* [< OFr. < L. < *novem,* nine: the ancient Roman year began with March] the eleventh month of the year, having 30 days: abbrev. **Nov.**

no·ve·na (nō vē′nə) *n.* [ML. < L. < *novem,* nine] *R.C.Ch.* a nine-day period of devotions

nov·ice (nov′is) *n.* [OFr. < L. *novicius* < *novus,* new] **1.** a person on probation in a religious group before taking vows **2.** a person new to a particular activity, etc.; beginner

no·vi·ti·ate (nō vish′ē it, -āt′; -vish′it) *n.* **1.** the period or state of being a novice **2.** a novice **3.** the quarters of religious novices: also sp. **no·vi′ci·ate**

No·vo·cain (nō′və kān′) [L. *novo(us),* new + (C)OCAIN(E)] a *trademark for* PROCAINE: also sp. **Novocaine**

now (nou) *adv.* [OE. *nu*] **1.** *a)* at the present time *b)* at once

2. at the time referred to; then; next [*now* the war began] **3.** *a*) very recently [he left just *now*] *b*) very soon [he's leaving just *now*] **4.** with things as they are [*now* I'll never know] *Now* is often used for emphasis or in making transitions [*now* look here] —*conj.* since; seeing that [*now* that you know] —*n.* the present time [that's all for *now*] —*adj.* of the present time [the *now* generation] —*interj.* an exclamation of warning, reproach, etc. —**now and then** sometimes: also **now and again**

now·a·days (nou′ə dāz′) *adv.* in these days; at the present time —*n.* the present time

no·way (nō′wā′) *adv.* in no manner; by no means; not at all; nowise: also **no′ways′** (-wāz′)

now·el, now·ell (nō el′) *n.* alt. sp. of NOEL

no·where (nō′wer′, -hwer′) *adv.* not in, at, or to any place; not anywhere —*n.* **1.** a place that is nonexistent, remote, etc. **2.** a place or state of obscurity —**get nowhere** [Colloq.] fail to make progress —**nowhere near** not nearly

no·wise (-wīz′) *adv.* in no manner; noway

nowt¹ (naut) *n.* [Dial.] nothing

nowt² (naut) *n. pl., sing* **nowt** [ME. < ON. *naut,* cattle: see NEAT²] [Chiefly Scot.] cattle; oxen

nox·ious (nok′shəs) *adj.* [< L. < *noxa,* injury < *nocere, to hurt*] harmful to health or morals; injurious; unwholesome —**nox′ious·ly** *adv.* —**nox′ious·ness** *n.*

noz·zle (noz′'l) *n.* [dim. of NOSE] a spout at the end of a hose, etc., for controlling a stream of liquid or gas

Np *Chem.* neptunium

N.P., n.p. Notary Public

N.P.A. National Publishers' Association

N.P.L. National Physical Laboratory

N.R. North Riding

N/S, n/s *Banking* not sufficient funds: also **N.S.F.**

N.S. **1.** New Style **2.** not specified: also **n.s.** **3.** Nova Scotia

N.S.B. National Savings Bank

N.S.P.C.C. National Society for the Prevention of Cruelty to Children

N.S.W. New South Wales

-n't a contracted form of *not* [aren't]

NT., NT, N.T. New Testament

N.T. **1.** Northern Territory **2.** National Trust

nth (enth) *adj.* **1.** expressing the ordinal equivalent to *n* **2.** of the indefinitely large or small quantity represented by *n* —**to the nth degree** (or **power**) **1.** to an indefinite degree or power **2.** to an extreme

N.T.P. Normal Temperature and Pressure

nt. wt. net weight

nu (nyo͞o) *n.* [Gr.] the thirteenth letter of the Greek alphabet (N, ν)

nu·ance (nyo͞o′äns; nyo͞o äns′) *n.* [Fr. < *nuer,* to shade, ult. < L. *nubes,* a cloud] a slight or delicate variation in tone, colour, meaning, etc. —**nu′anced** *adj.*

nub (nub) *n.* [var. of *knub,* for KNOB] **1.** *a*) a knob or lump *b*) small piece **2.** [Colloq.] the point of a story or gist of a matter

nub·ble (nub′'l) *n.* [dim. of NUB] a small knob or lump —**nub′bly** *adj.* **-bli·er, -bli·est**

nub·by (-ē) *adj.* **-bi·er, -bi·est** covered with small nubs, or lumps; having a rough, knotted surface [a *nubby* fabric] —**nub′bi·ness** *n.*

nu·bile (nyo͞o′bīl) *adj.* [Fr. < L. < *nubere,* to marry] marriageable: said of a young woman with reference to her age or physical development —**nu·bil′i·ty** *n.*

nu·cle·ar (nyo͞o′klē ər) *adj.* **1.** of, like, or forming a nucleus **2.** of or relating to atomic nuclei [*nuclear* energy] **3.** of or operated by atomic energy [*nuclear* weapons] **4.** of, having, or involving nuclear weapons [*nuclear* war]

nuclear bomb an atomic bomb or a hydrogen bomb

nuclear disarmament the reduction, or attempted elimination of nuclear weapons from a country's armament

nuclear family a basic social unit consisting of parents and their children living in one household: cf. EXTENDED FAMILY

nuclear fission the splitting of the nuclei of atoms, with conversion of part of the mass into energy, as in an atomic bomb

nuclear fusion the fusion of atomic nuclei into a nucleus of heavier mass, with a resultant loss in the combined mass, which is converted into energy, as in a hydrogen bomb

nuclear physics the branch of physics dealing with the structure of atomic nuclei and their interactions

nuclear reactor a device for initiating and maintaining a controlled nuclear chain reaction in a fissionable fuel for the production of energy or additional fissionable material

nu·cle·ase (nyo͞o′klē ās′) *n.* [NUCLE(C)- + -ASE] any of various enzymes that speed up the hydrolysis of nucleic acids

nu·cle·ate (-it; *also, & for v. always,* -āt′) *adj.* having a nucleus —*vt.* **-at′ed, -at′ing** to form into or around a nucleus —*vi.* to form a nucleus —**nu′cle·a′tion** *n.* —**nu′·cle·a′tor** *n.*

nu·cle·i (nyo͞o′klē ī′) *n. pl.* of NUCLEUS

nu·cle·ic acid (nyo͞o klē′ik) any of a group of complex

organic acids found esp. in the nucleus of all living cells and essential to life

nu·cle·o- a combining form meaning: **1.** nucleus **2.** nuclear **3.** nucleic acid Also **nu·cle-**

nu·cle·o·lus (nyo͞o klē′ə ləs) *n., pl.* **-li′** (-lī′) [ModL. < LL., dim. of L. *nucleus*] a conspicuous, usually spherical body in the nucleus of most cells: also **nu′cle·ole′—nu·cle′o·lar** *adj.*

nu·cle·on (nyo͞o′klē on′) *n.* [NUCLE(US) + (PROT)ON] a neutron or proton, either of the fundamental particles of the atomic nucleus —**nu′cle·on′ic** *adj.*

nu·cle·on·ics (nyo͞o′klē on′iks) *n.pl.* [*with sing. v.*] the branch of physics dealing with nucleons or with nuclear phenomena

nu·cle·us (nyo͞o′klē əs) *n., pl.* **-cle·i′** (-ī′), **-cle·us·es** [ModL. < L., a kernel] **1.** a central thing or part around which other things or parts are grouped **2.** any centre of growth or development **3.** *Astron.* the bright central part of a comet head **4.** *Biol.* the central, usually rounded mass of protoplasm in most plant and animal cells, necessary to growth, reproduction, etc. **5.** *Chem., Physics* the central part of an atom, the fundamental particles of which are the proton and neutron: it carries a positive charge **6.** *Organic Chem.* a stable arrangement of atoms that may occur in many compounds

nu·clide (-klīd) *n.* [NUCL(EUS) + -*ide* < Gr. *eidos,* form] a specific type of atom that exists for a measurable time and is characterized by a distinct nuclear structure —**nu·clid′ic** (-klid′ik) *adj.*

nude (nyo͞od) *adj.* [L. *nudus*] completely unclothed or uncovered; naked; bare —*n.* **1.** a nude person **2.** a nude figure in painting, sculpture, etc. **3.** the condition of being nude [in the *nude*] —**nude′ly** *adv.* —**nude′ness** *n.*

nudge (nuj) *vt.* **nudged, nudg′ing** [prob. akin to Norw. dial. *nyggja,* to push] to push gently, esp. with the elbow, so as to get attention, etc. —*n.* a gentle push with the elbow, etc. —**nudg′er** *n.*

nud·ism (nyo͞o′diz'm) *n.* the practice or cult of going nude in the belief that it benefits health —**nud′ist** *n., adj.*

nu·di·ty (-də tē) *n.* **1.** a being nude; nakedness **2.** *pl.* **-ties** a nude figure, as in art

nuff (nuf) *adj.* [Colloq.] enough; esp. in phrase **nuff said:** also **'nuff, nuf**

nu·ga·to·ry (nyo͞o′gə tər ē) *adj.* [< L. < pp. of *nugari,* to trifle] **1.** trifling; worthless **2.** inoperative; invalid

nug·get (nug′it) *n.* [prob. dim. of E. dial. *nug,* lump] a lump, esp. of native gold

nui·sance (nyo͞o′s'ns) *n.* [< OFr. < *nuisir* < L. *nocere,* to annoy] an act, thing, person, etc. causing trouble, annoyance, or inconvenience

nuisance value the value of a person or thing to irritate or provoke an opponent, etc., without necessarily achieving a positive result

N.U.J. National Union of Journalists

null (nul) *adj.* [< MFr. < L. *nullus,* none < *ne-,* not + *ullus,* any] **1.** without legal force; invalid: usually in **null and void** **2.** amounting to nought; nil **3.** of no value, effect, etc.; insignificant **4.** *Math.* designating, of, or being zero

nul·lah (nul′ə) *n.* [Hind. *nālā,* brook, ravine] in India, etc., a watercourse, esp. one that is often dry: also **nul′la**

nul·la-nul·la (nul′ə nul′ə) *n.* [< Abor.] [Aust.] a battle club of the aborigines made of hard wood

nul·li·fy (nul′ə fī′) *vt.* **-fied′, -fy′ing** [< LL. < L. *nullus,* none + *facere,* to make] **1.** to make legally null; make void **2.** to make valueless or useless **3.** to cancel out —**nul′·li·fi·ca′tion** *n.* —**nul′li·fi′er** *n.*

nul·li·ty (nul′ə tē) *n.* **1.** a being null **2.** *pl.* **-ties** anything that is null

null set *Math.* a set having no members: also **empty set**

Num. (the book of) Numbers

num. **1.** number **2.** numeral(s)

N.U.M. National Union of Mineworkers

numb (num) *adj.* [< ME. *nomen,* pp. of *nimen,* to take] weakened in or deprived of the power of feeling or moving; deadened; insensible —*vt.* to make numb —**numb′ly** *adv.* —**numb′ness** *n.*

num·bat (num′bat′) *n.* [< Abor.] a small, insect-eating marsupial found in SW Australia

num·ber (num′bər) *n.* [< OE. < L. *numerus*] **1.** a symbol or word, or a group of either of these, showing how many or which one in a series: see CARDINAL NUMBER, ORDINAL NUMBER **2.** the sum or total of persons or units **3.** a collection of persons or things; assemblage **4.** *a*) [often *pl.*] a large group *b*) [*pl.*] numerical superiority **5.** quantity, as consisting of units **6.** *a*) a single issue of a periodical [the May *number*] *b*) a single song, skit, etc. in a programme **7.** [Colloq.] a person or thing singled out [this hat is a smart *number*] **8.** *Gram. a*) the differentiation in form to show whether one or more than one is meant *b*) the form itself See SINGULAR, PLURAL **9.** [*pl.*] *a*) metrical form; metre *b*) metrical lines; verses —*vt.* **1.** to count; enumerate **2.** to give a number to; designate by number **3.** to include as one of a group (*among*) **4.** to limit the number of [his days are numbered] **5.** to comprise; total —**vi. 1.** to total; count **2.** to be numbered —**a number of** several or many —**beyond (or without) number** too many to be counted —**get (or have) one's number** [U.S. Slang] to discover (or know) one's true character or motives —**one's number is up** [Slang] one's time to die, suffer punishment, etc. has arrived —**num′ber·er** *n.*

num·ber·less (-lis) *adj.* **1.** innumerable; countless **2.** without a number or numbers

number one [Colloq.] *n.* oneself —*adj.* first in importance, urgency, etc. [*number one* priority]

number plate a plate mounted on the front and back of a motor vehicle bearing the registration number

Number Ten the official residence of the British Prime Minister in Downing Street: regarded as the centre of government

num·bles (num′b'lz) *n.pl.* [ME. *noumbles* < OFr. *nombles*, by dissimilation < L. *lumbles*, dim. of *lumbus*, loin] [Archaic] the heart, lungs, liver, etc. of a deer, etc., used for food

numb·skull (num′skul′) *n.* same as NUMSKULL

nu·mer·a·ble (nyōō′mər ə b'l) *adj.* that can be numbered or counted

nu·mer·a·cy (nyōō′mər ə sē) *n.* the ability to handle numbers

nu·mer·al (-mər əl) *adj.* [< LL. < L. *numerus*, number] of, expressing, or denoting a number or numbers —*n.* a figure, letter, or word, or a group of any of these, expressing a number: see ARABIC NUMERALS, ROMAN NUMERALS

nu·mer·ate (-mə rāt′) *vt.* -at′ed, -at′ing **1.** same as ENUMERATE **2.** to read as words (numbers expressed in figures) —*adj.* able to perform basic arithmetic operations

nu·mer·a·tion (nyōō′mə rā′shən) *n.* **1.** a numbering or counting **2.** a system of numbering **3.** a numerating (sense 2)

nu·mer·a·tor (nyōō′mə rāt′ər) *n.* **1.** a person or thing that numbers **2.** *Math.* the term above the line in a fraction, indicating how many of the specified parts of a unit are taken

nu·mer·i·cal (nyoo mer′i k'l) *adj.* **1.** of, or having the nature of, number **2.** in or by numbers **3.** denoting (a) number **4.** expressed by numbers, not letters —**nu·mer′i·cal·ly** *adv.*

nu·mer·ol·o·gy (nyōō′mə rol′ə jē) *n.* [< L. *numerus*, a number + -LOGY] divination based on assigning meanings to numbers, as those of birth dates

nu·mer·ous (nyōō′mər əs) *adj.* [< L. < *numerus*, a number] **1.** consisting of many **2.** very many —**nu′mer·ous·ly** *adv.* —**nu′mer·ous·ness** *n.*

nu·mis·mat·ic (nyōō′miz mat′ik; -mis-) *adj.* [< Fr. < L. *numisma*, a coin < Gr. < *nomizein*, to sanction < *nomos*, law] **1.** of coins or medals **2.** of or having to do with currency **3.** of numismatics —**nu′mis·mat′i·cal·ly** *adv.*

nu·mis·mat·ics (-iks) *n.pl.* [with sing. v.] the study or collection of coins, medals, etc. —**nu·mis·ma·tist** (nyōō miz′-mə tist; -mis′-) *n.*

num·skull (num′skul′) *n.* [NUM(B) + SKULL] a stupid person; dolt; dunce

nun (nun) *n.* [< OE. < LL. *nonna*] a woman devoted to a religious life, esp. in a convent under vows of poverty, chastity, and obedience

Nunc Di·mit·tis (nuŋk′di mit′is, noonk′) [L., now thou lettest depart] **1.** a hymn based on the words in Luke 2: 29–32 **2.** [n- d-] *a)* departure or farewell *b)* dismissal

nun·ci·a·ture (nun′shē ə chər, -sē-) *n.* [It. *nunziatura*] the office or term of office of a nuncio

nun·ci·o (nun′shē ō′, -sē-) *n.*, *pl.* **-ci·os′** [It. < L. *nuntius*, messenger] an ambassador of the Pope to a foreign government

nun·ner·y (nun′ər ē) *n.*, *pl.* **-ner·ies** a former name for CONVENT

N.U.P.E. National Union of Public Employees

nup·tial (nup′shəl) *adj.* [< L. < *nuptiae*, marriage < pp. of *nubere*, to marry] **1.** of marriage **2.** of mating —*n.* [pl.] a wedding

N.U.R. National Union of Railwaymen

nurse (nurs) *n.* [< OFr. < LL. < L. < *nutrix* < *nutrire*, to nourish] **1.** a woman hired to take full care of another's young child or children **2.** a person trained to take care of the sick or aged, assist doctors, etc. **3.** a person or thing that fosters, protects, etc. —*vt.* nursed, nurs′ing **1.** to give milk from the breast to (an infant) **2.** to suck milk from the breast of **3.** to take care of (a child or children) **4.** to bring up; rear **5.** to tend (the sick or aged) **6.** to nourish or foster [to nurse a grudge] **7.** to treat, or try to cure [to nurse a cold] **8.** *a)* to use, handle, etc. carefully, so as to avoid pain, etc. [to nurse an injured leg] *b)* to consume, spend, etc. slowly or carefully so as to conserve [to nurse a drink] **9.** to hold carefully **10.** to keep in touch with (a parliamentary constituency) **11.** to oversee and promote [to nurse a business along] —*vi.* **1.** to feed at the breast **2.** to suckle a child **3.** to tend the sick, etc. as a nurse —**nurs′er** *n.*

nurse·maid (-mād′) *n.* a woman hired to take care of a child or children: also **nurs′er·y·maid′**

nurs·er·y (nur′sə rē, nurs′rē) *n.*, *pl.* **-er·ies 1.** a room in a home, set aside for the children **2.** same as NURSERY SCHOOL **3.** a place where young trees or plants are raised for sale, etc. **4.** anything that nourishes, fosters, etc.

nurs·er·y·man (-mən) *n.*, *pl.* **-men** (-mən) one who owns, operates, or works for a nursery (sense 3)

nursery rhyme a short poem for children

nursery school a school for young children aged usually 3 to 5

nursery slopes gentle slopes used by beginners in skiing

nursery stakes a horse race for two-year-olds

nursing home a residence providing care for the infirm, chronically ill, disabled, etc.

nurs·ling (nurs′liŋ) *n.* **1.** a young baby still being nursed **2.** anything that is being carefully tended or cared for Also **nurse′ling**

nur·ture (nur′chər) *n.* [< OFr. < LL. pp. of L. *nutrire*, to nourish] **1.** anything that nourishes; food **2.** training, upbringing, fostering, etc.: also **nur′tur·ance 3.** the environmental influences on a person as distinguished from his nature, or heredity —*vt.* -tured, -tur·ing **1.** to nourish **2.** to train, rear, foster, etc. —**nur′tur·ant, nur′tur·al** *adj.* —**nur′tur·er** *n.*

N.U.S. National Union of Students

nut (nut) *n.* [OE. *hnutu*] **1.** a dry, one-seeded fruit, consisting of a kernel, often edible, in a woody or leathery shell, as the walnut, chestnut, etc. **2.** the kernel itself **3.** loosely, any hard-shelled fruit keeping more or less indefinitely, as a peanut **4.** a small, usually metal block with a centre threaded hole for screwing onto a bolt, etc. **5.** [Slang] a foolish, crazy, or eccentric person **6.** [Slang] *a)* the head *b)* [pl.] the testicles: a vulgar usage **7.** a small piece of coal See also NUTS —*vi.* nut′ted, nut′ting to hunt for or gather nuts —**do one's nut** [Slang] to be extremely angry or annoyed —**hard** (or **tough**) **nut to crack** a person or thing hard to understand or deal with —**off one's nut** [Slang] crazy

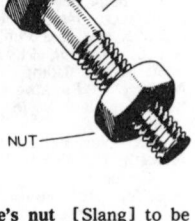

BOLT

NUT

N.U.T. National Union of Teachers

nu·ta·tion (nyōō tā′shən) *n.* [L. *nutatio* < *nutare*, to nod] **1.** the act of nodding the head **2.** a periodic variation from the vertical of the rotation axis, as of a top; specif. *Astron.* an oscillation of the earth's axis **3.** *Bot.* a slight rotary movement in the stem of a plant, due to the varying rates of growth in its parts —**nu·ta′tion·al** *adj.*

nut-brown (nut′broun′) *adj.* dark-brown, like some ripe nuts

nut case [Slang] an eccentric or insane person

nut·crack·er (-krak′ər) *n.* **1.** a device, usually hinged, for cracking the shells of nuts **2.** a white-spotted, dark-brown bird of the crow family, that feeds on nuts

nut-gall (-gôl′) *n.* a small, nut-shaped gall on the oak and other trees

nut·hatch (-hach′) *n.* a small, nut-eating bird with a sharp beak and short tail

nut house [Slang] a mental hospital or asylum

nut·meg (nut′meg′) *n.* [ME. *notemygge*, partial transl. of OFr. *noiz muscade*, lit., musky nut] **1.** the hard, aromatic seed of an East Indian tree: it is grated and used as a spice **2.** the tree

nu·tri·a (nyōō′trē ə) *n.* [Sp. < L. *lutra*, otter] **1.** a S. American water-dwelling rodent with webbed feet and a long, almost hairless tail **2.** its short-haired, soft, brown fur Also **coy′pu**

nu·tri·ent (nyōō′trē ənt) *adj.* [< L. prp. of *nutrire*, to nourish] nutritious; nourishing —*n.* anything nutritious

nu·tri·ment (-trə mənt) *n.* [< L. < *nutrire*, to nourish] anything that nourishes; food

nu·tri·tion (nyōō trish′ən) *n.* [< L. *nutrire*, to nourish] **1.** a nourishing or being nourished; esp., the series of processes by which an organism takes in and assimilates food for promoting growth and repairing tissues **2.** nourishment **3.** the science or study of proper diet —**nu·tri′tion·al** *adj.* —**nu·tri′tion·al·ly** *adv.* —**nu·tri′tion·ist** *n.*

nu·tri·tious (-əs) *adj.* nourishing; of value as food —**nu·tri′-tious·ly** *adv.* —**nu·tri′tious·ness** *n.*

nu·tri·tive (nyōō′trə tiv) *adj.* **1.** having to do with nutrition **2.** nutritious —**nu′tri·tive·ly** *adv.*

nuts (nuts) *adj.* [see NUT, 5] [Slang] crazy; foolish —*interj.* [Slang] an exclamation of disgust, scorn, refusal, etc.: often in the phrase **nuts to** (someone or something) —**be nuts about** [Slang] to love or like very much

nuts and bolts the practical, basic elements or mechanics of a situation or thing

nut·shell (nut′shel′) *n.* the shell enclosing the kernel of a nut —**in a nutshell** concisely

nut·ter (nut′ər) *n.* [NUT & -ER] [Slang] a mad or eccentric person

nut tree a nut-bearing tree
nut·ty (nut′ē) *adj.* -ti·er, -ti·est   1. containing or producing nuts   2. nutlike in flavour   3. [Slang] *a)* very enthusiastic *b)* crazy —**nut′ti·ly** *adv.* —**nut′ti·ness** *n.*
nux vom·i·ca (nuks′vom′i kə) [ML. < L. *nux*, nut + *vomere*, to vomit]   1. the poisonous seed of an Asiatic tree, containing strychnine   2. the tree
nuz·zle (nuz′'l) *vt.* -zled, -zling [< NOSE] to push against or rub with the nose, snout, etc. —*vi.*   1. to push or rub with the nose, etc. against or into something   2. to nestle; snuggle —**nuz′zler** *n.*
NW, N.W., n.w.   1. northwest   2. northwestern
N.W.T.   Northwest Territories
N.Y.C.   New York City
nyc·ta·lo·pi·a (nik′tə lō′pē ə) *n.* [LL. < Gr. < *nyx* (gen. *nyktos*), night + *alaos*, blind + *ōps*, eye]   *same as* NIGHT BLINDNESS —**nyc′ta·lop′ic** (-lop′ik) *adj.*
nye (nī) *n.* [< Ofr. *ni* < L. *nidus*, nest] a flock of pheasants
nyl·ghai (nil′gī) *n.*   *same as* NILGAI
ny·lon (nī′lon) *n.* [arbitrary coinage]   1. a synthetic polymeric amide made into fibre, bristles, etc. of great strength and elasticity   2. any of the materials made from nylon; specif., [*pl.*] stockings of nylon yarn
nymph (nimf) *n.* [< OFr. < L. < Gr. *nymphē*]   1. *Gr. & Rom. Myth.* any of a group of minor nature goddesses, represented as beautiful maidens living in rivers, trees, etc.   2. a lovely young woman   3. *Entomology* the young of an insect with incomplete metamorphosis —**nymph′al, nymph′e·an** *adj.*
nymph·et (nim′fət, nim fet′) *n.* [< Fr. dim. of *nymphe*: see prec.] a pubescent girl, esp. one who is sexually precocious —**nym·phet′ic** *adj.*
nym·pho (nim′fō) *n., pl.* -phos [contr. < *Nymphomaniac*] [Colloq.] a person who suffers from nymphomania
nym·pho·ma·ni·a (nim′fə mā′nē ə, -mān′yə) *n.* [ModL. < Gr. *nymphē*, bride, nymph + -MANIA] abnormal and uncontrollable desire by a woman for sexual intercourse —**nym′pho·ma′ni·ac′** (-ak′) *adj., n.*
N.Z., N.Zeal.   New Zealand

O

O, o (ō) *n., pl.* **O's, o's**   1. the fifteenth letter of the English alphabet   2. a sound of *O* or *o*   3. the numeral zero   4. an object shaped like O or o —*adj.* circular or oval in shape
O (ō) *interj.* an exclamation variously used: 1. in direct address [*O* Lord!]   2. to express surprise, fear, wonder, pain, etc.: now usually *oh*   3. at the end of a line in some ballads —*n., pl.* **O's** a use of this exclamation
o' (ə, ō) *prep.* an abbreviated form of: 1. of [o'clock]   2. [Archaic or Dial.] on
O' (ō) [Ir. ō, descendant] a prefix of some Irish surnames, meaning a descendant of [*O'Reilly*]
O   1. Linguis. Old [OFr.]   2. Chem. oxygen
Ω   *Physics the symbol for* ohm
O.   1. Ocean   2. Ontario
O., o.   1. octavo   2. old   3. [L. *octarius*] *Pharmacy* pint
oaf (ōf) *n. pl.* **oafs, oaves** (-vz) [< ON. *alfr*, elf] a stupid, clumsy fellow; lout —**oaf′ish** *adj.* —**oaf′ish·ly** *adv.* —**oaf′-ish·ness** *n.*
oak (ōk) *n.* see PLURAL, II, D, 3 [OE. *ac*]   1. a large hardwood tree or bush bearing nuts called *acorns*   2. its wood   3. any of various plants resembling an oak —*adj.* of oak: also **oak′en**
oak apple an applelike gall on oak trees
Oak apple day in Brit., May 29th, the anniversary of the Restoration (1660), once commemorated by the wearing of oak leaves (recalling the Boscobel oak, near Worcester, that was the hiding place of Charles II)
Oaks (ōks) *n.* an annual horse race for fillies held at Epsom since 1779 (preceded by *the*)
oa·kum (ō′kəm) *n.* [OE. *acumba* < *a*-, out + *camb*, a comb] loose, stringy, hemp fibre got by taking apart old ropes: used in caulking
OAP, O.A.P.   1. old age pensioner   2. old age pension
oar (ōr) *n.* [OE. *ar*]   1. a long pole with a broad blade at one end, used in rowing   2. a person who uses an oar; rower —*vt., vi.* to row —**put one's oar in** to meddle —**rest on one's oars** to stop to rest or relax —**oared** *adj.*
oar·fish (ōr′fish′) *n., pl.* -**fish′**, -**fish′es**: see FISH a narrow, serpentlike, deep-sea fish, up to 9 m long, with a fin the length of the back
oar·lock (-lok′) *n.*   *Chiefly U.S. term for* ROWLOCK
oars·man (ōrz′mən) *n., pl.* -**men** a man who rows; esp., an expert at rowing —**oars′man·ship′** *n.* —**oars′wom·an** *n. fem.*
OAS, O.A.S.   Organization of American States
o·a·sis (ō ā′sis; *occas.* ō′ə sis) *n., pl.* -**ses** (-sēz) [L. < Gr. *ōasis*: orig. Coptic]   1. a fertile place in a desert, due to the presence of water   2. any place or thing offering welcome relief in the midst of difficulty, dullness, etc.
oast (ōst) *n.* [ME. *ost* < OE. *ast*] a kiln for drying hops or malt —**oast′house** *n.*
oat (ōt) *n.* [OE. *ate*]   1. [*usually pl.*] *a)* a hardy cereal grass *b)* its edible grain   2. any related grass; esp., the wild oat   3. [Obs. or Poet.] a musical pipe made of an oat stalk —**feel one's oats** [Slang]   1. to be frisky   2. [U.S.] to feel and act important —**oat′en** *adj.*
oat·cake (-kāk′) *n.* a thin, flat cake of oatmeal
oath (ōth) *n., pl.* **oaths** (ōthz, ōths) [OE. *ath*]   1. *a)* a ritualistic declaration, as by appeal to God, that one will speak the truth, keep a promise, etc. *b)* the thing declared   2. the profane use of the name of God or of a sacred thing in anger or emphasis   3. a swearword —**take oath** to promise or declare with an oath
oat·meal (ōt′mēl′) *n.*   1. oats ground or rolled into meal or flakes   2. a brownish-yellow or greyish-yellow colour
O.A.U.   Organization of African Unity
ob- [< L. *ob*] a prefix meaning: 1. to, towards, before [*object*]   2. opposed to, against [*obnoxious*]   3. upon, over [*obfuscate*]   4. completely, totally [*obsolete*]   5. inversely, oppositely [*objurgate*]   In words of Latin origin, *ob*- assimilates to *o*- before *m*, *oc*- before *c*, *of*- before *f*, and *op*- before *p*
OB, O.B.   1. obstetrician   2. obstetrics
ob. [L. *obiit*] he (or she) died
O.B.   Outside Broadcast
ob·bli·ga·to (ob′lə gät′ō) *adj.* [It., lit., obliged < L.]   *Music* indispensable: said earlier of a required accompaniment but now, because of misunderstanding, usually of an optional one —*n., pl.* -**tos, -ti** (-ē) such an accompaniment
ob·du·rate (ob′dyoor ət) *adj.* [< L. pp. of *obdurare* < *ob*-, intens. + *durare*, to harden]   1. hardhearted   2. hardened and unrepenting   3. stubborn —**ob′du·ra·cy** (-ə sē) *n.* —**ob′-du·rate·ly** *adv.*
O.B.E.   Officer (of the Order of the) British Empire
o·be·ah (ō′bē ə) *n.* [of W Afr. orig.]   1. a form of witchcraft practised in Africa and the West Indies   2. a fetish used in such witchcraft
o·be·di·ence (ō bē′dē əns, ə-) *n.* the state, fact, or an instance of obeying; a being obedient
o·be·di·ent (-ənt) *adj.* [< L. prp. of *obedire*, OBEY] obeying or willing to obey; submissive —**o·be′di·ent·ly** *adv.*
o·bei·sance (ō bā′səns, -bē′-) *n.* [< OFr. < prp. of *obeir*, OBEY]   1. a gesture of respect or reverence, as a bow   2. homage; deference —**o·bei′sant** *adj.*
ob·e·lisk (ob′ə lisk) *n.* [< L. < Gr. *obeliskos*, dim. of *obelos*, a spit] a tall, four-sided stone pillar tapering towards its pyramidal top
o·bese (ō bēs′) *adj.* [< L. pp. of *obedere* < *ob*- (see OB-) + *edere*, to eat] very fat —**o·be′-si·ty** *n.*
o·bey (ō bā′, ə-) *vt.* [< OFr. < L. *obedire* < *ob*- (see OB-) + *audire*, to hear]   1. to carry out the orders of   2. to carry out (an order)   3. to be guided by [to *obey* one's conscience] —*vi.* to be obedient —**o·bey′er** *n.* —**o·bey′ing·ly** *adv.*
ob·fus·cate (ob′fəs kāt′, ob fus′kāt) *vt.* -**cat′ed, -cat′ing** [< L. pp. of *obfuscare* < *ob*- (see OB-) + *fuscare*, to obscure < *fuscus*, dark]   1. to darken; obscure   2. to muddle; confuse —**ob′-fus·ca′tion** *n.* —**ob′fus·ca′to·ry** *adj.*
o·bi (ō′bē) *n.* [Jap.] a broad sash with a bow at the back, worn with a Japanese kimono
o·bit (ō′bit, ob′it) *n.*   *same as* OBITUARY
ob·i·ter dic·tum (ob′i tər dik′təm, ō′bi-) *pl.* **ob′i·ter dic′ta** (-tə) [L.]   1. an incidental opinion expressed by a judge   2. any incidental remark, often irrelevant
o·bit·u·ar·y (ō bich′oo wer′ē, ə-: -bi′tyər-) *n., pl.* -**ar·ies** [< ML. < L. *obitus*, death < pp. of *obire*, to die < *ob*- (see OB-) + *ire*, to go] a notice of someone's death, usually with a brief biography —*adj.* of or recording a death or deaths
obj.   1. object   2. objection   3. objective

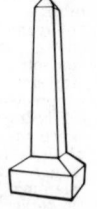

OBELISK

ob·ject (ob'jikt; *for v.* əb jekt', ob-) *n.* [< ML. *objectum*, something thrown in the way < L. pp. of *objicere* < *ob-* see OB-) + *jacere*, to throw] 1. a thing that can be seen or touched; material thing 2. a person or thing to which action, thought, or feeling is directed 3. aim; purpose; goal 4. *Gram.* a noun or substantive receiving the action of a verb (see DIRECT OBJECT, INDIRECT OBJECT), or one governed by a preposition 5. *Philos.* anything that can be perceived by the mind —*vt.* to state in opposition or disapproval —*vi.* 1. to put forward an objection; be opposed 2. to feel or express disapproval —**no object** not a hindrance or obstacle [money is *no object*] —**ob'ject·less** *adj.* —**ob·jec'tor** *n.*

object glass *same as* OBJECTIVE (*n.* 4)

ob·jec·ti·fy (əb jek'tə fī', ob-) *vt.* **-fied', -fy'ing** to make objective —**ob·jec'ti·fi·ca'tion** *n.*

ob·jec·tion (əb jek'shən, ob-) *n.* 1. an objecting 2. a feeling or expression of opposition, disapproval, or dislike 3. a reason for opposing, disapproving, or disliking

ob·jec·tion·a·ble (-ə b'l) *adj.* causing objection; disagreeable; offensive —**ob·jec'tion·a·bly** *adv.*

ob·jec·tive (əb jek'tiv, ob-) *adj.* 1. of or having to do with a known or perceived object that is not merely in the mind 2. having existence independent of the mind; real 3. concerned with the actual features of the thing dealt with rather than the thoughts, feelings, etc. of the artist, writer, or speaker [an *objective* description] 4. without bias or prejudice 5. being the aim or goal 6. minimizing subjective factors in answering and grading, as a multiple-choice or true-false test 7. *Gram.* designating or of the case of an object (sense 4) —*n.* 1. anything external to or independent of the mind; reality 2. aim; goal 3. *Gram.* a) the objective case b) a word in this case 4. *Optics* the lens or lenses nearest the object observed, as in a microscope or telescope —**ob·jec'tive·ly** *adv.* —**ob·jec'tive·ness** *n.*

ob·jec·tiv·i·ty (ob'jek tiv'ə tē) *n.* 1. the state or quality of being objective 2. objective reality

object lesson an actual or practical demonstration or exemplification of some principle

ob·jet d'art (ob'zhä där') *pl.* **ob·jets d'art** (ob'zhä-) [Fr.] a relatively small object of artistic value, as a figurine, vase, etc.

ob·jur·gate (ob'jər gāt', əb jur'gāt) *vt.* **-gat'ed, -gat'ing** [< L. pp. of *objurgare* < *ob-* (see OB-) + *jurgare*, to chide] to chide vehemently; upbraid sharply; berate —**ob'jur·ga'tion** *n.* —**ob·jur'ga·to·ry** (-gə tər ē) *adj.*

obl. 1. oblique 2. oblong

ob·late¹ (ob'lāt, ob lāt') *adj.* [ModL. *oblatus* < OB- + *-latus* as in *prolatus:* see PROLATE] *Geom.* flattened at the poles [an *oblate* spheroid]

ob·late² (ob'lāt) *n.* [< ML. *oblatus* < L. pp. of *offerre*, to OFFER] *R.C.Ch.* a person living in or associated with a religious community but not bound by vows

ob·la·tion (o blā'shən) *n.* [OFr. < L. < *oblatus*, pp. of *offerre:* see OFFER] an offering made to God or a god —**ob·la'tion·al** *adj.*

ob·li·gate (ob'lə gāt') *vt.* **-gat'ed, -gat'ing** [< L. pp. of *obligare:* see OBLIGE] to bind by a contract, promise, sense of duty, etc.

ob·li·ga·tion (ob'lə gā'shən) *n.* 1. an obligating or being obligated 2. a) a legal or moral responsibility b) the thing that such a responsibility binds one to do 3. binding power of a contract, promise, etc. 4. indebtedness for a favour, service, etc. —**ob'li·ga'tion·al** *adj.*

ob·li·ga·to (ob'lə gät'ō) *adj., n., pl.* **-tos, -ti** (-ē) *same as* OBBLIGATO

ob·lig·a·to·ry (ə blig'ə tər ē, ob'lig ə-) *adj.* legally or morally binding; required —**ob·lig'a·to·ri·ly** *adv.* —**ob·lig'·a·to·ri·ness** *n.*

o·blige (ə blīj', ō-) *vt.* **o·bliged', o·blig'ing** [< OFr. < L. *obligare* < *ob-* (see OB-) + *ligare*, to bind] 1. to compel by moral, legal, or physical force; constrain 2. to make indebted for a kindness; do a favour for —*vi.* to do a favour —**much obliged** thank you, an expression of appreciation —**o·blig'er** *n.*

o·blig·ing (ə blī'jin) *adj.* ready to do favours; helpful; accommodating —**o·blig'ing·ly** *adv.*

ob·lique (ə blēk', ō-) *adj.* [< L. *obliquus* < *ob-* (see OB-) + *liquis*, awry] 1. neither perpendicular nor horizontal; slanting 2. not straight to the point; indirect 3. evasive, underhanded, etc. 4. indirectly aimed at or attained 5. *Gram.* designating or of any case but the nominative and vocative —*n.* an oblique angle, muscle, etc. —*vi.* **-liqued', -liqu'ing** to veer from the perpendicular; slant —**ob·lique'·ly** *adv.* —**ob·liq·ui·ty** (ə blik'wə tē, ō-), **ob·lique'ness** *n.*

oblique angle any angle other than a right angle; acute or obtuse angle

ob·lit·er·ate (ə blit'ər āt, ō-) *vt.* **-at'ed, -at'ing** [< L. pp. of *obliterare*, to blot out < *ob-* (see OB-) + *litera*, a letter] 1. to blot out or wear away, leaving no traces; efface 2. to do away with; destroy —**ob·lit'er·a'tion** *n.* —**ob·lit'er·a'tive** *adj.* —**ob·lit'er·a'tor** *n.*

ob·liv·i·on (ə bliv'ē ən, ō-) *n.* [< OFr. < L. < *oblivisci*, to forget] 1. a forgetting or having forgotten; forgetfulness 2. a being forgotten [fall into *oblivion*]

ob·liv·i·ous (-əs) *adj.* 1. forgetful or unmindful (usually with *of* or *to*) 2. causing forgetfulness —**ob·liv'i·ous·ly** *adv.* —**ob·liv'i·ous·ness** *n.*

ob·long (ob'lôn) *adj.* [< L. < *ob-* (see OB-) + *longus*, long] longer than broad; elongated; specif., rectangular and longer in one direction than in the other —*n.* an oblong figure

ob·lo·quy (ob'lə kwē) *n., pl.* **-quies** [< LL. < *obloqui*, to speak against < *ob-* (see OB-) + *loqui*, to speak] 1. verbal abuse of a person or thing; esp., widespread censure 2. disgrace or infamy resulting from this

ob·nox·ious (əb nok'shəs, ob-) *adj.* [< L. < *obnoxius*, in danger < *ob-* (see OB-) + *noxa*, a harm] very unpleasant; objectionable; offensive —**ob·nox'ious·ly** *adv.* —**ob·nox'·ious·ness** *n.*

o·boe (ō'bō) *n.* [It. < Fr. *hautbois:* see HAUTBOY] a double-reed woodwind instrument having a high, penetrating, melancholy tone —**o'bo·ist** *n.*

Obs., obs. obsolete

ob·scene (ob sēn', əb-) *adj.* [< Fr. < L. *obscenus*, filthy, repulsive] 1. offensive to one's feelings, or to prevailing notions, of modesty or decency; lewd 2. disgusting; repulsive —**ob·scene'ly** *adv.*

ob·scen·i·ty (ob sen'ə tē) [< prec.] *n.* 1. the quality or condition of being obscene 2. *pl.* **-ties** anything obscene, esp. a swearword

ob·scu·rant·ism (ob skyoor'ənt iz'm, əb-; ob skyoor an'-) *n.* [< L. *obscurans*, obscuring] 1. opposition to human progress or enlightenment 2. the practice of being deliberately obscure or vague —**ob·scu'rant·ist** *n., adj.*

OBOE

ob·scure (əb skyoor', ob-) *adj.* [< OFr. < L. *obscurus*, lit., covered over] 1. lacking light; dim; dark [the *obscure* night] 2. not easily perceived; not clear or distinct [an *obscure* figure] 3. not easily understood; vague; ambiguous [an *obscure* answer] 4. in an inconspicuous position; hidden 5. not well-known [an *obscure* scientist] —*vt.* **-scured', -scur'ing** 1. to make obscure; specif., a) to darken; make dim b) to conceal from view c) to overshadow [success *obscured* his failures] d) to confuse [his testimony *obscured* the issue] 2. *Phonet.* to pronounce (a vowel) as (ə) or (i) —**ob·scure'ly** *adv.* —**ob·scure'ness** *n.*

ob·scu·ri·ty (-skyoor'ə tē) *n.* 1. the quality or condition of being obscure 2. *pl.* **-ties** an obscure person or thing —**ob'scu·ra'tion** *n.*

ob·se·quies (ob'sə kwēz) *n.pl.* [< OFr. < ML. *obsequiae* (pl.) (< L. *obsequium:* see ff.), substituted for L. *exsequiae*, funeral] funeral rites

ob·se·qui·ous (əb sē'kwē əs, ob-) *adj.* [< L. < *obsequium*, compliance < *obsequi*, to comply with] showing too great a willingness to serve or obey; fawning —**ob·se'qui·ous·ly** *adv.* —**ob·se'qui·ous·ness** *n.*

ob·serv·a·ble (əb zur'və b'l, ob-) *adj.* 1. that can be observed; visible; noticeable 2. deserving of attention 3. that can or must be kept or celebrated [an *observable* holiday] —**ob·serv'a·bly** *adv.*

ob·serv·ance (-vəns) *n.* 1. the act or practice of observing a law, duty, custom, etc. 2. a customary act, rite, etc. 3. observation 4. *R.C.Ch.* the rule to be observed by a religious order

ob·serv·ant (-vənt) *adj.* 1. strict in observing a rule, custom, etc. (often with *of*) 2. paying careful attention 3. perceptive or alert —**ob·serv'ant·ly** *adv.*

ob·ser·va·tion (ob'zər vā'shən) *n.* 1. *a)* the act, practice, or power of noticing *b)* something noticed 2. a being seen or noticed 3. *a)* a noting and recording of facts and events, as for some scientific study *b)* the data so noted and recorded 4. a comment based on something observed 5. the act of determining the altitude of the sun, a star, etc., in order to find a ship's position at sea —*adj.* for observing —**ob'·ser·va'tion·al** *adj.*

ob·serv·a·to·ry (əb zur'və tər ē, ob-) *n., pl.* **-ries** 1. a building or institution equipped for scientific observation, esp. one with a large telescope for astronomical research 2. any building or place providing an extensive view of the surrounding land

ob·serve (əb zurv', ob-) *vt.* **-served', -serv'ing** [< OFr. < L. *observare*, to watch < *ob-* (see OB-) + *servare*, to keep] 1. to adhere to or keep (a law, custom, duty, etc.) 2. to celebrate (a holiday, etc.) according to custom 3. a) to notice or perceive (something) b) to pay special attention to 4. to conclude after study 5. to say casually; remark 6. to examine scientifically —*vi.* 1. to take notice or make observations 2. to comment (*on* or *upon*) —**ob·serv'er** *n.* —**ob·serv'ing·ly** *adv.*

ob·sess (əb ses', ob-) *vt.* [< L. *obsessus*, pp. of *obsidere*, to besiege < *ob-* (see OB-) + *sedere*, to sit] to haunt or trouble in mind, esp. to an abnormal degree; preoccupy greatly —**ob·ses'sive** *adj.* —**ob·ses'sive·ly** *adv.* —**ob·ses'siveness** *n.*

ob·ses·sion (-sesh'ən) *n.* 1. the fact or state of being obsessed with an idea, desire, emotion, etc. 2. such a persistent idea, desire, etc. —**ob·ses'sion·al** *adj.*

ob·sid·i·an (əb sid'ē ən, ob-) *n.* [< ModL. < L. *Obsidianus*, a faulty reading for *Obsianus*, after Obsius, who, according to Pliny, discovered it] a hard, dark volcanic glass, used as a gemstone

ob·so·lesce (ob'sə les') *vi.* -lesced', -lesc'ing to be or become obsolete

ob·so·les·cent (-les'ənt) *adj.* in the process of becoming obsolete —**ob'so·les'cence** *n.* —**ob'so·les'cent·ly** *adv.*

ob·so·lete (ob'sə lēt') *adj.* [< L. pp. of *obsolescere* < *ob-* (see OB-) + *solere*, to become accustomed] 1. no longer in use or practice; discarded 2. out-of-date; passé —**ob'so·lete'ly** *adv.* —**ob'so·lete'ness** *n.*

ob·sta·cle (ob'sti k'l) *n.* [OFr. < L. *obstaculum* < *ob-* (see OB-) + *stare*, to stand] anything that gets in the way or hinders; obstruction

obstacle race a race in which competitors have to negotiate various obstacles

ob·stet·ric (əb stet'rik, ob-) *adj.* [< ModL. < L. < *obstetrix*, midwife, lit., she who stands before] of childbirth or obstetrics: also **ob·stet'ri·cal** —**ob·stet'ri·cal·ly** *adv.*

ob·ste·tri·cian (ob'stə trish'ən) *n.* a medical doctor who specializes in obstetrics

ob·stet·rics (əb stet'riks, ob-) *n.pl.* (with sing. v.) the branch of medicine concerned with the care and treatment of women in pregnancy, childbirth, and the period immediately following

ob·sti·na·cy (ob'stə nə sē) *n.* 1. the state or quality of being obstinate 2. *pl.* -cies an obstinate act, attitude, etc.

ob·sti·nate (ob'stə nit) *adj.* [< L. pp. of *obstinare*, to resolve on, ult. < *ob-* (see OB-) + *stare*, to stand] 1. unreasonably determined to have one's own way; stubborn; dogged 2. resisting treatment [an *obstinate* fever] 3. not easily subdued, ended, etc. —**ob'sti·nate·ly** *adv.* —**ob'sti·nate·ness** *n.*

ob·strep·er·ous (əb strep'ər əs, ob-) *adj.* [< L., ult. < *ob-* (see OB-) + *strepere*, to roar] noisy, boisterous, or unruly, esp. in resisting or opposing —**ob·strep'er·ous·ly** *adv.* —**ob·strep'er·ous·ness** *n.*

ob·struct (əb strukt', ob-) *vt.* [< L. pp. of *obstruere* < *ob-* (see OB-) + *struere*, to pile up] 1. to block (a passage) with obstacles; clog 2. to hinder (progress, an activity, etc.); impede 3. to block (the view) —**ob·struct'er, ob·struc'tor** *n.*

ob·struc·tion (əb struk'shən, ob-) *n.* 1. an obstructing or being obstructed 2. anything that obstructs; hindrance

ob·struc·tion·ist (-ist) *n.* anyone who obstructs progress; esp., a member of a legislature who hinders legislation by technical manoeuvres —*adj.* of obstructionists: also **ob·struc'tion·is'tic** —**ob·struc'tion·ism** *n.*

ob·struc·tive (əb strukt'iv, ob-) *adj.* causing or producing an obstruction, esp. deliberately hindering an activity or progress —*n.* an obstructive person or thing —**ob·struc'tive·ly** *adv.* —**ob·struc'tive·ness** *n.*

ob·tain (əb tān', ob-) *vt.* [< OFr. < L. *obtinere* < *ob-* (see OB-) + *tenere*, to hold] to get possession of by effort; procure —*vi.* to be in force or in effect; prevail [peace will obtain] —**ob·tain'a·ble** *adj.* —**ob·tain'er** *n.* —**ob·tain'ment** *n.*

ob·trude (əb trood', ob-) *vt.* -trud'ed, -trud'ing [< L. *obtrudere* < *ob-* (see OB-) + *trudere*, to thrust] 1. to thrust forward; push out; eject 2. to force (oneself, one's opinions, etc.) upon others unasked or unwanted —*vi.* to obtrude oneself (on or upon) —**ob·trud'er** *n.* —**ob·tru'sion** (-troo'zhən) *n.*

ob·tru·sive (-troo'siv) *adj.* 1. inclined to obtrude 2. obtruding itself —**ob·tru'sive·ly** *adv.* —**ob·tru'sive·ness** *n.*

ob·tuse (ob tyoos', əb-) *adj.* [< L. pp. of *obtundere*, to blunt < *ob-* (see OB-) + *tundere*, to strike] 1. not sharp or pointed; blunt 2. greater than 90 degrees and less than 180 degrees [an *obtuse* angle] 3. slow to understand or perceive; dull or insensitive 4. not acute [an *obtuse* pain] —**ob·tuse'ly** *adv.* —**ob·tuse'ness, ob·tu'si·ty** *n.*

OBTUSE ANGLES (ABE, DBE, CBE)

ob·verse (ob vurs', əb-; also & for n. always, ob'vurs) *adj.* [< L. pp. of *obvertere* < *ob-* (see OB-) + *vertere*, to turn] 1. turned towards the observer 2. narrower at the base than at the top [an *obverse* leaf] 3. forming a counterpart —*n.* 1. the side, as of a coin or medal, bearing the main design 2. the front or main surface of anything 3. a counterpart —**ob·verse'ly** *adv.*

ob·vi·ate (ob'vē āt') *vt.* -at'ed, -at'ing [< L. pp. of *obviare* < *obvius*: see OBVIOUS] to do away with or prevent by effective measures; make unnecessary —**ob'vi·a'tion** *n.*

ob·vi·ous (ob'vē əs) *adj.* [L. *obvius*, in the way: see OB- & VIA] easy to see or understand; evident —**ob'vi·ous·ly** *adv.* —**ob'vi·ous·ness** *n.*

oc- see OB-

o/c overcharge

Oc., oc. ocean

O.C. Officer Commanding

oc·a·ri·na (ok'ə rē'nə) *n.* [It., dim. of *oca* < LL. *auca*, a goose: from its shape] a small, simple wind instrument with finger holes and a mouthpiece: it produces soft, hollow tones

Oc·cam's razor (ok'əmz) [after William of *Occam*, 14th-c. Eng. philosopher] the principle that entities are not to be multiplied beyond necessity and that the simplest explanation of any phenomenon should be accepted

OCARINA

occas. 1. occasion 2. occasional 3. occasionally

oc·ca·sion (ə kā'zhən) *n.* [< OFr. < L. < pp. of *occidere* < *ob-* (see OB-) + *cadere*, to fall] 1. a favourable time; opportunity 2. a fact or event that makes something else possible 3. *a)* a happening; occurrence *b)* a particular time [on the *occasion* of his birth] 4. a special time or event, suitable for celebration 5. need arising from circumstances —*vt.* to give occasion to; cause —**on occasion** once in a while; sometimes —**rise to the occasion** to meet an emergency —**take (the) occasion** to use the opportunity (to do something)

oc·ca·sion·al (-'l) *adj.* 1. occurring on a particular occasion 2. of or for a special occasion 3. acting only on special occasions 4. happening now and then; infrequent —**oc·ca'sion·al·ly** *adv.*

occasional licence a licence to sell wines, spirits, etc. only at certain times and on specified occasions

oc·ci·dent (ok'sə dənt) *n.* [< OFr. < L. *occidens*, direction of the setting sun < *occidere*: see OCCASION] the west: now rare, except [O-] the part of the world west of Asia, esp. Europe and the Americas —**oc'ci·den'tal, Oc'ci·den'tal** *adj., n.*

oc·cip·i·tal (ok sip'ə t'l) *adj.* of the occiput or the occipital bone; —*n.* same as OCCIPITAL BONE —**oc·cip'i·tal·ly** *adv.*

occipital bone the bone that forms the back part of the skull

oc·ci·put (ok'si put') *n., pl.* **oc·cip'i·ta** (-sip'ə tə), -puts' [< MFr. < L. < *ob-* (see OB-) + *caput*, head] the back part of the skull or head

oc·clude (ə klood', o-) *vt.* -clud'ed, -clud'ing [< L. *occludere* < *ob-* (see OB-) + *claudere*, to shut] 1. to close or block (a passage) 2. to shut in or out 3. *Chem.* to retain or absorb (a gas, liquid, or solid) —*vi.* *Dentistry* to meet with the cusps fitting closely —**oc·clud'ent** *adj.* —**oc·clu'sion** (-kloo'zhən) *n.* —**oc·clu'sive** *adj.*

occluded front *Meteorol.* the front formed when a warm front is overtaken by a cold front and the warm air is forced up away from ground level

oc·cult (ə kult', o'kult) *adj.* [< L. pp. of *occulere*, to conceal < *ob-* (see OB-) + *celare*, hide] 1. hidden 2. secret; esoteric 3. beyond human understanding; mysterious 4. designating or of such alleged mystic arts as alchemy, astrology, etc. —*vt., vi.* to hide or become hidden —**the occult** the occult arts —**oc·cult'ism** *n.* —**oc·cult'ist** *n.* —**oc·cult'ly** *adv.* —**oc·cult'ness** *n.*

oc·cul·ta·tion (ok'ul tā'shən) *n.* 1. the state of becoming hidden or disappearing from view 2. *Astron.* an eclipse in which the eclipsed body seems much smaller than the eclipsing body

oc·cu·pan·cy (ok'yə pən sē) *n., pl.* -cies 1. an occupying; a taking or keeping in possession 2. *Law* the taking possession of a previously unowned object

oc·cu·pant (-pənt) *n.* 1. one who occupies a house, post, etc. 2. one who acquires possession by occupancy

oc·cu·pa·tion (ok'yə pā'shən) *n.* 1. an occupying or being occupied; specif., the seizure and control of a country or area by military forces 2. (one's) trade, profession, or business —**oc'cu·pa'tion·al** *adj.* —**oc'cu·pa'tion·al·ly** *adv.*

occupational disease a disease commonly acquired by people in a particular occupation [silicosis is an *occupational disease* of miners]

occupational therapy therapy by means of work, as arts and crafts, designed to divert the mind or to correct a physical defect

oc·cu·pi·er (ok'yə pī'ər) *n.* the person in possession; an occupant; a tenant

oc·cu·py (ok'yə pī') *vt.* -pied', -py'ing [< OFr. < L. *occupare*, to possess < *ob-* (see OB-) + *capere*, to seize] 1. to take possession of by settlement or seizure 2. to hold possession of by tenure; specif., *a)* to dwell in *b)* to hold (a position or office) **3.** to take up or fill up (space, time, etc.) **4.** to employ or busy (oneself, one's mind, etc.)

oc·cur (ə kur′) *vi.* **-curred′, -cur′ring** [< L. *occurrere* < *ob-* (see OB-) + *currere*, to run] **1.** to be found; exist [fish occur in most waters] **2.** to present itself; come to mind [an idea occurred to him] **3.** to take place; happen

oc·cur·rence (ə kur′əns) *n.* **1.** the act or fact of occurring **2.** something that occurs; event; incident **—oc·cur′rent** *adj.*

o·cean (ō′shən) *n.* [< OFr. < L. *oceanus* < Gr. *Okeanos*] **1.** the great body of salt water that covers about 71% of the earth's surface **2.** any of its five principal divisions: the Atlantic, Pacific, Indian, Arctic, or Antarctic Ocean **3.** any great expanse or quantity **—o·ce·an·ic** (ō′shē an′ik) *adj.*

o·cean·go·ing (-gō′iŋ) *adj.* of, having to do with, or made for travel on, the ocean

O·ce·a·nid (ō sē′ə nid) *n.,* pl. **O′ce·an′i·des′** (-an′ə dēz′) [Gr. *Okeanis* (gen. *Okeanidos*)] *Gr. Myth.* any of three thousand ocean nymphs

o·ce·a·nog·ra·phy (ō′shə nog′rə fē, ō′shē ə-) *n.* the study of the environment in the oceans **—o′ce·a·nog′ra·pher** *n.* **—o′ce·a·no·graph′ic** (-nə graf′ik), **o′ce·a·no·graph′i·cal** *adj.*

o·ce·a·nol·o·gy (-nol′ə jē) *n.* **1.** the study of the sea in all its aspects, including oceanography **2.** *same as* OCEANOGRAPHY **—o′ce·a·nol′o·gist** *n.*

ocean sunfish a large, sluggish ocean fish, with a globelike body and stumpy tail

o·cel·lus (ō sel′əs) *n.,* pl. **-li** (-ī) [L., dim. of *oculus*, an eye] **1.** the simple eyespot of certain invertebrates **2.** an eyelike spot **—o·cel′lar** *adj.*

o·ce·lot (os′ə lot′, ō′sə-) *n.,* pl. **-lots, -lot:** see PLURAL, II, D, 1 [Fr. < Nahuatl *ocelotl*, jaguar] a large cat of N. and S. America, with a yellow or grey coat marked with black spots

OCelt. Old Celtic

och (okh) *interj.* [Scot. & Ir.] an expression of regret, impatience, surprise, etc.

o·cher (ō′kər) *n., vt.* **o′chered, o′chering** *U.S. sp* of OCHRE **—o′cher·ous** (-kər əs, -krē əs) *adj.*

och·loc·ra·cy (ok lok′rə sē) *n.* [Fr. *ochlocratie* < Gr. *ochlos,* a mob + *-kratia,* -CRACY] government by the mob; mob rule **—och′lo·crat** (-ō krat′) *n.* **—och′lo·crat′ic** *adj.*

o·chre (ō′kər) *n.* [< L. < Gr. < *ōchres,* pale yellow] **1.** a yellow or reddish-brown clay coloured by iron oxide, used as a pigment **2.** the colour of ochre, esp., dark yellow **—vt.** **o′chred, o′chring** to colour with ochre **—o′chre·ous** *adj.*

-ock (ək) [OE. *-oc, -uc,* dim.] *a suffix used orig. to form the diminutive* [hillock]

o′clock (ə klok′, ō-) *adv.* **1.** of or according to the clock **2.** as if on a clock dial

oct- *same as:* **1.** OCTA- **2.** OCTO- Used before a vowel

Oct. October

oct. octavo

oc·ta- [Gr. *okta-* < *oktō,* eight] *a combining form meaning* eight [octagon]

oc·ta·gon (ok′tə gon′) *n.* [< L. < Gr.: see OCTA- & -GON] a plane figure with eight angles and eight sides **—oc·tag′o·nal** (-tag′ə n′l) *adj.* **—oc·tag′o·nal·ly** *adv.*

oc·ta·he·dron (ok′tə hē′drən) *n.,* pl. **-drons, -dra** (-drə) [< Gr.: see OCTA- & -HEDRON] a solid figure with eight plane surfaces **—oc′ta·he′dral** *adj.*

oc·tane (ok′tān) *n.* [< OCT(O)- + -ANE] an oily paraffin hydrocarbon, C_8H_{18}, found in petroleum

octane number (or **rating**) a number representing the antiknock quality of a fuel, etc.: the higher the number, the greater this quality

oc·tant (ok′tənt) *n.* [LL. *octans,* eighth part < L. *octo,* EIGHT] **1.** an eighth of a circle; 45° angle **2.** an instrument like the sextant, for measuring angles **3.** *Astron.* the position of one heavenly body when it is 45° distant from another **4.** *Math* one of eight parts into which space is divided by three planes at right angles intersecting at a point

oc·tave (ok′tiv, -tāv) *n.* [< OFr. < L. *octavus,* eighth < *octo,* eight] **1.** *a)* the eighth day inclusive following a church festival *b)* the period between the festival and this day **2.** the first eight lines of a sonnet **3.** any group of eight **4.** *Music a)* the eighth full tone above or below a given tone *b)* the interval of eight diatonic degrees between a tone and either of its octaves *c)* the series of tones (a full scale) within this interval, or the keys of an instrument producing such a series *d)* a tone and either of its octaves sounded together **—adj.** consisting of eight, or an octave **—oc·ta·val** (ok tā′v′l, ok′tə v′l) *adj.*

oc·ta·vo (ok tā′vō) *n.,* pl. **-vos** [< L. (*in*) *octavo,* (in) eight] **1.** the page size (c. 15x23 cm) of a book made from folding a sheet of paper three times to form eight leaves **2.** a book with pages of this size Also written **8vo** or **8°** **—adj.** with pages of this size

oc·tet, oc·tette (ok tet′) *n.* [< OCT(O)-+ (DU)ET] **1.** any group of eight; esp., an octave (sense 2) **2.** *Music a)* a composition for eight voices or eight instruments *b)* the eight performers of this

oc·to- [Gr. *oktō-* < *oktō,* eight] *a combining form meaning* eight

Oc·to·ber (ok tō′bər) *n.* [OE. < L. < *octo,* eight: it was the

eighth month of the ancient Roman year] the tenth month of the year, having 31 days: abbrev. **Oct.**

Oc·to·brist (ok tō′brist) *n.* a member of a Russian political party favouring the constitutional reforms granted in a manifesto issued by Nicholas II in Oct. 1905

oc·to·cen·te·nar·y (ok tō′sen tēn′ər ē) *n.* an 800th anniversary or its celebration **—oc·to·cen·ten′ni·al** *n.*

oc·to·ge·nar·i·an (ok′tə ji ner′ē ən) *adj.* [< L. < *octoginta,* eighty] eighty years old, or between the ages of eighty and ninety **—n.** a person of this age

oc·to·pus (ok′tə pəs) *n., pl.* **-pus·es, -pi′** (-pī′), **oc·top·o·des** (ok top′ə dēz′) [ModL. < Gr. < *oktō,* eight + *pous,* a foot] **1.** a mollusc with a soft body and eight arms covered with suckers **2.** anything suggesting an octopus; esp., a powerful organization with widespread influence and many branches

oc·to·roon (ok′tə rōōn′) *n.* [OCTO- + (QUAD)ROON] a person having one eighth Negro ancestry

O.C.T.U. Officer Cadets Training Unit

OCTOPUS
(diameter with out-spread arms, from 2 cm to 7.6 m)

oc·tu·ple (ok′tyoo p′l; ok tyōō′-) *adj.* [< L. < *octo,* eight + *-plus,* -fold] eightfold **—n.** something eight times as great as something else **—vt. -pled, -pling** to multiply by eight

oc·u·lar (ok′yə lər) *adj.* [< LL. < L. *oculus,* the eye] **1.** of, for, or like the eye **2.** by eyesight [an ocular demonstration] **—n.** the eyepiece of an optical instrument

oc·u·lar·ist (ok′yə lər ist) *n.* [< prec. + -IST] a maker of artificial eyes

oc·u·list (-list) *n.* [< Fr. < L. *oculus,* the eye] formerly, a specialist in eye diseases; ophthalmologist

OD, O.D. **1.** Officer of the Day **2.** olive drab **3.** outside diameter **4.** overdose

O.D. Ordnance Datum

o·da·lisque, o·da·lisk (ōd′ə lisk) *n.* [Fr. < Turk. *ōdalik,* chambermaid] a female slave or concubine in an Oriental harem

odd (od) *adj.* [< ON. *oddi,* triangle, hence (from the third angle) odd number] **1.** *a)* remaining or separated from a pair, a set, etc. [an odd glove, a few odd volumes of Dickens] *b)* remaining after the others are paired, grouped, taken, etc. **2.** having a remainder of one when divided by two; not even: said of numbers **3.** numbered with an odd number [the odd months] **4.** *a)* in addition to that mentioned in a round number [ten pounds and some odd change] *b)* with a relatively small number over that specified [thirty odd years ago] **5.** occasional; incidental [odd jobs] **6.** *a)* singular; peculiar *b)* queer; eccentric **7.** out-of-the-way [in odd corners] **—odd man out** a person or thing excluded from others forming a group, etc. **—odd′ly** *adv.* **—odd′ness** *n.*

odd·ball (-bôl) *n.* [ODD + BALL¹] [Chiefly U.S. Slang] an eccentric, unconventional, or nonconforming person **—adj.** strange or unconventional

odd·i·ty (od′ə tē) *n.* **1.** queerness; peculiarity **2.** *pl.* **-ties** an odd person or thing

odd·ment (-mənt) *n.* something odd or left over, often sold at a reduced price

odds (odz) *n.pl.* **1.** difference [it makes no odds] **2.** difference in favour of one side over the other; advantage **3.** an equalizing advantage given by a bettor or competitor in proportion to the assumed chances in his favour **4.** likelihood; probability **—against all** (or **appalling,** etc.) **odds** despite all (or appalling, etc.) difficulties **—at odds** in disagreement; quarrelling **—over the odds** more than is expected, necessary, etc. **—shout the odds** [Colloq.] to talk too loudly or too much **—take odds** to accept the bet offered **—the odds are** the likelihood is

odds and ends scraps; remnants; oddments

odds-on (-on′) *adj.* having better than an even chance of winning [an odds-on favourite]

ode (ōd) *n.* [Fr. < LL. < Gr. *ōidē,* song < *aeidein,* to sing] a lyric poem typically addressed to some person or thing and characterized by lofty feeling and dignified style **—od′ic** (ō′dik) *adj.*

-ode (ōd) [< Gr. *hodos*] *a suffix meaning* way, path

o·di·ous (ō′dē əs) *adj.* [< OFr. < L. < *odium:* see ff.] arousing or deserving hatred or loathing; disgusting **—o′di·ous·ly** *adv.* **—o′di·ous·ness** *n.*

o·di·um (-əm) *n.* [L. *odium,* hatred < *odi,* I hate] **1.** *a)* hatred *b)* a being hated **2.** the disgrace brought on by hateful action; opprobrium

o·dom·e·ter (ō dom′ə tər) *n.* [< Fr. < Gr. < *hodos,* way + *metron,* a measure] an instrument for measuring the distance travelled by a vehicle

-o·dont (ə dont′) [< Gr. *odōn* (gen. *odontos*)] *a combining form meaning* tooth

o·dont·o- [see prec.] *a combining form meaning* tooth or teeth: also, before a vowel, **odont-**

o·don·tol·o·gy (ō′don tol′ə jē) *n.* [< Fr.: see prec. & -LOGY] the science dealing with the structure, growth, and diseases of the teeth —**o·don′to·log′i·cal** (-tə loj′i k'l) *adj.* —**o·don′-to·log′i·cal·ly** *adv.* —**o·don′tol·o·gist** *n.*

o·dor (ō′dər) *n. U.S. sp. of* ODOUR

o·dor·if·er·ous (ō′də rif′ər əs) *adj.* giving off an odour, often, specif., a fragrant one —**o′dor·if′er·ous·ly** *adv.* —**o′dor·if′er·ous·ness** *n.*

o·dor·ous (ō′dər əs) *adj.* having an odour; esp., fragrant —**o′dor·ous·ly** *adv.* —**o′dor·ous·ness** *n.*

o·dour (ō′dər) *n.* [< OFr. < L.] **1.** *a)* that characteristic of a substance which makes it perceptible to the sense of smell *b)* a smell, whether pleasant or unpleasant; fragrance, stench, etc. **2.** [Archaic] a perfume —**be in bad** (or **ill**) **odour** to be in ill repute —**o′dour·less** *adj.*

-o·dus (ə das) [ModL. < Gr. *-odous* < *odōn*, tooth] *a combining form meaning* having teeth, toothed

-o·dyn·i·a (ə din′ē ə, -din′-) [ModL. < Gr. < *odynē*, pain] *a combining form meaning* pain in (a specified organ or part)

Od·ys·sey (od′ə sē) *n., pl.* **-seys** [after the Greek epic poem about the wanderings of Odysseus during the ten years after the fall of Troy] any extended wandering

oe- a variant spelling for many words of Gr. and L. origin now sometimes written with *e-*

OE., OE, O.E. Old English

O.E.C.D. Organization for Economic Cooperation and Development

OED, O.E.D. Oxford English Dictionary

oe·de·ma (i dē′mə) *n., pl.* **-mas, -ma·ta** (-mə tə) [ModL. < Gr. *Oidēma*, a swelling] **1.** an abnormal accumulation of fluid in tissues or cavities of the body, causing swelling **2.** a similar swelling in plants —**oe·dem·a·tous** (i dem′ə təs, i dē′-mə-) *adj.*

Oed·i·pal (ed′ə pəl, ē′də-) *adj.* [*also* o-] of or relating to the Oedipus complex

Oed·i·pus complex (-pəs) *Psychoanalysis* the unconscious tendency of a child, sometimes unresolved in adulthood, to be attached to the parent of the opposite sex and hostile towards the other parent

O.E.E.C. Organization for European Economic Cooperation (superseded 1961 by O.E.C.D.)

o′er (ôr) *prep., adv.* chiefly poet. contr. of OVER

oer·sted (ur′sted) *n.* [after Hans Christian *Oersted* (1777-1851), Dan. physicist] the cgs unit of magnetic intensity, equal to a force of one dyne acting on a unit magnetic pole in a vacuum: equivalent to $\pi/4 \times 10^3$ amperes per metre

oe·soph·a·gus (i sof′ə gəs) *n., pl.* **-gi′** (-jī′) [< OFr. < ML. < Gr. *oisophagos* < *oisein*, fut. inf. of *pherein*, to carry + *phagein*, to eat] the tube through which food passes from the pharynx to the stomach: see EPIGLOTTIS, illus. —**oe·soph·a·ge·al** (i sof′ə jē′əl) *adj.*

oes·tro·gen (ēs′trə jən) *n.* [< OESTRUS + -GEN] any of several female sex hormones or similar synthetic compounds —**oes′tro·gen′ic** (-jen′ik) *adj.*

oes·trous cycle (ē′trəs) the regular female reproductive cycle of most placental mammals that is under hormonal control and includes a period of heat

oes·trus (ēs′trəs) *n.* [ModL. < L. *oestrus* < Gr. *oistros*, frenzy] the periodic sexual excitement, or heat, of most female placental mammals, or the period of this Also **oes′-trum** (-trəm) —**oes′trous** *adj.*

of (uv, ov; *unstressed* əv, ə) *prep.* [OE., unstressed var. of *af, æf*, away (from)] **1.** from; specif., *a)* derived or coming from [men of Harlech] *b)* as relates to [how wise of her] *c)* resulting from; through [to die of fever] *d)* at a distance from [east of the city] *e)* proceeding as a product from; by [the poems of Poe] *f)* separated from [robbed of his money] *g)* from the whole constituting [part of the time] *h)* made from [a sheet of paper] **2.** belonging to [pages of a book] **3.** *a)* possessing [a man of property] *b)* containing [a bag of nuts] **4.** specified as [a height of two metres] **5.** with (something specified) as object, goal, etc. [a reader of books] **6.** characterized by [a man of honour] **7.** concerning; about [think well of me] **8.** set aside for [a day of rest] **9.** during [of late years] **10.** [Colloq.] indicating a day or part of a period of time when some activity habitually occurs [I go to the pub of an evening] **11.** [Archaic] by [rejected of men] *Of* is also used in various idiomatic expressions, many of which are entered in this dictionary under the key words

of- see OB-

off (of, ôf) *adv.* [LME. variant of *of*, OF] **1.** so as to be or keep away or at a distance [to move *off*, to ward *off*] **2.** so as to be measured, divided, etc. [to mark *off*] **3.** so as to be no longer on, attached, etc. [take *off* your hat] **4.** (a specified distance) away in space or time [200 yards *off*, two weeks *off*] **5.** so as to be no longer in operation, function, etc. [turn the motor *off*] **6.** so as to be less,

smaller, etc. [5 % *off* for cash] **7.** so as to lose consciousness [to doze *off*] **8.** away from one's work [take a day *off*] —*prep.* **1.** no longer (or not) on, attached, etc. [the car is *off* the road] **2.** away from [to live *off* the beaten track] **3.** *a)* from the substance of; on [to live *off* the land] *b)* at the expense of **4.** branching out from [a road *off* the High Street] **5.** free or relieved from [*off* duty] **6.** not up to the usual level, standard, etc. of [*off* one's game] **7.** [Colloq.] no longer using, supporting, etc. [to be *off* a diet] **8.** [Colloq.] from [to buy it *off* him] —*adj.* **1.** not on, attached, etc. [his hat is *off*] **2.** not in operation, function, etc. [the motor is *off*] **3.** on the way [be *off* to bed] **4.** less, smaller, etc. [sales are *off*] **5.** away from work, etc. [the maid is *off* today] **6.** not up to what is usual, standard, etc. [an *off* day] **7.** more remote; further [on the *off* chance] **8.** designating the horse on the right in double harness, etc. **9.** in (specified) circumstances [to be well *off*] **10.** not correct; in error [his figures are *off*] **11.** unfit for consumption; sour, rotten, etc. [the meat is *off*] **12.** *Cricket* designating the side of the field facing the batsman **13.** *Naut.* towards the sea —*n.* **1.** the fact or condition of being off **2.** *Horse Racing* the beginning of a race —*interj.* go away! stay away! —**a bit off** [Colloq.] **1.** slightly crazy **2.** irritating; unjust —**off and on** now and then —**off with!** take off! remove! —**off with you!** go away! depart! —**they're off!** a cry signifying that a race, esp. a horse race, has begun

off. **1.** office **2.** officer **3.** official

of·fal (of′'l) *n.* [ME. *ofall*, lit., off-fall] **1.** [*with sing. or pl. v.*] the entrails, etc. of a butchered animal **2.** refuse; garbage

off·beat (of′bēt′) *adj.* [< a rhythm in jazz music] [Colloq.] not conforming to the usual pattern or trend; unconventional, unusual, etc.

off-Broad·way (-brôd′wā′) *adj., adv.* outside the main commercial theatrical district in New York City —*n.* off-Broadway theatres and their productions Also written **Off Broadway**

off-col·our (-kul′ər) *adj.* **1.** varying from the usual, standard, or required colour **2.** not quite proper; risqué [an off-colour joke] **3.** slightly ill; unwell

off·cut (of′kut) *n.* an oddment of paper, timber etc. left after cutting that is usually sold at a lower price

of·fence (ə fens′) *n.* **1.** an offending; specif., *a)* a breaking of the law; sin or crime *b)* a creating of resentment, anger, etc. **2.** a being offended; esp. a feeling hurt, resentful, or angry **3.** [Rare] something that causes wrongdoing **4.** something that causes resentment, anger, etc. **5.** *a)* the act of attacking *b)* the action of seeking to score in any contest **6.** the person, army, etc. that is attacking —**give offence** to anger, insult, etc.; offend —**take offence** to become offended; feel hurt, angry, etc. —**of·fence′less** *adj.*

of·fend (ə fend′) *vi.* [< OFr. < L. *offendere* < *ob-* (see OB-) + *fendere*, to hit] **1.** to commit a sin or crime; do wrong **2.** to create resentment, anger, etc. —*vt.* **1.** to hurt the feelings of; make resentful, angry, etc. **2.** to be displeasing to (the taste, sense, etc.) —**of·fend′er** *n.* —**of·fend′ed·ly** *adv.*

of·fense (ə fens′) *n. U.S. sp. of* OFFENCE

of·fen·sive (ə fen′siv) *adj.* **1.** attacking; aggressive **2.** of or for attack **3.** unpleasant; disgusting; repugnant [an offensive odour] **4.** causing resentment, anger, etc.; insulting —*n.* **1.** attitude or position of attack **2.** an attack or hostile action, esp. by armed forces —**of·fen′sive·ly** *adv.* —**of·fen′sive·ness** *n.*

of·fer (of′ər) *vt.* [OE. *offrian* < LL. *offerre*, to sacrifice < *ob-* (see OB-) + *ferre*, to bring] **1.** to present in an act of worship [to offer prayers] **2.** to present for acceptance or consideration [to offer one's services, a suggestion, etc.] **3.** to express willingness or intention (to do something) [to offer to go] **4.** to show or give signs of [to offer resistance] **5.** *a)* to present for sale *b)* to bid (a price, etc.) —*vi.* **1.** to make a presentation in worship **2.** to occur; present itself [when the opportunity offers] —*n.* the act of offering or thing offered —**of′fer·er, of′fer·or** *n.*

of·fer·ing (-iŋ) *n.* **1.** the act of making an offer **2.** something offered; specif., *a)* a contribution *b)* a presentation made in an act of worship

of·fer·to·ry (of′ər tər ē) *n., pl.* **-ries** [< ML. < LL. *offertorium*, place for offerings < *offerre*, OFFER] [*often* O-] **1.** that part of Holy Communion during which the Eucharistic bread and wine are offered to God **2.** any collection of money at a church service, or the part of the service for this **3.** the prayers or music accompanying the offertory

off·hand (of′hand′) *adv.* without prior preparation; extemporaneously —*adj.* **1.** said or done offhand; extemporaneous **2.** casual, curt, etc. Also **off′hand′ed** —**off′hand′ed·ly** *adv.* —**off′hand′ed·ness** *n.*

of·fice (of′is) *n.* [< OFr. < L. *officium* < *opus*, a work + *facere*, to do] **1.** something done for another; (specified kind of) service [done through his good (or ill) offices] **2.** an assigned duty, esp. one that is an essential part of one's work; function; task **3.** a position of authority or trust, esp.

in a government, business, etc. **4.** a governmental department [the Foreign *Office*] **5.** a place where work or business that is clerical, administrative, professional, etc. is carried on **6.** a religious ceremony or rite; specif., a) [O-] *shortened form of* DIVINE OFFICE b) [often pl.] any special rites **7.** [pl] the rooms or buildings of a house or estate in which servants carry out their duties **8.** a hint or warning **9.** *a euphemistic term for* LAVATORY

office block a building, usually modern, containing premises of one or more businesses

office boy a boy who works in an office, doing odd jobs and errands

of·fi·cer (of'ə sər) *n.* **1.** anyone holding an office or position of authority in a government, business, society, etc. **2.** a policeman **3.** a person holding a position of authority in the armed forces; specif., *same as* COMMISSIONED OFFICER **4.** the captain or any of the mates of a nonnaval ship —*vt.* **1.** to provide with officers **2.** to command; direct

officer of the day the military officer in overall charge of the interior guard and security of his garrison for any given day

of·fi·cial (ə fish'əl) *adj.* **1.** of or holding an office, or position of authority **2.** by, from, or with the proper authority; authorized or authoritative [an *official* request] **3.** formal or ceremonious and often involving persons of authority **4.** formally set or prescribed [the *official* date of publication] —*n.* **1.** a person holding office **2.** *Sports* one who supervises an athletic contest —**of·fi′cial·ly** *adv.*

of·fi·cial·dom (-dəm) *n.* **1.** officials collectively **2.** the domain or position of officials

of·fi·cial·ese (ə fish'ə lēz') *n.* the pompous, wordy, and involved language typical of official communications and reports

of·fi·cial·ism (ə fish'əl iz'm) *n.* **1.** the characteristic, esp. bureaucratic, practices of officials **2.** officials collectively

Official Receiver a public official charged with certain duties in the winding-up of companies and the bankruptcy of individuals

of·fi·ci·ate (ə fish'ē āt') *vi.* -**at**'ed, -**at**'ing **1.** to perform the duties of an office **2.** to perform the functions of a priest, minister, rabbi, etc. at a religious ceremony **3.** *Sports* to act as referee, umpire, etc. —**of·fi′ci·a′tion** *n.* —**of·fi′ci·a′tor** *n.*

of·fi·cious (ə fish'əs) *adj.* [< L. < *officium*, OFFICE] offering unwanted advice or services; meddlesome —**of·fi′- cious·ly** *adv.* —**of·fi′cious·ness** *n.*

off·ing (ôf'iŋ) *n.* [< OFF] **1.** the distant part of the sea visible from the shore **2.** distance, or position at a distance, from the shore —**in the offing 1.** at some distance but in sight **2.** at some indefinite time in the future

off·ish (ôf'ish) *adj.* [Colloq.] aloof; standoffish —**off′ish·ly** *adv.* —**off′ish·ness** *n.*

off-key (ôf'kē') *adj.* **1.** not on the right note; flat or sharp **2.** not quite in accord with what is normal, fitting, etc.

off-li·cence (-līs′'ns) *n.* **1.** a shop, etc. where alcohol is sold in unopened containers for consumption elsewhere **2.** a licence permitting such sales

off-line (-līn') *adj.* designating equipment not directly controlled by the central processor of a computer

off-peak (-pēk') *adj.* of services used at times other than those of the highest demand [an *off-peak* railway return, an *off-peak* storage heater]

off-putting (-poot'iŋ) *adj.* tending to put one off; distracting, annoying, etc.

off·scour·ing (-skour'iŋ) *n.* [usually pl.] something scoured off; refuse, dregs, etc.

off·set (ôf'set'; *for v. usually* of set') *n.* **1.** an offshoot; extension; branch; spur **2.** anything that balances or compensates for something else **3.** a ledge formed in a wall by a reduction in its thickness above **4.** *Mech.* a bend in a pipe, etc. to permit it to pass an obstruction **5.** a) *same as* OFFSET PRINTING b) an impression made by this process —*adj.* **1.** of, relating to, or being an offset **2.** that is offset —*vt.* -**set**', -**set**'**ting 1.** to balance, compensate for, etc. **2.** to make an offset in **3.** to make (an impression) by offset printing —*vi.* to project or develop as an offset

offset printing a lithographic printing process in which the inked impression is first made on a rubber-covered roller, then transferred to paper

off·shoot (ôf'shoot') *n.* **1.** a shoot growing from the main stem of a plant **2.** anything that branches off, or derives from, a main source

off·shore (-shôr') *adj.* **1.** moving away from the shore **2.** at some distance from shore —*adv.* away from the shore

off·side (-sīd') *adj.* **1.** designating the side of a motor vehicle nearest the centre of the road [the *offside* headlight] **2.** *Sports* not in the proper position for play, as, in football, ahead of the ball when it is played

off-sid·er (-sī'dər) *n.* [Aust] a friend or companion

off·spring (-spriŋ') *n.*, *pl.* -**spring**', -**springs**' **1.** a child or animal as related to its parent **2.** progeny **3.** a result

off·stage (-stāj') *n.* that part of a stage, as the wings, not seen by the audience —*adj.* in or from the offstage —*adv.*

1. to the offstage **2.** when not actually appearing before the public

off-the-peg (-thə peg') *adj.* ready-to-wear, as opposed to made-to-order, said of clothing

off-white (-hwīt', -wīt') *adj.* of any of various shades of greyish-white or yellowish-white

OFr. Old French

oft (oft) *adv.* [OE.] *chiefly poet. var. of* OFTEN

of·ten (ôf'n, of't'n) *adv.* [ME. var. of prec.] many times; frequently —*adj.* [Archaic] frequent —**every so often** occasionally; from time to time

of·ten·times (-tīmz') *adv.* [Archaic] *same as* OFTEN: also [Chiefly Poet.] oft′times'

o·gee (ō'jē, ō jē') *n.* [< OFr. *ogive*] **1.** an S-shaped curve, line, moulding, etc. **2.** a pointed arch formed with the curve of an ogee on each side: also **ogee arch**

og·ham (og'əm) *n.* [Ir. < OFr. *ogam*] an ancient Irish alphabet of twenty characters: also **og′am**

o·gle (ō'g'l) *vi.*, *vt.* **o′gled**, **o′gling** [prob. < LowG. *oegeln* < *oog*, the eye] to keep looking (at) boldly and with obvious desire; make eyes (at) —*n.* an ogling look —**o′gler** *n.*

OGEE ARCH

o·gre (ō'gər) *n.* [Fr. < ? L. *Orcus*, Pluto, Hades] **1.** in fairy tales and folklore, a man-eating monster or giant **2.** a hideous or cruel man —**o′gre·ish**, **o′grish** *adj.* —**o′gress** *n.fem.*

oh (ō) *interj.* **1.** an exclamation of surprise, fear, wonder, pain, etc. **2.** a word used in direct address [oh, waiter!] —*n.*, *pl.* **oh's**, **ohs** any instance of this exclamation

OHG, OHG., O.H.G. Old High German

ohm (ōm) *n.* [after G. S. Ohm (1789-1854), G. physicist] the SI unit of electrical resistance, equal to the resistance of a circuit in which an electromotive force of one volt maintains a current of one ampere —**ohm′ic** *adj.*

ohm·me·ter (-mēt'ər) *n.* an instrument for measuring directly electrical resistance in ohms

ohm's law a law which states that the electric current through a conductor is directly proportional to the potential difference across it, and inversely proportional to the resistance of the conductor

O.H.M.S. On Her (or His) Majesty's Service

o·ho (ō hō') *interj.* [ME. *o ho!*: cf. O & HO] an exclamation expressing surprise, taunting, triumph, etc.

-oid (oid) [< Gr. < *eidos*, a form, shape] *a suffix meaning* like, resembling [crystalloid]

oil (oil) *n.* [< OFr. < L. *oleum* < Gr. *elaion*, (olive) oil] **1.** any of various greasy, combustible substances obtained from animal, vegetable, and mineral sources: oils are liquid at ordinary temperatures and soluble in certain organic solvents, as ether, but not in water **2.** *same as* PETROLEUM **3.** any of various substances with the consistency of oil **4.** *same as:* a) OIL COLOUR b) OIL PAINTING **5.** [Aust. & N.Z. Slang] news —*vt.* **1.** to lubricate or supply with oil **2.** to bribe [to *oil* someone's palm] —*adj.* of, from, or like oil, or having to do with the production or use of oil —**oil the wheels** to make things go more smoothly —**oil′er** *n.*

oil bomb a bomb containing oil that bursts into flames upon impact

oil cake a mass of crushed linseed, cottonseed, etc. from which the oil has been extracted, used as livestock feed and as a fertilizer

oil·cloth (-kloth') *n.* cloth made waterproof with oil or with heavy coats of paint

oil colour paint made by grinding a pigment in oil

oiled (oild) *adj.* **1.** treated with oil **2.** drunk, esp. in phrase **well oiled**

oil field a place where oil deposits of value are found, esp. one that is already being exploited

oil-fired (-fīrd') *adj.* using oil as a fuel [oil-fired central heating]

oil of vitriol *same as* SULPHURIC ACID

oil painting 1. a picture painted in oil colours **2.** the art of painting in oil colours

oil·pa·per (-pā'pər) *n.* paper made transparent and waterproof by treatment with oil

oil·skin (-skin') *n.* **1.** cloth made waterproof by treatment with oil **2.** [often pl.] a garment or outfit made of this

oil slick a film of oil on water, forming a smooth area

oil·stone (-stōn') *n.* a whetstone treated with oil

oil well a well bored through layers of rock, etc. to a supply of petroleum

oil·y (-ē) *adj.* **oil′i·er**, **oil′i·est 1.** of, like, or containing oil **2.** covered with oil; greasy **3.** too smooth; unctuous —**oil′- i·ly** *adv.* —**oil′i·ness** *n.*

oink (oiŋk) *n.* the grunt of a pig, or a sound imitating it —*vi.* to grunt as or like a pig

oint·ment (oint'mənt) *n.* [< OFr., ult. < L. *unguentum*: see UNGUENT] a fatty substance applied to the skin as a salve or cosmetic; unguent

Oir·each·tas (er'əkh təs) *n.* [Ir] the legislature of Ireland, consisting of the Dail Eireann (lower house) and the Seanad Eireann (upper house)

OK, O.K. (ō′kā′; *also, & for v. & n. usually,* ō′kā′) *adj., adv., interj.* [abbrev. for "oll korrect," jocular misspelling of *all correct:* popularized by use in name of Democratic *O.K.* Club in allusion to *Old Kinderhook,* native village of Martin Van Buren, the Democratic candidate for president] all right; correct —*n., pl.* **OK's, O.K.'s** approval —*vt.* **OK'd, O.K.'d, OK'ing, O.K.'ing** to put an OK on; approve

o·ka·pi (ō kä′pē) *n., pl.* **-pis, -pi:** see PLURAL, II, D, 1 [native Afr. name] an African animal related to the giraffe, but having a much shorter neck

o·kay (ō′kā′) *adj., adv., interj., n., vt. colloq. var. of* OK

o·kra (ō′krə) *n.* [< WAfr. name] 1. a tall plant with slender, ribbed, sticky green pods 2. the pods, used as a cooked vegetable, in soups, etc.

-ol¹ (ōl, ol) [< (ALCH)OL] *a suffix used in chemistry to mean* an alcohol or phenol [menthol]

-ol² (ōl, ôl) *var. of* -OLE

OL., O.L. Old Latin

OKAPI
(to 1.5 m high at shoulder)

old (ōld) *adj.* **old′er** or **eld′er, old′- est** or **eld′est** [OE. *ald*] 1. having lived or existed for a long time; aged 2. of or characteristic of aged people 3. of a certain age [a boy ten years *old*] 4. made some time ago; not new 5. known from the past [up to his *old* tricks] 6. [*often* O-] designating the earliest stage of a language [*Old* English] 7. worn out by age or use; shabby 8. former 9. having had long experience [an *old* hand at this work] 10. having existed long ago; ancient [an *old* civilization] 11. of long standing [an *old* joke] 12. designating the earlier or earliest of two or more [the *Old* World] 13. [Colloq.] dear: a term of affection [*old* boy] Also used as a colloquial intensive [a fine *old* time] —*n.* 1. time long past; yore [days of *old*] 2. a person of a specified age: used in hyphenated compounds [a six-year-*old*] 3. something old (with *the*) —**old′ish** *adj.* —**old′ness** *n.*

old age the advanced years of life, when strength and vigour decline: cf. MIDDLE AGE

old age pension a state pension paid to older people upon retirement —**old age pensioner**

Old Bailey popular name for the Central Criminal Court, London

Old Boy [*often* o- b-] [Colloq.] 1. a male ex-pupil of a school 2. *a)* familiar name used to refer to a man *b)* an old man Also **old girl** *fem.*

Old Contemptibles the British Expeditionary Force of 1914

old country the country from which an immigrant came

old·en (ōl′d'n) *adj.* [Poet.] (of) old; ancient

Old English the West Germanic, Low German language of the Anglo-Saxons, spoken in England from c. 400 to c. 1100 A.D.

old-fash·ioned (ōld′fash′ənd) *adj.* suited to or favouring the styles, ideas, etc. of past times; out-of-date —*n.* [U.S.] [*also* O- F-] a cocktail made with whisky, soda water, bitters, sugar, and fruit

old fogy, old fogey *see* FOGY

Old French the French language from c. 800 to c. 1550 A.D., esp. from the 9th to the 14th century

Old Guard [after Napoleon's imperial guard (1804)] 1. any group that has long defended a cause 2. the conservative element of a group, party, etc.

old hat [Slang] 1. old-fashioned 2. well-known to the point of being trite or commonplace

Old High German the High German language from the 8th to the 12th century

Old Hundredth a well-known setting of the hundredth psalm

old·ie, old·y (ōl′dē) *n., pl.* **old′ies** [Colloq.] an old joke, song, film, etc.

Old Irish Irish Gaelic before the 11th century

old lady [Slang] 1. one's mother 2. one's wife

Old Lady of Threadneedle Street the Bank of England

Old Latin the Latin language before c. 75 B.C.

Old Low German the Low German language from its earliest period to the 12th century A.D.

old maid 1. a woman, esp. an older woman, who has never married; spinster 2. a prim, prudish, fussy person —**old′-maid′ish** *adj.*

old man [Slang] 1. one's father 2. one's husband 3. [*usually* O- M-] any man in authority, as the head of a company, captain of a vessel, etc.

old man kangaroo [Aust.] a large male kangaroo

old master 1. any great European painter before the 18th cent. 2. a painting by any of these

old moon the moon in its last quarter, when it appears as a crescent curving to the left

Old Nick [prob. contr. < *Nicholas,* a masculine name] the Devil; Satan: also **Old Harry**

Old Norman French *same as* NORMAN FRENCH

Old Norse the North Germanic language of the Scandinavian peoples before the 14th century

Old Prussian a Baltic language which became extinct in the 17th century

old rose greyish or purplish red —**old′-rose′** *adj.*

Old Saxon a West Germanic language known chiefly from manuscripts of the 9th and 10th centuries A.D.

old school a group of people who cling to traditional or conservative ideas, methods, etc.

old school tie 1. a necktie striped in the distinctive colours of any of the British public schools 2. the system of mutual aid supposed to operate among former pupils of British public schools 3. the clannishness, etc. associated with this system

Old South the South of the U.S. before the Civil War

old·ster (ōld′stər) *n.* [Colloq.] a person who is no longer a youngster; old or elderly person

old style 1. an old style of type with narrow, light letters 2. [O- S-] the old method of reckoning time according to the Julian calendar, which was off one day every 128 years —**old′-style′** *adj.*

Old Testament *Christian designation for* the Holy Scriptures of Judaism, the first of the two general divisions of the Christian Bible

old-time (ōld′tīm′) *adj.* 1. of or like past times 2. of long standing or experience

old-tim·er (-tī′mər) *n.* [U.S. Colloq.] 1. a longtime resident, employee, etc. 2. an old-fashioned person

old wives' tale a silly story or superstition such as gossipy old women might pass around

old-wom·an·ish (-woom′ən ish) *adj.* like, typical of, or suitable for an old woman; fussy

Old World the Eastern Hemisphere, often esp. Europe —**old′-world′** *adj.*

-ole (ōl) [< L. *oleum,* oil] *a suffix used in chemistry indicating:* 1. a five-member, closed-chain compound 2. a compound without hydroxyl

o·le·ag·i·nous (ō′lē aj′i nəs) *adj.* [< Fr. < L. < *olea,* olive tree] oily; unctuous —**o′le·ag′i·nous·ness** *n.*

o·le·an·der (ō′lē an′dər) *n.* [ML.] a poisonous evergreen shrub with fragrant white, pink, or red flowers

o·le·ate (ō′lē āt′) *n.* a salt or ester of oleic acid

o·le·ic (ō lē′ik, ō′lē-) *adj.* [< L. *oleum,* oil + -IC] 1. of or from oil 2. of oleic acid

oleic acid an oily acid, present in most fats and oils as an ester, used in soaps, etc.

o·le·in (ō′lē in) *n.* [< Fr. < L. *oleum,* an oil] 1. a liquid glyceride, present in olive oil, etc. 2. the liquid part of a fat

o·le·o- [< L. *oleum,* an oil] *a combining form meaning* oil, olein, or oleic [oleomargarine]

o·le·o·mar·ga·rine, o·le·o·mar·ga·rin (ō′lē ō mär′jə rin) *n.* [< Fr.: see prec. & MARGARINE] [U.S.] *full name of* MARGARINE

o·le·o·res·in (ō′lē ō rez′'n) *n.* 1. a mixture of a resin and an essential oil, as turpentine, occurring naturally in various plants 2. a prepared solution of resin in an essential oil

o·le·um (ō′lē əm) *n., pl.* **o·le·a, o·le·ums** [L. *oleum,* oil] a solution of sulphur trioxide in concentrated sulphuric acid, forming a highly corrosive oily liquid

'O' level *clipped form of* ORDINARY LEVEL

ol·fac·tion (ol fak′shən, ōl-) *n.* [see ff.] 1. the sense of smell 2. the act of smelling

ol·fac·to·ry (-tər ē, -trē) *adj.* [< L. pp. of *olfacere,* to smell < *olere,* to have a smell + *facere,* to make] of the sense of smell: also **ol·fac′tive** —*n., pl.* **-ries** [*usually pl.*] an organ of smell

OLG, OLG., O.L.G. Old Low German

ol·i·garch (ol′ə gärk′) *n.* any of the rulers of an oligarchy

ol·i·gar·chy (-gär′kē) *n., pl.* **-chies** [Gr. *oligarchia:* see OLIGO- & -ARCHY] 1. a form of government with the ruling power belonging to a few 2. a state so governed 3. those ruling such a state —**ol′i·gar′chic, ol′i·gar′chi·cal, ol′i·gar′- chal** (-k'l) *adj.*

ol·i·go- [Gr. < *oligos,* small] *a combining form meaning* few, small, a deficiency of: also **olig-**

Ol·i·go·cene (ol′ə gō sēn′) *adj.* [< prec. + Gr. *kainos,* new] designating or of the third epoch of the Tertiary Period in the Cainozoic Era —**the Oligocene** the Oligocene Epoch or its rocks: see GEOLOGY, chart

ol·i·gop·o·ly (ol′ə gop′ə lē) *n., pl.* **-lies** [OLIG(O)-+ (MON)OPOLY] control of a commodity or service by a few companies or suppliers —**ol′i·gop′o·list** *n.* —**ol′i·gop′o·lis′- tic** *adj.*

o·li·o (ō′lē ō′) *n., pl.* **o′li·os′** [< Sp. *olla:* see OLLA] 1. a spicy stew 2. a medley or miscellany

ol·ive (ol′iv) *n.* [OFr. < L. *oliva* < Gr. *elaia*] 1. *a)* an evergreen tree of the olive family, native to S Europe and the Near East, with an edible fruit *b)* the small, oval fruit, eaten green or ripe, or pressed to extract its oil *c)* the wood of this tree 2. an olive branch or wreath 3. the dull, yellowish-green colour of the unripe fruit —*adj.* 1. of the olive 2. olive-coloured 3. designating a family of trees and shrubs with loose clusters of four-parted flowers, including the olives, ashes, lilacs, etc.

olive branch 1. the branch of the olive tree, a symbol of peace 2. any peace offering

olive drab 1. a shade of greenish brown 2. woollen cloth dyed this colour and used for U.S. Army uniforms 3. [*pl.*] such a uniform —**ol′ive-drab′** *adj.*

olive oil a light-yellow oil pressed from ripe olives, used in cooking, soap, etc.

ol·i·vine (ol′ə vēn′) *n.* [OLIV(E) + -INE⁴] a green silicate of magnesium and iron

ol·la (ol′ə; *Sp.* ôl′yä) *n.* [Sp. < L.] 1. a large-mouthed pot or jar 2. a spicy stew

ol·o·gy (ol′ə jē) *n., pl.* **-gies** [< -LOGY] a branch of learning; science: humorous usage

o·lo·ro·so (ō′lə rō′sō) *n., pl.* **-sos** [< Sp. *oloroso*, sweet-smelling] a medium-sweet sherry

O·lym·pi·ad (ō lim′pē ad′) *n.* [after the plain in Greece where the first Olympic Games were held] [*often* o-] 1. in ancient Greece, a four-year period between Olympic games 2. a celebration of the modern Olympic Games 3. an international contest in chess, mathematics, etc.

O·lym·pi·an (-ən) *n.* 1. *Gr. Myth.* any of the gods on Mount Olympus 2. a native of Olympia —*adj.* 1. of Olympia or Mount Olympus 2. exalted; majestic 3. of the ancient Olympic games

O·lym·pic (ō lim′pik, ə-) *adj.* *same as* OLYMPIAN —*n.* [*pl.*] the Olympic games (preceded by *the*)

Olympic games 1. an ancient Greek festival with contests in athletics, poetry, and music, held every four years at Olympia to honour Zeus 2. a modern international athletic competition generally held every four years in a selected city: usually athletics, swimming, etc. at one place and winter sports at another site and time

O.M. Order of Merit

-o·ma (ō′mə) [ModL. < Gr. *-ōma*]¯ a suffix *meaning* tumour [*sarcoma*]

o·ma·sum (ō mā′səm) *n., pl.* **-sa** (-sə) [ModL. < L., bullock's tripe < Gaul.] the third division in the stomach of a cud-chewing animal, as the cow

om·buds·man (om′bədz mən) *n., pl.* **-men** [Sw.] a public official appointed to investigate citizens' complaints against government officials, etc. that may be infringing on the rights of individuals

o·me·ga (ō′mə gə) *n.* [Gr. *o mega*, lit., great (i.e., long) *o*] 1. the twenty-fourth and final letter of the Greek alphabet (Ω, ω) 2. the last (of any series); end

om·e·lette, om·e·let (om′lit, om′ə let) *n.* [< Fr., ult. < L. *lamella*, small plate] eggs beaten up, often with water, cooked as a pancake in a frying pan and served usually folded over and often with a filling, as of mushrooms or jam

o·men (ō′mən) *n.* [L.] a thing or happening supposed to foretell a future event, either good or evil; augury —*vt.* to be an omen of; augur

om·i·cron, om·i·kron (ō mī′krən) *n.* [Gr. *o mikron*, lit., small *o*] the fifteenth letter of the Greek alphabet (O, o)

om·i·nous (om′ə nəs) *adj.* [L. *ominosus*] of or serving as an evil omen; threatening; sinister —**om′i·nous·ly** *adv.* —**om′-i·nous·ness** *n.*

o·mis·si·ble (ō mis′ə b'l) *adj.* that can be omitted

o·mis·sion (ō mish′ən) *n.* [< LL. *omissio*] 1. an omitting or being omitted 2. anything omitted

o·mit (ō mit′) *vt.* **o·mit′ted, o·mit′ting** [< L. *omittere* < *ob-* (see OB-) + *mittere*, to send] 1. to fail to include; leave out 2. to fail to do; neglect —**o·mit′ter** *n.*

om·ni- [L. < *omnis*, all] a combining form meaning all, everywhere [*omniscient*]

om·ni·bus (om′nə bəs, -ni bus′) *n., pl.* **-bus·es** [Fr. < L., lit., for all] 1. *same as* BUS (sense 1) 2. a one-volume collection of previously published works —*adj.* providing for many things at once

om·ni·far·i·ous (om′nə fer′ē əs) *adj.* [< L. *omnifarius* < *omnis*, all + *fari*, to speak] of all kinds, varieties, or forms

om·nif·ic (om nif′ik) *adj.* [ML. *omnificus* < L. *omnis*, all + *facere*, to make] creating all things: also **om·nif′i·cent** (-ə sənt)

om·nip·o·tence (om nip′ə təns) *n.* 1. the state or quality of being omnipotent 2. [O-] God

om·nip·o·tent (-tənt) *adj.* [OFr. < L. < *omnis*, all + *potens*, able] having unlimited power or authority; all-powerful —**the Omnipotent** God —**om·nip′o·tent·ly** *adv.*

om·ni·pres·ent (om′ni prez′ənt) *adj.* [< ML. < L. *omnis*, all + *praesens*, present] present in all places at the same time —**om′ni·pres′ence** *n.*

om·nis·cient (om nish′ənt, om nis′ə-) *adj.* [< ML. < L. *omnis*, all + prp. of *scire*, to know] knowing all things —**the Omniscient** God —**om·nis′cience** *n.* —**om·nis′cient·ly** *adv.*

om·ni·um-gath·er·um (om′nē əm ga*th*′ər əm) *n.* [L. *omnium*, all + Latinized form of GATHER] a miscellaneous collection of persons or things

om·niv·o·rous (om niv′ər əs) *adj.* [< L.: see OMNI- & -VOROUS] 1. eating any sort of food 2. taking in everything indiscriminately [an *omnivorous* reader] —**om·niv′o·rous·ly** *adv.* —**om·niv′o·rous·ness** *n.*

on (on) *prep.* [OE. *on, an*] 1. above, but in contact with and supported by; upon 2. in contact with; covering or attached 3. so as to be supported by [to lean *on* one's elbow] 4. in the surface of 5. near to [a cottage *on* the lake] 6. at the time of [*on* entering] 7. with (something specified) as the basis [*on* purpose] 8. connected with, as a part [*on* the committee] 9. engaged in [*on* a trip] 10. in a state of [*on* parole] 11. as a result of [a profit *on* the sale] 12. in the direction of [a light shone *on* us] 13. so as to affect [to put a curse *on* someone] 14. through the use or medium of [to live *on* bread] 15. concerning [an essay *on* war] 16. coming after [insult *on* insult] 17. [Colloq.] chargeable to [a drink *on* the house] 18. [Slang] using; addicted to [to be *on* drugs] 19. [Aust. Slang] at; in [to be *on* Ballarat] —*adv.* 1. in a situation of contacting, being supported by, or covering [put your shoes *on*] 2. in a direction toward [looked *on*] 3. forward; ahead [move *on*] 4. continuously [she sang *on*] 5. into operation or action [turn the light *on*] 6. *Theatre* on stage —*adj.* 1. in action or operation [the TV is *on*] 2. planned for [tomorrow's game is still *on*] 3. easily possible [his getting the post is *on*] —*n.* the fact or state of being on —**and so on** and more like the preceding —**be on at** [Colloq.] to nag —**on and off** intermittently —**on and on** continuously —**on time** promptly; punctually —**on to** [Colloq.] 1. aware of, esp. aware of the real nature of 2. nagging

-on (on) a suffix *designating:* 1. [< *-on* in *argon*] an inert gas [*radon*] 2. [< *-on* in *ion*] a subatomic particle [*electron*]

ON., ON, O.N. Old Norse

on·a·ger (on′ə jər) *n., pl.* **-gri′** (-grī′), **-gers** [ME. < L. < Gr. *onagros*, wild ass] 1. a wild ass of C Asia 2. a catapult for throwing stones, used in ancient and medieval warfare

o·nan·ism (ō′nə niz'm) *n.* [< *Onan* (Gen. 38:9)] 1. withdrawal in coition before ejaculation 2. masturbation —**o′nan·ist** *n.* —**o′nan·is′tic** *adj.*

O.N.C. Ordinary National Certificate

once (wuns) *adv.* [ME. *ones*, gen. of *on*, ONE] 1. one time; one time only 2. at any time; ever 3. formerly 4. by one degree [a cousin *once* removed] —*conj.* as soon as; if ever —*adj.* former —*n.* one time [go this *once*] —**all at once** 1. all at the same time 2. suddenly —**at once** 1. immediately 2. at the same time —**for once** for at least one time —**once and again** repeatedly —**once (and) for all** finally; decisively —**once in a while** occasionally —**once or twice** a few times —**once upon a time** long ago

once-o·ver (wuns′ō′vər) *n.* [Colloq.] 1. a swiftly appraising glance 2. a quick cleaning or going-over

onc·er (wuns′ər) *n.* [ONCE + -ER] [Slang] a £1 note

on·com·ing (on′kum′iŋ) *adj.* approaching [*oncoming* traffic] —*n.* approach

O.N.D. Ordinary National Diploma

on dit (oṅ′dē′) *n.* [Fr.] a rumour; gossip; hearsay

one (wun) *adj.* [OE. *an*] 1. being a single thing 2. forming a whole; united 3. designating a person or thing as contrasted with another [from *one* day to another] 4. being uniquely the person or thing specified [the *one* solution to the problem] 5. single in kind; the same [all of *one* mind] 6. a certain but unspecified [*one* day last week] —*n.* 1. the number expressing unity or designating a single unit; the first and lowest cardinal number; 1; I 2. a single person or thing 3. anything consisting of a single unit or numbered one —*pron.* 1. some or a certain person or thing 2. any person or thing 3. the person or thing previously mentioned —**all one** making no difference —**at one** in accord —**for one** an intensifier used in place of myself, himself, etc. [I, *for one*, couldn't go] —**one and all** everybody —**one another** each one the other; each other: see EACH OTHER, under EACH —**one of those things** something inevitable

-one (ōn) [arbitrary use of Gr. *-ōnē*] a suffix *used in chemistry, meaning* a ketone [*acetone*]

one-armed bandit (-ärmd′) [Slang] a term for a slot machine used for gambling

one-horse (wun′hôrs′) *adj.* 1. drawn by or using one horse 2. [U.S. Colloq.] small, unimportant, etc.

o·nei·ric (ō nī′rik) *adj.* [< Gr. *oneiros*, a dream + -IC] of or having to do with dreams

one·ness (wun′nis) *n.* 1. singleness; unity 2. unity of mind, feeling, etc. 3. sameness; identity

one-night stand (wun′nīt′) a single appearance in a town by a travelling show, lecturer, etc.

one-off (-off′) *n.* something that is carried out or made only once —*adj.* of something done only once [a *one-off* job]

on·er·ous (on′ər əs, ō′nər-) *adj.* [< MFr. < L. *onerosus* < *onus*, a load] burdensome; oppressive —**on′er·ous·ly** *adv.* —**on′er·ous·ness** *n.*

one·self (wun′self′, wunz′-) *pron.* a person's own self:

also **one's self** —**be oneself** 1. to function normally 2. to be natural —**by oneself** alone; unaccompanied —**come to oneself** to recover one's senses or capacity for judgment

one-sid·ed (wun'sīd'id) *adj.* 1. on, having, or involving only one side 2. larger, heavier, etc. on one side; lopsided 3. favouring one side; unfair 4. uneven or unequal [a *one-sided* race] —**one'sid'ed·ly** *adv.* —**one'sid'ed·ness** *n.*

one-step (-step') *n.* an old ballroom dance with quick walking steps in 2/4 time —*vi.* -**stepped'**, -**step'ping** to dance the one-step

one-time (-tīm') *adj.* at a past time; former

one-to-one (wun'tə wun') *adj.* 1. permitting the pairing of an element of one group uniquely with a corresponding element of another group 2. *Math.* with each member of one set having a partner in the other set

one-track (wun'trak') *adj.* 1. having a single track 2. [Colloq.] able or willing to deal with only one thing at a time [a *one-track* mind]

one-up (-up') *adj.* [Colloq.] having an advantage (over another): often in **be one-up on** —**one'-up'man·ship** *n.*

one-way (-wā') *adj.* 1. moving, or allowing movement, in one direction only [a *one-way* street] 2. without reciprocal action or obligation

on·go·ing (on'gō'in) *adj.* going on; in process

on·ion (un'yən) *n.* [< OFr. < L. *unio*, a kind of single onion] 1. a plant of the lily family with an edible bulb of close, concentric layers and of strong, sharp smell and taste 2. the bulb —**know one's onions** [Colloq.] to be fully acquainted with a subject —**off one's onion** [Slang] to be crazy

on·ion·skin (-skin') *n.* a tough, thin, translucent paper, often used for carbon copies

on-line (on'līn') *adj.* of equipment directly connected to and controlled by the computer unit that interprets and executes instructions

on·look·er (on'look'ər) *n.* one who watches without taking part; spectator —**on'look'ing** *adj., n.*

on·ly (ōn'lē) *adj.* [OE. *anlic* < *an*, one + *-lic*, -LY[1]] 1. alone of its or their kind; sole 2. alone in superiority; best —*adv.* 1. and no other; and no (or nothing) more; solely [drink water *only*] 2. (but) in what follows or at the end [to meet one crisis, *only* to face another] 3. as recently as [*only* last autumn] —*conj.* [Colloq.] except that; but [I'd go, *only* it's late] —**if . . . only** would that; I wish that —**only too** very

o.n.o. or nearest offer

on·o·mat·o·poe·ia (on'ə mat'ə pē'ə) *n.* [LL. < Gr. < *onoma*, a name + *poiein*, to make] 1. formation of a word by imitating the sound associated with an object or action (Ex.: *buzz*) 2. the use of such words, as in poetry —**on'o·mat·o·poe'ic**, **on'o·mat'o·po·et'ic** (-pō et'ik) *adj.*

ONormFr. Old Norman French

on·rush (on'rush') *n.* a headlong dash forwards; strong onward rush —**on'rush'ing** *adj.*

on·set (-set') *n.* 1. an attack 2. a beginning

on·shore (-shôr') *adj.* 1. moving onto or towards the shore 2. on land [an *onshore* patrol] —*adv.* towards the shore; landward

on·slaught (-slôt') *n.* [< Du. *annslag* < *slagen*, to strike] a violent, intense attack

on·to (on'tōō; -tə) *prep.* 1. to a position on 2. [Slang] aware of the real nature, etc. of [he's *onto* our schemes] Also **on to**

on·to- [< Gr. prp. of *einai*, to be] a combining form meaning: 1. being; existence 2. organism

on·tog·e·ny (on toj'ə nē) *n.* [prec. + -GENY] the development of an individual organism: distinguished from PHYLOGENY: also **on·to·gen·e·sis** (on'tə jen'ə sis) —**on'to·ge·net'ic** (-jə net'ik), **on'to·gen'ic** *adj.*

on·tol·o·gy (on tol'ə jē) *n.* the study of the nature of being or reality —**on·to·log·i·cal** (on'tə loj'i k'l) *adj.* —**on'to·log'i·cal·ly** *adv.* —**on·tol'o·gist** *n.*

o·nus (ō'nəs) *n.* [L.] 1. a hard or unpleasant task, duty, etc.; burden 2. responsibility for a wrong; blame 3. [clip. of L. *onus probandi;* burden of proving] same as BURDEN OF PROOF

on·ward (on'wərd) *adv.* towards or at a position ahead; forwards: also **on'wards** —*adj.* moving or directed ahead; advancing

on·yx (on'iks; *occas.* ō'niks) *n.* [< OFr. < L. < Gr. *onyx*, nail, claw: its colour resembles that of the fingernail] 1. a variety of agate with alternate coloured layers 2. a translucent, often banded, stalagmitic calcite: also **onyx marble**

o·o- [< Gr. *ōion*] a combining form meaning egg or ovum

oo·dles (ōō'd'lz) *n.pl.* [< ? HUDDLE] [Colloq.] a great amount; very many

o·o·lite (ō'ə līt') *n.* [< Fr.: see OO- & -LITE] 1. a tiny calcium carbonate particle with concentric layers, formed in the sea: also **o'o·lith** (-lith) 2. a rock of these —**o'o·lit'ic** (-lit'ik) *adj.*

o·ol·o·gy (ō ol'ə jē) *n.* [OO- + -LOGY] the study of birds' eggs —**o·o·log·i·cal** (ō'ə loj'i k'l) *adj.* —**o·ol'o·gist** *n.*

oo·long (ōō'lôn) *n.* [< Chin. *wulung*, lit., black dragon] a dark Chinese tea, partly fermented before being dried

oo·mi·ac, oo·mi·ak (ōō'mē ak') *n.* same as UMIAK

oom·pah, oom-pah (ōōm'pä') *n.* [echoic] the sound of a repeated, rhythmic bass figure played in a brass band —*adj.* of this sound Also **oom'-pah'-pah'**

oomph (ōōmf) *n.* [< ?] [Slang] 1. sex appeal 2. vigour; energy

o·o·pho·ro- (ō'ə fərō') [< Gr. *ōion*, an egg + *-phoros*, bearing] a combining form meaning ovary or ovaries: also, before a vowel, **oophor-**

oops (ōōps, oops) *interj.* same as WHOOPS

ooze[1] (ōōz) *n.* [OE. *wos*, sap] an oozing or something that oozes —*vi.* **oozed, ooz'ing** 1. to flow or leak out slowly, as through tiny holes; seep 2. to give forth moisture, as through pores —*vt.* to exude

ooze[2] (ōōz) *n.* [OE. *wase*] 1. soft mud or slime; esp., the sediment at the bottom of a lake, ocean, etc. 2. a muddy area; bog

oo·zle (ōō'z'l) *vt.* -**zled'**, -**zl'ing** [< ?] [Aust. Slang] to steal from someone

oo·zy[1] (ōō'zē) *adj.* -**zi·er**, -**zi·est** oozing moisture —**oo'zi·ly** *adv.* —**oo'zi·ness** *n.*

oo·zy[2] (ōō'zē) *adj.* -**zi·er**, -**zi·est** full of or like ooze; slimy —**oo'zi·ly** *adv.* —**oo'zi·ness** *n.*

op- see OB-

op. 1. opera 2. operation 3. opposite 4. opus

O.P. Order of Preachers (Dominicans)

O.P., OP, o.p., *op* 1. out of print 2. *Philately* over-print

o·pac·i·ty (ō pas'ə tē) *n.* 1. opaque state, quality, or degree 2. *pl.* -**ties** an opaque thing

o·pal (ō'p'l) *n.* [< L. < Gr. *opallios* < Sans. *upala*, precious stone] an amorphous silica, of various colours, typically iridescent: some varieties are used as semiprecious stones

o·pal·es·cent (ō'pə les'ənt) *adj.* iridescent like opal —**o'pal·esce'** *vi.* -**esced'**, -**esc'ing** —**o'pal·es'cence** *n.*

o·pal·ine (ō'pə lēn', -līn') *adj.* of or like opal —*n.* a translucent, milky glass

o·paque (ō pāk') *adj.* [L. *opacus*, shady] 1. not letting light through 2. not reflecting light or not shining 3. hard to understand; obscure 4. slow in understanding; obtuse —*n.* anything opaque —*vt.* **o·paqued'**, **o·paqu'ing** to make opaque —**o·paque'ly** *adv.* —**o·paque'ness** *n.*

op (**art**) (op) [< OP(TICAL)] a style of abstract painting using geometrical patterns to create various optical effects and illusions

op. cit. [L. *opere citato*] in the work cited

ope (ōp) *adj., vt., vi.* **oped, op'ing** [Poet.] open

OPEC (ō'pek) Organization of Petroleum Exporting Countries: also **O.P.E.C.**

o·pen (ō'p'n) *adj.* [OE.] 1. allowing access, entrance, or exit; not closed or shut 2. allowing freedom of view or passage; unenclosed or unobstructed 3. unsealed; unwrapped 4. *a)* not covered *b)* unprotected or undefended 5. spread out; unfolded 6. having spaces, gaps, etc. [open ranks] 7. free from ice 8. *a)* not excluding anyone [an *open* meeting] *b)* ready to admit customers, clients, etc. 9. free to be argued; not settled [an *open* question] 10. *a)* not prejudiced or narrow-minded *b)* liberal; generous 11. socially mobile, politically free, etc. [an *open* society] 12. in force or operation [an *open* account] 13. *a)* not already taken or engaged [the job is *open*] *b)* free to be accepted or rejected 14. accessible; available 15. not secret; public 16. frank; candid 17. *Music a)* not stopped by the finger: said of a string *b)* not closed at the top: said of an organ pipe *c)* produced by an open string or pipe or without a slide or key: said of a tone *d)* not muted 18. *Phonetics a)* low *b)* fricative *c)* ending in a vowel or diphthong: said of a syllable —*vt.* 1. to make open, or no longer closed, shut, obstructed, etc. 2. *a)* to make an opening in *b)* to produce (a hole, way, etc.) 3. to spread out; expand 4. to expose (to an influence or action) 5. to make available without restriction, fee, etc. 6. to reveal; disclose 7. to begin (bidding, a session, etc.) 8. to start operating, going, etc. [to open a new shop] —*vi.* 1. to become open 2. to spread out; expand; unfold 3. to become revealed, disclosed, etc. 4. to give access (with *to, into, on*, etc.) 5. to begin; start 6. to start operating, going, etc.; specif., in the stock exchange, to show an indicated initial price level [steel *opened* high] 7. to begin a series of performances, games, etc. —*n.* [usually O-] any of various golf tournaments for both professionals and amateurs —**be open with** to communicate frankly with —**open out** 1. to expand 2. to develop 3. to reveal —**open to** 1. willing to receive, discuss, etc. 2. liable to 3. available or accessible to or for —**open up** 1. to make or become open 2. to unfold 3. to start; begin 4. [Colloq.] to begin firing a gun or guns 5. [Colloq.] to speak freely 6. [Colloq.] to go or make go faster —**the open** 1. any open, unobstructed area 2. the outdoors 3. public knowledge —**o'pened** *adj.* —**o'pen·er** *n.* —**o'pen·ly** *adv.* —**o'pen·ness** *n.*

open access a system in a library where the public is able to remove the books from the shelves: also chiefly U.S. **open shelf**

open air the outdoors —**o'pen·air'** *adj.*

o·pen-and-shut (ō'p'n 'n shut') *adj.* easily decided; obvious [an *open-and-shut* case]

open-cast mining mining by excavating from the surface, as in quarrying

open chain the structural form of certain molecules in which the chain of atoms does not form a ring

open city a city left open to enemy occupation to gain immunity from attack

open door 1. unrestricted admission 2. equal, unrestricted opportunity for all nations to trade with a given nation —**o'pen-door'** *adj.*

o·pen-end·ed (-en'did) *adj.* 1. unrestricted in duration, scope, etc., as a discussion 2. open to change 3. allowing for a freely formulated answer rather than one chosen from among predetermined answers: said of a question —**o'pen-end'ed·ness** *n.*

o·pen-eyed (-īd') *adj.* with the eyes open or wide open, as in awareness or amazement

o·pen-faced (-fāst') *adj.* 1. having a frank, honest face 2. [Chiefly U.S.] designating a sandwich without a top slice of bread: also **o'pen-face'**

o·pen-hand·ed (-han'did) *adj.* generous —**o'pen-hand'-ed·ly** *adv.* —**o'pen-hand'ed·ness** *n.*

o·pen-heart·ed (-här'tid) *adj.* 1. not reserved; frank 2. kindly; generous —**o'pen-heart'ed·ly** *adv.* —**o'pen-heart'-ed·ness** *n.*

o·pen-hearth (-härth') *adj.* designating or using a furnace with a wide, saucer-shaped hearth and a low roof, for making steel

o·pen-heart surgery (-härt') heart surgery with the chest opened and the blood re-circulated and oxygenated by mechanical means

open house informal reception of visitors freely coming and going, at one's home, a school, etc.

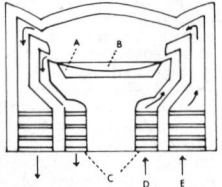

OPEN-HEARTH FURNACE
(A, lining; B, metal; C, heater ports; D, gas; E, air: fired alternately from either end)

o·pen·ing (-iŋ) *n.* 1. a becoming or making open 2. an open place; hole; gap 3. *a)* a beginning *b)* a first performance 4. an opportunity 5. a job available 6. *Chess, Draughts,* etc. the series of first moves

opening batsman *Cricket* one of the two batsmen beginning an innings

opening time the time at which public houses legally start selling alcoholic drinks

open letter a letter written as to a specific person but published in a newspaper, etc. for all to read

open market *same as* FREE MARKET

o·pen-mind·ed (-mīn'did) *adj.* open to new ideas; not biased —**o'pen-mind'ed·ly** *adv.* —**o'pen-mind'ed·ness** *n.*

o·pen-mouthed (-mouthd', -moutht') *adj.* 1. having the mouth open 2. gaping, as in astonishment

open-plan (-plan') *adj.* designating accommodation in which there are no, or relatively few, dividing walls or partitions between different areas

open punctuation punctuation characterized by relatively few commas or other marks

open sandwich a sandwich made from a slice of bread and meat, fish, etc., but no top slice

open sea 1. the expanse of sea away from coastlines, bays, inlets, etc. 2. *same as* HIGH SEAS

open secret something supposed to be secret but known to almost everyone

open sesame 1. magic words spoken to open the door of the thieves' den in the story of Ali Baba 2. any sure means of achieving an end

open shop a factory, business, etc. employing workers regardless of union membership

Open University a university founded in 1969 for mature students, teaching by radio, television, correspondence courses, etc.

o·pen·work (-wurk') *n.* ornamental work, as in cloth, with openings in the material

op·er·a[1] (op'ər ə, op'rə) *n.* [It. < L., a work] 1. a play with most or all the text sung to orchestral accompaniment and usually with elaborate costuming, sets, and choreography 2. the art of such plays 3. the score, libretto, or performance of an opera 4. a theatre for operas

o·pe·ra[2] (ō'pə rə, op'ər ə) *n. pl. of* OPUS

op·er·a·ble (op'ər ə b'l) *adj.* [< ML.: SEE OPERATE & -ABLE] 1. practicable 2. treatable surgically —**op'er·a·bil'i·ty** *n.* —**op'er·a·bly** *adv.*

‡o·pé·ra bouffe (ō pā rä bōōf'; *E.* op'ər ə bōōf') [Fr.] comic, esp. farcical, opera

opera glasses a small binocular telescope used at the opera, in theatres, etc.

opera hat a man's tall, collapsible silk hat

opera house a theatre chiefly for operas

op·er·ant (op'ər ənt) *adj.* operating, or producing an effect or effects —*n.* one that operates

op·er·ate (op'ə rāt') *vi.* -at'ed, -at'ing [< L. pp. of *operari,* to work < *opus* (gen. *operis),* a work] 1. to be in action; work 2. to produce a certain effect 3. to carry on military movements 4. to perform a surgical operation —*vt.* 1. [Now Rare] to effect 2. *a)* to put or keep in action; work (a machine, etc.) *b)* to conduct or manage (a business, etc.)

op·er·at·ic (op'ə rat'ik) *adj.* of or like the opera —**op'er·at'-i·cal·ly** *adv.*

operating theatre a room in a hospital, sometimes with a viewing gallery, set aside for surgical operations

op·er·a·tion (op'ə rā'shən) *n.* 1. the act, process, or method of operating 2. the condition of being in action or at work 3. a procedure that is part of a series in some work 4. any strategic military movement 5. any specific plan, project, etc. [*Operation* Overlord] 6. any surgical procedure to remedy a physical ailment or defect 7. *Math.* any process, as addition, involving a change in quantity —**in operation** 1. in action; working 2. in force

op·er·a·tion·al (-'l) *adj.* 1. of the operation of a device, system, process, etc. 2. *a)* that can be used or operated *b)* in use; operating 3. of or ready for use in a military operation —**op'er·a'tion·al·ly** *adv.*

operations research systematic, scientific analysis of problems, as in government, military, or business operations: also **operations analysis**

op·er·a·tive (op'ər ə tiv) *adj.* 1. capable of or in operation 2. effective 3. connected with physical work or mechanical action 4. of or resulting from a surgical operation —*n.* 1. a worker, esp. a skilled industrial worker —**op'er·a·tive·ly** *adv.*

op·er·a·tor (op'ə rāt'ər) *n.* 1. one who operates; specif., *a)* a person who effects something; agent *b)* a person who works a machine [a telephone *operator*] *c)* a person engaged in commercial or industrial operations or enterprises 2. [Slang] a clever person who generally manages to achieve his ends

o·per·cu·lum (ō pur'kyōō ləm) *n., pl.* -**la** (-lə), -**lums** [ModL. < L., lid, dim. < *operire,* to close] any of various covering flaps or lidlike structures in plants and animals, as the bony covering protecting the gills of fishes —**o·per'cu·lar** *adj.* —**o·per'cu·late** (-lit, -lāt'), **o·per'cu·lat'ed** *adj.*

op·er·et·ta (op'ə ret'ə) *n.* [It., dim. of *opera,* OPERA[1]] a light, amusing opera with spoken dialogue

oph·thal·mi·a (of thal'mē ə) *n.* [< LL. < Gr. < *ophthalmos,* the eye] severe inflammation of the eyeball or conjunctiva

oph·thal·mic (-mik) *adj.* of the eye; ocular

ophthalmic optician an optician who tests eyes, prescribes, and dispenses glasses

oph·thal·mo- [< Gr. *ophthalmos,* the eye] a combining form meaning the eye: also **oph·thalm-**

oph·thal·mol·o·gy (of'thal mol'ə jē, op'-; -thə-) *n.* the branch of medicine dealing with the structure, functions, and diseases of the eye —**oph'thal·mo·log'i·cal** (-mə loj'-i k'l) *adj.* —**oph'thal·mol'o·gist** *n.*

oph·thal·mo·scope (of thal'mə skōp', op-) *n.* [OPHTHALMO- & -SCOPE] an instrument for examining the interior of the eye —**oph'thal'mo·scop'ic** (-skop'ik) *adj.* —**oph'thal·mos'-co·py** (-thəl mos'kə pē) *n.*

-o·pi·a (ō'pē ə) [< Gr. < *ōps,* an eye] a combining form meaning a (specified kind of) eye defect

o·pi·ate (ō'pē it, -āt') *n.* 1. any medicine containing opium or any of its derivatives, and acting as a sedative and narcotic 2. anything quieting, soothing, etc. —*adj.* 1. containing opium 2. bringing sleep, quiet, etc.; narcotic

o·pine (ō pīn') *vt., vi.* o·pined', o·pin'ing [< MFr. < L. *opinari,* to think] to hold or express (some opinion)

o·pin·ion (ə pin'yən) *n.* [< OFr. < L. < *opinari,* to think] 1. a belief not based on certainty or knowledge but on what seems true, valid, or probable 2. an evaluation, estimation, etc. 3. an expert's formal judgment 4. *Law* the formal statement by a judge, court referee, etc. of the law bearing on a case

o·pin·ion·at·ed (-āt'id) *adj.* holding unreasonably or obstinately to one's own opinions —**o·pin'ion·at'ed·ly** *adv.* —**o·pin'ion·at'ed·ness** *n.*

o·pin·ion·a·tive (-āt'iv, -ə tiv) *adj.* 1. of, or of the nature of, opinion 2. opinionated —**o·pin'ion·a'tive·ly** *adv.* —**o·pin'-ion·a'tive·ness** *n.*

opinion poll *same as* POLL (sense 5a)

o·pi·um (ō'pē əm) *n.* [L. < Gr. < *opos,* vegetable juice] a narcotic drug made from the juice of the seed capsules of the opium poppy, used as an intoxicant and medicinally to relieve pain and produce sleep

opium poppy an annual poppy with large, white or purple flowers, the source of opium

o·pos·sum (ə pos′əm) *n., pl.* **-sums, -sum:** see PLURAL, II, D, 1 [< Algonquian, lit., white beast] 1. any of several American marsupials; esp., the **American** (or **Virginian**) **opossum,** a small, tree-dwelling mammal: it is active at night and pretends to be dead when trapped 2. any of various Australian phalangers

OPOSSUM
(body 30–50 cm long; tail 25–53 cm long)

opp. 1. opposed 2. opposite

op·po (op′pō) *n* [Slang] companion; friend

op·po·nent (ə pō′nənt) *n.* [< L. prp. of *opponere* < *ob-* (see OB-) + *ponere,* to set] one who opposes, as in a fight, game, etc.; adversary —*adj.* opposing; antagonistic

op·por·tune (op′ər tyōōn′, op′ər tōōn′) *adj.* [< MFr. < L. *opportunus,* lit., before the port < *ob-* (see OB-) + *portus,* a port] 1. right for the purpose: said of time 2. happening or done at the right time; timely —**op′por·tune′ly** *adv.* —**op′por·tune′ness** *n.*

op·por·tun·ism (-iz′m) *n.* the adapting of one's actions, judgments, etc. to circumstances, as in politics, for one's own benefit without regard for principles —**op′por·tun′ist** *n.* —**op′por·tun·is′tic** *adj.* —**op′por·tun·is′ti·cal·ly** *adv.*

op·por·tu·ni·ty (op′ər tyōō′nə tē) *n., pl.* **-ties** 1. a combination of circumstances favourable for the purpose 2. a good chance or occasion

op·pos·a·ble (ə pō′zə b'l) *adj.* 1. that can be resisted 2. that can be placed opposite something else —**op·pos′a·bil′i·ty** *n.*

op·pose (ə pōz′) *vt.* **-posed′, -pos′ing** [< OFr. < L. *opponere:* see OB- & POSITION] 1. to set against; place opposite, in balance or contrast 2. to contend with in speech or action; resist —*vi.* to act in opposition —**op·pos′er** *n.*

op·po·site (op′ə zit) *adj.* [OFr. < L. pp. of *opponere:* see prec.] 1. set against, facing, or back to back; at the other end or side (often with *to*) 2. hostile; resistant 3. entirely different; exactly contrary 4. *Bot.* growing in pairs, but separated by a stem —*n.* anything opposed or opposite —*adv.* on opposing sides or in an opposite position —*prep.* facing; across from —**op′po·site·ly** *adv.* —**op′po·site·ness** *n.*

opposite number a person holding an equivalent and corresponding position on the other side or in another situation; counterpart

op·po·si·tion (op′ə zish′ən) *n.* 1. an opposing 2. an opposed condition; resistance, contrast, etc. 3. anything that opposes; specif., [often O-] a political party opposing the party in power 4. *Astrol., Astron.* the position of two heavenly bodies 180° apart in longitude —**op′po·si′tion·al** *adj.* —**op′po·si′tion·ist** *n., adj.*

op·press (ə pres′) *vt.* [< OFr. < ML. < L. pp. of *opprimere* < *ob-* (see OB-) + *premere,* PRESS¹] 1. to weigh heavily on the mind, spirits, or senses of 2. to keep down by the cruel or unjust use of power; tyrannize over —**op·pres′sor** *n.*

op·pres·sion (ə presh′ən) *n.* 1. an oppressing or being oppressed 2. a thing that oppresses 3. physical or mental distress

op·pres·sive (ə pres′iv) *adj.* 1. hard to put up with 2. cruelly overbearing; tyrannical 3. weighing heavily on the mind, etc.; distressing 4. very hot and close [the day was *oppressive*] —**op·pres′sive·ly** *adv.* —**op·pres′sive·ness** *n.*

op·pro·bri·ous (ə prō′brē əs) *adj.* 1. expressing opprobrium; abusive 2. [Now Rare] disgraceful —**op·pro′bri·ous·ly** *adv.* —**op·pro′bri·ous·ness** *n.*

op·pro·bri·um (-əm) *n.* [L. < *opprobrare,* to reproach < *ob-* (see OB-) + *probrum,* a disgrace] 1. the disgrace or infamy attached to conduct viewed as grossly shameful 2. anything bringing shame or disgrace 3. reproachful contempt

op·pugn (o pyōōn′) *vt.* [M.E. *oppugnen* < L. *ob-* (see OB-) + *pugnare,* to fight] to oppose with argument; controvert

-op·sis (op′sis) [< Gr. < *opsis,* a sight] a combining form meaning sight or view

opt (opt) *vi.* [< Fr. < L. *optare*] to make a choice (often with *for*) —**opt out** (of) to choose not to be or continue in (an activity, group, etc.)

opt. 1. optical 2. optician 3. optional

op·ta·tive (op′tə tiv) *adj.* [< Fr. < LL. < L. *optare,* to desire] expressing wish or desire, as a mood in Greek grammar —*n.* the optative mood, or a verb in this mood —**op′ta·tive·ly** *adv.*

op·tic (op′tik) *adj.* [< Fr. < ML. < Gr. *optikos*] of the eye or sense of sight

op·ti·cal (-'l) *adj.* 1. of the sense of sight; visual 2. of optics 3. for aiding vision [*optical* instruments] —**op′ti·cal·ly** *adv.*

optical activity the ability of certain substances to rotate the plane of polarization when transmitting polarized light

op·ti·cian (op tish′ən) *n.* a person who makes or deals in optical instruments, esp. one who prepares and dispenses eyeglasses

op·tics (op′tiks) *n.pl.* [*with sing. v.*] [< OPTIC] the branch of physics dealing with the nature and properties of light and vision

op·ti·mal (op′tə məl) *adj.* most favourable or desirable; best; optimum —**op′ti·mal·ly** *adv.*

op·ti·mism (-miz′m) *n.* [< Fr. < L. *optimus,* best] 1. *Philos.* a) the doctrine that the existing world is the best possible b) the belief that good ultimately prevails over evil 2. the tendency to take the most hopeful or cheerful view of matters —**op′ti·mist** (-mist) *n.* —**op′ti·mis′tic** (-mis′tik), **op′ti·mis′ti·cal** *adj.* —**op′ti·mis′ti·cal·ly** *adv.*

op·ti·mize (-mīz′) *vi.* **-mized′, -miz′ing** to be given to optimism —*vt.* to make the most of —**op′ti·mi·za′tion** *n.*

op·ti·mum (-məm) *n., pl.* **-mums, -ma** (-mə) [L., neut. of *optimus,* best < *ops,* riches] the best or most favourable degree, condition, amount, etc. —*adj.* most favourable or desirable; best

op·tion (op′shən) *n.* [Fr. < L. *optio* < *optare,* to wish] 1. a choosing; choice 2. the right or liberty of choosing 3. something that is or can be chosen 4. the right to buy, sell, or lease at a fixed price, sign a contract, etc. within a specified time —**keep** (or **leave**) **one's options open** to be uncommitted to a course of action or policy

op·tion·al (-'l) *adj.* left to one's option, or choice; elective —**op′tion·al·ly** *adv.*

op·tom·e·try (op tom′ə trē) *n.* [see OPTIC & -METRY] 1. measurement of the range and power of vision 2. the profession of examining the eyes for errors in refraction and of prescribing glasses to correct such defects —**op·to·met·ric** (op′tə met′rik), **op′to·met′ri·cal** *adj.* —**op·tom′e·trist** *n.*

op·u·lent (op′yu lənt) *adj.* [< L. < *ops,* wealth] 1. wealthy; rich 2. abundant; profuse —**op′u·lence, op′u·len·cy** *n.* —**op′u·lent·ly** *adv.*

o·pus (ō′pəs) *n., pl.* **o·pe·ra** (ō′pə rə, op′ər ə), [L., a work] a work; composition; esp., any of the musical works of a composer numbered in order of composition or publication

-o·py (ō′pē) *same as* -OPIA

or¹ (ôr; *unstressed* ər) *conj.* [ME., in form a contr. of *other,* either, but actually < OE. *oththe*] a coordinating conjunction introducing: a) an alternative possibility [beer or wine, either go or stay] b) a synonymous term [ill, or sick]

or² (ôr) *n.* [Fr. < L. *aurum,* gold] *Heraldry* gold

-or (ər; *occas.* ôr) [< OFr. < L. *-or*] a suffix meaning: 1. a person or thing that [*inventor*] 2. quality or condition [*error*]: see also -OUR

O.R. operations research

or·a·cle (ôr′ə k'l) *n.* [OFr. < L. *oraculum* < *orare,* to pray < *os* (gen. *oris*), the mouth] 1. in ancient Greece and Rome, a) the place where, or medium by which, deities were consulted b) the revelation of a medium or priest 2. a) any person or agency believed to be in communication with a deity b) any person of, or supposed to be of, great wisdom: often an ironic usage c) opinion or statements of any such oracle

o·rac·u·lar (o rak′yōō lər) *adj.* of or like an oracle; wise, mysterious, etc. —**o·rac′u·lar′i·ty** (-yə lar′ə tē) *n.* —**o·rac′u·lar·ly** *adv.*

o·ral (ôr′əl) *adj.* [< L. *os* (gen. *oris*), the mouth] 1. uttered; spoken 2. of or using speech 3. of, at, or near the mouth 4. *Psychoanalysis* of an early stage of psychosexual development focusing on mouth functions —*n.* a spoken examination, as in a college —**o′ral·ly** *adv.*

oral society a people or tribe who have not yet developed a system of recording their traditions, myths, etc.; a pre-literate society

or·ange (ôr′inj) *n.* [< OFr. < Pr. *auranja* < Sp. < Ar. < Per. < Sans. *naranga*] 1. a reddish-yellow, round, edible citrus fruit with a sweet, juicy pulp 2. the evergreen tree it grows on 3. reddish-yellow —*adj.* 1. reddish-yellow 2. of oranges —**or′ang·y** (-in jē) *adj.*

or·ange·ade (-ād′) *n.* a drink made of orange juice and water, usually sweetened, often effervescent

orange blossom the flowers of the orange tree, traditionally worn by brides

Or·ange·man (ôr′inj mən) *n., pl.* **-men** [after the Prince of *Orange,* later William III] a member of a secret society organized in northern Ireland in 1795 to support Protestantism

Orangeman's Day July 12th, celebrated chiefly in Northern Ireland by Orangemen, esp. with parades, etc.

orange pekoe a black tea of Ceylon and India

or·ang·e·ry (ôr′inj ə rē′) *n., pl.* **-ries** [Fr. *orangerie* < *oranger,* orange tree] a hothouse or other sheltered place for growing orange trees in cooler climates

orange stick an orangewood stick, for manicuring

or·ange·wood (ôr′inj wood′) *n.* the wood of the orange tree —*adj.* of orangewood

o·rang·u·tan (ô raŋ'ōō tan', ə-; -taŋ') *n.* [< Malay < *oran*, man + *utan*, forest] an ape of Borneo and Sumatra, with shaggy, reddish-brown hair, very long arms, small ears, and a hairless face: also sp. **o·rang'ou·tang'** (-taŋ')

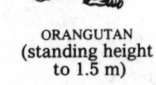

ORANGUTAN
(standing height to 1.5 m)

o·rate (ô rāt', ōr'āt) *vi.* **o·rat'ed, o·rat'ing** [< ff.] to make an oration; speak pompously or bombastically: a humorously derogatory term

o·ra·tion (ô rā'shən) *n.* [< L. *oratio* < *orare*, to speak] a formal speech, as at a ceremony

or·a·tor (or'ət ər) *n.* **1.** a person who delivers an oration **2.** an eloquent public speaker

or·a·tor·i·cal (or'ə tôr'i k'l) *adj.* **1.** of or characteristic of orators or oratory **2.** given to oratory —**or'a·tor'i·cal·ly** *adv.*

or·a·to·ri·o (or'ə tôr'ē ō') *n.*, *pl.* **-os** [It., small chapel: from performances at a chapel in Rome] a long, dramatic musical work, usually on a religious theme, consisting of arias, recitatives, choruses, etc. with orchestral accompaniment but without stage action, scenery, etc.

or·a·to·ry (or'ə tə rē) *n.*, *pl.* **-ries** [L. *oratoria*] **1.** the art of an orator; skill in public speaking **2.** [< LL. < L. *oratorius* < *orator*] a small chapel, esp. for private prayer

orb (ôrb) *n.* [L. *orbis*, a circle] **1.** a globe; sphere **2.** any heavenly sphere, as the sun or moon **3.** a small globe with a cross on top, as a royal symbol **4.** [Poet.] the eye —*vt.* **1.** to form into a sphere or circle **2.** [Poet.] to enclose or encircle —**orbed** *adj.* —**orb'y** *adj.*

or·bic·u·lar (ôr bik'yōō lər) *adj.* [< LL. < L. dim. of *orbis*, a circle] **1.** in the form of an orb; spherical or circular **2.** *Bot.* round and flat, as some leaves Also **or·bic'u·late** (-lit, -lāt') & **or·bic'u·lat'ed** (-lāt'id) —**or·bic'u·lar'i·ty** (-lar'ə tē) *n.* —**or·bic'u·lar·ly** *adv.*

or·bit (ôr'bit) *n.* [< MFr. < ML. < L. *orbita*, path < *orbis*, a circle] **1.** the bony cavity containing the eye; eye socket **2.** *a)* the path of a heavenly body in its revolution around another *b)* the path of an artificial satellite or spacecraft around a heavenly body **3.** the range of one's experience or activity —*vi.* to move in an orbit or circle —*vt.* **1.** to put into an orbit in space **2.** to move in an orbit around —**or'bit·al** *adj.* —**or'bit·er** *n.*

Or·cad·i·an (ôr kā'dē ən) *n.* [< L. *Orcades*, the Orkney Islands] a native or inhabitant of the Orkneys —*adj.* relating to the Orkneys

or·chard (ôr'chərd) *n.* [< OE. *ortgeard*, ult. < L. *hortus*, a garden + OE. *geard*, enclosure] **1.** an area of land where fruit trees or nut trees are grown **2.** such trees

or·ches·tra (ôr'kis trə, -kes'-) *n.* [L. < Gr. *orchēstra*, space for the chorus in front of the stage < *orcheisthai*, to dance] **1.** the space in front of and below the stage, where the musicians sit: in full, **orchestra pit 2.** [U.S.] *a)* the main-floor seats of a theatre, esp. the front section *b)* the main floor itself **3.** *a)* a group of musicians playing together; esp., *same as* SYMPHONY ORCHESTRA *b)* their instruments —**or·ches'tral** (-kes'trəl) *adj.* —**or·ches'tral·ly** *adv.*

or·ches·trate (ôr'kis trāt') *vt.*, *vi.* **-trat'ed, -trat'ing 1.** to compose or arrange (music) for an orchestra **2.** to furnish (a ballet, etc.) with an orchestral score **3.** to combine or arrange harmoniously —**or'ches·tra'tion** *n.* —**or'ches·tra'tor, or'ches·trat'er** *n.*

or·chid (ôr'kid) *n.* [< L.: see ff.] **1.** any of a family of plants having bulbous roots and flowers with three petals, one lip-shaped **2.** the flower **3.** a light bluish red —*adj.* of this colour

or·chis (ôr'kis) *n.* [L. < Gr. *orchis*, lit., testicle: from the shape of the roots] an orchid; specif., one with small flowers growing in spikes

ord. 1. order **2.** ordinal **3.** ordinance

or·dain (ôr dān') *vt.* [< OFr. < L. *ordinare* < *ordo*, an order] **1.** to decree; order; establish; enact **2.** to invest with the functions or office of a minister, priest, or rabbi —*vi.* to command; decree —**or·dain'er** *n.* —**or·dain'ment** *n.*

or·deal (ôr dēl'; ôr'dēl) *n.* [OE. *ordal*] **1.** an old method of trial exposing the accused to physical dangers from which he was supposedly protected if innocent **2.** a painful or severe trial

or·der (ôr'dər) *n.* [< OFr. < L. *ordo*, straight row] **1.** social position **2.** a state of peace; orderly conduct **3.** arrangement of things or events; series **4.** a fixed or definite plan; system **5.** a group set off from others by some quality **6.** a group of persons organized for military, monastic, or social purposes [the Masonic *Order*] **7.** *a)* a group of persons distinguished by having received a certain award or citation *b)* the group's insignia **8.** a condition in which everything is in its right place and functioning properly **9.** condition in general [in working *order*] **10.** a command, direction, etc., usually backed by authority **11.** class; kind; sort [sentiments of a high *order*] **12.** an established method, as of conduct in meetings, court, etc. **13.** *a)* a request or commission to supply something *b)* the goods supplied *c)* a single portion of some food, as in a restaurant **14.** *Archit. a)* any of several classical styles of structure, as Doric, determined chiefly by the type of column and entablature *b)* a style of building **15.** *Biol.* a classification ranking above a family and below a class **16.** *Finance* written instructions to pay money or surrender property **17.** *Theol. a)* any of the nine grades of angels *b)* any rank in the Christian clergy *c)* [*pl.*] the position of ordained minister [he was in holy *orders*] —*vt.* **1.** to put or keep in order; arrange **2.** *a)* to command *b)* to command to go (*to, out of*, etc.) **3.** to request or direct (something to be supplied) —*vi.* **1.** to give a command **2.** to request that something be supplied —**by order of** according to the command of —**call to order** to request to be quiet, as to start (a meeting) —**in** (or **out of**) **order 1.** in (or not in) proper sequence or position **2.** in (or not in) good condition **3.** in (or not in) accordance with the rules **4.** being (or not being) suitable to the occasion —**in order that** so that; to the end that —**in order to** as a means to —**in short order** without delay —**on order** ordered but not yet supplied —**on the order of 1.** similar to **2.** approximately —**to order 1.** as specified by the buyer **2.** when called upon —**or'der·er** *n.*

order in council an order issued by a British sovereign with the advice of the Privy Council

or·der·ly (ôr'dər lē) *adj.* **1.** *a)* neatly arranged *b)* conforming to some regular order; systematic **2.** well-behaved; law-abiding —*adv.* in proper order; methodically —*n.*, *pl.* **-lies 1.** *Mil.* an enlisted man assigned as a personal attendant or given a specific task **2.** a male hospital attendant —**or'der·li·ness** *n.*

Order of Merit a limited order, instituted in 1902, and awarded for outstanding achievement in any sphere, civil or military

or·di·nal (ôr'dən əl) *adj.* [< LL. *ordinalis* < L. *ordo*, order] **1.** expressing order, specif. of a number in a series: see ORDINAL NUMBER **2.** of an order of animals or plants —*n.* **1.** *same as* ORDINAL NUMBER **2.** [*often* O-] a book of religious rituals

ordinal number a number used to indicate order (e.g., ninth, 25th, etc.) in a series: distinguished from CARDINAL NUMBER

or·di·nance (ôr'dən əns) *n.* [< OFr. < *ordener*: see ORDAIN] **1.** an authoritative command **2.** an established practice, rite, etc.

or·di·nar·i·ly (ôr'd'n er'ə lē) *adv.* **1.** usually; as a rule **2.** in an ordinary way

or·di·nar·y (ôr'd'n ə rē) *n.*, *pl.* **-nar·ies** [< OFr. < ML. < L. *ordinarius*, an overseer < *ordo*, an order] **1.** an official of church or court whose power is original, not delegated **2.** [Archaic] *a)* a set meal at a fixed price *b)* an inn, etc. serving such meals **3.** *Eccles.* [*often* O-] the unvarying part of the Mass —*adj.* **1.** customary; usual **2.** unexceptional; common *b)* relatively inferior —**in ordinary** in regular service —**out of the ordinary** unusual —**or'di·nar'i·ness** *n.*

Ordinary Level a subject taken at the lower or basic standard of the General Certificate of Education, usually by people of about 16

ordinary rating see MILITARY RANKS, table

or·di·nate (ôr'din it, -āt') *n.* [< ModL. (*linea*) *ordinate* (*applicata*), line applied in an ordered manner] *Math.* in a system of coordinates, the distance of a point from the horizontal axis as measured along a line parallel to the vertical axis: cf. ABSCISSA

or·di·na·tion (ôr'din ā'shən) *n.* an ordaining or being ordained

ord·nance (ôrd'nəns) *n.* [contr. < ORDINANCE] **1.** cannon or artillery **2.** all military weapons together with ammunition, vehicles, equipment, etc. **3.** a military unit supplying and storing ordnance

ordnance datum mean sea level, as at Newlyn, Cornwall, used as basis for height on Ordnance Survey maps

Ordnance Survey the official map-making body of the British or Irish government

Or·do·vi·cian (ôr'də vish'ən) *adj.* [< L. *Ordovices*, a tribe in Wales] designating or of the second period of the Palaeozoic Era —**the Ordovician** the Ordovician Period or its rocks: see GEOLOGY, chart

or·dure (ôr'dyoor) *n.* [OFr. < *ord*, filthy < L. *horridus*, horrid] dung; excrement

ore (ôr) *n.* [OE. *ar*, brass, copper] **1.** any natural combination of minerals, esp. one from which a metal or metals can be profitably extracted **2.** a natural substance from which a nonmetallic material, as sulphur, can be extracted

ö·re (ö'rə) *n.*, *pl.* **ö're** [Sw., ult. < L. *aurum*, gold] *see* MONETARY UNITS, table (Sweden)

ø·re (ö'rə) *n.*, *pl.* **ö're** [Dan. & Norw.: see prec.] *see* MONETARY UNITS, table (Denmark, Norway)

o·re·ad (ôr′ē ad′) *n.* [< L. *oreas* < Gr. *oros*, mountain] *Gr. & Rom. Myth* a mountain nymph

o·reg·a·no (ô reg′ə nō, ə-; ô re gä′nō) *n.* [Sp. *orégano*, ult. < Gr. *origanon*] any of several labiate plants with fragrant leaves used for seasoning

or·gan (ôr′gən) *n.* [< OFr. & OE. < L. *organum* < Gr. *organon*, an instrument < *ergon*, work] 1. *a)* a large wind instrument consisting of various sets of pipes which, opened by keys on one or more keyboards, allow passage to a column of compressed air causing sound by vibration: also called **pipe organ** *b)* any of several musical instruments producing similar sounds, as a reed organ 2. in animals and plants, a part composed of specialized tissues and adapted to perform a specific function or functions 3. means for performing some action 4. a means of communicating ideas, as a periodical

or·gan·die, or·gan·dy (ôr′gən dē) *n., pl.* **-dies** [Fr. *organdi* < ?] a very sheer, crisp cotton fabric, used for dresses, curtains, etc.

or·gan·elle (ôr′gə nel′) *n.* [ult. < L. *organum*, a tool + *-ella*, dim. suffix] a specialized structure within a cell, as a chloroplast or cilium

organ grinder a person who makes a living by playing a barrel organ in the streets

or·gan·ic (ôr gan′ik) *adj.* 1. of or having to do with an organ 2. inherent; constitutional 3. made up of systematically interrelated parts; organized 4. *a)* designating or of any chemical compound containing carbon *b)* designating or of the branch of chemistry dealing with carbon compounds 5. of, like, or derived from living organisms 6. grown with only animal or vegetable fertilizers 7. *Law* designating or of fundamental, or constitutional, law 8. *Med.* producing or involving alteration in the structure of an organ: cf. FUNCTIONAL —**or·gan′i·cal·ly** *adv.*

or·gan·ism (ôr′gə niz′m) *n.* 1. any animal or plant with organs and parts that function together to maintain life 2. anything like a living thing in its complexity of structure or functions —**or′gan·is′mic** *adj.* —**or′gan·is′mi·cal·ly** *adv.*

or·gan·ist (ôr′gə nist) *n.* one who plays the organ

or·gan·i·za·tion (ôr′gə ni zā′shən, -nī-) *n.* 1. an organizing or being organized 2. the way in which the parts of a thing are organized 3. any unified group or systematized whole; esp., *a)* a body of persons organized for some purpose, as a club, union, etc. *b)* the administrative or executive structure of a business or political party —**or′gan·i·za′tion·al** *adj.* —**or′gan·i·za′tion·al·ly** *adv.*

or·gan·ize (ôr′gə nīz′) *vt.* **-ized′, -iz′ing** 1. to provide with an organic structure; esp., *a)* to arrange in an orderly way *b)* to bring into a unified, coherent form *c)* to make plans and arrange for 2. to bring into being; establish 3. to enlist in, or cause to form, a trade union 4. [Colloq.] to set (oneself) into an orderly state of mind —*vi.* 1. to become organized 2. [Chiefly U.S.] to form an organization, esp. a trade union —**or′gan·iz′a·ble** *adj.* —**or′gan·iz′er** *n.*

organ loft the gallery in a church, concert hall, etc. for an organ

or·gan·za (ôr gan′zə) *n.* [< ?] a stiff, sheer fabric of rayon, silk, etc.

or·gasm (ôr′gaz′m) *n.* [< Fr. < Gr. *orgasmos* < *organ*, to swell with moisture] a frenzy; esp., the climax of a sexual act —**or·gas′mic, or·gas′tic** *adj.*

or·geat (ôr′zhat; *Fr.* ôr′zhà′) *n.* [Fr. < Pr. *orjat* < *orge*, barley] a syrup or beverage, orig. made from barley, flavoured with almonds and orange flowers

or·gy (ôr′jē) *n., pl.* **-gies** [< Fr. < L. < Gr. *orgia*, pl., secret rites] 1. [*usually pl.*] in ancient Greece and Rome, wild celebration in worship of certain gods 2. any wild, licentious merrymaking 3. unrestrained indulgence in any activity —**or′gi·as′tic** (-as′tik) *adj.* —**or′gi·as′ti·cal·ly** *adv.*

o·ri·el (ôr′ē əl) *n.* [< OFr. < ? ML. *oriolum*, porch] a large window built out from a wall and resting on a bracket or corbel

o·ri·ent (ôr′ē ant; *also, and for v. usually*, -ent′) *n.* [OFr. < L. *oriens*, direction of the rising sun, prp. of *oriri*, to arise] the east: now rare, except [O-] the East, or Asia; esp., the Far East —*adj.* 1. shining, as pearls 2. [Poet.] *a)* eastern; oriental *b)* rising, as the sun —*vt.* 1. to arrange with reference to the east 2. to set (a map or chart) in agreement with the points of the compass 3. to adjust or adapt to a particular situation (often used reflexively)

ORIEL

o·ri·en·tal (ôr′ē en′t'l) *adj.* 1. [Poet.] eastern 2. [O-] of the Orient, its people, or their culture; Eastern —*n.* [*usually* O-] a native of the Orient or a member of a people native to that region

O·ri·en·tal·ism (-iz′m) *n.* 1. any trait, quality, etc. associated with people of the East 2. study of Eastern culture —**O′ri·en′tal·ist** *n.*

Oriental poppy a perennial poppy often grown for its red, pink, or white flowers

Oriental rug (or **carpet**) a carpet hand-woven in the Orient, usually with intricate, colourful designs

o·ri·en·tate (ôr′ē ən tāt′) *vt.* **-tat′ed, -tat′ing** *same as* ORIENT —*vi.* 1. to face east, or in any specified direction 2. to adjust to a situation

o·ri·en·ta·tion (ôr′ē ən tā′shən) *n.* 1. an orienting or being oriented 2. *a)* awareness of one's environment as to time, space, objects, and persons *b)* a period of introduction and adjustment [an *orientation* course]

or·i·en·teer·ing (ôr′ē ən tir′iŋ) *n.* [< Sw. *orientering*] a sport in which competitors race on foot over a course, usually rough country, with the aid of a map and compass

or·i·fice (ôr′ə fis) *n.* [Fr. < LL. *orificium* < L. *os* (gen. *oris*), mouth + *facere*, to make] an opening or mouth, as of a tube or cavity

or·i·flamme (ôr′ə flam′) *n.* [Fr. < OFr. < L. < *aurum*, gold + *flamma*, flame] 1. the ancient royal standard of France, a red silk banner with flame-shaped streamers 2. any battle standard

orig. 1. origin 2. original 3. originally

o·ri·ga·mi (ôr′ə gä′mē) *n.* [Jap.] 1. a traditional Japanese art of folding paper to form flowers, animal figures, etc. 2. an object so made

or·i·gin (ôr′ə jin) *n.* [< MFr. < L. *origo* (gen. *originis*) < *oriri*, to rise] 1. a coming into existence or use; beginning 2. parentage; birth; lineage 3. source; root 4. *Math.* the point at which coordinate axes intersect

o·rig·i·nal (ə rij′ə n'l) *adj.* 1. having to do with an origin; first; earliest 2. never having been before; new; novel 3. capable of creating something new, or thinking or acting in an independent, fresh way; inventive 4. coming from someone as the originator, maker, author, etc. 5. being that from which copies, reproductions, translations, etc. have been made —*n.* 1. a primary type that has given rise to varieties 2. an original work of art, writing, etc., as distinguished from a copy, etc. 3. the person or thing depicted in a painting, etc. 4. a person of original mind and unusual creativity —**o·rig′i·nal·ly** *adv.*

o·rig·i·nal·i·ty (ə rij′ə nal′ə tē) *n.* 1. a being original 2. the ability to be original, inventive, or creative

original sin *Christian Theology* sinfulness and depravity regarded as innate in man as a direct result of Adam's sin

o·rig·i·nate (ə rij′ə nāt′) *vt.* **-nat′ed, -nat′ing** to bring into being; esp., to create (something original); invent —*vi.* to come into being; begin; start —**o·rig′i·na′tion** *n.* —**o·rig′i·na′tive** *adj.* —**o·rig′i·na′tor** *n.*

o·ri·ole (ôr′ē ōl′) *n.* [< OFr. < ML. < L. *aureolus*, golden < *aurum*, gold] 1. any of a family of yellow and black birds found from Europe to Australia 2. any of a group of American birds, including the Baltimore oriole, that have orange and black plumage

O·ri·on (ə rī′ən, o-) an equatorial constellation near Taurus, containing the bright star Rigel

o·ri·son (ôr′i z'n; -s'n) *n.* [< OFr. < LL. *oratio*, a prayer < L.: see ORATION] a prayer

O·ri·ya (o rē′ə) *n.* 1. a people of India in E India on the Bay of Bengal 2. one of these people 3. their language, a member of the Indo-European family of languages

Or·lon (ôr′lon) [arbitrary coinage, after (RYL)ON] a trademark for a synthetic acrylic fibre somewhat like nylon, or a fabric made from this fibre —*n.* [o-] this fibre or fabric

or·lop (ôr′lop) *n.* [ME. *overlop* < Du. *over*, over + *loopen* to run: so called because it covers the hold] the lowest deck of a ship, esp. of a warship

or·mo·lu (ôr′mə lōō′) *n.* [< Fr. *or moulu*, ground gold] an imitation gold consisting of an alloy of copper and tin, used as decoration, etc.

or·na·ment (ôr′nə mənt; *for v.* -ment′) *n.* [< OFr. < L. *ornamentum* < *ornare*, to adorn] 1. anything that adorns; decoration; embellishment 2. a person whose character or talent adds lustre to his surroundings, society, etc. 3. an adorning or being adorned 4. mere external display 5. *Music* an embellishing trill, arpeggio, etc. —*vt.* to furnish with ornaments or be an ornament to; decorate —**or′na·ment′er** *n.*

or·na·men·tal (ôr′nə men′t'l) *adj.* serving as an ornament; decorative —*n.* something ornamental; specif., a decorative plant —**or′na·men′tal·ly** *adv.*

or·na·men·ta·tion (-men tā′shən) *n.* 1. an ornamenting or being ornamented 2. ornaments collectively

or·nate (ôr nāt′) *adj.* [< L. pp. of *ornare*, to adorn] 1. heavily ornamented; overadorned 2. showy or flowery, as some literary styles —**or·nate′ly** *adv.* —**or·nate′ness** *n.*

or·ner·y (ôr′nər ē) *adj.* [altered < ORDINARY] [U.S. Dial.] 1. having an ugly or mean disposition 2. obstinate 3. base; low —**or′ner·i·ness** *n.*

or·ni·thol·o·gy (ôr′nə thol′ə jē) *n.* [< ModL. < Gr. *ornis* (gen. *ornithos*), bird + -LOGY] the branch of zoology dealing with birds —**or·ni·tho·log·i·cal** (ôr′ni thə loj′i k'l) *adj.* —**or′ni·tho·log′i·cal·ly** *adv.* —**or′ni·thol′o·gist** *n.*

oro- (ôr′ō, -ə) [< Gr. *oros*, mountain] *a combining form meaning* mountain [*orography, orogeny*]

o·ro·tund (ôr′ə tund′) *adj.* [< L. *ore rotundo*, lit., with round mouth] **1.** clear, strong, and deep: said of the voice **2.** bombastic or pompous, as speech —**o′ro·tun′di·ty** *n.*

or·phan (ôr′fan) *n.* [< LL. < Gr. *orphanos*] a child whose parents are dead —*adj.* **1.** being an orphan **2.** of or for orphans —*vt.* to cause to become an orphan —**or′phan·hood** *n.*

or·phan·age (-ij) *n.* **1.** the state of being an orphan **2.** an institution housing orphans

Or·phic (ôr′fik) *adj.* **1.** of or characteristic of Orpheus **2.** [*also* **o-**] a) like the music attributed to Orpheus; entrancing b) mystic; occult Also **Or′phe·an** (ôr′fē ən)

or·pine (ôr′pin) *n.* [< MFr. < OFr. < L. *auripigmentum*, pigment of gold] a plant with fleshy leaves and white, yellow, or purple flowers

or·rer·y (ôr′ər ē) *n.,* pl. **-rer·ies** [after Charles Boyle, Earl of *Orrery* (1676-1731) for whom one was made] a mechanical apparatus which illustrates with balls of various sizes the relative motions and positions of the bodies in the solar system

or·ris (or′is) *n.* [prob. < MIt. < L. *iris*, iris] any of several European irises, esp. a species whose rootstocks yield orrisroot

or·ris·root (-rōōt′) *n.* the rootstock of the orris, ground and used in perfumery, tooth powders, etc.

or·tho- [< Gr. *orthos*, straight] *a combining form meaning:* **1.** straight [*orthodontics*] **2.** right angle [*orthoclase*] **3.** correct or standard [*orthography*] **4.** *Med.* correction of deformities [*orthopaedics*] Also, before a vowel, **orth-**

or·tho·clase (ôr′thə klās′, -klāz′) *n.,* [< G. < Gr. *orthos* (see ORTHO-) + *klasis*, fracture, of 90° cleavage] potassium feldspar, common in granitic rocks

or·tho·don·tics (ôr′thə dän′tiks) *n.pl.* [*with sing. v.*] [< ModL.: see ORTH(O)-, -ODONT, & -ICS] the branch of dentistry concerned with correcting irregularities of the teeth and poor occlusion: also **or′tho·don′ti·a** (-dän′shə, -shē ə) —**or′tho·don′tic** *adj.* —**or′tho·don′tist** *n.*

or·tho·dox (ôr′thə doks′) *adj.* [< Fr. < LL. < LGr. < Gr. *orthos*, correct + *doxa*, opinion < *dokein*, to think] **1.** conforming to the usual beliefs or established doctrines, esp. in religion; conventional; specif., a) conforming to the Christian faith as formulated in the early creeds b) [O-] strictly observing the rites and traditions of Judaism, such as kashrut, the Sabbath, etc. **2.** [O-] designating or of any church in the Orthodox Eastern Church —**or′tho·dox′y** *n.,* pl. **-dox′ies**

Orthodox Eastern Church the Christian church dominant in E Europe, W Asia, and N Africa, orig. made up of four patriarchates (Constantinople, Alexandria, Antioch, Jerusalem), now also including the autonomous churches of the Soviet Union, Greece, Romania, Bulgaria, etc.

or·tho·e·py (ôr′thō′ə pē, ôr′thō-) *n.* [< ModL. < Gr. < *orthos*, right + *epos*, a word] **1.** the study of pronunciation; phonology **2.** the standard pronunciation of a language —**or·tho·ep′ic** (ôr′thō ep′ik), **or′tho·ep′i·cal** *adj.* —**or′tho·ep′i·cal·ly** *adv.* —**or·tho′e·pist** *n.*

or·thog·ra·phy (ôr thog′rə fē) *n.,* pl. **-phies** [< MFr. < L. < Gr.: see ORTHO- & -GRAPHY] **1.** spelling in accord with accepted usage **2.** any method of spelling **3.** spelling as a subject for study —**or·thog′ra·pher** *n.* —**or·tho·graph·ic** (ôr′thə graf′ik), **or′tho·graph′i·cal** *adj.* —**or′tho·graph′i·cal·ly** *adv.*

or·tho·pae·dics (ôr′thə pē′diks) *n.pl.* [*with sing. v.*] [< Fr. < Gr. *orthos*, straight + *paideia*, training of children < *pais*, child] the branch of surgery dealing with the treatment of deformities, diseases, and injuries of the bones, joints, etc.: also U.S. sp. **orthopedics** —**or′tho·pae′dic** *adj.* —**or′tho·pae′dist** *n.*

or·thop·ter·an (ôr thop′tər ən) *n.* [< ORTHO- + Gr. *pteron*, wing] any of an order of insects, including crickets, grasshoppers, etc., having chewing mouthparts and hard forewings covering membranous hind wings —**or·thop′ter·ous** *adj.*

or·to·lan (ôr′tə lən) *n.* [Fr. < Pr. < It. < L. *hortulanus*, dim. of *hortus*, a garden] a European bunting, prized as choice food: also **ortolan bunting**

-o·ry (ər ē, ôr′ē) [< OFr. < L. *-orius, -oria, -orium*] a suffix meaning: **1.** of, having the nature of [*contradictory*] **2.** a place or thing for [*laboratory*]

o·ryx (ôr′iks) *n.,* pl. **o′ryx·es, o′ryx:** see PLURAL, II, D, 1 [ModL. < L., wild goat < Gr., lit., pickaxe] any of a group of large African and Asian antelopes, including the gemsbok, with long horns

‡**os¹** (os) *n.,* pl. **os′sa** (-ə) [L.] a bone

‡**os²** (os) *n.,* pl. **o·ra** (ôr′ə) [L.] a mouth; opening

Os *Chem.* osmium

OS, O.S. Old Style

OS., OS, O.S. Old Saxon

O·sage orange (ō sāj′, ō′sāj) [< *Osage*, AmInd. tribe] **1.** a North American thorny tree with hard, yellow wood, used for hedges, etc. **2.** its orangelike, inedible fruit

Os·car (os′kər) *n.* [< ?] [Slang] any of the statuettes awarded annually in the U.S. for achievements in films

os·car (os′kər) *n.* [< *Oscar Asche* (1871-1936), Aust. actor] [Aust. Slang] money, cash

os·cil·late (os′ə lāt′) *vi.* **-lat′ed, -lat′ing** [< L. pp. of *oscillare*, to swing] **1.** to swing back and forth **2.** to be indecisive; vacillate **3.** *Physics* to vary between maximum and minimum values, as electric current —*vt.* to cause to oscillate —**os′cil·la′tor** *n.* —**os′cil·la·to′ry** *adj.*

os·cil·la·tion (os′ə lā′shən) *n.* **1.** an oscillating **2.** fluctuation; instability **3.** *Physics* a) variation between maximum and minimum values, as of current b) a single swing of an oscillating object

os·cil·lo·graph (o sil′ə gräf′, ə-) *n.* [< L. *oscillare*, to swing + -GRAPH] an instrument for displaying or recording electrical oscillations in a wavy line (**oscillogram**) —**os·cil′lo·graph′ic** *adj.*

os·cil·lo·scope (-skōp′) *n.* [< L. *oscillare*, to swing + -SCOPE] a type of oscillograph that visually displays an electrical wave on a fluorescent screen, as of a cathode-ray tube —**os·cil′lo·scop′ic** (-skop′ik) *adj.*

os·cine (os′in, -īn) *adj.* [< ModL. < L. *oscen*, bird whose notes were used in divining] designating or of a group of perching birds, as the finches, larks, etc., typically with highly developed vocal organs —*n.* an oscine bird

os·ci·tan·cy (os′ē tən sē) *n.* [< L. *oscitans*, prp. of *oscitare*, to yawn < *os*, mouth + *citare*, to move] drowsiness, dullness, apathy, etc.

os·cu·lar (os′kyə lər) *adj.* [L. *osculum* (see ff.) + -AR] of the mouth or kissing

os·cu·late (os′kyə lāt′) *vt., vi.* **-lat′ed, -lat′ing** [< L. pp. of *osculari* < *osculum*, kiss, dim. of *os*, a mouth] **1.** to kiss: a jocular usage **2.** to touch closely **3.** *Biol.* to have (characteristics) in common —**os′cu·lant** *adj.* —**os′cu·la′-tion** *n.* —**os′cu·la·to·ry** *adj.*

-ose¹ (ōs) [Fr. < (*gluc*)*ose*: see GLUCOSE] a suffix designating: **1.** a carbohydrate [*sucrose*] **2.** the product of a protein hydrolysis [*proteose*]

-ose² (ōs) [L. *-osus*] a suffix meaning full of, having the qualities of, like [*verbose*]

o·sier (ō′zhər) *n.* [< OFr. < ML. *ausaria*, bed of willows] **1.** any of several willows whose branches or stems are used for baskets and furniture **2.** a willow branch used for wickerwork

-o·sis (ō′sis) [L. < Gr. *-ōsis*] a suffix meaning: **1.** state, condition, action [*osmosis*] **2.** an abnormal or diseased condition [*neurosis*]

-os·i·ty (os′ət ē) [< Fr. < L. *-ositas*] a suffix used to form nouns from adjectives ending in -OSE² and -OUS

Os·man·li (oz man′lē, os-) *n.* [Turk. < *Osman* (1259-1326), founder of Ottoman Empire] **1.** pl. **-lis** an Ottoman Turk **2.** *same as* TURKISH (n. 1) —*adj. same as* TURKISH

os·mics (oz′miks) *n.pl.* [*with sing. v.*] [< Gr. *osmē*, odour + -ICS] the science of smell

os·mi·um (oz′mē əm) *n.* [ModL. < Gr. *osmē*, odour: after the odour of one of its oxides] a very hard, bluish-white, metallic chemical element that occurs in the form of an alloy with platinum and iridium: symbol, Os; at. wt., 190.2; at. no., 76

os·mose (os′mōs, oz′-) *vt., vi.* **-mosed, -mos·ing** to undergo osmosis

os·mo·sis (os mō′sis, oz-) *n.* [ModL., ult. < Gr. *ōsmos*, impulse < *ōthein*, to push] **1.** the tendency of a solvent to pass through a semipermeable membrane, as the wall of a living cell, so as to equalize concentrations on both sides of the membrane **2.** the diffusion of fluids through a porous partition —**os·mot′ic** (-mot′ik) *adj.* —**os·mot′i·cal·ly** *adv.*

os·prey (os′prē) *n.,* pl. **-preys** [< L. *ossifraga*, lit., the bone-breaker < *os*, a bone + *frangere*, to break] a large diving bird of prey of the hawk family with a blackish back and white breast, that feeds solely on fish

‡**os·sa** (os′ə) *n.* pl. of OS¹

os·se·ous (os′ē əs) *adj.* [< L. < *os*, a bone] composed of, containing, or like bone; bony

os·si·fy (os′ə fī′) *vt., vi.* **-fied′, -fy′ing** [< L. *os* (gen. *ossis*), a bone + -FY] **1.** to change or develop into bone **2.** to settle or fix rigidly in a practice, custom, etc. —**os′si·fi·ca′tion** *n.*

OSPREY
(51-61 cm long)

os·te·al (os′tē əl) *adj.* osseous; bony

os·te·i·tis (os′tē īt′əs) *n.* [OSTE(O)- + -ITIS] inflammation of the bone or bony tissue

os·ten·si·ble (os ten′sə b'l, əs-) *adj.* [Fr. < ML. < L. *ostendere*, to show < *ob*(s)-, against + *tendere*, to stretch] apparent; seeming; professed —**os·ten′si·bly** *adv.*

os·ten·sive (os ten′siv) *adj.* **1.** directly pointing out; clearly demonstrative **2.** *same as* OSTENSIBLE —**os·ten′sive·ly** *adv.*

os·ten·ta·tion (os′tən tā′shən) *n.* [< L., ult. < *ostendere* see OSTENSIBLE] showy display, as of wealth, knowledge, etc.; pretentiousness —os'ten·ta'tious *adj.* —os'ten·ta'- tious·ly *adv.* —os'ten·ta'tious·ness *n.*

os·te·o- (os'tē ŏ',-ə) [ModL. < Gr. *osteon*] *a combining form meaning* a bone or bones [*osteopath*]: also, before a vowel, oste-

os·te·ol·o·gy (os'tē ol'ə jē) *n.* [ModL.: see prec. & -LOGY] the study of the structure and function of bones —os'- te·o·log'i·cal (-ə loj'i k'l) *adj.* —os'te·ol'o·gist *n.*

os·te·o·ma·la·cia (-ō mə lā'shə) *n.* [ModL. < OSTEO- + *malacia*, a softness of tissue] a bone disease characterized by a softening of the bones from a deficiency in calcium salts

os·te·o·my·e·li·tis (-ō mī' ə līt'is) *n.* [ModL.: see OSTEO- & MYELITIS] infection of bone marrow or structures

os·te·op·a·thy (os'tē op'ə thē) *n.* [ModL.: see OSTEO- & -PATHY] a school of medicine and surgery that seeks to cure ailments by manipulation of joints, esp. the spine —os'- te·o·path' (-ə path') *n.* —os'te·o·path'ic *adj.* —os'te·o·path'- i·cal·ly *adv.*

os·te·o·po·ro·sis (-ō pô rō'sis) *n.* [ModL. < OSTEO- + *porosis*, a porous condition] a bone disease characterized by brittleness in the bones accompanied by a loss of calcium

ost·ler (os'lər) *n.* [< HOSTELLER] one who takes care of horses at an inn, stable, etc.

os·tra·cism (os'trə siz'm) *n.* [see ff.] 1. in ancient Greece, the temporary banishment of a citizen by popular vote 2. an exclusion by general consent, as from society

os·tra·cize (-sīz') *vt.* -cized', -ciz'ing [Gr. *ostrakizein*, to exile by votes written on potsherds < *ostrakon*, a potsherd] to banish, exclude, etc. by ostracism

os·trich (os'trich) *n., pl.* -trich·es, -trich: see PLURAL, II, D, 1 [< OFr. < VL. < L. *avis*, bird + *struthio*, ostrich] 1. a swift-running, nonflying bird of Africa and the Near East, the largest living bird, with a long neck and legs and small wings 2. a person who refuses to recognize the truth, reality, etc.

OT., OT, O.T. Old Testament

O.T.C. Officer's Training Corps

oth·er (uth'ər) *adj.* [OE.] 1. being the remaining one or ones of two or more [Bill and the *other* boy(s)] 2. different or distinct from that or those implied [some *other* girl] 3. different [it is *other* than you think] 4. additional [to have no *other* coat] 5. former [in *other* times] —*pron.* 1. the other one [each loved the *other*] 2. some other person or thing [to do as *others* do] —*adv.* otherwise; differently [he can't do *other* than go] —of all others above all others —the other day (or night, etc.) not long ago —oth'er·ness *n.*

oth·er-di·rect·ed (-də rek'tid) *adj.* guided by or concerned with goals or ideals determined by others rather than oneself; conformist

oth·er·wise (-wīz') *adv.* 1. in another manner; differently [to believe *otherwise*] 2. in all other respects [an *otherwise* intelligent man] 3. in other circumstances —*adj.* different [his answer could not be *otherwise*]

other world a supposed world after death

oth·er-world·ly (-wurld'lē) *adj.* being apart from earthly or mundane interests; concerned with life in a future world —oth'er·world'li·ness *n.*

o·tic (ōt'ik, ot'-) *adj.* [Gr. *ōtikos* < *ous* (gen. *ōtos*), EAR[1]] of, or connected with the ear

-ot·ic (ot'ik) [Gr. *-ōtikos*] a suffix meaning: 1. of or affected with [*sclerotic*] 2. producing [*narcotic*]

o·ti·ose (ō'shē ōs', ōt'ē-) *adj.* [< L. < *otium*, leisure] 1. idle; indolent 2. ineffective; futile 3. useless; superfluous —o'ti·ose'ly *adv.* —o'ti·os'i·ty (-os'ə tē) *n.*

o·ti·tis (ō tīt'əs) *n.* [ModL.: see OTO- & -ITIS] inflammation of the ear

o·to- [< Gr. *ous* (gen. *ōtos*), the ear] *a combining form meaning* the ear [*otology*]: also, before a vowel, ot-

o·tol·o·gy (ō tol'ə jē) *n.* [OTO- + -LOGY] the branch of medicine dealing with the ear and its disorders —o·to·log'i·cal (ōt'ə loj'i k'l) *adj.* —o·tol'o·gist *n.*

o·to·scle·ro·sis (ōt'ō skli rō'sis) *n.* [OTO- + SCLEROSIS] a growth of spongy bone in the inner ear causing progressive deafness

ot·ter (ot'ər) *n., pl.* -ters, -ter: see PLURAL, II, D, 1 [OE. *otor*] 1. a furry, flesh-eating mammal related to the weasel and mink, with webbed feet and a long tail 2. its fur 3. *same as* SEA OTTER

ot·ter·hound (-hound) *n.* a breed of dog used in hunting otters

Ot·to·man (ot'ə mən) *adj.* [ult. < Ar. 'Uthmāni, of Osman: see OSMANLI] *same as* TURKISH —*n., pl.* -mans 1. a Turk 2. [o-] *a)* a low, cushioned seat or couch without a back or arms *b)* a cushioned footstool *c)* a container for blankets, often with a cushioned seat

O.U. 1. Open University 2. Oxford University

---

ou·bli·ette (oō'blē et') *n.* [Fr. < *oublier*, to forget] a concealed dungeon having a trap door in the ceiling as its only opening

ouch (ouch) *interj.* an exclamation of pain

ought[1] (ôt) *v.aux.* [orig., pt. of *owe* < OE. pp. of *agan*, to owe] an auxiliary used with infinitives to express obligation or duty [he *ought* to pay his debts] or desirability [you *ought* to eat more] or probability [it *ought* to be over soon], or advisibility [you *ought* to wear a hat]

ought[2] (ôt) *n.* [var. of AUGHT] anything whatever; aught —*adv.* [Archaic] to any degree; aught

ought[3] (ôt) *n.* [by faulty division of a *nought*] a nought; the figure zero (0)

ought·n't (-'nt) ought not

†oui (wē) *adv.* [Fr.] yes

Oui·ja (wē'jə, -jē) [Fr. *oui*, yes + G. *ja*, yes] a trademark for a device consisting of a planchette and a board bearing the alphabet and other symbols, used in spiritualistic séances, etc.

ounce[1] (ouns) *n.* [< OFr. < L. *uncia*, a twelfth] 1. a unit of weight equal to 1/16 pound avoirdupois, or 1/12 pound troy (28.35gm) 2. *same as* FLUID OUNCE 3. any small amount Abbrev. oz. (*sing. & pl.*)

ounce[2] (ouns) *n.* [< OFr. *l'once* < VL. < L. *lynx*, lynx] *same as* SNOW LEOPARD

O.U.P. Oxford University Press

our (our) *possessive pronominal adj.* [OE. *ure*] of, belonging to, made, or done by us

-our (ər; *occas.* ôr) [in OFr. -*eur*, L. -*or*] a *n.-forming suffix meaning* state, condition, or activity [*behaviour*, *labour*]: in U.S. usage, often -or

Our Father *same as* LORD'S PRAYER

ours (ourz) *pron.* that or those belonging to us: used without a following noun [*ours* are better]: also used after *of* to indicate possession [a friend of *ours*]

our·self (our self') *pron.* a form corresponding to OURSELVES, used, as in royal proclamations, by one person

our·selves (-selvz') *pron.* a form of the 1st pers. pl. pronoun, used: *a)* as an intensive [we went *ourselves*] *b)* as a reflexive [we hurt *ourselves*] *c)* as a quasi-noun meaning "our real or true selves" [we are not *ourselves* today]

-ous (əs) [< OFr. < L. -*osus*] *a suffix meaning*: 1. having, full of, characterized by [*dangerous*] 2. *Chem.* having a lower valence than is indicated by the suffix -*ic* [*nitrous*]

ou·sel (oō'z'l) *n. same as* OUZEL

oust (oust) *vt.* [< Anglo-Fr. < OFr. *ouster* < L. *ostare* < *ob-*, against + *stare*, to stand] to force or drive out; expel, dispossess, eject, etc.

oust·er (ou'stər) *n.* 1. a person or thing that ousts 2. *Law* an ousting or being ousted, esp. from freehold property; legal eviction or unlawful dispossession

out (out) *adv.* [OE. *ut*] 1. *a)* away or forth from a place, position, etc. [they live ten miles out] *b)* away from home *c)* away from shore *d)* on strike 2. into the open air [come out and play] 3. into existence or activity [disease broke out] 4. *a)* to a conclusion [fight it out] *b)* completely [tired out] *c)* in full bloom, or in leaf 5. into sight or notice [the moon came out] 6. *a)* into or in circulation [to put out a new style] *b)* into or in society [debutantes who come out] 7. from existence or activity [fade out] 8. so as to remove from power or office [vote them out] 9. aloud [sing out] 10. beyond a regular surface, condition, etc. [stand out, eke out] 11. away from the interior or midst [spread out] 12. from one state, as of composure, to another, as of annoyance [friends may fall out] 13. into disuse, discard, etc. [long skirts went out] 14. from a number or stock [pick out] 15. [Colloq.] into unconsciousness [to pass out] —*adj.* 1. external: usually in combination [*outpost*] 2. beyond regular limits 3. outlying 4. away from work, etc. 5. deviating from what is accurate 6. *a)* not in operation, use, etc. *b)* turned off; extinguished 7. not to be considered; not possible 8. not in power 9. [Colloq.] having suffered a loss [out five pounds] 10. [Colloq.] outmoded —*prep.* 1. out of; through to the outside 2. along the way of [to run out of a door] 3. [Poet.] forth from: usually after *from* —*n.* 1. something that is out 2. a person, group, etc. that is not in power, etc.: *usually used in pl.* 3. [U.S. Slang] a way out; means of avoiding 4. [U.S.] *Baseball* the failure of a batter or runner to reach base safely 5. *Tennis, Squash, etc.* a service or return that lands out of bounds —*vi.* to come out; esp., to become known —*vt.* to put out —*interj.* get out! —out and away by far; without comparison —out and out completely; thoroughly —out for making a determined effort to get or do —out of 1. from inside 2. from the number of 3. beyond 4. from (material, etc.) [made *out of* stone] 5. because of [out of spite] 6. having no [out of order] 7. not in a condition of [out of order] 8. so as to deprive [cheat out of money] —out to making a determined effort to

out- [< OUT] *a combining form meaning*: 1. at or from a

point away, outside [*outbuilding*] **2.** going away or forth, outward [*outbound*] **3.** better, greater, or more than [*outdo*]: a frequent usage as in the following self-explanatory terms:

outact	outhit	outscore
outbox	outperform	outshout
outfight	outproduce	outspend

out·age (out′ij) *n.* [OUT- + -AGE] an accidental suspension of operation, as of electric power

out-and-out (out′n out′) *adj.* complete; thorough

out·back (out′bak′) *n.* [*also* O-] the sparsely settled, flat, arid inland region of Australia

out·bal·ance (out′bal′əns) *vt.* -anced, -anc·ing to be greater than in weight, value, etc.

out·bid (-bid′) *vt.* -bid′, -bid′ding to bid or offer more than (someone else)

out·board (out′bôrd′) *adj., adv.* **1.** outside the hull or bulwarks of a ship or boat **2.** away from the fuselage or hull of an aircraft **3.** outside the main body of a spacecraft —*n.* **1.** *same as* OUTBOARD MOTOR **2.** a boat with an outboard motor

outboard motor a portable petrol engine mounted outboard on a boat to propel it

out·bound (-bound′) *adj.* outward bound

out·break (-brāk′) *n.* a breaking out; sudden occurrence, as of disease, war, rioting, etc.

out·build·ing (-bil′diŋ) *n.* a structure, as a garage, separate from the main building

out·burst (-burst′) *n.* a sudden release, as of feeling, energy, etc.

out·cast (-kast′) *adj.* driven out; rejected —*n.* a person or thing cast out or rejected

out·caste (-kāst′) *n.* in India, a person expelled from his caste, or one who belongs to no caste

out·class (out′kläs′) *vt.* to surpass; excel

out·come (out′kum′) *n.* result; consequence

out·crop (out′krop′; *for v.* -krop′) *n.* **1.** the emergence of a mineral from the earth so as to be exposed on the surface **2.** the mineral —*vi.* -cropped′, -crop′ping **1.** to emerge in this way **2.** to break forth

out·cry (-krī′) *n.*, *pl.* -cries′ **1.** a crying out **2.** a strong protest or objection

out·dat·ed (out′dāt′id) *adj.* no longer popular

out·dis·tance (-dis′təns) *vt.* -tanced, -tanc·ing to leave behind, as in a race

out·do (-dōō′) *vt.* -did′, -done′, -do′ing to exceed or surpass —**outdo oneself** to do one's best or better than expected

out·door (out′dôr′) *adj.* **1.** being or taking place outdoors **2.** of, or fond of, the outdoors

out·doors (-dôrz′) *adv.* in or into the open; outside —*n.* **1.** any area outside a building **2.** countryside, etc. where there are few houses

out·er (out′ər) *adj.* **1.** located farther out; exterior **2.** relatively far removed [*the outer regions*]

Outer House in Scotland, a court of Session where judges sit singly

out·er·most (-mōst′) *adj.* located furthest without

outer space **1.** space beyond the atmosphere of the earth **2.** space outside the solar system

out·er·wear (-wer′) *n.* outer garments, as overcoats

out·face (out′fās′) *vt.* -faced′, -fac′ing **1.** to subdue with a look or stare **2.** to defy or resist

out·fall (out′fôl′) *n.* the outlet of a river, sewer, etc.

out·field (out′fēld′) *n.* the playing area beyond the infield in Cricket & Baseball

out·field·er (-ər) *n.* *Baseball & Cricket* a player whose position is in the outfield

out·fit (-fit′) *n.* **1.** *a)* a set of articles for equipping *b)* the equipment used in any craft or activity **2.** articles of clothing worn together **3.** a group of people associated in some activity, as a military unit —*vt.* -fit′ted, -fit′ting to equip —*vi.* to obtain an outfit —**out′fit′ter** *n.*

out·flank (out′flaŋk′) *vt.* **1.** to go around and beyond the flank of (enemy troops) **2.** to thwart; outwit

out·flow (out′flō′) *n.* **1.** the act of flowing out **2.** *a)* that which flows out *b)* amount flowing out

out·fox (out′foks′) *vt.* to outwit; outsmart

out·gen·er·al (-jen′ər əl) *vt.* -alled, -al·ling to surpass, as in leadership

out·go (out′gō′; *for n.* out′gō′) *vt.* -went′, -gone′, -go′ing to surpass; go beyond —*n.*, *pl.* -goes′ **1.** a going out **2.** that which goes or is paid out; outflow or expenditure

out·go·ing (out′gō′iŋ) *adj.* **1.** going out; leaving **2.** sociable, friendly, etc. —*n.* **1.** the act of going out **2.** [*usually pl.*] an outlay; expenses

out·grow (out′grō′) *vt.* -grew′, -grown′, -grow′ing **1.** to grow faster or larger than **2.** to lose or get rid of by becoming mature **3.** to grow too large for

out·growth (out′grōth′) *n.* **1.** a growing out **2.** a result; consequence; development **3.** an offshoot

out·guess (out′ges′) *vt.* to outwit; anticipate

out·house (out′hous′) *n.* an outbuilding; esp. in U.S., a small outbuilding with a toilet over a pit

out·ing (-iŋ) *n.* **1.** a pleasure trip or holiday away from home **2.** an outdoor walk, ride, etc.

out·land·ish (out lan′dish) *adj.* **1.** very odd; fantastic **2.** remote; out-of-the-way —**out·land′ish·ly** *adv.*

out·last (-lāst′) *vt.* **1.** to endure longer than **2.** to outlive

out·law (out′lô′) *n.* [OE. *utlaga* < ON. *utlagr*] **1.** orig., a person deprived of legal rights and protection **2.** a notorious criminal who is a fugitive from the law —*vt.* **1.** orig., to declare to be an outlaw **2.** to declare illegal **3.** to bar, or ban —**out′law′ry** *n.*, *pl.* -ries

out·lay (out′lā′; *for v.*, *usually* out′lā′) *n.* **1.** a spending (of money, energy, etc.) **2.** money, etc. spent —*vt.* -laid′, -lay′ing to spend (money)

out·let (out′let′) *n.* **1.** a passage for letting something out **2.** a means of expression [*an outlet for rage*] **3.** a stream, river, etc. that flows out from a lake **4.** *a)* a market for goods *b)* a shop, etc. that sells the goods of a specific manufacturer or wholesaler **5.** [U.S.] an electric power point

out·line (-līn′) *n.* **1.** a line bounding the limits of an object **2.** a sketch showing the contours of an object **3.** [*also pl.*] an undetailed general plan **4.** a systematic listing of the important points of a subject —*adj.* providing an outline only; not detailed [*an outline proposal*] —*vt.* -lined′, -lin′ing **1.** to draw in outline **2.** to list the main points of

out·live (out′liv′) *vt.* -lived′, -liv′ing **1.** to live or endure longer than **2.** to live through; outlast

out·look (out′look′) *n.* **1.** *a)* a place for looking out *b)* the view from such a place **2.** a looking out **3.** viewpoint **4.** prospect; probable result

out·ly·ing (-lī′iŋ) *adj.* relatively far out from a certain point or centre; remote

out·man (out′man′) *vt.* -manned′, -man′ning to surpass in number of men

out·ma·noeu·vre (-mə nōō′vər) *vt.* -vred, -vring to manoeuvre with better effect than; outwit: also chiefly U.S. **outmaneuver**

out·match (-mach′) *vt.* to surpass; outdo

out·mod·ed (out′mōd′id) *adj.* no longer in fashion or accepted; obsolete

out·most (out′mōst′) *adj.* most remote; outermost

out·num·ber (out′num′bər) *vt.* to exceed in number

out-of-date (out′əv dāt′) *adj.* no longer in style or use; outmoded; old-fashioned

out-of-door (-dôr′) *adj.* *same as* OUTDOOR

out-of-doors (-dôrz′) *adv., n.* *same as* OUTDOORS

out-of-pock·et (-pok′it) *adj.* **1.** having lost money **2.** without money to spend **3.** designating unbudgeted expenses, or ready cash paid out, as for miscellaneous items

out-of-the-way (-thə wā′) *adj.* **1.** secluded **2.** unusual

out·pace (out′pās′) *vt.* -paced′, -pac′ing to surpass; exceed

out·pa·tient (out′pā′shənt) *n.* a patient, not an inmate, receiving treatment at a hospital

out·play (out′plā′) *vt.* to play better than

out·point (-point′) *vt.* to score more points than

out·post (out′pōst′) *n.* **1.** *Mil. a)* a small group stationed at a distance from the main force, to prevent a surprise attack *b)* the station so occupied *c)* any military base away from the home country **2.** *a)* a settlement on a frontier *b)* a place considered remote from the centre of an activity etc. [*outpost of learning*]

out·pour (out′pôr′; *for v.* out′pôr′) *n.* **1.** a pouring out **2.** outflow Also **out′pour′ing** —*vt., vi.* to pour out

out·put (out′poot′) *n.* **1.** the work done or amount produced, esp. over a given period **2.** in computers, *a)* information transferred or delivered *b)* the act or process of transferring or delivering this information *c)* any of various devices involved in this process **3.** *Elec. a)* the useful current delivered by amplifiers, generators, etc. or by a circuit *b)* the terminal where such energy is delivered

out·rage (out′rāj′) *n.* [< OFr. < *outre*, beyond < L. *ultra*] **1.** an extremely vicious or violent act **2.** a deep insult or offence **3.** great anger, indignation, etc. aroused by such an act or offence —*vt.* -raged′, -rag′ing **1.** to commit an outrage upon; specif., *a)* to offend, insult, or wrong *b)* to rape **2.** to cause great anger, etc. in

out·ra·geous (out rā′jəs) *adj.* **1.** involving or doing great injury or wrong **2.** very offensive or shocking **3.** violent in action or disposition —**out·ra′geous·ly** *adv.* —**out·ra′geous·ness** *n.*

out·rank (out′raŋk′) *vt.* to exceed in rank

‡**out·ré** (ōō trā′; *E.* -trā′) *adj.* [Fr.] **1.** exaggerated **2.** eccentric; bizarre

out·reach (out′rēch′; *for n.* out′rēch′) *vt., vi.* **1.** to reach farther (than); surpass **2.** to reach out; extend —*n.* **1.** a reaching out **2.** the extent of reach

out·ride (out′rīd′) *vt.* -rode′, -rid′den, -rid′ing **1.** to surpass in riding **2.** to endure successfully

out·rid·er (out′rīd′ər) *n.* **1.** an attendant on horseback who rides ahead of or beside a carriage **2.** a motorcyclist, who rides ahead of or beside a car, or group of cars **3.** a trailblazer; forerunner

out·rig·ger (-rig'ər) *n.* **1.** any framework extended beyond the rail of a ship, as a projecting brace for an oarlock **2.** a timber rigged out from the side of a native canoe to prevent tipping; also, a canoe of this type

out·right (out'rīt'; *for adv.* out'rīt') *adj.* **1.** without reservation; downright **2.** straightforward **3.** complete; whole —*adv.* **1.** entirely **2.** openly **3.** at once —**out'right'ness** *n.*

OUTRIGGER

out·run (out'run') *vt.* **-ran', -run', -run'ning 1.** to run faster or further than **2.** to exceed **3.** to escape (a pursuer) as by running

out·sell (-sel') *vt.* **-sold', -sell'ing 1.** to sell in greater amounts than **2.** to excel in salesmanship

out·set (out'set') *n.* a setting out; beginning

out·shine (out'shīn') *vt.* **-shone'-shin'ing 1.** to shine brighter or longer than (another) **2.** to surpass; excel —*vi.* to shine forth

out·shoot (out'shoot'; *for n.* out'shoot') *vt., vi.* **-shot', -shoot'ing** to shoot better than (another) —*n.* that which shoots out or protrudes

out·side (out'sīd', out'-; -sīd') *n.* **1.** the outer side, part, or surface; exterior **2.** *a)* outward aspect or appearance *b)* that which is obvious or superficial **3.** any place or area not inside —*adj.* **1.** of or on the outside; outer **2.** coming from or situated beyond given limits; from some other place, person, group, etc. [to accept no *outside* help] **3.** extreme [an *outside* estimate] **4.** mere; slight [an *outside* chance] —*adv.* **1.** on or to the outside **2.** beyond certain limits **3.** outdoors —*prep.* **1.** on or to the outer side of **2.** beyond the limits of —**at the outside** at the very most —**get outside of** [Colloq.] eat or drink —**outside of** [Chiefly U.S.] outside

outside broadcast *Radio & T.V.* a broadcast taking place away from the studio [the Cup Final was an *outside broadcast*]

out·sid·er (out'sīd'ər) *n.* one who is outside or not included; esp., one not a member of or in sympathy with a given group

out·sit (-sit') *vt.* **-sat', -sit'ting** to sit longer than or beyond the time of

out·size (out'sīz') *n.* **1.** an odd size; esp., an unusually large size **2.** a garment, etc. of such a size —*adj.* of nonstandard size; esp., unusually large: also **out'sized'**

out·skirts (-skurts') *n.pl.* the outer areas, as of a city

out·smart (out'smärt') *vt.* [Colloq.] to overcome by cunning or cleverness; outwit

out·spo·ken (out'spō'kən) *adj.* **1.** unrestrained in speech; frank **2.** spoken boldly or candidly —**out'spo'ken·ly** *adv.* —**out'spo'ken·ness** *n.*

out·spread (out'spred'; *for adj. & n.* out'spred') *vt., vi.* **-spread', -spread'ing** to spread out; extend; expand —*n.* a spreading out —*adj.* spread out; extended; expanded

out·stand·ing (out'stand'iŋ) *adj.* **1.** projecting **2.** prominent; distinguished **3.** unsettled **4.** unpaid **5.** that have been issued and sold: said of stocks and bonds —**out'stand'ing·ly** *adv.*

out·stare (-ster') *vt.* **-stared', -star'ing** to outdo in staring; stare down; outface

out·stay (-stā') *vt.* **1.** to stay longer than **2.** to stay beyond the time of; overstay

out·stretch (-strech') *vt.* **1.** to extend **2.** to stretch beyond —**out'stretched'** *adj.*

out·strip (-strip') *vt.* **-stripped', -strip'ping 1.** to go at a faster pace than; get ahead of **2.** to surpass; excel

out·talk (-tôk') *vt.* to talk more skilfully, loudly, or forcibly than; surpass in talking

out·think (-thiŋk') *vt.* **-thought', -think'ing 1.** to think deeper, faster, or more cunningly than **2.** to outwit by such thinking

out tray a receptacle in an office to hold papers, etc. that have been dealt with

out·vote (-vōt') *vt.* **-vot'ed, -vot'ing** to defeat or surpass in voting

out·ward (out'wərd) *adj.* **1.** having to do with the outside; outer **2.** readily seen; visible **3.** to or towards the outside **4.** having to do with the physical as opposed to the mind or spirit **5.** superficial or external —*adv.* **1.** towards the outside; away **2.** visibly; publicly Also **out'wards** —*n.* that which is outward —**out'ward·ness** *n.*

outward bound 1. travelling away from home, specif. a ship from its home port. **2.** [O- B-] a scheme to provide adventure training, such as mountaineering and sailing, for young people

out·ward·ly (-lē) *adv.* **1.** towards or on the outside **2.** with regard to outward appearance or action

out·wear (out'wer') *vt.* **-wore', -worn', -wear'ing 1.** to wear out **2.** to be more lasting than

out·weigh (-wā') *vt.* **1.** to weigh more than **2.** to be more important, valuable, etc. than

out·wit (-wit') *vt.* **-wit'ted, -wit'ting** to get the better of by cunning or cleverness

out·with (out'with') *adj.* [Scot.] outside; without; beyond

out·work (out'wurk'; *for v.* out'wurk') *n.* **1.** a lesser fortification built out beyond the main defences **2.** work brought from a factory, etc. to be done at home —*vt.* **-worked'** or **-wrought', -work'ing** to work better or harder than

ouz·el (oo'z'l) *n.* [OE. *osle*] any of several perching birds including the dippers, of Europe, Asia, and the Americas

ou·zo (oo'zō) *n.* [Mod Gr. *ouzon* < ?] a colourless Greek spirit flavoured with aniseed

o·va (ō'və) *n. pl. of* OVUM

o·val (ō'v'l) *adj.* [< Fr. < L. *ovum*, an egg] **1.** shaped like the cross section of an egg lengthways; elliptical **2.** having the form of an egg —*n.* anything oval —**o'val·ly** *adv.* —**o'val·ness** *n.*

o·var·i·ec·to·my (ō·ver'ē·ek'tə·mē) *n., pl.* **-mies** [see -ECTOMY] the surgical removal of one or both ovaries

o·va·ry (ō'vər·ē) *n., pl.* **-ries** [< ModL. < L. *ovum*, an egg] **1.** *Anat., Zool.* either of the pair of female reproductive glands producing eggs and, in vertebrates, sex hormones **2.** *Bot.* the enlarged hollow part of the pistil, containing ovules —**o·var·i·an** (ō·ver'ē·ən) *adj.*

o·vate (ō'vāt) *adj.* [< L. < *ovum*, an egg] **1.** egg-shaped **2.** *Bot.* shaped like the longitudinal section of an egg, esp. with the broader end at the base, as some leaves —**o'vate·ly** *adv.*

o·va·tion (ō·vā'shən) *n.* [L. *ovatio* < *ovare*, to celebrate a triumph] an enthusiastic outburst of applause or an enthusiastic public welcome

ov·en (uv'ən) *n.* [OE. *ofen*] a compartment or receptacle for baking or roasting food or for heating or drying things

ov·en·bird (-burd') *n.* **1.** any of several S American perching birds that build ovenlike nests **2.** a N American warbler that builds a domelike nest on the ground

o·ver (ō'vər) *prep.* [OE. *ofer*] **1.** *a)* in, at, or to a position up from; above *b)* across and down from [to fall *over* a cliff] **2.** while engaged in [discuss it *over* dinner] **3.** upon the surface of [spread icing *over* the cake] **4.** so as to cover [shutters *over* the windows] **5.** upon, as an effect or influence [he cast a spell *over* us] **6.** with care, concern, etc. for [watch *over* the flock] **7.** above in authority, power, etc. **8.** along or across, or above and to the other side of [fly *over* the lake] **9.** on the other side of [a city *over* the border] **10.** through all or many parts of [*over* the whole country] **11.** during [*over* a decade] **12.** more than [*over* ten pounds] **13.** up to and including [stay *over* Easter] **14.** [Chiefly U.S.] rather than **15.** concerning; about **16.** through the medium of [*over* the radio] —*adv.* **1.** *a)* above, across, or to the other side *b)* across the brim or edge **2.** more; beyond [three hours or *over*] **3.** longer or till a time later **4.** covering the entire area [the wound healed *over*] **5.** from start to finish [count the money *over*] **6.** *a)* from an upright position [he fell *over*] *b)* upside down [turn the cup *over*] **7.** at or on the other side, as of an intervening space [*over* in Spain] **8.** from one side, viewpoint, person, etc. to another [they won him *over*] —*adj.* **1.** upper, outer, superior, excessive, or extra: often in combination [*overcoat, overseer, oversupply*] **2.** finished; past [his life is *over*] **3.** having reached the other side **4.** [Colloq.] as a surplus; extra [an hour *over* for the week] —*n.* **1.** something in addition; surplus **2.** *Cricket a)* a set of six (or eight) balls bowled by one bowler from one end of the wicket *b)* the period of time during which this takes place —*interj.* turn the page, etc. over—**all over 1.** utterly finished **2.** over one's entire body [she blushed *all over*] **3.** typical; peculiar [that's men *all over*] **4.** [Colloq.] extremely attentive or affectionate towards —**over again** another time; anew —**over and above** besides; in addition —**over against** opposite; in front of; in contrast to —**over all** from end to end —**over and above** more than —**over and over (again)** repeatedly

o·ver- *a combining form meaning:* **1.** above in position, outer, upper, superior [*overhead, overlord*] **2.** passing across or beyond [*overrun*] **3.** involving a movement downward from above [*overflow*] **4.** excessive(ly), too much [*overload, oversell*]: the list below includes some common compounds formed with over- that can be understood if *too* or *too much* is added to the meaning of the base word

overabundance	overeager	overpeopled
overabundant	overeat	overpopulate
overactive	overemotional	overpraise
overambitious	overemphasize	overprecise
overanxious	overenthusiastic	overrefined
overattentive	overexercise	overreligious
overbold	overexert	overripe
overbuild	overexpand	oversensitive

overburden
overbusy
overbuy
overcapitalize
overcareful
overcareless
overcautious
overcompensate
overconfident
overconscientious
overconservative
overcook
overcritical
overcrowd
overdecorate
overdependent
overdye

overexpose
overfed
overfond
overgenerous
overgreedy
overhasty
overheat
overindulge
overindulgence
overinflate
overinvert
overladen
overlong
overnice
overorganize
overpay
overpayment

oversentimental
oversexed
oversolicitous
overspecialize
overstimulate
overstretch
overstrict
overstudy
oversubtle
oversufficient
oversuspicious
overtire
overuse
overvalue
overwind
overzealous

o·ver·act (ō'vər akt') *vt., vi.* to act with exaggeration
o·ver·age (ō'vər āj') *adj.* 1. over the age fixed as a standard 2. so old as to be of no use
o·ver·all (ō'vər ôl'; *for adv.* -ôl') *adj.* 1. from end to end 2. including everything; total —*adv.* 1. from end to end 2. in general —*n.* a garment worn over the ordinary clothing as a protection against dirt
o·ver·alls (-ôlz') *n.pl.* loose-fitting trousers, often with an attached bib, worn over other clothing to protect against dirt and wear
o·ver·arm (-ärm') *adj.* performed by raising the arm above the shoulder, as in swimming or cricket
o·ver·awe (ō'vər ô') *vt.* -awed', -aw'ing to overcome or subdue by inspiring awe
o·ver·bal·ance (ō'vər bal'əns; *for n.* ō'vər bal'əns) *vt.* -anced, -anc·ing 1. same as OUTWEIGH 2. to throw off balance —*n.* something that overbalances
o·ver·bear (ō'vər ber') *vt.* -bore', -borne', -bear'ing 1. to press down by weight or physical power 2. to dominate or subdue —*vi.* to be too fruitful
o·ver·bear·ing (-iŋ) *adj.* 1. arrogant or domineering 2. dominant or overriding —o'ver·bear'ing·ly *adv.* —o'·ver·bear'ing·ness *n.*
o·ver·bid (ō'vər bid'; *for n.* ō'vər bid') *vt., vi.* -bid', -bid'-ding 1. to outbid (another person) 2. to bid more than the worth of (a thing, as one's hand in bridge) —*n.* a higher or excessive bid
o·ver·blown¹ (ō'vər blōn') *adj.* past the stage of full bloom
o·ver·blown² (ō'vər blōn') *adj.* 1. stout; obese 2. *a)* overdone; excessive *b)* pompous; bombastic
o·ver·board (ō'vər bôrd') *adv.* 1. over a ship's side 2. from a ship into the water —go overboard [Colloq.] to go to extremes
o·ver·book (-book') *vt.* -booked', book'ing to make more bookings than there are vacancies, as for an aircraft flight
o·ver·cast (ō'vər kast'; *for v.* 1, *usually* ō'vər kast') *n.* a covering, esp. of clouds —*adj.* 1. cloudy: said of the sky or weather 2. *Sewing* made with overcasting —*vt., vi.* -cast', -cast'ing 1. to overcloud 2. *Sewing* to sew over (an edge) with long, loose stitches to prevent unravelling
o·ver·charge (ō'vər chärj'; *for n.* ō'vər chärj') *vt., vi.* -charged', -charg'ing 1. to charge too high a price 2. to overload 3. to exaggerate —*n.* 1. an excessive charge 2. too full or heavy a load
o·ver·cloud (-kloud') *vt., vi.* 1. to darken or cover over with clouds; dim 2. to make or become gloomy, angry, etc. in appearance
o·ver·coat (ō'vər kōt') *n.* a coat, esp. a heavy coat, worn over the usual clothing for warmth
o·ver·come (ō'vər kum') *vt.* -came', -come', -com'ing 1. to get the better of in competition, etc.; conquer 2. to master, prevail over, or surmount [to overcome obstacles] 3. to overpower or overwhelm [overcome by laughter] —*vi.* to win
o·ver·com·pen·sate (-kom'pən sāt') *vt.* -sat'ed, -sat'ing to give an excessive compensation to —*vt. Psychol.* to attempt to make up for or conceal a fault or character trait by overexaggerating its opposite
o·ver·de·vel·op (-di vel'əp) *vt.* 1. to develop too much 2. *Photog.* to develop (a film, plate, etc.) too long or in too strong a developer —o'ver·de·vel'op·ment *n.*
o·ver·do (-dōō') *vt.* -did', -done', -do'ing 1. to do too much, or to excess 2. to spoil the effect of by exaggeration 3. to cook too long 4. to exhaust; tire —*vi.* to do too much
o·ver·dose (ō'vər dōs'; *for v.* ō'vər dōs') *n.* too large a dose, esp. one causing death —*vt.* -dosed', -dos'ing to dose to excess
o·ver·draft (ō'vər draft') *n.* 1. an overdrawing of money from a bank 2. the amount overdrawn
o·ver·draw (ō'vər drô') *vt.* -drew', -drawn', -draw'ing 1. to spoil the effect of by exaggeration 2. to draw on in excess of the amount credited to the drawer
o·ver·dress (-dres') *vt., vi.* to dress too warmly, too showily, or too formally for the occasion

o·ver·drive (ō'vər drīv') *n.* a gear that automatically reduces an engine's power output without reducing its driving speed
o·ver·due (ō'vər dyōō') *adj.* 1. past or delayed beyond the time set for payment, arrival, etc. 2. that should have come about sooner
o·ver·es·ti·mate (-es'tə māt'; *for n.* -mit) *vt.* -mat'ed, -mat'-ing to set too high an estimate on or for —*n.* an estimate that is too high —o'ver·es'ti·ma'tion *n.*
o·ver·flow (ō'vər flō'; *for n.* ō'vər flō') *vt.* 1. to flow or spread across; flood 2. to flow over the brim or edge of 3. to cause to overflow by filling beyond capacity —*vi.* 1. to run over 2. to be superabundant —*n.* 1. an overflowing or being overflowed 2. the amount that overflows; surplus 3. an outlet for overflowing liquids
o·ver·fly (ō'vər flī') *vt.* -flew', -flown', -fly'ing to fly an aircraft over (a specified area) or beyond (a specified place), as for reconnaissance —o'ver·flight' *n.*
o·ver·grow (-grō') *vt.* -grew', -grown', -grow'ing 1. to overspread with growth or foliage so as to cover up 2. to outgrow —*vi.* 1. to grow too large or too fast 2. to grow beyond normal size —o'ver·grown' *adj.* —o'ver·growth' *n.*
o·ver·hand (ō'vər hand') *adj.* 1. with the hand over the object it grasps 2. done with the hand raised above the shoulder 3. designating or of sewing in which the stitches are passed over two edges to sew them together —*adv.* in an overhand manner —*vt.* to sew overhand —*n. Sports* an overhand stroke
o·ver·hang (ō'vər haŋ'; *for n.* ō'vər haŋ') *vt.* -hung', -hang'-ing 1. to hang or project over or beyond 2. to impend; threaten —*vi.* to project or jut out over something —*n.* 1. the projection of one thing over or beyond another 2. an overhanging or projecting part
o·ver·haul (ō'vər hôl'; *for n.* ō'vər hôl') *vt.* 1. to haul over, as for examination 2. *a)* to check thoroughly for needed repairs, adjustments, etc. *b)* to make such repairs, etc., as on a motor car, etc. 3. to catch up with or overtake —*n.* an overhauling
o·ver·head (ō'vər hed'; *for adv.* ō'vər hed') *adj.* 1. located or operating above the level of the head 2. in the sky 3. on a higher level, with reference to related objects —*n.* [*usually pl.*] the general, continuing costs of running a business, as of rent, maintenance, taxes, etc. —*adv.* above the head; aloft
o·ver·hear (ō'vər hir') *vt.* -heard', -hear'ing to hear (something spoken or a speaker) without the speaker's knowledge or intention
o·ver·joy (-joi') *vt.* to give great joy to; delight
o·ver·kill (ō'vər kil') *n.* 1. the capacity of a nation's nuclear weapon stockpile to kill many times the total population of any given nation 2. any capacity or treatment which is greater than that required
o·ver·land (-land', -lənd) *adv., adj.* by, on, or across land —*vt., vi.* [Aust.] to drive sheep or cattle or go overland for long distances —o'ver·land'er *n.*
o·ver·lap (ō'vər lap'; *for n.* ō'vər lap') *vt., vi.* -lapped', -lap'-ping to lap over; to extend over (something or each other) so as to coincide in part —*n.* 1. an overlapping 2. a part that overlaps 3. the extent or place of overlapping
o·ver·lay (ō'vər lā'; *for n.* ō'vər lā') *vt.* -laid', -lay'ing 1. to lay or spread over 2. to cover, as with a decorative layer —*n.* 1. a covering 2. a decorative layer or the like 3. a transparent flap showing additional details, areas of colour, etc. placed over a map, art work, etc.
o·ver·leaf (ō'vər lēf') *adj., adv.* on the other side of the page or sheet
o·ver·leap (ō'vər lēp') *vt.* 1. to leap over or across 2. to omit; pass over 3. to overreach (oneself) by leaping too far
o·ver·lie (-lī') *vt.* -lay', -lain', -ly'ing to lie on or over 2. to stifle or smother by lying on, esp. a newborn baby or animal
o·ver·load (ō'vər lōd'; *for n.* ō'vər lōd') *vt.* to put too great a load in or on —*n.* too great a load
o·ver·look (ō'vər look'; *for n.* ō'vər look') *vt.* 1. to look at from above 2. to give a view of from above 3. to rise above 4. *a)* to look beyond and not see *b)* to ignore; neglect 5. to pass over indulgently; excuse 6. to oversee; supervise —*n.* a height or the view from it
o·ver·lord (ō'vər lôrd') *n.* a lord ranking above other lords, esp. in the feudal system
o·ver·ly (-lē) *adv.* [Chiefly U.S. & Scot.] too or too much; excessively
o·ver·man (ō'vər man') *vt.* -manned', -man'ning to supply with more men than necessary
o·ver·mas·ter ((-mäs'tər) *vt.* to overcome; conquer
o·ver·match (-mach') *vt.* 1. to be more than a match for 2. to match against a superior opponent
o·ver·much (ō'vər much') *adj., adv.* too much —*n.* too great a quantity; excessive amount
o·ver·night (ō'vər nīt'; *for adj.* ō'vər nīt') *adv.* 1. during the night 2. on or during the previous evening 3. very suddenly —*adj.* 1. done or going on during the night 2. of

the previous evening **3.** for one night [an *overnight* guest]
4. of or for a brief trip [an *overnight* bag]

o·ver·pass (ō′vər pas′) *n.* a bridge or other passageway over a road, railway, etc.: see also FLYOVER (sense 1)

o·ver·play (ō′vər plā′) *vt.* **1.** to overact, overdo, or overemphasize **2.** *Card Games* to overestimate the strength of (one's hand)

o·ver·pop·u·late (-pop′yə lāt′) *vt.* **-lat′ed, -lat′ing** to populate (an area) too heavily for the available resources —**o′ver·pop′u·la′tion** *n.*

o·ver·pow·er (-pou′ər) *vt.* **1.** to get the better of; make helpless; subdue; overwhelm **2.** to supply with more power than is needed —**o′ver·pow′er·ing** *adj.* —**o′ver·pow′er·ing·ly** *adv.*

o·ver·print (ō′vər print′; *for n.* ō′vər print′) *vt.* to print over (a previously printed surface) —*n.* anything overprinted, as (on) a stamp

o·ver·pro·duce (ō′vər prə dyōōs′) *vt., vi.* **-duced′, -duc′ing** to produce in a quantity that exceeds the need or demand —**o′ver·pro·duc′tion** *n.*

o·ver·pro·tect (-prə tekt′) *vt.* to protect more than is necessary; specif., to seek to shield (one's child, etc.) from normal hurts or conflicts —**o′ver·pro·tec′tive** *adj.*

o·ver·rate (-rāt′) *vt.* **-rat′ed, -rat′ing** to rate or estimate too highly, esp. for rating purposes

o·ver·reach (-rēch′) *vt.* **1.** to reach beyond or above **2.** to reach too far for and miss **3.** to outwit or cheat —*vi.* to reach too far —**overreach oneself 1.** to fail because of trying more than one can do **2.** to fail because of being too crafty or eager —**o′ver·reach′er** *n.*

o·ver·re·act (-rē akt′) *vi.* to react in an extreme, highly emotional way, as by undue use of force

o·ver·ride (-rīd′) *vt.* **-rode′, -rid′den, -rid′ing 1.** to ride over **2.** to trample down **3.** to suppress or prevail over **4.** to disregard, overrule, or nullify **5.** to fatigue (a horse, etc.) by riding too long

o·ver·rid·er (ō′vər rīd′ər) *n.* an attachment fitted to the front bumper of a motor which prevents the bumper becoming locked together with another car's bumper in a crash

o·ver·rule (-rōōl′) *vt.* **-ruled′, -rul′ing 1.** to set aside or decide against, as by higher authority; rule against or rule out **2.** to prevail over

o·ver·run (-run′; *for n.* ō′vər run′) *vt.* **-ran′, -run′, -run′ning 1.** to spread out over so as to cover **2.** to swarm over, as vermin, or ravage, as an army **3.** to invade or conquer by a rapid advance **4.** to spread swiftly throughout, as ideas **5.** to run beyond (certain limits) —*vi.* **1.** to overflow **2.** to run beyond certain limits —*n.* **1.** an act or instance of overrunning **2.** the amount that overruns

o·ver·seas (ō′vər sēz′) *adv.* over or beyond the sea —*adj.* **1.** foreign **2.** over or across the sea Also **o′ver·sea′**

o·ver·see (ō′vər sē′) *vt.* **-saw′, -seen′, -see′ing 1.** to supervise; superintend **2.** [Now Rare] to catch sight of secretly or accidentally **3.** to survey; watch

o·ver·se·er (ō′vər sē′ər) *n.* a person who directs the work of others; supervisor

o·ver·sell (ō′vər sel′) *vt.* **-sold′, -sell′ing 1.** to sell more than can be supplied **2.** to promote to an extreme degree that defeats one's purposes

o·ver·set (ō′vər set′; *for n.* ō′vər set′) *vt.* **-set′, -set′ting 1.** to upset **2.** to overturn or overthrow —*vi.* to tip over —*n.* an overturning

o·ver·sew (ō′vər sō′, ō′vər sō′) *vt.* **sewed′** or **-sewn′, sew′-ing** to sew together (two pieces of material) by passing small, close stitches over their coinciding edges; sew overhand

o·ver·shad·ow (ō′vər shad′ō) *vt.* **1.** a) to cast a shadow over b) to darken **2.** to be, or appear to be, more significant or important than by comparison

o·ver·shoe (ō′vər shōō′) *n.* a kind of boot of rubber or fabric worn over the regular shoe to protect against cold or dampness; galosh

o·ver·shoot (ō′vər shōōt′) *vt.* **-shot′, -shoot′ing 1.** to shoot or pass over or beyond (a target, mark, etc.) **2.** to go farther than (an intended or normal limit); exceed —*vi.* to shoot or go too far

o·ver·shot (ō′vər shot′) *adj.* **1.** with the upper part or half extending past the lower [an *overshot* jaw] **2.** driven by water flowing onto the upper part [an *overshot* water wheel]

o·ver·sight (-sīt′) *n.* a careless mistake or omission

o·ver·sim·pli·fy (ō′vər sim′plə fī′) *vt., vi.* **-fied′, -fy′ing** to simplify to an extent that distorts, as by ignoring essential details —**o′ver·sim′pli·fi·ca′tion** *n.*

o·ver·size (ō′vər sīz′) *adj.* **1.** too large **2.** larger than the normal or usual Also **o′ver·sized′**—*n.* a size larger than regular sizes

o·ver·skirt (-skurt′) *n.* an outer skirt

o·ver·sleep (ō′vər slēp′) *vi.* **-slept′, -sleep′ing** to sleep past the intended time for getting up

o·ver·spend (ō′vər spend′) *vt.* **-spent′, spend′ing 1.**

[Rare] to use until worn out; exhaust **2.** to spend more than —*vt.* to spend more than one can afford

o·ver·spill (ō′vər spil′; *for v.* ō′vər spil′) *n.* something that spills over or is in excess, esp. a surplus population —*adj.* relating to an excess [*overspill* population] —*vi.* to have a surplus; overflow

o·ver·spread (-spred′) *vt.* **-spread′, -spread′ing** to spread over; cover the surface of

o·ver·state (-stāt′) *vt.* **-stat′ed, -stat′ing** to give a magnified account of (facts, truth, etc.); exaggerate —**o′-ver·state′ment** *n.*

o·ver·stay (-stā′) *vt.* to stay beyond the time, duration, or limits of

o·ver·step (-step′) *vt.* **-stepped′, -step′ping** to go beyond the limits of; exceed

o·ver·stock (ō′vər stok′; *for n.* ō′vər stok′) *vt.* to stock stock more of than is needed —*n.* too large a stock

o·ver·strung (ō′vər struŋ′) *adj.* too highly strung; tense

o·ver·stuff (-stuf′) *vt.* **1.** to stuff with too much of something **2.** to upholster (furniture) with deep stuffing —**o′ver·stuffed′** *adj.*

o·ver·sub·scribe (-səb skrīb′) *vt., vi.* **-scribed′, -scrib′ing** to subscribe for more (of) than is available or asked —**o′-ver·sub·scrip′tion** (-skrip′shən) *n.*

o·ver·sup·ply (-sə plī′) *vt.* **-plied′, -ply′ing** to supply in excess —*n., pl.* **-plies** too great a supply

o·vert (ō vurt′, ō′vurt) *adj.* [< MFr. pp. of *ovrir* < L. *aperire*, to open] **1.** not hidden; open **2.** *Law* done publicly, without attempt at concealment —**o·vert′ly** *adv.* —**o·vert′ness** *n.*

o·ver·take (ō′vər tāk′) *vt.* **-took′, -tak′en, -tak′ing 1.** to catch up with and, often, go beyond; pass [his car *overtook* the bus in front] **2.** to come upon unexpectedly or suddenly

o·ver·tax (-taks′) *vt.* **1.** to tax too heavily **2.** to make excessive demands on

o·ver·throw (ō′vər thrō′; *for n.* ō′vər thrō′) *vt.* **-threw′, -thrown′, -throw′ing 1.** to throw or turn over; upset **2.** to conquer; end **3.** to throw a ball, etc. beyond (the intended receiver or target) —*n.* **1.** an overthrowing or being overthrown **2.** destruction; end

o·ver·time (ō′vər tīm′; *for v.* -tīm′) *n.* **1.** time beyond the established limit, as of working hours **2.** pay for work done in such time —*adj., adv.* of, for, or during overtime —*vt.* **-timed′, -tim′ing** to allow too much time for (a photographic exposure, etc.)

o·ver·tone (ō′vər tōn′) *n.* **1.** any of the attendant higher tones heard with a fundamental musical tone **2.** an implication; nuance: *usually used in pl.* [a reply full of *overtones*]

o·ver·top (ō′vər top′) *vt.* **-topped′, -top′ping 1.** to rise above **2.** to excel; surpass

o·ver·ture (ō′vər chər, ō′və-) *n.* [< OFr. < L. *apertura*, APERTURE] **1.** an introductory proposal or offer **2.** a musical introduction to an opera, oratorio, etc.

o·ver·turn (ō′vər turn′; *for n.* ō′vər turn′) *vt.* **1.** to turn over; upset **2.** to conquer —*vi.* to tip over; capsize —*n.* an overturning or being overturned

o·ver·view (ō′vər vyōō′) *n.* a general survey

o·ver·ween·ing (ō′vər wē′niŋ) *adj.* [< OE. *oferwenan*: see OVER- & WEEN] **1.** arrogant; excessively proud **2.** exaggerated; excessive —**o′ver·ween′ing·ly** *adv.*

o·ver·weigh (-wā′) *vt.* **1.** same as OUTWEIGH **2.** to burden; oppress

o·ver·weight (ō′vər wāt′; *for adj. & v.,* ō′vər wāt′) *n.* extra or surplus weight —*adj.* above the normal, desirable, or allowed weight —*vt.* same as OVERWEIGH

o·ver·whelm (ō′vər hwelm′, -welm′) *vt.* [see OVER- & WHELM] **1.** to pour down on and bury beneath **2.** to crush; overpower —**o′ver·whelm′ing** *adj.* —**o′ver·whelm′ing·ly** *adv.*

o·ver·work (ō′vər wurk′; *for n.* ō′vər wurk′) *vt.* to work or use to excess —*vi.* to work too hard or too long —*n.* work that is severe or burdensome

o·ver·write (ō′vər rīt′) *vt., vi.* **-wrote′, -writ′ten, -writ′ing 1.** to write over (other writing) **2.** to write too much, or in a laboured style, about (some subject)

o·ver·wrought (ō′vər rôt′) *adj.* **1.** very nervous or excited **2.** with the surface adorned **3.** too elaborate

o·vi- [< L. *ovum*, an egg] *a combining form meaning egg or ovum* [*oviduct, oviform*]

o·vi·bos (ō′vi bōs′) *n.* [< L. *ovis*, a sheep + *bos*, an ox] an animal between a sheep and an ox; a musk ox —**o·vi′-bo·vine** (ō′vi bō′vīn) *adj.*

o·vi·duct (ō′vi dukt′) *n.* [< ModL.: see OVI- & DUCT] a duct or tube through which the ovum passes from an ovary to the uterus or to the outside

o·vi·form (-fôrm′) *adj.* [OVI- & -FORM] egg-shaped

o·vine (ō′vīn) *adj.* [LL. *ovinus* < L. *ovis*, sheep] of, or having the nature of, sheep

o·vip·a·rous (ō vip′ər əs) *adj.* [< L.: see OVI- & -PAROUS] producing eggs which hatch after leaving the body —**o·vip′-a·rous·ly** *adv.*

o·vi·pos·i·tor (ō′vi poz′i tər) *n.* [ModL. < OVI- + L. *positor,* one who places < *ponere*, to place] a special organ of many female insects, usually at the end of the abdomen, for depositing eggs

o·void (ō′void) *adj.* [OV(I)- + -OID] egg-shaped: also **o·void′al** —*n.* anything of ovoid form

o·vu·late (ō′vyə lāt′, ov′yə-) *vi.* -lat′ed, -lat′ing [OVUL(E) + -ATE[1]] to produce and discharge ova from the ovary —**o′vu·la′tion** *n.* —**o′vu·la·to·ry** (-lə tə rē) *adj.*

o·vule (ō′vyōōl, ov′yōōl) *n.* [Fr. < ModL. dim. of L. *ovum*, egg] a small egg or seed, esp. one in an early stage of development; specif., *a) Bot.* the part of a plant which develops into a seed *b) Zool.* the immature ovum —**o′vu·lar** *adj.*

o·vum (ō′vəm) *n.,* pl. **o·va** (ō′və) [L., an egg] *Biol.* a mature female germ cell

ow (ou) *interj.* a cry of pain

owe (ō) *vt.* **owed, ow′ing** [OE. *agan*, to own] **1.** to be indebted to (someone) for (a specified amount or thing) **2.** to feel the need to do, give, etc. **3.** to cherish (a feeling) towards another: only in **owe a grudge** —*vi.* to be in debt

O·wen·ite (ō′ən īt′) *n.* a follower of Robert Owen, believing in socialistic cooperation —**O·wen·ism** *n.*

ow·ing (ō′iŋ) *adj.* **1.** that owes **2.** due; unpaid [ten pounds *owing* on a bill] —**owing to** because of; as a result of

owl (oul) *n.* [OE. *ule*] any of many nocturnal birds of prey found throughout the world, having a large face, large eyes, a short, hooked beak, and feathered legs with sharp talons: applied figuratively to a person who looks solemn, dull, etc. —**owl′ish** *adj.* —**owl′ish·ly** *adv.* —**owl′like′** *adj.*

owl·et (-it) *n.* a young or small owl

own (ōn) *adj.* [OE. *agen*, pp. of *agan*, to possess] belonging or relating to oneself or itself: used to strengthen a preceding possessive [his *own* book] —*n.* that which belongs to oneself [the car is his *own*] —*vt.* **1.** to possess; have **2.** to admit; acknowledge —*vi.* to confess (*to*) —**come into one's own** to receive what properly belongs to one, esp. recognition —**of own's own** belonging strictly to oneself —**on one's own** [Colloq.] by one's own efforts; independent —**own up (to)** to confess (to) —**own′er** *n.* —**own′er·less** *adj.* —**own′er·ship′** *n.*

owner occupier someone who both occupies and owns a house

ox (oks) *n.,* pl. **ox′en,** rarely **ox:** see PLURAL, II, D, 1 [OE. *oxa*] **1.** any of several bovine mammals, as the buffalo, bison, yak, etc. **2.** a castrated bull, used as a draught animal —**ox′like′** *adj.*

ox·al·ic acid (ok sal′ik) [< Fr. < L. < Gr. *oxalis*, sorrel < *oxys*, acid] a colourless, poisonous, crystalline acid, (COOH)₂, found in many plants and used in dyeing, bleaching, etc.

ox·blood (oks′blud′) *n.* a deep red colour

ox·bow (-bō′) *n.* **1.** the U-shaped part of an ox yoke which passes under and around the animal's neck **2.** something shaped like this, as a bend in a river

Ox·bridge (oks′brij) *n.* [Ox(ford) + (Cam)bridge] the British universities of Oxford and Cambridge, esp. considered as influencing political, intellectual, and social life in Britain —*adj.* of, or relating to Oxbridge [an *Oxbridge* accent]

ox·en (ok′s'n) *n.* pl. of OX

ox·eye (oks′ī′) *n.* **1.** any of several composite plants **2.** any of various birds, as the dunlin

ox·eyed (-īd′) *adj.* having large, full eyes

oxeye daisy same as DAISY (sense 1)

Ox·fam (oks′fam′) *n.* Oxford Famine Relief Fund

ox·ford (oks′fərd) *n.* [after Oxford] [sometimes O-] **1.** a low shoe laced over the instep: also **oxford shoe 2.** a cotton or rayon fabric with a basketlike weave, used for shirts, etc.: also **oxford cloth**

Oxford bags trousers with very baggy legs, usually with turnups

Oxford grey a very dark grey, nearly black

Oxford movement a High-Church movement within the Anglican Church, begun at Oxford University in 1833: see TRACTARIANISM

ox·heart (oks′härt′) *n.* a large, heart-shaped cherry

ox·i·dant (ok′sə dənt) *n.* an oxidizing agent

ox·i·da·tion (ok′sə dā′shən) *n.* an oxidizing or being oxidized —**ox′i·da′tive** *adj.*

ox·ide (ok′sīd) *n.* [Fr. < Gr. *oxys*, sour + Fr. (ac)ide, acid]

a binary compound of oxygen with another element or a radical

ox·i·dize (ok′sə dīz′) *vt.* -dized′, -diz′ing [< prec. + -IZE] **1.** to unite with oxygen, as in burning or rusting **2.** to increase the positive valence or decrease the negative valence of (an element or ion) —*vi.* to become oxidized —**ox′i·diz′a·ble** *adj.* —**ox′i·diz′er** *n.*

ox·lip (oks′lip′) *n.* [< OE. < *oxa*, ox + *slyppe*, dropping] a perennial plant related to the primrose, having yellow flowers in early spring

Oxon. 1. Oxfordshire **2.** of Oxford (University)

Ox·o·ni·an (ok sō′nē ən) *adj.* of Oxford or Oxford University —*n.* **1.** a student or former student of Oxford University **2.** a native or inhabitant of Oxford

ox·tail (oks′tāl′) *n.* the tail of an ox, esp. when skinned and used in soup or stew

ox·ter (ok′stər) *n.* [ModE. *oxtere*, altered < OE. *ohsta*, akin to G. *Achsel*, shoulder] [Scot.] the armpit

ox·tongue (oks′tuŋ′) *n.* **1.** any of a number of plants, as alkanet, with rough, tongue-shaped leaves **2.** the tongue of an ox, braised or boiled as food: also **tongue**

oxy·¹ [< OXY(GEN)] a combining form meaning containing oxygen

oxy·² [< Gr. *oxys*, sharp] a combining form meaning sharp, pointed, or acid [oxymoron, oxygen]

ox·y·a·cet·y·lene (ok′sē ə set′əl ēn′) *adj.* of or using a mixture of oxygen and acetylene, as for producing an extremely hot flame used in welding or cutting metals [oxyacetylene torch]

ox·y·gen (ok′si jən) *n.* [< Fr.: see OXY·² & -GEN] a colourless, odourless, tasteless, gaseous chemical element, the most abundant of all elements: it occurs free in the atmosphere, forming one fifth of its volume, and is able to combine with nearly all other elements; it is essential to life processes and to combustion: symbol, O; at. wt., 15.9994; at. no., 8 —**ox′y·gen′ic** (-jen′ik) *adj.*

ox·y·gen·ate (ok′si jə nāt′) *vt.* -at′ed, -at′ing to mix, treat, or combine with oxygen: also **ox′y·gen·ize′, -ized′, -iz′ing** —**ox′y·gen·a′tion** *n.* —**ox′y·gen·a′tor** *n.*

oxygen tent a transparent enclosure into which oxygen is released, fitted around a bed-ridden patient to help him breathe

ox·y·haem·o·glo·bin (ok′si hē′mə glō′bin) *n.* [OXY·¹ + HAEMOGLOBIN] the bright-red substance found in the arterial blood, formed in the lungs by the union of oxygen with haemoglobin

ox·y·hy·dro·gen (ok′si hī′drə jən) *adj.* of or using a mixture of oxygen and hydrogen, as for producing a hot flame used in welding [oxyhydrogen torch]

ox·y·mo·ron (ok′si môr′on) *n.,* pl. -mo′ra (-ə) [LGr. < *oxys*, sharp + *moros*, dull] a figure of speech in which contradictory ideas or terms are combined (Ex.: sweet sorrow)

o·yer and ter·mi·ner (ō′yər'nd tur′mi nər) [ME. for Anglo-Fr. *oyer et terminer*, lit. to hear and determine] a commission issued to judges authorizing them to hear and determine criminal cases at the assizes

o·yez, o·yes (ō′yez′, -yes′, -yā′) *interj.* [Anglo-Fr., hear ye, ult. < L. *audire*, to hear] hear ye! attention!: usually cried out three times by an official to command silence before a proclamation is made —*n.* a cry of "oyez"

oys·ter (oi′stər) *n.* [< OFr. < L. *ostrea* < Gr. *ostreon*] **1.** a marine mollusc with an irregular, bivalve shell, found esp. on the ocean floor and widely used as food **2.** any of several similar bivalve molluscs

oyster bed a natural or artificially prepared place on the ocean floor for breeding oysters

oys·ter catch·er (-kach′ər) *n.* any of a family of wading birds with strong wedge-shaped beaks and stout legs

oyster crab any of various small crabs that live in the gill cavities of oysters, clams, etc.

oyster plant same as SALSIFY

oz. pl. **oz., ozs.** ounce

o·zone (ō′zōn) *n.* [Fr. < Gr. *ozein*, to smell] **1.** a pale-blue gas, O₃, with a strong odour: it is an allotropic form of oxygen, formed by a silent electrical discharge in air and used as a bleaching agent, water purifier, etc. **2.** [Colloq.] pure, fresh air —**o·zon′ic** (-zon′ik, -zō′nik) *adj.*

o·zon·ize (ō′zō nīz′) *vt.* -ized′, -iz′ing **1.** to change (oxygen) into ozone **2.** to treat with ozone —**o′zon·i·za′tion** *n.* —**o′zon·iz′er** *n.*

P

P, p (pē) *n.*, *pl.* **P's, p's** 1. the sixteenth letter of the English alphabet 2. the sound of *P* or *p* —**mind one's p's and q's** to be careful what one does
P 1. *Chess* pawn 2. *Chem.* phosphorus 3. police 4. *Physics* power or pressure
p penny; pence
P., p. 1. power 2. pressure
p. 1. *pl.* **pp.** page 2. participle 3. past 4. penny 5. per 6. piano 7. pint
pa¹ (pä) *n.* [Colloq.] father; papa
pa² (pä) *n.* [Maori] a fortified village in New Zealand: also **pah**
Pa¹ *Chem.* protactinium
Pa² *Physics the symbol for* pascal
P.A. public address (system)
pa·an·ga (pä äŋ´ä) *n.*, *pl.* **pa·an´ga** [Polynesian (Tongan), a kind of seedpod] *see* MONETARY UNITS, table (Tonga)
pab·u·lum (pab´yoo ləm) *n.* [L.] 1. food 2. nourishment for the mind
P.A.B.X. Private Automatic Branch Exchange
pace¹ (pās) *n.* [< OFr. *pas* < L. *passus*, a step] 1. a step in walking, running, etc. 2. the length of a step or stride (75 cm to 100 cm) 3. the rate of speed in walking, etc. 4. rate of movement, progress, development, etc. 5. a particular way of walking, etc.; gait 6. the gait of a horse in which both legs on the same side are raised together —*vt.* **paced, pac´ing** 1. to walk back and forth across 2. to measure by paces (often with *out*) 3. to train or guide the pace of (a horse) 4. to set the pace for (a runner, etc.) 5. to go before and lead 6. to cover (a certain distance) —*vi.* 1. to walk with regular steps 2. to raise both legs on the same side at the same time in moving: said of a horse —**change of pace** variation in tempo or mood or in speed of delivery —**keep pace (with)** to maintain the same speed or rate of progress (as) —**put through one's paces** to test one's abilities, etc. —**set the pace** 1. to go at a speed that others try to equal 2. to do or be something for others to emulate —**pac´er** *n.*
‡**pa·ce²** (pä´sē, pä´che) *prep.* [L. abl. of *pax*, PEACE] with all due respect to: used in polite disagreement
pace·mak·er (pās´mā´kər) *n.* 1. a) a runner, horse, etc. that sets the pace for others, as in a race b) a person, group, or thing that serves as a model Also **pace´set´ter** 2. *Med.* an electronic device surgically implanted in the body to stimulate or regulate the heartbeat —**pace´mak´ing** *n.*
pa·chi·si (pə chē´zē) *n.* [< Hindi < *pacīs*, twenty-five (the highest throw)] 1. in India, a game in which the moves of pieces around a board are determined by the throwing of cowrie shells 2. *same as* PARCHEESI
pach·y·derm (pak´ə dûrm´) *n.* [< Fr. < Gr. < *pachys*, thick + *derma*, a skin] 1. a large, thick-skinned, hoofed animal, as the elephant, rhinoceros, or hippopotamus 2. an insensitive, stolid person —**pach´y·der´mal, pach´y·der´mic** *adj.* —**pach´y·der´ma·tous, pach´y·der´mous** *adj.*
pach·y·san·dra (pak´ə san´drə) *n.* [ModL. < Gr. *pachys*, thick + ModL. *-andrus*, *-ANDROUS*] a low, dense-growing, hardy evergreen plant, often used for a ground cover
pa·cif·ic (pə sif´ik) *adj.* [< Fr. < L. < *pacificare*, PACIFY] 1. making or tending to make peace 2. peaceful; calm; tranquil —**pa·cif´i·cal·ly** *adv.*
pa·cif·i·cate (-ə kāt´) *vt.* **-cat´ed, -cat´ing** *same as* PACIFY —**pa·cif·i·ca·tion** (pas´ə fi kā´shən) *n.* —**pa·cif´i·ca´tor** *n.* —**pa·cif´i·ca·to·ry** (-kə tər ē) *adj.*
pac·i·fi·er (pas´ə fī´ər) *n.* 1. a person or thing that pacifies 2. [U.S.] a baby's dummy
pac·i·fism (-fiz´m) *n.* [< Fr.: see PACIFIC & -ISM] opposition to the use of force under any circumstances; specif., refusal for reasons of conscience to participate in war —**pac´i·fist** *n., adj.* —**pac´i·fis´tic** *adj.* —**pac´i·fis´ti·cal·ly** *adv.*
pac·i·fy (pas´ə fī´) *vt.* **-fied´, -fy´ing** [< Fr. < L. *pacificare* < *pax*, peace + *facere*, to make] 1. to make peaceful or calm; appease; tranquilize 2. a) to secure peace in (a nation, etc.) b) to seek to neutralize or win over (people in occupied areas) —**pac´i·fi´a·ble** *adj.*
pack¹ (pak) *n.* [MDu. *pak* < MFl. *pac*] 1. a bundle of things tied up for carrying, as on the back; load; burden 2. a container in which something may be stored compactly [parachute *pack*] 3. a group or set [a *pack* of lies or liars];

specif., *a*) a package of a standard number [a *pack* of cigarettes] *b*) a set of playing cards; deck *c*) a set of hunting hounds *d*) a group of wild animals living and hunting together *e*) *Rugby* the forwards of a team 4. *same as* PACK ICE 5. *a*) treatment by wrapping a patient in sheets, etc. that are wet or dry and hot or cold *b*) the sheets so used 6. a cosmetic paste applied to the skin and left to dry [*mudpack*] 7. *a*) the amount of food put in bottles, etc. in a season or year *b*) a method of packing or bottling —*vt.* 1. to make a pack of 2. *a*) to put together in a box, trunk, etc. *b*) to fill (a box, trunk, etc.) 3. to put (food) in (jars, etc.) for preservation 4. *a*) to crowd; cram [the hall was *packed*] *b*) to crowd (people) together 5. to fill in tightly, as for prevention of leaks [to *pack* valves] 6. to press together firmly [*packed* earth] 7. to load (an animal) with a pack 8. to carry (goods, etc.) in a pack: said of an animal 9. to send (*off*) 10. [Slang] to wear or carry (a gun, etc.) as part of one's equipment 11. [Slang] *a*) to deliver (a blow, punch, etc.) with force *b*) to provide or contain [a play that *packs* a message] —*vi.* 1. to make up packs 2. to put one's clothes, etc. into luggage for a trip 3. to crowd together in a small space 4. to admit of being folded compactly, put in a container, etc. [this suit *packs* well] 5. to settle into a compact mass —*adj.* 1. used in or suitable for packing 2. formed into packs 3. used for carrying packs, loads, etc. [a *pack* animal] —**pack it in** [Colloq.] to stop doing something —**pack up** [Colloq.] 1. stop working: said esp. of a machine 2. retire from a contest, activity, etc. —**send packing** to dismiss (a person) abruptly —**pack´a·bil´i·ty** *n.* —**pack´a·ble** *adj.*
pack² (pak) *vt.* [orig. unc., but infl. by prec.] to choose (a jury, court, etc.) dishonestly so as to get desired results
-pack (pak) *a combining form meaning* a carton of (a specified number of) bottles or cans, as of beer
pack·age (pak´ij) *n.* 1. orig., the act or process of packing 2. a wrapped or boxed thing; parcel 3. a number of items, plans, etc. offered as an inseparable unit —*vt.* **-aged, -ag·ing** to put into a package
package holiday a holiday with a fixed intinerary and at a price inclusive of travel and lodging
packed out [Colloq.] crowded; full
pack·er (pak´ər) *n.* a person or thing that packs; specif., *a*) one who packs goods for shipping, sale, etc. *b*) one whose business it is to pack goods, esp. processing and packing food
pack·et (-it) *n.* 1. a small package 2. *same as* PACKET BOAT 3. a container, wrapping, etc., esp. one in which a commodity is packed for sale 4. [Colloq.] a large sum of money —*vt.* to make up into a packet
packet boat a boat that travels on a regular route carrying passengers, freight, and mail
pack ice a large, floating expanse of ice masses frozen together
pack·ing (pak´iŋ) *n.* 1. the act or process of a person or thing that packs; specif., the large-scale processing and packaging of meats, fruits, etc. 2. any material used to pack
pack rat a N American rat that often hides small articles in its nest
pack·sad·dle (-sad´'l) *n.* a saddle with fastenings to secure the load carried by a pack animal
pack·thread (-thred´) *n.* strong, thick thread or twine for tying bundles, packages, etc.
pack train a procession of pack animals
pact (pakt) *n.* [< OFr. < L. < pp. of *paciscere*, to agree < *pax*, peace] an agreement between persons, groups, or nations; compact
pad¹ (pad) *n.* [echoic, but infl. by PAD³] the dull sound made by a footstep or staff on the ground
pad² (pad) *n.* [? var. of POD] 1. a soft, stuffed saddle 2. anything made of or stuffed with soft material to fill out a shape, protect from friction, jarring, blows, etc. [a shoulder *pad*] 3. a piece of folded gauze, etc. used as a dressing on a wound, etc. 4. *a*) the foot of certain animals, as the wolf, fox, etc. *b*) any of the cushionlike parts on the underside of such a foot 5. the floating leaf of a water plant, as the water lily 6. a tablet of paper for writing on 7. a small cushion soaked with ink for inking a rubber stamp: in full, **stamp pad** or **ink pad** 8. *same as* LAUNCHING PAD 9.

[Slang] the room, flat, etc. where one lives —*vt.* **pad′ded, pad′ding** 1. to stuff, cover, or line with a pad or padding 2. to lengthen (a speech or writing) with unnecessary material 3. to fill (an expense account, etc.) with invented or inflated entries

pad³ (pad) *vi.* **pad′ded, pad′ding** [< Du. *pad*, path] 1. to travel on foot; walk 2. to walk or run with a soft step

padded cell a room in a mental hospital, etc., with lined or padded surfaces, in which violent inmates are placed for their own protection

pad·ding (pad′iŋ) *n.* 1. the action of one who pads 2. any soft material used to pad, as cotton, felt, etc. 3. unnecessary material inserted in a speech, writing, etc. to make it longer

pad·dle¹ (pad′'l) *n.* [< ?] 1. a short oar with a wide blade, used without a rowlock 2. any of various implements shaped like this and used in washing clothes, working butter, etc. 3. any of the propelling boards in a water wheel or paddle wheel —*vt., vi.* **-dled, -dling** 1. to propel (a canoe, etc.) with a paddle 2. to stir, work, etc. with a paddle —**paddle one's own canoe** to depend entirely on oneself —**pad′dler** *n.*

pad·dle² (pad′'l) *vi.* **-dled, -dling** [prob. freq. of PAD³] 1. to move the hands or feet about in the water; dabble 2. to walk like a small child; toddle —**pad′dler** *n.*

pad·dle·fish (-fish′) *n., pl.* **-fish′, -fish′es**: see FISH a large fish of the Mississippi and Yangtse river systems, with a paddle-shaped snout

paddle wheel a wheel with paddles around it for propelling a steamboat

pad·dock (pad′ək) *n.* [< OE. *pearruc*, enclosure] 1. a small enclosure near a stable, in which horses are exercised 2. an enclosure at a race track, where horses are saddled and walked before a race 3. [Aust.] a large field or pasture, esp. one that is enclosed

pad·dy¹ (pad′ē) *n., pl.* **-dies** [Malay *padi*] 1. rice in the husk, growing or gathered 2. rice in general 3. a rice field: often **rice paddy**

pad·dy² (pad′ē) *n., pl.* **-dies** [< *Paddy*, a nickname for an Irishman] [Colloq.] a fit of temper; rage: also **pad′dy·whack** (-wak′, -hwak′)

pad·lock (pad′lok′) *n.* [< ME. < *pad* (< ?) + *lokke*, LOCK¹] a removable lock with a hinged link to be passed through a staple, chain, or eye —*vt.* to fasten or keep shut as with a padlock

pa·dre (pä′drā, -drē; *It.* -dre; *Sp.* -thre) *n., pl.* **-dres** (-dräz, -drēz; *Sp.* -thres;) It. **pa′dri** (-drē) [Sp., It., Port. < L. *pater*, a father] 1. father: the title of a priest in Italy, Spain, Portugal, and Latin America 2. [Slang] a priest or chaplain, esp. in the army

pae·an (pē′ən) *n.* [L. < Gr. < *Paian*, epithet of Apollo] a song of joy, triumph, praise, etc.

pae·di·a·tri·cian (pē′dē·ə·trish′ən) *n.* a specialist in paediatrics: also **pae·di·at·rist** (-at′rist)

pae·di·at·rics (-at′riks) *n.pl.* [*with sing. v.*] [< PAEDO- + -IATRICS] the branch of medicine dealing with the care of infants and children and the treatment of their diseases —**pae′di·at′ric** *adj.*

pae·do- *a combining form meaning* child, children: also **paed-**

pae·do·phil·i·a (pē′də·fil′ē·ə, -fil′yə) *n.* [PAEDO- + -PHILIA] a sexual desire in an adult for children

pa·el·la (pä·yel′ə; *Sp.* pä·e′lyä) *n.* [Catalan, lit., cooking pot < OFr. < L. *patella*, a small pan] a Spanish dish of rice cooked with chicken, seafood, etc. and seasoned with saffron

pa·gan (pā′gən) *n.* [LL. *paganus*, a heathen < L., a peasant < *pagus*, country] 1. anyone not a Christian, Moslem, or Jew; heathen 2. a person who has no religion —*adj.* 1. of pagans 2. not religious —**pa′gan·dom** *n.* —**pa′gan·ish** *adj.* —**pa′gan·ism** *n.*

pa·gan·ize (pā′gə·nīz′) *vt., vi.* **-ized, -iz′ing** to make or become pagan —**pa′gan·iz′er** *n.*

page¹ (pāj) *n.* [Fr. < L. *pagina* < base of *pangere*, to fasten] 1. a) one side of a leaf of a book, newspaper, etc. b) the printing or writing on it [the sports *pages*] c) an entire leaf in a book, etc. 2. [*often pl.*] a record of events [the *pages* of history] 3. an event or series of events that might fill a page [a colourful *page* in his life] —*vt.* **paged, pag′ing** to number the pages of —*vi.* to turn pages in scanning (*through* a book, etc.)

page² (pāj) *n.* [OFr. < It. *paggio*] 1. formerly, a boy training for knighthood 2. a boy attendant, esp. one serving a person of high rank, as in court 3. a boy, or sometimes a girl, who runs errands, carries messages, etc., as in a hotel, etc. —*vt.* **paged, pag′ing** 1. to attend as a page 2. to try to find (a person) by calling his name, as a hotel page does

PADDLE WHEEL

pag·eant (paj′ənt) *n.* [Anglo-L. *pagina*, scene displayed on a stage, stage < L., PAGE¹] 1. a spectacular exhibition, elaborate parade, etc., as a procession with floats 2. a drama, often staged outdoors, celebrating a historical event or events 3. empty pomp or display

pag·eant·ry (-ən·trē) *n., pl.* **-ries** 1. pageants collectively 2. grand spectacle; gorgeous display 3. empty show or display

page·boy (pāj′boi′) *n.* 1. a smooth medium-length hair style with the ends of the hair curled under 2. *same as* PAGE²

pag·i·nate (paj′ə·nāt′) *vt.* **-nat′ed, -nat′ing** to number the pages of (a book, etc.)

pag·i·na·tion (paj′ə·nā′shən) *n.* 1. the numbering of the pages of a book, etc. 2. the figures with which pages are numbered in sequence

pa·go·da (pə·gō′də) *n.* [< Port., prob. < Per. < *but*, idol + *kadah*, house] in the Orient, a temple that is a tapering tower with rooflike, upward curving projections between its several storeys

paid (pād) *pt. & pp.* of PAY¹

pail (pāl) *n.* [OE. *pægel*, small measure] 1. a cylindrical container, usually with a hoop-shaped handle, for carrying liquids, etc.; bucket 2. the amount held by a pail: also **pail′-ful′**, *pl.* **-fuls′**

pain (pān) *n.* [< OFr. < L. *poena*, punishment < Gr. *poinē*, penalty] 1. orig., penalty or punishment 2. a sensation of hurting caused by injury, disease, etc., transmitted by the nervous system 3. the distress or suffering caused by anxiety, grief, disappointment, etc. 4. [*pl.*] the labour of childbirth 5. [*pl.*] great care [to take *pains* with one's work] 6. [Colloq.] an annoyance —*vt.* to cause pain to; hurt —*vi.* to have or cause pain —**on** (or **upon** or **under**) **pain of** at the risk of bringing upon oneself (punishment, death, etc.) —**pain′less** *adj.* —**pain′less·ly** *adv.* —**pain′-less·ness** *n.*

pained (pānd) *adj.* 1. hurt or distressed; offended 2. showing hurt feelings or resentment

pain·ful (pān′fəl) *adj.* 1. causing pain; hurting; distressing 2. having pain; aching 3. exacting and difficult 4. extremely bad or irritating —**pain′ful·ly** *adv.* —**pain′ful·ness** *n.*

pain·kill·er (-kil′ər) *n.* a medicine that relieves pain; analgesic

pains·tak·ing (pānz′tā′kiŋ) *n.* great care or diligence —*adj.* 1. very careful; diligent 2. characterized by great care —**pains′tak′ing·ly** *adv.*

paint (pānt) *vt.* [< OFr. pp. of *peindre* < L. *pingere*] 1. a) to make a (picture, etc.) in colours applied to a surface b) to depict with paints [to *paint* a landscape] 2. to describe colourfully; depict in words 3. to cover or decorate with paint [to *paint* a wall] 4. to apply such cosmetics as lipstick, rouge, etc. to 5. to apply (a medicine, etc.) with a brush or swab —*vi.* 1. to practise the art of painting pictures 2. to use cosmetics —*n.* 1. a mixture of pigment with oil, water, etc. used as a covering or colouring or for making pictures on canvas, etc. 2. a dried coat of paint 3. a) colouring matter, as lipstick, rouge, etc., used as a cosmetic b) *same as* GREASEPAINT —**paint out** to cover up as with a coat of paint —**paint the town** (**red**) [Colloq.] to go on a boisterous spree —**paint′a·ble** *adj.* —**paint′y** *adj.* **paint′i·er, paint′i·est**

paint·brush (-brush′) *n.* a brush used for applying paint

painted lady a butterfly with brownish-red mottled wings

paint·er¹ (pān′tər) *n.* 1. an artist who paints pictures 2. a person whose work is covering surfaces, as walls, with paint

paint·er² (pān′tər) *n.* [< OFr., ult. < L. *pendere*, to hang] a rope attached to the bow of a boat for tying it to a dock, etc.

paint·ing (pān′tiŋ) *n.* 1. the work or art of one who paints 2. a picture made with paints

pair (per) *n., pl.* **pairs**; sometimes, after a number, **pair** [< OFr. < L. neut. pl. of *par*, equal] 1. two similar or corresponding things associated or used together [a *pair* of shoes] 2. a single thing with two joined corresponding parts [a *pair* of trousers] 3. two persons or animals; specif., a) a married, engaged, or courting couple b) two mated animals c) two people with something in common [a *pair* of thieves] d) a brace; span [a *pair* of oxen] e) two legislators on opposing sides of a question who agree to withhold their vote so as to offset each other; also, such an agreement 4. two playing cards of the same denomination —*vt.* 1. to make a pair of (two persons or things) or of (one *with* another) by matching, joining, etc. 2. to arrange in pairs —*vi.* 1. to form a pair; match 2. to mate —**pair off** 1. to join (two people or things) in a pair 2. to separate into pairs

pai·sa (pī′sä) *n., pl.* **-se** (-se) [Hindi *paisā*] *see* MONETARY UNITS, table (Bangladesh, India, Pakistan)

pais·ley (pāz´lē) *adj.* [after *Paisley*, burgh in Scotland where orig. made] [*also* **P-**] **1.** of or having an elaborate, colourful pattern of intricate, curved figures **2.** made of cloth having such a pattern —*n.* [*also* **P-**] a paisley cloth, shawl, etc.

pa·ja·mas (pəjam´əz, -jä´məz) *n.pl.* *U.S. sp. of* PYJAMAS

Pak (pak) *n.* [Slang] a Pakistani immigrant residing in Britain: a derogatory term: also **Pak´i**

pa·ke·ha (pä´kä ha) *n.* [Maori] a white man in New Zealand

Pa·ki·stan·i (pä´ki stä´nē, pak´- i stan´ē) *adj.* of Pakistan or its people —*n.* a native or inhabitant of Pakistan

PAISLEY PATTERN

pal (pal) *n.* [Eng. Romany < Sans. *bhrātr*, brother] [Colloq.] an intimate friend; comrade; chum —*vi.* **palled, pal´ling** [Colloq.] **1.** to associate as pals **2.** to be a pal (*with* another)

pal·ace (pal´is) *n.* [< OFr. < L. < *Palatium*, one of the seven hills of Rome, where Augustus lived] **1.** the official residence of a king, emperor, etc. **2.** any large, magnificent house or building

pal·a·din (pal´ə din) *n.* [< Fr. < It. < L. *palatinus*, a palace officer: see prec.] **1.** any of the twelve legendary peers of Charlemagne's court **2.** a knight or heroic champion

pa·lae·o- *same as* PALEO-: also **pa·lae-**

pa·la·fitte (pal´ə fit) *n.* [Fr.< It. *palafitta*, pile fence] a prehistoric lake dwelling, usually in Switzerland or N Italy

pal·an·quin, pal·an·keen (pal´ən kēn´) *n.* [< Port. < Jav. < Sans. *palyanka*] formerly in eastern Asia, a covered litter for one person, carried by poles on men's shoulders

pal·a·ta·ble (pal´it ə b'l) *adj.* [PALAT(E) + -ABLE] **1.** pleasant or acceptable to the taste **2.** acceptable to the mind —**pal´at·a·bil´i·ty, pal´at·a·ble·ness** *n.* —**pal´at·a·bly** *adv.*

pal·a·tal (pal´it 'l) *adj.* **1.** of the palate **2.** pronounced with the tongue raised against or near the hard palate, as *y* in *yes* —*n.* a palatal sound —**pal´a·tal·ly** *adv.*

pal·a·tal·ize (-īz´) *vt.* **-ized´, -iz´ing** to pronounce as a palatal [the *t* in *nature* is palatalized to *ch*] —**pal´a·tal·i·za´tion** *n.*

pal·ate (pal´it) *n.* [L. *palatum*] **1.** the roof of the mouth, consisting of a hard, bony forward part (the *hard palate*) and a soft, fleshy back part (the *soft palate*) **2.** taste

pa·la·tial (pə lā´shəl) *adj.* [see PALACE] **1.** of, suitable for, or like a palace **2.** large and ornate; magnificent —**pa·la´tial·ly** *adv.*

pa·lat·i·nate (pə lat´ən āt´, -it) *n.* the territory ruled by a palatine

pal·a·tine (pal´ə tin´, -tin) *adj.* [< OFr. < L. < *palatium*, palace] **1.** of a palace **2.** having royal privileges [a count *palatine*] **3.** of or belonging to a count palatine or earl palatine —*n.* a medieval vassal lord having the rights of royalty in his own territory, or palatinate

PALATE

pa·lav·er (pə läv´ər) *n.* [Port. *palavra*, a word, speech < LL. *parabola*, PARABLE] **1.** a conference, as orig. between African natives and European explorers **2.** talk; esp., idle chatter **3.** flattery; cajolery **4.** fuss; bother —*vi.* **1.** to talk, esp. idly or flatteringly **2.** to confer —*vt.* to flatter or wheedle

pale¹ (pāl) *adj.* [OFr. < L. < *pallere*, to be pale] **1.** of a whitish or colourless complexion; pallid; wan **2.** lacking intensity; faint: said of colour, light, etc. **3.** feeble; weak [a *pale* imitation] —*vi., vt.* **paled, pal´ing** to make or become pale —**pale´ly** *adv.* —**pale´ness** *n.* —**pal´ish** *adj.*

pale² (pāl) *n.* [< MFr. < L. *palus*, a stake] **1.** a narrow, pointed stake used in fences; picket **2.** a fence; enclosure; boundary: now chiefly figurative [beyond the *pale*] **3.** a district enclosed within bounds, esp. [P-] a) an area of English rule in Ireland b) an area of Russia to which Jews were restricted

pale·face (pāl´fās´) *n.* a white person: a term allegedly first used by N American Indians

pale·o- [< Gr. *palaios*, ancient] a *combining form* meaning ancient, prehistoric, primitive, etc. [*Paleozoic, paleolithic*]: also **pa·le-**

Pa·le·o·cene (pā´lē ə sēn´, pal´ē-) *adj.* [< prec. + Gr. *kainos*, recent] designating or of the first epoch of the Tertiary Period in the Cainozoic Era —**the Paleocene** the Paleocene Epoch or its rocks: see GEOLOGY, chart

pa·le·og·ra·phy (pā´lē og´rə fē, pal´ē-) *n.* **1.** ancient writing or forms of writing **2.** the study of describing or deciphering ancient writings —**pa´le·og´ra·pher** *n.* —**pa´le·o·graph´ic** (-ə graf´ik), **pa´le·o·graph´i·cal** *adj.*

pa·le·o·lith·ic (pā´lē ə lith´ik, pal´ē-) *adj.* [PALEO- + -LITHIC] designating or of the middle part of the early Stone Age, during which stone and bone tools were used

pa·le·on·tol·o·gy (-on tol´ə jē) *n.* [< Fr.: see PALE(O)- & ONTO- & -LOGY] the branch of geology that deals with prehistoric life through the study of fossils —**pa´le·on´to·log´i·cal** (-tə loj´i k'l), **pa´le·on´to·log´ic** *adj.* —**pa´le·on·tol´o·gist** *n.*

Pa·le·o·zo·ic (pā´lē ə zō´ik) *adj.* [PALEO- + ZO- + -IC] designating or of the era between the Precambrian and the Mesozoic —**the Paleozoic** the Paleozoic era or its rocks: see GEOLOGY, chart

Pal·es·tin·i·an (pal´əs tin´ē ən) *adj.* of the region on the E coast of the Mediterranean —*n.* an inhabitant, esp. an Arab, of this area

Palestinian Liberation Organization an organization dedicated to setting up an independent Palestine on the Arab lands now occupied by Israel

pal·ette (pal´it) *n.* [Fr. < L. *pala*, a shovel] **1.** a thin board with a hole for the thumb at one end, on which an artist arranges and mixes his paints **2.** the colours used, as by a particular artist

pal·frey (pôl´frē) *n., pl.* **-freys** [< OFr. < ML., ult. < Gr. *para*, beside + L. *veredus*, post horse] [Archaic] a saddle horse, esp. one for a woman

Pa·li (pä´lē) *n.* the Old Indic dialect which has become the religious language of Buddhism

pal·imp·sest (pal´imp sest´) *n.* [< L. < Gr. < *palin*, again + *psēn*, to rub smooth] a parchment, tablet, etc. that has been written upon several times, with previous, erased texts still partly visible

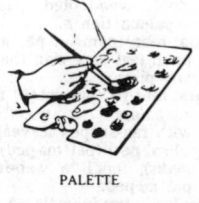

PALETTE

pal·in·drome (pal´in drōm´) *n.* [< Gr. < *palin*, again + *dramein*, to run] a word, phrase, or sentence that reads the same backwards or forwards (Ex.: madam) —**pal´in·drom´ic** (-drom´ik) *adj.*

pal·ing (pāl´iŋ) *n.* **1.** a fence made of pales **2.** the action of making such a fence **3.** a pale, or pales collectively

pal·i·sade (pal´ə sād´, pal´ə säd´) *n.* [< Fr. < Pr. < L. *palus*, a stake] **1.** any of a row of large pointed stakes set in the ground to form a fence as for fortification **2.** such a fence —*vt.* **-sad´ed, -sad´ing** to fortify or defend with a palisade

pall¹ (pôl) *vi.* **palled, pall´ing** [ME. *pallen*, short for *appallen*, APPAL] **1.** to become cloying, insipid, etc. **2.** to become satiated or bored —*vt.* to satiate, bore, or disgust —**pall on** cease to interest; become boring

pall² (pôl) *n.* [< OE. < L. *pallium*, a cover] **1.** a piece of velvet, etc. used to cover a coffin, hearse, or tomb **2.** a dark or gloomy covering [a *pall* of smoke] **3.** a cloth, or cardboard covered with cloth, used to cover the chalice in some Christian churches —*vt.* **palled, pall´ing** to cover as with a pall

pal·la·di·um¹ (pə lā´dē əm) *n., pl.* **-di·a** (-ə) [after the legendary statue of Pallas Athene in Troy] any safeguard

pal·la·di·um² (pə lā´dē əm) *n.* [ModL. < *Pallas*, the asteroid < Gr. *Pallas* (Athene), the goddess] a rare, silvery-white, metallic chemical element: it is used as a catalyst, or in alloys with gold, silver, etc.: symbol, Pd; at. wt., 106.4; at. no., 46

pall·bear·er (pôl´ber´ər) *n.* [PALL² + BEARER] one of the persons who bear the coffin at a funeral

pal·let¹ (pal´it) *n.* [< MFr.: see PALETTE] **1.** a wooden tool consisting of a flat blade with a handle; esp., such a tool for smoothing pottery **2.** *same as* PALETTE (sense 1) **3.** a low, portable platform for storing goods in warehouses, etc. **4.** any of the clicks or pawls in the escapement of a clock, etc. which engage the ratchet wheel to regulate the speed

pal·let² (pal´it) *n.* [< MFr. < OFr. *paille*, straw < L. *palea*, chaff] a small, inferior bed or a mattress filled as with straw and used on the floor

pal·li·asse (pal´ē as´, pal´ē äs´; pal´yas) *n.* [< Fr. < It. < L. *palea*, straw, chaff] a mattress filled with straw, sawdust, etc.

pal·li·ate (pal´ē āt´) *vt.* **-at´ed, -at´ing** [< LL. pp. of *palliare*, to conceal < *pallium*, a cloak] **1.** to lessen the pain or severity of without curing; alleviate **2.** to make appear less serious or offensive; excuse —**pal´li·a´tion** *n.* —**pal´li·a´tive** (-āt´iv, -ə tiv) *adj., n.* —**pal´li·a´tor** *n.*

pal·lid (pal´id) *adj.* [L. *pallidus*, PALE¹] faint in colour; pale —**pal´lid·ly** *adv.* —**pal´lid·ness** *n.*

pall-mall (pel´mel´) *n.* [MFr. < It. *pallamaglio* < *palla*, ball + *maglio*, hammer] **1.** an old game in which a boxwood ball was struck by a mallet through an iron ring at the end of an alley **2.** the alley in which this game was played

pal·lor (pal´ər) *n.* [L. < *pallere*: see PALE¹] lack of colour; unnatural paleness, as of the face

pal·ly (pal´ē) *adj.* [PAL + -Y²] [Colloq.] friendly

palm¹ (päm; *occas.* pälm) *n.* [OE. < L. *palma*: from its handlike fronds] 1. any of a family of tropical or subtropical trees with a tall, branchless trunk and a bunch of large leaves at the top 2. a leaf of this tree carried as a symbol of victory, triumph, etc. 3. victory; triumph —*adj.* designating or of a family of plants including the coconut palm, date palm, etc. —**bear** (or **carry off**) **the palm** to be the winner —**pal·ma·ceous** (pal mā'shəs) *adj.*

palm² (päm; *occas.* pälm) *n.* [< OFr. < L. *palma*] 1. the inner surface of the hand between the fingers and wrist 2. the part of a glove, etc. that covers the palm 3. the broad, flat part of an antler, as of a moose 4. a unit of measure based either on the width of the hand (3 to 4 inches; 7.5 to 10 cm) or its length (7 to 9 inches; 18 to 23 cm) 5. any broad, flat part at the end of an arm, handle, etc. —*vt.* to hide (something) in the palm or between the fingers, as in a sleight-of-hand trick —**have an itching palm** [Colloq.] to desire money greedily —**palm off** to pass off by fraud or deceit —**pal·mar** (pal'mər) *adj.*

pal·mate (pal'māt) *adj.* [< L. < *palma*, PALM²] shaped like a hand with the fingers spread; specif., a) *Bot.* having veins or lobes radiating from a common centre, as some leaves b) *Zool.* web-footed Also **pal'mat·ed** —**pal'mate·ly** *adv.* —**pal·ma'tion** *n.*

palm·er (päm'ər, päl'mər) *n.* 1. a pilgrim who carried a palm leaf as a sign that he had been to the Holy Land 2. any pilgrim

pal·met·to (pal met'ō) *n., pl.* -tos, -toes [Sp. *palmito*, dim. < *palma* < L., PALM¹] any of several new-world palms with fan-shaped leaves, as the cabbage palm

pal·mi·ped (pal'mə ped) *n.* [< L. *palma*, PALM² + *pes* (gen. *pedis*), foot] a web-footed bird —*adj.* web-footed Also **pal'mi·pede**

palm·is·try (päm'is trē, päl'mis-) *n.* [< ME., prob. contr. < *paume*, PALM² + *maistrie*, mastery] the pretended art of telling a person's fortune by the lines, etc. on the palm of his hand —**palm'ist** *n.*

pal·mit·ic acid (pal mit'ik) [< Fr.] a fatty acid found in many natural fats and oils

palm leaf the leaf of a palm tree, esp. of a palmetto, used to make fans, hats, etc.

palm oil an oil obtained from the fruit of certain palms, used in making soap, candles, etc.

Palm Sunday the Sunday before Easter, commemorating Jesus' triumphal entry into Jerusalem

palm·y (päm'ē, päl'mē) *adj.* **palm'i·er, palm'i·est** 1. abounding in or shaded by palm trees 2. of or like a palm 3. prosperous [*palmy* days]

pal·my·ra (pal mī'rə) *n.* [< Port. < *palma* < L., PALM¹] a palm tree grown in India, Ceylon, and Africa for its durable wood, its leaves used for thatching, etc.

pal·o·mi·no (pal'ə mē'nō) *n., pl.* -nos [AmSp. < Sp., dove-coloured ult. < L. *palumbes*, pigeon] a cream, golden, or light-chestnut horse with white mane and tail

palp¹ (palp) *n. same as* PALPUS —**pal'pal** *adj.*

palp² (palp) *vt.* palped, palp'ing [< L. *palpere*, to feel] to feel, or explore by touch

pal·pa·ble (pal'pə b'l) *adj.* [< LL. < L. *palpare*, to touch] 1. that can be touched, felt, etc.; tangible 2. easily perceived by the senses; recognizable, perceptible, etc. 3. obvious; plain —**pal'pa·bil'i·ty** *n.* —**pal'pa·bly** *adv.*

pal·pate (pal'pāt) *vt.* -pat·ed, -pat·ing [< L. pp. of *palpare*, to touch] to examine by touching, as for medical diagnosis —**pal·pa'tion** *n.*

pal·pe·bral (pal'pə brəl) *adj.* [LL. *palpebralis* < L. *palpebra*, an eyelid] of or having to do with the eyelids

pal·pi·tate (pal'pə tāt') *vi.* -tat'ed, -tat'ing [< L. pp. of *palpitare*, freq. of *palpare*, to feel] 1. to beat rapidly or flutter: said of the heart 2. to throb; quiver —**pal'pi·tant** *adj.* —**pal'pi·ta'tion** *n.*

pal·pus (pal'pəs) *n., pl.* **pal'pi** (-pī) [ModL. < L. *palpus*, the soft palm of the hand] a jointed organ or feeler for touching or tasting, attached to one of the head appendages of insects, lobsters, etc.

pal·sy (pôl'zē) *n., pl.* -sies [< OFr. < L. *paralysis*, PARALYSIS] paralysis of any voluntary muscle, sometimes accompanied by uncontrollable tremors —*vt.* -sied, -sy·ing to afflict with or as with palsy; paralyse

pal·ter (pôl'tər) *vi.* [< ?] 1. to talk or act insincerely; prevaricate 2. to trifle 3. to quibble

pal·try (pôl'trē) *adj.* -tri·er, -tri·est [prob. < LowG. *paltrig* < *palte*, a rag] worthless; trifling; petty —**pal'tri·ness** *n.*

pal·y·nol·o·gy (pal'ə nol'ə jē) *n.* [< Gr. *palynein*, to sprinkle + -LOGY] the study of living or fossil plant spores and pollen —**pal'y·no·log'i·cal** (-nə loj'i k'l) *adj.*

pam·pas (pam'pəz; *for adj., usually* -pəs) *n.pl.* [AmSp., pl. of *pampa* < Quechua, plain] the extensive treeless plains of S. America, esp. of Argentina —*adj.* of the pampas —**pam·pe·an** (pam'pē ən, pam pē'-) *adj., n.*

pampas grass any of several S American grasses grown for their large, feathery flower branches, which are used for bouquets

pam·per (pam'pər) *vt.* [< LowG. source] 1. orig., to feed too much; glut 2. to be overindulgent with; coddle [to *pamper* a child] —**pam'per·er** *n.*

pam·phlet (pam'flit) *n.* [< OFr. *Pamphilet*, popular name of a ML. poem] 1. a small, unbound booklet, usually with a paper cover 2. a treatise in this form, as on some topic of current interest

pam·phlet·eer (pam'flə tir') *n.* a writer of pamphlets, esp. those dealing with political or social issues —*vi.* to write or publish pamphlets

pan¹ (pan) *n.* [OE. *panne*] 1. any broad, shallow container, usually of metal, used in cooking, etc.: often in combination [*saucepan*] 2. a pan-shaped part or object; specif., a) a container for washing out gold, etc. from gravel b) either receptacle in a pair of scales 3. *same as* HARDPAN (sense 1) 4. the part holding the powder in a flintlock 5. the bowl of a lavatory —*vt.* panned, pan'ning 1. [Colloq.] to criticize unfavourably, as in reviewing 2. *Mining* a) to wash (gravel) in a pan b) to separate (gold, etc.) from gravel in this way —*vi. Mining* 1. to wash gravel in a pan 2. to yield gold in this process —**pan out** 1. *Mining* to yield gold, as gravel, a mine, etc. 2. [Colloq.] to turn out; esp., to turn out well

pan² (pan) *vt., vi.* panned, pan'ning [< PAN(ORAMA)] move (a film or television camera) so as to get a panoramic effect or follow a moving object —*n.* the act of panning

pan- [< Gr. *pan*, neut. of *pas*, all, every] *a combining form meaning:* 1. all [*pantheism*] 2. [P-] a) of, comprising, or common to every [*Pan-American*] b) (belief in) the union or cooperation of all members of (a specified group) [*Pan-Hellenism*] In sense 2, usually with a hyphen, as in the following words:

Pan-African	**Pan-European**
Pan-Arabic	**Pan-Islamic**
Pan-Asiatic	**Pan-Slavic**

pan·a·ce·a (pan'ə sē'ə) *n.* [L. < Gr. < *pan*, all + *akeisthai*, to cure] a supposed remedy or cure for all diseases or ills; cure-all —**pan'a·ce'an** *adj.*

pa·nache (pə nash') *n.* [Fr., ult. < LL. *pinnaculum*, plume] 1. a plume on a helmet 2. carefree self-confidence or style; flamboyance

pa·na·da (pə nä'də) *n.* [Sp. < L. *panis*, bread] 1. orig. a dish made of bread boiled to a pulp and flavoured 2. a paste of flour boiled in water or milk, and used as a binding agent, esp. in forcemeats

Pan·a·ma (**hat**) (pan'ə mä') [< *Panama* (city), once a main distributing centre] a fine, hand-plaited hat made from select leaves of a Central and South American plant

Pan-A·mer·i·can (pan'ə mer'ə kən) *adj.* of North, Central, and South America, collectively

Pan-A·mer·i·can·ism (-iz'm) *n.* a policy of political and economic cooperation, mutual cultural understanding, etc. among the Pan-American nations

pan·a·tel·a, pan·a·tel·la (pan'ə tel'ə) *n.* [AmSp., orig. a long biscuit < It., dim. of *pane*, bread] a long, slender cigar

pan·cake (pan'kāk') *n.* 1. a thin, flat cake of batter fried on both sides in a pan 2. [U.S.] a griddlecake or waffle 3. a landing in which the plane levels off, stalls, then drops almost vertically: in full, **pancake landing** —*vi., vt.* -caked', -cak'ing to make, or cause to make, a pancake landing

Pancake Day *same as* Shrove Tuesday (*see* SHROVETIDE)

pancake makeup a thin cake of compressed powder used as cosmetic or theatrical makeup

pan·chro·mat·ic (pan'krō mat'ik) *adj.* sensitive to light of all colours [*panchromatic* film] —**pan·chro·ma·tism** (pan krō'mə tiz'm) *n.*

pan·cre·as (pan'krē əs, pan'-) *n.* [ModL. < Gr. < *pan*, all + *kreas*, flesh] a large, elongated gland that secretes an alkaline digestive juice (**pancreatic juice**) into the small intestine: the pancreas of animals, used as food, is called *sweetbread* —**pan'cre·at'ic** (-at'ik) *adj.*

pan·cre·a·tin (pan'krē ə tin, pan'-) *n.* 1. any of the pancreatic enzymes or a mixture of these 2. a commercial preparation of pancreas extract used as an aid to digestion

pan·da (pan'də) *n.* [Fr. < native name in Nepal] *clipped form of:* 1. GIANT PANDA 2. LESSER PANDA

panda car a police patrol car, usually blue with a broad white stripe

pan·dem·ic (pan dem'ik) *adj.* [< LL. < Gr. < *pan*, all + *dēmos*, the people] epidemic over a large region —*n.* a pandemic disease

pan·de·mo·ni·um (pan'də mō'nē əm) *n.* [ModL. < Gr. *pan*, all + *daimon*, demon] wild disorder, noise, or confusion, or a place where this exists: after the capital of Hell in Milton's *Paradise Lost*

pan·der (pan'dər) *n.* [< L. *Pandarus*, who, in the story of Troilus and Cressida, acts as their go-between] 1. a go-between in a sexual intrigue; pimp 2. one who provides the means of helping to satisfy the ambitions, vices, etc. of another Also **pan'der·er** —*vi.* to act as a pander (to)

pan·dit (pun'dit, pan'-) *n.* [var. of PUNDIT] in India, a learned man: used [P-] as a title of respect

P. and L., P. & L. profit and loss

P and O Peninsular and Oriental (Steamship Company)

p. & p. postage and packing

pane (pān) *n.* [< OFr. < L. *pannus*, piece of cloth] 1. a flat piece, side, or face 2. *a)* a single division of a window, etc., consisting of a sheet of glass in a frame *b)* such a sheet of glass 3. a panel, as of a door

pan·e·gyr·ic (pan'ə jir'ik) *n.* [< Fr. < L. < Gr. *panēgyris*, public meeting < *pan*, all + *ageirein*, to bring together] 1. a formal speech or writing praising a person or event 2. high or exaggerated praise —**pan'e·gyr'i·cal** *adj.* —**pan'e·gyr'i·cal·ly** *adv.* —**pan'e·gyr'ist** *n.* —**pan'e·gy·rize'** (-jə rīz') *vt., vi.* -**rized', -riz'ing**

pan·el (pan'l) *n.* [< OFr., ult. < L. *pannus*, piece of cloth] 1. a section or division of a surface; specif., *a)* a flat piece, usually rectangular, forming a part of the surface of a wall, door, etc., usually raised, recessed, framed, etc. *b)* a similar piece used as a cover, a light diffuser, a built-in heating element, etc. *c)* a pane of a window *d)* a board, or flat surface, for instruments or controls 2. *a)* a thin board for an oil painting *b)* a painting on such a board *c)* a picture much longer than it is wide 3. *a)* a list of persons summoned for jury duty *b)* the jury itself *c)* Scots Law the accused 4. a group of persons selected for a specific purpose, as for judging a contest, discussing an issue, etc. 5. a lengthwise strip, as of contrasting material, in a skirt or dress —*vt.* -**elled, -el·ling** to provide, decorate, etc. with panels

panel discussion a discussion carried on by a selected group of speakers before an audience

panel game a quiz, etc. played by a group of people, esp. on radio or TV

pan·el·ling (-iŋ) *n.* 1. panels collectively; series of panels in a wall, etc. 2. sections of plastic, wood, etc. from which panels are cut Also U.S. sp. **pan'el·ing**

pan·el·list (-ist) *n.* a member of a panel (*n.* 4)

pan·e·tel·a, pan·e·tel·la (pan'ə tel'ə) *n.* *same as* PANATELA

pang (paŋ) *n.* [< ?] a sudden, sharp, brief pain, physical or emotional; spasm of distress

pan·ga (paŋ'gə) *n.* [< native name in E Africa] a long knife with a broad, hooked, sharp blade used in Africa as a cutting tool or as a weapon

pan·go·lin (paŋ gō'lin) *n.* [Malay *pěngulin*, roller < *gulin*, to roll] any of various toothless, scaly mammals of Asia and Africa, able to roll into a ball when attacked

pan·han·dle¹ (pan'han'd'l) *n.* 1. the handle of a pan 2. [U.S.] [often P-] a strip of land like the handle of a pan, as the northern extension of Texas

pan·han·dle² (pan'han'd'l) *vt., vi.* -**dled, -dling** [ult. < PAN¹ + HANDLE, *vt.*] [U.S. Colloq.] to beg (from), esp. on the streets —**pan'han'dler** *n.*

Pan·hel·len·ic (pan'hə len'ik) *adj.* of all the Greek peoples

pan·ic¹ (pan'ik) *n.* [L. *panicum*, kind of millet < *panus*, a swelling] any of several related grasses, as millet, used as fodder: also **panic grass**

pan·ic² (pan'ik) *adj.* [< Fr. < Gr. *panikos*, of Pan] 1. literally, of Pan or of sudden fear supposedly inspired by him 2. like, showing, or resulting from, panic —*n.* 1. a sudden, unreasoning, hysterical fear, often spreading quickly 2. a widespread fear of financial collapse, resulting in stock-market decline, withdrawals of bank deposits, etc. —*vt.* -**icked, -ick·ing** to affect with panic —*vi.* to give way to or show panic —**push** (or **press, hit,** etc.) **the panic button** [Slang] to react to a crisis by some frantic action —**pan'i·cal·ly** *adv.* —**pan'ick·y** *adj.*

pan·i·cle (pan'i k'l) *n.* [< L. dim. of *panus*, a swelling, ear of millet] a loose, irregularly branched flower cluster; compound raceme —**pan'i·cled, pa·nic·u·late** (pa nik'yə lit, -lāt') *adj.*

pan·ic-strick·en (pan'ik strik''n) *adj.* stricken with panic; badly frightened: also **panic-struck**

pan·jan·drum (pan jan'drəm) *n.* [arbitrary coinage] a self-important, pompous official

pan·nage (pan'ij) *n.* [< OFr. ult < L. *pastio*, pasture] 1. acorns, etc. as food for pigs 2. the privilege of pasturing pigs or the payment for the privilege

pan·nier (pan'yər, -ē ər) *n.* [< MFr. < L. *panarium*, breadbasket < *panis*, bread] 1. *a)* a large basket for carrying loads on the back *b)* either of a pair of baskets hung across the back of a donkey, horse, etc. 2. *a)* a framework, as of wire, used formerly to puff out a skirt at the hips *b)* a skirt so puffed

pan·ni·kin (pan'ə kin) *n.* a small pan or cup

pa·no·cha (pə nō'chə) *n.* [AmSp. < Sp. *pan*, bread < L. *panis*] a coarse Mexican sugar

PANICLE
OF OATS

pan·o·ply (pan'ə plē) *n., pl.* -**plies** [< Gr. < *pan*, all + *hopla*, arms] 1. a complete suit of armour 2. any complete or magnificent covering or array —**pan'o·plied** *adj.*

pan·op·tic (pan op'tik) *adj.* [PAN- + OPTIC] including in one view everything in sight

pan·o·ra·ma (pan'ə räm'ə) *n.* [< PAN- + Gr. *horama*, a view] 1. *a)* a picture unrolled in such a way as to give the impression of a continuous view *b)* *same as* CYCLORAMA (sense 1) 2. an open view in all directions 3. a full review of a subject 4. a constantly changing scene [the *panorama* of the waterfront] —**pan'o·ram'ic** (pan'ə ram'ik) *adj.* —**pan'o·ram'i·cal·ly** (-ram'ik əl ē) *adv.*

pan·pipe (pan'pīp') *n.* [also P-] a primitive musical instrument made of a row of reeds or tubes of graduated lengths, played by blowing across the open ends: also **panpipes, Pan's pipes**

pan·sy (pan'zē) *n., pl.* -**sies** [Fr. *pensée*, a thought < *penser*, to think] 1. a small, flowering plant with flat, broad, velvety petals in many colours 2. [Colloq.] a male homosexual

pant¹ (pant) *vi.* [prob. < OFr. *pantaisier*, ult. < L. *phantasia*, nightmare] 1. to breathe rapidly and heavily, as from running fast 2. to beat rapidly; throb 3. to yearn eagerly (with *for* or *after*) —*vt.* to gasp out —*n.* 1. any of a series of rapid, heavy breaths; gasp 2. a throb, as of the heart 3. a puff of an engine

pant² (pant) *n., adj.* *see* PANTS

pan·ta·lets, pan·ta·lettes (pan'tə lets') *n.pl.* [dim. of ff.] 1. long, loose drawers showing below the skirt, worn by women in the 19th cent. 2. detachable ruffles for the legs of drawers

pan·ta·loon (pan'tə lōōn') *n.* [< Fr. < It., ult. after the Venetian patron saint *Pantalone*] [P-] 1. a foolish old man in early Italian comedy, typically slender and in tightfitting trousers 2. a similar buffoon in modern pantomime —*n.* [*pl.*] 1. orig., tight trousers fastened below the calf or strapped under the boot 2. [Chiefly U.S.] trousers

pan·tech·ni·con (pan tek'ni kon', -kən) *n.* [PAN-+ Gr. *technikon* (neut. adj.), of the arts] 1. orig., a bazaar where all kinds of things were sold 2. a warehouse 3. a furniture removal van

pan·the·ism (pan'thē iz'm) *n.* 1. the belief that God is not a personality but the sum of all beings, things, forces, etc. in the universe 2. the worship of all gods —**pan'the·ist** *n.* —**pan'the·is'tic, pan'the·is'ti·cal** *adj.* —**pan'the·is'ti·cal·ly** *adv.*

pan·the·on (pan'thē on', -ən) *n.* [< L. < Gr. < *pan*, all + *theos*, a god] 1. a temple for all the gods; esp., [P-] a temple built in Rome in 27 B.C.: used since 609 A.D. as a Christian church 2. all the gods of a people 3. [often P-] a building in which the famous dead of a nation are entombed or commemorated

pan·ther (pan'thər) *n., pl.* -**thers, -ther:** see PLURAL, II, D, 1 [< OFr. < L. < Gr. *panthēr*] 1. a leopard; specif., *a)* a black leopard *b)* a leopard that is very large or fierce 2. [U.S.] *same as:* *a)* PUMA *b)* JAGUAR —**pan'ther·ess** *n.fem.*

pant·ies (pan'tēz) *n.pl.* women's or children's short undergarments

pan·ti·hose (pan'tē hōz) *n.pl.* a woman's undergarment combining pants with stockings; tights

pan·tile (pan'tīl') *n.* [PAN¹ + TILE] a roofing tile having an S curve, laid with the large curve of one tile overlapping the small of the next

pan·to (pan'tō) *n.* [Colloq.] *clipped form of* PANTOMIME

pan·to- [< Gr. *pantos*, gen. of *pan*, all, every] a combining form meaning all or every: also **pant-**

pan·to·graph (pan'tə gräf') *n.* [< Fr.: see prec. & -GRAPH] a mechanical device for reproducing a drawing on the same or a different scale

pan·to·mime (pan'tə mīm') *n.* [< L. < Gr. < *pantos* (see PANTO-) + *mimos*, a mimic] 1. *a)* a play, skit, etc. performed without words, using actions and gestures only *b)* the art of acting in this way 2. actions and gestures without words 3. a spectacular entertainment based usually on a fairy tale and performed at Christmas 4. a confused or farcical situation —*vt., vi.* -**mimed', -mim'ing** to express or act in pantomime —**pan'to·mim'ic** (-mim'ik) *adj.* —**pan'to·mim'ist** (-mī'mist, -mim'ist) *n.*

pan·to·then·ic acid (pan'tə then'ik) [< Gr. *pantothen*, from every side] a yellow, viscous oil, a member of the vitamin B complex, found in all living tissues

pan·try (pan'trē) *n., pl.* -**tries** [< OFr. < ML. *panetaria* < L. *panis*, bread] 1. a small room off the kitchen where cooking ingredients and utensils, china, etc. are kept; larder 2. *same as* BUTLER'S PANTRY

pants (pants) *n.pl.* [abbrev. of PANTALOON(S)] 1. [Chiefly U.S.] trousers 2. drawers, panties or underpants —**with one's pants down** unprepared; embarrassed, etc.

pan·ty (pan'tē) *n., pl.* -**ties** *same as* PANTIES

panty girdle a girdle with a crotch like panties

pan·zer (pan′zər; *G.* pän′tsər) *adj.* [G., armour] armoured [a *panzer* division]

pap[1] (pap) *n.* [prob. orig. < baby talk] [Archaic] a nipple or teat

pap[2] (pap) *n.* [orig. < baby talk] 1. any soft food for babies or invalids 2. any oversimplified or tasteless writing, ideas, etc.

pa·pa (pə pä′) *n.* [< baby talk, as also in Fr. & L. *papa*] father: a child's word

pa·pa·cy (pā′pə sē) *n.*, *pl.* **-cies** [< ML. < LL. *papa*, pope] 1. the position or authority of the Pope 2. the period during which a pope rules 3. the succession of popes 4. [*also* P-] the government of the Roman Catholic Church, headed by the Pope

pa·pal (pā′pəl) *adj.* [< MFr. < ML.: see POPE & -AL] 1. of the Pope or the papacy 2. of the Roman Catholic Church —**pa′pal·ly** *adv.*

pa·paw (pô′pô) *n.* [prob. < ff.] 1. *same as* PAPAYA 2. *a)* a tree of central and southern U.S. having a yellowish, edible fruit with many seeds *b)* its fruit

pa·pa·ya (pə pī′yə) *n.* [Sp. < Carib name] 1. a palmlike tropical American tree bearing a large, yellowish-orange fruit like a melon 2. its fruit

pa·per (pā′pər) *n.* [< OFr. < L. *papyrus*, PAPYRUS] 1. a thin, flexible material usually in sheets, made from wood pulp, rags, etc., and used for writing or printing on, for packaging, etc. 2. a single piece or sheet of this 3. a printed or written paper; specif., *a)* an official document *b)* an essay, dissertation, etc. *c)* a written examination, report, etc. 4. *same as* PAPER MONEY 5. *clipped form of:* a) NEWSPAPER *b)* WALLPAPER 6. a small wrapper of paper, usually including its contents [a *paper* of pins] 7. any material like paper, as papyrus 8. [*pl.*] *a)* documents identifying a person; credentials *b)* a collection of letters, writings, etc. —*adj.* 1. of paper; made of paper 2. like paper; thin 3. existing only in written form; theoretical [*paper* profits] —*vt.* 1. to cover with paper, esp. wallpaper 2. to wrap in paper —*vi.* to hang wallpaper —**on paper** 1. in written or printed form 2. in theory —**pa′per·er** *n.* —**pa′- per·like′, pa′per·y** *adj.*

pa·per·back (-bak′) *n.* a book bound in paper —**pa′- per·backed′, pa′per·bound′** (-bound′) *adj.*

paper birch the N American birch having white or ash-coloured paperlike bark

pa·per·boy (-boi′) *n.* a boy or man who sells or delivers newspapers —**pa′per·girl** (-gurl′) *n. fem.*

pa·per·chase (-chās′) *n.* a cross-country race in which runners follow a trail of torn-up pieces of paper

paper clip a flexible clasp of metal wire for holding loose sheets of paper together

paper cutter 1. *same as* PAPER KNIFE 2. a device for cutting and trimming several sheets of paper at a time

pa·per·hang·er (-haŋ′ər) *n.* a person whose work is covering walls with wallpaper —**pa′per·hang′ing** *n.*

paper knife a knifelike blade, as of metal, used to slit sealed envelopes and uncut bookpages

paper money noninterest-bearing notes, as pound notes, issued by a government or its banks, circulating as legal tender

paper nautilus an eight-armed mollusc related to the octopus: the female has a paperlike shell in which the young develop

paper tiger a person, nation, etc. that seems to pose a threat but is actually powerless

pa·per·weight (-wāt′) *n.* any small, heavy object set on papers to keep them from being scattered

paper work the keeping of records, filing of reports, etc. incidental to some work or task

Pa·phi·an (pā′fi ən) *adj.* [< L. *Paphius* + -AN] 1. of Paphos 2. [in reference to the worship of Aphrodite in Paphos] of sexual love; erotic

pa·pier-mâ·ché (pā′pər ma′shā, -mə shā′) *n.* [Fr. *papier*, paper + pp. of *mâcher*, to chew] a material made of paper pulp mixed with size, glue, etc. that is easily moulded when moist and dries strong and hard —*adj.* made of papier-mâché

pa·pil·la (pə pil′ə) *n.*, *pl.* **-lae** (-ē) [L., dim. of *papula*, pimple] 1. a small bulge of flesh, as at the root of a hair, a developing tooth, etc., or on the surface of the tongue 2. *Bot.* a tiny, protruding cell —**pap·il·lar·y** (pap′ə lər ē, pə pil′ər ē) *adj.* —**pap·il·late** (pap′ə lāt′, pə pil′it) *adj.*

pap·il·lo·ma (pap′ə lō′mə) *n.*, *pl.* **-ma·ta** (-mə tə), **-mas** [ModL.: see PAPILLA & -OMA] a benign tumour of the skin or mucous membrane, consisting of a thickened and enlarged papilla or group of papillae, as a corn or wart

pa·pist (pā′pist) *n.* [< ModL. < LL. *papa*, POPE] 1. one who believes in papal supremacy 2. a Roman Catholic —*adj.* Roman Catholic Usually a disparaging term

pa·poose (pa pōōs′, pə-) *n.* [< Algonquian *papoos*] a North American Indian baby

pap·pus (pap′əs) *n.*, *pl.* **pap′pi** (-ī) [ModL. < L. < Gr.

pappos, old man] *Bot.* a tuft of bristles, hairs, etc., as on dandelion seeds —**pap′pose** (-ōs), **pap′ous** (-əs) *adj.*

pa·pri·ka (pa prē′kə, pə-; pap′ri kə) *n.* [Hung. < Serb. < Gr. *peperi*, pepper] 1. mild, red condiment ground from the fruit of certain peppers 2. the fruit or plant from which this seasoning is obtained

Pap test (pap) [after G. *Papanicolaou* (1883-1962), U.S. anatomist] the microscopic examination of a smear (**Pap smear**) taken from the cervix of a woman: a test for uterine cancer

pap·ule (pap′yōōl) *n.* [L. *papula*] a pimple: also **pap′pu·la** —**pap′u·lar** (-lər) *adj.* —**pap′u·lose′** (-lōs′) *adj.*

pap·y·rol·o·gy (pap′ə rol′ə jē) *n.* the study and translation of ancient manuscripts written on papyrus —**pap′y·rol′- o·gist** *n.*

pa·py·rus (pə pī′rəs) *n.*, *pl.* **-ri** (-rī), **-rus·es** [L. < Gr. *papyros*, prob. < Egypt.] 1. a tall water plant abundant in the Nile region in Egypt 2. a writing material made from this plant by the ancient Egyptians, Greeks, and Romans 3. any ancient document or manuscript on papyrus

par (pär) *n.* [L., an equal] 1. the established value of the money of one country in terms of the money of another 2. an equal status, footing, level, etc.: usually in **on a par (with)** 3. the average state, condition, etc. [work that is above *par*] 4. *Commerce* the face value of shares, bonds, etc. 5. *Golf* the number of strokes established as a skilful score for a hole or course —*adj.* 1. of or at par 2. average; normal —*vt.* **parred, par′ring** *Golf* to score par on (a given hole or course)

par. 1. paragraph 2. parallel 3. parenthesis 4. parish

pa·ra (pä′rä′, pär′ə) *n.* [Turk. < Per. *pärah*, a piece] *see* MONETARY UNITS, table (Yugoslavia)

para- [< Gr. < *para*, at the side of] a prefix meaning: 1. by or at the side of, beyond, aside from [*paramilitary*] 2. *Med.* a) in a secondary capacity b) functionally disordered, abnormal c) like or resembling [*paratyphoid*]

par·a·a·mi·no·ben·zo·ic acid (par′ə ə mē′nō ben zō′ik, -am′ə nō′-) a crystalline compound considered a member of the vitamin B complex: needed for growth by many organisms

par·a·ba·sis (par′ə bā′sis) *n.* [< Gr. *para*, PARA- + *basis*, a going] an ode sung by the chorus in ancient Greek comedy

par·a·ble (par′ə b'l) *n.* [< MFr. < LL. < L. < Gr. *parabolē*, a comparing: ult. < *para*-, beside + *ballein*, to throw] a short, simple story teaching a moral or religious lesson

pa·rab·o·la (pə rab′ə lə) *n.* [ModL. < Gr. *parabolē*: see prec.] *Geom.* a plane curve formed by the intersection of a cone with a plane parallel to its side

par·a·bol·ic[1] (par′ə bol′ik) *adj.* of, like, or expressed by a parable: also **par′a·bol′i·cal** —**par′a·bol′i·cal·ly** *adv.*

par·a·bol·ic[2] (par′ə bol′ik) *adj.* 1. of or like a parabola 2. concave with the regular outline of a parabola, as a reflector —**par′a·bol′i·cal·ly** *adv.*

par·a·ce·ta·mol (par′ə sēt′ə mol′) *n.* [< *para-acetamidophenol*] a mild analgesic drug

pa·rach·ro·nism (pə ra′krə niz′m) *n.* [PARA- & Gr. *chronos*, time] an error in dating, esp. one in which the event is dated later than its actual occurrence

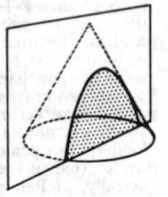

PARABOLA

par·a·chute (par′ə shōōt′) *n.* [Fr. < *para-* (< It. *parare*, to ward off) + *chute*, a fall] 1. a large cloth contrivance shaped like an umbrella when it opens up, used to retard the speed of a person or thing dropping from an aircraft, etc. 2. something shaped like or having the effect of a parachute —*vt.*, *vi.* **-chut′ed, -chut′ing** to drop or descend by parachute —**par′a·chut′ist** *n.*

pa·rade (pə rād′) *n.* [Fr. < Sp. *parada*, ult. < L. *parare*, to prepare] 1. ostentatious display 2. *a)* a military assembly; esp., a review of marching troops *b)* a place where troops assemble regularly for parade 3. any organized procession or march, as for display 4. *a)* a public walk or promenade *b)* persons promenading —*vt.* **-rad′ed, -rad′ing** 1. to bring together (troops, etc.) for inspection or display 2. to march or walk through (the streets, etc.), as for display 3. to show off [he *parades* his knowledge] —*vi.* 1. to march in a parade 2. to walk about ostentatiously 3. to assemble in military formation for review or display —**on parade** on display —**pa·rad′er** *n.*

par·a·digm (par′ə dīm) *n.* [< Fr. < LL. < Gr. < *para*, beside + *deigma*, example < *deiknynai*, to show] 1. a pattern, example, or model 2. *Gram.* an example of a declension or conjugation, giving all the inflectional forms of a word —**par′a·dig·mat′ic** (-dig mat′ik) *adj.*

par·a·dise (par′ə dīs′) *n.* [< OFr. < LL. < L. < Gr. *paradeisos*, a garden] 1. [P-] the garden of Eden 2. *same as* HEAVEN 3. any place or state of perfection, happiness, etc. —**par′a·di·si′a·cal** (-di sī′ə k'l), **par′a·dis′- i·ac′** (-dis′ē ak′) *adj.*

par·a·dox (par′ə doks′) *n.* [< L. < Gr. < *para*-, beyond + *doxa*, opinion < *dokein*, to think] **1.** a statement that seems contradictory, absurd, etc. but may be true in fact **2.** a statement that contradicts itself and is false **3.** a person, situation, etc. that seems inconsistent or full of contradictions —**par′a·dox′i·cal** *adj.* —**par′a·dox′i·cal·ly** *adv.* —**par′a·dox′i·cal·ness, par′a·dox′i·cal·i·ty** *n.*

par·af·fin (par′ə fin) *n.* [G. < L. *parum*, too little + *affinis*, akin: from its chemical inertness] **1.** a white, waxy substance consisting of a mixture of hydrocarbons, distilled from petroleum and used for making candles, sealing jars, etc. **2.** a liquid mixture of hydrocarbons used as a fuel in domestic heaters, etc. **3.** *Chem.* any hydrocarbon of the methane series —*vt.* to coat or impregnate with paraffin

paraffin series *same as* METHANE SERIES

paraffin wax *same as* PARAFFIN (*n.* 1)

par·a·gon (par′ə gon′, -gən) *n.* [MFr. < It. *paragone*, touchstone < Gr. < *para*-, against + *akonē*, whetstone] a model of perfection or excellence

par·a·graph (par′ə gräf′) *n.* [< OFr. < ML. < Gr. *paragraphos* < *para*-, beside + *graphein*, to write] **1.** a distinct section of a chapter, letter, etc. dealing with a particular point: it is begun on a new line, often indented **2.** a mark (¶) used as by proofreaders to indicate the beginning of a paragraph **3.** a brief item in a newspaper or magazine —*vt.* **1.** to write about in paragraphs **2.** to arrange in paragraphs — **par′a·graph′er, par′a·graph′ist** *n.* —**par′a·graph′ic** (par′ə graf′ik) *adj.*

Par·a·guay tea (par′ə gwī′) *same as* MATÉ

par·a·keet (par′ə kēt′) *n.* [MFr. *paroquet*, prob. < *perrot*, parrot] any of various small, slender parrots with a long, tapering tail

par·a·leip·sis (par′ə līp′sis) *n.* [Gr. *paraleipsis*, omission] a rhetorical device in which a point is stressed by suggesting that it is too obvious to mention (Ex.: "not to mention the expense"): also **par′a·lep′sis** (-lep′-), **par′a·lip′sis** (-lip′-)

par·al·lax (par′ə laks′) *n.* [< Fr. < Gr. < *para*-, beyond + *allassein*, to change] **1.** the apparent change in the position of an object resulting from a change in the viewer's position **2.** the amount of such change; specif., *Astron.* the apparent difference in the position of a heavenly body with reference to some point on the surface of the earth and some other point, as the centre of the earth —**par′al·lac′tic** *adj.*

par·al·lel (par′ə lel′, -ləl) *adj.* [< Fr. < L. < Gr. < *para*-, side by side + *allēlos*, one another] **1.** extending in the same direction and at a constant distance apart, so as never to meet, as lines, planes, etc. **2.** having parallel parts or movements, as some machines **3.** *a)* similar or corresponding, as in purpose, time, or essential parts *b)* having a balanced arrangement, esp. of phrases or clauses [*parallel* structure] **4.** *Elec.* designating a circuit in parallel —*adv.* in a parallel manner —*n.* **1.** a parallel line, surface, etc. **2.** any person or thing similar or corresponding to another; counterpart **3.** a being parallel **4.** any comparison showing likeness **5.** *a)* any of the imaginary lines parallel to the equator and representing degrees of latitude *b)* such a line drawn on a map or globe: in full, **parallel of latitude 6.** [*pl.*] a sign (‖) used as a reference mark **7.** *Elec.* a circuit connection in which the negative terminals are joined to one conductor and the positive to another: usually in phrase, **in parallel** —*vt.* **-al·lelled′, -al·lel′ling 1.** *a)* to make (one thing) parallel to another *b)* to make parallel to each other **2.** to be parallel to **3.** to compare (things) in order to show similarity **4.** to be or find a counterpart for; match

parallel bars two parallel, horizontal bars set on adjustable upright posts: used in gymnastics

par·al·lel·e·pi·ped (par′ə lel′ə pī′-pid, -pip′id) *n.* [< Gr. *parallēlos*, parallel + *epipedos*, plane] a solid with six faces, each of which is a parallelogram: also **par′al·lel′-e·pip′e·don′** (-pip′ə don′)

par·al·lel·ism (par′ə lel iz′m, -ləl-) *n.* **1.** the state of being parallel **2.** close resemblance; similarity **3.** use of parallel structure in writing

par·al·lel·o·gram (par′ə lel′ə gram′) *n.* [< Fr. < L. < Gr. < *parallēlos*, PARALLEL + *grammē*, a line] a plane figure with four sides, having the opposite sides parallel and equal

PARALLEL BARS

par·a·lyse (par′ə līz′) *vt.* **-lysed′, -lys′ing 1.** to cause paralysis in **2.** to make inactive, ineffective, or powerless —**par′a·ly·sa′tion** *n.* —**par′a·lys′er** *n.*

pa·ral·y·sis (pə ral′ə sis) *n., pl.* **-ses′** (-sēz′) [L. < Gr. < *paralyein*, to loosen at the side < *para*-, beside + *lyein*, to loose] **1.** partial or complete loss of the power of motion or

sensation, esp. voluntary motion, in some part or all of the body **2.** any condition of helpless inactivity or inability to act

par·a·lyt·ic (par′ə lit′ik) *adj.* **1.** relating to paralysis **2.** [Slang] drunk —*n.* a person affected with paralysis

par·a·mat·ta (par′ə mat′ə) *n.* [after *Parramatta*, city in SE Australia] a soft, lightweight dress fabric with a cotton warp and a filling of fine wool

par·a·me·ci·um (par′ə mē′shē əm, -sē əm) *n., pl.* **-ci·a** (-ə) [ModL. < Gr. *paramēkēs*, oval] a one-celled, elongated protozoan that moves by means of cilia and has a large mouth

par·a·med·ic (par′ə med′ik) *n.* [< PARA(CHUTE) + MEDIC[1]] a doctor, or other military medical attendant, who parachutes to combat or rescue areas

par·a·med·i·cal (par′ə med′i k'l) *adj.* [PARA- + MEDICAL] designating or of auxiliary medical personnel, as midwives, laboratory technicians, nurses' aides, etc.

pa·ram·e·ter (pə ram′ə tər) *n.* [< ModL. < Gr. *para*, alongside + *metron*, measure] **1.** *Math.* a quantity whose value varies with the circumstances of its application **2.** any constant, with variable values, used as a reference for other variables —**par·a·met′ric** (par′ə met′rik) *adj.*

par·a·mil·i·tar·y (par′ə mil′ə tər ē) *adj.* [PARA- + MILITARY] designating or of forces working along with, or in place of, a regular military organization, often as a semi-official or secret auxiliary

par·a·mount (par′ə mount′) *adj.* [< Anglo-Fr. < OFr. *par* (L. *per*), by + *amont* (< L. *ad montem*), uphill] ranking higher than any other; chief; supreme —*n.* a supreme ruler; overlord —**par′a·mount′cy** (-sē) *n.* —**par′a·mount′ly** *adv.*

par·a·mour (par′ə moor′) *n.* [< OFr. *par amour*, with love] **1.** a lover; esp., the illicit sexual partner of a married person **2.** [Archaic] a sweetheart

pa·rang (pä′rəŋ) *n.* [Malay] a heavy knife used by the Malays as a tool and weapon

par·a·noi·a (par′ə noi′ə) *n.* [ModL. < Gr. < *para*-, beside + *nous*, the mind] a mental disorder characterized by systematized delusions, as of grandeur or, esp., persecution —**par′a·noid′, par′a·noi′ac** (-ak) *adj., n.* —**par′a·noi′dal** *adj.*

par·a·pet (par′ə pit, -pet′) *n.* [Fr. < It. < *parare*, to guard + *petto*, breast < L. *pectus*] **1.** a wall or bank for screening troops from enemy fire **2.** a low wall or railing, as on a balcony or bridge

par·a·pher·na·li·a (par′ə fər nāl′yə, -fə nāl′-; -nā′lē ə) *n.pl.* [*often with sing. v.*] [ML. < LL. *parapherna* < Gr. < *para*-, beyond + *phernē*, a dowry] **1.** personal belongings **2.** equipment; apparatus; gear

par·a·phrase (par′ə frāz′) *n.* [Fr. < L. < Gr. *paraphrasis*, ult. < *para*, beyond + *phrazein*, to tell] a rewording of the meaning of something spoken or written. —*vt., vi.* **-phrased′, -phras′ing** to express in a paraphrase —**par′-a·phras′er, par′a·phrast′** (-frast′) *n.* —**par′a·phras′tic** *adj.*

par·a·ple·gi·a (par′ə plē′jē ə, -jə) *n.* [ModL. < Gr. *paraplēgia*, a stroke at one side: see PARA- & -PLEGIA] paralysis of the entire lower half of the body —**par′a·ple′gic** (-plē′jik, -plej′ik) *adj., n.*

par·a·psy·chol·o·gy (-sī kol′ə jē) *n.* [PARA- + PSYCHOLOGY] the study of such psychic phenomena as telepathy, ESP, etc.

par·a·quat (par′ə kwat′) *n.* [PARA- + QUAT(ERNARY)] a quick-acting weedkiller

Pa·rá rubber (pə rä′) crude rubber obtained from several tropical S American trees

par·a·site (par′ə sīt′) *n.* [< L. < Gr. *parasitos*, one who eats at the table of another < *para*-, beside + *sitos*, food] **1.** a person who lives at others' expense without making any useful return **2.** a plant or animal that lives on or within another from which it derives sustenance —**par′a·sit′ic** (-sit′ik), **par′a·sit′i·cal** *adj.* —**par′a·sit′i·cal·ly** *adv.* —**par′-a·sit′ism** (-iz′m) *n.*

par·a·sit·ize (-sī tīz′, -sī-) *vt.* **-ized′, -iz′ing 1.** to live on, in, or with as a parasite **2.** to infest with parasites

par·a·si·tol·o·gy (par′ə sī tol′ə jē, -si-) *n.* the science dealing with parasites —**par′a·si·tol′o·gist** *n.*

par·a·sol (par′ə sol′) *n.* [Fr. < It. < *parare*, to ward off + *sole*, the sun] a light umbrella carried as a sunshade

par·a·sym·pa·thet·ic (par′ə sim′pə thet′ik) *adj.* [PARA- + SYMPATHETIC] designating or of that part of the autonomic nervous system whose functions include the slowing of the heartbeat and stimulation of certain digestive glands: cf. SYMPATHETIC

par·a·thi·on (par′ə thī′on) *n.* [< Gr. *para*-, alongside + *theion*, sulphur] a poisonous insecticide

par·a·thy·roid (-thī′roid) *adj.* [PARA- + THYROID] designating or of any of four small glands located on or near the thyroid gland: their hormonal secretions help control the body's calcium-phosphorus balance —*n.* a parathyroid gland

par·a·troops (par′ə trōōps′) *n.pl.* [< PARA(CHUTE) + TROOP] troops trained and equipped to parachute into a combat area —**par'a·troop'** adj. —**par'a·troop'er** n.

par·a·ty·phoid (par'ə tī'foid) adj. [PARA- + TYPHOID] designating, of, or causing a disease similar to typhoid fever but milder and caused by various bacteria —n. paratyphoid fever

‡**par a·vion** (pàrà vyōn') [Fr.] by air mail

par·boil (pär'boil') vt. [< OFr. < par (< L. per), through + boullir (< L. bullire), to boil: meaning infl. by Eng. part] 1. to boil until partly cooked, as before roasting 2. to make uncomfortably hot

par·buck·le (pär'buk''l) n. [altered (after BUCKLE¹) < Early ModE. parbunkel] a sling for a log, barrel, etc. made by passing a doubled rope around the object and pulling the ends through the loop —vt. **-led, -ling** to raise or lower by using a parbuckle

Par·cae (pär'sē) n.pl. Rom. Myth. the three Fates

par·cel (pär's'l) n. [< MFr., ult. < L. particula: see PARTICLE] 1. a small, wrapped bundle; package 2. a quantity of items put up for sale 3. a group; pack [a parcel of fools] 4. a piece, as of land —vt. **-celled, -cel·ling** 1. to separate into parts and distribute (with out) 2. to make up in or as a parcel

parcel post a postal service for carrying and delivering parcels

parch (pärch) vt. [< ?] 1. to expose (corn, etc.) to great heat, so as to dry or roast 2. to make hot and dry 3. to make very thirsty —vi. to become very hot, dry, thirsty, etc.

par·chee·si (pär chē'zē) n. 1. a game like parchisi in which dice are thrown 2. the game of parchisi Also sp. **par·che'si**

parch·ment (pärch'mənt) n. [< OFr., ult. < L. (charta) Pergamena, (paper) of Pergamum, city in Asia Minor] 1. an animal skin, as of a sheep or goat, prepared as a surface for writing or painting 2. paper treated to resemble this 3. a manuscript, diploma, etc. on parchment

pard (pärd) n. [< OFr. < L. < Gr. pardos] [Archaic or Poet.] a leopard, or panther

par·da·lote (pär'də lōt') n. [ModL. < Gr. pardalōtos, spotted] an Australian bird with a brightly-coloured spotted plumage: also **diamond bird**

par·don (pär'd'n) vt. [< OFr. < LL. < L. per-, through + donare, to give] 1. to release (a person) from punishment 2. to cancel penalty for (an offence); forgive 3. to excuse (a person) for (a minor fault, discourtesy, etc.) —n. 1. a pardoning or being pardoned; forgiveness 2. an official document granting a pardon 3. R.C.Ch. same as INDULGENCE —**I beg your pardon** excuse me: a polite form of apology, disagreement, etc. —**par'don·a·ble** adj. —**par'don·a·bly** adv.

par·don·er (-ər) n. 1. in the Middle Ages, a person authorized to sell ecclesiastical pardons, or indulgences 2. a person who pardons

pare (per) vt. **pared, par'ing** [< MFr. < L. parare, to prepare] 1. to cut or trim away (the rind, skin, covering, etc.) of (anything); peel 2. to reduce gradually —**par'er** n.

par·e·gor·ic (par'ə gor'ik) n. [< LL. < Gr. < parēgoros, speaking, consoling < para-, beside + agora, assembly] 1. orig., a medicine that lessens pain 2. a camphorated tincture of opium, used to relieve diarrhoea —adj. [Archaic] soothing or lessening pain

pa·ren·chy·ma (pə reŋ'ki mə) n. [ModL. < Gr., ult. < para-, beside + en-, in + cheein, to pour] 1. Anat. the functional tissue of an organ, as distinguished from its connective tissue, etc. 2. Bot. a soft tissue of thin-walled cells in plant leaves and stems, fruit pulp, etc. —**pa·ren'chy·mal, par·en·chym·a·tous** (par'eŋ kim'ə təs) adj.

par·ent (per'ənt) n. [OFr. < L. parens, parent, orig. prp. of parere, to beget] 1. a father or mother 2. a progenitor or ancestor 3. any organism in relation to its offspring 4. a source; origin —**pa·ren·tal** (pə ren't'l) adj. —**pa·ren'tal·ly** adv. —**par'ent·hood'** n.

par·ent·age (-ij) n. 1. descent or derivation from parents or ancestors; lineage; origin 2. the position or relation of a parent; parenthood

pa·ren·the·sis (pə ren'thə sis) n., pl. **-ses** (-sēz') [LL. < Gr., ult. < para-, beside + entithenai, to insert] 1. a word, clause, remark, etc. added as an explanation or comment within a complete sentence and usually marked off by curved lines, commas, etc. 2. either or both of the curved lines ( ) so used 3. an episode or interlude —**par·en·thet·i·cal** (par'ən thet'i k'l), **par'en·thet'ic** adj. —**par'en·thet'i·cal·ly** adv.

pa·ren·the·size (-sīz') vt. **-sized', -siz'ing** 1. to insert (a word, etc.) as a parenthesis 2. to put into parentheses (sense 2)

parent teacher association an organisation formed by the parents of school children and their teachers to advance better relations between them

pa·re·sis (pə rē'sis, par'ə sis) n., pl. **-ses** (-sēz) [ModL. < Gr. < parienai, to relax] 1. partial or slight paralysis 2. a syphilitic brain disease marked by dementia, paralytic

attacks, etc.: in full, **general paresis** —**pa·ret'ic** (-ret'ik, -rē'-tik) n., adj.

par ex·cel·lence (pär ek'sə läns') [Fr.] in the greatest degree of excellence; beyond comparison

par·fait (pär'fã, pär fã') n. [Fr., lit., perfect] 1. a frozen dessert of cream, eggs, syrup, etc. in a tall, slender, short-stemmed glass 2. a dessert of layers of ice cream, crushed fruit, etc. in such a glass

par·he·li·on (pär hē'lē ən, -hēl'yən) n., pl. **-li·a** (-ə, -yə) [< L. < Gr. < para-, beside + hēlios, the sun] a bright, coloured spot of light on a solar halo —**par·he'lic, par'he·li'a·cal** (-hi lī'ə k'l) adj.

pa·ri·ah (pə rī'ə, par'ē ə) n. [< Tamil paraiyan, a drummer: the pariah was a hereditary drumbeater] 1. a member of one of the lowest social castes in India 2. any outcast

pa·ri·e·tal (pə rī'ə t'l) adj. [< Fr. < LL. < L. paries, a wall] Anat. of the walls of a cavity, etc.; esp., designating either of two bones forming part of the top and sides of the skull

pa·ri·mu·tu·el (par'ə myoo'choo wəl) n. [Fr., lit., a mutual bet] a system of betting on races in which the winning bettors share the total amount bet, minus a percentage for the track operators, taxes, etc.; totalizator

par·ing (per'iŋ) n. a thin piece or strip pared off

‡**pa·ri pas·su** (par'ē pas'ŏŏ) [L.] 1. with equal speed 2. in equal proportion

Par·is green (par'is) a poisonous, bright-green chemical powder used chiefly as an insecticide

par·ish (par'ish) n. [< OFr. < LL. < LGr. paroikia, diocese, ult. < Gr. para-, beside + oikos, dwelling] 1. a district of British local government 2. an administrative district of various churches, esp. a part of a diocese, under the charge of a priest or minister 3. a) the members of a church congregation b) the territory they live in 4. [U.S.] a civil division in Louisiana, corresponding to a county in other states of the U.S.

parish clerk an official appointed by a clergyman to perform certain duties in a parish

parish council a body elected to adminster the affairs of a parish

pa·rish·ion·er (pə rish'ə nər) n. a member of a parish

parish register a book in which all the births, baptisms, marriages and deaths in a particular parish are recorded

par·i·ty (par'ə tē) n., pl. **-ties** [< Fr. < L. < par, equal] 1. a being the same in power, value, etc.; equality 2. resemblance; similarity 3. equivalence in value of a currency in terms of another country's currency 4. equality of value at a given ratio between different kinds of money, commodities, etc.

park (pärk) n. [< OFr. < ML. parricus] 1. land with woods, lakes, etc., held as part of a private estate or as a hunting preserve 2. an area of public land for public recreation, usually with walks, playgrounds, etc. or a large area with natural scenery, preserved by a government 3. that arrangement in an automatic transmission of a motor vehicle that holds the vehicle in place when it is parked 4. Mil. an area for storing and servicing vehicles and other equipment —vt. 1. to enclose as in a park 2. to assemble (military equipment) in a park 3. to leave (a vehicle) in a certain place temporarily 4. to manoeuvre (a vehicle) into a space for parking 5. [Colloq.] to put, leave, or deposit in a certain place —vi. to park a vehicle —**park oneself** [Colloq.] sit down

par·ka (pär'kə) n. [Aleutian < Russ.] 1. a hip-length, pullover fur garment with a hood, worn in arctic regions 2. a similar hooded jacket

par·kin (pär'kin) n. [< ?] a moist, spicy ginger cake, usually containing oatmeal

parking meter a coin-operated timing device at a parking space to show the length of time that a parked vehicle may occupy that space

parking ticket the notice of a fine incurred by a motorist in violation of parking laws: often attached to the vehicle's windscreen

Par·kin·son's disease (pär'kin sənz) [after J. Parkinson (1755-1824), Brit. physician] a brain disease characterized by a tremor and muscular rigidity

Parkinson's Law [after C. Parkinson (1909-), Brit. economist] the idea, expressed facetiously as a law of economics, that work expands to fill the time allotted to it

park·land (-land) n. an open expanse of grass with trees dotted about in it

park·y (pär'kē) adj. **park'i·er, park'i·est** [Colloq.] chilly; cold: used esp. of the weather

Parl. 1. Parliament 2. Parliamentary

par·lance (pär'ləns) n. [< Anglo-Fr. < OFr. < parler, to speak] a style or manner of speaking or writing; language; idiom [military parlance]

par·lan·do (pär lan'dō) adj., adv. [It.] Music to be sung in a style suggesting or approximating speech

par·ley (pär'lē) vi. [< Fr. parler, to speak < LL. < parabola, PARABLE] to confer, esp. with an enemy —n., pl.

-leys a conference; specif., a military conference with an enemy to discuss terms

par·lia·ment (pär'lə mənt) *n.* [< OFr. *parlement* < *parler*: see prec.] 1. an official conference or council concerned with government 2. [P-] the national legislative body of Great Britain, composed of the House of Commons and the House of Lords 3. [P-] a similar body in other countries

par·lia·men·tar·i·an (pär'lə men ter'e ən, -mən-) *n.* a person skilled in parliamentary rules or debate

par·lia·men·ta·ry (pär'lə men'tə rē, -trē) *adj.* 1. of, like, or established by a parliament 2. conforming to the rules of a parliament or other public assembly 3. having or governed by a parliament; specif., of a government in which the prime minister holds office only so long as he commands a majority in the parliament

Parliamentary Private Secretary a member of parliament who helps the head of a government department

par·lour (pär'lər) *n.* [< OFr. < *parler*: see PARLEY] 1. *a)* orig., a room set aside for the entertainment of guests *b)* any living room: old-fashioned term 2. a small, semi-private room in a hotel, etc., used as for conferences 3. [Chiefly U.S.] a business establishment, esp. one with specialized services [a billiard *parlour*] U.S. sp. **parlor**

par·lous (pär'ləs) *adj.* [ME., contr. of *perilous*] [Chiefly Archaic] 1. perilous 2. cunning, shrewd, etc. —*adv.* [Chiefly Archaic] extremely

Par·me·san (cheese) (pär'mə zan', -zən) [Fr. < It. < *Parma*, city in Italy] a very hard, dry Italian cheese made from skim milk and usually grated for sprinkling on spaghetti, soup, etc.

Par·nas·sus (pär nas'əs) *n.* [after the mountain in C Greece sacred to Apollo and the Muses] 1. poetry or poets collectively 2. any centre of poetic or artistic activity —**Par·nas'si·an** (-ē ən) *adj.*

pa·ro·chi·al (pə rō'kē əl) *adj.* [OFr. < ML. < LL. *parochia*: see PARISH] 1. of or in a parish or parishes 2. narrow; provincial; limited —**pa·ro'chi·al·ism** *n.* —**pa·ro'chi·al·ist** *n.* —**pa·ro'chi·al·ly** *adv.*

par·o·dy (par'ə dē) *n.,* *pl.* **-dies** [< Fr. < L. < Gr. *parōidia* < *para-*, beside + *ōidē*, song] 1. a literary or musical composition imitating the style of a writer or composer in a nonsensical way, as in ridicule 2. a weak imitation —*vt.* **-died, -dy·ing** to make a parody of —**pa·rod·ic** (pə rod'ik), **pa·rod'i·cal** *adj.* —**par'o·dist** *n.* —**par'o·dis'tic** *adj.*

pa·role (pə rōl') *n.* [Fr. < L. < LL. *parabola*, PARABLE] 1. word of honour; esp., the promise of a prisoner of war not to fight further if released 2. the condition of being on parole 3. *a)* the release of a prisoner before his sentence has expired, on condition of future good behaviour *b)* the freedom thus granted, or its duration —*vt.* **-roled', -rol'ing** to release on parole —**on parole** at liberty under conditions of parole

pa·rol·ee (pə rō'lē') *n.* a person on parole from prison

pa·rot·id (pə rot'id) *adj.* [< ML. < L. < Gr. *parōtis* < *para-*, beside + *ous* (gen. *ōtos*), ear] designating or of either of the salivary glands below and in front of each ear —*n.* a parotid gland

par·o·ti·tis (par'ə tīt'əs) *n.* [< prec. & -ITIS] inflammation of the parotid gland; mumps

-par·ous (par əs) [< L. < *parere*, to bear] a combining form meaning bringing forth, producing, bearing [*viviparous*]

par·ox·ysm (par'ək siz'm) *n.* [< Fr. < ML. < Gr. < *para-*, beyond + *oxynein*, to sharpen < *oxys*, sharp] 1. a sudden attack, or intensification of the symptoms, of a disease, usually recurring periodically 2. a sudden outburst of laughter, rage, etc.; fit; spasm —**par'ox·ys'mal** (-siz'm'l) *adj.*

par·quet (pär'kā) *n.* [Fr. < MFr. dim. of *parc*, a park] a flooring of parquetry —*vt.* **-queted** (-kād), **-quet·ing** (-kā iŋ) 1. to use parquetry to make (a floor, etc.) 2. to decorate the floor of (a room) with parquetry

par·quet·ry (pär'kə trē) *n.* inlaid woodwork in geometric forms: used esp. in flooring

parr (pär) *n., pl.* **parrs, parr:** see PLURAL, II, D, 1 [< ?] a young salmon before it enters salt water

par·ra·keet (par'ə kēt') *n.* alt. sp. of PARAKEET

par·ra·mat·ta (par'ə mat'ə) *n.* alt. sp. of PARAMATTA

par·ri·cide (par'ə sīd') *n.* [Fr. < L. *parricida,* a relative + *-cida,* -CIDE] 1. a person who murders his parent or another near relative 2. the act of a parricide —**par'ri·ci'dal** *adj.*

PARQUETRY

par·rot (par'ət) *n.* [Fr. dial. *perrot*] 1. any of several related tropical or subtropical birds with a hooked bill, brightly coloured feathers, and feet having two toes pointing forwards and two backwards: some parrots can learn to imitate human speech 2. a person who mechanically repeats the words or acts of

others —*vt.* to repeat or imitate, esp. without understanding

par·rot-fash·ion (-fash'ən) *adv.* without regard for meaning; by rote

parrot fever same as PSITTACOSIS

parrot fish any of various related, brightly coloured, tropical ocean fishes with parrotlike jaws

par·ry (par'ē) *vt.* **-ried, -ry·ing** [prob. < imper. of Fr. *parer* < It. *parare,* to ward off < L. *parare,* to prepare] 1. to ward off or deflect (a blow, sword thrust, etc.) 2. to turn aside (a question, etc.) as by a clever or evasive reply —*vi.* to make a parry —*n., pl.* **-ries** 1. a warding off of a blow, etc. 2. an evasive reply

parse (pärs) *vt., vi.* **parsed, pars'ing** [< L. *pars* (orationis), part (of speech)] [Now Rare] 1. to separate (a sentence) into its parts, explaining the grammatical form, function, etc. of each part 2. to describe the form, part of speech, etc. of (a word in a sentence)

par·sec (pär'sek') *n.* [PAR(ALLAX) + SEC(OND)²] a unit of measure of astronomical distance, approximately 31 million million kilometres

Par·see, Par·si (pär'sē, pär sē') *n.* [Per. *Pārsī,* a Persian] a member of a Zoroastrian religious sect in India descended from Persian refugees from the Moslem persecutions of the 7th and 8th cent. —**Par'see·ism, Par'si·ism** *n.*

par·si·mo·ny (pär'sə mō'nē) *n.* [< L. *parcimonia* < *parcere,* to spare] a tendency to be very careful in spending; stinginess —**par'si·mo'ni·ous** *adj.* —**par'si·mo'ni·ous·ly** *adv.* —**par'si·mo'ni·ous·ness** *n.*

pars·ley (pärs'lē) *n.* [< OE. & OFr. < L. *petroselinum* < Gr. < *petros,* a rock + *selinon,* celery] an umbelliferous plant with aromatic, often curled leaves used to flavour or garnish some foods

pars·nip (pär'snip) *n.* [altered (after ME. *nepe,* turnip) < OFr. < L. *pastinaca* < *pastinare,* to dig up] 1. an umbelliferous plant with a long, thick, sweet, white root used as a vegetable 2. its root

par·son (pär's'n) *n.* [< OFr. < ML. *persona,* orig., person < L.: see PERSON] 1. a clergyman in charge of a parish 2. any clergyman

par·son·age (-ij) *n.* the dwelling provided by a church for the use of its parson

parson's nose the rump of a fowl

part (pärt) *n.* [OE. & OFr., both < L. *pars* (gen. *partis*)] 1. a division or portion of a whole; specif., *a)* any of several equal quantities, numbers, pieces, etc. into which something can be divided *b)* an essential, separable element [radio *parts*] *c)* a certain amount but not all *d)* a segment or organ as of the body 2. a share assigned or given; specif., *a)* duty [to do one's *part*] *b)* interest; concern [to have some *part* in a matter] *c)* [usually *pl.*] talent; ability [a man of *parts*] *d)* a role in a play *e)* Music any voice or instrument in an ensemble, or the score for it 3. a region; esp., [usually *pl.*] a portion of a country; district 4. one of the sides in a transaction, dispute, etc. —*vt.* [< OFr. < L. *partire* < the n.] 1. to break or divide into parts 2. to comb (the hair) so as to leave a parting 3. to break up or separate; break or hold apart 4. [Archaic] to apportion —*vi.* 1. to break or divide into parts 2. to separate and go different ways 3. to cease associating 4. *a)* to go away *b)* to die —*adj.* not total; partial —*adv.* not fully; partly —**for one's part** as far as one is concerned —**for the most part** mostly; generally —**in good part** good-naturedly —**in part** to some extent or degree; partly —**on the part of one** 1. as far as one is concerned 2. by or coming from one Also **on one's part** —**part and parcel** a fundamental or essential part —**part with** to give up; relinquish —**play a part** 1. to behave unnaturally in trying to deceive 2. to participate: also **take part** —**take someone's part** to side with someone

part. 1. participial 2. participle

par·take (pär tāk') *vi.* **-took, -tak'en, -tak'ing** [< *partaker,* contr. of *part taker*] 1. to take part (*in* an activity); participate 2. to take a portion; have, to eat or drink, esp. with others (usually with *of*) 3. to have or show a trace (*of*); have some of the qualities (*of*) —**par·tak'er** *n.*

par·terre (pär ter') *n.* [Fr. < *par,* on + *terre,* earth] 1. an ornamental garden area 2. the pit of a theatre

par·the·no·gen·e·sis (pär'thə nō jen'ə sis) *n.* [ModL. < Gr. *parthenos,* virgin + *genesis,* origin] reproduction by the development of an unfertilized ovum, seed, or spore, as in certain insects, algae, etc. —**par'the·no·ge·net'ic** (-jə net'ik) *adj.* —**par'the·no·ge·net'i·cal·ly** *adv.*

Par·thi·an shot (pär'thē ən) any hostile gesture or remark made in leaving: Parthian cavalrymen shot at the enemy while retreating or pretending to retreat

par·tial (pär'shəl) *adj.* [MFr. < ML. < L. *pars,* PART] 1. favouring one person, faction, etc. more than another; biased 2. not complete or total —**partial to** fond of —**par'tial·ly** *adv.*

par·ti·al·i·ty (pär'shē al'ə tē) *n.* 1. the state or quality of being partial; bias 2. particular fondness or liking

par·ti·ble (pär'tə b'l) *adj.* [LL. *partibilis* < L. *partiri,* to divide] that can be divided, separated, or parted, esp. of an inheritance

par·tic·i·pant (pär tis'ə pənt, pər-) *adj.* participating —*n.* a person who participates

par·tic·i·pate (-pāt') *vi.* -pat'ed, -pat'ing [< L. pp. of *participare* < *pars*, PART + *capere*, to take] to have or take a share with others (*in* an activity, etc.) —**par·tic'i·pa'tion**, —**par·tic'i·pance** *n.* —**par·tic'i·pa'tive** *adj.* —**par·tic'i·pa'tor** *n.* —**par·tic'i·pa·to·ry** (-pə tə rē) *adj.*

par·ti·cip·i·al (pär'tə sip'ē əl) *adj.* of, based on, or having the nature and use of a participle —**par'ti·cip'i·al·ly** *adv.*

par·ti·ci·ple (pär'tə sip''l) *n.* [OFr. < L. < *particeps*, partaking < *pars*, PART + *capere*, to take] a verbal form having the qualities of both verb and adjective Participles are used: *a*) in verb phrases (are *asking*) *b*) as verbs (*seeing* her, he stopped) *c*) as adjectives (the *beaten* path) *d*) as nouns (*seeing* is *believing*) *e*) as adverbs (*raving* mad) *f*) as connectives (*saving* those present)

par·ti·cle (pär'ti k'l) *n.* [< MFr. < L. *particula*, dim. of *pars*, PART] **1.** *a*) a tiny fragment *b*) the slightest trace; speck **2.** *Gram.* *a*) a short, usually uninflected part of speech used to show syntactical relationships, as an article, preposition, conjunction, or interjection *b*) an uninflected stem **3.** *Physics* a piece of matter so small as to be considered without magnitude

par·ti·col·oured (pär'tē kul'ərd) *adj.* [< Fr. pp. of *partir*: see PARTY] **1.** having different colours in different parts **2.** diversified

par·tic·u·lar (pər tik'yə lər) *adj.* [< MFr. < LL. < L. *particula*, PARTICLE] **1.** of or belonging to a single, definite person, group, or thing **2.** regarded separately; specific **3.** unusual; special **4.** itemized; detailed **5.** hard to please; exacting —*n.* **1.** a distinct fact, item, or instance **2.** a detail; item —**in particular** particularly; especially

par·tic·u·lar·i·ty (pər tik'yə lar'ə tē) *n.*, *pl.* -ties **1.** the state, quality, or fact of being particular; specif., *a*) individuality *b*) attention to detail **2.** something particular; specif., *a*) a peculiarity *b*) a minute detail

par·tic·u·lar·ize (-tik'yə lə rīz') *vt.* -ized', -iz'ing to specify; itemize —*vi.* to give particulars or details —**par·tic'u·lar·i·za'tion** *n.*

par·tic·u·lar·ly (-tik'yə lər lē) *adv.* **1.** in detail **2.** especially; unusually **3.** specifically

par·tic·u·late (pär tik'yə lit, -lāt') *adj.* [< L. *particula*, particle + -ATE¹] of or pertaining to tiny, separate particles —*n.* a tiny particle

part·ing (pärt'iŋ) *adj.* **1.** dividing; separating **2.** departing **3.** given, spoken, done, etc. at parting —*n.* **1.** a breaking or separating **2.** a dividing point or line **3.** something that separates or divides **4.** a leave-taking or departure **5.** death **6.** the dividing line made by combing the hair in different directions

parting of the ways **1.** a point at which a road is divided into two or more **2.** a falling-out; estrangement

par·ti·san (pärt'ə zən, -sən; pärt'ə zan') *n.* [MFr. < It. *partigiano* < L. *pars*, PART] **1.** a strong supporter of a side, party, or person; often, specif., an unreasoning, emotional adherent **2.** any of a group of guerrilla fighters, esp. in a civilian force —*adj.* of or like a partisan Also sp. **par'ti·zan** —**par'ti·san·ship'** *n.*

par·ti·ta (pär tēt'ə) *n.* [It. < fem. pp. of *partire*, to divide < L. *pars*, part] *Music* **1.** a kind of suite, esp. of the 18th cent. **2.** an air with variations

par·tite (pär'tīt) *adj.* [< L. pp. of *partire*, to part] in parts: often in compounds [*tripartite*]

par·ti·tion (pär tish'ən, pər-) *n.* [< L. *partitio*] **1.** division into parts **2.** something that divides, as a wall separating rooms **3.** a part or section —*vt.* **1.** to divide into parts **2.** to divide by a partition —**par·ti'tion·er** *n.*

par·ti·tive (pärt'ə tiv) *adj.* [< ML.: see PARTITE & -IVE] **1.** making a division **2.** *Gram.* restricting to or involving only a part of a whole —*n.* a partitive word —**par'ti·tive·ly** *adv.*

part·ly (pärt'lē) *adv.* in part; not fully

part·ner (pärt'nər) *n.* [altered (after *part*) < *parcener*, joint inheritor] one who takes part in an activity with another or others; specif., *a*) one of two or more persons heading the same business enterprise *b*) a husband or wife *c*) either of two persons dancing together *d*) either of two players on the same side or team playing against two others —*vt.* **1.** to join (others) together as partners **2.** to be or provide a partner for —**partner in crime** an associate, esp. in nefarious activity

part·ner·ship (-ship') *n.* **1.** the state of being a partner **2.** the relationship of partners; joint interest **3.** *a*) an association of partners in a business enterprise *b*) the contract for this

part of speech any of the classes of words of a given language, variously based on form, function, meaning, etc.: in traditional English grammar, the parts of speech are noun, verb, adjective, adverb, pronoun, preposition, conjunction, and interjection

par·took (pär took') *pt.* of PARTAKE

par·tridge (pär'trij) *n.*, *pl.* **-tridg·es, -tridge**: see PLURAL, II, D, 1 [< OFr. < L. < Gr. *perdix*] **1.** a quaillike game bird of Europe, with an orange-brown head, greyish neck, and rust-coloured tail **2.** [U.S.] any of various game birds like the partridge, as the pheasant

PARTRIDGE
(to 36 cm long;
wingspread to
33 cm)

part song a song for several voices singing in harmony, usually unaccompanied: also **part'-song'** *n.*

part-time (pärt'tim') *adj.* designating, of, or engaged in work, study, etc. for periods regarded as taking less time than a full schedule

part time as a part-time employee, student, etc. [to work *part time*]

par·tu·ri·ent (pär tyoor'ē ənt) *adj.* [< L. prp. of *parturire*, to be in labour < *parere*, to produce] **1.** giving birth or about to give birth to young **2.** of childbirth —**par·tu'ri·en·cy** *n.*

par·tu·ri·tion (pär'choo rish'ən, -tyoo-) *n.* [< L.: see prec.] a giving birth; childbirth

part·way (pärt'wā') *adv.* to some point, degree, etc.

par·ty (pär'tē) *n.*, *pl.* **-ties** [< OFr. < *partir*, to divide < L. < *pars*, PART] **1.** a group working to establish or promote certain principles of government: esp., a political group which tries to elect its candidates to office **2.** any group acting together to accomplish or do something [a surveying *party*] **3.** a gathering for social entertainment, or the entertainment itself [a cocktail *party*] **4.** a participant in an action, plan, etc. (often with *to*) [he is a *party* to the plan] **5.** either of the persons or sides concerned in a legal matter **6.** [Colloq.] a person —*adj.* **1.** of a political party **2.** for a social gathering [*party* clothes]

party line **1.** a single circuit connecting two or more telephone users with the exchange **2.** the line of policy followed by a political party —**par'ty-lin'er** *n.*

party wall a wall separating and common to two buildings or properties: each owner has a partial right in its use

par value the value of a stock, bond, etc. fixed at the time of its issue; face value

par·ve·nu (pär'və nyoo', -noo) *n.* [Fr., pp. of *parvenir* < L. *parvenire*, to arrive] a person who has suddenly acquired wealth or power and is considered an upstart —*adj.* like or characteristic of a parvenu

pas (pä) *n.*, *pl.* **pas** (päz; Fr. pä) [Fr. < L. *passus*, a step] a step or series of steps in dancing: in ballet, a **pas de deux** (pä'də dər') is a dance for two, a **pas de trois** (pät trwä') is for three, a **pas de qua·tre** (pät kä'tr') is for four

pas·cal (pas kal') [after Blaise *Pascal* (1623-62), Fr. mathematician] the SI unit of pressure; equivalent to 1 newton per square metre

Pasch (pask) *n.* [< OFr. < LL. < Gr. *pascha* < Heb. *pesah*, the Passover] *same as:* **1.** PASSOVER **2.** EASTER —**pas'·chal** (pas'k'l) *adj.*

pasch flower (pask) *same as* PASQUEFLOWER

pash (pash) *n.* [< PASSION] [Slang] hero-worship or infatuation; a crush

pa·sha (pä'shə, pash'ə) *n.* [Turk. *pasha*] formerly, in Turkey, **1.** a title of honour placed after the name **2.** a high official

Pash·to (push'tō, päsh'-) *n.* an Iranian language of Afghanistan and West Pakistan

pasque·flow·er (pask'flou'ər) *n.* [< MFr. < *passer*, PASS² + *fleur*, a flower, altered after Fr. *pasque*, PASCH] **1.** a kind of anemone with large, purple flowers **2.** any of several related N American plants, esp. a wildflower with cup-shaped bluish flowers

pas·quin·ade (pas'kwə nād') *n.* [Fr. < It. < *Pasquino*, classical statue in Rome to which it was the custom in the 16th cent. to attach satirical verses] a satire; lampoon, esp. one posted up in a public place

pass¹ (päs) *n.* [see PACE¹] a narrow passage or opening, esp. between mountains; gorge; defile

pass² (päs) *vi.* [< OFr. *passer*, ult. < L. *passus*, a step] **1.** to go forward, through, or out **2.** to extend; lead [a road *passing* near the house] **3.** to be handed on from person to person **4.** to go or be conveyed from one place, condition, possession, etc. to another **5.** to be exchanged between persons, as greetings **6.** *a*) to cease [the fever *passed*] *b*) to go away; depart **7.** to die (usually with *away, on*) **8.** to go by or past **9.** to slip by or elapse [an hour *passed*] **10.** to make a way (with *through* or *by*) **11.** to take place or be accepted without question **12.** to be sanctioned or approved, as by a legislative body **13.** *a*) to go through an examination, course, etc. successfully; satisfy requirements *b*) to be barely acceptable as a substitute **14.** to take place; happen **15.** to give a judgment, sentence, etc.; decide (*on* or *upon*) **16.** to be rendered or pronounced [the judgment *passed* against us] **17.** *Card Games* to decline a chance to bid, play, etc. **18.** *Sports* to make a pass of the ball, etc. —*vt.* **1.** to go by, beyond, past, over, or through; specif., *a*) to leave behind *b*) to undergo (usually with *through*) *c*) to go by without noticing *d*) to go through (a test, course, etc.) successfully *e*) to surpass; excel **2.** to cause or allow to go or move; specif., *a*) to send; dispatch *b*) to guide into position [to *pass* a rope around a stake] *c*) to cause to go through *d*) to make move past *e*) to cause or allow to get by an obstacle, etc. *f*) to ratify, enact, or approve *g*) to cause or allow to go through a test, course, etc. successfully *h*) to spend (time) *i*)to excrete; void **3.** to make move from place to place or person to person; specif., *a*) to hand to another *b*) to put into circulation [to *pass* a bad cheque] *c*) to throw or kick (a ball, etc.) from one player to another **4.** *a*) to give (an opinion or judgment) *b*) to utter (a remark) —*n.* **1.** an act of passing; passage **2.** the successful completion of a course or examination in school or university, etc. esp. without honours **3.** condition or situation [a strange *pass*] **4.** *a*) a ticket, etc. giving one free entry or exit *b*) a ticket that permits unlimited rides on a bus, etc. for a specified period *c*) *Mil.* a written leave of absence for a brief period **5.** a motion of the hands meant to deceive, as in card tricks **6.** a motion of the hand, as in hypnotism **7.** *a*) a motion of the hand as if to strike *b*) a tentative attempt **8.** [Slang] an attempt to embrace or kiss, often an over-familiar one **9.** *Aeron.* a flight over a specified point or at a target **10.** *Card Games* a declining of a chance to bid, play, etc. **11.** *Sports a*) an intentional transfer of the ball, etc. to another player during play *b*) a lunge or thrust in fencing —**bring to pass** to make happen —**come to pass** to happen —**pass away 1.** to disappear gradually **2.** to die —**pass for** to be accepted or looked upon as [it is a sham but *passes for* the real thing] —**pass off 1.** to cease **2.** to take place, as a transaction **3.** to be or cause to be accepted as genuine, etc., esp. through deceit **4.** to set aside or disregard —**pass out 1.** to distribute **2.** to faint **3.** to qualify for military commission —**pass over 1.** to disregard; ignore; omit **2.** to not consider (someone) for a promotion, etc. —**pass up** [Colloq.] to reject, refuse, or let go by, as an opportunity —**pass′er** *n.*

pass. 1. passenger **2.** passim **3.** passive

pass·a·ble (-ə b'l) *adj.* **1.** that can be passed, travelled over, or crossed **2.** that can be circulated, as coin **3.** barely satisfactory; fair **4.** that can be enacted, as a proposed law —**pass′a·ble·ness** *n.* —**pass′a·bly** *adv.*

pass·a·ca·glia (päs′ə käl′yə, pas′-) *n.* [pseudo-It. < Sp. *pasacalle*, < *pasar*, to pass + *calle*, street] **1.** formerly, a slow, stately Italian dance **2.** the music for this **3.** a musical form, based on this in 3/4 time

pas·sage (pas′ij) *n.* [OFr. < *passer*: see PASS² & -AGE] **1.** the act of passing; specif., *a*) migration *b*) transition *c*) the enactment of a law by a legislature **2.** permission, right, or a chance to pass **3.** a journey, esp. by water; voyage **4.** *a*) passenger accommodation, esp. on a ship *b*) the charge for this **5.** a way or means of passing; specif., *a*) a road or path *b*) a channel, duct, etc. *c*) a passageway **6.** an interchange, as of blows or words **7.** a short section of something written or spoken or of a musical composition

pas·sage·way (-wā′) *n.* a narrow way for passage, as a hall, corridor, or alley

pass·book (päs′book′) *n.* **1.** *same as* BANKBOOK **2.** a book recording deposits and withdrawals for a building society **3.** [S. Afr.] an official document carried by non-whites in urban areas: also **reference book**

pass degree an ordinary degree awarded at a university, without honours

pas·sé (pa sā′, pas′ā) *adj.* [Fr., lit., past] **1.** out-of-date; old-fashioned **2.** past

pas·sen·ger (pas′ən jər) *n.* [< MFr. < OFr. *passage*, PASSAGE] **1.** a person travelling in a vehicle, esp. when not operating it **2.** one who does not participate as fully as others in the work of a team —*adj.* of something designed for a passenger [*passenger* seat, *passenger* train]

passenger pigeon a N American pigeon formerly abundant but now extinct

passe-par·tout (päs′pär tōō′, pas′-) *n.* [Fr., lit., passes everywhere] **1.** that which allows passage everywhere **2.** a passkey **3.** a mat used in mounting pictures **4.** a picture mounting using gummed paper **5.** the gummed paper used for picture mounting

pass·er-by (päs′ər bī′) *n., pl.* **pass′ers-by′** a person who passes by

pas·ser·ine (pas′ə rīn′) *adj.* [< L. < *passer*, a sparrow] of the order of perching songbirds to which many birds belong —*n.* a bird of this order

‡**pas·sim** (pas′im) *adv.* [L.] here and there; in various parts (of a book, etc.)

pass·ing (päs′iŋ) *adj.* **1.** going by, beyond, past, over, or through **2.** only brief; momentary **3.** casual; incidental [a *passing* remark] —*adv.* [Chiefly Archaic] very —*n.* **1.** the act of one that passes; specif., death **2.** a means or place of passing —**in passing 1.** casually **2.** incidentally

pas·sion (pash′ən) *n.* [OFr. < L. < pp. of *pati*, to suffer] **1.** orig., suffering, as of a martyr **2.** [P-] the suffering of Jesus during the Crucifixion or after the Last Supper **3.** *a*) any emotion, as hate, grief, love, etc. *b*) [*pl.*] all of these

emotions **4.** extreme emotion; specif., *a*) rage; fury *b*) enthusiasm [a *passion* for music] *c*) strong love or affection *d*) sexual desire; lust **5.** the object of strong desire or fondness —**pas′sion·al** *adj.* —**pas′sion·less** *adj.*

pas·sion·ate (-it) *adj.* **1.** having or showing strong emotions **2.** hot-tempered **3.** intense; ardent **4.** readily aroused sexually —**pas′sion·ate·ly** *adv.*

pas·sion·flow·er (-flou′ər) *n.* [from the supposed resemblance of parts of the flowers to Jesus' wounds, crown of thorns, etc.] any of a number of tropical plants with variously coloured flowers and yellow or purple, egglike fruit (**passion fruit**)

Passion play a religious play representing the Passion of Jesus

pas·sive (pas′iv) *adj.* [< L. *passivus* < pp. of *pati*, to suffer] **1.** acted upon without acting in return **2.** not resisting; submissive **3.** taking no active part; inactive **4.** *Gram.* denoting the voice or form of a verb whose subject is the receiver (object) of the action of the verb —*n.* *Gram.* the passive voice —**pas′sive·ly** *adv.* —**pas′sive·ness**, **pas·siv·i·ty** (pa siv′ə tē) *n.*

passive resistance opposition, as to a government, by refusal to comply with orders, or by such nonviolent acts as fasting, public demonstrations, etc.

pass·key (päs′kē′) *n.* **1.** *same as:* *a*) MASTER KEY *b*) SKELETON KEY **2.** any private key

Pass·o·ver (päs′ō′vər) *n.* [PASS² & OVER] a Jewish holiday (*Pesach*) of eight (or seven) days commemorating the ancient Hebrews' deliverance from slavery in Egypt: Ex. 12

pass·port (-pôrt′) *n.* [< Fr. < *passer*, PASS² & *port*, PORT¹] **1.** a government document issued to a citizen for travel abroad, subject to visa requirements, certifying his identity and citizenship and entitling him to protection **2.** anything making a person accepted or admitted

pass·word (-wʉrd′) *n.* **1.** a secret word or phrase that must be uttered by someone wishing to pass a guard **2.** any means of gaining entrance, etc.

past (päst) *rare pp. of* PASS² —*adj.* **1.** gone by; ended **2.** of a former time **3.** just gone by [the *past* week] **4.** having served formerly [a *past* chairman] **5.** *Gram.* indicating a time or condition gone by or an action completed or in progress at a former time —*n.* **1.** time gone by **2.** the history or former life of a person, group, etc.: often used to indicate a hidden or questionable past [a woman with a *past*] **3.** *Gram. a*) the past tense *b*) a verb form in this tense —*prep.* **1.** later than **2.** further on than **3.** beyond in amount or degree **4.** beyond the extent, power, etc. of [*past* belief] —*adv.* to and beyond a point in time or space —**not put it past someone** to believe someone is not unlikely (to do a certain thing) [I would *not put it past* him to lie] —**past it** [Colloq.] incompetent because of age, etc.

pas·ta (pas′tə, päs′-) *n.* [It. < LL.: see ff.] **1.** dough made as of semolina and shaped and dried in the form of spaghetti, macaroni, etc. **2.** spaghetti, macaroni, etc. cooked in some way

paste (pāst) *n.* [OFr. < LL. *pasta* < Gr. *pastē*, barley porridge] **1.** dough for making rich pastry **2.** any soft, moist, smooth-textured substance [*toothpaste*] **3.** a foodstuff, pounded or ground until creamy [almond *paste*, meat *paste*] **4.** a mixture of flour or starch, water, resin, etc., used as an adhesive for paper, etc. **5.** the moistened clay used to make pottery or porcelain **6.** *a*) a hard, brilliant glass for making artificial gems *b*) such a gem or gems —*vt.* **past′ed**, **past′ing 1.** to fasten or make stick as with paste **2.** to cover with pasted material —**past′er** *n.*

paste·board (-bôrd′) *n.* a stiff material made of layers of paper pasted together or of pressed and dried paper pulp —*adj.* **1.** of pasteboard **2.** flimsy

pas·tel (pas′təl) *n.* [Fr. < It. *pastello* < LL. *pasta*, PASTE] **1.** a ground colouring matter formed into a crayon *b*) the crayon **2.** a picture drawn with such crayons **3.** drawing with pastels as an art form **4.** a soft, pale shade of any colour —*adj.* **1.** soft and pale: said of colours **2.** of pastel **3.** drawn with pastels —**pas′tel·ist**, **pas·tel′list** *n.*

pas·tern (pas′tərn) *n.* [< MFr. < *pasture*, a tether, ult. < L. *pastor*: see PASTOR] the part of a horse's foot between the fetlock and the hoof

paste-up (pāst′up′) *n.* *Printing* a pasted-up dummy that is photographed for making into a plate

pas·teur·i·za·tion (päs′chər ī zā′shən, pas′-tər-) *n.* a method of destroying and checking bacteria in milk, beer, etc. by heating the liquid to a specified temperature for a specified period of time

pas·teur·ize (päs′chə rīz′, pas′tə-) *vt.* **-ized′**, **-iz′ing** [after Louis *Pasteur* (1822-95), Fr. chemist] to subject (milk, beer, etc.) to pasteurization —**pas′teur·iz′er** *n.*

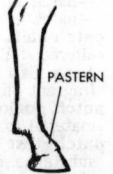

PASTERN

pas·tiche (pas tēsh′) *n.* [Fr. < It. *pasticcio*] **1.** *a*) a literary, artistic, or musical composition made up of bits from various sources; potpourri *b*) such a composition intended to imitate or ridicule another artist's style   **2.** a jumbled mixture; hotchpotch

pas·tie (pas'tē) *n.* *same as* PASTY²

pas·tille (pas tēl') *n.* [Fr. < L. *pastillus*, lozenge < *pascere*, to feed] **1.** a small tablet or lozenge containing medicine, flavouring etc. **2.** a pellet of aromatic paste, burned for fumigating or deodorizing Also **pas·til** (pas'til)

pas·time (păs'tīm') *n.* [transl. of Fr. *passe-temps*] a way of spending spare time pleasantly

past master **1.** a former master, as in a lodge **2.** an expert —**past mistress** *fem.*

pas·tor (păs'tər) *n.* [< OFr. < L., a shepherd < *pascere*, to feed] a clergyman, priest, etc. in charge of a church or congregation —**pas'tor·ship'** *n.*

pas·to·ral (-əl) *adj.* [< L. < *pastor*, a shepherd] **1.** of shepherds or their work, etc. **2.** of or characteristic of rural life idealized as peaceful, simple, and natural **3.** of a pastor or his duties —*n.* **1.** a poem, play, etc. having an idealized pastoral setting with shepherds, etc. **2.** a pastoral picture or scene **3.** a letter from a pastor or bishop to those in his charge **4.** *same as* PASTORALE —**pas'to·ral·ly** *adv.*

pas·to·rale (păs'tə ral', -rä'lē) *n.* [It., lit., pastoral] *Music* a composition suggesting rural scenes or life

pas·tor·al·ist (păs'tər ə list) *n.* [Aust.] a rancher; grazier

pas·tor·ate (păs'tər it) *n.* **1.** the position, rank, or term of office of a pastor **2.** a group of pastors

past participle a participle used: *a)* with auxiliaries and typically expressing completed action or a time or state gone by (as *started* in "he has started") *b)* as an adjective (as *grown* in "a grown man")

past perfect **1.** a tense indicating an action or state as completed before a specified or implied time in the past **2.** a verb form in this tense (Ex.: had gone)

pas·try (păs'trē) *n.*, *pl.* **-tries** [see PASTE & -ERY] **1.** *a)* flour dough made with fat, for pie crust, tarts, etc. *b)* foods made with this **2.** a single pie, tart, etc.

pas·tur·age (păs'chər ij) *n.* *same as* PASTURE

pas·ture (păs'chər) *n.* [OFr. < LL. *pastura* < L. *pascere*, to feed] **1.** grass or other growing plants used as food by grazing animals **2.** ground suitable, or a field set aside, for grazing —*vt.* **-tured, -tur·ing** **1.** to put (cattle, etc.) out to graze in a pasture **2.** to graze on (grass, etc.) —*vi.* to graze —**put out to pasture** **1.** to pasture (cattle) **2.** to cause to retire from work —**pas'tur·a·ble** *adj.* —**pas'tur·er** *n.*

past·y¹ (păs'tē) *adj.* **past'i·er, past'i·est** **1.** of or like paste in colour or texture **2.** pale or unhealthy-looking [*pasty-faced*] —**past'i·ness** *n.*

pas·ty² (pas'tē, päs'-) *n.*, *pl.* **pas'ties** [< OFr. < *paste*, PASTE] a round of pastry folded over a filling, often of meat, diced potatoes, and turnips

pat¹ (pat) *adj.* [prob. < ff.] **1.** apt; timely; opportune **2.** exactly suitable [a *pat* hand in poker] **3.** so glibly plausible as to seem contrived —*adv.* in a pat manner —**have (down) pat** [Colloq.] to know or have memorized thoroughly —**stand pat** to stick to an opinion, course of action, etc. —**pat'ly** *adv.* —**pat'ness** *n.*

pat² (pat) *n.* [prob. echoic] **1.** a gentle tap or stroke with the hand or other flat surface **2.** the sound made by this **3.** a small lump, as of butter —*vt.* **pat'ted, pat'ting** **1.** *a)* to tap or stroke gently, esp. with the hand, as in affection, sympathy, etc. *b)* to tap lightly with a flat surface **2.** to shape, apply, etc. by patting —*vi.* **1.** to pat a surface **2.** to move with a patting sound

pat. **1.** patent **2.** patented

patch (pach) *n.* [prob. < OFr. *pieche*, PIECE] **1.** a piece of material to cover or mend a hole or tear or to strengthen a weak spot **2.** a dressing for a wound **3.** a shield worn over an injured eye **4.** a differing part of a surface area [*patches* of blue sky] **5.** a small plot of ground [a potato *patch*] **6.** *a)* a scrap of material; remnant *b)* *same as* BEAUTY SPOT (sense 1) **7.** the area patrolled by a policeman **8.** *Mil.* a cloth insignia of unit identification worn high on the sleeve **9.** [Colloq.] a stage; period, etc. [to strike a bad *patch*] —*vt.* **1.** to put a patch on **2.** to be a patch for **3.** to make (a quilt, etc.) out of patches **4.** to make or put together crudely or hurriedly (often with *up* or *together*) **5.** *Electronics* to connect electrical circuits temporarily —**not a patch on** not nearly as good as; not to be compared with —**patch up** to end or settle (differences, a quarrel, etc.) —**patch'er** *n.*

patch·ou·li, patch·ou·ly (pach'ōō lē, pə chōō'lē) *n.* [Fr., altered < E. *patch leaf* < Tamil < *paccu*, green + *ilai*, leaf] **1.** an East Indian plant that yields a heavy, dark-brown, fragrant oil **2.** a perfume made from this oil

patch pocket a pocket made by sewing a patch of shaped material to the outside of a garment

patch test a test for determining allergy to a specific substance, made by attaching a sample of it to the skin and observing the reaction

patch·work (pach'wurk') *n.* **1.** anything made of odd, miscellaneous parts; jumble **2.** needlework, as a quilt, made of odd patches of cloth sewn together at the edges **3.** any design or surface like this

patch·y (pach'ē) *adj.* **patch'i·er, patch'i·est** **1.** of or like patches **2.** not consistent or uniform; irregular —**patch'i·ly** *adv.* —**patch'i·ness** *n.*

pate (pāt) *n.* [< ?] **1.** the head, esp. the top of the head **2.** the brain or intellect A humorous term

pâ·té (pa'tā) *n.* [Fr.] **1.** a pie **2.** a meat paste

pâ·té de foie gras (pa tä'də fwä'grä', pat'ā-) [Fr.] a paste made of the livers of fattened geese

pa·tel·la (pə tel'ə) *n.*, *pl.* **-las, -lae** (-ē) [L., dim. of *patina*, a pan < Gr. *patanē*] *same as* KNEECAP —**pa·tel'lar** *adj.*

pat·en (pat'ʼn) *n.* [< OFr. < L. *patina*: see prec.] a metal plate, esp. for the Eucharistic bread

pa·ten·cy (pāt'ən sē, pat'-) *n.* the state or quality of being patent, or obvious

pat·ent (pat'ʼnt; *for adj.* 2, 3, & 4, *esp.* pāt'-) *adj.* [MFr. < L. prp. of *patere*, to be open] **1.** *a)* open to public inspection: said of a document granting a right, esp. to an invention [letters *patent*] *b)* granted or appointed by letters patent **2.** generally accessible or available **3.** obvious; evident [a *patent* lie] **4.** open or unobstructed **5.** *a)* protected by a patent *b)* of or having to do with patents *c)* made or sold under a patent —*n.* **1.** an official document granting a right or privilege; letters patent; esp., document granting the exclusive right to produce, sell, or get a profit from an invention, process, etc. for a specific period **2.** *a)* the right so granted *b)* the thing so protected **3.** any exclusive right or licence —*vt.* **1.** to grant a patent to or for **2.** to get a patent for —**pat'ent·a·ble** *adj.* —**pat·ent·ee** (pat'ʼn tē', pāt'-) *n.* —**pat·en·tor** (pat'ʼn tər, pāt'-) *n.*

patent leather leather with a hard, glossy, usually black finish: formerly patented

pa·tent·ly (pāt'ənt lē, pat'-) *adv.* in a patent manner; clearly; obviously; openly

patent medicine a trademarked medical preparation obtainable without a prescription

patent office the government office which grants letters patent

patent rolls the annual register of letters patent

pa·ter (pāt'ər) *n.* [L.] [Colloq.] father

pa·ter·fa·mil·i·as (pāt'ər fə mil'ē əs, pāt'-) *n.* [L.] the father of a family

pa·ter·nal (pə tur'n'l) *adj.* [< ML. < L. < *pater*, father] **1.** of or like a father; fatherly **2.** derived or inherited from a father **3.** related through the father's side of the family [*paternal* grandparents] —**pa·ter'nal·ly** *adv.*

pa·ter·nal·ism (-iz'm) *n.* the system of controlling a country, employees, etc. as a father might his children —**pa·ter'nal·ist** *n., adj.* —**pa·ter'nal·is'tic** *adj.* —**pa·ter'·nal·is'ti·cal·ly** *adv.*

pa·ter·ni·ty (pə tur'nə tē) *n.* **1.** the state of being a father **2.** male parentage **3.** origin in general

pa·ter·nos·ter (pat'ər nos'tər) *n.* [L., our father] **1.** the Lord's Prayer, esp. in Latin: often **Pater Noster** **2.** each large bead on a rosary on which this is said

path (päth) *n.* [OE. *pæth*] **1.** a way worn by footsteps **2.** a walk for use by people on foot, as in a park **3.** a course along which something moves **4.** a course of conduct or procedure —**path'less** *adj.*

Pa·than (pə tän', pət hän') *n.* [Hindi *pathan* < Afghan *pĕstānĕ*, pl. of *pĕstūn*, an Afgan] a member of a Moslem, Indo-Iranian, Pashto-speaking people of Afghanistan and N Pakistan

pa·thet·ic (pə thet'ik) *adj.* [< LL. < Gr. *pathētikos*, akin to *pathos*, suffering] **1.** expressing or arousing pity, sympathy, etc.; pitiful **2.** pitifully unsuccessful, ineffective, etc. **3.** of the emotions: now only in PATHETIC FALLACY Also **pa·thet'i·cal** —**pa·thet'i·cal·ly** *adv.*

pathetic fallacy the ascribing of human feelings, etc. to nonhuman things (Ex.: the angry sea)

path·find·er (päth'fīn'dər) *n.* **1.** one who makes a way where none had existed, as in a wilderness **2.** an aircraft or parachutist that indicates the target area for bombing by dropping flares

-path·i·a (path'ē ə) [ModL.] *same as* -PATHY

-path·ic (path'ik) *a combining form used to form adjectives from nouns ending in* -PATHY

path·o- [< Gr. *pathos*, suffering] *a combining form meaning* suffering, disease, feeling: also, before a vowel, **path-**

path·o·gen (path'ə jən) *n.* [prec. + -GEN] any microorganism or virus that can cause disease —**path'·o·gen'ic** (-jen'ik) *adj.* —**path'o·gen'i·cal·ly** *adv.*

path·o·gen·e·sis (path'ə jen'ə sis) *n.* [ModL.: see PATHO- & GENESIS] the development of a disease: also **pa·thog·e·ny** (pə thoj'ə nē) —**path'o·ge·net'ic** (-jə net'ik) *adj.*

pa·thol·o·gy (pə thol'ə jē, pa-) *n.*, *pl.* **-gies** [< Fr. or ModL. < Gr.: see ff. & -LOGY] **1.** the branch of medicine dealing with the nature of disease, esp. with the structural and functional changes caused by disease **2.** all the conditions, processes, or results of a particular disease —**path·o·log·i·cal** (path'ə loj'i k'l), **path'o·log'ic** *adj.* —**path'o·log'i·cal·ly** *adv.* —**pa·thol'o·gist** *n.*

pa·thos (pā'thos) *n.* [Gr., suffering] **1.** the quality in something experienced or observed which arouses feelings of pity, sorrow, sympathy, or compassion 2. the feeling aroused

path·way (päth'wā') *n.* *same as* PATH

-pa·thy (pə thē) [< ModL. < Gr. < *pathos*, suffering] *a combining form meaning*: 1. feeling, suffering [*antipathy*] 2. disease, treatment of disease [*osteopathy*]

pa·tience (pā'shəns) *n.* [< OFr. < L. *patientia* < *pati*, to suffer] 1. the state, quality, or fact of being patient 2. any of many card games, played by one person

pa·tient (pā'shənt) *adj.* [< OFr. < L. prp. of *pati*, to suffer] 1. enduring pain, trouble, etc. with composure and without complaint 2. calmly tolerating insult, delay, confusion, etc. 3. showing calm endurance [a *patient* face] 4. diligent; persevering [a *patient* worker] —*n.* a person receiving medical care —**pa'tient·ly** *adv.*

pat·i·na (pat'ən ə) *n.* [Fr. < It.] 1. a fine greenish crust formed by oxidation on bronze or copper, often valued as ornamental 2. any surface change due to age, as on old wood 3. any fine layer, incrustation or film [a *patina* of frost]

pa·ti·o (pat'ē ō') *n.*, *pl.* **-ti·os**' [Sp.] 1. a courtyard or inner area open to the sky, as in Spanish and Spanish-American architecture 2. a paved area, as one next to a house, with chairs, tables, etc. for outdoor lounging, dining, etc.

pat·ois (pat'wä; *Fr.* pȧ twä') *n.*, *pl.* **-ois** (-wäz; *Fr.* -twä') [Fr.] 1. a form of a language differing from the accepted standard, as a local dialect 2. *same as* JARGON (sense 4)

pat. pend. patent pending

pat·ri- [L. < Gr. < *patēr*, father] *a combining form meaning* father

pa·tri·al (pā'trē əl) *n.* [< L. *patria*, native land] a person who has the right of residence in a given country because his parents or grandparents were born there —**pa·tri·al'-i·ty** *n.*

pa·tri·arch (pā'trē ärk') *n.* [< OFr. < LL. < Gr., ult. < *patēr*, father + *archein*, to rule] 1. the father and ruler of a family or tribe: in the Bible, Abraham, Isaac, Jacob, and Jacob's twelve sons were patriarchs 2. a person regarded as the founder of a religion, business, etc. 3. a man of great age and dignity 4. [*often* P-] a) any of certain bishops in the early Christian Church b) *R.C.Ch.* the Pope (**Patriarch of the West**), or any of certain Eastern bishops c) *Orthodox Eastern Ch.* the highest-ranking bishop at Constantinople, Alexandria, Antioch, Jerusalem, Moscow, etc. —**pa'tri·ar'-chal** *adj.*

pa·tri·ar·chate (-är'kit, -kāt) *n.* the position, rank, jurisdiction, etc. of a patriarch

pa·tri·ar·chy (-är'kē) *n.*, *pl.* **-chies** 1. a form of social organization in which the father is the head of the family or tribe, descent being traced through the male line 2. rule or domination by men —**pa'tri·ar'chic** *adj.*

pa·tri·cian (pə trish'ən) *n.* [< MFr. < L. *patricius* < *patres*, pl. of *pater*, father] 1. in ancient Rome, a) orig., a member of any of the Roman citizen families b) later, a member of the nobility 2. an aristocrat —*adj.* 1. of or characteristic of patricians 2. noble; aristocratic

pat·ri·cide (pat'rə sīd') *n.* [< ML.: see PATRI- & -CIDE] 1. the act of killing one's father 2. a person who kills his father —**pat'ri·ci'dal** *adj.*

pat·ri·mo·ny (pat'rə mō'nē) *n.*, *pl.* **-nies** [< OFr. < L. *patrimonium* < *pater*, father] 1. property inherited from one's father or ancestors 2. property endowed to a church, etc. 3. anything inherited; heritage —**pat'ri·mo'ni·al** *adj.*

pa·tri·ot (pā'trē ət'; pat'rē-) *n.* [< Fr. < LL. < Gr. < *patris*, fatherland] a person who loves and loyally or zealously supports his own country —**pa'tri·ot'ic** *adj.* —**pa'tri·ot'i·cal·ly** *adv.*

pa·tri·ot·ism (-ə tiz'm) *n.* love and loyal or zealous support of one's own country

pa·tris·tic (pə tris'tik) *adj.* [< G. < L. *patres*, pl. of *pater*, father] of the early leaders, or fathers, of the Christian Church or their writings, etc.: also **pa·tris'ti·cal** —**pa·tris'-ti·cal·ly** *adv.*

pa·trol (pə trōl') *vt.*, *vi.* **-trolled'**, **-trol'ling** [Fr. *patrouiller* < OFr. *patouiller*, to paddle] to make a regular, repeated circuit of (an area, camp, etc.), as in guarding—*n.* 1. a patrolling 2. a person or group patrolling 3. a group of ships, aircraft, etc. used in patrolling 4. a subdivision of a troop of Boy Scouts or Girl Guides —**pa·trol'ler** *n.*

pa·tron (pā'trən) *n.* [< OFr. < ML., ult. < L. *pater*, father] 1. a person who is like a father in some respects; protector; benefactor 2. a wealthy or influential person who sponsors and supports some person, activity, etc. 3. a regular customer —**pa'tron·ess** *n.fem.*

pa·tron·age (pā'trən ij) *n.* 1. a) the function or status of a patron b) support, sponsorship, etc. given by a patron 2. favour, courtesy, etc. shown to people considered inferior; condescension 3. a) clientele; customers b) business; trade 4. a) the power to appoint to office or grant other political favours b) the distribution of such offices or favours c) the offices, etc. thus distributed 5. the legal right to present a clergyman to an Anglican benefice

pa·tron·ize (pa'trə nīz') *vt.* **-ized'**, **-iz'ing** 1. to act as a patron towards: sponsor; support 2. to treat kindly but as an inferior 3. to be a regular customer of (a shop etc.)

patron saint a saint looked upon as the special guardian of a person, place, institution,etc.

pat·ro·nym·ic (pat'rə nim'ik) *n.* [< LL. < Gr. < *patēr*, father + *onyma*, a name] a name showing descent from a given person as by the addition of a prefix or suffix (e.g., *Stevenson*, son of Steven, *O'Brien*, descendant of Brien)

pa·troon (pə trōōn') *n.* [Du., protector < Fr. *patron*, PATRON] *U.S. History* a person who held an estate with manorial rights under the old Dutch governments of New York and New Jersey

pat·sy (pat'sē) *n.*, *pl.* **-sies** [prob. < It. *pazzo*, an insane person] [U.S. Slang] a person easily imposed upon or victimized

pat·ten (pat''n) *n.* [MFr. *patin*, a clog < *pate*, a paw] a thick wooden sandal or clog

pat·ter¹ (pat'ər) *vi.* [freq. of PAT²] to make, or move so as to make, a patter —*n.* a series of quick, light taps

pat·ter² (pat'ər) *vt.*, *vi.* [< *pater*, in PATERNOSTER] to speak rapidly or glibly; recite mechanically —*n.* 1. language peculiar to a group, class, etc.; jargon 2. glib, rapid speech, as of salesmen, comedians, etc. 3. idle, meaningless chatter

pat·ter³ (pat'ər) *n.* a person or thing that pats

pat·tern (pat'ərn) *n.* [< OFr. *patron*, patron, hence model, pattern] 1. a person or thing considered worthy of imitation or copying 2. a model, plan, or set of forms used as a guide in making things [a dress *pattern*] 3. something representing a class or type; sample 4. an arrangement of form; design [wallpaper *patterns*] 5. a regular, mainly unvarying way of acting [behaviour *patterns*] 6. a predictable or prescribed route, movement, etc. [traffic *pattern*] —*vt.* to make, do, shape, or plan in imitation of a model or pattern (with *on*, *upon*, or *after*) —**pat'tern·mak'-er** *n.*

pattern room the place in a factory or foundry where patterns for moulds are made: also **pattern shop**

pat·ty (pat'ē) *n.*, *pl.* **-ties** [Fr. *pâté*, a pie] 1. a small pie 2. [Chiefly U.S.] a small, flat cake of minced meat, fish, etc., usually fried

patty case a pastry case in which individual portions of creamed foods, etc. are served

pau·a (pou'ə) *n.* [Maori] a New Zealand shellfish; abalone

pau·ci·ty (pô'sə tē) *n.* [< MFr. < L. < *paucus*, few] 1. fewness; small number 2. scarcity; insufficiency

Pau·li exclusion principle (pou'lē) [after Wolfgang *Pauli* (1900-58), Austrian physicist] the principle that no two electrons can occupy the same orbit in the electron structure of an atom, i.e., have the same set of quantum numbers

Paul·ine (pôl'īn, -ēn) *adj.* [ModL. *Paulinus*] of the Apostle Paul, his writings, or doctrines

paunch (pônch) *n.* [< MFr. < L. *pantex*, belly] 1. the abdomen, or belly; esp., a potbelly 2. the first stomach of a cow or other ruminant —**paunch'i·ness** *n.* —**paunch'y** *adj.*

pau·per (pô'pər) *n.* [L., poor person] 1. a person who lives on charity, esp. public charity 2. an extremely poor person —**pau'per·ism, pau'per·dom** *n.*

pau·per·ize (pô'pə rīz') *vt.* **-ized'**, **-iz'ing** to make a pauper of —**pau'per·i·za'tion** *n.*

pause (pôz) *n.* [MFr. < L. < Gr. *pausis*, a stopping < *pauein*, to stop] 1. a temporary stop or rest, as in working or speaking 2. hesitation; delay [pursuit without *pause*] 3. *Music same as* FERMATA 4. *Prosody* a rhythm break or caesura —*vi.* **paused, paus'ing** 1. to make a pause; stop; hesitate 2. to dwell or linger (*on* or *upon*) —**give one pause** to make one hesitant or uncertain —**paus'er** *n.*

pav·ane (pə vän', pav'ən) *n.* [Fr. < Olt. < *Pavana*, lit., Paduan (dance)] 1. a slow, stately court dance of Spanish or Italian origin, performed by couples 2. the music for this Also **pav·an** (pav'ən)

pave (pāv) *vt.* **paved, pav'ing** [< OFr. *paver*, ult. < L. *pavire*, to beat] 1. to cover the surface of (a road, etc.), as with concrete, asphalt, etc. 2. to be the top surface of —**pave the way (for)** to prepare the way (for) —**pav'er** *n.*

pave·ment (pāv'mənt) *n.* 1. a paved surface, as of concrete, brick, etc.; specif., a paved path for pedestrians 2. the material used in paving

pavement artist 1. someone who draws pictures on the pavement, hoping that passers-by will reward him for his efforts 2. someone who exhibits paintings on the pavement

pa·vil·ion (pə vil'yən) *n.* [< OFr. < L. *papilio*, butterfly, also tent] 1. a large tent, usually with a peaked top 2. a building, often partly open, for exhibits, etc., as at a fair or park 3. part of a building jutting out 4. any of the separate or connected parts of a group of related buildings, as of a hospital 5. a building attached to a sports ground in which players change, refreshments are served, etc. —*vt.* to furnish with or shelter in a pavilion

pav·ing (pā'viŋ) *n.* 1. a pavement 2. material for a pavement

pav·lo·va (pav lō'və) *n.* [after Anna *Pavlova* (1885?-1931),

Russ. ballerina] a meringue cake topped with whipped cream and fruit, popular in Australia and New Zealand

paw (pô) *n.* [< OFr. *poue* < Frank.] **1.** the foot of a four-footed animal having claws **2.** [Colloq.] a hand —*vt.*, *vi.* **1.** to touch, dig, strike, etc. with the paws or feet [the horse *pawed* the air] **2.** to handle clumsily, roughly, or overintimately —**paw′er** *n.*

pawl (pôl) *n.* [akin ? to Du. *pal*, pole] a mechanical device allowing rotation in only one direction, as a hinged tongue which engages the notches of a ratchet wheel, preventing backward motion

pawn[1] (pôn) *n.* [< MFr. *pan*] **1.** anything given as security, as for a debt; pledge **2.** the state of being pledged [his ring was in *pawn*] **3.** the act of pawning —*vt.* **1.** to put in pawn **2.** to stake or risk —**pawn′age** *n.* —**pawn′er**, **pawn′or** *n.*

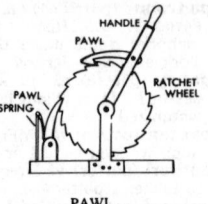

HANDLE
PAWL
PAWL SPRING
RATCHET WHEEL

PAWL

pawn[2] (pôn) *n.* [< OFr. < ML. *pedo*, foot soldier, ult. < L. *pes*, foot] **1.** a chessman of the lowest value **2.** a person used to advance another's purposes

pawn·bro·ker (-brō′kər) *n.* a person licensed to lend money at interest on personal belongings left with him as security —**pawn′bro′king** *n.*

pawn·shop (pôn′shop′) *n.* a pawnbroker's shop

pawn ticket a receipt for goods in pawn

paw·paw (pô′pô′) *n.* same as PAPAW

pax (paks) *n.* [ME. < ML. (Eccles.) < L., PEACE] **1.** the kiss of peace **2.** *R.C.Ch* a small tablet kissed during Mass —*interj.* [Slang] a call signalling a desire for or acceptance of an end to hostilities

P.A.X. Private Automatic Exchange

‡**pax vo·bis·cum** (paks vō bis′kəm, päks-) [L.] peace (be) with you

pay[1] (pā) *vt.* **paid** or obs. (except in phrase *pay out*, sense 2) **payed**, **pay′ing** [< OFr. < L. *pacare*, to pacify < *pax*, *peace*] **1.** to give to (a person) what is due, as for goods or services; remunerate **2.** to give (what is due) in return, as for goods or services **3.** to make a deposit or transfer of (money) [to *pay* £10 into savings] **4.** to settle (a debt, etc.) **5.** a) to give (a compliment, respects, etc.) b) to make (a visit, etc.) **6.** to yield as a recompense [this job *pays* £50] **7.** to be profitable to [it will *pay* him to listen] —*vi.* **1.** to give due compensation; make payment **2.** to be profitable **3.** to yield return as specified [that stock *pays* poorly] —*n.* **1.** a paying or being paid; payment **2.** money paid; esp., wages or salary —**in the pay of** employed and paid by —**pay as you go** to pay expenses as they arise —**pay back 1.** to repay **2.** to get even with —**pay for 1.** to undergo punishment because of **2.** to atone for —**pay off 1.** to pay all that is owed **2.** to take revenge on (a wrongdoer) or for (a wrong done) **3.** to turn out to be profitable —**pay out 1.** to give out (money, etc.) **2.** to let out a rope, cable, etc. gradually —**pay up** to pay in full or on time —**pay′er** *n.*

pay[2] (pā) *vt.* **payed**, **pay′ing** [ONormFr. *peier* < L. < *pix*, pitch] to coat (the seams of a vessel, etc.) as with tar, in order to make waterproof

pay·a·ble (pā′ə b'l) *adj.* **1.** that can be paid **2.** that is to be paid (on a specified date); due

pay-as-you-earn (-əz yōō urn′) a system by which income tax levied on wage earners is paid by employers directly to the government: also **P.A.Y.E.**

pay-bed (-bed) *n.* a hospital bed whose occupant is not treated under the National Health Service

pay·cheque (-chek′) *n.* a cheque in payment of wages, etc.

pay-day (-dā′) *n.* the day on which wages, etc. are paid

pay dirt [U.S.] soil, gravel, ore, etc. rich enough in minerals to make mining profitable —**hit** (or **strike**) **pay dirt** [U.S. Colloq.] discover a source of wealth, success, etc.

pay·ee (pā ē′) *n.* the person to whom a cheque, note, money, etc. is payable

paying guest same as LODGER: also **P.G.**

pay·load (pā′lōd′) *n.* **1.** a cargo, or the part of a cargo, producing income: also **pay load 2.** a) the warhead of a ballistic missile, the spacecraft launched by a rocket, etc. b) the weight of this

pay·mas·ter (-mäs′tər) *n.* the official in charge of paying employees —**pay′mis′tress** *n.fem.*

Paymaster General the government official appointed to make payments on behalf of various government departments

pay·ment (-mənt) *n.* **1.** a paying or being paid **2.** something paid **3.** penalty or reward

pay·nim (pā′nim) *n.* [< OFr. < LL. *paganismus*, paganism] [Archaic] **1.** a pagan or the pagan world **2.** a non-Christian; esp., a Moslem

pay-off (pā′of′) *n.* **1.** the act or time of payment **2.** settlement or reckoning **3.** that which is paid off;

recompense **4.** [Colloq.] a bribe **5.** [Colloq.] an unexpected or improbable climax or outcome

pay·o·la (pā ō′lə) *n.* [PAY[1] + *-ola*, as in *Pianola* (trademark for a mechanical piano)] [Slang] **1.** the paying of bribes or graft for commercial advantage or special favours, as to a disc jockey for promoting a song unfairly **2.** such a bribe or graft

pay packet 1. the envelope containing an employee's wages **2.** the wages themselves

pay·roll (pā′rōl′) *n.* **1.** a list of employees to be paid, with the amount due to each **2.** the total amount needed for this for a given period

payt., pay′t payment

Pb [L. *plumbum*] *Chem.* lead

PBX, P.B.X. [< *p(rivate) b(ranch) ex(change)*] the telephone connections on the switchboard of an office, company, etc.

pc. 1. piece **2.** price(s)

P.C. 1. Police Constable **2.** Privy Councillor

p.c. 1. percent: also **pct. 2.** post card

Pd *Chem.* palladium

pd. paid

P.D. per diem: also **p.d.**

P.D.S.A. People's Dispensary for Sick Animals

P.E. Physical Education

pea (pē) *n.*, *pl.* **peas**, archaic or dial. **pease** [< ME. *pese*, a pea, taken as pl. < OE. *pise* < L. < Gr. *pison*] **1.** a climbing plant with white or pinkish flowers and green seedpods **2.** its small, round seed, eaten as a vegetable **3.** any similar plant —**as like as two peas** (**in a pod**) exactly alike

peace (pēs) *n.* [< OFr. *pais* < L. *pax*] **1.** freedom from or a stopping of war **2.** a treaty or agreement to end war **3.** freedom from public disturbance; law and order **4.** harmony in a group; concord **5.** an undisturbed state of mind; serenity: in full, **peace of mind 6.** calm; quiet —*vi.* [Obs. except in imperative] to be or become silent or quiet —**at peace** free from war, conflict, etc. —**hold** (or **keep**) **one's peace** to be silent —**keep the peace** to maintain law and order —**make peace** to end hostilities

peace·a·ble (-ə b'l) *adj.* **1.** fond of or promoting peace; not quarrelsome **2.** at peace; peaceful — **peace′a·ble·ness** *n.* —**peace′a·bly** *adv.*

peace conference a conference for ending a war or for seeking ways to establish lasting peace

Peace Corps an agency of the U.S., established to provide volunteers skilled in teaching, construction, etc. to assist underdeveloped areas abroad: cf. VOLUNTARY SERVICE OVERSEAS

peace·ful (-fəl) *adj.* **1.** not quarrelsome; peaceable **2.** free from disturbance; calm **3.** of or characteristic of a time of peace —**peace′ful·ly** *adv.* —**peace′ful·ness** *n.*

peace·mak·er (-mā′kər) *n.* a person who makes peace, as by settling the quarrels of others —**peace′mak′ing** *n.*, *adj.*

peace offering [used to translate Heb. *shelem*, lit.,thankoffering] **1.** an offering or sacrifice in thanksgiving to God **2.** an offering made to maintain or bring about peace

peace pipe same as CALUMET

peace·time (-tīm′) *n.* a time of peace —*adj.* of or characteristic of such a time

peach[1] (pēch) *n.* [< OFr. < VL., ult. < L. *Persicum* (*malum*), Persian (apple)] **1.** a small tree with pink blossoms and round, juicy, orange-yellow fruit with a fuzzy skin and a rough stone **2.** its fruit **3.** the colour of this fruit **4.** [Slang] any person or thing well liked —**peach′-like′** *adj.*

peach[2] (pēch) *vi.* [ult. < OFr. *empechier*, IMPEACH] [Old Slang] to inform against another

peaches and cream having a creamy-coloured skin with soft pink cheeks

peach·y (pē′chē) *adj.* **peach′i·er**, **peach′i·est** peachlike, as in colour or texture —**peach′i·ness** *n.*

pea·cock (pē′kok′) *n.*, *pl.* **-cocks′**, **-cock′**: see PLURAL, II, 1 [< OE. *pea* < L. *pavo*, peacock + *cok*, COCK[1]] **1.** the male of a species of peafowls, with a crest and long tail coverts having rainbow-coloured, eyelike spots: these coverts can be erected and fanned out **2.** any male peafowl **3.** a vain, strutting person —*vi.* to display vanity in behaviour, dress, etc. —**pea′cock′ish**, **pea′cock′y** *adj.*

pea·fowl (-foul′) *n.*, *pl.* **-fowls′**, **-fowl′**: see PLURAL, II, D, 1 any of a genus of pheasantlike birds of S Asia and the East Indies, including the peacock that is widely domesticated

pea green a light yellowish green

pea·hen (-hen′) *n.* a female peafowl

pea jacket [< Du. < *pij*, coarse cloth + *jekker*, jacket] a hip-length, heavy woollen coat worn as by seamen: also **pea′coat′** *n.*

peak[1] (pēk) *n.* [var. of *pike* (summit)] **1.** a pointed end or top, as of a cap, roof, etc. **2.** a) the summit of a mountain ending in a point b) a mountain with such a summit **3.** the highest point or degree; maximum [the *peak* of production] **4.** *Naut.* a) the top rear corner of a fore-and-aft sail b) the upper end of the gaff c) the narrowed part of the hull, front or rear —*adj.* maximum *[peak production]* —*vt., vi.* **1.** to bring or come to a vertical position, as a sail yard **2.** to come or cause to come to a peak

peak² (pēk) *vi.* [< ?] to become sickly; waste away; droop

peaked (pēkt; *occas.* pē′kid) *adj.* **1.** having a peak; pointed **2.** *same as* PEAKY

peak hour the time at which a maximum occurs, either in the amount of traffic or the demand for gas, electricity, etc.

peak load the maximum demand for electricity in a power station

peak·y (pēk′ē) *adj.* **-i·er, -i·est** [< PEAK²] thin; sickly; emaciated

peal (pēl) *n.* [ME. *pele* < *apele*, appeal] **1.** the loud ringing of a bell or bells **2.** a set of bells; chimes **3.** any loud, prolonged sound, as of gunfire, laughter, etc. —*vt., vi.* to sound in a peal; resound; ring

pea·nut (pē′nut′) *n.* **1.** an annual vine of the legume family, with brittle pods ripening underground and containing edible seeds **2.** the pod or its seed **3.** [*pl.*] [Slang] a trifling sum

peanut butter a food paste or spread made by grinding roasted peanuts

pear (per) *n.* [< OE. < VL. *pira* < L. pl. of *pirum*] **1.** a tree with soft, juicy fruit, round at the base and narrowing towards the stem **2.** this fruit

PEANUT PLANT

pearl (purl) *n.* [< MFr., ult. < L. *perna*, a sea mussel] **1.** a smooth, hard, usually white or bluish-grey, roundish growth formed around a foreign body within the shell of some oysters and other molluscs: it is used as a gem **2.** *same as* MOTHER-OF-PEARL **3.** anything pearllike in size, colour, beauty, value, etc. **4.** the colour of some pearls, a bluish grey —*vt.* **1.** to decorate with pearls **2.** to make round, like pearls, esp. barley, etc. —*vi.* to fish for pearl-bearing molluscs —*adj.* **1.** of or having pearls **2.** like a pearl in shape or colour **3.** made of mother-of-pearl *[pearl* buttons*]* —**pearled** *adj.* —**pearl′er** *n.* —**pearl′i·ness** *n.* —**pearl′y** *adj.* **-i·er, -i·est**

pearl ash a refined potash

pearl barley barley seed rubbed down into small, round grains, used esp. in soups and stews: also **pearled barley**

pearl diver (or **fisher**) a person who dives for pearl-bearing molluscs

pearl grey a pale, bluish grey

Pearly Gates [Colloq.] the gates of heaven: cf. Rev. 21:21

pearly king the London costermonger whose ceremonial clothes display the most lavish collection of pearl buttons —**pearly queen**

pear-shaped (per′shāpt′) *adj.* **1.** shaped like a pear **2.** full, clear, and resonant: said of sung tones

peart (pirt) *adj.* [var. of PERT] [Dial.] lively, spirited, sprightly, smart, etc. —**peart′ly** *adv.* —**peart′ness** *n.*

peas·ant (pez′'nt) *n.* [< Anglo-Fr. < MFr. < OFr. < *pais*, country < LL. < *pagus*, district] **1.** any person of the class of small farmers or of farm labourers, as in Europe or Asia **2.** [Colloq.] a person regarded as coarse, boorish, ignorant, etc.

peas·ant·ry (-'n trē) *n.* peasants collectively

pease (pēz) *n.* **1.** *pl.* **peas′es, peas′en** (-'n) [Obs.] a pea **2.** *archaic* or *dial. pl. of* PEA

pease-cod, peas·cod (pēz′kod′) *n.* [Archaic] the pod of the pea plant

pease pudding a dish of split peas that have been soaked and boiled

pea soup 1. a heavy soup made from dried split peas **2.** [Colloq.] a dense, yellowish fog: also **pea′soup′er**

peat (pēt) *n.* [ML. *peta*, piece of turf < Celt.] **1.** partly decayed plant matter found in ancient bogs and swamps **2.** a dried block of this used as fuel —**peat′y** *adj.* **peat′i·er, peat′i·est**

peat bog marshland whose foundation is peat

peat moss 1. *same as* SPHAGNUM **2.** peat composed of residues of mosses, used as a mulch

peb·ble (peb′'l) *n.* [< OE. *papol(stan)*, pebble (stone)] **1.** a small stone worn smooth and round, as by the action of water **2.** clear, transparent quartz or a lens made from it **3.** a surface treated to make it irregular or indented, as on leather (**pebble leather**), paper, etc. —*vt.* **-bled, -bling 1.** to cover as with pebbles **2.** to stamp (leather) so as to give it a pebble surface

pebble dash a mortar containing pebbles used for surfacing exterior walls

peb·bly (-lē) *adj.* **-bli·er, -bli·est 1.** having many pebbles **2.** having a pebble surface

pec·ca·dil·lo (pek′ə dil′ō) *n., pl.* **-loes, -los** [< Sp. dim. of

pecado < L. < *peccare*, to sin] a minor or petty sin; slight fault

pec·cant (pek′ənt) *adj.* [< L. prp. of *peccare*, to sin] sinful; sinning —**pec′can·cy** *n., pl.* **-cies** —**pec′cant·ly** *adv.*

pec·ca·ry (pek′ər ē) *n., pl.* **-ries, -ry**: see PLURAL, II, D, 1 [AmSp. *pecari* < native Carib name] a greyish, piglike animal of N and S America, with sharp tusks and porklike flesh

peck¹ (pek) *vt.* [< ME. var. of *picken*, PICK²] **1.** to strike with a pointed object, as a beak **2.** to make by doing this *[to peck* a hole*]* **3.** to pick up or get by pecking —*vi.* **1.** to make strokes as with a pointed object —*n.* **1.** a stroke so made, as with the beak **2.** a mark made as by pecking **3.** [Colloq.] a quick, casual kiss —**peck at 1.** to make a pecking motion at **2.** [Colloq.] to eat very little of **3.** [Colloq.] to criticize constantly —**peck′er** *n.*

peck² (pek) *n.* [< OFr. *pek*] **1.** a unit of dry measure equal to 1/4 bushel, eight quarts or 9.092 litres **2.** any container that will hold a peck **3.** [Colloq.] a large amount, as of trouble

peck·er (pek′ər) *n.* **1.** a person or thing that pecks **2.** [Colloq.] courage; spirits: chiefly in the phrase **keep one's pecker up**

pecking order [trans < G. *Hackordnung*] **1.** the hierarchy formed among birds with the more aggressive birds pecking the less aggressive ones **2.** any hierarchical order, as among people in a particular group or society

peck·ish (-ish) *adj.* [PECK¹ + -ISH] [Colloq.] somewhat hungry —**peck′ish·ly** *adv.* —**peck′ish·ness** *n.*

pec·tin (pek′tin) *n.* [< Gr. *pēktos*, congealed + -IN¹] a water-soluble carbohydrate obtained from certain ripe fruits, which yields a gel that is the basis of jams —**pec′tic, pec′tin·ous** *adj.*

pec·to·ral (pek′tər əl) *adj.* [< L. < *pectus* (gen. *pectoris*), breast] **1.** of or located in or on the breast or chest **2.** worn on the chest or breast *[a pectoral cross]* —*n.* a pectoral fin or muscle

pectoral fin either of a pair of fins just behind the head of a fish

pec·u·late (pek′yə lāt′) *vt., vi.* **-lat′ed, -lat′ing** [< L. pp. of *peculari*, to embezzle] to steal or misuse (money or property in one's care); embezzle —**pec′u·la′tion** *n.* —**pec′-u·la′tor** *n.*

pe·cu·liar (pi kyōol′ē ər, -yər) *adj.* [< L. < *peculium*, private property] **1.** of only one person, thing, group, etc.; exclusive; special *[a matter of peculiar interest]* **3.** queer; odd; strange —**pe·cul′iar·ly** *adv.*

pe·cu·li·ar·i·ty (pi kyōol′ē ar′ə tē, -kyōol′yar′-) *n.* **1.** a being peculiar **2.** *pl.* **-ties** something that is peculiar, as a trait

pe·cu·ni·ar·y (pi kyōol′nē ər ē) *adj.* [< L. < *pecunia*, money] **1.** of or involving money **2.** involving a money penalty, or fine —**pe·cu′ni·ar·i·ly** *adv.*

ped- *same as* PEDI- Used before a vowel

ped·a·gog·ic (ped′ə goj′ik, -gō′jik) *adj.* [see ff.] of or characteristic of teachers or of teaching: also **ped′a·gog′-i·cal** —**ped′a·gog′i·cal·ly** *adv.*

ped·a·gogue (ped′ə gog′) *n.* [< OFr. < L. < Gr. *pais*, a child + *agein*, to lead] a teacher; often specif., a pedantic, dogmatic teacher

ped·a·go·gy (-gō′jē, -goj′ē) *n.* [see prec.] **1.** the profession of teaching **2.** the art or science of teaching; esp., instruction in teaching methods

ped·al (ped′'l) *adj.* [< L. < *pes* (gen. *pedis*), a foot] **1.** of the foot or feet **2.** of or operated by a pedal —*n.* a lever operated by the foot to transmit motion, as in a bicycle, or to change the tone or volume of an organ, harp, etc. —*vt., vi.* **-alled, -al·ling** to operate by a pedal or pedals; use the pedals (of)

pedal cycle *same as* BICYCLE

ped·al·o (ped′ə lō′) *n., pl.* **-os** [arbitrary extension of PEDAL] a small watercraft for one or two people with a paddle wheel propelled by foot pedals: also **ped′dal·o**

ped·ant (ped′ənt) *n.* [< Fr. < It. *pedante*, ult. < Gr. *paidagōgos*: see PEDAGOGUE] **1.** a person who emphasizes trivial points of learning, showing a scholarship lacking in judgment **2.** a narrow-minded teacher who insists on exact adherence to rules —**pe·dan·tic** (pi dan′tik) *adj.* —**pe·dan′-ti·cal·ly** *adv.*

ped·ant·ry (ped′ən trē) *n., pl.* **-ries 1.** the qualities, practices, etc. of a pedant; showy display of knowledge, or an instance of this **2.** adherence to rules

ped·ate (ped′āt) *adj.* [< L. < *pes*, foot] **1.** *Bot.* palmately divided into three main divisions **2.** *Zool.* a) having a foot or feet b) footlike

ped·dle (ped′'l) *vi.* **-dled, -dling** [back-formation < *peddler* < ? ME. *ped*, a basket] to go from place to place selling small articles —*vt.* **1.** to carry from place to place and offer for sale **2.** to deal out or circulate (gossip, etc.)

-pede (pēd) [< L. *pes*, a foot] a combining form meaning foot or feet *[centipede]*: also **-ped**

ped·er·as·ty (ped′ə ras′tē, pē′də-) *n.* [< ModL. < Gr. < *pais* (gen. *paidos*), boy + *eran*, to love] sodomy between males, esp. by a man with a boy: also sp. **paed′er·as′ty**

—**ped′er·ast′, paed′er·ast′** n. —**ped′er·as′tic** adj. —**ped′-er·as′ti·cal·ly** adv.

ped·es·tal (ped′is t'l) n. [< Fr. < It. < piè (< L. pes), a foot + di, of + stal (< Gmc. hyp. stal), a rest] 1. the bottom support of a column, statue, etc. 2. any foundation, base, etc. —vt. **-talled, -tal·ling** to furnish with a pedestal —**put (or set) on a pedestal** to idolize

pe·des·tri·an (pə des′trē ən) adj. [< L. pedester < pes (gen. pedis), a foot + -IAN] 1. going or done on foot 2. of or for pedestrians [a pedestrian crossing] 3. lacking interest or imagination; prosaic; dull —n. one who goes on foot; a walker —**pe·des′tri·an·ism** n.

pedestrian crossing a path across a road marked as a crossing for pedestrians

pe·des·tri·an·ize (pə des′trē ən īz) vt. **-ized, -iz′ing** to convert a street, etc., into an area solely for the use of pedestrians —**pe·des′tri·an·i·za′tion** n.

ped·i- [< L. pes (gen. pedis), a foot] a combining form meaning foot or feet [pedicure]

ped·i·cab (ped′i kab′) n. [PEDI- + CAB] a three-wheeled passenger vehicle, esp. in SE Asia, which the driver propels by pedalling like a bicycle

ped·i·cel (ped′i s'l) n. [< ModL. dim. of L. pediculus, dim. of pes, a foot] 1. Bot. the stalk of a single flower, fruit, grass spikelet, etc. 2. Zool. a) a small, stalklike structure b) a small, footlike part Also **ped′i·cle** (-k'l) —**ped′i·cel′late** (-sel′it, -āt) adj.

pe·dic·u·lo·sis (pi dik′yə lō′sis) n. [< L. dim. of pedis, a louse + -OSIS] infestation with lice —**pe·dic′u·lous** (-ləs) adj.

ped·i·cure (ped′i kyoor′) n. [< Fr. < L. pes, a foot + cura, care] 1. same as CHIROPODIST (see CHIROPODY) 2. care of the feet; esp., a trimming, polishing, etc. of the toenails —**ped′i·cur′ist** n.

ped·i·gree (ped′ə grē′) n. [< MFr. piè de grue, lit., crane's foot: from the lines in the genealogical tree] 1. a list of ancestors; family tree 2. descent; lineage 3. a recorded line of descent, esp. of a purebred animal —**ped′i·greed′** adj.

ped·i·ment (ped′ə mənt) n. [altered (after L. pes, gen. pedis, a foot) < earlier periment, prob. < PYRAMID] 1. a low-pitched gable on the front of some buildings of Grecian architecture 2. any similar triangular piece, as over a doorway, etc. —**ped′-i·men′tal** adj. —**ped′i·men′-ted** adj.

ped·i·palp (ped′i palp′) n. [< ModL.: see PEDI- & PALPUS] either of the second pair of appendages of arachnids, developed for grasping, sensing, etc.

PEDIMENT

ped·lar (ped′lər) n. one who peddles; hawker

pe·do- [< Gr. pais (gen. paidos), a child] same as PAEDO-

pe·dol·o·gy (pi dol′ə jē) n. [< Gr. pedon, the ground + -LOGY] the scientific study of soils —**pe·dol′o·gist** n.

pe·dom·e·ter (pi dom′ə tər) n. [< Fr. < L. pes (gen. pedis), a foot + Gr. metron, a measure] an instrument which measures the distance covered in walking by recording the number of steps

pe·dun·cle (pi dun′k'l, pē′dun k'l) n. [< ModL. dim. of L. pes, foot] 1. Anat., Med., Zool. a stalklike part 2. Bot. a stalk of a flower cluster or solitary flower —**pe·dun′cu·lar** (-kyə lər) adj. —**pe·dun′cu·late** (-kyə lit, -lāt′), **pe·dun′-cu·lat·ed** adj.

pee (pē) vi., vt. [orig. euphemistic use of P(ISS)] [Colloq.] to urinate —n. [Colloq.] 1. urine 2. the act of urinating

peek (pēk) vi. [< ?] to glance or look quickly and furtively, as through an opening —n. such a glance

peek·a·boo (pēk′ə boo′) n. a child's game in which someone hides his face, as behind his hands, and then suddenly reveals it, calling "peekaboo!" —adj. made of openwork or sheer fabric, as a blouse

peel¹ (pēl) vt. [< OFr. < L. pilare, to make bald < pilus, a hair] to cut away or strip off (the rind, skin, surface, etc.) of (anything); pare —vi. 1. to shed skin, bark, etc. 2. to come off in layers or flakes, as old paint 3. [Slang] to undress —n. the rind or skin of fruit —**peel off** Aeron. to veer away from a flight formation abruptly

peel² (pēl) n. [< OFr. < L. pala, a spade] a long shovellike tool used by bakers for moving bread into and out of ovens

peel³ (pēl) n. [ME. pel < AngloFr. < OFr, a fort, stake < L. palus: see PALE²] a fortified house or tower of a type built on the Scottish border during the 16th cent.

peel·er (pēl′ər) n. [after Sir Robert Peel (1788-1850), Brit. statesman who first organized the Irish and British constabulary] 1. [Old Slang] a policeman 2. formerly, one of the Irish constabulary

peel·ing (pēl′iŋ) n. a peeled-off strip, as of apple skin

peen (pēn) n. [prob. < Scand.] the part of certain hammer heads opposite to the flat striking surface: often ball-shaped

(ball peen) or wedge-shaped —vt. to hammer, bend, etc. with a peen

peep¹ (pēp) vi. [orig. echoic] 1. to make the short, high-pitched cry of a young bird 2. to speak in a weak voice, as from fear —n. 1. a short, high-pitched sound 2. a slight vocal sound

peep² (pēp) vi. [? akin to ME. piken, peek] 1. to look through a small opening or from a place of hiding 2. to peer slyly or secretly 3. to show or appear gradually or partially [stars peeped through the clouds] —vt. to cause to appear or protrude —n. 1. a brief look; secret or furtive glimpse 2. the first appearance, as of dawn

peep·er (-ər) n. 1. a person who peeps or pries 2. [Slang] [pl.] the eyes

peep·hole (-hōl′) n. a hole to peep through

peeping Tom [after the tailor who was struck blind after peeping at Lady Godiva] a person who gets pleasure, esp. sexual pleasure, from furtively watching others

peep show a pictured scene or group of objects, as in a box, viewed through a small opening, sometimes with a magnifying lens

peer¹ (pir) n. [< OFr. per < L. par, an equal] 1. one that has the same rank, value, etc. as another; specif., an equal before the law 2. a noble; esp., a British duke, marquis, earl, viscount, or baron —vt. 1. [Archaic] to match or equal 2. to make a nobleman of —**peer of the realm** a peer in the House of Lords

peer² (pir) vi. [? short for APPEAR] 1. to look closely, as in trying to see more clearly 2. to come partly into sight 3. [Poet.] to appear

peer·age (pir′ij) n. 1. all the peers of a particular country 2. the rank or dignity of a peer 3. a book or list of peers with their lineage

peer·ess (-is) n. 1. the wife of a peer 2. a woman having the rank of peer in her own right

peer group a group of people of about the same age and status and having the same set of values

peer·less (-lis) adj. without equal; unrivalled —**peer′less·ly** adv. —**peer′less·ness** n.

peeve (pēv) vt. peeved, peev′ing [< ff.] [Colloq.] to make peevish —n. [Colloq.] 1. an object of dislike; annoyance 2. a peevish state

pee·vish (pē′vish) adj. [< ?] 1. irritable; fretful 2. showing ill humour or impatience, as a remark —**pee′-vish·ly** adv. —**pee′vish·ness** n.

pee·wee (pē′wē′) n. [prob. echoic redupl. of WEE¹] [U.S. Colloq.] unusually small person or thing

pee·wit (pē′wit, pyoo′it) n. [echoic of its call] same as LAPWING

peg (peg) n. [prob. < LowG. source] 1. a short pin or bolt used to hold parts together, close an opening, hang things on, fasten ropes to, mark the score in a game, etc. 2. a) the distance between pegs b) a step or degree 3. any of the pins that regulate the tension of the strings of a violin, etc. 4. a point or prong for tearing, hooking, etc. 5. a point of reference, esp. an excuse or reason 6. clipped form of CLOTHESPEG 7. a small drink of wine or spirits 8. [Colloq.] the foot or leg 9. [Colloq.] an act of throwing —vt. pegged, peg′ging 1. to put a peg or pegs into so as to fasten, mark, etc. 2. to maintain (prices, etc.) at a fixed level 3. to score (points) in cribbage 4. [U.S. Colloq.] to identify or categorize [pegged him as a scholar] 5. [Colloq.] to throw (a ball) —vi. 1. to keep score with pegs, as in cribbage 2. to move energetically (with along, etc.) —**peg away (at)** to work steadily and persistently (at) —**round peg in a square hole** one in a position, office, for which he is unfitted: also **square peg in a round hole** —**take down a peg** to lower the pride or conceit of

Peg·a·sus (peg′ə səs) [after the winged horse Pegasus, in Gr. mythology] a large northern constellation

peg·board (peg′bôrd′) n. 1. a small board with holes in it for inserting scoring pegs for cribbage 2. a piece of boardlike material with rows of holes for hooks to hold displays, tools, etc.

peg leg [Colloq.] 1. a wooden leg 2. a person with a wooden leg

peg-top (peg′top′) adj. designating trousers that are full at the hips and narrow at the ankles

peg top 1. a child's spinning top, pear-shaped with a metal tip 2. [pl.] peg-top trousers

P.E.I. Prince Edward Island

peign·oir (pān wär′, pen-) n. [Fr. < peigner, to comb, ult. < L. pecten, a comb] a négligé

pe·jo·ra·tion (pē′jə rā′shən, pej′ə-) n. [see ff.] 1. a worsening 2. a change for the worse in the meaning of a word

pe·jo·ra·tive (pi jor′ə tiv, pej′ə rāt′iv) adj. [< L. pp. of pejorare, to make worse < pejor, worse] 1. declining; making or becoming worse: said of a word whose basic meaning has changed for the worse (Ex.: cretin) 2. disparaging or derogatory —n. a pejorative word or form

pek·an (pek′ən) *n.* [< Am.Ind. name] *same as* FISHER (sense 2)

peke (pēk) *n.* *clipped form of* PEKINGESE (sense 3)

Pe·king·ese (pē′kiŋ ēz′; *for n.* 3, *usually* -kə nēz′) *adj.* of Peking, China, or its people —*n.*, *pl.* **Pekingese** 1. a native or inhabitant of Peking 2. the Chinese dialect of Peking 3. a small dog with long, silky hair, short legs, and a pug nose Also **Pe′kin·ese′** (-kə nēz′)

Pe·king man (pē′kiŋ) a type of early man of the Pleistocene age, known from fossil remains found near Peking

pe·koe (pē′kō, pek′ō) *n.* [< Chin. *pek-ho*, lit., white down (on the young leaves used)] a black, small-leaved tea of Ceylon and India

Pe·la·gi·an (pi lā′jē ən) *n.* [LL. (Eccles.) *Pelagianus*] a follower of Pelagius, who denied the doctrine of original sin and maintained that man has freedom of will —*adj.* of Pelagius or his followers

pe·lag·ic (pi laj′ik) *adj.* [< L. < Gr. < *pelagos*, the sea] of the open sea or ocean

pel·ar·go·ni·um (pel′ər gō′nē əm) *n.* [ModL. < Gr. *pelargos*, stork] any of a group of plants with lobed leaves and showy flowers; geranium

pelf (pelf) *n.* [akin to MFr. *pelfre*, booty] 1. orig., booty 2. wealth regarded with contempt

pel·i·can (pel′i kən) *n.* [< OE. < LL. < Gr. *pelekan*] a large water bird with webbed feet and an expandable pouch in the lower bill for scooping up fish

pelican crossing a type of road crossing with pedestrian-operated traffic lights

pe·lisse (pə lēs′) *n.* [Fr., ult. < L. *pellicius*, made of skins < *pellis*, a skin] a long cloak or outer coat, esp. one made or lined with fur

pel·la·gra (pə lag′rə, -lā′grə) *n.* [It. < *pelle* (< L. *pellis*), the skin + -*agra* < Gr. *agra*, seizure] a chronic disease caused by a deficiency of niacin in the diet and characterized by skin eruptions and mental disorders —**pel·la′grous** *adj.*

pel·let (pel′ət) *n.* [< OFr. *pelote* < VL. dim. of L. *pila*, a ball] 1. a little ball, as of clay, paper, medicine, compressed food, etc. 2. *a)* a crude projectile, as used in a catapult *b)* a bullet, or imitation bullet *c)* a small lead shot —*vt.* 1. to make pellets of 2. to shoot or hit with pellets

pel·let·ize (-īz′) *vt.* -**ized′**, -**iz′ing** to make pellets of the iron-containing particles recovered from low-grade iron (ore) —**pel′let·i·za′tion** *n.*

pel·li·to·ry (pel′ə tər ē) *n.*, *pl.* -**ries** [altered < ME. *peritorie* < OFr. < L. *parietarius*, of walls] 1. any of various plants of the nettle family, common on old walls: in full **wall pellitory** 2. a Mediterranean plant of the composite family: in full **pellitory of Spain**

pell-mell, pell·mell (pel′mel′) *adv.*, *adj.* [< Fr. < OFr. *pesle mesle*, redupl. < *mesler*, to mix] 1. in a jumbled, confused mass or manner 2. in reckless haste; headlong —*n.* confusion; disorder

pel·lu·cid (pə lyōo′sid, -lōo′-) *adj.* [< L. < *pellucere* < *per*, through + *lucere*, to shine] 1. transparent or translucent; clear 2. clear and simple in style —**pel′lu·cid′i·ty, pel·lu′·cid·ness** *n.* —**pel·lu′cid·ly** *adv.*

pel·met (pel′mət) *n.* [? altered < Fr. *palmette*, a palm-leaf ornament on a cornice] a board or valance for concealing curtain fixtures

pelt¹ (pelt) *vt.* [? ult. < L. *pillare*, to drive] 1. to throw things at 2. to beat heavily and repeatedly 3. to throw (missiles) —*vi.* 1. to strike heavily or steadily, as hard rain 2. to hurry —*n.* a blow —(at) **full pelt** at full speed

pelt² (pelt) *n.* [prob. < PELTRY] 1. the skin of a fur-bearing animal, esp. after it is stripped from the carcass 2. the human skin: a humorous usage

pel·tate (pel′tāt) *adj.* [< L. *pelta*, light shield + -ATE¹] *Bot.* shield-shaped: having the stalk attached to the lower surface within the margin: said of a leaf —**pel′tate·ly** *adv.*

pelt·ry (pel′trē) *n.*, *pl.* -**ries** [< OFr. < *peletier*, furrier < *pel*, a skin] pelts, or fur-bearing skins, collectively

pel·vis (pel′vis) *n.*, *pl.* -**vis·es**, -**ves** (-vēz) [ModL. < L., a basin] *Anat.*, *Zool.* any basinlike structure; specif., *a)* the basinlike cavity in the posterior part of the trunk of man and many other vertebrates *b)* the ring of bones forming this cavity: also **pelvic girdle** —**pel′vic** *adj.*

Pemb. Pembrokeshire

pem·mi·can (pem′i kən) *n.* [< Cree *pemikkân*, fat meat < *pimiy*, fat] [U.S.] 1. dried lean meat, pounded into a paste with fat and preserved as pressed cakes 2. a concentrated food of dried beef, suet, dried fruit, etc., as for explorers

pen¹ (pen) *n.* [OE. *penn*] 1. a small enclosure for domestic animals 2. the animals inside it 3. any small enclosure 4. a special dock, usually with a bombproofed roof, for repairing submarines —*vt.* **penned** or **pent, pen′ning** to confine or enclose as in a pen

pen² (pen) *n.* [< OFr. < L. *penna*, a feather] 1. orig., a heavy quill trimmed to a split point, for writing with ink 2. any of various devices used in writing or drawing with ink,

often with a metal point split into two nibs: see also BALL POINT PEN, FOUNTAIN PEN 3. the metal point for this device 4. *a)* writing as a profession *b)* literary style —*vt.* **penned, pen′ning** to write as with a pen

pen³ (pen) *n.* [U.S. Slang] a penitentiary

pen⁴ (pen) *n.* [< ?] a female swan

Pen., pen. peninsula

P.E.N. International Association of Poets, Playwrights, Editors, Essayists, and Novelists

pe·nal (pē′n′l) *adj.* [< L. < *poena*, punishment] 1. of, for, or involving punishment, esp. legal punishment 2. making one liable to punishment, as an offence —**pe′nal·ly** *adv.*

penal code a body of law dealing with various crimes or offences and their legal penalties

pe·nal·ize (pē′nəl īz′, pen′əl-) *vt.* -**ized′**, -**iz′ing** 1. to set a penalty for 2. to impose a penalty on, as for breaking some rule 3. to put at a disadvantage —**pe′nal·i·za′tion** *n.*

pen·al·ty (pen′′l tē) *n.*, *pl.* -**ties** 1. a punishment fixed by law, as for a crime 2. the handicap, fine, forfeit, etc. imposed upon an offender or one who does not fulfil a contract or obligation 3. any unfortunate consequence 4. *Sports* a free shot at goal, free kick, etc. imposed for breaking a rule

pen·ance (pen′əns) *n.* [< OFr. < L. < *paenitens*: see PENITENT] 1. *R.C.Ch. & Orthodox Eastern Ch.* a sacrament involving the confession of sin, repentance, and submission to penalties imposed, followed by absolution 2. any voluntary suffering to show repentance for wrongdoing —*vt.* -**anced**, -**anc·ing** to impose a penance on —**do penance** to perform an act of penance

pen and ink writing materials

pe·na·tes (pi nät′ēz) *n.pl.* [L.] the household gods of the ancient Romans: see LARES AND PENATES

pence (pens; *in compounds*, pəns) *n.* *pl. of* PENNY: used also in compounds [*twopence*]

pen·chant (pen′chənt; *Fr.* pän shän′) *n.* [Fr. < *pencher*, to incline, ult. < L. *pendere*, to hang] a strong liking or fondness; inclination

pen·cil (pen′s′l) *n.* [< MFr. < L. *penicillus* < dim. of *penis*, a tail] 1. orig., an artist's brush 2. the style of a given artist 3. a pointed, rod-shaped instrument with a core of graphite or crayon, used for writing, drawing, etc. 4. something shaped or used as a pencil [a styptic *pencil*] 5. *a)* a series of lines coming to or spreading out from a point *b)* a set of rays, etc., as light rays converging at a point —*vt.* -**cilled**, -**cil·ling** 1. to write, draw, etc. as with a pencil 2. to use a pencil on —**pen′cil·ler** *n.*

pencil sharpener an instrument with a sharp edge that hones pencils by rotation

pend (pend) *vi.* [< OFr. < L. *pendere*, to hang] to await judgment or decision

pend·ant (pen′dənt) *n.* [< OFr. prp. of *pendre* < L. *pendere*, to hang] 1. an ornamental hanging object, as from an earring 2. anything hanging, as a chandelier 3. a decorative piece suspended from a ceiling or roof —*adj.* *same as* PENDENT —**pend′ant·ly** *adv.*

pend·ent (-dənt) *adj.* [see prec.] 1. suspended 2. overhanging 3. undecided; pending —*n.* *same as* PENDANT —**pend′en·cy** *n.* —**pend′ent·ly** *adv.*

pend·ing (pen′diŋ) *adj.* 1. not decided or established [patent *pending*] 2. impending —*prep.* 1. throughout the course of; during 2. while awaiting; until [*pending* his arrival]

pending tray a basket in an office containing papers awaiting answers, decisions, etc.

pen·drag·on (pen drag′ən) *n.* [W. *pen*, head + *dragon*, leader < L. *draco*, cohort's standard] supreme chief or leader: a title used in ancient Britain

pen·du·late (pen′dyōo lāt′) *vi.* [< PENDUL(UM) + -ATE] 1. to swing like a pendulum 2. to fluctuate

pen·du·line (pen′dyōo lin′) *adj.* [< L. *pendulus*, hanging + -INE¹] 1. hanging (of a nest) 2. designating a bird that builds such a nest

pen·du·lous (pen′dyōo ləs) *adj.* [L. *pendulus* < *pendere*, to hang] 1. hanging freely or loosely; suspended so as to swing 2. drooping —**pen′du·lous·ly** *adv.* —**pen′du·lous·ness** *n.*

pen·du·lum (pen′dyōo ləm) *n.* [ModL. < L.: see prec.] a body hung from a fixed point so as to swing freely to and fro under the combined forces of gravity and momentum: often used to regulate clock movements—**pen′du·lar** *adj.*

pe·ne·plain, pe·ne·plane (pē′nə plān′) *n.* [L. *pene, paene*, almost + PLAIN¹, PLANE²] land worn down by erosion almost to a level plain

pen·e·tra·ble (pen′i trə b′l) *adj.* that can be penetrated —**pen′e·tra·bil′i·ty, pen′e·tra·ble·ness** *n.* —**pen′e·tra·bly** *adv.*

pen·e·trate (pen′ə trāt′) *vt.* -**trat′ed**, -**trat′ing** [< L. pp. of *penetrare* < base of *penitus*, inward] 1. to find or force a way into or through; enter as by piercing 2. to see into the interior of 3. to have an effect throughout; permeate 4. to affect or move deeply 5. to understand —*vi.* 1. to make a way into or through something 2. to have a marked effect on the mind or emotions

pen·e·trat·ing (-trāt'iŋ) *adj.* l. that can penetrate [a *penetrating* oil] 2. sharp; piercing [a *penetrating* smell] 3. that has entered deeply [a *penetrating* wound] 4. discerning [a *penetrating* mind] Also **pen'e·tra'tive** —**pen'e·trat'ing·ly, pen'e·tra'tive·ly** *adv.*

pen·e·tra·tion (pen'ə trā'shən) *n.* l. a penetrating 2. the depth to which something penetrates 3. sharp discernment; insight

pen friend a person, esp. a stranger in another country with whom one arranges to exchange letters: also **pen pal**

pen·guin (peŋ'gwin, pen'-) *n.* [prob. < W. *pen gwyn,* lit., white head] any of a group of flightless birds of the Southern Hemisphere, having webbed feet and paddlelike flippers for swimming

pen·hold·er (pen'hōl'dər) *n.* l. the holder into which a pen point fits 2. a container for a pen

pen·i·cil·lin (pen'ə sil'in) *n.* [< ff. + -IN¹] any of several antibiotic compounds obtained from certain moulds or produced synthetically

pen·i·cil·li·um (-ē əm) *n., pl.* **-li·ums, -li·a** (-ə) [ModL. < L. *penicillus,* a brush: from the tuftlike ends] any of a group of fungi growing as green mould on stale bread, decaying fruit, etc.

PENGUIN
(to 120 cm high)

pen·in·su·la (pə nin'syoo lə) *n.* [< L. < *paene,* almost + *insula,* an isle] l. a land area almost entirely surrounded by water, connected with the mainland by an isthmus 2. any land area projecting into the water —**pen·in'su·lar** *adj.*

pe·nis (pē'nis) *n., pl.* **-nis·es, -nes** (-nēz) [L., a tail, penis] the male organ of sexual intercourse: in mammals it is also the organ through which urine is ejected by the male —**pe'nile** (-nīl) *adj.*

pen·i·tent (pen'ə tənt) *adj.* [< OFr. < L. prp. of *paenitere,* to repent] sorry for having done wrong and willing to atone; repentant —*n.* l. a penitent person 2. *R.C.Ch.* a person undergoing penance —**pen'i·tence** *n.* —**pen'i·tent·ly** *adv.*

pen·i·ten·tial (pen'ə ten'shəl) *adj.* of, constituting, or expressing penitence or penance —*n.* l. a penitent 2. a list or book of rules governing religious penance —**pen'i·ten'tial·ly** *adv.*

pen·i·ten·tia·ry (pen'ə ten'shə rē) *adj.* [< ML. < L.: see PENITENT] l. of or for penance 2. used in punishing and reforming —*n., pl.* **-ries** [U.S.] a prison; specif., a prison for persons convicted of serious crimes

pen·knife (pen'nīf') *n., pl.* **-knives** (-nīvz') a small pocketknife; orig., one used in making quill pens

pen·man (pen'mən) *n., pl.* **-men** l. a person employed to write or copy; scribe 2. a person skilled in penmanship 3. an author

pen·man·ship (-ship') *n.* l. handwriting as an art or skill 2. a style of handwriting

pen name a name used by an author in place of his true name; nom de plume

pen·nant (pen'ənt) *n.* [< PENNON, altered after PENDANT] any long, narrow flag

pen·ni (pen'ē) *n., pl.* **-ni·a** (-ə), **-nis, -ni** [Finn., akin to PENNY] *see* MONETARY UNITS, table (Finland)

pen·ni·less (pen'i lis) *adj.* without even a penny; extremely poor —**pen'ni·less·ness** *n.*

pen·non (pen'ən) *n.* [< OFr. < *penne:* see PEN²] l. a long, narrow, triangular or swallow-tailed flag used as an ensign by knights or lancers 2. any flag or pennant 3. a pinion; wing

Penn·syl·va·ni·a Dutch (pen's'l vā'nē ə) l. the descendants of early German immigrants, who settled mainly in E Pennsylvania 2. their High German dialect: also called **Pennsylvania German** 3. their folk art, featuring stylized decorations of flowers, birds, etc. —**Penn'syl·va'ni·a-Dutch'** *adj.*

Penn·syl·va·ni·an (pen's'l vān'yən, -vā'nē ən) *adj.* l. of Pennsylvania 2. [U.S.] corresponding to the Upper Carboniferous period of the Paleozoic era, in N America —*n.* a native or inhabitant of Pennsylvania —**the Pennsylvanian** the Pennsylvanian Period or its rocks

pen·ny (pen'ē) *n., pl.* **-nies;** for l (esp. collectively), **pence** [OE. *pening,* ult. < L. *pannus,* cloth (a medium of exchange)] l. in the United Kingdom and certain Commonwealth countries, *a)* formerly, a unit of currency equal to one twelfth of a shilling *b)* a unit of currency equal to one 100th part of a pound: in full, **new penny** 2. [U.S.] U.S. or Canadian cent 3. a sum of money —**a pretty penny** [Colloq.] a large sum of money —**spend a penny** [Colloq.] to urinate —**the penny dropped** comprehension dawned

-pen·ny (pen'ē, pə nē') a *combining form meaning* costing (a specified number of) pennies [*sixpenny*]

penny arcade a public amusement hall with various coin-operated game and vending machines

Penny Black the first postage stamp issued in Britain in 1840

pen·ny-dread·ful (pen'ē dred'fəl) *n., pl.* **-fuls** a cheap, often lurid book or magazine

pen·ny-far·thing (pen'ē fär'thiŋ) *n.* an early type of bicycle with a large front wheel and a small rear wheel

penny pincher a person who is extremely frugal or stingy —**pen'ny-pinch'ing** *n., adj.*

penny post a postal system charging one penny for all letters irrespective of distance, specif. that instituted in Britain in 1840

pen·ny-roy·al (pen'ē roi'əl) *n.* [< Anglo-Fr. < OFr. *poliol* (< L. *pulegium,* fleabane) + *real,* royal] l. a European mint with lavender flowers 2. a similar N American mint that yields an aromatic oil

pen·ny·weight (pen'ē wāt') *n.* a unit of weight, equal to 24 grains, 1/20 ounce troy weight or 1.55 gms

pen·ny-wise (pen'ē wīz') *adj.* careful or thrifty in small matters —**penny-wise and pound-foolish** thrifty in small matters but wasteful in major ones

pen·ny·wort (-wurt') *n.* [ME. *penywort:* see PENNY & WORT²] any of various plants with small round leaves growing in crevices of rocks and walls or in marshy places

pen·ny·worth (-wurth') *n.* l. the amount that can be bought for one penny 2. the value in money of something paid for 3. a small amount

pe·nol·o·gy (pē nol'ə jē) *n.* [Gr. *poinē,* penalty + -LOGY] the study of the reformation and rehabilitation of criminals and of prison management —**pe·no·log·i·cal** (pē'nə loj'i k'l) *adj.* —**pe·nol'o·gist** *n.*

pen pusher a person who writes a lot, esp. a clerk involved with boring paperwork —**pen-push·ing** *adj., n.*

pen·sion (pen'shən; *Fr.* pän syōn') *n.* [< MFr. < L. *pensio* < pp. of *pendere,* to pay] l. a regular payment, not wages, to one who has fulfilled certain requirements, as of service, age, disability, etc. 2. a regular payment, not a fee, given to an artist, etc. by his patron; subsidy 3. in France, etc., *a)* a boardinghouse *b)* room and board —*vt.* to grant a pension to —**pension off** to dismiss from service with a pension —**pen'sion·a·ble** *adj.* —**pen'sion·ar·y** *adj., n.* —**pen'sion·er** *n.*

pen·sive (pen'siv) *adj.* [< OFr. < *penser* < L. *pensare,* to consider, freq. of *pendere,* to weigh] l. thinking deeply, often of sad or melancholy things 2. expressing deep thoughtfulness, often with some sadness —**pen'sive·ly** *adv.* —**pen'sive·ness** *n.*

pen·stock (pen'stok') *n.* [PEN¹ + STOCK] a sluice for controlling the flow of water

pent (pent) *alt. pt. & pp. of* PEN¹ —*adj.* held or kept in; penned (often with *up*)

pen·ta- [Gr. *penta-* < *pente,* five] *a combining form meaning* five: also, before a vowel, **pent-**

pen·ta·cle (pen'tə k'l) *n.* [MFr. < ML. < Gr. *penta-,* five + L. *-culum,* dim, suffix] a symbol, usually a five-pointed star, formerly used in magic: also called **pen'ta·gram** (-gram'), **pen'ta·gle** (-əŋ'g'l)

pen·tad (-tad') *n.* [Gr. *pentas* < *pente,* FIVE] l. the number five 2. a group of five 3. a five-year period 4. *Chem.* an element or radical with a valence of five

pen·ta·gon (pen'tə gon') *n.* [< L. < Gr.: see prec. & -GON] a plane figure with five angles and five sides —**the Pentagon** a five-sided building in U.S.A., housing the Department of Defense; hence, the U.S. military establishment —**pen·tag'o·nal** (-tag'ə n'l) *adj.*

pen·ta·he·dron (pen'tə hē'drən) *n., pl.* **-drons, -dra** (-drə) [ModL.: see PENTA- & -HEDRON] a solid figure with five plane surfaces —**pen'ta·he'dral** *adj.*

pen·tam·er·ous (pen tam'ər əs) *adj.* [PENTA- + -MEROUS] *Biol.* made up of five parts: also written **5-merous**

pen·tam·e·ter (-ə tər) *n.* [L. < Gr.: see PENTA- & METER] a line of verse containing five metrical feet 2. verse consisting of pentameters —*adj.* having five metrical feet

Pen·ta·teuch (pen'tə tyōōk') *n.* [< LL. < Gr. < *penta-,* five + *teuchos,* a book] the first five books of the Bible

pen·tath·lon (pen tath'lon, -lən) *n.* [< Gr. < *penta-,* five + *athlon,* a contest] an athletic contest in which each contestant takes part in five events

pen·ta·ton·ic (pen'tə ton'ik) *adj.* [see PENTA- & TONIC] designating a musical scale having only five tones

pen·ta·va·lent (pen'tə vā'lənt) *adj.* l. having a valence of five 2. *same as* QUINQUEVALENT (sense l)

Pen·te·cost (pen'tə kost') *n.* [< LL. < Gr. *pentēkostē (hēmera),* the fiftieth (day) after Passover] a Christian festival on the seventh Sunday after Easter, celebrating the descent of the Holy Spirit upon the Apostles; Whitsunday —**Pen'te·cos'tal** *adj.*

pent·house (pent'hous') *n.* [< MFr. *apentis,* ult. < L. *appendere,* APPEND] l. a small structure with a sloping roof, or such a roof, attached to the side of a building 2. a flat or houselike structure built on the roof of a building

pen·to·bar·bi·tone sodium (pen'tə bär'bi tōn')　a barbiturate drug used in medicine as a sedative and hypnotic

pen·tode (pen'tōd) *n.* [PENT(A)- + -ODE] an electron tube containing five electrodes, usually a cathode, anode, and three grids

Pen·to·thal Sodium (pen'tə thol') *a trademark for* THIOPENTAL SODIUM: often clipped to **Pentothal**

pent-up (pent'up') *adj.* held in check; curbed; confined [*pent-up* emotion]

pe·nult (pē'nult, pi nult') *n.* [< L. < *paene,* almost + *ultimus,* last] the one next to the last; specif., the second last syllable in a word

pe·nul·ti·mate (pi nul'tə mit) *adj.* 1. next to the last 2. of the penult —*n. same as* PENULT —**pe·nul'ti·mate·ly** *adv.*

pe·num·bra (pi num'brə) *n., pl.* **-brae** (-brē), **-bras** [ModL. < L. *paene,* almost + *umbra,* shade] 1. the partly lighted area surrounding the complete shadow of a body, as the moon, in full eclipse 2. the less dark region around the central area of a sunspot 3. a vague, indefinite, or borderline area —**pe·num'bral** *adj.*

pe·nu·ri·ous (pə nyoor'ē əs) *adj.* 1. unwilling to part with money or possessions; miserly; stingy 2. characterized by penury; destitute —**pe·nu'ri·ous·ly** *adv.* —**pe·nu'ri·ous·ness** *n.*

pen·u·ry (pen'yoo rē, -yə-) *n.* [< L. *penuria,* want] lack of money, property, or necessities; destitution

pe·on (pē'on, -ən) *n.* [< Sp. < ML. *pedo,* foot soldier] 1. in Latin America, a person of the labouring class 2. in India, a messenger or attendant, esp. in an office 3. an exploited labourer —**pe'on·age** *n.*

pe·o·ny (pē'ə nē) *n., pl.* **-nies** [< OE. & OFr. < L. < Gr. *Paiōn,* epithet for Apollo, god of medicine: from its former medicinal use] 1. any of a group of plants with large pink, white, red, or yellow, showy flowers 2. the flower

peo·ple (pē'p'l) *n., pl.* **-ple;** for 1 & 10, **-ples** [< Anglo-Fr. < OFr. < L. *populus,* nation] 1. all the persons of a racial, national, religious, linguistic, or cultural group; nation, race, ethnic group, etc. 2. the persons belonging to a certain place, community, or class [*people* of wealth] 3. the persons under the leadership or control of a particular person or body 4. the members of (someone's) class, occupation, set, race, etc. [the miner spoke for his *people*] 5. one's relatives or ancestors; family 6. persons without wealth, privilege, etc.; populace 7. the electorate of a country, etc. 8. persons considered indefinitely [what will *people* say?] 9. human beings 10. a group of creatures [the ant *people*] —*vt.* **-pled, -pling** to populate

people's front *same as* POPULAR FRONT

pep (pep) *n.* [< PEPPER] [Colloq.] energy; vigour; liveliness —*vt.* **pepped, pep'ping** [Colloq.] to fill with pep; invigorate; stimulate (with *up*)

P.E.P. political and economic planning

pep·lum (pep'ləm) *n., pl.* **-lums, -la** (-lə) [L. < Gr. *peplos,* a shawl] 1. a large scarf worn draped about the body by women in ancient Greece 2. a flounce attached at the waist of a dress, jacket, blouse etc. and extending around the hips

pep·per (pep'ər) *n.* see PLURAL, II, D, 3 [< OE. < L. *piper* < Gr. *peperi*] 1. *a)* a pungent condiment obtained from the small, dried fruits of an East Indian plant: see BLACK PEPPER, WHITE PEPPER *b)* the plant itself 2. any of various plants possessing aromatic and pungent properties, used as flavouring 3. *a) same as* CAPSICUM *b)* the fruit of the capsicum: see RED PEPPER, GREEN PEPPER, SWEET PEPPER 4. any of various pungent spices, as cayenne pepper —*vt.* 1. to season with ground pepper 2. to sprinkle thickly 3. to shower with many small objects [a roof *peppered* with hailstones] 4. to beat or hit with quick jabs

pep·per-and-salt (-'n sôlt') *adj.* speckled with contrasting colours, esp. black and white

pep·per·corn (-kôrn') *n.* [OE. *piporcorn*] the dried berry of the black PEPPER (*n.* 1)

peppercorn rent rent, for a property, that is very low or nominal

pepper mill a hand mill used to grind peppercorns

pep·per·mint (-mint', -mənt) *n.* 1. a species of mint with lance-shaped leaves and whitish or purplish flowers 2. the pungent oil it yields, used for flavouring 3. a sweet flavoured with this oil

pepper pot 1. any of various stews or soups of vegetables, meat, etc. flavoured with hot spices, esp. in the West Indies 2. a container with a perforated top, for sprinkling ground pepper: also **pepper box**

pepper tree a S. American ornamental tree with loose clusters of yellowish flowers and pinkish-red berries

pep·per·y (-ē) *adj.* 1. of, like, or highly seasoned with pepper 2. sharp or fiery, as speech or writing 3. hot-tempered; irritable —**pep'per·i·ness** *n.*

pep pill [Slang] any of various pills containing a stimulant, esp. amphetamine

pep·py (pep'ē) *adj.* **-pi·er, -pi·est** [Colloq.] full of pep, or energy; brisk; vigorous; spirited —**pep'pi·ly** *adv.* —**pep'-pi·ness** *n.*

pep·sin (pep'sən) *n.* [G. < Gr. < *peptein,* to digest] 1. an enzyme secreted in the stomach, aiding in the digestion of proteins 2. an extract of pepsin from the stomachs of calves, etc., formerly used to help in digesting food

pep talk a talk, as to a football team by its manager, to instil enthusiasm, etc.

pep·tic (pep'tik) *adj.* [< L. < Gr. < *peptein,* to digest] 1. of or aiding digestion 2. of or relating to pepsin 3. related to, or caused to some extent by, digestive secretions [a *peptic* ulcer]

pep·tide (pep'tīd) *n.* [PEPT(ONE) + -IDE] any of a group of compounds formed from two or more amino acids by the linkage of amino groups of some of the acids, or by hydrolysis of proteins

pep·tone (-tōn) *n.* [< G. < Gr. *peptos,* digested] any of a group of soluble and diffusible derived proteins formed by the action of enzymes on proteins, as in digestion —**pep·ton'ic** (-ton'ik) *adj.*

per (pur; *unstressed* pər) *prep.* [L.] 1. through; by; by means of 2. for each [fifty pence *per* metre] 3. [Colloq.] according to [*per* his instructions] —**as per usual** as usual

per- [< L. *per,* through] *a prefix meaning:* 1. through; throughout [*perceive, percolate*] 2. thoroughly; very [*persuade*] 3. *Chem.* containing a specified element or radical in its maximum, or a relatively high, valence [*peroxide*]

Per. 1. Persia 2. Persian

per. 1. period 2. person

per·ad·ven·ture (pur'əd ven'chər) *adv.* [< OFr. < *par,* by + *aventure,* chance] [Archaic] 1. possibly 2. by chance —*n.* chance; doubt

per·am·bu·late (pər am'byoo lāt') *vt.* **-lat'ed, -lat'ing** [< L. pp. of *perambulare* < *per,* through + *ambulare,* to walk] to walk through, over, around, etc., as in inspecting —*vi.* to stroll —**per·am'bu·la'tion** *n.* —**per·am'bu·la·to·ry** (-lə tər ē, -lā tər ē) *adj.*

per·am·bu·la·tor (-lāt'ər) *n.* 1. a person who perambulates 2. a light carriage for wheeling a baby about

per an·num (pər an'əm) [L.] by the year; yearly

per·cale (pər kāl', -kal') *n.* [Fr. < Per. *pargāla*] closely woven cotton cloth, used for sheets, etc.

per cap·i·ta (pər kap'ə tə) [ML., lit., by heads] for each person

per·ceive (pər sēv') *vt., vi.* **-ceived', -ceiv'ing** [< OFr. < L. *percipere* < *per,* through + *capere,* to take] 1. to grasp or take in mentally 2. to become aware (of) through the senses —**per·ceiv'a·ble** *adj.* —**per·ceiv'a·bly** *adv.* —**per·ceiv'er** *n.*

per·cent (pər sent') *adv., adj.* [< It. < L. *per centum*] in or for every hundred [a 20 *percent* rate means 20 in every hundred]: symbol, % : also **per cent** or, now rare, **per cent., per cen·tum** (sen'təm) —*n.* 1. a hundredth part 2. [Colloq.] percentage 3. [*pl.*] bonds, etc. bearing regular interest of a (stated) percentage [the four *percents*]

per·cent·age (-ij) *n.* 1. a given part or amount in every hundred 2. any amount, as of interest, stated in percent 3. part; portion [a *percentage* of the audience] 4. [Colloq.] use; advantage; gain

per·cen·tile (pər sen'tīl) *n. Statistics* 1. any value in a series dividing the distribution of its members into 100 groups of equal frequency 2. any of these groups —*adj.* of a percentile

per·cept (pur'sept) *n.* [< PERCEPTION] a recognizable sensation or impression received by the mind through the senses

per·cep·ti·ble (pər sep'tə b'l) *adj.* that can be perceived —**per·cep'ti·bil'i·ty** *n.* —**per·cep'ti·bly** *adv.*

per·cep·tion (-shən) *n.* [< L. < pp. of *percipere:* see PERCEIVE] 1. *a)* the act of perceiving or the ability to perceive; awareness *b)* insight or intuition 2. the understanding, knowledge, etc. or a specific idea, concept, etc. got by perceiving —**per·cep'tion·al** *adj.* —**per·cep'tu·al** (-tyoo əl) *adj.*

per·cep·tive (-tiv) *adj.* 1. of or capable of perception 2. able to perceive quickly and easily —**per·cep'tive·ly** *adv.* —**per·cep'tive·ness, per·cep·tiv'i·ty** *n.*

perch¹ (purch) *n., pl.* **perch, perch'es:** see PLURAL, II, D, 2 [< OFr. < L. < Gr. *perkē*] 1. a small, spiny-finned, freshwater food fish 2. any of various bony, spiny-rayed, usually saltwater fishes

perch² (purch) *n.* [< OFr. < L. *pertica,* a pole] 1. a horizontal pole, branch, etc. serving as a roost for birds 2. any resting place, esp. a high or insecure one 3. *same as* ROD (sense 7) —*vi., vt.* to alight and rest, or place, on or as on a perch —**perch'er** *n.*

per·chance (pər chäns') *adv.* [< OFr. *par,* by + *chance,* chance] [Archaic] 1. by chance 2. perhaps; possibly

Per·che·ron (pur'chə ron', -shə-) *n.* [Fr. < *Perche,* region in France] a breed of large, fast-trotting draught horses: also **Percheron Norman**

per·cip·i·ent (pər sip'ē ənt) *adj.* perceiving, esp. keenly or

per·co·late (pur'kə lāt') **vt.** -lat'ed, -lat'ing [< L. pp. of *percolare* < *per*, through + *colare*, to strain] 1. to pass (a liquid) gradually through a porous substance; filter 2. to drain or ooze through (a porous substance); permeate 3. to brew (coffee) in a percolator —**vi.** 1. to ooze through a porous substance 2. to permeate 3. to start bubbling up, as percolated coffee —**per'co·la'tion n.**

per·co·la·tor (-lāt'ər) **n.** a coffeepot in which boiling water bubbles up through a tube and filters back down through the ground coffee

per·cuss (pər kus') **vt.** [< L. *percussus* pp. of *percutere*, to strike] to rap gently and firmly, as in medical diagnosis —**per·cus'sor n.**

per·cus·sion (pər kush'ən) **n.** [< L. < pp. of *percutere*, to strike] 1. the hitting of one body against another, as the hammer of a firearm against a powder cap 2. the impact of sound waves on the ear 3. percussion instruments collectively 4. *Med.* the tapping of the chest, back, etc. with the fingers to determine from the sound produced the condition of internal organs —**per·cus'sive adj.** —**per·cus'sive·ly adv.** —**per·cus'sive·ness n.**

percussion cap a small paper or metal container holding a charge that explodes when struck

percussion instrument a musical instrument in which the tone is produced when some part is struck, as the drums, cymbals, xylophone, etc.

per·cus·sion·ist (-ist) **n.** a musician who plays percussion instruments

per di·em (dē'əm, dī'əm) [L.] 1. by the day; daily 2. a daily allowance, as for expenses

per·di·tion (pər dish'ən) **n.** [< OFr. < LL. < L. pp. of *perdere*, to lose] 1. [Archaic] complete and irreparable loss; ruin 2. *Theol. a)* the loss of the soul; damnation *b) same as* HELL

‡**père** (per) **n.** [Fr.] father: often used after the surname, like English *Senior* [Dumas *père*]

per·e·gri·nate (per'ə gri nāt') **vt., vi.** -nat'ed, -nat'ing [< L. pp. of *peregrinari* < *peregrinus:* see PILGRIM] to travel, esp. walk (along or through) —**per'e·gri·na'tion n.** —**per'·e·gri·na'tor n.**

per·e·grine (falcon) (per'ə grin, -grēn') [see prec.] a very swift European falcon with a spotted breast: used in falconry

per·emp·to·ry (pə remp'tər ē) **adj.** [< LL. < L. < pp. of *perimere*, to destroy < *per-*, intens. + *emere*, to take] 1. *Law a)* barring further action, debate, etc.; final; decisive *b)* not requiring that any cause be shown [a *peremptory* challenge of a juror] 2. that cannot be denied, delayed, etc., as a command 3. intolerantly positive; dogmatic [a *peremptory* manner] —**per·emp'to·ri·ly adv.** —**per·emp'·to·ri·ness n.**

per·en·ni·al (pə ren'ē əl) **adj.** [< L. < *per*, through + *annus*, a year] 1. lasting or active throughout the whole year 2. continuing for a long time [a *perennial* youth] 3. becoming active again and again; perpetual 4. having a life cycle of more than two years: said of plants —**n.** a perennial plant —**per·en'ni·al·ly adv.**

perf. 1. perfect 2. perforated

per·fect (pur'fikt; *for v., usually* pər fekt') **adj.** [< OFr. < L. pp. of *perficere* < *per*, through + *facere*, to do] 1. complete in all respects; flawless 2. in a condition of excellence, as in skill or quality 3. completely accurate; exact [a *perfect* copy] 4. utter; absolute [a *perfect* fool] 5. *Gram.* expressing a state or action completed at the time of speaking or at the time indicated: verbs have three perfect tenses: present perfect, past perfect, and future perfect 6. *Music* designating an interval, as an octave, whose character is not altered by inversion and which has no alternative major and minor forms —**vt.** 1. to bring to completion 2. to make perfect or more nearly perfect according to a given standard, as by training, etc. —**n.** 1. the perfect tense 2. a verb form in this tense —**per·fect'er n.** —**per'fect·ness n.**

per·fect·i·ble (pər fek'tə b'l) **adj.** that can become, or be made, perfect or more nearly perfect —**per·fect'i·bil'i·ty n.**

per·fec·tion (pər fek'shən) **n.** 1. the act or process of perfecting 2. a being perfect 3. a person or thing that is the perfect embodiment of some quality —**to perfection** completely; perfectly

per·fec·tion·ism (-iz'm) **n.** extreme or obsessive striving for perfection, as in one's work —**per·fec'tion·ist n., adj.** —**per·fec'tion·is'tic adj.**

per·fect·ly (pur'fikt lē) **adv.** 1. to a perfect degree 2. completely; fully

perfect participle *same as* PAST PARTICIPLE

perfect pitch *a popular term for* ABSOLUTE PITCH

per·fer·vid (pər fur'vid) **adj.** extremely fervid

per·fi·dy (pur'fə dē) **n.,** *pl.* -dies [< Fr. < L. *perfidia* < *per fidem* (*decipi*), (to deceive) through faith] betrayal of trust;

treachery —**per·fid·i·ous** (pər fid'ē əs) **adj.** —**per·fid'i·ous·ly adv.**

per·fo·li·ate (pər fō'lē it, -āt') **adj.** [< ModL. < L. *per*, through + *folium*, a leaf] having a stem that seems to pass through it: said of a leaf —**per·fo'li·a'tion n.**

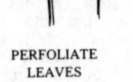

PERFOLIATE LEAVES

per·fo·rate (pur'fə rāt'; *for adj., usually* -rit) **vt., vi.** -rat'ed, -rat'ing [< L. pp. of *perforare* < *per*, through + *forare*, to bore] 1. to make a hole or holes through, as by punching or boring 2. to pierce with holes in a row, as a pattern, computer tape, etc. —**adj.** pierced with holes, esp. in a row, for easy tearing: also **per'fo·rat'ed** —**per'fo·ra·ble adj.** —**per'fo·ra'·tor n.**

per·fo·ra·tion (pur'fə rā'shən) **n.** 1. a perforating or being perforated 2. a hole made by piercing, ulceration, etc. 3. any of a series of punched holes, as those between postage stamps on a sheet

per·force (pər fôrs') **adv.** [< OFr.: see PER & FORCE¹] by or through necessity; necessarily

per·form (pər fôrm') **vt.** [< Anglo-Fr. < OFr. *parfournir*, to consummate < *par* (< L. *per-*, intens.) + *fornir*, to accomplish] 1. to act on so as to complete; do (a task, process, etc.) 2. to fulfil (a promise, etc.) 3. to render or enact (a piece of music, a dramatic role, etc.) —**vi.** to execute an action or process; esp., to act in a play, dance, etc. before an audience —**per·form'a·ble adj.** —**per·form'·er n.**

per·form·ance (-fôr'məns) **n.** 1. the act of performing; execution, accomplishment, etc. 2. functioning, usually with regard to effectiveness, as of a machine 3. a deed or feat 4. *a)* a formal exhibition or presentation before an audience, as a play; show *b)* one's part in this

per·fume (pər fyōōm'; *for n., usually* pur'fyōōm) **vt.** -fumed', -fum'ing [< MFr. < It. < L. *per-*, intens. + *fumare*, to smoke] 1. to fill with a pleasing odour 2. to put perfume on —**n.** 1. a sweet scent; fragrance 2. a substance producing a pleasing odour; esp., a volatile oil, as that extracted from flowers

per·fum·er (pər fyōō'mər) **n.** 1. one who makes or sells perfumes 2. one who or that which perfumes

per·fum·er·y (-ē) **n.,** *pl.* -er·ies 1. the trade or art of a perfumer 2. perfumes collectively 3. a place where perfume is made or sold

per·func·to·ry (pər funk'tər ē) **adj.** [< LL. < L. pp. of *perfungi* < *per-*, intens. + *fungi*, to perform] 1. done merely as a routine; superficial [a *perfunctory* examination] 2. without concern; indifferent [a *perfunctory* teacher] —**per·func'to·ri·ly adv.** —**per·func'to·ri·ness n.**

per·fuse (pər fyōōz') **vt.** -fused', -fus'ing [< L. *perfusus* pp. of *perfundere*, to pour through] to suffuse or permeate (a liquid, etc.) through or over (something)

per·go·la (pur'gə lə) **n.** [It., arbour < L. *pergula*, projecting cover] an arbour, esp. one with an open roof of cross rafters supported on columns, usually with climbing plants

per·gun·nah (pər gu'nə) **n.** [Hindi] a sub-division of a district in India

per·haps (pər haps', -aps') **adv.** [PER + *haps*, pl. of HAP] possibly; maybe

pe·ri (pir'ē) **n.** [Per. *parī*] *Persian Myth.* 1. a fairy or elf 2. any fairylike being

peri- [< Gr. < *peri*] *a prefix meaning:* 1. around, about [*periscope*] 2. near [*perigee*]

per·i·anth (per'ē anth') **n.** [< ModL. < Gr. *peri-*, around + *anthos*, a flower] the outer envelope of a flower, including the calyx and corolla

per·i·apt (-apt') **n.** [Fr. *périapte* < Gr. *periaptein*, to fit about] *same as* AMULET

per·i·car·di·tis (per'ə kär dīt'is) **n.** inflammation of the pericardium

per·i·car·di·um (-kär'dē əm) **n.,** *pl.* -di·a (-ə) [ModL. < Gr. < *peri-*, around + *kardia*, heart] in vertebrates, the thin, membranous sac around the heart —**per'i·car'di·al, per'·i·car'di·ac'adj.**

per·i·carp (per'ə kärp') **n.** [< ModL. < Gr.: see PERI- & -CARP] *Bot.* the wall of a ripened ovary —**per'i·car'pi·al adj.**

per·i·cra·ni·um (per'ə krā'nē əm) **n.,** *pl.* -ni·a (-ə) [ModL. < Gr. < *peri-*, around + *kranion*, skull] the tough membrane covering the skull

per·i·dot (per'ə dot') **n.** [Fr. *péridot* < MFr. *peritot* < ?] a variety of yellowish-green olivine, used as a gem

per·i·gee (per'ə jē') **n.** [< Fr. < ModL. < Gr. < *peri-*, near + *gē*, earth] 1. the point nearest to the earth, the moon, or another planet, in the orbit of a satellite or spacecraft around it 2. the lowest or nearest point —**per'i·ge'an, per'·i·ge'al adj.**

per·i·he·li·on (per'ə hē'lē ən, -hēl'yən) **n.,** *pl.* -li·ons, -li·a (-ə) [ModL. < Gr. *peri-*, around + *hēlios*, the sun] the point nearest the sun in the orbit around it of a planet, comet, or man-made satellite: cf. APHELION

per·il (per′əl) *n.* [OFr. < L. *periculum*, danger] **1.** exposure to harm or injury; danger **2.** something that may cause harm or injury —*vt.* **-illed, -il·ling** to expose to danger —**at your peril** accept the consequences of your action, etc.

per·il·ous (-əs) *adj.* involving peril or risk; dangerous —**per′il·ous·ly** *adv.* —**per′il·ous·ness** *n.*

per·i·lune (per′ə lōōn′) *n.* [< PERI- & L. *Luna*, the moon] the point nearest to the moon in the elliptical orbit of a man-made satellite in orbit around it

per·im·e·ter (pə rim′ə tər) *n.* [< L. < Gr. < *peri-*, around + *metron*, a measure] **1.** the outer boundary of a figure or area **2.** the total length of this —**per·i·met·ric** (per′ə met′- rik), **per′i·met′ri·cal** *adj.* —**per′i·met′ri·cal·ly** *adv.*

per·i·ne·um (per′ə nē′əm) *n., pl.* **-ne′a** (-ə) [ModL. < LL. < Gr. < *peri-*, around + *inein*, to discharge] the region between the thighs; specif., the small area between the anus and the vulva or the scrotum —**per′i·ne′al** *adj.*

pe·ri·od (pir′ē əd) *n.* [< MFr. < L. < Gr. *periodos*, a cycle < *peri-*, around + *hodos*, way] **1.** the interval between the successive occurrences of an astronomical event, as between two full moons **2.** a portion of time distinguished by certain processes, conditions, etc.; stage [a *period* of change] **3.** any of the portions of time into which a school day, etc. is divided **4.** the full course, or one of the stages, of a disease **5.** the menses **6.** an end or conclusion [death put a *period* to his plans] **7.** a subdivision of a geologic era **8.** *Gram.* a) a sentence, esp. a well-balanced sentence b) *Chiefly U.S.* name for FULL STOP **9.** *Physics* the interval of time necessary for a complete cycle of a regularly recurring motion —*adj.* of or like that of an earlier period or age [*period* furniture]

pe·ri·od·ic (pir′ē od′ik) *adj.* **1.** appearing or recurring at regular intervals [a *periodic* fever] **2.** occurring from time to time; intermittent **3.** of or characterized by periods **4.** of a sentence (**periodic sentence**) in which the essential elements are withheld until the end

pe·ri·od·i·cal (-i k′l) *adj.* **1.** *same as* PERIODIC **2.** published at regular intervals, as weekly, monthly, etc. **3.** of a periodical —*n.* a periodical publication —**pe′ri·od′i·cal·ly** *adv.*

periodic function *Math.* a function which repeats the same values, even though the value of the variable changes

pe·ri·o·dic·i·ty (pir′ē ə dis′ə tē) *n., pl.* **-ties** the tendency or fact of recurring at regular intervals

periodic law the law that properties of chemical elements recur periodically when the elements are arranged in order of their atomic numbers

periodic table an arrangement of the chemical elements according to their atomic numbers, to exhibit the periodic law

per·i·o·don·tal (per′ē ə don′t′l) *adj.* [PERI- + -ODONT + -AL] occurring around a tooth or affecting the gums

per·i·o·don·tics (-tiks) *n.pl.* [*with sing v.*] [see prec. & -ICS] the branch of dentistry concerned with diseases of the bone and tissue supporting the teeth

per·i·os·te·um (per′ē os′tē əm) *n., pl.* **-te·a** (-ə) [ModL. < L. < Gr. < *peri-*, around + *osteon*, a bone] the membrane of connective tissue covering all bones except at the joints —**per′i·os′te·al** *adj.*

per·i·pa·tet·ic (per′i pə tet′ik) *adj.* [< Fr. < L. < Gr., ult. < *peri-*, around + *patein*, to walk] **1.** [P-] of the philosophy or followers of Aristotle, who taught while walking about **2.** walking or moving about; itinerant **3.** of a teacher employed in more than one school, etc. and travelling from one to another —*n.* **1.** [P-] a follower of Aristotle **2.** a person who walks from place to place —**per′i·pa·tet′i·cal·ly** *adv.*

pe·riph·er·al (pə rif′ər əl) *adj.* **1.** of, belonging to, or forming a periphery **2.** *Anat.* of, at, or near the surface of the body **3.** merely incidental; tangential [of *peripheral* interest] —**pe·riph′er·al·ly** *adv.*

pe·riph·er·y (-ē) *n., pl.* **-er·ies** [< MFr. < LL. < Gr. < *peri-*, around + *pherein*, to bear] **1.** a boundary line or outside surface, esp. of a rounded figure **2.** surrounding space or area

pe·riph·ra·sis (pə rif′rə sis) *n., pl.* **-ses′** (-sēz′) [L. < Gr. < *peri-*, around + *phrazein*, to speak] the use of many words where a few would do; roundabout way of speaking: also **per·i·phrase** (per′ə frāz′)

per·i·phras·tic (per′ə fras′tik) *adj.* **1.** of, like, or expressed in periphrasis **2.** *Gram.* formed with a particle or auxiliary verb instead of by inflection, as the phrase *did sing* used for *sang* —**per′i·phras′ti·cal·ly** *adv.*

pe·rique (pə rēk′) *n.* [AmFr.] a strong, rich black tobacco grown in Louisiana, U.S, and used in blending

per·i·sarc (per′ə särk′) *n.* [< PERI- + Gr. *sarx*, flesh] the tough, nonliving, outer skeleton layer of many hydroid colonies

per·i·scope (per′ə skōp′) *n.* [PERI- + -SCOPE] an optical instrument consisting of a tube equipped with lenses and mirrors or prisms, so arranged that a person looking through one end can see objects reflected at the other end: used on submerged submarines, etc. —**per′i·scop′ic** (-skop′ik) *adj.*

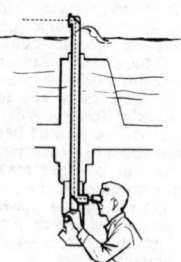

PERISCOPE

per·ish (per′ish) *vi.* [< OFr. < L. *perire*, to perish < *per-*, intens. + *ire*, to go] **1.** to be destroyed, ruined, or wiped out **2.** to die; esp., to die a violent or untimely death **3.** to decay; moulder: said esp. of rubber —*n.* [Aust.] a state of dying of thirst, hunger, etc. —**perish the thought!** do not even consider such a possibility!

per·ish·a·ble (-ə b′l) *adj.* that may perish; esp., liable to spoil, as some foods —*n.* something, esp. a food, liable to spoil or deteriorate —**per′ish·a·bil′i·ty, per′ish·a·ble·ness** *n.*

per·ish·er (-ər) *n.* [Colloq.] a person who is a nuisance, pest, etc., esp. a child

per·ish·ing (-iŋ) *adj.* **1.** extremely cold **2.** [Slang] blasted; confounded [a *perishing* nuisance]

pe·ris·so·dac·tyl (pə ris′ə dak′til) *adj.* [ModL. *perissodactylus* < Gr. *perissos*, uneven + *daktylos*, finger] having an uneven number of toes on each foot —*n.* any of a number of hoofed mammals with an uneven number of toes on each foot, including the horse, tapir, etc.

pe·ris·ta·lith (pə ris′tə lith) *n.* [< Gr. *peri*, around + *statos*, standing + *lithos*, a stone] a ring of standing stones round a prehistoric burial mound

per·i·stal·sis (per′ə stal′sis) *n., pl.* **-ses** (-sēz) [ModL. < Gr. < *peri-*, around + *stellein*, to place] the wavelike muscular contractions and dilations of the walls of the alimentary canal and certain other hollow organs, that move the contents onwards —**per′i·stal′tic** *adj.*

per·i·style (per′ə stīl′) *n.* [< Fr. < L. < Gr. < *peri-*, around + *stylos*, a column] **1.** a row of columns forming an enclosure or supporting a roof **2.** any area so formed, as a court —**per′i·sty′lar** (-stī′lər) *adj.*

per·i·to·ne·um (per′i tən ē′əm) *n., pl.* **-ne′a** (-ə), **-ne′ums** [LL. < Gr. < *peri-*, around + *teinein*, to stretch] the serous membrane lining the abdominal cavity and covering the visceral organs —**per′i·to·ne′al** *adj.*

per·i·to·ni·tis (-īt′əs) *n.* inflammation of the peritoneum

per·i·wig (per′ə wig′) *n.* [earlier *perwyke* < Fr. *perruque*, PERUKE] a wig, formerly worn by men

per·i·win·kle[1] (per′ə wiŋ′k′l) *n.* [< OE. < L. *pervinca*] a European creeper with blue, white, or pink flowers, grown as a ground cover

per·i·win·kle[2] (per′ə wiŋ′k′l) *n.* [OE. *pinewincle*] **1.** any of various small saltwater snails having a thick, cone-shaped shell **2.** such a shell

per·jure (pur′jər) *vt.* **-jured, -jur·ing** [< OFr. < L. < *per*, through + *jurare*, to swear] to make (oneself) guilty of perjury —**per′jur·er** *n.*

per·jured (-jərd) *adj.* guilty of, or characterized by, perjury: also **per·jur·i·ous** (pər jur′ē əs)

per·ju·ry (-jər ē) *n., pl.* **-ries** [< OFr. < L. < *perjurus*, false] **1.** the wilful telling of a lie while under oath **2.** the breaking of any oath

perk[1] (purk) *vt.* [< ? ONormFr. *perquer*, to perch] **1.** to raise (the head, ears, etc.) briskly (often with *up*) **2.** to make smart in appearance (often with *up* or *out*) **3.** to give or restore freshness, vivacity, etc. to (usually with *up*) —*vi.* **1.** to straighten one's posture jauntily (with *up*) **2.** to become lively or recover one's spirits (with *up*)

perk[2] (purk) *vt., vi.* *colloq. clip of* PERCOLATE

perk[3] (purk) *n.* *colloq. clip of* PERQUISITE

perk·y (pur′kē) *adj.* **perk′i·er, perk′i·est** **1.** aggressive; self-confident **2.** gay or lively; saucy —**perk′i·ly** *adv.* —**perk′i·ness** *n.*

perm[1] (purm) *n.* *colloq. clip of* PERMANENT WAVE —*vt.* [Colloq.] to give a permanent wave to

perm[2] (purm) *n.* *colloq. clip of* PERMUTATION (sense 2) —*vt.* [Colloq.] to make a permutation of

per·ma·frost (pur′mə frost′) *n.* [PERMA(NENT) + FROST] permanently frozen subsoil

per·ma·nence (pur′mə nəns) *n.* the state or quality of being permanent

per·ma·nen·cy (-nən sē) *n.* **1.** *same as* PERMANENCE **2.** *pl.* **-cies** something permanent

per·ma·nent (-nənt) *adj.* [MFr. < L. prp. of *permanere* < *per*, through + *manere*, to remain] lasting or intended to last indefinitely or for a relatively long time —**per′ma·nent·ly** *adv.*

permanent wave a hair wave, produced by applying heat or chemicals, that is relatively longlasting

permanent way the track of a railway, including the ballast, sleepers, rails, etc.

per·man·ga·nate (pər maŋ′gə nāt′) *n.* a salt of permanganic acid, generally dark purple

per·man·gan·ic acid (pur′man gan′ik) an unstable acid, HMnO₄, that is an oxidizing agent

per·me·a·bil·i·ty (pur′mē ə bil′ə tē) *n.* 1. a being permeable 2. *Physics* a) the measure of ease with which magnetic lines of force are carried b) the rate of diffusion of a fluid through a porous body

per·me·a·ble (pur′mē ə b'l) *adj.* that can be permeated, as by liquids —**per′me·a·bly** *adv.*

per·me·ate (-āt′) *vt.* -**at**′**ed**, -**at**′**ing** [< L. pp. of *permeare* < *per*, through + *meare*, to glide] to pass into or through and affect every part of; spread through [ink *permeates* blotting paper] —*vi.* to spread or diffuse (with *through* or *among*) —**per′me·a′tion, per′me·ance** *n.* —**per′me·a′tive** (-āt′iv) *adj.*

Per·mi·an (pur′mē ən) *adj.* [after *Perm*, former province of Russia] designating or of the seventh and last period of the Paleozoic Era —**the Permian** the Permian Period or its rocks: see GEOLOGY, chart

per·mis·si·ble (pər mis′ə b'l) *adj.* that can be permitted; allowable —**per·mis′si·bil′i·ty** *n.* —**per·mis′si·bly** *adv.*

per·mis·sion (pər mish′ən) *n.* the act of permitting; esp., formal consent; leave

per·mis·sive (-mis′iv) *adj.* 1. giving permission 2. allowing freedom; indulgent —**per·mis′sive·ly** *adv.* —**per·mis′sive·ness** *n.*

per·mit[1] (pər mit′; for n., usually pur′mit) *vt.* -**mit**′**ted**, -**mit**′-**ting** [< L. < *per*, through + *mittere*, to send] 1. to allow; consent to [smoking is not *permitted*] 2. to give permission to; authorize [to *permit* them to leave the country] 3. to give opportunity for [to *permit* light to enter] —*vi.* to give opportunity [if time *permits*] —*n.* 1. same as PERMISSION 2. a document granting permission; licence —**per·mit′ter** *n.*

per·mit[2] (pur′mit) *n.* [altered (after prec.) < Sp. *palometa*, orig. dim. of *paloma*, dove] an Atlantic pompano found esp. in the Caribbean

per·mit·tiv·i·ty (pur′mi tiv′ə tē) *n.* [< PERMIT + -IVE + -ITY] *Physics* the measure of the ability of a capacitor to store electrical energy

per·mu·ta·tion (pur′myoo tā′shən) *n.* 1. any radical alteration; total transformation 2. a fixed plan or combination for selection of results on football pools 3. *Math.* any one of the total number of groupings, or subsets, into which a group, or set, of elements can be arranged: the permutations of 1, 2, and 3 taken two at a time are 12, 21, 13, 31, 23, 32 —**per′mu·ta′tion·al** *adj.*

per·mute (pər myoot′) *vt.* -**mut**′**ed**, -**mut**′**ing** [< L. *permutare* < *per*-, intens. + *mutare*, to change] 1. to make different; alter 2. to rearrange the order or sequence of —**per·mut′a·ble** *adj.*

per·ni·cious (pər nish′əs) *adj.* [< Fr. < L. < *pernecare* < *per*, thoroughly + *necare*, to kill < *nex* (gen. *necis*), death] 1. causing great injury, destruction, or ruin 2. [Rare] wicked; evil —**per·ni′cious·ly** *adv.* —**per·ni′cious·ness** *n.*

pernicious anaemia a form of anaemia characterized by a reduction of the red blood cells and by gastrointestinal and nervous disturbances, etc.

per·nick·et·y (pər nik′ə tē) *adj.* [< Scot. dial] [Colloq.] 1. too particular or precise; fussy 2. showing or requiring careful treatment

per·o·ne·al (per′ə nē′əl) *adj.* [< ModL. *peroneus* (< Gr. *peronē*, a pin, fibula) + -AL] of or near the fibula

per·o·rate (per′ə rāt′) *vi.* -**rat**′**ed**, -**rat**′**ing** 1. to make a speech, esp. a lengthy oration 2. to sum up or conclude a speech

per·o·ra·tion (per′ə rā′shən) *n.* [< L. < pp. of *perorare* < *per*, through + *orare*, to speak] 1. the concluding part of a speech, including a summing up 2. a bombastic speech

per·ox·ide (pə rok′sīd) *n.* [PER- + OXIDE] any oxide containing the oxygen (O₂) group linked by a single bond; specif., hydrogen peroxide —*vt.* -**id·ed**, -**id·ing** to bleach (hair, etc.) with hydrogen peroxide —*adj.* bleached with hydrogen peroxide

per·pen·dic·u·lar (pur′pən dik′yə lər) *adj.* [< OFr. < L. < *perpendiculum*, plumb line < *per*-, intens. + *pendere*, to hang] 1. at right angles to a given plane or line 2. exactly upright; vertical 3. very steep 4. [P-] of the third and latest style of English Gothic architecture of the 14th to 16th cent., characterized by vertical lines in its tracery —*n.* 1. a line at right angles to another line or plane 2. a perpendicular position —**per′pen·dic′u·lar′i·ty** (-lar′-ə tē) *n.* —**per′pen·dic′u·lar·ly** *adv.*

PERPENDICULAR

per·pe·trate (pur′pə trāt′) *vt.* -**trat**′**ed**, -**trat**′**ing** [< L. pp. of *perpetrare* < *per*, thoroughly + *patrare*, to effect] 1. to do (something evil, criminal, or offensive) 2. to commit (a

blunder), impose (a hoax), etc. —**per′pe·tra′tion** *n.* —**per′-pe·tra′tor** *n.*

per·pet·u·al (pər pe′tyoo wəl, -pech′oo-) *adj.* [< OFr. < L. < *perpetuus*, constant] 1. lasting forever or for an indefinitely long time 2. continuing indefinitely without interruption; constant [a *perpetual* nuisance] —**per·pet′u·al·ly** *adv.*

perpetual check *Chess* the gaining of a draw by repeated checking of the king

perpetual motion the motion of a hypothetical device which, once set in motion, would operate indefinitely by creating its own energy

per·pet·u·ate (pər pe′tyoo wāt, -pech′oo-) *vt.* -**at**′**ed**, -**at**′**ing** to make perpetual; cause to continue or be remembered —**per·pet′u·a′tion** *n.* —**per·pet′u·a′tor** *n.*

per·pe·tu·i·ty (pur′pə tyoo′ə tē) *n.*, *pl.* -**ties** 1. a being perpetual 2. something perpetual, as a pension to be paid indefinitely 3. unlimited time; eternity —**in perpetuity** forever

per·plex (pər pleks′) *vt.* [< MFr. < L. *perplexus*, confused < *per*, through + pp. of *plectere*, to twist] 1. to make (a person) uncertain, hesitant, etc.; confuse 2. to make intricate or complicated —**per·plexed′** *adj.* —**per·plex′ing** *adj.* —**per·plex′ed·ly** *adv.* —**per·plex′ing·ly** *adv.*

per·plex·i·ty (-plek′sə tē) *n.* 1. the state of being perplexed; bewilderment 2. *pl.* -**ties** something that perplexes

per·qui·site (pur′kwə zit) *n.* [< ML. < pp. of *perquirere*, to obtain < L. < *per*-, intens. + *quaerere*, to seek] 1. something additional to regular profit or pay, resulting from one's employment 2. a tip or gratuity 3. a prerogative or right, by virtue of one's status, position, etc.

per·ry (per′ē) *n.* [ME. *pereye* < MFr. < L. *pirum*, pear] a fermented drink like cider, made from pear juice

Pers. 1. Persia 2. Persian

pers. 1. person 2. personal

per se (pur′sē′, sā′) [L.] by (or in) itself; intrinsically

per second per second for each second every second: used of a rate of acceleration

per·se·cute (pur′sə kyoot′) *vt.* -**cut**′**ed**, -**cut**′**ing** [< MFr. < L. < *persequi*, to pursue < *per*, through + *sequi*, to follow] 1. to afflict constantly so as to injure or distress, esp. for reasons of religion, politics, or race 2. to annoy constantly [*persecuted* by mosquitoes] —**per′se·cu′tion** *n.* —**per′-se·cu′tive** *adj.* —**per′se·cu′tor** *n.*

persecution complex *Psychol.* an acute irrational fear that other people are plotting one's downfall

Per·seus (pur′syoos, -sē əs) [after *Perseus* in Greek Myth. who slew Medusa] a N constellation

per·se·ver·ance (pur′sə vir′əns) *n.* 1. the act of persevering 2. persistence; steadfastness

per·sev·er·ate (pər sev′ə rāt′) *vi.* -**at**′**ed**, -**at**′**ing** to experience or display perseveration

per·sev·er·a·tion (pər sev′ə rā′shən) *n.* the tendency of an idea, experience, or response to persist in an individual

per·se·vere (pur′sə vir′) *vi.* -**vered**′, -**ver**′**ing** [< OFr. < L. < *perseverus* < *per*-, intens. + *severus*, severe] to continue in some effort, course of action, etc. in spite of difficulty, opposition, etc.; persist —**per′se·ver′ing·ly** *adv.*

Per·sian (-zhən, -shən) *adj.* of Persia, its people, their language, etc.; Iranian —*n.* 1. a native or inhabitant of Persia 2. the Iranian language of Iran

Persian cat a variety of domestic cat with long silky hair

Persian lamb 1. the lamb of the karakul sheep 2. the black or grey pelt of newborn karakul lambs, having small, tight curls

Persian rug (or carpet) an Oriental rug made in Persia, with a richly coloured, intricate pattern

per·si·flage (pur′sə fläzh′) *n.* [Fr. < *persifler*, to banter < *per*- (see PER-) + *siffler*, to whistle] 1. a light, frivolous style of writing or speaking 2. talk or writing of this kind

per·sim·mon (pər sim′ən) *n.* [< AmInd.] 1. any of various trees with white flowers, hard wood, and plumlike fruit 2. the fruit, sour and astringent when green, but sweet and edible when ripe

per·sist (pər sist′, -zist′) *vi.* [< MFr. < L. < *per*, through + *sistere*, to cause to stand] 1. to refuse to give up, esp. when faced with opposition 2. to continue insistently, as in repeating a question 3. to endure; remain; last

per·sist·ence (-sis′təns, -zis′-) *n.* 1. a persisting; stubborn continuance 2. a persistent or lasting quality; tenacity: also **per·sist′en·cy**

per·sist·ent (-tənt) *adj.* 1. continuing, esp. in the face of opposition, etc.; stubborn 2. continuing to exist or endure 3. constantly repeated; continued —**per·sist′ent·ly** *adv.*

per·son (pur′s'n) *n.* [< OFr. < L. *persona*, lit., actor's mask, hence a person] 1. a human being; individual man, woman, or child 2. a) a living human body b) bodily appearance [to be neat about one's person] 3. personality; self 4. *Gram.* a) division into three sets of pronouns (**personal pronouns**) and, usually, corresponding verb forms, to identify the subject: see FIRST PERSON, SECOND PERSON, THIRD PERSON b) any of these sets 5. *Law* any individual or incorporated group having certain legal rights and responsibilities —**in person** actually present

-per·son (pur's'n) *a combining form* meaning person (of either sex) in a specified activity: [chair-person]

per·so·na (pər sō'nə) *n.*, *pl.* **-nae** (-nē); for sense 2, **-nas** [L.: see PERSON] 1. [*pl.*] the characters of a drama, novel, etc. 2. *Psychol.* the outer personality presented to others by an individual

per·son·a·ble (pur'sən ə b'l) *adj.* having a pleasing appearance and personality; attractive —**per'son·a·ble·ness** *n.* —**per'son·a·bly** *adv.*

per·son·age (-ij) *n.* 1. an important person 2. any person 3. a character in history, a play, novel, etc.

‡**per·so·na gra·ta** (pər sō'nə grät'ə, grät'ə) [L.] a person who is acceptable or welcome

per·son·al (pur'sən əl) *adj.* 1. private; individual 2. done in person or by oneself [a *personal* interview] 3. involving human beings [*personal* relationships] 4. of the body or physical appearance 5. *a)* having to do with the character, conduct, etc. of a certain person [a *personal* remark] *b)* tending to make personal remarks [to get *personal* in an argument] 6. of or like a person or rational being 7. *Gram.* indicating grammatical person, as the inflectional endings of verbs in Latin and Greek 8. *Law* of property (**personal property**) that is movable or not attached to the land

personal column a part of a newspaper devoted to births, marriages, deaths, personal messages, etc.

per·son·al·i·ty (pur'sə nal'ə tē) *n.*, *pl.* **-ties** 1. the quality or fact of being a person 2. the quality or fact of being a particular person; individuality 3. *a)* distinctive individual qualities of a person, considered collectively *b)* such qualities applied to a group, nation, etc. 4. *a)* the sum of such qualities as impressing others *b)* personal attractiveness 5. a person; esp., a notable person 6. [*pl.*] any offensive remarks aimed at a person

per·son·al·ize (pur'sən ə līz') *vt.* **-ized'**, **-iz'ing** 1. to apply to a particular person, esp. to oneself 2. *same as* PERSONIFY 3. to have marked with one's name or initials [*personalized* stationery]

per·son·al·ly (-ə lē) *adv.* 1. without the help of others; in person 2. as a person [I dislike him *personally*, but admire his art] 3. in one's own opinion 4. as though directed at oneself [to take a remark *personally*]

per·son·al·ty (-əl tē) *n.*, *pl.* **-ties** *same as* PERSONAL PROPERTY: see PERSONAL (sense 8)

‡**per·so·na non gra·ta** (pər sō'nə non grät'ə, grät'ə) [L.] a person who is not acceptable

per·son·ate (pur'sə nāt') *vt.* **-at'ed**, **-at'ing** 1. to act the part of, as in a drama 2. *Law* to assume the identity of with intent to defraud —**per'son·a'tion** *n.* —**per'son·a'tive** *adj.* —**per'son·a'tor** *n.*

per·son·i·fi·ca·tion (pər son'ə fi kā'shən) *n.* 1. a personifying or being personified 2. a person or thing thought of as representing some quality, idea, etc.; perfect example [Cupid is the *personification* of love] 3. a figure of speech in which a thing or idea is represented as a person

per·son·i·fy (pər son'ə fī') *vt.* **-fied'**, **-fy'ing** 1. to think or speak of (a thing) as a person [to *personify* a ship by referring to it as "she"] 2. to symbolize (an abstract idea) by a human figure, as in art 3. to be a symbol or perfect example of (something); typify —**per·son'i·fi'er** *n.*

per·son·nel (pur'sə nel') *n.* [Fr.] 1. persons employed in any work, enterprise, service, etc. 2. a personnel department or office for hiring employees, etc. —*adj.* of or in charge of personnel

per·spec·tive (pər spek'tiv) *adj.* [< LL. < L. *perspicere* < *per*, through + *specere*, to look] 1. of perspective 2. drawn in perspective —*n.* 1. the art of picturing objects or a scene, e.g., by converging lines, so as to show them as they appear to the eye with reference to relative distance or depth 2. *a)* the appearance of objects as determined by their relative distance and positions *b)* the effect of relative distance and position 3. the relationship of the parts of a whole, regarded from a particular standpoint or point in time 4. *a)* a specific point of view in judging things or events *b)* the ability to see things in a true relationship —**per·spec'tive·ly** *adv.*

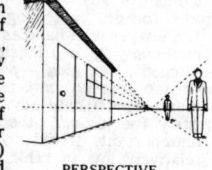

PERSPECTIVE

per·spex (pur'speks) *a trademark for* a hard transparent plastic, an acrylic resin —*n.* [p-] this plastic

per·spi·ca·cious (pur'spə kā'shəs) *adj.* [L. *perspicax* < *perspicere*: see PERSPECTIVE] having keen judgment or understanding; discerning —**per'spi·ca'cious·ly** *adv.* —**per'spi·cac'i·ty** (-kas'ə tē), **per'spi·ca'cious·ness** *n.*

per·spic·u·ous (pər spik'yoo wəs) *adj.* [L. *perspicuus*, transparent < *perspicere*: see PERSPECTIVE] clear in statement or expression; easily understood —**per·spi·cu·i·ty**

(pur'spə kyoo'ə tē), **per·spic'u·ous·ness** *n.* —**per·spic'- u·ous·ly** *adv.*

per·spi·ra·tion (pur'spə rā'shən) *n.* [Fr.] 1. a perspiring; sweating 2. sweat —**per·spir·a·to·ry** (pər spīr'ə tər ē) *adj.*

per·spire (pər spīr') *vt.*, *vi.* **-spired'**, **-spir'ing** [< Fr. < L. *perspirare* < *per*, through + *spirare*, to breathe] to give forth (a characteristic salty moisture) through the pores of the skin; sweat

per·suade (pər swād') *vt.* **-suad'ed**, **-suad'ing** [< MFr. < L. *persuadere* < *per*-, intens. + *suadere*, to urge] to cause to do something, esp. by reasoning, urging, etc.; induce; convince —**per·suad'a·ble**, **per·sua'si·ble** (-swā'sə b'l) *adj.* —**per·suad'er** *n.* —**per·sua'si·bil'i·ty** *n.*

per·sua·sion (pər swā'zhən) *n.* 1. a persuading or being persuaded 2. power of persuading 3. a strong belief; conviction 4. *a)* a particular religious belief *b)* a particular sect, group, etc. 5. [Colloq.] kind, sex, etc.: used jocularly

per·sua·sive (-siv) *adj.* having the power, or tending, to persuade —**per·sua'sive·ly** *adv.* —**per·sua'sive·ness** *n.*

P E R T Programme Evaluation and Review Technique

pert (purt) [aphetic for *apert* < OFr. < L. *apertus*, open] 1. bold or impudent in speech or behaviour; saucy 2. chic and jaunty 3. [Dial.] lively; brisk —**pert'ly** *adv.* —**pert'ness** *n.*

per·tain (pər tān') *vi.* [< OFr. < L. *pertinere*, to reach < *per*-, intens. + *tenere*, to hold] 1. to belong; be connected or associated; be a part, etc. 2. to be appropriate [conduct that *pertains* to a lady] 3. to have reference; be related [laws *pertaining* to the case]

per·ti·na·cious (pur'tə nā'shəs) *adj.* [< L. *pertinax* (gen. *pertinacis*), firm < *per*-, intens. + *tenax* < *tenere*, to hold] 1. holding firmly or stubbornly to some purpose, belief, or action 2. hard to get rid of; persistent —**per'ti·na'cious·ly** *adv.* —**per'ti·nac'i·ty** (-nas'ə tē) *n.*

per·ti·nent (pur'tən ənt) *adj.* [< MFr. < L. prp. of *pertinere*: see PERTAIN] of or connected with the matter at hand; relevant —**per'ti·nence**, **per'ti·nen·cy** *n.* —**per'ti·nent·ly** *adv.*

per·turb (pər turb') *vt.* [< MFr. < L. < *per*-, intens. + *turbare*, to disturb] 1. to cause to be alarmed, agitated, or upset; disturb or trouble greatly 2. to cause confusion in —**per·turb'a·ble** *adj.* —**per·turb'ed·ly** *adv.* —**per·turb'er** *n.*

per·tur·ba·tion (pur'tər bā'shən) *n.* 1. a perturbing or being perturbed 2. a disturbance 3. *Astron.* an irregularity in the orbit of a heavenly body, caused by the attraction of a body other than the one around which it orbits —**per'- tur·ba'tion·al** *adj.*

per·tus·sis (pər tus'is) *n.* [ModL. < L. *per*-, intens. + *tussis*, a cough] *same as* WHOOPING COUGH

Pe·ru Current (pə roo') a cold current flowing north along the coasts of Chile & Peru: also **Humboldt Current**

pe·ruke (pə rook') *n.* [< Fr. *perruque*] *same as* PERIWIG

pe·rus·al (pə roo'z'l) *n.* a perusing

pe·ruse (pə rooz') *vt.* **-rused'**, **-rus'ing** [prob. < L. *per*-, intens. + ME. *usen*, to use] 1. to read carefully; study 2. to read —**pe·rus'er** *n.*

per·vade (pər vād') *vt.* **-vad'ed**, **-vad'ing** [< L. *pervadere* < *per*, through + *vadere*, to go] 1. to pass through; spread throughout 2. to be prevalent throughout —**per·va'sion** (-vā'zhən) *n.* —**per·va'sive** *adj.* —**per·va'sive·ly** *adv.* —**per·va'sive·ness** *n.*

perve (purv) *n.* [back formation < PERVERT] [Aust. Slang] a pervert —*vi.* **perved**, **perv'ing** [Aust. Slang] to look at with erotic interest

per·verse (pər vurs') *adj.* [< OFr. < L. pp. of *pervertere*: see PERVERT] 1. deviating from what is considered right or good; improper; wicked, etc. 2. persisting in error; stubbornly contrary 3. obstinately disobedient 4. obstinate; stubborn —**per·verse'ly** *adv.* —**per·verse'ness**, **per·ver'si·ty** *n.*, *pl.* **-ties**

per·ver·sion (-vur'zhən, -shən) *n.* 1. a perverting or being perverted 2. something perverted 3. any sexual act or practice considered abnormal

per·vert (pər vurt'; *for n.* pur'vərt) *vt.* [< OFr. < L. < *per*-, intens. + *vertere*, to turn] 1. to lead astray from what is right or good; misdirect; corrupt 2. to misuse 3. to misinterpret; distort 4. to debase —*n.* a perverted person; esp., one who practises sexual perversion —**per·ver'sive** (-vur'siv) *adj.* —**per·vert'ed** *adj.* —**per·vert'er** *n.*

per·vi·ous (pur'vē əs) *adj.* [< L. < *per*, through + *via*, way] 1. allowing passage through; permeable 2. having a mind open to influence, argument etc. —**per'vi·ous·ly** *adv.* —**per'- vi·ous·ness** *n.*

pe·se·ta (pə sāt'ə; *Sp.* pe se'tä) *n.* [Sp., dim. of *peso*, PESO] the monetary unit and a coin of Spain and Equatorial Guinea: see MONETARY UNITS, table

pes·e·wa (pes'ə wä) *n.*, *pl.* **-e·was**, **-e·wa** [< native word *kpesaba*, a seed] *see* MONETARY UNITS, table (Ghana)

pes·ky (pes'kē) *adj.* **-ki·er**, **-ki·est** [prob. var. of *pesty* < PEST + -y²] [U.S. Colloq.] annoying; troublesome —**pes'ki·ly** *adv.* —**pes'ki·ness** *n.*

pe·so (pā'sō; *Sp.* pe'sō) *n.*, *pl.* **- sos** [Sp. < L. pp. of *pendere*, to weigh] the monetary unit of Argentina, Colombia, Cuba, Mexico, the Philippines, etc.: see MONETARY UNITS, table

peso bo·liv·i·a·no (bō lē'vyä'nō) *pl.* **pesos bolivianos** *see* MONETARY UNITS, table (Bolivia)

pes·sa·ry (pes'ər ē) *n.*, *pl.* **-ries** [< LL. < L. < Gr. *pessos*, pebble] a device worn in the vagina to support the uterus or prevent conception

pes·si·mism (pes'ə miz'm) *n.* [< Fr. < L. *pessimus*, superl. of *pejor*, worse] **1.** *a*) the belief that the existing world is the worst possible *b*) the belief that the evil in life outweighs the good **2.** the tendency to expect the worst outcome in any circumstance; a looking on the dark side of things —**pes'si·mist** *n.* —**pes'si·mis'tic** *adj.* —**pes'si·mis'ti·cal·ly** *adv.*

pest (pest) *n.* [< Fr. < L. *pestis*, a plague] **1.** a person or thing that causes trouble, annoyance, etc.; nuisance; specif., any destructive insect, small animal, weed, etc. **2.** [Rare] bubonic plague

pes·ter (pes'tər) *vt.* [< OFr. *empestrer*, orig., to hobble a horse: infl. by prec.] to annoy repeatedly with petty irritations; bother —**pes'ter·er** *n.*

pes·ti·cide (pes'tə sīd') *n.* any chemical used for killing insects, weeds, etc. —**pes'ti·ci'dal** *adj.*

pes·tif·er·ous (pes tif'ər əs) *adj.* [< L. < *pestis*, a plague + *ferre*, to bear] **1.** orig., *a*) bringing or carrying disease *b*) infected with an epidemic disease **2.** dangerous to the welfare of society; evil **3.** annoying; bothersome —**pes·tif'er·ous·ly** *adv.* —**pes·tif'er·ous·ness** *n.*

pes·ti·lence (pes'tə ləns) *n.* [see ff.] **1.** any contagious or infectious disease that is fatal or very harmful, esp. an epidemic of such disease, as bubonic plague **2.** anything, as a doctrine, regarded as harmful —**pes·ti·len'tial** (-tə-len'shəl) *adj.* —**pes'ti·len'tial·ly** *adv.*

pes·ti·lent (-ənt) *adj.* [< L. < *pestis*, plague] **1.** likely to cause death; deadly **2.** dangerous to the security and welfare of society; pernicious **3.** annoying; troublesome —**pes'ti·lent·ly** *adv.*

pes·tle (pes'l) *n.* [< OFr. < L. *pistillum* < *pinsere*, to pound] **1.** a tool used to pound or grind substances, as in a mortar **2.** a heavy bar used in pounding or stamping —*vt.*, *vi.* **-tled, -tling** to pound, grind, crush, etc. as with a pestle

pest·ol·o·gy (pest'ol'ə jē) *n.* the branch of science dealing with pests, esp. insects harmful to animal and plant life

pet¹ (pet) *n.* [orig. Scot. dial.] **1.** an animal that is domesticated and kept as a companion or treated with fondness **2.** a person who is liked or treated better than others; favourite —*adj.* **1.** kept or treated as a pet **2.** especially liked; favourite **3.** greatest; particular [one's pet hatred] **4.** showing fondness [a pet name] —*vt.* **pet'ted, pet'ting 1.** to stroke or pat gently; fondle; caress **2.** to pamper —*vi.* [Colloq.] to kiss, fondle intimately, etc. in making love —**pet'ter** *n.*

pet² (pet) *n.* [< obs. phr. *to take the pet* < ?] a state of sulky peevishness or ill humour

Pet. Peter

pet·al (pet'l) *n.* [< ModL. < Gr. < *petalos*, outspread] any of the component parts, or leaves, of a corolla —**pet'-alled** *adj.* —**pet'al·like'** *adj.* —**pet'al·ous** *adj.*

pe·tard (pi tärd') *n.* [< Fr. < *péter*, ult. < L. *pedere*, to break wind] a metal cone filled with explosives: formerly fastened to walls and gates and exploded to force an opening

pet·cock (pet'kok') *n.* [< obs. *pet*, breaking wind + COCK¹] a small valve for draining excess water or air from pipes, radiators, boilers, etc.

pe·ter¹ (pē'tər) *vi.* [< ?] [Colloq.] to become gradually smaller, weaker, etc. and cease (with *out*)

pe·ter² (pē'tər) *n.* [? < *Peter*, masculine name] [Slang] a safe

pe·ter·man (-mən) *n.* [< *Peter*, masculine name + -MAN] [Slang] a safebreaker

Peter Pan [after the main character in *Peter Pan* by J.M. Barrie] a youthful, boyish, or immature man

Peter's fish the haddock, from the spot on each shoulder, said to be the imprint of St. Peter's fingers

pe·ter·sham (pēt'ər shəm) *n.* [after Lord *Petersham*] **1.** a rough heavy woollen cloth **2.** formerly, an overcoat made of this **3.** a thick, corded ribbon used for stiffening belts, etc.

Peter's pence **1.** an annual tax, orig. of one penny, paid to the papal see by certain English property owners before the Reformation **2.** an annual voluntary donation made by Catholics everywhere to the papal treasury Also **Peter pence**

pet·i·ole (pet'ē ōl') *n.* [< ModL. < L. *petiolus*, dim. of *pes*, a foot] **1.** *Bot.* same as LEAFSTALK **2.** *Zool.* a stalklike part; peduncle —**pet'i·o·lar** (-ə lər) *adj.* —**pet'i·o·late'** (-ə lāt', -lit) *adj.*

pet·it (pet'ē; *Fr.* pə tē') *adj.* [< OFr.: see PETTY] same as PETTY (sense 4)

petit bourgeois **1.** the section of the middle class with the lowest social status and least wealth, as small shopkeepers, etc. **2.** a member of this strata Also **petite bourgeoise, petty bourgeoise**

pe·tite (pə tēt') *adj.* [Fr., fem. of *petit*] small and trim of figure: said of a woman —**pe·tite'ness** *n.*

pe·tit four (pet'ē fôr'; *Fr.* pə tē fōōr') *pl.* **pe·tits fours**

pe·tit fours (pet'ē fôrz'; *Fr.* pə tē fōōr',) **pe·tit fours** (pet'ē fôrz') [Fr. < *petit*, small + *four*, lit., oven] any of various small fancy cakes, usually decorated with fancy icing

pe·ti·tion (pə tish'ən) *n.* [< OFr. < L. *petitio* < *petere*, to ask] **1.** a solemn, earnest request to a superior or to those in authority; entreaty **2.** a formal document making such a request, often signed by a number of persons **3.** something that is asked or entreated **4.** *Law* a written plea asking for specific court action —*vt.* **1.** to address a petition to **2.** to ask for; solicit —*vi.* to make a petition —**pe·ti'tion·ar'y** *adj.* —**pe·ti'tion·er** *n.*

Petition of Rights a declaration by Parliament (1628) in the form of a petition accepted by Charles I the violation of which led to the Civil War

‡**pe·ti·ti·o prin·ci·pi·i** (pi tish'ē ō'prin sip'ē ī) [L., lit., begging of the question] *Logic* assuming the conclusion to be proved as one of the premises

petit jury same as PETTY JURY

petit larceny see LARCENY

pe·tit mal (pə tē'mal'; *Fr.* pə tē màl') [Fr. lit., small ailment] a type of epilepsy in which there are attacks of momentary unconsciousness without convulsions: distinguished from GRAND MAL

petit point **1.** a small diagonal needlepoint stitch used for fine detail **2.** work done with such stitches

pet·rel (pet'rəl) *n.* [? a dim. of masculine name *Peter*, in allusion to St. Peter's walking on the sea] any of various related small, dark, sea birds with long wings; esp., same as STORMY PETREL

pe·tri dish (pē'trē) [after J. *Petri* (1852-1921), G. bacteriologist] [*also* P- d-] a shallow, cylindrical, transparent dish with a cover, used for the culture of microorganisms

pet·ri·fy (pet'rə fī') *vt.* **-fied'**, **-fy'ing** [< Fr. < L. *petra*, a rock + *facere*, to make] **1.** to replace the normal cells of (organic matter) with silica, etc.; re-form as a stony substance **2.** to make rigid; harden or deaden **3.** to paralyse, as with fear; stun —*vi.* to become petrified —**pet'ri·fac'tion** (-fak'shən), **pet'ri·fi·ca'tion** *n.*

pet·ro- [< Gr. *petra* or *petros*] a combining form meaning rock or stone: also, before a vowel, **petr-**

pet·ro·chem·i·cal (pet'rō kem'i k'l) *n.* [PETRO(LEUM) + CHEMICAL] a chemical derived ultimately from petroleum, as ethylene glycol, etc. —**pet'ro·chem'is·try** (-is trē) *n.*

pet·ro·dol·lar (pet'rō dol'ər) *n.* [PETROLEUM + DOLLAR] the dollars earned by a petroleum-exporting country

pe·trog·ra·phy (pi trog'rə fē) *n.* [< ModL.: see PETRO- & -GRAPHY] the science of the description or classification of rocks —**pe·trog'ra·pher** *n.* —**pet'ro·graph·ic** (pet'rə graf'-ik), **pet'ro·graph'i·cal** *adj.*

pet·rol (pet'rəl) *n.* [< Fr. < ML. *petroleum*: see PETROLEUM] a volatile, highly flammable, colourless liquid produced by the distillation of petroleum and used chiefly as a fuel in internal-combustion engines

pet·ro·la·tum (pet'rə lāt'əm, -lat'-) *n.* [ModL. < ff. + -atus: see -ATE¹] a greasy, jellylike substance consisting of a mixture of hydrocarbons obtained from petroleum

pe·tro·le·um (pə trō'lē əm) *n.* [ML. < L. *petra*, a rock + *oleum*, oil] an oily, liquid solution of hydrocarbons, yellowish-green to black in colour, occurring naturally in certain rock strata: it yields paraffin, fuel oil, kerosine, petrol, benzine, etc.

petroleum jelly same as PETROLATUM

pe·trol·o·gy (pi trol'ə jē) *n.* [PETRO- + -LOGY] the study of the composition, structure, and origin of rocks —**pet·ro·log·ic** (pet'rə loj'ik), **pet'ro·log'i·cal** *adj.* —**pet'-ro·log'i·cal·ly** *adv.* —**pe·trol'o·gist** *n.*

pet·ti·coat (pet'i kōt') *n.* [< PETTY + COAT] **1.** a skirt, now esp. an underskirt, worn by women and girls **2.** [Colloq.] a woman or girl —*adj.* of or by women

pet·ti·fog·ger (pet'ē fog'ər) *n.* [PETTY + obs. *fogger* < ?] **1.** a lawyer who handles petty cases, esp. by using unethical methods **2.** a trickster **3.** a quibbler —**pet'ti·fog'** *vi.* **-fogged', -fog'ging** —**pet'ti·fog'ger·y** *n.*

pet·tish (pet'ish) *adj.* [< PET² + -ISH] peevish; petulant; cross —**pet'tish·ly** *adv.* —**pet'tish·ness** *n.*

pet·ty (pet'ē) *adj.* **-ti·er, -ti·est** [OFr. *petit*] **1.** relatively unimportant; trivial **2.** narrow-minded, mean, etc. **3.** relatively low in rank; subordinate **4.** insignificant: used chiefly in law —**pet'ti·ness** *n.*

petty cash a cash fund for incidental expenses

petty jury a group of twelve citizens picked to weigh evidence in and decide the issues of a trial in court: cf. GRAND JURY

petty larceny see LARCENY

petty officer see MILITARY RANKS, table

pet·u·lant (pet'yōō lənt) *adj.* [< L. *petulans* < *petere*, to attack] impatient or irritable, esp. over a petty annoyance —**pet'u·lance, pet'u·lan·cy** *n.* —**pet'u·lant·ly** *adv.*

pe·tu·ni·a (pə tyōōn'yə, -ē ə) *n.* [ModL. < Fr. < Tupi *petun*, tobacco] a plant of the nightshade family, with variously coloured, funnel-shaped flowers

pe·tun·tse (pi tun'tsi, -tōōn'-) *n.* [< Chin. *pe tun tzu*, from *pe*, white + *tun*, heap + *tzu*, offspring] a fine, white, porcelain clay

pew (pyōō) *n.* [< OFr. *puie* < L. pl. of *podium*, balcony < Gr. *podion* < *pous*, a foot] **1.** any of the benches with a back fixed in rows in a church **2.** any of the boxlike enclosures with seats, in some churches, for one family, etc.

pe·wee (pē'wē) *n.* [echoic of its call] any of several small N. American flycatchers

pew·ter (pyōō'tər) *n.* [< OFr. *peautre*] **1.** a dull, silvery-grey alloy of tin with brass, copper, or, esp., lead **2.** articles made of pewter —*adj.* made of pewter

pe·yo·te (pā ōt'ē; *Sp.* pe yô'te) *n.* [AmSp. < Nahuatl *peyotl*, caterpillar, in reference to the downy centre] *same as* MESCAL (sense 3): also **pe·yo'tl** (-'l; *Sp.* -t'l)

pf. 1. perfect **2.** preferred: also **pfd.**

pfen·nig (fen'ig; *G.* pfen'iH) *n.*, *pl.* **-nigs**, G. **-ni·ge** (-i gə) [G., akin to PENNY] *see* MONETARY UNITS, table (Germany)

pg. page

pH (pē'āch') [< Fr. *p(ouvoir)* h(ydrogène), hydrogen power] *a symbol for the degree of acidity* (values from 0 to 7) or alkalinity (values from 7 to 14)

pha·ton, pha·ë·ton (fā'ət'n, fā't'n) *n.* [< L. after the son of Helios in Greek and Roman Myth. who attempted to drive his father's sun chariot] a light four-wheeled carriage with front and back seats and, usually, a folding top

-phage (fāj) [< Gr. *phagein*, to eat] *a combining form meaning eating or destroying*

phag·o- [< Gr. *phagein*, to eat] *a combining form meaning:* **1.** eating or destroying [*phagocyte*] **2.** phagocyte Also, before a vowel, **phag-**

phag·o·cyte (fag'ə sīt') *n.* [prec. + -CYTE] any leucocyte that ingests and destroys other cells, microorganisms, etc. in the blood and tissues —**phag'o·cyt'ic** (-sit'ik) *adj.*

-phagous (fə gəs) [< Gr. *phagein*, to eat] *a combining form meaning that eats (a thing specified)*

-phagy (fə jē) [< ModL. < Gr. *phagein*, to eat] *a combining form meaning the practice of eating (a thing specified)*: also **-pha·gi·a** (fā'jē ə, -jə)

phal·ange (fal'ənj, fāl'-; fə lanj') *n.* [Fr. < *phalanges*, pl. of PHALANX] *same as* PHALANX (sense 4) —**pha·lan·ge·al** (fə lan'jēəl), **pha·lan'gal** (-lan'g'l) *adj.*

pha·lan·ger (fə lan'jər) *n.* [ModL. < Gr. *phalanx*, bone between two joints: with reference to the structure of the hind feet] any of various small Australian marsupials with a long, bushy tail

pha·lanx (fal'aŋks) *n.*, *pl.* **-lanx·es**; also, & for 4 always, **pha·lan·ges** (fə lan'jēz) [L. < Gr., line of battle] **1.** an ancient military formation of infantry in close ranks with shields together **2.** a massed group of individuals **3.** a group of individuals united for a common purpose **4.** any of the bones of the fingers or toes

phal·a·rope (fal'ə rōp) *n.* [Fr. < ModL. < Gr. *phalaris*, coot + *pous*, foot] any of various swimming and wading birds of fresh and salt waters

phal·lic (fal'ik) *adj.* **1.** of or like the phallus **2.** of or relating to phallicism **3.** *same as* GENITAL

phal·li·cism (fal'ə siz'm) *n.* worship of the phallus as a symbol of the male generative power: also **phal'lism**

phal·lus (fal'əs) *n.*, *pl.* **-li** (-ī), **-lus·es** [L. < Gr. *phallos*] an image of the penis as a symbol of generative power

phan·tasm (fan'taz'm) *n.* [< OFr. < L. < Gr. *phantasma* < *phantazein*, to show] **1.** a figment of the mind; esp., a spectre, or ghost **2.** a deceptive likeness —**phan·tas'mal, phan·tas'mic** *adj.*

phan·tas·ma·go·ri·a (fan taz'mə gôr'ē ə) *n.* [< Fr. < Gr. *phantasma*, phantasm + *ageirein*, to assemble] a rapidly changing series of things seen or imagined, as in a dream: also **phan·tas'ma·go'ry**, *pl.* **-ries** —**phan·tas'ma·go'ri·al, phan·tas'ma·go'ric, phan·tas'ma·go'ri·cal** *adj.*

phan·ta·sy (fan'tə sē) *n.*, *pl.* **-sies** *same as* FANTASY

phan·tom (fan'təm) *n.* [< OFr. *fantosme*: see PHANTASM] **1.** something not real that one seems to see; apparition; spectre **2.** something feared **3.** an illusion **4.** a person or thing that is something in appearance but not in fact [a *phantom* of a leader] **5.** any mental image or representation —*adj.* of, like, or constituting a phantom; illusory

phantom limb the illusion that an amputated limb has not been amputated and still experiences sensations, etc.

Phar·aoh (fer'ō) *n.* [ult. < Egypt. *pr-'o*, great house] the title of the rulers of ancient Egypt —**Phar'a·on'ic** (-ā on'-ik), **Phar'a·on'i·cal** *adj.*

Phar·i·sa·ic (far'ə sā'ik) *adj.* **1.** of the Pharisees **2.** [p-] a) observing the letter but not the spirit of religious law b) hypocritical: **phar'i·sa'i·cal** —**phar'i·sa'i·cal·ly** *adv.*

Phar·i·sa·ism (far'ə sā'iz'm) *n.* **1.** the beliefs and practices of the Pharisees **2.** [p-] pharisaic behaviour, character, principles, etc.

Phar·i·see (far'ə sē') *n.* **1.** a member of an ancient Jewish party that carefully observed the written and the oral, or traditional, law **2.** [p-] a pharisaic person —**Phar'i·see'-ism** *n.*

Pharm., pharm. 1. pharmaceutical **2.** pharmacist **3.** pharmacopeia **4.** pharmacy

phar·ma·ceu·ti·cal (fär'mə syōōt'i k'l, -sōōt'-) *adj.* [< LL. < Gr., ult. < *pharmakon*, a medicine] **1.** of pharmacy or pharmacists **2.** of or by drugs Also **phar'ma·ceu'tic** —**phar'ma·ceu'ti·cal·ly** *adv.*

phar·ma·ceu·tics (-iks) *n.pl.* [with sing. v.] *same as* PHARMACY (sense 1)

phar·ma·cist (fär'mə sist) *n.* a person licensed to practise pharmacy; pharmaceutical chemist

phar·ma·cog·no·sy (fär'mə kog'nə sē) *n.* [< Gr. *pharmakon*, a drug + -*gnosia* < *gnosis*, knowledge] the science dealing with properties of crude drugs

phar·ma·col·o·gy (-kol'ə jē) *n.* [< ModL. < Gr. *pharmakon*, a drug] **1.** the study of the preparation, qualities, and uses of drugs **2.** the science dealing with the effects of drugs —**phar'ma·co·log'i·cal** (-kə loj'i k'l), **phar'ma·co·log'ic** *adj.* —**phar'ma·co·log'i·cal·ly** *adv.* —**phar'ma·col'o·gist** *n.*

phar·ma·co·poe·ia (fär'mə kə pē'ə) *n.* [ModL. < Gr. < *pharmakon*, a drug + *poiein*, to make] an authoritative book containing a list of drugs and medicines and the lawful standards for their production, dispensation, etc. —**phar'ma·co·poe'ial** *adj.*

phar·ma·cy (fär'mə sē) *n.*, *pl.* **-cies** [< MFr. < LL. < Gr. < *pharmakon*, a drug] **1.** the art or profession of preparing and dispensing drugs and medicines **2.** a place where this is done; dispensary

pha·ros (fer'os) *n.* [after the lighthouse near Alexandria, Egypt, one of the Seven Wonders of the World] any lighthouse or marine beacon

phar·yn·gi·tis (far'in jīt'əs) *n.* inflammation of the mucous membrane of the pharynx; sore throat

phar·ynx (far'iŋks) *n.*, *pl.* **phar'ynx·es, pha·ryn·ges** (fə rin'-jēz) [ModL. < Gr. *pharynx*] the cavity leading from the mouth and nasal passages to the larynx and oesophagus: see EPIGLOTTIS, illus. —**pha·ryn·ge·al** (fə rin'jē əl, far'ən jē'əl), **pha·ryn'gal** (-riŋ'gəl) *adj.*

phase (fāz) *n.* [< ModL. < Gr. *phasis* < *phainesthai*, to appear] **1.** any stage in the illumination or appearance of the moon or a planet **2.** any stage or form in a series of changes, as in development **3.** aspect; side; part [a problem with many *phases*] **4.** a solid, liquid, or gaseous homogeneous form [ice is a *phase* of H_2O] **5.** the fractional part of a cycle through which a periodic wave, as of light, sound, etc., has advanced at any instant, with reference to a standard position **6.** a characteristic variation in the colour of an animal's fur or plumage, according to season, age, etc. —*vt.* **phased, phas'ing 1.** to plan, introduce, carry out, etc. in phases (often with *in, into*, etc.) **2.** to put in phase —**in** (or **out of**) **phase** in (or not in) synchronization —**phase out** to terminate (an activity) by stages —**pha·sic** (fā'zik) *adj.*

phase modulation *Radio* variation in the phase of a carrier wave in accordance with some signal, as speech

phase-out (fāz'out') *n.* [U.S.] a phasing out; gradual termination, withdrawal, etc.

phat·ic (fat'ik) *adj.* [< Gr. *phatos*, spoken + -IC] of formalistic talk, meaningless sounds, etc. used merely to establish social contact rather than to communicate ideas —**phat'i·cal·ly** *adv.*

Ph.D. [L. *Philosophiae Doctor*] Doctor of Philosophy

pheas·ant (fez''nt) *n.*, *pl.* **-ants, -ant:** see PLURAL, II, D, 1 [< Anglo-Fr. < OFr. < L. < Gr. *phasianos*, lit., (bird) of *Phasis*, river in Asia] **1.** a chickenlike game bird with a long tail and brilliant feathers **2.** any of various birds resembling the pheasant, as the lyre bird, francolin, etc.

phel·lem (fel'em) *n.* [< Gr. *phellos*] *same as* CORK (*n.* 4)

phen- [< Fr. < Gr. *phainein*, to show] *a combining form meaning of or derived from* benzene: also **phe·no-**

phe·nac·e·tin (fi nas'ə tin) *n.* [PHEN- + ACET(O) + -IN[1]] *same as* ACETOPHENETIDIN

PHEASANT
(to 89 cm long, including beak and tail)

phe·no·bar·bi·tal (fē'nə bär'bə tol') *n.* [PHENO- + BARBITAL] an odourless, white powder used as a sedative and antispasmodic: also **phe'no·bar'bi·tone** (-bə tōn)

phe·no·cryst (fē'nə krist, fen'ə-) *n.* [< Fr. < Gr. *phainein*, to show + *krystallos*, crystal] a conspicuous crystal found in porphyritic rock

phe·nol (fē'nol) *n.* [PHEN- + -OL[1]] a white crystalline compound, C_6H_5OH, produced from coal tar and used in making explosives, dyes, etc.: its dilute aqueous solution is commonly called carbolic acid —**phe·no'lic** *adj.*

phe·nol·phthal·ein (fē'nol thal'ēn -fthal'-; -ē ən) *n.* [< PHENOL + NAPHTHALENE] a white to pale-yellow, crystalline powder used as a laxative, in making dyes, and as an acid-base indicator in chemical analysis

phe·nom·e·na (fi nom'ə nə) *n.* *pl. of* PHENOMENON
phe·nom·e·nal (fi nom'ə n'l) *adj.* **1.** of or constituting a phenomenon or phenomena **2.** very unusual; extraordinary —**phe·nom'e·nal·ly** *adv.*
phe·nom·e·nal·ism (-iz'm) *n.* the philosophic theory that all knowledge comes from sense perceptions —**phe·nom'e·nal·ist** *n.*
phe·nom·e·non (fi nom'ə non', -nən) *n.,* *pl.* **-na** (-nə); also, esp. for 3 and 4, **-nons'** [< LL. < Gr. *phainomenon,* neut. prp. of *phainesthai,* to appear] **1.** any fact or experience that is apparent to the senses and can be scientifically described, as an eclipse **2.** the appearance of something experienced as distinguished from the thing in itself **3.** anything extremely unusual **4.** [Colloq.] a person who is extraordinary in some way
phe·no·type (fē'nə tīp') *n.* [G. *Phänotypus*] *Biol.* the manifest characters of an organism collectively, resulting from both its heredity and its environment —**phe'no·typ'ic** (-tip'ik), **phe'no·typ'i·cal** *adj.* —**phe'no·typ'i·cal·ly** *adv.*
phen·yl (fen'il, fē'nil) *n.* [PHEN- + -YL] the monovalent radical, C₆H₅, forming the basis of phenol, benzene, aniline, and some other compounds
phen·yl·al·a·nine (fen'il al'ə nēn', fē'nil-) *n.* an essential amino acid occurring in proteins
phen·yl·ke·to·nu·ri·a (-kēt'ə nyoor'ē ə) *n.* [PHENYL + KETON(E) + -URIA] a genetic disorder of phenylalanine metabolism, which, if untreated, causes severe mental retardation in infants
pher·o·mone (fer'ə mōn') *n.* [< Gr. *pherein,* BEAR¹ + E. -o- + (HOR)MONE] a chemical substance secreted by certain animals, as ants, that produces responses in other individuals in the same species
phew (fyōō, fyoo: *conventionalized pronun.*) *interj.* a breathy sound expressing disgust, surprise, etc.
phi (fī, fē) *n.* [MGr.] the 21st letter of the Greek alphabet (Φ, φ)
phi·al (fī'əl) *n.* [< OFr. < Pr. < ML. < L. < Gr. *phialē,* shallow bowl] a small glass bottle; vial
Phi Be·ta Kap·pa (fī'bāt'ə kap'ə, bēt'ə) **1.** an honorary society of U.S. college students of high scholastic rank founded in 1776 **2.** a member of this society
Phil. 1. Philippians **2.** Philippine
phil·a·del·phus (fil'ə del'fəs) *n.* [ModL. < Gr. *philadelphon,* mock orange] *same as* MOCK ORANGE
phi·lan·der (fi lan'dər) *vi.* [< Gr. < *philos,* loving + *anēr* (gen. *andros*), a man] to make love insincerely: said of a man —**phi·lan'der·er** *n.*
phil·an·throp·ic (fil'ən throp'ik) *adj.* of, showing, or constituting philanthropy; charitable; benevolent; humane: also **phil'an·throp'i·cal** —**phil'an·throp'i·cal·ly** *adv.*
phi·lan·thro·py (fi lan'thrə pē) *n.* [< LL. < Gr. < *philein,* to love + *anthrōpos,* man] **1.** a desire to help mankind, as by gifts to charitable or humanitarian institutions **2.** *pl.* **-pies** a philanthropic act, gift, institution, etc. —**phi·lan'thro·pist** *n.*
phi·lat·e·ly (fi lat'əl ē) *n.* [< Fr. < Gr. *philos,* loving + *ateleia,* exemption from (further) tax taken as equivalent of "postage prepaid"] the collection and study of postage stamps, postmarks, etc. —**phil·a·tel·ic** (fil'ə tel'ik) *adj.* —**phil'a·tel'i·cal·ly** *adv.* —**phi·lat'e·list** *n.*
-phile (fīl, fil) [< Gr. *philos,* loving] a combining form meaning loving, liking, favourably disposed to [*Anglophile*]: also **-phil** (fil)
phil·har·mon·ic (fil'här mon'ik, fil'ər-) *adj.* [< Fr. < Gr. *philos,* loving + *harmonia,* harmony] loving or devoted to music: used in the title of some symphony orchestras —*n.* a specific philharmonic choir, orchestra or society
phil·hel·lene (fil hel'ēn) *n.* [see PHILO- & HELLENE] a friend or supporter of the Greeks or Greece —**phil'hel·len'ic** (-hə len'ik) *adj.*
-phil·i·a (fil'ē ə, fil'yə) [< Gr. *philos,* loving] a combining form meaning **1.** tendency towards [*haemophilia*] **2.** abnormal attraction to [*necrophilia*]
Phi·lip·pic (fi lip'ik) *n.* **1.** any of the orations of Demosthenes against Philip, king of Macedon **2.** [p-] any bitter verbal attack
Phil·ip·pine (fil'ə pēn') *adj.* of the Philippine Islands or their people
Philippine mahogany the reddish wood of various trees of the Philippines and SE Asia
Phil·is·tine (fil'is tīn') *n.* **1.** a member of a non-Semitic people who lived in Philistia and repeatedly warred with the Israelites **2.** [*often* p-] a person regarded as smugly conventional, indifferent to cultural values, etc. —*adj.* **1.** of the ancient Philistines **2.** [*often* p-] smugly conventional, lacking in culture, etc. —**Phil'is·tin·ism** *n.*
Phil·lips (fil'əps) [after H. *Phillips* (? -1958), its U.S. developer] a screwdriver (**Phillips screwdriver**) with a tip that can be used on a screw (**Phillips screw**) that has two slots crossing at the centre of the head
phil·o- [< Gr. *philos,* loving] a combining form meaning loving, liking, having a predilection for [*philology*]: also, before a vowel, **phil-**

phil·o·den·dron (fil'ə den'drən) *n.* [ModL. < Gr. *philos,* loving + *dendron,* a tree] a tropical American climbing plant of the arum family, often with heart-shaped leaves
phi·log·y·ny (fi loj'ə nē) *n.* [< Gr. < *philein,* to love + *gynē,* woman] love of or fondness for women —**phi·log'y·nist** *n.* —**phi·log'y·nous** *adj.*
phi·lol·o·gy (fi lol'ə jē) *n.* [< Fr. < L. < Gr. *philologia,* love of literature < *philein,* to love + *logos,* a word] **1.** the study of literary texts, etc. in order to determine their authenticity, meaning, etc. **2.** *earlier term for* LINGUISTICS —**phil·o·log·i·cal** (fil'ə loj'i k'l), **phil'o·log'ic** *adj.* —**phil'o·log'i·cal·ly** *adv.* —**phi·lol'o·gist** *n.*
phil·o·mel (fil'ə mel') *n.* [< ME. *Philomene* < L. *Philomela* < Gr. *Philomela*] *poetic term for* NIGHTINGALE
philos. philosophy
phi·los·o·pher (fi los'ə fər) *n.* [< OFr. < L. < Gr. < *philos,* loving + *sophos,* wise] **1.** a person who studies or is learned in philosophy **2.** a person who lives by a system of philosophy **3.** *a)* a person who meets difficulties with calmness and composure *b)* a person who philosophizes
philosophers' (or **philosopher's**) **stone** an imaginary substance that alchemists believed would change base metals into gold or silver
phil·o·soph·ic (fil'ə sof'ik) *adj.* **1.** of a philosophy or philosopher **2.** devoted to or learned in philosophy **3.** calm, as in a difficult situation; rational Also **phil'o·soph'i·cal** —**phil'o·soph'i·cal·ly** *adv.*
phi·los·o·phize (fi los'ə fīz') *vi.* **-phized', -phiz'ing 1.** to deal philosophically with abstract matter; reason like a philosopher **2.** to express superficial philosophic ideas, truisms, etc.; esp., to moralize —**phi·los'o·phiz'er** *n.*
phi·los·o·phy (-fē) *n.,* *pl.* **-phies** [< OFr. < L. < Gr.: see PHILOSOPHER] **1.** theory or logical analysis of the principles underlying conduct, thought, knowledge, and the nature of the universe **2.** the general principles of a field of knowledge [the *philosophy* of economics] **3.** a particular system of principles for the conduct of life **4.** *a)* a study of human morals, character, etc. *b)* composure; calmness
-phi·lous (fi ləs) [< Gr. *philos,* loving] a combining form meaning loving, liking
phil·tre (fil'tər) *n.* [< MFr. < L. < Gr. *philtron* < *philein,* to love] **1.** a potion or charm thought to arouse sexual love, esp. towards a specific person **2.** any magic potion —*vt.* [Rare] to charm or arouse with a philtre
phiz (fiz) *n.* [contr. < PHYSIOGNOMY] [Old Slang] a face or facial expression
phle·bi·tis (fli bīt'is) *n.* [see ff. & -ITIS] inflammation of a vein —**phle·bit'ic** (-bit'ik) *adj.*
phleb·o- [< Gr. *phleps* (gen. *phlebos*), a vein] a combining form meaning vein: also, before a vowel, **phleb-**
phle·bot·o·my (fli bot'ə mē) *n.,* *pl.* **-mies** [< OFr. < LL. < Gr.: see prec. & -TOMY] the act of bloodletting as a therapeutic measure —**phle·bot'o·mist** *n.*
phlegm (flem) *n.* [< MFr. < LL. < Gr. *phlegma,* inflammation < *phlegein,* to burn] **1.** the thick secretion of the mucous glands of the respiratory tract, discharged from the throat, as during a cold **2.** [Obs.] that one of the four humours believed to cause sluggishness **3.** *a)* sluggishness *b)* calmness; composure —**phlegm'y** *adj.*
phleg·mat·ic (fleg mat'ik) *adj.* [ult. < Gr. *phlegma:* see prec.] hard to rouse to action; specif., *a)* sluggish; dull *b)* calm; cool Also **phleg·mat'i·cal** —**phleg·mat'i·cal·ly** *adv.*
phlo·em (flō'em) *n.* [G. < Gr. *phloos,* bark] the cell tissue serving as a path for the distribution of food material in a plant
phlo·gis·ton (flō jis'ton, -tən) *n.* [ModL., ult. < Gr. *phlegein,* to burn] an imaginary element formerly believed to cause combustion; principle of fire —**phlo·gis'tic** *adj.*
phlox (floks) *n.* [ModL. < L. < Gr. *phlox,* a flame < *phlegein,* to burn] any of a group of plants, with opposite leaves and white, pink, red, or bluish flowers
-phobe (fōb) [Fr. < L. < Gr. < *phobos,* a fear] a suffix meaning one who fears or hates [*xenophobe*]
pho·bi·a (fō'bē ə) *n.* [< Gr. *phobos,* a fear] an irrational, persistent fear of some particular thing or situation —**pho'bic** *adj.*
-pho·bi·a (fō'bē ə) [see prec.] a combining form meaning fear, dread, hatred [*claustrophobia*]
phoe·be (fē'bē) *n.* [echoic, with sp. after femininine name *Phoebe*] any of several American flycatchers with grey or brown back and a short crest

PHLOX

Phoe·ni·cian (fə nish'ən, -nē'shən) *adj.* of Phoenicia, its people, their language, etc. —*n.* **1.** a native of Phoenicia **2.** the extinct Semitic language of the Phoenicians
phoe·nix (fē'niks) *n.* [< OE. & OFr. *fenix* < L. *phoenix* < Gr. *phoinix*] *Egyptian Myth.* a beautiful bird which lived

for 500 or 600 years and then consumed itself in fire, rising renewed from the ashes: a symbol of immortality

phon (fon) *n.* [< Gr. *phōnē*, a sound] a measure of the apparent loudness of a sound

pho·nate (fō′nāt) *vi.* **-nat·ed, -nat·ing** [< Gr. *phōnē*, a voice + -ATE¹] to utter a voiced sound —**pho·na′tion** *n.*

phone¹ (fōn) *n.* [Gr. *phōnē*, a sound] any single speech sound: a phoneme is composed of phones

phone² (fōn) *n., vt., vi.* phoned, phon′ing *colloq. shortened form of* TELEPHONE

-phone (fōn) [< Gr. *phōnē*, a sound] *a combining form meaning:* **1.** a device producing or transmitting sound [*saxophone*] **2.** a telephone [*radiophone*] **3.** speaking a particular language [*Francophone*]

pho·neme (fō′nēm) *n.* [< Fr. < Gr. *phōnēma*, a sound < *phōnē*, a voice] *Linguis.* a set of similar sounds in a language that are heard as the same sound and represented in phonemic transcription by the same symbol, as the sounds of *p* in *pin, spin,* and *tip* —**pho·ne·mic** (fə nē′mik, fō-) *adj.*

pho·ne·mics (fə nē′miks, fō-) *n.pl.* [with *sing. v.*] **1.** the branch of language study dealing with the phonemic systems of languages **2.** the description and classification of the phonemes of a language —**pho·ne′mi·cist** (-mə sist) *n.*

pho·net·ic (fə net′ik, fō-) *adj.* [< ModL. < Gr. *phōnētos*, to be spoken, ult. < *phōnē*, a sound] **1.** of speech sounds **2.** of phonetics **3.** conforming to pronunciation [*phonetic spelling*] —**pho·net′i·cal·ly** *adv.*

pho·net·ics (-iks) *n.pl.* [with *sing. v.*] **1.** the branch of language study dealing with speech sounds, their production and combination, and their representation by written symbols **2.** the phonetic system of a particular language —**pho·ne·ti·cian** (fō′nə tish′ən), **pho·ne·tist** (fō′nə tist) *n.*

pho·ney (fō′nē) *adj., n.* [Colloq.] *same as* PHONY

phon·ic (fon′ik, fō′nik) *adj.* [< Gr. *phōnē*, a sound] **1.** of, or having the nature of, sound; esp., of speech sounds **2.** of phonics —**phon′i·cal·ly** *adv.*

phon·ics (fon′iks, fō′niks) *n.pl.* [with *sing. v.*] [< prec.] a method of teaching beginners to read by learning the usual sounds of certain letters or groups of letters

phono- [< Gr. *phōnē*, a sound] *a combining form meaning* sound, speech: also, before a vowel, **phon-**

pho·no·gram (fō′nə gram′) *n.* [prec. + -GRAM] a symbol representing a word, syllable, or sound, as in shorthand —**pho′no·gram′ic, pho′no·gram′mic** *adj.*

pho·no·graph (fō′nə graf′) *n.* [PHONO- + -GRAPH] **1.** [U.S.] a gramophone **2.** an early type of gramophone with a cylindrical record and external horn —**pho′no·graph′ic** (-graf′ik) *adj.* —**pho′no·graph′i·cal·ly** *adv.*

pho·nog·ra·phy (fō nog′rə fē) *n.* [PHONO- + -GRAPHY] **1.** a written representation of the sounds of speech **2.** any system of shorthand based on a phonetic transcription of speech

pho·nol·o·gy (fō nol′ə jē, fə-) *n.* [PHONO- + -LOGY] **1.** phonetics or phonemics or, esp., both considered as a system of speech sounds **2.** the study of the changes in speech sounds in a language or dialect —**pho·no·log·i·cal** (fō′nə loj′i k'l), **pho′no·log′ic** *adj.* —**pho′no·log′i·cal·ly** *adv.* —**pho·nol′o·gist** *n.*

pho·non (fō′non) *n.* [PHON(O)- + -on, as in PHOTON] a quantum of sound energy that is a carrier of heat

pho·ny (fō′nē) *adj.* **-ni·er, -ni·est** [< ?] [Colloq.] not genuine; false, counterfeit, pretentious, etc. —*n., pl.* **-nies** [Colloq.] **1.** something not genuine; fake **2.** a person who deceives, dissembles, is insincere, etc.; fraud —**pho′ni·ness** *n.*

-phony (fə nē) [< Gr. *phōnē*, a sound] *a combining form meaning* a (specified kind of) sound: also **-pho·ni·a** (fō′nē ə)

phooey (fōo′ē) *interj.* [echoic of spitting like (or ? <) G. *pfui*] an exclamation expressing contempt, scorn or disgust

-phore (fôr) [< ModL. < Gr. *-phoros* < *pherein*, to bear] *a combining form meaning* bearer, producer

-phor·ous (fər əs) [see prec.] *a combining form meaning* bearing, producing

phos·gene (fos′jēn) *n.* [< Gr. *phōs*, light + -gene (for -GEN)] a colourless, volatile liquid, COCl₂, used as a poison gas, in making dyes, etc.

phos·phate (fos′fāt) *n.* [Fr.] **1.** a salt or ester of phosphoric acid **2.** a fertilizer containing phosphates —**phos·phat′ic** (-fat′ik) *adj.*

phos·pha·tide (fos′fə tīd′) *n.* [PHOSPHAT(E) + -IDE] any of a group of fatty compounds, as lecithin, found in animal and plant cells

phos·phide (-fīd) *n.* a compound consisting of trivalent phosphorus with another element or a radical

phos·phite (-fīt) *n.* [Fr.] a salt or ester of phosphorous acid

phos·pho- [< PHOSPHORUS] *a combining form meaning* phosphorous or phosphoric acid: also **phosph-**

Phos·phor (fos′fər) [see PHOSPHORUS] [Poet.] the morning star, esp. Venus —*n.* [p-] **1.** *same as* PHOSPHORUS: now esp. in **phosphor bronze,** a bronze with a little phosphorus in it **2.** a phosphorescent or fluorescent substance

phos·pho·rate (-fə rāt′) *vt.* **-rat′ed, -rat′ing** to combine or impregnate with phosphorus

phos·pho·resce (fos′fə res′) *vi.* **-resced′, -resc′ing** to show or undergo phosphorescence

phos·pho·res·cence (-res′ns) *n.* [Fr.: see PHOSPHORUS & -ESCENCE] **1.** *a)* the condition or property of giving off light after exposure to radiant energy, as light, X-rays, etc. *b)* such light **2.** a giving off of light without noticeable heat, as from phosphorus —**phos′pho·res′cent** *adj.*

phos·pho·ret·ted (fos′fə ret′id) *adj.* combined or impregnated with phosphorus: also **phos′phut·ret′ted** (-fyoo-)

phos·phor·ic (fos for′ik) *adj.* of, like, or containing phosphorus, esp. with a valence of five

phosphoric acid any of several oxygen acids of phosphorus

phos·pho·ro- *a combining form meaning* phosphorus or phosphorescence: also **phosphor-**

phos·pho·rous (fos′fər əs) *adj.* of, like, or containing phosphorus, esp. with a valence of three

phosphorous acid a white or yellowish, crystalline acid, H₃PO₃, that absorbs oxygen readily

phos·pho·rus (fos′fər əs) *n.* [ModL. < L. *Phosphorus*, morning star < Gr. < *phōs*, a light + *pherein*, to bear] **1.** orig., any phosphorescent substance or object **2.** a nonmetallic chemical element, normally a white, phosphorescent, waxy solid, becoming yellow when exposed to light: it is poisonous and ignites spontaneously at room temperature: when heated in sealed tubes it becomes red, nonpoisonous, and less flammable: symbol, P; at. wt., 30.9738; at. no., 15: a radioactive isotope (**phosphorus 32**) is used in medical treatment, as a tracer in research, etc.

phot (fōt, fot) *n.* [< Gr. *phōs (gen. phōtos), a light*] the cgs unit of illumination, equal to one lumen per square centimetre

pho·tic (fōt′ik) *adj.* [< Gr. *phōs (gen. phōtos), a light* + -IC] **1.** of light, esp. in its effect on organisms **2.** designating or of the upper layer (**photic zone**) in a body of water into which daylight penetrates and influences living organisms

pho·to (fōt′ō) *n., pl.* **-tos** clipped form of PHOTOGRAPH

photo- [< Gr. *phos (gen. phōtos), a light*] *a combining form meaning:* **1.** of or produced by light [*photograph*] **2.** of a photograph or photography

pho·to·chem·is·try (fōt′ō kem′is trē) *n.* the branch of chemistry having to do with the effect of light, etc. in producing chemical action, as in photography —**pho′·to·chem′i·cal** (-i k'l) *adj.*

pho·to·com·po·si·tion (-kom′pə zish′ən) *n.* any of various methods of preparing matter for printing by projecting light images of the letters on a photosensitive surface to produce a negative from which plates can be made —**pho′·to·com·pose′** (-kəm pōz′) *vt.* **-posed′, -pos′ing**

pho·to·con·duc·tive (-kən duk′tiv) *adj.* designating or of a substance, as selenium, whose conductivity varies with the illumination striking it —**pho′to·con·duc′tor** *n.*

pho·to·cop·i·er (fōt′ə kop′ēər) *n.* an instrument which produces photographic copies of matter that is typed, handwritten, etc.

pho·to·cop·y (fōt′ə kop′ē) *n., pl.* **-cop′ies** a photographic copy of printed or other graphic material —*vt.* **-cop′ied, -cop′y·ing** to make a photocopy of

pho·to·de·tec·tor (fōt′ō di tek′tər) *n.* a demodulator that is sensitive to light

pho·to·e·lec·tric (-i lek′trik) *adj.* of or having to do with the electric effects produced by light or other radiation, esp. as in the emission of electrons by certain substances when subjected to radiation of suitable wavelength

photoelectric cell any device in which light controls the electron emission from a cathode, the electrical resistance of an element, etc.: usually used in an electric circuit for mechanical devices, as for opening doors, etc.; electric eye

pho·to·e·lec·tron (-i lek′tron) *n.* an electron emitted by a photoelectric effect

pho·to·en·grav·ing (-in grā′viŋ) *n.* **1.** a photomechanical process by which photographs are reproduced in relief on printing plates **2.** a plate so made **3.** a print from such a plate —**pho′to·en·grave′** *vt.* **-graved′, -grav′ing** —**pho′to·en·grav′er** *n.*

photo finish **1.** a race so close that the winner can be determined only from a photograph at the finish line **2.** any close finish of a game, contest, etc.

pho·to·flash (fōt′ə flash′) *adj. Photog.* designating or of a light, esp. a flashbulb, electrically synchronized with the shutter —*n.* a photoflash bulb, lamp, photograph, etc.

pho·to·flood (-flud′) *adj. Photog.* designating or of a high-intensity electric lamp used for sustained illumination —*n.* a photoflood bulb, lamp, photograph, etc.

photog. **1.** photographic **2.** photography

pho·to·gen·ic (fōt′ə jen′ik) *adj.* [PHOTO- + -GENIC] **1.** giving off light **2.** that looks or is likely to look attractive in photographs: said esp. of a person —**pho′to·gen′i·cal·ly** *adv.*

pho·to·graph (fōt′ə graf′) *n.* a picture made by photography —*vt.* to take a photograph of —*vi.* **1.** to take photographs **2.** to appear (as specified) in photographs [to *photograph* well] —**pho·tog·ra·pher** (fə tog′-rə fər) *n.*

pho·to·graph·ic (fōt′ə graf′ik) *adj.* 1. of or like a photograph or photography 2. used in or made by photography 3. retaining or recalling in precise detail [a *photographic* memory] —**pho′to·graph′i·cal·ly** *adv.*

pho·tog·ra·phy (fə tog′rə fē) *n.* [PHOTO- + -GRAPHY] the art or process of producing images of objects upon a photosensitive surface by the chemical action of light or other radiant energy

pho·to·gra·vure (fōt′ə grə vyoor′) *n.* [Fr.] 1. a photomechanical process by which photographs are reproduced on intaglio printing plates 2. a plate so made 3. a print from such a plate, usually with a satinlike finish

pho·to·li·thog·ra·phy (-li thog′rə fē) *n.* a printing process combining photography and lithography

pho·tol·y·sis (fō tol′ə sis) *n.* [see PHOTO- & -LYSIS] chemical decomposition caused by the action of light —**pho·to·lyt·ic** (fōt′ə lit′ik) *adj.*

pho·to·mechan·i·cal (fōt′ō mə kan′i k'l) *adj.* designating or of any process by which printing plates are made by a photographic method —**pho′to·me·chan′i·cal·ly** *adv.*

pho·tom·e·ter (fō tom′ə tər) *n.* [PHOTO- + -METER] a device used to measure the intensity of light

pho·tom·e·try (-trē) *n.* the measurement of the intensity of light, esp. as a branch of optics —**pho·to·met·ric** (fōt′ə met′-rik) *adj.* —**pho′to·met′ri·cal·ly** *adv.*

pho·to·mon·tage (fōt′ə mon täzh′) *n.* montage done in or with photographs

pho·to·mu·ral (-myoor′əl) *n.* a very large photograph used as a mural

pho·ton (fō′ton) *n.* [PHOT(O)- + (ELECTR)ON] a quantum of electromagnetic energy, as of light, X-rays, etc., having both particle and wave behaviour

pho·to·off·set (fōt′ō of′set′) *n.* a method of offset printing in which the pictures or text are photographically transferred to a metal plate from which inked impressions are made on the rubber roller

pho·to·re·cep·tor (-ri sep′tər) *n.* *Biol.* a sense organ, as an eye, specialized to detect light —**pho′to·re·cep′tive** *adj.*

pho·to·sen·si·tive (-sen′sə tiv) *adj.* reacting or sensitive to radiant energy, esp. to light —**pho′to·sen′si·tiv′i·ty** *n.* —**pho′to·sen′si·tize** (-tīz′) *vt.* -**tized′**, -**tiz′ing**

pho·to·set (fōt′ə set′) *vt.* -**set′**, -**set′ting** to set (matter for printing) by photocomposition

pho·to·sphere (fōt′ə sfir′) *n.* [PHOTO- + SPHERE] the visible surface of the sun —**pho′to·spher′ic** (-sfer′ik) *adj.*

Pho·to·stat (-stat′) [PHOTO- + -STAT] *a trademark for* a device for making photographic copies of printed matter, drawings, etc. directly as positives upon special paper —*n.* [p-] a copy so made —*vt.* [p-] -**stat′ted**, —**stat′ting** to make a photostat of —**pho′to·stat′ic** *adj.*

pho·to·syn·the·sis (fōt′ə sin′thə sis) *n.* the formation in green plants of organic substances, chiefly sugars, from carbon dioxide and water in the presence of light and chlorophyll —**pho′to·syn′the·size′** (-sīz′) *vt.*, *vi.* -**sized′**, -**siz′ing** —**pho′to·syn·thet′ic** (-sin thet′ik) *adj.* —**pho′-to·syn·thet′i·cal·ly** *adv.*

pho·tot·ro·pism (fō tot′rə piz′m) *n.* *Bot.* movement of a part of a plant towards or away from light sources: see HELIOTROPISM —**pho·to·trop·ic** (fōt′ə trop′ik) *adj.*

phrasal verb *Gram.* a phrase consisting of a verb and adverb whose meaning cannot be deduced from the constituents (Ex.: "take in" meaning "deceive")

phrase (frāz) *n.* [< L. *phrasis*, diction < Gr. < *phrazein*, to speak] 1. a manner or style of speech or expression 2. a short, colourful, or forceful expression 3. *Gram.* a sequence of two or more words conveying a single thought or forming a distinct part of a sentence but not containing a subject and predicate: cf. CLAUSE 4. *Music* a short, distinct passage, usually of two, four, or eight bars —*vt.* **phrased**, **phras′ing** 1. to express in words or in a phrase 2. *Music* to mark off (notes) into phrases —**phras′al** *adj.* —**phras′-al·ly** *adv.*

phra·se·o·gram (frā′zē ə gram′) *n.* [PHRASEO(LOGY) + -GRAM] a mark or symbol representing an entire phrase, as in Pitman shorthand

phra·se·ol·o·gy (frā′zē ol′ə jē) *n.*, *pl.* -**gies** [< ModL.: see PHRASE & -LOGY] choice and pattern of words; way of speaking or writing —**phra′se·o·log′i·cal** (-ə loj′i k'l) *adj.* —**phra′se·ol′o·gist** *n.*

phre·net·ic (fri net′ik) *adj.* [< OFr. < L. < Gr. *phrenētikos*, mad] *earlier sp. of* FRENETIC

phren·ic (fren′ik) *adj.* [< Gr. *phrēn* (gen. *phrenos*), midriff & -IC] 1. of the diaphragm 2. [Obs.] of the mind; mental

phre·nol·o·gy (fri nol′ə jē) *n.* [< Gr. *phrēn*, mind + -LOGY] a system, now rejected, by which character and mental faculties are analysed by studying the shape and protuberances of the skull —**phren·o·log·i·cal** (fren′ə loj′i k'l) *adj.* —**phre·nol′o·gist** *n.*

phren·sy (fren′zē) *n.*, *pl.* -**sies**, *vt.* -**sied**, -**sy·ing** *earlier sp. of* FRENZY

Phryg·i·an cap (frij′ē ən) a conical cap of soft material worn during ancient times that became the liberty cap during the French Revolution and was the origin of the papal tiara

phthi·sis (thī′sis, tī′-, fthī′-) *n.* [L. < Gr. < *phthiein*, to waste away] *old term for* any wasting disease, esp. tuberculosis of the lungs —**phthis·ic** (tiz′ik) *adj.*, *n.* —**phthis′i·cal, phthis′ick·y** *adj.*

phut (fut) *n.* [< Hind. *phatna*, to burst] 1. the sound made by a passing bullet 2. the sound of a bladder collapsing —**to go phut** [Colloq.] to collapse; to break down

phy·co·my·cete (fī′kō mī′sēt, -mī sēt′) *n.* [< Gr. *phykos*, seaweed + -MYCETE] any of a class of fungi resembling the algae —**phy′co·my·ce′tous** (-mī sēt′əs) *adj.*

phy·la (fī′lə) *n. pl. of* PHYLUM

phy·lac·ter·y (fi lak′tər ē, -trē) *n.*, *pl.* -**ter·ies** [< ML. < LL. < Gr. *phylaktērion*, a safeguard < *phylassein*, to guard] a small leather case holding slips inscribed with Scripture passages: one is worn on the forehead and one on the left arm by Orthodox or Conservative Jewish men during morning prayer

PHYLACTERIES

-**phyll** (fil) [ModL. < Gr. *phyllon*, a leaf] *a combining form meaning* leaf [*chlorophyll*]

phyl·lo- [< Gr. *phyllon*, a leaf] *a combining form meaning* leaf: also, before a vowel, **phyll-**

phyl·lo·tax·is (fil′ə tak′sis) *n.* [ModL. < prec. + Gr. *taxis*, arrangement] *Bot.* 1. the arrangement of leaves on a stem 2. the study or principles of such arrangement Also **phyl′lo·tax′y** (-sē) —**phyl′lo·tac′tic** (-tik) *adj.*

-**phyl·lous** (fil′əs) [see PHYLLO- & -OUS] *a combining form meaning* having (a specified number or kind of) leaves, leaflets, etc.

phyl·lox·e·ra (fil′ək sir′ə, fi lok′sər ə) *n.*, *pl.* -**rae** (-ē), -**ras** [ModL. < Gr. *phyllon*, a leaf + *xēros*, dry] any of various plant lice that attack the leaves and roots of certain plants, as grapevines

phy·lo- [< Gr. *phylon*, tribe] *a combining form meaning* tribe, race, phylum, etc.: also **phyl-**

phy·log·e·ny (fī loj′ə nē) *n.*, *pl.* -**nies** [< G.: see PHYLO- & -GENY] descent, development, or evolution, as of a species or race: distinguished from ONTOGENY Also **phy·lo·gen·e·sis** (fī′lə jen′ə sis) —**phy′lo·ge·net′ic** (-jə net′ik), **phy′lo·gen′ic** (-jen′ik) *adj.* —**phy′lo·ge·net′i·cal·ly** *adv.*

phy·lum (fī′ləm) *n.*, *pl.* -**la** (-lə) [< Gr. *phylon*, tribe] 1. any principal division of the animal kingdom: sometimes, unofficially, a main subdivision of the plant kingdom 2. *a*) a language stock *b*) loosely, a language family

phys. 1. physical 2. physician 3. physics

phys·ic (fiz′ik) *n.* [< OFr. < L. *physica*, natural science < Gr. < *physis*, nature < *phyein*, to produce] 1. [Archaic] medical science 2. a medicine, esp. a cathartic —*vt.* -**icked**, -**ick·ing** 1. to dose with medicine, esp. with a cathartic 2. to cure; heal

phys·i·cal (fiz′i k'l) *adj.* [< ML. < L.: see prec.] 1. of nature and all matter; natural; material 2. of natural science 3. of or according to the laws of nature 4. of, or produced by the forces of, physics 5. of the body as opposed to the mind —**phys′i·cal·ly** *adv.*

physical chemistry chemistry dealing with physical properties in relation to chemical properties

physical education instruction in the exercise, hygiene, etc. of the human body

physical geography the study of the features and nature of the earth's surface, atmosphere, climate, etc.

physical jerks [Colloq.] physical training

physical science any science dealing with inanimate matter or energy, as physics, chemistry, etc.

physical therapy *same as* PHYSIOTHERAPY

physical training a method of keeping fit by following a course of bodily exercises

phy·si·cian (fə zish′ən) *n.* [< OFr. < L.: see PHYSIC] 1. a person licensed to practise medicine 2. a medical doctor other than a surgeon 3. any person or thing that heals or relieves

phys·i·cist (fiz′ə sist) *n.* a specialist in physics

phys·ics (fiz′iks) *n.pl.* [with *sing. v.* in senses 1 & 2] [transl. of L. *physica*, physics] 1. orig., natural science 2. *a*) the science dealing with the properties, changes, etc. of matter and energy, with energy considered either as continuous (**classical physics**) or as discrete (**quantum physics**) *b*) a specific system of physics 3. physical properties or processes

phys·i·o- [< Gr. *physis*, nature] *a combining form meaning*: 1. nature; natural [*physiography*] 2. physical [*physiotherapy*] Also, before a vowel, **physi-**

phys·i·o·crat (fiz′ē ə krat′) *n.* [Fr.: see PHYSIO- & -CRAT] a believer in the 18th cent. French economic theory that land and its products are the only true sources of wealth, and advocating laissez faire in the economic sphere

phys·i·og·no·my (fiz´ē on´ə mē) *n.* [< MFr. < ML. < Gr. < *physis*, nature + *gnōmōn*, one who knows] **1.** the practice of trying to judge character and mental qualities by observation of bodily, esp. facial, features **2.** facial features, esp. as supposedly indicative of character **3.** outward features —**phys´i·og·nom´ic** (-ə nom´ik), **phys´- i·og·nom´i·cal** *adj.* —**phys´i·og·nom´i·cal·ly** *adv.* —**phys´- i·og´no·mist** *n.*

phys·i·og·ra·phy (fiz´ē og´rə fē) *n.* [PHYSIO- + -GRAPHY] **1.** a description of the features and phenomena of nature **2.** *same as* PHYSICAL GEOGRAPHY —**phys´i·og´ra·pher** *n.* —**phys´i·o·graph´ic** (-ə graf´ik), **phys´i·o·graph´i·cal** *adj.*

physiol. **1.** physiological **2.** physiology

phys·i·ol·o·gy (fiz´ē ol´ə jē) *n.* [< Fr. < L. < Gr.: see PHYSIO- & -LOGY] **1.** the study of the functions and vital processes of living organisms or their parts and organs **2.** the functions and vital processes (*of* an organism, etc.) —**phys´i·o·log´i·cal** (-ə loj´i k'l), **phys´i·o·log´ic** *adj.* —**phys´- i·o·log´i·cal·ly** *adv.* —**phys´i·ol´o·gist** *n.*

phys·i·o·ther·a·py (fiz´ē ō ther´ə pē) *n.* therapy using exercise, massage, heat, etc. instead of drugs —**phys´- i·o·ther´a·pist** *n.*

phy·sique (fi zēk´) *n.* [Fr.] the structure, constitution, strength, or appearance of the body

-phyte (fīt) [< Gr. *phyton*, a plant] *a combining form meaning:* **1.** a plant growing in a (specified) way or place [*sporophyte*] **2.** plantlike [*zoophyte*]

phy·to- [< Gr. *phyton*, a plant] *a combining form meaning* a plant, vegetation: also, before a vowel, **phyt-**

phy·to·pa·thol·o·gy (fīt´ō pa thol´ə jē) *n.* [PHYTO- + PATHOLOGY] the study of plant diseases and their control

pi¹ (pī) *n., pl.* **pies** [< PIE¹] *chiefly U.S. sp. of* PIE²

pi² (pī) *n.* [Gr.] **1.** the sixteenth letter of the Greek alphabet (Π, π) **2. a)** the symbol (π) designating the ratio of the circumference of a circle to its diameter **b)** this ratio, equal to 3.14159265+

pi³ (pī) *adj.* [contr. < PIOUS] [Slang] pious, esp. mawkishly religious

pi·affe (pyaf) *n.* [Fr. < *piaffer*, to strut, prob. of echoic origin] a dressage movement in which the horse performs a slow trot without gaining ground

pi·a ma·ter (pī´ə māt´ər) [ML., lit., gentle mother < L.] the vascular membrane that is the innermost of the three membranes around the brain and spinal cord

pi·an·ism (pē´ən iz'm) *n.* a pianist's technique —**pi·a·nis´tic** *adj.*

pi·a·nis·si·mo (pē´ə nis´ə mō) *adj., adv.* [It., superl. of *piano*, soft] *Music* very soft: a direction to the performer —*n., pl.* **-mos´, -mi´** (-mē´) a pianissimo note or passage

pi·an·ist (pē´ən ist) *n.* a person who plays the piano, esp. skilfully

pi·an·o¹ (pē an´ō, pyan´ō, pyä´nō) *n., pl.* **-os** [It., contr. < *pianoforte*] a large, stringed percussion instrument played from a keyboard: each key operates a felt-covered hammer that strikes and vibrates a rigid steel wire or set of wires

pi·a·no² (pē ä´nō, pyä´-) *adj., adv.* [It., soft, smooth < L. *planus*, smooth] *Music* soft: a direction to the performer —*n., pl.* **-nos** a note or passage played softly

piano accordion an accordion in which the right hand plays a piano-like keyboard rather than studs or buttons: see also ACCORDION

pi·an·o·for·te (pē an´ə fôr´tē) *n.* [It. < *piano*, soft + *forte*, strong] *same as* PIANO¹

Pi·a·no·la (pē´ə nō´lə) *a trademark for* a kind of mechanical piano —*n.* [p-] such a piano

pi·as·tre (pē as´tər) *n.* [< Fr. < It., ult. < L. *emplastrum*, plaster] a unit of currency in Lebanon, Sudan, Syria, and the United Arab Republic: see MONETARY UNITS, table Also, U.S. sp., **pi·as´ter**

pi·az·za (pyat´sə; *It.* pyät´tsä) *n.* [It. < L. *platea*: see PLACE] **1.** in Italy, an open public square, esp. with buildings around it **2.** a covered gallery or arcade **3.** [U.S.] a large, covered porch

pi·broch (pē´brok) *n.* [< Gael. *piobaireachd*, ult. < *piob*, bagpipe] a piece of music for the bagpipe, usually martial but sometimes dirgelike

pi·ca¹ (pī´kə) *n.* [< ? ML., directory: perhaps in reference to the type used in printing it] **1.** a size of type, 12 point **2.** the height of this type, about .42 cm or ¹/₆ inch: used as a measure

pi·ca² (pī´kə) *n.* [ModL. < L. magpie] an abnormal craving to eat substances not fit for food, as clay, paint, etc.

pi·ca·dor (pik´ə dôr´) *n.* [Sp. < *picar*, to prick] in bullfighting, any of the horsemen who prick the bull's neck with a lance to weaken him

pic·a·resque (pik´ə resk´) *adj.* [< Sp. < *pícaro*, a rascal] of or dealing with sharp-witted vagabonds and their adventures [*a picaresque novel*]

pic·a·roon (pik´ə rōōn´) *n.* [Sp. *picaron* < *pícaro*, a rascal] **1.** an adventurous rogue or vagabond: also **picaro** **2.** a pirate or pirate ship —*vt.* to act as a pirate

pic·a·yune (pik´ə yōōn´) *n.* [Fr. *picaillon*, small coin < Pr.] [U.S.] **1.** a coin of small value **2.** anything trivial or

worthless —*adj.* trivial; petty; small or small-minded: also **pic´a·yun´ish**

pic·ca·lil·li (pik´ə lil´ē) *n.* [prob. < PICKLE] a pickle of chopped vegetables, mustard, spices, etc.

pic·ca·nin·ny (pik´ə nin´ē) *n.* [? < Port. *pequenino*, tiny one] **1.** a small child **2.** a small Negro or Aboriginal child

pic·co·lo (pik´ə lō´) *n., pl.* **-los´** [It., small] a small flute, pitched an octave above the ordinary flute —**pic´co·lo´ist** *n.*

pice (pīs) *n., pl.* **pice** [Hindi *paisā*] *see* MONETARY UNITS, table (Nepal)

pick¹ (pik) *n.* [var. of PIKE⁴] **1.** a heavy tool with a long, pointed metal head set at a right angle to the handle, used for breaking up soil, rock, etc. **2.** a pointed instrument for picking [*toothpick*] **3.** *same as* PLECTRUM

pick² (pik) *vt.* [ME. *picken*, akin to ON. *pikka*, to pierce] **1.** to break up, pierce, or dig up (soil, rock, etc.) with something pointed **2.** to make (a hole) with something pointed **3. a)** to dig, probe, or scratch at in trying to remove *b)* to clear something from (the teeth, etc.) in this way **4.** to remove by pulling; specif., to gather (flowers, berries, etc.) **5.** to clear thus, as a tree of its fruit **6.** to eat sparingly or daintily **7.** to pull (fibres, rags, etc.) apart **8.** to choose **9.** to find occasion for (a quarrel or fight) **10. a)** to pluck (the strings on a guitar, etc.) *b)* to play (a guitar, etc.) thus **11.** to open (a lock) with a wire, etc. instead of a key **12.** to steal from (another's pocket, etc.) —*vi.* **1.** to eat sparingly or fussily **2.** to thieve **3.** to use a pick **4.** to gather growing berries, flowers, etc. **5.** to select, esp. in a fussy way —*n.* **1.** a stroke or blow with something pointed **2.** the act of choosing or a thing chosen **3.** the best or most desirable one(s) **4.** the amount of a crop gathered at one time —**pick and choose** to choose or select carefully —**pick apart** (or **to pieces**) **1.** to separate into many parts **2.** to find flaws in by examining critically —**pick a quarrel** to provoke a dispute —**pick at 1.** to eat small portions of, esp. in a fussy way **2.** [Colloq.] to find fault with —**pick off 1.** to pluck **2.** to hit with a carefully aimed shot —**pick on 1.** to choose **2.** [Colloq.] to single out for abuse, criticism, etc. —**pick one's way** to move slowly and cautiously —**pick out 1.** to choose **2.** to single out from among a group; distinguish **3.** to make out (meaning) **4.** to play (a tune) note by note —**pick over** to sort out, item by item —**pick up 1.** to grasp and lift **2.** to get or learn, esp. by chance or casually **3.** to stop for and take along **4.** to take into custody; arrest **5.** to gain (speed) **6.** to regain (health, power, etc.); improve **7.** to resume (an activity, etc.) after a pause **8.** to bring into range of sight, hearing, radio or TV reception, etc. **9.** [Colloq.] to get to know casually, esp. for lovemaking —**pick´er** *n.*

pick·a·back (pik´ə bak´, pik´ē-) *adv., adj.* [var. of *pickapack*, redupl. of PACK¹] *same as* PIGGYBACK

pick·axe (pik´aks´) *n.* [altered (after *axe*) < OFr. *picquois*] a pick with a point at one end of the head and a chisellike edge at the other —*vt., vi.* **-axed´, -ax´ing** to use a pickaxe (on)

PICKAXE

picked (pikt) *adj.* [< PICK²] **1.** selected with care **2.** gathered directly from plants, as berries

pick·er·el (pik´ər əl, pik´rəl) *n., pl.* **-el, -els:** see PLURAL, II, D, 2 [dim. of PIKE³] **1.** a young pike **2.** any of various small N American freshwater fishes related to the pike

pick·et (pik´it) *n.* [< Fr. dim. of *pic*, PIKE²] **1.** a stake, usually pointed, used in a fence, as a hitching post, etc. **2.** a soldier or soldiers stationed to guard troops from surprise attack **3.** a person stationed, as by a trade union, outside a factory, store, public building, etc. to demonstrate protest, keep strikebreakers out, etc. —*vt.* **1.** to enclose with a picket fence **2.** to hitch (an animal) to a picket **3. a)** to post as a military picket *b)* to guard (troops) with a picket **4.** to place pickets, or serve as a picket, at (a factory, etc.) —*vi.* to serve as a picket (sense 3) —**pick´- et·er** *n.* —**pick´et·ing** *n.*

picket fence a fence made of upright stakes

picket line a line of people serving as pickets

pick·ing (pik´in) *n.* **1.** the act of one that picks **2.** [*usually pl.*] something picked, or the amount of this; specif., *a)* small scraps that may be gleaned *b)* something got by effort; returns or spoils

pick·le (pik´'l) *n.* [< MDu. *pekel*] **1.** any brine, vinegar, or spicy solution used to preserve or marinate food **2.** [*usually pl.*] vegetables, such as onions, cucumbers, etc. so preserved **3.** a chemical bath to clear metal of scale, preserve wood, etc. **4.** [Colloq.] an awkward or difficult situation **5.** [Colloq.] a mischievous child —*vt.* **-led, -ling** to treat or preserve in a pickle solution —**pick´ler** *n.*

pick·led (-'ld) *adj.* [Slang] intoxicated; drunk

pick-me-up (pik'mē up') *n.* [Colloq.] a tonic, esp. an alcoholic drink, taken to raise one's spirits

pick·pock·et (-pok'it) *n.* a thief who steals from the pockets of persons, as in crowds

pick·up (pik'up') *n.* 1. a picking up 2. an increasing in speed; acceleration 3. [U.S.] a small, open truck for light loads 4. [Colloq.] a casual acquaintance, as for lovemaking 5. [Colloq.] improvement, as in business 6. [Colloq.] *a)* a stimulant *b)* stimulation 7. *a)* in an electric gramophone, a device producing audio-frequency currents from the vibrations of a needle in a record groove *b)* the pivoted arm holding this 8. *Radio & TV a)* reception of sound or light for conversion into electrical energy in the transmitter *b)* the apparatus used

pick·wick·i·an (pik wik'ē ən) *adj.* 1. relating to, or resembling Mr Pickwick in Charles Dickens' *The Pickwick Papers*, in being naïve or benevolent 2. used with an odd or unusual sense: said of a word or phrase

pick·y (pik'ē) *adj.* **pick'i·er, pick'i·est** [U.S. Colloq.] very fastidious or exacting; fussy

pic·nic (pik'nik) *n.* [< Fr., prob. < *piquer*, to pick + *nique*, a trifle] 1. a pleasure outing, with an outdoor meal 2. [Slang] *a)* a pleasant experience *b)* an easy task —*vi.* **-nicked, -nick·ing** to hold or attend a picnic —**pic'nick·er** *n.*

pi·co- [prob. < It. *piccolo*, small] *a combining form meaning* one billionth

pi·cot (pē'kō) *n., pl.* **-cots** (-kōz) [Fr., dim. of *pic*, a point] any of the small loops in an ornamental edging on lace, ribbon, etc. —*vt., vi.* **-coted** (-kōd), **-cot·ing** (-kō iŋ) to edge with these

pic·ric acid (pik'rik) [< Fr. < Gr. *pikros*, bitter] a poisonous, yellow, crystalline, bitter acid used in dyes, explosives, etc.

Pict (pikt) *n.* any of an ancient people of Great Britain, driven into Scotland by the Britons and Romans —**Pict'ish** *adj., n.*

pic·to·graph (pik'tə gräf') *n.* [< L. *pictus* (see PICTURE) + -GRAPH] 1. a picture or picturelike symbol representing an idea, as in ancient writing 2. a diagram using pictured objects to convey ideas, data, etc. Also **pic'to·gram** —**pic'·to·graph'ic** *adj.* —**pic'to·graph'i·cal·ly** *adv.* —**pic·tog'ra·phy** (-tog'rə fē) *n.*

pic·to·ri·al (pik tôr'ē əl) *adj.* 1. of, containing, or expressed in pictures 2. suggesting a mental image; graphic —*n.* a periodical featuring many pictures —**pic·to'ri·al·i·za'tion** *n.* —**pic·to'ri·al·ize'** *vt.* **-ized', -iz'ing** —**pic·to'ri·al·ly** *adv.*

pic·ture (pik'chər) *n.* [< L. *pictura* < *pictus*, pp. of *pingere*, to paint] 1. *a)* a likeness of an object, person, or scene produced on a flat surface, as by painting or photography *b)* a printed reproduction of this 2. anything resembling or typifying something else [he's the *picture* of health] 3. anything regarded as like a painting, etc. 4. a mental image; idea 5. a vivid description 6. all the facts of an event 7. *same as: a)* TABLEAU *b)* FILM (sense 4) 8. the image on a TV screen —*vt.* **-tured, -tur·ing** 1. to make a picture of by painting, drawing, etc. 2. to make visible; show clearly 3. to describe or explain 4. to imagine —**in** (or **out of**) **the picture** considered as involved (or not involved) in a situation

picture card *same as* COURT CARD

picture hat a woman's wide-brimmed hat with plumes, flowers, etc., like those seen in paintings by Reynolds and Gainsborough

picture moulding 1. the edging used to frame pictures 2. the rail near the ceiling from which framed pictures are hung: also **picture rail**

picture palace a cinema: also **picture house, picture theatre**

picture postcard a postcard with a picture on one side and writing space on the other

pictures (pik'chərz) *n.pl.* [Colloq.] the cinema or a film performance

pic·tur·esque (pik'chə resk') *adj.* 1. like a picture; specif., *a)* having a wild beauty, as mountain scenery *b)* pleasantly unfamiliar; quaint 2. suggesting a mental picture; vivid —**pic'tur·esque'ly** *adv.* —**pic'tur·esque'ness** *n.*

picture tube *same as* TELEVISION TUBE

picture window a large window, esp. in a living room, that seems to frame the outside view

picture writing writing that uses pictographs

pic·tur·ize (pik'chə rīz') *vt.* **-ized', -iz'ing** to portray in a picture, esp. a film —**pic'tur·i·za'tion** *n.*

pid·dle (pid''l) *vi.* **-dled, -dling** [< ?] 1. to trifle or deal in trifles 2. [Colloq.] to urinate —**pid'dler** *n.*

pid·dling (pid'liŋ) *adj.* [Colloq.] trifling; petty

pidg·in (pij'in) *n.* [a supposed Chin. pronun. of BUSINESS] a jargon, as pidgin English, incorporating the vocabulary of one or more languages

pidgin English 1. a simplified form of English with a Chinese or Melanesian syntax, used as a trade language 2. any jargon intermixed with English in a similar way

pi-dog *same as* PYE DOG

pie¹ (pī) *n.* [akin ? to PIE³] a baked dish consisting of fruit, meat, etc. with an under or upper crust, or both —**(as) easy as pie** [Colloq.] extremely easy

pie² (pī) *n.* [< ? prec.] 1. a mixed, disordered collection of printing type 2. any jumble or mixture — *vt.* **pied, pie'ing** to make jumbled; mix up (type)

pie³ (pī) *n.* [OFr. < L. *pica*] *same as* MAGPIE

pie·bald (pī'bôld') *adj.* [PIE³ + BALD] covered with patches or spots of two colours, esp. white and black —*n.* a piebald horse or other animal

piece (pēs) *n.* [OFr. *pece*, prob. < Gaul.] 1. a part broken or separated from the whole 2. a section or quantity of a whole, regarded as complete in itself 3. a single thing, specimen, etc.; specif., *a)* an artistic work, as of music *b)* an action or its result [a *piece* of business] *c)* a firearm *d)* a coin or token *e)* one of a set, as of china *f)* a counter as used in games 4. the quantity or size, as of cloth, manufactured as a unit 5. an amount of work constituting a single job 6. *Chess* any chessman other than a pawn 7. [Dial.] a packed lunch taken to work, esp. a sandwich 8. [Slang] a handgun —*vt.* **pieced, piec'ing** 1. to add pieces to, as in repairing or enlarging 2. to join (*together*) the pieces of, as in mending 3. to unite —**a piece of one's mind** frank criticism, esp. by way of rebuke, censure, etc. —**go to pieces** 1. to fall apart 2. to lose all self-control —**nasty piece of work** an unpleasant person —**of a** (or **one**) **piece** of the same sort; alike —**piece of cake** [Colloq.] something easily obtained or achieved —**piec'er** *n.*

‡pièce de ré·sis·tance (pyes'də rā zēs täns') [Fr., lit. piece of resistance] 1. the principal dish of a meal 2. the main item or event in a series

piece goods textiles made in standard width, usually sold by the metre, or yard

piece·meal (pēs'mēl') *adv.* [< ME. < *pece*, PIECE + -*mele*, a measure] 1. piece by piece; in small amounts or degrees 2. into pieces —*adj.* made or done in pieces or one piece at a time

piece of eight the obsolete Spanish dollar

piece·work (-wurk') *n.* work paid for at a fixed rate (**piece rate**) per piece —**piece'work'er** *n.*

pie chart a graph in the form of a circle divided into sectors in which relative quantities are indicated by the proportionately different sizes of the sectors

pied (pīd) *adj.* covered with spots or patches of two or more colours; piebald; variegated

‡pied-à-terre (pye tà ter') *n., pl.* **pied-à-terre** (pye-) [Fr., lit., foot on the ground] a lodging or dwelling, esp. one used only part time or temporarily

pied·mont (pēd'mont) *adj.* [after *Piedmont*, the region of NW Italy] at the base of a mountain —*n.* a piedmont area, etc.

pie-eyed (pī'īd') *adj.* [Slang] intoxicated; drunk

pie in the sky [Slang] 1. a promise of benefits or a reward in an afterlife or in the remote future 2. a Utopian plan or project

pier (pir) *n.* [ML. *pera*, ult. < ? or akin to L. *petra*, stone] 1. a heavy structure supporting the spans of a bridge 2. a structure built out over water and supported by pillars: used as a landing place, pavilion, etc. 3. *Archit. a)* a heavy supporting column *b)* the part of a wall between windows or other openings *c)* a buttress

pierce (pirs) *vt.* **pierced, pierc'ing** [OFr. *percer*, ult. < L. *per*, through + *tundere*, to strike] 1. to pass into or through as a pointed instrument does; stab 2. to affect sharply the senses or feelings of 3. to make a hole in; perforate; bore 4. to make (a hole), as by boring 5. to break into or through 6. to sound sharply through 7. to penetrate with the sight or mind —*vi.* to penetrate —**pierc'er** *n.* —**pierc'ing·ly** *adv.*

pier glass a tall mirror set in the pier, or wall section, between windows

Pi·er·rot (pē'ə rō'; *Fr.* pye rō') [Fr., dim. of *Pierre*, Peter] a stock comic character in old French pantomime, having a whitened face and loose white pantaloons and jacket

pi·e·tism (pī'ə tiz'm) *n.* religious piety, esp. when exaggerated —**pi'e·tis'tic, pi'e·tis'ti·cal** *adj.* —**pi'e·tis'·ti·cal·ly** *adv.*

pi·e·ty (pī'ə tē) *n., pl.* **-ties** [< OFr. < LL. *pietas* < L. < *pius*, pious] 1. devotion to religious duties and practices 2. loyalty and devotion to parents, family, etc. 3. a pious act, statement, etc.

piezoelectric effect the property exhibited by certain crystals of generating voltage when subjected to pressure, and, conversely, undergoing mechanical stress when subjected to voltage

pi·e·zo·e·lec·tric·i·ty (pē ā'zō i lek'tris'ə tē) *n.* [< Gr. *piezein*, to press + ELECTRICITY] electricity resulting from the piezoelectric effect —**pi·e'zo·e·lec'tric, pi·e'zo·e·lec'·tri·cal** *adj.* —**pi·e'zo·e·lec'tri·cal·ly** *adv.*

pif·fle (pif''l) *n.* [< ?] [Colloq.] talk, action, etc. regarded as insignificant or nonsensical —*interj.* nonsense! —*vi.* **-fled, -fling** to talk or behave in a silly manner —**pif'fling** *adj.*

pig (pig) *n.*, *pl.* **pigs, pig:** see PLURAL, II, D, 1 [ME. *pigge*, orig., young pig] **1.** a domesticated animal with a long, broad snout and a thick, fat body covered with coarse bristles; swine **2.** pork **3.** a person regarded as piggish or like a pig **4.** *a)* an oblong casting of iron, etc. poured from the smelting furnace *b)* the mould used *c)* *clipped form of* PIG IRON **5.** something that is difficult or unpleasant **6.** [Slang] a policeman: a derogatory term —*vi.* **pigged, pig'- ging 1.** to bear pigs **2.** to live like a pig, esp. in the phrase **pig it** —**buy a pig in a poke** to buy an article without prior sight or knowledge of it, usually something of no value

pi·geon¹ (pij'ən) *n.*, *pl.* **-geons, -geon:** see PLURAL, II, D, 1 [< MFr. < LL. *pipio*, chirping bird < *pipire*, to peep] **1.** any of various related birds with a small head, plump body, and short legs, larger than doves **2.** *same as* CLAY PIGEON **3.** a young woman **4.** [Slang] a dupe

pi·geon² (pij'ən) *n.* *same as* PIDGIN —**one's pidgeon** [Slang] one's special concern, or business

pigeon breast a deformity of the human chest, as from rickets, in which the sternum projects sharply like that of a pigeon —**pi'geon-breast'ed** *adj.*

pi·geon·hole (-hōl') *n.* **1.** a small recess for pigeons to nest in **2.** a small, open compartment, as in a desk, for filing papers —*vt.* **-holed', -hol'ing 1.** to put in the pigeonhole of a desk, etc. **2.** to put aside indefinitely; shelve **3.** to classify

pi·geon-toed (-tōd') *adj.* having the toes or feet turned in

pig·ger·y (pig'ər ē) *n.*, *pl.* **-ger·ies** *var. of* PIGSTY

pig·gish (pig'ish) *adj.* like a pig; gluttonous or filthy —**pig'- gish·ly** *adv.* —**pig'gish·ness** *n.*

pig·gy (pig'ē) *n.*, *pl.* **-gies** a little pig: also sp. **pig'gie** —*adj.* **-gi·er, -gi·est** *same as* PIGGISH

pig·gy·back (pig'ē bak') *adv.*, *adj.* [alt. of PICKABACK] on the shoulders or back

piggy bank any small savings bank, often in the form of a pig, with a slot for coins

pig·head·ed (-hed'id) *adj.* stubborn; obstinate —**pig'head'- ed·ly** *adv.* —**pig'head'ed·ness** *n.*

pig iron [see PIG, *n.* 6] crude iron, as it comes from the blast furnace

pig jump [Aust. Slang] to jump from all four legs, keeping them stiff: said of a horse

pig·let (pig'lit) *n.* a little pig, esp. a suckling

pig meat bacon, pork, or ham

pig·ment (pig'mənt) *n.* [< L. *pigmentum* < base of *pingere*, to paint] **1.** colouring matter, usually as an insoluble powder mixed with oil, water, etc. to make paints **2.** colouring matter in the cells and tissues of plants or animals —*vi.*, *vt.* to take on or make take on pigment: also **pig'- ment·ize', -ized', -iz'ing** —**pig'men·tar·y** (-mən tər ē) *adj.*

pig·men·ta·tion (pig'mən tā'shən) *n.* colouration in plants or animals due to pigment in the tissue

Pig·my (pig'mē) *adj.*, *n.*, *pl.* **-mies** *same as* PYGMY

pig·nut (pig'nut') *n.* **1.** any of several bitter-tasting hickory nuts **2.** any tree they grow on **3.** *same as* EARTHNUT

pig·pen (-pen') *n.* [U.S.] *same as* PIGSTY

pig·skin (-skin') *n.* **1.** the skin of a pig **2.** leather made from this

pig·stick·ing (-stik'iŋ) *n.* the hunting of wild boars, esp. on horseback with spears —**pig'stick'er** *n.*

pig·sty (-stī') *n.*, *pl.* **-sties'** a place or pen where pigs are confined

pig swill 1. kitchen or brewery swill given to pigs **2.** any unpleasant looking food Also **pig's wash, pig wash**

pig·tail (-tāl') *n.* **1.** tobacco in a twisted roll **2.** a plait or plaits of hair hanging at the back or sides of the head

pi jaw [Slang] a moral lecture, esp. if it is long and tedious

pi·ka (pī'kə) *n.* [< E. Siberian name] any of various small, rabbitlike mammals of rocky, usually high areas in western N America and in Asia

pike¹ (pīk) *n.* [< Fr. < *piquer*, to pierce < ? L. *picus*, woodpecker] a weapon, formerly used by foot soldiers, with a metal spearhead on a long, wooden shaft —*vt.* **piked, pik'ing** to pierce with a pike —**pike'man** *n.*, *pl.* **-men**

pike² (pīk) *n.*, *pl.* **pike, pikes:** see PLURAL, II, D, 2 [prob. < *pike* (see ff.), from the pointed head] **1.** a slender, voracious, freshwater game fish of northern waters, with a narrow, pointed head and sharp teeth **2.** any of several related fishes **3.** a fish resembling the true pike, as the walleyed pike

pike³ (pīk) *n.* [OE. *pic*, a pickaxe] a spike or point, as the pointed tip of a spear

pike⁴ (pīk) *n.* [ME. prob. < ON. *pik*, akin to OE. *pic*: see prec.] [Dial.] **1.** a peaked summit **2.** a mountain or hill with a peaked summit

pike·staff (pīk'staf') *n.*, *pl.* **-staves** (-stāvz') **1.** the shaft of a pike **2.** a traveller's staff with a sharp point

pi·laf, pi·laff (pi laf', pē'laf) *n.* [Pers. & Turk. *pilāw*] a dish of rice boiled in a seasoned liquid, and usually containing meat or fish

pi·las·ter (pi las'tər) *n.* [< Fr. < It. *pilastro* < L. *pila*, a pile] a rectangular support projecting partially from a wall and treated architecturally as a column, with a base, shaft, and capital

pi·lau, pi·law (pi lô') *n.* *same as* PILAF

pil·chard (pil'chərd) *n.* [earlier *pilcher* < ?] a small saltwater fish of the herring family, the commercial sardine of western Europe

pile¹ (pīl) *n.* [< MFr. < L. *pila*, a pillar] **1.** a mass of things heaped together **2.** a heap of wood, etc. on which a corpse or sacrifice is burned **3.** a large building or group of buildings **4.** [Colloq.] *a)* a large amount or number *b)* a lot of money **5.** *Elec. a)* orig., a series of alternate plates of unlike metals with acid-saturated cloth or paper between them, for making an electric current *b)* any similar arrangement that produces an electric current; battery **6.** *an earlier name for* NUCLEAR REACTOR —*vt.* **piled, pil'ing 1.** to put in a pile; heap up **2.** to cover with a pile; load **3.** to accumulate Often with *up* —*vi.* **1.** to form a pile or heap **2.** to move confusedly in a mass (with *in, out, on*, etc.) —**pile it on** to exaggerate —**pile on the agony** to try and make bad things worse

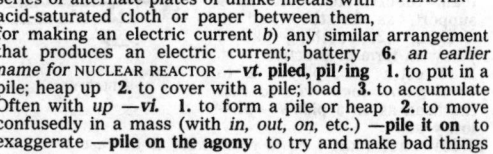

PILASTER

pile² (pīl) *n.* [< L. *pilus*, a hair] **1.** a soft, velvety, raised surface on a rug, fabric, etc., consisting of yarn loops that are often sheared **2.** soft, fine hair, as on wool, fur, etc. —**piled** *adj.*

pile³ (pīl) *n.* [OE. *pil*] **1.** a long, heavy beam driven into the ground, sometimes under water, to support a bridge, dock, etc. **2.** any similar support —*vt.* **piled, pil'ing 1.** to drive piles into **2.** to support with piles

pi·le·ate (pī'lē it, pil'ē-; -āt') *adj.* [< L. < *pileus*, cap] having a crest extending from the bill to the nape, as some birds Also **pi'le·at'ed** (-āt'id)

pile driver (or **engine**) a machine with a drop hammer for driving piles

pile dwelling a building supported by piles, usually in a lake

pi·le·ous (pī'lē əs, pil'ē-) *adj.* [< L. *pilus*, a hair + -EOUS] hairy or furry

piles (pīlz) *n.pl.* [< L. *piloe*, pl. of *pila*, a ball] *same as* HAEMORRHOIDS (see HAEMORRHOID)

pi·le·um (pī'lē əm, pil'ē-) *n.*, *pl.* **-le·a** (-ə) [ModL. < L. *pilleum*, felt cap] the top of a bird's head from the bill to the nape

pile-up (pīl'up') *n.* **1.** a piling up **2.** [Colloq.] a collision involving several vehicles

pi·le·us (pī'lē əs) *n.*, *pl.* **-le·i'** (-ī') [< L. *pilleus* (or *pilleum*), felt cap] *Bot.* the cap of a mushroom, or a similar part of other fungi

pil·fer (pil'fər) *vt.*, *vi.* [MFr. *pelfrer* < *pelfre*, booty] to steal (esp. small sums, petty objects, etc.) —**pil'fer·age** *n.* —**pil'fer·er** *n.*

pil·grim (pil'grim) *n.* [< OFr. < LL. < L. *peregrinus*, foreigner, ult. < *per*, through + *ager*, country] **1.** a wanderer **2.** a traveller to a shrine or holy place **3.** [P-] any member of the band of English Puritans who founded Plymouth colony in Massachusetts, U.S. in 1620

pil·grim·age (-ij) *n.* **1.** a pilgrim's journey, esp. to a shrine, etc. **2.** any similar long journey

Pilgrim Fathers the Pilgrims

pil·ing (pī'liŋ) *n.* **1.** piles collectively **2.** a structure of piles

Pil·i·pi·no (pil'ə pē'nō) *n.* [Tag. < obs. Sp. *Philippino*, FILIPINO] *same as* TAGALOG (sense 2): official national language of the Philippines

pill¹ (pil) *n.* [contr. < L. *pilula*, dim. of *pila*, a ball] **1.** a small ball, tablet, or capsule of medicine to be swallowed whole **2.** a thing that is unpleasant but unavoidable **3.** [Slang] a billiard ball, golf ball, etc. **4.** [Slang] an unpleasant person —*vt.* to dose with pills —**the pill** [Colloq.] a contraceptive taken as a pill by women

pill² (pil) *vt.*, *vi.* [ME. < OE. *pylian* (prob. < L. *pilare*, to make bare of hair) & MFr. *piller*, to rob] **1.** [Archaic] to pillage **2.** [Archaic or Dial.] to peel, skin, etc.

pil·lage (pil'ij) *n.* [< MFr. < *piller*, to rob] **1.** a plundering **2.** booty; loot —*vt.* **-laged, -lag·ing 1.** to deprive of money or property by violence; loot **2.** to take as booty or loot —*vi.* to take loot —**pil'lag·er** *n.*

pil·lar (pil'ər) *n.* [< OFr., ult. < L. *pila*, a column] **1.** a slender, vertical structure used as a support; column **2.** a column standing alone as a monument **3.** a person who is a main support of an institution, movement, etc. —*vt.* to support as with pillars —**from pillar to post** from one predicament, place of appeal, etc. to another

pillar box a pillar-shaped public letter box, usually red and often situated on a pavement

pill·box (pil'boks') *n.* **1.** a small, shallow box, often cylindrical, for pills **2.** a low, enclosed gun emplacement of concrete and steel

pil·lion (pil'yən) *n.* [< Gael. < *peall*, a hide, ult. < L. *pellis*, a skin] **1.** a cushion behind a saddle for an extra rider, esp.

a woman **2.** an extra saddle behind the driver's on a motorcycle —**ride pillion** to travel on the pillion, esp. of a motorcycle

pil·lo·ry (pil'ər ē) *n.*, *pl.* **-ries** [OFr. *pilori*] **1.** a wooden board with holes for the head and hands, in which petty offenders were formerly locked and exposed to public scorn **2.** any exposure to public scorn —*vt.* **-ried**, **-ry·ing 1.** to punish by placing in a pillory **2.** to lay open to public ridicule, scorn, or abuse

PILLORY

pil·low (pil'ō) *n.* [OE. *pyle*] **1.** a cloth case filled with feathers, foam rubber, etc., used as a support, as for the head in sleeping **2.** anything like a pillow in form or function —*vt.* **1.** to rest as on a pillow **2.** to be a pillow for —*vi.* to rest the head as on a pillow —**pil'-low·y** *adj.*

pil·low·case (-kās') *n.* a removable cloth case to cover a pillow: also **pil'low·slip'** (-slip')

pillow fight a mock fight in which participants hit each other with pillows

pi·lose (pī'lōs) *adj.* [< L. < *pilus*, a hair] covered with hair, esp. fine, soft hair: also **pi'lous** (-ləs) —**pi·los·i·ty** (pī-los'ə tē) *n.*

pi·lot (pī'lət) *n.* [< MFr. < It. *pilota*, ult. < Gr. *pēdon*, oar blade] **1.** a steersman; specif., a person licensed to direct or steer ships into or out of a harbour or through difficult waters **2.** a qualified operator of an aircraft **3.** a guide; leader **4.** a device guiding the action of a machine or machine part **5.** *same as* PILOT LIGHT —*vt.* **1.** to act as a pilot of, on, in, or over **2.** to guide; lead —*adj.* **1.** that guides or activates **2.** that serves as a testing unit —**pi'-lot·less** *adj.*

pi·lot·age (-ij) *n.* a piloting, or the fee for it

pilot balloon a small balloon sent up to determine the direction and velocity of the wind

pilot bird 1. a Caribbean sea bird **2.** an Australian bird

pilot fish any of various fishes seemingly acting as pilots, as the remora

pi·lot·house (-hous') *n.* *same as* WHEELHOUSE

pilot lamp an electric lamp placed in an electric circuit to indicate when the current is on

pilot light 1. a small gas burner kept lighted to rekindle a principal burner when needed: also **pilot burner 2.** *same as* PILOT LAMP

pilot officer *see* MILITARY RANKS, table

Pil·sener, Pil·sner (pilz'nər, pils'-) *adj.* [after Pilsen (*Plzeň*), city in Bohemia, where first made] [*often* p-] designating a light, Bohemian lager beer often served in a tall, conical glass (**Pilsener glass**)

pil·ule (pil'yo̅o̅l) *n.* [Fr. < L. *pilula*: see PILL¹] a small pill

pi·men·to (pi men'tō) *n.*, *pl.* **-tos** [< Sp. < L. *pigmentum*, lit., PIGMENT (in VL. & ML., spice)] *same as* ALL-SPICE

pi·mien·to (pi myen'tō, -men'-) *n.* [var. of PIMENTO] a sweet variety of the capsicum pepper, or its red fruit, used as a vegetable, etc.

pimp (pimp) *n.* [prob. < or akin to MFr. *pimper*, to allure] a man who is an agent for prostitutes —*vi.* to act as a pimp

pim·per·nel (pim'pər nel', -nəl) *n.* [< OFr. < LL., ult. < L. *piper*, PEPPER: its fruit resembles peppercorns] any of certain related plants with clustered flowers and leafless stems; esp., the **scarlet pimpernel**, with red, white, or blue, starlike flowers which close in bad weather

pimp·ing (pim'piŋ) *adj.* [< dial. prob. akin to Du. *pimpel*, weak man] **1.** petty; mean **2.** sickly; puny

pim·ple (pim'p'l) *n.* [prob. < or akin to OE. *piplian*, to break out in pimples] any small, rounded, usually inflamed swelling of the skin

pim·ply (pim'plē) *adj.* **-pli·er**, **-pli·est** having pimples: also **pim'pled** (-p'ld)

pin (pin) *n.* [OE. *pinn*] **1.** a peg of wood, metal, etc., used for fastening things together, as a support to hang things, etc. **2.** a little piece of stiff wire with a pointed end and flattened or rounded head, for fastening things together **3.** something worthless or insignificant; trifle **4.** *clipped form of* SAFETY PIN, COTTER PIN, etc. **5.** anything like a pin in form, use, etc. **6.** an ornament, badge, or emblem with a pin or clasp for fastening to clothes **7.** a peg for regulating the tension of a string in a piano, harp, etc. **8.** [Colloq.] the leg: *usually used in pl.* **9.** *Bowling* any of the wooden clubs at which the ball is rolled; skittle **10.** *Golf* a pole with a flag attached, in and marking the hole of a green **11.** *Naut.* a) *same as* THOLE b) a peg or bolt to fasten rigging —*vt.* **pinned**, **pin'ning 1.** to fasten as with a pin **2.** to pierce with a pin **3.** to hold firmly in one position —**pin down 1.** to get (someone) to commit himself as to his

opinion, plans, etc. **2.** to determine or confirm (a fact, details, etc.) —**pin** (something) **on someone** [Colloq.] to lay the blame for (something) on someone

pin·a·fore (pin'ə fôr') *n.* [PIN + AFORE] **1.** an apron, esp. a wraparound one or one with a bib **2.** a sleeveless dress, or skirt with straps and a bib, worn over a sweater or blouse: also **pinafore dress**

pin·ball machine (pin'bôl') a game machine with an inclined board having pins, holes, etc. marked with scores for a spring-driven ball to contact

pince-nez (pans'nā', pins'-; *Fr.* pans nā') *n.*, *pl.* **pince'-nez'** (-nāz'; *Fr.* -nā') [Fr., nose-pincher] eyeglasses without sidepieces, kept in place by a spring gripping the bridge of the nose

pin·cers (pin'sərz) *n.pl.* [*occas. with sing. v.*] [< OFr. *pincier*, to pinch] **1.** a tool with two pivoted parts for gripping or nipping things **2.** a grasping claw, as of a crab —**pin'cer·like'** *adj.*

PINCERS

pinch (pinch) *vt.* [ult. < OFr. *pincier*] **1.** to squeeze as between finger and thumb or between two edges **2.** to nip off the end of (a plant shoot) **3.** to press painfully upon (a part of the body) **4.** to cause distress or discomfort to **5.** to make thin, cramped, etc., as by hunger or cold **6.** to restrict closely; straiten: usually in the passive **7.** [Colloq.] a) to steal b) to arrest —*vi.* **1.** to squeeze painfully **2.** to be stingy or frugal —*n.* **1.** a pinching; squeeze **2.** a quantity graspable between finger and thumb; small amount **3.** distress; hardship **4.** an emergency **5.** [Slang] a) a theft b) an arrest —**pinch pennies** to be very frugal —**pinch'er** *n.*

pinch·beck (pinch'bek') *n.* [after C. *Pinchbeck*, 18th-cent. Brit. jeweller] **1.** an alloy of copper and zinc used to imitate gold in jewellery **2.** anything cheap or imitation —*adj.* of or like pinchbeck

pinch·ers (pin'chərz) *n.pl.* *same as* PINCERS

pinch-hit (pinch'hit') *vi.* **-hit'**, **-hit'ting** [U.S.] **1.** *Baseball* to bat in place of the batter whose turn it is, esp. when a hit is needed **2.** to act as a substitute (*for*) in an emergency —**pinch hitter**

pin·cush·ion (pin'koosh'ən) *n.* a small cushion to stick pins and needles in, to keep them handy

pine¹ (pīn) *n.* see PLURAL, II, D, 3 [OE. *pin* < L. *pinus*, pine tree] **1.** any of various evergreen trees of the pine family: many pines are valuable for wood and for resin, from which turpentine, tar, etc. are obtained **2.** the wood —*adj.* designating a family of trees with needlelike leaves and, usually, woody cones and valuable wood, including the pines, firs, hemlocks, etc.

pine² (pīn) *vi.* **pined**, **pin'ing** [OE. *pinian*, to torment < *pin* < L. *poena*, a pain] **1.** to waste (*away*) with grief, longing, etc. **2.** to have an intense desire; yearn (*for* or *after*)

pin·e·al body (pin'ē əl) [< Fr. < L. *pinea*, a pine cone] a small, cone-shaped body on the dorsal portion of the brain of all vertebrates: its function is obscure

pine·ap·ple (pīn'ap''l) *n.* [ME. *pinappel*, pine cone (see PINE¹ & APPLE)] **1.** a juicy, edible tropical fruit somewhat resembling a pine cone **2.** the plant it grows on, with spiny-edged leaves

pine cone the cone of a pine tree

pine tar a thick, dark liquid obtained from pine wood, used in disinfectants, tar paints, etc.

pin·ey (pī'nē) *adj.* **pin'i·er**, **pin'i·est 1.** abounding in pines **2.** of or like pines

pin·feath·er (pin'feth'ər) *n.* an undeveloped feather that is just emerging through the skin

pin·fold (-fōld') *n.* [OE *pundfald* < *pund*, pound + *fald*, fold] a place where stray animals are confined —*vt.* to gather or confine as if in a pinfold

ping (piŋ) *n.* [echoic] a sharp sound, as of a bullet striking, an engine knocking, etc. —*vi.*, *vt.* to make or cause to make such a sound

Ping-Pong (piŋ'poŋ') [echoic] a *trademark* for table tennis equipment —*n.* [p- p-] *same as* TABLE TENNIS

pin·head (pin'hed') *n.* **1.** the head of a pin **2.** anything tiny or trifling **3.** a stupid or silly person —**pin'head'ed** *adj.* —**pin'head'ed·ness** *n.*

pin·hole (-hōl') *n.* **1.** a tiny hole made as by a pin **2.** a hole into which a pin or peg goes

pin·ion¹ (pin'yən) *n.* [< Fr., ult. < L. *pinna*, bucket of a paddle wheel, lit., feather] a small cogwheel with teeth that fit into a gearwheel or rack

pin·ion² (pin'yən) *n.* [< OFr. < L. *pinna*, a feather] **1.** the end joint of a bird's wing **2.** a wing **3.** any wing feather —*vt.* **1.** to cut off or bind the pinions of (a bird) to keep it from flying **2.** to bind (the wings) **3.** to disable or impede by binding the arms of **4.** to confine

pink¹ (piŋk) *n.* [< ?] **1.** any of certain annual and perennial plants of the pink family **2.** the flower **3.** pale red **4.** the finest example, degree, etc. —*adj.* **1.** designating a family of plants with bright-coloured flowers, including the carnation, sweet william, etc. **2.** pale-red **3.** [Colloq.] somewhat radical politically —**in the pink** [Colloq.] in good physical condition; healthy —**pink′ish** adj. —**pink′-ness** n.

pink² (piŋk) vt. [akin ? to OE. pyngan, to prick] **1.** to ornament (cloth, paper, etc.) by making perforations in a pattern **2.** to cut a saw-toothed edge on (cloth, etc.) to prevent unravelling or for decoration **3.** to prick or stab **4.** to adorn or embellish —**pink′er** n.

pink³ (piŋk) n. [? akin to G. dial. pinke] a young salmon or minnow

pink⁴ (piŋk) n. [< ME. pynk < MDu. pinke] a ship with a narrow stern

pink⁵ (piŋk) vi. [echoic] to make a metallic knocking sound; to knock: said of an internal-combustion engine —**pink′-ing** n.

pink·eye (piŋk′ī′) n. an acute, contagious form of conjunctivitis, in which the eyeball also is inflamed

pink·ie, pink·y (piŋ′kē) n., pl. **pink′ies** [prob. < Du. dim. of pink, little finger] [U.S. & Scot.] the fifth, or smallest, finger

pink·ing shears (piŋ′kiŋ) shears with notched blades, for pinking the edges of cloth, etc.

pink salmon a widespread species of salmon, often tinned

pin money **1.** orig., an allowance given to a wife for small personal expenses **2.** any small sum of money, as for incidental minor expenses

pin·na (pin′ə) n., pl. **-nae** (-ē), **-nas** [L., a feather] **1.** Anat. the external ear **2.** Bot. a leaflet of a pinnately compound leaf **3.** Zool. a feather, wing, fin, etc. —**pin′nal** adj.

pin·nace (pin′is) n. [< Fr. < Sp., ult. < L. pinus, PINE¹] **1.** a small sailing ship **2.** a ship's boat

pin·na·cle (pin′ə k'l) n. [< MFr. < LL. dim. of L. pinna, wing] **1.** a small turret or spire on a buttress, etc. **2.** a slender, pointed formation, as a mountain peak **3.** the highest point; acme —vt. **-cled, -cling** **1.** to set on a pinnacle **2.** to furnish with pinnacles **3.** to form the pinnacle of

pin·nate (pin′āt, -it) adj. [ModL. < L. < pinna, a feather] **1.** resembling a feather **2.** Bot. with featherlike leaflets on each side of a common axis —**pin′nate·ly** adv. —**pin·na′-tion** n.

pin·ny (pin′ē) n. [Colloq.] a pinafore

pi·noch·le, pi·noc·le (pē′nuk′'l, -nok′'l) n. [earlier binochle < G. dial. < Fr. binocle, eyeglasses] [Chiefly U.S.] a card game using a 48-card pack made up of two of every card above the eight

pi·ñon (pin′yən, -yōn; Sp. pē nyôn′) n., pl. **-ñons;** Sp. **-ño′-nes** (-nyô′nes) [< AmSp. < Sp., ult. < L. pinus, PINE¹] **1.** any of several small pines with large, edible seeds, found in western N. America **2.** the seed

pin·point (pin′point′) vt. **1.** to show the location of (a place on a map, etc.) by sticking in a pin **2.** to locate, define, or focus on precisely —n. **1.** the point of a pin **2.** something trifling

pin·prick (-prik′) n. **1.** a tiny hole made as by a pin **2.** a minor irritation or annoyance

pins and needles a prickling feeling as in a numb limb —**on pins and needles** in anxious suspense

pin stripe **1.** a very thin stripe, as in some suits **2.** a pattern of such stripes in parallel

pint (pīnt) n. [< MFr. < ML. pinta: orig. prob. a painted spot marking the level of a measure] **1.** a measure of capacity (liquid or dry) equal to 1/2 quart (0.568 litre) **2.** a pint container Abbrev. **pt., p.**

pin·ta (pīn′tə) n. [< pint of] [Colloq.] a pint, esp. of milk

pin·tail (pin′tāl′) n., pl. **-tails′, -tail′:** see PLURAL, II, D, 1 **1.** any of several ducks, esp. one with long, pointed middle tail feathers **2.** a N American grouse with a long, pointed tail —**pin′tailed′** adj.

pin·tle (pin′t'l) n. [OE. pintel, penis] a pin or bolt upon which some other part pivots or turns

pin·to (pin′tō) adj. [AmSp. < Sp., ult. < L. pp. of pingere, to paint] [U.S.] marked with patches of white and another colour —n., pl. **-tos** [U.S.] a pinto horse

pint-size (pīnt′sīz′) adj. tiny: also **pint′-sized′**

pin tuck a very narrow, ornamental fold in the fabric of a shirt, dress, etc.

pin·up (pin′up′) adj. [Colloq.] designating or of a woman or man whose sexual attractiveness makes her or him a suitable subject for the kind of pictures often pinned up on walls, as of a barracks —n. [Colloq.] a pinup woman or man, picture, etc.

pin·wheel (-wēl′, -hwēl′) n. a firework that revolves when set off

pin·worm (-wurm′) n. a small, unsegmented worm sometimes parasitic in the human large intestine

PINTLE

pin·y (pī′nē) adj. **pin′i·er, pin′i·est** same as PINEY

pi·on (pī′on′) n. [PI² + (MES)ON] any of three mesons, positive, negative, or neutral, with a mass approximately 270 times that of an electron

pi·o·neer (pī′ə nir′) n. [< Fr. < OFr. peonier, foot soldier < peon: see PEON] one who goes before, preparing the way for others, as an early settler or a scientist in research —adj. of a pioneer —vi. to be a pioneer —vt. **1.** to prepare or open (a way, etc.) **2.** to be a pioneer in or of

pi·ous (pī′əs) adj. [L. pius] **1.** having or showing religious devotion **2.** springing from actual or pretended religious devotion **3.** virtuous in a hypocritical way **4.** sacred —**pi′-ous·ly** adv. —**pi′ous·ness** n.

pip¹ (pip) n. [contr. < PIPPIN] a small seed, as of an apple, pear, orange, etc.

pip² (pip) n. [earlier peep < ?] **1.** any of the spots on playing cards, dice, etc. **2.** same as BLIP (sense 1) **3.** the emblem worn by certain officers in the army indicating their rank

pip³ (pip) vi. **pipped, pip′ping** [prob. var. of PEEP¹] to peep or chirp, as a young bird —vt. to break through (the shell): said of a hatching bird

pip⁴ (pip) n. [< MDu., ult. < L. pituita, phlegm] **1.** a contagious disease of fowl, characterized by the secretion of mucus in the throat **2.** [Colloq.] any unspecified human ailment: a jocular usage **3.** [Slang] a bad temper or depression [he gives me the pip]

pip⁵ (pip) vt. **pipped, pip′ping** [< ?] [Colloq.] **1.** to wound, esp. with a gun **2.** to defeat, esp. when victory seemed certain [to pip at the post] **3.** to blackball

pip⁶ (pip) n. [< PIP³] a high-pitched sound, of which a sequence (**the pips**) acts as a time signal, esp. on the radio

pipe (pīp) n. [OE., ult. < L. pipare, to chirp] **1.** a cylindrical tube, as of wood or metal, into which air is blown to make musical sounds; specif., [pl.] same as: a) PANPIPE b) BAGPIPE **2.** any of the tubes in an organ that produce the tones **3.** a boatswain's whistle **4.** a high, shrill sound, as of a birdcall **5.** [often pl.] the vocal organs, esp. as used in singing **6.** a long tube of concrete, metal, etc., for conveying water, gas, oil, etc. **7.** a tubular organ of the body; esp., [pl.] the respiratory organs **8.** anything tubular in form **9.** a) a tube with a small bowl at one end, in which tobacco, etc. is smoked b) enough tobacco, etc. to fill such a bowl **10.** a) a cask holding about 105 gallons (447 litres) b) this volume as a unit of measure —vi. **piped, pip′ing** **1.** to play on a pipe **2.** to utter shrill sounds —vt. **1.** to play (a tune, etc.) on a pipe **2.** to utter in a shrill voice **3.** to bring, call, etc. by piping **4.** to convey (water, oil, etc.) by pipes **5.** to provide with pipes **6.** to trim (a dress, etc.) with piping —**pipe down** [Slang] to become quiet, stop shouting, etc. —**pipe up** **1.** to begin to play or sing (music) **2.** to speak up or say, esp. in a piping voice

pipe clay a white, plastic clay used for making tobacco pipes, whitening leather, etc.

pipe cleaner a short length of wires twisted to hold tiny tufts of yarn, for cleaning pipestems

pipe cutter a tool that is rotated around a metal pipe and cuts it by sharp discs in a curved jaw

pipe dream [Colloq.] a fantastic idea or vain hope, such as an opium smoker might have

pipe fitter a mechanic who installs and maintains plumbing pipes, etc. —**pipe fitting**

pipe·ful (pīp′fool′) n., pl. **-fuls′** the amount (of tobacco, etc.) put in a pipe at one time

pipe·line (-līn′) n. **1.** a line of pipes for conveying water, gas, oil, etc. **2.** any means whereby something is conveyed [a pipeline of information] —vt. **-lined′, -lin′ing** to convey by, or supply with, a pipeline

pipe major the non-commissioned officer in charge of a pipe band

pip emma [Colloq.] the army signallers term for P.M.

pipe organ same as ORGAN (sense 1a)

pip·er (-ər) n. a person who plays on a pipe; esp., a bagpiper —**pay the piper** to suffer the consequences of doing as one pleases

pipe rolls the record of Exchequer accounts kept between 1131 and 1833

pipe·stem (-stem′) n. **1.** the slender stem of a tobacco pipe **2.** anything like this in form

pi·pette (pi pet′) [Fr. dim. of pipe, a pipe] a slender tube for measuring or transferring small amounts of liquids

pi·pi (pē′pē) n. [Maori] a shellfish, in Australia and New Zealand, often mistakenly called cockle

pip·ing (pīp′iŋ) n. **1.** the act of one who pipes **2.** music made by pipes **3.** a shrill sound **4.** a system of pipes **5.** material used for pipes **6.** a narrow, rounded fold of material with which edges or seams are trimmed —adj. **1.** playing on a pipe **2.** shrill —**piping hot** so hot as to sizzle; very hot

pip·is·trelle (pip′i strel′) n. [Fr. < It. < L. vespertilio, bat < vesper, evening] any of various small bats that fly in the early evening

pip·it (pip′it) *n.* [echoic of its cry] a small songbird with a slender bill and streaked breast

pip·kin (pip′kin) *n.* [? dim. of PIPE, *n.* 10] a small earthenware pot

pip·pin (pip′in) *n.* [OFr. *pepin*, seed, pip] any of a number of varieties of apple

pip·sis·se·wa (pip sis′ə wə) *n.* [< Algonquian] a N American evergreen plant with jagged, leathery leaves formerly used in medicine: also called **wintergreen**

pip·squeak (pip′skwēk′) *n.* [PIP³ + SQUEAK] [Colloq.] a person, etc. regarded as small or insignificant

pi·quant (pē′kənt, -känt) *adj.* [Fr. prp. of *piquer*, to prick] **1.** pleasantly sharp or spicy to the taste **2.** exciting interest; stimulating; provocative —**pi′quan·cy** (-kən sē), **pi′quant·ness** *n.* —**pi′quant·ly** *adv.*

pique (pēk) *n.* [Fr. < *piquer*, to prick] **1.** resentment at being slighted; ruffled pride **2.** a fit of displeasure —*vt.* **piqued, piqu′ing** **1.** to arouse resentment in, as by slighting **2.** to arouse (one's curiosity, etc.)

pi·qué (pē kā′) *n.* [Fr., pp. of *piquer*, to prick] a firmly woven cotton fabric with ribbed wales

pi·quet (pi ket′, -kā′) *n.* [Fr. < *pic*, orig., a sting] a game of cards for two, played with 32 cards

pi·ra·cy (pī′rə sē) *n., pl.* **-cies** [< ML.: see PIRATE] **1.** robbery of ships on the high seas **2.** the unauthorized publication or use of a copyrighted or patented work

pi·ra·gua (pi rag′wə, -räg′-) *n.* [Sp. < WInd. (Carib) name] **1.** a canoe made by hollowing out a large log **2.** a flat-bottomed, two-masted sailing boat

pi·ra·nha (pi rän′yə) *n.* [Braz. Port. < Tupi, toothed fish] a small, fiercely voracious freshwater fish of South America

pi·rate (pī′rət) *n.* [< L. < Gr. *peiratēs* < *peirān*, to attack] **1.** a person who practises piracy; esp., a robber of ships on the high seas **2.** a pirates' ship —*vt., vi.* **-rat·ed, -rat·ing** **1.** to practise piracy (upon) **2.** to take (something) by piracy **3.** to publish or reproduce without authorization (a literary work, musical recording, etc.), esp. in violation of a copyright —**pi·rat·i·cal** (pī rat′i k'l), **pi·rat′ic** *adj.* —**pi·rat′i·cal·ly** *adv.*

pi·rogue (pi rōg′) *n.* [< Fr. < Sp. *piragua* < Carib] a canoe made by hollowing out a log

pir·ou·ette (pir′ōō wet′) *n.* [Fr., spinning top; prob. < dial. *piroue*, a top] a whirling around on one foot or the point of the toe, esp. in ballet —*vi.* **-et′ted, -et′ting** to do a pirouette

pis·ca·to·ri·al (pis′kə tôr′ē əl) *adj.* [< L. < *piscator*, fisherman] of fishermen or fishing: also **pis·ca·to·ry** —**pis′ca·to′ri·al·ly** *adv.*

Pis·ces (pī′sēz, pis′ēz) [L., pl. of *piscis*, a fish] **1.** a constellation south of Andromeda **2.** the twelfth sign of the zodiac: see ZODIAC, illus.

pis·ci- [< L. *piscis*, a fish] a combining form meaning fish [*pisciculture*]

pis·ci·cul·ture (pis′i kul′chər) *n.* [prec. + CULTURE] the breeding of fish as a science or industry

pis·cine¹ (pis′īn, -ēn; pī′sēn) *adj.* [< L. *piscis*, a fish] of or resembling fish

pis·cine² (pis′ēn) *n.* [Fr. < L. *pixina*, a tank, fishpond] a swimming pool

pish (psh, pish) *interj., n.* an exclamation of disgust or impatience —*vi., vt.* to make this exclamation (at)

pi·shogue (pi shōg′) *n.* [< Ir. *piseog*, witchcraft] **1.** spell; charm **2.** sorcery

pis·mire (pis′mīr′, piz′-) *n.* [< ME. < *pisse*, urine + *mire*, ant: from the odour of ants' formic acid] an ant

piss (pis) *vi.* [ME. *pissen* < OFr. *pissier*, prob. of echoic origin] to urinate —*vt.* to discharge as or with the urine —*n.* urine Often considered a vulgar term —**piss off** [Slang] *interj.* an expression of dismissal —*vt.* to annoy, irritate —*vi.* to go away; depart Usually considered a vulgar term

pissed (pist) *adj.* [Slang] drunk, intoxicated: often considered a vulgar term

pis·ta·chi·o (pi stä′shē ō′, -stash′ē ō′, -stash′ō) *n., pl.* **-chi·os** [< It. < L. < Gr. *pistakē* < OPer. *pistah*] **1.** a small tree related to the cashew **2.** its edible, greenish seed (**pistachio nut**) **3.** the flavour of this nut **4.** a light yellow-green colour

pis·til (pis′t'l) *n.* [Fr. < L. *pistillum*, PESTLE] the seedbearing organ of a flowering plant, consisting of one carpel or of several united carpels

pis·til·late (pis′tə lit, -lāt′) *adj.* having a pistil or pistils; specif., having pistils but no stamens

pis·tol (pis′t'l) *n.* [< Fr. < G. < Czech *pišt'al*, prob. < *pisk*, a whistling sound] **1.** a small firearm held and fired with one hand **2.** such a firearm in which the chamber is part of the barrel: cf. REVOLVER —*vt.* **-tolled, -tol·ling** to shoot with a pistol

PISTIL

pis·tole (pis tōl′) *n.* [Fr.] **1.** a former Spanish gold coin **2.** any similar obsolete European coin

pis·tol-whip (pis′t'l wip′, -hwip′) *vt.* **-whipped′, -whip′ping** to beat with a pistol, esp. about the head

pis·ton (pis′t'n) *n.* [Fr. < It. < *pistare*, to beat, ult. < L. *pinsere*, to pound] **1.** a disc or short cylinder closely fitted in a hollow cylinder and moved back and forth by the pressure of a fluid so as to transmit reciprocating motion to a rod (**piston rod**), or moved by the rod so as to exert pressure on the fluid **2.** *Music* a sliding valve moved in the cylinder of a brass instrument to change the pitch

piston ring a split metal ring placed around a piston to make it fit the cylinder closely

PISTON

pit¹ (pit) *n.* [Du. < MDu. *pitte*] [U.S.] the stone of various fruits

pit² (pit) *n.* [OE. *pytt*, ult. < L. *puteus*, a well] **1.** a hole in the ground **2.** an abyss **3.** hell: used with *the* **4.** a covered hole used to trap wild animals; pitfall **5.** any concealed danger; trap **6.** an enclosed area in which animals are kept or made to fight [a bear *pit*] **7.** a) the shaft of a coal mine b) the mine itself **8.** a hollow on a part of the human body [an *armpit*] **9.** a small hollow in a surface; specif., a smallpox scar on the skin **10.** a) the rear part of the ground floor of a theatre b) the spectators in that section **11.** the sunken section in front of the stage, where the orchestra sits **12.** [U.S.] the part of the floor of an exchange where a special branch of business is transacted [the corn *pit*] **13.** a) an area off the side of a motor racing circuit for servicing cars b) a sunken area in a garage for servicing cars —*vt.* **pit′ted, pit′ting** **1.** to put or store in a pit **2.** to make pits in **3.** to mark with small scars **4.** to set (cocks, etc.) in a pit to fight **5.** to set in competition (*against*) —*vi.* to become marked with pits —**pit of the stomach** the hollow depression below the breastbone

pit·a·pat (pit′ə pat′) *adv.* [echoic] with rapid beating; palpitatingly —*n.* a rapid succession of beats —*vi.* **-pat′ted, -pat′ting** to go pitapat

pitch¹ (pich) *n.* [OE. *pic* < L. *pix*] **1.** a black, sticky substance formed in the distillation of coal tar, petroleum, etc. and used for waterproofing, pavements, etc. **2.** natural asphalt **3.** a resin from certain evergreen trees —*vt.* to cover or smear as with pitch

pitch² (pich) *vt.* [ME. *picchen*] **1.** to set up [to *pitch* a tent] **2.** to throw; fling; toss **3.** to fix or set at a particular point, level, degree, etc. **4.** *Cricket* to throw a cricket ball, esp. at some specified point **5.** *Golf* to loft (a ball), esp. in making an approach **6.** *Music* to set the key of (a tune, an instrument, or the voice) —*vi.* **1.** to encamp **2.** to take up one's position; settle **3.** to hurl or toss anything, as hay, a ball, etc. **4.** to fall or plunge forwards or headlong **5.** to incline downwards; dip **6.** to toss with the bow and stern rising and falling: said of a ship **7.** to move in a like manner in the air: said of an aircraft —*n.* **1.** act or manner of pitching **2.** a throw; toss **3.** the pitching of a ship or aircraft in rough sea or air **4.** anything pitched **5.** the amount pitched **6.** a point or degree [emotion was at a high *pitch*] **7.** the degree of slope or inclination **8.** a vendor's station, esp. his position on a pavement **9.** [Slang] a line of talk, such as a salesman or hawker uses **10.** *Machinery* the distance between corresponding points, as on two adjacent gear teeth or on two adjacent threads of a screw **11.** *Music*, etc. a) that quality of a tone or sound determined by the frequency of vibration of the sound waves: the greater the frequency, the higher the pitch b) a standard of pitch for tuning instruments **12.** *Sports* the field of play, esp. in football and cricket —**pitch in** [Colloq.] **1.** to set to work energetically **2.** to make a contribution —**pitch into** [Colloq.] to attack

pitch-black (pich′blak′) *adj.* very black

pitch·blende (-blend′) *n.* [< G. < *Pech*, PITCH¹ + *Blende*, BLENDE] a brown to black lustrous mineral, the chief ore of uranium

pitch-dark (-därk′) *adj.* very dark

pitched battle (picht) **1.** a battle in which placement of troops and the line of combat are fixed before the action **2.** a hard-fought battle

pitch·er¹ (pich′ər) *n.* [< OFr. < VL. *bicarium*, a jug, cup: see BEAKER] a container, usually rounded with a narrow neck, often of earthenware, used mainly as a water container —**pitch′er·ful** (-fool′) *n., pl.* **-fuls′**

pitch·er² (pich′ər) *n.* [PITCH² + -ER] [U.S.] *Baseball* the player who pitches the ball to opposing batters

pitcher plant a plant with pitcherlike leaves which attract and trap insects

pitch·fork (pich′fôrk′) *n.* a large, long-handled fork used for lifting and tossing hay, etc. —*vt.* to lift and toss as with a pitchfork

pit·chi (pich′ē) *n.* [Abor.] [Aust.] a hollowed-out log used for collecting and carrying food

pitch pine a resinous pine from which pitch or turpentine is obtained

pitch pipe a small pipe which produces a fixed tone as a standard for tuning instruments, etc.

pitch·y (pich′ē) *adj.* **pitch′i·er, pitch′i·est** l. full of or smeared with pitch **2.** thick and sticky like pitch **3.** black —**pitch′i·ness** *n.*

pit·e·ous (pit′ē əs) *adj.* arousing or deserving pity —**pit′·e·ous·ly** *adv.* —**pit′e·ous·ness** *n.*

pit·fall (pit′fôl′) *n.* [< ME. < *pit*, PIT² + *falle*, a trap < OE. *fealle*] **1.** a lightly covered pit used as a trap for animals **2.** any hidden danger or difficulty

pith (pith) *n.* [OE. *pitha*] **1.** the soft, spongy tissue in the centre of certain plant stems **2.** any soft core, as of a bone **3.** the essential part; gist —*vt.* **1.** to remove the pith from (a plant stem) **2.** to pierce or sever the spinal cord of (an animal)

pit head the ground and machinery at the top of a mine shaft

Pith·e·can·thro·pus e·rec·tus (pith′ə kan′thrə pəs i rek′-təs, -kan thrō′pəs) [ModL. < Gr. *pithēkos*, an ape + *anthrōpos*, man] *an earlier name for* JAVA MAN

pith helmet a lightweight hat made of pith covered with white cotton and worn in hot climates

pith·y (pith′ē) *adj.* **pith′i·er, pith′i·est** **1.** of, like, or full of pith **2.** terse and full of substance or meaning —**pith′i·ly** *adv.* —**pith′i·ness** *n.*

pit·i·a·ble (pit′ē ə b'l) *adj.* arousing or deserving pity, sometimes mixed with scorn or contempt —**pit′i·a·ble·ness** *n.* —**pit′i·a·bly** *adv.*

pit·i·ful (pit′i fəl) *adj.* **1.** exciting or deserving pity **2.** deserving contempt; despicable —**pit′i·ful·ly** *adv.* —**pit′·i·ful·ness** *n.*

pit·i·less (-lis) *adj.* without pity; merciless —**pit′i·less·ly** *adv.* —**pit′i·less·ness** *n.*

pit·man (pit′mən) *n.*, *pl.* **-men** a person who works in a pit; esp., a coal miner

pi·ton (pē′ton; *Fr.* pē tōn′) *n.*, *pl.* **-tons** (-tonz; *Fr.* -tōn′) [Fr. < MFr., a spike] a metal spike that is driven into rock or ice for support in mountain climbing: it has an eye to which a rope can be secured

pit pony a pony used underground in mines, esp. coal mines

pit·tance (pit′əns) *n.* [< OFr. *pitance*, food allowed a monk, ult. < L. *pietas*, PIETY] **1.** a meagre allowance of money **2.** a small amount or share

pit·ter-pat·ter (pit′ər pat′ər) *n.* [echoic] a rapid succession of light beating or tapping sounds, as of raindrops —*adv.* with a pitter-patter —*vi.* to fall, etc. with a pitter-patter

pi·tu·i·tar·y (pi tyōō′ə tər ē) *adj.* [< L. < *pituita*, phlegm] of the pituitary gland —*n.*, *pl.* **-tar·ies** same as PITUITARY GLAND

pituitary gland (or **body**) a small, oval endocrine gland attached to the base of the brain: it secretes hormones influencing body growth, the activity of other endocrine glands, etc.

pit viper any of a family of poisonous American snakes, as the rattlesnake, copperhead, etc., with a pit on each side of the head

pit·y (pit′ē) *n.*, *pl.* **pit′ies** [< OFr. < L. *pietas*, PIETY] **1.** sorrow for another's suffering or misfortune; compassion **2.** a cause for sorrow or regret —*vt.*, *vi.* **pit′ied, pit′y·ing** to feel pity (for) —**have** (or **take**) **pity on** to show pity for —**pit′i·er** *n.* —**pit′y·ing·ly** *adv.*

‡**più** (pyōō) *adv.* [It.] more: a direction in music, as in *più allegro*, more quickly

piv·ot (piv′ət) *n.* [Fr.] **1.** a point, shaft, etc. on which something turns **2.** a person or thing on which something turns or depends **3.** a pivoting movement —*vt.* to provide with or mount on a pivot —*vi.* to turn as on a pivot

piv·ot·al (-'l) *adj.* **1.** of or acting as a pivot **2.** on which something turns or depends; crucial

pix¹ (piks) *n.* obs. var. of PYX

pix² (piks) *n.pl.* [< PIC(TURE)S] [Slang] **1.** films **2.** photographs

pix·ie, pix·y (pik′sē) *n.*, *pl.* **pix′ies** [< ?] a fairy or sprite, esp. one that is puckish —**pix′ie·ish, pix′y·ish** *adj.*

pix·i·lat·ed (pik′sə lāt′id) *adj.* [altered < *pixy-led*, lost] **1.** eccentric, daft, puckish, etc. **2.** drunk

piz·za (pēt′sə) *n.* [It.] an Italian dish made by baking a thin layer of dough covered with a spiced preparation of tomatoes, cheese, etc.

piz·ze·ri·a (pēt′sə rē′ə) *n.* [It.] a place where pizzas are prepared and sold

piz·zi·ca·to (pit′sə kät′ō; *It.* pēt′tsē kä′tō) *adj.* [It.] *Music* plucked: a direction to pluck the strings of a violin, viola, etc. —*adv.* in a pizzicato manner —*n.*, *pl.* **-ca′ti** (-ē; *It.* -tē) a note or passage played in this way

pk. *pl.* **pks.** **1.** pack **2.** park **3.** peak **4.** peck

pkg. package; packages

pl. **1.** place **2.** plate **3.** plural

P.L.A. Port of London Authority

plac·a·ble (plak′ə b'l, plā′kə-) *adj.* [< OFr. < L. < *placare*, to soothe] capable of being placated; forgiving —**plac′·a·bil′i·ty** *n.* —**plac′a·bly** *adv.*

plac·ard (plak′ärd, -ərd) *n.* [< MFr. < MDu. *placke*, a piece] **1.** a notice for display in a public place; poster **2.** a small card or plaque —*vt.* **1.** to place placards on or in **2.** to advertise by means of placards **3.** to display as a placard

pla·cate (plə kāt′) *vt.* **-cat′ed, -cat′ing** [< L. pp. of *placare*, to soothe] to stop from being angry; appease; pacify —**pla·cat′er** *n.* —**pla·ca′tion** *n.* —**pla′ca′tive** *adj.*—**pla·ca′to·ry** *adj.*

place (plās) *n.* [OFr. < L. < *platea* < Gr. *plateia*, a street < *platys*, broad] **1.** a square or court in a city **2.** a short street **3.** space; room **4.** a region or locality **5.** *a)* the part of space occupied by a person or thing *b)* situation or state **6.** a city, town, or village **7.** a residence; dwelling **8.** a building or space devoted to a special purpose [a *place* of amusement] **9.** a particular spot on or part of something [a sore *place* on the leg] **10.** a particular passage or page in a book, etc. **11.** position or standing, esp. one of importance [one's *place* in history] **12.** a step or point in a sequence [in the first *place*] **13.** the customary or proper position, time, or character **14.** a space reserved or occupied by a person, as a seat in a theatre, etc. **15.** a job or position; employment **16.** official position **17.** the duties of any position **18.** one's duty or business **19.** *Arith.* the position of an integer, as in noting decimals [the third decimal *place*] **20.** *Racing* the first, second, or third position at the finish, specif. the second position —*vt.* **placed, plac′ing 1.** *a)* to put in a particular place, condition, or relation *b)* to identify by associating with the correct place or circumstances **2.** to find employment or a position for **3.** to assign (a value) **4.** to offer for consideration, etc. **5.** to repose (trust, etc.) in a person or thing **6.** to finish in (a specified position) in a competition —**give place** **1.** to make room **2.** to yield —**go places** [Colloq.] to achieve success —**in** (or **out of**) **place** **1.** in (or out of) the customary or proper place **2.** being (or not being) fitting or timely —**in place of** instead of —**put someone in his place** to humble someone who is overstepping bounds —**take place** to occur —**take the place of** to be a substitute for

pla·ce·bo (plə sē′bō) *n.*, *pl.* **-bos, -boes** [L., I shall please] *Med.* a sugar pill given merely to humour a patient

place card a small card with the name of a guest, set at the place that he is to occupy at a table

place kick *Rugby* a kick made in which the ball is placed in position before it is kicked, sometimes being held in place by a teammate —**place′-kick′** *vi.*

place mat a small mat serving as an individual table cover for a person at a meal

place·ment (plās′mənt) *n.* **1.** a placing or being placed **2.** the finding of employment for a person **3.** location or arrangement

pla·cen·ta (plə sen′tə) *n.*, *pl.* **-tas, -tae** (-tē) [ModL. < L., lit., a cake, ult. < Gr. *plax*, a flat object] a vascular organ developed within the uterus, connected by the umbilical cord to the foetus and supplying it with nourishment —**pla·cen′tal, pla·cen′tate** *adj.*

plac·er¹ (plās′ər) *n.* a person who places

plac·er² (plas′ər) *n.* [AmSp. < Catal. < *plassa*, a place] a waterborne or glacial deposit of gravel or sand containing particles of gold, platinum, etc. that can be washed out

placer mining (plas′ər) mining in placer deposits by washing, dredging, etc.

place setting the china, cutlery, etc. for setting one place at a table for a person at a meal

pla·cet (plā′sit) *n.* [L. it pleases] a vote of assent expressed by saying *placet*

plac·id (plas′id) *adj.* [L. *placidus*] undisturbed; tranquil; calm —**pla·cid′i·ty** (plə sid′ə tē), **plac′id·ness** *n.* —**plac′id·ly** *adv.*

plack·et (plak′it) *n.* [prob. < PLACARD, in related obs. sense] a slit at the waist of a skirt or dress to make it easy to put on and take off

pla·gal (plā′gəl) *adj.* [ML. *plagalis* < Gr. *plagos*, a side] *Music* **1.** with its keynote in the middle of the compass as a mode **2.** of a cadence, moving from the subdominant chord to the tonic chord

plage (pläzh) *n.* [Fr. < It. < Gr. *plagios*, oblique] a bright area on the sun, visible in the light of hydrogen or ionized calcium

pla·gia·rism (plā′jə riz'm, -jē ə riz'm) *n.* [< L. *plagiarius*, kidnapper] **1.** the act of plagiarizing **2.** an idea, plot, etc. that has been plagiarized Also **pla′gia·ry**, *pl.* **-ries** —**pla′·gia·rist** *n.* —**pla′gia·ris′tic** *adj.*

pla·gia·rize (-rīz′) *vt.*, *vi.* **-rized′, -riz′ing** to take (ideas, writings, etc.) from (another) and pass them off as one's own —**pla′gia·riz′er** *n.*

pla·gi·o·clase (plā′jē ə klās′) *n.* [< G. < Gr. *plagios*, oblique

+ *klasis*, a cleaving] any of a series of common rock-forming feldspars

plague (plāg) *n.* [< MFr. < L. *plaga* < Gr. *plēgē*, misfortune] **1.** anything that afflicts or troubles; calamity **2.** any deadly epidemic disease; specif., *same as* BUBONIC PLAGUE **3.** [Colloq.] a nuisance —*vt.* **plagued, plagu'ing** **1.** to afflict with a plague **2.** to vex; torment —**plagu'er** *n.*

pla·guy (plā'gē) *adj.* [Dial. or Colloq.] annoying; vexatious —*adv.* [Dial. or Colloq.] annoyingly; disagreeably: also **pla'gui·ly**

plaice (plās) *n., pl.* **plaice, plaic'es:** see PLURAL, II. D. 2 [< OFr. < LL. *platessa*, flatfish < Gr. *platys*, broad] a kind of European or American flatfish

plaid (plad, plăd) *n.* [Gael. *plaide*, a blanket] **1.** a long woollen cloth with a crossbarred pattern, worn over the shoulder by Scottish Highlanders **2.** a fabric with such a pattern **3.** any pattern of this kind —*adj.* having such a pattern: also **plaid'ed**

plain[1] (plān) *adj.* [OFr. < L. *planus*, flat] **1.** orig., flat; level **2.** not obstructed; open [in *plain* view] **3.** clearly understood; obvious [his meaning was *plain*] **4.** a) outspoken; frank [*plain* talk] b) thoroughgoing [*plain* nonsense] **5.** not luxurious [a *plain* coat] **6.** not complicated; simple [*plain* sewing] **7.** homely [a *plain* face] **8.** unfigured, undyed, etc. [*plain* cloth] **9.** unmixed [*plain* soda] **10.** not of high rank; ordinary [a *plain* man] **11.** *Knitting* of or done in plain —*n.* **1.** an extent of level country **2.** a simple stitch in knitting —*adv.* clearly or simply —**as plain as a pikestaff** perfectly clear and obvious —**plain'ly** *adv.* —**plain'ness** *n.*

plain[2] (plān) *vi.* [ME. *pleynen*, < OFr. < L. *plangere*] [Archaic] to complain

plain chocolate eating chocolate with a slightly bitter taste and a dark colour

plain-clothes man (plăn'klōz', -klōth z') a police detective who wears civilian clothes on duty: also **plain'clothes'man** (-mən) *n., pl.* **-men**

plain sailing **1.** *Naut.* sailing in a body of water that is unobstructed **2.** smooth progress or advancement

plains·man (plānz'mən) *n., pl.* **-men** an inhabitant of the plains; esp., a frontiersman on the Great Plains of the U.S. and Canada

plain·song (plān'soŋ') *n.* early Christian church music, still used in some churches, in free rhythm and sung in unison: also **plain'chant'** (chănt')

plain-spo·ken (plān'spō'k'n) *adj.* speaking or spoken plainly or frankly —**plain'-spo'ken·ness** *n.*

plaint (plānt) *n.* [< OFr. < L. < pp. of *plangere*, to lament] **1.** [Poet.] lament **2.** a complaint

plain·tiff (plān'tif) *n.* [< OFr. < *plaindre*, to complain: see prec.] a person who brings a suit into a court of law; complainant

plain·tive (-tiv) *adj.* [< OFr.: see prec.] expressing sorrow or melancholy; sad —**plain'tive·ly** *adv.* —**plain'tive·ness** *n.*

plait (plat) *n.* [< OFr. < L. pp. of *plicare*, to fold] **1.** *same as* PLEAT **2.** a length of plaited hair —*vt.* **1.** to interweave three or more strands of (hair, straw, etc.) **2.** to make by such interweaving **3.** to arrange (the hair) in a plait or plaits

plan (plan) *n.* [Fr., plan: merging of *plan* (< L. *planus*, flat) with MFr. *plant* < It. *pianta* < L. *planta*, sole of the foot] **1.** a diagram showing the arrangement in horizontal section of a structure, piece of ground, etc. **2.** a) a scheme for making, doing, or arranging something; project, schedule, etc. b) a method of proceeding **3.** any outline or sketch —*vt.* **planned, plan'ning** **1.** to make a plan of (a structure, etc.) **2.** to devise a scheme for doing, making, etc. **3.** to have in mind as a project or purpose —*vi.* to make plans —**plan on** [Colloq.] intend to; aim to do —**plan'ner** *n.*

pla·nar (plā'nər) *adj.* **1.** of or relating to a plane **2.** laying in one plane; flat

plan·chet (plan'chit) *n.* [Fr. *planchete*, dim. of *planche*, PLANK] a disc of metal to be stamped as a coin

plan·chette (plan shet', plăn-) *n.* [Fr., dim. of *planche*, PLANK] a small, three-cornered device used on a Ouija board: it is believed to move without guidance to letters or words as the fingers rest on it

Planck's constant (plaŋks) [after Max *Planck* (1858-1947) Ger. physicist] *Physics* a fundamental constant equal to the energy of any quantum of radiation divided by its frequency

plane[1] (plān) *n.* [< MFr. < L. < Gr. < *platys*, broad: from its broad leaves] any of several trees with broad leaves and bark that comes off in large patches: also **plane tree**

plane[2] (plān) *adj.* [L. *planus*] **1.** flat; level **2.** *Math.* a) on a surface that is a plane b) of such surfaces —*n.* **1.** a surface that wholly contains a straight line joining any two points lying in it **2.** a flat or level surface **3.** a level of achievement, existence, etc. **4.** *clipped form of* AEROPLANE **5.** any aerofoil esp., a wing of an aeroplane

plane[3] (plān) *n.* [< OFr. < LL. < *planare*, to make level < L. *planus*, level] a carpenter's tool for shaving a wood surface to make it smooth, level, etc. —*vt.* **planed, plan'ing** **1.** to make smooth or level with a plane **2.** to remove with a plane (with *off* or *away*) —*vi.* **1.** to work with a plane **2.** to do the work of a plane —**plan'er** *n.*

PLANE

plane[4] (plān) *vi.* **planed, plan'ing** [Fr. *planer* < OFr. (term used in falconry)] **1.** to soar or glide **2.** to rise from the water, as a hydroplane does **3.** to travel by aircraft

plane geometry the branch of geometry dealing with plane figures

plan·et (plan'it) *n.* [< OFr. < LL. < Gr. *planētēs*, wanderer < *planan*, to wander] **1.** orig., any heavenly body with apparent motion, including the sun, moon, Venus, Mars, etc. **2.** now, any heavenly body shining by reflected sunlight and revolving about the sun: the major planets, in their order from the sun, are Mercury, Venus, Earth, Mars, Jupiter, Saturn, Uranus, Neptune, and Pluto **3.** *Astrol.* any heavenly body regarded as influencing human lives

plan·e·tar·i·um (plan'ə ter'ē əm) *n., pl.* **-i·ums, -i·a** (-ə) [ModL. < LL. *planeta*, PLANET + L. (*sol*)*arium*, SOLARIUM] **1.** an arrangement for projecting the images of the sun, moon, planets, and stars inside a large dome by means of a complex optical instrument that is revolved to show the celestial motions **2.** the room or building containing this

plan·e·tar·y (plan'ə tər ē) *adj.* **1.** of a planet or the planets **2.** terrestrial; global **3.** wandering; erratic **4.** moving in an orbit, like a planet **5.** designating or of an epicyclic train of gears, as in a motor car transmission **6.** *Astrol.* under the influence of a planet

plan·e·tes·i·mal (plan'ə tes'i m'l) *adj.* [PLANET + (INFINIT)ESIMAL] of very small bodies in space that move in planetary orbits: according to the **planetesimal hypothesis** the planets were formed by the uniting of planetesimals —*n.* any of these bodies

plan·et·oid (plan'ə toid') *n.* [PLANET + -OID] *same as* ASTEROID (*n.* 1)

plank (plaŋk) *n.* [< ONormFr. < OFr. < LL. *planca*, a board] **1.** a long, broad, thick board **2.** timber cut into planks **3.** something that supports —*vt.* **1.** to cover, lay, etc. with planks **2.** [Colloq.] a) to lay or set (*down*) with force b) to pay (usually with *down* or *out*) —**walk the plank** to walk off a plank projecting out from a ship's side, as pirates' victims were forced to do

plank·ing (-iŋ) *n.* **1.** the act of laying planks **2.** planks collectively

plank·ton (plaŋk'tən) *n.* [G. < Gr. *planktos*, wandering < *plazesthai*, to wander] the microscopic animal and plant life floating in bodies of water, used as food by fish —**plank·ton'ic** (-ton'ik) *adj.*

planned parenthood the planning of the number and spacing of the births of one's children

pla·no- [< L. *planus*, flat] *a combining form meaning:* **1.** plane, flat **2.** having one side plane and (the other as specified)

pla·no-con·cave (plā'nō kon kāv', -kon'kāv) *adj.* having one side plane and the other concave

pla·no-con·vex (-kon veks', -kon'veks) *adj.* having one side plane and the other convex

plan position indicator a circular radarscope on which the centre represents the location of the transmitter and echoes represent the location of objects

plant (plänt) *n.* [OE. *plante* < L. *planta*, a sprout] **1.** a living organism that, unlike an animal, cannot move voluntarily, synthesizes food from carbon dioxide, and has no sense organs **2.** a young tree, shrub, or herb, ready to put into other soil to mature **3.** a soft-stemmed organism of this kind, as distinguished from a tree or shrub **4.** the machinery, buildings, etc. of a factory **5.** the equipment, buildings, etc. of an institution, as a school **6.** the apparatus for a certain mechanical operation [a ship's power *plant*] **7.** [Slang] a person placed, or thing used, to trick or trap —*vt.* **1.** a) to put into the ground to grow b) to set plants in (a piece of ground) **2.** to set firmly in position **3.** to fix in the mind; implant **4.** to settle; found; establish **5.** to stock with animals **6.** to put a stock of (fish, etc.) in a body of water **7.** [Slang] to deliver (a punch, etc.) with force **8.** [Slang] a) to place (a person or thing) in such a way as to trick, trap, etc. b) to place (an ostensible news item) in a newspaper, etc. **9.** [Slang] to hide or conceal —**plant oneself** position oneself; take root somewhere —**plant'like'** *adj.*

plan·tain[1] (plan'tin) *n.* [OFr. < L. *plantago*] any of various related plants with leaves at the base of the stem and spikes of tiny, greenish flowers

plan·tain[2] (plan'tin) *n.* [< Sp. *plá(n)tano*, lit., plane tree <

L. *platanus:* see PLANE¹] **1.** a tropical banana plant with a coarse fruit eaten as a cooked vegetable **2.** this fruit

plantain lily a plant of the lily family, with broad leaves and white or bluish flowers

plan·tar (plan′tər) *adj.* [< L. < *planta*, sole of the foot] of or on the sole of the foot

plan·ta·tion (plan tā′shən) *n.* [< L. < *plantare*, to plant] **1.** formerly, a colony **2.** an area growing cultivated crops **3.** an estate cultivated by workers living on it **4.** a large, cultivated planting of trees

plant·er (plän′tər) *n.* **1.** the owner of a plantation **2.** a person or machine that plants **3.** a decorative container for house plants

plan·ti·grade (plan′tə grād′) *adj.* [Fr. < L. *planta*, sole + Fr. *-grade*, -GRADE] walking on the whole sole of the foot, as a bear, man, etc. —*n.* a plantigrade animal

plant louse *same as* APHID

plaque (pläk, plak) *n.* [Fr. < MDu. *placke*, a disc] **1.** *a)* any thin, flat piece of metal, wood, etc. with a design, etc. used as a wall ornamentation *b)* a wall tablet commemorating or identifying something **2.** a platelike brooch **3.** *a)* an abnormal patch on the skin, mucous membrane, etc. *b)* a thin, transparent film on a tooth surface

plash¹ (plash) *n.* [OE. *plæsc*, prob. echoic] a pool or puddle —**plash′y** *adj.* **plash′i·er, plash′i·est**

plash² (plash) *vt., vi., n.* [echoic] *same as* SPLASH

-pla·si·a (plā′zhə, -zhē ə) [ModL. < Gr. < *plassein*, to mould] a combining form meaning change, development

-plasm (plaz′'m) [see ff.] a combining form meaning: **1.** the fluid substances of an animal or vegetable cell **2.** protoplasm [ectoplasm]

plas·ma (plaz′mə) *n.* [G. < Gr., something moulded < *plassein*, to form] **1.** the fluid part of blood, without the corpuscles **2.** the fluid part of lymph, milk, or intramuscular liquid **3.** *same as* PROTOPLASM **4.** a high-temperature, ionized gas composed of nearly equal numbers of electrons and positive ions —**plas·mat′ic** (-mat′ik) *adj.*

plasma membrane a very thin living membrane surrounding the cytoplasm of a plant or animal cell

plas·ter (pläs′tər) *n.* [< OE. & OFr. < LL. *plastrum* < L. *emplastrum* < Gr. < *emplassein*, to daub over] **1.** a pasty mixture of lime, sand, and water, hard when dry, for coating walls, ceilings, etc. **2.** *same as* PLASTER OF PARIS **3.** a pasty preparation spread on cloth and applied to the body as a medicine **4.** a small prepared bandage of gauze and adhesive tape —*vt.* **1.** to cover, smear, etc. as with plaster **2.** to apply or affix like a plaster [to *plaster* posters on walls] **3.** to make lie smooth and flat **4.** [Colloq.] to affect or strike with force —**plas′ter·er** *n.* —**plas′ter·y** *adj.*

plas·ter·board (-bôrd′) *n.* a thin board formed of layers of plaster and gypsum, used in wide sheets

plas·tered (pläs′tərd) *adj.* [Slang] intoxicated; drunk

plaster of Paris [from use of gypsum from Paris, France] a heavy white powder, calcined gypsum, which, when mixed with water, forms a thick paste that sets quickly: used for casts, statuary, etc.

plas·tic (plas′tik, pläs′-) *adj.* [< L. < Gr. *plastikos* < *plassein*, to form] **1.** moulding or shaping matter; formative **2.** *a)* that can be moulded or shaped *b)* made of a plastic **3.** in a flexible state; impressionable **4.** dealing with moulding or modelling **5.** *Physics* capable of change of shape without breaking apart —*n.* any of various nonmetallic compounds, synthetically produced, which can be moulded and hardened, or formed into pliable sheets, etc. —**plas′ti·cal·ly** *adv.* —**plas·tic′i·ty** (-tis′ə tē) *n.*

-plas·tic (plas′tik, pläs′-) [< Gr.: see prec.] a combining form meaning forming, developing

plastic bomb a bomb made from an adhesive puttylike substance, used by guerrillas or terrorists

Plas·ti·cine (plas′tə sēn′, pläs′-) [PLASTIC + -INE⁴] a trademark for an oil-based modelling paste, used like clay or wax —*n.* [p-] this paste: also **plas′ti·cene′** (-sēn)

plas·ti·cize (-sīz′) *vt., vi.* **-cized′, -ciz′ing** to make or become plastic

plas·ti·ciz·er (-sī′zər) *n.* any substance added to a plastic material to keep it soft and viscous

plastic surgery surgery dealing with the repair of injured, deformed, or destroyed parts of the body, esp. by transferring skin, bone, etc. from other parts —**plastic surgeon**

plas·tid (plas′tid) *n.* [< G. < Gr. < *plastēs*, moulder < *plassein*, to form] a specialized protoplasmic structure in the cytoplasm of some plant cells

plas·tron (plas′trən) *n.* [Fr. < It. < *piastra*, thin plate of metal] **1.** a metal breastplate **2.** a chest protector for a fencer **3.** the under shell of a turtle

-plas·ty (plas′tē) [< Gr. < *plastos*, formed < *plassein*, to mould] a combining form meaning plastic surgery

plat¹ (plat) *vt.* **plat′ted, plat′ting** [see PLAIT] [Dial.] to plait —*n.* [Dial.] a plait

plat² (plat) *n.* [var. of PLOT] **1.** a small piece of ground **2.**

[U.S.] a map or plan, esp. of a piece of land divided into building lots —*vt.* **plat′ted, plat′ting** [U.S.] make a map or plan of

plate (plāt) *n.* [OFr., flat object, ult. < Gr. *platys*, flat] **1.** a smooth, flat, thin piece of metal, etc. **2.** *same as* SHEET METAL **3.** *a)* any of the thin sheets of metal used in one kind of armour (**plate armour**) *b)* such armour **4.** *a)* a thin, flat piece of metal on which an engraving is cut *b)* an impression taken from this **5.** a print of a woodcut, lithograph, etc. **6.** a full-page book illustration printed on special paper **7.** dishes, utensils, etc. of, or plated with, gold or silver **8.** a shallow dish from which food is eaten **9.** *same as* PLATEFUL **10.** a container passed in churches, etc. for donations of money **11.** a thin cut of beef from the forequarter, just below the short ribs **12.** a horse race with a silver or gold cup as a prize **13.** *Anat., Zool.* a thin layer or scale, as of horny tissue, etc. **14.** *Archit.* a horizontal wooden girder that supports the trusses of a roof **15.** *Dentistry a)* that part of a denture which fits to the mouth and holds the teeth *b)* [often pl.] loosely, a full set of false teeth **16.** [US.] *Elec. same as* ANODE (sense 1) **17.** *Geol.* a rigid sheet of rock in the outer crust of the earth **18.** *Philately* the impression surface from which a sheet of stamps is printed **19.** *Photog.* a sheet of glass, metal, etc. coated with a film sensitive to light, upon which the image is formed **20.** *Printing* a cast, to be printed from, made from a mould of set type by the electrotype or stereotype process —*vt.* **plat′ed, plat′ing 1.** to coat with gold, tin, etc. **2.** to cover with metal plates for protection **3.** *Printing* to make a stereotype or electrotype plate of —**on a plate** acquired without trouble —**on one's plate** waiting to be done or dealt with —**put up one's plate** start practising as a doctor, etc.

pla·teau (pla tō′) *n., pl.* **-teaus′, -teaux′** (-tōz′) [Fr. < OFr. < *plat:* see PLATE] **1.** an elevated tract of more or less level land **2.** a period of little change or progress, as represented by a flat extent on a graph, etc.

plat·ed (plāt′id) *adj.* **1.** protected with plates, as of armour **2.** coated with a metal [silver-*plated*]

plate·ful (-fool′) *n., pl.* **-fuls′** as much as a plate will hold

plate glass polished, clear glass in thick sheets, used for shop windows, mirrors, etc.

plate·lay·er (-lā′ər) *n.* one whose work is laying and repairing railway lines

plate·let (plāt′lit) *n.* [PLATE + -LET] any of certain roundish discs, smaller than a red blood cell, found in the blood of mammals and associated with blood clotting

plat·en (plat′'n) *n.* [< OFr. *platine*, flat plate < *plat:* see PLATE] **1.** a flat metal plate, as that in a printing press which presses the paper against the inked type **2.** in a typewriter, the roller against which the keys strike

plat·er (plāt′ər) *n.* **1.** a person or thing that plates **2.** an inferior racehorse

plate rack a kitchen device for holding plates that are draining or not in use

plat·form (plat′fôrm′) *n.* [Fr. *plate-forme*, lit., flat form: see PLATE & FORM] **1.** a raised horizontal surface; specif., *a)* a raised flooring beside a railway line, etc. *b)* a space at the entrance of a bus, etc. *c)* a raised stage for performers, speakers, etc. **2.** [Chiefly U.S.] a statement of principles, as of a political party —*adj.* **1.** designating a woman's shoe with a thick sole of cork, leather, etc. **2.** designating such a sole

platform ticket a ticket allowing entry to a railway platfrom but not allowing the holder to travel by train

plat·ing (plāt′in) *n.* **1.** the act or process of one that plates **2.** an external layer of metal plates **3.** a thin coating of gold, silver, tin, etc.

plat·i·nize (plat′ə nīz′) *vt.* **-nized′, -niz′ing** to coat or combine with platinum —**plat·i·ni·za′tion** *n.*

plat·i·num (plat′ə nəm) *n.* [ModL. < Sp. *platina* < *plata*, silver] a steel-grey, ductile metallic chemical element, resistant to corrosion and electrochemical attack: used as a chemical catalyst, for dental alloys, jewellery, etc.: symbol, Pt; at. wt., 195.09; at. no., 78

platinum blonde 1. a girl or woman with very light, silvery blonde hair **2.** such a colour

plat·i·tude (plat′ə tyōōd′) *n.* [Fr. < *plat*, flat (see PLATE), after *latitude*, etc.] **1.** dullness or triteness of ideas, etc. **2.** a trite remark, esp. one uttered as though it were fresh —**plat′i·tu′di·nous** *adj.* —**plat′i·tu′di·nous·ly** *adv.*

plat·i·tu·di·na·rian (plat′ə tyōō dən er′ē ən) *n.* [< PLATI-TUDIN(IZE) + -ARIAN] someone who frequently uses platitudes

plat·i·tu·di·nize (plat′ə tyōō′dən īz′) *vi.* **-nized′, -niz′ing** to write or speak platitudes

Pla·ton·ic (pla ton′ik, plā-) *adj.* **1.** of or characteristic of Plato or his philosophy **2.** idealistic or impractical **3.** [usually p-] not amorous or sexual, but purely spiritual or intellectual [platonic love] —**pla·ton′i·cal·ly** *adv.*

Platonic body *Geom.* one of the five regular solids:

tetrahedron, cube, octohedron, dodecahedron, and icosehedron: also **Platonic solid**

Pla·to·nism (plāt′ən iz′m) *n.* the philosophy of Plato or his school; Platonic idealism —**Pla′to·nist** *n.* —**Pla′to·nis′tic** *adj.*

Pla·to·nize (-īz′) *vi.* **-nized′**, **-niz′ing** to follow the philosophy of Plato; philosophize in a Platonic manner —*vt.* to make Platonic

pla·toon (plə tōōn′) *n.* [Fr. *peloton*, a ball, group < *pelote*, a ball] **1.** a military unit composed of two or more squads **2.** a group like this [a *platoon* of police]

Platt·deutsch (plät′doich′, plat′-) *n.* [G. < Du. *plat*, clear, lit., flat + *duitsch*, German, Dutch] any Low German vernacular dialect of N Germany

plat·ter (plat′ər) *n.* [< Anglo-Fr. < OFr. *plat:* see PLATE] a large, shallow dish, usually oval, from which food, esp. meat or fish, is served

plat·y- [< Gr. *platys*, flat] *a combining form meaning* broad or flat [*platypus*]: also, before a vowel, **plat-**

plat·y·hel·minth (plat′ē hel′minth) *n.* [prec. + HELMINTH] any of a large group of flattened worms, as the tapeworms, liver flukes, etc.: many are parasitic —**plat′y·hel·min′thic** *adj.*

plat·y·pus (plat′ə pəs) *n.*, *pl.* **-pus·es, -pi′** (-pī′) [ModL. < Gr. < *platys*, flat + *pous*, a foot] a small, aquatic, egg-laying mammal of Australia and Tasmania, with webbed feet, a tail like a beaver's, and a bill like a duck's: in full, **duckbill platypus**

PLATYPUS
(40-60 cm long,
including tail)

plau·dit (plô′dit) *n.* [< L. pl. imper. of *plaudere*, to applaud] [*usually pl.*] **1.** a round of applause **2.** any strong expression of approval or praise

plau·si·ble (plô′zə b′l) *adj.* [< L. *plausibilis* < *plaudere*, to applaud] **1.** seemingly true, acceptable, etc.: often implying disbelief **2.** seemingly honest, trustworthy, etc.: often implying distrust —**plau′si·bil′i·ty, plau′si·ble·ness** *n.* —**plau′si·bly** *adv.*

play (plā) *vi.* [OE. *plegan*] **1.** to move lightly, rapidly, etc. [sunlight *playing* on the waves] **2.** to have fun; amuse oneself **3.** to take part in a game or sport **4.** to gamble **5.** to handle or treat carelessly or lightly; trifle (*with* a thing or person) **6.** to perform on a musical instrument **7.** to give out musical sounds, etc.: said of an instrument, gramophone record, etc. **8.** *a)* to act in a specified way [to *play* fair] *b)* to pretend to be [to *play* dumb] **9.** to perform on the stage, etc. **10.** to be performed in a theatre, on the radio, etc. **11.** to impose (*on* another's feelings or weaknesses) —*vt.* **1.** *a)* to take part in (a game or sport) *b)* to be stationed at (a specified position) in a sport **2.** to oppose (a person, team, etc.) in a game or contest **3.** to use (a player, etc.) in a game **4.** to do (something), as in fun or to deceive [to *play* tricks] **5.** to bet **6.** to speculate in (the stock market) **7.** to cause to move, act, etc.; wield **8.** to put (a specified card) into play **9.** to cause or effect [to *play* havoc] **10.** to perform (music, a drama, etc.) **11.** *a)* to perform on (an instrument) *b)* to put (a gramophone, a recording, etc.) into operation **12.** to act the part of [to *play* Iago] **13.** to imitate the activities of for amusement [to *play* teacher, mothers and fathers, etc.] **14.** to give performances in [to *play* Newcastle] **15.** to direct (a light, a stream of water, etc.) repeatedly or continuously (*on, over,* or *along*) **16.** to let (a hooked fish) tire itself by tugging at the line **17.** to use or exploit (a person) [*played* him for a fool] —*n.* **1.** motion or activity, esp. when free and rapid **2.** freedom or looseness of movement in a mechanical part [too much *play* in a wheel] **3.** activity for amusement or recreation; sport, games, etc. **4.** fun; joking [to do a thing in *play*] **5.** the playing of, or the way of playing, a game **6.** gambling **7.** a dramatic composition or performance; drama —**in** (or **out of**) **play** *Sports* in (or not in) the condition for continuing play: said of a ball, etc. —**make a play for** [Colloq.] to employ one's arts or skills to obtain, win, etc.; court —**play along** (**with**) to cooperate (with), often just for expediency —**play around** (or **about**) **1.** to behave in a frivolous way **2.** to be sexually unfaithful or promiscuous —**play at 1.** to pretend to be engaged in **2.** to work at halfheartedly —**play by ear 1.** to play an instrument without music **2.** to take things as they come; follow one's instinct —**play down** to make seem not too important —**played out 1.** finished **2.** exhausted —**play into** (**someone's**) **hands** to act in a way that gives the advantage to (someone) —**play it** to act in a (specified) manner [to *play* it cool] —**play off 1.** to pit (one) against another **2.** to break (a tie) by playing once more —**play out 1.** to play to the finish; end **2.** to pay out (a rope, etc.) —**play up 1.** to give prominence **2.** to behave irritatingly

3. to become inflamed to —**play up to** [Colloq.] to try to please by flattery etc. —**play′a·ble** *adj.*

play·act (plā′akt′) *vi.* **1.** to act in a play **2.** to pretend **3.** to behave in an affected or dramatic manner —**play′act′-ing** *n.*

play·back (-bak′) *n.* the playing of a gramophone record or tape to listen to or check the sound recorded on it

play·bill (-bil′) *n.* **1.** a poster or circular advertising a play **2.** [U.S.] a programme of a play

play·boy (-boi′) *n.* a man of means who is given to pleasure-seeking, sexual promiscuity, etc.

play·er (-ər) *n.* **1.** a person who plays a game **2.** an actor **3.** a person who plays a musical instrument **4.** a gambler **5.** a thing that plays; specif., a RECORD PLAYER

player piano a piano that can play mechanically

play·ful (-fəl) *adj.* **1.** fond of play or fun; frisky; frolicsome **2.** said or done in fun; jocular —**play′ful·ly** *adv.* —**play′-ful·ness** *n.*

play·go·er (-gō′ər) *n.* a person who goes to the theatre frequently —**play′go′ing** *n., adj.*

play·ground (-ground′) *n.* a place, often part of a schoolground, for outdoor games and play

play·group (-grōōp′) *n.* a group of preschool children who meet for periods of supervised play: also **play′school′**

play hook·y (hōōk′ē) [*hooky* prob. < *hook it,* to run away] [U.S.] to stay away from school without permission

play·house (plā′hous′) *n.* **1.** a theatre **2.** [Chiefly U.S.] a small house for children to play in

playing cards cards used in playing various games, arranged in four suits (spades, hearts, diamonds, and clubs): a standard pack has 52 cards

playing field a field or open space used for sport

play·let (-lit) *n.* a short drama

play·mate (-māt′) *n.* a companion in games and recreation: also **play′fel′low** (-fel′ō)

play-off (-of′) *n.* a game played to break a tie or to decide a championship

play on words a pun or punning

play·pen (-pen′) *n.* a small, portable enclosure in which an infant can play, crawl, etc.

play·thing (-thiŋ′) *n.* a thing to play with; toy

play·time (-tīm′) *n.* time for play or recreation

play·wright (-rīt′) *n.* a writer of plays; dramatist

pla·za (plä′zə) *n.* [Sp. < L. *platea:* see PLACE] a public square in a city or town

plea (plē) *n.* [< OFr. < L. *placitum*, an opinion < pp. of *placere*, to please] **1.** a statement in defence; excuse **2.** an appeal; entreaty **3.** *Law* a defendant's statement, answering the charges against him or showing why he should not answer

plead (plēd) *vi.* **plead′ed** or **pled** or **plead** (pled), **plead′ing** [< OFr.: see PLEA] **1.** to present a case or a plea in a law court **2.** to make an appeal; beg [to *plead* for mercy] —*vt.* **1.** to argue (a law case) **2.** to declare oneself to be (guilty or not guilty) of a charge **3.** to offer as an excuse [to *plead* ignorance] —**plead′a·ble** *adj.* —**plead′er** *n.*

plead·ings (-iŋz) *n.pl.* the statements setting forth to the court the claims of the plaintiff and the answer of the defendant

pleas·ance (plez′əns) *n.* [< MFr. < *plaisant:* see ff.] a pleasant area or garden, as on an estate

pleas·ant (-ənt) *adj.* [< MFr. prp. of *plaisir*, to please] **1.** agreeable to the mind or senses; pleasing **2.** having an agreeable manner, appearance, etc. —**pleas′ant·ly** *adv.* —**pleas′ant·ness** *n.*

pleas·ant·ry (plez′ən trē) *n., pl.* **-ries 1.** pleasant jocularity in conversation **2.** *a)* a humorous remark or action *b)* a polite social remark

please (plēz) *vt.* **pleased, pleas′ing** [MFr. *plaisir* < L. *placere*] **1.** to be agreeable to; give pleasure to; satisfy **2.** to be the will or wish of [it *pleased* him to remain] —*vi.* **1.** to be agreeable; satisfy [to aim to *please*] **2.** to have the will or wish; like [to do as one *pleases*] *Please* is also used for politeness in requests to mean "be obliging enough (to)" [*please* sit down] —**if you please** if you wish or like

pleas·ing (plē′ziŋ) *adj.* giving pleasure; agreeable —**pleas′-ing·ly** *adv.* —**pleas′ing·ness** *n.*

pleas·ur·a·ble (plezh′ər ə b′l) *adj.* pleasant; enjoyable —**pleas′ur·a·ble·ness** *n.* —**pleas′ur·a·bly** *adv.*

pleas·ure (plezh′ər) *n.* **1.** a pleased feeling; enjoyment; delight **2.** one's wish, will, or choice [what is your *pleasure?*] **3.** a thing that gives delight or satisfaction **4.** sensual satisfaction **5.** amusement; fun —**with pleasure** willingly; happily; gladly —**pleas′ure·ful** *adj.*

pleat (plēt) *n.* [ME. *pleten:* cf. PLAIT] a flat double fold in cloth or other material, pressed or stitched in place —*vt.* to lay and press (cloth) in a pleat or series of pleats —**pleat′-er** *n.*

pleb (pleb) *n.* **1.** [Colloq.] a common, vulgar person **2.** *same as* PLEBEIAN —**pleb′by** *adj.*

ple·be·ian (pli bē′ən) *n.* [< L. < *plebs*, common people] **1.** a member of the ancient Roman lower class **2.** one of the common people **3.** a vulgar, coarse person —*adj.* **1.** of or characteristic of the lower class in ancient Rome or of the common people anywhere **2.** vulgar, coarse, or common

pleb·i·scite (pleb'ə sit', -sīt) *n.* [< Fr. < L. < *plebs,* common people + *scitum,* decree] a direct vote of the people on a political issue, as on a choice between independence for their region or union with another nation

plec·trum (plek'trəm) *n.,* *pl.* **-trums, -tra** (-trə) [L. < Gr. *plēktron* < *plēssein,* to strike] a thin piece of metal, bone, plastic, etc., used for plucking the strings of a guitar, mandolin, etc.

pled (pled) [U.S. & Scot.] *alt. pt. & pp. of* PLEAD

pledge (plej) *n.* [< OFr. or ML., ? < OS. *plegan,* to guarantee] **1.** the condition of being given or held as security for a contract, payment, etc. **2.** a person or thing given or held as such security; something pawned; hostage **3.** a token **4.** the drinking of a toast to someone **5.** a promise or agreement **6.** something promised, esp. money to be donated —*vt.* **pledged, pledg'ing 1.** to present as security, esp. for the repayment of a loan; pawn **2.** to drink a toast to **3.** to bind by a promise **4.** to promise to give (loyalty, a donation, etc.) —**take the pledge** to vow not to drink alcohol —**pledg'er** *n.*

pledg·ee (plej ē') *n.* a person to whom a pledge is delivered: distinguished from PLEDGOR

pledg·or (plej'ər) *n. Law* a person who delivers something as security

-ple·gia (plē'jē ə, -jə) [ModL. < Gr. < *plēgē,* a stroke] a combining form meaning paralysis [*paraplegia*]

Ple·ia·des (plē'ə dēz', plī'-) *n.pl., sing.* **Ple'iad** (-ad) **1.** *Gr. Myth.* the seven daughters of Atlas, placed by Zeus among the stars **2.** *Astron.* a cluster of stars in the constellation Taurus

Plei·o·cene (plī'ə sēn') *adj.* same as PLIOCENE

Pleis·to·cene (plīs'tə sēn') *adj.* [< Gr. *pleistos,* most + *kainos,* recent] designating or of the first epoch of the Quaternary Period in the Cainozoic Era —**the Pleistocene** the Pleistocene Epoch or its rocks: see GEOLOGY, chart

ple·na·ry (plē'nə rē, plen'ə-) *adj.* [< LL. < L. *plenus,* full] **1.** full; complete [*plenary* power] **2.** for attendance by all members [a *plenary* session] —**ple'na·ri·ly** (-rə lē) *adv.*

plenary indulgence *R.C.Ch.* an indulgence remitting in full the temporal punishment due a sinner

plen·i·po·ten·ti·ar·y (plen'i pə ten'shər ē) *adj.* [< ML. < LL. < L. *plenus,* full + *potens,* powerful] having or giving full authority —*n.,* *pl.* **-ar·ies** a person given full authority to act as diplomatic representative of a government

plen·i·tude (plen'ə tyōod') *n.* [OFr. < L. < *plenus,* full] **1.** fullness; completeness **2.** abundance; plenty —**plen'i·tu'·di·nous** *adj.*

plen·te·ous (plen'tē əs) *adj.* plentiful; abundant —**plen'·te·ous·ly** *adv.* —**plen'te·ous·ness** *n.*

plen·ti·ful (plen'ti fəl) *adj.* **1.** having or yielding plenty **2.** ample or abundant —**plen'ti·ful·ly** *adv.* —**plen'ti·ful·ness** *n.*

plen·ty (plen'tē) *n., pl.* **-ties** [< MFr. < L. *plenitas* < *plenus,* full] **1.** prosperity; opulence **2.** an ample supply; enough **3.** a large number [*plenty* of errors] —*adj.* [Chiefly U.S. Colloq.] ample; enough —*adv.* [Colloq.] abundantly; fully [that dress is *plenty* big enough]

ple·num (plē'nəm) *n., pl.* **-nums, -na** (-nə) [ModL. < L., neut. of *plenus,* FULL[1]] **1.** space filled with matter **2.** a full or general assembly **3.** fullness; plethora

ple·o·nasm (plē'ə naz'm) *n.* [< LL. < Gr. < *pleonazein,* to be in excess < *pleon,* more, compar. of *polys,* much] **1.** the use of more words than are necessary for the meaning; redundancy **2.** a redundant word or expression —**ple'·o·nas'tic** *adj.*

ple·si·o·saur (plē'sē ə sôr') *n.* [ModL. < Gr. *plēsios,* close + *sauros,* lizard] any of an extinct order of reptiles of the Mesozoic Era, with a small head, long neck, and four paddlelike limbs

pleth·o·ra (pleth'ə rə) *n.* [ML. < Gr. < *plēthos,* fullness] the state of being too full; overabundance; excess —**ple·thor·ic** (plə thor'ik, pleth'ə rik) *adj.*

pleu·ra (ploor'ə) *n., pl.* **-rae** (-ē) [ML. < Gr. *pleura,* a rib] the thin serous membrane lining each half of the chest cavity and covering a lung —**pleu'ral** *adj.*

pleu·ri·sy (ploor'ə sē) *n.* [< MFr. < LL. < L. < Gr. < *pleura,* a rib] inflammation of the pleura, characterized by painful breathing —**pleu·rit·ic** (ploo rit'ik) *adj.*

pleu·ro- [< Gr. *pleura,* a rib] a combining form meaning: **1.** on or near the side **2.** of, involving, or near the pleura Also, before a vowel, **pleur-**

Plex·i·glas (plek'sə glas) [< L. *plexus,* a twining + GLASS] a trademark for a lightweight, transparent, thermoplastic resin, used for aircraft canopies, lenses, etc. —*n.* this material: also **plex'i·glass'**

plex·or (plek'sər) *n.* [ModL. < Gr. *plēxis,* a stroke] *Med.* a small hammer with a soft head, as of rubber, used in percussion and testing reflexes: also **ple'sor**

plex·us (plek'səs) *n., pl.* **-us·es, -us** [ModL. < L. < pp. of

plectere, to twine] a network; specif., *Anat.* a network of blood vessels, nerves, etc.

pli·a·ble (plī'ə b'l) *adj.* [< MFr. < *plier,* to bend < L. *plicare,* to fold] **1.** easily bent; flexible **2.** easily influenced or persuaded **3.** adjusting readily; adaptable —**pli'a·bil'i·ty, pli'a·ble·ness** *n.* —**pli'a·bly** *adv.*

pli·ant (plī'ənt) *adj.* [see prec.] **1.** easily bent; pliable **2.** adaptable or compliant —**pli'an·cy, pli'ant·ness** *n.* —**pli'·ant·ly** *adv.*

pli·cate (plī'kāt) *adj.* [< L. pp. of *plicare,* to fold] having lengthwise folds —**pli·ca'tion** *n.*

pli·er (plī'ər) *n.* a person or thing that plies

pli·ers (plī'ərz) *n.pl.* [< PLY[1]] small pincers for gripping small objects, bending wire, etc.

plight[1] (plīt) *n.* [< Anglo-Fr. *plit,* for OFr. *pleit,* a fold] a condition or state of affairs; esp., an awkward, sad, or dangerous situation

plight[2] (plīt) *vt.* [OE. *plihtan,* to pledge < *pliht,* danger] to pledge or promise, or bind by a pledge —**plight one's troth** to make a promise of marriage

PLIERS

Plim·soll mark (or **line**) (plim'səl, -sol) [after S. *Plimsoll* (1824–98), Brit. statesman] a line or set of lines on the outside of merchant ships, showing the water level to which they may legally be loaded

plim·solls (plim'səlz, -solz) *n.* *pl.* [? < resemblance to a PLIMSOLL MARK] lightweight canvas shoes with rubber soles, used for play and sports: also **plim'soles**

plinth (plinth) *n.* [< L. < Gr. *plinthos,* a brick, tile] **1.** the square block at the base of a column, pedestal, etc. **2.** the base on which a statue rests

Pli·o·cene (plī'ə sēn') *adj.* [< Gr. *pleōn,* more + *kainos,* new] designating or of the last epoch of the Tertiary Period in the Cainozoic Era —**the Pliocene** the Pliocene Epoch or its rocks: see GEOLOGY, chart

plis·sé, plis·se (pli sā') *n.* [< Fr. < pp. of *plisser,* to pleat] **1.** a crinkled finish given to cotton, nylon, etc. with a caustic soda solution **2.** a fabric with this finish

PLO Palestinian Liberation Organization

plod (plod) *vi.* **plod'ded, plod'ding** [prob. echoic] **1.** to walk or move heavily and laboriously; trudge **2.** to work steadily and monotonously; drudge —*n.* **1.** the act of plodding **2.** the sound of a heavy step —**plod'der** *n.* —**plod'ding·ly** *adv.*

plonk[1] (plonk, plunk) *vt., vi., n.* same as PLUNK

plonk[2] (plonk) *n.* [? < Fr. *blanc,* white in *vin blanc,* white wine] alcohol, usually wine, esp. of an inferior quality

plop (plop) *vt., vi.* **plopped, plop'ping** [echoic] **1.** to drop with a sound like that of something flat falling into water **2.** to drop heavily —*n.* the act of plopping or the sound made by this —*adv.* with a plop

plo·sive (plō'siv) *adj.* [< (EX)PLOSIVE] *Phonet.* produced by the stoppage and sudden release of the breath, as the sounds of *k, p,* and *t* when used initially —*n.* a plosive sound

plot (plot) *n.* [OE., a piece of land] **1.** a small area of ground [a garden *plot*] **2.** [U.S.] a chart or diagram, as of a building or estate **3.** a secret, usually evil, scheme **4.** the plan of action of a play, novel, etc. —*vt.* **plot'ted, plot'ting 1.** *a)* to draw a plan of (a ship's course, etc.) *b)* to mark the position or course of on a map **2.** to make secret plans for **3.** to plan the action of (a story, etc.) **4.** *a)* to determine the location of (a point) on a graph by means of coordinates *b)* to represent (an equation) by joining points on a graph to form a curve —*vi.* to scheme or conspire —**plot'less** *adj.* —**plot'less·ness** *n.* —**plot'ter** *n.*

Plough the plough-shaped group of stars in the constellation Ursa Major (Great Bear): also called **Charles's Wain**

plough (plou) *n.* [ME. *ploh* < Late OE.] **1.** a farm implement used to cut and turn up the soil **2.** anything like this; specif., a SNOWPLOUGH —*vt.* **1.** to cut and turn up (soil) with a plough **2.** to make furrows in with or as with a plough **3.** to make as if by ploughing [he *ploughed* his way in] **4.** to cut a way through (water) —*vi.* **1.** to use a plough in tilling the soil **2.** to cut a way (*through* water, etc) **3.** to plod **4.** to begin work vigorously (with *into*) **5.** to collide forcefully (with *into*) —**plough a lonely furrow** to go one's own way; to continue without assistance from others —**plough back** to reinvest (profits) in the same business enterprise —**plough up 1.** to remove with a plough **2.** to till (soil) thoroughly —**plough'a·ble** *adj.* —**plough'er** *n.*

plough·man (-mən) *n., pl.* **-men 1.** a man who guides a plough **2.** a farm worker

plough·share (-sher′) *n.* the share, or cutting blade, of a mouldboard plough

plov·er (pluv′ər) *n., pl.* **plov′ers, plov′er:** see PLURAL, II, D, 1 [< OFr., ult. < L. *pluvia,* rain] a shore bird with a short tail, long, pointed wings, and a short beak

plow (plou) *n., vt., vi. U.S. sp.* of PLOUGH

ploy (ploi) *n.* [? < (EM)PLOY] 1. an action or manoeuvre intended to outwit or disconcert another person 2. any business, job, hobby, etc. with which one is occupied

PLP Parliamentary Labour Party

PLR Public Lending Right

pluck (pluk) *vt.* [OE. *pluccian*] 1. to pull off or out; pick 2. to drag or snatch 3. to pull feathers or hair from [to *pluck* a chicken, *pluck* eyebrows] 4. to pull at (the strings of a musical instrument) and release quickly to sound tones 5. [Slang] to rob or swindle —*vi.* 1. to pull; tug; snatch (often with *at*) 2. to pluck a musical instrument —*n.* 1. a pulling; tug 2. courage; fortitude —**pluck up** to rouse one's (courage); take heart —**pluck′er** *n.*

pluck·y (-ē) *adj.* **pluck′i·er, pluck′i·est** brave; spirited; resolute —**pluck′i·ly** *adv.* —**pluck′i·ness** *n.*

plug (plug) *n.* [MDu. *plugge*] 1. an object used to stop up a hole, drain, etc. 2. *a)* a cake of pressed tobacco *b)* a piece of chewing tobacco 3. a device, as with projecting prongs, for fitting into an electric outlet, appliance, etc. to make electrical contact 4. *same as* SPARKING PLUG 5. a handle for the release of a water-closet flushing mechanism 6. [Colloq.] a defective or shop-worn article 7. [Colloq.] an electric socket 8. [Colloq.] a boost, advertisement, etc., esp. on a radio or TV programme, in a magazine article, etc. —*vt.* **plugged, plug′ging** 1. to stop up (a hole, etc.) with a plug (often with *up*) 2. to insert (something) as a plug 3. [Colloq.] *a)* to promote (a song) by frequent performance *b)* to promote with a plug (*n.* 8) 4. [Slang] to shoot a bullet into —*vi.* [Colloq.] to work or study hard and steadily; plod —**plug in** to connect (an electrical device) with an outlet, etc. by inserting a plug in a socket or jack

plug-ugly (-ug′lē) *n., pl.* **-lies** [U.S. Slang] a ruffian or gangster

plum (plum) *n.* [OE. *plume*] 1. *a)* any of various small trees bearing a smooth-skinned, edible fruit with a flattened stone *b)* the fruit 2. a raisin, when used in pudding or cake 3. the dark bluish-red or reddish-purple colour of some plums 4. something choice or desirable

plum·age (plōō′mij) *n.* [MFr. *plombe* < L. *plumbe,* a feather] a bird's feathers

plumb[1] (plum) *n.* [< MFr. < L. *plumbum,* LEAD[2]] a lead weight (**plumb bob**) hung at the end of a line (**plumb line**), used to determine how deep water is or whether a wall, etc. is vertical —*adj.* perfectly vertical —*adv.* 1. straight down; directly; completely 2. [U.S. Colloq.] entirely; absolutely [*plumb* crazy] —*vt.* 1. to test or sound with a plumb 2. to discover the facts of; solve 3. to make vertical —**out of** (or **off**) **plumb** not vertical

plumb[2] (plum) *vt.* [< PLUMB(ER)] to install, or fit as part of, a plumbing system —*vi.* to work as a plumber

plumb·er (plum′ər) *n.* [< MFr. < L. < *plumbarius,* lead-worker < *plumbum,* LEAD[2]] a skilled worker who installs and repairs pipes, fixtures, etc., as of water or gas systems in a building

PLUMB

plumb·ing (plum′in) *n.* 1. the using of a plumb 2. the work of a plumber 3. the pipes and fixtures with which a plumber works

plumb rule a narrow rule equipped with a plumb line and bob, used by carpenters, masons, etc.

plume (plōōm) *n.* [OFr. < L. *pluma*] 1. *a)* a feather, esp. a large, showy one *b)* a cluster of these 2. an ornament made of such a feather or feathers, or a feathery tuft of hair, esp. when worn on a hat, helmet, etc. 3. a token of worth or achievement; prize 4. something like a plume in shape or lightness [a *plume* of smoke] —*vt.* **plumed, plum′ing** 1. to provide, cover, or adorn with plumes 2. to preen (its feathers): said of a bird 3. to pride (oneself) —**plume′let** *n.*

plum·met (plum′it) *n.* [< MFr. dim. of *plombe:* see PLUMB[1]] 1. a plumb 2. a thing that weighs heavily —*vi.* to fall or drop straight downwards

plum·my (plum′ē) *adj.* **-mi·er, -mi·est** 1. full of or tasting of plums 2. [Colloq.] good or desirable 3. [Colloq.] rich, full, and mellow: said of a sound or voice

plu·mose (plōō′mōs) *adj.* [< L. < *pluma,* a feather] 1. feathered 2. like a feather —**plu′mose·ly** *adv.* —**plu·mos·i·ty** (plōō mos′ə tē) *n.*

plump[1] (plump) *adj.* [< MDu. *plomp,* bulky] full and rounded in form; chubby —*vt., vi.* to make plump; fill out (sometimes with *up* or *out*) —**plump′ish** *adj.* —**plump′ly** *adv.* —**plump′ness** *n.*

plump[2] (plump) *vi.* [< MDu. *plompen:* orig. echoic] 1. to

fall or bump (*against*) suddenly or heavily 2. to offer strong support (*for* someone or something) —*vt.* to drop, throw, or put down heavily or all at once —*n.* a sudden or heavy fall or the sound of this —*adv.* 1. suddenly or heavily 2. straight down 3. in plain words; bluntly —*adj.* blunt; direct

plum pudding [orig. made with plums] a rich pudding made of raisins, currants, flour, suet, etc., boiled or steamed, as in a linen bag

plum-pudding dog *same as* DALMATIAN

plu·mule (plōōm′yōōl) *n.* [< L. dim. of *pluma,* a feather] 1. the growing stem tip of the embryo of a plant seed 2. a down feather

plum·y (plōō′mē) *adj.* **plum′i·er, plum′i·est** 1. covered or adorned with plumes 2. like a plume; feathery

plun·der (plun′dər) *vt.* [< G. *Plunder,* baggage] 1. to rob (a person or place) by force, esp. in warfare 2. to take (property) by force or fraud —*vi.* to engage in plundering —*n.* 1. the act of plundering; pillage 2. goods taken by force or fraud; loot; booty —**plun′der·er** *n.* —**plun′der·ous** *adj.*

plunge (plunj) *vt.* **plunged, plung′ing** [< OFr. *plongier,* ult. < L. *plumbum,* LEAD[2]] to thrust or throw suddenly (*into* a liquid, hole, condition, etc.) —*vi.* 1. to dive or rush, as into water, a fight, etc. 2. to move violently and rapidly downwards or forwards 3. to pitch, as a ship 4. to extend down in a revealing way [a *plunging* neckline] 5. [Colloq.] to spend, gamble, or speculate heavily —*n.* 1. *a)* a dive or downward leap *b)* a swim 2. any sudden, violent plunging motion 3. [Colloq.] a heavy, rash investment —**take the plunge** to start on some new and uncertain enterprise, esp. after some hesitation

plung·er (plun′jər) *n.* 1. a person who plunges 2. a large, rubber suction cup with a long handle, used to free clogged drains 3. any cylindrical device that operates with a plunging motion, as a piston

plunk (plunk) *vt.* [echoic] 1. to pluck or strum (a banjo, guitar, etc.) 2. to throw or put down heavily; plump —*vi.* 1. to give out a twanging sound, as a banjo 2. to fall heavily 3. [Colloq.] *same as* PLUMP[2] (*vi.* 2) —*n.* the act or sound of plunking —*adv.* with a twang or thud —**plunk′-er** *n.*

plu·per·fect (plōō pur′fikt) *adj.* [abbrev. of L. *plus quam perfectum,* more than perfect] designating a tense in any of certain languages corresponding to the past perfect in English —*n.* a pluperfect tense or a form in this tense

plu·ral (ploor′al) *adj.* [L. *pluralis* < *plus* (gen. *pluris*), more] 1. of or including more than one 2. of or involving a plurality of persons or things [*plural* marriage] 3. *Gram.* designating or of that category of number referring to more than one, or in languages having dual number, more than two —*n. Gram.* 1. the plural number 2. a plural form of a word 3. a word in plural form The plurals of nouns are formed in English according to the principles listed below. Words with alternative plurals in the regular -(e)s form are marked (*).

I. REGULAR ENGLISH PLURALS

A. Add -*s* in all cases except as noted below
B. Add -*es* after final -*ss,* -*sh,* -*ch,* -*s,* -*x,* -*z,* and -*zz: glass-es, ash-es, witch-es, gas-es, box-es, adz-es, buzz-es*
C. Add -*es* after -*y* preceded by a consonant or by -*qu-,* and change the -*y* to -*i: fly, fli-es; soliloquy, soliloqui-es;* etc. (Add -*s* after -*y* preceded by a vowel: *day, day-s; monkey, monkey-s;* etc.)
D. Add -*s* to most words ending in -*o* preceded by a consonant, and to all words ending in -*o* preceded by a vowel: *piano-s, radio-s, studio-s,* etc. (Add -*es* to some words ending in -*o* preceded by a consonant: *buffalo-s, *domino-es, echo-es, hero-es, potato-es,* etc.)

II. OTHER ENGLISH PLURALS

A. Change -*f* to -*v* in many words, and add -*es: half, self, life, leaf, *scarf*[1], *wharf,* etc.
B. Plural formed by:
 1. -*en: ox-en*
 2. -*ren: children*
 3. Vowel change: *man, men; foot, feet; mouse, mice;* etc.
C. Plural the same as the singular: *alms, barracks, Chinese, deer* (occas. *deers*), *forceps, gross, means, moose, sheep,* etc.
D. Plural either different from or the same as the singular:
 1. Plural usually different, but sometimes the same, esp. in the usage of hunters and fishermen: *antelope, badger, brant, buffalo, cougar, giraffe, mullet, shrimp, sturgeon, tarpon,* etc.
 2. Plural usually the same, but different if referring to different kinds, species, varieties, etc. [the *fishes* of the North Sea]: *cod, elk, gar, mackerel, shad, springbok, trout,* etc.
 3. Plural usually lacking, but given in -(*e*)*s* form when different kinds are referred to [the many *steels* produced]: *brass, coffee, fruit, iron, linen, wool,* etc.
 4. Plural and collective singular interchangeable: *seeds, seed:* etc.

III. FORMS SINGULAR OR PLURAL ONLY
A. Singular only (or when a generalized abstraction): *clearness, fishing, information, knowledge, luck, music, nonsense, truth,* etc.
B. Plural only (even when singular in meaning), including certain senses of nouns otherwise singular: *Balkans, blues* (depression), *glasses, overalls, pliers, remains* (corpse), *scissors, tongs, trousers,* etc.
C. Plural in form but used with singular verbs: *draughts* (game), *measles, mumps, news,* etc.
D. Nouns ending in *-ics* are singular when they denote scientific subjects, as *mathematics, physics,* etc., and plural when they denote activities or qualities, as *acrobatics, acoustics,* etc.

IV. LATIN AND GREEK PLURALS
A. With Latin suffix *-i* replacing singular ending *-us: alumnus, alumn-i;* **focus, foc-i;* **nucleus, nucle-i;* **radius, radi-i;* etc.
B. With Latin suffix *-ae* replacing singular ending *-a: alumna, alumn-ae;* **formula, formul-ae;* etc.
C. With suffix *-a* replacing singular ending:
1. Latin nouns in *-um:* **agendum, agend-a; datum, dat-a;* **medium, medi-a;* etc.
2. Greek nouns in *-on:* **criterion, criteri-a;* **phenomenon, phenomen-a;* etc.
D. With suffix *-es:*
1. Latin suffix *-ex* or *-ix* replaced by *-ices:* **appendix, append-ices;* **index, ind-ices;* etc.
2. Latin or Greek suffix *-is* replaced by *-es: analysis, analys-es; axis, ax-es;* etc
E. Miscellaneous Latin and Greek plurals: **phalanx, phalang-es;* **stigma, stigma-ta; corpus, corp-ora;* **genus, gen-era;* etc.

V. OTHER FOREIGN PLURALS
A. Hebrew: **cherub, cherub-im; kibbutz, kibbutz-im;* **matzo, matzo-t(h)*
B. Italian: **bandit, bandit-ti;* **dilettante, dilettant-i;* **virtuoso, virtuos-i;* etc.
C. French: *bijou, bijou-x;* **château, château-x;* **portmanteau, portmanteau-x;* etc.

VI. PLURALS OF NUMBERS LETTERS, SIGNS, WORDS (when thought of as things), etc. add *-'s* (or now often *-s*): *8's* (or *8s*), *B's* (or *Bs*), *&'s* (or *&s*), *but's* (or *buts*)

plu·ral·ism (ploor'əl iz'm) *n.* **1.** a being plural, or existing in more than one part or form **2.** the existence within a society of groups that differ ethnically, culturally, etc. **3.** the holding by one person of more than one office or church benefice at the same time **4.** *Philos.* the theory that reality is composed of a number of ultimate beings, principles, or substances —**plu′ral·ist** *n., adj.* —**plu′ral·is′tic** *adj.* —**plu′·ral·is′ti·cal·ly** *adv.*

plu·ral·i·ty (ploo ral′ə tē) *n., pl.* **-ties** **1.** a being plural or numerous **2.** a great number; multitude **3.** [U.S.] *a*) the total number of votes received by the leading candidate in an election *b*) the number of votes that the leading candidate of more than two obtains over the next highest candidate **4.** *same as* MAJORITY

plu·ral·ize (ploor′ə līz′) *vt., vi.* **-ized′, -iz′ing** to make or become plural —**plu′ral·i·za′tion** *n.* —**plu′ral·iz′er** *n.*

plu·ral·ly (-əl ē) *adv.* in the plural number

plural society one in which there are members of more than one race: see PLURALISM (sense 2)

plu·ri- [L. < *plus* (gen. *pluris*), several] *a combining form meaning* several or many

plus (plus) *prep.* [L., more] **1.** added to *[2 plus 2 equals 4]* **2.** in addition to *[salary plus bonus]* —*adj.* **1.** designating a sign (**plus sign**) indicating addition *[+ is a plus sign]* **2.** positive *[a plus quantity]* **3.** somewhat higher than *[a mark of B plus]* **4.** involving extra gain or advantage *[a plus factor]* **5.** [Colloq.] and more *[she has personality plus]* **6.** *Elec. same as* POSITIVE *[the plus terminal]* —*adv.* [Chiefly U.S. Colloq.] moreover *[he has the time plus he has the money]* —*n., pl.* **plus′es, plus′es** **1.** a plus sign **2.** an added or favourable quantity or thing **3.** a positive quantity

plus fours [orig. indicating added length of material for overlap below the knee] loose knickerbockers worn, esp. formerly, for active sports

plush (plush) *n.* [< Fr. < *peluche,* ult. < L. *pilus,* hair] a fabric with a soft, thick, deep pile —*adj.* **1.** of plush **2.** [Slang] luxurious, as in furnishings —**plush′i·ly** *adv.* —**plush′i·ness** *n.* —**plush′y** *adj.* **plush′i·er, plush′i·est**

Plu·to (ploot′ō) **1.** *Gr. & Rom. Myth.* the god ruling the lower world **2.** the outermost planet of the solar system: diameter, c. 5900 km. —**plu·to′ni·an** *adj.*

plu·toc·ra·cy (ploo tok′rə sē) *n., pl.* **-cies** [< Gr. < *ploutos,* wealth + *kratein,* to rule] **1.** government by the wealthy **2.** a group of wealthy people who control a government

plu·to·crat (ploot′ə krat′) *n.* **1.** a member of a wealthy ruling class **2.** a person whose wealth gives him control or great influence —**plu′to·crat′ic** *adj.* —**plu′to·crat′i·cal·ly** *adv.*

plu·tol·a·try (ploo tol′ə trē) *n.* the worship of wealth

plu·ton·ic (ploo ton′ik) *adj.* [after PLUTO] *Geol.* formed far below the surface of the earth by intense heat and slow cooling, as some rocks

plu·to·ni·um (ploo tō′nē əm) *n.* [ModL. after *Pluto* (planet)] a radioactive, metallic chemical element: symbol, Pu; at. wt., 239.05; at. no., 94

plu·vi·al (ploo′vē əl) *adj.* [< L. < *pluvia,* rain] **1.** *a*) of or having to do with rain *b*) having much rain **2.** *Geol.* formed by the action of rain

ply[1] (plī) *vt.* **plied, ply′ing** [< OFr. < L. *plicare,* to fold] [Now Rare] to bend, twist, fold, or mould —*n., pl.* **plies** **1.** a single thickness or layer, as of plywood, doubled cloth, etc. **2.** one of the twisted strands in rope, yarn, etc. **3.** bias or inclination —*adj.* having (a specified number of) layers, strands, etc. *[three-ply]*

ply[2] (plī) *vt.* **plied, ply′ing** [ME. *plien,* short for *applien,* APPLY] **1.** to work with; wield or use (a tool, faculty, etc.) **2.** to work at (a trade) **3.** to address (someone) urgently (*with* questions, etc.) **4.** to keep supplying (*with* gifts, food, etc.) **5.** to sail back and forth across *[boats ply the channel]* —*vi.* **1.** to keep busy or work (*at* something or *with* a tool, etc.) **2.** to travel regularly (*between* places): said of ships, buses, etc.

Ply·mouth Brethren (plim′əth) a Calvinistic religious sect, founded at Plymouth about 1830, recognizing the autonomy of each local church and with no ordained ministry

Plymouth Rock any of a breed of American chickens

ply·wood (plī′wood′) *n.* [PLY[1] + WOOD] a material made of thin layers of wood glued and pressed together, usually with the grains at right angles

Pm *Chem.* promethium

pm. **1.** phase modulation **2.** premium

P.M. **1.** Paymaster **2.** Postmaster **3.** Prime Minister

P.M., p.m., PM [L. *post meridiem*] after noon: used to designate the time from noon to midnight

p.m. post-mortem

PMG Postmaster General

PNdB Perceived Noise Decibel

PNEU Parents' National Educational Union

pneu·mat·ic (nyoo mat′ik) *adj.* [< L. < Gr. < *pneuma,* breath] **1.** of or containing wind, air, or gases **2.** *a*) filled with compressed air *[pneumatic tyre]* *b*) worked by compressed air *[pneumatic drill]* —**pneu·mat′i·cal·ly** *adv.*

pneu·mat·ics (-iks) *n.pl.* [with *sing. v.*] the branch of physics dealing with such properties of air and other gases as pressure, density, etc.

pneu·mo·coc·cus (nyoo′mə kok′əs) *n., pl.* **-coc′ci** (-kok′sī) [ModL. < Gr. *pneumōn,* a lung + COCCUS] a bacterium that is a causative agent of pneumonia —**pneu′mo·coc′cal** (-kok′′l), **pneu′mo·coc′cic** (-kok′sik) *adj.*

pneu·mo·en·ceph·a·lo·gram (-en sef′ə lō gram′) *n.* [< Gr. *pneumōn,* a lung + *en-,* in + *kephalē,* the head + -GRAM] an X-ray photograph of the brain made after cerebrospinal fluid has been replaced with air or oxygen

pneu·mo·nec·to·my (nyoo′mə nek′tə mē) *n., pl.* **-mies** [< Gr. *pneumōn,* a lung & -ECTOMY] the surgical removal of an entire lung

pneu·mo·ni·a (nyoo mōn′yə, -mō′nē ə) *n.* [ModL. < Gr. < *pneumōn,* a lung < *pnein,* to breathe] inflammation or infection of the alveoli of the lungs, caused by any of various agents, such as bacteria or viruses —**pneu·mon′ic** (-mon′ik) *adj.*

Po *Chem.* polonium

P.O., p.o. **1.** petty officer: also **PO** **2.** post office **3.** postal order

po (po) *n., pl.* **-pos** [< POT] *Colloq.* clipped form of CHAMBER POT

poach[1] (pōch) *vt.* [< MFr. < *poche,* a pocket: the yolk is "pocketed" in the white] to cook (fish, an egg without its shell, etc.) in water or other liquid near the boiling point, or in a small receptacle put over boiling water —**poach′er** *n.*

poach[2] (pōch) *vt.* [< Fr. < OFr. *pochier,* to tread upon < MHG. *puchen,* to plunder] **1.** to trample **2.** *a*) to trespass on (private property), esp. for shooting or fishing *b*) to hunt or catch (game or fish) illegally, esp. by trespassing **3.** to steal —*vi.* to hunt or fish illegally, esp. as a trespasser —**poach′er** *n.*

po·chard (pō′chərd, kərd) *n., pl.* **-chards, -chard:** see PLURAL, II, D 1 [< ? Fr. *pocher,* to pocket] **1.** a European diving sea duck with a brownish-red head **2.** any of various similar ducks

pock (pok) *n.* [OE. *pocc*] **1.** a pustule, esp. one caused by smallpox **2.** *same as* POCKMARK —**pocked** *adj.* —**pock′y** *adj.* **pock′i·er, pock′i·est**

pock·et (pok′it) *n.* [< Anglo-Fr. < ONormFr. dim. of *poque,* a bag] **1.** *a*) a little bag or pouch, now usually sewn into or on clothing, for carrying money and small articles *b*) any usually small container, compartment, pouch, etc. **2.** a cavity for holding something **3.** a small area or group *[a pocket of poverty]* **4.** a confining or frustrating situation **5.** funds *[a drain on one's pocket]* **6.** *Aeron. same as* AIR POCKET **7.** any of the pouches at the sides and corners of a billiard table **8.** *Geol. a*) a cavity filled with ore, oil, gas, or water *b*) a small deposit of ore, etc. —*adj.* **1.** *a*) that is or can be carried in a pocket *b*) smaller than standard **2.** not widespread; isolated *[pocket resistance]* —*vt.* **1.** to put into a pocket **2.** to provide with pockets **3.** to envelop; enclose **4.** to take dishonestly; appropriate (money, etc.) for one's own use **5.** to put up with (an insult, etc.) without answering or showing anger **6.** to hide, suppress, or set aside [*pocket* one's pride] **—out of pocket** having made a loss after a transaction

pocket battleship a small battleship within certain treaty limits as to tonnage and guns

pocket billiards [U.S.] *same as* POOL² (*n.* 2)

pock·et·book (-book′) *n.* **1.** a case, as of leather, for carrying money and papers in one's pocket; wallet **2.** monetary resources

pocket book [Chiefly U.S.] a book small enough to be carried in one's pocket

pocket borough before 1832, a borough whose representation in Parliament was controlled by one family or person

pock·et·ful (-fool′) *n., pl.* **-fuls** as much as a pocket will hold

pocket handkerchief **1.** a handkerchief small enough for a pocket **2.** anything small, esp. a small lawn

pock·et·knife (-nif′) *n., pl.* **-knives** (-nīvz′) a knife with blades that fold into the handle

pocket money cash for small expenses, esp. that given to children to buy sweets, etc.

pock·et·size (-sīz′) *adj.* of a small size; esp., of a size to fit in a pocket: also **pock′et-sized′**

pocket veto [U.S.] the indirect veto by the President of the U.S. of a bill presented to him by Congress within ten days of its adjournment, by his failing to sign and return the bill before Congress adjourns

pock·mark (pok′märk′) *n.* a scar or pit left by a pustule, as of smallpox, or any mark like this **—vt.** to cover with pockmarks **—pock′marked** *adj.*

po·co (pō′kō) *adv.* [It.] *Music* somewhat

pod (pod) *n.* [< ?] **1.** a dry fruit or seed vessel enclosing one or more seeds, as a legume **2.** a contoured enclosure, as the housing of a jet engine **—vi. pod′ded, pod′ding** **1.** to bear pods **2.** to swell out into a pod **—pod′like′** *adj.*

-pod (pod) [< Gr. *pous* (gen. *podos*), a foot] *a combining form meaning:* **1.** foot **2.** (one) having a (specified number or kind of) feet [*tripod*] Also **-pode** (pōd)

po·dag·ra (pə dag′rə, pod′ə grə) *n.* [L. < Gr. < *pous* (gen. *podos*) FOOT + *agra,* a seizure] gout, esp. in the big toe **—po·dag′ral, po·dag′ric** *adj.*

pod·ded (pod′id) *adj.* **1.** pod-bearing **2.** well-off; comfortable

pod·dy (pod′ē) *n.* [< ?] [Aust.] a calf, usually one that is stray or motherless

podg·y (poj′ē) *adj.* **podg·i·er, podg′i·est** *var. of* PUDGY

po·di·a·try (pō dī′ə trē, pə-) *n.* [< Gr. *pous* (see -POD) + -IATRY] *Chiefly U.S.* term for CHIROPODY **—po·di′a·trist** *n.* **—po′di·at′ric** *adj.*

po·di·um (pō′dē əm) *n., pl.* **-di·a** (-ə); for 1 usually, **-di·ums** [L. < Gr. *podion,* dim. of *pous* (see -POD)] **1.** a low platform, esp. for the conductor of an orchestra **2.** *Zool.* a foot or footlike structure

po·em (pō′əm) *n.* [< MFr. < L. < Gr. *poiēma* < *poiein,* to make] **1.** an arrangement of words written or spoken, traditionally a rhythmical or metrical composition, sometimes rhymed **2.** anything suggesting a poem in its effect

po·e·sy (pō′ə sē′, -zē′) *n., pl.* **-sies** [< OFr. < L. < Gr. *poiēsis* < *poiein,* to make] **1.** *old-fashioned var. of* POETRY **2.** [Obs.] a poem

po·et (pō′ət) *n.* [< OFr. < L. < Gr. *poiētēs* < *poiein,* to make] **1.** a person who writes poems **2.** a person who expresses himself with beauty of thought and language **—po′et·ess** [Now Rare] *n.fem.*

poet. **1.** poetic **2.** poetry

po·et·as·ter (pō′ə tas′tər) *n.* [see POET & -ASTER] a writer of mediocre verse; rhymester

po·et·ic (pō et′ik) *adj.* **1.** of, like, or fit for a poet or poetry **2.** written in verse **3.** having the beauty, imagination, etc. of poetry **4.** imaginative or creative Also **po·et′i·cal** **—po·et′i·cal·ly** *adv.*

po·et·i·cize (-ə sīz′) *vt.* **-cized′, -ciz′ing** **1.** to make poetic **2.** to express, or deal with, in poetry **—vi.** to write poetry

poetic justice justice, as in some plays, etc., in which good is rewarded and evil punished

poetic licence **1.** disregard of strict fact or of rigid form, as by a poet, for artistic effect **2.** freedom to do this

po·et·ics (pō et′iks) *n.pl.* [*with sing. v.*] **1.** *a)* the theory or structure of poetry *b)* a treatise on this **2.** the poetic theory or practice of a specific poet

po·et·ize (pō′ə tīz′) *vt., vi.* **-ized′, -iz′ing** *same as* POETICIZE

poet laureate *pl.* **poets laureate, poet laureates** **1.** the court poet of Britain, appointed for life by the monarch to write poems celebrating official occasions, national events, etc. **2.** any official poet of any nation, region, etc.

po·et·ry (pō′ə trē) *n.* [< OFr. < ML. < L. *poeta,* a poet] **1.** the art, theory, or structure of poems **2.** poems **3.** *a)* poetic qualities *b)* the expression or embodiment of such qualities

Poets' Corner that area of Westminster Abbey devoted to the graves and monuments of various poets

po-faced (-fast) *adj.* [< ? PO or changed for *poor-faced*] wearing a disapproving, stern expression: said of a person

po·go·not·o·my (pō gə not′ə mē) *n.* [< Gr. *pōgōnos,* beard + *tomy,* cutting] shaving

po·go stick (pō′gō) [arbitrary coinage] a stilt with pedals and a spring at one end, used as a toy on which one can move along in a series of bounds

po·grom (pō′grəm) *n.* [Russ., devastation] an organized persecution and massacre of a minority group, esp. of Jews (as in Czarist Russia)

poign·ant (poin′yənt, -ənt) *adj.* [MFr. prp. of *poindre* < L. *pungere,* to prick] **1.** *a)* sharp or pungent to the smell or, formerly, the taste *b)* keenly affecting the other senses [*poignant* beauty] **2.** *a)* sharply painful to the feelings *b)* evoking pity, compassion, etc. **3.** sharp, biting, etc. [*poignant* wit] **—poign′an·cy** *n.* **—poign′ant·ly** *adv.*

poi·kil·o·ther·mal (poi kil′ō thur′m'l) *adj.* [< Gr. *poikilos,* variegated + THERMAL] *Zool. same as* COLD-BLOODED (sense 1)

poin·ci·a·na (poin′sē an′ə, -ā′nə) *n.* [ModL., after M. de *Poinci,* a governor of the Fr. West Indies] any of various small tropical trees with showy red, orange, or yellow flowers

poin·set·ti·a (poin set′ē ə, -set′ə) *n.* [ModL., after J. R. *Poinsett* (d. 1851), U.S. ambassador to Mexico] a Mexican and Central American plant with yellow flowers surrounded by petallike red leaves

point (point) *n.* [OFr., a dot, prick < L. < *punctus,* pp. of *pungere,* to prick] **1.** a minute mark or dot **2.** a dot in print or writing, as a full stop, decimal point, etc. **3.** *a)* an element in geometry having definite position, but no size, shape, or extension *b)* a particular position, location, spot, etc. [*points* on an itinerary] **4.** *a)* the position of certain players, as in cricket [*cover point*] *b)* the player **5.** the exact moment [at the *point* of death] **6.** a stage, condition, level, or degree reached [a boiling *point*] **7.** an item [explain it *point* by *point*] **8.** *a)* a distinguishing characteristic *b)* a physical characteristic of an animal, used as a standard in judging breeding **9.** a unit, as of measurement, value, game scores, etc. **10.** *a)* a sharp end; tip *b)* something with a sharp end **11.** needlepoint lace **12.** a projecting piece of land; cape **13.** a branch of a deer's antler [a ten-*point* buck] **14.** *a)* the essential fact or idea under consideration *b)* the main idea or feature of a story, etc. **15.** aim; purpose; object [there's no *point* in going there!] *b)* [Chiefly U.S.] a helpful hint **16.** *a)* an impressive argument or fact [he has a *point* there!] *b)* [Chiefly U.S.] a helpful hint **17.** [often *pl.*] a movable section of railway line used in transferring a train from one line to another **18.** *Ballet* the position of being on the tips of the toes **19.** *Elec. a)* either of the two tungsten or platinum contacts that make or break the circuit in a distributor *b)* [Colloq.] *same as* POWER POINT **20.** *Finance* a standard unit of value used in quoting prices, as of stocks **21.** *Navigation a)* any of the 32 marks showing direction on a compass card *b)* the angle between two successive compass points **22.** *Printing* a measuring unit for type bodies and printed matter, equal to about ¹/₇₂ of an inch **—vt.** **1.** *a)* to put punctuation marks in *b)* to mark (off a sum, etc.) with (decimal) points **2.** to sharpen (a pencil, etc.) to a point **3.** to give (a story, remark, etc.) emphasis (sometimes with *up*) **4.** to show or call attention to (usually with *out*) [*point* the way] **5.** to aim or direct (a gun, finger, etc.) **6.** to extend the foot so as to bring (the toe) more nearly in line with the leg **7.** to show the location of (game) by standing still and facing towards it: said of gun dogs **8.** *Masonry* to rake out mortar from the joints of (brickwork) and finish with fresh mortar **—vi.** **1.** to direct one's finger (at or to) **2.** to call attention (to); hint (at) **3.** to aim or be directed (to or towards) **4.** to point game: said of a dog **—at the point of** very close to **—beside the point** not pertinent **—give points to** to show much more skill than **—in point of** in the matter of **—make a point of** **1.** to make (something) one's strict rule, practice, etc. **2.** to call special attention to **—on** (or **upon**) **the point of** on the verge of **—point out** to indicate or specify **—stretch** (or **strain**) **a point** to make an exception or concession **—to the point** pertinent; apt: also **in point** **—point′a·ble** *adj.*

point-blank (-blaŋk′) *adj.* [POINT + BLANK (white centre of the target)] **1.** aimed horizontally, straight at a mark **2.** straightforward; plain [a *point-blank* answer] **—adv.** **1.** in a direct line; straight **2.** without quibbling; bluntly [to refuse *point-blank*]

point duty the regulation of traffic by a policeman or traffic warden, stationed at a point, usually in the road

point·ed (poin′tid) *adj.* **1.** *a)* having a point, or sharp end *b)* tapering **2.** sharp; incisive, as an epigram **3.** aimed at someone [a *pointed* remark] **4.** very evident; emphasized **—point′ed·ly** *adv.* **—point′ed·ness** *n.*

point·er (-tər) *n.* **1.** a person or thing that points **2.** a long, tapered rod for pointing to things, as on a map **3.** an indicator on a clock, meter, etc. **4.** a large, lean dog with a smooth coat: it smells out game and then points **5.** [Colloq.] a helpful hint —**the Pointers** *Astron.* the two stars in the Plough that are almost in a line with the North Star

POINTER
(66 cm
at shoulder)

poin·til·lism (pwan′t'l iz′m, -tē iz′m; point′'l-) *n.* [Fr. < *pointiller*, to mark with dots ult. < L. *punctus*, point] the method of painting of certain French impressionists, using dots of pure colour on a white background, rather than mixing colours on the canvas

point·ing (-iŋ) *n.* [< POINT + -ING] **1.** punctuation **2.** the marks made by punctuation **3.** the act of filling the crevices of walls with mortar **4.** the material used for this

point lace needlepoint lace

point·less (point′lis) *adj.* **1.** without a point **2.** without meaning, relevance, or force; senseless —**point′less·ly** *adv.* —**point′less·ness** *n.*

point of honour a matter affecting one's honour

point of no return a point at which an irreversible commitment must be made to an action, progression, stance, etc.

point of order a question as to whether the rules of parliamentary procedure are being observed

point of view **1.** the place from which, or way in which, something is viewed; standpoint **2.** a mental attitude

points·man (-mən) *n., pl.* **-men** a railway employee who operates points

point-to-point (point′tə point′) *n.* a steeplechase organized by a hunt or some other body, usually restricted to amateurs riding hunters

point·y (poin′tē) *adj.* **point′i·er, point′i·est** **1.** that comes to a sharp point **2.** having many points

poise[1] (poiz) *n.* [< OFr. < VL. < L. *pensum*, something weighed < *pendere*, to weigh] **1.** balance; stability **2.** ease and dignity of manner; composure **3.** the condition of being calm or serene **4.** carriage; bearing, as of the body —*vt.* **poised, pois′ing** **1.** to balance; keep steady **2.** to suspend (usually passive or reflexive) —*vi.* **1.** to be suspended or balanced **2.** to hover

poise[2] (poiz) *n.* [Fr., after J. L. M. *Poisenille*, 19th-c. anatomist] the cgs unit of viscosity of a liquid, equal to one dyne-second per square centimetre (10⁻¹ newton seconds per square metre)

poi·son (poi′z'n) *n.* [< OFr. < L. *potio*, potion] **1.** a substance causing illness or death when eaten, drunk, or absorbed in small quantities **2.** anything harmful to happiness or welfare —*vt.* **1.** to harm or destroy by means of poison **2.** to put poison on or into **3.** to influence wrongfully [to *poison* one's mind] —*adj.* poisonous or poisoned —**what's your poison** [Colloq.] what are you drinking —**poi′son·er** *n.*

poison ivy any of several American plants having leaves of three leaflets and ivory-coloured berries: it can cause a severe rash on contact

poison oak *name variously used for:* **1.** POISON IVY **2.** POISON SUMAC

poi·son·ous (poi′z'n əs) *adj.* capable of injuring or killing by or as by poison; full of poison; venomous —**poi′son·ous·ly** *adv.* —**poi′son·ous·ness** *n.*

poi·son·pen (-pen′) *adj.* [Colloq.] concerning an abusive letter written out of spite or malice, usually anonymously, for the purpose of harassing the recipient

poison sumac an American swamp plant with clusters of greyish fruit and leaves made up of 7 to 13 leaflets: it can cause a severe rash on contact

poke[1] (pōk) *vt.* **poked, pok′ing** [MDu. or LowG. *poken*] **1.** a) to push or jab with a stick, finger, etc. b) [Slang] to hit with the fist **2.** to make (a hole, etc.) by poking **3.** to stir up (a fire) **4.** to thrust (something) forwards; intrude [to *poke* one's head out of a window] —*vi.* **1.** to jab with a stick, poker, etc. (at) **2.** to intrude; meddle **3.** to search (sometimes with *about* or *around*) **4.** to stick out; protrude —*n.* **1.** a) a poking; jab; thrust b) [Slang] a blow with the fist **2.** *same as* POKE BONNET —**poke fun (at)** to ridicule or deride

poke[2] (pōk) *n.* [OFr. *poke, poque* < Frank.] [Dial.] a sack or bag

poke bonnet a bonnet with a wide front brim

pok·er[1] (pō′kər) *n.* [< ?] a card game in which the players bet on the value of their hands, forming a pool to be taken by the winner: see DRAW POKER, STUD POKER

pok·er[2] (pō′kər) *n.* **1.** a person or thing that pokes **2.** a bar, as of iron, for stirring a fire

poker face [Colloq.] an expressionless face, as of a poker player hiding the nature of his hand

poke·weed (pōk′wēd′) *n.* [< AmInd. *puccoon*] a N American plant with purplish-white flowers, reddish-purple berries, and poisonous roots: also **poke′ber·ry**

poker work *same as* PYROGRAPHY

pok·y (pō′kē) *adj.* **pok′i·er, pok′i·est** [POKE[1] + -Y²] **1.** slow; dull **2.** small; stuffy [a *poky* room] **3.** shabbily dressed Also [U.S.] **pok′ey** —**pok′i·ly** *adv.* —**pok′i·ness** *n.*

Pol. **1.** Poland **2.** Polish

po·lar (pō′lər) *adj.* [< ML. < L. *polus:* see POLE²] **1.** of or near the North or South Pole **2.** of a pole or poles **3.** having polarity **4.** opposite in character, direction, etc. **5.** guiding, like the polestar

polar bear a large, white bear of the Arctic regions

polar circle *same as:* **1.** ARCTIC CIRCLE **2.** ANTARCTIC CIRCLE

po·lar·im·e·ter (pō′lə rim′ə tər) *n.* [POLARI(ZE) + -METER] an instrument for measuring the degree of polarization of light, or the amount of polarized light in a ray

Po·la·ris (pō lar′is) [ModL. < ML. (*stella*) *polaris*, polar (star)] *same as* POLESTAR (sense 1)

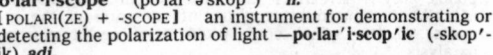

POLAR BEAR

po·lar·i·scope (pō′lər·ə skōp′) *n.* [POLARI(ZE) + -SCOPE] an instrument for demonstrating or detecting the polarization of light —**po·lar′i·scop′ic** (-skop′-ik) *adj.*

po·lar·i·ty (pō lar′ə tē) *n., pl.* **-ties** **1.** the tendency of bodies having opposite magnetic poles to become aligned so that their two extremities point to the two magnetic poles of the earth **2.** any tendency to turn, feel, etc. in a certain way, as if magnetized **3.** the having of two contrary qualities, powers, etc. **4.** the condition of being positive or negative with respect to some reference point or object

po·lar·i·za·tion (pō′lər i zā′shən) *n.* **1.** the producing or acquiring of polarity **2.** the accumulation of gases around the electrodes of an electric cell during electrolysis, causing a reduction in the flow of current **3.** *Optics* a condition, or the production of a condition, of light in which the transverse vibrations of the waves are in one plane or direction only

po·lar·ize (pō′lə rīz′) *vt.* **-ized, -iz′ing** [< Fr. < *polaire*, POLAR] to give polarity to; produce polarization in —*vi.* to acquire polarity; specif., to separate into diametrically opposed groups, etc. —**po′lar·iz′a·ble** *adj.* —**po·lar·iz′er** *n.*

Po·lar·oid (pō′lə roid′) [POLAR + -OID] *a trademark for:* **1.** a transparent material capable of polarizing light **2.** a camera that develops and prints snapshots: in full, **Polaroid (Land) camera**

pol·der (pol′dər) *n.* [Du., prob. akin to POOL¹] an area of low-lying land reclaimed from a sea, lake, or river, as by the building of dikes

Pole (pōl) *n.* a native or inhabitant of Poland

pole[1] (pōl) *n.* [OE. *pal* < L. *palus*, a stake] **1.** a long, slender piece of wood, metal, etc. [a tent *pole*] **2.** a unit of measure, equal to one rod or one square pole —*vt., vi.* **poled, pol′ing** **1.** to propel (a boat or raft) with a pole **2.** to impel, support, etc. (something) as with a pole —**up the pole 1.** slightly mad **2.** on the wrong track; in a dilemma

pole[2] (pōl) *n.* [L. *polus* < Gr. *polos*] **1.** either end of any axis, as of the earth, of the celestial sphere, etc. **2.** the region around the North Pole or South Pole **3.** either of two opposed forces, parts, etc., such as the ends of a magnet, the terminals of a battery, etc. **4.** *Geom.* the origin of a system of polar or spherical co-ordinates —**poles apart** widely separated, as in tastes, opinions, etc.

pole·axe (pōl′aks′) *n., pl.* **-ax′es** (-ak′siz) [< *pol*, POLL + *ax*, AXE] **1.** a long-handled battle-axe **2.** any axe with a spike, hook, etc. opposite the blade —*vt.* **-axed′, -ax′ing** to attack or fell as if with a poleaxe

pole·cat (pōl′kat′) *n., pl.* **-cats′, -cat′:** see PLURAL, II, D, 1 [prob. < OFr. *poule:* see PULLET & CAT] **1.** a small, weasellike carnivore of Europe **2.** [U.S.] *same as* SKUNK

po·lem·ic (pə lem′ik, pō-) *adj.* [< Fr. < Gr. *polemikos* < *polemos*, a war] **1.** of or involving dispute; controversial **2.** argumentative Also, esp. for 2, **po·lem′i·cal** **1.** an argument or controversial discussion **2.** a person inclined to argument —**po·lem′i·cal·ly** *adv.*

po·lem·ics (-iks) *n.pl.* [*with sing. v.*] the art or practice of disputation —**po·lem′i·cist** (-ə sist) *n.*

pole·star (pōl′stär′) *n.* **1.** Polaris, the North Star **2.** a guiding principle **3.** a centre of attraction

pole vault *Athletics* **1.** an event in which the contestants leap for height, vaulting over a bar with the aid of a long, flexible pole **2.** such a leap —**pole′-vault′** *vi.* —**pole′-vault′-er** *n.*

po·lice (pə lēs′, plēs′) *n.* [Fr. < LL. < Gr. *politeia*, the state < *politēs*, citizen < *polis*, city] **1.** the regulation of morals, safety, etc.; law enforcement **2.** the governmental department (of a city, county, etc.) for keeping order, enforcing the law, and preventing and detecting crimes **3.** [*with pl. v.*] the members of such a department, or of a private organization like this [security *police*] —*vt.* **-liced′,**

-lic′ing to control, protect, etc. with police or similar force [to *police* the streets]
police constable the lowest rank in the police force
police dog a dog specially trained to assist police; esp., in popular usage, an Alsatian
po·lice·man (-mən) *n., pl.* **-men** a member of a police force **—po·lice′wom′an** *n.fem., pl.* **-wom′en**
police state a government that uses a secret police force to suppress political opposition
police station the office or headquarters of the police force of a district
pol·i·clin·ic (pol′i klin′ik) *n.* [< G. < Gr. *polis*, city + G. *Klinik*, clinic] the department of a hospital where outpatients are treated
pol·i·cy¹ (pol′ə sē) *n., pl.* **-cies** [< OFr. < L. < Gr. *politeia*: see POLICE] 1. wise or prudent management 2. any governing principle, plan, etc.
pol·i·cy² (pol′ə sē) *n., pl.* **-cies** [< MFr. < It. *polizza* < ML., ult. < Gr. *apodeixis*, proof < *apodeiknynai*, to display] a written contract (**insurance policy**) in which one party guarantees to insure another against a specified loss, injury, etc.
po·li·o (pō′lē ō′) *n. clipped form of* POLIOMYELITIS
po·li·o·my·e·li·tis (pō′lē ō mī′ə līt′əs) *n.* [ModL. < Gr. *polios*, grey + MYELITIS] an acute infectious disease, esp. of children, caused by a virus inflammation of the grey matter of the spinal cord, often resulting in muscular paralysis
Pol·ish (pō′lish) *adj.* of Poland, its people, their language, or culture **—n.** the West Slavic language of the Poles
pol·ish (pol′ish) *vt.* [< OFr. < L. *polire*] 1. a) to smooth and brighten, as by rubbing *b*) to coat with wax, etc. and make glossy 2. to improve or refine (manners, etc.) by removing crudeness 3. to complete or embellish **—vi.** to take a polish; become glossy, refined, etc. **—n.** 1. a surface gloss 2. elegance; refinement 3. a substance used for polishing 4. a polishing or being polished **—polish off** [Colloq.] to finish or get rid of **—polish up** [Colloq.] to improve **—pol′ished** *adj.* **—pol′ish·er** *n.*
Po·lit·bu·ro (pol′it byoor′ō, pō′lit-) *n.* [< Russ. < *Polit(icheskoe) Byuro*, political bureau] the executive committee of the Communist Party of the Soviet Union and of certain other countries
po·lite (pə līt′) *adj.* [< L. pp. of *polire*, to polish] 1. polished; cultured; refined [polite society] 2. having good manners; courteous **—po·lite′ly** *adv.* **—po·lite′ness** *n.*
pol·i·tesse (pol′ə tes′) *n.* [Fr.] politeness
pol·i·tic (pol′ə tik) *adj.* [< MFr. < L. < Gr. < *politēs*: see POLICE] 1. having practical wisdom; prudent 2. crafty; unscrupulous 3. artful; expedient [a politic plan] 4. [Rare] political: see BODY POLITIC **—vi.** **-ticked, -tick·ing** to engage in political campaigning **—pol′i·tic·ly** *adv.*
po·lit·i·cal (pə lit′i k'l) *adj.* 1. of or concerned with government, politics, etc. 2. having a definite governmental organization 3. engaged in politics [political parties] 4. of or characteristic of political parties or politicians **—po·lit′-i·cal·ly** *adv.*
political economy *earlier name for* ECONOMICS
political prisoner someone imprisoned for political offences rather than criminal ones
political science the science of the principles, organization, and methods of government **—political scientist**
pol·i·ti·cian (pol′ə tish′ən) *n.* a person actively engaged in politics, often one holding or seeking political office: often used derogatorily of one who seeks only to advance himself or his party, as by scheming: cf. STATESMAN
po·lit·i·cize (pə lit′ə sīz′) *vi.* **-cized′, ciz′ing** to talk about, engage in politics **—vt.** to make political in tone, character, etc. **—po·lit′i·ci·za′tion** *n.*
po·lit·i·co (pə lit′i kō′) *n., pl.* **-cos′** [Sp. or It.] *same as* POLITICIAN
pol·i·tics (pol′ə tiks) *n.pl.* [with *sing.* or *pl.* v.] 1. the science of government; political science 2. political affairs 3. participation in political affairs 4. political methods, tactics, etc. 5. political opinions, principles, etc. 6. fractional scheming for power within a group
pol·i·ty (pol′ə tē) *n., pl.* **-ties** [< MFr. < L. *politia*: see POLICY¹] 1. the government organization of a state, church, etc. 2. a society or institution with a government; state
pol·ka (pōl′kə) *n.* [Czech ? < Pol. fem. of *Polak*, a Pole] 1. a fast dance for couples 2. music for this dance, in duple time **—vi.** to dance the polka
polka dot 1. one of the small round dots regularly spaced to form a pattern on cloth 2. a pattern or cloth with such dots **—pol′ka-dot′** *adj.*
poll (pōl) *n.* [< or akin to MDu. *pol*, head] 1. the head; esp., the crown, back, or hair of the head 2. a counting, listing, etc. of persons, esp. of voters 3. the number of votes recorded 4. *a*) a canvassing of a selected or random group to collect information, or to attempt to discover public opinion *b*) a report on this **—vt.** 1. to cut off or cut short 2. to trim the poll, horns, branches, etc. of 3. *a*) to

register the votes of *b*) [U.S.] to require each member of (a jury, etc.) to declare his vote individually 4. to receive (a certain number of votes) 5. to cast (a vote) 6. to canvass in a poll (sense 4 *a*) **—vi.** to vote in an election **—poll′er** *n.*
pol·lack (pol′ək) *n., pl.* **-lack, -lacks.** see PLURAL, II D. 2 [for early Scot. *podlok* < ?] various food fish of the cod family: also sp. **pol′lock**
pol·len (pol′ən) *n.* [ModL. < L., dust] the yellow, powderlike male sex cells on the stamens of a flower
pollen count a measure of the pollen grains present in the air over a 24 hour period, published for the benefit of hay fever sufferers
pol·lex (pol′əks) *n., pl.* **pol′li·ces** (-ə sēz′) [L., thumb, big toe] the innermost digit of a forelimb; esp., the thumb **—pol′li·cal** (-ə k′l) *adj.*
pol·li·nate (pol′ə nāt′) *vt.* **-nat′ed, -nat′ing** to transfer pollen from a stamen to a pistil of (a flower) **—pol′li·na′tion** *n.* **—pol′li·na′tor** *n.*
polling booth a voting place at an election
pol·li·wog (pol′ē wog′) *n.* [prob. < *pol*, POLL + *wigelen*, to WIGGLE] [U.S. Dial.] *same as* TADPOLE: also sp. **pol′ly·wog′**
poll·ster (pōl′stər) *n.* a person whose work is taking public opinion polls
poll tax a tax per head: in some states of the U.S. payment of a poll tax is a prerequisite for voting
pol·lu·tant (pə loot′'nt) *n.* something that pollutes, as a harmful chemical discharged into the air
pol·lute (pə loot′) *vt.* **-lut′ed, -lut′ing** [< L. pp. of *polluere*] to make unclean, impure, or corrupt; defile **—pol·lut′er** *n.* **—pol·lu′tion** *n.*
Pol·lux (pol′əks) [after the immortal twin of Castor in Gr. & Rom. Myth.] the brightest star in the constellation Gemini
Pol·ly·an·na (pol′ē an′ə) *n.* [the heroine of novels by Eleanor H. Porter (1868-1920), U.S. writer] a persistently optimistic person
po·lo (pō′lō) *n.* [prob. < Tibet. *pulu*, the ball] 1. a game played on horseback by two teams who try to drive a small wooden ball through the opponents' goal with long-handled mallets 2. *same as* WATER POLO **—po′lo·ist** *n.*
po·lo·naise (pol′ə nāz′) *n.* [Fr. < fem. of *polonais*, Polish] 1. a stately Polish dance in triple time 2. music for this dance
polo·neck (pō′lō -nek′) *n.* 1. a high, snugly fitting, turnover collar on a pullover, shirt, etc. 2. a sweater, shirt, etc. with such a neck
po·lo·ni·um (pə lō′nē əm) *n.* [ModL. < ML. *Polonia*, Poland: coinage of Marie Curie, its co-discoverer] a radioactive chemical element formed by the disintegration of radium: symbol, Po; at. wt., 210.05; at. no., 84
polo shirt a knitted pullover sports shirt
polo stick the long-handled mallet used to play polo
pol·ter·geist (pōl′tər gīst′) *n.* [G. < *poltern*, to make noise + *Geist*, GHOST] a ghost supposed to be responsible for rappings and other mysterious noisy disturbances
pol·troon (pol troon′) *n.* [< Fr. < It. *poltrone*, coward < *poltro*, colt] a thorough coward **—adj.** cowardly **—pol·troon′er·y** *n.*
Poly (pol′ē) *n. Colloq. clipped form of* POLYTECHNIC
pol·y- [ModL. < Gr. *poly-* < *polys*, much, many] a combining form meaning much, many, more than one
pol·y·an·dry (pol′ē an′drē, pol′ē an′-) *n.* [< Gr. < *poly-*, many + *anēr*, a man] the state or practice of having two or more husbands at the same time **—pol′y·an′dric** *adj.* **—pol′y·an′drist** *n.* **—pol′y·an′drous** *adj.*
pol·y·an·thus (pol′ē an′thəs) *n.* [ModL. < Gr. < *poly-*, many + *anthos*, a flower] 1. any of various primroses with many flowers 2. a sweet-scented narcissus with clusters of star-shaped flowers
pol·y·bas·ic (pol′i bā′sik) *adj.* [POLY- + BASIC] designating an acid having more than one replaceable hydrogen atom per molecule
pol·y·cen·tric (pol′i sen′trik) *adj.* [POLY- + CENTR(E) + -IC] of or relating to independent centres of power within a political system **—pol′y·cen′trism** *n.* **—pol′y·cen′trist** *adj., n.*
pol·y·chro·mat·ic (-krō mat′ik) *adj.* [POLY- + CHROMATIC] having various or changing colours
pol·y·clin·ic (-klin′ik) *n.* [POLY- + CLINIC] a clinic or hospital treating various kinds of diseases
pol·y·dac·tyl (-dak′t′l) *adj.* [Fr. < Gr. *polydactylos*, many-toed] having more than the normal number of fingers and toes **—n.** a polydactyl animal or person
pol·y·es·ter (pol′ē es′tər) *n.* [POLY(MER) + ESTER] any of several polymeric synthetic resins used in making plastics, fibres, etc.
pol·y·eth·yl·ene (pol′ē eth′ə lēn′) *n.* [POLY(MER) + ETHYLENE] any of several thermoplastic resins, $(C_2H_4)_n$, used in making plastics, films, etc.
po·lyg·a·my (pə lig′ə mē) *n.* [< Fr. < Gr.: see POLY- & -GAMY] the practice of having two or more wives or husbands at the same time **—po·lyg′a·mist** *n.* **—po·lyg′a·mous** *adj.* **—po·lyg′a·mous·ly** *adv.*
pol·y·gen·e·sis (pol′i jen′ə sis) *n.* [ModL.: see POLY- &

GENESIS] 1. derivation from more than one kind of germ cell 2. the theory that different species are descended from different ultimate ancestors —**pol′y·ge·net′ic** (-jə net′ik) *adj.* —**pol′y·ge·net′i·cal·ly** *adv.*

pol·y·glot (päl′i glät′) *adj.* [< Gr. < *poly-*, many + *glötta*, the tongue] 1. speaking or writing several languages 2. containing or written in several languages —*n.* 1. a polyglot person 2. a polyglot book

pol·y·gon (päl′i gän′) *n.* [< LL. < Gr.: see POLY- & -GON] a closed plane figure, esp. one with more than four sides and angles —**po·lyg·o·nal** (pə lig′ə n'l) *adj.*

pol·y·graph (-gräf′) *n.* 1. an early device for reproducing writings or drawings 2. an instrument for recording changes in blood pressure, pulse rate, etc.: see LIE DETECTOR —**pol′y·graph′ic** *adj.*

po·lyg·y·ny (pə lij′ə nē) *n.* [ModL. < POLY- + Gr. *gynē*, a woman] the practice of having two or more wives or concubines at the same time —**po·lyg′y·nous** (-nəs) *adj.*

pol·y·he·dron (päl′i hē′drən) *n.*, *pl.* **-drons, -dra** (-drə) [ModL. < Gr.: see POLY- & -HEDRON] a solid figure, esp. one with more than six plane surfaces —**pol′y·he′dral** *adj.*

Pol·y·hym·ni·a (-him′nē ə) *Gr. Myth.* the Muse of sacred poetry: also **Po·lym′ni·a** (pə lim′-)

pol·y·math (päl′i math′) *n.* [< Gr. < *poly-* (see POLY-) + *manthanein*, to learn] a person of great and diversified learning —**pol′y·math′ic** *adj.*

pol·y·mer (päl′i mər) *n.* [G. < Gr.: see POLY- & -MEROUS] a naturally occurring or synthetic substance made up of giant molecules formed by polymerization —**po·lym·er·ous** (pə lim′ə rəs) *adj.*

pol·y·mer·ic (päl′i mer′ik) *adj.* composed of the same chemical elements in the same proportions by weight, but differing in molecular weight —**pol′y·mer′i·cal·ly** *adv.*

po·lym·er·i·za·tion (pə lim′ər i zā′shən, päl′i mər-) *n.* the process of joining two or more like molecules to form a more complex molecule whose molecular weight is a multiple of the original and whose physical properties are different —**po·lym′er·ize′** (-īz′) *vt.*, *vi.* **-ized′, -iz′ing**

pol·y·mor·phous (päl′i môr′fəs) *adj.* [< Gr.: see POLY- & -MORPH] having, occurring in, or passing through several or various forms: also **pol′y·mor′phic** —**pol′y·mor′phism** *n.* —**pol′y·mor′phous·ly** *adv.*

Pol·y·ne·sian (päl′ə nē′zhən, -shən) *adj.* of Polynesia, its people, their language, etc. —*n.* 1. a member of the brown people of Polynesia, including the Hawaiians, Tahitians, Samoans, and Maoris 2. the group of Malayo-Polynesian languages of Polynesia

pol·y·no·mi·al (päl′i nō′mē əl) *n.* [POLY- + (BI)NOMIAL] 1. *Algebra* an expression consisting of two or more terms (Ex.: x³ + 3x + 2) 2. *Biol.* a species or subspecies name having two or more terms —*adj.* consisting of polynomials

pol·yp (päl′ip) *n.* [< Fr. < L. < Gr. < *poly-*, many + *pous*, a foot] 1. any of various coelenterates having a mouth fringed with tentacles at the top of a tubelike body, as the sea anemone, hydra, etc. 2. a projecting growth of mucous membrane inside the nose, bladder, etc. —**pol′yp·ous** *adj.*

pol·y·pep·tide (päl′i pep′tīd) *n.* [POLY- + PEPTIDE] a substance containing two or more amino acids in the molecule joined together by peptide linkages

pol·y·pet·al·ous (-pet′'l əs) *adj.* [POLY- + PETAL + -OUS] *Bot.* having separate petals

pol·y·phon·ic (päl′i fän′ik) *adj.* [< Gr.: see POLY- & -PHONE] 1. having or making many sounds 2. *Music* of or characterized by polyphony; contrapuntal Also **po·lyph·o·nous** (pə lif′ə nəs) —**pol′y·phon′i·cal·ly** *adv.*

po·lyph·o·ny (pə lif′ə nē) *n.* 1. multiplicity of sounds, as in an echo 2. *Music* a combining of a number of individual but harmonious melodies; counterpoint

pol·y·pro·pyl·ene (päl′i prō′pə lēn′) *n.* [POLY(MER) + PROPYLENE] polymerized propylene, a very light thermoplastic resin used in packaging, tubing, etc.

pol·y·se·my (päl′i sē′mē) *n.* [ModL. *polysemia* < Gr. *polysēmos* < *poly-*, POLY- & *sēma*, a sign] the fact of having or being open to several or many meanings —**pol′y·se·mous** (-məs) *adj.*

pol·y·some (päl′i sōm′) *n.* [POLY- + -SOME³] a group of ribosomes in which protein synthesis occurs

pol·y·so·mic (päl′i sō′mik) *adj.* [< prec. + -IC] *Genetics* having extra chromosomes, not in a set

pol·y·sty·rene (-stī′rēn) *n.* a tough plastic, a polymer of styrene, used to make containers, etc.

pol·y·syl·lab·ic (-si lab′ik) *adj.* 1. having several, esp. four or more, syllables 2. characterized by polysyllables Also **pol′y·syl·lab′i·cal** —**pol′y·syl·lab′i·cal·ly** *adv.*

pol·y·syl·la·ble (päl′i sil′ə b'l) *n.* a polysyllabic word

pol·y·tech·nic (päl′i tek′nik) *adj.* [< Fr. < Gr. < *poly-*,

many + *technē*, an art] of or providing instruction in many scientific and technical subjects —*n.* a polytechnic college, etc.

pol·y·the·ism (päl′i thē iz'm) *n.* [< Fr. < Gr. < *poly-*, many + *theos*, god] belief in more than one god —**pol′y·the·ist** *adj.*, *n.* —**pol′y·the·is′tic, pol′y·the·is′ti·cal** *adj.* —**pol′y·the·is′ti·cal·ly** *adv.*

pol·y·thene (päl′i thēn′) *n.* *var. of* POLYETHYLENE

pol·y·un·sat·u·rat·ed (päl′i un sach′ə rāt′id) *adj.* [POLY- + UNSATURATED] containing more than one double or triple bond in the molecule, as certain vegetable and animal fats and oils

pol·y·u·re·thane (-yoor′ə thān′) *n.* [POLY- + URETHANE] any of certain synthetic rubber polymers used in cushions, moulded products, etc.

pol·y·va·lent (-vā′lənt) *adj.* 1. designating a vaccine for two or more strains of the same microorganism 2. *Chem.* a) having a valence of more than two b) having more than one valence —**pol′y·va′lence** *n.*

poly vinyl chloride a polymer of vinyl chloride that is tough and resistant, used for pipes, films, etc.

pol·y·wa·ter (-wôt′ər) *n.* [POLY(MERIC) + WATER] a viscous substance variously identified as a new form of water, highly contaminated water, etc.

pom·ace (pum′is) *n.* [ML. *pomacium*, cider < L. *pomum*, a fruit] 1. the crushed pulp of apples or other fruit pressed for juice 2. the crushed matter of anything pressed, as seeds for oil

po·ma·ceous (pō mā′shəs) *adj.* [< L. *pomum*, a fruit] of or like apples or other pomes

po·made (po mäd′, pə-) *n.* [< Fr. < It. *pomata*, ult. < L. *pomum*, fruit: orig. perfumed with apple pulp] a perfumed preparation, as for grooming the hair: also **po·ma·tum** (pō mät′əm) —*vt.* **-mad′ed, -mad′ing** to apply pomade to

po·man·der (pō man′dər, pə man′-) *n.* [< MFr. *pome ambre* < *pome* (see POME) + *ambre*, amber] 1. a mixture of aromatic substances compressed in a ball, thought to be a safeguard against infection 2. a case for carrying this, esp. a hollow, perforated ball

pome (pōm) *n.* [OFr., ult. < L. *pomum*, fruit] any fleshy fruit with a core and seeds, as the apple, pear, etc.

pome·gran·ate (pom′ə gran′it, pom′gran-) *n.* [< OFr. < *pome*, apple + *granade* < L. *granatum*, lit., having seeds] 1. a round fruit with a thick, red rind and many seeds covered with red, juicy, edible flesh 2. the bush or small tree that bears it

Pom·er·a·ni·an (pom′ə rā′nē ən) *adj.* of Pomerania or its people —*n.* 1. a native or inhabitant of Pomerania 2. any of a breed of small dog with long, silky hair, pointed ears, and a bushy tail

pomfret cake (pum′frət, -frē) a small, cakelike sweet made of liquorice, originally made at Pontefract; also **pom′-fret-cake, pontefract cake**

pom·mel (pum′'l; *also, for n.,* pom′'l) *n.* [< OFr. dim. of *pome*: see POME] 1. a round knob on the end of some sword hilts 2. the rounded, upward-projecting front part of a saddle —*vt.* **-melled, -mel·ling** *same as* PUMMEL

Pom·my, Pom·mie (pom′ē) *n.*, *pl.* **-mies** [? < POMEGRANATE because of rosy cheeks of British immigrants or < P.O.M.E., Prisoner of Mother England] [also p-] [Aust. Slang] a Briton —*adj.* [also p-] [Aust. Slang] British

po·mol·o·gy (pō mol′ə jē) *n.* [< ModL.: see POME & -LOGY] the science of fruit cultivation —**po′mo·log′i·cal** (-mə loj′-i k'l) *adj.* —**po·mol′o·gist** *n.*

pomp (pomp) *n.* [< MFr. < L. < Gr. *pompē*, solemn procession] 1. stately display; splendour 2. ostentatious show or display

pom·pa·dour (pom′pə door′) *n.* [after Marquise de *Pompadour*, mistress of Louis XV] a hair style in which the hair is swept or brushed up high from the forehead

pom·pa·no (pom′pə nō′) *n.*, *pl.* **-no′, -nos′**: see PLURAL, II, D, 2 [Sp. *pámpano*] a spiny-finned, saltwater food fish of N America and the West Indies

pom-pom (pom′pom′) *n.* [echoic] 1. any of several rapid-firing automatic weapons 2. *same as* POMPON (sense 1): also **pom′pom′**

pom·pon (pom′pon′, -pom′) *n.* [Fr.] 1. an ornamental ball or tuft as of silk or wool, worn as on hats, shoes, etc. 2. *a*) a kind of chrysanthemum, dahlia, etc. with small, round flowers *b*) the flower

pom·pous (pom′pəs) *adj.* 1. full of pomp; magnificent 2. pretentious, as in speech or manner; self-important —**pom·pos′i·ty** (-pos′ə tē), *pl.* **-ties, pom′pous·ness** *n.* —**pom′pous·ly** *adv.*

ponce (pons) *n.* [< ?] [Slang] *same as* PIMP —*vi.* **ponced, ponc′ing** [Slang] 1. *same as* PIMP 2. to go around in a flashy or showy way [he ponced around the room]

pon·cho (pon′chō) *n.*, *pl.* **-chos** [< SAmInd.] 1. a cloak like a blanket with a hole in the middle for the head 2. a garment, esp. a raincoat, like this

pond (pond) *n.* [< ME. var. of POUND³] 1. body of standing water smaller than a lake, often man-made 2. the sea: a jocular usage

MOUTH

PERISARC

POLYP
(sense 1)

pon·der (pon′dər) *vt., vi.* [< MFr. < L. *ponderare*, to weigh < *pondus*, a weight] to think deeply (about); deliberate —**pon′der·a·bil′i·ty** *n.* —**pon′der·a·ble** *adj.* —**pon′der·er** *n.*

pon·der·ous (pon′dər əs) *adj.* [< L. < *pondus* (gen. *ponderis*), a weight] 1. very heavy 2. unwieldy because of weight 3. bulky; massive 4. laboured; dull [a *ponderous* style] —**pon′der·ous·ly** *adv.* —**pon′der·ous·ness, pon′-der·os′i·ty** (-os′ə tē) *n.*

pond lily *same as* WATERLILY

pond scum a mass of filamentous algae forming a green scum on the surface of ponds, etc.

pond·weed (pond′wēd′) *n.* any of various related water plants, with submerged or floating leaves

pone[1] (pōn) *n.* [< Algonquian] [Chiefly Southern U.S.] 1. maize bread in small, oval loaves 2. such a loaf

pone[2] (pōn) *n.* [< L. *ponere*, to put] *Cards* the player to the right of the dealer

pong (poŋ) *vi., n.* [prob. < Romany *pan*, to stink] [Slang] *same as* STINK

pon·gee (pon jē′) *n.* [< Chin. dial. *pen-chi*, domestic loom] 1. a soft, thin silk cloth, usually left in its natural light-brown colour 2. a cloth like this

pon·go (poŋ′gō) *n.* [Abor.] an Australian flying squirrel

pon·iard (pon′yərd) *n.* [< Fr., ult. < L. *pugnus*, fist] a dagger —*vt.* to stab with a poniard

pons (ponz) *n. pl.* **pon·tes** (pon′tēz) [L., a bridge] *Anat., Zool.* a piece of connecting tissue

pon·ti·fex (pon′tə feks′) *n., pl.* **pon·tif·i·ces** (pon tif′ə sēz′) [L.: see ff.] in ancient Rome, a member of the supreme college of priests

pon·tiff (pon′tif) *n.* [< Fr. < LL. *pontifex*, bishop < L., high priest] 1. a bishop; specif., [P-] the Pope (in full, **Supreme Pontiff**) 2. a high priest

pon·tif·i·cal (pon tif′i k'l) *adj.* 1. having to do with a high priest 2. celebrated by a bishop or other highranking prelate [a *pontifical* Mass] 3. papal 4. having the pomp, dogmatism, etc. of a pontiff; often, specif., arrogant or haughty —*n.* 1. [*pl.*] a pontiff's vestments and insignia 2. a book of rites as performed by a bishop —**pon·tif′i·cal·ly** *adv.*

pon·tif·i·cate (-kit; *also, and for v. always,* -kāt′) *n.* the office or tenure of a pontiff —*vi.* **-cat′ed, -cat′ing** 1. to officiate as a pontiff 2. to speak in a pompous or dogmatic way —**pon·tif′i·ca′tor** *n.*

pon·toon[1] (pon tōōn′) *n. same as* VINGT-ET-UN

pon·toon[2] (pon tōōn′) *n.* [Fr. < L. *ponto* < *pons*, a bridge] 1. a flat-bottomed boat 2. any of a number of these, or of hollow, floating cylinders, etc., used to support a temporary bridge (**pontoon bridge**) 3. a float on an aircraft

po·ny (pō′nē) *n., pl.* **-nies** [< Scot., prob. < OFr. dim of *poulain*, a colt, ult. < L. *pullus*, foal] 1. a small horse of any of several breeds, usually not over 1·3 m high at the withers 2.[U.S.] something small of its kind; specif., a small liqueur glass or its contents 3. [Colloq.] a sum of money in bookmaking, £25 4.[Slang] a racehorse

po·ny·tail (pō′nē tāl′) *n.* a hair style in which long hair, tied high at the back of the head, hangs free

pony trekking the pastime of travelling through the countryside on horseback, usually in an organized group

pooch (pōōch) *n.* [U.S. Slang] a dog

poo·dle (pōō′d'l) *n.* [G. *Pudel* < LowG. < *pudeln*, to splash] any of a breed of dog with a solid-coloured, curly coat

poof (poof, pōōf) *n.* [< Fr. *pouffe*, puff] [Colloq.] an effeminate man, esp. a male homosexual

pooh (pōō) *interj.* [prob. echoic] an exclamation of disdain, disbelief, or impatience

Pooh-Bah (pōō′bä′) *n.* [after *Pooh-Bah* in Gilbert & Sullivan's *The Mikado*] 1. an official holding several offices at once and fulfilling none of them 2. a pompous, self-important person

pooh-pooh (pōō′pōō′) *vt.* [redupl. of POOH] to minimize; make light of; belittle

pool[1] (pōōl) *n.* [OE. *pol*] 1. a small pond, as in a garden 2. a puddle 3. *same as* SWIMMING POOL 4. a deep, still spot in a river 5. a natural underground accumulation of oil or gas —*vi.* to form, or accumulate in, a pool

pool[2] (pōōl) *n.* [Fr. *poule* < LL. *pulla*, hen: associated in E. with *prec.*] 1. the total stakes played for, as in a single deal of a card game 2. *a)* a game of billiards for such a pool *b)* [Chiefly U.S.] a game of billiards played with object balls numbered 1 to 15 and a cue ball, on a table with six pockets 3. *a)* a combination of resources, funds, etc. for some common purpose *b)* the persons or parties forming it 4. a combination of business firms for creating a monopoly 5. a supply of equipment, personnel, etc. shared by a group —*vt., vi.* to contribute to a common fund; form a pool (of)

pools (pōōlz) *n. pl.* an organized gambling pool betting, mostly through the post, on the result of football matches: also **football pools**

poop[1] (pōōp) *n.* [< MFr., ult. < L. *puppis*] 1. orig., the stern of a ship 2. on sailing ships, a raised deck at the stern, sometimes forming the roof of a cabin: also **poop deck** —*vt.* to break over the poop or stern of: said of waves

poop[2] (pōōp) *vt.* [echoic] [U.S. Slang] to tire: usually in the passive voice —**poop out** [U.S. Slang] 1. to become exhausted 2. to cease functioning

poor (poor) *adj.* [< OFr. < L. *pauper*, poor] 1. *a)* having little or no means to support oneself; needy *b)* indicating or characterized by poverty [a *poor* relation] 2. lacking in some quality or thing; specif., *a)* scanty; inadequate [*poor* crops] *b)* barren; sterile [*poor* soil] *c)* lacking nourishment; feeble *d)* lacking excellence; inferior *e)* mean-spirited; contemptible *f)* lacking pleasure or comfort *g)* lacking skill [a *poor* cook] 3. worthy of pity; unfortunate —**the poor** poor, or needy, people —**poor′ly** *adv.* —**poor′ness** *n.*

poor·house (-hous′) *n.* formerly, an institution for paupers, supported from public funds

poor law formerly, a law providing for the relief or support of the poor from public, esp. parish, funds

poor man's weatherglass *same as* PIMPERNEL

poor white [U.S.] a white person, esp. in the South, who lives in great poverty: often an offensive term

pop[1] (pop) *n.* [echoic] 1. a sudden, short, light explosive sound 2. a shot with a revolver, rifle, etc. 3. any carbonated, nonalcoholic beverage —*vi.* **popped, pop′ping** 1. to make, or burst with, a pop 2. to move, go, come, etc. suddenly and quickly 3. to open wide suddenly, or protrude: said of the eyes 4. to shoot a pistol, etc. —*vt.* 1. [U.S.] to cause (maize) to pop, as by roasting, etc. 2. *a)* to fire (a pistol, etc.) *b)* to shoot 3. to put suddenly or quickly [to *pop* one's head in at the door] 4. to place in pawn —*adv.* with or like a pop —**pop off** [Slang] 1. to die suddenly 2. [U.S.] to speak or write emotionally, etc. 3. to leave hastily —**pop the question** [Colloq.] to propose marriage

pop[2] (pop) *n.* [< PAPA] [U.S. Slang] father: also a familiar term of address for any elderly man

pop[3] (pop) *adj.* *clipped form of* POPULAR

pop[4] (pop) *n.* [< POP(ULAR)] music popular among young people, characterized by strong rhythm and electronic amplification

pop. 1. popular 2. popularly 3. population

P.O.P. Post Office Preferred

pop (art) (pop) a realistic style of painting and sculpture, using techniques and popular subjects from commercial art and mass media, such as comic strips

pop concert 1. a popular concert, chiefly of semiclassical and light classical music 2. a concert at which rock music, reggae, etc. is played, esp. for young people

pop·corn (-kôrn′) *n.* 1. a variety of maize with small ears and hard grains which pop open in a white, puffy mass when heated 2. the popped grains, often salted for eating

pope (pōp) *n.* [OE. *papa* < LL., ult. < Gr. *pappas*, father] [*usually* P-] R.C.Ch. the bishop of Rome and head of the Church —**pope′dom** (-dəm) *n.*

pop·er·y (pōp′ər ē) *n.* the doctrines and rituals of the Roman Catholic Church: a hostile term

pop-eyed (pop′īd′) *adj.* having protruding eyes

pop·gun (-gun′) *n.* a toy gun that shoots pellets by air compression, with a pop

pop·in·jay (pop′in jā′) *n.* [< MFr. *papagai* < Ar. *babaghā*, parrot] a talkative, conceited person

pop·ish (pōp′ish) *adj.* having to do with popery: a hostile term —**pop′ish·ly** *adv.* —**pop′ish·ness** *n.*

pop·lar (pop′lər) *n.* [< OFr. *poplier*, ult. < L. *populus*] 1. any of various tall, fast-growing trees with alternate leaves and catkins 2. the wood of any of these 3. [U.S.] *same as: a)* TULIP TREE *b)* TULIPWOOD (sense 1)

pop·lin (pop′lin) *n.* [Fr. *papeline*, prob. < It. *papalina*, papal, after the papal city of Avignon] a sturdy fabric of cotton, rayon, etc. with fine ribbing

pop·per (-ər) *n.* 1. a person or thing that pops 2. [U.S.] a covered wire basket or pan for popping maize 3. [Colloq.] *same as* PRESS STUD

pop·pet (pop′it) *n.* [var. of PUPPET] 1. a valve that moves into and from its seat, as in an internal combustion engine: in full, **poppet valve** 2. [Colloq.] a little person: a term of endearment

popping crease *Cricket* the line 4 feet in front of the wicket at, or behind which, the batsman stands

pop·py (pop′ē) *n., pl.* **-pies** [OE. *popæg* < L. *papaver*] 1. any of various related plants with a milky juice and showy, variously coloured flowers 2. the flower of any of these 3. an extract, as opium, made from poppy juice 4. yellowish red, the colour of some poppies: also **poppy red**

pop·py·cock (-kok′) *n.* [Du. *pappekak*, dung] [Colloq.] nonsense

Poppy Day another name for Remembrance Day, because of the artificial poppies sold in aid of the Earl Haig Fund

poppy seed the small, dark seed of the poppy, used in baking, etc. as a flavouring or topping

pop shop [Colloq.] a pawnshop

pop·sy, pop·sie (pop′sē) *n., pl.* **-sies** [< *pop*, short for POPPET & -Y[1]] [Colloq.] a girl or young woman: a term of affection

pop·u·lace (pop′yə lis) *n.* [Fr. < It. < L. *populus*, PEOPLE]

1. the common people; the masses 2. *same as* POPULATION (sense 1a)

pop·u·lar (pop′yə lər) *adj.* [< L. < *populus*, PEOPLE] 1. of or carried on by people generally 2. suitable or intended for the general public [*popular music*] 3. within the means of the ordinary person [*popular* prices] 4. common; prevalent [a *popular* belief] 5. liked by very many people [a *popular* actor] 6. having many friends —**pop′u·lar′i·ty** (-lar′ə tē) *n.* —**pop′u·lar·ly** *adv.*

popular front a political coalition of left wing and liberal groups, as in France (1936–39) to combat fascism

pop·u·lar·ize (pop′yə lə rīz′) *vt.* **-ized′**, **-iz′ing** 1. to make popular 2. to make understandable to the general public —**pop′u·lar·i·za′tion** *n.* —**pop′u·lar·iz′er** *n.*

pop·u·late (pop′yə lāt′) *vt.* **-lat′ed**, **-lat′ing** [< ML. pp. of *populare* < L. *populus*, PEOPLE] 1. to inhabit 2. to supply with inhabitants

pop·u·la·tion (pop′yə lā′shən) *n.* 1. *a)* all the people in a country, region, etc. *b)* the number of these *c)* a (specified) part of the people in a given area [the Indian *population* of Glasgow] 2. a populating or being populated 3. *Biol.* all the organisms living in a given area 4. *Statistics* a group of persons or things

population explosion the very great and continuing increase in human population in modern times

pop·u·lous (pop′yə ləs) *adj.* full of people; thickly populated —**pop′u·lous·ly** *adv.* —**pop′u·lous·ness** *n.*

por·ce·lain (pôr′s'l in, pôrs′lin) *n.* [< Fr. < It. *porcellana*, a kind of shell, shaped like a pig, ult. < L. *porcus*, pig] 1. a hard, white, nonporous, translucent ceramic ware, made of kaolin, feldspar, and quartz or flint 2. porcelain dishes or ornaments, collectively —*adj.* made of porcelain —**por′cel·la′ne·ous** (-sə lā′nē əs) *adj.*

por·ce·lain·ize (-īz′) *vt.* **-ized′**, **-iz′ing** to coat with porcelain or a substance like it

porch (pôrch) *n.* [< OFr. < L. *porticus* < *porta*, a gate] 1. a structure projecting from the doorway of a building and forming a covered or enclosed entrance 2. [U.S.] a veranda 3. [Obs.] a portico

por·cine (pôr′sīn, -sin) *adj.* [< Fr. < L. < *porcus*, a pig] of or like pigs

por·cu·pine (pôr′kyə pīn′) *n.*, *pl.* **-pines′**, **-pine′**: see PLURAL, II, D, 1 [< MFr. < OIt. < L. *porcus*, a pig + *spina*, a spine] any of various large, related rodents having coarse hair mixed with long, stiff, sharp spines

pore[1] (pôr) *vi.* **pored**, **por′ing** [< ?] 1. to read or study carefully [to *pore* over a book] 2. to ponder (with *over*)

pore[2] (pôr) *n.* [< L. < Gr. *poros*, a passage] 1. a tiny opening, as in plant leaves, skin, etc., through which fluids may be absorbed or discharged 2. a similar tiny opening in rocks or other substances

por·gy (pôr′gē) *n.*, *pl.* **-gies, -gy**: see PLURAL, II, D, 1 [prob. < Sp. or Port. *pargo* < L. *pagrus* < Gr. *phagros*, sea bream] 1. a N. American saltwater food fish having spiny fins and a wide body, as the sea bream 2. any of various other fishes, as the menhaden

pork (pôrk) *n.* [< OFr. < L. *porcus*, a pig] the flesh of a pig used, fresh or cured, as food

pork barrel [U.S. Colloq.] government money spent for political patronage, as for local improvements to please the voters in a district

pork butcher 1. a butcher who specializes in selling pork 2. someone who kills pigs

pork·er (pôr′kər) *n.* a pig, esp. a young one, fattened for use as food

pork pie 1. a meat pie made with chopped pork 2. a man's soft hat with a round, flat crown: now often **pork′pie′***n.*, **porkpie hat**

pork·y (pôr′kē) *adj.* **pork′i·er**, **pork′i·est** 1. of or like pork 2. fat, as though overfed

porn (porn) *n.* *colloq.* clipped form of PORNOGRAPHY

porn·o (pôrn′ō) *n.*, *adj.* *colloq.* clipped form of: 1. PORNOGRAPHY 2. PORNOGRAPHIC (see PORNOGRAPHY)

por·nog·ra·phy (pôr nog′rə fē) *n.* [< Gr. < *porne*, a prostitute + *graphein*, to write] writings, pictures, etc. intended primarily to arouse sexual desire —**por·nog′ra·pher** *n.* —**por′no·graph′ic** (-nə graf′ik) *adj.* —**por′no·graph′i·cal·ly** *adv.*

po·rous (pôr′əs) *adj.* full of pores, through which fluids, air, or light may pass —**po·ros·i·ty** (pô ros′ə tē, pə-), **po′rous·ness** *n.* —**po′rous·ly** *adv.*

por·phyr·i·a (pô fir′ē ə) *n.* [ModL. < Gr. *porphyra*, purple + -IA] an inherited disorder of pigment metabolism with abnormal pigmentation of urine and sensitivity to sunlight

por·phy·ry (pôr′fər ē) *n.*, *pl.* **-ries** [< OFr. < ML., ult. < Gr. *porphyros*, purple] 1. orig., an Egyptian rock with large feldspar crystals in a purplish rock mass 2. any igneous rock resembling this —**por′phy·rit′ic** (-fə rit′ik) *adj.*

por·poise (pôr′pəs) *n.*, *pl.* **-pois·es, -poise**: see PLURAL, II, D, 1 [< OFr. *porpeis* < L. *porcus*, a pig + *piscis*, a fish] 1. any of a number of small, toothed whales with a blunt snout, found in most seas, esp. the **harbour porpoise** 2. a dolphin or any of several other small cetaceans

por·ridge (por′ij) *n.* [altered < POTTAGE by confusion with ME. *porrey* < OFr. < VL. *porrata*, leek broth < L. *porrum*, leek] a soft food made of cereal or oatmeal boiled in water or milk 2. [Slang] a prison term

por·rin·ger (-in jər) *n.* [< Fr. *potager*, soup dish: altered after prec.] a bowl for porridge, soup, etc., esp. one of metal used by children

port[1] (pôrt) *n.* [OFr. & OE. < L. *portus*, a haven] 1. a harbour 2. a city with a harbour where ships can load and unload cargo 3. *same as* PORT OF ENTRY

port[2] (pôrt) *n.* [< *Oporto*, city in Portugal] a sweet, fortified, usually dark-red wine

port[3] (pôrt) *vt.* [< MFr. < L. *portare*, to carry] to hold or place (a rifle or sword) diagonally in front of one, as for inspection —*n.* way of carrying the head and body

port[4] (pôrt) *n.* [prob. < PORT[1]] the left-hand side of a ship or aircraft as one faces forwards, towards the bow —*adj.* of or on the port —*vt., vi.* to move or turn (the helm) to the port side

port[5] (pôrt) *n.* [< OFr. < L. *porta*, a door] 1. *a) same as* PORTHOLE *b)* a porthole covering 2. an opening, as in a valve face, for the passage of steam, gas, etc.

Port. 1. Portugal 2. Portuguese

port·a·ble (pôr′tə b'l) *adj.* [< MFr. < LL. < L. *portare*, to carry] 1. that can be carried 2. *a)* easily carried or moved, esp. by hand [a *portable* TV] *b)* that can be used anywhere because battery-operated [a *portable* radio] —*n.* something portable —**port′a·bil′i·ty** *n.*

por·tage (pôr′tij; for n 2 & v., also Canad. pôr täzh′) *n.* [MFr. < ML. *portaticum* < L. *portare*, to carry] 1. the act of carrying 2. *a)* a carrying of boats and supplies overland between navigable rivers, lakes, etc. *b)* any route over which this is done —*vt., vi.* **-taged**, **-tag·ing** to carry (boats, etc.) over a portage

por·tal (pôr′t'l) *n.* [MFr. < ML. < L. *porta*, a gate] a doorway, gate, or entrance, esp. a large or imposing one

port authority the appointed or elected body responsible for the traffic, regulations, etc. of a port

port·cul·lis (pôrt kul′is) *n.* [< MFr. < *porte*, a gate + *coleïce*, sliding < L. *colare*, to filter] a heavy iron grating suspended by chains and lowered between grooves to bar the gateway of a castle or fortified town

Porte (pôrt) *n.* [Fr., in *la Sublime Porte*, transl. of Turk. *Babi Ali*, the imperial gate, regarded as the seat of government] the Ottoman Turkish government

porte-co·chere, porte-co·chère (pôrt′kō sher′) *n.* [Fr., coach gate] 1. a large gateway into a courtyard 2. [Chiefly U.S.] a kind of porch roof projecting over a driveway at an entrance to a house, etc.

por·tend (pôr tend′) *vt.* [< L. *portendere* < *por-*, akin to *per-*, through + *tendere*, to stretch] 1. to be an omen or warning of; foreshadow 2. to be an indication of; signify

por·tent (pôr′tent) *n.* 1. something that portends an event about to occur, esp. an unfortunate event; omen 2. a portending; significance 3. a marvel

por·ten·tous (pôr ten′təs) *adj.* 1. being a portent; ominous 2. marvellous; amazing 3. pompous —**por·ten′tous·ly** *adv.* —**por·ten′tous·ness** *n.*

por·ter[1] (pôr′tər) *n.* [< OFr. < LL. *portarius* < L. *porta*, a gate] a doorman or gatekeeper, esp. at a university or college —**port′ress** *n. fem.*

por·ter[2] (pôr′tər) *n.* [< OFr. < LL. < L. *portare*, to carry] 1. a man whose work is to carry luggage, as at a railway station 2. a man who sweeps, cleans, does errands, etc. in a hotel, shop, etc. 3. [abbrev. of *porter's ale*] a dark-brown beer

por·ter·house (-hous′) *n.* 1. [Chiefly U.S.] formerly, a place serving beer, porter, etc. (and sometimes steaks and chops) 2. a choice cut of beef from the loin just before the sirloin: in full, **porterhouse steak**

port·fo·li·o (pôrt fō′lē ō′) *n.*, *pl.* **-li·os′** [< It. *portafoglio* < L. *portare*, to carry + *folium*, a leaf] 1. a flat, portable case for carrying loose papers, drawings, etc. 2. such a case for state documents 3. the office of a minister of state [a minister without *portfolio*] 4. a list of an investor's stocks, bonds, etc.

port·hole (pôrt′hōl′) *n.* 1. an opening in a ship's side, as for admitting light and air 2. an opening to shoot through; embrasure 3. any similar opening

por·ti·co (pôr′tə kō′) *n.*, *pl.* **-coes′, -cos′** [It. < L. *porticus*: see PORCH] a porch or covered walk, consisting of a roof supported by columns

por·tière (pôr tyer′, -tē er′) *n.* [Fr. < *porte*, a door] a curtain hung in a doorway

por·tion (pôr′shən) *n.* [< OFr. < L. *portio* (gen. *portionis*)] 1. a part, esp. as allotted to a person, set aside for some purpose, etc.; share 2. the part of an estate received by an heir 3. a dowry 4. one's lot; destiny 5. a helping

PORTICO

of food —*vt.* **1.** to divide into portions **2.** to give as a portion to **3.** to give a portion to —**por'tion·er** *n.* —**por'tion·less** *adj.*

portland cement [concrete made from it resembles stone from the Isle of *Portland*] [*sometimes* P-] a kind of cement that hardens under water, made by burning limestone and clay

port·ly (pôrt'lē) *adj.* -**li·er**, -**li·est** [PORT³ + -LY¹] **1.** large and heavy in a dignified or stately way **2.** stout; corpulent —**port'li·ness** *n.*

port·man·teau (pôrt man'tō) *n., pl.* -**teaus**, -**teaux** (-tōz) [< Fr. < *porter*, to carry + *manteau*, a cloak] a stiff leather suitcase that opens like a book into two compartments

portmanteau word a word that is a combination of two others (Ex.: *smog*, from *smoke* and *fog*)

port of call 1. a port where ships stop regularly **2.** any place visited on a traveller's itinerary

port of entry any place where customs officials check people and foreign goods entering a country

por·trait (pôr'trit, -trāt) *n.* [MFr., pp. of *portraire*: see PORTRAY] **1.** a painting, photograph, etc. of a person, esp. of his face **2.** a description, portrayal, etc. of a person —**por'trait·ist** *n.*

por·trai·ture (pôr'tri chər) *n.* **1.** the making of portraits **2.** a portrait

por·tray (pôr trā') *vt.* [MFr. *portraire* < L. < *pro-*, forth + *trahere*, to draw] **1.** to make a picture or portrait of **2.** to make a word picture of; describe **3.** to play the part of in a play, film, etc. —**por·tray'a·ble** *adj.* —**por·tray'al** *n.* —**por·tray'er** *n.*

Por·tu·guese (pôr'chə gēz') *adj.* of Portugal, its people, their language, etc. —*n.* **1.** *pl.* -**guese'** a native or inhabitant of Portugal **2.** the Romance language spoken in Portugal and Brazil

Portuguese man-of-war a large, warm-sea animal having long, dangling tentacles that sting, and a large, bladderlike sac that enables it to float on water

por·tu·lac·a (pôr'chə lak'ə) *n.* [ModL. < L., purslane] a fleshy annual plant with yellow, pink, or purple flowers

pose¹ (pōz) *vt.* **posed, pos'ing** [< OFr. *poser* < VL. < LL. *pausare*, to pause: infl. by L. *positus*, pp. of *ponere*, to place] **1.** to put forth; assert [*to pose a claim*] **2.** to propose (a question, problem, etc.) **3.** to put (a model, photographic subject, etc.) in a certain attitude —*vi.* **1.** to assume a certain attitude, as in modelling for an artist **2.** to strike attitudes for effect [*look at her posing*] **3.** to pretend to be what one is not [*to pose as an officer*] —*n.* **1.** a bodily attitude, esp. one held for an artist, photographer, etc. **2.** behaviour or speech assumed for effect; pretence

pose² (pōz) *vt.* **posed, pos'ing** [< APPOSE, OPPOSE] to baffle, as by a difficult question

pos·er¹ (pō'zər) *n.* **1.** a person who poses **2.** a person who behaves in an affected way

pos·er² (pō'zər) *n.* a baffling question or problem

po·seur (pō zur') *n.* [Fr.] a person who assumes attitudes or manners merely for their effect upon others

posh (posh) *adj.* [prob. < obs. slang *posh*, a dandy] [Colloq.] luxurious and fashionable; elegant —**posh'ly** *adv.* —**posh'ness** *n.*

pos·it (poz'it) *vt.* [< L. *positus*, pp. of *ponere*, to place] **1.** to set in place or position; situate **2.** to set down or assume as fact; postulate

po·si·tion (pə zish'ən) *n.* [MFr. < L. *positio* < pp. of *ponere*, to place] **1.** the manner in which a person or thing is placed or arranged; attitude **2.** one's attitude towards or opinion on a subject; stand **3.** the place where a person or thing is, esp. in relation to others; location or situation **4.** the usual or proper place; station [*the players are in position*] **5.** a location or condition of advantage [*to jockey for position*] **6.** a person's relative place, as in society; rank; status **7.** a place high in society, business, etc. [*a man of position*] **8.** a post of employment; job; office —*vt.* to put in a particular position; place —**po·si'tion·al** *adj.* —**po·si'tion·er** *n.*

pos·i·tive (poz'ə tiv) *adj.* [< OFr. < L. *positivus* < pp. of *ponere*, to place] **1.** *a)* definitely set; explicit; specific [*positive instructions*] *b)* allowing no doubt; certain; sure **2.** *a)* sure in mind; confident; assured [*a positive person*] *b)* overconfident or dogmatic **3.** showing resolution or agreement; affirmative [*a positive answer*] **4.** tending in the direction regarded as that of increase, progress, etc. **5.** making a definite contribution; constructive [*positive criticism*] **6.** unrelated to anything else; absolute; unqualified **7.** having real existence in itself [*a positive good*] **8.** based on reality or facts [*positive proof*] **9.** concerned only with real things and experience; empirical; practical **10.** [Colloq.] complete; downright [*a positive fool*] **11.** *Biol.* directed towards the source of a stimulus [*positive tropism*] **12.** *Elec. a)* of, generating, or charged with POSITIVE ELECTRICITY *b)* having a deficiency of electrons **13.** *Gram.* of an adjective or adverb in its uninflected or

unmodified form or degree: neither comparative nor superlative **14.** *Math.* greater than zero; plus **15.** *Med.* indicating the presence or existence of a condition, symptoms, bacteria, etc. **16.** *Photog.* with the relation of light and shade the same as in the thing photographed —*n.* something positive, as a degree, quality, etc.; specif., *a)* the plate in a voltaic battery where the higher potential is *b)* *Gram.* the positive degree, or a word in it *c)* *Math.* a positive quantity *d)* *Photog.* a positive print —**pos'i·tive·ly** *adv.* —**pos'i·tive·ness** *n.*

positive electricity the kind of electricity in a glass body rubbed with silk; it is deficient in electrons

pos·i·tiv·ism (poz'ə tiv iz'm) *n.* **1.** a being positive; certainty; assurance **2.** overconfidence or dogmatism **3.** a system of philosophy based solely on observable scientific facts and rejecting speculation about ultimate origins —**pos'i·tiv·ist** *n., adj.* —**pos'i·tiv·is'tic** *adj.*

pos·i·tron (poz'ə tron') *n.* [POSI(TIVE) + (ELEC)TRON] the positive antiparticle of an electron, with about the same mass and magnitude of charge

poss. 1. possession **2.** possessive **3.** possibly

pos·se (pos'ē) *n.* [ML., short for *posse comitatus*, power of the country] [Now chiefly U.S.] a body of men summoned by a sheriff, to assist him in keeping the peace

pos·sess (pə zes') *vt.* [< MFr. < L. pp. of *possidere*] **1.** to have as something that belongs to one; own **2.** to have as an attribute, quality, etc. [*to possess wisdom*] **3.** to gain or keep influence or control over; dominate [*possessed* by an idea] **4.** to cause (someone) to have property, facts, etc. (usually with *of*) **5.** [Archaic] to seize; gain —**pos·ses'sor** *n.*

pos·sessed (pə zest') *adj.* **1.** owned **2.** controlled as by an evil spirit; crazed —**possessed of** having

pos·ses·sion (pə zesh'ən) *n.* **1.** a possessing or being possessed; ownership, hold, etc. **2.** anything possessed **3.** [*pl.*] property; wealth **4.** territory ruled by an outside country **5.** *Sports* actual control of the ball in play

pos·ses·sive (pə zes'iv) *adj.* **1.** of possession, or ownership **2.** showing or desiring possession [*a possessive person*] **3.** *Gram.* designating or of a case, form, or construction expressing possession (Ex.: *men's*, *of men*, *her*, *whose*) —*n.* *Gram.* **1.** the possessive case **2.** a possessive form —**pos·ses'sive·ly** *adv.* —**pos·ses'sive·ness** *n.*

pos·set (pos'it) *n.* [ME *poshote* < ?] a hot drink made of milk and ale, wine, etc., usually spiced

pos·si·bil·i·ty (pos'ə bil'ə tē) *n.* **1.** a being possible **2.** *pl.* -**ties** something that is possible —*adj.* same as POSSIBLE (sense 2)

pos·si·ble (pos'ə b'l) *adj.* [OFr. < L. < *posse*, to be able] **1.** that can be **2.** that may or may not happen **3.** that can be done, known, chosen, etc., depending on circumstances **4.** permissible —*n.* **1.** the highest attainable mark or score, esp. in shooting **2.** a candidate, etc. who has a good chance of winning, succeeding, being chosen, etc. [Smith was a *possible* for the job]

pos·si·bly (-blē) *adv.* **1.** by any possible means [*it can't possibly work*] **2.** perhaps; maybe

pos·sum (pos'əm) *n.* [Colloq.] same as OPOSSUM —**play possum** to feign death, unawareness, etc.

post¹ (pōst) *n.* [OE. < L. *postis*] **1.** a piece of wood, metal, etc., usually long and square or cylindrical, set upright to support a building, sign, fence, etc. **2.** the starting point of a horse race [*post* prices in the race] **3.** the finishing point of a race [first past the *post*] —*vt.* **1.** to put up (a notice, etc.) on (a wall, post, etc.) **2.** to announce or publicize thus [*post* a reward] **3.** to warn persons against trespassing on (grounds, etc.) by posted notices **4.** to put (a name) on a posted or published list

post² (pōst) *n.* [< Fr. < It., ult. < L. *positum*, neut. pp. of *ponere*, to place] **1.** the place where a soldier, guard, etc. is stationed **2.** *a)* a place where troops are stationed *b)* the troops there; garrison **3.** a place where a person or group is stationed, as at a machine **4.** an assigned or appointed position, job, or duty **5.** *clipped form of* TRADING POST **6.** either of two military bugle calls (**first** and **last post**) giving notice of the time to retire for the night —*vt.* **1.** to station at or assign to a post **2.** to announce as by means of a poster [to *post* banns]

post³ (pōst) *n.* [< Fr. < It. < L. fem. pp. of *ponere*: see prec.] **1.** *a)* formerly, any of a number of riders or runners posted at intervals to carry letters, etc. in relays along a route *b)* a stage of a post route *c)* a post horse *d)* a packet boat **2.** *a)* a single collection or delivery of mail *b)* a post office *c)* a postbox or pillar box *d)* the system or organization for the collection, transport, and delivery of letters, etc. —*vi.* **1.** formerly, to travel in posts or stages **2.** to travel fast **3.** to rise and sink back in the saddle in rhythm with the horse's trot —*vt.* **1.** to send by post **2.** to inform, as of events: usually passive [keep me *posted*] **3.** *Bookkeeping a)* to transfer (an item) to the ledger *b)* to enter all necessary items in (a ledger, etc.) —*adv.* **1.** by post or postal courier **2.** speedily

post- [L. < *post*, after] *a prefix meaning:* 1. after in time, following [*postglacial*] 2. after in space, behind

post·age (pōs'tij) *n.* [< POST³ + -AGE] the amount charged for delivering a letter or package, esp. as represented by stamps

postage meter [U.S.] a franking machine

postage stamp a government stamp for a letter or package, showing postage paid

post·al (pōs't'l) *adj.* having to do with mail or post offices

postal order a money order issued by one office authorizing payment at another post office

Postal Union an organization of the postal services of various countries that regulates international postal services

post bag a mailbag

post·bel·lum (pōst bel'əm) *adj.* [L.] after the war; specif., after the American Civil War

post·box (pōst'boks') *n.* a box, as on a street, into which mail is put for collection

post·card (-kärd') *n.* an unofficial card, often a picture card, for posting when a postage stamp is affixed: also **post card**

post chaise a closed, four-wheeled coach drawn by fast horses, formerly used to carry mail and passengers

post code a system devised to speed postal deliveries, under which the post office assigns a code to individual areas and places: also **postal code**

post·date (pōst'dāt') *vt.* -dat'ed, -dat'ing 1. to assign a later date to than the actual or current date 2. to put such a date on 3. to follow in time

post·er (pōs'tər) *n.* 1. a person who posts notices, bills, etc. 2. a large advertisement or notice, often illustrated, posted publicly 3. a large coloured picture, as of a pop or film star, used for decoration

poste res·tante (pōst'res'tänt) a department in a post office to which letters can be addressed to be kept till called for

pos·te·ri·or (pos tir'ē ər) *adj.* [L., compar. of *posterus*, following < *post*, after] 1. later; following after 2. coming after in order; succeeding 3. at or towards the rear; hinder; back: opposed to ANTERIOR —*n.* [formerly also pl.] the buttocks —**pos·te'ri·or·i·ty** (-or'ə tē) *n.* —**pos·te'ri·or·ly** *adv.*

pos·ter·i·ty (pos ter'ə tē) *n.* [< MFr. < L. < *posterus*: see prec.] 1. all of a person's descendants 2. all future generations

pos·tern (pōs'tərn, pos'-) *n.* [< OFr. < LL. *posterula* < *posterus*: see POSTERIOR] a back door or gate; private entrance at the side or rear —*adj.* of a postern; rear, etc.

poster paint a watercolour paint, used esp. for posters and frequently in schools

post-free (pōst'frē') *adj., adv.* 1. with the postage prepaid 2. free of postal charge

post·gla·cial (pōst'glā'shəl, -ē əl) *adj.* existing or happening after the disappearance of glaciers from a specific area

post·grad·u·ate (-grad'yoo wit, -wāt') *adj.* of or taking a course of study after graduation —*n.* a postgraduate student

post·haste (pōst'hāst') *adv.* with great haste

post horse formerly, a horse kept at an inn (**post house**) for couriers or for hire to travellers

post·hu·mous (pos'tyoo məs) *adj.* [< LL. < L. *postumus*, last, superl. of *posterus* (see POSTERIOR): altered after *humare*, to bury] 1. born after the father's death 2. published after the author's death 3. occurring or continuing after one's death [a *posthumous* award of the V.C.] —**post'hu·mous·ly** *adv.*

post·hyp·not·ic (pōst'hip not'ik) *adj.* of, or carried out in, the period following a hypnotic trance [*posthypnotic* suggestion]

pos·til·ion, pos·til·lion (pos til'yən) *n.* [Fr. < It. < *posta*, POST³] a person riding the left-hand leading horse of a four-horse carriage or the left-hand horse of a two-horse carriage

post·im·pres·sion·ism (pōst'im presh'ən iz'm) *n.* the theory or practice of some late 19th-cent. painters reacting against impressionism and emphasizing what is subjective or formal —**post'im·pres'sion·ist** *adj., n.* —**post'im·pres'sion·is'tic** *adj.*

post·lude (pōst'lood') *n.* [POST- + (PRE)LUDE] 1. a solo on the organ at the end of a church service 2. a concluding musical section

post·man (-mən) *n., pl.* -men one whose work is carrying and delivering the post

postman's knock a parlour game involving the exchange of kisses

post·mark (-märk') *n.* a post-office mark stamped on a piece of mail, cancelling the postage stamp and recording the date and place —*vt.* to stamp with a postmark

post·mas·ter (-mäs'tər) *n.* a person in charge of a post office —**post'mas'ter·ship'** *n.* —**post'mis'tress** *n.fem.*

postmaster general *pl.* postmasters general, postmaster generals the head of a government's postal system

post·me·rid·i·an (pōst'mə rid'ē ən) *adj.* [< L.: see POST- & MERIDIAN] of or in the afternoon

post me·ri·di·em (-ē əm) [L.] after noon: abbrev. **P.M.,** **p.m., PM**

post-mor·tem (pōst'môr'təm) *adj.* [L., after death] 1. happening or done after death 2. designating or of an examination of a human body after death —*n.* 1. a post-mortem examination: see AUTOPSY 2. a detailed evaluation of some event just ended

post·na·sal drip (pōst'nā'z'l) a dripping of mucus from behind the nose onto the pharynx

post·na·tal (pōst'nāt''l) *adj.* after birth

post-o·bit (-ō'bit, -ob'it) *adj.* [contr. < L. *post obitum*, after death] being, or to be, in effect after a specified person's death —*n.* a bond given by a borrower pledging to pay his debt upon the death of a specified person from whom he expects to inherit money

post office 1. the governmental department in charge of the postal and telecommunications services 2. an office or building where post is sorted, postage stamps are sold, etc.

post·op·er·a·tive (pōst'op'ər ə tiv, -op'rə-) *adj.* of or in the period after surgery —**post'op'er·a·tive·ly** *adv.*

post·paid (pōst'pād') *adj.* with the postage prepaid

post·pone (pōst pōn', pōs-) *vt.* -poned', -pon'ing [< L. *post*, after + *ponere*, to put] to put off until later; defer; delay —**post·pon'a·ble** *adj.* —**post·pone'ment** *n.* —**post·pon'er** *n.*

post·pran·di·al (pōst'pran'dē əl) *adj.* [< POST- + L. *prandium*, noonday meal] after a meal —**post'pran'di·al·ly** *adv.*

post road a road over which the post, or mail, is or formerly was carried

post·script (pōst'skript', pōs'-) *n.* [< ModL. < L. pp. of *postscribere* < *post-*, after + *scribere*, to write] a note, paragraph, etc. added below the signature of a letter, or to a book, speech, etc. to give more facts, ideas, etc.

pos·tu·lant (pos'chə lənt) *n.* [Fr. < L. prp. of *postulare*: see ff.] a petitioner, esp. for admission into a religious order

pos·tu·late (pos'chə lāt'; *for n.*, usually -lit) *vt.* -lat'ed, -lat'ing [< L. pp. of *postulare*, to demand] 1. to claim; demand; require 2. to assume without proof to be true, real, or necessary, esp. as a basis for argument 3. to take for granted; assume —*n.* 1. something postulated; assumption or axiom 2. a prerequisite 3. a basic principle —**pos'tu·la'tion** *n.* —**pos'tu·la'tor** (-ər) *n.*

pos·ture (pos'chər) *n.* [MFr. < It. < L. *positura* < *ponere*, to place] 1. the position or carriage of the body; bearing 2. a position assumed as in posing for an artist 3. the way things stand; condition [the *posture* of foreign affairs] 4. a) frame of mind b) an attitude assumed merely for effect —*vt.* -tured, -tur·ing to place in a posture; pose —*vi.* to assume a bodily or mental posture, esp. for effect; pose —**pos'tur·al** *adj.* —**pos'tur·er** *n.*

pos·tur·ize (-chə rīz') *vt., vi.* -ized', -iz'ing same as POSTURE

post·war (pōst'wôr') *adj.* after the (or a) war

po·sy (pō'zē) *n., pl.* -sies [contr. < POESY] 1. orig., a verse or motto inscribed inside a ring, etc. 2. a flower or bouquet: an old-fashioned usage

pot (pot) *n.* [OE. *pott*] 1. a round vessel of metal, etc., for holding liquids, cooking food, etc. 2. a pot with its contents 3. same as POTFUL 4. shortened form for FLOWERPOT, CHIMNEY POT, etc. 5. same as CHAMBERPOT 6. [Colloq.] a) all the money bet at a single time b) a large amount of money 7. [Colloq.] a potshot 8. [Colloq.] a cup or other prize 9. [Slang] same as MARIJUANA —*vt.* pot'ted, pot'ting 1. to put into a pot 2. to cook or preserve in a pot 3. to shoot (game) for food, not for sport 4. to hit or get as by a potshot —**go to pot** to go to ruin

po·ta·ble (pōt'ə b'l) *adj.* [Fr. < L. < L. *potare*, to drink] fit to drink; drinkable —*n.* something drinkable; beverage —**po'ta·bil'i·ty, po'ta·ble·ness** *n.*

‡**po·tage** (pô tazh') *n.* [Fr.] soup or broth

pot·ash (pot'ash') *n.* [< Du. < *pot*, pot + *asch*, ash] 1. same as: a) POTASSIUM CARBONATE b) POTASSIUM HYDROXIDE 2. any substance containing potassium; esp., any potassium compound used in fertilizers

po·tas·si·um (pə tas'ē əm) *n.* [ModL. < see prec.] a soft, silver-white, waxlike metallic chemical element: its native salts are used in fertilizers, glass, etc.: symbol, K; at. wt., 39.102; at. no., 19 —**po·tas'sic** *adj.*

potassium bromide a white, crystalline compound, KBr, used in photography, medicine, etc.

potassium carbonate an alkaline, crystalline compound, K_2CO_3, used in making soap, glass, etc.

potassium chlorate a crystalline salt, $KClO_3$, a strong oxidizing agent used in medicine and in making matches, etc.

potassium chloride a crystalline salt, KCl, used in fertilizers, as a source of potassium salts, etc.

potassium cyanide an extremely poisonous crystalline compound, KCN, used in metallurgy, in electroplating, etc.

potassium hydroxide a strongly alkaline, crystalline compound, KOH, used in making soap, glass, etc.

potassium nitrate a crystalline compound, KNO₃, used in fertilizers, gunpowder, etc. and as an oxidizing agent

potassium permanganate a dark-purple, crystalline compound, KMnO₄, used as an oxidizing agent, disinfectant, etc.

po·ta·tion (pō tā'shən) n. [< MFr. < L. < potare, to drink] 1. the act of drinking 2. a drink or draught, esp. or alcohol

po·ta·to (pə tāt'ō, -ə) n., pl. -toes [Sp. patata < WInd. name] 1. same as SWEET POTATO 2. a) the starchy tuber of a widely cultivated plant of the nightshade family, cooked as a vegetable b) the plant

potato beetle (or **bug**) same as COLORADO BEETLE

potato crisp a very thin slice of potato fried crisp and often salted and often flavoured: also, U.S., **potato chip**

pot·bel·ly (pot'bel'ē) n., pl. -lies a protruding belly —**pot'-bel·lied** adj.

pot·boil·er (-boil'ər) n. a piece of writing, etc., usually inferior, done quickly for money

pot-bound (-bound') adj. of a plant whose roots are too great for their container

po·teen (pō tēn', -tyēn') n. [Ir. poitin, dim. of pota, pot] illicitly distilled Irish whiskey, often made from potatoes: also **po·theen'**

po·tent (pōt'ənt) adj. [L. potens (gen. potentis), prp. of posse, to be able] 1. having authority or power; mighty 2. convincing; cogent 3. effective or powerful in action, as a drug 4. able to have an erection and hence to engage in sexual intercourse —**po'ten·cy**, pl. -cies, **po'tence** n. —**po'tent·ly** adv.

po·ten·tate (pōt''n tāt') n. a ruler; monarch

po·ten·tial (pə ten'shəl) adj. [< ML. < L.: see POTENT] 1. that can, but has not yet, come into being; possible; latent 2. Gram. expressing possibility, capability, etc. ["I can go" is in the potential mood] —n. 1. something potential 2. Elec. the relative voltage at a point in an electric circuit or field with respect to some reference point in the same circuit or field —**po·ten'tial·ly** adv.

potential difference the difference in electrical potential between two points in an electric field; voltage

potential energy inactive energy resulting from position or structure instead of motion, as in a coiled spring

po·ten·ti·al·i·ty (pə ten'shē al'ə tē) n. 1. possibility or capability of becoming, developing, etc.; latency 2. pl. -ties something potential

po·ten·ti·ate (pə ten'shē āt') vt. -at·ed, -at·ing [< L. potentia, potency + -ATE¹] to increase (the effect of a drug or toxin) by previous or simultaneous use of another drug or toxin —**po·ten'ti·a'tion** n. —**po·ten'ti·a'tor** n.

po·ten·ti·om·e·ter (pə ten'shē om'ə tər) n. [< POTENTIAL + -METER] an instrument for measuring, comparing, or controlling electric potentials

pot·ful (pot'fool') n., pl. -fuls' as much as a pot will hold

poth·er (poth'ər) n. [< ?] 1. a cloud of smoke, dust, etc. 2. a commotion or fuss —vt., vi. to fuss or bother

pot·herb (pot'hurb') n. any herb whose leaves and stems are boiled for food or used as a flavouring

pot·hole (-hōl') n. 1. a deep hole or pit 2. a rough hole in a road, made by wear and weathering

pot·hol·ing (-iŋ) n. the exploration of deep holes, esp. those with systems of passages occurring in limestone rocks

pot·hook (-hook') n. 1. an S-shaped hook for hanging a pot or kettle over a fire 2. a hooked rod for lifting hot pots, etc. 3. a curved mark in writing

pot·house (-hous') n. formerly, a small tavern

pot·hunt·er (-hun'tər) n. 1. a hunter who kills game indiscriminately, without regard for the rules of sport 2. a person who enters competitions merely to win prizes

po·tion (pō'shən) n. [< OFr. < L. < potare, to drink] a drink or liquid dose, as of medicine or poison

pot·latch (pot'lach', -lash') n. [< AmInd. (Chinook) patshatl, a gift] among American Indians of the N Pacific coast, a) a winter festival b) a distribution of gifts during such a festival

pot·luck (pot'luk') n. whatever the family meal happens to be [invited in to take potluck]

pot·o·roo (pot'ə rōō') n. [< Abor.] in Australia, the kangaroo rat

pot·pour·ri (pō'poo rē', pō poor'ē) n. [Fr. < pot, a pot + pp. of pourrir, to rot] 1. a mixture of dried flower petals with spices, kept in a jar for its fragrance 2. a medley, miscellany, or anthology

pot roast meat, usually a large cut of beef, cooked in one piece by braising

pot·sherd (pot'shurd') n. [see POT & SHARD] a piece of broken pottery

pot·shot (-shot') n. 1. an easy shot 2. a random shot 3. a haphazard try 4. a random criticism

pot·tage (pot'ij) n. [< MFr. < pot, a pot < Du.] a thick soup or stew of vegetables, or meat and vegetables

pot·ted (pot'id) adj. 1. put into a pot 2. cooked or preserved in a pot or can

pot·ter¹ (-ər) n. a maker of earthenware pots, dishes, etc.

pot·ter² (pot'ər) vi. [< OE. potian, to push] to busy oneself in an ineffective or aimless way; dawdle (often with around, etc.) —vt. to fritter (away)

Pot·ter·ies (pot'ər ēz) an area of W central England in which the china and earthenware industries are concentrated

potter's field [cf. Matt. 27:7] a burial ground for paupers or unknown persons

potter's wheel a rotating horizontal disc upon which clay is moulded into bowls, etc.

pot·ter·y (pot'ər ē) n., pl. -ter·ies [< MFr. < potier, a potter < pot, a pot] 1. a potter's workshop or factory 2. the art of a potter 3. pots, bowls, etc. made of clay hardened by heat; earthenware

potting shed a shed in the garden originally used to pot plants, now often used to store gardening equipment

pot·tle (pot''l) n. [< MFr. dim. of pot, a pot] formerly, a half-gallon liquid measure

pot·ty¹ (pot'ē) n., pl. -ties 1. a child's small chamber pot 2. a child's chair for toilet training, having an open seat with a pot beneath: in full, **potty chair** 3. a toilet: a child's word

POTTER'S WHEEL

pot·ty² (pot'ē) adj. -ti·er, -ti·est [Colloq.] 1. trivial 2. slightly crazy —**pot'ti·ness** n.

pouch (pouch) n. [MFr. < poche, var. of poque, a poke] 1. a small bag or sack, as for pipe tobacco 2. a mailbag 3. a pouchlike cavity, part, etc. 4. a) a saclike structure on the abdomen of some animals; marsupium b) a baglike part, as of some rodents' cheeks, for carrying food —vt. 1. to put into a pouch 2. to make into a pouch —vi. to form a pouch —**pouched** adj.

pouf (pōōf) n. [Fr., a puff: echoic] 1. an elaborate woman's hairstyle of the 18th cent., characterized by high rolls of hair 2. a large, solid cushion used as a seat; hassock Also sp. **pouff, pouffe**

poul·ter·er (pōl'tər ər) n. a dealer in poultry and game: also [Archaic] **poul'ter**

poul·tice (pōl'tis) n. [ML. pultes, orig. pl. of L. puls, pap] a hot, soft, moist mass, as of flour, mustard, etc., applied, sometimes on a cloth, to a sore part of the body —vt. -ticed, -tic·ing to apply a poultice to

poul·try (pōl'trē) n. [< MFr. < OFr. poulet: see PULLET] domestic fowls, as chickens, raised for meat or eggs

poul·try·man (-mən) n., pl. -men a person who raises or deals in poultry

pounce¹ (pouns) n. [< ? MFr. poinçon: see PUNCHEON¹] 1. a claw or talon of a bird of prey 2. the act of pouncing; swoop, leap, etc. —vi. pounced, pounc'ing to swoop down, spring, or leap (on, upon, or at) as in attacking —**pounc'er** n.

pounce² (pouns) n. [< Fr. < L. pumex, pumice] 1. a fine powder, as of cuttlefish bone, formerly used to keep ink from blotting 2. a fine powder sprinkled over a stencil to make a design, as on cloth —vt. pounced, pounc'ing to use pounce on

pound¹ (pound) n., pl. pounds, collectively pound [OE. pund < L. pondo, abl. of pondus, weight] 1. a unit of weight, equal to 16oz. (7000 grains) avoirdupois (.454 kgm) or 12 oz. (5760 grains) troy (.373 kgm): abbrev. **lb.** 2. the monetary unit of the United Kingdom, equal to 100 (new) pence: in full **pound sterling**: symbol £: see MONETARY UNITS, table 3. the monetary unit of various other countries, as of Ireland, Israel, etc.: see MONETARY UNITS, table —**pound of flesh** a literal, legal but unreasonable fulfilment of a bargain

pound² (pound) vt. [OE. punian] 1. to beat to a pulp, powder, etc. 2. to strike or drive with repeated heavy blows 3. to make by pounding —vi. 1. to deliver repeated, heavy blows (at or on a door, etc.) 2. to move with heavy steps, thumps, etc. 3. to beat heavily; throb —n. a pounding, or the sound of it —**pound out** 1. to flatten, smooth, etc. by pounding 2. to produce (musical notes, typed copy, etc.) with a very heavy touch

pound³ (pound) n. [< OE. pund-] 1. an enclosure maintained by a public authority for confining stray animals 2. an enclosure for keeping animals 3. an enclosure for trapping animals 4. a place of confinement, as for arrested persons 5. an enclosed area for catching or keeping fish

pound·age (poun'dij) n. 1. a tax, etc. per pound (sterling or weight) 2. weight in pounds

pound·al (poun'd'l) n. [< POUND¹] a unit of force producing an acceleration of one foot per second every second on a one-pound mass

pound·cake (pound'kāk') n. a rich cake made with a pound each of flour, butter, sugar, etc.

pound·er (poun'dər) n. a person or thing that pounds, esp. a pestle

-pound·er (poun'dər) a combining form meaning something weighing or worth (a specified number of pounds)

pound-fool·ish (pound′fōōl′ish) *adj.* not handling large sums of money wisely: see PENNY-WISE
pound note a banknote valued at one pound sterling; £1
pour (pôr) *vt.* [< ?] **1.** to make flow in a continuous stream **2.** to emit, utter, etc. profusely or steadily —*vi.* **1.** to flow freely, continuously, or copiously **2.** to rain heavily **3.** to swarm **4.** to act as a hostess by pouring tea, coffee, etc. for guests at a reception —*n.* **1.** a pouring **2.** a heavy rain —**pour cold water on** to discourage; disparage: said esp. of ideas, schemes, etc. —**pour′er** *n.*
‡**pour·boire** (pōōr bwàr′) *n.* [Fr. < *pour,* for + *boire,* to drink] a tip, or gratuity
pout[1] (pout) *vi.* [ME. *pouten*] **1.** to thrust out the lips, as in sullenness **2.** [U.S.] to sulk **3.** to protrude: said of the lips —*vt.* **1.** to thrust out (the lips) **2.** to utter with a pout —*n.* **1.** a pouting **2.** a fit of sulking: also **the pouts**
pout[2] (pout) *n., pl.* **pout, pouts**: see PLURAL, II, D, 2 [OE. *-pute*] any of several stout-bodied fishes, as the horned pout, eelpout, etc.
pout·er (-ər) *n.* **1.** a person who pouts **2.** any of a breed of pigeon that can distend its crop: also **pouter pigeon**
pov·er·ty (pov′ər tē) *n.* [< OFr. < L. < *pauper,* poor] **1.** the condition or quality of being poor; need **2.** inferiority; inadequacy **3.** scarcity
pov·er·ty-strick·en (-strik′′n) *adj.* very poor
pow (pou) *interj.* an exclamation suggesting the sound of a shot, explosion, etc.
POW, P.O.W. prisoner of war
pow·der (pou′dər) *n.* [< OFr. *poudre* < L. *pulvis*] **1.** any dry substance in the form of fine, dustlike particles, produced by crushing, grinding, etc. **2.** a specific kind of powder [face *powder*] **3.** *same as* GUNPOWDER —*vt.* **1.** to put powder on **2.** to make into powder —*vi.* **1.** to be made into powder **2.** to use powder as a cosmetic —**take a powder** [U.S. Slang] to run away; leave —**pow′der·er** *n.*
powder blue pale blue —**pow′der-blue′** *adj.*
powder burn a skin burn caused by gunpowder exploding at close range
powder horn a container made of an animal's horn, for carrying gunpowder
powder keg **1.** a small barrel used to hold gunpowder **2.** anything that may explode, lit. or fig.
powder puff a soft pad for applying cosmetic powder
powder room [U.S.] a lavatory for women
pow·der·y (pou′dər ē) *adj.* **1.** of, like, or in the form of, powder **2.** easily made into powder **3.** covered with or as if with powder
pow·er (pou′ər) *n.* [< OFr. *poeir,* earlier *poter,* ult. < L. *posse,* to be able] **1.** ability to do, act, or produce **2.** a specific ability or faculty [the *power* of sight] **3.** great ability to do, act, or affect; vigour; force **4.** a) the ability to control others; influence b) [pl.] special authority of a person or group in office c) legal authority **5.** a) physical force or energy [water *power*] b) the capacity to exert such force [200 *horsepower*] **6.** a person or thing of great influence, force, or authority **7.** a nation, esp. one dominating others **8.** a spirit or divinity **9.** military strength **10.** *Math.* a) the result of multiplying a quantity by itself [4 is the second *power* of 2 (2²)] b) *same as* EXPONENT (sense 3) **11.** *Optics* the degree of magnification of a lens, telescope, etc. —*vt.* to supply with power —*adj.* **1.** operated by electricity, etc. [*power* tools] **2.** using an auxiliary, engine-powered system [*power* steering] **3.** carrying electricity [*power* lines] —**in power** **1.** in authority **2.** in office —**the powers that be** the persons in control —**pow′ered** *adj.*
pow·er·boat (-bōt′) *n. same as* MOTORBOAT
power dive *Aeron.* a dive speeded by engine power —**pow′er-dive′** *vi., vt.* **-dived′, -div′ing**
pow·er·ful (-fəl) *adj.* having much power; strong —*adv.* [Dial.] very —**pow′er·ful·ly** *adv.* —**pow′er·ful·ness** *n.*
pow·er·house (-hous′) *n.* **1.** *same as* POWER STATION **2.** [Colloq.] a powerful person, team, etc.
pow·er·less (-lis) *adj.* without power; weak, impotent, etc. —**pow′er·less·ly** *adv.* —**pow′er·less·ness** *n.*
power of attorney a written statement legally authorizing a person to act for one
power pack *Radio* a unit in an amplifier that converts power-line or battery voltage to required voltages
power point **1.** an electrical socket mounted on, or recessed into, a wall **2.** such a socket designed to provide electric current for electrical appliances other than lights
power station a building where electric power is generated
power structure those persons or groups who hold the ruling power in a nation, organization, etc. because of their social, economic, and institutional position
pow·wow (pou′wou′) *n.* [< Algonquian *powwaw,* priest] **1.** a N American Indian ceremony to effect a cure, success in

war, etc. as by magic, attended by feasting, dancing, etc. **2.** a conference of or with N American Indians **3.** [Colloq.] any conference or gathering —*vi.* **1.** to hold a powwow **2.** [Colloq.] to confer
pox (poks) *n.* [for *pocks:* see POCK] **1.** a disease characterized by skin eruptions, as smallpox **2.** syphilis
pp., pp. *Music* pianissimo
pp. **1.** pages **2.** past participle
P.P., p.p. **1.** parcel post **2.** past participle **3.** postpaid **4.** prepaid
ppd. **1.** postpaid **2.** prepaid
PPI plan position indicator
ppm, p.p.m., PPM parts per million
ppr., p.pr. present participle
P.P.S., p.p.s. **1.** [L. *post postscriptum*] an additional postscript **2.** Parliamentary Private Secretary
P.Q. Province of Quebec
Pr *Chem.* praseodymium
Pr **1.** Prince **2.** Provençal
pr. **1.** pair(s) **2.** present **3.** price **4.** pronoun
PR Proportional Representation
P.R., PR **1.** Puerto Rico **2.** public relations
P.R.A. President of the Royal Academy
prac·ti·ca·ble (prak′ti kə b'l) *adj.* [< Fr. < *pratiquer:* see PRACTICE] **1.** that can be done or put into practice; feasible [a *practicable* plan] **2.** that can be used; usable [a *practicable* tool] —**prac′ti·ca·bil′i·ty, prac′ti·ca·ble·ness** *n.* —**prac′ti·ca·bly** *adv.*
prac·ti·cal (prak′ti k'l) *adj.* [obs. *practic* < LL. *practicus:* see PRACTICE] **1.** of or from practice or action [*practical* knowledge] **2.** a) usable; functional; useful and sensible [*practical* proposals] b) designed for use; utilitarian **3.** concerned with application to useful ends, rather than theory, speculation, etc. [*practical* science] **4.** given to actual practice [a *practical* farmer] **5.** of, concerned with, or realistic and sensible about everyday activities, work, etc. **6.** that is so in practice; virtual **7.** matter-of-fact —**prac′-ti·cal′i·ty** (-kal′ə tē), *pl.* **-ties, prac′ti·cal·ness** *n.*
practical joke a trick played on someone but meant in fun —**practical joker**
prac·ti·cal·ly (prak′tik lē, -tik 'l ē) *adv.* **1.** in a practical way **2.** from a practical viewpoint **3.** in effect; virtually **4.** [Colloq.] nearly
prac·tice (prak′tis) *n.* [< MFr. < *pratiquer* < ML. < LL. < Gr. *praktikos,* practical < *prassein,* to do] **1.** the act, result, etc. of practising; specif., a) a usual action; habit b) a usual method or custom; convention **2.** a) repeated action for gaining skill b) the resulting condition of being skilled [out of *practice*] **3.** knowledge put into action **4.** a) exercise of a profession b) a business based on this [to buy another's law *practice*] —*vt., vi.* **-ticed, -tic·ing** *U.S. sp. of* PRACTISE —**prac′tic·er** *n.*
prac·tise (-tis) *vt., vi.* **-tised, -tis·ing** [see PRACTICE] **1.** to do or engage in regularly; make a habit of [to *practise* thrift] **2.** to do repeatedly so as to gain skill **3.** a) to work at, esp. as a profession [to *practise* law] b) to observe, or adhere to (beliefs, ideals, etc.) [to *practise* one's religion] —*vi.* **1.** to do something repeatedly so as to gain skill **2.** to work at a profession
prac·tised (-tist) *adj.* **1.** skilled through practice **2.** learned or perfected by practice
prac·ti·tion·er (prak tish′ə nər) *n.* **1.** a person who practises a profession, art, etc., esp. medicine **2.** a Christian Science healer
prae- [L.: see PRE-] *same as* PRE-
prae·no·men (prē nō′mən) *n., pl.* **-no′mens, -nom′i·na** (-nom′i nə) [L. < *prae-,* before + *nomen,* a name] the first name of an ancient Roman
prae·sid·i·um (prī sid′ē əm) *same as* PRESIDIUM
prae·tor (prēt′ər) *n.* [L., ult. < *prae-,* before + *ire,* to go] an ancient Roman magistrate, next below a consul in rank —**prae·to·ri·al** (pri tôr′ē əl) *adj.*
prae·to·ri·an (pri tôr′ē ən) *adj.* **1.** of a praetor **2.** [often P-] designating or of the bodyguard (**Praetorian Guard**) of a Roman emperor
prag·mat·ic (prag mat′ik) *adj.* [< L. < Gr. *pragmatikos* < *pragma,* business < *prassein,* to do] **1.** concerned with actual practice, not with theory; practical **2.** dealing with historical facts as causally related **3.** of pragmatism Also, for senses 1 & 3, **prag·mat′i·cal** —**prag·mat′i·cal·ly** *adv.*
pragmatic sanction any of various royal decrees that had the force of fundamental law
prag·ma·tism (prag′mə tiz′m) *n.* **1.** the quality or condition of being pragmatic **2.** a philosophy that tests all concepts by practical results —**prag′ma·tist** *n., adj.*
prai·rie (prer′ē) *n.* [Fr. < OFr. *praerie* < *pré* < L. *pratum,* meadow + *-erie, -ERY*] a large area of level or slightly rolling grassland, esp. in S Canada & C U.S.
prairie chicken either of two brown-and-white henlike grouse, with a short, rounded tail, of N American prairies and the coast of the Gulf of Mexico: also **prairie hen**

POWDER HORN

prairie dog a small, squirrellike, burrowing rodent of N. America, with a barking cry

prairie schooner [U.S.] a large covered wagon used by pioneers to cross the American prairies

prairie wolf same as COYOTE

praise (prāz) vt. **praised, prais′ing** [< OFr. < LL. < L. pretium, worth] 1. to commend the worth of; express admiration of 2. to laud the glory of (God, etc.), as in song; glorify —n. a praising or being praised; commendation; glorification —**sing someone's praise** (or **praises**) to praise someone highly —**prais′er** n.

PRAIRIE DOG
(to 38 cm long, including tail)

praise·wor·thy (-wur′thē) adj. worthy of praise; laudable —**praise′wor′thi·ly** adv. —**praise′wor′thi·ness** n.

Pra·krit (prä′krit) n. [Sans. prākrta, natural < pra-, before + kr, to do] any of several Old Indic languages not of Sanskrit origin, spoken in ancient India

pra·line (prä′lēn) n. [Fr., after Marshal Duplessis-Praslin (1598–1675), whose cook created it] a crisp sweet made of almonds or other nuts browned in boiling sugar

pram¹ (pram) n. [Colloq.] a perambulator

pram² (präm) n. [Du. praam < MLowG. < Czech. pram] a small, flat-bottomed boat with square ends

prance (präns) vi. **pranced, pranc′ing** [< ?] 1. to rise up on the hind legs in a lively way, esp. while moving along: said of a horse 2. to ride on a prancing horse 3. to caper like a prancing horse 4. to swagger; strut —vt. to make (a horse) prance —n. a prancing —**pranc′er** n. —**pranc′ing·ly** adv.

prang (praŋ) vt., vi. [echoic] [Slang] 1. to cause (an aircraft, car, etc.) to crash 2. to collide with 3. to make by crashing 4. to bomb heavily —n. [Slang] 1. a collision 2. a bombing raid

prank¹ (praŋk) n. [< ? or akin ? to ff.] a playful trick, often one causing some mischief —**prank′ish** adj. —**prank′ish·ly** adv. —**prank′ish·ness** n. —**prank′ster** n.

prank² (praŋk) vt., vi. [prob. < LowG. source] to dress up or adorn showily

pra·se·o·dym·i·um (prā′zē ō dim′ē əm, -sē-) n. [ModL. < Gr. prasios, green + (DI)DYMIUM] a metallic chemical element of the rare-earth group, whose salts are generally green: symbol, Pr; at. wt., 140.907; at. no., 59

prate (prāt) vi. **prat′ed, prat′ing** [< MDu. praten; prob. echoic] to talk on and on, foolishly; chatter —vt. to tell idly; blab —n. chatter —**prat′er** n. —**prat′ing·ly** adv.

prat·fall (prat′fôl′) n. [U.S. Slang] a fall on the buttocks, esp. for comic effect, as in burlesque

pra·tie (prä′tē) n. [alt. < POTATO] [Dial. or Ir.] a potato

prat·tle (prat′'l) vi., vt. **-tled, -tling** [MLowG. pratelen] 1. same as PRATE 2. to speak childishly; babble —n. 1. idle chatter 2. childish babble —**prat′tler** n.

prau (prou, prä′oo) n. same as PROA

prawn (prôn) n. [< ?] any of various related edible, shrimplike crustaceans or larger shrimp

prax·is (prak′sis) n. [ML. < Gr. < prassein, to do] 1. practice as distinguished from theory 2. established practice; custom 3. a set of examples or exercises, as in grammar

pray (prā) vt. [< OFr. < LL. < L. precari < prex (gen. precis), prayer] 1. to implore: no longer used except in a shortened form of direct request [(I) pray (you) tell me] 2. to ask for by prayer; beg for imploringly 3. to recite (a prayer) 4. to effect, get, etc. by praying —vi. to make supplication or offer prayers

PRAWN
(from 2.54 cm to 61 cm long)

prayer¹ (prer) n. [< OFr. < ML. < L. precarius, got by begging < precari, to entreat] 1. the act of praying 2. an earnest request; entreaty 3. a) an earnest request to God, etc. b) an utterance of praise, etc. to God c) a set of words used in praying [evening prayer] 4. [often pl.] a religious prayer service 5. something prayed for —**prayer′ful** adj. —**prayer′ful·ly** adv. —**prayer′ful·ness** n.

pray·er² (prā′ər) n. a person who prays

prayer book a book of formal religious prayers

prayer mat the small carpet on which a Muslim kneels while saying his prayers: also **prayer rug**

prayer wheel a revolving drum with written prayers, used by Tibetan Buddhists, like a rosary, in counting prayers

praying mantis same as MANTIS

P.R.B. Pre-Raphaelite Brotherhood

pre- [< Fr. pré- or L. prae- < L. prae, before] a prefix

meaning: 1. before in time or, place [prewar] 2. preliminary to [preschool] 3. before in rank, superior, surpassing [preeminent]

preach (prēch) vi. [< OFr. < LL. < L. < prae-, before + dicare, to proclaim] 1. to give a sermon 2. to give moral or religious advice, esp. tediously —vt. 1. to teach, advocate, or urge as by preaching 2. to deliver (a sermon)

preach·er (prē′chər) n. a person who preaches; esp., a clergyman

preach·i·fy (-chə fī′) vi. **-fied′, -fy′ing** [Colloq.] to preach or moralize tiresomely

preach·ment (prēch′mənt) n. a preaching or sermon, esp. a long, tiresome one

preach·y (prē′chē) adj. **preach′i·er, preach′i·est** [Colloq.] given to or marked by preaching

pre·am·ble (prē am′b'l, prē′am′-) n. [< MFr., ult. < L. < prae-, before + ambulare, to go] 1. an introduction, esp. to a constitution, statute, etc., stating its reason and purpose 2. an introductory fact, event, etc.; preliminary

pre·am·pli·fi·er (prē am′plə fī′ər) n. in a radio, gramophone, etc., an amplifier to boost the voltage of a weak signal before it reaches the main amplifier

pre·ar·range (prē′ə rānj′) vt. **-ranged′, -rang′ing** to arrange beforehand —**pre′ar·range′ment** n.

preb·end (preb′ənd) n. [< MFr. < ML. praebenda, things to be supplied < L. praebere, to give] 1. the amount paid a clergyman by his cathedral or collegiate church 2. the church property yielding this amount 3. same as PREBENDARY

preb·en·dar·y (preb′ən dər ē) n., pl. **-dar·ies** a person receiving a prebend

prec. preceding

Pre·cam·bri·an (prē kam′brē ən) adj. designating or of the geologic era covering all the time before the Cambrian Period —**the Precambrian** the Precambrian Era or its rocks: see GEOLOGY, chart

pre·can·cel (prē kan′s'l) vt. **-celled, -cel·ling** to cancel (a postage stamp) before the letter, etc. is posted —n. a precancelled stamp

pre·can·cer·ous (-kan′sər əs) adj. that may or is likely to become cancerous

pre·car·i·ous (pri ker′ē əs) adj. [L. precarius: see PRAYER¹] 1. dependent upon circumstances; insecure [a precarious living] 2. dependent upon chance; risky [a precarious foothold] —**pre·car′i·ous·ly** adv. —**pre·car′i·ous·ness** n.

pre·cast concrete (prē′käst′) blocks, slabs, etc. of concrete cast into form before being put into position

pre·cau·tion (pri kô′shən) n. [< Fr. < LL. < L. pp. of praecavere < prae-, before + cavere, to take care] 1. care taken beforehand 2. a measure taken beforehand against possible danger, failure, etc. —**pre·cau′tion·ar·y** adj.

pre·cede (pri sēd′) vt., vi. **-ced′ed, -ced′ing** [< MFr. < L. < prae-, before + cedere, to go] to be, come, or go before in time, order, rank, importance, etc.

prec·e·dence (pres′ə dəns, pri sēd′'ns) n. 1. the act, right, or fact of preceding; priority in time, order, rank, etc. 2. a ranking of dignitaries in order of importance Also **prec′e·den·cy**

pre·ced·ent (pri sēd′'nt; for n. pres′ə dənt) adj. that precedes —n. 1. an act, decision, etc. that may serve as an example, reason, or justification for a later one 2. a practice resulting from such precedents

prec·e·den·tial (pres′ə den′shəl) adj. 1. of, like, or serving as a precedent 2. having precedence

pre·cen·tor (pri sen′tər) n. [< LL. < L. < prae, before + canere, to sing] a person who directs church singing —**pre·cen·to·ri·al** (prē′sen tôr′ē əl) adj.

pre·cept (prē′sept) n. [< L. < praecipere, to teach < prae-, before + capere, to take] 1. a direction meant as a rule of action or conduct (Ex.: Look before you leap) 2. a rule of moral conduct 3. a rule or direction, as in technical matters —**pre·cep′tive** adj.

pre·cep·tor (pri sep′tər) n. [see prec.] a teacher —**pre·cep·to·ri·al** (prē′sep tôr′ē əl) adj. —**pre·cep′tor·ship′** n. —**pre·cep′tress** n.fem.

pre·ces·sion (pri sesh′ən) n. 1. a preceding; precedence 2. Mech. a change in direction of the rotational axis of a spinning body, in which the axis describes a cone —**pre·ces′sion·al** adj.

pre·cinct (prē′siŋkt) n. [< ML. < L. pp. of praecingere, to encompass < prae-, before + cingere, to surround] 1. a) [usually pl.] an enclosure between buildings, walls, etc. b) an area in a town or city where vehicles are not allowed [a shopping precinct] 2. [pl.] environs; neighbourhood 3. [U.S.] a) a division of a city, as for police administration b) a subdivision of a ward, as for voting 4. any limited area 5. a boundary

pre·ci·os·i·ty (presh′ē os′ə tē) n., pl. **-ties** [see PRECIOUS] great fastidiousness or affectation, esp. in language

pre·cious (presh′əs) adj. [< OFr. < L. pretiosus < pretium, a price] 1. of great price or value; costly 2. much loved or cherished; dear 3. overrefined or affected 4. [Colloq.]

very great [a *precious* liar] —*adv.* [Colloq.] very —**pre′-cious·ly** —**pre′cious·ness** *n.*
precious metals any of gold, silver or platinum
precious stone a rare and costly gem
prec·i·pice (pres′ə pis) *n.* [< Fr. < L. < *praeceps,* headlong < *prae-,* before + *caput,* a head] a vertical, almost vertical, or overhanging rock face; steep cliff
pre·cip·i·tant (pri sip′ə tant) *adj.* [< L. prp. of *praecipitare:* see ff.] *same as* PRECIPITATE —*n.* a substance causing formation of a precipitate —**pre·cip′i·tan·cy,** *pl.* **-cies, pre·cip′i·tance** *n.* —**pre·cip′i·tant·ly** *adv.*
pre·cip·i·tate (pri sip′ə tāt′; *also, for adj. & n.,* -tit) *vt.* **-tat′-ed, -tat′ing** [< L. pp. of *praecipitare* < *praeceps:* see PRECIPICE] **1.** to throw headlong; hurl downwards **2.** to make happen before expected, needed, etc.; hasten **3.** *Chem.* to cause (a dissolved substance) to become insoluble and separate out from a solution, as by a reagent **4.** *Meteorol.* to condense (vapour) and make fall as rain, snow, etc. —*vi.* **1.** *Chem.* to be precipitated **2.** *Meteorol.* to condense and fall as rain, snow, etc. —*adj.* **1.** falling steeply, rushing headlong, etc. **2.** acting, happening, or done very hastily or rashly; impetuous **3.** very sudden; abrupt —*n.* a substance precipitated out from a solution —**pre·cip′i·tate·ly** *adv.* —**pre·cip′i·tate·ness** *n.* —**pre·cip′i·ta′-tive** *adj.* —**pre·cip′i·ta′tor** *n.*
pre·cip·i·ta·tion (pri sip′ə tā′shən) *n.* **1.** a precipitating or being precipitated **2.** sudden or rash haste **3.** *Chem.* a precipitating or precipitate **4.** *Meteorol.* a) rain, snow, etc. b) the amount of this
pre·cip·i·tous (pri sip′ə təs) *adj.* **1.** steep like a precipice **2.** having precipices **3.** *same as* PRECIPITATE —**pre·cip′-i·tous·ly** *adv.* —**pre·cip′i·tous·ness** *n.*
pré·cis (prā′sē) *n., pl.* **pré·cis′**(-sēz′, -sēz) [Fr.: see ff.] a summary or abstract —*vt.* to make a précis of
pre·cise (pri sīs′) *adj.* [MFr. *precis* < L. pp. of *praescidere,* to cut off < *prae-,* before + *caedere,* to cut] **1.** strictly defined; accurately stated; definite **2.** speaking definitely or distinctly **3.** minutely exact **4.** *a)* very careful or strict in following a procedure, rules, etc. *b)* finicky —**pre·cise′ly** *adv.* —**pre·cise′ness** *n.*
pre·ci·sion (pri sizh′ən) *n.* **1.** the quality of being precise; exactness, accuracy, etc. **2.** the degree of this —*adj.* characterized by precision, as in measurement, operation, etc. —**pre·ci′sion·ist** *n.*
pre·clude (pri klōōd′) *vt.* **-clud′ed, -clud′ing** [< L. *praecludere* < *prae-,* before + *claudere,* to shut] to make impossible, esp. in advance; shut out —**pre·clu′sion** (-klōō′zhən) *n.* —**pre·clu′sive** (-siv) *adj.* —**pre·clu′sive·ly** *adv.*
pre·co·cious (pri kō′shəs) *adj.* [L. *praecox,* ult. < *prae-,* before + *coquere,* to cook] **1.** matured beyond normal for one's age, esp. in mental capacity, talent, etc. **2.** of or showing premature development —**pre·co′cious·ly** *adv.* —**pre·co′cious·ness, pre·coc′i·ty** (-kos′ə tē) *n.*
pre·cog·ni·tion (prē′kog nish′ən) *n.* supposed perception, esp. extrasensory, of something before it occurs —**pre·cog′-ni·tive** (-nə tiv) *adj.*
pre·con·ceive (prē′kən sēv′) *vt.* **-ceived′, -ceiv′ing** to form a conception or opinion of beforehand —**pre′con·cep′tion** *n.*
pre·con·cert (-kən surt′) *vt.* to arrange or settle beforehand —**pre′con·cert′ed** *adj.* —**pre′con·cert′ed·ly** *adv.*
pre·con·di·tion (-kən dish′ən) *vt.* to prepare (someone or something) to react, etc. in a certain way under certain conditions —*n.* a condition required in advance for something to occur, be done, etc.
pre·co·nize (prē′kə nīz′) *vt.* **-nized′, -niz′ing** [ME. *preconism* < ML. < L. *praeco* (gen. *praeconis*), public crier + -IZE] **1.** proclaim in public **2.** to approve and announce the name of (a new bishop) publicly: said of the Pope
pre·cook (prē′kook′) *vt.* to cook partially or completely, for final preparation later
pre·cur·sor (pri kur′sər) *n.* [< L. < *praecurrere,* to run ahead] **1.** a person or thing that comes before and indicates, or prepares the way for, what will follow; forerunner **2.** a predecessor, as in office
pre·cur·so·ry (-sə rē) *adj.* **1.** serving as a precursor **2.** introductory; preliminary
pred. predicate
pre·da·cious (pri dā′shəs) *adj.* [< L. *praedari,* to prey upon < *praeda,* a prey + -ACEOUS] preying on other animals —**pre·dac′i·ty** (-das′ə tē), **pre·da′cious·ness** *n.*
pre·date (prē′dāt′) *vt.* **-dat′ed, -dat′ing** **1.** to date before the actual date **2.** to come before in date
pre·da·tion (pri dā′shən) *n.* [< L. < pp. of *praedari:* see PREDACIOUS] **1.** a plundering or preying **2.** the method of existence of predatory animals
pred·a·tor (pred′ə tər) *n.* a predatory person or animal
pred·a·to·ry (-tə rē) *adj.* [< L. < *praeda,* a prey] **1.** plundering, robbing, or exploiting **2.** capturing and feeding upon other animals —**pred′a·to·ri·ly** *adv.* —**pred′-a·to·ri·ness** *n.*

pre·de·cease (prē′di sēs′) *vt., vi.* **-ceased′, -ceas′ing** to die before (someone else)
pred·e·ces·sor (prē′di ses′ər) *n.* [< MFr. < LL. < L. *prae-,* before + *decessor,* retiring officer < *decessus:* see DECEASE] **1.** a person preceding another, as in office **2.** a thing replaced by another thing, as in use
pre·des·ig·nate (prē dez′ig nāt′) *vt.* **-nat′ed, -nat′ing** to designate beforehand —**pre·des′ig·na′tion** *n.*
pre·des·ti·nar·i·an (prē des′tə ner′ē ən) *adj.* [PREDESTIN(ATE) + -arian] believing in predestination —*n.* a person who believes in predestination
pre·des·ti·nate (prē des′tə nit; *for v.* -nāt′) *adj.* predestined or foreordained —*vt.* **-nat′ed, -nat′ing** to foreordain, specif., *Theol.,* by divine decree —**pre·des′ti·na′-tor** *n.*
pre·des·ti·na·tion (prē des′tə nā′shən) *n.* **1.** *Theol.* divine foreordaining of everything, specif. of certain souls to salvation and, esp. in Calvinism, of others to damnation **2.** destiny; fate
pre·des·tine (prē des′tin) *vt.* **-tined, -tin·ing** to destine or decree beforehand; foreordain
pre·de·ter·mine (prē′di tur′mən) *vt.* **-mined, -min·ing** **1.** to determine or decide beforehand **2.** to bias or prejudice beforehand —**pre′de·ter′mi·nate** (-mə nit) *adj.* —**pre′-de·ter′mi·na′tion** *n.*
pred·i·ca·ble (pred′i kə b'l) *adj.* that can be predicated —*n.* something predicable —**pred′i·ca·bil′i·ty, pred′i·ca·ble·ness** *n.* —**pred′i·ca·bly** *adv.*
pre·dic·a·ment (pri dik′ə mənt) *n.* [< LL. *praedicamentum* < L. *praedicare:* see PREACH] a condition or situation, esp. one that is difficult, embarrassing, or comical
pred·i·cant (pred′i kənt) *adj.* [L. *praedicans,* prp. of *praedicare,* to preach] preaching —*n.* a preacher, esp. formerly, a Dominican friar
pred·i·cate (pred′ə kāt′; *for n. and adj.,* -kit) *vt.* **-cat′ed, -cat′ing** [< L. pp. of *praedicare:* see PREACH] **1.** orig., to proclaim; affirm **2.** to affirm as a quality, attribute, etc. [to *predicate* the honesty of one's motives] **3.** [Chiefly U.S.] to base (something) *on* or *upon* facts, conditions, etc. **4.** to imply or connote —*vi.* to make an affirmation —*n.* **1.** *Gram.* the verb or verbal phrase, including any complements, objects, and modifiers, that is one of the two constituents of a sentence or clause, the other being the subject **2.** *Logic* something that is affirmed or denied about the subject of a proposition (Ex.: *green* in "grass is green") —*adj. Gram.* of, or having the nature of, a predicate —**pred′i·ca′tion** *n.* —**pred′i·ca′tive** *adj.* —**pred′-i·ca′tive·ly** *adv.*
pre·dict (pri dikt′) *vt., vi.* [< L. pp. of *praedicere* < *prae-,* before + *dicere,* to tell] to state (what one believes will happen); foretell —**pre·dict′a·bil′i·ty** *n.* —**pre·dict′a·ble** *adj.* —**pre·dict′a·bly** *adv.* —**pre·dic′tive** *adj.* —**pre·dic′tive·ly** *adv.* —**pre·dic′tor** *n.*
pre·dic·tion (pri dik′shən) *n.* **1.** a predicting or being predicted **2.** something predicted
pre·di·gest (prē′di jest′, -dī-) *vt.* to digest beforehand; specif., to treat (food) as with enzymes for easier digestion —**pre′di·ges′tion** *n.*
pred·i·kant (prēd′i kant′) *n.* [< Du < MFr. *predicant,* preacher] an ordained minister in the Dutch Reformed Church, esp. in South Africa
pre·di·lec·tion (prēd′ə lek′shən, prē′də-) *n.* [< Fr. < ML. < L. *prae-,* before + *diligere,* to prefer] a preconceived liking; partiality (*for*)
pre·dis·pose (prē′dis pōz′) *vt.* **-posed′, -pos′ing** to make receptive beforehand —**pre′dis·po·si′tion** (-pə zish′ən) *n.*
pre·dom·i·nant (pri dom′ə nənt) *adj.* **1.** having authority or influence over others; superior **2.** most frequent; prevailing —**pre·dom′i·nance, pre·dom′i·nan·cy** *pl.* **-cies** *n.* —**pre·dom′-i·nant·ly** *adv.*
pre·dom·i·nate (-nāt′; *for adj.* -nit) *vi.* **-nat′ed, -nat′ing** **1.** to have influence or authority (*over* others); hold sway **2.** to prevail; preponderate —*adj. same as* PREDOMINANT —**pre·dom′i·nate·ly** *adv.* —**pre·dom′i·na′tion** *n.*
pre·dy·nas·tic (prē′di nas′tik) *adj.* of the period in Egyptian history prior to the establishment of the first dynasty in the fourth millenium B.C.
pre·em·i·nent, pre-em·i·nent (prē em′ə nənt) *adj.* eminent above others; surpassing —**pre·em′i·nence, pre-em′-i·nence** *n.* —**pre·em′i·nent·ly, pre-em′i·nent·ly** *adv.*
pre·empt, pre-empt (-empt′) *vt.* [< ff.] **1.** to acquire (public land) by preemption **2.** to seize before anyone else can; appropriate —*vi. Bridge* to make a preemptive bid —**pre·emp′tor, pre-emp′tor** *n.*
pre·emp·tion, pre-emp·tion (-emp′shən) *n.* [< ML. pp. of *preemere* < L. *prae-,* before + *emere,* to buy] **1.** the act or right of buying land, etc. before, or in preference to, others **2.** action taken to check other action beforehand
pre·emp·tive, pre-emp·tive (-emp′tiv) *adj.* **1.** having to do with preemption **2.** *Bridge* designating a high bid intended to shut out opposing bids —**pre·emp′tive·ly, pre-emp′tive·ly** *adv.*
preen (prēn) *vt.* [< OE. < *proinen,* to prune (a tree, etc.)]

1. to clean and trim (the feathers) with the beak: said of birds 2. to dress up or adorn (oneself) 3. to show satisfaction with or vanity in (oneself) —*vi.* to primp —**preen'er** *n.*

pre·ex·ist, pre-ex·ist (prē'ig zist') *vt., vi.* to exist previously or before (another person or thing) —**pre'ex·ist'ence, pre'-ex·ist'ence** *n.* —**pre'ex·ist'ent, pre'-ex·ist'ent** *adj.*

pref. 1. preface 2. preference 3. prefix

pre·fab (prē'fab') *n.* [Colloq.] a prefabricated building

pre·fab·ri·cate (prē fab'rə kāt') *vt.* -cat'ed, -cat'ing 1. to fabricate beforehand 2. to make (houses, etc.) in standardized sections for shipment and quick assembly —**pre'fab·ri·ca'tion** *n.*

pref·ace (pref'is) *n.* [< MFr. < ML. < L. *prae-,* before + pp. of *fari,* to speak] 1. an introductory statement to an article, book, or speech, telling its subject, purpose, etc. 2. something introductory —*vt.* -aced, -ac·ing 1. to furnish or introduce with a preface 2. to be or serve as a preface to

pref·a·to·ry (pref'ə tôr ē) *adj.* of, like, or serving as a preface: also **pref'a·to'ri·al** —**pref'a·to'ri·ly** *adv.*

pre·fect (prē'fekt) *n.* [< OFr. < L. pp. of *praeficere,* to set over < *prae-,* before + *facere,* to make] 1. in ancient Rome, any of various officials in charge of governmental or military departments 2. any of various administrators; specif., the head of a department of France 3. in some schools, a pupil given certain duties and powers, esp. in order to help maintain discipline

pre·fec·ture (prē'fek tyoor, -chər) *n.* the office, authority, territory, or residence of a prefect —**pre·fec'tur·al** *adj.*

pre·fer (pri fur') *vt.* -ferred', -fer'ring [< MFr. < L. < *prae-,* before + *ferre,* BEAR¹] 1. to promote; advance 2. to put before a magistrate, court, etc. to be considered 3. to choose before another; like better —**pre·fer'rer** *n.*

pref·er·a·ble (pref'ər ə b'l, pref'rə-) *adj.* to be preferred; more desirable —**pref'er·a·bil'i·ty, pref'er·a·ble·ness** *n.* —**pref'er·a·bly** *adv.*

pref·er·ence (pref'ər əns, pref'rəns) *n.* 1. a preferring or being preferred 2. the right, power, etc. of prior choice or claim 3. something preferred 4. a giving of advantage to one person, country, etc. over others, as in granting credit or setting tariff rates

preference shares shares on which dividends must be paid before those of common stock: also, chiefly U.S., **preferred stock**

pref·er·en·tial (pref'ə ren'shəl) *adj.* 1. of, giving, or receiving preference 2. offering a preference —**pref'er·en'tial·ly** *adv.*

pre·fer·ment (pri fur'mənt) *n.* 1. a preferring 2. an advancement in rank or office; promotion 3. an office, rank, or honour to which a person is advanced

pre·fig·ure (prē fig'ər) *vt.* -ured, -ur·ing [< LL. < L. *prae-,* before + *figurare,* to fashion] 1. to be a type of or foreshadow (something that will appear later) 2. to imagine beforehand —**pre'fig·u·ra'tion** (-ə rā'shən) *n.* —**pre·fig'ur·a·tive** *adj.* —**pre·fig'ur·a·tive·ly** *adv.* —**pre·fig'ur·a·tive·ness** *n.* —**pre·fig'ure·ment** *n.*

pre·fix (prē'fiks, pre'-; *also, for v.,* prē fiks') *vt.* [< MFr. < L. pp. of *praefigere* < *prae-,* before + *figere,* to fix] to fix to the beginning of a word, speech, book, etc.; esp., to add as a prefix —*n.* 1. a syllable or group of syllables joined to the beginning of a word to alter its meaning or create a new word [*pre-* is a prefix added to *cool* to form *precool*] 2. a title before a person's name, as *Dr.* —**pre'fix·al** *adj.* —**pre·fix'ion** *n.*

pre·fron·tal (prē frunt''l) *adj.* of or situated near the front of the brain or of the head of a vertebrate

preg·gers (preg'ərz) *adj.* [Colloq.] *same as* PREGNANT

preg·na·ble (preg'nə b'l) *adj.* [< MFr. < *prendre,* to take] that can be captured or attacked —**preg'na·bil'i·ty** *n.*

preg·nant (preg'nənt) *adj.* [< L. *pregnans* (gen. *pregnantis*) < *prae-,* before + base of OL. *gnasci,* to be born] 1. having (an) offspring developing in the uterus; with young or with child 2. mentally fertile; inventive 3. productive of results; fruitful 4. full of meaning, significance, etc. 5. filled (*with*) or rich (*in*); abounding —**preg'nan·cy** *n., pl.* -cies —**preg'nant·ly** *adv.*

pre·hen·sile (pri hen'sil) *adj.* [< Fr. < L. pp. of *prehendere,* to take] adapted for seizing or grasping, esp. by wrapping itself around something, as a monkey's tail does —**pre·hen·sil·i·ty** (prē'hen sil'ə tē) *n.*

pre·hen·sion (-shən) *n.* [L. *prehensio:* see PREHENSILE] 1. the act of seizing or grasping 2. mental apprehension

pre·his·tor·ic (prē'his tor'ik) *adj.* of the period before recorded history: also **pre'his·tor'i·cal** —**pre'his·tor'i·cal·ly** *adv.*

pre·judge (prē juj') *vt.* -judged', -judg'ing [< Fr. < L.: see PRE- & JUDGE] to judge beforehand, or without all the evidence —**pre·judg'ment, pre·judge'ment** *n.*

prej·u·dice (prej'ə dis) *n.* [< MFr. < L. < *prae-,* before + *judicium,* judgment] 1. an opinion formed before the facts are known; preconceived idea, usually one that is unfavourable 2. *a*) an opinion held in disregard of facts that contradict it; unreasonable bias *b*) the holding of such

opinions 3. intolerance or hatred of other races, creeds, etc. 4. harm resulting as from some judgment or action of another. —*vt.* -diced, -dic·ing 1. to harm or damage, as by some judgment or action 2. to cause to have prejudice; bias

prej·u·di·cial (prej'ə dish'əl) *adj.* causing prejudice, or harm; injurious; detrimental —**prej'u·di'cial·ly** *adv.*

prel·a·cy (prel'ə sē) *n., pl.* -cies 1. *a*) the office or rank of a prelate *b*) prelates collectively Also **prel'a·ture** (-chər) 2. church government by prelates: often a hostile term: also **prel'a·tism** (-it iz'm)

prel·ate (-it) *n.* [< OFr. < LL. < L. pp. of *praeferre,* to PREFER] a high-ranking ecclesiastic, as a bishop —**prel'ate·ship'** *n.* —**pre·lat·ic** (pri lat'ik) *adj.*

pre·li·ba·tion (prē'lī bā'shən) *n.* [LL. < L. *praelibare* < *prae-,* PRE- + *libare,* to taste] a tasting beforehand; a foretaste

pre·lim (prē'lim) *n.* [Slang] *clipped form of* PRELIMINARY

prelim. preliminary

pre·lim·i·nar·y (pri lim'ə nər ē) *adj.* [< Fr. or ModL. < L. *prae-,* before + *liminaris* < *limen,* threshold] leading up to the main action, business, etc.; introductory; preparatory —*n., pl.* -nar'ies [*often pl.*] 1. a preliminary step, procedure, etc. 2. a preliminary examination 3. a contest before the main one —**pre·lim'i·nar·i·ly** *adv.*

prel·ude (prel'yōōd) *n.* [< Fr. < ML. < L. < *prae-,* before + *ludere,* to play] 1. a preliminary part; preface; opening 2. *Music a*) an introductory section of a suite, fugue, etc. *b*) since the 19th cent., any short, romantic composition —*vt., vi.* -ud·ed, -ud·ing 1. to serve as or be a prelude (to) 2. to play (as) a prelude —**pre·lu·di·al** (prē lyōō'dē əl, -lōō'-)

pre·mar·i·tal (prē mar'ə t'l) *adj.* before marriage

pre·ma·ture (prē'mə chər, -tyoor; pre-, -tyoor') *adj.* [< L.: see PRE- & MATURE] happening, done, arriving, or existing before the proper or usual time; specif., born before the full period of gestation —**pre'ma·ture'ly** *adv.* —**pre'ma·tu'ri·ty, pre'ma·ture'ness** *n.*

pre·med·i·cal (prē med'i k'l) *adj.* designating or of the studies preparatory to the study of medicine

pre·med·i·tate (pri med'ə tāt') *vt.* -tat'ed, -tat'ing to think out or plan beforehand —*vi.* to meditate beforehand —**pre·med'i·tat'ed** *adj.* —**pre·med'i·tat'ed·ly** *adv.* —**pre·med'i·ta'tive** *adj.* —**pre·med'i·ta'tor** *n.*

pre·med·i·ta·tion (pri med'ə tā'shən, prē'med-) *n.* 1. a premeditating 2. *Law* a degree of forethought sufficient to show intent to commit an act

prem·ier (prem'yər) *adj.* [MFr. < L. *primarius* < *primus,* first] 1. first in importance; chief 2. first in time —*n.* a chief official; specif., *the title of a*) the prime minister in Britain and certain other countries *b*) the governor of a Canadian province or Australian state —**pre·mier'ship** *n.*

pre·mière (prem'ē ər) *n.* [Fr., fem. of *premier:* see prec.] a first performance of a play, film, etc. —*adj.* 1. being the leading woman performer, as in ballet 2. *same as* PREMIER —*vt., vi.* -mièred'-mièr'ing to exhibit (a play, film, etc.) for the first time

prem·ise (prem'is; *for v., also* pri mīz') *n.* [< ML. < L. pp. of *praemittere* < *prae-,* before + *mittere,* to send] 1. a previous statement serving as a basis for an argument; specif., either of the two propositions of a syllogism from which the conclusion is drawn: also sp. **prem'iss** 2. [*pl.*] *a*) the part of a deed or lease that states the parties and property involved, etc. *b*) the property so mentioned 3. [*pl.*] a piece of real estate [keep off the *premises*] —*vt.* -ised, -is·ing 1. to state as a premise 2. to preface (a discourse, etc.) —*vi.* to make a premise —**on the premises** in the shop, business, etc., rather than elsewhere

pre·mi·um (prē'mē əm, prēm'yəm) *n., pl.* -ums [< L. < *prae-,* before + *emere,* to take] 1. a reward or prize, esp. as an added inducement to buy or do something 2. [U.S.] an amount paid in addition to the regular charge, interest, etc. 3. a payment, as for an insurance policy 4. very high value [to put a *premium* on honesty] 5. the amount by which one form of money exceeds another (of the same nominal value), as in exchange value —*adj.* rated as superior and higher in price —**at a premium** 1. at a value or price higher than normal 2. very valuable, as because of scarcity

Premium Savings Bonds bonds issued by the Treasury that yield no interest but give one the opportunity of winning cash prizes: also **premium bonds**

pre·mo·lar (prē mō'lər) *adj.* designating or of any bicuspid tooth in front of the molars —*n.* a premolar tooth

pre·mo·ni·tion (prē'mə nish'ən, prem'ə-) *n.* [< MFr. < LL. < L. < *prae-,* before + *monere,* to warn] 1. a forewarning 2. a foreboding —**pre·mon·i·to·ry** (pri mon'ə tər ē) *adj.*

pre·na·tal (prē nāt''l) *adj.* [PRE- + NATAL] existing or taking place before birth —**pre·na'tal·ly** *adv.*

pre·nup·tial (prē nup'shəl, -chəl) *adj.* 1. before a marriage or wedding 2. before mating

pre·oc·cu·pa·tion (prē ok'yə pā'shən) *n.* a preoccupying or being preoccupied: also **pre·oc'cu·pan·cy,** *pl.* -cies

pre·oc·cu·py (-ok'yə pī') *vt.* -pied', -py'ing [< MFr. < L.: see PRE- & OCCUPY] 1. to occupy completely the thoughts of; engross; absorb **2.** to occupy or take possession of before someone else or beforehand

pre·or·dain (prē′ôr dān′) *vt.* to ordain or decree beforehand —**pre′or·di·na′tion** (-dən ā′shən) *n.*

prep (prep) *n.* [Colloq.] **1.** *clipped form of* PREPARATION **2.** [Colloq.] *clipped form of* PREPARATORY SCHOOL

prep. **1.** preparation **2.** preparatory **3.** preposition

pre·pack·age (prē′pak′ij) *vt.* **-aged, -ag·ing** to package (goods, esp. foods) in certain amounts or weights before selling

pre·paid (prē′pād′) *pt. & pp. of* PREPAY

prep·a·ra·tion (prep′ə rā′shən) *n.* **1.** a preparing or being prepared **2.** a preparatory measure **3.** something prepared for a special purpose, as a medicine, cosmetic, etc. **4.** *a)* the act of doing homework *b)* homework

pre·par·a·tive (pri par′ə tiv) *adj. same as* PREPARATORY —*n. same as* PREPARATION (sense 2, 3)

pre·par·a·to·ry (-tər ē) *adj.* **1.** that prepares or serves to prepare; introductory **2.** undergoing preparation —**pre·par′·a·to·ri·ly** *adv.*

preparatory school a private school for children between the ages of 6 and 13, generally preparing them for public school **2.** [U.S.] a private secondary school for preparing students to enter college

pre·pare (pri per′) *vt.* **-pared′, -par′ing** [< MFr. < L. < *prae-*, before + *parare,* to get ready] **1.** to make ready or suitable **2.** to make receptive; dispose **3.** to equip or furnish; fit out **4.** to put together; construct; compound [to *prepare* a dinner or a medicine] —*vi.* **1.** to make things ready **2.** to make oneself ready —**be prepared to** to be ready to; be willing to —**pre·par′ed·ly** (-id lē) *adv.*

pre·par·ed·ness (-id nis) *n.* the state of being prepared, esp. for waging war, as by stockpiling weapons

pre·pay (prē′pā′) *vt.* **-paid′, -pay′ing** to pay or pay for in advance —**pre′pay′ment** *n.*

pre·pense (pri pens′) *adj.* [< OFr. < *pur-,* pro- + *penser,* to think] planned beforehand

pre·pon·der·ant (pri pon′dər ənt) *adj.* greater in amount, power, influence, etc.; predominant —**pre·pon′der·ance, pre·pon′der·an·cy** *n.* —**pre·pon′der·ant·ly** *adv.*

pre·pon·der·ate (-də rāt′) *vi.* **-at′ed, -at′ing** [< L. pp. of *praeponderare* < *prae-,* before + *ponderare,* to weigh < *pondus,* a weight] to be greater in amount, power, influence, etc.; predominate —**pre·pon′der·a′tion** *n.*

prep·o·si·tion (prep′ə zish′ən) *n.* [< L. < pp. of *praeponere* < *prae-,* before + *ponere,* to place] **1.** a relation word, as *in, by, for, with, to,* etc., that connects a noun or pronoun, or a noun phrase, to another element, as to another noun (Ex.: the sound *of* rain), to a verb (Ex.: he went *to* the shop), or to an adjective (Ex.: late *for* the tea party) **2.** any construction having a similar function (Ex.: *in the neighbourhood of,* equivalent to *near*) —**prep′o·si′tion·al** *adj.* —**prep′o·si′tion·al·ly** *adv.*

prepositional phrase a preposition and its object

pre·pos·sess (prē′pə zes′) *vt.* **1.** orig., to occupy beforehand or before another **2.** to preoccupy to the exclusion of later thoughts, feelings, etc. **3.** to prejudice or bias **4.** to impress favourably at once —**pre′pos·ses′sion** *n.*

pre·pos·sess·ing (-iŋ) *adj.* that prepossesses, or impresses favourably; pleasing —**pre′pos·sess′ing·ly** *adv.* —**pre′·pos·sess′ing·ness** *n.*

pre·pos·ter·ous (pri pos′tər əs) *adj.* [< L. < *prae-,* before + *posterus,* coming after < *post,* after] so contrary to nature, common sense, etc. as to be laughable; absurd —**pre·pos′ter·ous·ly** *adv.* —**pre·pos′ter·ous·ness** *n.*

pre·po·ten·cy (prē pōt′ən sē) *n.,* pl. **-cies** [L. < PRE- + POTENCY (see POTENT)] **1.** superiority in power, force, or influence **2.** *Biol.* the greater capacity of one parent to transmit certain characteristics to offspring —**pre·po′tent** *adj.*

pre-preference shares shares on which dividends must be paid before preference shares

prep school *Colloq. clipped form of* PREPARATORY SCHOOL

pre·puce (prē′pyoos) *n.* [< MFr. < L. *praeputium*] **1.** the fold of skin covering the end of the penis **2.** a similar fold over the end of the clitoris —**pre·pu′tial** (-pyoo′shəl) *adj.*

Pre-Raph·a·el·ite (prē′raf′ē ə lit′, -rā′fē-) *n.* **1.** a member of a society of artists (**Pre-Raphaelite Brotherhood**) formed in Britain in 1848 to revive the qualities of Italian art before Raphael **2.** any artist with similar aims —*adj.* of or like Pre-Raphaelites —**Pre-Raph′a·el·it′ism** *n.*

pre·re·cord (prē′ri kôrd′) *vt.* *Radio & TV* to record (an announcement, programme, etc.) in advance, for later broadcasting

pre·req·ui·site (pri rek′wə zit) *adj.* required beforehand, esp. as a necessary condition for something following —*n.* something prerequisite

pre·rog·a·tive (pri rog′ə tiv) *n.* [< MFr. < L. *praerogativa,* called upon to vote first, ult. < *prae-,* before + *rogare,* to ask] **1.** a prior or exclusive privilege, esp. one peculiar to a rank, class, etc. **2.** a superior advantage —*adj.* of or having a prerogative

Pres. **1.** Presbyterian: also **Presb.** **2.** President

pres. **1.** present **2.** presidency

pres·age (pres′ij; *for v., usually* pri sāj′) *n.* [< MFr. < L. < *prae-,* before + *sagire,* to perceive] **1.** a sign or warning of a future event; portent **2.** a foreboding **3.** foreshadowing quality [of ominous *presage*] —*vt.* **-aged′, -ag′ing** **1.** to give a warning of; portend **2.** to have a foreboding of **3.** to predict —*vi.* to make a prediction —**pres·ag′er** *n.*

pres·by·o·pi·a (prez′bē o′pē ə) *n.* [ModL. < Gr. *presbys,* old + *ops,* an eye] a form of longsightedness occurring after middle age caused by diminished elasticity of the eye lens

pres·by·ter (prez′bi tər, pres′-) *n.* [LL.: see PRIEST] **1.** in the early Christian church and in the Presbyterian Church, an elder **2.** in the Episcopal Church, a priest or minister —**pres′by·te′ri·al** (-bə tir′ē əl), **pres·byt′er·al** (-bit′ər əl) *adj.*

pres·by·te·ri·an (prez′bə tir′ē ən, pres′-) *adj.* **1.** having to do with church government by presbyters **2.** [P-] designating or of a church of a Calvinistic Protestant denomination governed by presbyters, or elders —*n.* [P-] a member of a Presbyterian church —**pres′by·te′ri·an·ism** *n.*

pres·by·ter·y (prez′bə tər ē, pres′-) *n.* pl. **-ter·ies** **1.** *a)* in Presbyterian churches, a governing body made up of all the ministers and an equal number of elders from all the churches in a district *b)* such a district **2.** the part of a church reserved for the officiating clergy

pre·school (prē′skool′) *adj.* designating, of, or for a child between infancy and school age, usually between the ages of two and five

pre·sci·ence (prē′shē əns, presh′əns, pre′sē əns) *n.* [< OFr. < LL., ult. < L. *prae-,* before + *scire,* to know] apparent knowledge of things before they happen; foreknowledge —**pre′sci·ent** *adj.* —**pre′sci·ent·ly** *adv.*

pre·scribe (pri skrib′) *vt.* **-scribed′, -scrib′ing** [< L. < *prae-,* before + *scribere,* to write] **1.** to set down as a rule or direction; order **2.** to order or advise as a medicine or treatment: said of doctors, etc. —*vi.* **1.** to set down or impose rules **2.** to give medical advice or prescriptions —**pre·scrib′er** *n.*

pre·script (pri skript′; *also, and for n. always,* prē′skript) *adj.* prescribed —*n.* something prescribed; direction; rule

pre·scrip·tion (pri skrip′shən) *n.* **1.** a prescribing **2.** something prescribed; order **3.** *a)* a doctor's or optician's, etc. direction for the preparation and use of a medicine, the grinding of spectacle lenses, etc. *b)* a medicine so prescribed —*adj.* made according to, or purchasable only with, a doctor's prescription —**pre·scrip′tive** *adj.* —**pre·scrip′tive·ly** *adv.*

pres·ence (prez′əns) *n.* **1.** the fact or condition of being present **2.** immediate surroundings [admitted to his *presence*] **3.** one that is present, esp. a person of high station or imposing appearance **4.** *a)* a person's bearing, appearance, etc. *b)* poised and confident bearing, as that of a performer before an audience (**stage presence**) **5.** a spirit or ghost felt to be present

presence chamber the room in which a great person, such as a monarch, receives guests, holds assemblies, etc.

presence of mind ability to think clearly and act quickly and intelligently in an emergency

pres·ent (prez′ənt; *for v.* pri zent′) *adj.* [OFr. < L. *praesens,* prp. of *praeesse* < *prae-,* before + *esse,* to be] **1.** *a)* being at the specified place; in attendance *b)* existing (*in a particular thing*) [nitrogen is *present* in the air] **2.** existing or happening now **3.** now being discussed, considered, etc. [the *present* writer] **4.** *Gram.* indicating action as now taking place (Ex.: he *goes*) or state as now existing (Ex.: the plums *are* ripe), action that is habitual (Ex.: he *speaks* softly), or action that is always true (Ex.: two and two *is* four) —*n.* **1.** the present time **2.** the present occasion **3.** *Gram.* the present tense or a verb in it **4.** [pl.] *Law* this very document [know by these *presents*] **5.** something presented, or given; gift —*vt.* [< OFr. < L. *praesentare,* to place in the presence of < *praesens:* see the *adj.*] **1.** to introduce (a person *to* someone) **2.** to offer for viewing or notice; exhibit; show **3.** to offer for consideration **4.** to give (a gift, award, etc.) to (someone) **5.** to hand over, send, etc. (a bill, credentials, etc.) to **6.** to point or aim (a weapon, etc.) —**present arms** *Mil.* **1.** to hold a rifle vertically in front of the body: a position of salute **2.** *a)* this position *b)* the command to assume it —**present oneself** appear as a candidate for a job, examination, etc. —**pre·sent′er** *n.*

pre·sent·a·ble (pri zen′tə b'l) *adj.* **1.** that can be presented; fit to be shown, given, etc. to others **2.** properly dressed for meeting people —**pre·sent′a·bil′i·ty, pre·sent′a·ble·ness** *n.* —**pre·sent′a·bly** *adv.*

pre·sen·ta·tion (prez′ən tā′shən) *n.* **1.** a presenting or being presented **2.** something presented, as a theatrical performance, a gift, etc. —**pre′sen·ta′tion·al** *adj.*

pres·ent-day (prez′ənt dā′) *adj.* of the present time

pre·sen·tient (prē zen′tē ənt) *adj.* [< L. *praesentiens,* prp. of *praesentire* < *prae-,* PRE- + *sentire,* to feel] characterized by, or experiencing a presentiment

pre·sen·ti·ment (pri zen′tə mənt) *n.* [MFr. < L.: see PRE- &

SENTIMENT] a feeling that something, esp. of an unfortunate nature, is about to take place; foreboding

pres·ent·ly (prez'ənt lē) *adv.* 1. in a little while; soon 2. [Chiefly U.S. & Scot.] at present; now 3. [Archaic] instantly

pre·sent·ment (pri zent'mənt) *n.* 1. *same as* PRESENTATION 2. [Now chiefly U.S.] a grand-jury report of an offence initiated by the jury without their having received a bill of indictment

present participle a participle used *a*) with auxiliaries to express present or continuing action or state of being [as *going* in "I am going"] *b*) as an adjective [as *going* in "a going concern"]

present perfect 1. a tense indicating an action or state as completed at the time of speaking but not at any definite time in the past 2. a verb form in this tense (Ex.: has gone)

pre·ser·va·tive (pri zur'və tiv) *adj.* preserving —*n.* anything that preserves; esp., a substance added to food to keep it from spoiling

pre·serve (pri zurv') *vt.* -served', -serv'ing [< MFr., ult. < L. *prae-*, before + *servare*, to keep] 1. to keep from harm, damage, etc.; protect; save 2. to keep from spoiling or rotting 3. to prepare (food), as by bottling, salting, etc., for future use 4. to keep up; maintain [to *preserve* liberty] —*vi.* to preserve fruit, etc. —*n.* 1. [*usually pl.*] fruit preserved whole or in large pieces by cooking with sugar; jam 2. a place where game, fish, etc. are maintained and protected, esp. for regulated hunting and fishing 3. the special domain or sphere of some person or group —**pre·serv'a·ble** *adj.* —**pres·er·va·tion** (prez'ər vā'shən) *n.* —**pre·serv'er** *n.*

pre·ses (prē'sēz) *n.* [L. *prae-*, PRE- + *sedere*, to sit] [Scot.] a chairman; president

pre·set (prē set') *vt.* -set', -set'ting to set (the controls of an automatic apparatus) beforehand

pre-shrunk (prē'shrunk') *adj.* shrunk by a special process in manufacture so as to minimize shrinkage in washing or dry cleaning

pre·side (pri zīd') *vi.* -sid'ed, -sid'ing [< Fr. < L. *praesidere* < *prae-*, before + *sedere*, to sit] 1. to be in charge of an assembly; act as chairman 2. to have authority, control, etc. (usually with *over*) —**pre·sid'er** *n.*

pres·i·den·cy (prez'i dən sē) *n.*, *pl.* -cies 1. the office, function, or term of president 2. [*often* P-] the office of president of the U.S.

pres·i·dent (prez'i dənt) *n.* [< MFr. < L. prp. of *praesidere*: see PRESIDE] 1. [Chiefly U.S.] the highest executive officer of a company, university, etc. 2. [*often* P-] the chief executive, or sometimes the formal head, of a republic 3. a person who presides over a council, society, etc. —**pres'i·den'tial** (-den'shəl) *adj.* —**pres'i·den'tial·ly** *adv.*

pre·sid·i·o (pri sid'ē ō') *n.*, *pl.* -os [Sp. < L. *praesidium*] a military post, esp. in Spain and Spanish America

pre·sid·i·um (pri sid'ē əm) *n.*, *pl.* -i·a (-ə), -i·ums [< Russ. < L. *praesidium*, a presiding over] 1. in the Soviet Union, *a*) any of a number of permanent administrative committees *b*) [P-] the permanent administrative committee of the Supreme Soviet 2. [P-] a chief administrative committee as in Albania, Romania, etc.

pre·sig·ni·fy (prē sig'nə fī') *vt.* -fied', -fy'ing to indicate beforehand; foreshadow

pre·so·crat·ic (prē'sə krat'ik) *adj.* of the philosophy of Greece prior to Socrates, the 5th cent. B.C. Greek philosopher

press[1] (pres) *vt.* [< MFr. < L. *pressare*, freq. of *premere*, to press] 1. to act on with steady force or weight; push steadily against; squeeze 2. to squeeze (juice, etc.) from (grapes, etc.) 3. *a*) to squeeze so as to make smooth, compact, etc.; compress *b*) to iron (clothes, etc.) with a heavy iron or a steam machine 4. to embrace closely 5. to force; compel; constrain 6. to urge persistently; entreat 7. to try to force acceptance of [she *pressed* the gift on us] 8. to lay stress on; emphasize 9. to distress or trouble [to be *pressed* for time] 10. to urge on 11. to shape (a gramophone record, plastic item, etc.), using a form 12. [Archaic] to crowd; throng 13. [Obs.] *same as* OPPRESS —*vi.* 1. to exert pressure; specif., *a*) to weigh down; bear heavily *b*) to go forwards with determined effort *c*) to force one's way *d*) to crowd; throng *e*) to be urgent or insistent *f*) *Golf* to put too much force into a stroke 2. to iron clothes, etc. 3. to undergo pressing in a specified way —*n.* 1. a pressing or being pressed; pressure, urgency, etc. 2. a crowd; throng 3. an instrument or machine by which something is crushed, stamped, smoothed, etc. by pressure 4. *a*) *clipped form of* PRINTING PRESS *b*) a printing or publishing establishment *c*) the art or business of printing *d*) newspapers, magazines, etc. or the persons who write for them *e*) publicity, criticism, etc., as in newspapers 5. an upright cupboard for clothes, etc. —**go to press** to start to be printed —**press'er** *n.*

press[2] (pres) *vt.* [altered (after prec.) < obs. *prest*, to enlist for military service by advance pay < OFr., ult. < L. *praes*, surety + *stare*, to stand] 1. to force into service, esp.

military or naval service 2. to use in a way different from the ordinary, esp. in an emergency

press agent a person whose work is to get publicity for an individual, organization, etc. —**press'-a'gent·ry** *n.*

press box a place reserved for reporters at sports events, etc.

press conference a collective interview granted to journalists as by a celebrity or personage

press gallery a section set apart for journalists in a chamber where a legislature, such as the House of Commons, meets

press gang [for *prest gang*: see PRESS[2]] formerly, a group who rounded up others and forced them into military or naval service

press·gang (pres'gan) *vt.* 1. formerly, to force (someone) to enlist for military service by a press gang 2. to induce (someone) to perform a duty, etc., by forceful persuasion

press·ing (pres'in) *adj.* calling for immediate attention; urgent —*n.* something stamped, squeezed, etc. with a press [a *pressing* of gramophone records] —**press'ing·ly** *adv.*

press·man (-mən) *n.*, *pl.* -men 1. an operator of a printing press 2. a newspaperman

press of sail (or **canvas**) the maximum amount of sail that a ship can safely carry under given conditions

press stud a fastening device, one part with a projecting knob that snaps into a hole on another part, used esp. to fasten clothing

press-up (pres'up') *n.* an exercise in which a person lying face down, with hands palm down under the shoulders, pushes the body up by straightening the arms and lowers it by bending the arms

pres·sure (presh'ər) *n.* [OFr. < L. *pressura* < pp. of *premere*, to PRESS[1]] 1. a pressing or being pressed; compression; squeezing 2. a state of distress or strain 3. a feeling as though a part of the body is being compressed 4. a compelling influence [social *pressure*] 5. pressing demands; urgency 6. *clipped form of: a*) AIR PRESSURE *b*) BLOOD PRESSURE 7. *Physics* the force pressing against a surface, expressed in units of force per unit of area —*vt.* -sured, -sur·ing to exert pressure on

pressure cooker an airtight container for quick cooking by steam under pressure —**pres'sure-cook'** *vt.*

pressure group any group exerting pressure on legislators and the public through lobbying, propaganda, etc. to affect legislation, etc.

pressure suit a type of G-suit designed to maintain normal respiration and circulation, esp. in space flights

pres·sur·ize (presh'ər īz') *vt.* -ized', -iz·ing 1. to keep nearly normal air pressure inside (an aircraft, space suit, etc.), as at high altitudes 2. to subject to high pressure —**pres'sur·i·za'tion** *n.* —**pres'sur·iz'er** *n.*

press·work (pres'wurk') *n.* 1. the operation of a printing press 2. work done by a printing press

Pres·ter John (pres'tər) a legendary medieval Christian king & priest said to have ruled either in the Far East or in Ethiopia

pres·ti·dig·i·ta·tion (pres'tə dij'i tā'shən) *n.* [Fr. < *preste* < It. *presto*, quick + L. *digitus*, a finger] the doing of tricks by quick, skilful use of the hands; sleight of hand —**pres'ti·dig'i·ta'tor** *n.*

pres·tige (pres tēzh') *n.* [Fr. < LL. *praestigium*, illusion, ult. < L. *praestringere*, to blind] 1. the power to impress or influence, as because of success, wealth, etc. 2. reputation based on high achievement, character, etc. —**pres·tige'ful**, **pres·ti'gious** (-tij'əs, -tē'jəs) *adj.*

pres·tis·si·mo (pres tis'ə mō') *adv., adj.* [It., superl. of *presto*: see ff.] *Music* very fast —*n.*, *pl.* -mos' a prestissimo passage or movement

pres·to (pres'tō) *adv., adj.* [It., quick < L. *praestus*, ready] 1. fast 2. *Music* in fast tempo —*n.*, *pl.* -tos *Music* a presto passage or movement

pre·stressed concrete (prē'strest') concrete containing steel cables, wires, etc. under tension to produce compressive stress and lend greater strength

pre·sume (pri zyoom') *vt.* -sumed', -sum'ing [< OFr. < L. < *prae-*, before + *sumere*, to take] 1. to take upon oneself without permission or authority; dare (to say or do something); venture 2. to take for granted, lacking proof; suppose 3. to constitute reasonable evidence for supposing [a signed invoice *presumes* receipt of goods] —*vi.* 1. to act presumptuously; take liberties 2. to rely too much (*on* or *upon*), as in taking liberties —**pre·sum'a·ble** *adj.* —**pre·sum'a·bly** *adv.* —**pre·sum'ed·ly** *adv.*

pre·sump·tion (pri zump'shən) *n.* 1. a presuming; specif., *a*) an overstepping of proper bounds; effrontery *b*) a taking of something for granted 2. the thing presumed; supposition 3. a ground or reason for presuming 4. *Law* the inference that a fact exists, based on other known facts

pre·sump·tive (-tiv) *adj.* 1. giving reasonable ground for belief [*presumptive* evidence] 2. based on probability; presumed [an heir *presumptive*] —**pre·sump'tive·ly** *adv.*

pre·sump·tu·ous (-choo wəs, -tyoo-) *adj.* too bold or

forward; overstepping proper bounds; showing presumption —**pre·sump′tu·ous·ly** *adv.* —**pre·sump′tu·ous·ness** *n.*

pre·sup·pose (prē′sə pōz′) *vt.* **-posed′, -pos′ing** 1. to suppose or assume beforehand; take for granted 2. to require or imply as a preceding condition —**pre′sup·po·si′tion** (-sup ə zish′ən) *n.*

pret. preterite

pre·tence (pri tens′, prē′tens) *n.* [< Anglo-Fr., ult. < L. pp. of *praetendere*: see PRETEND] 1. a claim; pretension [making no *pretence* to being rich] 2. a false claim or profession [a *pretence* of friendship] 3. a false show of something 4. a pretending, as at play; make-believe 5. a pretext 6. pretentiousness Also, U.S. sp., **pretense**

pre·tend (pri tend′) *vt.* [< MFr. < L. < *prae-*, before + *tendere*, to stretch] 1. to claim; profess [to *pretend* ignorance of the law] 2. to claim or profess falsely; feign [to *pretend* illness] 3. to make believe, as in play [to *pretend* to be astronauts] —*vi.* 1. to lay claim (with *to*) 2. to make believe in play or deception —**pre·tend′ed** *adj.*

pre·tend·er (-ten′dər) *n.* 1. a person who pretends 2. a claimant to a throne; specif., [P-] in British history, the son or grandson of James II 3. an aspirant

pre·ten·sion (pri ten′shən) *n.* [< ML. < L.: see PRETENCE] 1. a pretext or allegation 2. a claim, as to a right, title, etc. 3. assertion of a claim 4. pretentiousness

pre·ten·tious (-shəs) *adj.* [< Fr.] claiming or pretending to be more important, elegant, etc. than is really so; affectedly grand; ostentatious —**pre·ten′tious·ly** *adv.* —**pre·ten′tious·ness** *n.*

pret·er·ite (pret′ər it) *adj.* [< MFr. < L. pp. of *praeterire* < *praeter-*, beyond + *ire*, to go] *Gram.* expressing past action or state —*n.* 1. the past tense 2. a verb in this tense

pre·ter·mit (prēt′ər mit′) *vt.* **-mit′ted, -mit′ting** [< L. < *praeter-*, beyond + *mittere*, to send] to neglect, omit, or overlook —**pre′ter·mis′sion** *n.*

pre·ter·nat·u·ral (-nach′ər əl) *adj.* [< ML. < L. *praeter-*, beyond + *naturalis*, natural] 1. differing from or beyond what is natural; abnormal 2. same as SUPERNATURAL —**pre′ter·nat′u·ral·ism** *n.* —**pre′ter·nat′u·ral·ly** *adv.*

pre·text (prē′tekst) *n.* [< L. pp. of *praetexere*, to pretend: see PRE- & TEXTURE] 1. a false reason or motive put forth to hide the real one; excuse 2. a cover-up; front —*vt.* to allege as a pretext

pre·tor (prēt′ər) *n.* *Chiefly U.S. sp. of* PRAETOR —**pre·to·ri·al** (pri tôr′ē əl) *adj.* —**pre·to′ri·an** *adj., n.*

pret·ti·fy (prit′ə fī′) *vt.* **-fied′, -fy′ing** to make pretty

pret·ty (prit′ē) *adj.* **-ti·er, -ti·est** [< OE. *prætig*, crafty < *prætt, prætt*, a trick] 1. pleasing or attractive, esp. in a light, dainty, or graceful way 2. a) fine; nice: often used ironically [a *pretty* fix] b) skilful [a *pretty* move] 3. [Colloq.] considerable; quite large [a *pretty* price] —*adv.* fairly; somewhat; quite [*pretty* sure] —*n., pl.* **-ties** a pretty person or thing —*vt.* **-tied, -ty·ing** to make pretty (usually with *up*) —**pretty much** very nearly —**sitting pretty** [Slang] in a favourable position —**pret′ti·ly** *adv.* —**pret′ti·ness** *n.* —**pret′ty·ish** *adj.*

pret·ty-pret·ty (prit′ē prit′ē) *adj.* insipid; characterless; over pretty

pret·zel (pret′s'l) *n.* [G. *Brezel* < OHG., ult. < L. *brachium*, an arm] a hard, brittle biscuit usually in the form of a loose knot or stick, sprinkled with salt

pre·vail (pri vāl′) *vi.* [< L. < *prae-*, before + *valere*, to be strong] 1. to gain the advantage or mastery; be victorious (*over* or *against*) 2. to be effective; succeed 3. to be or become stronger or more widespread; predominate 4. to exist widely; be prevalent —**prevail on** (or **upon, with**) to persuade; induce

PRETZEL

pre·vail·ing (-iŋ) *adj.* 1. superior in strength, influence, or effect 2. most frequent; predominant 3. widely existing; prevalent —**pre·vail′ing·ly** *adv.*

prevailing wind the wind that occurs most frequently in a place [the *prevailing wind* was from the east]

prev·a·lent (prev′ə lənt) *adj.* [see PREVAIL] 1. [Rare] dominant 2. widely existing, practised, or accepted; common —**prev′a·lence** *n.* —**prev′a·lent·ly** *adv.*

pre·var·i·cate (pri var′ə kāt′) *vi.* **-cat′ed, -cat′ing** [< L. pp. of *praevaricari*, lit., to walk crookedly < *prae-*, before + *varicare*, to straddle, ult. < *varus*, bent] 1. to turn aside from, or evade, the truth; equivocate —**pre·var′i·ca′tion** *n.* —**pre·var′i·ca′tor** *n.*

pre·vent (pri vent′) *vt.* [< L. pp. of *praevenire* < *prae-*, before + *venire*, to come] 1. to stop or keep (*from* doing something) 2. to keep from happening; make impossible by prior action; hinder —**pre·vent′a·ble, pre·vent′i·ble** *adj.* —**pre·vent′er** *n.*

pre·ven·tion (pri ven′shən) *n.* 1. a preventing 2. [Now Rare] a means of preventing; preventive

pre·ven·tive (-tiv) *adj.* preventing or serving to prevent; esp., preventing disease —*n.* anything that prevents; esp.,

anything that prevents disease; prophylactic Also **pre·vent′a·tive** —**pre·ven′tive·ly** *adv.* —**pre·ven′tive·ness** *n.*

preventive detention prolonged imprisonment for habitual offenders, usually with corrective training, etc.

Preventive Service the Customs department concerned with preventing smuggling

pre·view (prē′vyōō) *vt.* to view or show beforehand —*n.* 1. a previous or preliminary view or survey 2. a) a restricted showing, as of a film, before exhibition to the public generally b) [U.S.] a showing of scenes from a film, TV show, etc. to advertise it

pre·vi·ous (prē′vē əs) *adj.* [< L. < *prae-*, before + *via*, way] 1. occurring before in time or order; prior 2. [Colloq.] too soon; premature —**previous to** before —**pre′vi·ous·ly** *adv.*

previous question the question, put as a motion, whether a matter under consideration by a parliamentary body should be voted on immediately

pre·vise (prē vīz′) *vt.* **-ised′, -is′ing** [< L. *praevidēre*, to forsee] 1. to be aware of in advance; forsee 2. to notify in advance

pre·vi·sion (prē vizh′ən) *n.* [< Fr. < ML. < L. pp. of *praevidere* < *prae-*, before + *videre*, to see] 1. foresight or foreknowledge 2. a prediction or prophecy —*vt.* to foresee —**pre·vi′sion·al, pre·vi′sion·ar·y** *adj.*

pre·war (prē′wôr′) *adj.* before a (or the) war

prey (prā) *n.* [OFr. *preie* < L. *praeda*] 1. orig., plunder; booty 2. an animal hunted for food by another animal 3. a person or thing that falls victim to someone or something 4. the mode of living by preying on other animals [a bird of *prey*] —*vi.* 1. to plunder; rob 2. to hunt other animals for food 3. to profit by swindling 4. to have a wearing or destructive influence Generally used with *on* or *upon* —**prey′er** *n.*

pri·ap·ic (prī ap′ik) *adj.* [after *Priapus*, the god personifying the male procreative power in Gr. & Rom. myth] 1. same as PHALLIC 2. excessively concerned with one's virility

price (prīs) *n.* [< OFr. < L. *pretium*] 1. the amount of money, etc. asked or paid for something; cost 2. value or worth 3. a reward for the capture or death of a person 4. the cost, as in life, labour, etc., of obtaining some benefit —*vt.* **priced, pric′ing** 1. to fix the price of 2. [Colloq.] to ask or find out the price of —**at any price** no matter what the cost —**beyond** (or **without**) **price** priceless; invaluable —**what price...?** 1. what is the possibility of...? [*what price* success?] 2. what do you think of...now? [*what price* freedom?] —**priced** *adj.* —**pric′er** *n.*

price control the setting of ceiling prices on basic commodities by a government, as to fight inflation

price fixing setting prices at a certain level, esp. by mutual agreement of competitors

price index see INDEX (sense 5 b)

price·less (prīs′lis) *adj.* 1. too valuable to be measured by price 2. [Colloq.] very amusing or absurd

price tag 1. a label on an item showing the cost 2. the cost of an enterprise, etc.

price·y (prī′sē) *adj.* [Colloq.] expensive; dear

prick (prik) *n.* [OE. *prica*, a dot] 1. a very small puncture or dot made by a sharp point 2. [Archaic] a pointed object, as a thorn 3. a pricking 4. a sharp pain caused as by being pricked —*vt.* 1. to make (a tiny hole) in (something) with a sharp point 2. to pain sharply [pricked by remorse] 3. to mark by dots, points, or punctures 4. to cause to point or stick up (with *up*) 5. [Archaic] to goad —*vi.* 1. to cause or feel a slight, sharp pain 2. to point or stick up: said esp. of ears —**prick up one's ears** to listen closely —**prick′er** *n.*

prick·et (-it) *n.* [ME. *pryket*, dim. of *prike*, PRICK] 1. a small spike on which to stick a candle 2. a candlestick having such a spike 3. a male deer in his second year, with straight, unbranched antlers

prick·le (prik′'l) *n.* [OE. *pricel* < base of *prica*, prick] 1. any sharp point; specif., a thornlike process on a plant 2. a prickly sensation; tingling —*vt.* **-led, -ling** 1. to prick as with a thorn 2. to cause to feel a tingling sensation —*vi.* to tingle

prick·ly (-lē) *adj.* **-li·er, -li·est** 1. full of prickles 2. stinging; tingling —**prick′li·ness** *n.*

prickly heat an itching skin disease with small eruptions caused by inflammation of the sweat glands

prickly pear 1. any of various cactus plants, some of which have barbed spines 2. its pear-shaped, edible fruit

pride (prīd) *n.* [OE. *pryte* < *prut*, proud] 1. a) a high opinion of oneself; exaggerated self-esteem b) haughtiness; arrogance 2. a sense of one's own dignity; self-respect 3. delight or satisfaction in one's achievements, one's children, etc. 4. a person or thing that one is proud of 5. the best of a class, group, etc.; pick 6. the best part; prime [in the *pride* of manhood] 7. a) a group or family (of lions) b) [Colloq.] any impressive group —*vt.* **prid′ed, prid′ing** [Rare] to make proud —**pride oneself on** to be proud of —**pride′ful** *adj.* —**pride′ful·ly** *adv.* —**pride′ful·ness** *n.*

pride of place 1. distinction of holding the most exalted place 2. the most exalted position

prie-dieu (prē′dyōo′) *n.* [Fr. < *prier*, to pray + *dieu*, God] a narrow, upright frame with a ledge for kneeling on at prayer and an upper ledge, as for a book

pri·er (prī′ər) *n.* same as PRYER

priest (prēst) *n.* [OE. *preost* < LL. *presbyter*, an elder < Gr. < *presbys*, old] 1. a person whose function is to make sacrificial offerings and perform other religious rites 2. in some Christian churches, a clergyman authorized to administer the sacraments 3. any clergyman —**priest′hood**′ *n.* —**priest′li·ness** *n.* —**priest′ly** *adj.* -li·er, -li·est

priest·ess (prēs′tis) *n.* a girl or woman priest, esp. of a pagan religion

priest-hole (-hōl) *n.* a secret chamber or other hiding place in certain houses; used to hide Catholic priests in the 16th and 17th cent.

prig (prig) *n.* [< 16th-c. slang] an annoying person who is excessively proper and smug in his moral behaviour and attitudes —**prig′ger·y**, **prig′gism** *n.* —**prig′gish** *adj.* —**prig′gish·ly** *adv.* —**prig′gish·ness** *n.*

prim (prim) *adj.* **prim′mer**, **prim′mest** [< ? MFr. *prim*, prime, sharp, neat < L. *primus*, first] stiffly formal, precise, moral, etc.; proper; demure —*vt.*, *vi.* **primmed**, **prim′ming** to get a prim look on (one's face or mouth) —**prim′ly** *adv.* —**prim′ness** *n.*

prim. 1. primary 2. primitive

pri·ma ballerina (prē′mə) [It., lit., first ballerina] the principal woman dancer in a ballet company

pri·ma·cy (prī′mə sē) *n.*, *pl.* **-cies** [< MFr. < ML. < LL. *primas*: see PRIMATE] 1. the state of being first in time, order, rank, etc. 2. the rank or authority of a primate

pri·ma don·na (prē′mə don′ə) *pl.* **pri′ma don′nas** [It., lit., first lady] 1. the principal woman singer, as in an opera 2. [Colloq.] a temperamental or arrogant person

pri·ma fa·ci·e (prī′mə fā′shi ē′, fā′shē) [L.] at first sight: used to designate legal evidence (**prima facie evidence**) that is enough to establish a fact unless refuted

pri·mal (prī′m′l) *adj.* [< ML. < L. *primus*, first] 1. first in time; original 2. first in importance; chief

pri·ma·quine (prī′mə kwēn′) *n.* a synthetic chemical compound used as a cure for malaria

pri·ma·ri·ly (prī′mə rə lē) *adv.* 1. at first; originally 2. mainly; principally

pri·ma·ry (prī′mər ē) *adj.* [< L. *primarius primus*, first] 1. first in time or order of development; primitive; original 2. a) from which others are derived; fundamental b) designating colours regarded as basic, from which all others may be derived: see COLOUR (n. 2 & 3) 3. first in importance; chief; principal [a *primary* concern] 4. firsthand; direct [a *primary* source of information] 5. *Elec.* designating or of an inducing current, input circuit, or input coil in a transformer, etc. 6. *Zool.* of the large feathers on the end joint of a bird's wing —*n.*, *pl.* **-ries** 1. something first in order, quality, etc. 2. in the U.S., a) a local meeting of voters of a given political party to nominate candidates for public office, etc. b) same as DIRECT PRIMARY ELECTION 3. any of the primary colours 4. *Elec.* a primary coil 5. *Zool.* a primary feather

primary accent (or **stress**) 1. the heavier stress or force given to one syllable in a spoken word or to one word in an utterance 2. the mark to show this (′)

primary cell a battery cell whose energy is derived from an essentially irreversible electrochemical reaction

primary education the education obtained in an elementary school, usually emphasizing reading, writing and simple mathematics

primary school a school for children below the age of 11, or 9 if there is a middle school, concerned with primary education

pri·mate (prī′māt; *also, for 1*, -mit) *n.* [< OFr. < LL. *primas* (gen. *primatis*), chief < L. *primus*, first] 1. an archbishop, or the highest-ranking bishop in a province, etc. 2. any of an order of mammals, including man, the apes, monkeys, lemurs, etc. —**pri′mate·ship′** *n.* —**pri·ma·tial** (prī mā′shal) *adj.*

Primate of All England the Archbishop of Canterbury

Primate of England the Archbishop of York

prime (prīm) *adj.* [MFr. < L. *primus*, first < OL. *pri*, before] 1. first in time; original; primitive 2. first in rank; chief [*prime* minister] 3. first in importance; principal [a *prime* advantage] 4. first in quality; first-rate [*prime* beef] 5. from which others are derived; fundamental 6. *Finance* designating the most favourable interest rate on bank loans [the *prime* rate was 8%] 7. *Math.* a) of or being a prime number b) having no factor in common except 1 [9 and 16 are *prime* to each other] —*n.* [OE. *prim* < L. *prima* (hora), first (hour): see the *adj.*] 1. [*often* P-] the first daylight canonical hour 2. the first or earliest part; dawn, springtime, youth, etc. 3. *a*) the best or most vigorous period or stage of a person or thing *b*) the best part; pick 4. *a*) any of a number of equal parts, usually sixty, into which a unit, as a degree, is divided *b*) the mark (′) indicating this:

it is also used to distinguish a letter, etc. from another of the same kind, as A′ 5. *Math.* same as PRIME NUMBER 6. *Music* same as UNISON —*vt.* **primed**, **prim′ing** 1. to make ready; prepare 2. to prepare (a gun) for firing or (a charge) for exploding by providing with priming or a primer 3. *a*) to get (a pump) into operation by pouring in water *b*) to get (an empty carburettor) into operation by pouring in petrol 4. to undercoat, size, etc. (a surface) for painting 5. to provide (a person) beforehand with information, answers, etc. 6. to ply (someone) with spirits or other liquor —*vi.* to prime a person or thing —**prime′ness** *n.*

prime meridian the meridian from which longitude is measured east and west; O° longitude: see GREENWICH TIME

prime minister [also P- M-] in parliamentary governments, the chief executive and, usually, head of the cabinet —**prime ministry**

prime mover 1. the originating force in a series of transmissions of force 2. in Aristotle's philosophy the first cause of all movement, itself unmovable 3. the original or primary force behind an idea, enterprise, etc.

prime number an integer that can be evenly divided by no other whole number than itself and 1, as 2, 3, 5, or 7

prim·er[1] (prī′mər) *n.* [< ML. < L. *primus*, first] 1. a simple book for first teaching children to read 2. a textbook giving the first principles of any subject

prim·er[2] (prī′mər) *n.* a person or thing that primes; specif., *a*) a small cap, tube, etc. containing an explosive, used to set off the main charge *b*) a preliminary coat of paint, etc.

pri·me·val (prī mē′v′l) *adj.* [< L. *primaevus* (< *primus*, first + *aevum*, an age) + -AL] of the earliest times or ages; primordial: also **prim·ae′val** —**pri·me′val·ly** *adv.*

prim·ing[1] (prī′miŋ) *n.* 1. the explosive used to set off the charge in a gun, etc. 2. paint, sizing, etc. used as a primer

prim·ing[2] (prī′miŋ) *n.* the progressive reduction of time between tides as the spring tide draws near

prim·i·tive (prim′ə tiv) *adj.* [< MFr. < L. *primitivus* < *primus*, first] 1. of or existing in the earliest times or ages; original 2. *a*) characteristic of the earliest ages *b*) crude, simple, etc. 3. not derivative; primary —*n.* 1. a primitive person or thing 2. *a*) an artist or a work of art of an early culture *b*) an artist or a work of art characterized by lack of formal training —**prim′i·tive·ly** *adv.* —**prim′i·tive·ness** *n.*

prim·i·tiv·ism (-iz′m) *n.* 1. belief in or practice of primitive ways, living, etc. 2. the qualities, etc. of primitive art or artists —**prim′i·tiv·ist** *n.*, *adj.*

pri·mo·gen·i·tor (prī′mə jen′i tər) *n.* [LL. < L. *primus*, first + *genitor*, a father] 1. an ancestor; forefather 2. the earliest ancestor of a family, race, etc.

pri·mo·gen·i·ture (-chər) *n.* [< ML. < L. *primus*, first + *genitura*, a begetting] 1. the condition or fact of being the firstborn of the same parents 2. *Law* the exclusive right of the eldest son to inherit his father's estate

pri·mor·di·al (prī môr′dē əl) *adj.* [< LL. < L. *primordium*, the beginning < *primus*, first + *ordiri*, to begin] 1. existing at or from the beginning; primitive 2. fundamental; original —**pri·mor′di·al·ly** *adv.*

primp (primp) *vt.*, *vi.* [prob. extension of PRIM] to groom or dress up in a fussy way

prim·rose (prim′rōz′) *n.* [< MFr. altered (after *rose*, ROSE[1]) < OFr. *primerole* < ML. *primula* < L. *primus*, first] 1. a spring-blooming plant with light yellow flowers 2. the flower of this plant 3. the light yellow of primroses —*adj.* 1. of the primrose 2. light yellow

Primrose Day the 19th April, anniversary of the death of Benjamin Disraeli, whose favourite flower was the primrose

Primrose League a Conservative association, founded by Lady Randolph Churchill in 1883

primrose path [cf. *Hamlet* I, iii] the path of pleasure, self-indulgence, etc.

prim·u·la (prim′yōo lə) *n.* [ML.] any of a genus of plants including the primrose, oxslip and polyanthus having variously coloured, tubelike flowers with five petals

Pri·mus (prī′məs) [arbitrary use of L. *primus*, first: see PRIME] a trademark for a small, portable stove (**Primus stove**) fuelled originally with kerosene but now usually with propane or butane —*n.* [p-] such a stove

prin. 1. principal 2. principle

prince (prins) *n.* [OFr. < L. *princeps*, chief < *primus*, first + *capere*, to take] 1. orig., any male monarch; esp., a king 2. a ruler whose rank is below that of a king; head of a principality 3. a nonreigning male member of a royal family 4. in Great Britain, a son or son's son of the sovereign 5. *a*) a preeminent person in any class or group [a merchant *prince*] *b*) [Colloq.] a fine, generous, helpful fellow —**prince′dom** *n.*

prince consort the husband of a queen or empress reigning in her own right

prince·ling (prins′liŋ) *n.* a young, small, or subordinate prince: also **prince′kin**, **prince′let**

prince·ly (-lē) *adj.* **-li·er**, **-li·est** 1. of a prince; royal 2. characteristic or worthy of a prince; magnificent; generous —**prince′li·ness** *n.*

Prince of Darkness a name sometimes given to SATAN

Prince of Peace *a name sometimes given to* JESUS
Prince of Wales *title conferred on* the oldest son and heir apparent of a British king or queen
Prince Rupert's drops the tadpole-like pieces of glass formed when drops of molten glass fall into cold water; if the tail is cut off they disintegrate making a loud noise
prin·cess¹ (prin′ses, prin ses′) *n.* 1. orig., any female monarch 2. a nonreigning female member of a royal family 3. in Great Britain, a daughter of the sovereign or of a son of the sovereign 4. the wife of a prince
prin·cess² (prin′ses, prin ses′) *adj.* [< Fr. *princesse,* a princess] of or designating a woman's one-piece, closefitting, gored dress, etc.: also **prin·cesse′** (-ses′)
princess royal the eldest daughter of a king or queen
prin·ci·pal (prin′sə pəl) *adj.* [OFr. < L. *principalis* < *princeps:* see PRINCE] 1. first in rank, authority, importance, etc. 2. that is or has to do with principal (*n.* 3) —*n.* 1. a principal person or thing; specif., *a*) a chief; head *b*) the head of some educational institutions *c*) a main actor or other kind of performer 2. any of the main end rafters of a roof 3. *Finance a*) the amount of a debt, investment, etc. minus the interest *b*) the face value of a share or bond *c*) the main portion of an estate, etc., as distinguished from income 4. *Law a*) one who employs another to act as his agent *b*) the one primarily responsible for an obligation *c*) one who commits a crime: cf. ACCESSORY —**prin′ci·pal·ly** *adv.* —**prin′ci·pal·ship′** *n.*
principal boy the actress who plays the principal male part in a pantomime
prin·ci·pal·i·ty (prin′sə pal′ə tē) *n.,* *pl.* **-ties** 1. the rank, dignity, or jurisdiction of a prince 2. the territory ruled by a prince 3. a country with which a prince's title is identified 4. [P-] Wales
principal parts the principal inflected forms of a verb, from which the other forms may be derived: in English, they are the present infinitive, the past tense, the past participle, and, sometimes, the present participle (Ex.: *drink, drank, drunk, drinking; go, went, gone, going*)
prin·ci·ple (prin′sə pəl) *n.* [< MFr. < L. *principium* < *princeps:* see PRINCE] 1. the ultimate source or cause 2. a natural or original tendency, faculty, etc. 3. a fundamental truth, law, etc., upon which others are based [moral *principles*] 4. *a*) a rule of conduct *b*) such rules collectively *c*) adherence to them; integrity [a man of *principle*] 5. an essential element or quality [the active *principle* of a medicine] 6. *a*) the scientific law that explains a natural action [the *principle* of cell division] *b*) the method of a thing's operation —**in principle** theoretically or in essence
prin·ci·pled (-pəld) *adj.* having or based on principles, as of conduct
prink (priŋk) *vt., vi.* [prob. < PRANK²] *same as* PRIMP
print (print) *n.* [< OFr. < pp. of *preindre* < L. *premere,* to PRESS¹] 1. a mark made on a surface by pressing or hitting with an object; imprint [the *print* of a heel] 2. an object for making such a mark, as a stamp, die, etc. 3. a cloth printed with a design 4. the condition of being printed 5. printed lettering 6. the impression made by inked type 7. a picture or design printed from a plate, block, etc., as an etching or lithograph 8. printed material [*newsprint*] 9. a photograph, esp. one made from a negative —*vt.* 1. to make a print on or in 2. to stamp or draw, trace, etc. (a mark, letter, etc.) on or in a surface 3. to produce on (paper) the impression of inked type, plates, etc. by means of a printing press 4. to produce (a book, etc.) by typesetting, presswork, etc. 5. to publish in print [to *print* a story] 6. to write in letters resembling printed ones 7. to produce (a photograph) from (a negative) 8. in computers, to deliver (information) by means of a printer: often with *out* 9. to impress upon the mind, memory, etc. —*vi.* 1. to practise the trade of a printer 2. to produce an impression, photograph, etc. 3. to write in letters resembling printed ones 4. to produce newspapers, books, etc. by means of a printing press —**in** (or **out of**) **print** still (or no longer) for sale by the publisher: said of books, etc. —**print′a·bil′i·ty** *n.* —**print′a·ble** *adj.*
printed circuit an electrical circuit formed by applying conductive material in fine lines or other shapes to an insulating surface
print·er (-ər) *n.* 1. one whose work or business is printing 2. a device that prints; esp., in computers, a device that produces information in printed form
printer's devil an apprentice in a printing shop
print·ing (-iŋ) *n.* 1. the act of a person or thing that prints 2. the production of printed matter 3. the art of a printer 4. something printed 5. *same as* IMPRESSION (sense 5 *b*) 6. written letters made like printed ones
printing press a machine for printing from inked type, plates, or rolls
print·out (-out′) *n.* the output of a computer presented in printed or typewritten form
print shop 1. a shop where printing is done: also **printing office** 2. a shop where prints, etchings, etc. are sold
pri·or (prī′ər) *adj.* [L., former, superior] 1. preceding in

time; earlier 2. preceding in order or importance [a *prior* choice] —*n.* [OE. & OFr., both < ML. < L.] 1. the head of a priory 2. in an abbey, the person in charge next below the abbot —**prior to** before in time —**pri′or·ate** (-it), **pri′-or·ship′** *n.* —**pri′or·ess** *n.fem.*
pri·or·i·tize (prī ôr′ə tīz′) *vt.* **-tized′, -tiz′ing** 1. to arrange (items) in order of priority 2. to assign (an item) to a particular level of priority
pri·or·i·ty (prī ôr′ə tē) *n.,* *pl.* **-ties** 1. a being prior; precedence 2. *a*) a right to precedence over others in obtaining, buying, or doing something *b*) an order granting this 3. something given or to be given prior attention
pri·o·ry (prī′ər ē) *n.,* *pl.* **-ries** a monastery governed by a prior, or a convent governed by a prioress, sometimes as a branch of an abbey
prise (prīz) *vt.* **prised, pris′ing** *same as* PRIZE² (*vt.* 2)
prism (priz′'m) *n.* [< LL. < Gr. *prisma,* lit., something sawed < *prizein,* to saw] 1. a solid figure whose ends are equal and parallel polygons and whose sides are parallelograms 2. anything that refracts light, as a drop of water 3. *Optics a*) a transparent body, as of glass, whose ends are equal and parallel triangles, and whose three sides are parallelograms: used for refracting or dispersing light, as into the spectrum *b*) any similar body of three or more sides

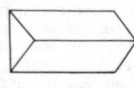

TRIANGULAR
PRISM

pris·mat·ic (priz mat′ik) *adj.* 1. of or like a prism 2. that refracts light as a prism 3. that forms prismatic colours 4. many-coloured; brilliant —**pris·mat′i·cal·ly** *adv.*
prismatic colours the colours of the visible spectrum; red, orange, yellow, green, blue, indigo, and violet
prism binoculars binoculars which use prisms instead of lenses in order to shorten their length
pris·on (priz′'n) *n.* [OFr. < L. *prensio,* for *prehensio* < *prehendere,* to take] 1. a place where persons are confined 2. a building, usually with cells, where persons convicted by trial or awaiting trial are confined 3. imprisonment
pris·on·er (priz′nər, -'ən ər) *n.* 1. a person confined in prison, as for some crime 2. a person held in custody 3. a person captured or held captive [a *prisoner* of love]
prisoner of state one confined for political rather than criminal reasons: also **State prisoner**
prisoner of war a member of the regular or irregular armed forces of a nation at war held captive by the enemy
prisoner's base a children's game played by two teams who chase and attempt to capture each other
pris·sy (pris′ē) *adj.* **-si·er, -si·est** [prob. PR(IM) + (S)ISSY] [Colloq.] very prim or precise; fussy, prudish, etc. —**pris′-si·ly** *adv.* —**pris′si·ness** *n.*
pris·tine (pris′tēn, -tīn) *adj.* [L. *pristinus,* former] 1. characteristic of the earliest period or condition; original 2. still pure; uncorrupted; unspoiled [*pristine* beauty] —**pris′-tine·ly** *adv.*
prith·ee (prith′ē) *interj.* [< *pray thee*] [Archaic] I pray thee; please
pri·va·cy (prī′və sē, priv′ə-) *n.,* *pl.* **-cies** 1. the quality or condition of being private; withdrawal from public view; seclusion 2. secrecy [told in strict *privacy*] 3. one's private life or personal affairs [an invasion of one's *privacy*]
pri·vate (prī′vit) *adj.* [< L. *privatus,* belonging to oneself, ult. < *privus,* separate] 1. of or concerning only one particular person or group; not general [*private* property, his *private* affairs] 2. not open to or controlled by the public [a *private* club] 3. for an individual person [a *private* room] 4. not holding public office [a *private* citizen] 5. away from public view; secluded [a *private* dining room] 6. secret; confidential [a *private* matter] 7. dealing with clients or patients who pay directly for services rendered [*private* medical practice] 8. working independently; self-employed [a *private* detective] —*n.* see MILITARY RANKS, table —**in private** not publicly —**pri′-vate·ly** *adv.*
private bill a bill presented to Parliament that affects an individual or company only
private company a limited company that does not issue shares for public subscription
private enterprise *same as* FREE ENTERPRISE
pri·va·teer (prī′və tir′) *n.* [< PRIVAT(E) + -EER] 1. a privately owned and manned armed ship commissioned in a war to attack and capture enemy ships, esp. merchant ships 2. a commander or crew member of a privateer: also **pri′-va·teers′man** (-tirz′mən), *pl.* **-men** —*vi.* to sail as a privateer
private eye [Colloq.] a private detective
private member's bill a parliamentary bill sponsored by a member of parliament who is not a government minister
private patient a patient not treated under the National Health Service
private school a school under the financial and managerial control of a private body or charitable trust, accepting pupils mostly on a fee paying basis

private secretary a secretary entrusted with the personal and confidential matters of a business executive

pri·va·tion (prī vā′shən) *n.* [< L. *privatio:* see PRIVATE] 1. deprivation; the loss or absence of some quality or condition 2. lack of the ordinary necessities of life

priv·a·tive (priv′ə tiv) *adj.* 1. depriving or tending to deprive 2. *Gram.* indicating negation, absence, or loss —*n. Gram.* a privative term or affix, as a-, un-, non-, or -less —**priv′a·tive·ly** *adv.*

priv·et (priv′it) *n.* [< ?] any of various shrubs of the olive family, with bluish-black berries and white flowers

priv·i·lege (priv′ə lij, priv′lij) *n.* [< OFr. < L. *privilegium,* a law for or against an individual < *privus,* separate + *lex* (gen. *legis*), a law] 1. a right, advantage, favour, etc. specially granted to a certain person, group, or class 2. a basic civil right, guaranteed by a government [the *privilege* of trial by jury] —*vt.* **-leged, -leg·ing** to grant a privilege to

priv·y (priv′ē) *adj.* [< OFr. < L. *privatus,* PRIVATE] 1. orig., private; personal 2. [Archaic] hidden, secret, etc. —*n., pl.* **priv′ies** a toilet; esp., one outside a house —**privy to** privately informed about —**priv′i·ly** *adv.*

privy council a body of advisers or confidential counsellors appointed by or serving a ruler —**privy councillor**

privy purse 1. an allowance from public revenue for the personal expenses of the monarch 2. the official responsible for dealing with the monarch's personal expenses: also **Keeper of the Privy Purse**

privy seal in Great Britain, the seal placed on documents which later received the great seal or which formerly were not important enough to receive it

prize¹ (prīz) *vt.* **prized, priz′ing** [see PRICE] 1. formerly, to price or appraise 2. to value highly; esteem —*n.* 1. something offered or given to the winner of a contest, lottery, etc. 2. a reward, premium, etc. 3. anything worth striving for; any highly valued possession —*adj.* 1. that has received a prize 2. worthy of a prize 3. given as a prize

prize² (prīz) *n.* [< OFr. *prise,* fem. pp. of *prendre* < L. *prehendere,* to take] something taken by force, as in war; esp., a captured enemy warship —*vt.* **prized, priz′ing** 1. to seize as a prize of war 2. to open by force, as with a crowbar

prize court a court that decides how captured property, esp. that taken at sea in wartime, is to be distributed

prize·fight (prīz′fīt′) *n.* a professional boxing match —**prize′fight′er** *n.* —**prize′fight′ing** *n.*

prize ring 1. a square platform, enclosed by ropes, for prizefights 2. prizefighting

pro¹ (prō) *adv.* [L., for] on the affirmative side; favourably —*adj.* favourable —*prep.* in favour of; for —*n., pl.* **pros** a reason, vote, position, etc. in favour of something [the *pros* and cons of a matter]

pro² (prō) *adj., n., pl.* **pros** *short form of* PROFESSIONAL

PRO, P.R.O. 1. Public Records Office 2. Public Relations Officer

pro-¹ [Gr. < *pro,* before] *a prefix meaning* before in place or time [*proboscis*]

pro-² [L. < *pro,* forward] *a prefix meaning:* 1. forward or ahead [*progress*] 2. forth [*produce*] 3. substituting for, acting for [*pronoun*] 4. supporting, favouring [*prolabour*]

pro·a (prō′ə) *n.* [Malay *prau*] a Malayan boat having a triangular sail and one outrigger

prob. 1. probable 2. probably 3. problem

prob·a·bil·i·ty (prob′ə bil′ə tē) *n., pl.* **-ties** 1. the quality or state of being probable; likelihood 2. a probable thing or event 3. *Math.* the ratio of the number of times a particular event can occur to the total number of likely events involved —**in all probability** very likely

prob·a·ble (prob′ə b'l) *adj.* [MFr. < L. < *probare,* to prove] 1. likely to occur or be; that can reasonably but not certainly be expected [the *probable* winner] 2. reasonably so, as on the basis of evidence, but not proved [the *probable* cause of a disease] —**prob′a·bly** *adv.*

pro·bate (prō′bāt) *n.* [< L. pp. of *probate:* see PROBE] 1. the act or process of proving or establishing that a document submitted for official certification and registration, as a will, is genuine 2. [U.S.] all matters coming under the jurisdiction of probate courts —*adj.* having to do with probate or a probate court —*vt.* **-bat·ed, -bat·ing** [U.S.] to establish officially the genuineness or validity of (a will) —**pro′ba·tive** (-bə tiv, prob′ə-), **pro′-ba·to·ry** (-tər ē) *adj.*

probate court a court having jurisdiction over matters

PROA

concerning the succession of personal property, esp. the administration of estates

pro·ba·tion (prō bā′shən) *n.* [< OFr. < L. < *probare:* see PROBE] 1. a testing or trial, as of a person's character, fitness for a position, etc. 2. the suspension of sentence of a person convicted but not imprisoned, on condition of continued good behaviour and regular reporting to a probation officer 3. *a)* the status of a person being tested or on trial *b)* the period of testing or trial —**pro·ba′tion·ary, pro·ba′tion·al** *adj.*

pro·ba·tion·er (-ər) *n.* a person on probation

probation officer an officer appointed by a court to supervise persons placed on probation

probe (prōb) *n.* [LL. *proba,* proof < L. *probare,* to test < *probus,* proper] 1. a slender, blunt surgical instrument for exploring a wound or the like 2. the act of probing 3. a searching examination; specif., *a)* [U.S.] an investigation, as by a legislative committee, into corruption, etc. *b)* an exploratory survey 4. an instrumented spacecraft for exploring the upper atmosphere, outer space, another planet, etc. —*vt.* **probed, prob′ing** 1. to explore (a wound, etc.) with a probe 2. to examine or investigate thoroughly —*vi.* to search; investigate —**prob′er** *n.*

pro·bi·ty (prō′bə tē, prob′ə-) *n.* [< L. < *probus,* good] uprightness; honesty; integrity

prob·lem (prob′ləm) *n.* [< MFr. < L. < Gr. *problēma* < *pro-,* forward + *ballein,* to throw] 1. a question or matter to be thought about or worked out [a maths *problem*] 2. a matter, person, etc. that is perplexing or difficult —*adj.* 1. depicting a social problem [a *problem* play] 2. very difficult to deal with, esp. to train or discipline [a *problem* child]

prob·lem·at·ic (prob′lə mat′ik) *adj.* 1. having the nature of a problem; hard to solve or deal with 2. uncertain Also **prob′lem·at′i·cal** —**prob′lem·at′i·cal·ly** *adv.*

‡**pro bo·no pu·bli·co** (prō bō′nō pub′li kō′) [ML.] for the public good or welfare

pro·bos·cid·e·an (prō′bə sid′ē ən) *n.* [see ff. & -AN] any of various large mammals having tusks and a long, flexible, tubelike snout, as the elephant or the extinct mastodon —*adj.* of the proboscidea

pro·bos·cis (prō bos′is) *n., pl.* **-cis·es, -ci·des′** (-ə dēz′) [L. < Gr. < *pro-,* before + *boskein,* to feed] 1. an elephant's trunk, or a long, flexible snout, as of a tapir 2. any tubular organ for sucking, food-gathering, sensing, etc., as of some insects, worms, and molluscs 3. a person's nose, esp. if large: a jocular usage

pro·caine (prō′kān) *n.* [PRO.² + (CO)CAINE] a synthetic crystalline compound used as a local anaesthetic

pro·ce·dure (prə sē′jər, prō-) *n.* 1. the act, method, or manner of proceeding in some action; esp., the order of steps to be followed 2. a particular course or method of action 3. the established way of carrying on the business of a legislature, law court, etc. —**pro·ce′dur·al** *adj.* —**pro·ce′-dur·al·ly** *adv.*

pro·ceed (prə sēd′, prō-) *vi.* [< MFr. < L. < *procedere* < *pro-,* forward + *cedere,* to go] 1. to advance or go on, esp. after stopping 2. to continue speaking, esp. after an interruption 3. to undertake and carry on some action [to *proceed* to build a fire] 4. to move along or be carried on [things *proceeded* smoothly] 5. to take legal action (often with *against*) 6. to come forth, issue, or arise (*from*)

pro·ceed·ing (-iŋ) *n.* 1. an advancing or going on with what one has been doing 2. the carrying on of an action or course of action 3. a particular action or course of action 4. [*pl.*] a record of the business transacted by a learned society, etc. 5. [*pl.*] legal action

pro·ceeds (prō′sēdz) *n.pl.* the sum or profit derived from a sale, venture, etc.

proc·ess¹ (prō′ses) *n.* [< OFr. < L. pp. of *procedere:* see PROCEED] 1. a series of changes by which something develops or is brought about [the *process* of digestion, growth, etc.] 2. a particular method of making or doing something, in which there are a number of steps 3. *Biol.* a projecting part of a structure or organism 4. *Law a)* an action or suit *b)* a written order, as a summons to appear in court —*vt.* to prepare by or subject to a special process —*adj.* prepared by a special process —**in process** in the course of being done —**in (the) process of** in or during the course of —**proc′es·sor, proc′ess·er** *n.*

pro·cess² (prə ses′) *vi.* [back-formation < PROCESSION] [Colloq.] to move along as if in a procession

processed cheese a cheese made by heating and blending together several natural cheeses with an emulsifying agent

pro·ces·sion (prə sesh′ən, prō-) *n.* [OFr. < L. < *procedere:* see PROCEED] 1. the act of proceeding, esp. in an orderly manner 2. a number of persons or things moving forwards, as in a parade, in an orderly, formal way

pro·ces·sion·al (-'l) *adj.* of or relating to a procession —*n.* 1. a hymn sung at the beginning of a church service during the entrance of the clergy 2. any musical composition to accompany a procession

process server *Law* a sheriff's officer or bailiff who serves legal documents as writs, warrants, etc., esp. when appearance in court is required

pro·chro·nism (prō′kron iz′m) *n.* [PRO¹-& Gr. *chronos*, time] an error in dating that places an event earlier than it actually occurred

pro·claim (prō klām′, prə-) *vt.* [< MFr. < L. < *pro*-, before + *clamare*, to cry out] 1. to announce to the public officially; announce to be 2. to show to be [acts that *proclaimed* him a friend] 3. to praise or extol

proc·la·ma·tion (prok′lə mā′shən) *n.* 1. a proclaiming or being proclaimed 2. something that is proclaimed

pro·clit·ic (prō klit′ik) *adj.* [ModL. *procliticus* < Gr. *proklinein*, to lean forwards] *Gram.* dependent for its stress on the following word: said of a word that forms a phonetic unit with the following, stressed word (eg., *for* in *once and for all*) —*n.* any such word or particle

pro·cliv·i·ty (prō kliv′ə tē) *n., pl.* **-ties** [L. *proclivitas* < *pro*-, before + *clivus*, a slope] a natural or habitual tendency or inclination

pro·con·sul (prō kon′s′l) *n.* [L. < *pro consule*, (acting) for the consul] a Roman official with consular authority who commanded an army in the provinces, often acting as provincial governor —**pro·con′sul·ar** (-syool ər) *adj.* —**pro·con′sul·ate** (-syool it), **pro·con′sul·ship′** *n.*

pro·cras·ti·nate (prō kras′tə nāt′, prə-) *vi., vt.* **-nat′ed, -nat′ing** [< L. pp. of *procrastinare*, ult. < *pro*-, forward + *cras*, tomorrow] to put off doing (something) until later; delay —**pro·cras′ti·na′tion** *n.* —**pro·cras′ti·na′tor** *n.*

pro·cre·ate (prō′krē āt′) *vt., vi.* **-at′ed, -at′ing** [< L. pp. of *procreare* < *pro*-, before + *creare*, to create] 1. to produce (young); beget 2. to produce or bring into existence —**pro′cre·ant** *adj.* —**pro′cre·a′tion** *n.* —**pro′cre·a′tive** *adj.* —**pro′cre·a′tor** *n.*

Pro·crus·te·an (prō krus′tē ən) *adj.* 1. of or like Procrustes, the giant in Greek Myth. who seized travellers, tied them to a bedstead, and either stretched them or cut off their legs to make them fit 2. like the actions of Procrustus 3. securing conformity at any cost

proc·tol·o·gy (prok tol′ə jē) *n.* [< Gr. *prōktos*, anus + -LOGY] the branch of medicine dealing with the rectum and anus and their diseases —**proc′to·log′ic** (-tə loj′ik), **proc′-to·log′i·cal** *adj.* —**proc·tol′o·gist** *n.*

proc·tor (prok′tər) *n.* [< ME., contr.: see PROCURATOR] 1. a person employed to manage another's affairs, esp. one engaged to conduct another's case in an ecclesiastical court 2. a college or university official who maintains order, discipline, etc. among students —*vt.* [U.S.] to supervise (an examination) —**proc·to·ri·al** (prok tôr′ē əl) *adj.* —**proc′-tor·ship′** *n.*

pro·cum·bent (prō kum′bənt) *adj.* [< L. prp. of *procumbere*, ult. < *pro*-, forward + *cubare*, to lie down] 1. lying face down 2. *Bot.* trailing along the ground: said of a stem

proc·u·ra·tor (prok′yə rāt′ər) *n.* [< OFr. < L. < *procurare*: see PROCURE] 1. in the Roman Empire, an administrator of a province 2. a person employed to manage another's affairs; agent —**proc′u·ra·to′ri·al** (-yər ə tôr′ē əl) *adj.*

procurator fiscal a legal officer in Scotland who performs the functions of public prosecutor and coroner

pro·cure (prō kyoor′, prə-) *vt.* **-cured′, -cur′ing** [< MFr. < L. < *pro*, for + *curare*, to attend to < *cura*, a care] 1. to get or bring about by some effort; obtain; secure 2. to obtain (women) for the purpose of prostitution —**pro·cur′-a·ble** *adj.* —**pro·cure′ment, pro·cur′ance, pro·cur′al** *n.*

pro·cur·er (-ər) *n.* a person who procures; specif., a man who obtains women for the purpose of prostitution; pimp —**pro·cur′ess** *n.fem.*

Pro·cy·on (prō′sē on′) [L. < Gr. < *pro*-, before + *kyōn*, dog: it rises before the Dog Star] a star of the first magnitude in Canis Minor

prod (prod) *vt.* **prod′ded, prod′ding** [< ?] 1. to jab or poke as with a pointed stick 2. to urge or stir into action —*n.* 1. a prodding; jab, poke, thrust, etc. 2. something that prods; specif., a rod or pointed stick used in driving cattle —**prod′-der** *n.*

prod·e·li·sion (prōd ē lizh′ən) *n.* the omission or elision of an initial vowel (eg., 're in *they're*)

prod·i·gal (prod′i gəl) *adj.* [MFr. < L. < *prodigere*, to waste < *pro*-, forth + *agere*, to drive] 1. wasteful in a reckless way 2. extremely generous; lavish 3. extremely abundant; profuse —*n.* a person who recklessly wastes his wealth, resources, etc. —**prod′i·gal′i·ty** (-gal′ə tē) *n., pl.* **-ties** —**prod′i·gal·ly** *adv.*

prodigal son *Bible* a wastrel son who repented and was welcomed home: Luke 15:11-32

pro·di·gious (prə dij′əs) *adj.* [< L.: see ff.] 1. wonderful; amazing 2. enormous; huge —**pro·di′gious·ly** *adv.* —**pro·di′gious·ness** *n.*

prod·i·gy (prod′ə jē) *n., pl.* **-gies** [L. *prodigium*, omen] a person or thing so extraordinary as to inspire wonder; specif., a child who is extremely talented or intelligent

pro·duce (prə dyoos′; *for n.* prod′yoos) *vt.* **-duced′, -duc′ing** [L. *producere* < *pro*-, forward + *ducere*, to lead] 1. to

bring to view; offer for inspection [to *produce* identification] 2. to bring forth; bear; yield [a well that *produces* oil] 3. *a*) to make or manufacture *b*) to create 4. to cause; give rise to [war *produces* devastation] 5. to get ready and present (a play, film, etc.); be the producer (sense 2) of 6. *Econ.* to create (anything having exchange value) 7. *Geom.* to extend (a line or plane) —*vi.* to bear, yield, create, manufacture, etc. something —*n.* something produced; yield; esp., fresh fruits and vegetables —**pro·duc′-i·bil′i·ty** *n.* —**pro·duc′i·ble** *adj.*

pro·duc·er (prə dyoos′ər) *n.* 1. a person or thing that produces; specif., one who produces goods and services: opposed to CONSUMER 2. *a*) a person in charge of the artistic direction of a play *b*) a person in charge of the financing and coordination of all activities in connection with the production of a film *c*) [U.S.] a person in charge of the financing, etc. of a play

prod·uct (prod′əkt) *n.* [< ML. < L. pp. of *producere*: see PRODUCE] 1. something produced by nature or by man 2. result; outgrowth 3. *Chem.* any substance resulting from a chemical change 4. *Math.* the quantity obtained by multiplying two or more quantities together

pro·duc·tion (prə duk′shən) *n.* 1. the act or process of producing 2. the rate of producing or the amount produced 3. *a*) something produced; product *b*) a work of art, literature, etc. *c*) a show, film, etc. 4. the creation of economic value; producing of goods and services

pro·duc·tive (-tiv) *adj.* 1. fertile 2. marked by abundant production or effective results 3. bringing as a result (with *of*) [war is *productive* of much misery] 4. of or engaged in the creating of economic value —**pro·duc′tive·ly** *adv.* —**pro·duc·tiv·i·ty** (prō′dək tiv′ə tē), **pro·duc′tive·ness** *n.*

pro·em (prō′em) *n.* [< MFr. < L. < Gr. < *pro*-, before + *oimē*, song] a brief introduction; preface

prof (prof) *n.* [Colloq.] *shortened form of* PROFESSOR

Prof. Professor

prof·a·na·tion (prof′ə nā′shən) *n.* a profaning or being profaned; desecration —**pro·fan·a·to·ry** (prə fan′ə tər ē, prō-) *adj.*

pro·fane (prə fān′, prō-) *adj.* [< MFr. < L. < *pro*-, before (i.e., outside) + *fanum*, a temple] 1. not connected with religion; secular [*profane* art] 2. not hallowed 3. showing disrespect or contempt for sacred things; irreverent —*vt.* **-faned′, -fan′ing** 1. to treat (sacred things) with disrespect or contempt 2. to put to a base or improper use —**pro·fane′ly** *adv.* —**pro·fane′ness** *n.* —**pro·fan′er** *n.*

pro·fan·i·ty (-fan′ə tē) *n.* 1. the state or quality of being profane 2. *pl.* **-ties** something profane; esp., profane language or the use of profane language

pro·fess (prə fes′, prō-) *vt.* [< L. pp. of *profiteri* < *pro*-, before + *fateri*, to avow] 1. to make an open declaration of; affirm [to *profess* one's love] 2. to claim to have (some feeling, knowledge, etc.): often connoting insincerity or pretence 3. to practise as one's profession 4. to declare one's belief in [to *profess* Christianity]

pro·fessed (-fest′) *adj.* 1. openly declared; avowed 2. insincerely avowed; pretended 3. having made one's profession (sense 4) 4. professing to be duly qualified [a *professed* economist] —**pro·fess′ed·ly** (-fes′id lē) *adv.*

pro·fes·sion (prə fesh′ən) *n.* 1. a professing or declaring; avowal, as of love, religious belief, etc. 2. a faith or religion professed 3. *a*) an occupation requiring advanced education and involving intellectual skills, as medicine, law, theology, engineering, teaching, etc. *b*) the body of persons in any such occupation *c*) loosely, any occupation 4. the act or ceremony of taking vows on entering a religious order —**the oldest profession** prostitution: a jocular usage

pro·fes·sion·al (-′l) *adj.* 1. of, engaged in, or worthy of the standards of, a profession 2. designating or of a school offering instruction in a profession 3. earning one's living from an activity, such as a sport, not normally thought of as an occupation 4. engaged in by professional players [*professional* boxing] 5. engaged in a specific occupation for pay [a *professional* writer] 6. being such in the manner of one practising a profession [a *professional* gossip] —*n.* 1. a person who is professional (esp. in sense 3) 2. a person who does something with great skill —**pro·fes′sion·al·ism** *n.* —**pro·fes′sion·al·ly** *adv.*

pro·fes·sion·al·ize (-′l īz′) *vt.* **-ized′, -iz′ing** to cause to have professional qualities, status, etc. —**pro·fes′-sion·al·i·za′tion** *n.*

pro·fes·sor (prə fes′ər) *n.* 1. a person who professes something 2. a teacher, esp. one holding a university chair —**pro·fes·so·ri·al** (prō′fə sôr′ē əl) *adj.* —**pro′fes·so·ri·al·ly** *adv.* —**pro·fes′sor·ship′, pro·fes′sor·ate** (-it) *n.*

prof·fer (prof′ər) *vt.* [< Anglo-Fr. & OFr. < *por*-, PRO.² + *offrir*, ult. < L. *offerre*, to offer] to offer (advice, friendship, etc.) —*n.* an offer or proposal

pro·fi·cient (prə fish′ənt) *adj.* [< L. prp. of *proficere*, to advance < *pro*-, forward + *facere*, to make] highly competent; skilled —*n.* an expert —**pro·fi′cien·cy** (-ən sē) *n., pl.* **-cies** —**pro·fi′cient·ly** *adv.*

pro·file (prō′fīl) *n.* [< It. < *profilare*, to outline < *pro*- (<

L. *pro-*), before + *filo* (< L. *filum*), a thread] 1. *a*) a side view of the face *b*) a drawing of this 2. outline [the *profile* of a hill] 3. a short, vivid biographical and character sketch 4. a graph, writing, etc. presenting data about a particular subject 5. *Archit.* a side or sectional elevation of a building, etc. —*vt.* -**filed**, -**fil·ing** to sketch, write, or make a profile of

prof·it (prof'it) *n.* [OFr. < L. pp. of *proficere*, to profit: see PROFICIENT] 1. advantage; gain; benefit 2. [*often pl.*] income from money invested in stocks, bonds, etc. 3. [*often pl.*] the sum remaining after all costs are deducted from the income of a business —*vi.* 1. to make a profit 2. to benefit; gain —*vt.* to be of profit or advantage to —**prof'it·er** *n.* —**prof'it·less** *adj.*

prof·it·a·ble (-əb'l) *adj.* yielding profit, gain, or benefit —**prof'it·a·bil'i·ty**, **prof'it·a·ble·ness** *n.* —**prof'it·a·bly** *adv.*

profit and loss *Bookkeeping* an account compiled at the end of a financial year showing that year's revenue and expense items and indicating gross and net profit or loss

prof·i·teer (prof'ə tir') *n.* [PROFIT + -EER] a person who makes an unfair profit by charging very high prices when there is a shortage of something that people need —*vi.* to be a profiteer

profit sharing the practice of dividing a share of the profits of a business among employees, in addition to paying them their wages —**prof'it-shar'ing** *adj.*

profit taking the selling of stocks, shares, etc. when the market value is high so as to make a profit

prof·li·gate (prof'lə git) *adj.* [< L. pp. of *profligare*, to rout, ruin < *pro-*, forward + *fligere*, to drive] 1. immoral and shameless; dissolute 2. recklessly extravagant —*n.* a profligate person —**prof'li·ga·cy** (-gə sē), **prof'li·gate·ness** *n.* —**prof'li·gate·ly** *adv.*

pro·found (prə faund') *adj.* [< OFr. < L. *profundus* < *pro-*, forward + *fundus*, bottom] 1. very deep or low [a *profound* abyss, sigh, etc.] 2. marked by intellectual depth [*profound* talk] 3. deeply or intensely felt [*profound* grief] 4. thoroughgoing; [*profound* changes] 5. unbroken [a *profound* silence] —**pro·found'ly** *adv.* —**pro·found'ness** *n.*

pro·fun·di·ty (-fun'də tē) *n., pl.* -**ties** 1. depth 2. intellectual depth 3. a profound idea, matter, etc.

pro·fuse (prə fyoos') *adj.* [< L. pp. of *profundere* < *pro-*, forth + *fundere*, to pour] 1. giving freely; generous [*profuse* in her apologies] 2. given or poured forth freely and abundantly —**pro·fuse'ly** *adv.* —**pro·fuse'ness** *n.*

pro·fu·sion (-fyoo'zhən) *n.* 1. a pouring forth with great liberality or wastefulness 2. great liberality or wastefulness 3. rich or lavish supply; abundance

pro·gen·i·tive (prō jen'ə tiv, prə-) *adj.* [see ff. & -IVE] capable of begetting offspring; reproductive

pro·gen·i·tor (prō jen'ə tər, prə-) *n.* [< MFr. < L., ult. < *pro-*, forth + *gignere*, to beget] 1. a forefather; ancestor in direct line 2. an originator or precursor

prog·e·ny (proj'ə nē) *n., pl.* -**nies** [< MFr. < L. < *progignere*: see prec.] children, descendants, or offspring

pro·ges·ter·one (prō jes'tə rōn') *n.* [PRO-¹ + *ge*(station) (see GESTATE) + STER(OL) + -ONE] a steroid hormone that prepares the uterus for the fertilized ovum and the mammary glands for milk secretion

prog·na·thous (prog nā'thəs) *adj.* [PRO-¹ + Gr. *gnathos*, a jaw] having the jaws projecting beyond the upper face: also **prog·nath'ic** (-nath'ik) —**prog'na·thism** *n.*

prog·no·sis (prog nō'sis) *n., pl.* -**no'ses** (-sēz) [< LL. < Gr. < *pro-*, before + *gignōskein*, to know] a forecast or forecasting; esp., a prediction of the probable course of a disease in an individual and the chances of recovery

prog·nos·tic (-nos'tik) *n.* [see prec.] 1. a sign; omen 2. a forecast —*adj.* 1. foretelling 2. *Med.* of, or serving as a basis for, prognosis

prog·nos·ti·cate (-nos'tə kāt') *vt.* -**cat'ed**, -**cat'ing** 1. to foretell or predict 2. to indicate beforehand —**prog·nos'ti·ca'tion** *n.* —**prog·nos'ti·ca'tive** (-kāt iv) *adj.* —**prog·nos'ti·ca'tor** *n.*

pro·gram (prō'gram, -grəm) *n.* [see ff.] 1. chiefly *U.S. sp.* of PROGRAMME 2. *a*) a sequence of operations to be performed by a digital computer, as in solving a problem *b*) the coded instructions and data for this —*vt.* -**gramed**, -**gram·ing** 1. chiefly *U.S. sp.* of PROGRAMME 2. *a*) to furnish (a computer) with a program *b*) to incorporate in a computer program —*vi.* to prepare a program —**pro'-gram·er** *n.*

pro·gram·a·ble, **pro·gram·ma·ble** (prō'grəm'ə b'l) *adj.* of a computer that can be programed

pro·gramme (prō'gram, -grəm) *n.* [< Fr. < LL. < Gr. *programma*, an edict < *pro-*, before + *graphein*, to write] 1. *a*) the acts, speeches, musical pieces, etc. that make up an entertainment, ceremony, etc. *b*) a printed list of these 2. a scheduled broadcast on radio or television 3. a plan or procedure 4. all the activities offered at a camp, resort, etc. 5. a statement of intentions, esp. that of a political party —*vt.* -**grammed** -**gram·ming** 1. to schedule in programme 2. [Chiefly *U.S.*] to prepare (a textbook) for use in

programmed learning —*vi.* to prepare a programme —**pro·gram·mat·ic** (prō'grə mat'ik) *adj.* —**pro'gram·mer** *n.*

programmed learning [Chiefly U.S.] learning that a pupil acquires on his own, step by step, from a textbook that has a series of questions with the answers given elsewhere in the book

programme music instrumental music that is meant to suggest a particular scene, story, etc.

prog·ress (prō'gres; *for v.* prə gres') *n.* [< L. pp. of *progredi* < *pro-*, before + *gradi*, to step] 1. a moving forwards or onwards 2. forward course; development 3. advance towards perfection; improvement —*vi.* 1. to move forwards or onwards 2. to move forwards towards completion, a goal, etc. 3. to advance towards perfection; improve —**in progress** going on

pro·gres·sion (prə gresh'ən) *n.* 1. a moving forwards or onwards 2. a succession, as of acts, happenings, etc. 3. *Math.* a series of numbers increasing or decreasing by a constant difference between terms: see ARITHMETIC PROGRESSION, GEOMETRIC PROGRESSION —**pro·gres'sion·al** *adj.*

pro·gres·sive (-gres'iv) *adj.* 1. moving forwards or onwards 2. continuing by successive steps 3. of, or concerned with, progression 4. designating a tax whose rate increases as the base increases 5. favouring or working for progress, as through political or social reform 6. of education that stresses self-expression, etc. 7. of a dance in which partners dance one figure with each other before moving on 8. *Gram.* indicating continuing action: said of certain verb forms, as *am working* 9. *Med.* becoming more severe: said of a disease —*n.* a person who is progressive, esp. one who favours political progress or reform —**pro·gres'sive·ly** *adv.* —**pro·gres'sive·ness** *n.*

progress report an account or report giving details of the progress made on a project, etc.

pro·hib·it (prō hib'it, prə-) *vt.* [< L. pp. of *prohibere* < *pro-*, before + *habere*, to have] 1. to refuse to permit; forbid by law or by an order 2. to prevent; hinder —**pro·hib'it·er**, **pro·hib'i·tor** *n.*

pro·hi·bi·tion (prō'ə bish'ən) *n.* 1. a prohibiting or being prohibited 2. an order or law that forbids 3. the forbidding by law of the manufacture or sale of alcohol specif., [P-] in the U.S., the period (1920–1933) of prohibition by Federal law —**pro'hi·bi'tion·ist** *n.*

pro·hib·i·tive (prō hib'ə tiv, prə-) *adj.* 1. prohibiting or tending to prohibit something 2. such as to prevent purchase, use, etc. [*prohibitive* prices] Also **pro·hib'i·to·ry** (-tər ē) —**pro·hib'i·tive·ly** *adv.*

proj·ect (proj'ekt, -ikt; *for v.* prə jekt') *n.* [< L. pp. of *projicere* < *pro-*, before + *jacere*, to throw] 1. a proposal; plan 2. an organized undertaking, as a special unit of work, research, etc. in school —*vt.* 1. to propose (a plan of action) 2. to throw forwards 3. *a*) to cause (one's voice) to be heard clearly and at a distance *b*) to get (ideas, feelings, etc.) across to others effectively 4. to send forth in one's imagination [to *project* oneself into the future] 5. to cause to jut out 6. to cause (a shadow, image, etc.) to fall upon a surface 7. *same as* EXTRAPOLATE 8. *Geom.* to transform the points of (a geometric figure) into the points of another figure, usually by lines of correspondence —*vi.* 1. to jut out 2. to project one's voice, ideas, etc.

pro·jec·tile (prə jek'til) *n.* 1. an object designed to be shot forwards, as a cannon shell, bullet, or rocket 2. anything thrown forwards —*adj.* 1. designed to be hurled forwards, as a javelin 2. hurling forwards [*projectile* energy]

pro·jec·tion (-shən) *n.* 1. a projecting or being projected 2. something that projects, or juts out 3. something that is projected; specif., in map making, the representation on a plane of all or part of the earth's surface or of the celestial sphere 4. an extrapolation 5. *Psychiatry* the unconscious act of ascribing to others one's own ideas, impulses, or emotions 6. *Photog.* the process of projecting an image, as from a transparent slide, upon a screen, etc. —**pro·jec'-tion·al** *adj.* —**pro·jec'tive** *adj.*

pro·jec·tion·ist (-ist) *n.* the operator of a film or slide projector

projective geometry the branch of geometry dealing with the properties of a figure that do not vary when the figure is projected

pro·jec·tor (prə jek'tər) *n.* a person or thing that projects; specif., a machine for throwing an image on a screen, as from a film

pro·lapse (prō'laps; *also, and for v. usually,* prō laps') *n.* [< ModL. < LL. < pp. of *prolabi* < *pro-*, forward + *labi*, to fall] *Med.* the slipping out of place of an internal organ, as the uterus: also **pro·lap'sus** (-lap'səs) —*vi.* -**lapsed'**, -**laps'-ing** *Med.* to slip out of place

pro·late (prō'lāt) *adj.* [< L. pp. of *proferre*, to bring forwards] extended or elongated at the poles [a *prolate* spheroid]

prole (prōl) *adj., n.* *colloq.* clipped form of proletarian (see PROLETARIAT)

pro·lep·sis (prō lep'sis) *n., pl.* -**lep'ses** (-sēz) [L. < Gr. *prolēpsis* < *prolambanein*, to take before] 1. a rhetorical device in which objections are anticipated and answered in advance 2. use of a word after a verb in anticipation of its becoming applicable through the action of the verb (eg., *flat* in *hammer it flat*)

pro·le·tar·i·at (prō'lə ter'ē ət) *n.* [< Fr. < L. *proletarius*, a citizen of the poorest class, who served the state only by having children < *proles*, offspring] 1. [Rare] the class of lowest status in any society 2. the working class; esp., the industrial working class —**pro'le·tar'i·an** *adj., n.*

pro·lif·er·ate (prō lif'ə rāt', prə-) *vt., vi.* -at'ed, -at'ing [ult. < ML. < L. *proles*, offspring + *ferre*, to bear] 1. to reproduce (new parts) in quick succession 2. to create in profusion; multiply rapidly —**pro·lif'er·a'tion** *n.* —**pro·lif'er·ous** (-rəs) *adj.*

pro·lif·ic (prə lif'ik, prō-) *adj.* [< Fr. < ML. < L. *proles*, offspring + *facere*, to make] 1. producing many young or much fruit 2. creating many products of the mind [a *prolific* poet] 3. fruitful; abounding (often with *in* or *of*) —**pro·lif'i·ca·cy** (-i kə sē) *n.* —**pro·lif'i·cal·ly** *adv.*

pro·lix (prō liks', prō'liks) *adj.* [< L. *prolixus*, extended] 1. so wordy as to be tiresome; verbose 2. long-winded —**pro·lix'i·ty** *n.* —**pro·lix'ly** *adv.*

pro·logue (prō'lôg) *n.* [< MFr. < L. < Gr. < *pro-*, before + *logos*, a discourse] 1. an introduction to a poem, play, etc.; esp., introductory lines spoken before a dramatic performance 2. the actor speaking such lines 3. any preliminary act, event, etc.

pro·long (prə lôŋ') *vt.* [< MFr. < LL. < L. *pro-*, forth + *longus*, long] to lengthen in time or space: also **pro·lon'gate** (-gāt) -gat·ed, -gat·ing —**pro·lon·ga·tion** (prō'-lôŋ gā'shən) *n.* —**pro·long'er** *n.*

prom (prom) *n.* [contr. < ff.] 1. *same as* PROMENADE (sense 2) 2. *clipped form of* PROMENADE CONCERT 3. [U.S. Colloq.] a formal dance held at a school or college

prom·e·nade (prom'ə nād'; *occas.* -näd') *n.* [Fr. < *promener*, to take for a walk < LL. < L. *pro-*, forth + *minare*, to herd] 1. a leisurely walk taken for pleasure, to display one's finery, etc. 2. a public place for such a walk esp. a paved walk along the front at a seaside resort 3. *a)* [U.S.] a ball, or formal dance *b)* a march of all the guests, beginning a formal ball 4. a walking figure in a square dance —*vi., vt.* -nad'ed, -nad'ing to take or perform a promenade (along or through); parade —**prom'e·nad'er** *n.*

promenade concert a musical performance at which some of the audience pay a low entrance fee to stand rather than sit

promenade deck an upper covered deck of a passenger ship for the use of passengers

pro·me·thi·um (prə mē'thē əm) *n.* [ModL. after *Prometheus*, the Titan in Gr. myth. who stole fire from heaven to benefit mankind] a metallic chemical element of the rare-earth group: symbol Pm; at. wt., 145(?); at.no. 61

prom·i·nence (prom'ə nəns) *n.* 1. a being prominent 2. something prominent

prom·i·nent (-nənt) *adj.* [< L. prp. of *prominere*, to project] 1. sticking out; projecting [a *prominent* chin] 2. noticeable at once; conspicuous 3. widely and favourably known [a *prominent* artist] —**prom'i·nent·ly** *adv.*

pro·mis·cu·ous (prə mis'kyoo wəs) *adj.* [< L. < *pro-*, forth + *miscere*, to mix] 1. consisting of different elements mixed together without sorting 2. showing little or no taste or care in choosing; specif., engaging in sexual intercourse with many persons casually 3. without plan or purpose; casual —**prom·is·cu·i·ty** (prom'is kyoo'ə tē), *pl.* -ties, **pro·mis'cu·ous·ness** *n.* —**pro·mis'cu·ous·ly** *adv.*

prom·ise (prom'is) *n.* [< L. *promissum*, ult. < *pro-*, forth + *mittere*, to send] 1. an agreement to do or not to do something; vow 2. a sign that gives reason for expecting success 3. something promised —*vi.* -ised, -is·ing 1. to make a promise 2. to give a basis for expectation —*vt.* 1. to make a promise of (something) *to* somebody 2. to engage or pledge (with an infinitive or clause) [to *promise* to go] 3. to give a basis for expecting 4. [Colloq.] to assure —**prom'is·er,** *Law* **prom'i·sor'** (-i sôr') *n.*

promised land a place where one expects to have a better life: after Canaan, the land promised by God in the Bible to Abraham and his descendants

prom·is·ing (prom'i siŋ) *adj.* showing promise of success, excellence, etc. —**prom'is·ing·ly** *adv.*

prom·is·so·ry (prom'i sər ē) *adj.* 1. containing a promise 2. stipulating conditions that must be complied with to keep an insurance contract valid

promissory note a written promise to pay a certain sum of money to a certain person or bearer on demand or on a specified date

prom·on·to·ry (prom'ən tər ē) *n., pl.* -ries [< LL. < L. *promunturium*, prob. < *prominere*, to project] a peak of high land that juts out into a body of water; headland

pro·mote (prə mōt') *vt.* -mot'ed, -mot'ing [< L. pp. of *promovere* < *pro-*, forward + *movere*, to move] 1. to raise or advance to a higher position or rank [she was *promoted* to manager] 2. to help bring about or further the growth or establishment of [to *promote* the general welfare] 3. to

further the popularity, sales, etc. of by publicizing and advertising [to *promote* a product] 4. to support the passage of a private bill in Parliament 5. *Chess* to move a pawn to the eighth rank and change it into a piece —**pro·mot'a·ble** *adj.*

pro·mot·er (-mōt'ər) *n.* a person or thing that promotes; specif., a person who begins, secures financing for, and helps to organize an undertaking, as a business

pro·mo·tion (-mō'shən) *n.* a promoting; specif., *a)* advancement in rank, grade, or position *b)* furtherance of an enterprise, cause, etc. —**pro·mo'tion·al** *adj.*

prompt (prompt) *adj.* [< MFr. < L. < pp. of *promere* < *pro-*, forth + *emere*, to take] 1. quick to act or to do what is required; ready, punctual, etc. 2. done, spoken, etc. at once or without delay —*n.* 1. a notice of payment due 2. a reminder, esp. one to an actor of forgotten lines —*vt.* 1. to urge into action 2. to remind (a person) of something he has forgotten; specif., to help (an actor, etc.) with a cue 3. to move or inspire by suggestion —**prompt'ly** *adv.* —**prompt'ness** *n.*

prompt box *Theatre* the seat, out of sight of the audience, where the prompter sits

prompt·er (promp'tər) *n.* a person who prompts; specif., one who cues performers when they forget their lines

promp·ti·tude (-tə tyōōd') *n.* the quality of being prompt; promptness

prom·ul·gate (prom'əl gāt') *vt.* -gat'ed, -gat'ing [< L. pp. of *promulgare*, to publish, altered < ? *pro-*, before + *vulgus*, the people] 1. to publish or make known officially (a decree, law, dogma, etc.) 2. to make widespread [to *promulgate* culture] —**prom'ul·ga'tion** *n.* —**prom'ul·ga'tor** *n.*

pron. 1. pronominal 2. pronoun 3. pronounced 4. pronunciation

pro·na·os (prō nā'os) *n., pl.* -na·oi (-nā'oi) [Gr. *pro-* , PRO-[1] & *naos*, a temple] an open porch in front of a Greek temple

pro·nate (prō'nāt) *vt., vi.* -nat·ed, -nat·ing [< LL. *pronatus* < L. *pronus*: see PRONE] to rotate (the hand or forearm) so that the palm faces down or towards the body —**pro·na'tion** *n.*

prone (prōn) *adj.* [< L. *pronus* < *pro*, before] 1. lying or leaning face downwards 2. lying flat or prostrate 3. having a natural bent; disposed or inclined (*to*) [prone to error] 4. grovelling —**prone'ly** *adv.* —**prone'ness** *n.*

prong (proŋ) *n.* [akin to MLowG. *prangen*, to pinch] 1. any of the pointed ends of a fork; tine 2. any pointed projecting part, as the tip of an antler —*vt.* to pierce or break up with a prong —**pronged** *adj.*

prong·horn (proŋ'hôrn') *n., pl.* -horns', -horn' : see PLURAL, II, D, 1 an antelopelike deer of Mexico and the western U.S., having curved horns

pro·nom·i·nal (prō nom'i n'l) *adj.* *Gram.* of, or having the function of, a pronoun —**pro·nom'i·nal·ly** *adv.*

pro·noun (prō'noun) *n.* [< MFr. < L. *pronomen* < *pro*, for + *nomen*, noun] *Gram.* a word that can assume the functions of a noun and be used in place of a noun: *I, you, them, it, ours, who, which, myself, anybody,* etc. are pronouns

pro·nounce (prə nouns') *vt.* -nounced', -nounc'ing [< OFr. < L. < *pro-*, before + *nuntiare*, to announce < *nuntius*, messenger] 1. to say officially, solemnly, etc. [the judge *pronounced* sentence] 2. to declare to be as specified [to *pronounce* a man guilty] 3. *a)* to utter or articulate (a sound or word) *b)* to utter in the required or standard manner [he couldn't *pronounce* my name] —*vi.* 1. to make a pronouncement (*on*) 2. to pronounce words, syllables, etc. —**pro·nounce'a·ble** *adj.* —**pro·nounc'er** *n.*

pro·nounced (-nounst') *adj.* 1. spoken or uttered 2. clearly marked; unmistakable; decided [a *pronounced* change] —**pro·nounc'ed·ly** (-noun'sid lē) *adv.*

pro·nounce·ment (-nouns'mənt) *n.* 1. a pronouncing 2. a formal statement of a fact, opinion, or judgment

pronouncing dictionary a dictionary in which the pronunciation of words is given rather than the meanings

pron·to (pron'tō) *adv.* [Sp. < L. *promptus*: see PROMPT] [Chiefly U.S. Slang] at once; quickly; immediately

pro·nun·ci·a·men·to (prə nun'sē ə men'tō, prō-) *n., pl.* -tos [Sp. < L.: see PRONOUNCE] 1. a public declaration; proclamation 2. *same as* MANIFESTO

pro·nun·ci·a·tion (-ā'shən) *n.* 1. the act or manner of pronouncing words 2. *a)* any of the accepted or standard pronunciations of a word *b)* the representation in phonetic symbols of such a pronunciation —**pro·nun'ci·a'tion·al** *adj.*

proof (prōōf) *n.* [< OFr. *prueve* < LL. *proba*: see PROBE] 1. a proving, testing, or trying of something 2. anything serving to establish the truth of something; conclusive evidence 3. the establishment of the truth of something [to work on the *proof* of a theory] 4. a test or trial of the truth, worth, quality, etc. of something 5. the state of having been tested or proved 6. tested or proved strength, as of armour 7. the relative strength of an alcoholic liquor with reference to the standard for proof spirit: see PROOF SPIRIT 8. *Law* all the facts, admissions, and conclusions which together operate to determine a verdict **9.** *Photog.* a trial print of a negative **10.** *Printing* an impression of composed type taken for checking errors and making changes —*adj.* **1.** of tested and proved strength **2.** able to resist, withstand, etc. (with *against*) [*proof* against criticism] **3.** used in proving or testing **4.** of standard strength: said of alcoholic liquors —*vt.* **1.** to make a proof of **2.** to render proof against, esp. to make materials impervious to water

-proof (proof) *a combining form meaning:* **1.** impervious to [*waterproof*] **2.** protected from [*rustproof*] **3.** resistant to [*fireproof*]

proof·read (proof'red') *vt., vi.* to read and mark corrections on (printers' proofs, etc.) —**proof'read'er·** *n.*

proof spirit an alcoholic liquor that is 100 proof and contains 57.10 of its volume of alcohol having a specific gravity of .919 at 15.6°C

prop¹ (prop) *n.* [MDu. *proppe*, a prop] **1.** a support, as a stake or pole, placed under or against a structure or part **2.** a person or thing that gives support to a person, institution, etc. —*vt.* propped, prop'ping **1.** to support or hold up, as with a prop (often with *up*) **2.** to place or lean (something) *against* a support **3.** to sustain or bolster

prop² (prop) *n.* *same as* PROPERTY (sense 5)

prop³ (prop) *n.* *clipped form of* PROPELLER

prop. 1. proper(ly) **2.** property **3.** proposition

pro·pae·deu·tic (pro'pi dyoot'ik) *n.* [< Gr. *propaideuein*, to teach beforehand] [*often pl.*] elementary or preparatory instruction basic to further study of an art or science —*adj.* of, relating to, or providing such instruction

prop·a·gan·da (prop'ə gan'də) *n.* [ModL., short for *congregatio de propaganda fide,* congregation for propagating the faith] **1.** [P-] R.C.Ch. a committee of cardinals in charge of the foreign missions **2.** the systematic, widespread promotion of a certain set of ideas, doctrines, etc., esp. to further one's own cause: also **prop'**-**a·gan'dism 3.** ideas, doctrines, or allegations so spread, esp. if regarded as spread by deception —**prop'a·gan'dist** *n., adj.* —**prop'a·gan·dis'tic** *adj.* —**prop'a·gan·dis'ti·cal·ly** *adv.*

prop·a·gan·dize (-dīz) *vt., vi.* -dized, -diz·ing **1.** to spread (certain ideas or propaganda) **2.** to subject (people) to propaganda

prop·a·gate (prop'ə gat') *vt.* -gat'ed, -gat'ing [< L. pp. of *propagare,* to peg down' < *propago,* slip (of a plant)] **1.** to cause (a plant or animal) to reproduce itself; raise or breed **2.** to reproduce (itself): said of a plant or animal **3.** to spread (ideas, customs, etc.) **4.** to extend or transmit (sound waves, etc.) through air or water —*vi.* to reproduce, as plants or animals —**prop'a·ga·ble** *adj.* —**prop'a·ga'tion** *n.* —**prop'a·ga'tive** *adj.* —**prop'a·ga'tor** *n.*

pro·pane (pro'pan) *n.* [PROP(YL) + (METH)ANE] a heavy, gaseous hydrocarbon, C₃H₈, of the methane series, used as a fuel, in refrigerants, etc.

‡**pro·pa·tri·a** (pro pä'tre ə) [L.] for (one's) country

pro·pel (prə pel') *vt.* -pelled', -pel'ling [< L. < *pro-,* forward + *pellere,* to drive] to push, drive, or impel onwards, forwards, or ahead —**pro·pel'lant** *n.* —**pro·pel**(**-lent** *adj., n.*

pro·pel·ler (-ər) *n.* a person or thing that propels; specif., a device (**screw propeller**) consisting of blades twisted to move in a spiral as they rotate with the hub, and serving to propel a ship or aircraft forwards

propelling pencil a pencil consisting of a metal case containing a pencil lead that by a screwing motion of the outer case can be moved forward and used to write

pro·pen·si·ty (prə pen'sə te) *n., pl.* -ties [< L. pp. of *propendere,* to hang forward + -ITY] a natural inclination or tendency; bent

prop·er (prop'ər) *adj.* [< OFr. < L. *proprius,* one's own] **1.** specially adapted or suitable; appropriate [the *proper* tool for a job] **2.** naturally belonging or peculiar (*to*) [weather *proper* to May] **3.** conforming to an accepted standard or to good usage; correct **4.** fitting; seemly; right **5.** decent or decorous or exceedingly respectable **6.** in its most restricted sense; strictly so called [the family *proper*] **7.** real; genuine [a *proper* gun] **8.** [Colloq.] complete; thorough [a *proper* scoundrel] **9.** [Archaic or Dial.] *a)* fine; excellent *b)* handsome **10.** *Gram.* designating a noun that names a specific individual, place, etc., is not used with an article, and is normally capitalized, as *Donald, London,* etc. —*adv.* [Dial.] completely; thoroughly —**prop'er·ly** *adv.* —**prop'er·ness** *n.*

proper fraction *Math.* a fraction in which the numerator is less than the denominator (Ex.: 2/5)

proper motion the very small, continuous change in the direction of motion of a star relative to the sun

prop·er·tied (prop'ər ted) *adj.* owning property

prop·er·ty (prop'ər te) *n., pl.* -ties [< OFr. < L. *proprietas* < *proprius,* one's own] **1.** *a)* the right to possess, use, and dispose of something; ownership *b)* something, as a piece of writing, in which copyright or other rights are held **2.** a

thing or things owned; possessions; esp., land or real estate owned **3.** a specific piece of land **4.** any trait or attribute proper to a thing; characteristic or essential quality [the *properties* of a chemical compound] **5.** any of the movable articles used as part of a stage setting or in a piece of stage business, except the costumes, backdrops, etc. **6.** [Chiefly Aust.] a ranch, esp. one smaller than a station —**prop'er·ty·less** *adj.*

property man a man in charge of the properties in a theatrical production: also **property master** —**property mistress** *fem.*

proph·e·cy (prof'ə se) *n., pl.* -cies [< OFr. < LL. < Gr. < *prophetes:* see PROPHET] **1.** prediction of the future by a prophet, as supposedly influenced by the guidance of God or a god **2.** any prediction **3.** something prophesied

proph·e·sy (-sī') *vt., vi.* -sied', -sy'ing **1.** to declare or predict (something) by or as by the influence of divine guidance; utter (prophecies) **2.** to predict (a future event) in any way —**proph'e·si'er** *n.*

proph·et (prof'it) *n.* [< OFr. < LL. < Gr. *prophetes,* interpreter of God's will < *pro-,* before + *phanai,* to speak] **1.** a person who claims to speak for God, or a religious leader who claims to be, or is thought to be, divinely inspired **2.** a spokesman for some cause, group, etc. **3.** a person who predicts the future —**the Prophet** *a name used for* Mohammed (by Moslems) —**the Prophets 1.** the prophetic books of the Bible that include Isaiah, Jeremiah, etc. **2.** the authors or subjects of these books —**proph'-et·ess** *n. fem.*

pro·phet·ic (prə fet'ik) *adj.* **1.** of, or having the powers of, a prophet **2.** of or containing a prophecy **3.** that predicts Also **pro·phet'i·cal** —**pro·phet'i·cal·ly** *adv.*

pro·phy·lac·tic (pro'fə lak'tik) *adj.* [< Gr., ult. < *pro-,* before + *phylassein,* to guard] preventive or protective; esp., preventing disease —*n.* a prophylactic medicine, device, etc.; esp. in U.S., a condom

pro·phy·lax·is (-sis) *n., pl.* -lax'es (-sez) the prevention of or protection from disease; prophylactic treatment

pro·pin·qui·ty (pro pin'kwə te) *n.* [< MFr. < L. *propinquus,* near] **1.** nearness in time or place **2.** nearness of relationship; kinship

pro·pi·on·ic acid (pro'pe on'ik) [PRO(TO)- + Gr. *pion,* fat + -IC] a colourless, sharp-smelling, liquid fatty acid produced in the distillation of wood: used in making artificial flavours, perfume esters, etc.

pro·pi·ti·ate (prə pish'e at') *vt.* -at'ed, -at'ing [< L. pp. of *propitiare* < *propitius:* see ff.] to win or regain the good will of; appease or conciliate —**pro·pi'ti·a·ble** *adj.* —**pro·pi'-ti·a'tion** *n.* —**pro·pi'ti·a'tor** *n.* —**pro·pi'ti·a·to·ry** (-ə tar e), **pro·pi'ti·a·tive** (-at'iv) *adj.*

pro·pi·tious (prə pish'əs) *adj.* [< OFr. < L. *propitius* < *pro-,* before + *petere,* to seek] **1.** favourably inclined; gracious [the *propitious* gods] **2.** favourable; auspicious [a *propitious* omen] **3.** that favours or furthers [*propitious* winds] —**pro·pi'tious·ly** *adv.* —**pro·pi'tious·ness** *n.*

prop·jet (prop'jet') *n.* *same as* TURBOPROP

prop·o·lis (prop'ə lis) *n.* [L. < Gr. *propolis,* suburb, bee glue < *pro-,* before + *polis,* city] a brownish, waxy substance collected from the buds of certain trees by bees and used by them to cement or caulk their hives

pro·po·nent (prə po'nənt) *n.* [< L. prp. of *proponere* < *pro-,* forth + *ponere,* to place] **1.** a person who makes a proposal or proposition **2.** a person who espouses or supports a cause, etc.

pro·por·tion (prə pôr'shən) *n.* [< MFr. < L. < *pro-,* for + *portio,* a part] **1.** the comparative relation between things with respect to size, amount, etc.; ratio **2.** a part, share, etc., esp. in its relation to the whole; quota **3.** balance or symmetry **4.** size, degree, etc. relative to a standard **5.** [*pl.*] dimensions **6.** *Math. a)* an equality between ratios (Ex.: 2 is to 6 as 3 is to 9): also called **geometrical proportion** *b) same as* RULE OF THREE —*vt.* **1.** to cause to be in proper relation, balance, etc. [*proportion* the penalty to the crime] **2.** to arrange the parts of (a whole) so as to be harmonious —**pro·por'tion·a·ble** *adj.* —**pro·por'tioned** *adj.* —**pro·por'tion·ment** *n.*

pro·por·tion·al (-'l) *adj.* **1.** of or determined by proportion; relative **2.** in proportion [pay *proportional* to work done] **3.** *Math.* having the same ratio —*n.* a quantity in a mathematical proportion —**pro·por'tion·al'i·ty** (-al'ə te) *n.* —**pro·por'tion·al·ly** *adv.*

pro·por·tion·al·ist (-ist) *n.* [< prec. + -IST] a person who favours proportional representation

proportional representation representation of parties and other groups in an elective body in proportion to the number of votes they receive

pro·por·tion·ate (prə pôr'shə nit; *for v.* -nat') *adj.* in proper proportion; proportional —*vt.* -at'ed, -at'ing to make proportionate —**pro·por'tion·ate·ly** *adv.*

pro·pos·al (prə po'z'l) *n.* **1.** a proposing **2.** a plan or action proposed **3.** an offer of marriage

pro·pose (prə poz') *vt.* -posed', -pos'ing [< OFr. < L. pp. of *proponere:* see PROPONENT] **1.** to put forth for consideration or acceptance **2.** to plan or intend **3.** to present as a toast in drinking **4.** to nominate for membership, office, etc. —*vi.* **1.** to make a proposal; form a purpose, etc. **2.** to offer marriage —**pro·pos'er** *n.*

prop·o·si·tion (prop'ə zish'ən) *n.* **1.** a proposing **2.** *a)* something proposed; plan *b)* [Colloq.] an immoral proposal, esp. in sexual relations **3.** [Colloq.] a proposed deal, as in business **4.** [Colloq.] a person, problem, etc. to be dealt with **5.** a subject to be discussed **6.** *Logic* an expression in which the predicate affirms or denies something about the subject **7.** *Math.* a theorem to be demonstrated or a problem to be solved —*vt.* [Colloq.] to make a proposition, esp. an improper one, to —**prop'o·si'tion·al** *adj.*

pro·pound (prə pound') *vt.* [< L. *proponere*: see PROPONENT] to put forth for consideration; propose —**pro·pound'er** *n.*

pro·pri·e·tar·y (prə prī'ə tər ē, -trē) *n. pl.* **-tar·ies** [< LL. < L. *proprietas*: see PROPERTY] **1.** a proprietor **2.** a group of proprietors **3.** proprietorship —*adj.* **1.** belonging to a proprietor **2.** holding property **3.** of property or proprietorship **4.** held under patent, trademark, or copyright [a *proprietary* medicine]

pro·pri·e·tor (prə prī'ə tər) *n.* [< PROPRIET(ARY) + -OR] **1.** a person who has exclusive right to some property; owner **2.** one who owns and operates a business establishment —**pro·pri'e·tor·ship'** *n.* —**pro·pri'e·tress** (-tris) *n.fem.*

pro·pri·e·ty (-ə tē) *n., pl.* **-ties** [< OFr.: see PROPERTY] **1.** the quality of being proper, fitting, etc.; fitness **2.** conformity with what is proper or fitting or with accepted standards of behaviour —**the proprieties** accepted standards of behaviour in polite society

pro·proc·tor (prō'prok'tər) *n.* the deputy or assistant of a university proctor

pro·pul·sion (prə pul'shən) *n.* [< L. pp. of *propellere* (see PROPEL) + -ION] **1.** a propelling or being propelled **2.** something that propels; propelling or driving force —**pro·pul'sive, pro·pul'so·ry** *adj.*

pro·pyl (prō'pil) *n.* [< PRO(TO)- + Gr. *piōn*, fat + -YL] the monovalent radical C₃H₇, occurring in two isomeric forms —**pro·pyl'ic** *adj.*

prop·y·lae·um (prop'ə lē'əm) *n., pl.* **-lae'a** (-lē'ə) [L. < Gr. *propylaion*, orig. neut. of *propylaios*, before the gate] *Gr. & Rom. Archit.* an ornamental structure in front of a temple or other enclosure; esp., [*pl.*] the entrance to the Acropolis

pro·pyl·ene (prō'pə lēn') *n.* [prec. + -ENE] a flammable, colourless gas, used in making polypropylene, synthetic glycerol, etc.

propylene glycol a colourless, viscous liquid used as antifreeze, in making polyester resins, etc.

pro ra·ta (prō rāt'ə, rät'ə) [L. *pro rata (parte)*, according to the calculated (share)] in proportion; proportionate or proportionally

pro·rate (prō rāt', prō'rāt') *vt., vi.* **-rat'ed, -rat'ing** [< prec.] [Chiefly U.S.] to divide, assess, or distribute proportionately —*vi.* —**pro·ra'tion** *n.*

pro·rogue (prō rōg') *vt., vi.* **-rogued', -rogu'ing** [< MFr. < L. *prorogare*, to defer < *pro-*, for + *rogare*, to ask] to discontinue or end a session of (a legislative assembly, esp. a parliament) —**pro'ro·ga'tion** (-rō gā'shən) *n.*

pro·sa·ic (prō zā'ik) *adj.* [< ML. < L. *prosa*, PROSE] **1.** of or like prose; unpoetic **2.** commonplace; dull —**pro·sa'i·cal·ly** *adv.* —**pro·sa'ic·ness** *n.*

pro·sce·ni·um (prō sē'nē əm) *n., pl.* **-ni·ums, -ni·a** (-ə) [L. < Gr. < *pro-*, before + *skēnē*, a tent] **1.** the apron of a stage **2.** the plane separating the stage proper from the audience and including the arch (*proscenium arch*) and its curtain

pro·sciut·to (prə shoōt'ō) *n.* [It. < *prosciugare*, to dry out] a spicy Italian ham, cured by drying and served in very thin slices

pro·scribe (prō skrīb') *vt.* **-scribed', -scrib'ing** [< L. < *pro-*, before + *scribere*, to write] **1.** in ancient Rome, to publish the name of (a person) condemned to death, banishment, etc. **2.** to deprive of the protection of the law; outlaw **3.** to banish; exile **4.** to denounce or forbid the practice of —**pro·scrib'er** *n.* —**pro·scrip'tion** (-skrip'shən) *n.* —**pro·scrip'tive** *adj.* —**pro·scrip'tive·ly** *adv.*

prose (prōz) *n.* [MFr. < L. *prosa*, for *prorsa (oratio)*, direct (speech), ult. < pp. of *provertere*, to turn forwards] **1.** the ordinary form of language, without rhyme or metre: cf. VERSE, POETRY **2.** dull, commonplace talk —*adj.* **1.** of or in prose **2.** dull; prosaic —*vt., vi.* prosed, pros'ing to speak or write in prose —**pros'er** *n.*

pros·e·cute (pros'ə kyoōt') *vt.* **-cut'ed, -cut'ing** [< L. pp. of *prosequi* < *pro-*, before + *sequi*, to follow] **1.** to pursue (something) to a conclusion [to *prosecute* a war] **2.** to carry on; engage in **3.** *a)* to conduct legal proceedings against, esp. in court for a crime *b)* to try to get, enforce, etc. by legal process —*vi.* to institute and carry on a legal action —**pros'e·cut'a·ble** *adj.* —**pros'e·cu'tor** *n.*

pros·e·cu·tion (pros'ə kyoō'shən) *n.* **1.** a prosecuting, or following up **2.** the conducting of a lawsuit **3.** the lawyers

acting for the Crown against the accused in criminal proceedings

pros·e·lyte (pros'ə līt') *n.* [< LL. < Gr. *prosēlytos*] a person who has been converted from one religion, belief, etc. to another —*vt., vi.* **-lyt'ed, -lyt'ing** **1.** to try to convert (a person), esp. to one's religion **2.** to persuade to do or join something —**pros'e·lyt'er** *n.* —**pros'e·lyt·ism** (-li tiz'm, -līt iz'm) *n.*

pros·e·lyt·ize (-li tīz') *vi., vt.* **-ized', -iz'ing** *same as* PROSELYTE —**pros'e·lyt·iz'er** *n.*

‡**pro·sit** (prō'zit; *E.* prō'sit) *interj.* [G. < L. *prodesse*, to do good] to your health: a toast, esp. among Germans

pros·o·dy (pros'ə dē) *n., pl.* **-dies** [< L. < Gr. *prosōidia*. tone, accent < *pros*, to + *ōidē*, song] **1.** the science or art of versification, including the study of metrical structure, rhyme, etc. **2.** a system of versification [Poe's *prosody*] —**pro·sod·ic** (prə sod'ik), **pro·sod'i·cal** *adj.* —**pro·sod'-i·cal·ly** *adv.* —**pros'o·dist** *n.*

pro·so·po·poe·ia (prə sō'pō pē'ə) *n.* [L. < Gr. < *prosōpon*, person, face, mask + *poiein*, to make] *Rhetoric* **1.** a figure of speech which represents a dead or imaginary person as speaking **2.** *same as* PERSONIFICATION

pros·pect (pros'pekt; *for v.* pros pekt') *n.* [L. *prospectus*, lookout, ult. < *pro-*, forward + *specere*, to look] **1.** *a)* a broad view; scene *b)* a place from which one can see such a view **2.** a mental view; survey **3.** the view from any particular point; outlook **4.** a looking forwards; anticipation **5.** *a)* something hoped for *b)* [*usually pl.*] apparent chance for success **6.** a likely customer, candidate, etc. —*vt., vi.* to explore or search (*for*) [to *prospect* for gold] —**in prospect** expected

pro·spec·tive (prə spek'tiv) *adj.* **1.** looking towards the future **2.** expected; likely —**pro·spec'tive·ly** *adv.*

pros·pec·tor (pros pek'tər) *n.* a person who prospects for valuable ores, oil, etc.

pro·spec·tus (prə spek'təs, pro-) *n.* [L.: see PROSPECT] a statement outlining the main features of a new work, business enterprise, etc. or of an established institution

pros·per (pros'pər) *vi.* [< MFr. < L. < *prosperus*, favourable] to succeed, thrive, grow, etc. vigorously —*vt.* [Archaic] to cause to prosper

pros·per·i·ty (pro sper'ə tē) *n.* prosperous condition; good fortune, wealth, success, etc.

pros·per·ous (pros'pər əs) *adj.* **1.** prospering; flourishing **2.** well-to-do; well-off **3.** conducive to success; favourable —**pros'per·ous·ly** *adv.*

pros·tate (pros'tāt) *adj.* [< ML. < Gr. *prostatēs*, one standing before, ult. < *pro-*, before + *histanai*, to stand] of or relating to the prostate gland: also **pros·tat'ic** (-tat'-ik) —*n. same as* PROSTATE GLAND

prostate gland a partly muscular gland surrounding the urethra at the base of the bladder in most male mammals

pros·the·sis (pros'thə sis; *for 2, often* pros thē'-) *n., pl.* **-the·ses** (-sēz') [< LL. < Gr. < *pros*, to + *tithenai*, to place] *Med.* **1.** the replacement of a missing limb, eye, etc. by an artificial substitute **2.** such a substitute —**pros·thet'ic** (-thet'ik) *adj.*

pros·thet·ics (pros thet'iks) *n.pl.* [with sing. v.] [< PROSTHESIS] the branch of surgery or dentistry concerned with the replacement of missing parts, esp. limbs, by artificial substitutes

pros·ti·tute (pros'tə tyoōt') *vt.* **-tut'ed, -tut'ing** [< L. pp. of *prostituere* < *pro-*, before + *statuere*, to make stand] **1.** to sell the services of (oneself or another) for purposes of sexual intercourse **2.** to sell (oneself, one's integrity, etc.) for unworthy purposes —*n.* **1.** a man or woman who engages in promiscuous sexual intercourse for pay **2.** someone who sells his or her services for unworthy purposes —**pros'ti·tu'tion** *n.* —**pros'ti·tu'tor** *n.*

pros·trate (pros'trāt; *for v.* pros trāt') *adj.* [< L. pp. of *prosternere* < *pro-*, before + *sternere*, to stretch out] **1.** lying with the face downwards in humility or submission **2.** lying flat, prone, or supine **3.** thrown or fallen to the ground **4.** *a)* laid low; overcome *b)* physically weak or exhausted **5.** *Bot.* trailing on the ground —*vt.* **-trat'ed, -trat'ing** **1.** to lay flat on the ground **2.** to lay low; overcome or exhaust —**pros·tra'tion** *n.*

pro·style (prō'stīl) *adj.* [< L. < Gr. < *pro*, before + *stylos*, pillar] having a portico with columns, usually four, across the front only —*n.* such a portico

pros·y (prō'zē) *adj.* **pros'i·er, pros'i·est** **1.** like, or having the nature of, prose **2.** prosaic, dull, etc. —**pros'i·ly** *adv.* —**pros'i·ness** *n.*

Prot. Protestant

pro·tac·tin·i·um (prō'tak tin'ē əm) *n.* [ModL.: see PROTO- & ACTINIUM] a rare, radioactive, metallic chemical element: symbol, Pa; at. wt., 231.10; at. no., 91

pro·tag·o·nist (prō tag'ə nist) *n.* [< Gr. *prōtos*, first + *agōnistēs*, actor] **1.** the main character in a drama, novel, or story **2.** a person playing a leading or active part

prot·a·sis (prot'ə sis) *n.* [LL. < Gr. < *pro-*, before + *teinein*, to stretch] *Gram.* the clause that expresses the condition in a conditional sentence: cf. APODOSIS

pro·te·a (prō′tē ə) *n.* [ModL., after *Proteus*, the sea god in Gr. Myth. who could change his shape at will: because of the large numbers of species] any of various shrubs found in S. Africa with large showy heads of flowers

pro·te·an (prōt′ē ən, prō tē′ən) *adj.* **1.** [P-] of or like Proteus, the sea god in Gr. Myth. who could change shape at will **2.** readily taking on different shapes or forms

pro·te·ase (prōt′ē ās′) *n.* [PROTE(IN) + (DIAST)ASE] an enzyme that digests proteins

pro·tect (prə tekt′) *vt.* [< L. pp. of *protegere* < *pro-*, before + *tegere*, to cover] **1.** to shield from injury, danger, or loss; defend **2.** to set aside funds for paying (a note, draft, etc.) at maturity **3.** *Econ.* to guard (domestic goods) by tariffs on imports —**pro·tect′a·ble** *adj.*

pro·tec·tion (prə tek′shən) *n.* **1.** a protecting or being protected **2.** a person or thing that protects **3.** a passport or safe conduct pass **4.** [Colloq.] money extorted by racketeers threatening violence **5.** *Econ.* the system of protecting domestic goods by taxing imports

pro·tec·tion·ism (-iz′m) *n. Econ.* the system, theory, or policy of protection —**pro·tec′tion·ist** *n., adj.*

pro·tec·tive (prə tek′tiv) *adj.* **1.** protecting or intended to protect **2.** *Econ.* intended to protect domestic products, industries, etc. in competition with foreign ones [a *protective* tariff] —**pro·tec′tive·ly** *adv.* —**pro·tec′tive·ness** *n.*

protective colouration (or **colouring**) natural colouration of certain organisms allowing them to blend in with the normal environment and escape detection by enemies

protective custody the detention of someone to protect him or to protect the public from his possible actions

pro·tec·tor (prə tek′tər) *n.* **1.** one that protects; guardian **2.** *a)* a person ruling a kingdom during the minority, incapacity, etc. of the sovereign *b)* [P-] the title (in full **Lord Protector**) held by Oliver Cromwell (1653-1658) and his son Richard (1658-1659), during the Protectorate —**pro·tec′tor·ship′** *n.* —**pro·tec′tress** (-tris) *n.fem.*

pro·tec·tor·ate (-it) *n.* **1.** government by a protector **2.** the office or term of a protector **3.** [P-] the government of England under the Protectors (1653-1659) **4.** *a)* the relation of a strong state to a weaker state under its control and protection *b)* a state so controlled

pro·té·gé (prōt′ə zhā′, prōt′ə zhā′) *n.* [Fr., pp. of *protéger* < L.: see PROTECT] a person receiving guidance and help, esp. in furthering his career, from an influential person —**pro′·té·gée** (-zhā′, -zhā′) *n.fem.*

pro·tein (prō′tēn, prōt′ē in) *n.* [G. < Fr. < Gr. *prōteios*, prime < *prōtos*, first] any of a class of complex nitrogenous substances occurring in all animal and vegetable matter and essential to the diet of animals

pro tem·po·re (prō tem′pə rē′) [L.] for the time (being); temporary or temporarily: shortened to **pro tem**

pro·te·ol·y·sis (prōt′ē ol′ə sis) *n.* [ModL.: see PROTEIN & -LYSIS] *Biochem.* the breaking down of proteins, as by gastric juices, into simpler substances —**pro′te·o·lyt′ic** (-ə lit′ik) *adj.*

pro·te·ose (prōt′ē ōs′) *n.* [PROTE(IN) + -OSE[1]] any of a class of water-soluble products, formed in the hydrolysis of proteins, that can be broken down into peptones

pro·test (prə test′; *for n.* prō′test) *vt.* [< MFr. < L. < *pro-*, forth + *testari*, to affirm < *testis*, a witness] **1.** to state positively; declare or affirm strongly **2.** [U.S.] to speak strongly against **3.** to make a written declaration of the nonpayment of (a promissory note, cheque, etc.) —*vi.* **1.** to make solemn affirmation **2.** to express disapproval; object —*n.* **1.** the act or an instance of protesting; objection **2.** a document formally objecting to something **3.** *Law* a formal declaration that a bill or note has not been honoured by the drawer —**under protest** while expressing one's objections; unwillingly —**pro·test′er, pro·tes′tor** *n.*

Prot·es·tant (prot′is tənt; *for n. 2 & adj. 2, also* prə tes′tənt) *n.* [Fr. < G. < L. prp. of *protestari*: see prec.] **1.** a member of any of the Christian churches resulting or deriving from the Reformation under the leadership of Luther, Calvin, Wesley, etc. **2.** [p-] a person who protests —*adj.* **1.** of Protestants or Protestant beliefs, practices, etc. **2.** [p-] protesting —**Prot′es·tant·ism** *n.*

prot·es·ta·tion (prō′tes tā′shən) *n.* **1.** a strong declaration or affirmation **2.** the act of protesting **3.** a protest; objection

pro·thal·li·um (prō thal′ē əm) *n., pl.* -li·a (-ə) [ModL. < Gr. *pro-*, before + *thallos*, a shoot] the part of a fern that bears the sex organs, a small, flat, greenish disc usually attached to the ground by hairlike roots: also **pro·thal′lus** (-əs), *pl.* -li (-ī), -lus·es

pro·throm·bin (prō throm′bin) *n.* [PRO-[1] + THROMBIN] a factor in the blood plasma that is converted into thrombin during blood clotting

pro·tist (prōt′ist) *n.* [< Gr. *prōtistos*, first] *Biol.* any of a large group of one-celled organisms having characteristics found in both plants and animals, including algae, bacteria, protozoans, etc.

pro·ti·um (prōt′ē əm) *n.* [ModL.: see ff. & -*ium*, a

n.-forming suffix] the most common isotope of hydrogen with mass number 1

pro·to- [< Gr. < *protōs*, first] *a combining form meaning:* **1.** first in time, original, primitive [*prototype*] **2.** first in importance, chief [*protagonist*] Also **prot-**

pro·to·col (prōt′ə kol′) *n.* [< MFr. < ML. < LGr. *prōtokollon*, first leaf glued to a manuscript (noting the contents) < Gr. *prōtos*, first + *kolla*, glue] **1.** an original draft or record of a document, negotiation, etc. **2.** the code of ceremonial forms and courtesies used in official dealings, as between heads of state or diplomats —*vt., vi.* -**colled′**, -**col′ling** to draw up, or state in, a protocol

proto hippus an extinct, horselike quadruped

pro·ton (prō′ton) *n.* [ModL. < Gr. neut. of *prōtos*, first] a fundamental particle in the nucleus of all atoms: it carries a unit positive charge of electricity and has a mass approximately 1836 times that of an electron: cf. NEUTRON

proton synchrotron a synchrotron for accelerating protons and other heavy particles to very high energies

pro·to·phyte (-fīt) *n.* [PROTO- & -PHYTE] a single-celled plant of the first or lowest order

pro·to·plasm (prōt′ə plaz′m) *n.* [< G.: see PROTO- & PLASMA] a semifluid, colloidal substance that is the living matter of all animal and plant cells —**pro′to·plas′mic** *adj.*

pro·to·type (prōt′ə tīp′) *n.* [see PROTO- & TYPE] **1.** the first thing or being of its kind; original **2.** a model for another of its kind —**pro′to·typ′al** (-tī′p′l), **pro′to·typ′ic** (-tip′ik), **pro′to·typ′i·cal** *adj.*

pro·to·zo·an (prōt′ə zō′ən) *n.* [ModL. Protozoa (see PROTO- & -ZOA) + -AN] any of a large group of mostly microscopic, one-celled animals living chiefly in water but sometimes parasitic: also **pro′to·zo′on** (-on), *pl.* -zo′a (-ə) —*adj.* of the protozoans: also **pro′to·zo′ic** (-ik)

pro·tract (prō trakt′) *vt.* [< L. pp. of *protrahere* < *pro-*, forward + *trahere*, to draw] **1.** to draw out in time; prolong **2.** to draw to scale, using a protractor and scale **3.** *Zool.* to thrust out; extend —**pro·tract′ed·ly** *adv.* —**pro·tract′ed·ness** *n.* —**pro·tract′i·ble** *adj.* —**pro·trac′tion** *n.* —**pro·trac′tive** *adj.*

pro·trac·tile (prō trak′t′l) *adj.* capable of being protracted or thrust out; extensible

pro·trac·tor (-tər) *n.* [ML.] **1.** a person or thing that protracts **2.** a graduated, semicircular instrument for plotting and measuring angles

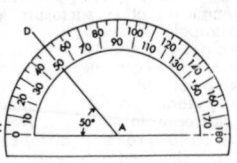

PROTRACTOR
(DAC, angle measured)

pro·trude (prō trōōd′) *vt., vi.* -**trud′ed**, -**trud′ing** [< L. < *pro-*, forth + *trudere*, to thrust] to thrust or jut out; project —**pro·tru′sion** (-trōō′zhən) *n.*

pro·tru·sile (-trōō′s′l) *adj.* that can be protruded, or thrust out, as a tentacle, etc.: also **pro·tru′si·ble**

pro·tru·sive (-trōō′siv) *adj.* **1.** protruding; jutting or bulging out **2.** *same as* OBTRUSIVE —**pro·tru′sive·ly** *adv.* —**pro·tru′sive·ness** *n.*

pro·tu·ber·ance (prō tyōō′bər əns) *n.* **1.** a being protuberant **2.** a part or thing that protrudes; projection; bulge; swelling Also **pro·tu′ber·an·cy** (-ən sē), *pl.* -**cies**

pro·tu·ber·ant (-ənt) *adj.* [< LL. prp. of *protuberare*, to bulge out < L. *pro-*, forth + *tuber*, a bump] bulging or swelling out; protruding; prominent —**pro·tu′ber·ant·ly** *adv.*

proud (proud) *adj.* [OE. prud < OFr. < LL. *prode*, beneficial < L. *prodesse*, to be useful] **1.** having or showing a proper pride in oneself, one's position, etc. **2.** having or showing an overweening opinion of oneself; haughty; arrogant **3.** feeling or causing great pride or joy [his *proud* parents, a *proud* moment] **4.** caused by pride; presumptuous **5.** stately; splendid [a *proud* fleet] **6.** spirited [a *proud* stallion] —**do oneself proud** [Colloq.] to do extremely well —**proud of** highly pleased with —**proud′ly** *adv.*

proud flesh [< the notion of swelling up] an abnormal growth of flesh around a healing wound

Prov. **1.** Provençal **2.** Proverbs **3.** Province

prov. **1.** province **2.** provincial **3.** provisional **4.** provost

prove (prōōv) *vt.* **proved, proved** or **prov′en, prov′ing** [< OFr. *prover* < L.: see PROBE] **1.** to test by experiment, a standard, etc.; try out **2.** to establish as true; demonstrate to be a fact **3.** to establish the validity of (a will, etc.) **4.** to show (oneself) to be capable, dependable, etc. **5.** *Math.* to test the correctness of (a calculation, etc.) —*vi.* to be found by experience or trial; turn out to be —**prov′a·bil′i·ty, prov′a·ble·ness** *n.* —**prov′a·ble** *adj.* —**prov′a·bly** *adv.* —**prov′er** *n.*

prov·e·nance (prov′ə nəns) *n.* [Fr. < L. < *pro-*, forth + *venire*, to come] origin; derivation; source

Pro·ven·çal (prov′ən säl′) *adj.* of Provence, its people, their language, etc. —*n.* **1.** the vernacular of S France, a Romance language which, in its medieval form, was an important literary language **2.** a native or inhabitant of Provence

prov·en·der (prov′ən dər) *n.* [< MFr. < ML. *praebenda*: see PREBEND] 1. dry food for livestock, as hay, corn, etc. 2. [Colloq.] provisions; food

prov·erb (prov′ərb) *n.* [< OFr. < L. < *pro-*, before + *verbum*, a word] 1. a short, popular saying that expresses some obvious truth; adage; maxim 2. a person or thing that has become commonly recognized as a type; byword

pro·ver·bi·al (prə vur′bē əl) *adj.* 1. of, or having the nature of, a proverb 2. expressed in a proverb 3. well-known because commonly referred to —**pro·ver′bi·al·ly** *adv.*

pro·vide (prə vīd′) *vt.* **-vid′ed, -vid′ing** [< L. < *pro-*, before + *videre*, to see] 1. to make available; supply 2. to supply (someone *with* something) 3. to state as a condition; stipulate —*vi.* 1. to prepare (*for* or *against*) a possible situation, event, etc. 2. to furnish the means of support (*for*) —**pro·vid′er** *n.*

pro·vid·ed (-vīd′id) *conj.* on the condition or understanding; if (often with *that*)

prov·i·dence (prov′ə dəns) *n.* [< MFr. < L. < prp. of *providere*: see PROVIDE] 1. a looking to, or preparation for, the future; provision 2. skill in management; prudence 3. a) the benevolent guidance of God or nature b) an instance of this 4. [P-] God

prov·i·dent (-dənt) *adj.* [< L. *providens*, prp. of *providere*: see PROVIDE] 1. providing for future needs or events 2. prudent or economical —**prov′i·dent·ly** *adv.*

prov·i·den·tial (prov′ə den′shəl) *adj.* of, by, or as if decreed by divine providence —**prov′i·den′tial·ly** *adv.*

provident society *same as* FRIENDLY SOCIETY

pro·vid·ing (prə vīd′iŋ) *conj.* on the condition or understanding; provided (often with *that*)

prov·ince (prov′ins) *n.* [< OFr. < L. *provincia*] 1. an outside territory governed by ancient Rome 2. an administrative division of a country, esp. of Canada and New Zealand 3. a) a territorial district; territory b) [pl.] the parts of a country removed from the capital and major cities 4. range of duties or functions 5. a field of knowledge, activity, etc. 6. a division of a country under the jurisdiction of an archbishop or metropolitan

pro·vin·cial (prə vin′shəl) *adj.* 1. of or belonging to a province 2. having the ways, speech, attitudes, etc. of a certain province 3. rural; countrified; rustic 4. narrow or limited in outlook; unsophisticated —*n.* 1. a native of a province 2. a provincial, esp. unsophisticated, person —**pro·vin′cial·ly** *adv.*

pro·vin·cial·ism (-iz′m) *n.* 1. a being provincial 2. narrowness of outlook 3. a provincial custom, characteristic, etc. 4. a word, phrase, etc. peculiar to a province Also **pro·vin′ci·al′i·ty** (-shē al′ə tē), *pl.* **-ties** —**pro·vin′cial·ist** *n.*

proving ground a place for testing new equipment, new theories, etc.

pro·vi·sion (prə vizh′ən) *n.* [MFr. < L. < pp. of *providere*: see PROVIDE] 1. a providing or supplying 2. something provided for the future; specif., [pl.] a stock of food 3. a preparatory arrangement or measure taken in advance 4. a clause, as in a legal document, stipulating some specific thing —*vt.* to supply with provisions —**pro·vi′sion·er** *n.*

pro·vi·sion·al (-′l) *adj.* 1. conditional or temporary, pending a permanent arrangement 2. [P-] relating to a faction of the IRA —*n.* [P-] a member of the Provisional IRA, advocating terrorism as a means to achieve Irish unity —**pro·vi′sion·al·ly** *adv.*

pro·vi·so (prə vī′zō) *n.*, *pl.* **-sos, -soes** [ML. *proviso* (*quod*), provided that] 1. a clause, as in a document, making some condition 2. a condition or stipulation

pro·vi·so·ry (-zər ē) *adj.* 1. containing a proviso; conditional 2. same as PROVISIONAL —**pro·vi′so·ri·ly** *adv.*

Pro·vo (prō′vō) *n.*, *pl.* **-vos** [PROV(ISIONAL) + *-o*, a suffix] *colloq.* clipped form of PROVISIONAL (*adj.* 2, *n.*)

prov·o·ca·tion (prov′ə kā′shən) *n.* 1. a provoking 2. something that provokes; esp., a cause of anger or irritation

pro·voc·a·tive (prə vok′ə tiv) *adj.* provoking or tending to provoke; stimulating, erotic, irritating, etc. —*n.* something that provokes —**pro·voc′a·tive·ly** *adv.* —**pro·voc′a·tive·ness** *n.*

pro·voke (prə vōk′) *vt.* **-voked′, -vok′ing** [< MFr. < L. < *pro-*, forth + *vocare*, to call] 1. to excite to some action or feeling 2. to anger or irritate 3. to stir up (action or feeling) 4. to evoke —**pro·vok′er** *n.* —**pro·vok′ing·ly** *adv.*

pro·vost (prov′əst; *esp. military* prə vō′) *n.* [< OE. & OFr., both < ML. *propositus*, for L. *praepositus*, chief, ult. < *prae-*, before + *ponere*, to place] 1. a superintendent; official in charge 2. the chief administrative official of a Scottish burgh 3. the head of a cathedral chapter or principal church 4. the head of some colleges —**pro′vost·ship** *n.*

provost marshal the officer in charge of military police, and thus responsible for military discipline in a camp, etc.

prow (prou) *n.* [< Fr., ult. < L. < Gr. *prōira*] 1. the forward part of a ship 2. anything like this

prow·ess (prou′is, prō′-) *n.* [< OFr. *prouesse* < *prou*,

brave, var. of *prud*: see PROUD] 1. bravery; valour 2. superior ability, skill, etc.

prowl (proul) *vi., vt.* [ME. *prollen* < ?] to roam about furtively as in search of prey —*n.* a prowling —**on the prowl** prowling about —**prowl′er** *n.*

prox. proximo

prox·i·mal (prok′sə m′l) *adj.* 1. proximate; next or nearest 2. situated near the point of attachment of a limb, etc. —**prox′i·mal·ly** *adv.*

prox·i·mate (prok′sə mit) *adj.* [< LL. pp. of *proximare*, to come near < L. *proximus*, nearest, superl. of *prope*, near] 1. next or nearest in space, order, time, etc. 2. approximate —**prox′i·mate·ly** *adv.*

prox·im·i·ty (prok sim′ə tē) *n.* [< MFr. < L. < *proximus*: see prec.] nearness in space, time, etc.

prox·i·mo (prok′sə mō′) *adv.* [L. *proximo* (*mense*), in the next (month)] in or of the next month [on the 9th *proximo*]

prox·y (prok′sē) *n.*, *pl.* **prox′ies** [ME. *prokecie* < *procuracie*, office of a procurator] 1. the function of a deputy 2. a) the authority to act for another, or a person given this authority b) a document giving this authority, as in voting at a stockholders' meeting

prs. pairs

P.R.S. President of the Royal Society

prude (prōōd) *n.* [Fr. < *prudefemme*, excellent woman] a person who is excessively modest or proper in behaviour, dress, speech, etc., esp. in a way that annoys others —**prud′ish** *adj.* —**prud′ish·ly** *adv.* —**prud′ish·ness** *n.*

pru·dence (prōōd′əns) *n.* 1. the quality or fact of being prudent 2. careful management; economy

pru·dent (prōōd′ənt) *adj.* [OFr. < L. *prudens*, for *providens*, PROVIDENT] 1. exercising sound judgment in practical matters, esp. as concerns one's own interests 2. cautious in conduct; sensible; not rash 3. managing carefully and with economy —**pru′dent·ly** *adv.*

pru·den·tial (prōō den′shəl) *adj.* 1. characterized by or exercising prudence 2. having an advisory function —**pru·den′tial·ly** *adv.*

prud·er·y (prōōd′ər ē) *n.* a being prudish

prune[1] (prōōn) *n.* [< MFr. < VL. < L. *prunum* < Gr. *proumnon*, plum] 1. a plum dried for eating 2. [Slang] a dull or otherwise unpleasant person

prune[2] (prōōn) *vt.* **pruned, prun′ing** [< MFr., prob. ult. < *provain* (< L. *propago*), a slip] 1. to remove dead or living parts from (a plant), as to increase fruit or flower production 2. to cut out as being unnecessary 3. to shorten by removing unnecessary parts [to prune a novel] —*vi.* to remove unnecessary parts —**prun′er** *n.*

prunes and prisms affectation; unnaturalness; insincerity, esp. a mincing way of talking

pruning hook a long tool or shears with a hooked blade, for pruning plants

pru·ri·ent (proor′ē ənt) *adj.* [L. *pruriens* < *prurire*, to itch, long for] 1. having lustful ideas or desires 2. full of or causing lust; lascivious; lewd —**pru′ri·ence, pru′ri·en·cy** *n.* —**pru′ri·ent·ly** *adv.*

pru·ri·tus (proo rīt′əs) *n.* [< L. pp. of *prurire*, to itch] intense itching without a rash —**pru·rit′ic** (-rit′ik) *adj.*

Prus·sian blue (prush′ən) any of a group of dark-blue iron pigments used in paints, printing inks, etc.

prus·sic acid (prus′ik) *same as* HYDROCYANIC ACID

pry[1] (prī) *n.*, *pl.* **pries** [back-formation < PRIZE[2]] [U.S.] 1. a lever or crowbar 2. leverage —*vt.* **pried, pry′ing** [U.S.] 1. to raise or move with a lever or crowbar 2. to draw forth with difficulty

pry[2] (prī) *vi.* **pried, pry′ing** [ME. *prien* < ?] to look (*into*) closely or inquisitively; peer or snoop —*n.*, *pl.* **pries** 1. a prying 2. a person who is too inquisitive

pry·er (prī′ər) *n.* a person who pries

pry·ing (-iŋ) *adj.* improperly curious or inquisitive —**pry′ing·ly** *adv.*

Ps., Psa. Psalm; Psalms

ps. pieces

P.S. 1. Police Sergeant 2. Private Secretary 3. Privy Seal 4. Public School

P.S., p.s., PS postscript

psalm (säm) *n.* [OE. *sealm* < LL. < Gr. *psalmos* < *psallein*, to pluck (a harp)] 1. a sacred song or poem 2. [usually P-] any of the sacred songs in praise of God that make up the Book of Psalms in the Bible

psalm-book (-book′) *n.* a collection of psalms for use in religious worship

psalm·ist (-ist) *n.* a composer of psalms —**the Psalmist** King David, to whom some or all of the Psalms are attributed

psal·mo·dy (säm′ə dē, sal′mə-) *n.* [< LL. < Gr. < *psalmos* (see PSALM) + *ōidē*, a song] 1. the singing of psalms 2. psalms collectively 3. the arrangement of psalms for singing —**psal′mo·dist** *n.*

Psal·ter (sôl′tər) *n.* [< OE. & OFr., both < L. < Gr. *psaltērion*, psaltery < *psallein*, to pluck] the Book of

Psalms —*n.* [*also* p-] a version of the Psalms for use in religious services

psal·te·ri·um (sôl tir′ē əm) *n.,* *pl.* **-ri·a** (-ə) [ModL. < L. *psalterium*, a stringed instrument, because of its many folds] *same as* OMASUM

psal·ter·y (sôl′tər ē, sôl′trē) *n.,* *pl.* **-ter·ies** [< OFr. < L.: see PSALTER] an ancient stringed instrument with a shallow sound box, played by plucking the strings

PSALTERY

pse·phol·o·gy (sē fol′ə jē) *n.* [< Gr. *psēphos*, pebble (used in voting) + -LOGY] the statistical evaluation of election returns or of political polls —**pse·pho·log′·i·cal** (-fə loj′i k′l) *adj.* —**pse·phol′o·gist** *n.*

pseud (syōōd) *n.* [< PSEUDO] [Colloq.] a false, artificial, or pretentious person; phoney —*adj.* *same as* PSEUDO

pseud. pseudonym

pseu·do (syōō′dō) *adj.* [see ff.] sham; false; spurious; pretended; counterfeit

pseu·do- [< LL. < Gr. < *pseudēs*, false < *pseudein*, to deceive] *a combining form meaning:* **1.** fictitious, sham [*pseudonym*] **2.** counterfeit, spurious **3.** closely or deceptively similar to (a specified thing): also **pseud-**

pseu·do·nym (syōō′də nim′) *n.* [< Fr. < Gr. < *pseudēs*, false + *onyma*, a name] a fictitious name, esp. one assumed by an author; pen name —**pseu′do·nym′i·ty** *n.* —**pseu·don′y·mous** (-don′ə məs) *adj.* —**pseu·don′y·mous·ly** *adv.*

pseu·do·po·di·um (syōō′də pō′dē əm) *n.,* *pl.* **-di·a** (-ə) [ModL.: see PSEUDO- & PODIUM] a temporary jutting out of a part of a single cell, as in an amoeba, by means of which it can move about or take in food: also **pseu′do·pod′** (-pod′) —**pseu·dop′o·dal** (-dop′ə dəl) *adj.*

pseu·do·sci·ence (-dō sī′əns) *n.* any system of theories that claims to be a science but has no scientific basis —**pseu′do·sci′en·tif′ic** *adj.*

psf, p.s.f. pounds per square foot

pshaw (shô) *interj., n.* an exclamation of impatience, disgust, contempt, etc.

psi (sī, psē) *n.* [LGr. < Gr.] the twenty-third letter of the Greek alphabet (Ψ, ψ)

psi, p.s.i. pounds per square inch

psi·lo·cy·bin (sī′lə sī′bin, sil′ə-) *n.* [< ModL. *Psilocybe*, genus of mushrooms] a hallucinogenic drug obtained from certain mushrooms

psit·ta·cine (sit′ə sīn′, -sin) *adj.* [L. < Gr. *psittakos*, a parrot + -*inus*, -INE¹] of, resembling or pertaining to parrots

psit·ta·co·sis (sit′ə kō′sis) *n.* [ModL. < L. < Gr. *psittakos*, a parrot + -OSIS] an acute, infectious virus disease of birds of the parrot family, often transmitted to man

pso·ri·a·sis (sə rī′ə sis) *n.* [ModL. < Gr. < *psōra*, an itch] a chronic skin disease in which scaly, reddish patches are formed —**pso·ri·at·ic** (sôr′ē at′ik) *adj.*

psst (pst) *interj.* a sound made to get someone's attention quickly and quietly

P.S.V. Public Service Vehicle

psy·che (sī′kē) *n.* [L. < Gr. < *psychē*, the soul] **1.** the human soul **2.** the human mind

psy·che·del·ic (sī′kə del′ik) *adj.* [< PSYCHE + Gr. *delein*, to make manifest] **1.** of or causing extreme changes in the conscious mind, with hallucinations, delusions, etc. **2.** of or like the intense, distorted sights, sounds, colours, etc. produced by such changes in the mind —*n.* a psychedelic drug —**psy′che·del′i·cal·ly** *adv.*

psy·chi·a·trist (sə kī′ə trist, sī-) *n.* a doctor of medicine specializing in psychiatry

psy·chi·a·try (-trē) *n.* [ModL.: see PSYCHO- & -IATRY] the branch of medicine dealing with disorders of the mind, including psychoses and neuroses —**psy·chi·at·ric** (sī′kē at′·rik), **psy′chi·at′ri·cal** *adj.* —**psy′chi·at′ri·cal·ly** *adv.*

psy·chic (sī′kik) *adj.* [< Gr. < *psychē*, the soul] **1.** of the psyche, or mind **2.** beyond natural or known physical processes **3.** apparently sensitive to supernatural forces Also **psy′chi·cal** —*n.* a person who is supposedly sensitive to supernatural forces —**psy′chic·ism** *n.* —**psy′chi·cal·ly** *adv.*

psy·cho (sī′kō) *adj., n.* *colloq.* clipped form of PSYCHOTIC, PSYCHOPATHIC, PSYCHOPATH

psy·cho- [< Gr. *psychē*, soul] *a combining form meaning* the mind or mental processes [*psychology*]: also, before a vowel, **psych-**

psy·cho·ac·tive (sī′kō ak′tiv) *adj.* [PSYCHO- + ACTIVE] designating or of a drug, chemical, etc. that has a strong or specific effect on the mind

psy·cho·an·a·lyse (-an′ə līz′) *vt.* **-lysed′, -lys′ing** to treat by means of psychoanalysis

psy·cho·a·nal·y·sis (sī′kō ə nal′ə sis) *n.* [ModL.: see PSYCHO- & ANALYSIS] a method or practice, originated by Freud, of treating neuroses and some other mental disorders through analysis of emotional conflicts, repressions, etc. by getting the patient to talk freely, analysing his dreams, etc. —**psy′·cho·an′a·lyt′ic** (-an′ə lit′ik), **psy′cho·an′a·lyt′i·cal** *adj.* —**psy′cho·an′a·lyt′i·cal·ly** *adv.*

psy·cho·an·a·lyst (-an′əl ist) *n.* a specialist in psychoanalysis

psy·cho·dra·ma (sī′kə drä′mə) *n.* a form of psychotherapy in which each patient in a group acts out situations related to his problem —**psy′cho·dra·mat′ic** (-drə mat′ik) *adj.*

psy·cho·dy·nam·ics (sī′kō dī nam′iks) *n.pl.* [*with sing. v.*] the study of the mental and emotional motives underlying human behaviour —**psy′cho·dy·nam′ic** *adj.* —**psy′·cho·dy·nam′i·cal·ly** *adv.*

psy·cho·gen·ic (sī′kə jen′ik) *adj.* [PSYCHO- + -GENIC] caused by mental conflicts; psychic —**psy′cho·gen′i·cal·ly** *adv.*

psy·cho·ki·ne·sis (sī′kō ki nē′sis) *n.* [PSYCHO- + Gr. *kinēsis*, motion] the supposed ability to influence physical objects or events by thought processes —**psy′cho·ki·net′ic** (-net′ik) *adj.*

psy·cho·lin·guis·tics (-lin gwis′tiks) *n.pl.* [*with sing. v.*] the study of the psychological factors involved in the perception of and response to linguistic phenomena

psy·cho·log·i·cal (sī′kə loj′i k′l) *adj.* **1.** of psychology **2.** of the mind; mental **3.** affecting or intended to affect the mind Also **psy′cho·log′ic** —**psy′cho·log′i·cal·ly** *adv.*

psychological moment **1.** the moment when one is mentally ready for something **2.** the critical moment

psychological warfare the use of psychological means, as propaganda, to influence the thinking of or undermine the morale of an enemy

psy·chol·o·gist (sī kol′ə jist) *n.* a specialist in psychology

psy·chol·o·gize (-ə jīz′) *vi.* **-gized′, -giz′ing** **1.** to study psychology **2.** to reason psychologically —*vt.* to analyse psychologically

psy·chol·o·gy (-jē) *n.,* *pl.* **-gies** [< ModL.: see PSYCHO- & -LOGY] **1.** a) the science dealing with the mind and with mental and emotional processes b) the science of human and animal behaviour **2.** the sum of a person's actions, traits, thoughts, etc. **3.** a system of psychology

psy·cho·neu·ro·sis (sī′kō nyoo rō′sis) *n.,* *pl.* **-ro′ses** (-sēz) [ModL.: see PSYCHO- & NEUROSIS] *same as* NEUROSIS —**psy′cho·neu·rot′ic** (-rot′ik) *adj., n.*

psy·cho·path (sī′kə path′) *n.* *same as* PSYCHOPATHIC PERSONALITY (sense 1)

psy·cho·path·ic (sī′kə path′ik) *adj.* characterized by psychopathy; mentally ill —**psy′cho·path′i·cal·ly** *adv.*

psychopathic personality **1.** a person with serious personality defects, whose behaviour is amoral and asocial (often criminal), generally without psychotic symptoms **2.** the personality of such a person

psy·cho·pa·thol·o·gy (sī′kō pə thol′ə jē) *n.* **1.** the science dealing with mental disorders **2.** the behaviour of the mentally ill —**psy′cho·path′o·log′i·cal** (-path′ə loj′ik′l) *adj.* —**psy′cho·pa·thol′o·gist** *n.*

psy·chop·a·thy (sī kop′ə thē) *n.* [PSYCHO- + -PATHY] mental disorder

psy·cho·phar·ma·col·o·gy (sī′kō fär′mə kol′ə jē) *n.* the study of the effects of drugs on the mind —**psy′cho·phar′·ma·co·log′i·cal** (-kə loj′i k′l), **psy′cho·phar′ma·co·log′ic** *adj.*

psy·cho·sex·u·al (-sek′shoo wəl) *adj.* having to do with the psychological aspects of sexuality in contrast to the physical aspects —**psy′cho·sex′u·al′i·ty** (-wal′ə tē) *n.*

psy·cho·sis (sī kō′sis) *n.,* *pl.* **-cho′ses** (-sēz) [ModL.: see PSYCHO- & -OSIS] a major mental disorder in which the personality is very seriously disorganized and one's sense of reality is usually altered

psy·cho·so·cial (sī′kō sō′shəl) *adj.* of the psychological development of an individual in relation to his social environment

psy·cho·so·mat·ic (-sō mat′ik) *adj.* [PSYCHO- + SOMATIC] **1.** designating or of a physical disorder originating in or aggravated by one's psychic or emotional processes **2.** designating a system of medicine using a coordinated psychological and physiological approach towards such disorders —**psy′cho·so·mat′i·cal·ly** *adv.*

psy·cho·sur·ger·y (-sur′jər ē) *n.* brain surgery performed in treating chronic mental disorder

psy·cho·ther·a·py (-ther′ə pē) *n.* [PSYCHO- + THERAPY] treatment of mental disorder by counselling, psycho-analysis, etc. —**psy′cho·ther′a·peu′tic** *adj.* —**psy′cho·ther′·a·pist** *n.*

psy·chot·ic (sī kot′ik) *adj.* of or having a psychosis —*n.* a person having a psychosis —**psy′chot′i·cal·ly** *adv.* '

psy·chot·o·mi·met·ic (sī kot′ō mi met′ik) *adj.* [< PSYCHOT(IC) + -*o*- + MIMETIC] designating or of certain drugs, as LSD and mescaline, that produce hallucinations, psychotic symptoms, etc. —*n.* a psychotomimetic drug

psy·cho·tox·ic (sī′kō tok′sik) *adj.* [PSYCHO- + TOXIC] of or pertaining to substances capable of damaging the brain

Pt *Chem.* platinum

P.T. **1.** Physical Therapy **2.** Physical Training **3.** Postal Telegraph

pt. *pl.* **pts.** 1. part 2. pint 3. point
p.t. 1. past tense 2. pro tempore
P.T.A. Parent/Teacher Association
ptar·mi·gan (tär′mə gən) *n.*, *pl.* **-gans, -gan:** see PLURAL, II, D, 1 [altered (after PTERO-) < Scot. *tarmachan*] any of several varieties of northern or alpine grouse, having feathered legs and undergoing seasonal colour changes
Pte. *Mil.* Private
pter·i·do·phyte (ter′ə dō fīt′) *n.* [< Gr. *pteris*, a fern + -PHYTE] a group of plants reproducing by means of spores and including the ferns —**pter′id·o·phyt′ic** (-fit′ik), **pter′-i·doph′y·tous** (-dof′i təs) *adj.*
pter·o- [ModL. < Gr. *pteron*] *a combining form meaning* feather, wing [*pterodactyl*]
pter·o·dac·tyl (ter′ə dak′təl) *n.* [< ModL.: see prec. & DACTYL] an extinct flying reptile, having wings of skin stretched between the hind limb and a long digit of the forelimb —**pter′o·dac′tyl·oid′**, **pter′-o·dac′tyl·ous** *adj.*
-pter·ous (tər əs) [see PTERO- & -OUS] *a combining form meaning* having (a specified number or kind of) wings [*homopterous*]
P.T.O., p.t.o. please turn over
Ptol·e·ma·ic (tol′ə mā′ik) *adj.* 1. of Ptolemy, the 2nd cent. A.D. Gr. astronomer, or his theory that the earth is the centre of the universe and that heavenly bodies move around it 2. of the Ptolemies who ruled Egypt
pto·maine (tō′mān) *n.* [< It. < Gr. *ptōma*, a corpse < *piptein*, to fall] any of a class of alkaloid substances, some of which are poisonous, formed in decaying animal or vegetable matter by bacteria
ptomaine poisoning *earlier term for* FOOD POISONING (erroneously thought to be from ptomaines)
Pty. [Aust., N.Z., S.Afr.] Proprietary
pty·a·lin (ti′ə lin) *n.* [< Gr. < *ptyein*, to spit + -IN¹] an enzyme in the saliva of man (and some animals) that converts starch to dextrin and maltose
Pu *Chem.* plutonium
pub (pub) *n.* *colloq.* clipped form of PUBLIC HOUSE (sense 2)
pub. 1. public 2. published 3. publisher 4. publishing
pub-crawl (pub′krôl) *vi.* [Slang] to make a drinking tour of a number of pubs —*n.* a drinking tour of a number of pubs or bars: also **pub crawl**
pu·ber·ty (pyōo′bər tē) *n.* [< L. < *puber*, adult] the state of physical development when sexual reproduction first becomes possible: the age is generally fixed in common law at 14 for boys and 12 for girls —**pu′ber·tal** *adj.*
pu·bes¹ (pyōo′bēz) *n.* [L., pubic hair] 1. the body hair appearing at puberty; esp., the hair surrounding the genitals 2. the region of the abdomen covered by such hair
pu·bes² (pyōo′bēz) *n.* *pl. of* PUBIS
pu·bes·cent (pyōo bes′′nt) *adj.* [Fr. < L. prp. of *pubescere*, to reach puberty < *pubes*, adult] 1. reaching or having reached puberty 2. covered with a soft down, as many plants and insects —**pu·bes′cence** *n.*
pu·bic (pyōo′bik) *adj.* of or in the region of the pubes
pu·bis (-bis) *n.*, *pl.* **pu′bes** (-bēz) [ModL. < L.: see PUBES¹] that part of either hipbone forming, with the other, the front arch of the pelvis
pub·lic (pub′lik) *adj.* [L. *publicus*, ult. < *populus*, the people] 1. of, belonging to, or concerning the people as a whole; of the community at large [the *public* welfare] 2. for the use or benefit of all; esp., government-supported [*public* transport] 3. acting in an official capacity on behalf of the people as a whole [the *public* prosecutor] 4. known by all or most people [a *public* figure] —*n.* 1. the people as a whole; community at large 2. a specific part of the people [the reading *public*] —**go public** *Finance* to offer company shares for sale to the public —**in public** openly; not in privacy or secret —**pub′lic·ly** *adv.*
pub·lic-ad·dress system (pub′lik ə dres′) an electronic amplification used to increase the sound level of speech or music at public gatherings: also **PA system**
pub·li·can (pub′li kən) *n.* 1. in ancient Rome, a tax collector 2. the licensee of a public house; innkeeper
pub·li·ca·tion (pub′lə kā′shən) *n.* [< L. < *publicare*: see PUBLISH] 1. a publishing or being published; public notification 2. the printing and distribution, usually for sale, of books, magazines, newspapers, etc. 3. something published, esp. a periodical
public company a limited company whose shares may be purchased by the public and traded freely on the open market
public convenience a public lavatory, esp. one situated in a public park, on the street, etc.

public domain the condition of being free, esp. from copyright or patent, and available to anyone
public enemy a hardened criminal or other person who is a menace to society
public house 1. an inn 2. an establishment where wines and spirits are served; bar
pub·li·cist (pub′lə sist) *n.* 1. a specialist in international law 2. a journalist who writes about public affairs 3. a specialist in public relations
pub·lic·i·ty (pə blis′ə tē) *n.* 1. a being public, or commonly known 2. *a*) any information that makes a person, place, etc. known or well-known to the public *b*) the work of handling such information 3. a being noticed by the public 4. any procedure or act intended to gain public notice
pub·li·cize (pub′lə sīz′) *vt.* **-cized′**, **-ciz′ing** to give publicity to; draw public attention to
public lending right the right campaigned for by authors to receive payment when their books are loaned out by public libraries
public library a library, usually supported by the rates, which the public can use without paying a fee
public opinion the opinion held by people generally
public relations relations of an organization with the public through publicity seeking to form public opinion
public school 1. an independent fee-paying school whose headmaster is a member of the Headmaster's Conference 2. in Scotland, an elementary or primary school, usually non-feepaying 3. [U.S.] any school that is part of the free local educational system
public servant an elected or appointed government official or a civil-service employee
pub·lic-spir·it·ed (pub′lik spir′i tid) *adj.* having or showing zeal for the public welfare
public transport vehicles, such as trains, buses, etc. that have fixed routes and are available to the general public
public utility an organization that supplies water, electricity, transportation, etc. to the public
public works works constructed by the government for public use or service, as roads, power stations, etc.
pub·lish (pub′lish) *vt.* [< OFr. < L. *publicare* < *publicus*, PUBLIC] 1. to make publicly known; announce; proclaim 2. *a*) to issue (a printed work, etc.) to the public, as for sale *b*) to issue the written work of (an author) —*vi.* 1. to issue books, newspapers, etc. to the public 2. to write books, etc. that are published —**pub′lish·a·ble** *adj.*
pub·lish·er (-ər) *n.* a person or firm that publishes books, newspapers, magazines, etc.
puce (pyōos) *n.* [Fr., lit., a flea] brownish purple
puck¹ (puk) *n.* [akin to POKE¹] *Ice Hockey* a hard rubber disc which the players try to drive into the opponents' goal
puck² (puk) *n.* [OE. *puca*] a mischievous sprite or elf, as [P-] the one in Shakespeare's *A Midsummer Night's Dream* —**puck′ish** *adj.* —**puck′ish·ly** *adv.* —**puck′ish·ness** *n.*
puck·a (puk′ə) *adj.* same as PUKKA
puck·er (puk′ər) *vt.*, *vi.* [freq. form of POKE²] to draw up into wrinkles or small folds —*n.* such a wrinkle or fold —**pucker up** to contract the lips as to kiss —**puck′er·y** *adj.*
pud *colloq.* clipped form of PUDDING (sense 4)
pud·ding (pood′iŋ) *n.* [akin ? to OE. *puduc*, a swelling] 1. a kind of boiled sausage [black *pudding*] 2. a soft, mushy food, usually made with a base of flour, cereal, etc. and boiled or baked [Yorkshire *pudding*] 3. a sweetened dessert of this kind, variously containing eggs, milk, fruit, etc. 4. the dessert course in a meal, following the main dish —**in the pudding club** [Slang] pregnant
pud·dle (pud′′l) *n.* [dim. < OE. *pudd*, a ditch] 1. a small pool of water, esp. stagnant or muddy water 2. a thick mixture of clay, and sometimes sand, with water —*vt.* **-dled**, **-dling** 1. to make muddy 2. to make a thick mixture of (wet clay and sand) 3. to keep water from penetrating by using this mixture 4. to treat (iron) by the puddling process —*vi.* to dabble or wallow in muddy water —**pud′dler** *n.* —**pud′dly** *adj.* **-dli·er, -dli·est**
pud·dling (-liŋ) *n.* the process of making wrought iron from pig iron by heating and stirring it in the presence of oxidizing agents
pu·den·dum (pyōo den′dəm) *n.*, *pl.* **-den′da** (-də) [ModL., ult. < L. *pudere*, to be ashamed] [*usually pl.*] the external human sex organs, esp. of the female —**pu·den′dal** (-d′l) *adj.*
pudg·y (puj′ē) *adj.* **pudg′i·er**, **pudg′i·est** [prob. < Scot. *pud*, belly] short and fat —**pudg′i·ness** *n.*
pueb·lo (pweb′lō) *n.*, *pl.* **-los**; also, for 2, **-lo** [Sp. < L. *populus*, people] 1. a type of Indian village of the SW U.S. and parts of S America in which the Indians live together in one or more terraced, flat-roofed structures of stone or adobe 2. [P-] an Indian living in a pueblo
pu·er·ile (pyōo′īl) *adj.* [< Fr. < L. < *puer*, boy] childish; silly; immature —**pu′er·ile·ly** *adv.* —**pu′er·il′i·ty** (-ə ril′ə tē) *n.*, *pl.* **-ties**
pu·er·per·al (pyōo ur′pər əl) *adj.* [< L. < *puer*, boy + *parere*, to bear] of or connected with childbirth

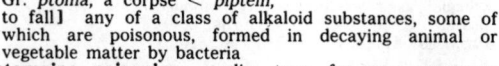

PTERODACTYL
(wingspread to 6 m)

puerperal fever septic poisoning occurring during childbirth: a term no longer used

puff (puf) *n.* [OE. *pyff* < the *v.*] **1.** *a)* a short, sudden gust, as of wind, or an expulsion, as of breath *b)* a small quantity of vapour, smoke, etc. expelled at one time **2.** a drawing into the mouth of smoke from a cigarette, etc. **3.** a swelling or protuberance **4.** a shell of light pastry filled with whipped cream, etc. **5.** a soft, bulging mass of material, gathered in at the edges **6.** a soft roll of hair on the head **7.** a soft pad for dabbing powder on the skin or hair **8.** undue or exaggerated praise, as in a book review **9.** one's breath [out of *puff*] —*vi.* [OE. *pyffan*] **1.** to blow in puffs, as the wind **2.** *a)* to give forth puffs of smoke, steam, etc. *b)* to breathe rapidly and hard **3.** to move (*away, out, in,* etc.), giving forth puffs **4.** to fill, become inflated, or swell (*out* or *up*), as with air or pride **5.** to take a puff or puffs on a cigarette, etc. —*vt.* **1.** to blow, drive, etc. in or with a puff or puffs **2.** to inflate; swell **3.** to praise unduly, as in a book review **4.** to smoke (a cigarette, etc.) **5.** to set (the hair) in puffs —**puff'i·ly** *adv.* —**puff'i·ness** *n.* —**puff'y** *adj.* **puff'i·er, puff'i·est**

puff adder a large, poisonous African snake which inflates its body when alarmed

puff·ball (-bôl') *n.* any of various round, white-fleshed fungi that burst at the touch when mature

puffed (puft) *adj.* **1.** breathless; winded **2.** swollen; puffy

puff·er (-ər) *n.* **1.** one that puffs **2.** any of various fishes that can expand the body by swallowing air or water

puf·fin (puf'in) *n.* [ME. *poffin* < ?] a northern sea bird with a short neck, ducklike body, and brightly coloured triangular beak

puff pastry a dough used for making a rich, flaky pastry for pies, pastries, etc.

puff-puff (puf'puf') *n.* [echoic] a child's name for a train

pug[1] (pug) *n.* [< ? PUCK[2]] **1.** a small, short-haired dog with a wrinkled face, snub nose, and curled tail **2.** *same as* PUG NOSE

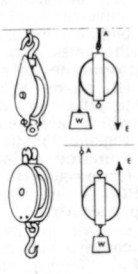

PUFFIN
(to 34.5 cm long)

pug[2] (pug) *vt.* **pugged, pug'ging** [< dial.: prob. echoic of pounding] **1.** to mix (wet, plastic clay) for making bricks, earthenware, etc. **2.** to fill in with clay, mortar, etc. for soundproofing —*n.* wet, plastic clay

pug[3] (pug) *n.* [Slang] a pugilist

pug·ging (pug'iŋ) *n.* **1.** the mixing of pug (wet clay) **2.** clay, mortar, etc. used for soundproofing

pug·gree (pug'rē) *n.* [Hindi *pagri*, a turban] **1.** in India, a turban **2.** a light scarf hanging round and down the back of a sun helmet to protect the back of the neck Also **pug'-ga·ree, pug'a·ree** (-ə·rē')

pu·gil·ism (pyōō'jə·liz'm) *n.* [< L. *pugil*, boxer, akin to *pugnare*, to fight + -ISM] *same as* BOXING —**pu'gil·ist** *n.* —**pu'gil·is'tic** *adj.*

pug·na·cious (pug·nā'shəs) *adj.* [< L. < *pugnare*, to fight + -OUS] eager and ready to fight; quarrelsome —**pug·na'cious·ly** *adv.* —**pug·nac'i·ty** (-nas'ə·tē), **pug·na'cious·ness** *n.*

pug nose a short, thick, turned-up nose —**pug'-nosed'** (-nōzd') *adj.*

pu·is·sant (pwis'ənt, pyōō'i·sənt) *adj.* [OFr. < *poeir*: see POWER] [Archaic] powerful; strong —**pu'is·sance** *n.* —**pu'is·sant·ly** *adv.*

puke (pyōōk) *n., vi., vt.* **puked, puk'ing** [akin ? to G. *spucken*, to spit] *same as* VOMIT

pu·ke·ko (pōō·kē'kō) *n.* [Maori] an Australian and New Zealand bird

puk·ka (puk'ə) *adj.* [Hindi *pakkā*, ripe] [Anglo-Indian] **1.** good or first-rate of its kind **2.** genuine; real

pul (pool) *n., pl.* **puls, pul** [< Per., ult. < L., orig., bellows, hence bag, moneybag] *see* MONETARY UNITS, table (Afghanistan)

pul·chri·tude (pul'krə·tyōōd') *n.* [< L. < *pulcher*, beautiful] physical beauty —**pul'chri·tu'di·nous** (-ən əs) *adj.*

pule (pyōōl) *vi.* **puled, pul'ing** [echoic] to whine or whimper, as a sick or fretful child

Pul·it·zer Prize (pool'it·sər) any of various yearly prizes established by Joseph Pulitzer, newspaper owner and philanthropist, for work in journalism, literature, and music in America

pull (pool) *vt.* [OE. *pullian*, to pluck] **1.** to exert force or influence on so as to make move towards or after the source of the force; drag, tug, draw, etc. **2.** *a)* to draw or pluck out; extract (a tooth, etc.) *b)* to pick or uproot (weeds, etc.) **3.** to draw apart; tear **4.** to strain and injure [to *pull* a muscle] **5.** [U.S. Colloq.] to carry out; perform [to *pull* a raid] **6.** [Colloq.] to restrain [to *pull* one's punches] **7.** [Colloq.] to take out (a gun, etc.) so as to threaten **8.** *Baseball, Golf* to hit (the ball) so it goes to the left or, if

left-handed, to the right **9.** *Printing* to take (a proof) on a hand press **10.** *Rowing* *a)* to work (an oar) by drawing it towards one *b)* to be rowed normally by [this boat *pulls* four oars] —*vi.* **1.** to exert force in or for dragging, tugging, or attracting something **2.** to take a deep draught of a drink, a puff on a cigarette, etc. **3.** to be capable of being pulled **4.** to move or drive a vehicle (*away, ahead, out,* etc.) —*n.* **1.** the act or force of pulling; specif., *a)* a dragging, tugging, attracting, etc. *b)* a drink, a puff on a cigarette, etc. *c)* a hard, steady effort *d)* the force to move something **2.** something to be pulled, as a drawer handle **3.** [Colloq.] *a)* influence or special advantage *b)* drawing power; appeal —**pull apart** to find fault with —**pull down 1.** to tear down **2.** to degrade; humble **3.** to reduce —**pull in 1.** to arrive **2.** to draw in **3.** to receive as payment **4.** [Slang] to arrest and take to a police station —**pull off** [Colloq.] to accomplish or do —**pull oneself together** to regain one's poise, courage, etc. —**pull one's socks up** [Colloq.] to try harder —**pull one's weight** to do a fair or proper share of a task —**pull out 1.** to depart **2.** to withdraw or retreat **3.** to escape from a responsibility, etc. —**pull over** to drive (a vehicle) to or towards the kerb —**pull strings** to exercise personal influence —**pull through** to get over (an illness, difficulty, etc.) —**pull up 1.** to uproot **2.** to bring or come to a stop **3.** to drive (a vehicle) to a specified place **4.** to check or rebuke —**pull'er** *n.*

pul·let (pool'it) *n.* [< OFr. dim. of *poule*, hen < L. *pullus*, chicken] a young hen, usually not more than a year old

pul·ley (pool'ē) *n., pl.* **-leys** [< OFr. < ML. *poleia*, ult. < Gr. dim. of *polos*, axis] **1.** a small wheel with a grooved rim in which a rope or chain runs, as to raise a weight attached at one end by pulling on the other end **2.** a combination of such wheels, used to increase the applied power **3.** a wheel that turns or is turned by a belt, rope, chain, etc., so as to transmit power

Pull·man (pool'mən) *n.* [after G. M. Pullman (1831–1897), U.S. inventor] a railway carriage with private compartments or seats that can be made up into berths for sleeping: also **Pullman car**

pull·out (pool'out') *n.* **1.** a pulling out; esp., a removal, withdrawal, etc. **2.** something to be pulled out, as a magazine insert

PULLEYS
(A, anchor;
E, energy;
W, weight)

pull·o·ver (-ō'vər) *n.* a garment, esp. a knitted sweater, put on by being pulled over the head

pul·lu·late (pul'yōō·lāt') *vi.* **-lat'ed, -lat'ing** [< L. *pullulatus*, pp. of *pullulare*, to spread out, sprout] **1.** to sprout; germinate **2.** to breed quickly **3.** to spring up in abundance; teem —**pul'lu·la'tion** *n.*

pull-up (pool'up') *n.* *Gym.* the act of chinning oneself

pul·mo·nar·y (pul'mə·nər ē, pool'-) *adj.* [< L. < *pulmo* (gen. *pulmonis*), a lung] **1.** of, like, or affecting the lungs **2.** having lungs **3.** designating the artery conveying blood from the heart to the lungs or any of the veins conveying blood from the lungs to the heart Also **pul·mon'ic** (-mon'ik)

pulp (pulp) *n.* [< Fr. < L. *pulpa*, flesh] **1.** a soft, moist, formless mass **2.** the soft, juicy part of a fruit **3.** the soft pith of a plant stem **4.** the soft, sensitive substance under the dentine of a tooth **5.** ground-up, moistened fibres of wood, rags, etc., from which paper is made **6.** [Chiefly U.S.] a magazine printed on rough, inferior paper, often featuring shocking stories about sex, crime, etc. —*vt.* **1.** to reduce to pulp **2.** to remove the pulp from —*vi.* to become pulp —**pulp'i·ly** *adv.* —**pulp'i·ness** *n.* —**pulp'y** *adj.* **pulp'i·er, pulp'i·est**

pul·pit (pool'pit) *n.* [L. *pulpitum*, a stage] **1.** a raised platform from which a clergyman preaches in a church **2.** preachers as a group

pulp·wood (pulp'wood') *n.* **1.** soft wood for making paper **2.** wood ground to pulp for paper

pul·que (pool'kē; *Sp.* pōōl'ke) *n.* [AmSp., prob. of Mex. Ind. origin] a fermented drink, popular in Mexico, made from the juice of an agave

pul·sar (pul'sär) *n.* [PULS(E) + -AR] any of several small heavenly objects in the Milky Way that emit radio pulses at regular intervals

pul·sate (pul'sāt, pul sāt') *vi.* **-sat·ed, -sat·ing** [< L. pp. of *pulsare*, to beat] **1.** to beat or throb rhythmically, as the heart **2.** to vibrate; quiver —**pul·sa'tion** *n.* —**pul'sa·tive** (-sə tiv) *adj.* —**pul'sa·tor** *n.* —**pul'sa·to·ry** *adj.*

pulse[1] (puls) *n.* [< OFr., ult. < L. pp. of *pellere*, to beat] **1.** the regular beating in the arteries, caused by the contractions of the heart **2.** any regular or rhythmical beat, signal, etc. **3.** the underlying feelings of a group, the public, etc. **4.** a brief surge of electric current **5.** a very short burst of radio waves —*vi.* **pulsed, puls'ing** to pulsate —*vt.* to make pulsate —**puls'er** *n.*

pulse² (puls) *n.* [< OFr. < L. *puls,* a pottage] 1. the edible seeds of peas, beans, lentils, and similar plants having pods 2. any such plant

pulse-jet (engine) (-jet') a jet engine in which the air-intake valves of the combustion chamber open and close in a pulselike manner

pul·ver·ize (pul'və rīz') *vt.* **-ized', -iz'ing** [< MFr. < LL. < L. *pulvis,* dust] 1. to crush, grind, etc. into a powder or dust 2. to demolish —*vi.* to be pulverized into a powder, or dust —**pul'ver·iz'a·ble, pul'ver·a·ble** (-vər ə b'l) *adj.* —**pul'ver·iz·a'tion** *n.* —**pul'ver·iz'er** *n.*

pu·ma (pyōō'mə) *n., pl.* **-mas, -ma:** see PLURAL, II, D, 1 [AmSp. < Quechua] a large tawny-brown animal of the cat family, with a long slender body

pum·ice (pum'is) *n.* [< OFr. < L. *pumex*] a light, porous, volcanic rock used in solid or powdered form to scour, smooth, and polish: also **pumice stone** —*vt.* **-iced, -ic·ing** to scour, etc. with pumice —**pu·mi·ceous** (pyōō mish'əs) *adj.*

pum·mel (pum'ʼl) *vt.* **-melled, -mel·ling** [< POMMEL] to beat or hit with repeated blows, esp. with the fist

pump¹ (pump) *n.* [< MDu. *pompe* < Sp. *bomba,* prob. of echoic origin] any of various machines that force a liquid or gas into or through, or draw it out of, something, as by suction or pressure —*vt.* 1. to move (fluids) with a pump 2. to remove water, etc. from, as with a pump 3. to drive air into, as with a pump 4. to force in, draw out, move up and down, etc. in the manner of a pump 5. to apply force to with a pumping motion 6. [Colloq.] *a)* to question closely and persistently *b)* to get (information) in this way —*vi.* 1. to work a pump 2. to move water, etc. with a pump 3. to move or go up and down like a pump handle 4. to flow in, out, or through by, or as if by, being pumped —**pump up** to inflate the tyre of a bicycle, motor car, etc. —**pump'er** *n.*

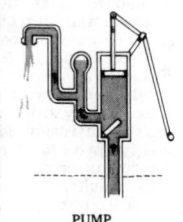

PUMP

pump² (pump) *n.* [< ? Fr. *pompe,* an ornament] 1. a low-cut, low-heeled shoe worn esp. for dancing 2. a rubber-soled shoe used in tennis, etc.; plimsoll

pump·er·nick·el (pum'pər nik'ʼl) *n.* [G.] a coarse, dark, sour bread made of unsifted rye

pump·kin (pum'kin, pump'-) *n.* [< MFr. < L. < Gr. *pepōn,* lit., ripe] 1. a large, round, orange-yellow fruit with many seeds, cooked and eaten in pies, etc. 2. the climbing plant on which it grows 3. any of several gourds

pun¹ (pun) *n.* [< ? It. *puntiglio,* fine point] the humorous use of words that have the same sound or spelling, but have different meanings; a play on words —*vi.* **punned, pun'ning** to make a pun or puns —**pun'ner** *n.*

pun² (pun) *vt.* **punned, pun'ning** [Dial. var. of POUND²] to form a hard, dense mass of earth, clay, etc. by pounding it —**pun'ner** *n.*

‡**pu·na** (pōō'nä) *n.* [AmSp. < Quechua] 1. a high, cold, arid plateau, as in the Andes 2. *same as* MOUNTAIN SICKNESS

Punch (punch) [< PUNCHINELLO] the hero of the puppet show **Punch and Judy,** a humpbacked figure with a hooked nose, constantly fighting with his wife, Judy —**pleased as Punch** greatly pleased

punch¹ (punch) *n.* [see PUNCHEON¹] 1. *a)* a tool driven or pressed against a surface that is to be shaped or stamped *b)* a tool driven against a nail, bolt, etc. that is to be worked in or out 2. a device or machine for making holes, cuts, etc. 3. the hole, cut, etc. so made —*vt.* 1. to pierce, stamp, etc. with a punch 2. to make (a hole, etc.) with a punch —**punch'er** *n.*

punch² (punch) *vt.* [ME. *punchen*] 1. to prod or poke with a stick 2. to strike with the fist —*n.* 1. a thrusting blow with the fist 2. [Colloq.] effective force; vigour —**pull one's punches** [Colloq.] to deliver blows, criticisms, etc. intended to have little or no effect —**punch a (time) clock** to insert a timecard into a time clock when arriving at or leaving work —**punch'er** *n.*

punch³ (punch) *n.* [Hindi *pāc,* five: it orig. had five ingredients] a sweet drink of fruit juices, carbonated beverages, etc., often mixed with wine or spirits, and served in cups from a large bowl (**punch bowl**)

punch ball a stuffed or inflated leather bag hung up in order to be punched for exercise or practice

punch card a card with holes or notches positioned in it, esp. by a key punch for data processing: also **punched card**

punch-drunk (-druŋk') *adj.* dazed, unsteady in gait, confused in speech, etc., as because of many blows to the head in boxing

pun·cheon¹ (pun'chən) *n.* [< MFr., ult. < L. pp. of *pungere,* to prick] 1. a short, upright wooden post used in

framework 2. a heavy piece of timber roughly dressed with one side flat 3. a device for punching, stamping, etc.

pun·cheon² (pun'chən) *n.* [OFr. *poincon*] a large cask of varying capacity (72-120 gallons, 320-540 litres), for beer, wine, etc.; also, as much as it will hold

pun·chi·nel·lo (pun'chə nel'ō) *n., pl.* **-los** [< a character's name in a Neapolitan puppet play] a buffoon; clown

punch line the line carrying the point of a joke

punch press a press in which dies are fitted for cutting, shaping, or stamping metal

punch-up (-up) *n.* [Slang] a fight, brawl, or violent argument

punch·y (pun'chē) *adj.* **punch'i·er, punch'i·est** [Colloq.] 1. forceful; vigorous 2. *same as* PUNCH-DRUNK

punc·til·i·o (puŋk til'ē ō') *n., pl.* **-os** [< Sp. or It., ult. < L. *punctum,* a point] 1. a nice point of conduct, ceremony, etc. 2. punctiliousness

punc·til·i·ous (-ē əs) *adj.* 1. very careful about every detail of behaviour, ceremony, etc. 2. very exact; scrupulous —**punc·til'i·ous·ly** *adv.* —**punc·til'i·ous·ness** *n.*

punc·tu·al (puŋk'tyoo wəl) *adj.* [< ML. *punctualis* < L. *punctus,* a point] on time; prompt —**punc'tu·al'i·ty** (-wal'ə tē) *n.* —**punc'tu·al·ly** *adv.* —**punc'tu·al·ness** *n.*

punc·tu·ate (puŋk'tyoo wāt') *vt.* **-at'ed, -at'ing** [< ML. pp. of *punctuare* < L. *punctus,* a point] 1. *a)* to insert punctuation marks in *b)* to function as a punctuation mark in 2. to break in on here and there [a speech *punctuated* with applause] 3. to emphasize; accentuate —*vi.* to use punctuation marks —**punc'tu·a'tor** *n.*

punc·tu·a·tion (puŋk'tyoo wā'shən) *n.* 1. a punctuating; specif., the use of standardized marks in writing and printing to separate sentences or sentence elements or to make meaning clearer 2. a punctuation mark or marks

punctuation mark any of the marks used in punctuation, as a full stop or comma

punc·ture (puŋk'chər) *n.* [< L. < *pungere,* to pierce] 1. a perforating or piercing 2. a hole made by a sharp point —*vt.* **-tured, -tur·ing** 1. to perforate or pierce with a sharp point 2. to reduce or put an end to [to *puncture* one's pride] —*vi.* to be punctured —**punc'tur·a·ble** *adj.*

pun·dit (pun'dit) *n.* [< Hindi < Sans. *pandita*] 1. in India, a Brahman learned in Sanskrit, Hindu philosophy, etc. 2. a person who has great learning 3. one speaking with authority: often used ironically

pun·gent (pun'jənt) *adj.* [< L. prp. of *pungere,* to prick] 1. producing a sharp sensation of taste or smell; acrid 2. sharp to the mind; poignant 3. sharply penetrating; biting [*pungent* language] 4. keenly clever —**pun'gen·cy** *n.* —**pun'gent·ly** *adv.*

Pu·nic (pyōō'nik) *adj.* [L. *Punicus* < *Poeni,* the Carthaginians] 1. of ancient Carthage or its people 2. like the Carthaginians, regarded by the Romans as faithless and treacherous —**Punic faith** treachery

pun·ish (pun'ish) *vt.* [< OFr. < L. *punire,* to punish < *poena,* punishment] 1. to cause to undergo pain, loss, or suffering for a crime or wrongdoing 2. to impose a penalty for (an offence) 3. to treat harshly 4. [Colloq.] to consume or use up —*vi.* to deal out punishment —**pun'-ish·a·bil'i·ty** *n.* —**pun'ish·a·ble** *adj.* —**pun'ish·er** *n.*

pun·ish·ment (-mənt) *n.* 1. a punishing or being punished 2. a penalty imposed on an offender for wrongdoing 3. harsh treatment

pu·ni·tive (pyōō'nə tiv) *adj.* inflicting or concerned with punishment: also **pu'ni·to·ry** (-tər ē) —**pu'ni·tive·ly** *adv.* —**pu'ni·tive·ness** *n.*

punitive damages *same as* EXEMPLARY DAMAGES

punk¹ (puŋk) *n.* [var. of SPUNK] any substance, as decayed wood, that smoulders when ignited, used as tinder; esp., a fungous substance shaped into slender, fragile sticks and used to light fireworks, etc.

punk² (puŋk) *n.* [< ?] 1. [Slang] a young hoodlum 2. [Slang] anyone, esp. a youngster, regarded as inexperienced, insignificant, etc. 3. a follower of punk rock, esp. one wearing old plastic bags, safety pins, etc., often with lurid makeup —*adj.* [Slang] poor or bad in quality 2. designating a form of rock music characterized by strong rhythm and supposedly anarchistic lyrics

pun·kah, pun·ka (pun'kə) *n.* [Hindi *pankhā*] in India, a large fan made from the palmyra leaf, or a large, swinging fan hung from the ceiling

pun·net (pun'ət) *n.* [< ?] a small, shallow chip basket for fruit, esp. strawberries

pun·ster (pun'stər) *n.* a person who is fond of making puns

punt¹ (punt) *n.* [< ?] *Rugby American football* a kick in which the ball is dropped from the hands and then kicked before it strikes the ground —*vt., vi.* to kick (a ball) in this way —**punt'er** *n.*

punt² (punt) *n.* [OE. < L. *ponto:* see PONTOON²] a flat-bottomed boat with square ends, usually propelled by a long pole —*vt.* 1. to propel (a boat) by pushing with a pole against the bottom of a shallow river or lake 2. to carry in a punt —*vi.* to go in a punt —**punt'er** *n.*

punt³ (punt) *vi.* [< Fr. < Sp. *punto* < L. *punctum*, a point] 1. in certain card games, to bet against the banker 2. to gamble; bet —**punt'er** *n.*

pu·ny (pyoo'nē) *adj.* -ni·er, -ni·est [< Fr. < OFr. *puis*, after + *né*, born] of inferior size, strength, or importance; weak —**pu'ni·ness** *n.*

pup (pup) *n.* 1. *a)* a young dog; puppy *b)* a young fox, wolf, etc. 2. a young seal, whale, etc. —*vi.* **pupped, pup'ping** to give birth to pups

pu·pa (pyoo'pə) *n., pl.* **-pae** (-pē), **-pas** [ModL. < L., a girl, doll] an insect in the stage between the larval and adult forms: some pupae are enclosed in cocoons —**pu'pal** *adj.*

pu·pate (-pāt) *vi.* -pat·ed, -pat·ing to go through the pupal stage —**pu·pa'-tion** *n.*

PUPA

pu·pil¹ (pyoo'p'l) *n.* [< MFr. < L. *pupillus* (dim. of *pupus*, boy), *pupilla* (dim. of *pupa*, girl), ward] a person being taught by a teacher or tutor, as in a school —**pu'pil·lage, pu'pil·age** *n.*

pu·pil² (pyoo'p'l) *n.* [< Fr. < L. *pupilla*, one's figure reflected in another's eye; special use of *pupilla*: see prec.] the contractile circular opening in the centre of the iris of the eye

pup·pet (pup'it) *n.* [< OFr., ult. < L. *pupa*, a girl, doll] 1. orig., a doll 2. a small, usually jointed figure, as of a human being, moved with the hands or by strings, wires, or rods, usually in a puppet show 3. a person whose actions, ideas, etc. are controlled by another

pup·pet·eer (pup'i tir') *n.* a person who operates or designs puppets or produces puppet shows

pup·pet·ry (pup'i trē) *n.* the art or work of a puppeteer

puppet show a play or performance with puppets

puppet state an apparently independent country that, in reality, is controlled by another country

pup·py (pup'ē) *n., pl.* **-pies** [< ? MFr. *popee*, doll < OFr.: see PUPPET] 1. a young dog 2. an insolent, conceited, or silly young man —**pup'py·ish** *adj.*

puppy fat the chubbiness associated with adolescence that usually disappears in adulthood

puppy love immature love between a boy and a girl

pu·ra·na (poo rä'nə) *n.* [Sans. lit., ancient] [*often* P-] any of a group of 18 Hindu epics dealing with creation, the gods, genealogy, etc. in fables, legends, and tales

Pur·beck stone (pur'bek) a very hard limestone found in Dorset and used in building: also **Purbeck marble**

pur·blind (pur'blīnd') *adj.* [ME. *pur blind*, quite blind] 1. orig., completely blind 2. partly blind 3. slow in perceiving or understanding —**pur'blind'ness** *n.*

pur·chase (pur'chəs) *vt.* -chased, -chas·ing [< OFr. < *pour*, for + *chacier*, to chase] 1. to get for money; buy 2. to get at a cost, as of suffering 3. *a)* to move or raise by applying mechanical power *b)* to get a fast hold on so as to do this —*n.* 1. anything obtained by buying 2. a buying 3. *a)* a fast hold applied to move something mechanically or to keep from slipping *b)* an apparatus for applying such a hold —**pur'chas·a·ble** *adj.* —**pur'chas·er** *n.*

purchase tax formerly, a tax levied on non-essential consumer goods and added to selling prices by retailers

pur·dah (pur'də) *n.* [Hindi & Per. *pardah*, a veil] a curtain or veil used by some Hindus and Moslems to hide their women from strangers; also, this practice of hiding women

pure (pyoor) *adj.* [< OFr. < L. *purus*] 1. *a)* free from any adulterant [*pure gold*] *b)* free from anything harmful [*pure water*] 2. simple; mere [*pure luck*] 3. utter; absolute 4. free from defects 5. free from sin or guilt 6. virgin or chaste 7. of unmixed stock; purebred 8. abstract or theoretical [*pure physics*] —**pure'ly** *adv.* —**pure'ness** *n.*

pure·bred (-bred') *adj.* belonging to a recognized breed through generations of unmixed descent —*n.* such a plant or animal

pu·rée (pyoor'ā) *n.* [Fr. < OFr. < L. < *purus*, pure] 1. food prepared by putting cooked vegetables, fruits, etc. through a sieve or liquidizer 2. a thick, smooth soup made with this —*vt.* **-réed', -rée'ing** to make a purée of Also sp. **puree**

pur·fle (pur'f'l) *vt.* -fled, -fling [ME. *purfilen*, < MFr. *pour*, for + *fil*, thread] 1. to decorate the border of 2. to adorn or edge with metallic thread, beads, lace, etc. —*n.* an ornamental border or trimming, as the inlaid border of a violin: also **pur'fling**

pur·ga·tion (pur gā'shən) *n.* the act of purging

pur·ga·tive (pur'gə tiv) *adj.* 1. that purges 2. causing bowel movement —*n.* a substance that purges; specif., a cathartic —**pur'ga·tive·ly** *adv.*

pur·ga·to·ry (pur'gə tər ē) *n., pl.* **-ries** [< OFr. < ML. < LL. < L. *purgare*: see ff.] 1. [*often* P-] in R.C. and other Christian doctrine, a state or place in which those who have died in the grace of God expiate their sins 2. any state or place of temporary punishment or remorse —**pur'ga·to'ri·al** (-tôr'-) *adj.*

purge (purj) *vt.* **purged, purg'ing** [< OFr. < L. *purgare* < *purus*, clean + *agere*, to do] 1. to cleanse of impurities, foreign matter, etc. 2. to cleanse of guilt, sin, etc. 3. to remove by cleansing 4. *a)* to rid (a nation, political party, etc.) of individuals regarded as disloyal or undesirable *b)* to kill or otherwise get rid of (such individuals) 5. *Med. a)* to empty (the bowels) *b)* to make the bowels of (a person) become empty —*vi.* 1. to become clean, clear, or pure 2. to have or cause a thorough bowel movement —*n.* 1. a purging 2. that which purges; esp., a cathartic —**purg'er** *n.*

pu·ri·fy (pyoor'ə fī) *vt.* **-fied', -fy'ing** [< OFr. < L. *purificare* < *purus*, pure + *facere*, to make] 1. to rid of impurities or pollution 2. to free from guilt, sin, corruption, etc. —*vi.* to become purified —**pu'ri·fi·ca'tion** *n.* —**pu·rif·i·ca·to·ry** (pyoo rif'ə kə tər ē) *adj.* —**pu'ri·fi'er** *n.*

Pu·rim (poor'im, poo rēm') *n.* [Heb. *pūrīm*, pl., lit., lots] a Jewish holiday celebrated around the beginning of March, commemorating the deliverance of the Jews by Esther from a massacre: also called **Feast of Lots**

pur·ism (pyoor'iz'm) *n.* 1. strict observance of or insistence on precise usage or style, as in applying formal rules of grammar, art, etc. 2. an instance of this —**pur'ist** *n.* —**pu·ris'tic, pu·ris'ti·cal** *adj.* —**pu·ris'ti·cal·ly** *adv.*

Pu·ri·tan (pyoor'ə t'n) *n.* [see PURITY & -AN] 1. a member of a Protestant group who, in the 16th and 17th centuries, wanted to make the Church of England simpler in its services and stricter about morals 2. [p-] a person regarded as excessively strict in morals and religion —*adj.* 1. of the Puritans 2. [p-] puritanical —**Pu'ri·tan·ism, pu'ri·tan·ism** *n.*

pu·ri·tan·i·cal (pyoor'ə tan'i k'l) *adj.* 1. [P-] of the Puritans 2. excessively strict in morals and religion Also **pu'ri·tan'ic** —**pu'ri·tan'i·cal·ly** *adv.*

pu·ri·ty (pyoor'ə tē) *n.* [< MFr. < LL. < L. *purus*, pure] the quality or condition of being pure; specif., *a)* freedom from adulterating matter *b)* cleanness; clearness *c)* innocence or chastity *d)* freedom from elements regarded as corrupting

purl¹ (purl) *vi.* [< ? Scand.] 1. to move in ripples or with a murmuring sound 2. to eddy; swirl —*n.* a stream or rill that purls, or its murmuring sound

purl² (purl) *vt., vi.* [prob. < a Romance source] 1. to edge (lace) with small loops 2. to invert (stitches) in knitting —*n.* 1. metal thread, for embroidery 2. a small loop or chain of loops on the edge of lace 3. an inversion of knitting stitches

purl³ (purl) *vt., vi.* [? < PURL²] spin around; fall heavily —*n.* a heavy fall

pur·ler (pur'lər) *n.* [< PURL³ + -ER] a blow or throw that causes one to fall forwards —**come a purler** to fall headlong, as from a horse

pur·lieu (pur'lyoo) *n.* [< Anglo-Fr. < OFr. < *pur-*, through + *aler*, to go] 1. orig., an outlying part of a royal forest, returned to private owners 2. a place one visits often 3. [*pl.*] *a)* bounds; limits *b)* environs 4. an outlying part

pur·lin, pur·line (pur'lin) *n.* [< ?] a horizontal timber supporting rafters of a roof

pur·loin (pər loin', pur'loin) *vt., vi.* [< OFr. < *pur-*, for + *loin*, far] to steal; filch —**pur·loin'er** *n.*

pur·ple (pur'p'l) *n.* [OE. < L. *purpura* < Gr. *porphyra*, shellfish yielding purple dye] 1. a dark colour that is a blend of red and blue 2. esp. formerly, *a)* deep crimson *b)* cloth or clothing of such colour: an emblem of royalty or high rank —*adj.* 1. of the colour purple 2. imperial; royal 3. *a)* flowery [*purple prose*] *b)* strong and often offensive [*purple language*] —*vt., vi.* **-pled, -pling** to make or become purple —**born to** (or **in**) **the purple** of royal or high birth —**pur'plish, pur'ply** *adj.*

Purple Heart [U.S.] a decoration awarded to members of the U.S. armed forces wounded in action

purple heart [Colloq.] a heart-shaped tablet consisting mainly of amphetamine

purple martin a large N American swallow with bluish-black plumage

pur·port (pər pôrt'; *also, & for n. always,* pur'pôrt) *vt.* [< Anglo-Fr. < OFr. < *por-*, forth + *porter*, to bear] 1. to profess or claim as its meaning or intent 2. to give the appearance, often falsely, of being, intending, etc. —*n.* meaning; main idea —**pur·port'ed** *adj.* —**pur·port'ed·ly** *adv.*

pur·pose (pur'pəs) *vt., vi.* **-posed, -pos·ing** [< OFr. var. of *proposer*, to PROPOSE] to plan, intend, or resolve —*n.* 1. what one plans to get or do; intention; aim 2. resolution; determination 3. the reason or use for something [a room with no *purpose*] —**on purpose** not by accident; intentionally —**to good purpose** advantageously —**to little** (or **no**) **purpose** with little or no effect —**to the purpose** apt; relevant —**pur'pose·less** *adj.* —**pur'pose·less·ly** *adv.* —**pur'pose·less·ness** *n.*

pur·pose·ful (-fəl) *adj.* 1. resolutely aiming at a specific goal 2. directed towards a specific end; not meaningless —**pur'pose·ful·ly** *adv.* —**pur'pose·ful·ness** *n.*

pur·pose·ly (-lē) *adv.* with a definite purpose; intentionally; deliberately

pur·pos·ive (pur′pə siv) *adj.* 1. serving a purpose 2. having purpose —**pur′pos·ive·ly** *adv.*

purr (pur) *n.* [echoic] 1. a low, vibratory sound made by a cat when it seems to be pleased 2. any sound like this —*vi., vt.* to make, or express by, such a sound

purse (purs) *n.* [OE. *purs* < ML. *bursa*, a bag < LL., a hide < Gr. *brysa*] 1. a small bag or pouch for carrying money 2. finances; money 3. a sum of money given as a present or prize 4. [U.S.] a woman's handbag —*vt.* **pursed, purs′ing** to pucker (one's lips, brows, etc.)

purse bearer 1. one who carries a purse for someone else 2. the official responsible for carrying the Great Seal in a bag, for the Lord Chancellor

purs·er (pur′sər) *n.* [ME., a purse bearer] a ship's officer in charge of accounts, freight, tickets, etc., esp. on a passenger vessel

purse strings a drawstring for certain purses —**hold the purse strings** to be in control of the money —**tighten (or loosen) the purse strings** to make funds less (or more) readily available

purs·lane (purs′lin, -lān) *n.* [< MFr. < LL. *porcilaca* < L. *portulaca*] any of a number of trailing weeds with pink, fleshy stems and small, yellow flowers; esp., an annual used as a potherb and in salads

pur·su·ance (pər syo̅o̅′əns) *n.* a pursuing, or carrying out, as of a project, plan, etc.

pur·su·ant (-ənt) *adj.* [Now Rare] pursuing —**pursuant to** 1. following upon 2. in accordance with

pur·sue (pər syo̅o̅′) *vt.* **-sued′, -su′ing** [< OFr. < VL. < L. < *pro-*, forth + *sequi*, to follow] 1. to follow in order to overtake, capture, etc.; chase 2. to follow or go on with (a specified course, action, etc.) 3. to strive for; seek after [to *pursue* success] 4. to have as one's occupation, profession, or study; devote oneself to 5. to keep on harassing; hound —*vi.* 1. to chase 2. to go on; continue —**pur·su′a·ble** *adj.* —**pur·su′er** *n.*

pur·suit (-syo̅o̅t′) *n.* 1. a pursuing 2. a career, interest, etc. to which one devotes oneself

pursuit plane a fighter plane: see FIGHTER (sense 3)

pursuit race *Cycling* a race in which riders start from opposite sides of the track, and riding in the same direction, attempt to overtake each other: also **pur·suit**

pur·sui·vant (pur′si vənt, -swi-) *n.* [< OFr. < *poursuir*: see PURSUE] 1. in Britain, an officer ranking below a herald 2. a follower; attendant

pur·sy¹ (pur′sē) *adj.* **-si·er, -si·est** [< Anglo-Fr. *pursif*, for OFr. *polsif* < *polser*, to push, pant < L. *pulsare*, to beat] 1. short-winded, esp. from being fat 2. fat —**pur′si·ness** *n.*

pur·sy² (pur′sē) *adj.* **-si·er, -si·est** pursed; puckered

pu·ru·lent (pyo̅o̅r′ə lənt, -yoo lənt) *adj.* [Fr. < L. < *pus* (gen. *puris*), pus] of, like, containing, or discharging pus —**pu′ru·lence, pu′ru·len·cy** *n.* —**pu′ru·lent·ly** *adv.*

pur·vey (pər vā′) *vt.* [< Anglo-Fr. < OFr. < L. *providere*: see PROVIDE] to supply (esp. food or provisions) —**pur·vey′ance** *n.* —**pur·vey′or** *n.*

pur·view (pur′vyo̅o̅) *n.* [< Anglo-Fr. *purvere* (*est*), (it is) provided, ult. < L. *providere*: see PROVIDE] 1. the body and scope of an act or bill 2. extent or range of control, activity, concern, etc.; province

pus (pus) *n.* [L.] the usually yellowish-white liquid matter produced in certain infections, consisting of bacteria, white corpuscles, serum, etc.

push (poosh) *vt.* [< MFr. < OFr. < L. *pulsare*, to beat < pp. of *pellere*, to drive] 1. *a)* to exert pressure or force against, esp. so as to move *b)* to move in this way *c)* to thrust, shove, or drive (*up, down, in, out,* etc.) 2. *a)* to urge on; impel *b)* to follow up vigorously; promote (a campaign, claim, etc.) *c)* to extend or expand (business activities, etc.) 3. to bring into a critical state; press [be *pushed* for time] 4. [Colloq.] to urge or promote the use, sale, etc. of 5. [Colloq.] to be near or close to [*pushing* sixty years] —*vi.* 1. to press against a thing so as to move it 2. to try hard to advance, succeed, etc. 3. to move forwards against opposition 4. to move by being pushed —*n.* 1. a pushing 2. a vigorous effort, campaign, etc. 3. pressure of circumstances 4. [Colloq.] enterprise; drive 5. [Aust. Slang] gang; set; clique —**push off** [Colloq.] to set out; depart —**push on** to go forwards; proceed —**the push** [Colloq.] dismissal from employment; the sack

push bike [Colloq.] a pedal cycle, rather than a motorcycle

push button a small knob or button that is pushed to cause something to operate, as by closing an electric circuit —**push′-but′ton** *adj.*

push·cart (poosh′kärt′) *n.* [U.S.] a barrow

push chair a light, chairlike baby carriage

push·er (-ər) *n.* 1. a person or thing that pushes 2. [Slang] a person peddling drugs, esp. narcotics, illegally

push·ing (-iŋ) *adj.* 1. aggressive; enterprising 2. forward; officious —**push′ing·ly** *adv.*

push·o·ver (poosh′ō′vər) *n.* [Slang] 1. anything very easy to do 2. a person, group, etc. easily persuaded, defeated, seduced, etc.

push-start (-stärt′) *n.* a way of starting a car engine by pushing it to turn the engine over —*vt.* **-start′ed, -start′ing** to start a motor car using this method

Push·tu (push′too̅) *n.* *same as* PASHTO

push-up, push·up (poosh′up′) *n.* [U.S.] a press up

push·y (poosh′ē) *adj.* **push′i·er, push′i·est** [Colloq.] annoyingly aggressive and persistent —**push′i·ness** *n.*

pu·sil·lan·i·mous (pyo̅o̅′sə lan′ə məs) *adj.* [< LL. < L. *pusillus*, tiny + *animus*, the mind] 1. timid or cowardly 2. proceeding from or showing a lack of courage —**pu′sil·la·nim′i·ty** (-ə nim′ə tē) *n.* —**pu′sil·lan′i·mous·ly** *adv.*

puss¹ (poos) *n.* [< ?] 1. a cat: pet name 2. a girl: term of affection

puss² (poos) *n.* [prob. < IrGael. *pus*, mouth] [Slang] 1. the face 2. the mouth

pus·sy¹ (pus′ē) *adj.* **-si·er, -si·est** containing or like pus

puss·y² (poos′ē) *n., pl.* **puss′ies** [dim. of PUSS¹] a cat, esp. a kitten: also **puss′y·cat′** (-kat′)

puss·y·foot (-foot′) *vi.* [Chiefly U.S. Colloq.] 1. to move with stealth, like a cat 2. to shy away from taking a definite opinion, taking a firm stand, etc. —**puss′y·foot′er** *n.*

pussy willow any of several willows bearing silvery, velvetlike catkins before the leaves appear

pus·tu·lant (pus′tyo̅o̅ lənt) *adj.* making pustules form

pus·tu·lar (-lər) *adj.* of, like, or covered with pustules: also **pus′tu·lous** (-ləs)

pus·tu·late (-lāt′; *for adj.* -lit) *vt., vi.* **-lat′ed, -lat′ing** [< LL. pp. of *pustulare* < *pustula*, a pustule] to form into pustules —*adj.* covered with pustules —**pus′tu·la′tion** *n.*

pus·tule (pus′tyo̅o̅l) *n.* [L. *pustula*] 1. a small swelling in the skin, containing pus 2. any small swelling like a blister or pimple

put (poot) *vt.* **put, put′ting** [< or akin to OE. *potian*, to push] 1. *a)* to drive or send by a blow, shot, or thrust *b)* to throw with an overhand thrust from the shoulder [put the shot] 2. to make do something; impel; force 3. to make be in a specified place, condition, relation, etc.; place; set [put her at ease] 4. to make undergo; subject 5. to impose (a burden, tax, etc.) 6. *a)* to bring to bear (on); apply (to) *b)* to bring in; add; inject *c)* to bring about; effect [put a stop to] 7. to attribute; assign; ascribe [put the blame on him] 8. to express; state [put it plainly] 9. to translate (into) 10. present for consideration, decision, etc. [put the question] 11. *a)* to estimate as being (with *at*) [to *put* the cost at £25] *b)* to fix or set (a price, value, etc.) on 12. to fit (words) to music 13. *a)* to bet (money) on *b)* to invest (money) *in* or *into* —*vi.* to go (*in, out, back,* etc.) —*n.* a cast or thrust —*adj.* [Colloq.] fixed [stay put] —**put about** 1. to turn from one tack or direction to another 2. to make widely known —**put across** [Colloq.] 1. to make understood or accepted 2. to carry out with success 3. [U.S.] to carry out by trickery —**put aside** (or **by**) 1. to keep for later 2. to discard —**put away** 1. *same as* PUT ASIDE 2. to return (things) to their proper place; tidy up 3. [Colloq.] *a)* to put in a jail, etc. *b)* to consume (food or drink) —**put down** 1. *a)* to crush; repress *b)* to strip of power, rank, etc.; degrade 2. to write down; record 3. to attribute (to) 4. to consider as; classify 5. to land (an aircraft) 6. to kill (a pet) to prevent suffering 7. [Slang] to belittle, reject, criticize, or humiliate —**put forth** 1. to grow (leaves, etc.) 2. to exert (effort, etc.) 3. to propose; offer 4. to leave port —**put in** 1. to enter a port or haven 2. to enter (a claim, etc.) 3. [Colloq.] to spend (time) —**put in for** to apply for —**put it (or something) across on someone** [Colloq.] to deceive; trick —**put off** 1. to postpone; delay 2. to evade or divert 3. to perturb; upset —**put on** 1. to clothe, adorn, or cover oneself with 2. to take on; add 3. to assume or pretend 4. to apply (a brake, etc.) 5. to stage (a play) —**put out** 1. to expel; dismiss 2. to stop from burning; extinguish (a fire or light) 3. to spend (money) 4. to disconcert or vex 5. to inconvenience 6. to publish, produce, or supply 7. *Sports* to cause (a batsman or runner) to be out —**put over** [Colloq.] *same as* PUT ACROSS —**put through** 1. to carry out successfully 2. to cause to do or undergo 3. to connect (someone) by telephone with someone else —**put to it** to place in a difficult situation; press hard —**put under** to render unconscious; knock out with a blow, anaesthetic —**put up** 1. to offer, as for consideration, decision, sale, etc. 2. to offer as a candidate 3. [Chiefly U.S.] to preserve or bottle (fruits, etc.) 4. to erect; build 5. to lodge, or provide lodgings for 6. *a)* to advance or provide (money) *b)* [Slang] to do or produce what is needed or wanted 7. to arrange (the hair) with curlers, hairgrips, etc. 8. to carry on [to *put up* a struggle] 9. [Colloq.] to incite (a person) *to* some action —**put upon** to impose on; victimize —**put up with** to tolerate; bear

pu·ta·tive (pyo̅o̅t′ə tiv) *adj.* [< L. < *putare*, to suppose] reputed; supposed —**pu′ta·tive·ly** *adv.*

put-down (poot′doun′) *n.* [Slang] a belittling remark or crushing retort

put-put (put'put') *n., vi.* put'-put'ted, put'-put'ting *same as* PUTT-PUTT

pu·tre·fac·tion (pyōō'trə fak'shən) *n.* [see ff.] the rotting of organic matter by bacteria, fungi, and oxidation, with resulting foul-smelling products —**pu'tre·fac'tive** *adj.*

pu·tre·fy (pyōō'trə fī') *vt., vi.* -fied', -fy'ing [< L. *putrefacere* < *putris*, putrid + *facere*, to make] to make or become putrid or rotten —**pu'tre·fi'er** *n.*

pu·tres·cent (pyōō tres'ənt) *adj.* [L. prp. of *putrescere*, to become rotten < *putris*, rotten] 1. rotting 2. of or relating to putrefaction —**pu·tres'cence** *n.*

pu·trid (pyōō'trid) *adj.* [< Fr. < L. *putridus* < *putrere*, to be rotten] 1. rotten and smelling bad 2. of or from decay 3. corrupt or depraved 4. [Colloq.] very unpleasant —**pu·trid'i·ty, pu'trid·ness** *n.* —**pu'trid·ly** *adv.*

‡**Putsch** (pooch) *n.* [G.] an uprising or rebellion, esp. an unsuccessful one

putt (put) *n.* [< PUT, *v.*] *Golf* a light stroke made on the putting green in trying to put the ball into the hole —*vt., vi.* to hit (the ball) thus

put·tee (pu tē', put'ē) *n.* [< Hindi *paṭṭī*, a bandage < Sans. *paṭṭa*, a strip of cloth] a cloth or leather legging or a cloth strip wound spirally to cover the leg from ankle to knee

putt·er[1] (poot'ər) *n.* a person or thing that puts

putt·er[2] (put'ər) *n.* *Golf* 1. a short, straight-faced club used in putting 2. a person who puts

putt·er[3] (put'ər) *vi.* [var. of POTTER[2]] *Chiefly U.S. var. of* POTTER[2]

putt·ing green (put'iŋ) *Golf* the area of smooth, closely mowed turf in which the hole is sunk

‡**put·to** (poot'tō) *n., pl.* put'ti (-tē) [It. < L. *putus*, var. of *pusus*, boy] a figure of a plump, young, male angel or cupid, as in baroque art

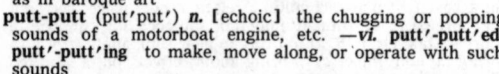

PUTTEES

putt-putt (put'put') *n.* [echoic] the chugging or popping sounds of a motorboat engine, etc. —*vi.* putt'-putt'ed, putt'-putt'ing to make, move along, or operate with such sounds

put·ty (put'ē) *n.* [< Fr. *potée*, lit., potful < *pot*, a pot] 1. a soft, plastic mixture of powdered chalk and linseed oil, used to hold glass panes in place, to fill small cracks, etc. 2. any similar substance —*vt.* -tied, -ty·ing to cement, fill, etc. with putty —**put'ti·er** *n.*

putty knife a knife with a broad blade used to apply putty

put-up (poot'up') *adj.* [Colloq.] planned secretly beforehand [a put-up job]

puz·zle (puz'l) *vt.* -zled, -zling [< ?] to perplex; bewilder —*vi.* 1. to be perplexed, etc. 2. to exercise one's mind, as on a problem —*n.* 1. a puzzled state 2. a puzzling problem, etc. 3. a toy or problem to test skill or ingenuity —**puzzle out** to solve by deep thought —**puzzle over** to give deep thought to —**puz'zle·ment** *n.* —**puz'zler** *n.*

P.V.C. Poly Vinyl Chloride

Pvt. Private

PW policewoman

pwt. pennyweight(s)

PX post exchange

pya (pyä) *n., pl.* **pyas** [Burmese] *see* MONETARY UNITS, table (Burma)

py·ae·mi·a (pī ē'mē ə) *n.* [ModL.: see PYO- & -AEMIA] blood poisoning caused by pus-producing organisms —**py·ae'mic** *adj.*

pye-dog (pī'dog') *n.* [prob. Anglo-Indian contr. of *pariah dog*] an undomesticated Asian dog, often roaming in packs in and around villages

Pyg·my (pig'mē) *n., pl.* -mies [< L. < Gr. *pygmaios*, of the length of the *pygmē*, forearm and fist] 1. a member of any of several African and Asian peoples of small stature 2. [p-] any abnormally undersized or insignificant person or thing —*adj.* 1. of Pygmies 2. [p-] very small

py·ja·mas (pə jäm'əz) *n.pl.* [< Hindi < Per. *pai*, a leg + *jāma*, a garment] a loosely fitting sleeping or lounging suit consisting of jacket and trousers

py·lon (pī'lon) *n.* [Gr. *pylōn*, gateway] 1. a gateway, as of an Egyptian temple 2. a towerlike structure, as for supporting electric lines, marking an aircraft course, etc.

py·lo·rus (pī lôr'əs, pə-) *n., pl.* -ri (-ī) [LL. < Gr. *pylōros*, gatekeeper < *pylē*, a gate + *ouros*, watchman] the opening from the stomach into the duodenum —**py·lor'ic** *adj.*

py·o- [< Gr. *pyon*, pus] *a combining meaning:* 1. pus 2. pus-forming Also **py-**

py·or·rhoe·a (pī'ə rē'ə) *n.* [ModL.: see PYO- & -RRHOEA] a discharge of pus; specif., *short for* PYORRHOEA ALVEOLARIS —**py'or·rhoe'al** *adj.*

pyorrhoea al·ve·o·la·ris (al vē'ə lãr'is) an infection of the gums and tooth sockets, in which pus forms and the teeth become loose

pyr·a·mid (pir'ə mid) *n.* [L. *pyramis* (gen. *pyramidis*) < Gr.] 1. any huge structure with a square base and four sloping, triangular sides meeting at the top, as those built for royal tombs in ancient Egypt 2. anything shaped like this 3. *Geom.* a solid figure the base of which is a polygon whose sides are the bases of triangular surfaces meeting at a common vertex —*vi., vt.* to build up or grow as in the form of a pyramid —**py·ram'i·dal** (pi ram'ə d'l) *adj.* —**py·ram'i·dal·ly** *adv.* —**pyr'a·mid'ic, pyr'a·mid'i·cal** *adj.*

EGYPTIAN PYRAMID

pyre (pīr) *n.* [< L. < Gr. < *pyr*, a fire] a pile, esp. of wood, for burning a corpse in a funeral rite

py·re·thrum (pī rē'thrəm) *n.* [ModL. < L. < Gr. *pyrethron*, feverfew] 1. any of several chrysanthemums, with white, pink, red, or purple flower heads 2. an insecticide made from the dried flower heads of certain chrysanthemums

py·ret·ic (pī ret'ik) *adj.* [< ModL. < Gr. *pyretos*, fever < *pyr*, a fire] of or causing fever

Py·rex (pī'reks) [arbitrary coinage < PIE[1] + -r- + -ex] *a trademark for* a heat-resistant glassware for cooking, etc.

pyr·i·dine (pir'ə dēn', -din) *n.* [PYR(O)- + -ID + -INE[4]] a flammable, liquid base with a sharp odour, produced by distilling coal tar, etc. and used in the synthesis of vitamins and drugs, etc.

pyr·i·dox·ine (pir'ə dok'sēn', -sin) *n.* [PYRID(INE) + OX(Y)- + -INE[4]] a pyridine derivative, a vitamin of the B complex, found in cereal grains, liver, yeast, etc.

py·rite (pī'rīt) *n., pl.* **py·ri·tes** (pə rīt'ēz, pi-; pī'rīts) [< L. < Gr. *pyrītēs*, flint < *pyr*, a fire] iron sulphide, FeS₂, a lustrous, yellow mineral that is an important ore of sulphur

py·ri·tes (pə rīt'ēz, pī-; pī'rīts) *n.* any of various native metallic sulphides, as pyrite —**py·rit'ic** (-rit'ik), **py·rit'i·cal** *adj.*

py·ro- [< Gr. *pyr*, a fire] *a combining form meaning* fire, heat [*pyromania*]: also **pyr-**

py·ro·gen·ic (pī'rə jen'ik) *adj.* [PYRO- + -GENIC] 1. producing or produced by heat 2. *Geol.* same as IGNEOUS

py·rog·ra·phy (pī rog'rə fē) *n.* [PYRO- + -GRAPHY] 1. the art of burning designs on wood or leather with heated tools 2. a design so made —**py·rog'ra·pher** *n.* —**py'ro·graph'ic** (-rə gräf'ik) *adj.*

py·ro·la·try (pī'rə lə trē') *n.* [PYRO- + -LATRY] fire worship

py·ro·ma·ni·a (pī'rə mā'nē ə, -mān'yə) *n.* [ModL.: see PYRO- & -MANIA] an uncontrollable desire to start destructive fires —**py'ro·ma'ni·ac'** (-nē ak') *n., adj.* —**py'ro·ma·ni'a·cal** (-mə nī'ə k'l) *adj.*

py·rom·e·ter (pī rom'ə tər) *n.* [PYRO- + -METER] an instrument for measuring unusually high temperatures —**py'ro·met'ric** (-rə met'rik) *adj.* —**py'ro·met'ri·cal·ly** *adv.* —**py·rom'e·try** (-trē) *n.*

py·ro·tech·nic (pī'rə tek'nik) *adj.* [< Fr. < Gr. *pyr*, fire + *technē*, art] 1. of fireworks 2. [U.S.] designating or of spacecraft devices or materials that ignite or explode to activate propellants, etc. 3. dazzling [*pyrotechnic* wit] Also **py'ro·tech'ni·cal** —**py'ro·tech'ni·cal·ly** *adv.*

py·ro·tech·nics (-niks) *n.pl.* 1. [with sing. v.] the art of making and using fireworks: also **py'ro·tech'ny** (-nē) 2. a) a display of fireworks b) fireworks; esp., rockets, flares, etc., as for signalling c) [U.S.] pyrotechnic devices in spacecraft 3. a dazzling display, as of eloquence —**py'ro·tech'nist** *n.*

py·rox·ene (pī rok'sēn, pī'rok sēn') *n.* [Fr. < Gr. *pyr*, fire + *xenus*, a stranger] *Geol.* a group of mineral silicates found in igneous rocks

py·rox·y·lin, py·rox·y·line (pī rok'sə lin) *n.* [< Fr. < Gr. *pyr*, fire + *xylon*, wood] nitrocellulose, esp. in less explosive forms than guncotton, used in making paints, lacquers, etc.

Pyr·rhic victory (pir'ik) [after *Pyrrhus*, king of Epirus, who defeated the Romans in 280 and 279 B.C., suffering extremely heavy losses] a victory that is too costly

Pyr·rho·nism (pir'ə niz'm) 1. the doctrine taught by Pyhrho (365?-275? B.C.), a Gr. sceptic, that all knowledge is uncertain 2. extreme scepticism —**pyr'rho·nic** *adj.*

Py·thag·o·ras' Theorem (pi thag'ər əs) [after *Pythagoras*, 6th cent. B.C. Gr. mathematician] the theorem that the square on the hypotenuse of a right-angled triangle is equal to the sum of the squares on the other two sides

Pyth·i·an (pith'ē ən) *adj.* [< L. < Gr. *Pythios*, of *Pythō*, older name for Delphi, Greek city] 1. of Apollo as patron of Delphi and the Delphic oracle 2. designating or of the games held at Delphi every four years in ancient Greece in honour of Apollo

py·thon (pī'thon, -thən) *n.* [< L. < Gr. *Pythōn*, a serpent slain by Apollo] 1. any of a group of large, nonpoisonous snakes of Asia, Africa, and Australia, that crush their prey to death 2. popularly, any large snake that crushes its prey

py·tho·ness (pī'thə nis) *n.* [< MFr. < ML. < LL. < Gr.,

Pythō: see PYTHIAN] **1.** a priestess of Apollo at Delphi **2.** any woman soothsayer; prophetess

pyx (piks) *n.* [< L. < Gr. *pyxis*, a box < *pyxos*, the box tree] **1.** the container in which the consecrated wafer of the Eucharist is kept or carried **2.** the chest in which selected coins from the Mint are placed to be tested for weight

pyx·is (pik'sis) *n., pl.* **pyx'i·des** (-sə dēz') [L.: see prec.] *Bot.* a dry fruit whose upper portion splits off as a lid

Q

Q, q (kyōō) *n., pl.* **Q's, q's** **1.** the seventeenth letter of the English alphabet **2.** the sound of *Q* or *q*

Q *Chess* queen

Q. **1.** Quebec **2.** Queen **3.** Question

q. **1.** quart **2.** quarter **3.** quarto **4.** queen **5.** question **6.** quetzal **7.** quintal: also **ql.** **8.** quire

Q.A.R.A.N.C. Queen Alexandra's Royal Army Nursing Corps

Q.A.R.N.N.S. Queen Alexandra's Royal Naval Nursing Service

Q.B. Queen's Bench

Q-boat (kyōō'bōt') *n.* [< *Q*, Query + BOAT] a boat with concealed guns used in anti-submarine warfare in World War I

Q.C. Queen's Counsel

Q.E.D. [L. *quod erat demonstrandum*] which was to be proved

qin·tar (kin tär') *n.* [Alb., ult. < L. *centum*, cent] see MONETARY UNITS, table (Albania)

Q'ld. Queensland

QM, Q.M. Quartermaster

Q.M.G. Quartermaster General

Q.P.M. Queen's Police Medal

qr. *pl.* **qrs.** **1.** quarter **2.** quire

qt. **1.** quantity **2.** quart(s)

Q.T., q.t. [Slang] quiet: usually in **on the Q.T.** (or **q.t.,**) in secret

qua (kwā, kwä) *adv.* [L. < *qui*, who] in the function or capacity of [the Queen *qua* Head of the Commonwealth]

quack[1] (kwak) *vi.* [echoic] to utter the sound or cry of a duck, or a sound like it —*n.* the sound made by it —**quack-quack** a child's name for a duck

quack[2] (kwak) *n.* [short for QUACKSALVER] **1.** a person who practises medicine without having been trained, licensed, etc. **2.** any person who pretends to have knowledge or skill that he does not have; charlatan —*adj.* **1.** characterized by grand claims that have little or no foundation **2.** dishonestly claiming to bring about a cure —*vi.* to engage in quackery —**quack'ish** *adj.* —**quack'ish·ly** *adv.*

quack·er·y (-ər ē) *n.* the claims or methods of a quack

quack·sal·ver (-sal'vər) *n.* [< MDu. < *quacken*, to brag + *zalf*, salve] [Now Rare] a quack; charlatan

quad[1] (kwod) *n.* *same as:* **1.** QUADRANGLE (of a college) **2.** QUADRUPLET

quad[2] (kwod) *n.* [< QUAD(RAT)] *Printing* a piece of type metal lower than the face of the type, used for spacing, etc. —*vt.* **quad'ded, quad'ding** to fill out (a line) with quads

Quad·ra·ges·i·ma (kwod'rə jes'i mə) *n.* [LL. < fem. of L. *quadragesimus*, fortieth] the first Sunday in Lent: also **Quadragesima Sunday**

quad·ran·gle (kwod'raŋ'g'l) *n.* [< MFr. < LL. < L.: see QUADRI- & ANGLE[1]] **1.** a plane figure with four angles and four sides **2.** *a)* an area surrounded on four sides by buildings *b)* the buildings themselves —**quad·ran'gu·lar** (-gyə lər) *adj.*

quad·rant (kwod'rənt) *n.* [< L. *quadrans*, fourth part] **1.** a fourth part of the circumference of a circle; an arc of 90° **2.** a quarter section of a circle **3.** an instrument for measuring altitudes or angular elevations in astronomy and navigation —**quad·ran'tal** (-ran't'l) *adj.*

quad·ra·phon·ic (kwod'rə fon'ik) *adj.* [< L. *quadra*, a square + PHONIC] designating or of sound reproduction, as on records or tapes or in broadcasting, using four channels to carry and reproduce through separate speakers a blend of sounds from separate sources

quad·rat (kwod'rat) *n.* [var. of ff.] **1.** *same as* QUAD[2] **2.** *Ecol.* a plot of ground used to study plant and animal life

quad·rate (-rāt; *also, for adj. & n.,* -rit) *adj.* [< L. pp. of *quadrare*, to make square, ult. < *quattuor*, four] square or nearly square —*n.* **1.** a square or rectangle **2.** a square or rectangular space, thing, etc. —*vi.* **-rat·ed, -rat·ing** to square; agree (*with*) —*vt.* to make square

quad·rat·ic (kwod rat'ik) *adj.* [< prec. + -IC] *Algebra* involving a quantity or quantities that are squared but none

that are raised to a higher power —*n.* *Algebra* a quadratic term, expression, or equation —**quad·rat'i·cal·ly** *adv.*

quadratic equation *Algebra* an equation in which the second power, or square, is the highest to which the unknown quantity is raised

quad·ra·ture (kwod'rə chər) *n.* [< LL. < L. pp. of *quadrare*: see QUADRATE] **1.** the act of squaring **2.** the determining of the dimensions of a square equal in area to a given surface **3.** *Astron.* the relative position of two heavenly bodies when 90° distant from each other

quad·ren·ni·al (kwod ren'ē əl) *adj.* [< L. < *quadri-* (see ff.) + *annus*, a year] **1.** lasting four years **2.** occurring once every four years —*n.* a quadrennial event —**quad·ren'·ni·al·ly** *adv.*

quad·ri- [L. < base of *quattuor*, four] *a combining form meaning* four times, fourfold: also, before a vowel, **quadr-**

quad·ri·lat·er·al (kwod'rə lat'ər əl) *adj.* [< L.: see QUADRI- & LATERAL] four-sided —*n.* **1.** *Geom.* a plane figure having four sides and four angles **2.** a four-sided area —**quad'ri·lat'er·al·ly** *adv.*

qua·drille[1] (kwə dril', kə-) *n.* [Fr. < Sp. *cuadrilla*, dim. < *cuadro*, a square] **1.** a square dance performed by four couples **2.** music for this dance

qua·drille[2] (kwə dril', kə-) *n.* [Fr., altered after prec. < Sp. *cuartillo* ult. < L. *quartus*: see QUART] a card game, popular in the 18th cent., played by four persons

QUADRILATERALS

quad·ril·lion (kwod ril'yən) *n.* [Fr. < *quadri-* (see QUADRI-) + (MI)LLION] **1.** in Great Britain and Germany, the number represented by 1 followed by 24 zeros **2.** in the U.S. and France, the number represented by 1 followed by 15 zeros —*adj.* amounting to one quadrillion in number —**quad·ril'·lionth** *adj., n.*

quad·ri·ple·gi·a (kwod'rə plē'jē ə, -jə) *n.* [ModL.: see QUADRI- & -PLEGIA] total paralysis of the body from the neck down —**quad'ri·ple'gic** (-plē'jik, -plej'ik) *adj., n.*

quad·ri·va·lent (kwod'rə vā'lənt, kwo driv'ə-) *adj.* **1.** having four valences **2.** *same as* TETRAVALENT (sense 1) —**quad'ri·va'lence, quad'ri·va'len·cy** *n.*

quad·roon (kwo drōōn') *n.* [< Sp. < *cuarto*, a fourth < L. *quartus*: see QUART] a person who has one Negro grandparent

quad·ru·ped (kwod'rōo ped') *n.* [< L. < *quadru-* (for *quadri-*), four + *pes*, a foot] an animal, esp. a mammal, with four feet —*adj.* having four feet —**quad·ru·pe·dal** (kwo drōō'pi d'l, kwod'rə ped'l) *adj.*

quad·ru·ple (kwo drōō'p'l, -drup'-'l; kwod'rōo-) *adj.* [MFr. < L. < *quadru-* (see prec.) + *-plus*, -fold] **1.** consisting of four **2.** four times as much or as many; fourfold **3.** *Music* having four beats to the bar —*n.* an amount four times as much or as many —*vt., vi.* **-pled, -pling** to make or become four times as much or as many

quad·ru·plet (kwo drup'lit, -drōō'plit; kwod'rōo plit) *n.* [dim. of prec.] **1.** any of four offspring born at a single birth **2.** a group of four, usually of one kind

quad·ru·pli·cate (kwo drōō'plə kāt'; *for adj. & n., usually* -kit) *vt.* **-cat'ed, -cat'ing** [< L. pp. of *quadruplicare* < *quadru-* (see QUADRUPED) + *plicare*, to fold] to make four identical copies of —*adj.* **1.** fourfold **2.** designating the fourth of identical copies —*n.* any of four identical copies —**in quadruplicate** in four identical copies —**quad·ru'pli·ca'tion, quad·ru'pli·ci·ty** *n.*

quaes·tor (kwēs'tər, kwes'-) *n.* [L. < pp. of *quaerere*, to inquire] in ancient Rome, **1.** orig., a judge in certain criminal cases **2.** later, any of certain state treasurers —**quaes·to'ri·al** (-tôr'ē əl) *adj.* —**quaes'tor·ship'** *n.*

quaff (kwof, kwäf) *vt., vi.* [prob. (by misreading of *-ss-* as *-ff-*) < LowG. *quassen*, to overindulge] to drink deeply in a hearty or thirsty way —*n.* **1.** a quaffing **2.** a drink that is quaffed —**quaff'er** *n.*

quag (kwag, kwog) *n.* [< ?] a bog or a marsh

quag·ga (kwag′ə) *n., pl.* **-ga, -gas** see PLURAL, II, D, 2 [Afrik. < native name] a striped wild ass of Africa, now extinct

quag·gy (kwag′ē, kwog′-) *adj.* **-gi·er, -gi·est** 1. like a quagmire; boggy; miry 2. soft; flabby

quag·mire (kwag′mīr′, kwog′-) *n.* [< earlier *quag*, a bog + MIRE] 1. wet, boggy ground, yielding under the feet 2. a difficult or dangerous situation from which it is hard to escape [a *quagmire* of debts]

qua·hog, qua·haug (kwô′hôg, kō′-; -hog) *n.* [< AmInd. name] an edible clam of the eastern coast of N. America, having a very hard, solid shell

quaich, quaigh (kwākh) *n.* [ScotGael. *cuach*] a small, shallow drinking cup, usually with two handles

Quai d'Or·say (kā′dôr′sā; *Fr.* ke dôrse′) 1. the quay on the Seine, in Paris, towards which the French Foreign Office building faces 2. the French Foreign Office

quail¹ (kwāl) *vi.* [prob. < OFr. *coaillier* < L. *coagulare*, to coagulate] to draw back in fear; lose courage; cower

quail² (kwāl) *n., pl.* **quails, quail:** see PLURAL, II, D, 1 [< OFr. < ML. *cuacula*, prob. < Gmc. echoic name] any of various small game birds, resembling partridges

quail hawk a New Zealand falcon

quaint (kwānt) *adj.* [< OFr. *cointe* < L. *cognitus*, known: see COGNITION] 1. unusual or old-fashioned in a pleasing way 2. unusual; curious 3. fanciful; whimsical —**quaint′ly** *adv.* —**quaint′ness** *n.*

quake (kwāk) *vi.* **quaked, quak′ing** [OE. *cwacian*] 1. to tremble or shake, as the ground does in an earthquake 2. to shudder or shiver, as from fear or cold —*n.* 1. a shaking or tremor 2. an earthquake

Quak·er (kwāk′ər) *n.* [orig. mocking: said to be from founder's admonition to "quake" at the word of the Lord] *a popular name for* a member of the Society of Friends: see SOCIETY OF FRIENDS —**Quak′er·ess** [Now Rare] *n.fem.* —**Quak′er·ish** *adj.* —**Quak′er·ism** *n.* —**Quak′er·ly** *adj., adv.*

Quaker bird *same as* SOOTY ALBATROSS

quaking aspen a N. American poplar with small, flat-stemmed leaves that tremble in the slightest breeze

quaking grass any of various annual or perennial grasses that have very thin stalks and tremble in the lightest breeze

quak·y (kwā′kē) *adj.* **quak′i·er, quak′i·est** inclined to quake; shaky —**quak′i·ly** *adv.* —**quak′i·ness** *n.*

qual·i·fi·ca·tion (kwol′ə fi kā′shən) *n.* 1. a qualifying or being qualified 2. a thing or condition that qualifies or limits; modification or restriction 3. any skill, knowledge, experience, etc. that fits a person for a position, office, etc. 4. a condition that must be met, as to be eligible

qual·i·fied (kwol′ə fīd′) *adj.* 1. having met conditions or requirements set 2. having the necessary or desirable qualities; competent 3. limited; modified [*qualified* approval] —**qual′i·fied′ly** *adv.* —**qual′i·fied′ness** *n.*

qual·i·fy (-fī′) *vt.* **-fied′, -fy′ing** [< Fr. < ML. < L. *qualis*, of what kind + *facere*, to make] 1. to describe by giving the qualities or characteristics of 2. to make fit for an office, position, etc. 3. to make legally capable; license 4. to modify; restrict; limit 5. to moderate; soften 6. to change the strength of (a spirit, etc.) 7. *Gram.* to modify the meaning of (a word) —*vi.* to be or become qualified —**qual′i·fi′a·ble** *adj.* —**qual′i·fi′er** *n.* —**qual′i·fy′ing·ly** *adv.*

qual·i·ta·tive (-tāt′iv) *adj.* having to do with quality or qualities —**qual′i·ta′tive·ly** *adv.*

qualitative analysis the branch of chemistry dealing with the determination of the elements or ingredients of which a compound or mixture is composed

qual·i·ty (kwol′ə tē) *n., pl.* **-ties** [< OFr. < L. < *qualis*, of what kind] 1. any of the features that make something what it is; characteristic; attribute 2. basic nature; character; kind 3. the degree of excellence which a thing possesses 4. excellence; superiority 5. [Archaic] *a)* high social position *b)* people of such position 6. the property of a tone determined by its overtones; timbre

quality control a system for maintaining desired standards in a product, esp. by inspecting samples

qualm (kwäm) *n.* [OE. *cwealm*, disaster] 1. a sudden feeling of sickness, faintness, or nausea 2. a sudden feeling of uneasiness or doubt; misgiving 3. a twinge of conscience; scruple —**qualm′ish** *adj.* —**qualm′ish·ly** *adv.* —**qualm′ish·ness** *n.*

quan·da·ry (kwon′drē, -dər ē) *n., pl.* **-ries** [< ? L. *quande*, how much] a state of perplexity; dilemma

quan·dong, quan·dang (kwon′doŋ′) *n.* 1. a small Australian tree whose edible fruit has a single stone containing an edible kernel 2. this fruit or stone Also **quan′tong′** (toŋ′)

quant (kwant, kwont) *n.* [< ?] a punting pole with a flat cap at the end to prevent its sinking in the mud —*vt., vi.* to propel (a boat) with a quant

quan·ta (kwon′tə) *n. pl. of* QUANTUM

quan·ti·fy (kwon′tə fī′) *vt.* **-fied′, -fy′ing** [ML. < L. *quantus*, how much + *facere*, to make] to determine or express the quantity of; measure —**quan′ti·fi′a·ble** *adj.* —**quan′ti·fi·ca′tion** *n.* —**quan′ti·fi′er** *n.*

quan·ti·ta·tive (kwon′tə tā′tiv) *adj.* 1. having to do with quantity 2. capable of being measured —**quan′ti·ta′tive·ly** *adv.* —**quan′ti·ta′tive·ness** *n.*

quantitative analysis the branch of chemistry dealing with the measurement of the amounts or percentages of the various components of a compound or mixture

quan·ti·ty (kwon′tə tē) *n., pl.* **-ties** [< OFr. < L. < *quantus*, how much] 1. an amount; portion 2. any bulk, weight, or number not definitely specified 3. the exact amount of something 4. [*also pl.*] a great amount 5. that property of anything which can be determined by measurement 6. the relative length of a vowel, syllable, musical tone, etc. 7. *Math. a)* a thing that has the property of being measurable in dimensions, amounts, etc. *b)* a number or symbol expressing a quantity

quantity surveyor a person who estimates the costs of materials and labour for builders

quan·tize (-tīz) *vt.* **-tized, -tiz·ing** [QUANT(UM) + -IZE] 1. *Math.* to express in multiples of a basic unit 2. *Physics* to restrict (a physical quantity) to one of a set of fixed values —**quan′ti·za′tion** *n.*

quan·tum (-təm) *n., pl.* **-ta** (-tə) [L., neut. sing. of *quantus*, how much] *Physics* an (or the) elemental unit, as of energy: the **quantum theory** states that energy is not absorbed or radiated continuously, but discontinuously, in quanta

quar·an·tine (kwor′ən tēn′) *n.* [It. *quarantina*, lit., forty days, ult. < L. *quadraginta*, forty] 1. *a)* the period, orig. 40 days, during which a vessel suspected of carrying contagious disease is detained in a port in isolation *b)* the place where such a vessel is stationed 2. any isolation or restriction on travel to keep contagious diseases, insect pests, etc. from spreading 3. a place where persons, animals, or plants having such diseases, etc. are isolated 4. the state of being quarantined —*vt.* **-tined′, -tin′ing** 1. to place under quarantine 2. to isolate politically, commercially, socially, etc. —**quar′an·tin′a·ble** *adj.*

quark (kwôrk, kwärk) *n.* [orig. a word coined by James Joyce in *Finnegan's Wake*] any of three proposed particles thought of as the building blocks of baryons and mesons

quar·rel¹ (kwor′əl) *n.* [< OFr., ult. < dim. of L. *quadrus*, a square] 1. a square-headed arrow shot from a crossbow 2. a small, diamond-shaped or square pane of glass

quar·rel² (kwor′əl) *n.* [< OFr. < L. *querela*, complaint < *queri*, to complain] 1. a cause for dispute 2. a dispute, esp. one marked by anger and resentment 3. a breaking up of friendly relations —*vi.* **-relled, -rel·ling** 1. to find fault; complain 2. to dispute heatedly 3. to have a breach in friendship —**quar′rel·ler** *n.*

quar·rel·some (-səm) *adj.* inclined to quarrel —**quar′rel·some·ly** *adv.* —**quar′rel·some·ness** *n.*

quar·ry¹ (kwor′ē) *n., pl.* **-ries** [< OFr. *cuiree*, altered (after *cuir*, a hide) < pp. of *curer*, to eviscerate] 1. an animal that is being hunted down 2. anything pursued

quar·ry² (kwor′ē) *n., pl.* **-ries** [< ML., ult. < L. *quadrare*, to square] a place where building stone, marble, or slate is excavated —*vt.* **-ried, -ry·ing** 1. to excavate from a quarry 2. to make a quarry in (land)

quar·ry·man (-mən) *n., pl.* **-men** a person who works in a stone quarry: also **quar·ri·er** (kwor′ē ər)

quarry tile a flooring tile that is unglazed

quart (kwôrt) *n.* [< MFr. < L. *quartus*, fourth < base of *quattuor*, four] 1. a liquid measure, equal to ¼ gallon (1.136 litres) 2. [U.S.] a dry measure, equal to ⅛ peck 3. any container that can hold one quart —**put (or pour) a quart into a pint pot** to attempt to perform the impossible

quar·ter (kwôr′tər) *n.* [< OFr. < L. *quartarius*, a fourth < *quartus*, fourth] 1. any of the four equal parts of something; fourth 2. one fourth of a year; three months college term, usually one fourth of a school year 3. *a)* one fourth of an hour; 15 minutes *b)* the moment marking the end of each fourth of an hour 4. a coin of the U.S. and Canada equal to 25 cents 5. any leg of a four-legged animal, with the adjoining parts 6. *a)* any of the four main points of the compass *b)* any of the regions of the earth thought of as under these 7. a particular district in a city [the Latin *quarter*] 8. [*pl.*] lodgings; place of abode 9. mercy granted to a surrendering foe 10. a particular person, group, place, etc., esp. one serving as a source [news from the highest *quarters*] 11. *a)* the period of time in which the moon makes one fourth of its revolution around the earth *b)* a phase of the moon when it is half lighted 12. *Basketball*, etc. any of the four periods into which a game is divided 13. *Heraldry a)* any of the four equal divisions of a shield *b)* the charge occupying such a division 14. *Naut. a)* the after part of a ship's side *b)* an assigned station or post —*vt.* 1. to divide into four equal parts 2. loosely, to separate into any number of parts 3. to dismember (the body of a person put to death) into four parts 4. to provide lodgings for; specif., to assign (soldiers) to lodgings 5. to pass over (an area) in many directions, as hounds do in searching for game 6. *Heraldry* to place (different coats of arms) on the quarters of a shield, or to add (a coat of arms) to a shield thus —*vi.* **1.** to be lodged or stationed (*at* or *with*) **2.** to range over a field, etc., as hounds in hunting **3.** *Naut.* to blow on the quarter of a ship: said of the wind —*adj.* constituting or equal to a quarter —**at close quarters** at close range —**cry quarter** to beg for mercy —**quarter of a century** a twenty-five year period —**quar′ter·ing** *adj.*

quar·ter·back (-bak′) *n.* *U.S. Football* the offensive player who directs the attacks

quarter day any of the four days regarded as beginning a new quarter of the year, when quarterly payments on rents, etc. are due

quar·ter-deck, quar·ter·deck (-dek′) *n.* the after part of a ship's upper deck, usually reserved for officers and official ceremonies

quar·tered (kwôr′tərd) *adj.* **1.** divided into quarters **2.** provided with quarters or lodgings **3.** quartersawn

quar·ter·fi·nal (kwôr′tər fī′n'l; *for n. usually* kwôr′tər fī′n'l) *adj.* coming just before the semifinals, as of a tournament —*n.* **1.** a quarterfinal match **2.** [*pl.*] a quarterfinal round —**quar′ter·fi′nal·ist** *n.*

quarter horse [U.S.] an American breed of horse with a low, compact, muscular body and great sprinting speed for distances up to a quarter of a mile

quar·ter·ing (-iŋ) *n.* **1.** the act of dividing in quarters **2.** the providing of quarters for soldiers, etc. **3.** *Heraldry a)* the marshalling of several coats of arms on one shield, usually representing family intermarriages *b)* such a coat of arms

quar·ter·light (-līt′) a small pivoted window in the door of a car, providing ventilation

quar·ter·ly (kwôr′tər lē) *adj.* **1.** occurring or appearing at regular intervals four times a year **2.** consisting of a quarter —*adv.* once every quarter of the year —*n.,* pl. **-lies** a publication issued every three months

quar·ter·mas·ter (-mäs′tər) *n.* **1.** *Mil.* an officer whose duty it is to provide troops with quarters, clothing, equipment, etc. **2.** a ship's petty officer who attends to navigation, signals, etc.

Quartermaster General *Mil.* an official in charge of supplies, etc. for the whole army

quar·ter·mil·er (-mīl′ər) *n.* one who competes in quarter-mile races

quar·tern (kwôr′tərn) *n.* [< OFr.: see QUART] **1.** orig., a fourth part **2.** one fourth of a pint, a peck, etc.

quarter note *Music* [U.S.] a crotchet: see NOTE, illus.

quar·ter·saw (kwôr′tər sô′) *vt.* **-sawed′, -sawn′** or **-sawed′, -saw′ing** to saw (a log) into quarters lengthwise and then into boards, in order to show off the grain of the wood

quarter section [U.S.] a division of public lands that is one fourth of a section and is half a mile square

quarter sessions **1.** in Britain, a court that sits quarterly in civil proceedings, with limited criminal jurisdiction **2.** in the U.S., any of various courts that sit quarterly

quar·ter·staff (-stäf′) *n.,* pl. **-staves′** (-stāvz′) a stout, iron-tipped wooden staff, six to eight feet long, formerly used as a weapon

quarter tone *Music* an interval of one half of a semitone

quar·tet, quar·tette (kwôr tet′) *n.* [< Fr. < It. dim. of *quarto* < L. *quartus,* a fourth] **1.** any group of four **2.** *Music a)* a composition for four voices or four instruments *b)* the four performers of such a composition

quar·to (kwôr′tō) *n.,* pl. **-tos** [< L. (*in*) *quarto,* (in) a fourth] **1.** the page size of a book made up of printer's sheets folded into four leaves **2.** a book with pages of this size —*adj.* with pages of this size

quartz (kwôrts) *n.* [G. *Quarz* < ?] a brilliant, crystalline mineral, silicon dioxide, SiO_2, occurring most often in a colourless, transparent form, but also as variously coloured semiprecious stones —**quartz·ose** (kwôrt′sōs) *adj.*

quartz clock a clock operated by the vibrations of a quartz crystal

quartz crystal *Electronics* a thin plate or rod cut from quartz and ground so as to vibrate at a particular frequency

quartz lamp a mercury-vapour lamp with a quartz tube for transmitting ultraviolet rays

qua·sar (kwā′sär, -zär, -sər) *n.* [< *quas*(*i-stell*)*ar* (*radio source*)] any of a number of extremely distant starlike objects that emit powerful radio waves

quash[1] (kwosh) *vt.* [< MFr. < LL. *cassare,* to destroy < L. *cassus,* empty] *Law* to annul or set aside (an indictment)

quash[2] (kwosh) *vt.* [< MFr. < L. *quassare,* to shatter < pp. of *quatere,* to break] to put down or overcome as by force; suppress; quell [*to quash an uprising*]

qua·si (kwä′sī, -zī; kwā′sē, -zē) *adv.* [L. < *quam,* as + *si,* if] as if; seemingly; in part —*adj.* seeming Often hyphenated as a prefix [*quasi-judicial*]

qua·si-stel·lar radio source (-stel′ər) same as QUASAR

quas·si·a (kwosh′ē ə, kwosh′ə) *n.* [ModL. < Graman *Quassi,* Surinam Negro who prescribed it for fever, c. 1730] **1.** any of a group of tropical trees related to the ailanthus **2.** the wood of certain of these or a drug extracted from it

qua·ter·na·ry (kwə tur′nər ē) *adj.* [< L. < *quaterni,* four each] **1.** consisting of four **2.** [Q-] designating or of the geologic period following the Tertiary in the Cainozoic Era —**the Quaternary** the Quaternary Period or its rocks: see GEOLOGY, chart

qua·ter·nion (kwə tur′nē ən) *n.* [ME. < LL. < L. *quaterni:* see QUATERNARY] **1.** a set of four **2.** *Math a)* an operator, containing four terms, three of which are complex, that changes one vector into another *b)* the calculus using the quaternion

quat·rain (kwo′trān) *n.* [Fr. < *quatre* < L. *quattuor,* four] a stanza or poem of four lines

quat·re·foil (kat′ər foil′, kat′rə-) *n.* [< MFr. < *quatre* (< L. *quattuor*), four + *feuille* (< L. *folium*), a leaf] **1.** a flower with four petals or a leaf with four leaflets **2.** *Archit.* a circular design of four converging arcs

quat·tro·cen·to (kwot′trō chen′tō) *n.* [It. four hundred: short for *mille quattrocento,* one thousand four hundred] the 15th cent. as a period in Italian art and literature

qua·ver (kwā′vər) *vi.* [ME. *cwafien*] **1.** to shake or tremble **2.** to be tremulous: said of the voice **3.** to make a trill in singing or playing —*vt.* **1.** to utter in a tremulous voice **2.** to sing or play with a trill —*n.* **1.** a tremulous quality in a voice or tone **2.** *Music* a note having one eighth the duration of a semibreve —**qua′ver·er** *n.* —**qua′ver·ing·ly** *adv.* —**qua′ver·y** *adj.*

quay (kē) *n.* [MFr. *cai* < Celt.] a wharf for loading and unloading ships, usually one of stone or concrete

Que. Quebec

quean (kwēn) *n.* [OE. *cwene*] **1.** a hussy **2.** a prostitute

quea·sy (kwē′zē) *adj.* **-si·er, -si·est** [ME. *qwesye* < ?] **1.** causing or feeling nausea **2.** squeamish; easily nauseated **3.** uncomfortable; uneasy —**quea′si·ly** *adv.* —**quea′si·ness** *n.*

Quech·ua (kech′wä, -wə) *n.* [Sp. < Quechua name] **1.** *pl.* **-uas, -ua** a member of any of a group of S. American Indian tribes dominant in the former Inca Empire **2.** their language, still widely spoken —**Quech′uan** *adj., n.*

queen (kwēn) *n.* [OE. *cwen*] **1.** the wife of a king **2.** a woman who rules over a monarchy in her own right **3.** a woman who is foremost among others, as in beauty or accomplishments **4.** a place or thing regarded as the finest of its kind **5.** the fully developed, reproductive female in a colony of bees, ants, etc. **6.** a playing card with a picture of a queen on it **7.** [Slang] a male homosexual, esp. one with feminine characteristics **8.** *Chess* the most powerful piece: it can move in any straight or diagonal direction —**Queen Anne is dead** that is stale news —**queen it** to act like a queen; domineer —**queen′dom** *n.* —**queen′hood′** *n.* —**queen′like′** *adj.*

Queen Anne's lace same as WILD CARROT

Queen Anne Style **1.** a style of English architecture of the early 18th cent., characterized by the use of red brick and simple, dignified ornamentation **2.** a style of furniture of the same period, characterized by simple, curved lines

queen-cake (-kāk′) *n.* a small, light cake

queen consort the wife of a reigning king

queen dowager the widow of a king

queen·ly (-lē) *adj.* **-li·er, -li·est** of, like, or fit for a queen; royal; regal —**queen′li·ness** *n.*

queen mother a queen dowager who is mother of a reigning sovereign

queen of puddings a pudding made from breadcrumbs and meringue

Queen of the May a young girl, crowned with flowers, who is the ruler of May Day celebrations

queen olive a large olive with a long, slender pit

queen post *Carpentry* either of two vertical posts set between the rafters and the base of a truss, at equal distances from the apex

Queens·ber·ry rules (kwēnz′-bər ē) the rules for boxing formulated by the Marquis of Queensberry (1844-1900)

queen's English see KING'S ENGLISH

QUEEN POSTS

queer (kwir) *adj.* [< ? G. *quer,* crosswise] **1.** differing from what is usual or ordinary: odd; strange **2.** slightly ill; giddy, queasy, etc. **3.** [Colloq.] doubtful; suspicious **4.** [Colloq.] having mental quirks; eccentric **5.** [Slang] counterfeit; not genuine **6.** [Slang] homosexual —*vt.* [Slang] **1.** to spoil the success of **2.** to put (oneself) into an unfavourable position —*n.* [Slang] **1.** counterfeit money **2.** an eccentric person **3.** a homosexual —**in** (or on) **queer street** in trouble or difficulty, esp. in a bad state financially —**queer the pitch for** to spoil someone's chances, esp. by underhand means —**queer′ish** *adj.* —**queer′ly** *adv.* —**queer′ness** *n.*

quell (kwel) *vt.* [OE. *cwellan,* to kill] **1.** to crush; subdue [*to quell a mutiny*] **2.** to quiet; allay [*to quell fears*] —**quell′er** *n.*

quench (kwench) *vt.* [OE. *cwencan,* caus. of *cwincan,* to go out] **1.** to extinguish; put out [*water quenched the fire*] **2.**

to overcome; subdue **3.** to satisfy; slake [he *quenched* his thirst] **4.** to cool (hot steel, etc.) suddenly by plunging into water, oil, etc. —**quench'a·ble** *adj.* —**quench'er** *n.* —**quench'less** *adj.*

quern (kwʉrn) *n.* [OE. *cweorn*] a primitive hand mill, esp. for grinding grain

quer·u·lous (kwer'ə ləs, -yə-) *adj.* [< L. < *queri*, to complain] **1.** inclined to find fault; complaining **2.** full of complaint; peevish —**quer'u·lous·ly** *adv.* —**quer'·u·lous·ness** *n.*

que·ry (kwir'ē) *n.,* pl. **-ries** [< L. *quaere*, 2nd pers. sing., imper., of *quaerere*, to ask] **1.** a question; inquiry **2.** a doubt. **3.** a question mark (?) —*vt.* **-ried, -ry·ing 1.** to call in question; ask about **2.** [U.S.] to question (a person) **3.** to question the accuracy of (written or printed matter) by marking with a question mark —*vi.* to ask questions or express doubt —**que'rist** *n.*

ques. question

quest (kwest) *n.* [< OFr. < ML., ult. < L. *quaesitus*, pp. of *quaerere*, to seek] **1.** a seeking; hunt; search **2.** a journey in search of adventure, etc., as those undertaken by knights-errant in medieval times **3.** the persons participating in a quest —*vi.* to go in search or pursuit —*vt.* to seek —**quest'er** *n.*

ques·tion (kwes'chən) *n.* [< Anglo-Fr. < OFr. < L. *quaestio* < pp. of *quaerere*, to ask] **1.** an asking; inquiry **2.** something asked; interrogative sentence **3.** doubt; uncertainty **4.** something in controversy before a court **5.** a problem; matter open to discussion or inquiry **6.** a matter or case of difficulty [not a *question* of money] **7.** a) a point being debated or a resolution brought up before an assembly b) the putting of such a matter to a vote —*vt.* **1.** to ask questions of; interrogate **2.** to express uncertainty about; doubt **3.** to dispute; challenge —*vi.* to ask a question or questions —**a question of** (only) a matter of; all that is necessary is... —**beside the question** not relevant —**beyond (all) question** without any doubt —**in question** being considered, debated, etc. —**out of the question** impossible; not to be considered —**ques'tion·er** *n.* —**ques'·tion·ing** *adj.*

ques·tion·a·ble (-ə b'l) *adj.* **1.** that can or should be questioned; open to doubt **2.** suspected with good reason of being immoral, dishonest, etc. **3.** uncertain [of *questionable* excellence] —**ques'tion·a·ble·ness** *n.* —**ques'·tion·a·bly** *adv.*

question mark 1. a mark of punctuation (?) put after a sentence, word, etc. to indicate a direct question, and also used to express doubt, uncertainty, etc. **2.** an unknown factor

ques·tion·naire (kwes'chə ner') *n.* [Fr.] a written or printed list of questions used in gathering information from one or more persons

question time in the British parliament, the time set aside each day for ministers' oral answers to questions from members

quet·zal (ket säl', kwet's'l) *n.* [AmSp. < Nahuatl < *quetzalli*, tail feather] **1.** a Central American bird, usually brilliant green above and red below, with long, streaming tail feathers in the male **2.** pl. **-zal'es** (-sä'les) *see* MONETARY UNITS, table (Guatemala)

queue (kyōō) *n.* [Fr.< OFr. *coue* < L. *cauda*, tail] **1.** a pigtail **2.** a line, as of persons waiting to be served —*vi.* **queued, queu'ing** to form in a line (often with *up*)

quib·ble (kwib'l) *n.* [< L. *quibus* (formerly common in legal documents), abl. pl. of *qui*, who, which] **1.** a petty evasion; cavil **2.** a petty objection or criticism —*vi.* **-bled, -bling** to evade the truth of a point under discussion by cavilling —**quib'bler** *n.*

quiche (kēsh) *n.* [Fr., ult. < G. *Kuchen*, cake] a savoury tart with a rich filling of eggs, milk, etc. to which bacon, cheese, onion, etc. are added

quick (kwik) *adj.* [OE. *cwicu*, living] **1.** [Archaic] living **2.** a) rapid in action; swift [a *quick* walk, a *quick* worker] b) prompt [a *quick* reply] **3.** lasting a short time [a *quick* look] **4.** prompt to understand or learn [she has *quick* wits] **5.** sensitive [a *quick* sense of smell] **6.** easily stirred; fiery [a *quick* temper] —*adv.* quickly; rapidly —*n.* **1.** the living, esp. in the **quick and the dead 2.** the sensitive flesh under a fingernail or toenail **3.** the deepest feelings [cut to the *quick*] —**quick'ly** *adv.* —**quick'ness** *n.*

quick-change artist an actor or other entertainer who undertakes several rapid costume changes

quick·en (kwik'ən) *vt.* **1.** to animate; enliven **2.** to stir; arouse; stimulate **3.** to make move more rapidly; hasten —*vi.* **1.** to become enlivened; revive **2.** a) to begin to show

signs of life b) to enter the stage of pregnancy in which the movement of the foetus can be felt **3.** to become more rapid; speed up [the pulse *quickens* with fear] —**quick'·en·er** *n.*

quick-freeze (-frēz') *vt.* **-froze', -froz'en, -freez'ing** to subject (food) to sudden freezing so that flavour and natural juices are retained and the food can be stored at low temperatures for a long time

quick·ie (-ē) *n.* [Colloq.] anything done or made quickly —*adj.* done or made quickly

quick·lime (-līm') *n.* lime, or calcium oxide, which gives off much heat in combining with water; unslaked lime

quick one [Colloq.] a speedily consumed alcholic drink: also **quick'ie**

quick·sand (-sand') *n.* [see QUICK & SAND] a deep deposit of loose, wet sand in which a person or heavy object may be easily engulfed

quick·set (-set') *n.* **1.** a live slip or cutting, as of hawthorn, planted, as for a hedge **2.** a hedge, as of hawthorn

quick·sil·ver (-sil'vər) *n.* the metal mercury —*vt.* to cover with mercury —*adj.* of or like mercury, esp. rapid or unpredictable in movement or change

quick·step (-step') *n.* **1.** the step used for marching in quick time **2.** a march in the rhythm of quick time **3.** a spirited dance step

quick-tem·pered (-tem'pərd) *adj.* easily angered

quick time the normal rate of marching: in the Army, 120 paces a minute

quick-wit·ted (-wit'id) *adj.* nimble of mind; alert —**quick'-wit'ted·ly** *adv.* —**quick'-wit'ted·ness** *n.*

quid[1] (kwid) *n.* [var. of *cud*] a piece, as of tobacco, to be chewed

quid[2] (kwid) *n.,* pl. **quid** [Slang] a sovereign, or one pound sterling

quid·di·ty (kwid'ə tē) *n.,* pl. **-ties** [< ML. < L. *quid*, what] **1.** essential quality **2.** a quibble

quid·nunc (kwid'nuŋk') *n.* [L., lit., what now?] an inquisitive, gossipy person; busybody

quid pro quo (kwid'prō kwō') [L.] **1.** one thing in return for another **2.** something equivalent; substitute

qui·es·cent (kwī es'ənt) *adj.* [< L. prp. of *quiescere*, to become quiet] quiet; still; inactive —**qui·es'cence** *n.* —**qui·es'cent·ly** *adv.*

qui·et (kwī'ət) *adj.* [< OFr. < L. *quietus*, pp. of *quiescere*, to keep quiet < quies (gen. *quietis*), rest] **1.** still; calm; motionless **2.** a) not noisy; hushed b) not speaking; silent **3.** not agitated; gentle [a *quiet* sea] **4.** not easily excited [a *quiet* disposition] **5.** not bright or showy [*quiet* furnishings] **6.** not forward; unobtrusive [a *quiet* manner] **7.** secluded [a *quiet* glade] **8.** peaceful; relaxing [a *quiet* evening] **9.** *Commerce* not busy [a *quiet* market] —*n.* **1.** a quiet state; calmness, stillness, etc. **2.** a quiet or peaceful quality —*vt., vi.* to make or become quiet —*adv.* in a quiet manner —**be quiet** a request for silence —**qui'et·er** *n.* —**qui'et·ly** *adv.* —**qui'et·ness** *n.*

qui·et·en (-ən) *vt., vi.* to make or become quiet

qui·et·ism (-iz'm) *n.* [It. *quietismo* < L. *quietus*: see QUIET & -ISM] **1.** a form of religious mysticism originating in Spain in the 17th cent., requiring complete passivity of the will **2.** tranquillity of the spirit or quietness of life —**qui'·et·ist** *n., adj.* —**qui'et·is'tic** *adj.*

qui·e·tude (kwī'ə tyōōd') *n.* a state of being quiet; rest; calmness

qui·e·tus (kwī ēt'əs) *n.* [< ME. *quietus* (*est*) < ML., (he is) quit < L., QUIET] **1.** discharge or release from debt, obligation, etc. **2.** discharge or release from life; death **3.** anything that kills

quiff (kwif) *n.* [< ? It. *cuffia*, a coif < LL. *cofea*: see COIF] a lock or tuft of hair, esp. one at the front of the head

quill (kwil) *n.* [prob. < MLowG. or MDu.] **1.** any of the large, stiff wing or tail feathers of a bird **2.** a) the hollow, horny stem of a feather b) anything made from this, as a pen or plectrum **3.** any of the spines of a porcupine or hedgehog —*vt.* **1.** to form with or into quillings **2.** to cover or pierce with quills, as of a hedgehog

quill·ing (kwil'iŋ) *n.* a band of material fluted into small ruffles so as to resemble a row of quills

quilt (kwilt) *n.* [< OFr. < L. *culcita*, a bed] **1.** a bedcover made of two layers of cloth filled with down, wool, etc. and stitched together in lines or patterns **2.** anything like or used as a quilt —*vt.* **1.** to stitch as or like a quilt [to *quilt* a tea cosy] **2.** to fasten between two pieces of material **3.** to line or pad with quilting —*vi.* to make a quilt or quilts —**quilt'er** *n.*

quilt·ing (-iŋ) *n.* **1.** the act of making quilts **2.** material for quilts

quin (kwin) *n.* *shortened form of* QUINTUPLET

quince (kwins) *n.* [orig. pl. of ME. *quyn* < OFr. < L. < Gr. *kydōnion*] **1.** a golden or greenish-yellow, hard, apple-shaped fruit used in jellies, preserves, etc. **2.** the tree that bears this fruit

quin·cunx (kwin'kuŋks) *n.* [L., lit. five twelfths < *quinque*, five + *uncia*, a twelfth] **1.** an arrangement of five objects in a square, with one at each corner and one in the middle **2.** *Bot.* an arrangement of five-petalled flowers, with two exterior petals, two interior and one part interior and part exterior

qui·nine (kwi nēn') *n.* [< *quina*, cinchona bark (< Sp. < Quechua name) + -INE[4]] **1.** a bitter, crystalline substance extracted from cinchona bark **2.** any compound of this used in medicine, esp. for treating malaria

quinine water *same as* TONIC (*n.* 2)

Quin·qua·ges·i·ma (kwin'kwə jes'i mə) *n.* [LL. *quinquagesima* (*dies*), fiftieth (day)] the Sunday before Lent: also **Quinquagesima Sunday**

quin·quen·ni·al (kwin kwen'ē əl) *adj.* [< L. < *quinque*, five + *annus*, year] **1.** lasting five years **2.** taking place every five years —*n.* a quinquennial event —**quin·quen'ni·al·ly** *adv.*

quin·que·reme (kwin'kwə rēm') *n.* [< L. *quinque*, five + *remus*, oared] an ancient galley having five tiers of rowers

quin·que·va·lent (kwin'kwə vā'lənt) *adj.* [L. *quinque*, five + -VALENT] **1.** having five valences **2.** *same as* PENTAVALENT (sense 1) —**quin'que·va'lence, quin'que·va'len·cy** *n.*

quin·sy (kwin'zē) *n.* [< ML. *quinancia* < LL. *cynanche* < Gr. *kynanchē*, lit., dog-choking < *kyōn*, dog + *anchein*, to choke] *an earlier term for* TONSILLITIS

quin·tain (kwin'tin) *n.* [ME. *quaintan* < OFr. < ML. ult. < L. *quintus* fifth] an object supported by a crosspiece on a post, used by knights as a target in tilting

quin·tal (kwin't'l) *n.* [< MFr. < ML. < Ar. *qintār*, ult. < L. *centenarius*: see CENTENARY] **1.** a hundredweight (112 lbs. in Great Britain, 100 lbs. in the U.S.) **2.** a metric unit of weight, equal to 100 kilogrammes

quin·tes·sence (kwin tes'əns) *n.* [< MFr. < ML. *quinta essentia*, fifth essence, or ultimate substance] **1.** the essence of something in its purest form **2.** the perfect type or example of something —**quin'tes·sen'tial** (-tə sen'shəl) *adj.*

quin·tet, quin·tette (kwin tet') *n.* [< Fr. < It. dim. of *quinto* < L. *quintus*, a fifth] **1.** any group of five **2.** *Music* a) a composition for five voices or five instruments b) the five performers of such a composition

quin·til·lion (kwin til'yən) *n.* [< L. *quintus*, a fifth + (M)ILLION] **1.** in Great Britain and Germany, the number represented by 1 followed by 30 zeros **2.** in the U.S. and France, the number represented by 1 followed by 18 zeros —*adj.* amounting to one quintillion in number —**quin·til'·lionth** *adj., n.*

quin·tu·ple (kwin tyōō'p'l, kwin'tyoo p'l) *adj.* [MFr. < LL. < L. *quintus*, a fifth + -*plex*, -fold] **1.** consisting of five **2.** five times as much or as many; fivefold —*n.* an amount five times as much or as many —*vt., vi.* -**pled, -pling** to make or become five times as much or as many

quin·tu·plet (kwin tyōō'plit, kwin'tyoo plit) *n.* [dim. of prec.] **1.** any of five offspring born at a single birth **2.** a group of five, usually of one kind

quip (kwip) *n.* [< L. *quippe*, indeed] **1.** a witty, or, esp. formerly, sarcastic remark; jest **2.** a quibble **3.** something curious or odd —*vi.* quipped, quip'ping to utter quips —**quip'ster** *n.*

quire[1] (kwīr) *n.* archaic var. of CHOIR

quire[2] (kwīr) *n.* [< OFr. < VL. *quaternum*, paper in sets of four < L. *quaterni*, four each] a set of 24 or 25 sheets of paper of the same size and stock

quirk (kwurk) *n.* [< ? ON. *kverk*, a bird's crop] **1.** a) a sudden twist, turn, etc. [a quirk of fate] b) a flourish in writing **2.** a quibble **3.** a peculiar trait or mannerism —**quirk'i·ly** *adv.* —**quirk'i·ness** *n.* —**quirk'y** *adj.* **quirk'i·er, quirk'i·est**

quirt (kwurt) *n.* [AmSp. *cuarta*] [U.S.] a riding whip with a braided leather lash and a short handle —*vt.* to strike with a quirt

quis·ling (kwiz'liŋ) *n.* [after Vidkun *Quisling* (1887-1945), Norw. collaborationist with the Nazis] a person who collaborates with enemy forces of occupation; a traitor

quit (kwit) *vt.* quit'ted, quit'ting [< OFr. < ML. *quietus*, free: see QUIET] **1.** to free (oneself) of **2.** to discharge (a debt); repay **3.** to give up **4.** to leave; depart from **5.** to stop, discontinue, or resign from —*vi.* **1.** a) to stop doing something b) to give up, as in discouragement **2.** to give up one's job; resign —*adj.* clear, free, or rid, as of an obligation

quitch (kwich) *n.* [< OE. < *cwicu*, alive] *same as* COUCH GRASS

quit·claim (kwit'klām') *n.* [< Anglo-Fr. & OFr.: see QUIT & CLAIM] **1.** the relinquishment of a claim, right, title, etc. **2.** a legal paper in which a person relinquishes to another a claim or title to some property or right: in full, **quitclaim deed** —*vt.* to give up a claim or title to

quite (kwīt) *adv.* [ME. form of QUIT, *adj.*] **1.** completely; entirely **2.** really; truly **3.** to a considerable degree or extent —**quite a few** (or **bit,** etc.) [Colloq.] more than a few (or bit, etc.) —**quite (so)!** certainly! —**quite something** an unusual or extraordinary thing

quit·rent (kwit'rent') *n.* a rent paid in lieu of feudal services: also **quit rent**

quits (kwits) *adj.* [prob. contr. < ML. *quittus*, var. of *quietus*: see QUIETUS] on even terms, as by paying a debt, retaliating, etc. —**call it quits** [Chiefly U.S. Colloq.] **1.** to stop working, playing, etc. **2.** to end an association or friendship; stop being intimate —**cry quits** to declare oneself even with another; agree to stop competing

quit·tance (kwit'əns) *n.* [see QUIT] **1.** a) payment of a debt or obligation b) a document certifying this; receipt **2.** recompense; repayment

quit·ter (kwit'ər) *n.* [Colloq.] a person who quits or gives up easily, without trying hard

quiv·er[1] (kwiv'ər) *vi.* to shake with a tremulous motion; tremble —*n.* the act or condition of quivering; tremor —**quiv'er·y** *adj.*

quiv·er[2] (kwiv'ər) *n.* [OFr. *coivre* < Gmc.] **1.** a case for holding arrows **2.** the arrows in it

‡**qui vive?** (kē vēv') [Fr., (long) live who? (i.e., whose side are you on?)] who goes there?: a sentry's challenge —**on the qui vive** on the lookout; on the alert

quix·ot·ic (kwik sot'ik) *adj.* **1.** [*often* Q-] of or like Don Quixote **2.** extravagantly chivalrous or romantically idealistic; visionary; impractical Also **quix·ot'i·cal** —**quix·ot'i·cal·ly** *adv.* —**quix'ot·ism** (-sə tiz'm) *n.*

quiz (kwiz) *n., pl.* **quiz'zes** [prob. arbitrary use of L. *quis,* what?] **1.** formerly, a) a queer or eccentric person b) a practical joke; hoax **2.** *same as* QUIZ PROGRAMME **3.** a short examination to test one's knowledge —*vt.* quizzed, quiz'zing **1.** [Obs.] to make fun of **2.** to ask questions of, as in interrogating —**quiz'zer** *n.*

quiz programme a radio or TV programme in which a group of people compete in answering questions posed by a master of ceremonies (**question master**)

quiz·zi·cal (kwiz'i k'l) *adj.* **1.** odd; comical **2.** teasing; bantering **3.** perplexed —**quiz'zi·cal'i·ty** (-kal'ə tē), **quiz'·zi·cal·ness** *n.* —**quiz'zi·cal·ly** *adv.*

quod (kwod) *n.* [prob. var. of *quad,* contr. < QUADRANGLE (of a prison)? [Slang] prison; jail

quoin (koin, kwoin) *n.* [var. of COIN] **1.** the external corner of a building; esp., any of the stones forming the corner of a building **2.** a wedgelike piece of stone, etc., such as the keystone of an arch **3.** a wedge-shaped wooden or metal block used to lock something in place

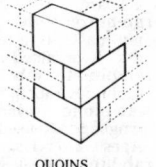

QUOINS

quoit (kwoit, koit) *n.* [< Anglo-Fr., prob. < OFr. *coite,* a cushion] **1.** a ring of rope or metal thrown at an upright peg: the object of the game is to encircle the peg with the ring **2.** [*pl., with sing. v.*] this game

quon·dam (kwon'dəm) *adj.* [L.] that was at one time; former [a quondam pacifist]

Quon·set hut (kwon'sit) [< *Quonset* Point, U.S., where first manufactured] a trademark for a U.S. military shelter, like a Nissen hut

quo·rum (kwôr'əm) *n.* [L., gen. pl. of *qui,* who] the minimum number of members required to be present at an assembly or meeting before it can validly transact business

quo·ta (kwōt'ə) *n.* [ML., short for L. *quota pars,* how large a part] **1.** a share which each of a number is to contribute or receive; proportional share **2.** the number or proportion that is allowed or admitted [quotas for immigrants to Britain]

quot·a·ble (kwōt'ə b'l) *adj.* worthwhile quoting or suitable for quotation —**quot'a·bil'i·ty** *n.* —**quot'a·bly** *adv.*

quo·ta·tion (kwō tā'shən) *n.* **1.** a quoting **2.** the words or passage quoted **3.** *Commerce* the current quoted price of a stock, bond, commodity, etc.

quotation mark either of a pair of punctuation marks (". . .") used to enclose a direct quotation, or of single marks ('. . .') for enclosing a quotation within a quotation

quote (kwōt) *vt.* quot'ed, quot'ing [< ML. *quotare,* to number (chapters, etc.) < L. *quotus,* of what number] **1.** to repeat a passage from or statement of **2.** to repeat (a passage, statement, etc.) **3.** to cite as an example or authority **4.** to state (the price of something) —*vi.* to make a quotation, as from a book —*n.* [Colloq.] *same as:* **1.** QUOTATION **2.** QUOTATION MARK —*interj.* I shall quote: used in speech before a quotation —**quot'er** *n.*

quoth (kwōth) *vt.* [< OE. < *cwethan,* to speak] [Archaic] said: followed by a subject in the first or third person

quoth·a (-ə) *interj.* [< *quoth he*] [Archaic] indeed!

quo·tid·i·an (kwō tid'ē ən) *adj.* [< OFr. < L. < *quotidie,* daily < *quot,* as many as + *dies,* day] **1.** daily; recurring every day **2.** everyday; ordinary —*n.* anything, esp. a fever, that recurs daily

quo·tient (kwō'shənt) *n.* [< L. *quoties,* how often < *quot,* how many] *Arith.* the result obtained when one number is divided by another

quo war·ran·to (kwō wo ran'tō) *pl.* **quo war·ran'tos** [ML., by what warrant] a legal proceeding undertaken to recover an office, franchise, etc. from the one in possession

Qu·ran (koo rän', -ran') *n. same as* KORAN

qursh (koorsh) *n., pl.* **qu·rush** (koo'rəsh) [< Ar. *taqrush,* to earn < *qrsh,* to collect] *see* MONETARY UNITS, table (Saudi Arabia)

q.v. [L. *quod vide*] which see

R

R, r (är) *n., pl.* **R's, r's** 1. the eighteenth letter of the English alphabet 2. a sound of *R* or *r*

R 1. *Chem.* radical 2. *Math.* ratio 3. *Elec.* resistance 4. *Chess* rook **—the three R's** reading, writing, and arithmetic, regarded as the basic studies

r 1. *Math.* radius 2. roentgen(s) 3. ruble

R. 1. Radical 2. Registered (Trademark) 3. [Chiefly U.S.] Republic(an) 4. *Chess* Rook

R., r. 1. [L. *Rex*] king 2. [L. *Regina*] queen 3. rabbi 4. radius 5. railway 6. right 7. river 8. road 9. ruble 10. *pl.* **Rs., Rs, rs.** rupee

r. 1. rare 2. retired 3. rod(s)

Ra *Chem.* radium

R.A. 1. Rear Admiral 2. Royal Academician 3. Royal Academy

R.A.A.F. Royal Australian Air Force

ra·bat (rab'ē, rəbat') *n.* [MFr.] a plain, black shirt front worn with a clerical collar by some clergymen: also **rebato** (ri bä'tō)

rab·bet (rab'it) *n.* [< OFr. < *rabattre:* see REBATE] a groove or cut made in the edge of a board, etc. so that another piece may be fitted into it to form a joint (**rabbet joint**) **—vt.** 1. to cut a rabbet in 2. to join by means of a rabbet **—vi.** to be joined by a rabbet

rabbet plane a plane for cutting a groove along the edge of a board

rab·bi (rab'ī) *n., pl.* **-bis, -bies** [< LL. < Gr. < Heb. *rabbī,* my master] a teacher of the Jewish law, now usually one that is ordained and the spiritual head of a congregation

rab·bin·ate (rab'i nit, -nāt') *n.* 1. the position or office of rabbi 2. rabbis as a group

Rab·bin·ic (rə bin'ik) *adj.* 1. designating the Hebrew language as used in the writings of rabbis of the Middle Ages 2. [r-] *same as* RABBINICAL

rab·bin·i·cal (-i k'l) *adj.* of the rabbis, their doctrines, learning, language, etc., esp. in the early Middle Ages **—rab·bin'i·cal·ly** *adv.*

rab·bit (rab'it) *n., pl.* **-bits, -bit:** see PLURAL, II, D, 1 [ME. *rabette*] 1. a burrowing mammal that is usually smaller than the hare, produces unfurred young, and has soft fur, long ears, and a stubby tail 2. its fur 3. [Colloq.] a novice or poor performer at a game **—vi.** to hunt rabbits

rabbit fever *same as* TULAREMIA

rabbit punch *Boxing* a sharp blow to the back of the neck

rab·ble (rab''l) *n.* [< ?] a noisy, disorderly crowd; mob **—vt. -bled, -bling** to attack by a rabble; mob **—the rabble** the common people; the masses: a term of contempt

rab·ble-rous·er (-rouz'ər) *n.* a person who tries to arouse people to violent action by appeals to emotions, prejudices, etc.; demagogue **—rab'ble-rous'ing** *adj., n.*

Rab·e·lais·i·an (rab'ə lā'zhən, -zē ən) *adj.* 1. of or relating to François Rabelais (1495?-1553) or his writings 2. coarsely humorous **—n.** a student or admirer of Rabelais

rab·id (rab'id; *for 3 occas.* rä'bid) *adj.* [< L. < *rabere,* to rage] 1. violent; raging 2. fanatical or unreasonably zealous 3. of or having rabies **—ra·bid'i·ty** (rə bid'ə tē), **rab'id·ness** *n.* **—rab'id·ly** *adv.*

ra·bies (rā'bēz) *n.* [L., madness] an infectious virus disease of mammals, passed on to man by the bite of an infected animal: it causes choking, convulsions, etc.

R.A.C. 1. Royal Armoured Corps 2. Royal Automobile Club

rac·coon (ra koon') *n., pl.* **-coons, -coon':** see PLURAL, II, D, 1 [< Algonquian *ärakun,* lit., scratcher] 1. a small, tree-climbing, chiefly flesh-eating mammal of N America, active largely at night and having long, yellowish-grey fur and a long, black-ringed tail 2. its fur

race[1] (rās) *n.* [< ON. *rās,* a running] 1. a competition of speed in running, riding, etc. 2. [*pl.*] a series of such competitions for horses, cars, etc., on a regular course 3. any contest likened to a race [the *race* for the moon] 4. a steady onward movement 5. a) a swift current of water b) a channel for this, esp. one built to use the water in industry [a *millrace*] 6. [Aust.] a narrow passageway in a sheep yard where sheep are gathered for individual treatment **—vi. raced, rac'ing** 1. to take part in a race 2. to go or

move very fast or too fast **—vt.** 1. to compete with in a race 2. to enter or run (a horse, etc.) in a race 3. to make go very fast or too fast 4. to run (an engine) at high speed with the transmission system not engaged

race[2] (rās) *n.* [Fr. < It. *razza*] 1. any of the different varieties of mankind, mainly the Caucasoid, Mongoloid, and Negroid groups, distinguished by kind of hair, colour of skin, stature, etc.: now often replaced in scientific use by *ethnic stock* or *group* 2. any geographical, national, or tribal ethnic grouping 3. any group of people having the same ancestry or the same habits, ideas, etc. 4. a) a subspecies, or variety b) *same as* BREED (*n.* 1) **—the (human) race** mankind

race card a programme giving information about the horses or dogs that are due to race

race·course (-kôrs') *n.* a course prepared for racing

race·horse (-hôrs') *n.* a horse bred and trained for racing

ra·ceme (rā sēm', rə-) *n.* [L. *racemus,* cluster of grapes] a flower cluster with individual flowers growing on small stems at intervals along one central stem, as in the lupin **—rac·e·mose** (ras'ə mōs') *adj.*

race meeting a regularly organized fixture for racing horses, dogs, etc.

ra·ce·mic (rə sē'mik) *adj.* [< RACEME + -IC, orig. tartaric acid found in grape juice] *Chem.* 1. consisting of an optically inactive mixture of the dextrorotary and laevorotary forms of certain substances 2. designating a compound formed of such a mixture **—rac·e·mism** (ras'ə miz'm) *n.*

rac·er (rās'ər) *n.* 1. any person, animal, vehicle, etc. that takes part in races 2. any of several slim, swift, harmless snakes found in N America

RA-
CEME

race relations the relations between members of two or more human races who are aware of their physical differences, esp. within a single community

race riot violence and fighting in a community, brought on by racial hostility

race track a racecourse, esp. an oval one

race·way (rās'wā') *n.* 1. a narrow channel for water 2. [U.S.] a) a race track for harness racing b) a race track for drag races, racing stock cars, etc.

ra·chi·tis (rə kīt'əs, ra-) *n.* [ModL. < Gr. *rhachitis,* inflammation of the spine < *rhachis,* spine] *same as* RICKETS **—ra·chit'ic** (-kit'ik) *adj.*

Rach·man·ism (rak'mə niz'm) *n.* [< Perec *Rachman* (1920-62), Brit. property owner, born in Poland] the practice of charging high rents for slum property

ra·cial (rā'shəl) *adj.* 1. of a race, or ethnic group 2. of or between races **—ra'cial·ly** *adv.*

ra·cial·ism (-iz'm) *n.* 1. a doctrine or teaching, without scientific support, that claims to find racial differences in character, intelligence, etc. and that seeks to maintain the supposed superiority and purity of some one race 2. *same as* RACISM (sense 2) **—ra'cial·ist** *n., adj.*

rac·ism (rā'siz'm) *n.* 1. *same as* RACIALISM (sense 1) 2. the practice of racial discrimination, segregation, etc., based on racialism **—rac'ist** *n., adj.*

rack[1] (rak) *n.* [prob. < MDu. *rek < recken,* to stretch] 1. a framework, stand, etc. for holding things [clothes *rack*] 2. [Chiefly U.S.] *same as* FRAME (*n.* 15) 3. a device for lifting a motor car for repairs from below 4. a toothed bar that meshes with a cogwheel, etc. 5. formerly, a frame on which a victim was tortured by stretching his limbs out of place 6. any great torment 7. a wrenching or upheaval, as by a storm **—vt.** 1. to put in or on a rack 2. to torture on a rack 3. to torment or afflict 4. to oppress, as by demanding excessive rent **—on the rack** in a very painful situation **—rack one's brains** (or **memory,** etc.) to try very hard to think of something

rack[2] (rak) *n., vi.* [< ?] *same as* SINGLE-FOOT

rack[3] (rak) *n.* [var. of WRACK] destruction: now only in **go to rack and ruin,** to become ruined

rack[4] (rak) *n.* [prob. < Scand.] a broken mass of clouds blown by the wind

rack[5] (rak) *vt.* [< ME. *rakken* < Pr. *arracar* < *raca,* husks and stems of grapes] to draw off (cider, wine, etc.) from the dregs

rack and pinion (-'nd pin'yən) *adj.* designating a type of steering in motor cars with a track rod that can engage with a pinion attached to the steering column

rack·et¹ (rak'it) *n.* [prob. echoic] **1.** a noisy confusion; uproar **2.** *a)* an obtaining of money illegally, as by fraud *b)* [Colloq.] any dishonest scheme **3.** [Slang] *a)* an easy, profitable source of income *b)* any business, profession, etc. *—vi.* to make a racket, or uproar **—rack'et·y** *adj.*

rack·et² (rak'it) *n.* [MFr. *raquette* < ML. *rasceta* < Ar. *rāḥah*, palm of the hand] **1.** a light bat for tennis, etc., with a network of catgut, nylon, etc. in an oval or round frame attached to a handle **2.** [*pl.*, with *sing. v.*] the game of racquets

rack·et·eer (rak'ə tir') *n.* [see RACKET¹ & -EER] one who gets money illegally, as by fraud, blackmail, or, esp., extortion *—vi.* to get money thus **—rack'·et·eer'ing** *n.*

racket press a wooden frame used for keeping tennis, etc. rackets taut and in shape

RACKETS (A, squash; B, tennis; C, badminton)

rack railway a steep mountain railway having a middle rail fitted with a rack that engages a corresponding pinion on the locomotive to provide traction

rack-rent (rak'rent') *n.* [RACK¹ + RENT] an excessively high rent *—vt.* to exact rack-rent from **—rack'-rent'er** (-ər) *n.*

rac·on·teur (rak'on tur') *n.* [Fr. < *raconter*, to recount] a person skilled at telling stories or anecdotes

ra·coon (ra koon') *n., pl.* **-coons', -coon' :** see PLURAL, II, D, 1 same as RACCOON

rac·quet (rak'it) *n.* **1.** *same as* RACKET² **2.** [*pl.*, with *sing. v.*] a game similar to court tennis: see TENNIS

rac·y (rā'sē) *adj.* **rac'i·er, rac'i·est** [RACE² + -Y²] **1.** having the taste or quality required to be genuine [*racy* flavour] **2.** lively; spirited **3.** piquant; pungent **4.** indecent; risqué **—rac'i·ly** *adv.* **—rac'i·ness** *n.*

rad¹ (rad) *n.* [< *rad*(*iation*)] the unit of absorbed dose of ionizing radiation, equal to 100 ergs of energy per gramme of matter

rad² *the symbol for* radian

rad. 1. radical **2.** radius.

RADA (rā'da) Royal Academy of Dramatic Art

ra·dar (rā'där) *n.* [*ra*(*dio*) *d*(*etecting*) *a*(*nd*) *r*(*anging*)] a system or device for sending out radio waves in order to detect an object by the waves reflected back from the object and thus find out its direction, distance, height, or speed: used also in mapping, navigation, etc. **—ra'dar·man** (-mən) *n., pl.* **-men**

ra·dar·scope (rā'där skōp') *n.* an instrument that displays on a screen the reflected radio waves picked up by radar

radar trap a device using to detect motorists who exceed the speed limit

RADC Royal Army Dental Corps

rad·dle (rad''l) *vt.* [var. of *ruddle*, < *rud*, red ochre < ME. *rude*] **1.** to colour or mark with red ochre, esp. to mark sheep thus **2.** to paint (the face) with rouge, esp. heavily or coarsely **—rad'dled** *adj.*

ra·di·al (rā'dē əl) *adj.* [< ML.: see RADIUS] **1.** of or like a ray or rays; branching out in all directions from a common centre **2.** of or like a radius **3.** *Anat.* of or near the radius *—n.* a radial part **—ra'di·al·ly** *adv.*

radial (ply) tyre a motor car tyre with the ply cords extending to the beads almost at right angles to the centre line of the tread

ra·di·ant (rā'dē ənt) *adj.* [< L. prp. of *radiare:* see RADIATE] **1.** shining brightly **2.** filled with light **3.** showing joy, love, well-being, etc. **4.** issuing (from a source) in or as in rays *—n.* a source of heat or light rays **—ra'di·ance, ra'di·an·cy** *n.* **—ra'di·ant·ly** *adv.*

radiant energy energy travelling in waves; esp., electromagnetic radiation, as heat, light, X-rays, etc.

ra·di·ate (rā'dē āt') *vi.* **-at'ed, -at'ing** [< L. pp. of *radiare* < *radius:* see RADIUS] **1.** to send out rays of heat, light, etc. **2.** to spread out in rays **3.** to branch out in lines from a centre *—vt.* **1.** to send out (heat, light, etc.) in rays **2.** to give forth (happiness, love, etc.) *—adj.* having rays or raylike parts; radial **—ra'di·ate·ly** *adv.*

ra·di·a·tion (rā'dē ā'shən) *n.* **1.** a radiating; specif., the process in which radiant energy is sent out from atoms and molecules as they undergo internal change **2.** such radiant energy **3.** energetic nuclear particles, as alpha and beta particles, etc. **—ra'di·a'tion·al** *adj.* **—ra'di·a'tive** *adj.*

radiation sickness sickness produced by overexposure to radiation from X-rays, nuclear explosions, etc. and resulting in nausea, diarrhoea, bleeding, etc.

ra·di·a·tor (rā'dē āt'ər) *n.* anything that radiates; specif., *a)* a series of pipes with hot water or steam circulating in them so as to radiate heat into a room, etc. *b)* a device of tubes and fins, as in a motor vehicle, through which circulating water passes so as to take away the extra heat and thus cool the engine

rad·i·cal (rad'i k'l) *adj.* [< LL. < L. *radix* (gen. *radicis*), a root] **1.** *a)* of or from the root or source; fundamental; basic *b)* extreme; thorough **2.** *a)* favouring basic or extreme change, as in the social or economic structure *b)* [R-] designating or of any of various modern political parties, as in Europe, ranging from moderate to conservative *—n.* **1.** *a)* a basic part of something *b)* a fundamental **2.** *a)* a person having radical views *b)* [R-] a member of a Radical party **3.** *Chem.* a group of two or more atoms that acts as a single atom and goes through a reaction unchanged, or is replaced by a single atom **4.** *Math. a)* an expression showing that a root is to be extracted *b)* *same as* RADICAL SIGN **—rad'i·cal·ly** *adv.* **—rad'·i·cal·ness** *n.*

rad·i·cal·ism (-iz'm) *n.* **1.** the quality or state of being radical **2.** radical principles, methods, or practices

rad·i·cal·ize (-īz') *vt., vi.* **-ized', -iz'ing** to make or become politically radical **—rad'i·cal·i·za'tion** *n.*

radical sign *Math.* the sign (√ or √‾) used before a quantity to show that its root is to be extracted

rad·i·cand (rad'i kand') *n.* *Math.* a quantity from which a root is to be extracted, shown with a radical sign

rad·i·cle (rad'i k'l) *n.* [< L. dim. of *radix*, a root] *Bot.* the lower part of the axis of an embryo seedling

ra·di·i (rā'dē ī') *n. pl. of* RADIUS

ra·di·o (rā'dē ō') *n., pl.* **-os'** [contr. < RADIOTELEGRAPH] **1.** a way of communicating over a distance by changing sounds or signals into electromagnetic waves that are sent through space, without wires, to a receiving set, which changes them back into sounds or signals **2.** such a receiving set **3.** broadcasting by radio as an industry, entertainment, etc. *—adj.* **1.** of, using, used in, or sent by radio **2.** of electromagnetic wave frequencies from c.10 kilohertz to c. 300 000 megahertz *—vt., vi.* **-oed', -o'ing** to send (a message, etc.) or communicate with (a person, etc.) by radio

ra·di·o- [Fr. < L. *radius*, ray: see RADIUS] a *combining form meaning:* **1.** ray, raylike **2.** by radio **3.** by means of radiant energy [*radiotherapy*] **4.** radioactive [*radioisotope*]

ra·di·o·ac·tive (rā'dē ō ak'tiv) *adj.* giving off radiant energy in particles or rays by the disintegration of the atomic nuclei: said of such elements as radium and uranium **—ra'di·o·ac'tive·ly** *adv.* **—ra'di·o·ac·tiv'i·ty** (-ak tiv'ə tē) *n.*

radio astronomy astronomy dealing with radio waves in space in order to get data about certain regions in the universe

radio beacon a radio transmitter that gives off special signals to help ships or aircraft determine their positions or come in safely, as in a fog

ra·di·o·broad·cast (-brôd'käst') *n.* a broadcast by radio *—vt., vi.* **-cast'** or **-cast'ed, -cast'ing** to broadcast by radio **—ra'di·o·broad'cast'er** *n.*

radio cab a taxi fitted out with a radio to aid communication

ra·di·o·car·bon (-kär'bən) *n.* *same as* CARBON 14: see CARBON

ra·di·o·chem·is·try (-kem'is trē) *n.* the branch of chemistry dealing with radioactive phenomena **—ra'di·o·chem'i·cal** (-ik'l) *adj.*

radio frequency any frequency between normally audible sound waves and infrared light, from c.10 kilohertz to c. 1 000 000 megahertz

ra·di·o·gram (rā'dē ō gram') *n.* **1.** a single unit consisting of a radio and a gramophone **2.** a message sent by radio: also **ra'di·o·tel'e·gram 3.** *same as* RADIOGRAPH

ra·di·o·graph (-gräf') *n.* a picture made on a sensitized film or plate by X-rays **—ra'di·og'ra·pher** (-og'rə fər) *n.* **—ra'·di·o·graph'ic** *adj.* **—ra'di·o·graph'i·cal·ly** *adv.* **—ra'di·og'·ra·phy** *n.*

ra·di·o·i·so·tope (rā'dē ō ī'sə tōp') *n.* a natural or artificial radioactive isotope of a chemical element

ra·di·ol·o·gy (rā'dē ol'ə jē) *n.* [RADIO- + -LOGY] the science dealing with X-rays and other radiant energy, esp. as used in medicine and surgery **—ra'di·o·log'i·cal** (-ə loj'i k'l) *adj.* **—ra'di·o·log'i·cal·ly** *adv.* **—ra'di·ol'o·gist** *n.*

ra·di·om·e·ter (-om'ə tər) *n.* an instrument for measuring radiant energy **—ra'di·om'e·try** *n.*

ra·di·o·pho·to (rā'dē ō fōt'ō) *n., pl.* **-tos** a photograph or picture transmitted by radio: also **ra'di·o·pho'to·graph'**

ra·di·os·co·py (-os'kə pē) *n.* [RADIO- + -SCOPY] the direct examination of the inside structure of opaque objects by radiation, as by X-rays **—ra'di·o·scop'ic** (-ə skop'ik) *adj.*

ra·di·o·sonde (rā'dē ō sond') *n.* [Fr. < *radio* (cf. RADIO) + *sonde*, a sounding line] a compact package made up of a radio transmitter and meteorological instruments sent into the upper atmosphere, as by balloon, to record and radio back temperature, pressure, and humidity data

radio spectrum the complete range of frequencies of electromagnetic radiation useful in radio, from c.10 kilohertz to c. 300 000 megahertz

ra·di·o·tel·e·graph (rā'dē ō tel'ə graf') *n.* same as WIRELESS TELEGRAPHY: also **ra'di·o·te·leg'ra·phy** (-tə leg'rə fē) —*vt., vi.* to send (a message, etc.) by radiotelegraph —**ra'di·o·tel'- e·graph'ic** *adj.*

ra·di·o·tel·e·phone (-tel'ə fōn') *n.* the equipment needed at one station for two-way voice communication by radio: also **ra'di·o·phone'**—**ra'di·o·tel'e·phon'ic** (-fon'ik) *adj.* —**ra'- di·o·te·leph'o·ny** (-tə lef'ə nē) *n.*

radio telescope a radio antenna or array of antennas for use in radio astronomy

ra·di·o·ther·a·py (-ther'ə pē) *n.* the treatment of disease by X-rays or by rays from a radioactive substance

rad·ish (rad'ish) *n.* [OE. rædic < L. radix, a root] 1. an annual plant of the cabbage family, with an edible root 2. the pungent root, eaten raw as a relish or in a salad

ra·di·um (rā'dē əm) *n.* [ModL. < L. radius, a ray] a radioactive metallic chemical element, found in uranium minerals, which undergoes spontaneous atomic disintegration: see also RADIUM THERAPY: symbol, Ra; at. wt., 226.00; at. no., 88

radium therapy the treatment of cancer or other diseases by the use of radium

ra·di·us (rā'dē əs) *n., pl.* **-di·i** (-ī'), **-us·es** [L., a spoke (of a wheel), hence ray (of light)] 1. a raylike part, as a spoke of a wheel 2. a) a straight line from the centre to the periphery of a circle or sphere b) its length 3. a) the circular area or distance within the sweep of such a line [no house within a *radius* of five miles] b) the distance a ship or aircraft can go and still get back without refuelling 4. any limited extent, scope, etc. [within the *radius* of one's experience] 5. the shorter and thicker of the two bones of the forearm on the same side as the thumb

ra·dome (rā'dōm') *n.* [RA(DAR) + DOME] a domed housing for a radar antenna, esp. on aircraft

ra·don (rā'don) *n.* [RAD(IUM) + -ON] a radioactive gaseous chemical element formed in the atomic disintegration of radium: symbol, Rn; at. wt., 222.00; at. no., 86

RAF, R.A.F. Royal Air Force

raf·fi·a (raf'ē ə) *n.* [< Malagasy native name] 1. a palm tree of Madagascar, with large, pinnate leaves 2. fibre from its leaves, woven into baskets, hats, etc.

raff·ish (raf'ish) *adj.* [(RIFF)RAFF + -ISH] 1. disreputable, rakish, etc. 2. tawdry; vulgar; low —**raff'ish·ly** *adv.* —**raff'ish·ness** *n.*

raf·fle (raf'l) *n.* [MFr. rafle, dice game < OHG. raffel, a rake] a lottery in which a chance or chances to win a prize are bought —*vt.* **-fled, -fling** to offer as a prize in a raffle (often with *off*) —**raf'fler** *n.*

raf·fle (raf'l) *n.* [prob. < Fr. < MFr. < MHG. raffen, to snatch, scrape together] a jumble or tangle, esp. of ropes, canvas, etc. on a ship

raft (räft) *n.* [< ON. raptr, a log] 1. a flat structure of logs, boards, etc. fastened together and floated on water 2. an inflatable boat or pad, as of rubber, for floating on water —*vt.* to carry on a raft —*vi.* to travel, work, etc. on a raft —**rafts'man** (-mən) *n., pl.* **-men**

raft (räft) *n.* [< Dial. raff, rubbish] [U.S. Colloq.] a large number, collection, or quantity; lot

raft·er (räf'tər) *n.* [OE. ræfter] any of the beams that slope from the ridge of a roof to the eaves and serve to support the roof

RAFVR Royal Air Force Volunteer Reserve

rag (rag) *n.* [ult. < ON. rögg, tuft of hair] 1. a waste piece of cloth, esp. an old or torn one 2. a small cloth for dusting, washing, etc. 3. anything regarded as having as little value as a rag 4. [pl.] a) old, worn clothes b) any clothes: humorous term 5. [Slang] any newspaper regarded with contempt —*adj.* made of rags —**chew the rag** [Slang] to chat —**rags to riches** poverty to prosperity [it was a *rags to riches* story]

RAFTERS

rag (rag) *vt.* **ragged, rag'ging** [< ?] [Slang] 1. to tease 2. to scold 3. to play a practical joke or jokes on —*n.* 1. [Slang] an act or instance of ragging 2. an organized student procession of floats, etc., usually to raise money for charity

rag (rag) *n.* 1. *clipped form of* RAGTIME 2. a composition in ragtime —*vt.* **ragged, rag'ging** to play in ragtime

ra·ga (rä'gə) *n.* [Sans. rāga, lit., colour] any of various traditional arrangements of notes used in improvising by Hindu musicians

rag·a·muf·fin (rag'ə muf'in) *n.* [< ? ME. Ragamoffyn, name of a demon in *Piers Plowman*, a poem attributed to William Langland] a dirty, ragged person; esp., a poor, ragged child

rag-and-bone man a man who buys, collects, and sells discarded clothing, furniture, and other household articles

rag·bag (rag'bag') *n.* 1. a bag for rags 2. a collection of odds and ends

rag doll a child's toy made of cloth and usually stuffed with rags

rage (rāj) *n.* [< OFr. < LL. < L. rabies, madness] 1. furious, uncontrolled anger; esp., a brief spell of raving fury 2. violence or intensity, as of the wind 3. strong emotion, enthusiasm, or desire —*vi.* **raged, rag'ing** 1. to show violent anger in action or speech 2. to be violent, uncontrolled, etc. [a *raging* sea] 3. to spread unchecked, as a disease —**(all) the rage** anything thought of as a fashion uncontrolled, etc. [a *raging* sea] 3. to spread unchecked, as or craze

rag·ged (rag'id) *adj.* 1. shabby or torn from wear 2. wearing shabby or torn clothes 3. uneven; rough 4. shaggy; unkempt [ragged hair] 5. not finished; imperfect 6. harsh; strident —**run ragged** to make (someone) exhausted —**rag'ged·ly** *adv.* —**rag'ged·ness** *n.*

rag·ged·y (rag'i dē) *adj.* somewhat ragged, or tattered

rag·i, rag·gee (rag'ē) *n.* [Hind. rāgī < Sans. rāgin, red] a cereal grass of Africa and India whose grain is a staple food

rag·lan (rag'lən) *n.* [after Lord Raglan (1788-1855), Brit. general] a loose overcoat without shoulder seams, each sleeve (**raglan sleeve**) continuing in one piece to the collar

rag·man (rag'man') *n., pl.* **-men'** a man who collects, buys, and sells rags, old paper, etc.

ra·gout (ra gōō') *n.* [< Fr. < ragoûter, to revive the appetite of] a highly seasoned stew of meat and vegetables —*vt.* **-gouted'** (-gōōd'), **-gout'ing** (-gōō'iŋ) to make into a ragout

rag·pick·er (rag'pik'ər) *n.* [U.S.] a ragman

rag·tag (and bobtail) (rag'tag') [RAG¹ + TAG] the lowest classes; the rabble: term of contempt

rag·time (rag'tīm') *n.* [prob. < ragged time] 1. a type of strongly syncopated music in fast, even time, popular 1890-1915 originating in U.S. 2. its rhythm

rag trade [Colloq.] the clothing business, esp. the manufacture and sale of clothes

rag·weed (rag'wēd') *n.* [from the tattered appearance of the leaves] 1. same as GROUNDSEL 2. any of a genus of chiefly N American plants of the composite family, having tassellike, greenish flowers with a pollen that is a major cause of hay fever

rag·wort (-wurt') *n.* [see prec.] a common wild flower with bright-yellow flowers on a tall, erect stem

rah (rä) *interj.* [U.S.] hurrah: used as a cheer

raid (rād) *n.* [< ROAD, in obs. sense "a riding"] 1. a sudden, hostile attack, as by troops, aircraft, bandits, etc. 2. any sudden invasion of some place by police, to discover violations of the law 3. an attempt by speculators to make stock market prices fall —*vt., vi.* to make a raid (on) —**raid'er** *n.*

rail (rāl) *n.* [< OFr. < L. regula, a rule] 1. a bar of wood, metal, etc. placed horizontally between posts as a barrier or support 2. a fence or railing 3. any of a series of parallel metal bars laid on sleepers, etc. to make a track for trains, etc. 4. a railway as a means of transportation [travel by *rail*] 5. the rim of a billiard table 6. a narrow wooden piece at the top of a ship's bulwarks —*vt.* to supply with rails or a railing; fence —**go off the rails** 1. to go off the proper course 2. to become insane 3. to start to behave in a manner considered to be unconventional, improper, etc.

rail (rāl) *vi.* [< MFr. railler < Pr., ult. < LL. ragere, to bellow] to complain violently (with *against* or *at*) —**rail'- er** *n.*

rail (rāl) *n., pl.* **rails, rail:** see PLURAL, II, D, 1 [< MFr. < raaler, to screech] any of a number of small, cranelike wading birds living in marshes and having short wings and tail, long toes, and a harsh cry

rail·ing (rāl'iŋ) *n.* 1. material for rails 2. rails collectively 3. a fence or balustrade

rail·ler·y (rāl'ər ē) *n., pl.* **-ler·ies** [Fr. raillerie: see RAIL² & -ERY] 1. light ridicule; banter 2. a teasing act or remark

rail·head (rāl'hed') *n.* 1. the furthest point to which rails have been laid in a railway 2. *Mil.* the point on a railway in a theatre of operations at which supplies are unloaded and distributed

rail·way (-wā') *n.* 1. a permanent way laid with parallel steel rails along which engines draw carriages in a train 2. a complete system of such tracks, including land, rolling stock, etc. 3. the company owning such a system

railway crossing the point at which a railway line crosses a road, usually equipped with barriers, lights, etc.

rai·ment (rā'mənt) *n.* [ME. rayment < arayment: see ARRAY & -MENT] [Archaic] clothing; wearing apparel

rain (rān) *n.* [OE. *regn*] 1. water falling in drops condensed from the moisture in the atmosphere 2. the falling of such drops; shower 3. *a)* rainy weather *b)* [*pl.*] the rainy season (preceded by *the*) 4. a rapid falling or propulsion of many small objects [a *rain* of ashes] —*vi.* 1. to fall: said of rain [it is *raining*] 2. to fall like rain 3. to cause rain to fall —*vt.* 1. to pour down (rain or something likened to rain) 2. to give in large quantities —**rain off** to cause (an event) to be postponed or cancelled because of rain —**rain′less** *adj.*

rain·bow (-bō′) *n.* an arc containing the colours of the spectrum in bands, formed in the sky by the refraction, reflection, and dispersion of the sun's rays in falling rain or in mist —*adj.* of many colours

rain check [U.S.] 1. the stub of a ticket to a baseball game, etc., entitling the holder to be admitted at a future date if the original event is rained off 2. a bid for, or an offer of, a future invitation in place of one turned down

rain·coat (rān′kōt′) *n.* a waterproof or water-repellent coat for giving protection from rain

rain·drop (-drop′) *n.* a single drop of rain

rain·fall (-fôl′) *n.* 1. a falling of rain; shower 2. the amount of water falling as rain, snow, etc. over a given area in a given time: measured in inches or centimetres of depth in an instrument (**rain gauge**) into which the water falls

rain forest a dense, evergreen forest in a tropical region having abundant rainfall throughout the year

rain·proof (rān′prōōf′) *adj.* not letting rain through —*vt.* to make rainproof

rain shadow a region of little rainfall on the lee slopes of mountains whose windward slopes receive the rain

rain·storm (-stôrm′) *n.* a storm with a heavy rain

rain·wa·ter (-wôt′ər) *n.* water that falls or has fallen as rain and is soft and fairly free of mineral matter

rain·wear (-wer′) *n.* rainproof clothing

rain·y (rā′nē) *adj.* **rain′i·er, rain′i·est** 1. that has rain or much rain [the *rainy* season] 2. wet with rain 3. bringing rain —**rain′i·ness** *n.*

rainy day a possible future time of difficulty or need

raise (rāz) *vt.* **raised, rais′ing** [< ON. *reisa*] 1. *a)* to make rise; lift *b)* to put upright 2. to construct (a building, etc.) 3. to stir up; arouse; incite [to *raise* a revolt] 4. to increase in size, value, amount, etc. [to *raise* prices] 5. to increase in degree, intensity, etc. [to *raise* one's voice] 6. to improve the position or rank of [to *raise* oneself from poverty] 7. to cause to arise, appear, or come; esp., to bring back as from death [to *raise* the dead] 8. to produce; provoke [the joke *raised* a laugh] 9. to bring forward for consideration [to *raise* a question] 10. to collect or procure (an army, money, etc.) 11. to utter (a cry, shout, etc.) 12. to bring to an end [to *raise* a siege] 13. to leaven (bread, etc.) 14. *a)* to make (vegetables, etc.) grow *b)* to breed (cattle, etc.) *c)* [Chiefly U.S.] to bring up (children) 15. to contact by radio 16. to make (a blister) form 17. to make (a nap on cloth) with teasels, etc. 18. *Bridge* to increase (one's partner's bid in a suit) 19. *Naut.* to come within sight of (land, etc.) 20. *Poker* to bet more than (the highest preceding bet or bettor) —*vi.* 1. [Dial.] to rise or arise 2. *Poker* to increase the bet —*n.* 1. a raising 2. [U.S.] a rise (in wages or salary) —**raise Cain** (or **the devil, hell, a rumpus, the roof,** etc.) [Slang] to create a disturbance; cause trouble —**raise the wind** obtain ready money

raised (rāzd) *adj.* 1. made in low relief; embossed 2. having a napped surface 3. leavened with yeast

rai·sin (rā′z'n) *n.* [< OFr. < L. *racemus*, cluster of grapes] a sweet, dried grape, usually seedless

rai·son d'être (rā′zōn det′, det′rə; *Fr.* re zōn de′tr′) [Fr.] reason for being; justification for existence

raj (räj) *n.* [see ff.] in India, rule; sovereignty; dominion

ra·jah, ra·ja (rä′jə) *n.* [< Hindi < Sans. *rājan* < *rāj*, to rule] 1. formerly, a prince or chief in India 2. esp. formerly, a Malay chief

Raj·put (räj′pōōt) *n.* [Hindi *rājpūt*, prince] a member of a Hindu people, the former ruling caste of northern India: also sp. **Raj′poot**

rake¹ (rāk) *n.* [OE. *raca*] a long-handled tool with teeth or prongs at one end, used for gathering loose grass, leaves, etc. —*vt.* **raked, rak′ing** 1. *a)* to gather with or as with a rake *b)* to make (a lawn, etc.) tidy with a rake 2. to gather with great care 3. to scratch or smooth as with a rake 4. to search through carefully 5. to direct gunfire along (a line of troops, etc.): often used figuratively —*vi.* 1. to use a rake 2. to search as if with a rake 3. to scrape or sweep (with *over, across,* etc.) —**rake in** to gather fast a great deal of —**rake up** to uncover facts or gossip about

rake² (rāk) *n.* [contr. of *rakeshell*, prob. < ME. *rakel*, rash] a man who leads a wild, dissolute life: also **rake′hell** (-hel′)

rake³ (rāk) *vi., vt.* **raked, rak′ing** [? akin to Sw. *raka,* to project] to be or make slightly inclined, as a ship's masts; slant —*n.* a slanting or inclining

rake-off (rāk′ôf) *n.* [Slang] a commission, rebate, or share, esp. one gained in a shady deal

rak·ish¹ (rā′kish) *adj.* [< RAKE³ + -ISH] 1. having a trim, neat appearance suggesting speed: said of a ship 2. dashing and gay; jaunty —**rak′ish·ly** *adv.* —**rak′ish·ness** *n.*

rak·ish² (rā′kish) *adj.* like a rake; wild and dissolute —**rak′ish·ly** *adv.* —**rak′ish·ness** *n.*

ral·len·tan·do (ral′ən tan′dō) *adj., adv.* [It., prp. of *rallentare,* to slow down] *Music* gradually slower: abbrev. **rall.**

ral·ly¹ (ral′ē) *vt.* **-lied, -ly·ing** [< Fr. < OFr. < *re-,* again + *alier,* to join: see ALLY] 1. to gather together (retreating troops) and restore to a state of order 2. to bring (persons) together for a common purpose 3. to revive (one's spirits, etc.) —*vi.* 1. to return to a state of order: said esp. of retreating troops 2. to come together for a common purpose 3. to come in order to help [to *rally* to a friend] 4. to revive; recover [to *rally* from a fever] 5. *Commerce* to rise in price after having fallen: said of stocks, etc. 6. *Sports* to come from behind in scoring 7. *Tennis,* etc. to take part in a rally —*n., pl.* **-lies** 1. a rallying or being rallied; specif., a mass meeting 2. an organized run, esp. of sports cars, over a course, designed to test driving skills 3. *Tennis,* etc. an exchange of several strokes before the point is won —**ral′li·er** *n.*

ral·ly² (ral′ē) *vt., vi.* **-lied, -ly·ing** [Fr. *rallier,* to RAIL²] to tease or mock playfully; banter

ram (ram) *n.* [OE. *ramm*] 1. a male sheep 2. *same as* BATTERING RAM 3. *a)* formerly, a sharp projection at a prow, for piercing enemy vessels *b)* a ship with this 4. *same as* HYDRAULIC RAM 5. the striking part of a pile driver 6. the plunger of a force pump —[R-] Aries —*vt.* **rammed, ram′ming** 1. to strike against with great force 2. to force into place 3. to force acceptance of (an idea, legislative bill, etc.) 4. to stuff or cram (*with* something) —*vi.* 1. to strike with force; crash (*into* someone or something) 2. to move rapidly —**ram′mer** *n.*

R.A.M. Royal Academy of Music

Ra·man effect (rä′mən) [after Sir C. *Raman* (1888-1970), Ind. physicist] the change in wavelength of light that is scattered by electrons within a material: used in spectroscopy to study the properties of molecules

Ra·ma·ya·na (rä mä′yə nə) one of the two great epics of India, written in Sanskrit after the Mahabharata

ram·ble (ram′b'l) *vi.* **-bled, -bling** [< ME. *romblen,* freq. of *romen,* to roam] 1. to roam about; esp., to stroll about idly 2. to talk or write aimlessly, without sticking to any point 3. to spread in all directions, as a vine —*vt.* to roam through —*n.* a rambling, esp. a stroll

ram·bler (ram′blər) *n.* 1. a person or thing that rambles 2. any of certain climbing roses

ram·bunc·tious (ram buŋk′shəs) *adj.* [altered < *robustious* < *robust*] [U.S.] wild, boisterous, unruly, etc. —**rambunc′tious·ly** *adv.* —**ram·bunc′tious·ness** *n.*

R.A.M.C. Royal Army Medical Corps

ram·e·kin, ram·e·quin (ram′ə kin) *n.* [Fr. *ramequin* < MDu. *rammeken,* cheese dish] 1. a food mixture, specif. of bread crumbs, cheese, and eggs, baked in individual baking dishes 2. a baking dish of this kind

ram·i·fi·ca·tion (ram′ə fi kā′shən) *n.* 1. a ramifying or being ramified 2. *a)* a branch or offshoot *b)* a derived effect, consequence, or result

ram·i·fy (ram′ə fī′) *vt., vi.* **-fied′, -fy′ing** [< Fr. < ML. < L. *ramus,* a branch + *facere,* to make] to divide or spread out into branches or branchlike divisions

ram·jet (engine) (ram′jet′) a jet engine in which the air for burning the fuel is compressed by being rammed into the inlet by the aircraft's velocity

ra·mose (rä′mōs, rə mōs′) *adj.* [< L. < *ramus,* a branch] 1. bearing many branches 2. branching —**ra′mose·ly** *adv.*

ra·mous (rä′məs) *adj.* 1. *same as* RAMOSE 2. branchlike

ramp¹ (ramp) *n.* [Fr. *rampe* < OFr.: see ff.] 1. a sloping walk, road, plank, etc. joining different levels 2. a wheeled staircase rolled up to an aircraft for use in getting on or off

ramp² (ramp) *vi.* [OFr. *ramper,* to climb] 1. to rear up on the hind legs; specif., *Heraldry* to be shown rampant 2. to rampage or rage —*n.* a ramping

ramp³ (ramp) *n.* [< ?] [Slang] a swindle —*vt., vi.* [Slang] to extort money by threats of violence —**ramp′er** *n.*

ram·page (ram pāj′; *also, and for n. always,* ram′pāj) *vi.* **-paged′, -pag′ing** [prob. < RAMP²] to rush violently or wildly about; rage —*n.* a rampaging: chiefly in **on the** (or **a**) **rampage** —**ram·pa′geous** *adj.* —**ram·pag′er** *n.*

ramp·ant (ram′pənt) *adj.* [< OFr.: see RAMP²] 1. growing or spreading unchecked; rife 2. violent and uncontrollable 3. standing up on the hind legs; specif., *Heraldry* shown so in profile, one forepaw above the other [a lion *rampant*] —**ramp′an·cy** *n.* —**ramp′ant·ly** *adv.*

ram·part (ram′pärt, -pərt) *n.* [Fr. < *re-,* again + *emparer* < Pr. *amparer,* to fortify < L. *ante,* before + *parare,* to prepare] 1. a defensive embankment round a castle, fort, etc., with a parapet at the top 2. any defence or bulwark

ram·rod (ram′rod′) *n.* a rod for ramming down the charge in a gun loaded through the muzzle

ram·shack·le (ram'shak''l) *adj.* [< freq. of RANSACK] loose and rickety; likely to fall to pieces

ran (ran) *pt. of* RUN

RAN, R.A.N. Royal Australian Navy

ranch (ränch) *n.* [< Sp. *rancho,* small farm] 1. [Chiefly U.S.] a large farm, esp. in western states, for raising many cattle, horses, or sheep 2. any large farm for raising a particular crop or livestock [a mink *ranch*] 3. *same as* RANCH HOUSE —*vi.* to work on or manage a ranch —**ranch'-er** *n.* —**ranch'man** (-mən) *n., pl.* -**men**

ranch house the owner's residence on a ranch

ran·cid (ran'sid) *adj.* [< L. < *rancere,* to be rank] having the bad smell or taste of spoiled fats or oils —**ran·cid'i·ty** (-sid'ə tē), **ran'cid·ness** *n.* —**ran'cid·ly** *adv.*

ran·cour (raŋ'kər) *n.* [OFr. < LL. < L. *rancere,* to be rank] a continuing and bitter hate or ill will; deep spite: also, U.S. sp., **ran'cor** —**ran'cor·ous** *adj.* —**ran'cor·ous·ly** *adv.*

rand[1] (rand, ränd) *n., pl.* **rand** [Afrik., orig., shield] 1. *see* MONETARY UNITS, table (Lesotho, South Africa) 2. [S.Afr.] high land above a river valley

rand[2] (rand) *n.* [OE. akin to OHG *rant,* edging] 1. in shoemaking, the leather strip put in the heel of a shoe before the lifts are put in 2. *a)* a strip or margin *b)* selvage

R and A *Golf* Royal and Ancient (Golf Club, St. Andrews)

R & B, r & b rhythm and blues

R & D, R. and D. research and development

ran·dom (ran'dəm) *n.* [< OFr. *randon,* violence, speed < *randir,* to run violently] haphazard movement: now only in **at random,** without careful choice, aim, plan, etc.; haphazardly —*adj.* 1. made, done, etc. in an aimless or haphazard way 2. not uniform 3. *Statistics* with each in a set or group having an equal opportunity of occurring or of occurring with a particular frequency —**ran'dom·ly** *adv.* —**ran'dom·ness** *n.*

ran·dom·ize (-īz') *vt.* **-ized', -iz'ing** to pick at random so as to get an unbiased result, often using a table of random numbers —**ran'dom·i·za'tion** *n.*

ran·dy (ran'dē) *adj.* **-di·er, -di·est** [prob. < *rand,* dial. var. of RANT + -Y[2]] sexually aroused; lustful —**ran'di·ness** *n.*

ra·nee (rä'nē) *n. alt. sp. of* RANI

rang (raŋ) *pt. of* RING[1]

rang·a·ti·ra (raŋ gə tē'rə) *n.* [Maori] a Maori chieftain: often extended to anyone of noble birth

range (rānj) *vt.* **ranged, rang'ing** [< OFr. var. of *rengier* < *renc,* a row] 1. to put in a certain order, esp. in a row or rows 2. to classify 3. to place with others in a cause, party, etc. [to *range* oneself with the rebels] 4. to aim (a gun, telescope, etc.) properly 5. to roam over or through 6. to move along parallel to [*ranging* the coastline] —*vi.* 1. to extend in a given direction [hills *ranging* south] 2. to wander about; roam 3. to vary between stated limits [ages *ranging* from 1 to 7] 4. *Biol., Zool.* to be native to a specified region —*n.* 1. a row, line, or series; rank 2. a class, kind, or order 3. a chain or single system of mountains 4. *a)* the firing distance, either maximum or to a target, of a weapon *b)* the flight path of a missile or rocket 5. the farthest distance a plane, etc. can go without refuelling 6. *a)* a place for shooting practice *b)* a place for testing rockets in flight 7. the full extent over which something moves or is heard, seen, effective, etc.; scope 8. the full extent of pitch, from highest to lowest tones, of a voice, instrument, etc. 9. [Chiefly U.S.] a large, open area of land for grazing livestock 10. the limits within which there are changes or differences in amount, degree, etc. [a wide *range* in price] 11. a cooking unit typically with an oven and surface heating units usually heated by solid fuel 12. *Biol., Zool.* the region to which a plant or animal is native —*adj.* of a range (sense 9)

range finder any of various instruments to determine the distance of a target or object from a gun, camera, etc.

rang·er (rān'jər) *n.* 1. one who ranges; roamer 2. [*often* R-] [Chiefly U.S.] a commando 3. *a)* in Britain, the chief official of a royal park or forest *b)* in the U.S., a warden patrolling government forests 4. [R-] a member of the senior branch of the Girl Guides

rang·y (rān'jē) *adj.* **rang'i·er, rang'i·est** 1. ranging about 2. long-limbed and slender 3. having range —**rang'i·ness** *n.*

ra·ni (rä'nē) *n.* [< Hindi < Sans. fem. of *rājan:* see RAJAH] the wife of a rajah

rank[1] (raŋk) *n.* [< MFr. < OFr. *renc*] 1. a row, line, or series; specif., a set of organ pipes of the same kind 2. an orderly arrangement 3. a social class [people from all *ranks* of life] 4. a high position in society [a man of *rank*] 5. an official grade [the *rank* of captain] 6. a relative position as measured by quality, etc. [a poet of the first *rank*] 7. a row of soldiers, etc., side by side 8. [*pl.*] all those in an organization, as the army, who are not officers or leaders [to rise from the *ranks*]: also **rank and file** —*vt.* 1. to place in a rank or ranks 2. to assign a relative position to 3. [U.S.] to outrank —*vi.* to hold a certain position [to *rank* third] —**pull (one's) rank** [Colloq.] to use one's higher rank to get others to obey, etc.

rank[2] (raŋk) *adj.* [OE. *ranc,* strong] 1. growing vigorously and coarsely; too luxuriant [*rank* grass] 2. producing a luxuriant crop, often to excess 3. very bad in smell or taste 4. coarse; indecent 5. utter; extreme [*rank* injustice] —**rank'ly** *adv.* —**rank'ness** *n.*

ran·kle (raŋ'k'l) *vi., vt.* **-kled, -kling** [< OFr. < *draoncle* < ML. *dracunculus,* a fester < L. dim. of *draco,* dragon] 1. orig., to fester 2. to cause or fill with long-lasting rancour, resentment, etc.

ran·sack (ran'sak) *vt.* [< ON. < *rann,* a house + *sækja,* search] 1. to search through every part of 2. to search through for plunder; pillage —**ran'sack·er** *n.*

ran·som (ran'səm) *n.* [< OFr. *raençon* < L. *redemptio,* REDEMPTION] 1. the securing of the release of a captive or of seized property by paying money or meeting other demands 2. the price so paid or demanded —*vt.* to get (a captive, etc.) released by paying the demanded price —**ran'som·er** *n.*

rant (rant) *vi., vt.* [< obs. Du. *ranten,* to rave] to talk or say in a loud, wild, extravagant way; declaim violently; rave —*n.* ranting talk —**rant'er** *n.* —**rant'ing·ly** *adv.*

R.A.O.C. Royal Army Ordnance Corps

rap[1] (rap) *vt.* **rapped, rap'ping** [prob. echoic] 1. to strike quickly and sharply; tap 2. [Colloq.] to criticize sharply —*vi.* 1. to knock quickly and sharply 2. [Chiefly U.S. Slang] to talk; chat —*n.* 1. a quick, sharp knock; tap 2. [Chiefly U.S. Slang] a talking; chat 3. [Slang] blame or punishment; specif., a judicial sentence, as to prison: usually in **beat** (escape) or **take** (receive) **the rap** —**rap out** to utter sharply —**rap'per** *n.*

rap[2] (rap) *n.* [< ?] [Colloq.] the least bit: in **not care** (or **give**) **a rap,** not care anything at all

ra·pa·cious (rə pā'shəs) *adj.* [< L. *rapax* (gen. *rapacis*) < *rapere,* to seize] 1. taking by force; plundering 2. greedy; voracious 3. living on captured prey; predatory —**ra·pa'cious·ly** *adv.* —**ra·pac·i·ty** (rə pas'ə tē), **ra·pa'cious·ness** *n.*

R.A.P.C. Royal Army Pay Corps

rape[1] (rāp) *n.* [ME. < L. *rapere,* to seize] 1. *a)* the crime of having sexual intercourse with a woman or girl forcibly and without her consent, or with a girl below the age of consent *b)* any sexual assault upon a person 2. [Now Rare] a seizing and carrying away by force 3. any violent or outrageous assault —*vt., vi.* **raped, rap'ing** to commit rape (on) —**rap'ist** *n.*

rape[2] (rāp) *n.* [L. *rapa, rapum,* turnip] an annual plant of the cabbage family, with seed (**rape'seed'**) yielding an oil (**rape oil, rapeseed oil**) and with leaves used for fodder

rape[3] (rāp) *n.* [Fr. *râpe* < ML. *raspa,* ult. < OHG *raspon,* to scrape together] the crushed pulp of grapes after the juice has been extracted

rape[4] (rāp) *n.* [< ?] a former administrative district of Sussex

rape cake a cattle cake made from rape seed

rap·id (rap'id) *adj.* [L. *rapidus* < *rapere,* to rush] moving, occurring, or acting with speed; swift; fast; quick —*n.* [*usually pl.*] a part of a river where the current is swift, as because of a narrowing of the river bed —**ra·pid·i·ty** (rə pid'ə tē), **rap'id·ness** *n.* —**rap'id·ly** *adv.*

rap·id-fire (-fīr') *adj.* 1. firing shots in rapid succession: said of guns 2. done, carried on, etc. in a swift, sharp way

rapid transit [U.S.] a system of rapid public transport in an urban area

ra·pi·er (rā'pē ər, rāp'yər) *n.* [Fr. *rapière*] 1. orig., a slender, two-edged sword with a large cup hilt 2. later, a light, sharp-pointed sword used only for thrusting

rap·ine (rap'in, īn) *n.* [OFr. < L. *rapina* < *rapere,* to seize] the act of seizing and carrying off by force others' property; plunder; pillage

rap·pa·ree (rap'ə rē') *n.* [Ir. *rapaire,* pikeman] 1. formerly, an Irish freebooting soldier 2. a plunderer or robber

rap·pel (ra pel', rə-) *n.* [Fr., lit., a recall] a descent down a steep cliff by a mountain climber using a double rope secured above —*vi.* **-pelled', -pel'ling** to make such a descent

rap·pen (rap'ən) *n., pl.* **-pen** [G. < *Rappe,* raven: after the eagle on an earlier Alsatian coin] *see* MONETARY UNITS, table (Liechtenstein)

rap·port (ra pôr', -pôrt') *n.* [Fr. < OFr. < *re-,* again + *aporter* < L. < *ad-,* to + *portare,* to carry] relationship, esp. of a sympathetic kind; agreement; harmony

rap·proche·ment (ra prosh'män; *Fr.* rä prôsh män') *n.* [Fr.] an establishing or restoring of friendly relations

rap·scal·lion (rap skal'yən) *n.* [< earlier *rascallion,* extension of RASCAL] a rascal; rogue

rapt (rapt) *adj.* [< L. pp. of *rapere,* to seize] 1. carried away with joy, love, etc.; full of or showing rapture 2. absorbed (*in* meditation, study, etc.)

rap·to·ri·al (rap tôr'ē əl) *adj.* [< L. < pp. of *rapere,* to seize] 1. predatory; specif., of or belonging to a group of birds of prey with a strong notched beak and sharp talons, as the eagle 2. adapted for seizing prey [*raptorial* claws]

rap·ture (rap'chər) *n.* [RAPT + -URE] 1. the state of being carried away with joy, love, etc.; ecstasy **2.** an expression of great joy, pleasure, etc. —**rap'tur·ous** *adj.* —**rap'·tur·ous·ly** *adv.*

ra·ra a·vis (rer'ə ā'vis) *pl.* **ra·rae a·ves** (rer'ē ā'vēz) [L., lit., strange bird] an unusual or extraordinary person or thing

rare[1] (rer) *adj.* **rar'er, rar'est** [MFr. < L. *rarus*] **1.** not often seen, done, found, etc.; uncommon **2.** unusually good; excellent [a *rare* teacher] **3.** not dense; thin [*rare* atmosphere] —**rare'ness** *n.*

rare[2] (rer) *adj.* **rar'er, rar'est** [OE. *hrere*] not fully cooked; partly raw: said esp. of meat —**rare'ness** *n.*

rare[3] (rer) *vi.* **rared, rar'ing** [Colloq.] to be eager, enthusiastic, etc.: used in prp. [*raring* to go]

rare·bit (rer'bit) *n.* *same as* WELSH RABBIT

rare earth 1. any of certain similar basic oxides; specif., any of the oxides of the rare-earth metals **2.** any of the rare-earth metals

rare-earth metals (or **elements**) (rer'urth') a group of rare metallic chemical elements with consecutive atomic numbers of 57 to 71 inclusive

ra·ree show (rer'ē) [< pronun. (by Savoyard showmen) of *rare show*] **1.** a portable peep show **2.** any street show

rar·e·fy (rer'ə fī') *vt., vi.* **-fied', -fy'ing** [< MFr. < L. < *rarus*, rare + *facere*, to make] **1.** to make or become thin, or less dense **2.** to make or become more refined, subtle, or lofty —**rar'e·fac'tion** (-fak'shən) *n.*

rare·ly (rer'lē) *adv.* **1.** not often; seldom **2.** beautifully, excellently, etc. **3.** uncommonly; unusually

rar·i·ty (rer'ə tē) *n.* **1.** a being rare; specif., *a)* uncommonness; scarcity *b)* excellence *c)* lack of density **2.** *pl.* **-ties** a rare or uncommon thing

ras·cal (räs'k'l) *n.* [OFr. *rascaille*, scrapings, ult. < L. pp. of *radere*, to scrape] a scoundrel; rogue; scamp: often used playfully, as of a mischievous child

ras·cal·i·ty (räs kal'ə tē) *n.* **1.** the character or behaviour of a rascal **2.** *pl.* **-ties** a low, mean, or dishonest act

ras·cal·ly (räs'k'l ē) *adj.* of or like a rascal; base; dishonest; mean —*adv.* in a rascally way

rase (rāz) *vt.* **rased, ras'ing** *alt. sp. of* RAZE

rash[1] (rash) *adj.* [ME. *rasch*] too hasty and careless; reckless —**rash'ly** *adv.* —**rash'ness** *n.*

rash[2] (rash) *n.* [MFr. *rasche*] **1.** a breaking out of red spots on the skin **2.** a sudden appearance of a large number [a *rash* of complaints]

rash·er (rash'ər) *n.* [< ? obs. *rash*, to cut] a thin slice of bacon or, rarely, ham, for frying or grilling

rasp (räsp) *vt.* [< OFr. < OHG. *raspon*, to scrape together] **1.** to scrape or rub as with a file **2.** to utter in a rough, grating tone **3.** to grate upon; irritate —*vi.* **1.** to scrape; grate **2.** to make a rough, grating sound —*n.* **1.** a type of rough file with sharp, projecting points **2.** a rough, grating sound —**rasp'er** *n.* —**rasp'ing·ly** *adv.*

rasp·ber·ry (räz'ber ē) *n., pl.* **-ries** [earlier *raspis berry* < *raspis*, raspberry] **1.** the small, juicy, edible fruit of various brambles of the rose family: it is a cluster of usually red drupelets **2.** the bramble bearing this **3.** [Slang] a jeering sound made by blowing out so as to vibrate the tongue between the lips

raspberry vinegar a cordial-like syrup made from vinegar and raspberries

rasp·y (räs'pē) *adj.* **rasp'i·er, rasp'i·est 1.** rasping; grating **2.** easily irritated —**rasp'i·ness** *n.*

Ras·ta·far·i·an (ras'tə fer'ē ən) *n.* a member of a Jamaican cult that regards the former emperor of Ethiopia, Haile Selasse, as spiritual leader

rat (rat) *n.* [OE. *ræt*] **1.** *a)* any of numerous long-tailed rodents resembling, but larger than, the mouse, very destructive, and carriers of disease *b)* any of various ratlike rodents **2.** [Slang] a treacherous, contemptible person; informer, traitor, etc. —*vi.* **rat'ted, rat'ting 1.** to hunt rats **2.** [Slang] *a)* to desert or betray a cause, movement, etc. *b)* to act as an informer —**rats!** [Slang] an exclamation of disgust, disappointment, etc. —**smell a rat** to suspect a trick, plot, etc.

ra·ta (rä'tə) *n.* [Maori] a New Zealand hardwood tree

rat·a·ble (rāt'ə b'l) *adj.* **1.** that can be rated, or estimated, etc. **2.** figured at a certain rate; proportional **3.** liable to payment of rates Also *sp.* **rate'a·ble** —**rat'a·bly, rate'a·bly** *adv.*

rat·a·fi·a (rat'ə fē'ə) *n.* [Fr., prob. of Creole origin] **1.** a cordial flavoured with almond or fruit kernels **2.** a macaroon: in full **ratafia biscuit**

ra·tan (ra tan') *n.* *alt. sp. of* RATTAN

rat-a-tat (rat'ə tat') *n.* [echoic] a series of sharp, quick rapping sounds: also **rat'-a-tat'-tat'**

rat·bag (rat'bag') *n.* [RAT + BAG] [Chiefly Aust. Slang] a contemptible person —**rat·bag'ger·y** *n.*

rat·catch·er (-kach'ər) *n.* someone who catches or kills rats

ratch·et (rach'it) *n.* [< Fr. < It. *rocchetto*, dim. of *rocca*, distaff] **1.** a toothed wheel (in full, **ratchet wheel**) or bar whose teeth slope in one direction so as to catch and hold a pawl, which thus prevents backward movement **2.** such a pawl **3.** such a wheel (or bar) and pawl as a unit

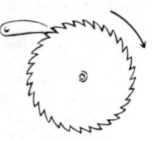

RATCHET WHEEL

rate[1] (rāt) *n.* [OFr. < L. *rata* (*pars*), reckoned (part) < pp. of *reri*, to reckon] **1.** the amount, degree, etc. of anything in relation to units of something else [the *rate* of pay per month] **2.** a fixed ratio; proportion [the *rate* of exchange] **3.** a price or value; specif., the cost per unit of some commodity, service, etc. **4.** speed of movement or action **5.** a class or rank [of the first *rate*] **6.** [often *pl.*] a tax on property levied by a local authority —*vt.* **rat'ed, rat'ing 1.** to estimate the value, capacity, skill, etc. of; appraise **2.** to assess the value of property for taxation purposes **3.** to put into a particular class or rank **4.** to consider; esteem **5.** to fix or determine the rates for **6.** [U.S. Colloq.] to deserve —*vi.* **1.** to be classed or ranked **2.** [Chiefly U.S.] to have value, status, or rating —**at any rate 1.** in any event **2.** anyway —**at this rate** this being so

rate[2] (rāt) *vt., vi.* **rat'ed, rat'ing** [ME. *raten*] to scold severely; chide

rateable value the value of property for rating purposes

rate·pay·er (rāt'pā'ər) *n.* one who pays rates

-rat·er (rāt'ər) a *combining form meaning* one of a (specified) rate, or class [first-*rater*]

rath·er (räth'ər; *for interj.* rä'th·ur') *adv.* [OE. *hrathor*, compar. of *hrathe*, quickly] **1.** more willingly; preferably **2.** with more justice, reason, etc. **3.** more accurately; more precisely **4.** on the contrary **5.** to some degree; somewhat —*interj.* certainly —**had** (or **would**) **rather 1.** would choose to **2.** would prefer that —**rather than** instead of

rat·i·fy (rat'ə fī') *vt.* **-fied', -fy'ing** [< MFr. < ML. < L. *ratus* (see RATE[1]) + *facere*, to make] to approve or confirm; esp., to give official sanction to —**rat'i·fi·ca'tion** *n.* —**rat'i·fi'er** *n.*

ra·ti·né (rat'ən ā') *n.* [Fr., frizzed: of the nap] a loosely woven fabric of cotton, wool, rayon, etc., with a nubby surface: also **ra·tine** (ra tēn')

rat·ing[1] (rāt'iŋ) *n.* **1.** a rank, class, or grade; specif., a classification of chiefly naval personnel **2.** a placement in a certain rank or class **3.** an evaluation of the credit or financial standing of a businessman, firm, etc. **4.** the assessment of the value of a property for taxation **5.** *Radio & TV* the relative popularity of a programme, determined by polls

rat·ing[2] (rāt'iŋ) *n.* [see RATE[2]] a scolding; sharp reprimand

ra·tio (rā'shē ō', -shō) *n., pl.* **-tios** [L.: see REASON] **1.** a fixed relation in degree, number, etc. between two similar things; proportion [a *ratio* of two boys to three girls] **2.** *Math.* the quotient of one quantity divided by another of the same kind, usually expressed as a fraction

ra·ti·o·ci·nate (rash'ē os'ə nāt', rat'ē-) *vi.* **-nat'ed, -nat'ing** [< L. pp. of *ratiocinari* < *ratio*: see REASON] to reason; esp. to reason using formal logic —**ra'ti·o'ci·na'tion** *n.* —**ra'ti·o'ci·na'tive** *adj.* —**ra'ti·o'ci·na'tor** *n.*

ra·tion (rash'ən) *n.* [MFr. < ML. < L. *ratio*: see REASON] **1.** a fixed portion; share; allowance **2.** a fixed allowance of food or provisions, as a daily allowance for one soldier, etc. **3.** [*pl.*] food or food supply —*vt.* **1.** to give rations to **2.** to distribute (food, clothing, etc.) in rations, as in times of scarcity —**ra'tion·ing** *n.*

ra·tion·al (rash'ən 'l) *adj.* [L. *rationalis* < *ratio*: see REASON] **1.** of or based on reasoning **2.** able to reason; reasoning **3.** showing reason; sensible [a *rational* plan] **4.** *Math.* designating or of a number that can be expressed as the quotient of two integers or as an integer —**ra'tion·al'i·ty** (-ə nal'ə tē) *n., pl.* **-ties** —**ra'tion·al·ly** *adv.*

ra·tion·a·le (rash'ə näl', -nä'lē) *n.* [L.: see prec.] **1.** the rational basis for something **2.** an explanation of reasons or principles

ra·tion·al·ism (rash'ən ə liz'm) *n.* the principle or practice of accepting reason as the only source of knowledge and as the only basis for forming one's opinions, beliefs, or course of action —**ra'tion·al·ist** *n., adj.* —**ra'tion·al·is'tic** *adj.* —**ra'·tion·al·is'ti·cal·ly** *adv.*

ra·tion·al·ize (rash'ən ə līz') *vt.* **-ized', -iz'ing 1.** to make rational; make conform to reason **2.** to explain on the basis of reason or logic **3.** to reorganize (an industry) so as to eliminate uneconomic units and increase productivity **4.** *Psychol.* to think of explanations for (one's acts, beliefs, etc.) that seem to make sense but do not truly reveal one's motives —*vi.* **1.** to think in a rational or rationalistic manner **2.** to rationalize one's acts, beliefs, etc. —**ra'·tion·al·i·za'tion** *n.* —**ra'tion·al·iz'er** *n.*

rat·ite (rat'īt) *adj.* [< L. < *ratis*, a raft] of a group of large, flightless birds having a flat breastbone without the keellike ridge of flying birds —*n.* any bird of this group, as the ostrich

rat·line (rat'lin) *n.* [altered by folk etym. < LME. *ratling* < ?] any of the small, thin pieces of tarred rope that join the shrouds of a ship and serve as a ladder: also sp. **rat'lin**

ra·toon (ra to͞on') *n.* [Sp. < *retoñar*, to sprout again < *re-*, again + *otonar*, to grow in autumn] a shoot growing from the root of a plant (esp. the sugar cane) that has been cut down —*vi.* to grow ratoons, or grow as a ratoon

rat race [Colloq.] a mad scramble or intense competitive struggle, as in the business world

rats·bane (rats'bān') *n.* [see BANE] 1. rat poison 2. any of various poisonous plants

rat·tail (rat'tāl') *adj.* shaped like a rat's tail; slim and tapering: also **rat'tailed'**

RATLINES

rat·tan (ra tan') *n.* [Malay *rotan* < *raut*, to strip] 1. a climbing palm with long, slender, tough stems 2. these stems, used in making wickerwork, etc. 3. a cane or switch made from such a stem

rat·ter (rat'ər) *n.* 1. a dog or cat skilled at catching rats 2. [Slang] a betrayer or informer

rat·tle (rat''l) *vi.* **-tled, -tling** [ME. *ratelen*: prob. echoic] 1. to make a rapid series of sharp, short sounds 2. to move with such sounds [a cart *rattled* over the stones] 3. to chatter (often with *on*) —*vt.* 1. to cause to rattle [he *rattled* the handle] 2. to utter or perform rapidly (usually with *off*) 3. to confuse or upset [catcalls *rattled* the speaker] —*n.* 1. a quick succession of short, sharp sounds 2. a rattling noise in the throat, as of a dying person 3. a noisy uproar 4. the series of horny rings at the end of a rattlesnake's tail 5. a device, as a baby's toy, intended to rattle when shaken —**rattle around in** to occupy (a place too big for one's needs) —**rattle the sabre** to be aggressive or warlike; menacing —**rat'tly** *adj.*

rat·tle·brain (-brān') *n.* a frivolous, talkative person: also **rat'tle·pate'** (-pāt') —**rat'tle·brained'** *adj.*

rat·tler (rat'lar) *n.* 1. a person or thing that rattles 2. [U.S.] a rattlesnake

rat·tle·snake (rat''l snāk') *n.* any of various poisonous American pit vipers having a series of horny rings at the end of the tail that rattle when shaken

rat·tle·trap (-trap') *n.* anything worn out, rickety, or rattling; esp., an old, worn-out motor car

rat·tling (rat'lin) *adj.* 1. that rattles 2. [Colloq.] very fast, good, etc. —*adv.* [Colloq.] very [a *rattling* good time]

rat·ty (rat'ē) *adj.* **-ti·er, -ti·est** 1. of, like, or full of rats 2. [Slang] irritable; annoyed 3. [U.S. Slang] shabby or run-down

rau·cous (rô'kəs) *adj.* [L. *raucus*] 1. hoarse; rough-sounding [a *raucous* shout] 2. loud and rowdy [a *raucous* party] —**rau'cous·ly** *adv.* —**rau'cous·ness** *n.*

raun·chy (rôn'chē) *adj.* **-chi·er, -chi·est** [< ?] [U.S. Slang] 1. dirty, cheap, sloppy, etc. 2. earthy, risqué, lustful, etc. —**raun'chi·ly** *adv.* —**raun'chi·ness** *n.*

rau·wol·fi·a (rô wool'fē ə, rou-) *n.* [ModL., after L. *Rauwolf*, 16th-c. G. botanist] 1. any of a group of tropical trees and shrubs, some of which yield medicinal substances 2. the root of one of these trees, a source of reserpine

rav·age (rav'ij) *n.* [Fr. < *ravir*: see RAVISH] 1. the act or practice of violently destroying 2. ruin; devastating damage —*vt.* **-aged, -ag·ing** to destroy violently; devastate; ruin —*vi.* to commit ravages —**rav'ag·er** *n.*

R.A.V.C. Royal Army Vetinary Corps

rave (rāv) *vi.* **raved, rav'ing** [prob. < OFr. *raver*] 1. to talk incoherently or wildly, as when delirious or demented 2. to talk with excessive enthusiasm (*about*) 3. to rage, as a storm —*vt.* to utter incoherently —*n.* 1. a raving 2. [Colloq.] an excessively enthusiastic commendation: often used before another noun [a *rave* review] —**rav'er** *n.*

rav·el (rav''l) *vt.* **-elled, -el·ling** [MDu. *ravelen*] 1. orig., to make complicated or tangled 2. to separate the parts, esp. threads, of; untwist 3. to make clear; disentangle —*vi.* to become separated into its parts, esp. threads; fray (*out*) —*n.* a ravelling, or a ravelled thread —**rav'el·ler** *n.*

rav·el·ling (rav''l in, rav'lin) *n.* anything unravelled, as a thread unravelled from knitted or woven fabric

ra·ven (rā'vən) *n.* [OE. *hræfn*] a large bird of the crow family, with shiny black feathers and a sharp beak —*adj.* black and shiny [*raven* locks]

rav·en·ing (rav'ən in) *adj.* [see RAVENOUS] greedily searching for prey

rav·e·nous (rav'ə nəs) *adj.* [< OFr. < *ravine* < L. *rapina*, RAPINE] 1. greedily hungry 2. greedy [*ravenous* for praise] 3. rapacious —**rav'e·nous·ly** *adv.* —**rav'e·nous·ness** *n.*

rav·er (rāv'ər) *n.* [Slang] someone with a hectic social life, usually being the life and soul of any party

rave-up (-up) *n.* [Slang] an enjoyable social event, usually an energetic party

ra·vine (ra vēn') *n.* [Fr., flood < OFr.: see préc.] a long, deep hollow in the earth's surface, worn by a stream; gorge

rav·ing (rā'vin) *adj.* 1. raging; delirious 2. [Colloq.] exciting raving admiration [a *raving* beauty] —*adv.* so as to cause raving [*raving* mad] —*n.* delirious, incoherent speech

ra·vi·o·li (rav'ē ō'lē) *n.pl.* [with sing. v.] [It.] small casings of pasta containing seasoned minced meat, cheese, etc., boiled and served usually in a savoury tomato sauce

rav·ish (rav'ish) *vt.* [< stem of OFr. *ravir*, ult. < L. *rapere*, to seize] 1. to seize and carry away forcibly 2. to rape 3. to enrapture —**rav'ish·er** *n.* —**rav'ish·ment** *n.*

rav·ish·ing (-in) *adj.* causing great joy or delight; entrancing —**rav'ish·ing·ly** *adv.*

raw (rô) *adj.* [OE. *hreaw*] 1. not cooked 2. in its natural condition; not changed by art, manufacture, etc. [*raw* silk] 3. not processed, edited, etc. [*raw data*] 4. inexperienced [a *raw* recruit] 5. with the skin rubbed off; sore and inflamed [a *raw* cut] 6. uncomfortably cold and damp [a *raw* wind] 7. [Chiefly U.S.] coarse; indecent 8. [Colloq.] harsh or unfair [a *raw* deal] —**in the raw** 1. in the natural state 2. naked —**raw'ly** *adv.* —**raw'ness** *n.*

raw·boned (rô'bōnd') *adj.* having little fat; lean; gaunt

raw·hide (-hīd') *n.* 1. an untanned or partially tanned cattle hide 2. a whip made of this

ray¹ (rā) *n.* [< OFr. < L. *radius*: see RADIUS] 1. any of the thin lines, or beams, of light that appear to come from a bright source 2. any of several lines coming out from a centre 3. a tiny amount [a *ray* of hope] 4. *Bot., Zool.* any part of a structure with parts coming like rays from a centre, as the petals of certain flowers, the limbs of a starfish, etc. 5. *Physics* a) a stream of particles given off by a radioactive substance, or any of the particles b) a straight line along which any part of a wave of radiant energy is regarded as travelling —*vi.* 1. to shine forth in rays 2. to radiate —*vt.* 1. to send out in rays 2. to supply with rays or radiating lines —**ray'less** *adj.* —**ray'like'** *adj.*

ray² (rā) *n.* [< MFr. < L. *raia*] any of several fishes, as the stingray, electric ray, skate, etc., having a horizontally flat body with both eyes on top, wide fins at each side, and a slender or whiplike tail

ray flower any of the flowers around the margin of the head of certain composite plants, as the daisy: also **ray floret**

ray·on (rā'on) *n.* [arbitrary coinage < RAY¹] 1. any of various synthetic textile fibres produced by pressing a cellulose solution through very small holes and solidifying it in the form of filaments 2. any fabric woven or knitted from such fibres

raze (rāz) *vt.* **razed, raz'ing** [< OFr. *raser*, ult. < L. pp. of *radere*, to scrape] to tear down completely; level to the ground; demolish

ra·zor (rā'zər) *n.* [< OFr. < *raser*: see prec.] 1. a sharp-edged cutting instrument for shaving off or cutting hair 2. an instrument used in shaving; esp. a device with a small electric motor that operates a set of cutters

ra·zor·back (-bak') *n.* 1. *same as* RORQUAL 2. a wild or semiwild pig of the S. U.S., with a ridged back and long legs 3. [Chiefly U.S.] a sharp ridge

ra·zor·bill (rā'zər bil') *n.* a black and white auk of the N Atlantic coasts with a black compressed bill

razor blade a sharp-edged cutting tool placed in a handle and used for shaving

razz (raz) *vt., vi.* [contr. < RASPBERRY] [U.S. Slang] to tease, ridicule, heckle, etc.

raz·zle-daz·zle (raz''l daz''l) *n.* [Slang] 1. a flashy display intended to confuse, bewilder, or deceive 2. a spree; frolic: also **razzle**

razz·ma·tazz (raz'mə taz') *n.* [Slang] 1. lively spirit; excitement 2. flashy display; showiness

Rb *Chem.* rubidium

R.C. 1. Red Cross 2. Roman Catholic

R.C.A. Royal College of Art

R.C.A.F., RCAF Royal Canadian Air Force

R.C.Ch. Roman Catholic Church

R.C.M. Royal College of Music

R.C.M.P., RCMP Royal Canadian Mounted Police

R.C.N. Royal Canadian Navy

R.C.P. Royal College of Physicians

R.C.S. 1. Royal College of Science 2. Royal College of Surgeons 3. Royal Corps of Signals

Rd., rd. 1. road 2. rod 3. round

R.D.C. Rural District Council

re¹ (rā) *n.* [It. < L. *re(sonare)*: see GAMUT] *Music* a syllable representing the second tone of the diatonic scale

re² (rē, rā) *prep.* [L., abl. of *res*, thing] in the case or matter of; as regards: short for *in re*

re- [< Fr. *re-, ré-* < L. *re-, red-*, back] a prefix meaning: 1. back [*repay*] 2. again, anew [*reappear*] It is used with a hyphen: 1) to distinguish between a word in which the prefix means *again* or *anew* and a word having a special meaning (Ex.: *re-sound*, resound) 2) to avoid ambiguity in forming nonce words [re-urge] 3) esp. formerly, before words beginning with an e [re-edit]: now usually solid [reedit] The following list contains some of the more common words in which re- means *again* or *anew*

reabsorb	recultivate	reinstruct
reabsorption	redecorate	reinsure
reaccuse	rededicate	reinterment
reaccustom	redefine	reinterpret
reacquaint	redefinition	reinterrogate
reacquire	redeliver	reintroduce
readapt	redemand	reintroduction
readdress	redeposit	reinvest
readjust	redescribe	reinvestigate
readmission	redesign	reinvigorate
readmit	redetermine	reinvite
readmittance	redevelop	reinvolve
readopt	rediscover	reissue
reaffiliate	rediscovery	rekindle
reaffirm	redistribute	reknit
reaffirmation	redistribution	relabel
realliance	redraft	relace
reallocation	redraw	relaunder
reallot	redry	relearn
reapperance	redye	relet
reapplication	reedit	relight
reapply	reelect	reload
reappoint	reelection	reman
reappointment	reembark	remarriage
rearrest	reembody	remarry
reascend	reembrace	rematch
reassemble	reemerge	remeasure
reassembly	reemergence	remelt
reassert	reemphasize	remerge
reassertion	reenact	remilitarize
reassess	reengage	remix
reassign	reenlist	remodify
reassociate	reenlistment	remould
reassume	reenter	rename
reassumption	reentrance	renegotiate
reattach	reequip	renominate
reattack	reestablish	renotify
reattain	reevaluate	renumber
reattempt	reexamination	reobtain
reawaken	reexamine	reoccupy
rebaptism	reexchange	reoccur
rebaptize	reexperience	reoccurrence
rebeautify	reexplain	reopen
rebid	reexport	reoppose
rebill	reface	reorient
rebind	refashion	repack
reborn	refasten	repaint
rebuild	refigure	repanel
rebury	refile	repaper
recalculate	refloat	repark
recapitalize	refocus	repartition
recarry	refold	repave
recertify	reformulate	rephotograph
rechannel	refortify	replan
recharge	reframe	replant
recharter	refreeze	replaster
recheck	refuel	replate
rechew	refurnish	replay
recirculate	regather	repolish
reclassification	regild	repopularize
reclassify	reglaze	repopulate
reclothe	reglorify	repot
recode	reglue	repour
recolour	regrade	re-present
recombine	regrind	reprice
recommence	regrow	reprocess
recommission	rehandle	reprosecute
recompose	rehang	re-prove
recompress	rehire	republication
recompute	rehospitalize	republish
recondense	rehouse	repurchase
reconduct	reignite	repurify
reconfine	reimpose	requalify
reconfirm	reimprisonment	reread
reconquer	reincorporate	rerecord
reconquest	reincur	reroll
reconsecrate	reinduce	resaddle
reconsign	reinfect	reschedule
reconsolidate	reinflate	rescore
reconstitute	reinform	rescreen
recontaminate	reinfuse	reseal
reconvene	reinoculate	reseed
reconvey	reinsert	reseize
recook	reinspect	resell
recopy	reinspire	resend
recross	reinstall	resentence
recrystallize	reinstitute	re-serve

resettle	restretch	retrial
resew	restrike	retrim
reshape	restringe	retry
resharpen	restudy	retune
reshine	restyle	retwist
reshow	resubmit	retype
reshuffle	resubscribe	reupholster
re-sign	resummon	reusuable
resilver	resupply	reuse
resituate	resurvey	revaccinate
resmooth	reswallow	revaluation
resolder	resynthesize	revalue
resolidify	retabulate	revarnish
re-solve	retack	reverify
re-sound	retape	revibrate
respace	reteach	revisit
respread	retelevise	revisualize
restabilize	retell	revitalize
restaff	retest	revote
restage	retestify	rewaken
restamp	rethread	rewarm
restart	retie	rewash
restimulate	retitle	reweave
restitch	retold	reweigh
restock	retrain	reweld
restraighten	retransfer	rewin
re-strain	retranslate	rework
restrengthen	re-treat	rezone

Re *Chem.* rhenium

R.E. Royal Engineers

reach (rēch) *vt.* [OE. *ræcan*] 1. to thrust out or extend (the hand, etc.) 2. to extend to, or touch, by thrusting out, etc. 3. to obtain and hand over [*reach* me the salt] 4. to go as far as; attain 5. to carry as far as [the news *reached* him late] 6. to add up to [to *reach* one million pounds] 7. to influence; affect 8. to get in touch with, as by telephone —*vi.* 1. to thrust out the hand, foot, etc. 2. to stretch, or be extended, in amount, influence, space, time, etc. 3. to carry, as sight, sound, etc. 4. to try to obtain something 5. *Naut.* to sail on a reach —*n.* 1. a stretching or thrusting out 2. the power of stretching, obtaining, etc. 3. the distance or extent covered in stretching, obtaining, etc. 4. a continuous extent or stretch, esp. of water 5. *Naut.* a tack sailed with the wind coming from abeam —**reach'a·ble** *adj.* —**reach'- er** *n.*

reach-me-downs (-mē dounz') *n.pl.* [Colloq.] second-hand or ready-made clothing

re·act (rē akt') *vi.* 1. to act in return or reciprocally 2. to act in opposition 3. to go back to a former condition, stage, etc. 4. to respond to a stimulus, influence, etc. 5. *Chem.* to act with another substance in producing a chemical change —*vt.* to produce a chemical change in

re-act (rē'akt') *vt.* to act or do again

re·act·ance (rē ak'təns) *n.* *Elec.* opposition to the flow of alternating current, caused by inductance or capacitance

re·act·ant (-tənt) *n.* any of the substances taking part in a chemical reaction

re·ac·tion (rē ak'shən) *n.* 1. a returning or opposing action, influence, etc. 2. a response, as to a stimulus 3. a movement back to a former or less advanced condition, stage, etc.; esp., such a movement in politics 4. *Chem.* a) the mutual action of substances undergoing chemical change b) a process that produces changes in an atomic nucleus 5. *Med.* a) an action induced by resistance to another action b) the effect produced by an allergen c) depression or exhaustion following nervous tension, overstimulation, etc. d) increased activity following depression —**re·ac'tion·al** *adj.* —**re·ac'tive** *adj.* —**re·ac'- tive·ly** *adv.* —**re'ac·tiv'i·ty** *n.*

re·ac·tion·ar·y (-shə ner ē) *adj.* of, showing, or favouring reaction, esp. in politics —*n., pl.* -ar·ies a reactionary person

reaction engine an engine, as a jet or rocket engine, that develops thrust by the reaction to the stream of gases ejected from it

reaction time *Psychol.* the time between stimulation and the beginning of the response

re·ac·ti·vate (rē ak'tə vāt') *vt.* -vat·ed, -vat·ing to make active again —**re·ac'ti·va'tion** *n.*

re·ac·tor (-tər) *n.* 1. a person or thing that reacts 2. same as NUCLEAR REACTOR

read[1] (rēd) *vt.* read (red), read·ing (rēd'iŋ) [OE. *rædan*, to counsel] 1. to get the meaning of (something written or printed) by interpreting its characters or signs [to *read* books, music, Braille, etc.] 2. to utter aloud (something written or printed) 3. to interpret movements of (the lips of a person speaking) 4. to know (a language) well enough to interpret its written form 5. to understand the nature, significance, or thinking of 6. to interpret (dreams, omens, etc.) or foretell (the future) 7. to interpret (a printed passage, a signal, etc.) as having a particular meaning **8.** to give as a reading in a certain passage [for "shew" *read* "show"] **9.** to study [to *read* law] **10.** to register [the thermometer *reads* 25°C] **11.** to put into a specified state by reading **12.** to obtain (information) from (punch cards, tape, etc.): said of a computer **13.** [Slang] to hear and understand [I *read* you loud and clear] —*vi.* **1.** to read something written or printed **2.** to utter aloud the words of written or printed matter **3.** to learn by reading (with *about* or *of*) **4.** to study **5.** to give a particular meaning when read **6.** to be drawn up in certain words [the sentence *reads* as follows] **7.** to admit of being read [it *reads* well] —*n.* something for reading or a spell of reading —**read between the lines** to deduce a meaning that is implied rather than openly stated —**read into** (or **in**) to interpret in a certain way —**read oneself in** in the Church of England, to assume possession of a benefice by publicly reading the Thirty-Nine Articles —**read out** to display or record with a readout device —**read (someone) a lecture** (or **lesson**) to scold or reprimand (someone) —**read up (on)** to become well informed (about) by reading

read² (red) *pt. & pp. of* READ¹ —*adj.* having knowledge got from reading; informed [well-*read*]

read·a·ble (rēd'ə b'l) *adj.* **1.** interesting or easy to read **2.** capable of being read; legible —**read'a·bil'i·ty, read'-a·ble·ness** *n.* —**read'a·bly** *adv.*

read·er (rēd'ər) *n.* **1.** a person who reads **2.** a person who reads lessons, prayers, etc. aloud in church **3.** *a)* a schoolbook containing stories, poems, etc. for use in teaching how to read *b)* an anthology of stories, essays, etc. **4.** a lecturer or instructor in a university **5.** in publishing, *a)* a person who reads and assesses the merit of manuscripts submitted *b)* a proofreader

read·er·ship (-ship') *n.* all the people who read a particular publication, author, etc.

read·ing (rēd'iŋ) *adj.* **1.** that reads **2.** of or for reading —*n.* **1.** the act or practice of one who reads **2.** the reciting of a literary work in public **3.** material read or to be read **4.** the extent to which a person has read **5.** the amount measured by a barometer, thermometer, etc. **6.** the way something is written, read, performed, understood, etc. [a superb *reading* of Hamlet] **7.** in legislative assemblies, esp. Parliament, a formal recital of a bill or enactment

reading matter books, magazines, etc. collectively

reading room a room (in a club, library, etc.) for reading and writing

read·out (rēd'out') *n.* **1.** a retrieving of information from storage in a digital computer **2.** this information, displayed visually or recorded, as by typewriter or on tape, for immediate use **3.** information immediately displayed or recorded from various electronic instruments

read·y (red'ē) *adj.* **read'i·er, read'i·est** [OE. *ræde*] **1.** prepared to act or be used immediately [*ready* to go, *ready* for occupancy] **2.** unhesitant; willing [a *ready* worker] **3.** *a)* likely or liable immediately [*ready* to cry] *b)* apt; inclined [always *ready* to blame others] **4.** done without delay; prompt [a *ready* reply] **5.** available immediately [*ready* cash] —*vt.* **read'ied, read'y·ing** to make ready (often used reflexively) —**at the ready** being prepared for immediate use [to hold a gun *at the ready*] —**make ready** to prepare —**ready up** [Aust. Slang] to prepare (something) for a dishonest purpose —**read'i·ly** *adv.* —**read'i·ness** *n.*

read·y-made (-mād') *adj.* made so as to be ready for immediate use or sale; not made-to-order: also, as applied to clothing, **read'y-to-wear'** (-tə wer')

ready reckoner a book of tabulated calculations, providing a quick and easy method of finding the amounts of money involved in commercial transactions

re·af·for·est (rē ə for'ist) *vt., vi.* to plant new trees on (land once forested) —**re'af·for·es·ta'tion** *n.*

re·a·gent (rē ā'jənt) *n.* [RE- + AGENT] *Chem.* a substance used to detect or measure another substance or to convert one substance into another

re·al¹ (rē'əl, rēl) *adj.* [OFr. < ML. *realis* < L. *res,* thing] **1.** existing or happening as or in fact; actual, true, etc. **2.** *a)* authentic; genuine *b)* not pretended; sincere **3.** designating wages or income as measured by purchasing power **4.** *Law* of or relating to permanent, immovable things [*real* property] **5.** *Philos.* existing objectively —**for real** [Slang] really

re·al² (rē'əl; *Sp.* re äl') *n., pl.* **re'als;** *Sp.* **re·al'es** (-ä'les) [Sp. & Port., lit., royal < L. *regalis:* see REGAL] a former silver coin of Spain

re·al³ (re äl') *n. sing. of* REIS

real estate land, including the buildings or improvements on it and its natural assets, as minerals, water, timber, etc.

re·a·lign (rē'ə līn') *vt., vi.* to align again; specif., to readjust alliances (between) —**re'a·lign'ment** *n.*

re·al·ism (rē'ə liz'm) *n.* **1.** a tendency to face facts and be practical **2.** the picturing in art and literature of people and things as they really appear to be, without idealizing **3.** *Philos. a)* the doctrine that universals are objectively actual

b) the doctrine that material objects exist in themselves apart from the mind's consciousness of them —**re'al·ist** *n.*

re·al·is·tic (rē'ə lis'tik) *adj.* **1.** of, having to do with, or in the style of, realism or realists **2.** tending to face facts; practical rather than visionary —**re'al·is'ti·cal·ly** *adv.*

re·al·i·ty (rē al'ə tē) *n., pl.* **-ties 1.** the quality or fact of being real **2.** a person or thing that is real; fact **3.** the quality of being true to life **4.** *Philos.* that which is real —**in reality** in fact; actually

re·al·ize (rē'ə līz') *vt.* **-ized', -iz'ing 1.** to make real; bring into being; achieve **2.** to make appear real **3.** to understand fully [to *realize* one's danger] **4.** to convert (assets, rights, etc.) into money **5.** to gain; obtain [to *realize* a profit] **6.** to be sold for, or bring as profit (a specified sum) —**re'al·iz'a·ble** *adj.* —**re'al·i·za'tion** *n.* —**re'al·iz'er** *n.*

re·al·ly (rē'ə lē, rēl'ē) *adv.* **1.** in reality; in fact; actually **2.** truly or genuinely [*really* hot] —*interj.* indeed —**not really 1.** not actually **2.** no

realm (relm) *n.* [< OFr. *reaume* < L. *regimen,* rule, infl. by L. *regalis,* REGAL] **1.** a kingdom **2.** a region; sphere; area [the *realm* of imagination]

real number *Math.* any rational or irrational number

real tennis an ancient form of tennis played in a walled indoor court: also **royal tennis**

real time 1. time in which the occurrence and recording of an event are almost simultaneous **2.** the actual time used by a computer to solve a problem the answer to which is immediately available to control a process that is going on at the same time

re·al·ty (rē'əl tē) *n.* [REAL¹ + -TY¹] *same as* REAL ESTATE

ream¹ (rēm) *n.* [< MFr. < Ar. *rizma,* a bale] **1.** a quantity of paper varying from 480 sheets (20 quires) to 516 sheets **2.** [*pl.*] [Colloq.] a great amount

ream² (rēm) *vt.* [OE. *reman,* akin to *ryman,* lit., to make roomy < base of *rum,* room] **1.** *a)* to enlarge or taper (a hole) *b)* to enlarge the bore of (a gun) **2.** to remove (a defect) by reaming **3.** to [U.S.] squeeze the juice from in a reamer

ream·er (-ər) *n.* a person or thing that reams; specif., *a)* a sharp-edged tool for enlarging or tapering holes *b)* [U.S.] a utensil in which oranges, etc. are squeezed for juice

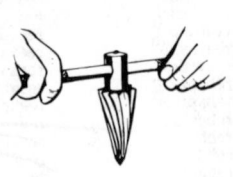

REAMER

re·an·i·mate (rē an'ə māt') *vt.* **-mat'ed, -mat'ing** to give new life, power, vigour, courage, etc. to —**re·an'i·ma'-tion** *n.*

reap (rēp) *vt.* [OE. *ripan*] **1.** to cut (grain) with a scythe, machine, etc. **2.** to gather (a crop, harvest, etc.) **3.** to harvest grain from (a field) **4.** to get as the result of action, work, etc. —*vi.* to reap a harvest, reward, etc.

reap·er (rē'pər) *n.* **1.** a person who reaps **2.** a machine for reaping grain —**the (Grim) Reaper** death

re·ap·por·tion (rē'ə pôr'shən) *vt.* to apportion again —**re'-ap·por'tion·ment** *n.*

re·ap·praise (-prāz') *vt.* **-praised', -prais'ing** to make a fresh appraisal of; reconsider —**re·ap·prais'al** *n.*

rear¹ (rir) *n.* [< ARREAR(S)] **1.** the back part **2.** the position behind or at the back **3.** the part of an army, etc. farthest from the battle front **4.** [Slang] the buttocks: also **rear end** —*adj.* of, at, or in the rear —**bring up the rear** to come at the end, as of a procession —**in the rear** behind

rear² (rir) *vt.* [OE. *ræran,* caus. of *risan,* to rise] **1.** to put upright; elevate **2.** to build; erect **3.** to grow or breed (animals or plants) **4.** to bring to maturity by educating, nourishing, etc. [to *rear* children] —*vi.* **1.** to rise on the hind legs, as a horse **2.** to rise (*up*) in anger, etc.

rear admiral *see* MILITARY RANKS, table

rear guard a military detachment to protect the rear of a main force or body

rear light a light, usually red, at the rear of a vehicle to warn other vehicles coming from behind

re·arm (rē ärm') *vt., vi.* **1.** to arm again **2.** to arm with new or more effective weapons —**re·ar'ma·ment** *n.*

rear·most (rir'mōst') *adj.* farthest in the rear

re·ar·range (rē'ə rānj') *vt.* **-ranged', -rang'ing 1.** to arrange again **2.** to arrange in a different manner —**re'-ar·range'ment** *n.*

rear-view mirror a mirror in a motor vehicle positioned so that the driver can see the traffic behind his vehicle

rear·ward (rir'wərd) *adj.* at, in, or towards the rear —*adv.* towards the rear: also **rear'wards**

rea·son (rē'z'n) *n.* [< OFr. < L. *ratio,* a reckoning < pp. of *reri,* to think] **1.** an explanation or justification of an act, idea, etc. **2.** a cause or motive **3.** the ability to think, draw conclusions, etc. **4.** sound thought or judgment; good sense **5.** normal mental powers; sanity —*vi.* **1.** to think logically **2.** to draw conclusions from facts known or assumed —*vt.* **1.** to think or talk in a logical way **1.** to think logically about analyze **2.** to argue, conclude, or infer [he *reasoned* that the method was too costly] **3.** to justify with reason **4.** to persuade by reasoning (*into* or *out of* something) —**by reason of** because of —**in** (or **within**) **reason** in accord with what is reasonable —**out of all reason** unreasonable —**stand to reason** to be logical or reasonable —**with reason** justifiably; rightly —**rea′son·er** *n.*

rea·son·a·ble (-ə b'l) *adj.* **1.** capable of reasoning or being reasoned with **2.** using or showing reason, or sound judgment; sensible **3.** *a)* not extreme or excessive *b)* not expensive —**rea′son·a·ble·ness** *n.* —**rea′son·a·bly** *adv.*

rea·son·ing (-iŋ) *n.* **1.** the drawing of inferences or conclusions from known or assumed facts **2.** the reasons, proofs, etc. used in this process

re·as·sure (rē′ə shoor′) *vt.* **-sured′, -sur′ing** **1.** to assure again or anew **2.** to restore to confidence **3.** to insure anew —**re′as·sur′ance** *n.* —**re′as·sur′ing·ly** *adv.*

Ré·au·mur (rā′ə myoor′; *Fr.* rā ō mür′) *adj.* [after R.A.F. *de Réaumur* (1683-1757), Fr. physicist] designating a temperature scale with the boiling point of water fixed at 80° and the freezing point at 0°

re·bate (rē′bāt; *also for v.* ri bāt′) *vt.* **-bat·ed, -bat·ing** [< OFr. < *re-*, re- + *abattre:* see ABATE] **1.** to give back (part of an amount paid) **2.** to make a deduction from (a bill) —*n.* a return of part of the amount paid, as for goods

re·bec, re·beck (rē′bek) *n.* [Fr. < OFr. *rebebe* < Ar. *rabāb*] a medieval pear-shaped instrument played with a bow like a violin

reb·el (reb′'l; *for v.* ri bel′) *n.* [< OFr. < L. < *re-*, again + *bellare,* to war < *bellum,* war] **1.** a person who takes up arms against the government of his own country **2.** a person who resists any authority or control —*adj.* **1.** rebellious **2.** of rebels —*vi.* **-elled′, -el′ling** **1.** to be a rebel against the government of one's country **2.** to resist any authority or control **3.** to feel or show strong aversion

re·bel·lion (ri bel′yən) *n.* [< MFr. < L.: see prec.] **1.** an act or state of armed, open resistance to one's government **2.** defiance of any authority or control

re·bel·lious (-yəs) *adj.* **1.** resisting authority; engaged in rebellion **2.** of or like rebels or rebellion **3.** opposing any control; defiant **4.** difficult to treat or handle —**re·bel′-lious·ly** *adv.* —**re·bel′lious·ness** *n.*

re·bid (rē′bid′) *vt., vi.* Cards to bid again, esp., in bridge, in the same suit as before —*n.* a rebidding

re·birth (rē burth′, rē′burth′) *n.* **1.** a new or second birth **2.** a reawakening; revival

re·bound (ri bound′; *also, & for n. usually,* rē′bound′) *vi.* **1.** to bound or spring back, as upon impact or in recovery **2.** to reecho —*vt.* to make bound or spring back —*n.* **1.** a rebounding; recoil **2.** a basketball or football that bounds back after hitting a wall, goal post, etc. —**on the rebound** **1.** after bouncing off the ground, a wall, etc. **2.** just after and while reacting to rejection, as in love

re·bo·zo (ri bō′zō; *Sp.* re bō′thō, -sō) *n., pl.* **-zos** (-zōz; *Sp.* -thôs, -sôs) [Sp., a shawl] a long scarf worn by women around the head and shoulders, as in Mexico

re·broad·cast (rē brôd′kast′) *vt., vi.* **-cast′** or **-cast′ed, -cast′ing** **1.** to broadcast again **2.** to broadcast (a programme, etc. received in a relay system from another station) —*n.* **1.** a rebroadcasting **2.** a programme that is being or has been rebroadcast

re·buff (ri buf′) *n.* [< MFr. < It. *rabbuffo,* ult. < Gmc.] **1.** a blunt refusal of offered help, advice, etc. **2.** any check or repulse —*vt.* **1.** to refuse bluntly; snub **2.** to check

re·buke (ri byook′) *vt.* **-buked′, -buk′ing** [< Anglo-Fr. < OFr. < *re-*, back + *buchier,* to beat] to blame or scold in a sharp way; reprimand —*n.* a sharp scolding or reprimand —**re·buk′er** *n.* —**re·buk′ing·ly** *adv.*

re·bus (rē′bəs) *n.* [L., lit., by things] a kind of puzzle consisting of pictures of things combined so as to suggest words or phrases [a picture of a bee plus the figure 4 is a *rebus* for "before"]

re·but (ri but′) *vt.* **-but′ted, -but′ting** [< Anglo-Fr. < OFr. < *re-*, back + *buter,* to push] to contradict or oppose, esp. in a formal manner by argument, proof, etc. —*vi.* to provide opposing arguments —**re·but′ta·ble** *adj.* —**re·but′-ter** *n.*

re·but·tal (-'l) *n.* a rebutting, as in law

rec (rek) *n. a shortened form of* RECREATION

rec. **1.** receipt **2.** recipe **3.** record(ed)

re·cal·ci·trant (ri kal′si trənt) *adj.* [< L. prp. of *recalcitrare* < *re-*, back + *calcitrare,* to kick < *calx,* a heel] **1.** refusing to obey authority, regulation, etc.; stubbornly defiant **2.** hard to handle or deal with —*n.* a recalcitrant person —**re·cal′ci·trance, re·cal′ci·tran·cy** *n.* —**re·cal′ci·trant·ly** *adv.*

re·ca·les·cence (rē′kə les′əns) *n.* [< L. *recalescere,* to grow hot again] a sudden and temporary increase in the glow and temperature of cooling iron

re·call (ri kôl′; *for n. also* rē′kôl′) *vt.* **1.** to call back; order to return **2.** to bring back to mind; remember **3.** to take back; revoke **4.** to bring back in awareness, attention, etc. —*n.* **1.** a recalling **2.** the ability to remember; memory **3.**

[U.S.] the process of removing, or the right to remove, a public official from office by popular vote —**re·call′a·ble** *adj.*

re·cant (ri kant′) *vt., vi.* [< L. < *re-*, back + *cantare,* freq. of *canere,* to sing] to take back or confess being wrong about (former beliefs, statements, etc.), esp. formally or publicly —**re·can·ta·tion** (rē′kan tā′shən) *n.*

re·cap¹ (rē kap′; *also, & for n. always,* rē′kap′) *vt.* **-capped′, -cap′ping** [RE- + CAP] [U.S.] same as REMOULD

re·cap² (rē′kap′) *n.* a recapitulation, or summary —*vi., vt.* **-capped′, -cap′ping** to recapitulate

re·ca·pit·u·late (rē′kə pich′ə lāt′) *vi., vt.* **-lat′ed, -lat′ing** [see RE- & CAPITULATE] to tell again briefly; summarize

re·ca·pit·u·la·tion (-pich′ə lā′shən) *n.* **1.** a recapitulating **2.** a summary, or brief restatement —**re′ca·pit′u·la′tive, re′-ca·pit′u·la·to·ry** (-lə tər ē) *adj.*

re·cap·ture (rē kap′chər) *vt.* **-tured, -tur·ing** **1.** to capture again; retake; reacquire **2.** to bring back by remembering —*n.* a recapturing or being recaptured

re·cast (rē kást′; *for n.* rē′kást′) *vt.* **-cast′, -cast′ing** **1.** to cast again or anew **2.** to improve the form of by redoing; reconstruct [to *recast* a sentence] —*n.* a recasting

rec·ce (rek′ē) *n. Mil. colloq. var. of* RECONNAISSANCE

recd., rec′d. received

re·cede¹ (ri sēd′) *vi.* **-ced′ed, -ced′ing** [< L.: see RE- & CEDE] **1.** to go or move back [the flood *receded*] **2.** to withdraw [to *recede* from a promise] **3.** to slope backwards [her chin *recedes*] **4.** to lessen, dim, etc.

re·cede² (rē′sēd′) *vt.* **-ced′ed, -ced′ing** to cede back

re·ceipt (ri sēt′) *n.* [< Anglo-Fr. < ML. < L. < pp. of *recipere:* see RECEIVE] **1.** *old-fashioned var. of* RECIPE **2.** a receiving or being received **3.** a written acknowledgment that something, as goods, money, etc., has been received **4.** [*pl.*] the thing or amount received, as of money taken in by a business —*vt.* **1.** to mark (a bill) paid **2.** [Chiefly U.S.] to write a receipt for (goods, etc.)

re·ceiv·a·ble (ri sē′və b'l) *adj.* **1.** that can be received **2.** suitable for acceptance **3.** due in payment from one's customers —*n.* [*pl.*] accounts or bills receivable

re·ceive (ri sēv′) *vt.* **-ceived′, -ceiv′ing** [< Anglo-Fr. < OFr. < L. *recipere* < *re-*, back + *capere,* to take] **1.** to take or get (something given, offered, sent, etc.) **2.** to meet with; experience [to *receive* acclaim] **3.** to undergo; suffer [to *receive* a blow] **4.** to take the force of; bear [each wheel *receives* equal weight] **5.** to react to as specified [the song was well *received*] **6.** to get knowledge of; learn [to *receive* news] **7.** to accept as authentic, valid, etc. **8.** *a)* to let enter; admit *b)* to have room for; contain **9.** to greet (visitors, etc.) —*vi.* **1.** to be a recipient **2.** to greet guests or visitors **3.** to buy and sell stolen goods **4.** *Radio & TV* to convert incoming electromagnetic waves into sound or light, thus reproducing the sounds or images being transmitted **5.** *Sports* to catch a ball or be prepared to return a thrown, kicked, etc. ball —**be on the receiving end** [Colloq.] **1.** to be the recipient of a gift **2.** to be the victim of an attack

Received Pronunciation the accent of standard British English as spoken by educated English people and used as a pronunciation norm for foreigners learning English

re·ceiv·er (ri sē′vər) *n.* **1.** a person who receives (in various senses); specif., *Law* a person appointed by the court to administer or hold in trust property in bankruptcy or in a lawsuit **2.** a thing that receives; specif., *a)* a receptacle *b)* an apparatus that converts electrical signals, etc. into sound or light, as a radio or television receiving set, or that part of a telephone held to the ear **3.** someone who receives stolen goods knowing that they are stolen

re·ceiv·er·ship (-ship′) *n. Law* **1.** the duties or office of a receiver **2.** the state of being administered or held by a receiver

receiving set an apparatus for receiving radio or television signals; receiver

re·cent (rē′s'nt) *adj.* [MFr. < L. *recens* < *re-*, again + base akin to Gr. *kainos,* new] **1.** done, made, etc. just before the present time; modern; new **2.** of a time just before the present **3.** [R-] designating or of the present epoch, extending from the close of the Pleistocene —**the Recent** the Recent Epoch or its rocks: see GEOLOGY, chart —**re′-cent·ly** *adv.* —**re′cent·ness** *n.*

re·cep·ta·cle (ri sep′tə k'l) *n.* [L. *receptaculum* < freq. of *recipere:* see RECEIVE] **1.** anything used to contain or hold something else; container **2.** *Bot. a)* the part of the stalk from which the flower grows *b)* a cuplike or dislike part supporting spores, seeds, etc.

re·cep·tion (ri sep′shən) *n.* [OFr. < L. < pp. of *recipere:* see RECEIVE] **1.** *a)* a receiving or being received *b)* the manner of this [a friendly *reception*] **2.** a social function, often formal, for the receiving of guests **3.** *Radio & TV* the manner of receiving, with reference to quality [poor *reception*]

re·cep·tion·ist (-ist) *n.* a person employed at a hotel, doctor's surgery, etc. to receive clients, arrange appointments, etc.

reception room **1.** a room in a house used to entertain visitors **2.** a room in an office, etc. for receiving visitors, clients, etc. as they arrive **3.** a living room in a house: term used chiefly by estate agents

re·cep·tive (ri sep'tiv) *adj.* **1.** receiving or tending to receive, admit, or contain **2.** able or ready to receive requests, suggestions, new ideas, etc. **3.** of reception or receptors —**re·cep'tive·ly** *adv.* —**re·cep'tiv'i·ty, re·cep'-tive·ness** *n.*

re·cep·tor (-tər) *n. Physiol.* a nerve ending specialized for the reception of stimuli; sense organ

re·cess (rē'ses; *also, and for v. usually,* ri seś') *n.* [< L. pp. of *recedere,* to recede] **1.** a receding or hollow place, as in a wall; niche **2.** a secluded or withdrawn place [the *recesses* of the subconscious] **3.** a temporary halting of work, study, etc. [the parliamentary *recess*] —*vt.* **1.** to place in a recess **2.** to form a recess in —*vi.* [U.S.] to take a recess

re·ces·sion¹ (ri sesh'ən) *n.* [L. *recessio* < pp. of *recedere,* to recede] **1.** a going backwards; withdrawal **2.** a departing procession, as of clergy and choir after a church service **3.** a receding part, as of a wall **4.** a temporary falling off of business activity during a prosperous period

re·ces·sion² (rē sesh'ən) *n.* [RE- + CESSION] a ceding back, as to a former owner

re·ces·sion·al (-'l) *adj.* of a recession —*n.* a hymn or other music sung or played during a church recession

re·ces·sive (ri ses'iv) *adj.* **1.** receding or tending to recede **2.** *Genetics* designating or of that one of any pair of allelic characters which, when both are present in the germ plasm, remains latent: opposed to DOMINANT —**re·ces'sive·ly** *adv.* —**re·ces'sive·ness** *n.*

re·charge (rē chärj'; *also & for n. always* rē'chärj) *vt., vi.* **-charged', -charg'ing** to charge again (in various senses) —*n.* the act of recharging —**re·charge'a·ble** *adj.* —**re·charg'-er** *n.*

re·cher·ché (rə sher'shā) *adj.* [Fr., pp. of *rechercher:* see RESEARCH] **1.** sought out with care; choice **2.** having refinement or contrived elegance **3.** too refined; too studied

re·cid·i·vism (ri sid'ə viz'm) *n.* [< L. < *recidere* < *re-,* back + *cadere,* to fall + -ISM] relapse, or tendency to relapse, esp. into crime or antisocial behaviour —**re·cid'i·vist** *n., adj.* —**re·cid'i·vis'tic, re·cid'i·vous** *adj.*

rec·i·pe (res'ə pē) *n.* [L., imperative of *recipere:* see RECEIVE] **1.** formerly, a medicinal prescription **2.** a list of ingredients and directions for preparing a dish or drink **3.** any procedure for bringing about a desired result

re·cip·i·ent (ri sip'ē ənt) *n.* [< L. prp. of *recipere:* see RECEIVE] a person or thing that receives —*adj.* receiving, or ready or able to receive —**re·cip'i·ence, re·cip'i·en·cy** *n.*

re·cip·ro·cal (ri sip'rə k'l) *adj.* [< L. *reciprocus,* returning] **1.** done, felt, given, etc. in return **2.** on both sides; mutual **3.** corresponding but reversed **4.** equivalent or interchangeable; complementary **5.** *Gram.* expressing mutual action or relation [each *other* is a *reciprocal* pronoun] **6.** *Math.* of reciprocals —*n.* **1.** anything that has a reciprocal relation to another; counterpart **2.** *Math.* the quantity resulting from the division of 1 by the given quantity [the *reciprocal* of 7 is 1/7] —**re·cip'ro·cal'i·ty** (-kal'ə tē) *n.* —**re·cip'ro·cal·ly** *adv.*

re·cip·ro·cate (-kāt') *vt., vi.* **-cat'ed, -cat'ing** [< L. pp. of *reciprocare* < *reciprocus:* see prec.] **1.** *a)* to give and get reciprocally *b)* to give, do, feel, etc. (something similar) in return **2.** to move alternately back and forth —**re·cip'-ro·ca'tion** *n.* —**re·cip'ro·ca'tive, re·cip'ro·ca·to·ry** (-kə tər ē) *adj.* —**re·cip'ro·ca'tor** *n.*

rec·i·proc·i·ty (res'ə pros'ə tē) *n., pl.* **-ties** [< Fr.] **1.** reciprocal state or relationship **2.** mutual exchange; esp., exchange of special privileges between two countries, as mutual reduction of tariffs

re·cit·al (ri sīt''l) *n.* **1.** *a)* a reciting; specif., a telling in detail *b)* the account, story, etc. told **2.** a detailed statement **3.** a musical or dance programme given by a soloist, soloists, or a small ensemble —**re·cit'al·ist** *n.*

rec·i·ta·tion (res'ə tā'shən) *n.* **1.** a recital (sense 1) **2.** *a)* the speaking aloud in public of something memorized *b)* the piece so presented **3.** [U.S.] a reciting by pupils of answers to questions on a prepared lesson, etc.

rec·i·ta·tive (res'ə tə tēv') *n.* [It. *recitativo* < L. *recitare,* to RECITE] *Music* **1.** a type of declamatory singing, free in rhythm and tempo, as in the dialogue of operas **2.** a work or passage in this style **3.** music for such passages —*adj.* in the style of recitative

re·cite (ri sīt') *vt., vi.* **-cit'ed, -cit'ing** [< OFr. < L. *recitare:* see RE- & CITE] **1.** to speak aloud, as from memory, (a lesson) in class or (a poem, etc.) before an audience **2.** to tell in detail or narrate (something) —**re·cit'er** *n.*

reck (rek) *vi., vt.* [OE. *reccan*] [Archaic] **1.** to have care or concern (for) or take heed (of) **2.** to concern or be of concern; matter (to)

reck·less (rek'lis) *adj.* [see prec. & -LESS] **1.** careless; heedless **2.** not regarding consequences; rash —**reck'-less·ly** *adv.* —**reck'less·ness** *n.*

reck·on (rek'ən) *vt.* [OE. *-recenian*] **1.** to count; add up;

compute **2.** *a)* to consider as; regard as being [*reckon* them friends] *b)* to judge; estimate **3.** [Colloq.] to suppose —*vi.* **1.** to count up; figure **2.** [Colloq.] to rely (with *on*) **3.** [Colloq.] to suppose —**reckon up** to add or total a bill, etc. —**reckon with 1.** to settle accounts with **2.** to take into consideration

reck·on·ing (-iŋ) *n.* **1.** the act of one who reckons; count or computation **2.** a calculated guess **3.** *a)* a bill; account *b)* settlement of an account **4.** the giving of rewards or punishments [day of *reckoning*] **5.** *Naut.* the determination of the position of a ship; esp., *short for* DEAD RECKONING —**out in one's reckoning** having made a mistake in one's calculations

re·claim (ri klām') *vt.* [< OFr. < L. *reclamare:* see RE- & CLAIM] **1.** to rescue or bring back (someone) from error, vice, etc. **2.** to make (marshland, etc.) capable of being cultivated or lived on, as by irrigating, etc. **3.** to recover (useful materials) from waste products —*n.* reclamation [beyond *reclaim*] —**re·claim'a·ble** *adj.* —**re·claim'ant, re·claim'er** *n.*

re-claim (rē'klām') *vt.* to claim back; demand the return of; try to get back

rec·la·ma·tion (rek'lə mā'shən) *n.* a reclaiming or being reclaimed, as of marshland or of useful materials from waste products

re·cline (ri klīn') *vt., vi.* **-clined', -clin'ing** [< L. < *re-,* back + *clinare,* to lean] to lie or cause to lie back or down; lean back —**rec·li·na·tion** (rek'lə nā'shən) *n.* —**re·clin'er** *n.*

rec·luse (ri klōōs') *adj.* [< OFr. < LL. < L. pp. of *recludere* < *re-,* back + *claudere,* to shut] secluded; solitary —*n.* a person who leads a secluded, solitary life —**re·clu·sion** (ri klōō'zhən) *n.* —**re·clu'sive** *adj.*

rec·og·ni·tion (rek'əg nish'ən) *n.* [< L. < pp. of *recognoscere:* see ff.] **1.** *a)* a recognizing or being recognized; acknowledgment *b)* approval, gratitude, etc. [in *recognition* of his services] **2.** formal acceptance by a government of the sovereignty of a newly established state or government **3.** identification of a person or thing as being known to one **4.** notice, as in passing; greeting —**re·cog·ni·to·ry** (ri kog'nə tər ē), **re·cog'ni·tive** *adj.*

re·cog·ni·zance (ri kog'ni zəns, -kon'i-) *n.* [< OFr. < L. < *re-,* again + *cognoscere,* to know: see COGNITION] *Law* **1.** a bond or obligation of record binding a person to some act, as to appear in court **2.** a sum of money that one must forfeit if this obligation is not fulfilled —**re·cog'ni·zant** *adj.*

rec·og·nize (rek'əg nīz') *vt.* **-nized', -niz'ing** [altered (after prec.) < OFr.: see prec.] **1.** to identify as known before **2.** to know by some detail, as of appearance **3.** to be aware of the significance of **4.** to acknowledge the existence, validity, etc. of [to *recognize* a claim] **5.** to accept as a fact; admit [to *recognize* defeat] **6.** to acknowledge as worthy of appreciation or approval **7.** to formally acknowledge the legal standing of (a government or state) **8.** to show acquaintance with (a person) by greeting **9.** [Chiefly U.S.] to grant (a person) the right to speak, as in a meeting —**rec'og·niz'a·bil'i·ty** *n.* —**rec'og·niz'a·ble** *adj.* —**rec'og·niz'a·bly** *adv.* —**rec'og·niz'er** *n.*

re·coil (ri kɔil'; *also for n., esp. of weapons,* rē'kɔil') *vi.* [< OFr. < *re-,* back + *cul* < L. *culus,* the buttocks] **1.** to draw, start, or shrink back, as in fear, surprise, disgust, etc. **2.** to fly back when released, as a spring, or kick back when fired, as a gun **3.** to return as to the starting point or source; react (on or upon) —*n.* **1.** a recoiling **2.** the state of having recoiled —**re·coil'er** *n.* —**re·coil'less** *adj.*

re-coil (rē'kɔil') *vt., vi.* to coil anew or again

rec·ol·lect (rek'ə lekt') *vt.* [< L.: see RE- & COLLECT¹] **1.** to call back to mind; remember, esp. with some effort **2.** to recall to (oneself) something temporarily forgotten —*vi.* to remember —**rec'ol·lec'tion** *n.* —**rec'ol·lec'tive** *adj.*

re-col·lect (rē'kə lekt') *vt.* **1.** to collect again (what has been scattered) **2.** to rally (one's courage, etc.) **3.** to compose (oneself): in this sense sometimes written **recollect**

rec·om·mend (rek'ə mend') *vt.* [< ML.: see RE- & COMMEND] **1.** to give in charge; entrust [*recommended* to his care] **2.** to suggest favourably as suited for some function, position, etc. **3.** to make acceptable or pleasing [his charm *recommends* him] **4.** to advise; counsel —**rec'-om·mend'a·ble** *adj.* —**rec'om·mend'a·to·ry** *adj.* —**rec'-om·mend'er** *n.*

rec·om·men·da·tion (-mən dā'shən) *n.* **1.** a recommending **2.** anything that recommends or makes favourable or pleasing impression; specif., a letter recommending a person or thing **3.** advice; counsel

re·com·mit (rē'kə mit') *vt.* **-mit'ted, -mit'ting 1.** to commit again **2.** to refer (a question, bill, etc.) back to a

rec·om·pense (rek'əm pens') *vt.* **-pensed', -pens'ing** [< MFr. < LL.: see RE- & COMPENSATE] **1.** to repay (a person, etc.); reward **2.** to compensate (a loss, injury, etc.) —*n.* **1.** something given or done in return for something else; requital, reward, etc. **2.** something given or done to make up for a loss, injury, etc.; compensation

rec·on·cile (rek'ən sīl') *vt.* **-ciled', -cil'ing** [< OFr. < L.: see RE- & CONCILIATE] **1.** to make friendly again **2.** to settle (a quarrel, etc.) **3.** to make (facts, ideas, texts, etc.) consistent or compatible **4.** to make content or acquiescent (*to*) —**rec'on·cil·a·bil'i·ty** *n.* —**rec'on·cil'a·ble** *adj.* —**rec'-on·cil'a·bly** *adv.* —**rec'on·cil'i·a'tion** (-sil'ē ā'shən), **rec'-on·cile'ment** *n.* —**rec'on·cil'i·a·to·ry** (-sil'ē ə tər ē) *adj.*

rec·on·dite (ri kon'dīt, rek'ən dīt') *adj.* [< L. pp. of *recondere* < *re*-, back + *condere*, to store up, hide] **1.** beyond the grasp of ordinary understanding; profound **2.** dealing with abstruse or difficult subjects **3.** obscure or concealed —**rec'on·dite'ly** *adv.* —**rec'on·dite'ness** *n.*

re·con·di·tion (rē'kən dish'ən) *vt.* to put back in good condition by cleaning, repairing, etc.

re·con·nais·sance (ri kon'ə səns, -zəns) *n.* [Fr.: see RECOGNIZANCE] an exploratory survey or examination, as in seeking information about enemy positions

rec·on·noi·tre (rē'kə noit'ər, rek'ə-) *vt., vi.* [< Fr. < OFr.: see RECOGNIZANCE] to make a reconnaissance (of): also, U.S. sp., **rec'on·noi'ter** —**rec'on·noi'trer** (-noi'trər) *n.*

re·con·sid·er (rē'kən sid'ər) *vt., vi.* to consider again; think over, as with a view to changing a decision —**re'con·sid'-er·a'tion** *n.*

re·con·sti·tute (rē kon'stə tyōōt') *vt.* -tut'ed, -tut'ing to constitute again or anew; specif., to restore (a dehydrated or condensed substance) to its full liquid form by adding water —**re·con'sti·tu'tion** *n.*

re·con·struct (rē'kən strukt') *vt.* **1.** to construct again; make over **2.** to build up again (something in its original form), as from remaining parts —**re'con·struc'tive** *adj.*

re·con·struc·tion (-struk'shən) *n.* **1.** a reconstructing **2.** something reconstructed

re·con·vert (rē'kən vurt') *vt., vi.* to change back, as to a former status, religion, etc. —**re'con·ver'sion** *n.*

re·cord (ri kôrd'; *for n.* & *adj.*, rek'ərd) *vt.* [< OFr. < L. *recordari*, to remember < *re*-, again + *cor* (gen. *cordis*), heart, mind] **1.** *a)* to put in writing, print, etc. for future use *b)* to make an official note of [*to record* a vote] **2.** *a)* to indicate automatically and permanently, as on a graph [a seismograph *records* earthquakes] *b)* to show, as on a dial **3.** to remain as evidence of **4.** *a)* to register (sound or visual images) in some permanent form, as on a gramophone record, magnetic tape, etc. for reproduction on a playback device *b)* to register the performance of in this way —*vi.* **1.** to record something **2.** to admit of being recorded —*n.* **1.** the condition of being recorded **2.** *a)* an account of events *b)* anything that serves as evidence of an event, etc. *c)* an official report of public proceedings, as in a court **3.** anything that written evidence is put on or in, as a register, monument, etc. **4.** *a)* the known facts about anyone or anything, as about one's career *b)* the recorded offences of a person who has been arrested one or more times **5.** a thin, flat, grooved disc for playing on a gramophone **6.** the best performance, highest speed, greatest amount, etc. achieved, esp. when officially recorded —*adj.* establishing a record as the best, largest, etc. [a *record* crop] —**for the record** officially —**go on record** to state one's opinions publicly or officially —**have a record** to have been convicted of criminal offences in the past —**off the record** confidential(ly) —**on (the) record** publicly declared

record changer a gramophone device that automatically sets in place each record from a stack placed on a spindle

re·cord·er (ri kôr'dər) *n.* **1.** a barrister or solicitor who is appointed to act as a magistrate or justice of the peace **2.** [Chiefly U.S.] a public officer who keeps records of deeds or other official papers **3.** a machine or device that records; esp., *same as* TAPE RECORDER **4.** an early form of flute

re·cord·ing (ri kôr'diŋ) *adj.* that records —*n.* **1.** the act of one that records **2.** *a)* what is recorded, as on a disc or tape *b)* the record itself

recording angel the angel supposedly in charge of writing down all misdeeds in a large book

Record Office 1. the state department responsible for public and state records **2.** the office where such records are stored

record player a gramophone having the pickup, turntable, amplifier, speaker, etc. operated electrically or or electronically

re·count (ri kount') *vt.* [< Anglo-Fr.: see RE- & COUNT[1]] to tell in detail; narrate; enumerate —**re·count'al** *n.*

re-count (rē'kount'; *for n.* rē'kount') *vt.* to count again —*n.* a second or additional count, as of votes: also written **recount**

re·coup (ri kōōp') *vt.* [< Fr. < *re*-, again + *couper*, to cut] **1.** *a)* to make up for [to *recoup* a loss] *b)* to regain [to *recoup* one's health] **2.** to pay back —*n.* a recouping —**re·coup'a·ble** *adj.* —**re·coup'ment** *n.*

re·course (ri kôrs') *n.* [< OFr. < L. *recursus*, a running back: see RE- & COURSE] **1.** a turning for aid, safety, etc. [he

had *recourse* to the law] **2.** that to which one turns seeking aid, safety, etc. [one's last *recourse*]

re·cov·er (ri kuv'ər) *vt.* [< OFr. < L. *recuperare*: see RECUPERATE] **1.** *a)* to get back (something lost, stolen, etc.) *b)* to regain (health, etc.) **2.** to compensate for [to *recover* losses] **3.** *a)* to get (oneself) back to a state of control, balance, etc. *b)* to save (oneself) from a slip, betrayal of feeling, etc. **4.** to reclaim (land from the sea, useful substances from waste, etc.) **5.** *Law* to get back by final judgment in a court —*vi.* **1.** to regain health, balance, control, etc. **2.** to save oneself from a slip, self-betrayal, etc. **3.** *Law* to receive judgment in one's favour —**re·cov'-er·a·ble** *adj.*

re-cov·er (rē'kuv'ər) *vt.* to cover again or anew

re·cov·er·y (ri kuv'ər ē) *n., pl.* -er·ies the act or an instance of recovering; specif., *a)* a regaining of something lost or stolen *b)* a return to health, consciousness, etc. *c)* a regaining of balance, composure, etc. *d)* a retrieval of a capsule, nose cone, etc. after a spaceflight *e)* the removal of valuable substances from waste material, byproducts, etc.

rec·re·ant (rek'rē ənt) *adj.* [OFr. prp. of *recreire*, to surrender allegiance < ML. < L. *re*-, back + *credere*, to beleive] **1.** *a)* orig., crying for mercy *b)* cowardly **2.** disloyal; traitorous —*n.* **1.** a coward **2.** a disloyal person; traitor —**rec're·an·cy** *n.* —**rec're·ant·ly** *adv.*

rec·re·ate (rek'rē āt', *vt.* -at'ed, -at'ing [< L. pp. of *recreare*: see RE- & CREATE] to refresh in body or mind —*vi.* to take recreation —**rec're·a'tive** *adj.*

re-cre·ate (rē'krē āt') *vt.* -at'ed, -at'ing to create anew —**re'-cre·a'tion** *n.* —**re'-cre·a'tive** *adj.*

rec·re·a·tion (rek'rē ā'shən) *n.* [see RECREATE] **1.** refreshment in body or mind, as after work, by some form of play, amusement, or relaxation **2.** any form of play, amusement, etc. used for this purpose, as games, sports, etc. —**rec're·a'tion·al** *adj.*

re·crim·i·nate (ri krim'ə nāt') *vi.* -nat'ed, -nat'ing [< ML.: see RE- & CRIMINATE] to answer an accuser by accusing him in return —**re·crim'i·na'tion** *n.* —**re·crim'i·na·to·ry** (-nə tə rē), **re·crim'i·na'tive** *adj.*

re·cru·desce (rē'krōō des') *vi.* -desced', -desc'ing [< L. < *re*-, again + *crudescere*, to become harsh < *crudus*, raw] to break out again after being relatively inactive —**re'-cru·des'cence** *n.* —**re'cru·des'cent** *adj.*

re·cruit (ri krōōt') *vt.* [< Fr. < pp. of *recroitre*, to grow again < L. *re*-, again + *crescere*, to grow] **1.** to raise or strengthen (an army, navy, etc.) by enlisting personnel **2.** to enlist (personnel) into an army or navy **3.** *a)* to enlist (new members) for a party, organization, etc. *b)* to hire or engage the services of —*vi.* to enlist new personnel, esp. for a military force —*n.* **1.** a recently enlisted soldier, sailor, etc. **2.** a new member of any group, etc. —**re·cruit'-er** *n.* —**re·cruit'ment** *n.*

rec·tal (rek't'l) *adj.* of, for, or near the rectum —**rec'tal·ly** *adv.*

rec·tan·gle (rek'taŋ'g'l) *n.* [Fr. < ML.: see RECTI- & ANGLE[1]] any four-sided plane figure with four right angles

rec·tan·gu·lar (rek taŋ'gyə lər) *adj.* **1.** shaped like a rectangle **2.** having right-angled corners, as a building **3.** right-angled —**rec'tan'gu·lar'i·ty** (-lar'ə tē) *n.* —**rec·tan'gu·lar·ly** *adv.*

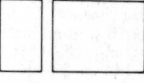

RECTANGLES

recti- [LL. < L. *rectus*] a combining form meaning straight, right [*rectilinear*]: also, before a vowel, **rect-**

rec·ti·fi·er (rek'tə fī'ər) *n.* **1.** a person or thing that rectifies **2.** *Elec.* a device that converts alternating current into direct current

rec·ti·fy (rek'tə fī') *vt.* -fied', -fy'ing [< MFr. < LL.: see RECTI- & -FY] **1.** to put right; correct **2.** *Chem.* to refine or purify (a liquid) by distillation **3.** *Elec.* to convert (alternating current) to direct current —**rec'ti·fi'a·ble** *adj.* —**rec'ti·fi·ca'tion** *n.*

rec·ti·lin·e·ar (rek'tə lin'ē ər) *adj.* [< LL. < *rectus*, straight + *linea*, LINE[1]] **1.** in or forming a straight line **2.** bounded, formed, or characterized by straight lines Also **rec'ti·lin'e·al** —**rec'ti·lin'e·ar·ly** *adv.*

rec·ti·tude (rek'tə tyōōd') *n.* [MFr. < LL. < L. *rectus*, straight] **1.** strict honesty; uprightness of character **2.** correctness of judgment or method

rec·to (rek'tō) *n., pl.* -tos [< ModL. (*folio*) *recto*, on (the page) to the right] *Printing* any right-hand page of a book; front side of a leaf: opposed to VERSO

Rec·tor (rek'tər) *n.* the nominal head of a Scottish university, elected by the students: also **Lord Rector**

rec·tor (rek'tər) *n.* [L. < pp. of *regere*, to rule] **1.** *Anglican Ch.* a clergyman in charge of a parish, in which the incumbent was formerly entitled to the whole of the tithes **2.** *R.C.Ch. a)* a priest in charge of a seminary, college, etc. *b)* the head priest of a parish **3.** in certain schools, colleges, etc., the head or headmaster —**rec'tor·ate** (-it) *n.* —**rec·to'-ri·al** (-tôr'ē əl) *adj.*

RECORDER

rec·to·ry (rek'tər ē) *n.*, *pl.* **-ries** the residence of a clergyman who is a rector

rec·tum (rek'təm) *n.*, *pl.* **-tums**, **-ta** (-tə) [ModL. < L. *rectum* (*intestinum*), straight (intestine)] the lowest, or last, segment of the large intestine, ending at the anus

re·cum·bent (ri kum'bənt) *adj.* [< L. < *re-*, back + *cumbere*, to lie down] 1. lying down; reclining 2. resting; idle —**re·cum'ben·cy** *n.* —**re·cum'bent·ly** *adv.*

re·cu·per·ate (ri kōō'pə rāt', -kyōō'-) *vt.* **-at'ed**, **-at'ing** [< L. pp. of *recuperare*, to recover] to get back, or recover (losses, health, etc.) —*vi.* 1. to get well again 2. to recover losses, etc. —**re·cu'per·a'tion** *n.* —**re·cu'per·a·tive** (-pə rāt'-iv, -pər ə tiv), **re·cu'per·a·to·ry** (-ə tər ē) *adj.* —**re·cu'per·a'tor** *n.*

re·cur (ri kur') *vi.* **-curred'**, **-cur'ring** [< L. *re-*, back + *currere*, to run] 1. to have recourse (*to*) 2. to return in thought, talk, etc. [to *recur* to a topic] 3. to occur again, as in memory 4. to happen or appear again or at intervals

re·cur·rent (ri kur'ənt) *adj.* 1. appearing again or periodically 2. turning back in the opposite direction, as some nerves —**re·cur'rence** *n.* —**re·cur'rent·ly** *adv.*

re·cur·sion (ri kur'zhən) *n.* [< L. *recurrere*: see RECUR] a return —*adj.* of a formula enabling successive terms to be computed from preceding terms

re·curve (ri kurv') *vt.*, *vi.* **-curved'**, **-curv'ing** to curve or bend back or backwards —**re·cur·vate** (ri kur'vit, -vāt) *adj.*

rec·u·sant (rek'yōō zənt, ri kyōō'z'nt) *n.* [L. *recusans*, prp. of *recusare*, to reject] a person who refuses to obey an established authority; specif., in England in the 16th to 18th cent., a Roman Catholic who refused to attend the services of the Church of England —**rec'u·san·cy** *n.*

re·cy·cle (rē sī'k'l) *vt.*, *vi.* **-cled**, **-cling** 1. to pass through a cycle again, as for treating 2. to use again and again, as a single supply of water

red¹ (red) *n.* [OE. *read*] 1. a primary colour varying in hue from that of blood to pink 2. a pigment producing this colour 3. [*often* R-] a political radical; esp., a communist 4. anything coloured red, as a red draughts piece —*adj.* **red'der**, **red'dest** 1. of the colour red 2. auburn or reddish-brown in colour: said of hair 3. *a*) having a reddish skin *b*) florid, flushed, or blushing *c*) bloodshot *d*) sore 4. [R-] *a*) politically radical; esp., communist *b*) of the Soviet Union —**in the red** in debt or losing money —**see red** [Colloq.] to be or become angry —**red'dish** *adj.* —**red'ly** *adv.* —**red'ness** *n.*

red² (red) *vt.*, *vi.* red, **red'ding** *var. of* REDD

re·dact (ri dakt') *vt.* [< L. pp. of *redigere*, to reduce to order] to arrange in proper form for publication; edit —**re·dac'tion** *n.* —**re·dac'tor** *n.*

red algae a group of red, brownish-red, pink, or purple algae that form shrublike masses in the depths of the oceans

red·bait (red'bāt') *vi.*, *vt.* [Chiefly U.S.] to denounce (a person or group) as being communist, esp. with little or no valid evidence —**red'bait'er** *n.*

red biddy a mixture of methylated spirit and cheap red wine

red·bird (-burd') *n.* any of several predominantly red-coloured birds, as the cardinal, scarlet tanager, etc.

red blood cell *same as* ERYTHROCYTE: also called **red blood corpuscle**

red-blood·ed (red'blud'id) *adj.* high-spirited and strong-willed; vigorous, lusty, etc.

red·breast (-brest') *n.* any of several birds with a reddish breast; esp., the European robin and the American robin

red·brick, red-brick (-brik') *adj.* [from the typical building material] of a British university of relatively recent foundation, esp. as distinguished from Oxford and Cambridge —*n.* a redbrick university or college

red·cap (-kap') *n.* 1. a military policeman 2. [U.S.] a porter in a railway station, air terminal, etc.

red carpet 1. a long red carpet laid out for important guests to walk on, as at a reception 2. a very grand welcome and entertainment (with *the*) —**roll out the red carpet** (for) to welcome and entertain in a very grand style —**red'-car'pet** *adj.*

red·coat (red'kōt') *n.* a British soldier in a uniform with a red coat

Red Crescent a Moslem organization equivalent to the Red Cross, whose symbol is a red crescent on a white background

Red Cross 1. a red cross on a white ground, emblem of neutrality in war, used since 1864 to mark hospitals, ambulances, etc. 2. *a*) an international society (in full, **International Red Cross**) for the relief of suffering in time of war or disaster *b*) any national branch of this

redd (red) *vt.*, *vi.* redd or **redd'ed**, **redd'ing** [< ? OE. *hreddan*, to free] [Colloq.] to make (a place) tidy (usually with *up*)

red deer 1. a deer native to Europe and Asia 2. the N American white-tailed deer in its reddish summer coat

red·den (red''n) *vt.* to make red —*vi.* to become red; esp., to blush or flush

rede (rēd) *n.* [ME. < OE. < *rædan*, to interpret] [Archaic] 1. counsel 2. a plan; scheme 3. a narration; interpretation

—*vt.* **red'ed**, **red'ing** [Archaic] 1. to advise 2. to interpret (dreams, etc.) 3. to narrate

re·deem (ri dēm') *vt.* [< MFr. < L. *redimere* < *re*(d)-, back + *emere*, to get] 1. to get or buy back; recover 2. to pay off (a mortgage, etc.) 3. *a*) to convert (paper money) into coin or bullion *b*) to convert (stocks, bonds, etc.) into cash *c*) to turn in (trading stamps or coupons) for a prize, premium, etc. 4. *a*) to set free by paying a ransom *b*) to deliver from sin and its penalties 5. to fulfil (a promise or pledge) 6. *a*) to make amends or atone for *b*) to restore (oneself) to favour by making amends *c*) to make worthwhile —**re·deem'a·ble, re·demp'ti·ble** (-demp'tə b'l) *adj.* —**re·deem'er** *n.*

re·demp·tion (ri demp'shən) *n.* [OFr. < L. < pp. of *redimere*: see prec.] 1. a redeeming or being redeemed 2. something that redeems —**re·demp'tion·al** *adj.* —**re·demp'-tive, re·demp'to·ry** *adj.*

red ensign the flag flown by the merchant navy: also **red duster**

re·de·ploy (rē'di ploi') *vt.*, *vi.* to move (troops, etc.) from one front or area to another —**re'de·ploy'ment** *n.*

red flag 1. the emblem of revolution 2. a danger signal

red fox the common European fox with reddish fur

Red Guard 1. a Chinese youth movement founded by Mao Tse Tung 2. a member of this movement

red-hand·ed (red'han'did) *adv.*, *adj.* 1. with hands covered with a victim's blood 2. in the very act of committing a crime 3. in a situation that makes one seem guilty

red hat a wide-brimmed, flat, red hat presented to a new cardinal by the pope as a symbol of the cardinal's rank

red·head (red'hed') *n.* a person with red hair —**red'head'-ed** *adj.*

red herring 1. a smoked herring 2. something used to turn attention away from the basic issue: from the act of drawing a herring across the trace in hunting, to confuse the hounds

red-hot (red'hot') *adj.* 1. hot enough to glow; very hot 2. very excited, angry, etc. 3. very new; up-to-the-minute [*red-hot* news]

red·in·gote (red'iŋ gōt') *n.* [Fr., altered < E. *riding coat*] 1. formerly, a man's long, full-skirted overcoat 2. a long, unlined, lightweight coat, open down the front, worn by women

red·in·te·grate (red in'tə grāt', ri din'-) *vt.* **-grat'ed**, **-grat'-ing** [< L. pp. of *redintegrare*: see RE- & INTEGRATE] to make whole again; reunite; re-establish —**red·in'te·gra'tion** *n.*

re·di·rect (rē'di rekt', -dī-) *vt.* to direct again or to a different place —*adj.* [U.S.] *Law* designating the examination of one's own witness again, after his cross-examination by the opposing lawyer —**re'di·rec'tion** *n.*

re·dis·count (rē dis'kount') *vt.* to discount (esp. commercial paper) for a second time —*n.* 1. a rediscounting 2. rediscounted commercial paper —**re'dis·count'a·ble** *adj.*

red lead red oxide of lead, used in making paint, in glassmaking, etc.

red-let·ter (red'let'ər) *adj.* designating a memorable or joyous day or event: from the custom of marking holidays on the calendar in red ink

red light 1. any warning signal 2. a red traffic light

red-light district (red'līt') a district (in a town or city) containing many brothels, formerly indicated by red lights

red man a North American Indian

red meat meat that is red before cooking; esp., beef or mutton as distinguished from pork, veal, poultry, etc.

re·do (rē dōō') *vt.* **-did'**, **-done'**, **-do'ing** 1. to do again 2. to redecorate (a room, etc.)

red·o·lent (red'ō lənt, red'əl ənt) *adj.* [OFr. < L. prp. of *redolere* < *re*(d)-, intens. + *olere*, to smell] 1. sweet-smelling; fragrant 2. smelling (*of*) [*redolent* of tar] 3. suggestive (*of*) —**red'o·lence, red'o·len·cy** *n.* —**red'o·lent·ly** *adv.*

re·dou·ble (rē dub''l) *vt.* **-bled**, **-bling** [MFr. *redoubler*: see RE- & DOUBLE] 1. *a*) to increase fourfold *b*) to make twice as much or twice as great *c*) to make much greater 2. to make echo or re-echo 3. to refold —*vi.* 1. *a*) to become twice as great or twice as much *b*) to increase fourfold 2. to reecho 3. to turn sharply backwards, as on one's tracks 4. *Bridge* to double a bid that an opponent has already doubled —*n.* *Bridge* a redoubling

re·doubt (ri dout') *n.* [< Fr. < It. *ridotto* < ML. *reductus*, orig. pp. of L. *reducere*: see REDUCE] 1. a breastwork outside or within a fortification 2. any stronghold

re·doubt·a·ble (-ə b'l) *adj.* [< MFr. < *redouter*, to fear < L. *re*-, intens. + *dubitare*, to doubt] 1. inspiring fear 2. commanding respect Also [Archaic] **re·doubt'ed** —**re·doubt'a·bly** *adv.*

re·dound (ri dound') *vi.* [< MFr. < L. *redundare*, to overflow < *re*(d)-, intens. + *undare*, to surge] 1. to have a result (*to* the credit or discredit of someone or something) 2. to come back; recoil (*upon*): said of honour or disgrace

re·dox (rē'doks) *n.* [< *red*(uction-) *ox*(idation)] *Chem.* a reaction involving both oxidation and reduction

red pepper 1. a plant with a red, many-seeded fruit, as the cayenne 2. the fruit 3. the ground fruit or seeds, used for seasoning

red·poll (red'pol') *n.* any of a number of finches the males of which usually have a red crown

red rag [Colloq.] anything which excites one to fury

re·dress (ri dres'; *for n., usually* rē'dres) *vt.* [< OFr.: see RE- & DRESS] 1. to set right; rectify, as by making compensation for (a wrong, etc.) 2. [Now Rare] to make amends to —*n.* 1. compensation, as for a wrong 2. a redressing —**re·dress'a·ble** *adj.* —**re·dress'er** *n.*

re-dress (rē'dres') *vt.* to dress again

red salmon *same as* SOCKEYE

red·shank (red'shaŋk') *n.* any of several common European sandpipers with red legs

red shift *Astron.* a shift towards longer wavelengths of the spectral lines of remote galaxies, thought to be due to the Doppler effect and therefore indicating an expanding universe

red·skin (-skin) *n.* [Colloq.] a North American Indian

red snapper a reddish, deep-water food fish, found in the Gulf of Mexico and in adjacent Atlantic waters

red spider a small, red, vegetarian mite

red squirrel a tree squirrel, with reddish fur

red·start (red'stärt') *n.* [RED¹ + obs. *start*, tail] 1. a small European warbler with a reddish tail 2. an American fly-catching warbler

red tape [from the tape used to tie official papers] 1. official forms and routines 2. rigid adherence to routine and regulations, causing delay in getting business done

red tide a reddish discolouration of sea waters, caused by large numbers of certain red protozoans that release poisons that kill fishes and other organisms

re·duce (ri dyōōs') *vt.* **-duced'**, **-duc'ing** [< L. < *re-*, back + *ducere*, to lead] 1. *a)* to lessen in any way, as in size, amount, value, price, etc. *b)* to put into a simpler or more concentrated form 2. to bring into a certain order; systematize 3. to change to a different form, as by melting, grinding, etc. 4. to lower, as in rank; demote 5. *a)* to bring to order, obedience, etc., as by persuasion or force *b)* to subdue or conquer 6. *a)* to bring into difficult circumstances [*reduced* to poverty] *b)* to compel by need [*reduced* to stealing] 7. to make thin 8. *Arith.* to change in denomination or form without changing in value [to *reduce* 4/8 to 1/2] 9. *Chem.* a) to decrease the positive valence of (an atom or ion) *b)* to increase the number of electrons of (an atom or ion) *c)* to remove the oxygen from *d)* to combine with hydrogen *e)* to bring into the metallic state by removing nonmetallic elements 10. *Photog.* to weaken the density of (a negative) 11. *Surgery* to restore to normal position [to *reduce* a fracture] —*vi.* 1. to become reduced 2. to lose weight, as by being on a diet —**re·duc'er** *n.* —**re·duc'i·bil'i·ty** *n.* —**re·duc'i·ble** *adj.* —**re·duc'i·bly** *adv.*

reducing agent *Chem.* any substance that reduces another substance and is itself oxidized in the process

†**re·duc·ti·o ad ab·sur·dum** (ri duk'tē ō' ad ab sur'dəm) [L., lit., reduction to absurdity] *Logic* the disproof of a proposition by showing the logical conclusions drawn from it to be absurd

re·duc·tion (ri duk'shən) *n.* 1. a reducing or being reduced *b)* the amount of this 2. anything made or brought about by reducing, as a smaller copy —**re·duc'tion·al** *adj.* —**re·duc'tive** *adj.* —**re·duc'tive·ly** *adv.*

re·duc·tion·ism (-iz'm) *n.* the belief that complex statements, data, etc. can be reduced to seemingly equivalent simple ones: usually a disparaging term —**re·duc'tion·ist** *n., adj.*

re·dun·dan·cy (ri dun'dən sē) *n., pl.* **-cies** 1. a being redundant 2. an overabundance 3. the use of redundant words 4. the part of a statement that is redundant or unnecessary Also **re·dun'dance**

redundancy payment a sum of money given to a worker who is made redundant by an employer

re·dun·dant (-dənt) *adj.* [< L. prp. of *redundare*: see REDOUND] 1. more than enough; excess; superfluous 2. wordy 3. unnecessary to the meaning: said of words and affixes 4. of a worker deprived of a job because he is no longer needed —**re·dun'dant·ly** *adv.*

re·du·pli·cate (ri dyōō'plə kāt'; *for adj. & n., usually* -kit) *vt.* **-cat'ed**, **-cat'ing** [< ML.: see RE- & DUPLICATE] 1. to redouble, double, or repeat 2. to double (a syllable or word) to form a new word (as *tom-tom*), sometimes with changes (as *chitchat*) —*vi.* to become reduplicated —*adj.* reduplicated; doubled —*n.* something reduplicated —**re·du'pli·ca'tion** *n.* —**re·du'pli·ca'tive** *adj.*

red·wing (red'wiŋ') *n.* a small European thrush with an orange-red patch on the underside of the wings

red·wood (-wood') *n.* 1. a giant N American evergreen having enduring, soft wood, found on the coast of California and S Oregon 2. the wood of these trees

ree·bok (rē'bok) *n.* *same as* RHEBOK

re·ech·o, re-ech·o (rē ek'ō) *vt., vi.* **-ech'oed, -ech'o·ing** to echo back or again; resound —*n., pl.* **-ech'oes** the echo of an echo

reed (rēd) *n.* [OE. *hreod*] 1. *a)* any of various tall, slender grasses growing in wet or marshy land *b)* the stem of any of these *c)* such plants collectively 2. a rustic musical pipe made from a hollow stem 3. *Music a)* a thin strip of some flexible substance placed within the opening of the mouthpiece of certain wind instruments, as the clarinet: when vibrated by the breath, it produces a musical tone *b)* an instrument with a reed *c)* in some organs, a similar device that vibrates in a current of air

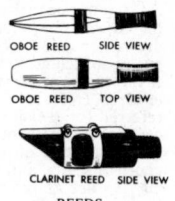

OBOE REED   SIDE VIEW

OBOE REED   TOP VIEW

CLARINET REED   SIDE VIEW

REEDS

reed bunting *same as* ORTOLAN

reed organ an organ with a set of free metal reeds instead of pipes to produce the tones

re·ed·u·cate, re-ed·u·cate (rē'ed'yoo kāt') *vt.* **-cat'ed, -cat'ing** to educate anew, esp. so as to rehabilitate or adapt to new situations —**re·ed'u·ca'tion, re-ed'u·ca'tion** *n.* —**re·ed'·u·ca'tive, re-ed'u·ca'tive** *adj.*

reed warbler a small, brown, European songbird that nests in reeds

reed·y (rēd'ē) *adj.* **reed'i·er, reed'i·est** 1. full of reeds 2. made of reed or reeds 3. like a reed; slender, fragile, etc. 4. sounding like a reed instrument; thin; piping —**reed'i·ly** *adv.* —**reed'i·ness** *n.*

reef¹ (rēf) *n.* [prob. < ON. *rif*, a rib] a ridge of rock, coral, or sand at or near the surface of the water

reef² (rēf) *n.* [< akin to prec.] 1. a part of a sail which can be folded and tied down to reduce the area exposed to the wind 2. the act of reefing —*vt.* 1. to reduce (a sail) by taking in part of it 2. to lower (a spar or mast) or reduce the projection of (a bowsprit)

reef·er (rē'fər) *n.* 1. a person who reefs 2. a short, thick, double-breasted coat like a seaman's jacket 3. [from the rolled appearance of a *reef* (of a sail)] [Slang] a marijuana cigarette

reef knot a double knot in which the free ends run parallel to the standing parts

reek (rēk) *n.* [OE. *rec*] 1. vapour; fume 2. a strong, unpleasant smell; stench —*vi.* 1. to fume 2. to have a strong, offensive smell 3. to be permeated with anything very unpleasant —*vt.* to emit or exude (vapour, fumes, etc.) —**reek'y** *adj.*

reel¹ (rēl) *vi.* [< the *n.*] 1. to give way or fall back; sway or stagger as from being struck 2. to lurch or stagger about, as from drunkenness 3. to go round and round; whirl 4. to feel dizzy —*vt.* to cause to reel —*n.* [OE. *hreol*] a reeling motion; whirl, stagger, etc.

reel² (rēl) *n.* [prob. < REEL¹, *n.*] 1. any of various lively Scottish dances 2. music for these

reel³ (rēl) *n.* [OE. *hreol*] 1. a frame or spool on which thread, wire, film, etc. is wound; esp. for sewing thread 2. such a frame on a fishing rod for winding line 3. the quantity of wire, thread, film, etc. usually wound on one reel; spool 4. in a lawn mower, a set of spiral steel blades rotating on a horizontal bar —*vt., vi.* to wind on a reel —**reel in** 1. to wind on a reel 2. to pull in (a fish) by winding a line on a reel —**reel off** to tell, write, etc. easily and quickly —**reel out** to unwind from a reel —**(right) off the reel** without hesitation

re·en·force, re-en·force (rē'in fôrs') *vt.* **-forced', -forc'ing** *same as* REINFORCE

re·en·try, re-en·try (rē en'trē) *n., pl.* **-tries** 1. a re-entering; specif., a coming back, as of a space vehicle, into the earth's atmosphere 2. a second or repeated entry 3. *Bridge, Whist* a card that will win a trick and regain the lead

reeve¹ (rēv) *n.* [OE. *gerefa*] 1. in English history, *a)* the chief officer of a town or district *b)* the overseer of a manor; steward 2. the elected head of a town council in certain Canadian provinces

reeve² (rēv) *vt.* **reeved** or **rove, rove** or **rov'en, reev'ing** [prob. < Du. *reven*] *Naut.* 1. to slip (a rope, etc.) through a block, ring, etc. 2. *a)* to pass in, through, or round something *b)* to fasten by so doing 3. to pass a rope through (a block or pulley)

reeve³ (rēv) *n.* [? < irreg. pl. of RUFF¹] the female of the ruff (sandpiper)

ref (ref) *n., vt., vi.* [Colloq.] *same as* REFEREE

ref. 1. referee 2. reference 3. reformed

re·fec·tion (ri fek'shən) *n.* [OFr. < L. < pp. of *reficere* < *re-*, again + *facere*, to make] 1. food or drink taken to refresh oneself 2. a light meal

re·fec·to·ry (-tər ē) *n., pl.* **-ries** a dining hall in a monastery, convent, college, etc.

refectory table a long, narrow, rectangular table, as that used in the dining hall of a monastery or convent

re·fer (ri fur') *vt.* **-ferred', -fer'ring** [< MFr. < L. *referre* < *re-*, back + *ferre*, to bear] 1. to assign or attribute (*to*) as cause or origin **2.** to assign or regard as belonging (*to* a kind, class, etc.) **3.** to submit (a quarrel, etc.) for settlement **4.** to direct (*to* someone or something) for aid, information, etc. —*vi.* **1.** to relate or apply (*to*) **2.** to direct attention, or make reference (*to*) [*to refer* to an earlier event] **3.** to turn for information, aid, etc. (*to*) [*to refer* to a map] —**refer to drawer** written by bankers on cheques when the account has insufficient funds available —**ref·er·a·ble** (ref'ər ə b'l), **re·fer'ra·ble, re·fer'ri·ble** (ri fur'-) *adj.* —**re·fer'rer** *n.*

ref·er·ee (ref'ə rē') *n.* **1.** a person to whom something is referred for decision **2.** an official who enforces the rules in certain sports contests **3.** someone who testifies to the good character of another **4.** *Law* a person appointed by a court to study, and report on, a matter —*vt., vi.* **-eed', -ee'-ing** to act as referee (in)

ref·er·ence (ref'ər əns, ref'rəns) *n.* **1.** a referring or being referred **2.** relation; regard [in *reference* to his letter] **3.** *a*) the direction of attention to a person or thing *b*) a mention or allusion **4.** *a*) an indication, as in a book, of some other work to be consulted *b*) the work so indicated *c*) a number or symbol (in full, **reference mark**) directing the reader to a footnote, etc. **5.** *a*) the giving of the name of a person who can offer information or recommendation *b*) the person so indicated *c*) a written statement giving the qualifications, abilities, etc. of someone seeking a position, etc. **6.** *a*) a source of information: often attributive [*reference* books] *b*) a book, etc. used for reference —*vt.* **-enced, -enc·ing** to provide with references —**make reference to** refer to; mention —**with reference to** concerning —**ref'er·en'tial** (-ə ren'shəl) *adj.* —**ref'er·en'-tial·ly** *adv.*

reference library a library where books may be consulted but not taken away by readers

ref·er·en·dum (ref'ə ren'dəm) *n., pl.* **-dums** or **-da** (-də) [ModL. < L., gerund of *referre*: see REFER] **1.** the submission of a law, proposed or already in effect, to a direct vote of the people **2.** the right of the people to vote on such laws, overruling the legislature **3.** the vote itself

ref·er·ent (ref'ər ənt) *n.* something referred to; specif., *Linguis.* the thing referred to by a term or expression

re·fer·ral (ri fur'əl) *n.* **1.** a referring or being referred, as for professional service **2.** a person who is referred or directed to another person, an agency, etc.

re·fill (rē fil'; *for n.* rē'fil) *vt., vi.* to fill again —*n.* a new filling; esp., *a*) a unit to replace the used-up contents of a container *b*) any additional filling of a prescription for medicine —**re·fill'a·ble** *adj.*

re·fi·nance (rē'fə nans', rē fī'nans) *vt.* **-nanced', -nanc'ing** to finance again; specif., to provide or obtain a new loan or more capital for

re·fine (ri fin') *vt., vi.* **-fined', -fin'ing** [RE- + FINE[1], v.] **1.** to free or become free from impurities, dross, etc.; purify **2.** to free or become free from imperfection, coarseness, etc.; make or become more polished **3.** to make or become more subtle, as in thinking or speaking —**refine on** (or **upon**) to improve, as by adding refinements —**re·fin'er** *n.*

re·fined (ri find') *adj.* **1.** made free from impurities; purified **2.** free from coarseness; cultivated; elegant **3.** characterized by great subtlety, precision, etc.

re·fine·ment (ri fin'mənt) *n.* **1.** *a*) a refining or being refined *b*) the result of this **2.** delicacy or elegance of language, speech, manners, etc.; polish **3.** a development; improvement; elaboration **4.** a fine distinction; subtlety

re·fin·er·y (ri fin'ər ē) *n., pl.* **-er·ies** an establishment or plant for refining, or purifying, such raw materials as oil, metal, sugar, etc.

re·fin·ish (rē fin'ish) *vt.* to give a new surface to (wood, etc.) —**re·fin'ish·er** *n.*

re·fit (rē fit'; *also for n.* rē'fit) *vt., vi.* **-fit'ted, -fit'ting** to make or be made ready or fit for use again, as by repairing, reequipping, etc. —*n.* an act or instance of refitting

refl. **1.** reflection **2.** reflex **3.** reflexive

re·flate (rē flāt') *vt., vi.* [< REFLATION] to inflate or be inflated again

re·fla·tion (rē flā'shən) *n.* [RE- + (IN)FLATION] **1.** an increase in money supply designed to cause an increase in economic activity **2.** the increase in economic activity, output, employment, investment, etc.

re·flect (ri flekt') *vt.* [< MFr. < L. < *re*-, back + *flectere*, to bend] **1.** to bend or throw back (light, heat, or sound) **2.** to give back an image of; mirror or reproduce **3.** to bring back as a consequence (with *on*) [deeds that *reflect* honour on him] **4.** to express or show [skills that *reflect* years of training] **5.** to recollect or realize after thought (*that*) **6.** to fold or turn back: *usually used in pp.* —*vi.* **1.** to be thrown back [light *reflecting* from the water] **2.** to throw back light, heat, etc. [a *reflecting* surface] **3.** *a*) to give back an image *b*) to be mirrored **4.** to think seriously; contemplate (*on* or *upon*) **5.** to cast blame or discredit (*on* or *upon*)

re·flec·tance (-flek'təns) *n.* *Physics* the ratio of the total electromagnetic radiation, usually light, reflected by a surface to the total striking the surface

re·flec·tion (ri flek'shən) *n.* **1.** a reflecting or being reflected **2.** the throwing back by a surface of sound, light, etc. **3.** anything reflected; specif., an image; likeness **4.** *a*) serious thought; contemplation *b*) an idea, remark, etc. that comes from such thought **5.** *a*) blame; discredit *b*) a statement casting, or an action bringing, blame or discredit **6.** *Anat.* a bending back on itself —**re·flec'tion·al** *adj.*

re·flec·tive (-tiv) *adj.* **1.** reflecting **2.** of or produced by reflection **3.** meditative; thoughtful —**re·flec'tive·ly** *adv.* —**re·flec'tive·ness, re·flec·tiv'i·ty** *n.*

re·flec·tor (-tər) *n.* **1.** a person or thing that reflects; esp., a surface, object, or device that reflects radiant energy, as light, sound, etc. **2.** a reflecting telescope: see TELESCOPE

re·flex (rē'fleks; *for v.* ri fleks') *n.* [< L. pp. of *reflectere*: see REFLECT] **1.** reflection, as of light **2.** a reflected image or reproduction **3.** *a*) *Physiol.* a reflex action *b*) any quick, automatic or habitual response *c*) [*pl.*] ability to react quickly and effectively [a boxer with good *reflexes*] —*adj.* **1.** turned or bent back **2.** coming in reaction; esp., *Physiol.* designating or of an involuntary action, as a sneeze, resulting when a stimulus carried to a nerve centre is directly transmitted to the muscle or gland that responds **3.** *Geom.* designating an angle greater than a straight angle (180°) —*vt.* to bend, turn, or fold back —**re'flex·ly** *adv.*

REFLEX ANGLES

re·flex·ion (ri flek'shən) *n.* *var. of* REFLECTION

re·flex·ive (-siv) *adj.* **1.** reflex **2.** *Gram. a*) designating a verb whose subject and direct object refer to the same person or thing (e.g., *wash* in "I wash myself") *b*) designating a pronoun used as the direct object of such a verb, as *myself* in the above example —*n.* a reflexive verb or pronoun —**re·flex'ive·ly** *adv.* —**re·flex'ive·ness, re·flex·iv'i·ty** (rē'flek siv'ə tē) *n.*

re·form (ri form') *vt.* [< OFr. < L. *reformare*: see RE- & FORM] **1.** to make better by removing faults; correct [to *reform* a calendar] **2.** *a*) to make better by stopping abuses, introducing better procedures, etc. *b*) to put a stop to (abuses, etc.) **3.** to cause (a person) to give up misconduct and behave better —*vi.* to become better; give up one's bad ways —*n.* **1.** a correction of faults or evils, as in government or society **2.** an improvement in character and conduct —*adj.* [R-] designating or of a movement in Judaism that emphasizes its ethical aspects rather than traditional ritual —**re·form'a·ble** *adj.* —**re·form'a·tive** *adj.*

re·form (rē'form') *vt., vi.* to form again

ref·or·ma·tion (ref'ər mā'shən) *n.* **1.** a reforming or being reformed **2.** [R-] the 16th-cent. religious movement that aimed at reforming the Roman Catholic Church and resulted in establishing the Protestant churches —**ref'or·ma'tion·al** *adj.*

re·form·a·to·ry (ri fôr'mə tər ē) *adj.* reforming or aiming at reform —*n., pl.* **-ries** formerly, an institution to which young offenders were sent for training and discipline intended to reform them: also **reform school**

re·formed (re fôrmd') *adj.* **1.** improved or corrected **2.** [R-] designating a Protestant church or churches, esp. Calvinist churches

re·form·er (ri fôr'mar) *n.* a person who seeks to bring about reform, esp. political or social reform

re·form·ism (-miz'm) *n.* the practice or advocacy of reform, esp. political or social reform —**re·form'ist** *n., adj.*

re·fract (ri frakt') *vt.* [< L. *refractus*, pp. of *refringere* < *re*-, back + *frangere*, to break] **1.** to cause (a ray or wave of light, heat, or sound) to undergo refraction **2.** *Optics* to measure the degree of refraction of (an eye or lens) —**re·frac'tive** *adj.* —**re·frac'tive·ly** *adv.* —**re·frac·tiv'i·ty** (rē'-frak tiv'ə tē), **re·frac'tive·ness** *n.*

re·frac·tion (ri frak'shən) *n.* **1.** the bending of a ray or wave of light, heat, or sound, as it passes obliquely from one medium to another of different density **2.** *Optics* the ability of the eye to refract light entering it, so as to form an image on the retina

refractive index *Physics* a measure of the extent to which a material refracts light; the ratio of the velocity of light in a vacuum to the velocity of light in the material

re·frac·tom·e·ter (rē'frak tom'ə tar) *n.* an instrument for measuring refraction, as of the eye

re·frac·tor (ri frak'tar) *n.* **1.** something that refracts **2.** a refracting telescope: see TELESCOPE

re·frac·to·ry (ri frak'tar ē) *adj.* [< L. < *refractus*: see REFRACT] **1.** hard to manage; stubborn; obstinate **2.** resistant to heat; hard to melt or work: said of ores or metals **3.** not yielding to treatment, as a disease —**re·frac'to·ri·ly** *adv.* —**re·frac'to·ri·ness** *n.*

re·frain[1] (ri frān') *vi.* [< OFr. < L. < *re*-, back + *frenare*, to curb < *frenum*, a rein] to hold back; keep oneself (*from* doing something); forbear

re·frain[2] (ri frān') *n.* [MFr., ult. < L. *refringere*: see REFRACT] **1.** a phrase or verse repeated at intervals in a song or poem, as after each stanza **2.** music for this

re·fran·gi·ble (ri fran'jə b'l) *adj.* [< RE- + L. *frangere*, to break + -IBLE] that can be refracted, as light rays —**re·fran'gi·bil'i·ty, re·fran'gi·ble·ness** *n.*

re·fresh (ri fresh') *vt.* [< OFr.: see RE- & FRESH¹] 1. to make fresh by cooling, wetting, etc. [rains *refreshing* parched plants] 2. to make (another or oneself) feel cooler, stronger, etc., as by food, drink, or sleep 3. to replenish, as by new supplies, etc. 4. to revive (the memory, etc.) —*vi.* 1. to become fresh again; revive 2. to take refreshment, as food or drink —**re·fresh'er** *n.* —**re·fresh'ing** *adj.* —**re·fresh'·ing·ly** *adv.*

refresher course a course of study reviewing material previously studied

re·fresh·ment (ri fresh'mənt) *n.* 1. a refreshing or being refreshed 2. something that refreshes, as food, drink, etc. 3. [*pl.*] food or drink or both, esp. when not a full meal

refreshment room a room where food and drinks are sold, esp. in a railway or coach station

re·frig·er·ant (ri frij'ər ənt) *adj.* 1. that refrigerates; cooling or freezing 2. reducing heat or fever —*n.* 1. a substance used to reduce fever 2. a substance used in refrigeration; specif., any of various liquids that vaporize at a low temperature, used in mechanical refrigeration

re·frig·er·ate (-ə rāt') *vt.* -at'ed, -at'ing [< L. pp. of *refrigerare* < *re*-, intens. + *frigerare*, to cool < *frigus*, cold] 1. to make or keep cool or cold; chill 2. to preserve (food, etc.) by keeping cold or freezing —**re·frig'er·a'tion** *n.* —**re·frig'er·a'tive, re·frig'er·a·to·ry** *adj.*

re·frig·er·a·tor (-rāt'ər) *n.* something that refrigerates; esp., a box, cabinet, or room in which food, etc. is kept cool, as by ice or mechanical refrigeration

reft (reft) *adj.* robbed or deprived (of something); bereft

re·fu·el (rē fyōō'l', -fyōō'əl) *vt.* -fu'elled, -fu'el·ling to supply again with fuel —*vi.* to take on a fresh supply of fuel

ref·uge (ref'yōōj) *n.* [< OFr. < L., ult. < *re*-, back + *fugere*, to flee] 1. shelter or protection from danger, difficulty, etc. 2. a place of safety; shelter; safe retreat

ref·u·gee (ref'yoo jē') *n.* a person who flees from his home or country to seek refuge elsewhere, as in a time of war, persecution, etc.

re·ful·gent (ri ful'jənt) *adj.* [< L. prp. of *refulgere*: see RE- & FULGENT] shining; radiant; resplendent —**re·ful'gence, re·ful'gen·cy** *n.* —**re·ful'gent·ly** *adv.*

re·fund¹ (ri fund'; *for n.* rē'fund') *vt., vi.* [< MFr. < L. < *re*-, back + *fundere*, to pour] to give back (money, etc.); repay —*n.* the act of refunding or the amount refunded; repayment —**re·fund'a·ble** *adj.*

re·fund² (rē'fund') *vt.* to fund again or anew; specif., *Finance* to use borrowed money, as from the sale of a bond issue, to pay back (a loan)

re·fur·bish (ri fur'bish) *vt.* [RE- + FURBISH] to brighten, freshen, or polish up again; renovate —**re·fur'bish·ment** *n.*

re·fus·al (ri fyōō'z'l) *n.* 1. the act of refusing 2. the right or chance to accept or refuse something before it is offered to another; option

re·fuse¹ (ri fyōōz') *vt.* -fused', -fus'ing [< OFr. *refuser*, ult. < L. pp. of *refundere*: see REFUND¹] 1. to decline to accept; reject 2. to decline to do, give, grant, obey, etc.; deny [to *refuse* a request, to *refuse* to go] 3. to stop short at (a fence, etc.) without jumping it: said of a horse —*vi.* to decline to accept, agree to, or do something —**re·fus'er** *n.*

ref·use² (ref'yōōs, -yōōz) *n.* [< OFr. pp. of *refuser*: see prec.] anything thrown away or rejected as worthless or useless; waste; rubbish —*adj.* thrown away or rejected as worthless or useless

re·fute (ri fyōōt') *vt.* -fut'ed, -fut'ing [L. *refutare*, to repel: see RE- & CONFUTE] 1. to prove (a person) to be wrong; confute 2. to prove (an argument or statement) to be false or wrong, by argument or evidence —**re·fut'a·ble** (-fyōōt'ə b'l, ref'yoo tə-) *adj.* —**re·fut'a·bly** *adv.* —**ref·u·ta·tion** (ref'yə tā'shən), **re·fut'al** *n.* —**re·fut'er** *n.*

reg. 1. regiment 2. region 3. register 4. registered 5. registrar 6. regular 7. regulation

re·gain (ri gān') *vt.* 1. to get back again; recover 2. to succeed in reaching again; get back to

re·gal (rē'gəl) *adj.* [MFr. < L. *regalis* < *rex* (gen. *regis*), a king] 1. of a king; royal 2. characteristic of, like, or fit for a king; splendid, stately, etc. —**re·gal·i·ty** (rē gal'ə tē) *n.* —**re'gal·ly** *adv.*

re·gale (ri gāl') *vt.* -galed', -gal'ing [< Fr. < *ré*- (see RE-) + OFr. *gale*, joy] 1. to entertain by providing a splendid feast 2. to delight with something pleasing or amusing —*vi.* to feast —**re·gale'ment** *n.* —**re·gal'er** *n.*

re·ga·li·a (ri gāl'yə, -gā'lē ə) *n.pl.* [L., neut. pl. of *regalis*: see REGAL] 1. the emblems and insignia of kingship, as a crown, sceptre, etc. 2. the insignia or decorations of any rank, society, etc. 3. [Colloq.] splendid clothes; finery

re·gard (ri gärd') *n.* [< OFr. < *regarder*: see RE- & GUARD] 1. a firm, fixed look; gaze 2. consideration; concern [have *regard* for your health] 3. respect and affection; esteem [to have high *regard* for one's teachers] 4. reference; relation [in *regard* to your plan] 5. [*pl.*] good wishes; respects [give my *regards* to Bill] —*vt.* 1. to look at with a firm,

steady gaze 2. to take into account; consider 3. [Archaic] to give attentive heed to 4. to hold in affection and respect 5. to think of in a certain light [to *regard* taxes as a burden] 6. to have relation to; concern [this *regards* your welfare] —*vi.* to look or pay heed —**as regards** concerning —**without regard to** without considering

re·gard·ful (-fəl) *adj.* 1. observant; heedful; mindful (*of*) 2. showing regard; respectful —**re·gard'ful·ly** *adv.*

re·gard·ing (-iŋ) *prep.* with regard to; concerning; about

re·gard·less (-lis) *adj.* without regard; heedless; careless —*adv.* [Colloq.] without regard for objections, difficulties, etc.; anyway —**regardless of** in spite of; notwithstanding —**re·gard'less·ly** *adv.*

re·gat·ta (ri gat'ə) *n.* [It.] 1. a boat race 2. a series of such races

regd. registered

re·gen·cy (rē'jən sē) *n., pl.* -cies 1. the position, function, or authority of a regent or group of regents 2. a group of men serving as regents 3. a country governed by a regent or a group of regents 4. the time during which a regent or regency governs; specif., [R-] in Britain, the period between 1811 and 1820

Regency stripes a fabric pattern with coloured stripes of equal width

re·gen·er·ate (ri jen'ər it; *for v.* -ə rāt') *adj.* [< L. pp. of *regenerare*: see RE- & GENERATE] 1. spiritually reborn 2. renewed or restored —*vt.* -at'ed, -at'ing 1. to cause to be spiritually reborn 2. to cause to be completely reformed or improved 3. to bring into existence again; reestablish 4. *Biol.* to grow anew (a part to replace one hurt or lost) 5. *Electronics* to increase the amplification of (a signal) by feeding energy back from an amplifier output to its input 6. *Physics* to restore (a battery, etc.) to its original state or properties —*vi.* 1. to form again, or be made anew 2. to be regenerated, or spiritually reborn —**re·gen'er·a·cy** (-ə sē) *n.* —**re·gen'er·a'tion** *n.* —**re·gen'er·a'tive** *adj.*

re·gent (rē'jənt) *adj.* [MFr. < ML. < L. prp. of *regere*, to rule] acting in place of a king or ruler [a prince *regent*] —*n.* 1. a person appointed to rule a monarchy when the sovereign is absent, too young, or incapacitated 2. a member of a governing board, as of a university —**re'·gent·ship'** *n.*

re·gent·bird (-burd) *n.* a bowerbird of Australia with a very beautiful plumage

Regent House the general assembly of resident senior members in Cambridge University

reg·gae (reg'ā) *n.* [< ?] a form of popular music of Jamaican origin, characterized by a strong rhythm and influenced by calypso and rock-and-roll

reg·i·cide (rej'ə sid') *n.* [< ML. < L. *rex* (see REGAL) + -*cida*: see -CIDE] 1. a person who kills a king, specif. [R-] one of those who tried and executed Charles I 2. the killing of a king —**reg'i·ci'dal** *adj.*

re·gime, ré·gime (rə zhēm', rā-) *n.* [< Fr. < L. *regimen*: see ff.] 1. *a)* a political system *b)* a form of government or rule 2. a social system or order 3. the period that a person or system is in power 4. *same as* REGIMEN

reg·i·men (rej'ə mən) *n.* [L., rule < *regere*, to rule] a regulated system of diet, exercise, rest, etc. for promoting the health

reg·i·ment (rej'ə mənt; *for v.* -ment') *n.* [< MFr. < LL. *regimentum*, government < L. *regere*, to rule] 1. a military unit consisting of two or more battalions 2. a large number (of persons, etc.) —*vt.* 1. to form into regiments 2. to assign to a regiment 3. to organize systematically, as into uniform groups 4. to organize in a rigid system under strict discipline and control —**reg'i·men'tal** *adj.* —**reg'i·men'·tal·ly** *adv.* —**reg'i·men·ta'tion** *n.*

reg·i·men·tals (rej'ə men't'lz) *n.pl.* 1. a regiment's uniform and insignia 2. military uniform

regimental serjeant major 1. *see* WARRANT OFFICER 2. *see* MILITARY RANKS, table

re·gi·na (ri jī'nə) *n.* [L., a queen] [*also* R-] queen [*Regina* vs. Jones]

re·gion (rē'jən) *n.* [< Anglo-Fr. < OFr. < L. *regio* < *regere*, to rule] 1. a part of the earth's surface, esp. a part having a specified position or feature [a coastal *region*, tropical *regions*] 2. any area, place, space, etc. or sphere, realm, etc. [the upper *regions* of the air, a *region* of research] 3. an administrative division of a country, as in Scotland, Italy, or the U.S.S.R. 4. a division or part of the body [the abdominal *region*] —**in the region of** approximately; about

re·gion·al (-'l) *adj.* 1. of a whole region, not just a locality 2. of some particular region, district, etc. —**re'gion·al·ly** *adv.*

re·gion·al·ism (-'l iz'm) *n.* 1. the division of a country into smaller administrative regions 2. regional quality or character 3. devotion to one's own geographical region

reg·is·ter (rej'is tər) *n.* [< MFr. < ML. *registrum* < LL. < L. pp. of *regerere*, to record] 1. *a)* a record or list of names, events, items, etc. *b)* a book in which this is kept *c)* an entry in such a record 2. registration; enrolment 3. a device, as a meter or counter, for recording fares paid, money deposited, etc. [a cash *register*] 4. an opening into a room by which the amount of air passing, as from a furnace, can be controlled **5.** *Music a)* a part of a range of tones of the human voice or of an instrument having a specified quality *b)* an organ stop, or the tone quality it produces **6.** *Printing* exact placing of lines, pages, colours, etc. —*vt.* **1.** to enter in or as in a record or list; enrol **2.** to indicate as on a scale [*a thermometer registers temperature*] **3.** to show, as by facial expression [*to register surprise*] **4.** to safeguard (a letter, etc.) by having its committal to the postal system recorded, for a fee **5.** *Printing* to cause to be in register —*vi.* **1.** to enter one's name, as in a hotel register, a list of eligible voters, etc. **2.** to enrol in a school, college, etc. **3.** to make an impression —**reg′is·tra·ble** (-trə b'l) *adj.* —**reg′is·trant** (-trant) *n.*

reg·is·tered (-tərd) *adj.* officially or legally recorded, enrolled, or certified

registered post 1. a postal service, by which, for a fee, either delivery of post or compensation for its loss is guaranteed **2.** letters, etc. sent using this service

reg·is·trar (rej′i strär′, rej′i strär′) *n.* **1.** an official who keeps records, as of the students in a college **2.** a hospital doctor senior to a houseman and junior to a consultant **3.** [Chiefly U.S.] a trust company that keeps the records of stock transfers, etc.

reg·is·tra·tion (rej′i strā′shən) *n.* **1.** a registering or being registered **2.** an entry in a register **3.** [Chiefly U.S.] the number of persons registered

registration plate *same as* NUMBER PLATE

reg·is·try (rej′is trē) *n.*, *pl.* **-tries 1.** *same as* REGISTRATION **2.** an office where registers are kept **3.** an official record or list; register **4.** a certificate showing the nationality of a merchant ship as recorded in an official register

registry office a government office where civil marriages are performed and births, marriages, and deaths are recorded

re·gi·us (rē′jē əs) *adj.* [ModL. < L. < *rex*, a king] designating certain professors at British universities holding chairs founded by royal charter

reg·nant (reg′nənt) *adj.* [< L. prp. of *regnare*, to reign] **1.** reigning; ruling **2.** predominant **3.** prevalent; widespread —**reg′nan·cy** *n.*

re·gorge (ri görj′) *vt.* **-gorged′**, **-gorg′ing** [< Fr.: see RE- & GORGE] to throw up or back; disgorge

re·gress (rē′gres; *for v.* ri gres′) *n.* [< L. pp. of *regredi* < *re-*, back + *gradi*, to go] **1.** a going or coming back **2.** backward movement; retrogression —*vi.* **1.** to go back; move backwards **2.** to revert to an earlier form or to earlier or more infantile behaviour patterns —**re·gres′sion** *n.* —**re·gres′sive** *adj.* —**re·gres′sive·ly** *adv.* —**re·gres′sor** *n.*

re·gret (ri gret′) *vt.* **-gret′ted**, **-gret′ting** [< OFr. *regreter*, to mourn < a Gmc. base] **1.** to be sorry about or mourn for (a person or thing gone, lost, etc.) **2.** to feel troubled or remorseful over (an occurrence, one's acts, etc.) —*n.* **1.** a troubled feeling or remorse, esp. over one's acts or omissions **2.** sorrow over a person or thing gone, lost, etc. —**(one's) regrets** a polite expression of regret, as at declining an invitation —**re·gret′ful** *adj.* —**re·gret′ful·ly** *adv.* —**re·gret′ful·ness** *n.* —**re·gret′ta·ble** *adj.* —**re·gret′ta·bly** *adv.* —**re·gret′ter** *n.*

re·group (rē grōōp′) *vt.*, *vi.* to group again; specif., *Mil.* to reorganize (one's forces), as after a battle

Regt. Regiment

reg·u·lar (reg′yə lər) *adj.* [< MFr. < L. < *regula*: see RULE] **1.** conforming in form or arrangement to a rule, principle, type, etc.; orderly; symmetrical **2.** characterized by conformity to a fixed principle or procedure **3.** usual; customary **4.** consistent, habitual, steady, etc. [*a regular customer*] **5.** recurring at set times or functioning in a normal way **6.** conforming to a generally accepted rule of conduct; proper **7.** properly qualified [*a regular doctor*] **8.** [Colloq.] thorough; absolute [*a regular nuisance*] **9.** [U.S. Colloq.] pleasant, friendly, etc. [*a regular fellow*] **10.** *Bot.* having all similar parts of the same shape and size: said of flowers **11.** *Eccles.* belonging to a religious order, etc. and adhering to its rule **12.** *Gram.* conforming to the usual type as in inflection **13.** *Math.* having all angles and sides equal, as a polygon, or all faces equal, as a polyhedron **14.** *Mil. a)* designating or of the standing army of a country *b)* designating soldiers recognized in international law as legitimate combatants in warfare —*n.* **1.** a member of a religious order **2.** a member of a regular army **3.** [Colloq.] a regular customer, visitor, etc. —**reg′u·lar′i·ty** (-lar′ə tē) *n.*, *pl.* **-ties** —**reg′u·lar·ly** *adv.*

Regular Army the permanent, or standing, army of any country, specif. that of Britain

reg·u·late (reg′yə lāt′) *vt.* **-lat′ed**, **-lat′ing** [< LL. pp. of *regulare* < L. *regula*: see RULE] **1.** to control or direct according to a rule, principle, etc. **2.** to adjust to a standard, rate, degree, etc. [*regulate price rises*] **3.** to adjust (a clock, etc.) so as to make operate accurately **4.** to make uniform, methodical, etc. —**reg′u·la·tive**, **reg′u·la·to·ry** (-lə tər ē) *adj.*

reg·u·la·tion (reg′yə lā′shən) *n.* **1.** a regulating or being

regulated **2.** a rule or law by which conduct, etc. is regulated —*adj.* **1.** required by regulation [*a regulation uniform*] **2.** usual; normal

reg·u·la·tor (reg′yə lāt′ər) *n.* a person or thing that regulates; specif., *a)* a mechanism for controlling the movement of machinery, fluids, etc.; governor *b)* the device in a watch or clock by which its speed is adjusted

re·gur·gi·tate (ri gur′jə tāt′) *vi.*, *vt.* **-tat′ed**, **-tat′ing** [< ML. pp. of *regurgitare* < *re-*, back + LL. *gurgitare*, to surge] to surge or flow back, or cause to do this; specif., to bring (partly digested food) from the stomach back to the mouth —**re·gur′gi·tant** *adj.* —**re·gur′gi·ta′tion** *n.*

re·ha·bil·i·tate (rē′hə bil′ə tāt′, rē′ə-) *vt.* **-tat′ed**, **-tat′ing** [< ML.: see RE- & HABILITATE] **1.** to restore to rank, privileges, reputation, etc. which one has lost **2.** to put back in good condition **3.** *a)* to restore to a normal state of health, etc. as by medical treatment *b)* to make (the handicapped or disadvantaged) able to be employed by giving them special training —**re′ha·bil′i·ta′tion** *n.* —**re′ha·bil′i·ta′tive** *adj.*

re·hash (rē hash′; *for n.* rē′hash) *vt.* [RE- + HASH¹] to work up again or go over again [*to rehash the same old arguments*] —*n.* the act or result of rehashing

re·hear (rē hir′) *vt.* **-heard′** (-hurd′), **-hear′ing** *Law* to hear (a case) a second time —**re·hear′ing** *n.*

re·hears·al (ri hurs′l) *n.* a rehearsing; specif., a practice performance of a play, concert, etc.

re·hearse (ri hurs′) *vt.* **-hearsed′**, **-hears′ing** [< OFr. < *re-*, again + *herser*, to harrow < *herse*, a harrow] **1.** to repeat aloud as heard or read; recite **2.** to tell in detail **3.** to perform (a play, concert, etc.) for practice in preparation for a public performance **4.** to drill (a person) in what he is to do —*vi.* to rehearse a play, etc.

re·heat (rē hēt′) *vt.* to heat again; specif., to add heat to (a fluid), as in an afterburner —**re·heat′er** *n.*

Reich (rīk; *G.* rīH) *n.* [G.] Germany or the German government; specif., the German fascist state under the Nazis from 1933 to 1945 (**Third Reich**)

reichs·mark (rīks′märk′; *G.* rīHs′mark′) *n.*, *pl.* **-marks′**, **-mark′** [G.] the monetary unit of Germany from 1924 to 1948

Reichs·tag (rīks′täg′; *G.* rīHs′takh′) *n.* [G.] formerly, the legislative assembly of Germany

re·i·fy (rē′ə fī′) *vt.* **-fied′**, **-fy′ing** [< L. *res*, thing + -FY] to treat (an abstraction) as substantially existing, or as a concrete material object —**re′i·fi·ca′tion** *n.*

reign (rān) *n.* [< OFr. < L. *regnum* < *regere*, to rule] **1.** royal power or rule **2.** dominance; prevalence [*the reign of fashion*] **3.** the period of rule, dominance, etc. —*vi.* **1.** to rule as a sovereign **2.** to be widespread; prevail [*peace reigns*]

reigning champion the present holder of a sporting, etc. title

re·im·burse (rē′im burs′) *vt.* **-bursed′**, **-burs′ing** [RE- + archaic *imburse*, after Fr. *rembourser*] **1.** to pay back (money spent) **2.** to compensate (a person) for expenses, damages, losses, etc. —**re′im·burs′a·ble** *adj.* —**re′im·burse′ment** *n.*

rein (rān) *n.* [< OFr. *resne*, ult. < L. *retinere*: see RETAIN] **1.** a narrow strip of leather attached to each end of a horse's bit and held by the rider or driver to control the animal: *usually used in pl.* **2.** [*pl.*] a means of guiding, controlling, etc. [*the reins of government*] —*vt.* to guide, control, etc. as with reins —*vi.* to stop or slow down as with reins (with *in* or *up*) —**draw rein** to slow down or stop: also **draw in the reins** —**give (free) rein to** to allow to act without restraint

REINS

re·in·car·nate (rē′in kär′nāt) *vt.* **-nat′ed**, (rē′in kär nāt′əd) **-nat′ing** to cause to undergo reincarnation

re·in·car·na·tion (-kär nā′shən) *n.* **1.** a rebirth of the soul in another body, as in Hindu religious belief **2.** a new incarnation **3.** the doctrine that the soul reappears after death in another and different bodily form

rein·deer (rān′dir′) *n.*, *pl.* **-deer′**, occas. **-deers′** [< ON. < *hreinn*, reindeer + *dyr*, deer] a large deer with branching antlers, found in northern regions: domesticated there as a beast of burden and for its milk, meat, and leather

reindeer moss an arctic lichen eaten by grazing animals

re·in·force (rē′in fôrs′) *vt.* **-forced′**, **-forc′ing** [RE- + var. of ENFORCE] **1.** to strengthen (a military or naval force) with more troops, ships, planes, etc. **2.** to strengthen, as by propping, adding new material, etc. **3.** to make stronger or more compelling [*to reinforce an argument*] —**re′in·forc′er** *n.*

reinforced concrete concrete masonry containing steel bars or mesh to increase its tensile strength

re·in·force·ment (-mənt) *n.* **1.** a reinforcing or being reinforced **2.** anything that reinforces; specif., [*pl.*] additional troops, ships, etc.

reins (rānz) *n.pl.* [< OFr. < L. pl. of *ren*, kidney]

[Archaic] **1.** the kidneys **2.** the loins, thought of as the seat of the emotions and affections

re·in·state (rē′in stāt′) *vt.* **-stat′ed, -stat′ing** to instate again; restore to a former condition, position, etc. **—re′-in·state′ment** *n.*

reis (rās) *n.pl., sing.* **re·al** (re äl′) [Port.] a former Portuguese and Brazilian money of account

re·it·er·ate (rē it′ər āt′) *vt.* **-at′ed, -at′ing** [< L. pp. of *reiterare*: see RE- & ITERATE] to say or do again or repeatedly **—re·it′er·a′tion** *n.* **—re·it′er·a′tive** (-ə rāt′iv, -ər ə tiv) *adj.* **—re·it′er·a′tive·ly** *adv.*

re·ject (ri jekt′; *for n.* rē′jekt) *vt.* [< L. pp. of *rejicere* < *re-*, back + *jacere*, to throw] **1.** to refuse to take, agree to, use, believe, etc. **2.** to discard or throw out as worthless **3.** to pass over (a gramophone record set by a record changer) **4.** to vomit **5.** to deny love or acceptance to (someone) **6.** *Physiol.* to be incompatible with (a part or organ transplanted into the body) **—n.** a rejected thing or person **—re·ject′ee′** *n.* **—re·ject′er, re·jec′tor** *n.* **—re·jec′tion** *n.* **—re·jec′tive** *adj.*

re·jig (rē′jig′) *vt.* **-jigged′, -jig′ging** [RE-+ JIG] **1.** to reequip a factory, etc. **2.** to change or rearrange (something), usually in an unethical or unscrupulous way

re·joice (ri jois′) *vi.* **-joiced′, -joic′ing** [< OFr. *rejoir* < *re-*, again + *joir* < L. *gaudere*, to rejoice] to be glad or happy (often with *at* or *in*) **—vt.** to make glad; delight **—re·joic′-ing·ly** *adv.*

re·join[1] (rē join′) *vt.* [< MFr.: see ff.] **1.** to come into the company of again **2.** to join together again; reunite **3.** to renew membership in (an organization) after a lapse **—vi.** to become joined together again

re·join[2] (ri join′) *vt.* [< Anglo-Fr. < MFr. *rejoindre*: see RE- & JOIN] to say in answer **—vi.** to answer

re·join·der (-dər) *n.* [< Anglo-Fr. substantive use of *rejoindre*: see prec.] **1.** *a)* an answer to a reply *b)* any answer **2.** *Law* the defendant's answer to the plaintiff's replication

re·ju·ve·nate (ri jōō′və nāt′) *vt.* **-nat′ed, -nat′ing** [<RE- + L. *juvenis*, young + -ATE[1]] **1.** to make young again; bring back to youthful strength, appearance, etc. **2.** to make seem new or fresh again **—re·ju′ve·na′tion** *n.* **—re·ju′ve·na′-tor** *n.*

re·lapse (ri laps′) *vi.* **-lapsed′, -laps′ing** [< L. pp. of *relabi*, to slip back: see RE- & LAPSE] to slip back into a former condition, esp. after improvement or seeming improvement **—n.** **1.** a relapsing **2.** the recurrence of a disease after apparent improvement **—re·laps′er** *n.*

re·late (ri lāt′) *vt.* **-lat′ed, -lat′ing** [< L. pp. of *referre*, to bring back: see REFER] **1.** to tell the story of; narrate **2.** to connect, as in thought or meaning; show a relation between [to *relate* theory and practice] **—vi.** **1.** *a)* to have some connection (*to*) *b)* to show sympathy and understanding **2.** to have reference (*to*) **—re·lat′a·ble** *adj.* **—re·lat′er, re·la′-tor** *n.*

re·lat·ed (-lāt′id) *adj.* **1.** narrated; told **2.** connected or associated, as by origin, kinship, marriage, etc.; of the same family **—re·lat′ed·ness** *n.*

re·la·tion (ri lā′shən) *n.* **1.** a narrating, telling, etc. **2.** what is narrated; recital **3.** connection, as in thought, meaning, etc. **4.** connection of persons by blood or marriage; kinship **5.** a person related to others by kinship; relative **6.** [*pl.*] *a)* the connections between or among persons, groups, nations, etc. *b)* sexual intercourse **7.** *Math.* an association between numbers, quantities, etc. **—in** (or **with**) **relation to** concerning; regarding **—re·la′tion·al** *adj.*

re·la·tion·ship (-ship′) *n.* **1.** the state or an instance of being related **2.** connection by blood or marriage; kinship

rel·a·tive (rel′ə tiv) *adj.* **1.** related each to the other; referring to each other **2.** having to do with; relevant **3.** regarded in relation to something else; comparative **4.** meaningful only in relationship ["cold" is a *relative* term] **5.** *Gram. a)* designating a word that introduces a subordinate clause and refers to an antecedent ["which" is a *relative* pronoun in "the hat which you bought"] *b)* introduced by such a word [a *relative* clause] **—n.** **1.** a relative word or thing **2.** a person related to others by kinship; member of the same family **—relative to** **1.** concerning; about **2.** corresponding to; in proportion to **—rel′a·tive·ness** *n.*

relative humidity *see* HUMIDITY

rel·a·tive·ly (-lē) *adv.* in a relative manner; in relation to or compared to something else; not absolutely [a *relatively* unimportant matter]

rel·a·tiv·ism (-iz′m) *n.* any theory of ethics or knowledge based on the idea that all values or judgments are relative, differing according to circumstances, persons, etc. **—rel′-a·tiv·ist** *n.* **—rel′a·tiv·is′tic** *adj.*

rel·a·tiv·i·ty (rel′ə tiv′ə tē) *n.* **1.** a being relative **2.** *Physics* the fact, principle, or theory of the relative, rather than absolute, character of motion, velocity, mass, time, etc.: as developed esp. by Albert Einstein, the theory includes the statements that: 1) the velocity of light is constant; 2) the mass of a body in motion varies with its velocity; 3) matter

and energy are interconvertible; 4) space and time are interdependent and form a four-dimensional continuum

re·lax (ri laks′) *vt., vi.* [< L. < *re-*, back + *laxare*, to loosen < *laxus*, loose] **1.** to make or become looser, or less firm, stiff, or tense **2.** to make or become less strict, severe, or intense, as discipline, effort, etc. **3.** to rest or give rest to, from work, worry, etc. **—re·laxed′** *adj.* **—re·lax′ed·ly** (-lak′-sid lē) *adv.* **—re·lax′er** *n.*

re·lax·ant (-ənt) *adj.* of or causing relaxation, esp. of muscular tension **—n.** a relaxant drug or agent

re·lax·a·tion (rē′lak sā′shən) *n.* **1.** a relaxing or being relaxed; loosening, lessening of severity, etc. **2.** *a)* a lessening of or rest from work, worry, etc. *b)* recreation or other activity for bringing this about

re·lay (rē′lā; *for v., also* ri lā′) *n.* [MFr. *relais* (pl.), orig. relays of hunting hounds < *re-*, back + *laier*, to leave] **1.** a fresh supply of horses, etc. ready to relieve others, as for a stage of a journey **2.** a crew of workers relieving others; shift **3.** *a)* same as RELAY RACE *b)* any of the laps of a relay race **4.** a conveying or transmitting as by relays **5.** same *as* SERVOMOTOR **6.** *Elec.* a device activated by variations in conditions in one electric circuit and controlling a larger current or activating other devices in the same or another circuit: used in telegraphy, etc. **—vt. -layed, -lay·ing** **1.** to convey by or as by relays [to *relay* news] **2.** *Elec.* to control, operate, or send on by a relay

re·lay (rē′lā′) *vt.* **-laid′, -lay′ing** to lay again or anew: also written **re′lay′**

relay race (rē′lā) a race between teams, each runner going in turn only part of the total distance

re·lease (ri lēs′) *vt.* **-leased′, -leas′ing** [< OFr. < L. *relaxare*: see RELAX] **1.** to set free, as from confinement, duty, work, etc. **2.** to let (a missile, etc.) go **3.** to permit to be issued, published, broadcast, etc. **4.** *Law* to give up to someone else (a claim, right, etc.) **—n.** **1.** a freeing or being freed, as from prison, pain, an obligation, etc. **2.** relief from tension as by expressing emotion freely **3.** a document authorizing release, as from prison, etc. **4.** a letting loose of something caught, held, etc. **5.** a device for releasing a catch, etc., as on a machine **6.** *a)* a releasing to the public, as of a book, film, news, etc. *b)* the book, film, news, etc. released **7.** *Law* a giving up of a claim or right *b)* the document by which this is done

re·lease (rē′lēs′) *vt.* **-leased′, -leas′ing** to lease again

rel·e·gate (rel′ə gāt′) *vt.* **-gat′ed, -gat′ing** [< L. pp. of *relegare* < *re-*, away + *legare*, to send] **1.** to exile or banish (*to*) **2.** to consign or assign to an inferior position, specif., *Football* to demote (a team) to a lower division [Chelsea were *relegated* this year] **3.** to assign to a class, sphere, etc. **4.** to refer, commit, or hand over for decision or action **—rel′e·ga′tion** *n.*

re·lent (ri lent′) *vi.* [ult. < L. < *re-*, again + *lentus*, pliant] to soften in temper, resolution, etc.; become less severe, stern, or stubborn **—re·lent′ing·ly** *adv.*

re·lent·less (-lis) *adj.* **1.** not relenting; harsh; pitiless **2.** persistent; unremitting **—re·lent′less·ly** *adv.* **—re·lent′-less·ness** *n.*

rel·e·vant (rel′ə vənt) *adj.* [< ML. prp. of *relevare*: see RELIEVE] bearing upon or relating to the matter in hand; pertinent; to the point **—rel′e·vance, rel′e·van·cy** *n.* **—rel′-e·vant·ly** *adv.*

re·li·a·ble (ri li′ə b′l) *adj.* that can be relied on; dependable **—re·li′a·bil′i·ty, re·li′a·ble·ness** *n.* **—re·li′a·bly** *adv.*

re·li·ance (-əns) *n.* **1.** the act of relying **2.** trust, dependence, or confidence **3.** a thing relied on

re·li·ant (-ənt) *adj.* having or showing trust, dependence, or confidence; dependent (*on*) **—re·li′ant·ly** *adv.*

rel·ic (rel′ik) *n.* [< OFr. < L. *reliquiae* (pl.), remains < *relinquere*: see RELINQUISH] **1.** *a)* an object, custom, etc. that has survived from the past *b)* a keepsake or souvenir **2.** [*pl.*] remaining fragments; ruins **3.** *R.C.Ch. & Orthodox Eastern Ch.* the bodily remains of a saint, martyr, etc., or an object associated with him, reverenced as a memorial

rel·ict (rel′ikt) *n.* [< L. pp. of *relinquere*: see RELINQUISH] [Archaic] a widow

re·lief (ri lēf′) *n.* [< OFr. *relever*: see ff.] **1.** an easing, as of pain, anxiety, a burden, etc. **2.** anything that lessens tension, or offers a pleasing change **3.** aid in the form of goods or money given esp., formerly, under the Poor Law **4.** any aid given in times of need, danger, or disaster, as supplies sent into a flooded area **5.** *a)* release from work or duty *b)* the person or persons bringing such release by taking over a post **6.** *a)* the projection of sculptured figures and forms from a flat surface, so that they stand wholly or partly free *b)* a work of art so made **7.** *a)* the differences in height, collectively, of land forms in any particular area *b)* these differences as shown by lines, colours, or raised areas on a map (**relief map**) **8.** *Law* the assistance sought by a complainant as in a court of equity **9.** *a)* *Painting* the apparent solidity or projection of objects *b)* distinctness of outline; contrast **—in relief** carved or moulded so as to project from a surface **—on relief** [U.S.] receiving relief from a government agency

re·lieve (ri lēv') vt. -lieved', -liev'ing [< OFr. < L. < re-, again + levare, to raise < levis, light] 1. a) to ease, lighten, or reduce (pain, anxiety, etc.) b) to free from pain, distress, etc. 2. to lighten (pressure, stress, etc.) on (something) 3. to give or bring aid or assistance to [to relieve a besieged city] 4. a) to set free from a burden, obligation, etc. b) to remove (a burden, etc.) 5. to set free from duty or work by replacing with oneself or another [to relieve a nurse] 6. to make less tedious, etc. by providing a pleasing change 7. to set off by contrast; make distinct or prominent 8. to ease (oneself) by urinating or defecating —**relieve someone of** to take from [the thief relieved him of his wallet] —**re·liev'a·ble** adj. —**re·liev'er** n.

re·lie·vo (ri lē'vō) n., pl. -vos same as RELIEF (SENSE 6)

re·li·gion (ri lij'ən) n. [< OFr. < L. religio < ? < re-, back + ligare, to bind] 1. a) belief in a superhuman power or powers to be obeyed and worshipped as the creator(s) and ruler(s) of the universe b) expression of this belief in conduct and ritual 2. any specific system of belief, worship, etc., often involving a code of ethics [the Christian religion] 3. the state or way of life of a person in a monastic order, etc. 4. any object that is seriously or zealously pursued

re·li·gi·os·i·ty (ri lij'ē os'ə tē) n. the quality of being excessively or mawkishly religious —**re·li·gi·ose'** (-ōs') adj.

re·li·gious (ri lij'əs) adj. 1. that believes in or supports a religion; devout; pious 2. of or concerned with religion [religious books] 3. belonging to a community of monks, nuns, etc. 4. conscientiously exact; scrupulous —n., pl. -gious a member of a community of monks, nuns, etc. —**re·li'gious·ly** adv. —**re·li'gious·ness** n.

re·line (rē lin') vt. -lined', -lin'ing 1. to mark with new lines 2. to provide with a new lining

re·lin·quish (ri liŋ'kwish) vt. [< OFr. < L. < re-, from + linquere, to leave] 1. to give up (a plan, policy, etc.) 2. to surrender (something owned, a right, etc.) 3. to let go (a grasp, etc.) —**re·lin'quish·ment** n.

rel·i·quar·y (rel'ə kwar ē) n., pl. -quar·ies [< Fr. < L.: see RELIC] a small box, casket, or shrine in which relics are kept and shown

rel·ique (rel'ik, re lēk') n. archaic var. of RELIC

rel·ish (rel'ish) n. [< OFr. relais, something remaining < relaisser: see RELEASE] 1. the distinctive flavour something has 2. a trace (of some quality) 3. an appetizing flavour; pleasing taste 4. a) pleasure; enjoyment b) liking or craving 5. anything that gives pleasure, zest, etc. 6. pickles, olives, etc. served with a meal to add flavour or make appetizing —vt. to enjoy; like —vi. 1. to have the flavour (of something) 2. to have a pleasing taste

re·live (rē liv') vt. -lived', -liv'ing to experience again (a past event) as in the imagination

re·lo·cate (rē lō kāt') vt., vi. -cat'ed, -cat'ing 1. to locate again 2. to move to a new location —**re'lo·ca'tion** n.

re·luc·tance (ri luk'təns) n. 1. a being reluctant; unwillingness 2. Elec. a measure of the opposition presented to the lines of force in a magnetic circuit

re·luc·tant (-tant) adj. [< L. prp. of reluctari < re-, against + luctari, to struggle] 1. unwilling or disinclined (to do something) 2. marked by unwillingness [a reluctant answer] —**re·luc'tant·ly** adv.

re·ly (ri lī') vi. -lied', -ly'ing [< OFr. < L. religare: see RELIGION] to have confidence; depend (with on or upon)

REM (rem) n., pl. **REMs** [r(apid) e(ye) m(ovement)] the periodic, rapid, jerky movement of the eyeballs under closed lids while asleep and dreaming

re·main (ri mān') vi. [< OFr. < L. < re-, back + manere, to stay] 1. to be left over when the rest has been taken away, destroyed, etc. 2. to stay on as while others go [to remain at home] 3. to go on being [to remain a cynic] 4. to continue to exist; persist [hope remains] 5. to be left to be dealt with, done, etc.

re·main·der (-dər) n. 1. those remaining 2. what is left when a part is taken away 3. a copy or copies of a book still held by the publisher when the sale has fallen off, usually disposed of at a very low price 4. Arith. a) what is left when a smaller number is subtracted from a larger b) what is left undivided when one number is not evenly divisible by another —vt. to sell (books, etc.) as remainders

re·mains (ri mānz') n.pl. 1. what is left after part has been used, destroyed, etc. 2. a dead body; corpse 3. writings left unpublished by an author at his death 4. relics from the past [Roman remains]

re·make (rē māk'; for n. rē'māk') vt. -made', -mak'ing to make again or anew —n. 1. a remaking 2. something remade, as a film

re·mand (ri mānd') vt. [< OFr., ult. < L. re-, back + mandare, to order] 1. to send back 2. Law a) to send (a prisoner or accused person) back into custody, as to await trial, etc. b) to send (a case) back to a lower court for further proceedings —n. a remanding or being remanded

remand home an institution to which juvenile offenders may be sent for detention while waiting to appear before a juvenile court or sent to an approved school

re·mark (ri märk') vt. [Fr. remarquer < re-, again +

marquer, to mark] 1. to notice; observe; perceive 2. to say or write as an observation or comment —vi. to make an observation or comment (with on or upon) —n. 1. a noticing or observing 2. something said briefly; comment

re·mark·a·ble (-ə b'l) adj. 1. worthy of remark or notice 2. unusual; extraordinary —**re·mark'a·ble·ness** n. —**re·mark'a·bly** adv.

R.E.M.E. Royal Electrical and Mechanical Engineers

re·me·di·a·ble (ri mē'dē ə b'l) adj. that can be remedied —**re·me'di·a·ble·ness** n. —**re·me'di·a·bly** adv.

re·me·di·al (-əl) adj. 1. providing, or intended to provide, a remedy 2. Educ. of or being for students having difficulty in a subject [remedial education] —**re·me'di·al·ly** adv.

rem·e·dy (rem'ə dē) n., pl. -dies [< Anglo-Fr. < OFr. < L. remedium < re-, again + mederi, to heal] 1. any medicine or treatment that cures, heals, or relieves a disease or tends to restore health 2. something that corrects or counteracts an evil or wrong; relief 3. a legal means by which a violation of a right is prevented or compensated for —vt. -died, -dy·ing to act as a remedy for; cure, counteract, correct, etc. —**rem'e·di·less** adj.

re·mem·ber (ri mem'bər) vt. [< OFr. < LL. < L. re-, again + memorare, to bring to mind < memor, mindful] 1. to have (an event, thing, person, etc.) come to mind again; think of again 2. to bring back to mind by an effort; recall 3. to bear in mind; be careful not to forget 4. to keep (a person) in mind for a present, legacy, etc. 5. to mention as sending greetings (to) [remember me to your sister] —vi. 1. to bear in mind or call back to mind 2. to have memory

re·mem·brance (-brəns) n. 1. a remembering or being remembered 2. the power to remember 3. a memory 4. the extent of time over which one can remember 5. a souvenir or keepsake 6. commemoration 7. [pl.] greetings

Remembrance Day the day commemorating those killed in World War I and World War II, celebrated on Armistice Day or the preceding Sunday: also **Remembrance Sunday**

re·mem·branc·er (-brən sər) n. [ME. < Anglo-Fr.: REMEMBRANCE & -ER] 1. a person who reminds another of something, esp. one appointed to do so 2. [usually R-] any of certain officials, specif. one responsible for collecting debts owed to the sovereign

re·mind (ri mīnd') vt., vi. [RE- + MIND, v.] to put (a person) in mind (of something); cause to remember —**re·mind'er** n.

re·mind·ful (-fəl) adj. reviving memory; reminding

rem·i·nisce (rem'ə nis') vi. -nisced', -nis'cing [< ff.] to think, talk, or write about one's past experiences

rem·i·nis·cence (-əns) n. [Fr. < LL. < L. prp. of reminisci < re-, again + memini, to remember] 1. a remembering of past experiences 2. a memory or recollection 3. [pl.] an account, written or spoken, of remembered experiences

rem·i·nis·cent (-ənt) adj. 1. characterized by or given to reminiscence 2. bringing to mind something else; suggestive (of) —**rem'i·nis'cent·ly** adv.

re·miss (ri mis') adj. [see REMIT] 1. careless in, or negligent about, carrying out a task 2. showing carelessness or negligence —**re·miss'ness** n.

re·mis·si·ble (-ə b'l) adj. that can be remitted

re·mis·sion (ri mish'ən) n. the act or an instance of remitting; forgiveness of sins or debts, lessening or leaving of pain or symptoms, etc. —**re·mis'sive** adj.

re·mit (ri mit') vt. -mit'ted, -mit'ting [< L. remittere (pp. remissus) < re-, back + mittere, to send] 1. to forgive or pardon (sins, etc.) 2. to free someone from (a debt, tax, penalty, etc.) 3. to let slacken; lessen [without remitting one's efforts] 4. to refer (a matter) for consideration, judgment, etc.; specif., Law same as REMAND 5. to send (money) in payment —vi. 1. a) to moderate; slacken b) to have its symptoms lessen or disappear: said of an illness 2. to send money in payment —**re·mit'ment** n. —**re·mit'ta·ble** adj. —**re·mit'ter** n.

re·mit·tal (-'l) n. same as REMISSION

re·mit·tance (-'ns) n. 1. the sending of money, as by post 2. the money sent

remittance man someone who lives abroad supported by remittances from home

re·mit·tent (-'nt) adj. remitting; abating for a while or at intervals, as a fever —**re·mit'tent·ly** adv.

rem·nant (rem'nənt) n. [< OFr. prp. of remaindre: see REMAIN] 1. what is left over 2. [often pl.] a small remaining part, amount, or number 3. a trace; vestige 4. a piece of cloth, ribbon, etc. left over, as at the end of the bolt —adj. remaining

re·mod·el (rē mod''l) vt. -elled, -el·ling 1. to model again 2. to make over; rebuild

re·mon·e·tize (rē mun'ə tiz') vt. -tized', -tiz'ing to reinstate as legal tender [to remonetize gold] —**re·mon'e·ti·za'tion** n.

re·mon·strance (ri mon'strəns) n. a remonstrating; protest, complaint, etc., or a statement of this

re·mon·strant (-strənt) adj. remonstrating —n. a person who remonstrates —**re·mon'strant·ly** adv.

re·mon·strate (-strāt; rem'ən strāt) vt. -strat·ed, -strat·ing [< ML. pp. of remonstrare < L. re-, again + monstrare, to show] to say or plead in protest, objection, etc. —*vi.* to present and urge reasons in opposition or complaint; protest —**re·mon·stra·tion** (rem′ən strā′shən) *n.* —**re·mon′stra·tive** (-strə tiv) *adj.* —**re·mon′stra·ting·ly,** —**re·mon′stra·tive·ly** *adv.* —**re·mon′stra·tor** (-strät ər) *n.*

rem·o·ra (rem′ər ə) *n.* [L., lit., hindrance] an ocean fish with a sucking disc on the head, by which it clings to sharks, ships, etc.

re·morse (ri môrs′) *n.* [< OFr. < LL. < L. pp. of *remordere* < *re-*, again + *mordere*, to bite] 1. a deep, torturing sense of guilt over a wrong one has done; self-reproach 2. pity: now only in *without remorse,* pitilessly —**re·morse′ful** *adj.*

REMORA
(c. 18-90 cm long)

—**re·morse′ful·ly** *adv.* —**re·morse′ful·ness** *n.* —**re·morse′· less** *adj.* —**re·morse′less·ly** *adv.* —**re·morse′less·ness** *n.*

re·mote (ri mōt′) *adj.* **-mot′er, -mot′est** [< L. pp. of *removere,* to remove] 1. distant in space or time; far off 2. far off and hidden; secluded 3. distant in connection, relation, etc. [a question *remote* from the subject] 4. distantly related [a *remote* cousin] 5. distant in manner; aloof 6. slight; faint [a *remote* chance] —**re·mote′ly** *adv.* —**re·mote′ness** *n.*

remote control control of aircraft, missiles, or other apparatus from a distance, as by radio waves

re·mould (rē′mōld′; *for n.* rē′mōld′) *vt.* **-mould′ed, -mould′· ing** [RE- + MOULD[1]] to cement, mould, and vulcanize a strip of rubber of the outer surface of (a worn tyre); tyre); retread —*n.* a remoulded tyre

re·mount (rē mount′; *for n. usually* rē′mount′) *vt., vi.* to mount again —*n.* a fresh horse to replace another

re·mov·a·ble (ri mōō′və b'l) *adj.* that can be removed —**re·mov′a·bil′i·ty** *n.* —**re·mov′a·bly** *adv.*

re·mov·al (ri mōō′v'l) *n.* a removing or being removed; esp., *a*) a taking away *b*) dismissal, as from an office *c*) a moving to somewhere else, as of a shop, household, etc.

removal man a person whose work or business is packing and conveying furniture, etc. for those moving house

re·move (ri mōōv′) *vt.* **-moved′, -mov′ing** [< OFr. < L. *removere:* see RE- & MOVE] 1. to move (something) from where it is; take away 2. to take off [*remove* your hat] 3. *a*) to kill *b*) to dismiss, as from an office *c*) to get rid of [to *remove* the causes of war] 4. to extract or separate (*from*) —*vi.* 1. [Poet.] to go away 2. to move away, as to another place of residence 3. to be removable [paint that *removes* easily] —*n.* 1. a removing 2. the space or time in which a move is made 3. any step, interval, or degree [but one *remove* from war] 4. a move to another residence or place of business 5. a class or form in certain schools —**re·mov′er** *n.*

re·moved (ri mōōvd′) *adj.* 1. distant by (a specified number of degrees of relationship) [one's first cousin once *removed* is the child of one's first cousin] 2. remote; distant (*from*)

re·mu·ner·ate (ri myōō′nə rāt′) *vt.* **-at′ed, -at′ing** [< L. pp. of *remunerari,* to reward < *re-*, again + *munus,* a gift] to pay (a person) for (a service, loss, etc.); reward; recompense —**re·mu′ner·a·ble** *adj.* —**re·mu′ner·a′tion** *n.* —**re·mu′ner·a·tive** (-nə rāt′iv, -nər ə tiv) *adj.* —**re·mu′ner·a·tive·ly** *adv.* —**re·mu′ner·a·tive·ness** *n.* —**re·mu′ner·a′tor** *n.*

ren·ais·sance (ri nā′səns) *n.* [Fr. < *re-*, again + *naître* (ult. < L. *nasci*), to be born] 1. a rebirth; revival 2. [R-] *a*) the great revival of art, literature, and learning in Europe in the 14th, 15th, and 16th centuries *b*) the period of this *c*) the style of art, literature, architecture, etc. of this period *d*) any similar revival —*adj.* [R-] of, or in the style of, the Renaissance

re·nal (rē′n'l) *adj.* [< Fr. < L. *renalis* < *renes,* kidneys] of or near the kidneys

re·nas·cence (ri nas′əns, -nãs′-) *n.* [*also* R-] same as RENAISSANCE

re·nas·cent (-ənt) *adj.* [< L.: see RE- & NASCENT] having or showing new life, strength, or vigour

rend (rend) *vt.* **rent, rend′ing** [OE. *rendan*] 1. to tear or pull with violence (with *from, off,* etc.) 2. to tear apart or split with violence: often figurative [a roar *rends* the air] —*vi.* to tear; split apart

ren·der (ren′dər) *vt.* [< OFr., ult. < L. < *re-*, back + *dare,* to give] 1. to hand over, or submit, as for approval, consideration, payment, etc. [*render* an account of your actions] 2. to give (*up*); surrender 3. to give in return [*render* good for evil] 4. to give or pay as due [to *render* thanks] 5. to cause to be; make [to *render* one helpless] 6. *a*) to give (aid, etc.) *b*) to do (a service, etc.) 7. to represent; depict 8. to recite (a poem, etc.), play (music), act (a role), etc. 9. to translate 10. to deliver (a judgment, verdict, etc.) 11. to melt down (fat) 12. *Masonry* to cover (brickwork, etc.) directly with a coat of plaster —**ren′· der·a·ble** *adj.* —**ren′der·er** *n.* —**ren′der·ing** *n.*

ren·dez·vous (ron′dā vōō′, -dē-, -də-) *n., pl.* **-vous** (-vōōz′) [< Fr. *rendez vous,* betake yourself] 1. a place set for a

meeting, as of troops, ships, spacecraft, etc. 2. a place where people gather; meeting place 3. *a*) an agreement to meet at a certain time or place *b*) the meeting itself —*vi., vt.* **-voused′** (-vōōd′), **-vous′ing** (-vōō′iŋ) to bring or come together at a rendezvous

ren·di·tion (ren dish′ən) *n.* a rendering or result of rendering; specif., *a*) a performance (*of* a piece of music, a role, etc.) *b*) a translation

ren·e·gade (ren′ə gād′) *n.* [< Sp. pp. of *renegar,* to deny, ult. < L. *re-*, again + *negare,* to deny] a person who abandons his religion, party, principles, etc. to join the other side; apostate; traitor —*adj.* disloyal; traitorous

re·nege (ri nēg′, -nāg′) *vi.* **-neged′, -neg′ing** [ML. *renegare:* see prec.] 1. to go back on a promise (often with *on*) 2. same as REVOKE —**re·neg′er** *n.*

re·new (ri nyōō′) *vt.* 1. to make new or as if new again; make fresh or strong again 2. to cause to exist again; reestablish 3. to begin again; resume 4. to go over again; repeat [*renew* a promise] 5. to replace as by a fresh supply of 6. to give or get an extension of [to *renew* a lease] —**re·new′a·bil′i·ty** *n.* —**re·new′a·ble** *adj.* —**re·new′al** *n.* —**re·new′ed·ly** *adv.* —**re·new′er** *n.*

ren·i- [< L. *renes,* kidneys] a combining form meaning kidney, kidneys

ren·i·form (ren′ə fôrm′, rē′nə-) *adj.* [ModL. *reniformis:* see RENI- & -FORM] shaped like a kidney

ren·net (ren′it) *n.* [< OE. *gerennan,* to coagulate] 1. *a*) the membrane lining the stomach of an unweaned animal, esp. the fourth stomach of a calf *b*) the contents of such a stomach 2. *a*) an extract of this membrane or of the stomach contents, used to curdle milk, as in making cheese or junket *b*) any substance used to curdle milk

ren·nin (ren′in) *n.* [RENN(ET) + -IN[1]] a coagulating enzyme that can curdle milk, found in rennet

re·nounce (ri nouns′) *vt.* **-nounced′, -nounc′ing** [OFr. < L. < *re-*, back + *nuntiare,* to tell < *nuntius,* messenger] 1. to give up formally (a claim, right, etc.) 2. to give up (a pursuit, practice, belief, etc.) 3. to cast off or disown [to *renounce* a son] —**re·nounce′ment** *n.*

ren·o·vate (ren′ə vāt′) *vt.* **-vat′ed, -vat′ing** [< L. pp. of *renovare* < *re-*, again + *novare,* to make new < *novus,* new] to make fresh or sound again, as though new; clean up, replace worn parts in, repair, rebuild, etc. —**ren′o·va′· tion** *n.* —**ren′o·va′tive** *adj.* —**ren′o·va′tor** *n.*

re·nown (ri noun′) *n.* [< Anglo-Fr. < OFr. < *re-*, again + *nom(m)er,* to name < L. < *nomen,* a name] great fame or reputation —**re·nowned′** *adj.*

rent[1] (rent) *n.* [< OFr. < LL. hyp. form for L. *reddita* (*pecunia*), paid (money)] 1. a stated payment at fixed intervals for the use of a house, land, etc. 2. *Econ.* income from the use of land —*vt.* 1. to get or give temporary possession of (a house, land, etc.) in return for rent 2. to get or give temporary use of (a car, tool, etc.) in return for a fee —*vi.* to be leased or let for rent or a fee —**for rent** available to be rented —**rent′a·ble** *adj.* —**rent′er** *n.*

rent[2] (rent) *pt. & pp.* of REND

rent[3] (rent) *n.* [n. use of obs. var. of REND] 1. a hole or gap made by tearing or splitting 2. a split in an organization; schism

rent·al (ren′t'l) *n.* 1. an amount paid or received as rent 2. [*Chiefly U.S.*] a house, car, etc. for rent —*adj.* of, in, or for rent

rent-free (rent′frē′) *adj., adv.* without payment of rent

†**ren·tier** (rän′tyä) *n.* [Fr. < *rente,* rent] a person who has a fixed income from lands, bonds, etc.

re·nun·ci·a·tion (ri nun′sē ā′shən) *n.* [< L.: see RENOUNCE] a renouncing, as of a right, claim, pursuit, etc. —**re·nun′· ci·a·tive, re·nun′ci·a·to·ry** (-ə tə rē) *adj.*

re·or·der (rē ôr′dər) *n.* a repeated order for the same goods —*vt.* 1. to order again 2. to put in order again —*vi.* to order goods again

re·or·gan·i·za·tion (rē ôr′gə ni zā′shən, rē′ôr-) *n.* 1. a reorganizing or being reorganized 2. a thorough reconstruction of a business corporation as effected after, or in anticipation of, a failure

re·or·gan·ize (rē ôr′gə nīz′) *vt., vi.* **-ized, -iz′ing** to organize again or anew; effect a reorganization (of) —**re·or′· gan·iz′er** *n.*

rep[1] (rep) *n.* [Fr. *reps* < Eng. *ribs*] a ribbed fabric of silk, wool, cotton, rayon, etc.: *also* **repp**

rep[2] (rep) *n.* clipped form of: 1. REPERTORY (THEATRE) 2. REPRESENTATIVE (sense 2) 3. REPUTATION

Rep. [U.S.] 1. Representative 2. Republic 3. Republican

rep. 1. repeat 2. report(ed) 3. reporter

re·pack·age (rē pak′ij) *vt.* **-aged, -ag·ing** to package again or anew, as in a more secure or attractive package

re·paid (rē pād′) *pt. & pp.* of REPAY

re·pair[1] (ri per′) *vt.* [< OFr. < L. < *re-*, again + *parare,* to prepare] 1. to put back in good condition after damage, decay, etc.; fix 2. to renew; restore (one's health, etc.) 3. to set right; remedy (a mistake, etc.) 4. to make amends for (a wrong, etc.) —*n.* 1. a repairing 2. [*usually pl.*] an instance of, or work done in, repairing 3. the state of being fit for use [a car kept in *repair*] **4.** state with respect to being repaired [in bad *repair*] —**re·pair′a·ble** *adj.* —**re·pair′-er** *n.*

re·pair² (ri per′) *vi.* [< OFr. < LL. *repatriare* < L. *re-*, back + *patria*, one's native country] to go (*to* a place)

re·pair·man (-mən, -man′) *n.*, *pl.* **-men** (-mən, -men′) a man whose work is repairing things

rep·a·ra·ble (rep′ər ə b'l) *adj.* that can be repaired, remedied, etc. —**rep′a·ra·bly** *adv.*

rep·a·ra·tion (rep′ə rā′shən) *n.* [< MFr. < LL. < pp. of L. *reparare*: see REPAIR¹] **1.** a repairing or being repaired **2.** a making up for a wrong or injury **3.** compensation; specif., [*usually pl.*] compensation by a defeated nation for damage done by it in a war, payable in money, goods, etc.

rep·ar·tee (rep′är tē′) *n.* [< Fr. pp. of *repartir*, to reply < *re-*, back + *partir*, to part] **1.** a quick, witty reply; retort **2.** a series of such retorts; banter **3.** skill in making witty replies

re·past (ri păst′) *n.* [< OFr. < *re-*, RE- + *past*, food < L. < pp. of *pascere*, to feed] food and drink; a meal

re·pa·tri·ate (rē pā′trē āt′; *for n.* usually -it) *vt.*, *vi.* -**at′ed**, **-at′ing** [< LL. pp. of *repatriare*: see REPAIR²] to send back or return to the country of birth, citizenship, or allegiance [to *repatriate* prisoners of war] —*n.* a person who has been repatriated —**re·pa′tri·a′tion** *n.*

re·pay (ri pā′) *vt.* -**paid′**, **-pay′ing** [OFr. *repaier*] **1.** *a)* to pay back (money); refund *b)* to pay back (a person) **2.** to make some return for [*repay* a kindness] **3.** to make some return to (a person), as for some service —*vi.* to make a repayment or return —**re·pay′a·ble** *adj.* —**re·pay′ment** *n.*

re·peal (ri pēl′) *vt.* [< OFr. *rapeler*: see RE- & APPEAL] to revoke; cancel; annul [to *repeal* a law] —*n.* the act of repealing —**re·peal′a·ble** *adj.* —**re·peal′er** *n.*

re·peat (ri pēt′) *vt.* [< OFr. < L. < *re-*, again + *petere*, to seek] **1.** to say or utter again **2.** to say over; recite, as a poem **3.** to say (something) as said by someone else **4.** to tell to others [to *repeat* a secret] **5.** to do or make again [*repeat* an operation] **6.** to say again what has been said before by (oneself) —*vi.* **1.** to say or do again what has been said or done before **2.** to occur again; recur **3.** to continue to be tasted, as because of belching: often with *on* —*n.* **1.** a repeating **2.** *a)* anything said or done again *b)* a rebroadcast of a radio or TV programme **3.** *Music a)* a passage repeated in playing *b)* a symbol for this —**re·peat′-a·bil′i·ty** *n.* —**re·peat′a·ble** *adj.*

re·peat·ed (-id) *adj.* said, made, or done over, or again and again —**re·peat′ed·ly** *adv.*

re·peat·er (-ər) *n.* **1.** a person or thing that repeats **2.** *same as* REPEATING FIREARM **3.** a watch that repeats the hour and the quarter just passed, when a spring is pressed

repeating decimal a decimal in which some digit or group of digits is repeated continuously (Ex.: .3333, .037037)

repeating firearm a firearm that can fire a number of shots (from a magazine or clip) without reloading

re·pel (ri pel′) *vt.* -**pelled′**, **-pel′ling** [< L. < *re-*, back + *pellere*, to drive] **1.** to drive back or force back [to *repel* an attack] **2.** to refuse, reject, or spurn [she *repelled* his attentions] **3.** to cause dislike in; disgust [the odour *repels* me] **4.** *a)* to be resistant to, or present an opposing force to [plastic *repels* water] *b)* to fail to mix with [water *repels* oil] —*vi.* to cause distaste, dislike, aversion, etc. —**re·pel′-ler** *n.*

re·pel·lent (-ənt) *adj.* **1.** that repels; pushing away or driving back **2.** causing distaste, dislike, etc. **3.** able to resist the absorption of liquid, esp. water, to a limited extent —*n.* something that repels; specif., *a)* a solution applied to fabric to make it water-repellent *b)* any substance used to repel insects Also **re·pel′lant** —**re·pel′lence**, **re·pel′len·cy** *n.* —**re·pel′lent·ly** *adv.*

re·pent¹ (ri pent′) *vi.*, *vt.* [< OFr. < VL. < L. *re-*, again + *paenitere*, to repent] **1.** to feel sorry for (a past error, sin, omission, etc.) **2.** to feel such regret over (some past act, intention, etc.) as to change one's mind —**re·pent′er** *n.*

re·pent² (rē′pant) *adj.* [L. *repens*, prp. of *repere*, to creep: see REPTILE] *Biol.* creeping or crawling

re·pent·ance (-əns) *n.* a repenting or being penitent; feeling of sorrow, etc., esp. for wrongdoing; remorse —**re·pent′ant** *adj.* —**re·pent′ant·ly** *adv.*

re·peo·ple (rē pē′p'l) *vt.* -**pled**, **-pling** to people anew; provide with new inhabitants

re·per·cus·sion (rē′pər kush′ən, rep′ər-) *n.* [< L. pp. of *repercutere*: see RE- & PERCUSSION] **1.** formerly, a recoil **2.** reflection, as of sound **3.** a reaction to some event or action: *usually used in pl.* —**re′per·cus′sive** *adj.*

rep·er·toire (rep′ər twär′, rep′ə-) *n.* [< Fr. < LL. *repertorium*: see ff.] **1.** the stock of plays, operas, roles, songs, etc. that a company, actor, singer, etc. knows and is ready to perform **2.** the stock of special skills of a certain person or group

rep·er·to·ry (rep′ər tər ē, rep′ə-) *n.*, *pl.* -**ries** [LL. *repertorium* < L. pp. of *reperire*, to discover] **1.** a storehouse, or the things in it **2.** *same as* REPERTOIRE **3.** the system of play production used by a repertory theatre

repertory company a commercial theatrical company that presents a repertoire of plays, usually at one theatre

repertory theatre a theatre with a repertoire of plays and a permanent company

rep·e·ti·tion (rep′ə tish′ən) *n.* [< MFr. < L. *repetitio*] **1.** a repeating; a doing or saying again **2.** something repeated **3.** a copy or imitation —**re·pet′i·tive** (ri pet′ə tiv) *adj.* —**re·pet′i·tive·ly** *adv.*

rep·e·ti·tious (-əs) *adj.* full of or using repetition, esp. tiresome or boring repetition —**rep′e·ti′tious·ly** *adv.* —**rep′-e·ti′tious·ness** *n.*

re·phrase (rē frāz′) *vt.* -**phrased′**, **-phras′ing** to phrase again, esp. in a different way

re·pine (ri pīn′) *vi.* -**pined′**, **-pin′ing** [RE- + PINE²] to feel or express discontent; complain; fret —**re·pin′er** *n.* —**re·pin′-ing·ly** *adv.*

re·place (ri plās′) *vt.* -**placed′**, **-plac′ing** **1.** to put back in a former or the proper place or position **2.** to take the place of **3.** to provide an equivalent for [*replace* a worn tyre] **4.** to put back or pay back; restore [*replace* stolen goods] —**re·place′a·ble** *adj.* —**re·plac′er** *n.*

re·place·ment (-mənt) *n.* **1.** a replacing or being replaced **2.** a person or thing that takes the place of another that is lost, worn out, dismissed, etc.

re·plen·ish (ri plen′ish) *vt.* [< OFr. < L. *re-*, again + *plenus*, full] **1.** to make full or complete again, as with a new supply **2.** to supply again with fuel, etc. —**re·plen′-ish·er** *n.* —**re·plen′ish·ment** *n.*

re·plete (ri plēt′) *adj.* [< OFr. < L. pp. of *replere* < *re-*, again + *plere*, to fill] **1.** well-filled; plentifully supplied **2.** stuffed with food and drink —**re·ple′tion** *n.*

re·plev·in (ri plev′in) *n.* [< OFr. < *re-*, again + *plevir*, to pledge] *Law* **1.** the recovery by a person of goods claimed to be his, on his promise to test the matter in court and give up the goods if defeated **2.** the writ by which this is done —*vt.* to take back (goods) under such a writ: usually **re·plev′y** -**plev′ied**, **-plev′y·ing**

rep·li·ca (rep′li kə) *n.* [It. < ML. < L. *replicare*: see REPLY] a reproduction or close copy, esp. of a work of art

rep·li·cate (rep′li kit; *for v.* -kāt′) *adj.* [L. *replicatus*, pp. of *replicare*: see REPLY] *Bot.* folded back on itself, as a leaf —*vt.* -**cat′ed**, **-cat′ing** **1.** to fold; bend back **2.** to repeat or duplicate —**rep′li·ca′tion** *n.*

re·ply (ri plī′) *vi.* -**plied′**, **-ply′ing** [< OFr. < L. *re-*, back + *plicare*, to fold] **1.** to answer in speech or writing **2.** to respond by some action [to *reply* to enemy fire] **3.** *Law* to answer a defendant's plea —*vt.* to say in answer [she *replied* that she agreed] —*n.*, *pl.* -**plies′** **1.** an answer in speech or writing **2.** a response by some action —**re·pli′-er** *n.*

re·port (ri pôrt′) *vt.* [< OFr. < L. < *re-*, back + *portare*, to carry] **1.** to give an account of; give information about; recount **2.** to carry and repeat (a message, etc.) **3.** to write an account of for publication, as in a newspaper **4.** to make known the presence, approach, etc. of **5.** to give an official account of **6.** to present (something referred for study, etc.) with conclusions, recommendations, etc. **7.** to make a charge about (an offence or offender) to a person in authority —*vi.* **1.** to make a report **2.** to work as a reporter **3.** to present oneself or make one's presence known [to *report* for duty] **4.** to be responsible (*to* a superior) —*n.* **1.** rumour; gossip [*report* has it that he will resign] **2.** reputation [a man of good *report*] **3.** a statement or account brought in and presented, often for publication **4.** a formal or official presentation of facts or of the record of an investigation, court case, etc. **5.** a statement of a child's progress in school sent to the parents **6.** a loud noise, esp. one made by an explosion —**report progress** notify (someone) of the developments that have occurred —**re·port′a·ble** *adj.* —**re·port′ed·ly** *adv.* —**re·port′-ing** *n.*

re·port·age (-ij) *n.* the reporting of news events

reported speech statement of what a person said, without quoting his exact words (Ex.: she said that she could not go)

re·port·er (-ər) *n.* a person who reports; specif., *a)* a person who reports legal or legislative proceedings *b)* a person who gathers information and writes reports for a newspaper, magazine, etc. *c)* a person who reports news on radio or TV —**re·por·to·ri·al** (rep′ər tôr′ē əl) *adj.* —**rep′or·to′ri·al·ly** *adv.*

report stage in Britain, the stage before the third reading in Parliament of a bill when, after it has been amended in committee, it is reported back to the chamber considering it

re·pose¹ (ri pōz′) *vt.* -**posed′**, **-pos′ing** [< OFr. < LL. < L. *re-*, again + LL. *pausare*, to rest] to lay or place for rest [to *repose* oneself on a bed] —*vi.* **1.** to lie at rest **2.** to rest from work, travel, etc. **3.** to rest in death or a grave **4.** to rest or be supported [the shale *reposes* on limestone] —*n.* **1.** a reposing, or resting **2.** *a)* rest *b)* sleep **3.** ease of manner; composure **4.** calm; peace —**re·pose′ful** *adj.* —**re·pose′ful·ly** *adv.*

re·pose² (ri pōz′) *vt.* -**posed′**, **-pos′ing** [< L. *repositus*: see ff.] **1.** to place (trust, etc.) in someone **2.** to place (power, etc.) in the control of someone

re·pos·i·to·ry (ri poz'ə tər ē) *n., pl.* **-ries** [< L. < pp. of *reponere* < *re-*, back + *ponere*, to place] **1.** a box, chest, cupboard, or room in which things may be placed for safekeeping **2.** a centre for storing [a *repository* of information] **3.** a person to whom something is confided
re·pos·sess (rē'pə zes') *vt.* to get possession of again; specif., to take back from a buyer who has failed to keep up payments —**re'pos·ses'sion** (-zesh'ən) *n.*
rep·re·hend (rep'ri hend') *vt.* [< L. < *re-*, back + *prehendere*, to take] **1.** to reprimand or rebuke (a person) **2.** to find fault with (something done) —**rep·re·hen·sion** (-hen'shən) *n.* —**rep're·hen'sive** *adj.* —**rep're·hen'sive·ly** *adv.*
rep·re·hen·si·ble (-hen'sə b'l) *adj.* deserving to be reprehended —**rep're·hen'si·bil'i·ty** *n.* —**rep're·hen'si·bly** *adv.*
rep·re·sent (rep'ri zent') *vt.* [< OFr. < L.: see RE- & PRESENT, *v.*] **1.** to present or picture to the mind **2.** to present or be a likeness of **3.** to describe or set forth, often in order to influence, persuade, etc. **4.** *a*) to be a sign or symbol for [x *represents* the unknown] *b*) to express by symbols, characters, etc. **5.** to be the equivalent of [a cave *represents* home to them] **6.** to act the part of (a character), as in a play **7.** to act in place of; be a substitute for **8.** to speak and act for by conferred authority, as a legislator for his constituents **9.** to serve as a specimen, example, type, etc. of —**rep're·sent'a·ble** *adj.*
rep·re·sen·ta·tion (rep'ri zen tā'shən) *n.* **1.** a representing or being represented **2.** legislative representatives, collectively **3.** a likeness, image, etc. **4.** [*often pl.*] an account of facts, arguments, etc. intended to influence action, etc. **5.** the production or performance of a play, etc.
rep·re·sen·ta·tion·al (-'l) *adj.* **1.** of representation **2.** designating or of art that represents in recognizable form objects in nature —**rep're·sen·ta'tion·al·ism** *n.* —**rep're·sen·ta'tion·al·ist** *n.* —**rep're·sen·ta'tion·al·ly** *adv.*
rep·re·sen·ta·tive (rep'rə zen'tə tiv) *adj.* **1.** representing; specif., *a*) picturing; portraying *b*) acting in the place of or on behalf of another or others; esp., serving as an elected delegate **2.** of or based on representation of the people by elected delegates [*representative* government] **3.** typical —*n.* **1.** an example or type **2.** a person authorized to act or speak for others, as an elected legislator or a salesman, agent, etc. **3.** [U.S.] [**R-**] a member of the lower house of Congress —**rep're·sent'a·tive·ly** *adv.* —**rep're·sent'a·tive·ness** *n.*
re·press (ri pres') *vt.* [< L. pp. of *reprimere*: see RE- & PRESS[1]] **1.** to hold back; restrain [to *repress* a sigh] **2.** to put down; subdue **3.** to control so strictly as to stifle free, natural behaviour [to *repress* a child] **4.** *Psychiatry a*) to force (painful ideas, impulses, etc.) into the unconscious *b*) to prevent (unconscious ideas, etc.) from becoming conscious —**re·press'er, re·press'sor** *n.* —**re·press'i·ble** *adj.* —**re·pres'sive** *adj.* —**re·pres'sive·ly** *adv.* —**re·pres'sive·ness** *n.*
re·press (rē'pres') *vt.* to press again; esp., to make new copies of (a recording) from the original master
re·pres·sion (ri presh'ən) *n.* **1.** a repressing or being repressed **2.** *Psychiatry* what is repressed
re·prieve (ri prēv') *vt.* **-prieved', -priev'ing** [ult. < Fr. pp. of *reprendre*, to take back] **1.** to postpone the punishment of; esp., to postpone the execution of (a condemned person) **2.** to give temporary relief to, as from pain —*n.* a reprieving or being reprieved; specif., *a*) a postponement of a penalty, esp. of execution *b*) a temporary relief, as from trouble or pain
rep·ri·mand (rep'rə mänd'; *also for v.,* rep'rə mänd') *n.* [< Fr. < L. *reprimendus*, that is to be repressed < *reprimere*, REPRESS] a severe or formal rebuke —*vt.* to rebuke severely or formally
re·print (rē print'; *for n. usually* rē'print') *vt.* to print again; print an additional impression of —*n.* something reprinted; specif., an additional impression or edition, as of an earlier book, pamphlet, etc.
re·pris·al (ri prī'z'l) *n.* [< MFr. < It. < *riprendere*, to take back < L. *reprehendere*: see REPREHEND] **1.** the use of force, short of war, against another nation to obtain redress of grievances **2.** injury done in return for injury received, esp. in war, as the killing of prisoners
re·prise (ri prēz') *n.* [< Fr. pp. of *reprendre*, to take back: see REPREHEND] in a musical play, the repetition of all or part of a song performed earlier —*vt.* **-prised', -pris'ing** to present a reprise (of a song)
re·pro (rē'prō) *n., pl.* **-pros** shortened form of REPRODUCTION PROOF: also **repro proof**
re·proach (ri prōch') *vt.* [OFr. *reprochier*: ult. < L. *re-*, back + *prope*, near] to accuse of and blame for a fault; rebuke; reprove —*n.* **1.** shame, disgrace, or blame, or a source or cause of this **2.** a blaming, or an expression of blame; rebuke —**re·proach'a·ble** *adj.* —**re·proach'er** *n.* —**re·proach'ing·ly** *adv.*
re·proach·ful (-fəl) *adj.* full of or expressing reproach —**re·proach'ful·ly** *adv.* —**re·proach'ful·ness** *n.*

rep·ro·bate (rep'rə bāt') *vt.* **-bat'ed, -bat'ing** [< LL. pp. of *reprobare*: see REPROVE] **1.** to disapprove of strongly; condemn **2.** to reject or abandon —*adj.* **1.** depraved; corrupt **2.** *Theol.* lost in sin; rejected by God —*n.* a reprobate person —**rep'ro·ba'tion** *n.* —**rep'ro·ba'tive** *adj.*
re·pro·duce (rē'prə dyo͞os') *vt.* **-duced', -duc'ing** to produce again; specif., *a*) to bring forth others of (its kind), esp. by sexual intercourse *b*) to make (a lost part or organ) grow again *c*) to make a copy, imitation, etc. of (a picture, sound, etc.) *d*) to repeat —*vi.* **1.** to produce offspring, esp. by sexual intercourse **2.** to undergo copying, duplication, etc. —**re'pro·duc'er** *n.* —**re'pro·duc·i·bil'i·ty** *adv.* —**re'pro·duc'i·ble** *adj.*
re·pro·duc·tion (rē'prə duk'shən) *n.* **1.** a reproducing or being reproduced **2.** something made by reproducing; copy **3.** the process by which animals and plants produce new individuals
reproduction proof an especially fine proof of type, etc. to be photographed for making a printing plate
re·pro·duc·tive (-tiv) *adj.* **1.** reproducing **2.** of or for reproduction —**re'pro·duc'tive·ly** *adv.* —**re'pro·duc'tive·ness** *n.*
re·prog·ra·phy (rep rog'rə fē) *n.* the art or process of copying, reprinting, or reproducing printed material
re·proof (ri pro͞of') *n.* a reproving or something said in reproving; rebuke: also **re·prov'al** (-pro͞o'v'l)
re·prove (ri pro͞ov') *vt.* **-proved', -prov'ing** [< OFr. < LL. *reprobare*: see RE- & PROVE] **1.** to speak to in disapproval; rebuke **2.** to express disapproval of (something done or said) —**re·prov'a·ble** *adj.* —**re·prov'er** *n.* —**re·prov'ing·ly** *adv.*
rep·tile (rep'tīl) *n.* [LL. < neut. of L. *reptilis*, crawling < pp. of *repere*, to creep] **1.** any of a group of coldblooded vertebrates having a body covered with scales or horny plates and including snakes, lizards, turtles, crocodiles, etc. and dinosaurs **2.** a contemptible, grovelling person —*adj.* of or like a reptile —**rep·til·i·an** (rep til'ē ən) *adj., n.*
re·pub·lic (ri pub'lik) *n.* [< MFr. < L. < *res*, thing + *publica*, public] **1.** a nation in which the supreme power rests in all the citizens entitled to vote and is exercised by representatives elected by them **2.** the government of such a state **3.** a nation with a president as its head **4.** any of certain divisions of the U.S.S.R. or Yugoslavia
re·pub·li·can (ri pub'li kən) *adj.* **1.** of or like a republic **2.** favouring a republic —*n.* **1.** a person who favours a republican form of government **2.** [U.S.] [**R-**] a member of the Republican Party
re·pub·li·can·ism (-iz'm) *n.* **1.** republican government **2.** republican principles, or adherence to them
Republican Party 1. [U.S.] one of the two major political parties in the U.S., organized in 1854 **2.** any of a number of political parties in various countries, organized to oppose monarchy
Republic day the day celebrating the founding of a republic, specif., January 26 in India
re·pu·di·ate (ri pyo͞o'dē āt') *vt.* **-at'ed, -at'ing** [< L. pp. of *repudiare*, to divorce < *repudium*, separation] **1.** to disown or cast off publicly **2.** *a*) to refuse to accept or support (a belief, treaty, etc.) *b*) to deny the truth of (a charge, etc.) **3.** to refuse to acknowledge or pay (a debt, etc.) —**re·pu'di·a'tion** *n.* —**re·pu'di·a'tor** *n.*
re·pug·nance (ri pug'nəns) *n.* [< MFr. < L. < prp. of *repugnare* < *re-*, back + *pugnare*, to fight] **1.** inconsistency **2.** extreme dislike or distaste Also **re·pug'nan·cy**
re·pug·nant (-nənt) *adj.* **1.** contradictory or opposed **2.** causing repugnance; offensive —**re·pug'nant·ly** *adv.*
re·pulse (ri puls') *vt.* **-pulsed', -puls'ing** [< L. pp. of *repellere*, REPEL] **1.** to drive back; repel (an attack, etc.) **2.** to repel with discourtesy, coldness, etc.; rebuff **3.** to be repulsive to —*n.* **1.** a repelling or being repelled **2.** a refusal, rejection, or rebuff
re·pul·sion (ri pul'shən) *n.* **1.** a repelling or being repelled **2.** strong dislike, distaste, or aversion **3.** *Physics* the mutual action by which bodies or particles of matter tend to repel each other: opposed to ATTRACTION
re·pul·sive (-siv) *adj.* **1.** tending to repel **2.** causing strong dislike or aversion **3.** of repulsion —**re·pul'sive·ly** *adv.* —**re·pul'sive·ness** *n.*
rep·u·ta·ble (rep'yoo tə b'l) *adj.* **1.** having a good reputation; respectable **2.** in proper or good usage [a *reputable* word] —**rep'u·ta·bil'i·ty** *n.* —**rep'u·ta·bly** *adv.*
rep·u·ta·tion (rep'yoo tā'shən) *n.* [< L. < pp. of *reputare*: see ff.] **1.** the regard, favourable or not, shown for a person or thing by the public, community, etc.; repute **2.** such regard when favourable [to lose one's *reputation*] **3.** fame; distinction
re·pute (ri pyo͞ot') *vt.* **-put'ed, -put'ing** [< MFr. < L. < *re-*, again + *putare*, to think] to consider to be as specified [he is *reputed* to be rich] —*n.* same as REPUTATION (senses 1, 3)
re·put·ed (-id) *adj.* generally regarded as being such [the *reputed* owner] —**re·put'ed·ly** *adv.*
re·quest (ri kwest') *n.* [< OFr. < ML., ult. < L. *requirere*:

see REQUIRE] 1. an asking for something; petition 2. something asked for 3. state of being asked for; demand [a song much in *request*] —*vt.* 1. to ask for, esp. in a polite or formal way 2. to ask (a person) to do something —**by request** in response to a request

request stop a point on a route at which public transport will stop only if signalled to do so

Re·qui·em (rek'wē əm) *n.* [L., acc. of *requies*, rest: first word of the Mass] [also r-] 1. R.C.Ch. a) a Mass for the repose of the dead b) a musical setting for this 2. a dirge

†**re·qui·es·cat in pa·ce** (rāk'wē es'kät in pä'chā, rek'-) [L.] may he (or she) rest in peace

re·quire (ri kwīr') *vt.* -**quired'**, -**quir'ing** [< OFr. < L. *requirere* < *re-*, again + *quaerere*, to ask] 1. to ask or insist upon, as by right or authority; demand 2. to order; command [to *require* him to go] 3. to need [to *require* help] 4. to call for as needed [the work *requires* skill] —*vi.* to make a demand

re·quire·ment (-mənt) *n.* 1. a requiring 2. something required or demanded 3. something needed; necessity

req·ui·site (rek'wə zit) *adj.* [< L. pp. of *requirere*: see REQUIRE] required; necessary; indispensable —*n.* something requisite

req·ui·si·tion (rek'wə zish'ən) *n.* 1. a requiring, as by authority 2. a formal written request, as for equipment 3. the state of being demanded for use —*vt.* 1. to demand or take, as by authority [to *requisition* food for troops] 2. to demand from 3. to submit a written request for (equipment, etc.)

re·quite (ri kwīt') *vt.* -**quit'ed**, -**quit'ing** [RE- + *quite*, obs. var. of QUIT] to repay or make return to (a person, group, etc.) for (a benefit, service, etc. or an injury, wrong, etc.) —**re·quit'al** *n.* —**re·quit'er** *n.*

rere·dos (rir'dos, rer'ə-) *n.* [< Anglo-Fr. < OFr. *arere* (see ARREARS) + *dos*, back] an ornamental screen or partition wall behind an altar in a church

re·route (rē rōot') *vt.* -**rout'ed**, -**rout'ing** to send by a new or different route

re·run (rē run'; for *n.* rē'run') *vt.* -**ran'**, -**run'ning** to run again —*n.* 1. a rerunning; esp., a repeat showing of a film, taped TV programme, etc. 2. the film, etc. so shown

res (räs, rēz) *n.*, *pl.* **res** [L., a thing] Law 1. a thing; object 2. matter; case; point; action

res. 1. reserve 2. residence 3. resides 4. resolution

re·sal·a·ble (rē sāl'ə b'l) *adj.* that can be sold again

re·sale (rē'sāl') *n.* the act of selling again

re·scind (ri sind') *vt.* [L. *rescindere* < *re-*, back + *scindere*, to cut] to revoke, repeal, or cancel (a law, order, etc.) —**re·scind'a·ble** *adj.* —**re·scind'er** *n.*

re·scis·sion (ri sizh'ən) *n.* a rescinding

re·script (rē'skript) *n.* [< L. < pp. of *rescribere* < *re-*, back + *scribere*, to write] an official decree or order

res·cue (res'kyōō) *vt.* -**cued**, -**cu·ing** [< OFr. < *re-*, again + *escorre*, to shake < L. < *ex-*, off + *quatere*, to shake] 1. to free or save from danger, evil, etc. 2. Law to take out of legal custody by force —*n.* a rescuing —**res'cu·a·ble** *adj.* —**res'cu·er** *n.*

re·search (ri surch'; for *n.* equally rē'surch) *n.* [< MFr.: see RE- & SEARCH] [sometimes *pl.*] systematic investigation in a field of knowledge, to discover or establish facts or principles —*vi.*, *vt.* to do research (on or in) —**re·search'·a·ble** *adj.* —**re·search'er**, **re·search'ist** *n.*

re·seat (rē sēt') *vt.* 1. to seat again or in another seat 2. to supply with a new seat or seats

re·sect (ri sekt') *vt.* [< L. pp. of *resecare* < *re-*, back + *secare*, to cut] Surgery to remove part of (an organ, bone, etc.) —**re·sec'tion** *n.*

re·sem·blance (ri zem'bləns) *n.* 1. a resembling; likeness 2. a point, degree, or sort of likeness

re·sem·ble (ri zem'b'l) *vt.* -**bled**, -**bling** [< OFr. < *re-*, again + *sembler* < L. *simulare*: see SIMULATE] to be like or similar to in appearance or nature

re·sent (ri zent') *vt.* [< Fr. < OFr. < *re-*, again + *sentir* < L. *sentire*, to feel] to feel or show hurt or indignation at (some act, etc.) or towards (a person), from a sense of being offended —**re·sent'ful** *adj.* —**re·sent'ful·ly** *adv.* —**re·sent'·ful·ness** *n.* —**re·sent'ment** *n.*

re·ser·pine (ri sur'pin, -pēn) *n.* [G. *Reserpin*] a crystalline alkaloid, obtained from the root of a rauwolfia: used in the treatment of hypertension and as a sedative

res·er·va·tion (rez'ər vā'shən) *n.* 1. a reserving or the thing reserved; specif., a) [U.S.] public land set aside for some special use [an Indian *reservation*] b) an arrangement by which a hotel room, theatre ticket, etc. is set aside for use at a certain time or until called for c) anything so reserved 2. a limiting condition or qualification, expressed or implied: see also MENTAL RESERVATION

re·serve (ri zurv') *vt.* -**served'**, -**serv'ing** [< OFr. < L. < *re-*, back + *servare*, to hold] 1. to keep back, store up, or set apart for later use or a special purpose 2. to hold over to a later time 3. to set aside or have set aside (a theatre seat, etc.) for someone 4. to retain for oneself [to *reserve* the right to refuse] —*n.* 1. something reserved 2. a

limitation: now rare except in **without reserve** (see below) 3. the practice of keeping one's thoughts, feelings, etc. to oneself; aloofness 4. reticence; silence 5. restraint in artistic expression; freedom from exaggeration 6. [*pl.*] a) manpower kept out of action and ready for emergency use or for replacing others b) military forces not on active duty but subject to call 7. cash, or any liquid assets, kept aside by a bank, business, etc. to meet expected or unexpected demands 8. land set apart for special use [a nature *reserve*] —*adj.* being, or having the nature of, a reserve —**in reserve** reserved for later use —**without reserve** subject to no limitation

reserve currency a foreign currency that is acceptable as a medium of international payments and that is, therefore, kept in reserve by many countries

re·served (ri zurvd') *adj.* 1. set apart for some purpose, person, etc. 2. showing reserve; aloof or reticent —**re·serv'·ed·ly** (-zur'vid lē) *adv.* —**re·serv'ed·ness** *n.*

reserved list Mil. a list of retired naval officers put on half-pay, but liable to be called upon in an emergency

reserve price the minimum price acceptable to the owner of property being auctioned

re·serv·ist (ri zur'vist) *n.* a member of a country's military reserves

res·er·voir (rez'ər vwär', -vwôr') *n.* [< Fr. < *réserver*: see RESERVE] 1. a place where anything is collected and stored; esp., a natural or artificial lake in which water is stored for use 2. a receptacle (in an apparatus) for a fluid, as oil or ink 3. a reserve supply

re·set (rē set'; for *n.* rē'set') *vt.* -**set'**, -**set'ting** to set again —*n.* 1. a resetting 2. something reset 3. a device for resetting something

re·ship (rē ship') *vt.* -**shipped'**, -**ship'ping** 1. to ship again 2. to transfer to another ship —**re·ship'ment** *n.*

re·shuf·fle (rē shuf'f'l) *n.* 1. an act of shuffling again 2. a reorganization, as in a reassignment of jobs within a government or cabinet —*vt.* to carry out a reshuffle

re·side (ri zīd') *vi.* -**sid'ed**, -**sid'ing** [< MFr. < L. *residere* < *re-*, back + *sedere*, to sit] 1. to dwell for a long time; live (in or at) 2. to be present or exist (in): said of qualities, etc. 3. to be vested (in): said of rights, powers, etc.

res·i·dence (rez'i dəns) *n.* 1. a residing 2. the fact or status of living or staying in a place while working or in training, at university, etc. 3. the place where one resides; one's abode; esp., a house or mansion 4. the time during which a person resides in a place

res·i·den·cy (-dən sē) *n.*, *pl.* -**cies** 1. same as RESIDENCE 2. [U.S.] a period of advanced, specialized medical or surgical training at a hospital 3. formerly, the official residence of a governor-general at the court of a native, Indian prince

res·i·dent (-dənt) *adj.* 1. having a residence (in or at); residing 2. being in residence (sense 2) 3. present or existing (in) 4. not migratory: said of birds, etc. —*n.* 1. a person who lives in a place and is not a visitor or transient 2. [U.S.] a person who is serving a residency 3. a nonmigratory bird, etc. 4. a representative of the British government in a British protectorate 5. formerly, a diplomatic representative ranking below an ambassador

res·i·den·tial (rez'ə den'shəl) *adj.* 1. of or connected with residence 2. of or suitable for residences, or homes [a *residential* area] 3. chiefly for residents rather than transients [a *residential* hotel] —**res'i·den'tial·ly** *adv.*

re·sid·u·al (ri zid'yoo wəl) *adj.* of or like a residue; leftover; remaining —*n.* 1. something remaining, as at the end of a process 2. [U.S.] [*pl.*] extra fees paid to performers for reruns, as on TV 3. Math. the difference between an actual and an estimated value —**re·sid'u·al·ly** *adv.*

re·sid·u·ar·y (-yoo wər ē) *adj.* 1. residual; leftover 2. Law a) relating to the residue of an estate b) receiving such a residue [a *residuary* legatee]

res·i·due (rez'ə dyōō') *n.* [< MFr. < L. neut. of *residuus*, remaining < *residere*: see RESIDE] 1. what is left after part is removed; remainder 2. Chem. matter remaining after evaporation, combustion, etc. 3. Law that part of a testator's estate left after all claims and bequests have been satisfied

re·sid·u·um (ri zid'yoo wəm) *n.*, *pl.* -**u·a** (-wə) [L.] same as RESIDUE

re·sign (ri zīn') *vt.*, *vi.* [< MFr. < L. < *re-*, back + *signare*, to sign] to give up or relinquish (a claim, office, position, etc.), esp. by formal notice (often with *from*) —**resign oneself** (to) to submit or become reconciled (to)

res·ig·na·tion (rez'ig nā'shən) *n.* 1. a) a resigning b) formal notice of this, esp. in writing 2. patient submission; acquiescence

re·signed (ri zīnd') *adj.* feeling or showing resignation —**re·sign'ed·ly** (-zīn'id lē) *adv.* —**re·sign'ed·ness** *n.*

re·sile (ri zīl') *vi.* -**siled'**, -**sil'ing** [MFr. *resiler* < L. *resilire*, to jump back] to bounce or spring back; specif. to come back into shape after being pressed or stretched: said of elastic bodies

re·sil·ience (ri zil'yəns, -ē əns) *n.* the quality of being resilient: also **re·sil'ien·cy**

re·sil·ient (-yənt, -ē ənt) *adj.* [< L. prp. of *resilire* < *re-*, back + *salire*, to jump] 1. springing back into shape, position, etc. after being stretched, bent, or compressed 2. recovering strength, spirits, etc. quickly —**re·sil′ient·ly** *adv.*

res·in (rez′'n) *n.* [< MFr. < L. *resina*] 1. a solid or semisolid, viscous, organic substance exuded from various plants and trees: natural resins are used in varnishes and lacquers 2. *same as:* a) SYNTHETIC RESIN b) ROSIN —*vt.* to treat or rub with resin: also **res′in·ate′** (-ə nāt′) -**at′ed**, -**at′ing** —**res′in·ous, res′in·y** *adj.*

re·sist (ri zist′) *vt.* [< MFr. < L. < *re-*, back + *sistere*, to set] 1. to withstand; fend off; stand firm against 2. a) to oppose actively; fight or work against b) to refuse to cooperate with, submit to, etc. 3. to keep from yielding to or enjoying —*vi.* to oppose or withstand something; offer resistance —*n.* a resistant substance, as a protective coating —**re·sist′er** *n.* —**re·sist′i·bil′i·ty** *n.* —**re·sist′i·ble** *adj.* —**re·sis′tive** *adj.* —**re·sis·tiv·i·ty** (rē′zis tiv′ə tē, ri zis′-) *n.*

re·sist·ance (ri zis′təns) *n.* 1. a resisting; opposition 2. power or capacity to resist; specif., the ability of an organism to ward off disease 3. opposition of some force, thing, etc. to another 4. a force that retards or opposes motion 5. [*often* R-] an underground movement in a country fighting against a foreign occupying power, etc. 6. *Elec.* a) the property by which a conductor opposes current flow and thus generates heat b) *same as* RESISTOR —**re·sist′-ant** *adj., n.*

re·sist·less (ri zist′lis) *adj.* 1. that cannot be resisted; irresistible 2. without power to resist —**re·sist′less·ly** *adv.* —**re·sist′less·ness** *n.*

re·sis·tor (ri zis′tər) *n. Elec.* a device, as a wire coil, used to produce resistance in a circuit

re·sole (rē′sōl′) *vt.* -**soled′, -sol′ing** to put a new sole on (a shoe, etc.) —*n.* a new sole for a shoe, etc.

re·sol·u·ble (ri zol′yoo b'l, rez′əl-) *adj.* that can be resolved or analysed; soluble —**re·sol′u·bil′i·ty, re·sol′u·ble·ness** *n.*

res·o·lute (rez′ə loot′, -lyoot′) *adj.* [< L. pp. of *resolvere*: see RE- & SOLVE] having or showing a fixed, firm purpose; determined; resolved —**res′o·lute′ly** *adv.* —**res′o·lute′-ness** *n.*

res·o·lu·tion (rez′ə loo′shən, -lyoo′-) *n.* 1. a) a resolving of something or breaking it up into its separate parts b) the result of this 2. a) a determining or deciding b) a decision as to future action 3. a resolute quality of mind 4. a formal statement of opinion adopted by a group 5. a solving or answering; solution 6. the unravelling of the plot in a drama or narrative 7. *Music* the process in harmony where a dissonant note or chord is followed by a consonant one 8. *Physics same as* RESOLVING POWER

re·solve (ri zolv′) *vt.* -**solved′, -solv′ing** [< L.: see RE- & SOLVE] 1. to break up into separate parts; analyse 2. to change or transform [the talk *resolved* itself into a dispute] 3. to cause to decide [this *resolved* him to go] 4. to reach as a decision; determine [to *resolve* to go] 5. a) to find an answer to; solve b) to make a decision about, esp. by vote or formally c) to explain or make clear (a problem, a fictional plot, etc.) d) to remove (doubt, etc.) 6. *Music* to make (a dissonant chord or tone) become consonant —*vi.* 1. to be resolved, as by analysis 2. to come to a decision —*n.* 1. a fixed purpose or intention 2. [U.S.] a formal resolution, as by a group —**re·solv′a·bil′i·ty** *n.* —**re·solv′a·ble** *adj.* —**re·solv′er** *n.*

re·solved (-zolvd′) *adj.* firm and fixed in purpose; resolute —**re·solv′ed·ly** (-zol′vid lē) *adv.*

resolving power 1. *Physics* the ability of a microscope, telescope, etc. to distinguish between adjoining points 2. *Photog.* the ability of an emulsion to show up fine detail in an image

res·o·nance (rez′ə nəns) *n.* 1. a being resonant 2. the reinforcing and prolonging of a sound or musical tone by reflection or by sympathetic vibration of other bodies 3. *Elec.* the condition arising in a circuit when an incoming current is at the same, or nearly the same, frequency as the circuit, thus producing much greater currents 4. *Physics* the effect produced when the natural vibration frequency of a body is greatly amplified by vibrations at this same frequency from another body

res·o·nant (-nənt) *adj.* [< L. prp. of *resonare*, to resound] 1. resounding or reechoing 2. producing resonance [*resonant* walls] 3. of, full of, or intensified by resonance [a *resonant* voice] —**res′o·nant·ly** *adv.*

res·o·nate (-nāt′) *vi., vt.* -**nat′ed, -nat′ing** to be or make resonant

res·o·na·tor (-nāt′ər) *n.* 1. a device for producing resonance or increasing sound by resonance 2. *Electronics* an apparatus or system that can be put into oscillation by oscillations in another system

re·sorb (ri sôrb′) *vt.* [< L. < *re-*, again + *sorbere*, to suck up] to absorb again —**re·sorp′tion** (-sôrp′shən) *n.*

res·or·cin·ol (ri zôr′si nol′) *n.* [< RES(IN) + It. *orcello*, a kind of lichen] a colourless crystalline compound used in making dyes, celluloid, pharmaceuticals, etc.: also **res·or′cin** (-sin)

re·sort (ri zôrt′) *vi.* [< OFr. < *re-*, again + *sortir*, to go out] 1. to go; esp., to go often 2. to have recourse; turn (*to*) for help, support, etc. —*n.* 1. a place people often go to for rest or recreation, as on a holiday 2. a frequent getting together or visiting [a place of general *resort*] 3. a person or thing one turns to for help, support, etc. 4. a turning for help, support, etc.; recourse —**as a** (or the) **last resort** as the last available means

re·sound (ri zound′) *vi.* [< OFr. < L. < *re-*, again + *sonare*, to sound] 1. to echo or be filled with sound; reverberate 2. to make a loud, echoing or prolonged sound 3. to be echoed 4. to be celebrated [an act that *resounded* through the ages] —*vt.* 1. to give back (sound); echo 2. to give forth or utter loudly

re·sound·ing (-iŋ) *adj.* 1. reverberating 2. thoroughgoing; complete [a *resounding* victory] 3. high-sounding —**re·sound′ing·ly** *adv.*

re·source (ri sôrs′, -zôrs′) *n.* [< Fr. < OFr. < *re-*, again + *sourdre*, to spring up < L. *surgere*, to rise] 1. something ready for use or available as needed 2. [*pl.*] wealth; assets 3. [*pl.*] something useful, as coal or oil, that a country, state, etc. has 4. a means to an end; expedient 5. [*pl.*] a source of strength or ability within oneself: in full, **inner resources** 6. a being resourceful

re·source·ful (ri sôrs′fəl, -zôrs′-) *adj.* full of resource; able to deal promptly and effectively with difficulties, etc. —**re·source′ful·ly** *adv.* —**re·source′ful·ness** *n.*

re·spect (ri spekt′) *vt.* [< L. pp. of *respicere* < *re-*, back + *specere*, to look at] 1. to hold in high regard; show honour or courtesy to 2. to show consideration for; avoid intruding upon, etc. [*respect* others′ privacy] 3. [Obs.] to concern; relate to —*n.* 1. a feeling of high regard; esteem 2. a being held in honour 3. deference or dutiful regard [*respect* for law] 4. courteous consideration 5. [*pl.*] courteous expressions of regard: now chiefly in **pay one′s respects,** to show polite regard as by visiting and **pay one′s last respects,** to attend someone′s funeral 6. a particular point or detail [right in every *respect*] 7. reference; relation [with *respect* to this] —**in respect of** with reference to —**re·spect′er** *n.*

re·spect·a·ble (ri spek′tə b'l) *adj.* 1. worthy of respect or esteem 2. socially acceptable; proper 3. fairly good in quality 4. fairly large 5. good enough to be seen, worn, etc. —**re·spect′a·bil′i·ty** *n.* —**re·spect′a·bly** *adv.*

re·spect·ful (ri spekt′fəl) *adj.* full of or showing respect; polite —**re·spect′ful·ly** *adv.* —**re·spect′ful·ness** *n.*

re·spect·ing (ri spek′tiŋ) *prep.* concerning; about

re·spec·tive (-tiv) *adj.* as relates individually to each of two or more [their *respective* merits]

re·spec·tive·ly (-tiv lē) *adv.* in regard to each in the order named [the first and second prizes went to Mary and George, *respectively*]

re·spell (rē spel′) *vt.* to spell again; specif., to spell differently in an attempt to show the pronunciation [to *respell* the word "calf" as (käf)]

res·pi·ra·tion (res′pə rā′shən) *n.* 1. act or process of respiring; breathing 2. the processes by which a living organism or cell takes in oxygen, distributes and utilizes it in oxidation, and gives off products, esp. carbon dioxide 3. a similar process in anaerobic organisms —**res′pi·ra′tion·al** *adj.*

res·pi·ra·tor (res′pə rāt′ər) *n.* 1. a device, as of gauze, worn over the mouth and nose, as to prevent the inhaling of harmful substances 2. an apparatus for giving artificial respiration

res·pi·ra·to·ry (res′pər ə tər ē, ri spir′ə-) *adj.* of, for, or involving respiration

re·spire (ri spir′) *vi., vt.* -**spired′, -spir′ing** [< OFr. < L. < *re-*, back + *spirare*, to breathe] to breathe; inhale and exhale (air)

res·pite (res′pit, -pit) *n.* [< OFr. < L. pp. of *respicere*: see RESPECT] 1. a delay or postponement, esp. in carrying out a death sentence; reprieve 2. a period of temporary relief, as from pain, work, etc. —*vt.* -**pit·ed, -pit·ing** to give a respite to

re·splend·ent (ri splen′dənt) *adj.* [< L. prp. of *resplendere* < *re-*, again + *splendere*, to shine] shining brightly; dazzling —**re·splend′ence, re·splend′en·cy** *n.* —**re·splend′-ent·ly** *adv.*

re·spond (ri spond′) *vi.* [< OFr. < L. < *re-*, back + *spondere*, to pledge] 1. to answer; reply 2. to act in return, as if in answer [to *respond* by issuing an invitation] 3. to react favourably, as to medical treatment 4. *Law* to be answerable or liable —*vt.* to say in answer

re·spond·ent (-spon′dənt) *adj.* responding; answering —*n.* 1. a person who responds 2. *Law* a defendant —**re·spond′-ence, re·spond′en·cy** *n.*

re·spond·er (-dər) *n.* 1. a person or thing that responds 2. *Electronics* a device, as a transponder, that indicates reception of a signal

re·sponse (ri spons′) *n.* [< ML. < L. pp. of *respondere*: see RESPOND] 1. something said or done in answer; reply or reaction **2.** *Eccles.* a word, phrase, etc. sung or spoken in answer, as by a congregation or choir in answer to an officiating clergyman **3.** *Electronics* the ratio of output to input of a device or system **4.** *Physiol., Psychol.* a reaction to a stimulus

re·spon·si·bil·i·ty (ri spon′sə bil′ə tē) *n.,* pl. **-ties 1.** a being responsible; obligation, accountability, etc. **2.** a person or thing that one is responsible for

re·spon·si·ble (ri spon′sə b'l) *adj.* [< MFr. < L.: see RESPONSE] **1.** expected or obliged to account (*for* something, *to* someone); answerable **2.** involving obligation or duties [a *responsible* job] **3.** that can be charged with being the cause, agent, etc. of something **4.** able to think and act rationally, and hence accountable for one's behaviour **5.** dependable or reliable, as in meeting obligations —**re·spon′si·ble·ness** *n.* —**re·spon′si·bly** *adv.*

re·spon·sive (-siv) *adj.* **1.** answering **2.** reacting readily, as to suggestion [a *responsive* audience] **3.** containing responses —**re·spon′sive·ly** *adv.* —**re·spon′sive·ness** *n.*

re·spray (rē sprā′) *vt.* [RE- & SPRAY¹] to spray again; specif., to spray a car or other vehicle with paint, changing its colour

rest¹ (rest) *n.* [OE.] **1.** *a)* peace, ease, and refreshment, as produced by sleep *b)* sleep or repose **2.** refreshing inactivity after work or exertion, or a period of this **3.** *a)* relief from anything distressing, tiring, etc. *b)* peace of mind **4.** the repose of death **5.** absence of motion **6.** a place for resting; lodging place, as for travellers **7.** a thing that supports [a foot *rest*] **8.** *Music a)* a measured interval of silence between tones *b)* a symbol for this —*vi.* **1.** *a)* to become refreshed by sleeping, lying down, ceasing work, etc. *b)* to sleep **2.** to be at ease or at peace **3.** to be dead **4.** to be quiet or still for a while **5.** to remain unchanged [let the matter *rest*] **6.** *a)* to lie, sit, or lean *b)* to be placed or based (*in, on,* etc.) **7.** to be or lie (where specified) [the fault *rests* with him] **8.** to be fixed [his eyes *rested* on her] **9.** to rely; depend **10.** *Law* to end voluntarily the introduction of evidence in a case —*vt.* **1.** to give rest to; refresh by rest **2.** to put or lay for ease, support, etc. [*rest* your head on the pillow] **3.** to base; ground [to *rest* an argument on facts] **4.** to fix (the eyes, etc.) **5.** to bring to rest; stop **6.** *Law* to cause (a case) to rest —**at rest 1.** asleep **2.** immobile **3.** free from distress, care, etc. **4.** dead —**be resting** [Theatrical Colloq.] to be out of work —**lay to rest** to bury —**rest on one's oars 1.** to stop rowing for a time **2.** to stop doing anything for a time —**set** (or **put**) **at rest 1.** to relieve (the mind) **2.** to remove anxiety —**rest′er** *n.*

MUSICAL RESTS
(A, semibreve; B, minim; C, crotchet; D, quaver; E, semiquaver)

rest² (rest) *n.* [< OFr. < L. *restare*, to remain < *re-*, back + *stare*, to stand] **1.** what is left; remainder **2.** [with pl. v.] the others Used with *the* —*vi.* to go on being [rest assured] —**for the rest** as regards all other matters —**rest with** to be the responsibility (of)

re·state (rē stāt′) *vt.* **-stat′ed, -stat′ing** to state again, esp. in a different way —**re·state′ment** *n.*

res·tau·rant (res′tə rənt) *n.* [Fr. < prp. of *restaurer*: see RESTORE] a place where meals can be bought and eaten

restaurant car *same as* DINING CAR

res·tau·ra·teur (res′tər ə tur′) *n.* [Fr.] a person who owns or operates a restaurant

rest cure 1. a medical treatment consisting of complete rest **2.** any complete rest [Army life is not a *rest cure*]

rest·ful (rest′fəl) *adj.* **1.** full of or giving rest **2.** quiet; peaceful **3.** having a soothing effect —**rest′ful·ly** *adv.* —**rest′ful·ness** *n.*

res·ti·tu·tion (res′tə tyōō′shən) *n.* [< MFr. < L. < pp. of *restituere*, to restore < *re-*, again + *statuere*, to set up] **1.** restoration to the rightful owner of something lost or taken away **2.** a making good for loss or damage **3.** a return to a former condition

res·tive (res′tiv) *adj.* [< OFr. < *rester*: see REST²] **1.** hard to control; unruly; balky, etc. **2.** nervous or impatient under restraint; restless —**res′tive·ly** *adv.* —**res′tive·ness** *n.*

rest·less (rest′lis) *adj.* **1.** unable to rest or relax **2.** giving no rest or relaxation; disturbed [*restless* sleep] **3.** never or seldom still; always moving **4.** seeking change; discontented —**rest′less·ly** *adv.* —**rest′less·ness** *n.*

res·to·ra·tion (res′tə rā′shən) *n.* **1.** a restoring or being restored, as of a person or thing to a former condition or position, or of something taken away or lost to its rightful owner **2.** a reconstruction of the original form of a building, fossil animal, etc. **3.** a restored thing —**the Restoration 1.** reestablishment of the monarchy in England in 1660 under Charles II **2.** the period of his reign (1660–85)

re·stor·a·tive (ri stor′ə tiv) *adj.* **1.** of restoration **2.** restoring or able to restore health, consciousness, etc. —*n.* a thing that restores

re·store (ri stôr′) *vt.* **-stored′, -stor′ing** [< OFr. < L.

restaurare, to rebuild] **1.** to give back (something taken away, lost, etc.) **2.** to bring back to a former or normal condition, as by repairing, rebuilding, etc. **3.** to put (a person) back into a position, rank, etc. **4.** to bring back to health, strength, etc. **5.** to bring back into being, use, etc. —**re·stor′a·ble** *adj.* —**re·stor′er** *n.*

restr. restaurant

re·strain (ri strān′) *vt.* [< OFr. < L. < *re-*, back + *stringere*, to draw tight] **1.** to hold back from action; check; curb **2.** to keep under control **3.** to deprive of physical liberty, as by shackling **4.** to limit; restrict —**re·strain′a·ble** *adj.* —**re·strain′ed·ly** *adv.* —**re·strain′er** *n.*

re·straint (ri strānt′) *n.* **1.** a restraining or being restrained **2.** a restraining influence or action **3.** a means of restraining **4.** loss or limitation of liberty **5.** control of emotions, impulses, etc.; reserve —**without restraint** freely; intemperately

restraint of trade restriction or prevention of business competition, as by monopoly, price fixing, etc.

re·strict (ri strikt′) *vt.* [< L. pp. of *restringere*: see RESTRAIN] to keep within certain limits; limit; confine

re·strict·ed (ri strik′tid) *adj.* limited; confined; specif., *a)* that may be seen only by authorized personnel [a *restricted* document] *b)* [Chiefly U.S.] excluding certain groups, esp. minorities

restricted area an area in which a speed limit is in operation

re·stric·tion (-shən) *n.* **1.** restricting or being restricted **2.** something that restricts; limitation

re·stric·tion·ism (-shən iz′m) *n.* the policy of favouring restriction, as of trade, immigration, etc. —**re·stric′tion·ist** *n., adj.*

re·stric·tive (ri strik′tiv) *adj.* **1.** restricting or tending to restrict **2.** *Gram.* designating a clause, phrase, or word felt as limiting what it modifies and so not set off with commas (Ex.: the man who spoke to us is my uncle) —**re·stric′tive·ly** *adj.* —**re·stric′tive·ness** *n.*

restrictive practice 1. any agreement that effects the supply of goods or production: also **restrictive trade practice 2.** any work practice that hinders the most efficent use of machinery, etc.: also **restrictive labour practice**

rest·room (rest′rōōm′) *n.* [U.S.] a room or rooms in a public building, with toilets, washbasins, and, sometimes, couches, etc.: also **rest room**

re·struc·ture (rē struk′chər) *vt.* **-tured, -tur·ing** to plan or provide a new structure or organization for

re·sult (ri zult′) *vi.* [< ML. < L. *resultare*, to rebound] **1.** to happen because of something else; follow as an effect (often with *from*) **2.** to end (*in* something) as an effect or development —*n.* **1.** *a)* what comes about from an action, process, etc.; consequence; outcome *b)* [pl.] desired effects **2.** the number, quantity, etc. obtained by mathematical calculation

re·sult·ant (-ənt) *adj.* that results —*n.* **1.** a result **2.** *Physics* a force, velocity, etc. with an effect equal to that of two or more such forces, etc. acting together

re·sume (ri zyōōm′) *vt.* **-sumed′, -sum′ing** [< MFr. < L. < *re-*, again + *sumere*, to take] **1.** to take or occupy again **2.** to begin again or go on with again after interruption —*vi.* to begin again or go on again

ré·su·mé (rez′yōō mā′) *n.* [Fr., pp. of *résumer*: see prec.] a summary; specif., in the U.S. a statement of a job applicant's previous employment experience, education, etc.

re·sump·tion (ri zump′shən) *n.* [< L. < pp. of *resumere*] the act of resuming

re·sur·face (rē sur′fis) *vt.* **-faced, -fac·ing** to put a new surface on —*vi.* to come to the surface again

re·surge (ri surj′) *vi.* **-surged′, -surg′ing 1.** to rise again; revive **2.** to surge back again

re·sur·gent (-sur′jənt) *adj.* rising or tending to rise again; resurging —**re·sur′gence** *n.*

res·ur·rect (rez′ə rekt′) *vt.* [< ff.] **1.** *Theol.* to bring back to life **2.** to bring back into notice, use, etc. —*vi.* *Theol.* to rise from the dead

res·ur·rec·tion (rez′ə rek′shən) *n.* [< OFr. < LL. < L. *resurrectus*, pp. of *resurgere*, to rise again] **1.** *Theol. a)* a rising from the dead, or coming back to life *b)* the state of having so risen **2.** a return to notice, use, etc.; revival —**the Resurrection** *Theol.* **1.** the rising of Jesus from the dead **2.** the rising of all the dead at the Last Judgment —**res′-ur·rec′tion·al** *adj.*

res·ur·rec·tion·ist (-ist) *n.* **1.** a person who stole bodies from graves, esp. for dissection: also **resurrection man 2.** a person who believes in resurrection

resurrection plant any of various small plants that curl up when dry and spread their branches or become green again when watered

re·sus·ci·tate (ri sus′ə tāt′) *vt., vi.* **-tat′ed, -tat′ing** [< L. pp. of *resuscitare* < *re-*, again + *suscitare*, to revive] to revive (someone who is unconscious, apparently dead, etc.) —**re·sus′ci·ta′tion** *n.* —**re·sus′ci·ta′tive** *adj.* —**re·sus′ci·ta′tor** *n.*

ret (ret) *vt.* **ret'ted, ret'ting** [MDu. *reten*] to dampen or soak (flax, hemp, etc.) in water to separate the fibres from woody tissue

ret. 1. retain 2. retired 3. return(ed)

re·tail (rē'tāl; *for vt. 2, usually* ri tāl') *n.* [< OFr. *retailler,* to cut up < *re-,* again + *tailler,* to cut] the sale of goods in small quantities directly to the consumer: cf. WHOLESALE —*adj.* having to do with the selling of goods in this way —*adv.* in small amounts or at a retail price —*vt.* 1. to sell as retail goods 2. to repeat or pass on (gossip, etc.) —*vi.* to be sold as retail goods —**re'tail·er** *n.*

re·tain (ri tān') *vt.* [< OFr. < L. < *re-,* back + *tenere,* to hold] 1. to keep in possession 2. to keep in a fixed state 3. to continue to hold (heat, etc.) 4. to continue to use, etc. 5. to keep in mind; remember 6. to engage (a lawyer, etc.) by an advance fee called a retainer —**re·tain'a·ble** *adj.* —**re·tain'ment** *n.*

re·tain·er (ri tā'nər) *n.* 1. a person or thing that retains 2. a servant, attendant, etc., as of a person or family of rank or wealth 3. *Law a)* the retaining of the services of a lawyer, consultant, etc. *b)* a fee paid in advance to make such services available when needed

retaining wall a wall built to hold back earth, water, loose rocks, etc.

re·take (rē tāk'; *for n.* rē'tāk') *vt.* **-took', -tak'en, -tak'ing** 1. to take again, take back, or recapture 2. to photograph again —*n.* 1. a retaking 2. a film scene, etc. rephotographed or to be rephotographed

re·tal·i·ate (ri tal'ē āt') *vi.* **-at'ed, -at'ing** [< L. pp. of *retaliare* < *re-,* back + *talio,* punishment in kind] to return like for like; esp., to pay back injury for injury —*vt.* to return in kind (an injury, wrong, etc. suffered) —**re·tal'i·a'tion** *n.* —**re·tal'i·a'tive, re·tal'i·a·to·ry** *adj.*

re·tard (ri tärd') *vt.* [< OFr. < L. < *re-,* back + *tardare,* to make slow < *tardus,* slow] to hinder, delay, or slow the advance or progess of —*n.* a retarding; delay

re·tard·ant (-ənt) *n.* something that retards; esp., a substance that delays a chemical reaction: also **re·tard'er** —*adj.* tending to retard

re·tar·da·tion (rē'tär dā'shən) *n.* 1. a retarding or being retarded 2. something that retards 3. *same as* MENTAL RETARDATION —**re·tard·a·tive** (ri tär'də tiv), **re·tard'a·to·ry** (-ter ē) *adj.*

re·tard·ed (ri tär'did) *adj.* delayed in development or progress, esp. because of mental retardation

retch (rech) *vi.* [OE. *hræcan,* to hawk, spit] to undergo the straining action of vomiting, esp. without bringing anything up

retd. 1. retained 2. retired 3. returned

re·ten·tion (ri ten'shən) *n.* 1. a retaining or being retained 2. power of or capacity for retaining 3. *a)* memory *b)* ability to remember

re·ten·tive (-tiv) *adj.* 1. retaining or able to retain 2. having good recall or a good memory —**re·ten'tive·ly** *adv.* —**re·ten'tive·ness, re·ten·tiv·i·ty** (rē'ten tiv'ə tē) *n.*

re·think (rē think') *vt.* **-thought', -think'ing** to think over again, with a view to changing; reconsider

ret·i·cence (ret'ə səns) *n.* quality, state, or instance of being reticent; reserve: also **ret'i·cen·cy**

ret·i·cent (-sənt) *adj.* [< L. prp. of *reticere* < *re-,* again + *tacere,* to be silent] 1. not willing to say much; tending to keep one's thoughts, etc. to oneself; reserved 2. having a restrained, quiet, or understated quality —**ret'i·cent·ly** *adv.*

ret·i·cle (ret'i k'l) *n.* [L. *reticulum:* see RETICULE] *Optics* a network of very fine lines, wires, etc, in the focus of the eyepiece of an optical instrument

re·tic·u·lar (ri tik'yə lər) *adj.* [see RETICULE] 1. netlike 2. intricate —**re·tic'u·lar·ly** *adv.*

re·tic·u·late (-lit; *also, and for v. always,* -lāt') *adj.* [< L. *reticulum:* see ff.] like a net or network, as the veins of some leaves: also **re·tic'u·lat'ed** —*vt., vi.* **-lat'ed, -lat'ing** to divide, mark, or be marked so as to look like network —**re·tic'u·late·ly** *adv.* —**re·tic'u·la'tion** *n.*

ret·i·cule (ret'ə kyool') *n.* [< Fr. < L. *reticulum,* dim. of *rete,* a net] formerly, a woman's drawstring handbag, orig. of net

re·tic·u·lum (ri tik'yə ləm) *n., pl.* **-la** (-lə) [L.: see RETICULE] 1. network 2. the second division of the stomach of cud-chewing animals, as cows

ret·i·na (ret''n ə) *n., pl.* **-nas, -nae'** (-ē') [ML., prob. < L. *rete,* a net] the innermost coat of the back part of the eyeball, on which the image is formed by the lens —**ret'i·nal** *adj.*

ret·i·nue (ret'ə nyoo') *n.* [< OFr. < pp. of *retenir:* see RETAIN] a body of assistants, servants, etc. attending a person of rank or importance; train of attendants

re·tir·al (ri tīr'əl) *n.* [Scot.] retirement

re·tire (ri tīr') *vi.* **-tired', -tir'ing** [< Fr. < *re-,* back + *tirer,* to draw] 1. to withdraw to a private or secluded place 2. to go to bed 3. to retreat, as in battle 4. to give up one's work, career, etc., esp. because of advanced age 5. to move back or away 6. *Cricket,* etc. to stop (batting) before one is out, as because of injury —*vt.* 1. to withdraw or move

(troops) in retreat 2. to take (money, paid-off bonds, etc.) out of circulation 3. to cause to retire from a job, etc. 4. to withdraw (an outdated or worn-out thing) from use —**retire into oneself** to become uncommunicative; keep to oneself

re·tired (ri tīrd') *adj.* 1. secluded or private 2. *a)* having given up one's work, etc., esp. because of advanced age *b)* of or for such retired persons

re·tire·ment (ri tīr'mənt) *n.* 1. a retiring or being retired, specif. from work, etc. 2. *a)* privacy; seclusion *b)* a place of privacy or seclusion

retirement pension 1. the pension an employee may receive from his employer when he retires 2. *same as* OLD AGE PENSION

re·tir·ing (-in) *adj.* 1. that retires 2. reserved; modest; shy

re·took (rē took') *pt. of* RETAKE

re·tool (rē tool') *vt., vi.* to adapt the machinery of (a factory) for making a different product by changing the tools and dies

re·tort¹ (ri tôrt') *vt., vi.* [< L. *retortus,* pp. of *retorquere* < *re-,* back + *torquere,* to twist] 1. to return in kind (an insult, etc. received) 2. to answer back, esp. in a sharp, quick, or clever way —*n.* a retorting or the response so made

re·tort² (ri tôrt') *n.* [< Fr. < ML. *retorta* < L. fem. pp.: see prec.] 1. a container for distilling, usually of glass and with a long tube 2. a vessel for heating ore to extract metal, coal to produce gas, etc.

re·touch (rē tuch'; *for n., also* rē'tuch') *vt.* to touch up or change details in (a painting, the negative or print of a photograph, etc.) —*n.* a retouching or thing retouched —**re·touch'er** *n.*

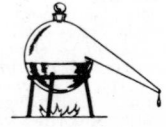

RETORT

re·trace (ri träs') *vt.* **-traced', -trac'ing** [Fr. *retracer:* see RE- & TRACE¹] 1. to go back over again, esp. in the reverse direction [to *retrace* one's steps] 2. to trace again the story of, from the beginning

re·trace (rē'träs') *vt.* **-traced', -trac'ing** to trace the lines of (a drawing, engraving, etc.) over again

re·tract (ri trakt') *vt., vi.* [< L.: ult. < *re-,* back + *trahere,* to draw] 1. to draw back or in [to *retract* claws] 2. to withdraw or take back (a statement, offer, charge, etc.); recant —**re·tract'a·bil'i·ty** *n.* —**re·tract'a·ble** *adj.* —**re·trac'-tion** *n.* —**re·trac'tive** *adj.*

re·trac·tile (ri trak'til) *adj.* [Fr.] that can be retracted, or drawn back or in, as the claws of a cat

re·trac·tor (-tər) *n.* one that retracts; esp., *a)* a muscle that retracts an organ, protruded part, etc. *b)* a surgical device for retracting a part or organ

re·tral (rē'trəl) *adj.* [< L. *retro,* backward + -AL] at, near, or towards the back —**re'tral·ly** *adv.*

re·tread (rē tred'; *for n.* rē'tred') *vt., vi. same as* REMOULD

re·tread (rē'tred') *vt.* **-trod', -trod'den** or **-trod', -tread'-ing** to tread again

re·treat (ri trēt') *n.* [< OFr., ult. < L. *re-,* back + *trahere,* to draw] 1. a going back or backwards; withdrawal in the face of opposition, etc. 2. withdrawal to a safe or private place 3. a safe, quiet, or secluded place 4. a period of seclusion, esp. for religious contemplation, often as part of a group 5. *Mil. a)* the forced withdrawal of troops under attack, or a signal for this *b)* a signal by bugle or drum at sunset for lowering the national flag, or this ceremony —*vi.* 1. to withdraw; go back 2. [Chiefly U.S.] to slope backwards —**beat a retreat** to retreat or withdraw in a hurry

re·trench (rē trench') *vt., vi.* [< MFr.: see RE- & TRENCH] to cut down or reduce (esp. expenses); curtail, economize, etc. —**re·trench'ment** *n.*

ret·ri·bu·tion (ret'rə byoo'shən) *n.* [< OFr. < LL., ult. < L. < *re-,* back + *tribuere,* to pay] deserved punishment for evil done, or, sometimes, reward for good done —**re·trib·u·tive** (ri trib'yoo tiv), **re·trib'u·to·ry** (-tər ē) *adj.* —**re·trib'u·tive·ly** *adv.*

re·triev·al (ri trē'v'l) *n.* 1. a retrieving 2. possibility of recovery or restoration

re·trieve (ri trēv') *vt.* **-trieved', -triev'ing** [< OFr. < *re-,* again + *trouver,* to find] 1. to get back; recover 2. to restore; revive [to *retrieve* one's spirits] 3. to rescue or save 4. to set right or repair (a loss, error, etc.) 5. to recall to mind 6. to recover (information) from data stored in a computer 7. to find and bring back (killed or wounded game): said of dogs 8. *Tennis,* etc. to return (a ball hard to reach) —*vi.* to retrieve game —*n.* a retrieving —**re·triev'-a·ble** *adj.*

re·triev·er (-ər) *n.* 1. a person or thing that retrieves 2. a dog trained to retrieve game; specif., any of several breeds of dog developed for this purpose

ret·ro (ret'rō) *n., pl.* **-ros** *clipped form of* RETROROCKET

ret·ro- [< L. *retro,* backward] *a combining form meaning* backward, back, behind [*retroactive*]

ret·ro·act (ret'rō akt') *vi.* [< L. *retroactus,* pp. of *retroagere,* to drive back, reverse] **1.** to act in opposition; react **2.** to have influence, etc. on things done in the past

ret·ro·ac·tive (ret'rō ak'tiv) *adj.* applying to, or going into effect as of, the preceding period [a retroactive pay increase] **—ret'ro·ac'tive·ly** *adv.* **—ret'ro·ac·tiv'i·ty** *n.*

ret·ro·cede (ret'rə sēd') *vi.* **-ced'ed, -ced'ing** [< L. < *retro-,* back + *cedere,* to yield, go] to go back; recede **—vt.** to cede (territory) back **—ret'ro·ces'sion** (-sesh'ən) *n.*

ret·ro·choir (ret'rō kwīr) *n.* [RETRO- + CHOIR, after ML. *retrochorus*] that part of a church which lies behind the choir and main altar

ret·ro·fire (ret'rə fīr') *vi., vt.* **-fired', -fir'ing** to ignite: said of a retrorocket **—n.** a retrofiring

ret·ro·fit (-fit') *n.* [RETRO- + FIT¹] a change in design, construction, etc., as of an aircraft, to incorporate later improvements **—vt., vi. -fit'ted, -fit'ting** to modify with a retrofit

ret·ro·flex (-fleks') *adj.* [< L.: see RETRO- & FLEX¹] **1.** bent or turned backwards **2.** *Phonet.* pronounced with the tip of the tongue raised and bent slightly backwards Also **ret'·ro·flexed' —n.** *Phonet.* a retroflex sound

ret·ro·grade (ret'rə grād') *adj.* [< L. *retrogradi:* see RETRO- & GRADE] **1.** moving or directed backwards **2.** going back to an earlier, esp. worse, condition **—vi. -grad'ed, -grad'ing 1.** to go or move backwards **2.** to deteriorate **—ret'·ro·gra·da'tion** (-grā dā'shən) *n.*

ret·ro·gress (ret'rə gres') *vi.* [< L. pp. of *retrogradi:* see prec.] to move backwards, esp. into an earlier or worse condition **—ret'ro·gres'sion** (-gresh'ən) *n.* **—ret'ro·gres'·sive** *adj.* **—ret'ro·gres'sive·ly** *adv.*

ret·ro·rock·et, ret·ro·rock·et (ret'rō rok'it) *n.* a small rocket on a larger rocket or spacecraft, used to produce thrust against flight direction so as to reduce speed

ret·ro·spect (ret'rə spekt') *n.* [< L. pp. of *retrospicere* < *retro-,* back + *specere,* to look] a looking back on or thinking about things past **—in retrospect** in reviewing the past **—ret'ro·spec'tion** *n.*

ret·ro·spec·tive (ret'rə spek'tiv) *adj.* **1.** looking or directed back, to the past, etc. **2.** retroactive **—n.** an art show of typical works of an artist over all or part of his lifetime **—ret'ro·spec'tive·ly** *adv.*

ret·rous·sé (rə trōō'sā) *adj.* [Fr., turned up] turned up at the tip [a retroussé nose]

ret·si·na (ret'si nə) *n.* [ModGr.] a wine of Greece, flavoured with pine resin

re·turn (ri tɜrn') *vi.* [< OFr. *retourner:* see RE- & TURN] **1.** to go or come back **2.** to answer; retort **—vt. 1.** to bring, send, carry, or put back **2.** to pay back by doing or giving the same; reciprocate [to return a visit, a compliment, etc.] **3.** to produce (a profit, revenue, etc.); yield **4.** to report officially or formally **5.** to elect or reelect **6.** to render (a verdict, etc.) **7.** *Sports* to hit back or throw back (a ball) **—n. 1.** a coming or going back **2.** a bringing, sending, carrying, or putting back **3.** something returned **4.** repayment; requital; reciprocation **5.** *a)* profit made on an exchange of goods *b)* [often *pl.*] yield or profit, as from investments **6.** an answer; retort **7.** *a)* an official or formal report *b)* [usually *pl.*] a report on a vote count [election returns] *c)* a form for reporting income tax due: in full, **(income) tax return —adj. 1.** of or for returning [a return ticket] **2.** given, sent, done, etc. again or in return [a return visit] **3.** returning or returned **—in return** as a return; as an equivalent, response, etc. **—re·turn'a·ble** *adj.* **—re·turn'er** *n.*

returning officer an official in charge of an election in a district

return ticket 1. a ticket entitling a passenger to travel to his destination and back again **2.** the part of the ticket used for the return journey

re·u·ni·fy (rē yōō'nə fī') *vt., vi.* **-fied', -fy'ing** to unify again after being divided **—re'u·ni·fi·ca'tion** *n.*

re·un·ion (rē yōōn'yən) *n.* **1.** a reuniting **2.** a gathering of persons after separation [a family reunion]

re·u·nite (rē'yoo nīt') *vt., vi.* **-nit'ed, -nit'ing** to unite again; bring or come together again

Reu·ters (roit'ərz) *n.* [after Baron Paul Julius von *Reuter* (1816-99), the founder] a private British agency for gathering and distributing news among member newspapers: also **Reuter's News Agency**

rev (rev) *n.* [Colloq.] a revolution, as of an engine **—vt., vi.** **revved, rev'ving** [Colloq.] to speed up (an engine, motor, etc.): usually with **up**

Rev. 1. *Bible* Revelation **2.** *pl.* **Revs.** Reverend

rev. 1. revenue **2.** reverse **3.** review(ed) **4.** revise(d) **5.** revision **6.** revolution **7.** revolving

re·val·u·ate (rē val'yoo wāt') *vt.* **-at'ed, -at'ing** to make a new valuation or appraisal of **—re·val'u·a'tion** *n.*

re·vamp (rē vamp') *vt.* **1.** to put a new vamp on (a shoe or boot) **2.** to renovate; revise **—n.** a revamping

re·vanch·ism (rə vänsh'iz'm, -vänch'-) *n.* [< Fr. *revanche,* revenge + -ISM] the revengeful spirit moving a defeated nation to aggressively seek restoration of territories, etc. **—re·vanch'ist** *adj., n.*

Revd. Reverend

re·veal (ri vēl') *vt.* [< OFr. < L. *revelare,* lit., to draw back the veil < *re-,* back + *velum,* a veil] **1.** to make known (something hidden or secret); disclose **2.** to expose to view; show; display **—re·veal'a·ble** *adj.* **—re·veal'er** *n.* **—re·veal'·ment** *n.*

re·veil·le (ri val'ē, -vel'-) *n.* [< Fr. imper. of (*se*) *réveiller,* to wake up, ult. < L. *re-,* again + *vigilare,* to watch] *Mil.* **1.** a signal on a bugle, drum, etc. early in the morning to wake soldiers or sailors or call them to first assembly **2.** the first assembly of the day

rev·el (rev''l) *vi.* **-elled, -el·ling** [< MFr. < L. *rebellare:* see REBEL] **1.** to make merry; be noisily festive **2.** to take much pleasure (*in*) [to revel in sports] **—n. 1.** merrymaking; revelry **2.** [often *pl.*] an occasion of merrymaking **—rev'el·ler** *n.*

rev·e·la·tion (rev'ə lā'shən) *n.* **1.** a revealing, or disclosing **2.** something disclosed, especially when it comes as a great surprise **3.** *Theol.* God's revealing of himself and his will to man **—[R-]** the last book of the New Testament (in full, **The Revelation of Saint John the Divine**): also **Revelations** **—rev'e·la'tor** *n.* **—rev'e·la·to·ry** (-lə tar ē) *adj.*

rev·el·ry (rev''l rē) *n., pl.* **-ries** revelling; noisy merrymaking; boisterous festivity

re·venge (ri venj') *vt.* **-venged', -veng'ing** [< OFr. *re-,* again + *vengier,* to take vengeance < L. *vindicare:* see VINDICATE] **1.** to inflict injury or punishment in return for (an injury, insult, etc.) **2.** to avenge (a person, oneself, etc.) **—n. 1.** a revenging; vengeance **2.** what is done in revenging **3.** desire to take vengeance **4.** a chance to retaliate, as by a return match after a defeat **—be revenged** to get revenge **—re·veng'er** *n.* **—re·veng'ing·ly** *adv.*

re·venge·ful (-fəl) *adj.* full of or desiring revenge **—re·venge'ful·ly** *adv.* **—re·venge'ful·ness** *n.*

rev·e·nue (rev'ə nyōō') *n.* [< MFr. < *re-,* back + *venir* < L. *venire,* to come] **1.** the income or return from property or investment **2.** a source of income **3.** the income of a government from taxes, licences, etc. **4.** the government department responsible for the collection of government revenue

revenue officer someone employed to collect customs and excise duties and to prevent smuggling

re·ver·ber·ant (ri vur'bər ənt) *adj.* reverberating

re·ver·ber·ate (-bə rāt') *vt.* **-at'ed, -at'ing** [< L. < *re-,* again + *verberare,* to beat < *verber,* a lash] **1.** to cause (a sound) to reecho **2.** to reflect (light, heat, etc.) **—vi. 1.** to reecho or resound **2.** to be reflected, as light or sound waves **3.** to recoil; rebound

re·ver·ber·a·tion (ri vur'bə rā'shən) *n.* **1.** a reverberating or being reverberated; reflection of light or sound waves, etc. **2.** something reverberated, as reechoed sound **—re·ver'·ber·a'tive** (-bə rāt'iv, -bər ə tiv) *adj.* **—re·ver'ber·a'tive·ly** *adv.* **—re·ver'ber·a·to·ry** (-bər ə tar ē) *adj.*

re·vere¹ (ri vir') *vt.* **-vered', -ver'ing** [< Fr. < L. < *re-,* again + *vereri,* to fear] to regard with deep respect, love, and awe; venerate

re·vere² (ri vir') *n.* same as REVERS

rev·er·ence (rev'ər əns, rev'rəns) *n.* **1.** a feeling or attitude of deep respect, love, and awe; veneration **2.** a manifestation of this; specif., a bow or curtsy **3.** [R-] a title used in speaking to or of a clergyman: preceded by *your* or *his* **—vt. -enced, -enc·ing** to treat with reverence

rev·er·end (-ər ənd, -rənd) *adj.* [< MFr. < L. *reverendus,* gerundive of *revereri:* see REVERE¹] worthy of reverence: used [usually **the R-**] as a title of respect for a clergyman, often before the name **—n.** *colloq.* term for CLERGYMAN

rev·er·ent (-ər ənt, -rənt) *adj.* feeling or showing reverence **—rev'er·ent·ly** *adv.*

rev·er·en·tial (rev'ə ren'shəl) *adj.* showing or caused by reverence **—rev'er·en'tial·ly** *adv.*

rev·er·ie (rev'ər ē) *n.* [< Fr. < MFr. < *rever,* to wander] **1.** dreamy thinking, esp. of agreeable things; daydreaming **2.** a fanciful notion or daydream

re·vers (ri vir', -ver') *n., pl.* **-vers** (-virz', -verz') [Fr. < L. *reversus:* see REVERSE] a part (of a garment) turned back to show the reverse side or facing, as a lapel

re·ver·sal (ri vur's'l) *n.* a reversing or being reversed

re·verse (ri vurs') *adj.* [< OFr. < L. pp. of *revertere:* see REVERT] **1.** *a)* turned backwards; opposite or contrary, as in position, direction, etc. *b)* with the back showing **2.** reversing the usual effect, as to show white letters on a black background **3.** acting or moving in a way opposite or contrary to the usual **4.** causing movement backwards or in the opposite direction **—n. 1.** the opposite or contrary **2.** the back, as the side of a coin or medal that does not show the main design **3.** a reversing; esp., a change from good fortune to bad; defeat; check **4.** a mechanism, etc. for reversing, as a gear or an arrangement in an automatic transmission that causes a machine or motor vehicle to run backwards: also **reverse gear —vt. -versed', -vers'ing 1.** to turn in an opposite position or direction, upside down, or inside out **2.** to change to the opposite **3.** to cause to go in an opposite direction **4.** to transfer (the charges for a telephone call) to the party being called **5.** *Law* to revoke or annul (a decision, etc.) —*vi.* **1.** to go or turn in the opposite direction **2.** to put a motor, engine, etc. in reverse —**the reverse of** far from; the opposite of —**re·verse′ly** *adv.* —**re·vers′er** *n.*

re·vers·i·ble (ri vur′sə b'l) *adj.* **1.** that can be reversed, as cloth, coats, etc. finished so that either side can be used as the outer side **2.** that can reverse, as a chemical reaction —*n.* a reversible coat, jacket, etc. —**re·vers′i·bil′i·ty** *n.* —**re·vers′i·bly** *adv.*

reversing light a small light attached to the rear of a motor vehicle that is illuminated when the vehicle is reversed

re·ver·sion (ri vur′zhən, -shən) *n.* **1.** a return, as to a former state, custom, etc. **2.** *Biol.* a return to a former or primitive type; atavism **3.** *Law a)* the right of succession, future possession, etc. *b)* the return of an estate to the grantor and his heirs after a grant terminates —**re·ver′sion·ar·y, re·ver′sion·al** *adj.*

re·vert (ri vurt′) *vi.* [< OFr. < L. < *re-*, back + *vertere*, to turn] **1.** to go back; return, as to a former practice, subject, etc. **2.** *Biol.* to return to an earlier type **3.** *Law* to go back to a former owner or his heirs —**re·vert′i·ble** *adj.*

rev·er·y (rev′ər ē) *n., pl.* **-er·ies** *same as* REVERIE

re·vet·ment (ri vet′mənt) *n.* [< Fr. < OFr., ult. < L. *re-*, again + *vestire*, to clothe] **1.** a facing of stone, cement, etc., as to protect an embankment **2.** *same as* RETAINING WALL

re·view (ri vyoo′) *n.* [< MFr. < L. < *re-*, again + *videre*, to see] **1.** a looking at or looking over again **2.** a general survey or report **3.** a looking back, as on past events **4.** reexamination, as by a higher court of the decision of a lower court **5.** a critical report and evaluation, as in a newspaper, of a book, play, concert, etc. **6.** a magazine containing articles of criticism and evaluation [a law *review*] **7.** [U.S.] revision (sense 3) **8.** *same as* REVUE **9.** a formal inspection, as of troops on parade —*vt.* **1.** to look back on (past events, etc.) **2.** to survey in thought, speech, or writing **3.** to inspect (troops, etc.) formally **4.** to give or write a critical report of (a book, play, etc.) **5.** to reexamine (a lower court's decision) —*vi.* to review books, plays, etc.

re·view·er (-ər) *n.* a person who reviews; esp., one who reviews books, plays, etc. as for a newspaper

re·vile (ri vīl′) *vt., vi.* **-viled′, -vil′ing** [< OFr. *reviler,* to treat as vile: see RE- & VILE] to call bad names in talking (to or about) —**re·vile′ment** *n.* —**re·vil′er** *n.*

re·vise (ri vīz′) *vt.* **-vised′, -vis′ing** [< Fr. < L. < *re-*, back + *visere*, to survey, freq. of *videre*, to see] **1.** to read (a manuscript, etc.) over carefully and correct and improve it **2.** to change or amend **3.** to go over (lessons, etc.) again —*n.* a revising or a revision —**re·vis′al** *n.* —**re·vis′er,** **re·vi′sor** *n.*

Revised Standard Version a mid-20th-cent. revision of an earlier version of the Bible, made by certain U.S. scholars

Revised Version a late 19th-cent. revision of the Authorized Version of the Bible, made by a committee of British and U.S. scholars

re·vi·sion (ri vizh′ən) *n.* **1.** act, process, or work of revising **2.** a revised form, as of a book, etc. **3.** the act of going over a lesson or lessons again —**re·vi′sion·ar·y, re·vi′sion·al** *adj.*

re·vi·sion·ist (-ist) *n.* a person who favours the revision of some accepted theory, etc. —*adj.* of revisionists —**re·vi′sion·ism** *n.*

re·vi·so·ry (ri vī′zər ē) *adj.* of, or having the nature or power of, revision

re·vi·tal·ize (rē vīt′l′līz′) *vt.* **-ized′, -iz′ing** to bring vitality, vigour, etc. back to after a decline

re·viv·al (ri vīv′l) *n.* **1.** a reviving or being revived; specif., *a)* a bringing or coming back into use, being, etc. *b)* a new presentation of an earlier play, film, etc. *c)* restoration to vigour and activity *d)* a bringing or coming back to life or consciousness *e)* a stirring up of religious feelings, usually by the excited preaching of evangelists at public meetings *f)* a series of such meetings

re·viv·al·ist (-ist) *n.* a person who promotes or conducts religious revivals —**re·viv′a·lism** *n.* —**re·viv′a·lis′tic** *adj.*

re·vive (ri vīv′) *vi., vt.* **-vived′, -viv′ing** [< OFr. < L. < *re-*, again + *vivere*, to live] **1.** to come or bring back to life or consciousness **2.** to come or bring back to health and vigour **3.** to come or bring back into use, operation, or attention **4.** to come or bring to mind again **5.** to present (a play or film) in a revival —**re·viv′a·bil′i·ty** *n.* —**re·viv′a·ble** *adj.* —**re·viv′er** *n.*

re·viv·i·fy (ri viv′ə fī′) *vt., vi.* **-fied′, -fy′ing** to give or acquire new life or vigour; revive —**re·viv′i·fi·ca′tion** *n.* —**re·viv′i·fi′er** *n.*

rev·o·ca·ble (rev′ə kə b'l) *adj.* that can be revoked: also **re·vok·a·ble** (ri vō′kə b'l) —**rev′o·ca·bil′i·ty** *n.* —**rev′o·ca·bly** *adv.*

rev·o·ca·tion (rev′ə kā′shən) *n.* a revoking or being revoked; repeal; annulment

rev·o·ca·to·ry (rev′ə kə tər ē) *adj.* revoking or tending to revoke

re·voke (ri vōk′) *vt.* **-voked′, -vok′ing** [< MFr. < L. < *re-*, back + *vocare*, to call] to withdraw, repeal, or cancel (a law, permit, etc.) —*vi.* *Card Games* to play a card of another suit, against the rules, when holding any of the suit called for —*n.* *Card Games* an act of revoking —**re·vok′-er** *n.*

re·volt (ri vōlt′) *n.* [< Fr. < It., ult. < L. *revolvere:* see REVOLVE] **1.** a rising up against the government; rebellion **2.** any refusal to submit to authority **3.** the state of a person or persons revolting [the slaves were in *revolt]* —*vi.* **1.** to rise up against the government **2.** to refuse to submit to authority; rebel **3.** to be disgusted or shocked (with *at* or *against*) —*vt.* to disgust —**re·volt′er** *n.*

re·volt·ing (-vōl′tiŋ) *adj.* **1.** rebellious **2.** causing revulsion; disgusting —**re·volt′ing·ly** *adv.*

rev·o·lu·tion (rev′ə loo′shən) *n.* [< OFr. < LL. < L. pp. of *revolvere:* see REVOLVE] **1.** *a)* movement of a body in an orbit or circle *b)* the time taken for a body to go around an orbit **2.** a turning motion of a body round its centre or axis; rotation **3.** a complete cycle of events **4.** complete or radical change of any kind **5.** overthrow of a government or social system, with another taking its place

rev·o·lu·tion·ar·y (-ər ē) *adj.* **1.** of, like, favouring, or causing a revolution in a government or social system **2.** bringing about a very great change **3.** [R-] *a)* having to do with the French Revolution *b)* [U.S.] having to do with the War of American Independence **4.** revolving or rotating —*n., pl.* **-ar·ies** a revolutionist

revolution counter *same as* TACHOMETER: also **rev counter**

rev·o·lu·tion·ist (-ist) *n.* a person who favours or takes part in a revolution

rev·o·lu·tion·ize (-īz′) *vt.* **-ized′, -iz′ing** **1.** to make a complete and basic change in **2.** [Rare] to bring about a political revolution in

re·volve (ri volv′) *vt.* **-volved′, -volv′ing** [< L. < *re-*, back + *volvere*, to roll] **1.** to turn over in the mind; reflect on **2.** to cause to travel in a circle or orbit **3.** to cause to rotate —*vi.* **1.** to move in a circle or orbit **2.** to rotate **3.** to seem to move (*around* or *about* something) **4.** to recur at intervals **5.** to be pondered on —**re·volv′a·ble** *adj.*

re·volv·er (ri vol′vər) *n.* a handgun with a revolving cylinder holding several bullets which can be fired without reloading

re·volv·ing (-viŋ) *adj.* **1.** that revolves **2.** designating a fund that is regularly replenished, for making loans, etc. **3.** designating credit, as with a credit card, renewed by regular payments to maintain a specified amount

revolving door a door consisting of four vanes hung on a central axle, and turned around by pushing on a vane

re·vue (ri vyoo′) *n.* [Fr.: see REVIEW] a musical show consisting of skits, songs, and dances, often poking fun at personages, fashions, etc.

re·vul·sion (ri vul′shən) *n.* [< Fr. < L. < pp. of *revellere* < *re-*, back + *vellere*, to pull] **1.** a sudden, complete, and violent change of feeling **2.** extreme disgust —**re·vul′sive** *adj.*

re·ward (ri wôrd′) *n.* [< ONormFr. (for OFr. *regarde*) < *regarder:* see REGARD] **1.** something given in return for good or, sometimes, evil, or for service or merit **2.** money offered, as for the capture of a criminal, etc. **3.** compensation; profit —*vt.* **1.** to give a reward to **2.** to give a reward for (service, etc.) —**re·ward′a·ble** *adj.* —**re·ward′er** *n.* —**re·ward′less** *adj.*

re·ward·ing (-iŋ) *adj.* giving a sense of reward, or return —**re·ward′ing·ly** *adv.*

re·wa-re·wa (rā′wä rā′wä) *n.* [Maori] a New Zealand timber-producing tree

re·wind (rē wīnd′) *vt.* **-wound′, -wind′ing** to wind again; specif., to wind (film, tape, etc.) back on the reel —*n.* **1.** something rewound **2.** a rewinding

re·wire (-wīr′) *vt., vi.* **-wired′, -wir′ing** to wire again; specif., to put new wires in or on (a house, motor, etc.)

re·word (rē wurd′) *vt.* to state again in other words; change the wording of

re·work (-wurk′) *vt.* to work again; specif., *a)* to rewrite or revise *b)* to process (something used) for use again

re·write (rē rīt′; *for n.* rē′rīt′) *vt., vi.* **-wrote′, -writ′ten, -writ′ing** **1.** to write again **2.** to revise **3.** to write (news turned in by a reporter) in a different form for publication —*n.* an article so written —**re·writ′er** *n.*

rex (reks) *n.* [L., a king] [*also* R-] king

rex·ine (rek′sēn) *n.* [REX + -INE⁴] a kind of imitation leather

Reyn·ard (ren′ərd, re′närd, rā′närd) [OFr. *Renard* < OHG.] the fox in the medieval beast epic *Reynard the Fox;* hence, a name for any fox

RF, R.F., r.f. **1.** radio frequency **2.** rapid-fire

R.F.C. Rugby Football Club

R.G.S. Royal Geographical Society

Rh **1.** *see* RH FACTOR **2.** *Chem.* rhodium

r.h. relative humidity

r.h., R.H., RH right hand

R.H.A. Royal Horse Artillery

rhab·do·man·cy (rab′də man′sē) *n.* [LL. < Gr.

rhabdomanteia < *rhabdos*, a rod + *manteia*, divination] divination by a rod or wand, esp. finding underground water, ores, etc. by means of a divining rod; dowsing

Rhad·a·man·thine (rad'ə man'thin,-thīn) *adj.* [after *Rhadamanthus* in Gr. Myth. who became a judge of the dead in the lower world after he died] judicially strict, impartial, and severe

rhap·sod·ic (rap sod'ik) *adj.* of, or having the nature of, rhapsody; extravagantly enthusiastic: also **rhap·sod'i·cal** —**rhap·sod'i·cal·ly** *adv.*

rhap·so·dize (rap'sə dīz') *vi., vt.* -**dized'**, -**diz'ing** to speak, write, or recite in a rhapsodic manner or form —**rhap'·so·dist** *n.*

rhap·so·dy (-dē) *n., pl.* -**dies** [< Fr. < L. < Gr. *rhapsōidia*, ult. < *rhaptein*, to stitch together + *ōidē*, song] **1.** any ecstatic or extravagantly enthusiastic speech or writing **2.** great delight **3.** *Music* an instrumental composition of free, irregular form, suggesting improvization

rhe·a (rē'ə) *n.* [after *Rhea*, in Gr. Myth. the mother of Zeus and wife of Cronus] a large S. American nonflying bird, resembling the African ostrich but smaller and having a feathered neck and head

rhe·bok (rē'bok) *n.* [Afrik. *reebok* < MDu. *reeboc*, male roe deer] a rare South African antelope with woolly, brownish-grey hair

Rhen·ish (ren'ish) *adj.* of the Rhine or the regions around it —*n.* [Now Rare] same as RHINE WINE

rhe·ni·um (rē'nē əm) *n.* [ModL. < L. *Rhenus*, Rhine] a rare metallic chemical element resembling manganese: symbol, Re; at. wt., 186.2; at no., 75

rheo- [< Gr. *rheos*, current < *rhein*, to flow] a combining form meaning a flow, current [*rheostat*]

rhe·ol·o·gy (rē ol'ə jē) *n.* [RHEO- + -LOGY] the study of the change in form and the flow of matter —**rhe'o·log'i·cal** (-ə loj'i k'l) *adj.*

rhe·o·stat (rē'ə stat') *n.* [RHEO- + -STAT] a device for varying the resistance of an electric circuit without interrupting the circuit, used as to dim or brighten electric lights —**rhe'o·stat'ic** *adj.*

rhe·sus (rē'səs) *n.* [ModL. < L. < Gr. proper name] a brownish-yellow macaque of India, often kept in zoos and used in medical research: in full, **rhesus monkey**

rhet·o·ric (ret'ər ik) *n.* [< OFr. < L. < Gr. *rhētorikē* (*technē*), oratorical (art) < *rhētōr*, orator] **1.** the art of using words effectively in speaking or writing; esp., now, the art of prose composition **2.** a book on this **3.** artificial eloquence; showiness in literary style

rhe·tor·i·cal (ri tor'i k'l) *adj.* **1.** of, having the nature of, or according to rhetoric **2.** artificially eloquent; showy and elaborate in literary style —**rhe·tor'·i·cal·ly** *adv.*

rhetorical question a question asked only to produce an effect, no spoken answer being expected

RHESUS
MONKEY
(head & body
to 46 cm; tail
to 20 cm)

rhet·o·ri·cian (ret'ə rish'ən) *n.* **1.** a person skilled in using or teaching the art of rhetoric **2.** a person who speaks or writes in a showy, elaborate way

rheum (rōōm) *n.* [< OFr. < L. < Gr. *rheuma*, a flow] **1.** any watery discharge from the mucous membranes, as of the mouth, eyes, or nose **2.** a cold; rhinitis —**rheum'y** *adj.* **rheum'i·er, rheum'i·est**

rheu·mat·ic (rōō mat'ik) *adj.* of, caused by, or having rheumatism —*n.* a person who has rheumatism —**rheu·mat'i·cal·ly** *adv.*

rheumatic fever a disease in which there is fever, the joints ache and swell, and the heart becomes inflamed

rheu·ma·tism (rōō'mə tiz'm) *n.* [< L. < Gr. *rheumatismos*: see RHEUM] a popular term for any of various painful conditions in which the joints and muscles become inflamed and stiff, including rheumatoid arthritis, bursitis, etc.

rheu·ma·toid (-toid') *adj.* of or like rheumatism

rheumatoid arthritis a chronic disease in which the joints become inflamed, painful, and swollen often to the extent that fingers, toes, etc. become deformed

Rh factor (är'āch') [RH(ESUS): first discovered in rhesus monkeys] a group of antigens, usually present in human red blood cells, which may cause haemolytic reactions during pregnancy or after tranfusion of blood containing this factor into someone lacking it: people who have this factor are **Rh positive**; those who lack it are **Rh negative**

R.H.G. Royal Horse Guards

rhi·nal (rī'n'l) *adj.* [RHIN(O)- + -AL] of the nose; nasal

rhine·stone (rīn'stōn') *n.* [transl. of Fr. *caillou du Rhin*: so called because orig. made at Strasbourg (on the Rhine)] a bright, artificial gem made of hard, colourless glass, often cut to imitate a diamond

Rhine wine (rīn) **1.** any of various wines produced in the

Rhine Valley, esp. a light, dry white wine **2.** a wine like this produced elsewhere

rhi·ni·tis (rī nīt'əs) *n.* [ModL.: see RHINO- & -ITIS] inflammation of the mucous membrane of the nose

rhi·no¹ (rī'nō) *n., pl.* -**nos**, -**no** shortened form of RHINOCEROS

rhi·no² (rī'nō) *n.* [< ?] [Slang] money; cash

rhi·no- [< Gr. *rhis* (gen. *rhinos*), the nose] a combining form meaning nose: also, before a vowel, **rhin-**

rhi·noc·er·os (rī nos'ər əs) *n., pl.* -**os·es**, -**os**: see PLURAL, II, D, 1 [< L. < Gr. < *rhis* (see prec.) + *keras*, horn] any of various large, thick-skinned, plant-eating mammals of Africa and Asia, with one or two upright horns on the snout

INDIAN
RHINOCEROS
(0.9-2 m high
at shoulder)

rhi·zo- [< Gr. *rhiza*, a root] a combining form meaning root: also, before a vowel, **rhiz-**

rhi·zoid (rī'zoid) *adj.* [prec. + -OID] rootlike —*n.* any of the rootlike filaments in a moss, fern, etc. that attach the plant to the substratum —**rhi·zoi'dal** *adj.*

rhi·zome (rī'zōm) *n.* [ModL. < Gr., ult. < *rhiza*, a root] a creeping stem lying, usually horizontally, at or under the surface of the soil: it has scale leaves, bears leaves or aerial shoots near its tips, and produces roots from its undersurface —**rhi·zom'a·tous** (-zom'ə təs, -zō'mə-) *adj.*

rhi·zo·pod (rī'zə pod') *n.* [RHIZO- + -POD] any of a class of one-celled animals with pseudopodia, including the amoebas, foraminifers, etc. —**rhi·zop'o·dous** (-zop'ə dəs) *adj.*

rho (rō) *n.* [Gr.] the seventeenth letter of the Greek alphabet (P, ρ)

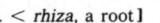
RHIZOME
OF GRASS

Rhode Island Red (rōd) any of a breed of American chickens with reddish-brown feathers and a black tail

Rho·de·sian man (rō dē'zhən) [skeletal remains found in Northern *Rhodesia* in Southern Africa] a form of primitive man of the later Pleistocene, with massive brow ridges

Rhodes scholarship (rōdz) any of a number of scholarships for a period of study at Oxford University established by the will of C.J. Rhodes (1853-1902), Brit. financier, for selected students (**Rhodes scholars**) from the Commonwealth and the United States

rho·di·um (rō'dē əm) *n.* [ModL. < Gr. *rhodon*, a rose: from the colour of its salts in solution] a hard, grey-white metallic chemical element, used in alloys with platinum and gold: symbol, Rh; at. wt., 102.905; at no., 45

rho·do- [< Gr. *rhodon*, a rose] a combining form meaning rose, rose-red: also, before a vowel, **rhod-**

rho·dop·sin (rō dop'sin) *n.* [< Gr. *rhodon*, rose + *opsis*, appearance + -IN¹] a purplish protein pigment, contained in the rods of the retina that is necessary for vision in dim light

rho·do·den·dron (rō'də den'drən) *n.* [L. < Gr. < *rhodon*, a rose + *dendron*, a tree] any of a genus of trees and shrubs, mainly evergreen, with showy flowers of pink, white, or purple

rhom·bo·he·dron (rom'bə hē'drən) *n., pl.* -**drons**, -**dra** (-drə) [ModL.: see RHOMBUS & -HEDRON] a six-sided prism each face of which is a rhombus

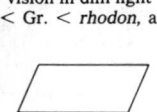
RHOMBOID

rhom·boid (rom'boid) *n.* [< Fr. < L. < Gr.: see RHOMBUS & -OID] a parallelogram with oblique angles and only the opposite sides equal —*adj.* shaped like a rhomboid or rhombus: also **rhom·boi'dal**

rhom·bus (rom'bəs) *n., pl.* -**bus·es**, -**bi** (-bī) [L. < Gr. *rhombos*, turnable object] an equilateral parallelogram, esp. one with oblique angles: also **rhomb** —**rhom'bic** *adj.*

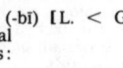
RHOMBUS

R.H.S. **1.** Royal Historical Society **2.** Royal Horticultural Society **3.** Royal Humane Society

rhu·barb (rōō'bärb) *n.* [< OFr. < ML. < LL. < Gr. *rhēon*, rhubarb + *barbaron*, foreign] **1.** a perennial plant having large leaves whose long, thick, sour stalks are cooked or baked in pies, etc. **2.** the roots or rhizomes of certain Asiatic varieties, used as a cathartic **3.** [Colloq.] [from noise made by actors repeating this word in crowd scenes] murmurous conversation

rhumb (rum, rumb) *n.* [< Port. & Sp. *rumbo*, prob. < L. *rhombus*, RHOMBUS] any of the points of a mariner's compass

rhum·ba (rum'bə) *n.* alt. sp. of RUMBA

rhumb line a course keeping a constant compass direction, charted as a line cutting all meridians at the same angle

rhyme (rīm) *n.* [< OFr. < *rimer*, to rhyme, prob. < Frank.

hyp. *rim*, a row: form infl. by L. *rhythmus*, rhythm] **1.** likeness of sounds at the ends of words or lines of verse **2.** a word that has the same end sound as another ["lazy" is a *rhyme* for "daisy"] **3.** a poem, or verse in general, using such end sounds —*vi.* **rhymed, rhym'ing 1.** to make verse, esp. rhyming verse **2.** to form a rhyme ["more" *rhymes* with "door"] **3.** to be composed in metrical form with rhymes: said of verse —*vt.* **1.** to put into rhyme **2.** to compose in metrical form with rhymes **3.** to use as a rhyme [to *rhyme* "new" with "true"] —**rhyme or reason** order or sense: preceded by *without, no,* etc. —**rhym'er n.**
rhyme scheme the pattern of rhymes used in a piece of verse, usually indicated by letters
rhyme·ster (rīm'stər) *n.* a maker of simple or inferior verse or rhymes; poetaster
rhyming dictionary a dictionary in which words are grouped according to the sounds of their last syllable(s)
rhyming slang 1. a word or phrase that rhymes with, and is a slang term for, a particular word (Ex.: *bees and honey* for *money*) **2.** such words or phrases collectively
rhythm (ri﬋'m, ri﬋'əm) *n.* [< Fr. < L. < Gr. *rhythmos*, measure < *rhein*, to flow] **1.** *a)* flow or movement having a regularly repeated pattern of accents, beats, etc. [the *rhythm* of the waves, of dancing, of the heartbeat, etc.] *b)* the pattern of this **2.** *Biol.* a periodic occurrence in living organisms of specific physiological changes **3.** *Music a)* regular, repeated grouping of strong and weak beats, or heavily and lightly accented tones *b)* the form or pattern of this [waltz *rhythm*] **4.** *Prosody* the form or pattern of the regularly repeated stressed and unstressed or long and short syllables [iambic *rhythm*] —**rhyth'mic** (ri﬋'mik), **rhyth'mi·cal.** —**rhyth'mi·cal·ly** *adv.*
rhythm and blues a form of popular music, influenced by the blues and having a strong beat
rhythm method a method of seeking birth control by abstaining from sexual intercourse during the woman's probable monthly ovulation period
rhythm section those instruments in a band, as the drums, piano, etc. that mainly supply rhythm
R.I. 1. [L. *Rex et Imperator*] King and Emperor **2.** [L. *Regina et Imperatrix*] Queen and Empress **3.** Royal Institute
ri·al (rī'əl) *n.* [Per. < Ar. < Sp. *real*, REAL[2]] *see* MONETARY UNITS, table (Iran and Oman)
ri·al·to (rē al'tō) *n., pl.* **-tos** [< *Rialto*, a bridge in Venice, Italy] a trading area or marketplace
rib (rib) *n.* [OE. *rib*] **1.** any of the curved bones attached to the backbone and enclosing the chest cavity: in man there are twelve pairs of such bones: see TRUE RIBS, FALSE RIBS, FLOATING RIBS **2.** a cut of meat having one or more ribs, as spareribs **3.** a raised ridge in woven or knitted material **4.** any riblike piece used to form a framework, or to shape or strengthen something [an umbrella *rib*] **5.** any of the main veins of a leaf —*vt.* **ribbed, rib'bing 1.** to provide, form, or strengthen with ribs **2.** [Slang] to tease playfully —**ribbed** *adj.* —**rib'ber n.** —**rib'less** *adj.*
R.I.B.A. Royal Institute of British Architects
rib·ald (rib'əld) *adj.* [OFr. *ribaud*, debauchee, ult. < MHG. *riban*, to copulate] characterized by coarse joking; esp., dealing with sex in a humorously earthy or direct way —*n.* a ribald person
rib·ald·ry (-əl drē) *n.* ribald language or humour
rib·and (rib'ənd, -ən) *n. archaic var. of* RIBBON
rib·bing (rib'iŋ) *n.* an arrangement or series of ribs, as in knitted fabric, a ship's framework, etc.
rib·bon (rib'ən) *n.* [MFr. *riban*] **1.** a narrow strip as of silk or rayon, used for decorating or tying, for badges, etc. **2.** anything suggesting such a strip [a *ribbon* of blue sky] **3.** [*pl.*] torn strips or shreds; tatters [a sleeve torn to *ribbons*] **4.** a narrow strip of cloth inked for use in a typewriter, etc. —*vt.* **1.** to decorate, trim, or mark with ribbons **2.** to tear into ribbonlike shreds —*vi.* to extend in a ribbonlike strip —**rib'bon·like'** *adj.*
ribbon development the siting of houses in a continuous row on one or both sides of a main road
ri·bo·fla·vin (rī'bə flā'vin) *n.* [< *ribose*, a sugar + FLAVIN] a factor of the vitamin B complex, found in milk, eggs, liver, fruits, leafy vegetables, etc.: lack of riboflavin in the diet causes stunted growth, loss of hair, etc.
ri·bo·nu·cle·ase (rī'bō nyōō'klē ās') + NUCLEASE] any of various enzymes that split ribonucleic acid
ri·bo·nu·cle·ic acid (-nyōō klē'ik) [RIBO(SE) + NUCLEIC ACID] an essential component in the cytoplasm of all living cells, composed of long chains of phosphate and ribose along with several bases bonded to the ribose: one form carries the genetic information needed for protein synthesis in the cell
ri·bose (rī'bōs) *n.* [< G. *Rib(onsäure)*, an acid containing four OH radicals + -OSE[1]] a sugar derived from nucleic acids
ri·bo·some (rī'bə sōm') *n.* [RIBO(SE) + -SOME[3]] any of the minute particles composed of RNA and proteins, found in cell cytoplasm and functioning in the production of proteins —**ri'bo·so'mal** *adj.*

-ric (rik) [OE. *rice*, reign] a combining form meaning jurisdiction, realm [bishopric]
Ri·car·di·an (ri kä'dē ən) *adj.* [after David *Ricardo* (1772-1823), Brit. economist] of or pertaining to Ricardo or his economic teachings —*n.* a follower of Ricardo's economics theory
rice (rīs) *n.* [OFr. *ris* < It. < L. < Gr. *oryza*: of Oriental origin] **1.** a cereal grass of warm climates, planted in ground under water **2.** its starchy seeds or grain, used as food —*vt.* **riced, ric'ing** [U.S.] to form (cooked potatoes, etc.) into ricelike granules
rice bowl an area that produces a lot of rice
rice paper 1. a thin paper made from the straw of rice **2.** a fine, delicate paper made by cutting and pressing the pith of an Asian plant (the **rice-paper plant**)
rich (rich) *adj.* [OE. *rice*, noble, powerful < OFr. < Gmc.] **1.** having much money or property; wealthy **2.** having abundant natural resources [a *rich* region] **3.** well-supplied (*with*); abounding (*in*) **4.** valuable [a *rich* prize] **5.** costly and elegant; sumptuous [*rich* gifts] **6.** *a)* containing much butter (or other fat), cream, sugar, flavouring, etc. [*rich* foods] *b)* strong and flavourful [*rich* wine] **7.** *a)* full and mellow: said of sounds, the voice, etc. *b)* deep; vivid: said of colours *c)* very fragrant: said of odours **8.** abundant; ample [a *rich* fund of stories] **9.** yielding in abundance, as soil, etc. **10.** [Colloq.] *a)* very amusing *b)* absurd —**the rich** wealthy people collectively —**rich'ly** *adv.* —**rich'ness n.**
rich·en (rich''n) *vt.* to make rich or richer
rich·es (-iz) *n.pl.* [ME. *richess*, n. sing. < OFr. *richesse*] valuable possessions; much money, property, etc.; wealth
Rich·ter scale (rik'tər) [devised by C. *Richter* (1900—), U.S. seismologist] a scale for measuring the magnitude of earthquakes, with each of its 10 steps about 60 times greater than the preceding step
rick[1] (rik) *n.* [OE. *hreac*] a stack of hay, straw, etc. in a field, esp. one covered for protection from rain —*vt.* to pile (hay, etc.) into ricks
rick[2] (rik) *vt.* [var. of WRICK] to sprain or wrench —*n.* a sprain or wrench
rick·ets (rik'its) *n.* [altered < ? RACHITIS] a disease, chiefly of children, characterized by a softening and, often, bending of the bones: it is caused by lack of vitamin D
rick·ett·si·a (ri ket'sē ə) *n., pl.* **-si·ae'** (-ē'), **-si·as** [ModL., after H. T. *Ricketts* (1871-1910), U.S. pathologist] any of a genus of microorganisms that cause certain diseases, as typhus, and are transmitted by the bite of certain lice and ticks —**rick·ett'si·al** *adj.*
rick·et·y (rik'it ē) *adj.* **1.** of or having rickets **2.** weak in the joints; tottering **3.** liable to fall apart or break down; shaky —**rick'et·i·ness n.**
rick·rack (rik'rak') *n.* [redupl. of RACK[1]] flat, zigzag braid for trimming dresses, etc.
rick·shaw, rick·sha (rik'shô) *n.* same as JINRIKISHA
ric·o·chet (rik'ə shā', rik'ə shä', -shet') *n.* [Fr.] **1.** the rebound or skipping of a bullet, stone, etc. after striking a surface at an angle **2.** a bullet, etc. that ricochets —*vi.* **-cheted** (-shād') or **-chet'ted** (-shet'id), **-chet'ing** (-shā'iŋ) or **-chet'ting** (-shet'iŋ) to move with such a motion
ri·cot·ta (ri kot'ə; It. rē kôt'tä) *n.* [It. < L. pp. of *recoquere*, to boil again] a soft, dry or moist Italian cheese made from whey left from making other cheeses
R.I.C.S. Royal Institute of Chartered Surveyors
ric·tus (rik'təs) *n.* [ModL. < L. open mouth < pp. of *ringi*, to open the mouth wide] **1.** a sustained gaping, as of a bird's beak or animal's mouth **2.** the opening so produced —**ric'tal** *adj.*
rid (rid) *vt.* **rid** or **rid'ded, rid'ding** [ON. *rythja*, to clear (land)] to free, clear, or relieve, as of something undesirable [to *rid* a garden of weeds] —**be rid of** to be freed from —**get rid of 1.** to get free from **2.** to do away with; dispose of
rid·dance (rid''ns) *n.* a ridding or being rid; clearance or removal, as of something undesirable —**good riddance!** welcome relief or deliverance!
rid·den (rid''n) *pp. of* RIDE —*adj.* controlled or obsessed (by the thing specified) [fear-ridden]
rid·dle[1] (rid''l) *n.* [OE. *rædels*, akin to *rædan*, to guess] **1.** a puzzle in the form of a question or statement with an ingenious meaning or answer that is hard to guess; conundrum **2.** any puzzling or perplexing person or thing; enigma —*vt.* **-dled, -dling** to solve or explain (a riddle) —*vi.* to utter riddles —**rid'dler n.**
rid·dle[2] (rid''l) *n.* [OE. *hriddel*] a coarse sieve —*vt.* **-dled, -dling 1.** to sift through a riddle **2.** *a)* to make many holes in, as with gun shot *b)* to affect every part of [riddled with errors]
ride (rīd) *vi.* **rode** or archaic **rid** (rid), **rid'den** or archaic **rid** or **rode, rid'ing** [OE. *ridan*] **1.** *a)* to sit on and control a horse or other animal in motion *b)* to be carried along (*in* a vehicle, *on* a bicycle, bus, etc.) *c)* to move along as if so carried *d)* to be carried or supported in motion (*on* or *upon*) [tanks *ride* on treads] **2.** to admit of being ridden [the car *rides* smoothly] **3.** to move, lie, or float on the water **4.** to

be dependent (*on*) [the change *rides* on his approval] **5.** to be placed as a bet (*on*) **6.** [Colloq.] to continue undisturbed, with no action taken —*vt.* **1.** to sit on or in and control so as to move along [to *ride* a horse] **2.** to move along on or be carried or supported on [to *ride* the waves] **3.** to move over, along, or through (a road, area, etc.) by horse, car, etc. **4.** to cover (a specified distance) by riding **5.** to engage in by riding [to *ride* a race] **6.** to cause to ride **7.** to control, dominate, or oppress [*ridden* by fear] **8.** [U.S. Colloq.] to torment or tease, as with ridicule, criticism, etc. —*n.* **1.** *a*) a riding; esp., a journey by horse, car, bicycle, etc. *b*) a way or chance to ride *c*) the way a car, etc. rides **2.** a road, etc. for riding —**ride down 1.** to knock down by riding against **2.** to overtake by riding **3.** to overcome **4.** to exhaust (a horse, etc.) by riding —**ride out** to withstand or endure (a storm, crisis, etc.) successfully —**ride up** to move upwards out of place, as an article of clothing —**take for a ride** [Slang] **1.** to take somewhere, as in a car, and kill **2.** to cheat or swindle —**rid′a·ble, ride′-a·ble** *adj.*

rid·er (-ər) *n.* **1.** a person who rides **2.** *a*) an addition or amendment to a contract, jury verdict, etc. *b*) a clause added to a legislative bill **3.** any of various pieces moving or resting on something else —**rid′er·less** *adj.*

ridge (rij) *n.* [OE. *hrycg*] **1.** the long, narrow top or crest of something, as of an animal's back, a wave, etc. **2.** a long, narrow elevation of land or similar range of hills or mountains **3.** any narrow, raised strip, as on fabric **4.** the horizontal line formed by the meeting of two sloping surfaces [the *ridge* of a roof] —*vt., vi.* ridged, ridg′ing to form into or mark with a ridge or ridges —**ridge′like** *adj.* —**ridg′y** *adj.*

ridge·pole (-pōl′) *n.* **1.** the horizontal timber or beam at the ridge of a roof: also **ridge′-piece′ 2.** the horizontal pole forming the apex of a tent

RIDGEPOLE

rid·i·cule (rid′i kyōōl′) *n.* [Fr. < L. *ridiculum*, a jest, ult. < *ridere*, to laugh] **1.** the act of making someone or something the object of scornful laughter by joking, mocking, etc.; derision **2.** words or actions used in doing this —*vt.* -culed′, -cul′ing to make fun of or make others laugh at; deride; mock

ri·dic·u·lous (ri dik′yə ləs) *adj.* deserving ridicule; absurd —**ri·dic′u·lous·ly** *adv.* —**ri·dic′-u·lous·ness** *n.*

rid·ing¹ (rīd′in) *adj.* **1.** that rides or is ridden **2.** of or for riders on horseback —*n.* the act of one that rides

rid·ing² (rīd′in) *n.* [OE. *-thrithing*, a third part] any of the three former administrative divisions of Yorkshire

riding crop a short whip with a looped lash used when riding horses

riding-light (-līt) *n.* a white light hung in the rigging of a vessel at anchor during the night, indicating its position

ri·el (rē el′, rēl) *n.* [cf. RIAL, REAL²] *see* MONETARY UNITS, table (Cambodia)

Ries·ling (rēz′lin) *n.* [Gr. < Early ModG. *rüssling* < ?] [*also* **r-**] a dry, white wine made from the riesling grape in the Rhine valley, Austria, Hungary, and Yugoslavia

rife (rīf) *adj.* [OE. *ryfe*] **1.** frequently or commonly occurring; widespread [gossip was *rife*] **2.** *a*) abundant *b*) abounding; filled [*rife* with error] —**rife′ness** *n.*

riff (rif) *n.* [prob. altered < REFRAIN²] *Jazz* a repeated musical phrase —*vi. Jazz* to perform a riff

rif·fle (rif′'l) *n.* [< ? or akin to G. *Riffel*, a groove] **1.** the act or a method of riffling cards **2.** [U.S.] *a*) a shoal, reef, etc. in a stream, producing a stretch of ruffled or choppy water *b*) a stretch of such water, or a ripple on it —*vt., vi.* -fled, -fling **1.** to leaf rapidly (through) by releasing pages, sheets, etc. along their edge with the thumb **2.** to shuffle (playing cards) by holding part of the pack in each hand and mixing the cards together with riffling motions

riff·raff (rif′raf′) *n.* [< OFr. *rif* and *raf* < *rifler*, to scrape + *rafle*, a raking in] **1.** those people regarded as worthless, insignificant, etc.; rabble **2.** worthless rubbish

ri·fle¹ (rī′f'l) *vt.* -fled, -fling [Fr. *rifler*, to scrape < OFr. < MHG. *riffeln*, to scratch] **1.** to cut spiral grooves on the inside of (a gun barrel, etc.) **2.** to hurl or throw with great speed —*n.* **1.** a shoulder gun with spiral grooves cut into the inner surface of the barrel: see RIFLING **2.** [*pl.*] troops armed with rifles

ri·fle² (rī′f'l) *vt.* -fled, -fling [< OFr. *rifler*, to plunder, orig. to scratch: see prec.] **1.** to ransack and rob; pillage; plunder **2.** to take as plunder; steal —**ri′fler** *n.*

ri·fle·man (-mən) *n., pl.* -men **1.** a soldier armed with a rifle **2.** a man who uses a rifle

rifle range a place for target practice with a rifle

ri·fle·ry (-rē) *n.* the skill or practice of shooting at targets with rifles

ri·fling (rī′flin) *n.* **1.** the cutting of spiral grooves within a gun barrel, to make the projectile spin when fired **2.** a system of such grooves

rift (rift) *n.* [Dan., a fissure < *rive*, to tear] **1.** an opening caused by splitting; fissure; cleft **2.** an open break in friendly relations —*vt., vi.* to burst open; split

rift valley a long narrow sunken area thought to result from the subsidence of land between two parallel faults

rig (rig) *vt.* rigged, rig′ging [< Scand.] **1.** *a*) to fit (a ship, mast, etc.) with sails, shrouds, etc. *b*) to fit (a ship's sails, shrouds, etc.) to the masts, yards, etc. **2.** to fit (out); equip **3.** to prepare for use, esp. in a hurry (often with *up*) **4.** to arrange in a dishonest way [to *rig* a contest] **5.** [Colloq.] to dress; clothe (usually with *out*) —*n.* **1.** the arrangement of sails, masts, etc. on a vessel **2.** equipment; gear **3.** equipment for drilling an oil well: also **oil rig 4.** a frolic; trick; dodge —**in full rig** neatly dressed, often in dress or ceremonial uniform

rig·a·ma·role (rig′ə mə rōl′) *n. var. of* RIGMAROLE

Ri·gel (rī′g'l, -j'l) [Ar. *rijl*, foot: in the left foot of Orion] a bright, bluish star, brightest in the constellation Orion

rig·ging (rig′in) *n.* **1.** the chains, ropes, etc. used for supporting and working the masts, sails, etc. of a vessel **2.** equipment; gear

right (rīt) *adj.* [OE. *riht*] **1.** orig., straight [a *right* line] **2.** *a*) formed by a straight line perpendicular to a base [a *right* angle] *b*) having the axis perpendicular to the base [a *right* cylinder] **3.** in accordance with justice, law, morality, etc.; virtuous [*right* conduct] **4.** in accordance with fact, reason, etc.; correct; true [the *right* answer] **5.** *a*) fitting; suitable *b*) most convenient or favourable **6.** designating the side meant to be seen [the *right* side of cloth] **7.** having sound physical or mental health **8.** *a*) designating or of that side of one's body which is towards the east when one faces north *b*) designating or of the corresponding side of anything *c*) closer to the right side of a person facing the thing mentioned [the top *right* drawer] **9.** of the bank of a river on the right of a person facing downstream **10.** of the political right; conservative or reactionary **11.** [Colloq.] complete; real; utter [a *right* idiot] —*n.* **1.** what is right, or just, lawful, proper, etc. **2.** *a*) a power, privilege, etc. that a person has or gets by law, nature, tradition, etc. [the *right* of free speech] *b*) [*often pl.*] an interest in property, real or intangible **3.** the true report, as of a happening (with *the*) **4.** *a*) the right side *b*) a turn towards the right side **5.** *Boxing a*) the right hand *b*) a blow delivered with the right hand **6.** [*often* R-] *Politics* a conservative or reactionary position, party, etc. (often with *the*): from the location of their seats in some European legislatures —*adv.* **1.** in a straight line; directly [go *right* home] **2.** in a way that is correct, proper, just, favourable, etc.; well **3.** completely [soaked *right* through his coat] **4.** [Colloq.] exactly [*right* here] **5.** [Colloq.] immediately [come *right* down] **6.** on or towards the right hand **7.** very [he knows *right* well]: colloquial except in certain titles [the *right* reverend] —*interj.* agreed! I understand! —*vt.* **1.** to put in or restore to an upright position [we *righted* the boat] **2.** to correct **3.** to put in order [she *righted* the room] **4.** to make amends for —*vi.* to regain an upright position —**bang to rights** in the act; red-handed —**by right** (or **rights**) in justice; properly —**in one's own right** through one's own status, ability, etc. —**in the right** on the side supported by truth, justice, etc. —**on the right side of 1.** to be approved of (by someone) **2.** to be less than [on the *right* side of forty] —**right and left** on all sides —**right away** (or **off**) without delay; at once —**to rights** [Colloq.] in or into proper condition or order —**right′a·ble** *adj.* —**right′er** *n.* —**right′ness** *n.*

right·a·bout (rīt′ə bout′) *n.* **1.** *same as* RIGHTABOUT-FACE **2.** the direction faced after turning completely about —*adv., adj.* with, in, or by a rightabout-face

right·a·bout-face (-fās′) *n.* **1.** a turning directly about so as to face the opposite direction **2.** a complete reversal of belief, conduct, etc. —*interj.* a military command to perform a rightabout-face

right angle an angle of 90 degrees, made by the meeting of two straight lines perpendicular to each other

right-an·gled (rīt′an′g'ld) *adj.* having or forming one or more right angles; rectangular: also **right′-an′gle**

rightangled triangle a triangle with one right angle

right arm a reliable helper [Smith was the chairman's *right arm*]

RIGHT ANGLE

right·eous (rī′chəs) *adj.* [altered < OE. *rihtwis*: see RIGHT & -WISE] **1.** acting justly; doing what is right; upright; virtuous [a *righteous* man] **2.** morally right or having a sound moral basis [*righteous* anger] —**right′eous·ly** *adv.* —**right′eous·ness** *n.*

right·ful (rīt′fəl) *adj.* 1. fair; just; right 2. having a just, lawful claim, or right [the *rightful* owner] 3. belonging or owned by just or lawful claim [a *rightful* rank] 4. proper; fitting —**right′ful·ly** *adv.* —**right′ful·ness** *n.*

right-hand (rīt′hand′) *adj.* 1. on or directed towards the right 2. of, for, or with the right hand 3. most helpful or reliable [the managing director's *right-hand* man]

right-hand·ed (-han′did) *adj.* 1. using the right hand more skilfully than the left 2. done with the right hand 3. made for use with the right hand 4. turning from left to right; clockwise —*adv.* with the right hand [to bat *right-handed*] —**right′-hand′ed·ly** *adv.* —**right′-hand′ed·ness** *n.* —**right′-hand′er** *n.*

right·ist (rīt′ist) *n.* a person whose political position is conservative or reactionary; member of the right —*adj.* conservative or reactionary —**right′ism** *n.*

right·ly (rīt′lē) *adv.* 1. with justice; fairly 2. properly; suitably 3. correctly

right-mind·ed (rīt′mīn′did) *adj.* thinking or believing what is right; having correct views or sound principles —**right′-mind′ed·ly** *adv.* —**right′-mind′ed·ness** *n.*

right·o (rīt′ō, rī′tō′) *interj.* [Colloq.] yes; certainly

right of asylum the right of a nation to extend protection to refugees, esp. political refugees, from another nation

right of way 1. the legal right to move in front of others, as at a traffic intersection 2. *a)* the right to use a certain route, as over another's property *b)* a path marking such a route 3. [Chiefly U.S.] *a)* a strip of land used by a railway for its lines *b)* land over which a public road, an electric power line, etc. passes Also **right′-of-way′**

right-on (rit′on′) *adj.* [U.S. Slang] sophisticated, informed, current, etc.

Right Reverend the form of address used for bishops

rights issue an issue of new shares offered by a company to its existing shareholders on favourable terms

right·ward (-wərd) *adv., adj.* on or towards the right: also **right′wards** *adv.*

right whale a large-headed whalebone whale without teeth or dorsal fin

right wing [see RIGHT, *n.* 6] the more conservative or reactionary section of a political party, group, etc. —**right′-wing′** *adj.* —**right′-wing′er** *n.*

rig·id (rij′id) *adj.* [< L. < *rigere*, to be stiff] 1. not bending or flexible; stiff [a *rigid* metal girder] 2. not moving; set 3. severe, strict, or rigorous [a *rigid* taskmaster, a *rigid* rule] 4. *Aeron.* having a rigid framework that encloses containers for the gas, as a dirigible —**ri·gid·i·ty** (ri jid′ə tē), **rig′id·ness** *n.* —**rig′id·ly** *adv.*

ri·gid·i·fy (ri jid′ə fī′) *vt., vi.* -**fied′**, -**fy′ing** to make or become rigid —**ri·gid′i·fi·ca′tion** *n.*

rig·ma·role (rig′mə rōl′) *n.* [< *ragman roll* < ME. *rageman rolle*, a document] 1. rambling talk; nonsense 2. a fussy or time-wasting procedure

rig·or mor·tis (rig′ər môr′tis) [ModL., stiffness of death] the stiffening of the muscles after death

rig·or·ous (rig′ər əs) *adj.* 1. very strict or harsh [*rigorous* rules] 2. very severe or sharp [a *rigorous* climate] 3. exactly precise or accurate [*rigorous* scholarship] —**rig′-or·ous·ly** *adv.* —**rig′or·ous·ness** *n.*

rig·our (rig′ər) *n.* [< MFr. < L. *rigere*, to be rigid] 1. harshness or severity; specif., *a)* strictness [the *rigour* of martial law] *b)* extreme hardship [the *rigours* of life] 2. exact precision or accuracy 3. a severe, harsh, or oppressive act, etc. 4. stiffness or rigidity, esp. in the body tissues Also U.S. sp., **rig′or**

rig-out (rig′out′) *n.* [Colloq.] a person's clothing or costume, esp. when it appears strange

Rig-Ve·da (rig′vā′də, -vē′də) [Sans. *Rigveda* < *ric*, praise + *veda*, knowledge] the Veda of Verses (Psalms), the oldest and most important of the Hindu Vedas

rile (rīl) *vt.* **riled**, **ril′ing** [var. of ROIL] [Colloq.] to anger; irritate

rill (ril) *n.* [< Du. *ril* or LowG. *rille*] 1. a little brook 2. a small gulley, as formed by soil erosion 3. one of many cracks or valleys on the surface of the moon, forming a long series of craters

rim (rim) *n.* [OE. *rima*, an edge] 1. an edge, border, or margin, esp. of something circular 2. *a)* the outer part of a wheel *b)* the metal flange of a motor car wheel, on which the tyre is mounted 3. *Basketball, Netball*, etc. the metal hoop to which the net is attached —*vt.* **rimmed**, **rim′ming** 1. to put a rim on or around 2. to roll around the rim of [the golf ball *rimmed* the hole] —**rim′less** *adj.*

rime¹ (rīm) *n., vt., vi.* **rimed**, **rim′ing** *same as* RHYME —**rim′-er** *n.*

rime² (rīm) *n.* [OE. *hrīm*] a white frost on grass, leaves, etc.; hoarfrost —*vt.* **rimed**, **rim′ing** to coat with rime —**rim′y** *adj.*

ri·mu (rē′mōō) *n.* [Maori] a coniferous New Zealand tree: also called **red pine**

rind (rīnd) *n.* [OE.] a thick, hard, or tough outer layer or coating, as on fruit, cheese, bacon, etc.

rin·der·pest (rin′dər pest′) *n.* [G. *Rinder*, cattle + *Pest*, a plague] an acute infectious disease of cattle and, often, sheep and goats

ring¹ (riŋ) *vi.* **rang** or now chiefly dial. **rung**, **rung**, **ring′ing** [OE. *hringan*] 1. to give forth the clear, resonant sound of a bell 2. to produce, as by sounding, a specified impression [promises that *ring* false] 3. to cause a bell to sound, esp. as a summons [to *ring* for a maid] 4. to sound loudly; resound [the room *rang* with laughter] 5. to have a sensation as of ringing, etc.: said of the ears or head —*vt.* 1. to cause (a bell, etc.) to ring 2. to sound (a peal, knell, etc.) as by ringing a bell 3. to signal, announce, etc. as by ringing 4. to call by telephone (often with *up*) —*n.* 1. the sound of a bell 2. any similar sound, esp. when loud and continued 3. a characteristic sound or impression [the *ring* of sincerity] 4. the act of ringing a bell, etc. 5. [Colloq.] a telephone call: chiefly in **give (someone) a ring**, to telephone (someone) —**ring a bell** to stir up a memory —**ring down** (or **up**) **the curtain** 1. to signal for a theatre curtain to be lowered (or raised) 2. to end (or begin) something —**ring in** 1. to report to someone by telephone 2. to accompany or escort the arrival of (a person or thing) with bells, esp. in **ring in the new year** —**ring off** to terminate a telephone conversation —**ring up** 1. to record (a specified amount) on a cash register 2. to telephone (someone)

ring² (riŋ) *n.* [OE. *hring*] 1. a small, circular band, esp. of precious metal, to be worn on the finger 2. any similar band used for some special purpose [a key *ring*] 3. a circular line, mark, or figure 4. the outer edge, or rim, as of a wheel 5. any of the circular marks seen in the cross section of a tree trunk: each ring represents a year's growth: in full, **annual ring** 6. a number of people or things grouped in a circle 7. a group of people working together to advance their own selfish interests, as in antique auctions, etc. 8. an enclosed area, often circular, for contests, exhibitions, etc. [a circus *ring*] 9. *a)* an enclosure, now a square, in which boxing and wrestling matches are held *b)* prizefighting (with *the*) 10. [U.S.] a contest: often used in **throw one's hat into the ring**, to enter a contest, esp. one for political office 11. *Chem.* a number of atoms united in such a way that they can be represented as a ring —*vt.* **ringed**, **ring′ing** 1. to encircle as with a ring 2. to form into, or furnish with, a ring or rings 3. in some games, to toss a ring, horseshoe, etc. so that it encircles (a peg) 4. to cut a circle of bark from (a tree) —*vi.* to form in a ring or rings —**run rings around** [Colloq.] 1. to run much faster than 2. to excel greatly —**ringed** *adj.*

ring·bolt (-bōlt′) *n.* a bolt with a ring at the head

ring·dove (-duv′) *n.* 1. the European wood pigeon 2. a small dove of Europe and Asia, with a dark ring around the neck

ring·er¹ (riŋ′ər) *n.* 1. a horseshoe, quoit, etc. thrown so that it encircles the peg 2. such a throw

ring·er² (riŋ′ər) *n.* 1. a person or thing that rings a bell, chime, etc. 2. [Slang] *a)* [Chiefly U.S.] a horse, player, etc. fraudulently entered, or substituted for another, in a competition *b)* a person or thing very closely resembling another

ring finger the finger next to the little finger, esp. of the left hand, on which a wedding ring is usually worn

ring·lead·er (riŋ′lēd′ər) *n.* a person who leads others, esp. in unlawful acts, etc.

ring·let (-lit) *n.* 1. a little ring 2. a curl of hair, esp. a long one —**ring′let·ed** *adj.*

ring main a domestic electrical wiring system consisting of a ring circuit supplied by mains electricity

ring·mas·ter (riŋ′mäs′tər) *n.* a man who directs the performances in a circus ring

ring-necked pheasant (-nekt′) an Asian game fowl with a whitish collar around the neck in the male, now widespread in Europe and N America

ring road a road encircling a busy town centre; bypass

ring·side (-sīd′) *n.* 1. the place just outside the ring, as at a boxing match or circus 2. any place that provides a close view of something

ring·tail (-tāl) *n.* 1. a female hen-harrier 2. a young golden eagle 3. a ring-tailed opossum, lemur, or phalanger 4. *Naut.* an additional sail used in light winds

ring·worm (-wurm′) *n.* any contagious skin disease caused by a fungus that produces ring-shaped patches

rink (riŋk) *n.* [< Scot. < ? OFr. *renc*, RANK¹] 1. a smooth expanse of ice, often enclosed, for ice skating or for playing ice hockey 2. a smooth floor, usually of wood and enclosed, for roller-skating 3. a building enclosing either of such rinks 4. a section of the green or ice used for play in bowls and curling

rinse (rins) *vt.* **rinsed**, **rins′ing** [< OFr. *rincer*, ult. < L. *recens*, fresh] 1. to wash lightly, as by dipping into clear water 2. to remove (soap, dirt, etc.) by such washing 3. to flush (the mouth or teeth), as with clear water 4. *a)* to dip (fabrics, etc.) into a dye solution *b)* to use a rinse on (the hair) —**vi.** to undergo rinsing —**n.** 1. a rinsing 2. the water or solution used in rinsing 3. a substance mixed with water and used to tint hair —**rins′er** n.

ri·ot (rī′ət) n. [OFr. riote < rihoter, to make a disturbance] 1. wild or violent disorder, confusion, etc.; tumult 2. a violent, public disturbance of the peace by a number of persons (in law, usually three or more) assembled together 3. a brilliant display [a riot of colour] 4. [Now Rare] a) debauchery b) unrestrained revelry or a wild revel 5. [Colloq.] an extremely amusing person, thing, or event —vi. 1. to take part in a riot or public disturbance 2. [Now Rare] to revel —**run riot** 1. to act in a wild, unrestrained manner 2. to grow in profusion —**ri′ot·er** n.

Riot Act a law passed in 1715 stating that if twelve or more people disturbing the peace do not disperse on the reading of the act then they are guilty of a felony —**read the riot act** to warn or reprimand severely, esp. using the threat of punishment

ri·ot·ous (rī′ət əs) adj. 1. a) having the nature of a disturbance of the peace b) engaging in rioting 2. disorderly or boisterous 3. debauched; immoral [riotous living] 4. luxuriant or profuse —**ri′ot·ous·ly** adv. —**ri′ot·ous·ness** n.

rip[1] (rip) vt. ripped, rip′ping [prob. < or akin to Fl. rippen, to tear] 1. a) to cut or tear apart roughly b) to remove as by cutting or tearing (with off, out, etc.) c) to make (a hole) in this way d) to slash with a sharp instrument e) to cut or tear (stitches) so as to open (a seam, hem, etc.) 2. to saw or split (wood) along the grain —vi. 1. to become torn or split apart 2. [Colloq.] to move with speed or violence —n. a torn place or burst seam; split —**let rip** to act or speak without restraint or control —**rip into** [Colloq.] to attack violently, often with words —**rip off** [Slang] 1. to steal or rob 2. to cheat, exploit, etc. —**rip out** [Colloq.] to utter sharply, as in anger —**rip′per** n.

rip[2] (rip) n. [< ? prec.] an extent of rough water caused by cross currents or tides meeting

rip[3] (rip) n. [var. of rep, prob. abbrev. of REPROBATE] [Colloq.] a debauched, dissipated person

R.I.P. abbrev. of REQUIESCAT IN PACE

ri·par·i·an (ri per′ē ən, rī-) adj. [< L. < ripa, a bank] of, adjacent to, or living on the bank of a river or, sometimes, of a lake, pond, etc.

rip cord a cord, etc. pulled to open a parachute during descent

ripe (rīp) adj. [OE.] 1. fully grown or developed; specif., ready to be harvested for food, as grain or fruit 2. like ripe fruit, as in being ruddy and full [ripe lips] 3. sufficiently processed to be ready for use [ripe cheese] 4. fully or highly developed; mature [ripe wisdom] 5. advanced in years [the ripe age of ninety] 6. fully prepared [ripe for marriage] 7. ready for some treatment or process [a boil ripe for lancing] 8. far enough along (for some purpose): said of time —**ripe′ly** adv. —**ripe′ness** n.

rip·en (rī′pən) vi., vt. to become or make ripe; mature, age, cure, etc. —**rip′en·er** n.

rip-off (rip′ôf′) n. [Slang] a stealing, robbing, cheating, exploiting, etc.

ri·poste, ri·post (ri pōst′, -post′) n. [< Fr. < It. risposta < L. responderе: see RESPOND] 1. Fencing a sharp, swift thrust made after parrying an opponent's lunge 2. a sharp, swift retort —vi. -post′ed, -post′ing to make a riposte

rip·ping (rip′iŋ) adj. 1. that rips or tears 2. [Slang] excellent; fine —**rip′ping·ly** adv.

rip·ple (rip′'l) vi. -pled, -pling [prob. < RIP[1] + -le, freq. suffix] 1. a) to form or have little waves on the surface, as water stirred by a breeze b) to flow with such waves on the surface 2. to give the effect of rippling water, as by alternately rising and falling [laughter rippling through the hall] —vt. to cause to ripple —n. 1. a small wave or undulation, as on the surface of water 2. a movement, appearance, etc. like this 3. a sound like that of rippling water —**rip′pler** n. —**rip′ply** (-lē) adj. -pli·er, -pli·est

ripple mark any of the ripply lines on the surface of sand, mud, etc. caused by waves, wind, or both

rip-roaring (-rôr′iŋ) adj. [Slang] boisterous; uproarious

rip-saw (-sô′) n. [RIP[1] + SAW[1]] a saw with coarse teeth, for cutting wood along the grain

rip·tide (-tīd′) n. [RIP[2] + TIDE] a tide opposing another tide, producing rough waters

rise (rīz) vi. rose, ris·en (riz′'n), ris′ing [OE. risan] 1. to stand or assume an erect or nearly erect position after sitting, lying, etc. 2. to get up after sleeping or resting 3. to rebel; revolt 4. to end an official assembly or meeting 5. to return to life after dying 6. to go to a higher place or position; ascend 7. to appear above the horizon [the moon rose] 8. to attain a higher level [the river is rising] 9. to advance in status, rank, etc.; become rich, famous, etc. 10. to become erect or rigid 11. to extend or incline upwards [hills rising steeply] 12. to increase in amount, degree, etc. 13. to become louder, shriller, etc. 14. to become stronger, more vivid, etc. 15. to become larger and puffier, as dough

with yeast 16. to originate; begin 17. to have its source: said of a stream 18. to happen; occur 19. to become apparent to the senses or the mind [land rising ahead of the ship] 20. to become aroused [to make one's temper rise] 21. to be built [the house rose quickly] —vt. to cause to rise, as birds from cover —n. 1. the appearance of the sun, moon, etc. above the horizon 2. upward motion; ascent 3. an advance in status, rank, etc. 4. the appearance of a fish at the water's surface 5. a piece of rising ground; hill 6. a slope upwards 7. the vertical height of something, as a staircase 8. a) an increase in height, as of water level b) an increase in pitch of a sound c) an increase in degree, amount, etc. 9. a beginning, origin, etc. 10. an increase in wages —**get a rise out of** [Slang] to draw a desired response from, as by teasing —**give rise to** to bring about; begin —**rise and shine** [Colloq.] to get out of bed —**rise to** to prove oneself capable of coping with [to rise to the occasion]

ris·er (rīz′ər) n. 1. a person or thing that rises 2. a vertical piece between the steps in a stairway

ris·i·bil·i·ty (riz′ə bil′ə tē) n., pl. -ties 1. the quality or state of being risible 2. [usually pl.] a sense of the ridiculous or amusing

ris·i·ble (riz′ə b'l) adj. [Fr. < LL. < L. pp. of ridere, to laugh] 1. able or inclined to laugh 2. of or connected with laughter 3. causing laughter; laughable; funny

ris·ing (rī′ziŋ) adj. 1. that rises; ascending, advancing, etc. 2. growing; maturing [the rising generation] 3. [Colloq. or Dial.] somewhat more than; also, approaching [a man rising fifty] —n. 1. the act of one that rises; esp., an uprising; revolt 2. something that rises; projection

risk (risk) n. [Fr. risque < It. risco] 1. the chance of injury, damage, or loss; dangerous chance; hazard 2. a) the chance or likelihood that a person or thing insured may suffer injury, damage, or loss b) the person or thing insured, in relation to such chance or likelihood —vt. 1. to expose to risk; hazard [to risk one's life] 2. to take the chance of [to risk a fight] —**at risk** in a dangerous position —**run** (or **take**) **a risk** to expose oneself to a risk; take a chance —**risk′er** n.

risk capital capital invested in an issue of ordinary shares, esp. of a risky or speculative enterprise

risk·y (ris′kē) adj. risk′i·er, risk′i·est involving risk; hazardous; dangerous —**risk′i·ly** adv. —**risk′i·ness** n.

ris·qué (ris kā′) adj. [Fr., pp. of risquer, to risk] very close to being improper or indecent; daring; suggestive

ris·sole (ris′ōl; Fr. rē sôl′) n. [Fr. ult. < LL. russeolus, < L. russus, red] a small ball of minced meat mixed with breadcrumbs, eggs, etc., often fried

ri·tar·dan·do (rē′tär dan′dō) adj., adv. [It., gerund of ritardare, to delay: see RETARD] Music becoming gradually slower

rite (rīt) n. [L. ritus] 1. a solemn or ceremonial act or observance in accordance with prescribed rule, as in religious use [marriage rites] 2. any formal, customary observance, practice, or procedure [the rites of courtship] 3. a) a particular system or form of ceremonial procedure; ritual b) [often R-] liturgy; esp., any of the forms of the Eucharistic service 4. [often R-] either of the two major divisions (Eastern Rite and Western Rite) of the Christian (Catholic) Church, according to the liturgy used

rite of passage a ceremony performed in some countries at times when an individual changes his status, as at puberty and marriage

rit·u·al (rich′ōō wəl) adj. [L. ritualis] of, having the nature of, or done as a rite —n. 1. a system of rites, religious or otherwise 2. the observance of set forms or rites, as in worship 3. a book containing rites 4. a practice, service, or procedure done as a rite —**rit′u·al·ly** adv.

rit·u·al·ism (-iz'm) n. 1. the observance of ritual 2. an excessive devotion to ritual 3. the study of religious ritual —**rit′u·al·ist** n., adj. —**rit′u·al·is′tic** adj. —**rit′u·al·is′ti·cal·ly** adv.

ritual murder the sacrifice of someone, usually in a tribal religious ceremony

ritz·y (rit′sē) adj. ritz′i·er, ritz′i·est [< the Ritz hotels] [Colloq.] luxurious, fashionable, elegant, etc. —**ritz′i·ness** n.

ri·val (rī′v'l) n. [Fr. < L. rivalis, orig., one using the same stream as another < rivus, a brook] 1. a person who tries to get the same thing as another, or to equal or surpass another; competitor 2. an equal or a satisfactory substitute [plastics are rivals of many metals] —adj. acting as a rival; competing —vt. -valled, -val·ling 1. to try to equal or surpass 2. to equal —vi. [Archaic] to be a rival

ri·val·ry (-rē) n., pl. -ries the act of rivalling or the fact or state of being a rival or rivals; competition

rive (rīv) vt., vi. rived, rived or riv·en (riv′'n), riv′ing [ON. rifa] 1. to tear apart; rend 2. to split; cleave

riv·er (riv′ər) n. [< OFr. < VL. < L. riparius: see RIPARIAN] 1. a natural flow of water larger than a stream and emptying into an ocean, a lake, or another river 2. any plentiful stream or flow —**sell down the river** to betray, deceive, etc. —**up the river** [U.S. Slang] to or confined in a prison

river basin the area drained by a river and its tributaries

riv·er·bed (riv′ər bed′) *n.* the channel in which a river flows or has flowed

riv·er·side (riv′ər sīd′) *n.* the bank of a river —*adj.* on or near the bank of a river

riv·et (riv′it) *n.* [< MFr. < *river*, to clinch] 1. a metal bolt with a head on one end, used to fasten beams together by being inserted through holes: the plain end is then hammered into a head 2. a similar device used to strengthen seams, as on work clothes —*vt.* 1. to fasten with rivets 2. to hammer the end of (a bolt, etc.) into a head 3. to fasten firmly 4. to hold (the eyes, attention, etc.) firmly —**riv′et·er** *n.*

riv·u·let (riv′yoo lit) *n.* [< It. *rivoletto*, ult. < L. *rivus*, a brook] a little stream

ri·yal (rē yäl′) *n.*, *pl.* -**yals**′[Ar. *riyāl* < Sp. *real:* see REAL²] *see* MONETARY UNITS, table (Qatar, Saudi Arabia, Yemen)

R.L. Rugby League

rly. railway

rm. *pl.* **rms.** 1. ream 2. room

R.M. 1. Royal Mail 2. Royal Marines

R.M.A. Royal Military Academy

rms, r.m.s. root mean square

Rn *Chem.* radon

R.N. Royal Navy

RNA ribonucleic acid

R.N.A.S. Royal Naval Air Service

R.N.L.I. Royal National Lifeboat Institution

R.N.(V.)R. Royal Naval (Volunteer) Reserve

R.N.Z.A.F. Royal New Zealand Air Force

R.N.Z.N. Royal New Zealand Navy

roach¹ (rōch) *n.*, *pl.* **roach, roach′es:** see PLURAL, II, D, 2 [OFr. *roche*, prob. < Gmc.] a freshwater fish of the carp family, found in N Europe

roach² (rōch) *n.* [< ?] *Naut.* the curve at the foot of a square sail

road (rōd) *n.* [OE. *rad*, a ride < *ridan*, to ride] 1. a way made for travelling between places by motor car, horseback, etc. 2. a way; path; course [the *road* to fortune] 3. [U.S.] a railway 4. [often *pl.*] a protected place near shore where ships can ride at anchor —**one for the road** [Colloq.] a last alcoholic drink before leaving —**on the road** 1. travelling, as a salesman 2. on tour, as actors —**take to the road** to start travelling —**the road** the cities visited by touring theatrical companies

road·bed (rōd′bed′) *n.* 1. a layer of crushed rock, cinders, etc. on which the sleepers and rails of a railway are laid 2. the foundation of a road

road·block (-blok′) *n.* 1. a blockade set up in a road to prevent movement of vehicles 2. any hindrance in one's way

road fund the money from motor licence fees, supposed to be used for the maintenance of main roads and bridges

road fund licence [Colloq.] vehicle excise tax disc

road hog a selfish, dangerous, or aggressive driver

road·hold·ing (-hōld′iŋ) *n.* the stability of a motor vehicle under varied driving conditions, as high speeds, wet roads, etc.

road·house (-hous′) *n.* a restaurant, hotel, etc. situated on a country road

road runner a long-tailed, crested desert bird of the southwestern U.S. and northern Mexico, that can run swiftly

road·show (-shō′) *n.* 1. a show presented by a theatrical company on tour 2. a discotheque that tours the area, esp. one associated with a radio station

road·side (-sid′) *n.* the side of a road —*adj.* on or at the side of a road [a *roadside* park]

road·stead (-sted′) *n.* same as ROAD (sense 4)

road·ster (-star) *n.* a type of open motor car with front seats only

road test a test of a vehicle, tyres, etc. under actual operating conditions —**road′-test′** *vt.*

road·way (-wā′) *n.* 1. a road 2. that part of a road intended for cars, lorries, and other vehicles to travel on

road works repairs to, and maintenance of, the roads

roam (rōm) *vi.* [ME. *romen*] to travel from place to place, esp. with no special plan or purpose; wander —*vt.* to wander over or through [to *roam* the streets] —*n.* the act of roaming; ramble —**roam′er** *n.*

roan (rōn) *adj.* [OFr. < OSp. *roano*, ult. < *ravus*] of a solid colour, as reddish-brown, black, etc., with a thick sprinkling of white hairs: said chiefly of horses —*n.* 1. a roan colour 2. a roan horse or other animal

roar (rôr) *vi.* [OE. *rarian*] 1. to utter a loud, deep, rumbling sound, as a lion 2. to talk or laugh loudly and boisterously 3. to operate with a loud noise, as a motor or gun 4. to resound with a noisy din —*vt.* 1. to utter with a roar 2. to

make, put, etc. by roaring [to *roar* oneself hoarse] —*n.* 1. a loud, deep, rumbling sound, as of a lion, bull, crowd shouting, etc. 2. a loud noise, as of waves, a motor, etc.; din —**roar′er** *n.*

roar·ing (rôr′iŋ) *n.* 1. the act of an animal, etc. that roars 2. the sound of a roar —*adj.* [Colloq.] very active or successful; brisk [a *roaring* business] —*adv.* to the point of being noisy, boisterous, etc. [*roaring* drunk]

roast (rōst) *vt.* [OFr. *rostir* < Frank.] 1. to cook (something) with little or no moisture, as in an oven or over an open fire 2. to dry, parch, or brown (coffee, etc.) by exposure to heat 3. to expose to great heat 4. to heat (ore, etc.) in a furnace in order to remove impurities or cause oxidation 5. [U.S. Colloq.] to criticize or ridicule severely —*vi.* 1. to be cooked by being roasted 2. to be or become very hot —*n.* 1. roasted meat 2. a cut of meat for roasting 3. a roasting or being roasted —*adj.* roasted [*roast* pork] —**roast′ing** *adj.*

roast·er (rōs′tar) *n.* 1. a person or thing that roasts 2. a pan, oven, etc. for roasting meat 3. a young pig, chicken, etc. suitable for roasting

rob (rob) *vt.* **robbed, rob′bing** [OFr. *rober* < Gmc.] 1. *a)* *Law* to take personal property, money, etc. from unlawfully by using or threatening force *b)* popularly, to steal something from in any way 2. to deprive (someone) *of* something belonging to or due him [the accident *robbed* him of his health] —*vi.* to commit robbery —**rob′ber** *n.*

rob·ber·y (rob′ər ē) *n.*, *pl.* -**ber·ies** a robbing; specif., the committing of a crime by taking another's property while he is present, by violence or threat of violence

robe (rōb) *n.* [OFr., a robe, orig., booty < Gmc.] 1. a long, loose outer garment; specif., *a)* such a garment worn on formal occasions, to show rank or office, as by a judge *b)* [U.S.] a bathrobe or dressing gown 2. [*pl.*] [Archaic] clothes; costume —*vt., vi.* **robed, rob′ing** to dress in or cover with a robe

rob·in (rob′in) *n.* [< OFr. dim. of *Robert*] 1. a small European warbler with an orange-red breast 2. a large N American thrush with a dull-red breast and belly Also **robin redbreast**

Robin Good·fel·low (good′fel′ō) *Eng. Folklore* a mischievous elf or fairy: identified with Puck

Robin Hood *Eng. Legend* an outlaw of the 12th cent. who lived with his followers in Sherwood Forest and robbed the rich to help the poor

Rob·in·son Cru·soe (rob′in s′n kroo′sō) the hero of Defoe's novel (1719) of the same name, a sailor who is shipwrecked on a tropical island

ro·bot (rō′bət, -bot) *n.* [< Czech *robota*, forced labour · < OBulg. < *rabu*, servant] 1. *a)* any manlike mechanical being, as those in Karel Capek's play *R.U.R.* *b)* any mechanical device operated automatically, esp. by remote control, to perform in a seemingly human way 2. an automaton; esp., a person who acts or works mechanically —**ro′bot·ism** *n.*

robot bomb a small, jet-propelled bomb with wings, steered by an automatic pilot and carrying high explosives

ro·bust (rō bust′) *adj.* [L. *robustus* < *robur*, hard variety of oak] 1. *a)* strong and healthy; hardy *b)* strongly built; muscular or sturdy 2. suited to or requiring physical strength [*robust* work] 3. rough; coarse; boisterous 4. full and rich, as in flavour [a *robust* port wine] —**ro·bust′ly** *adv.* —**ro·bust′ness** *n.*

ro·bus·tious (rō bus′chas) *adj.* [prec. + -IOUS] 1. rough; boisterous 2. [Archaic] strong; robust

roc (rok) *n.* [< Ar. < Per. *rukh*] *Arabian & Persian Legend* a fabulous bird, so huge and strong that it could carry off large animals

R.O.C. Royal Observer Corps

Ro·chelle salt (rō shel′) [after La *Rochelle*, France] a colourless, crystalline compound used as a piezoelectric material, etc.

roch·et (roch′it) *n.* [< OFr. < *roc*, a cloak < MHG. < OHG. *roch*] a vestment of lawn or linen, like a surplice, worn by bishops

rock¹ (rok) *n.* [< OFr. *roche*] 1: a large mass of stone 2. *a)* a large stone detached from the mass; boulder *b)* broken pieces of any size of such stone 3. *a)* mineral matter formed in masses in the earth's crust *b)* a particular kind or mass of this 4. anything like a rock, as in strength; esp., a firm support, basis, etc. 5. a hard sweet made in sticks 6. [Slang] a diamond or other gem —**on the rocks** [Colloq.] 1. in a condition of ruin or catastrophe 2. bankrupt 3. served undiluted over ice cubes: said of spirits, wine, etc. —**the Rock** Gibraltar

rock² (rok) *vt.* [OE. *roccian*] 1. to move backwards and forwards or from side to side (a cradle, a child in the arms, etc.) 2. to make or put by moving this way [to *rock* a baby to sleep] 3. *a)* to sway strongly; shake [the explosion *rocked* the house] *b)* to upset emotionally —*vi.* 1. to move backwards and forwards or from side to side 2. to sway strongly; shake —*n.* 1. a rocking 2. a rocking motion **3.** *a)* *same as* ROCK-AND-ROLL *b)* popular music evolved from rock-and-roll, variously containing elements of folk music, country music, etc. —**rock the boat** to make things difficult for others

rock-and-roll (rok'ʼn rōl') *n.* a form of popular music, having a strong and regular rhythm, which evolved from jazz and the blues: also sp. **rock 'n' roll**

rock bottom the lowest level or point; very bottom —**rock'·bot'tom** *adj.*

rock-bound (-bȯund') *adj.* surrounded or covered by rocks [a *rock-bound* coast]

rock cake a small cake containing dried fruit whose rough surface resembles a rock

rock crystal a transparent, esp. colourless, quartz

rock dove the wild ancestor of the domestic pigeons, now much interbred with them

rock·er (rok'ər) *n.* **1.** either of the curved pieces on the bottom of a cradle, rocking chair, etc. **2.** *same as* ROCKING CHAIR **3.** any of various devices that work with a rocking motion —**off one's rocker** [Slang] crazy; insane

rock·er·y (rok'ər ē) *n.,* *pl.* **-er·ies** rocks and soil arranged for growing a rock garden

rock·et (rok'it) *n.* [It. *rocchetta,* a spool, orig. dim. of *rocca,* a distaff < OHG.] **1.** any of various devices, typically cylindrical, containing a combustible substance which when ignited produces gases that escape through a rear vent and drive the container forwards by the principle of reaction: rockets are used as fireworks and projectile weapons and to propel spacecraft **2.** a spacecraft, missile, etc. propelled by a rocket **3.** [Colloq.] a severe reprimand —*vi.* **1.** to dart ahead swiftly like a rocket **2.** to travel in a rocket **3.** to soar [prices *rocketed*] —*vt.* to convey in a rocket —**rock·e·teer** (rok'ə tir') *n.*

rock·et·ry (rok'ə trē) *n.* **1.** the science of designing, building, and launching rockets **2.** rockets collectively

rock garden a garden with flowers and plants growing among rocks variously arranged

rocking chair a chair mounted on rockers or springs, so as to allow a rocking movement

rocking horse a toy horse mounted on rockers or springs and big enough for a child to ride

rocking stone *same as* LOGAN

rock lobster *same as* SPINY LOBSTER

rock plant a plant which thrives in dry exposed places among stones and rocks

rock·rose (-rōz') *n.* a small plant with wiry stems and yellow flowers —*adj.* designating a family of bushy plants

rock salmon the name used for dogfish by fishmongers

rock salt common salt in solid masses

rock wool a fibrous material that looks like spun glass, made from molten rock or slag through which steam is forced: it is used for insulation, esp. in buildings

rock·y¹ (rok'ē) *adj.* **rock'i·er, rock'i·est 1.** full of rocks **2.** consisting of rock **3.** like a rock; firm, hard, unfeeling, etc. **4.** full of obstacles [the *rocky* road to success] —**rock'·i·ness** *n.*

rock·y² (rok'ē) *adj.* **rock'i·er, rock'i·est 1.** *a)* inclined to rock, or sway *b)* uncertain; shaky **2.** [Colloq.] weak and dizzy; groggy —**rock'i·ness** *n.*

Rocky Mountain goat a white, goatlike antelope of the mountains of northwest N America

ro·co·co (rə kō'kō; *occas.* rō'kō kō') *n.* [Fr. < *rocaille,* shell work] a style of architecture and decoration using elaborate ornamentation imitating foliage, shell work, scrolls, etc.: popular in the 18th cent. —*adj.* **1.** of or in rococo **2.** too elaborate; florid and tasteless

rod (rod) *n.* [OE. *rodd*] **1.** *Bible* a branch of a family or tribe **2.** any straight stick, bar, etc., as of wood, metal, etc. [curtain *rods*] **3.** *a)* a stick for beating as punishment *b)* punishment **4.** *a)* a staff, sceptre, etc., carried as a symbol of office or rank *b)* power; authority **5.** *same as* FISHING ROD **6.** a stick used to measure something **7.** *a)* a measure of length equal to 5¹/₂ yards (5m) *b)* a square rod, equal to 30¹/₄ square yards (25m²) **8.** [U.S. Slang] a pistol or revolver **9.** [U.S. Slang] *same as* HOT ROD **10.** *Biol.* a rod-shaped cell, microorganism, etc. —**rod'like**'*adj.*

rode (rōd) *pt.* & *archaic pp. of* RIDE

ro·dent (rōd'ʼnt) *adj.* [< L. prp. of *rodere,* to gnaw] **1.** gnawing **2.** of or like rodents —*n.* any of various gnawing mammals, including rats, mice, beavers, etc., that have constantly growing incisors; esp., a rat or mouse

rodent officer an official ratcatcher

ro·de·o (rō'dē ō'; *also, esp. for 1,* rō dā'ō) *n.,* *pl.* **-de·os**'[Sp. < *rodear,* surround < L. *rotare:* see ROTATE] [U.S. & Canad.] **1.** [Now Rare] a roundup of cattle **2.** a public exhibition of the skills of cowboys, as broncobusting, lassoing, etc.

rod·o·mon·tade (rod'ə mon tād', -täd') *n.* [Fr. < It. *Rodomonte,* boastful Saracen leader in *Orlando Furioso,* 16th-c. epic] arrogant boasting or blustering talk —*adj.* arrogantly boastful —*vi.* **-tad'ed, -tad'ing** to boast

roe¹ (rō) *n.* [akin to or < ? ON. *hrogn*] fish eggs, esp. when still massed in the ovarian membrane

roe² (rō) *n.,* *pl.* **roe, roes:** see PLURAL, II, D, 2 [OE. *ra*] a small, agile, graceful European and Asian deer

roe·buck (rō'buk') *n.,* *pl.* **-bucks', -buck':** see PLURAL, II, D, 1 the male of the roe deer

roent·gen (rent'gən, ren'chən) *n.* [after W. K. *Roentgen* (1845-1923), Ger. physicist who discovered X-rays] the international unit used in measuring ionizing radiation, as X-rays or gamma rays

Roentgen ray [*also* r-] *same as* X-RAY

ro·ga·tion (rō gā'shən) *n.* [< L. < *rogare,* to ask] a supplication or prayer, esp. as chanted during Rogation days

Rogation days the three days before Ascension Day, during which supplications are chanted

Rogation Sunday the Sunday before Ascension Day

Rog·er (roj'ər) *interj.* [< conventional name of international signal flag for R] [*also* r-] **1.** received: term used in radiotelegraphy to indicate reception of a message **2.** [Colloq.] right!; OK!

rogue (rōg) *n.* [< ?] **1.** formerly, a vagabond **2.** a scoundrel **3.** a fun-loving, mischievous person **4.** an animal that wanders alone and is fierce and wild [*rogue* elephant] —*vt.* **rogued, rogu'ing** to cheat —*vi.* to live or act like a rogue

ro·guer·y (rō'gər ē) *n.,* *pl.* **-guer·ies** the behaviour of a rogue; specif., *a)* trickery; cheating *b)* playful mischief

rogues' gallery a collection of photographs of criminals, as used by police in identification

ro·guish (rō'gish) *adj.* of or like a rogue; specif., *a)* dishonest; unscrupulous *b)* playfully mischievous —**ro'·guish·ly** *adv.* —**ro'guish·ness** *n.*

roil (roil) *vt.* [< ?] **1.** to make (a liquid) cloudy, muddy, etc. by stirring up the sediment **2.** to stir up; agitate **3.** to make angry or irritable —*vi.* to be agitated —**roil'y** *adj.* **roil'i·er, roil'i·est**

roist·er (rois'tər) *vi.* [< OFr. < L. *rusticus:* see RUSTIC] **1.** to boast or swagger **2.** to be lively and noisy; revel boisterously —**roist'er·er, roist'er·ing** *n.* —**roist'er·ous** *adj.*

role, rôle (rōl) *n.* [Fr. *rôle,* a roll: from roll containing actor's part] **1.** a part, or character, that an actor plays **2.** a function assumed by someone [an advisory *role*]

roll (rōl) *vi.* [OFr. *roller,* ult. < L. *rotula* (or *rotulus*), dim. of *rota,* wheel] **1.** to move by turning over and over **2.** *a)* to move on wheels *b)* to travel in a wheeled vehicle **3.** to pass [the years *rolled* by] **4.** to move in a periodical revolution: said of stars, planets, etc. **5.** *a)* to flow, as water, in a full, sweeping motion *b)* to be carried in a flow **6.** to extend in gentle swells or undulations **7.** to make a loud, rising and falling sound [thunder *rolls*] **8.** to rise and fall in a full, mellow cadence, as speech **9.** to trill or warble **10.** to be wound into a ball or cylinder, as yarn **11.** to turn in a circular motion [with eyes *rolling*] **12.** to rock from side to side, as a ship **13.** to walk by swaying **14.** to become spread under a roller **15.** to make progress; advance **16.** to start operating [the presses *rolled*] **17.** [Colloq.] to abound (*in*) [*rolling* in wealth] —*vt.* **1.** to move by turning over and over **2.** to move on wheels or rollers **3.** to cause to start operating **4.** to beat (a drum) with light, rapid blows **5.** to utter with a full, flowing sound **6.** to say with a trill [to *roll* one's r's] **7.** to give a swaying motion to **8.** to move around or from side to side [to *roll* one's eyes] **9.** to wind into a ball or cylinder [to *roll* a cigarette] **10.** to wrap or enfold **11.** to make flat or spread out, by using a roller, etc. **12.** to iron (sleeves, etc.) without forming a crease **13.** [U.S. Slang] to rob (a drunken or sleeping person) **14.** *Printing* to spread ink on (type, a forme, etc.) with a roller —*n.* **1.** the act or an instance of rolling **2.** *a)* a scroll *b)* something that is, or looks as if, rolled up **3.** *a)* a register; catalogue *b)* the official list of solicitors **4.** a list of names for checking attendance **5.** a measure of something rolled into a cylinder [a *roll* of wallpaper] **6.** a cylindrical mass of something **7.** any of various small cakes of bread, etc. **8.** a roller (in various senses) **9.** a swaying motion **10.** a rapid succession of light blows on a drum **11.** a loud, reverberating sound, as of thunder **12.** a trill **13.** a slight swell on the surface of something, as land —**roll back 1.** to move back **2.** [Chiefly U.S.] to reduce (prices) to a previous level by government action —**roll in** to arrive or appear, usually in large numbers or amounts —**roll out** to spread out by unrolling —**roll round** to recur, as in a cycle —**roll up 1.** to increase by accumulation **2.** [Colloq.] to arrive in or as if in a vehicle —**strike off** (or **from**) **the rolls** to expel from membership

roll·a·way (rōl'ə wā') *adj.* [Chiefly U.S.] having rollers for easy moving and storing when not in use [a *rollaway* bed]

roll bar a heavy metal bar reinforcing the roof of a motor car to reduce injury if the car should roll over

roll call the reading aloud of a roll, as in military formations, to find out who is absent

rolled gold brass or other base metal covered with a thin layer of gold

roll·er (rōl′lər) *n.* 1. a person or thing that rolls 2. *a)* a cylinder on which something is rolled up [a hair *roller*] *b)* a heavy rolling cylinder used to crush, smooth, or spread something 3. a long bandage in a roll 4. a long, heavy wave that breaks on the shoreline 5. a canary that trills its notes

roller bearing a bearing in which the shaft turns on rollers in a ringlike track

roller coaster [U.S.] a switchback

roller skate a skate with wheels: see SKATE[1] (sense 2) —**roll′er-skate′** *vi.* -skat′ed, -skat′ing —**roller skater**

roller towel a towel whose ends are sewn together and which is hung on a roller

rol·lick (rol′ik) *vi.* [< ? FROLIC] to play or behave in a gay, carefree way —**rol′lick·ing, rol′lick·some** (-səm) *adj.*

roll·ing (rōl′iŋ) *adj.* 1. that rolls; specif., rotating or revolving, recurring, swaying, surging, resounding, trilling, etc. 2. [Colloq.] to be wealthy —*n.* the action, motion, or sound of something that rolls —**rolling in** [Colloq.] having an ample supply of (money, etc.)

rolling mill 1. a factory in which metal bars, sheets, etc. are rolled out 2. a machine used for such rolling

rolling pin a heavy, smooth cylinder of wood, glass, etc., usually with a handle at each end, used to roll out pastry, etc.

rolling stock *a)* all the engines, coaches, etc. of a railway *b)* [U.S.] all the lorries etc. of a trucking company

rolling stone a person who is incapable of settling down in any one place

roll-mop (rōl′mop′) *n.* [G. *Rollmops* < *rollen*, to ROLL + *Mops*, a pug dog] a fillet of fresh herring rolled around an onion and marinated

roll-on (rōl′on) *n.* 1. a liquid, esp. a deodorant, that is packed in a container having an applicator consisting of a revolving ball 2. [Colloq.] a woman's foundation garment —*adj.* 1. dispensed by rolling the applicator over the flesh or other surface 2. designed to allow vehicles to be driven aboard: said of a ferry, cargo ship, etc.

Rolls-Royce (rōlz′rois′) *n.* [after Charles Stewart *Rolls* (1877-1910) & Sir Frederick Henry *Royce* (1863-1933), the Brit. engineers] a make of motor car, famed for its luxury

roll-top (rōl′top′) *adj.* made with a flexible top of parallel slats that slides back [a *roll-top desk*]

ro·ly-po·ly (rō′lē pō′lē) *adj.* [redupl. of ROLL] short and plump; pudgy —*n., pl.* -lies 1. a roly-poly person or thing 2. a pudding made of rich dough spread with jam, rolled up, and boiled, steamed, etc.

rom, Rom. roman (type)

Rom. 1. Roman 2. Romance 3. Romania 4. Romanian 5. Romanic 6. Romans (Epistle to the Romans)

Ro·ma·ic (rō mā′ik) *n.* the everyday language of modern Greece —*adj.* of this language

ro·maine (rō mān′, rō′mān) *n.* [Fr. < fem. of *romain*, Roman] [U.S.] cos lettuce

Ro·man (rō′mən) *adj.* 1. of or characteristic of ancient or modern Rome, its people, etc. 2. of the Roman Catholic Church 3. [*usually* r-] designating or of the usual upright style of printing types; not italic —*n.* 1. a native, citizen, or inhabitant of ancient or modern Rome 2. [*usually* r-] roman type or characters

‡**roman à clef** (rô män nà klā′) [Fr., lit., novel with a key] a novel in which real persons appear under fictitious names

Roman alphabet the alphabet of the ancient Romans, used with little change in most modern European languages

Roman arch a semicircular arch

Roman candle a firework consisting of a long tube that sends out balls of fire, sparks, etc.

Roman Catholic 1. of the Roman Catholic Church 2. a member of this church —**Roman Catholicism**

Roman Catholic Church the Christian church headed by the Pope

Ro·mance (rō mans′, rō′mans) *adj.* [see ff.] designating or of any of the languages derived from Vulgar Latin, as Italian, Spanish, French, etc. —*n.* these languages

ro·mance (rō mans′; *also, for n.*, rō′mans) *n.* [OFr. *romanz*, Roman (i.e., the vernacular, not Latin), ult. < L. *Romanicus*, Roman] 1. a long verse or prose narrative, orig. written in one of the Romance languages, about knights and chivalric deeds, adventure, and love 2. a novel of love, adventure, etc. 3. excitement, love, and adventure of the kind found in such literature 4. the tendency to enjoy romantic adventures 5. an exaggeration or fabrication 6. a love affair —*vi.* -manced′, -manc′ing 1. to write or tell romances 2. to think or talk about romantic things —*vt.* [Colloq.] to woo; court —**ro·manc′er** *n.*

Roman Curia *R.C.Ch. see* CURIA (sense 2)

Roman Empire empire established by Augustus around the Mediterranean: it existed from 27 B.C. until 395 A.D.

Ro·man·esque (rō′mə nesk′) *adj.* designating or of a style of European architecture of the 11th and 12th cent., based on the Roman and using round arches and vaults, massive walls, etc. —*n.* this style of architecture

Roman holiday [after the ancient Roman gladiatorial contests] entertainment at the expense of others' suffering, or a spectacle yielding such entertainment

Ro·man·ic (-man′ik) *adj., n. same as* ROMANCE

Ro·man·ism (rō′mən iz′m) *n.* Roman Catholicism: hostile usage

Ro·man·ize (-īz′) *vt.* -ized′, -iz′ing 1. to make or become Roman in character, spirit, etc. 2. to make or become Roman Catholic —**Ro′man·i·za′tion** *n.*

Roman nose a nose with a prominent bridge

Roman numerals the Roman letters used as numerals until the 10th cent. A.D.: in Roman numerals I = 1, V = 5, X = 10, L = 50, C = 100, D = 500, M = 1000 The value of a symbol following another of the same or greater value is added (e.g., III = 3, XV = 15); the value of a symbol preceding one of greater value is subtracted (e.g., IX = 9)

Ro·ma·no- (rō mä′nō) *a combining form meaning* Roman (*Romanobritish*)

ro·man·tic (rō man′tik) *adj.* 1. of, like, or characterized by romance 2. without a basis in fact; fanciful or fictitious 3. not practical; visionary [a *romantic* scheme] 4. full of thoughts, feelings, etc. of romance 5. *a)* of or concerned with idealized lovemaking *b)* suited for romance, or lovemaking [a *romantic* night] 6. [*often* R-] of or associated with the ROMANTIC MOVEMENT —*n.* a romantic person —**ro·man′ti·cal·ly** *adv.*

ro·man·ti·cism (rō man′tə siz′m) *n.* 1. romantic spirit, outlook, etc. 2. *a) same as* ROMANTIC MOVEMENT *b)* the spirit, style, etc. of, or adherence to, the Romantic Movement: contrasted with CLASSICISM, etc. —**ro·man′·ti·cist** *n.*

ro·man·ti·cize (-sīz′) *vt.* -cized′, -ciz′ing to treat or regard romantically —*vi.* to have romantic ideas, attitudes, etc. —**ro·man′ti·ci·za′tion** *n.*

Romantic Movement the revolt in the 18th and 19th cent. against neoclassicism in literature, music, art, etc.: it emphasized freedom of form, full expression of feeling, etc.

Rom·a·ny (rom′ə nē, rō′mə-) *n.* [Romany *romani*, Gypsy < *rom*, a man < Sans.] 1. *pl.* -ny, -nies a Gypsy 2. the Indic language of the Gypsies —*adj.* of the Gypsies, their language, etc. Also sp. **Rom′ma·ny**

Rom. Cath. Roman Catholic

Rome (rōm) *same as* ROMAN CATHOLIC CHURCH

Ro·me·o (rō′mē ō′) *n., pl.* -os [after the hero of Shakespeare's tragedy *Romeo and Juliet*] a man who is an ardent lover

romp (romp) *n.* [< earlier *ramp*, prob. < OFr. *ramper*: see RAMP[2]] 1. a person who romps, esp. a girl 2. boisterous, lively play 3. *a)* an easy, winning gait in a race *b)* an easy victory —*vi.* 1. to play in a boisterous, lively way 2. to win with ease, etc. [he *romped* home]

romp·er (rom′pər) *n.* 1. one who romps 2. [*pl.*] a young child's loose-fitting, one-piece outer garment with bloomerlike pants

ron·deau (ron′dō) *n., pl.* -deaux (-dōz) [Fr. < *rondel* < *rond*, round] a short lyrical poem of thirteen (or ten) lines and an unrhymed refrain that consists of the opening words and is used in two places

ron·del (-d′l, -del) *n.* [OFr.: see prec.] a kind of rondeau, usually with fourteen lines, two rhymes, and the first two lines used as a refrain in the middle and at the end

ron·do (ron′dō) *n., pl.* -dos [It. < Fr.: see RONDEAU] *Music* a composition or movement having its principal theme stated three or more times, separated by subordinate themes

rone (rōn) *n.* [< ?] [Scot.] a gutter or drainpipe that carries rainwater from a roof

roo (rōō) *n.* [(KANGA)ROO] [Aust. Colloq.] a kangaroo

rood (rōōd) *n.* [OE. *rod*] 1. a crucifix 2. formerly, a measure of area usually equal to 1/4 acre (40 square rods)

rood screen a screen, usually carved or ornamented and surmounted by a rood, dividing the choir or chancel of a church from its nave

roof (rōōf) *n., pl.* **roofs** [OE. *hrof*] 1. the outside top covering of a building 2. figuratively, a house or home 3. anything like a roof [the *roof* of the mouth] —*vt.* to cover as with a roof —**hit** (or **go through**) **the roof** to become extremely angry —**raise the roof** [Colloq.] to be very noisy, as in anger or joy —**roof′less** *adj.*

roof·er (-ər) *n.* a person who builds or repairs roofs

roof garden 1. a garden on the flat roof of a building 2. [U.S.] the roof or top floor of a building, decorated as a garden and used as a restaurant, etc.

roof·ing (-iŋ) *n.* 1. the act of covering with a roof 2. material for roofs 3. a roof

roof rack a rack attached to the roof of a motor vehicle and used to carry luggage, etc.

roof·top (-top′) *n.* the roof of a building

roof·tree (-trē′) *n.* 1. the ridgepole of a roof 2. a roof

rook[1] (rōōk) *n.* [OE. *hroc*] 1. a crowlike European bird 2. a swindler; cheat —*vt., vi.* to swindle; cheat

rook[2] (rōōk) *n.* [< OFr. *roc* < Ar. < Per. *rukh*] *Chess* either of the two corner pieces shaped like a castle tower, movable only in a vertical or horizontal line; castle

rook·er·y (rook′ər ē) *n., pl.* **-er·ies** 1. a breeding place or colony of rooks, or of seals, penguins, etc. 2. [Now Rare] an overcrowded, slum tenement

rook·ie (rook′ē) *n.* [altered < ? RECRUIT] [Slang] an inexperienced recruit in the army

room (room, room) *n.* [OE. *rum*] 1. space to contain something or in which to do something [*room* for one more] 2. opportunity [*room* for doubt] 3. a space within a building enclosed or set apart by walls 4. [*pl.*] living quarters; lodgings 5. the people in a room [the whole *room* was silent] —*vi., vt.* [U.S.] to have, or provide with, lodgings

room and board lodging and meals

room·er (room′mər) *n.* [U.S.] a lodger

room·ful (room′fool′, room′-) *n., pl.* **-fuls** 1. as much or as many as will fill a room 2. the people or objects in a room, collectively

rooming house [U.S.] a lodging house

room·mate (-māt′) *n.* a person with whom one shares a room or rooms

room service the service provided by hotels serving food, etc. in the guest's room

room·y (-ē) *adj.* **room′i·er, room′i·est** having plenty of room; spacious —**room′i·ly** *adv.* —**room′i·ness** *n.*

roost[1] (room) *n.* [OE. *hrost*] 1. a perch on which birds, esp. domestic fowls, can rest or sleep 2. a place with perches for birds 3. a place for resting, sleeping, etc. —*vi.* 1. to sit, sleep, etc. on a perch 2. to settle down, as for the night —**come home to roost** to come back in an unfavourable way to the doer; boomerang —**rule the roost** to be master

roost[2] (room) *n.* [< ON. *rōst*] a tidal race found esp. around the Orkney and Shetland Islands

roos·ter (room′tər) *n.* [Chiefly U.S.] a cock

root[1] (room) *n.* [Late OE. *rote* < ON. *rot*] 1. the part of a plant, usually below the ground, that lacks nodes, shoots, and leaves, holds the plant in place, and draws water and food from the soil 2. loosely, any underground part of a plant 3. the embedded part of a bodily structure, as of the teeth, hair, etc. 4. the source or cause of an action, quality, condition, etc. 5. an ancestor 6. [*pl.*] the close ties one has with some place or people as through birth, upbringing, long association, etc. 7. a supporting part; base 8. an essential or basic part; core [the *root* of the matter] 9. *Math. a)* a quantity that, multiplied by itself a specified number of times, produces a given quantity [4 is the square *root* (4 × 4) of 16 and the cube *root* (4 × 4 × 4) of 64] *b)* a number that, when substituted for the unknown quantity in an equation, will satisfy the equation 10. *Music* the basic tone of a chord 11. *Linguis.* same as BASE[1] (*n.* 10) —*vi.* 1. to begin to grow by putting out roots 2. to become fixed, settled, etc. —*vt.* 1. to fix the roots of in the ground 2. to establish; settle —**root up** (or **out, away**) to pull out by the roots; remove completely —**take root** 1. to begin growing by putting out roots 2. to become settled —**root′i·ness** *n.* —**root′y** *adj.*

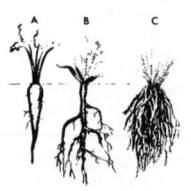

ROOTS
(A, B, taproot;
C, fibrous)

root[2] (room) *vt.* [OE. *wrotan* < *wrot*, snout] to dig (*up* or *out*) with or as with the snout —*vi.* 1. to dig in the ground, as with the snout 2. to search about; rummage 3. [U.S. Colloq.] *a)* to encourage a contestant or team by applauding and cheering *b)* to lend moral support to one seeking success, recovery, etc. Usually with *for* —**root′er** *n.*

root beer [U.S.] a carbonated drink made of extracts from the roots and bark of certain plants, etc.

root canal a small, tubular channel, normally filled with pulp, in the root of a tooth

root crop a crop, as turnips, beets, etc., grown for the edible roots

root hair *Bot.* any of the hairlike tubular outgrowths from a growing root, which absorb water and minerals from the soil

root·le (room′'l) *vi.* [< ROOT[2]] to search out; burrow

root·less (-lis) *adj.* having no roots or ties —**root′less·ly** *adv.* —**root′less·ness** *n.*

root·let (-lit) *n.* a little root

root mean square the square root of the averages of a set of numbers

root·stock (-stok′) *n. Bot.* 1. same as RHIZOME 2. a plant onto which another is grafted as a new top

rope (rōp) *n.* [OE. *rap*] 1. a thick, strong cord made of intertwisted strands of fibre, wires, etc. 2. *a)* a noose for hanging a person *b)* death by hanging: with *the* 3. [U.S.] same as LASSO 4. a ropelike string of things [a *rope* of

pearls] 5. a ropelike, sticky formation, as in a liquid —*vt.* **roped, rop′ing** 1. to fasten or tie with a rope 2. to connect by a rope 3. to mark off or enclose with a rope (usually with *in, off,* or *out*) —*vi.* to become ropelike and sticky, as toffee —**know the ropes** [Colloq.] to know the details or procedures, as of a job —**on the ropes** 1. *Boxing* knocked against the ropes 2. [Colloq.] near collapse or ruin —**rope in** 1. to persuade someone to do something 2. [U.S.] to trick into doing something —**the end of one's rope** the end of one's endurance, resources, etc. —**rop′er** *n.*

rope ladder a ladder made entirely of rope

rope·walk (-wôk′) *n.* a long, low, narrow shed, etc. in which ropes are made

rope·walk·er (-ər) *n.* a performer who walks or does tricks on a tightrope: also **rope′danc′er** (-dän′sər) —**rope′walk′ing** *n.*

rop·y (rō′pē) *adj.* **rop′i·er, rop′i·est** 1. forming sticky threads, as some liquids 2. like rope 3. inferior; inadequate —**rop′i·ness** *n.*

Roque·fort (cheese) (rok′fôr) [< *Roquefort*, France, where orig. made] a strong cheese with a bluish mould, made from goats' and ewes' milk

ror·qual (rôr′kwəl) *n.* [Fr. < Norw. *röyrkval* < ON. *reytharhvalr*, lit., red whale] any of the whalebone whales with a well-developed dorsal fin, esp. a finback whale with lengthwise furrows on its belly and throat

Ror·schach test (rôr′shäk) [after H. *Rorschach* (1884-1922), Swiss psychiatrist] *Psychol.* a test for personality analysis, in which the person being tested tells what is suggested to him by a standard series of inkblot designs: his responses are then interpreted

rort (rôrt) *n.* [< foll.] [Slang] a trick, scheme, or racket —**rort′er** *n.*

ror·ty (rôr′tē) *adj.* [19th cent. < ?] [Slang] gay; enjoyable

ro·sa·ceous (rō zā′shəs) *adj.* 1. of the rose family of plants, as the strawberry, plum, etc. 2. like a rose 3. rose-coloured

ro·sa·ry (rō′zər ē) *n., pl.* **-ries** [L. *rosarium*, ult. < *rosa*, a rose] *R.C.Ch.* 1. a string of beads used to keep count in saying certain prayers 2. [*also* R-] the prayers said with these beads

rose[1] (rōz) *n.* [OE. < L. *rosa*] 1. any of a genus of shrubs with prickly stems and five-parted, usually fragrant flowers of red, pink, white, yellow, etc. 2. the flower of any of these 3. any of several related plants 4. pinkish red or purplish red 5. anything like a rose in form, as a rosette, the perforated nozzle of a watering can, a round cut of gem with many facets and a flat base, etc. —*adj.* 1. of or having to do with roses 2. rose-coloured 3. rose-scented 4. designating a large family of wild and cultivated flowers, shrubs, and trees, including the hawthorns, roses, strawberries, apples, peaches, almonds, etc. —*vt.* **rosed, ros′ing** to make rose-coloured —**under the rose** same as SUB ROSA —**rose′like′** *adj.*

rose[2] (rōz) *pt. of* RISE

ro·sé (rō zā′) *n.* [Fr., lit., pink] a light, pink wine made by removing the grape husks after partial fermentation

ro·se·ate (rō′zē it, -āt′) *adj.* 1. rose-coloured; rosy 2. cheerful or optimistic —**ro′se·ate·ly** *adv.*

rose bay 1. a willow herb with showy spikes of large pink or purple flowers 2. *same as: a)* OLEANDER *b)* RHODODENDRON

rose·bud (rōz′bud′) *n.* the bud of a rose

rose·bush (-boosh′) *n.* a shrub that bears roses

rose chafer a small beetle that feeds on the leaves and flowers of roses and other plants

rose-col·oured (-kul′ərd) *adj.* 1. pinkish-red or purplish-red 2. cheerful or optimistic —**through rose-coloured glasses** (or **spectacles**) with excessive optimism

ro·sel·la (rō zel′ə) *n.* [< corruption of *Rose Hill* N.S.W., where originally found] any of various brightly-coloured Australian parrots

rose·mar·y (-mə rē) *n.* [altered (after ROSE[1] & *Mary,* a feminine name) ult. < L. *ros marinus*, lit., dew of the sea] an evergreen plant with small, light-blue flowers and fragrant leaves used in perfumery, cooking, etc.

rose of Sharon 1. a plant with white, red, pink, or purplish, bell-shaped flowers 2. a Saint Johnswort shrub with large, yellow flowers

ro·se·o·la (rō zē′ə lə) *n.* [ModL., dim. < L. *roseus,* rosy] any of various rose-coloured skin rashes

rose tree same as ROSE[1] (*n.* 1)

Ro·set·ta stone (rō zet′ə) a stone tablet, found in 1799 at Rosetta, Egypt, bearing inscriptions that provided a key for deciphering Egyptian hieroglyphics

ro·sette (rō zet′) *n.* [Fr. < OFr., dim. of *rose,* ROSE[1]] an ornament, arrangement, etc. resembling or suggesting a rose [a *rosette* of ribbon]

rose water a preparation consisting of water and attar of roses, used as a perfume

rose window a circular window with roselike tracery or mullions arranged like the spokes of a wheel

rose·wood (rōz′wŏŏd′) *n.* [from its odour] **1.** any of a number of valuable hard, reddish, black-streaked woods, used in making furniture, etc. **2.** a tropical tree yielding such wood

Rosh Ha·sha·na (rōsh′hə shä′nə) the Jewish New Year, celebrated in late September or early October: also sp. **Rosh Hashona, Rosh Hashanah**, etc.

Ro·si·cru·cian (rō′zə krōō′shən) *n.* [*Rosicruc-* < Latinized form of G. pseudonym of founder, Christian *Rosenkreuz* + -IAN] **1.** a member of a secret society in the 17th and 18th cent. said to have various sorts of occult lore and power **2.** a member of any of several later groups supposed to be based on the original society —*adj.* of or characteristic of the Rosicrucians —**Ros′si·cru′cian·ism** *n.*

ros·in (roz′in) *n.* [altered < MFr. *resine*, RESIN] the hard, brittle resin, light-yellow to almost black, left after the distillation of crude turpentine: it is rubbed on violin bows, used in making varnish, etc. —*vt.* to rub with rosin; put rosin on —**ros′in·ous, ros′in·y** *adj.*

ROSPA Royal Society for the Prevention of Accidents

ros·ter (ros′tər) *n.* [Du. *rooster*, orig., gridiron, hence a list (from ruled paper used for lists)] [Chiefly U.S] **1.** a list of military or naval personnel, with their assignments, duties, etc. **2.** any list; roll

ros·trum (ros′trəm) *n., pl.* **-trums, -tra** (-trə) [L., (ship's) beak, hence the speakers' platform in the Forum, decorated with ramming beaks taken from captured ships] **1.** any platform for public speaking **2.** public speaking, or public speakers collectively —**ros′tral** *adj.*

ros·y (rō′zē) *adj.* **ros′i·er, ros′i·est** **1.** like a rose, esp. in colour; rose-red or pink [*rosy* cheeks] **2.** [Archaic] made with roses **3.** bright, promising, cheerful, etc. [a *rosy* future] —**ros′i·ly** *adv.* —**ros′i·ness** *n.*

rot (rot) *vi.* **rot′ted, rot′ting** [OE. *rotian*] **1.** to decompose gradually by the action of bacteria, etc.; decay **2.** to become unhealthy, etc. [to *rot* in prison] **3.** to become morally corrupt —*vt.* **1.** to cause to rot, or decompose **2.** *same as* RET —*n.* **1.** a rotting or being rotten; decay **2.** something rotting or rotten **3.** any of various plant and animal diseases, esp. of sheep, causing decay **4.** [Colloq.] nonsense —*interj.* an exclamation of disgust, anger, etc.

ro·ta (rōt′ə) *n.* [L., a wheel: see ROLL] **1.** a list or register of names, esp. one listing the rotation of duties **2.** [R-] *R.C.Ch.* the supreme ecclesiastical tribunal for judging cases brought before the Holy See

ro·ta·ry (rōt′ər ē) *adj.* [< ML. < L. *rota*, a wheel] **1.** turning around a central point or axis, as a wheel; rotating **2.** *a)* having a rotating part or parts *b)* having blades that rotate on a hub [a *rotary* lawn mower] —*n., pl.* **-ries** a rotary machine or engine

Rotary Club any local organization of an international club (**Rotary International**) of business and professional men, founded in 1905 to promote community welfare —**Ro·tar·i·an** (rō ter′ē ən) *n., adj.* —**Ro·tar′i·an·ism** *n.*

rotary press a printing press with curved plates mounted on rotating cylinders, for printing on paper fed from a roll

ro·ta·ry-wing aircraft (-wiŋ′) an aircraft, as the helicopter, sustained in the air by rotors

ro·tate (rō tāt′) *vi., vt.* **-tat′ed, -tat′ing** [< L. pp. of *rotare* < *rota*, a wheel] **1.** to move or turn around, as a wheel **2.** to go or cause to go in a regular and recurring succession of changes [to *rotate* crops] —**ro·tat′a·ble** *adj.* —**ro·ta·tive** (rō′tāt iv, rōt′ə tiv) *adj.*

ro·ta·tion (rō tā′shən) *n.* **1.** a rotating or being rotated **2.** regular and recurring succession of changes —**ro·ta′tion·al** *adj.*

rotation of crops a system of rotating in a fixed order the kinds of crops grown in the same field, to maintain soil fertility

ro·ta·tor (rō tāt′ər) *n.* [L.] a person or thing that rotates; specif., *Anat. pl.* **ro·ta·to·res** (rō′tə tôr′ēz) a muscle that serves to rotate a part of the body

ro·ta·to·ry (rō′tə tər ē, rōt′ə-) *adj.* **1.** of, or having the nature of, rotation **2.** rotating; rotary **3.** going or following in rotation **4.** causing rotation

rote (rōt) *n.* [< ?] a fixed, mechanical way of doing something; routine —**by rote** by memory alone, without thought

ro·te·none (rōt′ə nōn) *n.* [Jap. *roten*, an East Indian plant + -ONE] a white, odourless, crystalline substance used in insecticides

rot·gut (rot′gut′) *n.* [ROT + GUT] [Slang] raw, low-grade whisky or other spirit

ro·ti·fer (rōt′ə fər) *n.* [ModL. < L. *rota*, wheel + -FER] any of various microscopic, invertebrate freshwater animals,

having a ring or rings of cilia at the front end of the body —**ro·tif′er·al** (rō tif′ər əl), **ro·tif′er·ous, ro·tif′er·an** *adj.*

ro·tis·ser·ie (rō tis′ər ē) *n.* [Fr. < MFr., ult. < *rostir*, to ROAST] **1.** a shop where roasted meats are sold **2.** a grill with a spit, often electrically turned

ro·to·gra·vure (rōt′ə grə vyŏŏr′) *n.* [< L. *rota*, a wheel + GRAVURE] **1.** a printing process using photogravure cylinders on a rotary press **2.** [Chiefly U.S.] a print or newspaper pictorial section printed by this process

ro·tor (rōt′ər) *n.* [< ROTATE] **1.** the rotating part of a motor, dynamo, etc. **2.** a device, as on a helicopter, consisting of generally horizontal aerofoils with their hub

ro·to·va·tor (rōt′ə vāt′ər) *n.* [< *rotavator* < ROTA(RY) + (CULTI)VATOR] a motorized cultivator with rotary blades —**ro′to·vate′** *vt.*

rot·ten (rot′n) *adj.* [ON. *rotinn*] **1.** decayed; decomposed; spoiled **2.** smelling of decay; putrid **3.** morally corrupt or offensive; dishonest, etc. **4.** unsound or weak, as if decayed within **5.** [Colloq.] very bad, disagreeable, etc. [a *rotten* show] **6.** [Colloq.] unwell; in a deplorable state —**rot′-ten·ly** *adv.* —**rot′ten·ness** *n.*

rotten borough before 1832, a borough with only a few voters but with the right to send a representative to Parliament

rot·ter (rot′ər) *n.* [< ROT] [Colloq.] a despicable fellow; cad; bounder

ro·tund (rō tund′) *adj.* [L. *rotundus*, akin to *rota*, a wheel] **1.** round or rounded out; plump or stout **2.** full-toned; sonorous [a *rotund* voice] —**ro·tun′di·ty, ro·tund′ness** *n.* —**ro·tund′ly** *adv.*

ro·tun·da (rō tun′də) *n.* [< It. < L. fem. of *rotundus*, rotund] a round building, hall, or room, esp. one with a dome

rou·ble (rōō′b'l) *n.* *same as* RUBLE

rou·é (rōō ā′) *n.* [Fr., pp. of *rouer*, to break on the wheel < L. *rota*, a wheel] a dissipated man; debauchee; rake

rouge (rōōzh) *n.* [Fr., red < L. *rubeus*] **1.** any of various reddish cosmetic powders, pastes, etc. for colouring the cheeks and lips **2.** a reddish powder, mainly ferric oxide, for polishing jewellery, metal, etc.—*vi., vt.* **rouged, roug′ing** to use cosmetic rouge (on)

rough (ruf) *adj.* [OE. *ruh*] **1.** *a)* not smooth or level; uneven [a *rough* surface] *b)* not easily travelled; overgrown, wild, etc. [*rough* country] **2.** shaggy [a *rough* coat] **3.** moving violently; agitated; specif., *a)* stormy; tempestuous [*rough* weather] *b)* boisterous or disorderly [*rough* play] **4.** harsh, rude, brutal, etc. [a *rough* temper] **5.** sounding, feeling, or tasting harsh **6.** lacking comforts and conveniences [the *rough* life of pioneers] **7.** not refined or polished [a *rough* diamond] **8.** not finished, perfected, etc. [a *rough* sketch, a *rough* estimate] **9.** needing strength rather than skill or intelligence [*rough* work] **10.** [Colloq.] difficult, severe, etc. [a *rough* time] **11.** [Colloq.] ill or physically upset **12.** *Phonet.* pronounced with an aspirate; having the sound of *h* —*n.* **1.** rough ground **2.** rough material or condition **3.** a rough sketch or draft **4.** a rough person; rowdy **5.** *Golf* any part of the course where grass, weeds, etc. grow uncut —*adv.* in a rough manner —*vt.* **1.** to make rough; roughen **2.** to treat roughly (often with *up*) **3.** to make or shape roughly (usually with *in* or *out*) [*rough* out a scheme] —*vi.* to behave roughly —**in the rough** in a rough or crude state —**rough edge** (or **side**) **of one's tongue** harsh or severe words —**rough it** to live without comforts and conveniences —**rough up** [Slang] to attack someone violently —**rough′ish** *adj.* —**rough′ly** *adv.* —**rough′ness** *n.*

rough·age (ruf′ij) *n.* **1.** rough or coarse substance; specif., coarse food or fodder, as bran, straw, etc., serving as a stimulus to peristalsis

rough-and-read·y (ruf′′n red′ē) *adj.* **1.** rough, or crude, rude, etc., but effective [*rough-and-ready* methods] **2.** characterized by rough vigour rather than refinement, formality, etc.

rough-and-tum·ble (-tum′b'l) *adj.* violent and disorderly, with no concern for rules —*n.* a fight or struggle of this kind

rough·cast (ruf′käst′) *n.* **1.** a coarse plaster for covering outside surfaces, as walls **2.** a rough pattern or crude model —*vt.* **-cast′, -cast′ing** **1.** to cover (walls, etc.) with roughcast **2.** to make or shape in a rough form

rough diamond **1.** a diamond in its natural state **2.** a person or thing of fine quality but lacking polish

rough-dry (-drī′) *vt.* **-dried′, -dry′ing** to dry (washed laundry) without ironing: also **rough′dry′**—*adj.* washed and dried but not ironed

rough·en (ruf′'n) *vt., vi.* to make or become rough

rough grazing uncultivated pasturage

rough-hew (ruf′hyōō′) *vt.* **-hewed′, -hewed′** or **-hewn′, -hew′ing** **1.** to hew (timber, stone, etc.) roughly, or without finishing or smoothing **2.** to form roughly Also **rough′hew′**

rough·house (ruf′hous′) *n.* [Slang] rough or boisterous play, fighting, etc. —*vt.* **-housed′, -hous′ing** [Slang] to

treat roughly or boisterously —*vi.* [Slang] to take part in roughhouse
rough·neck (-nek') *n.* [U.S. Slang] a rough person; rowdy
rough·rid·er (-rīd'ər) *n.* 1. a person who breaks horses for riding 2. a person who does much hard, rough riding 3. [U.S. history] [R-] a member of Theodore Roosevelt's volunteer cavalry regiment in the Spanish-American War: also **Rough Rider**
rough·shod (-shod') *adj.* shod with horseshoes that have metal points to prevent slipping —**ride roughshod over** to treat in a harsh, arrogant, inconsiderate manner
rough stuff [Slang] rowdy, wild, or violent behaviour
rou·lade (rōō läd') *n.* [Fr. < *rouler*, to ROLL] 1. a rapid series of tones sung to one syllable 2. a slice of meat rolled and cooked
rou·lette (rōō let') *n.* [Fr. < OFr. dim. of *roele*, a small wheel, ult. < L. *rota*, a wheel] 1. a gambling game played by rolling a small ball around a shallow bowl with a revolving inner disc (**roulette wheel**) with red and black numbered compartments 2. a small toothed wheel for making rows of marks or dots, as between postage stamps —*vt.* **-let'ted, -let'ting** to make marks, dots, etc. in with a roulette
Rou·ma·nian (rōō mān'yən, -mā'nē ən) *same as* RUMANIAN
round (round) *adj.* [< OFr. < L. *rotundus*, rotund] 1. shaped like a ball; spherical 2. *a)* shaped like a circle, ring, etc.; circular or curved *b)* shaped like a cylinder; cylindrical 3. plump or stout 4. with or involving a circular motion [a *round* dance] 5. full; complete [a *round* dozen] 6. expressed by a whole number, or in tens, hundreds, etc. 7. large in amount, size, etc. [a *round* sum] 8. mellow and full in tone; sonorous 9. brisk; vigorous [a *round* pace] 10. outspoken; plain and blunt 11. *Phonet.* pronounced with the lips forming an oval [a *round* vowel] —*n.* 1. something round; thing that is spherical, circular, curved, etc. 2. a rung of a ladder or a chair 3. [Chiefly U.S.] the part of a beef animal between the rump and the leg: in full, **round of beef** 4. movement in a circular course 5. *same as* ROUND DANCE 6. a series or succession of actions, events, etc. [a *round* of parties] 7. the complete extent [the *round* of human beliefs] 8. [*often pl.*] a regular, customary circuit, as by a watchman of his station 9. a single serving, as of drinks, for each in a group 10. a single slice of bread [a *round* of toast] 11. *a)* a single shot from a rifle, etc. or from a number of rifles fired together *b)* ammunition for such a shot 12. a single outburst, as of applause 13. *Games & Sports* a single period or division of action; specif., *a)* *Boxing* any of the timed periods of a fight *b)* *Golf* a number of holes as a unit of competition 14. *Music* a short song for two or more persons or groups, in which the second starts when the first reaches the second phrase, etc. —*vt.* 1. to make round 2. to pronounce with rounded lips 3. to make plump 4. to express as a round number (usually with *off*) 5. to complete; finish 6. to make a circuit of [we *rounded* the island] 7. to make a turn about [to *round* a corner] —*vi.* 1. to make a complete or partial circuit 2. to turn; reverse direction 3. to become round or plump —*adv.* 1. in a circle; along a circular course 2. through a recurring period of time [to work the year *round*] 3. from one person or place to another [the peddler came *round*] 4. for each of several [not enough to go *round*] 5. in circumference 6. on all sides; in every direction 7. about; near 8. in a roundabout way 9. here and there 10. with a rotating movement 11. in or to the opposite direction 12. in or to an opposite viewpoint —*prep.* 1. so as to encircle or surround 2. on the circumference or border of 3. on all sides of 4. in the vicinity of 5. in a circuit or course through 6. here and there in 7. so as to make a curve or circuit about —**go the round** (or **rounds**) 1. to be circulated widely, as a story, rumour, etc. 2. to walk one's regular circuit: also **make one's rounds** —**in the round** 1. with the audience, etc. seated all around a central stage, etc. 2. in full and completely rounded form, not in relief: said of sculpture 3. in full detail —**round about** 1. in or to the opposite direction 2. in every direction around —**round down** (or **up**) to lower (or raise) a number or price to the nearest whole or convenient number —**round on** to attack, esp. verbally —**round up** 1. to drive together in a herd, group, etc. 2. [Colloq.] to gather or assemble —**round'ish** *adj.* —**round'ness** *n.*
round·a·bout (round'ə bout') *adj.* 1. not straight or straightforward; indirect [*roundabout* methods] 2. encircling; enclosing 3. approximately —*n.* 1. something that is indirect or circuitous 2. a road junction where traffic flows around a central island 3. a circular, revolving platform with wooden animals and seats on it, used in a funfair, etc.
round dance 1. a dance with the dancers moving in a circle 2. any of several dances, as the waltz, polka, etc., in which the couples make circular movements
round·ed (roun'did) *adj.* 1. made round 2. having variety in tastes, abilities, etc. [a well-*rounded* person]
roun·del (roun'd'l) *n.* [ME. < OFr. *rondel*, orig. dim. of

roond, ROUND] 1. orig., something round 2. a small circular window, pane, panel, medallion, etc. 3. a variant of the rondel 4. a dance in a circle
roun·de·lay (roun'də lā') *n.* [< MFr. dim. of *rondel*, a rondel] a simple song in which some phrase, line, etc. is continually repeated
round·er (roun'dər) *n.* 1. a complete circuit of bases in the game of rounders 2. [*pl. with sing. v.*] a bat-and-ball game in which players run between bases when the ball is hit, scoring if they run round all four bases
Round·head (round'hed') *n.* a member of the Parliamentary, or Puritan, party in England during the English civil war (1642–52)
round·house (-hous') *n.* 1. [U.S.] a building, generally circular, with a turntable in the centre, for storing and repairing railway engines 2. a cabin on the after part of a ship's quarter-deck 3. *Boxing* a wide swing or hook, as to the head
round·ly (-lē) *adv.* 1. in a round form 2. in a round manner; specif., *a)* vigorously, severely, etc. *b)* fully
round robin 1. a petition, protest, etc. with the signatures written in a circle to conceal the order of signing 2. [U.S.] a tournament in which every entrant is matched with every other one
round-shoul·dered (-shōl'dərd) *adj.* stooped because the shoulders are bent forwards
Round Table 1. the table around which King Arthur and his knights sat 2. King Arthur and his knights, collectively 3. [r- t-] *a)* an informal discussion group *b)* the informal discussion—**round'-ta'ble** *adj.*
round-the-clock (-*th*ə klok') *adj., adv.* continuously
round trip a trip to a place and back again —**round'-trip'** *adj.*
round·up (-up') *n.* 1. *a)* the act of driving cattle, etc. together on the range and collecting them in a herd, as for branding *b)* [U.S.] the cowboys, horses, etc. that do this work 2. any similar driving together or collecting 3. a summary, as of news
round·worm (-wurm') *n.* 1. *same as* NEMATODE 2. a species of nematode worms, living as parasites, esp. in the intestines of man and other mammals
rouse (rouz) *vt.* **roused, rous'ing** [prob. < Anglo-Fr. or OFr.] 1. to stir up (game) from cover to flight or attack 2. to stir up, as to anger or action; excite 3. to wake —*vi.* 1. to leave cover: said of game 2. to wake —*n.* a rousing —**rous'er** *n.* —**rous'ing** *adj.* —**rous'ing·ly** *adv.*
roust·a·bout (roust'ə bout') *n.* [*roust*, dial. var. of ROUSE + ABOUT] 1. [U.S.] *a)* a deckhand or waterfront labourer *b)* an unskilled or transient labourer, as in a circus 2. [Aust.] an odd-job man on a sheep station
rout¹ (rout) *n.* [< OFr. < L. *rupta*: see ROUTE] 1. a disorderly crowd; rabble 2. a disorderly flight, as of defeated troops 3. an overwhelming defeat 4. [Archaic] a group of people; company —*vt.* 1. to put to disorderly flight 2. to defeat overwhelmingly
rout² (rout) *vi.* [var. of ROOT²] 1. to dig for food with the snout, as a pig 2. to poke or rummage about —*vt.* 1. to dig up with the snout 2. to force out —**rout out** 1. to expose to view 2. to scoop, gouge, or hollow out 3. to make (a person) get out, esp. of bed —**rout up** to get by poking about —**rout'er** *n.*
route (rōōt) *n.* [OFr. < L. *rupta* (via), broken (path) < pp. of *rumpere*, to break] 1. a road, etc. for travelling 2. *a)* any regularly followed course or way *b)* [U.S.] a regular course travelled as in delivering post, milk, etc. —*vt.* **rout'ed, rout'ing** to send by a specified route [to *route* goods through Birmingham]
route march a training march undertaken by troops
rou·tine (rōō tēn') *n.* [Fr. < *route*: see prec.] 1. a regular, unvarying procedure, customary, prescribed, or habitual, as of work 2. a theatrical skit 3. a series of dance steps 4. a set of coded instructions for a computer —*adj.* having the nature of or using routine —**rou·tine'ly** *adv.* —**rou·tin'ism** *n.* —**rou·tin'ize** *vt.* **-ized, -iz'ing**
roux (rōō) *n.* [Fr. *roux* (*beurre*), reddish-brown (butter)] a cooked mixture of butter (or other fat) and flour, used for thickening sauces, soups, gravies, etc.
rove¹ (rōv) *vi.* **roved, rov'ing** [< ME. *roven*, (in archery) to shoot at a target chosen at random] 1. to wander about; roam 2. to look around: said of the eyes —*vt.* to wander over; roam through [he *roved* the woods] —*n.* a roving; ramble
rove² (rōv) *vt.* [< ?] to twist (fibres) together and draw out into a strand (**roving**) before spinning
rove³ (rōv) alt. pt. & pp. of REEVE²
rov·en (rōv''n) alt. pp. of REEVE²
rov·er (rō'vər) *n.* [ROVE¹ + -ER] 1. a person or thing that roves 2. [R-] former name for VENTURE SCOUT 3. *Archery* a mark or target chosen at random
roving commission the authorization to go wherever necessary to conduct an enquiry or transact business
row¹ (rō) *n.* [OE. *ræw*] 1. a number of people or things

arranged in a line   **2.** any of the lines of seats side by side in a theatre, etc.   **3.** a street with a line of buildings, as of a specified nature, on either side —*vt.* to arrange or put in rows —**hard** (or **long**) **row to hoe** anything hard or tiring to do —**in a row** one after the other

row² (rō) *vt.* [OE. *rowan*] **1.** to move (a boat, etc.) on water by using oars   **2.** to carry in a rowing boat [*row* us across the lake]   **3.** to use (oarsmen, a stroke, etc. as specified) in rowing   **4.** to take part in (a race) by rowing —*vi.* **1.** to use oars in moving a boat   **2.** to be moved by oars: said of a boat —*n.* **1.** a rowing   **2.** a trip made by rowing boat —**row′er** *n.*

row³ (rau) *n.* [< ? ROUSE] a noisy quarrel, dispute, or disturbance; squabble or brawl —*vi.* to take part in a row

row·an (rō′ən, rou′-) *n.* [< Scand.] **1.** the mountain ash, a tree with white flowers and reddish berries   **2.** its fruit: also **row′an·ber·ry,** *pl.* **-ries**

row·dy (rou′dē) *n., pl.* **-dies** [< ? ROW³] a person whose behaviour is rough, quarrelsome, and disorderly; hoodlum —*adj.* **-di·er, -di·est** of or like a rowdy —**row′di·ly** *adv.* —**row′di·ness** *n.* —**row′dy·ish** *adj.* —**row′dy·ism** *n.*

row·el (rou′əl) *n.* [< OFr. *roele:* see ROULETTE] a small wheel with sharp projecting points, forming the end of a spur —*vt.* **-elled, -el·ling** to spur or prick (a horse) with a rowel

rowing boat a boat made to be rowed: U.S. **row′boat**

row·lock (rō′lok′, rol′ək) *n.* [altered (after ROW²) < OARLOCK] a device, often U-shaped, for holding the oar in place in rowing

roy·al (roi′əl) *adj.* [< OFr. < L. *regalis:* see REGAL] **1.** of a king, queen, or other sovereign [a *royal* edict, the *royal* family]   **2.** having the rank of a king or queen   **3.** of a kingdom, its government, etc. [the *royal* fleet]   **4.** *a)* founded or supported by a king or queen *b)* in the service of the Crown   **5.** suitable for a king or queen; magnificent, stately, regal, etc.   **6.** unusually large, fine, etc. —*n.* a small sail set on the royal mast —**roy′al·ly** *adv.*

Royal Air Force the airborne branch of the British armed forces

royal blue a deep, vivid blue

Royal British Legion, the an organization founded in 1921 to help former members of the armed forces

Royal Family the reigning monarch and the members of his or her family

royal flush the highest poker hand, consisting of the ace, king, queen, jack, and ten of the same suit

roy·al·ist (-ist) *n.* a person who supports a king or monarchy, esp. in times of revolution —**roy′al·ism** *n.*

royal jelly a highly nutritious food fed by worker bees to all very young larvae and continued to be fed to larvae chosen to be queens

Royal Marines a branch of the Armed Forces trained for land and sea combat

royal mast a small mast above the topgallant mast

Royal Navy the seafaring branch of the British armed forces

royal palm any of a genus of tall, ornamental palm trees

Royal prerogative the special privilege of a sovereign to act at his own unrestricted discretion

Roy·als (roi′əlz) *n.* **1.** formerly, the regiment of the Royal Scots, the first foot regiment in the British Army   **2.** [Colloq.] members of the Royal Family

roy·al·ty (roi′əl tē) *n., pl.* **-ties** **1.** the rank, status, or power of a king or queen   **2.** a royal person or, collectively, royal persons   **3.** a kingdom   **4.** royal quality or character; regalness, nobility, etc.   **5.** [*usually pl.*] a right, privilege, etc. of a monarch   **6.** *a)* a share of the proceeds paid to the owner of a right, as a patent, for its use *b)* such a share paid to one who leases out lands rich in oil or minerals *c)* a share of the proceeds from his work paid to an author, composer, etc.

royal warrant the authorization for a tradesman to advertise that he supplies goods to a member of the royal family

Roy·ston crow (roi′stən) *same as* HOODED CROW

roz·zer (roz′ər) *n.* [< ?] [Slang] a policeman

rpm, r.p.m. revolutions per minute

-rrha·gi·a (rā′jē ə) [ModL. < Gr. < *rhēgnynai,* to burst] a combining form meaning abnormal discharge or flow: also **-rrhage** (rij), **-rrhag′y** (rā′jē)

-rrhoe·a (rē′ə) [ModL. < Gr. < *rhein,* to flow] a combining form meaning a flow, discharge: also U.S. **-rrhea**

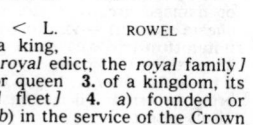

ROWEL

ROYAL PALM

rubidium

Rs, rs. rupees

R.S. Royal Society

R.S.A. **1.** Royal Scottish Academy   **2.** Royal Society of Arts

R.S.F.S.R., RSFSR Russian Soviet Federated Socialist Republic

R.S.M. regimental sergeant major

R.S.P.C.A. Royal Society for the Prevention of Cruelty to Animals

RSV, R.S.V. Revised Standard Version (of the Bible)

R.S.V.P., r.s.v.p. [Fr. *répondez s'il vous plâit*] please reply

rt. right

Rt. Hon. Right Honourable

Ru *Chem.* ruthenium

R.U. Rugby Union

rub (rub) *vt.* **rubbed, rub′bing** [ME. *rubben,* akin to Dan. *rubbe*] **1.** to move (one's hand, a cloth, etc.) back and forth over (something) firmly   **2.** to spread or apply (polish, salve, etc.) on a surface   **3.** to move (a thing) against something else, or move (things) over each other with pressure and friction   **4.** to put into a specified condition by applying pressure and friction [*rub* it dry]   **5.** to make sore by rubbing   **6.** to remove by rubbing (out, off, etc.) —*vi.* **1.** to move with pressure and friction (on, against, etc.)   **2.** to rub something   **3.** to admit of being rubbed or removed by rubbing (often with *off, out,* etc.) —*n.* **1.** a rubbing   **2.** an obstacle or difficulty   **3.** something that irritates, annoys, etc. —**rub down 1.** to massage   **2.** to smooth, polish, etc. by rubbing —**rub it in** [Colloq.] to keep reminding someone of his failure or mistake —**rub off on** to be left on as a mark, as by rubbing or, figuratively, by close contact —**rub out 1.** to erase, usually with a rubber   **2.** [Chiefly U.S. Slang] to kill —**rub salt into a wound** to make a bad thing worse —**rub shoulders with** to come into contact with socially —**rub up the wrong way** to annoy or irritate

ru·ba·to (rōō bät′ō) *adj., adv.* [It. < (*tempo*) *rubato,* stolen (time)] *Music* with some notes lengthened and others shortened in dropping strict tempo in a passage for effect —*n., pl.* **-tos** **1.** the use of rubato   **2.** a rubato passage, phrase, etc.

rub·ber¹ (rub′ər) *n.* **1.** a person or thing that rubs   **2.** [from use as an eraser] an elastic substance produced from the milky sap of various tropical plants or synthetically   **3.** something made of this substance; specif., a piece of rubber used for erasing writing, typing etc. —*adj.* made of rubber —**rub′ber·like′** *adj.* —**rub′ber·y** *adj.*

rub·ber² (rub′ər) *n.* [< ?] **1.** *Bridge* a series limited to three games, two of which must be won to win the series   **2.** any game played to break a tie in games won: usually **rubber game**

rubber band a narrow, continuous band of rubber as for holding small objects together

rubber cement an adhesive made of unvulcanized rubber in a quickly evaporating solvent

rub·ber·ize (-īz′) *vt.* **-ized′, -iz′ing** to coat or impregnate with rubber

rub·ber·neck (-nek′) *n.* [Colloq.] a person who gazes about in curiosity, as a sightseer —*vi.* to gaze about in this way

rubber plant **1.** any plant yielding latex from which crude rubber is formed   **2.** a house plant with large, glossy, leathery leaves

rubber stamp **1.** a stamp made of rubber, inked on a pad and used for printing signatures, dates, etc.   **2.** [Colloq.] *a)* a person, bureau, etc. that approves something in a routine way, without thought *b)* any routine approval —**rub′-ber-stamp′** *vt., adj.*

rub·bing (rub′iŋ) *n.* an impression of a raised or incised design, etc. taken by placing a paper over it and rubbing with graphite, wax, etc.

rub·bish (rub′ish) *n.* [? ult. < base of RUB] **1.** any material thrown away as worthless; waste food, etc.   **2.** worthless, foolish ideas, statements, etc.; nonsense —**rub′bish·y** *adj.*

rub·ble (rub′'l) *n.* [akin to RUBBISH, RUB] **1.** rough, broken pieces of stone, brick, etc.   **2.** masonry made of such pieces: also **rub′ble·work′**   **3.** debris from buildings, etc., resulting from earthquake, bombing, etc. —**rub′bly** *adj.*

rub·down (rub′doun′) *n.* a massage

rube (rōōb) *n.* [*Reuben,* the masculine name] [U.S. Slang] a country person regarded as simple, unsophisticated, etc.

ru·bel·la (rōō bel′ə) *n.* [ModL. < L. *rubellus* < *ruber,* red] a contagious virus disease, characterized by swollen glands of the neck and small red spots on the skin; German measles

ru·be·o·la (rōō bē′ə lə, rōō′bē ō′lə) *n.* [ModL., neut. dim. of L. *rubeus,* red] *same as* MEASLES (sense 1)

Ru·bi·con (rōō′bi kon′) small river in N Italy crossed by Caesar to march on Rome with his army (49 B.C.), starting a civil war —**cross the Rubicon** to make a decisive move that cannot be undone

ru·bi·cund (rōō′bi kund′) *adj.* [< Fr. < L. < *ruber,* red] reddish; ruddy —**ru′bi·cun′di·ty** *n.*

ru·bid·i·um (rōō bid′ē əm) *n.* [ModL. < L. *rubidus,* red (from red lines in its spectrum)] a soft, silvery-white metallic chemical element, resembling potassium: symbol, Rb; at. wt., 85.47; at. no., 37

ru·big·i·nous (rōō bij′ə nəs) *adj.* [LL. *rubiginosus* < L. *rubigo,* rust] rust-coloured; reddish-brown

ru·ble (rōō′b'l) *n.* [Russ. *rubl'*] the monetary unit of the U.S.S.R.: see MONETARY UNITS, table

ru·bric (rōō′brik) *n.* [< MFr. < L. *rubrica,* rubric < *ruber,* red] 1. in early books and manuscripts, a chapter heading, initial letter, etc. printed or written in red, decorative lettering, etc. 2. a heading, title, etc., as of a chapter, a law, etc. 3. a direction in a prayer book 4. a note of comment; gloss 5. an established rule of procedure —**ru′bri·cal** *adj.* —**ru′bri·cal·ly** *adv.*

ru·by (rōō′bē) *n.,* pl. **-bies** [< OFr. *rubi,* ult. < L. *rubeus,* red] 1. a clear, deep-red variety of corundum, valued as a precious stone 2. deep red —*adj.* deep-red

ruby wedding a couple's fortieth wedding anniversary

R.U.C. Royal Ulster Constabulary

ruche (rōōsh) *n.* [Fr., lit., beehive < OFr. < Celt.] a fluting or pleating of lace, ribbon, net, etc. for trimming garments, esp. at the neck or wrist

ruch·ing (rōō′shiŋ) *n.* 1. ruches collectively 2. material used to make ruches

ruck¹ (ruk) *n.* [ME. *ruke,* a heap < ON. *hroki,* a heap, pile] 1. orig. a heap or stack 2. a large quantity, mass or crowd, esp., of undistinguished people or things 3. the horses left behind by the leaders in a race 4. *Rugby* a loose scrimmage —*vi.* *Rugby* to try to win the ball by scrimmaging

ruck² (ruk) *n., vt., vi* [prop. via dial. < ON. *hrukka*] crease, fold, wrinkle, or pucker: also **ruck′le**

ruck·sack (ruk′sak′) *n.* [G. < *Rücken,* the back + *Sack,* a sack] a kind of knapsack

ruc·tion (ruk′shən) *n.* [altered < INSURRECTION] [Colloq.] noisy confusion; uproar; row; disturbance: also chiefly U.S. **ruck′us**

rud·der (rud′ər) *n.* [OE. *rother,* steering oar] 1. a broad, flat, movable piece of wood or metal hinged vertically at the stern of a boat or ship, used for steering 2. a piece like this on an aircraft, etc. —**rud′der·less** *adj.*

rud·der·post (-pōst′) *n.* the sternpost or the vertical shaft to which the rudder is fastened

rud·dy (rud′ē) *adj.* **-di·er, -di·est** [OE. *rudig*] 1. having a healthy red colour 2. red or reddish —**rud′di·ness** *n.*

rude (rōōd) *adj.* **rud′er, rud′est** [OFr. < L. *rudis*] 1. crude or rough in form [a *rude* hut] 2. barbarous or ignorant [*rude* savages] 3. lacking refinement; coarse, uncouth, etc. 4. discourteous; impolite [a *rude* reply] 5. rough; harsh [a *rude* awakening] 6. harsh in sound; discordant 7. simple or primitive 8. not carefully worked out —**rude′ly** *adv.* —**rude′ness** *n.*

ru·di·ment (rōō′də mənt) *n.* [L. *rudimentum* < *rudis,* rude] 1. a first principle or element, as of a subject to be learned [the *rudiments* of physics] 2. a first slight beginning of something 3. *Biol.* an incompletely developed or vestigial organ or part

ru·di·men·ta·ry (rōō′də men′tər ē, -men′trē) *adj.* 1. of rudiments or first principles; elementary 2. incompletely developed 3. vestigial Also **ru′di·men′tal** —**ru′di·men′ta·ri·ly** *adv.* —**ru′di·men′ta·ri·ness** *n.*

rue¹ (rōō) *vi,* **rued, ru′ing** [OE. *hreowan*] to feel sorrow or remorse (for); regret; repent —*n.* [Archaic] sorrow or regret

rue² (rōō) *n.* [< OFr. < L. *ruta* < Gr. *rhytē*] a strong-scented herb with yellow flowers and bitter-tasting leaves formerly used in medicine

rue·ful (rōō′fəl) *adj.* 1. causing sorrow or pity 2. feeling or showing sorrow or regret, esp. in a wry way —**rue′ful·ly** *adv.* —**rue′ful·ness** *n.*

ruff¹ (ruf) *n.* [contr. of RUFFLE¹, *n.*] 1. a high, frilled, stiff collar worn by men and women in the 16th and 17th cents. 2. a ring of feathers or fur standing out about the neck of a bird or animal 3. a Eurasian sandpiper the male of which grows a ruff in the breeding season —**ruffed** *adj.*

ruff² (ruf) *n.* [< OFr. *roffle*] *Card Games* the act of trumping —*vt., vi. Card Games* to trump

ruffed grouse a N. American game bird with neck feathers that can be spread into a ruff

ruf·fi·an (ruf′ē ən, ruf′yən) *n.* [< Fr. < It. *ruffiano,* a pander] a brutal, lawless person; bully —*adj.* brutal and lawless: also **ruf′fi·an·ly** —**ruf′fi·an·ism** *n.*

ruf·fle (ruf′'l) *vt.* **-fled, -fling** [< ON. or MLowG.] 1. to disturb the smoothness of; ripple [wind *ruffling* the water] 2. to gather into ruffles 3. to put ruffles on 4. to make (feathers, etc.) stand up as in a ruff 5. to disturb or annoy 6. *a)* to turn (pages) rapidly *b)* to shuffle (cards) —*vi.* 1. to

RUDDER

RUFF

become uneven 2. to become disturbed, annoyed, etc. —*n.* 1. a strip of cloth, lace, etc. gathered in pleats or puckers and used for trimming 2. a bird's ruff 3. a disturbance; annoyance 4. a ripple —**ruf′fly** *adj.* **-fli·er, -fli·est**

ruf·fle² (ruf′'l) *n.* [prob. echoic] a low, continuous beating of a drum —*vi., vt.* **-fled, -fling** to beat (a drum, etc.) with a ruffle

ru·fous (rōō′fəs) *adj.* [L. *rufus,* red] brownish-red

rug (rug) *n.* [< Scand.] 1. a piece of thick, often napped fabric, woven strips of rag, an animal skin, etc. used as a floor covering 2. a heavy blanket, etc., laid over the lap and legs for warmth

Rug·by (rug′bē) *n.* [first played at *Rugby,* a boys' school in Warwickshire] a kind of football in which there are 15 (**Rugby Union**) or 13 (**Rugby League**) players on each side, action is continuous, and the oval ball may be kicked, thrown laterally, or run with: also **Rugby Football, rug′ger**

rug·ged (rug′id) *adj.* [< Scand.] 1. having a surface that is uneven, rough, craggy, etc. [*rugged* ground] 2. strong, irregular, and lined [a *rugged* face] 3. stormy [*rugged* weather] 4. sounding harsh 5. severe; hard [a *rugged* life] 6. not polished or refined; rude 7. [Chiefly U.S.] strong; robust; vigorous; hardy 8. [Colloq.] requiring skill, endurance, etc. —**rug′ged·ly** *adv.* —**rug′ged·ness** *n.*

ru·in (rōō′in) *n.* [< OFr. < L. *ruina* < *ruere,* to fall] 1. [*pl.*] the remains of a fallen building, city, etc., or of something destroyed, devastated, decayed, etc. 2. anything that has been destroyed, etc. 3. the state of being destroyed, dilapidated, etc. 4. downfall, destruction, decay, etc., as of a thing or person, or the cause of this [gambling was his *ruin*] —*vt.* to bring to ruin; specif., *a)* to destroy, or damage greatly *b)* to make bankrupt *c)* to seduce (a chaste woman) —*vi.* to go or come to ruin

ru·in·a·tion (rōō′ə nā′shən) *n.* 1. a ruining or being ruined 2. anything that ruins

ru·in·ous (rōō′ə nəs) *adj.* 1. falling or fallen into ruin 2. bringing ruin; disastrous —**ru′in·ous·ly** *adv.* —**ru′in·ous·ness** *n.*

rule (rōōl) *n.* [< OFr. < L. *regula,* a guiding line < *regere,* to lead straight] 1. *a)* an authoritative regulation for conduct, method, procedure, etc. *b)* an established practice that serves as a guide [*rules* of grammar] 2. a set of regulations in a religious order 3. a habit; custom 4. customary course of events [famine is the *rule* following war] 5. *a)* government; reign *b)* the period of a particular reign 6. a ruler 7. *Law a)* a court regulation *b)* a decision, order, etc. made by a judge or court in regard to a specific question or point *c)* a legal principle 8. *Printing* a thin strip of metal as high as type, used to print lines —*vt.* **ruled, rul′ing** 1. to have an influence over; guide 2. to keep under control 3. to have authority over; govern 4. to settle by decree; determine 5. to mark (lines) on (paper, etc.) as with a ruler —*vi.* 1. to govern 2. to prevail 3. to issue a formal decree about a question —**as a rule** usually —**rule out** 1. to decide to leave out from consideration 2. to make impossible; prevent —**rule the roost** to be in control

rule of three *Math.* the method of finding the fourth term of a proportion when three terms are given: the product of the first and last is equal to the product of the second and third

rule of thumb 1. a rule based on experience or practice rather than on scientific knowledge 2. any practical, though crude, method of estimating

rul·er (rōō′lər) *n.* 1. a person or thing that rules or governs 2. a thin strip of wood, metal, etc. with a straight edge, used in drawing lines, measuring, etc. —**rul′er·ship′** *n.*

rul·ing (-liŋ) *adj.* that rules; governing, predominating, etc. —*n.* 1. a governing 2. a decision made by a court 3. *a)* the making of ruled lines *b)* the lines so made

rum¹ (rum) *n.* [short for rumbullion, orig. a dial. term, tumult < ?] 1. a spirit distilled from fermented sugar cane, molasses, etc. 2. [Chiefly U.S.] alcohol in general

rum² (rum) *adj.* [< obs. *rum,* good] [Colloq.] 1. odd; strange 2. bad, poor, etc. [a *rum* joke] —**rum′my** *adj.* —**rum′ly** *adv.* —**rum′ness** *n.*

rum³ (rum) *n.* same as RUMMY

Ru·ma·ni·an (rōō mān′yən, -mā′nē ən) *adj.* of Rumania, its people, language, etc. —*n.* 1. a native or inhabitant of Rumania 2. the Romance language of the Rumanians

rum·ba (rum′bə, room′-; *Sp.* rōōm′bä) *n.* [AmSp., prob. of Afr. origin] 1. a dance of Cuban Negro origin 2. a ballroom adaptation of this, characterized by rhythmic movements of the lower part of the body 3. music for this dance —*vi.* to dance the rumba

rum·ble¹ (rum′b'l) *vi.* **-bled, -bling** [prob. < MDu. *rommelen*] 1. to make a deep, heavy rolling sound, as thunder 2. to move with such a sound —*vt.* 1. to cause to make, or move with, such a sound 2. to utter with such a sound —*n.* 1. a deep, heavy rolling sound 2. a widespread expression of discontent 3. [U.S. Slang] a gang fight —**rum′bler** *n.*

rum·ble² (rum′b'l) *vt.* [< ?] to see through; understand; grasp

rum·bus·tious (rum bus′chəs) *adj.* [altered (? after RUM¹) < ROBUSTIOUS] boisterous, unruly, etc.

ru·men (rōō′min) *n., pl.* **-mi·na** (-mi nə) [ModL. < L., gullet] the first stomach of a ruminant

ru·mi·nant (rōō′mə nənt) *adj.* [< L. prp. of *ruminare*, to ruminate < *rumen*, RUMEN] 1. chewing the cud 2. of the cud-chewing animals 3. meditative —*n.* any of a large group of four-footed, hoofed, even-toed, cud-chewing mammals, as the cow, sheep, goat, deer, camel, etc. —**ru′- mi·nant·ly** *adv.*

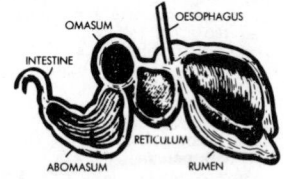

STOMACH OF A RUMINANT

ru·mi·nate (-nāt′) *vt., vi.* **-nat′ed, -nat′ing** [< L. pp. of *ruminare*: see prec.] 1. to chew (the cud), as a cow does 2. to meditate (on); muse —**ru′mi·na′tion** *n.* —**ru′mi·na′tive** *adj.*

rum·mage (rum′ij) *n.* [< MFr. < *arrumer*, to stow cargo < *run*, ship's hold < Frank.] 1. odds and ends 2. a rummaging search —*vt.* **-maged, -mag·ing** 1. to search through (a place, etc.) thoroughly by moving the contents about 2. to get or turn up by searching thoroughly (with *up* or *out*) —*vi.* to make a thorough search —**rum′mag·er** *n.*

rummage sale [U.S.] a jumble sale

rum·my (rum′ē) *adj.* **-mi·er, -mi·est** [RUM² + -Y²] [Colloq.] odd; strange; queer —*n.* any of certain card games in which the object is to match cards into sets of the same denomination or sequences of the same suit

ru·mour (rōō′mər) *n.* [< OFr. < L., noise] 1. general talk not based on definite knowledge; hearsay 2. an unconfirmed report, story, etc. in general circulation —*vt.* to tell or spread by rumour Also U.S. sp., **ru′mor**

rump (rump) *n.* [ON. *rumpr*] 1. the hind part of an animal, where the legs and back join 2. a cut of beef from this part 3. the buttocks 4. the last and unimportant part; remnant

rum·ple (rum′p'l) *n.* [< MDu. < *rompe*, a wrinkle] an uneven fold or crease; wrinkle —*vt., vi.* **-pled, -pling** 1. to make rumples (in); crumple 2. to make or become dishevelled —**rum′ply** *adv.*

Rump Parliament the remainder of the Long Parliament after Pride's Purge, which sat from 1648–1653 and from 1659–1660

rum·pus (rum′pəs) *n.* [< ?] [Colloq.] noisy disturbance

run (run) *vi.* **ran** or dial. **run, run, run′ning** [ON. *rinna* & OE. *rinnan*] 1. to go by moving the legs faster than in walking 2. a) to move swiftly [we *ran* to her aid] b) to go (*to*) for help [*run* to the doctor] 3. to associate (*with*) 4. to go, move, etc. easily and freely, without hindrance 5. to flee 6. to make a quick trip (*up to, down to,* etc.) for a brief stay 7. a) to take part in a contest or race b) to be a candidate in an election 8. to swim in migration: said of fish 9. to go, as on a schedule [a train *runs* between London and Liverpool] 10. to pass lightly and rapidly [his eyes *ran* over the page] 11. to circulate [a rumour *ran* through the town] 12. to climb or creep, as a vine 13. to unravel; ladder [her stocking *ran*] 14. to operate with parts that revolve or slide [the machine is *running*] 15. to flow [rivers *run* to the sea] 16. to melt and flow, as wax 17. a) to spread over cloth, etc. when moistened, as colours b) to be subject to this spreading, as fabric 18. to be wet with a flow [her eyes *ran* with tears] 19. a) to discharge pus, mucus, etc. b) to leak, as a tap 20. a) to appear in print, as in a newspaper b) to appear continuously [the play *ran* for a year] 21. a) to continue in effect [the law *runs* for ten years] b) to continue to occur [talent *runs* in the family] 22. to show a preference for (with *to*) [his taste *runs* to sweets] 23. a) to extend in a continuous line [a fence *runs* through the woods] b) to extend in scope (*from* one thing *to* another) 24. to pass into a specified condition, etc. [to *run* into trouble] 25. to be written, expressed, etc. in a specified way [the adage *runs* like this] 26. to be or continue at a specified size, price, etc. —*vt.* 1. to follow (a specified course) 2. to travel over [horses *ran* the range] 3. to perform as by running [to *run* a race] 4. to incur (a risk) 5. to get past [to *run* a blockade] 6. to hunt, chase (game, etc.) 7. to compete with as in a race 8. a) to enter (a horse, etc.) in a race b) to put up as a candidate for election 9. a) to make run, move, etc. b) to cause to go between points, as on a schedule c) to cause (an engine, etc.) to idle for a while 10. to bring or force into a specified condition by running [to *run* oneself into debt] 11. a) to convey, as in a vehicle b) to smuggle 12. to drive or force (an object) into, against, etc. (something) 13. to make pass, flow, etc., esp. rapidly, in a specified way, place, etc. [to *run* water into a glass] 14. a) to manage [to *run* a household] b) to conduct (a test, etc.) 15. to mark or draw (lines, as on a map) 16. to trace [to *run* a story back to its source] 17. to undergo (a fever, etc.) 18. to melt or smelt (ore) 19. to cast or mould; found 20. to publish (a story, etc.) as

in a newspaper 21 *Billiards,* etc. to complete successfully (a sequence of shots, etc.) 22. *Bridge* to lead (a suit) taking a series of tricks 23. *Cricket* to score (a run) by hitting the ball —*n.* 1. a) an act or period of running b) a running pace 2. the distance covered or time spent in running 3. a trip; journey; esp., a regular trip, as of an aeroplane b) a route for making deliveries 4. a) movement onwards; progression b) a continuous course or period [a *run* of good luck] 5. a continuous course of performances, etc., as of a play 6. a continued series of demands, as for specified goods 7. a continuous series or extent 8. a flow or rush of water, etc., as of the tide 9. [U.S.] a small, swift stream 10. a) a period during which some fluid flows readily b) the amount of flow 11. a) a period of operation of a machine b) the output during this period 12. a) a kind or class, as of goods b) the usual or average kind 13. a) an inclined pathway or course [a ski *run*] b) an enclosed area for domestic animals [a chicken *run*] 14. freedom to move about at will [to have the *run* of the house] 15. a) a large number of fish migrating together b) such migration 16. [Chiefly U.S.] a ladder, as in a stocking 17. [Aust.] a tract of land for grazing livestock 18. *Cricket* a score of one made by running from one wicket to the other after hitting the ball 19. *Billiards,* etc. a sequence of successful shots, etc. 20. *Mil.* the approach to the target made by an aeroplane in bombing, etc. 21. *Music* a rapid succession of tones —*adj.* 1. melted 2. poured while in a melted state [*run* metal] —**a run for one's money** 1. powerful competition 2. satisfaction for what one has expended —**in the long run** in the final outcome; ultimately —**on the run** 1. running 2. running away —**run across** to encounter by chance —**run along** to depart —**run around** 1. to transport someone, usually by motor car 2. to associate with someone of the opposite sex —**run a temperature** to be feverish —**run away** 1. to flee 2. to desert one's home or family 3. to escape and run loose —**run away with** 1. to steal 2. to carry out of control [his anger *ran away* with him] 3. a) to outdo all others in (a contest, etc.) b) to get (a prize, etc.) in this way —**run down** 1. to stop operating 2. to run or drive against so as to knock down 3. to pursue and capture or kill 4. to search out the source of 5. to speak of with disapproval 6. to make or become run-down 7. to read through rapidly —**run for it** to run to escape something —**run in** 1. to include (something additional) 2. to run a car engine for a specified period of time 3. [Slang] to arrest —**run in the family** to be a hereditary characteristic —**run into** 1. to encounter by chance 2. to collide with 3. to add up to (a large sum of money) —**run off** 1. to print, make copies of, etc. 2. to cause to be run, played, etc. 3. to drive (trespassers) away 4. to drain 5. *same as* RUN AWAY —**run on** 1. to continue or be continued 2. to add (something) at the end 3. to talk continuously —**run out** 1. to come to an end; expire 2. to drive out 3. *cricket* to dismiss (a batsman) while he is running between the wickets —**run out of** to use up —**run out on** [Colloq.] to abandon or desert —**run over** 1. to ride or drive over 2. to overflow 3. to go beyond a limit 4. to examine, rehearse, etc. rapidly —**run through** 1. to use up or spend quickly or recklessly 2. to pierce 3. to examine, rehearse, etc. rapidly —**run to** 1. to extend to or be sufficient for 2. to be able to afford 3. to show inclination towards —**run up** 1. to raise, rise, or make rapidly 2. to let (bills, etc.) go without paying them 3. to sew with a rapid succession of stitches

run·a·bout (run′ə bout′) *n.* 1. a person who runs about from place to place 2. a light, one-seated, open carriage or motor car 3. a light motorboat

run·a·round (-ə round′) *n.* [U.S. Colloq.] a series of evasive excuses, delays, etc.: usually in **get** (or **give**) **the runaround**

run·a·way (-ə wā′) *n.* 1. a fugitive 2. a horse, etc. that runs away 3. a running away —*adj.* 1. running away or having run away 2. of or done by runaways 3. easily won, as a race 4. a) rising rapidly, as prices b) having an uncontrolled rise of prices [*runaway* inflation]

run·ci·ble spoon (run′sə b'l) [coined by E. Lear in *The Owl and the Pussycat* (1871)] a utensil with broad prongs in a spoonlike shape

run·dale (run′dāl′) *n.* [Scot. *ryndale* < *ryn,* RUN + *dale,* DOLE¹] a system of land tenure in which each holder has several strips of land not contiguous to one another

run-down (-doun′) *adj.* 1. not wound and therefore not running, as a clock 2. in poor physical condition, as from overwork 3. fallen into disrepair

run-down (-doun′) *n.* 1. a concise summary 2. a decrease in numbers, esp. of employees

rune (rōōn) *n.* [OE. *run*] 1. any of the characters of an ancient Germanic alphabet 2. something inscribed in such characters 3. a) a Finnish or Old Norse poem or canto b) [Poet.] any poem, song, etc. that is mystical or obscure

rung¹ (ruŋ) *n.* [OE. *hrung,* a staff] 1. any sturdy stick, bar, or rod used as a crossbar, support, etc.; specif., a) any of the steps of a ladder b) a crosspiece between the legs of a chair, or across the back, etc. **2.** a degree, as of social status, success, etc.

rung² (ruŋ) *pp. & chiefly dial. pt.* of RING¹

ru·nic (rōō′nik) *adj.* **1.** consisting of or set down in runes **2.** like runes in decorative effect **3.** mystical; obscure

run-in (run′in′) *adj. Printing* made continuous without a break or paragraph —*n.* **1.** *Printing* run-in matter **2.** [Colloq.] a quarrel, fight, etc.

run·nel (run′'l) *n.* [OE. *rynel* < *rinnan*, to run] a small stream; little brook: also **run′let** (-lit)

run·ner (run′ər) *n.* **1.** one that runs; specif., an athlete **2.** a messenger, as for a bank or broker **3.** a smuggler **4.** a person who operates a machine, etc. **5.** a long, narrow cloth or rug **6.** a long, trailing stem, as of a strawberry, that puts out roots along the ground, thus producing new plants **7.** something on or in which something else moves **8.** either of the long, narrow pieces on which a sledge or sleigh slides **9.** the blade of a skate

runner bean any of various strains of the common garden bean that grow twining about supports

run·ner-up (-up′) *n., pl.* **-ners-up′** a person or team that finishes second in a race, contest, etc.

run·ning (run′iŋ) *n.* **1.** the act of one that runs; racing, managing, etc. **2.** that which runs, or flows —*adj.* **1.** moving or advancing rapidly **2.** flowing [*running* water] **3.** cursive: said of handwriting **4.** melting; becoming liquid **5.** discharging pus [a *running* sore] **6.** creeping or climbing: said of plants **7.** in operation, as machinery **8.** in a straight line [a *running* foot] **9.** without interruption; continuous [a *running* commentary] **10.** prevalent **11.** current [a *running* account] **12.** simultaneous [a *running* translation] **13.** moving easily or smoothly **14.** slipping or sliding easily, as a knot **15.** moving when pulled, as a rope **16.** done in or by a run [a running jump] **17.** of the normal run (of a train, bus, etc.) [running time] —*adv.* in succession [for ten days *running*] —**in** (or **out of**) **the running** in (or out of) the competition

running board esp. formerly, a footboard along the lower part of the side of some motor cars

running fire a rapid succession of shots fired, remarks made, questions asked, etc.

running head (or **title**) a heading or title printed at the top of every, or every other, page: also **running headline**

running knot same as SLIPKNOT

running lights the lights that a ship or aircraft travelling at night is required to display

running mate [U.S.] a candidate for a lesser office, as for the vice-presidency, in his relationship to the candidate for the greater office

running repairs minor repairs, usually performed without stopping the machinery, engine, etc.

run·ny (run′ē) *adj.* **-ni·er, -ni·est** **1.** that flows, esp. too freely **2.** that keeps on discharging mucus [a runny nose]

run-off (run′ôf′) *n.* **1.** a deciding, final race, election, etc., as in the case of a tie **2.** [U.S.] something that runs off, as rain in excess of the amount absorbed by the ground

run-of-the-mill (run′əv thə mil′) *adj.* [see RUN, *n.*, 12 *b*] not selected or special; ordinary

run-on (run′on′) *adj. Printing* continuous without a break or new paragraph —*n.* run-on matter

runt (runt) *n.* [< ?] **1.** a stunted or undersized animal, plant, thing, or (usually in a contemptuous sense) person **2.** the smallest animal of a litter —**runt′i·ness** *n.* —**runt′y** *adj.* **runt′i·er, runt′i·est**

run-through (run′thrōō′) *n.* a full rehearsal without stopping

run-up (run′up′) *n.* **1.** an approach run by an athlete for a long jump, etc. **2.** any preliminary or preparatory period before some major event

run·way (-wā′) *n.* a channel, track, chute, etc. in, on, or along which something moves; specif., *a)* a strip of levelled, usually paved ground for use by aircraft in taking off and landing *b)* a narrow extension of a stage out into the audience

ru·pee (rōō pē′, rōō′pē) *n.* [< Hindi < Sans. *rūpya*, wrought silver] the monetary unit of India, Pakistan, Sri Lanka, etc.: see MONETARY UNITS, table

ru·pi·ah (rōō pē′ə) *n.* [< Hindi] *see* MONETARY UNITS, table (Indonesia)

rup·ture (rup′chər) *n.* [< MFr. < L. < pp. of *rumpere*, to break] **1.** a breaking apart or being broken apart **2.** a breaking off of friendly or peaceful relations **3.** a hernia —*vt., vi.* **-tured, -tur·ing** **1.** to break apart or burst **2.** to affect with or undergo a rupture

ru·ral (roor′əl) *adj.* [< MFr. < LL. *ruralis* < L. *rus* (gen. *ruris*, the country)] **1.** of or like the country, country folk, etc.; rustic **2.** living in the country **3.** having to do with farming —**ru′ral·ly** *adv.*

rural dean a senior clergyman or parish priest having authority over a group of parishes in a specified area

rural district formerly, an administrative district formed by a group of country parishes: cf. URBAN DISTRICT

ru·ral·ism (-iz'm) *n.* **1.** rural quality **2.** rural life **3.** a rural

idiom, feature, etc. Also **ru·ral·i·ty** (roo ral′ə tē), *pl.* **-ties** —**ru′ral·ist** (-ist) *n.*

ru·ral·ize (roor′ə līz′) *vt.* **-ized′, -iz′ing** to make rural —*vi.* to live for a time in the country —**ru′ral·i·za′tion** *n.*

Ru·ri·ta·ni·an (roor′ə tā′nē ən) *adj.* [after *Ruritania*, imaginary kingdom in novels by A. Hope (1863-1933)] of or characteristic of some quaint, romantic, unreal place

ruse (rōōz) *n.* [< MFr. < OFr. *reuser*, to deceive < L. *recusare*, to refuse] a stratagem or trick

rush¹ (rush) *vi.* [< Anglo-Fr. < MFr. < OFr. *reuser*: see prec.] **1.** *a)* to move swiftly or impetuously *b)* to dash recklessly **2.** to make a sudden attack (on or upon) **3.** to pass, come, go, etc. swiftly or suddenly —*vt.* **1.** to move, send, push, etc. swiftly or violently **2.** to do, make, move, etc. with unusual speed or haste **3.** *a)* to attack suddenly *b)* to overcome or capture thus **4.** [U.S. Colloq.] to lavish attentions on, as in courting —*n.* **1.** a rushing **2.** an eager movement of many people to get to a place **3.** intense activity; haste; hurry **4.** a sudden attack **5.** great pressure, as of much business requiring quick or hasty attention **6.** [*usually pl.*] *Cinema* a first print of a scene or scenes, of a film shown for the director, etc. to inspect —*adj.* necessitating haste [rush orders] —**rush one's fences** to act hastily, usually without due consideration —**with a rush** suddenly and forcefully —**rush′er** *n.*

rush² (rush) *n.* [OE. *risc*] **1.** any of a genus of grasslike plants usually growing in wet places and having, in some species, round stems and pliant leaves used in making baskets, mats, etc. **2.** any of various similar plants, as bulrushes —**rush′y** *adj.* **rush′i·er, rush′i·est**

rush hour a time of the day when business, traffic, etc. are especially heavy —**rush′-hour′** *adj.*

rush job something done in great haste

rush light a primitive candle made from the pith of various types of rush dipped in tallow: also **rush candle**

rusk (rusk) *n.* [Sp. *rosca*, twisted bread roll] **1.** raised bread toasted in an oven until crisp, usually after being sliced **2.** a piece of this

Russ. **1.** Russia **2.** Russian

rus·set (rus′it) *n.* [< OFr. < L. *russus*, reddish] **1.** yellowish (or reddish) brown **2.** a coarse, brownish cloth, formerly used for clothing by country folk **3.** a winter apple with a rough, mottled skin —*adj.* yellowish-brown or reddish-brown

Russia leather a fine, smooth leather, usually dyed dark red, orig. made in Russia: used in bookbinding, etc.

Rus·sian (rush′ən) *adj.* of Russia, its people, their language, etc. —*n.* **1.** *a)* a native or inhabitant of Russia, specif. of the R.S.F.S.R. *b)* popularly, any citizen of the U.S.S.R. **2.** a member of the chief Slavic people of Russia **3.** the East Slavic language of the Russians; esp., its principal dialect **(Great Russian)**, the official language of the U.S.S.R.

Rus·sian·ize (-īz′) *vt.* **-ized′, -iz′ing** to make Russian in character —**Rus′sian·i·za′tion** *n.*

Russian roulette a deadly game of chance in which a person spins the cylinder of a revolver holding only one bullet, aims at his head, and pulls the trigger

Russian salad a salad of cold, diced, cooked vegetables mixed with a dressing of mayonnaise, pickles, etc.

Russian wolfhound same as BORZOI

Rus·si·fy (rus′ə fī′) *vt.* **-fied′, -fy′ing** same as RUSSIANIZE

Rus·so- *a combining form meaning:* **1.** Russia or Russian **2.** Russian and [*Russo-Japanese*]

rust (rust) *n.* [OE.] **1.** the reddish-brown coating (mainly ferric oxide) formed on iron or steel by oxidation, as during exposure to air and moisture **2.** any similar coating on other metals **3.** any stain or formation resembling iron rust **4.** any habit, influence, etc. injurious to usefulness, to the mind, etc. **5.** inactivity; idleness **6.** a reddish brown **7.** *a)* any of various plant diseases caused by parasitic fungi that produce reddish spots on stems and leaves *b)* such a fungus: in full, **rust fungus** —*vi., vt.* **1.** to affect or be affected by a rust fungus **2.** to become or cause to be coated with rust **3.** to spoil, as from lack of use **4.** to become or make rust-coloured —**rust′-col′oured** *adj.* —**rust′less** *adj.*

rus·tic (rus′tik) *adj.* [< MFr. < L. *rusticus* < *rus*: see RURAL] **1.** of or living in the country, as distinguished from cities or towns; rural **2.** not refined or sophisticated; specif., *a)* simple, plain, or artless *b)* awkward, uncouth, or boorish **3.** made of bark-covered branches or roots [rustic furniture] —*n.* a country person, esp. one regarded as simple, awkward, uncouth, etc. —**rus′ti·cal·ly** *adv.* —**rus·tic′i·ty** (-tis′ə tē) *n.*

rus·ti·cate (rus′ti kāt′) *vi.* **-cat′ed, -cat′ing** **1.** to go to the country **2.** to live in the country —*vt.* **1.** to send to live in the country **2.** to suspend (a student) temporarily from a university **3.** to make rustic —**rus′ti·ca′tion** *n.* —**rus′ti·ca′tor** *n.*

rus·tle¹ (rus′'l) *vi., vt.* **-tled, -tling** [ult. < WGmc. echoic base] to make or cause to make soft sounds, as of leaves moved by a breeze —*n.* a series of such sounds

rus·tle² (rus′'l) *vi., vt.* **-tled, -tling** [< ? RUSH¹ + HUSTLE] [U.S. Colloq.] **1.** to work with, or move or get by, energetic action 2. to steal (cattle, etc.) —**rustle up** [Colloq.] to collect or get together, as by foraging around —**rus′tler** *n.*

rust·proof (rust′prŏŏf′) *adj.* resistant to rust —*vt.* to make rustproof

rust·y (rus′tē) *adj.* **rust′i·er, rust′i·est** 1. coated with rust, as a metal, or affected by rust, as a plant 2. of or caused by rust 3. not working freely because of or as if because of rust 4. *a)* impaired by disuse, neglect, etc. *b)* having lost one's skill through lack of practice 5. rust-coloured 6. faded, old-looking, or shabby —**rust′i·ly** *adv.* —**rust′i·ness** *n.*

rut[1] (rut) *n.* [< ? MFr. *route*, ROUTE] 1. a track or furrow, esp. one made by wheeled vehicles 2. a fixed, routine procedure, way of acting, thinking, etc. —*vt.* **rut′ted, rut′ting** to make a rut or ruts in —**in a rut** to be fixed in a routine

rut[2] (rut) *n.* [< OFr. < L. < *rugire*, to roar] 1. the periodic sexual excitement of certain mammals, esp. males 2. the period of this —*vi.* **rut′ted, rut′ting** to be in rut

ru·ta·ba·ga (rŏŏt′ə bā′gə) *n.* [Sw. dial. *rotabagge*] [U.S.] *same as* SWEDE

ruth (rŏŏth) *n.* [ult. < OE. *hreowian*, to rue] [Now Rare] 1. pity; compassion 2. sorrow; grief; remorse

ru·the·ni·um (rŏŏ thē′nē əm) *n.* [ModL. < ML. *Ruthenia*, Russia, where first found] a rare, very hard, silvery-grey metallic chemical element, used in alloys and as a catalyst: symbol, Ru; at. wt., 101.07; at. no., 44

ruth·ful (rŏŏth′fəl) *adj.* [Now Rare] full of ruth, or pity, sorrow, etc. —**ruth′ful·ly** *adv.* —**ruth′ful·ness** *n.*

ruth·less (-lis) *adj.* without ruth; pitiless and relentless, as in seeking some goal —**ruth′less·ly** *adv.* —**ruth′less·ness** *n.*

rut·ty (rut′ē) *adj.* **-ti·er, -ti·est** having or full of ruts [a *rutty* road] —**rut′ti·ness** *n.*

R.V. Revised Version (of the Bible)

Rwy., Ry. Railway

-ry (rē) *shortened form of* -ERY [*dentistry*]

rye (rī) *n.* see PLURAL, II, D, 3 [OE. *ryge*] 1. a hardy cereal grass widely grown for its grain and straw 2. the grain or seeds of this plant, used for making flour and whisky, and as feed for livestock 3. whisky distilled from this grain

rye bread bread made altogether or partly of rye flour

rye·grass (-gräs′) *n.* any of various grasses that are annuals or that live for only a few years

ry·ot (rī′ət) *n.* [Hindi *raiyat* < Ar. *ra'iyah*, a flock] in India, a peasant or tenant farmer

S

S, s (es) *n.,* *pl.* **S's, s's** 1. the nineteenth letter of the English alphabet 2. a sound of *S* or *S*

S (es) *n.* something shaped like an *S* —*adj.* shaped like *S*

S *Chem.* sulphur

S *Physics the symbol for* siemens

-s [alt. form of -ES] 1. the plural ending of most nouns [*hips, shoes*] 2. the ending of the third person singular, present indicative, of verbs [*gives, runs*] 3. a suffix used to form some adverbs [*betimes, nights*]

-'s[1] [OE. *-es*] the ending of the possessive singular of nouns (and some pronouns) and of the possessive plural of nouns not ending in *s* [*boy's, one's, women's*]

-'s[2] *the unstressed and assimilated form of:* 1. is [*he's here*] 2. has [*she's eaten*] 3. does [*what's it matter?*] 4. us [*let's go*]

S, S., s, s. 1. south 2. southern

S. 1. Saturday 2. September 3. Sunday

S., s. 1. *pl.* **SS., ss.** saint 2. school

s. 1. second(s) 2. shilling(s) 3. singular

S.A. 1. Salvation Army 2. [Slang] sex appeal 3. South Africa 4. South America 5. South Australia

Sab·ba·tar·i·an (sab′ə ter′ē ən) *adj.* of the Sabbath and its observance —*n.* 1. a person, esp. a Christian, who observes the Sabbath (sense 1) 2. a Christian favouring rigid observance of Sunday as the Sabbath —**Sab′ba·tar′i·an·ism** *n.*

Sab·bath (sab′əth) *n.* [< OFr. & OE. *sabat*, both < L. < Gr. < Heb. < *shābath*, to rest] 1. the seventh day of the week (Saturday), observed as a day of rest and worship by Jews and some Christian sects 2. Sunday as the usual Christian day of rest and worship —*adj.* of the Sabbath

Sab·bat·i·cal (sə bat′i k'l) *adj.* [< Fr. < LL. < Gr. *sabbatikos*: see prec.] 1. of or suited to the Sabbath 2. [s-] designating a year or shorter period of absence for study, rest, or travel, given at intervals, orig. every seven years, as to some university teachers —*n.* [s-] a sabbatical year or leave Also **Sab·bat′ic**

sab·ba·tize (sab′ə tīz′) *vi., vt.* [ME. < LL. *sabbatizare* < Gr. *sabbatizō*, see SABBATH] to keep as, or as if, the Sabbath

S.A.B.C. South African Broadcasting Corporation

sa·ber (sā′bər) *n.* U.S. sp. of SABRE

Sa·bi·an (sāb′i ən) *adj.* 1. relating to a sect mentioned in the Koran as believers in the True God 2. relating to the worship of heavenly bodies: an erroneous usage —*n.* a member of such a sect

Sa·bine (sā′bīn) *n.* a member of an ancient tribe living in central Italy, conquered by the Romans, 3rd century B.C.

sa·ble (sā′b'l) *n., pl.* **-bles, -ble:** see PLURAL, II, D, 1 [OFr. < ML. *sabelum*, ult. < Russian *sobol'*] 1. *same as* MARTEN; esp., *a)* the **European marten,** with light-coloured underfur *b)* the **American marten,** with a darker pelt 2. *a)* the costly fur of the sable *b)* [*pl.*] a coat, etc. of this 3. *Heraldry* the colour black —*adj.* 1. made of or with the fur of the sable 2. black or dark brown; dark

sable antelope a large antelope of Southern Africa, with long, ringed horns

sa·bot (sab′ō, sa bō′) *n.* [Fr., ult. < Ar. *sabbât,* sandal] 1. a shoe shaped from a single piece of wood 2. a heavy leather shoe with a wooden sole

sab·o·tage (sab′ə täzh′) *n.* [Fr. < *saboter,* to damage < *sabot:* see prec. & -AGE: from damage done to machinery by wooden shoes] 1. intentional destruction of machines, waste of materials, etc., as during labour disputes 2. destruction of railways, bridges, etc. as by enemy agents or an underground resistance 3. deliberate obstruction of or damage to any cause, effort, etc. —*vt.* **-taged′, -tag′ing** to injure or destroy by sabotage —*vi.* to engage in sabotage

SABOT

sab·o·teur (sab′ə tur′) *n.* [Fr.] a person who sabotages

sa·bra (sä′brə) *n.* [ModHeb. *sābrāh,* lit., prickly fruit of a native cactus] a native-born Israeli

sa·bre (sā′bər) *n.* [< Fr. < G. *Sabel* < MGH. < Pol. & Hung.] a heavy cavalry sword with a slight curved blade —*vt.* to cut wound, or kill with a sabre

sabre rattling a threatening of war, or a menacing show of armed force

sac (sak) *n.* [Fr. < L. *saccus:* see SACK[1]] a pouchlike part in a plant or animal, esp. one filled with fluid —**sac′like′** *adj.*

S.A.C. Senior Aircraftman

sac·cha·ride (sak′ə rīd′) *n.* [see ff.] any of the carbohydrates; esp., any of the sugars, as glucose

sac·cha·rim·e·ter (sak′ə rim′ə tər) *n.* [Fr. *saccharimètre:* see SACCHARO- & -METER] an instrument used to determine the amount of sugar in a solution, esp. one using polarized light

sac·cha·rin (sak′ə rin) *n.* [< L. *saccharum,* sugar < Gr. *sakcharon,* ult. < Sans.] a white, crystalline coal-tar compound, about 500 times sweeter than cane sugar, used as a sugar substitute in diabetic diets, etc.

sac·cha·rine (-rin, -rīn′) *adj.* [see prec.] 1. of, like, or producing sugar 2. too sweet or syrupy [a *saccharine* voice] —*n.* *same as* SACCHARIN —**sac′cha·rine·ly** *adv.* —**sac′cha·rin′i·ty** (-rin′ə tē) *n.*

sac·cha·ro- (sak′ə rō′) [< L. *saccharum,* sugar: see SACCHARIN] a *combining form meaning* sugar

sac·er·do·tal (sas′ər dōt′'l, sak′-) *adj.* [< MFr. < L. < *sacerdos,* priest] of priests or the office of priest; priestly —**sac′er·do′tal·ly** *adv.*

sa·chem (sā′chəm) *n.* [< Algonquian *sâchimau*] among some N. American Indian tribes, the chief

sa·chet (sash′ā) *n.* [Fr. < OFr., dim. of *sac:* see SAC] 1. a small bag, pad, etc. filled with perfumed powder and put in drawers, etc. to scent clothing 2. such powder: also **sachet powder** 3. a small, sealed envelope containing shampoo, cream etc.

sack[1] (sak) *n.* [OE. *sacc* < L. *saccus* < Gr. < Heb. *śaq*] 1. *a)* a bag, esp. a large bag of coarse cloth, for holding grain, foodstuffs, etc. *b)* the contents or capacity of a sack 2. a loose-fitting jacket or dress 3. [Slang] dismissal from a job (with *the*) 4. [Chiefly U.S. Slang] a bed, bunk, etc. —*vt.*

1. to put into sacks 2. [Slang] to dismiss from a job; fire —**hit the sack** [Slang] to go to bed

sack² (sak) *n.* [< MFr. < It. *sacco*, plunder, lit., bag < L. *saccus*: see prec.] the plundering of a captured city, etc. —*vt.* to plunder (a city, etc.)

sack³ (sak) *n.* [< Fr. (*vin*) *sec*, dry (wine) < L. *siccus*, dry] any of various dry white wines from Spain or the Canary Islands

sack·but (sak'but') *n.* [Fr. *saquebute* < OFr. *saquer*, to pull + *bouter*, to push] a medieval wind instrument, forerunner of the trombone: the word is also incorrectly used in the King James Version of the Bible to translate an Aramaic word for a kind of lyre

sack·cloth (-kloth') *n.* 1. *same as* SACKING 2. a rough cloth worn as a symbol of mourning or penitence —**in sackcloth and ashes** in a state of great mourning or penitence

sack coat a man's loose-fitting, straight-backed coat, usually part of a suit

sack·ful (sak'fool') *n., pl.* -**fuls'** 1. the amount a sack holds 2. a large quantity

sack·ing (-iŋ) *n.* a cheap, coarse cloth of flax, hemp, jute, etc., used esp. for sacks

sa·cral¹ (sā'krəl) *adj.* [< L. neut. of *sacer*, sacred] of or for religious rites or observances

sa·cral² (sā'krəl) *adj.* [< ModL.: see SACRUM & -AL] of, or in the region of, the sacrum

sac·ra·ment (sak'rə mənt) *n.* [< OFr. < LL. *sacramentum*, ult. < L. *sacer*, sacred] 1. any of certain rites variously observed by Christians as ordained by Jesus, as baptism, Holy Communion, etc. 2. [*sometimes* S-] the Eucharist, or Holy Communion; also, the consecrated bread and wine, or sometimes the bread alone 3. something regarded as sacred —**take the sacrament** to receive holy communion

sac·ra·men·tal (sak'rə men't'l) *adj.* of, like, or used in a sacrament —*n.* R.C.Ch. something like a sacrament but instituted by the Church, as holy water —**sac'ra·men'tal·ly** *adv.* — **sac'ra·men'tal·ism** *n.* —**sac'ra·men'tal·ist** *n.*

sa·cred (sā'krid) *adj.* [< OFr. < L. *sacer*, holy] 1. consecrated to a god or deity; holy 2. having to do with religion or religious rites 3. given the respect accorded holy things; venerated 4. dedicated to a person, place, purpose, etc. [*sacred* to his memory] 5. that must not be broken, ignored, etc.; inviolate [a *sacred* promise] —**sa'cred·ly** *adv.* —**sa'cred·ness** *n.*

sacred cow any person or thing regarded as above criticism

sac·ri·fice (sak'rə fīs') *n.* [< OFr. < L. *sacrificium* < *sacer*, sacred + *facere*, to make] 1. a) an offering of the life of a person or animal, or of an object, in homage to a deity b) the thing offered 2. a) a giving up, destroying, etc. of one thing for the sake of another b) the thing given up, etc. 3. a) a selling or giving up of a thing at less than its value b) the loss incurred 4. —*vt.* -**ficed'**, -**fic'ing** 1. to offer as a sacrifice to a deity 2. to give up, destroy, etc. for the sake of another thing 3. to sell at less than value 4. *Chess* to allow one's opponent to gain a piece in order to advance one's attack —*vi.* to make a sacrifice

sac·ri·fi·cial (sak'rə fish'əl) *adj.* of, like, or used in a sacrifice —**sac'ri·fi'cial·ly** *adv.*

sac·ri·lege (sak'rə lij) *n.* [< MFr. < L. < *sacrilegus*, temple robber < *sacer*, sacred + *legere*, to take away] 1. misuse or violation of what is consecrated to God or religion 2. a desecrating of anything held sacred

sac·ri·le·gious (sak'rə lij'əs) *adj.* 1. that is or involves sacrilege 2. guilty of sacrilege —**sac'ri·le'gious·ly** *adv.* —**sac'ri·le'gious·ness** *n.*

sac·ris·tan (sak'ris tən) *n.* a person in charge of a sacristy: also **sa'crist** (sā'krist)

sa·cris·ty (-tē) *n., pl.* -**ties** [< Fr. < ML. < L. < *sacrista*, sacristan] a room in a church where the sacred vessels, vestments, etc. are kept

sa·cro·il·i·ac (sā'krō il'ē ak', sak'rō-) *adj.* [< SACRUM + *iliac*, of or near the ilium] of the sacrum and the ilium; esp., designating the joint between them —*n.* the sacroiliac joint

sac·ro·sanct (sak'rō saŋkt') *adj.* [< L. < *sacer*, sacred + *sanctus*, holy] very sacred, holy, or inviolable —**sac'ro·sanc'ti·ty** *n.*

sa·crum (sā'krəm, sak'rəm) *n., pl.* -**cra** (-krə, -rə) or -**crums** [ModL. < LL. (*os*) *sacrum*, sacred (bone): ? anciently used in sacrifices] a thick, triangular bone joining the ilia (see ILIUM) at the lower end of the spinal column

S.A.C.W. Senior Aircraftwoman

sad (sad) *adj.* **sad'der**, **sad'dest** [OE. *sæd*, sated] 1. having or expressing low spirits or sorrow; unhappy; sorrowful 2. causing or characterized by sorrow, dejection, etc. 3. dark or dull in colour; drab 4. [Colloq.] very bad; deplorable —**sad'ly** *adv.* —**sad'ness** *n.*

sad·den (sad''n) *vt., vi.* to make or become sad

sad·dle (sad''l) *n.* [OE. *sadol*] 1. a seat, usually of padded leather, for a rider on a horse, bicycle, etc. 2. a padded part of a harness worn over a horse's back 3. the part of an animal's back where a saddle is put 4. anything like a saddle in form, position, etc. 5. a ridge between two peaks 6. a cut of lamb, etc. including part of the backbone and the two loins —*vt.* -**dled**, -**dling** 1. to put a saddle upon 2. to burden (a person) with (a debt, responsibility, obligation, etc.) —*vi.* to put a saddle on a horse and mount it (often with *up*) —**in the saddle** 1. seated on a saddle 2. having control

sad·dle-backed (-bakt') *adj.* 1. having a low, hollow back curved like a saddle, as some horses 2. having a concave outline, as a ridge between peaks —**sad'dle·back** *n.*

sad·dle·bag (-bag') *n.* 1. a large bag, usually one of a pair, carried on either side of the back of a horse, etc., just behind the saddle 2. a similar bag carried over the back wheel of a motorcycle, etc.

sad·dle·bow (-bō') *n.* the arched front part of a saddle, the top of which is the pommel

sad·dle·cloth (-kloth') *n.* a thick cloth placed under a saddle on an animal's back

saddle horse a horse trained for riding

sad·dler (sad'lər) *n.* a person whose work is making, repairing, or selling saddles, harnesses, etc.

saddle roof a roof with two gables and a ridge

sad·dler·y (sad'lə rē) *n., pl.* -**dler·ies** 1. the work of a saddler 2. articles made by a saddler 3. a shop where these are sold

saddle soap a mild soap with neat's-foot oil in it, for cleaning and softening leather

sad·dle·tree (sad'l trē') *n.* [ME. *sadetre*] the frame of a saddle

sad dog a reprobate, rake, or black sheep

Sad·du·cee (sad'yoo sē') *n.* a member of an ancient Jewish party accepting only the written law and rejecting the oral, or traditional, law —**Sad'du·ce'an** *adj.*

sa·dhu (sä'doo) *n.* [Sans. < *sādhu*, straight] a Hindu holy man

sad·i·ron (sad'ī'ərn) *n.* [SAD, in obs. sense, heavy + IRON] a heavy flatiron, pointed at both ends

sad·ism (sā'diz'm, sad'iz'm) *n.* [Fr., after Marquis de *Sade* (1740-1814), Fr. soldier & novelist] the getting of pleasure, specif. sexual pleasure, from hurting or mistreating another or others —**sad'ist** *n.* —**sa·dis·tic** (sə dis'tik, sā-) *adj.* —**sa·dis'ti·cal·ly** *adv.*

sad·o·mas·o·chism (sā'dō mas'ə kiz'm, sad'ō-; -maz'-) *n.* sadism and masochism in the same individual —**sad'o·mas'o·chist** *n.* —**sad'o·mas'o·chis'tic** *adj.*

sad sack [U.S. Slang] a person who means well but is always blundering and in trouble

s.a.e. stamped addressed envelope

sa·fa·ri (sə fär'ē) *n., pl.* -**ris** [Swahili < Ar. < *safara*, to travel] a journey or hunting expedition, esp. in E Africa

safari park an enclosed park, often attached to a stately home, where wild animals can be viewed

safe (sāf) *adj.* **saf'er**, **saf'est** [OFr. *sauf* < L. *salvus*] 1. a) free from danger, damage, etc.; secure b) having escaped injury; unharmed 2. a) giving protection b) trustworthy 3. unable to cause trouble or damage [*safe* in jail] 4. taking or involving no risks —*n.* 1. a strong, locking metal container for valuables 2. any compartment, box, etc. to store food, etc. —**on the safe side** allowing extra in case of error, etc. —**safe'ly** *adv.* —**safe'ness** *n.*

safe-con·duct (-kon'dukt) *n.* 1. permission to travel through a dangerous area, as in time of war, with protection against arrest or harm 2. a written pass giving this

safe·crack·ing (-krak'iŋ) *n.* the breaking open and robbing of safes: also **safe'break'ing** (-brāk'iŋ) —**safe'crack'er** *n.*

safe-de·pos·it (-di poz'it) *adj.* designating or of a box or vault, esp. in a bank, for storing valuables: also **safe'ty-de·pos'it**

safe·guard (-gärd') *n.* any person or thing that protects or guards against loss or injury; a precaution or protection —*vt.* to protect or guard

safe·keep·ing (-kēp'iŋ) *n.* a keeping or being kept in safety; protection or custody

safe seat a parliamentary seat which is unlikely to be lost by a particular political party

safe·ty (sāf'tē) *n., pl.* -**ties** 1. a being safe; security 2. a device to prevent accident, as a locking device (also **safety catch**, **safety lock**) on a firearm —*adj.* giving safety

safety belt 1. a belt attaching a person working at heights to something to prevent falling 2. *same as* SEAT BELT

safety curtain a fire-resistant curtain between the stage and the auditorium

safety glass glass made to be shatterproof by fastening together two sheets of glass with a transparent, plastic substance between them

safety lamp a miner's lamp designed to avoid fire, etc.

safety match a match that will light only when it is struck on a prepared surface

safety pin a pin bent back on itself so as to form a spring, the point being held with a guard

safety razor a razor with guards for the blade to protect the skin from cuts

safety valve 1. an automatic valve for a steam boiler, etc., to release steam if the pressure is too great 2. any outlet for emotion, energy, etc.

saf·fi·an leather (saf′ē ən) [G. *saffian*, ult. < Per. *säht*, hard] leather of sheepskin or goatskin tanned with sumac

saf·flow·er (saf′lou′ər) *n.* [< Du. or MFr., ult. < Ar. *as far*, a yellow plant] a thistlelike annual plant of the composite family, with orange flower heads yielding a dyestuff and with seeds yielding oil used in paints, foods, etc.

saf·fron (saf′rən) *n.* [< OFr. *safran*, ult. < Ar. *za'farān*] 1. a perennial species of crocus with funnel-shaped purplish flowers having orange stigmas 2. the dried, aromatic stigmas, used in flavouring and colouring foods 3. orange yellow: also **saffron yellow** —*adj.* orange-yellow

saffron cake a cake flavoured with saffron, made chiefly in the West Country

S. Afr. 1. South Africa 2. South African

sag (sag) *vi.* **sagged, sag′ging** [prob. < Scand.] 1. to sink or bend, esp. in the middle, from weight or pressure 2. to hang down unevenly 3. to lose firmness, strength, etc.; weaken 4. to decline in price, sales, etc. —*vt.* to cause to sag —*n.* 1. a sagging 2. a sunken place; depression

sa·ga (sä′gə) *n.* [ON., a tale] 1. a medieval Scandinavian story of battles, etc., generally telling the legendary history of a Norse family 2. any long story relating heroic deeds or complicated adventures

sa·ga·cious (sə gā′shəs) *adj.* [< L. *sagax* (gen. *sagacis*), wise] keenly perceptive or discerning, farsighted, etc. —**sa·ga′cious·ly** *adv.* —**sa·ga′cious·ness** *n.*

sa·gac·i·ty (sə gas′ə tē) *n.,* *pl.* **-ties** the quality or an instance of being sagacious

sag·a·more (sag′ə môr′) *n.* [< AmInd. *sägimau*] a chief of second rank among certain tribes of N American Indians

sage[1] (sāj) *adj.* **sag′er, sag′est** [< OFr., ult. < L. *sapiens*, orig. prp. of *sapere*, to know] having or showing wisdom or good judgment —*n.* a very wise man, esp. an old man respected for his wisdom, experience, etc. —**sage′ly** *adv.* —**sage′ness** *n.*

sage[2] (sāj) *n.* [< OFr. < L. < *salvus*, safe: it reputedly had healing powers] 1. any of various plants, esp. the **garden sage**, with leaves dried for seasoning meats, etc. [*sage* and onion stuffing] 2. *same as* SAGEBRUSH

sage·brush (-brush′) *n.* any of certain plants of the composite family, common in dry, alkaline areas of the western U.S.; esp., the **big sagebrush**, with small, aromatic leaves

sag·gy (sag′ē) *adj.* **-gi·er, -gi·est** inclined to sag

Sag·it·ta·ri·us (saj′i ter′ē əs) [L., archer] 1. a large S constellation in the Milky Way 2. the ninth sign of the zodiac: see ZODIAC, illus.

sag·it·tate (saj′ə tāt′) *adj.* [< ModL. < L. *sagitta*, arrow] in the shape of an arrowhead, as some leaves

sa·go (sā′gō) *n.,* *pl.* **-gos** [Malay *sägü*] 1. an edible starch prepared from certain palm trees and other plants 2. a milk pudding made from this 3. a palm tree yielding sago: also **sago palm**

sa·gua·ro (sə gwä′rō, -wä′-) *n.,* *pl.* **-ros** [MexSp. < native name] a giant cactus of southwestern N America: also **sa·hua′ro** (-wä′-)

sa·hib (sä′ib, -hib, -ēb, -hēb) *n.* [< Hindi < Ar. *sähib*, master] sir; master: title formerly used by natives in colonial India when speaking to or of a European

said (sed) *pt. & pp. of* SAY —*adj.* aforesaid; named before

sail (sāl) *n.* [OE. *segl*] 1. any of the shaped sheets of canvas, etc. spread to catch the wind and so drive certain vessels forward 2. sails collectively 3. a sailing vessel or vessels 4. a trip in a ship or boat 5. anything like a sail, as an arm of a windmill —*vi.* 1. to be moved forward by means of sails or a propeller, etc. 2. to travel on water 3. to begin a trip by water 4. to manage a sailing boat as in racing 5. to glide through the air 6. to move smoothly, like a ship sailing 7. [Colloq.] to move quickly 8. [Colloq.] to throw oneself (*into*) with energy 9. [Colloq.] to attack or criticize someone severely (with *into*) —*vt.* 1. to move through or upon (a body of water) in a boat or ship 2. to manage or navigate (a boat or ship) —**in sail** with sails set —**make sail** 1. to spread out a ship's sail 2. to begin a trip by water —**sail close to the wind** 1. to sail a course almost directly into the wind 2. to run great risks, esp. by nearly breaking a moral position or law —**set sail** 1. to hoist the sails for departure 2. to begin a trip by water —**take in sail** to lower sails —**under sail** sailing; with sails set —**sail′ing** *n., adj.*

sail arm the rotating arm of a windmill

sail·cloth (-klôth′) *n.* canvas or other cloth used in making sails, tents, etc.

sail·er (-ər) *n.* a ship or boat, esp. one with sails, specif. with regard to its speed, etc.

sail·fish (-fish′) *n.,* *pl.* **-fish′, -fish′es:** see FISH a large, tropical marine fish with a large, saillike dorsal fin and a sword-shaped upper jaw

SAILFISH
(to 3.4 m long)

sail·or (-ər) *n.* 1. a person who makes his living by sailing; seaman 2. *a)* a man in the navy below the rank of officer *b)* anyone in the navy 3. a voyager on water, as affected by seasickness [a bad *sailor*] 4. a straw hat with a low, flat crown and flat brim —**sail′or·ing** *n.* —**sail′or·ly** *adj.*

sail·plane (sāl′plān′) *n.* a light glider designed for soaring —*vi.* **-planed′, -plan′ing** to fly a sailplane

sain·foin (sān′foin) *n.* [Fr. < *sain*, wholesome (< L. *sanus*, healthy) + *foin* (< L. *faenum*), hay] a Eurasian perennial plant cultivated as a forage or cover crop

saint (sānt) *n.* [< OFr. < LL. < L. *sanctus*, holy] 1. a holy person 2. a person who is unusually charitable, patient, etc. 3. [*pl.*] those, esp. holy persons, who have died and are believed to be with God 4. *a)* in the New Testament, any Christian *b)* [S-] a member of any religious group calling themselves Saints 5. in certain Christian churches, a deceased person officially recognized as having lived an exceptionally holy life —*vt.* to make a saint of —**saint′hood′** *n.*

Saint Ag·nes's Eve (ag′nis iz) the night of January 20, when a girl's future husband was supposed to be revealed to her if she performed certain rites

Saint Ber·nard (bur′nərd) a large, reddish-brown and white dog of a breed formerly trained by monks at the St. Bernard hospice, in the Swiss Alps, to rescue travellers

saint·ed (sān′tid) *adj.* 1. of or fit for a saint; saintly 2. regarded as a saint 3. holy; sacred

Saint El·mo's fire (or **light**) (el′mōz) [after *St. Elmo*, patron saint of sailors] a visible electric discharge from tips of masts, spires, trees, etc. as during electrical storms

Saint James (jāmz) [after the palace in Pall Mall, London, which was a residence of Brit. monarchs (1697-1837)] the British court: also **St. James**

Saint Johns·wort (jonz′wurt′) [< ?] any of various plants with usually yellow flowers and spotted leaves

Saint Leg·er (lej′ər) an annual horse race run at Doncaster; one of the classics of the flat-racing season Also **St. Leger**

saint·ly (sānt′lē) *adj.* **-li·er, -li·est** like or suitable for a saint —**saint′li·ness** *n.*

Saint Pat·rick's Day (pat′riks) March 17, observed by the Irish in honour of Saint Patrick, the patron saint of Ireland

saint·paul·ia (sānt pôl′yə, -ē ə) *n.* [Mod L. after Baron W. von *Saint Paul* (died 1910), G. colonial administrator] 1. the genus to which African violets belong 2. *same as* AFRICAN VIOLET

Saint Swi·thin's Day (swi′thinz) July 15, observed in honour of Saint Swithin, a 9th cent. bishop of Winchester; if it rains on this day it is commonly believed that it will rain for the next forty days

Saint Val·en·tine's Day (val′ən tīnz′) February 14, observed in honour of a martyr of the 3rd cent. and, coincidentally, as a day for sending valentines to sweethearts, etc.

Saint Vi·tus' dance (vī′təs) [after *St. Vitus*, patron saint of persons having convulsive fits] *same as* CHOREA

saith (seth) archaic 3rd pers. sing., pres. indic., *of* SAY

saithe (sāth) *n.* [ON. *seithr*] a food fish like cod whose skin blackens the fingers as if it were coal: also called **coalfish**

sake[1] (sāk) *n.* [OE. *sacu*, suit at law] 1. purpose or reason; motive [for the *sake* of peace] 2. advantage; behalf; benefit [for my *sake*] —**for heaven's** (or **gosh** or **Pete's**) **sake!** a mild exclamation of surprise, annoyance, etc.

sa·ke[2] (sä′kē) *n.* [Jap.] a Japanese alcoholic beverage made from fermented rice: also sp. **sa′ki**

sal (sal) *n.* [L.] *Pharmacy* salt

sa·laam (sə läm′) *n.* [Ar. *salām*, peace] 1. a Moslem greeting ("peace") 2. an Oriental greeting made by bowing low with the palm of the right hand placed on the forehead 3. a greeting showing respect —*vt., vi.* to greet with, or make, a salaam

sal·a·ble (sāl′ə b'l) *adj.* *same as* SALEABLE

sa·la·cious (sə lā′shəs) *adj.* [< L. < *salire*, to leap] 1. lecherous; lustful 2. obscene; pornographic —**sa·la′cious·ly** *adv.* —**sa·la′cious·ness, sa·lac′i·ty** (-las′ə tē) *n.*

sal·ad (sal′əd) *n.* [< MFr. < Pr. < L. pp. of *salare*, to salt < *sal*, salt] 1. a dish, usually cold, of vegetables, usually raw, or fruits, often served with a dressing 2. any green plant or herb used for such a dish

salad days time of youth and inexperience

salad dressing a preparation of olive oil or other vegetable oil, vinegar, spices, etc. served with a salad

sal·a·man·der (sal′ə man′dər) *n.* [< OFr. < L. *salamandra* < Gr.] 1. a mythological reptile that was said to live in fire

2. any of a group of tailed amphibians related to frogs and toads, with a soft, moist skin

sa·la·mi (sə lä′mē) *n.* [It., pl., preserved meat, ult. < L. *sal*, salt] a highly spiced, salted sausage, orig. Italian, of pork and beef, or of beef alone

sal ammoniac *same as* AMMONIUM CHLORIDE

sal·a·ri·at (sə ler′ē ət) *n.* [< SALARY after PROLETARIAT] the class of salary earners

sal·a·ried (sal′ə rēd) *adj.* 1. receiving a salary 2. yielding a salary [a *salaried* position]

sal·a·ry (sal′ə rē) *n., pl.* **-ries** [< L. *salarium*, orig., part of a Roman soldier's pay for buying salt < *sal*, salt] a fixed payment at regular intervals for services, esp. when clerical or professional

sale (sāl) *n.* [< OE. < ON. *sala*] 1. a selling; the exchange of property or a service for an agreed sum of money or its equivalent 2. opportunity to sell; market 3. an auction 4. a selling at prices lower than usual 5. [pl.] receipts in business 6. [pl.] the work, department, etc. of selling [a job in *sales*] —**for** (or on) **sale** to be sold —**put up for sale** to offer for sale, esp. for auction —**sale or return** an arrangement whereby the retailer can return any goods left unsold to the wholesaler

sale·a·ble (sāl′ə b'l) *adj.* that can be sold

sale of work a sale of articles, usually made by the contributors, to raise funds for some specific charity, fund, etc.

sal·e·ra·tus (sal′ə rāt′əs) *n.* [ModL. *sal aeratus*, aerated salt] [U.S.] sodium bicarbonate; baking soda

sale·room (sāl′rōōm) *n.* a room in which goods are shown and offered for sale, esp. by auction

sales·clerk (sālz′klärk′) *n.* [Chiefly U.S.] a person employed to sell goods in a shop

sales·man (sālz′mən) *n., pl.* **-men** 1. a man who is employed to sell goods in a shop 2. a travelling agent who sells goods or services

sales·man·ship (-ship′) *n.* the ability, skill, or technique of selling

sales resistance resistance of potential customers to efforts aimed at getting them to buy

sales talk any persuasion or argument used in trying to sell something or to persuade one to do something

sales·wom·an (-woom′ən) *n., pl.* **-wom′en** (-wim′in) a woman who sells goods in a shop: also **sales′la′dy** (-lā′dē), *pl.* **-dies, sales′girl′** (-gurl′)

Sa·li·an (sā′lē ən) *adj.* [< LL. *Salii*, Salian Franks < the Gmc. name] of a tribe of Franks who settled near the Ijssel river in the Netherlands in the 4th cent. A.D. —*n.* a Salian Frank

Sal·ic law (sal′ik, sā′lik) [< ML. < LL. *Salii*, a tribe of Franks] 1. a code of laws of Germanic tribes, or any of these laws 2. a law excluding women from succession to the throne in the French and Spanish monarchies

sa·lic·y·late (sə lis′ə lāt′, -it) *n.* any salt or ester of salicylic acid

sal·i·cyl·ic acid (sal′ə sil′ik) [< Fr. *salicyle* (radical of the acid) < L. *salix*, willow + -IC] a white, crystalline compound used in making aspirin, as a food preservative, etc.

sa·li·ent (sā′lē ənt) *adj.* [< L. prp. of *salire*, to leap] 1. leaping 2. pointing outwards; projecting 3. standing out; noticeable; prominent —*n.* 1. the part of a battle line, fort, etc. projecting farthest towards the enemy 2. a projecting angle, part, etc. —**sa′lience** *n.* —**sa′lien·cy** *n., pl.* **-cies** —**sa′lient·ly** *adv.*

sa·li·en·ti·an (sā′lē en′she ən) *n.* [Mod L. < L. *saliens*, prp. of *salire*, to leap + -AN] any of a subclass of tailless amphibians, including frogs and toads —*adj.* of the salientians

sa·line (sā′līn; *for n. l also* sə lin′) [< L. < *sal*, salt] of, like, or containing salt; salty —*n.* 1. a salt lake, salt marsh, etc. 2. a salt of an alkali metal or of magnesium, used as a cathartic 3. a saline solution —**sa·lin·i·ty** (sə lin′ə tē) *n.*

sal·i·nom·e·ter (sal′ə nom′ə tər) *n.* [see SALINE & -METER] any device for measuring the amount of dissolved salts in a solution

sa·li·va (sə lī′və) *n.* [L.] the thin, watery, slightly viscid fluid secreted by the salivary glands: it aids digestion by moistening and softening food, and contains an enzyme that converts starch to dextrin and maltose

sal·i·var·y (sal′ə vər ē) *adj.* of or secreting saliva

sal·i·vate (-vāt′) *vt.* **-vat′ed, -vat′ing** [< L. pp. of *salivare*] to produce an excessive flow of saliva in —*vi.* to secrete saliva —**sal′i·va′tion** *n.*

saliva test a test for drug use in athletes, racehorses, etc. made by sampling the saliva

Salk vaccine (sôlk) [after J.E. *Salk* (1914-), U.S. bacteriologist] a vaccine for injection to prevent poliomyelitis

sal·lee (sal′ē) *n.* [< Abor.] 1. a type of eucalyptus that grows in S Australia 2. any of various Australian acacias

sal·low (sal′ō) *adj.* [OE. *salu*] of a sickly, pale-yellowish complexion —*vt.* to make sallow —**sal′low·ness** *n.*

sal·ly (sal′ē) *n., pl.* **-lies** [MFr. *saillie*, ult. < L. *salire*, to leap] 1. a sudden rushing forth, as of troops to attack besiegers 2. any sudden start into activity 3. a quick witticism; quip 4. an excursion; jaunt —*vi.* **-lied, -ly·ing** 1. to make a sally 2. *a)* to go outdoors *b)* to set out on a trip Used with *forth* or *out*

Sally Lunn (lun) [said to be name of 18th-c. Brit. woman who first made these at Bath] [*also* s- l-] a type of sweetened tea-cake, usually served hot

sally port a postern gate or underground passage allowing the defenders to make a sally

sal·ma·gun·di (sal′ma gun′dē) *n.* [Fr. *salmigondis* < ? It. *salame conditi*, pickled meat] 1. a dish of chopped meat, eggs, etc. flavoured with onions, anchovies, etc. 2. mixture or medley

salm·on (sam′ən) *n., pl.* **-on, -ons:** see PLURAL, II, D, 2 [< MFr. < OFr. *saumon* < L. *salmo*] 1. any of various bony fishes; specif., any of several varieties of game and food fishes of the N Hemisphere, with silver scales and flesh that is pink when cooked: salmon spawn in fresh water but usually live in salt water 2. yellowish pink: also **salmon pink**

sal·mo·nel·la (sal′mə nel′ə) *n., pl.* **-nel′lae** (-ē), **-nel′la, -nel′las** [ModL.: after D. *Salmon* (d. 1914), U.S. veterinarian] any of certain rod-shaped bacteria that cause various diseases, as typhoid fever, food poisoning, etc.

salmon ladder a series of steps to enable a salmon to move upstream to its breeding grounds: also **salmon stair, salmon leap**

sa·lon (sal′on; Fr. sȧ lōn′) *n.* [Fr.: see SALOON] 1. a large reception hall 2. a drawing room of a French private home 3. a regular gathering of distinguished persons, writers, artists, etc. in a celebrity's home 4. *a)* an art gallery *b)* an art exhibition 5. a shop or business place specially equipped for performing some personal service [beauty *salon*]

sa·loon (sə lōōn′) *n.* [Fr. *salon* < It. < *sala*, a hall] 1. any large room or hall for receptions, exhibitions, etc.; specif., the main social cabin of a passenger ship 2. a room in a public house that is supposed to be quieter and more comfortable than the public bar: also **saloon bar** 3. [U.S.] a place where alcoholic drinks are sold to be drunk on the premises 4. an enclosed motor car with two or four doors, and usually a wide seat in the rear: also **saloon car**

sa·loon·keep·er (-kēp′ər) *n.* [U.S.] a person who operates a saloon (sense 3)

sal·si·fy (sal′sə fē′, -fī′) *n.* [< Fr. < It. *sassefrica*] a plant of the composite family, with white, edible, fleshy roots

sal soda crystallized sodium carbonate

SALT (sôlt) Strategic Arms Limitation Talks

salt (sôlt) *n.* [OE. *sealt*] 1. sodium chloride, NaCl, a white, crystalline substance found in natural beds, in sea water, etc., and used for seasoning and preserving food, etc. 2. a chemical compound derived from an acid by replacing hydrogen, wholly or partly, with a metal or an electropositive radical 3. that which lends tang or piquancy, as pungent wit 4. *same as* SALTCELLAR 5. [pl.] mineral salts used as a cathartic (as **Epsom salts**), to soften bath water (**bath salts**), as a restorative (**smelling salts**), etc. 6. [Colloq.] a sailor —*adj.* 1. containing salt 2. preserved with salt 3. tasting or smelling of salt 4. *a)* flooded with salt water *b)* growing in salt water —*vt.* 1. to sprinkle, season, or preserve with salt 2. to treat or provide with salt 3. to give tang to 4. to put minerals in (a mine), oil in (a well), etc. so as to deceive prospective buyers —**salt away** (or **down**) 1. to pack and preserve with salt 2. [Colloq.] to store or save (money, etc.) —**the salt of the earth** [after Matt 5:13] any person or persons regarded as the finest, noblest, etc. —**with a grain** (or **pinch**) **of salt** with allowance or reserve; sceptically —**worth one's salt** worth one's wages, etc. —**salt′er** *n.* —**salt′ish** *adj.* —**salt′-like′** *adj.* —**salt′ness** *n.*

salt-and-pep·per (-'n pep′ər) *adj.* *same as* PEPPER-AND-SALT

salt·cel·lar (-sel′ər) *n.* [< ME. < *salt*, salt + MFr. *salière*, saltcellar] 1. a small dish or shaker for salt at the table 2. the hollow in the neck above the collarbone

salt lick 1. an exposed natural deposit of rock salt which animals come to lick 2. a block of rock salt placed in a pasture for cattle, etc. to lick

salt marsh grassland over which salt water flows at intervals: also **salt meadow**

salt mine 1. a mine where rock salt is obtained 2. any place where hard labour is necessary

salt·pe·tre (sôlt′pēt′ər) *n.* [< L. *sal*, salt + *petra*, a rock] 1. *same as* POTASSIUM NITRATE 2. *see* CHILE SALTPETRE

salt pork pork cured in salt

salt·shak·er (sôlt′shā′kər) *n.* a container for salt, with a perforated top for shaking out the salt

sal·tus (sal′təs) *n., pl.* **-tus·es** [< L. *saltus*, a leap] a break in the continuity of a sequence; a sudden transition

salt·wa·ter (-wôt′ər) *adj.* of, having to do with, or living in saltwater or the sea

salt·works (-wurks') *n., pl.* **-works'** a place where salt is made, as by evaporation of natural brines

salt·wort (-wurt') *n.* any of a genus of plants of the goosefoot family, growing on seashores or saline soils

salt·y (sôl'tē) *adj.* **salt'i·er, salt'i·est** 1. of, tasting of, or containing salt 2. smelling of or suggesting the sea 3. *a*) sharp; piquant *b*) coarse or earthy —**salt'i·ly** *adv.* —**salt'i·ness** *n.*

sa·lu·bri·ous (sə lōō'brē əs) *adj.* [L. *salubris* < *salus*, health] promoting health or welfare; healthful, wholesome, salutary, etc. —**sa·lu'bri·ous·ly** *adv.* —**sa·lu'bri·ty** (-brə tē), **sa·lu'bri·ous·ness** *n.*

Sa·lu·ki (sə lōō'kē) *n.* [Ar. *salūqīy* < *Satuq*, ancient Arabian city] any of an ancient breed of dog shaped like a greyhound but having long ears and silky hair

sal·u·tar·y (sal'yōō tər ē) *adj.* [< Fr. < L. < *salus* (gen. *salutis*), health] 1. promoting health; healthful 2. promoting some good purpose; beneficial —**sal'u·tar·i·ly** *adv.* —**sal'u·tar·i·ness** *n.*

sal·u·ta·tion (sal'yōō tā'shən) *n.* [< MFr. < L. < pp. of *salutare*: see SALUTE] 1. the act of greeting, addressing, etc. by gestures or words 2. certain words serving as a greeting or as the opening of a letter, as "Dear Sir"

sa·lu·ta·to·ry (sə lōōt'ə tər ē) *adj.* of or expressing a salutation

sa·lute (sə lōōt') *vt.* **-lut'ed, -lut'ing** [< L. *salutare* < *salus*: see SALUTARY] 1. to greet in a friendly way, as by bowing, tipping the hat, etc. 2. to honour ceremonially and officially by firing cannon, raising the right hand to the forehead, etc. 3. to present itself to, as if in greeting 4. to acknowledge with praise; commend —*vi.* to make a salute —*n.* 1. an act, remark, or gesture made in saluting 2. *Mil.* the position of the hand, etc. assumed in saluting —**take the salute** to receive a formal salute, usually from a parade or procession as it passes

Sal·va·do·ran (sal'və dôr'ən) *adj.* of El Salvador, its people, or culture —*n.* a native or inhabitant of El Salvador Also **Sal'va·do'ri·an** (-dôr'ē ən)

sal·vage (sal'vij) *n.* [Fr. < MFr. < *salver*, to SAVE[1]] 1. *a*) the rescue of a ship and cargo at sea from fire, shipwreck, etc. *b*) compensation paid for such rescue *c*) the ship or cargo so rescued *d*) the bringing up of a sunken ship or its cargo by divers, caissons, etc. 2. *a*) the saving of any goods, etc. from destruction or waste *b*) goods, etc. so saved *c*) the proceeds from sale of such goods, etc. as in settling insurance claims —*vt.* **-vaged, -vag·ing** to save or rescue from shipwreck, destruction or loss; engage or succeed in the salvage of (ships, goods, etc.) —**sal'vage·a·bil'i·ty** *n.* —**sal'vage·a·ble** *adj.* —**sal'vag·er** *n.*

sal·va·tion (sal vā'shən) *n.* [< OFr. < LL. < L. pp. of *salvare*, to SAVE[1]] 1. a saving or being saved 2. a person or thing that saves or rescues 3. *Theol.* spiritual rescue from the consequences of sin —**sal·va'tion·al** *adj.*

Salvation Army a Christian organization that works to bring religion and help to the very poor —**Sal·va'tion·ist** *n.*

salve[1] (säv, salv) *n.* [OE. *sealf*] 1. any soothing or healing ointment applied to wounds, burns, sores, etc. 2. anything that soothes or heals; balm —*vt.* **salved, salv'ing** to soothe

salve[2] (salv) *vt.* **salved, salv'ing** *same as* SALVAGE

sal·ver (sal'vər) *n.* [< Fr. < Sp. *salva* < *salvar*, to taste (so as to prove food wholesome) < L. *salvare*, to SAVE[1]] a tray on which something is served or presented

sal·vi·a (sal'vē ə) *n.* [ModL., genus name < L.] *same as* SAGE[2] (sense 1)

sal·vo (sal'vō) *n., pl.* **-vos, -voes** [< It. < L. *salve*, hail!] 1. a discharge of a number of guns in succession or at the same time, either in salute or at a target 2. the release of a load of bombs or the launching of several rockets at the same time 3. a burst of cheers or applause

sal vo·la·ti·le (vō lat'əl ē') [ModL., volatile salt] ammonium carbonate, used in smelling salts

SAM (sam) surface-to-air missile

Sam. Samuel

sam·a·ra (sam'ər ə) *n.* [ModL. < L., elm seed] a dry, winged, seeded fruit, as of the ash

Sa·mar·i·tan (sə mar'ət'n) *n.* 1. a native or inhabitant of Samaria 2. *see* GOOD SAMARITAN —*adj.* of Samaria or its people

sa·mar·i·um (sə mer'ē əm, -mar'-) *n.* [ModL. < *samarskite*, a mineral, ult. < Col. *Samarski*, Russ. mining official] a metallic chemical element of the rare-earth group: symbol, Sm; at. wt., 150.35; at. no., 62

sam·ba (sam'bə) *n.* [Port., prob. of Afr. origin] 1. a Brazilian dance of African origin 2. music for this dance —*vi.* to dance the samba

Sam Browne belt (sam'broun') [after 19th-c. Brit. Gen. *Samuel J.*

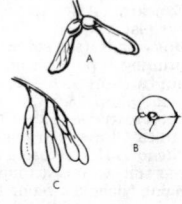

SAMARAS
A, sycamore;
B, ash; C, elm

Browne] a military officer's belt with a diagonal strap across the right shoulder

same (sām) *adj.* [ON. *samr*] 1. being the very one; identical 2. alike in kind, quality, amount, etc.; corresponding 3. unchanged; not different [he looks the *same*] 4. before-mentioned; just spoken of [one and the *same*] —*pron.* the same person or thing —*adv.* 1. in the same way 2. nevertheless The *adj.* & *pron.* are usually used with *the, this,* or *that;* the *adv.,* with *the* —**all the same** 1. nevertheless: also **just the same** 2. indifferent —**same'ness** *n.*

sam·fu (sam'fōō) *n.* [< Cantonese] a style of dress worn by Chinese women consisting of a waisted blouse and trousers: also **sam'foo**

Sa·mi·an (sā'mē ən) *adj.* of Samos or its people —*n.* a native or inhabitant of Samos

Samian ware a fine earthenware pottery, made chiefly in Gaul and widely distributed throughout the Roman Empire including Britain

sam·i·sen (sam'ə sen') *n.* [Jap. < Chin. *san hsien,* three strings] a three-stringed Japanese musical instrument, somewhat like a banjo

sam·ite (sam'īt, sā'mīt) *n.* [< MFr. < ML. < MGr. < *hexamitos,* woven with six threads] a heavy silk fabric interwoven with gold or silver threads, worn in the Middle Ages

‡**sam·iz·dat** (sam'iz dat') *n.* [Russ., lit., self-published] a system by which manuscripts denied official publication in Russia are circulated clandestinely

sam·o·var (sam'ə vär', sam'ə vär') *n.* [Russ., lit., self-boiler] a Russian metal urn with an internal tube for heating water for tea

Sam·o·yed, Sam·o·yede (sam'oi yed') *n.* [Russ.] 1. any of a Uralic people of Siberia 2. their language 3. any of a strong breed of Siberian dog, with a thick, white coat —*adj.* of the Samoyeds or their language: also **Sam'o·yed'ic**

sam·pan (sam'pan) *n.* [Chin. *san-pan* < ? *san,* three + *pan,* a plank] any of various small boats used in China and Japan, rowed with a scull from the stern, and often having a sail and a small cabin formed of mats

sam·phire (sam'fīr') *n.* [earlier *sampire,* altered < Fr. (*herbe de*) *Saint Pierre,* St. Peter's (herb)] 1. a seashore plant with fleshy divided leaves and small clusters of yellowish flowers. 2. *same as* GLASSWORT

SAMOVAR

sam·ple (säm'p'l) *n.* [< OFr.: see EXAMPLE] 1. a part, piece, or item that shows what the whole thing or group is like; specimen or example [samples of wallpaper, a *sample* of his humour] 2. *Statistics* a selected part of the population studied to gain knowledge of the whole —*vt.* **-pled, -pling** to take or test a sample of —*adj.* being a sample; typical

sam·pler (-plər) *n.* 1. a person who prepares or tests samples 2. a cloth embroidered with designs, mottoes, etc. in different stitches

Sam·son (sam's'n) *n.* [LL. < Gr.: after *Samson,* an Israelite noted for his great strength: Judges 13-16] a man of outstanding strength

sam·u·rai (sam'ə rī') *n., pl.* **-rai** [Jap.] 1. a member of a military class in feudal Japan 2. a Japanese army officer or member of the military caste

‡**-san** (sän) [Jap.] a Japanese honorific suffix added to names, titles, etc.

san·a·tive (san'ə tiv) *adj.* [ME. < LL. *sanativus* < L. *sanatus,* prp. of *sanare,* to heal] having the power to heal or cure; curative: also **san'a·to·ry** (-tər ē)

san·a·to·ri·um (san'ə tôr'ē əm) *n., pl.* **-ri·ums, -ri·a** (-ə) [ModL. < LL. *sanatorius,* giving health < L. *sanare,* to heal] a nursing home, hospital, etc. for the treatment of invalids or convalescents

sanc·ti·fied (saŋk'tə fīd') *adj.* 1. made holy; consecrated 2. sanctimonious

sanc·ti·fy (saŋk'tə fī') *vt.* **-fied', -fy'ing** [< OFr. < LL. *sanctificare:* see SAINT & -FY] 1. to make holy; specif., *a*) to set apart as holy; consecrate *b*) to make free from sin; purify 2. to make binding or inviolable by sanction —**sanc'ti·fi·ca'tion** *n.* —**sanc'ti·fi'er** *n.*

sanc·ti·mo·ni·ous (saŋk'tə mō'nē əs) *adj.* pretending to be very pious; affecting sanctity or righteousness —**sanc'ti·mo'ni·ous·ly** *adv.* —**sanc'ti·mo'ni·ous·ness** *n.*

sanc·ti·mo·ny (saŋk'tə mō'nē) *n.* [< OFr. < L. *sanctimonia* < *sanctus,* holy] affected piety or righteousness

sanc·tion (saŋk'shən) *n.* [< Fr. < L. < *sanctus,* holy] 1. the confirming or ratifying of an action by authority; authorization 2. support; approval 3. something that gives binding force to a law, as the penalty for breaking it or a reward for carrying it out 4. something, as a moral principle or influence, that makes a rule of conduct, etc.

binding **5.** [*usually pl.*] a boycott, blockade, or similar coercive measure, as against one nation by others to enforce international law —*vt.* to give sanction to; specif., *a)* to ratify or confirm *b)* to authorize or permit —**sanc'tion·a·ble** *adj.*

sanc·ti·ty (saŋk'tə tē) *n., pl.* **-ties** [< L. < *sanctus*, holy] **1.** saintliness or holiness **2.** a being sacred or inviolable **3.** anything held sacred

sanc·tu·ar·y (saŋk'tyo̅o̅ wər ē) *n., pl.* **-ar·ies** [< MFr. < LL. < L. *sanctus*, sacred] **1.** a holy place, as a building set aside for worship; specif., *a)* the ancient Temple at Jerusalem *b)* any church, temple, etc. *c)* a holy place within a church, temple, etc., as the part around the altar, the holy of holies, etc. **2.** a place of refuge or protection [she took *sanctuary* in the Abbey] **3.** refuge; immunity from punishment **4.** a reservation where animals or birds may not be hunted or trapped

sanc·tum (saŋk'təm) *n., pl.* **-tums, -ta** (-tə) [L., neut. of *sanctus*, holy] **1.** a sacred place **2.** a study or private room where one is not to be disturbed

sanctum sanc·to·rum (saŋk tôr'əm) [LL.] **1.** *same as* HOLY OF HOLIES **2.** a place of utmost privacy

sand (sand) *n.* [OE.] **1.** loose, gritty grains of disintegrated rock, as on beaches, in deserts, etc. **2.** [*usually pl.*] an area of sand; beach **3.** the sand in an hourglass **4.** [*pl.*] moments of time [the *sands* were running out] —*vt.* **1.** to sprinkle, fill, or mix with sand **2.** to smooth or polish with sand or sandpaper —**sand'ed** *adj.* —**sand'er** *n.*

san·dal[1] (san'd'l) *n.* [< L. < Gr. dim. of *sandalon*] **1.** a kind of footwear consisting of a sole fastened in various ways to the foot by straps over the instep or toes, or round the ankles **2.** any of various low slippers —**san'dalled** *adj.*

san·dal[2] (san'd'l) *n. same as* SANDALWOOD

san·dal·wood (-wood') *n.* [< MFr. < ML., ult. < Sans. *candana*] **1.** the hard, sweet-smelling heartwood of any of certain Asiatic trees, used for carving and cabinetmaking or burned as incense **2.** any tree yielding such wood

sand·bag (sand'bag') *n.* **1.** a bag filled with sand and used for ballast, in fortifications, for embankments against floods, etc. **2.** a small, sand-filled bag used as a bludgeon —*vt.* **-bagged', -bag'ging 1.** to place sandbags in or around **2.** to hit with a sandbag **3.** [U.S. Colloq.] to force into doing something —**sand'bag'ger** *n.*

sand bar a ridge or narrow shoal of sand formed in a river or along a shore by the action of currents or tides: also **sand·bank** (-baŋk') *n.*

sand·blast (-bläst') *n.* **1.** a current of air or steam carrying sand at a high velocity, used in etching glass and in cleaning surfaces as of metals, stone, etc. **2.** the machine used to apply this blast —*vt.* to engrave, clean, etc. with a sandblast —**sand'blast'er** *n.*

sand·box (-boks') *n.* **1.** a box on a locomotive from which sand is released to improve the traction on the rails **2.** [U.S.] a sandpit

sand·cas·tle (-käs''l) *n.* the edifice resembling a castle constructed by children out of sand

sand·er·ling (san'dər liŋ) *n.* [prob. < SAND + OE. *yrthling*, farmer, kind of bird] a bird of the sandpiper family found on sandy beaches

sand flea 1. any of various crustaceans found on sandy beaches, that jump like fleas **2.** *same as* CHIGOE

sand·man (-man') *n.* in fairy tales, etc. a person supposed to make children sleepy by dusting sand in their eyes

sand martin a European bird of the swallow family, mostly brown, that nests in sand burrows in river banks, etc.

sand·pa·per (-pā'pər) *n.* a strong paper with sand glued on one side, used for smoothing and polishing—*vt.* to smooth or polish with sandpaper

sand·pip·er (-pī'pər) *n., pl.* **-pip'ers, -pip'er:** see PLURAL, II, D, 1 a small wading bird with a long, soft-tipped bill

sand·pit (-pit) *n.* **1.** a box containing sand for children to play in **2.** a pit from which sand is extracted

sand·stone (sand'stōn') *n.* a common sedimentary rock much used for building, composed largely of sand grains, mainly quartz, cemented together by silica, etc.

sand·storm (-stôrm') *n.* a windstorm in which large quantities of sand are blown about

sand trap a hollow filled with sand, serving as a hazard on a golf course; bunker

sand·wich (sand'wich, san'-) *n.* [< 4th Earl of *Sandwich* (1718–1792)] two or more slices of bread with a filling of meat, cheese, etc. between them —*vt.* to place between other persons, things, materials, etc.

sandwich course a course of study in which academic study is alternated with practical experience in industry, etc.

sandwich man a man who walks the streets with two signboards (**sandwich boards**) hung from his shoulders, in front and behind

sand·y (san'dē) *adj.* **sand'i·er, sand'i·est 1.** composed of, full of, or covered with sand **2.** like sand; gritty, shifting,

etc. **3.** pale brown or dark yellow [*sandy hair*] —**sand'i·ness** *n.*

sand yacht a vehicle mounted on wheels that uses sails to skim over stretches of firm sand

sandy blight [Aust.] a form of ophthalmia that causes the eyes to feel full of sand

sane (sān) *adj.* [L. *sanus*, healthy] **1.** having a normal, healthy mind; able to make sound, rational judgments **2.** showing good sense; sensible [a *sane* policy] —**sane'ly** *adv.* —**sane'ness** *n.*

San·for·ize (san'fə rīz') *vt.* **-ized', -iz'ing** [from the trademark *Sanforized*, applied to fabrics so treated: after *Sanford* L. Cluett (1874–1968), the inventor] to preshrink (cloth) permanently by a patented process before making garments

sang (saŋ) *pt. of* SING

‡**sang-de-boeuf** (sän'də bœf') *adj.* [Fr. lit., ox-blood] of a dark red colour found on antique Chinese porcelain —*n.* this dark red colour

sang-froid (säg'frwä'; Fr. sän frwä') *n.* [Fr., lit., cold blood] cool self-possession or composure

San·graal (san grāl') *n.* [ME. < OFr. *saint graal*, holy grail] *same as* GRAIL: also **Sangreal, Sangrail**

‡**san·gri·a** (sän grē'ä) *n.* [Sp. lit., bleeding < L. *sanguis*, blood] a Spanish punch made with red wine and fruit

san·gui·nar·y (saŋ'gwi nər ē) *adj.* [< L. < *sanguis*: see ff.] **1.** with much bloodshed or killing **2.** of or stained with blood **3.** bloodthirsty —**san'gui·nar·i·ly** *adv.* —**san'gui·nar·i·ness** *n.*

san·guine (saŋ'gwin) *adj.* [< OFr. < L. < *sanguis* (gen. *sanguinis*), blood] **1.** of the colour of blood; ruddy **2.** [from medieval notion about those in whom blood is the main humour] cheerful; confident; optimistic —**san'guine·ly** *adv.* —**san'guine·ness** *n.*

san·guin·e·ous (saŋ gwin'ē əs) *adj.* [see prec.] *same as:* **1.** SANGUINARY **2.** SANGUINE

San·he·drin (san hed'rin, -hē'drin) *n.* [< Heb. < Gr. < *syn-*, together + *hedra*, seat] the highest court and council of the ancient Jewish nation, having religious and civic functions

san·i·tar·i·um (san'ə ter'ē əm) əm) *n., pl.* **-i·ums, -i·a** (-ə) [ModL. < *sanitas*, health] *U.S. var of* SANATORIUM

san·i·tar·y (san'ə tər ē, -trē) *adj.* [< Fr. < L. *sanitas*, health] **1.** of health or the rules and conditions of health; esp., promoting health by getting rid of dirt and things that bring disease **2.** free from dirt, etc. that could bring disease; clean; hygienic —**san'i·tar·i·ly** *adv.* —**san'i·tar·i·ness** *n.*

sanitary engineering that branch of civil engineering concerned with sewage disposal, water supply, etc. —**sanitary engineer**

sanitary napkin an absorbent pad of cotton, etc. worn by women during menstruation

san·i·ta·tion (san'ə tā'shən) *n.* **1.** the science and work of bringing about healthful and hygienic conditions **2.** drainage and disposal of sewage

san·i·tize (san'ə tīz') *vt.* **-tized', -tiz'ing** to make sanitary, as by sterilizing —**san'i·tiz'er** *n.*

san·i·ty (san'ə tē) *n.* [< OFr. < L. *sanitas*, health] **1.** the condition of being sane; soundness of mind; mental health **2.** soundness of judgment

sank (saŋk) *pt. of* SINK

sans (sanz; Fr. sän) *prep.* [< OFr. *sanz* (Fr. *sans*) < L. *sine*, without] without; lacking

Sans. Sanskrit

sans-cu·lotte (sanz'kyo̅o̅ lot') *n.* [Fr., without breeches] a revolutionary: term of contempt applied by the aristocrats to the republicans in the French Revolution, who wore pantaloons instead of knee breeches

san·se·vi·e·ri·a (san'sə vir'ē ə, -vi ē'rē ə) *n.* [ModL., after the Prince of *Sanseviero* (1710–71)] any of a genus of succulent plants with thick, lance-shaped leaves

San·skrit (san'skrit) *n.* [< Sans. *samskrta*, lit., made together, well arranged] the classical Old Indic literary language: important in the study of comparative Indo-European linguistics —*adj.* of or written in Sanskrit Also sp. **San'scrit** —**San·skrit'ic** *adj.* —**San'·skrit·ist** *n.*

sans-ser·if (san ser'if) *n.* [see SANS & SERIF] a style of printing type with no serifs: also **san·ser'if**

San·ta (san'tə; *for adj., also* sän'tä) *short for* SANTA CLAUS —*adj.* [Sp. & It., saint, fem.] holy or saint: used in combinations [*Santa Maria*]

San·ta Claus (san'tə klôz) [< Du. dial. < *Sant Nikolass*, St. Nicholas] *Folklore* a fat, white-bearded, jolly old man in a red suit, who distributes gifts at Christmas time: also called **Saint Nicholas, Saint Nick**

sap[1] (sap) *n.* [OE. *sæp*] **1.** the juice that circulates through a plant, esp. a woody plant, bearing water, food, etc. **2.** any fluid considered vital to life or health **3.** vigour; energy **4.** [Slang] a stupid person: in full, **sap'head'** (-hed') or **sap'skull'**—*vt.* **sapped, sap'ping** to drain of sap

sap² (sap) *n.* [MFr. *sappe*, a spade < It. *zappe*] a trench for approaching or undermining an enemy position —*vt.* **sapped, sap′ping** 1. to undermine by digging away foundations 2. to undermine in any way; weaken; exhaust —*vi.* 1. to dig saps 2. to approach a position by saps

sap green 1. a paint made from buckthorn berries 2. the light green colour of this paint

sap·id (sap′id) *adj.* [L. *sapidus* < *sapere*, to have a taste] 1. having a taste, esp. a pleasing one 2. interesting; engaging —**sa·pid′i·ty** (sə pid′ə tē)

sa·pi·ent (sā′pē ənt) *adj.* [< L. prp. of *sapere*, to taste, know] full of knowledge; wise; discerning —**sa′pi·ence** *n.* —**sa′pi·ent·ly** *adv.*

sa·pi·en·tial (sā′pē en′shəl) *adj.* [see prec.] having, providing, or expounding wisdom

sap·ling (sap′liŋ) *n.* 1. a young tree 2. a youth

sap·o·dil·la (sap′ə dil′ə) *n.* [< Sp. < Nahuatl *tzapotl*] 1. a tropical American evergreen tree, yielding chicle and having a brown fruit with a yellowish pulp 2. the fruit

sap·o·na·ceous (sap′ə nā′shəs) *adj.* [< ModL. < L. *sapo*, soap] soapy or soaplike

sa·pon·i·fy (sə pon′ə fī′) *vt.* **-fied′, -fy′ing** [< Fr. < L. *sapo* (gen. *saponis*), soap + *facere*, to make] to convert (a fat) into soap by reaction with an alkali —*vi.* to be made into soap —**sa·pon′i·fi′a·ble** *adj.* —**sa·pon′i·fi·ca′tion** *n.*

sap·per (sap′ər) *n.* 1. a soldier employed in digging saps, laying mines, etc., esp. a soldier in the Royal Engineers 2. a private of the Royal Engineers 3. a person or thing that saps

Sap·phic (saf′ik) *adj.* [L. *Sapphicus* < Gr. *Sapphikos* < *Sapphō*] 1. of Sappho 2. of certain metres used by or named after Sappho 3. of, or relating to, a lesbian relationship —*n.* a Sapphic verse

sap·phire (saf′īr) *n.* [< OFr. < L. < Gr. *sappheiros*] 1. a hard, transparent precious stone of a clear, deep-blue corundum 2. its colour 3. a hard variety of corundum, varying in colour 4. a gem made of this —*adj.* deep-blue

sap·py (sap′ē) *adj.* **-pi·er, -pi·est** 1. full of sap; juicy 2. [Slang] foolish; silly; fatuous —**sap′pi·ness** *n.*

sap·ro- (sap′rō, -rə) [< Gr. *sapros*, rotten] a *combining form meaning* dead, decaying: also, before a vowel, **sapr-**

sap·ro·phyte (sap′rə fīt′) *n.* [< Gr. *sapros*, rotten + -PHYTE] any organism that lives on dead or decaying organic matter, as some fungi —**sap′ro·phyt′ic** (-fit′ik) *adj.*

sap·wood (sap′wood′) *n.* the soft wood between the inner bark of a tree and the heartwood, serving to conduct water

sar·a·band (sar′ə band′) *n.* [< Fr. < Sp., ult. < Per. *sarband*, kind of dance] 1. a graceful, stately, slow Spanish dance in triple time 2. music for this dance

Sar·a·cen (sar′ə s'n) *n.* any Arab or any Moslem, esp. at the time of the Crusades —*adj.* of the Saracens

sar·casm (sär′kaz'm) *n.* [< LL. < Gr. < *sarkazein*, to tear flesh like dogs < *sarx*, flesh] 1. a taunting or sneering remark; gibe or jeer, generally ironical 2. the making of such remarks 3. sarcastic quality

sar·cas·tic (sär kas′tik) *adj.* 1. of, like, or full of sarcasm; sneering 2. using sarcasm —**sar·cas′ti·cal·ly** *adv.*

sar·co- [< Gr. *sarx*, flesh] a *combining form meaning* flesh: also, before a vowel, **sarc-**

sar·co·carp (sär′kə kärp′) *n.* [prec. + -CARP] the fleshy part of a stone fruit, as in the plum

sar·co·ma (sär kō′mə) *n.,* pl. **-mas, -ma·ta** (-mə tə) [ModL. < Gr. < *sarx*, flesh] any of various malignant tumours that begin in connective tissue —**sar·co′ma·to′sis** (-tō′sis) *n.* —**sar·co′ma·tous** (-təs) *adj.*

sar·coph·a·gus (sär kof′ə gəs) *n.,* pl. **-gi′** (-jī′, -gī′), **-gus·es** [L. < Gr. < *sarx*, flesh + *phagein*, to eat: because the limestone orig. used hastened disintegration] a stone coffin, esp. one on display, as in a monumental tomb

sar·cous (sär′kəs) *adj.* [SARCO- + -OUS] *Zool.* of or composed of flesh or muscle

sard (särd) *n.* [L. *sarda*] a very hard, deep orange-red variety of chalcedony, used in jewellery, etc.

sar·dine¹ (sär dēn′) *n.,* pl. **-dines′, -dine′:** see PLURAL, II, D, 1 [< MFr. < L. < *sarda*, kind of fish] any of various small ocean fishes preserved in tightly packed tins for eating; specif., *same as* PILCHARD —**like sardines** closely packed; crowded together

sar·dine² (sär′din, -dīn) *adj.* *same as* SARD

sar·don·ic (sär don′ik) *adj.* [< Fr. < L. < Gr. < *sardanios*, bitter, scornful] disdainfully or bitterly sneering or sarcastic [a *sardonic* smile] —**sar·don′i·cal·ly** *adv.*

sar·do·nyx (sär′də niks) *n.* [L. < Gr. < *sardios*, sard + *onyx*, onyx] a variety of onyx made up of layers of white chalcedony and sard, used as a gem

sar·gas·sum (sär gas′əm) *n.* [ModL. < Port. < *sarga*, kind of grape] any of various floating, brown seaweeds having special branches with berrylike air sacs: also **sar·gas′so** (-ō), pl. **-sos,** sargasso weed

sarge (särj) *n.* *colloq.* shortened form of SERGEANT

sa·ri (sä′rē) *n.* [< Hindi < Sans.] an outer garment of Hindu women, a long cloth wrapped around the body with one end over the shoulder: also sp. **sa′ree**

SARI

sa·rod, sa·rode (sə rōd′) *n.* [Hindi *sarod* < Per.] a lutelike musical instrument of India, with many strings

sa·rong (sə roŋ′) *n.* [Malay *sarung*] a garment of men and women in the Malay Archipelago, the East Indies, etc., consisting of a long cloth, often brightly coloured and printed, worn like a skirt

sar·sa·pa·ril·la (säs′pə ril′ə, sär′sə-) *n.* [< Sp. < *zarza*, bramble + dim. of *parra*, vine] 1. a tropical American plant with fragrant roots 2. its dried root, or an extract 3. a carbonated drink flavoured with sarsaparilla

sarse·net (särs′net) *n.* [ME. < Anglo-Fr. *sarzinett*, dim < OFr. *Sarrazin*, SARACEN] a soft, silk cloth, formerly used for ribbons, linings, etc.: also **sarce′net**

sar·to·ri·al (sär tôr′ē əl) *adj.* [< LL. *sartor*, a tailor] 1. of tailors or their work 2. of men's clothing or dress —**sar·to′·ri·al·ly** *adv.*

sar·to·ri·us (-əs) *n.* [ModL. < LL. *sartor*, a tailor: in reference to the traditional cross-legged position of tailors at work] a narrow muscle of the thigh, the longest in the human body, used to rotate the knee to enable someone to sit cross-legged

S.A.S.E., s.a.s.e. Self-Addressed Stamped Envelope

sash¹ (sash) *n.* [Ar. *shāsh*, muslin] an ornamental ribbon or scarf worn over the shoulder or around the waist

sash² (sash) *n.* [taken as sing. of earlier *shashes* < Fr. *châssis*, a frame] a frame for holding the glass pane of a window or door, esp. a sliding frame as in a **sash window** —*vt.* to furnish with sashes

sa·shay (sa shā′) *vi.* [altered < *chassé* (dance)] [U.S. Colloq.] to move, walk, or go, esp. casually

sash cord a cord attached to either side of a sliding sash, having balancing weights (**sash weights**) for raising or lowering the window easily

sass (sas) *n.* [var. of SAUCE] [U.S. Colloq.] impudent talk —*vt.* [U.S. Colloq.] to talk impudently to

sas·sa·fras (sas′ə fras′) *n.* [Sp. *sasafras*] 1. a small eastern N. American tree bearing small, bluish fruits 2. the dried root bark of this tree, used as a flavouring

Sas·se·nach (sas′ə nak′, -'n akh) *n.* [Ir. *Sasanach* or Gael. *Sasunach* < Gael. *Sasunn*, Saxon] an Englishman: term used, often disparagingly by Scots & occasionally Irish

sass·y (sas′ē) *adj.* **sass′i·er, sass′i·est** [dial. var. of SAUCY] [U.S. Colloq.] impudent; saucy —**sass′i·ly** *adv.* —**sass′i·ness** *n.*

sat (sat) *pt. & pp.* of SIT

Sat. 1. Saturday 2. Saturn

Sa·tan (sāt′'n) [OE., ult. < Heb. *sātān*, to plot against] *Christian Theol.* the chief evil spirit; the Devil

sa·tang (sa taŋ′) *n.,* pl. **-tang** [Siamese *satāṇ*] *see* MONETARY UNITS, table (Thailand)

sa·tan·ic (sā tan′ik, sə-) *adj.* of or like Satan; devilish; wicked: also **sa·tan′i·cal** —**sa·tan′i·cal·ly** *adv.*

Sa·tan·ism (sāt′'n iz′m) *n.* [chiefly after Fr. *satanisme*] worship of Satan —**Sa′tan·ist** *n.*

S.A.T.B. *Music* Soprano, Alto, Tenor, Bass

satch·el (sach′əl) *n.* [< OFr. < L. dim. of *saccus*, a sack] a small bag for carrying clothes, books, etc., usually having a shoulder strap

sate¹ (sāt) *vt.* **sat′ed, sat′ing** [prob. < L. *satiare*, to fill full] 1. to satisfy (an appetite, desire, etc.) to the full 2. to satiate; surfeit; glut

sate² (sat, sāt) *archaic pt. & pp.* of SIT

sa·teen (sa tēn′, sə-) *n.* [< SATIN] a smooth, glossy cotton cloth, made to imitate satin

sat·el·lite (sat′əl īt′) *n.* [Fr. < L. *satelles*, an attendant] 1. a) an attendant of some important person *b)* an obsequious follower 2. *a)* a small planet revolving round a larger one *b)* a man-made object put into orbit round the earth, the moon, or some other heavenly body 3. a small state that is economically dependent on a larger state

sa·tia·ble (sā′shə b'l, sā′shē ə-) *adj.* that can be sated or satiated —**sa′tia·bil′i·ty** *n.* —**sa′tia·bly** *adv.*

sa·ti·ate (sā′shē āt′) *adj.* [< L. pp. of *satiare*, to satisfy < *satis*, enough] having had enough or more than enough —*vt.* **-at′ed, -at′ing** 1. [Rare] to sate; satisfy fully 2. to provide with more than enough, so as to weary or disgust; glut; surfeit —**sa′ti·a′tion** *n.*

sa·ti·e·ty (sə tī′ə tē) *n.* a being satiated; surfeit

sat·in (sat′in) *n.* [< MFr. < Sp. < Ar. *zaitūnī*, of *Zaitūn*, former name of a Chinese seaport] a fabric of silk, nylon, rayon, etc. with a smooth, glossy finish on one side —*adj.* of or like satin; smooth and glossy [a *satin* finish] —**sat′in·y** *adj.*

satin flower any of various flowers including: **1.** HONESTY **2.** CHICKWEED

sat·in·wood (sat'in wood') *n.* **1.** any of several smooth, hard woods used in fine furniture, etc. **2.** a tree yielding such wood, esp. one in the East or one in the West Indies

sat·ire (sa'tīr) *n.* [Fr. < L. *satira* or *satura*, a poetic medley < (*lanx*) *satura*, (dish) of fruits] **1.** a literary work in which vices, follies, etc. are held up to ridicule and contempt **2.** such works collectively **3.** the use of ridicule, sarcasm, irony, etc. to attack or deride vices, follies, etc.

sa·tir·i·cal (sə tir'i k'l) *adj.* **1.** of, like, or containing satire **2.** using satire Also **sa·tir'ic** —**sa·tir'i·cal·ly** *adv.*

sat·i·rist (sat'ə rist) *n.* **1.** a writer of satires **2.** a person given to satirizing

sat·i·rize (-rīz') *vt.* -**rized'**, -**riz'ing** to attack, ridicule, or criticize with satire —**sat'i·riz'er** *n.*

sat·is·fac·tion (sat'is fak'shən) *n.* **1.** a satisfying or being satisfied **2.** something that satisfies; specif., *a)* anything that brings pleasure or contentment *b)* settlement of debt *c)* reparation for injury or insult —**give satisfaction 1.** to satisfy **2.** to accept a challenge to duel or fight

sat·is·fac·to·ry (-fak'tər ē, -trē) *adj.* satisfying; fulfilling a need, wish, requirement, etc. adequately —**sat'is·fac'to·ri·ly** *adv.* —**sat'is·fac'to·ri·ness** *n.*

sat·is·fy (sat'is fī') *vt.* -**fied'**, -**fy'ing** [< OFr. < L. < *satis*, enough + *facere*, to make] **1.** to fulfil the needs or desires of; gratify **2.** to fulfil the requirements of **3.** to comply with (rules or obligations) **4.** *a)* to free from doubt; convince *b)* to answer (a doubt, etc.) adequately **5.** *a)* to give what is due to *b)* to discharge (a debt, etc.) **6.** to make reparation to or for —*vi.* to be adequate, sufficient, etc. —**satisfy the examiners** to attain the minimum standard necessary to pass a university examination —**sat'is·fi'a·ble** *adj.* —**sat'is·fi'er** *n.*

sa·to·ri (sə tôr'ē) *n.* [Jap.] *Zen Buddhism* spiritual enlightenment or illumination

sa·trap (sat'rap) *n.* [< L. < Gr. *satrapēs* < OPer.] **1.** the governor of a province in ancient Persia **2.** a ruler of a dependency, esp. a petty tyrant

sa·trap·y (sat'rə pē) *n.,* *pl.* -**trap·ies** the government, authority, or province of a satrap

Sat·su·ma (sat'soo mə) *n.* [< Jap. *Satsuma* Peninsula, where pottery was made] **1.** a variety of Japanese pottery **2.** [s-] a small, loose-skinned variety of orange

sat·u·ra·ble (sach'ər ə b'l) *adj.* that can be saturated —**sat'-u·ra·bil'i·ty** *n.*

sat·u·rate (sach'ə rāt') *vt.* -**rat'ed**, -**rat'ing** [< L. pp. of *saturare*, to fill up < *satur*, full] **1.** to cause to be thoroughly soaked **2.** to cause to be so completely filled or supplied that no more can be taken up **3.** *Chem. a)* to cause (a substance) to combine to its full capacity with another *b)* to dissolve the maximum amount of (a gas, liquid, or solid) in a solution —**sat'u·ra'tor** *n.*

sat·u·ra·tion (sach'ə rā'shən) *n.* **1.** a saturating or being saturated **2.** the degree to which a colour is free from mixture with white; intensity of hue

saturation point 1. the point at which the maximum amount of something has been absorbed **2.** the limit beyond which something cannot be continued, endured, etc.

Sat·ur·day (sat'ər di, -dā') *n.* [OE. *Sæterdæg*, Saturn's day] the seventh and last day of the week

Sat·ur·days (-diz, -dāz') *adv.* [Colloq.] on or during every Saturday

Sat·urn (sat'ərn) **1.** *Rom. Myth.* the god of agriculture: identified with the Greek god Cronus **2.** a planet in the solar system, sixth in distance from the sun: diameter, c. 1 900 000 km —**Sa·tur·ni·an** (sə tur'nē ən) *adj.*

Sat·ur·na·li·a (sat'ər nā'lē ə, -nāl'yə) *n.pl.* **1.** the ancient Roman festival of Saturn, held about December 17, with general feasting and revelry **2.** [s-] [often with sing. v. & with a pl. -li·as] a period of unrestrained revelry

sat·ur·nine (sat'ər nīn') *adj.* **1.** *Astrol.* born under the supposed influence of the planet Saturn **2.** sluggish, grave, taciturn, etc. —**sat'ur·nine'ly** *adv.*

‡**Sat·ya·gra·ha** (sat'yə gru'hə) *n.* [< Hindi; lit., a grasping for truth] the political doctrine of Gandhi, which favoured passive resistance and noncooperation in opposing British rule in India

sat·yr (sat'ər) *n.* [< L. < Gr. *satyros*] **1.** *Gr. Myth.* a lecherous woodland deity, attendant on Bacchus, represented as having pointed ears, short horns, the head and body of a man, and the legs of a goat **2.** a lecherous man

sat·y·ri·a·sis (sat'ə rī'ə sis) *n.* [LL. < Gr. *satyriasis*: see prec.] abnormal and uncontrollable desire by a man for sexual intercourse

sauce (sôs) *n.* [< OFr. < L. *salsa*, salted food, ult. < *sal*, salt] **1.** *a)* a liquid or soft dressing served with food as a relish *b)* a flavoured syrup put on ice cream, etc. **2.** something that adds interest or zest **3.** [Colloq.]

impudence —*vt.* **sauced, sauc'ing 1.** to flavour with a sauce **2.** to give flavour to **3.** [Colloq.] to be impudent or saucy to —**sauce for the goose is sauce for the gander** an appeal for consistency: often used as a retort in an argument

sauce·pan (-pən) *n.* a small pot with a projecting handle, used for cooking

sau·cer (sô'sər) *n.* [MFr. *saussier* < *sause*, SAUCE] **1.** a small, round, shallow dish, esp. one with an indentation to hold a cup **2.** anything round and shallow like a saucer [flying *saucer*] —**sau'cer·ful** *n.*

sau·cy (sô'sē) *adj.* -**ci·er**, -**ci·est** [SAUC(E) + -Y²] **1.** rude; impudent **2.** pert; sprightly [a *saucy* smile] **3.** stylish or smart —**sau'ci·ly** *adv.* —**sau'ci·ness** *n.*

sau·er·kraut (sour'krout') *n.* [G. *sauer*, sour + *Kraut*, cabbage] chopped cabbage fermented in a brine of its own juice with salt

sau·ger (sô'gər) *n.* [< ?] a small American pikeperch

sau·na (sô'nə) *n.* [Finn.] **1.** a Finnish bath, consisting of exposure to very hot, relatively dry air, with light beating of the skin with birch or cedar boughs **2.** the enclosure for such a bath

saun·ter (sôn'tər) *vi.* [< ?] to walk about idly; stroll —*n.* **1.** a leisurely and aimless walk **2.** a slow, leisurely gait —**saun'ter·er** *n.*

sau·ri·an (sôr'ē ən) *n.* [< Gr. *sauros*, a lizard] any of those reptiles that are lizards —*adj.* of or like lizards

-sau·rus (sôr'əs) [see prec.] a combining form meaning lizard

sau·sage (sô'sij) *n.* [< ONormFr. < VL. < L. *salsus*: see SAUCE] pork or other meat, finely chopped, highly seasoned, and stuffed into membranous casings —**not a sausage** [Colloq.] nothing whatsoever

sausage dog [Colloq.] a dachshund

sausage roll a small roll of pastry filled with sausage meat

sau·té (sō tā') *adj.* [Fr., pp. of *sauter*, to leap] fried quickly in a little fat —*vt.* -**téed'**, -**té'ing** to fry quickly in a pan with a little fat —*n.* a sautéed dish

sau·terne (sō turn') *n.* [< *Sauternes*, town in France] a white, usually sweet table wine

sav·age (sav'ij) *adj.* [< OFr. < VL. < L. *silvaticus*, wild < *silva*, a wood] **1.** wild; uncultivated [a *savage* jungle] **2.** fierce; untamed [a *savage* tiger] **3.** without civilization; barbarous [a *savage* tribe] **4.** crude; rude **5.** cruel; pitiless —*n.* **1.** a member of a primitive society or savage tribe **2.** a fierce, brutal person —*vt.* -**aged**, -**ag·ing** to attack violently, either physically or verbally —**sav'age·ly** *adv.* —**sav'age·ness** *n.*

sav·age·ry (-rē) *n.,* *pl.* -**ries 1.** the condition of being savage, wild, primitive, etc. **2.** savage act or behaviour

sa·van·na, sa·van·nah (sə van'ə) *n.* [< Sp. < *zavana* < native name] a treeless plain or a grassland with scattered trees, esp. in or near the tropics

sa·vant (sav'ənt) *n.* [Fr., orig. prp. of *savoir* < L. *sapere*, to know] a learned person

save¹ (sāv) *vt.* **saved, sav'ing** [< OFr. *salver* < L. < *salvus*, safe] **1.** to rescue or preserve from harm or danger **2.** to preserve for future use (often with *up*) **3.** to prevent loss or waste of [to *save* time] **4.** to avoid or lessen [to *save* wear and tear] **5.** to treat carefully in order to preserve, lessen wear, etc. **6.** *Theol.* to deliver from sin and punishment —*vi.* **1.** to avoid expense, loss, waste, etc.; economize to keep something or someone from danger, harm, etc. **3.** to hoard money or goods **4.** *Theol.* to exercise power to redeem from sin —*n.* *Sports* an action that keeps an opponent from scoring or winning —**sav'a·ble, save'a·ble** *adj.* —**sav'er** *n.*

save² (sāv) *prep.* [< OFr. *sauf*, lit., SAFE] except; but —*conj.* **1.** except; but **2.** [Archaic] unless

save-as-you-earn (sāv'əz yoo urn) *n.* a way of saving by having regular deposits made into a savings account from a salary or wage

sav·ing¹ (sā'viŋ) *adj.* that saves; specif., *a)* rescuing *b)* economical *c)* containing an exception [a *saving* clause] *d)* compensating; redeeming [a *saving* grace] —*n.* **1.** the act of one that saves **2.** [often pl. with sing. v.] any reduction in expense, time, etc. [a *saving(s)* of 10%] **3.** *a)* anything saved *b)* [pl.] sums of money saved

sav·ing² (sā'viŋ) *prep.* [Now Rare] **1.** with due respect for **2.** except; save —*conj.* [Now Rare] save

savings bank a bank in which savings may be deposited and earn interest for the depositor

savings certificate a certificate, issued by the government to savers, that also pays interest on the deposit

sav·iour (sāv'yər) *n.* [< OFr. < LL. *salvator* < *salvare*, to SAVE¹] a person who saves —**the Saviour** Jesus Christ Also U.S. sp., **sav'ior**

sa·voir-faire (sav'wär fer') *n.* [Fr., to know (how) to do] ready knowledge of what to do or say, and of when and how to do or say it; social poise and tact

sa·vor·y (sā'vər ē) *n.* [< OFr. *savoreie*, altered (prob. after

savour, SAVOUR] < L. *satureia,* savoury] a fragrant herb of the mint family, used in cooking

sa·vour (sā′vər) *n.* [< OFr. < L. *sapor*] **1.** the taste or smell of something; flavour **2.** characteristic quality **3.** noticeable trace **4.** power to excite interest, zest, etc. —*vi.* **1.** to have the particular taste, smell, or quality; smack (*of*) **2.** to show traces or signs (*of*) —*vt.* **1.** to season or flavour **2.** to taste or smell, esp. with relish **3.** to dwell on with delight; relish Also, U.S. sp., **savor** —**sa′vour·er** *n.* —**sa′vour·less** *adj.* —**sa′vour·ous** *adj.*

sa·vour·y (sā′vər ē) *adj.* -**vour·i·er,** -**vour·est** [< OFr. pp. of *savourer,* to taste < *savour,* SAVOUR] **1.** pleasing to the taste or smell **2.** pleasant, agreeable, etc. **3.** morally acceptable; respectable **4.** salty or piquant [a *savoury* relish] —*n., pl.* -**vour·ies** a small, highly seasoned portion of food served at the end of a meal or as an appetizer Also, U.S. sp., **savory** —**sa′vour·i·ness** *n.*

sa·voy (sə voi′) *n.* [Fr. *(chou de) Savoie,* (cabbage of) Savoy] a type of cabbage with a compact head

Sa·voy·ard (sə voi′ärd) *n.* [< the *Savoy,* London theatre] an actor, producer, or admirer of Gilbert and Sullivan operas

sav·vy (sav′ē) *vi.* -**vied,** -**vy·ing** [altered < Sp. *sabe* (*usted*), do (you) know? < *saber,* to know] [Slang] to understand; get the idea —*n.* [Slang] **1.** shrewd understánding **2.** skill or know-how —*adj.* [Chiefly U.S. Slang] shrewd or discerning

saw[1] (sô) *n.* [OE. *sagu*] **1.** a cutting tool having a thin, metal blade or disc with sharp teeth along the edge **2.** a machine that operates a saw —*vt.* **sawed, sawed** or **sawn, saw′ing 1.** to cut or shape with a saw **2.** to make sawlike cutting motions through or with (something) or produce with such motions **3.** to play a violin, viola, etc. with a bow —*vi.* **1.** to cut with a saw or as a saw does **2.** to be cut with a saw [wood that *saws* easily] **3.** to make sawlike cutting motions —**saw′er** *n.*

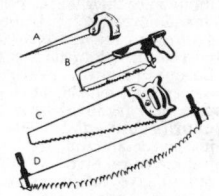

SAWS
(A, keyhole; B, hacksaw; C, handsaw; D, crosscut)

saw[2] (sô) *n.* [OE. *sagu*] an old saying; maxim

saw[3] (sô) *pt. of* SEE[1]

saw·bones (sô′bōnz′) *n.* [Slang] a surgeon

saw·buck (-buk′) *n.* [Du. *zaagbok*] [Chiefly U.S.] a sawhorse with the legs projecting above the crossbar

saw·dust (-dust′) *n.* tiny bits of wood formed in sawing

saw·fish (sô′fish′) *n., pl.* -**fish′, -fish′es:** see FISH any of a genus of tropical giant rays having a long, flat, sawlike snout edged with teeth on both sides

saw·fly (-flī′) *n., pl.* -**flies′** any of a group of four-winged insects the female of which has a pair of sawlike organs that cut into plants, the eggs being then deposited in the cuts

saw·horse (-hôrs′) *n.* a rack on which wood is placed while being sawed

saw·mill (-mil′) *n.* **1.** a place where logs are sawed into boards **2.** a large sawing machine

sawn (sôn) *pp. of* SAW[1]

sawn-off (sôn′of′) *adj.* **1.** designating a shotgun with the barrel cut off short **2.** [Colloq.] short in stature Also **sawed-off**

saw-toothed (sô′tooth′) *adj.* having notches like the teeth of a saw; serrate: also **saw′tooth′**

saw·yer (sô′yər) *n.* a person whose work is sawing wood, as into planks and boards

sax (saks) *n.* [Colloq.] a saxophone

sax·a·tile (sak′sə til, -tīl) *adj.* [L. *saxatilis* < *saxum,* a rock] *Biol., Ecol.* living or growing among rocks

sax·horn (saks′hôrn′) *n.* [after A. J. *Sax* (1814–1894), Belgian inventor] any of a group of valved brass wind instruments with a full, even tone

sax·i·frage (sak′sə frij) *n.* [MFr. < L. < *saxum,* a rock + base of *frangere,* to break: the plant grows in rock crevices] any of a group of plants with white, yellow, purple, or pinkish small flowers, and leaves often at the base of the plant

Sax·on (sak′s'n) *n.* **1.** a member of an ancient Germanic people of northern Germany: some Saxons conquered parts of England in the 5th and 6th cent. A.D. **2.** *same as* ANGLO-SAXON (*n.* 1 & 4) **3.** a native or inhabitant of modern Saxony **4.** any of the Low German dialects of the Saxon peoples —*adj.* **1.** of the Saxons, their language, etc. **2.** of Saxony

sax·o·phone (sak′sə fōn′) *n.* [Fr., after A. J. *Sax* (see SAXHORN) & -PHONE] a single-reed, keyed wind instrument having a curved metal body —**sax′o·phon′ist** *n.*

SAXOPHONE

say (sā) *vt.* **said, say′ing;** 3rd pers. sing., pres. indic., **says** (sez), archaic **saith** [OE. *secgan*] **1.** to utter; speak **2.** to express in words; state; declare **3.** to state positively or as an opinion [who can *say* what will be?] **4.** to indicate or show [the clock *says* ten] **5.** to recite; repeat [to *say* one's prayers] **6.** to estimate [he is, I'd *say,* forty] **7.** to allege; report [they *say* he's guilty] **8.** to communicate (an idea, feeling, etc.) [the painting *says* nothing] —*vi.* to make a statement; speak; express an opinion —*n.* **1.** a chance to speak [to have one's *say*] **2.** authority, as to make a final decision: often with *the* —*adv.* **1.** for example [any fish, *say* perch] **2.** about; nearly [costing, *say,* £5] —*interj.* [Chiefly U.S.] an exclamation expressing surprise, admiration, etc. —**go without saying** to be too obvious to need explanation —**not to say** as well as; and indeed —**says you** [Colloq.] an exclamation of disagreement —**that is to say** in other words; that means —**to say the least** to understate —**say′er** *n.*

S.A.Y.E. Save As You Earn

say·ing (sā′iŋ) *n.* something said; esp., an adage, proverb, or maxim

‡**sa·yo·na·ra** (sä′yô nä′rä) *n., interj.* [< Jap.] farewell

say-so (sā′sō′) *n.* [Colloq.] **1.** (one's) word, opinion, assurance, etc. **2.** right of decision; authority

Sb [L. *stibium*] *Chem.* antimony

S.B.N. Standard Book Number

Sc *Chem.* scandium

Sc. 1. Scotch **2.** Scots **3.** Scottish

sc. 1. scene **2.** science **3.** scilicet

S.C. Special Constable

s.c. *Printing* small capitals

scab (skab) *n.* [ON. *skabb*] **1.** a crust that forms over a sore or wound as it is healing **2.** a mangy skin disease, esp. of sheep **3.** a plant disease characterized by roughened, scablike spots **4.** *a*) [Old Slang] a scoundrel *b*) a worker who refuses to join a union *c*) a worker who refuses to strike, or who takes the place of a striking worker —*vi.* **scabbed, scab′bing 1.** to become covered with a scab **2.** to work or act as a scab

scab·bard (skab′ərd) *n.* [< Anglo-Fr. *escaubers* (pl.) < ? OHG. *scar,* sword + *bergan,* to hide] a sheath or case to hold the blade of a sword, dagger, etc.

scab·by (skab′ē) *adj.* -**bi·er, -bi·est 1.** covered with or consisting of scabs **2.** low; base; mean —**scab′bi·ly** *adv.* —**scab′bi·ness** *n.*

sca·bies (skā′bēz, -bē ēz) *n.* [L., itch < *scabere,* to scratch] a contagious skin disease caused by mites that burrow under the skin to deposit eggs, causing intense itching

sca·bi·o·sa (skā′bē ō′sə) *n.* [ModL., genus name < ML. < L.: see prec.: once considered a remedy for scabies] any of various related plants having showy flowers in flattened or dome-shaped heads

sca·bi·ous[1] (skā′bē əs) *adj.* [< Fr. < L. *scabiosus* < *scabies,* itch] **1.** covered with scabs; scabby **2.** of or like scabies

sca·bi·ous[2] (skā′bē əs) *n.* *same as* SCABIOSA

scab·rous (skā′brəs) *adj.* [< LL. < L. *scabere,* to scratch] **1.** rough, like a file; scaly, scabby, etc. **2.** full of difficulties **3.** indecent, scandalous, etc. —**scab′rous·ly** *adv.* —**scab′rous·ness** *n.*

scad (skad) *n.* [< ?] [usually *pl.*] [Chiefly U.S. Colloq.] a very large number or amount [*scads* of money]

scaf·fold (skaf′'ld, -ōld) *n.* [OFr. *escafalt:* prob. akin to CATAFALQUE] **1.** a temporary framework for supporting workmen during the erecting, repairing, or painting of a building, etc. **2.** a raised platform on which criminals are executed, as by hanging **3.** any raised framework —*vt.* to furnish or support with a scaffold

scaf·fold·ing (-′l diŋ) *n.* **1.** the materials that form a scaffold **2.** a scaffold or scaffolds

sca·lar (skā′lər) *adj.* **1.** in, on, or of a scale **2.** *Math.* designating or of a quantity that has magnitude but no direction in space, as volume or temperature —*n.* a scalar quantity: distinguished from VECTOR (sense 2 *a*)

scal·a·wag (skal′ə wag′) *n.* [< ?] a scamp; rascal; also sp. **scallawag**

scald[1] (skôld) *vt.* [< ONormFr. < OFr. < LL. *excaldare* < L. *ex-,* intens. + *calidus,* hot] **1.** to burn with hot liquid or steam **2.** to heat almost to the boiling point [*scalded* milk] **3.** to use boiling liquid on, as in sterilizing, etc. —*vi.* to be or become scalded —*n.* **1.** a burn caused by scalding **2.** the act or an instance of scalding **3.** any of various plant diseases characterized by a whitening or browning of tissues

scald² (skôld) *n.* *var. of* SKALD —**scald'ic** *adj.*

scale¹ (skāl) *n.* [< LL. *scala* < L., a ladder] **1.** orig., a ladder or flight of stairs **2.** *a)* a series of marks along a line, as at regular intervals, used in measuring or registering something [the *scale* of a thermometer] *b)* any instrument or ruler so marked **3.** *a)* the proportion that a map, model, etc. bears to the thing that it represents [a *scale* of one centimetre to a kilometre] *b)* a line marked off on a map to show this ratio **4.** *a)* a system of classifying in a series of degrees according to relative size, amount, rank, etc. [a wage *scale*] *b)* any point, level, or degree in such a series **5.** *Math.* a number system having a specified base [the binary *scale*] **6.** *Music* a sequence of tones, rising or falling in pitch, in accordance with any of various systems of intervals —*vt.* **scaled, scal'ing 1.** to climb up or over **2.** to make according to a scale —*vi.* **1.** to climb; go up **2.** to go up in a graduated series —**in scale** in proportion or balance with —**on a large** (or **small**) **scale** to a relatively large (or small) degree or extent —**scale down** (or **up**) to reduce (or increase) according to a ratio —**to scale** to a particular scale; of uniform reduction or enlargement —**scal'er** *n.*

scale² (skāl) *n.* [< OFr. *escale,* husk & *escaille,* shell: both < Gmc.] **1.** any of the thin, flat, overlapping, horny plates forming the outer covering of many fishes and reptiles **2.** any thin, flaky or platelike layer or piece that forms part of, or peels off from, a surface **3.** a coating that forms on metals when heated or rusted [*scale* on the inside of a boiler] **4.** any small scalelike leaf or bract; esp., such a modified leaf covering the bud of a seed plant —*vt.* **scaled, scal'ing 1.** to strip or scrape scales from **2.** to remove in thin layers; pare down **3.** to cause scales to form on —*vi.* **1.** to flake or peel off in scales **2.** to become covered with scale or scales —**scales fell from his eyes** he was no longer blinded to a particular situation, etc. —**scale'less** *adj.*

scale³ (skāl) *n.* [ON. *skäl,* bowl] **1.** either of the shallow dishes or pans of a balance **2.** [often *pl.*] a balance or other weighing device —*vt.* **scaled, scal'ing 1.** to weigh in scales **2.** to have a weight of —*vi.* to be weighed —**the Scales** *same as* LIBRA —**turn** (or **tip**) **the scales** to determine; decide

scale insect any of a large group of small, homopterous insects destructive to plants: the females secrete a round, wax scale under which they live and lay their eggs

sca·lene (skā lēn′, skā′lēn) *adj.* [< LL. < Gr. *skalēnos,* uneven] *Geom.* **1.** having unequal sides and angles: said of a triangle **2.** having the axis not perpendicular to the base: said of a cone, etc.

scaling ladder a ladder used for climbing high walls

scal·lion (skal′yən) *n.* [< ONormFr. *escalogne,* ult. < L. *(caepa) Ascalonia,* (onion of) Ascalon (in Phillistia)] [Chiefly U.S.] any of three varieties of onion; specif., *a)* the shallot *b)* the leek *c)* a green onion with an almost bulbless root

scal·lop (skal′əp) *n.* [OFr. *escalope* < *escale:* see SCALE²] **1.** a kind of mollusc with two deeply grooved, curved shells, that swims by means of a large muscle that rapidly snaps its shells together **2.** this muscle, used as food **3.** a single shell of such a mollusc specif., one used as a baking dish **4.** any of a series of curves, projections, etc. forming an ornamental edge on cloth, lace, etc. —*vt.* **1.** to cut the edge or border of in scallops **2.** to bake with a milk sauce and bread crumbs; escallop —*vi.* to gather scallops —**scal'lop·er** *n.*

SCALLOP (sense 1)

scal·ly·wag (skal′ē wag′) *n.* *same as* SCALAWAG

scalp (skalp) *n.* [< Scand.] **1.** the skin on the top and back of the head, usually covered with hair **2.** a part of this, cut or torn from the head of an enemy for a trophy, as by certain N. American Indians, frontiersmen, etc. **3.** a symbol of victory, prowess, etc. —*vt.* **1.** to cut or tear the scalp from **2.** [Chiefly U.S.] *a)* to cheat or rob *b)* to defeat decisively **3.** *a)* [Chiefly U.S. Colloq.] to buy and sell in order to make small, quick profits *b)* to buy (theatre tickets, etc.) and sell later at higher than regular prices —*vi.* [Chiefly U.S. Colloq.] to scalp tickets, etc. —**scalp'er** *n.*

scal·pel (skal′pəl) *n.* [< L. dim. of *scalprum,* a knife < *scalpere,* to cut] a small, light, straight knife with a very sharp blade, used by surgeons and in anatomical dissections

scal·y (skā′lē) *adj.* **scal'i·er, scal'i·est** having, covered with, or resembling scales —**scal'i·ness** *n.*

scamp¹ (skamp) *n.* [< obs. *scamp,* to roam < MFr. *escamper,* to flee, ult. < L. *ex-,* out + *campus,* battlefield] a mischievous or roguish fellow; rascal —**scamp'ish** *adj.*

scamp² (skamp) *vt.* [akin to or < ON. *skammr,* short] to do in a careless, inadequate way —**scamp'er** *n.*

scam·per (skam′pər) *vi.* [prob. freq. of obs. *scamp:* see SCAMP¹] to run or go hurriedly or quickly —*n.* the act of scampering —**scam'per·er** *n.*

scam·pi (skam′pē) *n.,* *pl.* -**pi,** -**pies** [It., pl. of *scampo*] a kind of large prawn, valued as food

scan (skan) *vt.* **scanned, scan'ning** [< L. *scandere,* to climb] **1.** to analyse (verse), as by marking off the metrical feet and showing the rhythmic structure **2.** to look at closely or in a broad, searching way; scrutinize **3.** to glance at quickly **4.** in computers, to examine in sequence (data), esp. with an electronic device **5.** *Radar* to traverse (a region) with a succession of transmitted radar beams **6.** *TV* to traverse (a surface) rapidly and point by point with a beam of light or electrons in transmitting or reproducing an image —*vi.* **1.** to scan verse **2.** to be in a certain poetic metre —*n.* a scanning —**scan'na·ble** *adj.* —**scan'ner** *n.*

Scan., Scand. 1. Scandinavia **2.** Scandinavian

scan·dal (skan′d'l) *n.* [< OFr. < LL. *scandalum,* cause for stumbling < Gr. *skandalon,* a snare] **1.** any act, person, or thing that offends or shocks the moral feelings of people and leads to disgrace **2.** a reaction of shame, outrage, etc. caused by such an act, person, etc. **3.** disgrace or ignominy **4.** talk that harms a reputation; wicked gossip

scan·dal·ize (skan′də līz′) *vt.* -**ized', -iz'ing** to outrage the moral feelings of by improper conduct —**scan'dal·iz'er** *n.*

scan·dal·mon·ger (skan′d'l muŋ′gər) *n.* a person who gossips maliciously and spreads scandal

scan·dal·ous (-əs) *adj.* **1.** causing scandal; shocking to people's moral feelings; shameful **2.** consisting of or spreading slander; libellous —**scan'dal·ous·ly** *adv.* —**scan'·dal·ous·ness** *n.*

scandal sheet [Colloq.] a newspaper, magazine, etc. that features sensationalism, gossip, or the like

Scan·di·na·vi·an (skan′də nā′vē ən) *adj.* of Scandinavia, its people, their languages, etc. —*n.* **1.** any of the people of Scandinavia **2.** the subbranch of the Germanic languages spoken by them; North Germanic

scan·di·um (skan′dē əm) *n.* [ModL. < ML. < L. *Scandia,* N European lands] a rare metallic chemical element: symbol, Sc; at. wt., 44.956; at. no., 21

scan·sion (skan′shən) *n.* the act of scanning verse

scant (skant) *adj.* [< ON. < *skammr,* short] **1.** inadequate in size or amount; not enough; meagre **2.** not quite up to full measure —*vt.* **1.** to limit in size or amount; stint **2.** to fail to give full measure of **3.** to treat in an inadequate manner —*adv.* scarcely; barely —**scant'ly** *adv.* —**scant'·ness** *n.*

scant·ling (skant′liŋ) *n.* [< ONormFr. < OFr. *eschandillon,* a measure] a small beam or timber; esp., a small upright timber, as in the frame of a structure

scant·y (skan′tē) *adj.* **scant'i·er, scant'i·est** [SCANT + -Y²] **1.** barely sufficient; not ample; meagre **2.** insufficient; not enough —**scant'i·ly** *adv.* —**scant'i·ness** *n.*

scape (skāp) *n., vt., vi.* **scaped, scap'ing** [Archaic] *same as* ESCAPE: also **'scape**

-scape (skāp) [< (LAND)SCAPE] *a combining form meaning* (a drawing, etc. of) a specified view or scene [seascape]

scape·goat (skāp′gōt′) *n.* [SCAPE + GOAT] **1.** a goat over which the high priest of the ancient Jews confessed the sins of the people, after which it was allowed to escape: Lev. 16:7-26 **2.** a person, group, or thing upon whom the blame for the mistakes or crimes of others is thrust

scape·grace (-grās′) *n.* [SCAPE + GRACE] a graceless, unprincipled fellow; scamp; rogue

scap·u·la (skap′yoo lə) *n.,* *pl.* -**lae'** (-lē′), -**las** [ModL. < L.] *same as* SHOULDER BLADE

scap·u·lar (-lər) *adj.* of the shoulder or scapula —*n.* **1.** a sleeveless outer garment falling from the shoulders, worn by monks **2.** two small pieces of cloth joined by strings, worn on the chest and back, under the clothes, by some Roman Catholics as a token of religious devotion

scar¹ (skär) *n.* [< MFr. < LL. < Gr. *eschara,* orig., fireplace] **1.** a mark left after a wound, burn, ulcer, etc. has healed **2.** any mark like this, as on a plant where a leaf was attached **3.** the lasting mental or emotional effects of suffering —*vt., vi.* **scarred, scar'ring** to mark with or form a scar

scar² (skär) *n.* [ME. *skerre* < ON. *sker*] **1.** a precipitous rocky place or cliff **2.** a projecting or isolated rock, as in the sea Also **scaur**

scar·ab (skar′əb) *n.* [< Fr. < L. *scarabaeus*] **1.** any of various beetles, mostly stout-bodied and often brilliantly coloured **2.** *a)* the black, winged dung beetle, held sacred by the ancient Egyptians *b)* an image of this beetle, cut from a stone or gem and formerly worn as a charm

scar·a·bae·id (skar′ə bē′id) *n.* [< ModL. family name] *same as* SCARAB (sense 1) —*adj.* of the scarab beetles

Scar·a·mouch (skar′ə mōōch′) [< Fr. < It. *Scaramuccia,* lit., a skirmish] a stock character in old Italian comedy, depicted as a braggart and a coward

scarce (skers) *adj.* [ONormFr. *escars,* ult. < L. *excerpere,* to select] **1.** not common; rarely seen **2.** not plentiful; hard to get —*adv.* literary var. of SCARCELY —**make oneself scarce** [Colloq.] to go or stay away —**scarce'ness** *n.*

scarce·ly (-lē) *adv.* **1.** hardly; not quite **2.** probably not or certainly not [scarcely true]

scar·ci·ty (sker′sə tē) *n., pl.* **-ties** 1. the condition of being scarce; inadequate supply 2. rarity; uncommonness

scare (sker) *vt.* **scared, scar′ing** [ON. *skirra*, to scare < *skjarr*, timid] to fill with fear or terror; esp., to frighten suddenly —*vi.* to become frightened, esp. suddenly —*n.* 1. a sudden fear or panic 2. a state of widespread fear or panic *[a war scare]* —**scare up** [U.S. Colloq.] to produce or gather quickly

scare·crow (-krō′) *n.* 1. a figure of a man, etc. made with sticks, old clothes, etc., put in a field to frighten birds away from crops 2. anything that frightens one but is harmless 3. a person who is dressed like a scarecrow

scare·mon·ger (-muŋ′gər) *n.* a person who circulates alarming rumours —**scare′mon′ger·ing** *n.*

scarf[1] (skärf) *n., pl.* **scarfs, scarves** [ONormFr. *escarpe*, a purse hung from the neck < ML. < L. < *scirpus*, a bulrush] a long or broad piece of cloth worn about the neck, head, etc. for warmth or decoration —*vt.* to cover as with a scarf

scarf[2] (skärf) *n., pl.* **scarfs** [prob. < Scand.] 1. a joint made by notching, grooving, or otherwise cutting the ends of two pieces and fastening them so that they join firmly into one continuous piece: also **scarf joint** 2. the ends of a piece so cut —*vt.* 1. to join by a scarf 2. to make a scarf in the end of

scarf·pin (-pin) *n.* an ornamental pin worn in a scarf

scar·i·fy (skar′ə fi′) *vt.* **-fied′, -fy′ing** [< MFr., ult. < Gr. *skariphasthai*, to scratch < *skariphos*, a stylus] 1. to make a series of small cuts or punctures in (the skin), as in surgery 2. to criticize sharply 3. *Agric.* to loosen or stir (the topsoil) —**scar′i·fi·ca′tion** *n.* —**scar′i·fi′er** *n.*

scar·la·ti·na (skär′lə tē′nə) *n.* [ModL. < ML. (*febris*) *scarlatina*] popular term for a mild form of SCARLET FEVER

scar·let (skär′lət) *n.* [< OFr. < ML. *scarlatum*, scarlet cloth < Per. < Ar., ult. < Gr. *kyklas*, encircling] 1. very bright red with a slightly orange tinge 2. cloth or clothing of this colour —*adj.* 1. of this colour 2. sinful

scarlet fever an acute contagious disease in which one has a sore throat, fever, and a scarlet rash

scarlet letter a scarlet letter A worn in earlier times by a person convicted of adultery, esp. in Puritan communities in the U.S.

scarlet runner (bean) a climbing bean plant originating in tropical America, having scarlet flowers, and pods with red-and-black seeds

scarlet woman [after the woman mentioned in Revelations 17] any sexually promiscuous woman, esp. a prostitute

scarp (skärp) *n.* [< It. *scarpa*] 1. a steep slope; specif., an escarpment or cliff along the edge of a plateau 2. the outer slope of a rampart, or a rear slope of a ditch below the rampart —*vt.* to make into a steep slope

scar·per (skär′pər) *vi.* [ult. < It. *scappare*, escape] [Slang] to run away or depart; decamp

scar tissue the fibrous, contracted tissue of a scar

scarves (skärvz) *n.* alt. *pl.* of SCARF[1]

scar·y (sker′ē) *adj.* **scar′i·er, scar′i·est** [Colloq.] 1. causing fear 2. easily frightened —**scar′i·ness** *n.*

scat[1] (skat) *vi.* **scat′ted, scat′ting** [? a hiss + CAT] [Colloq.] to go away: usually in the imperative

scat[2] (skat) *adj.* [< ?] *Jazz* designating or of singing in which meaningless syllables are used, often to imitate the sounds of a musical instrument —*n.* such singing —*vi.* **scat′ted, scat′ting** to engage in scat singing

scathe (skāth) *vt.* **scathed, scath′ing** [< ON. < *skathi*, harm] 1. [Archaic] *a)* to injure *b)* to wither or sear 2. to denounce fiercely —*n.* (Archaic) injury or harm —**scathe′-less** *adj.*

scath·ing (skā′thiŋ) *adj.* searing; harsh or caustic *[scathing remarks]* —**scath′ing·ly** *adv.*

sca·tol·o·gy (skə tol′ə jē) *n.* [< Gr. *skōr* (gen. *skatos*), excrement + -LOGY] obsession with the obscene, esp. with excrement or excretion, in literature —**scat·o·log·i·cal** (skat′ə loj′i k'l), k'l), **scat′o·log′ic** *adj.*

scat·ter (skat′ər) *vt.* [ME. *skateren*] 1. to throw here and there or strew loosely; sprinkle 2. to separate and drive in many directions; disperse —*vi.* to separate and go off in several directions *[the crowd scattered]* —*n.* 1. a scattering 2. what is scattered about —**scat′ter·er** *n.*

scat·ter·brain (-brān′) *n.* a person who is flighty and not able to think in a serious way —**scat′ter·brained′** *adj.*

scat·ty (skat′ē) *adj.* **-ti·er, -ti·est** [contr. < ? SCATTERBRAIN(ED)] [Slang] silly, foolish, or crazy

scaup (skôp) *n., pl.* **scaups, scaup:** SEE PLURAL, II, D, 1 [obs. var. of *scalp*, mussel bed] any of several wild ducks related to the pochard: also **scaup duck**

scav·enge (skav′inj) *vt.* **-enged, -eng·ing** [< ff.] 1. to clean (streets, etc.); remove rubbish from 2. to salvage (usable goods) by rummaging through refuse —*vi.* 1. to act as a scavenger 2. to look for food

scav·en·ger (-in jər) *n.* [< Anglo-Fr., ult. < Fl. *scawen* or OFrank. *scouwon*, to peer at] 1. a person who gathers things that have been discarded by others 2. any animal that eats refuse and decaying organic matter

Sc.D. [L. *Scientiae Doctor*] Doctor of Science

S.C.E. Scottish Certificate of Education

sce·nar·i·o (si ner′ē ō′, -när′-) *n., pl.* **-i·os′** [It. < L. < *scaena*, stage, SCENE] 1. a synopsis of a play, opera, or the like 2. the script of a film esp. the shooting script 3. any sequence of events, esp. an imagined one —**sce·nar′ist** *n.*

scene (sēn) *n.* [< MFr. < L. < Gr. *skēnē*, tent, stage] 1. the place in which any event occurs *[the scene of the crime]* 2. the setting of the action of a play, story, etc. *[the scene of Hamlet is Denmark]* 3. a division of a play, usually part of an act 4. a part of a play, story, etc. that constitutes a unit of action *[a deathbed scene]* 5. same as SCENERY (sense 1) 6. a view of people or places 7. a display of strong feeling before others *[she made a scene in court]* 8. an episode or event, real or imaginary, esp. as described 9. [Colloq.] the locale or environment for a specified activity *[the poetry scene]* —**behind the scenes** 1. backstage 2. in private or in secrecy —**make the scene** [Chiefly U.S. Slang] 1. to be present 2. to participate actively or successfully —**set the scene** to describe the background, location etc. of an event, story, etc.

scene painter someone who paints the flats etc. for theatrical performances —**scene painting**

sce·ner·y (sē′nər ē) *n., pl.* **-ner·ies** 1. painted screens, backdrops, hangings, etc., used on the stage to represent places 2. the general appearance of a place; features of a landscape

scene shifter the person responsible for moving scenery between scenes of a theatrical performance —**scene shifting**

sce·nic (sē′nik, sen′ik) *adj.* 1. *a)* of the stage; theatrical *b)* relating to stage effects or stage scenery 2. *a)* having to do with natural scenery *b)* having beautiful scenery 3. representing an action, event, etc. —**sce′ni·cal·ly** *adv.*

scenic railway a small railway passing through areas with a scenic view, often artifically contrived

scent (sent) *vt.* [< OFr. < L. *sentire*, to feel] 1. to smell 2. to get a hint of; suspect 3. to fill with an odour; perfume —*vi.* to hunt by the sense of smell —*n.* 1. a smell; odour 2. the sense of smell 3. a perfume 4. an odour left by an animal, by which it is tracked 5. a track followed in hunting 6. any clue by which something is followed —**put** (or **throw**) **off the scent** to mislead wilfully —**scent′ed** *adj.* —**scent′less** *adj.*

scep·ter (sep′tər) *n., vt.* U.S. sp. of SCEPTRE

scep·tic (skep′tik) *adj.* [< L. < Gr. *skeptikos*, inquiring] *var. of* SCEPTICAL —*n.* 1. [S-] a member of any of the ancient Greek philosophical schools that denied the possibility of real knowledge 2. a believer in philosophical scepticism 3. one who habitually doubts or questions matters generally accepted 4. one who doubts religious doctrines

scep·ti·cal (skep′ti k'l) *adj.* 1. of or characteristic of sceptics or scepticism 2. not easily convinced; doubting; questioning; 3. doubting the fundamental doctrines of religion —**scep′ti·cal·ly** *adv.*

scep·ti·cism (-siz′m) *n.* 1. [S-] the doctrines of the ancient Greek Sceptics 2. the philosophical doctrine that the truth of all knowledge must always be in question 3. sceptical attitude; doubt, esp. about religious doctrines

scep·tre (sep′tər) *n.* [< OFr. < L. < Gr. *skēptron*, staff] 1. a staff held by rulers on ceremonial occasions as a symbol of sovereignty 2. royal authority —*vt.* to furnish with a sceptre; invest with royal authority

sched·ule (shed′yool, shej′ool) *n.* [< OFr. < LL. dim. of L. *scheda*, a leaf of paper < Gr. *schidē*, splinter of wood] 1. a list or catalogue of details, as of a bill of sale 2. a list of times of recurring events, arriving and departing trains, etc. 3. a timed plan for a project —*vt.* **-uled, -ul·ing** 1. to place in a schedule 2. to make a schedule of 3. to plan for a certain time

Scheduled Castes the groups of people in India formerly belonging to the class of untouchables

scheduled territories *same as* STERLING AREA

sche·ma (skē′mə) *n., pl.* **-ma·ta** (-mə tə) [Gr.: see SCHEME] an outline, diagram, scheme, plan, etc.

sche·mat·ic (skē mat′ik, skə-) *adj.* of, or having the nature of, a scheme, schema, plan, diagram, etc. —*n.* a diagram, as of the wiring of an electric circuit —**sche·mat′i·cal·ly** *adv.*

sche·ma·tize (-tīz′) *vi., vt.* **-tized′, -tiz′ing** [< Gr. *schēmatizein*, to form] to form, form into, or arrange according to, a scheme or plan —**sche′ma·ti·za′tion** *n.*

scheme (skēm) *n.* [< L. < Gr. *schēma*, a form] 1. *a)* a systematic programme for attaining some object *b)* a secret or underhanded plan; plot *c)* a visionary plan 2. an orderly combination of things on a definite plan *[a colour scheme]* 3. an outline showing different parts of an object or system —*vt.* schemed, schem′ing to plan as a scheme; devise; contrive; plot —*vi.* 1. to make schemes 2. to plot; intrigue —**schem′er** *n.*

schem·ing (skē′miŋ) *adj.* given to forming schemes or plots; crafty, tricky, etc. —**schem′ing·ly** *adv.*

scher·zan·do (sker tsan′dō) *adj.* [It. < *scherzo*: see ff.] *Music* playful —*adv. Music* playfully

scher·zo (sker'tsō) *n., pl.* **-zos, -zi** (-tsē) [It., a jest] a lively, playful movement, as of a sonata, in 3/4 time

Schick test (shik) [after B. *Schick* (1877-1967), U.S. paediatrician] a test for immunity to diphtheria, made by injecting dilute diphtheria toxin into the skin

schil·ling (shil'iŋ) *n.* [G.] *see* MONETARY UNITS, table (Austria)

schism (siz''m; *now occas.* skiz'm) *n.* [< OFr. < LL. < Gr. *schisma* < *schizein*, to cleave] **1.** a split in an organized group, esp. a church, because of difference of opinion, of doctrine, etc. **2.** the offence of trying to cause a split in a church

schis·mat·ic (siz mat'ik; *now occas.* skiz-) *adj.* **1.** of or having the nature of schism **2.** tending to or causing schism Also **schis·mat'i·cal** —*n.* a person who causes or participates in schism —**schis·mat'i·cal·ly** *adv.*

schist (shist) *n.* [< Fr. < Gr. *schistos*, easily cleft < *schizein*, to cleave] any metamorphic rock of a type that splits easily into thin leaves —**schist'ose** (-ōs) *adj.*

schis·to·so·mi·a·sis (shis'tə sō mī'ə sis) *n.* [ModL. < Gr. *schistos*, cleft + *sōma*, body + -IASIS] a chronic disease, caused by parasitic flukes in the bloodstream, that produces disorders of the liver, bladder, lungs, etc.

schiz·an·thus (skiz an'thəs) *n.* [ModL. < Gr. *schizein*, to cut + *anthos*, flower] an annual plant, native to Chile, with divided leaves

schizo (skiz'ō, skit'sō) *n.* *Colloq.* shortened form of schizophrenic, *see* SCHIZOPHRENIA

schiz·o- [< Gr. *schizein*, to cleave] a combining form meaning split, division: also, before a vowel, **schiz-**

schiz·o·carp (skit'sə karp', skiz'ə-) *n.* [prec. + -CARP] *Bot.* a dry fruit that splits into one-seeded carpels —**schiz'o·car'pous, schiz'o·car'pic** *adj.*

schiz·oid (skiz'oid) *adj.* **1.** of, like, or having schizophrenia **2.** designating or of a type of person who is withdrawn, introverted, etc. —*n.* a schizoid person

schiz·o·phre·ni·a (skit'sə frē'nē ə, skiz'ə-) *n.* [ModL. < SCHIZO- + Gr. *phrēn*, the mind] a major mental disorder of unknown cause in which, typically, a person's emotions are displayed by bizarre behaviour, his sense of reality is distorted by delusions and hallucinations, etc. —**schiz'·o·phren'ic** (-fren'ik) *adj., n.*

schmaltz (shmalts, shmôlts) *n.* [via Yid. < G. *schmalz*, lit., melted fat] [Slang] **1.** highly sentimental and banal music, literature, etc. **2.** banal sentimentalism Also **schmalz** —**schmaltz'y** *adj.* **schmaltz'i·er, schmaltz'i·est**

schnapps (shnaps) *n., pl.* **schnapps** [G., a dram] any strong spirit, esp. Hollands gin: also sp. **schnaps**

schnau·zer (shnou'zər) *n.* [G. < *schnauzen*, to snarl] any of a breed of small active terrier with a close, wiry coat

schnor·kle (shnôr'k'l) *n.* same as SNORKEL

schnoz·zle (shnoz''l) *n.* [via Yid. < G. *Schnauze*] [Chiefly U.S. Slang] the nose: also **schnoz**

schol·ar (skol'ər) *n.* [< OE. or OFr., both ult. < L. *schola*, a SCHOOL[1]] **1.** *a)* a learned person *b)* a specialist in a particular branch of learning, esp. in the humanities **2.** a student given scholarship aid **3.** any student or pupil

SCHNAUZER
(43-51 cm high at shoulder)

schol·ar·ly (-lē) *adj.* **1.** of or relating to scholars **2.** showing much knowledge and critical ability **3.** devoted to learning; studious —*adv.* [Obs.] like a scholar

schol·ar·ship (-ship') *n.* **1.** the quality of knowledge and learning shown by a student **2.** the systematized knowledge of a learned man, or of scholars collectively **3.** a gift of money or other aid to help a student

scho·las·tic (skə las'tik) *adj.* [< L. < Gr. < *scholazein*, to be at leisure < *scholē*, a SCHOOL[1]] **1.** of schools, colleges, students, teachers, etc.; academic **2.** [*also* **S-**] of or relating to scholasticism Also **scho·las'ti·cal** —*n.* [*also* **S-**] **1.** *same as* SCHOOLMAN (sense 1) **2.** a person who favours Scholasticism —**scho·las'ti·cal·ly** *adv.*

scho·las·ti·cism (-tə siz'm) *n.* **1.** [*often* **S-**] a medieval system of Christian thought based on Aristotelian logic **2.** an insistence upon traditional doctrines and methods

scho·li·ast (skō'lē əst) *n.* [< ModL. < MGr. < Gr. *scholion*, a comment < *scholē*, a SCHOOL[1]] an ancient interpreter and annotator of the classics —**scho'li·as'tic** *adj.*

school[1] (skōol) *n.* [OE. *scol* < L. *schola* < Gr. *scholē*, leisure, school] **1.** a place or institution for teaching and learning, as a grammar school, dancing school, infant or secondary school etc. **2.** *a)* the building or buildings, classrooms, etc. of a school *b)* all of its students and teachers *c)* a regular session of teaching at a school **3.** *a)* attendance at a school [to miss *school* for a week] *b)* the process of being educated at a school [he finished *school*] **4.** any situation or experience through which one gains

knowledge, training, etc. [the *school* of hard knocks] **5.** a particular division of an institution of learning, esp. of a university [the *school* of law] **6.** a group following the same teachings, beliefs, methods, etc. [the Impressionist *school*] **7.** a way of life [a gentleman of the old *school*] **8.** [*pl.*] [**S-**] *a)* a degree examination, esp. at Oxford *b)* a collective term for medieval universities, their teachers, and teaching —*vt.* **1.** to teach; instruct; educate **2.** to discipline or control —*adj.* of a school or schools —**at school** to be attending school

school[2] (skōol) *n.* [Du., a crowd] a large number of fish or water animals of the same kind swimming or feeding together —*vi.* to move together in such a school

school age the years during which attendance at school is required or customary —**school'-age'** *adj.*

school·bag (-bag') *n.* a bag, usually of cloth, in which a pupil at a school carries his books, pens, etc.

school·book (skōol'book') *n.* a book used for study in schools

school·boy (-boi') *n.* a boy attending school

school·child (-chīld') *n., pl.* **-chil'dren** (-chil'drən) a child attending school

school·fel·low (-fel'ō) *n.* *same as* SCHOOLMATE

school·girl (-gurl') *n.* a girl attending school

school·house (-hous') *n.* **1.** a building used as a school **2.** a building, often attached to a school, where a schoolmaster lives

school·ing (-iŋ) *n.* **1.** training or education; esp., formal instruction at school **2.** cost of attending school

school leaver a school child who leaves school, either at the minimum age possible or any later stage

school·man (-mən) *n., pl.* **-men** (-mən; *for 2, often* -men') **1.** [*often* **S-**] any of the medieval teachers of scholasticism **2.** [U.S.] a teacher or educator

school·marm (-märm') *n.* [Chiefly U.S. Colloq] a woman schoolteacher, hence any person, who tends to be oldfashioned and prudish: also **school'ma'am** (-mäm', -mam')

school·mas·ter (-mäs'tər) *n.* **1.** a man who teaches in a school **2.** a headmaster —**school'mis'tress** (-mis'tris) *n.fem.*

school·mate (-māt') *n.* a person going to the same school at the same time as another

school·room (-rōom') *n.* a classroom either in a school or private house

school·teach·er (-tē'chər) *n.* a person whose work is teaching in a school

school·work (-wurk') *n.* lessons worked on in classes at school or done as homework

school year the part of a year when schools are in session, usually from September to June

schoon·er (skōo'nər) *n.* [< ? Scot. dial. *scun*, to skip a flat stone across water] **1.** a ship with two or more masts, rigged fore and aft **2.** a large sherry glass **3.** [U.S.] a large beer glass

schot·tische (shot ish') *n.* [< G. (*der*) *schottische* (*Tanz*), (the) Scottish (dance)] **1.** a form of round dance in 2/4 time, similar to the polka **2.** music for this —*vi.* **-tisched, -tisch·ing** to dance a schottische

schuss (shoos) *n.* [G., lit., shot, rush] a straight run down a hill in skiing —*vi.* to make such a run

schwa (shwä) *n.* [G. < Heb. *sh'wā*] **1.** the neutral vowel sound of most unstressed syllables in English; sound of *a* in *ago, e* in *agent*, etc. **2.** the symbol (ə) for this sound

sci. **1.** science **2.** scientific

sci·at·ic (sī at'ik) *adj.* [< MFr. < ML. < L. < Gr. *ischiadikos* < *ischion*, the hip] of, near, or affecting the hip or its nerves

sci·at·i·ca (sī at'i kə) *n.* any painful condition in the region of the hip and thighs; esp., neuritis of the long nerve (**sciatic nerve**) passing down the back of the thigh

sci·ence (sī'əns) *n.* [< OFr. < L. < prp. of *scire*, to know] **1.** orig., knowledge **2.** systematized knowledge derived from observation, study, and experimentation **3.** a branch of knowledge, esp. one concerned with establishing and systematizing facts, principles, and methods [the *science* of mathematics] **4.** *a)* the systematized knowledge of nature *b)* any branch of this See NATURAL SCIENCE **5.** skill based upon systematized training [the *science* of cooking]

science fiction highly imaginative or fantastic fiction typically involving real or imagined scientific phenomena

sci·en·tif·ic (sī'ən tif'ik) *adj.* **1.** of, dealing with, or used in science [*scientific* study, *scientific* apparatus] **2.** *a)* based on, or using, the principles and methods of science; systematic and exact *b)* designating a method in which theories are based on data collected systematically and tested objectively **3.** *a)* done according to methods gained by systematic training [*scientific* boxing] *b)* having or showing such training —**sci'en·tif'i·cal·ly** *adv.*

sci·en·tism (sī'ən tiz'm) *n.* **1.** the techniques, beliefs, etc. characteristic of scientists **2.** the uncritical application of scientific methods to any field of study —**sci·en·tis'tic** *adj.*

sci·en·tist (sī′ən tist) *n.* a specialist in science, as in biology, chemistry, etc.

sci-fi (sī′fī′) *adj., n.* *same as* SCIENCE FICTION

scil·i·cet (sīl′i set′) *adv.* [L., contr. of *scire licet*, it is permitted to know] namely; that is to say

scim·i·tar, scim·i·ter (sim′ə tər) *n.* [It. *scimitarra* < ?] a short, curved sword with an edge on the convex side, used chiefly by Turks, Arabs, etc.

scin·til·la (sin til′ə) *n.* [L.] 1. a spark 2. the least trace

scin·til·late (sin′til āt′) *vi.* -lat′ed, -lat′ing [< L. pp. of *scintillare* < *scintilla*, a spark] 1. to give off sparks; flash; sparkle 2. to sparkle with wit 3. to twinkle, as a star —scin′til·lant *adj.* —scin′til·la′tor *n.*

scin·til·la·tion (sin′til ā′shən) *n.* 1. a scintillating, or flashing, twinkling, sparkling, etc. 2. a spark or flash 3. the flash of light made by ionizing radiation upon striking a crystal detector or a phosphor

scintillation counter an instrument for detecting and measuring the scintillations induced by ionizing radiation in a crystal or phosphor

sci·o·lism (sī′ə liz′m) *n.* [< L. dim. of *scius*, knowing < *scire*, to know] superficial knowledge or learning —sci′·o·list *n.* —sci′o·lis′tic *adj.*

sci·on (sī′ən) *n.* [OFr. *cion* < ?] 1. a shoot or bud of a plant, esp. one for grafting 2. a descendant; offspring

scis·sion (sizh′ən, sish′-) *n.* [Fr. < LL. < L. pp. of *scindere*, to cut] a cutting or splitting, or the state of being cut

scis·sor (siz′ər) *vt.* to cut with scissors

scis·sors (siz′ərz) *n.pl.* [< OFr. < LL. pl. of *cisorium*, cutting tool < L. *caedere*, to cut] 1. a cutting instrument, smaller than shears, with two opposing blades which are pivoted together so that they work against each other: also **pair of scissors** 2. [*with sing. v.*] a) a gymnastic feat in which the legs are moved in a way suggestive of scissors b) *same as* SCISSORS HOLD

scissors hold a wrestling hold in which one contestant clasps the other with his legs

scissors kick a swimming kick in which one leg is bent at the knee and the other thrust backward, then both brought together with a snap

scis·sor·tail (siz′ər tāl′) *n.* a pale grey and pink variety of flycatcher of S N. America

scle·ra (sklir′ə) *n.* [< Gr. *sklēros*, hard] the tough, white, fibrous membrane covering all of the eyeball except the area covered by the cornea

scle·ren·chy·ma (skli reŋ′kə mə) *n.* [ModL. < Gr. *sklēros*, hard + *enchyma*, infusion] *Bot.* plant tissue of uniformly thick-walled, dead cells, as in nut shells

scle·ro- [< Gr. *sklēros*, hard] a combining form meaning: 1. hard 2. of the sclera Also, before a vowel, **scler-**

scle·ro·sis (skli rō′sis) *n., pl.* -ses (-sēz) [< ML. < Gr. < *sklēros*, hard] 1. an abnormal hardening of body tissues, esp. of the nervous system or the walls of arteries 2. a disease characterized by such hardening

scle·rot·ic (-rot′ik) *adj.* 1. hard 2. of, characterized by, or having sclerosis 3. of the sclera

S.C.M. 1. State Certified Midwife 2. Student Christian Movement

scoff[1] (skof) *n.* [prob. < Scand.] 1. an expression of scorn or derision; jeer 2. an object of mocking contempt, scorn, etc. —*vt.* to mock at or deride —*vi.* to show scorn or derision; jeer (*at*) —scoff′er *n.* —scoff′ing·ly *adv.*

scoff[2] (skof) *n.* [< Dial. *scaff* < ?] [Slang] food or rations —*vt., vi.* [Slang] 1. to eat or devour 2. to plunder or seize

scold (skōld) *n.* [< ON. *skald*, poet (prob. because of satirical verses)] a person, esp. a woman, who habitually uses abusive language —*vt.* to find fault with angrily; rebuke —*vi.* 1. to find fault angrily 2. to use abusive language habitually —scold′er *n.* —scold′ing *adj., n.*

scol·lop (skol′əp) *n., vt.* var. of SCALLOP

sconce[1] (skons) *n.* [< OFr., ult. < L. *abscondere*, to hide] a bracket attached to a wall for holding a candle, etc.

sconce[2] (skons) *n.* [Du. *schans*, a fortress, orig. wickerwork] a small fort, bulwark, etc. —*vt.* sconced, sconc′ing [Archaic] 1. to provide with a sconce 2. to shelter or protect

scone (skōn, skon) *n.* [Scot., contr. < ? MDu. *schoonbrot*, fine bread] sweet or savoury cake made from an unyeasted light dough often baked on a griddle

scoop (sklōp) *n.* [< MDu. *schope*, bailing vessel & *schoppe*, a shovel] 1. any of various small, shovellike utensils; specif., *a*) a kitchen utensil used to take up sugar, flour, etc. *b*) a small utensil with a round bowl, for dishing up ice cream, mashed potatoes, etc. 2. the deep shovel of a dredge or steam shovel, which takes up sand, etc. 3. the act or motion of taking up with or as with a scoop 4. the amount taken up at one time by a scoop 5. a hollowed-out place 6. [Colloq.] a large profit made by speculation 7. [Colloq.] *a*) advantage gained over a competitor by being first, specif. as in the publication of a news item *b*) such a news item —*adj.* designating a rounded, somewhat low neckline in a dress, etc. —*vt.* 1. to take up or out as with a scoop 2. to dig (*out*); hollow (*out*) 3. to make by digging

out 4. to gather (*in* or *up*) as if with a scoop 5. [Colloq.] to effect a scoop (*n.* 7) in competition with —scoop′er *n.*

scoop·ful (-fool′) *n., pl.* -fuls′ as much as a scoop will hold

scoot (sklōt) *vi., vt.* [prob. < ON. *skjōta*, to shoot] [Colloq.] to go or move quickly; hurry (off); dart —*n.* [Colloq.] the act of scooting

scoot·er (-ər) *n.* [< prec.] 1. a child's toy for riding on, consisting of a low footboard with a wheel or wheels at each end, and a raised handlebar for steering: it is moved by pushing one foot against the ground 2. a similar vehicle with a seat, propelled by a motor: in full, **motor scooter** 3. [Chiefly U.S.] a sailing boat with runners, for use on water or ice

scope (sklōp) *n.* [< It. < L. < Gr. *skopos*, distant object viewed, watcher] 1. the extent of the mind's grasp; range of understanding 2. the range or extent of action, content, etc., or of an activity, concept, etc. [the *scope* of a book] 3. room or opportunity for action or thought 4. *short for* TELESCOPE, MICROSCOPE, RADARSCOPE, etc.

-scope (sklōp) [< Gr. < *skopein*, to see] a combining form meaning an instrument, etc. for seeing or observing [*telescope*]

-sco·pic (sko′pik) [< -SCOPE & -IC] a combining form meaning: 1. related to an instrument with the suffix -*scope* [*telescopic*] 2. related to use of sight or vision [*macroscopic*]

sco·pol·a·mine (skō pol′e mēn′, -min) *n.* [< G. < ModL. *Scopolia*, a genus of plants, after G. A. *Scopoli* (1723–1788), It. naturalist + G. *Amin*, amine] an alkaloid, $C_{17}H_{21}O_4N$, used in medicine as a sedative, hypnotic, etc.

scops (skops) *n.* [< ModL. < Gr. *skops*, a horned owl] any of several small species of owl with ear-tufts: also **scops owl**

-sco·py (ska pē′) [< Gr. < *skopein*, to see] a combining form meaning a seeing, observing [*bioscopy*]

scor·bu·tic (skôr byōot′ik) *adj.* [< ModL. < ML. *scorbutus*, scurvy < ? Russ. *skórbnut*, to wither] of, like, or having scurvy: also **scor·bu′ti·cal**

scorch (skôrch) *vt.* [< ? Scand.] 1. *a*) to char or discolour the surface of by superficial burning *b*) to parch or shrivel by heat 2. to criticize very sharply 3. to burn and destroy everything in (an area) before yielding it to the enemy [a *scorched*-earth policy] —*vi.* 1. to become scorched 2. [Slang] to drive or ride very fast —*n.* a superficial burning or burn

scorch·er (-ər) *n.* anything that scorches; esp., [Colloq.] *a*) a very hot day *b*) a withering remark

score (skôr) *n.* [OE. *scoru* < ON. *skor*] 1. *a*) a scratch, mark, incision, etc. *b*) a drawn line, as one to mark a starting point *c*) notches, marks, etc. made to keep tally or account 2. an amount due; debt 3. a grievance one seeks to settle or get even for 4. a reason or ground 5. the number of points made in a game, contest, quiz, etc. 6. *a*) twenty people or things *b*) [*pl.*] very many 7. [Colloq.] a successful action, remark, etc. 8. [Chiefly U.S. Colloq.] the way things really are: chiefly in **know the score** 9. *Music a*) a written or printed copy of a composition, showing all parts for the instruments or voices *b*) the music for a stage production, film, etc. —*vt.* scored, scor′ing 1. to mark or mark out with notches, lines, gashes, etc. 2. to crease or partly cut (paper, etc.) for accurate folding or tearing 3. to keep account of by lines or notches 4. *a*) to make (runs, goals, etc.) in a game *b*) to record the score of *c*) to add (points) to one's score 5. to gain [to *score* a success] 6. *Music* to arrange in a score —*vi.* 1. to make points, as in a game 2. to run up a score 3. to keep score in a game 4. to succeed in getting what one wants, esp. to purchase drugs illegally —**on that score** on that matter, subject, etc. —**score out** to cross out —**score points off** to gain the advantage over: also **score off** —scor′er *n.*

score·board (-bôrd′) *n.* a large board for posting the score and other details of a game, as at a cricket ground

score card 1. a card for recording the score of a game, match, etc. 2. a card printed with the names, positions, etc. of the players of competing teams Also **score′card′n.**

score·keep·er (-kēp′ər) *n.* a person keeping score, esp. officially, at a game, competition, etc.

score·less (-lis) *adj.* with no points scored

sco·ri·a (skôr′ē ə) *n., pl.* -ri·ae′ (-ē′) [L. < Gr. < *skōr*, dung] 1. the refuse left after metal is smelted from ore 2. cinderlike lava —sco′ri·a′ceous (-ā′shəs) *adj.*

sco·ri·fy (skôr′ə fī′) *vt.* -fied′, -fy′ing to remove impurities from metal by forming slag

scorn (skôrn) *n.* [< OFr. < *escharnir*, to scorn] 1. great contempt for someone or something, often with some indignation 2. expression of this feeling 3. the object of such contempt —*vt.* 1. to regard with scorn; treat with contempt 2. to refuse or reject as wrong or disgraceful —*vi.* [Obs.] to scoff; mock —**laugh to scorn** to ridicule

scorn·ful (-fəl) *adj.* filled with or showing scorn or contempt —scorn′ful·ly *adv.* —scorn′ful·ness *n.*

Scor·pi·o (skôr′pē ō′) [L.] 1. a S constellation: also **Scor′·pi·us** (-əs) 2. *Astrol.* the eighth sign of the zodiac: see ZODIAC, illus.

scor·pi·on (-ən) *n.* [OFr. < L. < Gr. *skorpios*] 1. any of various arachnids found in warm regions, with a long tail ending in a curved, poisonous sting 2. *Bible* a whip or scourge —[S-] *same as* SCORPIO

Scot (skot) *n.* 1. any member of a Gaelic tribe of northern Ireland that migrated to Scotland in the 5th cent. A.D. 2. a native or inhabitant of Scotland

SCORPION
(to 25 cm long)

scot (skot) *n.* [ON. *skot,* tribute] money assessed or paid; tax; levy —**scot and lot** formerly, a comprehensive parish tax, assessed according to ability to pay

Scot. 1. Scotch 2. Scotland 3. Scottish

Scotch (skoch) *adj.* of Scotland, its people, their language, etc.: cf. SCOTTISH —*n. same as:* 1. SCOTTISH 2. SCOTCH WHISKY

scotch[1] (skoch) *vt.* [prob. < Anglo-Fr. < OFr. *coche,* a notch] 1. to cut; scratch; notch 2. to wound without killing; maim 3. to put an end to; stifle [to *scotch* a rumour] —*n.* a cut or scratch

scotch[2] (skoch) *vt.* [< ?] to block (a wheel, log, etc.) with a wedge to prevent movement —*n.* such a wedge or block that prevents movement

Scotch broth a broth of mutton and vegetables, thickened with barley

Scotch egg a hard-boiled egg enclosed in sausage meat and breadcrumbs and deep-fried

Scotch-Irish (-ī′rish) *adj.* designating or of those people of northern Ireland descended from Scottish settlers, esp. those who emigrated to America

Scotch·man (-mən) *n., pl.* -men *var. of* SCOTSMAN

Scotch mist a thick, wetting haze; a drizzle

Scotch pine a hardy Eurasian pine, with yellow wood

Scotch terrier *same as* SCOTTISH TERRIER

Scotch whisky whisky, often having a smoky flavour, distilled in Scotland from malted barley

sco·ter (skōt′ər) *n., pl.* -ters, -ter: see PLURAL, II, D, 1 [< ?] any of several large, dark-coloured sea ducks found chiefly along the N coasts of Europe and N America

scot-free (skot′frē′) *adj.* 1. free from payment of scot, or tax 2. unharmed or unpunished; free from penalty

Sco·tia (skō′shə) *n. poet. term for* Scotland

Scotland Yard 1. headquarters of the metropolitan London police: officially, **New Scotland Yard** 2. the London police, esp. the detective bureau

Scots (skots) *adj., n. same as* SCOTTISH

Scots·man (skots′mən) *n., pl.* -men a native or inhabitant of Scotland, esp. a man: *Scotsman* or *Scot* is preferred to *Scotchman* in Scotland —**Scots′wom′an** *n.fem., pl.* -wom′-en

Scot·ti·cism (skot′ə siz′m) *n.* a Scottish idiom, expression, word, pronunciation, etc.

Scot·tie, Scot·ty (skot′ē) *n., pl.* -ties *colloq. name for* SCOTTISH TERRIER

Scot·tish (skot′ish) *adj.* of Scotland, its people, their English dialect, etc. *Scottish* is preferred in formal usage, but with some words, *Scotch* is almost invariably used (e.g., tweed, whisky), with others, *Scots* (e.g., law) —*n.* the dialect of English spoken in Scotland —**the Scottish** the Scottish people

Scottish Certificate of Education the Scottish equivalent of the GENERAL CERTIFICATE OF EDUCATION

Scottish Gaelic the Celtic language of the Scottish Highlands: see GAELIC

Scottish terrier any of a breed of terriers with short legs, a squarish muzzle, rough, wiry hair, and pointed, erect ears

scoun·drel (skoun′drəl) *n.* [prob. < Anglo-Fr. *escoundre,* ult. < L. *abscondere,* ABSCOND] a mean, immoral, or wicked person; villain; rascal —*adj.* characteristic of a scoundrel; mean: also **scoun′drel·ly**

scour[1] (skour) *vt.* [MDu. *scuren* < ? OFr. *escurer* < VL. < L. *ex-,* intens. + *curare,* to take care of] 1. to clean or polish by vigorous rubbing, as with abrasives 2. to remove dirt and grease from (wool, etc.) 3. *a)* to wash or clear as by a swift current of water; flush *b)* to wash away; erode 4. to clear of (something undesirable) —*vi.* 1. to clean things by rubbing and polishing 3. to become clean and bright by being scoured —*n.* 1. the act of scouring 2. the place scoured, esp. by running water 3. [*usually pl., with sing. v.*] dysentery in cattle, etc. —**scour′er** *n.*

scour[2] (skour) *vt.* [< ? OFr. *escourre,* to run forth < VL. < L. *ex-,* out + *currere,* to run] to pass over quickly, or range over or through, as in search or pursuit [to *scour* a town for an escaped convict] —*vi.* to run or range about, as in search or pursuit —**scour′er** *n.*

scourge (skurj) *n.* [< OFr. < L. *ex-,* off + *corrigia,* a whip] 1. a whip or other instrument for flogging 2. any means of severe punishment or any cause of great suffering [the

scourge of war] —*vt.* **scourged, scourg′ing** 1. to whip or flog 2. to punish or make suffer severely —**scourg′er** *n.*

scour·ings (skour′inz) *n.pl.* dirt, refuse, or remains removed by or as if by scouring

scouse (skous) *n.* [< (LOB)SCOUSE] [sometimes S-] 1. lobscouse as traditionally prepared in Liverpool 2. the dialect of Liverpool —*adj.* of or from Liverpool —**scous′er** *n.*

scout[1] (skout) *n.* [< OFr. < *escouter,* to hear < L. *auscultare,* to listen] 1. a soldier, plane, etc. sent to spy out the strength, movements, etc. of the enemy 2. a person sent out to learn the tactics of an opponent, to search out new talent, etc. [a talent *scout*] 3. a member of the Boy Scouts or, in the U.S., Girl Scouts 4. the . act of reconnoitring 5. [Slang] fellow; person —*vt.* 1. to follow closely so as to spy upon 2. to look for; watch 3. to find by looking around (often with *out, up*) —*vi.* 1. to go out in search of information about the enemy; reconnoitre 2. to go in search of something [*scout* around for some firewood] 3. to work as a scout (*n.* 2) 4. to be active in the Boy Scouts or, in the U.S., Girl Scouts —**scout′ing** *n.*

scout[2] (skout) *vt.* [prob. < ON. *skuti,* a taunt] to reject as absurd; scoff at —*vi.* to scoff (*at*)

scout·er (skout′ər) *n.* the adult leader of a troop of Boy Scouts: also **scout′mast′er**

scow (skou) *n.* [Du. *schouw*] a large, flat-bottomed boat with square ends, used for carrying coal, sand, etc. and often towed by a tug

scowl (skoul) *vi.* [prob. < Scand.] 1. to contract the eyebrows and lower the corners of the mouth in showing displeasure; look angry, sullen, etc. 2. to have a threatening look; lower —*vt.* to affect or express with a scowl —*n.* the act or expression of scowling; angry frown —**scowl′er** *n.*

scrab·ble (skrab′'l) *vi.* -bled, -bling [Du. *schrabbelen* < *schrabben,* to scrape] 1. to scratch, scrape, or paw as though looking for something 2. to struggle 3. to scribble —*vt.* 1. to scrape together quickly 2. *a)* to scribble *b)* to scribble on —*n.* a scrabbling; a scramble, scribble, etc. —[S-] *a trademark for* a word game played with lettered tiles placed as in a crossword puzzle —**scrab′bler** *n.*

scrag (skrag) *n.* [prob. < ON.] 1. a thin, scrawny person, animal, or plant 2. the neck, or back of the neck, of mutton, veal, etc.: also **scrag end** 3. [Slang] the neck —*vt.* **scragged, scrag′ging** [Slang] to choke or wring the neck of

scrag·gly (skrag′lē) *adj.* -gli·er, -gli·est [see ff. & -LY[1]] sparse, scrubby, irregular, uneven, ragged, or the like [a *scraggly* beard] —**scrag′gli·ness** *n.*

scrag·gy (skrag′ē) *adj.* -gi·er, -gi·est [< SCRAG] 1. rough or jagged 2. lean; bony; skinny —**scrag′gi·ly** *adv.*

scram (skram) *vi.* **scrammed, scram′ming** [contr. of ff.] [Slang] to leave or get out, esp. in a hurry

scram·ble (skram′b'l) *vi.* -bled, -bling [< ? SCAMPER + SCRABBLE] 1. to climb, crawl, or clamber hurriedly 2. to scuffle or struggle for something 3. to rush pell-mell, as to get something highly prized [to *scramble* for political office] 4. to get aircraft into the air quickly, esp. to intercept enemy aircraft —*vt.* 1. *a)* to throw together haphazardly; jumble *b) Electronics* to modify (transmitted auditory or visual signals) so as to make unintelligible without special receiving equipment 2. to cook (eggs) while stirring the mixed whites and yolks —*n.* 1. a hard, hurried climb or advance as over difficult ground 2. a disorderly struggle or rush, as for something prized 3. a jumble 4. a motorcycle race over rough country —**scram′bler** *n.*

scrap[1] (skrap) *n.* [< ON. *skrap*] 1. a small piece; fragment; bit 2. a bit of something written 3. *a)* discarded metal suitable only for reprocessing *b)* discarded articles of rubber, leather, paper, etc. 4. [*pl.*] bits of leftover food —*adj.* 1. in the form of pieces, leftovers, etc. 2. used and discarded —*vt.* **scrapped, scrap′ping** 1. to make into scrap 2. to discard —**scrap′per** *n.*

scrap[2] (skrap) *n.* [prob. < *scrape,* orig., nefarious scheme] [Colloq.] a fight or quarrel —*vi.* **scrapped, scrap′ping** [Colloq.] to fight or quarrel —**scrap′per** *n.*

scrap·book (-book′) *n.* a book of blank pages for mounting newspaper cuttings, pictures, etc.

scrape (skrāp) *vt.* **scraped, scrap′ing** [< ON. *skrapa*] 1. to rub over the surface of with something rough or sharp 2. to make smooth or clean by rubbing with a tool or abrasive 3. to remove by rubbing with something sharp or rough (with *off, out,* etc.) 4. to scratch or abrade by a rough, rubbing contact 5. to rub with a harsh, grating sound [chalk *scraping* a blackboard] 6. to gather slowly and with difficulty [to *scrape* up some money] —*vi.* 1. to rub against something harshly; grate 2. to give out a harsh, grating noise 3. to gather goods or money slowly and with difficulty 4. to manage to get by (with *through, along, by*) 5. to draw the foot back along the ground in bowing —*n.* 1. a scraping 2. a scraped place; abrasion 3. a harsh, grating sound 4. a disagreeable situation; predicament 5. a fight or conflict —**scrape the bottom of the barrel** to use the last or weakest of one's resources —**scrap′er** *n.*

scrap·ing (skrā′pin) *n.* 1. the act of a person or thing that

scrapes **2.** the sound of this **3.** [*usually pl.*] something scraped off, together, or up

scrap merchant a dealer in scrap, esp. scrap metal

scrap metal discarded or waste pieces of iron, etc., to be recast

scrap·py (skrap'ē) *adj.* **-pi·er, -pi·est** [SCRAP¹ + -Y²] **1.** made of scraps **2.** disconnected [*scrappy* memories] —**scrap'pi·ly** *adv.* —**scrap'pi·ness** *n.*

Scratch (skrach) [altered (after ff.) < ON. *skratti,* devil] [*sometimes* s-] the Devil: usually **Old Scratch**

scratch (skrach) *vt.* [prob. altered < ME. *scratten,* to scratch, after *cracchen*] **1.** to mark or cut the surface of slightly with something pointed or sharp **2.** to tear or dig with the nails or claws **3.** to scrape lightly to relieve itching, etc. **4.** to rub or scrape with a grating noise **5.** to write or draw hurriedly or carelessly **6.** to strike out (writing, etc.) **7.** to gather with difficulty; scrape (*together* or *up*) **8.** [U.S.] *Politics* to strike out the name of (a candidate) on (a party ticket or ballot) **9.** *Sports* to withdraw (an entry) from a contest, specif. from a horse race —*vi.* **1.** to use nails or claws in digging or wounding **2.** to scrape the skin lightly to relieve itching, etc. **3.** to manage to get by **4.** to make a harsh, scraping noise **5.** to withdraw from a race or contest **6.** *Billiards, Snooker,* etc. to commit a scratch —*n.* **1.** the act of scratching **2.** a mark, tear, or slight wound made by scratching **3.** a grating or scraping sound **4.** a scribble **5.** the starting line of a race **6.** [Slang] money **7.** *Billiards, Snooker,* etc. a) a shot that results in a penalty b) a miss **8.** *Sports* a) the starting point or time of a contestant who receives no handicap b) such a contestant c) an entry withdrawn from a contest —*adj.* **1.** [Chiefly U.S.] used for hasty notes, preliminary figuring, etc. [*scratch* paper] **2.** having no handicap in a contest **3.** put together hastily, without selection —**from scratch 1.** from the starting line, as in a race **2.** from nothing; without advantage —**scratch one's head** to be puzzled or worried —**scratch the surface** to do, consider, or affect something superficially —**up to scratch** [Colloq.] up to a standard —**scratch'er** *n.*

scratch·y (-ē) *adj.* **scratch'i·er, scratch'i·est 1.** made with scratches **2.** making a scratching noise **3.** scratched together; haphazard **4.** that chafes, itches, etc. [*scratchy* cloth] —**scratch'i·ly** *adv.* —**scratch'i·ness** *n.*

scrawl (skrôl) *vt., vi.* [< ?] to write, draw, or mark hastily, carelessly, or awkwardly —*n.* **1.** sprawling handwriting, often hard to read **2.** something scrawled —**scrawl'er** *n.* —**scrawl'y** *adj.* **scrawl'i·er, scrawl'i·est**

scraw·ny (skrô'nē) *adj.* **-ni·er, -ni·est** [prob. < Scand.] **1.** very thin; skinny and bony **2.** stunted or scrubby —**scraw'ni·ness** *n.*

scream (skrēm) *vi.* [akin to WFl. *schreemen,* to scream, G. *schrei,* a cry] **1.** to utter or make a shrill, piercing cry or sound **2.** to laugh loudly or hysterically **3.** to have a startling effect; be obvious **4.** to shout or yell in anger, hysteria, etc. —*vt.* **1.** to utter with or as with a scream **2.** to bring into a specified state by screaming [to *scream* oneself hoarse] —*n.* **1.** a sharp, piercing cry or sound **2.** [Colloq.] a hilariously funny person or thing

scream·er (-ər) *n.* **1.** a person who screams **2.** any of various long-toed S. American wading birds

scream·ing (-iŋ) *adj.* **1.** that screams **2.** startling in effect **3.** causing screams of laughter —**scream'ing·ly** *adv.*

scree (skrē) *n.* [back-formation < pl. *screes* < ON. *skritha,* a landslide] a pile of rock debris at the foot of a rock face, often forming a sloping heap

screech (skrēch) *vi.* [ON. *skraekja*] to utter or make a shrill, high-pitched, harsh shriek or sound —*vt.* to utter with a screech —*n.* a shrill, high-pitched, harsh shriek or sound —**screech'er** *n.* —**screech'y** *adj.* **screech'i·er, screech'i·est**

screech owl 1. same as BARN OWL **2.** a small, N American owl with an eerie, wailing cry

screed (skrēd) *n.* [ME. *screde,* var. of *schrede,* shred] a long, tiresome speech or piece of writing

screen (skrēn) *n.* [< OFr. *escren* < Gmc.] **1.** a curtain or movable partition, as a covered frame, used to separate, conceal, protect, etc. **2.** anything that functions to shield, conceal, etc. [a smoke *screen*] **3.** a coarse mesh of wire, etc. used as a sieve, as for grading coal **4.** a system for screening or testing persons **5.** [Chiefly U.S.] a frame covered with a mesh, as of wire, used, as on a window, to keep insects out **6.** a) a white surface upon which films, slides, etc. are projected b) the film industry **7.** the surface area of a television or radar receiver on which the light pattern is traced —*vt.* **1.** to separate, conceal, or protect, as with a screen **2.** to enclose or provide with a screen **3.** to sift through a screen **4.** a) to interview or test in order to separate according to skills, personality, etc. b) to separate in this way (usually with *out*) **5.** a) to project (films, etc.) upon a screen b) to photograph with a film camera c) to adapt (a story, play, etc.) as for a film —*vi.* to be screened or adapted for screening, as in films —**screen off** to hide from view by means of a screen —**screen'a·ble** *adj.* —**screen'er** *n.* —**screen'less** *adj.*

screen·ing (-iŋ) *n.* **1.** the act of one that screens **2.** [U.S.] a) a screen or set of screens b) mesh used in a screen **3.** [*pl.*] material separated out by a sifting screen

screen·play (-plā') *n.* a story written, or adapted from a novel, etc., for production as a film

screen printing same as SILK-SCREEN printing

screw (skrōō) *n.* [MFr. *escroue,* hole in which a screw turns < L. *scrofa,* sow] **1.** a) a cylindrical or conical piece of metal for fastening things by being turned: it is threaded evenly with an advancing spiral ridge and usually has a slotted head: also called **male** (or **external**) **screw** b) the internal thread, as of a nut, into which a male screw can be turned: also called **female** (or **internal**) **screw** c) a turning of such a screw **2.** any of various devices operating or threaded like a screw, as a screw propeller **3.** [Slang] a prison guard **4.** [Colloq.] a stingy person **5.** [Colloq.] a salary —*vt.* **1.** to twist; turn; tighten **2.** to fasten, tighten, insert, etc. as with a screw or screws **3.** to twist out of shape; contort **4.** to make stronger (often with *up*) **5.** to force or compel, as if by using screws **6.** [Slang] to cheat; swindle **7.** [Slang] to have sexual intercourse with —*vi.* **1.** to go together or come apart by being turned like a screw [a lid *screws* on] **2.** to be fitted for screws **3.** to twist; turn; wind **4.** to cheat; swindle —**have a screw loose** [Slang] to be eccentric, odd, etc. —**put the screws on** to subject to force or great pressure —**screw up** [Slang] to make a mess of; bungle

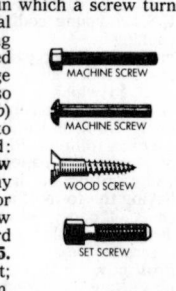
MACHINE SCREW
MACHINE SCREW
WOOD SCREW
SET SCREW

screw·ball (-bôl') *n.* [U.S. Slang] a person who seems irrational, unconventional, unbalanced, etc. —*adj.* [U.S. Slang] peculiar; irrational

screw·driv·er (-drī'vər) *n.* **1.** a tool used for turning screws, having an end that fits into the slot in the head of a screw **2.** a cocktail of orange juice and vodka

screwed (skrōōd) *adj.* **1.** having threads like a screw **2.** twisted **3.** [Slang] drunk

screw eye a screw with a loop for a head

screw hook a screw with a hook for a head

screw propeller see PROPELLER

screw thread the spiral ridge of a screw

screw top a bottle top that screws on allowing a container to be resealed after use —**screw-top** *adj.*

screw·y (skrōō'ē) *adj.* **screw'i·er, screw'i·est** [Slang] **1.** mentally unbalanced; crazy **2.** peculiar, odd, etc. in a confusing way —**screw'i·ness** *n.*

scrib·ble (skrib''l) *vt., vi.* **-bled, -bling** [< ML. < L. *scribere,* to write] **1.** to write carelessly, hastily, or illegibly **2.** to cover with or make marks that are meaningless or hard to read —*n.* scribbled writing, marks, etc.; scrawl —**scrib'·bler** *n.*

scribbling pad a pad of paper used for jottings, etc.

scribe (skrib) *n.* [L. *scriba,* public writer < *scribere,* to write] **1.** a penman who copied manuscripts before the invention of printing **2.** a writer; author **3.** a person learned in the Jewish law who makes handwritten copies of the Torah **4.** a person employed by the public to write letters, etc. —*vi.* scribed, scrib'ing to work as a scribe —**scrib'al** *adj.*

scrim (skrim) *n.* [< ?] a light, sheer, loosely woven cotton or linen cloth, often used for bookbinding or curtains

scrim·mage (skrim'ij) *n.* [altered < SKIRMISH] **1.** a tussle; confused struggle **2.** *American Football* the play that follows the pass from centre —*vi.* **-maged, -mag·ing** to take part in a scrimmage

scrimp (skrimp) *vt.* [prob. < Scand.] **1.** to make too small, short, etc.; skimp **2.** to treat stingily; stint —*vi.* to be sparing and frugal —**scrimp'er** *n.* —**scrimp'ing·ly** *adv.*

scrimp·y (skrim'pē) *adj.* **scrimp'i·er, scrimp'i·est 1.** skimpy; scanty; meagre **2.** frugal or economical —**scrimp'·i·ly** *adv.* —**scrimp'i·ness** *n.*

scrim·shank (skrim'shaŋk') *vi.* [< ?] to be workshy; to shirk a duty —**scrim'shank·er** *n.*

scrim·shaw (skrim'shô') *n.* [< ?] **1.** carving done on shells, bone, ivory, etc., esp. by sailors **2.** an article or articles so made

scrip (skrip) *n.* [contr. < SCRIPT] **1.** a note, list, receipt, etc. **2.** a negotiable document which acts as proof of ownership of a holding in a joint stock company

script (skript) *n.* [< MFr. < L. *scriptum,* neut. pp. of *scribere,* to write] **1.** handwriting, or a style of this **2.** *Printing* a typeface that looks like handwriting **3.** an original manuscript **4.** a copy of the text of a play or film, or of a radio or television show **5.** the written work of an examination candidate —*vt.* [Colloq.] to write the script for (a film, etc.)

scrip·ture (skrip'chər) *n.* [< L. < *scriptus:* see SCRIPT] **1.**

[**S-**] [*often pl.*] a) the sacred writings of the Jews, identical with the Old Testament of the Christians b) the Christian Bible; Old and New Testaments **2.** any sacred writing —**scrip′tur·al** *adj.* —**scrip′tur·al·ist** *n.* —**scrip′tur·al·ly** *adv.*

script·writ·er (skript′rīt′ər) *n.* a person who writes scripts for films, television shows, etc.

scrive·ner (skriv′nər, -'nər) *n.* [< OFr., ult. < L. *scriba*, a SCRIBE] [Archaic] **1.** a scribe or clerk **2.** a notary

scrod (skrod) *n.* [prob. < MDu. *schrode*, strip] [Chiefly U.S.] a young codfish or haddock, split and prepared for cooking

scrof·u·la (skrof′yə lə) *n.* [ML. < L. < dim. of *scrofa*, a sow] tuberculosis of the lymphatic glands, esp. of the neck, in which the glands become enlarged —**scrof′u·lous** *adj.* —**scrof′u·lous·ly** *adv.* —**scrof′u·lous·ness** *n.*

scroll (skrōl) *n.* [altered (? after *roll*) < ME. *scrowe* < OFr. *escroue*, roll of writings] **1.** a roll of parchment, paper, etc., usually with writing on it **2.** anything having the form of a loosely rolled sheet of paper, as an ornamental design in coiled or spiral form —**scrolled** *adj.*

SCROLL

scroll saw a thin, ribbonlike saw for cutting thin wood into spiral or ornamental designs

scroll·work (-wurk′) *n.* **1.** ornamental work marked by scrolls **2.** ornamental work done with a scroll saw

Scrooge (skrōōj) *n.* [after *Scrooge*, a character in Dickens' *A Christmas Carol*] [*also* **s-**] a hard, miserly old man

scro·tum (skrōt′əm) *n., pl.* **-ta** (-ə), **-tums** [L.] in most male mammals, the pouch of skin containing the testicles —**scro′tal** *adj.*

scrounge (skrounj) *vt.* scrounged, scroung′ing [< ?] [Colloq.] **1.** to get or find by hunting around **2.** to get by begging or sponging **3.** to pilfer —*vi.* [Colloq.] to search (*around*) for something —**scroung′er** *n.*

scrub[1] (skrub) *n.* [dial. var. of *shrub*, infl. ? by ON. *skroppa*, a lean creature] **1.** a) short, stunted trees or bushes growing thickly together b) land covered with such growth **2.** any person, animal, or thing smaller than the usual, or considered inferior —*adj.* **1.** mean; poor; inferior **2.** undersized; stunted

scrub[2] (skrub) *vt.* scrubbed, scrub′bing [prob. < Scand.] **1.** to clean or wash by rubbing hard **2.** to rub hard **3.** to cleanse (a gas) of impurities **4.** [Colloq.] a) to cancel or call off b) to get rid of —*vi.* to clean something by rubbing, as with a brush —*n.* **1.** the act of scrubbing **2.** a person who scrubs —**scrub up** the act of a surgeon in washing his hands and arms thoroughly before an operation

scrub·ber[1] (skrub′ər) *n.* [Aust.] a bullock which has escaped into the scrub and becomes wild

scrub·ber[2] (skrub′ər) *n.* **1.** a person or thing that scrubs, esp. a device for cleaning a gas **2.** [Slang] a promiscuous girl, usually unintelligent and unattractive

scrubbing brush a brush with extra strong bristles, used for scrubbing floors, etc.

scrub·by (skrub′e) *adj.* -bi·er, -bi·est **1.** undersized or inferior; stunted **2.** covered with brushwood **3.** paltry, shabby, etc. —**scrub′bi·ly** *adv.* —**scrub′bi·ness** *n.*

scrub typhus an acute febrile rickettsial disease occurring mainly in the W Pacific

scruff (skruf) *n.* [< ON. *skrufr*, tuft of hair] the back of the neck; nape

scruff·y (skruf′ē) *adj.* scruff′i·er, scruff′i·est [< dial. *scruff*, var. of SCURF + -Y[2]] shabby, unkempt, or untidy; grubby —**scruff′i·ly** *adv.* —**scruff′i·ness** *n.*

scrum·mage (skrum′ij) *n.* [dial. var. of SCRIMMAGE] *Rugby* a play in which the two sets of forwards, lined up facing each other, try to kick the ball back to their teammates —*vi.* -maged, -mag·ing to take part in a scrummage Also **scrum**

scrump (skrump) *vi.,vt.* [< SCRUMPY] to steal (apples) from an orchard or garden

scrump·tious (skrump′shəs) *adj.* [? < SUMPTUOUS] [Colloq.] very pleasing, attractive, etc. —**scrump′tious·ly** *adv.* —**scrump′tious·ness** *n.*

scrump·y (skrum′pē) *n.* [< dial. *scrump*, withered apple] a rough cider, brewed mainly in the West Country

scru·ple (skrōō′p'l) *n.* [< MFr. < L. *scrupulus*, small sharp stone] **1.** a very small quantity **2.** an apothecaries' weight equal to 1/3 dram (20 grains) **3.** a doubt arising from difficulty in deciding what is right, proper, etc.; qualm —*vt., vi.* -pled, -pling to hesitate (at) from doubt; have scruples (*about*) —**make no scruple(s)** to do, or plan to do, with an easy conscience

scru·pu·lous (skrōō′pyoo ləs) *adj.* **1.** having or showing scruples; conscientiously honest **2.** demanding or using precision, care, and exactness —**scru′pu·los′i·ty** (-los′e tē), *pl.* -ties, **scru′pu·lous·ness** *n.* —**scru′pu·lous·ly** *adv.*

scru·ti·nize (skrōō′tin īz′) *vt.* -nized′, -niz′ing to look at carefully or examine closely —**scru′ti·niz′er** *n.*

scru·ti·ny (-in ē) *n., pl.* -nies [< LL. < L. *scrutari*, to search

into carefully] **1.** a close examination **2.** a careful, continuous watch **3.** a lengthy, searching look

scu·ba (skōō′bə) *n.* [*s*(elf-)*c*(ontained) *u*(nderwater) *b*(reathing) *a*(pparatus)] a diver's apparatus with compressed-air tanks connected to a mouthpiece for breathing under water

scud (skud) *vi.* scud′ded, scud′ding [prob. < ON.] **1.** to move swiftly **2.** to be driven before the wind —*n.* **1.** a scudding **2.** spray, rain, or snow driven by the wind **3.** very low, dark, swiftly moving clouds

scuff (skuf) *vt.* [prob. < or akin to ON. *skufa*, to shove] **1.** to scrape (one's feet) on the ground, etc. **2.** to wear a rough place on the surface of **3.** to scrape (the ground, etc.) with the feet —*vi.* **1.** to walk without lifting the feet; shuffle **2.** to become scraped or worn in patches —*n.* **1.** a noise or act of scuffing **2.** a worn or rough spot **3.** a loose-fitting slipper, esp. one without a back

scuf·fle (skuf′'l) *vi.* -fled, -fling [freq. of prec.] **1.** to struggle or fight in rough confusion **2.** to move in a confused hurry **3.** to drag one's feet —*n.* **1.** a rough, confused fight **2.** the act or sound of feet shuffling

scul·dud·der·y, scul·dug·ger·y (skul dug′ər ē) *same as* SKULDUGGERY

scull (skul) *n.* [prob. < Scand.] **1.** an oar mounted at the stern and worked from side to side to move a boat forward **2.** either of a pair of light oars used by a single rower **3.** a light racing boat for one, two, or four rowers —*vt., vi.* to propel with a scull or sculls —**scull′er** *n.*

scul·ler·y (skul′ər ē) *n., pl.* -ler·ies [< OFr., ult. < *escuelle*, a dish < L. *scutella*, a tray] a room adjoining the kitchen, where pots and pans are cleaned, etc.

scul·lion (skul′yən) *n.* [< OFr. < L. *scopa*, a broom] [Archaic] a servant doing the rough, dirty work in a kitchen

scul·pin (skul′pin) *n., pl.* -pin, -pins: see PLURAL, II, D, 2 [prob. < Fr. *scorpene* < L. *scorpaena*: see SCORPION] any of certain spiny sea fishes with a big head and wide mouth

sculpt (skulpt) *vt., vi.* [Fr. *sculpter*, ult. < L. *sculpere*: see SCULPTURE] **1.** to carve or model as a sculptor **2.** to give sculpturelike form to (hair, fabric, etc.) Also **sculp**

sculp·tor (skulp′tər) *n.* [L. < *sculpere*, to carve] an artist who models, carves, or fashions figures or forms of clay, stone, metal, wood, etc. —**sculp′tress** *n. fem.*

sculp·ture (-chər) *n.* [< L. < pp. of *sculpere*, to carve] **1.** the art of carving wood, chiselling stone, casting or welding metal, modelling clay, etc. into statues, figures, or the like **2.** any work or works of sculpture —*vt.* -tured, -tur·ing **1.** to carve, chisel, etc. into statues, figures, etc. **2.** to portray in sculpture **3.** to form like sculpture **4.** to decorate with sculpture —*vi.* to work as a sculptor —**sculp′tur·al** *adj.* —**sculp′tur·al·ly** *adv.*

sculp·tur·esque (skulp′chə resk′) *adj.* like sculpture

scum (skum) *n.* [< MDu. *schum*] **1.** a thin layer of impurities which forms on the top of liquids **2.** worthless parts or things; refuse **3.** a mean, despicable person, or such people collectively —*vi.* scummed, scum′ming to form scum

scum·my (skum′ē) *adj.* -mi·er, -mi·est of, like, or covered with scum

scun·ner (skun′ər) *vi.* [LME. (Northern dialect) < ?] to feel disgust or strong aversion —*n.* a strong dislike or disgust: chiefly in **take a scunner**

scup (skup) *n., pl.* scup, scups: see PLURAL, II, D, 2 [< AmInd.] a brown-and-white perchlike fish of the N Atlantic

scup·per[1] (skup′ər) *n.* [< ?] **1.** an opening in a ship's side to allow water to run off the deck **2.** an opening in a wall to allow water to run off a floor or roof

scup·per[2] (skup′ər) *vt.* [< ?] [Colloq.] to annihilate or disable, as by a surprise attack

scurf (skurf) *n.* [< ON. hyp. *skurfr*] **1.** little, dry scales shed by the skin, as dandruff **2.** any scaly coating —**scurf′y** *adj.* **scurf′i·er, scurf′i·est**

scur·ril·ous (skur′ə ləs) *adj.* [< L. < *scurra*, buffoon] using or containing coarse, vulgar, or abusive language —**scur·ril′i·ty** (skə ril′ə tē) *n., pl.* -ties —**scur′ril·ous·ly** *adv.* —**scur′ril·ous·ness** *n.*

scur·ry (skur′ē) *vi.* -ried, -ry·ing [< HURRY-SCURRY] to run hastily —*vt.* to cause to scurry —*n.* a scurrying

scur·vy (skur′vē) *adj.* -vi·er, -vi·est [< SCURF] low; mean; contemptible —*n.* a disease resulting from a deficiency of vitamin C in the body and causing weakness, anaemia, spongy gums, bleeding from the mucous membranes, etc.—**scur′vi·ly** *adv.* —**scur′vi·ness** *n.*

scut (skut) *n.* [< ?] a short, stumpy tail, esp. of a rabbit or deer

scu·tage (skyōōt′ij) *n.* [ML. *scutagium* < L. *scutum*, a shield] a tax paid by the holder of a knight's fee, usually in lieu of feudal military service

scu·tate (skyōō′tāt) *adj.* [ModL. < L. < *scutum*, a shield] **1.** *Bot.* same as PELTATE **2.** *Zool.* covered by bony or horny plates or scales

scutch·eon (skuch′ən) *n. same as* ESCUTCHEON

scu·tel·lum (skyōō tel′əm) *n., pl.* -tel′la (-ə) **1.** [ModL. mistaken for L. dim. of *scutum*, a shield] *Bot.* any shield-shaped part   **2.** [ModL. < L. *scutella*: see ff.] *Zool.* a small, horny scale or plate

scut·tle[1] (skut''l) *n.* [OE. *scutel*, a dish < L. *scutella*] a kind of bucket used for pouring coal on a fire: in full, **coal scuttle**

scut·tle[2] (skut'')1 *vi.* **-tled, -tling** [prob. akin to SCUD] to scurry, esp. away from trouble, etc. —*n.* a scurry

scut·tle[3] (skut'')1 *n.* [< MFr. < Sp. *escotilla*, dim. of *escote*, a notch] **1.** a small, covered opening in the hull or deck of a ship   **2.** [U.S.] an opening in a wall or roof, fitted with a cover —*vt.* **-tled, -tling** **1.** to make or open holes in the hull of (a ship) below the waterline; esp., to sink in this way   **2.** to abandon (a plan, undertaking, etc.)

scut·tle·butt (-but') *n.* [orig. < *scuttled butt*, lidded cask] **1.** *Naut.* a water butt on board a ship   **2.** [Colloq.] rumour or gossip

scu·tum (skyōot'əm) *n., pl.* **scu'ta** (-ə) [L.] **1.** the long, leather-covered, wooden shield of Roman infantrymen   **2.** *Zool.* a heavy, horny scale, as on certain reptiles or insects: also **scute** (skyōot)

Scyl·la (sil'ə) a dangerous rock on the southern Italian coast, opposite the whirlpool Charybdis —**between Scylla and Charybdis** facing danger or evil on either hand

scythe (sīth) *n.* [altered (after L. *scindere*, to cut) < OE. *sithe*] a tool with a long, single-edged blade on a bent wooden shaft, used in cutting tall grass, grain, etc. by hand —*vt.* **scythed, scyth'ing** to cut with a scythe

Scyth·i·an (sith'ē ən) *adj.* of Scythia, ancient region in SE Europe, on the N coast of the Black Sea —*n.* **1.** an inhabitant of Scythia   **2.** the language of Scythia

SCYTHE

S.D.R. Special Drawing Right (from the International Monetary Fund)

Se *Chem.* selenium

SE, S.E., s.e. **1.** southeast   **2.** southeastern

sea (sē) *n.* [OE. sæ] **1.** the ocean   **2.** a large body of salt water wholly or partly enclosed by land [the Red Sea]   **3.** a large body of fresh water [the Sea of Galilee]   **4.** the condition of the ocean's surface [a calm sea]   **5.** a heavy swell or wave   **6.** a very great amount or expanse   **7.** *Astron.* same as MARE[2] (sense 2) —*adj.* of, connected with, or for use at sea —**at sea** **1.** on the open sea   **2.** uncertain; bewildered —**follow the sea** to be a sailor —**go to sea** to become a sailor —**put (out) to sea** to sail away from land

sea anchor a large, canvas-covered frame, usually conical, let out from a ship as a drag to reduce drifting or to keep the ship heading into the wind

sea anemone a sea polyp having a firm, gelatinous body topped with coloured, petallike tentacles

sea bag a large, cylindrical bag in which a sailor carries his clothes and personal belongings

sea bass **1.** any of numerous sea fishes; esp., a) the **black sea bass,** a food fish with large scales and a wide mouth, found in the W Atlantic b) the **giant sea bass,** found in the E Pacific   **2.** any of various similar fishes, as the **white sea bass**

sea bird a bird living on or near the sea: also **sea fowl**

sea·board (-bôrd') *n.* land or coastal region bordering on the sea —*adj.* bordering on the sea

sea·borne (-bôrn') *adj.* **1.** carried on or by the sea   **2.** afloat: said of ships

sea breeze a breeze blowing inland from the sea

sea cabbage *same as* SEA KALE

sea·coast (-kōst') *n.* land bordering on the sea

sea cow **1.** any of several sea mammals, as the dugong or manatee   **2.** *earlier name for* WALRUS

sea cucumber an echinoderm with a cucumber-shaped, flexible body and long tentacles around the mouth

sea dog **1.** an experienced sailor   **2.** any of various seals

sea elephant a large seal that is hunted for oil: the male has a long proboscis

sea·far·er (-fer'ər) *n.* a traveller by sea; esp., a sailor

sea·far·ing (-fer'iŋ) *adj.* of or engaged in life at sea —*n.* **1.** the occupation of a sailor   **2.** travel by sea

sea·food (-fōōd') *n.* food prepared from or consisting of saltwater fish or shellfish

sea·girt (-gurt') *adj.* surrounded by the sea

sea·go·ing (-gō'iŋ) *adj.* **1.** made for use on the open sea [a seagoing schooner]   **2.** same as SEAFARING

sea green a pale bluish green —**sea'-green'** *adj.*

sea gull *same as* GULL[1]; esp., any gull living along a seacoast

sea horse **1.** a small, semitropical marine fish with a slender tail, plated body, and a head somewhat like that of a horse   **2.** a mythical sea creature, half fish and half horse

sea kale [from growing near the coast] a fleshy, European, coastal plant whose young shoots are eaten as a vegetable

seal[1] (sēl) *n.* [< OFr. < L. *sigillum*, a seal, dim. of *signum*, a sign] **1.** a design, initials, etc. placed on a letter, document, etc. to prove it is authentic: letters were once commonly sealed with a molten wax wafer impressed with such a design   **2.** a stamp or signet ring for making such an impression   **3.** a wax wafer, piece of paper, etc. bearing an impressed design recognized as official   **4.** a) something that closes or fastens tightly or securely b) a tight closure, as against the passage of air or water   **5.** anything that guarantees; pledge   **6.** a sign; token [a handshake as a *seal* of friendship]   **7.** an ornamental paper stamp [a Christmas *seal*] —*vt.* **1.** to mark with a seal   **2.** to secure the contents of (a letter, etc.) by closing with a wax seal, a gummed flap, etc.   **3.** to confirm the truth of (a promise, etc.) by some action   **4.** to certify as being official, accurate, exact, etc. by or as by fixing a seal to   **5.** to settle or determine finally [to *seal* one's fate]   **6.** a) to close, etc. as with a seal [to *seal* one's lips]   b) to close completely as to make airtight or watertight c) to apply a nonpermeable coating to (a porous surface, as a wood) —**seal off** **1.** to close completely   **2.** to surround with barriers, a cordon, etc. —**set one's seal to** **1.** to mark with one's seal   **2.** to endorse —**the seals** symbols or marks of office, esp. of public office —**seal'a·ble** *adj.* —**seal'er** *n.*

seal[2] (sēl) *n., pl.* **seals, seal:** see PLURAL, II, D, 1 [OE. *seolh*] **1.** a sea mammal with a sleek coat and four flippers: it lives in cold waters and eats fish   **2.** the fur of a fur seal   **3.** leather made from sealskin —*vi.* to hunt seals

sea lane a commonly used route for travel by sea

seal·ant (sēl'ənt) *n.* [SEAL[1] + -ANT] a substance, as a wax, plastic, silicone, etc., used for sealing

sea legs the ability to walk without loss of balance on board ship, esp. in a rough sea

FUR SEAL (1·5-2 m long)

seal·er·y (sēl'ər ē) *n., pl.* **-er·ies** **1.** a place where seals are hunted   **2.** the work of hunting seals Also **seal fishery**

sea level the level of the surface of the sea, esp. the mean level between high and low tide: used as a standard in measuring heights and depths

sea lily a stalked and attached crinoid

sealing wax a hard mixture of resin and turpentine used for sealing letters, dry cells, etc.: it softens when heated

sea lion a large, eared seal of the N Pacific

Sea Lord a naval member of the Board of Admiralty

seal ring *same as* SIGNET RING

seal·skin (sēl'skin') *n.* **1.** the skin of the seal; esp., the soft undercoat dyed dark-brown or black   **2.** a garment made of this —*adj.* made of sealskin

Sea·ly·ham terrier (sē'lē əm) [< *Sealyham*, an estate in Wales] any of a breed of small, white terrier with short legs and square jaws

seam (sēm) *n.* [OE. *seam*] **1.** the line formed by sewing together two pieces of material   **2.** any line marking joining edges, as of boards   **3.** a mark, line, etc. like this, as a scar, wrinkle, etc.   **4.** a layer or stratum of ore, coal, etc. —*vt.* **1.** to join together so as to form a seam   **2.** to mark with a seamlike line, crack, etc. —**seam'less** *adj.*

sea·man (sē'mən) *n., pl.* **-men** **1.** a sailor   **2.** man ranking below a petty officer in the navy —**sea'man·like'** *adj.*

sea·man·ship (-ship') *n.* skill in sailing, navigating, or working a ship

seam bowler *Cricket* a bowler who makes the ball swing during its flight and after it hits the ground

seam·stress (sēm'stris) *n.* a woman who sews expertly or who makes her living by sewing

seam·y (sē'mē) *adj.* **seam'i·er, seam'i·est** **1.** having or showing seams   **2.** unpleasant, squalid, or sordid [the seamy side of life] —**seam'i·ness** *n.*

Sean·ad Eir·eann (san'äd er'ən) [Ir., lit., senate of Ireland] in the Republic of Ireland, the upper chamber of parliament

sé·ance (sā'äns) *n.* [Fr. < OFr. *seoir* < L. *sedere*, to sit] a meeting at which spiritualists seek or profess to communicate with the dead

sea otter a web-footed sea mammal, found along the N Pacific coast of the U.S.: its dark-brown fur is valuable

sea pie **1.** a sailor's pie made from salt meat, vegetables, etc.   **2.** the oystercatcher: also **sea pilot**

sea·plane (sē'plān') *n.* any aircraft designed to land on and take off from water

sea·port (-pôrt') *n.* **1.** a port or harbour used by ocean ships   **2.** a town or city having such a port

sear (sir) *adj.* [OE.] withered; sere —*vt.* **1.** to dry up; wither   **2.** to scorch or burn the surface of   **3.** to brand with a hot iron **4.** to make callous or unfeeling —*n.* a mark produced by searing —**sear′ing·ly** *adv.*

search (surch) *vt.* [< OFr. *cercher* < LL. *circare,* to go about < *circus,* ring] **1.** to go over and look through in order to find something [*search* the records] **2.** to examine (a person) for something concealed **3.** to examine carefully; probe [to *search* one's soul] —*vi.* to make a search —*n.* the act of searching; examination —**in search of** trying to find —**search me** [Slang] I do not know —**search out** to seek and find by searching —**search′a·ble** *adj.* —**search′er** *n.*

search·ing (-iŋ) *adj.* **1.** examining thoroughly **2.** keen; piercing —**search′ing·ly** *adv.*

search·light (-līt′) *n.* **1.** an apparatus on a swivel, that projects a strong, far-reaching beam of light **2.** such a beam

search party a group of people taking part in a search, as for a lost or missing person

search warrant a legal document authorizing a police search, as for stolen articles, etc.

sea·scape (sē′skāp′) *n.* [SEA + (LAND)SCAPE] **1.** a view of the sea **2.** a drawing, painting, etc. of this

Sea Scout a member of the branch of the Boy Scouts that emphasizes seamanship

sea·shell (-shel′) *n.* the shell of any saltwater mollusc

sea·shore (-shôr′) *n.* land along the sea; seacoast

sea·sick·ness (-sik′nis) *n.* nausea, dizziness, etc. caused by the rolling or pitching of a ship at sea —**sea′sick′** *adj.*

sea·side (-sīd′) *n.* land along the sea; seashore —*adj.* at or of the seaside

sea·son (sē′z'n) *n.* [< OFr. < L. *satio,* sowing time < base of *serere,* to sow] **1.** any of the four divisions into which the year is divided; spring, summer, autumn, or winter **2.** the time of the year when something specified takes place, is popular, permitted, at its best, etc. [the harvest *season,* the hunting *season*] **3.** a period of time [the busy *season* in a factory] **4.** the fitting or convenient time **5.** the time of a specified festival or holiday [the Easter *season*] —*vt.* **1.** to make (food) more tasty by adding salt, spices, etc. **2.** to add zest or interest to **3.** to make more fit for use, as by aging, curing, etc. **4.** to make used to; accustom [a *seasoned* traveller] **5.** to temper; soften —*vi.* to become seasoned, as wood by drying —**for a season** for a while —**in season 1.** available fresh for use as food **2.** at the legally established time for being hunted or caught: said of game, etc. **3.** in or at the proper time **4.** early enough: also **in good season 5.** in heat: said of animals —**out of season** not in season —**sea′son·er** *n.*

sea·son·a·ble (-ə b'l) *adj.* **1.** suitable to or usual for the time of year **2.** timely; opportune —**sea′son·a·ble·ness** *n.* —**sea′son·a·bly** *adv.*

sea·son·al (-əl) *adj.* of or depending on a season or the seasons [*seasonal* rains, *seasonal* work] —**sea′son·al·ly** *adv.*

sea·son·ing (-iŋ) *n.* anything that adds zest; esp., salt, spices, etc. added to food to make it more tasty

season ticket a ticket or set of tickets as for a series of concerts, sports events, etc. or for transportation, etc. for a given period of time

seat (sēt) *n.* [ON. *sæti*] **1.** the manner of sitting, as on horseback **2.** *a)* a place to sit, or the right to such a place, esp. as shown by a ticket *b)* a thing to sit on; chair, bench, etc. **3.** *a)* the buttocks *b)* the part of a garment covering the buttocks *c)* the part of a chair, etc. that supports the buttocks **4.** the right to sit as a member; membership [a *seat* on the stock exchange] **5.** a part or surface on which another part rests or fits **6.** the chief location, or centre [the *seat* of government] **7.** a place of abode, esp. a country house **8.** a parliamentary constituency —*vt.* **1.** to put or set in or on a seat **2.** to lead to a seat **3.** to have seats for [the car *seats* six] **4.** to put a seat in or on; reseat **5.** to put in a certain place, position, etc. —*vi.* **1.** to stretch or sag as a result of wear: said of skirts, etc. —**be seated 1.** to get in a seat; sit down: also **take a seat 2.** to be sitting **3.** to be located, settled, etc. —**by the seat of one's pants** instinctively; intuitively —**seat′less** *adj.*

seat belt anchored straps buckled across the hips, to protect a seated passenger, as in a motor car or aircraft

-seat·er (sēt′ər) *a combining form meaning* a vehicle, etc. having (a specified number of) seats [a two-*seater*]

seat·ing (-iŋ) *n.* **1.** a providing with a seat or seats **2.** material for covering chair seats, etc. **3.** the arrangement of seats

SEATO (sē′tō) Southeast Asia Treaty Organization

sea urchin a small sea animal with a round body in a shell covered with long, movable spines

sea wall a wall made to break the force of the waves and to protect the shore from erosion

sea·ward (sē′ward) *adj., adv.* towards the sea: also, for *adv.,* **sea′wards** —*n.* a seaward direction or position

sea·way (-wā′) *n.* **1.** a way or route by sea **2.** a ship's headway **3.** a rough sea **4.** an inland waterway to the sea for ocean ships

sea·weed (-wēd′) *n.* **1.** any sea plant or plants; esp., any

marine alga: in full, **marine seaweed 2.** any similar freshwater plant: in full, **freshwater seaweed**

sea·wor·thy (-wur′thē) *adj.* fit to travel in on the open sea; sturdy: said of a ship —**sea′wor′thi·ness** *n.*

se·ba·ceous (si bā′shəs) *adj.* [< L. < *sebum,* tallow] of or like fat, tallow, or sebum; esp., designating certain skin glands that secrete sebum

se·bum (sē′bəm) *n.* [L., tallow] the semiliquid, greasy secretion of the sebaceous glands

Sec. Secretary

‡**sec** (sek) *adj.* [Fr.] dry; not sweet: said of wine

SEC, S.E.C. [U.S.] Securities and Exchange Commission

sec secant

sec. 1. second(s) **2.** secondary **3.** secretary **4.** section(s) **5.** sector **6.** security

se·cant (sē′kant, -kant) *adj.* [< L. prp. of *secare,* to cut] cutting; intersecting —*n.* **1.** *Geom.* any straight line intersecting a curve at two or more points **2.** *Trigonometry* the ratio of the hypotenuse of a right-angled triangle to either of the other two sides with reference to the enclosed angle

sec·a·teurs (sek′ə tərz) *n. pl* [Fr. *secateur* < L. *secare,* to cut + Fr. *-ateur*] shears used esp. for pruning

se·cede (si sēd′) *vi.* **-ced′ed, -ced′ing** [< L. < *se-,* apart + *cedere,* to go] to withdraw formally from a larger body, as from a political union —**se·ced′er** *n.*

se·ces·sion (si sesh′ən) *n.* **1.** a seceding **2.** [*often* S-] the withdrawal of the Southern States from the Federal Union at the start of the American Civil War —**se·ces′sion·al** *adj.* —**se·ces′sion·ism** *n.* —**se·ces′sion·ist** *n.*

se·clude (si klōōd′) *vt.* **-clud′ed, -clud′ing** [< L. *secludere* < *se-,* apart + *claudere,* to shut] **1.** to keep away or shut off from others; isolate **2.** to make private or hidden

se·clud·ed (-klōōd′id) *adj.* shut off or kept apart from others; isolated; withdrawn —**se·clud′ed·ly** *adv.*

se·clu·sion (si klōō′zhən) *n.* **1.** a secluding or being secluded; retirement; isolation **2.** a secluded spot —**se·clu′sive** *adj.* —**se·clu′sive·ly** *adv.* —**se·clu′sive·ness** *n.*

sec·ond[1] (sek′and; *also for vt.* 4 si kond′) *adj.* [OFr. < L. *secundus* < *sequi,* to follow] **1.** coming next after the first in order; 2nd **2.** another; other; additional [a *second* helping] **3.** being of the same kind as another [a *second* Caesar] **4.** alternate [every *second* day] **5.** next below the first in rank, value, merit, etc. **6.** *Music a)* lower in pitch *b)* performing a part lower in pitch —*n.* **1.** the second person, thing, class, place, etc. **2.** the next after the first **3.** an article of merchandise that is not of the first quality **4.** an aid or assistant, as to a duellist or boxer **5.** the second forward gear ratio of a motor vehicle **6.** an honours degree between a first-class and third-class degree: also **second-class honours** degree **7.** [Slang] [*pl.*] a second helping of food —*vt.* **1.** to act as an aid to; assist **2.** to give support or encouragement to; reinforce **3.** to indicate formal support of (a motion, etc.) so that it may be discussed or voted on **4.** to transfer (someone, esp. a military officer) from his regular service to special service, civil or military —*adv.* in the second place, group, etc. —**second to none** unsurpassed —**upper (lower) second** designating a degree that is in the upper (lower) division of second-class honours —**sec′ond·er** *n.*

sec·ond[2] (sek′and) *n.* [ML. (*pars minuta*) *secunda,* second (small part): from being a further division (i.e., beyond the minute)] **1.** 1/60 of a minute of time **2.** 1/60 of a minute of angular measurement **3.** a very short time; instant **4.** a specific point in time **5.** the SI unit of time, defined as the duration of 9 192 631 770 periods of radiation corresponding to the transition between two hyperfine levels of the ground state of caesium-133

Second Advent *same as* SECOND COMING

sec·ond·ar·y (sek′an dər ē) *adj.* **1.** second, or below the first, in rank, importance, place, etc.; subordinate; minor **2.** *a)* coming from something considered primary or original; derivative *b)* second-hand; not original [a *secondary* source of information] *c)* designating colours derived by mixing two primary colours: see COLOUR (*n.* 3) **3.** coming after the first in a series of processes, events, stages, etc. **4.** *Elec.* designating or of an induced current or its circuit **5.** *Zool.* designating or of the long flight feathers on the second joint of a bird's wing —*n., pl.* **-ar·ies 1.** a person or thing that is secondary, subordinate, etc. **2.** any of the secondary colours **3.** *Elec.* an output winding of a transformer from which the power is taken —**sec′ond·ar·i·ly** *adv.*

secondary accent (or stress) 1. any accent, or stress, that is weaker than the full, or primary, accent **2.** a mark (in this dictionary, ′) to show this

secondary education formal education that succeeds primary education and precedes a university education

secondary school a school, as a comprehensive school, coming after primary school

secondary sexual characteristics any of the physical

characteristics that differentiate males and females and are not directly related to reproduction

second ballot a system of election by which, if the leading candidate does not poll more than half the votes cast, a second ballot is held in which he and the next most successful candidate are voted upon

second best something of the quality next below the best —**sec′ond-best′** adj.

second chamber the higher or revising body or house in a bicameral system of government

second childhood feeble and childish state due to old age

sec·ond-class (sek′ənd kläs′) adj. 1. of the class, rank, quality, etc. next below the highest 2. designating or of a class of travel accommodation next below the best 3. designating or of a class of letters that is handled more slowly than first-class post 4. inferior, inadequate, etc. —adv. 1. with second-class accommodation 2. as or by second-class post

Second Coming in the theology of some Christian sects, the expected return of Christ, at the Last Judgment

second cousin the child of one's parent's first cousin

second growth tree growth on land stripped of virgin forest

sec·ond-guess (sek′ənd ges′) vt., vi. [Chiefly U.S. Colloq.] to use hindsight in criticizing (someone or something), remaking (a decision), etc. —**sec′ond-guess′er** n.

sec·ond-hand (-hand′) adj. 1. not direct from the original source; not original 2. used or worn previously by another; not new 3. of or dealing in merchandise that is not new —adv. not firsthand; not directly

second hand the hand (of a clock or watch) that indicates the seconds and moves around the dial once every minute

second lieutenant see MILITARY RANKS, table

sec·ond·ly (sek′ənd lē) adv. in the second place; second

second nature acquired habits, etc. fixed so deeply as to seem part of a person's nature

second person that form of a pronoun (as you) or verb (as are) which refers to the person(s) spoken to

sec·ond-rate (-rāt′) adj. 1. second in quality, rank, etc.; second-class 2. inferior; mediocre —**sec′ond-rat′er** n.

second sight the supposed ability to see things not physically present, to foresee the future, etc.

sec·ond-string (-striŋ′) adj. [Chiefly U.S. Colloq.] 1. Sports that is the second or a substitute choice for play at a specified position 2. second-rate; inferior —n. a second or alternative course of action

second wind 1. the return of normal ease in breathing after the feeling one has at first of being exhausted from hard exercise 2. recovered capacity for continuing any effort

se·cre·cy (sē′krə sē) n., pl. -cies 1. a being secret 2. the practice or habit of being secretive —**in secrecy** secretly; confidentially; privately

se·cret (sē′krit) adj. [< OFr. < L. pp. of secernere < se-, apart + cernere, to sift, discern] 1. kept from the knowledge of others 2. remote; secluded 3. keeping one's affairs to oneself; secretive 4. beyond general understanding; mysterious 5. concealed from sight or notice; hidden [a secret drawer] 6. acting in secret [a secret society] —n. 1. something known only to some and kept from the knowledge of others 2. something not understood or explained; mystery 3. the true explanation, regarded as not obvious [the secret of success] —**in secret** without the knowledge of others; secretly —**se′cret·ly** adv.

secret agent a person who engages in espionage or similar work of a secret nature, as for a government

sec·re·taire (sek′rə ter′) n. same as ESCRITOIRE

sec·re·tar·i·at (sek′rə ter′ē ət) n. 1. the office, position, or quarters of a secretary of high position in a government, etc. 2. a staff headed by a secretary-general

sec·re·tar·y (sek′rə tər ē, -trē) n., pl. -tar·ies [ML. secretarius, one entrusted with secrets < L. secretum: see SECRET] 1. a) a person whose work is keeping records, handling correspondence, etc. as for an executive in a business office b) an officer of a company, club, etc. having somewhat similar duties 2. an official in charge of a department of government 3. a writing desk, esp. one topped with a small bookcase —**sec′re·tar′i·al** adj. —**sec′re·tar·y·ship′** n.

secretary bird [from the penlike feathers of its crest] a large, greyish-blue and black African bird of prey with a long neck and long legs

sec·re·tar·y-gen·er·al (-jen′ər əl) n., pl. -tar·ies-gen′er·al the chief administrative officer of an organization, in charge of a secretariat, esp. [S- G-] the chief administrative officer of the United Nations

secretary of state 1. the head of any of several British government departments 2. [U.S.] the foreign minister

secret ballot a vote in which the decision of the individual voter is not made public

se·crete (si krēt′) vt. -cret′ed, -cret′ing [< L. pp. of

secernere: see SECRET] 1. to hide; conceal 2. to form and release (a specified secretion) as a gland, etc. does

se·cre·tion (si krē′shən) n. 1. a hiding or concealing of something 2. a) the process by which a substance is formed from the blood or sap and then released for use by the organism or as a waste product b) such a substance

se·cre·tive (sē′krə tiv; also, & for 2 always, si krēt′iv) adj. [SECRET + -IVE] 1. keeping one's affairs to oneself; not frank; reticent 2. same as SECRETORY —**se′cre·tive·ly** adv. —**se′cre·tive·ness** n.

se·cre·to·ry (si krēt′ər ē) adj. of, or having the function of, secretion —n. a secretory gland, etc.

secret police a police force that operates secretly, esp. in order to suppress opposition to the government

secret service a government service that carries on secret investigation

sect (sekt) n. [< MFr. < L. < sequi, to follow] 1. a religious denomination, esp. one that has broken away from an established church 2. a group of people or a faction having a common leadership, philosophy, etc.

sec·tar·i·an (sek ter′ē ən) adj. 1. of or relating to a sect 2. devoted to one sect 3. narrow-minded —n. 1. a member of any religious sect 2. a person who is blindly devoted to a sect —**sec·tar′i·an·ism** n.

sec·ta·ry (sek′tər ē) n., pl. -ries a member of a sect

sec·tion (sek′shən) n. [< L. < pp. of secare, to cut] 1. a cutting or separating by cutting; specif., an incision in surgery 2. a part separated by cutting; slice; division 3. a) a division of a book, newspaper, etc. b) a numbered paragraph of a law etc. 4. any distinct or separate part [a bookcase in sections] 5. a segment of an orange, etc. 6. [U.S.] a division of public lands that is a mile square 7. a drawing, etc. of a thing as it would appear if cut straight through in a given plane 8. Railways a division of the right of way maintained by a single crew 9. Printing a mark (§) used to indicate a section in a book, etc., or as a reference mark: also **section mark** —vt. 1. to divide into sections 2. to represent in sections

sec·tion·al (sek′shən 'l) adj. 1. of or devoted to a given section or district 2. made up of or divided into sections —**sec′tion·al·ly** adv.

sec·tion·al·ism (-iz'm) n. narrow-minded concern shown for one section of a country —**sec′tion·al·ist** adj., n.

sec·tor (sek′tər) n. [LL. < L., cutter < secare, to cut] 1. part of a circle bounded by any two radii and the included arc 2. a mathematical instrument, as for measuring angles, consisting of two scaled rulers jointed together at one end 3. any of the districts into which an area is divided for military operations 4. a distinct part of a society or of an economy, group, etc. —vt. to divide into sectors —**sec′tor·al, sec·to′ri·al** (-tôr′ē əl) adj.

sec·u·lar (sek′yə lər) adj. [< OFr. < LL. < L. < saeculum, an age, generation] 1. a) not related to church or religion; not sacred or religious; temporal; wordly b) of secularism 2. living in the outside world and not bound by a monastic vow [the secular clergy] 3. a) occurring only once in an age or century b) lasting for an age or ages —n. a member of the secular clergy —**sec′u·lar·ly** adv.

sec·u·lar·ism (-iz'm) n. 1. worldly spirit, views, etc.; esp., a system of beliefs and practices that rejects any form of religious faith 2. the belief that religion should be strictly separated from the state or government, esp. from education —**sec′u·lar·ist** n., adj. —**sec′u·lar·is′tic** adj.

sec·u·lar·ize (sek′yə lə rīz′) vt. -ized′, -iz′ing 1. to change from religious to civil ownership or use 2. to deprive of religious character, influence, etc. 3. to convert to secularism —**sec′u·lar·i·za′tion** n.

se·cure (si kyoor′) adj. [< L. < se-, free from + cura, care] 1. free from fear, care, doubt, etc.; not worried, troubled, etc. 2. free from danger; safe 3. in safekeeping 4. firm; stable [make the knot secure] 5. reliable; dependable —vt. -cured′, -cur′ing 1. to make secure, or safe; protect 2. to make sure or certain; guarantee, as with a pledge [to secure a loan] 3. to make firm, fast, etc. [secure the bolt] 4. to obtain; acquire; get [to secure aid] 5. to capture —vi. to give security —**se·cur′a·ble** adj. —**se·cur′ance** n. —**se·cure′ly** adv. —**se·cure′ment** n. —**se·cur′er** n.

se·cu·ri·ty (si kyoor′ə rĭz′) n., pl. -ties 1. the state of being or feeling free from fear, anxiety, danger, doubt, etc. 2. protection or defence, as against attack, espionage, etc. [funds for national security] 3. a) something given as a pledge of repayment, etc. b) a person who promises to pay another's debt if he fails to pay it 4. a stock certificate or bond: usually used in pl.

Security Council the United Nations council responsible for maintaining international peace and security

security risk a person thought to be a threat to state security, usually because of his political beliefs

secy., sec′y. secretary

se·dan (si dan′) n. [< ? L. sedere, to sit] 1. same as SEDAN CHAIR 2. [U.S.] a saloon car

sedan chair an enclosed chair for one person, carried on poles by two men

se·date[1] (si dāt′) *adj.* [< L. pp. of *sedare,* to settle] calm or composed; esp., serious and unemotional; decorous —**se·date′ly** *adv.* —**se·date′ness** *n.*

se·date[2] (si dāt′) *vt.* **-dat′ed, -dat′ing** [< SEDATIVE] to dose with a sedative

se·da·tion (si dā′shən) *n.* *Med.* **1.** the reducing of excitement, nervousness, or irritation by means of sedatives **2.** the calm state produced by sedatives

SEDAN CHAIR

sed·a·tive (sed′ə tiv) *adj.* [see SEDATE[1]] tending to soothe or quiet; specif., *Med.* producing sedation —*n.* a sedative medicine

sed·en·tar·y (sed′'n tər ē, -trē) *adj.* [< Fr. < L. < prp. of *sedere,* to sit] **1.** *a)* tending to sit much of the time *b)* keeping one seated much of the time [a *sedentary* job] **2.** *a)* not migratory, as some birds *b)* fixed to one spot, as a barnacle —**sed′en·tar·i·ly** *adv.* —**sed′en·tar·i·ness** *n.*

Se·der (sā′dər) *n., pl.* **Se·dar·im** (sə där′im), **Se′ders** [Heb. *sēdher,* arrangement] *Judaism* the Passover feast commemorating the exodus of the Jews from Egypt

sedge (sej) *n.* [OE. *secg*] any of several coarse, grasslike plants often found on wet ground or in water —**sedg′y** *adj.*

sedge warbler a common European songbird

sed·i·ment (sed′ə mənt) *n.* [< Fr. < L. < *sedere,* to sit] **1.** matter that settles to the bottom of a liquid **2.** *Geol.* matter deposited by water or wind —**sed′i·men′tal** (-men′t'l) *adj.* —**sed′i·men·ta′tion** (-men tā′shən) *n.*

sed·i·men·ta·ry (sed′ə men′tər ē) *adj.* **1.** of, like, or containing sediment **2.** formed by the deposit of sediment, as certain rocks —**sed′i·men′ta·ri·ly** *adv.*

se·di·tion (si dish′ən) *n.* [OFr. < L. < *sed-,* apart + *itio,* a going < *ire,* to go] a stirring up of rebellion against the government —**se·di′tion·ist** *n.*

se·di·tious (si dish′əs) *adj.* **1.** of, like, or constituting sedition **2.** stirring up rebellion —**se·di′tious·ly** *adv.* —**se·di′tious·ness** *n.*

se·duce (si dyōōs′) *vt.* **-duced′, -duc′ing** [< LL. < L. < *se-,* apart + *ducere,* to lead] **1.** *a)* to persuade to do something disloyal, disobedient, etc. *b)* to tempt to evil or wrongdoing; lead astray *c)* to persuade to engage in unlawful sexual intercourse, esp. for the first time **2.** to entice —**se·duce′ment** *n.* —**se·duc′er** *n.* —**se·duc′i·ble** *adj.*

se·duc·tion (si duk′shən) *n.* **1.** a seducing or being seduced **2.** something that seduces

se·duc·tive (-tiv) *adj.* tending to seduce, or lead astray; enticing —**se·duc′tive·ly** *adv.* —**se·duc′tive·ness** *n.*

se·duc·tress (-tris) *n.* a woman who seduces

sed·u·lous (sed′yōō ləs) *adj.* [L. *sedulus,* ult. < *se-,* apart + *dolus,* trickery] working hard and steadily; diligent and persistent —**se·du·li·ty** (si dyōōl′ə tē), **sed′u·lous·ness** *n.* —**sed′u·lous·ly** *adv.*

se·dum (sē′dəm) *n.* [ModL., genus name < L.] any of a genus of plants found on rocks and walls, with fleshy stalks and leaves and white, yellow, or pink flowers

see[1] (sē) *vt.* **saw, seen, see′ing** [OE. *seon*] **1.** *a)* to get knowledge of through the eyes; look at *b)* to picture mentally; imagine **2.** *a)* to grasp mentally; understand *b)* to accept as suitable or possible [I can't *see* him as president] *c)* to consider; judge [*saw* it as his duty] **3.** to find out; learn [*see* who's there] **4.** to know by experience [has *seen* better days] **5.** to look over; inspect **6.** to make sure [*see* that he goes] **7.** *a)* to escort [to *see* someone home] *b)* to date someone **8.** to encounter; meet **9.** to call on; visit or consult [*see* a lawyer] **10.** to admit to one's presence; receive [too ill to *see* anyone] **11.** to be a spectator at; view or attend [*see* a show] **12.** *Card Games* to meet (a bet) of (another) by staking an equal sum —*vi.* **1.** to have the power of sight **2.** to discern objects, colours, etc. by using the eyes [able to *see* far] **3.** *a)* to take a look *b)* to investigate or inquire **4.** to understand **5.** to think something over; reflect [let's *see,* where is it?] —*interj.* behold! look! —**see about 1.** to inquire into **2.** to attend to —**see after** to take care of —**see fit (to)** to think it is proper (to do something) —**see into 1.** to look into **2.** to perceive the true meaning or nature of —**see off** to go with and watch (another) leave by aircraft, boat, bus, etc. —**see out 1.** to go through with; finish **2.** to wait till the end of —**see through 1.** to perceive the true meaning or character of **2.** to carry out to the end; finish **3.** to help through a time of difficulty —**see to** to attend to —**see′a·ble** *adj.*

see[2] (sē) *n.* [< OFr. *sie* < L. *sedes,* a seat] **1.** the official seat, or centre of authority, of a bishop **2.** the position, authority, or jurisdiction of a bishop

seed (sēd) *n., pl.* **seeds, seed:** see PLURAL, II, D, 4 [OE. *sæd*] **1.** the part of a flowering plant that contains the embryo and will develop into a new plant if sown **2.** loosely, *a)* any part, as a bulb, from which a new plant will grow *b)* a small,

seedlike fruit **3.** seeds used for sowing **4.** source; origin [the *seeds* of revolt] **5.** family stock; ancestry **6.** descendants; posterity **7.** *same as* SPAT[4] **8.** seed-bearing condition [in *seed*] **9.** *same as* SPORE (*n.* 2) **10.** sperm or semen **11.** something tiny, like a seed; esp., *a)* a tiny crystal or particle *b)* a tiny bubble, as in glassware **12.** *Sports* a seeded player —*vt.* **1.** to plant with seeds **2.** to sow (seeds) **3.** to remove the seeds from **4.** to sprinkle particles of dry ice, silver iodide, etc. into (clouds), as in trying to produce rainfall **5.** to provide with the means or stimulus for growing or developing **6.** *Sports a)* to distribute the names of contestants in (the draw for position in a tournament) so as to avoid matching the most skilled too early *b)* to treat (any of the most skilled players) thus —*vi.* **1.** to become ripe and produce seeds **2.** to shed seeds **3.** to sow seeds —**go** (or **run**) **to seed 1.** to shed seeds after flowering **2.** to become weak, useless, etc.; to dissipate one's talents —**seed′ed** *adj.* —**seed′er** *n.* —**seed′less** *adj.*

seed·bed (-bed′) *n.* a bed of soil, usually covered with glass, in which seedlings are grown for transplanting

seed·case (-kās′) *n. same as* SEED VESSEL

seed coral fragments of coral used in ornaments

seed leaf, seed lobe *same as* COTYLEDON

seed·ling (-liŋ) *n.* **1.** a plant grown from a seed, rather than from a cutting, etc. **2.** any young plant; esp., a young tree less than three feet high

seed money [Chiefly U.S.] money made available to begin the financing of, or to attract additional funds for, a long-term project

seed oysters oyster spat; very young oysters, esp. at the stage suitable for relocation

seed pearl a very small pearl, often imperfect

seed plant *same as* SPERMATOPHYTE

seed·pod (-pod′) *n.* a carpel or pistil, enclosing ovules or seeds in angiosperms

seeds·man (sēdz′mən) *n., pl.* **-men 1.** a sower of seeds **2.** a dealer in seeds

seed·time (sēd′tīm′) *n.* the season for sowing seeds

seed vessel any dry, hollow fruit, as a pod, containing seed

seed·y (sēd′ē) *adj.* **seed′i·er, seed′i·est 1.** containing many seeds **2.** gone to seed **3.** shabby, run-down, or looking bad, ill, etc. —**seed′i·ly** *adv.* —**seed′i·ness** *n.*

see·ing (sē′iŋ) *n.* **1.** the sense or power of sight **2.** the use of the eyes to see —*adj.* having the sense of sight —*conj.* considering; inasmuch as

seeing eye dog a guide dog, specif. one trained to guide the blind

seek (sēk) *vt.* **sought, seek′ing** [OE. *secan*] **1.** to try to find; look for **2.** to go to; resort to [to *seek* the woods for peace] **3.** *a)* to try to get or find out by asking or searching [to *seek* an answer] *b)* to request; ask for **4.** to try for; aim at [*seeking* perfection] **5.** to try: used with an infinitive [to *seek* to please] —*vi.* to look for someone or something —**seek out 1.** to go to find **2.** to look hard for —**seek′er** *n.*

seem (sēm) *vi.* [prob. < ON. *sæma,* to conform to] **1.** *a)* to appear to be [to *seem* glad] *b)* to appear: usually used with an infinitive [he *seems* to know] *c)* to have the impression; think: used with an infinitive [I *seem* to recall] **2.** to appear to exist [there *seems* no end] **3.** to be apparently true [it *seems* he was here]

seem·ing (-iŋ) *adj.* that seems real, true, etc. without necessarily being so; apparent [her *seeming* anger] —*n.* outward appearance; semblance —**seem′ing·ly** *adv.*

seem·ly (sēm′lē) *adj.* **-li·er, -li·est** [< ON. < *sæmr,* fitting] **1.** pleasing in appearance **2.** suitable, proper, decorous, etc. —*adv.* in a seemly way —**seem′li·ness** *n.*

seen (sēn) *pp.* of SEE[1]

seep (sēp) *vi.* [OE. *sipian,* to soak] to leak, drip, or flow out slowly through small openings; ooze —*n.* **1.** a seeping **2.** liquid that seeps —**seep′age** (-ij) *n.* —**seep′y** *adj.*

seer[1] (sē′ər *for l;* sir *for 2*) *n.* **1.** a person who sees **2.** a person with the supposed power to foretell the future

seer[2] (sir) *n.* [Hind. *sēr*] a unit of weight in Nepal, Pakistan, Aden, etc.

seer·suck·er (sir′suk′ər) *n.* [< Hindi < Per. *shir u shakar,* lit., milk and sugar] a light fabric of cotton, etc. woven with alternating crinkled stripes in various patterns

see·saw (sē′sô′) *n.* [redupl. of SAW[1]] **1.** a plank balanced at the middle, used by children at play, who ride the ends so that when one goes up, the other comes down **2.** such a riding **3.** any up-and-down or back-and-forth movement or change —*adj.* moving up and down or back and forth —*vt., vi.* to move on a seesaw or like a seesaw

seethe (sēth) *vt.* **seethed, seeth′ing** [OE. *sēothan*] **1.** to cook by boiling **2.** to soak or saturate in liquid —*vi.* **1.** to boil or to surge, foam, etc. as if boiling **2.** to be violently agitated —*n.* a seething

seg·ment (seg′mənt; *for v.* -ment) *n.* [L. *segmentum* < *secare,* to cut] **1.** any of the parts into which something is separated or separable; section **2.** *Geom.* any part, esp. of a circle or sphere, cut off by a line or plane —*vt., vi.* to divide into segments —**seg·men'tal** (-men't'l), **seg'-men·tar'y** *adj.* —**seg·men'tal·ly** *adv.*

seg·men·ta·tion (seg'mən tā'shən, -men-) *n.* 1. a dividing or being divided into segments 2. *Biol.* the progressive growth and cleavage of a single cell into others to form a new organism

seg·re·gate (seg'rə gāt'; *for adj. usually* -git) *adj.* [< L. pp. of *segregare* < *se-*, apart + *grex* (gen. *gregis*), a flock] separate; set apart —*vt.* -**gat'ed, -gat'ing** to set apart from others; isolate; specif., to impose a system of segregation on (racial groups, social facilities, etc.) —*vi.* to become segregated —**seg're·gat'ive adj.**

seg·re·gat·ed (seg'rə gāt'id) *adj.* conforming to a system that segregates racial groups

seg·re·ga·tion (seg'rə gā'shən) *n.* a segregating or being segregated; specif., the policy or practice of compelling racial groups to live apart from each other, go to separate schools, etc. —**seg're·ga'tion·ist *n., adj.***

se·gue (seg'wā, sā'gwā) *vi.* -**gued, -gue·ing** [< It., ult. < L. *sequi*, to follow] to continue without break (*to* or *into*) the next part or what follows —*n.* a segueing

seich (sāsh) *n.* [< Swiss-Fr.] an oscillation of the water in a lake caused by changes in atmospheric pressure

sei·del (zī'd'l, sī'-) *n., pl.* -**dels, -del** [G. < MHG. < L. *situla*, a bucket] a large beer mug, often with a hinged lid

Seid·litz powder (sed'lits) [its properties are said to resemble those of natural spring water from Sedlčany (G. *Seidlitz*), Czechoslovakia] a laxative powder, dissolved in water and drunk while effervescing

sei·gneur (sān yur', sēn-) *n.* [Fr. < MFr.: see SEIGNIOR] 1. *same as* SEIGNIOR 2. the owner of a seigneury (sense 2) —**sei·gneur'i·al** (-ē əl) *adj.*

sei·gneur·y (sān'yər ē, sēn'-) *n., pl.* -**gneur·ies** 1. *same as* SEIGNIORY (sense 1) 2. in French Canada, an estate granted by royal decree to 17th-cent. French settlers

sei·gnior (sēn'yər) *n.* [< Anglo-Fr. < OFr. < L. *senior*: see SENIOR] a lord or noble; specif., the lord of a fief

sei·gnio·ri·al, sei·gno·ri·al (sān yôr'ē əl) *adj.* of or relating to a seignior: also **sei·gnior·al, sei·gnor·al** (sān'yər al)

sei·gnior·y (sān'yər ē, sēn'-) *n., pl.* -**gnior·ies** 1. the estate of a seignior 2. the rights or authority of a feudal lord

seine (sān) *n.* [OE. *segne*, ult. < L. < Gr. *sagēnē*] a large fishing net with floats along the top edge and weights along the bottom —*vt., vi.* **seined, sein'ing** to fish with a seine

seise (sēz) *vt.* **seised, seis'ing** [see SEIZE] 1. orig. to give a feudal holding to 2. to give ownership to: in the passive voice [*seised* of the lands]

seis·mic (sīz'mik, sīs'-) *adj.* [< Gr. *seismos*, an earthquake < *seiein*, to shake] of, relating to, or caused by an earthquake or earthquakes or similar, but man-made, tremors —**seis'mi·cal·ly adv.**

seis·mo- [< Gr. *seismos*: see prec.] a combining form meaning earthquake [*seismogram*]

seis·mo·gram (sīz'mə gram', sīs'-) *n.* the chart of an earthquake as recorded by a seismograph

seis·mo·graph (-grāf', -graf') *n.* an instrument that records the intensity and duration of earthquakes and similar tremors —**seis·mog·ra·pher** (sīz mog'rə fər, sīs-) *n.* —**seis'mo·graph'ic adj.** —**seis'mog'ra·phy n.**

seis·mol·o·gy (sīz mol'ə jē, sīs-) *n.* [SEISMO- + -LOGY] a geophysical science dealing with earthquakes and related phenomena —**seis'mo·log'ic** (-mə loj'ik), **seis'mo·log'i·cal adj.** —**seis'mo·log'i·cal·ly adv.** —**seis·mol'o·gist n.**

seize (sēz) *vt.* **seized, seiz'ing** [< OFr. *saisir* < ML. *sacire*, prob. < Frank.] 1. [U.S.] seise 2. *a)* to take possession of by legal power; confiscate [to *seize* contraband] *b)* to capture and put into custody; arrest; apprehend 3. to take forcibly or quickly; grasp [to *seize* a weapon, to *seize* power] 4. *a)* to suddenly fill the mind of [an idea *seized* him] *b)* to grasp with the mind, esp. suddenly 5. to afflict suddenly [*seized* with tremors] 6. *Naut.* to bind with cord, etc. —**seized of** 1. to be in legal possession of: also **seised of** 2. to be aware of —**seize on** (or **upon**) to grasp or take eagerly —**seize up** to stop working; to become jammed: usually said of a machine —**seiz'a·ble adj.** —**seiz'-er n.**

sei·zin (sē'zin) *n.* [< OFr.: see prec.] legal possession, esp. of a freehold estate —**sei'zor n.**

sei·zure (sē'zhər) *n.* 1. a seizing or being seized 2. a sudden attack, as of disease

sel. 1. selected 2. selection(s)

sel·dom (sel'dəm) *adv.* [OE. *seldan*] not often; rarely —*adj.* rare; infrequent —**sel'dom·ness n.**

se·lect (sə lekt') *adj.* [L. *selectus*, pp. of *seligere* < *se-*, apart + *legere*, to choose] 1. chosen in preference to others; specially picked 2. choice; excellent 3. careful in choosing; discriminating 4. limited to certain people or groups; exclusive —*vt., vi.* to choose, as for excellence —**se·lect'ness n.** —**se·lec'tor n.**

select committee a number of members of parliament chosen to investigate a matter of public interest

se·lec·tion (sə lek'shən) *n.* 1. a selecting or being selected 2. *a)* a thing, person, or group chosen *b)* a variety to choose

from 3. *Biol.* any process by which certain organisms or genetic characters naturally survive over others or are bred to do so: see NATURAL SELECTION

se·lec·tive (-tiv) *adj.* 1. of or characterized by selection 2. having the power of selecting, or tending to select 3. *Radio* excluding undesired frequencies when tuned to a specific station —**se·lec'tive·ly adv.** —**se·lec'tive·ness n.**

selective employment tax a tax levied on employers in certain industries, according to the number of employees

se·lec·tiv·i·ty (sə lek'tiv'ə tē) *n.* 1. the state or quality of being selective 2. the degree to which a radio receiver is selective

sel·e·nite (sel'ə nīt) *n.* [< L. < Gr. *selēnitēs* (*lithos*), lit., moon (stone)] a kind of gypsum in crystalline form

se·le·ni·um (sə lē'nē əm) *n.* [ModL. < Gr. *selēnē*, the moon] a nonmetallic chemical element whose electrical conductivity varies with the intensity of light: used in photoelectric devices, etc.: symbol, Se; at. wt., 78.96; at. no., 34

sel·e·no- (sel'ə nō) [< Gr. *selēnē*, the moon] a combining form meaning moon

self (self) *n., pl.* **selves** [OE.] 1. the identity, character, or essential qualities of a person or thing 2. one's own person or being as apart from all others 3. one's own well-being or advantage —*pron.* [Colloq.] myself, himself, herself, or yourself [tickets for *self* and wife] —*adj.* 1. uniform throughout 2. of the same kind, colour, material, etc. as the rest [a *self* lining]

self- *a prefix used in hyphenated compounds, meaning:* 1. of oneself or itself [*self*-restraint] 2. by oneself or itself [*self*-starting] 3. in oneself or itself [*self*-centred] 4. to, with, or for oneself or itself [*self*-addressed, *self*-pity]

self-a·base·ment (self'ə bās'mənt) *n.* abasement or humiliation of oneself

self-ab·ne·ga·tion (-ab'nə gā'shən) *n.* lack of consideration for oneself; self-denial

self-ab·sorp·tion (-əb zôrp'shən, -sôrp'-) *n.* absorption in one's own interests, affairs, etc. —**self'-ab·sorbed' adj.**

self-a·buse (-ə byoos') *n.* a euphemism for masturbation, (see MASTURBATE)

self-act·ing (-ak'tiŋ) *adj.* working by itself; automatic

self-ad·dressed (-ə drest') *adj.* addressed to oneself [a *self*-addressed envelope]

self-ad·vance·ment (-əd vāns'mənt) *n.* the advancing or promoting of one's own interests

self-ag·gran·dize·ment (-ə gran'diz mənt) *n.* the act of making oneself powerful, wealthy, etc., esp. in a ruthless way —**self-ag·gran'diz'ing** (-dīz'iŋ) *adj.*

self-ap·point·ed (-ə poin'tid) *adj.* acting as such on one's own, but not recognized as such by others [a *self*-appointed censor]

self-as·ser·tion (-ə sur'shən) *n.* the act or fact of demanding recognition for oneself or of insisting upon one's rights, claims, etc. —**self'-as·ser'tive, self'-as·sert'ing adj.**

self-as·sur·ance (-ə shoor'əns) *n.* confidence in oneself, one's own ability, talent, etc. —**self'-as·sured' adj.**

self-cen·tred (-sen'tərd) *adj.* occupied or concerned only with one's own affairs; egocentric; selfish

self-col·oured (-kul'ərd) *adj.* 1. of only one colour 2. of the natural or original colour, as a fabric

self-com·mand (-kə mänd') *n.* same as SELF-CONTROL

self-com·pla·cent (-kəm plā's'nt) *adj.* self-satisfied, esp. in a smug way —**self'-com·pla'cen·cy n.**

self-con·ceit (-kən sēt') *n.* too high an opinion of oneself; conceit —**self'-con·ceit'ed adj.**

self-con·fessed (-kən fest') *adj.* being such by one's own admission [a *self*-confessed thief]

self-con·fi·dence (-kon'fə dəns) *n.* confidence in oneself, one's own abilities, etc. —**self'-con'fi·dent adj.** —**self'con'-fi·dent·ly adv.**

self-con·scious (-kon'shəs) *adj.* 1. unduly conscious of oneself as an object of notice; embarrassed or ill at ease 2. showing embarrassment [a *self*-conscious cough] —**self'-con'scious·ly adv.** —**self'-con'scious·ness n.**

self-con·tained (-kən tānd') *adj.* 1. keeping one's affairs to oneself; reserved 2. showing self-control 3. having all working parts, complete with motive power, in an enclosed unit: said of machinery 4. having within oneself or itself all that is necessary; self-sufficient, as a community 5. (of a flat) having its own kitchen, bathroom, etc. —**self'-con·tain'ment n.**

self-con·tent·ed (-kən ten'tid) *adj.* contented with what one is or has —**self'-con·tent', self'-con·tent'ment n.**

self-con·tra·dic·tion (-kon'trə dik'shən) *n.* 1. contradiction of oneself or itself 2. any statement or idea containing elements that contradict each other —**self'con'tra·dic'to·ry adj.**

self-con·trol (-kən trōl') *n.* control of oneself, or of one's own emotions, desires, actions, etc.

self-de·cep·tion (-di sep'shən) *n.* the deceiving of oneself as to one's true feelings, motives, circumstances, etc.: also **self'-de·ceit', self'-de·lu'sion** (-di lōō'zhən) —**self'de·ceiv'-ing adj.**

self-de·feat·ing (-di fēt'iŋ) *adj.* that unwittingly defeats its own purpose or interests

self-de·fence (-di fens') *n.* 1. defence of oneself, one's rights, etc. 2. boxing: usually in **manly art of self-defence** —**self'-de·fen'sive** *adj.*

self-de·ni·al (-di nī'əl) *n.* denial or sacrifice of one's own desires or pleasures —**self'-de·ny'ing** *adj.*

self-de·struc·tion (-di struk'shən) *n.* destruction of oneself or itself; specif., suicide —**self'-de·struc'tive** *adj.*

self-de·ter·mi·na·tion (-di tur'mi nā'shən) *n.* 1. determination or decision according to one's own mind or will, without outside influence 2. the right of a people to decide upon its own political status or form of government —**self'-de·ter'mined** *adj.* —**self'-de·ter'min·ing** *adj.*

self-dis·ci·pline (-dis'ə plin) *n.* the disciplining or controlling of oneself, one's actions, etc. —**self'-dis'·ci·plined** *adj.*

self-doubt (-dout') *n.* lack of self-confidence

self-drive (-drīv') *adj.* relating to a hired car that is driven by the hirer

self-ed·u·cat·ed (-ed'joo kāt'id) *adj.* educated by oneself, with little or no formal teaching

self-ef·face·ment (-i fās'mənt) *n.* modest, retiring behaviour —**self'-ef·fac'ing** *adj.*

self-em·ployed (-im ploid') *adj.* working for oneself, with direct control over work, services, fees, etc. —**self'em·ploy'ment** *n.*

self-es·teem (-ə stēm') *n.* 1. belief in oneself; self-respect 2. undue pride in oneself; conceit

self-ev·i·dent (-ev'ə dənt) *adj.* evident without need of proof or explanation —**self'-ev'i·dent·ly** *adv.*

self-ex·am·i·na·tion (-ig zam'ə nā'shən) *n.* examination or analysis of oneself and one's conduct, motives, etc.

self-ex·ist·ent (-ig zis'tənt) *adj.* existing of or by itself without external cause —**self'-ex·ist'ence** *n.*

self-ex·plan·a·to·ry (-ik splan'ə tər ē) *adj.* explaining itself: also **self'-ex·plain'ing**

self-ex·pres·sion (-ik spresh'ən) *n.* expression of one's own personality or emotions, as in the arts

self-ful·fil·ment (-fəl fil'mənt) *n.* fulfilment of one's aspirations, hopes, etc. through one's own efforts

self-gov·ern·ment (-guv'ər mənt, -ərn-) *n.* government of a group by its own members, as in electing representatives —**self'-gov'ern·ing** *adj.*

self-hate (-hāt') *n.* hate directed against oneself or one's own people, often in despair: also **self'-ha'tred**

self-heal (-hēl') *n.* any of various plants supposed to have healing properties; esp., a common weed with purple flowers

self-help (-help') *n.* care or betterment of oneself by one's own efforts, as through study

self-hyp·no·sis (-hip nō'sis) *n.* *same as* AUTOHYPNOSIS

self-im·age (-im'ij) *n.* one's concept of oneself and one's identity, abilities, worth, etc.

self-im·por·tant (-im pôr't'nt) *adj.* having or showing an exaggerated opinion of one's own importance; pompous or officious —**self'-im·por'tance** *n.*

self-im·posed (-im pōzd') *adj.* imposed on oneself by oneself, as a duty

self-im·prove·ment (-im proov'mənt) *n.* improvement of one's status, mind, etc. by one's own efforts

self-in·crim·i·na·tion (-in krim'ə nā'shən) *n.* incrimination of oneself by one's own statements or answers —**self'-in·crim'i·nat'ing** *adj.*

self-in·duced (-in dyoost') *adj.* 1. induced by oneself or itself 2. produced by self-induction

self-in·duc·tion (-in duk'shən) *n.* induction of a voltage in a circuit by the variation of current in that circuit

self-in·dul·gence (-in dul'jəns) *n.* indulgence of one's own desires, impulses, etc. —**self'-in·dul'gent** *adj.*

self-in·flict·ed (-in flik'tid) *adj.* inflicted on oneself by oneself, as an injury

self-in·ter·est (-in'trist, -in'tər ist) *n.* 1. one's own interest or advantage 2. an exaggerated regard for this, esp. at the expense of others

self·ish (sel'fish) *adj.* 1. too much concerned with one's own welfare or interests, with little or no thought or care for others 2. showing or prompted by self-interest —**self'ish·ly** *adv.* —**self'ish·ness** *n.*

self-jus·ti·fi·ca·tion (self'jus'tə fi kā'shən) *n.* the justifying or explaining away of one's actions or motives

self·less (self'lis) *adj.* devoted to others' welfare or interests and not one's own; unselfish —**self'less·ly** *adv.* —**self'less·ness** *n.*

self-load·ing (self'lōd'iŋ) *adj.* loading again by its own action [a *self-loading* gun]

self-love (-luv') *n.* love of self or regard for oneself and one's own interests

self-made (-mād') *adj.* 1. made by oneself or itself 2. successful, rich, etc. through one's own efforts

self-o·pin·ion·at·ed (-ə pin'yə nāt'id) *adj.* stubborn or conceited with regard to one's own opinions

self-pit·y (-pit'ē) *n.* pity for oneself

self-pol·li·na·tion (-pol'ə nā'shən) *n.* pollination of a flower by itself or by another flower on the same plant —**self'-pol'li·nat'ed** *adj.*

self-por·trait (-pôr'trit, -trāt) *n.* a painting, drawing, etc. of oneself, done by oneself

self-pos·ses·sion (-pə zesh'ən) *n.* full control of one's feelings, actions, etc.; self-control; composure —**self'-pos·sessed'** *adj.*

self-pres·er·va·tion (-prez'ər vā'shən) *n.* 1. preservation of oneself from danger, injury, or death 2. the urge to preserve oneself, regarded as instinctive

self-pro·nounc·ing (-prə noun'siŋ) *adj.* showing pronunciation by marks added to the original spelling, not by phonetic respelling

self-pro·pelled (-prə peld') *adj.* propelled by its own motor or power: also **self'-pro·pel'ling**

self-rais·ing (-rāz'iŋ) *adj.* rising by itself: said specif. of flour sold with a raising agent blended in

self-re·al·i·za·tion (-rē'ə li zā'shən) *n.* fulfilment of oneself, one's capabilities, etc.

self-re·cord·ing (-ri kôr'diŋ) *adj.* recording its own operations automatically, as a seismograph

self-re·gard (-ri gärd') *n.* 1. concern for oneself and one's own interests 2. *same as* SELF-RESPECT

self-reg·u·lat·ing (-reg'yə lāt'iŋ) *adj.* regulating oneself or itself automatically or without outside control —**self'reg'·u·la'tion** *n.*

self-re·li·ance (-ri lī'əns) *n.* reliance on oneself, one's abilities, etc. —**self'-re·li'ant** *adj.*

self-re·proach (-ri prōch') *n.* blame of oneself; guilt feeling —**self'-re·proach'ful** *adj.*

self-re·spect (-ri spekt') *n.* proper respect for oneself and one's worth as a person —**self'-re·spect'ing** *adj.*

self-re·straint (-ri strānt') *n.* restraint of oneself; self-control —**self'-re·strained'** *adj.*

self-re·veal·ing (-ri vēl'iŋ) *adj.* revealing one's innermost thoughts, feelings, etc.: also **self'-rev'e·la·to·ry** (-rev'ə lə tər ē) —**self'-rev'e·la'tion** *n.*

self-right·eous (-rī'chəs) *adj.* thinking oneself more righteous or moral than others —**self'-right'eous·ly** *adv.* —**self'-right'eous·ness** *n.*

self-ris·ing (-rīz'iŋ) *adj.* [U.S.] self-raising

self-rule (-rool') *n.* *same as* SELF-GOVERNMENT

self-sac·ri·fice (-sak'rə fīs') *n.* sacrifice of oneself or one's interests to benefit others —**self'-sac'ri·fic'ing** *adj.*

self·same (-sām') *adj.* exactly the same; identical; (the) very same —**self'same'ness** *n.*

self-sat·is·fied (-sat'is fīd') *adj.* excessively pleased with oneself or with what one has done —**self'-sat'is·fac'tion** *n.*

self-sat·is·fy·ing (-sat'is fī'iŋ) *adj.* satisfying to oneself

self-seal·ing (-sēl'iŋ) *adj.* 1. automatically sealing punctures, etc., as some tyres 2. sealable by pressure alone, as some envelopes

self-seek·er (-sē'kər) *n.* a person seeking only or mainly to further his own interests —**self'-seek'ing** *n.*, *adj.*

self-serv·ice (-sur'vis) *n.* the practice of serving oneself in a shop, cafeteria, etc. and then paying a cashier —*adj.* operating thus

self-serv·ing (-sur'viŋ) *adj.* serving one's own selfish interests, esp. at the expense of others

self-sown (-sōn') *adj.* sown by wind, water, or other natural means, as some weeds

self-start·er (-stärt'ər) *n.* an electric motor connected to, and used for automatically starting, an internal-combustion engine

self-styled (-stīld') *adj.* so named by oneself [he is a *self-styled* expert]

self-suf·fi·cient (-sə fish'ənt) *adj.* able to get along without help; independent —**self'-suf·fi'cien·cy** *n.*

self-sup·port (-sə pôrt') *n.* support of oneself or itself without aid or reinforcement —**self'-sup·port'ing** *adj.*

self-sus·tain·ing (-sə stān'iŋ) *adj.* 1. supporting or able to support oneself or itself 2. able to continue once begun

self-taught (-tôt') *adj.* 1. having taught oneself 2. learned by oneself without instruction

self·ward (-wərd) *adv.* towards oneself: also **self'wards** —*adj.* directed towards oneself

self-willed (-wild') *adj.* stubborn about getting one's own way; wilful —**self'-will'** *n.*

self-wind·ing (-wīn'diŋ) *adj.* winding automatically, as certain wristwatches

Sel·juk (sel jook') *n.* [Turk. *Seljūq*, legendary ancestor of the dynasties] a member of any of the several dynasties of the Seljuk Turks, that expanded westward from Turkestan in the 11th cent. —*adj.* of these dynasties or the Seljuk Turks Also **Sel·juk'i·an** (-joo'kē ən)

sell (sel) *vt.* **sold**, **sell'ing** [OE. *sellan*, to give] 1. to exchange (property, goods, services, etc.) for money or its equivalent 2. to offer for sale; deal in 3. *a)* to deliver (a person) to his enemies, into slavery, etc. *b)* to betray (a country, cause, etc.) 4. to give up (one's honour etc.) for profit, etc. 5. to promote the sale of [television *sells* many products] 6. [Colloq.] *a)* to establish confidence or belief in [to *sell* oneself to the public] *b*) [Chiefly U.S.] to persuade (someone) of the value of something (with *on*) [*sell* him on the idea] **7.** [Slang] to cheat or dupe —*vi.* **1.** to sell something **2.** to work or act as a salesclerk or salesperson **3.** to be a popular item on the market **4.** to be sold (*for* or *at*) [belts *selling* for two pounds] **5.** [Colloq.] to be accepted, approved, etc. [a scheme that won't *sell*] —*n.* [Slang] **1.** a trick or hoax **2.** selling or salesmanship [hard *sell*] —**sell out 1.** to dispose of completely by selling **2.** [Colloq.] to betray (someone, a cause, etc.) —**sell short 1.** to sell securities, etc. not yet owned, expecting to cover later at a lower price **2.** to undervalue —**sell up 1.** to sell all of (the land or goods) of (a debtor) so as to satisfy his debts **2.** to dispose of one's house, business, etc., on leaving —**sell'er** *n.*

selling race a horse race immediately after which the winner is auctioned and the losers may be claimed for prices previously set

sell-off (-ôf') *n.* a price decline for all or certain stocks and bonds, caused by pressure to sell

Sel·lo·tape (sel'ō tāp) *a trademark for* an adhesive tape, usually transparent —*n.* [**s-**] any similar adhesive tape —*vt.* to stick or fix something with sellotape

sell-out (-out') *n.* [Colloq.] **1.** a selling out, or betrayal **2.** a show, etc. for which all seats have been sold

Selt·zer (selt'sər) *n.* [< *Niederselters*, village near Wiesbaden, Germany] **1.** natural mineral water that is effervescent **2.** [*often* **s-**] any carbonated water Also **Seltzer water**

sel·vage, sel·vedge (sel'vij) *n.* [< SELF + EDGE, after MDu. *selfegge*] **1.** a specially woven edge to keep cloth from unravelling **2.** an edge of material or paper that is to be trimmed off or covered

selves (selvz) *n. pl. of* SELF

Sem. 1. Seminary **2.** Semitic

se·man·tic (sə man'tik) *adj.* [Gr. *sēmantikos*, significant < *sēmainein*, to show < *sēma*, a sign] **1.** of meaning, esp. in language **2.** of semantics —**se·man'ti·cal·ly** *adv.*

se·man·tics (-tiks) *n.pl.* [*with sing. v.*] [see prec.] **1.** the branch of linguistics dealing with the meanings given to words and the changes that occur to these meanings as time goes on **2.** the relationships between symbols and the ideas given to them by their users **3.** loosely, the twisting of meaning to mislead or confuse, as in some advertising and propaganda —**se·man'ti·cist** (-tə sist) *n.*

sem·a·phore (sem'ə fôr') *n.* [< Fr. < Gr. *sēma*, a sign + *-phoros*: see -PHOROUS] any device or system for signalling as by lights, flags, mechanical arms, etc. —*vt., vi.* -**phored', -phor'ing** to signal by semaphore —**sem'a·phor'ic** *adj.* —**sem'a·phor'ist** *n.*

se·ma·si·ol·o·gy (simā'sēol'əjē) *n.* [< Gr. *sēmasia*, signification of a word + -LOGY] same as SEMANTICS (senses 1 & 2)

sem·blance (sem'blans) *n.* [< OFr. < *sembler*, to seem, ult. < L. *similis*, like] **1.** outward look or show; seeming likeness **2.** a likeness, image, or representation **3.** a false, assumed, or deceiving form or appearance

SEMAPHORE

sem·eme (sem'ēm) *n.* [coined < Gr. *sēma*, a sign + (MORPH)EME] Linguis. **1.** the meaning of a morpheme **2.** a minimum unit of meaning: also **se·man'teme**

se·men (sē'mən) *n.* [ModL. < L., a seed] the fluid secreted by the male reproductive organs, containing the spermatozoa

sem·i (sem'ē) *n. Colloq. clipped form of* SEMI-DETACHED house

sem·i- (sem'i, -ē, -ə) [L.] *a prefix meaning:* **1.** half [*semicircle*] **2.** partly [*semiskilled*] **3.** twice in a (specified period) [*semiannually*]

sem·i·an·nu·al (sem'ē an'yoo wal) *adj.* **1.** happening, presented, etc. every half year **2.** lasting only half a year —**sem'i·an'nu·al·ly** *adv.*

sem·i·a·quat·ic (-ə kwat'ik) *adj. Biol.* **1.** growing in or near water **2.** spending some time in water, as certain animals

sem·i·au·to·mat·ic (-ôt'ə mat'ik) *adj.* **1.** partly automatic and partly hand-controlled: said of machinery **2.** operating like an automatic firearm but requiring a trigger pull for each shot fired —*n.* a semiautomatic firearm

sem·i·base·ment (sem'i bās'mənt) *n.* a living area partly underground and partly above ground

sem·i·breve (sem'i brēv') *n.* [It.] Music a note having four times the duration of a crotchet: see NOTE, illus.

sem·i·cho·rus (-kôr'əs) *n.* **1.** a section of a choir **2.** the part to be sung by this section

sem·i·cir·cle (sem'ē sur'k'l) *n.* a half circle —**sem'i·cir'cu·lar** (-kyə lər) *adj.*

semicircular canal any of the three loop-shaped, tubular structures of the inner ear that serve to maintain balance in the organism

sem·i·co·lon (sem'ē kō'lən) *n.* a mark of punctuation (;) showing more separation than that marked by the comma and less than that marked by the full stop, etc.: used chiefly between units containing elements separated by commas and between some coordinate clauses

sem·i·con·duc·tor (sem'ē kən duk'tər) *n.* a substance, as silicon, whose conductivity is improved by minute additions of certain substances or by application of heat, light, or voltage: used in transistors, etc.

sem·i·con·scious (-kon'shəs) *adj.* not fully conscious or awake —**sem'i·con'scious·ness** *n.*

sem·i·dem·i·sem·i·qua·ver (sem'i dem'i sem'i kwä'vər) *n. Music* a note having one sixty-fourth the duration of a semi-breve: see NOTE, illus.

sem·i·de·tached (-di tacht') *adj.* partly separate, as two houses joined by a common wall

sem·i·fi·nal (sem'i fi'n'l) *adj.* coming just before the final match, as of a tournament —*n.* **1.** a semifinal match **2.** [*pl.*] a semifinal round —**sem'i·fi'nal·ist** *n.*

sem·i·flu·id (sem'i floo'id) *adj.* heavy or thick but able to flow —*n.* a semifluid substance

sem·i·lit·er·ate (-lit'ər it) *adj.* knowing how to read and write a little, or knowing only how to read —*n.* a person who barely knows how to read and write

sem·i·lu·nar (-loo'nər) *adj.* [ModL. *semilunaris*: see SEMI- & LUNAR] shaped like a half-moon

sem·i·month·ly (-munth'lē) *adj.* coming, happening, done, etc. twice a month —*n., pl.* -**lies** something coming, appearing, issued, etc. twice a month —*adv.* twice a month

sem·i·nal (sem'ə n'l) *adj.* [< MFr. < L. < *semen*, a seed] **1.** of or containing seed or semen **2.** of reproduction **3.** being a source; able to develop or be developed further —**in the seminal state** capable of development; rudimentary —**sem'i·nal·ly** *adv.*

sem·i·nar (sem'ə när) *n.* [G. < L.: see ff.] **1.** *a*) a group of supervised students doing advanced study *b*) a course for such a group **2.** any similar group discussion

sem·i·nar·y (sem'ə när ē) *n., pl.* -**nar·ies** [< L. neut. of *seminarius*, of seed < *semen*, a seed] **1.** a school: an old-fashioned term **2.** a school or college where priests, ministers, or rabbis are trained —**sem'i·nar'i·an** (-ner'ē ən) *n.*

sem·i·nif·er·ous (sem'ə nif'ər əs) *adj.* [< L. *semen*, a seed + -FEROUS] **1.** seed-bearing **2.** containing or conveying semen

sem·i·of·fi·cial (sem'ē ə fish''l) *adj.* having some, but not full, official authority —**sem'i·of·fi'cial·ly** *adv.*

se·mi·ot·ics (sē'mē ot'iks) *n.pl.* [< Gr. < *sēmeion*, a sign] [*with sing. v.*] Philos. a general theory of signs and symbols; esp., the analysis of signs used in language: also **se'mi·ol'o·gy** —**se'mi·ot'ic** *adj.*

sem·i·per·ma·nent (-pur'mə nənt) *adj.* not permanent but (esp. of buildings) expected to remain in use for some time

sem·i·per·me·a·ble (sem'i pur'mē ə b'l) *adj.* allowing some substances to pass; permeable to smaller molecules but not to larger ones

sem·i·pre·cious (-presh'əs) *adj.* designating gems, as garnets and opals, of lower value than precious gems

sem·i·pri·vate (-prī'vit) *adj.* partly but not completely private; specif., designating or of a hospital room with two, three, or, sometimes, four beds

sem·i·pro·fes·sion·al (sem'i prə fesh'ən 'l) *adj.* not fully professional; specif., *a*) engaging in a sport, etc. for pay but not as a regular occupation *b*) engaged in by semiprofessional players, etc. —*n.* a semiprofessional player, etc. —**sem'i·pro·fes'sion·al·ly** *adv.*

sem·i·qua·ver (sem'i kwā'vər) *n. Music* a note having one sixteenth the duration of a semibreve: see NOTE, illus.

sem·i·rig·id (sem'i rij'id) *adj.* somewhat or partly rigid; specif., designating an airship with a rigid internal keel

sem·i·skilled (-skild') *adj.* **1.** partly skilled **2.** of or doing manual work that requires only limited training

sem·i·soft (-soft') *adj.* soft but firm and easily cut

sem·i·sol·id (-sol'id) *adj.* viscous and slowly flowing, as asphalt —*n.* a semisolid substance

sem·i·sweet (-swēt') *adj.* only slightly sweetened

Sem·ite (sē'mīt) *n.* [prob. < Fr. < ModL. < *Semiticus*: see ff.] a member of any people speaking a Semitic language, as a Hebrew, Arab, etc.

Se·mit·ic (sə mit'ik) *adj.* [< G. < ModL. *Semiticus*, ult. < Gr. *Sem* < Heb. *Shēm*, SHEM] **1.** of or like the Semites **2.** designating or of a major division of a family of languages of SW Asia and N Africa, including Hebrew, Arabic, etc. —*n.* this division, or any member of it

Sem·i·tism (sem'ə tiz'm) *n.* **1.** a Semitic word or idiom **2.** traits, customs, etc. of the Semites

sem·i·tone (sem'i tōn') *n. Music* the difference in pitch between any two immediately adjacent keys on the piano —**sem'i·ton'ic** (-ton'ik), **sem'i·ton'al** (-tō'n'l) *adj.*

sem·i·trail·er (-trā′lər) *n.* a detachable trailer designed to be attached by a coupling to the rear part of a tractor (sense 2), on which it is partly supported

sem·i·trop·i·cal (sem′i trop′i k′l) *adj.* somewhat like the tropics; nearly tropical: also **sem′i·trop′ic**

sem·i·vow·el (sem′i vou′əl) *n.* *Phonet.* a glide at the beginning of a syllable, as the sound of *w* in *wall*

sem·i·week·ly (sem′i wēk′lē) *adj.* appearing, happening, done, etc. twice a week —*n.,* *pl.* **-lies** a semiweekly publication —*adv.* twice a week

sem·i·year·ly (-yir′lē) *adj.* coming, happening, done, etc. twice a year —*adv.* twice a year

sem·o·li·na (sem′ə lē′nə) *n.* [< It. dim. of *semola*, bran] 1. particles of coarsely ground durum, used in making macaroni, puddings, etc. 2. a milk pudding made with this

sem·pi·ter·nal (sem′pi tur′n′l) *adj.* [< ML. < L. < *semper*, always + *aeternus*, ETERNAL] everlasting; eternal —**sem′·pi·ter′nal·ly** *adv.* —**sem′pi·ter′ni·ty** *n.*

sem·pre (sem′prē; *It.* sem′pre) *adv.* [It., always < L. *semper*, always] *Music* always; throughout

semp·stress (sem′stris) *n.* *var.* of SEAMSTRESS

sen (sen) *n.,* *pl.* **sen** [Jap.] *see* MONETARY UNITS, table (Cambodia, Indonesia, Japan)

sen. 1. senate 2. senator 3. senior

S.E.N. State Enrolled Nurse

sen·ate (sen′it) *n.* [< OFr. < L. *senatus* < *senex,* old] 1. the supreme council of the ancient Roman state 2. a lawmaking assembly │ 3. [S-] the upper branch of the legislature of the U.S., France, etc. 4. a governing body, as in some universities

sen·a·tor (sen′ə tər) *n.* a member of a senate —**sen′a·to′·ri·al** (-tôr′ē əl) *adj.*

send (send) *vt.* **sent, send′ing** [OE. *sendan*] 1. *a)* to cause to go or be carried; convey *b)* to dispatch or transmit (a message) by post, radio, etc. 2. to direct or command to go [*send him home*] 3. to enable to go or attend [*to send one's son to college*] 4. to cause to move by hitting, throwing, etc. [*he sent the ball over the fence*] 5. to drive into some condition [*sent him to his ruin*] 6. to cause to happen, come, etc. [*joy sent by the gods*] 7. [Slang] to excite; thrill —*vi.* 1. to send a message, messenger, etc. [*to send for help*] 2. to transmit, as by radio —**send away** to dispatch or banish —**send down** to suspend or expel from a university —**send flying** 1. to dismiss hurriedly 2. to knock over, as with a blow 3. to put to flight 4. to scatter abruptly in all directions —**send for** 1. to order to come; summon 2. to request or order delivery of —**send forth** to give out or forth; produce, emit, etc. —**send in** 1. to dispatch or send to one receiving 2. to put (a player) in a game —**send off** 1. to dispatch (a letter, gift, etc.) 2. to dismiss, esp. in some sporting event as football 3. to give a send-off to —**send on** 1. to send in advance 2. to redirect to another place —**send up** 1. to cause to rise 2. to parody or satirize 3. [U.S. Colloq.] to sentence to prison —**send′·er** *n.*

send-off (send′ôf′) *n.* [Colloq.] 1. a demonstration of friendly feeling towards someone starting out on a journey, career, etc. 2. a start given to someone or something

send-up (-up′) *n.* a parody or imitation, esp. a disrespectful one

se·nes·cent (sə nes′′nt) *adj.* [< L. prp. of *senescere*, to grow old] growing old; aging —**se·nes′cence** (-′ns) *n.*

sen·es·chal (sen′ə shəl) *n.* [< OFr. < Frank. *siniskalk,* oldest servant] a steward in a medieval household

se·nile (sē′nīl) *adj.* [L. *senilis* < *senex,* old] 1. of or typical of old age 2. showing the deterioration, esp. the mental confusion, memory loss, etc., often accompanying old age —**se′nile·ly** *adv.* —**se·nil·i·ty** (si nil′ə tē) *n.*

sen·ior (sēn′yər) *adj.* [L., compar. of *senex,* old] 1. the older 2. of higher rank or longer service —*n.* 1. an older person 2. a person of greater rank or longer service 3. [U.S.] student in the last year of a high school or college —**one's senior** a person older than oneself

senior aircraftman *see* MILITARY RANKS, table

senior citizen an elderly person, esp. one who is retired

senior common room the room used by senior members of a college or university

sen·ior·i·ty (sēn i or′ə tē) *n.,* *pl.* **-ties** 1. a being senior, as in age or rank 2. status, priority, etc. achieved by length of service in a given job

senior service the Royal Navy

senior tutor the college official in charge of arranging the teaching

se·ni·ti (se nit′ē) *n.,* *pl.* **se·ni′ti** [Polynesian (Tongan), cent] *see* MONETARY UNITS, table (Tonga)

sen·na (sen′ə) *n.* [< ML. < Ar. *sanā*] 1. any of a genus of plants of the legume family, with yellow flowers 2. the dried leaflets of various sennas, used, esp. formerly, as a laxative

sen·night, se′n·ight (sen′īt) *n.* [ME. *sennyt* < OE. *seofen nichta,* seven nights] [Archaic] a week

‡**se·ñor** (se nyôr′) *n.,* *pl.* **se·ño′res** (-nyô′res) [Sp. < L.

senior: *see* SENIOR] a man; gentleman: Spanish title equivalent to *Mr.* or *Sir*

‡**se·ño·ra** (se nyô′rä) *n.,* *pl.* **se·ño′ras** (-räs) [Sp.] a married woman: Spanish title equivalent to *Mrs.* or *Madam*

‡**se·ño·ri·ta** (se′nyô rē′tä) *n.,* *pl.* **se·ño·ri′tas** (-täs) [Sp.] an unmarried woman or girl: Spanish title equivalent to *Miss*

sen·sa·tion (sen sā′shən) *n.* [< LL. < *sensatus,* intelligent < L. *sensus,* sense] 1. the power or process of receiving conscious sense impressions through direct stimulation of the bodily organism [the *sensations* of hearing, seeing, etc.] 2. a conscious feeling or sense impression [a *sensation* of cold] 3. a generalized feeling [a *sensation* of joy] 4. *a)* a state or feeling of general excitement [the play caused a *sensation*] *b)* the action, event, person, etc. causing this

sen·sa·tion·al (-′l) *adj.* 1. of the senses or sensation 2. *a)* intensely interesting or exciting *b)* intended to startle, shock, thrill, etc. 3. [Colloq.] unusually good, fine, etc. —**sen·sa′tion·al·ize′** (-′l īz′) *vt.* **-ized′, -iz′ing** —**sen·sa′·tion·al·ly** *adv.*

sen·sa·tion·al·ism (-′l iz′m) *n.* 1. the use of subject matter, style, etc. intended to shock, thrill, etc. 2. *Philos.* the belief that all knowledge is acquired through the senses —**sen·sa′·tion·al·ist** *n.* —**sen·sa′tion·al·is′tic** *adj.*

sense (sens) *n.* [< Fr. < L. *sensus* < *sentire,* to feel] 1. ability to receive and react to stimuli, as light, sound, etc.; specif., any of five faculties of receiving impressions through certain body organs (sight, touch, taste, smell, and hearing) 2. these faculties collectively 3. *a)* feeling, impression, or perception through the senses [a *sense* of warmth] *b)* a generalized feeling [a *sense* of longing] 4. an ability to judge external conditions, sounds, etc. [a *sense* of direction, pitch, etc.] 5. an ability to feel, appreciate, or understand some quality [a *sense* of humour, honour, etc.] 6. *a)* sound thinking; normal intelligence and judgment *b)* something wise or reasonable [to talk *sense*] 7. [*pl.*] normal ability to think or reason soundly [to come to one's *senses*] 8. *a)* meaning; esp., any of several meanings of the same word or phrase *b)* essential meaning; gist 9. the general opinion or attitude of a group —*vt.* **sensed, sens′ing** 1. to be aware of; perceive 2. to understand 3. to detect automatically, as by sensors —**in a sense** from one aspect; to a limited degree —**make sense** to be intelligible or logical —**take the sense of the meeting** take a vote, etc.

sense datum that which is directly perceived as the direct effect of stimulus on a sense organ

sense·less (-lis) *adj.* 1. unconscious 2. not showing good sense; stupid 3. having no real point; meaningless —**sense′·less·ly** *adv.* —**sense′less·ness** *n.*

sense organ any organ or structure, as an eye or a taste bud, that receives specific stimuli and transmits them as sensations to the brain

sen·si·bil·i·ty (sen′sə bil′ə tē) *n.,* *pl.* **-ties** [< MFr. < LL. < L.: see ff.] 1. the capacity for physical sensation; ability to feel 2. [*often pl.*] *a)* the capacity for being affected emotionally or intellectually *b)* sensitive responsiveness to intellectual, moral, or aesthetic values

sen·si·ble (sen′sə b′l) *adj.* [< MFr. < L. *sensibilis* < pp. of *sentire,* to feel] 1. that can cause physical sensation 2. perceptible to the intellect 3. easily perceived or noticed; striking 4. capable of receiving sensation 5. having appreciation or understanding; aware 6. showing good sense or sound judgment; wise —**sen′si·bly** *adv.*

sen·si·tive (sen′sə tiv) *adj.* [< MFr. < ML. *sensitivus* < L. *sensus:* see SENSE] 1. of the senses or sensation; sensory 2. receiving and responding to stimuli 3. keenly susceptible to stimuli [a *sensitive* ear] 4. easily hurt; tender 5. highly responsive to whatever is stimulating intellectually, artistically, etc. 6. easily offended, shocked, irritated, etc. 7. highly responsive as to light, radio signals, etc. [*sensitive* equipment] 8. indicating or measuring small changes or differences 9. of or dealing with secret or delicate government matters —**sen′si·tive·ly** *adv.* —**sen′si·tiv′i·ty** (-ə tē), **sen′si·tive·ness** *n.*

sensitive plant a tropical American plant with purplish flowers, whose leaflets fold and leafstalks droop when touched

sen·si·tize (sen′sə tīz′) *vt.* **-tized′, -tiz′ing** to make sensitive —**sen′si·ti·za′tion** *n.* —**sen′si·tiz′er** *n.*

sen·si·tom·e·ter (sen′sə tom′ə tər) *n.* [*sensit(ivity),* SENSITIVE + *-o-* + -METER] an instrument used for measuring sensitivity, as of photographic film

sen·sor (sen′sər, -sôr) *n.* [< L. pp. of *sentire,* to feel + -OR] a device designed to detect, measure, or record physical phenomena, as radiation, and to respond, as by transmitting information or operating controls

sen·so·ri·mo·tor (sen′sə rē mōt′ər) *adj.* [< SENSORY + MOTOR] *Physiol., Psychol.* of or involving both sensory and motor functions

sen·so·ri·um (sen sôr′ē əm) *n.,* *pl.* **-ri·ums, -ri·a** (-rē ə) [LL. < L. *sensus,* SENSE] 1. the supposed seat of physical sensations in the brain 2. the whole sensory apparatus of the body

sen·so·ry (sen′sər ē) *adj.* 1. of the senses or sensation 2.

connected with the reception and transmission of sense impressions Also **sen·so'ri·al** (-sôr'ē əl)

sen·su·al (sen'shoo wəl) *adj.* [L. *sensualis* < *sensus*, SENSE] 1. of the body and the senses as distinguished from the intellect or spirit 2. *a)* connected or preoccupied with bodily or sexual pleasures *b)* lustful; lewd —**sen'su·al·ly** *adv.*

sen·su·al·ism (-iz'm) *n.* 1. frequent or excessive indulgence in sensual pleasures 2. *a)* the belief that sensual pleasures are the greatest good for mankind *b)* expression of this belief, esp. in art —**sen'su·al·ist** *n.*

sen·su·al·i·ty (sen'shoo wal'ə tē) *n.* 1. a being sensual; fondness for or indulgence in sensual pleasures 2. lasciviousness; lewdness

sen·su·al·ize (sen'shoo wə līz') *vt.* -ized', -iz'ing to make sensual —**sen'su·al·i·za'tion** *n.*

sen·su·ous (sen'shoo wəs) *adj.* 1. of, based on, or appealing to the senses 2. enjoying or readily affected by sense impressions —**sen'su·ous·ly** *adv.* —**sen'su·ous·ness** *n.*

sent (sent) *pt. & pp. of* SEND

sen·tence (sen'təns) *n.* [< OFr. < L. *sententia*, opinion, ult. < prp. of *sentire*, to feel] 1. *a)* a decision or judgment, as of a court; esp., the determination by a court of a convicted person's punishment *b)* the punishment 2. *Gram.* a word or group of words stating, asking, commanding, or exclaiming something, usually having a subject and predicate: in writing, it begins with a capital letter and ends with a full stop, question mark, etc. —*vt.* -tenced, -tenc·ing to pronounce judgment upon (a convicted person); condemn (*to* a specified punishment) —**sen·ten'tial** (-ten'shəl) *adj.*

sen·ten·tious (sen ten'shəs) *adj.* [< L. < *sententia*: see prec.] 1. expressing much in few words; short and pithy 2. full of, or fond of using, maxims, proverbs, etc., esp. in a pompously trite or moralizing way —**sen·ten'tious·ly** *adv.*

sen·tient (sen'shənt, -shē ənt) *adj.* [< L. prp. of *sentire*, to feel] of, having, or capable of feeling or perception; conscious —**sen'tience, sen'tien·cy** *n.* —**sen'tient·ly** *adv.*

sen·ti·ment (sen'tə mənt) *n.* [< OFr. < ML. < L. *sentire*, to feel] 1. a complex combination of feelings and opinions 2. an opinion, attitude, etc.: *often used in the pl.* 3. susceptibility to emotional appeal; sensibility 4. appeal to the emotions in literature or art 5. sentimentality; maudlin emotion 6. a short sentence expressing some thought or wish 7. the real thought or meaning behind something

sen·ti·men·tal (sen'tə men't'l) *adj.* 1. having or showing tender or delicate feelings, as in literature or art, often in an excessive or maudlin way 2. influenced more by emotion than reason 3. of or resulting from sentiment —**sen'·ti·men'tal·ism** *n.* —**sen'ti·men'tal·ist** *n.* —**sen'ti·men'tal·ly** *adv.*

sen·ti·men·tal·i·ty (sen'tə men tal'ə tē) *n.* 1. the quality or condition of being sentimental, esp. in a maudlin way 2. *pl.* -ties any expression of this

sen·ti·men·tal·ize (-men'tə līz') *vi.* -ized', -iz'ing to be sentimental —*vt.* to regard or treat sentimentally —**sen'·ti·men'tal·i·za'tion** *n.*

sentimental value the value of an object having no intrinsic worth but prized because of its associations

sen·ti·nel (sen'ti n'l) *n.* [< Fr. < It. *sentinella*, ult. < L. *sentire*, to feel] a person or animal set to guard a group; specif., a sentry —*vt.* -nelled, -nel·ling 1. to guard as a sentinel 2. to furnish with a sentinel 3. to post as a sentinel

sen·try (sen'trē) *n., pl.* -tries [< ? obs. *centery*, guardhouse] a sentinel; esp., any member of a military guard posted to guard against, and warn of, danger

sentry box a small boxlike structure serving as a shelter for a sentry on duty during bad weather

se·pal (sep'l) *n.* [< Fr. < ModL. *sepalum*, arbitrary blend < Gr. *skepē*, a covering + L. *petalum*, petal] *Bot.* any of the usually green, leaflike parts of the calyx —**se'palled** *adj.*

-sep·al·ous (sep'l əs) a *combining form meaning* having (a specified number or kind of) sepals

sep·a·ra·ble (sep'ər ə b'l, sep'rə-) *adj.* that can be separated —**sep'a·ra·bil'i·ty** *n.* —**sep'a·ra·bly** *adv.*

sep·a·rate (sep'ə rāt'; *for adj. & n.* sep'ər it, sep'rit) *vt.* -rat'ed, -rat'ing [< L. pp. of *separare* < *se-*, apart + *parare*, to arrange] 1. to set apart into groups, sets, units, etc.; divide 2. to tell apart; distinguish between 3. to keep apart by being between (a wall *separates* the gardens) 4. to bring about a separation between (a man and wife) 5. to set apart from others; segregate 6. to take away (a part or ingredient) from a combination or mixture —*vi.* 1. to withdraw or secede 2. to part, become disconnected, etc. 3. to part company; go in different directions 4. to stop living together as man and wife but without getting a divorce 5. to become distinct or disengaged, as from a mixture —*adj.* 1. set apart or divided from the rest or others 2. not associated with others; distinct; individual 3. having individual form or function 4. not shared or held in common —*n.* [*pl.*] articles of dress designed to be worn as a set or separately —**sep'a·rate·ly** *adv.* —**sep'a·rate·ness** *n.* —**sep·a·ra·tive** (sep'ə rā'tiv, -ər ə tiv), sep'a·ra·to·ry (-ər ə tər ē) *adj.* —**sep'a·ra'tor** *n.*

sep·a·ra·tion (sep'ə rā'shən) *n.* 1. a separating or being separated 2. the place where this occurs; break; division 3. something that separates 4. an arrangement by which a man and wife live apart by agreement or court decree: also **judicial** (or **legal**) **separation**

sep·a·ra·tism (sep'ər ə tiz'm) *n.* a policy of or movement for political, religious, or racial separation —**sep'a·ra·tist** (-ər ə tist) *n., adj.*

Se·phar·dim (sə fär'dim, -fär dēm') *n.pl., sing.* **Se·phard** (sə färd'), **Se·phar·di** (-fär'dē, -fär dē') [< Heb.: cf. Obad. 20] the Jews of Spain and Portugal before the Inquisition, or their descendants —**Se·phar'dic** *adj.*

se·pi·a (sē'pē ə) *n.* [L., cuttlefish < Gr. *sēpia* < *sēpein*, to cause to rot (from the inky fluid)] 1. a dark-brown pigment prepared from the inky secretion of cuttlefish 2. a dark reddish-brown colour 3. a photographic print in this colour —*adj.* 1. of sepia 2. dark reddish-brown

se·poy (sē'poi) *n.* [Port. *sipae* < Hindi & Per. *sipāhī* < *sipāh*, army] formerly, a native of India serving in the British army

sep·pu·ku (se poo'koo) *n.* [Jap.] *same as* HARA-KIRI

sep·sis (sep'sis) *n.* [ModL. < Gr. < *sēpein*, to make putrid] poisoning caused by the absorption into the blood of certain microorganisms and their products

sept (sept) *n.* [var. of SECT] 1. a clan, or subdivision of a clan, as in Ireland and Scotland 2. any similar group based on supposed descent from a common ancestor

Sept. 1. September 2. Septuagint

sep·ta (sep'tə) *n. alt. pl. of* SEPTUM

sep·tal (-t'l) *adj.* 1. of or forming a septum or septa 2. of septs

Sep·tem·ber (sep tem'bər, səp-) *n.* [< L. < *septem*, seven: the early Romans reckoned from March] the ninth month of the year, having 30 days

sep·te·nar·y (sep'tə nər ē) *adj.* [< L. *septum*, SEVEN] 1. related to the number seven 2. consisting of seven —*n., pl.* -nar·ies 1. a group of seven, esp. seven years 2. a line of verse of seven feet

sep·ten·ni·al (sep ten'ē əl) *adj.* [< L. < *septum*, seven + *annus*, year] 1. lasting seven years 2. coming, happening, etc. every seven years —**sep·ten'ni·al·ly** *adv.*

sep·tet, sep·tette (sep tet') *n.* [G. < L. *septem*, seven + G. *(du)ett*] 1. a group of seven persons or things 2. *Music a)* a composition for seven voices or instruments *b)* the performers of this

sep·tic (sep'tik) *adj.* [< L. < Gr. *sēptikos* < *sēpein*, to make putrid] caused by or involving microorganisms that are infecting or putrefying —**sep'ti·cal·ly** *adv.* —**sep·tic·i·ty** (sep tis'i tē) *n.*

sep·ti·ce·mi·a (sep'tə sē'mē ə) *n.* [< Gr. *sēptikos*, putrefactive + *haima*, blood] a systemic disease caused by certain microorganisms and their toxic products in the blood —**sep'ti·ce'mic** *adj.*

septic tank an underground tank in which waste matter is putrefied and decomposed through bacterial action

sep·til·lion (sep til'yən) *n.* [Fr. < L. *septem*, seven + Fr. *(m)illion*] 1. in Great Britain and Germany, the number represented by 1 followed by 42 zeros 2. in the U.S. and France, the number represented by 1 followed by 24 zeros —*adj.* amounting to one septillion in number

sep·tu·a·ge·nar·i·an (sep'tyoo wə ji ner'ē ən) *adj.* [< LL. < L. *septuageni*, seventy each < *septuaginta*, seventy] seventy years old, or between the ages of seventy and eighty —*n.* a person of this age

Sep·tu·a·gint (sep'tyoo wə jint) [< L. *septuaginta*, seventy: in tradition, done by 70 or 72 translators] a Greek translation of the Hebrew Scriptures made in the 3rd cent. B.C.

sep·tum (sep'təm) *n., pl.* -tums, -ta (-tə) [ModL. < L. *sepire*, to enclose < *saepes*, a hedge] *Biol.* a part that separates two cavities or masses of tissue, as in the nose, a fruit, etc.; partition —**sep'tal** *adj.*

sep·tu·ple (sep tyoo'p'l) *adj. adj.* [LL. *septuplus* < L. *septem*, seven] 1. consisting of seven 2. seven times as much or as many —*vt., vi.* -pled, -pling to multiply by seven

sep·ul·cher (sep''l kər) *n., vt. U.S. sp. of* SEPULCHRE

se·pul·chral (sə pul'krəl) *adj.* 1. of sepulchres, burial, etc. 2. suggestive of the grave, etc.; dismal; gloomy 3. deep and melancholy: said of sound —**se·pul'chral·ly** *adv.*

sep·ul·chre (sep''l kər) *n.* [< OFr. < L. *sepulchrum* < *sepelire*, to bury] a vault for burial; grave; tomb —*vt.* to bury in a sepulchre

sep·ul·ture (sep''l chər) *n.* burial; interment

seq. [L. *sequentes* or *sequentia*] the following: also **seqq.**

se·quel (sē'kwəl) *n.* [< MFr. < L. *sequela* < *sequi*, to follow] 1. something that follows; continuation 2. a result or consequence 3. any literary work complete in itself but continuing a story begun in an earlier work

se·quence (sē′kwəns) *n.* [< MFr. < LL. < L. *sequens:* see ff.] **1.** *a)* the following of one thing after another; succession or continuity *b)* the order in which this occurs **2.** a continuous or related series **3.** a resulting event; consequence **4.** *Math.* an ordered set of quantities or elements **5.** *Cinema* the series of shots forming a single, uninterrupted episode

se·quent (-kwənt) *adj.* [L. *sequens,* prp. of *sequi,* to follow] **1.** following in time or order; subsequent **2.** following as a result; consequent —*n.* something sequent; consequence

se·quen·tial (si kwen′shəl) *adj.* **1.** *same as* SEQUENT **2.** characterized by or forming a regular sequence of parts —**se·quen′tial·ly** *adv.*

se·ques·ter (si kwes′tər) *vt.* [< MFr. < LL. *sequestrare,* to remove < L. *sequester,* trustee] **1.** to set apart; separate **2.** to take possession of (property) as security for a debt, claim, etc. **3.** to confiscate; seize, esp. by authority **4.** to withdraw; seclude —**se·ques′tered** *adj.*

se·ques·trate (-trāt) *vt.* -trat·ed, -trat·ing *same as* SEQUESTER —**se′ques·tra′tor** *n.*

se·ques·tra·tion (sē′kwes trā′shən) *n.* **1.** a sequestering or being sequestered; seclusion; separation **2.** *a)* the legal seizure of property for security *b)* confiscation of property, as by court action

se·quin (sē′kwin) *n.* [Fr. < It. *zecchino* < *zecca,* a mint < Ar. *sikkah,* a stamp] **1.** an obsolete Italian gold coin **2.** a small, shiny spangle, as a metal disc, esp. one of many sewn on material for decoration —*vt.* -quined or -quinned, -quin·ing or -quin·ning to adorn with sequins

se·quoi·a (si kwoi′ə) *n.* [ModL., genus name: after *Sequoya,* Am. Indian (c. 1760–1843) who devised the Cherokee syllabary] either of two giant evergreen trees; specif., *a)* BIG TREE *b)* REDWOOD

se·ra·gli·o (si räl′ē ō, -yō) *n., pl.* -lios [It. *serraglio,* enclosure (infl. by Turk. *serai,* palace), ult. < LL. *serare,* to lock < *sera,* a lock] **1.** the part of a Moslem's household where his wives or concubines live; harem **2.** the palace of a Turkish sultan

se·rang (se raŋ′) *n.* [< Per *sarhang,* commander] the boatswain of a lascar crew

se·ra·pe (sə rä′pē) *n.* [MexSp.] a woollen blanket, often brightly coloured, worn as an outer garment by men in Spanish-American countries

ser·aph (ser′əf) *n., pl.* -aphs, -a·phim′ (-ə fim′) [< LL. < Heb. *sĕrāphīm,* pl.] *Bible* one of the heavenly beings mentioned in Isaiah as surrounding the throne of God —**se·raph·ic** (sə raf′ik) *adj.* —**se·raph′i·cal·ly** *adv.*

Serb (sʉrb) *n.* **1.** a native or inhabitant of Serbia **2.** *same as* SERBIAN (*n.* 1) —*adj. same as* SERBIAN

Ser·bi·an (-ən) *adj.* of Serbia, the Serbs, or their language —*n.* **1.** Serbo-Croatian as spoken in Serbia **2.** *same as* SERB (*n.* 1)

Ser·bo-Cro·a·tian (sʉr′bō krō ā′shən) *n.* the major South Slavic language of Yugoslavia: it is generally written in the Roman alphabet in Croatia and in the Cyrillic alphabet in Serbia —*adj.* of this language or the people who speak it

SERAPE

sere¹ (sir) *n.* [< SERIES] *Ecol.* the complete series of communities occurring in succession in an area

sere² (sir) *adj.* [var. of SEAR] [Poet.] withered

ser·e·nade (ser′ə nād′) *n.* [< Fr. < It. *serenata,* ult. < L. *serenus,* clear] **1.** the act of playing or singing music outdoors at night, esp. by a lover under the window of his sweetheart **2.** music suitable for this —*vt., vi.* -nad′ed, -nad′ing to play or sing a serenade (*to*) —**ser′e·nad′er** *n.*

ser·en·dip·i·ty (ser′ən dip′ə tē) *n.* [after the princes in a Per. fairy tale, *The Three Princes of Serendip,* who make such discoveries] a seeming gift for making fortunate discoveries accidentally —**ser′en·dip′i·tous** *adj.*

se·rene (sə rēn′) *adj.* [L. *serenus*] **1.** clear; unclouded [a *serene* sky] **2.** untroubled; calm, peaceful, etc. **3.** [S-] exalted: in titles [His *Serene* Highness] —**se·rene′ly** *adv.* —**se·ren′i·ty** (-ren′ə tē), **se·rene′ness** *n.*

serf (sʉrf) *n.* [OFr. < L. *servus,* a slave] **1.** a person in a slavelike condition under the feudal system, bound to his master's land and transferred with it **2.** a person treated like a slave —**serf′dom, serf′hood′** *n.*

Serg., serg. sergeant

serge (sʉrj) *n.* [< OFr. < L. < *sericus,* silken, lit., of the *Seres,* prob. the Chinese, prob. ult. < Chin. *se,* silk] a strong, twilled material made of wool, silk, rayon, etc. and used for suits, coats, linings, etc. —*vt.* serged, serg′ing to finish off (a cut or unravelling edge) with overcast stitches

ser·geant (sär′jənt) *n.* [< OFr. < L. *serviens,* serving < *servire,* to serve] **1.** *same as* SERGEANT-AT-ARMS **2.** *see* MILITARY RANKS, table **3.** a police officer ranking next below an inspector —**ser′gean·cy,** *pl.* -cies, **ser′geant·ship′** *n.*

ser·geant-at-arms (-ət ärmz′) *n., pl.* **ser′-**

geants-at-arms′ an officer appointed to keep order in a legislative body, court, etc.: also **serjeant-at-arms**

Sergeant Baker a type of fish found around New South Wales

sergeant major *pl.* **sergeants major** the chief administrative noncommissioned officer of a military headquarters: see also note at WARRANT OFFICER

Sergt., sergt. sergeant

se·ri·al (sir′ē əl) *adj.* [< ModL. < L. *series,* a row, SERIES] **1.** of, arranged in, or forming a series [*serial* numbers] **2.** appearing or published in a series of continuing parts at regular intervals **3.** of a serial or serials **4.** *same as* TWELVE-TONE —*n.* a story presented in serial form, as in magazines, films, radio, TV, etc. —**se′ri·al·ly** *adv.*

se·ri·al·ize (-īz′) *vt.* -ized′, -iz′ing to put or publish (a story, etc.) in serial form —**se′ri·al·i·za′tion** *n.*

serial number any of a series of numbers given to a person (as a soldier) or thing (as an engine) for identification

se·ri·ate (sir′ē it) *adj.* [ML. *seriatus,* pp. of *seriare,* to arrange in a series] arranged or occurring in a series —**se′ri·a′tion** *n.*

se·ri·a·tim (sir′ē āt′im) *adv., adj.* [ML. < L. *series*] one after another in order; serial(ly)

se·ries (sir′ēz) *n., pl.* -ries [L. < *serere,* to join together] **1.** a number of similar things arranged in a row [a *series* of arches] **2.** a number of similar persons, things, or events coming one after another; sequence **3.** a number of things produced as a related group; set **4.** *Elec.* a circuit connection in which the components are joined end to end, forming a single path for the current: usually in the phrase **in series 5.** *Geol.* a subdivision of a geologic system **6.** *Math.* a sequence, often infinite, of terms to be added or subtracted —*adj.* designating or of a circuit in series

ser·if (ser′if) *n.* [< Du. *schreef,* a stroke < *schrijven,* to write < L. *scribere*] *Printing* a fine line projecting from a main stroke of a letter

ser·i·graph (ser′ə graf′) *n.* [< L. *sericum,* silk + -GRAPH] a colour print made by the silk-screen process and printed by the artist himself —**se·rig′ra·phy** (sə rig′rə fē) *n.*

ser·in (ser′in) *n.* [Fr.] a small, domesticated, yellow or yellowish-green European finch, related to the canary

se·ri·o·com·ic (sir′ē ō kom′ik) *adj.* partly serious and partly comic —**se′ri·o·com′i·cal·ly** *adv.*

se·ri·ous (sir′ē əs) *adj.* [< ML. *seriosus* < L. *serius*] **1.** earnest, grave, sober, or solemn [a *serious* man] **2.** *a)* meaning what one says; not joking or trifling *b)* meant in earnest [*serious* thought] **3.** concerned with grave, important matters; weighty [a *serious* novel] **4.** requiring careful consideration [a *serious* problem] **5.** giving cause for concern [a *serious* wound] —**se′ri·ous·ly** *adv.* —**se′ri·ous·ness** *n.*

se·ri·ous-mind·ed (-mīn′did) *adj.* having or showing earnestness of purpose, etc.; not frivolous, jocular, etc. —**se′ri·ous-mind′ed·ly** *adv.* —**se′ri·ous-mind′ed·ness** *n.*

ser·jeant (sär′jənt) *n. var. of* SERGEANT

ser·mon (sʉr′mən) *n.* [OFr. < LL. < L. *sermo,* a discourse] **1.** a speech, esp. by a clergyman during services, on some religious topic or on morals **2.** any serious or boring talk on one's behaviour, responsibilities, etc. —**ser·mon′ic** (-mon′-ik) *adj.*

ser·mon·ize (-mə nīz′) *vi., vt.* -ized′, -iz′ing to preach (to); lecture —**ser′mon·iz′er** *n.*

Sermon on the Mount the sermon given by Jesus to his disciples: Matt. 5–7, Luke 6:20–49

se·rol·o·gy (si rol′ə jē) *n.* [< SERUM + -LOGY] the science dealing with the properties and actions of serums —**se·ro·log·ic** (sir′ə loj′ik), **se′ro·log′i·cal** *adj.* —**se·rol′-o·gist** *n.*

se·rous (sir′əs) *adj.* **1.** of or containing serum **2.** like serum; thin and watery

ser·pent (sʉr′pənt) *n.* [OFr. < L. < prp. of *serpere,* to creep] **1.** a snake, esp. a large or poisonous one **2.** a sly, treacherous person **3.** *Music* an obsolete, coiled wind instrument, covered with leather

ser·pen·tine (sʉr′pən tēn′, -tīn′) *adj.* of or like a serpent; esp., *a)* evilly cunning; treacherous *b)* coiled, twisted, or winding —*n.* **2.** a green or brownish-red mineral, magnesium silicate

ser·rate (ser′āt; *for v. usually* sə rāt′) *adj.* [L. *serratus* < *serra,* a saw] having sawlike notches along the edge, as some leaves: also **ser·rat′ed** —*vt.* -rat′ed, -rat′ing to make serrate

ser·ra·tion (sə rā′shən) *n.* **1.** the condition of being serrate **2.** a single tooth or notch in a serrate edge **3.** a formation of these Also **ser·ra·ture** (ser′ə chər)

ser·ried (ser′ēd) *adj.* [pp. of obs. *serry* < Fr. *serrer,* to crowd < LL. *serare:* see SERAGLIO] placed close together; compact, as soldiers in ranks

ser·um (sir′əm) *n., pl.* -rums, -ra (-ə) [L., whey] **1.** any watery animal fluid, esp. the yellowish fluid that is left after blood clots: in full, **blood serum 2.** blood serum used as an antitoxin, taken from an animal made immune to a specific disease by inoculation **3.** whey **4.** watery plant fluid

serum albumin the most abundant protein of blood serum, serving to regulate osmotic pressure and used in the emergency treatment of shock

serv·ant (sʉr′vənt) *n.* [OFr. < prp. of *servir* < L. *servire*, to serve] **1.** a person hired to work in another's home as a maid, cook, chauffeur, etc. **2.** a person who works for a government [a civil *servant*] **3.** a person who works earnestly for a cause, etc.

servants' hall formerly, the room in which the household servants ate

serve (sʉrv) *vt.* **served, serv′ing** [< OFr. < L. *servire*, to serve < *servus*, a slave] **1.** to work for as a servant **2.** *a)* to do services for; aid; help *b)* to give reverence to, as God **3.** to do military or naval service for **4.** to pass or spend (a term of imprisonment, military service, etc.) **5.** to carry out the duties of (a position, office, etc.) **6.** to provide (customers) with (goods or services) **7.** to prepare and offer (food, etc.) to (a person or persons) **8.** *a)* to meet the needs of [a tool to *serve* many purposes] *b)* to promote or further [to *serve* the national interest] **9.** to be used by [one hospital *serves* the town] **10.** to function for [my memory *serves* me well] **11.** to treat [she was cruelly *served*] **12.** to deliver (a summons, subpoena, etc.) to (someone) **13.** to hit (a tennis ball, etc.) to one's opponent in order to start play **14.** to operate (a large gun) **15.** to copulate with (a female): said of an animal **16.** *Naut.* to put a binding around in order to strengthen (rope, etc.) —*vi.* **1.** to work as a servant **2.** to be in service [to *serve* in the navy] **3.** to carry out the duties of an office or position **4.** to be of service; function **5.** to meet needs or satisfy requirements **6.** to wait at table **7.** to be suitable: said of weather, wind, etc. **8.** to start play by hitting the ball, etc. —*n.* the act or manner of serving the ball in tennis, etc., or one's turn to serve —**it will serve** although not the right thing for the job, it can be used for the present —**serve (someone) right** to be what (someone) deserves, as for doing something wrong —**serve (one's) time 1.** to undergo imprisonment **2.** to serve an apprenticeship

serv·er (sʉr′vər) *n.* **1.** a person who serves, as a waiter, etc. **2.** a thing used in serving, as a tray, cart, etc.

ser·ver·y (sʉr′vər ē) *n.* a pantry communicating with a dining room from which meals are served

serv·ice (sʉr′vis) *n.* [< OFr. < L. *servitium* < *servus*, a slave] **1.** the occupation or condition of a servant **2.** *a)* employment, esp. public employment *b)* a branch of this, including the people in it; specif., the armed forces **3.** work done or duty performed for others [repair *service*] **4.** a religious ceremony, esp. a meeting for prayer **5.** *a)* an act of assistance *b)* the result of this; benefit *c)* [*pl.*] friendly help; also, professional aid [a fee for *services*] **6.** the act or manner of serving food **7.** a set of utensils used in serving [a tea *service*] **8.** [often *pl.*] a system or method of providing people with electric power, water, transportation, etc. **9.** installation, maintenance, repairs, etc. provided to customers by a dealer, etc. **10.** the act or manner of serving the ball in tennis, etc., or one's turn to serve **11.** *Law* notification of legal action, esp. through the serving of a writ, etc. **12.** *Naut.* any material, as wire, used in serving (ropes, etc.) —*adj.* **1.** of, for, or in service **2.** of, for, or used by servants, tradespeople, etc. [a *service* entrance] —*vt.* **-iced, -ic·ing 1.** to furnish with a service **2.** to copulate with (a female): said of an animal **3.** to make or keep fit for service, as by adjusting, repairing, etc. —**at one's service 1.** ready to serve one **2.** ready for one's use —**has seen service 1.** to have been a member of the armed forces in wartime **2.** to have been put to long and usually hard use —**in service 1.** in use; functioning **2.** in the armed forces **3.** working as a servant —**of service** helpful; useful

serv·ice·a·ble (sʉr′vis ə b'l) *adj.* **1.** that can be of service; useful **2.** that will give good service; durable —**serv′-ice·a·bil′i·ty, serv′ice·a·ble·ness** *n.* —**serv′ice·a·bly** *adv.*

service area a place on a motorway providing facilities for motorway users, as a restaurant, garage, etc.

service bus [Aust. & N.Z.] a motor coach

service charge a percentage added to a bill in a restaurant etc. to pay for service

service flat a self-contained flat where the management provides certain services, as cleaning, washing, etc.

serv·ice·man (sʉr′vis man′, -mən) *n., pl.* **-men** (-men′, -mən) **1.** a member of the armed forces **2.** a person whose work is servicing or repairing something: also **service man** —**serv′ice·wom·an** *n.fem.,* **-wom·en**

service station a place selling petrol and oil, for motor vehicles

service tree [ME. *serves* pl. of obs. *serve* ult < L. *sorbus*] a European tree of the rose family, resembling the mountain ash and having small, edible fruits

ser·vi·ette (sʉr′vē et′) *n.* [Fr. < MFr. < *servir*, to serve] a table napkin

ser·vile (sʉr′vil) *adj.* [< L. < *servus*, a slave] **1.** of a slave or slaves **2.** like that of slaves or servants [*servile* employment] **3.** humbly yielding or submissive; cringing

—ser′vile·ly *adv.* **—ser·vil·i·ty** (sər vil′ə tē), *pl.* **-ties, ser′-vile·ness** *n.*

serv·ing (-viŋ) *n.* a helping of food —*adj.* used for serving food [a *serving* spoon]

ser·vi·tor (sʉr′və tər) *n.* a servant, attendant, etc.

ser·vi·tude (sʉr′və tyōōd′) *n.* [MFr. < L. < *servus*, a slave] **1.** slavery or bondage **2.** work imposed as punishment for crime

ser·vo (sʉr′vō) *n., pl.* **-vos** *clipped form of:* **1.** SERVOMECHANISM **2.** SERVOMOTOR —*adj.* of, or controlled by, a servomechanism [*servo* brakes]

ser·vo·mech·a·nism (sʉr′vō mek′ə niz′m) *n.* [SERVO(MOTOR) + MECHANISM] an automatic control system in which the output is compared with the input through feedback so that any error in control is corrected

ser·vo·mo·tor (sʉr′vō mōt′ər) *n.* [< Fr. *servo-moteur* < L. *servus*, slave + Fr. *moteur*, MOTOR] a device, as an electric motor, that is controlled by an amplified signal as from a servomechanism

ses·a·me (ses′ə mē′) *n.* [< L. < Gr. *sēsamon*, of Sem. orig.] **1.** an East Indian plant whose flat seeds yield an edible oil **2.** its seeds, used for flavouring bread, rolls, etc. See also OPEN SESAME

ses·qui- [< L. < *semis*, half + *que*, and] a combining form meaning one and a half [*sesquicentennial*]

ses·qui·cen·ten·ni·al (ses′kwi sen ten′ē al) *adj.* of or ending a period of 150 years —*n.* a 150th anniversary or its celebration

ses·sile (ses′il) *adj.* [< L. pp. of *sedere*, to sit] **1.** *Anat., Zool.* attached directly by its base **2.** *Bot.* attached directly to the main stem

ses·sion (sesh′ən) *n.* [< L. *sessio* < *sedere*, to sit] **1.** *a)* the sitting together or meeting of a court, legislature, council, etc. *b)* a continuous series of such meetings *c)* the period a session lasts **2.** an academic year or period of study, classes, etc. **3.** the governing body of a Presbyterian church **4.** any period of activity [a *session* of golf] —**in session** meeting —**ses′sion·al** *adj.*

SESSILE LEAVES
(A, trillium; B, Solomon's seal)

ses·terce (ses′tərs) *n.* [L. *sestertius* (*nummus*), for *semis tertius*, two and a half because originally equal in value to two and a half asses] an old Roman coin, orig. of silver, equal to 1/4 denarius

ses·tet (ses tet′) *n.* [< It. dim. of *sesto*, sixth < L. < *sex*, six] **1.** *Music* same as SEXTET **2.** *a)* the final six lines of a sonnet *b)* a poem of six lines

set (set) *vt.* **set, set′ting** [OE. *settan*] **1.** to cause to sit; seat **2.** *a)* to cause (a fowl) to sit on eggs to hatch them *b)* to put (eggs) under a fowl to hatch them **3.** to put in a certain or designated place or position [*set* the book on the table, *set* the wheel on the axle] **4.** to bring (something) into contact with something else [to *set* a match to paper] **5.** to affix (one's signature, etc.) to a document **6.** to cause to be in some condition or relation **7.** to cause to be in working or proper condition; arrange; fix; specif., *a)* to fix (a net, trap, etc.) to catch animals *b)* to fix (a sail) to catch the wind *c)* to adjust; regulate [to *set* a clock] *d)* to place (oneself) in readiness for action *e)* to arrange (a table) with tableware for a meal *f)* to put (a dislocated or fractured bone) into normal position **8.** *a)* to put into a fixed position [he *set* his jaw] *b)* to cause (one's mind, etc.) to be fixed, determined, etc. *c)* to cause to become firm [pectin *sets* jam] *d)* to make (a colour) fast in dyeing *e)* to mount (gems) in jewellery *f)* to decorate (jewellery) with gems *g)* to arrange (hair) in a certain style with lotion, hairpins, etc. **9.** to cause to take a specified direction; direct [he *set* his face towards home] **10.** to appoint; establish; specif., *a)* to station (a person) for certain duties *b)* to fix (limits or boundaries) *c)* to fix (a time) for (an event) *d)* to establish (a rule, record, etc.) *e)* to furnish (an example) for others *f)* to introduce (a fashion, etc.) *g)* to fix (a quota) for a given period *h)* to begin to apply (oneself) to a task *i)* to assign (a task etc.) for work or study **11.** *a)* to fix (the amount of a price, fine, etc.) *b)* to fix or put as an estimate [to *set* little store by someone] **12.** to point towards (game): said of dogs **13.** *Baking* to put aside (leavened dough) to rise **14.** *Bridge* to prevent (one's opponents) from making their bid **15.** *Music* to write or fit (words *to* music or music *to* words) **16.** *Printing a)* to arrange (type) for printing *b)* to put (manuscript) into type **17.** *Theatre a)* to place (a scene) in a given locale *b)* to arrange the scenery and properties on (the stage) —*vi.* **1.** to sit on eggs: said of a fowl **2.** to become firm or hard [the cement *set*] **3.** to become fast, as a dye **4.** *a)* to begin to move, travel, etc. (with *out, forth, on, off,* etc.) *b)* to get started [to *set* to work] **5.** to have a certain direction; tend **6.** *a)* to sink below the horizon *b)* to wane; decline **7.** to grow together: said of a broken bone **8.** *Bot.* to begin to develop into a fruit —*adj.* **1.** fixed in advance [a *set* time] **2.** established, as by authority [a *set* book] **3.** deliberate; intentional **4.** conventional [a *set* speech] **5.** fixed; rigid **6.** *a)* resolute *b)* obstinate **7.** firm in consistency **8.** ready [get *set*] **9.** formed; built —*n.* **1.** a setting or being set; specif., the act of a dog in setting game **2.** the way or position in which a thing is set; specif., *a)* direction, as of a current *b)* tendency; inclination *c)* warp; bend *d)* the position of a part of the body [the *set* of her head] **3.** something which is set; specif., *a)* a twig, young bulb, etc. for planting or grafting *b)* the constructed scenery for a play, film, etc. **4.** *a)* the act or a style of arranging hair *b)* the lotion, etc. used for this: in full, **hair set 5.** a group of persons or things classed or belonging together [the social *set*, a *set* of tools, books, china, etc.] **6.** assembled equipment for radio or television reception **7.** *Math.* a collection of elements or objects that satisfy a given condition **8.** *Tennis* a group of games of which the winner must win a specified number, usually (and at least) six —**all set** [Colloq.] prepared; ready —**set about** to begin; start doing —**set against 1.** to balance **2.** to compare **3.** to make hostile towards —**set aside 1.** to reserve for a purpose: also **set apart 2.** to discard; reject **3.** to annul —**set back 1.** to reverse or hinder the progress of **2.** [Slang] to cost (a person) a specified sum of money —**set down 1.** to put down **2.** to land (an aircraft) **3.** to put in writing or print **4.** to establish (rules, etc.) **5.** to ascribe —**set eyes on** to behold; to see —**set forth 1.** to publish **2.** to express in words —**set in 1.** to begin **2.** to insert **3.** to become established —**set little (much) by** to regard or esteem little (highly) —**set off 1.** to start (a person) doing something **2.** to make begin **3.** to make prominent by contrast **4.** to enhance **5.** to cause to explode —**set on 1.** to incite to attack **2.** to attack: also **set upon** —**set one's sights on** to train upon; determine upon —**set out 1.** to display, as for sale **2.** to plant **3.** to undertake —**set sail 1.** to hoist the sails into position **2.** to begin a voyage, esp. a sea voyage —**set the fashion** (or **pace**) to be responsible for deciding what is fashionable —**set to 1.** to get to work; begin **2.** to begin fighting —**set up 1.** to place in an upright position **2.** to raise to power, a high position, etc. **3.** to present as specified: also **set up as 4.** to put together or erect (a tent, machine, etc.) **5.** to establish; found **6.** to make detailed plans for **7.** to begin **8.** to make successful, etc. —**set upon** to attack, esp. with violence

se·ta (sēt'ə) *n.*, *pl.* **-tae** (-ē) [ModL. < L., a stiff hair] *Bot.*, *Zool.* a bristle or bristlelike part or organ

set·back (set'bak') *n.* **1.** a reversal or check in progress; relapse **2.** a steplike recessed section, as in the upper part of a wall

set·off (set'ôf') *n.* **1.** a thing that makes up for something else; counterbalance **2.** *a)* a debt claimed by a debtor against his creditor *b)* a claim for this

set piece 1. an artistic composition intended to impress others **2.** a scenic display of fireworks **3.** any situation carefully planned beforehand

set·screw (set'skrōō') *n.* a machine screw passing through one part and against or into another to prevent movement, as of a ring around a shaft

set·tee[1] (se tē') *n.* [prob. altered < SETTLE[1]] **1.** a seat or bench with a back **2.** a couch or sofa

set·tee[2] (se tē') *n.* [< It. *soettia*, < L. *sagitta*, arrow] a single-decked, two-masted vessel used esp. formerly in the Mediterranean

set·ter (set'ər) *n.* **1.** a person who sets or a thing used in setting **2.** any of several breeds of long-haired gun dogs trained to find game and point it out by standing rigid: see ENGLISH SETTER, IRISH SETTER

set·ting (set'iŋ) *n.* **1.** the act of one that sets **2.** the position of something, as a dial, that has been set **3.** a thing in or on which something, as a gem, has been set **4.** time and place, environment, etc. of an event, story, play, etc. **5.** actual physical surroundings, real or artificial **6.** the music for a set of words **7.** the eggs in the nest of a setting hen **8.** *same as* PLACE SETTING

set·tle[1] (set'l) *n.* [OE. *setl*] a long wooden bench with a back and armrests

set·tle[2] (set'l) *vt.* **-tled, -tling** [OE. < *setl*, a seat] **1.** to put in order; arrange as desired [to *settle* one's affairs] **2.** to set in place firmly or comfortably **3.** to establish as a resident or residents [he *settled* his family in London] **4.** to migrate to; colonize [New York was *settled* by the Dutch] **5.** to cause to sink and become more compact [the rain *settled* the dust] **6.** to clarify (a liquid) by causing the sediment to sink to the bottom **7.** to free (the mind, nerves, stomach, etc.) from disturbance **8.** to establish in business, marriage, etc. **9.** to fix definitely; decide (something in doubt) **10.** to end (a dispute) **11.** to pay (a bill, debt, etc.) **12.** to make over (property, etc.) to someone by legal action (with *on* or *upon*) **13.** to decide (a legal dispute) without court action —*vi.* **1.** to stop moving and stay in one place **2.** to cast itself, as fog over a landscape or gloom over a person **3.** to become localized in a part of the body: said of

pain or disease **4.** to take up permanent residence **5.** to move downwards; sink [the car *settled* in the mud] **6.** to become more dense by sinking, as sediment **7.** to become clearer by the settling of dregs **8.** to become more stable or composed **9.** *a)* to reach a decision (with *with*, *on*, or *upon*) *b)* to accept something less than what is hoped for [he'll *settle* for any kind of work] **10.** to pay a bill or debt —**settle down 1.** to take up permanent residence, a regular job, etc. **2.** to become less nervous, erratic, etc. **3.** to apply oneself steadily —**settle up** to pay any outstanding amount —**settle with 1.** to pay a debt or bill **2.** to make an agreement with

set·tle·ment (-mənt) *n.* **1.** a settling or being settled **2.** a new colony **3.** a village **4.** a community established by a religious or social group **5.** an agreement, adjustment, etc. **6.** *a)* the disposition of property for the benefit of a person *b)* this property **7.** an institution, usually in a depressed neighbourhood, offering social services and recreational and educational activities: also **settlement house 8.** sinking or subsidence in all or part of a building **9.** the fortnightly settlement of accounts on the Stock Exchange

set·tler (set'lər) *n.* **1.** a person or thing that settles **2.** one who settles in a new country

settler's clock [Aust.] the laughing jackass

set·tlings (-liŋz) *n.pl.* sediment; dregs

set-to (set'tōō') *n.*, *pl.* **-tos** (-tōōz') [Colloq.] **1.** a fight or struggle **2.** any brisk or vigorous contest

set-up (set'up') *n.* **1.** the way in which something is set up; specif., *a)* plan, makeup, etc., as of equipment, an organization, etc. *b)* details of a plan of action, etc. **2.** bodily posture; carriage

sev·en (sev'n) *adj.* [OE. *seofon*] totalling one more than six —*n.* **1.** the cardinal number between six and eight; 7; VII **2.** anything having seven units or members, or numbered seven

seven deadly sins *same as* DEADLY SINS

sev·en·fold (-fōld') *adj.* [see -FOLD] **1.** having seven parts **2.** having seven times as much or as many —*adv.* seven times as much or as many

seven seas all the oceans of the world

sev·en·teen (sev'n tēn') *adj.* [OE. *seofentyne*] seven more than ten —*n.* the cardinal number between sixteen and eighteen; 17; XVII

sev·en·teenth (-tēnth') *adj.* **1.** preceded by sixteen others in a series; 17th **2.** designating any of the seventeen equal parts of something —*n.* **1.** the one following the sixteenth **2.** any of the seventeen equal parts of something; 1/17

sev·enth (sev'nth) *adj.* [< ME. < *seoven* + -TH[2]] **1.** preceded by six others in a series; 7th **2.** designating any of the seven equal parts of something —*n.* **1.** the one following the sixth **2.** any of the seven equal parts of something; 1/7 **3.** *Music a)* the seventh tone of an ascending diatonic scale, or a tone six degrees above or below a given tone *b)* the interval between two such tones, or a combination of them —**sev'enth·ly** *adv.*

seventh-day (-dā') *adj.* **1.** of the seventh day (Saturday) **2.** [*often* S- D-] observing the Sabbath on Saturday [*Seventh-Day* Adventists]

seventh heaven 1. in certain ancient cosmologies, the outermost of the spheres enclosing the earth, in which God and his angels are **2.** a state of perfect happiness

sev·en·ti·eth (sev'n tē ith) *adj.* **1.** preceded by sixty-nine others in a series; 70th **2.** designating any of the seventy equal parts of something —*n.* **1.** the one following the sixty-ninth **2.** any of the seventy equal parts of something; 1/70

sev·en·ty (-tē) *adj.* seven times ten —*n.*, *pl.* **-ties** the cardinal number between sixty-nine and seventy-one; 70; LXX —**the seventies** the numbers or years, as of a century, from seventy to seventy-nine

sev·er (sev'ər) *vt.*, *vi.* [< OFr., ult. < L. *separare*] **1.** to separate; divide **2.** to part or break off; cut in two [to sever a cable, to *sever* a relationship] —**sev'er·a·ble** *adj.*

sev·er·al (sev'ər əl, sev'rəl) *adj.* [< Anglo-Fr. < ML. < L. *separ*, separate] **1.** separate; distinct **2.** different; respective [parted and went their *several* ways] **3.** more than two but not many; few —*n.* [with *pl.* v.] an indefinite but small number (*of* persons or things) —*pron.* [with *pl.* v.] several persons or things; a few

sev·er·al·ly (-ē) *adv.* **1.** separately; distinctly **2.** respectively; individually

sev·er·al·ty (-tē) *n.*, *pl.* **-ties** [ME. *severalte* < Anglo-Fr. *severauté*: see SEVERAL < -TY[1]] **1.** the condition of being several or distinct **2.** property owned by individual right, not shared with any other

sev·er·ance (sev'ər əns, sev'rəns) *n.* a severing or being severed

severance pay extra pay given to an employee dismissed through no fault of his own

se·vere (sə vir') *adj.* **-ver'er, -ver'est** [< MFr. < OFr. < L. *severus*] **1.** harsh or strict, as in treatment; stern **2.** serious; grave [a *severe* glance, a *severe* wound] **3.** rigidly accurate or demanding **4.** extremely plain or simple [a severe style*]* **5.** keen; intense *[severe* pain*]* **6.** difficult; rigorous *[a severe* test*]* —**se·vere′ly** *adv.* —**se·vere′ness** *n.*

se·ver·i·ty (sə ver′ə tē) *n.* **1.** a being severe; specif., a) strictness; harshness b) seriousness; gravity c) rigid accuracy d) extreme plainness, as in style e) keenness, as of pain f) rigorousness **2.** *pl.* **-ties** something severe

Se·ville orange (sə vil′) **1.** a bitter orange used esp. for making marmalade **2.** the tree bearing this orange

Sè·vres (sev′rə) *n.* [< *Sèvres,* suburb of Paris*]* a type of fine French porcelain

sew (sō) *vt.* **sewed, sewn** or **sewed, sew′ing** [OE. *siwian*] **1.** to join or fasten with stitches made with needle and thread **2.** to make, mend, etc. by such means —*vi.* to work with needle and thread or at a sewing machine —**sew up 1.** to close together the edges of with stitches **2.** [Colloq.] to complete or negotiate successfully

sew·age (soo′ij, syoo′-) *n.* the waste matter carried off by sewers or drains

sewage farm an establishment where sewage is treated to provide innocuous sludge or manure

sew·er[1] (soo′ər, syoo′-) *n.* [MFr. *essewéur,* ult. < L. *ex,* out + *aqua,* water] a pipe or drain, usually underground, for carrying off water and waste matter

sew·er[2] (sō′ər) *n.* a person or thing that sews

sew·er·age (soo′ər ij, syoo′-) *n.* **1.** removal of surface water and waste matter by sewers **2.** a system of sewers **3.** *same as* SEWAGE

sew·ing (sō′iŋ) *n.* **1.** the act or occupation of a person who sews **2.** material for sewing; needlework

sewing machine a machine with a mechanically driven needle used for sewing and stitching

sewn (sōn) *alt. pp.* of SEW

sex (seks) *n.* [L. *sexus* < ? *secare,* to divide] **1.** either of the two divisions, male or female, of persons, animals, or plants, with reference to their reproductive functions **2.** the character of being male or female **3.** anything connected with sexual gratification or reproduction; esp., the attraction of one sex for the other **4.** sexual intercourse —*adj.* [Colloq.] *same as* SEXUAL —*vt.* to ascertain the sex of

sex- [< L. *sex,* six] *a combining form meaning* six

sex·a·ge·nar·i·an (sek′sə ji ner′ē ən) *adj.* [< L. < *sexageni,* sixty each] sixty years old, or between the ages of sixty and seventy —*n.* a person of this age

sex appeal the physical attractiveness and erotic charm that attracts members of the opposite sex

sex chromosome a sex-determining chromosome in the germ cells of most animals and a few plants: in most animals, all the eggs carry an X chromosome and the spermatozoa either an X or Y chromosome, and an egg receiving an X chromosome at fertilization will develop into a female (XX) while one receiving a Y will develop into a male (XY)

sexed (sekst) *adj.* **1.** of or having sex **2.** having (a specified degree of) sexuality

sex hormone any hormone, as testosterone, oestrogen, etc., having an effect upon the reproductive organs, sexual characteristics, etc.

sex·ism (sek′siz′m) *n.* [SEX + (RAC)ISM] the economic exploitation and social domination of members of one sex by the other, specif. of women by men —**sex′ist** *adj., n.*

sex·less (seks′lis) *adj.* **1.** lacking the characteristics of sex; asexual **2.** lacking in normal sexual appetite or appeal —**sex′less·ly** *adv.* —**sex′less·ness** *n.*

sex linkage *Genetics* the phenomenon by which inherited characters are determined by genes carried on one of the sex chromosomes —**sex′-linked′** (-liŋkt′) *adj.*

sex maniac someone who is considered to be oversexed and/or perverted

sex·ol·o·gy (sek sol′ə jē) *n.* the science dealing with human sexual behaviour —**sex·o·log·i·cal** (sek′sə loj′i kəl) *adj.* —**sex·ol′o·gist** *n.*

sex-starved (-stärvd′) *adj.* of or relating to someone who is not obtaining sufficient sexual gratification

sext (sekst) *n.* [< ML. < L. *sexta* (*hora*), sixth (hour)] [*often* S-] the fourth of the canonical hours, orig. set for the sixth hour of the day (counting from 6 A.M.), or noon

sex·tant (seks′tənt) *n.* [ModL. *sextans,* arc of a sixth part of a circle < L. < *sextus,* sixth] an instrument used by navigators for measuring the angular distance of the sun, a star, etc. from the horizon, as in finding the position of a ship

sex·tet, sex·tette (seks tet′) *n.* [altered (after L. *sex,* six) < SESTET] **1.** any group of six **2.** *Music* a) a composition for six voices or instruments b) the six performers of this

sex·til·lion (seks til′yən) *n.* [Fr. < L. *sextus,* sixth + Fr. (m)*illion*] **1.** in Great Britain and Germany, the number represented by 1 followed

SEXTANT

by 36 zeros **2.** in the U.S. and France, the number represented by 1 followed by 21 zeros —*adj.* amounting to one sextillion in number

sex·ton (seks′tən) *n.* [< OFr. < ML. *sacristanus,* SACRISTAN] a church official in charge of the maintenance of church property, who often acts as gravedigger, etc.

sex·tu·ple (seks tyoo′p′l, seks′tyoo p′l) *adj.* [< L. *sextus,* sixth, after QUADRUPLE] **1.** consisting of six **2.** six times as much or as many **3.** *Music* having six beats to the bar —*n.* an amount six times as much or as many —*vt., vi.* -**pled, -pling** to multiply by six

sex·tu·plet (seks′tyoo plit; seks tyoo′plit) *n.* [dim. of prec.] **1.** any of six offspring born at a single birth **2.** a group of six, usually of one kind

sex·u·al (sek′shoo wəl) *adj.* **1.** of or involving sex, the sexes, the organs of sex and their functions, etc. **2.** *Biol.* a) having sex b) designating or of reproduction by the union of male and female germ cells —**sex′u·al′i·ty** (-wal′ə tē) *n.* —**sex′u·al·ly** *adv.*

sex·y (sek′sē) *adj.* **sex′i·er, sex′i·est** [Colloq.] exciting or intended to excite sexual desire; erotic —**sex′i·ly** *adv.* —**sex′i·ness** *n.*

sez (sez) *vi.* [Slang] *same as* says (see SAY), esp. in **sez you**

s.f., sf, SF science fiction

sf., sfz. sforzando

S.F.A. Scottish Football Association

sfor·zan·do (sfôr tsän′dō) *adj., adv.* [It. < *sforzare,* to force] *Music* with emphasis: abbrev. **sf., sfz.** —*n., pl.* -**dos** a sforzando note or chord Also **sfor·za′to** (-tsä′tō)

S.G. 1. Solicitor General **2.** Specific Gravity

sgd. signed

sgraf·fi·to (skra fē′tō) *n., pl.* -**fi′ti** (-tē) [It. < *sgraffiare,* to scratch] **1.** the producing of a design on ceramics, stuccoed façades, etc. by incising the outer coating to reveal a ground of different colour **2.** such a design or the object bearing it

Sgt, Sgt. Sergeant

sh (sh: *a lengthened sound*) *interj.* hush!

sh. 1. share(s) **2.** shilling(s)

shab·by (shab′ē) *adj.* -**bi·er, -bi·est** [< dial. *shab,* scab < OE. *sceabb*] **1.** run down; dilapidated **2.** a) showing much wear; threadbare: said of clothing b) wearing such clothing **3.** beggarly; unworthy *[a shabby* offering*]* **4.** shameful *[shabby* treatment*]* —**shab′bi·ly** *adv.* —**shab′bi·ness** *n.*

shab·by-gen·teel (-jen tēl′) *adj.* shabby but genteel in trying to keep up appearances

shack (shak) *n.* [prob. < Scot. dial. *shachle,* a shanty] a small, crudely built cabin; shanty —**shack up with** [Slang] to share living quarters with (one's lover)

shack·le (shak′′l) *n.* [OE. *sceacul*] **1.** a metal fastening, usually one of a linked pair, for the wrist or ankle of a prisoner; fetter; manacle **2.** [*usually pl.*] anything that keeps one from acting, thinking, or developing freely **3.** any of several devices for fastening or coupling —*vt.* -**led, -ling** to bind, fasten, or hinder with or as with shackles —**shack′ler** *n.*

shad (shad) *n., pl.* **shad, shads:** see PLURAL, II, D, 2 [OE. *sceadd*] **1.** any of several herringlike saltwater food fishes that spawn in rivers **2.** any of various similar fishes, esp. the **gizzard**

SHACKLES

shad, often stocked in fresh waters as food for other fish

shade (shād) *n.* [OE. *sceadu*] **1.** slight darkness caused by a more or less opaque object cutting off rays of light, as from the sun **2.** an area less brightly lighted than its surroundings, as an open place sheltered from sunlight **3.** [Archaic] a) a shadow b) [*often pl.*] a secluded place **4.** a representation of darkness in a painting, etc. **5.** degree of darkness of a colour **6.** a) a small difference *[shades of* opinion*]* b) a slight amount or degree; trace *[a shade of* humour in his voice*]* **7.** [Chiefly Literary] a) a ghost b) anything lacking reality **8.** any device used to protect or screen from light, esp. a partial cover for an electric lamp, etc.: in full, **lamp shade** —*vt.* **shad′ed, shad′ing 1.** to protect or screen from light or heat **2.** to provide with a shade **3.** to hide or screen as with a shadow **4.** to darken; dim **5.** a) to represent the effects of shade in (a painting, etc.) b) to mark with gradations of light or colour **6.** to change by very slight degrees or gradations **7.** to lessen (a price) slightly —*vi.* **1.** to change or vary slightly or by degrees —**in** (or **into**) **the shade 1.** in or into darkness or shadow **2.** in or into comparative obscurity —**shades of (something)!** how suggestive of (something past)! *[shades of* my father*]* —**the shades 1.** the increasing darkness, as of evening **2.** Hades —**shade′less** *adj.*

shad·ing (-iŋ) *n.* **1.** a shielding against light **2.** the representation of light or shade in a picture **3.** any small variation, as in quality

sha·doof (shə doof′) *n.* [Ar. *shādūf*] a device used in the Near East for irrigating the land consisting of a pivoted pole with a bucket on one end and a weight on the other

shad·ow (shad′ō) *n.* [< dat. & gen. of OE. *sceadu*, shade] 1. the darkness or the dark shape cast upon a surface by something cutting off light from it 2. [*pl.*] the growing darkness after sunset 3. *a*) gloom, sadness, etc. *b*) anything causing gloom, doubt, etc. 4. a dark or shaded area, as in a picture 5. *a*) something imagined, not real *b*) a ghost; apparition 6. a vague indication or omen 7. *a*) a faint suggestion or appearance; trace [a *shadow* of hope] *b*) remnant; vestige 8. a constant companion 9. a person who trails another closely, as a spy —*vt.* 1. to throw a shadow upon 2. to make dark or gloomy 3. to foreshadow (often with *forth*) 4. to follow closely, esp. in secret —*adj.* designating a member of the parliamentary opposition in Britain who would be a minister if his party were in power —**in** (or **under**) **the shadow of** 1. very close to 2. under the influence of —**under the shadow of** 1. *see prec. phrase* 2. in danger of —**shad′ow·er** *n.* —**shad′ow·less** *adj.*
shad·ow·box (-boks′) *vi.* to spar with an imaginary opponent, esp. in training as a boxer —**shad′ow·box′ing** *n.*
shadow cabinet members of the opposition party in the British Parliament selected to form a cabinet that is a counterpart of the one in power
shad·ow·y (shad′ə wē) *adj.* 1. that is or is like a shadow; specif., *a*) without reality; illusory *b*) dim; indistinct 2. shaded or full of shadow —**shad′ow·i·ness** *n.*
shad·y (shād′ē) *adj.* **shad′i·er**, **shad′i·est** 1. giving shade 2. shaded, as from the sun; full of shade 3. [Colloq.] of questionable character or honesty —**on the shady side of** beyond (a given age) —**shad′i·ly** *adv.* —**shad′i·ness** *n.*
shaft (shäft) *n.* [OE. *sceaft*] 1. *a*) the long stem or handle of an arrow or spear *b*) an arrow or spear 2. a missile or something like a missile [*shafts* of light, wit, etc.] 3. a long, slender part or object; specif., *a*) the stem of a feather *b*) a column or obelisk; also, the main, usually cylindrical, part between the ends of a column *c*) a flagpole *d*) a handle, as on some tools or implements *e*) either of the two poles between which an animal is harnessed to a vehicle *f*) a bar supporting, or transmitting motion to, a mechanical part [the drive *shaft* of an engine] 4. a long, narrow opening sunk into the earth [a mine *shaft*] 5. a vertical opening through the floors of a building 6. a conduit for air, as in heating —*vt.* [U.S. Slang] to cheat, trick, exploit, etc.
shag¹ (shag) *n.* [OE. *sceacga*, akin to ON. *skegg*, a beard] 1. *a*) a heavy, rough nap, as on some woollen cloth *b*) cloth with such a nap 2. any disordered, tangled mass 3. coarse, shredded tobacco —*vt.* **shagged**, **shag′ging** to make shaggy or rough
shag² (shag) *n.* [< prec.: prob. with reference to the rough crest] any of various cormorants, esp. a very dark-green bird common along Brit. coasts
shag³ (shag) *vt.* [< ?] 1. to have sexual intercourse with: usually regarded as a vulgar usage 2. [Slang] to exhaust: esp. in **shagged out**
shag·bark (shag′bärk′) *n.* 1. a N American hickory tree with grey, shredding bark 2. its wood 3. its edible nut
shag·gy (shag′ē) *adj.* **-gi·er**, **-gi·est** 1. covered with long, coarse hair or wool 2. carelessly groomed; unkempt 3. of tangled, coarse growth; straggly 4. having a rough nap or surface —**shag′gi·ly** *adv.* —**shag′gi·ness** *n.*
shaggy dog (story) a long, rambling joke, usually having an irrelevant conclusion
sha·green (shə grēn′) *n.* [Fr. *chagrin* < Turk. *saghri*, hide] 1. rawhide with a rough, granular surface, made from the skin of a horse, seal, etc. 2. the hard, rough skin of the shark or dogfish
shah (shä) *n.* [Per. *shāh*] a title of the ruler of Iran
Shak. Shakespeare
shake (shāk) *vt.* **shook**, **shak′en**, **shak′ing** [OE. *sceacan*] 1. to cause to move up and down, back and forth, or from side to side with short, quick movements 2. to bring, force, mix, scatter, etc. by abrupt, brisk movements [*shake* the medicine before taking it, *shake* salt on the steak] 3. to cause to tremble 4. *a*) to cause to totter or become unsteady *b*) to unnerve; upset [he was *shaken* by the news] 5. to brandish; wave 6. to clasp (another's hand), as in greeting 7. [U.S. Colloq.] to get away from or rid of [to *shake* one's pursuers] 8. *Music* same as TRILL —*vi.* 1. to move quickly up and down, back and forth, etc.; vibrate 2. to tremble, quiver, etc., as from cold or fear 3. to become unsteady; totter 4. to clasp each other's hand, as in greeting 5. *Music* same as TRILL —*n.* 1. an act of shaking 2. an unsteady movement; tremor 3. a natural fissure in rock or timber 4. a long shingle split from a log 5. [Colloq.] an earthquake 6. *short for* MILKSHAKE 7. [*pl.*] [Colloq.] a convulsive trembling (usually with *the*) 8. [Colloq.] a moment [be back in a *shake*] 9. *Music* same as TRILL —**no great shakes** [Colloq.] not outstanding or unusual —**shake down** 1. to bring down or cause to fall by shaking 2. to cause to settle by shaking 3. to test or condition (new equipment, etc.) 4. to go to bed, esp. to a makeshift bed 5. [Chiefly U.S. Slang] to extort money from —**shake hands** to clasp each other's hand as a token of agreement or friendship, or in parting or greeting —**shake**

off to get away from or rid of —**shake out** to make fall out, empty, straighten out, etc. by shaking —**shake up** 1. to shake, esp. so as to mix or loosen 2. to disturb or rouse by or as by shaking 3. to jar or shock 4. to reorganize as by shaking —**shak′a·ble, shake′a·ble** *adj.*
shake·down (shāk′doun′) *n.* 1. a makeshift bed 2. [Chiefly U.S. Colloq.] an extortion of money, as by blackmail 3. [Chiefly U.S. Colloq.] a thorough search of a person or place —*adj.* for testing the performance, acclimatizing the personnel, etc. [the *shakedown* cruise for a ship]
shak·en (-′n) *pp. of* SHAKE
shak·er (shā′kər) *n.* 1. a person or thing that shakes 2. a device used in shaking [a cocktail *shaker*] 3. [S-] [short for earlier *Shaking Quaker*: from trembling under emotional stress of devotions] a member of a former religious sect practising celibacy, communal living, etc.
Shakespearean sonnet a sonnet composed of three quatrains and a final couplet
shake-up (shāk′up′) *n.* a shaking up; specif., an extensive reorganization, as in policy or personnel
shak·o (shak′ō) *n., pl.* **shak′os** [< Fr. < Hung. *csákó* < ? G. *Zacke, a peak*] a stiff, cylindrical military dress hat, usually with a flat top and a plume
shak·y (shā′kē) *adj.* **shak′i·er**, **shak′i·est** 1. not firm, substantial, etc.; weak, unsound, etc., as a structure, belief, etc. 2. *a*) trembling *b*) nervous or jittery 3. not dependable or reliable; questionable [*shaky* evidence] —**shak′i·ly** *adv.* —**shak′i·ness** *n.*
shale (shāl) *n.* [OE. *scealu*, a shell] a fine-grained rock formed largely by the hardening of clay: it splits easily into thin layers —**shal′y** *adj.* **shal′i·er**, **shal′i·est**

SHAKO

shall (shal; *unstressed* shəl) *v., pt.* **should** [OE. *sceal*, inf. *sceolan*] 1. an auxiliary sometimes used to express the simple future in the first person [I *shall* tell him] and determination, obligation, etc. in the second and third persons [you *shall* obey]: see also WILL² 2. an auxiliary regularly used: *a*) in questions in the first person asking for agreement [*shall* we dance?] *b*) in laws and resolutions [the fine *shall* not exceed £100]
shal·lop (shal′əp) *n.* [< Fr., prob. orig. fig. use of *chaloupe*, nutshell, ult. < OFr. *escalope*, SCALLOP] any of various former small open boats fitted with oars or sails or both
shal·lot (shə lot′) *n.* [obs. Fr. *eschalotte*, altered < OFr. *eschaloigne*, scallion] a small onion whose clustered bulbs, like garlic but milder, are used for flavouring
shal·low (shal′ō) *adj.* [ME. *shalow* < OE. hyp. *scealw*] 1. not deep [a *shallow* lake] 2. lacking depth of character or intellect; superficial —*n.* [usually *pl.*, often with sing. *v.*] a shallow place in water; shoal —*vt., vi.* to make or become shallow —**shal′low·ly** *adv.* —**shal′low·ness** *n.*
sha·lom (shä lōm′, sha-) *n., interj.* [Heb. *shālōm*, lit., peace] a word used as the traditional Jewish greeting or farewell
shalt (shalt; *unstressed* shalt) *archaic 2nd pers. sing., pres. indic., of* SHALL
sham (sham) *n.* [prob. < a dial. var. of SHAME] 1. *a*) an imitation that is meant to deceive *b*) a hypocritical action, false appearance, etc. 2. one who falsely affects a certain character —*adj.* not genuine or real; false; fake —*vt., vi.* to fake; pretend —**sham′mer** *n.*
sha·man (sham′ən) *n., pl.* **-mans** [Russ., ult. < Prakrit *śamana*, Buddhist monk] a priest or medicine man of shamanism —**sha·man·ic** (shə man′ik) *adj.*
sha·man·ism (-iz′m) *n.* 1. a religion of northeast Asia, based on a belief in spirits who are influenced only by shamans 2. a similar religion of some American Indians —**sha′man·ist** *n.* —**sha′man·is′tic** *adj.*
sham·a·teur (sham′ə tər) *n.* [SHAM + (AM)ATEUR] a sports player who although technically an amateur makes gains from his sport
sham·ble (sham′b'l) *vi.* **-bled, -bling** [orig. *adj.*, in *shamble legs*, prob. < ff., in obs. sense of stool] to walk in a clumsy manner, barely lifting the feet —*n.* a shambling walk
sham·bles (-b'lz) *n.pl.* [with sing. *v.*] [OE. *scamol*, a bench, ult. < L. *scamellum*, dim. < *scamnum*, a bench] 1. a slaughterhouse 2. a scene of great slaughter or bloodshed 3. any scene or condition of great destruction or disorder [the children left the room a *shambles*]
shame (shām) *n.* [OE. *scamu*] 1. a painful feeling of having lost the respect of others because of the improper behaviour, incompetence, etc. of oneself or another 2. a capacity for such feeling 3. dishonour or disgrace 4. a person or thing that brings dishonour or disgrace 5. something unfortunate or outrageous —*vt.* **shamed, sham′ing** 1. to cause to feel shame 2. to dishonour or disgrace 3. to force by a sense of shame [*shamed* into apologizing] —**for shame!** you

ought to be ashamed! —**put to shame** 1. to cause to feel shame 2. to do much better than; surpass

shame·faced (-fāst′) *adj.* [altered < OE. < *scamu,* shame + *fæst,* fast] 1. shy or bashful 2. showing a feeling of shame; ashamed —**shame·fac·ed·ly** (shām′fās′id lē, shām′- fāst′lē) *adv.* —**shame′fac′ed·ness** *n.*

shame·ful (-fəl) *adj.* 1. bringing or causing shame or disgrace; disgraceful 2. not just, moral, or decent; offensive —**shame′ful·ly** *adv.* —**shame′ful·ness** *n.*

shame·less (-lis) *adj.* having or showing no shame, modesty, or decency; brazen —**shame′less·ly** *adv.* —**shame′- less·ness** *n.*

sham·my (sham′ē) *n., pl.* **-mies;** *adj., vt.* **-mied, -my·ing** *same as* CHAMOIS (*n.* 2, *adj.* 1, *vt.*)

sham·poo (sham pōō′) *vt.* **-pooed′, -poo′ing** [Hindi *chāmpo,* imper. of *chāmpnā,* to press] 1. formerly, to massage 2. to wash (the hair and scalp), esp. with shampoo 3. to wash the hair and scalp of 4. to wash (a rug, upholstery, etc.) with a shampoo —*n.* 1. the act of washing hair, a rug, etc. 2. a special soap, or soaplike preparation, that produces suds —**sham·poo′er** *n.*

sham·rock (sham′rok′) *n.* [< Ir. dim. of *seamar,* clover] any of certain clovers or cloverlike plants with leaflets in groups of three: the emblem of Ireland

shan·dy (shan′dē) *n.* [< ?] a drink of beer mixed with ginger beer or lemonade: also **shan′dy-gaff** (-gaf′)

shang·hai (shaŋ hī′) *vt.* **-haied′, -hai′ing** [< *Shanghai,* seaport in E China, in allusion to such kidnapping for crews on the China run] 1. to kidnap, usually by drugging, for service aboard ship 2. [Slang] to induce (another) to do something through force or underhanded methods —**shang·hai′er** *n.*

Shan·gri-La (shaŋ′grə lä′) *n.* [< the scene of J. Hilton's novel, *Lost Horizon*] any imaginary, idyllic utopia or hidden paradise

shank (shaŋk) *n.* [OE. *scanca*] 1. the part of the leg between the knee and the ankle in man or a corresponding part in animals 2. the whole leg 3. a cut of meat from the leg of an animal 4. a straight, narrow part between other parts, as *a)* the part of a tool between the handle and the working part *b)* the narrow part of a shoe sole 5. a projection on some buttons by which they are sewn to fabric 6. the body of a piece of type —**ride** (or **go**) **on shank's mare** to walk: also **ride** (or **go**) **on shank's pony**

shan't (shant) shall not

shan·tey (shan′tē) *n., pl.* **-teys** *var. of* SHANTY

shan·tung (shan tuŋ′, shan′tuŋ′) *n.* [< *Shantung,* province of NE China] a fabric of silk with an uneven surface

shan·ty¹ (shan′tē) *n., pl.* **-ties** [< CanadFr. *chantier,* workshop] a small, shabby dwelling; hut

shan·ty² (shan′tē) *n., pl.* **-teys** [< ? Fr.: see CHANT] a song that sailors sing in rhythm with their actions while working

shan·ty·town (-toun′) *n.* the section of a city where there are many ramshackle houses

shape (shāp) *n.* [< OE. (ge)*sceap,* form, akin to *scieppan,* to create] 1. the way a thing looks because of its outline; outer form 2. the form of a particular person or thing, or class of things 3. the contour of the body; figure 4. assumed appearance; guise [a foe in the *shape* of a friend] 5. a phantom 6. a mould used for shaping 7. definite or regular form [to bring to take *shape*] 8. [Colloq.] *a)* condition; state [a patient in poor *shape*] *b)* good physical condition [exercises that keep one in *shape*] —*vt.* **shaped, shap′ing** 1. to give definite shape to; make 2. to arrange, express, or devise (a plan, answer, etc.) in definite form 3. to adapt [*shape* your plans to your abilities] 4. to direct or conduct (one's life, the course of events, etc.) —*vi.* [Colloq.] to take shape —**shape up** [Colloq.] 1. to develop to a definite form, condition, etc. 2. to develop satisfactorily 3. to behave as required —**take shape** to begin to have definite form —**shap′er** *n.*

SHAPE (shāp) Supreme Headquarters Allied Powers, Europe

shape·less (-lis) *adj.* 1. without distinct or regular form 2. without a pleasing shape; unshapely —**shape′less·ly** *adv.* —**shape′less·ness** *n.*

shape·ly (-lē) *adj.* **-li·er, -li·est** having a pleasing shape; well-proportioned: used esp. of a woman —**shape′li·ness** *n.*

shard (shärd) *n.* [OE. *sceard*] 1. a fragment or broken piece, esp. of pottery; potsherd 2. *Zool.* a hard covering, as a shell, plate, or scale

share¹ (sher) *n.* [OE. *scearu*] 1. a part or portion that belongs to an individual, or the part contributed by one 2. a just or full part [to do one's *share* of work] 3. any of the parts into which the ownership of a property is divided; esp., any of the equal parts of the capital stock of a corporation —*vt.* **shared, shar′ing** 1. to distribute in shares 2. to receive, use, experience, etc. in common with another or others —*vi.* 1. to have a share; participate (often with *in*) 2. to share or divide something equally (often with *out* or *with*) —**go shares** to take part jointly, as in an enterprise —**share and share alike** with each having an equal share —**shar′er** *n.*

share² (sher) *n.* [OE. *scear*] the part of a plough or other agricultural tool that cuts the soil

share·crop (sher′krop′) *vi., vt.* **-cropped′, -crop′ping** [Chiefly U.S.] to work (land) for a share of the crop, esp. as a tenant farmer —**share′crop′per** *n.*

share·hold·er (sher′hōl′dər) *n.* a person who holds or owns a share or shares, esp. in a corporation

share list a list of prices of shares of companies, etc.

share-out (-out) *n.* a distribution of goods, profits, etc.

shark¹ (shärk) *n.* [prob. < G. *Schurke,* scoundrel] a person who victimizes others, as by swindling

shark² (shärk) *n.* [? akin to prec.] any of numerous, usually large, mostly marine fishes with a tough, slate-grey skin: most sharks are fish-eaters and some will attack man

shark·skin (-skin′) *n.* 1. leather made from the skin of a shark 2. a cloth of cotton, wool, rayon, etc. with a smooth, silky surface 3. a fabric woven with a pebbly pattern

SHARK
(13.5 m maximum
length)

sharp (shärp) *adj.* [OE. *scearp*] 1. having a very thin edge or fine point, suitable for cutting or piercing; keen 2. having a point or edge; not rounded [a *sharp* ridge] 3. not gradual; abrupt [a *sharp* turn] 4. clearly defined; distinct [a *sharp* contrast] 5. quick or acute in perception or intellect; specif., *a)* acutely sensitive in seeing, hearing, etc. *b)* clever 6. attentive; vigilant [a *sharp* lookout] 7. crafty; underhanded 8. harsh, biting, or severe [*sharp* criticism] 9. violent [a *sharp* attack] 10. brisk; active [a *sharp* run] 11. severe; intense [a *sharp* pain] 12. strong; pungent, as in taste 13. high-pitched; shrill [a *sharp* sound] 14. cold and cutting [a *sharp* wind] 15. [Slang] attractively dressed or groomed 16. *Music a)* higher in pitch by a semitone [C *sharp* (C♯)] *b)* above true pitch —*n.* 1. a long thin needle with a sharp point 2. *same as* SHARK¹, SHARPER 3. *Music a)* a tone one semitone above another *b)* the symbol (♯) indicating this —*adv.* 1. in a sharp manner; specif., *a)* keenly; piercingly *b) Music* above true pitch 2. precisely [one o'clock *sharp*] —**sharp′ish** *adj.* —**sharp′ly** *adv.* —**sharp′ness** *n.*

sharp·en (shär′p'n) *vt., vi.* to make or become sharp or sharper —**sharp′en·er** *n.*

sharp·er (-pər) *n.* a person, esp. a gambler, who is dishonest in dealing with others; swindler

sharp practice unscrupulous, underhand, usually dishonest dealings

sharp-set (-set) *adj.* 1. set to give an acute cutting edge 2. hungry; ravenous 3. keen or eager

sharp·shoot·er (shärp′shōōt′ər) *n.* a person who shoots with great accuracy; good marksman —**sharp′shoot′ing** *n.*

sharp-tongued (-tuŋd′) *adj.* using or characterized by sharp or harshly critical language

sharp-wit·ted (-wit′id) *adj.* having or showing keen intelligence; thinking quickly and effectively —**sharp′-wit′- ted·ly** *adv.* —**sharp′-wit′ted·ness** *n.*

shas·ter (shas′tər) *n.* [< Sans. *śāstra*] one of Vedas or other books of the Brahmanic scriptures: also **shas′tra** (-trə)

shat·ter (shat′ər) *vt.* [ME. *schateren,* to scatter] 1. to break into pieces suddenly, as with a blow 2. to damage severely [to *shatter* one's health] —*vi.* to burst into pieces

shat·ter·proof (-prōōf′) *adj.* that will resist shattering

shave (shāv) *vt.* **shaved, shav′en, shav′ing** [OE. *sceafan*] 1. to cut or scrape away thin slices from [to *shave* the edge of a door] 2. *a)* to cut off (hair, esp. the beard) at the surface of the skin (often with *off* or *away*) *b)* to cut the hair to the surface of [to *shave* the chin, the legs, etc.] *c)* to cut the beard of (a person) 3. to barely touch or almost touch in passing; graze 4. to trim (grass, etc.) closely —*vi.* to cut off hair with a razor; shave oneself —*n.* 1. a tool used for cutting off thin slices 2. something shaved off; shaving 3. the act or an instance of shaving the beard

shav·en (shā′v'n) *alt. pp. of* SHAVE —*adj.* 1. shaved or tonsured 2. closely trimmed

shav·er (-vər) *n.* 1. a person who shaves 2. *same as* RAZOR (sense 2) 3. [Colloq.] a boy; lad

Sha·vi·an (shā′vē ən) *adj.* [< ModL. *Shavius,* Latinized < G. B. *Shaw,* Brit. dramatist] of or characteristic of George Bernard Shaw or his work —*n.* an admirer of Shaw or his work

shav·ing (shā′viŋ) *n.* 1. the act of one that shaves 2. a thin piece of wood, metal, etc. shaved off

shawl (shôl) *n.* [prob. via Urdu < Per. *shāl*] an oblong or square cloth worn, esp. by women, as a covering for the head or shoulders

shawm (shôm) *n.* [< MFr., ult. from L. *calamus,* a reed] an early double-reed wind instrument resembling the oboe

shay (shā) *n.* [back-formation < CHAISE, assumed as pl.] [Dial.] a light carriage; chaise

she (shē; *unstressed* shi) *pron.* *for pl. see* THEY [prob. after OE. *seo*, fem. def. article, replacing OE. *heo*, she] the woman, girl, or female animal (or the object regarded as female) previously mentioned: *she* is the nominative case form of the feminine third personal pronoun —*n.*, *pl.* **shes** a woman, girl, or female animal

shead·ing (shēd'iŋ) *n.* [*var. of shedding:* see SHED²] any of the six constituencies of the Isle of Man

sheaf (shēf) *n.*, *pl.* **sheaves** [OE. *sceaf*] 1. a bunch of cut stalks of grain, etc. bound together 2. a collection, as of papers, bound in a bundle —*vt.* *same as* SHEAVE²

shear (shir) *vt.* **sheared**, **sheared** or **shorn**, **shear'ing** [OE. *scieran*] 1. to cut as with shears 2. *a)* to remove (the hair, wool, etc.) by cutting *b)* to cut the hair, wool, etc. from 3. to tear (*off*) by shearing stress 4. to move through as if cutting 5. to strip (*of* a power, right, etc.) —*vi.* 1. to use shears, etc. in cutting wool, metal, etc. 2. to break under a shearing stress 3. to move as if by cutting —*n.* 1. *a) rare var. of* SHEARS *b)* a single blade of a pair of shears 2. a machine used in cutting metal 3. the act or result of shearing; specif., the shearing of wool from an animal [a sheep of three *shears*] 4. *same as* SHEARING STRESS —**shear'er** *n.*

sheared (shird) *adj.* subjected to shearing: said esp. of fur trimmed to give it an even surface

shearing stress the force causing two contacting parts to slide upon each other in opposite directions parallel to their plane of contact

shear·ling (shir'liŋ) *n.* [see SHEAR & -LING¹] 1. a sheep that has been sheared once, usually a yearling 2. lambskin or sheepskin from an animal killed not long after being sheared

shears (shirz) *n.pl.* [*also with sing. v.*] 1. large scissors: also called **pair of shears** 2. any of several large tools or machines with two opposed blades, used to cut metal, etc.

shear·wa·ter (shir'wôt'ər) *n.* any of various black-and-white sea birds, related to the albatrosses, that skim the water in flight

sheath (shēth) *n.*, *pl.* **sheaths** (shēthz, shēths) [OE. *sceath*] 1. a case for the blade of a knife, sword, etc. 2. a covering resembling this, as the membrane round a muscle, etc. 3. a woman's closefitting dress —*vt.* *same as* SHEATHE

sheathe (shēth) *vt.* **sheathed**, **sheath'ing** 1. to put into a sheath or scabbard 2. to enclose in a case or covering

sheath·ing (shē'thiŋ) *n.* something that sheathes, as the inner covering of boards or waterproof material on a roof

sheath knife a knife carried in a sheath

sheave¹ (shēv, shiv) *n.* [ME. *scheve*] a wheel with a grooved rim, as in a pulley block

sheave² (shēv) *vt.* **sheaved**, **sheav'ing** [< SHEAF] to gather and fix (grain, papers, etc.) in a sheaf or sheaves

sheaves¹ (shēvz) *n.* *pl. of* SHEAF

sheaves² (shēvz) *n.* *pl. of* SHEAVE¹

she·bang (shə baŋ') *n.* [U.S. Colloq.] an affair, business, contrivance, thing, etc.: chiefly in **the whole shebang**

she·been (shi bēn') *n.* [Anglo-Ir. < Ir. *síbín*, little mug] a house or establishment in Ireland or Scotland where alcohol is sold without a licence

shed¹ (shed) *n.* [OE. *scead*] 1. a small, rough building or lean-to, used for shelter or storage 2. a large, barnlike or hangarlike structure for storage

shed² (shed) *vt.* **shed**, **shed'ding** [OE. *sceadan*, to separate] 1. to pour out; emit 2. to cause to flow; let fall in drops [to *shed* tears] 3. to send forth or spread about; radiate [to *shed* confidence] 4. to cause to flow off without going through; repel [oilskin *sheds* water] 5. to cast off (a natural growth or covering, as leaves, hair, etc.) —*vi.* to shed leaves, hair, etc. —*n.* [ME. *schede*, division] a ridge of high ground; specif., *same as* WATERSHED —**shed blood** to kill in a violent way —**shed'der** *n.*

she'd (shēd) 1. she had 2. she would

sheen (shēn) *n.* [< the adj.] 1. brightness; lustre 2. bright attire —*adj.* [OE. *sciene*, beautiful] [Archaic] of shining beauty; bright

sheep (shēp) *n.*, *pl.* **sheep** [OE. *sceap*] 1. a cud-chewing mammal related to the goats with heavy wool and edible flesh called mutton 2. leather made from sheepskin 3. a person who is meek, stupid, timid, etc. 4. a member of a church's congregation —**make** (or **cast**) **sheep's eyes at** to look shyly but amorously at

sheep·cote (-kōt') *n.* [cf. COTE] *var. of* SHEEPFOLD: also **sheep'cot'** (-kot')

sheep·dip (-dip') *n.* any chemical preparation used as a bath, as to free sheep from vermin or to clean the fleece

sheep dog any dog trained to herd and protect sheep

sheep·fold (-fōld') *n.* a pen or enclosure for sheep

sheep·ish (-ish) *adj.* 1. *a)* embarrassed by being caught in a mistake, lie, etc. *b)* awkwardly shy or bashful 2. meek, timid, etc. like sheep —**sheep'ish·ly** *adv.* —**sheep'ish·ness** *n.*

sheep run grazing land for sheep, esp. in Australia

sheep·shank (-shaŋk') *n.* a knot used for shortening a rope

sheep·skin (-skin') *n.* 1. the skin of a sheep, esp. with the fleece left on 2. parchment or leather made from the skin of a sheep 3. [U.S. Colloq.] *same as* DIPLOMA

sheep·walk (-wôk') *n.* a tract of land for grazing sheep

sheer¹ (shir) *vi.* [var. of SHEAR] to turn aside from a course; swerve; deviate —*vt.* to cause to sheer —*n.* 1. deviation from a course 2. the oblique heading of a ship riding at a single bow anchor 3. the upward curve of a ship's deck lines as seen from the side

sheer² (shir) *adj.* [ON. *skærr*] 1. very thin; transparent: said of textiles 2. not mixed with anything else; pure 3. absolute; downright [*sheer* persistence] 4. extremely steep, as the face of a cliff —*adv.* 1. completely; utterly 2. very steeply —*n.* thin, fine material —**sheer off** fight shy of; keep away from —**sheer'ly** *adv.* —**sheer'ness** *n.*

sheet¹ (shēt) *n.* [OE. *sceat*] 1. a large piece of cotton, linen, etc., used on a bed 2. *a)* a single piece of paper *b)* a large piece of paper with a number of pages printed on it, to be folded into a signature for binding into a book: *usually used in pl. c)* [Colloq.] a newspaper [a scandal *sheet*] 3. a broad, continuous surface or layer, as of flame, water, etc. 4. a broad, thin piece of any material, as glass, metal, etc. 5. [Chiefly Poet.] a sail 6. *Philately* a complete page of stamps, printed by a single impression of a plate —*vt.* to cover or provide with, or form into, a sheet or sheets —*adj.* in the form of a sheet [*sheet* iron] —**sheet'like'** *adj.*

sheet² (shēt) *n.* [short for OE. *sceatline*] 1. a rope for controlling the set of a sail, attached to a lower corner 2. [*pl.*] the spaces not occupied by thwarts, at the bow and stern of an open boat —**three sheets in** (or **to**) **the wind** [Slang] very drunk

sheet anchor 1. a large anchor used only in emergencies 2. a person or thing to be relied upon in emergency

sheet bend *Naut.* a knot used in fastening a rope to the bight of another rope or to an eye

sheet·ing (shēt'iŋ) *n.* 1. cotton or linen material used for making sheets 2. material used in covering or lining a surface [copper *sheeting*]

sheet metal metal rolled thin in the form of a sheet

sheet music music printed on unbound sheets of paper

sheik, sheikh (shāk, shēk) *n.* [Ar. *shaikh*, old man] 1. the chief of an Arab family, tribe, or village 2. an official in the Moslem religious organization —**sheik'dom, sheikh'dom** *n.*

shei·la (shē'lə) *n.* [< *Sheila*, a feminine name] [Aust. Colloq.] a girl or young woman

shek·el (shek'l) *n.* [< Heb. < *shāqal*, to weigh] 1. among the ancient Hebrews, Babylonians, etc., a unit of weight (about 15 gm), or a gold or silver coin of this weight 2. [*pl.*] [Slang] money

shel·duck (shel'duk) *n.*, *pl.* **-drakes', -drake':** see PLURAL, II, D,1 [prob. < a ME. cognate of MDu. *schillede*, variegated + *drake*, drake] a large wild duck found in Europe, Asia, etc., that feeds on fish, etc. and nests in burrows: the plumage is variegated: also **shel'drake'** (-drāk')

shelf (shelf) *n.*, *pl.* **shelves** [prob. < MLowG. *schelf*] 1. a thin, flat length of wood, metal, etc. fixed horizontally to a wall, or in a cupboard, etc., used for holding things 2. the contents or capacity of a shelf 3. something like a shelf; specif., *a)* a flat ledge of rock *b)* a sand bar or reef —**on the shelf** 1. out of use, circulation, etc. 2. unmarried, said esp. of a woman —**shelf'like'** *adj.*

shelf life the length of time a packaged food, etc. can be stored without deteriorating

shell (shel) *n.* [OE. *sciel*] 1. a hard outer covering, as of a turtle, egg, nut, etc. 2. something like a shell in being hollow, empty, a covering, etc., as the hull of a boat, the framework of a building, etc. 3. a shy or uncommunicative manner [to come out of one's *shell*] 4. a light, long, narrow racing boat rowed by a team of oarsmen 5. an explosive artillery projectile containing high explosives and sometimes shrapnel, chemicals, etc. 6. a small-arms cartridge —*vt.* 1. to remove the shell or covering from [to *shell* peas] 2. to fire shells at from large guns; bombard —*vi.* 1. to separate from the shell or covering 2. to fall or peel off, as a shell —**shell out** [Colloq.] to pay out (money) —**shell'-like'** *adj.* —**shell'y** *adj.*

she'll (shēl; *unstressed* shil) 1. she shall 2. she will

shel·lac (shə lak') *n.* [SHEL(L) + LAC, used as transl. of Fr. *laque en écailles*, lac in fine sheets] 1. refined lac, a resin usually produced in thin, flaky layers, used in making varnish, gramophone records, etc. 2. a thin varnish containing this resin and alcohol —*vt.* **-lacked', -lack'ing** 1. to apply shellac to; cover with shellac 2. [U.S. Slang] to beat or defeat decisively

shell·back (shel'bak') *n.* [prob. referring to the shell of the sea turtle] 1. an old, experienced sailor 2. anyone who has crossed the equator by ship

-shelled (sheld) a *combining form meaning* having a (specified kind of) shell [soft-*shelled* crab]

shell·fire (shel'fīr') *n.* the firing of large shells

shell·fish (-fish') *n.*, *pl.* **-fish', -fish·es:** see FISH any aquatic animal with a shell, esp. an edible one, as the clam, lobster, etc.

shell game [U.S.] *same as* THIMBLERIG

shell·proof (-prōōf') *adj.* proof against damage from shells or bombs

shell shock *an earlier term for* COMBAT FATIGUE —**shell'-shocked'** *adj.*

shel·ta (shel'tə) *n.* [earlier *sheldru*, shelter ? ult. < OIr. *bēlre*, speech] a jargon based on Gaelic and used by tinkers, etc.

shel·ter (shel'tər) *n.* [< ? OE. *sceldtruma*, troop protected by interlocked shields < *scield*, shield + *truma*, a troop] **1.** something that covers or protects; place of protection against the elements, danger, etc. [a bus *shelter*] **2.** a being covered, protected, etc.; refuge —*vt.* to provide shelter or refuge for; protect —*vi.* to find shelter or refuge —**shel'-ter·er** *n.* —**shel'ter·less** *n.*

shel·tie, shel·ty (shel'tē) *n., pl.* **-ties** [prob. < Orkney pronun. of ON. *hjalti*, Shetlander] *same as:* **1.** SHETLAND PONY **2.** SHETLAND SHEEPDOG

shelve (shelv) *vi.* **shelved, shelv'ing** [< SHELF] to slope gradually —*vt.* **1.** to furnish with shelves **2.** to put on a shelf or shelves **3.** *a)* to lay aside [to *shelve* a discussion] *b)* to dismiss from active service

shelves (shelvz) *n. pl.* of SHELF

shelv·ing (shel'viŋ) *n.* **1.** material for shelves **2.** shelves collectively **3.** the condition or degree of sloping

she·nan·i·gan (shi nan'i gən) *n.* [altered < ? Ir. *sionna-chuighim*, I play the fox] [*usually pl.*] [Colloq.] nonsense; trickery; mischief

She·ol (shē'ōl, shē ōl') [< Heb. < *shā'al*, to dig] *Bible* a place in the depths of the earth conceived of as the dwelling of the dead

shep·herd (shep'ərd) *n.* [OE. *sceaphyrde*: see SHEEP & HERD²] **1.** a person who herds sheep **2.** a leader of a group; esp., a clergyman —*vt.* to herd, guard, lead, etc. as a shepherd —**shep'herd·ess** *n.fem.*

shepherd dog *same as* SHEEP DOG

shepherd's check (or **plaid**) **1.** a pattern of small checks formed by stripes of black and white **2.** fabric woven in this pattern

shepherd's pie a meat pie with mashed potatoes on top

shepherd's purse a small weed of the cabbage family, with triangular, pouchlike pods

Sher·a·ton (sher'ə tən) *adj.* [after T. *Sheraton* (1751–1806), Brit. cabinetmaker] designating or of a style of furniture having simplicity of form, straight lines, etc.

sher·bet (shur'bət) *n.* [< Turk. < Ar. *sharbah*, a drink] **1.** a beverage made of watered fruit juice and sugar **2.** a fruit-flavoured powder that effervesces when water is added **3.** [Chiefly U.S.] a frozen dessert like an ice cream but with gelatin and, often, milk added

sherd (shurd) *n. same as* SHARD (sense 1)

she·rif (shə rēf') *n.* [Ar. *sharif*, noble] **1.** a descendant of Mohammed through his daughter Fatima **2.** an Arab prince or chief

sher·iff (sher'if) *n.* [< OE. < *scir*, shire + *gerefa*, reeve] **1.** in England, esp. formerly, any of various officers of a shire, or county **2.** in Scotland, a judge or chief magistrate **3.** in the U.S., the chief law-enforcement officer of a county —**sher'iff·dom** *n.*

Sher·lock Holmes (shur'lok hōmz') [after *Sherlock Holmes*, the main character in many stories by A. Conan Doyle] any skilful detective or logical reasoner

Sher·pa (shur'pə) *n., pl.* **-pas, -pa** a member of a Tibetan people from the southern slopes of the Himalayas, famous as mountain climbers

sher·ry (sher'ē) *n., pl.* **-ries** [< earlier *sherris* < *Xeres* (now Jerez), Spain] **1.** a strong, yellow or brownish Spanish wine **2.** any similar wine made elsewhere esp. in S Africa or Cyprus

she's (shēz) **1.** she is **2.** she has

Shet·land pony (shet'lənd) any of a breed of sturdy ponies with a rough coat and long tail and mane, orig. from the Shetland Islands

Shetland sheep·dog (shēp'dog) any of a breed of dogs closely resembling collies but smaller: orig. from the Shetland Islands

shew (shō) *n., vt., vi.* **shewed, shewn** or **shewed, shew'ing** *archaic sp. of* SHOW

shew·bread (-bred') *n.* [prec. + BREAD, transl. of Heb. *lehem pānīm*, presence bread] *Ancient Judaism* the unleavened bread placed at the altar in the ancient Temple as an offering every Sabbath by the priests

shib·bo·leth (shib'ə ləth) *n.* [LL. < Heb. *shibbōleth*, a stream] something said or done that is a sign or test of belonging to a certain group, class, or party: after the test word used, in the Bible, by the men of Gilead to distinguish the escaping Ephraimites, who pronounced the initial (sh) as (s): Judg. 12:4-6

shied (shīd) *pt. & pp. of* SHY²

shi·cer (shī'sur) *n.* [< G. *scheissen*, to defecate] [Aust.] **1.** formerly, an unprofitable claim **2.** a man who does not pay his gambling debts

shield (shēld) *n.* [OE. *scield*] **1.** a broad piece of armour carried in the hand or worn on the forearm to ward off blows or missiles **2.** any person or thing that guards or protects **3.** anything shaped like a triangular shield, broad at the top and with curved sides, as an escutcheon, badge,

etc. **4.** a safety screen or guard, as over the moving parts of machinery **5.** a pad worn at the armpit to protect a garment from perspiration: also **dress shield** —*vt., vi.* to be a shield (for); defend; protect —**shield'er** *n.*

shiel·ing (shē'liŋ) *n.* [< Scot. *shiel*, hut + -ING] [Scot.] **1.** a grazing ground; pasture **2.** a rude hut or cottage Also **sheal'ing**

shift (shift) *vt.* [OE. *sciftan*, to divide] **1.** to move or transfer as from one person, place, direction, etc. to another **2.** to replace by another or others; change or exchange **3.** [Chiefly U.S.] to change the arrangement of (gears) in driving a motor vehicle **4.** [Colloq.] to move very quickly —*vi.* **1.** to change position, direction, form, etc. **2.** to get along; manage [to *shift* for oneself] **3.** to use tricky or expedient methods **4.** [Chiefly U.S.] to change from one gear arrangement to another **5.** in typing, to change from small letters, etc. to capitals, etc. by depressing a key (**shift key**) —*n.* **1.** the act of shifting; change [a *shift* in public opinion, a *shift* in the wind] **2.** a plan of conduct, esp. for an emergency; expedient; stratagem **3.** a deceitful scheme; trick **4.** a group of people working in relay with other groups, or the work period involved [the night *shift*] **5.** the displacement of a series or group [red *shift* in the Doppler Effect, vowel *shift*] **6.** *a)* [Now Rare] a woman's slip *b)* a loose dress that hangs straight with no waistline —**make shift** to manage or do the best one can (*with* whatever means are at hand) —**shift'a·ble** *adj.* —**shift'er** *n.*

shift·less (-lis) *adj.* lazy or careless —**shift'less·ly** *adv.* —**shift'less·ness** *n.*

shift·y (shif'tē) *adj.* **shift'i·er, shift'i·est** having or showing a nature that is not to be trusted; full of shifts; tricky—**shift'i·ly** *adv.* —**shift'i·ness** *n.*

shil·le·lagh, shil·la·lah (shi lā'lē, -lə) *n.* [< *Shillelagh*, Irish village] a club or cudgel: also sp. **shil·le'lah**

shil·ling (shil'iŋ) *n.* [OE. *scylling*] **1.** a British money of account and silver coin, equal to 1/20 of a pound: symbol, /: coinage discontinued in 1971 **2.** a money of account used in several other countries: see MONETARY UNITS, table

shil·ly-shal·ly (shil'ē shal'ē) *vi.* **-lied, -ly·ing** [a redupl. of *shall I?*] to be unable to make up one's mind; show indecision; vacillate —*n.* the act of shilly-shallying

shim (shim) *n.* [< ?] a thin piece of wood, metal, etc. used for filling space, levelling, etc. —*vt.* **shimmed, shim'ming** to fit with a shim or shims

shim·mer (shim'ər) *vi.* [OE. *scymrian*] **1.** to shine with an unsteady light; glimmer **2.** to form a wavering image, as by reflection from waves of heat —*n.* a shimmering light

shim·my (shim'ē) *n.* [< CHEMISE] **1.** a jazz dance of the 1920's, with much shaking of the body **2.** a shaking or wobbling, as in the front wheels of a motor car —*vi.* **-mied, -my·ing** to shake or wobble

shin (shin) *n.* [OE. *scinu*] **1.** the front part of the leg between the knee and the ankle **2.** the lower foreleg in beef —*vt., vi.* **shinned, shin'ning** to climb (a rope, pole, etc.) by gripping with both hands and legs: often with *up*

shin·bone (shin'bōn') *n. same as* TIBIA

shin·dig (shin'dig') *n.* [folk-etym. form of colloq. SHINDY] [Colloq.] a dance, party, or other social affair

shin·dy (shin'dē) *n., pl.* **-dies** [< ?] [Colloq.] a noisy disturbance; commotion

shine (shīn) *vi.* **shone, shin'ing** [OE. *scinan*] **1.** to give off or reflect light; gleam; glow **2.** to excel; be eminent **3.** to show itself clearly [to *shine* from her face] —*vt.* **1.** to direct the light of [to *shine* a flashlight] **2.** to make shiny by polishing —*n.* **1.** brightness; radiance **2.** lustre; polish; gloss **3.** [Chiefly U.S.] *short for* SHOESHINE **4.** splendour; brilliance **5.** sunshine; fair weather —**shine up to** [U.S. Slang] to curry favour with —**take a shine to** [Colloq.] take a liking to (someone)

shin·er (-ər) *n.* **1.** a person or thing that shines **2.** *pl.* **-ers, -er:** see PLURAL, II, D, **1** any of a number of freshwater minnows with silvery scales **3.** [Slang] a black eye, as from a blow

shin·gle¹ (shiŋ'g'l) *n.* [prob. < Scand.] **1.** coarse, waterworn gravel, as on a beach **2.** an area covered with this —**shin'gly** *adj.* **-gli·er, -gli·est**

shin·gle² (shiŋ'g'l) *n.* [prob. altered < OE. *scindel*, ult. < L. *scindula*, a shingle] **1.** a thin, wedge-shaped piece of wood, slate, etc. laid with others in a series of overlapping rows as a covering for roofs, etc. **2.** a woman's short haircut with the hair over the nape shaped close to the head **3.** [U.S. Colloq.] a small signboard, as that of a doctor or lawyer —*vt.* **-gled, -gling** **1.** to cover (a roof, etc.) with shingles **2.** to cut (hair) in shingle style

shin·gles (shiŋ'g'lz) *n.* [< ML. < L. *cingulum*, a girdle < *cingere*, to gird] *same as* HERPES ZOSTER

shin·ing (shīn'iŋ) *adj.* **1.** giving off or reflecting light; bright **2.** brilliant; splendid [a *shining* example]

Shin·to (shin'tō) *n.* [Jap. < Chin. *shin*, god + *tao*, way] a religion of Japan, emphasizing worship of nature and of ancestors —**Shin′to·ism** *n.* —**Shin′to·ist** *n., adj.* —**Shin′-to·is′tic** *adj.*

shin·ty (shin′tē) *n., pl.* **-ties** [prob. < SHIN] **1.** a simple form of hockey played esp. by the Scots **2.** the curved stick used in this game

shin·y (shīn′ē) *adj.* **shin′i·er, shin′i·est 1.** bright; shining **2.** highly polished; glossy **3.** rubbed smooth, and having a glossy finish —**shin′i·ness** *n.*

ship (ship) *n.* [OE. *scip*] **1.** any large vessel navigating deep water **2.** a sailing vessel with a bowsprit and at least three square-rigged masts **3.** a ship's officers and crew **4.** [Chiefly U.S.] an aircraft —*vt.* **shipped, ship′ping 1.** to put or take on board a ship **2.** to send or transport by any carrier [to *ship* coal by rail] **3.** to take in (water) over the side, as in a heavy sea **4.** to put or fix in its proper place on a ship or boat [*ship* the oars] **5.** to hire for work on a ship **6.** [Colloq.] to send (*away, out*, etc.); get rid of —*vi.* **1.** to go aboard ship; embark **2.** to be hired to serve on a ship **3.** to travel by ship —**when** (or **if**, etc.) **one's ship comes in** (or **home**) when (or if, etc.) one's fortune is made —**ship′-pa·ble** *adj.*

-ship (ship) [OE. *-scipe*] *a suffix meaning:* **1.** the quality or state of [*friendship*] **2.** *a*) the rank or office of [*governorship*]   *b*) one having the rank of [*lordship*] **3.** ability as [*leadership*] **4.** all individuals (of the specified class) collectively [*readership*]

ship biscuit *same as* HARDTACK

ship·board (ship′bôrd′) *n.* a ship: chiefly in **on shipboard**, aboard a ship —*adj.* done, happening, used, etc. on a ship [a *shipboard* romance]

ship·build·er (-bil′dər) *n.* one whose business is building ships —**ship′build′ing** *n.*

ship canal a canal large enough for seagoing ships

ship·load (-lōd′) *n.* the load of a ship

ship·mas·ter (-mäs′tər) *n.* the officer in command of a merchant ship; captain

ship·mate (-māt′) *n.* a fellow sailor on the same ship

ship·ment (-mənt) *n.* **1.** the shipping or transporting of goods **2.** goods shipped

ship money a former tax levied on English ports, maritime countries, etc. to provide money for warships

ship of the desert a camel

ship of the line formerly, a warship of the largest class, having a position in the line of battle

ship·own·er (-ō′nər) *n.* an owner of a ship or ships

ship·pen (ship′ən) *n.* [OE. *scypen*] [Dial.] a stable; byre: also **ship′pon**

ship·per (-ər) *n.* a person who ships goods

ship·ping (-iŋ) *n.* **1.** the act or business of transporting goods **2.** ships collectively, as of a nation or port, esp. with reference to tonnage

shipping agent the person who arranges the shipment of goods or passengers

shipping bill the invoice of goods shipped

ship's articles the agreement reached by the captain and crew on conditions of service

ship·shape (-shāp′) *adj.* having everything neatly in place, as on board ship; trim —*adv.* in a neat and orderly manner

ship·side (-sīd′) *n.* the area on a pier alongside a ship

ship·worm (-wurm′) *n.* any of various small molluscs with wormlike bodies: they burrow into submerged wood

ship·wreck (-rek′) *n.* **1.** the remains of a wrecked ship **2.** the loss or destruction of a ship through storm, collision, etc. **3.** any ruin or destruction —*vt.* **1.** to cause to undergo shipwreck **2.** to destroy, ruin, or wreck

ship·wright (-rīt′) *n.* a man, esp. a carpenter, whose work is the construction and repair of ships

ship·yard (-yärd′) *n.* a place where ships are built and repaired

shire (shīr) *n.* [OE. *scir*, office] **1.** any of the former Anglo-Saxon districts in Great Britain coinciding generally with the modern county **2.** any of the counties of Great Britain with a name ending in *-shire* —**the Shires** the Midland counties of England

shire horse any of a breed of large, powerful, draught horses, orig. raised in the Shires

shirk (shurk) *vt., vi.* [? akin to G. *Schurke*, rascal] to neglect or evade doing (something that should be done) —**shirk′er** *n.*

shirr (shur) *n.* [< ?] *same as* SHIRRING —*vt.* **1.** to make shirring in (cloth or a garment) **2.** to bake (eggs) with crumbs or cream in small buttered dishes

shirr·ing (-iŋ) *n.* **1.** a gathering made in cloth by drawing the material up on parallel rows of short, running stitches **2.** any trim made by shirring

shirt (shurt) *n.* [OE. *scyrte*] *a*) the usual sleeved garment worn by men on the upper part of the body, often under a suit jacket, typically having a collar and a buttoned opening down the front *b*) a similar garment for women —**keep one's shirt on** [Slang] to remain patient or calm —**lose**

one's shirt [Slang] to lose everything —**put one's shirt on** [Slang] to support to the fullest extent possible

shirt·ing (-iŋ) *n.* material for making shirts

shirt-sleeve (-slēv′) *adj.* **1.** in, or suitable for being in, one's shirt sleeves **2.** plain; informal

shirt·tail (shurt′tāl′) *n.* the part of a shirt extending below the waist

shirt·waist·er (-wāst′ər) a dress with a bodice like a shirt

shirt·y (shur′tē) *adj.* **shirt′i·er, shirt′i·est** [< SHIRT + -Y³] [Slang] ill-tempered, cross, angry, etc.

shish ke·bab (shish′kə bab′) [< Arm., ult. < Ar. *shīsh*, skewer + *kabāb*, kebab] a dish consisting of small chunks of meat, esp. lamb, placed on skewers alternately with tomatoes, onions, etc., and grilled: also **shish′ka·bob′**

shit (shit) *vi.* **shat**, or **shit′ted, shit′ting** [OE. *scītan*, dung] to defecate —*n.* **1.** excrement **2.** [Slang] rubbish, nonsense **3.** [Slang] a contemptible person —**shit′ty** *adj.*

shiv (shiv) *n.* [prob. < Romany *chiv*, a blade] [Slang] a knife, esp. one with a narrow blade used as a weapon

shiv·a·ree (shiv′ə rē′, shiv′ə rē′) *n.* U.S. sp. of CHARIVARI

shiv·er¹ (shiv′ər) *n.* [ME. *schivere*] a fragment or splinter of something broken, as glass —*vt., vi.* to break into many fragments or splinters; shatter [*shiver* my timbers] —**shiv′-er·y** *adj.*

shiv·er² (shiv′ər) *vi.* [ME. *cheveren* < ? OE. *ceafl*, a jaw] to shake, tremble, etc., as from fear or cold —*n.* a shaking, trembling, etc., as from fear or cold —**the shivers** a fit of shivering —**shiv′er·y** *adj.*

shoal¹ (shōl) *n.* [OE. *scolu*] **1.** a large group; mass; crowd **2.** a large school of fish —*vi.* to come together in or move about as a shoal

shoal² (shōl) *n.* [OE. *sceald*, shallow] **1.** a shallow place in a river, sea, etc. **2.** a sand bar, etc. forming a shallow place that is a danger to navigation, esp. one visible at low water **3.** [*usually pl.*] hidden snags or difficulties —*vt., vi.* to make or become shallow —**shoal′y** *adj.* **shoal′i·er, shoal′i·est**

shoat (shōt) *n.* [< ?] a young, weaned pig

shock¹ (shok) *n.* [< Fr. < MFr. *choquer*, prob. < MDu. *schokken*, to collide] **1.** *a*) a sudden, powerful blow, shake, disturbance, etc. *b*) the effect of this **2.** *a*) a sudden and strong upsetting of the mind or feelings *b*) something causing this [her accident was a *shock* to us] **3.** the violent effect on the body of an electric current passed through it **4.** [Colloq.] *short for* SHOCK ABSORBER: *used in pl.* **5.** *Med.* a disorder caused by severe injury or damage to the body, loss of blood, etc., and marked by a sharp drop in blood pressure, a rapid pulse, etc. —*vt.* **1.** to disturb emotionally; astonish, horrify, etc. **2.** to affect with physical shock **3.** to produce electric shock in —*vi.* to be shocked, distressed, etc. [one who does not *shock* easily] —**shock′er** *n.*

shock² (shok) *n.* [prob. via MDu. or MLowG. *schok*] a number of grain sheaves, as of corn or wheat, stacked together on end to cure and dry —*vt., vi.* to gather in shocks

shock³ (shok) *n.* [< ? prec.] a thick, bushy or tangled mass, as of hair [*shockheaded*]

shock absorber a device, as on the springs of a car, that lessens or absorbs the force of shocks

shock·er (shok′ər) *n.* **1.** a person or thing that shocks **2.** a sensational story, play, etc.

shock·ing (shok′iŋ) *adj.* **1.** causing great surprise **2.** very bad or terrible **3.** of a garish colour [*shocking* pink] —**shock′ing·ly** *adv.*

SHOCKS OF CORN

shock·proof (-prōōf′) *adj.* able to absorb shock without being damaged [a *shockproof* watch]

shock therapy a method of treating certain psychotic conditions by injecting certain drugs or by applying electric current to the brain, which results in convulsion or coma: also **shock treatment**

shock troops troops especially chosen, trained, and equipped to lead an attack

shod (shod) *alt. pt. & pp.* of SHOE

shod·den (shod′'n) *alt. pp.* of SHOE

shod·dy (shod′ē) *n., pl.* **shod′dies** [< ?] **1.** an inferior woollen yarn or cloth made from fibres of used fabrics **2.** anything of less worth than it seems to have; specif., an inferior imitation —*adj.* **shod′di·er, shod′di·est 1.** *a*) made of shoddy *b*) made of any inferior material *c*) poorly done or made **2.** sham **3.** contemptible; low [a *shoddy* trick] —**shod′di·ly** *adv.* —**shod′di·ness** *n.*

shoe (shōō) *n.* [OE. *sceoh*] **1.** an outer covering for the foot, made of leather, canvas, etc. and usually having a stiff sole and a heel **2.** something like a shoe in shape or use; specif., *a*) *short for* HORSESHOE, BRAKE SHOE *b*) the metal strip along the bottom of a sledge runner c) the casing of a pneumatic tyre —vt. **shod** or **shoed, shod** or **shoed, shoe'ing** to furnish with shoes —**fill one's shoes** to take one's place —**in another's shoes** in another's position

shoe·black (-blak') n. a person whose work is shining shoes and boots

shoe·horn (-hôrn') n. an implement of metal, horn, plastic, etc. with a troughlike blade, inserted at the back of a shoe to help in slipping the heel in

shoe·lace (-lās') n. a length of cord, leather, etc. used for lacing and fastening a shoe

shoe leather 1. leather suitable for the manufacture of shoes 2. shoes, in general

shoe·mak·er (-māk'ər) n. a person whose business is making or repairing shoes —**shoe'mak'ing** n.

sho·er (shōō'ər) n. a person who shoes horses; blacksmith; farrier

shoe·shine (-shīn') n. the cleaning and polishing of a pair of shoes

shoe·string (-striŋ') n. 1. same as SHOELACE 2. a small amount of money as capital [the business was started on a shoestring] —adj. precarious; barely sufficient [a shoestring victory]

shoe tree a form, as of wood or metal, put into a shoe to stretch it or preserve its shape

sho·gun (shō'gun', -gōōn') n. [Jap. < Chin. chiang-chun, leader of an army] any of the military governors of Japan who, until 1868, exercised absolute rule —**sho'gun·ate** (-it, -gə nāt') n.

shone (shon) pt. & pp. of SHINE

shoo (shōō) interj. [echoic] 1. an exclamation used in driving away chickens and other animals 2. go away! get out! —vi. **shooed, shoo'ing** to cry "shoo" —vt. to drive away abruptly, by or as by crying "shoo"

shoo-in (shōō'in') n. [SHOO + -IN¹] [U.S. Colloq.] someone or something expected to win easily in an election, a race, etc.

shook (shook) pt. and dial. pp. of SHAKE —**shook up** [Chiefly U.S. Slang] upset; disturbed

shoon (shōōn) n. archaic or dial. pl. of SHOE

shoot (shōōt) vt. **shot, shoot'ing** [OE. sceotan] 1. a) to move swiftly over, by, etc. [to shoot the rapids in a canoe] b) to make move with great force [the crash shot her out of her seat] 2. to pour, empty out, or dump, as down a chute 3. a) to hurl or thrust out [volcanoes shooting molten rock] b) to cast (an anchor, net, etc.) 4. to slide (a door bolt) into or out of its fastening 5. a) to streak or fleck (with another colour or substance) [blue shot with orange] b) to vary (with something different) [a story shot with humour] 6. to put forth (a branch, leaves, etc.) 7. a) to launch (a rocket), discharge (a bullet, arrow, etc.), or fire (a gun, bow, etc.) b) to discharge (rays) with force 8. to send forth (a question, fist, etc.) swiftly or with force 9. to hit, wound, kill, or destroy with a bullet, arrow, etc. 10. to take the altitude of (a star), as with a sextant 11. to photograph or film 12. to inject, as with drugs 13. Games, Sports a) to throw or drive (a ball, etc.) towards the objective b) [Chiefly U.S.] to score (a goal, points, etc.) c) to play (golf, pool, etc.) —vi. 1. a) to move swiftly, as an arrow from a bow b) to spurt or gush 2. to be felt suddenly and keenly, as pain, etc. 3. to grow or sprout rapidly 4. to jut out; project 5. to fire a missile, gun, etc. 6. to use guns, bows and arrows, etc., as in hunting 7. a) to photograph a scene b) to start film cameras working 8. Sports to propel a ball, etc. towards the objective —n. 1. a) the act of shooting b) a party organized to hunt game usually with guns c) the ground over which game is hunted 2. the act of sprouting 3. a new growth; sprout or twig 4. a sloping trough; chute 5. a spasm of pain —interj. [Chiefly U.S.] begin talking! —**shoot at** (or **for**) [Colloq.] to strive for —**shoot from the hip** to act or talk in a rash, impetuous way —**shoot it out** to settle a problem etc. by violent action, as a gunfight, etc. —**shoot off one's** (or **at the**) **mouth** [Slang] 1. to speak without caution; blab 2. to boast; brag —**shoot the cat** [Slang] to vomit —**shoot the moon** [Colloq.] to decamp by night without paying rent due —**shoot'er** n.

shooting box (or **lodge**) a house or lodge used by hunters during the shooting season

shooting brake same as ESTATE CAR

shooting star same as METEOR

shooting stick a canelike stick with a spike at one end and a narrow, folding seat at the top for resting on

shop (shop) n. [OE. sceoppa, booth] 1. a) a place where certain goods or services are offered for sale b) a specialized department in a large store [the gourmet shop] 2. a place where a particular kind of work is done [a printing shop] —vi. **shopped, shop'ping** to visit shops so as to examine or buy merchandise —vt. [Slang] to inform on or betray to the police —**all over the shop** [Colloq.] 1. everywhere 2. in disorder 3. wildly —**come to the wrong shop** [Slang] to have made a mistake; to be in the wrong place for

sympathy, etc. —**set up shop** to start a business —**shop around** 1. to go from shop to shop, looking for bargains or special items 2. to search for a good or better job, idea, etc. —**talk shop** to discuss one's work

shop assistant someone who is employed to assist customers in a shop or store

shop floor 1. the part of a factory where goods are actually produced 2. the workers as opposed to the management of a business concern

shop·girl (shop'gurl') n. same as SALESWOMAN

shop·keep·er (shop'kē'pər) n. a person who owns or operates a shop —**shop'keep'ing** n.

shop·lift·er (-lif'tər) n. a person who steals articles from a store during shopping hours —**shop'lift'vt., vi.**

shop·per (shop'ər) n. 1. a person who shops 2. [U.S.] a person hired by a store to compare competitors' merchandise and prices

shopping centre a complex of stores, restaurants, etc. with an adjoining car park

shop-soiled (-soild') adj. 1. soiled, faded, etc. from having been displayed in a shop 2. drab, dull, trite, etc.

shop steward a person elected by his fellow workers in a union shop to represent them in dealing with the employer

shop·talk (shop'tôk') n. 1. the specialized vocabulary of a particular occupation, etc. 2. conversation about one's work, esp. after hours

Shor·an (shôr'an) n. [Sho(rt) Ra(nge) N(avigation)] [also s-] a radar system for locating the position of an aircraft etc. by signals from a pair of transponders on the ground

shore¹ (shôr) n. [< OE. hyp. score < or akin to scorian, to jut out] 1. land at the edge of a body of water 2. land as opposed to water [shore-based]

shore² (shôr) n. [akin to MDu. schore, Olce. skortha, a prop] a beam, etc. placed under or against something as a prop —vt. **shored, shor'ing** to support or make stable as with shores (usually with up)

shore leave leave granted to a ship's crew for going ashore

shore·line (-līn') n. the edge of a body of water

shore·ward (-wərd) adv. towards the shore: also **shore'-wards** —adj. moving towards the shore

shor·ing (shôr'iŋ) n. 1. the act of supporting with shores 2. a system of shores used for support

shorn (shôrn) alt. pp. of SHEAR

short (shôrt) adj. [OE. scort] 1. not extending far from end to end; not long 2. not great in range or scope [a short journey, view, etc.] 3. low in height; not tall 4. lasting but a little time; brief 5. not retentive [a short memory] 6. condensed or concise 7. brief to the point of rudeness; curt 8. less than a sufficient or correct amount [short notice] 9. not far enough to reach the objective [the shot fell short] 10. having a tendency to crumble, as pastry 11. a) not possessing at the time of sale the commodity or security one is selling b) designating or of a sale of commodities or securities which the seller does not have but expects to buy later at a lower price 12. Phonet. & Prosody comparatively brief in duration, as sounds, syllables, etc. —n. 1. something short; specif., a short sound or syllable 2. a drink of whisky, gin, etc. as opposed to a drink of beer 3. [pl.] a) formerly, knee breeches b) short trousers reaching partway to the knee c) [U.S.] a man's undergarment of similar form 4. [pl.] a byproduct of wheat milling that consists of bran, germ, and coarse meal 6. clipped form of SHORT CIRCUIT —adv. 1. abruptly; suddenly 2. rudely; curtly 3. briefly; concisely 4. so as to be short 5. by surprise; unawares [caught short] 6. by a short sale —vt., vi. 1. to give less than what is needed, usual, etc. 2. clipped form of SHORT-CIRCUIT —**fall** (or **come**) **short** 1. to be insufficient 2. to fail to reach —**in short** 1. in summing up 2. briefly —**run short** to have less than enough —**short for** being an abbreviation of —**short of** 1. not equalling; less than 2. lacking 3. without actually resorting to —**the short end of the stick** the worst of a deal —**short'ish** adj. —**short'ness** n.

short·age (-ij) n. a deficiency in the quantity or amount needed or expected; deficit

short·bread (-bred') n. a rich, crumbly biscuit made with a lot of butter or fat

short·cake (-kāk') n. 1. same as SHORTBREAD 2. [Chiefly U.S.] a light biscuit or a sweet cake served with fruit, etc. as a dessert

short·change (-chānj') vt., vi. **-changed', -chang'ing** [Colloq.] 1. to give less money than is due in change 2. to cheat —**short'chang'er** n.

short-cir·cuit (-sur'kit) vt. 1. Elec. to make a short circuit in 2. to bypass (an obstruction, custom, etc.) 3. to thwart —vi. to develop a short circuit

short circuit 1. a usually accidental low-resistance connection between two points in an electric circuit that deflects the current or causes excessive current flow 2. popularly, a disrupted electric circuit resulting from this

short·com·ing (-kum'iŋ) *n.* a falling short of what is expected or required; defect or deficiency

short·cut (-kut') *n.* **1.** a shorter way to get to the same place **2.** any way of saving time, effort, expense, etc.

short-dat·ed (-dāt'əd) *adj.* (of a bill, bond, etc.) having a short time to run

short·en (shôrt''n) *vt.* **1.** to make short or shorter **2.** to furl or reef (a sail) **3.** to add shortening to (pastry, etc.) —*vi.* to become short or shorter —**short'en·er** *n.*

short·en·ing (shôrt'n iŋ, shôrt'niŋ) *n.* **1.** a making or becoming short or shorter **2.** fat used to make pastry, etc. crisp or flaky

short·hand (-hand') *n.* any system of special symbols for letters, words, and phrases for taking notes, dictation, etc. rapidly —*adj.* written in or using shorthand

short-hand·ed (-han'did) *adj.* short of workers or helpers

shorthand typist a person skilled in taking dictation and later transcribing it on a typewriter

short-head·ed (shôrt'hed'id) *adj.* having a short or broad head —**short'head'ed·ness** *n.*

short·horn (-hôrn') *n.* any of a breed of cattle with short, curved horns: they are raised for both beef and milk

"THIS IS A SAMPLE OF SHORTHAND WRITING"

short list the candidates left for a position, etc. after preliminary tests, interviews, etc. —**short'-list** *vt.* to include on a short list

short-lived (-livd') *adj.* having or tending to have a short life span or existence

short·ly (-lē) *adv.* **1.** in a few words; briefly **2.** in a short time; soon **3.** abruptly and rudely; curtly

short-range (shôrt'rānj') *adj.* **1.** having a range of short distance **2.** not looking far into the future [*short-range plans*]

short shrift very little care or attention, as from lack of patience or sympathy —**make short shrift of** to dispose of quickly and impatiently: also **give short shrift**

short-sight·ed (shôrt'sīt'id) *adj.* **1.** having better vision for near things than for far ones; myopic **2.** having or showing a lack of foresight —**short'sight'ed·ly** *adv.* —**short'sight'ed·ness** *n.*

short story a kind of story shorter than the novel or novelette, developing a single theme and more limited in scope and number of characters

short-tem·pered (-tem'pərd) *adj.* having a tendency to lose one's temper; easily or quickly angered

short-term (-turm') *adj.* **1.** for a short time **2.** designating or of a capital gain, loan, etc. that involves a relatively short period

short ton in the US., Canada, and S. Africa, ton that is 2000 pounds avoirdupois

short-waist·ed (-wās'tid) *adj.* with a high waistline

short·wave (-wāv') *n.* **1.** a radio wave sixty metres or less in length **2.** a radio or radio band for broadcasting or receiving shortwaves: in full, **shortwave radio**

short-wind·ed (-win'did) *adj.* **1.** easily put out of breath by exertion **2.** breathing with quick, laboured breaths **3.** brief or concise —**short'wind'ed·ness** *n.*

short·ie, short·ie (-ē) *n., pl.* **short'ies** [Colloq.] a person or thing of less than average height or size

Sho·sho·ne (shō shō'nē) *n.* **1.** *pl.* **-sho'nes, -sho'ne** any member of a group of N. American Indians scattered over Idaho, Nevada, Utah, Wyoming, and California **2.** their Shoshonean language Also sp. **Sho·sho'ni**

shot¹ (shot) *n.* [OE. *sceot*] **1.** the act of shooting; discharge of a missile, esp. from a gun **2.** *a)* the distance a missile travels *b)* range; scope **3.** an attempt to hit with a missile **4.** *a)* any attempt or try *b)* a guess **5.** a pointed, critical remark **6.** the flight or path of an object thrown, driven, etc. in any of several games **7.** *a)* a projectile to be discharged from a firearm, esp. a solid ball or bullet *b)* such projectiles collectively **8.** a small pellet or pellets of lead, used for a charge of a shotgun **9.** the ball used in the shot put: see SHOT PUT **10.** a blast **11.** a marksman [*a fair shot*] **12.** *a)* a single photograph *b)* a sequence or view taken by a single continuous run of a film or TV camera **13.** a hypodermic injection, as of vaccine **14.** a drink of alcohol, esp. whisky **15.** [Colloq.] a bet, with reference to the odds given [*a ten-to-one shot*] —*vt.* **shot'ted, shot'ting** to load or weight with shot —**a shot in the arm** something that bolsters up, encourages, etc. —**call the shots 1.** to give orders **2.** to control what happens —**have** (or **take**) **a shot at** [Colloq.] to make a try at —**like a shot 1.** quickly or suddenly **2.** eagerly or willingly —**shot across the bows** a warning —**shot in the dark** a wild guess or conjecture

shot² (shot) *pt. & pp.* of SHOOT —*adj.* **1.** variegated, streaked, etc. with another colour or substance **2.** varied with something different **3.** [Chiefly U.S. Colloq.] ruined or worn out

shot³ (shot) *n.* [OE. *scot*] a reckoning; one's share of expenses incurred

shot·gun (shot'gun') *n.* a smoothbore gun for firing a charge of small shot at short range

shot put (poot') **1.** a contest in which a heavy metal ball is propelled by an overhand thrust from the shoulder **2.** a single put of the shot —**shot'-put'ter** *n.* —**shot'-put'ting** *n.*

should (shood; *unstressed, often* shəd) *v.* [OE. *sceolde*, pt. of *sceal*, I am obliged] **1.** *pt.* of SHALL **2.** an auxiliary used to express: *a)* obligation, duty, etc. [*he should help her*] *b)* expectation or probability [*he should be here soon*]: equivalent to *ought to c)* futurity from the standpoint of the past in indirect quotations: replaceable by *would* [I said I *should* (or *would*) be home late] *d)* futurity in polite requests or in statements implying doubt: replaceable by *would* [I *should* (or *would*) think he'd like it] *e)* a future condition [if I *should* die tomorrow] *f)* a past condition replaceable by *would* [I *should* (or *would*) have gone had you asked me] In the usage of some grammarians, the distinctions between *should* and *would* are the same as those between *shall* and *will: see* WILL²

shoul·der (shōl'dər) *n.* [OE. *sculdor*] **1.** *a)* the joint connecting the arm or forelimb with the body *b)* the part of the body including this joint, extending to the base of the neck **2.** [*pl.*] the two shoulders and the part of the back between them **3.** a cut of meat consisting of the upper foreleg and attached parts **4.** the part of a garment that covers the shoulder **5.** a shoulderlike projection **6.** the strip along the edge of a paved road; berm —*vt.* **1.** to push along or through, as with the shoulder **2.** to carry upon the shoulder **3.** to assume the burden of —*vi.* to push with the shoulder —**cry on someone's shoulder** to tell one's troubles to someone in seeking sympathy —**put one's shoulder to the wheel** to set to work vigorously —**shoulder arms** to rest a rifle against the shoulder, supporting the butt with the hand —**shoulder to shoulder 1.** side by side and close together **2.** working together —**straight from the shoulder 1.** moving straight forward from the shoulder: said of a blow **2.** without reserve; frankly —**turn** (or **give**) **a cold shoulder to** to treat with disdain; avoid

shoulder blade either of two flat bones in the upper back

shoulder knot an ornament of braided cord worn on the shoulders of full-dress uniforms

shoulder strap 1. a strap, usually one of a pair, worn over the shoulder to support a garment **2.** a strap worn over the shoulder for carrying an attached bag, camera, etc. **3.** a flap of cloth on the shoulder of a uniform, coat, etc.

should·n't (shood''nt) should not

shouldst (shoodst) *archaic 2nd pers. sing. pt.* of SHALL: used with thou: also **should·est** (shood'ist)

shout (shout) *n.* [ME. *schoute*] **1.** a loud, sudden cry, call, or outburst **2.** [Chiefly Aust. Colloq.] a turn to pay, esp. for a round of drinks —*vt., vi.* **1.** to utter in a shout or cry out loudly **2.** [Aust. Colloq.] to treat (someone), as to a drink —**shout down** to silence by loud shouting —**shout for** to obtain (something or someone) by shouting —**shout'er** *n.*

shove (shuv) *vt., vi.* **shoved, shov'ing** [OE. *scufan*] **1.** to push, as along a surface **2.** to push roughly —*n.* a push or thrust —**shove off 1.** to push (a boat) away from shore **2.** [Colloq.] to start off; leave —**shov'er** *n.*

shove-half·pen·ny (-hăp'nē) *n.* a game in which halfpennies are propelled by hand to certain lined sections of a wooden board

shov·el (shuv''l) *n.* [OE. *scofl*] **1.** *a)* a tool with a broad scoop or blade and a long handle: used in lifting and moving loose material *b)* any machine with a shovellike device **2.** same as SHOVELFUL —*vt.* **-elled, -el·ling 1.** to lift and move with a shovel **2.** to dig out (a path, etc.) with a shovel **3.** to put in large quantities [to *shovel* food in one's mouth] —*vi.* to use a shovel

shov·el·board (shuv'əl bôrd) *n.* **1.** *same as* SHUFFLEBOARD **2.** the board on which the game is played

shov·el·ler (shuv''l ər, shuv'lər) *n.* **1.** a person or thing that shovels **2.** a freshwater duck with a long, broad, flattened bill: also **shov'el·ler, shov'el·er**

shov·el·ful (shuv''l fool') *n., pl.* **-fuls'** as much as a shovel will hold

show (shō) *vt.* **showed, shown** or **showed, show'ing** [OE. *sceawian*, to look] **1.** to bring or put in sight; make visible; exhibit; display **2.** to guide; conduct [*show* him to his room] **3.** to direct attention to; point out [we *showed* him the sights] **4.** to reveal, manifest, etc. [to *show* anger] **5.** to explain, prove, or demonstrate [to *show* how it works] **6.** to register [a clock *shows* the time] **7.** to grant or bestow (favour, mercy, etc.) —*vi.* **1.** to be or become seen; appear **2.** to be noticeable [the scratch won't *show*] **3.** [Colloq.] to come or arrive as expected —*n.* **1.** showing or demonstration [a *show* of passion] **2.** a display or exhibition, esp. in public or for the public **3.** a spectacular, pompous display **4.** a trace as of metal, coal, etc. in the earth **5.** something false; pretence [her sorrow was mere *show]* **6.** a ridiculous spectacle **7.** a presentation of entertainment, as a TV programme or a film **8.** a thing or affair, esp. in **good show, bad show 9.** [U.S.] third position at the finish of a horse or dog race —**for show** in order to attract attention —**good show!** an exclamation of appreciation and congratulations on another's accomplishment —**show off 1.** to make a display of **2.** to do something meant to attract attention —**show one's hand 1.** *Cards* to show opponents one's cards **2.** to reveal one's intentions, plans, etc. —**show up 1.** to expose or be exposed **2.** to come; arrive **3.** to embarrass —**show willing** to appear cheerful, helpful, etc.

show·boat (-bōt′) *n.* a boat with a theatre in which plays are presented for people who live in river towns

show·bread (-bred′) *n. same as* SHEWBREAD

show business the theatre, cinema, television, etc. as a business or industry: also [Colloq.] **show biz**

show·case (-kās′) *n.* **1.** a glass-enclosed case for protecting things on display **2.** a means of displaying to good advantage [the revue was a *showcase* for new talent] —*vt.* **-cased′, -cas′ing** [U.S.] to display to good advantage

show·down (-doun′) *n.* [Colloq.] **1.** *Poker* the laying down of the cards face up to see who wins **2.** any action that brings matters to a climax or settles them

show·er[1] (shō′ər) *n.* a person who shows something

show·er[2] (shou′ər) *n.* [OE. *scur*] **1.** a brief fall of rain, hail, sleet, or snow **2.** a sudden, abundant fall or flow, as of tears, rays, sparks, etc. **3.** [Chiefly U.S.] a party at which gifts are presented to the guest of honour **4.** *a)* a bath in which the body is sprayed with fine streams of water from a perforated nozzle: in full, **shower bath** *b)* an apparatus, or a room or enclosure, for this *c)* a bath taken there **5.** [Slang] a group of people, esp. a disreputable one —*vt.* **1.** to make wet as with a spray of water **2.** to pour forth as in a shower [*showered* with praise] —*vi.* **1.** to fall or come as a shower **2.** to bathe under a shower —**show′er·y** *adj.*

show·girl (shō′gurl′) *n. same as* CHORUS GIRL

show·ing (shō′in) *n.* an exhibition, display, or performance

show·jump·ing (shō′jum′pin) *n.* a horse-riding competition in which skill in jumping over or between various obstacles is demonstrated

show·man (shō′mən) *n., pl.* **-men 1.** a person whose business is producing or presenting shows **2.** a person skilled at this or at presenting anything in a striking manner —**show′man·ship** *n.*

shown (shōn) *alt. pp. of* SHOW

show·off (shō′of′) *n.* a person who shows off

show·piece (-pēs′) *n.* **1.** something exhibited **2.** something that is a fine example of its kind

show·place (-plās′) *n.* **1.** a place that is exhibited to the public for its beauty, etc. **2.** any place that is beautiful, lavishly furnished, etc.

show·room (-rōōm′) *n.* a room where merchandise is displayed, as for advertising or sale

show window a shop window for displaying goods

show·y (-ē) *adj.* **show′i·er, show′i·est 1.** of striking appearance **2.** attracting attention in a gaudy or flashy way —**show′i·ly** *adv.* —**show′i·ness** *n.*

shrank (shrank) *alt. pt. of* SHRINK

shrap·nel (shrap′n'l) *n.* [after H. *Shrapnel* (1761–1842), Brit. general who invented it] **1.** an artillery shell filled with an explosive charge and many small metal balls, set to explode in the air **2.** these metal balls or the shell fragments scattered by any exploding shell

shred (shred) *n.* [OE. *screade*] **1.** a long, narrow strip or piece cut or torn off **2.** a very small piece or amount; fragment [not a *shred* of truth] —*vt.* **shred′ded** or **shred, shred′ding** to cut or tear into shreds —**shred′der** *n.*

shrew (shrōō) *n.* [OE. *screawa*] **1.** a small, mouselike mammal with soft, brown fur and a long snout: also **shrew′-mouse**′, *pl.* **-mice**′ **2.** a nagging, bad-tempered woman —**shrew′ish** *adj.* —**shrew′ish·ly** *adv.* —**shrew′ish·ness** *n.*

shrewd (shrōōd) *adj.* [< ME. pp. of *schrewen*, to curse < *schrewe*, shrew] keen-witted, clever, or sharp in practical affairs; astute —**shrewd′ly** *adv.* —**shrewd′ness** *n.*

shriek (shrēk) *vi.* [prob. < ON.] to make a loud, sharp, piercing cry or sound; screech; scream —*vt.* to utter with a shriek —*n.* a loud, piercing cry or sound —**shriek′er** *n.*

shriev·al·ty (shrēv′'l tē) *n., pl.* **-ties 1.** a sheriff's office or term of office **2.** the district served by a sheriff —**shriev′al** *adj.*

shrift (shrift) *n.* [OE. *scrift* < *scrifan*, to shrive] [Archaic] **1.** confession to and absolution by a priest **2.** the act of shriving See also SHORT SHRIFT

shrike (shrīk) *n.* [OE. *scric*] any of several shrill-voiced birds with hooked beaks: most types feed on insects, some on small birds, frogs, etc., which are sometimes impaled on thorns

shrill (shril) *adj.* [ME. *schrille*: echoic] **1.** having or producing a high, thin, piercing tone; high-pitched **2.** characterized or accompanied by shrill sounds **3.** irritatingly insistent —*vt., vi.* to utter with or make a shrill sound —**shrill′ness** *n.* —**shril′ly** *adv.*

shrimp (shrimp) *n., pl.* **shrimps, shrimp:** see PLURAL, II, D, 1 [< base of OE. *scrimman*, to shrink] **1.** a small, long-tailed crustacean, valued as food **2.** [Colloq.] a small, slight person —*vi.* to fish for shrimp —**shrimp′er** *n.*

SHRIMP
(to 23 cm long)

shrine (shrīn) *n.* [OE. *scrin* < L. *scrinium*, box] **1.** a container holding sacred relics **2.** the tomb of a saint or revered person **3.** a place of worship, usually one whose centre is a sacred scene or object **4.** a place or thing hallowed or honoured because of its history or associations

shrink (shrink) *vi.* **shrank** or **shrunk, shrunk** or **shrunk′en, shrink′ing** [OE. *scrincan*] **1.** to contract, as from heat, cold, wetness, etc. **2.** to lessen, as in amount, worth, etc. **3.** to draw back in fear, dislike, etc.; cower or flinch —*vt.* to cause to shrink or contract —*n.* **1.** a shrinking **2.** [< (*head*)*shrink*(*er*)] [Slang] a psychiatrist: also **shrink′er** —**shrink′a·ble** *adj.*

shrink·age (shrin′kij) *n.* **1.** the act or process of shrinking, as of a fabric in washing **2.** decrease in value; depreciation **3.** the amount of shrinking, decrease, etc.

shrinking violet a very shy or modest person

shrive (shrīv) *vt., vi.* **shrived** or **shrove, shriv′en** (shriv′'n) or **shrived, shriv′ing** [OE. *scrifan*, ult. < L. *scribere*, to write] [Archaic] **1.** to hear the confession of (a person) and, usually after penance, give absolution **2.** to get absolution for (oneself) by confessing and doing penance

shriv·el (shriv′'l) *vt., vi.* **-elled, -el·ling** [prob. < Scand.] **1.** to shrink and make or become wrinkled or withered **2.** to make or become helpless, useless, etc.

shroud (shroud) *n.* [OE. *scrud*] **1.** a cloth used to wrap a corpse for burial **2.** something that covers, protects, or screens; veil **3.** any of the ropes stretched from a ship's side to a masthead to offset lateral strain on the mast **4.** any of the lines from a parachute's canopy to the harness: in full, **shroud line** —*vt.* **1.** to wrap (a corpse) in a shroud **2.** to hide; cover; screen

shrove (shrōv) *alt. pt. of* SHRIVE

Shrove·tide (shrōv′tīd′) *n.* the three days before Ash Wednesday (**Shrove Sunday, Monday,** and **Tuesday**), formerly set aside as a period of confession and of festivity just before Lent

shrub[1] (shrub) *n.* [OE. *scrybb*, brushwood] a low, woody plant with several permanent stems instead of a single trunk; bush —**shrub′like**′ *adj.*

shrub[2] (shrub) *n.* [< Ar. *sharāb*, drink] a drink made of fruit juice, sugar, and, usually, rum or brandy

shrub·ber·y (shrub′ər ē) *n., pl.* **-ber·ies** a group or heavy growth of shrubs, as around a house

shrub·by (-ē) *adj.* **-bi·er, -bi·est 1.** covered with shrubs **2.** like a shrub —**shrub′bi·ness** *n.*

shrug (shrug) *vt., vi.* **shrugged, shrug′ging** [ME. *schruggen*, orig., to shiver] to draw up (the shoulders), as in expressing indifference, doubt, disdain, etc. —*n.* the gesture so made —**shrug off** to dismiss in a carefree way

shrunk (shrunk) *alt. pt. & pp. of* SHRINK

shrunk·en (-'n) *alt. pp. of* SHRINK —*adj.* contracted in size; shrivelled

shuck (shuk) *n.* [< ?] [Chiefly U.S.] **1.** a shell, pod, or husk **2.** the shell of an oyster or clam —*vt.* [Chiefly U.S.] **1.** to remove shucks from (maize, clams, etc.) **2.** to remove like a shuck [to *shuck* one's clothes] —**shuck′er** *n.*

shucks (shuks) *interj.* [Chiefly U.S.] an exclamation of mild disappointment, embarrassment, etc.

shud·der (shud′ər) *vi.* [ME. *schoderen*] to shake or tremble suddenly and violently, as in horror —*n.* a shuddering; sudden, strong tremor —**shud′der·ing·ly** *adv.* —**shud′der·y** *adj.*

shuf·fle (shuf′'l) *vt.* **-fled, -fling** [prob. < or akin to LowG. *schuffeln* < base of SHOVE] **1.** to move (the feet) with a dragging gait **2.** to mix (playing cards) so as to change their order **3.** to mix together in a jumbled mass **4.** to shift (things) about from one place to another **5.** to bring, put, or thrust (*into* or *out of*) clumsily —*vi.* **1.** to move by dragging or scraping the feet, as in walking or dancing **2.** to act in a shifty, underhand, or dishonest manner **3.** to shift repeatedly from one position or place to another **4.** to shuffle playing cards —*n.* **1.** the act of shuffling **2.** a deceptive action; evasion; trick **3.** *a)* a shuffling of the feet *b)* a gait, dance, etc. characterized by this **4.** *a)* a shuffling of playing cards *b)* one's turn at this —**lose in the shuffle** to leave out in the confusion of things —**shuffle off** to get rid of —**shuf′fler** *n.*

shuf·fle·board (-bôrd′) *n.* [< earlier *shovel board*, after the shape of the cues] **1.** a game in which large discs are pushed with a cue along a smooth lane toward numbered squares **2.** the surface on which it is played

shuf·ty (shuf'tē) *n.* [< Ar.] [Slang] a look or peep
shun (shun) *vt.* **shunned, shun'ning** [OE. *scunian*] to keep away from; avoid strictly **—shun'ner** *n.*
'shun (shun) *interj. clipped form of* ATTENTION
shunt (shunt) *vt., vi.* [< ? or akin to SHUN] **1.** to move or turn to one side; turn aside or out of the way **2.** to switch (a train, etc.) from one line to another **3.** *Elec.* to divert or be diverted by a shunt —*n.* **1.** a shunting **2.** a railway switch **3.** [Slang] a collision between motor vehicles, esp. in a car race **4.** *Elec.* a conductor connecting two points in a circuit and diverting part of the current from the main circuit **—shunt'er** *n.*
shush (shush) *interj.* [echoic] hush! be quiet! —*vt.* to say "shush" to; tell (another) to be quiet
shut (shut) *vt.* **shut, shut'ting** [OE. *scyttan* < base of *sceotan,* to shoot] **1.** *a)* to move (a door, window, lid, etc.) into a position that covers the opening to which it is fitted *b)* to fasten (a door, etc.) securely, as with a bolt or catch **2.** to close (an opening, container, etc.) **3.** *a)* to prevent entrance to or exit from; bar *b)* to confine or enclose (*in* a room, cage, etc.) **4.** to fold up or close the parts of (an umbrella, a book, the eyes, etc.) **5.** to stop or suspend the operation of (a school, business, etc.) —*vi.* to be or become shut —*adj.* closed, fastened, etc. —*n.* the act or time of shutting **—shut down 1.** to close by lowering **2.** to close (a factory, etc.), usually temporarily **—shut in** to surround or enclose **—shut off 1.** to prevent the passage of (water, electricity, etc.) **2.** to prevent passage through (a road, tap, etc.) **3.** to separate; isolate **—shut out 1.** to deny entrance to; exclude (sound, a view, etc.) **2.** [U.S.] to prevent (the opposition) from scoring in a game **—shut up 1.** to enclose, confine, or imprison **2.** to close all the entrances to **3.** [Colloq.] *a)* to stop or cause to stop talking *b)* to prevent from speaking or writing freely; censor
shut·down (-doun') *n.* a stoppage or suspension of work or activity, as in a factory
shut·eye (-ī') *n.* [Slang] sleep
shut·in (-in') *n.* [Chiefly U.S.] a person who is too ill, weak, etc. to go out —*adj.* not able to go out
shut·off (-ôf') *n.* **1.** something that shuts off a flow, as a valve **2.** a stoppage or interruption
shut·out (-out') *n.* [U.S.] **1.** a preventing of the opposing team from scoring **2.** a game in which this occurs
shut·ter (shut'ər) *n.* **1.** a person or thing that shuts **2.** a movable, usually hinged cover for a window **3.** anything used to cover an opening; specif., a device for opening and closing the aperture of a camera lens to expose the film or plate —*vt.* to close or furnish with shutters **—put up the shutters** (of a shop) to close for the night or permanently
shut·tle (shut''l) *n.* [OE. *scytel,* missile: from being cast back and forth] **1.** *a)* a device used to pass the woof thread back and forth between the warp threads in weaving *b)* any of several devices having a similar use or motion, as the device that carries the lower thread back and forth on a sewing machine **2.** a bus, train, helicopter, aircraft, etc. making frequent trips back and forth over a short route —*vt., vi.* **-tled, -tling 1.** to move rapidly to and fro **2.** to go by means of a shuttle
shut·tle·cock (-kok') *n.* **1.** a rounded piece of cork having a flat end stuck with feathers: it is struck back and forth across a net by players in badminton or in battledore and shuttlecock **2.** the game of battledore and shuttlecock —*vt., vi.* to go, send, or bandy back and forth
shuttle service a transport service, esp. an airline, operating over a short distance with a limited number of vehicles
shy[1] (shī) *adj.* **shy'er** or **shi'er, shy'est** or **shi'est** [OE. *sceoh*] **1.** easily frightened or startled; timid **2.** not at ease with other people; bashful **3.** distrustful; wary **4.** [Slang] lacking in amount; short (*on* or *of*) —*vi.* **shied, shy'ing 1.** to move or pull back suddenly when startled; start **2.** to be or become cautious or unwilling; draw back (often with *at* or *from*) —*n., pl.* **shies** an act of shying; start, as of a horse **—fight shy of** to avoid or evade **—shy'er** *n.* **—shy'ly** *adv.* **—shy'ness** *n.*
shy[2] (shī) *vt., vi.* **shied, shy'ing** [< ? or akin to prec.] to fling, esp. sidewise with a jerk [*shying* stones at a target] —*n., pl.* **shies** a shying; fling
Shy·lock (shī'lok') *n.* [after *Shylock,* the moneylender in Shakespeare's *Merchant of Venice*] an exacting creditor
shy·ster (shī'stər) *n.* [< ?] [Chiefly U.S. Slang] a person, esp. a lawyer, who uses unethical or underhand methods
si (sē) *n. Music same as* TI
‡**si** (sē) *adv.* [Sp.] yes: also [It.] **sì**
Si *Chem.* silicon
Si·a·mese (sī'ə mēz', -mēs') *n., pl.* **Si'a·mese'** *same as* THAI —*adj. same as* THAI
Siamese cat a breed of short-haired cat characterized by blue eyes and a fawn-coloured coat shading to a darker colour at the face, ears, paws, and tail
Siamese twins [after such a pair born in Siam] any pair of twins born joined to each other

sib (sib) *n.* [OE. *sibb*] **1.** blood relatives; kin **2.** a blood relative **3.** a brother or sister —*adj.* related by blood
sib·i·lant (sib'ə lənt) *adj.* [< L. < *sibilare,* to hiss] having or making a hissing sound —*n. Phonet.* a consonant characterized by a hissing sound, as (s), (z), (sh), (zh), (ch), and (j) —**sib'i·lance, sib'i·lan·cy** *n., pl.* **-cies** —**sib'i·lant·ly** *adv.*
sib·i·late (-āt') *vt., vi.* **-lat'ed, -lat'ing** [< L. *sibitatus* pp. of *sibilare:* see prec.] to hiss or pronounce with a hissing sound —**sib'i·la'tion** *n.*
sib·ling (sib'liŋ) *n.* [20th-c. readoption of OE. *sibling,* a relative] one of two or more persons born of the same parents, or, sometimes, having one parent in common; brother or sister
sib·yl (sib''l) *n.* [< L. < Gr. *sibylla*] **1.** any of certain women consulted as prophetesses or oracles by the ancient Greeks and Romans **2.** a prophetess; fortuneteller —**sib'yl·line** (-'l īn', -ēn', -in) *adj.*
‡**sic**[1] (sik) *adv.* [L.] thus; so: used within brackets, [*sic*], to show that a quoted passage, esp. one containing some error, is shown exactly as in the original
sic[2] (sik) *vt.* [var. of SEEK] **sicked, sick'ing 1.** to pursue and attack: said esp. of or to a dog **2.** to urge to attack [*sic* a dog on someone]
Si·cil·i·an (si sil'yən, -ē ən) *adj.* designating or of Sicily, an island of Italy, off its S tip —*n.* a native or inhabitant of Sicily
sick[1] (sik) *adj.* [OE. *seoc*] **1.** suffering from disease; physically or mentally ill **2.** having nausea; vomiting or about to vomit **3.** characteristic of sickness [a *sick* expression] **4.** of or for sick people [*sick* leave] **5.** deeply disturbed, as by grief, failure, etc. **6.** disgusted by reason of excess [*sick* of his excuses]: often **sick and tired 7.** unsound **8.** having a great longing (*for*) [*sick* for the hills] **9.** [Colloq.] sadistic, morbid, etc. [a *sick* joke] —*vt.* [Colloq.] to vomit (*up*) **—take sick** to become ill **—the sick** sick people collectively
sick[2] (sik) *vt. same as* SIC[2]
sick bay a room or area for treating the sick, as on a ship, at a school, etc.
sick·bed (sik'bed') *n.* the bed of a sick person
sick benefit the allowance made (under the National Health Service) to a person sick and off work
sick call *Mil.* **1.** a daily formation for those who wish to receive medical attention **2.** the time for this
sick·en (sik''n) *vt., vi.* to make or become sick, disgusted, etc. **—sick'en·er** *n.*
sick·en·ing (-iŋ) *adj.* **1.** causing sickness or nausea **2.** disgusting **—sick'en·ing·ly** *adv.*
sick headache 1. any headache accompanied by nausea **2.** *same as* MIGRAINE
sick·ish (sik'ish) *adj.* **1.** somewhat sick or nauseated **2.** somewhat sickening or nauseating **—sick'ish·ly** *adv.*
sick·le (sik''l) *n.* [OE. *sicol,* ult. < L. *secula* < *secare,* to cut] a tool consisting of a crescent-shaped blade with a short handle, for cutting tall grass, etc.
sick leave leave from work granted for illness, often with pay (**sick pay**) for a limited number of days

SICKLE

sickle cell anaemia an inherited chronic anaemia found chiefly among Negroes, characterized by an abnormal red blood cell (**sickle cell**) containing a defective form of haemoglobin that causes the cell to become sickle-shaped when deprived of oxygen: also **sickle cell disease**
sick list a list of sick persons, esp. in the armed services
sick·ly (sik'lē) *adj.* **-li·er, -li·est 1.** in poor health; sick much of the time **2.** of or produced by sickness [a *sickly* pallor] **3.** producing illness; unhealthful **4.** sickening, as an odour **5.** faint; feeble [a *sickly* light] **6.** weak; insipid [a *sickly* smile] —*adv.* in a sick manner: also **sick'li·ly** **—sick'·li·ness** *n.*
sick·ness (-nis) *n.* **1.** a being sick or diseased; illness **2.** a particular disease or illness **3.** nausea
sick·room (-rōōm') *n.* the room to which a sick person is confined
side (sīd) *n.* [OE.] **1.** the right or left half of a human or animal body **2.** a position beside one **3.** *a)* any of the lines or surfaces that bound something [a square has four *sides*] *b)* either of the two bounding surfaces of an object that are not the front, back, top, or bottom **4.** either of the two surfaces of paper, cloth, etc. **5.** a particular or specified surface [the visible *side* of the moon] **6.** a particular part or quality of a person or thing [his cruel *side,* the bright *side* of life] **7.** the slope of a hill, bank, etc. **8.** any location, area, space, etc. with reference to a central point or line, or to the speaker **9.** the ideas, opinions, or position of one person or faction opposing another [his *side* of the argument] **10.** one of the parties in a contest, conflict, etc. **11.** line of descent through either parent **12.** any of the pages containing an actor's part in a play **13.** [Slang]

superior or patronizing manner **14.** *Billiards* a spinning motion given to a ball, as by striking it on one side —*adj.* **1.** of, at, or on a side [a *side* door] **2.** to or from one side [a *side* glance] **3.** done, happening, etc. incidentally [a *side* effect] **4.** not main; secondary [a *side* issue] —*vt.* **sid′ed, sid′ing** to furnish with sides or siding —**let the side down** to do or say something that causes embarrassment or frustration among one's colleagues —**on the side** in addition to the main thing, part, etc. —**side by side** beside each other; together —**side with** to support (one of opposing factions, etc.) —**take sides** to support one of the parties in a dispute, etc.

side arms weapons of the kind that may be worn at the side or at the waist, as a sword, pistol, etc.

side-board (sīd′bôrd′) *n.* a piece of dining-room furniture for holding table linen, silver, china, etc.

side-boards (-bôrds′) *n.pl.* the hair growing on a man's face just in front of the ears, esp. when the rest of the beard is cut off

side-burns (-bʉrnz′) *n.pl. Chiefly U.S. var. of* SIDEBOARDS

side-car (-kär′) *n.* a small car attached to the side of a motorcycle, for carrying a passenger, parcels, etc.

sid-ed (sīd′id) *adj.* having (a specified number or kind of) sides [six-*sided*]

side dish any food served along with the main course, usually in a separate dish

side-door (-dôr′) *n.* **1.** a side entrance to a house, etc. **2.** a circuitous or oblique method of approaching something

side-kick (-kik′) *n.* [Chiefly U.S. Slang] **1.** a companion; close friend **2.** a partner; confederate

side-light (-līt′) *n.* **1.** a light coming from the side **2.** a bit of incidental information on a subject

side-line (-līn′) *n.* a line along the side; specif., *a)* either of the two lines marking the side limits of a playing area, as in football or basketball *b)* [*pl.*] the areas just outside these lines *c)* a line, as of merchandise or work, in addition to one's main line —**sit on the sidelines** to be only passively involved —**side′lin′er** *n.*

side-long (-lôŋ′) *adv.* **1.** towards the side; obliquely **2.** on the side —*adj.* **1.** inclined; slanting **2.** directed to the side, as a glance

side-man (-man′) *n., pl.* **-men′** (-men′) [as distinguished from the *front man*, or leader] a member of a jazz or dance band other than the leader

side-piece (-pēs′) *n.* a piece forming, or attached to, the side of something

si-de-re-al (sī dir′ē əl) *adj.* [< L. < *sidus* (gen. *sideris*), a star] **1.** of the stars or constellations; astral **2.** with reference to the stars —**si-de′re-al-ly** *adv.*

sidereal day the time between two successive passages of the vernal equinox over the upper meridian: it measures one rotation of the earth and is equal to 23 hours, 56 minutes, 4.091 seconds of mean solar time

sidereal year *see* YEAR (sense 3)

sid-er-ite (sid′ə rīt′) *n.* [< G. < L. < Gr. < *sidēros*, iron] a yellowish to light-brown iron ore, FeCO₃ —**sid′er-it′ic** (-rit′ik) *adj.*

side-sad-dle (sīd′sad′'l) *n.* a saddle for women wearing skirts, upon which the rider sits with both legs on the same side of the animal —*adv.* on or as if on a sidesaddle

side-show (-shō′) *n.* **1.** a small show apart from the main show, as of a circus **2.** activity of minor importance

side-slip (-slip′) *vi.* **-slipped′, -slip′ping 1.** to slip sideways, as on skis **2.** *Aeron.* to move in a sideslip —*vt.* to cause to sideslip —*n.* **1.** a slip or skid to the side **2.** *Aeron.* a sideways and downwards movement towards the inside of a turn by an aircraft in a sharp bank

sides-man (sīd′zmən) *n., pl.* **-men** *Church of England* a man who helps the church warden, esp. in taking the collection

side-split-ting (-split′iŋ) *adj.* **1.** very hearty: said of laughter **2.** causing hearty laughter

side-step (-step′) *vt.* **-stepped′, -step′ping** to avoid by or as by stepping aside; dodge [to *sidestep* a difficulty] —*vi.* to step to one side

side step a step to one side, as to avoid something, or a step taken sideways

side-swipe (-swīp′) *vt., vi.* **-swiped′, -swip′ing** [U.S.] to hit along the side in passing —*n.* [U.S.] a glancing blow of this kind

side-track (-trak′) *vt., vi.* **1.** to switch (a train, etc.) to a siding **2.** to turn away from the main issue —*n.* a railway siding

side-walk (-wôk′) *n.* [U.S.] pavement

side-wall (-wôl′) *n.* the side of a motor car tyre between the tread and the rim of a wheel

side-ward (-wərd) *adv., adj.* directed or moving towards one side: also **side′wards** *adv.*

side-ways (-wāz′) *adv.* **1.** from the side **2.** with one side forwards **3.** towards one side; obliquely —*adj.* turned or moving towards or from one side

side-wheel (sīd′hwēl′, -wēl′) *adj.* designating a steamboat having a paddle wheel on each side —**side′-wheel′er** *n.*

side whiskers whiskers at the side of the face

sid-ing (sīd′iŋ) *n.* **1.** a short railway track connected with a main track by a switch and used for unloading, bypassing, etc. **2.** [US.] boards, panels, etc. forming the outside covering of a frame building

si-dle (sī′d'l) *vi.* **-dled, -dling** [< *sideling*, sideways] to move sideways, esp. in a shy or stealthy manner —*vt.* to make go sideways —*n.* a sidling movement

SIDS Sudden Infant Death Syndrome

siege (sēj) *n.* [OFr., ult. < L. *obsidere*, to besiege < *ob-*, against + *sedere*, to sit] **1.** the surrounding of a city, fort, etc. by an enemy army trying to capture it by continued blockade and attack **2.** any stubborn and continued effort to win or control something **3.** [Chiefly U.S.] a long, distressing period [a *siege* of illness] **4.** [Obs.] a seat; throne —*vt.* **sieged, sieg′ing** *same as* BESIEGE —**lay siege to** to subject to a siege

sie-mens (sē′mənz) *n.* [after Sir William *Siemens* (1823-83), Brit. engineer & inventor] the SI unit of electrical conductance; the reciprocal of one ohm

si-en-na (sē en′ə) *n.* [It. *terra di Siena*, lit., earth of Siena, city in Italy] **1.** a yellowish-brown earth pigment containing iron and manganese **2.** a reddish-brown pigment made by burning this; burnt sienna **3.** either of these colours

si-er-ra (sē er′ə) *n.* [Sp. < L. *serra*, a saw] a range of mountains with a saw-toothed appearance

si-es-ta (sē es′tə) *n.* [Sp. < L. *sexta* (*hora*), sixth (hour), noon] a brief nap or rest taken after the noon meal, esp. in Spain and some Latin American countries

‡**sieur** (syėr) *n.* [OFr., inflected form of *sire*, SIRE] *archaic French title of respect meaning* SIR

sieve (siv) *n.* [OE. *sife*] a utensil having many small openings, used to strain solids from liquids or to separate fine particles from coarser ones; strainer; sifter —*vt., vi.* **sieved, siev′ing** to pass through a sieve

sift (sift) *vt.* [OE. *siftan*] **1.** to pass through a sieve so as to separate the coarse from the fine particles, or to break up lumps, as of flour **2.** to scatter by or as by the use of a sieve **3.** to examine with care; weigh (evidence, etc.) **4.** to separate; screen [to *sift* fact from fable] —*vi.* **1.** to sift something **2.** to pass through or as through a sieve —**sift′-er** *n.*

sift-ings (-iŋz) *n.pl.* sifted matter

sigh (sī) *vi.* [OE. *sican*] **1.** to take in and let out a long, deep, sounded breath, as in sorrow, relief, fatigue, etc. **2.** to make a sound like a sigh [trees *sighing* in the wind] **3.** to long or lament (*for*) —*vt.* to express with a sigh —*n.* the act or sound of sighing —**sigh′er** *n.*

sight (sīt) *n.* [OE. (ge)*siht* < base of *seon*, to see] **1.** *a)* something seen; view *b)* a remarkable view; spectacle *c)* a thing worth seeing: *usually used in pl.* [the *sights* of the city] **2.** the act of seeing **3.** a look; glimpse **4.** any device used to aid the eyes in lining up a gun, optical instrument, etc. on its objective **5.** aim or an observation taken as with a sextant, gun, etc. **6.** the ability to see; vision; eyesight **7.** range of vision **8.** one's thinking or opinion [a hero in her *sight*] **9.** a person or thing not pleasant to look at **10.** [Colloq. or Dial.] a large amount; lot [a *sight* better than fighting] —*vt.* **1.** to observe or examine by taking a sight **2.** to catch sight of; see **3.** *a)* to furnish with a sighting device *b)* to adjust the sights of **4.** to aim (a gun, etc.) at (a target), using the sights —*vi.* **1.** to take aim or an observation with a sight **2.** to look carefully [*sight* along the line] —**a sight for sore eyes** [Colloq.] a welcome sight —**at first sight** when seen or considered for the first time —**at** (or **on**) **sight** when or as soon as seen —**by sight** by recognizing but not through being acquainted —**catch sight of** to see, esp. briefly; glimpse —**lose sight of 1.** to see no longer **2.** to forget —**not by a long sight 1.** not nearly **2.** not at all —**out of sight** (**of**) **1.** not in sight (of) **2.** far off (from) —**sight unseen** without seeing (the thing) beforehand

sight-ed (-id) *adj.* **1.** having sight; not blind **2.** having (a specified kind of) sight: used in combination [longsighted]

sight-less (-lis) *adj.* **1.** blind **2.** unseen —**sight′less-ly** *adv.* —**sight′less-ness** *n.*

sight-ly (-lē) *adj.* **-li-er, -li-est 1.** pleasant to the sight **2.** providing a fine view —**sight′li-ness** *n.*

sight reading the act or skill of performing unfamiliar written music, or of translating something written in a foreign language, without previous study —**sight′-read′** *vt., vi.*

sight-screen (-skrēn′) *n. Cricket* a white screen placed near the boundary behind the bowler to help the batsman see the ball

sight-see-ing (-sē′iŋ) *n.* the act of visiting places and things of interest —*adj.* for or engaged in seeing sights —**sight′-se′er** *n.*

sig-il-late (sij′ə lāt′) *adj.* [< L. *sigillatus* < *sigillum*, dim. of *signum*, sign] **1.** (of pottery) having stamped, impressed decorations **2.** *Bot.* having seal-like markings or scars

sig-la (sig′lə) *n.pl.* [< L., pl. of *siglum* dim. of *signum*, sign] the list of symbols used in a book, usually found at the beginning of the book

sig·ma (sig′mə) *n.* [Gr.] the eighteenth letter of the Greek alphabet (Σ, σ, ς)

sig·moid (-moid) *adj.* having a double curve like the letter S: also **sig·moi′dal** —**sig·moi′dal·ly** *adv.*

sigmoid flexure 1. *Anat.* the last curving part of the colon, ending in the rectum 2. *Zool.* an S-shaped curve

sign (sīn) *n.* [< OFr. < L. *signum*] 1. something that indicates a fact, quality, etc. [black is a *sign* of mourning] 2. *a)* a gesture that tells something specified [a nod is a *sign* of approval] *b)* any of the gestures used in sign language 3. a mark or symbol having a specific meaning [the *sign* £ for pounds] 4. a publicly displayed board, placard, etc. bearing information, advertising, etc. 5. any visible trace or indication [the *signs* of spring] 6. an omen 7. *same as* SIGN OF THE ZODIAC —*vt.* 1. to mark with a sign, esp. of the cross as in blessing 2. to write one's name on, as in agreement, authorization, etc. 3. to write (one's name) as a signature 4. to hire by written contract —*vi.* 1. to write one's signature, as in confirming something 2. to make a sign; signal —**sign away** (or **over**) to transfer ownership of (something) by signing a document —**sign in** (or **out**) to sign a register on arrival (or departure) —**sign off** to stop broadcasting, as for the day —**sign on** to hire or be hired —**sign up** 1. *same as* SIGN ON 2. to enlist in military service —**sign′er** *n.*

sig·nal (sig′n'l) *n.* [< OFr. < VL. *signale*, ult. < L. *signum*, a sign] 1. any sign, event, etc. that is a call to some kind of action [a bugle *signal* to attack] 2. *a)* a sign given by gesture, a device, etc. to convey a command, direction, warning, etc. *b)* an object or device providing such a sign 3. *Card Games* a bid or play designed to guide one's partner 4. *Telegraphy, Radio & TV*, etc. the electrical impulses, sound or picture elements, etc. transmitted or received —*adj.* 1. not ordinary; notable 2. used as a signal —*vt., vi.* -**nalled**, -**nal·ling** 1. to make a signal or signals (to) 2. to communicate by signals —**sig′nal·ler** *n.*

signal box a building from which railway signals are operated

sig·nal·ize (-īz′) *vt.* -**ized′**, -**iz′ing** 1. to make notable 2. to draw attention to —**sig′nal·i·za′tion** *n.*

sig·nal·ly (-ē) *adj.* notably; remarkably

sig·nal·man (-mən, -man′) *n., pl.* -**men** (-mən, -men′) a person responsible for signalling or receiving signals

sig·nar·y (sig′nə rē) *n.* [< L. *signare*, sign + -ARY] a list or system of symbols, as a syllabary or an alphabet

sig·na·to·ry (sig′nə tər ē, -trē) *adj.* that has or have joined in the signing of something —*n., pl.* -**ries** any of the persons, states, etc. that have signed a document

sig·na·ture (sig′nə chər) *n.* [< LL. < L. *signare*, to sign] 1. a person's name written by himself 2. the act of signing one's name 3. an identifying characteristic or mark 4. *Music* a sign or signs placed at the beginning of a staff to show key or time 5. *Printing a)* a large sheet on which pages are printed in some multiple of four, and which, when folded to page size, forms one section of a book *b)* a letter or number on the first page of each sheet showing in what order that section is to be bound

signature tune an identifying song or melody used by a danceband, etc., or for a radio or television series

sign·board (sīn′bôrd′) *n.* a board bearing a sign, esp. one advertising a business, product, etc.

sig·net (sig′nit) *n.* [MFr. dim. of *signe*, a sign] 1. a small seal used in marking documents as official, etc. 2. a mark made by a signet

signet ring a finger ring containing a signet, often in the form of an initial or a monogram

sig·nif·i·cance (sig nif′ə kəns) *n.* 1. that which is signified; meaning 2. the quality of being significant; suggestiveness; expressiveness 3. importance; consequence Also **sig·nif′-i·can·cy**

sig·nif·i·cant (-kənt) *adj.* [< L. prp. of *significare*, to signify] 1. *a)* having or expressing a meaning *b)* full of meaning 2. important; momentous 3. having or expressing a special or hidden meaning 4. of a difference too large to be due to chance, as in statistics Also **sig·nif′i·ca′tive** (-kāt′iv) —**sig·nif′i·cant·ly** *adv.*

significant figure 1. a figure of a number that expresses a magnitude to a specified degree of accuracy 2. the number of such figures [3.142 has four *significant figures*]

sig·ni·fi·ca·tion (sig′nə fi kā′shən) *n.* 1. significance; meaning 2. a signifying; indication

sig·ni·fy (sig′nə fī′) *vt.* -**fied′**, -**fy′ing** [< OFr. < L. *significare* < *signum*, a sign + *facere*, to make] 1. to be a sign or indication of; mean 2. to show or make known by a sign, words, etc. —*vi.* to be significant; matter —**sig′ni·fi′-er** *n.*

sign language communication of thoughts or ideas by means of signs and gestures of the hands and arms

sign of the times an indication of some present state of affairs or the tendency of events, etc.

sign of the zodiac any of the twelve divisions of the zodiac, each represented by a symbol: see ZODIAC

‡**si·gnor** (sē nyôr′; *E.* sēn′yôr) *n., pl.* **si·gno′ri** (-nyô′rē); *E.* **si′gnors** [It.] 1. [S-] Mr.: Italian title of respect, used before the name 2. a gentleman; man

‡**si·gno·ra** (sē nyô′rä; *E.* sēn nyô′rə) *n., pl.* **si·gno′re** (-re); *E.* **si·gno′ras** [It.] 1. [S-] Mrs.; Madam: Italian title of respect 2. a married woman

‡**si·gno·re** (sē nyô′re) *n., pl.* **si·gno′ri** (-rē) [It.] 1. [S-] Sir: Italian title of respect, used in direct address without the name 2. a gentleman; man

‡**si·gno·ri·na** (sē′nyô rē′nä; *E.* sēn′yə rē′nə) *n., pl.* -**ri′ne** (-ne); *E.* -**ri′nas** [It.] 1. [S-] Miss: Italian title of respect 2. an unmarried woman or girl

sign painter someone who paints signs for inns, shops, etc.

sign·post (sīn′pōst′) *n.* 1. a post with a sign on it, as for showing a route or direction 2. a clear indication; obvious clue, symptom, etc.

si·ka deer (sē′kə) a small, reddish-brown deer, introduced into Europe from Japan and Manchuria

Sikh (sēk) *n.* [Hindi, a disciple] a member of a monotheistic Hindu religious sect that rejects the caste system —*adj.* of Sikhs —**Sikh′ism** *n.*

si·lage (sī′lij) *n.* [contr. (after SILO) < ENSILAGE] green fodder stored in a silo

sild (sild) *n., pl.* **sild, silds:** see PLURAL, II, D, 2 [Norw., herring] any of several small or young herrings canned as Norwegian sardines

si·lence (sī′ləns) *n.* 1. the state or fact of keeping silent or still 2. absence of any sound or noise; stillness 3. a withholding of knowledge or omission of mention 4. failure to communicate, write, etc. 5. oblivion or obscurity —*vt.* -**lenced, -lenc·ing** 1. to make silent 2. to put down; repress 3. to put (enemy guns) out of action —*interj.* be silent!

si·lenc·er (sī′lən sər) *n.* 1. one that silences 2. a device for muffling the report of a firearm 3. a device for silencing noises, as a section in the exhaust pipe of an internal-combustion engine

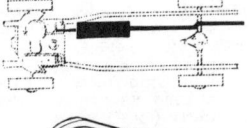

si·lent (sī′lənt) *adj.* [< L. < prp. of *silere*, to be silent] 1. making no vocal sound; mute 2. seldom speaking; not talkative 3. free from sound or noise; quiet; still 4. not spoken, expressed, etc. [*silent* grief, the *silent* "b" in "debt"] 5. making no mention, explanation, etc. 6. not active [factories now *silent*] 7. designating or of films without synchronized sound —**si′lent·ly** *adv.*

SILENCER

silent majority those who are presumed to support the status quo but rarely make their views known

si·le·nus (sī lē′nəs) *n., pl.* -**ni** (nī) [after *Silenus*, in Gr. Myth. the foster father and tutor of Dionysus and leader of the satyrs] any of a group of woodland deities resembling the satyrs

si·lex (sī′leks) *n.* [L.] 1. silica, esp. in the form of flint or quartz 2. heat-resistant glass of fused quartz

sil·hou·ette (sil′ŏŏ wet′) *n.* [Fr., after E. de *Silhouette*, 18th-c. Fr. minister of finance] 1. *a)* a profile portrait in black or in some solid colour, often a cutout mounted on a light background *b)* any dark shape seen against a light background 2. the outline of a figure, garment, etc.; contour —*vt.* -**et′ted, -et′ting** to show or project in silhouette

sil·i·ca (sil′i kə) *n.* [ModL. < L. *silex*, flint] the dioxide of silicon, SiO_2, a hard, glassy mineral found in various forms, as in quartz, sand, opal, etc.

sil·i·cate (sil′i kit, -kāt′) *n.* a salt or ester derived from silica or a silicic acid

si·li·ceous (sə lish′əs) *adj.* 1. of, containing, or like silica 2. growing in soil that has much silica in it

SILHOUETTE

si·lic·ic (sə lis′ik) *adj.* of, like, or derived from silicon

silicic acid 1. any of several jellylike precipitates formed by acidifying sodium silicate solution 2. any of the hypothetical acids of which the mineral silicates may be regarded as salts

sil·i·con (sil′i kən, -kon′) *n.* [ModL., ult. < L. *silex*, flint] a nonmetallic chemical element second only to oxygen in its abundance in nature and found always in combination, as in silica: symbol, Si; at. wt., 28.086; at. no., 14

sil·i·cone (-kōn′) *n.* [SILIC(ON) + -ONE] any of a group of polymerized, organic silicon compounds highly resistant to heat, water, etc. and used in lubricants, polishes, etc.

silicone rubber a rubberlike polymer made from certain silicones: it keeps its elasticity over a wide temperature range and is used in gaskets, insulation, etc.

si·li·co·sis (sil'ə kō'sis) *n.* [ModL.: see SILICON & -OSIS] a chronic lung disease caused in miners, stonecutters, etc. by inhaling silica dust over a long time

silk (silk) *n.* see PLURAL, II, D, 3 [OE. *seoluc*, ult. < ? L. *sericus*: see SERGE] 1. the fine, soft, shiny fibre produced by silkworms 2. thread or fabric made from this 3. a garment or other article of such fabric 4. any silklike filament or substance 5. *a)* [*pl.*] a distinctive silk uniform, as of a jockey *b)* the silk gown worn by a King's (or Queen's) counsel in the law courts on formal occasions *c)* a King's or Queen's Counsel —*adj.* of or like silk —**take silk** to become a Queen's or King's counsel

silk cotton same as KAPOK

silk·en (sil'k'n) *adj.* 1. made of silk 2. dressed in silk 3. like silk, as in being soft, smooth, glossy, or luxurious

silk hat a tall, cylindrical hat covered with silk or satin, worn by men in formal dress

silk-screen (silk'skrēn') *adj.* 1. designating or of a stencil process of printing a design through a screen of silk or other fine cloth, parts of the screen being blocked as with an impermeable film 2. designating a print made by this process —*vt.* to print by this process

silk·worm (-wurm') *n.* any of certain moth caterpillars that produce cocoons of silk fibre

silk·y (sil'kē) *adj.* **silk'i·er, silk'i·est** 1. of or like silk; soft, smooth, lustrous, etc. 2. having fine, soft hairs, as some leaves —**silk'i·ly** *adv.* —**silk'i·ness** *n.*

sill (sil) *n.* [OE. *syll*] 1. a heavy, horizontal timber or line of masonry supporting a house wall, etc. 2. a horizontal piece forming the bottom frame of the opening into which a window or door is set 3. *Geol.* an intrusive body of igneous rock

sil·la·bub (sil'ə bub') *n.* var. of SYLLABUB

sil·ler (sil'ər) *adj., n.* [< SILVER] [Scot.] silver; money

sil·ly (sil'ē) *adj.* **-li·er, -li·est** [OE. *sælig*, happy, blessed < *sæl*, happiness (sense development: happy → blissful → unaware of reality → foolish)] 1. having or showing little sense or judgment; foolish, absurd, etc. 2. frivolous or trivial 3. [Colloq.] dazed or senseless, as from a blow 4. *Cricket* of a fielder standing close to a batsman [*silly* mid-on] —*n., pl.* **-lies** a silly person —**sil'li·ly** (or **sil'ly**) *adv.* —**sil'li·ness** *n.*

silly season a period, usually during August, when newspapers are filled with frivolous news items

si·lo (sī'lō) *n., pl.* **-los** [Fr. < Sp. < L. < Gr. *siros*] 1. an airtight pit or tower in which grain or green fodder is stored 2. an underground structure for storing and launching a long-range ballistic missile —*vt.* **-loed, -lo·ing** to store in a silo

silt (silt) *n.* [prob. < Scand.] earthy sediment made up of fine particles carried or laid down by moving water —*vt., vi.* to fill or choke up with silt —**silt·ta·tion** (sil tā'shən) *n.* —**silt'y** *adj.* **silt'i·er, silt'i·est**

Si·lu·ri·an (si loor'ē ən, sī; -lyoor'-) *adj.* [< L. *Silures*, ancient tribe in Wales] designating or of the geological period after the Ordovician in the Paleozoic Era —**the Silurian** the Silurian Period or its rocks: see GEOLOGY, chart

sil·va (sil'və) *n.* [ModL. < L., a forest] 1. the forest trees of an area 2. *pl.* **-vas, -vae** (-vē) a book or treatise describing these

sil·van (sil'vən) *adj., n.* same as SYLVAN

sil·ver (sil'vər) *n.* [OE. *seolfer*] 1. a white, metallic chemical element that is extremely ductile and malleable and takes a high polish: it is a precious metal and is used in coins, jewellery, etc.: symbol, Ag; at. wt., 107.868; at. no., 47 2. *a)* silver coin *b)* money; riches 3. articles, esp. tableware, made of or plated with silver 4. the lustrous, greyish-white colour of silver 5. something having this colour, as the coating for a mirror 6. an award given to mark the attainment of a high standard in certain sports, dancing, etc. —*adj.* 1. of or containing silver; silvery 2. of or advocating silver as a currency standard 3. having a silvery colour, tone, etc. 4. eloquent [a *silver* tongue] 5. marking the 25th anniversary [a *silver* wedding anniversary] —*vt.* 1. to cover with silver 2. to make silvery in colour —*vi.* to become silvery

silver band a brass band with silver-plated instruments

silver birch 1. a tree found in Europe, Asia, etc., with a silvery-white, peeling bark 2. same as PAPER BIRCH

sil·ver·fish (-fish') *n.* 1. *pl.* **-fish', -fish'es:** see FISH any of various unrelated fishes of silvery colour 2. *pl.* **-fish'** a wingless insect with silvery scales and long feelers, found in damp, dark places

silver fox 1. a N. American fox with white-tipped black fur 2. this fur

silver iodide a yellow powder, AgI, that darkens in light: used in photography, to seed clouds, etc.

silver jubilee a 25th anniversary of an event, esp. the accession of a sovereign

silver lining anything seen as hopeful or comforting in the midst of despair, misfortune, etc.

silver medal a medal awarded to an entrant who is placed second in a competition

silver nitrate a colourless, crystalline salt, $AgNO_3$, used in silver-plating, photography, medicine, etc.

sil·ver-plate (-plāt') *vt.* **-plat'ed, -plat'ing** to coat with silver, esp. by electroplating

silver plate tableware, etc., made of, or plated with, silver

silver salmon same as COHO

silver screen 1. a screen onto which films are projected in cinemas 2. films collectively

sil·ver·side (-sīd') *n.* 1. a cut of beef from the upper round 2. any of certain small, mostly saltwater fishes with silver stripes along the sides: also **sil'ver·sides'**

sil·ver·smith (-smith') *n.* a skilled worker who makes articles of silver

silver standard a monetary standard in which the basic currency unit is made equal to and redeemable by a specified quantity of silver

silver stick an officer of the Life Guards on duty at the royal palace whose insignia of office is a silver wand

sil·ver·ware (-wer') *n.* articles, esp. tableware, made of or plated with silver

sil·ver·y (sil'vər ē) *adj.* 1. like silver, as in colour or lustre 2. covered with or containing silver 3. soft and clear, like the sound of a silver bell —**sil'ver·i·ness** *n.*

sil·vi·cul·ture (sil'vi kul'chər) *n.* [Fr. *sylviculture* < L. *silva*, forest + *culta*, CULTURE] the art of cultivating a forest; forestry —**sil'vi·cul'tur·ist** *n.*

sim·i·an (sim'ē ən) *adj.* [< L. *simia*, an ape, prob. < *simus*, flat-nosed < Gr.] of or like an ape or monkey —*n.* an ape or monkey

sim·i·lar (sim'ə lər) *adj.* [< Fr. < L. *similis*] 1. nearly but not exactly the same or alike 2. *Geom.* having the same shape, but not the same size or position —**sim'i·lar·ly** *adv.*

sim·i·lar·i·ty (sim'ə lar'ə tē) *n.* 1. a being similar; likeness 2. *pl.* **-ties** a point, feature, or instance in which things are similar

sim·i·le (sim'ə lē) *n.* [L., a likeness < *similis*, like] a figure of speech in which one thing is likened to another, dissimilar thing by using *like, as,* etc. (Ex.: a voice like thunder): cf. METAPHOR

si·mil·i·tude (sə mil'ə tyood') *n.* [MFr. < L. *similitudo*] 1. [Obs.] a person or thing resembling another; counterpart 2. the form or likeness (*of* some person or thing) 3. [Rare] a simile 4. similarity; likeness

sim·mer (sim'ər) *vi.* [prob. of echoic origin] 1. to remain at or just below the boiling point 2. to be about to break out, as in anger, revolt, laughter, etc. —*vt.* 1. to make (a liquid) simmer 2. to cook in such a liquid —*n.* a simmering —**simmer down** 1. to simmer, as a liquid, until the volume is reduced 2. to become calm; cool off

sim·nel (sim'n'l) *n.* [ME. *simenel* < OFr. < L. *simila*, fine wheat flour] 1. formerly, a kind of bread or roll prepared by boiling, or boiling and baking 2. a rich fruit cake eaten in mid-Lent or at Easter or Christmas

si·mon-pure (sī'mən pyoor') *adj.* [after *Simon Pure,* a Quaker in S. Centlivre's play *A Bold Stroke for a Wife* (1718)] genuine; authentic

si·mo·ny (sī'mə nē) *n.* [< OFr. < ML. *simonia* < *Simon Magus,* a Samaritan magician who offered money for instruction in the rite of imparting the Holy Ghost: Acts 8:9-24] the buying or selling of sacred or spiritual things, as church offices

si·moom (si moom') *n.* [< Ar. < *samma,* to poison] a hot, violent, sand-laden wind of the African and Asiatic deserts: also **si·moon'** (-moon')

sim·pa·ti·co (sim pät'i kō, -pat'-) *adj.* [< It. *simpatico* or Sp. *simpático*] compatible or congenial

sim·per (sim'pər) *vi.* [akin to MDu. *simperlijc,* dainty, affected] to smile in a silly or affected way —*vt.* to say with a simper —*n.* a silly or affected smile —**sim'per·er** *n.* —**sim'per·ing·ly** *adv.*

sim·ple (sim'p'l) *adj.* **-pler, -plest** [OFr. < L. *simplex*] 1. having only one part, feature, etc.; not compound or complex 2. having few parts, etc.; not complicated or involved 3. easy to do, solve, or understand, as a task, question, etc. 4. without additions or qualifications [the *simple* facts] 5. *a)* not ornate; unadorned [*simple* clothes] *b)* not luxurious; plain [*simple* tastes] 6. pure; unadulterated 7. without guile or deceit 8. *a)* not showy or affected *b)* not sophisticated; naive 9. of low rank or position; lowly or ordinary 10. insignificant; unimportant 11. *a)* stupid or foolish *b)* uneducated or ignorant 12. *Chem.* elementary or unmixed 13. *Law* unconditional [in fee *simple*] 14. *Zool.* not divided into parts; not compounded —*n.* 1. an ignorant or foolish person 2. [Archaic] a medicinal plant or herb, or a medicine made from it —**sim'ple·ness** *n.*

simple fraction a fraction in which both numerator and denominator are whole numbers, as 1/2

simple fracture a bone fracture in which the broken ends of bone do not pierce the skin

sim·ple-heart·ed (-här'tid) *adj.* artless or unsophisticated

simple interest interest computed on principal alone, not on principal plus interest

simple interval *Music* an interval of less than an octave

simple machine any of the basic mechanical devices, including the lever, wheel and axle, pulley, wedge, screw, and inclined plane, essential to any complex machine

sim·ple-mind·ed (-mīn'did) *adj.* **1.** artless; unsophisticated **2.** foolish; stupid; silly **3.** mentally retarded —**sim'·ple-mind'ed·ly** *adv.* —**sim'ple-mind'ed·ness** *n.*

simple sentence a sentence having one main clause and no subordinate clauses (Ex.: The boy ran home.)

sim·ple·ton (sim'p'l tən) *n.* [< SIMPLE] a person who is stupid or easily deceived; fool

‡**sim·plic·i·ter** (sim plis'i tər) *adv.* [L.] simply; not relatively; unconditionally

sim·plic·i·ty (sim plis'ə tē) *n.,* *pl.* **-ties** **1.** a being simple; freedom from complexity or intricacy **2.** absence of luxury, elegance, etc.; plainness **3.** freedom from affectation **4.** lack of sense; foolishness

sim·pli·fy (sim'plə fī') *vt.* **-fied'**, **-fy'ing** to make simpler, easier, less complex, etc. —**sim'pli·fi·ca'tion** *n.* —**sim'·pli·fi'·er** *n.*

sim·plist (sim'plist) *n.* a person given to simplistic explanations, theories, etc. —*adj.* same as SIMPLISTIC —**sim'plism** *n.*

sim·plis·tic (sim plis'tik) *adj.* making complex problems seem to be simple; oversimplifying or oversimplified —**sim·plis'ti·cal·ly** *adv.*

sim·ply (sim'plē) *adv.* **1.** in a simple way **2.** merely; only [*simply* trying to help] **3.** absolutely; completely

sim·u·la·crum (sim'yoo lā'krəm) *n.,* *pl.* **-cra** (-krə) [L. < *simulare:* see ff.] **1.** an image; likeness **2.** false appearance; semblance **3.** a mere pretence sham

sim·u·late (sim'yoo lāt') *vt.* **-lat'ed**, **-lat'ing** [< L. pp. of *simulare,* to feign < *simul,* likewise] **1.** to give a false appearance of; feign [to *simulate* an interest] **2.** *a)* to look or act like [an insect *simulating* a twig] *b)* to represent a physical system, as a traffic flow, esp. by a computer program —**sim'u·la'tion** *n.* —**sim'u·la'tive** *adj.*

sim·u·la·tor (-lāt'ər) *n.* one that simulates; specif., a training device that duplicates artificially the conditions likely to be encountered in some operation, as in a spacecraft [a flight *simulator*]

si·mul·cast (sī'm'l kåst') *vt.* **-cast'** or **-cast'ed**, **-cast'ing** [SIMUL(TANEOUS) + (BROAD)CAST] to broadcast (a programme, event, etc.) simultaneously by radio and television —*n.* a programme, etc. so broadcast

si·mul·ta·ne·ous (sī'm'l tā'nē əs, -tän'yəs) *adj.* [< ML., ult. < L. *simul,* at the same time] occurring, done, existing, etc. together or at the same time —**si'mul·ta·ne'i·ty** (-tə nē'ə tē), **si'mul·ta·ne·ous·ness** *n.* —**si'mul·ta·ne·ous·ly** *adv.*

sin (sin) *n.* [OE. *synne*] **1.** *a)* the breaking of religious or moral law, esp. through a wilful act *b)* the state of committing sins **2.** any offence or fault —*vi.* **sinned**, **sin'·ning** to commit a sin

sin sine

since (sins) *adv.* [< OE *siththan,* ult. < *sith,* after + *thon,* instrumental form of *thæt,* that] **1.** from then until now [he came on Monday and has been here ever *since*] **2.** at some time or any time between then and now [he was ill last week but has *since* recovered] **3.** before now; ago [gone long *since*] —*prep.* **1.** continuously from (the time given) until now [out walking *since* noon] **2.** during the period following [he's written twice *since* May] —*conj.* **1.** after the time that [two years *since* he died] **2.** continuously from the time when [lonely ever *since* he left] **3.** inasmuch as; because [*since* you're tired, let's go home]

sin·cere (sin sir') *adj.* **-cer'er**, **-cer'est** [< MFr. < L. *sincerus,* clean] **1.** without deceit or pretence; truthful; honest **2.** genuine; real [*sincere* grief] —**sin·cere'ly** *adv.* —**sin·cere'ness** *n.*

sin·cer·i·ty (sin ser'ə tē) *n.,* *pl.* **-ties** a being sincere; honesty, genuineness, etc.

sine (sīn) *n.* [ML. *sinus* (< L., a curve), used as transl. of Ar. *jaib,* bosom of a garment] *Trigonometry* the ratio between the side opposite a given acute angle in a right triangle and the hypotenuse

‡**si·ne** (sī'nē, si'nā) *prep.* [L.] without

si·ne·cure (sī'nə kyoor, sin'ə-) *n.* [< ML. < L. *sine,* without + *cura,* care] **1.** a church benefice not involving spiritual care of members **2.** any position that brings profit without involving much work, responsibility, etc. —**si'ne·cur'ism** *n.* —**si'ne·cur'ist** *n.*

sine curve a graphic representation of the sine ratio; specif., the graph of $y = \text{sine } x$

si·ne di·e (sī'nē dī'ē, sin'ā dē'ā) [LL.] without (a) day (being set for meeting again); for an indefinite period of time [to adjourn an assembly *sine die*]

si·ne qua non (sī'nē kwä non', sin'ā kwä nōn') [L., without which not] something essential or indispensable

sin·ew (sin'yōō) *n.* [OE. *seonwe,* oblique form < nom. *seonu*] **1.** a tendon **2.** muscular power; strength **3.** [often *pl.*] any source of power or strength —*vt.* to strengthen as with sinews

sine wave any oscillation, such as a sound wave, whose waveform is that of a sine curve

sin·ew·y (sin yoo wē) *adj.* **1.** of or like sinew; tough **2.** having many sinews, as a cut of meat **3.** having good muscular development **4.** vigorous; powerful

sin·ful (sin'fəl) *adj.* full of or characterized by sin; wicked —**sin'ful·ly** *adv.* —**sin'ful·ness** *n.*

sing (siŋ) *vi.* **sang** or now rarely **sung**, **sung**, **sing'ing** [OE. *singan*] **1.** *a)* to produce musical sounds with the voice *b)* to perform musical selections vocally **2.** to use song in description, praise, etc. [of thee I *sing*] **3.** *a)* to make musical sounds like those of the human voice, as a songbird *b)* to whistle, buzz, hum, etc., as a kettle, bee, etc. **4.** to admit of being sung **5.** to rejoice [his heart *sang*] **6.** to have a sensation of ringing, etc., esp. in the ears —*vt.* **1.** to render or utter by singing **2.** to chant **3.** to describe, proclaim, etc. in song **4.** to bring or put, as to sleep, by singing —*n.* **1.** a sound of whistling, humming, etc. **2.** [Colloq.] a singing by a group gathered for the purpose —**sing out** [Colloq.] to speak or call out loudly —**sing'·a·ble** *adj.* —**sing'er** *n.*

sing. singular

sing-a-long (siŋ'ə loŋ') *n.* [Colloq.] an informal gathering of people to join in the singing of songs

singe (sinj) *vt.* **singed**, **singe'ing** [OE. *sengan*] **1.** to burn superficially or slightly **2.** to expose (a carcass) to flame in removing bristles or feathers —*n.* **1.** a singeing **2.** a slight burn —**sing'er** *n.*

Singh (siŋ) *n.* [Sans. *sinhá,* a lion] a title assumed by a Sikh after being initiated as a full member of the community

Sin·gha·lese (siŋ'gə lēz', -lēs') *adj., n., pl.* **-lese'** same as SINHALESE

sin·gle (siŋ'g'l) *adj.* [< OFr. < L. *singulus*] **1.** *a)* one only; one and no more *b)* distinct from others of the same kind [every *single* time] *c)* designating a ticket valid for a journey in one direction only **2.** without another; alone **3.** of or for one person or family, as a house **4.** between two persons only [*single* combat] **5.** unmarried **6.** having only one part; not double, compound, etc. **7.** the same for all; uniform **8.** unbroken **9.** having only one set of petals **10.** sincere —*vt.* **-gled**, **-gling** to select from others (usually with *out*) —*n.* **1.** a single person or thing; specif., *a)* a ticket for a bus, train, etc., entitling the passenger to travel only to his destination, without returning *b)* a gramophone record with one short piece of music on each side **2.** *Cricket* a hit by which one run is scored **3.** [*pl.*] *Tennis,* etc. a match with only one player on each side —**sin'·gle·ness** *n.*

sin·gle-breast·ed (-bres'tid) *adj.* overlapping over the breast just enough to be fastened with one button or one row of buttons, as a coat

sin·gle-deck·er (-dek'ər) *n.* a bus, etc., with only one passenger deck

single entry a system of bookkeeping in which a single account is kept, usually of cash and of debts owed to and by the concern in question

single file **1.** a single column of persons or things, one directly behind another **2.** in such a column

sin·gle-foot (-foot') *n.* the gait of a horse in which the legs move in lateral pairs, each foot falling separately —*vi.* to move with this gait

sin·gle-hand·ed (-han'did) *adj.* **1.** having only one hand **2.** using or requiring the use of only one hand **3.** done or working alone —*adv.* **1.** by means of only one hand **2.** without help —**sin'gle-hand'ed·ly** *adv.* —**sin'gle-hand'·ed·ness** *n.*

sin·gle-heart·ed (-här'tid) *adj.* honest; sincere —**sin'·gle-heart'ed·ly** *adv.* —**sin'gle-heart'ed·ness** *n.*

sin·gle-mind·ed (-mīn'did) *adj.* **1.** *same as* SINGLE-HEARTED **2.** with only one aim or purpose —**sin'gle-mind'ed·ly** *adv.* —**sin'gle-mind'ed·ness** *n.*

sin·gle-space (-spās') *vt., vi.* **-spaced'**, **-spac'ing** to type (copy) so as to leave no line space between lines

sin·gle·stick (-stik') *n.* **1.** a swordlike stick formerly used for fencing **2.** the sport of fencing with such sticks

sin·glet (siŋ'glit) *n.* **1.** a man's sleeveless vest **2.** a sleeveless top worn by athletes and boxers

sin·gle·ton (siŋ'g'l tən) *n.* **1.** the only playing card held by a player in a given suit **2.** a single thing, all by itself

sin·gle-track (-trak') *adj.* **1.** of a road or railway, carrying only one vehicle at a time **2.** *same as* ONE-TRACK

sin·gle·tree (-trē') *n.* [U.S. and Aust.] *same as* SWINGLETREE

sin·gly (siŋ'glē) *adv.* **1.** as a single, separate person or thing; alone **2.** one by one **3.** without help; unaided

sing·song (siŋ'soŋ') *n.* **1.** *a)* an unvarying rise and fall of tone *b)* speech, tones, etc. marked by this **2.** *a)* monotonous rhyme or rhythm in verse *b*) verse with this —*adj.* monotonous because done in singsong

sin·gu·lar (siŋ′gyə lər) *adj.* [< OFr. < L. < *singulus*, single] 1. being the only one of its kind; unique 2. extraordinary; remarkable [*singular* beauty] 3. strange; odd [a *singular* remark] 4. [Archaic] separate; individual 5. *Gram.* designating or of that category of number referring to only one —*n. Gram.* 1. the singular number 2. the singular form of a word 3. a word in singular form —**sin′gu·lar′i·ty** (-lar′ə tē) *n., pl.* **-ties** —**sin′gu·lar·ly** *adv.*

sin·gu·lar·ize (siŋ′gyə lə rīz′) *vt.* **-ized′, -iz′ing** to make singular

sinh (shīn) *n. Math.* hyperbolic sine

Sin·ha·lese (sin′hə lēz′, sin′ə-; -lēs′) *adj.* of Ceylon, its principal people, their language, etc. —*n.* 1. *pl.* **-lese′** any member of the Sinhalese people 2. their language

sin·is·ter (sin′is tər) *adj.* [< L. *sinister*, left-hand or unlucky (side)] 1. of or on the left-hand side (on a coat of arms, the right of the viewer) 2. threatening harm, evil, etc.; ominous 3. evil or dishonest, esp. in a dark, mysterious way [a *sinister* plot] 4. unfortunate or disastrous [a *sinister* fate] —**sin′is·ter·ly** *adv.* —**sin′is·ter·ness** *n.*

sin·is·tral (sin′is trəl) *adj.* [OFr. < L.: see prec.] 1. on the left-hand side; left 2. left-handed —**sin′is·tral′i·ty** (-i stral′ə tē) *n.* —**sin′is·tral·ly** *adv.*

sin·is·trorse (sin′is trôrs′) *adj.* [< ModL. < L. < *sinister*, left + pp. of *vertere*, to turn] *Bot.* twining upwards to the left, as the stems of some plants

Si·nit·ic (si nit′ik) *n.* [see SINO-, -ITE, & -IC] a branch of Sino-Tibetan, including Chinese languages —*adj.* of China, the Chinese, their languages, etc.

sink (siŋk) *vi.* **sank** or **sunk, sunk** or obs. **sunk′en, sink′-ing** [OE. *sincan*] 1. to go beneath the surface of water, snow, etc. and be partly or completely covered 2. *a*) to go down slowly *b*) to seem to descend, as the sun 3. to become lower in level, as a lake 4. to decrease in degree, volume, or strength, as wind, flames, a sound, etc. 5. to become less in value or amount, as prices 6. to become hollow; recede, as the cheeks 7. to pass gradually (*into* sleep, despair, etc.) 8. to approach death; fail 9. *a*) to lose social position, wealth, etc. *b*) to lose or abandon one's moral values and stoop (*to* an unworthy action) 10. to become absorbed; penetrate —*vt.* 1. to cause to sink; make go beneath a surface, make go down, make lower, etc. 2. to make (a well, design, etc.) by digging, drilling, or cutting 3. *a*) to invest (money, capital, etc.) *b*) to lose by investing 4. to hold back, suppress, or conceal (evidence, identity, etc.) 5. to pay up (a debt) 6. to defeat; undo; ruin 7. *Sports* to put (a basketball) through the basket or (a golf ball) into the hole, and so score —*n.* 1. a cesspool or sewer 2. any place or thing considered morally filthy 3. a basin, as in a kitchen, with a drainpipe and, usually, a water supply 4. *Geol. a*) an area of slightly sunken land, esp. one in which water collects *b*) same as SINKHOLE (sense 2) —**sink in** [Colloq.] to be grasped mentally, esp. with difficulty —**sink′a·ble** *adj.*

sink·er (siŋ′kər) *n.* 1. a person or thing that sinks 2. a lead weight for fishing 3. [U.S. Colloq.] a doughnut

sink·hole (siŋk′hōl′) *n.* 1. same as CESSPOOL 2. *Geol.* a hollow into which surface water flows and sinks: also **swallowhole**

sinking fund a fund made up of sums of money set aside at intervals, usually invested at interest, to pay a debt, meet expenses, etc.

sin·less (sin′lis) *adj.* without sin; innocent —**sin′less·ly** *adv.* —**sin′less·ness** *n.*

sin·ner (-ər) *n.* a person who sins; wrongdoer

Sinn Fein (shin′fān′) [Ir., we ourselves] 1. formerly, an Irish revolutionary movement working for independence and to revive Irish culture 2. a political movement for the unification of Ireland —**Sinn′ Fein′er**

Si·no- (sī′nō, sin′ō) [< Fr. < LL. < Gr. *Sinai*, an Oriental people] a combining form meaning: 1. of the Chinese people or language 2. Chinese and

Si·nol·o·gy (sī nol′ə jē, si-) *n.* [SINO- + -LOGY] the study of Chinese languages, customs, etc. —**Si·no·log·i·cal** (sī′nə loj′-i k′l, sin′ə-) *adj.* —**Si·nol′o·gist, Si·no·logue** (sī′nə log′) *n.*

Si·no-Ti·bet·an (sī′nō ti bet′′n, sin′ō-) *adj.* designating or of a family of languages of C and SE Asia, including Sinitic, Tibetan, and Burmese —*n.* this family

sin·u·ate (sin′yoo wit; *also, and for v.* al′wāts, -wāt′) *adj.* [< L. pp. of *sinuare*, to bend < *sinus*, a bend] 1. same as SINUOUS 2. *Bot.* having an indented, wavy margin, as some leaves —*vi.* **-at′ed, -at′ing** to wind in and out —**sin′-u·ate·ly** *adv.* —**sin′u·a′tion** *n.*

sin·u·ous (sin′yoo wəs) *adj.* [< L. < *sinus*, a bend] 1. bending or winding in and out 2. not straightforward; devious —**sin′u·os′i·ty** (-wos′ə tē) *n., pl.* **-ties** —**sin′-u·ous·ly** *adv.*

si·nus (sī′nəs) *n.* [L., a bent surface] 1. a bend or curve 2. a cavity, hollow, or passage; specif., *Anat., Zool. a*) any air cavity in the skull opening into a nasal cavity *b*) a channel

for venous blood 3. a channel leading from a pus-filled cavity

si·nus·i·tis (sī′nə sīt′əs) *n.* [ModL.: see prec. & -ITIS] inflammation of a sinus or sinuses, esp. of the skull

si·nu·soi·dal projection (sī′nə soi′d′l) [< ML. *sinus* < L.: see SINUS] a map projection showing the entire surface of the earth, with straight lines of latitude and curved lines of longitude

Si·on (sī′ən) *var. of* ZION

-sion (shən; *sometimes* zhən) [< L. *-sio*] a suffix meaning act, quality, condition, or result of [*discussion, confusion*]

Siou·an (sōō′ən) *adj.* designating or of a language family of N American Indians of the west central U.S., central Canada, etc.: it includes Dakota, Crow, etc. —*n.* this family of languages

sip (sip) *vt., vi.* **sipped, sip′ping** [akin to LowG. *sippen*] to drink a little at a time —*n.* 1. a sipping 2. a small quantity sipped —**sip′per** *n.*

si·phon (sī′fən) *n.* [Fr. < L. < Gr. *siphōn*, a tube] 1. a bent tube for carrying liquid out over the edge of a container to a lower level through the atmospheric pressure on the surface of the liquid 2. same as SIPHON BOTTLE 3. a tubelike organ, as in a cuttlefish, for drawing in or ejecting liquids —*vt., vi.* to draw off, or pass, through a siphon —**si′phon·al** (-′l), **si·phon′ic** (-fon′ik) *adj.*

siphon bottle a heavy, sealed bottle with a tube inside connected at the top with a valve and nozzle used to release the pressurized, carbonated water within

SIPHON

si·phon·et (sī′fən et) *n.* [SIPHON + -ET] the honeydew tube of an aphid

sir (sur) *n.* [< *sire*: see ff.] 1. [*sometimes* S-] a respectful term of address used to a man: not followed by the name: often used in the salutation of a letter 2. [S-] the title used before the name of a knight or baronet 3. [Archaic] a term of address used with the title of a man's office, etc. [*sir* judge]

sir·car (sur′kär) *n.* [< Urdu *sirkar* < Per. *sarkār*] 1. in India, the supreme authority; government 2. a Hindu clerk or accountant

sir·dar (sur′där) *n.* [Hindi *sardār*] 1. in India, *a*) a chief or noble *b*) a high military officer 2. in India, anyone holding an important position

sire (sīr) *n.* [< OFr., a master < L. *senior*: see SENIOR] 1. a title of respect used in addressing a king 2. [Poet.] a father or forefather 3. the male parent of an animal —*vt.* **sired, sir′ing** to beget: said esp. of animals

si·ren (sī′rən) *n.* [< OFr., ult. < Gr. *Seirēn*] 1. *Gr. & Rom. Myth.* any of several sea nymphs who lured sailors to their death on rocky coasts by seductive singing 2. a seductive woman 3. a device using steam or air driven against a rotating, perforated disc to make a loud, wailing sound, esp. as a warning signal —*adj.* of or like a siren; dangerously seductive

Sir·i·us (sir′ē əs) [L. < Gr. *Seirios*, lit., the scorcher] same as DOG STAR (sense 1)

sir·loin (sur′loin) *n.* [< MFr. < OFr. *sur*, over < *loigne*, loin] a choice cut, esp. of beef, from the loin end just in front of the rump

si·roc·co (sə rok′ō) *n., pl.* **-cos** [It. < Ar. *sharq*, the east] 1. a hot, steady wind blowing from the Libyan deserts into S Europe 2. any wind like this Also **sci·roc·co**

sir·rah (sir′ə) *n.* [< SIR] [Archaic] a contemptuous term of address used to a man

sir·ree, sir·ee (sə rē′) *interj.* [< SIR] [Chiefly U.S.] an interjection used for emphasis after *yes* or *no*

sis (sis) *n.* [U.S. Colloq.] shortened *form of* SISTER

si·sal (sī′s′l) *n.* [< *Sisal*, Yucatán, a former seaport] 1. a strong fibre obtained from a widely cultivated agave native to S Mexico, used for making rope, insulation, etc. 2. the agave itself Also **sisal hemp**

sis·kin (sis′kin) *n.* [< G. *Zeischen*] a European and Asiatic finch with green plumage and black and yellow markings

sis·sy (sis′ē) *n., pl.* **-sies** [dim. of SIS] [Colloq.] 1. an effeminate man or boy 2. a coward —*adj.* [Colloq.] of or like a sissy: also **sis′si·fied′** (-ə fīd′) —**sis′sy·ish** *adj.*

sis·ter (sis′tər) *n.* [ON. *systir*] 1. a female as she is related to other children of her parents 2. a close friend who is like a sister 3. a female fellow member of the same race, creed, profession, organization,etc. 4. a member of a female religious order; nun 5. one of the same kind, model, etc. 6. a nurse, esp. a head nurse —*adj.* related as sisters

sis·ter·hood (-hood′) *n.* 1. the state of being a sister or sisters 2. an association of women united in a common interest, work, creed, etc.

sis·ter-in-law (-in lô′) *n., pl.* **sis′ters-in-law′** 1. the sister of one's husband or wife 2. the wife of one's brother 3. the wife of the brother of one's husband or wife

sis·ter·ly (-lē) *adj.* 1. of or like a sister 2. friendly, kind, affectionate, etc. —**sis′ter·li·ness** *n.*

Sis·y·phe·an (sis′ə fē′ən) *adj.* [L. < Gr.] 1. of or like

Sisyphus, in Greek mythology a greedy king doomed forever in Hades to roll uphill a heavy stone which always rolled down again **2.** endless and laborious

sit (sit) *vi.* **sat, sit′ting** [OE. *sittan*] **1.** *a)* to rest the body on the buttocks, as on a chair *b)* to rest on the haunches with forelegs braced, as a dog *c)* to perch, as a bird **2.** to cover eggs for hatching **3.** *a)* to occupy a seat as a judge, member of parliament, etc. *b)* to be in session, as a court **4.** to pose, as for a portrait **5.** to be inactive **6.** to be located [a house *sitting* on a hill] **7.** to hang on the wearer [a coat *sitting* loosely] **8.** to rest or lie as specified [cares *sit* lightly on him] **9.** to take an examination [*for* a degree, etc.] **10.** same as BABY-SIT —*vt.* **1.** to cause to sit **2.** to stay seated on (a horse, etc.) **3.** to have seating space for —*n.* [Colloq.] the time spent seated —**sit back 1.** to relax **2.** to be passive —**sit down** to take a seat —**sit in 1.** to take part; attend (often with *on*) **2.** to take the place of temporarily; deputize (often with *for*) **3.** to take part in a sit-in —**sit on** (or **upon**) **1.** to be on (a jury, committee, etc.) **2.** to confer on **3.** [Colloq.] to suppress, check, etc. **4.** [Colloq.] to rebuke; snub **5.** [Colloq.] to hold (something) back from being considered or acted upon —**sit out 1.** to stay until the end of **2.** to stay seated during or take no part in (a dance, game, etc.) —**sit tight 1.** to wait patiently **2.** to refuse to move or be moved —**sit up 1.** to rise to a sitting position **2.** to sit erect **3.** to put off going to bed **4.** [Colloq.] to become suddenly alert

si·tar (si tär′, si′tär) *n.* [Hindi *sitār*] a lutelike instrument of India with a long, fretted neck, a resonating gourd or gourds, and strings that vibrate along with those being played —**si·tar′ist** *n.*

sit·com (sit′kom′) *n.* Colloq. *clipped form of* SITUATION COMEDY

sit-down (sit′doun′) *n.* **1.** *clipped form of* SIT-DOWN STRIKE **2.** a form of civil disobedience in which demonstrators sit down in streets, etc. and resist being moved —**sit′-down′er** *n.*

SITAR

sit-down strike a strike in which employees stop work but refuse to leave their place of employment

site (sīt) *n.* [< L. *situs*, position < pp. of *sinere*, to put down] **1.** a piece of land considered for a certain purpose [a good *site* for a town] **2.** the place or scene of anything —*vt.* **sit′ed, sit′ing** to locate on a site

sith (sith) *adv., conj., prep.* [OE. *siththa*] *archaic form of* SINCE

sit-in (sit′in′) *n.* a sit-down inside a public place by a group demonstrating for civil rights, against war, etc.

sit·ter (sit′ər) *n.* one that sits; specif., *a) short for* BABY SITTER *b)* a brooding hen *c)* a person who is posing for a portrait

sit·ting (sit′iŋ) *n.* **1.** the act or position of one that sits **2.** a session or meeting, as of a court **3.** a period of being seated at some activity **4.** *a)* a brooding upon eggs *b)* a clutch of eggs being hatched **5.** a space to be seated in **6.** one of two or more times at which a meal is served —*adj.* that sits; seated

sitting duck [Colloq.] a person or thing especially vulnerable to attack: also **sitting target**

sitting room *same as* LIVING ROOM

sitting tenant a tenant already living in a house, flat, etc.

sit·u·ate (sit′yoo wāt′) *vt.* **-at′ed, -at′ing** [< ML. pp. of *situare*, to place < L. *situs*, SITE] to put in a certain place or position; place; locate

sit·u·at·ed (-id) *adj.* **1.** placed as to site or position; located **2.** placed as to circumstances

sit·u·a·tion (sit′yoo wā′shən) *n.* **1.** location; position **2.** a place; locality **3.** condition with regard to circumstances **4.** *a)* a combination of circumstances at a given time in real life or in the plot of a play, novel, etc. *b)* a difficult state of affairs **5.** a position of employment

sit·u·a·tion·al (-′l) *adj.* of, resulting from, or determined by a specific situation —**sit′u·a·tion·al·ly** *adv.*

situation comedy a comedy, esp. one on television, in which the humour arises from the characters and situations in which they find themselves

sit-up, sit·up (sit′up′) *n.* an exercise in which a person lying flat on the back rises to a sitting position without using the hands and keeping the legs straight

sit-up·on (-ə pon′) *n.* [Colloq.] the backside or buttocks

sitz bath (sits, zits) [< G. *Sitzbad*, a sitting bath] a hip-bath

SI Units [< Fr. *Système Internationale*] international system of units (based on the metre and kilogramme) adopted as the metric system for Britain

six (siks) *adj.* [OE. *sex*] totalling one more than five —*n.* **1.** the cardinal number between five and seven; 6; VI **2.** a group of six; half a dozen **3.** anything having six units or members, or numbered six —**at sixes and sevens** [Colloq.]

1. in confusion or disorder **2.** disagreeing —**hit** (or **knock**) **for six** to stun; overwhelm completely

six·fold (-fōld′) *adj.* [see -FOLD] **1.** having six parts **2.** having six times as much or as many —*adv.* six times as much or as many

six·pence (-pəns) *n.* **1.** the sum of six British (old) pennies **2.** a British coin of this value, now worth $2^1/_2$ pence

six-shoot·er (-shoot′ər) *n.* [Colloq.] a revolver that fires six shots without reloading: also **six′-gun′**

six·teen (siks′tēn′) *adj.* [OE. *syxtene*] six more than ten —*n.* the cardinal number between fifteen and seventeen; 16; XVI

six·teenth (siks′tēnth′) *adj.* **1.** preceded by fifteen others in a series; 16th **2.** designating any of the sixteen equal parts of something —*n.* **1.** the one following the fifteenth **2.** any of the sixteen equal parts of something; 1/16

sixteenth note [U.S.] *Music* a semiquaver

sixth (siksth) *adj.* [OE. *sixta*] **1.** preceded by five others in a series; 6th **2.** designating any of the six equal parts of something —*n.* **1.** the one following the fifth **2.** any of the six equal parts of something; 1/6 **3.** *Music a)* the sixth tone of an ascending diatonic scale, or a tone five degrees above or below any given tone *b)* the interval between two such tones, or a combination of them —**sixth′ly** *adv.*

sixth sense a power to perceive by intuition, thought of as a sense in addition to the commonly accepted five senses

six·ti·eth (siks′tē ith) *adj.* **1.** preceded by fifty-nine others in a series; 60th **2.** designating any of the sixty equal parts of something —*n.* **1.** the one following the fifty-ninth **2.** any of the sixty equal parts of something; 1/60

six·ty (siks′tē) *adj.* [OE. *sixtig*] six times ten —*n., pl.* **-ties** the cardinal number between fifty-nine and sixty-one; 60; LX —**the sixties** the numbers or years, as of a century, from sixty to sixty-nine

six·ty-fourth note (-fôrth′) [U.S.] *Music* a hemi-demisemiquaver

siz·a·ble (sī′za b'l) *adj.* quite large or bulky: also **size′a·ble** —**siz′a·ble·ness** *n.* —**siz′a·bly** *adv.*

size[1] (sīz) *n.* [< OFr. *sise*, short for *assise*: see ASSIZE] **1.** that quality of a thing which determines how much space it occupies; dimensions **2.** any of a series of graded classifications for goods [*size* ten shoes] **3.** *a)* extent, amount, etc. *b)* sizable amount, dimensions, etc. **4.** [Colloq.] true state of affairs —*vt.* **sized, siz′ing 1.** to make in accordance with a given size **2.** to arrange according to size —**of a size** of one or the same size —**size up** [Colloq.] **1.** to estimate; judge **2.** to meet requirements —**that's the size of it** [Colloq.] that is right; that is a true account —**siz′er** *n.*

size[2] (sīz) *n.* [ME. *syse*] any thin, pasty or gluey substance used as a glaze or filler on porous materials, as on paper or cloth —*vt.* **sized, siz′ing** to apply size to

-sized (sīzd) *a combining form meaning* having (a specified) size [small-*sized*]: also **-size** [life-*size*]

siz·ing (sī′ziŋ) *n.* **1.** *same as* SIZE[2] **2.** the act or process of applying such size

siz·zle (siz′′l) *vi.* **-zled, -zling** [echoic] **1.** to make a hissing sound when in contact with heat, as water on hot metal **2.** to be extremely hot **3.** to simmer with suppressed emotion, esp. with rage —*vt.* to make sizzle —*n.* a sizzling sound —**siz′zler** *n.*

S.J. Society of Jesus

S.J.A. Saint John's Ambulance (Brigade or Association)

skald (skôld) *n.* [ON. *skāld*] any ancient Scandinavian poet, specif., of the Viking period —**skald′ic** *adj.*

skate[1] (skāt) *n.* [assumed sing. < Du. *schaats*, a skate < ONormFr. < OFr. *eschace*, stilt < Frank.] **1.** *a)* a bladelike metal runner in a frame to be fastened to a shoe, used for gliding on ice *b)* a shoe with this attached Also **ice skate 2.** a frame or shoe with two small wheels at the toe and two at the heel, for gliding on a pavement, etc.: also **roller skate 3.** a skating —*vi.* **skat′ed, skat′ing** to move along on skates —**skate on thin ice** to place oneself in a dangerous or delicate situation —**skat′er** *n.*

skate[2] (skāt) *n., pl.* **skates, skate:** see PLURAL, II, D, 1 [ON. *skata*] any of various rays with a broad, flat body and short, spineless tail

skate·board (skāt′bôrd′) *n.* a short, oblong board with two wheels at each end, which one rides on, usually while standing —*vi.* **-board′ed, -board′ing** to ride on a skateboard

skean (skēn) *n.* [ScotGael. *sgian*, akin to MIr. *scïan*, a knife] formerly, a kind of dagger or short sword used in Ireland and Scotland —**skean-dhu** (-doo′) the dagger worn in the stocking as part of Highland dress

ske·dad·dle (ski dad′′l) *vi.* **-dled, -dling** [19th-c. < ?] [Colloq.] run off; leave fast

skeet (skēt) *n.* [ult. < ON. *skeyti*, a projectile] trapshooting in which the shooter fires from different angles, usually eight, at clay discs

skein (skān) *n.* [< MFr. *escaigne*] **1.** a quantity of thread or yarn wound in a coil **2.** a coil of hair, etc.

skel·e·ton (skel′ət'n) *n.* [ModL. < Gr. *skeleton* (*sōma*), dried (body) < *skeletos*, dried up] **1.** the hard framework of an animal, supporting the tissues and protecting the organs; specif., all the bones or bony framework of a human being or other vertebrate **2.** anything like a skeleton; specif., *a*) a very lean or thin person or animal *b*) a supporting framework, as of a ship *c*) an outline, as of a novel —*adj.* of or like a skeleton; greatly reduced [a *skeleton* force] —**skeleton in the cupboard** some fact, as about a relative, kept secret because of shame —**skel′e·tal** (-t'l) *adj.*

skeleton crew a minimum number of people employed to perform essential duties

skel·e·ton·ize (-īz′) *vt.* **-ized′, -iz′ing** **1.** to reduce to a skeleton **2.** to outline **3.** to reduce greatly in number or size

skeleton key a key with much of the bit filed away so that it can open any of various simple locks

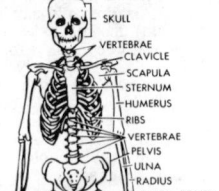

SKULL
VERTEBRAE
CLAVICLE
SCAPULA
STERNUM
HUMERUS
RIBS
VERTEBRAE
PELVIS
ULNA
RADIUS
CARPAL BONES
PHALANGES
FEMUR
PATELLA
TIBIA
FIBULA
TARSAL BONES
PHALANGES

HUMAN SKELETON

skep·tic (skep′tik) *adj., n.* *chiefly U.S. sp.* of SCEPTIC —**skep′ti·cal** *adj.* —**skep′ti·cal·ly** *adv.* —**skep′ti·cism** *n.*

sketch (skech) *n.* [Du. *schets* < It. *schizzo* < L. < Gr. *schedios*, extempore] **1.** a simple, rough drawing or design, done rapidly **2.** a brief plan; outline **3.** a short, light, informal story, description, skit, etc. —*vt., vi.* to make a sketch (of) —**sketch′a·ble** *adj.* —**sketch′er** *n.*

sketch·book (-book′) *n.* **1.** a book of drawing paper for making sketches **2.** a book of literary sketches Also **sketch book**

sketch·y (-ē) *adj.* **sketch′i·er, sketch′i·est** **1.** having the form of a sketch; not detailed **2.** not complete; inadequate —**sketch′i·ly** *adv.* —**sketch′i·ness** *n.*

skew (skyoo) *vi.* [< ONormFr. *eskiuer*, altered < OFr. < OHG.: see ESCHEW] **1.** to take a slanting course; swerve **2.** to glance sideways (*at*) —*vt.* **1.** to make slanting or oblique **2.** to bias or distort —*adj.* **1.** slanting; oblique **2.** not symmetrical —*n.* **1.** a slant or twist **2.** a slanting part or movement —**skew′ness** *n.*

skew·bald (skyoo′bôld′) *adj.* [< ME. *skewed*, piebald + BALD] having large patches of white and brown or any other colour except black —*n.* a skewbald horse

skew·er (skyoo′ər) *n.* [< ON. *skifa*, a slice] **1.** a long pin used to hold meat together while cooking or as a brochette **2.** any similar pin or rod —*vt.* to fasten or pierce as with skewers

skew·whiff (skyoo′wif′) *adj.* askew; awry

ski (skē) *n.,* *pl.* **skis, ski** [Norw. < ON. *skith*, snowshoe, strip of wood] **1.** either of a pair of long, thin runners of wood, metal, etc., fastened to the shoes for gliding over snow **2.** a water ski: see WATER-SKI —*vi.* **skied** (skēd), **ski′ing** **1.** to glide on skis, as down snow-covered hills **2.** *short for* WATER-SKI —**ski′er** *n.*

SKEWERS

ski·a·gra·phy (skī ag′rə fē) *n.* [Gr. *skia*, shadow + -GRAPH + -Y²] **1.** X-ray radiography **2.** the art of representing objects using shading Also **sci·ag·raphy** —**ski·a·graph** (skī′ə graf′) *n.*

skid (skid) *n.* [prob. < ON. *skith:* see SKI] **1.** [Chiefly U.S.] a plank, log, etc. used as a support or as a track to slide or roll a heavy object on **2.** a low, movable platform for holding loads or stacks **3.** [*pl.*] a protective wooden fender put against the side of a ship **4.** a runner in place of a wheel on some aircraft landing gear **5.** a sliding wedge or drag used to check a vehicle's motion by pressure against a wheel **6.** a skidding —*vt.* **skid′ded, skid′ding** **1.** to brake or lock (a wheel) with a skid **2.** to support or move on skids **3.** to cause (a wheel, vehicle, etc.) to skid —*vi.* **1.** to slide without turning, as a wheel when brakes are applied on a slippery surface **2.** to slide, as a vehicle not gripping an icy road **3.** to decline sharply, as prices —**be on** (or **hit**) **the skids** [Slang] to be in decline —**on the skids** [Colloq.] to be ready for launching —**put the skids on** (or **under**) [Slang] to thwart or cause to fail —**skid′der** *n.*

skid·dy (-ē) *adj.* **-di·er, -di·est** having a slippery surface on which vehicles are liable to skid

skid row [altered < *skid road,* a trail for dragging logs, hence a section of town where loggers gathered] [Chiefly U.S.] a section of a city where vagrants, derelicts, etc. gather

skiff (skif) *n.* [< MFr. < It. *schifo* < Gmc.] **1.** any light

rowing boat **2.** a long, narrow rowing boat, esp. one with a centreboard, outrigger, and a small sail

skif·fle (skif′'l) *n.* [< ?] a form of popular music in the 1950's played with guitars and percussion instruments

ski jump **1.** a jump made by a skier after skiing down a long incline or track **2.** such an incline or track

skil·ful (skil′fəl) *adj.* having or showing skill; accomplished; expert —**skil′ful·ly** *adv.* —**skil′ful·ness** *n.*

ski lift a motor-driven, endless cable, typically with seats attached, to carry skiers up a slope

skill (skil) *n.* [ON. *skil,* distinction] **1.** great ability or proficiency; expertness **2.** an art, craft, or science, esp. one involving the use of the hands or body **3.** ability in such an art, craft, or science

skilled (skild) *adj.* **1.** having skill; skilful **2.** having or requiring an ability gained by special experience or training

skil·let (skil′it) *n.* [< ? OFr. dim. of *escuelle,* basin < L. *scutella,* dim. of *scutra,* a dish] **1.** a pot or kettle with a long handle **2.** a frying pan

skil·ly (skil′ē) *n.* a watery soup or gruel

skim (skim) *vt.* **skimmed, skim′ming** [prob. akin to SCUM] **1.** *a*) to clear (a liquid) of floating matter *b*) to remove (floating matter) from a liquid **2.** [Chiefly U.S.] to coat with a thin layer [a pond *skimmed* with ice] **3.** to look through (a book, etc.) hastily **4.** *a*) to glide swiftly over *b*) to throw so as to make ricochet lightly [*skim* a flat stone across water] —*vi.* **1.** to move along swiftly and lightly; glide **2.** to read hastily (*through* or *over* a book, etc.) **3.** [Chiefly U.S.] to become thinly coated, as with scum —*n.* **1.** something skimmed **2.** a skimming **3.** a thin coating

skim·mer (-ər) *n.* **1.** one that skims **2.** a utensil for skimming liquids

skim milk milk from which cream has been removed: also **skimmed milk**

skimp (skimp) *vi.* [prob. altered < SCRIMP] [Colloq.] **1.** to give or allow too little; be stingy **2.** to keep expenses very low —*vt.* [Colloq.] **1.** to do poorly or carelessly **2.** to be stingy in or towards; specif., to make too small, too short, etc.

skimp·y (skim′pē) *adj.* **skimp′i·er, skimp′i·est** [Colloq.] barely or not quite enough; scanty —**skimp′i·ly** *adv.* —**skimp′i·ness** *n.*

skin (skin) *n.* [ON. *skinn*] **1.** the outer covering of the animal body **2.** this covering removed and prepared for use; pelt **3.** a skinlike outer layer, as fruit rind, a film or scum, etc. **4.** a container made of animal skin, for holding liquids **5.** [Slang] [*pl.*] a set of drums —*vt.* **skinned, skin′ning** **1.** to cover as with skin **2.** to remove skin from **3.** to injure by scraping (one's knee, etc.) **4.** [Colloq.] to defraud; swindle **5.** [U.S. Colloq.] to urge on (a mule, ox, etc.), esp. by whipping —**by the skin of one's teeth** by the tiniest margin; barely —**get under one's skin** [Colloq.] to anger or irritate one —**have a thick** (or **thin**) **skin** to be insensitive (or very sensitive) to criticism, etc. —**save one's skin** [Colloq.] to avoid death or injury —**skin′ner** *n.*

skin and bone very thin; skinny

skin-deep (-dēp′) *adj.* **1.** penetrating no deeper than the skin **2.** without real significance; superficial —*adv.* so as to be skin-deep

skin diving underwater swimming in which the swimmer, without lines to the surface, is variously equipped with a face mask, flipperlike footgear, a snorkel or scuba equipment, etc. —**skin′-dive′** (-dīv′) *vi.* **-dived′, -div′ing** —**skin diver**

skin-flick (-flik′) *n.* [Slang] a pornographic film

skin·flint (-flint′) *n.* [lit., one who would skin a flint for economy] a niggardly person; miser

skin·ful (-fool′) *n.,* *pl.* **-fuls′** **1.** as much as a skin container will hold **2.** [Colloq.] enough alcohol to make one drunk

skin grafting the surgical transplanting of skin (**skin graft**) to replace skin destroyed, as by burning

skin·head (-hed′) *n.* [Slang] any of a group of working-class youths of the late 1960's with closely cropped hair, often engaging in rowdyism

skink (skiŋk) *n.* [< L. < Gr. *skinkos*] a lizard with a very long, shiny body and short legs

skin·less (skin′lis) *adj.* without a skin, casing, etc.

skinned (skind) *adj.* having skin (of a specified kind) [dark-*skinned*]

skin·ny (skin′ē) *adj.* **-ni·er, -ni·est** **1.** of or like skin **2.** without much flesh; emaciated; thin **3.** inferior; inadequate —**skin′ni·ness** *n.*

skint (skint) *adj.* [< *skinned,* pp. of SKIN] [Slang] penniless; broke

skin test any test for detecting the presence of a disease or allergy from the reaction of the skin to a test substance

skin·tight (skin′tīt′) *adj.* clinging closely to the skin; tightfitting [a *skintight* dress]

skip¹ (skip) *vi.* **skipped, skip′ping** [prob. < Scand.] **1.** to leap, jump, etc. lightly; specif., to move along by hopping lightly on one foot and then the other **2.** to be deflected from a surface; ricochet **3.** to pass from one point to another, omitting what lies between **4.** [Chiefly U.S.

Colloq.] to leave hurriedly; abscond —*vt.* **1.** to leap lightly over **2.** to pass over or omit **3.** to fail to attend a session of (school, church, etc.) **4.** to cause to skip or ricochet **5.** [Chiefly U.S. Colloq.] to leave (a town, etc.) hurriedly —*n.* **1.** *a)* an act of skipping; leap *b)* a skipping gait alternating light hops on each foot **2.** a passing over or omitting —**skip it!** it doesn't matter!

skip² (skip) *n.* [< OE. *skeppa*, a basket] a large, open, metal container in which refuse from building operations is put

ski pants trousers that fit snugly at the ankles, worn for skiing and other winter sports

skip·jack (-jak') *n., pl.* **-jacks'**, **-jack'**: see PLURAL, II, D, 1 any of several kinds of fish that play at the surface of the water

ski·plane (skē'plān') *n.* an aircraft with skis for landing gear, for use on snow

ski pole either of a pair of light poles with a sharp tip, used by skiers as a help in climbing, keeping balance, etc.

skip·per¹ (skip'ər) *n.* **1.** a person or thing that skips **2.** any of various skipping insects

skip·per² (skip'ər) *n.* [MDu. *schipper* < *schip*, a ship] **1.** the captain of a ship **2.** any leader, director, or captain —*vt.* to act as skipper of

skipping rope a length of rope, often with handles, used by children and athletes in skipping

skirl (skurl) *vt., vi.* [prob. < Scand.] [Scot. & Dial.] to sound in shrill, piercing tones, as a bagpipe —*n.* a shrill sound, as of a bagpipe

skir·mish (skur'mish) *n.* [< MFr. < It. < *schermire*, to fight < Gmc.] **1.** a brief fight between small groups, usually an incident of a battle **2.** any slight, unimportant conflict —*vi.* to take part in a skirmish —**skir'mish·er** *n.*

skirt (skurt) *n.* [ON. *skyrt*, shirt] **1.** that part of a dress, coat, robe, etc. that hangs below the waist **2.** a woman's garment that hangs down from the waist **3.** something like a skirt, as a flap hanging from a saddle or a hovercraft **4.** a cut of beef from the flank **5.** [*pl.*] the outer parts; outskirts, as of a city **6.** [Old Slang] a girl or woman [a bit of *skirt*] —*vt.* **1.** to lie along or form the edge of **2.** *a)* to move along the edge of or pass round *b)* to miss narrowly **3.** to avoid (a difficult issue, problem, etc.) **4.** to border or edge with something —*vi.* to be on, or move along, the edge —**skirt'ed** *adj.* —**skirt'er** *n.*

skirting board a board or moulding covering the edge of a wall next to the floor

skit (skit) *n.* [prob. < Scand. var. of ON. *skjota*, to shoot] **1.** a short piece of satirical or humorous writing **2.** a short, comic theatrical sketch

ski tow a kind of ski lift enabling skiers to glide up the slope on their skis, towed by the endless cable

skit·ter (skit'ər) *vi.* [freq. of dial. *skite*, to dart about < Scand.] to skip or move along quickly or lightly, esp. over water —*vt.* to cause to skitter

skit·tish (skit'ish) *adj.* [see SKIT & -ISH] **1.** lively or playful, esp. in a coy way **2.** easily frightened; jumpy **3.** fickle; undependable —**skit'tish·ly** *adv.* —**skit'tish·ness** *n.*

skit·tle (skit''l) *n.* [prob. < Scand. cognate of SHUTTLE] **1.** [*pl. with sing. v.*] a form of ninepins in which a wooden disc or ball is used to knock down the pins **2.** any of these pins —**(not) all beer and skittles** (not) pure pleasure —**skittle out** *Cricket* to bowl out batsmen in rapid succession

skive (skīv) *vt.* skived, skiv'ing [< Scand.] **1.** to slice off (leather, rubber, etc.) in thin layers **2.** [Slang] to shirk or evade (work or responsibility) —*vi.* [Slang] to evade work —**skive off** [Slang] to depart, so as to evade work, etc. —**skiv'er** *n.*

skiv·vy (skiv'ē) *n., pl.* **-vies** [< ?] a servant, esp. a housemaid; a drudge —*vi.* to work as a housemaid, etc.

skoal (skōl) *interj.* [Dan. & Norw. *skaal*, a cup < ON. *skāl*, a bowl] to your health!: a toast

Skr., Skrt., Skt. Sanskrit

sku·a (sky$\overline{oo}$'ə) *n.* [ModL., ult. < ON. *skūfr*, a tuft] any of several large, brown and white, rapacious sea gulls, found in cold seas

skul·dug·ger·y, skull·dug·ger·y (skul dug'ər ē) *n.* [< ?] [Colloq.] underhand, dishonest behaviour; trickery

skulk (skulk) *vi.* [prob. < LowG. *schulken* or Dan. *skulke*] **1.** to move about in a stealthy or sinister manner; slink **2.** to avoid work or responsibility; shirk —*n.* a person who skulks —**skulk'er** *n.* —**skulk'ing·ly** *adv.*

skull (skul) *n.* [< Scand.] **1.** the bony framework of the head, enclosing the brain and sense organs **2.** the human head or mind

skull and crossbones a representation of two crossed thighbones under a human skull, used as a symbol of death or extreme danger or, formerly, piracy

skull·cap (-kap') *n.* a light, closefitting, brimless cap, usually worn indoors

skunk (skuŋk) *n.* [< AmInd. *segonku*] **1.** *a) pl.* **skunks, skunk:** see PLURAL, II, D, 1 a bushy-tailed mammal about the size of a cat: it has black fur with white stripes down its back, and ejects a foul-smelling liquid when molested *b)* its fur **2.** [Colloq.] a despicable, offensive person

skunk cabbage a plant having large, cabbagelike leaves and a disagreeable smell

sky (skī) *n., pl.* **skies** [ON., a cloud] **1.** [*often pl.*] the upper atmosphere, esp. with reference to its appearance [blue *skies*, a cloudy *sky*] **2.** the heavens, apparently arching over the earth; firmament **3.** heaven —*vt.* skied or skyed, sky'ing [Colloq.] to hit, throw, etc. high in the air —**out of a clear (blue) sky** without warning —**to the skies** without reserve

sky blue a blue colour like that of the sky on a clear day —**sky'-blue'** *adj.*

sky diving the sport of jumping from an aircraft and executing free-fall manoeuvres before opening the parachute —**sky'-dive'** (-dīv') *vi.* -dived', -div'ing —**sky diver**

Skye terrier any of a breed of small terrier with long hair, a long body, and short legs

sky-high (skī'hī') *adj., adv.* **1.** very high **2.** so as to be completely blasted; to pieces

sky·jack (-jak') *vt.* [Colloq.] to hijack (an aircraft) —**sky'jack'er** *n.* —**sky'jack'ing** *n.*

sky·lark (-lärk') *n.* a Eurasian lark, famous for the song it utters as it soars towards the sky —*vi.* [SKY + LARK²] to play about boisterously; frolic

sky·light (-līt') *n.* a window in a roof or ceiling

sky·line (-līn') *n.* **1.** the line along which sky and earth seem to meet **2.** the outline, as of a city, seen against the sky

sky pilot [Slang] a clergyman; esp., a military chaplain

sky·rock·et (-rok'it) *n.* a firework rocket that explodes in midair, with coloured flame, sparks, etc. —*vi., vt.* to rise or cause to rise rapidly to a great height, success, price, etc.

sky·sail (skī'sāl', -s'l) *n.* the small sail set above the royal at the top of a square-rigged mast

sky·scrap·er (-skrā'pər) *n.* a very tall building

sky·ward (-wərd) *adv., adj.* towards the sky: also **sky'-wards** *adv.*

sky·ways (-wāz') *n.pl.* routes of air travel

sky·writ·ing (-rīt'iŋ) *n.* the tracing of words, etc. in the sky by trailing smoke from an aircraft in flight —**sky'write'** *vi., vt.* -wrote', -writ'ten, -writ'ing —**sky'writ'er** *n.*

slab (slab) *n.* [ME. *sclabbe*] **1.** a piece that is flat, broad, and fairly thick [a *slab* of concrete] **2.** a rough piece cut from the outside of a log —*vt.* slabbed, slab'bing to cut the slabs from (a log)

slack¹ (slak) *adj.* [OE. *slæc*] **1.** slow; sluggish **2.** barely moving, as a current of air **3.** not busy or active; dull [a *slack* period] **4.** loose; not tight or taut **5.** weak; lax **6.** careless or negligent [a *slack* workman] —*vt.* **1.** to make slack **2.** to slake —*vi.* **1.** to be or become slack; slacken **2.** to be idle, careless, or negligent —*adv.* in a slack manner —*n.* **1.** a part that is slack or hangs loose **2.** a lack of tension **3.** a stoppage of movement in a current **4.** a dull period; lull —**slack off** to slacken —**slack up** to go more slowly —**slack'ly** *adv.* —**slack'ness** *n.*

slack² (slak) *n.* [akin to Fl. *slecke*, dross, Du. *slak*] a mixture of small pieces of coal, coal dust, and dirt left from the screening of coal

slack·en (slak''n) *vt., vi.* **1.** to make or become less active, intense, etc. **2.** to relax or loosen —**slack'en·er** *n.*

slack·er (-ər) *n.* a person who shirks his work or duty

slacks (slaks) *n.pl.* trousers for men or women; esp., trousers that are not part of a suit

slack water the period between tides when the water is still, esp. at low tide

slag (slag) *n.* [MLowG. *slagge*] **1.** the fused refuse separated from a metal in smelting **2.** lava resembling this —*vt., vi.* slagged, slag'ging to form into slag —**slag'gy** *adj.* -gi·er, -gi·est

slag heap a large pile of waste matter from coal-mining or metal-smelting

slain (slān) *pp.* of SLAY

slake (slāk) *vt.* slaked, slak'ing [OE. *slacian* < *slæc*, slack] **1.** to make (thirst, desire, etc.) less intense by satisfying **2.** to put out (a fire) **3.** to produce a chemical change in (lime) by combination with water —*vi.* to become slaked

slaked lime *same as* CALCIUM HYDROXIDE

sla·lom (slä'ləm) *n.* [Norw., sloping trail] a downhill skiing race over a zigzag course —*vi.* to ski in a slalom

slam¹ (slam) *vt.* slammed, slam'ming [prob. < Scand.] **1.** to shut with force and noise [to *slam* a door] **2.** to hit, put, etc. with force and noise [to *slam* a football over the fence] **3.** [Colloq.] to criticize severely —*vi.* to shut, go into place, etc. with force and noise —*n.* **1.** *a)* a heavy impact, shutting, etc. *b)* the noise made by this **2.** [Colloq.] severe criticism

slam² (slam) *n.* [< ?] *Bridge* shortened form of GRAND SLAM or LITTLE SLAM

slan·der (slän'dər) *n.* [< Anglo-Fr. < LL. *scandalum*: see SCANDAL] **1.** the utterance of a falsehood damaging to a person's character or reputation: cf. LIBEL **2.** such a spoken falsehood —*vt.* to utter a slanderous statement about —**slan′der·er** *n.*

slan·der·ous (-əs) *adj.* **1.** containing slander **2.** uttering slander —**slan′der·ous·ly** *adv.*

slang (slaŋ) *n.* [18th-c. cant < ?] **1.** orig., the specialized vocabulary of criminals, tramps, etc.: now usually called CANT[1] **2.** the specialized vocabulary of those in the same work, way of life, etc. **3.** highly informal language, usually short-lived and of a vigorous or colourful nature, that is usually avoided in formal speech and writing: it consists of both coined words and those with new meanings —*vi.* to use slang or abusive talk —*vt.* to abuse; criticize

slang·y (-ē) *adj.* **slang′i·er, slang′i·est** **1.** of, like, or containing slang **2.** given to using slang —**slang′i·ly** *adv.* —**slang′i·ness** *n.*

slant (slänt) *vt., vi.* [< Scand.] **1.** to turn or lie in a direction that is not straight up and down or straight across; slope **2.** to write or tell so as to appeal to a particular interest or to express a particular bias —*n.* **1.** *a)* a slanting surface, line, etc.; slope *b)* *same as* VIRGULE **2.** a point of view or attitude, or one that shows bias —*adj.* oblique; sloping —**slant′ing** *adj.* —**slant′ing·ly** *adv.*

slant·ways (-wāz′) *adv.* so as to slant or slope; obliquely: also **slant′wise′** —*adj.* slanting; oblique

slap (slap) *n.* [LowG. *sklapp:* echoic] **1.** *a)* a blow with something flat, as the palm of the hand *b)* the sound of this, or a sound like it **2.** an insult; rebuff —*vt.* **slapped, slap′-ping** **1.** to strike with something flat **2.** to put, hit, etc. carelessly or with force **3.** [Colloq.] to apply in large quantities [she *slapped* some make-up on] —*vi.* to make a dull, sharp noise, as upon impact —*adv.* **1.** [Colloq.] straight; directly **2.** [Colloq.] abruptly —**slap down** [Colloq.] to rebuke or rebuff sharply —**slap in the face** a snub or rebuff —**slap′per** *n.*

slap and tickle [Colloq.] rowdy, boisterous behaviour, esp. of a sexual nature

slap·dash (-dash′) *n.* something done carelessly and hastily —*adv.* in a hasty, careless manner —*adj.* hasty, careless, impetuous, etc.

slap-hap·py (-hap′ē) *adj.* [Slang] **1.** dazed, as by blows to the head **2.** silly or giddy

slap·stick (-stik′) *n.* **1.** a device, formerly used by stage comedians, made of two wooden slats that slap together loudly when hit against something **2.** crude comedy full of violent activity, horseplay etc. —*adj.* characterized by such comedy

slap-up (-up′) *adj.* [Colloq.] stylish; lavish; elegant

slash (slash) *vt.* [< ? OFr. *esclachier,* to break] **1.** to cut or wound with sweeping strokes, as of a knife **2.** to whip viciously; lash **3.** to cut slits in (a fabric, dress, etc.), esp. so as to expose underlying material **4.** to reduce drastically [to *slash* prices] **5.** to criticize severely —*vi.* to make a sweeping motion with or as with something sharp —*n.* **1.** a sweeping stroke made as with a knife **2.** a cut made by such a stroke; gash **3.** *same as* VIRGULE **4.** a slit in a fabric, dress, etc. **5.** *a)* an open place in a forest, cluttered with branches, chips, etc. as from the cutting of timber *b)* such debris **6.** [Slang] an act of urinating: usually considered a vulgar term —**slash′er** *n.*

slash·ing (-iŋ) *adj.* **1.** severe; violent **2.** dashing; spirited —*n.* *same as* SLASH —**slash′ing·ly** *adv.*

slat (slat) *n.* [OFr. *esclat,* fragment] a thin, narrow strip of wood, metal, etc. [*slats* of a Venetian blind] —*vt.* **slat′ted, slat′ting** to provide or make with slats

slate[1] (slāt) *n.* [< OFr. fem. of *esclat:* see prec.] **1.** a hard, fine-grained rock that separates easily into thin, smooth layers **2.** its bluish-grey colour: also **slate blue** **3.** a thin piece of slate, esp. one used as a roofing tile or as a tablet for writing on with chalk **4.** [Chiefly U.S.] a list of candidates proposed for nomination or election —*vt.* **slat′-ed, slat′ing** **1.** to cover with slate **2.** [Chiefly U.S.] to choose or schedule, as for a list of candidates, appointments, etc. —**a clean slate** a clean record without blemish —**slat′y** *adj.*

slate[2] (slāt) *vt.* **slat′ed, slat′ing** [prob. < ON. *sleita (akin to OE. slætan,* to bait)] [Colloq.] to scold or criticize harshly —**slat′ing** *n.*

slat·er (slāt′ər) *n.* **1.** a person who slates **2.** any of various isopod crustaceans; esp. *same as* WOOD LOUSE

slat·tern (slat′ərn) *n.* [< dial. *slatter,* to slop] **1.** a woman who is careless and sloppy in her habits, appearance, etc. **2.** a slut —**slat′tern·li·ness** *n.* —**slat′tern·ly** *adj., adv.*

slaugh·ter (slôt′ər) *n.* [ON. *slātr,* lit., slain flesh] **1.** the killing of animals for food; butchering **2.** the brutal killing of a human being **3.** the killing of people in large numbers, as in battle —*vt.* **1.** to kill (animals) for food; butcher **2.** to kill (people) brutally or in large numbers —**slaugh′ter·er** *n.* —**slaugh′ter·ous** *adj.*

slaugh·ter·house (-hous′) *n.* a place where animals are butchered for food; abattoir

Slav (släv, slav) *n.* a member of any of a group of Slavic-speaking peoples of E, SE, and C Europe, including the Russians, Ukrainians, Serbs, Croats, Bulgars, Czechs, Poles, Slovaks, etc. —*adj.* *same as* SLAVIC

Slav. Slavic

slave (slāv) *n.* [< OFr. < ML. *sclavus,* slave, orig. Slav < LGr. *Sklabos:* first applied to captive Slavs] **1.** a human being who is owned as property by another and is under his absolute control **2.** a person who is dominated by some influence, habit, person, etc. [*slaves* to fashion] **3.** a person who slaves; drudge **4.** any ant enslaved by ants of other species: also **slave ant** **5.** a device actuated or controlled by another, similar device —*vi.* **slaved, slav′ing** **1.** to work like a slave; drudge **2.** to deal in slaves —**slave′like** *adj.*

slave driver **1.** a person who oversees the work of slaves **2.** any merciless taskmaster

slave·hold·er (-hōl′dər) *n.* a person who owns slaves —**slave′hold′ing** *adj., n.*

slav·er[1] (slav′ər) *vi.* [< Scand.] to let saliva run from the mouth; drool —*n.* saliva drooling from the mouth —**slav′-er·er** *n.*

slav·er[2] (slā′vər) *n.* **1.** a ship used in the slave trade: also **slave ship** **2.** a person who deals in slaves

slav·er·y (slā′və rē, slāv′rē) *n.* **1.** the owning of slaves as a practice or institution **2.** the condition of being a slave; bondage **3.** a condition of domination by some influence, habit, etc. **4.** hard work or toil; drudgery

slave state any of the southern states of the U.S. in which slavery was legal before the American Civil War

slave trade traffic in slaves; specif., the transportation of African Negroes to America for sale as slaves

slav·ey (slā′vē) *n., pl.* **-eys** [Colloq.] a female domestic servant who does menial work

Slav·ic (släv′ik) *adj.* of the Slavs, their languages, etc. —*n.* a principal branch of the Indo-European family of languages, including Russian, Ukrainian, Byelorussian (**East Slavic**); Old Church Slavic, Bulgarian, Serbo-Croatian, Slovenian (**South Slavic**); and Polish, Sorbian, Czech, Slovak (**West Slavic**) Also **Sla·von·ic** (slə von′ik)

slav·ish (slā′vish) *adj.* **1.** of or like slaves; specif., *a)* servile *b)* laborious **2.** blindly dependent [*slavish* imitation] —**slav′ish·ly** *adv.* —**slav′ish·ness** *n.*

slaw (slô) *n.* short for COLESLAW

slay (slā) *vt.* **slew** or for **2 slayed, slain, slay′ing** [OE. *slean*] **1.** to kill by violent means **2.** [Colloq.] to impress or evoke admiration from **3.** [Chiefly U.S. Slang] to delight, amuse, etc. greatly —**slay′er** *n.*

sleave (slēv) *n.* [OE. *-slæfan,* to separate] **1.** [Obs.] silk floss that tangles easily **2.** [Rare] any tangle

slea·zy (slē′zē) *adj.* **-zi·er, -zi·est** [< ?] **1.** flimsy or thin in substance [a *sleazy* fabric] **2.** shoddy, cheap, etc. **3.** vulgar, sordid, etc. —**slea′zi·ly** *adv.* —**slea′zi·ness** *n.*

sled (sled) *n.* [MLowG. or MDu. *sledde*] *same as* SLEDGE[2]

sledge[1] (slej) *n., vt., vi.* **sledged, sledg′ing** [OE. *slecge* < base of *slean,* to strike] *same as* SLEDGEHAMMER

sledge[2] (slej) *n.* [MDu. *sleedse*] a vehicle mounted on runners for carrying loads or people over snow or ice —*vt.* **sledged, sledg′ing** to carry or ride on a sledge

sledge·ham·mer (-ham′ər) *n.* [see SLEDGE[1]] a long, heavy hammer, usually held with both hands —*vt., vi.* to strike as with a sledgehammer —*adj.* crushingly powerful

sleek (slēk) *adj.* [var. of SLICK] **1.** smooth and shiny; glossy [*sleek* fur] **2.** having a healthy, glowing, well-groomed appearance **3.** speaking or acting in a smooth but insincere way **4.** luxurious, elegant, etc. —*vt.* to make sleek: also **sleek′en** —**sleek′ly** *adv.* —**sleek′ness** *n.*

sleep (slēp) *n.* [OE. *slæp*] **1.** *a)* a condition of rest for the body and mind at regular times, during which the eyes stay closed and there is dreaming *b)* a period of sleeping **2.** any state like sleep, as a coma —*vi.* **slept, sleep′ing** **1.** to be in the state of sleep; slumber **2.** to be in a state like sleep, as hibernation **3.** [Colloq.] to have sexual intercourse (*with*) —*vt.* **1.** to have (a specified kind of sleep) [to *sleep* the sleep of the just] **2.** to provide sleeping accommodations for —**last sleep** death —**put to sleep** **1.** to drug or anaesthetize **2.** to kill painlessly, esp. a pet animal —**sleep around** [Colloq.] to have promiscuous sexual relations —**sleep away** to spend in sleep —**sleep in** **1.** to sleep at the place where one is in domestic service **2.** to sleep later than usual in the morning —**sleep off** to rid oneself of by sleeping —**sleep on it** to give extended consideration, esp. overnight —**sleep over** [Chiefly U.S. Colloq.] to spend the night at another's home

sleep·er (slē′pər) *n.* **1.** one who sleeps, esp. as specified [a light *sleeper*] **2.** a beam laid flat for supporting something **3.** any of the parallel crossbeams to which the rails of a railway are fastened **4.** *a)* *same as* SLEEPING CAR *b)* a compartment in a sleeping car **5.** something that achieves an unexpected success, importance, etc. **6.** [U.S.] [usually *pl.*] pyjamas for a young child that enclose the feet

sleeping bag a large bag with a warm lining, for sleeping in, esp. outdoors

sleeping car a railway coach with berths, compartments, etc. for passengers to sleep in: also **sleeping carriage**

sleeping partner a partner who shares in financing but not in managing a business, firm, etc.

sleeping pill a pill or capsule containing a drug, esp. a barbiturate, that helps bring on sleep

sleeping sickness 1. an infectious disease, esp. of tropical Africa, transmitted by the bite of the tsetse fly: it is characterized by fever, lethargy, and coma, usually ending in death **2.** inflammation of the brain, caused by a virus and inducing drowsiness, etc.

sleep·less (slēp'lis) *adj.* **1.** with little or no sleep [a *sleepless* night] **2.** always alert or active —**sleep'less·ly** *adv.* —**sleep'less·ness** *n.*

sleep·walk·ing (slēp'wôk'iŋ) *n.* the act or practice of walking while asleep; somnambulism —**sleep'walk'** *vi.* —**sleep'walk'er** *n.*

sleep·y (slē'pē) *adj.* **sleep'i·er, sleep'i·est 1.** ready or likely to fall asleep; drowsy **2.** not very active; dull; quiet [a *sleepy* little town] **3.** causing or showing drowsiness —**sleep'i·ly** *adv.* —**sleep'i·ness** *n.*

sleet (slēt) *n.* [< OE. hyp. *sliete*] **1.** rain that freezes as it falls **2.** a mixture of rain and snow **3.** [Chiefly U.S.] the icy coating formed when rain freezes on trees, streets, etc. —*vi.* to shower in the form of sleet —**sleet'y** *adj.*

sleeve (slēv) *n.* [OE. *sliefe*] **1.** that part of a garment that covers an arm or part of an arm **2.** a tube or tubelike part fitting around another part **3.** an envelope for a gramophone record —*vt.* **sleeved, sleev'ing** to provide with sleeves —**up one's sleeve** hidden but ready at hand —**sleeved** *adj.* —**sleeve'less** *adj.*

sleeve board a shaped board used in pressing sleeves, esp. suit sleeves

sleigh (slā) *n.* [Du. *slee,* contr. of *slede,* sled] a carriage with runners instead of wheels, for travel over snow and ice —*vi.* to ride in or drive a sleigh —**sleigh'ing** *n.*

sleight (slīt) *n.* [< ON. *slœgth < slœgr,* crafty] **1.** cunning used in deceiving **2.** skill or dexterity

sleight of hand 1. skill in using the hands so as to confuse those watching, as in doing magic tricks **2.** the performance of tricks that deceive in or as in this way

slen·der (slen'dər) *adj.* [< ?] **1.** long and thin **2.** having a slim, trim figure **3.** small in amount, size, degree, etc.; slight [*slender* earnings, *slender* hope] —**slen'der·ly** *adv.* —**slen'der·ness** *n.*

slen·der·ize (-īz') *vt.* **-ized', -iz'ing** to make or cause to seem slender —*vi.* to become slender

slept (slept) *pt. & pp.* of SLEEP

sleuth (slōōth) *n.* [ON. *sloth,* a track, spoor] **1.** a bloodhound: in full, **sleuth'hound'** **2.** [Colloq.] a detective —*vi.* to act as a detective

slew¹ (slōō) *n.* [U.S.] *same as* SLOUGH² (sense 4)

slew² (slōō) *vt., vi.* slewed, slew'ing [< ?] to turn or swing round a fixed point —*n.* **1.** the act of slewing **2.** the position to which a thing has been slewed

slew³ (slōō) *n.* [Ir. *sluagh,* a host] [U.S. Colloq.] a large number or amount; a lot

slew⁴ (slōō) *pt.* of SLAY

slice (slīs) *n.* [OFr. *esclice,* ult. < Frank. *slizzan,* to slice] **1.** a thin, broad piece cut from something [a *slice* of cake] **2.** a part or share [a *slice* of the profits] **3.** a spatula or knife with a broad, flat blade **4.** *a)* the path of a hit ball that curves away to the right from a right-handed player or to the left from a left-handed player *b)* a ball that follows such a path —*vt.* **sliced, slic'ing 1.** to cut into slices **2.** *a)* to cut as a slice (with *off, from, away,* etc.) *b)* to cut through like a knife **3.** to separate into parts or shares **4.** to hit (a ball) in a slice —*vi.* to cut (*through*) like a knife —**slic'er** *n.*

slick (slik) *vt.* [OE. *slician*] **1.** to make sleek or smooth **2.** [U.S. Colloq.] to make smart, neat, or tidy (with *up*) —*adj.* **1.** sleek; smooth **2.** accomplished; adept **3.** [Chiefly U.S.] deceptively plausible **4.** [Colloq.] showing skill in technique but little depth of feeling [a *slick* style of writing] —*n.* **1.** a smooth area on the surface of water, as resulting from a film of oil **2.** such a film of oil —**slick'ly** *adv.* —**slick'ness** *n.*

slick·er (-ər) *n.* [U.S.] **1.** a loose, waterproof coat **2.** [Colloq.] a person with smooth, plausible ways

slide (slīd) *vi.* **slid** (slid), **slid'ing** [OE. *slidan*] **1.** to move along in constant contact with a smooth surface, as on ice **2.** to move quietly and smoothly; glide **3.** to move stealthily or unobtrusively **4.** to slip [it *slid* from his hand] **5.** to pass gradually (*into* or *out of* some condition, habit, etc.) —*vt.* **1.** to cause to slide **2.** to move or slip quietly or stealthily (*in* or *into*) —*n.* **1.** an act of sliding **2.** a smooth, sloping track, surface, or chute down which to slide **3.** something that works by sliding **4.** a piece of film with a photograph on it, mounted for use with a viewer or projector **5.** a small glass plate on which objects are mounted for microscopic study **6.** *a)* the fall of a mass of rock, snow, etc. down a slope *b)* the mass that falls **7.** a

U-shaped section of tubing which is moved to change the pitch of a trombone, etc. **8.** an ornamental clip of metal, plastic, etc. to hold sections of hair in place —**let slide** to fail to take care of (some matter) —**slide over** barely to deal with or refer to (some matter) —**slid'er** *n.*

slide rule an instrument consisting of a ruler with a central sliding piece, both marked with logarithmic scales: used for rapid mathematical calculations

sliding scale a scale or schedule, as of costs, wages, etc., that varies with given conditions or standards

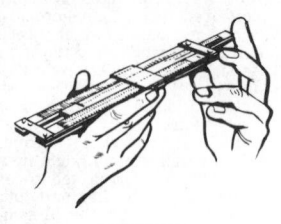

SLIDE RULE

slight (slīt) *adj.* [OE. *sliht*] **1.** *a)* light in build; slender *b)* frail; fragile **2.** having little weight, strength, substance, or significance **3.** small in amount or extent [a *slight* fever] —*vt.* **1.** to do carelessly or poorly; neglect **2.** to treat with disrespect or indifference **3.** to treat as unimportant —*n.* a slighting or being slighted by pointedly discourteous treatment —**slight'ing** *adj.* —**slight'ing·ly** *adv.* —**slight'ly** *adv.* —**slight'ness** *n.*

sli·ly (slī'lē) *adv.* *var.* of slyly (see SLY)

slim (slim) *adj.* **slim'mer, slim'mest** [Du., crafty, bad] **1.** small in girth in proportion to height or length; slender **2.** small in amount, degree, or extent; slight; scant; meagre —*vt., vi.* **slimmed, slim'ming** to make or become slim —**slim'ly** *adv.* —**slim'ness** *n.*

slime (slīm) *n.* [OE. *slim*] any soft, moist, slippery, often sticky matter, as thin mud, the mucous coating on fish, etc.; specif., any such matter considered disgusting —*vt.* **slimed, slim'ing 1.** to cover with slime **2.** to clean slime from

slim·y (slī'mē) *adj.* **slim'i·er, slim'i·est 1.** of or like slime **2.** covered with slime **3.** disgusting; repulsive —**slim'i·ly** *adv.* —**slim'i·ness** *n.*

sling¹ (sliŋ) *n.* [ME. *slinge(n),* prob. < ON. *slyngva,* to throw] **1.** *a)* a primitive instrument for throwing stones, etc., consisting of a piece of leather tied to cords that are whirled for releasing the missile *b)* *same as* SLINGSHOT **2.** a throwing as with a sling; cast; fling **3.** *a)* a looped or hanging band, strap, etc., used in raising or lowering a heavy object, carrying a rifle, etc. *b)* a wide piece of cloth looped from the neck under an injured arm for support —*vt.* **slung, sling'ing 1.** to throw (stones, etc.) with a sling **2.** to throw, cast, fling, etc. **3.** to raise, lower, etc. in a sling **4.** to hang loosely or in a sling; suspend —**sling'er** *n.*

sling² (sliŋ) *n.* [< ?] a drink made with spirits, esp. gin or rum, water, sugar, and lemon juice

sling·shot (sliŋ'shot') *n.* [U.S.] *same as* CATAPULT (sense 2)

slink¹ (sliŋk) *vi.* **slunk, slink'ing** [OE. *slincan,* to creep] to move in a fearful or stealthy way, or as if ashamed —**slink'ing·ly** *adv.*

slink² (sliŋk) *vt.* **slinked** or **slunk, slink'ing** [prob. < SLING¹] to expel (a foetus) prematurely: said of animals —*n.* an animal, esp. a calf, born prematurely

slink·y (sliŋ'kē) *adj.* **slink'i·er, slink'i·est 1.** sneaky in movement **2.** sinuous and graceful in movement, line, etc. —**slink'i·ness** *n.*

slip¹ (slip) *vi.* **slipped, slip'ping** [MLowG. *slippen*] **1.** to go quietly or secretly [to *slip* out of a room] **2.** *a)* to move or pass smoothly, quickly, or easily *b)* to get (*into* or *out of* clothes) quickly **3.** to pass gradually into or out of some condition, habit, etc. [to *slip* off to sleep] **4.** to escape from one's mind, power, etc. [to let a chance *slip* by] **5.** to shift or slide from position [the plate *slipped* from my hand] **6.** to slide accidentally, lose footing, etc. [to *slip* on ice] **7.** to make a mistake; err **8.** to become worse; weaken, lower, etc. [my memory is *slipping,* prices have *slipped*] —*vt.* **1.** to put or move smoothly, easily, or quickly [to *slip* a bolt into place, to *slip* one's shoes off, to *slip* in a snide remark] **2.** to escape (one's mind) **3.** to get loose from [the dog *slipped* his lead] **4.** to let loose; release **5.** to transfer (a stitch) from one needle to another without knitting it, as in forming patterns **6.** to put out of joint; dislocate —*n.* **1.** *a)* an inclined plane leading down to water, on which ships are built or repaired: also **slip'way** *b)* a water channel between piers or wharves for ship docking **2.** *a)* a woman's sleeveless undergarment, suspended from shoulder straps to the hemline of the skirt *b)* a petticoat; half slip **3.** a pillowcase **4.** a slipping or falling down **5.** an error or mistake in judgment, conduct, speech, etc., esp. one made by accident in speaking, writing, etc. [a *slip* of the tongue] **6.** an accident or mishap **7.** *Cricket* a fielder placed behind the wickets on the off side **8.** *Geol.* *a)* a movement resulting in a small fault or landslide *b)* a smooth surface where such movement has taken place —**give someone the slip** to evade or escape from someone —**let slip** to say without intending to —**slip off** to leave quietly, often without mentioning one's departure: also **slip away** —**slip one over on** [Colloq.] to trick; hoodwink —**slip up** to make a mistake

slip² (slip) *n.* [< MDu. < *slippen*, to cut] 1. a stem, root, twig, etc. cut off for planting or grafting 2. a young, slim person [a slip of a girl] 3. a long, narrow piece; strip 4. a small piece of paper, esp. one for a specific use [an order slip] —*vt.* **slipped, slip′ping** to take a slip from (a plant) for planting or grafting

slip³ (slip) *n.* [OE. *slypa*, a paste] *Ceramics* clay thinned to a watery paste for decorating, casting, or cementing

slip·case (-kās′) *n.* a boxlike container for a book or set of books, open at one end to expose the spine or spines

slip·cov·er (-kuv′ər) *n.* [U.S.] a loose cover

slip·knot (-not′) *n.* a knot made so that it will slip along the rope, etc. around which it is tied

slip-on (-on′) *adj.* easily put on or taken off, as shoes without laces, or a garment to be slipped on or off over the head —*n.* a slip-on shoe or garment

slip·o·ver (-ō′vər) *adj., n.* same as PULLOVER

slip·page (slip′ij) *n.* 1. a slipping, as of one gear past another 2. the amount of this

slipped disc a herniated disc between two vertebrae, esp. in the lumbar region, often causing sciatica

slip·per (slip′ər) *n.* 1. a light, low shoe easily slipped on the foot, esp. one for indoor wear 2. a shoe worn for dancing 3. a drag or brake for a wagon wheel —**slip′pered** *adj.*

slipper bath a slipper-shaped bath which is partially covered

slip·per·y (slip′ər ē, slip′rē) *adj.* **-per·i·er, -per·i·est** [OE. *slipur*] 1. causing or liable to cause slipping, as a wet surface 2. tending to slip away, as from the grasp 3. not reliable; untrustworthy —**slip′per·i·ness** *n.*

slippery elm 1. a N. American elm with sticky inner bark and hard wood 2. the wood or bark

slip·py (slip′ē) *adj.* [Colloq.] alert; sharp; quick

slip road a fairly narrow road used for joining and leaving a motorway

slip·shod (slip′shod′) *adj.* [SLIP¹ + SHOD] 1. wearing shoes with worn-down heels 2. careless; slovenly

slip·stream (-strēm′) *n.* the current of air thrust backward by the spinning propeller of an aircraft

slipt (slipt) *archaic or poetic pt. of* SLIP¹

slip-up (slip′up′) *n.* [Colloq.] an error, oversight, or mishap

slip·ware (slip′wer′) *n.* [SLIP³ + WARE] a pottery decorated with slip and glazed

slit (slit) *vt.* **slit, slit′ting** [akin to OE. *slitan*, to cut] 1. to cut or split open, esp. by a straight, lengthwise incision 2. to cut lengthwise into strips —*n.* 1. a long, straight cut or tear 2. a narrow opening or crack —**slit′ter** *n.*

slith·er (slith′ər) *vi.* [< OE. *sliderian*, freq. < base of *slidan*, to slide] 1. to slip or slide on a loose, broken surface, as a gravelly slope 2. to move along by sliding or gliding, as a snake —*vt.* to cause to slither or slide —*n.* a slithering motion —**slith′er·y** *adj.*

slit trench a narrow, relatively shallow trench for protecting a soldier from shellfire, bombs, etc.

sliv·er (sliv′ər) *n.* [OE. *slifan*, to cut] 1. a thin, sharp piece that has been cut, split, or broken off; splinter 2. a loose, thin, continuous fibre, as of flax, ready to be drawn and twisted —*vt., vi.* to cut or break into slivers

sli·vo·vitz (sliv′ə vits′) *n.* [Serb. *sljivovica* < *sliva*, plum] a usually colourless plum brandy drunk esp. in E Europe

slob (slob) *n.* [Ir. *slab*, mud < Scand.] [Colloq.] a sloppy, coarse, or gross person

slob·ber (slob′ər) *vi.* [< or akin to LowG. *slubberen*, to swig] 1. to let saliva, food, etc. run from the mouth; slaver 2. to speak, write, etc. in a gushy or maudlin way —*vt.* to smear or dribble on with saliva —*n.* 1. saliva, etc. running from the mouth 2. gushy talk or writing —**slob′ber·er** *n.* —**slob′ber·y** *adj.*

sloe (slō) *n.* [OE. *sla*] 1. same as BLACKTHORN (sense 1) 2. the small, blue-black, plumlike fruit of the blackthorn

sloe-eyed (-īd′) *adj.* 1. having large, dark eyes 2. having almond-shaped eyes

sloe gin a red liqueur made of gin flavoured with sloes

slog¹ (slog) *vt., vi.* **slogged, slog′ging** [var. of SLUG⁴] to hit hard; slug —**slog′ger** *n.*

slog² (slog) *vt., vi.* **slogged, slog′ging** [ME. *sluggen*: see SLUGGARD] 1. to make (one's way) with great effort; plod 2. to work hard (at something); toil —**slog′ger** *n.*

slo·gan (slō′gən) *n.* [< Gael. < *sluagh*, a host + *gairm*, a call] 1. orig., a battle cry of Scottish Highland and Irish clans 2. a catchword or motto associated with a political party or other group 3. a catch phrase used to advertise a product

sloid, slojd (sloid) *n.* same as SLOYD

sloop (sloop) *n.* [< Du. < LowG. < *slupen*, to glide] a fore-and-aft rigged, single-masted sailing vessel

slop (slop) *n.* [OE. *sloppe* (only in comp.)] 1. watery snow or mud; slush 2. a splash or puddle of spilled liquid 3. liquid or semiliquid food that is unappetizing or of poor quality 4. [often *pl.*] a) liquid waste of any kind [tea slops] b) kitchen swill, used for feeding pigs —*vi.* **slopped, slop′ping** 1. to spill or splash 2. to walk or splash through slush or mud 3. to make a slapping or tapping noise: said of water —*vt.* 1. to spill liquid on 2. to spill 3. to feed swill or slops to (pigs, etc.) —**slop over** 1. to overflow or spill 2. [Colloq.] to display sentimentality; gush

SLOOP

slop bowl (or **basin**) a bowl into which the dregs from tea cups are emptied at table

slope (slōp) *n.* [< OE. pp. of *aslupan*, to slip away < *slupan*, to glide] 1. ground that slants up or down, as a hillside 2. any inclined line, surface, position, etc.; slant 3. amount or degree of slant —*vi., vt.* **sloped, slop′ing** to slant or cause to slant up or down —**slope arms** *Mil.* to hold a rifle resting on the shoulder with the butt in the hand —**slop′er** *n.*

slop·py (slop′ē) *adj.* **-pi·er, -pi·est** 1. wet and splashy; muddy or slushy 2. splashed or spotted with liquids 3. a) very untidy; slovenly or messy b) careless; slipshod 4. [Colloq.] gushingly sentimental —**slop′pi·ly** *adv.* —**slop′-pi·ness** *n.*

slops (slops) *n.pl.* [< OE. *-slop*, as in *oferslop*, loose outer garment] 1. loose-fitting outer garments, esp. overalls 2. clothing, bedding, etc. issued or sold to seamen 3. cheap, ready-made clothing 4. same as SLOP (*n.* 4)

slosh (slosh) *vt.* [var. of SLUSH] 1. to shake or agitate (a liquid or something in it) 2. to apply (a liquid) carelessly or lavishly 3. [Slang] to hit violently —*vi.* 1. to splash or move clumsily through water, mud, etc. 2. to splash about: said of a liquid —*n.* 1. same as SLUSH 2. the sound of liquid splashing about —**slosh′y** *adj.*

sloshed (slosht) *adj.* [Slang] drunk

slot¹ (slot) *n.* [< OFr. *esclot*, the hollow between the breasts] 1. a narrow notch, groove, or opening, as a slit for a coin in a vending machine 2. [Colloq.] a position in a group, series, schedule, etc. —*vt.* **slot′ted, slot′ting** 1. to make a slot in 2. [Colloq.] to place in a series, schedule, etc.

slot² (slot) *n.* [OFr. *esclot* < ? ON. *sloth*: cf. SLEUTH] a track or trail of an animal, esp. a deer

sloth (slōth) *n.* [OE. *slæwth* < *slaw*, slow] 1. the condition of not liking to work or be active; indolence; laziness 2. any of several slow-moving mammals of Central and South America that live in trees, often hanging upside down from the branches

sloth·ful (-fəl) *adj.* characterized by sloth; indolent; lazy —**sloth′ful·ly** *adv.* —**sloth′ful·ness** *n.*

slot machine a machine, esp. a gambling device, worked by putting a coin in a slot

slouch (slouch) *n.* [ON. *slōkr*, lazy fellow < *slōka*, to droop] 1. a) a drooping or bending forward of the head and shoulders b) slovenly posture in general 2. a drooping, as of a hat brim 3. [Chiefly U.S.] a) a person who is awkward or lazy b) [Colloq.] a person who lacks skill [he's no slouch at golf] —*vi.* 1. to sit, stand, walk, etc. in a slouch 2. to droop, as a hat brim —*vt.* to cause to slouch

slouch·y (-ē) *adj.* **slouch′i·er, slouch′i·est** slouching, esp. in posture —**slouch′i·ly** *adv.* —**slouch′i·ness** *n.*

slough¹ (sluf) *n.* [ME. *slouh*] 1. the skin of a snake, esp. the outer, castoff layer 2. any castoff layer, covering, etc.: often used figuratively 3. *Med.* the dead tissue that separates from living tissue or an ulceration —*vi.* 1. to be shed, cast off, etc. 2. to shed skin or other covering 3. *Med.* to separate from the surrounding tissue Often with *off* —*vt.* 1. to shed or throw (off); get rid of 2. *Bridge* to discard (a card considered valueless) —**slough over** to gloss over; minimize —**slough′y** *adv.*

slough² (slou) *n.* [OE. *sloh*] 1. a place full of soft, deep mud 2. [< *Slough of Despond*, a swamp in Bunyan's *Pilgrim's Progress*] deep, hopeless discouragement 3. moral corruption 4. a swamp, bog, etc., esp. as part of an inlet —**slough′y** *adj.*

Slo·vak (slō′vak) *n.* 1. any of a Slavic people living chiefly in Slovakia 2. their West Slavic language, related to Czech —*adj.* of Slovakia, the Slovaks, or their language

slov·en (sluv′ən) *n.* [prob. < MDu. *slof*, lax] a person who is careless in his appearance, habits, work, etc.; dirty or untidy person

Slo·ve·ni·an (slō vē′nē ən, -vēn′yən) *n.* 1. any of a Slavic

people living chiefly in Slovenia   2. their South Slavic language —*adj.* of Slovenia, Slovenians, or their language Also **Slo·vene** (slō′vēn, slō vēn′)
slov·en·ly (sluv′ən lē) *adj.* **-li·er, -li·est** of or like a sloven; careless in appearance, habits, work, etc.; untidy —*adv.* in a slovenly manner —**slov′en·li·ness** *n.*
slow (slō) *adj.* [OE. *slaw*] 1. not quick or clever in understanding; dull; obtuse 2. taking a longer time than is expected or usual [a *slow* puncture] 3. marked by low speed, etc.; not fast 4. making speed difficult [a *slow* track, a *slow* cricket pitch] 5. showing a time that is behind the correct time: said of a timepiece 6. *a*) passing slowly or tediously *b*) not lively; dull 7. not active; slack [*slow* trading] 8. lacking in energy; sluggish 9. burning so as to give off low heat [a *slow* fire] 10. *Photog.* adapted to a relatively long exposure time —*vt., vi.* to make or become slow or slower (often with *up* or *down*) —*adv.* in a slow manner —**slow′ly** *adv.* —**slow′ness** *n.*
slow·coach (-kōch′) *n.* [Colloq.] a person who acts or moves slowly
slow handclap slow rhythmic clapping, used to show impatience or dissatisfaction
slow-mo·tion (-mō′shən) *adj.* 1. moving below usual speed 2. designating a film or taped television sequence in which the action is made to appear much slower than the actual action
slow poison a poison which is only dangerous after many doses; a poison that has a cumulative effect
slow-worm (-wurm′) *n.* [altered (after SLOW) < ME. *slaworm* < OE. *slawyrm*] a legless lizard found in Europe and Asia: also called **blind′worm′**
sloyd (sloid) *n.* [Sw. *slöjd*, skill] a system of manual training originating in Sweden, based upon the use of hand tools in woodcarving
slub (slub) *n.* [< ?] 1. a roll of fibre twisted slightly for use in spinning 2. a thick, irregular place in yarn
sludge (sluj) *n.* [var. of *slutch*, mud] 1. mud, mire, or ooze 2. spongy lumps of drift ice 3. any heavy, slimy deposit, sediment, or mass, as the waste resulting from oil refining, the sediment in a crankcase, the precipitate in a sewage tank, etc. —**sludg′y** *adj.* **sludg′i·er, sludg′i·est**
sludge·worm (-wurm′) *n.* a small, freshwater worm able to live where there is little oxygen, as in polluted waters
slue[1] (slōō) *vt., vi.* **slued, slu′ing** same as SLEW[2]
slue[2] (slōō) *n.* same as SLEW[3]
slug[1] (slug) *n.* [ME. *slugge*, clumsy one < Scand.] 1. a small mollusc resembling a land snail, but usually having only a rudimentary internal shell 2. rarely, a larva resembling a slug 3. a person, vehicle, etc. that moves slowly
slug[2] (slug) *n.* [prob. < prec.] 1. a small piece of metal; specif., a bullet 2. [Chiefly U.S.] a piece of metal used in place of a coin in automatic coin machines 3. *Printing a*) a strip of nonprinting metal used to space between lines *b*) a line of type made in one piece, as by a linotype machine
slug[3] (slug) *n.* [prob. < or akin to Dan. *sluge*, to gulp] [Chiefly U.S. Slang] a single drink, esp. of spirits
slug[4] (slug) *vt.* **slugged, slug′ging** [ON. *slag*] [Colloq.] to hit hard, esp. with the fist or a bat —*n.* [Colloq.] a hard blow or hit —**slug′ger** *n.*
slug·gard (slug′ərd) *n.* [< ME. < *sluggen*, to be lazy] a habitually lazy or idle person —*adj.* lazy or idle: also **slug′-gard·ly**
slug·gish (-ish) *adj.* [SLUG[1] + -ISH] 1. lacking energy or alertness; slothful 2. slow or slow-moving 3. below normal —**slug′gish·ly** *adv.* —**slug′gish·ness** *n.*
sluice (slōōs) *n.* [< OFr. *escluse* < LL. < pp. of L. *excludere*, EXCLUDE] 1. an artificial channel for water, with a gate at its head to regulate the flow, as in a canal 2. the water held back by such a gate 3. such a gate: also **sluice gate** 4. any channel, esp. one for excess water 5. a sloping trough through which water is run, as in carrying logs, etc. —*vt.* **sluiced, sluic′ing** 1. to draw off as by means of a sluice 2. to wash with water from or as from a sluice 3. to carry (logs, etc.) in a sluice —*vi.* to run or flow as in a sluice
sluit (slōōt) *n.* [Afrik. < Du. *sloot*, ditch] in South Africa, a narrow channel draining the fields during the rainy season
slum (slum) *n.* [< cant: orig. sense, a room < ?] a heavily populated area of a city having much poverty, poor housing, etc. —*vi.* **slummed, slum′ming** 1. to visit or tour slums 2. to experience slum conditions: also **slum it** —**slum′mer** *n.* —**slum′my** *adj.* **-mi·er, -mi·est**
slum·ber (slum′bər) *vi.* [< OE. < *sluma*, slumber] 1. to sleep 2. to be quiet or inactive —*vt.* to spend in sleeping —*n.* 1. sleep 2. an inactive state —**slum′ber·er** *n.*
slum·ber·ous (-əs) *adj.* 1. inclined to slumber; sleepy 2. suggestive of slumber 3. causing sleep 4. calm; quiet [a *slumberous* town] Also **slum′brous** (-brəs)
slum clearance the clearing of slum areas and the constructing of new housing

slump (slump) *vi.* [prob. < or akin to MLowG. *slumpen*, to come about by accident] 1. to fall or sink suddenly 2. to decline suddenly, as in value, etc. 3. to have a drooping posture —*n.* 1. a sudden or sharp fall, decline, etc. 2. a drooping posture 3. a period during which a player, team, etc. performs below normal
slung (sluŋ) *pt. & pp.* of SLING[1]
slunk (sluŋk) *pt. & pp.* of SLINK
slur (slur) *vt.* **slurred, slur′ring** [prob. < MDu. *sleuren*, to drag] 1. to pass (*over*) quickly and carelessly 2. to pronounce rapidly in an unclear way 3. to discredit or belittle 4. *Music a*) to sing or play (successive notes) by gliding from one to another without a break *b*) to mark (notes) with a slur —*n.* 1. a slurring 2. something slurred, as a pronunciation 3. a remark that is harmful to a person's reputation; aspersion 4. *Music* a curved symbol (⌢) or (⌣) connecting slurred notes —**slur′ring·ly** *adv.*
slurp (slurp) *vt., vi.* [Du. *slurpen*, to sip] [Slang] to drink or eat noisily —*n.* [Slang] a loud sipping noise
slush (slush) *n.* [prob. < Scand.] 1. partly melted snow or ice 2. soft mud; mire 3. grease 4. excessively sentimental talk or writing —*vi.* to walk or move through slush —**slush′i·ness** *n.* —**slush′y** *adj.* **slush′i·er, slush′i·est**
slush fund [Chiefly U.S.] money used for bribery, influencing politicians, voters, etc., or other corrupt purposes
slut (slut) *n.* [prob. akin to MLowG. *slote*, ditch] 1. a dirty, slovenly woman; slattern 2. a sexually promiscuous woman 3. a female dog; bitch —**slut′tish** *adj.* —**slut′tish·ly** *adv.* —**slut′tish·ness** *n.*
sly (slī) *adj.* **sli′er** or **sly′er, sli′est** or **sly′est** [ON. *slœgr*] 1. skilful at tricking or fooling others, in a secretive or underhanded way 2. tricking or teasing in playful way —**on the sly** secretly —**sly′ly** *adv.* —**sly′ness** *n.*
sly·boots (-bōōts′) *n.* [SLY + *boots*, see BOOT[1]] a person who is clever or crafty in an appealing or engaging way
Sm *Chem.* samarium
S.M. Sergeant Major
smack[1] (smak) *n.* [OE. *smæc*] 1. a slight but distinctive taste or flavour 2. *a*) a small amount; bit *b*) a trace; touch —*vi.* to have a smack (*of*) [actions that *smack* of treason]
smack[2] (smak) *n.* [< ? or akin to MDu. *smack*, of echoic orig.] 1. a sharp noise made by parting the lips suddenly 2. a loud kiss 3. *a*) a sharp blow with a flat object; slap *b*) the sound of this —*vt.* 1. to part (the lips) suddenly so as to make a smack 2. to slap loudly —*vi.* to make a loud, sharp noise, as when hitting something —*adv.* 1. with a smack; violently 2. directly; squarely: also [Colloq.]
smack′-dab′—smack in the eye a snub or rebuff
smack[3] (smak) *n.* [prob. < Du. *smak*] 1. a small sailing boat, usually rigged as a sloop and used for fishing 2. [U.S.] a fishing boat with a well for keeping fish alive
smack·er (-ər) *n.* 1. a person or thing that smacks 2. [Slang] a loud kiss; smack 3. [Slang] a pound note
small (smôl) *adj.* [OE. *smæl*] 1. comparatively little in size; not large 2. *a*) little in quantity, extent, value, duration, etc. [a *small* income] *b*) consisting of relatively few units; low in numbers [a *small* crowd] 3. of little importance; trivial 4. young [*small* children] 5. having relatively little investment, capital, etc. [a *small* business] 6. small-minded; petty 7. of low or inferior rank 8. gentle and low; soft, as a sound —*adv.* 1. in small pieces 2. in a low tone; softly 3. in a small manner —*n.* 1. the small or narrow part [the *small* of the back] 2. [*pl.*] small articles 3. [*pl.*] underclothes —**feel small** to feel shame or humiliation —**small′ish** *adj.* —**small′ness** *n.*
small arms firearms of small calibre, held in the hand or hands when fired, as pistols, rifles, etc.
small beer 1. weak, light, inferior beer 2. people or things of no importance
small change 1. coins, esp. those of low denomination 2. something of little value
small-clothes (smôl′klōthz′, -klōz′) *n.pl.* [Archaic] closefitting knee breeches of the 18th cent.
smallest room a euphemism for LAVATORY
small fry 1. unimportant people or things 2. a young child or children 3. a group of young or small fishes
small-goods (smôl′ goodz) *n.* [Aust.] meats sold in a delicatessen
small-hold·ing (-hōld′iŋ) *n.* a holding of agricultural land smaller than a farm, usually rented and worked by one man —**small′hold·er** *n.*
small hours the first few hours after midnight
small-mind·ed (-mīn′did) *adj.* selfish, petty, prejudiced, narrow-minded, etc. —**small′-mind′ed·ly** *adv.* —**small′-mind′ed·ness** *n.*
small·pox (-poks′) *n.* an acute, highly contagious virus disease causing fever, vomiting, and pustular eruptions that often leave pitted scars, or pockmarks
small-scale (-skāl′) *adj.* 1. drawn to a small scale 2. of limited scope; not extensive [*small-scale* trading]

small talk light conversation about common, everyday things; chitchat

small-time (-tīm′) *adj.* [Colloq.] of little importance or significance; minor or petty

smarm (smärm) *vt.* [< ?] [Colloq.] 1. to flatten the hair with grease 2. to flatter or ingratiate oneself

smarm·y (smär′mē) *adj.* **smarm′i·er, smarm′i·est** [SMARM + -Y²] [Colloq.] flattering in an oily, insincere manner

smart (smärt) *vi.* [OE. *smeortan*] 1. *a)* to cause sharp, stinging pain, as a slap, wound, etc. *b)* to feel such pain 2. to feel mental distress, as in resentment, remorse, etc. —*vt.* to cause to smart —*n.* a smarting sensation or distress —*adj.* 1. causing sharp or stinging pain [a *smart* slap] 2. sharp or stinging, as pain 3. brisk; lively [a *smart* pace] 4. *a)* intelligent, alert, clever, witty, etc. *b)* shrewd or sharp, as in one's dealings 5. neat; trim; spruce 6. in fashion; stylish 7. [Colloq.] impertinent, flippant, or saucy —*adv.* in a smart way —**smart′ly** *adv.* —**smart′ness** *n.*

smart al·eck, smart al·ec (al′ik) [SMART + *Aleck*, dim. of *Alexander*, a personal name] [Colloq.] a conceited, cocky person —**smart′-al′eck, smart′-al′eck·y** *adj.*

smart·en (smärt′'n) *vt.* to make smart or smarter; specif., *a)* to improve in appearance *b)* to make more alert, aware, etc. Usually with *up*

smart set sophisticated, fashionable people

smart·y (smär′tē) *n., pl.* **smart′ies** [Colloq.] *same as* SMART ALECK: also [Chiefly U.S.] **smart′y-pants′**

smash (smash) *vt.* [prob. < *s-*, intens. + MASH] 1. to break into pieces with noise or violence 2. to hit (a tennis ball, etc.) with a hard overhand stroke 3. to hit with a hard, heavy blow 4. to ruin completely; destroy —*vi.* 1. to break into pieces 2. to be destroyed 3. to move or collide with force —*n.* 1. a hard, heavy hit; specif., a hard overhand stroke, as in tennis 2. *a)* a violent, noisy breaking *b)* the sound of this 3. *a)* a violent collision *b)* a wreck 4. total failure, esp. in business 5. an overwhelming popular success —*adj.* that is a smash (*n.* 5) —**go to smash** [Colloq.] 1. to become smashed 2. to fail completely —**smash′er** *n.*

smash-and-grab raid (-'n grab′) daylight robbery in which thieves smash a shop-window and grab the goods on display

smashed (smasht) *adj.* [Slang] drunk; intoxicated

smash·ing (smash′iŋ) *adj.* 1. that smashes 2. [Colloq.] very good; extraordinary —**smash′ing·ly** *adv.*

smash·up (-up′) *n.* 1. a violent wreck or collision 2. total failure; ruin 3. any disaster

smat·ter (smat′ər) *vi.* [prob. akin to MHG. *smetern*, to chatter] [Now Rare] to speak, study, or learn superficially —*n. same as* SMATTERING

smat·ter·ing (-iŋ) *n.* 1. slight or superficial knowledge 2. a small number

smear (smir) *vt.* [OE. *smerian*, to anoint] 1. to cover or soil with something greasy, sticky, etc. 2. to apply (something greasy, sticky, etc.) 3. to make an unwanted mark on, or to obscure, by rubbing 4. to make a smear with (the hand, a rag, etc.) 5. to harm the reputation of; slander 6. [U.S. Slang] to overwhelm or defeat decisively —*vi.* to be or become smeared —*n.* 1. a mark made by smearing 2. a small quantity of some substance smeared on a slide for microscopic study, etc. 3. a slandering

smear·y (smir′ē) *adj.* **smear′i·er, smear′i·est** 1. covered with smears; smeared 2. tending to smear, as wet ink —**smear′i·ness** *n.*

smell (smel) *vt.* **smelled** or **smelt, smell′ing** [ME. *smellen*] 1. to be aware of by means of the nose and the olfactory nerves; detect the odour of 2. to sense the presence of [to *smell* trouble] 3. to test by the odour; sniff [*smell* the milk to tell if it's sour] —*vi.* 1. to use the sense of smell; sniff (often with *at* or *of*) 2. *a)* to have a scent or odour *b)* to have an unpleasant odour 3. to have the odour or a suggestion (*of*) [it *smells* of garlic] 4. [Colloq.] *a)* to lack ability, worth, etc. *b)* to be foul, corrupt, etc. —*n.* 1. that one of the five senses by which a substance is perceived through the stimulation of nerves (*olfactory nerves*) in the nasal cavity 2. the stimulation of any specific substance upon the olfactory nerves; odour; scent 3. an act of smelling 4. that which suggests the presence of something; trace —**smell out** to look for or find as by smelling —**smell′er** *n.*

smelling salts carbonate of ammonium, inhaled to relieve faintness, headaches, etc.

smell·y (smel′ē) *adj.* **smell′i·er, smell′i·est** having an unpleasant smell —**smell′i·ness** *n.*

smelt¹ (smelt) *n., pl.* **smelts, smelt:** see PLURAL, II, D, 1 [OE.] a small, silvery, salmonlike food fish found in northern seas

smelt² (smelt) *vt.* [MDu. or MLowG. *smelten*] 1. to melt or fuse (ore, etc.) so as to separate impurities from pure metal 2. to refine or extract (metal) in this way —*vi.* to be smelted

smelt·er (smel′tər) *n.* 1. a person engaged in the work of

smelting 2. a place where smelting is done: also **smelt′-er·y,** *pl.* **-er·ies**

smew (smyōō) *n.* [var. of *smee*, akin to obs. Du. *smeente*, kind of small duck] a duck of N Europe and Asia related to the goosander

smidg·en (smij′ən) *n.* [prob. < dial. *smidge*, var. of *smitch*, a particle] [U.S. Colloq.] a small amount; a bit: also **smidg′in, smidg′eon**

smi·lax (smī′laks) *n.* [L. < Gr. *smilax*, bindweed] 1. *same as* CAT BRIER 2. a twining greenhouse plant of the lily family, with bright green leaves

smile (smīl) *vi.* **smiled, smil′ing** [ME. *smilen*] 1. to show pleasure, amusement, affection, irony, etc. by an upward curving of the corners of the mouth and a sparkling of the eyes 2. to regard with favour (with *on* or *upon*) —*vt.* 1. to express with a smile 2. to affect by smiling —*n.* 1. the act or facial expression of smiling 2. a favourable or agreeable appearance —**smile away** to get rid of by smiling —**smil′er** *n.* —**smil′ing·ly** *adv.*

smirch (smurch) *vt.* [prob. < OFr. *esmorcher*, to hurt] 1. to soil or smear as with grime 2. to dishonour (a reputation) —*n.* 1. a smudge; smear 2. a stain on a reputation

smirk (smurk) *vi.* [OE. *smearcian*, to smile] to smile in a conceited or self-satisfied way —*n.* such a smile —**smirk′-er** *n.* —**smirk′ing·ly** *adv.*

smite (smīt) *vt.* **smote, smit′ten** or **smote, smit′ing** [OE. *smitan*] 1. [Now Rare] *a)* to hit or strike hard *b)* to defeat, punish, or kill 2. to attack with disastrous effect 3. to affect strongly and suddenly (*with*) [*smitten* with dread] 4. to distress [*smitten* by conscience] 5. to impress favourably [*smitten* with her charms] —*vi.* [Now Rare] to hit or strike hard —**smit′er** *n.*

smith (smith) *n.* [OE.] 1. a person who makes or repairs metal objects; metalworker: usually in combination [*silversmith*] 2. shortened form of BLACKSMITH

smith·er·eens (smith′ə rēnz′) *n.pl.* [Ir. *smidirīn*] [Colloq.] small fragments; bits

smith·er·y (smith′ə rē) *n., pl.* **-er·ies** 1. the work or craft of a smith 2. *same as* SMITHY

smith·y (smith′ē; smith′ē) *n., pl.* **smith′ies** [OE. *smiththe*] 1. the workshop of a smith, esp. a blacksmith 2. *same as* BLACKSMITH

smit·ten (smit′'n) *alt. pp. of* SMITE

smock (smok) *n.* [OE. *smoc* or ON. *smokkr*] a loose, shirtlike, outer garment worn to protect the clothes —*vt.* 1. to dress in a smock 2. to decorate with smocking

smock·ing (smok′iŋ) *n.* shirred, decorative stitching used in gathering cloth, as to make it hang in even folds

smog (smog) *n.* [SM(OKE) + (F)OG¹] a harmful mixture of fog and smoke —**smog′gy** *adj.* **-gi·er, -gi·est**

smoke (smōk) *n.* [OE. *smoca*] 1. *a)* the vaporous matter, with suspended particles of carbon, arising from something burning *b)* a cloud of this 2. any vapour, fume, etc. resembling smoke 3. *a)* an act or period of smoking tobacco, etc. [time for a *smoke*] *b)* something to smoke, as a cigarette 4. something fleeting, unreal, or obscuring —*vi.* **smoked, smok′ing** 1. to give off smoke or a smokelike substance 2. to discharge smoke excessively or improperly, as a fuel, a fireplace, etc. 3. *a)* to draw the smoke of tobacco, etc. into the mouth and blow it out again *b)* to be a habitual smoker —*vt.* 1. to stain or colour with smoke 2. to cure (meat, fish, etc.) with smoke 3. to fumigate as with smoke 4. to force out with smoke [to *smoke* an animal from its lair] 5. to use (tobacco, a pipe, etc.) in smoking —**go up in smoke** 1. to burn vigorously 2. to come to nothing 3. to flare up in anger —**smoke out** to force out of hiding, secrecy, etc. —**smok′a·ble, smoke′a·ble** *adj.*

smoked glass glass that has been darkened with smoke, usually so that the sun can be viewed through it

smoke-ho (-hō) *n.* [Aust. & N.Z. Colloq.] a period of rest from work for a smoke; tea-break

smoke·house (-haus′) *n.* a building where meats, fish, etc. are cured or flavoured with smoke

smoke·less (-lis) *adj.* having or making little or no smoke

smok·er (smō′kər) *n.* 1. a person or thing that smokes; specif., a person who habitually smokes tobacco [*smoker's* cough] 2. a railway coach or compartment reserved esp. for smoking: also **smoking car** 3. an informal party for men only

smoke screen 1. a cloud of smoke spread to screen the movements of troops, ships, etc. 2. anything said or done to conceal or mislead

smoke·stack (smōk′stak′) *n.* a pipe for the discharge of smoke from a steamship, factory, etc.

smoking jacket a man's lounging jacket for wear at home

smo·ko (smō′kō) *n. same as* SMOKE-HO

smok·y (smō′kē) *adj.* **smok′i·er, smok′i·est** 1. giving off smoke, esp. excessive smoke 2. like, of, or as of smoke [a *smoky* haze] 3. filled with smoke 4. having the colour of smoke **5.** flavoured by smoking **6.** darkened or soiled by smoke —**smok′i·ly** *adv.* —**smok′i·ness** *n.*

smol·der (smōl′dər) *vi., n.* *U.S. sp. of* SMOULDER

smolt (smōlt) *n.* [LME. (Scot.)] a young salmon when it first leaves fresh water and descends to the sea

smooch[1] (smōōch) *vt., n.* same as SMUTCH

smooch[2] (smōōch) *n.* [ult. akin to SMACK[2]] [Slang] a kiss —*vi., vt.* [Slang] to kiss or pet —**smooch′y** *adj.*

smoodge (smōōj) *vi.* [see SMOOCH[2]] [Aust. Colloq.] **1.** to toady; curry favour **2.** to engage in lovemaking

smooth (smōōth) *adj.* [OE. *smoth*] **1.** having an even surface with no roughness or projections **2.** without lumps [a *smooth* paste] **3.** even or gentle in flow or movement [a *smooth* voyage] **4.** free from interruptions, difficulties, etc. [*smooth* progress] **5.** calm; serene [a *smooth* temper] **6.** free from hair, beard, etc. **7.** not harsh to the taste **8.** having an easy, flowing rhythm or sound **9.** suave, polished, or ingratiating, esp. in an insincere way **10.** *Phonet.* not aspirated —*vt.* **1.** to make level or even **2.** to remove the lumps from **3.** to free from interruptions, difficulties, etc. **4.** to make calm; soothe **5.** to make less crude; refine —*vi.* to become smooth —*adv.* in a smooth manner —*n.* **1.** a smooth part **2.** an act of smoothing —**smooth away** to remove (difficulties, etc.) —**smooth down** to make or become smooth, or even, calm, etc. —**smooth over** to gloss over or make light of (an unpleasant situation) —**smooth′er** *n.* —**smooth′ly** *adv.* —**smooth′ness** *n.*

smooth·bore (-bôr′) *adj.* not rifled or grooved inside the barrel: said of guns —*n.* a smoothbore gun

smooth·en (-′n) *vt., vi.* to make or become smooth

smooth·ie (smōō′thē) *n.* [Slang] a glib, attractive person, esp. a man

smoothing iron *same as* IRON (n. sense 2a)

smooth muscle unstriated involuntary muscle, occurring in the walls of the uterus, intestines, etc.

smooth-shav·en (-shā′v′n) *adj.* wearing no beard or moustache

smooth-spo·ken (-spō′k′n) *adj.* speaking in a pleasing, persuasive, or polished manner

smooth-tongued (-tuŋd′) *adj.* smooth-spoken, esp. in a plausible or flattering way

smor·gas·bord, smör·gås·bord (smôr′gəs bôrd′, smur′-) *n.* [Sw.] a wide variety of appetizers, cheeses, fishes, meats, salads, etc., served buffet style

smote (smōt) *pt. & alt. pp. of* SMITE

smoth·er (smuth′ər) *vt.* [ME. *smorthren* < *smorther,* dense smoke] **1.** to keep from getting enough air to breathe, or kill in this way; suffocate; stifle **2.** to cover (a fire), causing it to smoulder or go out **3.** to cover over thickly [liver *smothered* in onions] **4.** to hide or suppress, as a rumour —*vi.* **1.** to be kept from getting enough air to breathe, or to die in this way **2.** to be hidden or suppressed —*n.* dense, suffocating smoke, dust, etc. —**smoth′er·er** *n.* —**smoth′er·y** *adj.*

smothered mate *Chess* the type of checkmate of a king by a knight

smoul·der (smōl′dər) *vi.* [ME. *smoldren* < GMC.] **1.** to burn and smoke without flame **2.** to exist in a suppressed state **3.** to have or show suppressed anger or hate —*n.* the act or condition of smouldering

smudge (smuj) *n.* [prob. < ME. *smogen*] **1.** a stain, smear, etc.; dirty spot **2.** [U.S.] *a)* a fire made to produce dense smoke *b)* such smoke produced by burning a substance in containers (**smudge pots**), esp. for driving away insects or protecting plants from frost —*vt.* **smudged, smudg′ing** **1.** to make dirty; soil **2.** [U.S.] to protect (an orchard, etc.) with smudge —*vi.* **1.** to blur or smear **2.** to become smudged —**smudg′y** *adj.*

smug (smug) *adj.* **smug′ger, smug′gest** [prob. < LowG. *smuk,* trim] **1.** orig., neat, trim, etc. **2.** so pleased with oneself, one's opinions, etc. as to be annoying to others; too self-satisfied —**smug′ly** *adv.* —**smug′ness** *n.*

smug·gle (smug′'l) *vt.* **-gled, -gling** [< LowG. *smuggeln*] **1.** to bring into or take out of a country secretly or illegally **2.** to bring, take, etc. secretly —*vi.* to smuggle forbidden or taxable goods —**smug′gler** *n.*

smut (smut) *n.* [< or akin to LowG. *smutt*] **1.** *a)* sooty matter *b)* a particle of this **2.** a soiled spot **3.** pornographic or obscene talk, writing, etc. **4.** *Bot. a)* a plant disease in which certain fungi form masses of black spores that break up into a fine powder *b)* any fungus causing smut —*vt., vi.* **smut′ted, smut′ting** to make or become smutty

smutch (smuch) *vt.* [akin to prec.] to smudge; soil —*n.* **1.** a dirty mark; smudge **2.** soot, dirt, etc. —**smutch′y** *adj.*

smut·ty (smut′ē) *adj.* **-ti·er, -ti·est** **1.** soiled with smut **2.** affected with plant smut **3.** pornographic or obscene —**smut′ti·ly** *adv.* —**smut′ti·ness** *n.*

Sn [L. *stannum*] *Chem.* tin

snack (snak) *n.* [prob. < MDu. *snacken,* to snap] a light meal or refreshment taken between regular meals —*vi.* to eat a snack or snacks

snack bar a lunch counter, cafeteria, etc. serving snacks

snaf·fle (snaf′'l) *n.* [prob. < Du. < ODu. dim. of *snabbe,* bill of a bird] a bit, usually light and jointed, attached to a bridle and having no curb —*vt.* **-fled, -fling** **1.** to fit with or control by a snaffle **2.** [Colloq.] to steal

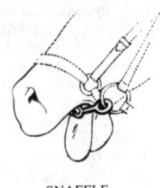

SNAFFLE

sna·fu (sna fōō′, snaf′ōō) *adj.* [orig. military slang for phrase *s(ituation) n(ormal), a(ll) f(ouled)*—a euphemism— *u(p)*] [U.S. Slang] in disorder or confusion; completely mixed up —*vt.* **-fued′, -fu′ing** [U.S. Slang] to throw into confusion

snag (snag) *n.* [< Scand.] **1.** a sharp part, point, etc. that sticks out and may catch on things **2.** an underwater tree stump or branch dangerous to navigation **3.** a snaggletooth **4.** a small branch of an antler **5.** a tear or a pulled, looped-out thread in fabric, made by or as by a snag **6.** an unexpected or hidden difficulty —*vt.* **snagged, snag′ging** **1.** to catch, tear, etc. on a snag **2.** to hinder; impede **3.** [Chiefly U.S.] to catch quickly —*vi.* **1.** to strike a snag in water **2.** to develop a snag —**snag′gy** *adj.* **-gi·er, -gi·est**

snag·gle·tooth (snag′'l tōōth′) *n., pl.* **-teeth′** [< prec.] **1.** a tooth that sticks out beyond the others **2.** a crooked or broken tooth —**snag′gle·toothed′** *adj.*

snail (snāl) *n.* [OE. *snægl*] **1.** a slow-moving gastropod mollusc living on land or in water and having a spiral protective shell **2.** any lazy, slow-moving person or animal

snail's pace a very slow speed

snake (snāk) *n.* [OE. *snaca*] **1.** any of various limbless reptiles with a long, scaly body, lidless eyes, and a tapering tail: some species have a poisonous bite **2.** a treacherous or deceitful person **3.** a long, flexible rod of spiralled wire, used by a plumber to clear blocked pipes, etc. **4.** the band within which EEC currencies are allowed to fluctuate —*vi.* **snaked, snak′ing** to move, twist, etc. like a snake —*vt.* [U.S. Colloq.] to drag, pull, or jerk —**snake′like′** *adj.*

snake charmer a person who, as an entertainer, appears to hypnotize snakes by body movements and music

snake dance an informal parade in which the celebrants join hands in a long, winding line

snake in the grass a treacherous person or harmful thing that is hidden or seemingly harmless

snake·root (-rōōt′) *n.* **1.** any of various plants reputed to be remedies for snake bites **2.** the roots of any of these plants

snakes and ladders a children's board game in which tossed dice determine how far counters move either to climb ladders or slide down snakes

snake·skin (-skin′) *n.* a snake's skin or leather from it

snak·y (snā′kē) *adj.* **snak′i·er, snak′i·est** **1.** of or like a snake or snakes **2.** sinuous; winding; twisting **3.** cunningly treacherous or evil **4.** infested with snakes

snap (snap) *vi., vt.* **snapped, snap′ping** [< MDu. or MLowG. *snappen*] **1.** to bite suddenly (often with *at*) **2.** to snatch or grasp quickly or eagerly (often with *at* or *up*) **3.** to speak or say in a sharp, abrupt way [to *snap* out orders, to *snap* back at a person in anger] **4.** to break or part suddenly, esp. with a sharp, cracking sound **5.** to break down suddenly under strain, as nerves, resistance, etc. **6.** to make or cause to make a sudden, sharp, cracking sound [to *snap* one's fingers] **7.** to close, fasten, etc. with a sound like this, as a lock **8.** to move or cause to move suddenly and smartly [to *snap* to attention] **9.** to take a snapshot (of) —*n.* **1.** a sudden bite, grasp, snatch, etc. **2.** a sudden breaking or parting **3.** a sudden, sharp cracking or clicking sound **4.** a short, angry utterance or way of speaking **5.** a brief spell of cold weather **6.** any clasp or fastening that closes with a click **7.** a hard, thin biscuit [gingersnaps] **8.** a simple card game in which cards can be won by the first person to say snap on seeing two identical cards **9.** same as SNAPSHOT **10.** [Colloq.] alertness, vigour, or energy —*adj.* **1.** made or done quickly without deliberation [a *snap* decision] **2.** that fastens with a snap —*adv.* with, or as with, a snap —**not a snap** not at all —**snap back** to recover quickly from an illness, disappointment, etc. —**snap one's fingers at** to show lack of concern for —**snap out of it** to recover quickly or regain one's senses

snap·drag·on (-drag′ən) *n.* [SNAP + DRAGON: from the mouth-shaped flowers] **1.** same as ANTIRRHINUM **2.** a Christmas game in which raisins are snatched from a bowl of burning brandy

snap fastener *same as* PRESS STUD

snap·per (-ər) *n.* **1.** a person or thing that snaps **2.** *pl.* **-pers, -per:** see PLURAL, II, D, 1 *a)* same as SNAPPING TURTLE *b)* any of various bony fishes of warm seas

snapping turtle any of several large, freshwater turtles of N America, with powerful jaws that snap with great force

snap·pish (snap'ish) *adj.* 1. likely to snap or bite 2. cross or irritable; sharp-tongued —**snap'pish·ly** *adv.* —**snap'pish·ness** *n.*

snap·py (snap'ē) *adj.* **-pi·er, -pi·est** 1. snappish; cross 2. that snaps; snapping 3. [Colloq.] *a)* brisk, vigorous, or lively [a *snappy* pace] *b)* sharply chilly [*snappy* weather] —**make it snappy** [Slang] be quick; hurry —**snap'pi·ly** *adv.* —**snap'pi·ness** *n.*

snap·shot (-shot') *n.* a photograph taken with brief exposure by snapping the shutter of a hand camera

snare (sner) *n.* [OE. *sneare* < ON. *snara*] 1. a trap for small animals, usually consisting of a noose which jerks tight upon the release of a spring trigger 2. anything dangerous, risky, etc. that tempts or attracts; trap 3. *a)* a length of spiralled wire or of gut strung across the bottom of a snare drum for added vibration *b)* [pl.] a set of snare drums —*vt.* **snared, snar'ing** 1. to catch in a trap or snare 2. to lure into a situation that is dangerous, risky, etc. —**snar'er** *n.*

snare drum a small, double-headed drum with snares

snark (snärk) *n.* an imaginary animal created by Lewis Carroll in his poem *The Hunting of the Snark*

snarl¹ (snärl) *vi.* [< earlier *snar*, to growl] 1. to growl fiercely, baring the teeth, as a threatening dog 2. to speak sharply, as in anger —*vt.* to utter with a snarl —*n.* 1. a fierce, harsh growl 2. a harsh, angry utterance —**snarl'er** *n.* —**snarl'ing·ly** *adv.* —**snarl'y** *adj.*

SNARE DRUM

snarl² (snärl) *vt.* [ME. *snarlen*, akin to SNARE] 1. to make (thread, hair, etc.) knotted or tangled 2. to make disordered or confused [to *snarl* traffic] —*vi.* to become knotted or tangled —*n.* 1. a tangle or knot 2. a confused, disordered state or situation; confusion —**snarl'y** *adj.*

snatch (snach) *vt.* [prob. var. of ME. *snakken*, to seize] 1. to grasp or seize suddenly, eagerly, or without right, warning, etc.; grab 2. to remove abruptly or hastily 3. to take, get, etc. hastily or while there is a chance 4. [U.S. Slang] to kidnap —*vi.* to try to seize a thing suddenly; grasp (*at* something) —*n.* 1. the act of snatching 2. a short time [to sleep in *snatches*] 3. a fragment; bit [*snatches* of gossip] —**snatch'er** *n.*

snatch·y (-ē) *adj.* **snatch'i·er, snatch'i·est** done in snatches; not complete or continuous; disconnected

snaz·zy (snaz'ē) *adj.* **-zi·er, -zi·est** [< ? SN(APPY) + (j)azzy, gaudy, showy < JAZZ] [Slang] stylishly or showily attractive —**snaz'zi·ly** *adv.*

sneak (snēk) *vi.* **sneaked, sneak'ing** [prob. < OE. hyp. *snecan*, akin to *snican*, to crawl] 1. to move quietly and stealthily so as to avoid notice 2. to act in an underhanded or cowardly manner —*vt.* to give, put, take, etc. secretly or in a sneaking manner —*n.* 1. one who sneaks; sneaking, underhanded, contemptible person, esp. an informer 2. an act of sneaking —*adj.* without warning [a *sneak* attack] —**sneak out of** to avoid (a duty, etc.) craftily —**sneak'er** *n.*

sneak·ing (-kiŋ) *adj.* 1. cowardly, stealthy, underhanded, or furtive 2. not admitted; secret [a *sneaking* fondness for chocolate] —**sneaking suspicion** a slight or growing suspicion —**sneak'ing·ly** *adv.*

sneak thief a person who commits thefts in a sneaking way, without the use of force or violence

sneak·y (snē'kē) *adj.* **sneak'i·er, sneak'i·est** of or like a sneak; underhanded —**sneak'i·ly** *adv.* —**sneak'i·ness** *n.*

sneer (snir) *vi.* [ME. *sneren*] 1. to look scornful or sarcastic, as by curling the lip 2. to express scorn, derision, etc. in speech or writing —*vt.* to utter in a sneering way —*n.* 1. an act of sneering 2. a sneering look, remark, etc. —**sneer'er** *n.* —**sneer'ing·ly** *adv.*

sneeze (snēz) *vi.* **sneezed, sneez'ing** [ME. *snesen*, altered < *fnesen* < OE. *fneosan*] to exhale breath from the nose and mouth in a sudden, uncontrolled way, as because the mucous membrane of the nose has been irritated —*n.* an act of sneezing —**not to be sneezed at** not to be disregarded —**sneez'er** *n.* —**sneez'y** *adj.*

snick¹ (snik) *n.* [prob. < *snick or snee*, combat with knives] 1. a small cut or notch; nick 2. *Cricket* a glancing blow —*vt.* to nick 2. *Cricket* to hit the ball with a snick

snick² (snik) *n., vt., vi.* [echoic] *same as* CLICK

snick·er (snik'ər) *vi.* [echoic] to laugh in a sly or partly stifled manner, as in disrespect or embarrassment —*vt.* to utter with a snicker —*n.* a snickering laugh —**snick'er·ing·ly** *adv.*

snide (snīd) *adj.* [orig., counterfeit < thieves' slang, prob. of Du. dial. or G. origin] slyly malicious or derisive [a *snide* remark] —**snide'ly** *adv.* —**snide'ness** *n.*

sniff (snif) *vi.* [echoic] 1. to draw air up the nose with enough force to be heard, as when trying to smell something 2. to express disdain, scepticism, etc. by sniffing —*vt.* 1. to draw (air, an inhalant, etc.) up the nose with some force 2.

to smell (a substance) by sniffing 3. to detect, perceive, etc. as by sniffing (often with *out*) —*n.* 1. an act or sound of sniffing 2. something sniffed —**sniff at** 1. to smell 2. to express disdain or contempt —**sniff'er** *n.*

snif·fle (snif''l) *vi.* **-fled, -fling** to sniff repeatedly, as in checking mucus running from the nose —*n.* an act or sound of sniffling —**the sniffles** [Colloq.] a head cold, etc. in which there is much sniffling —**snif'fler** *n.*

sniff·y (-ē) *adj.* **sniff'i·er, sniff'i·est** [Colloq.] characterized by or having a tendency to sniff: also **sniff'ish** —**sniff'i·ly** *adv.* —**sniff'i·ness** *n.*

snif·ter (snif'tər) *n.* 1. a small alcoholic drink, usually of brandy 2. [U.S.] a globe-shaped goblet with a small opening to concentrate the aroma, as of brandy

snig·ger (snig'ər) *vi., vt., n.* [echoic] *same as* SNICKER

snip (snip) *vt.* **snipped, snip'ping** [Du. *snippen*] 1. to cut with scissors, etc. in a short, quick stroke or strokes 2. to remove by such cutting —*vi.* to make a short, quick cut or cuts —*n.* 1. a small cut made with scissors, etc. 2. the sound of this 3. a small piece cut off 4. [pl.] heavy hand shears for cutting sheet metal, etc. 5. [Colloq.] a bargain 6. [Colloq.] a young, small, or insignificant person, esp. one regarded as impudent —**snip'per** *n.*

snipe (snīp) *n.* [ON. *snipa*] 1. *pl.* **snipes, snipe**: see PLURAL, II, D, 1 any of certain wading birds with a long, flexible bill, living chiefly in marshy places 2. a shot from a hidden position —*vi.* **sniped, snip'ing** 1. to hunt or shoot snipe 2. to shoot from a hidden position at individuals of an enemy force 3. to direct an attack (*at* someone) in a sly or underhanded way —**snip'er** *n.*

snip·pet (snip'it) *n.* [dim. of SNIP] 1. a small scrap or fragment, specif. of information, a writing, etc. 2. [Colloq.] *same as* SNIP (*n.* 5) —**snip'pet·y** *adj.*

snip·py (snip'ē) *adj.* **-pi·er, -pi·est** 1. made up of small scraps or snips; fragmentary 2. [U.S. Colloq.] curt, sharp, etc., esp. in a rude or insolent way —**snip'pi·ly** *adv.* —**snip'pi·ness** *n.*

snitch (snich) *vt.* [< 18th-c. thieves' slang: orig. sense "a nose"] [Slang] to steal (usually something of little value); pilfer —*vi.* [Slang] to be an informer; tattle (*on*) —*n.* [Slang] an informer: also **snitch'er**

sniv·el (sniv''l) *vi.* **-lled, -el·ling** [akin to OE. *snofl*, mucus] 1. to have mucus running from the nose 2. to cry and sniffle 3. to complain in a whining, tearful manner 4. to make a tearful, often false display of grief, sympathy, etc. —*n.* 1. nasal mucus 2. a sniffling 3. a snivelling display of grief, etc. —**sniv'el·er** *n.*

snob (snob) *n.* [< ? ON. *snāpr*, dolt] 1. a person who attaches great importance to wealth, social position, etc., having contempt for those he considers inferior 2. a person who feels and acts in a smugly superior way about his particular tastes or interests [an intellectual *snob*] —**snob'ber·y** *n., pl.* **-ber·ies** —**snob'bish** *adj.* —**snob'bish·ly** *adv.* —**snob'bish·ness** *n.* —**snob'bism** *n.*

snog (snog) *vi.* [< ?] [Slang] to kiss and cuddle —*n.* [Slang] the act of kissing and cuddling

snood (snood) *n.* [OE. *snod*] a baglike net worn at the back of a woman's head to hold the hair —*vt.* to bind (the hair) with a snood

snook¹ (snook) *n., pl.* **snook, snooks**: see PLURAL, II, D, 2 [Du. *snoek*, pike] a pikelike fish of warm seas; esp., a game and food fish of the tropical Atlantic

snook² (snook) *n.* [< ?] the gesture of thumbing one's nose in defiance or derision: used chiefly in the phrase **cock a snook at**

snook·er (snook'ər) *n.* [< ?] 1. a variety of the game of pool played with fifteen red balls and six other balls 2. a position in this game in which the object ball is masked by a ball of a different colour —*vt.* 1. to put (someone) into a snooker position 2. [Colloq.] to close off all avenues of escape for; defeat

snoop (snoop) *vi.* [Du. *snoepen*, to eat snacks on the sly] [Colloq.] to look about in a furtive, prying way —*n.* [Colloq.] 1. one who snoops: also **snoop'er** 2. the act of snooping —**snoop'i·ness** *n.* —**snoop'y** *adj.* **snoop'i·er, snoop'i·est**

snoot (snoot) *n.* [see SNOUT] [Colloq.] the nose —*vt.* to snub

snoot·y (-ē) *adj.* **snoot'i·er, snoot'i·est** [prec. + -Y²] [Colloq.] haughty; snobbish —**snoot'i·ly** *adv.* —**snoot'i·ness** *n.*

snooze (snooz) *n.* [< ? LowG. *snusen*, to snore] [Colloq.] a brief sleep; nap —*vi.* **snoozed, snooz'ing** [Colloq.] to take a brief sleep; nap —**snooz'er** *n.*

snore (snôr) *vi.* **snored, snor'ing** [echoic] to breathe, while asleep, with harsh sounds caused by vibration of the soft palate, usually with the mouth open —*n.* the act or sound of snoring —**snor'er** *n.*

snor·kel (snôr′k'l) *n.* [G. *Schnörkel*, spiral] **1.** a device for submarines, with air intake and exhaust tubes, permitting submergence for long periods **2.** a breathing tube extending above the surface of the water, used in swimming just below the surface —*vi.* **-kelled, -kel·ling** to move or swim under water using a snorkel —**snor′kel·ler** *n.*

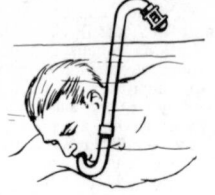

SNORKEL

snort (snôrt) *vi.* [ME. *snorten,* akin to SNORE] **1.** to force breath from the nose in a sudden and noisy way **2.** to express anger, scorn, etc. by a snort **3.** to make a noise like a snort, as in laughing boisterously —*vt.* to express or utter with a snort —*n.* **1.** the act or sound of snorting **2.** [U.S. Slang] a drink of spirits, taken in one gulp —**snort′ing·ly** *adv.*

snort·er (snôrt′ər) *n.* **1.** a person or thing that snorts **2.** [Slang] something excellent **3.** [Slang] something difficult; a problem

snot (snot) *n.* [OE. *(ge)snot,* mucus] **1.** nasal mucus: a vulgar term **2.** [Slang] a contemptible person

snot·ty (-ē) *adj.* **-ti·er, -ti·est 1.** of, like, or dirtied with snot **2.** [Slang] *a)* offensive; contemptible *b)* impudent, insolent, etc. **3.** [Slang] *a)* short-tempered *b)* snobbish —**snot′ti·ly** *adv.* —**snot′ti·ness** *n.*

snout (snout) *n.* [prob. < MDu. *snute*] **1.** the projecting nose and jaws, or muzzle, of an animal **2.** something like an animal's snout, as a nozzle or spout **3.** [Colloq.] a human nose, esp. a large one

snout beetle *same as* WEEVIL

snow (snō) *n.* [OE. *snaw*] **1.** particles of water vapour which when frozen in the upper air fall to earth as soft, white, crystalline flakes **2.** *a)* a falling of snow *b)* snowy weather **3.** a mass of fallen snow **4.** [Poet.] whiteness **5.** fluctuating spots appearing on a TV screen as a result of a weak signal **6.** [Slang] cocaine or heroin —*vi.* to fall as or like snow —*vt.* **1.** to shower or let fall as or like snow **2.** to cover, obstruct, etc. with or as with snow (usually with *in, under,* etc.) —**snow under** to overwhelm as with work, esp. paperwork

snow·ball (-bôl′) *n.* **1.** a mass of snow packed together into a ball **2.** *same as* GUELDER-ROSE —*vi.* **1.** to increase rapidly and out of control like a ball of snow rolling downhill **2.** to throw snowballs —*vt.* **1.** to throw snowballs at **2.** to cause to increase rapidly

snow·bank (-baŋk′) *n.* a large mound of snow

snow·ber·ry (-ber′ē) *n., pl.* **-ries 1.** a hardy N. American plant with small, pink flowers and soft, white berries **2.** any of various other plants with white berries **3.** any of these berries

snow·blind (-blīnd′) *adj.* blinded temporarily by ultraviolet rays of the sun reflected from snow —**snow blindness** *n.*

snow·bound (-bound′) *adj.* shut in or blocked off by snow

snow bunting a small finch inhabiting cold regions in the Northern Hemisphere

snow·cap (-kap′) *n.* a cap of snow, as on a mountain, the top of a tree, etc. —**snow′capped′** *adj.*

snow·drift (-drift′) *n.* **1.** a smooth heap of snow blown together by the wind **2.** snow blown along by the wind

snow·drop (-drop′) *n.* a low-growing, bulbous plant with small, bell-shaped white flowers

snow·fall (-fôl′) *n.* **1.** a fall of snow **2.** the amount of snow that falls in a given area or period of time

snow·field (-fēld′) *n.* a large expanse of snow

snow·flake (-flāk′) *n.* **1.** a single crystal of snow **2.** *same as* SNOW BUNTING **3.** a European bulbous plant with drooping white flowers

snow goose a white goose that breeds in the Arctic, having a red bill and black wing tips

snow leopard a large, whitish cat of the mountains of C Asia, having many dark blotches on its fur

snow line the lower boundary of a high region in which snow never melts

snow·man (-man′) *n., pl.* **-men′** (-men′) a crude human figure made of snow packed together

snow·mo·bile (-mō bēl′) *n.* a motor vehicle for travelling over snow, usually with steerable runners at the front and tractor treads at the rear

snow·plough (snō′plou′) *n.* **1.** any ploughlike machine used to clear snow off a road, railway, etc. **2.** *Skiing* a stemming of both skis, as for stopping, with the tips of the skis pointed at each other —*vi.* to stem with both skis

snow·shoe (-shoō′) *n.* a racket-shaped frame of wood crisscrossed with strips of leather, etc., worn on the feet to prevent sinking in deep snow —*vi.* **-shoed′, -shoe′ing** to use snowshoes in walking —**snow′shoe′er** *n.*

snow·slide (-slīd′) *n.* an avalanche of mainly snow

snow·storm (-stôrm′) *n.* a storm with a heavy snowfall

snow tyre a tyre with a deep tread, and sometimes protruding studs, for added traction on snow or ice

snow-white (-wīt′, -hwīt′) *adj.* white as snow

SNOWSHOES

snow·y (snō′ē) *adj.* **snow′i·er, snow′i·est 1.** of or characterized by snow **2.** covered or filled with snow **3.** like snow; specif., *a)* pure; spotless *b)* white —**snow′i·ly** *adv.* —**snow′i·ness** *n.*

SNP Scottish National Party

snub (snub) *vt.* **snubbed, snub′bing** [ON. *snubba,* to chide] **1.** orig., to check with sharp words **2.** to treat with scorn, disregard, etc.; slight **3.** *a)* to check suddenly the movement of (a rope, etc.) by turning it around a post *b)* to make (a boat, etc.) fast in this way —*n.* **1.** scornful, slighting action or treatment **2.** a snubbing, or checking —*adj.* short and turned up; pug: said of the nose —**snub′ber** *n.*

snub·by (-ē) *adj.* **-bi·er, -bi·est 1.** turned up; snub **2.** tending to snub or slight

snub-nosed (-nōzd′) *adj.* having a snub nose

snuff¹ (snuf) *n.* [< ?] the charred end of a candle wick —*vt.* **1.** to trim off the charred end of (a candle wick) **2.** to put out (a candle) —**snuff it** [Colloq.] to die —**snuff out 1.** to put out (a candle, etc.); extinguish **2.** to destroy or cause to die suddenly

snuff² (snuf) *vt.* [MDu. *snuffen*] **1.** to inhale strongly through the nose; sniff **2.** to smell or sniff at —*vi.* **1.** to sniff or snort **2.** [Rare] to use snuff —*n.* **1.** the act or sound of snuffing; sniff **2.** *a)* a preparation of powdered tobacco taken up into the nose by sniffing or applied to the gums *b)* a pinch of this —**up to snuff** [Colloq.] **1.** up to the usual standard **2.** not easily deceived

snuff·box (-boks′) *n.* a small box for holding snuff

snuff·er (-ər) *n.* **1.** a device with a cone on the end of a handle, for putting out a burning candle: in full, **candle snuffer 2.** [*pl.*] an instrument like shears, for snuffing a candle: also **pair of snuffers**

snuf·fle (snuf′'l) *vi.* **-fled, -fling** [freq. of SNUFF²] **1.** to breathe audibly and with difficulty or by constant sniffing, as a dog in trailing; sniffle **2.** to speak or sing in a nasal tone —*vt.* to utter by snuffling —*n.* **1.** the act or sound of snuffling **2.** a nasal tone or twang —**the snuffles** *same as* the sniffles, (see SNIFFLE) —**snuf′fler** *n.*

snuff·y (snuf′ē) *adj.* **snuff′i·er, snuff′i·est 1.** like snuff, as in colour or texture **2.** soiled with snuff **3.** disagreeable; unattractive

snug (snug) *adj.* **snug′ger, snug′gest** [prob. ult. < Scand.] **1.** protected from the weather; warm and cosy **2.** compact and convenient [a *snug* cottage] **3.** large enough to provide ease: said of an income [a *snug* income] **4.** tight in fit [a *snug* coat] **5.** well-built; seaworthy **6.** hidden or concealed [to lie *snug*] —*vt.* **snugged, snug′ging** to make snug or secure —*n.* a bar in certain public houses —**snug′ly** *adv.* —**snug′ness** *n.*

snug·ger·y (-ər ē) *n., pl.* **-ger·ies** a snug or comfortable room; esp. a small private room in a public house

snug·gle (-'l) *vi.* **-gled, -gling** [freq. of SNUG] to lie closely and comfortably; cuddle, as for warmth, in affection, etc. —*vt.* to cuddle

so¹ (sō) *adv.* [OE. *swa*] **1.** in the way shown, expressed, understood, etc. [hold the bat just *so*] **2.** *a)* to such an extent [why are you *so* late?] *b)* very [they are *so* happy] *c)* [Colloq.] very much [she *so* wants to go] **3.** for the reason specified; therefore [they were tired, and *so* left] **4.** more or less; approximately [fifty pounds or *so*]: in this sense often regarded as a pronoun **5.** also; likewise [I'm going and *so* are you] **6.** then [and *so* to bed] —*conj.* **1.** in order that; with the purpose that: usually followed by *that* [talk louder *so* (that) all may hear] **2.** [Colloq.] with the result that [he smiled, *so* I did too] **3.** if only; as long as (*that*) —*pron.* that which has been specified or named [he is a friend and will remain *so*] —*interj.* an exclamation of surprise, approval, triumph, etc. —*adj.* **1.** true; in reality [that's *so*] **2.** in proper order [everything must be just *so*] —**and so on** (or **forth**) and the rest; et cetera (etc.) —**so as** with the purpose or result (followed by an infinitive) —**so be it** an expression of acceptance or resignation —**so much** to an unspecified but limited degree, amount, etc. [paid *so much* per day] —**so much for** no more need be said about [*so much for* that] —**so to say** as it were; in a manner of speaking —**so what?** [Colloq.] even if so, what then?: used to express disregard, challenge, etc.

so² (sō) *n.* *Music same as* SOL²

So. 1. south 2. southern

soak (sōk) *vt.* [OE. *socian*] 1. to make thoroughly wet; drench or saturate 2. to submerge in a liquid, as for thorough wetting, softening, soothing, etc. 3. *a)* to take in (liquid) by absorbing (usually with *up*) *b)* to absorb by exposure to it [to *soak* up sunshine] 4. to take in mentally [to *soak* up knowledge] —*vi.* 1. to stay immersed in liquid for wetting, softening, etc. 2. to pass (*into* or *through*) as a liquid does [rain *soaking* through his coat] 3. to become absorbed mentally [the fact *soaked* into his head] —*n.* 1. a soaking or being soaked 2. liquid used for soaking 3. [Slang] a drunkard

soak·a·way (-ə wā') *n.* a depression in the ground where rainwater is drained away through the soil

so-and-so (sō'ən sō') *n.*, *pl.* **so'-and-sos'** [Colloq.] some person or thing whose name is not specified: often used to avoid vulgar or offensive name-calling

soap (sōp) *n.* [OE. *sape*] 1. a substance used with water to produce suds for washing, usually produced by the action of an alkali, as caustic soda or potash, on fats or oils 2. any metallic salt of a fatty acid —*vt.* to lather, scrub, etc. with soap —**no soap** [Slang] 1. (it is) not acceptable 2. to no avail

soap·ber·ry (-ber'ē) *n.*, *pl.* **-ries** 1. any of various trees with fruits containing a soapy material 2. the globe-shaped fruit, with yellowish flesh and a large, round seed

soap·box (-boks') *n.* 1. a box for soap 2. any improvised platform used by a person (**soapbox orator**) making an informal, often impassioned speech to a street audience

soap flakes soap in the form of flakes used esp. for washing delicate clothes

soap opera [Colloq.] a radio or TV serial drama of a melodramatic, sentimental nature: originally, many of the sponsors were soap companies

soap powder a powder used for washing clothes, usually containing additives as well as soap

soap·stone (-stōn') *n.* same as STEATITE

soap·suds (-sudz') *n.pl.* 1. soapy water, esp. when stirred into a foam 2. the foam on soapy water

soap·y (sō'pē) *adj.* **soap'i·er, soap'i·est** 1. covered with or containing soap 2. of or like soap 3. [Slang] suave; oily —**soap'i·ly** *adv.* —**soap'i·ness** *n.*

soar (sôr) *vi.* [OFr. *essorer*, ult. < L. *ex-*, out + *aura*, air] 1. to rise or fly high into the air 2. to sail or glide along high in the air, as a glider does on air currents 3. to rise above the ordinary level [*soaring* prices] —*n.* 1. soaring range 2. the act of soaring —**soar'er** *n.*

sob (sob) *vi.* **sobbed, sob'bing** [ME. *sobben*] 1. to weep aloud with short, gasping breaths 2. to make a sound like this, as the wind —*vt.* 1. to put (oneself), as to sleep, by sobbing 2. to utter with sobs —*n.* the act or sound of sobbing —**sob'bing·ly** *adv.*

so·ber (sō'bər) *adj.* [< OFr. < L. *sobrius*] 1. temperate, esp. in the use of alcohol 2. not drunk 3. serious, solemn, sedate, etc. 4. quiet; plain: said of colour, clothes, etc. 5. not distorted [the *sober* truth] 6. showing mental and emotional balance —*vt.*, *vi.* to make or become sober (often with *up* or *down*) —**so'ber·ly** *adv.* —**so'ber·ness** *n.*

so·ber-mind·ed (-mīn'did) *adj.* sensible and serious —**so'-ber-mind'ed·ly** *adv.* —**so'ber-mind'ed·ness** *n.*

so·bri·e·ty (sə brī'ə tē, sō-) *n.* a being sober; specif., *a)* temperance, esp. in the use of alcohol *b)* seriousness; sedateness

so·bri·quet (sō'brə kā', sō'brə kā') *n.* [Fr.] 1. a nickname 2. an assumed name

sob story [Colloq.] a very sad story, esp. an account of personal troubles meant to arouse sympathy

Soc., soc. 1. social 2. socialist 3. society

soc·age (sok'ij) *n.* [ME.: see SOKE & -AGE] a medieval system of land tenure in which a tenant held land in return for a fixed payment or for certain stated nonmilitary services to his lord: also **soc'cage**

so-called (sō'kôld') *adj.* 1. popularly known by this term [the *so-called* nuclear powers] 2. inaccurately regarded as such [a *so-called* liberal]

soc·cer (sok'ər) *n.* [alt. < (AS)SOC(IATION FOOTBALL)] same as ASSOCIATION FOOTBALL

so·cia·ble (sō'shə b'l) *adj.* [Fr. < L. < *socius*: see ff.] 1. enjoying or requiring the company of others; friendly; affable 2. characterized by pleasant, informal conversation and companionship —**so'cia·bil'i·ty**, *pl.* **-ties**, —**so'-cia·ble·ness** *n.* —**so'cia·bly** *adv.*

so·cial (sō'shəl) *adj.* [< Fr. < L. *socialis* < *socius*, companion] 1. of or having to do with human beings living together in a situation or group relation affecting their common welfare [*social* problems] 2. living in this way [man as a *social* being] 3. of or having to do with the ranks of society, specif. the more fashionable ranks [a *social* event] 4. getting along well with others; sociable 5. of or for companionship 6. of or engaged in welfare work

[a *social* worker] 7. living in groups or communities [the ant is a *social* insect] —*n.* an informal gathering for recreation; party —**so'cial·ly** *adv.*

social climber a person who seeks higher social status by getting acquainted with distinguished or wealthy people

social contract an agreement among individuals forfeiting some of their individual liberties for greater security, found in the political theories of Locke and Rousseau —[**S- C-**] an agreement operating in Britain between the government and the Trade Unions

social disease any venereal disease

so·cial·ism (sō'shəl iz'm) *n.* 1. any of various theories of the ownership and operation of the means of production and distribution by society rather than by private individuals, with all members of society sharing in the work and the products 2. [often **S-**] *a)* a political movement for establishing such a system *b)* the doctrines, etc. of the Socialist parties 3. the stage of society, in Marxist doctrine, coming between the capitalist stage and the communist stage (see COMMUNISM, sense 2), in which private ownership of the means of production and distribution has been eliminated

so·cial·ist (-ist) *n.* 1. an advocate or supporter of socialism 2. [**S-**] a member of a Socialist Party —*adj.* 1. of or like socialism or socialists 2. advocating or supporting socialism 3. [**S-**] designating or of a political party advocating Socialism Also **so'cial·is'tic** —**so'cial·is'ti·cal·ly** *adv.*

so·cial·ite (sō'shə līt') *n.* a person who is prominent in fashionable society

so·ci·al·i·ty (sō'shē al'ə tē) *n.* 1. a being social or sociable 2. *pl.* **-ties** the tendency to form social groups

so·cial·ize (sō'shə līz') *vt.* **-ized', -iz'ing** 1. to make social or fit for cooperative group living 2. to adapt to the common needs of a social group 3. to put under government ownership 4. to cause to become socialist —*vi.* to take part in social activity —**so'cial·i·za'tion** *n.* —**so'cial·iz'er** *n.*

socialized medicine [Chiefly U.S.] any system supplying complete medical and hospital care, through public funds, for all the people in a community, district, or nation

social science 1. the study of people living together in groups, families, etc. 2. any of several studies, as history, economics, civics, etc., dealing with society and the activity of its members —**social scientist**

social secretary a secretary employed by an individual to handle his social appointments and correspondence

social security a State system of old-age, unemployment, or disability insurance, financed by a fund maintained jointly by employees, employers, and the government

social service same as SOCIAL WORK —**so'cial-serv'ice** *adj.*

social studies a course of study, esp. in schools, including history, civics, geography, etc.

social welfare 1. the welfare of society, esp. of those who are underprivileged or disadvantaged because of poverty, unemployment, etc. 2. same as SOCIAL WORK

social work any activity designed to promote the welfare of the community and the individual, as through counselling services, recreation and rehabilitation centres, aid for the needy and aged, etc. —**social worker**

so·ci·e·ty (sə sī'ə tē) *n.*, *pl.* **-ties** [< MFr. < L. *societas* < *socius*, companion] 1. a group of persons regarded as forming a single community, esp. as forming a distinct social or economic class 2. the system or condition of living together in such a group [an agrarian *society*] 3. all people, collectively, regarded as a community of mutually dependent individuals 4. companionship 5. one's friends or associates 6. any organized group of people with work, interests, etc. in common [a medical *society*] 7. a group of persons regarded as a dominant class because of their wealth, birth, etc. —*adj.* of or involving society (*n.* 7) —**so·ci'e·tal** *adj.* —**so·ci'e·tal·ly** *adv.*

Society of Friends a Christian religious sect founded in England c. 1650 by George Fox: the Friends have no formal creed, rites, liturgy, or priesthood, and reject violence in human relations, including war

Society of Jesus see JESUIT

so·ci·o- (sō'sē ō', -shē-, -ə) [Fr. < L. *socius*, companion] a combining form meaning social, society, sociological

so·ci·o·e·co·nom·ic (-ē'kə nom'ik, -ek'ə-) *adj.* of or involving both social and economic factors

so·ci·o·lin·guis·tics (sō'sē ō lin gwis'tiks) *n.* *pl.* [with sing. v.] the study of language in relation to its social context —**so'ci·o·lin·guis'tic** *adj.*

so·ci·ol·o·gy (sō'sē ol'ə jē, -shē-) *n.* [< Fr.: see SOCIO- & -LOGY] the science of human society and of social relations, organization, and change; specif., the study of the beliefs, values, etc. of groups in society —**so'ci·o·log'i·cal** (-ə loj'-i k'l), **so'ci·o·log'ic** *adj.* —**so'ci·o·log'i·cal·ly** *adv.* —**so'ci·ol'-o·gist** *n.*

so·ci·om·e·try (-om'ə trē) *n.* [SOCIO- + -METRY] the quantitative study of group relationships —**so'ci·o·met'ric** (-ə met'rik) *adj.*

so·ci·o·path (sō'sē ə path', -shē-) *n.* [SOCIO- + (PSYCHO)PATH] a psychopathic personality whose behaviour is aggressively antisocial —**so'ci·o·path'ic** *adj.*

so·ci·o·po·lit·i·cal (sō'sē ō pə lit'i k'l, -shē-) *adj.* of or involving both social and political factors

sock[1] (sok) *n.* [OE. *socc* < L. *soccus*, a light, low-heeled shoe] 1. a light shoe worn by comic characters in ancient Greek and Roman drama 2. comic drama 3. a short stocking reaching only part way to the knee 4. an insole put in a shoe to make it fit better —**put a sock in it** [Slang] to stop talking, complaining, etc.

sock[2] (sok) *vt.* [Slang] to hit with force, esp. with the fist —*n.* [Slang] a blow —**sock it to (someone)** 1. to attack or assault (someone) 2. [Slang] a meaningless catch phrase

sock·et (sok'it) *n.* [< Anglo-Fr., dim. < OFr. *soc*, ploughshare < Gaul.] a hollow part into which something fits [an eye *socket*, the *socket* for a light bulb] —*vt.* to fit into a socket

sock·eye (sok'ī') *n.* [< AmInd. *suk-kegh*] a salmon of the N Pacific with red flesh, often tinned

So·crat·ic (sə krat'ik, sō-) *adj.* of or relating to Socrates (470?-399 B.C.), Athenian philosopher —*n.* a follower of Socrates

Socratic method a method of teaching, as used by Socrates, in which a series of questions leads the answerer to a logical conclusion foreseen by the questioner

sod[1] (sod) *n.* [prob. < MDu. or MLowG. *sode*] 1. a surface layer of earth containing grass plants with their matted roots; turf 2. a piece of this layer —*vt.* **sod'ded, sod'ding** to cover with sod or sods —**under the sod** dead and buried

sod[2] (sod) *n.* [clip of SODOMITE] [Slang] 1. *same as* SODOMITE 2. any obnoxious person 3. anyone: an affectionate term

so·da (sō'də) *n.* [ML., ult. < Ar. *suwwād*, a plant burned to produce soda] 1. *a)* sodium oxide, Na₂O *b) same as:* (1) SODIUM BICARBONATE (2) SODIUM CARBONATE (3) SODIUM HYDROXIDE 2. *a) same as* SODA WATER *b)* [U.S.] a drink of soda water flavoured with syrup

soda ash crude sodium carbonate (sense 1)

soda cracker [U.S.] a light, crisp cracker, usually salted, made from a dough of flour, water, baking soda, and cream of tartar

soda fountain 1. [U.S.] a counter for making and serving soft drinks, sundaes, etc. 2. an apparatus for making soda water, with taps for drawing it off

so·dal·i·ty (sō dal'ə tē) *n., pl.* **-ties** [< L. < *sodalis*, companion] 1. fellowship; companionship 2. an association or brotherhood 3. R.C.Ch. a devotional or charitable lay society

soda water water charged under pressure with carbon dioxide gas, used as a drink, with or without spirits

sod·den (sod''n) *obs. pp. of* SEETHE —*adj.* 1. soaked through 2. soggy from improper baking or cooking, as bread 3. dull or stupefied, as from drunkenness —*vt., vi.* to make or become sodden —**sod'den·ly** *adv.* —**sod'-den·ness** *n.*

so·di·um (sō'dē əm) *n.* [ModL. < SODA] a silver-white, alkaline metallic chemical element, found in nature only in combined form: symbol, Na; at. wt., 22.9898; at. no., 11

sodium benzoate a sweet, white powder, the sodium salt of benzoic acid, used as a food preservative

sodium bicarbonate a white, crystalline compound, NaHCO₃, used in baking powder, as an antacid, etc.

sodium carbonate 1. the anhydrous sodium salt of carbonic acid, Na₂CO₃ 2. any of the hydrated carbonates of sodium; esp., *same as* SAL SODA

sodium chloride common salt, NaCl

sodium cyanide a white, highly poisonous salt, NaCN, used in electroplating, as an insecticide, etc.

sodium hydroxide a white, strongly caustic substance, NaOH, used in chemistry, etc.

sodium hyposulphite *see* SODIUM THIOSULPHATE

sodium nitrate a clear, crystalline salt, NaNO₃, used in manufacturing explosives, fertilizers, etc.

sodium pentothal *same as* THIOPENTAL SODIUM

sodium thiosulphate a white, crystalline salt used as a fixing agent in photography, etc.: popularly but incorrectly called (*sodium*) hyposulphite or hypo

Sod·om (sod'əm) *n.* any place that is notorious for vice & depravity: after the city described in the Bible as being destroyed by fire, together with a neighbouring city, Gomorrah, because of the sinfulness of its people: Gen. 18-19

sod·om·ite (-īt') *n.* a person who practises sodomy

sod·om·y (-ē) *n.* [see SODOM] any sexual intercourse held to be abnormal, as between a person and an animal or between two persons of the same sex

so·ev·er (sō ev'ər) *adv.* 1. in any way [how dark *soever* it may be] 2. of any kind; at all [no rest *soever*]

-so·ev·er (sō ev'ər) a combining form added for emphasis or generalization to who, what, when, where, how, etc., *and* meaning any (person, thing, time, place, or manner) of all those possible

so·fa (sō'fə) *n.* [Fr. < Ar. *ṣuffah*] an upholstered couch with fixed back and arms

S. of Sol. Song of Solomon

soft (soft) *adj.* [OE. *softe*] 1. giving way easily under pressure, as a feather pillow or moist clay 2. easily cut, shaped, or worn away [a *soft* wood or metal] 3. not as hard as is normal, desirable, etc. [*soft* butter] 4. smooth to the touch 5. *a)* bland; not acid, sour, or sharp *b)* easy to digest because free from roughage: said of a diet 6. nonalcoholic: said of drinks 7. having few or none of the mineral salts that interfere with the lathering of soap: said of water 8. *a)* mild or temperate, as a breeze, climate, etc. *b)* rainy; drizzling; misty [*soft* weather] 9. *a)* weak; not strong or vigorous *b)* having flabby muscles 10. requiring little effort; easy [a *soft* job] 11. *a)* kind or lenient; not severe *b)* easily influenced or imposed upon 12. not bright; subdued: said of colour or light 13. showing little contrast or distinctness, as an etching 14. gentle; low: said of sound 15. not addictive: said of drugs 16. *Finance* unstable and declining: said of a market, prices, etc. 17. *Phonet. a)* sibilant: said of *c* and *g*, as in *cent* and *germ b)* voiced —*adv.* softly; gently; quietly —*n.* something soft; soft part —*interj.* [Archaic] hush! stop! —**be soft on** 1. to treat gently 2. to feel amorous towards —**soft in the head** stupid or foolish —**soft'ish** *adj.* —**soft'ly** *adv.* —**soft'ness** *n.*

sof·ta (sof'tə) *n.* [< Turk.] a Muslim student of theology

soft·ball (soft'bôl') *n.* [U.S.] a game like baseball played on a smaller diamond and with a larger and softer ball

soft-boiled (-boild') *adj.* boiled only a short time so that the yolk is still soft: said of an egg

soft coal *same as* BITUMINOUS COAL

soft-cov·er (-kuv'ər) *n. same as* PAPERBACK —*adj.* bound as a paperback

soft drink a nonalcoholic, esp. carbonated drink

soft·en (sof''n) *vt., vi.* 1. to make or become soft or softer 2. to make or become less resistant —**sof'ten·er** *n.*

soft furnishings fabrics, etc. for curtains, cushions & furniture coverings

soft·goods (soft'goodz') *n.pl.* goods that last a relatively short time, esp. textile products: also **soft goods**

soft·head·ed (-hed'id) *adj.* stupid or foolish —**soft'head'-ed·ly** *adv.* —**soft'head'ed·ness** *n.*

soft·heart·ed (-här'tid) *adj.* 1. full of compassion or tenderness 2. not strict or severe, as in discipline —**soft'-heart'ed·ly** *adv.* —**soft'heart'ed·ness** *n.*

soft landing a safe landing, as of a spacecraft on the moon, in which the craft and its contents remain unharmed

soft palate the soft, fleshy part at the rear of the roof of the mouth; velum

soft paste artificial porcelain made from clay, ground glass, etc.: cf. HARD PASTE

soft-ped·al (-ped'l) *vt.* **-alled, -al·ling** 1. to soften the tone of (a musical instrument) by use of a special pedal (**soft pedal**) 2. [Colloq.] to tone down; make less emphatic, less noticeable, etc.

soft sell selling that relies on subtle suggestion rather than high-pressure salesmanship —**soft'-sell'** *adj.*

soft-shell (-shel') *adj.* 1. having a soft shell 2. having an unhardened shell as the result of recent moulting Also **soft'-shelled'**

soft-shoe (-shoo') *adj.* designating a kind of tap dancing done without metal taps on the shoes

soft shoulder soft ground along the edge of a road

soft-soap (-sōp') *vt.* 1. to apply soft soap to 2. [Colloq.] to flatter —**soft'-soap'er** *n.*

soft soap 1. soap in liquid or semifluid form 2. [Colloq.] flattery or smooth talk

soft-spo·ken (-spō'k'n) *adj.* 1. speaking or spoken with a soft, low voice 2. smooth; suave

soft spot particular affection for someone or something [he has a *soft spot* for children]

soft touch [Slang] a person who is easily persuaded to give or lend money

soft·ware (-wer') *n.* the programs, data, routines, etc. for a computer: cf. HARDWARE (3b)

soft·wood (-wood') *n.* 1. *a)* any light, easily cut wood *b)* a tree yielding such wood 2. *Forestry* wood from a needle-bearing conifer

soft·y, soft·ie (sof'tē) *n., pl.* **soft'ies** [Colloq.] a person who is too sentimental or trusting

SOGAT Society of Graphical and Allied Trades

sog·gy (sog'ē) *adj.* **-gi·er, -gi·est** [prob. < or akin to ON. *sog*, lit., a sucking] 1. saturated with moisture; soaked 2. moist and heavy; sodden [a *soggy* cake] 3. dull and boring —**sog'gi·ly** *adv.* —**sog'gi·ness** *n.*

soil[1] (soil) *n.* [Anglo-Fr. < OFr. < L. *solum*] 1. the surface layer of earth, supporting plant life 2. any place for growth or development 3. land; country [foreign *soil*] 4. ground or earth —**the soil** life and work on a farm

soil[2] (soil) *vt.* [< OFr., ult. < L. *suculus*, dim. of *sus*, pig] 1. to make dirty 2. to smirch or stain 3. to bring disgrace upon 4. to corrupt or defile —*vi.* to become soiled —*n.*

1. a soiled spot; stain **2.** excrement, sewage, etc. **3.** a soiling or being soiled

soil³ (soil) *vt.* [altered < ? OFr. *saoler* < L. *salullare*, to satiate] **1.** to feed (livestock) on green crops **2.** to purge (livestock) by means of green grass

soi·ree, soi·rée (swä´rā´) *n.* [< Fr. < *soir*, evening] a party or gathering in the evening

so·journ (sō´jurn) *vi.* [< OFr. < L. *sub-*, under + *diurnus*, of a day < *dies*, day] to live somewhere temporarily; stay for a while —*n.* a brief stay; visit —**so·journ·er** *n.*

soke (sōk) *n.* [ME. < ML. *soca* < OE. *socn*, jurisdiction < base of *secan*, to SEEK] *Eng. History* **1.** the right to hold court and dispense justice within a given territory **2.** the territory under the jurisdiction of such a court

so·kol (sō´kôl) *n.* [Czech, lit., falcon] an organization promoting physical health, esp. through gymnastics

Sol (säl) [L.] **1.** *Rom. Myth.* the sun god: identified with the Greek god Helios **2.** the sun personified

sol¹ (sōl; *Sp.* sôl) *n., pl.* **sols,** *Sp.* **so·les** (sô´les) [Sp., lit., sun] *see* MONETARY UNITS, table (Peru)

sol² (sōl) *n.* [< ML. *sol*(ve): see GAMUT] *Music* a syllable representing the fifth tone of the diatonic scale

sol³ (sol, sōl) *n.* a liquid colloidal solution

so·la (sō´lə) *n.* [< Hindi *shola*] an Indian plant, whose pith is used for making topees

sol·ace (sol´is) *n.* [< OFr. < L. < *solari*, to comfort] **1.** an easing of grief, loneliness, etc. **2.** something that eases or relieves; comfort; relief Also **sol´ace·ment** —*vt.* **-aced, -ac·ing 1.** to give solace to; comfort **2.** to lessen (grief, sorrow, etc.) —**sol´ac·er** *n.*

so·lan (sō´lən) *n.* [Scot. < ME. *soland* < ON. *sūla*, gannet + *ọnd, -and*, duck] *same as* GANNET

so·lar (sō´lər) *adj.* [L. *solaris* < *sol*, the sun] **1.** of or having to do with the sun **2.** produced by or coming from the sun [*solar* energy] **3.** depending upon the sun's light or energy [*solar* heating] **4.** measured by the earth's motion with relation to the sun [mean *solar* time]

solar battery an assembly of devices (**solar cells**) that convert the energy of sunlight into electricity

solar flare a short-lived increase of intensity in the light of the sun, usually near a sunspot

so·lar·i·um (sō·ler´ē əm, sə-) *n., pl.* **-i·a** (-ə) [L. < *sol*, the sun] a glassed-in porch, room, etc. where people sun themselves, as in treating illness

solar plexus 1. a network of nerves in the abdominal cavity behind the stomach **2.** [Colloq.] the area of the belly just below the sternum

solar system the sun and all the heavenly bodies that revolve around it

solar wind streams of ionized gas particles constantly emitted by the sun

sold (sōld) *pt. & pp. of* SELL —**be sold on** [Slang] to be uncritically attached to or interested in

sol·der (sold´ər) *n.* [< OFr. < L. *solidare*, to make firm] **1.** a metal alloy used when melted to join or patch metal parts or surfaces **2.** anything that joins or fuses; bond —*vt., vi.* **1.** to join (things) with solder **2.** to unite or become united —**sol´der·er** *n.*

sol·der·ing iron (sold´ər iŋ) a pointed metal tool heated for use in melting and applying solder

sol·dier (sōl´jər) *n.* [< OFr. < *solde*, pay < LL. *solidus*, a coin] **1.** a member of an army **2.** such a person as distinguished from an officer **3.** a man of much military experience **4.** a person who works for a specified cause —*vi.* **1.** to serve as a soldier **2.** to shirk one's duty, as by pretending to work, to be ill, etc. —**soldier on** to persist tenaciously; carry on regardless of other events —**sol´dier·li·ness** *n.* —**sol´dier·ly** *adj.*

soldier of fortune 1. a mercenary soldier, esp. one seeking adventure or excitement **2.** any adventurer

sol·dier·y (-ē) *n., pl.* **-dier·ies 1.** soldiers collectively **2.** military science: also **sol´dier·ship´**

sole¹ (sōl) *n.* [< OFr., ult. < L. *solum*, a base, bottom] **1.** the bottom surface of the foot **2.** the part of a shoe, sock, etc. corresponding to this **3.** the bottom surface of various objects, as a golf club —*vt.* **soled, sol´ing** to furnish (a shoe, etc.) with a sole, esp. a new sole

sole² (sōl) *adj.* [< OE. < L. *solus*] **1.** *a)* without another; single; one and only *b)* acting, working, etc. alone without help **2.** of or having to do with only one (specified) person or group **3.** not shared; exclusive [*sole* rights to a patent] **4.** [Archaic] alone; solitary

sole³ (sōl) *n., pl.* **sole, soles:** *see* PLURAL, II, D, 2 [OFr. < L. *solea*, sole of a shoe, kind of fish: named from its shape] any of certain sea flatfishes, highly valued as food

sol·e·cism (sol´ə siz'm) *n.* [< L. < Gr. < *soloikos*, speaking incorrectly < dialect used in Soloi, city in Asia Minor] **1.** a violation of the conventional usage, grammar, etc. of a language (Ex.: "We done it" for "We did it") **2.** a mistake in etiquette —**sol´e·cist** *n.* —**sol´e·cis´tic** *adj.* —**sol´e·cis´ti·cal·ly** *adv.*

sole·ly (sōl´lē) *adv.* **1.** without another or others; alone **2.**

only, exclusively, merely, or altogether [to read *solely* for pleasure]

sol·emn (sol´əm) *adj.* [< OFr. < L. *sollemnis*, yearly < *sollus*, all + *annus*, year] **1.** *a)* observed or done according to ritual, as religious rites, etc. *b)* sacred **2.** according to strict form; formal **3.** serious; deeply earnest **4.** awe-inspiring; very impressive **5.** sombre because dark in colour —**sol´emn·ly** *adv.* —**sol´emn·ness** *n.*

so·lem·ni·fy (sə lem´nə fī´) *vt.* **-fied, -fy´ing** to make solemn

so·lem·ni·ty (-tē) *n., pl.* **-ties 1.** solemn ceremony, ritual, etc. **2.** seriousness; gravity

sol·em·nize (sol´əm nīz´) *vt.* **-nized´, -niz´ing 1.** to celebrate formally or according to ritual **2.** to perform the ceremony of (marriage, etc.) **3.** to make serious, grave, etc. —**sol´em·ni·za´tion** *n.* —**sol´em·niz´er** *n.*

so·le·noid (sō´lə noid´, sol´ə-) *n.* [< Fr. < Gr. *sōlēn*, a channel + *eidos*, a form] a coil of wire carrying an electric current and acting like a magnet —**so´le·noi´dal** *adj.*

sole·plate (sōl´plāt´) *n.* [SOLE¹ + PLATE] the ironing surface of an iron

sol·fa (sōl´fä´) *n.* [It. *solfa* < *sol* + *fa*: see GAMUT] **1.** the syllables *do, re, mi, fa, sol, la, ti, do,* used for the tones of a scale, regardless of key **2.** the use of these syllables in vocal exercises —*vt., vi.* **-faed´** (-fäd´), **-fa´ing** to sing (a scale, etc.) to these syllables —**sol´-fa´ist** *n.*

sol·feg·gio (sol fej´ō, -fej´ē ō´) *n., pl.* **-feg´gios, -feg´gi** (-fej´ē) [It. < *solfa*: see prec.] **1.** voice practice in which scales are sung to the sol-fa syllables **2.** the use of these syllables in singing

so·lic·it (sə lis´it) *vt.* [< MFr. < L.: see SOLICITOUS] **1.** to ask or seek earnestly; appeal to or for **2.** to entice (someone to do wrong) **3.** to approach for some immoral purpose, as a prostitute does —*vi.* to solicit someone or something —**so·lic´i·tant** (-i tənt) *n., adj.* —**so·lic´i·ta´tion** *n.*

so·lic·i·tor (-ər) *n.* **1.** a person who solicits **2.** in the English legal system, a member of the legal profession who is not a barrister **3.** in the U.S., a lawyer serving as official law officer for a city, department, etc.

solicitor general *pl.* **solicitors general, solicitor generals 1.** a law officer ranking next below the attorney general **2.** [U.S.] the chief law officer in some states

so·lic·i·tous (sə lis´ə təs) *adj.* [L. *sollicitus* < *sollus*, whole + pp. of *ciere*, to set in motion] **1.** showing care, attention, or concern [*solicitous* for her welfare] **2.** showing anxious desire; eager [*solicitous* to make friends] **3.** full of anxiety —**so·lic´i·tous·ly** *adv.* —**so·lic´i·tous·ness** *n.*

so·lic·i·tude (-tyo͞od´) *n.* the state of being solicitous; care, concern, etc.

sol·id (sol´id) *adj.* [< MFr. < L. *solidus*] **1.** tending to keep its form rather than to flow or spread out like a liquid or gas; relatively firm or compact **2.** not hollow **3.** having the three dimensions of length, breadth, and thickness **4.** firm and strong; substantial; sturdy **5.** serious; not trivial **6.** complete [*solid* satisfaction] **7.** having no breaks or divisions **8.** with no pauses [to talk for a *solid* hour] **9.** of one or the same colour, material, etc. throughout **10.** showing unity; unanimous [a *solid* vote] **11.** thick or dense, as a fog **12.** firm or dependable [a *solid* friendship] **13.** [U.S. Colloq.] having a firmly favourable relationship **14.** [Colloq.] healthful and filling [a *solid* meal] **15.** [Chiefly U.S. Slang] excellent **16.** *Printing* set without leads between the lines of type —*n.* **1.** a substance that is solid, not a liquid or gas **2.** an object or figure having length, breadth, and thickness —**go** (or **be**) **solid for** to be united, esp. in defence of someone or something —**sol´id·ly** *adv.* —**sol´id·ness** *n.*

sol·i·dar·i·ty (sol´ə dar´ə tē) *n., pl.* **-ties** agreement of all elements or individuals, as of a group; complete unity

solid fuel 1. a rocket fuel in solid form, consisting of both fuel and oxidizer combined or mixed **2.** fuel, as coal, coke, etc. used in central heating furnaces, solid fuel stoves, etc.

solid geometry geometry dealing with solid figures

so·lid·i·fy (sə lid´ə fī´) *vt., vi.* **-fied´, -fy´ing 1.** to make or become solid, firm, hard, etc. **2.** to crystallize **3.** to make or become solid, strong, or united —**so·lid´i·fi·ca´tion** *n.*

so·lid·i·ty (-tē) *n.* a being solid; firmness, hardness, etc.

sol·id-state (sol´id stāt´) *adj.* designating or of electronic devices, as semiconductors, that can control current without heated filaments, moving parts, etc.

so·lid·un·gu·late (sol´id uŋ´gyo͞o lāt) *adj.* [< L. *solidus*, SOLID + *ungula*, a hoof] having a solid hoof, not a cloven one, as the horse

sol·i·dus (sol´i dəs) *n., pl.* **-i·di** (-dī´) [LL. < L.] **1.** a gold coin of the Late Roman Empire **2.** *a)* a slant line (/) used to separate shillings from pence (Ex.: 7/6) *b)* same as VIRGULE

so·lil·o·quize (sə lil´ə kwīz´) *vi.* **-quized´, -quiz´ing** to deliver a soliloquy; talk to oneself —*vt.* to utter in a soliloquy —**so·lil´o·quist** (-kwist) *n.*

so·lil·o·quy (-kwē) *n., pl.* **-quies** [< LL. < L. *solus*, alone + *loqui*, to speak] **1.** a talking to oneself **2.** lines in a drama in which a character reveals his thoughts to the audience by speaking as if to himself

sol·ip·sism (sol'ip siz'm) *n.* [< L. *solus,* alone + *ipse,* self + -ISM] **1.** the theory that the self can be aware only of its own experiences or states **2.** the theory that nothing exists but the self —**sol'ip·sist** *n.* —**sol'ip·sis'tic** *adj.*

sol·i·taire (sol'ə tēr') *n.* [< Fr. < L.: see ff.] **1.** a single gem, esp. a diamond, set by itself **2.** any of many games, played by one person **3.** [U.S.] the game of patience

sol·i·tar·y (sol'ə tə rē) *adj.* [< OFr. < L. *solitarius* < *solus,* alone] **1.** living or being alone **2.** single; only [a *solitary* example] **3.** lacking companions; lonely **4.** with few or no people; remote [a *solitary* place] **5.** done in solitude —*n., pl.* -tar·ies **1.** a person who lives by himself; esp., a hermit **2.** [Colloq.] *same as* SOLITARY CONFINEMENT —**sol'i·tar·i·ly** *adv.* —**sol'i·tar·i·ness** *n.*

solitary confinement confinement of a prisoner, usually as extra punishment, away from all others

sol·i·tude (sol'ə tyōōd') *n.* [< MFr. < L. *solitudo* < *solus,* alone] **1.** a being solitary, or alone; seclusion **2.** a secluded place —**sol'i·tu'di·nous** *adj.*

sol·mi·za·tion (sol'mi zā'shən) *n.* [< Fr. < *sol* + *mi:* see GAMUT] solfeggio, or any similar use of a system of syllables in singing

so·lo (sō'lō) *n., pl.* -los; for *n.* 1 & 3, sometimes -li (-lē) [It. < L. *solus,* alone] **1.** a musical piece or passage to be played or sung by one person **2.** an aircraft flight made by a pilot alone **3.** any performance by one person alone **4.** any card game in which there are no partners —*adj.* **1.** for or by a single voice, person, or instrument **2.** performing a solo —*adv.* alone —*vi.* to make a solo flight —**so'lo·ist** *n.*

Sol·o·mon (sol'ə mən) *n.* [after *Solomon,* king of Israel, son & successor of David and noted for his wisdom] a very wise man

Solomon's seal 1. the Star of David used as a mystic symbol in the Middle Ages **2.** any of various plants with broad, waxy leaves and blue or black berries

So·lon (sō'lon) *n.* [after *Solon* (640?-559? B.C.), Athenian statesman and lawgiver] [sometimes s-] a wise lawmaker

so long *colloq. term for* GOODBYE

sol·stice (sol'stis) *n.* [MFr. < L. *solstitium* < *sol,* the sun + *sistere,* to make stand still < *stare,* to stand] **1.** either of two points on the sun's ecliptic at which it is farthest north or farthest south of the celestial equator **2.** the time of reaching either of these points: see SUMMER SOLSTICE, WINTER SOLSTICE —**sol·sti'tial** (-stish'əl) *adj.*

sol·u·ble (sol'yoo b'l) *adj.* [MFr. < L. *solubilis* < *solvere:* see SOLVE] **1.** that can be dissolved; capable of passing into solution **2.** that can be solved —**sol'u·bil'i·ty** *n., pl.* -ties —**sol'u·bly** *adv.*

so·lus (sō'ləs) *adj.* [L., SOLE²] alone: usually a stage direction

sol·ute (sol'yōōt) *n.* the substance dissolved in a solution —*adj.* dissolved; in solution

so·lu·tion (sə lōō'shən) *n.* [< OFr. < L. < pp. of *solvere:* see SOLVE] **1.** *a)* the solving of a problem *b)* the answer to a problem *c)* an explanation, etc. [the *solution* of a mystery] **2.** *a)* the dispersion of one or more substances in another, usually a liquid, so as to form a homogeneous mixture; a dissolving *b)* a being dissolved *c)* the mixture, usually a liquid, so produced **3.** a breaking up; dissolution

solution set *Math.* the root or values that satisfy a given equation or inequality

solve (solv) *vt.* **solved, solv'ing** [< L. *solvere,* to loosen < *se-,* apart + *luere,* to let go] to find a satisfactory answer for (a problem, mystery, etc.); make clear; explain —**solv'a·bil'i·ty** *n.* —**solv'a·ble** *adj.* —**solv'er** *n.*

sol·vent (sol'vənt) *adj.* [< L. prp. of *solvere:* see SOLVE] **1.** able to pay all one's debts **2.** that can dissolve another substance —*n.* **1.** a substance that can dissolve another substance **2.** something that solves or explains —**sol'ven·cy** *n.*

Som. Somerset

so·ma¹ (sō'mə) *n., pl.* **so'ma·ta** (-mə tə) [ModL. < Gr. *sōma,* body] the entire body of a plant or animal, excepting the germ cells

so·ma² (sō'mə) *n.* [Sans.] **1.** an intoxicating drink referred to in Vedic ritual **2.** an East Indian plant yielding an intoxicating drink

So·ma·li (sō mä'lē, sə-) *n.* **1.** *pl.* -lis, -li a member of an Islamic, pastoral people of Somalia and nearby regions **2.** their Eastern Cushitic language

so·mat·ic (sō mat'ik) *adj.* [Gr. *sōmatikos* < *sōma,* the body] **1.** of the body; corporeal; physical **2.** of the cells (**somatic cells**) of an organism that become differentiated into the tissues, organs, etc. of the body **3.** of the outer walls of the body —**so·mat'i·cal·ly** *adv.*

som·bre (som'bər) *adj.* [Fr. *sombre,* ult. < L. *sub,* under + *umbra,* shade] **1.** dark and gloomy or dull **2.** mentally depressed or depressing; melancholy **3.** solemn; grave Also, U.S. sp., **som'ber** —**som'bre·ly** *adv.* —**som'bre·ness** *n.*

som·bre·ro (som brer'ō) *n., pl.* **-ros** [Sp. < *sombra,* shade: see prec.] a broad-brimmed felt or straw hat, worn in Mexico, the southwest of the U.S., etc.

SOMBRERO

some (sum; *unstressed* səm) *adj.* [OE. *sum*] **1.** being a certain one or ones not specified or known [*some* people smoke, *some* idiot hit my car] **2.** being of a certain unspecified quantity, degree, etc. [have *some* butter] **3.** about [*some* ten of us] **4.** [Chiefly U.S. Colloq.] remarkable; striking [it was *some* fight] —*pron.* **1.** a certain one or ones not specified or known [*some* agree] **2.** a certain unspecified number, quantity, etc. [take *some*] —*adv.* about [*some* ten men] —**and then some** [U.S. Colloq.] and more than that

-some¹ (səm) [OE. -sum] *a suffix meaning* like, tending to, tending to be [tiresome, wholesome]

-some² (səm) [< ME. *sum,* SOME] *a suffix meaning* (a specified) number together [twosome]

-some³ (sōm) [< Gr. *sōma,* body] *a combining form meaning* body [chromosome]

some·bod·y (sum'bəd ē) *pron.* a person unknown or not named; some person; someone —*n., pl.* -bod'ies a person of importance

some·day (-dā') *adv.* at some future time

some·how (-hou') *adv.* in a way not known, stated, or understood [it was damaged *somehow*]: often in **somehow or other**

some·one (-wun', -wən) *pron. same as* SOMEBODY

some·place (-plās') *adv.* [U.S.] in, to, or at some place; somewhere

som·er·sault (sum'ər sôlt') *n.* [altered < MFr. *sombresault* < L. *supra,* over + *saltus,* a leap] an acrobatic stunt done by turning the body one full revolution, heels over head: often used figuratively, as of a complete reversal of opinion —*vi.* to do a somersault Also **som'er·set'** (-set')

some·thing (sum'thin) *n.* **1.** a thing not definitely known, understood, etc. [*something* went wrong] **2.** some thing or things, definite but unspecified [have *something* to eat] **3.** a bit; a little [*something* over an hour] **4.** [Colloq.] a remarkable person or thing —**something like 1.** approximately; about **2.** [Colloq.] striking; impressive —*adv.* **1.** somewhat **2.** [Colloq.] really [sounds *something* awful] Also used after a figure to indicate a fraction beyond [the bus leaves at six *something*] —**make something of 1.** to find a use for **2.** to treat as of great importance **3.** [Colloq.] to treat as a point of dispute —**something else** [Chiefly U.S. Slang] a really remarkable person or thing

some·time (-tīm') *adv.* **1.** at some time not known or specified **2.** at some future time **3.** [Archaic] *a)* sometimes *b)* formerly —*adj.* **1.** former [his *sometime* friend] **2.** occasional [his wit is a *sometime* thing]

some·times (-tīmz') *adv.* at times; occasionally

some·way (-wā') *adv.* in some way or manner; somehow or other

some·what (-hwot', -wot', -wət) *n.* some degree, amount, part, etc. [*somewhat* of a surprise] —*adv.* to some extent, degree, etc.

some·where (-hwer', -wer') *adv.* **1.** in, to, or at some place not known or specified **2.** at some time, degree, age, figure, etc. (with *about, in,* etc.)—*n.* an unspecified or undetermined place

som·me·lier (sum'əl yā') *n.* [Fr. < MFr., orig., person in charge of pack animals] a wine steward

som·nam·bu·late (som nam'byoo lāt', səm-) *vt.* **-lat'ed, -lat'ing** [< L. *somnus,* sleep + pp. of *ambulare,* to walk] to walk in a trancelike state while asleep —**som·nam'bu·lant** *adj.* —**som·nam'bu·la'tion** *n.* —**som·nam'bu·la'tor** *n.*

som·nam·bu·lism (-liz'm) *n.* [see prec.] **1.** the act or practice of sleepwalking **2.** the trancelike state of a sleepwalker —**som·nam'bu·list** *n.* —**som·nam'bu·lis'tic** *adj.*

som·nif·er·ous (som nif'ər əs, səm-) *adj.* [< L. < *somnus,* sleep + *ferre,* to bring] causing sleep; soporific: also **som·nif'ic** —**som·nif'er·ous·ly** *adv.*

som·no·lent (som'nə lənt) *adj.* [< MFr. < L. *somnolentus* < *somnus,* sleep] **1.** sleepy; drowsy **2.** causing drowsiness —**som'no·lence** *n.* —**som'no·lent·ly** *adv.*

son (sun) *n.* [OE. *sunu*] **1.** a boy or man as he is related to either or both parents: sometimes also used of animals **2.** a male descendant **3.** *a)* a son-in-law *b)* a stepson **4.** a male thought of as if in the relation of child to parent or to a formative influence [a *son* of revolution] **5.** a familiar form of address to a boy or younger man —**the Son** Jesus Christ, as the second person of the Trinity

so·nant (sō'nənt) *adj.* [< L. prp. of *sonare,* to SOUND¹] **1.** of sound **2.** having sound; sounding —**so'nance** *n.*

so·nar (sō'när) *n.* [*so*(und) *n*(avigation) *a*(nd) *r*(anging)] an apparatus that transmits high-frequency sound waves through water and registers the vibrations reflected back from an object: used to locate submarines, find depths, etc.

so·na·ta (sə nät′ə) *n.* [It. < L. *sonare*, to SOUND[1]] a musical composition for one or two instruments, usually in three or four movements in different tempos, etc.

sonde (sond) *n.* [Fr., a sounding line] any of various devices for measuring and telemetering meteorological data during ascent and descent through the atmosphere

‡son et lu·mière (sōn nä lü myer′) [Fr., lit., sound and light] a historical spectacle at night before a monument, etc., using special lighting effects, narration, music, etc.

song (sôŋ) *n.* [OE. *sang*] 1. the act or art of singing 2. a piece of music sung or as if for singing 3. *a)* poetry; verse *b)* a ballad or lyric that is or can be set to music 4. a musical sound like singing [the *song* of the lark] —**for a song** cheaply —**song and dance** 1. singing and dancing, esp. in the music halls 2. [Colloq.] a fuss, esp. about something trivial —**song′ful** *adj.* —**song′less** *adj.*

song·bird (-bʉrd′) *n.* a bird that makes vocal sounds that are like music

song·ster (sôŋ′stər) *n.* [OE. *sangestre*] 1. a singer 2. a writer of songs or poems 3. a songbird —**song′stress** *n.fem.*

song thrush a European songbird with brown wings and a white breast

song·writ·er (-rīt′ər) *n.* a person who writes words or music or both for songs, esp. popular songs

son·ic (sän′ik) *adj.* [< L. *sonus*, SOUND[1] + -IC] 1. of or having to do with sound 2. designating or of a speed equal to the speed of sound (about 340 metres per second through air at sea level at 0˚C)

sonic barrier same as SOUND BARRIER

sonic boom an explosive sound generated by the accumulation of pressure in a wave preceding an aircraft moving at or above the speed of sound

sonic depth finder same as FATHOMETER

son-in-law (sun′in lô′) *n.,* pl. **sons′-in-law′** the husband of one's daughter

son·net (sän′it) *n.* [Fr. < It. < Pr. dim. of *son*, a song < L. *sonus*, SOUND[1]] a poem normally of fourteen lines (typically in iambic pentameter) in any of several fixed verse and rhyme schemes, expressing a single theme: see SHAKESPEAREAN SONNET —*vt., vi.* to write sonnets (about): also **son′net·ize** (-ə tīz′) **-ized′, -iz′ing**

son·net·eer (sän′ə tir′) *n.* a person who writes sonnets

son·ny (sun′ē) *n.,* pl. **-nies** little son: used in addressing any young boy in a familiar way

son·o·buoy (sän′ō boi′) *n.* [< L. *sonus*, SOUND[1] + BUOY] a buoy that transmits amplified sound signals picked up under water

so·no·rant (sə nôr′ənt, sō-) *n.* [SONOR(OUS) + (CONSON)ANT] *Phonet.* a voiced consonant that is less sonorous than a vowel but more sonorous than an unvoiced plosive, as *l, m, n, r, y, w*: sonorants may occur as syllabics

so·nor·i·ty (sə nôr′ə tē, sō-) *n.,* pl. **-ties** the quality or state of being sonorous; resonance

so·no·rous (sə nôr′əs, sän′ər əs) *adj.* [< L. < *sonor*, a sound] 1. producing or capable of producing sound, esp. a full, deep, or rich sound; resonant 2. full, deep, or rich: said of sound 3. high-sounding; impressive [sonorous prose] —**so·no′rous·ly** *adv.* —**so·no′rous·ness** *n.*

sons of men mankind

son·sy, son·sie (sän′sē) *adj.* [< dial. *sonse*, prosperity < Gael. *sonas*, good fortune + -Y[2]] [Scot.] 1. buxom; handsome 2. good-natured

sool (sōōl) *vt.* [< ?] [Aust. Colloq.] 1. to incite a dog 2. to worry; to tease

soon (sōōn) *adv.* [OE. *sona*, at once] 1. in a short time; shortly [we will *soon* be there] 2. promptly; quickly [as *soon* as possible] 3. ahead of time; early [he left too *soon*] 4. readily; willingly [I would as *soon* go as stay] —**had sooner** would rather —**sooner or later** eventually

soot (soot) *n.* [OE. *sot*] a black substance consisting chiefly of carbon particles formed by the incomplete combustion of burning matter —*vt.* to cover, soil, or treat with soot

sooth (sōōth) *adj.* [OE. *soth*] 1. [Archaic] true 2. [Poet.] soothing; smooth —*n.* [Archaic] truth —**in sooth** [Archaic] in truth —**sooth′ly** *adv.*

soothe (sōōth) *vt.* **soothed, sooth′ing** [OE. *sothian* < *soth*, truth] 1. to make calm or composed, as by gentleness, flattery, etc. 2. to relieve (pain, etc.) —*vi.* to have a soothing effect —**sooth′er** *n.* —**sooth′ing** *adj.* —**sooth′-ing·ly** *adv.*

sooth·say·er (sōōth′sā′ər) *n.* a person who claims to foretell the future —**sooth′say·ing** *n.*

soot·y (soot′ē) *adj.* **soot′i·er, soot′i·est** 1. of, like, or covered with soot 2. dark or black like soot —**soot′i·ness** *n.*

sooty albatross a brownish-black albatross found in the S hemisphere

sop (sop) *n.* [OE. *sopp*] 1. a piece of food, as bread, soaked in milk, gravy, etc. 2. *a)* something given by way of appeasement, etc. *b)* a bribe —*vt.* **sopped, sop′ping** 1. to soak, steep, etc. in or with liquid 2. to take (*up*), as liquid,

by absorption —*vi.* 1. to soak (*in, into,* or *through* something) 2. to be or become thoroughly wet

SOP, S.O.P. standing (or standard) operating procedure

sop. soprano

soph·ism (sof′iz'm) *n.* [< OFr. < L. < Gr. < *sophos*, clever] clever and reasonable argument that is, however, faulty or misleading; fallacy or sophistry

soph·ist (-ist) *n.* [< L. < Gr. *sophistēs*, wise man] 1. [often S-] in ancient Greece, any of a group of teachers of rhetoric, philosophy, etc., some of whom were notorious for their clever, specious arguments 2. a learned person 3. any person practising clever, specious reasoning

so·phis·ti·cal (sə fis′ti k'l) *adj.* 1. of or characteristic of sophists or sophistry 2. clever and plausible but misleading Also **so·phis′tic** —**so·phis′ti·cal·ly** *adv.*

so·phis·ti·cate (sə fis′tə kāt′; *for n. usually* -kit) *vt.* **-cat′ed, -cat′ing** [< ML. < L. *sophisticus*, sophistical] 1. to change from being natural, simple, naive, etc. to being artificial, worldly-wise, etc. 2. to bring to a more developed, complex, or refined form, level, etc. —*n.* a sophisticated person

so·phis·ti·cat·ed (-kāt′id) *adj.* 1. not simple, natural, or naive; wise in the ways of the world; knowledgeable, subtle, etc. 2. appealing to sophisticated people 3. highly complex, refined, etc.; of an advanced form, technique, etc. —**so·phis′ti·cat′ed·ly** *adv.*

so·phis·ti·ca·tion (sə fis′tə kā′shən) *n.* 1. the act or process of sophisticating 2. the state or quality of being sophisticated

soph·is·try (sof′is trē) *n.,* pl. **-tries** 1. unsound or misleading but subtle argument or reasoning 2. the methods of the Sophists

soph·o·more (sof′ə môr′) *n.* [altered (after Gr. *sophos*, wise + *mōros*, foolish) < obs. *sophumer*, lit., sophist] [U.S.] a student in his second year in college —*adj.* of or for sophomores —**soph′o·mor′ic, soph′o·mor′i·cal** *adj.* —**soph′-o·mor′i·cal·ly** *adv.*

So·phy (sō fē′) *n.* [< Per. *safi*, name of Arab dynasty] 1. the title of Persian monarchs 2. the Persian monarch

-so·phy (sə fē) [< Gr. *sophia*, skill, wisdom] a combining form meaning knowledge [philosophy]

sop·o·rif·ic (sop′ə rif′ik) *adj.* [< Fr. < L. *sopor*, sleep + -FIC] 1. causing or tending to cause sleep 2. sleepy —*n.* a drug, etc. that causes sleep

sop·ping (sop′iŋ) *adj.* thoroughly wet; drenched

sop·py (sop′ē) *adj.* **-pi·er, -pi·est** 1. very wet; sopping 2. [Colloq.] sentimental —**sop′pi·ness** *n.*

so·pra·no (sə prä′nō) *n.,* pl. **-nos, -ni** (-prä′nē) [It. < *sopra*, above] 1. the highest singing voice of women, girls, and young boys 2. *a)* a voice or singer with this range *b)* a musical instrument with this range *c)* a part for a soprano —*adj.* of, for, or having the range of a soprano

so·ra (sôr′ə) *n.* [< ? AmInd.] a small, N. American, short-billed wading bird of the rail family, living in marshes: also **sora rail**

Sorb (sôrb) *n.* [G. *Sorbe*, of Slav. origin] any member of an old Slavic people living in an enclave in East Germany; Wend —**Sor·bi·an** (sôr′bē ən) *adj., n.*

sorb (sôrb) *n.* [Fr. *sorbe* < L. *sorbum*, serviceberry] 1. one of a number of European trees of the rose family, as the rowan and the service tree 2. the fruit of any of these trees

sor·bet (sôr′bā) *n.* [Fr. < It. < Turk. < Arab. *sharbah*, a drink] a mixture of crushed fruit, sugar, etc. frozen to make water ice

sor·bic acid (sôr′bik) [ult. < L. *sorbus*, a kind of tree] a white, crystalline solid used as a food preservative, fungicide, etc.

sor·bi·tol (sôr′bi tōl′) *n.* [see prec.] a white, sweet, crystalline alcohol used as a moistening agent in lotions, etc., and as a sugar substitute

sor·bo (sôr′bō) *n.* [< (AB)SORB] a type of sponge rubber

sor·cer·er (sôr′sər ər) *n.* a person who practises sorcery; wizard —**sor′cer·ess** *n.fem.*

sor·cer·y (-ē) *n.,* pl. **-cer·ies** [< OFr. < *sorcier*, sorcerer < L. *sors*, lot, share] 1. the supposed use of magical power by means of charms, spells, etc., usually for an evil purpose; witchcraft; black magic 2. seemingly magical power, charm, etc. —**sor′cer·ous** *adj.* —**sor′cer·ous·ly** *adv.*

sor·did (sôr′did) *adj.* [< Fr. < L. < *sordes*, filth] 1. *a)* dirty; filthy *b)* squalid; depressingly wretched 2. *a)* base; ignoble *b)* meanly selfish or grasping —**sor′did·ly** *adv.* —**sor′did·ness** *n.*

sore (sôr) *adj.* **sor′er, sor′est** [OE. *sar*] 1. *a)* giving pain; painful [a *sore* throat] *b)* feeling pain, as from bruises, etc. 2. *a)* filled with sadness, grief, etc. *sore* at heart] *b)* causing sadness, grief, etc. [sore hardships] 3. provoking irritation [a *sore* point] 4. [U.S. Colloq.] angry; offended —*n.* 1. a sore, usually infected spot on the body, as an ulcer or blister 2. a source of pain, distress, etc. —*adv.* [Archaic] sorely —**sore′ness** *n.*

sore·head (-hed′) *n.* [U.S. Colloq.] a person who is angry, resentful, disgruntled, etc., or one easily made so

sore·ly (-lē) *adv.* 1. grievously; painfully [*sorely* vexed] 2. urgently; extremely [*sorely* needed]

sor·ghum (sôr′gəm) *n.* [< It. *sorgo*] 1. any of several tropical cereal grasses grown for grain, syrup, fodder, etc. 2. a syrup made from the sweet juices of a variety (**sorgo**) of sorghum

sor·op·ti·mist (sə rop′tə mist) *n.* a member of one of an international association of women's clubs

so·ror·al (sə rôr′′l) *adj.* [see ff.] of or like a sister or sisters; sisterly —**so·ror′al·ly** *adv.*

so·ror·i·ty (sə ror′ə tē) *n., pl.* **-ties** [< ML. < L. *soror,* sister] [Chiefly U.S.] a group of women or girls joined together for social or professional reasons

sorp·tion (sôrp′shən) *n.* [back-formation < ABSORPTION & ADSORPTION] absorption or adsorption

sor·rel[1] (sor′əl,) *n.* [< OFr. < Frank. *sur,* sour] 1. any of several plants with sour, fleshy leaves; dock 2. *same as* WOOD SORREL

sor·rel[2] (sor′əl,) *n.* [< OFr. < *sor,* light brown < ML. *saurus* < Gmc.] 1. light reddish brown 2. a horse, etc. of this colour —*adj.* light reddish-brown

sor·row (sor′ō) *n.* [OE. *sorg*] 1. mental suffering caused by loss, disappointment, etc.; sadness, grief, or regret 2. that which produces such suffering; trouble, misfortune, etc. 3. the outward expression of such suffering; mourning 4. earnest repentance —*vi.* to feel or show sorrow; grieve —**sor′row·er** *n.* —**sor′row·ing·ly** *adv.*

sor·row·ful (-ə fəl) *adj.* feeling, causing, or expressing sorrow; sad —**sor′row·ful·ly** *adv.* —**sor′row·ful·ness** *n.*

sor·ry (sor′ē) *adj.* **-ri·er, -ri·est** [OE. *sarig* < *sar,* sore] 1. full of sorrow, pity, sympathy, etc.: also used in apologizing or in showing mild regret 2. a) inferior in worth or quality; poor b) wretched, pitiful, miserable, etc. —**sor′ri·ly** *adv.* —**sor′ri·ness** *n.*

sort (sôrt) *n.* [< MFr., ult. < L. *sors* (gen. *sortis*), a lot] 1. any group related by having something in common; kind; class 2. quality or type; nature [remarks of that *sort*] —*vt.* to arrange according to class or kind (often with *out*) —**of sorts** 1. of various kinds 2. of an inferior kind: also **of a sort —out of sorts** [Colloq.] cross, irritable, or ill —**sort of** [Colloq.] somewhat —**sort out** 1. to separate out 2. to find a solution [to *sort out* his problems] 3. [Slang] to punish someone, esp. by beating them —**sort′a·ble** *adj.* —**sort′er** *n.*

sor·tie (sôr′tē) *n.* [Fr. < *sortir,* to issue] 1. a sudden attack or raid by troops from a besieged place; sally 2. one mission by a single military plane

SOS (es′ō′es′) 1. a signal of distress in code (. . . ─ ─ ─ . . .) used internationally in wireless telegraphy, as by ships 2. [Colloq.] any urgent call for help

so-so (sō′sō′) *adv.* indifferently; just passably —*adj.* neither too good nor too bad; just fair Also **so so**

sos·te·nu·to (sos′tə nōōt′ō) *n., adj., adv.* [It.] *Music* sustained or prolonged in tempo

sot (sot) *n.* [< Late OE. *sott* or OFr. *sot,* a fool < VL. *sottus*] a drunkard —**sot′tish** *adj.* —**sot′tish·ly** *adv.*

so·te·ri·ol·o·gy (sō tir′ē ol′ə jē) *n.* [< Gr. *sōtēriā,* deliverance < *sōtēr,* a deliverer + -LOGY] the branch of theology concerned with spiritual salvation, esp. that believed to have been accomplished through Jesus

sot·ted (sot′id) *adj.* besotted; stupefied

sot·to vo·ce (sot′ō vō′chē) [It., under the voice] in an undertone, so as not to be overheard

sou (sōō) *n., pl.* **sous** (sōōz; *Fr.* sōō) [Fr. < OFr. *sol* < LL. *solidus,* SOLIDUS] 1. any of several former French coins, esp. one equal to five centimes 2. a very small amount of money

sou·brette (sōō bret′) *n.* [Fr. < Pr. < *soubret,* sly, ult. < L. *superare,* to be above] *Theatre* 1. the role of a lady's maid, esp. one involved in intrigue, or of any pretty, flirtatious young woman 2. an actress who plays such roles

sou·bri·quet (sōō′brə kā′) *n. var. of* SOBRIQUET

souf·flé (sōō′flā) *adj.* [Fr. < pp. of *souffler,* to blow] made light and puffy in cooking: also **souf·fléed′** (-flād′) —*n.* a baked food made light and puffy by adding beaten egg whites before baking [a cheese *soufflé*]

sough (sou, suf) *n.* [< OE. *swogan,* to sound] a soft, murmuring, sighing, or rustling sound —*vi.* to make a sough

sought (sôt) *pt. & pp. of* SEEK

souk (sōōk) *n.* [Ar. *sūq*] an open-air marketplace in North Africa and the Middle East

soul (sōl) *n.* [OE. *sawol*] 1. the part of one's being that is thought of as the centre of feeling, thinking, will, etc. apart from the body: in some religions the soul is believed to go on after death 2. the moral or emotional nature of man 3. spiritual or emotional warmth, force, etc. 4. vital or essential part, quality, etc. 5. the central or leading figure [Marx was the *soul* of Communism] 6. embodiment; personification [the very *soul* of kindness] 7. a person [a town of 1000 *souls*] 8. [Colloq.] a) among U.S. Negroes, a sense of racial pride and social and cultural solidarity b) *short for* SOUL FOOD *or* SOUL MUSIC —*adj.* [Colloq.] of, for,

like, or characteristic of U.S. Negroes —**upon my soul!** an exclamation of surprise

soul-de·stroy·ing (-di stroi′iŋ) *adj.* monotonous; dreary; tedious

soul food [Colloq.] items of food popular orig. in the Southern U.S. esp. among Negroes, as chitterlings, ham hocks, yams, turnip greens, etc.

soul·ful (sōl′fəl) *adj.* full of or showing deep feeling —**soul′-ful·ly** *adv.* —**soul′ful·ness** *n.*

soul·less (-lis) *adj.* lacking soul, sensitivity, or deep feeling —**soul′less·ly** *adv.* —**soul′less·ness** *n.*

soul mate [Colloq.] a person, esp. of the opposite sex, with whom one has a very close relationship

soul music [Colloq.] a form of RHYTHM AND BLUES (with added elements of U.S. Negro gospel singing)

soul-search·ing (-sur′chiŋ) *n.* a close, honest examination of one's true feelings, motives, etc.

sound[1] (sound) *n.* [< OFr. *son* < L. *sonus*] 1. a) vibrations in air, water, etc. that act on the nerves of the inner ear and produce the sensation of hearing b) the sensation that these vibrations stimulate in the ear 2. a) any identifiable noise, tone, vocal utterance, etc. [the *sound* of a violin, speech *sounds*] b) such effects transmitted by or recorded for radio, television, films etc. 3. the distance within which a sound may be heard; earshot 4. the impression made by something said, etc.; drift [the *sound* of his report] 5. meaningless noise —*vi.* 1. to make a sound 2. to seem or appear through sound or utterance [to *sound* troubled] —*vt.* 1. a) to cause to sound b) to produce the sound of c) to utter distinctly [to *sound* one's r's] 2. to express, signal, proclaim, etc. [*sound* the alarm, *sound* his praises] 3. to examine (the chest) by percussion, etc. —**sound off** [Slang] 1. to give free voice to complaints, opinions, etc. 2. to speak in a loud or offensive way —**sound′er** *n.*

sound[2] (sound) *adj.* [OE. (ge)*sund*] 1. free from defect, damage, or decay [*sound* timber] 2. normal and healthy [a *sound* body and mind] 3. firm and safe; stable; secure [a *sound* bank] 4. based on valid reasoning; sensible [*sound* advice] 5. agreeing with established views or beliefs [*sound* doctrine] 6. thorough, complete, forceful, etc. [a *sound* defeat] 7. deep and undisturbed: said of sleep 8. morally strong; honest, loyal, etc. 9. *Law* valid —*adv.* completely; deeply [*sound* asleep] —**sound′ly** *adv.* —**sound′ness** *n.*

sound[3] (sound) *n.* [< OE. & ON. *sund*] 1. a wide channel linking two large bodies of water or separating an island from the mainland 2. a long arm of the sea 3. the air bladder of certain fishes

sound[4] (sound) *vt.* [< MFr. *sonder* < VL. *subundare* < L. *sub,* under + *unda,* a wave] 1. a) to measure the depth of (water), esp. with a weighted line (**sounding line**) b) to examine (the bottom of the sea, etc.) with a line that brings up particles that stick to it c) to probe (the atmosphere or space) so as to gain data 2. to try to find out the opinions of (a person): often with *out* 3. *Med.* to examine with a sound, or probe —*vi.* 1. to sound water 2. to dive suddenly downwards through the water: said esp. of whales, etc. 3. to try to find out something —*n. Med.* a long probe used in examining body cavities —**sound′a·ble** *adj.* —**sound′er** *n.*

sound barrier the large increase in resistance encountered by an aircraft approaching the speed of sound

sound box the resonating chamber of the hollow body of a violin, guitar, etc.

sound effects sounds, as of thunder, animals, etc., produced artificially or by recording as for radio, TV, etc.

sound·ing[1] (soun′diŋ) *adj.* 1. giving forth sound 2. resonant; sonorous 3. high-sounding; bombastic

sound·ing[2] (soun′diŋ) *n.* 1. a) the act of measuring the depth of water b) depth so measured c) [pl.] a place, usually less than 180 metres in depth, where a sounding line will touch bottom 2. a) an examination of the atmosphere, as with a radiosonde b) a probe of space, as with a rocket 3. [pl.] measurements or data learned by sounding 4. [often pl.] a sampling, as of public opinion

sounding board 1. a thin plate of wood, etc. built into a musical instrument to increase its resonance: also **sound′-board′** *n.* 2. any structure designed to reflect sound 3. a person on whom one tests one's ideas, opinions, etc.

sound·less (sound′lis) *adj.* without sound; noiseless —**sound′less·ly** *adv.* —**sound′less·ness** *n.*

sound·proof (-prōōf′) *adj.* able to keep sound from coming through —*vt.* to make soundproof

sound track the area along one side of a film, carrying the sound record of the film

sound wave *Physics* a pressure wave transported by an elastic medium, as air; esp., such a wave vibrating at a frequency that can be heard

soup (sōōp) *n.* [Fr. *soupe* < OFr., soup: of Gmc. origin] 1. a liquid food made by cooking meat, vegetables, etc. in water, milk, etc. 2. [Colloq.] a heavy fog 3. [U.S. Slang] nitroglycerin —**in the soup** [Colloq.] in trouble —**soup up**

[Slang] to increase the power, capacity for speed, etc. of (an engine, etc.) —**soup′y** adj. **soup′i·er, soup′i·est**

soup·çon (sō̅o̅p sōn′, sō̅o̅p′sōn′) n. [Fr.] 1. a suggestion or trace, as of a flavour 2. a tiny amount; bit

soupe du jour (sō̅o̅p′doo zhoor′) [Fr., lit., soup of the day] the featured soup on a menu for that day: also **soup du jour**

soup kitchen a place where hot soup or the like is given to people in dire need

soup plate a large, deep plate from which soup is eaten

soup·spoon (sō̅o̅p′spō̅o̅n′) n. a large-bowled spoon for eating soup

sour (sour) adj. [OE. sur] 1. having the sharp, acid taste of lemon juice, vinegar, etc. 2. made acid or spoiled by fermentation [sour milk] 3. cross, bad-tempered, peevish, bitter, etc. 4. below what is usual; poor [his game has gone sour] 5. distasteful or unpleasant 6. gratingly wrong or off pitch [a sour note] 7. excessively acid: said of soil —n. 1. something sour 2. [Chiefly U.S.] a cocktail made with lime or lemon juice [a whisky sour] —vt., vi. to make or become sour —**sour′ish** adj. —**sour′ly** adv. —**sour′ness** n.

source (sôrs) n. [< OFr. < pp. of sourdre < L. surgere, to rise] 1. a spring, etc. from which a stream arises 2. that from which something originates, develops, etc. 3. a) that by which something is supplied b) a person, book, etc. that provides information 4. the point from which light rays, sound waves, etc. come forth

source·book (-book′) n. a collection of selections from documents giving fundamental information about a subject to be studied or written about; also, a diary, journal, etc. giving such information

sour·dough (sour′dō′) n. [Chiefly U.S.] 1. [Dial.] fermented dough saved from one baking to the next, for use as leaven 2. a prospector in the western U.S. or Canada: so called from his using sourdough

sour grapes [from Aesop's fable in which the fox, after futile efforts to reach some grapes, scorns them as being sour] a scorning or belittling of something only because it cannot be had or done

sour·puss (sour′poos′) n. [Colloq.] a gloomy or disagreeable person

sou·sa·phone (sō̅o̅′zə fōn′) n. [after J.P. Sousa (1854-1932), U.S. composer, who suggested its form] a brass instrument of the tuba family

souse (sous) n. [< OFr. < OHG. sulza, brine] 1. a pickled food, esp. the feet, ears, and head of a pig 2. liquid for pickling; brine 3. a plunging into a liquid 4. [Slang] a drunkard —vt., vi. **soused, sous′ing** 1. to pickle 2. to plunge or steep in a liquid 3. to make or become soaking wet 4. [Slang] to make or become intoxicated

sou·tane (sō̅o̅ tan′, -tän′) n. [Fr. < It. sottana] same as CASSOCK

south (south) n. [OE. suth] 1. the direction to the left of a person facing the sunset (180° on the compass, opposite north) 2. a region or district in or towards this direction 3. [often S-] the southern part of the earth, esp. the antarctic regions —adj. 1. in, of, to, or towards the south 2. from the south 3. [S-] designating the southern part of a country, etc. —adv. in or towards the south —**the South** 1. that part of England south of the Humber 2. that part of the U.S. south of the Mason-Dixon line

South African Dutch 1. the Boers 2. same as AFRIKAANS

south·bound (south′bound′) adj. going southwards

South·down (south′doun′) n. [after the South Downs, hills in SE England] any of a breed of English sheep having short wool and bred chiefly for their meat

south·east (south′ēst′; nautical sou-) n. 1. the direction halfway between south and east; 45° east of due south 2. a region or district in or towards this direction —adj. 1. in, of, to, or towards the southeast 2. from the southeast, as a wind —adv. in, towards, or from the southeast —**the Southeast** the southeastern part of England, esp. Kent and Sussex

south·east·er (south′ēs′tər; nautical sou-) n. a storm or strong wind from the southeast

south·east·er·ly (-tər lē) adj., adv. 1. in or towards the southeast 2. from the southeast

south·east·ern (-tərn) adj. 1. in, of, or towards the southeast 2. from the southeast 3. [S-] of or characteristic of the Southeast —**South′east′ern·er** n.

south·east·ward (-ēst′ward) adv., adj. towards the southeast: also **south′east′wards** adv. —n. a southeastward direction, point, or region

south·east·ward·ly (-ward lē) adj., adv. 1. towards the southeast 2. from the southeast, as a wind

south·er (sou′thər) n. a storm or wind from the south

south·er·ly (suth′ər lē) adj., adv. 1. towards the south 2. from the south

south·ern (suth′ərn) adj. 1. in, of, or towards the south 2. from the south 3. [S-] of or characteristic of the South —**south′ern·most** adj.

Southern Cross a small constellation in the S hemisphere with four bright stars in the form of a cross

south·ern·er (suth′ər nər, -ə nər) n. a native or inhabitant of the south, specif. [S-] of the southern part of the U.S.

Southern Hemisphere that half of the earth south of the equator

southern lights same as AURORA AUSTRALIS

south·land (south′land′, -lənd) n. [also S-] the southern region of a country —**south′land′er** n.

south·paw (-pô′) n. [SOUTH + PAW: in the Chicago baseball park (c. 1885) the pitcher's left arm was towards the south] [Slang] a person who is left-handed; esp., a left-handed boxer —adj. [Slang] left-handed

South Pole the southern end of the earth's axis

South Sea Islands islands in temperate or tropical parts of the South Pacific —**South Sea Islander**

South Seas 1. the South Pacific 2. all the seas located south of the equator

south-south·east (south′south′ēst′; nautical sou′sou-) n. the direction halfway between due south and southeast; 22°30′ east of due south —adj., adv. 1. in or towards this direction 2. from this direction

south-south·west (-west′) n. the direction halfway between due south and southwest; 22°30′ west of due south —adj., adv. 1. in or towards this direction 2. from this direction

south·ward (south′wərd; nautical suth′ərd) adv., adj. towards the south: also **south′wards** adv. —n. a southward direction, point, or region

south·ward·ly (-lē) adj., adv. 1. towards the south 2. from the south

south·west (south′west′; nautical sou-) n. 1. the direction halfway between south and west; 45° west of due south 2. a district or region in or towards this direction —adj. 1. in, of, to, or towards the southwest 2. from the southwest —adv. in, towards, or from the southwest —**the Southwest** the southwestern part of England, esp. Devon and Cornwall

south·west·er (south′wes′tər; nautical sou-) n. 1. a storm or strong wind from the southwest 2. a sailor's waterproof hat, having a broad brim at the back

south·west·er·ly (-tər lē) adj., adv. 1. in or towards the southwest 2. from the southwest

south·west·ern (-tərn) adj. 1. in, of, or towards the southwest 2. from the southwest 3. [S-] of or characteristic of the Southwest —**South′west′ern·er** n.

south·west·ward (-west′wərd) adv., adj. towards the southwest: also **south′west′wards** adv. —n. a southwestward direction, point, or region

SOUTHWESTER

south·west·ward·ly (-lē) adj., adv. 1. towards the southwest 2. from the southwest, as a wind

sou·ve·nir (sō̅o̅′və nir′, sō̅o̅′və nir′) n. [Fr., orig. inf., to remember < L. subvenire, to come to mind] something kept as a reminder of a place, person, or occasion; keepsake; memento

sou′·west·er (sou wes′tər) n. same as SOUTHWESTER

sov. sovereign

sov·er·eign (sov′rən) adj. [< OFr. soverain, ult. < L. super, above] 1. above or superior to all others; greatest 2. supreme in power, rank, etc. 3. of or being a ruler; reigning 4. independent of all others [a sovereign state] 5. excellent 6. very effectual, as a remedy —n. 1. a person having sovereign authority; specif., a monarch or ruler 2. formerly, a British gold coin valued at 20 shillings or one pound sterling —**sov′er·eign·ly** adv.

sov·er·eign·ty (-tē) n., pl. **-ties** 1. a being sovereign 2. the status, rule, power, etc. of a sovereign 3. supreme and independent political authority 4. a sovereign state

so·vi·et (sō′vē it, -et′; sov′-) n. [Russ., lit., council] 1. in the Soviet Union, any of various elected governing councils, ranging from village and town soviets to the Supreme Soviet of the whole country 2. [S-] [pl.] the Soviet people or their officials —adj. 1. of a soviet or soviets 2. [S-] of or connected with the Soviet Union —**so′vi·et·ism** n.

so·vi·et·ize (sō′vē ə tīz′) vt. **-ized′, -iz′ing** [often S-] 1. to change to a soviet form of government 2. to make conform to the system, principles, etc. of the Soviets —**so′vi·et·i·za′·tion** n.

sow¹ (sou) n. [OE. sugu] 1. an adult female pig 2. an adult female of certain other mammals, as the bear

sow² (sō) vt. **sowed, sown** (sōn) or **sowed, sow′ing** [OE. sawan] 1. to scatter or plant (seed) for growing 2. to plant (a field, etc.) with seed 3. to spread or scatter; disseminate 4. to plant in the mind —vi. to sow seed —**sow′er** n.

sow bug (sou) same as WOODLOUSE

soy (soi) n. [Jap., colloq. for shōyu < Chin. < chiang, salted bean + yu, oil] 1. a dark, salty sauce made from fermented soyabeans steeped in brine, used esp. with Chinese and

Japanese dishes: also **soy sauce** 2. the soyabean plant or its seeds Also **soy·a** (soi'ə)

soy·a·bean (soi'yə bēn') *n.* 1. a plant of the legume family, native to China and Japan but widely grown for forage and cover and for its seeds, rich in protein and oil 2. its seed: also **soybean**

soz·zled (soz''ld) *adj.* [pp. of dial. *sozzle*, to mix in a sloppy manner] [Colloq.] drunk; intoxicated

Sp. 1. Spain 2. Spaniard 3. Spanish

sp. 1. special 2. *pl.* **spp.** species 3. spelling

S.P. Starting Price

spa (spä) *n.* [< *Spa*, a health resort in Belgium] 1. a spring of mineral water 2. a place, esp. a health resort, with such a spring

space (späs) *n.* [< OFr. < L. *spatium*] 1. *a)* the continuous, boundless expanse extending in all directions or in three dimensions, within which all things exist *b) same as* OUTER SPACE 2. *a)* the distance, expanse, or area between, over, or within things *b)* area or room for something [parking *space*] 3. an interval or period of time 4. *Music* the open area between any two lines of a staff 5. *Printing a)* a blank piece of type metal used to separate characters, etc. *b)* the area left vacant by this on a printed or typed line —*adj.* of space —*vt.* **spaced, spac'ing** to arrange with spaces between —**space'less** *adj.* —**spac'er** *n.*

Space Age [*also* s- a-] the period, since 1957, in which artificial satellites and manned space vehicles have been launched —**space'-age' adj.**

space bar a bar, as on a typewriter keyboard, pressed to leave a blank space or spaces between words, etc.

space·craft (späs'kräft') *n., pl.* **-craft'** a spaceship or satellite for use in outer space

space·flight (-flīt') *n.* a flight through outer space

space·man (-man', -mən) *n., pl.* **-men'** (-men', -mən) an astronaut or any of the crew of a spaceship

space·port (-pôrt') *n.* a centre where spacecraft are assembled, tested, and launched

space·ship (-ship') *n.* a rocket-propelled vehicle for travel in outer space

space shuttle a spacecraft designed to transport persons and equipment between earth and an orbiting space station

space station (or **platform**) a structure designed to orbit in space as a launching pad or as an observation centre

space·suit (-sōōt') *n. same as* G-SUIT, esp. one modified for use in spaceflights

space-time (continuum) (-tīm') a continuum having the three dimensions of space and that of time, in which any event can be located

space·walk (-wôk') *n.* the act of an astronaut in moving about in space outside his spacecraft —*vi.* to engage in a spacewalk —**space'walk'er** *n.*

spa·cial (spä'shəl) *adj.* alt. sp. of SPATIAL

spac·ing (spä'siŋ) *n.* 1. the arrangement of spaces 2. space or spaces, as between printed words 3. the act of a person or thing that spaces

spa·cious (spä'shəs) *adj.* 1. having more than enough space or room; vast; extensive 2. not confined or limited; large —**spa'cious·ly** *adv.* —**spa'cious·ness** *n.*

spade[1] (späd) *n.* [OE. *spadu*] a heavy, long-handled digging tool with a flat blade that is pressed with the foot —*vt., vi.* **spad'ed, spad'ing** to dig or cut as with a spade —**call a spade a spade** to use plain, blunt words —**spade'ful** *n.*

spade[2] (späd) *n.* [Sp. *espada*, sword (sign used on Spanish cards) < L. *spatha*, SPATULA] 1. the black figure (♠) marking one of the four suits of playing cards 2. [*pl.*] this suit 3. a card of this suit 4. [Slang] a Negro: a derogatory term

spade·work (späd'wurk') *n.* work done to get a project started, esp. when tiresome or difficult

spa·dix (spä'diks) *n., pl.* **-dix·es, -di·ces'** (spä'də sēz', spä di'sēz) [ModL. < L., a palm branch < Gr. *spadix*] a fleshy spike of tiny flowers, usually enclosed in a spathe

spa·ghet·ti (spə get'ē) *n.* [It., dim. pl. of *spago*, small cord] long, thin strings of pasta, cooked by boiling or steaming and served with a sauce

spaghetti junction [after the junction between the M1 and M6 at Birmingham] [also S- J-] a junction formed by a large number of intersecting roads usually used by high-speed through traffic

spaghetti western [Slang] a cowboy film produced by the Italian film industry

spake (späk) *archaic pt. of* SPEAK

Spam (spam) *a trademark for* a kind of tinned meat, made chiefly from pork

span[1] (span) *n.* [OE. *sponn*] 1. a measure of length, equal to nine inches (23 cm), based on the distance between the tips of the extended thumb and little finger 2. *a)* the full amount or extent between any two limits *b)* the distance between ends or supports [the *span* of an arch] *c)* the full duration, as of attention 3. a part between two supports [a bridge of four *spans*] 4. *shortened form of* WINGSPAN —*vt.* **spanned, span'ning** 1. to measure, esp. by the hand with

the thumb and the little finger extended 2. to encircle with the hand or hands, as in measuring 3. to extend, reach, or pass over or across [a bridge *spans* the river]

span[2] (span) *archaic pt. of* SPIN

Span. 1. Spaniard 2. Spanish

span·dex (span'deks) *n.* [< EXPAND] an elastic fibre, chiefly a polymer of polyurethane, used in girdles, etc.

span·drel (span'drəl) *n.* [< dim. of Anglo-Fr. *spaundre* < OFr. *espandre*, to expand] 1. the space between the exterior curve of an arch and a rectangular frame enclosing it 2. any of the spaces between a series of arches and a cornice above

span·gle (spaŋ'g'l) *n.* [< dim. of ME. *spang*, a clasp < OE.] 1. a small piece of bright metal, esp. any of those sewn on fabric for decoration 2. any small, glittering object —*vt.* **-gled, -gling** to cover with spangles —*vi.* to glitter as with spangles —**span'gly** *adj.* **-gli·er, -gli·est**

Span·iard (span'yard) *n.* a native or inhabitant of Spain

span·iel (span'yəl) *n.* [< MFr. *espagnol*, lit., Spanish, ult. < L. *Hispania*, Spain] 1. any of several breeds of dog with a silky coat, drooping ears, and short legs and tail 2. a servile, fawning person

Span·ish (span'ish) *adj.* of Spain, its people, their language, etc. —*n.*, the Romance language of Spain and of Spanish America —**the Spanish** the people of Spain

Spanish America Mexico and those countries in Central and South America in which Spanish is the chief language

SPRINGER SPANIEL
(46 cm high at shoulder)

Span·ish-A·mer·i·can (-ə mer'ə kən) *adj.* 1. of both Spain and America 2. of Spanish America or its people —*n.* a native or inhabitant of Spanish America, esp. one of Spanish descent

Spanish fly 1. a bright green blister beetle of S Europe 2. the crushed bodies of these beetles used as a diuretic, aphrodisiac, etc.

Spanish Main 1. orig., the coastal region of the Americas along the Caribbean Sea; esp., the N coast of S America 2. later, the Caribbean Sea itself, or that part of it adjacent to the N coast of S America

Spanish moss a rootless epiphytic plant often growing in long, graceful strands from the branches of trees in the SE U.S. and tropical America

Spanish omelette an omelette, often open, with a sauce of chopped onion, green pepper, and tomato

Spanish rice boiled rice cooked with tomatoes and chopped onions, green peppers, etc.

spank (spaŋk) *vt.* [echoic] to strike with something flat, as the open hand, esp. on the buttocks, in punishment —*vi.* to move along swiftly —*n.* a smack given in spanking

spank·er (spaŋ'kər) *n.* 1. a person or thing that spanks 2. [Colloq.] an unusually fine, large, etc. person or thing 3. *Naut. a)* a fore-and-aft sail on the after mast of a square-rigged vessel *b)* the after mast and its sail on a schooner-rigged vessel of more than three masts

spank·ing (-kiŋ) *adj.* 1. rapid 2. brisk: said of a breeze 3. [Colloq.] unusually fine, large, etc. —*adv.* [Colloq.] altogether; completely [spanking new] —*n.* a series of smacks given by one who spanks

span·ner (span'ər) *n.* 1. one that spans 2. a tool used to tighten nuts, bolts, etc; wrench

spar[1] (spär) *n.* [< MDu. or MLowG. *spar*] any shiny, crystalline mineral that cleaves easily into chips or flakes —**spar'ry** *adj.* **-ri·er, -ri·est**

spar[2] (spär) *n.* [< ON. *sparri* or MDu. *sparre*] 1. any pole, as a mast, yard, or boom, for supporting the sails on a ship 2. a lengthwise support for the ribs of an aircraft wing —*vt.* **sparred, spar'ring** to equip with spars

spar[3] (spär) *vi.* **sparred, spar'ring** [prob. < MFr. < It. *sparare*, to kick < *parare*, to parry] 1. to fight with the feet and spurs: said of a fighting cock 2. to box with jabbing or feinting movements, landing few heavy blows, as in practice matches 3. to dispute; argue —*n.* a sparring match

spare (sper) *vt.* **spared, spar'ing** [OE. *sparian*] 1. to treat with mercy; refrain from killing, hurting, etc. 2. to save or free (a person) from (something) [spare me the trouble] 3. to omit, avoid using, or use frugally [spare no effort] 4. to part with or give up (money, time, etc.) without trouble to oneself —*vi.* 1. to be frugal 2. to show mercy —*adj.* 1. not in regular use; extra [a spare room] 2. not taken up by regular work or duties; free [spare time] 3. meagre; scanty [spare rations] 4. not fleshy; lean —*n.* 1. an extra part, thing, etc. 2. *Bowling a)* a knocking down of all the pins in two consecutive rolls of the ball *b)* a score so made —**go**

spare [Colloq.] to become extremely angry, annoyed, etc. —**(something) to spare** a surplus of (something) —**spare′ly** *adv.* —**spare′ness** *n.* —**spar′er** *n.*

spare·ribs (sper′ribz′) *n.pl.* [altered (after SPARE, *adj.*) < MLowG. *ribbesper*] a cut of meat, esp. pork, consisting of the thin end of the ribs with most of the meat cut away

spare tyre 1. an extra tyre carried in a motor car in case of punctures 2. [Colloq.] the roll of fat that many people have just above the waist

spar·ing (sper′iŋ) *adj.* 1. that spares 2. frugal 3. scanty; meagre —**spar′ing·ly** *adv.* —**spar′ing·ness** *n.*

spark[1] (spärk) *n.* [OE. *spearca*] 1. a glowing bit of matter, esp. one thrown off by a fire 2. any flash or sparkle of light like this 3. a tiny beginning or vestige, as of life, interest, etc.; particle or trace 4. liveliness; vivacity 5. *Elec.* a) a very brief flash of light accompanying an electric discharge through air or some other insulating material b) such a discharge, as in a spark plug —*vi.* 1. to make or throw off sparks 2. to come forth as or like sparks —*vt.* to stir into action; be the force that enlivens —**spark′er** *n.*

spark[2] (spärk) *n.* [ON. *sparkr*, lively] 1. a dashing, gallant young man 2. a beau or lover —*vt., vi.* [Colloq.] to court, woo, pet, etc. An old-fashioned term

spark gap a space between two electrodes through which a spark discharge may take place

sparking plug a piece fitted into a cylinder of an internal-combustion engine to make sparks that ignite the fuel mixture within: also **spark plug**

spar·kle (spär′k'l) *vi.* -**kled**, -**kling** [< ME. freq. of *sparken*, to SPARK[1]] 1. to throw off sparks 2. to shine with flashes of light; glitter, as jewels 3. to be brilliant and lively 4. to bubble or effervesce, as some wines —*vt.* to make sparkle —*n.* 1. a spark, or glowing particle 2. a sparkling, or glittering 3. brilliance; liveliness

spar·kler (-klər) *n.* one that sparkles; specif., a) a pencil-shaped firework that burns with bright sparks b) [Colloq.] a diamond or similar gem

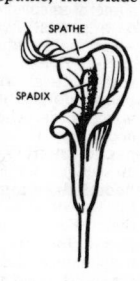
SPARKING PLUG
(cutaway model)
TERMINAL
INSULATOR
ELECTRODES
GAP

Sparks (spärks) *n.* [< SPARK[1]] [with sing. v.] [Colloq.] 1. an electrician 2. a radio officer, esp. on a ship

sparring partner 1. any person with whom a prizefighter boxes for practice 2. an opponent, usually a friend, in argument

spar·row (spar′ō) *n.* [OE. *spearwa*] any of several finch-like birds, esp. of a genus including the HOUSE SPARROW

sparrow grass (spar′ō grās′) *n.* [altered by folk etym. < ASPARAGUS] *dial. var. of* ASPARAGUS

sparrow hawk 1. a small European hawk with short wings 2. a small American falcon

sparse (spärs) *adj.* [< L. pp. of *spargere*, to scatter] thinly spread or scattered; not dense —**sparse′ly** *adv.* —**sparse′ness, spar·si·ty** (spär′sə tē) *n.*

Spar·tan (spär′t'n) *adj.* 1. of ancient Sparta, its people, or their culture 2. like or characteristic of the Spartans; brave, stoical, frugal, highly disciplined, strict, etc. —*n.* 1. a citizen of Sparta 2. a person with Spartan traits —**Spar′tan·ism** *n.*

spasm (spaz′m) *n.* [< MFr. < L. < Gr. *spasmos* < *span*, to pull] 1. a convulsive, involuntary contraction of a muscle or muscles 2. any short, sudden burst of activity, feeling, etc.

spas·mod·ic (spaz mod′ik) *adj.* [ModL. *spasmodicus* < Gr. < *spasmos*: see prec.] of, like, or characterized by a spasm or spasms; sudden, violent, and temporary; fitful; intermittent Also **spas·mod′i·cal** —**spas·mod′i·cal·ly** *adv.*

spas·tic (spas′tik) *adj.* [< L. < Gr. *spastikos*, pulling < *span*: see SPASM] of, marked by, or having spasm or spastic paralysis —*n.* a person with spastic paralysis —**spas′ti·cal·ly** *adv.*

spastic paralysis a condition, as in cerebral palsy, in which certain muscles stay contracted and movements are more or less uncontrollable

spat[1] (spat) *n.* [prob. echoic] [U.S.] 1. a quick, slapping sound 2. [Colloq.] a brief, petty quarrel or dispute —*vi.* **spat′ted, spat′ting** [U.S.] 1. to strike with a spat 2. [Colloq.] to have a spat, or quarrel

spat[2] (spat) *n.* [contr. < SPATTERDASH] a short gaiter for the instep and ankle

spat[3] (spat) *alt. pt. & pp. of* SPIT[2]

spat[4] (spat) *n.* [Anglo-Fr. < ?] 1. the spawn of the oyster or other bivalve shellfish 2. a young oyster or young oysters —*vi.* **spat′ted, spat′ting** to spawn: said of oysters

spate (spāt) *n.* [ME. < ?] 1. a sudden flood or heavy rain 2. a large outpour, as of words

spathe (spā*th*) *n.* [< ModL. < L. < Gr. *spathē*, flat blade] a large, leaflike part or pair of such parts enclosing a flower cluster (esp. a spadix)

SPATHE
SPADIX

spa·tial (spā′shəl) *adj.* [< L. *spatium*, space] 1. of space 2. happening or existing in space —**spa′ti·al′i·ty** (-shē al′ə tē) *n.* —**spa′tial·ly** *adv.*

spa·ti·o·tem·po·ral (spā′shē ō tem′pər əl) *adj.* 1. existing in both space and time 2. of space-time —**spa′ti·o·tem′po·ral·ly** *adv.*

spat·ter (spat′ər) *vt.* [akin to Fris. freq. of *spatten*, to splash] 1. to scatter in drops or small blobs 2. to splash with these 3. to defame —*vi.* 1. to be scattered in drops, etc., as fat in frying 2. to fall or strike as in a shower, as raindrops or pellets —*n.* 1. a) a spattering b) its sound 2. a mark made by spattering

spat·ter·dash (-dash′) *n.* [prec. + DASH] a long legging formerly worn to protect the stocking or trouser leg, as in wet weather

spat·u·la (spach′ə lə) *n.* [L., dim. of *spatha*, flat blade] a knifelike implement with a flat, flexible blade used for spreading or blending foods, paints, etc., for scraping, etc.

spav·in (spav′in) *n.* [MFr. *esparvain*] a disease of horses in which a deposit of bone (**bone spavin**) or an infusion of lymph (**bog spavin**) develops in the hock joint, usually causing lameness —**spav′ined** *adj.*

spawn (spôn) *vt., vi.* [< Anglo-Fr. < OFr. *espandre*, to shed < L.: see EXPAND] 1. to produce or deposit (eggs, sperm, or young) 2. to bring into being (esp. something regarded with contempt and produced in great quantity) —*n.* 1. the mass of eggs or young produced by fishes, molluscs, amphibians, etc. 2. something produced; specif., offspring or progeny: usually contemptuous

spay (spā) *vt.* [< Anglo-Fr. < OFr. < *espee*, sword < L. *spatha*: see SPATHE] to sterilize (a female animal) by removing the ovaries

SPCK Society for Promoting Christian Knowledge

speak (spēk) *vi.* **spoke** or archaic **spake**, **spo′ken** or archaic **spoke, speak′ing** [OE. *specan*, earlier *sprecan*] 1. to utter words with the ordinary voice; talk 2. to express opinions, feelings, ideas, etc. by or as by talking 3. [Chiefly U.S.] to make a request or reservation (*for*): usually in the passive [a seat not yet *spoken* for] 4. to make a speech; discourse 5. to be a spokesman (*for*) 6. to converse 7. to give out sound —*vt.* 1. to make known by or as by speaking 2. to use or be able to use (a given language) in speaking 3. to utter (words) orally —**so to speak** that is to say —**speak for itself** to be self-evident —**speak out** (or **up**) 1. to speak audibly or clearly 2. to speak freely or forcefully —**speak volumes** 1. to be significant 2. to be clearly understandable —**speak well for** to indicate something favourable about —**to speak of** worthy of mention [no gains *to speak of*] —**speak′a·ble** *adj.*

speak·eas·y (-ē′zē) *n.,* *pl.* -**eas′ies** [SPEAK + EASY: so named from the secretive atmosphere] [U.S. Slang] a place selling alcoholic drinks illegally, esp. during Prohibition in the U.S.

speak·er (spē′kər) *n.* 1. a person who speaks or makes speeches 2. a person who serves as presiding officer of a lawmaking body; specif., [S-] the presiding officer of the House of Commons: in full, **Speaker of the House** 3. a loudspeaker —**speak′er·ship′** *n.*

speak·ing (-kiŋ) *adj.* 1. that speaks, or seems to speak; expressive; vivid 2. in or for speech —*n.* 1. the act or art of one who speaks 2. utterance; discourse —**generally (strictly) speaking** in the common (strict) sense of the words —**on speaking terms** friendly enough to carry on conversation

speaking clock a telephone service by which the correct time is given to the one who telephones

speaking in tongues *same as* GLOSSOLALIA

spear (spir) *n.* [OE. *spere*] 1. a weapon with a long shaft and sharp head, for thrusting or throwing 2. any spearlike, often forked implement, as one used in fishing 3. [var. of SPIRE] a long blade or shoot, as of grass —*vt.* 1. to pierce or stab as with a spear 2. to catch (fish, etc.) as with a spear —*vi.* 1. to pierce like a spear 2. to sprout into a long stem —**spear′er** *n.*

spear·head (-hed′) *n.* 1. the pointed head of a spear 2. the person or persons leading an activity, esp. a military attack —*vt.* to lead (an attack, etc.)

spear·man (-mən) *n., pl.* -**men** a fighting man armed with a spear

spear·mint (-mint′) *n.* [from its flower spikes] a fragrant plant of the mint family, used for flavouring

spec. 1. special 2. specification 3. speculation

spe·cial (spesh′əl) *adj.* [< OFr. < L. < *species*, kind] 1. different, distinctive, or unique 2. exceptional; extraordinary 3. highly regarded [a *special* friend] 4. of or for a particular occasion, purpose, etc. [a *special* edition]

5. not general or regular; specific [*special* legislation] —*n.* something special, as a featured item on a menu or in a sale, or a special TV programme not part of a regular series —**spe′cial·ly** *adv.*

Special Branch the branch of the police force that deals with political offences and security

special constable someone, not a regular member of the police force, who becomes a temporary member for special occasions

special delivery delivery of mail by special postal messenger, for an extra fee

special drawing rights the right of member countries of the IMF to draw reserve currency from a fund operated by the IMF

spe·cial·ist (-ist) *n.* a person who specializes in a particular branch of study, professional work, etc. —*adj.* of a specialist: also **spe′cial·is′tic** —**spe′cial·ism** *n.*

spe·ci·al·i·ty (spesh′ē al′ə tē) *n.* **1.** a special quality, feature, etc. **2.** a special field of study, branch of a profession, etc. **3.** the state of being special **4.** a product or service given special attention to make it attractive, superior, etc. [curry was the restaurant's *speciality*]

spe·cial·ize (spesh′ə līz′) *vt.* **-ized′, -iz′ing 1.** to make special or specific **2.** to direct towards a specific end **3.** *Biol.* to adapt (parts or organs) to a special condition, use, etc. —*vi.* **1.** to make a speciality of something; specif., to take up a special study or work in a special branch of a profession **2.** *Biol.* to become specialized —**spe′cial·i·za′tion** *n.*

special licence a licence that is issued to allow a marriage to take place although the banns have not been called

spe·cial·ty (-əl tē) *n., pl.* **-ties 1.** *Chiefly U.S. var. of* SPECIALITY **2.** *Law* a formal contract under seal

spe·ci·a·tion (spē′shē ā′shən, -sē-) *n. Biol.* the process of developing new species through evolution —**spe′ci·ate′** (-āt′) *vi.* **-at′ed, -at′ing**

spe·cie (spē′shē, -sē) *n.* [abl. of L. *species*, kind: cf. use in phr. below] coin, as distinguished from paper money —**in specie 1.** in kind **2.** in coin

spe·cies (-shēz, -sēz) *n., pl.* **-cies** [L., appearance, shape, kind, etc.] **1.** a distinctive kind; sort; variety; class **2.** *Biol.* a group of highly similar plants or animals that is part of a genus and that can reproduce fertile offspring only among themselves **3.** *Logic* a class of things with distinctive common attributes, grouped with similar classes in a genus **4.** *R.C.Ch. a)* the outward form of the consecrated Eucharistic bread and wine *b)* the bread or wine —**the species** the human race

specif. specifically

spe·cif·ic (spi sif′ik) *adj.* [LL. *specificus* < L. *species* (see SPECIES) + *-ficus*, -FIC] **1.** specifying or specified; precise; definite; explicit **2.** of or forming a species **3.** peculiar to or characteristic of something [*specific* traits] **4.** of a particular sort **5.** *Med. a)* specially indicated as a cure for a particular disease [a *specific* remedy] *b)* produced by a particular microorganism [a *specific* disease] **6.** *Physics* designating a constant characteristic in relation to a fixed standard —*n.* **1.** something specially suited for a given use or purpose **2.** a specific cure or remedy **3.** a distinct item or detail; particular —**spe·cif′i·cal·ly** *adv.* —**spec·i·fic·i·ty** (spes′ə fis′ə tē) *n.*

spec·i·fi·ca·tion (spes′ə fi kā′shən) *n.* **1.** a specifying; detailed mention **2.** [*usually pl.*] a statement of particulars as to size, materials, etc. [*specifications* for a new building] **3.** something specified; specified item, etc.

specific gravity the ratio of the weight or mass of a given volume of a substance to that of an equal volume of another substance (water for liquids and solids, air or hydrogen for gases) used as a standard

spec·i·fy (spes′ə fī′) *vt.* **-fied′, -fy′ing** [< OFr. < LL. < *specificus*, SPECIFIC] **1.** to mention or describe in detail; state definitely or explicitly **2.** to include as an item in a set of specifications —**spec′i·fi′a·ble** *adj.* —**spec′i·fi′er** *n.*

spec·i·men (spes′ə mən) *n.* [L. < *specere*, to see] **1.** a part of a whole, or one individual of a group, used as a sample of the rest **2.** [Colloq.] a (specified kind of) individual or person [an odd *specimen*] **3.** *Med.* a sample, as of urine, for analysis

spe·cious (spē′shəs) *adj.* [< L. *speciosus* < *species*, appearance] seeming good, sound, etc., but not really so [*specious* logic] —**spe′cious·ly** *adv.* —**spe′cious·ness** *n.*

speck (spek) *n.* [OE. *specca*] **1.** a small spot or mark **2.** a tiny bit; particle —*vt.* to mark with specks

speck·le (spek′′l) *n.* [dim. of ME. *specke*, SPECK] a small mark of contrasting colour; speck —*vt.* **-led, -ling** to mark with speckles

specs (speks) *n.pl.* [Colloq.] **1.** spectacles; eyeglasses **2.** specifications: see SPECIFICATION (sense 2)

spec·ta·cle (spek′tə k'l) *n.* [< OFr. < L. < *spectare*, freq. of *specere*, to see] **1.** something to look at, esp. a remarkable sight **2.** a public show on a grand scale **3.** [*pl.*] eyeglasses —**spec′ta·cled** *adj.*

spec·tac·u·lar (spek tak′yə lər) *adj.* of or like a spectacle; strikingly grand or unusual —**spec·tac′u·lar·ly** *adv.*

spec·ta·tor (spek tāt′ər) *n.* [L. < pp. of *spectare*, to behold] a person who watches something without taking part; onlooker [*spectators* at sports events]

spectator sport a sport, such as football, that attracts large numbers of spectators

spec·tra (spek′trə) *n. alt. pl. of* SPECTRUM

spec·tral (-trəl) *adj.* **1.** of or like a spectre; ghostly **2.** of a spectrum —**spec′tral′i·ty** (-tral′ə tē), **spec′tral·ness** *n.* —**spec′tral·ly** *adv.*

spec·tre (spek′tər) *n.* [< Fr. < L. *spectrum*, appearance, apparition < *spectare*, to behold] **1.** a ghost; apparition **2.** any object of dread Also U.S. sp., **spec′ter**

spec·tro- [< SPECTRUM] *a combining form meaning:* **1.** of radiant energy as shown in a spectrum **2.** of or by a spectroscope

spec·tro·gram (spek′trə gram′) *n.* a photograph of a spectrum

spec·tro·graph (-graf′) *n.* an instrument for breaking up light into a spectrum and photographing the spectrum —**spec′tro·graph′ic** *adj.* —**spec′tro·graph′i·cal·ly** *adv.*

spec·trom·e·ter (spek trom′ə tər) *n.* an instrument for measuring spectral wavelengths —**spec′tro·met′ric** (-trə met′rik) *adj.* —**spec·trom′e·try** (-ə trē) *n.*

spec·tro·scope (spek′trə skōp′) *n.* an optical instrument for breaking up light from any source into a spectrum so that it can be studied —**spec′tro·scop′ic** (-skop′ik) *adj.* —**spec′tro·scop′i·cal·ly** *adv.*

spec·tros·co·py (spek tros′kə pē) *n.* the study of spectra by use of the spectroscope —**spec·tros′co·pist** *n.*

spec·trum (spek′trəm) *n., pl.* **-tra** (-trə), **-trums** [ModL., special use of L. *spectrum*: see SPECTRE] **1.** the series of coloured bands into which white light is broken up by passing through a prism, etc.: it is arranged according to wavelength, from red, the longest wave visible, to violet, the shortest **2.** any like series of bands or lines formed from other kinds of radiant energy **3.** a range or extent, as of opinion **4.** *same as* RADIO SPECTRUM

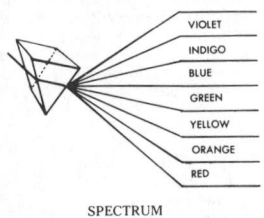

SPECTRUM
[VIOLET / INDIGO / BLUE / GREEN / YELLOW / ORANGE / RED]

spectrum analysis analysis of substances or bodies through study of their spectra

spec·u·late (spek′yə lāt′) *vi.* **-lat′ed, -lat′ing** [< L. pp. of *speculari*, to view < *specula*, watch tower < *specere*, to see] **1.** to think about the various aspects of a subject; ponder; esp., to conjecture **2.** to buy or sell stocks, land, etc., hoping to gain from price changes; also, to engage in any risky venture for possible huge profits —**spec′u·la′tion** *n.* —**spec′u·la·tive** (-lāt′iv, -lə tiv) *adj.* —**spec′u·la′tive·ly** *adv.* —**spec′u·la′tor** *n.*

spec·u·lum (spek′yə ləm) *n., pl.* **-la** (-lə), **-lums** [L. < *specere*, to look] **1.** a mirror, esp. one of polished metal used as a reflector in a telescope, etc. **2.** a patch of distinctive colour on the wings of some birds **3.** *Med.* an instrument used to dilate a passage for easier examination —**spec′u·lar** (-lər) *adj.* —**spec′u·lar·ly** *adv.*

sped (sped) *alt. pt. & pp. of* SPEED

speech (spēch) *n.* [OE. *spæc, spræc* < base of *sprecan*, to speak] **1.** the act of speaking **2.** the power or ability to speak **3.** the manner of speaking **4.** what is spoken; utterance, talk, etc. **5.** a talk given to an audience **6.** the language or dialect used by a certain group of people **7.** [U.S.] the study of the theory and practice of speaking

speech day a prize-giving event in most schools, usually held annually

speech·i·fy (spē′chə fī′) *vi.* **-fied′, -fy′ing** to make a speech: used humorously or contemptuously —**speech′i·fi′-er** *n.*

speech·less (spēch′lis) *adj.* **1.** not able to speak **2.** silent, as from shock **3.** not expressed or expressible in words —**speech′less·ly** *adv.* —**speech′less·ness** *n.*

speed (spēd) *n.* [OE. *spæd*, success] **1.** the act or state of moving rapidly; swiftness **2.** *a)* the rate of movement; velocity *b)* the rate or rapidity of any action [reading *speed*] **3.** an arrangement of gears for the drive of a bicycle [a *three-speed* bicycle] **4.** [Slang] any of various amphetamine compounds **5.** [Archaic] luck; success —*adj.* of speed —*vi.* **sped** or **speed′ed, speed′ing 1.** to go fast, esp. at a speed greater than the legal limit **2.** [Archaic] *a)* to get along; fare *b)* to prosper —*vt.* **1.** to help succeed; aid **2.** to wish Godspeed to **3.** to cause to go, move, etc. swiftly —**speed up** to go or make go faster —**speed′er** *n.*

speed·boat (-bōt′) *n.* a motorboat built for speed

speed limit the legal limit of speed of any vehicle on any given road

speed·o (spēd′ō) *n. Colloq.* clipped form of SPEEDOMETER

speed·om·e·ter (spi dom′ə tər) *n.* [< SPEED + -METER] a device attached to a motor vehicle, etc. to indicate speed, as in kilometres or miles per hour

speed·up (-up′) *n.* an increase in speed; esp., an increase in the rate of output, etc., as required by an employer

speed·way (-wā′) *n.* 1. a track for racing cars or motorcycles 2. [U.S.] a road for high-speed traffic

speed·well (-wel′) *n.* any of various plants of the figwort family, with spikes of white or bluish flowers

speed·y (spēd′ē) *adj.* **speed′i·er, speed′i·est** 1. rapid; swift 2. without delay; quick; prompt [a *speedy* reply] —**speed′i·ly** *adv.* —**speed′i·ness** *n.*

spe·le·ol·o·gy (spē′lē ol′ə jē) *n.* [< L. < Gr. *spēlaion*, a cave + -LOGY] the scientific study and exploration of caves —**spe·le·ol′o·gist** *n.*

spell¹ (spel) *n.* [OE., a saying] 1. a word or formula supposed to have some magic power 2. magical power or irresistible influence; charm; fascination —**cast a spell on** to enchant —**under a spell** enchanted

spell² (spel) *vt.* **spelled** or **spelt, spell′ing** [< OFr. *espeller,* to explain < Frank. *spellōn*] 1. to name, write, or signal, esp. correctly, the letters of (a word, etc.) 2. to make up, or form (a word, etc.): said of specified letters 3. to mean [red *spells* danger] —*vi.* to spell words, etc. —**spell out** 1. to read letter by letter or with difficulty 2. to discern as if by close reading 3. to explain in detail

spell³ (spel) *vt.* **spelled, spell′ing** [OE. *spelian*] [Colloq.] to work in place of (another) while he rests; relieve —*n.* 1. a turn of working in place of another 2. any period of work, duty, etc. 3. a period (*of* being in some state) [a *spell* of gloom] 4. a period of specified weather [a cold *spell*] 5. [Aust. & Dial.] a period or interval of rest 6. [Colloq.] a period of time that is indefinite, short, etc. 7. [Colloq.] a period of some illness

spell·bind (spel′bīnd′) *vt.* **-bound′, -bind′ing** to hold or affect as by a spell; fascinate; enchant —**spell′bind′er** *n.*

spell·er (-ər) *n.* 1. a person who spells words [a good *speller*] 2. an exercise book used to teach spelling

spell·ing (-iŋ) *n.* 1. the act of one who spells words 2. the way a word is spelled

spelling bee a spelling contest in which each contestant who misspells a word must drop out

spelt¹ (spelt) *alt. pt. & pp. of* SPELL²

spelt² (spelt) *n.* [OE. < LL. *spelta*] a species of wheat with grains that do not thresh free of chaff

spe·lunk·er (spi luŋ′kər) *n.* [< obs. *spelunk,* a cave (ult. < Gr. *spēlynx*) + -ER] [U.S.] a person who explores caves as a hobby —**spe·lunk′ing** *n.*

spen·cer¹ (spen′sər) *n.* [after the 2nd Earl *Spencer* (1758-1834)] 1. a short jacket worn in the early 19th cent. 2. a woman's knitted vest

spen·cer² (spen′sər) *n.* [< personal name *Spencer*] a trysail on a gaff

Spen·ce·ri·an (spen sir′ē ən) *adj.* [< Herbert *Spencer* (1820-1903), Brit. philosopher] pertaining to Spencer or to his philosophy —*n.* a follower of Spencer

spend (spend) *vt.* **spent, spend′ing** [< OE. *spendan* (in comp.) < ML. < L. *expendere,* to expend] 1. to use up, exhaust, etc. [his fury was *spent*] 2. to pay out (money) 3. to give or devote (time, effort, etc.) to something 4. to pass (time) [*spending* hours alone] 5. to waste; squander —*vi.* to pay out or use up money, etc. —**spend a penny** [Colloq.] to expel bodily wastes —**spend′a·ble** *adj.* —**spend′er** *n.*

spend·thrift (-thrift′) *n.* a person who spends money carelessly; squanderer —*adj.* wasteful; extravagant

Spen·se·ri·an (spen sir′ē ən) *adj.* [< Edmund *Spenser* (1551?-99), Eng. poet] of or characteristic of Spenser or his poetry —*n.* a student or imitator of Spenser

spent (spent) *pt. & pp. of* SPEND —*adj.* 1. tired out; physically exhausted 2. used up; worn out

sperm¹ (spurm) *n.* [< MFr. < LL. < Gr. *sperma,* seed < *speirein,* to sow] 1. the fluid from the male reproductive organs; semen 2. *same as* SPERMATOZOON

sperm² (spurm) *n.* shortened form of: 1. SPERMACETI 2. SPERM OIL 3. SPERM WHALE

-sperm (spurm) [see SPERM¹] a combining form meaning seed [gymnosperm]

sper·ma·ce·ti (spur′mə set′ē, -sēt′ē) *n.* [ML. < LL. *sperma,* SPERM¹ + L. *ceti,* gen. of *cetus,* a whale] a white, waxlike substance from oil in the head of a sperm whale or dolphin, used in making cosmetics, ointments, candles, etc.

-sper·mal (spur′m′l) *same as* -SPERMOUS

sper·mat·ic (spər mat′ik) *adj.* of, like, or having to do with sperm or sperm cells

sper·ma·tid (spur′mə tid) *n.* [SPERMAT(O)- + -ID] *Zool.* any of the four cells formed by division of a spermatocyte that develop into a spermatozoa

sper·mat·o- [< Gr. *sperma* (gen. *spermatos*), SPERM¹] a combining form meaning seed or sperm

sper·mat·o·phyte (spər mat′ə fīt′, spur′mə tə-) *n.* [SPERMATO- + -PHYTE] any seed-bearing plant —**sper·mat′o·phyt′ic** (-fit′ik) *adj.*

sper·mat·o·zo·on (spər mat′ə zō′on, -ən; spur′mə tə-) *n.,* *pl.* **-zo′a** (-ə) [ModL. < SPERMATO- + Gr. *zōion,* animal] the male germ cell, found in semen: it penetrates and fertilizes the egg of the female —**sper·mat′o·zo′al, sper·mat′o·zo′an, sper·mat′o·zo′ic** *adj.*

sperm·i·cide (spur′mə sīd′) *n.* [SPERM¹ + -i- + -CIDE] an agent that kills spermatozoa —**sperm′i·ci′dal** *adj.*

sperm oil a lubricating oil from the sperm whale

-sper·mous (spur′məs) a combining form meaning having (a specified number or kind of) seed

sperm whale a large, toothed whale of warm seas: a closed cavity in its roughly square head contains sperm oil

spew (spyoō) *vt., vi.* [OE. *spiwan*] 1. to throw up from or as from the stomach; vomit 2. to flow or gush forth —*n.* something spewed —**spew′er** *n.*

sp. gr. specific gravity

sphag·num (sfag′nəm) *n.* [ModL. < Gr. *sphagnos,* kind of moss] 1. a spongelike moss found in bogs 2. a mass of such mosses, used to improve soil, to pot plants, etc. —**sphag′nous** (-nəs) *adj.*

sphal·er·ite (sfal′ə rīt′) *n.* [< G. < Gr. *sphaleros,* deceptive] native zinc sulphide, ZnS, the principal ore of zinc, usually brownish with a resinous lustre

sphe·noid (sfē′noid) *adj.* [< ModL. < Gr. < *sphēn,* a wedge + -OID] *Anat.* designating or of the wedge-shaped compound bone at the base of the skull: also **sphe·noi′dal** —*n.* the sphenoid bone

sphere (sfir) *n.* [< OFr. < L. < Gr. *sphaira*] 1. any round body with a surface equally distant from the centre at all points; globe; ball 2. a star or planet 3. the visible heavens; sky 4. short for CELESTIAL SPHERE 5. any of a series of transparent shells that ancient astronomers imagined as revolving one within another around the earth and containing the stars, planets, sun, and moon 6. the place or range of action, knowledge, etc.; compass 7. place in society —*vt.* **sphered, spher′ing** [Chiefly Poet.] 1. to put in or as in a sphere 2. to put among the heavenly spheres 3. to form into a sphere

-sphere (sfir) a combining form meaning: 1. of or like a sphere [hydrosphere] 2. of any of the layers of gas around the earth [ionosphere]

spher·i·cal (sfer′i k′l) *adj.* 1. shaped like a sphere; globular 2. of a sphere or spheres Also **spher′ic** —**spher′i·cal·ly** *adv.* —**sphe·ric·i·ty** (sfi ris′ə tē) *n.*

sphe·roid (sfir′oid) *n.* a body that is almost but not quite a sphere —*adj.* of this shape: also **sphe·roi′dal**

sphinc·ter (sfiŋk′tər) *n.* [LL. < Gr. *sphinktēr* < *sphingein,* to draw close] *Anat.* a ring-shaped muscle that surrounds a natural opening in the body and can open or close it by expanding or contracting —**sphinc′ter·al** *adj.*

sphinx (sfiŋks) *n., pl.* **sphinx′es, sphin′ges** (sfin′jēz) [L. < Gr. *sphinx,* lit., the strangler] 1. any ancient Egyptian statue having a lion's body and the head of a man, ram, or hawk; specif., [S-] a huge statue of this kind with a man's head, near Cairo, Egypt 2. *a)* Gr. Myth. a winged monster with a lion's body and a woman's head and breasts; specif., [S-] such a monster at Thebes, who killed passers-by unable to solve its riddle *b)* a person who is hard to know or understand

sphra·gis·tics (sfrə jis′tiks) *n.pl.* [with *sing. v.*] [< LGr. *sphragistikos,* of seals < Gr. *sphragis,* a seal] the study of engraved seals and signets

sphyg·mo·ma·nom·e·ter (sfig′mō mə nom′ə tər) *n.* [< Gr. *sphygmos,* the pulse + MANOMETER] a manometer with an attached inflatable band wrapped around an upper arm to compress the artery, used to measure blood pressure

spi·cate (spī′kāt) *adj.* [L. *spicatus,* spiked] Bot., Zool. formed or arranged like a spike or spikes

spice (spīs) *n.* [OFr. *espice* < L. *species,* sort] 1. *a)* any of several vegetable substances, as clove, cinnamon, pepper, etc., used to season food *b)* such substances collectively 2. a spicy aroma 3. that which adds zest or interest —*vt.* **spiced, spic′ing** 1. to season or flavour with spice 2. to add zest or interest to

spice·bush (-boosh′) *n.* an aromatic E N. American plant with small, yellowish flowers and red fruit

spick-and-span (spik′′n span′) *adj.* [< *spick,* var. of SPIKE¹ + *span-new* < ON. < *spānn,* a chip + *nyr,* new] 1. new or fresh 2. neat and clean

spic·ule (spik′yoōl) *n.* [< ModL. < ML. < L. dim. of *spica,* a point] 1. Bot. a small spike 2. Zool. a small, hard, needlelike piece or process, as in the skeleton of a sponge: also **spic′u·lum** (-yə ləm), *pl.* **-la** (-lə) —**spic′u·late** (-yə lāt′), **spic′u·lar** (-lər) *adj.*

spic·y (spī′sē) *adj.* **spic′i·er, spic′i·est** 1. containing or full of spices 2. having the flavour or aroma of spice 3. lively, interesting, etc. 4. risqué; racy —**spic′i·ly** *adv.* —**spic′i·ness** *n.*

spi·der (spī′dər) *n.* [ME. *spithre,* ult. < OE. *spinnan,* to spin] 1. any of various small arachnids with a body in two parts, the front part bearing the legs and the back part having organs that spin threads for making nests, cocoons, or webs 2. a cluster of elastic straps used for holding loads on car racks, bicycles, etc. —**spi′der·y** *adj.*

spider monkey a monkey of South and Central America with long, spidery limbs and a long tail

spi·der·wort (-wʉrt′) *n.* any of various fleshy perennial plants with grasslike leaves and showy purplish, white, or pink flowers

spiel (spēl) *n.* [G., play] [Chiefly U.S. Slang] a talk or harangue, as in selling —*vi.* [Chiefly U.S. Slang] to give a spiel —**spiel′er** *n.*

spi·er (spī′ər) *n.* a person who spies

spiff·y (spif′ē) *adj.* **spiff′i·er, spiff′i·est** [< dial. *spiff*, well-dressed person] [Slang] spruce, smart, excellent or dapper

spig·ot (spig′ət) *n.* [ME. *spigote*] 1. a plug or peg used to stop the vent in a barrel, etc. 2. a tap

spike[1] (spīk) *n.* [< ON. *spīkr* or < MDu. & MLowG. *spīker*] 1. a long, heavy nail 2. a sharp-pointed projection, as along the top of an iron fence 3. *a)* any of the pointed metal projections on the bottoms of shoes used in athletics, golf, etc. *b)* [*pl.*] a pair of such shoes —*vt.* **spiked, spik′ing** 1. to fasten or equip as with a spike or spikes 2. to pierce, cut, etc. with, or impale on, a spike or spikes 3. [U.S.] to thwart or block (a scheme, etc.) 4. [Slang] to add alcohol to (a drink) —**spik′y** *adj.*

spike[2] (spīk) *n.* [L. *spica*] 1. an ear of grain 2. a long flower cluster with flowers attached directly to the stalk —**spiked** *adj.*

spike·let (-lit) *n.* a small spike, as in a flower cluster

spike·nard (-närd′) *n.* [< LL. < L. *spica*, ear of grain + *nardus*, NARD] 1. a fragrant ointment used in ancient times 2. the Asiatic plant from which it is made

spile (spīl) *n.* [MDu., a splinter] 1. a plug or spigot, as for a barrel 2. a heavy stake driven into the ground as a support 3. [Chiefly U.S.] a tap driven into a maple tree to draw off sap —*vt.* **spiled, spil′ing** 1. to furnish with spiles, or stakes 2. to set a spile into (a tree, barrel, etc.) 3. to plug (a hole) with a spile

SPIKES
(left, plantain; right, great mullein)

spill[1] (spil) *vt.* **spilled** or **spilt, spill′ing** [OE. *spillan*, to destroy] 1. to let or make fall or flow over from a container, esp. without intending to 2. to shed (blood) 3. to lessen the pressure of (wind) on (a sail) 4. to scatter at random from a container 5. [Colloq.] to let (a secret) become known 6. [Colloq.] to make (a rider, load, etc.) fall off —*vi.* to be spilled from a container —*n.* 1. a spilling 2. what is spilled 3. a spillway 4. [Colloq.] a fall; tumble —**spill over** to overflow —**spill the beans** to disclose a secret

spill[2] (spil) *n.* [prob. via dial. *spil* < ON. *spila*, a splinter] 1. a splinter 2. a thin roll of paper, thin stick, etc. set on fire to light a pipe, candle, etc.

spil·li·kin (spil′i k'n) *n.* [< MDu. *spilleken*, dim. of *spille*: see SPILE] 1. any of the strips used in playing spillikins 2. [*pl. with sing. v.*] a game played by tossing a number of strips into a jumbled heap and trying to remove them one at a time without moving any of the others

spill·way (spil′wā′) *n.* [SPILL[1] + WAY] a channel to carry off excess water, as around a dam

spilth (spilth) *n.* [SPIL(L)[1] + -TH[1]] 1. the act of spilling 2. that which is spilled, esp. profusely

spin (spin) *vt.* **spun** or archaic **span, spun, spin′ning** [OE. *spinnan*] 1. *a)* to draw out and twist fibres of (wool, cotton, etc.) into thread *b)* to make (thread, yarn, etc.) thus 2. to make (a web, cocoon, etc.) from a viscous fluid extruded from the body as a thread: said of spiders, etc. 3. to produce in a way that suggests spinning 4. to draw *out* (a story, etc.) to great length 5. to make whirl [to *spin* a top] 6. to make (wheels of a vehicle) rotate without traction, as on ice 7. to extract water from (clothes) in a washing machine or spin dryer by swift rotation —*vi.* 1. to spin thread, etc. 2. to fish with a spinning reel 3. to whirl 4. to feel dizzy and seem to be spinning 5. to go into a spin: said of an aircraft 6. to move along swiftly and smoothly 7. to rotate freely without traction —*n.* 1. the spinning or rotating of something, as a cricket ball 2. a moving along swiftly and smoothly 3. a ride in a motor vehicle 4. the descent of an aircraft nose first along a spiral path 5. any sudden, steep downward movement —**spin off** 1. to produce as a secondary development 2. to get rid of

spi·na bi·fi·da (spī′nə bif′ə də) a defect in which the spine fails to fuse in the embryonic stage

spin·ach (spin′ich, -ij) *n.* [< MFr. < OSp. *espinaca* < Ar. < Per. *aspanākh*] 1. a plant of the goosefoot family, with large, dark-green, edible leaves 2. the leaves

spi·nal (spī′n'l) *adj.* of the spine or spinal cord —*n.* a spinal anaesthetic —**spi′nal·ly** *adv.*

spinal anaesthesia anaesthesia of the lower part of the

body by injection of an anaesthetic into the spinal cord, usually in the lumbar region —**spinal anaesthetic**

spinal column the series of joined vertebrae forming the axial support for the skeleton; spine

spinal cord the thick cord of nerve tissue of the central nervous system, in the spinal column

spin bowler *Cricket* a bowler who imparts a twisted motion to the balls he bowls

spin·dle (spin′d'l) *n.* [< OE. *spinel* < *spinnan*, to spin] 1. a slender rod or pin for twisting, winding, or holding the thread in spinning by hand, on a spinning wheel, or in a spinning machine 2. something spindle-shaped, as a slender, decorative rod in some chair backs 3. any rod, pin, or shaft that revolves or serves as an axis for a revolving part 4. in a lathe, a shaftlike part that rotates (**live spindle**) or does not rotate (**dead spindle**) while holding the thing to be turned 5. [Chiefly U.S.] a metal spike on a base, to stick papers on for temporary filing: also **spindle file** 6. *Naut.* a metal rod or pipe topped with a lantern, etc. and fastened to a rock, shoal, etc. to warn vessels —*adj.* of or like a spindle —*vi.* **-dled, -dling** to grow in or into a long, slender shape or stem —*vt.* to form into a spindle

spin·dle-legs (-legz′) *n.pl.* 1. thin legs 2. [*with sing. v.*] [Colloq.] a person with thin legs —**spin′dle-leg′ged** (-leg′id, -legd′) *adj.*: also **spin′dle-shanked′** (-shaŋkt′)

spin·dly (spin′dlē) *adj.* **-dli·er, -dli·est** long or tall and very thin or slender: also **spin′dling** (-dliŋ)

spin·drift (spin′drift′) *n.* [< Scot. var. of *spoondrift* < *spoon*, to scud (< ?) + DRIFT] spray blown from a rough sea or surf

spin·dry (-drī′) *vt.* **-dried, -dry′ing** to dry washing by centrifugal force in a spin dryer

spin dryer a device that extracts water from clothes, etc. by spinning them in a perforated drum: also **spin drier**

spine (spīn) *n.* [< OFr. < L. *spina*, a thorn] 1. any of the short, sharp, woody projections on a cactus, etc. 2. *a)* a sharp process of bone *b)* any of the sharp, stiff projections on certain animals, as a porcupine quill *c)* anything like either of these 3. the spinal column; backbone 4. anything suggesting a backbone, as *a)* the crest of a hill *b)* the narrow back part of a bound book

spine-chill·ing (-chil′iŋ) *adj.* thrilling; lurid; frightening

spi·nel (spi nel′) *n.* [< MFr. < It. dim. of *spina*, spine < L. (see prec.)] a hard, crystalline mineral found in various colours: a red variety (**ruby spinel**) is used as a gem

spine·less (spīn′lis) *adj.* 1. having no backbone; invertebrate 2. having a weak backbone 3. lacking courage, willpower, etc. 4. having no spines or thorns —**spine′less·ly** *adv.* —**spine′less·ness** *n.*

spin·et (spin et′, spin′it) *n.* [< MFr. < It. *spinetta*, prob. < *spina*, a thorn] 1. an obsolete, small harpsichord 2. [U.S.] a small upright piano or electronic organ

spin·i·fex (spin′i feks′) *n.* [ModL. < L. *spina*, a thorn + *facere*, to make] any of a genus of Australian grasses with pointed leaves and bristly seed heads

spin·na·ker (spin′ə kər) *n.* [said to be altered < *Sphinx*, name of a yacht that carried the sail] a large, triangular forward sail used on some racing yachts

spin·ner (spin′ər) *n.* a person or thing that spins; specif., *a)* a fishing lure having blades that revolve or flutter when drawn through the water; also, any of its blades *b)* a spin dryer *c)* a ball bowled with a spinning motion *d)* a spin bowler

spin·ner·et (spin′ə ret′) *n.* [dim. of SPINNER] 1. the organ used by spiders, caterpillars, etc. to spin their silky threads 2. a device with tiny holes through which a solution is forced in making synthetic fibres

spin·ney (spin′ē) *n., pl.* **-neys, -nies** [ME. *spenne*, a thorn hedge] a copse or small grove of trees

spin·ning (spin′iŋ) *n.* 1. the act of making thread, etc. from fibres or filaments 2. fishing done with a rod that has a fixed spool, a light line, and light lures —*adj.* that spins or is used in spinning

spinning jenny an early spinning machine with several spindles, for spinning more than one thread at a time

spinning wheel a simple spinning machine with a single spindle driven by a large wheel

spin-off (spin′of) *n.* a secondary benefit, development, etc. [Teflon was a *spinoff* of the space programme]

spi·nose (spī′nōs) *adj.* [< L. < *spina*, spine] full of or covered with spines: also **spi′nous** (-nəs) —**spi′nose·ly** *adv.* —**spi·nos′i·ty** (-nos′ə tē) *n., pl.* **-ties**

spin·ster (spin′stər) *n.* [ME. < *spinnen*, to spin + -STER] 1. a woman who spins thread or yarn 2. an unmarried woman, esp. an older one; old maid —**spin′ster·hood′** *n.* —**spin′ster·ish** *adj.*

spin·y (spī′nē) *adj.* **spin′i·er, spin′i·est** 1. covered with spines or thorns 2. full of difficulties; troublesome 3. spine-shaped —**spin′i·ness** *n.*

spiny anteater same as ECHIDNA

spin·y-finned (spī′nē find′) *adj.* having fins supported by pointed, stiff spines

spiny lobster a sea crustacean similar to the common lobster, but lacking large pincers and having a spiny shell
spi·ra·cle (spī'rə k'l, spir'ə-) *n.* [L. *spiraculum* < *spirare*, to breathe] *Zool.* an opening for breathing, as one of the tracheal openings of arthropods, or the blowhole of a whale
spi·ral (spī'rəl) *adj.* [< ML. < L. *spira*, a coil < Gr. *speira*] 1. circling or coiling around a central point in a flat curve that constantly increases (or decreases) in size 2. circling an axis in a curve of conical or cylindrical form; helical —*n.* 1. a spiral curve occurring in a single plane 2. a spiral curve occurring in a series of planes; helix 3. something having a spiral form 4. a spiral path or flight 5. a section of a spiral 6. a continuous, widening decrease or increase [an inflationary *spiral*] —*vi., vt.* **-ralled, -ral·ling** to move in or form (into) a spiral —**spi'ral·ly** *adv.*
spi·rant (spī'rənt) *n., adj.* [< L. prp. of *spirare*, to breathe] *same as* FRICATIVE
spire (spīr) *n.* [OE. *spir*] 1. a sprout, spike, or stalk of a plant, blade of grass, etc. 2. the top part of a pointed, tapering object or structure, as a mountain peak 3. anything that tapers to a point, as a steeple —*vi.* **spired, spir'ing** to extend upwards, tapering to a point
spi·re·a (spī rē'ə) *n.* [< ModL. genus name < L. < Gr. < *speira*, a coil] any of several plants of the rose family, with dense clusters of small, pink or white flowers: also sp. **spi·rae'a**
spi·ril·lum (spī ril'əm) *n., pl.* **-la** (-ə) [ModL., dim. of L. *spira* (see SPIRAL)] a bacterium having the form of a spiral thread and moving by means of flagella
spir·it (spir'it) *n.* [< OFr. < L. *spiritus*, breath < *spirare*, to breathe] 1. the life principle or the soul, esp. in man, sometimes regarded as immortal 2. the thinking, feeling part of man; mind; intelligence 3. [*also* S-] life, will, thought, etc., regarded as separate from matter 4. a supernatural being, as a ghost, angel, demon, fairy, etc. 5. an individual person or personality [a brave *spirit*] 6. [*usually pl.*] disposition; mood [high *spirits*] 7. vivacity, courage, enthusiasm, etc. 8. enthusiasm and loyalty [school *spirit*] 9. real meaning; true intention [to follow the *spirit* if not the letter of the law] 10. an essential quality or prevailing tendency [the *spirit* of the Renaissance] 11. [*usually pl.*] distilled alcoholic liquor 12. [*often pl.*] any liquid produced by distillation 13. an alcoholic solution of a volatile substance [*spirits* of camphor] —*vt.* 1. to inspirit, encourage, cheer, etc. 2. to carry (*away, off,* etc.) secretly and swiftly —*adj.* 1. of spirits or spiritualism 2. operating by the burning of alcohol [a *spirit* lamp] —**out of spirits** sad; depressed —**the Spirit** *same as* HOLY SPIRIT —**spir'it·less** *adj.* —**spir'it·less·ly** *adv.* —**spir'it·less·ness** *n.*
spir·it·ed (-id) *adj.* 1. full of spirit; lively; vigorous; animated 2. having a (specified) character, mood, or disposition [low-*spirited*] —**spir'it·ed·ly** *adv.* —**spir'it·ed·ness** *n.*
spirit gum a solution of gum arabic in ether used to attach false hair, whiskers, etc. to the face
spir·it·ism (-iz'm) *n.* *same as* SPIRITUALISM —**spir'it·ist** *n., adj.* —**spir'it·is'tic** *adj.*
spirit lamp a lamp in which alcohol, usually methylated spirits, is burned
spirit level *same as* LEVEL (*n.* 1)
spir·it·ous (spir'i təs) *adj.* *same as* SPIRITUOUS
spirits of ammonia a 10% solution of ammonia in alcohol: also **spirit of ammonia**
spir·it·u·al (spir'i tyoōl, -tyoō wəl) *adj.* 1. of the spirit or soul as distinguished from the body or material matters 2. of or consisting of spirit; not corporeal 3. refined in thought or feeling 4. of religion or the church; sacred, devotional, etc. 5. spiritualistic or supernatural —*n.* 1. a religious folk song of U.S. Negro origin 2. [*pl.*] religious or church matters —**spir'it·u·al'i·ty** (-wal'ə tē), *pl.* **-ties, spir'it·u·al·ness** *n.* —**spir'it·u·al·ly** *adv.*
spir·it·u·al·ism (-iz'm) *n.* 1. the belief that the dead survive as spirits which can communicate with the living, esp. with the help of a medium 2. the philosophical doctrine that all reality is in essence spiritual 3. spiritual quality —**spir'it·u·al·ist** *n.* —**spir'it·u·al·is'tic** *adj.*
spir·it·u·al·ize (spir'i tyoōl līz') *vt.* **-ized', -iz'ing** 1. to make spiritual; remove worldliness from 2. to give a spiritual sense or meaning to —**spir'it·u·al·i·za'tion** *n.*
‡**spi·ri·tu·el** (spē rē tü el'; *E.* spir'i choo wel') *adj.* [Fr.] having or showing a refined nature or, esp., a quick, graceful wit or mind —**spi·ri·tu·elle'** *adj. fem.*
spir·it·u·ous (spir'it yoos, -tyoō wəs) *adj.* of, like, or containing alcohol: said of distilled beverages —**spir'it·u·os'i·ty** (-wos'ə tē) *n.*
spi·ro- [< Gr. *speira*, a coil] *a combining form meaning* spiral or coil [*spirochaete*]
spi·ro·chaete (spī'rə kēt') *n.* [< ModL. < Gr. *speira*, a spiral + *chaitē*, hair] any of various spiral-shaped bacteria, some of which cause disease: also Chiefly U.S. sp. **spi'ro·chete'**
spi·ro·graph (spī'rə gräf') *n.* [< L. *spirare*, to breathe +

-GRAPH] an instrument for recording the movements of breathing
spirt (spurt) *n., vt., vi.* *same as* SPURT
spir·y (spīr'ē) *adj.* **spir'i·er, spir'i·est** 1. of, or having the form of, a spire 2. having many spires
spit¹ (spit) *n.* [OE. *spitu*] 1. a thin, pointed rod on which meat is impaled for roasting over a fire or other direct heat 2. a narrow point of land, or a narrow reef or shoal, extending into a body of water —*vt.* **spit'ted, spit'ting** to impale as on a spit —**spit'ter** *n.*
spit² (spit) *vt.* **spit** or **spat, spit'ting** [OE. *spittan*] 1. to eject from the mouth 2. to throw (*out*), emit, or utter explosively [to *spit* out an oath] —*vi.* 1. to eject saliva from the mouth; expectorate 2. to make an explosive hissing noise, as an angry cat 3. to express contempt by spitting saliva (*on* or *at*) 4. to sputter, as frying fat —*n.* 1. the act of spitting 2. saliva 3. a salivalike, frothy secretion of certain insects 4. [Colloq.] the perfect likeness, as of a person: in **spit and image** (spit''n im'ij) —**spit it out** 1. to speak with venom 2. to divulge some information without more delay —**spit up** to bring up from the stomach or throat —**spit'ter** *n.*
spit and polish formal or ceremonial, sometimes superficial, orderliness, neatness, etc. as in the military
spite (spīt) *n.* [short for DESPITE] 1. a mean or evil feeling towards another, with a desire to hurt, humiliate, etc.; malice 2. an instance of this; a grudge —*vt.* **spit'ed, spit'ing** to show one's spite for by hurting, frustrating, etc. —**in spite of** regardless of —**spite'ful** *adj.* —**spite'ful·ly** *adv.* —**spite'ful·ness** *n.*
spit·fire (spit'fīr') *n.* a person, esp. a woman or girl, who is easily aroused to violent outbursts of temper
spit·ting im·age (spit''n im'ij) *alteration of* SPIT AND IMAGE: see SPIT²
spit·tle (spit''l) *n.* [< OE. *spætl*, var of *spatl*] saliva; spit
spit·toon (spi toōn') *n.* a container to spit into
spitz (spits) *n.* [G. < *spitz*, pointed] a small Pomeranian dog with pointed muzzle and ears and a long, silky coat
spiv (spiv) *n.* [? dial. var. of the 19th c. slang *spiff*, a dandy] [Colloq.] a man who lives by his wits, without doing any honest work, esp. one engaged in petty, shady dealings
splash (splash) *vt.* [intens. extension of PLASH²] 1. to cause (a liquid) to scatter and fall in drops 2. to dash or scatter a liquid, mud, etc. on, so as to wet or soil 3. to cause to splash a liquid [to *splash* the oars] 4. to make (one's way) by splashing 5. to mark as by splashing [*splashed* with sunlight] 6. to display conspicuously [scandal was *splashed* on the front page] —*vi.* 1. to dash or scatter a liquid about 2. to move, fall, strike, or scatter with a splash —*n.* 1. the act or sound of splashing 2. a mass of splashed water, mud, etc. 3. a spot or mark made as by splashing 4. a patch of colour, light, etc. 5. a small quantity [a *splash* of soda] —**make a splash** [Colloq.] to attract great, often brief, attention —**splash'er** *n.* —**splash'i·ness** *n.* —**splash'y** *adj.*
splash·down (-doun') *n.* the landing of a spacecraft on water
splat¹ (splat) *n.* [via dial. < base of SPLIT] a thin, flat piece of wood, esp. as used in the back of a chair
splat² (splat) *n., interj.* a splattering or wet, slapping sound
splat·ter (-ər) *n., vt., vi.* [< SPATTER] spatter or splash
splay (splā) *vt., vi.* [< ME. *displaien*, to display] 1. to spread out or apart; extend (often with *out*) 2. to slope —*n.* 1. a sloping surface or angle 2. a spreading; expansion —*adj.* 1. sloping, spreading, or turning outwards 2. broad and flat 3. awkward
splay·foot (-foot') *n., pl.* **-feet'** 1. a foot that is flat and turned outwards 2. the condition of having such feet —*adj.* of or having splayfoot: also **splay'foot'ed**
spleen (splēn) *n.* [< OFr. < L. < Gr. *splen*, spleen] 1. a large, vascular, lymphatic organ in the upper left part of the abdomen: it modifies the blood structure and was formerly regarded as the seat of certain emotions 2. malice; spite; bad temper —**spleen'ful, spleen'ish, spleen'y** *adj.*
spleen·wort (-wurt') *n.* any of various ferns including the maidenhair
splen·did (splen'did) *adj.* [L. *splendidus* < *splendere*, to shine] 1. having or showing splendour; specif., a) shining; brilliant b) magnificent; gorgeous 2. worthy of high praise; grand; glorious; illustrious 3. [Colloq.] very good; excellent —**splen'did·ly** *adv.* —**splen'did·ness** *n.*
splen·dif·er·ous (splen dif'ər əs) *adj.* [Colloq.] gorgeous; splendid: used jokingly —**splen·dif'er·ous·ly** *adv.* —**splen·dif'er·ous·ness** *n.*
splen·dour (splen'dər) *n.* [< OFr. < L. < *splendere*, to shine] 1. great lustre; brilliance 2. magnificent richness or glory; pomp; grandeur Also, U.S. sp., **splen'dor** —**splen'dor·ous, splen'drous** *adj.*
sple·net·ic (spli net'ik) *adj.* [LL. *spleneticus*] 1. of the spleen 2. irritable; peevish; spiteful Also **sple·net'i·cal** —*n.* a spleenful person —**sple·net'i·cal·ly** *adv.*
splen·ic (splen'ik, splēn'-) *adj.* [< L. < Gr. *splēnikos*] 1. of or having to do with the spleen 2. in or near the spleen

splice (splīs) *vt.* **spliced, splic′ing** [MDu. *splissen*] 1. to join (ropes or rope ends) by weaving together the end strands 2. to join the ends of (timbers) by overlapping and binding or bolting together 3. to fasten the ends of (wire, film, tape, etc.) together, as by cementing, twisting, etc. 4. [Colloq.] to join in marriage —*n.* 1. a joint or joining made by splicing 2. the wedge-shaped end of a cricket bat handle —**splic′er** *n.*

spline (splīn) *n.* [< E. Anglian dial., prob. akin to Norw. dial. *splindra*, a large flat splinter] 1. a long, flat, pliable strip, as of wood or metal 2. *a)* a flat key or strip that fits into a groove or slot between parts *b)* the groove or slot into which it fits —*vt.* **splined, splin′ing** 1. to fit with a spline 2. to cut a groove for a spline

SHORT
SPLICE

splint (splint) *n.* [MDu. or MLowG. *splinte*] 1. a thin strip of wood or cane woven together with others to make baskets, chair seats, etc. 2. a thin, rigid strip of wood, metal, etc. used to keep a broken bone in place or to keep a part of the body in a fixed position —*vt.* to fit, support, or hold in place as with a splint or splints

splin·ter (splin′tər) *vt., vi.* akin to *splinte*, splint] 1. to break or split into thin, sharp pieces 2. to break into groups with opposing views —*n.* 1. a thin, sharp piece of wood, bone, etc., made by splitting or breaking 2. a splinter group —*adj.* designating a group that separates from a main party, church, etc. because of opposing views —**splin′ter·y** *adj.*

split (split) *vt.* **split, split′ting** [MDu. *splitten*] 1. to separate, cut, etc. along the grain or length into two or more parts 2. to break or tear apart by force 3. to divide into parts or shares 4. to divide voting between two candidates of one party, etc. allowing a third to win 5. to cause (a group, political party, etc.) to separate into factions 6. *a)* to break (a molecule) into atoms or into smaller molecules *b)* to produce nuclear fission in (an atom) 7. *Finance* to divide (stock) by substituting some multiple of the original shares —*vi.* 1. to separate lengthwise into two or more parts 2. to break apart; burst 3. to separate because of failure to agree (often with *up*) 4. [U.S. Slang] to leave a place; depart —*n.* 1. the act or result of splitting; specif., *a)* a break; crack *b)* a division in a group, between persons, etc. 2. a splinter 3. a confection made of a split banana or other fruit with ice cream, sauces, nuts, etc. 4. same as DEVONSHIRE SPLIT 5. [*pl.*] the feat of spreading the legs apart until they lie flat on the floor, the body remaining upright 6. [Colloq.] a small bottle of wine, etc., usually about six ounces 7. [Colloq.] a share, as of loot 8. *Tenpin Bowling* an arrangement of pins after the first bowl, so separated as to make a spare extremely difficult —*adj.* 1. separated along the length or grain 2. divided; separated —**split off** to break off or separate as by splitting —**split′ter** *n.*

split infinitive *Gram.* an infinitive with the verb and the *to* separated by an adverb (Ex.: he decided *to gradually change* his style): despite objections to this construction, many writers use it to avoid ambiguity or wrong emphasis

split-lev·el (-lev′′l) *adj.* designating or of a type of house with floor levels so staggered that each level is about a half storey above or below the adjacent one

split pea a green or yellow pea that has been shelled, dried, and split: used esp. for making soup

split personality *a popular name for* SCHIZOPHRENIA

split second a fraction of a second —**split′-sec′ond** *adj.*

split shift a shift, or work period, separated into two parts by a period longer than the usual one for a meal or rest

split·ting (split′iŋ) *adj.* 1. that splits 2. *a)* aching severely: said of the head *b)* severe, as a headache

split-up (-up′) *n.* a breaking up or separating into two or more parts, units, groups, etc.

splotch (sploch) *n.* [prob. a fusion of SPOT & BLOTCH] a spot, splash, or stain, esp. one that is irregular —*vt., vi.* to mark or be marked with splotches —**splotch′y** *adj.*

splurge (splurj) *n.* [echoic] [Colloq.] 1. any very showy display or effort 2. a spell of extravagant spending —*vi.* **splurged, splurg′ing** [Colloq.] 1. to make a splurge 2. to spend money extravagantly —**splurg′er** *n.*

splut·ter (splut′ər) *vi.* [var. of SPUTTER] 1. to make hissing or spitting sounds; sputter 2. to speak hurriedly and confusedly, as when excited —*vt.* 1. to utter hurriedly and confusedly 2. to spatter —*n.* a spluttering sound or utterance —**splut′ter·er** *n.* —**splut′ter·y** *adj.*

Spode (spōd) *n.* a fine porcelain or chinaware produced by Josiah Spode (1754-1827), British potter

spoil (spoil) *vt.* **spoiled** or **spoilt, spoil′ing** [< MFr. < L. *spoliare* < *spolium*, plunder] 1. to damage or injure so as to make useless, valueless, etc.; destroy 2. to impair the enjoyment, quality, etc. of [rain *spoiled* the picnic] 3. to let (a person) have his own way so much that he demands or expects it —*vi.* to be damaged or injured so as to become useless, valueless, etc.; decay, as food —*n.* 1. [*usually pl.*] *a)* goods, territory, etc. taken by plunder; booty *b)* public offices to which the political party that wins has the power to appoint people 2. an object of plunder; prey —**be spoiling for a fight** to be aggressively eager for a fight, etc. —**spoil′a·ble** *adj.* —**spoil′er** *n.*

spoil·age (-ij) *n.* 1. a spoiling or being spoiled 2. something spoiled or the amount spoiled

spoil·sport (spoil′spôrt′) *n.* a person who behaves in such a way as to ruin the pleasure of others

spoils system [Chiefly U.S.] the practice of treating public offices as the booty of the political party that wins an election, to be distributed among party workers

spoke¹ (spōk) *n.* [OE. *spaca*] 1. any of the braces extending from the hub to the rim of a wheel 2. a ladder rung 3. any of the handholds along the rim of a ship's steering wheel —*vt.* **spoked, spok′ing** to equip with spokes

spoke² (spōk) *pt. & archaic pp. of* SPEAK

spo·ken (spō′k'n) *pp. of* SPEAK —*adj.* 1. uttered; oral 2. characterized by a (specified) kind of voice [soft-*spoken*]

spoke·shave (spōk′shāv′) *n.* a planing tool consisting of a blade with a handle at either end, used for shaping rounded surfaces, as, formerly, spokes

spokes·man (spōks′mən) *n., pl.* **-men** a person who speaks or gives information for another or for a group

spo·li·a·tion (spō′lē·ā′shən) *n.* [L. *spoliatio*] 1. robbery; plundering 2. the act of spoiling or damaging —**spo′li·a′tive** *adj.*

spon·dee (spon′dē) *n.* [< L. < Gr. < *spondē*, solemn libation (one accompanied by a solemn melody)] a metrical foot consisting of two long or heavily accented syllables —**spon·da′ic** (-dā′ik) *adj.*

spon·du·licks (spon dyoo′liks) *n.* [< ?] [Slang] money: also **spon·du′lix**

sponge (spunj) *n.* [OE. < L. < Gr. *spongia*] 1. a plantlike sea animal having a porous structure and a tough, fibrous skeleton and growing fixed to surfaces under water 2. the skeleton of such animals, light in weight and highly absorbent, used for washing surfaces, in bathing, etc. 3. any substance like this; specif., *a)* a piece of spongy plastic, cellulose, etc. *b)* a pad of gauze or cotton, as used in surgery *c)* a light, porous pudding *d)* a raised bread dough *e)* same as SPONGECAKE 4. [Colloq.] a person who lives upon others as a parasite —*vt.* **sponged, spong′ing** 1. to use a sponge on so as to dampen, wipe clean, etc. 2. to remove as with a damp sponge (with *out, off,* etc.) 3. to absorb with or like a sponge (often with *up*) 4. [Colloq.] to get as by begging, imposition, etc. —*vi.* 1. to gather sponges from the sea 2. to take up liquid like a sponge 3. [Colloq.] to be a parasite (often with *off* or *on*) —**throw** (or **toss,** etc.) **in the sponge** [Colloq.] to admit defeat; give up —**sponge′like′** *adj.* —**spong′er** *n.* —**spon′gi·ness** *n.* —**spon′gy** *adj.*

sponge bag a small bag, usually made of plastic, that holds toilet articles, esp. for use when travelling

sponge bath a bath taken by using a wet sponge or cloth without getting into water or under a shower

sponge·cake (-kāk′) *n.* a light cake of spongy texture made of flour, beaten eggs, sugar, etc., but no fat: also **sponge cake**

sponge rubber rubber processed to have a spongelike texture denser than foam rubber: used for gaskets, etc.

spon·sion (spon′shən) *n.* [L. *sponsio* < *spondere*, to promise] 1. a formal pledge, esp. the one made by a godparent 2. the act of standing surety for someone

spon·son (spon′sən) *n.* [altered < ? EXPANSION] 1. a structure that projects over the side of a ship or boat, as a gun platform 2. a winglike piece attached to the hull of a seaplane to give stability in the water

spon·sor (spon′sər) *n.* [L. < *spondere*, to promise solemnly] 1. a person or agency that acts as endorser, proponent, adviser, surety, etc. for a person, group, or activity 2. a godparent; person who answers for a child, as at baptism, making the promises prescribed 3. a business firm or other agency that alone or with others pays for a radio or TV programme on which it advertises or promotes something —*vt.* to act as sponsor for —**spon·so′ri·al** (-sôr′ē·əl) *adj.* —**spon′sor·ship′** *n.*

spon·ta·ne·i·ty (spon′tə nē′ə tē, -nā′-) *n.* 1. the state or quality of being spontaneous 2. *pl.* **-ties** spontaneous behaviour, movement, action, etc.

spon·ta·ne·ous (spon tā′nē əs) *adj.* [< LL. < L. *sponte*, of free will] 1. moved by a natural feeling or impulse, without constraint, effort, or forethought 2. acting by internal energy, force, etc. 3. growing naturally; wild —**spon·ta′ne·ous·ly** *adv.* —**spon·ta′ne·ous·ness** *n.*

spontaneous combustion the process of catching fire as a result of heat generated by internal chemical action

spontaneous generation the theory, now discredited, that living organisms can originate from nonliving matter

spoof (spoof) *n.* [coined c. 1889] [Slang] 1. a hoax, joke, or deception 2. a light parody or satire —*vt., vi.* [Slang] 1. to fool; deceive 2. to satirize in a playful manner

spook (spook) *n.* [Du.] [Colloq.] 1. a spectre; ghost 2. any person suggestive of a spectre, as an eccentric, a secret agent, etc.—*vt.*, *vi.* [Colloq.] to startle or be startled, frightened, etc. —**spook′i·ly** *adv.* —**spook′i·ness** *n.* —**spook′y** *adj.* **spook′i·er, spook′i·est**

spool (spōōl) *n.* [< MFr. < MDu. *spoele*] **1.** a cylinder, often hollowed and with a rim at either end, upon which thread, wire, etc. is wound **2.** something like a spool —*vt.* to wind on a spool

spoon (spōōn) *n.* [OE. *spon*, a chip] **1.** a utensil consisting of a small, shallow bowl with a handle, used for eating or stirring food or drinks **2.** something shaped like a spoon, as a shiny, curved fishing lure, usually of metal —*vt.* to take up as with a spoon —*vi.* [Colloq.] to make love, as by kissing or caressing: an old-fashioned term

spoon·bill (-bil′) *n.* **1.** *same as* SHOVELLER **2.** any of various other birds with a bill that is spoon-shaped at the tip

spoon·drift (-drift′) *n.* early form of SPINDRIFT

spoon·er·ism (spōōn′ər iz′m) *n.* [after Rev. W. A. *Spooner* (1844-1930), of Oxford Univ.] an unintentional interchange of sounds in two or more words (Ex.: "a well-boiled icicle" for "a well-oiled bicycle")

spoon·feed (spōōn′fēd′) *vt.* **-fed′, -feed′ing 1.** to feed with a spoon **2.** to pamper; coddle **3.** to treat, instruct, etc. so as to discourage independent thought and action

spoon·ful (-fool′) *n.*, *pl.* **-fuls′** as much as a spoon will hold

spoon·y, spoon·ey (spōō′nē) *adj.* **spoon′i·er, spoon′i·est** [Colloq.] silly or foolish; sentimental —*n.*, *pl.* **spoon′ies** [Colloq.] a spoony person

spoor (spoor, spôr) *n.* [Afrik. < MDu.] the track or trail of a wild animal hunted as game —*vt.*, *vi.* to hunt by following a spoor

spo·rad·ic (spə rad′ik, spo-) *adj.* [< ML. < Gr. *sporadikos* < *sporas*, scattered] **1.** happening from time to time; not regular **2.** appearing singly, apart, or in isolated instances —**spo·rad′i·cal·ly** *adv.*

spo·ran·gi·um (spə ran′jē əm) *n.*, *pl.* **-gi·a** (-ə) [ModL. < *spora* (see ff.) + Gr. *angeion*, vessel] *Bot.* an organ or single cell producing spores —**spo·ran′gi·al** *adj.*

spore (spôr) *n.* [ModL. *spora* < Gr. *spora*, a seed] a small reproductive body, usually a single cell, produced by bacteria, mosses, ferns, certain protozoans, etc. and capable of giving rise to a new individual —*vi.* **spored, spor′ing** to develop spores

spore case *same as* SPORANGIUM

spo·ro- a combining form meaning spore [*sporophyte*]: also, before a vowel, **spor-**

spo·ro·go·ni·um (spôr′ə gō′nē əm) *n.*, *pl.* **-ni·a** (-ə) [ModL.: see SPORO- & -GONIUM] the sporophyte in mosses and liverworts, usually a spore-bearing capsule on a stalk

spo·ro·phyll (spôr′ə fil) *n.* [SPORO- + -PHYLL] a leaf or leaflike part producing one or more sporangia —**spo′ro·phyl′la·ry** (-fil′ə rē) *adj.*

spo·ro·phyte (-fīt′) *n.* [SPORO- + -PHYTE] the asexual spore-bearing phase of some plants: cf. GAMETOPHYTE —**spo′ro·phyt′ic** (-fit′ik) *adj.*

spor·ran (spor′ən) *n.* [ScotGael. *sporan*] a leather pouch or purse, usually fur-covered, worn hanging from the belt in the dress costume of Scottish Highlanders

sport (spôrt) *n.* [short for DISPORT] **1.** any recreational activity; diversion **2.** such an activity requiring bodily exertion and carried on according to a set of rules, whether outdoors, as golf, or indoors, as tenpin bowling **3.** fun or play **4.** *a)* an object of ridicule; laughingstock *b)* a thing or person buffeted about, as though a plaything **5.** [Colloq.] *a)* a person who is sportsmanlike [be a *sport!*] *b)* a person judged according to his ability to take defeat, teasing, etc. [a good (or poor) *sport*] **6.** [Chiefly U.S. Colloq.] a pleasure-loving person **7.** a plant or animal showing some marked variation from the normal type —*vt.* [Colloq.] to wear or display [to *sport* a loud tie] —*vi.* **1.** to play or frolic **2.** *a)* to joke or jest *b)* to trifle or play (*with*) —**in** (or **for**) **sport** in joke or jest —**make sport of** to ridicule —**sport′er** *n.* —**sport′ful** *adj.* —**sport′ful·ly** *adv.*

sport·ing (-iŋ) *adj.* **1.** of, interested in, or taking part in sports **2.** sportsmanlike; fair **3.** having to do with games, races, etc. involving gambling or betting **4.** *Biol.* inclined to mutate —**sport′ing·ly** *adv.*

sporting chance [Colloq.] a fair or even chance

spor·tive (spôr′tiv) *adj.* **1.** fond of or full of sport or merriment **2.** done in fun or play, not in earnest —**spor′tive·ly** *adv.* —**spor′tive·ness** *n.*

sports (spôrts) *adj.* **1.** of or for sports, esp. athletics [*sports day*] **2.** suitable for informal, casual wear

sports car a low, small motor car, typically with seats for two and a high-compression engine

sports·cast (spôrts′kast′) *n.* a radio or TV broadcast of sports news —**sports′cast′er** *n.*

sports·man (-mən) *n.*, *pl.* **-men 1.** a man who is interested in or takes part in sports, esp. in hunting, fishing, etc. **2.** a person who plays fair and can take defeat without complaint or victory without gloating —**sports′man·like′, sports′man·ly** *adj.* —**sports′man·ship′** *n.*

sports·wear (-wer′) *n.* clothes worn while engaging in sports or for informal, casual wear

sports·wom·an (-woom′ən) *n.*, *pl.* **-wom′en** (-wim′ən) a woman who is interested in or takes part in sports

sports·writ·er (-rīt′ər) *n.* a reporter who writes about sports or sports events

sport·y (spôrt′ē) *adj.* **sport′i·er, sport′i·est** [Colloq.] **1.** sportsmanlike **2.** characteristic of a sport or sporting man **3.** loud, flashy, or showy, as clothes —**sport′i·ly** *adv.* —**sport′i·ness** *n.*

spor·ule (spo′rool) *n.* a small spore

spot (spot) *n.* [< or akin to MDu. *spotte*] **1.** a small area differing from the surrounding area, as in colour **2.** a mark, stain, blot, speck, etc. **3.** *a)* a skin blemish, as a pimple *b)* a flaw, as in character; fault **4.** a locality; place [a good fishing *spot*] **5.** shortened form of SPOTLIGHT **6.** [Colloq.] a small quantity; bit [a *spot* of tea] **7.** [Colloq.] a position or job **8.** [Colloq.] a position in a schedule —*vt.* **spot′ted, spot′ting 1.** to mark with spots **2.** to stain; blemish **3.** to place in or on a given spot or spots; locate **4.** *a)* to pick out; recognize [to *spot* someone in a crowd] *b)* to determine the location of (a target, the enemy, etc.) **5.** [Chiefly U.S. Colloq.] to allow as a handicap [I *spotted* him two points] —*vi.* **1.** to become marked with spots **2.** to make a stain, as ink, etc. —*adj.* **1.** *a)* ready; on hand [*spot* cash] *b)* involving immediate payment of cash **2.** made at random or by sampling [a *spot* survey] **3.** *a)* broadcast from the place of occurrence [*spot* news] *b)* inserted between regular radio or TV programmes [a *spot* announcement] —**hit the spot** [Colloq.] to satisfy a craving —**in a** (**bad** or **tight**) **spot** [Colloq.] in trouble —**on the spot 1.** at the place mentioned **2.** at once **3.** [Colloq.] in trouble or in a demanding situation **4.** [U.S. Slang] in danger, esp. of being murdered —**spot′less** *adj.* —**spot′less·ly** *adv.* —**spot′less·ness** *n.*

spot-check (-chek′) *vt.* to check or examine at random or by sampling —*n.* an act or instance of such checking

spot·light (-līt′) *n.* **1.** a strong beam of light focused on a particular person, thing, etc., as on a stage **2.** a lamp used to project such a light, as on a motor car **3.** public notice —*vt.* to focus a spotlight on

spot-on (-on′) *adj.* absolutely correct; very accurate

spot·ted (-id) *adj.* **1.** marked with spots **2.** stained; blemished; sullied

spotted dick a steamed suet pudding containing dried fruit: also **spotted dog**

spotted fever any of various diseases accompanied by fever and skin eruptions

spot·ter (spot′ər) *n.* a person who spots; specif. *a)* a person who watches for, and reports, enemy aircraft *b)* a person who notes down locomotive engine numbers [a train *spotter*]

spot·ty (-ē) *adj.* **-ti·er, -ti·est 1.** having, occurring in, or marked with spots **2.** not uniform or consistent, as in quality; uneven —**spot′ti·ly** *adv.* —**spot′ti·ness** *n.*

spot welding a process in which metal pieces are held together between two electrodes and welded by a powerful surge of current —**spot′-weld′** *vt.*, *vi.* —**spot′-weld′er** *n.*

spous·al (spou′z'l) *n.* [< ESPOUSAL] [often *pl.*] [Now Rare] a marriage ceremony —*adj.* [Now Rare] of marriage

spouse (spous; also, esp. for vt., spouz) *n.* [< OFr. < L. pp. of *spondere*: see SPONSOR] a partner in marriage —*vt.* **spoused, spous′ing** [Archaic] to marry

spout (spout) *n.* [ME. *spute* < *spouten*, to spout] **1.** a lip or projecting tube, as of a teapot, drinking fountain, gutter, by which a liquid is poured or discharged **2.** a stream, jet, etc. as of liquid from a spout **3.** *same as* WATERSPOUT —*vt.* **1.** to shoot out (liquid, etc.) from a spout **2.** to utter in a loud, pompous manner —*vi.* **1.** to shoot out with force in a jet: said of liquid, etc. **2.** to discharge liquid, etc. as from a spout **3.** to spout words, esp. (usually **spout off**) in a hasty or rash way —**up the spout** [Slang] **1.** in pawn **2.** in straits; ruined; lost **3.** pregnant —**spout′er** *n.*

SPQR [L. *S(enatus) P(opulus) q(ue) R(omanus)*] the Senate and the people of Rome

Spr. Sapper

sprag (sprag) *n.* [prob. < Scand., as in Dan. *sprag*, a twig] **1.** a roof prop used in a coal mine **2.** a device for preventing a vehicle from rolling backwards down a slope

sprain (sprān) *vt.* [< ? OFr. *espreindre*, to strain < L. < *ex-*, out + *premere*, to press] to wrench or twist a ligament or muscle of (a joint, as the ankle) without dislocating the bones —*n.* **1.** an act of spraining **2.** an injury resulting from this

sprang (spraŋ) *pt. of* SPRING

sprat (sprat) *n.* [OE. *sprott*] **1.** a small, sardinelike, European fish of the herring family **2.** any of several other small herrings

sprawl (sprôl) *vi.* [OE. *spreawlian*] **1.** *a*) to spread the limbs in a relaxed or awkward position *b*) to sit or lie in such a position **2.** to crawl awkwardly **3.** to spread out in a straggling, irregular fashion as handwriting, a line of men, etc. —*vt.* to cause to sprawl —*n.* a sprawling movement or position —**sprawl'er** *n.* —**sprawl'y** *adj.*

spray¹ (sprā) *n.* [< or akin to MDu. *spraeien*, to spray] **1.** a cloud or mist of fine liquid particles, as of water from breaking waves **2.** *a*) a jet of such particles, as from a spray gun *b*) a device for shooting out such a jet **3.** something likened to a spray [a *spray* of gunfire] —*vt., vi.* **1.** to direct a spray (upon) **2.** to shoot out in a spray —**spray'er** *n.*

spray² (sprā) *n.* [ME.] **1.** a small branch or sprig of a tree or plant, with leaves, berries, flowers, etc. **2.** a design or ornament like this

spray gun a device that shoots out a spray of liquid, as paint or insecticide, by air pressure

spread (spred) *vt.* **spread, spread'ing** [OE. *sprædan*] **1.** to open or stretch out so as to cover more space; unfold; unfurl **2.** to lay out in display **3.** to move apart (the fingers, arms, wings, etc.) **4.** *a*) to distribute over an area; scatter *b*) to distribute among a group **5.** *a*) to distribute in a thin layer; smear *b*) to cover by smearing (*with* something) **6.** to extend or prolong in time **7.** to cause to be widely or more widely known, felt, existent, etc. **8.** to cover or deck (*with* something) **9.** *a*) to set (a table) for a meal *b*) to set (food) on a table **10.** to push apart or farther apart —*vi.* **1.** to extend itself; be expanded **2.** to become distributed **3.** to be made widely or more widely known, felt, etc. **4.** to be pushed apart or farther apart **5.** to admit of being smeared, as butter —*n.* **1.** the act of spreading; extension **2.** *a*) the extent to which something can be spread *b*) the interval between the highest and lowest figures of a set **3.** an expanse; extent [middle-aged *spread*] **4.** *a*) two facing pages of a magazine, etc., treated as a single sheet *b*) printed matter set across a page or several columns of a newspaper, etc. **5.** a cover for a bed; bedspread **6.** any soft substance, as jam, paste, etc. used for spreading on bread **7.** [Colloq.] a meal, esp. one with a wide variety of food **8.** [U.S.] a ranch —**spread oneself** [Colloq.] **1.** to exert oneself in order to make a good impression, etc. **2.** to show off —**spread oneself thin** to try to do too many things at once —**spread'er** *n.*

spread-ea·gle (spred'ē'g'l) *adj.* having the figure of an eagle with the wings and legs spread —*vt.* **-gled, -gling** to stretch out in the form of a spread eagle, as for a flogging

spree (sprē) *n.* [18th-c. slang for earlier *spray* < ?] **1.** a lively, noisy frolic **2.** a drinking bout **3.** a period of unrestrained activity [a shopping *spree*] —**on the spree** taking part in a frolic, drinking bout, etc.

sprig (sprig) *n.* [ME. *sprigge*] **1.** *a*) a little twig or spray *b*) a design or ornament like this **2.** a young fellow; stripling —*vt.* **sprigged, sprig'ging** to decorate with a design of sprigs —**sprig'gy** *adj.* **-gi·er, -gi·est**

spright·ly (sprīt'lē) *adj.* **-li·er, -li·est** [< *spright*, var. of SPRITE + -LY¹] gay, lively, brisk, etc. —*adv.* in a sprightly manner —**spright'li·ness** *n.*

spring (spriŋ) *vi.* **sprang** or **sprung, sprung, spring'ing** [OE. *springan*] **1.** to move suddenly and rapidly; specif., *a*) to leap; bound *b*) to appear suddenly *c*) to be resilient; bounce **2.** to arise as from some source; specif., *a*) to grow or develop *b*) to come into existence [towns *sprang* up] **3.** to become bent, warped, split, etc. [the door has *sprung*] **4.** to rise up above surrounding objects; tower Often followed by *up* —*vt.* **1.** to cause to leap forth suddenly **2.** to cause to snap shut, as by a spring **3.** *a*) to cause to warp, bend, split, etc., as by force *b*) to stretch (a spring, etc.) too far **4.** to make known suddenly [to *spring* a surprise] **5.** [Slang] to organize an escape from jail —*n.* **1.** a springing; specif., *a*) a jump or leap, or the distance so covered *b*) a sudden darting or flying back **2.** *a*) elasticity; resilience *b*) energy or vigour, as in one's walk **3.** a device, as a coil of wire, that returns to its original form after being forced out of shape: used to absorb shock, etc. **4.** *a*) a flow of water from the ground, the source of a stream *b*) any source or origin **5.** *a*) that season of the year when plants begin to grow after lying dormant all winter *b*) any period of beginning **6.** *Naut.* a split or break, as in a mast —*adj.* **1.** of, for, appearing in, or planted in the spring **2.** of or like a spring; elastic; resilient **3.** having, or supported on, springs

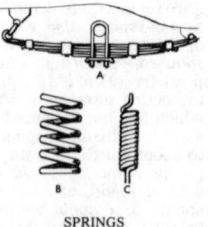

SPRINGS
(A, leaf; B, helical;
C, expansion)

[a *spring* mattress] **4.** coming from a spring [*spring* water] —**spring a leak** to begin to leak suddenly

spring balance a device for measuring weight by the compression or extension of a spiral spring

spring·board (spriŋ'bôrd') *n.* **1.** a flexible, springy board used by acrobats as a takeoff in leaping **2.** *same as* DIVING BOARD **3.** a starting point

spring·bok (-bok') *n., pl.* **-bok', -boks'**: see PLURAL, II, D, 2 [Afrik. < Du. *springen*, to spring + *bok*, a buck] **1.** a South African gazelle that leaps high in the air when startled: also **spring'buck'** (-buk') **2.** [Colloq.] [S-] a native or inhabitant of South Africa

spring chicken 1. [Chiefly U.S.] a young chicken, esp. one only a few months old, used for grilling or frying **2.** [Slang] a young or inexperienced person

spring·clean·ing (-klēn'iŋ) *n.* a thorough cleaning of the interior of a house, etc. as conventionally done in spring

spring·er (-ər) *n.* **1.** a person or thing that springs **2.** *short for* SPRINGER SPANIEL

springer spaniel a breed of field spaniel used for flushing, or springing, game

spring fever the laziness and listlessness that many people feel during the first warm days of spring

spring lock a lock in which the bolt is snapped into place automatically by a spring

spring tide 1. a tide occurring at the new and the full moon, normally the highest tide of the month **2.** any great flow, rush, or flood

spring·time (spriŋ'tīm') *n.* the season of spring: also **spring'tide'** (-tīd')

spring·y (-ē) *adj.* **spring'i·er, spring'i·est 1.** flexible; elastic **2.** having many springs of water —**spring'i·ly** *adv.* —**spring'i·ness** *n.*

sprin·kle (spriŋ'k'l) *vt.* **-kled, -kling** [ME. *sprinklen*] **1.** to scatter (water, salt, etc.) in drops or particles **2.** *a*) to scatter drops or particles upon *b*) to dampen before ironing **3.** to distribute at random —*vi.* **1.** to scatter something in drops or particles **2.** to fall in drops or particles **3.** to rain lightly —*n.* **1.** the act of sprinkling, or a small amount sprinkled **2.** a light rain —**sprin'kler** *n.*

sprin·kling (-kliŋ) *n.* **1.** a small number or amount, esp. when thinly distributed **2.** the act of one that sprinkles

sprint (sprint) *vi.* [< Scand.] to run or race at full speed, esp. for a short distance —*n.* **1.** the act of sprinting **2.** a short race at full speed **3.** a brief period of intense activity —**sprint'er** *n.*

sprit (sprit) *n.* [OE. *spreot*] a pole or spar extended diagonally upwards from a mast to the topmost corner of a fore-and-aft sail

sprite (sprīt) *n.* [< OFr. *esprit* < L. *spiritus*: see SPIRIT] **1.** an elf, pixie, fairy, or goblin **2.** an elflike person

sprit·sail (sprit'sāl', -s'l) *n.* a sail extended by a sprit

sprock·et (sprok'it) *n.* [< ?] **1.** any of the teeth or points, as on the rim of a wheel, arranged to fit into the links of a chain **2.** a wheel fitted with sprockets: in full, **sprocket wheel**

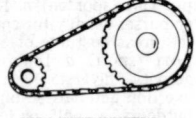

SPROCKET WHEELS

sprout (sprout) *vi.* [OE. *sprutan*] **1.** to begin to grow or germinate; give off shoots or buds **2.** to grow or develop rapidly —*vt.* to cause to sprout or grow —*n.* **1.** a young growth on a plant, as a stem or branch; shoot **2.** a new growth from a bud, rootstock, etc. **3.** any offshoot or scion **4.** [pl.] shortened form of BRUSSELS SPROUTS

spruce¹ (sproōs) *n.* [< OFr. < ML. *Prussia*: prob. because first known as from Prussia] **1.** any of various evergreen trees of the pine family, having slender needles **2.** its wood

spruce² (sproōs) *adj.* **spruc'er, spruc'est** [ME. *Spruce*, Prussia, esp. in phr. *Spruce leather*, fine leather imported from Prussia] neat and trim; smart; dapper —*vt., vi.* **spruced, spruc'ing** to make or become spruce (usually with *up*) —**spruce'ly** *adv.* —**spruce'ness** *n.*

sprung (spruŋ) *pp. & alt. pt. of* SPRING —*adj.* **1.** having the springs broken, overstretched, or loose **2.** provided with or mounted on springs

spry (sprī) *adj.* **spri'er** or **spry'er, spri'est** or **spry'est** [< Scand.] full of life; active, brisk, and agile, esp. though elderly —**spry'ly** *adv.* —**spry'ness** *n.*

spt. seaport

spud (spud) *n.* [prob. < Scand.] **1.** a sharp spade for rooting out weeds, etc. **2.** [Colloq.] a potato —*vt., vi.* **spud'ded, spud'ding** to dig, etc. with a spud —**spud'der** *n.*

spue (spyoō) *vt., vi.* **spued, spu'ing** *same as* SPEW

spume (spyoōm) *n.* [< MFr. < L. *spuma*] foam, froth, or scum —*vt., vi.* **spumed, spum'ing** to foam or froth —**spu'mous, spum'y** *adj.*

spun (spun) *pt. & pp. of* SPIN —*adj.* formed by or as if by spinning

spunk (spuŋk) *n.* [IrGael. *sponc*, tinder < L. *spongia*, sponge] 1. wood or fungus that smoulders when ignited; punk 2. [Colloq.] courage; spirit

spunk·y (spuŋ′kē) *adj.* **spunk′i·er, spunk′i·est** [Colloq.] having spunk; courageous; spirited —**spunk′i·ly** *adv.* —**spunk′i·ness** *n.*

spur (spur) *n.* [OE. *spura*] 1. a pointed device worn on the heel by horsemen and used to urge the horse forward 2. anything that urges or incites; stimulus to action 3. something like a spur; specif., *a)* a spinelike process, as on the wings or legs of certain birds *b)* a spinelike outgrowth of bone, as on the human heel, resulting from injury, disease, etc. *c)* a sharp metal device attached as a weapon to the leg of a gamecock *d)* a short branch or shoot of a tree, etc. 4. a ridge projecting from the main mass of a mountain or mountain range 5. a short side track (**spur track**) connected with the main track of a railway 6. *Bot.* a slender, tubelike structure formed by an extension of one or more petals or sepals, often holding nectar —*vt.* **spurred, spur′ring** 1. to prick with spurs 2. to urge on; incite; stimulate 3. to provide with a spur or spurs —*vi.* 1. to spur one's horse 2. to hurry; hasten —**on the spur of the moment** abruptly and impulsively —**win one's spurs** to gain distinction or honour —**spur′like′** *adj.* —**spur′rer** *n.*

spurge (spurj) *n.* [< MFr. < *espurger*, to purge < L. *expurgare*: see EXPURGATE] any of a genus of plants having a milky juice and small white flowers —*adj.* designating a family of plants, usually with milky juice and diclinous flowers, including the poinsettia, cassava, rubber tree, etc.

spur gear 1. a gearwheel with radial teeth parallel to the axle: also **spur wheel** 2. gearing having this kind of gearwheel: also **spur gearing**

spu·ri·ous (spyoor′ē əs) *adj.* [L. *spurius*] 1. [Now Rare] illegitimate 2. not true or genuine; false; counterfeit —**spu′ri·ous·ly** *adv.* —**spu′ri·ous·ness** *n.*

spurn (spurn) *vt.* [OE. *spurnan*] 1. to push or drive away as with the foot 2. to reject in a scornful way —*n.* 1. a kick 2. scornful treatment or rejection —**spurn′er** *n.*

spurred (spurd) *adj.* having, wearing, or fitted with spurs or spurlike parts

spurt (spurt) *vt.* [OE. *spryttan* < base of *sprutan*, to sprout] to expel suddenly in a stream or gushing flow; squirt; jet —*vi.* 1. to gush forth in a stream or jet 2. to show a sudden, brief burst of energy or increased activity —*n.* 1. a sudden gushing or shooting forth; jet 2. a sudden, brief burst of energy, etc.

sput·nik (spoot′nik, sput′-) *n.* [Russ., lit., co-traveller] an artificial satellite of the earth; specif., [S-] any of those put into orbit by the U.S.S.R. beginning in 1957

sput·ter (sput′ər) *vi.* [Du. *sputteren*] 1. to spit out bits of saliva, food, etc., as when talking excitedly; splutter 2. to talk in an excited, confused way, spitting out one's words 3. to make sharp, sizzling or spitting sounds, as frying fat —*vt.* 1. to spit out (bits or drops) in an explosive manner 2. to utter by sputtering —*n.* 1. the act or noise of sputtering 2. matter thrown out in sputtering 3. hasty, confused utterance —**sput′ter·ing·ly** *adv.*

spu·tum (spyoot′əm) *n.*, *pl.* **spu′ta** (-ə) [< L. < pp. of *spuere*, to SPIT²] saliva, usually mixed with mucus, ejected from the mouth

spy (spī) *vt.* **spied, spy′ing** [< OFr. < OHG. *spehōn*, to examine] to catch sight of; see —*vi.* 1. to watch closely and secretly; act as a spy 2. to look carefully —*n.*, *pl.* **spies** 1. a person who keeps close and secret watch on another or others 2. a person employed by a government to get secret information about the affairs, esp. military affairs, of another government, as of an enemy in wartime —**spy out** to discover or seek to discover by looking carefully

spy·glass (-gläs′) *n.* a small telescope

sq. 1. squadron 2. square

sq. ft., sq. in., square foot, square inch, etc.

squab (skwob) *n.* [prob. < Scand.] 1. a very young pigeon 2. a short, stout person 3. a stuffed cushion or couch —*adj.* short and stout: also **squab′by**

squab·ble (skwob′'l) *vi.* **-bled, -bling** [< Scand.] to quarrel noisily over a small matter; wrangle —*n.* a noisy, petty quarrel; wrangle —**squab′bler** *n.*

squad (skwod) *n.* [< Fr. < Sp. *escuadra*, or It. *squadra*, a square, both ult. < L.: see SQUARE] 1. a small group of soldiers assembled for drill, duty, etc. 2. *a)* any small group of people working together (flying squad) *b)* an athletic or football team —*vt.* **squad′ded, squad′ding** 1. to form into a squad 2. to assign to a squad

squad·ron (-rən) *n.* [< It. < *squadra*: see SQUAD] 1. a group of warships assigned to special duty 2. a unit of cavalry consisting of from two to four troops, etc. 3. in various airforces a unit of a number of aircraft 4. any organized group

squadron leader *see* MILITARY RANKS, table

squails (skwālz) *n.pl.* [< Du *kagel*, a nine pin] a game in which discs are flipped towards a mark in the centre of a board (**squail-board**)

squal·id (skwol′id) *adj.* [< L. < *squalere*, to be foul] 1. foul; filthy 2. wretched; sordid —**squa·lid′i·ty, squal′id·ness** *n.* —**squal′id·ly** *adv.*

squall¹ (skwôl) *n.* [< Scand.] 1. a brief, violent windstorm, usually with rain or snow 2. [Colloq.] trouble or disturbance —*vi.* to storm briefly —**squall′y** *adj.*

squall² (skwôl) *vi., vt.* [ON. *skvala*, to cry out] to cry or scream loudly or harshly —*n.* a harsh, shrill cry or loud scream —**squall′er** *n.*

squal·or (skwol′ər) *n.* [L., foulness] a being squalid; filth and wretchedness

squa·ma (skwā′mə) *n.,* *pl.* **-mae** (-mē) [L., a scale] a scale or scalelike part of an animal or plant —**squa′mate** (-māt), **squa′mous** (-məs), **squa′mose** (-mōs) *adj.*

squan·der (skwon′dər) *vt., vi.* [prob. < dial. *squander*, scatter] to spend or use (money, time, etc.) wastefully

square (skwer) *n.* [< OFr., ult. < L. *ex-*, out + *quadrare*, to square < *quadrus*, a square < *quattuor*, four] 1. a plane figure having four equal sides and four right angles 2. anything shaped like or nearly like this 3. an open area bounded by several streets, used as a park, plaza, etc. 4. an instrument having two sides that form a 90° angle, used for drawing or testing right angles 5. a solid piece with at least one face that is square [a cake cut into *squares*] 6. the product of a number multiplied by itself [9 is the *square* of 3] 7. [Slang] a person who is square (*adj.* 11) —*vt.* **squared, squar′ing** 1. *a)* to make into a square *b)* to make into any rectangle 2. to test or adjust with regard to straightness or evenness 3. to bring to or near to the form of a right angle [*square* your shoulders] 4. *a)* to settle; adjust [to *square* accounts] *b)* to settle the accounts of 5. to make equal [to *square* the score of a game] 6. to bring into agreement [to *square* a statement with the facts] 7. to mark off (a surface) in squares 8. to bring into the correct position, as with reference to a line, course, etc. 9. to multiply (a quantity) by itself 10. to determine the square that is equal in area to (a figure) —*vi.* to fit; agree; accord (*with*) —*adj.* 1. *a)* having four equal sides and four right angles *b)* more or less cubical, as a box 2. forming a right angle, or having a rectangular part or cross section 3. correctly adjusted; straight, level, even, etc. 4. *a)* leaving no balance; balanced *b)* even in score; tied 5. just; fair; honest 6. clear; direct; straightforward [a *square* refusal] 7. *a)* designating or of a unit of surface measure in the form of a square with sides of a specified length *b)* given or stated in terms of such measure 8. having a shape broad for its length or height, with a solid, sturdy appearance [a *square* build] 9. designating a number that is the product of another number multiplied by itself 10. [Colloq.] satisfying; substantial [a *square* meal] 11. [Slang] old-fashioned or unsophisticated —*adv.* 1. honestly; fairly 2. so as to be or form a square; at right angles 3. directly; exactly 4. so as to face 5. firmly; solidly —**get square with** to settle with, esp. with a creditor —**on the square** 1. at right angles 2. [Colloq.] honest(ly), fair(ly), genuine(ly), etc. —**square away** to bring a ship's yards around so as to sail before the wind —**square off** [Chiefly U.S.] to get into position for attacking or for defending —**square the circle** 1. to find a square equal in area to a circle: an insoluble problem 2. to do or attempt something that seems impossible —**square up** 1. to make a settlement, as by payment 2. to assume a posture of opposition (*to* an adversary) —**square′ly** *adv.* —**square′ness** *n.* —**squar′er** *n.* —**squar′ish** *adj.*

square·bash·ing (-bash′iŋ) *n.* [Slang] military drill as performed on the parade ground

square bracket *same as* BRACKET (n. 5)

square dance a lively dance with various steps and figures, the couples forming squares, etc. —**square′-dance′** *vi.* **-danced′, -danc′ing**

square deal [Colloq.] any dealing that is honest and fair

squared paper *same as* GRAPH PAPER

square knot a reef knot

square leg *Cricket* 1. a fielding position on the batsman's left 2. the person who fields in this position

square measure a system of measuring area, esp. the system in which 10 000 square centimetres = 1 square metre or that in which 144 square inches = 1 square foot: see TABLE OF WEIGHTS AND MEASURES in Supplement

square-rigged (-rigd′) *adj.* having square sails as principal sails —**square′-rig′ger** *n.*

square root the number that is multiplied by itself to produce a given number [3 is the *square root* of 9]

square sail a four-sided sail

square shooter [U.S. Colloq.] an honest, just person

square-shoul·dered (-shōl′dərd) *adj.* having shoulders jutting out squarely from the body's axis

squar·son (skwär'sən) *n.* [< SQU(IRE) +(P)ARSON] a squire or landed proprietor who is also a clergyman: used humorously

squash¹ (skwosh) *vt.* [< OFr. *esquasser*, ult. < L. *ex-*, intens. + pp. of *quatere*, to shake] **1.** *a*) to crush into a soft or flat mass *b*) to press tightly or too tightly **2.** to suppress; quash **3.** [Colloq.] to silence (another) crushingly —*vi.* **1.** to be squashed by pressure, etc. **2.** to make a sound of squashing **3.** to force one's way; squeeze —*n.* **1.** something squashed; crushed mass **2.** the act or sound of squashing **3.** either of two games (**squash rackets, squash tennis**) played in a four-walled court with rackets and a rubber ball **4.** a drink made from fruit juice diluted with water —*adv.* with a squash

squash² (skwosh) *n.* [< Algonquian] [U.S.] **1.** the fleshy fruit of various plants of the gourd family, cooked as a vegetable **2.** a plant, usually a trailing one, bearing this fruit

squash·y (-ē) *adj.* **-i·er, -i·est 1.** soft and wet; mushy **2.** easily squashed, as overripe fruit —**squash'i·ly** *adv.* —**squash'i·ness** *n.*

squat (skwot) *vi.* **squat'ted, squat'ting** [< MFr. *esquatir*, ult. < L. *ex-*, intens. + *coactus*, pp. of *cogere*, to force] **1.** to crouch, with the knees bent and the weight on the balls of the feet **2.** to crouch close to the ground, as an animal **3.** to settle on land, or occupy property, without any right or title to it **4.** to settle on public land under government regulation so as to get title to it —*adj.* **1.** crouched in a squatting position **2.** short and thick: also **squat'ty** —*n.* **1.** the act or position of squatting **2.** [Colloq.] premises that are, or could be, occupied by squatters —**squat'ly** *adv.* —**squat'ness** *n.*

squat·ter (-ər) *n.* **1.** a person or animal that squats **2.** someone who illegally occupies property **3.** [Aust.] *a*) a person who occupies land as a tenant of the Crown *b*) a sheep farmer

squaw (skwô) *n.* [< Algonquian] a N American Indian woman, esp. a wife

squawk (skwôk) *vi.* [echoic] **1.** to utter a loud, harsh cry, as a parrot **2.** [Colloq.] to complain or protest —*vt.* to utter in a squawk —*n.* **1.** a squawking cry **2.** [Colloq.] a complaint —**squawk'er** *n.*

squawk box [Slang] an intercom speaker or loudspeaker

squaw man a white man married to a N American Indian woman, esp. one living with her tribe

squeak (skwēk) *vi.* [prob. akin to ON. *skvakka*, to gurgle] **1.** to make or utter a short, sharp, high-pitched sound or cry —*vt.* to utter with a squeak —*n.* a short, shrill sound or cry —**narrow** (or **close**) **squeak** [Colloq.] a narrow escape —**squeak through** (or by, etc.) [Colloq.] to barely manage to succeed, survive, etc. —**squeak'er** *n.* —**squeak'i·ly** *adv.* —**squeak'y** *adj.* **-i·er, -i·est**

squeal (skwēl) *vi.* [prob. akin to ON. *skvala*: see SQUALL²] **1.** to make or utter a long, shrill sound or cry **2.** [Slang] to inform against, or tell on, someone —*vt.* to utter with a squeal —*n.* a long, shrill sound or cry —**squeal'er** *n.*

squeam·ish (skwēm'ish) *adj.* [< Anglo-Fr. *escoimous*, orig., shy] **1.** easily nauseated **2.** easily shocked or offended; prudish **3.** too fastidious —**squeam'ish·ly** *adv.* —**squeam'ish·ness** *n.*

squee·gee (skwē'jē) *n.* [prob. akin to SQUEEZE] a T-shaped tool with a blade of rubber, etc., for wiping liquid off a surface —*vt.* **-geed, -gee·ing** to use a squeegee on

squeeze (skwēz) *vt.* **squeezed, squeez'ing** [OE. *cwysan*, to squeeze] **1.** to press hard or closely, esp. from two or more sides **2.** *a*) to press so as to extract liquid, etc. [to *squeeze* oranges] *b*) to extract (liquid, etc.) by pressure **3.** to force (*into, out,* etc.) as by pressing **4.** to get or extort by force or unfair means **5.** to oppress with taxes, etc. **6.** to put pressure on (someone) to do something, as to pay money **7.** to embrace closely; hug —*vi.* **1.** to yield to pressure [a wet sponge *squeezes* easily] **2.** to exert pressure **3.** to force one's way by pushing or pressing (*in, out, through,* etc.) —*n.* **1.** a squeezing or being squeezed **2.** *a*) a close embrace; hug *b*) a firm handclasp **3.** the state of being closely pressed or packed; crush **4.** a difficult situation; pinch **5.** a quantity extracted by squeezing **6.** [Colloq.] pressure exerted, as in extortion: esp. in **put the squeeze on** —**squeeze through** (or by, etc.) [Colloq.] to barely manage to succeed, survive, etc. —**squeez'er** *n.*

squelch (skwelch) *n.* [prob. echoic] **1.** the sound of liquid, mud, etc. moving under pressure or suction, as in wet shoes **2.** [Colloq.] a suppressing or silencing; esp., a crushing retort, rebuke, etc. —*vt.* **1.** to crush as by stamping upon; squash **2.** [Colloq.] to suppress or silence completely and crushingly —*vi.* **1.** to walk heavily through mud, etc., making a splashing sound **2.** to make such a sound —**squelch'er** *n.*

squib (skwib) *n.* [prob. echoic] **1.** a firework that hisses before exploding **2.** a short, witty writing that criticizes, etc. —*vt., vi.* **squibbed, squib'bing 1.** to shoot off (a squib) **2.** to put out a squib (against); criticize —**a damp squib** a plan or project that comes to nothing

squid (skwid) *n., pl.* **squids, squid:** see PLURAL, II, D, 1 [prob. akin to SQUIRT] any of various cephalopod molluscs having a slender body and ten arms, two arms being much longer than the others

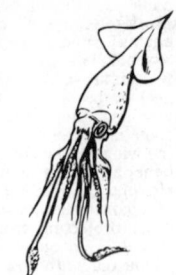

SQUID
(small species to 22 cm long)

squif·fy (skwif'ē) *adj.* **-fi·er, -fi·est** [< dial. *skew-whiff*, askew, tipsy + -y³] [Slang] drunk; intoxicated

squig·gle (skwig''l) *n.* [SQU(IRM) + (W)IGGLE] **1.** a short curved or wavy line; curlicue **2.** an illegible or meaningless scribble —*vt.* **-gled, -gling** to form into or write as a squiggle or squiggles —*vi.* **1.** to make squiggles **2.** to squirm along; wriggle —**squig'gly** *adj.*

squil·gee (skwē'jē; skwil'jē *is a sp. pron.*) *n., vt.* **-geed, -gee·ing** *sailors' var. of* SQUEEGEE

squill (skwil) *n.* [< L. < Gr. *skilla*] **1.** *a*) the dried bulb of a plant of the lily family, formerly used in medicine *b*) this plant **2.** a strain of this plant having red bulbs that yield a powder used chiefly in rat poison

squinch (skwinch) *n.* [var. of *scunch* < LME. *scuncheon* < OFr. *escoinson* < *es-*, EX- & *coin*, corner] an interior corner support, as a small arch supporting a weight, as of a spire resting on it: also **squinch arch**

squint (skwint) *vi.* [see ASQUINT] **1.** to peer with the eyes partly closed, as in too strong light **2.** to look sidelong or askance **3.** to be cross-eyed —*vt.* to keep (the eyes) partly closed in peering —*n.* **1.** a squinting **2.** an inclination **3.** a being cross-eyed **4.** [Colloq.] a glance, often sidelong —*adj.* **1.** looking sidelong or askance **2.** cross-eyed —**squint'er** *n.* —**squint'y** *adj.*

squire (skwīr) *n.* [< OFr. *esquier*: see ESQUIRE] **1.** a young man of high birth who attended a knight **2.** in England, a country gentleman who owns much land, esp. the main landowner in a rural community **3.** an attendant; esp., a man escorting a woman —*vt., vi.* to act as a squire (to)

squire·ar·chy (skwīr'är kē) *n.* [< prec. + -ARCHY, after HIERARCHY] **1.** country gentry or large landowners collectively **2.** government by such persons Also sp. **squir'ar·chy**

squir·een (skwīr ēn') *n.* [SQUIRE + Ir. dim. suffix -*een* < Gaelic -*in*] [Ir.] a small landowner; petty squire

squirm (skwurm) *vi.* [prob. echoic, infl. by WORM] **1.** to twist and turn the body in a snakelike movement; wriggle; writhe **2.** to show or feel distress, as from embarrassment —*n.* a squirming —**squirm'y** *adj.* **-i·er, -i·est**

squir·rel (skwir'əl) *n., pl.* **-rels, -rel:** see PLURAL, II, D, 1 [< OFr., ult. < L. *sciurus* < Gr. < *skia*, a shadow + *oura*, tail] **1.** any of a group of small, tree-dwelling rodents with heavy fur and a long, bushy tail, esp. the grey squirrel or the red squirrel **2.** the fur of some of these animals —*vt.* **-relled, -rel·ling** to store or hide (*away*)

squirt (skwurt) *vt.* [prob. < or akin to LowG. & Du. *swirtjen*, to squirt] **1.** to shoot out (a liquid) in a jet or narrow stream **2.** to wet with liquid thus shot out —*vi.* to be squirted out; spurt —*n.* **1.** a device for squirting, as a syringe **2.** a squirting **3.** a small amount of squirted liquid; jet **4.** [Colloq.] a small or young person, esp. one who is impudent —**squirt'er** *n.*

squirt gun a toy gun that shoots a stream of water

squish (skwish) *vi.* to make a soft, splashing sound when walked on, squeezed, etc. —*vt.* [Colloq.] to squeeze into a soft mass; squash —*n.* **1.** a squishing sound **2.** [Colloq.] a squashing; squash —**squish'y** *adj.*

squit (skwit) *n.* [*akin to* SQUIRT] [Slang] an insignificant, often contemptible person

Sr *Chem.* strontium

Sr *the symbol for* steradian

Sr. **1.** Senior **2.** [Sp.] *Señor* **3.** Sister

Sra. [Sp.] *Señora*

S.R.C. Science Research Council

S.R.N. State Registered Nurse

S.R.O. standing room only

Srta. [Sp.] *Señorita*

SS. [L. *Sancti*] Saints

S.S., SS, S/S steamship

S.S.A.F.A. Soldiers', Sailors', and Airmen's Family Association

SSE, S.S.E., s.s.e. south-southeast

S.S.R., SSR Soviet Socialist Republic

S.S.R.C. Social Science Research Council

SST Supersonic Transport

SSW, S.S.W., s.s.w. south-southwest

-st *same as* -EST

St. **1.** Saint **2.** Strait **3.** Street

St., st. **1.** statute(s) **2.** stratus

st. **1.** stone **2.** *Cricket* stumped (by)

stab (stab) *n.* [ME. *stabbe*, prob. < var. of *stubbe*, stub] **1.**

a wound made by piercing with a knife, dagger, etc. **2.** a thrust, as with a knife **3.** a sudden, sharp hurt or pain —*vt.* **stabbed, stab'bing 1.** to pierce or wound as with a knife **2.** to thrust (a knife, etc.) into something **3.** to go into in a sharp, thrusting way —*vi.* **1.** to make a thrust or piercing wound as with a knife **2.** to feel like a stabbing knife: said of pain —**make** (**or take**) **a stab at** to make an attempt at —**stab in the back** to harm (someone) by treachery —**stab'ber** *n.*

sta·bile (stā'bil *also, and for n. usually,* -bil) *adj.* [L. *stabilis:* see STABLE[1]] stable; stationary —*n.* a large stationary abstract sculpture, usually a construction of metal, wire, wood, etc.

sta·bil·i·ty (stə bil'ə tē) *n., pl.* **-ties 1.** a being stable, or fixed; steadiness **2.** firmness of character, purpose, etc. **3.** resistance to change **4.** the capacity of an object to return to equilibrium

sta·bi·lize (stā'bə līz') *vt.* **-lized', -liz'ing 1.** to make stable, or firm **2.** to keep from changing, as in price **3.** to give stability to (an aircraft, ship, etc.) with a stabilizer —*vi.* to become stabilized —**sta'bi·li·za'tion** *n.*

sta·bi·liz·er (-lī'zər) *n.* a person or thing that stabilizes; specif., *a)* an aerofoil to keep an aircraft steady in flight, specif. the horizontal part of the tail *b)* a gyrostabilizer or other device to steady a ship in rough waters *c)* any additive used in a substance to keep it stable, retard deterioration, etc.

sta·ble[1] (stā'b'l) *adj.* **-bler, -blest** [< OFr. < L. *stabilis* < *stare*, to stand] **1.** *a)* not easily moved or put off balance; firm; steady *b)* not likely to break down, fall apart, etc. **2.** firm in character, purpose, etc.; steadfast **3.** not likely to change or be affected adversely; enduring **4.** capable of returning to equilibrium **5.** *Chem., Physics* not readily decomposing —**sta'bly** *adv.*

sta·ble[2] (stā'b'l) *n.* [< OFr. < L. *stabulum* < *stare*, to stand] **1.** *a)* a building in which horses or cattle are sheltered and fed *b)* a group of animals kept in such a building **2.** *a)* all the racehorses of one owner *b)* the people who take care of and train these horses **3.** [Colloq.] all the athletes, performers, etc. under one management —*vt., vi.* **-bled, -bling** to keep or be kept in a stable

sta·ble·boy (-boi') *n.* a boy who works in a stable: also **sta'ble·lad**

sta·ble·mate (-māt') *n.* **1.** a horse from the same stable **2.** someone who has the same lodgings, club, school, etc. as someone else Also **stable companion**

stac·ca·to (stə kät'ō) *adj.* [It., detached] **1.** *Music* with distinct breaks between successive tones **2.** made up of abrupt, distinct elements or sounds —*adv.* so as to be staccato —*n., pl.* **-tos** something staccato

stack (stak) *n.* [ON. *stakkr*] **1.** a large pile of straw, hay, etc., esp. one neatly arranged, as in the form of a cone **2.** any somewhat orderly pile **3.** a number of arms, esp. three rifles, leaned together on end to form a cone **4.** *a)* a grouping of chimney flues *b) same as* SMOKESTACK **5.** a measure of wood (30.58 m³, 108 cubic feet) **6.** [Colloq.] a large amount —*vt.* **1.** to pile in a stack **2.** to load with stacks **3.** to assign (aircraft) to various altitudes for circling before landing **4.** to arrange in advance underhandedly for a desired result [to *stack* a jury, to *stack* the cards] —**stack up 1.** to come to as a total **2.** [Chiefly U.S.] to stand in comparison (*with* or *against*) —**stack'a·ble** *adj.* —**stack'er** *n.*

stacked (stakt) *adj.* [Chiefly U.S. Slang] having a full, shapely figure; curvaceous: said of a woman

stacked heel a heel on a woman's shoe of several layers alternating in shade

stack·up (stak'up') *n.* an arrangement of circling aircraft at various altitudes awaiting their turn to land

sta·di·um (stā'dē əm) *n., pl.* **-di·a** (-ə) *also, and for sense 2 usually,* **-di·ums** [L. < Gr. *stadion*, fixed standard of length] **1.** in ancient Greece and Rome, a track for footraces, about 220 metres long, with tiers of seats for spectators **2.** a large, open structure for football, athletics, etc. with tiers of seats for spectators

staff[1] (stäf) *n., pl.* **staffs;** *also, for senses* 1 & 5, **staves** [OE. *stæf*] **1.** a stick, rod, or pole used as for support, a weapon, a symbol of authority, a measure, etc. **2.** a group of people assisting a leader **3.** a group of officers serving a commanding officer as advisers and administrators **4.** a specific group of workers [a teaching *staff*] **5.** *Music* the five horizontal lines and four intermediate spaces on which music is written —*adj.* of, by, for, or on a staff —*vt.* to provide with a staff, as of workers

staff[2] (staf) *n.* [< G. *staffieren*, to fill out, decorate] a building material of plaster and fibre, used for temporary decorative work

staff nurse a nurse who is second in command of a ward to a sister

staff officer an officer on a staff

staff of life bread, regarded as the basic food

Staffs. Staffordshire

staff sergeant *see* MILITARY RANKS, table

stag (stag) *n., pl.* **stags, stag:** *see* PLURAL, II, D, 1 [OE.

stagga] **1.** *a)* a full-grown male deer *b)* the male of various other animals **2.** a male animal castrated in maturity **3.** *a)* a man who attends a social gathering unaccompanied by a woman *b)* [U.S.] a social gathering for men only **4.** *Finance* a speculator who applies to buy shares in a new company, hoping to sell immediately at a profit —*adj.* for men only

stag beetle any of a family of large beetles of which the male has long, branched mandibles

stage (stāj) *n.* [< OFr. *estage*, ult. < L. pp. of *stare*, to stand] **1.** a platform or dock **2.** a workmen's scaffold **3.** a level, floor, or storey **4.** *a)* a platform on which plays, speeches, etc. are presented *b)* any area, as in an arena theatre, in which actors perform *c)* the whole working section of a theatre, including the acting area, the backstage area, etc. *d)* the theatre as a profession (with *the*) **5.** the scene of an event or events **6.** a stopping point on a route, esp. formerly for a stagecoach **7.** the distance between two such points **8.** *shortened form of* STAGECOACH **9.** a period or degree in a process of development, change, etc. **10.** any of two or more propulsion units used in sequence as the rocket of a spacecraft, etc. **11.** *Radio* an element or part in a complex arrangement —*vt.* **staged, stag'ing 1.** to present as on a stage **2.** to plan and carry out [stage an attack] —*vi.* to be presented on the stage, as a play —**by easy stages** a little at a time, with many stops to rest

stage·coach (-kōch') *n.* formerly, a horse-drawn coach moving by steps along a set route

stage·craft (-kräft') *n.* skill in writing or staging plays

stage door an outside door leading to the backstage part of a theatre, used by actors, production staff, etc.

stage fright nervousness felt when appearing as a speaker or performer before an audience

stage·hand (-hand') *n.* a person who helps to set and remove scenery and furniture, operate the curtain, etc. for a stage performance

stage·man·age (-man'ij) *vt.* **-aged, -ag·ing 1.** to be stage manager for **2.** to arrange or display with dramatic effect, esp. as if from behind scenes

stage manager an assistant to the director of a play, in overall charge backstage during an actual performance

stag·er (-ər) *n.* [STAG(E) + -ER] **1.** a veteran, human or animal (usually with *old*) **2.** [Archaic] an actor

stage-struck (-struk') *adj.* having an intense desire to act or otherwise work in the theatre

stage whisper 1. a loud whisper by an actor on the stage, thought of as being heard only by the audience and not by his fellow actors **2.** any similar loud whisper made at a social gathering

stag·fla·tion (stag flā'shən) *n.* [< *stag(nation)*, see STAGNATE + (IN)FLATION] a period of high inflation and no increase in productivity

stag·ger (stag'ər) *vi.* [ON. *stakra*, to totter] **1.** to totter, sway, or reel, as from a blow, fatigue, drunkenness, etc. **2.** to waver in purpose, etc. —*vt.* **1.** to make stagger **2.** to affect strongly, as with astonishment **3.** to set alternately, as on either side of a line; make zigzag **4.** to arrange (duties, holidays, etc.) so as to avoid crowding —*n.* **1.** a staggering, tottering, etc. **2.** a staggered arrangement **3.** [*pl., with sing. v.*] a disease or toxic condition of horses, cattle, etc., marked by loss of coordination, staggering, etc. —**stag'ger·er** *n.* —**stag'ger·ing** *adj.* —**stag'ger·ing·ly** *adv.*

stag·ing (stā'jiŋ) *n.* **1.** a temporary structure used for support; scaffolding **2.** the business of operating stagecoaches **3.** travel by stagecoach **4.** the act or process of presenting a play on the stage **5.** shelving used for plants in greenhouses

stag·nant (stag'nənt) *adj.* [< L. prp. of *stagnare*, to stagnate] **1.** not flowing or moving **2.** foul from lack of movement: said of water, etc. **3.** lacking activity, etc.; sluggish —**stag'nan·cy** (-nən sē) *n.* —**stag'nant·ly** *adv.*

stag·nate (stag nāt', stag'nāt) *vi., vt.* **-nat·ed, -nat·ing** [< L. pp. of *stagnare*, to stagnate < *stagnum*, a swamp] to become or make stagnant —**stag·na'tion** *n.*

stag·ni·col·ous (stag ni'kəl əs) *adj.* [ModL.< L. *stagnum*, pool + L. *colere*, to inhabit + -OUS] inhabiting standing water or swamps

stag party a party for men only, esp. one held for a bachelor just before he is married

stag·y (stā'jē) *adj.* **stag'i·er, stag'i·est 1.** of the stage; theatrical **2.** affected; not real Also **stage'y** —**stag'i·ly** *adv.* —**stag'i·ness** *n.*

staid (stād) *archaic pt. & pp. of* STAY[3] —*adj.* sober; sedate —**staid'ly** *adv.* —**staid'ness** *n.*

stain (stān) *vt.* [< OFr. < L. *dis-*, from + *tingere*, to colour] **1.** to spoil the appearance of by discolouring or spotting **2.** to disgrace or dishonour (one's character, reputation, etc.) **3.** to change the appearance of (wood, glass, etc.) by applying a dye, pigment, etc. **4.** to treat (material for microscopic study) with a colouring matter, as to make transparent parts visible —*vi.* to impart or take a stain —*n.* **1.** a discolouration, spot, etc. resulting from staining **2.** a moral blemish; dishonour **3.** a dye, pigment, etc. for staining wood or for staining material for microscopic study —**stain'a·ble** *adj.* —**stain'er** *n.*

stain·less (-lis) *adj.* 1. without a stain 2. that resists staining, rusting, etc. 3. made of stainless steel —**stain'less·ly** *adv.*

stainless steel steel alloyed with chromium, etc., virtually immune to rust and corrosion

stair (ster) *n.* [OE. *stæger*] 1. [*usually pl.*] a flight of steps; staircase 2. one of a series of steps leading from one level to another

stair·case (-kās') *n.* a flight of stairs with a supporting structure and a handrail: also **stair'way'** (-wā')

stair·well (-wel') *n.* a vertical shaft (in a building) containing a staircase: also **stair well**

staith, staithe (stāth) *n.* [ME. *stathe* < OE. *stæth*, shore] [Dial.] a wharf equipped to load and unload (coal, etc.) from railway wagons into vessels

stake (stāk) *n.* [OE. *staca*] 1. a length of wood or metal pointed at one end for driving into the ground, as for marking a boundary 2. *a*) the post to which a person was tied for execution by burning *b*) such execution 3. any of the posts fitted into sockets at the edge of a flat truck or railway wagon to help hold a load 4. [*often pl.*] something, esp. money, risked in a wager, game, or contest 5. [*often pl.*] a prize given a winner, as in a race 6. [*pl., with sing. v.*] a race in which a prize is offered 7. a share or interest, as in property 8. [U.S. Colloq.] grubstake —*vt.* **staked, stak'ing** 1. *a*) to mark the boundaries of as with stakes *b*) to establish (a claim) thus 2. to support (a plant, etc.) by tying to a stake 3. to tether to a stake 4. to risk; gamble 5. [U.S. Colloq.] *a*) to furnish with money or resources *b*) to grubstake —**at stake** being risked —**pull up stakes** [U.S. Colloq.] to change one's place of residence, business, etc. —**stake out** [U.S.] to station (police, etc.) in an attempt to capture a suspected criminal at (a specified place)

stake·hold·er (-hōl'dər) *n.* one who holds money, etc. bet by others and pays it to the winner

Sta·kha·no·vism (stə khä'nə viz'm) *n.* [< A. G. *Stakhanov*, Soviet miner] in the Soviet Union, a system of working in teams to get higher production through greater efficiency, with bonuses, etc. given for success —**Sta·kha'no·vite'** (-vīt') *adj., n.*

sta·lac·tite (stə lak'tīt') *n.* [ModL. < Gr. *stalaktos*, dripping < *stalassein*, to drip] an icicle-shaped deposit hanging from the roof of a cave, formed by evaporation of dripping water full of lime —**stal·ac·tit·ic** (stal'ək tit'-ik) *adj.*

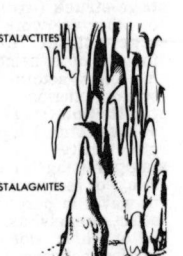

STALACTITES

‡**sta·lag** (shtä'lak; *E.* stal'ag) *n.* [G *Sta(mm)lag(er)* < *Stamm*, a base + *Lager*, a camp] a German prisoner-of-war camp for soldiers from the ranks

sta·lag·mite (stal'əg mīt') *n.* [ModL. < Gr. *stalagmos*, a dropping < *stalassein*, to drip] a cone-shaped deposit built up on the floor of a cave by dripping water full of lime, often from a stalactite above —**stal·ag·mit·ic** (stal'əg mit'-ik) *adj.*

STALAGMITES

stale (stāl) *adj.* **stal'er, stal'est** [prob. < LowG.] 1. having lost freshness; specif., *a*) flat; tasteless *b*) hard and dry, as bread *c*) having little oxygen; stagnant [*stale* air] *d*) beginning to decay, as eggs 2. no longer new or interesting; trite [a *stale* joke] 3. ineffective, weakened, etc. from too much or too little activity —*vt., vi.* staled, stal'ing to make or become stale —**stale'ly** *adv.* —**stale'ness** *n.*

stale·mate (stāl'māt') *n.* [OFr. *estal*, a fixed location + *mate* (to checkmate)] 1. *Chess* any situation in which a player cannot move without placing his king in check: it results in a draw 2. a deadlock; standstill —*vt.* -**mat'ed, -mat'ing** to bring into a stalemate

Sta·lin·ism (stä'lin iz'm) *n.* the theory and form of government associated with Joseph Stalin (1879-1953), Soviet statesman & premier

stalk¹ (stôk) *vi.* [OE. *stealcian* < *stealc*, steep] 1. *a*) to walk in a stiff, haughty, or grim manner *b*) to advance or spread grimly [plague *stalks* across the land] 2. to pursue or approach game, etc. stealthily —*vt.* 1. to pursue or approach (game, etc.) stealthily 2. to stalk through —*n.* 1. a slow, stiff, or haughty stride 2. a stalking of game, etc. —**stalk'er** *n.*

stalk² (stôk) *n.* [akin to OE. *stela*, stalk] 1. any stem or stemlike part 2. *Bot. a*) the main stem or axis of a plant *b*) a lengthened part on which an organ grows or is supported, as the petiole of a leaf 3. *Zool.* a lengthened support for an animal organ or for a whole body —**stalked** *adj.* —**stalk'i·ness** *n.* —**stalk'less** *adj.* —**stalk'y** *adj.* -**i·er, -i·est**

stalk·ing-horse (stôk'iŋ hôrs') *n.* 1. a horse, or a figure of one, used as cover by a hunter 2. anything used to hide intentions, schemes, etc. 3. [Chiefly U.S.] a person put forth as a political candidate until the candidate actually preferred is announced

stall¹ (stôl) *n.* [OE. *steall*] 1. *a*) formerly, a stable *b*) a compartment for one animal in a stable 2. any of various compartments, sections, etc.; specif., *a*) a booth, etc. where goods are sold, as at a fair *b*) an enclosed seat in a church *c*) a theatre seat near the stage *d*) a small, enclosed space, as for taking a shower *e*) any of the spaces marked off for parking cars in a garage, etc. 3. a protective sheath for a finger 4. a stopping or standing still due to failure to work properly 5. the tendency of an aircraft to drop or go out of control because of loss of lift and increase of drag —*vt., vi.* 1. to put, keep, or be kept in a stall 2. to stick fast, as in mud 3. to stop as from failure to work properly, as a motor car 4. to put (an aircraft) into a stall, or go into a stall

stall² (stôl) *vi.* [< obs. *stale*, a decoy < Anglo-Fr. *estale*] to act or speak evasively so as to deceive or delay —*vt.* to put off or delay by stalling (usually with *off*) —*n.* [Colloq.] any trick used in stalling

stal·lion (stal'yən) *n.* [OFr. *estalon* < Gmc. *stal*, a stall] an uncastrated male horse, esp. one used as a stud

stal·wart (stôl'wərt) *adj.* [OE. *stælwyrthe* < *stathol*, foundation + *wyrthe*, worth] 1. sturdy; robust 2. brave; valiant 3. resolute; firm —*n.* 1. a stalwart person 2. a firm supporter of a cause —**stal'wart·ly** *adv.* —**stal'wart·ness** *n.*

sta·men (stā'mən) *n.*, *pl.* -**mens, stam·i·na** (stam'ə nə) [ModL. < L., a thread, orig., warp] a pollen-bearing organ in a flower, made up of a slender stalk (*filament*) and a pollen sac (*anther*)

stam·i·na (stam'ə nə) *n.* [L., *pl.* of *stamen*: see STAMEN] resistance to fatigue, illness, hardship, etc.; endurance

stam·i·nate (stam'ə nāt') *adj.* 1. having stamens but no pistils, as male flowers 2. having stamens

stam·mer (stam'ər) *vt., vi.* [OE. *stamerian*] to speak or say with pauses that one cannot control, often with rapid repetitions of syllables or initial sounds, as because of excitement, embarrassment, or mental conflicts —*n.* the act or habit of stammering —**stam'mer·er** *n.* —**stam'mer·ing·ly** *adv.*

stamp (stamp) *vt.* [ME. *stampen*] 1. to bring (the foot) down forcibly on the ground, a floor, etc. 2. *a*) to strike down on forcibly with the foot *b*) to beat, crush, etc. by treading on heavily *c*) to remove by stamping the feet [*stamped* the snow from his boots] *d*) to pulverize (ore, etc.) by grinding or crushing 3. *a*) to imprint or cut out (a design, lettering, etc.) by bringing a form forcibly against a material *b*) to cut out or make as by applying a die to metal 4. to impress or imprint with a design, etc., as to decorate, show ownership, etc. 5. to impress distinctly or indelibly [a face *stamped* with grief] 6. to put an official seal or a stamp on (a document, letter, etc.) 7. to characterize or reveal distinctly, as if by imprinting —*vi.* 1. to bring the foot down forcibly on the ground, etc. 2. to walk with loud, heavy steps —*n.* 1. a stamping 2. a machine, tool, etc. for stamping or crushing ore, etc. 3. *a*) any implement, as a die, that is brought forcibly against something to mark or shape it *b*) the mark or form so made 4. a mark, seal, etc. used to show officially that a tax has been paid, authority given, etc. 5. *a*) a small piece of paper, distinctively imprinted and usually gummed, sold by a government and required to be put on a letter, parcel, document, etc. to show that the prescribed fee has been paid *b*) any similar piece of paper, issued by an organization, business, etc. [trading *stamps*] 6. a characteristic sign or impression [the *stamp* of truth] 7. character; kind; class; type —**stamp on** subdue; suppress —**stamp out** 1. to crush or put out (a fire, etc.) by treading on forcibly 2. to crush or put down (a revolt, etc.) —**stamp'er** *n.*

stamp-col·lect·ing (-kə lekt'iŋ) *n.* same as PHILATELY —**stamp'-col·lec'tor** *n.*

stam·pede (stam pēd') *n.* [AmSp. *estampida* < Sp. < *estampar*, to stamp < Gmc.] 1. a sudden, headlong running away of a herd of frightened horses, cattle, etc. 2. a confused, headlong rush of many people 3. any sudden, spontaneous mass movement —*vi.* -**ped'ed, -ped'ing** to move in a stampede —*vt.* to cause to stampede —**stam·ped'er** *n.*

stamp·ing ground (stam'piŋ) [Colloq.] a regular or favourite gathering place or resort

stance (stans, stäns) *n.* [< OFr., ult. < L. prp. of *stare*, to stand] 1. a particular way of standing, esp. in regard to placing the feet 2. an attitude adopted for dealing with a situation

stanch (stänch) *vt., vi., adj.* see STAUNCH

stan·chion (stän'shən, stan'-) *n.* [< OFr. < *estance*: see STANCE] 1. an upright bar, post, etc. used as a support 2. a restraining device in a stall, fitted loosely about a cow's neck —*vt.* 1. to support with stanchions 2. to confine with a stanchion

stand (stand) *vi.* **stood, stand'ing** [OE. *standan*] 1. *a*) to be or stay upright on the feet *b*) to be or stay upright on its base, bottom, etc., as a vase *c*) to grow upright: said of plants **2.** to rise to an upright position, as from sitting **3.** *a)* to take, or be in, a (specified) upright position *[stand at ease]* *b)* to take, keep, or be in a (specified) position or attitude *[I stand opposed]* **4.** to have a (specified) height when standing *[he stands six feet]* **5.** *a)* to be situated *b)* to stay where situated **6.** to gather and remain: said of a liquid **7.** to remain unchanged, valid, etc. *[the law still stands]* **8.** to be in a (specified) condition *[they stood in awe, he stands to lose]* **9.** to be of a (specified) rank, degree, etc. *[to stand first on the list]* **10.** to remain resolute *[to stand firm]* **11.** to make resistance **12.** *a)* to halt *b)* to remain stationary **13.** to show the (specified) relative position of those involved *[the score stands at 2 to 1]* **14.** to be a candidate, as for office; run **15.** *Naut.* to take or hold a certain course —*vt.* **1.** to make stand; put upright **2.** to put up with; endure **3.** to be unaffected by; withstand *[to undergo [to stand trial]* **5.** to do the duty of *[stand watch]* **6.** [Colloq.] *a)* to bear the cost of (a meal, etc.), as when treating *b)* to treat (a person) to food, drink, etc. —*n.* **1.** a standing; esp., a halt or stop; specif., *a)* a stopping to counterattack, resist, etc., as in retreat *b)* a halt by a touring theatrical company to give a performance; also, the place stopped at **2.** the place where one stands or is supposed to stand; position **3.** a view, opinion, etc., as on an issue **4.** a structure to stand or sit on; specif., *a)* a raised platform for a band, etc. *b)* [*often pl.*] a set of benches in tiers, as for spectators *c)* [U.S.] the place where a witness testifies in a courtroom **5.** *a)* a booth, stall, etc. where goods are sold *b)* a parking space reserved for taxicabs, etc. *c)* **6.** a rack, small table, etc. for holding things **7.** a standing growth of trees or plants —**make a stand 1.** to take a position for defence or opposition **2.** to support a definite position, opinion, etc. —**stand a chance** to have a chance —**stand by 1.** to be near and ready to act as needed **2.** to aid or support **3.** to keep (a promise, etc.) **4.** to be present, esp. as an onlooker —**stand corrected** to admit correction by someone else —**stand for 1.** to be a symbol for or sign of; represent **2.** to be a candidate for (office) **3.** [Colloq.] to put up with; endure —**stand in for** to substitute for —**stand off 1.** to keep at a distance **2.** to put off or evade **3.** to discharge (an employee) temporarily —**stand on 1.** to be founded on **2.** to insist upon (ceremony, one's rights, etc.) —**stand one's ground** to maintain one's position —**stand out 1.** to project **2.** to show up clearly **3.** to be prominent or outstanding **4.** to refuse to give in —**stand surety** to go bail for (someone) —**stand to 1.** to abide by or adhere to **2.** *Mil.* to be on the alert in expectation of enemy attack —**stand up 1.** to rise to or be in a standing position **2.** to prove valid, durable, etc. **3.** [Slang] to fail to keep an engagement with —**stand up for** to defend; support —**stand up to** to confront fearlessly —**stand'er** *n.*

stand·ard (stan'dərd) *n.* [OFr. *estendard*, ult. < Gmc.] **1.** a flag, banner, etc. used as an emblem or symbol of a leader, people, military unit, etc. **2.** something established as a rule or basis of comparison in measuring or judging quantity, quality, value, etc. **3.** a usage or practice that is generally accepted or followed; criterion *[moral standards]* **4.** an upright support **5.** a piece of music that has remained popular for many years **6.** a tree or shrub with a single, tall stem —*adj.* **1.** used as or conforming to an established rule, model, etc. **2.** generally accepted as reliable or authoritative *[standard reference books]* **3.** regular or typical; ordinary *[standard procedure]* **4.** of or in accord with speech or writing that is more or less formal; not slang, dialectal, obsolete, etc. *[standard English]*

stand·ard-bear·er (-ber'ər) *n.* **1.** a person carrying the standard, or flag, as of a military group **2.** a leader of a movement, political party, etc.

standard gauge 1. a width of 56½ inches (143.8 cm) between the rails of a railway track **2.** such a track, or a locomotive or railway carriage for it —**stand'ard-gauge'** *adj.*

stand·ard·ize (stan'dər dīz') *vt.* -**ized'**, -**iz'ing 1.** to make standard or uniform; make the same in all cases **2.** to test by or adjust to a standard —**stand'ard·i·za'tion** *n.* —**stand'-ard·iz'er** *n.*

standard lamp an electric light fixed to a tall support standing on the floor

standard of living level of daily living, as of a nation, class, or person, with regard to the adequacy of necessities and comforts

standard time the time in any of the 24 time zones, each an hour apart, into which the earth is divided: it is based on distance east or west of Greenwich, of a line of longitude passing through or near the centre of the area

stand·by (stand'bī') *n.,* *pl.* -**bys' 1.** a person or thing that can always be depended on, or one ready to be used if needed **2.** a person waiting to board an aeroplane, etc. if space becomes available —*adj.* of, for, or being a standby —**on standby** ready or waiting as a standby

stand-in (stand'in') *n.* **1.** a person who stands in a performer's place in films, etc. while lights, cameras, etc. are being adjusted **2.** any substitute for another

stand·ing (stan'diŋ) *n.* **1.** the act, state, or position of one that stands **2.** status, rank, or reputation *[in good standing]* **3.** the time that something lasts; duration *[of long standing]* —*adj.* **1.** that stands; upright **2.** in or from a standing position *[a standing jump]* **3.** not flowing; stagnant **4.** lasting; permanent **5.** stationary **6.** not in use; idle, as a machine

standing army a permanent army

standing order 1. an order, remaining in effect indefinitely until cancelled or modified **2.** [*often pl.*] a rule or order governing procedure in a formally constituted body, as parliament **3.** an instruction to a bank requesting regular payments, as for insurance premiums, mortgage payments, etc.: also **banker's order**

standing room room in which to stand, esp. when there are no vacant seats, as in a theatre

standing stones unhewn stones, standing singly or in groups, as at Stonehenge, erected in prehistoric days, possibly as centres of worship

standing wave an oscillatory motion with a definite wavelength and having stationary, regular spaced points where there is no motion

stand·off (stand'of') *n.* **1.** a standing off or being stood off **2.** an equalizing effect **3.** [U.S.] a tie or draw in a contest —*adj.* **1.** that stands off **2.** *same as* STANDOFFISH

stand·off·ish (stand'of'ish) *adj.* reserved and cool; aloof —**stand'off'ish·ly** *adv.* —**stand'off'ish·ness** *n.*

stand·pipe (-pīp') *n.* a large vertical pipe or cylindrical tank for storing water

stand·point (-point') *n.* the point or position from which something is seen or judged; point of view

stand·still (-stil') *n.* a stop, halt, or cessation

stand-up (-up') *adj.* **1.** upright; erect **2.** done, taken, etc. in a standing position **3.** designating or of a comedian who delivers monologues

stan·hope (stan'hōp, -əp) *n.* [after F. *Stanhope*, 19th-c. Brit. clergyman] a light, open carriage with two or four wheels and usually one seat

stank (staŋk) *alt. pt. of* STINK

stan·na·ry (stan'ər ē) *n.,* *pl.* -**ries** [ML. *stannaria* < LL. *stannum*, tin] a region of tin mines and tinworks; specif., [*usually pl.*] such a region in Devon and Cornwall

stan·nic (stan'ik) *adj.* [< LL. *stannum*, tin + -IC] of or containing tin, specif. with a valence of four

stan·nous (-əs) *adj.* [< LL. *stannum*, tin + -OUS] of or containing tin, specif. with a valence of two

stan·za (stan'zə) *n.* [It., room, ult. < L. *stare*, to stand] a group of lines of verse, usually four or more and regular in pattern, forming one of the divisions of a poem or song —**stan·za·ic** (-zā'ik) *adj.*

sta·pe·li·a (stə pē'lē ə) *n.* [ModL. after Jan Bode van *Stapel* (died 1636), Du. botanist & physician] any of various cactuslike African plants with bad-smelling flowers

sta·pes (stā'pēz) *n.,* *pl.* **sta'pes, sta·pe·des** (stə pē'dēz, stā'-pə dēz') [ModL. < ML., a stirrup, prob. < Gmc.] *Anat.* a small, stirrup-shaped bone, the innermost of the three bones in the middle ear

staph (staf) *n.* *shortened form of* STAPHYLOCOCCUS

staph·y·lo·coc·cus (staf'ə lō kok'əs) *n.,* *pl.* -**coc'ci** (-kok'sī) [ModL. < Gr. *staphylē*, bunch of grapes + -COCCUS] any of a genus of spherical bacteria that generally occur in clusters or chains and cause pus to form in abscesses, etc. —**staph'y·lo·coc'cal** (-kok''l), **staph'y·lo·coc'cic** (-kok'-sik) *adj.*

sta·ple¹ (stā'p'l) *n.* [< OFr. < MDu. *stapel*, mart] **1.** a chief commodity made, grown, etc. in a particular place **2.** a chief item or element **3.** raw material **4.** any common, regularly stocked item of trade, as salt, flour, etc. **5.** the fibre of cotton, wool, etc. with regard to length and fineness —*adj.* **1.** regularly stocked **2.** produced or consumed regularly and in quantity **3.** chief; main *[a staple industry]* —*vt.* -**pled, -pling** to sort (wool, cotton, etc.) according to staple —**sta'pler** *n.*

sta·ple² (stā'p'l) *n.* [OE. *stapol*, a post] **1.** a U-shaped piece of metal with sharp-pointed ends, driven into a surface to hold a hook, wire, etc. in place **2.** a similar piece of thin wire driven through papers, etc. so that the ends bend over as a binding —*vt.* -**pled, -pling** to fasten with a staple or staples —**sta'pler** *n.*

star (stär) *n.* [OE. *steorra*] **1.** any heavenly body seen as a point of light in the night sky; specif., *Astron.* any self-luminous, gaseous, spheroidal heavenly body, as the sun, seen (except for the sun) as a fixed point of light **2.** a flat figure with usually five or six projecting points, representing a star **3.** a mark, emblem, etc. resembling such a figure, used as an award, insigne, etc. **4.** an asterisk **5.** *a)* *Astrol.* a planet, etc. regarded as influencing human fate *b)* [*often pl.*] fate; destiny **6.** a person who excels, esp. in a sport **7.** a leading actor or actress —*vt.* **starred, star'ring 1.** to decorate with stars **2.** to mark with a star or stars as a grade of quality **3.** to mark with an asterisk **4.** to present (a performer) in a leading role —*vi.* **1.** to excel, esp. in a sport **2.** to have a leading role —*adj.* **1.** excelling [a star athlete] **2.** of a star or stars —**star'less** *adj.* —**star'like'** *adj.*

star·board (stär'bərd, -bôrd') *n.* [< OE. < *steoran*, to steer (with a large oar used on the ship's right side) + *bord*, board] the right-hand side of a ship or aircraft as one faces forwards, towards the bow —*adj.* of or on the starboard —*vt., vi.* to move or turn (the helm) to the starboard side

starch (stärch) *n.* [ult. < OE. *stearc*, stiff] **1.** a white, tasteless, odourless food substance found in potatoes, grain, etc.: it is a complex carbohydrate ($C_6H_{10}O_5)_n$ **2.** a powdered form of this, used in laundering to stiffen cloth, etc. **3.** [*pl.*] starchy foods **4.** stiff formality —*vt.* to stiffen as with starch —**starch'a·ble** *adj.* —**starch'less** *adj.*

starch·y (stär'chē) *adj.* **starch'i·er, starch'i·est 1.** of, containing, or like starch **2.** stiffened with starch **3.** formal; unbending —**starch'i·ly** *adv.* —**starch'i·ness** *n.*

star-crossed (stär'krost') *adj.* [see STAR (*n.* 5)] ill-fated

star·dom (-dəm) *n.* **1.** the status of a star of stage, screen, etc. **2.** such stars collectively

stare (ster) *vi.* **stared, star'ing** [OE. *starian*] to look with a steady, fixed gaze, eyes wide open, as in wonder, curiosity, dullness, etc. —*vt.* to inspect or affect in a given way by staring —*n.* a staring look —**stare down** to stare back at (another) until he looks away —**stare one in the face** to be pressing or inescapable; obvious —**star'er** *n.*

star·fish (stär'fish') *n.*, *pl.* **-fish', -fish'es:** see FISH a small sea animal with a hard, spiny skeleton and five or more arms or rays arranged like the points of a star

star·gaze (-gāz') *vi.* **-gazed', -gaz'ing 1.** to gaze at the stars **2.** to daydream —**star'gaz'er** *n.*

stark (stärk) *adj.* [OE. *stearc*] **1.** *a)* stiff or rigid, as a corpse *b)* harsh; severe **2.** sharply outlined or prominent [one *stark* tree] **3.** bleak; desolate **4.** *a)* emptied; stripped *b)* totally naked **5.** grimly blunt; not softened, embellished, etc. [*stark* realism] **6.** sheer; utter [*stark* terror] —*adv.* in a stark way; esp., utterly [*stark* mad] —**stark'ly** *adv.* —**stark'ness** *n.*

stark·ers (-ərz) *adj.* [Slang] stark-naked

star·let (stär'lit) *n.* **1.** a small star **2.** a young actress being promoted as a possible future star

star·light (-līt') *n.* light from the stars

star·ling (stär'liŋ) *n.* [OE. *stærlinc*, dim. of *stær*, starling] any of a family of short-tailed, dark-coloured birds, esp. the **common starling,** with iridescent plumage, of Europe, N America, Australia, etc.

star·lit (stär'lit') *adj.* lighted by the stars

Star of David a six-pointed star formed of two equilateral triangles: a symbol of Judaism

star prisoner a convict serving his first prison term

star·ry (stär'ē) *adj.* **-ri·er, -ri·est 1.** set or marked with stars **2.** shining like stars; bright **3.** star-shaped **4.** lighted by or full of stars **5.** of, from, or like stars —**star'ri·ness** *n.*

star·ry-eyed (-īd') *adj.* with the eyes sparkling in a glow of wonder, romance, visionary dreams, etc.

Stars and Stripes the red, white, and blue flag of the United States, with 13 stripes and 50 stars

STAR OF DAVID

Star-Span·gled Banner (stär'spaŋ'g'ld) the United States national anthem

star-stud·ded (-stud'əd) *adj.* **1.** covered with many stars **2.** containing many leading entertainers [the cast was *star-studded*]

start (stärt) *vi.* [OE. *styrtan* & cognate ON. *sterta*] **1.** to make a sudden, involuntary movement, as when startled **2.** to become displaced, loose, warped, etc. **3.** to stick out or seem to stick out [eyes *starting* in fear] **4.** *a)* to go into action or motion; begin to do something or go somewhere *b)* to make or have a beginning; commence **5.** to be among the beginning entrants in a race, players in a game, etc. **6.** to spring into being, activity, etc. —*vt.* **1.** to make move suddenly; rouse or flush (game) **2.** to displace, loosen, warp, etc. **3.** *a)* to enter upon; begin doing, etc. *b)* to set into motion, action, etc. **4.** to introduce (a topic, etc.) **5.** to cause to be among those starting in a race, game, etc. —*n.* **1.** a sudden, brief shock or fright **2.** a sudden, startled movement; leap, jerk, etc. **3.** [*pl.*] brief bursts of activity: usually in **by fits and starts** *a)* a part that is loosened, warped, etc. *b)* the resulting break or gap **5.** the act of starting, or beginning **6.** *a)* the place or time of a beginning; starting point *b)* a lead or other advantage, as the beginning of a race **7.** an opportunity to begin a career, etc. —**start in** to begin a task, activity, etc. —**start out** (or **off**) to begin a journey, action, etc. —**start up 1.** to spring up **2.** to cause (an engine, etc.) to begin running

start·er (-ər) *n.* a person or thing that starts; specif., *a)* the first in a series, as the first course of a meal *b)* one starting in a race, etc. *c)* one giving the signal to start *d)* any of various devices for starting an internal-combustion engine

starting gate a movable barrier that lifts automatically at the start of a horse race

starting handle a crank that can be inserted into the engine of a motor car to turn the engine over and start the car

starting price the odds offered on a horse or greyhound immediately before the start of the race

starting stalls a movable set of stalls with gates that open simultaneously at the start of a horse race

star·tle (stärt'l) *vt.* **-tled, -tling** [< ME. freq. of *sterten*, to start] to surprise, frighten, or alarm suddenly; esp., to make jump, jerk, etc. as from sudden fright —*vi.* to be startled —*n.* a startled reaction —**star'tler** *n.* —**star'tling** *adj.* —**star'tling·ly** *adv.*

star turn the principal performer in an entertainment, esp. in a variety show

starve (stärv) *vi.* **starved, starv'ing** [OE. *steorfan*, to die] **1.** *a)* to die from lack of food *b)* to suffer or get weak from hunger *c)* [Colloq.] to be very hungry **2.** to suffer great need (with *for*) [*starving* for affection] —*vt.* **1.** to cause to starve **2.** to force by starving [to *starve* an enemy into submission —**star·va'tion** *n.*

starve·ling (-liŋ) *n.* a starving person or animal —*adj.* **1.** starving **2.** impoverished

stash (stash) *vt.* [prob. a blend of STORE & CACHE] [Colloq.] to put or hide in a secret or safe place —*n.* [U.S.Slang] **1.** a place for hiding things **2.** something hidden away

sta·sis (stā'sis, stas'is) *n.*, *pl.* **-ses** (-sēz) [ModL. < Gr., a standing] **1.** *a)* a stoppage of the flow of a bodily fluid, as of blood *b)* reduced peristalsis of the intestines **2.** a state of equilibrium or stagnancy

-stat (stat) [< ModL. < Gr. *-statēs*] a combining form meaning stationary, making stationary [*thermostat*]

state (stāt) *n.* [< OFr. < L. *status* < pp. of *stare*, to stand] **1.** a set of circumstances or attributes characterizing a person or thing at a given time; condition [a *state* of poverty] **2.** a particular mental or emotional condition [a *state* of bliss] **3.** condition as regards structure, form, etc. [liquid *state*] **4.** *a)* social status; esp., high rank *b)* ceremonious display; pomp **5.** [*sometimes* S-] *a)* a body of people politically organized under one government within a definite territory *b)* the authority represented by such a body of people **6.** [*sometimes* S-] any of the political units together constituting a federal government, as in the U.S., Australia, etc. **7.** the territory of a state (senses 5*a* & 6) **8.** civil government [church and *state*] **9.** the sphere of highest governmental authority [matters of *state*] —*adj.* **1.** ceremonial **2.** [*sometimes* S-] of the government or a state —*vt.* **stat'ed, stat'ing 1.** to set or establish by specifying [the *stated* hour] **2.** to set forth or express in a specific, definite, or formal way [to *state* one's objections, *stating* a musical theme] —**in** (or **into**) **a state** [Colloq.] in (or into) an agitated emotional condition —**lie in state** to be displayed formally to the public before burial —**the States** the United States of America —**stat'a·ble** *adj.* —**state'less** *adj.*

state apartment a public room in a palace used for social receptions on ceremonial occasions

state·craft (-kräft') *n.* the ability of a statesman

state·house (-hous') *n.* the official meeting place of the legislature of a State of the U.S.: also **state house** or **state capitol**

state·ly (-lē) *adj.* **-li·er, -li·est** dignified, imposing, grand, or the like —**state'li·ness** *n.*

stately home a large, usually historic, house, esp. one open to the public

state·ment (-mənt) *n.* **1.** *a)* the act of stating *b)* the thing stated or said **2.** *a)* a summary of a financial account *b)* a listing of charges for goods, etc.

State Registered Nurse a nurse who had completed extensive training and has passed a State examination qualifying her to perform complete nursing services

state·room (stāt'rōōm') *n.* **1.** a private cabin on a ship **2.** *same as* STATE APARTMENT

state school any school which is maintained by the state and in which education is free

state·side (stāt'sīd') *adj.* [Chiefly U.S. Colloq.] of or having to do with the U.S. (as viewed from abroad) —*adv.* [Chiefly U.S. Colloq.] in, to, or towards the U.S.

states·man (stāts'mən) *n.*, *pl.* **-men** a person who shows wisdom and skill in conducting state affairs or dealing with public issues, or one experienced in the business of government —**states'man·like', states'man·ly** *adj.* —**states'man·ship'** *n.*

state socialism the theory, doctrine, or practice of an economy planned and controlled by the state, based on state ownership of banks, utilities, basic industries, etc.

stat·ic (stat'ik) *adj.* [< ModL. < Gr. *statikos*, causing to stand < *histanai*, to cause to stand] **1.** acting through weight only: said of the pressure exerted by a motionless body **2.** of masses, forces, etc. at rest or in equilibrium: opposed to DYNAMIC **3.** at rest; inactive; stationary **4.** *Elec.* designating, of, or producing stationary electrical charges, as from friction **5.** *Radio* of or having to do with static Also **stat'i·cal** —*n. a)* electrical discharges in the atmosphere that interfere with radio or TV reception, etc. *b)* interference or noises produced by such discharges —**stat'i·cal·ly** *adv.*

static electricity electricity at rest, as opposed to dynamic or current electricity

stat·ics (-iks) *n.pl.* [*with sing. v.*] [see prec.] the branch of mechanics dealing with bodies, masses, or forces at rest or in equilibrium

sta·tion (stā'shən) *n.* [< OFr. < L. < pp. of *stare*, to stand] **1.** the place where a person or thing stands or is located, esp. an assigned post, position, etc. [a guard's *station*, a police *station*] **2.** in Australia, a sheep run or cattle ranch **3.** *a)* a regular stopping place, as on a bus route or railway *b)* the building or buildings at such a place **4.** social standing or position **5.** a place equipped to transmit or receive radio waves; esp., the studios, technical installations, etc. of an establishment for radio or television transmission —*vt.* to assign to a station; post

sta·tion·ar·y (stā'shə nər ē) [< L. < *statio:* see STATION] **1.** not moving or movable; fixed **2.** unchanging in condition, value, etc. **3.** not migratory or itinerant —*n., pl.* **-ar·ies** a person or thing that is stationary

stationary engineer a person who operates and maintains stationary engines, such as steam boilers, turbines, etc.

stationary wave *same as* STANDING WAVE

sta·tion·er (stā'shə nər) *n.* [< ML. *stationarius* < L., STATIONARY] a person who sells office supplies, greeting cards, some books, etc.

Stationer's Hall the hall of the old Company of Stationers who formerly registered every book, etc. published in Britain

sta·tion·er·y (-nər ē) *n.* [see prec. & -ERY] writing materials; specif., paper and envelopes used for letters

Stationery Office in Britain, the government department responsible for the supply of stationery and the publication of all official reports, etc.

station house a building used as a station, esp. by police or firemen, or as a railway station

sta·tion·mas·ter (stā'shən mäs'tər) *n.* an official in charge of a railway station

station sergrant a police sergeant in charge of a police station

station wagon [U.S.] an estate car

stat·ism (stāt'iz'm) *n.* the doctrine or practice of vesting economic control and planning in a centralized state government —**stat'ist** *n., adj.*

sta·tis·tic (stə tis'tik) *adj.* rare var. of STATISTICAL —*n.* a statistical item or element

sta·tis·ti·cal (-ti k'l) *adj.* of, having to do with, consisting of, or based on statistics —**sta·tis'ti·cal·ly** *adv.*

stat·is·ti·cian (stat'is tish'ən) *n.* an expert or specialist in statistics

sta·tis·tics (stə tis'tiks) *n.pl.* [< G. < ModL. *statisticus* < L. *status:* see STATE] **1.** facts or data of a numerical kind, assembled and classified so as to present significant information **2.** [*with sing. v.*] the science of compiling such facts

sta·tor (stāt'ər) *n.* [ModL. < L. < pp. of *stare*, to stand] the fixed part, as the housing, of a motor, dynamo, etc.

stat·o·scope (stat'ə skōp') *n.* [< Gr. *statos*, standing + -SCOPE] a highly sensitive aneroid barometer, esp. one used to show the altitude of aircraft

stat·u·ar·y (stat'yoo wər ē) *n.* **-ar·ies** **1.** statues collectively **2.** the art of making statues —*adj.* of or suitable for statues

stat·ue (stach'oo, -tyoo) *n.* [< OFr. < L. < *statuere*, to place < *stare*, to stand] the form of a person or animal carved in stone, wood, etc., modelled in clay, etc., or cast in plaster, bronze, etc., esp. when done in the round

stat·u·esque (stach'oo wesk', stə'tyoo-) *adj.* like a statue; specif., *a)* tall and well-proportioned *b)* having a stately grace and dignity —**stat'u·esque'ly** *adv.* —**stat'u·esque'ness** *n.*

stat·u·ette (-wet') *n.* a small statue

stat·ure (stach'ər) *n.* [OFr. < L. *statura* < *statuere:* see STATUE] **1.** the height of the body in a natural standing position **2.** growth or level of attainment, esp. as worthy of esteem [moral *stature*]

sta·tus (stāt'əs) *n., pl.* **-tus·es** [L.: see STATE] **1.** condition or position with regard to law [the *status* of a minor] **2.** *a)* position; rank [high *status*] *b)* high position; prestige [seeking *status*] **3.** state or condition, as of affairs

status quo (kwō') [L., lit., the state in which] the existing state of affairs: also **status in quo**

status symbol a possession, practice, etc. regarded as a mark of social status, esp. of high social status

stat·ute (stach'oot, sta'tyoot) *n.* [< OFr. < LL. < L. pp. of *statuere:* see STATUE] **1.** an established rule **2.** *a)* a law passed by a legislative body and set forth in a formal document *b)* such a document

statute book a book or other record of the body of statutes of a particular jurisdiction

statute law law established by a legislative body

statute mile a unit of measure (5280 feet, 1.609 km): see MILE

statute of limitations a statute limiting the period within which a specific legal action may be taken

stat·u·to·ry (sta'tyoo tər ē, -trē; stach'oo-) *adj.* **1.** of, or having the nature of, a statute **2.** fixed, authorized, or established by statute **3.** declared by statute to be punishable: said of an offence

staunch (stônch, stänch) *vt.* [OFr. *estanchier*, ult. < L. *stans:* see STANCE] **1.** to stop or check (the flow of blood or of tears, etc.) from (a wound, opening, etc.) **2.** *a)* to stop or lessen (a drain of resources, etc.) *b)* to stop up (a source of leakage, etc.) —*vi.* to cease flowing —*adj.* **1.** watertight; seaworthy [a *staunch* ship] **2.** firm; steadfast [a *staunch* supporter] **3.** strong; solidly made Also **stanch** For the *adj.*, **staunch** is now the prevailing form; for the *v.*, usage is about evenly divided between **staunch** and **stanch** —**staunch'ly** *adv.* —**staunch'ness** *n.*

stave (stāv) *n.* [ME., taken as sing. of *staves*, pl. of *staf*, STAFF] **1.** *a)* any of the thin, shaped strips of wood, metal, etc. set edge to edge to form the wall of a barrel, bucket, etc. *b)* any similar slat, bar, rung, etc. **2.** a stick or staff **3.** a set of lines of a poem or song; stanza **4.** *Music same as* STAFF —*vt.* **staved** or **stove, stav'ing** **1.** to puncture or smash, esp. by breaking in staves **2.** to furnish with staves —*vi.* to be or become stove in, as a boat —**stave in** to break or crush inwards —**stave off** to ward off or hold off, as by force, cleverness, etc.

STAVE

stave rhyme the alliterative rhyme found in poetry, esp. old Germanic poetry

staves (stāvz) *n.* **1.** *alt. pl. of* STAFF **2.** *pl. of* STAVE

stay¹ (stā) *n.* [OE. *stæg*] a heavy rope or cable, usually of wire, used as a brace, as for a mast of a ship; guy —*vt.* **1.** to brace or support with stays **2.** to put (a ship) on the other tack —*vi.* to tack: said of a ship

stay² (stā) *n.* [MFr. *estaie* < Frank.] **1.** a support; prop **2.** a strip of stiffening material used in a corset, shirt collar, etc. —*vt.* **1.** to support, or prop up **2.** to comfort in spirit **3.** to cause to rest (*on, upon, or in*)

stay³ (stā) *vi.* **stayed** or *archaic* **staid, stay'ing** [< Anglo-Fr. < OFr. *ester* < L. *stare*, to stand] **1.** to continue in the place or condition specified; remain; keep [to *stay* at home, to *stay* healthy] **2.** to live, dwell, or reside, esp. temporarily **3.** to stop; halt **4.** to pause; wait; delay **5.** [Colloq.] to continue or endure; last **6.** [Colloq.] to keep up (*with* another contestant in a race, etc.) —*vt.* **1.** to stop, halt, or check **2.** to hinder, impede, or detain **3.** to postpone or delay (legal action) **4.** to satisfy for a time (thirst, appetite, etc.) **5.** *a)* to remain through (often with *out*) [to *stay* the week (out)] *b)* to be able to last through [to *stay* the distance] —*n.* **1.** *a)* a stopping or being stopped *b)* a halt, check, or pause **2.** a postponement in legal action [a *stay* of execution] **3.** the action of remaining, or the time spent, in a place [a long *stay* in Spain] —**stay for** [Colloq.] remain waiting for —**stay put** [Colloq.] to remain in place or unchanged

stay-at-home (-ət hōm') *adj.* domesticated; untravelled —*n.* a person who is unadventurous

staying power ability to last or endure; endurance

stay·mak·er (-māk'ər) *n.* [STAY² + MAKER] a corset maker

stay·sail (-sāl', -s'l) *n.* a sail, esp. a triangular sail, fastened on a stay

STC [India] State Trading Corporation

STD. **1.** [L. *Sacrae Theologiae Doctor*] Doctor of Sacred Theology **2.** Subscriber Trunk Dialling

Ste. [Fr. *Sainte*] Saint (female)

stead (sted) *n.* [OE. *stede*] the place or position of a person or thing as filled by a substitute or successor [he came in my *stead*] —**stand (one) in good stead** to give (one) good use, service, etc.

stead·fast (sted'fäst', -fəst) *adj.* [OE. *stedefæste*] **1.** firm, fixed, or established **2.** not changing or wavering; constant —**stead'fast'ly** *adv.* —**stead'fast'ness** *n.*

stead·ing (-iŋ) *n.* [ME. *steding*] *same as* FARMSTEAD

stead·y (sted'ē) *adj.* **stead'i·er, stead'i·est** [see STEAD & -Y²] **1.** that does not shake, totter, etc.; firm; stable **2.** constant, regular, or continuous; not changing, faltering, etc. [a *steady* gaze] **3.** constant in behaviour, loyalty, etc. **4.** habitual or regular [a *steady* customer] **5.** not easily excited; calm and controlled [*steady* nerves] **6.** sober; staid; reliable **7.** keeping almost upright, as in a rough sea: said of a ship —*interj.* keep calm! —*vt., vi.* **stead'ied, stead'y·ing** to make or become steady —*n.* [Colloq.] one's regular sweetheart —**go steady** [Colloq.] to be sweethearts —**stead'i·ly** *adv.* —**stead'i·ness** *n.*

stead·y-state (-stāt') *adj.* of a system, etc. that does not change with time or that maintains a state of relative equilibrium

stead·y-state theory a theory of cosmology holding that as the universe expands, new matter is continuously created

steak (stāk) *n.* [ON. *steik* < base of *steikja*, to roast on a spit] a slice of meat, esp. beef, or of a large fish, cut thick for grilling or frying

steak·house (-hous′) *n.* a restaurant that specializes in steaks

steak tar·tare (tär tär′) [*tartare*, pseudo-Fr. for TARTAR: hence, steak in Tartar style] raw sirloin steak minced and mixed with chopped onion, raw egg, salt, and pepper, and eaten uncooked

steal (stēl) *vt.* **stole, stol′en, steal′ing** [OE. *stælan*] **1.** to take (another's property, etc.) dishonestly, esp. in a secret manner **2.** to take slyly, surreptitiously, etc. [to *steal* a look] **3.** to gain slyly or artfully [he *stole* her heart] **4.** to be the outstanding performer in (a scene, act, etc.), esp. in a subordinate role **5.** to move, put, or convey stealthily (*in, into, from, away,* etc.) —*vi.* **1.** to be a thief **2.** to move, pass, etc. stealthily, quietly, etc. —*n.* [U.S. Colloq.] something obtained at an unusually low cost; a bargain —**steal a march on** to obtain an advantage, esp. by a trick —**steal′er** *n.*

stealth (stelth) *n.* [ME. *stelthe* < base of *stelen*, to steal] secret, furtive, or artfully sly action or behaviour —**stealth′·i·ly** *adv.* —**stealth′i·ness** *n.* —**stealth′y** *adj.* **stealth′i·er, stealth′i·est**

steam (stēm) *n.* [OE.] **1.** orig., a vapour **2.** *a)* water as converted into a vapour or gas by being heated to the boiling point: used for heating, as a source of power, etc. *b)* the power supplied by steam under pressure *c)* [Colloq.] driving force; energy **3.** condensed water vapour; mist —*adj.* **1.** using steam; heated, operated, etc. by steam **2.** containing or conducting steam —*vi.* **1.** to give off steam or a vapour **2.** to be given off as steam **3.** to become covered with condensed steam, as a window (usually with *up*) **4.** to generate steam **5.** to move by steam power **6.** [Colloq.] to proceed quickly; make progress [to *steam* ahead] —*vt.* to expose to the action of steam, as in cooking —**get up steam 1.** (of a ship, etc.) to work up a sufficient head of steam to move **2.** to work oneself into a state of anger or excitement —**let** (or **blow**) **off steam** [Colloq.] to release pent-up emotion

steam·boat (-bōt′) *n.* a steamship, esp. a small one

steam engine 1. an engine using steam under pressure to supply mechanical energy **2.** a locomotive powered by steam

steam·er (stē′mər) *n.* **1.** something operated by steam power, as a steamship **2.** a container in which things are cooked, cleaned, etc. with steam

steam fitter a mechanic whose work (**steam fitting**) is installing and maintaining boilers, pipes, etc. in steam pressure systems

steam heat heat given off by steam in a closed system of pipes and radiators

steam iron an electric iron that releases steam through vents in the soleplate onto material being pressed

steam radio [Colloq.] *same as* RADIO (*n.* 2 & 3)

steam·roll·er (stēm′rōl′ər) *n.* **1.** a heavy, steam-driven roller used in building and repairing roads **2.** power which crushes opposition or forces its way relentlessly —*vt.* to crush, override, or force as if with a steamroller **3.** to move or act with overwhelming, crushing force Also **steam′·roll′** —*adj.* relentlessly overpowering

steam·ship (-ship′) *n.* a ship driven by steam power

steam shovel a large, mechanically operated digger, powered by steam: also **steam navvy**

steam train a train powered by steam rather than diesel or electricity

steam turbine a turbine turned by steam moving under pressure

steam·y (stē′mē) *adj.* **steam′i·er, steam′i·est 1.** of or like steam **2.** filled with steam **3.** giving off steam —**steam′i·ly** *adv.* —**steam′i·ness** *n.*

ste·ap·sin (stē ap′sin) *n.* [< Gr. *stea(r)*, fat + (PE)PSIN] the lipase present in pancreatic juice

ste·ar·ic acid (stē ar′ik) [< Fr. < Gr. *stear*, tallow] a colourless, fatty acid found in many animal and vegetable fats, and used in making candles, soaps, etc.

ste·a·rin (stē′ə rin, stir′in) *n.* [< Fr. < Gr.: see prec. & -INE⁴] a white, crystalline substance found in the solid portion of most animal and vegetable fats: also **ste′a·rine** (-rin, -rēn′)

ste·a·tite (stē′ə tīt′) *n.* [L. *steatitis* < Gr. *stear*, tallow] a compact, massive variety of talc; soapstone —**ste′a·tit′ic** (-tit′ik) *adj.*

ste·a·to·pyg·i·a (stē′ə tō pij′ē ə) *n.* [ModL. < Gr. *stear*, fat + *pygē*, buttocks] a protuberance of the buttocks, caused by fatty deposits, as among Hottentot women

sted·fast (sted′fäst′, -fəst) *adj.* earlier var. *of* STEADFAST —**sted′fast′ly** *adv.* —**sted′fast′ness** *n.*

steed (stēd) *n.* [OE. *steda*] a horse; esp., a high-spirited riding horse: literary term

steel (stēl) *n.* see PLURAL, II, D, 3 [OE. *stiele*] **1.** a hard, tough metal composed of iron alloyed with a small percentage of carbon and often variously with other metals, as nickel, chromium, etc., to produce hardness, etc. **2.** something made of steel; specif., [Poet.] a sword or dagger **3.** great strength or hardness —*adj.* of or like steel —*vt.* **1.** to cover or edge with steel **2.** to make hard, tough, unfeeling, etc. —**steel′i·ness** *n.* —**steel′y** *adj.* **-i·er, -i·est**

steel band a percussion band, originating in Trinidad, using steel oil drums modified to produce varying pitches

steel blue a metallic blue colour like that of tempered steel —**steel′-blue′** *adj.*

steel grey a bluish-grey colour —**steel′-grey′** *adj.*

steel wool long, hairlike shavings of steel in a pad or ball, used for scouring, smoothing, and polishing

steel·work·er (stēl′wur′kər) *n.* a worker in a steel works

steel·works (-wurks′) *n.* a place where steel is made, processed, and shaped

steel·yard (stēl′yärd′, stil′yərd) *n.* [STEEL & YARD¹ (in obs. sense of "rod")] a scale consisting of a metal arm suspended from above: the object to be weighed is hung from the shorter end and a weight is moved along the graduated longer end until the arm balances

steen·bok (stēn′bok′, stän′-) *n., pl.* **-bok′, -boks′:** see PLURAL, II, D, 2 [Afrik. < Du. *steen*, a stone + *bok*, a buck] *same as* STEINBOK: also **steen′buck′** (-buk′)

steep¹ (stēp) *adj.* [OE. *steap*, lofty] **1.** having a sharp rise or slope; precipitous [a *steep* incline] **2.** [Colloq.] *a)* unreasonably high or great; excessive [a *steep* price] *b)* extreme —*n.* a steep slope —**steep′ly** *adv.* —**steep′ness** *n.*

steep² (stēp) *vt.* [akin to ON. *steypa*] **1.** to soak in liquid, as in order to extract the essence of **2.** to immerse, saturate, imbue, etc. [*steeped* in folklore] —*n.* **1.** a steeping or being steeped **2.** liquid in which something is steeped —*vi.* to be steeped, as tea leaves

steep·en (-'n) *vt., vi.* to make or become steep or steeper

stee·ple (stē′p'l) *n.* [OE. *stepel*] **1.** a tower rising above the main structure of a building, esp. of a church, usually capped with a spire **2.** *same as* SPIRE —**stee′pled** *adj.*

stee·ple·chase (-chās′) *n.* [the race orig. had as its goal a distant, visible steeple] **1.** orig., a horse race run across country **2.** a horse race run over a prepared course obstructed with ditches, hedges, etc. —*vi.* **-chased′, -chas′-ing** —**stee′ple·chas′er** *n.*

stee·ple·jack (-jak′) *n.* a person whose work is building, painting, or repairing steeples, smokestacks, etc.

steer¹ (stir) *vt.* [OE. *stieran*] **1.** to guide (a ship or boat) by means of a rudder **2.** to direct the course of (a motor car, etc.) **3.** to oversee; direct [he *steered* our efforts] **4.** to set and follow (a course) —*vi.* **1.** to steer a ship, motor car, etc. **2.** to be steered [the car *steers* easily] **3.** to set and follow a course —**steer clear of** to avoid —**steer′a·ble** *adj.* —**steer′er** *n.*

steer² (stir) *n.* [OE. *steor*] **1.** a castrated male of the cattle family **2.** loosely, any male of beef cattle

steer·age (stir′ij) *n.* **1.** *a)* the act of steering *b)* the response of a ship to the helmsman's guidance **2.** formerly, a section in some passenger ships occupied by passengers paying the lowest fare

steer·age·way (-wā′) *n.* the minimum forward speed needed to make a ship respond to the helmsman's guidance

steer·ing committee (stir′in) a committee, as of a legislative body, appointed to arrange the order of business

steering wheel a wheel turned by the driver of a vehicle to change direction

steers·man (stirz′mən) *n., pl.* **-men** a person who steers a ship or boat; helmsman

stein (stīn) *n.* [G.] **1.** an earthenware beer mug, or a similar mug of pewter, glass, etc. **2.** the amount that a stein will hold

stein·bok (stīn′bok′) *n., pl.* **-bok′, -boks′:** see PLURAL, II, D, 2 [< G.] a small, reddish antelope found in grassy areas of S and E Africa

ste·le (stē′lē; *also, & for 2 usually,* stēl) *n.* [< L. < Gr. *stēlē*, a slab] **1.** an upright stone slab with an inscription or design, as a grave marker **2.** a prepared surface with an inscription or design, as on a façade Also **ste·la** (stē′lə)

stel·lar (stel′ər) *adj.* [< LL. < L. *stella*, a star] **1.** of the stars or a star **2.** like a star, as in shape **3.** [U.S.] leading; chief [a *stellar* role]

stel·late (stel′āt, -it) *adj.* [< L. pp. of *stellare*, to cover with stars < *stella*, a star] star-shaped; coming out in rays or points from a centre: also **stel′lat·ed** —**stel′late·ly** *adv.*

stel·lu·lar (stel′yoo lər) *adj.* [< LL. *stellula*, dim. of L. *stella*, STAR + -AR] **1.** shaped like a small star or stars **2.** covered with small stars

stem¹ (stem) *n.* [OE. *stemn*] **1.** the main stalk or trunk of a tree, shrub, or other plant, extending above the ground and bearing the leaves, flowers, etc. **2.** any stalk supporting leaves, flowers, or fruit **3.** a stemlike part; specif., *a)* the slender part of a tobacco pipe attached to the bowl *b)* a narrow supporting part above the foot of a wineglass, goblet, etc. *c)* the shaft projecting from a watch, with a knob for winding the spring *d)* the thick stroke of a letter, as in printing *e)* the vertical line of a musical note **4.** the prow of a ship; bow **5.** a branch of a family **6.** the part of a word to which inflectional endings are added *—vt.* **stemmed, stem′ming 1.** to remove the stem from (a fruit, etc.) **2.** to make headway against [to row upstream, *stemming* the current] *—vi.* to originate or derive *—from* **stem to stern 1.** from one end of a ship to another **2.** through the length of anything *—stem′less adj. —stem′-like′ adj.*

stem² (stem) *vt.* **stemmed, stem′ming** [ON. *stemma*] **1.** to stop or check; esp., to dam (a river, etc.), or to stop or check as if by damming **2.** to turn (a ski) in stemming *—vi.* to stop or slow down in skiing by turning the tip of the ski(s) inwards

stem·ma (stem′ə) *n.* [Gr. *stemma*, a garland] **1.** a family tree; pedigree **2.** *Zool.* a simple eye

stemmed (stemd) *adj.* **1.** having a stem [a thin-*stemmed* goblet] **2.** with the stem or stems removed

stem stitch an embroidery stitch used esp. for forming flower stems

stem-wind·ing (stem′wīn′diŋ) *adj.* [Chiefly U.S.] wound, as a watch, by turning a knurled knob at the outer end of the stem *—stem′-wind′er n.*

stench (stench) *n.* [OE. *stenc*] an offensive smell; stink

sten·cil (sten′s'l) *vt.* **-cilled, -cil·ling** [< OFr. < *estencele,* ult. < L. *scintilla,* a spark] to make, mark, or paint with a stencil *—n.* **1.** a thin sheet, as of paper or metal, perforated or cut through in such a way that when ink, paint, etc. is applied to the sheet, the patterns, designs, letters, etc. are marked on the surface beneath **2.** a pattern, design, etc. made by stencilling *—sten′cil·ler n.*

sten gun a lightweight machine gun

sten·o- [< Gr. *stenos,* narrow] *a combining form meaning* narrow, thin, small, etc. [*stenography*]

ste·nog·ra·pher (stə nog′rə fər) *n.* a person skilled in stenography

ste·nog·ra·phy (-fē) *n.* [STENO- + -GRAPHY] shorthand writing; specif., the skill or work of writing down dictation, testimony, etc. in shorthand and later transcribing it, as on a typewriter *—sten·o·graph·ic* (sten′ə graf′ik), **sten′o·graph′-i·cal** *adj. —sten′o·graph′i·cal·ly adv.*

sten·o·type (sten′ə tīp′) *n.* [STENO- + -TYPE] **1.** a symbol or symbols used in stenotypy **2.** a keyboard machine used in stenotypy *—vt.* **-typed′, -typ′ing** to record by stenotype

sten·o·typ·y (-tī′pē) *n.* shorthand in which symbols representing sounds, words, or phrases are typed on a keyboard machine *—sten′o·typ′ist n.*

sten·tor (sten′tôr) *n.* [after *Stentor,* a Greek herald in the *Iliad* having a very loud voice] [*sometimes* S-] a person having a very loud voice

sten·to·ri·an (sten tôr′ē ən) *adj.* [< *Stentor:* see prec] very loud

step (step) *n.* [OE. *stepe*] **1.** the act of moving and placing the foot, as in walking, dancing, climbing, etc. **2.** the distance covered by such a movement **3.** a short distance **4.** *a)* a manner of stepping; gait *b)* any pace or stride in marching [the goose *step*] *c)* a sequence of movements in dancing, usually repeated in a set pattern **5.** the sound of stepping; footfall **6.** a mark made by stepping; footprint **7.** a rest for the foot in climbing, as a stair or the rung of a ladder **8.** [*pl.*] a flight of stairs or a step ladder **9.** something resembling a stair step, as a raised frame supporting a mast **10.** a degree; rank; level; stage **11.** any of a series of acts, processes, etc. **12.** *Music* [Chiefly U.S.] *a)* a degree of the staff or scale *b)* the interval between two consecutive degrees *—vi.* **stepped, step′ping 1.** to move by executing a step **2.** to walk, esp. a short distance **3.** to move with measured steps, as in dancing **4.** to move quickly: often with *along* **5.** to come or enter (*into* a situation, etc.) **6.** to put or press the foot down (*on* something) [*step* on the brake] *—vt.* **1.** to take (one or more strides or paces) **2.** *a)* to set (the foot) down *b)* to move across or over by foot **3.** to execute the steps of (a dance) **4.** to measure by taking steps: usually with *off* [*step* off ten paces] **5.** to provide with steps; specif., *a)* to cut steps in *b)* to arrange in a series of degrees or grades *—break step* **1.** to stop marching in cadence **2.** to cease to conform *—in step* **1.** keeping to a set rhythm in marching, dancing, etc. **2.** in conformity or agreement *—keep step* to stay in step *—out of step* not in step *—step by step* by degrees; gradually *—step down* **1.** to resign (*from* an office, etc.) **2.** to decrease, as in rate *—step in* **1.** to start to participate; intervene *—step on it* [Colloq.] to go faster; hurry *—step out* **1.** to go outside (a building), esp. briefly **2.** to begin to walk more quickly **3.** to go out for a good time *—step up* **1.** to approach **2.** to advance **3.** to increase, as in rate *—take steps* to adopt certain measures *—watch one's step* [Colloq.] to be careful: also *mind one's step*

step·broth·er (step′bruth′ər) *n.* one's stepparent's son by a former marriage

step·child (-chīld′) *n., pl.* **-chil′dren** [OE. *steop-,* orphaned: orig. used of orphaned children] a child that one's husband or wife had by a former marriage

step·daugh·ter (-dôt′ər) *n.* a female stepchild

step-down (-doun′) *adj.* that steps down, or decreases, power, speed, etc., as a transformer, gear, etc. *—n.* a decrease, as in intensity, etc.

step·fa·ther (-fä′thər) *n.* a male stepparent

steph·a·no·tis (stef′ə nōt′is) *n.* [ModL. < Gr. < *stephanos,* a crown] a woody climbing plant grown for its white, waxy, sweet-scented flowers

step-in (step′in′) *adj.* put on by being stepped into *—n.* a step-in garment or [*pl.*], esp. formerly, undergarment

step·lad·der (-lad′ər) *n.* a four-legged ladder having broad, flat steps

step·moth·er (-muth′ər) *n.* a female stepparent

step·par·ent (-per′ənt) *n.* [see STEPCHILD] the person who has married one's parent after the death or divorce of the other parent

steppe (step) *n.* [< Russ. *step′*] **1.** any of the great plains of SE Europe and Asia, having few trees **2.** any similar plain

stepped-up (stept′up′) *adj.* increased, as in tempo

step·per (step′ər) *n.* a person or animal that steps in a specified manner, as a dancer or a horse

step·ping·stone (step′iŋ stōn′) *n.* **1.** a stone, usually one of a series, used to step on, as in crossing a stream, etc. **2.** a means of advancement Also **stepping stone**

step·sis·ter (-sis′tər) *n.* one's stepparent's daughter by a former marriage

step·son (-sun′) *n.* a male stepchild

step-up (-up′) *adj.* that steps up, or increases, power, speed, etc., as a transformer, gear, etc. *—n.* an increase, as in intensity, etc.

-ster (stər) [OE. *-estre,* orig. a fem. agent suffix] *a suffix meaning:* **1.** a person who is, does, or creates (something specified) [*punster*]: often derogatory [*rhymester*] **2.** a person associated with (something specified) [*gangster*]

stere (stir) *n.* [Fr. *stère* < Gr. *stereos,* solid, cubic] a cubic metre

ster·e·o (ster′ē ō′) *n., pl.* **-os′ 1.** *a)* a stereophonic record player, radio, record, tape, etc. *b)* a stereophonic system **2.** a stereoscope or a stereoscopic picture, etc. **3.** *shortened form of:* a) STEREOTYPE b) STEREOTYPY *—adj.* shortened *form of* STEREOPHONIC

ster·e·o- [< Gr. *stereos,* hard, firm] *a combining form meaning* solid, firm, three-dimensional [*stereoscope*]

ster·e·o·chem·is·try (ster′ē ō kem′is trē) *n.* [STEREO- + CHEMISTRY] the branch of chemistry dealing with the spatial arrangement of groups of atoms forming molecules

ster·e·o·i·so·mer (ster′ē ō ī′sə mər) *n.* [STEREO- + ISOMER] any of two or more isomers, differing only in the spatial arrangements of their atoms

ster·e·o·phon·ic (ster′ē ə fon′ik) *adj.* [prec. + PHONIC] designating or of sound reproduction, as in films, records, tapes, or broadcasting, using two or more channels to carry and reproduce through separate speakers a blend of sounds from separate sources *—ster′e·o·phon′i·cal·ly adv.*

ster·e·op·ti·con (-op′ti kən, -kon′) *n.* [< STEREO + *optikon,* of sight] a kind of slide projector that allows one view to fade out while the next is fading in

ster·e·o·scope (ster′ē ə skōp′) *n.* [STEREO- + -SCOPE] an instrument that gives a three-dimensional effect to photographs viewed through it: it has two eyepieces, through which two slightly different views of the same scene are viewed side by side *—ster′e·o·scop′ic* (-skop′ik) *adj. —ster′e·o·scop′i·cal·ly adv.*

ster·e·os·co·py (ster′ē os′kə pē) *n.* the science of stereoscopic effects and techniques

ster·e·o·type (ster′ē ə tīp′) *n.* [< Fr.: see STEREO- & -TYPE] **1.** a printing plate cast in type metal from a mould (*matrix*), as of a page of set type **2.** *same as* STEREOTYPY **3.** a fixed idea or popular conception, as about how a certain type of person looks, acts, etc. *—vt.* **-typed′, -typ′ing 1.** to make a stereotype of **2.** to print from stereotypes *—ster′e·o·typ′-er, ster′e·o·typ′ist n.*

ster·e·o·typed (-tīpt′) *adj.* **1.** having the nature of a stereotype; esp., hackneyed; trite; not original **2.** printed from stereotype plates

ster·e·o·typ·y (-tī′pē) *n.* the process of making or printing from stereotype plates

ster·ile (ster′il) *adj.* [L. *sterilis*] **1.** incapable of producing others of its kind; barren **2.** producing little or nothing [*sterile* soil] **3.** lacking in interest or vitality [a *sterile* style] **4.** free from living microorganisms; esp., aseptic *—ster′ile·ly adv. —ste·ril·i·ty* (stə ril′ə tē) *n.*

ster·i·lize (ster′ə līz′) *vt.* **-lized′, -liz′ing** to make sterile; specif., *a)* to make incapable of producing others of its kind *b)* to make (land) unproductive *c)* to free from living microorganisms, as by subjecting to great heat *—ster′-i·li·za′tion n. —ster′i·liz′er n.*

ster·ling (stur'liŋ) *n.* [ME. *sterlinge*, Norman silver penny < ?] **1.** sterling silver or articles made of it **2.** the standard of fineness of legal British coinage: for silver, 0.500; for gold, 0.91666 **3.** British money —*adj.* **1.** of standard quality: said of silver that is at least 92.5 percent pure **2.** of or payable in British money **3.** made of sterling silver **4.** worthy; excellent

sterling area a group of countries, including most of the Commonwealth, that use sterling as a medium for international payments

stern[1] (sturn) *adj.* [OE. *styrne*] **1.** hard; severe; strict [*stern* measures] **2.** grim; forbidding [a *stern* face] **3.** unrelenting; inexorable [*stern* reality] **4.** unshakable; firm [*stern* determination] —**stern'ly** *adv.* —**stern'ness** *n.*

stern[2] (sturn) *n.* [ON. *stjorn*, steering < *styra*, to steer] **1.** the rear end of a ship, boat, etc. **2.** the rear end of anything

stern·most (sturn'mōst') *adj.* **1.** nearest the stern **2.** farthest astern; rearmost

stern·post (sturn'pōst') *n.* the main, upright piece at the stern of a vessel, usually supporting the rudder

ster·num (stur'nəm) *n., pl.* **ster'nums, ster'na** (-nə) [ModL. < Gr. *sternon*] a thin, flat structure of bone and cartilage to which most of the ribs are attached in the front of the chest in most vertebrates; breastbone —**ster'nal** *adj.*

ster·nu·ta·tion (stur'nyoo tā'shən) *n.* [< L. < freq. of *sternuere*, to sneeze] a sneeze or the act of sneezing —**ster·nu·ta·to·ry** (stər nyoo'tə tôr ē), **ster'nu·ta'tive** *adj.*

ster·nu·ta·tor (sturn'nyoo tāt'ər) *n.* a gas designed to incapacitate by severely irritating the respiratory passages

stern·ward (sturn'wərd) *adv., adj.* towards the stern; astern: also **stern'wards** *adv.*

stern·way (-wā') *n.* backwards movement of a ship

stern-wheel·er (-wēl'ər, -hwēl'ər) *n.* a steamer propelled by a paddle wheel at the stern

ster·oid (ster'oid) *n.* [STER(OL) + -OID] any of a group of compounds including the sterols, sex hormones, etc., having the ring structure of the sterols —**ste·roi'dal** *adj.*

ster·ol (stir'ol, ster'-; -ōl) *n.* [< (CHOLE)STEROL] any of a group of solid cyclic alcohols, as cholesterol, found in plant and animal tissues

ster·to·rous (stur'tə rəs) *adj.* [< L. *stertere*, to snore] characterized by loud, laboured breathing, or snoring —**ster'to·rous·ly** *adv.* —**ster'to·rous·ness** *n.*

stet (stet) [L.] let it stand: a printer's term used to indicate that matter previously struck out is to remain —*vt.* **stet'ted, stet'ting** to cancel a change in or deletion of (a word, line, etc.), as by writing "stet" in the margin

steth·o·scope (steth'ə skōp') *n.* [< Fr. < Gr. *stēthos*, the chest + -SCOPE] *Med.* a hearing instrument placed against the body for examining the heart, lungs, etc. by listening to the sounds they make —**steth'o·scop'ic** (-skop'ik), **steth'·o·scop'i·cal** *adj.* —**steth·os'co·py** (sta thos'kə pē) *n.*

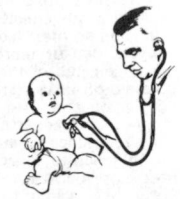

STETHOSCOPE

Stet·son (stet's'n) [U.S.] *a trademark for* hats of various kinds —*n.* [*often* s-] a man's hat, worn esp. by cowboys, usually of felt, with a broad brim and a high crown

ste·ve·dore (stē'və dôr') *n.* [< Sp. < *estivar*, to stow < L. *stipare*, to cram] a person employed at loading and unloading ships —*vt., vi.* **-dored', -dor'ing** to load or unload the cargo of (a ship)

stew[1] (styoo) *vt.* [< MFr. *estuver*, ult. < L. *ex*, out + Gr. *typhos*, steam] to cook by simmering slowly for a long time —*vi.* **1.** to undergo cooking in this way **2.** to be oppressed with heat; swelter —*n.* **1.** a dish, esp. of meat and vegetables, cooked by stewing **2.** a state of anxiety or worry, esp. in phrase **in a stew** —**stew in one's own juice** to suffer from one's own actions

stew[2] (styoo) *n.* [OE. *stow*, a place] **1.** a fish pond **2.** an oyster bed **3.** a breeding place for pheasants

stew·ard (styoo'ərd) *n.* [OE. *stiweard* < *stig*, enclosure + *weard*, a keeper] **1.** a person in charge of the affairs of a large household, who supervises the kitchen and servants, manages the accounts, etc. **2.** one who acts as an administrator, as of finances and property, for another **3.** a person variously responsible for the food and drink, the service personnel, etc. in a club, restaurant, etc. **4.** a person in charge of arrangements for a ball, race, etc. **5.** an attendant on a ship, aircraft, etc. who looks after the passengers' comfort **6.** *short for* SHOP STEWARD —*vi.* to act as a steward —**stew'ard·ship'** *n.*

stew·ard·ess (-ər dis) *n.* a woman steward (esp. sense 5)

stewed (styood) *adj.* **1.** cooked by stewing, as food **2.** [Slang] drunk; intoxicated

stew·pan (styoo'pan') *n.* a pan for stewing

stg. sterling

stick (stik) *n.* [OE. *sticca*] **1.** a twig or small branch broken or cut off, esp. a dead and dry one **2.** a long, slender piece of wood, often shaped for a specific purpose, as a wand, staff, club, cane, rod, etc. **3.** a stalk, as of celery **4.** something shaped like a stick [a *stick* of chewing gum] **5.** a separate article [every *stick* of furniture] **6.** an implement for striking a ball, puck, etc. [a hockey *stick*] **7.** punishment, esp. beating **8.** the power of adhering or making adhere **9.** [*usually pl.*] something made of sticks, as a racing hurdle **10.** [Colloq.] a dull or stupid person **11.** *Aeron.* a lever that controls the altitude and movement of an aircraft: in full, **control stick** —*vt.* **stuck** or for vt. 8 **sticked, stick'ing 1.** to pierce or puncture, as with a pointed instrument **2.** to kill by stabbing **3.** to pierce something with (a knife, pin, etc.) **4.** to thrust or push (*in, out*, etc.) **5.** *a)* to fasten or attach by gluing, pinning, etc. *b)* to decorate with things fastened in this way **6.** to transfix or impale **7.** to obstruct, bog down, etc.; also, to detain, delay, etc.: usually used in the passive [the wheels were *stuck*, he was *stuck* in town] **8.** to prop (a plant etc.) up with a stick **9.** [Colloq.] to place; put; set **10.** [Slang] to force or impose something unpleasant, as paying a bill [I was *stuck* with the bill] **11.** [Slang] endure; bear; tolerate —*vi.* **1.** to be fixed by a pointed end, as a nail, etc. **2.** to be attached by adhesion; adhere **3.** *a)* to remain in the same place; stay [to *stick* at home] *b)* to remain fixed in the memory *c)* to remain in effect [to make charges *stick*] **4.** to keep or stay close [friends *stick* together, *stick* to the trail] **5.** to persevere [to *stick* at a job] **6.** to remain firm; endure **7.** to become fixed, blocked, embedded, jammed, etc. [my shoe *stuck* in the mud, the gears *stuck*] **8.** to be puzzled **9.** to hesitate; scruple [he'll *stick* at nothing] **10.** to protrude or extend (with *out, up*, etc.) —**stick around** [Slang] to stay near at hand —**stick by** (or **to**) to remain loyal to —**stick fast** to be incapable of moving or being moved —**stick it out** [Slang] to endure something to the end —**stick out a mile** [Colloq.] to be very obvious —**stick to one's ribs** to be nourishing: said of food —**stick to someone's fingers** [Colloq.] to be stolen, embezzled, etc.: usually said of money —**stick up** [Slang] to commit armed robbery upon —**stick up for** [Colloq.] to uphold; defend —**stuck with** [Colloq.] unable to dispose of, esp. something unpleasant —**the sticks** [Colloq.] the rural districts —**stick'like'** *adj.*

stick·er (-ər) *n.* a person or thing that sticks; specif., *a)* a bur, barb, or thorn *b)* a gummed label *c)* [Slang] a knife used as a weapon

sticking plaster adhesive material for covering a slight wound, usually a thin cloth with gum on one side

stick insect an insect resembling a twig

stick-in-the-mud (stik''n *th*ə mud') *n.* [Colloq.] a· person who resists change or progress, new ideas, etc.

stick·le (-'l) *vi.* **-led, -ling** [prob. < ME. *stightlen*, to dispose, ult. < OE. *stihtan*, to arrange] **1.** to raise objections, haggle, etc., esp. in a stubborn way, usually about trifles **2.** to scruple (*at*)

stick·le·back (stik''l bak') *n.* [< OE. *sticel*, a prick + ME. *bak*, back] a small, scaleless fish with sharp spines: the male builds a nest for the eggs

stick·ler (stik'lər) *n.* [cf. STICKLE] **1.** a person who insists on strict observance of something [a *stickler* for discipline] **2.** [U.S. Colloq.] something puzzling to solve

stick shift [U.S.] gear lever

stick-up (stik'up') *n. slang term for* HOLDUP (sense 2)

stick·y (-ē) *adj.* **stick'i·er, stick'i·est 1.** that sticks; adhesive; clinging **2.** covered with an adhesive substance **3.** [Colloq.] hot and humid **4.** [Colloq.] difficult; troublesome [a *sticky* problem] **5.** [Colloq.] very unpleasant, esp. in **to come to a sticky end** —**stick'i·ly** *adv.* —**stick'i·ness** *n.*

stick·y·beak (-bēk) *n.* [Aust. Slang] an inquisitive or nosy person —*vt.* to pry; be nosy

sticky wicket 1. *Cricket* a damp area between wickets, making play difficult and slow **2.** a difficult or awkward situation

stiff (stif) *adj.* [OE. *stif*] **1.** hard to bend or stretch; rigid; firm **2.** hard to move or operate; not free or limber **3.** stretched tight; taut **4.** *a)* sore or limited in movement: said of joints or muscles *b)* having such joints or muscles **5.** not fluid or loose; thick; dense [a *stiff* sauce] **6.** moving swiftly, as a breeze **7.** containing much alcohol: said of a drink **8.** of high potency [a *stiff* dose of medicine] **9.** harsh [a *stiff* punishment] **10.** difficult [a *stiff* climb] **11.** constrained or awkward; not easy or graceful **12.** resolute or stubborn, as a person, a fight, etc. **13.** [Colloq.] high [a *stiff* price] —*adv.* **1.** to a stiff condition **2.** [Colloq.] completely [scared *stiff*] —*n.* [U.S. Slang] a corpse —**stiff'ish** *adj.* —**stiff'ly** *adv.* —**stiff'ness** *n.*

stiff·en (stif'n) *vt., vi.* to make or become stiff or stiffer —**stiff'en·er** *n.*

stiff-necked (stif'nekt') *adj.* stubborn; obstinate

sti·fle (stī'f'l) *vt.* **-fled, -fling** [ult. < MFr. *estouffer*, to smother] **1.** to suffocate; smother **2.** to suppress or check; stop [to *stifle* a sob] —*vi.* **1.** to die from lack of air **2.** to suffer from lack of fresh, cool air —**sti'fling** *adj.*

stig·ma (stig′mə) *n., pl.* **-mas;** also, and for 4, 5, & 6 usually, **stig·ma·ta** (stig mät′ə, stig′mə te) [L. < Gr., lit., a prick with a pointed instrument] **1.** formerly, a brand, as on a criminal **2.** a mark of disgrace or reproach **3.** a mark, sign, etc. indicating that something is not considered normal **4.** a small mark, scar, opening, etc., as a pore, on the surface of a plant or animal **5.** a spot on the skin, esp. one that bleeds as because of nervous tension **6.** [*pl.*] marks resembling the Crucifixion wounds of Jesus **7.** *Bot.* the upper tip of the style of a flower, on which pollen falls —**stig·mat′ic** (-mat′ik), **stig·mat′i·cal** *adj.*
stig·ma·tize (stig′mə tīz′) *vt.* **-tized′, -tiz′ing 1.** to mark with a stigma **2.** to mark as disgraceful —**stig′ma·ti·za′·tion** *n.*
stile¹ (stīl) *n.* [OE. *stigel* < *stigan,* to climb] **1.** a step or set of steps used in climbing over a fence or wall **2.** *shortened form of* TURNSTILE
stile² (stīl) *n.* [Du. *stijl,* doorpost] a vertical piece in a panel or frame, as of a door or window
sti·let·to (sti let′ō) *n., pl.* **-tos, -toes** [It., dim. of *stilo,* a dagger < L. *stilus:* see STYLE] **1.** a small dagger with a slender, tapering blade **2.** a sharp instrument for making eyelet holes in cloth **3.** a high, very thin heel on a woman's shoe: also **stiletto heel**
still¹ (stil) *adj.* [OE. *stille*] **1.** without sound; quiet; silent **2.** hushed, soft, or low in sound **3.** not moving; motionless: following *stand, sit, lie,* etc., sometimes regarded as an adverb **4.** calm; tranquil; unruffled [*still* water] **5.** not effervescent: said of wine, etc. **6.** *Cinema* designating or of a single posed photograph or one made from a single frame of a film, for use as in publicity —*n.* **1.** silence; quiet [in the *still* of the night] **2.** a still photograph —*adv.* **1.** at or up to the time indicated, whether past, present, or future **2.** even; yet [*still* colder] **3.** nevertheless; yet [rich but *still* unhappy] **4.** [Archaic] ever; constantly —*conj.* nevertheless; yet —*vt.* to make still; specif., *a)* to make silent *b)* to make motionless *c)* to calm; relieve —*vi.* to become still —**still′ness** *n.*
still² (stil) *n.* [< obs. *still,* DISTIL] **1.** an apparatus used for distilling liquids, esp. spirits **2.** same as DISTILLERY
still·born (stil′bôrn′) *adj.* **1.** dead at birth **2.** unsuccessful from the beginning; abortive —**still′birth′** *n.*
still life 1. an arrangement of objects, as fruit in a bowl, flowers in a vase, etc. as the subject of a painting, drawing, etc. **2.** *pl.* **still lifes** such a painting, etc. —**still′-life′** *adj.*
still·room (-rōom′) *n.* [STILL² + ROOM] **1.** a room containing a still **2.** a housekeeper's storeroom for preserves, liquors, etc.
Still·son wrench (stil′s'n) [after its U.S. inventor (in 1869), D. *Stillson*] *a trademark for* a wrench with a jaw that moves through a collar pivoted to the shaft, used for turning pipes, etc.: the jaw tightens as pressure is applied to the handle
still·y (stil′ē; *for adv.* stil′lē) *adj.* **still′i·er, still′i·est** [Literary] still; silent; calm —*adv.* in a still manner; quietly
stilt (stilt) *n.* [prob. < MLowG. or MDu. *stelte*] **1.** either of a pair of poles, each with a footrest somewhere along its length, used for walking with the feet above the ground, as in play **2.** any of a number of long posts used to hold a building, etc. above the ground or out of the water **3.** *pl.* **stilts, stilt:** see PLURAL, II, D, 1 any of several wading birds of the avocet family
stilt·ed (stil′tid) *adj.* **1.** raised on or as on stilts **2.** formal or dignified in a way that is not natural; pompous —**stilt′-ed·ly** *adv.* —**stilt′ed·ness** *n.*
Stil·ton (cheese) (stil′t'n) [< *Stilton,* village in EC England] a rich, crumbly cheese with veins of blue-green mould
stim·u·lant (stim′yə lənt) *adj.* stimulating —*n.* anything that stimulates; specif., *a)* any drug, etc. that temporarily speeds up the heartbeat or some other body process *b)* popularly, an alcoholic drink: actually alcohol is a body depressant
stim·u·late (-lāt′) *vt.* **-lat′ed, -lat′ing** [< L. pp. of *stimulare,* to prick < *stimulus,* a goad] **1.** to make active or more active; stir up or spur on; arouse; excite **2.** to invigorate as by an alcoholic drink **3.** *Med., Physiol.* to excite (an organ, etc.) to activity or increased activity —*vi.* to act as a stimulant or stimulus —**stim′u·lat′er, stim′u·la′tor** *n.* —**stim′u·la′tion** *n.* —**stim′u·la′tive** *adj., n.*
stim·u·lus (-ləs) *n., pl.* **-u·li** (-lī′) [L., a goad] **1.** something that stirs to action or increased activity; incentive

2. *Physiol., Psychol.* any action or agent that causes or changes an activity in an organism, organ, etc.
sti·my (stī′mē) *n., pl.* **-mies,** *vt.* **-mied, -my·ing** same as STYMIE
sting (stiŋ) *vt.* **stung, sting′ing** [OE. *stingan*] **1.** to prick or wound with a sting: said of plants and insects **2.** to cause sharp, sudden, smarting pain to [cold wind *stings* the face] **3.** to cause to suffer mentally [his conscience *stung* him] **4.** to stimulate suddenly and sharply [*stung* into action] **5.** [Slang] to cheat; esp., to overcharge —*vi.* **1.** to use a sting **2.** to cause or feel sharp, smarting pain, either physical or mental —*n.* **1.** the act or power of stinging **2.** a pain or wound resulting from or as from stinging **3.** a thing that stimulates; goad **4.** a sharp-pointed organ, as in insects, used to prick, wound, or inject poison **5.** any of the stinging, hollow hairs on some plants, as nettles —**sting′er** *n.* —**sting′ing·ly** *adv.* —**sting′less** *adj.*
stinging nettle same as NETTLE
sting·ray (stiŋ′rā′) *n.* a large ray (fish) having a whiplike tail with a sharp spine or spines that can inflict painful wounds: also [U.S. & Aust.] **sting·a·ree** (stiŋ′ə rē′ stiŋ′ə rē′)
stin·gy¹ (stin′jē) *adj.* **stin′gi·er, stin′gi·est** [akin to STING] **1.** giving or spending grudgingly; miserly **2.** less than needed or expected —**stin′gi·ly** *adv.* —**stin′gi·ness** *n.*
sting·y² (stiŋ′ē) *adj.* stinging or capable of stinging
stink (stiŋk) *vi.* **stank** or **stunk, stunk, stink′ing** [OE. *stincan*] **1.** to give off a strong, bad smell **2.** to be offensive or hateful **3.** [Slang] to be no good, or of low quality —*vt.* [Slang] to smell; notice the stink of —*n.* **1.** a strong, bad smell; stench **2.** [Slang] a strong public reaction, as of outrage, censure, or protest **3.** [*pl.*] [Colloq.] chemistry —**stink out** to drive out by a strong, bad smell —**stink up** to cause to stink
stink·ard (-ərd) *n.* **1.** same as STINKER **2.** a kind of badger
stink bomb a device made to burn or explode and give off an offensive smell
stink·er (-ər) *n.* **1.** a person or thing that stinks **2.** [Slang] *a)* a person regarded with disgust *b)* a difficult task, problem, etc. *c)* something of poor quality
stink·ing (-iŋ) *adj.* **1.** that stinks **2.** [Slang] *a)* very bad, unsatisfactory, etc. *b)* offensive, disgusting, etc. —*adv.* [Slang] to an excessive or offensive degree —**cry stinking fish** to denigrate one's own goods or products —**stink′-ing·ly** *adv.*
stink·o (stiŋk′ō) *adj.* [Slang] drunk; intoxicated
stink·weed (-wēd′) *n.* any of several foul-smelling plants
stint¹ (stint) *vt.* [OE. *styntan,* to blunt] to limit to a certain, usually small, quantity or share —*vi.* to be sparing in giving or using —*n.* **1.** restriction; limit **2.** a task or share of work to be done —**stint′er** *n.* —**stint′ing·ly** *adv.*
stint² (stint) *n.* [LME. *stynte* < ?] any of various small sandpipers
stipe (stīp) *n.* [Fr. < L. *stipes,* tree trunk] a stalk, as that supporting a mushroom cap, fern frond, etc.
sti·pend (stī′pend, -pənd) *n.* [L. *stipendium* < *stips,* small coin + *pendere,* to weigh out, pay] **1.** a regular or fixed payment for services, as a salary **2.** any periodic payment, as an allowance
sti·pen·di·ar·y (stī pen′dē ər ē) *adj.* **1.** receiving, or performing services for, a stipend **2.** paid for by a stipend [*stipendiary* services] —*n., pl.* **-ar·ies** a person who receives a stipend
stipendiary magistrate a lawyer who is a paid magistrate in one of the larger towns, as London
stip·ple (stip′'l) *vt.* **-pled, -pling** [< Du. < *stippel,* a speckle] **1.** to paint, draw, engrave, or apply in small dots rather than in lines or solid areas **2.** to mark with dots; fleck —*n.* **1.** *a)* the art of painting, drawing, etc. in dots *b)* the effect so produced, or an effect like it, as in nature **2.** stippled work Also **stip′pling** *n.* —**stip′pler** *n.*
stip·u·late (stip′yə lāt′) *vt.* **-lat′ed, -lat′ing** [< L. pp. of *stipulari,* to bargain] **1.** to arrange definitely, as in a contract **2.** to specify as an essential condition of an agreement —*vi.* to make a specific demand (for something) as a condition of an agreement —**stip′u·la′tion** *n.* —**stip′u·la·tor** *n.* —**stip′u·la·to·ry** (-lə tər ē) *adj.*
stip·ule (stip′yōōl) *n.* [ModL. *stipula* < L., a stalk] either of a pair of small, leaflike parts at the base of some leafstalks —**stip′u·lar** (-yōō lər) *adj.* —**stip′u·late** (-lāt′), **stip′u·lat′-ed** *adj.*
stir¹ (stur) *vt.* **stirred, stir′ring** [OE. *styrian*] **1.** to move, shake, etc., esp. slightly **2.** to rouse from sleep, lethargy, etc. **3.** to make move or be active [*stirring* oneself to finish the work] **4.** to mix (a liquid, etc.) by moving a spoon, fork, spatula, etc. around **5.** to excite the feelings of; move deeply **6.** to incite or provoke (often with *up*) **7.** to evoke,

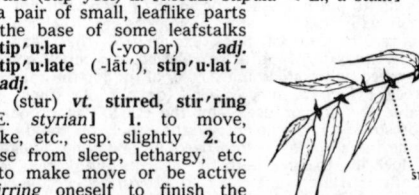

STIPULE

or call up [to *stir* memories] —*vi.* **1.** to move, esp. only slightly **2.** to be busy and active **3.** to begin to show signs of activity **4.** to do or undergo mixing —*n.* **1.** a stirring, or the sound of this **2.** movement; activity **3.** excitement or commotion —**stir one's stumps** [Colloq.] to move, esp. to increase one's pace in walking —**stir'rer** *n.*

stir² (stur) *n.* [? ult. < Romany] [Slang] a prison; imprisonment

stir·cra·zy (-krā'zē) *adj.* [see STIR²] [Slang] suffering nervous strain from being confined for a long time

stirk (sturk) *n.* [ME. < OE *stierc*, akin to Goth. *stairo*, barren] [Dial.] a bullock or heifer, esp. one between one and two years old

stirps (sturps) *n., pl.* **stir·pes** (stur'pēz) [L., lit., a stalk] **1.** a family or branch of a family **2.** *Law* the person from whom a family or branch of a family is descended

stir·ring (stur'iŋ) *adj.* **1.** active; busy **2.** that stirs one's feelings; moving; rousing [*stirring* music]

stir·rup (stir'əp) *n.* [OE. *stigrap*] **1.** a flat-bottomed ring hung by a strap (**stirrup leather**) from a saddle and used as a footrest **2.** any of various stirruplike supports, clamps, etc.

stirrup (bone) *same as* STAPES

stirrup cup 1. a farewell drink taken by a rider mounted to depart **2.** any farewell drink

stirrup pump a hand pump for putting out fires, set in a bucket and held by a stirrup or bracket, for one foot

stitch (stich) *n.* [OE. *stice*, a puncture] **1.** *a)* a single complete in-and-out movement of a threaded needle in sewing *b)* *same as* SUTURE (*n.* 3c) **2.** a single loop of yarn worked off a needle in knitting, crocheting, etc. **3.** a loop, knot, etc. made by stitching **4.** a particular kind of stitch or stitching **5.** a sudden, sharp pain, as in the side **6.** a bit, as of work, or piece, as of clothing [not wearing a *stitch*] —*vi.* to make stitches; sew —*vt.* to fasten, repair, adorn, etc. with stitches; sew —**in stitches** laughing uproariously —**stitch'er** *n.* —**stitch'ing** *n.*

stitch·er·y (-ər ē) *n.* [Chiefly U.S.] ornamental needlework, as embroidery, crewelwork, etc.

sti·ver (stī'vər) *n.* [Du. *stuiver*] **1.** a former Dutch coin equal to 1/20 of a guilder **2.** a trifling sum

Stn. station

sto·a (stō'ə) *n., pl.* **sto'ae** (-ē) [Gr. *stoa*] a portico or covered walk with columns on one side, as in ancient Greece

stoat (stōt) *n., pl.* **stoats, stoat:** see PLURAL, II, D, 1 [ME. *stote*] a large European weasel, esp. in its brown summer coat: see ERMINE (sense 1)

stock (stok) *n.* [OE. *stocc*] **1.** the trunk of a tree **2.** [Archaic] *a)* a tree stump *b)* a wooden block or log **3.** anything lacking life, motion, or feeling **4.** *a)* a plant stem into which a graft is inserted *b)* a plant from which cuttings are taken **5.** a rhizome or rootstock **6.** any of certain plants of the cabbage family **7.** *a)* the first of a line of descent *b)* a line of descent; ancestry or family *c)* a strain, race, or other related group of animals or plants *d)* a group of related languages or families of languages **8.** a supporting or main part, as of an implement, etc., to which the working parts are attached, as the butt of a whip, the frame of a plough, the part of a rifle holding the barrel, etc. **9.** [*pl.*] a framework; specif., *a)* a former instrument of punishment consisting of a wooden frame with holes for confining an offender's ankles and, sometimes, his wrists *b)* a frame of timbers supporting a ship during construction **10.** raw material **11.** water in which meat, fish, etc. has been boiled or stewed, used as a base for soup or gravy **12.** a store or supply; specif., *a)* all the animals, equipment, etc. kept on a farm *b)* short for LIVESTOCK *c)* the total amount of goods on hand in a store, etc.; inventory **13.** *a)* the capital invested in a company or corporation by individuals through the purchase of shares *b)* the proportionate share in the ownership of a company or corporation held by an individual stockholder, as represented by shares of this capital in the form of stock certificates **14.** [U.S.] a stock company (sense 2), or its repertoire **15.** a former type of wide, stiff cravat **16.** reputation; estimation [his *stock* increased because of the fight] —*vt.* **1.** to attach to a stock [to *stock* a plough] **2.** *a)* to furnish (a farm) with stock or (a shop, etc.) with stock *b)* to supply with [to *stock* a pond with fish] **3.** to keep a supply of, as for sale or for future use —*vi.* to put in a stock, or supply (often with *up*) —*adj.* **1.** continually kept in stock [*stock* sizes] **2.** common, hackneyed, or trite [a *stock* excuse] **3.** that deals with stock [a *stock* boy] **4.** of or relating to a stock company **5.** for breeding [a *stock* mare] **6.** of, or for the raising of, livestock [*stock* farming] —**in** (or **out of**) **stock** (not) available for sale or use —**on the stocks** in preparation —**take stock 1.** to inventory the stock on hand **2.** to examine the situation before deciding or acting —**take** (or **put**) **stock in** to have faith in, regard as important, etc.

stock·ade (sto kād') *n.* [< Fr. < Pr. *estacado* < *estaca*, a stake] **1.** a barrier of stakes driven into the ground side by side, for defence against attack **2.** an enclosure, as a fort, made with such stakes —*vt.* **-ad'ed, -ad'ing** to surround with a stockade

stock·breed·er (stok'brēd'ər) *n.* a breeder and raiser of livestock —**stock'breed'ing** *n.*

stock·bro·ker (stok'brō'kər) *n.* a person who acts as an agent for others in buying and selling stocks and bonds —**stock'bro'ker·age, stock'bro'king** *n.*

stock car 1. [U.S.] a railway car for carrying livestock **2.** a passenger motor car of standard make, modified in various ways for use in racing

stock company a company or corporation whose capital is divided into shares

stock dividend 1. a dividend in the form of additional shares of the same stock **2.** the payment of such a dividend

stock exchange 1. a place where stocks and shares are regularly bought and sold **2.** an association of stockbrokers who meet together for buying and selling stocks and shares according to regulations, esp. [**S- E-**] the group who occupy the Stock Exchange building in London

stock·fish (stok'fish') *n., pl.* **-fish', -fish'es:** see FISH [< MDu. < *stok*, stick + *visch*, fish] a fish split and dried without salt in the open air

stock·hold·er (-hōl'dər) *n.* a person owning stock or shares in a given company

stock·i·nette, stock·i·net (stok'ə net') *n.* [prob. for earlier *stocking net*] an elastic, machine-knitted cloth used for making stockings, underwear, etc.

stock·ing (stok'iŋ) *n.* [< STOCK, in obs. sense of leg covering + -ING] **1.** a closefitting covering, usually knitted, for the foot and, usually, most of the leg **2.** something like this, as a patch of colour on an animal's leg —**in one's stocking feet** wearing stockings or socks but no shoes

stocking cap a long, tapered knitted cap

stocking filler a small Christmas present, usually one small enough to go into a stocking that is hung up

stocking mask a nylon stocking pulled over a criminal's head for disguise

stock in trade 1. merchandise stocked in a shop **2.** tools, materials, etc. used in carrying on a trade or business **3.** any of the resources, practices, or devices always in use by a person or group

stock·ist (-ist) *n.* one who keeps a supply of certain goods

stock·job·ber (-job'ər) *n.* an operator in the stock exchange who deals only with brokers not with the public —**stock'-job'bing** (-iŋ) *n.*

stock·man (-man; *also, esp. for* 2, -man') *n., pl.* **-men** (-mən, -men') **1.** a man who tends livestock **2.** [U.S.] a man who works in a stockroom or warehouse

stock market 1. *same as* STOCK EXCHANGE **2.** the business carried on at a stock exchange **3.** the prices quoted on stocks and shares

stock·pile (-pīl') *n.* a supply of goods, raw material, etc., stored up esp. in anticipation of future shortage or emergency —*vt., vi.* **-piled', -pil'ing** to accumulate a stockpile (of) —**stock'pil'er** *n.*

stock·pot (-pot') *n.* a pot used for preparing soup stock

stock·room (-room') *n.* a room in which a store of goods, materials, etc. is kept: also **stock room**

stock split the act or result of splitting stock: see SPLIT (*vt.* 7)

stock-still (-stil') *adj.* perfectly motionless

stock·tak·ing (-tāk'iŋ) *n.* **1.** the act of preparing an inventory or valuation of goods in a shop, store, etc. **2.** an assessment of one's current situation

stock·y (stok'ē) *adj.* **stock'i·er, stock'i·est** heavily built; sturdy; short and thickset —**stock'i·ness** *n.*

stock·yard (stok'yärd') *n.* **1.** an enclosure for stock on a farm **2.** an enclosure with pens, sheds, etc. where cattle, pigs, etc. are kept just before slaughter or shipment

stodge (stoj) *n.* [? < STUFF & *podge*, short, fat person] [Colloq.] **1.** heavy, filling food, often unpalatable **2.** a boring person or thing —*vi., vt.* [Colloq.] to cram (oneself) with food

stodg·y (stoj'ē) *adj.* **stodg'i·er, stodg'i·est** [< dial. *stodge*, heavy food + -y²] **1.** heavily built; bulky and slow in movement **2.** dull; uninteresting **3.** drab, unfashionable, or unattractive **4.** very old-fashioned or conventional —**stodg'i·ly** *adv.* —**stodg'i·ness** *n.*

Sto·ic (stō'ik) *n.* [< L. < Gr. < *stoa*, colonnade: Zeno taught under a colonnade at Athens] **1.** a member of a Greek school of philosophy founded by Zeno about 308 B.C., holding that all things, properties, relations, etc. are governed by unchanging natural laws, and that the wise man should be indifferent to the external world and to passion or emotion **2.** [**s-**] a stoical person —*adj.* **1.** of the Stoics or their philosophy **2.** [**s-**] *same as* STOICAL

sto·i·cal (-i k'l) *adj.* **1.** showing austere indifference to joy, grief, pain, etc.; calm and unflinching under suffering, bad fortune, etc. **2.** [**S-**] *same as* STOIC —**sto'i·cal·ly** *adv.*

Sto·i·cism (-siz'm) *n.* **1.** the philosophy of the Stoics **2.** [**s-**] indifference to pleasure or pain

stoke (stōk) *vt., vi.* **stoked, stok'ing** [< STOKER] **1.** to stir up and feed fuel to (a fire) **2.** to tend (a furnace, boiler, etc.) **3.** to feed or eat large quantities of food; fill (*up*)

stoke·hold (-hōld′) *n.* **1.** the room containing the boilers on a ship **2.** *same as* STOKEHOLE (sense 2)

stoke·hole (-hōl′) *n.* **1.** the opening in a furnace or boiler through which the fuel is put **2.** a space in front of a furnace or boiler from which the fire is tended, as on a ship

stok·er (stō′kər) *n.* [Du. < *stoken*, to poke < *stok*, a stick] **1.** a man who tends a furnace, specif. of a steam boiler, as, esp. formerly, on a ship or steam locomotive **2.** a mechanical device that stokes a furnace

STOL (stōl) *adj.* [*s*(hort) *t*(ake) *o*(ff and) *l*(anding)] of or for an aircraft that can take off and land on a short runway —*n.* a STOL aircraft

stole[1] (stōl) *n.* [OE. < L. < Gr. *stolē*, a garment] **1.** a long, decorated strip of cloth worn like a scarf by officiating clergymen of various churches **2.** a woman's long scarf of cloth or fur worn around the shoulders, with the ends hanging in front

stole[2] (stōl) *pt. of* STEAL

stol·en (stō′lən) *pp. of* STEAL

stol·id (stol′id) *adj.* [L. *stolidus*, slow] having or showing little or no emotion or sensitivity; unexcitable —**sto·lid·i·ty** (stə-lid′ə tē), **stol′id·ness** *n.* —**stol′id·ly** *adv.*

sto·lon (stō′lon) *n.* [ModL. *stolo* (gen. *stolonis*) < L., a shoot] *Bot.* a runner; esp., a stem running underground

sto·ma (stō′ma) *n., pl.* **-ma·ta** (-mə tə), **-mas** [ModL. < Gr. *stoma*, mouth] **1.** a microscopic opening in the epidermis of plants, serving for gaseous exchange **2.** *Zool.* a mouth or mouthlike opening —**sto·ma·tal** (stō′mə t'l, stom′ə-) *adj.*

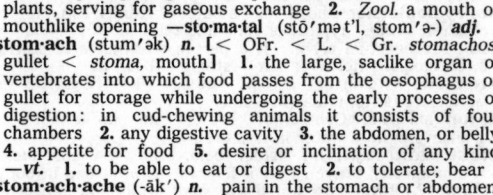

STOLE

stom·ach (stum′ək) *n.* [< OFr. < L. < Gr. *stomachos*, gullet < *stoma*, mouth] **1.** the large, saclike organ of vertebrates into which food passes from the oesophagus or gullet for storage while undergoing the early processes of digestion: in cud-chewing animals it consists of four chambers **2.** any digestive cavity **3.** the abdomen, or belly **4.** appetite for food **5.** desire or inclination of any kind —*vt.* **1.** to be able to eat or digest **2.** to tolerate; bear

stom·ach·ache (-āk′) *n.* pain in the stomach or abdomen

stom·ach·er (-ər) *n.* an ornamented, triangular piece of cloth formerly worn, esp. by women, as a covering for the chest and abdomen

sto·mach·ic (stə mak′ik) *adj.* **1.** of or having to do with the stomach **2.** acting as a digestive tonic Also **sto·mach′i·cal** —*n.* a digestive tonic —**sto·mach′i·cal·ly** *adv.*

stomach pump a suction pump with a flexible tube that can be placed in the stomach to remove the contents

stomach upset a slight digestive disorder

-stome (-stōm) [< Gr. *stoma*, mouth] *a combining form meaning* mouth

-sto·mous (-stə məs) [< Gr. *stoma*, mouth] *a combining form meaning* having a (specified kind of) mouth

stomp (stomp) *vt., vi.* *var. of* STAMP —*n.* formerly, **1.** a jazz tune with a lively rhythm and a strong beat **2.** a dance to this music

-sto·my (-stə mē) [< Gr. < *stoma*, mouth] *a combining form meaning* a surgical opening into (a specified part)

stone (stōn) *n.* [OE. *stan*] **1.** the hard, solid, nonmetallic mineral matter of which rock is composed **2.** a small piece of rock **3.** a piece of rock shaped for some purpose; specif., *a)* a building block *b)* a gravestone *c)* a milestone *d)* a grindstone **4.** *a)* the stonelike seed of certain fruits, as of a date *b)* the hard endocarp and the enclosed seed of a drupe, as of a peach **5.** *short for* PRECIOUS STONE **6.** *pl.* **stone** formerly, a unit of weight equal to 14 pounds **7.** *Med.* *same as* CALCULUS (sense 1) —*vt.* **stoned, ston′ing** **1.** to throw stones at or kill with stones **2.** to furnish, pave, line, etc. with stones **3.** to remove the stone from (a peach, etc.) —*adj.* of stone or stoneware —**cast the first stone** to be the first to censure or criticize —**leave no stone unturned** to do everything possible —**stone the crows** [Slang] an expression of surprise —**ston′er** *n.*

stone- [< prec., with the sense of "like a stone"] *a combining form used in hyphenated compounds, meaning* very, completely [*stone*-blind]

Stone Age the early period in human culture during which stone implements were used

stone-blind (stōn′blīnd′) *adj.* completely blind

stone·chat (-chat′) *n.* [from its cry, like the sound of pebbles knocked together] any of various small, insect eating birds, esp. a European bird with a black head

stone-cold (-kōld′) *adj.* quite or completely cold

stone·crop (-krop′) *n.* *popular name for* SEDUM

stone·cut·ter (-kut′ər) *n.* a person or machine that cuts stone and makes it smooth —**stone′cut′ting** *n.*

stoned (stōnd) *adj.* **1.** having the stones removed [*stoned* peaches] **2.** [Slang] *a)* drunk; intoxicated *b)* under the influence of a drug

stone-dead (stōn′ded′) *adj.* completely dead; lifeless

stone-deaf (-def′) *adj.* completely deaf

stone·fly (-flī′) *n., pl.* **-flies′** any of various soft-bodied, winged insects in an undeveloped stage that live under stones in swift streams

stone fruit any fruit, as a plum, having a stone

stone·ma·son (-mā′s'n) *n.* a person who cuts stone to shape and uses it in making walls, buildings, etc. —**stone′-ma′son·ry** (-rē) *n.*

stone's throw a relatively short distance

stone·wall (stōn′wôl′) *vi.* **1.** *Cricket* to play only a defensive game in order to gain a draw: said of a batsman **2.** [Colloq.] to obstruct a debate, negotiation, etc.

stone·ware (stōn′wer′) *n.* a coarse, dense pottery containing much silica or sand and flint

stone·work (-wurk′) *n.* **1.** the art or process of working in stone **2.** something made or built in stone **3.** [*pl.*] a place where stonecutting is done

stonk·ered (stoŋ′kərd) *adj.* [< *stonker*, to beat or make useless < ?] [Aust. Slang] completely exhausted; worn-out

ston·y (stō′nē) *adj.* **ston′i·er, ston′i·est** **1.** covered with or having many stones **2.** of or like stone; specif., *a)* hard *b)* unfeeling; pitiless *c)* cold; fixed; rigid Also **ston′ey** —**ston′-i·ly** *adv.* —**ston′i·ness** *n.*

ston·y-broke (-brōk′) *adj.* [STONY + BROKE] [Slang] having no money at all; penniless

stood (stood) *pt. & pp. of* STAND

stooge (stooj) *n.* [< ?] [Colloq.] **1.** an actor who aids a comedian by feeding him lines, being the victim of pranks, etc. **2.** anyone who acts as a foil, underling, etc. —*vi.* **stooged, stoog′ing** [Colloq.] to be a stooge (*for* someone)

stool (stool) *n.* [OE. *stol*] **1.** *a)* a single seat having no back or arms *b)* *same as* FOOTSTOOL **2.** a toilet, or water closet **3.** the faecal matter eliminated in a single bowel movement **4.** *a)* a root or tree stump sending out shoots *b)* a cluster of such shoots —*vi.* **1.** to put out shoots in the form of a stool **2.** [Chiefly U.S. Colloq.] to act as a stool pigeon

stool ball an early form of cricket played with a short-handled bat and one upright stick as a wicket

stool pigeon **1.** a pigeon or other bird used as a decoy **2.** a person serving as a decoy **3.** [Chiefly U.S. Colloq.] a spy or informer, esp. for the police: also **stool·ie** (stool′ē) *n.*

stoop[1] (stoop) *vi.* [OE. *stupian*] **1.** to bend the body forward or in a crouch **2.** to carry the head and shoulders habitually bent forward **3.** to lower one's dignity or do something beneath one's dignity **4.** to swoop down, as a bird of prey —*vt.* to bend (the head, etc.) forward —*n.* **1.** the act or position of stooping the body, esp. habitually **2.** a lowering of one's dignity **3.** a swoop, as by a hawk at prey —**stoop′er** *n.* —**stoop′ing·ly** *adv.*

stoop[2] (stoop) *n.* [Du. *stoep*] [U.S.] a small porch or platform with steps, at the door of a house

stop (stop) *vt.* **stopped, stop′ping** [< OE. *-stoppian* (in comp.) < WGmc. *stoppōn*, ult. < Gr. *styppē*, tow fibres] **1.** to close by filling, shutting off, covering, etc. **2.** to staunch (a wound, etc.) **3.** to block up (a passage, pipe, etc.); obstruct: often with *up* **4.** to close (a bottle, etc.) as with a cork **5.** to cause to cease motion, activity, etc. **6.** to prevent the passage of (water, light, etc.); block **7.** to halt the progress of (a person, vehicle, etc.) **8.** *a)* to check (a blow, stroke, etc.); parry; counter *b)* to defeat (an opponent) **9.** to fill (a decayed tooth) **10.** to cease; desist from (with a gerund) [*stop* talking] **11.** to cause to end [*stop* that racket] **12.** to cause (an engine, machine, etc.) to cease operation **13.** to close (a finger hole of a wind instrument) or press down (a violin string, etc.) to produce a desired tone **14.** to keep from beginning, acting, etc.; prevent **15.** to notify one's bank to withhold payment on (one's cheque): also **stop payment** —*vi.* **1.** to cease moving, walking, etc.; halt **2.** to leave off doing something; desist **3.** to cease operating or functioning **4.** to come to an end **5.** to become clogged **6.** to tarry or stay for a while (often with *at* or *in*) —*n.* **1.** a stopping or being stopped; check; cessation **2.** a finish; end **3.** a stay or brief visit **4.** a place stopped at, as on a bus route **5.** something that stops; obstruction; specif., *a)* a plug or stopper *b)* an order to withhold payment on a cheque *c)* a mechanical part that stops or regulates motion *d)* a punctuation mark, esp. a full stop **6.** *a)* a stopping of a violin string, finger hole of a wind instrument, etc. to produce a desired pitch *b)* such a hole **7.** *a)* a tuned set of organ pipes, reeds, or electronic devices of the same type and tone quality *b)* a pull, lever, or key for putting such a set into or out of operation **8.** *Phonet.* *a)* a complete stopping of the outgoing breath, as with the lips, tongue, or velum *b)* a consonant formed in this way, as *p, b, k, g, t,* and *d* —*adj.* that stops or is meant to stop [a *stop* signal] —**pull out all (the) stops** **1.** to use all the stops in playing an organ **2.** to make an all-out effort —**put a stop to** to cause to cease —**stop at nothing** to be merciless or ruthless —**stop off** to stop for a short visit on the way to a place —**stop out** **1.** to cover part of a page so that it does not print **2.** to remain out of a house, esp. overnight —**stop over** **1.** to visit for a while: also **stop in** **2.** to break a journey, as for rest

stop·cock (-kok′) *n.* a valve for stopping or regulating the flow of a fluid, as through a pipe

stope (stōp) *n.* [prob. < MLowG. *stōpe*] a steplike excavation formed by removing ore from around a mine shaft —*vt.*, *vi.* stoped, stop′ing to mine in stopes

stop·gap (stop′gap′) *n.* a person or thing serving as a temporary substitute —*adj.* used as a stopgap

stop·light (-līt′) *n.* [U.S.] a traffic light, esp. when red and signalling vehicles to stop

stop·o·ver (-ō′vər) *n.* 1. a brief stop or stay at a place in the course of a journey 2. a place for such a stop Also **stop′-off′**

stop·page (-ij) *n.* 1. a stopping or being stopped 2. an obstructed condition; block 3. a period during which a factory, etc. is inactive, as because of a strike 4. [*often pl.*] a deduction at source from wages, esp. for tax purposes

stop·per (-ər) *n.* 1. a person or thing that stops 2. something inserted to close an opening; plug —*vt.* to close with a plug or stopper

stopping train a train which stops at most of the minor stations as well as the major ones

stop·ple (-'l) *n.* [< ME. dim. < *stoppen*, to stop] a stopper, or plug —*vt.* -pled, -pling to close with a stopple

stop press 1. the news put into a newspaper, generally in a special column after printing has begun 2. the space left blank for such news

stop·watch (stop′woch′) *n.* a watch with a hand that can be started and stopped instantly so as to indicate fractions of seconds, as for timing races, etc.

stor·age (stôr′ij) *n.* 1. a storing or being stored 2. *a)* a place or space for storing goods *b)* the cost of keeping goods stored 3. *same as* MEMORY (sense 7)

storage battery a battery of electrochemical cells for generating electric current: the cells can be recharged by passing a current through them in the direction opposite to the discharging flow of current

storage heater a heater, usually electric, that stores off-peak electricity, etc. for later use

CURRENT FLOW

LEAD DIOXIDE PLATE

LEAD PLATE

WATER AND SULPHURIC ACID

STORAGE BATTERY CELL (current flow when charging)

store (stôr) *vt.* stored, stor′ing [< OFr. *estorer* < L. *instaurare*, to restore] 1. to put aside for use when needed 2. to furnish with a supply or stock 3. to put in a warehouse, etc. for safe-keeping 4. to be a place for the storage of 5. to put or keep (information) in a computer memory unit —*vi.* to undergo storage in a specified manner —*n.* 1. a supply (*of* something) for use when needed; reserve 2. [*pl.*] supplies, esp. of food, clothing, etc. 3. a large shop where a variety of goods are regularly offered for sale 4. a storehouse; warehouse 5. a great amount; abundance —*adj.* of a kind sold in stores —**in store** set aside for, or awaiting one in, the future —**set** (or **put** or **lay**) **store by** to value; esteem —**stor′a·ble** *adj.*

store·house (-haus′) *n.* a place where things are stored; esp., a warehouse

store·keep·er (-kē′pər) *n.* 1. a person in charge of stores, or supplies 2. [U.S.] a shopkeeper

store·room (-rōōm′) *n.* a room where things are stored

sto·rey (stôr′ē) *n.*, *pl.* **-reys** [ML. *historia*, a picture (< L.: see HISTORY): prob. from use of "storied" windows or friezes marking the outside of different floors] 1. a horizontal division of a building extending from a floor to the ceiling directly above [*ten storeys tall*] 2. all the rooms on the same level of a building

stor·eyed (stôr′ēd) *adj.* having storeys or floors: usually in hyphenated compounds [*many-storeyed*]

sto·ried (stôr′ēd) *adj.* 1. ornamented with designs showing scenes from history, a story, etc. 2. famous in story or history

stork (stôrk) *n.*, *pl.* **storks**, **stork**: see PLURAL, II, D, 1 [OE. *storc*] a large, long-legged wading bird, having a long neck and bill

storm (stôrm) *n.* [OE.] 1. a disturbance of the atmosphere in which there is a strong wind usually along with rain, snow, etc. and often with thunder and lightning 2. any heavy fall of snow, rain, etc. 3. anything resembling a storm [*a storm of bullets*] 4. a strong emotional outburst 5. a strong disturbance or upheaval of a political or social nature 6. a sudden, strong attack on a fortified place 7. *Meteorol.* a wind of force 11 on the Beaufort scale (c. 103-117 km/h) —*vi.* 1. to blow violently, rain, snow, etc. 2. to rage; rant 3. to rush or move violently [*to storm into a room*] —*vt.* 1. to attack (someone) in a vigorous or angry outburst 2. to capture or attempt to capture (a fortified place) with a sudden, strong attack

storm·bound (-bound′) *adj.* halted, delayed, or cut off by storms

storm centre 1. the shifting centre of a cyclone 2. a centre or focus of trouble or disturbance

storm door (or **window**) an extra door (or window) placed outside the regular one as added protection against winter weather

storm lantern *same as* HURRICANE LAMP

storm trooper a member of Hitler's Nazi party militia, notorious for their brutal methods

storm·y (stôr′mē) *adj.* **storm′i·er**, **storm′i·est** 1. of, characteristic of, or affected by storms 2. having or characterized by storms 3. violent, raging, turbulent, etc. —**storm′i·ly** *adv.* —**storm′i·ness** *n.*

stormy petrel 1. any of several small petrels whose presence is thought to warn of coming storms: also **storm petrel** 2. a person thought to bring trouble wherever he goes

Stor·ting, Stor·thing (stôr′tiŋ′) *n.* [Norw. < *stor*, great + *ting*, assembly] the parliament of Norway

sto·ry¹ (stôr′ē) *n.*, *pl.* **-ries** [< OFr. < L. < Gr. *historia*: see HISTORY] 1. the telling of an event or series of events, whether true or fictitious; account; narration 2. an anecdote or joke 3. *a)* a fictitious literary composition shorter than a novel; narrative; tale *b)* such tales as a form of literature 4. the plot of a novel, play, etc.: also **story line** 5. *a)* a report or rumour *b)* [Colloq.] a falsehood or fib 6. romantic legend or history 7. a news event or a report of it, as in the newspapers —*vt.* -ried, -ry·ing to decorate with paintings, etc. of scenes from history or legend

sto·ry² (stôr′ē) *n.*, *pl.* **-ries** *var. sp. of* STOREY

sto·ry·book (stôr′ē book′) *n.* a book of stories, esp. one for children —*adj.* typical of romantic tales in storybooks

sto·ry·tell·er (-tel′ər) *n.* 1. a person who narrates stories 2. [Colloq.] a fibber or liar —**sto′ry·tell′ing** *n.*

sto·tin·ka (stō tiŋ′kə) *n.*, *pl.* **-tin′ki** (-kē) [Bulg.] see MONETARY UNITS, table (Bulgaria)

stoup (stōōp) *n.* [ON. *staup*] 1. a drinking cup; tankard 2. a basin for holy water in a church

stout (staut) *adj.* [OFr. *estout*, bold, prob. < Frank. *stolt*] 1. courageous; brave [*a stout fellow*] 2. *a)* strong in body; sturdy *b)* firm; substantial [*a stout wall*] 3. powerful; forceful 4. fat; thickset; corpulent —*n.* a heavy, dark-brown brew like porter, but with a higher percentage of hops —**stout′ish** *adj.* —**stout′ly** *adv.* —**stout′ness** *n.*

stout·heart·ed (-här′tid) *adj.* courageous; brave —**stout′-heart′ed·ly** *adv.* —**stout′heart′ed·ness** *n.*

stove¹ (stōv) *n.* [MDu., a heated room] an apparatus using fuel or electricity for heating, cooking, etc.

stove² (stōv) *alt. pt. & pp. of* STAVE

stove·pipe (stōv′pīp′) *n.* 1. a metal pipe used to carry off smoke or fumes from a stove 2. [Colloq.] a man's tall silk hat: in full, **stovepipe hat**

stow (stō) *vt.* [OE. *stow*, a place] 1. to pack or store away; esp., to pack in an orderly, compact way 2. to fill by packing thus 3. to hold: said of a container, etc. 4. [Slang] to stop [*stow the chatter!*] —**stow away** 1. to put or hide away 2. to be a stowaway

stow·age (-ij) *n.* 1. a stowing or being stowed 2. place or room for stowing 3. something stowed 4. charges for stowing

stow·a·way (-ə wā′) *n.* a person who hides aboard a ship, aircraft, etc. to get free passage, evade port officials, etc.

STP 1. [L. *Sanctae Theologiae Professor*] Professor of Sacred Theology 2. Standard Temperature and Pressure

stra·bis·mus (strə biz′məs) *n.* [ModL. < Gr. < *strabizein*, to squint < *strabos*, twisted] a disorder of the muscles of the eyes, as cross-eye, in which both eyes cannot be focused on the same point at the same time —**stra·bis′mal**, **stra·bis′mic** *adj.* —**stra·bis′mal·ly** *adv.*

Strad (strad) *n.* *clipped form of* STRADIVARIUS

strad·dle (strad′'l) *vt.* -dled, -dling [freq. of STRIDE] 1. to place oneself with a leg on either side of 2. to spread (the legs) wide apart 3. to take or appear to take both sides of (an issue); avoid committing oneself on —*vi.* 1. to sit, stand, or walk with the legs wide apart 2. to be spread apart: said of the legs 3. [Chiefly U.S.] to straddle an issue, etc. —*n.* 1. the act or position of straddling 2. a refusal to commit oneself definitely —**strad′dler** *n.*

Strad·i·var·i·us (strad′ə ver′ē əs) *n.* [after A. *Stradivari* (1644-1737), It. violin maker] a string instrument, esp. a violin, made by A. Stradivari or his sons

strafe (sträf) *vt.* strafed, straf′ing [< G. phr. *Gott strafe England* (God punish England!)] to attack with machine-gun fire from low-flying aircraft —**straf′er** *n.*

strag·gle (strag′'l) *vi.* -gled, -gling [prob. < ME. freq. of *straken*, to roam] 1. to stray from the course or wander from the main group 2. to be scattered over a wide area; ramble 3. to leave, arrive, etc. at scattered irregular intervals 4. to hang in an untidy way, as hair, clothes, etc. —*n.* a straggly arrangement or group —**strag′gler** *n.*

strag·gly (-lē) *adj.* -gli·er, -gli·est spread out in a straggling, irregular way

straight (strāt) *adj.* [< ME. pp. of *strecchen*, to STRETCH]
1. having the same direction throughout its length [a *straight* line] 2. not crooked, bent, wavy, etc. [straight hair] 3. upright; erect [straight posture] 4. level; even [a *straight* hemline] 5. direct; undeviating, uninterrupted, etc. [to hold a *straight* course] 6. following a direct course of reasoning, etc.; methodical 7. in order; properly arranged, etc. 8. *a)* honest; sincere *b)* reliable [straight information] 9. outspoken; frank 10. *a)* without anything added; undiluted [a *straight* shot of whisky] *b)* [U.S.] not blended with neutral grain spirits 11. not qualified, slanted, etc. [a *straight* denial] 12. serious; without music, dancing, etc.: said of drama 13. [Slang] normal or conventional; specif., not a homosexual, not a drug addict, etc. —*adv.* 1. in a straight line or direction; unswervingly 2. upright; erectly 3. *a)* without detour, delay, etc. *b)* directly [tell it *straight*] *c)* without alteration, etc. [play the role *straight*] —*n.* 1. a being straight 2. something straight; specif., *a)* the straight part of a race track *b)* Poker a hand consisting of any five cards in sequence —**go straight** to reform, esp. to abandon former criminal activities —**straight away** (or **off**) at once; without delay —**the straight and narrow (path)** a strict code of morals —**straight′ly** *adv.* —**straight′ness** *n.*
straight angle an angle of 180 degrees
straight chair a chair with a back that is straight, or almost vertical, and not upholstered
straight·edge (-ej′) *n.* a piece of wood, etc. with a straight edge used in drawing straight lines, testing plane surfaces, etc.
straight·en (-'n) *vt., vi.* to make or become straight —**straighten out** 1. to make or become less confused, easier to deal with, etc. 2. [Chiefly U.S.] to correct or reform the behaviour of —**straight′en·er** *n.*
straight face a facial expression showing no amusement or other emotion —**straight′-faced′** *adj.*
straight fight an election with only two opposing candidates
straight·for·ward (strāt′fôr′wərd) *adj.* 1. moving or leading straight ahead; direct 2. honest; frank; open —*adv.* in a straightforward manner: also **straight′for′wards** —**straight′for′ward·ly** *adv.* —**straight′for′ward·ness** *n.*
straight·jack·et (strāt′jak′it) *n.* same as STRAITJACKET
straight-laced (-lāst′) *adj.* same as STRAIT-LACED (sense 2)
straight man an actor who serves as a foil for a comedian, feeding him lines
straight-out (-out′) *adj.* [U.S. Colloq.] 1. straightforward 2. unrestrained 3. thoroughgoing; unqualified
straight·way (-wā′) *adv.* at once; without delay
strain¹ (strān) *vt.* [< OFr. < L. *stringere*, to draw tight] 1. to draw or stretch tight 2. to exert, use, or tax to the utmost [to *strain* every nerve] 3. to injure by overexertion; wrench [to *strain* a muscle] 4. to injure or weaken by force, pressure, etc. [the wind *strained* the roof] 5. to stretch beyond the normal limits 6. *a)* to pass through a screen, sieve, etc.; filter *b)* to remove by filtration, etc. 7. to hug: now only in **to strain to one's bosom** (or **heart**, etc.) —*vi.* 1. to make violent efforts; strive hard 2. to be or become strained 3. to be subjected to great stress or pressure 4. to pull or push with force 5. to filter, ooze, etc. —*n.* 1. a straining or being strained 2. great effort, exertion, etc. 3. an injury to a part of the body as a result of overexertion [heart *strain*] 4. stress or force 5. a great or excessive demand on one's emotions, resources, etc. —**strain oneself** 1. to injure oneself after a physical effort 2. to exert oneself to do something
strain² (strān) *n.* [OE. *streon*, procreation < base of *strynan*, to produce] 1. ancestry; lineage 2. the descendants of a common ancestor; race; stock; line 3. a group of individuals within a species, different in one or more characters from others in the species 4. an inherited character or tendency 5. a trace; streak 6. the style or tone of a speech, book, action, etc. 7. [often *pl.*] a passage of music; tune; air
strained (strānd) *adj.* 1. being strained 2. unnatural; forced
strain·er (strān′ər) *n.* a person or thing that strains; specif., a device for straining, sifting, or filtering; sieve, filter, etc.
strait (strāt) *adj.* [< OFr. < L. pp. of *stringere*: see STRICT] 1. [Archaic] *a)* narrow; tight *b)* strict; rigid 2. [Now Rare] difficult; distressing —*n.* 1. [often *pl.*] a narrow waterway connecting two large bodies of water 2. [often *pl.*] difficulty; distress 3. [Rare] an isthmus
strait·en (strāt′'n) *vt.* 1. esp. formerly, *a)* to make strait or narrow *b)* to restrict or confine; hamper 2. to bring into difficulties: usually in the phrase **in straitened circumstances**, lacking sufficient money
strait·jack·et (-jak′it) *n.* a coatlike device that binds the arms tight against the body: used to restrain persons in a violent state
strait-laced (-lāst′) *adj.* 1. formerly, tightly laced, as a corset 2. narrowly strict in behaviour or moral views
strake (strāk) *n.* [akin to STRETCH] a single line of planking or plating extending along the length of a ship

strand¹ (strand) *n.* [OE.] shore, esp. ocean shore —*vt., vi.* 1. to run or drive aground [a ship *stranded* by the storm] 2. to leave or be put into a difficult, helpless position [*stranded* in a strange city with no money]
strand² (strand) *n.* [< ?] 1. any of the threads, fibres, wires, etc. that are twisted together to form a string, rope, or cable 2. a ropelike length of anything [a *strand* of pearls, *strands* of hair] 3. any of the parts that are bound together to form a whole [the *strands* of one's life] —*vt.* to form (a rope, etc.) by twisting strands together —**strand′-er** *n.*
strange (strānj) *adj.* **strang′er, strang′est** [< OFr. < L. *extraneus*, foreign < *extra*, outside] 1. foreign; alien 2. not previously known, seen, heard, etc.; unfamiliar 3. unusual; extraordinary 4. peculiar; odd 5. reserved, distant, or cold in manner 6. lacking experience; unaccustomed [*strange* to the job] —**feel strange** to feel odd, esp. to feel dizzy, etc. —**strange′ly** *adv.* —**strange′ness** *n.*
stran·ger (strān′jər) *n.* 1. an outsider or newcomer 2. a person not known or familiar to one 3. a person unaccustomed (*to* something) [a *stranger* to hate] 4. someone not a member of, or official in, the House of Commons, esp. in the phrase **I spy strangers**
stran·gle (straŋ′g'l) *vt.* **-gled, -gling** [< OFr. < L. *strangulare* < Gr. < *strangalē*, halter] 1. to kill by squeezing the throat as with the hands, a noose, etc., so as to shut off the breath 2. to choke or suffocate in any way 3. to suppress, stifle, or repress —*vi.* to be strangled; choke —**stran′gler** *n.*
stran·gle·hold (-hōld′) *n.* 1. an illegal wrestling hold that chokes off an opponent's breath 2. any force that restricts or suppresses freedom
stran·gles (-g'lz) *n.* an infectious disease of horses characterized by inflammation of the respiratory tract
stran·gu·late (straŋ′gyoo lāt′) *vt.* **-lat′ed, -lat′ing** [< L. pp. of *strangulare*] 1. same as STRANGLE 2. Med. to cause (an intestine or other tube) to become squeezed so that a flow, as of blood, is cut off —*vi.* Med. to be strangulated —**stran′gu·la′tion** *n.*
strap (strap) *n.* [dial. form of STROP] 1. a narrow strip of leather, plastic, cloth, etc. often with a buckle at one end, for tying or holding things together 2. any of several straplike parts or things, as a shoulder strap, a razor strop, etc. 3. punishment with a strap —*vt.* **strapped, strap′ping** 1. to fasten with a strap 2. to beat with a strap 3. to strop (a razor) —**strap′less** *adj.* —**strap′per** *n.*
strap·hang·er (-haŋ′ər) *n.* [Colloq.] a standing passenger, as on a crowded bus, who supports himself by holding onto a hanging strap, etc.
strap·ping (strap′iŋ) *adj.* [Colloq.] tall and sturdy; robust
strap·work (strap′wurk′) *n.* Archit. ornamentation consisting of interlaced bands
stra·ta (strāt′ə) *n.* alt. pl. of STRATUM
strat·a·gem (strat′ə jəm) *n.* [< L. < Gr. *stratēgēma*, act of a general < *stratos*, army + *agein*, to lead] 1. a trick, scheme, or plan for deceiving an enemy in war 2. any trick or scheme for achieving some purpose
stra·te·gic (strə tē′jik) *adj.* 1. of or having to do with strategy 2. sound in strategy; advantageous 3. *a)* needed for carrying out military strategy or carrying on war [*strategic* materials] *b)* directed against the military and industrial installations of the enemy [*strategic* bombing] Also **stra·te′gi·cal** —**stra·te′gi·cal·ly** *adv.*
strat·e·gist (strat′ə jist) *n.* one skilled in strategy
strat·e·gy (-jē) *n., pl.* **-gies** [< Fr. < Gr. < *stratēgos*, general: see STRATAGEM] 1. *a)* the science of planning and directing large-scale military operations *b)* a plan or action based on this 2. *a)* skill in managing or planning, esp. by using stratagems *b)* an ingenious or artful means to some end Also, esp. for sense 1, **strat·e·gics** (strə tē′jiks)
strath (strath) *n.* [< ScotGael. *srath*] a wide river valley
strat·i·fy (strat′ə fī′) *vt.* **-fied′, -fy′ing** [< Fr. < ModL. < L. *stratum*, layer + *facere*, to make] 1. to form or arrange in layers or strata 2. to classify (people) into groups graded according to status as determined by birth, income, education, etc. —*vi.* to become stratified —**strat′i·fi·ca′tion** (-fi kā′shən) *n.*
stra·to·cu·mu·lus (strat′ō kyoom′yə ləs) *n., pl.* **-li** (-lī′) [ModL.: see STRATUS & CUMULUS] a cloud type arranged in horizontal patterns, with parts that are rounded, roll-shaped, etc.
strat·o·sphere (strat′ə sfir′) *n.* [< Fr. < ModL. *stratum*, STRATUM + Fr. *sphère*, SPHERE] the atmospheric zone extending from about 9 kilometres to about 24 kilometres above the earth's surface, in which the temperature ranges from about -45°C to -75°C —**strat′o·spher′ic** (-sfer′-ik,-sfir′-) *adj.*
stra·tum (strāt′əm) *n., pl.* **stra′ta** (-ə), **-tums** [ModL. < L. < *stratus*, pp. of *sternere*, to spread] 1. a horizontal layer of material, esp. any of several lying one upon another; specif., Geol. a single layer of sedimentary rock 2. a section, level, or division, as of the atmosphere or ocean,

regarded as like a stratum **3.** any of the socioeconomic groups of a society as determined by birth, income, education, etc. —**stra·tal** (strät′'l) *adj.*

stra·tus (-əs) *n., pl.* **stra′ti** (-ī) [L., a strewing: see prec.] a cloud type extending in a long, low, grey layer with an almost uniform base

straw (strô) *n.* [OE. *streaw*] **1.** hollow stalks of grain after threshing, used for bedding, for weaving hats, baskets, etc. **2.** a single one of such stalks **3.** a tube used for sucking beverages **4.** something, as a hat, made of straw **5.** a worthless trifle —*adj.* **1.** straw-coloured; yellowish **2.** made of straw **3.** worthless; meaningless —**a straw in the wind** a sign of what may happen —**grasp** (or **clutch, catch**) **at a straw** (or **straws**) to try anything that offers even the slightest hope —**straw′y** *adj.*

straw·ber·ry (-ber′ē) *n., pl.* **-ries** [< OE. < *streaw,* straw + *berige,* berry: prob. so called from the small achenes on the fruit] **1.** the small, red, fleshy fruit of a low plant of the rose family that puts out runners **2.** this plant

strawberry blonde reddish blonde

strawberry leaves the badge of rank of a duke, after the ornamentation on his coronet

strawberry mark a small, red birthmark

straw·board (strô′bôrd′) *n.* a coarse cardboard made of straw pulp

straw colour a pale-yellow colour —**straw′-col′oured** *adj.*

straw·flow·er (-flou′ər) *n.* an annual plant whose brightly coloured flower heads are dried for winter bouquets

straw man **1.** a scarecrow made of straw **2.** a weak argument, opponent, etc. set up by one so that he may in attacking gain an easy, showy victory **3.** a person used to disguise another's activities, etc.; blind

straw vote [U.S.] an unofficial vote or poll for sampling popular opinion on candidates or on an issue

stray (strā) *vi.* [< OFr. *estraier,* prob. ult. < L. *extra vagari,* to wander outside] **1.** to wander from a given place, course, etc.; roam **2.** to go wrong; deviate (*from* what is right) **3.** to wander from the subject; be inattentive or digress —*n.* a person or thing that strays; esp., a domestic animal wandering at large —*adj.* **1.** having strayed; lost **2.** isolated, occasional, or incidental [a few *stray* words] —**stray′er** *n.*

streak (strēk) *n.* [OE. *strica*] **1.** a line or long, thin mark; stripe or smear **2.** a ray of light or a flash, as of lightning **3.** a thin layer, as of fat in meat or ore in rock **4.** a tendency in one's nature [a jealous *streak*] **5.** a period, spell, or run [a *streak* of victories] —*vt.* to mark with streaks —*vi.* **1.** to become streaked **2.** to move swiftly —**like a streak** [Colloq.] swiftly

streak·y (-ē) *adj.* **streak′i·er, streak′i·est** marked with or occurring in streaks; uneven —**streak′i·ness** *n.*

streaky bacon bacon with alternating strips of fat and lean meat

stream (strēm) *n.* [OE.] **1.** a current or flow of water; specif., a small river **2.** a steady flow of any fluid [a *stream* of cold air] or of rays of energy [a *stream* of light] **3.** a moving line of things [a *stream* of cars] **4.** a trend or course [the *stream* of events] **5.** *Educ.* any of the sections formed by grouping children of similar ability together —*vi.* **1.** to flow as in a stream **2.** to flow (*with*) [eyes *streaming* with tears] **3.** to move steadily or swiftly **4.** to float or fly, as a flag in the breeze —*vt.* to cause to stream

stream·er (strē′mər) *n.* **1.** something that streams **2.** a long, narrow flag **3.** any long, narrow, flowing strip of material **4.** a stream of light extending up from the horizon **5.** a newspaper headline across the full page

stream·let (strēm′lit) *n.* a small stream; rivulet

stream·line (-līn′) *vt.* **-lined′, -lin′ing** to make streamlined —*adj.* same as STREAMLINED

stream·lined (-līnd′) *adj.* **1.** having a contour designed to offer the least resistance in moving through air, water, etc. **2.** arranged so as to be more efficient [a *streamlined* programme] **3.** with no excess, as of weight, decoration, etc.; trim [a *streamlined* figure or design]

stream of consciousness individual conscious experience regarded as having continuity and flow: a principle made use of in novels, etc. in presenting the thoughts, inner feelings, etc. of a character in a natural, unrestrained flow

stream·y (strē′mē) *adj.* **stream′i·er, stream′i·est** **1.** full of streams or currents **2.** flowing; streaming

street (strēt) *n.* [OE. *stræt* < LL. < L. *strata* (*via*), paved (road)] **1.** a public road in a city or town; esp., a paved thoroughfare with buildings along the sides **2.** such a road apart from its pavements **3.** the people living, working, etc. in the buildings along a given street —*adj.* **1.** of, in, on, or near the street [the *street* door] **2.** suitable for everyday wear in public [*street* clothes] —**(right) up one's street** [Colloq.] (just) what one knows or likes best —**streets ahead** [Colloq.] far superior to

street·car (-kär′) *n.* [U.S.] a tram (sense 2)

street cries the calls of street traders

street·walk·er (-wôk′ər) *n.* a prostitute who solicits customers along the streets —**street′walk′ing** *n.*

strength (streŋkth, streŋth) *n.* [OE. *strengthu*] **1.** the state or quality of being strong; power; force; vigour **2.** the power to resist strain, stress, etc.; toughness; durability **3.** the power to resist attack **4.** legal, moral, or intellectual force **5.** *a*) capacity for producing an effect *b*) potency or concentration, as of drugs, spirits, etc. **6.** intensity, as of sound, colour, etc. **7.** force as measured in numbers [an army at full *strength*] **8.** vigour of feeling or expression **9.** a source of strength or support —**on the strength of** based or relying on

strength·en (-'n) *vt., vi.* to make or become stronger —**strength′en·er** *n.*

stren·u·ous (stren′yŏŏ wəs) *adj.* [L. *strenuus*] **1.** requiring or characterized by great effort or energy **2.** vigorous, arduous, zealous, etc. —**stren′u·ous·ly** *adv.* —**stren′-u·ous·ness** *n.*

strep (strep) *n.* shortened form of STREPTOCOCCUS

strep·to·coc·cus (strep′tə kok′əs) *n., pl.* **-coc′ci** (-kok′sī) [ModL., genus name < Gr. *streptos,* twisted + COCCUS] any of a group of spherical bacteria that occur generally in chains: some species cause serious diseases —**strep′to·coc′-cal** (-kok′əl), **strep′to·coc′cic** (-kok′sik) *adj.*

strep·to·my·cin (-mī′sin) *n.* [< Gr. *streptos,* twisted + *mykēs,* fungus] an antibiotic drug used in the treatment of various bacterial diseases, as tuberculosis

stress (stres) *n.* [< OFr., ult. < L. *strictus,* STRICT] **1.** strain or straining force; specif., force exerted upon a body, that tends to strain or deform its shape **2.** emphasis; importance **3.** *a*) mental or physical tension or strain *b*) urgency, pressure, etc. causing this **4.** *a*) the relative force of utterance given a syllable or word in pronunciation or, according to the metre, in verse *b*) an accented syllable **5.** *Music* emphasis on a note or chord —*vt.* **1.** to put stress, pressure, or strain on **2.** to give stress or accent to **3.** to emphasize —**stress′ful** *adj.* —**stress′ful·ly** *adv.*

-stress (stris) [< -STER + -ESS] a feminine suffix corresponding to -STER [*songstress*]

stretch (strech) *vt.* [OE. *streccan*] **1.** to reach out; extend [to *stretch* out a helping hand] **2.** to cause (the body or limbs) to reach out to full length, as in relaxing, etc. **3.** to pull or spread out to full extent or to a greater size **4.** to cause to extend over a given space, distance, or time [to *stretch* pipelines across a desert] **5.** *a*) to extend farther or too far *b*) to strain in interpretation, scope, etc. to questionable or unreasonable limits [to *stretch* a rule] **6.** to make tense with effort; strain (a muscle, etc.) —*vi.* **1.** *a*) to spread out to full extent or beyond normal limits *b*) to extend over a given space, distance, or time **2.** *a*) to extend the body or limbs to full length, as in relaxing, etc. *b*) to lie down at full length (usually with *out*) **3.** to become stretched to greater size, as any elastic substance —*n.* **1.** a stretching or being stretched **2.** *a*) an unbroken period [a *stretch* of ten days] *b*) [Slang] a term served in prison **3.** the extent to which something can be stretched **4.** an unbroken length, tract, etc. [a *stretch* of beach] —*adj.* made of elasticized fabric —**stretch a point** to make a concession —**stretch one's legs** to go for a short walk —**stretch′a·bil′i·ty** *n.* —**stretch′a·ble** *adj.*

stretch·er (-ər) *n.* **1.** one that stretches; specif., *a*) a brick or stone laid lengthwise in the face of a wall *b*) any of various devices for stretching or shaping garments, etc. **2.** *a*) a light frame covered with canvas, etc. and used for carrying the sick, injured, or dead *b*) any similar device, as a wheeled cot used in ambulances

stretch·er·bear·er (-ber′ər) *n.* a person who helps carry a stretcher, esp. from an accident or in military combat

stretch marks the marks left on a woman's abdomen after pregnancy

stretch·y (-ē) *adj.* **stretch′i·er, stretch′i·est** **1.** that can be stretched; elastic **2.** tending to stretch too far —**stretch′-i·ness** *n.*

strew (strŏŏ) *vt.* **strewed, strewed** or **strewn, strew′ing** [OE. *streawian*] **1.** to spread about here and there; scatter **2.** to cover as by scattering **3.** to be scattered over (a surface)

strewth (strŏŏth) *interj.* [< *God's truth*] an exclamation of surprise, indignation, etc.

stri·a (strī′ə) *n., pl.* **stri′ae** (-ē) [L.] **1.** a narrow groove or channel **2.** any of a number of parallel lines, stripes, furrows, etc.; specif., any of the cylindrical fibres in voluntary muscles

stri·ate (strī′āt; *for adj. usually* -it) *vt.* **-at·ed, -at·ing** [< L. pp. of *striare,* to groove] to mark with striae; stripe, furrow, etc. —*adj.* same as STRIATED —**stri·a′tion** *n.*

stri·at·ed (strī′āt id) *adj.* marked with striae, as the voluntary muscles; striped, furrowed, etc.

strick·en (strik′'n) *alt. pp. of* STRIKE —*adj.* **1.** struck or wounded **2.** suffering, as from pain, trouble, etc.

strict (strikt) *adj.* [< L. pp. of *stringere,* to draw tight] **1.** exact or precise [a *strict* translation] **2.** perfect; absolute [the *strict* truth] **3.** *a*) enforcing rules with great care *b*) closely enforced or rigidly maintained *c*) disciplining severely —**strict′ly** *adv.* —**strict′ness** *n.*

stric·ture (strik'chər) *n.* [< L. < pp. of *stringere*, to draw tight] **1.** strong criticism; censure **2.** a limiting or restricting condition; restriction **3.** *Med.* an abnormal narrowing of a passage in the body —**stric'tured** *adj.*

stride (strīd) *vi., vt.* strode, strid'den, strid'ing [OE. *stridan*] **1.** to walk with long steps, esp. in a vigorous or swaggering manner **2.** to cross with a single, long step [he *strode* over the log] **3.** to straddle —*n.* **1.** the act of striding **2.** a long step **3.** *a)* a full step in a gait, as of a horse *b)* the distance covered by such a step **4.** [usually *pl.*] progress; advancement [great *strides* in industry] —**get into one's stride** to reach one's normal level of efficiency —**take in one's stride** to cope with easily and without undue effort —**strid'er** *n.*

stri·dent (strīd'nt) *adj.* [< L. prp. of *stridere*, to rasp] harsh-sounding; shrill; grating —**stri'dence, stri'den·cy** *n.* —**stri'dent·ly** *adv.*

strid·u·late (stri'dyoo lāt') *vi.* -lat'ed, -lat'ing [< ModL. pp. of *stridulare* < L. < *stridere*, to rasp] to make a shrill, grating or chirping sound by rubbing certain body parts together, as some insects do —**strid'u·la'tion** *n.*

strid·u·lous (-ləs) *adj.* making a shrill, grating or chirping sound: also **strid'u·lant** (-lənt)

strife (strīf) *n.* [OFr. *estrif*] **1.** the act of striving; contention or competition **2.** the act or state of fighting or quarrelling; struggle; conflict

strig·il (strij'əl) *n.* [L. *strigilis*, a scraper] an instrument of bone, metal, etc. used by the Greek and Romans for scraping the skin during a bath

strike (strīk) *vt.* struck, struck or occas. (but for *vt.* 12 commonly and for *vt.* 8 & 16 usually) **strick'en, strik'ing** [OE. *strican*, to go, proceed] **1.** *a)* to give a blow to; hit; smite *b)* to give (a blow, etc.) *c)* to remove as by a blow [he *struck* the gun from her hand] *d)* to make by stamping, printing, etc. [to *strike* coins in a mint] *e)* to pierce or penetrate [struck in the head by a bullet] **2.** to produce (a tone or chord) by hitting (a key or keys) or touching (a string or strings) on a musical instrument **3.** to announce (time), as with a bell: said of clocks, etc. **4.** *a)* to cause to come into forceful contact [to *strike* one's head on a beam] *b)* to thrust (a weapon, etc.) in or into something *c)* to bring forcefully into contact [to *strike* cymbals together] *d)* to ignite (a match) by friction **5.** to produce (a light, etc.) by friction **6.** to come into forceful contact with; crash into [the stone *struck* his head] **7.** to wound with the fangs: said of snakes **8.** to afflict, as with disease, pain, or death **9.** to attack **10.** to come into contact with; specif., *a)* to fall on; shine on, as light *b)* to reach (the eye or ear) *c)* to come upon [we *struck* the main road] *d)* to make (a path, etc.) as one goes along *e)* to notice or find suddenly *f)* to discover, as after drilling [to *strike* oil] **11.** to affect as if by contact, a blow, etc.; specif., *a)* to occur to [struck by an idea] *b)* to impress (one's fancy, sense of humour, etc.) *c)* to seem to [it *strikes* me as silly] *d)* to cause to become suddenly [to be *struck* dumb] *e)* to overcome suddenly with strong feeling [to be *struck* with amazement] *f)* to arouse [to *strike* terror to the heart] **12.** to remove (from a list, record, minutes, etc.) **13.** *a)* to make and ratify (a bargain, truce, etc.) *b)* to arrive at by figuring, etc. [to *strike* a balance] **14.** *a)* to lower (a sail, flag, etc.) *b)* to take down (a tent, etc.) *c)* to abandon (a camp) as by taking down tents **15.** to refuse to continue to work at (a factory, company, etc.) until certain demands have been met **16.** to level the top of (a measure of grain, etc.) as with a stick **17.** to assume (a pose, etc.) **18.** to put forth (roots): said of plants **19.** *Theatre a)* to dismantle (a set) *b)* to turn (a light) down or off —*vi.* **1.** to deliver or aim a blow; hit (*at*) **2.** *a)* to attack *b)* to take part in a fight (*for* some objective) **3.** *a)* to make sounds as by being struck: said of a bell, clock, etc. *b)* to be announced by the striking of a bell, etc.: said of the time **4.** *a)* to hit; collide (*against, on,* or *upon*) *b)* to make an impression on the mind **5.** to ignite, as a match **6.** to seize a bait: said of a fish **7.** to dart in an attempt to wound, as a snake **8.** to penetrate or pierce (*to, through,* etc.) **9.** to come suddenly (*on* or *upon*) [we *struck* on an idea] **10.** to run upon a reef, rock, etc.: said of a ship **11.** *a)* to lower sail *b)* to lower a flag in token of surrender **12.** to refuse to continue to work until certain demands are met **13.** to take root: said of a plant **14.** to proceed, esp. in a new way or direction **15.** to move or pass quickly —*n.* **1.** the act of striking; blow; specif., a military attack **2.** *a)* a concerted refusal by employees to go on working, in an attempt to get higher wages, better working conditions, etc. *b)* any similar refusal to do something, undertaken as a form of protest [a hunger *strike*] **3.** the discovery of a rich deposit of oil, coal, minerals, etc. **4.** any sudden success **5.** the pull on the line by a fish seizing bait **6.** *Baseball* a pitched ball judged to be good but which is struck at but missed, or not struck at: three strikes put the batter out **7.** *Tenpin Bowling a)* the act of knocking down all the pins on the first bowl *b)* the score so made —(**out**) **on strike** striking (*vi.* 12) —**strike back** to retaliate —**strike camp** to take down all tents at the end of a period of encampment

—**strike dumb** to amaze; astound —**strike home** **1.** to deliver an effective blow **2.** to have the desired effect —**strike it rich** **1.** to discover a rich deposit of ore, oil, etc. **2.** to become rich or successful suddenly Also **strike lucky** —**strike off** **1.** to remove as by a cut or blow **2.** to print, stamp, etc. **3.** to erase or remove from a list, record, etc. —**strike out** **1.** to remove from a record, etc.; erase **2.** to start out —**strike up** **1.** to begin playing, singing, etc. **2.** to begin (a friendship, etc.)

strike·bound (-bound') *adj.* closed or hampered because of striking employees

strike·break·er (-brā'kər) *n.* a person who tries to break up a strike, as by working —**strike'break'ing** *n.*

strike pay an allowance paid by a trade union to workers on strike

strik·er (strī'kər) *n.* **1.** a person who strikes; specif., a worker who is on strike **2.** a thing that strikes, as the clapper in a bell, etc.

strik·ing (strī'kiŋ) *adj.* **1.** that strikes or is on strike **2.** impressive; outstanding; remarkable —**strik'ing·ly** *adv.*

Strine (strīn) *n.* [supposed pron. of *Australian*] the language formed by transliteration of Australian (Ex. *goodonyer* for *good on you*)

string (striŋ) *n.* [OE. *streng*] **1.** *a)* a thin length of twisted fibre or wire, nylon, etc. used for tying, pulling, etc. *b)* a narrow strip of leather or cloth for fastening shoes, clothing, etc. **2.** a length of things on a string [a *string* of pearls] **3.** a line, row, or series of things [a *string* of houses, a *string* of victories] **4.** a number of business enterprises under one ownership **5.** *a)* a slender cord of wire, gut, nylon, etc., stretched on a violin, guitar, etc., and bowed, plucked, or struck to make a musical sound *b)* [pl.] all the stringed instruments of an orchestra, or their players **6.** a strong, slender, stringlike organ, structure, etc.; specif., a fibre of a plant **7.** [Colloq.] a condition or limitation attached to a plan, offer, etc.: *usually used in pl.* —*vt.* strung, strung or rare stringed, string'ing **1.** to provide with strings **2.** to thread on a string **3.** to tie, pull, hang, etc. with a string **4.** to adjust or tune the strings of (a musical instrument) **5.** to make nervous or keyed (*up*) **6.** to remove the strings from (beans, etc.) **7.** to arrange in a row or series **8.** to extend like a string [to *string* a cable] —*vi.* **1.** to form into a string or strings **2.** to stretch out in a line —**on a** (or **the**) **string** completely under one's control —**pull strings** **1.** to get someone to use influence on one's behalf, often secretly **2.** to direct action of others, often secretly —**string along** [Colloq.] **1.** to agree **2.** to fool or deceive —**string along with** [Colloq.] to follow closely or accompany —**string up** [Colloq.] to kill by hanging —**string'less** *adj.* —**string'like'** *adj.*

string alphabet an alphabet developed for the blind using knotted string

string bag a bag made of string, esp. one used to carry shopping, etc.

string·board (-bôrd') *n.* a board placed along the side of a staircase to cover the ends of the steps

string·course (-kôrs') *n.* a decorative, horizontal band of brick or stone set in the wall of a building

stringed (striŋd) *rare pp. of* STRING —*adj.* having strings, as certain musical instruments

strin·gent (strin'jənt) *adj.* [< L. prp. of *stringere*, to draw tight] **1.** strict; severe **2.** tight in loan or investment money [a *stringent* money market] **3.** compelling; convincing —**strin'gen·cy** *n., pl.* -cies —**strin'gent·ly** *adv.* —**strin'gent·ness** *n.*

STRINGBOARD

string·er (striŋ'ər) *n.* **1.** a person or thing that strings **2.** a long piece of timber used as a support, as to connect upright posts in a frame **3.** a long structural member of an aircraft fuselage, wing, etc. **4.** a journalist retained by a newspaper to cover events in a particular town or area

string·halt (striŋ'hôlt') *n.* a condition in horses causing the hind legs to jerk spasmodically in walking

string·piece (-pēs') *n.* a long, horizontal timber for supporting a framework

string quartet a quartet of or for players on stringed instruments, usually first and second violins, a viola, and a violoncello

string tie a narrow necktie, usually tied in a bow

string vest an undergarment made from a large-meshed material

string·y (striŋ'ē) *adj.* string'i·er, string'i·est **1.** like a string or strings; long, thin, wiry, etc. **2.** consisting of strings or fibres **3.** having tough fibres [stringy meat, celery, etc.] **4.** forming strings; ropy [stringy paint] —**string'i·ness** *n.*

strip[1] (strip) *vt.* stripped, strip'ping [OE. *strypan* (in comp.)] **1.** to remove (the clothing, covering, etc.) of or from (a person); make naked **2.** to dispossess (a person) of (honours, titles, attributes, etc.) **3.** to plunder; rob **4.** to peel or take off (the covering, skin, etc.) from (something)

5. to make bare or clear by removing fruit, growth, removable parts, etc. [to *strip* a room of furniture] **6.** to take apart **7.** to break or damage the thread of (a nut, bolt, etc.) or the teeth of (a gear) —*vi.* **1.** to take off all clothing; undress **2.** to perform a striptease—**strip down 1.** to remove paint from a surface so as to prepare it for repainting **2.** to take an engine apart so as to clean or repair it —**strip'per n.**

strip² (strip) *n.* [altered (after prec.) < STRIPE] **1.** a long, narrow piece, as of land, ribbon, wood, etc. **2.** *short for* COMIC STRIP **3.** a runway for the takeoff and landing of aircraft; landing strip —*vt.* to cut or tear into strips

strip cartoon *same as* COMIC STRIP

strip club a nightclub, etc. that has regular performances of striptease

stripe (strīp) *n.* [MLowG. & MDu. *strīpe*] **1.** a long, narrow band, mark, or streak, differing as in colour from the area around it **2.** [*often pl.*] a fabric or garment with a pattern of parallel stripes **3.** a strip of cloth or braid worn on the sleeve of a uniform to show rank, years served, etc. **4.** [Chiefly U.S.] type; kind; sort [a man of his *stripe*] **5.** [Archaic] *a)* a stroke with a whip, etc. *b)* a long welt on the skin —*vt.* **striped, strip'ing** to mark with stripes

strip lighting electric lighting by means of long fluorescent tubes or tubes with long filaments —**strip light**

strip·ling (strip'liŋ) *n.* a grown boy; youth

strip mining [U.S.] opencast mining

stript (stript) *rare pt. & pp. of* STRIP¹

strip·tease (strip'tēz') *n.* an act, as in variety shows, clubs, etc., in which a woman takes off her clothes slowly, usually while music is being played —**strip'tease' vi. -teased', -teas'ing** —**strip'teas'er n.**

strip·y (strī'pē) *adj.* **strip'i·er, strip'i·est** characterized by, like, or marked with stripes

strive (strīv) *vi.* **strove** *or* **strived, striv·en** (striv''n) *or* **strived, striv'ing** [< OFr. < *estrif*, effort < Gmc.] **1.** to make great efforts; try very hard [to *strive* to win] **2.** to struggle; contend [to *strive* against tyranny] —**striv'er n.**

strobe (strōb) *n.* **1.** *shortened form of* STROBOSCOPE **2.** an electronic tube that can emit extremely rapid, brief, and brilliant flashes of light: used in photography, the theatre, etc.: also **strobe light**

stro·bi·lus (strō bi'ləs) *n., pl.* **-li** (-lē) [ModL. < LL. < Gr. *strobilos*, pine cone] *same as* CONE (*n.* 3): also **stro'bile** (-bīl)

stro·bo·scope (strō'bə skōp', strob'ə-) *n.* [< Gr. *strobos*, a twisting round + -SCOPE] **1.** an instrument for studying motion by illuminating a moving body, machine, etc. very briefly at frequent intervals **2.** *same as* STROBE (*n.* 2) —**stro'bo·scop'ic** (-skop'ik), **stro'bo·scop'i·cal** *adj.* —**stro'·bo·scop'i·cal·ly** *adv.*

strode (strōd) *pt. of* STRIDE

stro·ga·noff (strō'gə nof', strō'-) *adj.* [prob. after S. *Stroganoff*, 19th-c. Russ. gourmet] cooked with sour cream, bouillon, mushrooms, etc.: placed after the word it modifies [beef *stroganoff*]

stroke (strōk) *n.* [akin to OE. *strican*, to hit] **1.** a striking of one thing against another; blow of an axe, whip, etc. **2.** a sudden action resulting as if from a blow [a *stroke* of lightning, a *stroke* of luck] **3.** a sudden attack, esp. of apoplexy or paralysis **4.** *a)* a single effort to do or produce something, esp. a successful one *b)* something accomplished by such an effort *c)* a distinctive effect in an artistic, esp. literary, work **5.** the sound of striking, as of a clock **6.** *a)* a single movement, as with some tool, club, pen, etc. *b)* any of a series of repeated rhythmic motions made against water, air, etc. *c)* a type, manner, or rate of such a movement **7.** a mark made by a pen, etc. **8.** a beat of the heart **9.** a gentle, caressing motion with the hand **10.** *Mech.* any of the continuous, reciprocating movements of a piston, etc. **11.** *Rowing* the rower who sits nearest the stern and sets the rate of rowing —*vt.* **stroked, strok'ing 1.** to draw one's hand, a tool, etc. gently over the surface of **2.** to mark with strokes **3.** to hit (a ball), as in tennis, snooker, etc. **4.** to set the rate of rowing for (a crew) —*vi.* **1.** to hit a ball in tennis, etc. **2.** to act as stroke (*for*) in rowing —**at a stroke** with one operation; by a single action —**keep stroke** to make strokes in rhythm —**on the stroke** punctually; precisely —**strok'er n.**

stroll (strōl) *vi.* [prob. < SwissG. dial. *strolen*] **1.** to walk in an idle, leisurely manner; saunter **2.** to go from place to place; wander —*vt.* to stroll along or through —*n.* a strolling; leisurely walk

stroll·er (-ər) *n.* **1.** a person who saunters **2.** *a)* formerly, an itinerant actor *b)* a vagrant **3.** [U.S.] a push chair

stro·ma (strō'mə) *n., pl.* **-ma·ta** (-tə) [ModL. < L. < Gr. *strōma*, mattress] the connective tissue forming the substance or foundation of an organ or cell —**stro·mat'ic** (-mat'ik) *adj.*

strong (stroŋ) *adj.* [OE. *strang*] **1.** *a)* physically powerful; having great muscular strength; robust *b)* healthy; sound; hale **2.** *a)* performing well [a *strong* heart] *b)* not easily upset [a *strong* stomach] **3.** morally or intellectually

powerful [a *strong* will or mind] **4.** having special ability (*in* a specified area) [to be *strong* in French] **5.** governing firmly; authoritarian **6.** *a)* tough; firm; durable; able to resist *b)* holding firmly [a *strong* grip] *c)* binding tightly [*strong* glue] **7.** having many resources; powerful in wealth, numbers, supplies, etc. **8.** of a specified number [a force 6000 *strong*] **9.** having a powerful effect; drastic [*strong* measures] **10.** having a large amount of its essential quality; not diluted [*strong* coffee] **11.** affecting the senses powerfully [*strong* light, odour, etc.] **12.** rancid; rank [*strong* butter] **13.** firm and loud [a *strong* voice] **14.** intense in degree or quality; specif., *a)* ardent; passionate *b)* forceful; persuasive *c)* felt deeply; decided [a *strong* opinion] *d)* zealous [a *strong* socialist] *e)* vigorous; forthright [*strong* language] *f)* distinct; marked [a *strong* resemblance] *g)* having emphasis or stress [a *strong* beat] **15.** moving rapidly and with force [a *strong* wind] **16.** magnifying highly [*strong* lenses] **17.** tending towards higher prices [a *strong* market] **18.** *Chem.* having a high ion concentration, as some acids and bases **19.** *Gram.* expressing variation in tense by internal change of vowel rather than by inflectional endings; irregular (Ex.: *swim, swam, swum*) —**come on strong** [Slang] to make a striking impression —**strong'ish** *adj.* —**strong'ly** *adv.*

strong-arm (stroŋ'ärm') *adj.* [Colloq.] using physical force —*vt.* [Colloq.] to use force upon, esp. in robbing

strong·box (-boks') *n.* a heavily made box or safe for storing valuables

strong·hold (-hōld') *n.* **1.** a place having strong defences; fortified place **2.** a place where a group having certain views, attitudes, etc. is concentrated

strong language emphatic language; specif., swearing or cursing

strong-mind·ed (-mīn'did) *adj.* having a strong, unyielding mind or will; determined —**strong'-mind'ed·ly** *adv.* —**strong'-mind'ed·ness n.**

strong·room (-rōom') *n.* a strongly built room used for the safekeeping of valuables

strong-willed (-wild') *adj.* having a strong or obstinate will

stron·ti·um (stron'tē əm) *n.* [ModL. < *Strontian*, in Scotland, where first found] a pale-yellow, metallic chemical element resembling calcium in properties and found only in combination: symbol, Sr; at. wt., 87.62; at. no., 38: a deadly radioactive isotope of strontium (**strontium 90**) is present in the fallout of nuclear explosions —**stron'tic** *adj.*

strop (strop) *n.* [OE., ult. < L. *struppus* < Gr. *strophos*, a twisted band] **1.** *same as* STRAP **2.** a device, esp. a thick leather band, used for putting a fine edge on razors —*vt.* **stropped, strop'ping** to sharpen on a strop —**strop'per n.**

stro·phe (strō'fē) *n.* [< Gr. < *strephein*, to turn] **1.** in the ancient Greek theatre, *a)* a turning of the chorus from right to left *b)* that part of the song sung by the chorus during this **2.** a stanza —**stroph·ic** (strof'ik, strō'fik), **stroph'i·cal** *adj.*

strop·py (strop'ē) *adj.* [< OBSTREPEROUS] [Slang] angry, irritated, or awkward

strove (strōv) *alt. pt. of* STRIVE

strow (strō) *vt.* **strowed, strown** (strōn) *or* **strowed, strow'-ing** *archaic form of* STREW

struck (struk) *pt. & pp. of* STRIKE —*adj.* [Chiefly U.S.] closed or affected by a labour strike

struc·tur·al (struk'chər əl) *adj.* **1.** of, having, or characterized by structure **2.** used in construction or building —**struc'tur·al·ly** *adv.*

structural formula a chemical formula that illustrates the arrangement of atoms and bonds in a molecule

struc·tur·al·ist (-ist) *n.* an advocate of structural principles, as in the analysis or application of social, economic, or linguistic theory —*adj.* of structuralists or their theories —**struc'tur·al·ism n.**

structural linguistics the study of a language as a coherent, uniform system without comparing it to other languages or to its forms in early periods —**structural linguist**

struc·ture (struk'chər) *n.* [< L. < pp. of *struere*, to arrange] **1.** manner of building, constructing, or organizing **2.** something built or constructed, as a building or dam **3.** the arrangement of all the parts of a whole [the *structure* of the atom] **4.** something composed of interrelated parts —*vt.* **-tured, -tur·ing** to put together according to a system; construct; organize —**struc'ture·less** *adj.*

stru·del (strōō'd'l; *G.* shtrōō'dəl) *n.* [G.] a kind of pastry made of a very thin sheet of dough filled with apple slices, cheese, etc., rolled up, and baked

strug·gle (strug''l) *vi.* **-gled, -gling** [ME. *strogelen* < ?] **1.** to contend or fight violently with an opponent **2.** to make great efforts; strive **3.** to make one's way with difficulty —*n.* **1.** great effort; exertion **2.** conflict; strife —**strug'-gler n.** —**strug'gling·ly** *adv.*

strum (strum) *vt., vi.* **strummed, strum'ming** [echoic] to play (a guitar, banjo, etc.), esp. in a casual way, or without much skill—*n.* the act or sound of this —**strum'mer n.**

stru·ma (str$\overline{oo}$′mə) *n., pl.* **-mae** (-mē) [L., a scrofulous tumour] 1. *Bot.* a cushionlike swelling on a plant organ 2. *Med. same as:* a) GOITRE b) SCROFULA

strum·pet (strum′pit) *n.* [ME. < ?] a prostitute

strung (struŋ) *pt. & alt. pp. of* STRING

strut (strut) *vi.* **strut′ted, strut′ting** [OE. *strutian,* to stand rigid] to walk in a vain, stiff, swaggering manner —*vt.* 1. to provide with a strut or brace 2. to make a display of —*n.* 1. a vain, swaggering walk 2. a brace fitted into a framework to resist pressure in the direction of its length —**strut′ter** *n.* —**strut′ting·ly** *adv.*

'struth (str$\overline{oo}$th) *interj. same as* STREWTH

stru·thi·ous (str$\overline{oo}$′thē əs) *adj.* [<L. *struthio* < Gr. *strouthion,* ostrich) + -OUS] designating any of an order of large, flightless birds, as the emu, ostrich, etc.

strych·nine (strik′nēn) *n.* [Fr. < ModL. genus name < L. < Gr. *strychnos,* nightshade] a highly poisonous crystalline alkaloid, obtained from nux vomica and related plants: used in small doses as a stimulant

stub (stub) *n.* [OE. *stybb*] 1. a tree stump 2. a short piece remaining after the main part has been removed or used up [a cigar *stub*] 3. any short projection: a short piece of a ticket or of a leaf in a cheque book kept as a record —*vt.* **stubbed, stub′bing** 1. to root out (weeds, etc.) 2. to clear (land) of stumps 3. to strike (one's toe, etc.) against something by accident 4. to put out (a cigarette, etc.) by pressing the end against a surface: often with *out*

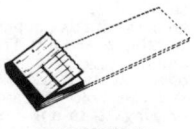

STUB (SENSE 4)

stub·ble (stub′'l) *n.* [OFr. *estouble* < VL. < L. *stipula,* a stalk] 1. the short stumps of grain left standing after harvesting 2. any growth like this [a *stubble* of beard] —**stub′bled** *adj.* —**stub′bly** *adj.,* **-bli·er, -bli·est**

stub·born (stub′ərn) *adj.* [? < OE. *stubb,* var. of *stybb,* STUB] 1. refusing to yield, obey, or comply; resisting; resolute or obstinate 2. done or carried on in an obstinate or persistent manner [a *stubborn* campaign] 3. hard to handle, treat, or deal with [a *stubborn* cold] —**stub′born·ly** *adv.* —**stub′born·ness** *n.*

stub·by (stub′ē) *adj.* **-bi·er, -bi·est** 1. covered with stubs or stubble 2. short and heavy or dense 3. short and thickset —**stub′bi·ly** *adv.* —**stub′bi·ness** *n.*

stuc·co (stuk′ō) *n., pl.* **-coes, -cos** [It., prob. < Gmc.] 1. plaster or cement, either fine or coarse, used for surfacing inside or outside walls, etc. 2. work done in this: also **stuc′co·work′** —*vt.* **-coed, -co·ing** to cover with stucco

stuck (stuk) *pt. & pp. of* STICK —*adj.* 1. baffled, nonplussed [to be *stuck* on the second question] 2. [Slang] keen on; infatuated by [I'm not really *stuck* on the idea] —**get stuck in** [Slang] 1. to start working hard 2. to start eating: used esp. as a command

stuck-up (stuk′up′) *adj.* [Colloq.] snobbish; conceited

stud¹ (stud) *n.* [OE. *studu,* post] 1. any of a series of small knobs or rounded nailheads used to ornament a surface 2. a small, buttonlike device used as an ornament or fastener on a shirt front 3. an upright piece in the frame of a building, to which panels, laths, etc. are nailed 4. a metal crossbar bracing a link, as in a chain cable 5. a projecting pin or peg used as a support, pivot, etc., or, as in a motor car tyre, to increase traction on ice —*vt.* **stud′ded, stud′ding** 1. to set or decorate with studs or studlike objects 2. to be set thickly on [rocks *stud* the hillside] 3. to scatter or cluster (something) thickly 4. to provide (a building) with studs

stud² (stud) *n.* [OE. *stod*] 1. a) a number of horses kept for breeding b) the place where these are kept 2. a) *same as* STUDHORSE b) any male animal used esp. for breeding 3. [Slang] a virile, sexually promiscuous man —*adj.* of or having to do with a stud —**at stud** available for breeding: said of male animals

stud·book (-book′) *n.* a register of purebred animals, esp. racehorses: also **stud book**

stud·ding (stud′iŋ) *n.* 1. studs collectively, esp. for walls 2. material used for or as studs

stud·ding·sail (stud′iŋ sāl′, stun′s'l) *n.* [< ?] a light, auxiliary sail set at the edge of a working sail in light weather: also **studding sail**

stu·dent (sty$\overline{oo}$′dənt) *n.* [< OFr.< L. prp. of *studere,* to study] 1. a person who studies something 2. a person who is enrolled for study in a university, college, etc. —**stu′dent·ship′** *n.*

stud·horse (stud′hôrs′) *n.* a stallion kept for breeding

stud·ied (stud′ēd) *adj.* 1. prepared by careful study 2. planned beforehand; deliberate [*studied* indifference] —**stud′ied·ly** *adv.* —**stud′ied·ness** *n.*

stu·di·o (sty$\overline{oo}$′dē ō′) *n., pl.* **-di·os** [It. < L. *studium,* a study] 1. a place where an artist or photographer does his work 2. a place where dancing or music lessons are given 3. a place where films are made 4. a place where radio or television programmes are produced or where recordings are made

studio couch a kind of couch that can be opened into a full-sized bed

stu·di·ous (sty$\overline{oo}$′dē əs) *adj.* 1. fond of study 2. showing close attention 3. zealous; wholehearted —**stu′di·ous·ly** *adv.* —**stu′di·ous·ness** *n.*

stud poker a form of poker in which each player is dealt some cards face down and some face up

stud·y (stud′ē) *n., pl.* **stud·ies** [< OFr. < L. < *studere,* to study] 1. the application of the mind to acquire knowledge, as by reading, investigating, etc. 2. careful and critical examination of a subject, event, etc. 3. a branch of learning 4. [pl.] formal education; schooling 5. an essay or thesis presenting results of an investigation 6. a work of literature or art treating a subject in careful detail 7. a first sketch for a story, picture, etc. 8. *same as* ÉTUDE 9. an earnest effort or intention 10. a reverie; deep absorption 11. a room designed for study, writing, etc. 12. the object, etc. to be studied [the *study* of mankind is man] 13. a person, esp. an actor, with reference to his memorizing ability [a quick *study*] —*vt.* **stud′ied, stud′y·ing** 1. to try to learn by reading, thinking, etc. 2. a) to investigate carefully [to *study* the problem of crime] b) to look at carefully; scrutinize [to *study* a map] 3. a) to read (a book, lesson, etc.) so as to know and understand it b) to memorize 4. to take a course in at a university or college 5. to give attention or thought to —*vi.* 1. to study something 2. to be a student 3. to try hard 4. to meditate

stuff (stuf) *n.* [< OFr. < *estoffer,* to cram, prob. < Frank.] 1. the material out of which anything is or can be made 2. basic elements; essence; character 3. any kind of matter, unspecified 4. cloth, esp. woollen cloth 5. a) household goods b) personal belongings c) things; objects 6. a) a medicine b) [Slang] a drug, as heroin 7. worthless objects; junk 8. a) talk or action of a specified kind b) foolish or worthless ideas, words, etc. [*stuff* and nonsense] 9. [Slang] money —*vt.* 1. to fill the inside of (something); pack; specif., a) to fill (a cushion, etc.) with padding b) to fill the skin of (a dead animal, etc.) in order to mount and preserve it c) to fill (a fowl, etc.) with seasoning, bread crumbs, etc. before roasting 2. a) to fill too full; cram b) to fill to excess with food 3. to pack or cram with 4. to fill with information, ideas, etc. 5. a) to plug; block b) to choke or stop up, as with phlegm 6. to force or push [to *stuff* money into a purse] —*vi.* to eat too much —**do one's stuff** do what is expected of one —**stuff oneself** to eat one's fill, esp. greedily —**stuff′er** *n.*

stuffed (stuft) *adj.* 1. filled with stuffing [*stuffed* duck] 2. [Colloq.] full-up, esp. with food —**get stuffed** [Slang] a vulgar exclamation of dismissal

stuffed shirt [Slang] a pompous, pretentious person

stuff·ing (-iŋ) *n.* 1. the action of one that stuffs 2. something used to stuff; specif., a) soft, springy material used as padding in cushions, etc. b) a seasoned mixture for stuffing fowl, etc.

stuff·y (stuf′ē) *adj.* **stuff′i·er, stuff′i·est** 1. poorly ventilated; having little fresh air; close 2. having the nasal passages stopped up, as from a cold 3. [Colloq.] a) dull; stodgy; old-fashioned b) prim; strait-laced c) pompous; pretentious —**stuff′i·ly** *adv.* —**stuff′i·ness** *n.*

stul·ti·fy (stul′tə fī′) *vt.* **-fied′, -fy′ing** [< LL. < L. *stultus,* foolish + *facere,* to make] 1. a) to cause to appear foolish, stupid, absurd, etc. b) to make dull or sluggish 2. to render worthless or useless —**stul′ti·fi·ca′tion** *n.*

stum·ble (stum′b'l) *vi.* **-bled, -bling** [< Scand.] 1. to trip in walking, running, etc. 2. to walk unsteadily, as when old and weak 3. to speak, act, etc. in a confused, blundering manner 4. to sin or err; do wrong 5. to come by chance; happen [to *stumble* across a clue] —*vt.* 1. to cause to stumble 2. to perplex; confound —*n.* a stumbling —**stum′·bler** *n.* —**stum′bling·ly** *adv.*

stumbling block an obstacle or difficulty

stu·mer (sty$\overline{oo}$′mər) *n.* [< ?] 1. a forgery or cheat, esp. a worthless cheque 2. [Ir.] a bad buy

stump (stump) *n.* [prob. < or akin to MLowG. *stump*] 1. the lower end of a tree or plant left in the ground after most of the stem or trunk has been cut off 2. a) the part of an arm, leg, tooth, etc. left after the rest has been cut off or broken off b) a butt; stub [the *stump* of a pencil] 3. [U.S.] the place where a political speech is made 4. a) the sound of a heavy, tramping step b) such a step 5. *Cricket* any of the three upright sticks of a wicket —*vt.* 1. to reduce to a stump; lop 2. to remove stumps from (land) 3. [U.S.] to travel over (a district), making political speeches 4. [Colloq.] to puzzle; baffle 5. *Cricket* to dismiss (a batsman) by hitting the stumps with a ball —*vi.* 1. to walk heavily or clumsily, as with a wooden leg 2. [U.S.] to travel about, making political speeches —**stump up** [Colloq.] to hand over money due; pay up —**stump′er** *n.* —**stump′like** *adj.*

stump·y (stum′pē) *adj.* **stump′i·er, stump′i·est** 1. covered with stumps **2.** like a stump; short and thickset; stubby —**stump'i·ness** *n.*

stun (stun) *vt.* **stunned, stun'ning** [< OFr. *estoner*, to stun: see ASTONISH] **1.** to make senseless or unconscious, as by a blow **2.** to shock deeply; daze; astound **3.** to overpower as by a loud noise or explosion —*n.* the effect or condition of being stunned

stung (stuŋ) *pt. & pp.* of STING

stunk (stuŋk) *pp. & alt. pt.* of STINK

stun·ner (stun'ər) *n.* [Colloq.] a remarkably attractive, excellent, etc. person or thing

stun·ning (-iŋ) *adj.* **1.** that stuns **2.** [Colloq.] remarkably attractive, excellent, etc. —**stun'ning·ly** *adv.*

stun·sail, stun's'le (stun's'l) *n. same as* STUDDINGSAIL

stunt[1] (stunt) *vt.* [OE. *stunt*, stupid] **1.** to check the growth or development of; dwarf **2.** to hinder (growth or development) —*n.* **1.** a stunting **2.** something stunted

stunt[2] (stunt) *n.* [< ?] **1.** a display of skill or daring; trick **2.** something done to attract attention, etc. —*vi.* to perform a stunt or stunts

stunt man a professional acrobat who takes the place of an actor when dangerous scenes involving falls, leaps, etc. are filmed

stu·pa (stoo'pə) *n.* [Sans.] a towerlike Buddhist shrine

stu·pe·fac·tion (styoo'pə fak'shən) *n.* **1.** a stupefying or being stupefied **2.** stunned amazement or utter bewilderment

stu·pe·fy (styoo'pə fī') *vt.* **-fied', -fy'ing** [< Fr. < L. < *stupere*, to be stunned + *facere*, to make] **1.** to make dull or lethargic; stun **2.** to amaze; astonish; bewilder —**stu'-pe·fi'er** *n.*

stu·pen·dous (styoo pen'dəs) *adj.* [< L. gerundive of *stupere*, to be stunned] **1.** astonishing; overwhelming **2.** astonishingly great or large —**stu·pen'dous·ly** *adv.* —**stu·pen'dous·ness** *n.*

stu·pid (styoo'pid) *adj.* [L. *stupidus* < *stupere*, to be stunned] **1.** dazed; stunned; stupefied **2.** lacking normal intelligence; slow-witted; dull **3.** showing or resulting from a lack of intelligence; foolish **4.** dull and boring [a *stupid* party] —*n.* a stupid person —**stu·pid'i·ty**, *pl.* **-ties, stu'-pid·ness** *n.* —**stu'pid·ly** *adv.*

stu·por (styoo'pər) *n.* [L.] **1.** a state in which the mind and senses are so dulled, as by a drug, that one can barely think, act, feel, etc. **2.** mental or moral dullness or apathy —**stu'-por·ous** *adj.*

stur·dy (stur'dē) *adj.* **-di·er, -di·est** [OFr. *estourdi*, stunned] **1.** firm; resolute; unyielding **2.** strong; hardy **3.** strongly built —**stur'di·ly** *adv.* —**stur'di·ness** *n.*

stur·geon (stur'jən) *n., pl.* **stur'geons, stur'geon:** see PLURAL, II, D, 1 [OFr. *esturjon* < Frank.] any of several large food fishes having rows of spiny plates along the body and a projecting snout: valuable as a source of caviar and isinglass

STURGEON
(to 2 m long)

stut·ter (stut'ər) *vt., vi.* [freq. of dial. *stut*, to stutter < ME. *stutten*] **1.** *same as* STAMMER **1.** to make (a series of repeated sounds) [stuttering machine guns] —*n.* the act or an instance of stuttering —**stut'ter·er** *n.*

sty[1] (stī) *n., pl.* **sties** [OE. *sti, stig*] **1.** a pen for pigs **2.** any foul or depraved place —*vt., vi.* **stied, sty'-ing** to lodge in or as in a sty

sty[2]**, stye** (stī) *n., pl.* **sties** [< obs. dial. *styany* (taken as *sty on eye*) < dial. *styan*, rising < OE. *stigend*, prp. of *stigan*, to climb] a small, inflamed swelling of a sebaceous gland on the rim of the eyelid

Styg·i·an (stij'ē ən) *adj.* **1.** of or like the river Styx and the infernal regions **2.** [*also* s-] a) infernal or hellish b) dark or gloomy

style (stīl) *n.* [L. *stilus*] **1.** a pointed instrument used by the ancients in writing on wax tablets **2.** any device similar in shape or use; specif., a) [Obs.] a pen b) an etching needle c) an engraving tool d) the pointer on a dial, chart, etc. e) *Bot.* the stalklike part of a carpel between the stigma and the ovary **3.** a) manner of expression in writing or speaking b) characteristic manner of expression, execution, or design, in any art, period, etc. [Gothic *style*] **4.** distinction, originality, etc. in artistic or literary expression [this author lacks *style*] **5.** the way in which anything is made or done; manner **6.** a) the current, fashionable way of dressing, acting, etc. b) something stylish c) a fashionable, luxurious manner [to dine in *style*] **7.** elegance of manner and bearing **8.** form of address; title [entitled to the *style* of Mayor] **9.** sort; kind; type **10.** a way of reckoning times, dates, etc.: see OLD STYLE (sense 2), NEW STYLE **11.** *Printing* a particular manner of dealing with spelling, punctuation, etc. —*vt.* **styled, styl'ing 1.** to name; call **2.** to design the style of **3.** to make conform to a particular style —**style'less** *adj.* —**styl'er** *n.*

style·book (-book') *n.* a book consisting of examples or rules of style (esp. sense 11)

styl·ish (stī'lish) *adj.* conforming to current style in dress, decoration, etc.; smart; fashionable —**styl'ish·ly** *adv.* —**styl'ish·ness** *n.*

styl·ist (-list) *n.* **1.** a writer, etc. whose work has style (sense 4) **2.** a person who designs, or advises on, current styles, as in dress —**sty·lis·tic** (stī lis'tik), **sty·lis'ti·cal** *adj.* —**sty·lis'ti·cal·ly** *adv.*

styl·ize (stī'līz) *vt.* **-ized, -iz·ing** to make conform to a given style rather than to nature; conventionalize —**styl'i·za'tion** *n.* —**styl'iz·er** *n.*

sty·lo (stī'lō) *n. clipped form of* STYLOGRAPH

sty·lo·bate (stī'lə bāt') *n.* [L. < Gr. *stylobatēs* < *stylos*, column + *bainein*, to go] *Archit.* a continuous base or coping for a row of columns

sty·lo·graph (-gräf') *n.* [< STYLUS & -GRAPH] a fountain pen having a pierced conical point, rather than a nib, through which the ink flows

sty·lus (stī'ləs) *n., pl.* **-lus·es, -li** (-lī) [L., for *stilus*, pointed instrument] **1.** a style or other needlelike marking device **2.** any of various pointed tools, as for marking mimeograph stencils **3.** a) a sharp, pointed device for cutting the grooves of a gramophone record b) a gramophone needle

sty·mie (stī'mē) *n.* [? < Scot. *stymie*, a person partially blind] **1.** *Golf* the situation on a putting green when an opponent's ball lies in a direct line between the player's ball and the hole **2.** any frustrating situation —*vt.* **-mied, -mie·ing 1.** to obstruct with a stymie **2.** to block; impede

sty·my (stī'mē) *n., pl.* **-mies, vt. -mied, -my·ing** *same as* STYMIE

styp·tic (stip'tik) *adj.* [< L. < Gr. *styptikos* < *styphein*, to contract] tending to halt bleeding by contracting the tissues or blood vessels; astringent —*n.* any styptic substance

sty·rene (stī'rēn) *n.* [< L. *styrax*, a kind of tree + -ENE] a colourless or yellowish, aromatic liquid used in the manufacture of synthetic rubber and plastics

Sty·ro·foam (stī'rə fōm') *a trademark for* rigid, lightweight, cellular polystyrene, used in insulation, commercial displays, etc. —*n.* [s-] this substance

sua·sion (swā'zhən) *n.* [< L. < pp. of *suadere*, to persuade] *same as* PERSUASION: now chiefly in **moral suasion**, a persuading by appealing to one's sense of morality —**sua'-sive** (-siv) *adj.* —**sua'sive·ly** *adv.* —**sua'sive·ness** *n.*

suave (swäv) *adj.* [MFr. < L. *suavis*, sweet] smoothly gracious or polite; polished; urbane —**suave'ly** *adv.* —**suave'ness** *n.* —**suav·i·ty** (swä'və tē, swav'ə-) *n.*

sub (sub) *n.* **1.** *shortened form of:* a) SUBMARINE b) SUBSCRIPTION c) SUBSTITUTE **2.** [Colloq.] an advance payment of wages or salary —*vi.* **subbed, sub'bing** [Colloq.] **1.** to be a substitute (*for* someone) **2.** to grant or receive (an advance payment of wages or salary)

sub- [< L. *sub*, under] *a prefix meaning:* **1.** under, beneath [*subsoil*] **2.** lower in rank or position than [*subaltern*] **3.** to a lesser degree than; somewhat [*subtropical*] **4.** by or forming a division into smaller parts [*subsection*] **5.** *Chem.* with less than the normal amount of (the specified substance) In words of Latin origin, sub- is assimilated to *suc-* before *c*, *suf-* before *f*, *sug-* before *g*, *sum-* before *m*, *sup-* before *p*, and *sur-* before *r*: sub- often changes to *sus-* before *c*, *p*, and *t*

sub. 1. substitute(s) **2.** suburb(an)

sub·ac·id (sub as'id) *adj.* slightly acid —**sub'a·cid'i·ty** (-ə sid'ə tē) *n.* —**sub·ac'id·ly** *adv.*

su·bah·dar, su·ba·dar (soob'ə där') *n.* [< Urdu < Hindi *subal*, a province + *dar*, a master] formerly, a native officer commanding a company in an Indian regiment

sub·al·pine (-al'pīn) *adj.* [L. *subalpinus*, lit., lying near the Alps] **1.** of the region at the foot of the Alps **2.** of or growing in mountain regions below the timberline

sub·al·tern (sub'al tərn) *adj.* [< Fr. < LL. < L. *sub-*, under + *alternus*, alternate] **1.** subordinate **2.** holding an army commission below that of captain —*n.* **1.** a subordinate **2.** a subaltern officer

sub·ant·arc·tic (sub'ant ärk'tik, -är'-) *adj.* designating or of the area surrounding the Antarctic Circle

sub·a·qua (sub'a'kwä) *adj.* of or designating underwater sports

sub·a·que·ous (sub ā'kwē əs) *adj.* [SUB- + AQUEOUS] **1.** adapted for underwater use or existence **2.** living or occurring underwater

sub·arc·tic (sub ärk'tik, -är'-) *adj.* designating or of the area surrounding the Arctic Circle

sub·at·om (sub at'əm) *n.* one of the parts that make up an atom —**sub'a·tom'ic** (-ə tom'ik) *adj.*

sub·base·ment (sub'bās'mənt) *n.* any floor or room below the principal basement

sub·branch (-bränch') *n.* a division of a branch

sub·class (-kläs') *n.* **1.** a division of a class; specif., *Biol.* any main natural subdivision of a class of plants or animals **2.** *Math. same as* SUBSET

sub·cla·vi·an (sub klā'vē ən) *adj.* situated under the clavicle

sub·clin·i·cal (sub klin′i k′l) *adj.* without obvious clinical symptoms, as a disease in its early stages

sub·com·mit·tee (sub′kə mit′ē) *n.* any of the small committees with special duties into which a main committee may be divided

sub·con·scious (sub kon′shəs) *adj.* 1. occurring with little or no conscious perception on the part of the individual: said of mental processes and reactions 2. not fully conscious —**the subconscious** the subconscious mental activity —**sub·con′scious·ly** *adv.* —**sub·con′scious·ness** *n.*

sub·con·ti·nent (-kon′tə nənt) *n.* a large land mass, smaller than a continent, often a subdivision of a continent regarded as a political or geographical unit

sub·con·tract (-kon′trakt; *also, for v.,* sub′kən trakt′) *n.* a secondary contract undertaking some or all of the obligations of a primary or previous contract —*vt., vi.* to make a subcontract (for) —**sub·con·trac′tor** *n.*

sub·crit·i·cal (-krit′i k′l) *adj.* unable to sustain a fission chain reaction: said of a nuclear reactor, etc.

sub·cul·ture (sub′kul′chər) *n.* 1. a group of people of the same age, social or economic status, ethnic background, etc. and having its own interests, goals, etc. 2. the distinct cultural patterns of such a group —**sub·cul′tur·al** *adj.*

sub·cu·ta·ne·ous (sub′kyoo tā′nē əs) *adj.* being, used, or introduced beneath the skin —**sub′cu·ta′ne·ous·ly** *adv.*

sub·dea·con (sub dē′k′n) *n.* a cleric ranking below a deacon

sub·di·vide (sub′di vīd′, sub′di vid′) *vt., vi.* -vid′ed, -vid′ing 1. to divide further after previous division 2. to divide (land) into small parcels for sale —**sub′di·vid′er** *n.*

sub·di·vi·sion (sub′di vizh′ən, sub′di vizh′ən) *n.* 1. a subdividing or being subdivided 2. one of the parts resulting from subdividing 3. [U.S.] a large tract of land subdivided into small parcels for sale

sub·dom·i·nant (sub dom′ə nənt) *adj.* less than or only partly dominant —*n.* 1. something that is subdominant 2. *Music* the fourth tone of a diatonic scale

sub·due (səb dyōō′) *vt.* -dued′, -du′ing [< OFr. < L. *subducere,* to remove] 1. to win control of; conquer; vanquish 2. to overcome, as by persuasion or training; control 3. to make less intense; diminish; soften 4. to repress (emotions, passions, etc.) —**sub·du′a·ble** *adj.*

sub·ed·i·tor (-ed′i tər) *n.* a person who writes and checks copy, esp. on a newspaper

sub·fam·i·ly (sub′fam′ə lē) *n., pl.* -lies 1. any main natural subdivision of a family of plants or animals 2. a subdivision of a language family

sub·freez·ing (sub′frē′ziŋ) *adj.* below freezing

sub·fusc (sub fusk′) *adj.* [L. *subfuscus* < *sub-,* below + *fuscus,* dark brown] having a dull or dark, often drab, colour —*n.* subfusc clothing

sub·ge·nus (sub′jē′nəs) *n., pl.* -gen·er·a (-jen′ər ə) any main natural subdivision of a genus of plants or animals

sub·head (sub′hed′) *n.* 1. the title of a subdivision of a chapter, article, etc. 2. a subordinate heading or title Also **sub′head′ing**

sub·hu·man (sub′hyōō′mən) *adj.* 1. less than human 2. nearly human

sub·in·dex (-in′deks) *n., pl.* -di·ces′ (-də sēz′) *same as* SUBSCRIPT

subj. 1. subject 2. subjunctive

sub·ja·cent (sub jā′s′nt) *adj.* [< L. prp. of *subjacere* < *sub-,* under + *jacere,* to lie] beneath; underlying —**sub·ja′cen·cy** *n.* —**sub·ja′cent·ly** *adv.*

sub·ject (sub′jikt; *for v.* səb jekt′) *adj.* [< OFr. < L. pp. of *subjicere* < *sub-,* under + *jacere,* to throw] 1. under the authority or control of, or owing allegiance to, another 2. having a disposition or tendency (to) [subject to fits of anger] 3. liable to receive [subject to censure] 4. contingent upon [subject to his approval] —*n.* 1. a person under the authority or control of another; esp., a person who owes allegiance to a ruler, government, etc. 2. someone or something undergoing a treatment, experiment, etc. 3. something dealt with in discussion, study, writing, painting, etc.; theme 4. the main theme of a musical composition 5. a cause; reason 6. a branch of learning 7. *Gram.* the noun, noun phrase, or noun substitute in a sentence about which something is said 8. *Philos.* the mind, or ego, that thinks or feels, as distinguished from everything outside the mind —*vt.* 1. to bring under the authority or control of 2. to make liable or vulnerable [to subject one to contempt] 3. to cause to undergo something —**sub·jec′tion** *n.*

subject catalogue a library catalogue with entries arranged by subject rather than author

sub·jec·tive (səb jek′tiv) *adj.* 1. of or resulting from the feelings of the subject, or person thinking; not objective; personal [a subjective opinion] 2. determined by and emphasizing the ideas, feelings, etc. of the artist or writer 3. *Gram. same as* NOMINATIVE 4. *Med.* designating or of a symptom perceptible only to the patient —**sub·jec′tive·ly** *adv.* —**sub·jec·tiv·i·ty** (sub′jek tiv′ə tē), **sub·jec′tive·ness** *n.* —**sub·jec′tiv·ism** (-iz′m) *n.*

sub·join (səb join′) *vt.* [< MFr. < L.: see SUB- & JOIN] to add (something) at the end of a statement

sub·ju·gate (sub′joo gāt′) *vt.* -gat′ed, -gat′ing [< L. pp. of *subjugare* < *sub-,* under + *jugum,* a yoke] 1. to bring under control or subjection; conquer 2. to cause to become submissive —**sub′ju·ga′tion** *n.* —**sub′ju·ga′tor** *n.*

sub·junc·tive (səb juŋk′tiv) *adj.* [< LL. < L. pp. of *subjungere,* to SUBJOIN] designating or of that mood of a verb used to express supposition, desire, possibility, etc., rather than to state a fact [were in "if I were you" is in the subjunctive mood] —*n.* 1. the subjunctive mood 2. a verb in this mood —**sub·junc′tive·ly** *adv.*

sub·lease (sub′lēs′; *for v.* sub lēs′) *n.* a lease granted by a lessee to another person of all or part of the property—*vt.* -leased′, -leas′ing to grant, obtain, or hold a sublease of —**sub′les·see′** (-les ē′) *n.* —**sub·les·sor** (sub les′ôr, sub′les ôr′) *n.*

sub·let (sub let′, sub′let′) *vt.* -let′, -let′ting to let to another (property which one is renting)

sub·lieu·ten·ant (sub′lef-ten′ənt) *n. see* MILITARY RANKS, table

sub·li·mate (sub′lə māt′; *for adj. & n., also* -mit) *vt.* -mat′-ed, -mat′ing [< L. pp. of *sublimare:* see ff.] 1. to sublime (a substance) 2. to have an ennobling effect on 3. to express (impulses, esp. sexual impulses, regarded as unacceptable) in ways that are acceptable —*vi.* to undergo subliming —*adj.* sublimated —*n.* a substance that is the product of subliming —**sub′li·ma′tion** *n.*

sub·lime (sə blīm′) *adj.* [< L. < *sub-,* up to + *limen,* lintel] 1. noble; exalted; majestic 2. inspiring awe or admiration through grandeur, beauty, etc. —*vt.* -limed′, -lim′ing 1. to make sublime 2. to purify (a solid) by heating directly to a gaseous state and condensing the vapour back into solid form —*vi.* to go through this process —**the sublime** a sublime quality or thing —**sub·lime′ly** *adv.* —**sub·lim·i·ty** (sə blim′ə tē), —**sub·lime′ness** *n.*

sub·lim·i·nal (sub lim′ə n′l) *adj.* [< SUB- + L. *limen,* threshold + -AL] below the threshold of consciousness; specif., involving stimuli intended to take effect subconsciously through repetition —**sub·lim′i·nal·ly** *adv.*

sub·lin·gual (sub liŋ′gwəl) *adj.* [ML. < L. *sub-,* below & *linguis,* the tongue] situated under the tongue

Sub. Lt. sub-lieutenant

sub·ma·chine gun (sub′mə shēn′) a portable, automatic or semiautomatic firearm with a short barrel and a stock, using pistol ammunition and fired from the shoulder or hip

sub·mar·gin·al (sub mär′ji n′l) *adj.* 1. below minimum requirements or standards 2. not yielding a satisfactory return [submarginal land] —**sub·mar′gin·al·ly** *adv.*

sub·ma·rine (sub′mə rēn′; *for n. usually* sub′mə rēn′) *adj.* being, living, used, etc. beneath the surface of the sea —*n.* 1. a submarine plant or animal 2. a kind of warship, armed with torpedoes, etc., that can operate under water

sub·max·il·lar·y (sub mak sil′ə rē) *adj.* [see SUB- & MAXILLARY] of or below the lower jaw; esp., designating or of either of two salivary glands, one on each side, beneath the lower jaw

sub·merge (səb murj′) *vt.* -merged′, -merg′ing [< L. < *sub-,* under + *mergere,* to plunge] 1. to place under or as under water, etc. 2. to cover over; suppress; hide 3. to sink below a decent level of life —*vi.* to sink or plunge beneath the surface of water, etc. —**sub·mer′gence** *n.* —**sub·mer′gi·ble** *adj.*

sub·merse (-murs′) *vt.* -mersed′, -mers′ing [< L. pp. of *submergere*] *same as* SUBMERGE —**sub·mer′sion** *n.*

sub·mers·i·ble (-mur′sə b′l) *adj.* that can be submersed —*n.* any of various ships that can operate under water

sub·min·i·a·ture (sub min′ē ə chər, -min′ə chər) *adj.* designating or of a camera, electronic component, etc., smaller than one described as "miniature"

sub·mis·sion (səb mish′ən) *n.* [OFr. < L. < pp. of *submittere*] 1. a submitting, yielding, or surrendering 2. a submissive quality or state; resignation; obedience 3. a submitting of something to another for decision, consideration, etc.

sub·mis·sive (-mis′iv) *adj.* having or showing a tendency to submit without resistance; docile —**sub·mis′sive·ly** *adv.* —**sub·mis′sive·ness** *n.*

sub·mit (-mit′) *vt.* -mit′ted, -mit′ting [< L. < *sub-,* under + *mittere,* to send] 1. to present to others for decision, consideration, etc. 2. to yield to the control, power, etc. of another; also, to allow to be subjected to treatment, analysis, etc.: often used reflexively 3. to offer as an opinion; suggest —*vi.* 1. *a*) to yield to the power, control, etc. of another *b*) to allow oneself to be subjected (to treatment, analysis, etc.) 2. to defer to another's judgment or decision 3. to be submissive, obedient, etc. —**sub·mit′-ta·ble** *adj.* —**sub·mit′tal** *n.* —**sub·mit′ter** *n.*

sub·nor·mal (sub nôr′m′l) *adj.* below the normal; less than normal, esp. in intelligence —*n.* a subnormal person —**sub′nor·mal′i·ty** (-mal′ə tē) *n.* —**sub·nor′mal·ly** *adv.*

sub·nu·cle·ar (sub nyōō′klē ər) *adj.* in or of something smaller than an atom

sub·or·bit·al (sub ôr'bit 'l) *adj.* 1. of a spaceflight in which the spacecraft follows a steep, short-range trajectory, instead of orbiting 2. beneath the orbit of the eye

sub·or·di·nate (sə bôr'də nit; *for v.* -nāt') *adj.* [< ML. pp. of subordinare < L. *sub-*, under + *ordinare*, to order] 1. below another in rank, power, importance, etc.; secondary 2. under the power or authority of another 3. subservient or submissive 4. *Gram.* functioning as a noun, adjective, or adverb within a sentence [a *subordinate* phrase]: cf. SUBORDINATE CLAUSE —*n.* a subordinate person or thing —*vt.* -nat'ed, -nat'ing 1. to place in a subordinate position 2. to make obedient or subservient (*to*) —**sub·or'di·nate·ly** *adv.* —**sub·or'di·na'tion** *n.* —**sub·or'di·na'tive** (-nāt'iv) *adj.*

subordinate clause in a complex sentence, a clause that cannot function syntactically as a complete sentence by itself; dependent clause (Ex.: She will visit us *if she can*)

subordinating conjunction a conjunction that connects subordinate words, phrases, or clauses to some other sentence element (Ex.: *if, as, so, unless, although, when*): also **subordinate conjunction**

sub·orn (sə bôrn') *vt.* [< MFr. < L. *sub-*, under + *ornare*, to furnish] 1. to get by bribery or other illegal methods 2. to induce or urge (another) to do something illegal, esp. to commit perjury —**sub·or·na·tion** (sub'ôr nā'shən) *n.* —**sub·or'na·tive** *adj.* —**sub·orn'er** *n.*

sub·plot (sub'plot') *n.* a secondary or subordinate plot in a play, novel, etc.

sub·poe·na (sə pē'nə, səb pē'-) *n.* [< ML. < L. *sub poena*, lit., under penalty: see SUB- & PAIN] a written legal order directing a person to appear in court to give testimony, etc. —*vt.* -naed, -na·ing to summon with such an order

sub·ro·gate (sub'rə gāt') *vt.* -gat'ed, -gat'ing [< L. pp. of subrogare, surrogate: see SURROGATE] to substitute (one person) for another; esp., to substitute (one creditor) for another —**sub'ro·ga'tion** *n.*

sub ro·sa (sub rō'zə) [L., under the rose, an ancient symbol of secrecy] secretly; privately

sub·rou·tine (sub'rōō tēn') *n.* a short set of instructions, often used repeatedly, that directs a digital computer in the solution of part of a problem

sub·scribe (səb skrīb') *vt.* -scribed', -scrib'ing [L. subscribere: see SUB- & SCRIBE] 1. to sign (one's name) at the end of a document, etc. 2. to write one's signature on (a document, etc.) as an indication of consent, etc. 3. to support; consent to 4. to promise to contribute (money) —*vi.* 1. to sign one's name to a document, etc. 2. to give support or approval (*to*) 3. to promise to contribute, or to give, a sum of money 4. to agree to receive and pay for a periodical, theatre tickets, etc. for a specified period (with *to*) —**sub·scrib'er** *n.*

sub·script (sub'skript) *adj.* [< L. pp. of subscribere, SUBSCRIBE] written below —*n.* a figure, letter, or symbol written below and to the side of another [in Y₃ and X₂, 3 and *a* are *subscripts*]

sub·scrip·tion (səb skrip'shən) *n.* 1. a subscribing 2. something subscribed; specif., *a*) a written signature *b*) a signed document, etc. *c*) consent or sanction, esp. in writing *d*) an amount of money subscribed *e*) a formal agreement to receive and pay for a periodical, theatre tickets, etc. for a specified period *f*) the membership dues paid to a club or society

sub·se·quent (sub'si kwənt, -kwent') *adj.* [< L. prp. of subsequi < *sub-*, after + *sequi*, to follow] coming after; following in time, place, or order —**subsequent to** after; following —**sub'se·quence'** *n.* —**sub'se·quent·ly** *adv.*

sub·serve (səb surv') *vt.* -served', -serv'ing to be useful or helpful to (a cause, etc.); serve; aid

sub·ser·vi·ent (-sur'vē ənt) *adj.* 1. that is useful or of service, esp. in a subordinate capacity 2. submissive; obsequious —**sub·ser'vi·ence, sub·ser'vi·en·cy** *n.* —**sub·ser'vi·ent·ly** *adv.*

sub·set (sub'set') *n.* a mathematical set containing some or all of the elements of a given set

sub·side (səb sīd') *vi.* -sid'ed, -sid'ing [< L. < *sub-*, under + *sidere*, to settle] 1. to sink to the bottom; settle 2. to sink to a lower level 3. to become less active, intense, etc.; abate —**sub·sid'ence** (-sīd'ns, sub'si dəns) *n.*

sub·sid·i·ar·y (səb sid'ē ər ē, -sid'jər ē) *adj.* [< L. < subsidium: see SUBSIDY] 1. giving aid, service, etc.; acting as a supplement; auxiliary 2. being in a subordinate capacity 3. of, constituting, or maintained by a subsidy or subsidies —*n., pl.* -ar·ies a person or thing that is subsidiary; specif., a company (**subsidiary company**) controlled by another company that owns all or most of its shares —**sub·sid'i·ar·i·ly** *adv.*

sub·si·dize (sub'sə dīz') *vt.* -dized', -diz'ing 1. to support with a subsidy 2. to buy the aid of with a subsidy —**sub'·si·di·za'tion** *n.* —**sub'si·diz'er** *n.*

sub·si·dy (sub'sə dē) *n., pl.* -dies [< Anglo-Fr. < L. subsidium, reserve troops, support] a grant of money; specif., *a*) a grant of money from one government to another *b*) a government grant to a private enterprise considered of benefit to the public

sub·sist (səb sist') *vi.* [< L. < *sub-*, under + *sistere*, to stand] 1. *a*) to continue to be or exist *b*) to continue to be in use, force, etc. 2. to continue to live (*on* sustenance, *by* specific means, etc.) 3. to consist (*in*) —*vt.* to maintain with sustenance

sub·sist·ence (-sis'təns) *n.* 1. existence; being 2. the act of providing sustenance 3. means of support or livelihood; specif., the barest means needed, as just enough food, to sustain life —**sub·sist'ent** *adj.*

subsistence farming a type of farming in which most of the produce is eaten by the farmer leaving little to sell or trade

sub·soil (sub'soil') *n.* the layer of soil beneath the surface soil —*vt.* to turn up the subsoil of —**sub'soil'er** *n.*

sub·son·ic (-son'ik) *adj.* [SUB- + SONIC] of a velocity less than the speed of sound

sub·spe·cies (-spē'shēz) *n.* any natural subdivision of a species that exhibits small variations in form from other subdivisions of the same species living in different regions

sub·stance (sub'stəns) *n.* [< OFr. < L. < substare < *sub-*, under + *stare*, to stand] 1. the real or essential part of anything; essence 2. *a*) the physical matter of which a thing consists; material *b*) matter of a particular kind or chemical composition 3. *a*) solid quality *b*) consistency; body 4. the real content or meaning of something said or written 5. material possessions; property; wealth —**in substance** 1. essentially 2. actually; really

sub·stand·ard (sub stan'dərd) *adj.* below standard; specif., *a*) below a legal standard *b*) *same as* NONSTANDARD: specif., designating or of a dialect regarded as below that used by educated speakers ["he don't" and "we ain't" are considered *substandard*]

sub·stan·tial (səb stan'shəl) *adj.* 1. of or having substance 2. real; actual; true 3. strong; solid; firm 4. ample; large 5. of considerable value; important 6. well-to-do 7. with regard to essential elements —**sub·stan'ti·al'i·ty** (-shē al'ə tē), **sub·stan'tial·ness** *n.* —**sub·stan'tial·ly** *adv.*

sub·stan·ti·ate (səb stan'shē āt') *vt.* -at'ed, -at'ing 1. to give substance to 2. to give concrete form or body to 3. to show to be true or real by giving evidence; prove —**sub·stan'ti·a'tion** *n.* —**sub·stan'ti·a'tive** *adj.* —**sub·stan'ti·a'tor** *n.*

sub·stan·tive (sub'stən tiv) *adj.* [< LL. < L. substantia, SUBSTANCE] 1. existing independently 2. of considerable amount 3. actual; real 4. *a*) essential *b*) having direct bearing on a matter 5. *Gram. a*) of or expressing existence [the *substantive* verb "to be"] *b*) of or used as a substantive —*n.* 1. something substantive 2. a noun or any word or group of words functioning as a noun —**sub'·stan·ti'val** (-tī'v'l) *adj.* —**sub'stan·ti·val·ly, sub'·stan·tive·ly** *adv.* —**sub'stan·tive·ness** *n.*

sub·sta·tion (sub'stā'shən) *n.* a subordinate station, esp. one that steps down the voltage from a power station

sub·sti·tute (sub'stə tyōōt') *n.* [< L. pp. of substituere < *sub-*, under + *statuere*, to put] a person or thing serving or used in place of another —*vt., vi.* -tut'ed, -tut'ing to put, use, or serve in place of another —*adj.* being a substitute —**sub'sti·tut'a·ble** *adj.* —**sub'sti·tu'tive** *adj.*

sub·sti·tu·tion (sub'stə tyōō'shən) *n.* the substituting of one person or thing for another —**sub'sti·tu'tion·al, —sub'·sti·tu'tion·ar·y** *adj.*

sub·stra·tum (sub'strāt'əm) *n., pl.* -ta (-ə), -tums [< L. pp. of substernere < *sub-*, under + *sternere*, to strew] 1. a part, substance, etc. which lies beneath and supports another 2. any basis or foundation 3. loosely, *same as* SUBSOIL

sub·struc·ture (-struk'chər) *n.* a structure acting as a support, base, or foundation —**sub·struc'tur·al** *adj.*

sub·sume (səb syōōm') *vt.* -sumed', -sum'ing [< ModL. < L. *sub-*, under + *sumere*, to take] 1. to include within a larger class, group, etc. 2. to show (an idea, instance, etc.) to be covered by a rule, principle, etc.

sub·sur·face (sub'sur'fis) *adj.* lying below the surface, esp. of the earth, the oceans, etc. —*n.* a subsurface part

sub·sys·tem (-sis'təm) *n.* any system that is part of a larger system; component system

sub·tem·per·ate (sub tem'pər it) *adj.* of or occurring in the colder areas of the temperate zones

sub·ten·ant (-ten'ənt) *n.* one who rents from a tenant; tenant of a tenant —**sub·ten'an·cy** *n.*

sub·tend (səb tend') *vt.* [< L. < *sub-*, under + *tendere*, to stretch] 1. to extend under or be opposite to in position [each side of a triangle *subtends* the opposite angle] 2. *Bot.* to enclose in an angle, as between a leaf and its stem

sub·ter- [L. < *subter*, below, beneath] a prefix meaning below, under, less than, secretly

sub·ter·fuge (sub'tər fyōōj') *n.* [< LL. < L. < *subter-*, below + *fugere*, to flee] any plan, action, etc. used to hide one's true objective, evade a difficult situation, etc.

sub·ter·ra·ne·an (sub'tə rā'nē ən) *adj.* [< L. < *sub-*, under + *terra*, earth] 1. lying beneath the earth's surface; underground 2. secret; hidden Also **sub'ter·ra'ne·ous** —*n.* one who lives underground —**sub'ter·ra'ne·an·ly** *adv.*

sub·tile (sut''l) *adj. now rare var. of* SUBTLE —**sub'tile·ly** *adv.* —**sub'tile·ness** *n.* —**sub'til·ty, sub·til·i·ty** (sə til'ə tē) *n., pl.* -**ties**

sub·til·ize (sut'əl īz') *vt., vi.* -**ized'**, -**iz'ing** to make or become subtle; esp., to discuss or argue in a subtle way —**sub'til·i·za'tion** *n.*

sub·ti·tle (sub'tīt''l) *n.* **1.** a secondary title of a book, play, etc. **2.** a unit of lines of dialogue or description flashed on a cinema or TV screen, esp. at the bottom in translation —*vt.* -**ti'tled, -ti'tling** to add a subtitle or subtitles to

sub·tle (sut'''l) *adj.* **sub'tler** (-lər, -'l ər), **sub'tlest** (-list, -'l ist) [< OFr. < L. *subtilis*, orig., closely woven < *sub*-, under + *tela*, web] **1.** thin; tenuous; not dense **2.** making fine distinctions or marked by mental keenness **3.** delicately skilful; deft **4.** crafty; sly **5.** not grossly obvious [*a subtle hint*] **6.** not easily detected [*a subtle poison*] —**sub'tle·ness** *n.* —**sub'tly** *adv.*

sub·tle·ty (-tē) *n.* **1.** the quality or condition of being subtle **2.** *pl.* -**ties** something subtle, as a fine distinction

sub·ton·ic (sub ton'ik) *n. Music* the seventh tone of a diatonic scale

sub·top·ic (sub'top'ik) *n.* a topic that is a division of a main topic

sub·to·tal (-tōt'''l) *n.* a total forming part of a final, complete total —*vt., vi.* -**talled, -tal·ling** to add up so as to form a subtotal

sub·tract (səb trakt') *vt., vi.* [< L. pp. of *subtrahere* < *sub*-, under + *trahere*, to draw] to take away or deduct (a part from a whole) or (one number or quantity from another) —**sub·tract'er** *n.* —**sub·trac'tive** *adj.*

sub·trac·tion (-trak'shən) *n.* a subtracting or being subtracted; esp., the mathematical process of finding the difference between two numbers or quantities

sub·tra·hend (sub'trə hend') *n.* [< L. gerundive of *subtrahere*: see SUBTRACT] a number or quantity to be subtracted from another

sub·trop·i·cal (sub trop'i k'l) *adj.* designating, of, or characteristic of regions bordering on the tropical zone; nearly tropical: also **sub·trop'ic**

sub·trop·ics (-iks) *n.pl.* subtropical regions

sub·urb (sub'ərb) *n.* [< L. < *sub*-, under, near + *urbs*, town] **1.** a residential district on the outskirts of a city or town **2.** [*pl.*] a region of such districts (with *the*)

sub·ur·ban (sə bur'bən) *adj.* **1.** of or living in a suburb or the suburbs **2.** characteristic of the suburbs or suburbanites —**sub·ur'ban·ize'** (-īz') *vt., vi.* -**ized', -iz'ing**

sub·ur·ban·ite (-īt') *n.* a person living in a suburb

sub·ur·bi·a (sə bur'bē ə) *n.* the suburbs or suburbanites collectively: used to connote suburban values, attitudes, etc.

sub·ven·tion (səb ven'shən) *n.* [< OFr. < LL. < L. < *sub*-, under + *venire*, to come] a grant of money; subsidy

sub·ver·sion (səb vur'zhən, -shən) *n.* a subverting or being subverted; ruin; overthrow

sub·ver·sive (-siv) *adj.* tending or seeking to subvert —*n.* a person regarded as subversive —**sub·ver'sive·ly** *adv.* —**sub·ver'sive·ness** *n.*

sub·vert (səb vurt') *vt.* [< MFr. < L. < *sub*-, under + *vertere*, to turn] **1.** to overthrow or destroy (something established) **2.** to undermine or corrupt, as in morals —**sub·vert'er** *n.*

sub·way (sub'wā) *n.* **1.** an underground way, esp. for pedestrians **2.** [U.S.] an underground (sense 3)

suc- *same as* SUB-: used before *c*

suc·ceed (sək sēd') *vi.* [L. *succedere* < *sub*-, under + *cedere*, to go] **1.** *a)* to come next after another *b)* to follow another into office, possession, etc., as by inheritance, election, etc. (often with *to*) **2.** to happen or turn out as planned **3.** to accomplish something planned or tried **4.** to have success; do well; attain wealth, fame, etc. —*vt.* **1.** to follow into office, etc. **2.** to come after; follow

suc·cess (sək ses') *n.* [< L. < pp. of *succedere*: see prec.] **1.** *a)* a favourable outcome *b)* something having a favourable outcome **2.** the gaining of wealth, fame, etc. **3.** a successful person

suc·cess·ful (-fəl) *adj.* **1.** turning out to be as was hoped for **2.** having gained wealth, fame, etc. —**suc·cess'ful·ly** *adv.* —**suc·cess'ful·ness** *n.*

suc·ces·sion (sək sesh'ən) *n.* **1.** a succeeding or coming after another in sequence or to an office, title, etc. **2.** the right to succeed to an office, title, etc. **3.** a number of persons or things coming one after another; series; sequence **4.** *a)* a series of heirs or rightful successors *b)* the order or line of such a series —**in succession** one after another —**suc·ces'sion·al** *adj.*

suc·ces·sive (sək ses'iv) *adj.* **1.** coming one after another; consecutive **2.** of succession —**suc·ces'sive·ly** *adv.* —**suc·ces'sive·ness** *n.*

suc·ces·sor (-ər) *n.* a person or thing that succeeds, or follows, another; esp., one who succeeds to a throne, title, office, etc.

suc·cinct (sək siŋkt') *adj.* [< L. pp. of *succingere*, to tuck up < *sub*-, under + *cingere*, to gird] **1.** clearly and briefly stated; terse **2.** concise and to the point in speaking —**suc·cinct'ly** *adv.* —**suc·cinct'ness** *n.*

suc·co·tash (suk'ə tash') *n.* [< AmInd.] [U.S.] a dish consisting of lima beans and kernels of maize cooked together

suc·cour (suk'ər) *vt.* [< OFr. < L. *succurrere* < *sub*-, under + *currere*, to run] to aid in time of need or distress —*n.* **1.** aid; help **2.** a person or thing that succours Also, U.S. sp. **suc'cor**

suc·cu·bus (suk'yoo bəs) *n., pl.* -**bi** (-bī') [< ML., ult. < L. *sub*-, under + *cubare*, to lie] a female demon thought in medieval times to have sexual intercourse with sleeping men: also **suc'cu·ba** (bə), *pl.* -**bae'** (-bē')

suc·cu·lent (suk'yoo lənt) *adj.* [L. *succulentus* < *sucus*, juice] **1.** juicy **2.** full of interest, vigour, etc. **3.** *Bot.* having thick, fleshy tissues for storing water, as a cactus· —*n.* a succulent plant —**suc'cu·lence, suc'cu·len·cy** *n.* —**suc'cu·lent·ly** *adv.*

suc·cumb (sə kum') *vi.* [L. *succumbere* < *sub*-, under + *cumbere*, to lie] **1.** to give way (*to*); yield; submit **2.** to die [*to succumb* to a plague *]*

such (such) *adj.* [OE. *swilc, swelc*] **1.** *a)* of the kind mentioned or implied [*one such* as he *]* *b)* of the same or a similar kind [*pens, pencils, and such* supplies *]* **2.** certain but not specified; whatever [*at such* time as you go *]* **3.** so extreme; so much, etc. [*such* fun! *] Such* is used, with *as* or *that*, in making comparisons [*such* wit *as* his is rare *]* An article may occur between *such* and the noun it modifies [*such* a fool! *]* **4.** to so great a degree [*such* good news *]* —*pron.* such a one or ones —**all such** all of these —**as such 1.** as being what is indicated **2.** in itself —**such a one** someone or something similar to —**such as 1.** for example **2.** like or similar to (what is specified)

such and such (being) something particular but not specified [he went to *such and such* a place *]*

such·like (-līk') *adj.* of such a kind; of similar kind —*pron.* persons or things of such kind

suck (suk) *vt.* [OE. *sucan*] **1.** *a)* to draw (liquid) into the mouth by making a vacuum with the lips, cheeks, and tongue *b)* to draw up (water, oil, etc.) by the action of a pump **2.** to take up or in as by sucking; absorb, inhale, etc. [*to suck* air into the lungs *]* **3.** to suck liquid from (a breast, fruit, etc.) **4.** to hold (a sweet, etc.) in the mouth and lick it **5.** to place (the thumb, etc.) in the mouth and draw on as if sucking —*vi.* **1.** to suck something in or up **2.** to suck milk from the breast or udder **3.** to make a sucking sound or movement —*n.* **1.** the act or sound of sucking **2.** *a)* something drawn in by sucking *b)* [Colloq.] the amount sucked at one time —**suck in** to compress and pull inwards [*to suck in* one's belly *]* —**suck up to** [Slang] to flatter or fawn upon

suck·er (-ər) *n.* **1.** one that sucks **2.** a carplike freshwater fish with a mouth adapted for sucking **3.** a part used for sucking; specif., *a)* a tube through which something is sucked *b)* the piston or piston valve of a suction *c)* an organ used by the leech, octopus, etc. for sucking or holding fast to a surface by suction **4.** [Colloq.] *a)* a person easily fooled or cheated; dupe *b)* a person readily drawn to specified attractions **5.** *Bot.* a shoot from a root bud or stem bud —*vt.* **1.** to remove suckers, or shoots, from **2.** [Colloq.] to make a dupe of; trick —*vi.* to bear suckers, or shoots

·SUCKERS

suck·le (suk'''l) *vt.* -**led, -ling** [prob. < ff.] **1.** to give milk to from a breast or udder; nurse **2.** to nourish; foster —*vi.* to suck milk from its mother

suck·ling (-liŋ) *n.* [see SUCK & -LING[1]] an unweaned child or young animal

sucks (suks) *interj.* [Colloq.] an expression of derision

su·cre (soo'kre) *n.* [AmSp. after A.J. de *Sucre*, 19th-c. S. American liberator] *see* MONETARY UNITS, table (Ecuador)

su·crose (soo'krōs) *n.* [< Fr. *sucre*, sugar + -OSE[1]] *Chem.* pure crystalline sugar extracted from sugar cane or sugar beets: it can be broken down into glucose and fructose

suc·tion (suk'shən) *n.* [OFr. < L. *suctus*, pp. of *sugere*, to suck] **1.** the act or process of sucking **2.** the drawing of air out of a space to make a vacuum that will suck in surrounding air, liquid, etc. or cause something to stick to the surface **3.** the force so created —*adj.* causing or operating by suction

suction pump a pump that draws liquid up by suction created by pistons fitted with valves

suc·to·ri·al (suk tôr'ē əl) *adj.* [< ModL. < L.: see SUCTION] sucking or adapted for sucking

Su·da·nese (soo dä nēz') *adj.* designating or of the Sudan —*n., pl.* -**nese'** a native or inhabitant of the Sudan

su·dar·i·um (syoo der'ē əm) *n., pl.* -**i·a** (-ə) [L. < *sudor*, sweat] in ancient Roman civilization, a cloth for wiping the face

su·da·to·ry (syōō'də tər ē, -trē) *adj.* [L. *sudatorius* < *sudor,* sweat] of or producing perspiration —*n., pl.* **-ries** an agent that causes sweating

sudd (sud) *n.* [Ar.] floating masses of weeds, etc. often obstructing navigation on the White Nile

sud·den (sud''n) *adj.* [OFr. *sodain* < L. *subitaneus,* ult. < *sub-,* under + *ire,* to go] **1.** *a)* happening or coming unexpectedly; not foreseen *b)* sharp or abrupt [a *sudden* turn] **2.** done, coming, or taking place quickly or abruptly —**all of a sudden** without warning; quickly —**sud′den·ly** *adv.* —**sud′den·ness** *n.*

sudden death *Sports* an extra period added to a drawn game, the game ending as soon as one side scores or goes ahead

su·dor·if·er·ous (syōō'də rif'ər əs) *adj.* [ModL. < L. *sudor,* sweat] secreting sweat

su·dor·if·ic (syōō'də rif'ik) *adj.* [< ModL. < L. *sudor,* sweat + *facere,* to make] causing or increasing sweating —*n.* a sudorific drug, etc.

suds (sudz) *n.pl.* [prob. < MDu. *sudse,* marsh water] **1.** foamy, soapy water **2.** foam, froth, or lather —*vi.* to make suds —**suds′y** *adj.* **-i·er, -i·est**

sue (sōō) *vt.* **sued, su′ing** [OFr. *sivre, suir,* ult. < L. *sequi,* to follow] **1.** to appeal to; petition **2.** to bring a lawsuit in court against **3.** [Archaic] to woo —*vi.* **1.** to petition; plead (*for* or *to*) **2.** [Archaic] to woo **3.** to bring legal suit —**su′er** *n.*

suede, suède (swād) *n.* [Fr. *Suède,* Sweden, in *gants de Suède,* Swedish gloves] **1.** tanned leather with the flesh side buffed into a nap **2.** a kind of cloth made to resemble this: also **suede cloth**

su·et (sōō'it, sōō'it) *n.* [dim. < Anglo-Fr. *sue* < OFr. < L. *sebum,* fat] hard fat from around the kidneys and loins of cattle and sheep: used in cooking and as a source of tallow —**su′et·y** *adj.*

suet pudding any of various sweet or savoury puddings made with suet and steamed or boiled

suf- same as SUB-: used before f

suf·fer (suf'ər) *vt.* [< Anglo-Fr. < OFr. < L. *sufferre* < *sub-,* under + *ferre,* to bear] **1.** to undergo (something painful or unpleasant) **2.** to undergo (any process) **3.** to allow; tolerate **4.** to bear; endure —*vi.* to undergo pain, harm, loss, punishment, etc. —**suf′fer·a·ble** *adj.* —**suf′fer·er** *n.* —**suf′fer·ing** *n.*

suf·fer·ance (suf'ər əns, suf'rəns) *n.* **1.** power or capacity to endure pain, etc. **2.** consent, toleration, etc. implied by failure to interfere or prohibit —**on sufferance** allowed or tolerated but not supported or encouraged

suf·fice (sə fīs') *vi.* **-ficed′, -fic′ing** [< OFr. < L. *sufficere* < *sub-,* under + *facere,* to make] to be enough —*vt.* [Archaic] to be enough for

suf·fi·cien·cy (sə fish'ən sē) *n.* **1.** sufficient means, ability, or resources; an amount that is enough **2.** a being sufficient; adequacy

suf·fi·cient (-'nt) *adj.* [see SUFFICE] as much as is needed; enough —**suf·fi′cient·ly** *adv.*

suf·fix (suf'iks; *also for v.* sə fiks') *n.* [< ModL. < L. pp. of *suffigere* < *sub-,* under + *figere,* to fix] a syllable or group of syllables added at the end of a word or word base to change its meaning or give it grammatical function (Ex.: *-ish* in *smallish, -ed* in *walked*) —*vt.* to add as a suffix —**suf′fix·al** *adj.* —**suf·fix′ion** *n.*

suf·fo·cate (suf'ə kāt') *vt.* **-cat′ed, -cat′ing** [< L. pp. of *suffocare* < *sub-,* under + *fauces,* throat] **1.** to kill by cutting off the supply of oxygen to the lungs, gills, etc. **2.** to hinder the free breathing of **3.** to smother, suppress, etc. —*vi.* **1.** to die by being suffocated **2.** to be unable to breathe freely; choke, etc. —**suf′fo·cat′ing·ly** *adv.* —**suf′fo·ca′tion** *n.* —**suf′fo·ca′tive** *adj.*

suf·fra·gan (suf'rə gən) *n.* [MFr. < ML. < L. *suffragari,* to support] **1.** a bishop assisting another bishop **2.** a bishop as a subordinate of his archbishop —*adj.* **1.** designating or of such a bishop **2.** subordinate to a larger see

suf·frage (suf'rij) *n.* [MFr. < ML. < L. *suffragium,* a vote < *sub-,* under + *fragor,* loud applause] **1.** a short prayer of supplication **2.** a vote or voting **3.** the right to vote in political elections

suf·fra·gette (suf'rə jet') *n.* formerly, a woman who worked for women's right to vote —**suf′fra·get′tism** *n.*

suf·fra·gist (suf'rə jist) *n.* a person who believes in extending the right to vote, esp. to women

suf·fuse (sə fyōōz') *vt.* **-fused′, -fus′ing** [< L. pp. of *suffundere* < *sub-,* under + *fundere,* to pour] to overspread so as to fill with a glow, colour, fluid, etc.: said of light, a blush, air, etc. —**suf·fu′sion** *n.* —**suf·fu′sive** (-siv) *adj.*

sug- same as SUB-: used before g

sug·ar (shoog'ər) *n.* [OFr. *sucre,* ult. < Per. *šakar* < Sans. *šárkarā*] **1.** any of a class of sweet, soluble, crystalline carbohydrates, including sucrose, lactose, maltose, glucose, fructose, etc. **2.** sucrose in crystalline or powdered form: it

is the common sugar used to sweeten food **3.** a lump or spoonful of sugar [three *sugars* please] **4.** [Chiefly U.S. Colloq.] sweetheart —*vt.* **1.** to put sugar on or in **2.** to make seem pleasant or less bad —*vi.* **1.** to form sugar **2.** to boil down maple syrup to form maple sugar (usually with *off*) —**sug′ar·less** *adj.* —**sug′ar·like′** *adj.*

sugar basin a bowl or container for sugar at table

sugar beet a variety of beet with a white root from which common sugar is obtained

sugar cane a very tall, tropical grass cultivated as the main source of common sugar

sug·ar·coat (-kōt') *vt.* **1.** to coat with sugar **2.** [Chiefly U.S.] to make seem less unpleasant [to 'sugarcoat bad news']

sugar diabetes *popular term for* DIABETES MELLITUS

sugar loaf 1. a conical mass of crystallized sugar **2.** a similarly shaped hill, etc.

sugar maple an E N American maple valued for its hard wood and for its sap, which yields maple syrup

sug·ar·plum (-plum') *n.* **1.** a crystallized plum **2.** a round or oval sugary sweet; bonbon

sugar shaker a device for sprinkling sugar on cakes, fruit, etc.

SUGAR CANE

sugar tongs small tongs for serving lumps of sugar

sug·ar·y (shoog'ər ē) *adj.* **1.** of, like, or containing sugar; sweet, granular, etc. **2.** too sweet or sentimental —**sug′ar·i·ness** *n.*

sug·gest (sə jest') *vt.* [< L. pp. of *suggerere* < *sub-,* under + *gerere,* to carry] **1.** to mention as something to think over, act on, etc.; bring to the mind for consideration **2.** to call to mind through association of ideas [objects *suggested* by the shapes of clouds] **3.** to propose (someone or something) as a possibility **4.** to imply; intimate —**sug·gest′er** *n.*

sug·gest·i·ble (-jes'tə b'l) *adj.* easily influenced by suggestion —**sug·gest′i·bil′i·ty** *n.*

sug·ges·tion (-jes'chən) *n.* **1.** a suggesting or being suggested **2.** something suggested **3.** the process by which one idea leads to another through association of ideas **4.** a faint hint; trace **5.** *Psychol.* the inducing of an idea that is accepted or acted on readily without questioning

suggestions box a box into which suggestions for improvements in a firm, etc. may be placed

sug·ges·tive (-jes'tiv) *adj.* **1.** that suggests or tends to suggest ideas **2.** tending to suggest something considered improper or indecent —**sug·ges′tive·ly** *adv.* —**sug·ges′tive·ness** *n.*

su·i·ci·dal (sōō'ə sīd'əl) *adj.* **1.** of, involving, or leading to suicide **2.** having an urge to commit suicide **3.** rash to the point of being dangerous —**su·i·ci′dal·ly** *adv.*

su·i·cide (sōō'ə sīd') *n.* [L. *sui,* of oneself + -CIDE] **1.** the intentional killing of oneself **2.** ruin of one's interests through one's own actions **3.** a person committing suicide

su·i ge·ne·ris (sōō'ē jen'ər is, sōō'ī) [L., lit., of his (or her or its) own kind] altogether unique

su·il·line (syōō'ə līn) *adj.* [L. < *sus,* a pig & -INE[1]] pertaining to pigs; pig-like

suit (sōōt, syōōt) *n.* [OFr. *suite,* ult. < L. *sequi,* to follow] **1.** *a)* a set of clothes to be worn together; esp., a coat and trousers (or skirt), usually of the same material *b)* any complete outfit [a *suit* of armour] **2.** a set or series of similar things; specif., any of the four sets of thirteen playing cards each (*spades, clubs, hearts, diamonds*) in a pack **3.** a lawsuit **4.** a suing, pleading, or wooing —*vt.* **1.** to meet the needs of; be right for or becoming to **2.** to make fit; adapt [a dance *suited* to the music] **3.** to please; satisfy **4.** to furnish with clothes, esp. with a suit —*vi.* to be suitable, convenient, or satisfactory —**bring suit** to start legal action; sue —**follow suit 1.** to play a card of the same suit as the card led **2.** to follow the example set —**suit oneself** to do as one pleases

suit·a·ble (-ə b'l) *adj.* right for the purpose, occasion, etc.; fitting; appropriate —**suit′a·bil′i·ty, suit′a·ble·ness** *n.* —**suit′a·bly** *adv.*

suit·case (-kās') *n.* a travel case for clothes, etc., esp. a rectangular one that opens into two hinged compartments

suite (swēt) *n.* [Fr.: see SUIT] **1.** a group of attendants or servants; retinue **2.** a set or series of related things; specif., *a)* a unit of connected rooms *b)* a set of matched furniture for a room [a bedroom *suite*] **3.** *Music* an instrumental composition made up of several movements or, in earlier times, dances

suit·ing (sōōt'iŋ, syōōt'-) *n.* cloth for making suits

suit·or (-ər) *n.* **1.** a person who sues, petitions, pleads, etc. **2.** a man courting or wooing a woman

su·ki·ya·ki (sōō′kē yä′kē) *n.* [Jap.] a Japanese dish of thinly sliced meat, onions, and other vegetables cooked quickly, often at table, with soya sauce, sake, sugar, etc.

sulf- *chiefly U.S. var. sp. of* SULPH-

sul·fur (sul′fər) *n. U.S. var. sp. of* SULPHUR

sulk (sulk) *vi.* [back-formation < ff.] to be sulky —*n.* **1.** a sulky mood or state: also **the sulks 2.** a sulky person

sulk·y (sul′kē) *adj.* **sulk′i·er, sulk′i·est** [prob. < OE. *solcen* (in comp.), idle] sullen in a pouting or peevish way [a *sulky child*] —*n., pl.* **sulk′ies** a light, two-wheeled carriage for one person, esp., now, one used in trotting races in the U.S. —**sulk′i·ly** *adv.* —**sulk′i·ness** *n.*

sul·len (sul′ən) *adj.* [ult. < L. *solus,* alone] **1.** silent and keeping to oneself because one feels angry, bitter, hurt, etc. **2.** gloomy; dismal; depressing **3.** sombre; dull **4.** sluggish —**sul′len·ly** *adv.* —**sul′len·ness** *n.*

sul·ly (sul′ē) *vt.* **-lied, -ly·ing** [prob. < OFr. *souiller:* see SOIL²] to soil, stain, etc., now esp. by disgracing

sulph- *a combining form meaning of* or containing sulphur

sul·pha (sul′fə) *adj.* designating or of a family of drugs that are sulphonamides, used in combatting certain bacterial infections: also, esp. U.S., **sul·fa**

sul·pha·di·a·zine (sul′fə dī′ə zēn′, -zin) *n.* [prec. + DI-¹ + AZ(O) + -INE⁴] a sulpha drug, used in treating certain pneumococcal, streptococcal, and staphylococcal infections

sul·pha·nil·a·mide (-nil′ə mīd′) *n.* [< SULPH- + ANIL(INE) + AMIDE] a white, crystalline compound formerly used in the treatment of bacterial infections

sul·phate (sul′fāt) *n.* a salt or ester of sulphuric acid —*vt.* —**phat′ed, -phat′ing** [U.S.] **1.** to treat with sulphuric acid or a sulphate **2.** to convert into a sulphate **3.** to form a lead sulphate deposit on (negative storage battery plates) —*vi.* to become sulphates —**sul·pha′tion** *n.*

sul·phide (sul′fīd) *n.* a compound of sulphur with another element or a radical

sul·phite (-fīt) *n.* a salt or ester of sulphurous acid

sul·phon·a·mide (sul fon′ə mīd, -mid) *n.* [< *sulphon(yl),* the radical SO₂ + AMIDE] a compound, as sulphadiazine, containing the univalent radical -SO₂NH₂

sul·phur (sul′fər) *n.* [L. *sulphur*] **1.** a pale-yellow, nonmetallic chemical element found in crystalline or amorphous form: it burns with a blue flame and a stifling odour: symbol, S; at. wt., 32.064; at. no., 16 **2.** any of numerous butterflies with dark-bordered, yellow or orange wings **3.** a greenish-yellow colour —*vt.* to sulphurize

sul·phu·rate (sul′fōō rāt′, -fə-) *vt.* **-rat′ed, -rat′ing** *same as* SULPHURIZE —**sul′phu·ra′tion** *n.*

sul·phur·bot·tom (sul′fər bot′əm) *n. same as* BLUE WHALE

sulphur dioxide a heavy, colourless, suffocating gas, SO₂, easily liquefied and used as a bleach, preservative, etc.

sul·phu·re·ous (sul fyoor′ē əs) *adj.* **1.** of, like, or containing sulphur **2.** greenish-yellow

sul·phu·ret (sul′fyōō ret′) *vt.* **-ret′ted, -ret′ting** *same as* SULPHURIZE

sul·phu·ric (sul fyoor′ik) *adj.* **1.** of or containing sulphur, esp. sulphur with a valence of six **2.** of or derived from sulphuric acid

sulphuric acid an oily, colourless, corrosive liquid, H₂SO₄, used in making explosives, fertilizers, chemicals, etc.

sul·phu·rize (sul′fyoo rīz′, -fə-) *vt.* **-rized′, -riz′ing** to combine or treat with sulphur or a sulphur compound —**sul′phu·ri·za′tion** *n.*

sul·phu·rous (sul′fər əs; *for 1 usually* sul fyoor′əs) *adj.* **1.** of or containing sulphur, esp. sulphur with a valence of four **2.** like burning sulphur in odour, colour, etc. **3.** of or suggesting the fires of hell **4.** violently emotional; fiery —**sul′phu·rous·ly** *adv.* —**sul′phu·rous·ness** *n.*

sulphurous acid a colourless acid known only in the form of its salts or in solution in water, and used as a chemical reagent, a bleach, etc.

sul·phur·y (sul′fər ē) *adj.* of or like sulphur

sul·tan (sul′t′n) *n.* [Fr. < Ar. *sultan*] a Moslem ruler; esp., [S-] formerly, the ruler of Turkey

sul·tan·a (sul tä′nə) *n.* **1.** a sultan's wife, mother, sister, or daughter: also **sul′tan·ess** (-tən is) **2.** a small, white, seedless grape or raisin

sultana bird a bird of Australia, West Indies and Southern U.S.

sul·tan·ate (sul′tən it, -āt′) *n.* the authority, office, reign, or dominion of a sultan

sul·try (sul′trē) *adj.* **-tri·er, -tri·est** [var. of *sweltry:* see SWELTER] **1.** oppressively hot and moist; sweltering **2.** fiery **3.** inflamed with passion, lust, etc. —**sul′tri·ly** *adv.* —**sul′tri·ness** *n.*

sum (sum) *n.* [< MFr. < L. *summa,* fem. of *summus,* highest] **1.** an amount of money **2.** the whole amount; totality [the *sum* of one's experiences] **3.** gist; summary: usually in **sum and substance 4.** *a)* the result obtained by adding numbers or quantities *b)* a series of numbers to be added up, or any problem in arithmetic —*vt.* **summed, sum′-ming 1.** to add up **2.** to summarize —*vi.* to get, or come to, a total —**in sum** to put it briefly; in short —**sum up 1.**

to add up or collect into a whole or total **2.** to summarize **3.** to form a quick opinion of

sum- *same as* SUB-: used before *m*

su·mac, su·mach (shōō′mak, sōō′-) *n.* [MFr. < Ar. *summāq*] **1.** *a)* any of various non-poisonous plants with compound leaves and cone-shaped clusters of hairy, red fruit *b)* the powdered leaves of some of these plants, used in tanning and dyeing **2.** any of several poisonous plants, as poison ivy

SUMAC

Su·mer·i·an (sōō mir′ē ən, -mer′-) *adj.* designating or of an ancient, non-Semitic people of Sumer —*n.* **1.** any of the Sumerian people **2.** the language of the Sumerians

‡sum·ma cum lau·de (soom′ə koom lou′de, sum′ə kum lô′dē) [L.] [Chiefly U.S.] with the greatest praise: phrase used to signify graduation with the highest honours from a college or university

sum·ma·rize (sum′ə rīz′) *vt.* **-rized′, -riz′ing** to make or be a summary of —**sum′ma·ri·za′tion** *n.* —**sum′ma·riz′er** *n.*

sum·ma·ry (sum′ə rē) *adj.* [< ML. < L. *summa,* a sum] **1.** briefly giving the general idea; concise; condensed **2.** *a)* prompt and informal *b)* hasty and arbitrary —*n., pl.* **-ries** a brief account covering the main points; digest —**sum·mar·i·ly** (sum′ə rə lē, sə mer′ə lē) *adv.*

summary jurisdiction *Law* the right a court has to adjudicate immediately upon some matter arising during its proceedings

sum·ma·tion (sə mā′shən) *n.* **1.** a summing up, to find a total **2.** a total or aggregate **3.** a final summing up

sum·mer (sum′ər) *n.* [OE. *sumor*] **1.** the warmest season of the year, following spring **2.** a year as reckoned by this season **3.** any period regarded, like summer, as a time of growth, development, etc. —*adj.* of, typical of, or suitable for summer —*vi.* to pass the summer —*vt.* to keep or feed during the summer —**sum′mer·y** *adj.*

sum·mer·house (-hous′) *n.* a small, open structure in a garden, park, etc., for providing a shady rest

summer house a house or cottage, as in the country, used during the summer

summer pudding a dessert made with a bread casing and fruit, usually raspberries or blackberries, as filling

sum·mer·sault (sum′ər sôlt′) *n., vi. var. of* SOMERSAULT

summer school a session at a college or university held during the summer (or long) vacation

summer solstice the time in the Northern Hemisphere when the sun is farthest north of the celestial equator; June 21 or 22

sum·mer·time (-tīm′) *n.* **1.** the season of summer **2.** any daylight-saving time, esp. British Summer Time

sum·ming·up (sum′iŋ up′) *n.* [Colloq.] a summarizing

sum·mit (sum′it) *n.* [< OFr., ult. < L. *summus,* highest] **1.** the highest point or part; top; apex **2.** the highest degree or state; acme **3.** *a)* a top level of officials; specif., in diplomacy, the level restricted to heads of government *b)* a conference at this level: also **summit meeting** —*adj.* of the heads of government

sum·mon (sum′ən) *vt.* [< OFr., ult. < L. *summonere,* to remind secretly < *sub-,* secretly + *monere,* to warn] **1.** to call together; order to meet **2.** to call for or send for with authority or urgency **3.** to order, as by a summons, to appear in court **4.** to call upon to do something **5.** to call forth; rouse (often with *up*) [*summon* up strength] —**sum′-mon·er** *n.*

sum·mons (-ənz) *n., pl.* **-mons·es** [< Anglo-Fr. *somonse* < OFr.: see prec.] **1.** an order to come or do something; specif., *Law* an official order to appear in court, specif. as a defendant; also, the writ containing such an order **2.** a call, knock, etc. that summons —*vt.* [Colloq.] to serve a court summons upon

‡sum·mum bo·num (soom′əm bō′nəm) [L.] the highest, or supreme, good

su·mo (wrestling) (sōō′mō) [Jap. *sumō*] [*sometimes* S-] stylized Japanese wrestling engaged in by a hereditary class of large, extremely heavy men

sump (sump) *n.* [ME. *sompe,* a swamp] a pit, cistern, cesspool, etc. for draining or collecting liquid, esp. oil from a motor vehicle engine

sump pump a pump for removing liquid from a sump

sump·ter (sump′tər) *n.* [< OFr. *sometier* < LL. *sagma,* packsaddle] a pack animal

sump·tu·ar·y (sump′choo wər ē, -tyoo-) *adj.* [< L. < *sumptus,* expense < pp. of *sumere,* to take] of or regulating expenses or expenditures

sump·tu·ous (sump′choo wəs, -tyoo-) *adj.* [< OFr. < L. < *sumptus:* see prec.] **1.** involving great expense; costly; lavish **2.** magnificent, as in furnishings —**sump′tu·ous·ly** *adv.* —**sump′tu·ous·ness** *n.*

sum total 1. the total arrived at by adding up a sum or sums 2. everything involved or included

sun (sun) *n.* [OE. *sunne*] 1. *a)* the self-luminous, gaseous sphere about which the earth and other planets revolve and which furnishes light, heat, and energy for the solar system: it is about 149 600 000 kilometres from earth and about 1 392 400 kilometres in diameter *b)* its heat or light 2. any star that is the centre of a planetary system 3. something like the sun, as in warmth, brilliance, etc. 4. [Poet.] *a)* a day *b)* a year *c)* a clime; climate —*vt., vi.* **sunned, sun'ning** to expose or be exposed to the sun so as to warm, tan, bleach, etc. —**place in the sun** a prominent or favourable position —**take the sun** 1. to sunbathe 2. *Naut.* to find the sun's altitude in order to find one's latitude —**under the sun** on earth; in the world

Sun. Sunday

sun·baked (-bākt') *adj.* 1. baked by the sun's heat, as bricks 2. parched, cracked, etc. by the sun's heat

sun bath exposure of the body to sunlight or a sunlamp

sun·bathe (-bāth') *vi.* **-bathed', -bath'ing** to take a sun bath —**sun'bath'er** *n.*

sun·beam (-bēm') *n.* a ray or beam of sunlight

sun·bon·net (-bon'it) *n.* a large-brimmed bonnet with a back flap, worn to shade the face and neck from the sun, esp. formerly, by women and girls

sun·burn (-burn') *n.* an inflammation of the skin resulting from prolonged exposure to the sun's rays or a sunlamp —*vi., vt.* **-burned'** or **-burnt', -burn'ing** to get or cause to get a sunburn

sun·burst (-burst') *n.* 1. a burst of sunlight, as between clouds 2. a decoration suggesting the sun and its rays

sun-cured (-kyoord') *adj.* cured, as meat or fruit, by drying in the sun

sun·dae (sun'dā, -dē) *n.* [prob. < SUNDAY] a serving of ice cream covered with syrup, fruit, nuts, etc.

Sun·day (sun'dē, -dā) *n.* [OE. *sunnandæg*, lit., day of the sun] the first day of the week, observed by most Christians as a day of worship or as the Sabbath —*adj.* 1. of or typical of Sunday 2. done, worn, etc. on Sunday

Sunday best [Colloq.] one's best clothes

Sun·days (-dēz, -dāz) *adv.* [Colloq.] on or during every Sunday

Sunday school 1. a school giving religious instruction on Sunday at a church or synagogue 2. the teachers and pupils of such a school

sun·der (sun'dər) *vt., vi.* [OE. *sundrian* < *sundor*, asunder] to break apart; split —**in sunder** into parts or pieces —**sun'der·a·ble** *adj.* —**sun'der·ance** *n.*

sun·di·al (sun'dī'əl, -dīl') *n.* an instrument that shows time by the shadow of a pointer or gnomon cast by the sun on a dial marked in hours

sun disc a disc flanked by two serpents and set in a pair of outspread wings: a symbol of the Egyptian god, Ra

sun·dog (-dog') *n.* same as PARHELION

sun·down (-doun') *n.* same as SUNSET

SUNDIAL

sun·down·er (-ər) *n.* 1. [Aust. Colloq.] a tramp or vagrant 2. [Colloq.] an alcoholic drink taken at sunset

sun dress a dress designed with the minimum covering for the upper torso, allowing maximum exposure to the sun

sun-dried (-drīd') *adj.* dried by the sun

sun·dries (sun'drēz) *n.pl.* sundry items; miscellaneous things

sun·dry (-drē) *adj.* [OE. *syndrig*, separate < *sundor*, apart] various; miscellaneous [*sundry* articles of clothing] —*pron.* [with pl. v.] sundry persons or things: chiefly in **all and sundry** everybody; one and all

sun·fast (sun'fāst') *adj.* [U.S.] not fading in sunlight

sun·fish (-fish') *n., pl.* **-fish', -fish'es:** see FISH 1. any of a large family of N American freshwater fishes 2. same as OCEAN SUNFISH

sun·flow·er (-flou'ər) *n.* any of various tall plants of the composite family, with large, yellow, daisylike flowers containing edible seeds from which an oil is extracted

sung (suŋ) *pp. & rare pt. of* SING

sun·glass (sun'glās') *n.* 1. same as BURNING GLASS 2. [pl.] eyeglasses with special lenses, usually tinted, to protect the eyes from the sun's glare

sun god 1. the sun personified and worshipped as a god 2. any god associated or identified with the sun

sunk (suŋk) *pp. & alt. pt. of* SINK —*adj.* 1. same as SUNKEN 2. [Colloq.] utterly ruined, disgraced, etc.

sunk·en (-ən) *obs. pp. of* SINK —*adj.* 1. submerged [a *sunken* ship] 2. below the level of the surrounding or adjoining area [a *sunken* patio] 3. fallen in; hollow [*sunken* cheeks] 4. dejected

sunk fence same as HA-HA

sun·lamp (sun'lamp') *n.* an electric lamp that radiates ultraviolet rays like those of sunlight

sun·less (-lis) *adj.* without sun or sunlight; dark

sun·light (-līt') *n.* the light of the sun

sun·lit (-lit') *adj.* lighted by the sun

sun lounge a room or porch with large windows positioned so as to receive as much sunlight as possible

Sun·na, Sun·nah (sun'ə) *n.* [Fr. *sunnah*, lit., a form, tradition] Moslem law based according to tradition on the teachings and practices of Mohammed: a supplement to the Koran

sun·ny (sun'ē) *adj.* **-ni·er, -ni·est** 1. bright with sunlight; full of sunshine 2. bright and cheerful 3. of or suggestive of the sun —**on the sunny side of** somewhat younger than (a specified age) —**sun'ni·ly** *adv.* —**sun'ni·ness** *n.*

sun·rise (-rīz') *n.* 1. the daily appearance of the sun above the eastern horizon 2. the time of this 3. the colour of the sky at this time

sun·set (-set') *n.* 1. the daily disappearance of the sun below the western horizon 2. the time of this 3. the colour of the sky at this time

sun·shade (-shād') *n.* a parasol, awning, etc. used for protection against the sun's rays

sun·shine (-shīn') *n.* 1. the shining of the sun, or its light and heat 2. cheerfulness, joy, etc., or a source of this —**sun'shin'y** *adj.*

sun·spot (-spot') *n.* any temporarily cooler region appearing from time to time as a dark spot on the sun

sun·stroke (-strōk') *n.* heatstroke caused by excessive exposure to the sun —**sun'struck'** (-struk') *adj.*

sun·suit (-sōot', -syōot') *n.* a garment consisting of short pants with a bib and shoulder straps, for babies and children

sun·tan (-tan') *n.* a darkened condition of the skin resulting from exposure to the sun or a sunlamp —**sun'-tanned'** *adj.*

sun·up (-up') *n.* [U.S.] same as SUNRISE

sun·ward (-wərd) *adv.* towards the sun: also **sun'wards** —*adj.* facing the sun

sup¹ (sup) *n., vt., vi.* **supped, sup'ping** [OE. *supan*, to drink] same as SIP

sup² (sup) *vi.* **supped, sup'ping** [< OFr. *souper* < *soupe*, soup] to have supper

sup- same as SUB-: used before *p*

sup. 1. superior 2. superlative 3. supine 4. supplement 5. supplementary 6. supply

su·per (sōo'pər) *n.* [< ff.] 1. *shortened form of:* a) SUPERNUMERARY b) SUPERINTENDENT 2. [Colloq.] a product that is superior, extra large, etc.: a trade term —*adj.* 1. outstanding; exceptionally fine 2. great, extreme, or excessive —*interj.* [Colloq.] good; excellent

su·per- [L. < *super*, above] a prefix meaning: 1. over, above, on top of [*superstructure*] 2. higher in rank than, superior to [*superintendent*] 3. *a)* surpassing [*superfine*] *b)* greater or better than others of its kind [*supermarket*] 4. to a degree greater than normal [*supersaturate*] 5. extra, additional [*supertax*]

su·per·a·ble (sōo'pər ə b'l) *adj.* that can be overcome; surmountable —**su'per·a·bly** *adv.*

su·per·a·bound (sōo'pər ə bound') *vi.* to be greatly or excessively abundant

su·per·a·bun·dant (-ə bun'dənt) *adj.* excessively abundant —**su'per·a·bun'dance** *n.* —**su'per·a·bun'dant·ly** *adv.*

su·per·an·nu·ate (-yōo wāt') *vt.* **-at'ed, -at'ing** [back-formation < ff.] 1. to set aside as old-fashioned or obsolete 2. to retire, esp. with a pension, because of old age or infirmity —**su'per·an'nu·a'tion** *n.*

su·per·an·nu·at·ed (-id) *adj.* [< ML. pp. of *superannuari* < L. *super*, beyond + *annus*, year] 1. *a)* too old for further work *b)* retired because of old age or infirmity 2. obsolete; old-fashioned; outdated

su·perb (sōo purb', soo-) *adj.* [L. *superbus*, proud < *super*, above] 1. noble, grand, or majestic 2. rich; splendid 3. excellent —**su·perb'ly** *adv.* —**su·perb'ness** *n.*

su·per·car·go (sōo'pər kär'gō) *n., pl.* **-goes, -gos** [< Sp. *sobrecargo* < *sobre*, over + *cargo*, CARGO] an officer on a merchant ship who has charge of the cargo, representing the shipowner

su·per·ce·les·tial (-sə les'chəl) *adj.* 1. above or beyond the heavens 2. more than heavenly

su·per·charge (-chärj') *vt.* **-charged', -charg'ing** 1. to increase the power of (an engine), as with a supercharger 2. same as PRESSURIZE (sense 1)

su·per·charg·er (-chär'jər) *n.* a blower or compressor used to increase the power of an internal-combustion engine by increasing the supply of air or fuel mixture to the cylinders

su·per·cil·i·ous (sōo'pər sil'ē əs) *adj.* [< L. < *supercilium*, eyebrow, hence (with reference to raised brows), haughtiness < *super*, above + *cilium*, eyelid] full of or showing pride or contempt; haughty —**su'per·cil'i·ous·ly** *adv.* —**su'per·cil'i·ous·ness** *n.*

su·per·con·duc·tiv·i·ty (-kon'dək tiv'ə tē) *n. Physics* the ability of certain metals and alloys to conduct electricity continuously without resistance when chilled to near absolute zero: also **su'per·con·duc'tion** (-kən duk'shən)

—**su·per·con·duct·ing, su·per·con·duc·tive** *adj.* —**su'·per·con·duc'tor** *n.*

su·per·cool (-kōōl') *vt.* to lower the temperature of (a liquid) to below its freezing point without causing solidification —*vi.* to become supercooled

su·per·crit·i·cal (krit'i k'l) *adj.* *Physics* of or having more than a critical mass

su·per·e·go (sōō'pər ē'gō) *n.,* *pl.* **-gos** *Psychoanalysis* that part of the psyche which is critical of the self or ego and enforces moral standards

su·per·em·i·nent (-em'ə nənt) *adj.* eminent beyond others —**su'per·em'i·nence** *n.* —**su'per·em'i·nent·ly** *adv.*

su·per·er·o·ga·tion (-er'ə gā'shən) *n.* [< LL. < pp. of *supererogare* < *super*, above + *erogare*, to pay out] the act of doing more than what is required or expected

su·per·e·rog·a·to·ry (-i rog'ə tər ē) *adj.* **1.** done beyond the degree required or expected **2.** superfluous

su·per·fat·ted (-fat'əd) *adj.* having a greater proportion of fat than usual

su·per·fi·cial (-fish'əl) *adj.* [< L. < *superficies*, a surface < *super-*, above + *facies*, face] **1.** *a)* of or being on the surface *b)* of surface area; plane **2.** concerned with and understanding only the easily apparent and obvious; not profound; shallow **3.** quick and cursory **4.** merely apparent [a superficial resemblance] —**su'per·fi'ci·al'i·ty** (-ē al'ə tē) *n.,* *pl.* **-ties** —**su·per·fi'cial·ly** *adv.* —**su'per·fi·cial·ness** *n.*

su·per·fine (sōō'pər fīn', sōō'pər fīn') *adj.* **1.** too subtle, delicate, or refined **2.** of very fine quality

su·per·flu·i·ty (sōō'pər flōō'ə tē) *n.,* *pl.* **-ties** **1.** a being superfluous **2.** a quantity beyond what is needed; excess **3.** something superfluous

su·per·flu·ous (soo pur'floo wəs) *adj.* [< L. < *superfluere* < *super-*, above + *fluere*, to flow] **1.** being more than is needed or wanted; excessive **2.** not needed; unnecessary —**su·per'flu·ous·ly** *adv.* —**su·per'flu·ous·ness** *n.*

su·per·heat (sōō'pər hēt'; *for n.* sōō'pər hēt') *vt.* **1.** to make too hot **2.** to heat (a liquid) above its boiling point without its vaporizing **3.** to heat (steam not in contact with water) beyond its saturation point, so that a drop in temperature will not cause it to turn back to water

su·per·het·er·o·dyne (sōō'pər het'ər ə dīn') *adj.* [SUPER(SONIC) + HETERODYNE] designating or of radio reception in which some amplification is done at an intermediate supersonic frequency —*n.* a radio set for this kind of reception

su·per·high frequency (sōō'pər hī') any radio frequency between 3000 and 30 000 megahertz

su·per·hu·man (-hyōō'mən) *adj.* **1.** having a nature above that of man; divine **2.** greater than normal for a human being —**su'per·hu'man·ly** *adv.* —**su'per·hu'man·ness** *n.*

su·per·im·pose (-im pōz') *vt.* **-posed', -pos'ing** **1.** to put or lay on top of something else **2.** to add as a feature that dominates or does not properly fit with the rest

su·per·in·duce (-in dyōōs') *vt.* **-duced', -duc'ing** to bring in as an addition —**su'per·in·duc'tion** (-duk'shən) *n.*

su·per·in·tend (-in tend') *vt.* to act as superintendent of; supervise —**su'per·in·tend'ence, su'per·in·tend'en·cy** *n.*

su·per·in·tend·ent (-in ten'dənt) *n.* [< LL. prp. of *superintendere:* see SUPER- & INTEND] **1.** a person in charge of a department, institution, etc.; supervisor **2.** a police officer ranking above an inspector **3.** [U.S.] the caretaker of a building, etc. —*adj.* that superintends

su·pe·ri·or (sə pir'ē ər, soo-) *adj.* [OFr. < L., compar. of *superus*, that is above] **1.** higher in space; placed higher up **2.** higher or greater in order, status, rank, numbers, etc. **3.** greater in quality or value than (with *to*) **4.** above average; excellent **5.** refusing to be affected by (something painful): with *to* **6.** haughty —*n.* **1.** a superior person or thing **2.** the head of a religious community —**su·pe'ri·or'i·ty** (-ôr'ə tē) *n.*

superl. superlative

su·per·la·tive (sə pur'lə tiv, soo-) *adj.* [< MFr. < LL. < L. < *super-*, above + *latus*, pp. of *ferre*, to carry] **1.** excelling all others; supreme **2.** excessive **3.** *Gram.* designating or of the extreme degree of comparison of adjectives and adverbs: usually indicated by the suffix *-est* (*hardest*) or by the use of *most* (*most beautiful*) —*n.* **1.** the highest degree; acme **2.** something superlative **3.** *Gram.* a) the superlative degree *b)* a word or form in this degree —**su·per'la·tive·ly** *adv.* —**su·per'la·tive·ness** *n.*

su·per·man (sōō'pər man') *n.,* *pl.* **-men** (-men') **1.** in Nietzsche's philosophy, a type of superior man regarded as the goal of the evolutionary struggle **2.** an apparently superhuman man

su·per·mar·ket (-mär'kit) *n.* a large, self-service, retail food store, often one of a chain, selling food, household goods, etc.

su·per·mun·dane (-mun'dān) *adj.* **1.** being above the world **2.** being superior to worldly matters

su·per·nal (soo pur'n'l) *adj.* [MFr. < L. *supernus*, upper] celestial, heavenly, or divine —**su·per'nal·ly** *adv.*

su·per·nat·u·ral (sōō'pər nach'ər əl) *adj.* **1.** existing outside man's normal experience or the known laws of nature; specif., of or involving God or a god, or ghosts, the occult, etc. **2.** extraordinary —**the supernatural** supernatural beings, forces, happenings, etc. —**su'per·nat'u·ral·ly** *adv.*

su·per·nat·u·ral·ism (-iz'm) *n.* **1.** a supernatural quality or state **2.** a belief that some supernatural, or divine, force controls nature and the universe —**su'per·nat'u·ral·ist** *n.,* *adj.* —**su'per·nat'u·ral·is'tic** *adj.*

su·per·no·va (-nō'və) *n.,* *pl.* **-vae** (-vē), **-vas** [ModL.: see SUPER- & NOVA] an extremely bright nova that suddenly increases 10 million to 100 million times in brightness

su·per·nu·mer·ar·y (-nyōō'mə rər ē) *adj.* [< LL. < L. *super*, above + *numerus*, number] beyond the regular or needed number; extra or superfluous —*n.,* *pl.* **-ar·ies** **1.** a supernumerary person or thing **2.** *Theatre* a person with a small, nonspeaking part, as in a crowd scene

su·per·pa·tri·ot (-pā'trē ət) *n.* a person who is or professes to be a devout patriot, often to the point of fanaticism —**su'per·pa'tri·ot'ic** (-pā'trē ot'ik) *adj.* —**su'per·pa'tri·ot·ism** *n.*

su·per·phos·phate (-fos'fāt) *n.* an acid phosphate; esp. one made by treating phosphate rock with sulphuric acid, and used as a fertilizer

su·per·pose (-pōz') *vt.* **-posed', -pos'ing** [< Fr. < L. pp. of *superponere:* see SUPER- & POSE] **1.** to lay or place on, over, or above something else **2.** *Geom.* to place (one figure) on top of another that is congruent so that corresponding sides coincide —**su'per·pos'a·ble** *adj.* —**su'per·po·si'tion** *n.*

su·per·pow·er (sōō'pər pou'ər) *n.* any of the few most powerful nations of the world competing for spheres of influence

su·per·sat·u·rate (sōō'pər sach'ə rāt') *vt.* **-rat'ed, -rat'ing** to saturate beyond the normal point for the given temperature —**su'per·sat'u·ra'tion** *n.*

su·per·scribe (-skrīb') *vt.* **-scribed', -scrib'ing** [< L.: see SUPER- & SCRIBE] to write or mark (an inscription, name, etc.) at the top or on an outer surface of something —**su'per·scrip'tion** (-skrip'shən) *n.*

su·per·script (sōō'pər skript') *adj.* written above —*n.* a figure, letter, or symbol written above and to the side of another [in y^2 and x^n, 2 and n are *superscripts*]

su·per·sede (sōō'pər sēd') *vt.* **-sed'ed, -sed'ing** [< MFr. < L. *supersedere*, to preside over < *super-*, above + *sedere*, to sit] **1.** to cause to be set aside as inferior or obsolete and be replaced **2.** to take the place or office of; succeed **3.** to replace; supplant —**su'per·sed'er** *n.* —**su'per·se'dure** (-sē'jər), **su'per·sed'ence** *n.*

su·per·sen·si·tive (-sen'sə tiv) *adj.* highly sensitive or too sensitive —**su'per·sen'si·tiv'i·ty** *n.*

su·per·son·ic (-son'ik) *adj.* [SUPER- + SONIC] **1.** designating, of, or moving at a speed in a surrounding fluid greater than that of sound in the same fluid: cf. SONIC **2.** same as ULTRASONIC —**su'per·son'i·cal·ly** *adv.*

su·per·son·ics (-son'iks) *n.pl.* [with sing. v.] the science dealing with supersonic phenomena

su·per·sti·tion (sōō'pər stish'ən) *n.* [< MFr. < L. *superstitio*, ult. < *super-*, over + *stare*, to stand] **1.** any belief, based on fear or ignorance, that is not in accord with the known laws of science or with what is considered true and rational; esp., such a belief in charms, omens, the supernatural, etc. **2.** any action or practice based on such a belief **3.** such beliefs collectively

su·per·sti·tious (-əs) *adj.* **1.** of, characterized by, or resulting from superstition **2.** having superstitions —**su'per·sti'tious·ly** *adv.* —**su'per·sti'tious·ness** *n.*

su·per·store (-stôr') *n.* a large supermarket; hypermarket

su·per·struc·ture (sōō'pər struk'chər) *n.* **1.** a structure built on top of another **2.** that part of a building above the foundation **3.** that part of a ship above the main deck

su·per·tank·er (sōō'pər tan'kər) *n.* an extremely large tanker, of about 300 000 tons or more

su·per·tax (-taks') *n.* an additional tax; esp., a surtax

su·per·ter·res·tri·al (-tə res'trē əl) *adj.* same as SUPERMUNDANE (sense 1)

su·per·vene (sōō'pər vēn') *vi.* **-vened', -ven'ing** [< L. < *super-*, over + *venire*, to come] to come or happen as something added or not expected —**su'per·ven'ient** (-vēn'yənt) *adj.* —**su'per·ven'tion** (-ven'shən), **su'per·ven'ience** (-vēn'yəns) *n.*

su·per·vise (sōō'pər vīz') *vt.,* *vi.* **-vised', -vis'ing** [< ML. pp. of *supervidere* < L. *super-*, over + *videre*, to see] to oversee, direct, or manage (work, workers, a project, etc.); superintend —**su'per·vi'sion** (-vizh'ən) *n.*

su·per·vi·sor (-vī'zər) *n.* **1.** a person who supervises; manager; director **2.** a university tutor supervising student's work **3.** [U.S.] in certain schools, an official in charge of the courses and teachers for a particular subject —**su'per·vi'so·ry** *adj.*

su·pine (sōō pīn') *adj.* [L. *supinus*] **1.** lying on the back, face upwards **2.** showing no concern or doing nothing about matters —**su·pine'ly** *adv.* —**su·pine'ness** *n.*

supp., suppl. **1.** supplement **2.** supplementary

sup·per (sup'ər) *n.* [OFr. *souper*, orig. inf., to SUP²] an evening meal, as a dinner, or a late, light meal, as one eaten after the theatre —**sup'per·less** *adj.*

sup·plant (sə plänt') *vt.* [< OFr. < L. *supplantare*, to trip up < *sub-*, under + *planta*, sole of the foot] **1.** to take the place of, esp. through force or plotting **2.** to remove and replace with something else —**sup·plan·ta·tion** (sup'-lan tā'shən) *n.* —**sup·plant'er** *n.*

sup·ple (sup''l) *adj.* [< OFr. < L. *supplex*, humble] **1.** bending easily; flexible **2.** lithe; limber [a *supple* body] **3.** changing easily, as under new conditions or strong influences **4.** adaptable or yielding: said of the mind, etc. —*vt., vi.* **-pled, -pling** to make or become supple —**sup'-ple·ly** *adv.* —**sup'ple·ness** *n.*

sup·ple·ment (sup'lə mənt; *for v.* -ment') *n.* [< L. < *supplere:* see SUPPLY[1]] **1.** something added, esp. to make up for a lack **2.** a section added to a book, etc., as to give additional information **3.** a separate newspaper section containing feature stories, illustrations, articles, etc. **4.** *Math.* the number of degrees to be added to an angle or arc to make 180 degrees —*vt.* to provide a supplement to; add to —**sup'ple·men·ta'tion** *n.* —**sup'ple·ment'er** *n.*

sup·ple·men·ta·ry (sup'lə men'tər ē) *adj.* supplying what is lacking; additional: also **sup'ple·men'tal** —*n., pl.* **-ries** a supplementary person or thing

supplementary angle either of two angles that together form 180 degrees

sup·pli·ant (sup'lē ənt) *n.* [MFr., prp. of *supplier* < L.: see SUPPLICATE] a person who supplicates; beseeching —**sup'pli·ance** *n.* —**sup'-pli·ant·ly** *adv.*

sup·pli·cant (sup'lə kənt) *adj., n.* same as SUPPLIANT

sup·pli·cate (sup'lə kāt') *vt.* **-cat'ed, -cat'ing** [< L. pp. of *supplicare,* to kneel down

SUPPLEMENTARY ANGLES (angle BCA and angle DCB are supplementary

< *sub-,* under + *plicare,* to fold] **1.** to ask for humbly, as by prayer **2.** to make a humble request of —*vi.* to make a humble request, esp. in prayer —**sup'pli·ca'tion** *n.* —**sup'-pli·ca'tor** *n.* —**sup'pli·ca·to·ry** (-kə tər ē) *adj.*

sup·ply[1] (sə plī') *vt.* **-plied', -ply'ing** [< MFr. < L. *supplere,* to fill up < *sub-,* under + *plere,* to fill] **1.** to give, furnish, or provide (what is needed) **2.** to meet the needs or requirements of **3.** to make up for (a deficiency, etc.) **4.** to act as a substitute in [to *supply* another's pulpit] —*vi.* to serve as a substitute —*n., pl.* **-plies'** **1.** the act of supplying **2.** an amount available for use; stock; store **3.** [*pl.*] materials, provisions, etc. for supplying an army, a business, etc. **4.** a substitute, as for a minister, teacher, etc. **5.** *Econ.* the amount of a commodity available for purchase at a given price —*adj.* **1.** having to do with a supply or supplies **2.** serving as a substitute —**sup·pli'er** *n.*

sup·ply[2] (sup'lē) *adv.* in a supple manner; supply

sup·port (sə pôrt') *vt.* [< MFr. < LL. < L. < *sub-,* under + *portare,* to carry] **1.** *a)* to carry or bear the weight of; hold up *b)* to carry or bear (a specified weight, pressure, etc.) **2.** to give courage or faith to; help; comfort **3.** to give approval to or be in favour of; uphold **4.** to provide for (a person, institution, etc.) with money or subsistence **5.** to help prove or vindicate [evidence to *support* a claim] **6.** to bear; endure; tolerate **7.** to keep up; maintain; specif., to maintain (the price of a commodity) as by purchases **8.** *Theatre* to act a subordinate role with (a specified star) —*n.* **1.** a supporting or being supported **2.** a person or thing that supports; specif., *a)* a prop, base, brace, etc. *b)* a means of subsistence *c)* an elastic device to support or bind a part of the body —**sup·port'a·ble** *adj.* —**sup·port'a·bly** *adv.*

sup·port·er (-ər) *n.* **1.** a person who supports; advocate; adherent **2.** a thing that supports; esp., an elastic device to support the back, abdomen, etc.

supporting film a film that is not the main attraction but forms part of a cinema programme

sup·port·ive (-iv) *adj.* that gives support, help, or approval

sup·pose (sə pōz') *vt.* **-posed', -pos'ing** [< MFr. < ML. *supponere,* ult. < L. *sub-,* under + *ponere,* to place] **1.** to take to be true, as for the sake of argument, etc. [*suppose* A equals B] **2.** to believe, think, guess, etc. **3.** to involve as a preceding condition; presuppose **4.** to consider as a suggested possibility [*suppose* he doesn't come] **5.** to expect or obligate: always in the passive [she's *supposed* to telephone] —*vi.* to think or guess; conjecture —**sup·pos'-a·ble** *adj.* —**sup·pos'a·bly** *adv.* —**sup·pos'er** *n.*

sup·posed (sə pōzd') *adj.* **1.** regarded as true, possible, etc., without actual knowledge **2.** merely imagined —**sup·pos'-ed·ly** *adv.*

sup·po·si·tion (sup'ə zish'ən) *n.* **1.** the act of supposing **2.** something supposed; assumption Also **sup·pos·al** (sə pōz''l) —**sup'po·si'tion·al** *adj.* —**sup'po·si'tion·al·ly** *adv.*

sup·pos·i·tious (-əs) *adj.* [L. *suppositicius* < *suppositus,* pp. of *supponere:* see SUPPOSE] **1.** substituted with intent to

deceive **2.** hypothetical Also **sup·pos·i·ti·tious** (sə poz'ə-tish'əs)

sup·pos·i·to·ry (sə poz'ə tər ē) *n., pl.* **-ries** [< ModL. < L. < pp. of *supponere:* see SUPPOSE] a small, shaped piece of medicated substance, inserted into the rectum, vagina, etc., where it is melted and spread by the body heat

sup·press (sə pres') *vt.* [< L. pp. of *supprimere* < *sub-,* under + *premere,* to press] **1.** to put down by force or authority; quell **2.** to keep from appearing or being known, published, etc. [to *suppress* a news story, a book, etc.] **3.** to keep back; restrain; check [to *suppress* a laugh, cough, etc.] **4.** to check the flow, secretion, etc. of **5.** *Electronics, Radio,* etc. to eliminate (an unwanted signal, etc.) **6.** *Psychiatry* to consciously dismiss (unacceptable ideas, impulses, etc.) from the mind —**sup·press'i·ble** *adj.* —**sup·pres'sive** *adj.* —**sup·pres'sive·ly** *adv.* —**sup·pres'-sor** *n.*

sup·pres·sion (sə presh'ən) *n.* **1.** a suppressing or being suppressed **2.** *Psychiatry a)* the mechanism by which unacceptable ideas, impulses, etc. are suppressed *b)* something suppressed in this way

sup·pu·rate (sup'yoo rāt') *vi.* **-rat'ed, -rat'ing** [< L. pp. of *suppurare* < *sub-,* under + *pus* (gen. *puris*), pus] to form or discharge pus; fester —**sup'pu·ra'tion** *n.* —**sup'pu·ra'-tive** *adj.*

su·pra- [< L. *supra,* above, over] a prefix meaning above, over, beyond [*suprarenal*]

su·pra·na·tion·al (soo'prə nash'ə n'l) *adj.* of, for, involving, or over all or a number of nations [*supranational* authority] —**su'pra·na'tion·al·ism** *n.*

su·pra·re·nal (-rē'n'l) *adj.* [< ModL.: see SUPRA- & RENAL] on or above the kidney; specif., designating or of an adrenal gland —*n.* an adrenal gland

su·prem·a·cist (soo prem'ə sist, syoo-, sə-) *n.* a person who believes in or promotes the supremacy of a particular group [a white *supremacist*]

su·prem·a·cy (soo prem'ə sē, syoo-, sə-) *n., pl.* **-cies** **1.** the quality or state of being supreme **2.** supreme power or authority

su·preme (soo prēm', syoo-) *adj.* [L. *supremus,* superl. of *superus,* that is above] **1.** highest in rank, power, etc. **2.** highest in quality, achievement, performance, etc.; most excellent **3.** highest in degree; utmost [a *supreme* fool] **4.** final; ultimate —**su·preme'ly** *adv.* —**su·preme'ness** *n.*

Supreme Being God

Supreme Court the highest Federal court in the U.S.A., consisting of nine judges

supreme sacrifice the sacrifice of one's life

Supreme Soviet the parliament of the Soviet Union

su·pre·mo (soo'prēm'ō) *n.* [< SUPREM(E) + -o] a person with overall authority or control [the drought *supremo*]

Supt., supt. Superintendent

sur-[1] [OFr. < L. *super,* over, above] a prefix meaning over, upon, above, beyond [*surcharge*]

sur-[2] same as SUB-: used before *r*

Su·ra (soor'ə) *n.* [Ar. *sūrah,* lit., step, degree] any of the main divisions or chapters of the Koran

su·rah (soor'ə) *n.* [< *Surat,* a seaport in India] a soft, twilled fabric of silk or rayon

sur·cease (sur sēs'; *for n. usually* sur'sēs) *vt., vi.* **-ceased', -ceas'ing** [< OFr. *sursis,* pp. of *surseoir,* to pause < L. *supersedere,* to refrain from] [Archaic] to stop; end —*n.* end; cessation

sur·charge (sur'chärj; *also for v.* sur chärj') *vt.* **-charged', -charg'ing** [< OFr.: see SUR-[1] & CHARGE] **1.** to overcharge **2.** to overload **3.** to fill to excess **4.** to mark (a postage stamp) with a surcharge —*n.* **1.** *a)* an additional charge *b)* an overcharge **2.** an extra or excessive load **3.** a new face value overprinted on a postage stamp

sur·cin·gle (sur'siŋ'g'l) *n.* [< MFr. < *sur-,* over + L. *cingulum,* a belt] a strap passed around a horse's body to bind on a saddle, pack, etc.

sur·coat (-kōt') *n.* [< MFr.: see SUR-[1] & COAT] an outer coat; esp., a short cloak worn over a knight's armour

surd (surd) *adj.* [L. *surdus,* deaf, mute] same as: **1.** *Math.* IRRATIONAL **2.** *Phonet.* VOICELESS —*n.* **1.** *Math.* an irrational number or quantity, as a root that cannot be determined exactly [√5 is a *surd*] **2.** *Phonet.* voiceless sound

sure (shoor) *adj.* **sur'er, sur'est** [< OFr. < L. *securus:* see SECURE] **1.** orig., secure or safe **2.** that will not fail; always effective [a *sure* method] **3.** that can be relied upon; trustworthy [a *sure* friend] **4.** that cannot be doubted, questioned, etc.; absolutely true **5.** having no doubt; positive; confident [to be *sure* of the facts] **6.** that can be counted on to be or happen [a *sure* defeat] **7.** bound to do, experience, etc. [*sure* to lose] **8.** never missing [a *sure* aim] —*adv.* [Chiefly U.S. Colloq.] **1.** surely; inevitably **2.** certainly; indeed: used as an intensive [*sure,* I'll go] —**for sure** certain(ly); without doubt —**make sure** to be or cause to be certain —**sure enough** [Colloq.] certainly; without doubt —**to be sure** surely; certainly —**sure'ness** *n.*

sure-fire (-fīr′) *adj.* [Colloq.] sure to be successful or as expected; that will not fail

sure-foot·ed (-foot′id) *adj.* not likely to stumble, fall, or err —**sure′-foot′ed·ly** *adv.* —**sure′-foot′ed·ness** *n.*

sure·ly (-lē) *adv.* 1. with confidence; in a sure, unhesitating manner 2. without a doubt; certainly [*surely* you don't believe that!] 3. without risk of failing : chiefly in **slowly but surely**

sure thing [Chiefly U.S. Colloq.] 1. something certain to win, succeed, etc. 2. all right; O.K.: used as an interjection

sure·ty (shoor′ə tē, shoor′tē) *n., pl.* **-ties** 1. a being sure; assurance 2. something sure; certainty 3. something that makes sure or gives assurance, as against loss, default, etc.; security 4. a person who makes himself responsible for another; specif., *Law* one who makes himself liable for another's debts, etc. —**sure′e·ty·ship′** *n.*

surf (surf) *n.* [earlier *suffe*, prob. var. of SOUGH] 1. the waves of the sea breaking on the shore or a reef 2. the foam or spray caused by this —*vi.* to engage in the sport of surfing —**surf′er** *n.*

sur·face (sur′fis) *n.* [Fr. < *sur-* (see SUB-) + *face*, a face] 1. *a*) the outside or outer face of a thing *b*) any side of a thing having several sides *c*) the area of such a side 2. outward appearance 3. *Aeron.* an aerofoil 4. *Geom.* an extent or magnitude having length and breadth, but no thickness —*adj.* 1. of, on, or at the surface 2. functioning or carried on land or sea, rather than in the air or under water [*surface* forces, *surface* mail] 3. seeming such on the surface; superficial —*vt.* -**faced′, -fac·ing** 1. to treat the surface of, esp. so as to make smooth or level 2. to give a surface to, as in paving 3. to bring (a submarine, etc.) to the surface of the water —*vi.* 1. to rise to the surface of the water 2. to become known, esp. after being concealed —**sur′fac·er** *n.*

sur·face-ac·tive (-ak′tiv) *adj. Chem.* designating or of a substance, as a detergent, that lowers the surface tension of the solvent in which it is dissolved

surface density *Physics* the amount of electric charge per unit area

surface printing printing from a plate in relief instead of from one with incised lines

surface tension a property of liquids in which the surface tends to contract to the smallest possible area, so that the surface seems like a thin, elastic film under tension

sur·fac·tant (sur fak′tənt) *n.* [*surf*(ace)-*act*(ive) *a*(ge)*nt*] a surface-active substance

surf·board (surf′bôrd′) *n.* a long, narrow board used in the sport of surfing —*vi.* to engage in this sport —**surf′-board′er** *n.* —**surf′board′-ing** *n.*

surf·boat (-bōt′) *n.* a sturdy, light boat used in heavy surf

surf-cast (-kãst′) *vi.* -**cast′, -cast′ing** to fish by casting into the ocean surf from or near the shore —**surf′-cast′er** *n.*

SURFBOARD

sur·feit (sur′fit) *n.* [< OFr. < *sorfaire*, to overdo < *sur-* (< L. *super*), over + *faire* (< L. *facere*) to make] 1. too great an amount or supply; excess [a *surfeit* of compliments] 2. an indulging in too much food, drink, etc. 3. disgust, nausea, etc. resulting from this —*vt.* to feed or supply to excess —*vi.* [Rare] to overindulge

surf·ing (sur′fiŋ) *n.* the sport of riding in towards shore on the crest of a wave, esp. on a surfboard

surf·rid·ing (-rīd′iŋ) *n.* same as SURFING

surg. 1. surgeon 2. surgery 3. surgical

surge (surj) *n.* [prob. < OFr. < L. *surgere*, to rise] 1. a large wave of water, or the swelling or rushing motion of such a wave or series of waves 2. any sudden strong rush [a *surge* of energy, electric power, etc.; the *surge* of the crowd] —*vi.* **surged, surg′ing** to move in a surge

sur·geon (sur′jən) *n.* a doctor who specializes in surgery

surgeon fish (-fish′) *n., pl.* -**fish, -fish′es**: see FISH any of various edible, brightly coloured, tropical sea fishes with movable spines on the base of the tail

sur·ger·y (sur′jər ē) *n., pl.* -**ger·ies** [< OFr. *cirurgie* < L. < Gr. *cheirourgia*, handicraft < *cheir*, the hand + *ergein*, to work] 1. *a*) the treatment of disease, injury, etc. by operations with the hands or instruments, as the removal of diseased parts by cutting, the setting of broken bones, etc. *b*) the branch of medicine dealing with this 2. the consulting rooms of a dentist, doctor, etc. 3. [Chiefly U.S.] the operating room of a surgeon or hospital 4. [Colloq.] the place or time when members of parliament can be visited by their constituents

sur·gi·cal (-ji k′l) *adj.* 1. of surgeons or surgery 2. used in or connected with surgery 3. resulting from surgery —**sur′-gi·cal·ly** *adv.*

surgical spirit methylated spirit for use as a cleanser in operations, etc.

sur·ly (sur′lē) *adj.* -**li·er, -li·est** [earlier *sirly*, imperious < *sir*, SIR] bad-tempered; sullenly rude; uncivil —**sur′li·ly** *adv.* —**sur′li·ness** *n.*

sur·mise (sər mīz′; *for n. also* sur′mīz) *n.* [< OFr. pp. of *surmettre* < *sur-* (< L. *super*), upon + *mettre*, to put < L. *mittere*, to send] 1. an idea or opinion that is only a guess, based on a few facts; conjecture 2. the act of surmising —*vt., vi.* -**mised′, -mis′ing** to imagine or infer (something) without conclusive evidence; guess —**sur·mis′er** *n.*

sur·mount (sər mount′) *vt.* [OFr. *surmonter*: see SUR-[1] & MOUNT[2]] 1. to overcome (a difficulty) 2. to be or lie at the top of; be or rise above 3. to climb up and across (a height, obstacle, etc.) —**sur·mount′a·ble** *adj.*

sur·name (sur′nām′; *for v. also* sur′nām′) *n.* [< OFr. < *sur-* (see SUR-[1]) + *nom* < L. *nomen*, name] 1. the family name, or last name, as distinguished from a Christian name 2. a name or epithet added to a person's given name (Ex.: Ivan *the Terrible*) —*vt.* -**named′, -nam′ing** to give a surname to

sur·pass (sər päs′) *vt.* [< MFr. < *sur-* (see SUR-[1]) + *passer*, to PASS[2]] 1. to be better or greater than; excel 2. to exceed in quantity, degree, etc. 3. to go beyond the limit, capacity, range, etc. of [riches *surpassing* belief] —**sur·pass′a·ble** *adj.* —**sur·pass′er** *n.*

sur·pass·ing (-iŋ) *adj.* that surpasses the average or usual; exceeding or excelling; unusually excellent —*adv.* [Archaic] exceedingly —**sur·pass′ing·ly** *adv.*

sur·plice (sur′plis) *n.* [< Anglo-Fr. < OFr. < ML. < L. *super-*, above + *pelliceum*, fur robe] a loose, white, wide-sleeved outer vestment worn by the clergy and choir in some churches —**sur′pliced** *adj.*

surplice fee a fee paid to clergy for performing baptisms, marriages, and funerals

SURPLICE

sur·plus (sur′plus, -pləs) *n.* [OFr. < *sur-*, above + L. *plus*, more] 1. a quantity over and above what is needed or used; excess 2. the excess of the assets of a business over its liabilities —*adj.* that is a surplus; excess

surplus value in Marxist economics, the amount by which the value of the worker's product exceeds that of his pay

sur·prise (sər prīz′) *vt.* -**prised′, -pris′ing** [< OFr. pp. of *sorprendre* < *sur-* (see SUR-[1]) + *prendre* < L. *prehendere*, to take] 1. to come upon suddenly or unexpectedly; take unawares 2. to attack or capture without warning 3. *a*) to cause to feel astonishment by being unexpected *b*) to present (someone) unexpectedly with a gift, etc. 4. *a*) to cause by some unexpected action to do or say something unintended: often with *into* *b*) to bring out (something) by such means —*n.* 1. [Rare] a surprising 2. an unexpected seizure or attack 3. a being surprised; astonishment 4. something that surprises because unexpected, unusual, etc. —**take by surprise** 1. to come upon suddenly or without warning 2. to amaze; astound —**sur·pris′ed·ly** *adv.* —**sur·pris′er** *n.*

surprise package 1. a package or parcel containing something unexpected, usually something pleasant 2. any unexpected surprise

sur·pris·ing (-iŋ) *adj.* causing surprise; amazing —**sur·pris′-ing·ly** *adv.*

sur·re·al·ism (sə rē′ə liz′m) *n.* [< Fr.: see SUR-[1] & REALISM] a modern movement in art and literature, in which an attempt is made to portray the workings of the subconscious mind, as by arranging material in unexpected, fantastic ways —**sur·re′al, sur·re′al·is′tic** *adj.* —**sur·re′al·ist** *adj., n.* —**sur·re′al·is′ti·cal·ly** *adv.*

sur·ren·der (sə ren′dər) *vt.* [< MFr. < *sur-* (see SUR-[1]) + *rendre*, to RENDER] 1. to give up possession of or power over; yield to another on compulsion 2. to give up or abandon [to *surrender* all hope] 3. to yield or resign (oneself) to an emotion, influence, etc. —*vi.* 1. to give oneself up, esp. as a prisoner; yield 2. to give in (*to*) [to *surrender* to a whim] —*n.* the act of surrendering —**surrender to one's bail** to appear in court in order to discharge one's bail —**sur·ren′der·er** *n.*

sur·rep·ti·tious (sur′əp tish′əs) *adj.* [< L. < pp. of *surripere* < *sub-*, under + *rapere*, to seize] 1. done, got, made, etc. in a secret, stealthy way; clandestine 2. acting in a secret, stealthy way —**sur′rep·ti′tious·ly** *adv.*

sur·rey (sur′ē) *n., pl.* -**reys** [< *Surrey*, county of S England, where it was originally made] [U.S.] a light pleasure carriage having four wheels, two seats, and usually a flat top

sur·ro·gate (sur′ə gāt; *for n. also* -git) *n.* [< L. pp. of *surrogare* < *sub-*, in place of + *rogare*, to elect] 1. a deputy or substitute for another person 2. a clergyman acting as a deputy of a bishop in granting special licences for marriages —*vt.* -**gat′ed, -gat′ing** to put in another's place as a substitute or deputy

sur·round (sə round') *vt.* [< OFr. < LL. < L. *super*, over + *undare*, to rise < *unda*, a wave] 1. to encircle on all or nearly all sides; enclose; encompass 2. to cut off (a military unit, etc.) from communication or retreat by encircling —*n.* something that surrounds

sur·round·ing (-roun'diŋ) *n.* that which surrounds; esp., [*pl.*] the things, conditions, influences, etc. that surround a given place or person; environment —*adj.* that surrounds

sur·tax (sur'taks; *for v. also* sur'taks') *n.* an extra tax on something already taxed, esp., a graduated tax on the amount by which an income exceeds a given figure —*vt.* to levy a surtax on

sur·tout (sər tōō', -tōōt') *n.* [Fr. < *sur*, over + *tout*, all] formerly, a man's long, closefitting overcoat

sur·veil·lance (sər vā'ləns, -vāl'yəns) *n.* [Fr. < *sur-* (see SUR-¹) + *veiller*, to watch < L. *vigilare*, to watch] 1. watch kept over a person, esp. a suspect 2. supervision —**sur·veil'lant** *n.*

sur·vey (sər vā'; *also, & for n. usually,* sur'vā) *vt.* [< Anglo-Fr. < OFr. < *sur-* (see SUR-¹) + *veoir* < L. *videre*, to see] 1. to examine, inspect, or consider carefully 2. to look at or consider, esp. in a comprehensive way 3. to determine the location, form, or boundaries of (a tract of land) by measuring lines and angles with a chain, transit, etc. —*vi.* to survey land —*n., pl.* **-veys** 1. a detailed study made by gathering and analysing information 2. a comprehensive study or examination [a *survey* of Italian art] 3. *a)* the process of surveying a tract of land *b)* a plan or written description of the area surveyed

sur·vey·ing (sər vā'iŋ) *n.* 1. the act of one who surveys 2. the science or profession of surveying land

sur·vey·or (-ər) *n.* a person who surveys, esp. one whose work is surveying land

surveyor's measure a system of measurement used in surveying, based on the chain (**surveyor's chain**) as a unit: see CHAIN (*n.* 3)

sur·viv·al (sər vī'v'l) *n.* 1. the act, state, or fact of surviving 2. someone or something that survives, esp. an ancient belief, custom, usage, etc.

survival of the fittest *popular term for* NATURAL SELECTION

sur·vive (sər vīv') *vt.* **-vived', -viv'ing** [< OFr. < L. < *super-*, above + *vivere*, to live] 1. to live or exist longer than; outlive 2. to continue to live after or in spite of [to survive a wreck] —*vi.* to continue living or existing —**sur·viv'a·bil'i·ty** *n.* —**sur·viv'a·ble** *adj.* —**sur·vi'vor** *n.*

sus (sus) *n.* [SUS(PICION), SUS(PECT)] [Colloq.] suspicion —*vt.* [Colloq.] to suspect —**sus out** [Colloq.] to puzzle out; to work out

sus·cep·ti·bil·i·ty (sə sep'tə bil'ə tē) *n., pl.* **-ties** 1. a being susceptible 2. [*pl.*] sensitive feelings 3. a susceptible temperament

sus·cep·ti·ble (sə sep'tə b'l) *adj.* [< ML. < L. pp. of *suscipere*, to receive < *sus-* (see SUB-), under + *capere*, to take] easily affected emotionally; having sensitive feelings —**susceptible of** admitting; allowing [testimony *susceptible* of error] —**susceptible to** easily influenced by or affected with [*susceptible to* disease] —**sus·cep'ti·ble·ness** *n.* —**sus·cep'ti·bly** *adv.*

sus·lik (sus'lik) *n.* [Russ.] a small, thickset rodent of the Balkans and E Europe

sus·pect (sə spekt'; *for adj. usually, & for n. always,* sus'-pekt) *vt.* [< L. pp. of *suspicere* < *sus-* (see SUB-), under + *spicere*, to look] 1. to believe to be guilty of something specified, on little or no evidence 2. to believe to be bad, wrong, harmful, etc.; distrust 3. to think it likely; surmise; suppose —*vi.* to be suspicious —*adj.* viewed with suspicion; suspected —*n.* a person who is suspected, esp. one suspected of a crime, etc.

sus·pend (sə spend') *vt.* [< OFr. < L. < *sus-* (see SUB-), under + *pendere*, to hang] 1. to remove (someone) from a position, office, club membership, etc., usually for a specified time, as a punishment 2. to cause to become inoperative for a time 3. to defer or hold back (judgment, a sentence, etc.) 4. to hang by a support from above 5. to hold (dust in the air, etc.) in suspension 6. to keep in suspense, wonder, etc. —*vi.* 1. to stop temporarily 2. to fail to pay debts or obligations 3. to be suspended; hang —**sus·pend'i·ble** *adj.*

suspended animation a temporary cessation of the vital functions resembling death

suspended sentence a prison sentence that is only served if the guilty party does not behave

suspender belt a wide belt, usually of elastic fibre, with suspenders hanging from it, worn by women

sus·pend·ers (sə spen'dərz) *n.pl.* 1. garters for holding up stockings 2. [U.S.] braces

sus·pense (sə spens') *n.* [< MFr. < ML. < L. pp. of *suspendere*, to SUSPEND] 1. the state of being undecided 2. a state of usually anxious uncertainty, as in awaiting a decision 3. the growing excitement felt as a story, play, etc. builds to a climax

sus·pen·sion (sə spen'shən) *n.* 1. a suspending or being suspended; specif., *a)* a temporary removal from a position,

privilege, etc. *b)* a temporary stoppage of payment, etc. *c)* a temporary cancelling, as of rules *d)* a deferring of action on a sentence *e)* a holding back of a judgment, etc. 2. a supporting device upon or from which something is suspended 3. the system of springs, etc. supporting a vehicle upon its undercarriage 4. *Chem. a)* the condition of a substance whose particles are dispersed through a fluid but not dissolved in it *b)* a substance in this condition *c)* a mixture of tiny, solid particles that are suspended in a liquid and settle out on standing 5. *Music a)* the continuing of one or more tones of one chord into a following chord while the others are changed, creating a temporary dissonance *b)* the tone(s) so continued

suspension bridge a bridge suspended from cables anchored at either end and supported by towers at intervals

sus·pen·sive (-siv) *adj.* 1. that suspends, defers, or temporarily stops something 2. tending to suspend judgment; undecided 3. of, characterized by, expressing, or in suspense —**sus·pen'sive·ly** *adv.*

sus·pen·so·ry (-sə rē) *adj.* 1. suspending, supporting, etc. [a *suspensory* muscle] 2. suspending or delaying, esp. so as to leave something undecided —*n., pl.* **-ries** a suspensory muscle, bandage, etc.: also **sus·pen'sor**

sus·pi·cion (sə spish'ən) *n.* [< OFr. < LL. < L. < *suspicere*, to SUSPECT] 1. a suspecting or being suspected 2. the feeling or state of mind of a person who suspects 3. a very small amount or degree; trace —**above suspicion** not to be suspected; honourable —**on suspicion** on the basis of suspicion —**under suspicion** suspected

sus·pi·cious (-əs) *adj.* 1. arousing or likely to arouse suspicion 2. showing suspicion 3. *a)* feeling suspicion *b)* tending habitually to suspect evil, etc. —**sus·pi'cious·ly** *adv.* —**sus·pi'cious·ness** *n.*

sus·tain (sə stān') *vt.* [< OFr. < L. *sustinere* < *sus-* (see SUB-), under + *tenere*, to hold] 1. to keep in existence; maintain or prolong [to *sustain* a mood] 2. to provide for the support of; specif., to provide nourishment for 3. to support; carry the weight of 4. to strengthen the spirits, courage, etc. of; comfort 5. to endure; withstand 6. to undergo; suffer (an injury, loss, etc.) 7. to uphold the validity of [to *sustain* a verdict] 8. to confirm; corroborate —**sus·tain'a·ble** *adj.* —**sus·tain'er** *n.* —**sus·tain'ment** *n.*

sus·te·nance (sus'ti nəns) *n.* 1. a sustaining or being sustained 2. means of livelihood; maintenance; support 3. that which sustains life; nourishment; food

su·sur·rate (sōō sur'āt, syōō-) *vi.* **-rat'ed, -rat'ing** [L. *susurratus*, pp. of *susurrare*, to whisper] to whisper; murmur; rustle —**su·sur·ra·tion** (sōō'sə rā'shən) *n.*

sut·ler (sut'lər) *n.* [< ModDu. < *soetelen*, to do dirty work] formerly, a person following an army to sell food, drink, esp. alcohol, etc. to its soldiers

su·tra (sōō'trə) *n.* [Sans. *sutra*, a thread] 1. *Brahmanism a)* a precept or maxim *b)* a collection of these 2. *Buddhism* a scriptural narrative; esp. a sermon of the Buddha

sut·tee (su tē', sut'ē) *n.* [< Hindi < Sans. *satī*, virtuous wife] 1. a Hindu widow who threw herself alive, and was cremated, on her husband's funeral pyre 2. the former custom of such self-cremation: also **sut·tee'ism**

su·ture (sōō'chər) *n.* [< L. < pp. of *suere*, to sew] 1. *a)* the act of joining together by or as by sewing *b)* the line along which such a joining is made 2. *Anat.* the line of junction of two bones, esp. of the skull 3. *Surgery a)* the stitching together of the two edges of a wound or incision *b)* the gut, thread, wire, etc. used in such stitching *c)* any of the stitches so made —*vt.* **-tured, -tur·ing** to join together as with sutures —**su'tur·al** *adj.*

su·ze·rain (sōō'zə rān') *n.* [Fr. < *sus*, above < L. *sursum*, upwards + ending of Fr. *souverain*, SOVEREIGN] 1. a feudal lord 2. a state in its relation to another state over which it has political control —**su'ze·rain·ty** *n., pl.* **-ties**

s.v. [L. *sub verbo*] under the word (specified)

svelte (svelt) *adj.* [Fr. < It., ult. < L. *evellere*, to pluck out] 1. slender and graceful 2. suave, polished, etc.

SW, S.W., s.w. 1. southwest 2. southwestern

Sw. 1. Sweden 2. Swedish

swab (swob) *n.* [contr. < *swabber* < ModDu. *zwabber* < *zwabben*, to do dirty work] 1. a mop for cleaning decks, floors, etc. 2. *a)* a small piece of cotton, sponge, etc. used to apply medicine to, or clean discharged matter from, the throat, mouth, etc. *b)* matter collected in this way 3. a brush for cleaning the barrel of a gun 4. [Slang] a clumsy, loutish person —*vt.* **swabbed, swab'bing** to clean, medicate, etc. with a swab —**swab'ber** *n.*

swad·dle (swod''l) *vt.* **-dled, -dling** [OE. *swethel*] 1. to wrap (a newborn baby) in long, narrow bands of cloth (**swaddling clothes** or **bands**), as in former times 2. to bind in or as in bandages; swathe —*n.* [U.S.] a cloth or bandage used for swaddling

swag (swag) *vi.* **swagged, swag'ging** [< or akin to Norw. *svagga*, to sway] 1. to sway or lurch 2. to sink down; sag —*vt.* 1. to decorate with swags 2. to hang in a swag 3. [Aust. Colloq.] to carry a bundle of personal possessions —*n.* 1. a swaying or lurching 2. a curtain, garland, chain, etc. hanging decoratively in a loop or curve **3.** [Slang] *a*) loot; plunder *b*) goods; valuables; money **4.** [Aust. Colloq.] a bundle containing one's personal belongings

swage (swāj) *n.* [OFr. *souage*] **1.** a tool for bending or shaping metal **2.** a die or stamp for shaping metal by hammering —*vt.* **swaged, swag′ing** to shape, etc. with a swage

swag·ger (swag′ər) *vi.* [prob. < Norw. dial. *svagra*, freq. of *svagga*, to sway] **1.** to walk with a bold, arrogant stride; strut **2.** to boast, brag, or show off in a loud, superior manner —*n.* swaggering walk, manner, or behaviour —*adj.* stylish, esp. in an elegant way —**swag′ger·er** *n.* —**swag′ger·ing·ly** *adv.*

swagger stick a short stick or cane as carried by some army officers, etc.: also **swagger cane**

swag·man (-mən) *n., pl.* **-men** [Aust. Colloq.] a vagrant worker, carrying his possessions on his back: also **swag′-ger** *n.*

Swa·hi·li (swä hē′lē) *n.* **1.** *pl.* **-lis, -li** any of a Bantu people of Zanzibar and the nearby mainland **2.** their Bantu language, widely used as a lingua franca in E and C Africa

swain (swān) *n.* [< ON. *sveinn*, boy] [Poet. or Archaic] **1.** a country youth **2.** a young rustic lover or gallant **3.** a lover —**swain′ish** *adj.* —**swain′ish·ness** *n.*

swal·low[1] (swol′ō) *n.* [OE. *swealwe*] **1.** any of various small, swift-flying birds with long, pointed wings and a forked tail, known for their regular migrations **2.** any of certain swifts resembling swallows —**swal′low·like′** *adj.*

swal·low[2] (swol′ō) *vt.* [OE. *swelgan*] **1.** to pass (food, etc.) from the mouth through the oesophagus into the stomach **2.** to take in; absorb; engulf (often with *up*) **3.** to take back (words said); retract **4.** to put up with; tolerate [to *swallow* insults] **5.** to refrain from expressing; suppress [to *swallow* one's pride] **6.** to utter (words) indistinctly **7.** [Colloq.] to accept as true without question —*vi.* to move the muscles of the throat as in swallowing, esp. when emotionally upset —*n.* **1.** the act of swallowing **2.** the amount swallowed at one time **3.** the throat or gullet —**swal′low·er** *n.*

SWALLOW
(to 19 cm long)

swallow dive a forward dive in which the legs are held straight and together, the back is arched, and the arms are stretched out to the sides

swal·low·tail (-tāl′) *n.* **1.** something having a forked shape like that of a swallow's tail **2.** a butterfly having taillike points on the hind wings

swal·low-tailed coat (-tāld′) a man's full-dress coat, with long, tapering tails at the back

swam (swam) *pt.* of SWIM[1] & SWIM[2]

swa·mi (swä′mē) *n., pl.* **-mis** [< Hindi < Sans. *svāmin*, a lord] **1.** master: a title of respect for a Hindu religious teacher **2.** a learned man

swamp (swomp) *n.* [< dial. var. of ME. *sompe*, SUMP] a piece of wet, spongy land; marsh; bog: also **swamp′-land**—*adj.* of or native to a swamp —*vt.* **1.** to plunge in a swamp, deep water, etc. **2.** to flood with or as with water **3.** to overwhelm; ruin [*swamped* by debts] **4.** to sink (a boat) by filling with water —*vi.* to sink as in a swamp —**swamp′i·ness** *n.* —**swamp′ish** *adj.* —**swamp′y** *adj.* **swamp′i·er, swamp′i·est**

swamp fever same as MALARIA

swan (swon) *n.* [OE.] *pl.* **swans, swan:** see PLURAL, II, D, 1 **1.** a large-bodied water bird with webbed feet, long, graceful neck, and, usually, pure white feathers **2.** a poet or singer of great ability: cf. SWAN SONG —**swan′like′** *adj.*

swan dive [U.S.] a swallow dive

swank (swaŋk) *n.* [akin to OE. *swancor*, pliant, supple] [Colloq.] **1.** stylish display or showiness in dress, etc. **2.** swaggering, showy behaviour, speech, etc. —*adj.* [Chiefly U.S. Colloq.] stylish in a showy way —*vi.* [Slang] to show off; boast

swank·pot (-pot′) *n.* [Colloq.] a person conducting himself with swank

swank·y (swaŋ′kē) *adj.* **swank′i·er, swank′i·est** [Colloq.] stylish or expensive in a showy way —**swank′i·ly** *adv.* —**swank′i·ness** *n.*

Swan River daisy a native, annual plant of Western Australia

swan's-down (swonz′doun′) *n.* **1.** the soft, fine underfeathers, or down, of a swan, used for trimming clothes, etc. **2.** a soft, thick fabric of wool and silk, rayon, or cotton, used for making baby clothes, etc. **3.** a soft cotton flannel Also **swans′down′**

swan song 1. the sweet song supposed in ancient legend to be sung by a dying swan **2.** the last act, final creative work, etc. of a person

swan-up·ping (swon′up′iŋ) *n.* [< SWAN + UP[1], *v.*] the practice of marking young swans with a notch in the upper beak as a sign of ownership

swap (swop) *vt., vi.* **swapped, swap′ping** [ME. *swappen*, to strike: hands were struck to conclude a bargain] [Colloq.] to exchange, trade, or barter —*n.* [Colloq.] *a*) an exchange, trade, or barter *b*) the thing exchanged or bartered —**swap′per** *n.*

swa·raj (swə räj′) *n.* [Hindi < Sans. *svarāj*, self-ruling] in India, home rule: during the period of British rule, [S-] the name of the political party seeking Indian independence —**swa·raj′ism** *n.*

sward (swôrd) *n.* [OE. *sweard*, skin] grass-covered soil; turf —*vt.* to cover with sward

sware (swer) *archaic pt.* of SWEAR

swarm[1] (swôrm) *n.* [OE. *swearm*] **1.** a large number of bees, led by a queen, leaving a hive to start a new colony **2.** a colony of bees in a hive **3.** a moving mass or crowd —*vi.* **1.** to fly off in a swarm: said of bees **2.** to move, collect, etc. in large numbers; throng **3.** to be filled or crowded; teem —*vt.* to crowd; throng —**swarm′er** *n.*

swarm[2] (swôrm) *vi., vt.* [orig. nautical word < ?] to climb (a tree, mast, etc.); shin (*up*)

swart (swôrt) *adj.* [OE. *sweart*] *var. of* SWARTHY

swarth (swôrth) *n.* dial. var. of SWARD —*adj.* same as SWARTHY

swarth·y (swôr′*th*ē, -thē) *adj.* **swarth′i·er, swarth′i·est** [< dial. *swarth*, var. of SWART + -Y[2]] having a dark complexion; dusky —**swarth′i·ly** *adv.* —**swarth′i·ness** *n.*

swash (swosh) *vi.* [echoic] **1.** to dash, strike, wash, etc. with a splashing sound; splash **2.** to swagger —*vt.* to splash (a liquid), as in a container —*n.* **1.** a channel of water cutting through or behind a sandbank **2.** the splashing of water **3.** a swaggering action

swash·buck·ler (-buk′lər) *n.* [prec. + BUCKLER] a blustering, swaggering fighting man —**swash′buck′ling** *n., adj.*

swas·ti·ka (swos′ti kə) *n.* [< Sans. < *svasti*, well-being] **1.** a design or ornament of ancient origin in the form of a cross with four equal arms, each bent in a right-angle extension **2.** this design with the extensions bent clockwise: used as the Nazi emblem

swat (swot) *vt.* **swat′ted, swat′ting** [*var. of* SQUAT] [Colloq.] to hit with a quick, sharp blow —*n.* [Colloq.] a quick, sharp blow —**swat′ter** *n.*

swatch (swoch) *n.* [orig., a cloth tally < ?] **1.** a sample piece of cloth or other material **2.** a small amount or number in a cluster, bunch, or patch

swath (swôth) *n.* [OE. *swathu*, a track] **1.** the space covered with one cut of a scythe, etc. **2.** the strip or band of grass, wheat, etc. cut in a single trip across a lawn or field by a mower, etc. **3.** any long strip —**cut a wide swath** to make a big or showy impression

swathe[1] (swā*th*) *vt.* **swathed, swath′ing** [OE. *swathian*] **1.** to wrap or bind up in a bandage **2.** to wrap (a bandage, etc.) around something **3.** to surround or envelop —*n.* a bandage or wrapping —**swath′er** *n.*

swathe[2] (swā*th*) *n.* same as SWATH

sway (swā) *vi.* [ON. *sveigja*, to bend] **1.** *a*) to swing or move from side to side or to and fro *b*) to vacillate between one opinion, etc. and another **2.** *a*) to lean or incline to one side; veer *b*) to incline in judgment or opinion —*vt.* **1.** to cause to sway, or swing to and fro, vacillate, incline to one side, etc. **2.** to change the thinking or actions of; influence in a certain direction [*swayed* by promises] **3.** [Archaic] to rule over; control —*n.* **1.** a swaying or being swayed; a swinging, leaning, etc. **2.** influence or control **3.** rule; dominion —**hold sway** to reign or prevail —**sway′er** *n.* —**sway′ing·ly** *adv.*

sway·backed (-bakt′) *adj.* having an abnormal sagging of the spine, usually as a result of strain or overwork, as some horses, etc. —**sway′back′** *n.*

swear (swer) *vi.* **swore, sworn, swear′ing** [OE. *swerian*] **1.** to make a solemn declaration, supporting it with an appeal to God or to something held sacred [to *swear* on one's honour] **2.** to make a solemn promise; vow **3.** to use profane or vulgar, offensive language; curse **4.** *Law* to give evidence under oath —*vt.* **1.** to declare solemnly in the name of God or of something held sacred **2.** to pledge or vow on oath **3.** to assert with great emphasis **4.** to take (an oath) by swearing **5.** to administer a legal oath to —**swear by 1.** to name (something held sacred) in taking an oath **2.** to have great faith in —**swear for** to give assurance for; guarantee —**swear in** to administer an oath to (a person taking office, a witness, etc.) —**swear off** to promise to give up [to *swear off* smoking] —**swear to** to be certain of [I couldn't *swear* to his presence] —**swear′er** *n.*

swear·word (-wurd′) *n.* a word or phrase used in swearing or cursing; profane or vulgar, offensive word

sweat (swet) *vi.* **sweat′ed, sweat′ing** [OE. *swætan* < *swat*, sweat] **1.** to give out a salty moisture through the pores of the skin; perspire **2.** *a*) to give out moisture in droplets on its surface, as a ripening cheese *b*) to condense water in droplets on its surface [a glass of iced water *sweats*] **3.** to ferment: said of tobacco leaves, etc. **4.** to come out in drops through pores; ooze **5.** to work hard enough to cause sweating **6.** [Colloq.] to suffer distress, anxiety, etc. —*vt.* **1.** *a)* to give out (moisture) through a porous surface *b)* to condense (moisture) on the surface **2.** to cause to perspire, as by drugs, exercise, etc. **3.** to cause to give out moisture; esp., to ferment **4.** to make wet with perspiration **5.** to heat (an alloy) so as to extract an easily fusible constituent **6.** to unite (metal parts) by heating the solder applied to the ends until it melts **7.** *a)* to cause to work so hard as to sweat *b)* to cause (employees) to work long hours at low wages under poor working conditions **8.** [Colloq.] to get information from by torture or gruelling questioning **9.** [Slang] to try hard or too hard to get or achieve —*n.* **1.** the clear, salty liquid given out through the pores in the skin **2.** moisture given out or collected in droplets on a surface **3.** a sweating or being sweated **4.** a condition of eagerness, anxiety, impatience, etc. **5.** hard work; drudgery —**sweat blood** [Slang] **1.** to work very hard; overwork **2.** to be impatient, anxious, etc. —**sweat off** to get rid of (weight) by sweating —**sweat out** [Slang] **1.** to suffer through (something) **2.** to wait anxiously or impatiently for

sweat·band (-band′) *n.* a band of leather, etc. inside a hat to protect it against sweat from the brow

sweat·er (swet′ər) *n.* **1.** a person or thing that sweats **2.** a knitted outer garment for the upper part of the body **3.** an employer of underpaid, overworked employees

sweat gland any of the many, tiny tubular glands just beneath the skin that secrete sweat

sweating sickness an infectious, fatal disease, epidemic in Europe in the 15th and 16th cent., characterized by fever and sweating

sweat shirt [Chiefly U.S.] a heavy, long-sleeved cotton jersey, worn to absorb sweat during or after exercise, sometimes with loose trousers (**sweat pants**) of the same material

sweat·shop (-shop′) *n.* a shop where employees work long hours at low wages under poor working conditions

sweat·y (-ē) *adj.* **sweat′i·er, sweat′i·est** **1.** wet with sweat; sweating **2.** of sweat [a *sweaty* odour] **3.** causing sweat [*sweaty* work] —**sweat′i·ly** *adv.* —**sweat′i·ness** *n.*

Swed. **1.** Sweden **2.** Swedish

Swede (swēd) *n.* a native or inhabitant of Sweden

swede (swēd) *n.* a turnip with a large, yellow root

Swed·ish (swē′dish) *adj.* of Sweden, its people, their language, etc. —*n.* the North Germanic language of the Swedes —**the Swedish** the people of Sweden

Swedish turnip *same as* SWEDE

sweep (swēp) *vt.* **swept, sweep′ing** [akin to (or ? altered <) OE. *swapan*: see SWOOP] **1.** to clear or clean as by brushing with a broom [to *sweep* a floor] **2.** to remove or clear away (dirt, debris, etc.) as with a broom or brushing movement **3.** to strip, carry away, or destroy with forceful movement **4.** to carry along with a sweeping movement **5.** to touch or brush in moving across **6.** to pass swiftly over or across **7.** *a)* to drag (a river, pond, etc.) with a net, grapple, etc. *b)* to clear (waters) with a mine sweeper **8.** to rake with gunfire **9.** to win overwhelmingly [to *sweep* a constituency] —*vi.* **1.** to clean a surface, room, etc. as with a broom **2.** to move or progress steadily with speed, force, or gracefulness [birds *swept* across the sky] **3.** to trail, as skirts or the train of a gown **4.** to extend in a long curve or line [a road *sweeping* up the hill] —*n.* **1.** the act of sweeping, as with a broom **2.** a steady sweeping movement or stroke [the *sweep* of a scythe] **3.** a trailing, as of skirts **4.** range or scope **5.** extent or stretch [a *sweep* of meadow] **6.** a line, contour, curve, etc. that gives an impression of flow or movement **7.** a person whose work is sweeping; specif., *short for* CHIMNEY SWEEP **8.** [usually pl.] sweepings **9.** complete victory or success, as in a series of contests **10.** a long oar **11.** a long pole mounted on a pivot, with a bucket at one end, used for raising water **12.** *Electronics* a crossing by an electron beam of the screen of a cathode-ray tube —**sweep the board** to win all the possible prizes, etc. —**sweep′er** *n.*

sweep·ing (-iŋ) *adj.* **1.** that sweeps **2.** extending over a wide range **3.** *a)* extensive; comprehensive *b)* complete *c)* indiscriminate —*n.* **1.** [pl.] things swept up, as dirt from a floor **2.** the act, work, etc. of one that sweeps —**sweep′-ing·ly** *adv.*

sweep-net (swēp′net′) *n.* a large fishing net usually used from the shore

sweep·stakes (-stāks′) *n., pl.* **-stakes′** **1.** a lottery in which each participant puts up money in a common fund from which the money for the winners comes **2.** *a)* a contest, esp. a horse race, which determines the winners of such a lottery *b)* the prize or prizes won **3.** any of various other lotteries Also **sweep′stake′, sweeps**

sweet (swēt) *adj.* [OE. *swete*] **1.** *a)* having a taste of, or like that of, sugar *b)* containing sugar in some form [*sweet* wines] **2.** *a)* pleasant in taste, smell, sound, looks, etc. *b)* gratifying [*sweet* praise] *c)* having a friendly, pleasing

disposition *d)* sentimental *e)* [Colloq.] good, delightful, nice, etc. **3.** *a)* not rancid, spoiled, or sour [*sweet* milk] *b)* not salty or salted: said of water or butter *c)* free from sourness or acidity: said of soil **4.** *Jazz* characterized by rather strict adherence to melody, blandness, moderate tempo, etc. —*n.* **1.** a being sweet; sweetness **2.** something sweet; specif., *a)* a sweet food, or small piece of sweet food, usually made from sugar or syrup, with flavouring, fruit, chocolate, nuts, etc. added *b)* a sweet dessert *c)* [usually pl.] pleasure or a pleasurable experience **3.** a sweetheart; darling —**be sweet on** [Colloq.] to be in love with —**sweet′ish** *adj.* —**sweet′ly** *adv.*

sweet alyssum a short garden plant with small spikes of tiny flowers

sweet·bread (swēt′bred′) *n.* the thymus (**heart,** or **throat, sweetbread**) or the pancreas (**stomach sweetbread**) of a calf, lamb, etc., when used as food

sweet·bri·er, sweet·bri·ar (-brī′ər) *n.* *same as* EGLANTINE

sweet cherry *1.* a cherry tree, widely grown in Europe & Asia for its sweet fruit **2.** its fruit

sweet clover any of various plants of the legume family, with small white or yellow flowers, and leaflets in groups of three: grown for hay, forage, etc.

sweet corn any of various strains of maize with kernels rich in sugar, eaten as a cooked vegetable

sweet·en (swēt′'n) *vt.* **1.** to make sweet with or as with sugar **2.** to make pleasant or agreeable **3.** to make less harsh, less acidic, etc. —*vi.* to become sweet

sweet·en·er (-ər) *n.* a sweetening agent, esp. a synthetic substance, such as saccharin

sweet·en·ing (-iŋ) *n.* **1.** the process of making sweet **2.** something that sweetens

sweet flag a perennial marsh plant with sword-shaped leaves, small, green flowers, and a sweet-scented rhizome

sweet·heart (swēt′härt′) *n.* **1.** a lover **2.** darling: a term of endearment —*vt., vi.* to court; to be engaged in lovemaking

sweet·ing (-iŋ) *n.* **1.** a variety of sweet apple **2.** *archaic var. of* SWEETHEART

sweet marjoram *see* MARJORAM

sweet·meat (-mēt′) *n.* a bit of sweet food, esp. a sweet, candied fruit, or other sweetened delicacy

sweet·ness (-nis) *n.* the quality of being sweet, kind, reasonable, etc. esp. in the phrase **sweetness and light**

sweet pea a climbing annual plant of the legume family, with butterfly-shaped flowers

sweet pepper *1.* a variety of the red pepper producing a large, mild fruit **2.** the fruit

sweet potato *1.* a tropical, trailing plant with purplish flowers and a fleshy, orange or yellow, tuberlike root used as a vegetable **2.** its root

sweet·shop (-shop′) *n.* a shop whose main business is selling confectionery

sweet-talk (-tôk′) *vt., vi.* [U.S. Colloq.] to talk in a flattering or blandishing way (to)

sweet tooth [Colloq.] a fondness or craving for sweets

sweet wil·liam, sweet William (wil′yəm) a perennial pink with dense, flat clusters of small flowers

swell (swel) *vi.* **swelled, swelled** or **swol′len, swell′ing** [OE. *swellan*] **1.** to become larger as a result of pressure from within; expand **2.** to curve out; bulge; protrude **3.** to extend above the normal level **4.** to form swells, or large waves: said of the sea **5.** to be filled (*with* pride, etc.) **6.** to increase within one [his anger *swelled*] **7.** to increase in size, force, intensity, etc. **8.** to increase in loudness —*vt.* to cause to swell; specif., *a)* to cause to increase in size, volume, etc. *b)* to cause to bulge *c)* to fill with pride, etc. *d)* to cause to increase in loudness —*n.* **1.** a part that swells; bulge; specif., *a)* a large wave that moves steadily without breaking *b)* a piece of rising ground **2.** a swelling or being swollen **3.** an increase in size, amount, degree, etc. **4.** [Colloq.] a person, esp. a man, of wealth and fashion: old-fashioned term **5.** *Music* *a)* a crescendo usually followed by a decrescendo *b)* a sign (< >) indicating this *c)* a device for controlling the loudness of tones, as in an organ —*adj.* [Chiefly U.S. Slang] first-rate; excellent: used in a general way to show approval

swell box a chamber enclosing one or more sets of organ pipes and fitted with movable shutters that regulate the loudness of tone

swelled head [Colloq.] great self-conceit

swell·ing (-iŋ) *n.* **1.** an increasing or being increased in size, volume, etc. **2.** a swollen part, as on the body

swel·ter (swel′tər) *vi.* [OE. *sweltan,* to die] to be or feel oppressively hot; sweat and wilt from great heat —*vt.* to cause to swelter —*n.* **1.** a sweltering **2.** oppressive heat

swel·ter·ing (-iŋ) *adj.* very hot, sweaty, sticky, etc.: also **swel′try** (-trē), **-tri·er, -tri·est** —**swel′ter·ing·ly** *adv.*

swept (swept) *pt. & pp. of* SWEEP

swept·back (swept′bak′) *adj.* having a backward slant, as the wings of an aircraft

swept·wing (-wiŋ′) *adj.* *Aeron.* having sweptback wings

swerve (swurv) *vi., vt.* **swerved, swerv′ing** [OE. *sweorfan,* to scour] to turn aside suddenly from a straight line, course, etc. —*n.* the act or degree of swerving —**swerv'er** *n.*

S.W.G. standard wire gauge

swift (swift) *adj.* [OE.] 1. moving or capable of moving with great speed; fast 2. coming, happening, or done quickly 3. acting or responding quickly; prompt [swift to help] —*adv.* in a swift manner —*n.* an insect-eating, swift-flying bird resembling the swallow —**swift'ly** *adv.* —**swift'ness** *n.*

swig (swig) *vt., vi.* **swigged, swig'ging** [< ?] [Colloq.] to drink in big gulps or amounts —*n.* [Colloq.] a big gulp, esp. of alcoholic liquor —**swig'ger** *n.*

swill (swil) *vt.* [OE. *swilian*] 1. to flood with water so as to wash 2. to drink greedily 3. to feed swill to (pigs, etc.) —*vi.* to drink in large quantities —*n.* 1. garbage, etc. mixed with liquid and fed to pigs, etc. 2. garbage or slop 3. the act of swilling 4. a swig

swim[1] (swim) *vi.* **swam, swum, swim'ming** [OE. *swimman*] 1. to move through water by movements of the arms and legs, or of flippers, fins, etc. 2. to move along smoothly 3. to float on the surface of a liquid 4. to be immersed in a liquid 5. to overflow [eyes *swimming* with tears] —*vt.* 1. to move in or across (a body of water) by swimming 2. to cause to swim 3. to perform (a specified stroke) in swimming —*n.* an act, spell, or distance of swimming —**in the swim** conforming to the current fashions, or active in the main current of affairs —**swim with the tide** to side with the majority opinion —**swim'ma·ble** *adj.* —**swim'mer** *n.*

swim[2] (swim) *n.* [OE. *swima*] the condition of being dizzy —*vi.* **swam, swum, swim'ming** 1. to be dizzy 2. to have a hazy, reeling, or whirling appearance

swim bladder a gas-filled sac in the body cavity of most bony fishes, giving buoyancy to the body

swim·mer·et (swim'ə ret') *n.* any of the small abdominal appendages in certain crustaceans, used for swimming, etc.

swimming bath an indoor swimming pool

swim·ming·ly (swim'iŋ lē) *adv.* easily and with success

swimming pool a pool of water for swimming; esp., a tank specially built for the purpose

swim·suit (swim'sōōt') *n.* a garment worn for swimming: also **swimming costume**

swin·dle (swin'd'l) *vt.* **-dled, -dling** [< G. *schwindeln,* to cheat] 1. to get money or property from (another) under false pretenses; cheat; defraud 2. to get by fraud —*vi.* to engage in swindling others —*n.* an act of swindling —**swin'dler** *n.*

swindle sheet *slang term for* EXPENSE ACCOUNT

swine (swin) *n., pl.* **swine** [OE. *swin*] 1. a pig: usually used collectively 2. a vicious, contemptible, or disgusting person

swine fever an infectious disease of pigs, with high fever, refusal to eat, and weight loss

swine·herd (-hurd') *n.* one who tends swine

swing (swiŋ) *vi.* **swung, swing'ing** [OE. *swingan*] 1. to sway or move backwards and forwards, as a freely hanging object 2. to walk, trot, etc. with freely swaying movements 3. to strike (at) 4. to turn, as on a hinge or swivel 5. *a)* to hang; be suspended *b)* [Colloq.] to be hanged in execution 6. to move on a swing (n. 10) 7. to have an exciting rhythmic quality [music that really *swings*] 8. [Slang] to be very fashionable, active, etc., esp. in the pursuit of pleasure —*vt.* 1. *a)* to move (a weapon, bat, etc.) with a sweeping motion; flourish *b)* to lift with a sweeping motion 2. to cause (a freely hanging object) to move backwards and forwards 3. to cause to turn or pivot, as on a hinge 4. to cause to hang freely [to *swing* a scaffold from the roof] 5. to cause to move in a curve [to *swing* a car around a corner] 6. [Colloq.] to cause to come about successfully; manage with the desired results [to *swing* a vote] 7. to play (music) in the style of swing —*n.* 1. the act of swinging 2. the arc through which something swings 3. the manner of swinging, as with a golf club, cricket bat, etc. 4. freedom to do as one wishes 5. a relaxed motion, as in walking 6. a sweeping blow or stroke 7. the course or movement of some activity, etc. 8. the force behind something swung; impetus 9. rhythm, as of poetry or music 10. a seat hanging from ropes or chains, on which one can sit and swing 11. the amount that a thing swings [the *swing* to Labour in the election] 12. a style of jazz music of about 1935 to 1945, characterized by large bands, improvised counterpoint, etc. —*adj.* of, in, or playing swing (music) —**in full swing** 1. in complete and active operation 2. going on without restraint —**swing the lead** [Colloq.] to try and evade a job, duty, etc.

swing boat a boat-shaped gondola, suspended from a frame, used for swinging in at a fair

swinge (swinj) *vt.* **swinged, swing'ing** [ME. < OE. *swengan,* causative of *swingan,* to SWING] [Archaic] to punish with blows; beat; whip

swinge·ing (-iŋ) *adj.* [prp. of prec.] [Colloq.] huge; very large

swing·er (swiŋ'ər) *n.* 1. a person or thing that swings 2. [Slang] someone thought to be sophisticated, etc.

swin·gle (swiŋ'g'l) *vt.* **-gled, -gling** [< MDu. < *swinghel,* a swingle] to beat and clean (flax or hemp) with a swingle —*n.* a wooden, swordlike tool for beating and cleaning

swin·gle·tree (-trē') *n.* [< ME. *swingle,* a rod + *tre,* a tree] a pivoted crossbar at the front of a wagon, etc., to which the traces of a horse's harness are hooked

swing shift [U.S. Colloq.] the evening work shift in some factories, from midafternoon to about midnight

swin·ish (swin'ish) *adj.* of, like, or fit for swine; beastly, piggish, etc. —**swin'ish·ly** *adv.* —**swin'ish·ness** *n.*

swipe (swip) *n.* [prob. var. of SWEEP] [Colloq.] a hard, sweeping blow —*vt.* **swiped, swip'ing** 1. [Colloq.] to hit with a hard, sweeping blow 2. [Slang] to steal —*vi.* to make a sweeping blow or stroke

swirl (swurl) *vi.* [ME. *swyrl,* prob. < Norw. dial. *sverra,* to whirl] 1. to move with a whirling motion 2. to be dizzy —*vt.* to cause to swirl —*n.* 1. a whirl; eddy 2. a twist; curl; whirl —**swirl'ing·ly** *adv.* —**swirl'y** *adj.*

swish (swish) *vi.* [echoic] 1. to move with a sharp, hissing sound, as a cane swung through the air 2. to rustle, as skirts —*vt.* to cause to swish —*n.* 1. a hissing or rustling sound 2. a movement that makes this sound —*adj.* [Colloq.] fashionable; smart [a *swish* car] —**swish'y** *adj.* **swish'i·er, swish'i·est**

Swiss (swis) *adj.* of Switzerland, its people, or its culture —*n., pl.* **Swiss** a native or inhabitant of Switzerland —**the Swiss** the people of Switzerland

Swiss chard *same as* CHARD

Swiss (cheese) a pale-yellow, hard cheese with many large holes, originally made in Switzerland

swiss roll a flat sponge cake rolled up while hot with jam or cream inside

switch (swich) *n.* [prob. < MDu. or LowG.] 1. a thin, flexible twig, stick, etc. used for whipping 2. the bushy part of the tail of a cow, etc. 3. a tress of detached hair used by women as part of a coiffure 4. a sharp, lashing movement, as with a whip 5. a device used to open, close, or divert an electric circuit 6. a shift or transference, esp. if sudden —*vt.* 1. to whip as with a switch 2. to jerk or swing sharply [a cow *switches* its tail] 3. to shift; change; turn aside 4. *a)* to operate the switch of (an electric current) *b)* to turn (an electric light, etc.) *on* or *off* in this way 5. to transfer (a train, etc.) from one line to another by means of a switch 6. [Colloq.] to change or exchange [to *switch* places] —*vi.* 1. to move as from one line to another 2. to shift; transfer 3. to swing sharply; lash —**switch'er** *n.*

switch·back (-bak') *n.* 1. a steep mountain road or railway with hairpin bends 2. an amusement ride in which small, open cars move on tracks that dip and curve sharply

switch-blade knife (-blād') a large pocketknife that snaps open when a release button on the handle is pressed

switch·board (-bôrd') *n.* a panel equipped with apparatus for controlling the operation of a system of electric circuits, as in a telephone exchange

switch·man (-mən) *n., pl.* **-men** [U.S.] a pointsman

switch-over (-ō'vər) *n.* a changeover; exchange

swith·er (swith'ər) *vi.* [? < OE. *swithrian,* to dwindle, fall] to hesitate; to vacillate

Switz·er (swit'sər) *n.* 1. a Swiss 2. a Swiss mercenary soldier

swiv·el (swiv'l) *n.* [< base of OE. *swifan,* to revolve] a coupling device that allows free turning of the parts attached to it; specif., a chain link in two parts, one piece fitting like a collar below the bolt head of the other and turning freely about it —*vt.* **-elled, -el·ling** 1. to cause to turn as on a swivel 2. to fit or support with a swivel —*vi.* to turn as on a swivel

swivel chair a chair whose seat turns horizontally on a pivot in the base

swizz (swiz) *n.* [< ?] [Slang] a fraud; a great disappointment: also **swiz**

swiz·zle (swiz''l) *n.* [< ?] 1. an alcoholic drink containing rum or gin 2. [Slang] *same as* SWIZZ —*vt.* to drink excessively

swizzle stick (swiz''l) [< ?] a small rod for stirring mixed drinks

swob (swob) *n., vt.* **swobbed, swob'bing** *var. sp. of* SWAB

swol·len (swō'lən) *alt. pp. of* SWELL —*adj.* blown up; distended; bulging

swoon (swōōn) *vi.* [< OE. *geswogen,* unconscious] 1. to faint 2. to feel strong, esp. rapturous emotion —*n.* an act of swooning —**swoon'er** *n.* —**swoon'ing·ly** *adv.*

swoop (swōōp) *vt.* [OE. *swapan,* to sweep along] to snatch or seize suddenly: often with *up* —*vi.* to pounce or sweep (*down* or *upon*) —*n.* the act of swooping

swoosh (swōōsh) *vi., vt.* [echoic intens. of SWISH] to move, pour, etc. with a sharp, rustling or whistling sound —*n.* such a sound

swop (swop) *n., vt., vi.* **swopped, swop'ping** *var. sp. of* SWAP

sword (sôrd) *n.* [OE. *sweord*] 1. a hand weapon having a long, sharp, pointed blade, set in a hilt **2.** *a)* power; esp. military power *b)* war —**at swords' points** ready to quarrel or fight —**cross swords 1.** to fight **2.** to argue —**put to the sword 1.** to kill with a sword **2.** to slaughter, esp. in war —**sword'like'** *adj.*

sword·bear·er (-ber'ər) *n.* someone who carries a sword, esp. the person who carries the sword of state on ceremonial occasions

sword dance any dance, esp. by men, involving the use of swords, esp. one performed around bare swords laid on the ground —**sword dancer**

sword·fish (-fish') *n., pl.* **-fish', -fish'es:** see FISH a large marine food and game fish with the upper jawbone extending in a long, flat, swordlike projection

sword grass any of a number of sedges or grasses with toothed or sword-shaped leaves

sword guard that part of a sword hilt that protects the hand

sword knot a loop of leather, ribbon, etc. attached to a sword hilt as an ornament or, orig., as a wrist support

sword of Dam·o·cles (dam'ə-klēz') [after the courtier of ancient Syracuse who was seated at a feast under a sword hanging from a hair] any imminent danger

SWORDFISH
(to 4.6 m long)

sword of state the sword carried in front of the sovereign on state occasions

sword·play (-plā') *n.* the act or skill of using a sword in fencing or fighting

swords·man (sôrdz'mən) *n., pl.* **-men 1.** a person who uses a sword in fencing or fighting **2.** a person skilled in using a sword Also [Archaic] **sword·man** (sôrd'mən), *pl.* **-men** —**swords'man·ship'** *n.*

sword·stick (-stik') *n.* a walking stick that contains a slender sword

sword·swal·low·er (-swol'ō ər) *n.* someone who swallows, or appears to swallow, swords in a circus, etc.

swore (swôr) *pt. of* SWEAR

sworn (swôrn) *pp. of* SWEAR —*adj.* bound, pledged, promised, etc. by or as by an oath

swot[1] (swot) *n., vt.* **swot'ted, swot'ting** *var. sp. of* SWAT

swot[2] (swot) *vi., vt.* **swot'ted, swot'ting** [dial. var. of SWEAT] [Colloq.] to study hard —*n.* [Colloq.] **1.** a person who studies hard **2.** something demanding hard study

swum (swum) *pp. of* SWIM[1] & SWIM[2]

swung (swung) *pp. & pt. of* SWING

syb·a·rite (sib'ə rīt') *n.* [< Sybarite, a native of Sybaris, an ancient Greek city in S Italy, famed for its luxury] anyone very fond of luxury and self-indulgence —**syb'a·rit'ic** (-rit'-ik) *adj.* —**syb'a·rit'i·cal·ly** *adv.*

syc·a·more (sik'ə môr') *n.* [< OFr. < L. < Gr. *sykomoros*] **1.** a shade tree native to Egypt and Asia Minor, with edible, figlike fruit **2.** a maple shade tree found in Europe and Asia **3.** [U.S.] *same as* PLANE[1]

sy·co·ni·um (sī kō'nē əm) *n., pl.* **-ni·a** (-ə) [ModL. < Gr. *sykon*, a fig] *Bot.* a pear-shaped, fleshy, false fruit, as of the fig, containing many flowers

syc·o·phant (sik'ə fant) *n.* [< L. < Gr. *sykophantēs*, informer < *sykon*, a fig + *phainein*, to show] a person who seeks favour by flattering people of wealth or influence; toady —**syc'o·phan·cy** *n., pl.* **-cies** —**syc'o·phan'-tic** (-fan'tik) *adj.* —**syc'o·phant'ish** *adj.* —**syc'o·phan'ti·cal·ly, syc'o·phant'ish·ly** *adv.*

syl- *same as* SYN-: used before *l*

syl·la·bar·y (sil'ə bər ē) *n., pl.* **-bar·ies** [< ModL. < L. *syllaba*: see SYLLABLE] **1.** a table of syllables **2.** a set of the written characters of a language representing syllables

syl·lab·ic (si lab'ik) *adj.* **1.** of a syllable or syllables **2.** forming a syllable or the nucleus of a syllable; specif., standing by itself as the nucleus of a syllable without an accompanying vowel: said of a consonant, as the *l* in *tattle* **3.** pronounced with the syllables distinct —*n.* a syllabic sound —**syl·lab'i·cal·ly** *adv.*

syl·lab·i·cate (si lab'ə kāt') *vt.* **-cat'ed, -cat'ing** *same as* SYLLABIFY —**syl·lab'i·ca'tion** *n.*

syl·lab·i·fy (si lab'ə fī') *vt.* **-fied', -fy'ing** [< *syllabification* < L. *syllaba*, syllable + -FICATION] to form or divide into syllables —**syl·lab'i·fi·ca'tion** *n.*

syl·la·ble (sil'ə b'l) *n.* [< OFr. < L. < Gr. *syllabē*, ult. < *syn-*, together + *lambanein*, to hold] **1.** a word or part of a word pronounced with a single, uninterrupted sounding of the voice **2.** any of the parts into which a written word is divided, in fairly close relation to its spoken syllables, to show where the word can be broken at the end of a line **3.** the least bit of detail, as of something said —*vt., vi.* **-bled, -bling** to pronounce in or as in syllables

syl·la·bub (sil'ə bub') *n.* [< ?] a dessert or beverage made of sweetened milk or cream mixed with wine or cider and beaten to a froth

syl·la·bus (sil'ə bəs) *n., pl.* **-bus·es, -bi** (-bī) [LL., a list < L. < Gr. *sillybos*, parchment label] a summary or outline, esp. of a course of study

syl·lep·sis (si lep'sis) *n., pl.* **-lep'ses** (-sēz) [L. < Gr. *syllēpsis*, a putting together] *Gram.* the agreement of a verb or adjective with one of two or more nouns, with any of which it might agree

syl·lo·gism (sil'ə jiz'm) *n.* [< MFr. < L. < Gr. *syn-*, together + *logizesthai*, to reason] **1.** a form of reasoning in which two statements or premises are made and a logical conclusion drawn from them Ex: All mammals are warm-blooded (*major premise*); whales are mammals (*minor premise*); therefore, whales are warmblooded (*conclusion*) **2.** reasoning from the general to the particular —**syl'lo·gis'tic, syl'lo·gis'ti·cal** *adj.* —**syl'lo·gis'ti·cal·ly** *adv.*

sylph (silf) *n.* [ModL. *sylphus* < L., a spirit < ?] **1.** an imaginary being supposed to live in the air **2.** a slender, graceful woman or girl —**sylph'like'** *adj.*

syl·van (sil'vən) *adj.* [< ML. < L. *silva*, a wood] **1.** of or characteristic of the woods or forest **2.** living, found, or carried on in the woods or forest **3.** wooded —*n.* one who lives in the woods

sym- *same as* SYN-: used before *m, p,* and *b*

sym·bi·ont (sim'bī ont) *n.* [G. < Gr. *symbiountos*, prp. of *symbioun*: see ff] an organism living in a state of symbiosis

sym·bi·o·sis (sim'bī ō'sis, -bē-) *n.* [ModL. < Gr. *symbioun* < *syn-*, together + *bioun*, to live] **1.** *Biol.* the intimate living together of two kinds of organisms, esp. where such association is of mutual advantage **2.** a similar relationship in which persons or groups are dependent on each other —**sym'bi·ot'ic** (-ot'ik) *adj.*

sym·bol (sim'b'l) *n.* [< Fr. < L. < Gr. *symbolon*, token, ult. < *syn-*, together + *ballein*, to throw] **1.** an object used to represent something abstract [the dove is a symbol of peace] **2.** a mark, letter, abbreviation, etc. standing for an object, quality, process, quantity, etc., as in music, chemistry, mathematics, etc. —*vt.* **-bolled, -bol·ling** *same as* SYMBOLIZE

sym·bol·ic (sim bol'ik) *adj.* **1.** of or expressed in a symbol, or symbols **2.** that serves as a symbol (*of something*) **3.** using symbolism Also **sym·bol'i·cal** —**sym·bol'i·cal·ly** *adv.*

symbolic logic a modern type of formal logic using special mathematical symbols for propositions and relationships among propositions

sym·bol·ism (sim'bal iz'm) *n.* **1.** the representation of things by use of symbols, esp. in art or literature **2.** a system of symbols **3.** symbolic meaning

sym·bol·ist (-ist) *n.* **1.** a person who uses symbols **2.** a person who practises symbolism in representing ideas, etc., esp. in art or literature —**sym'bol·is'tic** *adj.* —**sym'bol·is'-ti·cal·ly** *adv.*

sym·bol·ize (-īz') *vt.* **-ized', -iz'ing 1.** to be a symbol of; typify; stand for **2.** to represent by a symbol or symbols —*vi.* to use symbols —**sym'bol·i·za'tion** *n.* —**sym'bol·iz'-er** *n.*

sym·me·try (sim'ə trē) *n., pl.* **-tries** [< MFr. < L. < Gr., ult. < *syn-*, together + *metron*, a measure] **1.** similarity of form or arrangement on either side of a dividing line or plane; correspondence of opposite parts in size, shape, and position **2.** balance or beauty of form resulting from such correspondence —**sym·met·ri·cal** (si met'ri k'l), **sym·met'ric** *adj.* —**sym·met'ri·cal·ly** *adv.*

sym·pa·thet·ic (sim'pə thet'ik) *adj.* **1.** of, resulting from, feeling, or showing sympathy; sympathizing **2.** in agreement with one's tastes, mood, etc.; congenial **3.** showing favour, approval, etc. [to be *sympathetic* to a plan] **4.** *Physiol.* designating or of that part of the autonomic nervous system involved in the involuntary response to alarm, as by speeding the heart rate, dilating the pupils of the eyes, etc. **5.** *Physics* designating or of vibrations caused by other vibrations having the same period that are transmitted from a neighbouring vibrating body —**sym'-pa·thet'i·cal·ly** *adv.*

sympathetic magic a type of magic in which a small-scale ceremony is thought to produce a large-scale effect, as pouring water on an altar to induce rain

sym·pa·thize (sim'pə thīz') *vi.* **-thized', -thiz'ing 1.** to share or understand the feelings or ideas of another; be in sympathy **2.** to feel or express sympathy, esp. in pity or compassion; commiserate **3.** to be in harmony or accord —**sym'pa·thiz'er** *n.* —**sym'pa·thiz'ing·ly** *adv.*

sym·pa·thy (sim'pə thē) *n., pl.* **-thies** [< L. < Gr. < *syn-*, together + *pathos*, feeling] **1.** sameness of feeling; affinity between persons **2.** agreement in qualities; harmony; accord **3.** a mutual liking or understanding arising from sameness of feeling **4.** a sharing of, or the ability to share, another person's mental state, emotions, etc.; esp., [*often pl.*] pity or compassion felt for another's trouble, suffering, etc. **5.** a feeling of approval of an idea, cause, etc.

sympathy (or **sympathetic**) **strike** a strike by a group of workers in support of another group on strike

symphonic poem a composition of programme music for

full symphony orchestra, interpreting particular poetic or descriptive ideas, and free in form

sym·pho·ny (sim′fə nē) *n.*, *pl.* **-nies** [< OFr. < L. < Gr. *syn-*, together + *phōnē*, a sound] 1. harmony of sounds, esp. of instruments 2. any harmony, as of colour 3. *Music* a) an extended composition for full orchestra, having several (usually four) movements related in subject, but varying in form and execution b) [U.S.] *short for* SYMPHONY ORCHESTRA —**sym·phon·ic** (sim fon′ik) *adj.* —**sym·phon′- i·cal·ly** *adv.*

symphony orchestra a large orchestra of string, wind, and percussion sections for playing symphonic works

sym·po·si·arch (sim pō′zē ärk′) *n.* [Gr. *symposiarchos*, master of a feast] the master or director of a symposium, esp. in ancient Greece

sym·po·si·um (sim pō′zē əm) *n.*, *pl.* **-si·ums, -si·a** (-ə) [L. < Gr. *syn-*, together + *posis*, a drinking] 1. any meeting or social gathering at which ideas are freely exchanged 2. a conference organized for the discussion of some particular subject 3. a collection of opinions, esp. a group of essays, on a given subject —**sym·po′si·ac′** (-ak′) *adj.*

symp·tom (simp′təm) *n.* [< ML. < LL. < Gr. *symptōma*, ult. < *syn-*, together + *piptein*, to fall] any circumstance, event, or condition that accompanies something and indicates its existence or occurrence; sign; specif., *Med.* any condition accompanying a disease or a physical disorder and serving as an aid in diagnosis —**symp′to·mat′ic** (-tə mat′ik) *adj.* —**symp′to·mat′i·cal·ly** *adv.*

symp·tom·a·tize (-tə mə tīz′) *vt.* **-tized′, -tiz′ing** to be a symptom or sign of: also **symp′tom·ize′**

syn- [Gr. < *syn*, with] *a prefix meaning* with, together with, at the same time, by means of: *syn-* is assimilated to *syl-* before *l; sym-* before *m, p, b;* and *sys-* before *s* and aspirate *h*

syn. 1. synonym 2. synonymous 3. synonymy

syn·aes·the·si·a (sin′əs thē′zē ə) *n.* [ModL.: see SYN- & AESTHESIA] 1. *Physiol.* sensation felt in one part of the body when another part is stimulated 2. *Psychol.* a sense impression accompanying the stimulation of another sense, for instance a colour producing a specific smell sensation

syn·a·gogue (sin′ə gog′) *n.* [< OFr. < LL. < Gr. *synagōgē*, an assembly, ult. < *syn-*, together + *agein*, to bring] 1. an assembly of Jews meeting for worship and religious study 2. a building or place used for such an assembly 3. the Jewish religion as organized in such local congregations —**syn′a·gog′al** (-gog′′l), **syn′a·gog′i·cal** (-goj′i k′l) *adj.*

syn·apse (si naps′) *n.* [ModL. < Gr. *synapsis*, a union] the point of contact between adjacent neurons, where nerve impulses are transmitted from one to the other —**syn·ap′tic** (-nap′tik) *adj.*

syn·ap·sis (si nap′sis) *n.*, *pl.* **-ses** (-sēz) [ModL. < Gr. *synapsis*, a junction] 1. *Genetics* the association of chromosome pairs in the early stages of meiosis 2. *Physiol.* same as SYNAPSE

sync, synch (siŋk) *vt., vi., n.* *shortened form of:* 1. SYNCHRONIZE 2. synchronization (see SYNCHRONIZE)

syn·chro·mesh (siŋ′krə mesh′) *adj.* designating or employing a device by which gears to be meshed are automatically brought to the same speed of rotation before the change is completed —*n.* a synchromesh gear system

syn·chro·nism (siŋ′krə niz′m) *n.* 1. the fact or state of being synchronous; occurrence at the same time 2. a chronological listing of persons or events in history, showing existence or occurrence at the same time —**syn′- chro·nis′tic** *adj.* —**syn′chro·nis′ti·cal·ly** *adv.*

syn·chro·nize (siŋ′krə nīz′) *vi.* **-nized′, -niz′ing** [< Gr. < *synchronos*, contemporary < *syn-*, together + *chronos*, time] to move or occur at the same time or rate; be synchronous —*vt.* 1. to cause to agree in time or rate of speed; regulate (clocks, action and dialogue, etc.) so as to make synchronous 2. to assign (events, etc.) to the same date or period —**syn′chro·ni·za′tion** *n.* —**syn′chro·niz′er** *n.*

syn·chro·nous (-nəs) *adj.* [< LL. < Gr.: see prec.] 1. happening at the same time; simultaneous 2. having the same period between movements, occurrences, etc.; having the same rate and phase, as vibrations Also **syn′chro·nal** —**syn′chro·nous·ly** *adv.* —**syn′chro·nous·ness** *n.*

syn·chro·tron (-tron′) *n.* [SYNCHRO(NOUS) + (ELEC)TRON] a circular machine for accelerating charged particles, esp. electrons, to very high energies through the use of a low-frequency magnetic field in combination with a high frequency electrostatic field

syn·cline (siŋ′klīn) *n.* [< *synclinal* < Gr. *syn-*, together + *klinein*, to incline] *Geol.* a down fold in stratified rocks from whose central axis the beds rise upwards and outwards in opposite directions: opposed to ANTICLINE —**syn·cli′nal** (sin klī′n′l, siŋ′kli n′l) *adj.*

syn·co·pate (siŋ′kə pāt′) *vt.* **-pat′ed, -pat′ing** [< ML. pp. of *syncopare*, to cut short < LL., to swoon < *syncope*: see SYNCOPE] 1. to shorten (a word) by syncope 2. *Music* a) to shift (the regular accent) as by beginning a tone on an unaccented beat and continuing it through the next accented beat, or on the last half of a beat and continuing it through

the first half of the following beat b) to use such shifted accents in (a composition, etc.) —**syn′co·pa′tor** *n.*

syn·co·pa·tion (siŋ′kə pā′shən) *n.* 1. a syncopating or being syncopated 2. syncopated music, a syncopated rhythm, etc. 3. *Gram.* same as SYNCOPE

syn·co·pe (siŋ′kə pē) *n.* [LL. < Gr. < *syn-*, together + *koptein*, to cut] 1. the dropping of sounds or letters from the middle of a word, as in *Wooster* for *Worcester* 2. a fainting caused by an inadequate flow of blood to the brain

syn·cre·tism (siŋ′krə tiz′m) *n.* [Fr. *syncrétisme* < ModL. ult. < Gr. *synkrētizein*, to combine] 1. the reconciliation of differing beliefs, etc. in religion, philosophy, etc. 2. *Linguis.* the merging of two or more differently inflected forms

syn·cre·tize (siŋ′krə tīz′) *vt., vi.* **-tized′, -tiz′ing** [< ModL. < Gr. *synkrētizein*] to combine, unite, or reconcile

syn·dic (sin′dik) *n.* [Fr. < LL. < Gr. *syndikos*, advocate < *syn-*, together + *dikē*, justice] 1. a business manager, esp. of a university 2. a government official in Andorra, etc. —**syn′di·cal** *adj.*

syn·di·cal·ism (-di kə liz′m) *n.* a theory of trade unionism in which all means of production and distribution would be brought under the control of federations of trade unions by the use of general strikes, etc. —**syn′di·cal·ist** *adj., n.*

syn·di·cate (sin′də kit; *for v.* -kāt′) *n.* [Fr. *syndicat* < *syndic*, SYNDIC] 1. a council of syndics 2. a) an association of individuals or corporations formed to carry out some financial project requiring much capital b) any group organized to further some undertaking [crime *syndicate*] c) a group of similar organizations, as of newspapers, owned as a chain 3. an organization that sells articles or features for publication by many newspapers —*vt.* **-cat′ed, -cat′ing** 1. to manage as or form into a syndicate 2. to sell (an article, etc.) through a syndicate for publication in many newspapers, etc. —*vi.* to form a syndicate —**syn′di·ca′tion** *n.* —**syn′di·ca′tor** *n.*

syn·drome (sin′drōm) *n.* [ModL. < Gr. < *syn-*, with + *dramein*, to run] 1. a set of symptoms characterizing a disease 2. any set of characteristics identifying a type, condition, etc.

syne (sīn) *adv., conj., prep.* [Scot.] since; ago

syn·ec·do·che (si nek′də kē) *n.* [< ML. < L. < Gr., ult. < *syn-*, together + *ekdechesthai*, to receive] a figure of speech in which a part is used for a whole, an individual for a class, a material for a thing, or the reverse of any of these (Ex.: *bread* for *food, the army* for *a soldier*, or *copper* for a *penny*)

syn·e·col·o·gy (sin′i kol′ə jē) *n.* [G. *Synökologie* < *syn-*, SYN- + *ökologie*, ECOLOGY] the ecological study of different natural communities

syn·er·gism (sin′ər jiz′m) *n.* [< ModL. < Gr. < *syn-*, together + *ergon*, work] the simultaneous action of separate agencies which, together, have greater total effect than the sum of their individual effects: said esp. of drugs: also **syn′er·gy** (-jē) —**syn′er·gis′tic** *adj.*

syn·od (sin′əd) *n.* [OE. *sinoth*, ult. < Gr. *synodos*, lit., a meeting < *syn-*, together + *hodos*, way] 1. a council of churches or church officials; specif., a high governing body in any of certain Christian churches 2. any assembly or council —**syn′od·al** *adj.*

syn·od·i·cal (si nod′i k′l) *adj.* 1. of a synod 2. *Astron.* of or having to do with conjunction, esp. with the interval between two successive conjunctions of the same heavenly bodies Also **syn·od′ic** —**syn·od′i·cal·ly** *adv.*

syn·o·nym (sin′ə nim) *n.* [< L. < Gr. < *syn-*, together + *onyma*, a name] 1. a word having the same or nearly the same meaning as another in the same language 2. a word used in metonymy —**syn′o·nym′ic, syn′o·nym′i·cal** *adj.*

syn·on·y·mous (si non′ə məs) *adj.* [see prec.] of the same or nearly the same meaning —**syn·on′y·mous·ly** *adv.*

syn·on·y·my (-mē) *n., pl.* **-mies** 1. the study of synonyms 2. a list or listing of synonyms, esp. one in which the terms are discriminated from one another 3. the quality of being synonymous; sameness or near sameness of meaning

syn·op·sis (si nop′sis) *n., pl.* **-ses** (-sēz) [LL. < Gr. < *syn-*, together + *opsis*, a seeing] a short outline or review of the main points, as of a story; summary

syn·op·size (-sīz) *vt.* **-sized, -siz·ing** to make a synopsis of

syn·op·tic (-tik) *adj.* 1. of or giving a synopsis, summary, or general view 2. giving an account from the same point of view: said, esp. [*often* S-] of the first three Gospels Also **syn·op′ti·cal** —**syn·op′ti·cal·ly** *adv.*

syn·o·vi·a (si nō′vē ə) *n.* [ModL. < ?] the clear, albuminous lubricating fluid secreted by the membranes of joint cavities, tendon sheaths, etc. —**syn·o′vi·al** *adj.*

syn·tac·tic (sin tak′tik) *adj.* of or in accordance with syntax: also **syn·tac′ti·cal** —**syn·tac′ti·cal·ly** *adv.*

syn·tag·ma (sin′tag′mə) *n.* [LL. < Gr. *syntagma*, an ordering] 1. a systematic body of statements forming a whole 2. a phrase or word forming a syntactic unit

syn·tax (sin′taks) *n.* [< Fr. < LL. < Gr., ult. < *syn-*, together + *tassein*, to arrange] *Gram.* 1. the arrangement of words as elements in a sentence to show their relationship to one another 2. the organization and relationship of word groups, phrases, clauses, and sentences; sentence structure **3.** the branch of grammar dealing with this

syn·the·sis (sin'thə sis) *n., pl.* **-ses'** (-sēz') [Gr. < *syn-*, together + *tithenai*, to place] **1.** the putting together of parts or elements so as to form a whole **2.** a whole formed in this way **3.** *Chem.* the formation of a complex compound by the combining of two or more simpler compounds, elements, or radicals —**syn'the·sist** *n.*

syn·the·size (-sīz') *vt.* **-sized'**, **-siz'ing 1.** to bring together into a whole by synthesis **2.** to form by bringing together separate parts; specif., *Chem.* to produce by synthesis rather than by extraction, refinement, etc.

syn·the·siz·er (-sī'zər) *n.* a person or thing that synthesizes; specif., an electronic music device that produces sounds not made by ordinary musical instruments

syn·thet·ic (sin thet'ik) *adj.* **1.** of, involving, or using synthesis **2.** produced by synthesis; specif., produced by chemical synthesis, rather than of natural origin **3.** not real or genuine; artificial **4.** using inflection rather than word order and separate words to express syntactic relationships [Latin is a *synthetic* language] Also **syn·thet'i·cal** —*n.* something synthetic —**syn·thet'i·cal·ly** *adv.*

synthetic resin any of a large class of complex organic compounds formed from simpler molecules by polymerization, used esp. in making plastics

syph·i·lis (sif'ə lis) *n.* [ModL. < *Syphilus*, hero of a Latin poem (1530)] a disease, caused by a spirochete and usually passed on during sexual intercourse or obtained in the womb before birth —**syph'i·lit'ic** *adj., n.*

sy·phon (sī'fən) *n., vi., vt. var. sp. of* SIPHON

Syr. 1. Syria **2.** Syriac **3.** Syrian

Syr·i·ac (sir'ē ak') *n.* the ancient Aramaic language of Syria, used from the 3rd cent. to the 13th

Syr·i·an (sir'ē ən) *adj.* of Syria, its people, their language, etc. —*n.* **1.** a member of the Semitic people of Syria **2.** their modern Arabic dialect

sy·rin·ga (sə riŋ'gə) *n.* [ModL., genus name < Gr. *syrinx* (see ff.): from former use in making pipes] **1.** *same as* LILAC (senses 1 & 2) **2.** *same as* MOCK ORANGE

sy·ringe (sə rinj', sir'inj) *n.* [< ML. < Gr. *syrinx* (gen. *syringos*), a reed, pipe] **1.** a device consisting of a narrow tube fitted at one end with a rubber bulb or piston by means of which a liquid can be drawn in and then pushed out in a stream: used to inject fluids into, or extract fluids from, body cavities, to cleanse wounds, etc. **2.** *short for* HYPODERMIC SYRINGE —*vt.* **-ringed'**, **-ring'ing** to cleanse, inject, etc. with a syringe

syr·inx (sir'iŋks) *n., pl.* **sy·rin·ges** (sə rin'jēz), **syr'inx·es** [ModL. < Gr., a pipe] **1.** the vocal organ of songbirds, at or near the base of the trachea **2.** *same as* PANPIPE

SYRINGE

syr·up (sir'əp) *n.* [< OFr. < ML. < Ar. *sharāb*, a drink] **1.** any sweet, thick liquid; specif., *a*) a solution made by boiling sugar with water and, often, flavoured *b*) any such solution used in preparing medicines **2.** cloying sentimentality —**syr'up·y** *adj.*

sys·tal·tic (sis tal'tik) *adj.* [< LL. < Gr. *systaltikos*, drawing together] characterized by alternate contraction and dilation, as the action of the heart

sys·tem (sis'təm) *n.* [< LL. < Gr. *systēma*, ult. < *syn-*, together + *histanai*, to set] **1.** a group of things or parts working together or connected in some way so as to form a whole [a solar *system, system* of motorways] **2.** a set of principles, rules, etc. linked in an orderly way to show a logical plan [an economic *system*] **3.** a method or plan of classification or arrangement [the metric *system*] **4.** *a*) an established way of doing something; method; procedure *b*) orderliness or methodical planning in one's way of proceeding **5.** *a*) the body considered as a functioning organism *b*) a number of organs acting together to perform one of the main bodily functions [the nervous *system*] **6.** a related series of natural objects or elements, as rivers **7.** *Geol.* a major division of stratified rocks comprising the rocks laid down during a period —**get it out of one's system** [Colloq.] to free oneself of an obsession, etc.

sys·tem·at·ic (sis'tə mat'ik) *adj.* **1.** based on or forming a system [*systematic* theology] **2.** according to a system, method, or plan; regular; orderly **3.** orderly in planning or doing things; methodical **4.** of or having to do with classification Also **sys'tem·at'i·cal** —**sys'tem·at'i·cal·ly** *adv.*

sys·tem·a·tize (sis'təm ə tīz') *vt.* **-tized'**, **-tiz'ing** to form into a system; arrange according to a system; make systematic —**sys'tem·a·ti·za'tion** *n.* —**sys'tem·a·tiz'er** *n.* —**sys'tem·a·tism** *n.*

sys·tem·ic (sis tem'ik) *adj.* of a system; specif., *Physiol.* of or affecting the entire organism or bodily system —*n.* any of a group of pesticides that are absorbed into the tissues of plants, making the plants poisonous to insects, etc. that feed on them —**sys·tem'i·cal·ly** *adv.*

sys·tem·ize (sis'tə mīz') *vt.* **-ized'**, **-iz'ing** *same as* SYSTEMATIZE —**sys'tem·i·za'tion** *n.*

systems analysis an engineering technique that breaks down complex technical, social, etc. problems into basic elements whose interrelations are evaluated and programmed into a complete and integrated system —**systems analyst**

systems engineering a branch of engineering using computer science, facts from systems-analysis studies, etc. to design integrated operational systems for specific organizations —**systems engineer**

sys·to·le (sis'tə lē') *n.* [ModL. < Gr. *systolē*; ult. < *syn-*, together + *stellein*, to send] the usual rhythmic contraction of the heart, esp. of the ventricles, during which the blood is driven onward from the chambers —**sys·tol·ic** (sis tol'ik) *adj.*

syz·y·gy (siz'ə jē) *n., pl.* **-gies** [LL. < Gr. *syzygia*, yoked together] **1.** a pair of things, esp. of opposites **2.** *Astron.* the conjunction or opposition of a celestial body

T

T, t (tē) *n., pl.* **T's, t's 1.** the twentieth letter of the English alphabet **2.** the sound of *T* or *t*

T (tē) *n.* an object shaped like *T* —*adj.* shaped like T —**to a T** to perfection; exactly

T *Physics* the symbol for tesla

t tonne(s)

't it: a contraction, as in *'twas, do't*

-t *var. of* -ED (in some past participles and adjectives derived from them) [*slept, gilt*]

T. Testament

t. 1. temperature **2.** tense **3.** time **4.** ton(s) **5.** transitive **6.** troy

ta (tä) *interj.* [Colloq.] thank you: orig. a child's term

Ta *Chem.* tantalum

tab¹ (tab) *n.* [< ?] **1.** a small, flat loop or strap fastened to something for pulling it, hanging it up, etc. **2.** an attached or projecting piece of a card or paper, useful in filing —*vt.* **tabbed, tab'bing 1.** to provide with tabs **2.** to choose or select

tab² (tab) *n.* [prob. < TABULATE] [U.S. Colloq.] a bill for a meal or drinks, esp. in a restaurant —**keep tabs** (or **a tab**) **on** [Colloq.] to follow or watch every move of; check on

tab³ (tab) *n. shortened form of:* **1.** TABLET **2.** TABULATOR —*vt.* **tabbed, tab'bing** [Colloq.] to use the tabulator on a typewriter

tab·ard (tab'ərd) *n.* [OFr. *tabart*] **1.** a loose, heavy jacket worn outdoors as by peasants in the Middle Ages **2.** a short-sleeved, blazoned cloak worn by a knight over his armour **3.** a herald's official coat, blazoned with his lord's arms

Ta·bas·co (tə bas'kō) [< *Tabasco*, a Mexican state] *a trademark for* a hot sauce made from a kind of red pepper

tab·by (tab'ē) *n., pl.* **-bies** [< Fr. < ML. < Ar. *'attābi*, quarter of Baghdad where it was made] **1.** a silk taffeta with wavy markings **2.** a grey or brown cat with dark stripes **3.** any pet cat, esp. a female **4.** [Colloq.] *a*) an old maid *b*) a malicious gossip —*adj.* having dark stripes over grey or brown

tab·er·nac·le (tab'ər nak''l) *n.* [< LL. < L. *tabernaculum*, a tent, dim. of *taberna*, a hut] **1.** formerly, a temporary shelter, as a tent   **2.** [T-] a) the portable sanctuary carried by the Jews in their wanderings from Egypt to Palestine: Ex. 25-27 b) later, the Jewish Temple   **3.** a shrine, niche, etc. with a canopy   **4.** a place of worship, esp. one seating many people   **5.** a cabinetlike enclosure on an altar, for consecrated Hosts   —vi. **-led, -ling** to dwell temporarily —vt. to place in a tabernacle **—tab'er·nac'u·lar** (- yə lər) adj.

ta·bes dor·sa·lis (tā'bēz dôr sā'lis, -sal'is) [ModL. < L. tabes, a wasting away + dorsualis, of the back] a chronic disease of the nervous system, usually caused by syphilis and characterized by loss of reflexes and of muscular coordination, etc.

ta·ble (tā'b'l) n. [OFr. < L. tabula, a board, tablet] **1.** orig., a thin slab of metal, stone, or wood, used for inscriptions; tablet   **2.** a) a piece of furniture consisting of a flat, horizontal top set on legs b) such a table set with food for a meal c) food served at table d) the people seated at a table **3.** a large, flat-topped piece of furniture or equipment used for games, as a working surface, etc. [billiard table, sewing table]   **4.** a) a compact, orderly list of details, contents, etc. b) a compact, orderly arrangement of facts, figures, etc., usually in rows and columns [the multiplication table]   **5.** same as TABLELAND   **6.** any of various flat surfaces, layers, or parts, as the upper, flat facet of a gem   **7.** Archit. a) any horizontal, projecting piece, as a moulding or cornice b) a rectangular panel set into or raised on a wall **—adj. 1.** of, for, or on a table   **2.** fit for serving at table [table salt]   —vt. **-bled, -bling 1.** orig., to tabulate   **2.** to put on a table   **3.** to put up for consideration (a motion, bill, etc.)   **4.** [U.S.] to set aside the consideration of (a motion, bill, etc.) **—at table** at a meal **—the tables** laws, as the Ten Commandments, inscribed on flat stone slabs **—turn the tables** to reverse a situation completely **—under the table** [Colloq.] **1.** [Chiefly U.S.] secretly, as a bribe   **2.** drunk to the point of unconsciousness

tab·leau (tab'lō) n., pl. **-leaux** (-lōz), **-leaus** [Fr. < OFr. tablel, dim. of table: see prec.] **1.** a striking, dramatic scene or picture   **2.** a representation of a scene, picture, etc. by a person or group posed in costume: also **tab·leau vi·vant** (vē vän')

ta·ble·cloth (tā'b'l klôth') n. a cloth for covering a table, esp. at meals

ta·ble d'hôte (tā'b'l dōt', tab'l) pl. **ta'bles d'hôte** (-b'lz, -'lz) [Fr., lit., table of the host] a complete meal with courses as specified, served at a restaurant or hotel for a set price: distinguished from À LA CARTE

ta·ble·land (-land') n. a high, broad, level region; plateau

table licence a licence permitting alcoholic drinks to be served with meals only

table linen tablecloths, napkins, etc.

ta·ble·spoon (-spōōn') n. **1.** a large spoon used for serving at table   **2.** a spoon used as a measuring unit in cookery   **3.** same as TABLESPOONFUL

ta·ble·spoon·ful (-fool) n., pl. **-fuls** as much as a tablespoon will hold

tab·let (tab'lit) n. [< MFr. dim. of table: see TABLE] **1.** a flat, thin piece of stone, metal, etc., esp. one with an inscription   **2.** a smooth, flat leaf of wood, metal, etc., used to write on   **3.** a writing pad containing sheets of paper fastened at one edge   **4.** a small, flat piece of some hard substance, as medicine, soap, etc.

table talk informal conversation, as that at meals

table tennis a game somewhat like tennis in miniature, played on a table, with a small celluloid or plastic ball and short-handled, wooden bats

ta·ble·turn·ing (-tur'niŋ) n. the movement of a table attributed by spiritualists to supernatural power

ta·ble·ware (tā'b'l wer') n. dishes, glassware, silverware, etc. for use at table

Tab·loid (tab'loid) [TABL(ET) + -OID] a trademark for a small tablet of medicine **—n.** [t-] a newspaper with pages about half the ordinary size, and often carrying many pictures and short, often sensational, news stories **—adj.** [t-] condensed; short

ta·boo (ta bōō', tə-) n. [Tongan tabu] **1.** a) among some Polynesian peoples, a sacred prohibition which makes certain people or things untouchable, unmentionable, etc. b) the system of such prohibitions   **2.** any social restriction resulting from convention or tradition **—adj. 1.** sacred and forbidden by taboo   **2.** forbidden by tradition, etiquette, etc. —vt. **1.** to put under taboo   **2.** to prohibit or forbid

ta·bor (tā'bər) n. [OFr. tabur < Per. tabīrah] a small drum, formerly used by a fife player to beat out his own rhythmic accompaniment Also sp. **ta'bour**

tab·ou·ret (tab'ər it, tab'ə ret') n. [OFr., a stool, dim. of tabur: see prec.] **1.** a small tabor   **2.** a stool Also sp. **tab'-o·ret**

ta·bu (ta bōō', tə-) n., adj., vt. var. sp. of TABOO

tab·u·lar (tab'yə lər) adj. [< L. < tabula: see TABLE] **1.** flat like a table   **2.** a) of or arranged in tables or columns b) calculated by using tables **—tab'u·lar·ly** adv.

tab·u·late (tab'yə lāt'; for adj. -lit) vt. **-lat'ed, -lat'ing** [< L. tabula (see TABLE) + -ATE¹] to put (facts, statistics, etc.) in a table or columns; arrange systematically **—adj.** having a flat surface **—tab'u·la'tion** n.

tab·u·la·tor (-lāt'ər) n. **1.** a person or thing that tabulates; specif., a device or key for setting stops on a typewriter carriage, as for typing columns

tac·a·ma·hac (tak'ə mə hak') n. [< Sp. < Nahuatl tecomahca] **1.** a strong-smelling gum resin used in ointments and incenses   **2.** any of several trees yielding this resin

tach·ism, tach·isme (tash'iz'm; Fr. tà shēz'm') n. [Fr. < tache, a spot] a method of action painting in which paint is splashed onto the canvas in apparently random patterns

ta·chis·to·scope (tə kis'tə skōp') n. [< Gr. tachistos, swiftest + -SCOPE] an apparatus that exposes words, pictures, etc. for a fraction of a second, used to increase reading speed, etc.

tach·o·graph (tak'ō gräf') n. [< Gr. tachos, speed + -GRAPH] an instrument for recording the speed and distance travelled by a motor vehicle, esp. a heavy goods vehicle

ta·chom·e·ter (ta kom'ə tər, tə-) n. [< Gr. tachos, speed + -METER] a device that indicates or measures the revolutions per minute of a revolving shaft **—ta·chom'e·try** n.

tach·y·car·di·a (tak'i kär'dē ə) n. [ModL. < Gr. tachys, swift + kardia, heart] an abnormally fast heartbeat

ta·chyg·ra·phy (ta kig'rə fē, tə-) n. [< Gr. tachys, swift + -GRAPHY] shorthand, esp. of the ancient Greeks or Romans

ta·chym·e·ter (ta kim'ə tər, tə-) n. [< Gr. tachys, swift + -METER] a surveying instrument for rapid determination of distances, elevations, etc.

tac·it (tas'it) adj. [< Fr. < L. pp. of tacere, to be silent] **1.** making no sound; saying nothing   **2.** unspoken; silent   **3.** not expressed openly, but implied or understood [tacit approval] **—tac'it·ly** adv. **—tac'it·ness** n.

tac·i·turn (tas'ə turn') adj. [< Fr. < L. < tacere: see prec.] almost always silent; not liking to talk **—tac'i·tur'ni·ty** n. **—tac'i·turn'ly** adv.

tack (tak) n. [MDu. tacke, a twig, point] **1.** a short nail or pin with a sharp point and a somewhat large, flat head   **2.** a) a fastening, esp. in a slight or temporary way b) Sewing a stitch for marking darts, etc. from a pattern, clipped and later removed: in full, **tailor's tack**   c) stickiness **3.** a zigzag course, or movement in such a course   **4.** a course of action or policy   **5.** Naut. a) a rope for holding securely the forward lower corner of some sails b) the corner thus held c) the direction in which a ship is moving in relation to the position of the sails d) a change of direction made by changing the position of the sails e) a course against the wind f) any of a series of zigzag movements in such a course   **6.** a horse's equipment, as saddles, bridles, etc. **—vt. 1.** to fasten with tacks   **2.** to attach temporarily, as with long stitches   **3.** to attach as a supplement [to tack an amendment onto a bill] **4.** Naut. a) to change the course of (a ship) by turning its head to the wind b) to manoeuvre (a ship) against the wind by a series of tacks **—vi. 1.** a) to tack a ship b) to change its course by being tacked: said of a ship   **2.** to go in a zigzag course   **3.** to change suddenly one's course of action **—tack'er** n.

WIND

TACKING

tack·le (tak''l; in nautical usage, often tā'k'l) n. [MDu. takel, pulley, rope] **1.** apparatus; equipment; gear [fishing tackle]   **2.** a system of ropes and pulleys, used to lower, raise, or move weights   **3.** the act or an instance of tackling, as in football   **4.** Naut. the running rigging and pulleys used to operate a ship's sails **—vt. tack'led, tack'ling 1.** to fasten by means of tackle   **2.** to harness (a horse)   **3.** to take hold of; seize   **4.** to undertake to do, solve, or deal with [to tackle a problem]   **5.** Football, etc. to stop or throw (an opponent in possession of the ball) **—vi.** Football, etc. to tackle an opponent **—tackle low** Rugby to tackle an opponent at or below the waist **—tack'ler** n.

tack·y¹ (tak'ē) adj. **tack'i·er, tack'i·est** [TACK (n. 2) + -y²] sticky, as varnish, glue, etc. before completely dry **—tack'-i·ness** n.

tack·y² (tak'ē) adj. **tack'i·er, tack'i·est** [< tacky, a hillbilly < ?] [U.S. Colloq.] dowdy or shabby, as in appearance **—tack'i·ness** n.

ta·co (tä'kō) n., pl. **-cos** [AmSp.] a Mexican dish consisting of a fried, folded tortilla filled with chopped meat, shredded lettuce, etc.

tact (takt) n. [Fr. < L. pp. of tangere, to touch] a sense of the right thing to say or do without offending; skill in dealing with people

tact·ful (takt'fəl) adj. having or showing tact **—tact'ful·ly** adv. **—tact'ful·ness** n.

tac·tic (tak'tik) *n.* [< ModL. < Gr.: see TACTICS] **1.** *same as* TACTICS **2.** a detail or branch of tactics

tac·ti·cal (tak'ti k'l) *adj.* **1.** of or having to do with tactics, esp. in military or naval manoeuvres **2.** characterized by or showing skill in tactics —**tac'ti·cal·ly** *adv.*

tac·ti·cian (tak tish'ən) *n.* an expert in tactics

tac·tics (tak'tiks) *n.pl.* [Gr. (*ta*) *taktika*, lit., (the) matters of arrangement < *tassein*, to arrange] **1.** *a*) [*with sing. v.*] the science of manoeuvring military and naval forces in action, esp. with reference to short-range objectives *b*) actions in accord with this science **2.** any methods used to gain an end; esp., skilful methods

tac·tile (tak'til) *adj.* [Fr. < L. *tactilis* < *tangere*, to touch] **1.** that can be perceived by the touch; tangible **2.** of, having, or related to the sense of touch —**tac·til'i·ty** (-til'ə tē) *n.*

tact·less (takt'lis) *adj.* not having or showing tact —**tact'-less·ly** *adv.* —**tact'less·ness** *n.*

tad·pole (tad'pōl') *n.* [ME. *tadde*, toad + *poll*, head] the larva of certain amphibians, as frogs and toads, having gills and a tail and living in water

tael (tāl) *n.* [Port. < Malay *tahil*, a weight] **1.** any of various units of weight of E Asia **2.** formerly, a Chinese unit of money

ta'en (tān) [Poet.] taken

tae·ni·a (tē'nē ə) *n., pl.* **-ni·ae** (-ē') [L. < Gr. *tainia*, ribbon] **1.** an ancient Greek headband **2.** *Anat.* a ribbonlike structure, as of nerve tissue **3.** *Archit.* a band between the frieze and the architrave of a Doric entablature **4.** *Zool.* a tapeworm

taf·fe·ta (taf'i tə) *n.* [< OFr., ult. < Per. < *tāftan*, to weave] a fine, rather stiff fabric of silk, nylon, acetate, etc., with a sheen —*adj.* like or made of taffeta

taff·rail (taf'rāl') *n.* [< Du. *tafereel*, a panel, ult. < L. *tabula*: see TABLE] the rail around a ship's stern

Taf·fy (taf'ē) *n.* [< *Dafydd*, W form of *David*, masculine name] [Colloq.] a Welshman

tag (tag) *n.* [prob. < Scand.] **1.** orig., a hanging end, as on a torn skirt **2.** any hanging part or loosely attached end **3.** a hard-tipped end, as of metal, on a cord or lace **4.** a card, paper, ticket, etc. attached to something as a label or for identification, etc. **5.** an epithet **6.** the sentence or sentences ending a speech, story, play, etc. **7.** a children's game in which one player, called "it," chases the others until he touches, or tags, one of them, making him "it" in turn —*vt.* **tagged, tag'ging 1.** to provide with a tag; put a tag on **2.** to identify by an epithet **3.** to choose or select **4.** to overtake and touch as in the game of tag **5.** [Colloq.] to follow close behind —*vi.* [Colloq.] to follow close behind a person or thing (usually with *along, after,* etc.) —**tag'ger** *n.*

Ta·ga·log (tə gä'log) *n.* **1.** *pl.* **-logs, -log** a member of a Malayan people of the Philippine ʻ Islands **2.** their Indonesian language

tag end the last part of anything

ta·get·es (ta jē'tēz) *n.* [< L. *Tages*, an Etruscan god] a genus of plants of the aster family, with brilliant yellow or orange flowers, as the marigold

tah·sil (tə sēl') *n.* [Urdu < Ar. collection] an administrative division in certain states in India

Tai (tī) *n., adj.* *same as* THAI

tai·ga (tī'gə) *n.* [Russ.] the coniferous forests in the far northern regions of Eurasia and North America

tail[1] (tāl) *n.* [OE. *tægel*] **1.** the rear end of an animal's body, esp. when forming a distinct, flexible appendage to the trunk **2.** anything like an animal's tail in form or position [the *tail* of a shirt] **3.** a luminous train behind a comet **4.** the hind, last, bottom, or inferior part of anything **5.** [often *pl.*] the reverse side of a coin **6.** a long tress of hair **7.** *a*) the rear section of an aircraft, rocket, or missile *b*) a set of stabilizing planes at the rear of an aircraft **8.** [*pl.*] [Colloq.] *a*) a swallow-tailed coat *b*) full-dress attire for men **9.** [Colloq.] a person or vehicle that follows another, esp. in surveillance —*adj.* **1.** at the rear **2.** from the rear [a *tail* wind] —*vt.* **1.** to provide with a tail **2.** to form the tail or end of, as a procession **3.** to fasten at or by the tail **4.** to fasten one end of (a brick, board, etc.) into a wall, etc. **5.** [Slang] to follow stealthily **6.** [Aust.] to herd or tend sheep or cattle —*vi.* **1.** to become gradually smaller or fainter (with *off* or *away*) **2.** to form, or become part of, a line or tail **3.** [Colloq.] to follow close behind —**on one's tail** following one closely —**the tail wags the dog** the less important person, party, etc. controls that which is more important —**turn tail** to run from danger, difficulty, etc. —**with one's tail between one's legs** in defeat, esp. with fear or dejection —**tail'less** *adj.* —**tail'like** *adj.*

tail[2] (tāl) *n.* [< OFr. < *taillier*: see TAILOR] *same as* ENTAIL (*n.* 2 & 3) —*adj.* limited in a specific way as to inheritance

tail·back (-bak) *n.* an accumulation or buildup of vehicles in a traffic jam

tail·board (tāl'bôrd') *n.* a board or gate at the back of a lorry, wagon, etc.: it can be removed or swung down for loading, etc.

tail coat *same as* SWALLOW-TAILED COAT

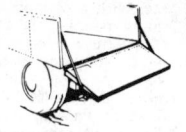

TAILBOARD

tailed (tāld) *adj.* having a (specified kind of) tail: usually in combination [*bobtailed*]

tail·gate (tāl'gāt') *n.* **1.** a gate at the lower end of a lock **2.** [Chiefly U.S.] *same as* TAILBOARD **3.** a door at the rear of a hatchback vehicle —*vi., vt.* **-gat'ed, -gat'ing** to drive too closely behind (another vehicle) —**tail'gat'er** *n.*

tail·ing (-iŋ) *n.* **1.** [*pl.*] refuse left in milling, mining, etc. **2.** the part of a projecting brick, stone, etc. fastened into a wall

tail·light (tāl'līt') *n.* a light, usually red, at the rear of a vehicle to warn vehicles coming from behind

tai·lor (tā'lər) *n.* [< OFr. < *taillier*, to cut < LL. *taliare*, to split < L. *talea*, a twig] a person who makes, repairs, or alters clothes, esp. men's suits, coats, etc. —*vi.* to work as a tailor —*vt.* **1.** to make (clothes) by tailor's work **2.** to make clothes for **3.** to form, alter, etc. so as to meet certain conditions [a novel *tailored* to popular taste] **4.** to fashion (women's garments) with trim, simple lines —**tai'lor·ing** *n.*

tai·lor·bird (-bɵrd') *n.* any of several small Asiatic and African birds that stitch leaves together to camouflage and hold their nests

tai·lored (tā'lɵrd) *adj.* having trim, simple lines, as some women's garments, or specially fitted, as loose covers

tai·lor-made (tā'lɵr mād') *adj.* made by or as by a tailor; specif., *a*) having trim, simple lines; tailored *b*) made-to-order *c*) made in a factory rather than rolled by hand: said of cigarettes *d*) exactly suited to its purpose

tail·piece (tāl'pēs') *n.* **1.** a part forming the end of something **2.** the piece of wood at the lower end of a violin, etc., to which the strings are attached **3.** a short beam with one end tailed in a wall and the other supported by a header **4.** *Printing* an ornamental design at the end of a chapter, etc.

tail·pipe (-pīp') *n.* **1.** an exhaust pipe at the rear of a motor vehicle **2.** the exhaust duct of a jet engine

tail·plane (-plān') *n.* a horizontal aerofoil at the tail of an aircraft to provide longitudinal stability

tail·race (-rās') *n.* the lower part of a millrace, through which water flows after going over a water wheel

tail·skid (-skid') *n.* a device underneath the tail of an aircraft protecting it from damage while landing or taking off

tail·spin (-spin') *n.* **1.** *same as* SPIN (*n.* 4): also **tail spin** **2.** a state of rapidly increasing depression or confusion

tail wind a wind blowing in the same direction as the course of a ship or aircraft

taint (tānt) *vt.* [prob. a merging of ME. *taynten*, to touch + Anglo-Fr. *teinter*, to colour, ult. < L. *tingere*, to wet] **1.** to affect with something injurious, unpleasant, etc.; spoil; infect **2.** to make morally corrupt —*vi.* to become tainted —*n.* **1.** a trace of corruption, disgrace, etc. **2.** an infectious or contaminating trace —**taint'less** *adj.*

tai·pan (tī'pan') *n.* [Abor.] a large, highly venomous Australian snake

take (tāk) *vt.* **took, tak'en, tak'ing** [OE. *tacan* < ON. *taka*] **1.** to get possession of by force or skill; capture, seize, etc. **2.** *a*) to win (a game, a trick at cards, etc.) *b*) to capture (an opponent's piece in chess or draughts) **3.** to get hold of; grasp or catch **4.** to affect; attack [*taken* with a fit] **5.** to capture the fancy of **6.** to obtain, acquire, assume, etc. **7.** to get into one's hand or hold **8.** to eat, drink, etc. for nourishment or as medicine **9.** to enter into a special relationship with [to *take* a wife] **10.** to rent, lease, etc. [to *take* a cottage] **11.** to get regularly by paying for [to *take* a newspaper] **12.** to assume as a responsibility, task, etc. [to *take* a job, *take* a vow] **13.** to assume (a symbol of duty or office, etc.) [the president *took* the chair] **14.** to join or support (one side in a contest, disagreement, etc.) **15.** to assume as if granted or due one [to *take* the blame] **16.** to get, adopt, etc. by selection or choice **17.** to use [*take* a mop to the floor] **18.** *a*) to travel by [to *take* a bus] *b*) to set out on [*take* that path] **19.** to go to for shelter, safety, etc. [to *take* cover] **20.** to consider [to *take* a matter seriously] **21.** *a*) to occupy [*take* a chair] *b*) to use up [it *took* all day] **22.** to require; need [it *takes* money] **23.** to derive (a name, quality, etc.) from something or someone **24.** to extract, as for quotation [he *took* a verse from the Bible] **25.** to obtain by observation, experiment, etc. [*take* a vote] **26.** to be studying as a student in (a course, etc.) **27.** to write down [to *take* notes] **28.** to make (a photograph, picture, etc.) **29.** to make an impression of [*take* his fingerprints] **30.** to win (a prize, etc,) **31.** to undergo [to *take* one's punishment] **32.** to occupy oneself or engage in [to *take* a nap] **33.** to accept (an offer, bet, etc.) **34.** to have a specified reaction to [to *take* a joke in earnest] **35.** to confront and get over, etc. [the horse *took* the jump] **36.** to be affected by [he *took* cold] **37.** to absorb (a dye, polish, etc.) **38.** to understand **39.** to suppose [he *took* her to be a clerk] **40.** to have or feel (an emotion, etc.) [*take* pity] **41.** to make (an objection, etc.) as the result of thought **42.** to conduct; lead [this path *takes* you home] **43.** to escort [*take* a friend to lunch] **44.** to carry [to *take* a book with one] **45.** to remove as by stealing **46.** to remove by death **47.** to subtract [*take* two from four] **48.** to direct (oneself) **49.** [Colloq.] to aim (a specified action) [he *took* a jab at me] **50.** *Gram.* to be used with in construction [a transitive verb *takes* an object] —*vi.* **1.** to get possession **2.** to take root: said of a plant **3.** to catch [the fire *took* rapidly] **4.** to gain public favour; be popular **5.** to be effective in action, etc. [the vaccination *took*] **6.** to detract (*from*) [nothing *took* from the scene's beauty] **7.** to go [to *take* to the hills] **8.** [Colloq. or Dial.] to become (ill) —*n.* **1.** the act or process of taking **2.** something taken **3.** *a*) the amount taken [the day's *take* of fish] *b*) [Chiefly U.S. Slang] money received; receipts **4.** a film scene photographed with an uninterrupted run of the camera **5.** a recording or tape of a performance —**have what it takes** [Colloq.] to possess the attributes necessary for success, popularity, etc. —**take after** to be, act, or look like —**take amiss** to become offended at (an act) as because of a misunderstanding —**take a person out of himself** to distract someone from his preoccupations, anxieties, etc. —**take a person up on** to accept someone's offer —**take as read** to accept (minutes, etc.) without the formality of reading or further discussion —**take back** to retract (something said, etc.) —**take down 1.** to take apart **2.** to humble (a person) **3.** to put in writing; record —**take five** (or **ten**, etc.) [Chiefly U.S.] take a five (or ten, etc.) minute break, as from working —**take for 1.** to consider to be **2.** to mistake for —**take in 1.** to admit; receive **2.** to make smaller **3.** to include **4.** to understand **5.** to cheat; trick **6.** to visit [to *take in* the sights] **7.** to escort in to dinner —**take it** [Slang] to withstand hardship, ridicule, etc. —**take it or leave it** [Colloq.] accept it or not —**take it out of** to sap the energy of; exhaust —**take it out on** [Colloq.] to make (another) suffer for one's own anger, irritation, etc. —**taken short** [Colloq.] to be in sudden need of evacuating the bowels —**take off 1.** to remove (a garment, etc.) **2.** to deduct **3.** to leave the ground or water in flight: said of an aircraft **4.** to spend as a holiday [he *took* Thursday *off*] **5.** [Colloq.] to start **6.** [Colloq.] to mimic —**take on 1.** to acquire; assume **2.** to employ **3.** to undertake (a task, etc.) **4.** to play against; oppose **5.** [Colloq.] to show violent emotion, esp. anger or sorrow —**take oneself off** [Colloq.] to go away, leave —**take one's time** to be unhurried —**take out 1.** to remove **2.** to apply for and get **3.** [Colloq.] to escort **4.** *Bridge* to bid higher than (one's partner) but in a different suit —**take over** to begin controlling, managing, etc. —**take the biscuit** (or **bun,** or **cake**) [Colloq.] to exceed all others (often used ironically) —**take to 1.** to apply oneself to (work, etc.) **2.** to become fond of **3.** to develop a habit of doing **4.** to go to, as for hiding, rest, etc. —**take up 1.** to make tighter or shorter **2.** to pay off (a mortgage, etc.) **3.** to absorb (a liquid) **4.** to accept (a challenge, etc.) **5.** to become interested in (an occupation, belief, etc.) **6.** to occupy (space or time) **7.** to interrupt in disapproval, rebuke, etc. **8.** to resume (something interrupted) —**take upon** (or **on**) **oneself 1.** to take the responsibility for **2.** to undertake Also **take upon** (or **on**) **one** —**take up with** [Colloq.] to become a friend or companion of —**tak′a·ble** *adj.* —**tak′er** *n.*

take·a·way (tāk′ə wā′) *adj.* designating or of prepared food sold by a restaurant to be eaten away from the premises —*n.* an establishment which sells such food

take-home pay (tāk′hōm′) wages or salary after deductions for income tax, national insurance, etc. have been made

tak·en (tāk′'n) *pp.* of TAKE

take-off (-ôf′) *n.* **1.** the act of leaving the ground, as in jumping or flight **2.** the place from which one leaves the ground **3.** the starting point or early stages of something **4.** [Colloq.] an amusing or mocking imitation; burlesque Also **take′-off′**

take·o·ver (-ō′vər) *n.* the act of seizing power or assuming control in a nation, organization, etc.: also **take′-o′ver**

tak·ing (-iŋ) *adj.* attractive; winning —*n.* **1.** the act of one that takes **2.** something taken; catch **3.** [*pl.*] earnings; profits —**tak′ing·ly** *adv.*

tal·a·poin (tal′ə poin′) *n.* [Port. *talapões* < Burmese *tala pôi,* my lord] **1.** a Buddhist monk **2.** a small, long-tailed West African monkey

ta·la·ri·a (tə ler′ē ə) *n. pl.* [L. < *talaris* < *talus,* an ankle] *Myth.* winged sandals or wings on the ankles

talc (talk) *n.* [Fr. < Ar. *ṭalq*] **1.** a soft mineral, magnesium silicate, used to make talcum powder, lubricants, etc. **2.** shortened form of TALCUM POWDER —*vt.* **talcked** or **talced, talck′ing** or **talc′ing** to use talc on

tal·cum (powder) (tal′kəm) a powder for the body and face made of powdered, purified talc, usually perfumed

tale (tāl) *n.* [OE. *talu*] **1.** something told or related **2.** a story of true or fictitious events; narrative **3.** a piece of idle or malicious gossip **4.** a falsehood; lie

tale·bear·er (-ber′ər) *n.* a person who spreads gossip, tells secrets, etc. —**tale′bear′ing** *adj., n.*

tal·ent (tal′ənt) *n.* [OE. *talente* < L. < Gr. *talanton,* a unit of money, weight] **1.** any of various large units of weight or of money in ancient Greece, Rome, the Middle East, etc. **2.** any natural ability or power **3.** a special, superior ability in an art, science, craft, etc. **4.** people who have talent **5.** [Slang] people of the opposite sex —**tal′ent·ed** *adj.*

talent scout a person whose work is recruiting persons of superior ability in the theatre, sports, etc.

ta·ler (tä′lər) *n., pl.* **ta′ler** [G.: see DOLLAR] a former German silver coin

ta·les·man (tālz′mən, tā′lēz-) *n., pl.* **-men** [ME. < ML. *tales* (*de circumstantibus*) such (of the bystanders), phr. in writ summoning them] *Law* a person summoned to fill a vacancy in a jury when the regular jury panel lacks the proper number

ta·li (tā′lī) *n. alt. pl.* of TALUS[1]

tal·i·pes (tal′ə pēz′) *n.* [ModL. < L. *talus,* an ankle + *pes,* a foot] *same as* CLUBFOOT

tal·i·pot (tal′ə pot′) *n.* [Beng. *tālipāt,* palm leaf < Sans.] a palm tree of the East Indies, with gigantic leaves used for fans, umbrellas, etc., and seeds used for buttons: also **talipot palm**

tal·is·man (tal′is mən, -iz-) *n., pl.* **-mans** [Fr. < Ar. < MGr. *telesma,* a consecrated object] **1.** a ring, stone, etc. bearing engraved figures supposed to bring good luck, keep away evil, etc. **2.** anything supposed to have magic power; a charm —**tal′is·man′ic, tal′is·man′i·cal** *adj.*

talk (tôk) *vi.* [ME. *talken,* prob. freq. based on OE. *talian,* to reckon] **1.** to put ideas into, or exchange ideas by, spoken words; speak **2.** to express ideas by speech substitutes [*talk* by signs] **3.** to speak trivially; chatter **4.** to gossip **5.** to confer; consult **6.** to make noises suggestive of speech **7.** to reveal secret information **8.** to make a somewhat informal speech —*vt.* **1.** to put into spoken words **2.** to use in speaking [to *talk* Spanish, to *talk* nonsense] **3.** to discuss **4.** to put into a specified condition by talking [to *talk* oneself hoarse] —*n.* **1.** *a*) the act of talking *b*) conversation **2.** an informal speech **3.** [*often pl.*] a conference **4.** gossip **5.** the subject of conversation, gossip, etc. **6.** empty, frivolous discussion **7.** a particular kind of speech; dialect, etc. **8.** sounds, as by an animal, suggestive of speech —**big talk** [Slang] a bragging —**now you're talking** [Colloq.] you are proposing something acceptable —**talk back** to answer impertinently —**talk big** [Slang] to boast —**talk down 1.** to silence by talking louder, longer, or more effectively than **2.** to instruct (an aircraft) by radio to enable it to land in poor visibility —**talk down to** to talk to (a person) as if he were one's inferior in rank, intellect, etc. —**talk into** to persuade —**talk out 1.** to discuss (a problem, etc.) at length in an effort to reach understanding **2.** to block (a bill, etc.) in a legislative body by lengthy discussion —**talk over 1.** to discuss **2.** to persuade (a person) by talking —**talk round** to persuade to one's opinion —**talk shop** to speak about one's work, esp. when meeting socially rather than at work —**talk up 1.** to promote or praise in discussion **2.** to speak loudly, boldly, etc. —**you can** (or **can't**) **talk** [Colloq.] you are not in a position to comment, criticize, etc. —**talk′er** *n.*

talk·a·thon (tôk′ə thon′) *n.* [TALK + (MAR)ATHON] [Chiefly U.S.] any prolonged period of talking

talk·a·tive (-tiv) *adj.* talking, or fond of talking, a great deal; loquacious —**talk′a·tive·ness** *n.*

talking book a recording of a reading of a book, etc. for use esp. by the blind

talking picture *earlier name for* a film with a synchronized sound track: also [Colloq.] **talk′ie** (-ē) *n.*

talk·ing-to (tôk′iŋ tōō′) *n.* [Colloq.] a rebuke; scolding

tall (tôl) *adj.* [< OE. (ge)tæl, swift] **1.** of more than normal height or stature **2.** having a specified height [five feet *tall*] **3.** [Colloq.] hard to believe; exaggerated [a *tall* story] —**tall′ish** *adj.* —**tall′ness** *n.*

tal·lage (tal′ij) *n.* [ME. *taillage* < OFr.] in feudalism, **1.** a tax levied by kings upon towns and crown lands **2.** a tax levied by feudal lords upon their tenants

tall·boy (tôl′boi) *n.* a high chest of drawers, sometimes in two parts, one above the other, or supported on legs

tal·lit, tal·lith (ta lēt′, tal′is) *n.* [< LHeb. < *tālal,* to cover] *Judaism* a fringed shawl worn by men during morning prayer: cf. Deut. 22:12

tall order a demand which is difficult to fulfil

tal·low (tal′ō) *n.* [prob. < MLowG. *talg*] the pale yellow solid fat extracted from the natural fat of cattle, sheep, etc., used in making candles, soaps, lubricants, etc. —*vt.* to cover or smear with tallow —**tal′low·y** *adj.*

tal·ly (tal′ē) *n.*, *pl.* **-lies** [Anglo-L. *talia* < L. *talea*, a stick] **1.** *a)* orig., a stick with notches representing the amount of a debt *b)* anything used as a record for an account or score **2.** an account, reckoning, or score **3.** *a)* either of two corresponding parts; counterpart *b)* agreement; correspondence **4.** an identifying tag or label —*vt.* **-lied**, **-ly·ing 1.** to put on or as on a tally **2.** to count (usually with *up*) **3.** to put a label or tag on —*vi.* **1.** to tally something **2.** to agree; correspond

tal·ly·ho (tal′ē hō′; *for n. & v.*, tal′ē hō′) *interj.* [altered < Fr. *taiaut*] the cry of a hunter on sighting the fox —*n.*, *pl.* **-hos′ 1.** a cry of "tallyho" **2.** a coach drawn by four horses —*vi.* to cry "tallyho"

tal·ly-sys·tem (-sis′tam) *n.* a method of trading by which goods are obtained on credit to be paid for at stipulated intervals, a tally being kept of the account

Tal·mud (tal′mood, -mad) *n.* [LHeb. *talmūdh*, lit., learning < *lāmadh*, to learn] the writings constituting the Jewish civil and religious law —**Tal·mud′ic, Tal·mud′i·cal** *adj.* —**Tal′·mud·ism** *n.* —**Tal′mud·ist** *n.*

tal·on (tal′an) *n.* [< ÒFr., ult. < L. *talus*, an ankle] **1.** the claw of a bird of prey, or, sometimes, of an animal **2.** a human finger or hand when like a claw in appearance or grasp —**tal′oned** *adj.*

ta·lus¹ (tā′las) *n.*, *pl.* **-lus·es, -li** (-lī) [ModL. < L., an ankle] **1.** the anklebone **2.** the entire ankle

ta·lus² (tā′las) *n.* [Fr. ? < OFr. *talu* < L. *talutium*, surface indication of gold under the earth] **1.** a slope **2.** the sloping face of a wall in a fortification **3.** *same as* SCREE

tam (tam) *n.* *short for* TAM-O′-SHANTER

ta·ma·le (ta mä′lē) *n.* [< MexSp. < Nahuatl *tamalli*] a native Mexican food of minced meat and red peppers rolled in maize flour, wrapped in maize husks, and cooked by baking, steaming, etc.

ta·man·dua (ta′man′dwa, tä′män dwä′) *n.* [Port. < Braz. (Tupi) < *taixi*, ant + *mondē*, to catch] a small, tree-dwelling anteater of tropical America

tam·a·rack (tam′a rak′) *n.* [< Algonquian] **1.** an American larch tree, usually found in swamps **2.** its wood

tam·a·rin (tam′a rin) *n.* [Fr. < the native (Carib) name] any of several South American marmosets with long, silky fur

tam·a·rind (tam′a rind) *n.* [< Sp. < Ar. *tamr hindī*, date of India] **1.** a tropical leguminous tree with yellow flowers and brown pods with an acid pulp **2.** its fruit, used in foods, medicine, etc.

tam·a·risk (tam′a risk) *n.* [< ME. < LL. *tamariscus*, for L. *tamarix*] any of a genus of trees or shrubs with slender branches and feathery flower clusters, common near salt water

tam·ba·la (tam bä′la) *n.*, *pl.* **ma′tam·ba′la** (mä′-) [native term, lit., rooster] *see* MONETARY UNITS, table (Malawi)

tam·bour (tam′boor) *n.* [< MFr. < OFr. < Ar. *tanbūr*, stringed instrument < Per.] **1.** a drum **2.** an embroidery frame of two hoops, one closely fitting inside the other, that hold the cloth stretched between them **3.** a door, panel, etc. as in a cabinet, made of narrow, wooden slats that glide flexibly in grooves, as around curves **4.** a drum-shaped stone forming part of a pillar **5.** vestibule in a church designed to exclude draughts **6.** a palisade constructed to defend a gateway —*vt.*, *vi.* to embroider on a tambour

tam·bou·rin (tam′ba rin) *n.* [Fr., dim. of *tambour*, drum] **1.** a small drum **2.** a Provençal folk dance **3.** the music for this

tam·bou·rine (tam′ba rēn′) *n.* [Fr., dim. of *tambour*: see TAMBOUR] a shallow, single-headed hand drum having jingling metal discs in the rim: played by shaking, hitting with the knuckles, etc. —**tam′bou·rin′ist** *n.*

tame (tām) *adj.* **tam′er, tam′est** [OE. *tam*] **1.** changed from a wild state, as an animal, for use by man **2.** gentle; docile **3.** crushed as by domestication; submissive **4.** without force or spirit; dull —*vt.* **tamed, tam′ing 1.** to make tame, or domestic **2.** to make gentle, docile, or spiritless **3.** to make less intense; soften —**tam′able, tame′able** *adj.* —**tame′ly** *adv.* —**tame′ness** *n.* —**tam′er** *n.*

tame·less (-lis) *adj.* **1.** not tamed **2.** not tamable

Tam·il (tam′l, tum′-) *n.* **1.** *pl.* **-ils, -il** any of a Tamil-speaking people of S India and N Ceylon **2.** the Dravidian language of the Tamils, ancient or modern

TAMBOURINE

tam-o′-shan·ter (tam′a shan′tar) *n.* [< main character of R. Burns's poem *Tam o'Shanter*] a Scottish cap with a round, flat top and, often, a centre tassel

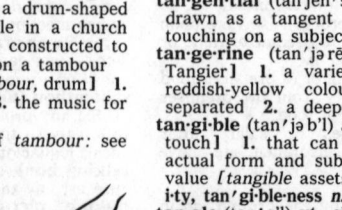

TAM-O′-SHANTER

tamp (tamp) *vt.* [< ? TAMPION] **1.** in blasting, to pack clay, sand, etc. around the charge in (the drill hole) **2.** to pack or pound (*down*) by a series of blows or taps

tamp·er¹ (tam′par) *n.* a person or thing that tamps; specif., any of various instruments or tools for tamping

tam·per² (tam′par) *vi.* [var. of TEMPER] [Archaic] to plot; scheme —**tamper with 1.** to make secret, illegal arrangements with, as by bribing **2.** to meddle with, esp. so as to damage, etc. —**tam′per·er** *n.*

tam·pi·on (tam′pē an) *n.* [< Fr. *tampion* < *tapon*, a bung < Frank.] a plug or stopper put in the muzzle of a gun not in use

tam·pon (tam′pan) *n.* [Fr.: see prec.] a plug of cotton or other absorbent material put into a body cavity, wound, etc. to stop bleeding or absorb secretions —*vt.* to put a tampon into

tam-tam (tam′tam) *n.* [< Hindi] **1.** a large gong **2.** a tom-tom

tan (tan) *n.* [MFr. < ML. *tannum*] **1.** *same as* TANBARK **2.** tannin or a solution made from it **3.** *a)* a yellowish-brown colour *b)* such a colour given to fair skin as by exposure to the sun —*adj.* **tan′ner, tan′nest** yellowish-brown —*vt.* **tanned, tan′ning 1.** to change (hide) into leather by soaking in tannin **2.** to produce a tan colour in, as by exposure to the sun **3.** [Colloq.] to whip severely; flog —*vi.* to become tanned

tan tangent

tan·a·ger (tan′a jar) *n.* [ModL. *tanagra* < Port. < Tupi *tangara*] any of various small, American songbirds: the males usually are brilliantly coloured

Tan·a·gra (tan′a gra; ta nag′ra) *n.* [< *Tanagra*, town in Boeotia, in ancient Greece] a terra cotta figurine found in tombs near Tanagra

tan·bark (tan′bärk′) *n.* any bark containing tannin, used to tan hides and, after the tannin has been extracted, to cover circus rings, etc.

tan·dem (tan′dam) *adv.* [orig. punning use of L. *tandem*, at length (of time)] one behind another; in single file —*n.* **1.** a two-wheeled carriage drawn by horses harnessed tandem **2.** a team, as of horses, harnessed tandem **3.** a bicycle with two seats and sets of pedals placed tandem

tang (taŋ) *n.* [ON. *tangi*, a sting] **1.** a projecting point or prong on a knife, file, etc. that fits into the handle **2.** a strong, penetrating taste or odour **3.** a touch or trace (*of*) **4.** a special or characteristic flavour, quality, etc. —*vt.* to provide (a knife, etc.) with a tang

tan·ge·lo (tan′ja lō′) *n.*, *pl.* **-los′** [TANG(ERINE) + (*pom*)*elo*, grapefruit] a fruit produced by crossing a tangerine with a grapefruit

tan·gent (tan′jant) *adj.* [< L. prp. of *tangere*, to touch] **1.** touching **2.** *Geom.* touching and not intersecting a curved line or surface at one point only: said of a line or plane —*n.* **1.** *Geom.* a tangent line, curve, or surface **2.** *Trigonometry* the ratio of the side opposite a given acute angle in a right triangle to the adjacent side —**go** (or **fly**) **off at** (or **on**) **a tangent** to change suddenly from one line of action, or conversation, etc. to another —**tan′gen·cy** *n.*

tan·gen·tial (tan jen′shal) *adj.* **1.** of or like a tangent **2.** drawn as a tangent **3.** going off at a tangent **4.** merely touching on a subject —**tan·gen′tial·ly** *adv.*

tan·ge·rine (tan′ja rēn′, tan′ja rēn′) *n.* [< Fr. *Tanger*, Tangier] **1.** a variety of mandarin orange with a deep, reddish-yellow colour and segments that are easily separated **2.** a deep, reddish-yellow colour

tan·gi·ble (tan′ja b'l) *adj.* [< LL. *tangibilis* < L. *tangere*, to touch] **1.** that can be touched or felt by touch; having actual form and substance **2.** that can be appraised for value [*tangible* assets] **3.** definite; objective —**tan′gi·bil′·i·ty, tan′gi·ble·ness** *n.* —**tan′gi·bly** *adv.*

tan·gle (tan′g′l) *vt.* **-gled, -gling** [prob. var. of ME. *taglen*, to entangle] **1.** to hinder, obstruct, or confuse by encircling, entwining, etc. **2.** to catch as in a net or snare; trap **3.** to make a confused muddle of; intertwist —*vi.* **1.** to become tangled **2.** [Colloq.] to quarrel or fight —*n.* **1.** an intertwisted, confused mass, as of string, branches, etc; snarl **2.** a jumbled, confused condition **3.** a perplexed state —**tan′gler** *n.* —**tan′gly** *adj.*

tan·go (tan′gō) *n.*, *pl.* **-gos** [AmSp.] **1.** a S American dance with long gliding steps and dips **2.** music for this —*vi.* **-goed, -go·ing** to dance the tango

tang·y (taŋ′ē) *adj.* **tang′i·er, tang′i·est** having a tang, or sharp flavour —**tang′i·ness** *n.*

tan·ist (tan′ist) *n.* [Ir. & Gael. *tanaiste*, next heir] in ancient Ireland, the elected heir of a living Celtic chief in a system (**tanistry**) limiting the choice to the chief's kin

tank (taŋk) *n.* [< Sp. & Port. *tanque* < *estancar*, to stop the flow of] 1. any large container for liquid or gas [an oil *tank*] 2. [name chosen to conceal secret manufacture] an armoured, self-propelled combat vehicle armed with guns and moving on tractor treads —*vt.* to put or store in a tank —**tank up** [Colloq.] 1. to supply with or get a full tank of petrol 2. to drink much liquor —**tank'ful** *n., pl.* **-fuls'**
tan·ka (taŋ'kə) *n.* [Jap.] a Japanese verse form of 31 syllables in five unrhymed lines, the first and third having five syllables each and the others seven
tank·age (taŋ'kij) *n.* 1. the capacity of a tank or tanks 2. a) the storage of fluids, gases, etc. in tanks b) the charge for such storage 3. slaughterhouse waste from which the fat has been rendered in tanks, dried, and ground for use as fertilizer
tank·ard (taŋ'kərd) *n.* [ME.] a large drinking cup with a handle and, often, a hinged lid
tank car a large tank on wheels, for carrying liquids and gases by rail
tank·er (taŋ'kər) *n.* 1. a ship or lorry for carrying a cargo of oil or other liquids in large tanks 2. a plane which refuels another plane in flight
tank farming *same as* HYDROPONICS
tan·ner (tan'ər) *n.* a person whose work is tanning hides
tan·ner·y (-ē) *n., pl.* **-ner·ies** a place where hides are tanned
tan·nic (tan'ik) *adj.* of, like, or obtained from tanbark or tannin
tannic acid a yellowish, astringent substance, derived from oak bark, gallnuts, etc. and used in tanning, medicine, etc.
tan·nin (tan'in) *n.* *same as* TANNIC ACID
tan·sy (tan'zē) *n., pl.* **-sies** [OFr. *tanesie*, ult. < LL. *tanacetum* < ? Gr. *athanasia*, immortality] any of various strong-smelling plants with clusters of small, yellow flowers
tan·ta·lite (tan'tə līt') *n.* [G. *Tantalit*: see TANTALUM + -ITE[1]] a heavy, black, crystalline mineral, the principal ore of tantalum
tan·ta·lize (tan'tə līz') *vt.* **-lized, -liz'ing** [< *Tantalus*: see TANTALUS] to tease or disappoint by promising or showing something and then withholding it —**tan'ta·li·za'tion** *n.* —**tan'ta·liz'er** *n.* —**tan'ta·liz'ing·ly** *adv.*
tan·ta·lum (tan'tə ləm) *n.* [ModL. < *Tantalus*: see TANTALUS: from the difficulty in extracting it from its ore] a rare, steel-blue, metallic chemical element that resists corrosion, used to make surgical instruments, parts for radio valves, etc.: symbol, Ta; at. wt., 180.948; at.no., 73
tan·ta·lus (tan'tə ləs) *n.* [after *Tantalus*, in Gr. Myth. a king doomed in the lower world to stand surrounded by inaccessible water and fruit] a case or stand in which bottles or decanters may be locked with their contents visible
tan·ta·mount (tan'tə mount') *adj.* [< Anglo-Fr. < OFr. *tant* (< L. *tantus*, so much) + *amonter* (see AMOUNT)] having equal value, effect, etc.; equivalent (*to*)
tan·ta·ra (tan'tə rə; tan tar'ə, -tär'ə) *n.* [echoic] a trumpet blast or fanfare
tan·tiv·y (tan tiv'ē) *adv.* [prob. echoic of sound of horse galloping] at full gallop; headlong —*n., pl.* **-tiv'ies** 1. a gallop 2. a hunting cry
tan·tra (tan'trə, tun'-) *n.* [Sans., a doctrine] [*often* T-] any of a class of Hindu or Buddhist religious writings that are mystical in nature
tan·trum (tan'trəm) *n.* [< ?] a violent, wilful outburst of annoyance, rage, etc.; childish fit of bad temper
tan·yard (tan'yärd') *n.* a tannery
Taoi·seach (tē'shakh) [Ir., lit., leader] the prime minister of the Republic of Ireland
Tao·ism (tä'ō iz'm, tou'iz'm) *n.* [Chin. *tao*, the way + -ISM] a Chinese religion and philosophy based on the doctrines of Lao-tse and advocating simplicity, selflessness, etc. —**Tao'-ist** *n., adj.* —**Tao·is'tic** *adj.*
tap[1] (tap) *vt.* **tapped, tap'ping** [OFr. *taper*, prob. echoic] 1. to strike lightly 2. to strike something lightly with 3. to make or do by tapping [to *tap* a message] 4. [U.S.] to repair (a shoe) by adding a thickness of leather, etc. to the heel or sole —*vi.* 1. to strike a light, rapid blow 2. to perform a tap dance 3. to move with a tapping sound —*n.* 1. a light, rapid blow, or the sound made by it 2. a small metal plate attached to the heel or toe of a shoe, as for tap dancing —**tap'per** *n.*
tap[2] (tap) *n.* [OE. *tæppa*] 1. a device for controlling the flow of liquid from a pipe, etc. 2. a plug, cork, etc. for stopping a hole in a container holding a liquid 3. liquor of a certain kind, as drawn from a certain tap 4. a draining of liquid from a body cavity 5. a tool used to cut threads in a female screw 6. the act of wiretapping 7. a place in an electrical circuit where a connection can be made —*vt.* **tapped, tap'ping** 1. to put a tap or spigot on 2. to make a hole in for drawing off liquid 3. to pull out the plug from 4. to draw (liquid) from a container, cavity, etc. 5. to make use of [to *tap* new resources] 6. to make a connection with (an electric circuit, telephone line, etc.); specif., to wiretap (a telephone line) 7. to cut the inner threads of (a nut, etc.) 8. [Slang] to borrow or get money from —**on tap** 1. in a

tapped cask and ready to be drawn 2. [Colloq.] ready for consideration or action —**tap'per** *n.*
ta·pa (tä'pə) *n.* [< native Polynesian name] an unwoven cloth made in the Pacific islands from the treated inner bark of a mulberry tree
tap dance a dance performed with sharp, loud taps of the foot, toe, or heel at each step —**tap'-dance'** *vi.* **-danced', -danc'ing** —**tap'-danc'er** *n.*
tape (tāp) *n.* [OE. *tæppe*, a fillet] 1. a strong, narrow, woven strip of cotton, linen, etc. used for binding, tying, etc. 2. a narrow strip or band of steel, paper, etc. 3. a strip of cloth stretched above the finishing line of a race 4. *short for: a)* TAPE MEASURE *b)* ADHESIVE TAPE, MASKING TAPE, etc. 5. *a) short for* MAGNETIC TAPE *b)* a recording on magnetic tape —*vt.* **taped, tap'ing** 1. to put tape on or around, as for binding, tying, etc. 2. to measure by using a tape measure 3. to record (sound, video material, computer data, etc.) on magnetic tape —**have** (someone or something) **taped** to have a shrewd idea of (a person's character, a situation) —**tap'er** *n.*
tape deck a simplified magnetic-tape assembly, without an amplifier or speaker but having tape reels, drive, and recording and playback heads
tape machine a telegraphic device that records stock market quotations, etc., on paper tape
tape measure a tape with marks showing lengths, used for measuring: also **tape'line'** (-līn') *n.*
ta·per (tā'pər) *n.* [OE. *tapur*] 1. a slender candle 2. a long wick coated with wax, used for lighting candles, lamps, etc. 3. any feeble light 4. *a)* a gradual decrease in width or thickness [the *taper* of a pyramid] *b)* a gradual decrease in action, power, etc. —*adj.* gradually decreased in size to a point —*vt., vi.* 1. to decrease gradually in width or thickness 2. to lessen; diminish Often with *off*
tape-re·cord (tāp'ri kôrd') *vt.* to record on magnetic tape
tape recorder a device for recording on magnetic tape and, usually, reproducing the sound: see MAGNETIC RECORDING
tape recording 1. the act of recording on magnetic tape 2. the magnetic tape used in recording 3. the sounds recorded on magnetic tape
tap·es·try (tap'is trē) *n., pl.* **-tries** [< MFr. < OFr. *tapis*, a carpet, ult. < Gr. dim. of *tapēs*, a carpet] a heavy woven cloth with decorative designs and pictures, used as a wall hanging, furniture covering, etc. —*vt.* **-tried, -try·ing** to decorate as with a tapestry: usually in the pp.
tape·worm (tāp'wurm') *n.* any of various flatworms that live as parasites in the intestines of man and other vertebrates
tap·i·o·ca (tap'ē ō'kə) *n.* [Port. & Sp. < Tupi < *ty*, juice + *pya*, heart + *oc*, to squeeze out] a starchy, granular substance prepared from the root of the cassava plant, used for puddings, etc.
ta·pir (tā'pər) *n., pl.* **ta'pirs, ta'pir:** see PLURAL, II, D, 1 [Sp. < Tupi *tapyra*] any of various large, piglike mammals found mostly in tropical America: tapirs have flexible snouts
tap·pet (tap'it) *n.* [TAP[1] + -ET] in an engine or machine, a projection or lever that moves or is moved by recurring contact, as with a cam
tap·room (tap'rōm') *n.* a room with a bar at which alcoholic drinks are served

TAPIR
(0.7-1.0 m high at shoulder)

tap·root (-rōōt', -root') *n.* [TAP[2] + ROOT[1]] a main root, growing almost vertically downwards, from which branch roots spread out
taps (taps) *n.* [< TAP[1], because orig. a drum signal] 1. [U.S.] a bugle call to put out the lights for the night, as in an army camp: also sounded at a military funeral 2. a song sung at the conclusion of an evening gathering by Girl Guides and Boy Scouts
tap·ster (tap'stər) *n.* [ME. < OE. *tæppestre*, barmaid] [Now Rare] a barman
ta·pu (tä'pōō) *adj.* [Maori] [N.Z.] *same as* TABOO
tar[1] (tär) *n.* [OE. *teru*] 1. a thick, sticky, brown to black liquid obtained by the destructive distillation of wood, coal, etc.: tars are used for protecting and preserving surfaces, in making many organic compounds, etc. 2. loosely, any of the solids in smoke, as from tobacco —*vt.* **tarred, tar'ring** to cover or smear with or as with tar —*adj.* 1. of or like tar 2. tarred —**tar and feather** to cover (a person) with tar and feathers, as in punishment by mob action —**tarred with the same brush** (or **stick**) having the same faults or obnoxious traits
tar[2] (tär) *n.* [< TAR(PAULIN)] [Colloq.] a sailor
tar·a·did·dle, tarr·a·did·dle (tar'ə did''l) *n.* [prob. < DIDDLE[2]] [Colloq.] 1. a petty lie; fib 2. nonsense
ta·ran·tass (tä'rän täs') *n.* [Russ. *tarantas*] a large, low, four-wheeled Russian carriage without springs

tar·an·tel·la (tar'ən tel'ə) *n.* [It., dim. of *Taranto*, town of SE Italy] **1.** a fast, whirling southern Italian dance for couples **2.** music for this

ta·ran·tu·la (tə ran'tyoo lə) *n., pl.* **-las, -lae** (-lē) [< ML. < It. *Taranto*, town of SE Italy] **1.** a large, hairy, somewhat poisonous spider of S Europe **2.** a similar spider of the SW U.S. and tropical America

ta·rax·a·cum (tə raks'ə kəm) *n.* [< ML. < Ar. *tarakhshaqūn*, wild chicory < ? Per.] **1.** any of various plants of the genus Taraxacum, as the dandelion **2.** the root of the dandelion, used in medicine

tar·boosh (tär boosh') *n.* [Ar. *tarbūsh*] a brimless cap of cloth or felt shaped like a truncated cone, worn by Moslem men

Tar·de·noi·si·an (tär'də noi'zēən) *adj.* [after *Fère-en-Tardenois*, town in NE France, where implements were found] of a mesolithic culture characterized by small flint implements of geometric form

tar·di·grade (tär'də grād') *n.* [Fr. < L. *tardigradus*, slow-moving] any of various minute water animals with segmented bodies and four pairs of unsegmented legs

tar·dy (tär'dē) *adj.* **-di·er, -di·est** [< OFr. < L. *tardus*, slow] **1.** slow in moving, acting, etc. **2.** late, delayed, or dilatory —**tar'di·ly** *adv.* —**tar'di·ness** *n.*

tare¹ (ter) *n.* [< or akin to MDu. *tarwe*, wheat] **1.** any of several vetches **2.** the seed of any of these plants **3.** *Bible* a weed, perhaps the darnel

tare² (ter) *n.* [< MFr. < It. < Ar. *taraha*, to reject] deduction of the weight of a container, wrapper, etc. from the total weight to determine the weight of the contents —*vt.* **tared, tar'ing** to find. out, allow for, or mark the tare of

tar·get (tär'git) *n.* [< MFr. dim. of *targe*, a shield < Frank.] **1.** orig., a small, round shield **2.** *a*) a round, flat board, straw coil, etc., marked as with concentric circles, aimed at in archery, rifle practice, etc. *b*) any object that is shot at, bombarded, etc. **3.** an objective; goal **4.** an object of attack, criticism, or ridicule

Tar·gum (tär'goom) *n., pl.* **Tar'gums:** Heb. **Tar·gu·mim** (tär goom'im) [< Heb. < Aram. *targūm*, lit., interpretation] any of several translations or paraphrases of parts of the Hebrew Scriptures, written in the vernacular (Aramaic) of Judea

tar·iff (tar'if) *n.* [< It. < Ar. *ta'rif*, information] **1.** a list or system of taxes upon exports or, esp., imports **2.** a tax of this kind, or its rate **3.** any list of prices, charges, etc. **4.** [Colloq.] any bill, charge, etc. —*vt.* **1.** to set a tariff on **2.** to fix the price of according to a tariff

tar·la·tan, tar·le·tan (tär'lə tən) *n.* [Fr. *tarlatane*] a thin, stiff, open-weave muslin

tar·mac (tär'mak) *n.* [< TAR¹ & J. L. McAdam (1756—1836), Brit. engineer] **1.** *a trademark for* a paving material of crushed stone rolled and bound with a mixture of tar and bitumen **2.** a road, airport runway, etc. paved with tarmac —*vt.* to cover (a surface) with tarmac Also **tar'mac·ad'am**

tarn (tärn) *n.* [< or akin to ON. *tjörn*] a small mountain lake

tar·na·tion (tär nā'shən) *interj., n.* [prob. < dial form of ETERNAL + (DAM)NATION] *U.S. dial. var. of* DAMNATION: used as an intensive [what in *tarnation* is that?]

tar·nish (tär'nish) *vt.* [< MFr. *ternir*, to make dim, prob. < OHG. *tarnjan*, to conceal] **1.** to dull the lustre of (a metal) by exposure to the air **2.** to sully (a reputation, etc.) —*vi.* **1.** to lose lustre; discolour, as from oxidation **2.** to become sullied —*n.* **1.** a being tarnished; dullness **2.** the film of discolouration on a tarnished surface **3.** a stain; blemish —**tar'nish·a·ble** *adj.*

ta·ro (tä'rō) *n., pl.* **-ros** [Tahitian] **1.** a large, tropical Asiatic plant, cultivated for its edible tubers, the source of poi **2.** the tuber of this plant

tar·ot (tar'ō, ta rō') *n.* [Fr., ? ult. < Ar. *taraha*, to remove] [*often* T-] any of a set of playing cards with pictures of symbolic figures, used in fortunetelling

tarp (tärp) *n.* [U.S. & Aust. Colloq.] *shortened form of* TARPAULIN

tar·pan (tär'pan) *n.* [Tatar] a small horse, now extinct, of the Russian steppes

tar paper a heavy paper impregnated with tar, used as a base for roofing, etc.

tar·pau·lin (tär pô'lin) *n.* [TAR¹ + -*paulin*, prob. < *palling* < PALL²] **1.** canvas coated with a waterproofing compound **2.** a sheet of this spread over something to keep it dry **3.** a hat made of, or covered with, this fabric **4.** [Obs.] a sailor

tar·pon (tär'pən, -pon) *n., pl.* **-pons, -pon:** see PLURAL, II, D, 1 [< ?] a large, silvery game fish of the herring group, found in the warmer parts of the W Atlantic

tar·ra·gon (tar'ə gən) *n.* [Sp. < Ar. < Gr. *drakōn*, dragon] **1.** a wormwood whose fragrant leaves are used for seasoning **2.** these leaves

tar·ry¹ (tar'ē) *vi.* **-ried, -ry·ing** [prob. < OE. *tergan*, to vex, merged with OFr. *targer*, to delay < L. *tardus*, slow] **1.** to

delay, linger, etc. **2.** to stay for a time, esp. longer than intended **3.** to wait —**tar'ri·er** *n.*

tar·ry² (tär'ē) *adj.* **-ri·er, -ri·est** **1.** of or like tar **2.** covered or smeared with tar —**tar'ri·ness** *n.*

tar·sal (tär's'l) *adj.* of the tarsus —*n.* a tarsal bone or plate

tar·si·er (tär'sē ər) *n.* [Fr. < *tarse*, TARSUS, from the foot structure] any of several small primates of the East Indies and the Philippines, with very large eyes and a long tail: they live in trees and are active at night

tar·sus (tär'səs) *n., pl.* **-si** (-sī) [ModL. < Gr. *tarsos*, flat of the foot] **1.** the human ankle, consisting of seven bones **2.** *Zool.* a) a group of bones in the ankle region of the hind limbs of vertebrates having four limbs b) the fifth segment from the base of an insect leg **3.** the connective tissue supporting the free edge of each eyelid

tart¹ (tärt) *adj.* [OE. *teart*] **1.** sharp in taste; sour; acid **2.** sharp in meaning; cutting [a *tart* answer] —**tart'ly** *adv.* —**tart'ness** *n.*

tart² (tärt) *n.* [MFr. *tarte*] **1.** a small shell of pastry filled with jam, custard, etc. **2.** a pie filled with fruit or other sweet filling having a top crust

tart³ (tärt) *n.* [< prec., orig. slang term of endearment] a prostitute or any woman of loose morals —**tart up** [Slang] to clothe, decorate, etc., often in a cheap and showy way

tar·tan (tär't'n) *n.* [prob. < MFr. *tiretaine*, a cloth of mixed fibres] **1.** woollen cloth with a woven plaid pattern, esp. as worn in the Scottish Highlands, where each clan has its own pattern **2.** any plaid cloth or pattern —*adj.* of or made of tartan

Tar·tar (tär'tər) *n.* [< ML. *Tartarus* < Per. *Tātār*] **1.** *same as* TATAR **2.** [*usually* t-] a bad-tempered person hard to deal with —*adj.* of Tatary or the Tatars —**catch a tartar** to attack or oppose someone too strong for one

tar·tar (tär'tər) *n.* [< ML. < MGr. *tartaron* < ? Ar.] **1.** a potassium salt of tartaric acid forming a reddish, crustlike deposit in wine casks: in purified form called CREAM OF TARTAR **2.** a hard deposit on the teeth, consisting of saliva proteins, food deposits, calcium phosphate, etc.

Tar·tar·e·an (tär ter'ē ən) *adj.* designating or of Tartarus, in Greek mythology an abyss below Hades, or Hades itself

tartar emetic a poisonous salt of tartaric acid used in medicine to cause vomiting, in dyeing as a mordant, etc.

tar·tar·ic (tär tar'ik, -tär'-) *adj.* of, containing, or derived from tartar or tartaric acid

tartaric acid a colourless, crystalline acid found in fruit juices, etc. and obtained from tartar: it is used in dyeing, photography, medicine, etc.

tar·tar sauce (tär'tər) [< Fr.] a sauce, as for seafood, consisting of mayonnaise with chopped pickles, olives, capers, etc.: also sp. **tartare sauce**

tar·trate (tär'trāt) *n.* a salt or ester of tartaric acid

tar·whine (tär'wīn) *n.* [Abor.] an edible Australian fish

Tar·zan (tär'zən, -zan) *n.* [after *Tarzan*, jungle-raised hero of stories by E. R. Burroughs (1875-1950), U.S. writer] [*also* t-] a very strong, virile, and agile man: often used humorously

task (täsk) *n.* [< ONormFr. < ML. *tasca*, for *taxa*, a tax < L. *taxare*, to rate, TAX] **1.** a piece of work that one must do **2.** any piece of work **3.** any difficult undertaking —*vt.* **1.** to assign a task to **2.** to put a strain on; tax —**take to task** to reprimand or scold

task force a specially trained, self-contained military unit assigned a specific mission or task

task·mas·ter (-mäs'tər) *n.* a person who assigns tasks to others, esp. when exacting or severe

Tasmanian devil a badgerlike, voracious, flesh-eating marsupial of Tasmania

Tasmanian wolf (or **tiger**) a fierce, flesh-eating marsupial of Tasmania

Tass (tas) [< the initial letters of the full name] a Soviet agency for gathering and distributing news

tass (tas) *n.* [< ME. *tasse* < MFr. < Ar. *tassa* < Per. *tast*, a cup] [Obs. or Scot.] **1.** a small cup **2.** a small draught

tas·sel (tas''l) *n.* [OFr., a knob] **1.** an ornamental tuft of threads, cords, etc. of equal length, hanging loosely from a knob or knot **2.** something resembling this; specif., a tassellike tuft, as of corn silk on an ear of corn —*vt.* **-selled, -sel·ling** to put tassels on —*vi.* [Chiefly U.S.] to grow tassels, as maize

taste (tāst) *vt.* **tast'ed, tast'ing** [OFr. *taster*, to touch, taste] **1.** to test the flavour of by putting a little in one's mouth **2.** to detect the flavour of by the sense of taste **3.** to eat or drink, esp. a small amount of **4.** to experience; have [to *taste* defeat] —*vi.* **1.** to tell flavours by the sense of taste **2.** to eat or drink a small amount (*of*) **3.** to have the specific flavour (*of*) [the salad *tastes* of garlic] **4.** to have a

TARSIER
(head & body
7-17 cm long;
tail 12-25 cm
long)

sensation or limited experience (*of* something) —*n.* **1.** the sense by which the taste buds on the tongue, when stimulated by a substance, distinguish it as sweet, sour, salty, or bitter **2.** the quality perceived through this sense; flavour; savour **3.** a small amount put into the mouth to test the flavour **4.** a slight experience of something; sample **5.** a bit; trace; touch **6.** *a)* the ability to appreciate and judge what is beautiful, appropriate, or excellent in art, dress, etc. *b)* a specific preference [a *taste* for red ties] *c)* a style or way that shows such ability or preferences **7.** a liking; inclination —**in bad, poor,** etc. (or **good, excellent,** etc.) **taste** in a form, style, or manner showing a bad (or good) sense of beauty, excellence, fitness, etc. —**to one's taste 1.** pleasing to one **2.** so as to please one

taste bud any of the cells in the epithelium of the tongue that are the sense organs of taste

taste·ful (tāst'fəl) *adj.* having or showing good taste [*tasteful* décor] —**taste'ful·ly** *adv.* —**taste'ful·ness** *n.*

taste·less (-lis) *adj.* **1.** *a)* without taste or flavour; flat; insipid *b)* dull; uninteresting **2.** lacking good taste; in poor taste —**taste'less·ly** *adv.* —**taste'less·ness** *n.*

tast·er (tās'tər) *n.* **1.** a person who tastes; specif., *a)* one employed to test the quality of wines, teas, etc. by tasting *b)* a servant, as in a royal house, who tastes his master's food and drink to detect poisoning **2.** any of several devices used for tasting, sampling or testing

tast·y (-tē) *adj.* **tast'i·er, tast'i·est 1.** that tastes good; appetizing **2.** [Now Rare] *same as* TASTEFUL —**tast'i·ly** *adv.* —**tast'i·ness** *n.*

tat¹ (tat) *vt.* **tat'ted, tat'ting** [< TATTING] to make by tatting —*vi.* to do tatting

tat² (tat) *n.* [< ? TAP¹] *see* TIT FOR TAT

tat³ (tat) *n.* [*back formation from* TATTY] [Colloq.] a person or thing that is tatty

ta·ta (ta tä') *interj.* [Colloq.] goodbye: orig. a child's term

ta·ta·mi (tə tä'mē) *n., pl.* **-mi, -mis** [Jap.] a floor mat woven of rice straw, used traditionally in Japanese homes for sitting on, as when eating

Ta·tar (tät'ər) *n.* [Per.] **1.** a member of any of the Mongolian and Turkic tribes that invaded W Asia and E Europe in the Middle Ages **2.** any of a Turkic people living in a region of EC European Russia and in parts of Asia **3.** any of their Turkic languages —*adj.* of the Tatars or their languages

'ta·ter, ta·ter (tät'ər) *n. dial. form of* POTATO: also **ta·tie** (-tē), **ta·tie** (tat'ē)

tat·ler (tat'lər) *n. obs. sp. of* tattler (*see* TATTLE)

tat·ter (tat'ər) *n.* [prob. < ON. *töturr*, rags] **1.** a torn and hanging shred or piece, as of a garment **2.** a separate shred; rag **3.** [*pl.*] torn, ragged clothes —*vt., vi.* to reduce to tatters; make or become ragged —**tat'tered** *adj.*

tat·ter·de·mal·ion (tat'ər di māl'yən, -mal'-) *n.* [< prec. + ?] a person in torn, ragged clothes; ragamuffin

tat·ting (tat'iŋ) *n.* [prob. < dial. *tat*, to tangle] **1.** a fine lace made by looping and knotting thread that is wound on a hand shuttle **2.** the act of making this

tat·tle (tat'l) *vi.* **-tled, -tling** [prob. < MDu. *tatelen*, of echoic origin] **1.** to talk idly; chatter **2.** to tell others' secrets —*n.* idle talk; chatter —**tat'tler** *n.*

TATTING

tat·tle·tale (-tāl') *n.* an informer; talebearer

tat·too¹ (ta tōō') *vt.* **-tooed', -too'ing** [< Tahitian *tatau*] **1.** to puncture (the skin) with a needle and insert indelible colours so as to leave permanent marks or designs **2.** to make (marks or designs) on the skin this way —*n., pl.* **-toos'** a tattooed mark or design —**tat·too'er, tat·too'ist** *n.*

tat·too² (ta tōō') *n., pl.* **-toos'** [< Du. < *tape toe*, shut the tap: a signal for closing barrooms] **1.** *a)* a signal on a drum, bugle, etc. summoning soldiers, etc. to their quarters at night *b)* a military spectacle featuring marching, etc. **2.** any continuous drumming, rapping, etc. —*vt., vi.* **-tooed', -too'ing** to beat or tap

tat·ty (tat'ē) *adj.* **-ti·er, -ti·est** [prob. akin to OE. *taetteca*, a rag] shabby, decrepit, tawdry, etc. —**tat'ti·ly** *adv.* —**tat'ti·ness** *n.*

tau (tou) *n.* [Gr.] the nineteenth letter of the Greek alphabet (T, τ)

taught (tôt) *pt. & pp. of* TEACH

taunt (tônt) *vt.* [< ? Fr. *tant pour tant*, tit for tat] **1.** to reproach in scornful or sarcastic language; jeer at **2.** to drive or provoke by taunting —*n.* a scornful or jeering remark; gibe —**taunt'ing·ly** *adv.*

taupe (tōp) *n.* [Fr. < L. *talpa*, a mole] a dark, brownish grey, the colour of moleskin —*adj.* of such a colour

tau·rine (tôr'īn, -in) *adj.* [L. *taurinus < taurus*, a bull] **1.** of or like a bull **2.** of Taurus (sense 2)

Tau·rus (tôr'əs) [L., a bull] **1.** a N constellation containing

the Pleiades **2.** the second sign of the zodiac: see ZODIAC, illus.

taut (tôt) *adj.* [ME. *toght*, tight, prob. < pp. of *togen*, to pull] **1.** tightly stretched, as a rope **2.** strained; tense [a *taut* smile] **3.** trim, tidy, etc. [a *taut* ship] —**taut'ly** *adv.* —**taut'ness** *n.*

taut·en (tôt'ən) *vt., vi.* to make or become taut

tau·to- [< Gr. < *to auto,* the same] a combining form meaning the same [*tautology*]

tau·tog (tô tog') *n.* [< Algonquian pl. of *tautau*, a blackfish] a black or greenish food fish found off the Atlantic coast of the U.S.

tau·tol·o·gy (tô tol'ə jē) *n., pl.* **-gies** [< LL. < Gr.: see TAUTO- & -LOGY] **1.** needless repetition of an idea in a different word, phrase, etc.; redundancy (Ex.: "necessary essentials") **2.** an instance of this **3.** *Math.* a statement, etc., that cannot be denied; necessary truth (Ex.: *a circle is round*) —**tau'to·log'i·cal** *adj.* —**tau'to·log'i·cal·ly** *adv.*

tau·tom·er·ism (tô tom'ər iz'm) *n.* [< TAUTO- + Gr. *meros*, a part + -ISM] *Chem.* the property of some substances of being in a condition of equilibrium between two isomeric forms and reacting readily to form either —**tau·to·mer** (tôt'ə mər) *n.* —**tau·to·mer·ic** (tô'tə mer'ik) *adj.*

tav·ern (tav'ərn) *n.* [< OFr. < L. *taberna*] **1.** a place where wines, spirits, beer, etc. are sold and drunk; saloon; bar **2.** an inn

taw¹ (tô) *n.* [< ?] **1.** a fancy marble used to shoot with in playing marbles **2.** *a)* the game of marbles *b)* the line from which the players shoot

taw² (tô) *vt.* [ME. *tawen* < OE. *tawian*, to prepare] to make (skins) into leather by treating with alum, salt, etc.

taw·dry (tô'drē) *adj.* **-dri·er, -dri·est** [< *St. Audrey*, esp. in *St. Audrey laces*, sold at St. Audrey's fair, Norwich, Norfolk] cheap and showy; gaudy; sleazy —**taw'dri·ly** *adv.* —**taw'dri·ness** *n.*

taw·ny (tô'nē) *adj.* **-ni·er, -ni·est** [< OFr. pp. of *tanner*, to tan] brownish-yellow; tan —*n.* tawny colour —**taw'ni·ness** *n.*

tawny owl a common European owl with short wings and a hooting call

tawse (tôz) *n.* [prob. pl. of obs. *taw*, a thong, tawed leather < TAW²] [Scot.] a leather thong split into strips at the end, used for corporal punishment: also sp. **taws**

tax (taks) *vt.* [< MFr. < L. *taxare*, to appraise < base of *tangere*, to touch] **1.** orig., to determine the value of; assess **2.** to require (a person) to pay a percentage of his income, property value, etc. for the support of a government **3.** to assess a tax on (income, property, purchases, etc.) **4.** to put a burden or strain on **5.** to accuse; charge [to be *taxed* with negligence] —*n.* **1.** a compulsory payment, usually a percentage of income, purchase price, etc., for the support of a government **2.** a heavy demand; burden; strain —**tax·a·bil'i·ty** *n.* —**tax'a·ble** *adj.* —**tax'er** *n.*

tax·a·tion (tak sā'shən) *n.* **1.** a taxing or being taxed **2.** the principle of levying taxes **3.** a tax or tax levy **4.** revenue from taxes

tax-de·duct·i·ble (taks'di duk'tə b'l) *adj.* allowed as a deduction in computing income tax

tax-free (-frē) *adj.* exempt from taxation; that may not be taxed

tax·i (tak'sē) *n., pl.* **tax'is** *shortened form of* TAXICAB —*vi.* **tax'ied, tax'i·ing** or **tax'y·ing 1.** to go in a taxi **2.** to move slowly along the ground or on water as an aircraft does before taking off or after landing —*vt.* **1.** to carry in a taxi **2.** to cause (an aircraft) to taxi

tax·i·cab (-kab') *n.* [< *taxi(meter) cab*] a motor car in which passengers are carried for a fare shown on a meter

tax·i·der·my (tak'si dur'mē) *n.* [< Gr. *taxis*, arrangement + *derma*, a skin] the art of preparing, stuffing, and mounting the skins of animals so as to give a lifelike effect —**tax'i·der'mal, tax'i·der'mic** *adj.* —**tax'i·der'mist** *n.*

tax·i·me·ter (tak'sē mēt'ər) *n.* [Fr. *taximètre* < G. < ML. *taxa*, a tax + *-meter*, -METER] an automatic device in taxicabs that registers fares due

taxi rank a place where taxicabs are stationed for hire

tax·is (tak'sis) *n.* [Gr. *taxis*, arrangement] **1.** in ancient Greece, a unit of troops, of varying size **2.** *Biol.* the movement of an organism in response to an external stimulus **3.** *Surgery* the replacement by hand of some displaced part, as a hernia, without cutting any tissues

tax·on (tak'son) *n., pl.* **tax'a** (-sə) [< TAXONOMY] a taxonomic category or unit, as a species, genus, etc.

tax·on·o·my (tak son'ə mē) *n.* [< Fr. < Gr. *taxis,* arrangement + *nomos,* a law] the science of classification, esp. of plants and animals into natural, related groups such as species and genera —**tax'o·nom'ic** (-sə nom'ik), **tax'o·nom'i·cal** *adj.* —**tax'o·nom'i·cal·ly** *adv.* —**tax·on'o·mist** *n.*

tax·pay·er (taks'pā'ər) *n.* a person who pays taxes

tax return *see* RETURN (sense n. 6c)

taz·za (tät'sə) *n.* [It. < Ar. *tassa:* see TASS] a shallow, ornamental cup or vase, usually with a pedestal

Tb *Chem.* terbium

TB, T.B., tb, t.b. tuberculosis

T-bone steak (tē′bōn′) a steak from the loin, with a T-shaped bone

tbs., tbsp. tablespoon; tablespoons

Tc *Chem.* technetium

tch *interj., n.* a clicking sound made with the tongue, to express disapproval, sympathy, etc. —*vi.* to utter "tchs"

Te *Chem.* tellurium

te (tē) *n. same as* TI

tea (tē) *n.* see PLURAL, II, D, 3 [Chin. dial. *t'e,* for Mandarin *ch'a,* tea] 1. a white-flowered, evergreen shrub grown in warm parts of Asia for its young leaves, which are prepared by drying, etc. for use in making a common drink 2. the dried, prepared leaves 3. the drink made by steeping these in hot water, etc. 4. a tealike plant, or the tealike beverage made from it or from a meat extract [camomile *tea,* beef *tea*] 5. a light meal, usually with tea, in the late afternoon; also **afternoon tea** 6. *same as* HIGH TEA —**tea and sympathy** [Colloq.] kind and understanding treatment of someone in trouble

tea bag a small, porous bag with tea leaves in it, for making an individual cup of tea

tea ball a hollow, perforated metal ball used to hold tea leaves in making tea

tea·cake (-kāk′) *n.* a flat, round, slightly sweetened bun, usually served hot and buttered

teach (tēch) *vt.* taught, teach′ing [OE. *tæcan*] 1. to show or help to learn how to do something; instruct 2. to give lessons to; guide the study of 3. to give lessons in (a subject) 4. to give knowledge, insight, etc. to; cause to know, understand, etc. [the accident *taught* her to be careful] —*vi.* to be a teacher —**teach′a·bil′i·ty, teach′-a·ble·ness** *n.* —**teach′a·ble** *adj.*

teach·er (-char) *n.* a person who teaches, esp. in a school —**teach′er·ship′** *n.*

tea-chest (tē′chest′) *n.* a large, square wooden box lined with foil, for exporting tea

teach·ing (tē′chiŋ) *n.* 1. the action of one who teaches; profession of a teacher 2. something taught; precept, doctrine, etc.: *usually in pl.*

tea-cloth (-kloth′) *n.* 1. a small tablecloth 2. a towel for drying dishes after they have been washed: also **tea towel**

tea·co·sy (-kō′zē) *n.* a padded cover for a teapot to keep the contents hot

tea·cup (tē′kup′) *n.* 1. a cup for drinking tea, etc. 2. a teacupful —**a storm in a teacup** a great commotion over a small problem

tea·cup·ful (-fōōl′) *n., pl.* **-fuls′** as much as a teacup will hold

tea-fight (tē fit) *n.* [Colloq.] a tea party

tea-gown (-goun′) *n.* a loose gown worn for tea at home

tea·house (-hous′) *n.* in the Orient, a place where tea and other refreshments are served

teak (tēk) *n.* [< Port. < native word *tēkka*] 1. a large East Indian tree with hard, yellowish-brown wood used for shipbuilding, furniture, etc. 2. its wood: also **teak′wood′**

tea·ket·tle (tē′ket″l) *n.* a covered container with a spout and handle, used to boil water for tea, etc.

teal (tēl) *n.* [ME. *tele*] 1. *pl.* **teals, teal:** see PLURAL, II, D, 1 any of several small, short-necked freshwater wild ducks 2. a dark greenish blue: also **teal blue**

team (tēm) *n.* [OE., offspring] 1. two or more horses, oxen, etc. harnessed to the same vehicle or plough 2. a draught animal or animals and the vehicle drawn 3. a group of people working together on a project or playing together against opponents in games —*vt., vi.* to join together in a team (often with *up*)

team·mate (tēm′māt′) *n.* a fellow team member

team spirit concern for the benefit of the group as a whole rather than for individual interest

team·ster (-star) *n.* 1. a driver of a team of horses 2. [U.S.] a lorry driver

team teaching teaching by several teachers working together with a group of students to explore relationships among various subject areas

team·work (-wurk′) *n.* the action or effort of people working together as a group

tea party a social gathering at which tea is served

tea·pot (tē′pot′) *n.* a pot with a spout, handle, and lid, for brewing and pouring tea

tear[1] (ter) *vt.* tore, torn, tear′ing [OE. *teran,* to rend] 1. to pull apart by force; rip; rend [to *tear* limb from limb] 2. to make (a hole, etc.) by tearing 3. to wound by tearing; lacerate 4. to split into factions; disrupt [ranks *torn* by dissension] 5. to divide by doubt, etc. [*torn* between duty and desire] 6. to remove as by tearing, pulling, etc. (with *up, out, off,* etc.) —*vi.* 1. to be torn 2. to move with force or speed; rush —*n.* 1. the act of tearing 2. a torn place; rip 3. a violent outburst —**tear at** to pull at violently in an effort to tear or remove —**tear down** to take apart; wreck, demolish, etc. —**tear into** [Colloq.] to attack or criticize violently —**tear′er** *n.*

tear[2] (tir) *n.* [OE.] 1. a drop of the salty fluid that keeps the eyeball moist and flows from the eye in weeping 2. any

tearlike drop 3. [*pl.*] sorrow; grief —**in tears** weeping —**tear′less** *adj.*

tear·drop (tir′drop′) *n.* a tear —*adj.* tear-shaped

tear·ful (-fal) *adj.* 1. in tears; weeping 2. causing tears; sad —**tear′ful·ly** *adv.* —**tear′ful·ness** *n.*

tear gas (tir) a gas that makes the eyes sore and blinds them with tears —**tear′-gas′** *vt.* **-gassed′, -gas′sing**

tear-jerk·er (-jur′kar) *n.* [Slang] a play, film, etc. that is sad in a too sentimental way —**tear′-jerk′ing** *adj.*

tea·room (tē′rōōm′) *n.* a restaurant that serves tea, coffee, light lunches, etc.: also **tea-shop**

tea rose a pale yellow rose supposed to have the scent of tea

tear·y (tir′ē) *adj.* **-i·er, -i·est** 1. tearful; crying 2. of or like tears —**tear′i·ly** *adv.* —**tear′i·ness** *n.*

tease (tēz) *vt.* teased, teas′ing [OE. *tæsan*] 1. a) to card or comb (flax, wool, etc.) b) to raise a nap on (cloth) with teasels 2. to bother or annoy by mocking, poking fun, etc. 3. [U.S.] to pester with repeated requests 4. to tantalize —*vi.* to tease someone —*n.* 1. a teasing or being teased 2. a person who teases

tea·sel (tē′z'l) *n.* [< OE. < base of *tæsan,* to tease] 1. a bristly plant (esp. the **fuller's teasel**) with prickly, cylindrical flower heads 2. a dried flower head of the fuller's teasel, used to raise a nap on cloth 3. any device for raising a nap on cloth —*vt.* **-seled** or **-selled, -sel·ing** or **-sel·ling** to nap (cloth) with teasels —**tea′sel·er, tea′sel·ler** *n.*

teas·er (tē′zar) *n.* 1. a person or thing that teases 2. an annoying or puzzling problem

tea·spoon (tē′spōōn′) *n.* 1. a spoon for stirring tea, coffee, etc. and eating some soft foods 2. *same as* TEASPOONFUL

tea·spoon·ful (-fōōl′) *n., pl.* **-fuls′** as much as a teaspoon holds

teat (tēt, tit) *n.* [< OFr. *tete* < Gmc.] 1. the nipple of a breast or udder 2. a rubber device resembling this, as on a feeding bottle

tea tree [Aust.] any of various shrubs whose leaves were, formerly, infused as a substitute for tea

tea·zel, tea·zle (tē′z'l) *n., vt. same as* TEASEL

tech. 1. technical 2. technology

tech·ne·ti·um (tek nē′shē əm) *n.* [ModL. < Gr. < *technē,* an art] a metallic chemical element obtained in the fission of uranium: symbol, Tc; at. wt., 97(?); at. no., 43

tech·nic (tek′nik; *for n. 1 also* tek nēk′) *adj.* [< Gr. < *technē,* an art] *same as* TECHNICAL —*n.* 1. *same as* TECHNIQUE 2. [*pl., with sing. or pl. v.*] the study or principles of an art

tech·ni·cal (tek′ni k'l) *adj.* [prec. + -AL] 1. dealing with the practical, industrial, or mechanical arts or the applied sciences [a *technical* college] 2. of, used in, or peculiar to a specific science, art, craft, etc. [*technical* terms] 3. of or showing technique [*technical* skill] 4. according to principles or rules [a *technical* difference] 5. involving or using technicalities —**tech′ni·cal·ly** *adv.*

tech·ni·cal·i·ty (tek′nə kal′ə tē) *n., pl.* **-ties** 1. the state or quality of being technical 2. a technical point, term, method, etc. 3. a minute, formal point or detail brought to bear upon a main issue

technical knockout *Boxing* a victory won when the opponent, though not knocked out, is so badly hurt that the referee stops the match

tech·ni·cian (tek nish′ən) *n.* a person skilled in the technicalities of some subject or in the technique of some art or science

Tech·ni·col·or (tek′ni kul′ər) *a trademark for* a certain process of making colour films —*n.* [t-] 1. this process 2. bright colours —**tech′ni·col′ored** *adj.*

tech·nique (tek nēk′) *n.* [Fr. < Gr.: see TECHNIC] 1. the method of procedure (as to practical or formal details) in creating an artistic work or carrying out a scientific or mechanical operation 2. the degree of expertness shown in this 3. any method of doing a thing

tech·no- [< Gr. *technē,* an art] *a combining form meaning:* 1. art, science, skill 2. technical, technological [*technocracy*]

tech·noc·ra·cy (tek nok′rə sē) *n.* [prec. + -CRACY] government by scientists and engineers —**tech′-no·crat′** (-nə krat′) *n.* —**tech′no·crat′ic** *adj.*

tech·no·log·i·cal (tek′nə loj′i k'l) *adj.* 1. of technology 2. resulting from technical progress in the use of machinery and automation Also **tech′no·log′ic** —**tech′no·log′i·cal·ly** *adv.*

tech·nol·o·gy (tek nol′ə jē) *n.* [Gr. *technologia,* systematic treatment] 1. the science or study of the practical or industrial arts, applied sciences, etc. 2. the terms used in a science, art, etc. 3. applied science 4. a method, process, etc. for handling a specific technical problem —**tech·nol′-o·gist** *n.*

tec·ton·ic (tek ton′ik) *adj.* [< LL. < Gr. < *tektōn,* a builder] 1. of or relating to building 2. designating, of, or pertaining to the processes that produce changes in the earth's crust

tec·ton·ics (-iks) *n. pl.* [*with sing. v.*] [see prec.] 1. the constructive arts in general **2.** *Geol.* the study of the earth's crystal structure and the forces that produce changes in it

tec·trix (tek′triks) *n.*, *pl.* **-tri·ces** (trə sēz′) [ModL. < L. *tectus*, pp. of *tegere* to cover] a wing covert of a bird

Ted (ted) *n.* a clipped form of TEDDY BOY

ted (ted) *vt.* **ted′ded, ted′ding** [prob. < ON. *tethja*, to manure] to spread or scatter (newly cut grass) for drying as hay **—ted′der** *n.*

ted·dy bear (ted′ē) [< *Teddy* (*Theodore*) Roosevelt] a child's stuffed toy made to look like a bear cub

Teddy Boy [< *Teddy*, < *Edward*, referring to the Edwardian dress] a youth of the 1950's who wore mock Edwardian fashions, and was often characterized by violent behaviour

Te De·um (tē dē′əm, tā dā′oom) [LL.] **1.** a Christian hymn beginning *Te Deum laudamus* (We praise thee, O God) **2.** music for this hymn

te·di·ous (tē′dē əs) *adj.* full of tedium; tiresome; boring **—te′di·ous·ly** *adv.* **—te′di·ous·ness** *n.*

te·di·um (-dē əm) *n.* [L. *taedium* < *taedet*, it offends] the condition or quality of being tiresome, boring, or monotonous

tee¹ (tē) *n.*, *pl.* **tees** **1.** the letter T, t **2.** anything shaped like a T **—adj.** shaped like a T **—to a tee** exactly

tee² (tē) *n.* [< prec.: the mark was orig. T-shaped] a mark aimed at in quoits, curling, etc.

tee³ (tē) *n.* [prob. < Scot. dial. *teaz*] **1.** a small, pointed holder of wood, plastic, etc. on which a golf ball is put to be driven **2.** the place at each hole from which a golfer makes his first stroke **—vt., vi. teed, tee′ing** to put (a ball) on a tee **—tee off 1.** to play a golf ball from a tee **2.** to begin

tee-hee (tē′hē′) *interj., n.* [ME.: echoic] the sound of a titter or snicker **—vi. -heed′, -hee′ing** to titter or snicker

teem¹ (tēm) *vi.* [OE. *tieman*, to bear < base of *team*, progeny] to be full; abound; swarm [a river *teeming* with fish]

teem² (tēm) *vt.* [ON. *taema*] to empty; pour out **—vi.** to pour [a *teeming* rain]

teen (tēn) *n.* [< OE. *tien*, ten] [*pl.*] the years from thirteen to nineteen (of a person's age)

teen-age (-āj′) *adj.* **1.** in one's teens **2.** of, like, or for persons in their teens Also **teen′age′**

teen-ag·er (-āj′ər) *n.* a person in his teens

tee·ny (tē′nē) *adj.* **-ni·er, -ni·est** *colloq. var. of* TINY: also **teen′sy**

teen·y-bop·per (tē′nē bop′ər) *n.* [TEEN + -Y¹ + BOP + -ER] [Slang] a young teen-ager, esp. a girl following the latest fads

tee·ny-wee·ny (-wē′nē) *adj.* [Colloq.] very small; tiny: also **teen·sy-ween·sy** (tēn′sē wēn′sē)

tee·pee (tē′pē) *n.* alt. sp. of TEPEE

tee shirt same as T-SHIRT

tee·ter (tēt′ər) *vi.* [dial. *titter* < ON. *titra*, to tremble] to totter, wobble, etc. **—vt.** to cause to teeter **—n.** [U.S.] *shortened form of* TEETER-TOTTER

tee·ter-tot·ter (-tot′ər) *n., vi.* U.S. name for SEESAW

teeth (tēth) *n.* pl. of TOOTH

teethe (tēth) *vi.* **teethed, teeth′ing** to grow teeth; cut one's teeth

teeth·ing (tēth′iŋ) *n.* the stage during which a baby cuts teeth

teething ring a ring of ivory, plastic, etc. for teething babies to bite on

teething troubles 1. discomfort suffered by a baby while teething **2.** difficulties experienced in the early stages of a project, etc.

teeth·ridge (tēth′rij′) *n.* the ridge of gum along the inside of the upper front teeth

tee·to·tal (tē tōt′'l, tē′tōt′'l) *adj.* [formed by redupl. of initial letter of TOTAL] **1.** of, or in favour of teetotalism **2.** [U.S. Colloq.] entire; complete **—tee·to′tal·ler** *n.* **—tee·to′tal·ly** *adv.*

tee·to·tal·ism (-iz′m) *n.* the principle or practice of never drinking any alcoholic liquor **—tee·to′tal·ist** *n.*

teff (tef) *n.* [< Amharic *tēf*] a kind of Abyssinian cereal-grass

Tef·lon (tef′lon) a trademark for a tough, insoluble polymer used in making nonstick coatings for cooking utensils, etc.

teg (teg) *n.* [< ?] a sheep in its second year: also sp. **tegg**

teg·u·ment (teg′yoo mənt) *n.* [< L. < *tegere*, to cover] same as INTEGUMENT

te-hee (tē′hē′) *interj., n., vi.* **-heed′, -hee′ing** var. of TEE-HEE

tek·tite (tek′tīt) *n.* [< Gr. *tēktos*, molten < *tēkein*, to melt + -ITE] any of certain small, dark green to black glassy bodies, assumed to have come to earth from outer space

tel- same as: **1.** TELE-. **2.** TELO-.

tel. 1. telegram **2.** telegraph **3.** telephone

tel·aes·the·si·a (tel′əs thē′zē ə, -zhə) *n.* [ModL.: see TELE- + aesthesia] extrasensory perception of distant objects,events, etc. **—tel′aes·thet′ic** *adj.*

tel·a·mon (tel′ə mon′) *n.*, *pl.* **tel′a·mo′nes** (-mō′nēz) [L. < Gr. *telamōn*, bearer] *Archit.* a supporting column in the form of a man's figure: see also ATLANTES, CARYATID

tel·e- a combining form meaning: **1.** [< Gr. < *tēle*, far off] at, over, from, or to a distance [*telegraph*] **2.** [< TELE(VISION)] of or by television [*telecast*]

tel·e·cast (tel′ə kāst) *vt., vi.* **-cast′** or **-cast′ed, -cast′ing** [TELE- + (BROAD)CAST] to broadcast by television **—n.** a television broadcast **—tel′e·cast′er** *n.*

tel·e·com·mu·ni·ca·tion (tel′ə kə myoo′nə kā′shən) *n.* [*also pl.*, *with sing. or pl. v.*] communication by radio, telephone, telegraph, television, etc.

tel·e·du (tel′ə doo′) *n.* [Malay] a small, flesh-eating, badgerlike mammal of Java, Borneo and Sumatra, that emits a vile-smelling fluid when molested

tel·e·gen·ic (tel′ə jen′ik) *adj.* [TELE- + -GENIC] looking or likely to look attractive on television

tel·e·gram (tel′ə gram′) *n.* [TELE- + -GRAM] a message transmitted by telegraph

tel·e·graph (-graf′) *n.* [< Fr.: see TELE- & -GRAPH] an apparatus or system for sending messages, orig. in Morse code, by electric impulses through a wire or by means of radio waves **—vt. 1.** to send (a message) by telegraph to (someone) **2.** to let another know without meaning to (something one plans to do), as by a look **—vi.** to send a telegram **—tel·e·leg·ra·pher** (tə leg′rə fər), **te·leg·ra·phist** *n.* **—tel′e·graph′ic** *adj.* **—tel′e·graph′i·cal·ly** *adv.*

telegraph plant a tropical Asian plant, so called because the two lateral leaflets of each leaf move like a semaphore signal

te·leg·ra·phy (tə leg′rə fē) *n.* **1.** the operation of telegraph apparatus **2.** the sending of messages by telegraph

tel·e·ki·ne·sis (tel′ə ki nē′sis) *n.* [ModL. < TELE- + Gr. *kinēsis*, motion] the causing of an object to move supposedly by means of psychic forces **—tel′e·ki·net′ic** (-net′ik) *adj.*

tel·e·mark (tel′ə märk′) *n.* [after *Telemark*, region in S Norway] *Skiing* a turning movement during which the outer ski is advanced and turned in at a widening angle

tel·e·me·ter (tel′ə mēt′ər, tə lem′ə tər) *n.* [TELE- + -METER] a device for measuring temperature, radiation, etc. at a remote point, as in outer space, and transmitting the information, esp. by radio, to a distant receiver on earth **—vt., vi.** to transmit by telemeter **—tel′e·met′ric** (-met′rik) *adj.* **—tel′e·met′ri·cal·ly** *adv.* **—te·lem·e·try** (tə lem′ə trē) *n.*

tel·e·ol·o·gy (tē′lē ol′ə jē, tel′ē-) *n.* [ModL. < Gr. *telos*, an end + -*logia* (see -LOGY)] **1.** the fact or quality of having an ultimate purpose or goal **2.** a belief that what happens or occurs in nature is determined by an overall design or purpose, not just by mechanical causes **—te′le·o·log′i·cal** (-ə loj′i k'l) *adj.* **—te′le·ol′o·gist** *n.*

tel·e·ost (tel′ē ost′, tē′lē-, tel′i-) *n.* [< Gr. *teleos*, complete < *telos*, an end + *osteon*, bone] any of a large subclass of bony fishes, including most fishes extant

te·lep·a·thy (tə lep′ə thē) *n.* [TELE- + -PATHY] supposed communication between minds by some means other than the normal functioning of the senses **—tel·e·path·ic** (tel′ə path′ik) *adj.* **—tel′e·path′i·cal·ly** *adv.* **—te·lep′-a·thist** *n.*

tel·e·phone (tel′ə fōn′) *n.* [TELE- + -PHONE] an instrument or system for conveying speech over distances by converting sound into electric impulses sent through a wire **—vi. -phoned′, -phon′ing** to talk over a telephone **—vt. 1.** to convey (a message) by telephone **2.** to speak to or reach (a person) by telephone **—tel′e·phon′er** *n.* **—tel′e·phon′ic** (-fon′ik) *adj.* **—tel′e·phon′i·cal·ly** *adv.*

telephone box a booth in a public place containing a telephone, usually operated by inserting coins: also **telephone booth, telephone kiosk**

telephone directory a book in which are listed alphabetically the names of persons, businesses, etc. having telephones in a specified area, with their addresses and telephone numbers

tel·e·phon·ist (tə lef′ə nist) *n.* a telephone switchboard operator

te·leph·o·ny (tə lef′ə nē) *n.* the science of communication by telephone

tel·e·pho·to (tel′ə fōt′ō) *adj.* **1.** telephotographic **2.** designating or of a camera lens producing a large image of a distant object

tel·e·pho·to·graph (tel′ə fōt′ə graf′) *n.* **1.** a photograph taken with a telephoto lens **2.** a photograph transmitted by telephotography **—vt., vi. 1.** to take (photographs) with a telephoto lens **2.** to transmit (photographs) by telephotography

tel·e·pho·tog·ra·phy (-fə tog′rə fē) *n.* **1.** photography done with a telephoto lens **2.** the science or process of transmitting photographs over distances by converting light rays into electric signals which are sent over wire or radio channels **—tel'e·pho'to·graph'ic** (-fōt'ə graf'ik) *adj.*

tel·e·print·er (tel'ə print'ər) *n.* a form of telegraph in which the message is typed on a keyboard that sends electric signals to a machine that prints the words

Tel·e·promp·ter (tel'ə promp'tər) *a trademark for* an electronic device that, unseen by the audience, unrolls a prepared script line by line, as a prompting aid to a speaker on television

tel·e·ran (tel'ə ran') *n.* [*tele*(*vision*) *r*(*adar*) *a*(*ir*) *n*(*avigation*)] the televised transmission to aircraft of data received by radar concerning terrain, etc., as an aid to navigation

tel·e·scope (tel'ə skōp') *n.* [< It. < ModL. < Gr.: see TELE-& -SCOPE] an instrument for making distant objects, as stars, appear nearer and larger: it consists of a tube or tubes containing lenses In a *refracting telescope*, the image is focused directly on a lens; in a *reflecting telescope*, the image is focused on a concave mirror **—adj.** having parts that slide one inside another **—vi. -scoped', -scop'ing** to slide or be forced one inside another like tubes of a collapsible telescope **—vt. 1.** to cause to telescope **2.** to condense; shorten

tel·e·scop·ic (tel'ə skop'ik) *adj.* **1.** of a telescope **2.** seen or obtained by a telescope **3.** visible only through a telescope **4.** having sections that slide one inside another Also **tel'e·scop'i·cal —tel'e·scop'i·cal·ly** *adv.*

te·les·co·py (tə les'kə pē) *n.* the art or practice of using a telescope **—te·les'co·pist** *n.*

tel·e·thon (tel'ə thon') *n.* [TELE(VISION) + (MARA)THON] [U.S.] a campaign, as on a lengthy telecast, asking for support for a cause, as by pledged donations made by telephone

Tel·e·type (tel'ə tīp') *a trademark for* a form of teleprinter **—n.** [often t-] communication by means of Teletype **—vt., vi. -typed', -typ'ing** [often t-] to send (messages) by Teletype **—tel'e·typ'er, tel'e·typ'ist** *n.*

tel·e·type·writ·er (tel'ə tīp'rīt'ər) *n. U.S. name for* TELEPRINTER

tel·e·view (tel'ə vyoō') *vt., vi.* to view or watch by television **—tel'e·view'er** *n.*

tel·e·vise (tel'ə vīz') *vt., vi. -vised', -vis'ing* to transmit by television **—tel'e·vi'sor** *n.*

tel·e·vi·sion (-vizh'ən) *n.* [TELE- + VISION] **1.** the process of transmitting scenes or views by radio waves or, sometimes, by wire, in which light rays are converted by a camera tube into electric signals that are transmitted to a receiver that changes the signals into electron beams that are projected against the screen of a picture tube, reproducing the original image **2.** television broadcasting as an industry, art, etc.; also, its facilities and related activities **3.** a television receiving set **—adj.** of, in, or by television

television tube a cathode-ray tube specifically designed to reproduce television pictures

tel·ex (tel'eks) *n.* [TEL(ETYPEWRITER) + EX(CHANGE)] **1.** an international telegraph service in which teleprinters are rented out to subscribers for direct communication **2.** a message sent by telex **—vt.** to send (a message) by telex

tell (tel) *vt.* **told, tell'ing** [OE. *tellan*, lit., to calculate] **1.** orig., to enumerate; count **2.** to give an account of (a story, etc.) in speech or writing; narrate; relate **3.** to express in words; utter [to *tell* the truth] **4.** to report; announce **5.** to make known; disclose **6.** to recognize; distinguish [I can *tell* the difference] **7.** to decide; know [he can't *tell* when to go] **8.** to let know; inform **9.** to request; order [*tell* him to leave] **10.** to assure emphatically [it's there, I *tell* you] **—vi. 1.** to give an account or description (*of* something) **2.** to be evidence or an indication (*of* something) **3.** to reveal something, esp. secrets **4.** to produce a result or have a marked effect **—tell a tale** reveal someting of interest or importance **—tell it to the marines** [Colloq.] an expression of disbelief **—tell off 1.** to count and separate from the total **2.** [Colloq.] to rebuke severely **—tell on 1.** to make weary, worn-out, etc. **2.** [Colloq.] to inform against **—tell tales (out of school)** to reveal secrets, esp. in order to stir up trouble **—tell the tale** [Colloq.] to give an exaggerated account, esp. in order to gain sympathy **—you're telling me** [Slang] I know that very well already **—tell'a·ble** *adj.*

tell·er (tel'ər) *n.* **1.** a person who tells (a story, etc.) **2.** a person who counts; specif., *a)* one who counts votes *b)* a bank clerk who pays out or receives money

tell·ing (tel'iŋ) *adj.* **1.** having an effect; forceful; striking **2.** that tells or reveals much **—tell'ing·ly** *adv.*

tell·tale (-tāl') *n.* **1.** a talebearer or informer **2.** an outward indication of a secret **3.** a device that indicates or records information **—adj.** revealing a secret

tel·lu·ri·an (te lyoor'ē ən) *adj.* [< L. *tellus*, gen. *telluris*, the earth] of the earth **—n.** an inhabitant of the earth

tel·lu·ric¹ (te lyoor'ik) *adj.* of tellurium, esp. tellurium of a high valence

tel·lu·ric² (te lyoor'ik) *adj.* **1.** of the earth; terrestrial **2.** of or arising from the soil

tel·lu·ri·um (te lyoor'ē əm) *n.* [ModL. < L. *tellus*, the earth] a rare, tin-white, brittle, nonmetallic chemical element: symbol, Te; at. wt., 127.60; at. no., 52

tel·ly (tel'ē) *n.* [Colloq.] television

tel·o- [< Gr. *telos*, an end] *a combining form meaning* end

tel·pher (tel'fər) *n.* [< TEL(E)- + Gr. *pherein*, to BEAR¹] an electrically driven car suspended from and run on overhead cables **—tel'pher·age** *n.*

tel·son (tel'sən) *n.* [ModL. < Gr. *telson*, a limit] the last segment, or an appendage on it, of the body of a crustacean or arachnid

Tel·u·gu (tel'ə goō') *n.* **1.** a Dravidian language of S India **2.** *pl.* **-gus', -gu'** a member of a Dravidian people speaking this language **—adj.** of Telugu or the Telugus Also **Tel'e·gu'**

tem·blor (tem'blôr, -blar; *Sp.* tem blôr') *n., pl.* **-blors;** *Sp.* **-blo'res** (-blô'res) [Sp. < *temblar*, to tremble] [U.S.] *same as* EARTHQUAKE

te·mer·i·ty (tə mer'ə tē) *n.* [< L. < *temere*, rashly] foolish or rash boldness; recklessness

temp (temp) *n.* [shortened form of TEMPORARY] [Colloq.] a temporary employee

temp. 1. temperature **2.** temporary **3.** [L. *tempore*] in the time of

tem·per (tem'pər) *vt.* [< OE. & OFr., both < L. *temperare*, to regulate < *tempus*, a period] **1.** to make suitable or free from excess by mingling with another thing; moderate [*temper* criticism with reason] **2.** *a)* to bring to the proper texture, hardness, etc. by treating in some way [to *temper* steel by heating and sudden cooling] *b)* to toughen, as by hardship **3.** *Music* to adjust the pitch of (a note, instrument, etc.) to some temperament **—vi.** to become tempered **—n. 1.** a being tempered; specif., the degree of hardness and resiliency of a metal **2.** frame of mind; disposition **3.** mental calm; composure: now only in **lose** (or **keep**) **one's temper, out of temper 4.** a tendency to get angry **5.** anger; rage **6.** something used to temper a mixture, etc.

tem·per·a (tem'pər ə) *n.* [It. < *temperare* < L.: see prec.] **1.** *a)* a way of painting that uses pigments mixed with size, casein, or egg to produce a dull finish *b)* the paint so used **2.** an opaque, water-base paint used as for posters

tem·per·a·ment (tem'prə mənt, -pər ə mənt) *n.* [L. *temperamentum*, proper mixing < *temperare*: see TEMPER] **1.** one's customary frame of mind or natural disposition **2.** a nature that is excitable, moody, etc. **3.** *Music* a system of adjustment of the intervals between the tones of an instrument

tem·per·a·men·tal (tem'prə men't'l, -pər ə men't'l) *adj.* **1.** of or caused by temperament **2.** excitable by temperament; easily upset **3.** erratic in behaviour **—tem'per·a·men'tal·ly** *adv.*

tem·per·ance (tem'pər əns, -prəns) *n.* [< MFr. < L. < prp. of *temperare*: see TEMPER] **1.** a being temperate or moderate; self-restraint **2.** moderation in drinking alcoholic liquor, or, esp., the avoiding of alcoholic liquor completely

temperance hotel a hotel in which no alcoholic drink is obtainable

tem·per·ate (tem'pər it, -prit) *adj.* [< L. pp. of *temperare*, to TEMPER] **1.** moderate in indulging the appetites; abstemious, esp. in using alcoholic liquor **2.** moderate in one's actions, speech, etc. **3.** characterized by restraint [a *temperate* reply] **4.** neither very hot nor very cold: said of a climate, etc. **—tem'per·ate·ly** *adv.* **—tem'per·ate·ness** *n.*

Temperate Zone either of two zones of the earth (**North Temperate Zone** and **South Temperate Zone**) between the tropics and the polar circles

tem·per·a·ture (tem'prə chər, tem'pər ə-) *n.* [< L. < *temperatus*, temperate] the degree of hotness or coldness of anything, usually as measured on a thermometer; specif., *a)* the degree of heat of a living body; also, an excess of this over the normal (about 98.4°F or 36.8°C in man) *b)* the degree of heat of the atmosphere

tem·pered (tem'pərd) *adj.* **1.** having been given the desired texture, hardness, etc. **2.** modified by other qualities, etc. **3.** having a (specified) temper [bad-*tempered*] **4.** *Music* adjusted to a temperament

tem·pest (tem'pist) *n.* [< OFr., ult. < L. *tempestas*, portion of time, weather < *tempus*, time] **1.** a violent storm with high winds, esp. one accompanied by rain, hail, or snow **2.** a violent outburst; tumult

tem·pes·tu·ous (tem pes'tyoō wəs) *adj.* **1.** of or like a tempest; stormy **2.** violent; turbulent **—tem·pes'tu·ous·ly** *adv.* **—tem·pes'tu·ous·ness** *n.*

tem·plate, tem·plet (tem'plit) *n.* [< Fr., dim. of *temple* < L. *templum*, small timber] **1.** a pattern, usually a thin plate, for forming an accurate copy of an object or shape **2.** *Archit.* *a)* a short stone or timber placed under a beam to help distribute the pressure *b)* a beam for supporting joists over a doorway, etc.

tem·ple[1] (tem′p'l) *n.* [< OE. & OFr., both < L. *templum*, orig., space marked out] 1. a building for the worship of a god or gods 2. [T-] any of three buildings for worshipping Jehovah, successively built by the Jews in ancient Jerusalem 3. a Christian church 4. a building, usually of imposing size, serving some special purpose [a Masonic *temple*] —tem′pled *adj.*

tem·ple[2] (tem′p'l) *n.* [< OFr. < VL. < L. *tempora*, the temples, pl. of *tempus*, temple of the head] the flat area at either side of the forehead, above and behind the eye

temple[3] (tem′p'l) *n.* [< ME. < MFr.: see TEMPLATE] a device for keeping the cloth in a loom stretched to its correct width during weaving

tem·po (tem′pō) *n., pl.* -pos, -pi (-pē) [It. < L. *tempus*, time] 1. the speed at which a piece of music is performed 2. rate of activity; pace [the *tempo* of modern living]

tem·po·ral[1] (tem′pər əl, -prəl) *adj.* [L. *temporalis* < *tempus*, time] 1. lasting only for a time; transitory; not eternal 2. of this world; not spiritual 3. civil or secular; not ecclesiastical 4. of or limited by time —*n.* a temporal thing, power, etc. —tem′po·ral·ly *adv.*

tem·po·ral[2] (tem′pər əl, -prəl) *adj.* [LL. *temporalis* < L. *tempora*: see TEMPLE[2]] of or near the temple or temples (of the head)

temporal bone either of a pair of compound bones forming the sides of the skull

tem·po·ral·i·ty (tem′pə ral′ə tē) *n., pl.* -ties 1. the quality or state of being temporal 2. [usually pl.] secular properties of a church

tem·po·rar·y (tem′pə rer ē) *adj.* [< L. < *tempus*, time] lasting only for a time; not permanent —tem·po·rar·i·ly (tem′pə rar ə lē, tem′pə rer′ə lē) *adv.* —tem′po·rar·i·ness *n.*

tem·po·rize (tem′pə rīz′) *vi.* -rized′, -riz′ing [MFr. *temporiser* < ML. < L. *tempus*, time] 1. to act or speak in a way one thinks is expedient, ignoring principle 2. *a)* to put off making a decision, or to agree for a while, so as to gain time *b)* to bargain or deal (*with* a person) so as to gain time —tem′po·ri·za′tion *n.* —tem′po·riz′er *n.*

tempt (tempt) *vt.* [< OFr. < LL. *temptare* < L., to try the strength of] 1. orig., to test; try 2. to entice (a person) to do or want something that is wrong, forbidden, etc. 3. to be inviting or enticing to; attract 4. to provoke or risk provoking (fate, etc.) —tempt′a·ble *adj.* —tempt′er *n.* —tempt′ress *n.fem.*

temp·ta·tion (temp tā′shən) *n.* 1. a tempting or being tempted 2. something that tempts

tempt·ing (temp′tiŋ) *adj.* that tempts; enticing; attractive —tempt′ing·ly *adv.*

tem·pu·ra (tem′poo rə, tem poor′ə) *n.* [Jap., lit., fried food] a Japanese dish of seafood or vegetables dipped in an egg batter and deep-fried [shrimp *tempura*]

‡tem·pus fu·git (tem′pəs fyoo′jit) [L.] time flies

ten (ten) *adj.* [OE.] totalling one more than nine —*n.* 1. the cardinal number between 9 and 11; 10; X 2. anything having ten units or members, or numbered ten

ten. 1. tenor 2. *Music* tenuto

ten·a·ble (ten′ə b'l) *adj.* [Fr. < OFr. < *tenir*: see TENANT] that can be held, defended, or believed —ten′a·bil′i·ty, ten′a·ble·ness *n.* —ten′a·bly *adv.*

ten·ace (ten′ās) *n.* [< Sp. *tenaza*, lit., pincers] *Bridge* an imperfect sequence of high cards in the same suit, as the ace and queen without the king

te·na·cious (tə nā′shəs) *adj.* [< L. *tenax* (gen. *tenacis*) < *tenere*, to hold] 1. holding firmly [a *tenacious* grip] 2. that retains well [a *tenacious* memory] 3. holding together strongly; cohesive 4. clinging; adhesive 5. persistent —te·na′cious·ly *adv.* —te·na′cious·ness *n.*

te·nac·i·ty (tə nas′ə tē) *n.* the quality or state of being tenacious

te·nac·u·lum (tə nak′yoo ləm) *n., pl.* -la (lə) [LL., instrument for holding < L. *tenere*, to hold] *Surgery* a pointed, hooked instrument for lifting and holding parts, as blood vessels

ten·an·cy (ten′ən sē) *n., pl.* -cies 1. occupancy or duration of occupancy by a tenant 2. any holding of property, an office, etc.

ten·ant (ten′ənt) *n.* [OFr., orig. prp. of *tenir*, to hold < L. *tenere*] 1. a person who pays rent to occupy or use land, a building, etc. 2. an occupant of or dweller in a specified place —*vt.* to occupy as a tenant —ten′ant·a·ble *adj.* —ten′ant·less *adj.*

tenant farmer a person who farms land owned by another and pays rent in cash or in a share of the crops

ten·ant·ry (ten′ən trē) *n., pl.* -ries 1. a body of tenants 2. occupancy by a tenant

tench (tench) *n., pl.* tench′es, tench: see PLURAL, II, D, 1 [ME. & OFr. *tenche* < LL. *tinca*] a common European freshwater fish of the carp family

Ten Commandments *Bible* the ten laws forming the fundamental moral code of Israel, given to Moses by God on Mount Sinai: Ex. 20:2-17; Deut. 5:6-22

tend[1] (tend) *vt.* [see ATTEND] 1. to take care of; watch over; attend to 2. to be in charge of; manage

tend[2] (tend) *vi.* [< OFr. < L. *tendere*, to stretch] 1. to move or extend [to *tend* eastwards] 2. to be likely or apt; incline [*tending* to boast] 3. to lead (*to* or *towards* a specified result)

tend·en·cy (ten′dən sē) *n., pl.* -cies [< ML. < L. prp. of *tendere*, to stretch] 1. an inclination to move or act in a particular direction or way; leaning; bias 2. a course toward some purpose, object, or result; drift 3. a definite purpose or point of view in something said or written

ten·den·tious (ten den′shəs) *adj.* [< G., ult. < ML. *tendentia*, TENDENCY] showing a deliberate tendency or aim; esp., advancing a definite point of view: also sp. **ten·den′cious** —ten·den′tious·ly *adv.* —ten·den′tious·ness *n.*

ten·der[1] (ten′dər) *adj.* [< OFr. < L. *tener*, soft] 1. soft or delicate and easily chewed, broken, cut, etc. 2. physically weak; frail 3. immature; young [the *tender* age of five] 4. of soft quality or delicate tone 5. needing careful handling; ticklish [a *tender* subject] 6. gentle or light, as a touch 7. *a)* affectionate, loving, etc. [a *tender* smile] *b)* careful; considerate 8. *a)* that is hurt or feels pain easily; sensitive [a *tender* skin] *b)* sensitive to impressions, emotions, etc. [a *tender* conscience] *c)* sensitive to others' feelings; compassionate [a *tender* heart] —ten′der·ly *adv.* —ten′der·ness *n.*

ten·der[2] (ten′dər) *vt.* [< Fr. < L. *tendere*, to stretch] 1. to offer in payment of an obligation 2. to present for acceptance; offer (an invitation, apology, etc.) —*vi.* to make an offer or estimate for a particular job (with *for*) —*n.* 1. an offer of money, services, etc. made to satisfy an obligation 2. a formal offer to supply specified goods or services at a stated cost —put out to tender to invite and compare tenders for a particular job —ten′der·er *n.*

tend·er[3] (ten′dər) *n.* 1. a person who tends, or has charge of, something 2. *a)* a ship to supply or service another ship, a submarine, etc. *b)* a boat for carrying passengers, etc. to or from a ship close to shore 3. the vehicle behind a steam locomotive for carrying its coal and water

ten·der·foot (-foot′) *n., pl.* -foots′, -feet′ 1. a newcomer, specif. to the hardships of ranching in the W U.S. 2. formerly, a beginner in the Boy Scouts

ten·der·heart·ed (-härt′id) *adj.* having a tender heart; quick to feel pity —ten′der·heart′ed·ly *adv.* —ten′der·heart′ed·ness *n.*

ten·der·ize (ten′də rīz′) *vt.* -ized′, -iz′ing to make (meat) tender, as by adding a substance that softens tissues —ten′der·iz′er *n.*

ten·der·loin (ten′dər loin′) the tenderest muscle of a loin of pork

ten·di·ni·tis (ten′də nīt′əs) *n.* [< ModL.: see TENDON & -ITIS] inflammation of a tendon

ten·don (ten′dən) *n.* [ML. *tendo* (gen. *tendinis*) < Gr. < *teinein*, to stretch] any of the cords of tough, fibrous tissue connecting muscles to bones or other parts; sinew —ten′di·nous (-də nəs) *adj.*

ten·dril (ten′drəl) *n.* [prob. < OFr. *tendrum*, ult. < L. *tener*, soft] a threadlike part of a climbing plant, serving to support it by clinging to or coiling around an object

ten·e·brous (ten′ə brəs) *adj.* [< L. < *tenebrae*, darkness] dark; gloomy: also **te·neb·ri·ous** (tə neb′rē əs)

ten·e·ment (ten′ə mənt) *n.* [< OFr. < ML. < L. *tenere*, to hold] 1. *Law* land, buildings, etc. held by tenure 2. a dwelling house 3. a separately tenanted room or flat 4. a large building divided into rooms or flats for rent, now often one that is run-down and overcrowded; also **tenement building** —ten′e·men′tal, ten′e·men′ta·ry *adj.*

TENDRIL

te·nes·mus (ti nez′məs, -nes′-) *n.* [ML. < L. < Gr. *teinein*, to stretch] *Med.* painful and futile straining to evacuate the bowels or bladder

ten·et (ten′it) *n.* [L., he holds] a principle, doctrine, or belief held as a truth, as by some group

ten·fold (ten′fōld′) *adj.* 1. having ten parts 2. having ten times as much or as many —*adv.* ten times as much or as many

ten-gal·lon hat (ten′gal′ən) a wide-brimmed felt hat with a high, round crown, orig. worn by cowboys

ten·ner (ten′ər) *n.* [Colloq.] a ten-pound note

ten·nis (ten′is) *n.* [prob. < Anglo-Fr. *tenetz*, hold (imperative) < OFr. *tenir*: see TENANT] 1. a game (officially **lawn tennis**), usually played outdoors, in which two or four players using rackets hit a ball back and forth over a net dividing a marked rectangular area (**tennis court**) 2. a similar but more complex old indoor game (**real tennis**), the ball being in addition bounced against walls

tennis shoe a canvas shoe with a heelless, soft rubber sole

Ten·ny·so·ni·an (ten'ə sō'nē ən) *adj.* [after Alfred, Lord Tennyson (1809-92), Brit. poet] of or in the style of Tennyson

ten·on (ten'ən) *n.* [< MFr. < *tenir*: see TENANT] a part of a piece of wood, etc. cut to stick out so that it will fit into a hole (*mortise*) in another piece to make a joint: see MORTISE, illus. —*vt., vi.* 1. to make a tenon (on) 2. to joint by mortise and tenon

ten·or (ten'ər) *n.* [< OFr. < L. < *tenere*, to hold] 1. general course or tendency 2. general meaning; drift 3. general character or nature 4. [because the tenor voice "held" the melody] *a)* the highest usual adult male voice, or its range: see also COUNTERTENOR *b)* a part for this voice *c)* a singer or instrument having this range —*adj.* of, in, or for the tenor

tenor clef *see* C CLEF

tenpin bowling a form of bowling in which bowls are rolled down a lane to knock over the ten target pins: also [esp. U.S.] **tenpins**

ten·rec (ten'rek) *n.* [Fr. < Malagasy *tàndraka*] a small, burrowing, hedgehoglike mammal of Madagascar: also **tanrac**

tense¹ (tens) *adj.* **tens'er, tens'est** [< L. pp. of *tendere*, to stretch] 1. stretched tight; strained; taut 2. feeling, showing, or causing mental strain; anxious —*vt., vi.* **tensed, tens'ing** to make or become tense —**tense'ly** *adv.* —**tense'ness** *n.*

tense² (tens) *n.* [< OFr. < L. *tempus*, time] any form or set of forms of a verb that show the time of the action or condition

ten·sile (ten'sil) *adj.* 1. of or under tension 2. capable of being stretched: also **ten'si·ble** (-sə b'l) —**ten·sil'i·ty** (-sil'ə tē) *n.*

tensile strength the lengthwise stress that a given substance can bear without tearing apart

ten·sim·e·ter (ten sim'ə tər) *n.* [TENS(ION) + -METER] an instrument that measures changes in gas or vapour pressure

ten·sion (ten'shən) *n.* 1. a tensing or being tensed 2. mental or nervous strain; tense feeling 3. a state of strained relations 4. a device to regulate tautness of thread, etc. 5. *same as* VOLTAGE 6. *a)* stress on a material by forces tending to cause extension *b)* a force exerting such stress —*vt.* to subject to tension —**ten'sion·al** *adj.*

ten·sor (ten'sər, -sôr) *n.* [ModL. < L. pp. of *tendere*, to stretch] 1. any muscle that stretches a body part 2. *Math.* a generalized type of vector used, for example, in the description of the stress in continuous media and the inertia of rigid bodies

tent (tent) *n.* [< OFr. < L. pp. of *tendere*, to stretch] 1. a portable shelter consisting of canvas, etc. stretched over poles and attached to stakes 2. anything like a tent; specif., *short for* OXYGEN TENT —*adj.* of or like a tent —*vi.* to live in a tent —*vt.* 1. to lodge in tents 2. to cover as with a tent

ten·ta·cle (ten'tə k'l) *n.* [ModL. *tentaculum* < L. *tentare*, to touch] 1. any of various slender, flexible growths at or near the head or mouth, as of some invertebrates, used for grasping, feeling, moving, etc. 2. *Bot.* any of the sensitive hairs on the leaves of insect-eating plants —**ten·tac'u·lar** (-tak'yə lər) *adj.*

ten·ta·tive (ten'tə tiv) *adj.* [LL. *tentativus* < pp. of L. *tentare*, to try] made or done as a test or for the time being; not definite or final —**ten'ta·tive·ly** *adv.* —**ten'ta·tive·ness** *n.*

tent-bed (tent'bed) *n.* 1. a camp-bed 2. a bed with a canopy hanging from a central point

ten·ter (ten'tər) *n.* [see TENT] a frame to stretch cloth on for even drying —*vt.* to stretch on a tenter

ten·ter·hook (-hook') *n.* any of the hooked nails that hold cloth stretched on a tenter —**on tenterhooks** in suspense

tenth (tenth) *adj.* [OE. *teogotha*] 1. preceded by nine others in a series; 10th 2. designating any of the ten equal parts of something —*n.* 1. the one following the ninth 2. any of the ten equal parts of something; 1/10 —**tenth'ly** *adv.*

tent stitch [< ? TENT] an embroidery stitch forming a series of parallel slanting lines

ten·u·is (ten'yoo wis) *n., pl.* **-u·es** (-yoo wēz') [L., thin: used as transl. of Gr. *psilos*, unaspirated] a voiceless stop (p, t, or k)

ten·u·ous (ten'yoo wəs) *adj.* [< L. *tenuis*, thin + -OUS] 1. slender or fine, as a fibre 2. not dense; rare, as air high up 3. slight; flimsy [*tenuous* evidence] —**te·nu'i·ty** (tə nyōo'ə tē) *n.* —**ten'u·ous·ness** *n.* —**ten'u·ous·ly** *adv.*

ten·ure (ten'yər, -yoor) *n.* [< MFr. < *tenir*: see TENANT] 1. the act or right of holding property, an office, etc. 2. the period or conditions of this 3. [U.S.] the holding of a position in teaching, etc. on a permanent basis after meeting specified requirements

te·nu·to (tə nōōt'ō) *adj.* [It., pp. of *tenere*, to hold] *Music* held for the full value, as a note

te·o·cal·li (tē'ə kal'ē) *n., pl.* **-cal'lis** (-ēz) [Nahuatl < *teotl*, god + *calli*, house] an Aztec temple, usually a building on a truncated pyramid

te·pee (tē'pē) *n.* [< Siouan < *ti*, to dwell + *pi*, used for] a cone-shaped tent of animal skins, used by the American Indians

tep·id (tep'id) *adj.* [< L. < *tepere*, to be slightly warm] 1. slightly warm; lukewarm 2. unenthusiastic; apathetic —**te·pid'i·ty** (tə pid'ə tē), **tep'id·ness** *n.* —**tep'id·ly** *adv.*

te·qui·la (tə kē'lə) *n.* [AmSp. < Nahuatl *Tequila*, a Mexican district] 1. a strong alcoholic liquor of Mexico, distilled from pulque or mescal 2. a Mexican agave that is a source of tequila and mescal

ter. 1. terrace 2. territory

ter·a- (ter'ə) [< Gr. *teras*, monster] a combining form meaning one billion

ter·a·tism (ter'ə tiz'm) *n.* [< Gr. *teras* . (gen. *teratos*), a monster] an abnormally formed foetus; monstrosity

ter·bi·um (tur'bē əm) *n.* [ModL. < *Ytterby*, town in Sweden] a metallic chemical element of the rare-earth group: symbol, Tb; at. wt., 158.924; at. no., 65

terce (turs) *n.* [< OFr. < L. *tertia*, fem. of *tertius*, third] [*often* T-] *Eccles.* the third of the seven canonical hours

ter·cel (tur's'l) *n.* var. of TIERCEL

ter·cen·te·nar·y (tur'sen ten'ər ē, tər sen'tə ner'ē) *adj., n., pl.* **-nar·ies** [L. *ter*, three times + CENTENARY] *same as* TRICENTENNIAL: also **ter'cen·ten'ni·al** (-ten'ē əl)

ter·cet (tur'sit, tər set') *n.* [Fr. < It. dim. of *terzo*, a third < L. *tertius*] a group of three lines that rhyme or are connected by rhyme with an adjacent triplet

ter·e·bene (ter'ə bēn') *n.* [< Fr. < TERE(BINTH) + -ENE] a mixture of terpenes obtained by the action of sulphuric acid on spirits of turpentine; used as an expectorant, etc.

ter·e·binth (ter'ə binth') *n.* [< MFr., ult. < Gr. *terebinthos*] a small European tree whose cut bark yields a turpentine

ter·e·bra (ter'ə brə) *n., pl.* **-brae** (-brē) [L., a borer] an organ with which certain insects simultaneously bore holes and lay their eggs within them

te·re·do (tə rē'dō) *n., pl.* **-dos, -di·nes'** (-də nēz') [ME. < L. < Gr. *terēdon*, borer] a marine mollusc that bores into and destroys submerged wood; shipworm

te·rete (tə rēt', ter'ēt) *adj.* [< L. *teres*, gen. *teretis*, smooth] *Biol.* cylindrical and tapered

ter·gi·ver·sate (tur'ji vər sāt') *vi.* **-sat'ed, -sat'ing** [< L. pp. of *tergiversari* < *tergum*, the back + *versari*, to turn] 1. to desert a cause, party, etc. 2. to use evasions or subterfuge —**ter'gi·ver·sa'tion** *n.* —**ter'gi·ver·sa'tor** *n.*

term (turm) *n.* [< OFr. < L. *terminus*, a limit] 1. a set date, as for payment, termination of tenancy, etc. 2. *a)* a set period of time [a *term* of office] *b)* a division of an academic year, during which a school, etc., is in session *c)* the normal period between conception and birth; also, the end of this period; childbirth 3. [*pl*] *a)* conditions of a contract, sale, etc. that limit or define it *b)* charges; prices 4. [*pl.*] personal relations [on speaking *terms*] 5. a word or phrase having definite meaning in some science, art, etc. 6. a word or phrase of a specified kind [a colloquial *term*] 7. [*pl.*] words that express ideas in a specified form [to speak in derogatory *terms*] 8. *Archit.* a boundary post, esp. one consisting of a pedestal topped by a bust 9. *Law a)* the time a court is in session *b)* the length of time for which an estate is granted *c)* the estate itself *d)* time allowed a debtor to pay 10. *Logic a)* either of two concepts with a stated relation, as the subject and predicate of a proposition *b)* any one of the three parts of a syllogism 11. *Math. a)* either of the two quantities of a fraction or ratio *b)* each quantity in a series or in an algebraic expression —*vt.* to call by a term; name —**bring to terms** to force to agree —**come to terms** to arrive at an agreement —**in terms of** 1. regarding; concerning 2. used as a basis for expression 3. taking as a likely estimate —**term'less** *adj.*

ter·ma·gant (tur'mə gənt) *n.* [< OFr. *Tervagant*, alleged Moslem deity] a quarrelsome, scolding woman; shrew

ter·mi·na·ble (tur'mi nə b'l) *adj.* 1. that can be terminated 2. that terminates after a specified time, as a contract —**ter'·mi·na·bil'i·ty, ter'mi·na·ble·ness** *n.* —**ter'mi·na·bly** *adv.*

ter·mi·nal (tur'mən 'l) *adj.* [L. *terminalis*] 1. of, at, or forming the end or extremity of something 2. occurring at the end of a series; concluding; final 3. of or in the final stages of a fatal disease [*terminal* cancer] 4. in or of a term or set period of time 5. of, at, or forming the end of a transport route —*n.* 1. a terminating part; end; extremity 2. a connective device or point on an electric circuit or conductor 3. *a)* a terminus for trains or long-distance buses *b)* a building at an airport where passengers await departure 4. *Archit. a)* an ornamental carving at the end of a structure *b) same as* TERM (sense 8) —**ter'mi·nal·ly** *adv.*

terminal velocity *Physics* the unchanging velocity reached by a falling body when the frictional resistance of the enveloping medium is equal to the force of gravity

ter·mi·nate (-nāt') *vt.* **-nat'ed, -nat'ing** [< L. pp. of *terminare*, to end < *terminus*, a limit] 1. to form the end

TEPEE

or limit of; finish or bound **2.** to put an end to; stop —*vi.* to come to an end —**ter'mi·na'tive** *adj.* —**ter'mi·na'tor** *n.*
ter·mi·na·tion (turʹmə nāʹshən) *n.* **1.** a terminating or being terminated **2.** the end or limit **3.** *Linguis.* the end of a word; specif., an inflectional ending —**ter'mi·na'tion·al** *adj.*
ter·mi·nol·o·gy (turʹmə nolʹə jē) *n., pl.* **-gies 1.** the terms or special words used in some science, art, work, etc. **2.** the study of terms —**ter'mi·no·log'i·cal** (-nə lojʹi kʹl) *adj.* —**ter'mi·no·log'i·cal·ly** *adv.* —**ter'mi·nol'o·gist** *n.*
ter·mi·nus (turʹmə nəs) *n., pl.* **-ni** (-nīʹ), **-nus·es** [L., a limit] **1.** a boundary or limit **2.** a boundary stone or marker **3.** an end; final point or goal **4.** *a)* either end of a railway line, bus route, etc. *b)* a station or town at such a point
ter·mi·tar·i·um (turʹmi terʹē əm) *n.* [< ff.] **1.** a colony of termites **2.** the conical mound-dwelling built by termites, often 3-3.5 m high Also **ter·mi·tar·y** (turʹmit ər ē)
ter·mite (turʹmīt) *n.* [L. *termes* (gen. *termitis*), wood-boring worm] a pale-coloured, soft-bodied, antlike insect that lives in colonies and is very destructive to wooden structures
terms of trade the ratio of export prices to import prices
tern (turn) *n.* [< ON. *therna*] any of several sea birds related to the gulls, but smaller, with a more slender body and beak and a deeply forked tail
ter·na·ry (turʹnər ē) *adj.* [< L. < *terni*, three each] **1.** threefold; triple **2.** third in rank, etc.
ter·nate (turʹnāt) *adj.* [ModL., ult. < L. *terni*, three each] **1.** consisting of three **2.** arranged in threes, as some leaves —**ter'nate·ly** *adv.*
terne·plate (turnʹplāt') *n.* [Fr. *terne*, dull + PLATE] steel plate coated with an alloy of lead and a small amount of tin
ter·pene (turʹpēn) *n.* [G. *terpen*] any of a series of isomeric hydrocarbons of the general formula $C_{10}H_{16}$, found in resins, etc.
Terp·sich·o·re (tarp sikʹə rē) *Gr. Myth.* the Muse of dancing
terp·si·cho·re·an (turpʹsi kə rēʹən) *adj.* **1.** [T-] of Terpsichore **2.** having to do with dancing —*n.* a dancer: now only in humorous use
ter·race (terʹəs) *n.* [OFr., walled platform < It. *terrazzo* < L. *terra*, earth] **1.** *a)* a raised, flat mound of earth with sloping sides *b)* any of a series of flat platforms of earth with sloping sides, rising one above another, as on a hillside *c)* a geological formation of this nature *d)* [*usually pl.*] unroofed tiers round a football pitch on which the spectators stand **2.** an unroofed, paved area adjoining a house and overlooking a lawn or garden **3.** a gallery, portico, etc. **4.** a flat roof, esp. of a house of Spanish or Oriental architecture **5.** *a)* a row of houses on ground raised from the street *b)* a street in front of such houses —*vt.* **-raced, -rac·ing** to form into or surround with a terrace
terraced house a house forming one of a row of identical houses with common dividing walls
ter·ra cot·ta (terʹə kotʹə) [It., lit., baked earth < L.] **1.** a hard, brown-red, usually unglazed earthenware used for pottery, sculpture, etc. **2.** its brown-red colour —**ter'-ra-cot'ta** *adj.*
terra fir·ma (furʹmə) [L.] firm earth; solid ground
ter·rain (tə rānʹ, terʹān) *n.* [Fr. < L. < *terra*, earth] ground or a tract of ground, esp. with regard to its features or fitness for some use
ter·ra in·cog·ni·ta (terʹə in kogʹni tə) [L.] an unknown or unexplored area
ter·ra·pin (terʹə pin) *n.* [< Algonquian] **1.** any of several American freshwater turtles **2.** its edible flesh
ter·ra·que·ous (ter āʹkwē əs) *adj.* [< L. *terra*, earth + AQUEOUS] consisting of land and water
ter·rar·i·um (tə rerʹē əm) *n., pl.* **-i·ums, -i·a** (-ə) [ModL. < L. *terra*, earth + *-arium* as in *aquarium*] **1.** an enclosure for keeping small land animals **2.** a glass container for a garden of small plants
ter·raz·zo (tə razʹō, tə rätʹsō) *n.* [It., lit., TERRACE] flooring of small chips of marble set in cement and polished
ter·rene (te rēnʹ, terʹēn) *adj.* [ME. < L. *terrenus* < L. *terra*, earth] **1.** of earth; earthy **2.** worldly; mundane —*n.* **1.** the earth **2.** a land; territory
terre·plein (terʹplān') *n.* [Fr. < It. *terrapienare*, to terrace] a level platform behind a parapet, rampart, etc., where guns are mounted
ter·res·tri·al (tə resʹtrē əl) *adj.* [< L. *terrestris* < *terra*, earth] **1.** of this world; worldly; mundane **2.** of or constituting the earth **3.** consisting of land as distinguished from water **4.** living on land rather than in water, in the air, in trees, etc. **5.** growing in the ground —*n.* an inhabitant of the earth —**ter·res'tri·al·ly** *adv.*
ter·ret (terʹit) *n.* [< OFr. *toret*, dim. of *tour*, a turn] **1.** a ring for attaching a leash, as on a dog collar **2.** any of the rings on a harness, through which the reins pass
ter·ri·ble (terʹə bʹl) *adj.* [OFr. < L. *terribilis* < *terrere*, to frighten] **1.** causing terror; fearful; dreadful **2.** [Colloq.] extreme; intense; severe **3.** [Colloq.] very bad, unpleasant, disagreeable, etc. —**ter'ri·ble·ness** *n.* —**ter'ri·bly** *adv.*

ter·ric·o·lous (te rikʹə ləs) *adj.* [< L. *terricola*, earth dweller] *Biol.* living in or on the ground
ter·ri·er[1] (terʹē ər) *n.* [MFr. (*chien*) *terrier*, hunting (dog) < *terrier*, hillock, ult. < L. *terra*, earth] any of various breeds of active, typically small dog; orig. bred to burrow after small game
ter·ri·er[2] (terʹē ər) *n.* [ME. < MFr. < ML. *terrarius* (*liber*), (book) concerning the land] a detailed inventory of the landholdings of persons or corporations
ter·rif·ic (tə rifʹik) *adj.* [< L. < base of *terrere*, to frighten + -FIC] **1.** causing great fear; terrifying; dreadful **2.** [Colloq.] *a)* unusually great, intense, etc. *b)* unusually fine, enjoyable, etc. —**ter·rif'i·cal·ly** *adv.*
ter·ri·fy (terʹə fī') *vi.* **-fied', -fy'ing** [L. *terrificare* < *terrificus*, TERRIFIC] to fill with terror; frighten greatly; alarm —**ter'ri·fy'ing·ly** *adv.*
ter·rine (te rēnʹ) *n.* [Fr.: see TUREEN] **1.** a small earthenware container in which table delicacies are prepared or packed **2.** a paté
ter·ri·to·ri·al (terʹə tôrʹē əl) *adj.* **1.** of territory or land **2.** of or limited to a specific territory or district **3.** [T-] of a Territory or Territories **4.** [*often* T-] organized regionally for home defence —*n.* [T-] a member of a Territorial force —**ter'ri·to·ri·al'i·ty** (-al'ə tē) *n.* —**ter'ri·to·ri·al·ly** *adv.*
Territorial Army formerly, a voluntary, locally organised home-defence force in Britain, formed (1907-8) to serve as second line to the regular army
territorial waters the area of sea over which a nation has jurisdiction, conventionally within three miles of shore
ter·ri·to·ry (terʹə tor'ē, -trē) *n., pl.* **-ries** [L. *territorium* < *terra*, earth] **1.** the land and waters under the jurisdiction of a nation, state, ruler, etc. **2.** a part of a country or empire without the full status of a principal division; specif., *a)* [T-] formerly, a part of the U.S. without the status of a state and having an appointed governor *b)* [T-] a similar region in Canada or Australia **3.** any large tract of land; region **4.** an assigned area, as of a travelling salesman **5.** a sphere of action, existence, etc. **6.** the area occupied by an animal or pair of animals as for breeding, foraging, etc.
ter·ror (terʹər) *n.* [< MFr. < L. < *terrere*, to frighten] **1.** intense fear **2.** *a)* a person or thing causing intense fear *b)* the quality of causing dread; terribleness **3.** [*often* T-] a period, as during the French Revolution, characterized by a programme of terrorism **4.** [Colloq.] a very annoying or unmanageable person, esp. a child
ter·ror·ism (-iz'm) *n.* **1.** the use of force and violence to intimidate, subjugate, etc., esp. as a political policy **2.** the intimidation produced in this way —**ter'ror·ist** *n., adj.* —**ter'ror·is'tic** *adj.*
ter·ror·ize (-īz') *vt.* **-ized', -iz'ing 1.** to fill with terror **2.** to coerce, make submit, etc. by filling with terror —**ter'-ror·i·za'tion** *n.* —**ter'ror·iz'er** *n.*
ter·ry (terʹē) *n., pl.* **-ries** [prob. < Fr. pp. of *tirer*, to draw] cloth having a pile in which the loops are left uncut: also **terry cloth**
terse (turs) *adj.* **ters'er, ters'est** [< L. pp. of *tergere*, to wipe] free of superfluous words; concise; succinct —**terse'-ly** *adv.* —**terse'ness** *n.*
ter·tial (turʹshəl) *adj.* [< L. *tertius*, third] designating or of the third row of flight feathers on a bird's wing —*n.* a tertial feather
ter·tian (turʹshən) *adj.* [< L. < *tertius*, third] occurring every other day —*n.* a tertian fever or disease
ter·ti·ar·y (turʹshē ər ē, -sha rē) *adj.* [< L. < *tertius*, third] **1.** of the third rank, order, formation, etc.; third **2.** [T-] *Geol.* designating or of the first period in the Cainozoic Era **3.** *Zool.* same as TERTIAL —*n., pl.* **-ar'ies** *Zool.* same as TERTIAL —**the Tertiary** the Tertiary Period or its rocks: see GEOLOGY, chart
Ter·y·lene (terʹə lēn') [arbitrary blend of *ter*(*ephthalate*) + (*polyeth*)*ylene*, components in its production] *a trademark for* a synthetic, polyester, textile fibre
ter·za ri·ma (tertʹsə rē'mə) [It., lit., third rhyme] a verse form of Italian origin, made up of tercets, the second line of each tercet rhyming with the first and third lines of the next one (*aba, bcb, cdc,* etc.)
tes·la (tesʹlə) *n.* [after N. *Tesla* (1856-1943), U.S. inventor] the SI unit of magnetic flux density; the density of one weber of magnetic flux per square metre
tes·sel·late (tesʹə lāt'; *for adj.* -lit) *vt.* **-lat'ed, -lat'ing** [< L. < *tessella*, little square stone] to lay out or pave in a mosaic pattern of small, square blocks —*adj.* tessellated
tes·ser·a (tesʹər ə) *n., pl.* **-ser·ae** (-ē) [L. < Gr. *tesseres* (for *tessares*), four] **1.** in ancient Rome, a small tablet of ivory, etc., used as a token, ticket, etc. **2.** any of the small pieces used in mosaic work
test[1] (test) *n.* [OFr., cup used in assaying < L. *testum*, earthen vessel < *testa*, shell] **1.** *a)* an examination or trial, as to prove the value or find out the nature of something *b)* a method or process, or a standard or criterion, used in this **2.** an event, situation, etc. that tries a person's qualities **3.** a set of questions, problems, etc. for determining a person's knowledge, abilities, etc.; examination **4.** a vessel in which

metals are refined **5.** [Colloq.] *same as* TEST MATCH **6.** *Chem. a*) a trial or reaction for identifying a substance *b*) the reagent used in the procedure *c*) a positive indication obtained by it —**vt.** to subject to a test; try —**vi.** to give or take a test for diagnosis, function, etc. [to *test* for blood sugar] —**test′a·ble** *adj.*

test² (test) *n.* [L. *testa*: see prec.] the hard outer covering of certain invertebrate animals, as the shell of clams

Test. Testament

tes·ta (tes′tə) *n., pl.* **-tae** (-tē) [ModL. < L., a shell] *Bot.* the hard outer covering of a seed

tes·ta·ceous (tes tā′shəs) *adj.* [< L. *testaceus,* made of shell or tile] **1.** of or like shells **2.** hard-shelled **3.** *Biol.* light reddish-brown in colour, like earthenware

tes·ta·ment (tes′tə mənt) *n.* [< LL. < L., ult. < *testis,* a witness] **1.** orig., a covenant, esp. one between God and man **2.** [T-] *a*) either of the two parts of the Christian Bible, the *Old Testament* and the *New Testament b*) [Colloq.] a copy of the New Testament **3.** *a*) a proof; testimonial [a *testament* to liberty] *b*) an affirmation of beliefs, etc. **4.** *Law* a will: now rare except in last will and testament —**tes′ta·men·ta·ry** (-men′tə rē), **tes′ta·men′tal** *adj.*

tes·tate (tes′tāt) *adj.* [< L. pp. of *testari,* to testify, make a will] having made and left a legally valid will —**n.** a person who has died testate

tes·ta·tor (tes′tāt ər, tes tāt′-) *n.* a person who has made a will, esp. one who has died leaving a valid will —**tes·ta′trix** (-tā′triks) *n.fem., pl.* **-tri·ces′** (-trī sēz′)

test ban an agreement between or among nuclear powers to forgo tests of nuclear weapons, esp. in the atmosphere

test case *Law* a case that is likely to be used as precedent

test·er¹ (tes′tər) *n.* a person or thing that tests

test·er² (tes′tər) *n.* [< OFr. *testiere,* headpiece < L. *testa:* see TEST¹] a canopy, as over a bed

tes·ti·cle (tes′ti k'l) *n.* [< L. dim. of *testis,* testicle] either of two oval sex glands in the male that are suspended in the scrotum and secrete spermatozoa —**tes·tic′u·lar** (-tik′yōo lər) *adj.*

tes·ti·fy (tes′tə fī′) *vi.* **-fied′, -fy′ing** [< L. *testificari* < *testis,* a witness + *facere,* to make] **1.** to bear witness or give evidence, esp. under oath in court **2.** to be evidence or an indication [his look *testifies* to his rage] —**vt.** **1.** to bear witness to; affirm; give as evidence, esp. under oath in court **2.** to be evidence of; indicate —**tes′ti·fi·ca′tion** *n.* —**tes′ti·fi′er** *n.*

tes·ti·mo·ni·al (tes′tə mō′nē əl) *n.* **1.** a statement testifying to a person's qualifications, character, etc. or to the merits of some product, etc. **2.** something given or done as an expression of gratitude or appreciation

tes·ti·mo·ny (tes′tə mō′nē) *n., pl.* **-nies** [< L. < *testis,* a witness] **1.** a statement made under oath in court to establish a fact **2.** any affirmation or declaration **3.** any form of evidence; indication [his smile was *testimony* of his joy] **4.** public avowal, as of faith

tes·tis (tes′tis) *n., pl.* **-tes** (-tēz) [L.] *same as* TESTICLE

test match a cricket or Rugby League match which is one of a series between international sides

tes·tos·ter·one (tes tos′tə rōn′) *n.* [TEST(IS) + -o- + STER(OL) + -ONE] a male sex hormone, a crystalline steroid obtained from animal testes or synthesized: used in medicine

test paper **1.** a paper on which a test has been written **2.** paper, as litmus paper, prepared with a reagent for making chemical tests

test pilot a pilot who tests new or newly designed aircraft in flight, to determine their fitness for use

test-tube (tes′tyōob′) *adj.* **1.** made in or as in a test tube; experimental **2.** produced by artificial insemination [a *test-tube* baby]

test tube a tube of thin, clear glass closed at one end, used in chemical experiments, etc.

tes·tu·di·nal (tes tyōod′'n əl) *adj.* [< ff.] of or like a tortoise

tes·tu·do (tes tyōo′dō) *n., pl.* **-di·nes′** (-də nēz′) [L., tortoise (shell)] in ancient Rome, **1.** a movable, roofed shelter used by soldiers **2.** a protection formed by a group of soldiers by overlapping shields above their heads

tes·ty (tes′tē) *adj.* **-ti·er, -ti·est** [< Anglo-Fr. < OFr. *teste,* the head < L. *testa:* see TEST¹] irritable; touchy; peevish —**tes′ti·ly** *adv.* —**tes′ti·ness** *n.*

tet·a·nus (tet′'n əs) *n.* [L. < Gr. *tetanos,* spasm, lit., stretched] an acute infectious disease, often fatal, caused by the toxin of a bacillus which usually enters the body through wounds: characterized by spasmodic contractions and rigidity of muscles; lockjaw —**te·tan·ic** (ti tan′ik) *adj.*

tetch·y (tech′ē) *adj.* **tetch′i·er, tetch′i·est** [prob. < OFr. *teche,* a spot + -y²] touchy; irritable; peevish —**tetch′i·ly** *adv.* —**tetch′i·ness** *n.*

tête-à-tête (tāt′ə tāt′) *n.* [Fr., lit., head-to-head] **1.** a private conversation between two people **2.** an S-shaped seat on which two people can sit facing each other —**adj.** for or of two people in private —**adv.** together privately [to speak *tête-à-tête*]

teth·er (teth′ər) *n.* [prob. < ON. *tjöthr*] **1.** a rope or chain fastened to an animal so as to keep it within certain bounds **2.** the limit of one's abilities, resources, etc. —**vt.** to fasten with a tether —**at the end of one's tether** at the end of one's endurance, resources, etc.

tet·ra- [Gr. < base of *tettares,* four] *a combining form meaning* four: also, before a vowel, **tetr-**

tet·ra·chord (tet′rə kôrd′) *n.* [< Gr.: see TETRA- & CHORD²] *Music* a series of four tones within the interval of a fourth —**tet′ra·chor′dal** *adj.*

tet·ra·cy·cline (tet′rə sī′klin, -klīn) *n.* [< TETRA- + CYCL(IC) + -INE⁴] a yellow, crystalline powder, prepared synthetically or obtained from certain microorganisms: used as an antibiotic

tet·rad (tet′rad) *n.* [< Gr. *tetras,* four] a group or set of four

tet·ra·eth·yl lead (tet′rə eth′'l) a heavy, colourless, poisonous compound of lead, added to petrol to increase power and prevent engine knock

tet·ra·gon (tet′rə gon′) *n.* [< LL. < Gr.: see TETRA- + -GON] *Crystallography* a plane figure with four angles and four sides

te·trag·o·nal (te trag′ə n'l) *adj.* **1.** of a tetragon **2.** of a system of crystallization in which the three axes intersect at right angles and the two horizontal axes are equal

tet·ra·he·dron (-hē′drən) *n., pl.* **-drons, -dra** (-drə) [ModL. < LGr.: see TETRA- & -HEDRON] a solid figure with four triangular faces —**tet′-ra·he′dral** *adj.*

te·tral·o·gy (te tral′ə jē) *n., pl.* **-gies** [< Gr.: see TETRA- & -LOGY] any series of four related plays, operas, novels, etc.

te·tram·er·ous (te tram′ər əs) *adj.* [TETRA- + -MEROUS] *Biol.* made up of four parts or divisions

te·tram·e·ter (te tram′ə tər) *n.* [< LL. < Gr.: see TETRA- & -METER] **1.** a line of verse containing four metrical feet **2.** verse consisting of tetrameters —**adj.** having four metrical feet

TETRAHEDRON

tet·ra·pod (-pod′) *n.* [TETRA- + -POD] an organism or object with four feet —**adj.** having four feet

te·trap·ter·ous (te trap′tər əs) *adj.* [TETRA- + -PTEROUS] *Zool.* having four wings

te·trarch (te′trärk, tē′-) *n.* [< LL. < L. < Gr.: see TETRA- & -ARCH] **1.** in the ancient Roman Empire, the ruler of part (orig. a fourth part) of a province **2.** a subordinate prince, governor, etc. —**te·trarch′ic** *adj.*

tet·rarch·y (-trär kē) *n., pl.* **-trarch·ies** **1.** the rule or territory of a tetrarch **2.** government by four persons

tet·ra·va·lent (tet′rə vā′lənt) *adj.* **1.** having a valence of four **2.** *same as* QUADRIVALENT (sense 1)

tet·rode (tet′rōd) *n.* [TETR(A)- + -ODE] a thermionic valve having four electrodes

te·trox·ide (te trok′sīd) *n.* any oxide with four atoms of oxygen in each molecule

tet·ter (tet′ər) *n.* [OE. *teter*] any of various skin diseases, as eczema, characterized by itching

Teut. **1.** Teuton **2.** Teutonic

Teu·ton (tyōot′ən) *n.* **1.** a member of the Teutones **2.** a member of any Teutonic people; esp., a German

Teu·to·nes (-ēz′) *n.pl.* [L.] an ancient tribe, either Teutonic or Celtic, that lived in Jutland

Teu·ton·ic (tyōo ton′ik) *adj.* **1.** of the ancient Teutons **2.** German **3.** designating or of a group of north European peoples including the German, Scandinavian, Dutch, English, etc. **4.** *Linguis.* earlier var. of GERMANIC —**Teu·ton′i·cal·ly** *adv.*

Tex·as tower (tek′səs) [from its resemblance to oil rigs off the *Texas* coast] an offshore platform on foundations planted in the sea bottom, for beacons, radar installations, etc.

text (tekst) *n.* [< OFr. < L. *textus,* fabric < pp. of *texere,* to weave] **1.** the exact or original words of an author or speaker, as distinguished from notes, paraphrase, etc. **2.** any of the forms, versions, or editions in which a written work exists **3.** the principal matter on a printed page, as distinguished from notes, pictures, etc. **4.** the words of a song, etc. **5.** *a*) a Biblical passage used as the topic of a sermon *b*) any topic or subject dealt with

text·book (-book′) *n.* a book giving instructions in the principles of a subject of study

tex·tile (teks′tīl) *adj.* [< L. *textilis* < *textus:* see TEXT] **1.** having to do with weaving or woven fabrics **2.** that has been or can be woven —**n.** **1.** a fabric made by weaving, knitting, etc.; cloth **2.** raw material suitable for this, as cotton, wool, nylon, etc.

tex·tu·al (teks′choo wəl) *adj.* of, contained in, or based on a text —**tex′tu·al·ly** *adv.*

tex·tu·al·ism (-iz′m) *n.* **1.** strict adherence to the text, esp. of the Scriptures **2.** the art of textual criticism —**tex′-tu·al·ist** *n.*

tex·ture (teks′chər) *n.* [< L. < *texere:* see TEXT] **1.** the character of a fabric as determined by the arrangement, size, etc. of its threads **2.** the structure or composition of anything, esp. in the way it looks or feels on the surface —*vt.* **-tured, -tur·ing** to cause to have a particular texture —**tex′tur·al** *adj.* —**tex′tur·al·ly** *adv.*

T.G.W.U. Transport and General Workers' Union

-th¹ [< OE.] *a suffix meaning:* **1.** the act of [*stealth*] **2.** the state or quality of being or having [*wealth*]

-th² [< OE.] a suffix used in forming ordinal numerals [*fourth*]: also, after a vowel, **-eth**

-th³ [< OE.: see -ETH²] *contracted form of* -ETH² [*hath, doth*]

Th *Chem.* thorium

Th. Thursday

Thai (tī) *n.* **1.** a group of Asian languages considered to belong to the Sino-Tibetan language family **2.** the official language of Thailand **3.** *pl.* **Thais, Thai** *a)* a member of a group of Thai-speaking peoples of SE Asia *b)* a native or inhabitant of Thailand —*adj.* of Thailand, its people, culture, etc.

thal·a·mus (thal′ə məs) *n.*, *pl.* **-mi′** (-mī′) [ModL. < L. < Gr. *thalamos,* inner room] **1.** *Anat.* a mass of grey matter at the base of the brain, involved in the transmission of certain sensations **2.** *Bot.* the receptacle of a flower —**tha·lam·ic** (thə lam′ik) *adj.*

tha·las·sic (thə las′ik) *adj.* [< Fr. < Gr. *thalassa,* sea] **1.** of the sea, esp. bays, gulfs and inland seas

Tha·li·a (thə lī′ə, thāl′yə) *Gr. Myth.* **1.** the Muse of comedy and pastoral poetry **2.** one of the three Graces

tha·lid·o·mide (thə lid′ə mīd′) *n.* [< (ph)thali(mi)do (glutari)mide] a drug formerly used as a sedative and hypnotic: found to be responsible for severe birth deformities when taken during pregnancy

thal·li·um (thal′ē əm) *n.* [ModL. < Gr. *thallos,* green shoot: from its green spectrum line] a rare, bluish-white, soft, metallic chemical element: symbol, Tl; at. wt., 204.37; at. no., 81

thal·lo·phyte (-ə fīt′) *n.* [see ff. & -PHYTE] any of a primary division of plants including the bacteria, algae, fungi, and lichens —**thal′lo·phyt′ic** (-fit′ik) *adj.*

thal·lus (-əs) *n.,* *pl.* **-li** (-ī), **-lus·es** [ModL. < Gr. *thallos,* young shoot] the plant body of a thallophyte, showing no clear distinction of roots, stem, or leaves —**thal′loid** (-oid) *adj.*

thal·weg (täl′veg) *n.* [G., obs. sp. of *Talweg,* lit., valley way] *Geog., Geol.* the longitudinal profile of a valley

than (than; *unstressed* thən, th′n) [< OE. *thenne,* orig., then] a particle used: *a)* to introduce the second element in a comparison [A is taller *than* B] *b)* to express exception [none other *than* Sam] —*prep.* compared to: in *than whom, than which* [a writer *than whom* there is none finer]

than·a·top·sis (than′ə top′sis) *n.* [< Gr. *thanatos,* death + *opsis,* a view] a musing upon death

thane (thān) *n.* [OE. *thegen*] **1.** in early England, one of a class of freemen who held land of the king or a lord in return for military services **2.** in early Scotland, a person of rank who held land of the king

thank (thaŋk) [OE. *thancian*] **1.** to express appreciation to, as by saying "thank you" **2.** to hold responsible; blame: an ironic use [he can be *thanked* for our failure] —**thank you** *shortened form of* I thank you

thank·ful (-fəl) *adj.* feeling or expressing thanks —**thank′-ful·ly** *adv.* —**thank′ful·ness** *n.*

thank·less (-lis) *adj.* **1.** not feeling or expressing thanks; ungrateful **2.** unappreciated [a *thankless* task] —**thank′-less·ly** *adv.* —**thank′less·ness** *n.*

thanks (thaŋks) an expression of gratitude —*interj.* I thank you —**thanks to** **1.** thanks be given to **2.** on account of

thanks·giv·ing (thaŋks′giv′iŋ) **1.** *a)* a giving of thanks *b)* an expression of this; esp., a formal, public expression of thanks to God **2.** [T-] *a)* a U.S. holiday on the fourth Thursday of November: it commemorates the Pilgrim Fathers' celebration of the good harvest of 1621 *b)* a similar Canadian holiday on the second Monday of October In full, **Thanksgiving Day**

thar (tär) *n.* [Nepali] the goat-antelope of Nepal

that (that; *unstressed* thət) *pron.,* *pl.* **those** [OE. *thæt*] *as a demonstrative pronoun:* **1.** the person or thing mentioned or understood [*that* is John] **2.** the thing further away [this is larger than *that* over there] **3.** something being contrasted [this possibility is more likely than *that*] **4.** [*pl.*] certain people [*those* who know] *as a relative pronoun:* **1.** who, whom, or which: generally in restrictive clauses [the road (*that*) we took] **2.** where; at which [the cupboard *that* I found it in] **3.** when; in which [the year *that* he died] —*adj.,* *pl.* **those 1.** designating the one mentioned or understood [*that* man is John] **2.** designating the thing farther away [this house is larger than *that* one] **3.** designating something being contrasted [this possibility is more likely than *that* one] **4.** designating a person or thing not described but well known [*that* certain feeling] —*conj.* used: **1.** to introduce a noun clause [*that* he's gone is obvious] **2.** to introduce an adverbial clause expressing purpose [they died *that* we might live] **3.** to

introduce an adverbial clause expressing result [he ran so fast *that* I lost him] **4.** to introduce an adverbial clause expressing cause [I'm sorry *that* I won] **5.** to introduce an incomplete sentence expressing surprise, desire, etc. [oh, *that* he were here!] —*adv.* **1.** to that extent; so [I can't see *that* far] **2.** [Colloq.] very; so very [I don't like skating *that* much]: also used colloquially or in dialect before an adjective modified by a clause showing result [I'm *that* tired I could drop] —**all that** [Colloq.] **1.** so very [he isn't *all that* rich] **2.** everything of the same sort [sex and *all that*] —**at that** [Colloq.] **1.** at that point: also **with that 2.** all things considered; even so —**that is 1.** to be specific **2.** in other words —**that's that!** that is settled!

thatch (thach) *n.* [OE. *thæc*] **1.** *a)* a roof or roofing of straw, rushes, palm leaves, etc. *b)* material for such a roof: also **thatch′ing 2.** anything resembling thatch as: *a)* [Colloq.] the hair of the head *b)* a matted layer of leaves, etc. between growing vegetation and the soil **3.** any of various palms whose leaves are used for thatch: also **thatch palm** —*vt.* [OE. *theccan*] to cover with or as with thatch —**thatch′y** *adj.* **thatch′i·er, thatch′i·est**

thau·ma·tur·gy (thô′mə tur′jē) *n.* [< Gr. < *thauma* (gen. *thaumatos*), a wonder + *ergon,* work] the supposed working of miracles; magic —**thau′ma·tur′gic, thau′-ma·tur′gi·cal** *adj.* —**thau′ma·turg·ist** *n.*

thaw (thô) *vi.* [OE. *thawian*] **1.** *a)* to melt: said of ice, snow, etc. *b)* to pass to an unfrozen state: said of frozen foods **2.** to rise in temperature above freezing, so that snow, etc. melts: with *it:* said of weather [it *thawed* today] **3.** *a)* to get rid of the chill, stiffness, etc. resulting from extreme cold (often with *out*) *b)* to lose coldness or reserve of manner —*vt.* to cause to thaw —*n.* **1.** a thawing **2.** a spell of weather warm enough to allow thawing **3.** a becoming less reserved

Th.D. [L. *Theologiae Doctor*] Doctor of Theology

the (tha; *before vowels* thi, thē) *adj., definite article* [OE. *se,* *the*] **1.** the (as opposed to *a, an*) refers to a particular person or thing, as *a)* that (one) being spoken of [the story ended] *b)* that (one) which is present, close, etc. [the day is hot] *c)* that (one) designated, as by a title [the Mersey] *d)* that (one) considered outstanding, etc. [that's the hotel in town]: usually italicized in print *e)* that (one) belonging to a person previously mentioned [take me by the hand] *f)* that (one) considered as a unit of purchase, etc. [fifty pence the dozen] *g)* one specified period of time [the fifties] *h)* [Colloq.] that (one) in a specified relationship to one [the wife] **2.** the is used to refer to that one of a number of persons or things which is identified by a modifier, as by an attributive adjective, a relative clause, prepositional phrase, etc. **3.** the is used to refer to a person or thing considered generically, as *a)* one taken as the representative of the entire genus or type [the cow is a domestic animal] *b)* an adjective used as a noun [the good, the true] —*adv.* **1.** that much; to that extent [the better to see you with] **2.** by how much . . . by that much; to what extent . . . to that extent: used in a correlative construction expressing comparison [the sooner, the better]

the·an·throp·ic (thē an throp′ik) *adj.* [< Gr. *theanthrōpas* < *theos,* god + *anthropos* man] having both godlike and human attributes

the·ar·chy (thē′är kē) *n.* [< Gr. *theos,* god + -ARCHY] **1.** government by gods **2.** a company of gods

the·a·ter (thē′ə tər) *n.* U.S. var. sp. of THEATRE

the·a·tre (thē′ə tər) *n.* [< OFr. < L. < Gr. *theatron* < base of *theasthai,* to view] **1.** a place or structure where plays, films, etc. are presented **2.** any place like a theatre, having ascending rows of seats **3.** any scene of events [the Asian *theatre* of war] **4.** *a)* the art of writing or putting on plays *b)* people engaged in putting on plays, esp. live plays on a stage **5.** theatrical technique with reference to its effectiveness [a play that is good *theatre*]

the·a·tre-in-the-round (-in thə round′) *n.* a theatre having a central stage without a proscenium, surrounded by seats

theatre sister a nurse who assists a surgeon in the operating theatre

the·at·ri·cal (thē at′ri k'l) *adj.* **1.** having to do with the theatre, the drama, a play, etc. **2.** characteristic of the theatre; dramatic; esp. (in disparagement), melodramatic or affected Also **the·at′ric** —**the·at′ri·cal·ism, the·at′ri·cal′i·ty** (-kal′ə tē) *n.* —**the·at′ri·cal·ly** *adv.*

the·at·ri·cals (-k'lz) *n.pl.* performances of stage plays, esp. by amateurs

the·at·rics (thē at′riks) *n.pl.* **1.** [with sing. v.] the art of the theatre **2.** something done or said for theatrical effect; histronics

The·ban (thē′bən) *adj.* **1.** of an ancient city in S. Egypt, on the Nile **2.** of an important city of ancient Boeotia, EC Greece —*n.* an inhabitant of Thebes

the·ca (thē′kə) *n.,* *pl.* **-cae** (-sē) [ModL. < L. < Gr. *thēkē,* a case] **1.** *Bot.* a spore case, sac, or capsule **2.** *Zool., Anat.* any sac enclosing an organ or a whole organism, as the covering of an insect pupa —**the′cal** *adj.* —**the′cate** (-kit) *adj.*

thee (*thē*) *pron.* [OE. *the*] *objective case of* THOU[1]: also used in place of *thou* by Friends (Quakers) [*thee* is kind]

theft (theft) *n.* [OE. *thiefth*] the act or an instance of stealing; larceny

thegn (thān) *n.* [OE.] *var. of* THANE

the·ine (thē'in, -ēn) *n.* [< ModL. < *thea*, tea] caffeine, esp. as found in tea

their (*th*er; *unstressed th*ər) *possessive pronominal adj.* [ON. *theirra*] of, belonging to, made by, or done by them: often used colloquially after a singular subject [everyone has had *their* lunch]

theirs (*th*ərz) *pron.* that or those belonging to them: used without a following noun [that cat is *theirs*, *theirs* are better]: also used after *of* to indicate possession [a friend of *theirs*]

the·ism (thē'iz'm) *n.* [THE(O)- + -ISM] 1. belief in a god or gods 2. belief in one God who is creator and ruler of the universe —**the'ist** *n., adj.* —**the·is'tic**, **the·is'ti·cal** *adj.* —**the·is'ti·cal·ly** *adv.*

them (*th*em; *unstressed th*əm, *th*'m, əm) *pron.* [ON. *theim*] *objective case of* THEY: also used colloquially as a predicate complement with a linking verb (Ex.: that's *them*)

theme (thēm) *n.* [< OFr. < L. < Gr. *thema* < base of *tithenai*, to put] 1. *a*) a topic, as of a lecture, essay, etc. *b*) a recurring, unifying subject or idea; motif 2. [U.S.] a short essay, esp. one written as a school assignment 3. *a*) a short melody used as the subject of a musical composition *b*) a musical phrase upon which variations are developed —**the·mat·ic** (thē mat'ik) *adj.* —**the·mat'i·cal·ly** *adv.*

theme song 1. a recurring song in a film, etc., that becomes popularly associated with the work 2. [Chiefly U.S.] *same as* SIGNATURE TUNE

them·selves (*th*em selvz', *th*əm-) *pron.* a form of the 3rd pers. pl. pronoun, used: *a*) as an intensive [they went *themselves*] *b*) as a reflexive [they hurt *themselves*] *c*) as a quasi-noun meaning "their real or true selves" [they are not *themselves* today]

then (*th*en) *adv.* [see THAN] 1. at that time [he was young *then*] 2. soon afterwards; next in time [he took his hat and *then* left] 3. next in order [first comes one and *then* two] 4. in that case; accordingly [if it rains, *then* I will get wet] 5. besides; moreover [I like to walk, and *then* it's cheaper] 6. at another time [now it's warm, *then* cold] —*adj.* being such at that time [the *then* director] —*n.* that time [by *then*, they were gone] —**but then** but on the other hand —**then and there** at that time and in that place; at once —**what then?** what would happen in that case?

the·nar (thē'när) *n.* [ModL. < Gr.] 1. the palm of the hand or, sometimes, the sole of the foot 2. the bulge at the base of the thumb

thence (*th*ens, thens) *adv.* [OE. *thanan*] 1. from that place 2. from that time; thenceforth 3. on that account; therefore

thence·forth (-fôrth') *adv.* from that time onwards; thereafter: also **thence'for'ward**, **thence'for'wards**

the·o- [< Gr. *theos*, god] *a combining form meaning* a god or God: also, before a vowel, **the-**

the·o·bro·mine (thē'ə brō'mēn, -min) *n.* [< ModL. *Theobroma*, a genus of trees (< Gr. *theos*, god + *brōma*, food) + -INE[4]] a bitter, crystalline alkaloid extracted from the cacao plant and used in medicine

the·oc·ra·cy (thē ok'rə sē) *n., pl.* -cies [< Gr.: see THEO- & -CRACY] 1. lit., the rule of a state by God or a god 2. government by priests or clergy claiming to rule with divine authority 3. a country so governed —**the·o·crat** (thē'ə krat') *n.* —**the'o·crat'ic**, **the'o·crat'i·cal** *adj.* —**the'o·crat'i·cal·ly** *adv.*

the·od·i·cy (thē od'ə sē) *n.* [< Gr. *theos*, god + *dike*, justice] a system of natural theology aimed at seeking to vindicate divine justice in allowing evil to exist

the·od·o·lite (thē od'əl īt') *n.* [ModL. *theodelitus*] a surveying instrument used to measure vertical and horizontal angles —**the·od'·o·lit'ic** (-ə lit'ik) *adj.*

theol. 1. theologian 2. theology

the·o·lo·gi·an (thē'ə lō'jən, -jē ən) *n.* a student of or a specialist in theology or a theology

the·o·log·i·cal (-loj'i k'l) *adj.* of, based on, or offering instruction in, theology or a theology: also **the'o·log'ic** —**the'o·log'·i·cal·ly** *adv.*

theological virtues *Theol.* the three virtues (faith, hope, and charity) having God as their object

the·ol·o·gize (thē ol'ə jīz') *vt.* -gized', -giz'-ing to put into theological terms —*vi.* to speculate theologically —**the·ol'o·giz'er** *n.*

the·ol·o·gy (thē ol'ə jē) *n., pl.* -gies [< LL. < Gr.: see THEO-& -LOGY] 1. the study of God and of religious doctrines and matters of divinity 2. a specific system of this study

the·om·a·chy (thē om'ə kē) *n.* [< Gr. *theos*, god + *mache*, a battle] battle against, or among, the gods

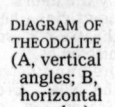

DIAGRAM OF THEODOLITE (A, vertical angles; B, horizontal angles)

the·o·phyl·line (thē'ə fil'ēn, -in) *n.* [< ModL. *thea*, tea + -PHYLL + -INE[4]] a colourless, crystalline alkaloid found in tea leaves; an isomer of theobromine

the·o·rem (thē'ə rəm, thir'əm) *n.* [< Fr. < L. < Gr. *theōrēma* < *theōrein*, to view] 1. a proposition that is not self-evident but that can be proved from accepted premises and so is established as a law or principle 2. an expression of relations in an equation or formula 3. *Math., Physics* a proposition embodying something to be proved —**the'·o·re·mat'ic** (-rə mat'ik) *adj.*

the·o·ret·i·cal (thē'ə ret'i k'l) *adj.* 1. of or constituting theory 2. limited to or based on theory; not practical; hypothetical 3. tending to theorize; speculative Also **the'·o·ret'ic** —**the'o·ret'i·cal·ly** *adv.*

the·o·re·ti·cian (thē'ə rə tish'ən) *n.* a person who specializes in the theory of some art, science, etc.: also **the'·o·rist** (-rist)

the·o·rize (thē'ə rīz') *vi.* -rized', -riz'ing to form a theory or theories; speculate —**the'o·ri·za'tion** *n.* —**the'o·riz'er** *n.*

the·o·ry (thē'ə rē, thir'ē) *n., pl.* -ries [< Fr. < LL. < Gr. < *theōrein*, to view] 1. a speculative idea or plan as to how something might be done 2. a systematic statement of principles involved [the *theory* of counterpoint in music] 3. a formulation of apparent relationships or underlying principles of certain observed phenomena which has been verified to some degree 4. that branch of an art or science consisting in a knowledge of its principles and methods rather than in its practice 5. popularly, a mere conjecture, or guess

theory of games *same as* GAME THEORY

the·os·o·phy (thē os'ə fē) *n., pl.* -phies [< ML. < LGr., ult. < Gr. *theos*, god + *sophos*, wise] 1. any of various philosophies or religions that propose to establish direct, mystical contact with divine principle through contemplation, revelation, etc. 2. [*often* T-] the doctrines of a modern sect (**Theosophical Society**) that incorporates elements of Buddhism and Brahmanism —**the'o·soph'ic** (-ə sof'ik), **the'o·soph'i·cal** *adj.* —**the'o·soph'i·cal·ly** *adv.* —**the·os'o·phist** *n.*

ther·a·peu·tic (ther'ə pyoot'ik) *adj.* [ModL. < Gr., ult. < *therapeuein*, to nurse] 1. *a*) serving to cure or heal; curative *b*) serving to preserve health 2. of therapeutics Also **ther'a·peu'ti·cal** —**ther'a·peu'ti·cal·ly** *adv.*

ther·a·peu·tics (-iks) *n.pl.* [*with sing. v.*] the branch of medicine that deals with the treatment and cure of diseases; therapy

ther·a·py (ther'ə pē) *n., pl.* -pies [ModL. < Gr. < *therapeuein*, to nurse] the treatment of disease or of any physical or mental disorder by medical or physical means: often used in compounds [hydrotherapy] —**ther'a·pist** *n.*

Ther·a·va·da (ther'ə vä'də) [Pali, lit., doctrine of the elders] a form of Buddhism stressing the original monastic discipline

there (*th*er) *adv.* [OE. *ther*] 1. at or in that place: often used as an intensive [John *there* is a good boy] 2. towards, to, or into that place [go *there*] 3. at that point in action, speech, etc. 4. in that matter, respect, etc. [*there* you are wrong] 5. right now [*there* goes the whistle] *There* is also used: *a*) in interjectional phrases of approval, etc. [*there's* a fine fellow!] *b*) in impersonal constructions in which the real subject follows the verb [*there* are three men here] —*n.* that place or point [we left *there* at six] —*interj.* an exclamation expressing defiance, dismay, satisfaction, sympathy, etc. [*there, there!* don't worry] —**(not) all there** [Colloq.] (not) mentally sound

there·a·bouts (*th*er'ə bouts') *adv.* 1. near that place 2. near that time 3. near that number, amount, degree, etc. Also **there'a·bout'**

there·af·ter (*th*er af'tər) *adv.* 1. after that; subsequently 2. [Archaic] accordingly

there·at (-at') *adv.* 1. at that place; there 2. at that time 3. for that reason

there·by (-bī') *adv.* 1. by that means 2. connected with that [*thereby* hangs a tale]

there·for (-fôr') *adv.* [Archaic] for this; for that; for it

there·fore (*th*er'fôr') *adv.* for this or that reason; consequently; hence: often used as a conjunction

there·from (*th*er from') *adv.* from this; from that; from it

there·in (-in') *adv.* 1. in there; in or into that place or thing 2. in that matter, detail, etc.

there·in·to (*th*er in'too) *adv.* [Archaic] 1. into that place or thing 2. into that matter, condition, etc.

there·of (-ov') *adv.* 1. of that 2. concerning that 3. from that as a cause, reason, etc.

there·on (-on') *adv.* [Archaic] 1. on that 2. *same as* THEREUPON

there's (*th*erz) 1. there is 2. there has

there·to (*th*er too') *adv.* 1. to that place, thing, etc.: also **there'un'to** 2. [Archaic] besides

there·to·fore (*th*er'tə fôr', *th*er'tə fôr') *adv.* up to then; until that time; before that

there·un·der (*th*er un'dər) *adv.* [Archaic] 1. under that; under it 2. under the terms stated there

there·up·on (*th*er'ə pon', *th*er'ə pon') *adv.* 1. immediately following that **2.** as a consequence of that **3.** concerning that subject, etc.

there·with (*th*er with′, -wi*th*′) *adv.* [Archaic] **1.** along with that **2.** in addition to that **3.** by that method or means **4.** immediately thereafter

there·with·al (*th*er′wi*th* ôl′) *adv.* **1.** in addition; besides **2.** [Obs.] along with that

therm (thurm) *n.* a unit of heat equal to 100 000 British thermal units (105 506 000 joules)

ther·mal (thur′m′l) *adj.* [Fr. < Gr. *thermē*, heat] **1.** having to do with heat, hot springs, etc. **2.** warm or hot —*n.* a rising column of warm air, caused by the uneven heating of the earth or sea by the sun —**ther′mal·ly** *adv.*

thermal barrier the speed limit beyond which the high temperatures caused by atmospheric friction would damage or destroy a given spacecraft, rocket, etc.

thermal capacity *same as* HEAT CAPACITY

thermal spring a spring whose water has a temperature higher than that of the air in the place where it is located; also **hot spring**

ther·mic (thur′mik) *adj.* of or caused by heat

therm·i·on·ic valve (thurm′ī on′ik, thur′mē-) [THERM(O)- + ION + -IC] an electron tube having a cathode electrically heated in order to cause electron or ion emission; also [esp. U.S.] **thermionic tube**

therm·is·tor (thar mis′tar, thur′mis′-) *n.* [THERM(O)- + (RES)ISTOR] a resistor made of semiconductor material, whose resistance decreases as temperature rises: used to measure temperature, microwave power, etc.

Ther·mit (thur′mit) [G. < Gr. *thermē*, heat + G. *-it*, -ITE] a trademark for a mixture of finely granulated aluminium with an oxide of iron or other metal, which produces great heat and is used in welding and incendiary bombs: also **Ther·mite** (-mīt)

ther·mo- [< Gr. *thermē*, heat] a combining form meaning: **1.** heat [*thermodynamics*] **2.** thermoelectric [*thermocouple*]. Also, before a vowel, **therm-**

ther·mo·chem·is·try (thur′mō kem′is trē) *n.* the branch of chemistry that deals with the relationship of heat to chemical change

ther·mo·cou·ple (thur′mə kup′′l) *n.* a pair of dissimilar conductors joined together at their ends: when this junction is heated, the voltage across it is in proportion to the rise in temperature: also called **thermoelectric couple**

ther·mo·dy·nam·ic (thur′mō dī nam′ik) *adj.* **1.** of or having to do with thermodynamics **2.** caused or operated by heat converted into motive power —**ther′mo·dy·nam′i·cal·ly** *adv.*

ther·mo·dy·nam·ics (-dī nam′iks) *n.pl.* [with sing. v.] the branch of physics dealing with the reversible transformation of heat into other forms of energy, esp. mechanical energy, and with the laws governing such conversions of energy

ther·mo·e·lec·tric (-i lek′trik) *adj.* of or having to do with the direct relations between heat and electricity: also **ther′-mo·e·lec′tri·cal** —**ther′mo·e·lec′tri·cal·ly** *adv.*

ther·mo·e·lec·tric·i·ty (-i lek′tris′ə tē) *n.* electricity produced by heating the junction between two dissimilar conductors so as to produce an electromotive force

ther·mo·gen·e·sis (-jen′ə sis) *n.* [ModL.: see THERMO- & -GENESIS] the production of heat, esp. by physiological action in an animal

ther·mo·gram (thur′mə gram′) *n.* [THERMO- + -GRAM] a record made by a thermograph

ther·mo·graph (-graf′) *n.* [THERMO- + -GRAPH] a thermometer for recording variations in temperature automatically

ther·mo·junc·tion (thur′mō juŋk′shən) *n.* the point of contact between the two conductors of a thermocouple

ther·mo·lu·mi·nes·cence (-lōō′mə nes′′ns) *n.* [THERMO- + LUMINESCENCE] the release in the form of light of stored energy from a substance when it is heated

ther·mom·e·ter (thər mom′ə tər) *n.* [< Fr.: see THERMO- & -METER] an instrument for measuring temperatures, as one consisting of a sealed glass tube, marked off in degrees, in which mercury, coloured alcohol, etc. rises or falls as it expands or contracts from changes in temperature: see FAHRENHEIT, CELSIUS —**ther·mo·met·ric** (thur′mə met′rik) *adj.* —**ther′mo·met′ri·cal·ly** *adv.*

ther·mo·nu·cle·ar (thur′mō nyōō′klē ər) *adj.* *Physics* **1.** designating or of a reaction in which light atomic nuclei fuse at temperatures of millions of degrees into heavier nuclei **2.** designating, of, or employing the heat energy released in nuclear fusion

ther·mo·pile (thur′mə pīl′) *n.* [THERMO- + PILE¹] a device consisting of a series of thermocouples, used for measuring minute changes in temperature or for generating thermoelectric current

ther·mo·plas·tic (thur′mə plas′tik) *adj.* soft and mouldable when subjected to heat: said of certain plastics —*n.* a thermoplastic substance

Ther·mos (thur′məs) [Gr. *thermos*, hot] a trademark for a type of flask or jug with two walls enclosing a vacuum, used for keeping liquids at almost their original temperature for several hours —*n.* such a flask, or jug: in full **Thermos flask** (or **jug**)

ther·mo·set·ting (thur′mō set′iŋ) *adj.* becoming permanently hard and unmouldable when once subjected to heat: said of certain plastics

ther·mo·sta·ble (-stā′b′l) *adj.* [THERMO- + STABLE¹] retaining its characteristic properties when heated

ther·mo·stat (thur′mə stat′) *n.* [THERMO- + -STAT]¹ **1.** an apparatus for regulating temperature, esp. one that automatically controls a heating unit **2.** a device that sets off a sprinkler, etc. at a certain heat —**ther′mo·stat′ic** *adj.* —**ther′mo·stat′i·cal·ly** *adv.*

ther·mo·tax·is (-tak′sis) *n.* [< THERMO + Gr. *taxis*, arrangement] **1.** *Biol.* movement of an organism towards or away from heat **2.** *Physiol.* the normal regulation of body temperature

ther·mot·ro·pism (thər mot′rə piz′m) *n.* [THERMO- + -TROPISM] *Biol.* growth or movement towards or away from a source of heat —**ther·mo·trop·ic** (thur′mə trop′ik) *adj.*

the·sau·rus (thi sôr′əs) *n.*, *pl.* **-ri** (-ī), **-rus·es** [L. < Gr. *thēsauros*, a treasure] **1.** a treasury or storehouse **2.** a book containing a store of words; specif., a book of synonyms and antonyms

these (thēz) *pron., adj.* *pl. of* THIS

the·sis (thē′sis) *n.*, *pl.* **the′ses** (-sēz) [L. < Gr. *thesis*, a placing < base of *tithenai*, to put] **1.** a proposition defended in argument **2.** a formal and lengthy research paper, esp. one presented as part of the requirements for a degree **3.** *Logic* an unproved statement assumed as a premise

Thes·pi·an (thes′pē ən) *adj.* [after *Thespis*, Greek poet of 6th c. B.C.] [often t-] having to do with the drama; dramatic —*n.* [often t-] an actor or actress: a humorous or pretentious term

Thess. Thessalonians

the·ta (thēt′ə) *n.* the eighth letter of the Greek alphabet (Θ, θ)

the·ur·gy (thē′ər jē) *n.* [< LL. < LGr. < Gr. *theos*, god + *ergon*, work] **1.** supernatural intervention in human affairs **2.** magic; sorcery

thews (thyōōz) *n.pl.*, *sing.* **thew** [OE. *theaw*, custom, habit] **1.** muscular power; bodily strength **2.** muscles or sinews —**thew′y** *adj.* **thew′i·er, thew′i·est**

they (thā) *pron.* *for sing. see* HE, SHE, IT¹ [< ON. *their*] **1.** the persons, animals, or things previously mentioned **2.** people in general [*they* say it's so] *They* is the nominative case form of the third personal plural pronoun

they'd (thād) **1.** they had **2.** they would

they'll (thāl, th el) **1.** they will **2.** they shall

they're (th er, thā′ər) they are

they've (thāv) they have

thi- *same as* THIO-

thi·a·mine (thī′ə mēn′, -min) *n.* [altered < THI(O)- + (VIT)AMIN] vitamin B₁, a white, crystalline compound found in cereal grains, egg yolk, liver, etc., or prepared synthetically: a deficiency of this vitamin results in beriberi and certain nervous disorders: also **thi′a·min** (-min)

thick (thik) *adj.* [OE. *thicce*] **1.** of relatively great depth or extent from one surface or side to the other [a *thick* board] **2.** having large diameter in relation to length [a *thick* pipe] **3.** measured between opposite surfaces [a wall nine centimetres *thick*] **4.** dense; compact; specif., *a)* marked by profuse, close growth; luxuriant [*thick* woods] *b)* great in number and close together [a *thick* crowd] *c)* having much body; not thin [*thick* soup] *d)* dense and heavy [*thick* smoke] *e)* covered [a road *thick* with mud] *f)* studded profusely [a sky *thick* with stars] **5.** dark or obscure [*thick* shadows] **6.** *a)* slurred, muffled, or husky [*thick* speech, a *thick* voice] *b)* strongly marked [a *thick* accent] *c)* muzzy; fuddled [a *thick* head] **7.** [Colloq.] stupid **8.** [Colloq.] close in friendship **9.** [Colloq.] too much to be tolerated [that's a bit *thick*] —*adv.* in a thick way —*n.* the thickest part or the period of greatest activity [in the *thick* of the fight] —**lay it on thick** [Slang] to exaggerate, esp. to flatter excessively —**the thick end of the stick** the inferior part of any transaction, etc. —**through thick and thin** in good times and bad times —**thick′ish** *adj.* —**thick′ly** *adv.*

thick·en (thik′ən) *vt., vi.* **1.** to make or become thick or thicker **2.** to make or become more complex or involved —**thick′en·er** *n.*

thick·en·ing (-iŋ) *n.* **1.** the action of one that thickens **2.** a substance used to thicken **3.** the thickened part

thick·et (thik′it) *n.* [OE. *thiccet* < *thicce*, thick] a thick growth of shrubs or small trees

thick·head·ed (thik′hed′id) *adj.* stupid —**thick′head′-ed·ness** *n.*

thick·ness (-nis) *n.* **1.** the quality of being thick **2.** the measure of how thick a thing is **3.** a layer [three *thicknesses* of cloth]

thick·set (-set′) *adj.* **1.** planted thickly or closely **2.** thick in body; stocky —*n.* [Archaic] a thicket

thick-skinned (-skind′) *adj.* **1.** having a thick skin **2.** not easily hurt by criticism, insults, etc.

thief (thēf) *n., pl.* **thieves** (thēvz) [OE. *theof*] a person who steals, esp. secretly

thieve (thēv) *vt., vi.* **thieved, thiev′ing** [OE. *theofian* < *theof,* a thief] to steal —**thiev′ish** *adj.* —**thiev′ish·ly** *adv.* —**thiev′ish·ness** *n.*

thiev·er·y (thēv′ər ē) *n., pl.* **-er·ies** the act or practice of stealing or an instance of this; theft

thigh (thī) *n.* [OE. *theoh*] the part of the leg between the knee and the hip

thigh·bone (-bōn′) *n.* the largest and longest bone in the body, from the hip to the knee; femur: also **thigh bone**

thill (thil) *n.* [OE. *thille*, a stake, pole] either of the two shafts between which a horse is hitched to a wagon

thim·ble (thim′b'l) *n.* [OE. *thymel* < *thuma*, a thumb] **1.** a small cap of metal, plastic, etc. worn as a protection on the finger that pushes the needle in sewing **2.** anything like this; esp., a grooved metal ring inserted in a loop of rope, etc. to prevent wear

thim·ble·ful (-fool′) *n., pl.* **-fuls** **1.** as much as a thimble will hold **2.** a very small quantity

thim·ble·rig (-rig′) *n.* a swindling game in which the victim bets that a pea is under one of three thimble-shaped containers manipulated by sleight of hand —*vt., vi.* **-rigged′, -rig′ging** to cheat or swindle, as in this game —**thim′-ble·rig′ger** *n.*

thin (thin) *adj.* **thin′ner, thin′nest** [OE. *thynne*] **1.** of relatively little depth or extent from one surface or side to the other [a *thin* board] **2.** having small diameter in relation to length [*thin* thread] **3.** having little fat or flesh; slender **4.** not dense or compact; specif., a) scanty in growth; sparse [*thin* hair] b) small in size or number [*thin* receipts] c) lacking body; watery [*thin* soup] d) not dense or heavy [*thin* smoke] e) rarified, as air at high altitudes **5.** not deep and strong; weak [*thin* colours, a *thin* voice] **6.** light or sheer, as fabric **7.** easily seen through; flimsy [a *thin* excuse] **8.** slight, weak, vapid, etc. [a *thin* plot, a *thin* argument] **9.** [Colloq.] dull; miserable [to have a *thin* time] —*adv.* in a thin way —*vt., vi.* **thinned, thin′-ning** to make or become thin or thinner: often with *out, down,* etc. —**thin on the ground** [Colloq.] small in number —**thin on top** [Colloq.] going bald —**thin′ly** *adv.* —**thin′-ness** *n.* —**thin′nish** *adj.*

thine (thīn) *pron.* [OE. *thin*] [Archaic or Poet.] that or those belonging to thee (you): absolute form of THY [a friend of *thine*, this is *thine*] —*possessive pronominal adj.* [Archaic or Poet.] thy: used before a word beginning with a vowel or unvoiced *h*

thing[1] (thing) *n.* [OE., a council, hence, "matter discussed, thing"] **1.** any matter, affair, or concern **2.** a happening, act, deed, incident, etc. [to do great *things*] **3.** an end to be achieved, a step in a process, etc. [the next *thing* is to mix thoroughly] **4.** an individual, distinguishable entity; specif., a) a tangible object, as distinguished from a quality, concept, etc. b) a lifeless object c) an item, detail, etc. [look at each *thing* on the list] d) the object or concept referred to by a word, symbol, or sign e) an object of thought; idea **5.** a) [pl.] personal belongings; also, clothes or clothing b) a dress,garment, etc. [not a *thing* to wear] **6.** a person or creature [poor *thing!*] **7.** something mentioned but unnamed [where did you buy that *thing?*] **8.** [Colloq.] a point of dispute; issue [he made a *thing* of it] **9.** [Colloq.] a strong, often neurotic liking, fear, aversion, etc. [to have a *thing* about flying] —**do one's (own) thing** [Colloq.] to express one's unique personality in one's own way of life, activities, etc. —**see things** [Colloq.] to have hallucinations —**the thing 1.** that which is wise, essential, etc. **2.** that which is the height of fashion

‡**thing**[2] (ting; *E.* thing) *n.* [ON., assembly] a Scandinavian legislative body

thing·a·ma·bob, thing·um·a·bob (thing′ə mə bob′) *n.* [Colloq.] *same as* THINGAMAJIG: also **thing′um·bob′, thing′-a·my, thing′um·my**

thing·a·ma·jig, thing·um·a·jig (-jig′) *n.* [extension of older *thingum*, THING[1]] [Colloq.] any device or gadget: jocular substitute for a name not known, temporarily forgotten, or deliberately withheld

think[1] (thingk) *vt.* **thought, think′ing** [OE. *thencan*] **1.** to form or have in the mind [*think* good thoughts] **2.** to judge; consider [I *think* her charming] **3.** to believe; surmise; expect [I *think* I can go] **4.** to determine, work out, etc. by reasoning [to *think* a problem through] **5.** [Now Rare] to intend [*thinking* to do right] **6.** a) to have in mind; form an idea of [*think* what may be] b) to recall; recollect [*think* what joy was ours] —*vi.* **1.** to use the mind; reflect or reason [*think* before you act] **2.** to have an opinion, belief, judgment, etc. [I just *think* so, we *think* highly of him] **3.** to remember (with *of* or *about*) **4.** to consider or be considerate (with *of* or *about*) **5.** to invent; conceive (*of*) **6.** to focus the attention on being [*think* big] —*n.* [Colloq.] the act of thinking [give it a good *think*] —*adj.* [Colloq.] having to do with thinking —**think (all)**

the world of to admire or love greatly —**think better of 1.** to form a more favourable opinion of **2.** to make a more sensible decision about, after reconsidering —**think fit** to regard as proper —**think little (or nothing) of 1.** to attach little (or no) importance to **2.** to have little (or no) hesitancy about —**think on (or upon)** [Archaic] to give thought to —**think out 1.** to think about to a conclusion: also **think through 2.** to work out by thinking —**think out loud** to speak one's thoughts as they occur: also **think aloud** —**think over** to give thought to; ponder well —**think twice** to consider carefully before deciding —**think up** to invent, contrive, etc. by thinking —**think′a·ble** *adj.* —**think′-er** *n.*

think[2] (thingk) *v.impersonal* *pt.* **thought** [OE. *thyncan*] to seem: obs., except in archaic METHINKS, METHOUGHT

think·ing (-ing) *adj.* **1.** that thinks or can think; rational **2.** given to thought; reflective —*n.* thought —**put on one's thinking cap** give serious consideration to a matter

think tank (or factory) [Colloq.] a group of experts organized to do intensive research and problem solving, often using computers, etc.

thin·ner (thin′ər) *n.* a person or thing that thins; esp., a substance added, as turpentine to paint, for thinning

thin-skinned (-skind′) *adj.* **1.** having a thin skin **2.** easily hurt by criticism, insults, etc.

thi·o- [< Gr. *theion*, brimstone] *a combining form meaning* sulphur, used to indicate the replacement of oxygen by sulphur

Thi·o·kol (thī′ə kol′, -kōl′) [arbitrary coinage] *a trademark for* any of various synthetic rubbery compounds used as sealants and sealing adhesives

thi·o·pen·tal (sodium) (thī′ə pen′tal, -tol, -t'l) [THIO- + PENT(A)- + -AL] a yellowish-white powder, injected intravenously in solution as a general anaesthetic and hypnotic

thi·o·sul·phate (thī′ō sul′fāt) *n.* a salt of thiosulphuric acid; esp., sodium thiosulphate

thi·o·sul·phu·ric acid (-sul fyoor′ik) [THIO- + SULPHURIC] an unstable acid, $H_2S_2O_3$, whose salts are used in photography, bleaching, etc.

third (thurd) *adj.* [OE. *thridda*] **1.** preceded by two others in a series; 3rd **2.** next below the second in rank, value, merit, etc. **3.** designating any of the three equal parts of something —*adv.* in the third place, rank, group, etc. —*n.* **1.** the one following the second **2.** any person, thing, class, etc. that is third **3.** any of the three equal parts of something; 1/3 **4.** the third forward gear ratio of a motor vehicle **5.** an honours degree of the third, and usually the lowest, class **6.** *Music* a) the third tone of an ascending diatonic scale, or a tone two degrees above or below any given tone in such a scale b) the interval between two such tones, or a combination of them —**third′ly** *adv.*

third-class (thurd′kläs′) *adj.* of the class, rank, excellence, etc. next below the second

third degree [Colloq.] harsh, gruelling treatment and questioning of a prisoner in order to force a confession or information —**third′-de·gree′** *adj.*

third dimension 1. a) the dimension of depth in something b) the quality of having, or of seeming to have, depth, or solidity **2.** the quality of being true to life or seeming real —**third′-di·men′sion·al** *adj.*

third man *Cricket* **1.** a fielding position on the off side near the boundary behind the batsman's wicket **2.** a player in this position

third party a person other than the principals in a case or matter

third person 1. that form of a pronoun (as *he*) or verb (as *is*) which refers to the person or thing spoken of **2.** narration characterized by the general use of such forms

third rail an extra rail used on some electric railway lines for supplying power

third-rate (-rāt′) *adj.* **1.** third in quality or other rating; third-class **2.** inferior; very poor —**third′-rat′er** *n.*

third world [often T- W-] the underdeveloped or emergent countries of the world, esp. of Africa and Asia

thirst (thurst) *n.* [OE. *thurst*] **1.** the discomfort or distress caused by a desire or need for water, characterized generally by dryness in the mouth and throat **2.** [Colloq.] a craving for a specific liquid, esp. for alcoholic liquor **3.** any strong desire; craving —*vi.* **1.** to be thirsty **2.** to have a strong desire or craving

thirst·y (thur′stē) *adj.* **thirst′i·er, thirst′i·est** **1.** feeling thirst **2.** lacking water or moisture; dry [*thirsty* fields] **3.** [Colloq.] causing thirst [*thirsty* work] **4.** having a strong desire; craving —**thirst′i·ly** *adv.* —**thirst′i·ness** *n.*

thir·teen (thur′tēn′) *adj.* [OE. *threotyne*] three more than ten —*n.* the cardinal number between twelve and fourteen; 13; XIII

thir·teenth (-tēnth′) *adj.* **1.** preceded by twelve others in a series; 13th **2.** designating any of the thirteen equal parts of something —*n.* **1.** the one following the twelfth **2.** any of the thirteen equal parts of something; 1/13

thir·ti·eth (thur′tē ith) *adj.* **1.** preceded by twenty-nine others in a series; 30th **2.** designating any of the thirty equal parts of something —**n.** **1.** the one following the twenty-ninth **2.** any of the thirty equal parts of something; 1/30

thir·ty (thurt′ē) *adj.* [OE. *thritig* < *thri,* three + *-tig,* -TY²] three times ten —**n., pl. -ties** the cardinal number between twenty-nine and thirty-one; 30; XXX —**the thirties** the numbers or years, as of a century, from thirty to thirty-nine

Thirty-nine Articles a set of formulas defining the doctrinal position of the Church of England

thir·ty-sec·ond note (thurt′ē sek′ənd) *Music U.S.* name for DEMISEMIQUAVER

this (*th*is) *pron., pl.* **these** [OE. *thes,* masc., *this,* neut.] **1.** the person or thing mentioned or understood [*this* is John] **2.** the thing that is nearer than another referred to as "that" [*this* is larger than that] **3.** the less remote in thought of two contrasted things [*this* is more likely than that] **4.** the fact, idea, etc. that is being, or is about to be, presented, etc. [now listen to *this*] —**adj., pl. these 1.** designating the person or thing mentioned or understood [*this* man is John] **2.** designating the thing that is nearer than the one referred to as "that" [*this* desk is smaller than that one] **3.** designating the less remote in thought of two contrasted things [*this* possibility is more likely than that] **4.** designating something that is being, or is about to be, presented, etc. [look at *this* picture] **5.** [Colloq.] designating a particular but unspecified person or thing [there's *this* lady in London] —**adv.** to this extent; so [it was *this* big]

this·tle (this′'l) *n.* [OE. *thistel*] any of various plants of the composite family, with prickly leaves and heads of white, purple, etc. flowers; esp., the **Scotch thistle** with white down and lavender flowers —**this·tly** (this′lē) *adj.*

this·tle·down (-doun′) *n.* the down attached to the flower head of a thistle

thith·er (thi*th*′ər, thith′-) *adv.* [OE. *thider*] to or towards that place; there —*adj.* on or towards that side; farther

thith·er·to (-tōō′; thith′ər tōō′, thith′-) *adv.* until that time; till then

thith·er·ward (-wərd) *adv.* [Rare] towards that place; thither: also **thith′er·wards**

thix·ot·ro·py (thik sot′rə pē) *n.* [< Gr. *thixis,* touching + -TROPY] the property of becoming fluid when agitated and setting again when left at rest

tho, tho' (*th*ō) *conj., adv.* shortened *sp.* of THOUGH

thole (thōl) *n.* [OE. *thol*] a pin or either of a pair of pins set vertically in the gunwale of a boat to serve as a fulcrum for an oar: also **thole′pin′** (-pin′)

Tho·mism (tō′miz'm) *n.* the theological and philosophical doctrines of Thomas Aquinas

Thompson submachine gun [< the co-inventor, J. T. *Thompson* (1860-1940), U.S. army officer] a trademark for a type of submachine gun: see SUBMACHINE GUN

thong (thôŋ) *n.* [OE. *thwang*] **1.** a narrow strip of leather, etc. used as a lace, strap, etc. **2.** a whiplash, as of braided strips of hide

tho·rac·ic (thô ras′ik, thə-) *adj.* of, in, or near the thorax

tho·ra·co- (thôr′ə kō) a combining form meaning the thorax (chest): also, before a vowel, **thorac-**

tho·rax (thôr′aks) *n., pl.* **-rax·es, -ra·ces′** (-ə sēz′) [L. < Gr. *thorax*] **1.** in man and other higher vertebrates, the part of the body between the neck and the abdomen; chest **2.** the middle one of the three main segments of an insect's body

tho·ri·um (thôr′ē əm) *n.* [ModL. < *Thor,* Scand. god of thunder] a rare, greyish, radioactive chemical element, used in making electronic equipment and as a nuclear fuel: symbol, Th; at. wt., 232.038; at. no., 90 —**tho′ric** *adj.*

thorn (thôrn) *n.* [OE.] **1.** a) a very short, hard, leafless branch or stem with a sharp point b) any small tree or shrub bearing thorns; esp., same as HAWTHORN **2.** anything that keeps troubling, vexing, or irritating one: usually in the phrase **thorn in one's side** (or **flesh**) **3.** in Old English, the runic character (þ), corresponding to either the voiced or unvoiced sound of English *th*

thorn apple 1. a poisonous annual weed of the nightshade family, with foul-smelling leaves, prickly fruit and trumpet-shaped flowers **2.** a haw

thorn·y (thôr′nē) *adj.* **thorn′i·er, thorn′i·est 1.** full of thorns; prickly **2.** difficult or full of obstacles, vexations, pain, etc. —**thorn′i·ness** *n.*

tho·ron (thôr′on) *n.* [ModL. < THORIUM] a radioactive isotope of radon, resulting from the disintegration of thorium

thor·ough (thur′ə) *prep., adv.* [ME. *thoruh,* a var. of *through,* THROUGH] *obs. var.* of THROUGH —*adj.* **1.** done or proceeding through to the end; complete [a *thorough* checkup] **2.** that is completely (the thing specified); absolute [a *thorough* rascal] **3.** very exact, accurate, or painstaking, esp. about details —**thor′ough·ly** *adv.* —**thor′-ough·ness** *n.*

thorough bass *Music* a form of musical notation in which the chording in the bass part is indicated by figures: also **figured bass**

thor·ough·bred (thur′ə bred′) *adj.* **1.** purebred, as a horse or dog; pedigreed **2.** thoroughly trained, cultured, etc.; well-bred —*n.* **1.** a thoroughbred animal; specif., [T-] any of a breed of racehorses **2.** a cultured, well-bred person

thor·ough·fare (-fer′) *n.* a public street open at both ends, esp. one through which there is much traffic; main road

thor·ough·go·ing (-gō′iŋ) *adj.* very thorough; specif., *a)* precise and painstaking *b)* absolute; out-and-out

thorp, thorpe (thôrp) *n.* [ME. < OE.] a village; hamlet: now mainly in place names

Thos. Thomas

those (*th*ōz) *adj., pron.* [OE. *thas*] *pl.* of THAT

thou¹ (*th*ou) *pron.* [OE. *thu*] the nominative second person singular of the personal pronoun: formerly used in familiar address but now replaced by *you* except in poetic, religious, and some dialectal use

thou² (thou) *n. Colloq.* clipped form of **1.** THOUSAND **2.** THOUSANDTH

though (*th*ō) *conj.* [< OE. *theah* & cognate ON. *tho*] **1.** in spite of the fact that; notwithstanding that [*though* it rained, he went] **2.** and yet; nevertheless; however [they will probably win, *though* no one thinks so] **3.** even if; supposing that [*though* he may fail, he will have tried] —*adv.* however; nevertheless [she sings well, *though*]

thought¹ (thôt) *n.* [OE. *thoht*] **1.** the act or process of thinking **2.** the power of reasoning; intellect; imagination **3.** what one thinks; idea, opinion, plan, etc. **4.** the ideas, opinions, etc. prevailing at a given time or place or among a given people [modern *thought* in education] **5.** attention; consideration [give it a moment's *thought*] **6.** intention or expectation [no *thought* of leaving] **7.** a little; trifle [be a *thought* more careful]

thought² (thôt) *pt & pp.* of THINK¹

thought·ful (-fəl) *adj.* **1.** full of thought; meditative **2.** characterized by thought; serious **3.** heedful, careful, etc.; esp., considerate of others —**thought′ful·ly** *adv.* —**thought′-ful·ness** *n.*

thought·less (-lis) *adj.* **1.** not stopping to think; careless **2.** not given thought; rash **3.** not considerate of others **4.** [Rare] stupid —**thought′less·ly** *adv.* —**thought′less·ness** *n.*

thought-read·ing (-rēd′iŋ) *n.* the supposed ability to know another person's thoughts by telepathy —**thought′-read′er** *n.*

thou·sand (thou′z'nd) *n.* [OE. *thusend*] **1.** ten hundred; 1000; M **2.** an indefinite but very large number **3.** [Colloq.] a thousand pounds —*adj.* amounting to one thousand in number

thou·sand·fold (-fōld′) *adj.* [see -FOLD] having a thousand times as much or as many —*adv.* a thousand times as much or as many: with a

Thousand Island dressing a salad dressing made of mayonnaise with ketchup, minced pickles, etc.

thou·sandth (thou′z'ndth) *adj.* **1.** coming last in a series of a thousand **2.** designating any of the thousand equal parts of something —*n.* **1.** the thousandth one of a series **2.** any of the thousand equal parts of something; 1/1000

Thra·cian (thrā′shən) *adj.* designating or of: *a)* an ancient region in the E Balkan Peninsula *b)* a modern region in the SE Balkans divided between Greece and Turkey —*n.* a native or inhabitant of Thrace

thrall (thrôl) *n.* [OE. *thræl* < ON.] **1.** orig., a slave or bondman **2.** a person under the moral or psychological domination of someone or something **3.** slavery

thrall·dom, thral·dom (-dəm) *n.* the condition of being a thrall; servitude; slavery

thrash (thrash) *vt.* [OE. *therscan,* to beat] **1.** same as THRESH **2.** to make move violently or wildly **3.** to give a severe beating to; flog —*vi.* **1.** same as THRESH **2.** to move or toss about violently [*thrashing* in agony] **3.** to make one's way by thrashing —*n.* the act of thrashing —**thrash out** to settle by much discussion —**thrash′er** *n.*

thread (thred) *n.* [OE. *thræd*] **1.** *a)* a light, fine, stringlike length of two or more fibres or strands of spun cotton, silk, etc. twisted together and used in sewing *b)* a similar fine length of synthetic material, as of plastic, or of glass or metal *c)* the fine, stringy filament produced from itself by a spider, silkworm, etc. *d)* a fine, stringy length of syrup, etc. **2.** any thin line, stratum, vein, ray, etc. **3.** something like a thread in its length, sequence, etc. [the *thread* of a story] **4.** the spiral or helical ridge of a screw, bolt, nut, etc. —*vt.* **1.** *a)* to put a thread through the eye of (a needle, etc.) *b)* to arrange thread for use on (a sewing machine) **2.** to string (beads, etc.) on or as if on a thread **3.** to fashion a thread (sense 4) on or in (a screw, pipe, etc.) **4.** to interweave with or as if with threads **5.** *a)* to pass through by twisting, turning, or weaving in and out [to *thread* the streets] *b)* to make (one's way) in this fashion —*vi.* **1.** to go along in a winding way **2.** to form a thread when dropped from a spoon: said of boiling syrup beginning to thicken —**thread′-er** *n.* —**thread′like′** *adj.*

THISTLE

thread·bare (-ber') *adj.* 1. worn down so that the threads show; having the nap worn off 2. wearing worn-out clothes; shabby 3. that has lost freshness or novelty; stale

thread mark a line made of silk fibre and put into bank notes to prevent forgery

thread·y (-ē) *adj.* **thread'i·er, thread'i·est** 1. of or like a thread; stringy; fibrous 2. forming threads; viscid: said of liquids 3. thin, weak, feeble, etc. [a *thready* pulse] —**thread'i·ness** *n.*

threat (thret) *n.* [OE. *threat*, a throng] 1. an expression of intention to hurt, destroy, punish, etc., as in intimidation 2. *a*) a sign of something dangerous or harmful about to happen [the *threat* of war] *b*) a source of possible danger, harm, etc.

threat·en (thret''n) *vt.* [OE. *threatnian*] 1. *a*) to make threats against *b*) to express one's intention to inflict (punishment, injury, etc.) 2. *a*) to be a sign of (danger, harm, etc.) [clouds *threatening* snow] *b*) to be a source of possible danger, harm, etc. to [an epidemic *threatens* the city] —*vi.* 1. to make threats 2. to be a sign or source of possible danger, etc. —**threat'en·er** *n.* —**threat'en·ing·ly** *adv.*

three (thrē) *adj.* [OE. *threo, thrie*] totalling one more than two —*n.* 1. the cardinal number between two and four; 3; III 2. anything having three units or members, or numbered three

three-colour process (kul'ər) a method of full-colour printing using three separate plates, each reproducing one primary colour

3-D (thrē'dē') *adj.* producing or designed to produce an effect of three dimensions [a *3-D* film] —*n.* a system or effect that adds a three-dimensional appearance to visual images, as in films

three-deck·er (-dek'ər) *n.* 1. a ship with three decks 2. any structure with three levels 3. [Colloq.] a sandwich made with three slices of bread

three-di·men·sion·al (-də men'shən 'l) *adj.* 1. *a*) of or having three dimensions *b*) appearing to have depth or thickness in addition to height and width 2. having a lifelike quality

three·fold (-fōld') *adj.* [see -FOLD] 1. having three parts 2. having three times as much or as many —*adv.* three times as much or as many

three-legged race (-leg'id) a race in which competitors run in pairs with their adjoining legs tied together

three·pen·ny (thrip'ə nē, throop'-, thrup'-) *adj.* 1. worth or costing threepence 2. of small worth; cheap

threepenny bit a former British coin, twelve-sided, and worth three (old) pennies

three-ply (-plī') *adj.* having three thicknesses, interwoven layers, strands, etc.

three-point landing (-point') an aircraft landing in which the main wheels and the tail wheel touch the ground simultaneously

three-point turn (-point') a complete turn of a motor vehicle made in three backwards-and-forwards movements

three-quar·ter (-kwôr'tər) *adj.* of or involving three fourths —*n.* Rugby any of the players between the full back and the half backs

three·score (thrē'skôr') *adj.* sixty

three·some (-səm) *n.* a group of three persons

thren·o·dy (thren'ə dē) *n.,* pl. **-dies** [< Gr. < *thrēnos*, lamentation + *ōidē*, song] a song of lamentation; dirge: also **thre·node** (thrē'nōd, thren'ōd) —**thre·nod·ic** (thri nod'-ik) *adj.* —**thren'o·dist** *n.*

thresh (thresh) *vt.* [earlier form of THRASH] 1. to beat out (grain) from its husk, as with a flail 2. to beat grain out of (husks) 3. to beat or strike as with a flail —*vi.* 1. to thresh grain 2. to toss about; thrash —**thresh out** to settle by much discussion; thrash out

thresh·er (-ər) *n.* 1. a person who threshes 2. a machine for threshing grain: also **threshing machine** 3. a large shark with a long tail

thresh·old (thresh'ōld, -hōld) *n.* [OE. *therscold* < base of *therscan* (see THRASH)] 1. same as DOORSILL 2. the entrance or beginning point of something 3. *Physiol.,* *Psychol.* the point at which a stimulus is just strong enough to be perceived or produce a response [the *threshold* of pain]

threw (thrōō) *pt.* of THROW

thrice (thrīs) *adv.* [ME. *thries*] 1. three times 2. threefold 3. greatly; highly

thrift (thrift) *n.* [ON. < *thrifast*, to THRIVE] 1. orig., a thriving 2. careful management of one's money or resources; economy; frugality 3. a small plant with narrow leaves and small white, pink, red, or purplish flowers —**thrift'less** *adj.* —**thrift'less·ly** *adv.* —**thrift'less·ness** *n.*

thrift·y (-ē) *adj.* **thrift'i·er, thrift'i·est** 1. practising or showing thrift; economical 2. thriving; prospering —**thrift'i·ly** *adv.* —**thrift'i·ness** *n.*

thrill (thril) *vi., vt.* [OE. *thyr(e)lian*, to pierce < *thyrel*, hole < *thurh*, through] 1. to feel or cause to feel keen emotional excitement; tingle with excitement 2. to quiver or cause to quiver; tremble; vibrate —*n.* 1. a thrilling or being thrilled;

tremor of excitement 2. the quality of thrilling, or the ability to thrill 3. something that causes emotional excitement 4. a vibration; tremor; quiver

thrill·er (-ər) *n.* a suspenseful novel, film, etc., esp. one dealing with crime and detection

thrips (thrips) *n.,* pl. **thrips** [L. < Gr. *thrips*, wood-worm] any of various small, usually winged, insects that suck the juices of plants

thrive (thrīv) *vi.* **thrived** or **throve, thrived** or **thriv·en** (thriv''n), **thriv'ing** [< ON. *thrifast*, to prosper < *thrifa*, to grasp] 1. to prosper or flourish; be successful, esp. by practising thrift 2. to grow vigorously or luxuriantly

thro', thro (thrōō) *prep., adv., adj.* archaic shortened sp. of THROUGH

throat (thrōt) *n.* [OE. *throte*] 1. the front part of the neck 2. the upper part of the passage from the mouth and nose to the stomach and lungs, including the pharynx, upper larynx, trachea, and oesophagus 3. any narrow, throatlike passage or part —**cut one another's throats** [Colloq.] to ruin each other, as by underselling in business —**jump down someone's throat** [Colloq.] to attack or criticize someone suddenly and violently —**stick in one's throat** to be hard for one to say, as from reluctance —**thrust** (or **ram**) **down a person's throat** to insist that someone listens, pays attention, etc., to something

-throat·ed (thrōt'id) a combining form meaning having a (specified kind of) throat [red-throated]

throat·y (-ē) *adj.* **throat'i·er, throat'i·est** 1. produced in the throat, as some sounds or tones 2. characterized by such sounds; husky [a *throaty* voice] —**throat'i·ly** *adv.* —**throat'i·ness** *n.*

throb (throb) *vi.* **throbbed, throb'bing** [ME. *throbben*] 1. to beat, pulsate, vibrate, etc. 2. to beat strongly or fast; palpitate, as the heart under exertion 3. to tingle or quiver with excitement —*n.* 1. the act of throbbing 2. a beat or pulsation, esp. a strong one of the heart —**throb'ber** *n.* —**throb'bing·ly** *adv.*

throe (thrō) *n.* [prob. < OE. *thrawu*, pain] a spasm or pang of pain: usually used in pl. [the *throes* of childbirth, death *throes*] —**in the throes of** in the act of struggling with (a problem, task, etc.)

throm·bin (throm'bin) *n.* [< Gr. *thrombos*, a clot] the enzyme of the blood, formed from prothrombin, that causes clotting by forming fibrin

throm·bo·sis (throm bō'sis) *n.* [ModL. < Gr. < *thrombos*, a clot] coagulation of the blood in the heart or a blood vessel, forming a clot —**throm·bot·ic** (-bot'ik) *adj.*

throne (thrōn) *n.* [< OFr. < L. < Gr. *thronos*, a seat] 1. the chair on which a king, cardinal, etc. sits on formal or ceremonial occasions 2. the power or rank of a king, etc.; sovereignty 3. a sovereign ruler, etc. [orders from the *throne*] —*vt., vi.* **throned, thron'ing** to enthrone or be enthroned

throng (throng) *n.* [OE. (ge)*thrang* < *thringan*, to crowd] 1. a great number of people gathered together; crowd 2. any great number of things massed or considered together; multitude —*vi.* to gather together, move, or press in a throng; crowd —*vt.* to crowd into; fill with a multitude

thros·tle (thros''l) *n.* [ME. < OE.] 1. same as SONG THRUSH 2. a spinning machine

throt·tle (throt''l) *n.* [prob. dim. of THROAT] 1. [Rare] the throat or windpipe 2. the valve that regulates the amount of fuel vapour entering an internal-combustion engine or controls the flow of steam in a steam line: also **throttle valve** 3. the lever or pedal that controls this valve —*vt.* **-tled, -tling** 1. to choke; strangle 2. to stop the utterance or action of; suppress 3. *a*) to reduce the flow of (fuel vapour, etc.) by means of a throttle *b*) to lessen the speed of (an engine, vehicle, etc.) by this or similar means (often with *back* or *down*) —*vi.* to choke or suffocate —**throt'tler** *n.*

through (thrōō) *prep.* [OE. *thurh*] 1. in one side and out the other side of; from end to end of 2. in the midst of; among 3. by way of 4. over the entire extent of 5. to various places in; around [touring *through* France] 6. *a*) from the beginning to the end of *b*) [U.S.] up to and including [*through* Friday] 7. without making a stop for [to go *through* a red light] 8. past the difficulties of [to come *through* hard times] 9. by means of 10. as a result of; because of —*adv.* 1. in one side and out the other; from end to end 2. from the beginning to the end 3. completely to the end [see it *through*] 4. thoroughly; completely: also **through and through** [soaked *through*] —*adj.* 1. extending from one place to another [a *through* road] 2. travelling to the destination without stops [a *through* train] 3. arrived at the end; finished 4. [Colloq.] at the end of one's usefulness, resources, etc. [*through* as a politician] 5. [Colloq.] having no further dealings, etc. (*with* someone or something)

through·out (thrōō out') *prep.* all the way through; in or during every part of —*adv.* 1. in or during every part; everywhere 2. in every respect

through·put (thrōō'poot') *n.* the amount of material put through a process in a given period, as by a computer

throve (thrōv) *alt. pt. of* THRIVE

throw (thrō) *vt.* **threw, thrown, throw′ing** [OE. *thrawan*, to twist] **1.** to twist strands of (silk, etc.) into thread or yarn **2.** to cause to fly through the air by releasing from the hand while the arm is in rapid motion; cast; hurl **3.** to discharge through the air from a catapult, gun, etc. **4.** to cause to fall; upset [*thrown* by a horse] **5.** to move or send rapidly [they *threw* troops into the battle] **6.** to put suddenly and forcibly into a specified place, condition, or situation [*thrown* into confusion] **7.** *a*) to cast (dice) *b*) to make (a specified cast) at dice [to *throw* a five] **8.** to cast off; shed [snakes *throw* their skins] **9.** to move (the lever of a switch, clutch, etc.) or connect, disconnect, etc. by so doing **10.** *a*) to direct, cast, turn, etc. (with *at, on, upon*, etc.) [to *throw* a glance, a light, a shadow, etc.] *b*) to deliver (a punch) **11.** to cause (one's voice) to seem to come from some other source **12.** to put (blame *on*, obstacles *before*, etc.) **13.** [U.S. Colloq.] to lose (a game, race, etc.) deliberately **14.** [Colloq.] to give (a party, dance, etc.) **15.** [Colloq.] to have (a fit, tantrum, etc.) **16.** [Colloq.] to confuse or disconcert [the question *threw* him] **17.** *Ceramics* to shape on a potter's wheel —*vi.* to cast or hurl something —*n.* **1.** the act of one who throws; a cast **2.** the distance something is or can be thrown [a stone's *throw*] **3.** *a*) the motion of a moving part, as a cam, eccentric, etc. *b*) the extent of such a motion —**throw a spanner in the works** to obstruct by interference; cause difficulties —**throw away 1.** to rid oneself of; discard **2.** to waste **3.** to fail to make use of **4.** to deliver (a line or lines) in an offhand way: said of an actor or comedian —**throw back 1.** to stop from advancing **2.** to revert to the type of an ancestor —**throw back on** to force (someone) to depend on or utilise [*thrown* back on his own resources] —**throw cold water on** to discourage by showing no interest or by criticizing —**throw in 1.** to interpolate (a remark, suggestion, etc. **2.** to add extra or free **3.** to add to others —**throw in one's lot with** to give one's allegiance to —**throw off 1.** *a*) to rid oneself of *b*) to recover from **2.** to mislead **3.** to expel, emit, etc. **4.** to write or utter quickly, in an offhand manner —**throw on** to put on (a garment) hastily —**throw oneself at** to try very hard to win the affection or love of —**throw oneself into** to engage in with great vigour —**throw oneself on** (or **upon**) **1.** to rely on for support for aid **2.** to assault —**throw one's hand in** to give up all attempt to succeed —**throw open 1.** to open completely and suddenly **2.** to remove all restrictions from —**throw out 1.** to discard **2.** to reject or remove, often with force **3.** to emit **4.** to put forth or utter (a hint or suggestion) **5.** to throw into confusion; disconcert —**throw over 1.** to give up; abandon **2.** to jilt —**throw together 1.** to make or assemble hurriedly **2.** to cause to become acquainted —**throw up 1.** to give up or abandon **2.** to vomit **3.** to construct rapidly **4.** to mention repeatedly (*to* someone), as in reproach —**throw′er** *n.*

throw·a·way (thrō′ə wā′) *adj.* **1.** designed to be discarded after use [a *throwaway* bottle] **2.** said or done incidentally, or as an aside [a *throwaway* remark]

throw·back (-bak′) *n.* **1.** reversion to an ancestral type **2.** instance of this

thru (thrōō) *prep., adv., adj.* shortened U.S. sp. of THROUGH

thrum¹ (thrum) *n.* [OE., a ligament] **1.** *a*) the row of warp thread ends left on a loom when the web is cut off *b*) any of these ends **2.** any short end thread or fringe

thrum² (thrum) *vt., vi.* **thrummed, thrum′ming** [echoic] **1.** to strum (a guitar, banjo, etc.) **2.** to drum (on) with the fingers —*n.* the act or sound of thrumming

thrush¹ (thrush) *n.* [OE. *thrysce*] any of a large group of songbirds, often plain-coloured, including the blackbird, nightingale etc., esp. the SONG THRUSH and MISTLE THRUSH

thrush² (thrush) *n.* [prob. akin to Dan. *trøske*] **1.** a disease, esp. of infants, caused by a fungus that forms milky white lesions on the mouth, lips, and throat **2.** a disease of the frog of a horse's foot, characterized by the formation of pus

thrust (thrust) *vt.* **thrust, thrust′ing** [ON. *thrysta*] **1.** to push with sudden force; shove **2.** to pierce; stab **3.** to force or impose (oneself or another) upon someone else or into some position or situation —*vi.* **1.** to push or shove against something **2.** to make a stab or lunge, as with a sword **3.** to force one's way (*into, through*, etc.) **4.** to extend, as in growth —*n.* **1.** a thrusting force; a sudden, forceful push *b*) a stab, as with a sword *c*) any sudden attack *d*) a remark intended to annoy or hurt someone **2.** continuous pressure of one part against another, as of a rafter against a wall **3.** *a*) the driving force of a propeller in the line of its shaft *b*) the forward force produced by the gases escaping rearwards from a jet or rocket engine **4.** *a*) forward movement; impetus *b*) energy; drive —**thrust′er** *n.*

thud (thud) **thud′ded, thud′ding** [prob. ult. < OE. *thyddan*, to strike] to hit or fall with a dull sound —*n.* **1.** a heavy blow **2.** a dull sound, as of a heavy object dropping on a soft, solid surface

thug (thug) [Hindi *thag* < Sans. *sthaga*, a rogue] **1.** [also

T-] a member of a former religious organization in India that murdered and robbed **2.** a rough, brutal hoodlum, gangster, robber, etc. —**thug′ger·y** *n.* —**thug′gish** *adj.*

thu·li·um (thyōō′lē əm) *n.* [ModL. < (ULTIMA) THULE] a metallic chemical element of the rare-earth group: symbol, Tm; at. wt., 168.934; at. no., 69

thumb (thum) [OE. *thuma*] **1.** the short, thick finger of the human hand that is nearest the wrist **2.** a corresponding part in some other animals **3.** that part of a glove, etc. which covers the thumb —*vt.* **1.** to handle, turn, soil, etc. as with the thumb **2.** [Colloq.] to ask for or get (a ride) or make (one's way) in hitchhiking by gesturing with the thumb extended —**all thumbs** clumsy; fumbling —**thumb one's nose** to raise one's thumb to the nose in a coarse gesture of defiance or contempt—**thumbs down** a signal of disapproval —**thumbs up** a signal of approval —**under one's thumb** under one's influence

thumb index an index to the sections of a reference book, consisting of a series of rounded notches cut in the front edge of a book with a labelled tab at the base of each notch —**thumb′-in′dex** *vt.*

thumb·nail (-nāl′) *n.* **1.** the nail of the thumb **2.** something as small as a thumbnail —*adj.* very small or brief [a *thumbnail* sketch]

thumb·screw (-skrōō′) *n.* **1.** a screw with a head shaped in such a way that it can be turned with the thumb and forefinger **2.** a former instrument of torture for squeezing the thumbs

thump (thump) [echoic] **1.** a blow with something heavy and blunt **2.** the dull sound made by such a blow —*vt.* **1.** to strike with a thump or thumps **2.** to thrash; beat severely —*vi.* **1.** to hit or fall with a thump **2.** to make a dull, heavy sound; pound; throb —**thump out** [Colloq.] to play on the piano loudly and without sensitivity —**thump′er** *n.*

THUMBSCREW

thump·ing (thum′pin) **1.** that thumps **2.** [Colloq.] very large; whopping —**thump′ing·ly** *adv.*

thun·der (thun′dər) *n.* [OE. *thunor*] **1.** the sound that is heard after a flash of lightning, caused by the sudden heating and expansion of air by electrical discharge **2.** any loud, rumbling sound like this **3.** an outburst of threatening or angry words Also used in mild oaths [yes, by *thunder!*]: also **thun′der·a′tion** —*vi.* **1.** to produce thunder [it is *thundering*] **2.** to make, or move with, a sound like thunder **3.** to make strong denunciations, etc. —*vt.* to utter, attack, etc. with a thundering sound —**steal someone's thunder** to lessen the effectiveness of someone's statement or action by anticipating him in its use —**thun′der·er** *n.*

thun·der·bolt (-bōlt′) *n.* **1.** a flash of lightning with the thunder heard after it **2.** something that stuns or acts with sudden force or violence **3.** the imagined agency of destruction produced by a flash of lightning **4.** *Myth.* the missile wielded by several gods, esp. the Greek god Zeus

thun·der·clap (-klap′) *n.* **1.** a clap, or loud crash, of thunder **2.** anything like this in being sudden, startling, violent, etc.

thun·der·cloud (-kloud′) *n.* a storm cloud charged with electricity and producing lightning and thunder

thun·der·head (-hed′) *n.* a round mass of cumulus clouds coming before a thunderstorm

thun·der·ing (-in) *adj.* **1.** that thunders **2.** [Colloq.] very large or excessive

thun·der·ous (-əs) *adj.* **1.** full of or making thunder **2.** making a noise like thunder —**thun′der·ous·ly** *adv.*

thun·der·storm (stôrm′) *n.* a storm with thunder and lightning

thun·der·struck (-struk′) *adj.* amazed or shocked as if struck by a thunderbolt: also **thun′der·strick′en** (-strik′'n)

thu·ri·ble (thyoor′ə b'l) *n.* [< L. < *thus* (gen. *thuris*), incense < Gr. *thyos*, sacrifice] same as CENSER

Thurs., Thur. Thursday

Thurs·day (thurz′dē, -dā) *n.* [< OE. < ON. *Thorsdagr*, Thor's day] the fifth day of the week

Thurs·days (-dēz, -dāz) *adv.* [Colloq.] on or during every Thursday

thus (thus) [OE.] **1.** in this or that manner; in the way just stated or in the following manner **2.** to this or that degree or extent; so **3.** consequently; therefore; hence: often used with conjunctive force **4.** for example

thwack (thwak) *vt.* [prob. echoic] to strike with something flat; whack —*n.* a blow with something flat

thwaite (thwāt) *n.* [< ON. *thveit*] a piece of ground reclaimed as arable land: now mainly in place names

thwart (thwôrt) *adj.* [ON. *thvert*, transverse] lying across something else —*adv., prep.* archaic var. of ATHWART —*n.* **1.** a rower's seat extending across a boat **2.** a brace extending across a canoe —*vt.* to keep from doing or being done; block or hinder (a person, plans, etc.)

thy (thī) *possessive pronominal adj.* [ME. *thi*, contr. < *thin*,

thy] of, belonging to, or done by thee: archaic or poet. var. of *your*: see also THINE, THOU[1]

thyme (tīm) *n.* [< MFr. < L. < Gr. *thymon* < *thyein*, to offer sacrifice] any of various shrubby plants or aromatic herbs with white, pink, or red flowers and fragrant leaves used for seasoning —**thym′ic** *adj.*

thy·mine (thī′mēn, -min) *n.* [G. *thymin* < Gr. *thymos*, spirit + G. -*in*, -INE[4]] a white, crystalline base, one of the substances forming the genetic code in DNA molecules

thy·mol (thī′môl, -mōl) *n.* [THYM(E) + -OL[1]] a colourless compound extracted from thyme or made synthetically: used as an antiseptic, as in mouthwashes, etc.

thy·mus (thī′məs) *n.* [ModL. < Gr. *thymos*] a ductless, glandlike body near the throat, that has no known function and disappears in the adult: see also SWEETBREAD: also **thymus gland** —**thy′mic** *adj.*

thy·roid (thī′roid) *adj.* [ModL. < Gr. < *thyreos*, door-shaped shield < *thyra*, door + -*eidēs*, -OID] **1.** designating or of a large ductless gland near the trachea, secreting the hormone thyroxine, which regulates body growth and metabolism **2.** designating or of the principal cartilage of the larynx, forming the Adam's apple —*n.* **1.** the thyroid gland **2.** the thyroid cartilage **3.** a preparation of the thyroid gland of certain animals, used in treating goitre, etc.: also **thyroid extract**

thy·rox·ine (thī rok′sēn, -sin) *n.* [THYR(OID) + OX(Y)-[1] + -INE[4]] a colourless, crystalline compound the active hormone of the thyroid gland, used in treating goitre, etc.: also **thy·rox′in** (-sin)

thyr·sus (thur′səs) *n., pl.* -**si** (-sī) [L. < Gr. *thyrsos*] **1.** *Gr. Myth.* a staff tipped with a pine cone and sometimes entwined with ivy, carried by Dionysus, the satyrs, etc. **2.** *Bot.* a flower cluster in which the main stem is racemose and the secondary stems are cymose, as in the lilac: also **thyrse** (thurs)

thy·self (thī self′) *pron.* reflexive or intensive form of THOU: an archaic or poet. var. of *yourself*

ti (tē) *n.* [altered < *si*: see GAMUT, SOL-FA] *Music* a syllable representing the seventh tone of the diatonic scale

Ti *Chem.* titanium

ti·ar·a (tē är′ə) *n.* [L. < Gr. *tiara*] **1.** an ancient Persian headdress **2.** the Pope's triple crown **3.** a woman's coronetlike headdress, often jewelled

Ti·bet·an (ti bet′'n) *adj.* of Tibet, its people, their language, etc. —*n.* **1.** a member of the Mongolic people of Tibet **2.** the Sino-Tibetan language of Tibet

tib·i·a (tib′ē ə) *n., pl.* -**i·ae** (-i ē′), -**i·as** [L.] **1.** the inner and thicker of the two bones of the leg below the knee; shinbone **2.** a corresponding bone in the leg of other vertebrates —**tib′i·al** *adj.*

tic (tik) *n.* [Fr. < ?] a twitching of a muscle, esp. of the face, that is not consciously controlled

tick[1] (tik) *n.* [prob. < Gmc. echoic base] **1.** a light clicking or tapping sound, as that made by a clock **2.** a mark made to check off, or indicate the correctness of, items; check mark (√, ', etc.) **3.** [Colloq.] a moment; instant —*vi.* **1.** to make a tick or ticks, as a clock **2.** [Colloq.] to function; work [what makes him *tick*?] —*vt.* **1.** to indicate or count by a tick or ticks **2.** to check off (an item in a list, etc.) with a tick (usually with *off*) —**tick off** [Colloq.] to reprimand —**tick over** to run very slowly; to idle: said of an engine, etc.

tick[2] (tik) *n.* [OE. *ticia*] any of a large group of bloodsucking arachnids that are parasitic on man, cattle, sheep, etc., including many species that transmit diseases

tick[3] (tik) *n.* [ult. < L. < Gr. *thēkē*, a case] **1.** the cloth case that is filled with cotton, feathers, etc. to form a mattress or pillow **2.** [Colloq.] *same as* TICKING

tick[4] (tik) *n.* [contr. < TICKET] [Colloq.] credit; trust [to buy something on *tick*]

TICK
(c. 0.5 cm long)

tick·er (tik′ər) *n.* a person or thing that ticks; specif., *a)* [Old Slang] a watch *b)* [Slang] the heart *c)* [Chiefly U.S.] *same as* TAPE MACHINE

ticker tape a continous paper ribbon on which a tape machine prints

tick·et (tik′it) *n.* [< obs. Fr. *etiquet* (now *étiquette*), a ticket] **1.** a printed card or piece of paper that gives one a specified right, as to attend a theatre, ride on a bus, etc. **2.** a label or tag, as on a piece of merchandise, giving the size, price, etc. **3.** [U.S.] *a)* the policy or principles of a political party *b)* the list of candidates nominated by a political party in an election **4.** a licence or certificate, as of a ship's captain or an aircraft pilot **5.** [Colloq.] a summons to court for a traffic violation —*vt.* **1.** to label or tag with a ticket **2.** to issue a ticket to —**that's the ticket!** [Colloq.] that's the correct or proper thing

tick·et·col·lec·tor (-kə lek′tər) *n.* the railway official who checks and takes in passengers' tickets

ticket day the day preceding settlement day on the Stock Exchange

tick·et·off·ice (-of′is) *n.* a place where tickets, as for transport, may be brought

tick·et·of·leave man (-əv lēv′) formerly, a person on parole from prison

tick·ing (tik′iŋ) *n.* [see TICK[3]] a strong, heavy cloth, often striped, used for casings of mattresses, pillows, etc.

tick·le (tik′'l) *vt.* -**led**, -**ling** [ME. *tikelen*] **1.** to please, gratify, etc.: often used in the passive voice with colloquial intensives, as **tickled pink** (or **silly, to death**, etc.) **2.** to amuse [the joke really *tickled* her] **3.** to touch or stroke lightly so as to cause twitching, laughter, etc. [to *tickle* someone's ear] —*vi.* **1.** to have a scratching or tingling sensation [a throat that *tickles*] —*n.* **1.** a tickling or being tickled **2.** a tickling sensation

tick·ler (tik′lər) *n.* a a person or thing that tickles

tick·lish (-lish) *adj.* **1.** sensitive to tickling **2.** very sensitive or easily upset; touchy **3.** needing careful handling; delicate —**tick′lish·ly** *adv.* —**tick′lish·ness** *n.*

tick-tack (tik′tak′) *n.* a system of signalling with the hands and arms used by bookmakers at race courses

tick-tock (tik′tok′) *n.* the sound made by a clock —*vi.* to make this sound

tid·al (tīd′'l) *adj.* of, having, caused by, determined by, or dependent on a tide or tides —**tid′al·ly** *adv.*

tidal wave 1. in popular usage, an unusually great, destructive wave sent inshore by an earthquake or a very strong wind **2.** any great, widespread movement, expression of feeling, etc.

tid·dler (tid′lər) *n.* [< ? Dial. *tittlebat*, stickleback, influenced by *tiddly*, little] [Colloq.] anything very small, specif., a stickleback

tid·dly, tid·dley (tid′lē) *adj.* [< ? dial.] [Slang] **1.** little **2.** slightly drunk

tid·dly·winks (tid′lē wiŋks′, tid′'l ē-) *n.* a game in which the players try to snap little coloured discs into a cup by pressing their edges with a larger disc: also **tid′-dle·dy·winks′** (-'l dē wiŋks′)

tide (tīd) *n.* [OE. *tid*, time] **1.** a period of time: now only in combination [*Eastertide*] **2.** *a)* the alternate rise and fall of the surface of oceans, seas, etc., caused by the attraction of the moon and sun: it occurs twice in each period of 24 hours and 50 minutes *b)* *same as* FLOOD TIDE **3.** something that rises and falls like the tide **4.** a stream, current, trend, etc. [the *tide* of public opinion] **5.** [Archaic] an opportune time —*adj.* *same as* TIDAL —*vi.* **tid′ed, tid′ing 1.** to surge like a tide **2.** *Naut.* to drift with the tide, esp. in moving into or out of a harbour, etc. —*vt.* to carry as with the tide —**tide over** to help along temporarily, as through a period of difficulty —**turn the tide** to reverse a condition

tide·land (-land′, -land) *n.* [U.S.] **1.** land covered by water at high tide and uncovered at low tide **2.** [*pl.*] loosely, land under water just beyond this and within territorial limits

tide·mark (-märk′) *n.* **1.** the high-water mark or, sometimes, the low-water mark of the tide **2.** [Colloq.] a dirty line indicating the extent of washing

tide-rip (-rip′) *n.* *same as* RIPTIDE

tide-ta·ble (-tā′b'l) *n.* a table giving times of high and low water at a particular place

tide-wait·er (-wāt′ər) *n.* formerly, a customs official who boarded and inspected incoming ships

tide·wa·ter (-wôt′ər) *n.* **1.** water that advances and recedes with the tide **2.** [U.S.] an area of coastal land drained by tidal streams —*adj.* [U.S.] of or along a tidewater

ti·dings (tī′diŋz) *n.pl.* [*sometimes with sing.* v.] [OE. *tidung*] news; information

ti·dy (tī′dē) *adj.* -**di·er**, -**di·est** [ult. < *tid*, time] **1.** neat in personal appearance, ways, etc.; orderly **2.** neat in arrangement; in order; trim **3.** [Colloq.] rather large; considerable [a tidy sum] —*vt., vi.* -**died**, -**dy·ing** to make (things) tidy (often with *up*) —*n., pl.* -**dies 1.** *same as* ANTIMACASSAR **2.** a small receptacle for scraps or oddments [a sink tidy] —**ti′di·ly** *adv.* —**ti′di·ness** *n.*

tie (tī) *vt.* **tied, ty′ing** [OE. *tigan* < base of *teag*, a rope] **1.** to fasten or bind together or to something else, as with string or rope made secure by knotting, etc. **2.** to tighten and knot the laces, strings, etc. of [to *tie* one's shoes] **3.** *a)* to make (a knot or bow) *b)* to make a knot or bow in [to *tie* a necktie] **4.** to join or bind in any way [tied by common interests] **5.** to confine; restrict **6.** to equal (the score, record, etc.) of (opponents, a rival, etc.) **7.** *Music* to connect with a tie —*vi.* to make a tie —*n.* **1.** a string, cord, etc. used to tie things **2.** something that joins, binds, etc.; bond **3.** something that confines or restricts [legal *ties*] **4.** *same as* NECKTIE **5.** a beam, rod, etc. that holds together and strengthens parts of a building **6.** *a)* an equality of scores, votes, etc. in a contest *b)* a contest in which scores, etc. are equal **7.** *Music* a curved line joining two notes of the same pitch, indicating that the tone is to be held unbroken —**tie down** to confine; restrain; restrict —**tie in 1.** to bring into or have a connection **2.** to make or be consistent, harmonious, etc. —**tie off** to close off passage through by tying with something —**tie up** 1. to tie securely 2. to wrap up and tie with string, etc. 3. to moor (a ship or boat) to a dock 4. to block or hinder 5. to cause to be already in use, committed, etc.

tie beam a horizontal beam serving as a tie (*n*. 5)

tie clasp a decorative clasp for fastening a necktie to the shirt front: also **tie clip, tie bar**

tied cottage a dwelling occupied by a tenant only as long as he is employed by its owner

tied house a public house restricted to dealing with one particular brewery for its supplies

tie-dye (tī′dī′) *n.* 1. a method of dyeing designs on cloth by tightly tying bunches of it with thread, etc. so that the dye affects only exposed parts 2. cloth so decorated or a design so made —*vt.* **-dyed′, -dye′ing** to dye in this way Also **tie-and-dye**

tie line a telephone line between two private exchanges that may pass through a main exchange but does not receive incoming calls

tie·pin (tī′pin′) *n.* an ornamental pin used to fasten a necktie to a shirt front

tier[1] (tir) *n.* [< MFr. *tire,* order] any of a series of layers or rows, as of seats, arranged one above or behind another —*vt., vi.* to arrange or be arranged in tiers

ti·er[2] (tī′ər) *n.* a person or thing that ties

tierce (turs) *n.* [*often* T-] *same as* TERCE

tier·cel (tir′səl) *n.* [ME. *tercel* < OFr. < L. *tertius,* third: reason for name uncertain] *Falconry* a male hawk, esp. the male peregrine

tie-up (tī′up′) *n.* 1. connection, relation, or involvement 2. [U.S.] a temporary stoppage or interruption

tiff (tif) *n.* [< ?] 1. a slight fit of anger or bad humour 2. a slight quarrel —*vi.* to be in or have a tiff

tif·fa·ny (tif′ə nē) *n.* [OFr. *tiphanie* Epiphany: ? so called because worn on Epiphany] a thin, gauze of silk or muslin

tif·fin (tif′in) *n., vi.* *Anglo-Ind.* *term for* LUNCH

tig (tig) *n.* *same as* TAG (*n.* 7)

ti·ger (tī′gər) *n., pl.* **-gers, -ger:** see PLURAL, II, D, 1 [< OE. & OFr., both < L. < Gr. *tigris*] 1. a large, flesh-eating animal of the cat family, native to Asia, having a tawny coat striped with black 2. *a*) a very energetic or persevering person *b*) a fierce, belligerent person 3. a servant in livery, esp. a groom riding at the back of a light carriage —**have a tiger by the tail** [U.S.] to find oneself in a situation more difficult to handle than one expected —**ti′ger·ish** *adj.*

tiger beetle any of various brightly coloured, often striped beetles with larvae that burrow in soil and feed on other insects

tiger lily a lily having orange flowers with purplish-black spots

tiger moth any of a group of stout-bodied moths with brightly striped or spotted wings

tiger's eye a semiprecious, yellow-brown stone: also **ti′-ger-eye′** *n.*

tight (tīt) *adj.* [< OE. *-thight,* strong] 1. made so that water, air, etc. cannot pass through [a *tight* boat] 2. drawn, packed, spaced, etc. closely together [a *tight* weave] 3. [Archaic or Dial.] snug; trim; neat 4. fixed securely; firm [a *tight* joint] 5. fully stretched; taut 6. fitting so closely as to be uncomfortable 7. strict [*tight* control] 8. difficult to manage: esp. in the phrase **a tight corner** (or **squeeze,** etc.), a difficult situation 9. showing strain [a *tight* smile] 10. almost even or tied [a *tight* race] 11. sharp: said of a spiral, turn, etc. 12. *a*) difficult to get; scarce *b*) characterized by such scarcity [a *tight* market] 13. concise: said of language, style, etc. 14. [Colloq.] stingy 15. [Colloq.] drunk —*adv.* in a tight manner; esp., *a*) securely or firmly [hold *tight*] *b*) [Colloq.] soundly [sleep *tight*] —**sit tight** to maintain one's opinion or position —**tight′ly** *adv.* —**tight′ness** *n.*

-tight (tīt) [< prec.] *a combining form meaning* not letting (something specified) in or out [water*tight,* air*tight*]

tight·en (tīt′'n) *vt., vi.* to make or become tight or tighter —**tight′en·er** *n.*

tight-fist·ed (tīt′fis′tid) *adj.* stingy

tight-fit·ting (-fit′iŋ) *adj.* fitting very tightly

tight-knit (-nit′) *adj.* 1. tightly knit 2. well organized or put together in an efficient way

tight-lipped (-lipt′) *adj.* 1. having the lips closed tightly 2. not saying much; taciturn or secretive

tight·rope (-rōp′) *n.* a rope stretched tight on which acrobats do balancing acts

tights (tīts) *n.pl.* 1. a garment that fits tightly over the legs and the lower part of the body, worn by acrobats, dancers, etc. 2. a similar garment, usually made of nylon, worn by women: pantihose

ti·glon (tī′glon′, -glən) *n.* [TIG(ER) + L(I)ON] the offspring of a male tiger and a female lion: also **ti′gon** (-gon′, -gən)

ti·gress (tī′gris) *n.* a female tiger

tike (tik) *n.* *same as* TYKE

til·bu·ry (til′bər ē) *n., pl.* **-ries** [< *Tilbury,* a London coach builder] a light, two-wheeled carriage for two persons

til·de (til′də) *n.* [Sp. < L. *titulus,* title, sign] a diacritical mark (~) used in various ways, as in Spanish over an *n* to indicate a palatal nasal sound (ny), as in *señor*

tile (tīl) *n.* [OE. *tigele,* ult. < L. *tegula*] 1. *a*) a thin piece of glazed or unglazed, fired clay, stone, etc. used for roofing, flooring, decorative borders, bathroom walls, etc. *b*) a similar piece of plastic, cork, etc., used to cover floors, walls, etc. 2. tiles collectively 3. a drain of semicircular tiles or earthenware pipe 4. burnt-clay, hollow blocks, used variously in construction 5. any of the pieces in mah-jongg or some other games —*vt.* **tiled, til′ing** to cover with tiles —**til′er** *n.*

til·ing (tīl′iŋ) *n.* 1. the action of a person who tiles 2. tiles collectively 3. a covering of tiles

till[1] (til) *prep., conj.* [OE. *til*] *same as* UNTIL

till[2] (til) *vt., vi.* [OE. *tilian,* lit., to strive for] to work (land) in raising crops, as by ploughing, fertilizing, etc.; cultivate—**till′a·ble** *adj.*

till[3] (til) *n.* [< ? ME. *tillen,* to draw] 1. a drawer or tray, as in a shop counter, for keeping money 2. ready cash

till[4] (til) *n.* [< ?] stiff clay containing stones, gravel, etc., the debris of glacial action; boulder clay

till·age (til′ij) *n.* 1. the tilling of land 2. land that is tilled

till·er[1] (til′ər) *n.* [< OFr. < ML. *telarium,* weaver's beam < L. *tela,* a web] a bar or handle for turning a boat's rudder

till·er[2] (til′ər) *n.* a person who tills the soil

till·er[3] (til′ər) *n.* [< OE. *telgor,* a twig] a shoot growing from the base of the stem of a plant

tilt (tilt) *vt.* [prob. < OE. *tealt,* shaky] 1. to cause to slope or slant; tip 2. *a*) to poise or thrust (a lance) in or as in a tilt *b*) to charge at (one's opponent) in a tilt —*vi.* 1. to slope; incline 2. to poise or thrust one's lance (*at* one's opponent) in a tilt 3. to take part in a tilt or joust 4. to dispute, argue, contend, etc. 5. to forge with a tilt hammer —*n.* 1. a medieval contest in which two horsemen thrust with lances in an attempt to unseat each other 2. any spirited contest, dispute, etc. between persons 3. *a*) the act of tilting, or sloping *b*) a slope or slant (at) **full tilt** at full speed; with the greatest force —**tilt′er** *n.*

tilth (tilth) *n.* [OE. < *tilian:* see TILL[2]] 1. a tilling of land 2. tilled land

tilt hammer a heavy drop hammer used in forging

tilt·yard (tilt′yärd′) *n.* a place where tilts were held

Tim. Timothy

tim·bal (tim′b'l) *n.* [< Fr. < Sp. < Ar. < *al,* the + *tabl,* drum] *same as* KETTLEDRUM

tim·bale (tam bäl′) *n.* [Fr.: see prec.] 1. a dish made with chicken, lobster, fish, etc. baked in a small drum-shaped mould 2. a type of fried or baked pastry shell, filled with a cooked food

tim·ber (tim′bər) *n.* [OE.] 1. wood suitable for building houses, ships, etc. 2. a large, heavy, dressed piece of wood used in building; beam 3. wood sawn into planks, boards, etc. of convenient sizes 4. trees or forests collectively 5. a wooden rib of a ship —*vt.* to provide, build, or prop up with timbers —*adj.* of or for timber —*interj.* a warning shout by a lumberman that a cut tree is about to fall —**tim′-bered** *adj.* —**tim′ber·ing** *n.*

timber hitch *Naut.* a knot used for tying a rope to a spar

tim·ber·line (-līn′) *n.* the line above or beyond which trees do not grow, as on mountains or in polar regions

timber wolf *same as* GREY WOLF

tim·bre (tam′bər, tim′-) *n.* [Fr., earlier, sound of a bell < MFr. < OFr., ult. < Gr. *tympanon,* a drum] the quality of sound, apart from pitch or intensity, that makes one voice or musical instrument different from another

tim·brel (tim′brəl) *n.* [< OFr.: see prec.] an ancient type of tambourine

Tim·buk·tu (tim′buk tōō′) *n.* [after *Timbuktu,* town in W Africa] [Colloq.] any very distant place

time (tīm) *n.* [OE. *tima*] 1. duration in which things happen in the past, present, and future; every minute there has been or ever will be 2. a system of measuring the passing of hours [solar *time,* standard *time*] 3. the period between two events or during which something exists, happens, or acts 4. [*usually* *pl.*] a period of history [medieval *times,* Gladstone's *time*] 5. *a*) a period characterized by a prevailing condition or specific experience [a *time* of peace, have a good *time*] *b*) [*usually* *pl.*] prevailing conditions [*times* are bad] 6. a set period or term, as a lifetime or a term of imprisonment, apprenticeship, military service, etc. 7. a period necessary,

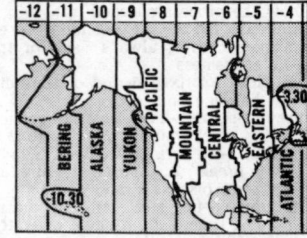

TIME ZONES

sufficient, measured, etc. for something [*time* for play, a baking *time* of ten minutes] **8.** a) the period worked or to be worked by an employee b) the hourly rate of pay for the regular working hours **9.** rate of speed in marching, etc. **10.** a precise instant, minute, hour, day, year, etc., determined by clock or calendar **11.** the point at which something happens; occasion **12.** the usual or appointed moment for something to happen, begin, or end [*time* to get up] **13.** the suitable or proper moment [now is the *time* to act] **14.** any one of a series of moments at which something recurs [for the fifth *time, time* and *time* again] **15.** *Music* a) the grouping of rhythmic beats into measures of equal length b) the characteristic rhythm of a piece of music in terms of this grouping c) the rate of speed at which a composition is played; tempo d) the duration of a note or rest —*interj.* **1.** a word called out by a publican indicating that it is closing time **2.** *Sports* a signal that a period of play or activity is ended or that play is temporarily suspended —*vt.* **timed, tim'ing 1.** to arrange the time of so as to be acceptable or suitable, opportune, etc. **2.** to adjust, set, etc. so as to coincide in time [*time* your entry to coincide with his exit] **3.** to set the duration of (a syllable or musical note) as a unit of rhythm **4.** to record the pace, speed, etc. of [to *time* a runner] —*adj.* **1.** having to do with time **2.** set to explode, open, etc. at a given time [a *time* bomb] **3.** payable later —**abreast of the times 1.** up to date **2.** informed about current matters —**against time** trying to finish in a given time —**ahead of time** sooner than due; early —**at one time 1.** together **2.** formerly —**at the same time 1.** together **2.** nonetheless; however —**at times** occasionally; sometimes —**behind the times** out of date; old-fashioned —**behind time** late —**do time** [Colloq.] to serve a prison term —**for the time being** for the present; temporarily —**from time to time** at intervals; now and then —**have no time** for [Colloq.] to dislike —**in good time 1.** at the proper time **2.** in a short time —**in no time** very quickly —**in time 1.** eventually **2.** before it is too late **3.** keeping the set tempo, pace, etc. —**make time** to find often occasion or opportunity (with *for*) —**many a time** often; frequently —**on time 1.** at the appointed time; punctual(ly) —**pass the time of day** to exchange a few words of greeting, etc. —**time after time** again and again; continually: also **time and again** —**time of one's life** [Colloq.] an experience of great pleasure for one —**time on one's hands** an interval with nothing to do —**time out of mind** time so long past as to be vague: also **time immemorial** —**time was** there was a time

time and a half a rate of payment one and a half times the usual rate, as for working overtime

time and motion study the study of operational or production procedures and the time consumed by them, with the intention of increasing efficiency and productivity: also **time and motion, time study**

time capsule a container holding articles of the present time, buried or preserved for a future age

time clock a clock with a mechanism for recording on a card (**timecard**) the time at which an employee begins and ends a work period

time exposure 1. a relatively long exposure of photographic film, generally for more than half a second **2.** a photograph taken in this way

time-hon·oured (tīm'on'ərd) *adj.* honoured because in existence or usage for a long time

time·keep·er (-kē'pər) *n.* **1.** a watch, clock, etc. judged in terms of its accuracy [good *timekeeper*] **2.** a person who keeps time; specif., a) one who keeps account of the hours worked by employees b) one who keeps account of the elapsed time in the periods of play in certain sports

time-lapse (-laps') *adj.* of a technique of photographing a slow process on film by exposing single frames at widely spaced intervals: the film is projected at regular speed to show the process speeded up

time·less (-lis) *adj.* **1.** unending **2.** eternal **3.** restricted to no specific time; always valid or true —**time'less·ly** *adv.* —**time'less·ness** *n.*

time limit a fixed period of time during which something must be done or ended

time·ly (-lē) *adj.* **-li·er, -li·est** happening, done, said, etc. at a suitable time; well-timed; opportune —**time'li·ness** *n.*

time·out (-out') *n.* [Chiefly U.S.] **1.** a period of rest or leisure; break **2.** *Sports*, etc. any temporary suspension of play, as to discuss strategy, etc.

time·piece (-pēs') *n.* any apparatus for measuring and recording time; esp., a clock or watch

tim·er (tī'mər) *n.* **1.** *same as* STOPWATCH **2.** a device for timing, or automatically starting and stopping, some mechanism

times (tīmz) *prep.* multiplied by: symbol, × [two *times* three is six]

time-sav·ing (tīm'sā'viŋ) *adj.* that saves time because of greater efficiency, etc. —**time'sav'er** *n.*

time-serv·er (-sur'vər) *n.* a person who seeks to advance himself by altering his principles to suit the times or to gain support or favour —**time'serv'ing** *n., adj.*

time signature *Music* a sign, usually like a numerical fraction, after the key signature, indicating the time, or tempo

time·ta·ble (-tā'b'l) *n.* **1.** a schedule of the times for things to happen, esp. of the times of arrival and departure of planes, trains, buses, etc. **2.** a tabulated list of the periods allotted to different subjects at school, etc. —*vt.* to assign to a period or time on a timetable —*vi.* to draw up a timetable

time-test·ed (-tes'tid) *adj.* having value proved by long use or experience

time·worn (-wôrn') *adj.* **1.** showing signs of wear or disrepair because of long use or existence **2.** hackneyed; trite

time zone a region throughout which the same standard time is used

tim·id (tim'id) *adj.* [< L. < *timere*, to fear] **1.** easily frightened; shy **2.** showing lack of self-confidence —**ti·mid·i·ty** (tə mid'ə tē), **tim'id·ness** *n.* —**tim'id·ly** *adv.*

tim·ing (tī'miŋ) *n.* **1.** a) the regulation of the speed with which something is performed so as to produce the most effective results b) the pacing of scenes, as of a play, for total effect **2.** measurement of time

tim·or·ous (tim'ər əs) *adj.* [< MFr. < ML. < L. *timor*, fear] **1.** full of or subject to fear; timid **2.** showing or caused by timidity —**tim'or·ous·ly** *adv.* —**tim'or·ous·ness** *n.*

tim·o·thy (tim'ə thē) *n.* [after Timothy Hanson, who took the seed to the Carolinas, c. 1720] a perennial grass with dense, cylindrical spikes, widely grown for hay

tim·pa·ni (tim'pə nē) *n.pl., sing.* **-pa·no'** (-nō') [It.: see TYMPANUM] kettledrums; esp., a set of kettledrums of different pitches played by one performer in an orchestra —**tim'pa·nist** *n.*

tin (tin) *n.* [OE.] **1.** a soft, silver-white, metallic chemical element, easily shaped at ordinary temperatures: symbol, Sn; at. wt., 118.69; at. no., 50 **2.** *same as* TIN PLATE **3.** a container made of tinned iron or other metal, in which foods or other perishable goods are sealed for preservation **4.** the contents of a tin; tinful **5.** a container made of tin and used for storing food, etc. [a biscuit *tin*] **5.** a rectangular-shaped loaf of bread —*vt.* **tinned, tin'ning 1.** to plate with tin **2.** to put in tins for preservation

tin·a·mou (tin'ə mōō') *n.* [Fr. < Carib name, *tinamu*] a bird of South and Central America resembling the partridge and quail, but related to the ostrich

tin can 1. a tin used for preserving food **2.** [Slang] *same as* DESTROYER (sense 2)

tinc·to·ri·al (tiŋk tôr'ē əl) *adj.* [< L. *tinctorius* < *tingere*: see ff.] having to do with colour, dyeing or staining

tinc·ture (tiŋk'chər) *n.* [< L. *tinctura* < pp. of *tingere*, to dye] **1.** orig., a dye **2.** a light colour; tint; tinge **3.** a slight trace, smattering, etc. **4.** a medicinal substance in a solution of alcohol or alcohol and water —*vt.* **-tured, -tur·ing 1.** to colour lightly; tint; tinge **2.** to imbue lightly or give a slight trace to

tin·der (tin'dər) *n.* [OE. *tynder*] any dry, easily flammable material, esp. as formerly used for starting a fire from a spark made by flint and steel struck together

tin·der·box (-boks') *n.* **1.** formerly, a metal box for holding tinder, flint, and steel **2.** any highly flammable object, structure, etc. **3.** any place or situation in which trouble, war, etc. is likely to flare up

tine (tīn) *n.* [OE. *tind*] a sharp, projecting point; prong [the *tines* of a fork] —**tined** *adj.*

tin·foil (tin'foil') *n.* a very thin sheet or sheets of tin or an alloy of tin and lead, etc. used as a wrapping for food products, in insulation, etc.

ting (tiŋ) *n.* [echoic] a single, light, ringing sound, as of a small bell being struck —*vt., vi.* to make or cause to make a ting

ting-a-ling (tiŋ'ə liŋ') *n.* the sound of a small bell ringing repeatedly

tinge (tinj) *vt.* **tinged, tinge'ing** or **ting'ing** [L. *tingere*, to dye] **1.** to colour slightly; give a tint to **2.** to give a trace, slight flavour or odour, shade, etc. to [joy *tinged* with sorrow] —*n.* **1.** a slight colouring; tint **2.** a slight trace, flavour, odour, etc.

tin·gle (tiŋ'g'l) *vi.* **-gled, -gling** [< ME. var. of *tinklen*, to tinkle] **1.** to have a prickling or stinging feeling, as from cold, excitement, etc. **2.** to cause this feeling —*n.* this feeling —**tin'gler** *n.* —**tin'gling·ly** *adv.* —**tin'gly** *adj.* **-gli·er, -gli·est**

tin god a person unworthy of the honour or respect he demands or receives

tin·ker (tiŋ'kər) *n.* [< ?] **1.** a person who mends pots, pans, etc., usually travelling at his trade **2.** a person who can make all kinds of minor repairs **3.** a clumsy or unskilful worker; bungler —*vi.* **1.** to work as a tinker **2.** to make clumsy attempts to mend something **3.** to potter aimlessly —*vt.* to mend as a tinker —**tin'ker·er** *n.*

tinker's damn (or **dam** or **cuss**) [< prec. + DAMN: with reference to the lowly status and profane speech of tinkers] something of no value: esp. in **not worth a tinker's damn**

tin·kle (tiŋ'k'l) vi. **-kled, -kling** [echoic] to make a series of light, clinking sounds like those of a very small bell —vt. **1.** to cause to tinkle **2.** to indicate, signal, etc. by tinkling —n. the act or sound of tinkling —**give someone a tinkle** [Colloq.] to phone someone up —**tin'kler** n. —**tin'kly** adj. **-kli·er, -kli·est**

tin liz·zie (liz'ē) [orig. nickname of an early model of Ford car] any cheap or old car

tin·ner (tin'ər) n. **1.** a tin miner **2.** same as TINSMITH

tin·ni·tus (ti nīt'əs) n. [< L. *tinnire*, to tinkle, of echoic origin] any ringing in the ears not caused by an external stimulus

tin·ny (tin'ē) adj. **-ni·er, -ni·est 1.** of or yielding tin **2.** like tin; bright but cheap; not durable **3.** of or like the sound made in striking a tin object —**tin'ni·ly** adv. —**tin'ni·ness** n.

Tin Pan Alley 1. the centre of popular music publishing in New York City **2.** the publishers, writers, and promoters of popular music

tin plate thin sheets of iron or steel plated with tin —**tin'-plate'** vt. **-plat'ed, -plat'ing**

tin·pot (tin'pot') adj. [Colloq.] worthless; inferior

tin·sel (tin's'l) n. [< MFr. *estincelle* < OFr.: see STENCIL] **1.** formerly, a cloth interwoven with glittering threads of gold, silver, etc. **2.** thin sheets, strips, or threads of tin, metal foil, etc., used for decoration, as on Christmas trees **3.** something that looks showy and fine but is really cheap and of little value —adj. **1.** of or decorated with tinsel **2.** showy; gaudy —vt. **-selled, -sel·ling 1.** to make glitter as with tinsel **2.** to give a showy, gaudy look to —**tin'sel·ly** adj.

tin·smith (tin'smith') n. a person who works in tin or tin plate; maker of tinware: also **tin'man**, pl. **-men**

tin·stone n. same as CASSITERITE

tint (tint) n. [< L. pp. of *tingere*, to dye] **1.** a delicate colour or hue; tinge **2.** a colour or shading of a colour, esp. with reference to its mixture with white **3.** a dye for the hair **4.** Engraving an even shading produced by fine parallel lines —vt. to give a tint to —**tint'er** n.

tin·tin·nab·u·la·tion (tin'ti nab'yoo lā'shən) n. [< L. *tintinnabulum*, little bell] the ringing sound of bells

tin·type (tin'tīp') n. an old kind of photograph taken directly on a sensitized plate of enamelled tin or iron

tin·ware (-wer') n. pots, pans, etc. of tin plate

ti·ny (tī'nē) adj. **-ni·er, -ni·est** [< ME. *tine*, a little (something)] very small; diminutive —**ti'ni·ly** adv. —**ti'-ni·ness** n.

-tion (shən) [< Fr. < OFr. < L. *-tio* (gen. *-tionis*)] a suffix meaning: **1.** the act of [*correction*] **2.** the state of being [*elation*] **3.** the thing that is [*creation*]

-tious (shəs) [< Fr. < L. *-tiosus*] a suffix used to form adjectives from nouns ending in -TION [*cautious*]

tip¹ (tip) n. [ME. *tippe*] **1.** the pointed or rounded end or top of something **2.** something attached to the end, as a cap, ferrule, etc. **3.** a top or apex, as of a mountain —vt. **tipped, tip'ping 1.** to make a tip on **2.** to cover the tip or tips of (*with* something) **3.** to serve as the tip of —**tip in** to insert (a map, picture, etc.) by pasting along the inner edge in bookbinding

tip² (tip) vt. **tipped, tip'ping** [akin ? to prec.] **1.** to strike lightly and sharply; tap **2.** to give a small present of money to (a waiter, porter, etc.) for some service **3.** [Colloq.] to give secret information to (often with *off*) —vi. to give a tip or tips —n. **1.** a light, sharp blow; tap **2.** a piece of secret information [*a tip on the race*] **3.** a suggestion, hint, warning, etc. **4.** a small present of money given to a waiter, porter, etc. for services; gratuity —**tip one's hand** (or mitt) [Slang] to reveal one's plans, etc., often without intending to —**tip'per** n.

tip³ (tip) vt. **tipped, tip'ping** [< ?] **1.** to overturn or upset (often with *over*) **2.** to cause to tilt or slant **3.** to raise (one's hat) slightly in greeting someone —vi. **1.** to tilt or slant **2.** to overturn or topple (often with *over*) —n. **1.** a tipping or being tipped; tilt; slant **2.** a place where rubbish is deposited; dump **3.** [Colloq.] a dirty or untidy place —**tip the scales** to weigh (a specified amount)

tip-off (tip'of') n. a giving of secret information, a hint, warning, etc.

tip·pet (tip'it) n. [prob. dim. of *tip*, TIP¹] **1.** formerly, a long, hanging part of a hood, cape, or sleeve **2.** a scarflike garment of fur, wool, etc. for the neck and shoulders, hanging down in front, esp. as worn by clergymen

tipper lorry a lorry that is unloaded by tilting the body backwards with the tailboard down

tip·ple (tip''l) vi., vt. **-pled, -pling** [prob. < ME. *tipelar*, tavern-keeper < ?] to drink (alcoholic liquor) habitually —n. strong drink —**tip'pler** n.

tip·staff (tip'stäf) n., pl. **-staffs, -staves 1.** formerly, a metal-tipped staff used as a badge of office **2.** an official in a law court

tip·ster (tip'stər) n. [Colloq.] a person who sells tips, as to people betting on horse races, speculating in stocks, etc.

tip·sy (tip'sē) adj. **-si·er, -si·est 1.** that tips easily; not steady **2.** crooked; awry **3.** somewhat drunk —**tip'si·ly** adv. —**tip'si·ness** n.

tip·toe (tip'tō') n. the tip of a toe or the tips of the toes —vi. **-toed', -toe'ing** to walk stealthily or cautiously on one's tiptoes —adj. standing on one's tiptoes —adv. on tiptoe —**on tiptoe 1.** on one's tiptoes **2.** eager or eagerly **3.** silently; stealthily

tip·top (-top') n. [TIP¹ + TOP¹] **1.** the highest point; very top **2.** [Colloq.] the highest in quality or excellence; best —adj., adv. **1.** at the highest point, or top **2.** [Colloq.] at the highest point of excellence, health, etc.

ti·rade (tī rād', tir-) n. [Fr. < It. *tirata*, a volley < pp. of *tirare*, to fire] a long, vehement speech or denunciation; harangue

tire¹ (tīr) vt., vi. **tired, tir'ing** [OE. *tiorian*] **1.** to make or become weary or fatigued, as by exertion **2.** to make or become bored or impatient, as by dull talk

tire² (tīr) n. U.S. sp. of TYRE

tired (tīrd) adj. **1.** fatigued; weary **2.** stale; hackneyed —**tired'ly** adv. —**tired'ness** n.

tire·less (tīr'lis) adj. that does not become tired —**tire'-less·ly** adv. —**tire'less·ness** n.

tire·some (-səm) adj. **1.** tiring; boring **2.** annoying; irksome —**tire'some·ly** adv. —**tire'some·ness** n.

tire·wom·an (tīr'woom'ən) n. [ME. *tiren* < *atiren*, to attire] [Archaic] a lady's maid

ti·ro (tī'rō) n., pl. **-ros** var. sp. of TYRO

'tis (tiz) it is

ti·sane (ti zan') n. [ME. < MFr. *tisane* < L. < Gr. *ptisanē*, peeled barley] an infusion of herbs; herb tea

tis·sue (tish'ōō, tis'yōō) n. [< OFr. *tissu* < pp. of *tistre* < L. *texere*, to weave] **1.** cloth; esp., light, thin cloth, as gauze **2.** a tangled mass or series; mesh; network; web [a *tissue* of lies] **3.** a piece of soft, absorbent paper, used as disposable handkerchief, as toilet paper, etc. **4.** a) same as TISSUE PAPER b) a sheet of tissue paper **5.** Biol. a) the substance of an organic body or organ, consisting of cells and the material between them b) any substance of this kind having a particular function [epithelial *tissue*] —vt. **-sued, -su·ing** to cover with tissue

tissue paper very thin, unglazed, nearly transparent paper, as for wrapping things, making tracings, etc.

tit¹ (tit) n. [TIT(MOUSE)] any of various small birds, as the blue tit, coal tit, etc.

tit² (tit) n. [OE.] **1.** same as TEAT **2.** breast: a vulgar usage

Tit. Titus

ti·tan (tīt''n) n. [after the *Titans*, in Gr. Myth. giants who were overthrown by the Olympian gods] any person or thing of great size or power —adj. same as TITANIC —**Ti'-tan·ess** n.fem.

Ti·tan·ic (tī tan'ik) adj. **1.** of or like the Titans **2.** [t-] of great size, strength, or power —**ti·tan'i·cal·ly** adv.

ti·ta·ni·um (tī tā'nē əm, ti-) n. [ModL. < Gr. pl. of *Titan*, a Titan] a silvery or dark-grey, lustrous, metallic chemical element found in various minerals and used as a deoxidizing agent in molten steel: symbol, Ti; at. wt., 47.90; at. no., 22

titanium dioxide a compound, TiO_2, used esp. as a white pigment

tit·bit (tit'bit') n. [< dial *tid*, small object + BIT²] a choice piece of food, gossip, etc.

tit·fer (tit'fər) n. [< ff.: rhyming slang] [Slang] a hat

tit for tat [var. of earlier *tip for tap*: see TIP²] this in return for that, as blow for blow

tithe (tīth) n. [OE. *teothe*, a tenth] **1.** one tenth of the annual produce of one's land or of one's annual income, paid as a contribution to support a church or its clergy **2.** a) a tenth part b) any small part **3.** any tax or levy —vt. **tithed, tith'ing 1.** to pay a tithe of (one's income, etc.) **2.** to levy a tithe —vi. to pay a tithe —**tith'a·ble** adj. —**tith'er** n.

tithe barn a barn where the parish tithe corn was stored

ti·tian (tish'ən) adj., n. [from the hair colour in many of *Titian's* portraits] reddish yellow

tit·il·late (tit'əl āt') vt. **-lat'ed, -lat'ing** [< L. pp. of *titillare*, to tickle] **1.** same as TICKLE **2.** to excite or stimulate pleasurably —**tit'il·lat'er** n. —**tit'il·la'tion** n. —**tit'il·la'tive** adj.

tit·i·vate, tit·ti·vate (tit'ə vāt') vt., vi. **-vat'ed, -vat'ing** [prob. < TIDY, with quasi-Latin suffix] to dress up; spruce up —**tit'i·va'tion, tit'ti·va'tion** n.

tit·lark (tit'lärk') n. [TIT¹ + LARK¹] same as PIPIT

ti·tle (tīt''l) n. [OFr. < L. *titulus*] **1.** the name of a book, chapter, poem, picture, piece of music, play, etc. **2.** a) short for TITLE PAGE b) a literary work having a particular title [50 new *titles* published in the autumn] **3.** a descriptive name; epithet **4.** a word used to show the rank, office, occupation, etc. of a person ["Duke," "Mayor," and "Dr." are *titles*] **5.** a claim or right **6.** Law a) a right to ownership, esp. of real estate b) evidence of such right c) a document stating such a right; title deed **7.** a championship, esp. in sports **8.** Cinema TV words shown on the screen that give credits, translations, etc. —vt. **-tled, -tling** to give a title to; name; entitle

ti·tle·hold·er (-hōl′dər) *n.* the holder of a title; specif., the winner of a championship, as in some sport

title page the page in the front of a book that gives the title, author, publisher, etc.

title role (or **part** or **character**) the character in a play, film, etc. whose name is used as or in its title

tit·mouse (tit′mous′) *n.*, *pl.* **-mice** (-mīs·) [ME. *titemose*, prob. < *tit-*, little + OE. *mase*, titmouse] *same as* TIT[1]

ti·trate (tī′trāt) *vt.*, *vi.* **-trat·ed**, **-trat·ing** [< Fr. *titrer* < *titre*, a standard < OFr. *title*, TITLE + -ATE[1]] to test by or be subjected to titration

ti·tra·tion (tī trā′shən) *n.* *Chem.* the process of finding out how much of a substance is in a known volume of a solution by measuring the volume of a solution of known concentration added to produce a given reaction

ti·tre (tīt′ər, tet′-) *n.* [Fr., lit., standard, title] *Chem.* the concentration of a dissolved substance as determined by titration

tit·ter (tit′ər) *vi.* [echoic] to laugh in a half-suppressed way, suggestive of silliness, nervousness, etc.; giggle —*n.* the act or an instance of tittering —**tit′ter·er** *n.*

tit·tle (tit′'l) *n.* [ME. *title*, orig. same word as TITLE] 1. formerly, a dot or other small mark used as a diacritic 2. a very small particle; iota; jot

tit·tle-tat·tle (tit′'l tat′'l) *n.*, *vi.* **-tled**, **-tling** [redupl. of *tattle*] gossip; chatter

tit·tup (tit′əp) *n.* [prob. echoic of hoofbeats] a lively movement; caper —*vi.* **-tuped** or **-tupped**, **-tup·ing** or **-tup·ping** to move in a frolicsome way; prance

tit·u·lar (tit′yə lər) *adj.* [< L. *titulus*, title] 1. of, or having the nature of, a title 2. having a title 3. existing only in title; in name only [a *titular* leader] 4. from whom or which the title or name is taken —**tit′u·lar·ly** *adv.*

tiz·zy (tiz′ē) *n.*, *pl.* **-zies** [< ?] *Colloq.* a state of frenzied excitement, esp. over some trivial matter

TKO, T.K.O. *Boxing abbrev. of* TECHNICAL KNOCKOUT

Tl *Chem.* thallium

T.L.S. Times Literary Supplement

Tm *Chem.* thulium

tme·sis (tə mē′sis) *n.* [LL. < Gr. *tmēsis*, a cutting] separation of the parts of a compound word by an intervening word or words (Ex.: *what person soever* for *whatsoever person*)

tn. ton(s)

TNT, T.N.T. trinitrotoluene

to (tōō; *unstressed* too, tə) *prep.* [OE.] 1. *a*) in the direction of; towards [turn *to* the left] *b*) in the direction of and reaching [he went *to* London] 2. as far as [wet *to* the skin] 3. into a condition of [a rise *to* fame] 4. on, onto, against, at, next, etc. [tie it *to* the post] 5. *a*) until [from noon *to* night] *b*) before [the time is ten *to* six] 6. for the purpose of [come *to* my aid] 7. *a*) as concerns; in respect of [open *to* attack] *b*) in the opinion of [it seems *to* me] 8. producing or resulting in [torn *to* pieces] 9. with; along with [add this *to* the rest] 10. belonging with [the key *to* this house] 11. as compared with; as against [a score of 7 *to* 0] 12. *a*) in agreement or correspondence with [not *to* my taste] *b*) in response to [come *to* my call] 13. constituting; in [ten *to* the pound] 14. to the limit of [moderate *to* high prices] 15. with (a specified person or thing) as the recipient, or indirect object, of the action [give the book *to* her] 16. in honour of [a toast *to* you] *To* is also used as a sign of the infinitive (Ex.: it is easy *to* read) —*adv.* 1. forward; in the normal or desired position or direction; esp., shut or closed [the door was blown *to*] 2. to the matter at hand [let's all fall *to*] —**to and fro** back and forth

toad (tōd) *n.* [OE. *tade*] 1. any of a group of tailless, leaping amphibians with a rough, warty skin, that live on moist land rather than in water, except during breeding 2. a person regarded as loathsome, contemptible, etc.

toad·fish (-fish′) *n.*, *pl.* **-fish′**, **-fish′·es**: see FISH 1. any of various scaleless fishes with froglike heads, found in shallows off the Atlantic coast of N America 2. any of various similar Australian fish, some of which are poisonous

TOAD
(1-22 cm long)

toad·flax (-flaks′) *n.* a perennial plant with yellow-orange flowers; also called **butter and eggs**

toad in the hole sausages baked in batter

toad·stool (-stōōl′) *n.* a mushroom; esp., in popular usage, any poisonous mushroom

toad·y (tōd′ē) *n.*, *pl.* **toad′ies** [short for *toadeater*, quack doctor's assistant who pretended to eat toads and then drank the quack's cure-all] a person who flatters and serves others in any way to gain favour: also **toad′eat′er** —*vt.*, *vi.* **toad′ied**, **toad′y·ing** to be a toady (to); flatter —**toad′y·ism** *n.*

to-and-fro (tōō′ən frō′) *adj.* moving forwards and backwards; back-and-forth

toast[1] (tōst) *vt.* [< OFr., ult. < L. pp. of *torrere*, to parch] 1. to brown the surface of (bread, etc.) by heating 2. to warm thoroughly [toast yourself by the fire] —*vi.* to become toasted —*n.* sliced bread browned by heat —**toast′er** *n.*

toast[2] (tōst) *n.* [< the toasted spiced bread formerly put in the wine, and the idea that the person honoured also added flavour] 1. a person, thing, idea, etc. in honour of which glasses of wine, etc. are raised and drunk 2. *a*) a proposal to drink to some person, etc. *b*) such a drink 3. any person greatly acclaimed —*vt.*, *vi.* to propose or drink a toast (to) —**toast′er** *n.*

toast·mas·ter (tōst′mäs′tər) *n.* the person at a banquet who proposes toasts, introduces after-dinner speakers, etc. —**toast′mis′tress** (-mis′trəs) *n.fem.*

toast-rack (-rak′) *n.* a small, partitioned stand of metal, china, etc., for serving toasted bread

Tob. Tobit

to·bac·co (tə bak′ō) *n.*, *pl.* **-cos** [Sp. *tobaco* < WInd., pipe in which the Indians smoked the plant] 1. any of various plants of the nightshade family, with large leaves and white, yellow, greenish, or purple flowers, esp. a species widely cultivated for its leaves 2. these leaves, prepared for smoking, chewing, or snuffing 3. cigars, cigarettes, snuff, etc. 4. the use of tobacco for smoking, etc.

to·bac·co·nist (tə bak′ə nist) *n.* a dealer in tobacco and other smoking supplies

-to-be (tōō bē′) *adj.* about to be; future: used in combination [a mother-to-be]

to·bog·gan (tə bog′ən) *n.* [CanadFr. *tabagan* < Algonquian] a long, narrow, flat sledge without runners, curved back at the front end: now used for riding downhill —*vi.* 1. to ride, travel, etc. on a toboggan 2. to decline rapidly —**to·bog′gan·er**, **to·bog′gan·ist** *n.*

To·by (tō′bē) *n.*, *pl.* **-bies** [< *Toby*, dim. of *Tobias*, ult. < Heb. *tōbhīyāh*, lit., the lord is good] a jug or mug for ale or beer shaped like a stout man with a three-cornered hat: also **Toby jug**

TOBOGGAN

toc·ca·ta (tə kät′ə) *n.* [It. < pp. of *toccare*, to touch < L.] a composition in free style for the organ, piano, etc., often used as a prelude of a fugue

Toc H (-äch′) [< the former telegraphic code for *T.H.*, initials of *Talbot House*, Poperinghe, Belgium, the original headquarters] a society formed after World War I to promote a spirit of Christian comradeship

to·coph·er·ol (tō kof′ə rol′) *n.* [< Gr. *tokos*, childbirth + *pherein*, to BEAR[1] + -OL[1]] any of the four related oils that compose vitamin E and occur chiefly in wheat-germ oil, lettuce, etc.

toc·sin (tok′sin) *n.* [Fr. < MFr. < Pr. < *toc*, a stroke + *senh*, a bell < L. *signum*, a sign] 1. *a*) an alarm bell *b*) its sound 2. any alarm

tod (tod) *n.* [< ? *Tod Sloan*, rhyming slang] [Colloq.] one's own; oneself: only in **on one's tod**

to·day (tə dā′) *adv.* [OE. *to dæg*] 1. on or during the present day 2. in the present time or age; nowadays —*n.* 1. the present day 2. the present time or period Also, esp. formerly, **to-day**

tod·dle (tod′'l) *vi.* **-dled**, **-dling** [? freq. of TOTTER] to walk with short, uncertain steps, as a child —*n.* a toddling —**tod′dler** *n.*

tod·dy (tod′ē) *n.*, *pl.* **-dies** [Anglo-Ind. < Hindi *tārī*, fermented sap < *tār*, palm tree] 1. the sweet or fermented sap of various East Indian palms, used as a beverage 2. a drink of brandy, whisky, etc. mixed with hot water, sugar, etc.: also **hot toddy**

to-do (tə dōō′) *n.* [Colloq.] a commotion; fuss

toe (tō) *n.* [OE. *ta*] 1. *a*) any of the digits of the foot *b*) the forepart of the foot *c*) that part of a shoe, sock, etc. which covers the toes 2. anything like a toe in location, shape, or function —*vt.* **toed**, **toe′ing** 1. to touch, kick, etc. with the toes 2. *a*) to drive (a nail) slantingly *b*) to fasten with nails so driven; toenail —*vi.* to stand, walk, or be formed so that the toes are in a specified position [to *toe* in] —**on one's toes** [Colloq.] mentally or physically alert —**step** (or **tread**) **on someone's toes** to offend someone, esp. by intruding on his rights —**toe the line** (or **mark**) to follow orders, rules, etc. strictly —**turn up one's toes** [Slang] to die —**toe′like′** *adj.*

toe·cap (tō′kap) *n.* a reinforced covering on the toe of a shoe

toed (tōd) *adj.* having (a specified kind or number of) toes: usually in hyphenated compounds [pigeon-*toed*]

toe dance a dance performed on the tips of the toes, as in ballet —**toe′-dance′** *vi.* **-danced′**, **-danc′ing** —**toe′-danc′er** *n.*

toe·hold (tō′hōld′) *n.* 1. a small space or ledge for supporting the toe of the foot in climbing, etc. 2. any means of surmounting obstacles, gaining entry, etc. 3. a

toe·less (-lis) *adj.* 1. having no toe or toes 2. having the toe open [*toeless* shoes]

toe·nail (-nāl´) *n.* 1. the nail of a toe 2. *Carpentry* a nail driven slantingly —*vt.* *Carpentry* to fasten with a toenail

toff (tof) *n.* [< *toft*, var. of TUFT] [Slang] a fashionable, upper-class person; esp., a dandy

tof·fee, tof·fy (to´fē) *n.* [var. of earlier *taffy*] a hard, chewy sweet made from sugar or treacle boiled at a high temperature, often with butter, nuts, etc. —**for toffee** [Colloq.] at all; by any means [he can't dance *for toffee*]

toffee apple a toffee-coated apple held on a stick

tof·fee-nosed (-nōz´d) *adj.* [Slang] snobbish; pretentious

toft (toft) *n.* [ME. < OE. < ON. *topt*, homestead] 1. *a)* a homestead *b)* a homestead with its arable land 2. [Dial.] a hillock

tog (tog) *n.* [prob. ult. < L. *toga*, TOGA] [*pl.*] [Colloq.] clothes —*vt., vi.* **togged, tog´ging** [Colloq.] to dress (usually with *up* or *out*)

to·ga (tō´gə) *n., pl.* **-gas, -gae** (-jē) [L. < *tegere*, to cover] 1. in ancient Rome, a loose, one-piece outer garment worn in public by citizens 2. a robe of office —**to´gaed** (-gəd) *adj.*

to·geth·er (tə geth´ər) *adv.* [< OE. < *to* (see TO) + *gædre*, together < base of *gaderian*, to gather] 1. in or into one gathering, group, or place [the family ate *together*] 2. in or into contact, collision, union, etc. [the cars skidded *together*] 3. considered collectively [he won more than all of us *together*] 4. *a)* with one another; in association [to live *together*] *b)* by joint effort [*together* they lifted the sofa] 5. at the same time [shots fired *together*] 6. in succession; continuously [he worked for two days *together*] 7. in or into agreement, cooperation, etc. [let's get *together*] 8. in or into a unified whole

to·geth·er·ness (-nis) *n.* the spending of much time together, as by a family in leisure-time activities, esp. in an effort to make the family more stable and unified; a feeling of closeness

tog·ger·y (tog´ər ē) *n.* [Colloq.] clothes; togs

tog·gle (tog´'l) *n.* [prob. < dial. *tuggle*, freq. of TUG] 1. a rod, pin, or bolt for insertion through a loop of a rope, a link of a chain, etc. to make an attachment, prevent slipping, etc. 2. a toggle joint or a device having one —*vt.* **-gled, -gling** to provide or fasten with a toggle

toggle joint a knee-shaped joint consisting of two bars pivoted together at one end: pressure put on the joint to straighten it transmits opposite, outward pressure to the open ends

toggle switch a switch consisting of a projecting lever moved back and forth through a small arc to open or close an electric circuit

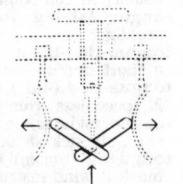

TOGGLE JOINT
(arrows indicate
direction of
pressure)

toil¹ (toil) *vi.* [Anglo-Fr. *toiler*, to strive < OFr. < L. *tudiculare*, to stir about, ult. < *tudes*, mallet] 1. to work hard and continuously 2. to go or move slowly with pain or effort [to *toil* up a hill] —*vt.* [Now Rare] to accomplish with great effort [to *toil* one's way] —*n.* 1. hard, exhausting work or effort 2. a task performed by such effort —**toil´er** *n.*

toil² (toil) *n.* [OFr. *toile* < L. *tela*, a web] 1. [Archaic] a net for trapping 2. [*pl.*] any snare suggestive of a net

toile (twäl) *n.* [Fr.: see prec.] any of various linen or sheer cotton fabrics

toi·let (toi´lit) *n.* [MFr. *toilette* < *toile*, cloth: see prec.] 1. formerly, a dressing table 2. the act of dressing or grooming oneself 3. dress; attire 4. *a)* a room, shelter, etc. for discharging wastes from the body; specif., a small room with a bowl-shaped fixture for this purpose that flushes with water *b)* such a fixture —*adj.* 1. of or for grooming oneself 2. for a toilet (*n.* 4b) —**make one's toilet** [Now Rare] to bathe, dress, arrange one's hair, etc.

toilet paper (or **tissue**) soft, absorbent paper, for cleaning oneself after discharging waste from the body

toilet roll a roll of toilet paper

toi·let·ry (toi´lə trē) *n., pl.* **-ries** soap, lotion, cologne, etc. used in cleaning and grooming oneself

toi·lette (twä let´, toi-) *n.* [Fr.: see TOILET] 1. the process of grooming oneself, including bathing, hairdressing, dressing, etc.: said of women 2. dress or manner of dress; attire

toilet training the training of a young child to use a toilet when he needs to discharge bodily waste

toilet water a perfumed, slightly alcoholic liquid applied to the skin after bathing, etc.

toil·some (toil´səm) *adj.* requiring toil; laborious —**toil´-some·ly** *adv.* —**toil´some·ness** *n.*

toil·worn (-wôrn´) *adj.* worn out by toil

To·kay (tō kā´) *n.* 1. a sweet, rich wine made in Tokay, Hungary 2. any wine like this 3. a large, sweet grape used for the wine

to·ken (tō´k'n) *n.* [OE. *tacn*] 1. a sign, indication, or symbol [a *token* of one's affection] 2. something serving as a sign of authority, identity, etc. 3. a distinguishing mark or feature 4. a keepsake 5. a metal disc with a face value higher than its real value, issued as a substitute for currency, for use in a slot machine, etc. 6. a voucher which can be exchanged for goods of a particular value [a record *token*] —*vt.* to be a token of —*adj.* 1. by way of a token, symbol, etc. 2. merely simulated; slight [*token* resistance] —**by the same** (or **this**) **token** following from this —**in token of** as evidence of

to·ken·ism (-iz'm) *n.* a pretending to act on a principle by doing so in a very small way

token money coins of greater face value than the value of their metal content

told (tōld) *pt. & pp. of* TELL —**all told** all (being) counted; in all [there were ten *all told*]

tole (tōl) *n.* [Fr. *tôle*, sheet iron < *table*, TABLE] a type of lacquered or enamelled metalware used for trays, lamps, etc.

To·le·do (tə lē´dō) *n., pl.* **-dos** [after *Toledo*, Spain, where they were made] a fine-tapered sword or sword blade

tol·er·a·ble (tol´ər ə b'l) *adj.* 1. that can be tolerated; endurable 2. fairly good; passable 3. [Colloq.] in fairly good health —**tol´er·a·bil´i·ty, tol´er·a·ble·ness** *n.* —**tol´-er·a·bly** *adv.*

tol·er·ance (-əns) *n.* 1. a tolerating or being tolerant of others' beliefs, practices, etc. 2. the amount of variation allowed from a standard, accuracy, etc.; specif., the difference between the allowable maximum and minimum sizes of some mechanical part 3. *Med.* the ability to resist the effects of a drug, etc. taken over a period of time or in larger and larger doses

tol·er·ant (-ənt) *adj.* 1. having or showing tolerance of others' beliefs, practices, etc. 2. *Med.* of or having tolerance —**tol´er·ant·ly** *adv.*

tol·er·ate (tol´ə rāt´) *vt.* **-at´ed, -at´ing** [< L. pp. of *tolerare*, to bear] 1. to allow; permit 2. to recognize and respect (others' beliefs, practices, etc.) without sharing them 3. to put up with; bear 4. *Med.* to have tolerance for (a specific drug, etc.) —**tol´er·a´tive** *adj.* —**tol´er·a´tor** *n.*

tol·er·a·tion (tol´ə rā´shən) *n.* tolerance; esp., freedom to hold religious views that differ from the established ones

toll¹ (tōl) *n.* [OE., prob. ult. < Gr. *telos*, tax] 1. a tax or charge for a privilege, esp. for permission to use a bridge, road, etc. 2. the right to demand toll 3. a charge for some service 4. the number lost, taken, etc. [the storm took a heavy *toll* of lives] [Now Rare] 1. to impose a toll on 2. to gather (something) as toll

toll² (tōl) *vt.* [< ? OE. *-tillan*, to touch] 1. to ring (a church bell, etc.) slowly but with regular strokes, as for announcing a death 2. to sound (the hour, a knell, etc.) by this 3. to announce, summon, etc. by this —*vi.* to sound or ring slowly: said of a bell —*n.* 1. the act or sound of tolling a bell 2. a single stroke of the bell —**toll´er** *n.*

toll bar a bar, gate, etc. for stopping travel at a point where toll is taken

toll bridge a bridge at which toll is paid for passage

toll·gate (-gāt´) *n.* a gate for stopping travel at a point where toll is taken

toll·keep·er (-kēp´ər) *n.* a person who collects tolls at a tollgate

toll road a road on which toll must be paid

Tol·tec (tol´tek, tôl´-) *adj.* designating or of a group of Nahuatl Indians who were dominant in Mexico before the rise of the Aztecs

to·lu (balsam) (tō lōō´) [< Sp. < *Tolú*, seaport in Colombia] a fragrant resin obtained from a S American tree: it is used in cough syrups, etc.

tol·u·ene (tol´yōō wēn´) *n.* [TOLU + (BENZ)ENE] a liquid hydrocarbon, C_7H_8, obtained from tolu balsam but now from coal tar, petroleum, etc.: it is used in making dyes, explosives, etc.: also **tol´u·ol´** (-wol´)

tom (tom) *n.* [< *Tom*, dim. of the name *Thomas*] the male of some animals, esp. the cat —*adj.* male

tom·a·hawk (tom´ə hôk´) *n.* [< Algonquian] 1. a light axe with a head of stone, used by North American Indians as a tool and a weapon 2. [Aust.] a hatchet; axe —*vt.* to hit, cut, or kill with a tomahawk

Tom and Jerry (jer´ē) a hot drink made of rum, etc., beaten eggs, sugar, water or milk, and nutmeg

to·ma·to (tə māt´ō) *n., pl.* **-toes** [< Sp. < Nahuatl *tomatl*] 1. a red or yellowish fruit with a juicy pulp, used as a vegetable: botanically it is a berry 2. the plant that it grows on

tomb (tōōm) *n.* [< Anglo-Fr. < LL. < Gr. *tymbos*] 1. a vault, chamber, or grave for the dead 2. a burial monument —**the tomb** death —**tomb´less** *adj.* —**tomb´like´** *adj.*

tom·bac, tom·bak (tom´bak) *n.* [Fr. < Port. < Malay *tĕmbaga*, copper] an alloy of copper and zinc, used in making cheap jewellery

tom·bo·la (tom bō´la, tom´bə lə) *n.* [It., prob. < *tombolare*, to tumble] a kind of lottery in which numbered tickets are bought, some of which entitle the possessor to prizes

tom·boy (tom'boi') *n.* a girl who behaves or plays like an active boy —**tom'boy'ish** *adj.* —**tom'boy'ish·ly** *adv.* —**tom'boy'ish·ness** *n.*

tomb·stone (tōōm'stōn') *n.* a stone, usually with an inscription, marking a tomb or grave

Tom Collins *see* COLLINS

Tom, Dick, and Harry everyone; anyone: usually preceded by *every* and used disparagingly

tome (tōm) *n.* [Fr. < L. < Gr. *tomos,* piece cut off] 1. orig., any volume of a work of several volumes 2. a book, esp. a large or ponderous one

to·men·tum (tō men'təm) *n., pl.* -**ta** (tə) [L., a stuffing (of hair, etc.)] 1. a growth of short, matted, woolly hairs, as on the leaves of some plants 2. a network of small blood vessels

tom·fool (tom'fool') *n.* a foolish, stupid, or silly person —*adj.* foolish, stupid, or silly

tom·fool·er·y (-ər ē) *n., pl.* -**er·ies** foolish or silly behavior; nonsense

Tom·my (tom'ē) *n., pl.* -**mies** [< *Tommy Atkins* (for *Thomas Atkins,* fictitious name used in Brit. army sample forms)] 1. [*also* t-] *epithet for* a private in the British army 2. [t-] bread; provisions, esp. as formerly given to workmen instead of pay

Tommy gun *alternate trademark for* THOMPSON SUBMACHINE GUN —*n.* a submachine gun

tom·my·rot (tom'ē rot') *n.* [Slang] nonsense; foolishness

to·mog·ra·phy (tə mog'rə fē) *n.* [< Gr. *tomos,* a piece cut off + -GRAPHY] a technique of X-ray photography by which a single plane is photographed, with the outline of structures in other planes eliminated

to·mor·row (tə mor'ō) *adv.* [OE. *to morgen*] 1. on the day after today 2. at some time in the future —*n.* 1. the day after today 2. some time in the future Also, esp. formerly, **to-morrow**

Tom Thumb 1. a tiny hero of English folk tales 2. any midget or small person

tom·tit (tom'tit') *n.* any of various tits, esp. the blue tit

tom-tom (tom'tom') *n.* [Hindi *tam-tam*] a simple kind of deep drum with a small head, usually beaten with the hands

-to·my (tə mē) [< Gr. < *temnein,* to cut] a combining form meaning: 1. a dividing [*dichotomy*] 2. a surgical operation [*lithotomy*]

ton (tun) *n.* [var. of TUN] 1. a unit of weight equal to 2,240 pounds avoirdupois, or 1016 kilogrammes, used in Britain: in full, **long ton** 2. a unit of weight equal to 2,000 pounds avoirdupois, or 746 kilogrammes, used in the U.S., Canada, South Africa, etc.: in full, **short ton** 3. *same as* TONNE 4. a unit of internal capacity of ships, equal to 100 cubic feet: in full, **register ton** 5. a unit of carrying capacity of ships, usually equal to 40 cubic feet: in full, **measurement ton, freight ton** 6. a unit for measuring displacement of ships, equal to 35 cubic feet: it is nearly equal to the volume of long ton of sea water: in full, **displacement ton** 7. [*often pl.*] [Colloq.] a very large amount or number 8. [Slang] *a)* £100 *b)* a speed of 100 m.p.h. Abbrev. **T., t., tn.** (*sing. & pl.*)

ton·al (tō'n'l) *adj.* of a tone or tonality —**ton'al·ly** *adv.*

to·nal·i·ty (tō nal'ə tē) *n., pl.* -**ties** 1. a quality of tone 2. *Art* the colour scheme in a painting 3. *Music a) same as* KEY[1] *b)* tonal character as determined by the relationship of the tones to the keynote

ton·do (ton'dō) *n., pl.* -**di** (-dē), -**dos** [It., a plate] a round painting

tone (tōn) *n.* [< OFr. < L. < Gr. *tonos* < *teinein,* to stretch] 1. *a)* a vocal or musical sound *b)* its quality 2. an intonation, pitch, modulation, etc. of the voice that expresses a particular feeling [a *tone* of contempt] 3. a way of wording or expressing things that shows a certain attitude [the friendly *tone* of her letter] 4. normal resilience [rubber that has lost its *tone*] 5. *a)* the style, character, spirit, etc. of a place or period *b)* distinctive style; elegance 6. a quality of colour; tint or shade 7. *Linguis.* the relative height of pitch with which a syllable, word, etc. is pronounced 8. *Music a)* a sound of distinct pitch (as distinguished from a noise) that may be put into harmonic relation with other such sounds *b)* the simple tone of a musical sound as distinguished from its overtones *c)* any one of the full intervals of a diatonic scale 9. *Painting* the effect produced by the combination of light, shade, and colour 10. *Physiol.* the condition of an organism, organ, muscle, etc. with reference to its normal, healthy functioning: see also TONUS —*vt.* **toned, ton'ing** 1. [Rare] *same as* INTONE 2. to give a tone to 3. to change the tone of —*vi.* to take on a tone —**tone down** 1. to make or become less bright, sharp, etc.; soften 2. to make (something written or said) less harsh —**tone in with** to harmonize with —**tone up** 1. to give a more intense tone to 2. to become strengthened or heightened —**tone'less** *adj.* —**tone'less·ly** *adv.* —**tone'less·ness** *n.* —**ton'er** *n.*

tone arm the pivoted arm containing the pickup on a record player

tone colour *same as* TIMBRE

tone-deaf (-def') *adj.* not able to distinguish accurately differences in musical pitch —**tone'-deaf'ness** *n.*

tone poem *same as* SYMPHONIC POEM

tone row (or **series**) *see* TWELVE-TONE

tong (toŋ) *n.* [Chin. *t'ang,* a meeting place] a Chinese association, society, etc.

ton·ga (toŋ'gə) *n.* [Hindu *tāngā*] a light, two-wheeled carriage used in India

Ton·gan (toŋ'gən) *n.* 1. a native of Tonga 2. the Polynesian language of the Tongans

tongs (toŋz) *n.pl.* [*sometimes with sing. v.*] [OE. *tange*] a device for seizing or lifting objects, with two arms pivoted or hinged together: also called **pair of tongs**

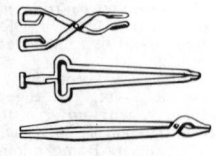

TONGS

tongue (tuŋ) *n.* [OE. *tunge*] 1. the movable muscular structure attached to the floor of the mouth: it is used in eating, tasting, and (in man) speaking 2. an animal's tongue used as food 3. *a)* talk; speech *b)* a manner of speaking in regard to tone, diction, etc. [a glib *tongue*] 4. a language or dialect 5. [*pl.*] *see* GLOSSOLALIA 6. something like a tongue in shape, position, motion, or use; specif., *a)* the flap under the laces of a shoe *b)* the clapper of a bell *c)* the harnessing pole of a horse-drawn vehicle, etc. *d)* the projecting tenon of a tongue-and-groove joint *e)* the vibrating end of the reed in a wind instrument *f)* a narrow strip of land extending into a sea, river, etc. *g)* a long, narrow flame —*vt.* **tongued, tongu'ing** 1. [Archaic] to speak 2. to touch, lick, etc. with the tongue 3. *Music* to play by tonguing: see TONGUING —*vi.* 1. to project like a tongue 2. *Music* to use tonguing: see TONGUING —**find one's tongue** to recover the ability to talk, as after shock —**hold one's tongue** to keep from speaking —**on everyone's tongue** spoken as common gossip —**on the tip of one's** (or **the**) **tongue** almost said or remembered —**with one's tongue in one's cheek** with a double meaning; ironically; humorously —**tongue'less** *adj.* —**tongue'like** *adj.*

tongue-and-groove joint (tuŋ'n grōōv') a kind of joint in which a tongue or tenon on one board fits exactly into a groove in another

tongued (tuŋd) *adj.* having a (specified kind of) tongue: usually in compounds [*sharp-tongued*]

tongue·lash·ing (tuŋ'lash'iŋ) *n.* [Colloq.] a thorough scolding

tongue-tie (-tī') *n.* limited motion of the tongue, caused by a short frenum —*vt.* **-tied', -ty'ing** to make tongue-tied

tongue-tied (-tīd') *adj.* 1. having a condition of tongue-tie 2. speechless from embarrassment, etc.

tongue twister a phrase or sentence hard to speak fast (Ex.: six sick sheiks)

tongu·ing (tuŋ'iŋ) *n.* the use of the tongue in playing a musical wind instrument, esp. for more accurate intonation of rapid notes

ton·ic (ton'ik) *adj.* [< Gr. < *tonos:* see TONE] 1. *a)* of or producing good muscle tone, or tension *b)* characterized by continuous muscular contraction [a *tonic* spasm] 2. invigorating to the body or mind 3. *Music* designating or based on a keynote —*n.* 1. anything that invigorates or stimulates; specif., *a)* a drug, medicine, etc. for increasing body tone *b)* a hair or scalp dressing 2. a carbonated beverage flavoured with a little quinine and served in a mixed drink with gin, vodka, etc.; tonic water 3. *Music* the basic tone of a diatonic scale; keynote —**ton'i·cal·ly** *adv.*

to·nic·i·ty (tō nis'ə tē) *n.* the quality or condition of being tonic; esp., normal muscle tension; tonus

to·night (tə nīt') *adv.* [OE. *to niht*] on or during the present or coming night —*n.* this night or the night about to come Also, esp. formerly, **to-night**

ton·nage (tun'ij) *n.* 1. a duty or tax on ships, based on tons carried 2. the total shipping, in tons, of a country or port 3. the amount in tons a ship can carry 4. weight in tons

tonne (tun) *n.* a measure of weight equal to 1000 kilogrammes

ton·neau (tu nō') *n., pl.* -**neaus', -neaux'** (-nōz') [Fr., lit., a cask] an enclosed rear compartment for passengers in an early type of motor car

to·nom·e·ter (tō nom'ə tər) *n.* [< Gr. *tonos,* tone + -METER] 1. an instrument for determining the pitch of a tone, as a tuning fork 2. an instrument for measuring vapour pressure 3. *Med.* an instrument for measuring tension or pressure, as blood pressure

ton·sil (ton's'l) *n.* [L. *tonsillae, pl.*] either of a pair of oval masses of lymphoid tissue, one on each side of the throat at the back of the mouth —**ton'sil·lar** *adj.*

ton·sil·lec·to·my (ton'sə lek'tə mē) *n., pl.* -**mies** the surgical removal of the tonsils

ton·sil·li·tis (-līt'əs) *n.* inflammation of the tonsils —**ton'sil·lit'ic** (-lit'ik) *adj.*

ton·so·ri·al (ton sôr′ē əl) *adj.* [< L. < *tonsor*, clipper < pp. of *tondere*, to clip] of a barber or barbering: often used humorously

ton·sure (ton′shər) *n.* [< MFr. < L. *tonsura* < pp. of *tondere*, to clip] 1. the act of shaving a man's head, esp. on top, when he becomes a priest or monk 2. the part of the head left bare by doing this —*vt.* **-sured, -sur·ing** to shave the head of, esp. in this way

ton·tine (ton′tēn, ton tēn′) *n.* [Fr. < It., after L. *Tonti*, 17th-c. banker of Naples] a fund to which a group of persons contribute, benefits finally going to the last survivor or to those surviving after a specified time

ton-up boy (tun′up) *n.* [Colloq.] a motorcyclist who habitually rides very fast

to·nus (tō′nəs) *n.* [ModL. < L. < Gr. *tonos*: see TONE] the slight continuous contraction of a normal muscle at rest

too (tōō) *adv.* [< TO] 1. in addition; also 2. more than enough; excessively, etc. [the hat is *too* big] 3. very; extremely [it's *too* good!] Often used as an adjective with *much*, *many* [*too* much to see]

took (took) *pt. of* TAKE

tool (tōōl) *n.* [OE. *tol*] 1. any implement, instrument, etc. held in the hand and used for some work, as a knife, saw, or shovel 2. *a)* the working part of a power-driven machine, as a drill, jigsaw blade, etc. *b)* the whole machine; machine tool 3. anything that serves as a means to get something done [books are *tools* of education] 4. a person used by another to accomplish his purposes, esp. when these are illegal or unethical —*vt.* 1. to shape or work with a tool 2. to provide tools or machinery for (a factory, etc.): often with *up* 3. to impress designs, etc. on (leather, etc.) with tools —*vi.* 1. to use a tool or tools 2. to get or install the tools, equipment, etc. needed (often with *up*) 3. to go in a vehicle —**tool′er** *n.* —**tool′ing** *n.*

tool·box (-boks′) *n.* a box or chest in which tools are kept: also **tool chest**

tool·mak·er (-mā′kər) *n.* a machinist who makes, maintains, and repairs machine tools —**tool′mak′ing** *n.*

tool·room (-rōōm′) *n.* a room, as in a machine shop, where tools are stored, kept in repair, issued to workmen, etc.

toot (tōōt) *vi.* [prob. via LowG. *tuten* < echoic base] 1. to blow a horn, whistle, etc. in short blasts: said of a horn, etc. —*vt.* 1. to cause to sound in short blasts 2. to sound (tones, etc.) as on a horn —*n.* a short blast of a horn, etc.

tooth (tōōth) (*for v. also* tōōth) *n., pl.* **teeth** (tēth) [OE. *toth*] 1. *a)* any of a set of hard, bonelike structures in the jaws of most vertebrates, used for biting, tearing, and chewing *b)* any similar structure in invertebrates *c)* [*pl.*] teeth as DENTURE 2. a toothlike part, as on a saw, comb, gearwheel, etc. 3. an appetite or taste for something [a sweet *tooth*] 4. something biting, piercing, etc. like a tooth [the *teeth* of the storm] 5. an effective means of enforcing something [to put *teeth* into a law] —*vt.* 1. to provide with teeth 2. to make jagged; indent —*vi.* to mesh or interlock, as gears —**armed** (or **dressed**) **to the teeth** as armed (or dressed up) as one can be —**by the skin of one's teeth** narrowly; only just —**get** (or **sink**) **one's teeth into** to become fully occupied with —**in the teeth of** 1. directly against 2. defying —**long in the tooth** [Colloq.] old —**tooth and nail** with all one's strength or resources —**tooth′less** *adj.*

CROWN
DENTIN
PULP
ROOT

TOOTH

tooth·ache (-āk′) *n.* pain in or near a tooth

tooth·brush (-brush′) *n.* a brush for cleaning the teeth

tooth-comb (-kōm) *n.* a small comb with teeth close together —**to go through** (something) **with a fine tooth-comb** to examine (something) with meticulous care

toothed (tōōtht, tōōthd) *adj.* 1. having teeth: often used in hyphenated compounds (big-*toothed*) 2. notched

toothed whale any of a main division of whales, as the sperm whale, that have cone-shaped teeth

tooth·paste (tōōth′pāst′) *n.* a paste used in cleaning the teeth with a toothbrush

tooth·pick (-pik′) *n.* a very small, pointed stick for getting bits of food free from between the teeth

tooth powder a powder used like toothpaste

tooth·some (-səm) *adj.* pleasing to the taste; tasty —**tooth′some·ly** *adv.* —**tooth′some·ness** *n.*

tooth·y (-ē) *adj.* **tooth′i·er, tooth′i·est** showing prominent teeth —**tooth′i·ly** *adv.* —**tooth′i·ness** *n.*

too·tle (tōōt′'l) *vi.* **-tled, -tling** [freq. of TOOT] to keep tooting softly —*n.* the act or sound of tootling

top¹ (top) *n.* [OE.] 1. the head or the crown of the head [from *top* to toe] 2. the *b)* a part, point, or surface of anything 3. the part of a plant growing above the ground [beetroot *tops*] 4. an uppermost part or covering; specif., *a)* a lid, cap, cover, etc. *b)* a folding roof of a motor car *c)* the upper part of a two-piece garment *d)* any garment, esp. for women, which extends from the shoulder to the waist or hips *e)* platform around the head of each lower mast on a sailing ship 5. one first in order, excellence, importance, etc.; specif., *a)* the highest degree, pitch, rank, position, etc. *b)* a person of highest rank, etc. *c)* the choicest part; pick [the *top* of the morning] *d)* the beginning, as of a piece of music [take it from the *top*] 6. *Sports a)* a stroke hitting the ball near its top *b)* the forward spin given the ball by such a stroke 7. *same as* TOP GEAR —*adj.* of or at the top; highest, greatest, foremost, etc. —*vt.* **topped, top′ping** 1. to take off the top of (a plant, etc.) 2. to put a top on [to *top* a cake with icing] 3. to be a top for 4. to reach or go over the top of 5. to exceed in amount, height, etc. [the fund *topped* £75] 6. to be better, more effective, etc. than; outdo 7. to be at the top of; head; lead 8. *Sports* to hit (a ball) near its top, giving it a forward spin —*vi.* to top someone or something —**off the top of one's head** speaking offhand, without careful thought —**on top** at the top; successful —**on top of** 1. on or at the top of 2. resting upon 3. in addition to; besides 4. right after 5. controlling successfully —**over the top** 1. over the front of a trench, as in attacking 2. exceeding the quota or goal —**(the) tops** [Slang] the very best —**top off** to complete by adding a finishing touch —**top out** 1. to complete the skeleton of a building, esp. by adding the highest part 2. [U.S.] to level off —**top up** to raise the level of a liquid, etc., in a container, usually filling it

top² (top) *n.* [OE.] a child's cone-shaped toy, spun on its pointed end —**sleep like a top** to sleep soundly

to·paz (tō′paz) *n.* [< OFr. < L. < Gr. *topazos*] 1. a crystalline mineral that is a silicate of aluminium and fluorine; esp., a clear, yellow variety used as a gem 2. a yellow variety of quartz

top boot a boot reaching to just below the knee, esp. such a boot topped with a band of contrasting colour

top brass *same as* BRASS (sense 7)

top·coat (top′kōt′) *n.* a lightweight overcoat

top dog [Slang] the person, company, etc. in a dominant or leading position, esp. in a competitive situation

top-drawer (-drôr′) *adj.* of first importance, esp. in social position

top-dress·ing (-dres′iŋ) *n.* material applied to a surface, as fertilizer —**top′-dress′** *vt.*

tope¹ (tōp) *vt., vi.* **topped, top′ing** [< ? Fr. *toper*, to accept a bet] [Archaic] to drink much (alcoholic liquor)

tope² (top) *n.* [< ? Cornish] 1. a small, grey, European shark 2. an Australasian shark

to·pee (tō pē′, tō′pē) *n.* [Hindi *topi*] in India, a pith helmet worn as a sunshade

top·er (tō′pər) *n.* a person who topes; drunkard

top-flight (top′flīt′) *adj.* [Colloq.] best; first-rate

top·gal·lant (top′gal′ənt; *naut.* tə gal′-) *adj.* next above the topmast —*n.* a topgallant mast, sail, etc.

top gear the gear ratio of a motor vehicle transmission which produces the highest speed

top hat a tall, black, cylindrical hat, usually of silk, worn by men in formal dress

top-heav·y (top′hev′ē) *adj.* too heavy at the top and so likely to fall over —**top′-heav′i·ness** *n.*

top-hole (-hōl′) *adj.* [Old Slang] excellent

to·pi (tō pē′, tō′pē) *n.* *same as* TOPEE

to·pi·ar·y (tō′pē ər ē) *adj.* designating or of the art of trimming and training shrubs or trees into unnatural, ornamental shapes —*n., pl.* **-ar·ies** topiary art or work

top·ic (top′ik) *n.* [< L. < Gr. *ta topika*, title of work by Aristotle, lit. < *topos*, a place] 1. the subject of a writing, speech, discussion, etc. 2. a heading or item in an outline

top·i·cal (-i k′l) *adj.* 1. of a particular place; local 2. of, using, or arranged by topics 3. having to do with topics of the day; of current or local interest 4. *Med.* of or for a particular part of the body [a *topical* lotion] —**top′i·cal′i·ty** (-kal′ə tē) *n.* —**top′i·cal·ly** *adv.*

top·knot (top′not′) *n.* 1. a knot of feathers, ribbons, etc. worn as a headdress 2. a tuft of hair or feathers on the crown of the head 3. any of several small European flatfish

top·less (-lis) *adj.* without a top; specif., designating or wearing a costume that exposes the breasts

top-lev·el (top′lev′'l) *adj.* 1. of or by persons of the highest office or rank 2. in highest office or rank

top·loft·y (-lof′tē) *adj.* [Colloq.] lofty in manner; haughty —**top′loft′i·ly** *adv.* —**top′loft′i·ness** *n.*

top·mast (top′məst, -mäst′) *n.* the second mast above the deck of a sailing ship, supported by the lower mast

top·most (top′mōst′) *adj.* at the very top

top-notch (-noch′) *adj.* [Colloq.] first-rate; excellent

to·pog·ra·phy (tə pog′rə fē) *n., pl.* **-phies** [< LL. < Gr.: see TOPIC & -GRAPHY] 1. *a)* the science of showing on maps, charts etc. the surface features of a region, such as hills, rivers, and roads *b)* such features 2. surveying done to discover and measure such features 3. a study of some part or system of the body showing the relationship, size, shape, etc. of its parts 4. a similar study of some whole, as the mind or the atom, in relation to its parts —**to·pog′ra·pher** *n.*

—top·o·graph·ic (top'ə graf'ik), **top'o·graph'i·cal** *adj.* **—top'o·graph'i·cal·ly** *adv.*

to·pol·o·gy (tə pol'ə jē) *n., pl.* **-gies** [< Gr. *topos*, a place + -LOGY] **1.** *same as* TOPOGRAPHY (senses 3 & 4) **2.** *Math.* the study of those properties of geometric figures that remain unchanged even when under distortion **—top·o·log·i·cal** (top'ə loj'i k'l) *adj.* **—to·pol'o·gist** *n.*

top·per (top'ər) *n.* **1.** a person or thing that tops or excels **2.** [Colloq.] *same as* TOP HAT

top·ping (-iŋ) *n.* something that forms the top of, or is put on top of, something else, as a sauce on food **—adj.** [Colloq.] excellent; first-rate

top·ple (top''l) *vi.* **-pled, -pling** [< TOP[1], *v.* + freq. *-le*] **1.** to fall (*over*) from top-heaviness, etc. **2.** to lean as if about to fall over; totter **—vt.** **1.** to cause to topple **2.** to overthrow

top·sail (top's'l, -sāl') *n.* **1.** in a square-rigged vessel, the square sail, or either of a pair of square sails, next above the lowest sail on a mast **2.** in a fore-and-aft-rigged vessel, the small sail set above the gaff

top·se·cret (-sē'krit) *adj.* designating or of the most highly restricted military or government information

top·side (-sīd') *n.* **1.** [*usually pl.*] the part of a ship's side above the waterline **2.** a lean cut of beef from the thigh containing no bone **—adv.** on or to an upper deck or the main deck of a ship

top·soil (-soil') *n.* the upper layer of soil, usually darker and richer than the subsoil

top·sy·tur·vy (top'sē tur've) *adv. adj.* [prob. < *top*, highest part + ME. *terven*, to roll] **1.** upside down; reversed **2.** in confusion or disorder **—n.** a topsy-turvy condition **—top'sy·tur'vi·ly** *adv.* **—top'sy·tur'vi·ness** *n.*

toque (tōk) *n.* [Fr.] **1.** a small, plumed hat of the 16th cent. **2.** a woman's small, round hat **3.** a monkey with toque-like hair on its head

tor (tor) *n.* [ME. < OE. *torr*] a high, rocky hill; crag

to·rah (tō'rə, tō rä') *n.* [Heb.] *Judaism* **1.** *a*) learning, law, instruction, etc. *b*) [*also* T-] the whole of Jewish religious literature, including the Scripture, the Talmud, etc. **2.** [*usually* T-] *a*) the Pentateuch *b*) *pl.* **-roth, -rot** (-rəs, -rōt') a parchment scroll containing the Pentateuch

torch (tôrch) *n.* [OFr. *torche*, ult. < L. *torquere*, to twist] **1.** a portable light consisting of a long piece of resinous wood, etc. flaming at one end **2.** a portable electric light, usually operated by batteries **3.** anything viewed as enlightening, inspiring, etc. **3.** a portable device for producing a very hot flame, used in welding, etc. **—carry a** (or **the**) **torch for** [Slang] to love (someone), esp. without having one's love returned

torch·bear·er (-ber'ər) *n.* **1.** a person who carries a torch **2.** a person or leader who enlightens or inspires others

tor·chere (tôr sher') *n.* [Fr. < *torche*, torch] a tall, ornamental stand for a candle, lamp, etc.

torch·light (tôrch'līt') *n.* the light of a torch or torches **—adj.** done or carried on by torchlight

tore (tôr) *pt. of* TEAR[1]

tor·e·a·dor (tôr'ē ə dôr') *n.* [Sp. < *torear*, to fight bulls, ult. < L. *taurus*, a bull] a bullfighter: term no longer used in bullfighting

to·re·ro (tô rer'ō; *sp.* tô re'rō) *n., pl.* **-ros** (-rōz; *Sp.* -rôs) [Sp. < LL. < L. *taurus*, a bull] a bullfighter, esp. a matador

to·ri·i (tôr'i ē') *n., pl.* **-ri·i'** [Jap.] a gateway at the entrance to a Shinto temple, consisting of two uprights supporting a curved horizontal beam, with a straight crosspiece just below

tor·ment (tôr'ment; *for v., usually* tôr ment') *n.* [< OFr. < L. *tormentum*, a rack, torture < *torquere*, to twist] **1.** great pain, physical or mental; agony **2.** a source of pain, anxiety, or annoyance **—vt.** **1.** to make suffer greatly, in body or mind **2.** to annoy, harass, or tease **—tor·ment'·ing·ly** *adv.* **—tor·men'tor** *n.*

tor·men·til (tôr'men til') *n.* [< Ofr. < ML. *tormentilla*] a perennial plant with yellow flowers and rhizomes used in tanning and dyeing

torn (tôrn) *pp. of* TEAR[1]

tor·na·do (tôr nā'dō) *n., pl.* **-does, -dos** [< Sp. *tronada*, thunder < L. *tonare*, to thunder] **1.** a rapidly whirling column of air, usually seen as a slender, funnel-shaped cloud that usually destroys everything in its narrow path **2.** any whirlwind or hurricane **—tor·nad'ic** (-nad'ik) *adj.*

tor·pe·do (tôr pē'dō) *n., pl.* **-does** [L., numbness < *torpere*, to be stiff] **1.** *same as* ELECTRIC RAY **2.** a large, cigar-shaped, self-propelled projectile launched under water against enemy ships as from a submarine: it explodes on contact **3.** [U.S.] any of various other explosive devices, as an underwater mine **—vt. -doed, -do·ing** to attack, destroy, etc. as with a torpedo

torpedo boat a small, fast warship for attacking with torpedoes

torpedo tube a tube for launching torpedoes, esp. from a submarine

tor·pid (tôr'pid) *adj.* [< L. < *torpere*, to be numb] **1.** having lost temporarily all or part of the power of sensation

or motion, as a hibernating animal; dormant **2.** sluggish or slow and dull **—tor·pid'i·ty, tor'pid·ness** *n.* **—tor'pid·ly** *adv.*

tor·por (tôr'pər) *n.* **1.** a state of being dormant or inactive **2.** sluggishness; dullness; apathy

tor·quate (tôr'kwāt) *adj.* [L. *torquatus*] *Zool.* having a distinctive collar or ring, as of a different colour from the rest of the body

torque (tôrk) *n.* [< L. *torques*, a twisted metal necklace] **1.** *Physics* a twisting effect exerted on a body by a force acting at a distance, equal to the force times its distance from the centre of rotation **2.** popularly, any force that causes rotation

torr (tôr) *n.* [after E. *Torricelli* (1608-47), It. physicist] a unit of pressure equivalent to 133.322 newtons per square metre: it is sufficient to support a column of mercury one millimetre high under standard conditions

tor·re·fy (tor'ə fī) *vt.* **-fied', -fy'ing** [< Fr. < L. *torrefacere*, to dry by heat] to dry (certain drugs or ores) by heat **—tor're·fac'tion** *n.*

tor·rent (tor'ənt) *n.* [Fr.< L. *torrens*, burning, rushing, prp. of *torrere*, to parch] **1.** a swift, violent stream, esp. of water **2.** a flood or rush of words, questions, etc. **3.** [*often pl.*] a very heavy fall of rain **—tor·ren·tial** (tô ren'shəl, tə-) *adj.* **—tor·ren'tial·ly** *adv.*

tor·rid (tor'id) *adj.* [< L. < *torrere*, to parch] **1.** dried by or subjected to intense heat, esp. of the sun; scorched; parched; arid **2.** so hot as to parch or scorch **3.** highly passionate, ardent, etc. **—tor·rid·i·ty** (tə rid'ə tē), **tor'·rid·ness** *n.* **—tor'rid·ly** *adv.*

Torrid Zone the area of the earth's surface between the Tropic of Cancer & the Tropic of Capricorn and divided by the equator

tor·sion (tôr'shən) *n.* [< MFr. < LL. < pp. of L. *torquere*, to twist] **1.** a twisting or being twisted **2.** *Mech.* a) the stress produced in a rod, wire, etc. from having one end twisted while the other is held firm or twisted in the opposite direction b) the tendency of a rod, etc. so twisted to untwist again **—tor'sion·al** *adj.* **—tor'sion·al·ly** *adv.*

tor·so (tôr'sō) *n., pl.* **-sos, -si** (-sē) [It. < L. < Gr. *thyrsos*, a stem] **1.** the trunk of the human body **2.** a statue representing this, esp. one lacking head and limbs

tort (tôrt) *n.* [< OFr. < ML. < L. pp. of *torquere*, to twist] *Law* a wrongful act, injury, or damage (not involving a breach of contract), for which a civil action can be brought

torte (tôrt) *n.* [G. < It. < LL. *torta*, a twisted bread] a rich cake, variously made, as of eggs, chopped nuts, and crumbs

tor·til·la (tôr tē'ə) *n.* [Sp., dim. of *torta*, a cake: see TORTE] a griddlecake of unleavened maize, now sometimes of flour: a staple food throughout Mexico

tor·toise (tôr'təs) *n., pl.* **-tois·es, -toise:** see PLURAL, II, D, 1 [< ML. *tortuca*, ult. < ? LGr. *tartarouchos*, demon] a toothless land reptile or turtle, having a soft body encased in a dome-shaped shell, and clawed limbs: cf. TURTLE

tortoise shell **1.** the hard, mottled, yellow-and-brown shell of some turtles used, esp. formerly, in making combs, etc. **2.** a synthetic substance like this **—tor'toise-shell'** *adj.* mottled with black, cream, and brownish markings like tortoise shell

tor·tu·ous (tôr'chōō wəs) *adj.* [Anglo-Fr. < L. *tortuosus* < pp. of *torquere*, to twist] **1.** full of twists and turns; winding; crooked **2.** not straightforward; devious or deceitful **—tor'tu·os'i·ty** (-wos'ə tē) *n., pl.* **-ties** **—tor'·tu·ous·ly** *adv.* **—tor'tu·ous·ness** *n.*

tor·ture (tôr'chər) *n.* [Fr. < LL. *tortura* < pp. of L. *torquere*, to twist] **1.** the inflicting of severe pain, as to force information or confession **2.** a method of doing this **3.** any severe physical or mental pain, or a cause of it **—vt. -tured, -tur·ing** **1.** to subject to torture **2.** to cause extreme physical or mental pain to **3.** to twist (meaning, etc.) **—tor'tur·er** *n.* **—tor'tur·ous** *adj.* **—tor'tur·ous·ly** *adv.*

to·rus (tôr'əs) *n., pl.* **-ri** (-ī) [L., a bulge] **1.** a large, convex moulding used at the base of columns, etc. **2.** *Anat.* a ridge or rounded projection **3.** *Bot.* the the receptacle of a flower stalk **4.** *Geom.* a surface, or its enclosed solid, generated by the revolution of a conic, esp. a circle, about any line in its plane and external to it

To·ry (tôr'ē) *n., pl.* **-ries** [< Ir. *tōruidhe*, robber < *tōir*, to pursue] **1.** formerly, a member of one of the two major political parties of England: orig. opposed to Whig: changed officially c. 1830 to *Conservative* **2.** a member of the Conservative Party in Britain or Canada **3.** in the American War of Independence a person who showed or favoured continued loyalty to Britain **4.** [*often* t-] any very conservative person **—adj.** [*also* t-] of or being a Tory **—To'ry·ism** *n.*

tosh (tosh) *n., interj.* [< ?] [Slang] nonsense

toss (tos) *vt.* [prob. < Scand.] **1.** to throw or pitch about; buffet [a boat *tossed* by a storm] **2.** to mix (a salad, etc.) lightly so as to coat the ingredients with a dressing **3.** to disturb; agitate **4.** to throw; specif., to throw upwards lightly from the hand **5.** to throw in or bandy (ideas, remarks, etc.) **6.** to lift quickly; jerk upwards [*tossed* her head in disdain] **7.** to toss up with (someone *for* something): see phrase below —*vi.* **1.** to be tossed or thrown about **2.** to fling oneself about in sleep, etc. **3.** to toss up: see phrase below —*n.* **1.** a tossing or being tossed **2.** a tossing up: see phrase below **3.** the distance that something is or can be tossed **4.** a fall from a horse [she took a *toss*] —**toss a pancake** to fling a pancake up so that it returns to the pan on its other side —**toss off 1.** to make, do, write, etc. quickly and casually **2.** to drink up in one draught —**toss up** to toss a coin to decide something according to which side lands uppermost —**toss′er** *n.*

toss·up (-up′) *n.* **1.** the act of tossing a coin to decide something according to which side lands uppermost **2.** an even chance

tost (tost) *archaic pt. & pp. of* TOSS

tot¹ (tot) *n.* [prob. < Scand.] **1.** a young child **2.** a small drink of alcohol

tot² (tot) *vt., vi.* **tot′ted, tot′ting** [contr. < TOTAL] [Colloq.] to add; total (usually with *up*)

to·tal (tōt′'l) *adj.* [< MFr. < ML. < L. *totus*, all] **1.** constituting the (or a) whole; entire **2.** complete; utter —*n.* the whole amount or number —*vt.* **-talled, -tal·ling 1.** to find the total of; add **2.** to equal a total of; add up to —*vi.* to amount (*to*) as a whole —**to′tal·ize′** *vt.* —**to′tal·ly** *adv.*

total abstinence complete abstention from all alcoholic drink

to·tal·i·tar·i·an (tō tal′ə ter′ē ən, tō′tal ə-) *adj.* [TOTAL + (AUTHOR)ITARIAN] designating, of, or like a government or state in which one political group maintains complete control under a dictatorship and bans all others —*n.* a person favouring such a government or state —**to·tal′i·tar′i·an·ism** *n.*

to·tal·i·ty (tō tal′ə tē) *n., pl.* **-ties 1.** the fact or condition of being total **2.** the total amount or sum

to·tal·i·za·tor (tōt′əl i zāt′ər) *n.* a machine used in parimutuel betting to register bets and, usually, compute odds and payoffs while bets are being placed: also **to′tal·i·sa′tor, to′tal·iz′er**

tote¹ (tōt) *vt.* **tot′ed, tot′ing** [prob. of Afr. orig.] [Chiefly U.S. Colloq.] to carry or haul **2.** to be armed with (a gun, etc.) —*n.* **1.** [Chiefly U.S. Colloq.] *a)* a toting *b)* something toted; load —**tot′er** *n.*

tote² (tōt) *n.* *shortened form of* TOTALIZATOR

tote bag a large, open bag of cloth, straw, etc.: also **tote**

tote board [Colloq.] a large board facing the grandstand at a race track, on which the bets, odds, and payoffs recorded by a totalizator are flashed

to·tem (tōt′əm) *n.* [< Algonquian] **1.** among primitive peoples, an animal or natural object considered to be related by blood to a given family or clan and taken as its symbol **2.** an image of this —**to·tem·ic** (tō tem′ik) *adj.* —**to′tem·ism** *n.* —**to′tem·ist** *n.*

totem pole a pole or post carved and painted with totems, often erected in front of their dwellings, by Indian tribes of northwestern N America

toth·er, t′oth·er, 'toth·er (tuth′ər) *adj., pron.* [Chiefly Dial.] that (or the) other

tot·ter (tot′ər) *vi.* [prob. < Scand.] **1.** to rock or shake as if about to fall **2.** to be on the point of collapse **3.** to be unsteady on one's feet; stagger —*n.* a tottering —**tot′ter·ing** *adj.* —**tot′ter·ing·ly** *adv.* —**tot′ter·y** *adj.*

tou·can (tōō′kan) *n.* [Fr. < Port. < Tupi *tucana*] a brightly coloured, fruit-eating bird of tropical America, with a very large beak

TOTEM POLE

touch (tuch) *vt.* [OFr. *tochier*] **1.** to put the hand, finger, etc. on, so as to feel **2.** to bring into contact with something else [*touch* a match to kindling] **3.** to be or come into contact with **4.** to border on; adjoin **5.** to strike lightly **6.** to affect by contact [water won't *touch* these grease spots] **7.** to injure slightly [frost *touched* these plants] **8.** to give a light tint, aspect, etc. to [clouds *touched* with pink] **9.** to stop at (a port, etc.) in passing: said of a ship **10.** to lay hands on; handle; use **11.** to manhandle or molest **12.** to partake of [didn't *touch* his supper] **13.** to come up to; reach **14.** to compare with; equal [cooking that can't *touch* hers] **15.** to take or use wrongfully **16.** to deal with or refer to, esp. in passing **17.** to affect; concern [a subject that *touches* our welfare] **18.** to arouse an emotion in, esp. one of sympathy or gratitude **19.** to hurt the feelings of; pain [*touched* him to the quick] **20.** [Slang] to ask for, or get by asking, a loan or gift of money from **21.** *Geom.* to be tangent to —*vi.* **1.** to touch a person or thing **2.** to be or come in contact **3.** to

approach; verge (*on, upon*) **4.** to pertain; bear (*on, upon*) **5.** to treat a topic slightly or in passing (with *on, upon*) **6.** to stop briefly (*at* a port, etc.) during a voyage **7.** *Geom.* to be tangent —*n.* **1.** a touching or being touched; specif., a light tap, stroke, etc. **2.** the sense by which physical objects are felt **3.** a sensation so caused; feel **4.** a special quality, skill, or manner [he lost his *touch*] **5.** an effect of being touched; specif., *a)* a mark, impression, etc. left by touching *b)* a subtle change or addition in a painting, story, etc. **6.** a very small amount, degree, etc.; specif., *a)* a trace, tinge, etc. [a *touch* of humour] *b)* a slight attack [a *touch* of the flu] **7.** formerly, a touchstone **8.** any test or criterion **9.** contact or communication [keep in *touch*] **10.** [Slang] *a)* the act of asking for a loan or gift of money, or a getting of it thus *b)* money so obtained *c)* a person with regard to how easily money can be so obtained from him [he's a soft *touch*] **11.** *Music a)* the way that a performer strikes the keys of a piano, etc. *b)* the way that the keys of a piano, etc. respond to the fingers —**touch down 1.** to land: said of an aircraft or spacecraft **2.** *Rugby* to place the ball behind the goal line, as when scoring a try —**touch off 1.** to represent accurately or aptly **2.** to make explode; fire **3.** to produce (esp. a violent reaction, etc.) —**touch up** to improve or finish (a painting, story, etc.) by minor changes or additions —**touch wood** to place one's hand on a wooden object in the superstitious hope of averting ill fortune —**touch′a·bil′i·ty** *n.* —**touch′a·ble** *adj.* —**touch′er** *n.*

touch and go an uncertain, risky, or dangerous situation —**touch-and-go** (tuch′ən gō′) *adj.*

touch·down (-doun′) *n.* **1.** a touching down, or landing **2.** *Rugby* the act of touching down

tou·ché (tōō shā′) *interj.* [Fr.] *Fencing* touched: said when one's opponent scores a point by a touch: also used in congratulating someone for his witty reply, etc.

touched (tucht) *adj.* **1.** emotionally moved **2.** [Colloq.] slightly unbalanced mentally: also **touched in the head**

touch·hole (tuch′hōl′) *n.* in early firearms, the hole in the breech through which the charge was touched off

touch·ing (tuch′in) *adj.* arousing tender emotion; affecting —*prep.* with regard to —**touch′ing·ly** *adv.*

touch-judge (-juj′) *n.* the linesman at a rugby match

touch-line (-līn′) *n.* either of the lines marking the sides of a football or rugby pitch

touch-mark (-märk′) *n.* a maker's mark stamped on pewter

touch-pa·per (-pā′pər) *n.* paper soaked in saltpetre to make it burn slowly and formerly used in firing a cannon

touch·stone (-stōn′) *n.* **1.** a black stone formerly used to test the purity of gold or silver by the streak left on it when it was rubbed with the metal **2.** any test of genuineness

touch-type (-tīp′) *vi.* **-typed′, -typ′ing** to type without looking at the keys, by a system (**touch system**) in which a given key is touched with a specific finger —**touch′-typ′ist** *n.*

touch·wood (-wood′) *n.* dried, decayed wood or dried fungus used as tinder

touch·y (tuch′ē) *adj.* **touch′i·er, touch′i·est** [TOUCH + -Y²] **1.** easily offended or irritated; oversensitive **2.** very risky —**touch′i·ly** *adv.* —**touch′i·ness** *n.*

tough (tuf) *adj.* [OE. *toh*] **1.** strong but pliant; that will bend, twist, etc. without tearing or breaking **2.** not easily cut or chewed [*tough* steak] **3.** sticky; viscous [*tough* putty] **4.** *a)* physically strong; hardy *b)* mentally or morally firm **5.** hard to influence; stubborn **6.** practical and realistic **7.** over aggressive; rough **8.** *a)* very difficult *b)* vigorous or violent [a *tough* fight] **9.** [Colloq.] unfavourable; bad [a *tough* time] —*n.* a tough person; thug —**tough′ly** *adv.* —**tough′ness** *n.*

tough·en (-'n) *vt., vi.* to make or become tough or tougher

tough·ie, tough·y (-ē) *n., pl.* **-ies** [Chiefly U.S. Colloq.] **1.** a tough person; ruffian **2.** a difficult problem or situation

tough-mind·ed (-mīn′did) *adj.* shrewd and unsentimental; practical; realistic —**tough′-mind′ed·ness** *n.*

tou·pee (tōō pā′, tōō′pā) *n.* [Fr. *toupet*, dim. of OFr. *toup*, tuft of hair] a man's wig, esp. one for a small bald spot

tour (toor) *n.* [< MFr. < OFr. < *tourner*, to TURN] **1.** a turn or shift of work; esp., a period of duty or military service at a single place: in full, **tour of duty 2.** a long journey, for sightseeing **3.** any journey, as for inspection; round; circuit; specif., a journey, as by a theatrical company, to give performances, etc. in various cities —*vi.* to go on a tour —*vt.* **1.** to take a tour through **2.** to take (a play, etc.) on tour —**on tour** touring, as to give performances, lectures, etc.

tou·ra·co (toor′ə kō′) *n., pl.* **-cos** [prob. < Fr. < W Afr. native name] a brightly-coloured, tropical forest bird of Africa

tour de force (toor′ də fôrs′) *pl.* **tours′ de force′** (toor) [Fr.] an unusually skilful or ingenious production, performance, etc., sometimes a merely clever one

touring car an early type of open motor car, often with a folding top, seating five or more passengers

tour·ism (toor'iz'm) *n.* tourist travel, esp. when regarded as a business —**tour·is'tic** *adj.*

tour·ist (-ist) *n.* **1.** a person who makes a tour, esp. for pleasure **2.** tourist class —*adj.* **1.** of or for tourists **2.** designating or of the lowest-priced accommodation, as on a ship: also **tourist class** —*adv.* in or by means of tourist class

tour·ist·y (toor'ist ē) *adj.* [Colloq.] designed to be attractive to tourists: often a derogatory term

tour·ma·line (toor'mə lin, -lēn') *n.* [Fr., ult. < Sinh. *tōramalli,* a carnelian] a crystalline mineral that is a complex silicate, commonly black but also coloured or transparent, used as a gemstone and in optical equipment

tour·na·ment (toor'nə mənt) *n.* [< OFr. < *torneier:* see TOURNEY] **1.** in the Middle Ages, a contest in which knights on horseback tried to unseat one another with lances **2.** a series of contests in a sport, chess, or bridge, usually a competition for championship

‡**tour·ne·dos** (toor'nə dō) *n.,* pl. **-dos**'(-dō') [Fr.] a thick round beefsteak, served in a variety of ways

tour·ney (toor'nē, tur'-) *n.,* pl. **-neys** [< OFr. *torneier* < base of *tourner:* see TURN] *same as* TOURNAMENT —*vi.* to take part in a tournament; joust

tour·ni·quet (toor'nə kit, tur'-; -kā') *n.* [Fr. < MFr. *turniquet,* coat of mail < OFr. *tunicle* < L. dim. of *tunica,* tunic] any device for compressing a blood vessel to stop bleeding, as a bandage twisted about a limb or a pad pressed down by a screw

tou·sle (tou'z'l) *vt.* **-sled, -sling** [freq. of ME. *tusen* (in comp.), to pull] to disorder, dishevel, rumple, etc. —*n.* a tousled condition, mass of hair, etc.

tout (tout) *vi., vt.* [OE. *totian,* to peep] [Colloq.] **1.** to solicit (customers, votes, etc.) (often with *for*) **2.** *a*) to spy on (racehorses) to get betting tips *b*) to provide such tips on (racehorses) —*n.* [Colloq.] a person who touts —**tout'er** *n.*

‡**tout de suite** (tōot swēt') [Fr.] immediately

tou·zle (tou'z'l) *n., vt.* **-zled, -zling** *var. of* TOUSLE

tow[1] (tō) *vt.* [OE. *togian*] to pull as by a rope or chain —*n.* **1.** a towing or being towed **2.** something towed **3.** a towline —**in tow 1.** being towed **2.** as one's companion or follower **3.** under one's control

tow[2] (tō) *n.* [OE. *tow-,* for spinning] the coarse and broken fibres of hemp, flax, etc. before spinning

to·ward (tō'ərd; *also, and for prep. usually,* tə wôrd') *adj.* [OE. *toweard:* see TO & -WARD] [Archaic or Rare] **1.** favourable **2.** docile **3.** at hand **4.** in progress —*prep. same as* TOWARDS

to·wards (tə wôrdz') *prep.* [see prec.] **1.** in the direction of **2.** facing **3.** in a way aimed at or tending to [steps *towards* peace] **4.** concerning; regarding [my attitude *towards* it] **5.** close to [*towards* noon] **6.** in order to get; for [saving *towards* a car] **7.** so as to help pay for [to contribute *towards* a new library]

tow·boat (tō'bōt') *n. same as* TUGBOAT

tow·el (tou'l, toul) *n.* [< OFr. *toaille* < Frank.] a piece of absorbent cloth or paper for wiping or drying things —*vt.* **-elled -el·ling** to wipe or dry with a towel —**throw** (or **toss,** etc.) **in the towel** [Colloq.] to admit defeat —**towel off** to dry oneself, as after bathing

tow·el·ling (-iŋ) *n.* material for making towels

tow·er[1] (tou'ər) *n.* [OE. *torr* & OFr. *tur,* both < L. *turris*] **1.** a structure that is relatively high for its length and width, either standing alone or as part of another building **2.** such a structure used as a fortress or prison **3.** a person or thing like a tower in height, strength, etc. —*vi.* to rise high or stand high like a tower —**a tower of strength** an unfailing support in time of trouble —**tow'ered** *adj.*

tow·er[2] (tō'ər) *n.* a person or thing that tows

tower block (tou'ər) a tall building of many storeys, as for offices or flats

tow·er·ing (tou'ər iŋ) *adj.* **1.** that towers; very high or tall **2.** very great, intense, etc. [a *towering* rage]

tow·head (tō'hed') *n.* **1.** a head of pale-yellow hair **2.** a person having such hair **3.** a person with untidy, tousled hair —**tow'head'ed** *adj.*

tow·line (tō'līn') *n.* a rope, chain, etc. for towing

town (toun) *n.* [OE. *tun*] **1.** a group of houses and buildings, larger than a village but smaller than a city **2.** city or other thickly populated urban place **3.** [U.S.] a territorial unit of local government that is smaller than a county; township **4.** the business centre of a city **5.** the people of a town —*adj.* of or for a town —**go to town** [Slang] to act enthusiastically —**on the town** [Colloq.] out for a good time

town clerk the chief administrative officer of a town or city

town crier a person who formerly cried public announcements through the streets of a village or town

town·ee (tou'nē) *n.* [Colloq.] a town dweller: often a derogatory term

town gas a manufactured gas for domestic and industrial use, made from coal gas mixed with water gas or natural gas

town hall a building in a town, housing the offices of public officials, the council chamber, etc.

town house 1. a city residence, esp. of a person who also owns a country residence **2.** a dwelling, usually of two or more storeys, that is one of a number of dwellings

town planning the comprehensive planning of the physical and social development of a town

town·ship (-ship') *n.* **1.** orig., in England, a parish or division of a parish **2.** in parts of the U.S., a division of a county constituting a unit of local government **3.** a unit of territory in the U.S. land survey, generally six miles square **4.** in Canada, a subdivision of a province **5.** in Australia, a village; small town

towns·man (tounz'mən) *n.,* pl. **-men 1.** a person who lives in, or has been reared in, a town **2.** a person who lives in the same town as one

towns·peo·ple (-pē'p'l) *n.pl.* **1.** the people of a town **2.** people reared in a town or city Also **towns'folk'** (-fōk')

tow·path (tō'päth') *n.* a path beside a canal, for men or animals towing canal boats

tow·rope (-rōp') *n.* a rope used in towing

tox·ae·mi·a (tok sē'mē ə) *n.* [ModL.: see TOXIC & -AEMIA] a condition in which poisonous substances, esp. toxins from bacteria, etc., are in the bloodstream —**tox·ae'mic** (-mik) *adj.*

tox·ic (tok'sik) *adj.* [< ML. < L. *toxicum,* a poison < Gr. *toxikon,* orig., poison for arrows < *toxon,* a bow] **1.** of, affected by, or caused by a toxin **2.** acting as a poison —**tox'i·cal·ly** *adv.* —**tox·ic'i·ty** (-sis'ə tē) *n.*

tox·i·co- [< Gr. *toxikon:* see prec.] a combining form meaning poison: also, before a vowel, **tox'ic-**

tox·i·col·o·gy (tok'si kol'ə jē) *n.* [< Fr.: see TOXIC & -LOGY] the science of poisons, their effects, antidotes, etc. —**tox'·i·co·log'ic** (-kəloj'ik), **tox'i·co·log'i·cal** *adj.* —**tox'i·co·log'·i·cal·ly** *adv.* —**tox'i·col'o·gist** *n.*

tox·in (tok'sin) *n.* [TOX(IC) + -IN[1]] **1.** any of various poisonous compounds produced by some microorganisms and causing certain diseases **2.** any of various similar poisons produced by certain plants or animals Toxins injected into animals or man usually cause antitoxins to form

tox·oid (tok'soid) *n.* [TOX(IN) + -OID] a toxin that has been treated, as with chemicals, so that its toxic qualities are removed but it can still act as an antigen

tox·oph·i·lite (tok sof'ə lit') *n.* [< Gr. *toxon,* bow + *philos,* lover] a student of, or expert in, archery

toy (toi) *n.* [< ? MDu. *toi,* finery] **1.** a thing of little value or importance; trifle **2.** a bauble; trinket **3.** a plaything, esp. one for children **4.** anything small; specif., a dog of a small breed —*adj.* **1.** being or like a toy **2.** of or for toys **3.** made as a toy or as a small model [a *toy* stove] —*vi.* to play or trifle (*with* a thing, idea, etc.)

toy·shop (toi'shop') *n.* a shop where toys are sold

T-R transmit-receive

tr. 1. trace **2.** transitive **3.** translated **4.** translation **5.** translator **6.** transpose **7.** treasurer **8.** trustee

trace[1] (trās) *n.* [< OFr. < *tracier,* ult. < L. pp. of *trahere,* to draw] **1.** a mark, footprint, etc. left by the passage of a person, animal, or thing **2.** a beaten path or trail **3.** a perceptible mark left by a past person, thing, or event; sign [*traces* of war] **4.** a barely perceptible amount [a *trace* of anger] **5.** something traced, drawn, recorded, etc. **6.** the visible line or spot moving across the face of a cathode-ray tube —*vt.* **traced, trac'ing 1.** [Now Rare] to move along (a path, route, etc.) **2.** to follow the trail of; track **3.** *a*) to follow the development or history of *b*) to determine (a source, date, etc.) thus **4.** to discover by investigating traces of (a prehistoric thing, etc.) **5.** to draw, outline, etc. **6.** to ornament with tracery **7.** to copy (a drawing, etc.) by following its lines on a transparent sheet placed over it **8.** to record by a curved, broken, or wavy line, as in a seismograph —*vi.* **1.** to follow a path, route, etc. **2.** to go back or date back (*to* something past) —**trace'a·bil'i·ty, trace'a·ble·ness** *n.* —**trace'a·ble** *adj.* —**trace'a·bly** *adv.*

trace[2] (trās) *n.* [< OFr. *trais* pl. of *trait:* see TRAIT] either of two straps, chains, etc. connecting a draught animal's harness to the vehicle drawn —**kick over the traces** to shake off control

trace element 1. a chemical element, as iron, copper, zinc, etc., essential in nutrition, but only in minute quantities **2.** any element present in minute quantities in an organism, soil, water, etc.

trac·er (trā'sər) *n.* **1.** one that traces; specif., *a*) a person who traces designs, etc. on transparent paper *b*) an instrument for tracing designs on cloth, etc. **2.** *same as* TRACER BULLET (OR SHELL) **3.** an element or other substance used to follow biochemical reactions, as in an animal body, to locate diseased cells, etc.

tracer bullet (or **shell**) a bullet or shell that leaves a trail of smoke or fire to mark its course and help in adjusting aim

trac·er·y (-ē) *n., pl.* **-er·ies** [TRACE¹ + -ERY] any graceful design of lines that come together or cross in various ways, as in a stained glass window

tra·che·a (trə kē'ə, trā'kē ə) *n., pl.* **-che·ae'** (-ē'), **-che·as** [ML. < LL. < Gr. *tracheia* (*arteria*), rough (windpipe)] 1. the tube through which most land vertebrates breathe, coming from the larynx and dividing into the bronchi 2. any of the minute tubes branching through the bodies of insects, etc. and bringing in air —**tra'che·al, tra'che·ate** *adj.*

tra·che·o- [< prec.] *a combining form* meaning: 1. of the trachea 2. the trachea and [*tracheobronchial*] Also, before a vowel, **trache-**

tra·che·o·bron·chi·al (trā'kē ō broŋ'kē əl) *adj.* relating to the trachea and bronchi   TRACERY

tra·che·ot·o·my (trā'kē ot'ə mē) *n., pl.* **-mies** [see -TOMY] surgical incision of the trachea

tra·cho·ma (trə kō'mə) *n.* [< Gr. < *trachys*, rough] a contagious infection of the conjunctiva and cornea, caused by a virus and producing granulation —**tra·cho'ma·tous** (-kom'ə təs, -kō'mə-) *adj.*

tra·chyte (trā'kīt, trak'īt) *n.* [Fr. < Gr. *trachys*, rough] a fine-grained, light-coloured, igneous rock

trac·ing (trā'siŋ) *n.* 1. the action of one that traces 2. something made by tracing, as a copy of a drawing, or a line traced by a recording instrument

track (trak) *n.* [MFr. *trac*, a track] 1. a mark or marks left by a person, animal, or thing, as a footprint or rut 2. a trace or vestige 3. a beaten path or trail 4. a course or line of motion or action; route 5. a sequence of ideas, events, etc. 6. a path or circuit laid out for running, horse racing, etc. 7. a pair of parallel metal rails on which trains, etc. run 8. the distance in inches between parallel wheels, as of a motor car 9. either of the two endless belts on tanks, some tractors, etc. on which they move 10. a course for running or racing 11. *a*) *same as* SOUND TRACK *b*) the part of a magnetic tape or drum passing under a given recording or reading head —*vt.* 1. *a*) to follow the track or footprints of *b*) to follow (a path, etc.) 2. to trace by means of vestiges, evidence, etc. 3. to plot the path of and record data from (an aircraft, spacecraft, etc.) using a telescope, radar, etc. 4. to tread or travel —*vi.* to be in alignment, as wheels, or a gramophone pickup in a record groove —**in one's tracks** where one is at the moment —**keep track of** to keep an account of; stay informed about —**lose track of** to fail to stay informed about —**make tracks** [Colloq.] to go or leave hurriedly —**on** (or **off**) **the track** keeping to (or straying from) the subject or goal —**track down** 1. to pursue until caught 2. to investigate fully —**track'er** *n.* —**track'less** *adj.*

track event an athletic sport performed on a track, as running, hurdling, etc.

track record [Colloq.] the past performance or achievements of a person or organization, esp. when put to the test

track shoe a spiked shoe worn by athletes in track events

track suit a warm suit worn over their sports kit by athletes, as before a race

tract¹ (trakt) *n.* [< L. < pp. of *trahere*, to draw] 1. formerly, *a*) duration of time *b*) a period of time 2. a continuous expanse of land, etc. 3. *Anat., Zool.* a system of parts or organs having some special function [the digestive *tract*]

tract² (trakt) *n.* [< LL. < L. *tractatus* pp. of *tractare*: see ff.] a pamphlet, esp. one on a religious or political subject

trac·ta·ble (trak'tə b'l) *adj.* [< L. < *tractare*, to drag, freq. of *trahere*, to draw] 1. easily managed, taught, etc.; docile 2. easily worked or shaped; malleable —**trac'ta·bil'i·ty, trac'ta·ble·ness** *n.* —**trac'ta·bly** *adv.*

Trac·tar·i·an·ism (trak ter'ē ən iz'm) *n.* the principles of the Oxford Movement, advocating a return to early Catholic doctrines and practices in the Church of England **Trac·tar'·i·an** *n., adj.*

trac·tion (trak'shən) *n.* [< ML. < L. *tractus*, pp. of *trahere*, to draw] 1. a pulling or drawing, as of a load, or a being pulled or drawn 2. the power used by a locomotive, etc. 3. the power, as of tyres on a road, to grip or hold to a surface while moving, without slipping —**trac'tive** *adj.*

traction engine a steam locomotive for pulling heavy wagons, farm equipment, etc. on roads or in fields

trac·tor (trak'tər) *n.* [ModL. < L.: see prec.] 1. a powerful, motor-driven vehicle with large rear wheels or endless belt treads, for pulling farm machinery, hauling loads, etc. 2. a vehicle with a driver's cab and no body, for hauling one or more trailers

trad (trad) *n.* [Colloq.] traditional jazz —*adj.* [Colloq.] traditional

trade (trād) *n.* [MLowG., a track < OS. *trada*, a trail] 1. *a*) a means of earning one's living; occupation *b*) skilled work;

craft *c*) all the persons or companies in a particular line of business 2. buying and selling, or bartering; commerce 3. business of a specified kind [the tourist *trade*] 4. customers; clientele 5. an exchange; swap 6. [*pl.*] the trade winds —*adj.* 1. of trade or commerce 2. of, by, or for the trade (*n.* 1c) [a *trade* journal] 3. of the members in the trades, or crafts, etc. [*trade* unions]: also **trades** —*vi.* **trad'ed, trad'ing** 1. to carry on a business 2. to have business dealings (*with* someone) 3. to make an exchange (*with* someone) —*vt.* 1. to exchange; barter 2. to buy and sell (stocks, etc.) —**trade in** to give (one's used car, etc.) as part of the purchase price of a new one —**trade on** (or **upon**) to take advantage of; exploit —**trad'a·ble, trade'-a·ble** *adj.*

trade-in (trād'in') *n.* 1. a used car, etc. given or taken as part payment towards a new one 2. a deal involving such a car, etc. 3. the amount allowed as part payment

trade·mark (-märk') *n.* a symbol, design, word, etc. used by a manufacturer or dealer to distinguish his products from those of competitors: usually registered and protected by law —*vt.* 1. to put a trademark on (a product) 2. to register (a symbol, word, etc.) as a trademark

trade name 1. the name by which a commodity is commonly known in trade 2. a name, often a trademark or service mark, used by a company to describe a product, service, etc. 3. the name under which a company carries on business

trade price the price of commodities as sold by wholesalers to retailers

trad·er (trā'dər) *n.* 1. a person who trades; merchant 2. a ship used in trade

trade route a regular route used by trading ships, caravans, etc.

trad·es·can·ti·a (trad'is kan'shē ə) *n.* [ModL., after John *Tradescant* (1608-62), Eng. naturalist] any of various plants native to America but widely cultivated as house plants for their variegated leaves

trade secret a secret formula, process, etc. known to and used to advantage by only one manufacturer or trade

trades·man (trādz'mən) *n., pl.* **-men** a person engaged in trade; esp., a shopkeeper —**trades'wom'an** *n.fem., pl.* **-wom'en**

trades·peo·ple (-pē'p'l) *n.pl.* people engaged in trade; esp., shopkeepers or craftsmen: also **trades'folk'**

Trades Union Congress the major association of British trade unions

trade union an association of workers to promote and protect the welfare, interests and rights of its members, mainly by collective bargaining: also **trades union** —**trade'-un'ion** *adj.* —**trade unionism** —**trade unionist**

trade wind [earlier *trade*, adv., steadily, in phr. *to blow trade*] a wind that blows steadily towards the equator from the northeast in the tropics north of the equator and from the southeast in the tropics south of the equator

trading estate *same as* INDUSTRIAL ESTATE

trading post a store or station in an outpost, settlement, etc., where trading is done, as with natives

trading stamp a stamp given by some retail organizations as a premium to customers, redeemable in merchandise

tra·di·tion (trə dish'ən) *n.* [< MFr. < L. < pp. of *tradere*, to deliver] 1. *a*) the handing down orally of beliefs, customs, stories, etc. from generation to generation *b*) a belief, custom, etc. so handed down 2. any long-established custom or practice 3. any unwritten religious teachings regarded as coming from the founder or earliest prophet of a religion —**tra·di'tion·less** *adj.*

tra·di·tion·al (-'l) *adj.* of, handed down by, or conforming to tradition; conventional: also **tra·di'tion·ar·y** (-ər ē) —**tra·di'tion·al·ly** *adv.*

tra·di·tion·al·ism (-'l iz'm) *n.* the following of tradition or a clinging to traditions —**tra·di'tion·al·ist, tra·di'tion·ist** *n.* —**tra·di'tion·al·is'tic** *adj.*

tra·duce (trə dyōōs') *vt.* **-duced', -duc'ing** [L. *traducere*, to disgrace < *tra(ns)*, across + *ducere*, to lead] 1. to say untrue or mean things about; defame 2. to turn against; betray —**tra·duce'ment** *n.* —**tra·duc'er** *n.*

traf·fic (traf'ik) *n.* [< Fr. < It. < *trafficare*, to trade < L. *trans*, across + It. *ficcare*, to bring] 1. buying and selling; trade, sometimes of a wrong or illegal kind [*traffic* in drugs] 2. dealings or business (*with* someone) 3. *a*) the movement or number of cars along a street, pedestrians along a pavement, etc. *b*) the cars, pedestrians, etc. 4. the amount of business done in a given period, as measured by the number of passengers or customers, the amount of goods handled, etc. —*adj.* of traffic or its regulation —*vi.* **-ficked, -fick·ing** 1. to carry on traffic (*in* something) 2. to have dealings (*with* someone) —**traf'fick·er** *n.*

traf·fi·ca·tor (traf'i kā'tər) *n.* formerly, a small arm at the side of a motor vehicle which could be raised to indicate a forthcoming turn to right or left

traffic island a small, raised area in the middle of a road to separate lanes of traffic and serve as a stopping place for pedestrians who are crossing

traffic light (or **signal**) a set of signal lights at intersections of streets to regulate traffic

traffic warden an official who aids the police in duties concerning the controlling of road traffic

trag·a·canth (trag'ə kanth') *n.* [< Fr. < L. < Gr. < *tragos*, goat + *akantha*, thorn] 1. a tasteless gum used as a thickener and emulsifier in foodstuffs, drugs, etc. 2. any of certain Asiatic plants that yield this gum

tra·ge·di·an (trə jē'dē ən) *n.* an actor of tragedy

tra·ge·di·enne (trə jē'dē en') *n.* an actress of tragedy

trag·e·dy (traj'ə dē) *n., pl.* **-dies** [< MFr. < L. < Gr. *tragōidia* < *tragos*, goat + *ōidē*, song: prob. from the goatskin dress of the performers representing satyrs] 1. serious play having a sad or disastrous ending brought about by fate, moral weakness in a character, social pressures, etc. 2. the branch of drama consisting of such plays 3. the writing or acting of such plays 4. a novel or any narrative having a tragic theme, tone, etc. 5. the tragic element in literature or life 6. a very sad or tragic event

trag·ic (traj'ik) *adj.* 1. of, like, or having to do with tragedy 2. bringing great harm, suffering, etc.; very sad, disastrous, etc. 3. suitable to tragedy [a *tragic* voice] Also **trag′i·cal** —*n.* the tragic element in art or life —**trag′i·cal·ly** *adv.* —**trag′i·cal·ness** *n.*

tragic irony the use in tragic drama of words which convey a deeper meaning (usually prophetic) to the audience than to the speaker

trag·i·com·e·dy (traj'ə kom'ə dē) *n., pl.* **-dies** 1. a play, novel, etc. combining tragic and comic elements 2. a situation or incident in life like this —**trag′i·com′ic, trag′-i·com′i·cal** *adj.* —**trag′i·com′i·cal·ly** *adv.*

trail (trāl) *vt.* [< MFr., ult. < L. *tragula*, sledge < *trahere*, to drag] 1. *a)* to drag or let drag behind one   *b)* to bring along behind [*trailing* exhaust fumes]   *c)* to pull or tow 2. *a)* to make (a path, etc.), as by treading down   *b)* to make a path in (grass, etc.) 3. to follow the tracks of 4. to hunt by tracking 5. to follow or lag behind (another or others) in movement, a contest, etc. 6. *Mil.* to carry (a rifle, etc.) at the full length of one arm, in a horizontal position with the muzzle to the fore —*vi.* 1. to be drawn along behind one, as the train of a gown 2. to grow along the ground, etc., as some plants 3. to extend in an irregular line; straggle 4. to flow behind in a long, thin stream, wisp, etc., as smoke 5. *a)* to follow or lag behind   *b)* to be losing, as in a sports contest 6. to track game: said of hounds 7. to grow gradually weaker, dimmer, etc. (with *off* or *away*) —*n.* 1. something that trails behind 2. a mark, scent, etc. left by a person, animal, or thing that has passed 3. a rough path made across country, as by repeated passage 4. a train of events, etc. following something [a *trail* of debts followed his illness] 5. a part of a gun carriage, which may be lowered to the ground to form a rear brace

trail·blaz·er (-blā'zər) *n.* 1. a person who blazes a trail 2. a pioneer in any field —**trail′blaz′ing** *n.*

trail·er (trā'lər) *n.* 1. one that trails another 2. a cart or van designed to be pulled by a motor vehicle (esp. a tractor, n. 2) 3. *U.S. name for a* CARAVAN (sense 3a) 4. a selection of scenes from a coming film used to advertise it 5. a trailing plant

trail·ing arbutus (trā'liŋ) *same as* ARBUTUS (sense 2)

trailing edge *Aeron.* the rear edge of an aerofoil, propeller blade, etc.

train (trān) *n.* [< OFr. < *trahiner*, to draw on, ult. < L. *trahere*, to pull] 1. something that drags along behind, as a part of a gown that trails 2. a group of followers or attendants in a procession; retinue 3. a group of persons, animals, vehicles, etc. moving in a line; procession; caravan 4. the persons, vehicles, etc. carrying supplies, ammunition, food, etc. for combat troops 5. a series of events that follow some happening [war brought famine in its *train*] 6. any connected sequence; series [a *train* of thought] 7. a line of gunpowder used to set off an explosive charge 8. a series of connected parts for transmitting motion [a gear *train*] 9. a line of connected railway coaches or wagons pulled or pushed by a locomotive —*vt.* 1. to guide the growth of (a plant) by tying, pruning, etc. 2. to subject to certain action, exercises. so as to bring to a desired condition 3. to guide the mental, moral, etc. development of; bring up; rear 4. to teach so as to make fully skilled [to *train* aircraft pilots] 5. to discipline (animals) to do tricks or obey commands 6. to make fit for some sport, as by exercise, practice, etc. 7. to aim (a gun, binoculars, etc.) at something (usually with *on*) —*vi.* to give or get training —**train′a·ble** *adj.*

train·band (-band') *n.* formerly, a body of citizens trained for home defence

train·bear·er (-ber'ər) *n.* a person who carries the train of an official's robe, a bride's dress, etc.

train·ee (trā nē') *n.* a person undergoing vocational training, military training, etc. —**train·ee′ship** *n.*

train·er (trā'nər) *n.* 1. a person who trains, specif., *a)* a person who trains animals, as racehorses   *b)* a person who

trains athletes 2. an apparatus used in training, as, in aeronautics, a flight simulator

train·ing (trā'niŋ) *n.* 1. the lessons, practice, drills, etc. given by one who trains or received by one who is being trained 2. the process of being trained for some sport, as by exercise, practice, etc.

train oil whale oil, or, formerly, oil from seals, codfish, etc.

train spotter a person who collects the numbers of railway locomotives

traipse (trāps) *vi., vt.* **traipsed, traips′ing** [< ?] [Dial. or Colloq.] to walk, wander, tramp, or gad —*n.* [Dial. or Colloq.] the act of traipsing

trait (trā, trāt) *n.* [Fr., a line < L. pp. of *trahere*, to draw] a distinct quality or feature, as of personality

trai·tor (trāt'ər) *n.* [OFr. < L. < pp. of *tradere*, to betray] a person who betrays his country, cause, friends, etc.; one guilty of treason or treachery —**trai′tress** *n.fem.*

trai·tor·ous (-əs) *adj.* 1. of or like a traitor; treacherous 2. of or involving treason; treasonable —**trai′tor·ous·ly** *adv.* —**trai′tor·ous·ness** *n.*

tra·jec·to·ry (trə jek'tə rē) *n., pl.* **-ries** [< ML. < L. pp. of *trajicere* < *tra*(*ns*), across + *jacere*, to throw] 1. the curved path of something hurtling through space, esp. that of a projectile 2. *Geom.* a curve that cuts a family of curves or surfaces at a constant angle

tram (tram) *n.* [prob. < LowG. *traam*, a beam] 1. an open railway car used in mines 2. a public vehicle running on rails laid in the road also **tram′car**

tram·line (tram'līn) *n.* 1. [often *pl.*] the tracks on which a tram runs: also **tram′way** 2. the route taken by a tram 3. [often *pl.*] the parallel markings along the sides of a tennis court

tram·mel (tram′l) *n.* [< MFr. < ML. *tremaculum*, kind of fishing net < L. *tres*, three + *macula*, a mesh] 1. *a)* a three-ply fishing net   *b)* a fowling net Also **trammel net** 2. a shackle for a horse 3. [usually *pl.*] something that hinders freedom of action 4. a device with links, etc. for hanging a pothook in a fireplace 5. an instrument for drawing ellipses —*vt.* **-melled -mel′ling** 1. to entangle as in a trammel 2. to hinder, restrain, or shackle —**tram′-mel·ler** *n.*

tra·mon·ta·na (trä'mən tä'nə) *n.* [It., < L. *transmontanus*, from beyond the mountains] a cold north wind of the Adriatic

tramp (tramp) *vi.* [< or akin to LowG. *trampen*, to trample] 1. *a)* to walk with heavy steps   *b)* to step heavily (*on* something); stamp 2. *a)* to travel about on foot; hike   *b)* to travel as or like a vagabond —*vt.* 1. to step on heavily; trample 2. to walk or ramble through —*n.* 1. a person who travels about on foot doing odd jobs or begging; vagrant 2. the sound of heavy steps 3. a journey on foot; hike 4. a freight ship that has no regular schedule, arranging for cargo, etc. as it goes along 5. [Slang] a sexually promiscuous woman —**tramp′er** *n.*

tram·ple (tram′p'l) *vi.* **-pled, -pling** [< ME. freq. of *trampen*: see prec.] to tread heavily —*vt.* to crush, destroy, etc. as by treading heavily on —*n.* the sound of trampling —**trample under foot** 1. to crush or hurt by or as by trampling 2. to treat with contempt Also **trample on** (or **upon**) —**tram′pler** *n.*

tram·po·line (tram'pə lēn', -lin; tram'pə lēn') *n.* [< It. *trampolino*, a springboard] a sheet of strong canvas stretched tightly on a frame, used as a kind of springboard in acrobatic tumbling, gymnastics, etc. —**tram′po·lin′er, tram′po·lin′ist** *n.*

trance (träns) *n.* [< OFr. < L. *transire*, to die: see TRANSIT] 1. a state brought on by hysteria, hypnosis, etc., in which a person seems to be conscious but is unable to move or act of his own will 2. any daze, stupor, etc. 3. the condition of being completely lost in thought or meditation 4. the state a spiritualist medium is in while allegedly communicating with the dead —*vt.* **tranced, tranc′ing** *Chiefly poet. var. of* ENTRANCE[2]

tran·nie (tran'ē) *n.* [Colloq.] a transistor radio

tran·quil (traŋ'kwəl, tran'-) *adj.* [L. *tranquillus*] free from disturbance or agitation; calm, quiet, peaceful, etc. [*tranquil* waters, a *tranquil* mood] —**tran′quil·ly** *adv.*

tran·quil·li·ty (traŋ kwil'ə tē, tran-) *n.* the quality or state of being tranquil; calmness, etc.

tran·quil·lize (traŋ'kwə līz', tran'-) *vt., vi.* **-ized′, -iz′ing** to make or become tranquil; specif., to calm by the use of a tranquilizer —**tran′quil·li·za′tion** *n.*

tran·quil·liz·er (-li'zər) *n.* any of certain drugs used in calming persons suffering from nervous tension, anxiety, etc.

trans- [L. < *trans*, across] a prefix meaning: 1. on or to the other side of, over, across, through [*transatlantic*] 2. so as to change thoroughly [*transliterate*] 3. above and beyond, transcending

trans. 1. transaction(s) 2. transitive 3. translated 4. translation 5. transport

trans·act (tran sakt', -zakt') *vt.* [< L. pp. of *transigere* < *trans-*, across + *agere*, to drive] to carry on, conduct, or complete (business, etc.) —**trans·ac′tor** *n.*

trans·ac·tion (-sak'shən, -zak'-) *n.* 1. a transacting or being transacted 2. something transacted; specif., *a)* a business deal *b)* [*pl.*] a record of the proceedings of a society, etc. —**trans·ac'tion·al** *adj.*

trans·al·pine (trans al'pīn, tranz-; -pin) *adj.* on the other (the northern) side of the Alps, from Rome

trans·at·lan·tic (trans'ət lan'tik, tranz'-) *adj.* 1. crossing or spanning the Atlantic 2. on the other side of the Atlantic

trans·ceiv·er (tran sē'vər) *n.* [TRANS(MITTER) + (RE)CEIVER] an apparatus in a single housing, functioning alternately as a radio transmitter and receiver

tran·scend (tran send') *vt.* [L. *transcendere* < *trans-*, over + *scandere*, to climb] 1. to go beyond the limits of; exceed [his story *transcends* belief] 2. to be superior to; surpass; excel —*vi.* to be transcendent

tran·scend·ent (-sen'dənt) *adj.* 1. transcending; surpassing; excelling 2. *Theol.* existing apart from the material universe —**tran·scend'ence, tran·scend'en·cy** *n.* —**tran·scend'ent·ly** *adv.*

tran·scen·den·tal (tran'sen den't'l) *adj.* 1. *same as: a)* TRANSCENDENT (sense 1) *b)* SUPERNATURAL 2. abstract; metaphysical 3. of transcendentalism 4. *Math. a)* not capable of being a root of any algebraic equation with rational coefficients *b)* designating a function that is not expressible algebraically in terms of the variables and constants —**tran'scen·den'tal·ly** *adv.*

tran·scen·den·tal·ism (-iz'm) *n.* 1. any of various philosophies seeking to discover the nature of reality by investigating the process of thought rather than the things that are thought about 2. the philosophical ideas of Emerson, the 19th cent. U.S. philosopher, based on a search for reality through spiritual intuition 3. popularly, any obscure, visionary, or idealistic thought —**tran'scen·den'-tal·ist** *n., adj.*

transcendental meditation intense meditation with the object of bringing relief from tension and of increasing awareness

trans·con·ti·nen·tal (trans'kon tə nen't'l) *adj.* 1. that crosses a (or the) continent 2. on the other side of a (or the) continent —**trans'con·ti·nen'tal·ly** *adv.*

tran·scribe (tran skrīb') *vt.* -scribed', -scrib'ing [< L. < *trans-*, over + *scribere*, to write] 1. to write or type out in full (shorthand notes, a speech, etc.) 2. to translate or transliterate 3. to arrange (a piece of music) for an instrument, etc. other than that for which it was originally written 4. *Radio & TV* to record (a programme, commercial, etc.) for broadcast later —**tran·scrib'er** *n.*

tran·script (tran'skript') *n.* 1. something made by transcribing; written, typewritten, or printed copy 2. any copy or reproduction, esp. one that is official —**tran·scrip'-tive** *adj.*

tran·scrip·tion (tran skrip'shən) *n.* 1. the act or process of transcribing 2. a transcript; copy 3. an arrangement of a piece of music for an instrument, voice, etc. other than that for which it was originally written 4. a recording made for radio or television broadcasting; also, the act of using such recordings —**tran·scrip'tion·al** *adj.*

trans·duc·er (trans dyōōs'ər, tranz-) *n.* [< L. *transducere*, to lead across] any of various devices that transmit energy from one system to another, sometimes one that converts the energy in form

tran·sect (tran sekt') *vt.* [< TRANS- + pp. of L. *secare*, to cut] to cut across —**tran·sec'tion** *n.*

tran·sept (tran'sept) *n.* [< ModL. < L. *trans-*, across + *septum*, enclosure] 1. the part of a cross-shaped church at right angles to the long, main section, or nave 2. either arm of this part, outside the nave

trans·fer (trans fur'; *also, & for n. always,* trans'fər) *vt.* -ferred', -fer'ring [< L. < *trans-*, across + *ferre*, to bear] 1. to convey, carry, send, etc. from one person or place to another 2. to make over (title to property, etc.) to another 3. to move (a picture, design, etc.) from one surface to another, as by making wet and pressing 4. *Football* to sell or release a player to another club —*vi.* 1. to transfer oneself or be transferred; move 2. to change from one group, football club, etc. to another 3. [U.S.] to change from one bus, train, etc. to another —*n.* 1. a transferring or being transferred 2. one that is transferred; specif., a picture or design transferred or to be transferred from one surface to another 3. a document effecting a transfer 4. a person who transfers or is transferred —**trans·fer'a·ble, trans·fer'ra·ble** *adj.* —**trans·fer'ence** *n.* —**trans·fer'rer, Law trans·fer'or** *n.*

trans·fer·ee (trans'fär ē') *n.* a person who is transferred or to whom something is transferred

transfer fee a sum of money paid for the transfer of a professional football player from one club to another

trans·fer·rin (trans fer'in) *n.* [< TRANS- + L. *ferrum*, iron + -IN¹] a protein in blood important as an iron carrier

trans·fig·u·ra·tion (trans fig'yoo rā'shən, trans'fig-) *n.* a transfiguring or being transfigured —[**T-**] 1. *Bible* the change in the appearance of Jesus on the mountain: Matt. 17 2. a church festival (Aug. 6) commemorating this

trans·fig·ure (trans fig'ər) *vt.* -ured, -ur·ing [L. *transfigurare*: see TRANS- & FIGURE] 1. to change the figure, form, or appearance of; transform 2. to transform so as to exalt or glorify —**trans·fig'ur·er** *n.*

trans·fix (trans fiks') *vt.* [< L. pp. of *transfigere* < *trans-*, through + *figere*, to fix] 1. to pierce through as with something pointed 2. to fasten in this way; impale 3. to make unable to move, as if impaled [*transfixed* with horror] —**trans·fix'ion** *n.*

trans·form (trans fôrm') *vt.* [L. *transformare*, ult. < *trans-*, over + *forma*, a shape] 1. to change the form or appearance of 2. to change the condition, character, or function of 3. *Elec.* to change (voltage, current, etc.) by use of a transformer 4. *Math.* to change (an algebraic expression or equation) to a different form having the same value 5. *Physics* to change (one form of energy) into another —*vi.* [Rare] to be or become transformed —**trans·form'a·ble** *adj.* —**trans'for·ma'tion** *n.* —**trans'-for·ma'tion·al** *adj.* —**trans·form'a·tive** *adj.*

trans·form·er (-fôr'mər) *n.* 1. a person or thing that transforms 2. *Elec.* a device for transferring electric energy from one alternating-current circuit to another, usually with a change in voltage, current, etc.

trans·fuse (trans fyōōz') *vt.* -fused', -fus'ing [< L. pp. of *transfundere* < *trans-*, across + *fundere*, to pour] 1. to pour in or spread through; instil, imbue, infuse, permeate, etc. 2. *Med. a)* to transfer or introduce (blood, saline solution, etc.) into a blood vessel, usually a vein *b)* to give a transfusion to —**trans·fus'er** *n.* —**trans·fus'i·ble** *adj.* —**trans·fu'sive** *adj.*

trans·fu·sion (-fyōō'zhən) *n.* a transfusing, esp. of blood

trans·gress (trans gres', tranz-) *vt.* [< Fr. < L. pp. of *transgredi* < *trans-*, over + *gradi*, to step] 1. to overstep or break (a law, commandment, etc.) 2. to go beyond (a limit, boundary, etc.) —*vi.* to break a law, commandment, etc.; sin —**trans·gres'sive** *adj.* —**trans·gres'sor** *n.*

trans·gres·sion (-gresh'ən) *n.* a transgressing; breach of a law, duty, etc.; sin

tran·ship (tran ship') *vt.* *var. sp. of* TRANSSHIP

trans·hu·mance (trans hyōō'məns, tranz-) *n.* [Fr. < Sp. < L. *trans*, across + *humus*, earth] seasonal movement of livestock between two regions, as lowlands and highlands

tran·si·ent (tran'zē ənt) *adj.* [< L. prp. of *transire*: see TRANSIT] 1. *a)* passing away with time; temporary; transitory *b)* passing quickly; fleeting; ephemeral 2. staying for only a short time [a *transient* lodger] —*n.* a transient person or thing —**tran'sience, tran'sien·cy** *n.* —**tran'sient·ly** *adv.*

tran·sis·tor (tran zis'tər, -sis'-) *n.* [TRAN(SFER) + (RE)SISTOR] 1. a small, solid-state electronic device used instead of a thermionic valve 2. *same as* TRANSISTOR RADIO

tran·sis·tor·ize (-tə rīz') *vt.* -ized', -iz'ing to equip with transistors

transistor radio a portable radio powered by transistors

trans·it (tran'sit, -zit) *n.* [< L. pp. of *transire* < *trans-*, over + *ire*, to go] 1. *a)* passage through or across *b)* a transition; change 2. a carrying or being carried from one place to another [goods in *transit*] 3. a surveying instrument for measuring horizontal angles: in full, **transit theodolite** 4. *Astron. a)* the apparent passage of a heavenly body across a given meridian or through the field of a telescope *b)* the apparent passage of a smaller heavenly body across the disc of a larger one —*vt., vi.* to make a transit (through or across)

transit camp camp in which refugees, soldiers, etc. live temporarily

tran·si·tion (tran zish'ən, -sish'-, -sizh'-) *n.* 1. *a)* a passing from one condition, activity, place, etc. to another *b)* the period of this 2. a word, phrase, sentence, etc. that relates one element or topic to another that follows 3. *Archit.* the change from Norman to Early English style 4. *Music a)* a shifting from one key to another; modulation *b)* *same as* BRIDGE¹ (*n.* 9) —**tran·si'tion·al** *adj.* —**tran·si'tion·al·ly** *adv.*

tran·si·tive (tran'sə tiv, -zə-) *adj.* taking a direct object to complete the meaning: said of certain verbs —*n.* a transitive verb —**tran'si·tive·ly** *adv.* —**tran'si·tive·ness** *n.*

tran·si·to·ry (tran'sə tər ē, -zə-) *adj.* of a passing nature; not enduring; temporary; fleeting —**tran'si·to·ri·ly** *adv.* —**tran'si·to·ri·ness** *n.*

transl. 1. translated 2. translation

trans·late (trans lāt', tranz-) *vt.* -lat'ed, -lat'ing [< L. *translatus*, used as pp. of *transferre*, to TRANSFER] 1. to change from one place or condition to another; specif., *Theol.* to carry up to heaven without death 2. to put into the words of a different language 3. to change into another medium or form [*translate* ideas into action] 4. to put into different words; rephrase 5. *Mech.* to impart translation to —*vi.* 1. to make a translation into another language 2. to be capable of being translated —**trans·lat'a·ble** *adj.* —**trans·la'tor** *n.*

trans·la·tion (-lā'shən) *n.* 1. a translating or being translated 2. writing or speech translated into another language 3. *Mech.* motion in which every point of the moving object has simultaneously the same velocity and direction —**trans·la′tion·al** *adj.*

trans·lit·er·ate (trans lit′ə rāt′, tranz-) *vt.* **-at′ed, -at′ing** [< TRANS- + L. *litera*, letter + -ATE¹] to write or spell (words, etc.) in corresponding characters of another alphabet —**trans·lit′er·a′tion** *n.* —**trans·lit′er·a·tor** *n.*

trans·lu·cent (trans lōō′sənt, tranz-) *adj.* [< L. prp. of *translucere* < *trans-*, through + *lucere*, to shine] **1.** orig., shining through **2.** letting light pass but diffusing it so that objects on the other side cannot be clearly distinguished, as frosted glass: also **trans·lu′cid** (-sid) —**trans·lu′cence, trans·lu′cen·cy** *n.* —**trans·lu′cent·ly** *adv.*

trans·lu·nar·y (trans lōō′nə rē) *adj.* [TRANS- + LUNAR] **1.** lying beyond the moon **2.** unworldly; ethereal Also **trans·lu′nar**

trans·mi·grate (-mī′grāt′) *vi.* **-grat′ed, -grat′ing** [< L. pp. of *transmigrare:* see TRANS- & MIGRATE] **1.** to move from one habitation, country, etc. to another **2.** in some religions, to pass into another body at death: said of the soul —**trans′mi·gra′tion** *n.* —**trans·mi·gra′tor** *n.* —**trans·mi′gra·to·ry** (-grə tər ē) *adj.*

trans·mis·si·ble (trans mis′ə b'l, tranz-) *adj.* capable of being transmitted —**trans·mis′si·bil′i·ty** *n.*

trans·mis·sion (-mish′ən) *n.* **1.** *a)* a transmitting or being transmitted *b)* something transmitted **2.** the part of a motor car, etc. that transmits motive force from the engine to the wheels, as by gears **3.** the passage of radio waves through space between the transmitting station and the receiving station —**trans·mis′sive** *adj.*

trans·mit (-mit′) *vt.* **-mit′ted, -mit′ting** [< L. < *trans-*, over + *mittere*, to send] **1.** to send or cause to go from one person or place to another; transfer; convey **2.** to pass along (a disease, etc.) **3.** to hand down to others by heredity, inheritance, etc. **4.** to communicate (news, etc.) **5.** *a)* to cause (light, heat, etc.) to pass through some medium *b)* to conduct [water *transmits* sound] **6.** to convey (force, movement, etc.) from one mechanical part to another **7.** to send out (radio or television broadcasts, etc.) by electromagnetic waves —*vi.* to send out radio or television signals —**trans·mit′tal, trans·mit′tance, trans·mit′tan·cy** *n.* —**trans·mit′ti·ble, trans·mit′ta·ble** *adj.*

trans·mit·ter (trans mit′ər; *for 2, often* trans′mit ər, tranz′-) *n.* **1.** a person who transmits **2.** a thing that transmits; specif., *a)* the part of a telegraphic instrument by which messages are sent *b)* the part of a telephone, behind the mouthpiece, that converts sound into electric impulses for transmission *c)* the apparatus that generates, modulates, and sends out radio waves

trans·mog·ri·fy (tranz mog′rə fī′, trans-) *vt.* **-fied′, -fy′ing** [humorous pseudo-Latin formation] to transform, esp. in a grotesque or strange manner

trans·mu·ta·tion (trans′myōō tā′shən, tranz′-) *n.* **1.** a transmuting or being transmuted **2.** the conversion of base metals into gold and silver as sought in alchemy **3.** *Chem.* the conversion of atoms of one element into atoms of a different isotope, or element, as by nuclear bombardment —**trans′mu·ta′tion·al** *adj.* —**trans·mut′a·tive** (-myōōt′ə tiv) *adj.*

trans·mute (trans myōōt′, tranz-) *vt., vi.* **-mut′ed, -mut′ing** [< L. < *trans-*, over + *mutare*, to change] to change from one form, nature, substance, etc. into another; transform —**trans·mut′a·bil′i·ty** *n.* —**trans·mut′a·ble** *adj.* —**trans·mut′a·bly** *adv.*

trans·na·tion·al (trans nash′ə n'l, tranz-) *adj.* transcending the limits, interest, etc. of a single nation

trans·o·ce·an·ic (trans′ō shē an′ik, tranz′-) *adj.* **1.** crossing or spanning the ocean **2.** from or on the other side of the ocean

tran·som (tran′səm) *n.* [prob. < L. *transtrum*, crossbeam] **1.** a horizontal crossbar across the top or middle of a window or the top of a door **2.** a small window directly over a door or window, usually hinged to the transom **3.** any crosspiece, as the horizontal beam of a gallows

tran·son·ic (tran son′ik) *adj.* designating, of, or moving at a speed within the range of change from subsonic to supersonic speed

trans·pa·cif·ic (trans′pə sif′ik) *adj.* **1.** crossing or spanning the Pacific **2.** on the other side of the Pacific

trans·par·en·cy (trans par′ən sē) *n.* **1.** a transparent state or quality: also **trans·par′ence 2.** *pl.* **-cies** *a)* something specif., a piece of material having a picture, etc. that is visible when light shines through it *b)* a positive photograph to be projected or viewed against the light

trans·par·ent (-ənt) *adj.* [< ML. prp. of *transparere* < L. *trans-*, through + *parere*, to appear] **1.** transmitting light rays so that objects on the other side may be distinctly seen **2.** so fine in texture or open in mesh as to be seen through; sheer; gauzy **3.** easily understood, recognized, or detected; obvious **4.** open; frank —**trans·par′ent·ly** *adv.* —**trans·par′ent·ness** *n.*

tran·spire (tran spīr′) *vt.* **-spired′, -spir′ing** [< Fr. < ML. < L. *trans-*, through + *spirare*, to breathe] to cause (vapour, moisture, etc.) to pass through tissue or other

permeable substances, esp. through the pores of the skin or the surface of leaves, etc. —*vi.* **1.** to give off vapour, moisture, etc. as through pores **2.** to be given off, exhaled, etc. **3.** to leak out; become known **4.** [Colloq.] to come to pass; happen: regarded by some as a loose usage —**tran′spi·ra′tion** (-spə rā′shən) *n.* —**tran·spi′ra·to·ry** (-tər ē) *adj.*

trans·plant (trans plänt′; *for n.* trans′plänt′) *vt.* [< LL.: see TRANS- & PLANT] **1.** to remove from one place and plant or put in another **2.** to remove (people) from one place and resettle in another **3.** *Surgery* to transfer (tissue or an organ) from one individual or part of the body to another; graft —*vi.* to be capable of being transplanted —*n.* **1.** a transplanting **2.** something transplanted, as a body organ or seedling —**trans·plant′a·ble** *adj.* —**trans′plan·ta′tion** *n.* —**trans·plant′er** *n.*

tran·spon·der (tran spon′dər) *n.* [TRAN(SMITTER) (RE)SPONDER] a radio or radar transceiver that automatically transmits electrical signals when actuated by a specific signal

trans·port (trans pôrt′; *for n.* trans′pôrt) *vt.* [< MFr. < L. < *trans-*, over + *portare*, to carry] **1.** to carry from one place to another, esp. over long distances **2.** to carry away with emotion; enrapture **3.** to banish or deport to a penal colony, etc. —*n.* **1.** a transporting; transportation **2.** *a)* a means or system of conveyance *b)* the work or business of conveying passengers or goods **3.** strong emotion, esp. of delight or joy **4.** a ship, aircraft, train, etc. used for transporting soldiers, goods, etc. **5.** a transported convict —**trans·port′a·bil′i·ty** *n.* —**trans·port′a·ble** *adj.* —**trans·port′er** *n.*

trans·por·ta·tion (trans′pər tā′shən) *n.* **1.** a transporting or being transported **2.** banishment for crime, as to a penal colony

transport café a cheap eating place on a main road, used chiefly by long-distance lorry drivers

trans·pose (trans pōz′) *vt.* **-posed′, -pos′ing** [MFr. *transposer:* see TRANS- & POSE¹] **1.** to change the usual, relative, or respective order or position of; interchange **2.** to transfer (an algebraic term) from one side of an equation to the other, reversing the plus or minus value **3.** to rewrite or play (a musical composition) in a different key —*vi.* to play music in a different key —**trans·pos′a·bill′i·ty, trans·pos′a·ble·ness** *n.* —**trans·pos′a·ble** *adj.* —**trans·pos′er** *n.* —**trans′po·si′tion** (-pə zish′ən) *n.*

trans·sex·u·al (tran sek′shōō wəl, trans-) *n.* a person who tends to identify with the opposite sex, or one whose sex has been changed by means of surgery and hormone injections —**trans·sex′u·al·ism** *n.*

trans·ship (tran ship′, trans-) *vt.* **-shipped′, -ship′ping** to transfer from one ship, train, etc. to another for reshipment —*vi.* to leave one ship, etc. and board another —**trans·ship′ment** *n.*

trans·son·ic (-son′ik) *adj.* *same as* TRANSONIC

tran·sub·stan·ti·a·tion (tran′sab stan′shē ā′shən) *n.* [< ML. < pp. of *transubstantiare* < L. *trans-*, over + *substantia*, substance] **1.** a changing of one substance into another **2.** *R.C. & Orthodox Eastern Ch.* the doctrine that, in the Eucharist, the whole substance of the bread and wine is changed into the body and blood of Christ, while only the appearance, taste, etc. of bread and wine remain

tran·sude (tran syōōd′) *vi.* **-sud′ed, -sud′ing** [< ModL. < L. *trans*, across + *sudare*, to sweat] to ooze through pores or interstices

trans·u·ran·ic (trans′yoo ran′ik, tranz′-) *adj.* designating or of the elements, as plutonium, having atomic numbers higher than that of uranium: also **trans′u·ra′ni·um** (-rā′nē əm)

trans·ver·sal (trans vur′səl) *adj.* *same as* TRANSVERSE —*n.* a line that intersects two or more other lines —**trans·ver′sal·ly** *adv.*

trans·verse (trans vurs′, tranz-; *also, and for n. usually,* trans′vurs, tranz′-) *adj.* [< L. pp. of *transvertere:* see TRAVERSE] lying, situated, placed, etc. across; crosswise —*n.* a transverse part, beam, etc. —**trans·verse′ly** *adv.*

transverse colon the central portion of the large intestine, crossing the abdomen: see INTESTINE, illus.

trans·ves·tite (trans ves′tīt, tranz-) *n.* [< TRANS- + L. *vestire*, to clothe + -ITE] a person who derives sexual pleasure from dressing in the clothes of the opposite sex —**trans·vest′** *vt.* —**trans·ves′tism, trans·ves′ti·tism** *n.*

trap¹ (trap) *n.* [OE. *træppe*] **1.** any device for catching animals; gin, snare, etc. **2.** any stratagem or ambush designed to catch or trick unsuspecting persons **3.** any of various devices for preventing the escape of gas, offensive odours, etc., as a U-shaped part in a drainpipe **4.** an apparatus for throwing discs into the air to be shot at in trapshooting **5.** a light, two-wheeled carriage with springs **6.** *same as* TRAPDOOR **7.** [*pl.*] the cymbals, blocks, etc. attached to a set of drums, as in a jazz band **8.** [Slang] the mouth **9.** *Golf same as* BUNKER **10.** *Greyhound Racing* a box-like stall from which the greyhound is released —*vt.* **trapped, trap′ping 1.** to catch as in a trap; entrap **2.** to

hold back or seal off by a trap **3.** to furnish with a trap or traps —*vi.* to set traps to catch animals, esp. for their furs
trap² (trap) *n.* [< Sw. < *trappa*, stair] **1.** any of several dark-coloured, igneous rocks; esp., such a rock, as basalt, used in road making **2.** a geologic structure enclosing oil or gas Also **trap′rock′** —**trap′e·an** *adj.*
trap³ (trap) *vt.* **trapped, trap′ping** [< OFr. *drap*, cloth] to cover with trappings; caparison —*n.* [*pl.*] [Colloq.] personal belongings, clothes, etc.
trap·door (trap′dôr′) *n.* a hinged or sliding door in a roof, ceiling, or floor
tra·peze (tra pēz′, tra-) *n.* [Fr. < ModL.: see ff.] a short horizontal bar, hung at a height by two ropes, on which gymnasts, acrobats, etc. swing and perform acrobatics
tra·pe·zi·um (tra pē′zē əm) *n.*, *pl.* **-zi·ums, -zi·a** (-ə) [ModL. < Gr. dim. of *trapeza*, table < *tra-*, for *tetra*, four + *peza*, a foot] **1.** a plane figure with four sides only two of which are parallel **2.** [U.S.] *same as* TRAPEZOID (sense 1) **3.** a small bone of the wrist near the base of the thumb

TRAPEZIUM

trap·e·zoid (trap′ə zoid′) *n.* [ModL. < Gr.: see prec. & -OID] **1.** a plane figure with four sides no two of which are parallel **2.** [U.S.] *same as* TRAPEZIUM (sense 1) **3.** a small bone of the wrist near the base of the index finger —*adj.* shaped like a trapezoid: also **trap′e·zoi′dal**

TRAPEZOID

trap·per (trap′ər) *n.* a person who traps; esp., one who traps fur-bearing animals for their skins
trap·pings (-iŋz) *n.pl.* [see TRAP³] **1.** a highly decorated covering for a horse; caparison **2.** highly decorated clothing **3.** extra benefits [*trappings* of success]
Trap·pist (trap′ist) *n.* [< Fr. < (La) *Trappe*, abbey in Normandy] a monk of a branch of the Cistercian order, living under a vow of silence —*adj.* of the Trappists
trap·shoot·ing (trap′shōōt′iŋ) *n.* the sport of shooting at clay pigeons, or discs, sprung into the air from traps —**trap′shoot′er** *n.*
trash (trash) *n.* [prob. < Scand.] **1.** parts that have been broken off, stripped off, etc., esp. leaves, twigs, etc. **2.** discarded or worthless things; rubbish **3.** worthless, unnecessary, offensive, or foolish matter [literary *trash*] **4.** the refuse of sugar cane after the juice has been squeezed out **5.** [Chiefly U.S.] a person or people regarded as disreputable —*vt.* to trim (trees and plants, esp. sugar cane) of outer leaves and branches
trash·y (-ē) *adj.* **trash′i·er, trash′i·est** containing, consisting of, or like trash; worthless —**trash′i·ness** *n.*
trass (tras) *n.* [G. < Du. *tras*] a volcanic rock, used in making a hydraulic cement
‡trat·tor·i·a (trät′tô rē′ä) *n.*, *pl.* **-i·e** (-e) [It. < *trattore*, innkeeper] a small, inexpensive restaurant in Italy
trau·ma (trô′mə, trou′-) *n.*, *pl.* **-mas, -ma·ta** (-mə tə) [ModL. < Gr.] **1.** *Med.* a bodily injury, wound, or shock **2.** *Psychiatry* an emotional shock which has a lasting effect on the mind —**trau·mat′ic** (-mat′ik) *adj.* —**trau·mat′i·cal·ly** *adv.*
trau·ma·tize (-tīz′) *vt.* **-tized′, -tiz′ing** **1.** *Med.* to injure or wound (tissues) **2.** *Psychiatry* to subject to a trauma
trav·ail (trav′āl, trə vāl′) *n.* [OFr. < VL. *tripalium*, a torture device < *tria*, three + *palus*, a stake] [Obs.] **1.** very hard work **2.** the pains of childbirth **3.** intense pain; agony —*vi.* [Obs.] **1.** to toil **2.** to suffer the pains of childbirth
trav·el (trav′'l) *vi.* **-elled, -el·ling** [var. of prec.] **1.** to go from one place to another; make a journey **2.** to go from place to place as a travelling salesman **3.** to walk or run **4.** to move, pass, or be transmitted **5.** to move in a given course: said of mechanical parts, etc. **6.** to be capable of withstanding deterioration, damage, etc. if transported **7.** to advance or progress **8.** *Basketball* to move (usually more than two steps) while holding the ball **9.** [Colloq.] to move with speed —*vt.* to make a journey over or through —*n.* **1.** the act or process of travelling **2.** [*pl.*] journeys, tours, etc. **3.** movement of any kind **4.** *a)* mechanical motion, esp. reciprocating motion *b)* the distance of a mechanical stroke, etc. —**trav′el·ler** *n.*
travel agency an agency that makes travel arrangements for tourists or other travellers, as for hotels, itineraries, etc. —**travel agent**
trav·elled (-'ld) *adj.* **1.** that has travelled much **2.** much used by travellers [a *travelled* road]
traveller's cheque a cheque, usually one of a set, issued by a bank, etc. and sold to a traveller who signs it when it is issued and again in the presence of the one cashing it
traveller's tale an exaggerated account; a tall story
travelling salesman *same as* COMMERCIAL TRAVELLER
trav·e·logue (trav′ə log′) *n.* **1.** a lecture on travels, accompanied by the showing of pictures **2.** a film of travels
trav·erse (tra vʉrs′, trə-; *also, & for* n.

& *adj. always,* trav′ərs) *vt.* **-ersed′, -ers′ing** [< OFr. < L. pp. of *transvertere* < *trans-*, over + *vertere*, to turn] **1.** *a)* to pass or extend over, across, or through *b)* to go back and forth over or along **2.** to go counter to; oppose **3.** to survey or examine carefully **4.** to turn (a gun, etc.) laterally **5.** *Law* to deny formally (an allegation) —*vi.* **1.** to cross over **2.** to move back and forth over a place, etc. **3.** to swivel or pivot **4.** to move across a mountain slope, as in skiing, in an oblique direction —*n.* **1.** something that traverses or crosses; specif., *a)* a crossbar, crossbeam,etc. *b)* a gallery, loft, etc. crossing a building **2.** a traversing or passing across **3.** a device that causes a traversing movement **4.** a way across **5.** a zigzag course taken by a vessel —*adj.* extending across —**trav·ers′a·ble** *adj.* —**trav·ers′al** *n.* —**trav·ers′er** *n.*
trav·er·tine (trav′ər tēn′, -tin) *n.* [< It., ult. < L. (*lapis*) *Tiburtinus*, (stone) by Tibur, ancient It. city] a light-coloured limestone deposited around limy springs, lakes, etc.
trav·es·ty (trav′is tē) *n.*, *pl.* **-ties** [< Fr. pp. of *travestir*, to disguise < It. < L. *trans-*, over + *vestire*, to dress] **1.** a grotesque or exaggerated imitation for purposes of ridicule; burlesque **2.** a crude or ridiculous representation —*vt.* **-tied, -ty·ing** to make a travesty of
trawl (trôl) *n.* [< ? MDu. *traghel*, a dragnet] **1.** a large, baglike net dragged by a boat along the bottom of a fishing bank: also **trawl′net′** **2.** [U.S.] a long line supported by buoys, from which many short fishing lines are hung: also **trawl line** —*vt., vi.* to fish or catch with a trawl
trawl·er (trô′lər) *n.* a boat used in trawling
tray (trā) *n.* [OE. *treg*, wooden board] **1.** a flat receptacle with low sides, for holding or carrying articles **2.** a tray with its contents [a *tray* of food] **3.** a shallow, removable compartment of a trunk, cabinet, etc.
treach·er·ous (trech′ər əs) *adj.* **1.** full of or showing treachery; traitorous **2.** untrustworthy; unreliable [*treacherous* rocks] —**treach′er·ous·ly** *adv.* —**treach′-er·ous·ness** *n.*
treach·er·y (-ē) *n.*, *pl.* **-er·ies** [< OFr. < *trichier*, to trick, cheat] **1.** betrayal of trust, faith, or allegiance; disloyalty or treason **2.** an act of disloyalty or treason
trea·cle (trē′k'l) *n.* [< OFr. < L. < Gr. *thēriakē*, remedy for venomous bites < *thērion*, dim. of *thēr*, wild beast] **1.** a thick, usually dark brown syrup produced during the refining of sugar: also called **black treacle 2.** [Colloq.] *same as* GOLDEN SYRUP **3.** (fig.) anything sweet and cloying —**trea′cly** (-klē) *adj.*
tread (tred) *vt.* **trod, trod′den** or **trod, tread′ing** [OE. *tredan*] **1.** to walk on, in, along, over, etc. **2.** to do or follow by walking, dancing, etc. [to *tread* the measures gaily] **3.** to press or beat with the feet; trample **4.** to oppress or subdue **5.** to copulate with: said of male birds —*vi.* **1.** to move on foot; walk **2.** to set one's foot (*on, across,* etc.) **3.** to trample (*on* or *upon*) **4.** to copulate: said of birds —*n.* **1.** the act, manner, or sound of treading **2.** something on which a person or thing treads or moves, as the part of a shoe sole, wheel, etc. that touches the ground, the endless belt over cogged wheels of a tractor, etc., the horizontal surface of a stair step, etc. **3.** *a)* the thick outer layer of a motor car tyre *b)* the depth or pattern of grooves in this layer —**tread the boards** to act in plays —**tread on air** to be very happy —**tread on a person's toes** (or **corns**) **1.** to offend someone's sensibilities **2.** to encroach on someone's rights —**tread on the heels** of to follow immediately after —**tread out 1.** to extinguish, as a fire **2.** to extract the juice of grapes by treading on them —**tread water** to keep the body upright and the head above water in swimming by moving the legs up and down —**tread′er** *n.*
trea·dle (tred′'l) *n.* [< OE. < *tredan*: see prec.] a lever or pedal moved by the foot as to turn a wheel —*vi.* **-dled, -dling** to work a treadle
tread·mill (tred′mil′) *n.* **1.** a mill wheel turned by persons treading steps built around its outer edge, or by an animal treading an endless belt **2.** any monotonous routine of duties, work, etc.
treas. **1.** treasurer **2.** treasury
trea·son (trē′z'n) *n.* [< OFr. < L. < pp. of *tradere*, to deliver up < *trans-*, over + *dare*, to give] **1.** [Now Rare] betrayal of trust or faith **2.** betrayal of one's country, esp. by helping the enemy in time of war
trea·son·a·ble (-ə b'l) *adj.* of or involving treason; traitorous: also **trea′son·ous** —**trea′son·a·ble·ness** *n.* —**trea′son·a·bly** *adv.*
treas·ure (trezh′ər) *n.* [< OFr. < L. < Gr. *thēsauros*] **1.** accumulated wealth, as money, gold, jewels, etc. **2.** any person or thing considered valuable —*vt.* **-ured, -ur·ing** **1.** to save up (money, etc.) for future use **2.** to value greatly; cherish
treasure hunt a game in which successive clues direct players to a hidden prize
treas·ur·er (trezh′ər ər) *n.* a person in charge of a treasure or treasury; specif., an officer in charge of the funds of a company, society, etc. —**treas′ur·er·ship′** *n.*

treas·ure-trove (-trōv′) *n.* [< Anglo-Fr. < OFr. *tresor, treasure* + *trové*, pp. of *trover,* to find] **1.** treasure found hidden, the original owner of which is not known **2.** any valuable discovery

treas·ur·y (-ē) *n., pl.* **-ur·ies 1.** a place where treasure is kept **2.** a place where public or private funds are kept, recorded, etc. **3.** the funds or revenues of a country, company, etc. **4.** [T-] the governmental department in charge of revenue, taxation, etc. **5.** a collection of treasures in art, literature, etc.

Treasury Bench the front row of seats to the right of the speaker in the House of Commons, occupied by the principal members of the government

treasury note 1. a currency note for £1 or 10 shillings, issued (1914-28) by the British Treasury **2.** [U.S.] any of the interest-bearing notes or obligations of the U.S. Treasury

treat (trēt) *vi.* [< OFr. *traiter* < L. *tractare,* freq. of *trahere,* to draw] **1.** to discuss terms (*with* a person or *for* a settlement) **2.** to deal with a subject; speak or write (*of*) **3.** to stand the cost of another's entertainment: also **stand treat** —*vt.* **1.** to deal with (a subject) in writing, music, etc. in a specified style **2.** to act towards (a person, animal, etc.) in a specified manner **3.** to regard in a specified way [he *treated* it as a joke] **4.** *a*) to pay for the food, drink, etc. of (another) *b*) to provide with something that pleases **5.** to subject to some process or substance, as in a chemical procedure **6.** to give medical or surgical care to (someone) or for (some disorder) —*n.* **1.** a meal, drink, etc. paid for by someone else **2.** anything that gives great pleasure **3.** *a*) the act of treating or entertaining *b*) one's turn to treat —**treat′a·bil′i·ty** *n.* —**treat′a·ble** *adj.* —**treat′er** *n.*

trea·tise (trēt′is) *n.* [< Anglo-Fr., ult. < OFr. *traiter:* see TREAT] a formal, systematic article or book dealing with some subject in a detailed way

treat·ment (-mənt) *n.* **1.** act, manner, method, etc. of treating **2.** medical or surgical care

trea·ty (trēt′ē) *n., pl.* **-ties** [< OFr. *traité,* ult. < pp. of L. *tractare,* to manage] **1.** a formal agreement between two or more nations, relating to peace, alliance, trade, etc. **2.** a document embodying such an agreement

tre·ble (treb′'l) *adj.* [< OFr. < L. *triplus,* triple] **1.** threefold; triple **2.** of, for, or performing the treble **3.** high-pitched or shrill —*n.* **1.** the highest part in musical harmony; soprano **2.** a singer or instrument that takes this part **3.** a high-pitched voice or sound —*vt., vi.* **-bled, -bling** to make or become threefold —**tre′bly** *adv.*

treble chance a method of competing in the football pools, by selecting from a list of matches those that will end in a draw, home and away wins counting less

treble clef *Music* a sign on a staff, indicating the position of G above middle C on the second line

treb·u·chet (treb′yoo shet′) *n.* [ME. < OFr. < *trebucher,* to stumble] a medieval engine of war for hurling large stones: also **tre·buck·et** (trē′buk it)

tre·cen·to (trā chen′tō) *n.* [It., lit., three hundred, short for *mil trecento,* one thousand three hundred] the 14th cent. as a period in Italian art and literature

tree (trē) *n.* [OE. *treow*] **1.** a large, woody perennial plant with one main trunk which develops many branches **2.** a treelike bush or shrub **3.** a wooden beam, bar, post, etc. **4.** anything resembling a tree; specif., *short for* FAMILY TREE —*vt.* **treed, tree′ing 1.** to chase up a tree **2.** to stretch on a shoe tree —**up a tree** [Colloq.] in a situation without escape; cornered —**tree′less** *adj.* —**tree′like′** *adj.*

tree creeper a small long-beaked bird that climbs tree-trunks in search of insects

tree fern a tropical fern with a woody trunk

tree frog any of various frogs that live in trees: many are called *tree toads*

tree line *same as* TIMBERLINE

tree·nail (trē′nāl′; tren′'l, trun′-) *n.* [< ME. < *tre,* wood + *nayle,* nail] a dry wooden peg used to join timbers, esp. in shipbuilding: it swells when wet so as to fit tightly

tree of heaven a fast-growing ailanthus

tree ring *same as* ANNUAL RING

tree surgery treatment of damaged trees as by filling cavities, pruning, etc. —**tree surgeon**

tree toad *see* TREE FROG

tree·top (trē′top′) *n.* the topmost part of a tree

tre·foil (trē′foil) *n.* [< Anglo-Fr. < L. < *tri-,* three + *folium,* a leaf] **1.** a plant with leaves divided into three leaflets, as the clover **2.** any ornamental figure shaped like such a leaf

trek (trek) *vi.* **trekked, trek′king** [Afrik. < Du. *trekken,* to draw] **1.** in South Africa, to travel by ox wagon **2.** to travel slowly or laboriously **3.** [Colloq.] to go, esp. on foot —*n.* **1.** in South Africa, a journey made by ox wagon **2.** a journey or leg of a journey **3.** a migration **4.** [Chiefly U.S. Colloq.] a short trip, esp. on foot —**trek′ker** *n.*

trel·lis (trel′is) *n.* [< OFr., ult. < L. *trilix,* triple-twilled] an openwork structure of thin, crossed strips, esp. of wood, on which climbing plants are trained; lattice —*vt.* **1.** to furnish with, or train on, a trellis **2.** to cross or interweave like a trellis

trem·a·tode ′(trem′ə tōd′, trē′mə-) *n.* [< ModL. < Gr. < *trēma* (gen. *trēmatos*), a hole + *eidos,* form] any of various parasitic flatworms; fluke —*adj.* of a trematode

trem·ble (trem′b′l) *vi.* **-bled, -bling** [< OFr. < VL., ult. < L. < *tremere*] **1.** to shake involuntarily from cold, fear, excitement, etc.; shiver **2.** to feel great fear or anxiety **3.** to quake, totter, vibrate, etc. **4.** to quaver [a *trembling* voice] —*n.* **1.** a trembling **2.** [*sometimes pl.*] a fit or state of trembling —**trem′bling·ly** *adv.* —**trem′bly** *adj.*

trem·bler (-blər) *n.* **1.** a person or thing that trembles **2.** any of several West Indian birds **3.** *Elec.* an automatic device for breaking a circuit

tre·men·dous (tri men′dəs) *adj.* [< L. *tremendus* < *tremere,* to TREMBLE] **1.** such as to make one tremble; terrifying **2.** *a*) very large; great *b*) [Colloq.] wonderful, amazing, etc. —**tre·men′dous·ly** *adv.* —**tre·men′dous·ness** *n.*

trem·o·lo (trem′ə lō′) *n., pl.* **-los′** [It. < L.: see TREMULOUS] **1.** a trembling effect produced by rapidly repeating the same musical tone **2.** a device, as in an organ, for producing such a tone

trem·or (trem′ər; *occas.* trē′mər) *n.* [< OFr. < L. < *tremere,* to TREMBLE] **1.** a trembling, shaking, etc. **2.** a vibratory motion **3.** a nervous thrill; trembling sensation **4.** a trembling sound —**trem′or·ous** *adj.*

trem·u·lous (trem′yoo ləs) *adj.* [L. *tremulus* < *tremere,* to TREMBLE] **1.** trembling; quivering **2.** fearful; timid **3.** marked by or showing trembling or quivering Also **trem′u·lant** —**trem′u·lous·ly** *adv.* —**trem′u·lous·ness** *n.*

tre·nail (trē′nāl′; tren′'l, trun′-) *n. same as* TREENAIL

trench (trench) *vt.* [< OFr. < ? L. *truncare,* to cut off] **1.** to cut, slice, gash, etc. **2.** to dig a ditch or ditches in **3.** to surround or fortify with trenches —*vi.* **1.** to dig a ditch or ditches **2.** to infringe (*on* or *upon* another's land, rights, etc.) **3.** to verge or border (*on*); come close —*n.* **1.** a deep furrow **2.** a long, narrow ditch with earth banked in front as a parapet, used in battle for cover, etc.

trench·ant (tren′chənt) *adj.* [< OFr.: see prec.] **1.** orig., cutting; sharp **2.** keen; penetrating; incisive [*trenchant* words] **3.** forceful; vigorous [a *trenchant* argument] **4.** clear-cut; distinct [a *trenchant* style] —**trench′an·cy** *n.* —**trench′ant·ly** *adv.*

trench coat a belted raincoat in a military style

trench·er (tren′chər) *n.* [Archaic] **1.** a wooden platter for carving and serving meat **2.** *a*) food served on a trencher *b*) a supply of food

trench·er·man (-mən) *n., pl.* **-men** an eater; esp., one who eats much and heartily

trench fever an infectious disease transmitted by body lice, in which there is remittent fever, muscular pains, etc.

trench foot a diseased condition of the feet resulting from prolonged exposure to wet and cold, as of soldiers in trenches

trench mortar (or **gun**) any of various portable mortars for shooting projectiles at a high trajectory and short range

trench warfare warfare in which each side entrenches itself in lines facing the enemy

trend (trend) *vi.* [OE. *trendan*] **1.** to extend, turn, bend, etc. in a specific direction **2.** to have a general tendency: said of events, opinions, etc. —*n.* **1.** the general direction of a river, road, etc. **2.** the general tendency or course, as of events, a discussion, etc. **3.** a vogue, or current style, as in fashions

trend·set·ter (-set′ər) *n.* any person or innovation that creates or is likely to create a new trend or fashion —**trend′- set′ting** *adj.*

trend·y (-ē) *adj.* **trend′i·er, trend′i·est** [Colloq.] of or in the latest style, or trend —**trend′i·ly** *adv.* —**trend′i·ness** *n.*

tre·pan (tri pan′) *n.* [< ML. < Gr. < *trypan,* to bore] **1.** an early form of the trephine **2.** a heavy boring tool —*vt.* **-panned′, -pan′ning** *same as* TREPHINE —**trep·a·na·tion** (trep′ə nā′shən) *n.*

tre·pang (tri pang′) *n.* [Malay *tēripang*] a boiled, smoked, and dried sea cucumber, used in the Orient for making soup

tre·phine (tri fīn′, -fēn′) *n.* [formed (after TREPAN) < L. *tres,* three + *fines,* ends] a type of small circular saw used in surgery to remove discs of bone from the skull —*vt.* **-phined′, -phin′ing** to operate on with a trephine —**treph·i·na·tion** (tref′ə nā′shən) *n.*

trep·i·da·tion (trep′ə dā′shən) *n.* [< L. < pp. of *trepidare,* to tremble < *trepidus,* disturbed] **1.** tremulous or trembling movement **2.** fearful uncertainty or anxiety

tres·pass (tres′pəs; *also, esp. for v.,* -pas′) *vi.* [< OFr., ult. < L. *trans-,* across + *passus,* a step] **1.** to go beyond the limits of what is considered right or moral; transgress **2.** to go on another's property without permission or right **3.** to intrude; encroach **4.** *Law* to commit a trespass —*n.* a trespassing; specif., *a*) a moral offence *b*) an encroachment; intrusion *c*) *Law* an illegal act done with force against another's person, rights, or property —**tres′pass·er** *n.*

tress (tres) *n.* [< OFr. < ? Frank.] **1.** orig., a braid of hair **2.** a lock of human hair **3.** [*pl.*] a woman's or girl's hair, esp. when long and falling loosely

-tress (tris) a suffix meaning female [actress]: see also -ESS

tres·tle (tres'′l) *n.* [< OFr., ult. < L. *transtrum*, a beam] 1. a frame consisting of a horizontal beam fastened to two pairs of spreading legs, used to support planks to form a table, etc. 2. a framework of uprights and crosspieces, supporting a bridge, etc.; also, such a bridge

TRESTLE

tres·tle·work (-wurk′) *n.* a system of trestles for supporting a bridge, etc.
trews (trooz) *n.pl.* [Scot. Gael, *triubhus*] *Scot.* close-fitting trousers, orig. of tartan
trey (trā) *n.* [< OFr. < L. *tres*, three] 1. a playing card with three spots 2. the side of a die bearing three spots, or a throw of the dice totalling three
T.R.H. Their Royal Highnesses
tri- [< Fr., L., or Gr.] *a combining form meaning:* 1. having or involving three [*triangular*] 2. triply, in three ways [*trilingual*] 3. three times, into three [*trisect*] 4. every third [*triannual*] 5. *Chem.* having three atoms, groups, or equivalents of (the thing specified) [*tribasic*]
tri·a·ble (trī′ə b'l) *adj.* 1. that can be tried or tested 2. subject to trial in a law court —**tri′a·ble·ness** *n.*
tri·ac·e·tate (trī as′ə tāt′) *n.* a compound containing three acetate radicals in the molecule
tri·ad (trī′ad) *n.* [< LL. < Gr. < *treis*, three] 1. a group of three persons, things, etc. 2. a musical chord of three tones, esp. one consisting of a root tone and its third and fifth: a triad with a major third and perfect fifth is called a *major triad*; a triad with a minor third and perfect fifth is called a *minor triad* 3. a person with triple grouping, common in Celtic literature —**tri·ad′ic** *adj.*
tri·age (trē äzh′) *n.* [Fr. < *trier*, to sift] a system of deciding in what order battlefield casualties will receive medical treatment, according to urgency, chance of survival, etc.
tri·al (trī′əl, trīl) *n.* [Anglo-Fr. < *trier*, to try] 1. *a)* a trying, testing, etc.; test *b)* a testing of qualifications, progress, etc.; probation *c)* an experiment 2. *a)* a being tried by suffering, temptation, etc. *b)* suffering, hardship, trouble, etc., or the cause of this 3. a formal examination of the facts of a case by a court of law to decide the validity of a charge or claim 4. an attempt; effort —*adj.* 1. of a trial 2. of or for trying, testing, etc. —**on trial** in the process of being tried
trial and error a trying or testing over and over again until the right result is found —**tri′al-and-er′ror** *adj.*
trial balance a statement of the debit and credit balances of all open accounts in a double-entry bookkeeping ledger to test their equality
trial balloon an action, statement, etc. made to test public opinion on an issue
trial run an initial test or rehearsal of something new or untried, as a vehicle, a play, etc., to gauge its effectiveness
tri·an·gle (trī′aŋ′g'l) *n.* [< MFr. < L.: see TRI- & ANGLE¹] 1. a plane figure having three angles and three sides 2. any three-sided or three-cornered figure, area, etc. 3. a situation involving three persons 4. a musical instrument consisting of a steel rod bent in a triangle: it makes a high-pitched, tinkling sound when struck —**tri·an′gu·lar** (-aŋ′gyə lər) *adj.* —**tri·an′gu·lar′i·ty** (-lar′ə tē) *n.*

TRIANGLES

tri·an·gu·late (trī aŋ′gyə lāt′; *for adj. usually* -lit) *vt.* **-lat′ed, -lat′ing** 1. to divide into triangles 2. to survey (a region) by triangulation 3. to make triangular 4. to measure by trigonometry —*adj.* of, like, or marked with triangles
tri·an·gu·la·tion (trī aŋ′gyə lā′shən) *n.* a triangulating or being triangulated; specif., *Surveying* the determining of distance between points on the earth's surface by calculations based on the division of an area into connected triangles and the measurement of their angles
tri·an·te·lope (trī an′tə lōp) *n.* [humorous var. of TARANTULA] a large, harmless Australian spider
Tri·as·sic (trī as′ik) *adj.* [< ModL. < LL. *trias*, TRIAD (because divisible into three groups) + -IC] designating or of the first period of the Mesozoic Era —**the Triassic** the Triassic Period or its rocks: see GEOLOGY, chart
tri·a·tom·ic (trī′ə tom′ik) *adj.* designating *a)* a molecule having three atoms *b)* a molecule containing three replaceable atoms or groups
trib·al·ism (trī′b'l iz'm) *n.* tribal organization, culture, loyalty, etc. —**trib′al·ist** *n., adj.* **trib′al·is′tic** *adj.*
tribe (trīb) *n.* [L. *tribus*, any of the divisions (orig. three) of the ancient Romans] 1. a group of persons, families, or clans believed to have a common ancestor: many tribes form a close community under a leader or chief 2. any group of people with the same occupation, ideas, etc. 3. a subdivision of a subfamily of plants or animals 4. loosely, any group of plants or animals classified together 5.

[Colloq.] *a)* a family *b)* [*pl.*] large numbers —**trib′al** *adj.* —**trib′al·ly** *adv.*
tribes·man (trībz′mən) *n., pl.* **-men** a member of a tribe
tri·brach (trī′brak, trib′rak) *n.* [< L. < Gr. < TRI- + *brachus*, short] a metrical foot of three short syllables
trib·u·la·tion (trib′yə lā′shən) *n.* [< OFr. < LL. < *tribulare*, to afflict < L., to press < *tribulum*, threshing sledge] 1. great misery or distress, as from oppression 2. the cause of this; affliction; trial
tri·bu·nal (trī byōō′n'l, tri-) *n.* [L.: see TRIBUNE¹] 1. the judge's bench 2. a court of justice 3. any seat of judgment
tri·bune¹ (trib′yōōn) *n.* [< L. *tribunus* < *tribus*, tribe] 1. in ancient Rome, *a)* any of several magistrates whose duty it was to protect the rights and interests of the plebeians *b)* any of six officers rotating command over a legion 2. a champion of the people —**trib′une·ship′** *n.*
tri·bune² (trib′yōōn) *n.* [Fr. < It. < L.: see TRIBUNAL, sense 1] a raised platform or dais for speakers
trib·u·tar·y (trib′yoo tar ē) *adj.* 1. paying tribute 2. under another's control; subject [a *tributary* nation] 3. owed or paid as tribute 4. *a)* making additions; contributory *b)* flowing into a larger one [a *tributary* stream] —*n., pl.* **-tar·ies** 1. a tributary nation or ruler 2. a tributary stream or river
trib·ute (trib′yōōt) *n.* [< MFr. < L. pp. of *tribuere*, to allot, pay < *tribus*, tribe] 1. money that one nation is forced to pay to another, more powerful nation 2. any forced payment 3. the obligation to pay tribute 4. something given, done, or said to show gratitude, honour, or praise
trice (trīs) *vt.* **triced, tric′ing** [MDu. *trisen*, to pull < *trise*, windlass] to haul up and secure (a sail, etc.): usually with *up* —*n.* [< *at a trice*, with one pull] a very short time; instant: now only in **in a trice**
tri·cen·ten·ni·al (trī′sen ten′ē əl) *adj.* happening once in, or lasting for, 300 years —*n.* a 300th anniversary
tri·ceps (trī′seps) *n., pl.* **-ceps·es, -ceps** [ModL. < L. < *tri-*, three + *caput*, a head] a muscle having three points of origin, esp. the muscle at the back of the upper arm that extends the forearm
tri·chi·na (tri kī′nə) *n., pl.* **-nae** (-nē) [ModL. < Gr. *trichinos*, hairy < *thrix*, hair] a very small worm whose larvae infest the intestines and muscles of man, pigs, etc., causing trichinosis —**trich·i′nal** *adj.*
trich·i·no·sis (trik′ə nō′sis) *n.* a trichinal disease marked by fever, diarrhoea, muscular pains, etc. and usually acquired by eating undercooked infested pork
tri·chlo·ride (trī klôr′īd) *n.* a chloride having three chlorine atoms to the molecule
tri·chot·o·my (trī kot′ə mē) *n.* [< Gr. *tricha*, threefold + -TOMY] division into three parts —**tri·chot′o·mize** *vt.* —**tri·chot′o·mous** *adj.*
tri·chro·mat·ic (trī′krō mat′ik) *adj.* [TRI- + CHROMATIC] 1. of, having, or using three colours 2. designating normal vision, in which three primary colours are distinguished —**trī·chro′matism** (-krō′mə tiz'm) *n.*
trick (trik) *n.* [ONormFr. *trique* < OFr. *trichier*, to cheat] 1. something that is done to fool, cheat, outwit, etc.; ruse; stratagem 2. *a)* a piece of playful mischief; prank *b)* a deception or illusion [the light played a *trick* on his eyes] 3. a freakish, foolish, or mean act 4. a clever or skilful act intended to amuse; specif., *a)* an act of jugglery, sleight of hand, etc. *b)* a feat done by a trained animal 5. the art or knack of doing a thing easily, skilfully, quickly, etc. 6. a personal mannerism 7. a turn at the helm of a ship 8. *Card Games* the cards played and won in a single round —*vt.* to deceive, cheat, outwit, fool, etc. —*adj.* 1. of, for, or using tricks [*trick* photography] 2. that tricks —**do the trick** to bring about the desired result —**how's tricks?** [Slang] how are things going? how are you? —**trick out** (or **up**) to dress up; adorn
trick cyclist 1. a cyclist who does tricks, as in a circus 2. [Slang] a psychiatrist
trick·er·y (-ər ē) *n., pl.* **-er·ies** the use of tricks to cheat, outwit, etc.; deception; stratagem
trick·le (trik′'l) *vi.* **-led, -ling** [prob. < freq. of ME. *striken*, to strike] 1. to flow slowly in a thin stream or fall in drops 2. to move little by little [the crowd *trickled* away] —*vt.* to cause to trickle —*n.* 1. a trickling 2. a thin flow or drip
trick·ster (trik′stər) *n.* a person who tricks; cheat
trick·sy (-sē) *adj.* **-si·er, -si·est** 1. mischievous; prankish 2. *same as* TRICKY —**trick′si·ness** *n.*
trick·y (trik′ē) *adj.* **trick′i·er, trick′i·est** 1. given to or full of trickery 2. intricate; difficult 3. needing special skill or care —**trick′i·ly** *adv.* —**trick′i·ness** *n.*
tri·clin·ic (trī klin′ik) *adj.* [< TRI- + Gr. *klinein*, to incline + -IC] designating a crystalline form that has three unequal axes intersecting at oblique angles
tri·clin·i·um (trī klin′ē əm, tri-) *n.* [L. < Gr. < *tri*, TRI- + *klinē*, a couch] in ancient Roman civilization, 1. a couch extending round three sides of a dining table, for reclining at meals 2. a dining room
tri·col·our (trī′kə lər, trī′kul′ər) *n.* a flag consisting of

three stripes, each of a different colour, esp. the flag of France —*adj.* having three colours

tri·corn, tri·corne (-kôrn') *adj.* [< Fr. < L. < *tri-*, three + *cornu*, horn] having three horns or corners —*n.* a tricorn hat

tri·cot (trē'kō) *n.* [Fr. < *tricoter*, to knit, ult. < MDu.] 1. a thin fabric that is knitted or woven to look knitted 2. a type of ribbed cloth for dresses

tri·cus·pid (trī kus'pid) *adj.* [< L.: see TRI- & CUSP] 1. having three cusps, or points [a *tricuspid* tooth]: also **tri·cus'pi·date** (-pə dāt') 2. designating or of a valve with three flaps, between the right auricle and right ventricle of the heart —*n.* a tricuspid tooth or valve

tri·cy·cle (trī'si k'l) *n.* [Fr.] a light, three-wheeled vehicle worked by pedals, esp. one for children —**tri'cy·clist** *n.*

tri·dent (trīd''nt) *n.* [< L. < *tri-*, three + *dens* (gen. *dentis*), a tooth] a three-pronged spear

tri·den·tate (trī den'tāt) *adj.* having three teeth, prongs, or points

Tri·den·tine (trī den'tin, -tīn, -tēn) *adj.* [< ML. < *Tridentum*, Trent] 1. of Trent, Italy 2. of the Council of Trent, held intermittently at Trent, 1545-63, or its decrees

tried (trīd) *pt. & pp. of* TRY —*adj.* 1. tested; proved 2. trustworthy; faithful 3. having endured trials and troubles

tri·en·ni·al (trī en'ē əl) *adj.* [< L. < *tri-*, three + *annus*, a year] 1. happening every three years 2. lasting three years —*n.* a triennial event —**tri·en'ni·al·ly** *adv.*

tri·en·ni·um (-əm) *n., pl.* **-ni·ums, -ni·a** (-ə) [L., see prec.] a period of three years

tri·er (trī'ər) *n.* a person or thing that tries

tri·fa·cial (trī fā'shəl) *adj., n. same as* TRIGEMINAL

tri·fid (trī'fid) *adj.* [< L. < *tri-*, three + base of *findere*, to divide] divided into three lobes by deep clefts, as some leaves

tri·fle (trī'f'l) *n.* [< OFr. dim. of *truffe*, deception] 1. something of little value or importance 2. a small amount; bit 3. a small sum of money 4. a cold dessert of sponge cake spread with fruit or jam, soaked in sherry and covered with custard and cream —*vi.* -**fled, -fling** 1. to talk or act in a joking way; deal lightly [not a person to *trifle* with] 2. to play or toy (*with* something) —*vt.* to spend idly; waste [*trifling* time away] —**tri'fler** *n.*

tri·fling (-fliŋ) *adj.* 1. frivolous; fickle 2. trivial

tri·fo·cal (trī fō'k'l, trī'fō'-) *adj.* having three focal lengths —*n.* 1. a lens with one part ground for close focus, one for intermediate focus, and one for distant focus 2. [*pl.*] a pair of glasses with such lenses

tri·fo·ri·um (trī fôr'ē əm) *n., pl.* -**ri·a** (-ə) [ML. < L. *tri*, TRI- + *foris*, door] a gallery or arcade in the wall above the arches of the nave, choir, or transept of a church

tri·fur·cate (trī fur'kit, -kāt) *adj.* [< L. < *tri*, TRI- + *furca*, a fork + -ATE¹] having three forks or branches

trig¹ (trig) *adj.* [< ON. *tryggr*, true] 1. trim; neat 2. in good condition —*vt.* **trigged, trig'ging** [Chiefly Dial.] to make trig (often with *out, up*)

trig² (trig) *n. shortened form of* TRIGONOMETRY

trig. 1. trigonometric(al) 2. trigonometry

tri·gem·i·nal (trī jem'ə n'l) *adj.* [< ModL. < L. < *tri-*, three + *geminus*, twin] designating or of either of a pair of cranial nerves, each dividing into three branches supplying the head and face —*n.* a trigeminal nerve

trig·ger (trig'ər) *n.* [< Du. < *trekken*, to pull] a lever, etc. which when pulled or pressed releases a catch, spring, etc.; esp., the small lever pressed back by the finger in firing a gun —*vt.* 1. to fire or set into action with a trigger 2. to set off (an action) (often with *off*) [the fight *triggered* off a riot] —**quick on the trigger** [Colloq.] 1. quick to fire a gun 2. quick to act, retort, etc.; alert

trig·ger·fish (-fish') *n., pl.* -**fish', -fish'es:** see FISH [because depression of the second spine of the fin causes the first to snap down] a brightly coloured tropical fish with a prominent first dorsal fin

trig·ger-hap·py (-hap'ē) *adj.* [Colloq.] quick to resort to force, make war, etc.

tri·glyc·er·ide (trī glis'ər īd') *n.* [TRI- + GLYCERIDE] any of a group of esters of fatty acids and glycerol, found in the blood and thought to be a factor in atherosclerosis

tri·glyph (trī'glif) *n.* [< L. < Gr. < *tri*, TRI- + *glyphē*, carving] a triple-grooved rectangle in the frieze of a Doric column, repeated at equal intervals

trig·o·nom·e·try (trig'ə nom'ə trē) *n.* [< ModL. < Gr. *trigōnon*, triangle + *-metria*, measurement] the branch of mathematics dealing with the ratios between the sides of a right-angled triangle with reference to either acute angle (*trigonometric functions*), the relations between these ratios, and use of these facts in finding the unknown sides or angles of any triangle —**trig·o·no·met·ric** (-nə met'rik), **trig'o·no·met'ri·cal** *adj.* —**trig'o·no·met'ri·cal·ly** *adv.*

tri·graph (trī'graf', -gräf') *n.* [TRI- + -GRAPH] three letters representing one sound (Ex.: *eau* in *bureau*)

tri·he·dral (trī hē'drəl) *adj.* [TRI- + -HEDRAL] having three sides or faces [a *trihedral* angle] —*n.* a figure formed by three lines, each in a different plane, that intersect at a point

tri·he·dron (-drən) *n.* [TRI- + HEDRON] a figure determined by the intersection of three planes

trike (trīk) *n.* [Colloq.] *same as* TRICYCLE

tri·lat·er·al (trī lat'ər əl) *adj.* three-sided

tril·by (tril'bē) *n.* [orig. worn in a stage version of the novel *Trilby*, by George Du Maurier (1834-96)] a man's soft, felt hat with an indented crown

tri·lin·gual (-liŋ'gwəl) *adj.* in or using three languages

tri·lit·er·al (-lit'ər əl) *adj.* [< TRI- + L. *litera*, letter + -AL] consisting of three letters, esp. three consonants

tri·lith (trī'lith) *n.* [< Gr. *tri*, TRI- + *lithos*, a stone] an ancient monument of two upright stones and a third resting across the top, as at Stonehenge: also **tri'lith·on** —**tri·lith'ic** *adj.*

trill (tril) *n.* [< It. < *trillare*, of echoic origin] 1. a rapid alternation of a tone with one just above it 2. a bird's warble 3. *a*) a rapid vibration of the tongue or uvula, as in pronouncing *r* in some languages *b*) an *r*, etc. so pronounced —*vt., vi.* to sound with a trill —**trill'er** *n.*

tril·lion (tril'yən) *n.* [Fr. < *tri-*, TRI- + (*mi*)*llion*] 1. in Britain and Germany, the number represented by 1 followed by 18 zeros 2. in the U.S. and France, the number represented by 1 followed by 12 zeros —*adj.* amounting to one trillion —**tril'lionth** *adj., n.*

tril·li·um (tril'ē əm) *n.* [ModL., genus name < L. *tri-*, three] a N American plant of the lily family with an erect stem bearing a whorl of three leaves and a single, three-petalled flower

tri·lo·bate (trī lō'bāt) *adj.* having three lobes, as some leaves: also **tri·lo'bat·ed, tri'·lobed'** (-lōbd')

tri·lo·bite (trī'lə bīt') *n.* [< ModL.: see TRI-, LOBE, & -ITE] an extinct sea arthropod with the body divided by two furrows into three parts: a common fossil in Paleozoic rocks —**tri'·lo·bit'ic** (-bit'ik) *adj.*

tri·loc·u·lar (trī lok'yoo lər) *adj.* [< TRI- + L. *loculus*, small place] having three cells

tril·o·gy (tril'ə jē) *n., pl.* -**gies** [Gr. *trilogia*: see TRI- & -LOGY] a set of three plays, novels, etc. which form a related group, although each is a complete work

TRILLIUM

trim (trim) *vt.* **trimmed, trim'ming** [OE. *trymman*, to make firm < *trum*, strong] 1. to put in proper order; make neat or tidy, esp. by clipping, etc. [to *trim* hair] 2. to clip, lop, cut, etc. [to *trim* dead branches off a tree] 3. to cut (something) down to the required size or shape 4. to decorate with ornaments, colourful materials, etc. [to *trim* a hat] 5. *a*) to balance (a ship) by shifting cargo, etc. *b*) to put (sails, etc.) in order for sailing 6. to balance (an aircraft in flight) by adjusting stabilizers, etc. 7. [Colloq.] *a*) to scold *b*) to beat, thrash, etc. *c*) to defeat *d*) to cheat —*vi.* 1. *a*) to take a middle position between opposing sides *b*) to change one's opinions, policy, etc. in a way that is expedient 2. to keep a ship, etc. in balance —*n.* 1. condition or order [in proper *trim*] 2. good condition or order [keep in *trim*] 3. a trimming by clipping, cutting, etc. 4. *a*) decorative moulding or borders, esp. around windows and doors *b*) the interior furnishings or ornamental metalwork of a motor car *c*) any ornamental trimming 5. *a*) the condition of being ready to sail: said of a vessel *b*) the position of a vessel in relation to the horizontal *c*) correct position in the water: a ship is **in trim** if stable and floating on an even keel, **out of trim** if not *d*) the adjustment of sails, etc. in a vessel 6. something trimmed off —*adj.* **trim'mer, trim'mest** 1. orderly; neat 2. well-proportioned; smartly designed 3. in good condition —*adv.* in a trim way —**trim one's sails** to adjust one's opinions, actions, etc. to meet changing conditions —**trim'ly** *adv.* —**trim'ness** *n.*

tri·ma·ran (trī'mə ran') *n.* [TRI- + (CATA)MARAN] a boat resembling a catamaran, but with three parallel hulls

trim·er·ous (trim'ər əs) *adj.* [TRI- + -MEROUS] 1. having parts in sets of three 2. having three parts

tri·mes·ter (trī mes'tər, trī'mes-) *n.* [Fr. < L. < *tri-*, three + *mensis*, month] 1. a three-month period 2. [U.S.] in some colleges and universities, any of three periods into which the academic year is divided

trim·e·ter (trim'ə tər) *n.* [< L. < Gr.: see TRI- & METRE] 1. a line of verse containing three metrical feet 2. verse consisting of trimeters —*adj.* having three metrical feet

trim·mer (trim'ər) *n.* 1. a person, machine, etc. that times 2. a transverse beam that receives the ends of headers, as round a stair well 3. a person who alters his opinions on the grounds of expediency

trim·ming (trim'iŋ) *n.* 1. the action of one that trims 2. that which trims; specif., *a*) decoration *b*) [*pl.*] vegetables, sauces, etc. served as the usual accompaniments of a main dish 3. [*pl.*] parts trimmed off

tri·month·ly (trī munth'lē) *adj.* happening or appearing every three months

tri·mor·phism (trī môr'fiz'm) *n.* [< Gr. *trimorphos*] **1.** existence in three different forms, as certain flowers, insects, etc. **2.** crystallizing in any of three different forms

tri·nal (trī'n'l) *adj.* [< LL. < L. *trinus*, triple < *tres*, three] threefold; triple: also **tri'na·ry** (-nər ē), **trine** (trīn)

Trin·i·tar·i·an (trin'ə ter'ē ən) *adj.* **1.** of, about, or believing in the Trinity **2.** [t-] of a trinity —*n.* one who believes in the Trinity —**Trin'i·tar'i·an·ism** *n.*

tri·ni·tro·tol·u·ene (trī nī'trō tol'yoo wēn') *n.* [TRI- + NITRO- + TOLUENE] a high explosive derived from toluene and used for blasting, in artillery shells, etc.: also **tri·ni'-tro·tol'u·ol'** (-wal'): abbrev. **TNT**

trin·i·ty (trin'ə tē) *n., pl.* **-ties** [< OFr. < L. < *trinus*, triple] **1.** a unit formed of three persons or things **2.** [T-] *Christian Theol.* the union of the three divine persons (Father, Son, and Holy Spirit, or Holy Ghost) in one Godhead

Trinity Brethren the members of Trinity House, an association responsible for the licensing of pilots, and the upkeep and inspection of lighthouses, buoys, etc. along the British coast

Trinity Sunday the Sunday after Whitsunday, dedicated to the Trinity

Trinity term the summer term at certain universities

trin·ket (triŋ'kit) *n.* [ONormFr. *trenquet*] **1.** a small piece of cheap jewellery, etc. **2.** a trifle or toy

tri·no·mi·al (trī nō'mē əl) *adj.* [TRI- + (BI)NOMIAL] composed of three terms —*n.* **1.** a mathematical expression consisting of three terms connected by plus or minus signs **2.** a three-word scientific name of a plant or animal, noting the genus, species, and subspecies

tri·o (trē'ō) *n., pl.* **tri'os** [Fr. < It. < *tri-*, TRI- (after *duo*, DUO)] **1.** a group of three **2.** *Music a)* a composition for three voices or instruments *b)* the three performers of such a composition *c)* the middle section of a minuet, scherzo, etc., orig. for three parts

tri·ode (trī'ōd) *n.* [TRI- + (ELECTR)ODE] a thermionic valve containing three electrodes (an anode, cathode, and control grid)

tri·oe·cious (trī ē'shəs) *adj.* [< TRI-+ LL. *oecus*, a room] *Bot.* having male, female and bisexual flowers on separate plants

tri·o·let (trī'ə lit, trē'ə let') *n.* [Fr., a little trio] a poem of eight lines and two rhymes, the first line being repeated as the fourth and seventh, and the second as the eighth (*a b a a a b a b*)

tri·ox·ide (trī ok'sīd) *n.* an oxide having three oxygen atoms to the molecule

trip (trip) *vi.* **tripped, trip'ping** [OFr. *treper* < Gmc.] **1.** to walk, run, or dance with light, rapid steps; skip; caper **2.** to stumble, esp. by catching the foot **3.** to make a mistake **4.** to go past an escapement catch: said of an escape wheel tooth —*vt.* **1.** to make stumble **2.** to cause to make a mistake **3.** to catch in a lie, error, etc. (often with *up*) **4.** *a)* to release (a spring, wheel, etc.), as by moving a catch *b)* to start or operate by such action —*n.* **1.** a light, quick tread **2.** a going to or from a place, or to a place and returning; journey, esp. for pleasure **3.** *a)* a stumble *b)* a manoeuvre to cause this **4.** a mistake **5.** *a)* a contrivance, as a pawl, to trip a part *b)* its action **6.** [Slang] the hallucinations, sensations, etc. produced by a psychedelic drug, esp. LSD —**trip the light fantastic** to dance

tri·par·tite (trī pär'tīt) *adj.* [< L. < *tri-*, three + *partitus*, PARTITE] **1.** divided into three parts **2.** having three corresponding parts or copies **3.** made or existing between three parties, as an agreement —**tri·par'tite·ly** *adv.*

tripe (trīp) *n.* [< MFr. < ?] **1.** part of the stomach of an ox, etc., used as food **2.** [Colloq.] nonsense; rubbish

trip·ham·mer (trip'ham'ər) *n.* a heavy, power-driven hammer with a tripping device making it alternately rise and fall: also **trip hammer**

tri·phib·i·ous (trī fib'ē əs) *adj.* [TRI- + (AM)PHIBIOUS] that can operate on land, at sea, or in the air

triph·thong (trif'thoŋ, trip'-) *n.* [TRI- + (DI)PTHONG] **1.** one syllable composed of three continuous vowel sounds (Ex.: *fire*) **2.** *loose term for* TRIGRAPH

TRIPHAMMER

tri·pin·nate (trī pin'it, -āt) *adj.* *Bot.* having pinnate leaves that are bipinnately arranged

tri·plane (trī'plān') *n.* an early type of aeroplane with three sets of wings one above the other

tri·ple (trip''l) *adj.* [Fr. < L. *triplus:* see the *v.*] **1.** consisting of three; threefold **2.** done, said, etc. three times **3.** three times as much, as many, etc. **4.** *Music* having three beats to the measure [*triple* time] —*n.* a triple amount, number, etc. —*vt.* **tri'pled, tri'pling** [< ML. < L. *triplus*, threefold < *tri-*, TRI- + *-plus*, as in *duplus*, double]

to make three times as much or as many —*vi.* to be tripled —**tri'ply** *adv.*

triple jump an athletic event in which the competitor has to perform a hop, a step, and a jump in a continuous movement

triple point *Chem.* the temperature and pressure at which the three phases of a substance are in equilibrium

tri·ple-space (-spās') *vt., vi.* **-spaced', -spac'ing** to type (copy) so as to leave two full spaces between lines

trip·let (trip'lit) *n.* [TRIPL(E) + -ET] **1.** a group of three, usually of one kind; specif., *a)* a group of three lines of poetry, usually rhyming *b)* a group of three musical notes to be performed in the time of two of the same value **2.** any of three offspring born at a single birth

Tri·plex (trī'pleks) *a trademark for* a laminated safety glass

trip·li·cate (trip'lə kit; *for v.* -kāt') *adj.* [< L. pp. of *triplicare*, to treble < *triplex*, threefold] **1.** threefold **2.** designating the third of identical copies —*n.* any of three identical copies —*vt.* **-cat'ed, -cat'ing** to make three identical copies of —**in triplicate** in three identical copies —**trip'li·ca'tion** *n.*

trip·loid (trip'loid) *adj.* [< L. *triplus*, TRIPLE + -OID] *Biol.* having three times the haploid number of chromosomes

tri·pod (trī'pod) *n.* [< L. < Gr. < *tri-*, three + *pous*, a foot] **1.** a three-legged cauldron, stool, etc. **2.** a three-legged support for a camera, etc. —**tri'pod·al** *adj.*

tri·pos (trī'pos) *n.* [< L. *tripus*, tripod: referring to the three-legged stool on which a graduate formerly sat at the graduation ceremony] the final examinations in various subjects taken for an honours degree at Cambridge University

trip·per (trip'ər) *n.* **1.** one that trips; specif., a device for tripping or releasing a catch, pawl, etc. **2.** a tourist

trip·ping (-iŋ) *adj.* moving lightly and quickly —**trip'ping·ly** *adv.*

trip·tych (trip'tik) *n.* [< Gr. *triptychos*, threefold < *tri-*, three + *ptychē*, a fold] **1.** an ancient writing tablet of three leaves hinged together **2.** a set of three panels with pictures, carvings, etc., often hinged and used as an altarpiece

tri·reme (trī'rēm) *n.* [< L. < *tri-*, three + *remus*, an oar] an ancient Greek or Roman galley, usually a warship, with three banks of oars on each side

tri·sect (trī sekt') *vt.* [< TRI- + L. pp. of *secare*, to cut] **1.** to cut into three parts **2.** *Geom.* to divide into three equal parts —**tri·sec'tion** *n.* —**tri·sec'tor** *n.*

tri·shaw (trī'shô') *n.* [< TRI- + (JINRIKI)SHA] *same as* PEDICAB

†triste (trēst) *adj.* [Fr.] sad

tri·syl·la·ble (trī sil'ə b'l, trī'sil'-) *n.* a word of three syllables —**tri·syl·lab·ic** (trī'si lab'ik) *adj.*

trite (trīt) *adj.* **trit'er, trit'est** [L. *tritus*, pp. of *terere*, to wear out] worn out by constant use; no longer fresh, original, etc. —**trite'ly** *adv.* —**trite'ness** *n.*

tri·the·ism (trī'thē'iz'm) *n.* [< TRI- + Gr. *theos*, god] **1.** belief in three gods **2.** belief that the Father, Son and Holy Ghost are three distinct gods

trit·i·um (trit'ē əm, trish'-) *n.* [ModL. < Gr. *tritos*, third] a radioactive isotope of hydrogen with an atomic weight of 3: it decays by beta-particle emission and is used in thermonuclear bombs, as a radioactive tracer, etc.

Tri·ton (trīt''n) **1.** *Gr. Myth.* a sea god with the head and upper body of a man and the tail of a fish **2.** the larger of Neptune's two moons —*n.* [t-] **1.** a sea snail with a long, spiral shell **2.** the shell

trit·u·rate (trich'ə rāt', trit'yoo rāt') *vt.* **-rat'ed, -rat'ing** [< LL. pp. of *triturare*, to grind < L. < *tritus:* see TRITE] to rub, crush, or grind into very fine particles; pulverize —*n.* something triturated —**trit'u·ra·ble** (-ər ə b'l) *adj.* —**trit'-u·ra'tion** *n.* —**trit'u·ra'tor** *n.*

tri·umph (trī'əmf) *n.* [< OFr. < L. *triumphus*, akin to Gr. *thriambos*, hymn to Bacchus] **1.** in ancient Rome, procession celebrating a victorious general's return **2.** a victory; success **3.** exultation or joy over a victory, etc. —*vi.* **1.** to be victorious, successful, etc. **2.** to rejoice or exult over victory, etc. —**tri·um'phal** (-um'f'l) *adj.*

tri·um·phant (trī um'fənt) *adj.* **1.** victorious; successful **2.** exulting in victory, etc. —**tri·um'phant·ly** *adv.*

tri·um·vir (trī um'vər) *n., pl.* **-virs, -vi·ri'** (-vi rī') [L. < *trium virum*, of three men] in ancient Rome, any of three administrators sharing authority equally —**tri·um'vi·ral** *adj.*

tri·um·vi·rate (-it) *n.* **1.** the office or term of a triumvir **2.** government by three men **3.** any association of three in authority **4.** any group of three

tri·une (trī'yoon) *adj.* [< TRI- + L. *unus*, one] being three in one [a *triune* God] —**tri·u'ni·ty** *n.*

tri·va·lent (trī vā'lənt) *adj.* [TRI- + -VALENT] **1.** having a valence of three **2.** having three valences —**tri·va'lence, tri·va'len·cy** *n.*

triv·et (triv'it) *n.* [OE. *trefet* < L. *tripes*, tripod] **1.** a three-legged stand for holding pots, kettles, etc. over or near a fire **2.** [U.S.] a short-legged plate for hot dishes to rest on —**as right as a trivet** in perfect condition: orig. with reference to the stability of a trivet

triv·i·a (triv′ē ə) *n.pl.* [*often with sing. v.*] [ModL. < ff.] unimportant matters; trivialities

triv·i·al (triv′ē əl, triv′yəl) *adj.* [L. *trivialis*, of the crossroads, commonplace < *tri-*, three + *via*, a road] of little value or importance; trifling —**triv′i·al·ly** *adv.*

triv·i·al·i·ty (triv′ē al′ə tē) *n.* 1. a being trivial 2. *pl.* -**ties** a trivial thing, idea, etc.; trifle

triv·i·al·ize (triv′ē ə līz′) *vt., vi.* -**ized′, -iz′ing** to treat as or make seem trivial —**triv′i·al·i·za′tion** *n.*

triv·i·um (triv′ē əm) *n., pl.* -**i·a** (-ə) [ML. < L.: see TRIVIAL] in the Middle Ages the arts of grammar, logic and rhetoric

-trix (triks) *pl.* -**trix·es, -tri·ces′** (tri sēz′, trī′sēz) [L.] an ending of some feminine nouns of agent

tro·car (trō′kär) *n.* [< Fr. < *trois*, three + *carre*, a side] a surgical instrument used to drain off fluid, as in dropsy

tro·chal (trō′k′l) *adj.* [< Gr. *trochos*, a wheel] *Zool.* resembling a wheel

tro·che (trō′kē) *n.* [< Fr. < LL. *trochiscus*, a pill < Gr. < *trochos*, a wheel] a small, usually round, medicinal lozenge

tro·chee (trō′kē) *n.* [< L. < Gr. *trochaios*, running < *trechein*, to run] a metrical foot of two syllables, the first accented and the other unaccented, as in English verse (Ex.: "Pĕtĕr Pīpĕr pícked ă pĕppĕr") —**tro·cha′ic** (-kā′ik) *adj.*

troch·le·a (trok′lē ə) *n., pl.* -**le·ae′** (-lē ē′) [< L., a pulley-block] *Anat.* a pulley-shaped part or structure

trod (trod) *pt. & alt. pp. of* TREAD

trod·den (-′n) *alt. pp. of* TREAD

trode (trōd) *archaic pt. of* TREAD

trog·lo·dyte (trog′lə dīt′) *n.* [< L. < Gr. < *trōglē*, a cave + *dyein*, to enter] 1. any of the prehistoric people who lived in caves 2. a person who lives alone in seclusion 3. an anthropoid ape —**trog′lo·dyt′ic** (-dit′ik), **trog′lo·dyt′i·cal** *adj.*

tro·gon (trō′gon) *n.* [ModL. < Gr. prp. of *trōgein*, to gnaw] any of various bright-coloured tropical birds

troi·ka (troi′kə) *n.* [Russ. < *troe*, three] 1. *a)* a Russian vehicle drawn by three horses abreast *b)* the horses 2. any group of three; esp., an association of three in authority

Tro·jan (trō′jən) *adj.* of ancient Troy, its people, etc. —*n.* 1. a native or inhabitant of ancient Troy 2. a strong, hard-working, determined person

Trojan horse [after the hollow, wooden horse filled with Greek soldiers and left at the gates of Troy: when the Trojans brought it into the city, the soldiers crept out and opened the gates to the Greek army] a person, device, etc. intended as a trap to deceive or undermine an enemy

troll[1] (trōl) *vt., vi.* [ME. *trollen*, to roll, wander] 1. to roll; revolve 2. *a)* to sing the parts of (a round, etc.) in succession *b)* to sing in a strong or full voice 3. *a)* to fish (*for* or *in*) with a moving line, esp. with a revolving bait trailed from a moving boat *b)* to move (bait etc.) thus —*n.* 1. a trolling 2. bait, or bait and line, used in trolling —**troll′-er** *n.*

troll[2] (trōl) *n.* [ON.] in Scandinavian folklore, any of certain supernatural beings, giants or dwarfs, living underground or in caves

trol·ley (trol′ē) *n., pl.* -**leys** [< TROLL[1]] 1. a wheeled carriage, basket, etc. that runs suspended from an overhead track 2. a device, as a grooved wheel at the end of a pole, to carry electric current from an overhead wire to the motor of an electric tram, etc. 3. a small table on wheels or castors used for conveying food and drink 4. a low, wheeled stand for transporting luggage, etc. 5. a low cart, as for carring groceries in a supermarket

trolley bus an electric bus that gets its power from overhead wires by means of trolleys but does not run on tracks

trolley car [U.S.] an electric tram that gets its power from an overhead wire by means of a trolley

trol·lop (trol′əp) *n.* [prob. < G. *Trolle*, a wench] a sexually promiscuous woman; specif., a prostitute

trol·ly (trol′ē) *n., pl.* -**lies,** *vt., vi.* -**lied, -ly·ing** *var. of* TROLLEY

trom·bone (trom bōn′, trom′bōn) *n.* [It. < *tromba*, a trumpet < OHG. *trumba*] a large brass instrument with a bell mouth and a long tube bent parallel to itself twice and having either a section that slides in or out (**slide trombone**) or valves (**valve trombone**) —**trom·bon′-ist** *n.*

trom·mel (trom′′l) *n.* [G., a drum] a sieve, usually revolving and cylindrical, used in screening ore, coal, etc.

tro·mom·e·ter (trō mom′ē tər) *n.* [< Gr. *tromos*, trembling + -METER] an instrument for recording minor earth tremors

‡trompe l'oeil (trōn p lĕ′y′) [Fr., lit., trick of the eye] 1. a painting, etc.

TROMBONE

so realistic that it gives the illusion of being the actual thing depicted 2. any such illusion or effect

-tron (tron) [Gr. *-tron*, suffix of instrument] a combining form meaning instrument

troop (trōop) *n.* [< Fr. < OFr. < ML. *troppus*, a flock] 1. a group of persons or animals; band, herd, etc. 2. loosely, a great number; lot 3. [*pl.*] *a)* a body of soldiers *b)* soldiers [45 *troops*] 4. a subdivision of a cavalry regiment, corresponding to an infantry company 5. a unit of Boy Scouts under an adult leader —*vi.* 1. to gather or go as in a group 2. to walk, go, etc. —*vt.* to form into troops —**trooping the colour** a ceremony held at the public mounting of garrison guards when colours are transferred and carried along the ranks

troop·er (trōo′pər) *n.* [prec. + -ER] 1. a cavalryman 2. a cavalry horse 3. a troopship 4. *a)* [U.S. & formerly Aust.] a mounted policeman *b)* [U.S. Colloq.] a member of a state police force

troop·ship (trōop′ship′) *n.* a ship for carrying troops

trope (trōp) *n.* [< L. < Gr. *tropos*, a turning < *trepein*, to turn] 1. a figure of speech 2. the use of figures of speech

tro·phy (trō′fē) *n., pl.* -**phies** [< MFr. < L. < Gr. *tropaion*, token of an enemy's defeat, ult. < *trepein*, to turn] 1. something taken from a defeated enemy and kept as a memorial of victory 2. an animal skin, head, etc. displayed to show one's hunting prowess 3. a prize, usually a silver cup, awarded in a sports contest, etc. 4. any memento

-tro·phy (trə fē) [Gr. *-trophia* < *trephein*, to nourish] a combining form meaning nutrition, growth [*hypertrophy*]

trop·ic (trop′ik) *n.* [< LL. < Gr. *tropikos*, of a turn (of the sun at the solstices) < *tropē*, a turn] 1. *Astron.* either of two circles of the celestial sphere (the **Tropic of Cancer,** c. 23¹/₂° north and the **Tropic of Capricorn,** c. 23¹/₂° south) parallel to the celestial equator: they are the limits of the apparent north-and-south journey of the sun 2. *Geog. a)* either of two parallels of latitude corresponding to these, on either side of the earth's equator *b)* [*also* T-] [*pl.*] the region of the earth between these latitudes, noted for its hot climate —*adj.* of the tropics; tropical

-trop·ic (trop′ik, trō′pik) [< Gr. < *trepein*, to turn + -IC] a combining form meaning turning, changing, or otherwise responding to a (specified kind of) stimulus [*phototropic*]: also **-troph·ic** (trof′ik)

trop·i·cal (träp′i k′l) *adj.* of, in, characteristic of, or suitable for the tropics —**trop′i·cal·ly** *adv.*

tropical fish any of various usually brightly coloured fish, orig. from the tropics, kept in an aquarium (**tropical aquarium**) maintained at a constant, warm temperature

Tropical Zone *same as* TORRID ZONE

tropic bird any of various tropical sea birds having white feathers with black markings and a pair of long tail feathers

tro·pism (trō′piz'm) *n.* [< ff.] the tendency of a plant or animal to grow or turn towards or away from an external stimulus such as light —**tro·pis′tic** *adj.*

-tro·pism (trə piz'm) [< Gr. *-tropos* (see TROPE) + -ISM] a combining form meaning tropism [*heliotropism*]: also **-tro·py** (trə pē)

trop·o·pause (trop′ə pôz, trō′pə-) *n.* [TROPO- (SPHERE) + PAUSE] a transition zone between the troposphere and the stratosphere, at which the drop in temperature with increasing height ceases

trop·o·sphere (trop′ə sfir′, trō′pə-) *n.* [< Fr. < Gr. *tropos* (see TROPE) + Fr. *sphère* (see SPHERE)] the atmosphere from the earth's surface to the stratosphere, reaching from 9 to 18 km, in which clouds form and in which temperature usually decreases as altitude increases —**trop′o·spher′ic** (-sfer′ik) *adj.*

‡trop·po (trôp′pô) *adv.* [It.] too; too much so: a direction in music, as in *allegro non troppo,* not too fast

trot (trot) *vi.* **trot′ted, trot′ting** [< OFr. < OHG. *trottōn,* to tread] 1. to move, ride, go, etc. at a trot 2. to hurry; run —*vt.* to make trot —*n.* 1. a gait of a horse, etc. in which the legs are lifted in alternating diagonal pairs 2. a person's gait between a walk and a run 3. a horse race for trotters 4. [*pl.*] [Colloq.] an attack of diarrhoea —**on the trot** [Colloq.] 1. busy; moving about 2. one after the other; successively [for six days *on the trot*] —**trot out** [Colloq.] to present or parade for, or as for, others to see, or admire, or consider

troth (trōth, troth) *n.* [ult. < OE. *treowth,* truth] [Archaic] 1. faithfulness; loyalty 2. truth: chiefly in **in troth,** truly; indeed 3. one's pledged word; promise: see also PLIGHT ONE'S TROTH (at PLIGHT[2]) —*vt.* [Archaic] to pledge to marry

trot·line (trot′līn′) *n.* a strong fishing line suspended over the water and hung with short lines bearing baited hooks

Trot·sky·ite (trot′skē īt′) *adj.* designating or of the theories of Leon Trotsky (1879-1940), Russian revolutionist and writer —*n.* a follower of Trotsky —**Trot′sky·ism** *n.*

trot·ter (trot′ər) *n.* 1. an animal that trots; esp., a horse bred and trained for trotting races 2. the foot of a sheep or pig used as food

trou·ba·dour (trōo′bə dôr′) *n.* [Fr. < Pr. < *trobar,* to compose in verse] any of a class of lyric poets who lived in southern France and northern Italy in the 11th, 12th, and 13th cent. and wrote poems of love and chivalry

trou·ble (trub´'l) *vt.* **-bled, -bling** [OFr. *trubler*, ult. < LL. *turbidare*, to trouble < L. *turbidus*, turbid] **1.** to disturb or agitate [*troubled* waters] **2.** to worry; harass; perturb **3.** to cause pain or discomfort to [*troubled* by headaches] **4.** to cause difficulty or inconvenience to **5.** to annoy, tease, bother, etc. —*vi.* to take pains; bother [don't *trouble* to return it] —*n.* **1.** a state of mental distress; worry **2.** *a)* a misfortune or mishap *b)* a difficult situation *c)* a condition of needing to be repaired, etc. [tyre *trouble*] **3.** a cause of annoyance, distress, etc. **4.** public disturbance **5.** bother; pains [he took the *trouble* to listen] **6.** an illness —**in(to) trouble** [Colloq.] pregnant when unmarried [she got *into trouble*] —**trou´bler** *n.*

trou·ble·mak·er (-mā´kər) *n.* a person who habitually makes trouble for others —**trou´ble·mak´ing** *n.*

trou·ble-shoot·er (-shōōt´ər) *n.* a person whose work is to find and repair or eliminate mechanical breakdowns or other sources of trouble —**trou´ble·shoot´ing** *n.*

trou·ble·some (-səm) *adj.* full of or causing trouble —**trou´-ble·some·ly** *adv.* —**trou´ble·some·ness** *n.*

trou·blous (trub´ləs) *adj.* [Chiefly Literary] **1.** troubled; disturbed **2.** *same as* TROUBLESOME

trough (trof) *n.* [OE. *trog*] **1.** a long, narrow, open container for holding water or food for animals **2.** a vessel of similar shape, as for kneading something **3.** a gutter; channel **4.** a long, narrow hollow, as between waves **5.** a low point in business activity, etc. **6.** a long, narrow area of low barometric pressure

trounce (trouns) *vt.* **trounced, trounc´ing** [< ?] **1.** to beat; thrash **2.** [Colloq.] to defeat —**trounc´er** *n.*

troupe (trōōp) *n.* [Fr.] a group, esp. of actors, singers, etc.; company —*vi.* **trouped, troup´ing** to travel as a member of a troupe —**troup´er** *n.*

trou·sers (trou´zərz) *n.pl.* [< obs. *trouse* < ScotGael. *triubhas*] an outer garment, esp. for men and boys, reaching from the waist usually to the ankles and divided into separate coverings for the legs —**trou´ser** *adj.*

trous·seau (trōō´sō, trōō sō´) *n., pl.* **-seaux** (-sōz), **-seaus** [Fr. < OFr., dim. of *trousse*, a bundle] a bride's outfit of clothes, linen, etc.

trout (trout) *n., pl.* **trout, trouts:** see PLURAL, II, D, 2 [OE. *truht* < LL. < Gr. *trōktēs*, kind of fish < *trōgein*, to gnaw] any of various food and game fishes related to but smaller than the salmon and found chiefly in fresh water

trove (trōv) *n.* *short for* TREASURE-TROVE

trow (trō, trou) *vi., vt.* [OE. *treowian* < *treow*, faith] [Archaic] to believe, think, suppose, etc.

trow·el (trou´al) *n.* [< MFr. < L. < L. *trulla* < *trua*, ladle] **1.** a tool with a thin, flat, rectangular blade for smoothing plaster **2.** a tool with a thin, flat, pointed blade for applying and shaping mortar **3.** a tool with a pointed scoop for digging holes in a garden —*vt.* **-elled, -el·ling** to spread, smooth, shape, dig, etc. with a trowel

TROWELS
(A, mortar; B, garden)

troy (troi) *adj.* by or in troy weight

troy weight [< *Troyes*, a city in France] a system of weights for gold, silver, precious stones, etc.: see TABLES OF WEIGHTS AND MEASURES in Supplement

tru·ant (trōō´ant) *n.* [OFr., a beggar < Celt.] **1.** a pupil who stays away from school without permission **2.** a person who shirks his duties —*adj.* **1.** that is a truant **2.** idle; shiftless **3.** errant; straying —*vi.* to be truant —**tru´an·cy** (-ən sē) *n., pl.* **-cies** —**tru´ant·ly** *adv.*

truce (trōōs) *n.* [OE. *treow*, compact, faith] **1.** a period during a war in which the nations or peoples engaged in it agree to stop fighting for a time **2.** any pause in quarrelling, conflict, etc.

truck[1] (truk) *n.* [prob. < L. < Gr. *trochos*, a wheel < *trechein*, to run] **1.** a small solid wheel, esp. for a gun carriage **2.** a small wooden disc with holes for halyards, esp. at the top of a flagpole or mast **3.** a frame with wheels at one end and handles at the other, used to carry trunks, crates, etc.: also **hand truck** **4.** a low frame or platform on wheels, for carrying heavy loads **5.** an open railway wagon **6.** a swivelling frame, with two or more pairs of wheels, under each end of a railway carriage, etc. **7.** [Chiefly U.S.] a lorry —*vt.* to carry on a truck —*vi.* [U.S.] to drive a truck as one's work

truck[2] (truk) *vt., vi.* [MFr. *troquer* < ?] to exchange; barter —*n.* **1.** *same as* BARTER **2.** payment of wages in goods instead of money **3.** small commercial articles **4.** small articles of little value **5.** [Colloq.] dealings [to have no *truck* with] **6.** [Colloq.] rubbish

truck·er (-ər) *n.* [U.S.] **1.** a lorry driver **2.** a person or company doing trucking Also **truck´man** (-mən), *pl.* **-men**

truck·ing (-iŋ) *n.* [U.S.] the business of carrying goods by lorry

truck·le (truk´'l) *n.* [< OFr. < L. *trochlea*, a pulley < Gr. < *trochos*, a wheel] **1.** orig., a small wheel **2.** *short for* TRUCKLE BED —*vi.* **-led, -ling** to give in or yield too easily (*to*)

truckle bed a low bed on castors, that can be rolled under a higher bed when not in use

truck system formerly, a system of forcing workers to accept payment in kind rather than in money, or in money which must be spent at a shop (**truck shop**) organized by their employers

truc·u·lent (truk´yoo lənt) *adj.* [< L. < *trux* (gen. *trucis*)] **1.** fierce; savage **2.** rude; harsh; scathing **3.** ready to fight —**truc´u·lence, truc´u·len·cy** *n.* —**truc´u·lent·ly** *adv.*

trudge (truj) *vi.* **trudged, trudg´ing** [< ?] to walk, esp. wearily or laboriously —*n.* a trudging —**trudg´er** *n.*

trudg·en stroke (truj´ən) [after J. *Trudgen*, Brit. amateur who introduced it (1868)] a swimming stroke in which a double overarm motion and a scissors kick are used

true (trōō) *adj.* **tru´er, tru´est** [OE. *treowe*] **1.** faithful; loyal **2.** reliable; certain **3.** in accordance with fact; not false **4.** *a)* conforming to an original, standard, etc. *b)* exact; accurate; correct **5.** rightful; lawful [the *true* heirs] **6.** accurately fitted, placed, or shaped [the board is *true*] **7.** *a)* genuine; authentic *b)* rightly so called [a *true* scholar] **8.** determined by the poles of the earth's axis, not by the earth's magnetic poles [*true* north] **9.** [Archaic] honest, virtuous, or truthful —*adv.* truly, truthfully, accurately, etc. —*vt.* **trued, tru´ing** or **true´ing** to fit, place, or shape accurately (often with *up*) —*n.* that which is true; truth or reality (with *the*) —**come true** to happen as predicted or expected —**in** (or **out of**) **true** that is (or is not) properly set, adjusted, etc. —**true to form** behaving as might be expected —**true´ness** *n.*

true bill in the U.S., and formerly in Britain, a bill of indictment endorsed by a grand jury

true-blue (trōō´blōō´) *adj.* **1.** very loyal; staunch **2.** staunchly Conservative in politics

true·bred (-bred´) *adj.* *same as:* **1.** WELL-BRED **2.** PURE-BRED

true·heart·ed (-här´tid) *adj.* **1.** loyal; faithful **2.** honest or sincere —**true´heart´ed·ness** *n.*

true-life (-lif´) *adj.* like what happens in real life; true to reality [a *true-life* story]

true·love (-luv´) *n.* (one's) sweetheart; a loved one

truelove knot a kind of bowknot that is hard to untie, a symbol of lasting love: also **true´-lov´er's knot**

true ribs ribs that are attached by cartilage directly to the breastbone; in man, the upper seven pairs of ribs

truf·fle (truf´'l) *n.* [< Fr. < OIt. *truffa*, ult. < L. *tuber*, a knob] any of certain related fleshy, edible fungi that grow underground, esp. a European kind regarded as a delicacy

trug (trug) *n.* [< ? dial. var. of TROUGH] a shallow, broad, gardener's basket made of strips of wood

tru·ism (trōō´iz'm) *n.* a statement the truth of which is obvious and well known —**tru·is´tic** *adj.*

trull (trul) *n.* [G. *Trolle*] a prostitute or trollop

tru·ly (trōō´lē) *adv.* **1.** in a true manner; genuinely, faithfully, rightfully, etc. **2.** really; indeed

trump[1] (trump) *n.* [altered < TRIUMPH] **1.** any playing card of a suit that ranks higher than any other suit during the playing of a hand **2.** [*occas. pl. with sing. v.*] a suit of trumps **3.** any advantage held in reserve until needed **4.** [Colloq.] a fine person —*vt.* **1.** to take (a trick, card, etc.) with a trump **2.** to outdo; surpass —*vi.* to play a trump —**trump up** to make up (a charge against someone, an excuse, etc.) in order deceive —**turn up trumps** to end more favourably than was expected

trump[2] (trump) *n., vi., vt.* [OFr. *trompe*] *archaic or poet. var. of* TRUMPET

trump·er·y (trum´pər ē) *n., pl.* **-er·ies** [< MFr. < *tromper*, to deceive] **1.** something showy but worthless **2.** nonsense —*adj.* showy but worthless

trum·pet (trum´pit) *n.* [< MFr. dim. of *trompe*, trumpet] **1.** a brass instrument with a blaring tone, consisting of a tube in an oblong loop or loops, flared at the end opposite the mouthpiece **2.** something shaped like a trumpet; esp., *same as* EAR TRUMPET **3.** a sound like that of a trumpet —*vi.* **1.** to blow a trumpet **2.** to make a sound like a trumpet —*vt.* **1.** to sound on or as on a trumpet **2.** to proclaim loudly

trum·pet·er (-ər) *n.* **1.** a trumpet player **2.** a person who proclaims or heralds something **3.** a long-legged, long-necked S. American bird having a loud cry **4.** *same as* TRUMPETER SWAN **5.** a domestic pigeon with feathered feet and a

TRUMPET

rounded crest **6.** any of numerous ocean fishes, esp. a large, edible Australian fish

trumpeter swan a N American wild swan with a loud cry

trumpet major the head trumpeter in a cavalry regiment

trun·cate (truŋ kāt′, truŋ′kāt) vt. **-cat·ed, -cat·ing** [< L. pp. of truncare, to cut off < truncus, a stem] to shorten by cutting; lop —adj. same as TRUNCATED —**trun·ca′tion** n.

trun·cat·ed (-id) adj. **1.** cut short or appearing as if cut short **2.** having the vertex cut off by a plane

trun·cheon (trun′chən) n. [< OFr., ult. < L. truncus, a stem] **1.** a staff carried as a symbol of authority **2.** a policeman's stick

trun·dle (trun′d′l) n. [OE. trendel, a circle < trendan, to roll] **1.** a small wheel **2.** short for TRUNDLE BED —vt., vi. **-dled, -dling** to roll along

trundle bed same as TRUCKLE BED

trunk (truŋk) n. [< OFr. < L. trucus, trunk, orig., mutilated] **1.** the main stem of a tree **2.** a human body or animal body, not including the head and limbs **3.** the thorax of an insect **4.** the main body of a nerve, blood vessel, etc. **5.** a long, flexible snout, as of an elephant **6.** a large, reinforced box for carrying a traveller's clothes, etc. **7.** a large, long, boxlike pipe, etc. that conveys air, water, etc. **8.** [pl.] same as TRUNK HOSE **9.** [pl.] men's shorts worn as for boxing, swimming, etc. **10.** short for TRUNK LINE **11.** [U.S.] the boot of a motor vehicle **12.** Archit. the shaft of a column

trunk call a long-distance telephone call

trunk·fish (-fish′) n., pl. **-fish′, -fish′es**: see FISH a tropical fish whose body is encased in fused bony plates

trunk hose full, baggy breeches reaching about halfway down the thigh, worn in the 16th and 17th cent.

trunk line a main line of a railway, telephone system, etc.

trunk road a main road connecting important centres

trun·nion (trun′yən) n. [Fr. trognon, a stump] either of two projecting pins on each side of a cannon, on which it pivots

truss (trus) vt. [OFr. trousser] **1.** orig., to tie into a bundle **2.** to tie or bind (often with up) **3.** to skewer or bind the wings, etc. of (a fowl) before cooking **4.** to support or strengthen with a truss —n. **1.** a bundle or pack, esp. one of hay or straw in any of various unit weights **2.** an iron band around a mast, to which a yard is fastened **3.** a rigid framework of beams, struts, etc. for supporting a roof, bridge, etc. **4.** an appliance worn for supporting a hernia, usually a pad on a belt **5.** a flower cluster growing at the tip of a stem

trust (trust) n. [ON. traust] **1.** a) firm belief in the honesty, reliability, etc. of another b) the one trusted **2.** confident expectation, hope, etc. [have trust in the future] **3.** a) the fact of having confidence placed in one b) the responsibility resulting from this **4.** care; custody **5.** something entrusted to one; charge **6.** confidence in a purchaser's intention or future ability to pay for goods etc.; credit **7.** an industrial or business combination of companies, with control vested in a single board of trustees who are able to eliminate competition, fix prices, etc. **8.** Law a) confidence placed in a person by giving him nominal ownership of property that he is to keep, use, or administer for another's benefit b) the property involved —vi. **1.** to have trust or faith; be confident **2.** to hope (for) **3.** to give business credit —vt. **1.** to have trust in; rely on, etc. **2.** to commit (to a person's care) **3.** to put something confidently in the charge of [to trust a lawyer with one's case] **4.** to allow to do something without fear of the outcome **5.** to believe or suppose **6.** to hope **7.** to grant business credit to —adj. **1.** relating to a trust or trusts **2.** held in trust **3.** acting as a trustee —**in trust** in the condition of being entrusted to another's care —**take on trust** to accept or believe without requiring corroboration —**trust to** to rely on —**trust′a·ble** adj. —**trust′er** n.

trus·tee (trus tē′) n. **1.** a person to whom another's property or the management of another's property is entrusted **2.** a nation under whose control a trust territory is placed **3.** any of a group of persons appointed to manage the affairs of a charity, hospital, etc.

trus·tee·ship (-ship′) n. **1.** the position or function of a trustee **2.** a) a commission from the United Nations to a country to administer a trust territory b) the state or fact of being a trust territory

trust·ful (trust′fəl) adj. full of trust or confidence in another or others; trusting —**trust′ful·ly** adv. —**trust′ful·ness** n.

trust fund money, stock, etc. held in trust

trust·ing (trus′tiŋ) adj. that trusts; trustful —**trust′ing·ly** adv. —**trust′ing·ness** n.

trust territory a territory placed by the United Nations under the control of a country that manages the affairs of the territory

trust·wor·thy (trust′wur′thē) adj. **-thi·er, -thi·est** worthy of trust; dependable; reliable —**trust′wor′thi·ly** adv. —**trust′wor′thi·ness** n.

trust·y (trus′tē) adj. **trust′i·er, trust′i·est** that can be relied upon; dependable —n., pl. **trust′ies** a trusted person;

specif., a convict granted special privileges as a trustworthy person —**trust′i·ly** adv. —**trust′i·ness** n.

truth (trōōth) n., pl. **truths** (trōōthz, trōōths) [OE. treowth] **1.** the quality or state of being true; specif., a) orig., loyalty b) sincerity; honesty c) the quality of being in agreement with reality or facts d) reality; actual existence e) agreement with a standard, rule, etc.; correctness **2.** that which is true **3.** an established or verified fact, etc. **4.** a particular belief or teaching regarded by the speaker as the true one (often with the) —**in truth** truly; in fact —**of a truth** certainly

truth drug an anaesthetic or hypnotic, as sodium pentothal, regarded as tending to make a person taking it willing to answer questions: also **truth serum**

truth·ful (trōōth′fal) adj. **1.** telling the truth; honest **2.** agreeing with fact or reality —**truth′ful·ly** adv. —**truth′ful·ness** n.

try (trī) vt. **tried, try′ing** [OFr. trier, ult. < ? L. pp. of terere, to thresh grain] **1.** to melt or render (fat, etc.) to get (the oil): usually with out **2.** a) to examine and decide (a case) in a law court b) to determine legally the guilt or innocence of (a person) **3.** to put to the proof; test **4.** to test the faith, patience, etc. of; afflict [he was sorely tried] **5.** to subject to a severe test or strain **6.** to test the effect of; experiment with [try this recipe] **7.** to attempt; endeavour [try to forget] —vi. **1.** to make an effort, attempt, etc. **2.** to experiment —n., pl. **tries** an attempt; effort; trial —**try it on** Colloq. to see how far one can go before being found out, or reprimanded —**try on** to test the fit, etc. of (a garment) by putting it on —**try one's hand at** to attempt (to do something), esp. for the first time —**try out** **1.** to test the quality, value, etc. of, as by using **2.** to test one's fitness, as to be on a team, act a role, etc.

try·ing (-iŋ) adj. that tries one's patience; annoying; exasperating; irksome —**try′ing·ly** adv.

try·out (trī′out′) n. [Colloq.] a chance to prove, or a test to determine, one's fitness to be in a team, act a role, etc.

tryp·a·no·some (trip′ə nə sōm′) n. [< Gr. trypanon, borer + -SOME³] a parasitic, flagellate protozoan transmitted to the blood of vertebrates by insect bites, and often causing serious disease, as sleeping sickness

tryp·sin (trip′sin) n. [G., prob. < Gr. tryein, to wear away + G. (Pe)psin: see PEPSIN] a digestive enzyme in the pancreatic juice: it changes proteins into polypeptides —**tryp′tic** adj.

tryp·to·phan (trip′tə fan′) n. [< Gr. tryein, to wear away + phanein, to show] a crystalline, essential amino acid, produced synthetically and in digestion by the action of trypsin on proteins

try·sail (trī′s′l, -sāl′) n. [< naut. phr. a try, position of lying to in a storm] a small, stout, fore-and-aft sail used for keeping a vessel's head to the wind in a storm

try square an instrument for testing the accuracy of square work and for marking off right angles

tryst (trist, trīst) n. [OFr. triste, hunting station] **1.** an appointment to meet at a specified time and place, esp. one made secretly by lovers **2.** a) a meeting held by appointment b) the place of such a meeting: also **trysting place** —**tryst′er** n.

tsar (tsär, zär) n. var. sp. of CZAR —**tsar′dom** n. —**tsar′ism** n. —**tsar′ist** adj., n.

tset·se fly (tset′sē, tet′-) [Afrik. < the Bantu name] any of several small flies of central and southern Africa, including the one that carries sleeping sickness

T-shirt (tē′shurt′) n. [so named because T-shaped] a collarless pullover shirt with short sleeves

tsk interj., n. a clicking or sucking sound made with the tongue, to express disapproval, sympathy, etc. —vi. to utter "tsks"

tsp. **1.** teaspoon(s) **2.** teaspoonful(s)

T square a T-shaped ruler for drawing parallel lines

T-strap (tē′strap′) n. **1.** a T-shaped strap over the instep of a shoe **2.** a woman's or girl's shoe with such a strap

tsu·na·mi (tsōō nä′mē) n. [Jap. < tsu, a harbour + nami, wave] a huge sea wave caused by a disturbance under water, as an earthquake: popularly, but inaccurately, called tidal wave —**tsu·na′mic** (-mik) adj.

Tswa·na (tswä′nə) n. **1.** any of a people of S Africa, living chiefly in Botswana **2.** their language

T.T. **1.** teetotal **2.** teetotaller **3.** Tourist Trophy **4.** tuberculin tested

T.U. trade union

Tu. Tuesday

‡**tu·an** (tōō wän′) n. [Malay] sir; master

tu·a·ta·ra (tōō′ə tä′rə) n. [< Maori < tua, back + tara, spine] a primitive, lizardlike reptile of islands near New Zealand, with a row of spines in the middle of the back

tub (tub) n. [MDu. tubbe] **1.** a) a round, open, wooden container, usually formed of staves and hoops fastened around a flat bottom b) any large, open container of metal, etc., as for washing c) as much as a tub will hold **2.** a) short for BATHTUB b) [Colloq.] a bath in a tub **3.** [Colloq.] a slow-moving, clumsy ship or boat —vt., vi. **tubbed, tub′-**

bing 1. [Colloq.] to wash in a tub 2. [Colloq.] to bath (oneself) —**tub′ba·ble** *adj.* —**tub′ber** *n.*

tu·ba (tyo͞o′bə) *n., pl.* **tu′bas, tu′bae** (-bē) [L., a trumpet] a large, brass musical instrument having three to five valves

tub·by (tub′ē) *adj.* **-bi·er, -bi·est** 1. shaped like a tub 2. short and fat —**tub′bi·ness** *n.*

tube (tyo͞ob) *n.* [Fr. < L. *tubus,* a pipe] 1. *a)* a slender, hollow cylinder or pipe of metal, glass, rubber, etc., in which gases and liquids can flow or be kept *b)* an instrument, part, organ, etc. resembling a tube [a bronchial *tube*] 2. a rubber casing inflated with air and used, esp. formerly, with an outer casing to form a tyre for a motor vehicle 3. an enclosed, hollow cylinder of thin, pliable metal, etc. with a screw cap at one end, used for holding pastes or semiliquids 4. *short for: a)* ELECTRON TUBE *b)* CATHODE-RAY TUBE 5. *a)* [Colloq.] [*often* T-] an underground railway system, esp. that in London (often preceded by *the*) *b)* an underground tunnel for such a railway —*vt.* **tubed, tub′ing** 1. to provide with, place in, or pass through a tube or tubes 2. to make tubular —**tub′al** *adj.* —**tu′bate** *adj.* —**tube′like** *adj.*

tube foot any of numerous projecting, water-filled tubes in most echinoderms, used in moving about, handling food, etc.

tube·less tyre (-lis) a tyre for a motor vehicle, consisting of a single air-filled unit without an inner tube

tu·ber (tyo͞o′bər) *n.* [L., lit., a swelling] 1. a short, thickened, fleshy part of an underground stem, as a potato 2. a tubercle or swelling

tu·ber·cle (-k'l) *n.* [L. *tuberculum,* dim. of *tuber*: see prec.] 1. a small, rounded part growing out from a bone or from the root of a plant 2. any abnormal hard nodule or swelling; specif., the typical nodular lesion of tuberculosis

tubercle bacillus the bacterium causing tuberculosis

tu·ber·cu·lar (tyo͞o bur′kyə lər) *adj.* 1. of, like, or having tubercles 2. of or having tuberculosis 3. caused by the tubercle bacillus Also **tu·ber′cu·lous** (-ləs) —*n.* a person having tuberculosis

tu·ber·cu·late (-kyə lāt) *adj.* 1. having a tubercle or tubercles 2. *same as* TUBERCULAR —**tu·ber′cu·la′tion** *n.*

tu·ber·cu·lin (-lin) *n.* a sterile solution prepared from a culture of the tubercle bacillus and injected into the skin as a test for tuberculosis

tuberculin tested produced by cows that have been certified as free of tuberculosis: said of milk, etc.

tu·ber·cu·lo·sis (tyo͞o bur′byə lō′sis) *n.* [ModL.: see TUBERCLE & -OSIS] an infectious disease caused by the tubercle bacillus and causing tubercles to form in body tissues; specif., tuberculosis of the lungs; consumption

tu·ber·ose (tyo͞ob′ər ōz′, tyo͞ob′rōz′) *n.* [ModL. < L. *tuberosus,* TUBEROUS] a perennial Mexican plant with a tuberous rootstock and white, sweet-scented flowers

tu·ber·ous (tyo͞o′bər əs) *adj.* [< Fr. < L. *tuberosus*: see TUBER & -OUS] 1. covered with rounded, wartlike swellings; knobby 2. of, like, or having a tuber or tubers Also **tu′-ber·ose′** (-ōs′) —**tu′ber·os′i·ty** (-bə ros′ə tē) *n., pl.* **-ties**

tu·bi·fex (tyo͞o′bə feks′) *n., pl.* **-fex′es, -fex** [ModL. < L. *tubus,* a pipe + *-fex* < *facere,* to make] a small freshwater worm, found esp. in polluted waters and often used as food for aquarium fish

tub·ing (tyo͞ob′iŋ) *n.* 1. a series or system of tubes 2. material in the form of a tube 3. a piece or length of tube

tub·thump·er (-thum′pər) [Colloq.] a ranting public speaker

tu·bu·lar (tyo͞o′byə lər) *adj.* [< L. dim. of *tubus,* a pipe] 1. of or shaped like a tube 2. made with tubes Also **tu′bu·late** (-lit) —**tu′bu·lar′i·ty** (-lar′ə tē) *n.* —**tu′bu·lar·ly** *adv.*

tu·bule (tyo͞ob′yo͞ol) *n.* a small tube

T.U.C. Trades Union Congress

tuck (tuk) *vt.* [< MDu. *tucken,* to tuck & cognate OE. *tucian,* to tug] 1. to pull up or gather up in a fold or folds, as to make shorter 2. to sew a fold or folds in (a garment) 3. *a)* to thrust the edges of (a sheet, napkin, etc.) under or in, in order to make secure (usually with *up, in,* etc.) *b)* to cover or wrap snugly (with *up*) 4. to put or press snugly into a small space; cram [to *tuck* shoes in a suitcase] 5. to put into a secluded, empty, or isolated spot: often used in the passive [a cottage *tucked* away in the hills] —*vi.* 1. to draw together; pucker 2. to make tucks —*n.* 1. a sewn fold in a garment 2. [Slang] food, esp. sweets, cakes, etc. —**tuck away** 1. to eat or drink heartily 2. to put aside, as for future use —**tuck in** 1. to pull in or contract (one's chin, stomach, etc.) 2. to eat or drink heartily

tuck·er¹ (tuk′ər) *n.* 1. a person or device that makes tucks 2. a neck and shoulder covering formerly worn with a low-cut bodice by women 3. [Aust. Slang] food

tuck·er² (tuk′ər) *vt.* [prob. < *tuck,* in obs. sense "to punish, rebuke"] [U.S. Colloq.] to tire (*out*); weary

tuck-in (-in′) *n.* [Slang] a large meal

tuck shop a shop selling sweets, cakes, etc., esp. to schoolchildren

Tu·dor (tyo͞o′dər) *adj.* 1. designating or of the Tudors, the ruling family of England (1485-1603) 2. designating or of a style of architecture characterized by shallow mouldings, extensive panelling, half-timbering, etc.

Tues. Tuesday

Tues·day (tyo͞oz′dē; -dā) *n.* [OE. *Tiwes dæg,* lit., day of the god of war *Tiw*] the third day of the week

Tues·days (-dēz, -dāz) *adv.* [Colloq.] on or during every Tuesday

tu·fa (tyo͞o′fə) *n.* [It. *tufo* < L. *tofus*] a porous rock formed of calcium carbonate, etc. deposited by springs —**tu·fa′-ceous** (-fā′shəs) *adj.*

tuff (tuf) *n.* [< Fr. < It. *tufo,* TUFA] a porous rock formed from volcanic ash, dust, etc. —**tuff·a′ceous** (-ā′shəs) *adj.*

tuf·fet (tuf′ət) *n.* [< TUFT] 1. a tuft of grass 2. [by misunderstanding of a nursery rhyme] a low stool

tuft (tuft) *n.* [OFr. *tufe,* prob. < L. *tufa,* helmet crest] 1. a bunch of hairs, feathers, grass, etc. growing or tied closely together 2. *a)* the fluffy ball forming the end of any of the clusters of threads drawn tightly through a quilt, etc. to hold the padding in place *b)* a decorative button to which such a tuft is fastened —*vt.* 1. to provide or decorate with a tuft or tufts 2. to keep the padding of (a quilt, mattress, etc.) in place by regularly spaced tufts —*vi.* to grow in or form into tufts —**tuft′ed** *adj.* —**tuft′er** *n.* —**tuft′y** *adj.*

tug (tug) *vi.* **tugged, tug′ging** [prob. < ON. *toga,* to draw] to pull hard (often with *at*) —*vt.* 1. to pull at with force; strain at 2. to drag; haul 3. to tow with a tugboat —*n.* 1. a hard pull 2. a great effort or a struggle, strain, etc. 3. a rope, chain, strap, etc. used for pulling 4. *shortened form of* TUGBOAT —**tug′ger** *n.* —**tug′ging·ly** *adv.*

tug·boat (-bōt′) *n.* a small, powerful boat used for towing or pushing ships, barges, etc.

tug of war 1. a contest in which two teams pull at opposite ends of a rope, each trying to drag the other across a central line 2. any power struggle between two parties

tu·grik (to͞o′grik) *n.* [Mongol. *dughurik,* lit., wheel] *see* MONETARY UNITS, table (Mongolia)

tu·i·tion (tyo͞o wish′ən) *n.* [< OFr. < L. *tuitio,* protection < pp. of *tueri,* to protect] 1. the fee for instruction, esp. at a college or private school 2. [Now Rare] teaching; instruction —**tu·i′tion·al** *adj.*

tu·la·rae·mi·a (to͞o′lə rē′mē ə) *n.* [ModL. < *Tulare* County, California, U.S. + -AEMIA] an infectious disease of rodents, esp. rabbits, sometimes transmitted to man: U.S. var. sp. **tu′la·re′mi·a** —**tu′la·rae′mic** *adj.*

tu·lip (tyo͞o′lip) *n.* [< Fr. < Turk. *tülbend,* TURBAN: the flower resembles a turban] 1. any of various spring-blooming bulb plants, with long, pointed leaves and a large, cup-shaped flower 2. the flower or bulb

tulip tree a tree of the magnolia family with tulip-shaped, greenish-yellow flowers, and long, conelike fruit: also called **tulip poplar**

tu·lip·wood (-wo͞od′) *n.* 1. the light, soft wood of the tulip tree, used for furniture, etc. 2. any of several woods having streaks of colour

tulle (tyo͞ol; *Fr.* tül) *n.* [< *Tulle,* city in France] a thin, fine netting of silk, rayon, nylon, etc., used for veils, scarfs, etc.

tum·ble (tum′b'l) *vi.* **-bled, -bling** [OE. *tumbian,* to jump, dance] 1. to do somersaults, handsprings, or similar acrobatic feats 2. *a)* to fall suddenly or helplessly *b)* to undergo a sudden drop or downfall [prices *tumbled,* the government *tumbled*] 3. to stumble or trip 4. to toss or roll about 5. to move in a hasty, disorderly manner 6. [Colloq.] to understand suddenly (with *to*) —*vt.* 1. to cause to tumble 2. to put into disorder as by tossing here and there —*n.* 1. a tumbling; specif., *a)* a somersault, handspring, etc. *b)* a fall 2. disorder; confusion 3. a confused heap

tum·ble·bug (-bug′) *n.* [U.S.] any of various beetles that roll balls of dung, in which they deposit their eggs and in which the larvae develop

tum·ble·down (-doun′) *adj.* ready to tumble down; dilapidated

tum·bler (tum′blər) *n.* 1. an acrobat or gymnast who does somersaults, handsprings, etc. 2. a kind of pigeon that does somersaults in flight 3. *a)* an ordinary drinking glass with no foot or stem *b)* its contents 4. a part of a lock whose position must be changed by a key in order to release the bolt 5. a device for tumbling things about

tum·bler-dri·er (-drī′ər) *n.* a machine which dries laundered articles by tumbling them about in hot air: also **tum′ble-dri′er**

tum·ble·weed (tum′b'l wēd′) *n.* any of various American plants which break off near the ground in autumn and are blown about by the wind

tum·brel, tum·bril (tum′brəl) *n.* [< MFr. < *tomber,* to fall] 1. a farmer's cart that can be tilted for emptying 2. any of the carts used to carry the condemned to the guillotine during the French Revolution

tu·me·fy (tyo͞o′mə fī′) *vt., vi.* **-fied′, -fy′ing** [< Fr., ult. < L. < *tumere,* to swell + *facere,* to make] to swell or cause to swell —**tu′me·fac′tion** (-fak′shən) *n.*

tu·mes·cence (tyo͞o mes′'ns) *n.* [< L. prp. of *tumescere,* to swell up] 1. a swelling; distention 2. a swollen or distended part —**tu·mes′cent** *adj.*

tu·mid (tyo͞o′mid) *adj.* [< L. < *tumere,* to swell] 1.

swollen; bulging **2.** inflated; pompous —**tu·mid′i·ty, tu′-mid·ness** *n.* —**tu′mid·ly** *adv.*

tum·my (tum′ē) *n., pl.* **-mies** stomach: a child's word

tummy button [Colloq.] the navel

tu·mour (tyōō′mər) *n.* [L. < *tumere*, to swell] an abnormal growth of tissue in some part of the body, that is either benign or malignant: U.S. sp. **tu′mor** —**tu′mor·ous** *adj.*

tump·line (tump′lin) *n.* [*tump*, a tumpline < AmInd.] [U.S. and Canad.] a broad band passed across the forehead and behind across the shoulders to support a pack on the back

tu·mult (tyōō′mult) *n.* [< MFr. < L. *tumultus* < *tumere*, to swell] **1.** noisy commotion, as of a crowd; uproar **2.** confusion; agitation; disturbance **3.** great emotional disturbance

tu·mul·tu·ous (tyōō mul′tyōō wəs, tyōō-) *adj.* **1.** full of or characterized by tumult; wild and noisy; uproarious **2.** making a tumult **3.** greatly disturbed —**tu·mul′tu·ous·ly** *adv.* —**tu·mul′tu·ous·ness** *n.*

tu·mu·lus (tyōō′myə ləs) *n., pl.* **-li** (-lī′), **-lus·es** [L., a mound] an artificial mound, esp. an ancient burial mound

tun (tun) *n.* [OE. *tunne*, large cask & OFr. *tonne*, both < ML. *tunna* prob. < Celt.] **1.** a large cask for liquids **2.** a measure of capacity for liquids, usually 252 wine gallons —*vt.* **tunned, tun′ning** to store in a tun or tuns

tu·na[1] (tyōō′nə) *n., pl.* **tu′na, tu′nas:** see PLURAL, II, D, 2 [AmSp. < Sp. < Ar. < L. *thunnus:* see TUNNY] **1.** a large, ocean, food and game fish of the mackerel group: also called **bluefin tuna 2.** any of various related fishes, as the albacore **3.** the flesh of the tuna, often tinned for food: also called **tuna fish**

tu·na[2] (tōō′nä, tyōō′-) *n.* [Sp., of WInd. origin] any of various prickly pears

tun·a·ble (tyōōn′ə b'l) *adj.* capable of being tuned: also sp. **tune′a·ble** —**tun′a·ble·ness** *n.*

tun·dra (toon′drə, tun′-) *n.* [Russ.] any of the vast, nearly level, treeless plains of the arctic regions

tune (tyōōn) *n.* [ME., var. of *tone*, TONE] **1.** a succession of musical tones forming a rhythmic, catchy whole; melody; air **2.** the condition of having correct musical pitch, or of being in key; also, harmony; concord: now chiefly in phrases **in tune, out of tune** —*vt.* **tuned, tun′ing 1.** to adjust (a musical instrument) to some standard of pitch **2.** to adapt (music, the voice, etc.) to some pitch, tone, etc. **3.** to adapt to some condition, mood, etc. **4.** to adjust (an electronics circuit, a motor, etc.) to the proper or desired performance —*vi.* to be in tune; harmonize —**call the tune** to be in control —**change one's tune** to change one's attitude or manner: also **sing a different tune** —**to the tune of** [Colloq.] to the amount of —**tune in 1.** to adjust a radio or television receiver to a given frequency or channel so as to receive (a specified station, programme, etc.) **2.** [Slang] to become or make aware, knowing, etc. —**tune out** to adjust a radio or television receiver so as to get rid of (interference, etc.) —**tune up 1.** to adjust (musical instruments) to the same pitch **2.** to put (an engine) into good working condition —**tun′er** *n.*

tune·ful (-fəl) *adj.* full of tunes or melody; musical; melodious —**tune′ful·ly** *adv.* —**tune′ful·ness** *n.*

tune·less (-lis) *adj.* not musical or melodious —**tune′less·ly** *adv.* —**tune′less·ness** *n.*

tune-up, tune-up (-up′) *n.* an adjusting, as of an engine, to the proper condition

tung oil (tung) [< Chin. *yu-t′ung* < *yu*, oil + *t′ung*, name of the tree] a fast-drying oil from the seeds of a subtropical tree (**tung tree**), used in paints, varnishes, etc.

tung·sten (tung′stən) *n.* [Sw. < *tung*, heavy + *sten*, stone] a hard, heavy, grey-white, metallic chemical element, used in steel, electric lamp filaments, etc.: symbol, W; at. wt., 183.85; at. no., 74 —**tung′stic** (-stik) *adj.*

tu·nic (tyōō′nik) *n.* [L. *tunica*] **1.** a loose, gownlike garment worn by men and women in ancient Greece and Rome **2.** a blouselike garment extending to the hips or lower, often belted **3.** a short coat forming part of the uniform of soldiers, policemen, etc. **4.** a short vestment worn by a subdeacon **5.** *Biol.* a covering membrane or tissue

tu·ni·cate (tyōō′ni kit, -kāt′) *adj.* [< L. pp. of *tunicare*, to put on a tunic] *Bot., Zool.* covered with or having a tunic or tunics: also **tu′ni·cat′ed** (-kat′id) —*n.* any of several sea animals having a saclike body enclosed by a thick cellulose tunic

tuning fork a small steel instrument with two prongs, which when struck sounds a certain fixed tone: it is used as a guide in tuning instruments, etc.

tun·nage (tun′ij) *n.* same as TONNAGE

tun·nel (tun′'l) *n.* [MFr. *tonnelle*, vault < OFr. dim. of *tonne*, a tun] **1.** an underground or underwater passageway for motor cars, trains, etc. **2.** an animal's burrow **3.** any tunnellike passage, as one in a mine —*vt.* **-nelled, -nel·ling 1.** to make a tunnel through or under **2.** to make (one's way) by digging a tunnel —*vi.* to make a tunnel —**tun′nel·ler** *n.*

tun·ny (tun′ē) *n., pl.* **-nies, -ny:** see PLURAL, II, D, 1 [< MFr. < Pr. < L. < Gr. *thynnos*] same as TUNA[1] (senses 1 & 2)

tup (tup) *n.* [ME. *tupe*] **1.** a male sheep; ram **2.** the striking part of a pile driver or steam hammer —*vt.* **tupped, tup′ping** to copulate with (a ewe)

Tu·pa·ma·ro (tōō′pə mä′rō) [< *Tupac Amaru,* Peruvian Indian leader against the Spaniards] a member of a left-wing urban guerrilla movement in Uruguay

tu·pe·lo (tōō′pə lō′, tyōō′-) *n., pl.* **-los′** [< Creek Indian *ito,* tree + *opilwa,* a swamp] **1.** any of several gum trees of the southern U.S. **2.** the fine-textured wood of any of these trees

Tu·pi (tōō′pē, tōō′pē) *n.* [Tupi, comrade] **1.** *pl.* **Tu·pis′, Tu·pi′** any member of a group of S. American Indian tribes living chiefly along the lower Amazon **2.** their language

tup·pence (tup′'ns) *n.* same as TWOPENCE

tuque (tōōk, tyōōk) *n.* [CanadFr. < Fr. *toque,* a cap] a kind of knitted winter cap

Tu·ra·ni·an (tyōō rā′nē ən) *adj.* [< Per. *Tūrān,* region beyond the Oxus] of the languages known as Ural-Altaic that are neither Semitic nor Indo-European

tur·ban (tur′bən) *n.* [< MFr. < It. or Port. < Turk. *tülbend,* dial. form of *dūlbend* < Per.] **1.** a headdress of Moslem origin, consisting of a cloth wound in folds about the head, often over a cap **2.** any head covering or hat made like or resembling this —**tur′baned** *adj.*

TURBAN

tur·ba·ry (tur′bə rē) *n.* [ME. < OFr. < ML. < *turba,* turf] **1.** land where peat is dug **2.** the legal right to cut peat on common land or on another person's land

tur·bid (tur′bid) *adj.* [< L. *turba,* a crowd] **1.** muddy or cloudy from having the sediment stirred up **2.** thick or dark, as clouds or smoke **3.** confused or perplexed; muddled —**tur·bid′i·ty, tur′bid·ness** *n.* —**tur′bid·ly** *adv.*

tur·bi·nate (tur′bi nit, -nāt′) *adj.* [< L. < *turbo,* a whirl] **1.** shaped like a cone resting on its apex; top-shaped **2.** shaped like a scroll or spiral

tur·bine (tur′bin, -bin) *n.* [Fr. < L. *turbo,* a whirl] an engine driven by the pressure of steam, water, air, etc. against the curved vanes of a wheel on a shaft

tur·bo- [< TURBINE] *a combining form meaning* consisting of or driven by a turbine

tur·bo·fan (tur′bō fan′) *n.* **1.** a turbojet engine in which additional thrust is obtained from the part of the air that bypasses the engine and is accelerated by a fan: in full, **turbofan engine 2.** a fan driven by a turbine

tur·bo·jet (-jet′) *n.* **1.** a jet engine with a turbine-driven air compressor that compresses air for fuel combustion, the resulting hot gases being used to rotate the turbine before forming the propulsive jet: in full, **turbojet engine 2.** an aircraft propelled by such an engine

tur·bo·prop (-prop′) *n.* [TURBO- + PROP(ELLER)] **1.** a turbojet engine whose turbine shaft drives a propeller that develops most of the thrust, some being added by a jet of the turbine exhaust gases: in full, **turboprop engine 2.** an aircraft propelled by such an engine

tur·bot (tur′bət) *n., pl.* **-bot, -bots:** see PLURAL, II, D, 2 [< OFr. *tourbout*] **1.** a large European flatfish, highly regarded as food **2.** any of several American flounders

tur·bu·lent (tur′byə lənt) *adj.* [Fr. < L. < *turba,* a crowd] full of commotion or wild disorder; specif., *a)* marked by or causing turmoil; disorderly *b)* violently agitated or excited *c)* marked by wildly irregular motion —**tur′bu·lence, tur′bu·len·cy** *n.* —**tur′bu·lent·ly** *adv.*

turd (turd) *n.* [ME. < OE. *tord*] a piece of excrement: now a vulgar term

tu·reen (tyōō rēn′, tə-) *n.* [MFr. *terrine,* earthen vessel, ult. < L. *terra,* earth] a large, deep dish with a lid, for serving soup, etc.

turf (turf) *n., pl.* **turfs, turves** (turvz) [OE.] **1.** *a)* a surface layer of earth containing grass plants with their matted roots; sod *b)* a piece of this layer **2.** peat —*vt.* to cover with turf —**the turf 1.** a track for horse racing **2.** the sport of horse racing —**turf out** [Colloq.] to throw out

turf accountant same as BOOKMAKER

turf·man (-mən) *n., pl.* **-men** an owner, trainer, etc. of racehorses

tur·ges·cent (tur jes′'nt) *adj.* [< L. prp. of *turgescere,* to swell up] becoming turgid or swollen —**tur·ges′cence** *n.*

tur·gid (tur′jid) *adj.* [< L. *turgidus* < *turgere,* to swell] **1.** swollen; distended **2.** bombastic; grandiloquent —**tur·gid′-i·ty, tur′gid·ness** *n.* —**tur′gid·ly** *adv.*

tur·gor (tur′gər) *n.* [LL. < L. *turgere,* to swell] turgidity; rigidity, esp. of plant cell after absorption of water

tur·i·on (tyōōr′ē ən) *n.* [< Fr. < L. *turio,* a shoot] a scaly shoot budded from a subterranean stem and growing independently above ground

Turk (turk) *n.* 1. a native or inhabitant of Turkey; esp., a member of the Moslem people of Turkey or, formerly, of the Ottoman Empire 2. a member of any of the peoples speaking Turkic languages See also YOUNG TURK

Turk. 1. Turkey 2. Turkish

tur·key (tur'kē) *n., pl.* **-keys, -key:** see PLURAL, II, D, 1 [orig. applied to the guinea fowl, sometimes imported through Turkey and for a time identified with the Am. fowl] *a)* a large, wild or domesticated, N. American bird with a small head and spreading tail, bred as poultry in many countries *b)* its flesh —**talk turkey** [U.S. Colloq.] to talk bluntly and directly

turkey buzzard a dark-coloured vulture of temperate and tropical America, having a naked, reddish head: also called **turkey vulture**

Turkey carpet a deep-piled, soft, woollen carpet, usually brightly patterned

turkey cock 1. a male turkey 2. an arrogant, conceited person

Tur·ki (tur'kē) *n.* 1. the Turkic languages collectively or any Turkic language 2. a member of any Turkic people —*adj.* designating or of the Turkic languages or the peoples who speak them

Tur·kic (tur'kik) *adj.* 1. designating or of a subfamily of Altaic languages, including Turkish 2. designating or of the peoples who speak any of these languages

Turk·ish (tur'kish) *adj.* of Turkey, the Turks, their language, etc. —*n.* 1. the Turkic language of Turkey: in full, **Ottoman-Turkish** 2. loosely, *same as* TURKIC

Turkish bath 1. a public bath in which the bather, after a period of heavy perspiration in a room of hot air or steam, is washed and massaged 2. [*sometimes pl.*] an establishment where such a bath is obtainable

Turkish coffee very strong, black, usually sweetened coffee

Turkish delight a jelly-like sweet, usually cube-shaped, delicately flavoured and covered in icing sugar

Turkish towel [*also* t-] a thick cotton towel of terry cloth

Tur·ko- *a combining form meaning:* 1. of Turkey or the Turks 2. Turkey and 3. the Turks and Also **Tur'co-**

tur·mer·ic (tur'mər ik) *n.* [< MFr. < ML. *terra merita*, lit., deserving earth < ?] 1. an East Indian plant whose rhizome in powdered form is used as a yellow dye, seasoning, etc. 2. this rhizome or the powder made from it

tur·moil (tur'moil) *n.* [*tur-* (< ? TURBULENT) + MOIL] a very excited or confused condition; tumult; commotion; uproar

turn (turn) *vt.* [< OE. *turnian* & OFr. *tourner*, both < L. *tornare*, to turn in a lathe, ult. < Gr. *tornos*, a lathe] 1. to make (a wheel, etc.) move about a centre or axis; revolve 2. to move round or partly round [to *turn* a key, handle, etc.] 3. to do (a somersault, cart wheel, etc.) 4. to give a rounded shape to, as on a lathe 5. to give a graceful form to [to *turn* a pretty phrase] 6. to change the position or direction of [*turn* your chair round] 7. to revolve in the mind; ponder (often with *over*) 8. *a)* to bend, fold, etc. [*turn* the sheet back] *b)* to twist (one's ankle) 9. to move so that the underside is on top, and vice versa; reverse; invert [to *turn* pages, a collar, the soil, etc.] 10. to make topsy-turvy 11. to upset (the stomach) 12. to deflect; divert 13. *a)* to convert or persuade *b)* to prejudice 14. to go round (a corner, etc.) 15. to reach or pass (a certain age, amount, etc.) 16. to reverse the course of; repel or make recoil [to *turn* an attack] 17. to drive, set, let go, etc. in some way [the dog was *turned* loose] 18. to direct, point, aim, etc. [eyes *turned* ahead, thoughts *turned* to the past] 19. to put to a specified use; apply [he *turned* his hand to writing] 20. to change from one form, condition, etc. to another [to *turn* cream into butter] 21. to exchange for [to *turn* produce into hard cash] 22. to translate or paraphrase 23. to derange, distract, or infatuate 24. to make sour 25. to affect in some way 26. to change the colour of —*vi.* 1. to rotate, revolve, pivot, etc. 2. to move round or partly round 3. to reel; whirl [my head is *turning*] 4. to become curved or bent 5. to become reversed or inverted 6. to become upset, as the stomach 7. to change or reverse one's or its course or direction [the tide *turned*] 8. to refer (*to*) 9. to go or apply (*to*) for help 10. to direct or shift one's attention, abilities, etc. [he *turned* to music] 11. to make a sudden attack (*on* or *upon*) [the dog *turned* on him] 12. to reverse one's feelings, allegiance, etc. [he *turned* against his sister] 13. to depend or hinge (*on* or *upon*) 14. to become [to *turn* bitter with age] 15. to change into another form [the rain *turned* into sleet] 16. to become rancid, sour, etc. 17. to change colour, as leaves in the autumn —*n.* 1. a turning round; rotation, as of a wheel, handle, etc. 2. a single twist, coil, winding, etc. 3. a musical ornament of four tones, with the tones above and below the principal tone alternating with it 4. a change or reversal of position, course, or direction 5. a short walk or ride around an area, as for exercise or inspection 6. the place where a change in direction occurs; bend; curve 7. *a)* a change in trend, events, health, etc. *b) same as* TURNING POINT 8. the time of change [the *turn* of the century] 9. a sudden, brief shock 10. an action or deed [a good *turn*] 11. a spell of activity 12. an attack of illness, dizziness, etc. 13. the right, duty, or chance to do something, esp. in regular order [his *turn* to bat] 14. an act in a variety show 15. a distinctive form, manner, detail, etc. [a quaint *turn* of speech] 16. natural inclination [a curious *turn* of mind] —**at every turn** in every instance; constantly —**by turns** one after another in regular order —**in turn** in proper sequence or succession —**out of turn** 1. not in proper sequence or order 2. imprudently [to talk *out of turn*] —**take turns** to speak, do, etc. one after another in regular order —**to a turn** perfectly —**turn and turn about** alternately —**turn down** 1. to reject (the request, etc. of someone) 2. to lessen the intensity or volume of 3. to fold down (a page, sheet, etc.) —**turn in** 1. to make a turn into; enter 2. to deliver; hand in 3. to inform on or hand over, as to the police 4. to give back 5. [Colloq.] to go to bed 6. [Colloq.] to give up; conclude (an activity, plan, etc.) —**turn off** 1. *a)* to leave (a road, etc.) *b)* to branch off: said of a road, etc. 2. to shut off; stop from functioning 3. to stop displaying suddenly [to *turn off* a smile] 4. to discharge (an employee) 5. [Slang] to cause (someone) to become uninterested, annoyed, etc. —**turn on** 1. to start; make go on or start functioning 2. to display suddenly [to *turn on* the charm] 3. [Slang] to stimulate with or as with a psychedelic drug; make elated, euphoric, etc. —**turn out** 1. to put out (a light) 2. to put outside 3. to dismiss; drive out 4. to come or gather [to *turn out* for a picnic] 5. to produce 6. to result 7. to prove to be 8. to become 9. to equip, dress, etc. 10. [Colloq.] to get out of bed 11. to clear or clean out the contents of [he *turned out* his pockets] —**turn over** 1. to change or reverse the position of 2. to change one's position 3. to begin, or make begin, to operate, as an engine 4. to consider; ponder 5. to hand over; give 6. to convert 7. to sell and replenish (a stock of goods) 8. to do business to the amount of —**turn to** to get to work —**turn up** 1. to fold back or over upon itself 2. to lift up or turn face up 3. to increase the speed, intensity, etc. of, as by turning a control 4. to make a turn onto or into (a street, etc.) 5. to have an upward direction 6. to happen 7. to arrive 8. to find or be found —**turn'er** *n.*

turn·a·bout (turn'ə bout') *n.* 1. a turning about, as to face the other way 2. a shift or reversal of allegiance, opinion, etc.; about-face

turn·buck·le (-buk''l) *n.* a metal loop with opposite internal threads in each end for the threaded ends of two rods or ringbolts, forming a coupling that can be turned to tighten or loosen the rods or two wires attached to the ringbolts

TURNBUCKLE

turn·coat (-kōt') *n.* a person who goes over to the opposite side or party; renegade; traitor

turn cock (-kok') *n.* a person who operates the stopcock on a water-main, etc.

turn·down (-doun') *adj.* 1. that can be turned down 2. having the upper part folded down [a turndown collar]

turn·ing (tur'niŋ) *n.* 1. the action of a person or thing that turns 2. *a)* a road that joins another [the fourth *turning* on the right] *b)* the point where this occurs 3. the art or process of shaping things on a lathe

turning circle the smallest circle in which it is possible to turn a motor vehicle round in one forward movement

turning point 1. a point at which something turns or changes direction 2. a point in time at which a decisive change occurs; crisis

tur·nip (tur'nip) *n.* [prob. < TURN or < Fr. *tour*, in sense of "round" + ME. *nepe* < OE. < L. *napus*, a turnip] 1. *a)* a plant of the cabbage family, with edible, hairy leaves and a roundish, light-coloured root used as a vegetable *b) same as* SWEDE 2. the root of either of these plants

turn·key (turn'kē') *n., pl.* **-keys'** a person in charge of the keys of a prison; warder; jailer

turn·out (-out') *n.* 1. a turning out 2. *a)* a gathering of people, as for a meeting *b)* the number of people 3. an amount produced 4. a carriage with its horse or horses 5. *a)* equipment *b)* a set of clothes

turn·o·ver (-ō'vər) *n.* 1. a turning over; specif., *a)* an upset *b)* a change from one side, opinion, etc. to another 2. a small, semi-circular or triangular pastry made by folding one half of the crust over the other with a filling in between 3. *a)* the selling out and replacing of a stock of goods *b)* the amount of business done during a given period in terms of the money used in buying and selling 4. *a)* the number of workers hired as replacements during a given period *b)* the ratio of this to the average number of workers employed —*adj.* that turns over

turn·pike (-pīk') *n.* [ME. *turnpyke*, a spiked barrier across a road: see TURN & PIKE⁴] 1. *same as* TOLLGATE 2. [Obs.] a toll road: also **turnpike road 3.** [U.S.] a road, esp. an expressway, for the use of which a toll is charged

turn·spit (-spit') *n.* **1.** formerly, a person or a small dog that turned a spit **2.** a spit that can be turned

turn·stile (-stīl') *n.* a post with revolving horizontal bars, often coin-operated, used at an entrance to admit persons one at a time

turn·stone (-stōn') *n.* a small, shore bird of the sandpiper family that turns over pebbles to seek food

turn·ta·ble (-tā'b'l) *n.* a circular rotating platform; specif., *a)* such a platform for supporting a gramophone record being played *b)* such a platform carrying tracks to turn a locomotive round

turn·up (turn'up') *n.* something turned up specif., a turned-up fold at the bottom of a trouser leg —*adj.* that turns up or is turned up —**a turnup for the book** [Colloq.] an unexpected happening

tur·pen·tine (tur'pən tīn') *n.* [< OFr. < L., ult. < Gr. *terebinthos*, a tree yielding turpentine] **1.** any of the various oleoresins obtained from pines and other coniferous trees: in full, **gum turpentine 2.** a colourless, volatile oil distilled from such oleoresins and used in paints, in medicine, etc.: in full, **spirits** (or **oil**) **of turpentine** —*vt.* **-tined'**, **-tin'ing** to apply turpentine to —**tur'pen·tin'ic** (-tin'ik), **tur'pen·tin'ous** (-tī'nəs) *adj.*

tur·pi·tude (tur'pə tyōōd') *n.* [MFr. < L. < *turpis*, vile] the condition of being wicked, evil, or depraved

turps (turps) *n.pl.* [with sing. v.] same as TURPENTINE (*n.* 2)

tur·quoise (tur'kwoiz, -koiz) *n.* [< MFr. fem. of OFr. *turqueis*, Turkish: orig. brought to W Europe through Turkey] **1.** a greenish-blue, semiprecious stone, a hydrous phosphate of aluminium containing a small amount of copper **2.** a greenish blue —*adj.* greenish-blue Also sp. **tur'quois**

tur·ret (tur'it) *n.* [< OFr. dim. of *tour*: see TOWER¹] **1.** a small tower projecting from a building, usually at a corner **2.** *a)* a low, armoured, usually revolving, towerlike structure for guns, as on a warship, tank, etc. *b)* a transparent dome for a gun and gunner, as on a bomber **3.** an attachment for a lathe, drill, etc., consisting of a block holding several cutting tools, which may be rotated to present any of the tools to the work: also **tur'ret·head'** —**tur'ret·ed** *adj.*

turret lathe same as CAPSTAN LATHE

tur·tle (tur't'l) *n.*, *pl.* **-tles, -tle:** see PLURAL, II, D, 1 [altered (after TURTLEDOVE) < Fr. *tortue*, tortoise] **1.** any of various land and water reptiles having a toothless beak and a soft body encased in a hard shell into which, in most species, it can pull its head, tail, and four legs: popularly, the term is restricted to the marine species which have flippers, land species being usually called *tortoise* **2.** the flesh of some turtles, used as food **3.** archaic var. of TURTLEDOVE —*vi.* **-tled, -tling** to hunt for turtles —**turn turtle** to turn upside down

tur·tle·back (-bak') *n.* an arched structure over the deck of a ship as a protection against heavy seas

tur·tle·dove (-duv') *n.* [OE. *turtle* < L. *turtur*, of echoic origin] any of several wild doves noted for their sad cooing and the devotion that the mates seem to show toward each other

tur·tle·neck (-nek') *n.* **1.** a high, snugly fitting collar on a sweater, etc. **2.** a sweater, etc. with such a neck

tusk (tusk) *n.* [OE. *tucs*] **1.** in elephants, wild boars, etc., a long, pointed tooth, usually one of a pair, that sticks out of the mouth **2.** any tusklike tooth or part —*vt.* to dig, gore, etc. with a tusk or tusks —**tusked** *adj.* —**tusk'like'** *adj.*

tusk·er (-ər) *n.* an animal with tusks, esp. very long ones

tus·ser (tus'ə) *n.* [< Hindi < Sans. *tasara*, lit., a shuttle] **1.** an Asiatic silkworm that produces a coarse, tough silk **2.** this silk: also **tusser silk** Also sp. **tus'sore, tus'sor** (tus'ôr), and chiefly U.S., **tus'sah** (tus'ə)

tus·sle (tus'l) *n.*, *vi.* **-sled, -sling** [LME. freq. of *tusen*, to pull] struggle; wrestle; scuffle

tus·sock (tus'ək) *n.* [prob. < ME. (to)*tusen*, to rumple + -OCK] a thick tuft or clump of grass, twigs, etc. —**tus'sock·y** (-ē) *adj.*

tut (tut) *interj.*, *n.* an exclamation of impatience, annoyance, rebuke, etc. —*vi.* **tut'ted, tut'ting** to utter "tuts"

tu·te·lage (tyōōt'əl ij) *n.* [< L. *tutela*, protection] **1.** guardianship; care, protection, etc. **2.** teaching; instruction **3.** the condition of being under a guardian or tutor

tu·te·lar·y (ə·tē) *adj.* [< L. < *tutela*: see prec.] **1.** that watches over or protects **2.** of or serving as a guardian Also **tu'te·lar** (-ər) —*n.*, *pl.* **-lar·ies** a tutelary god, spirit, etc.

tu·tor (tyōōt'ər) *n.* [< MFr. < L. < pp. of *tueri*, to guard] **1.** a teacher who teaches one student at a time **2.** a legal guardian of a minor **3.** in some universities, etc., *a)* a member of staff in charge of the studies of a number of students *b)* a member of staff responsible for the general welfare of a number of students **4.** in some U.S. colleges, a teacher ranking below an instructor —*vt.* **1.** to act as a tutor to; esp., to teach (students) one at a time **2.** to

discipline; admonish —*vi.* to act as a tutor —**tu'tor·age, tu'tor·ship'** *n.*

tu·to·ri·al (tyōō tôr'ē əl) *n.* a period of intensive tuition given by a tutor to an individual student or a small group of students —*adj.* of a tutor

tut·ti (tōōt'ē) *adj.* [It., ult. < L. *totus*, all] *Music* for all instruments or voices —*n.*, *pl.* **-tis 1.** a passage played or sung by all performers **2.** the tonal effect of such a passage

tut·ti-frut·ti (tōōt'ē frōōt'ē) *n.* [It., all fruits] **1.** ice cream or other sweet food containing bits of candied fruits **2.** a flavouring combining a number of fruit flavors

tut·ty (tut'ē) *n.* [< ME. *tutie* < MFr. < Ar. *tūtujā*, zinc oxide] crude zinc oxide

tu·tu (tōō'tōō) *n.* [Fr.] a very short, full, projecting skirt worn by women ballet dancers

tu-whit tu-whoo (tōō hwit'tōō hwōō'; -wit', -wōō') the sound made by an owl

tux·e·do (tək sē'dō) *n.*, *pl.* **-dos** [< the name of a country club near *Tuxedo* Lake, New York State] [U.S.] a dinner jacket

tu·yere (twē yer', tōō-; twir) *n.* [Fr., a nozzle] the pipe through which air is forced into a blast furnace, etc.: also **twy·er**

TV (tē'vē') *n.*, *pl.* **TVs, TV's** television or a television receiving set

twa (twô) *adj.*, *n.* [OE.] *Scot.* var. of TWO

twad·dle (twod''l) *n.* [prob. akin to TATTLE] foolish, empty talk or writing; nonsense —*vt.*, *vi.* **-dled, -dling** to talk or write in a foolish or senseless manner; prattle —**twad'dler** *n.*

twain (twān) *n.*, *adj.* [OE. *twegen*, two] archaic var. of TWO

twang (twaŋ) *n.* [echoic] **1.** a quick, sharp, vibrating sound, as of a plucked string **2.** *a)* a sharp, nasal speech sound *b)* a dialect using such sounds —*vi.*, *vt.* **1.** to make or cause to make a twang, as a bowstring, banjo, etc. **2.** to speak or say with a twang **3.** to shoot or be released with a twang, as an arrow —**twang'y** *adj.*

'twas (twoz; *unstressed* twaz) it was

twat (twat) *n.* [< ?] **1.** the female genitals; generally considered a vulgar term **2.** [Slang] a stupid person

twat·tle (twot''l) *n.*, *vi.*, *vt.* **-tled, -tling** var. of TWADDLE

tway·blade (twā'blād') *n.* [archaic *tway*, two + BLADE] any of various orchids with opposite, paired leaves

tweak (twēk) *vt.* [OE. *twiccan*, to twitch] to give a sudden, twisting pinch to (someone's nose, ear, cheek, etc.) —*n.* such a pinch

twee (twē) *adj.* [< *tweet*, child's pronun. of SWEET] [Colloq.] affectedly pretty, dainty, or quaint

tweed (twēd) *n.* [< misreading of *tweel*, Scot. form of TWILL: later assoc. with the *Tweed*, river in Scotland] **1.** a wool fabric with a rough surface, in a twill weave of two or more colours **2.** a suit, etc. of this **3.** [pl.] clothes of tweed

twee·dle (twēd''l) *vi.*, *vt.* **-dled, -dling** [echoic] **1.** to pipe, whistle, etc. shrilly **2.** to cajole or wheedle —*n.* a shrill, piping sound

twee·dle·dum and twee·dle·dee (twēd''l dum'n twēd''l dē') [< prec. + *dum* & *dee*, echoic of musical notes] two persons or things so much alike that it is hard to tell them apart

tweed·y (twēd'ē) *adj.* **tweed'i·er, tweed'i·est 1.** of or like tweed **2.** having the casually tailored look, fondness of the outdoors, heartiness, etc. of a person given to wearing tweeds —**tweed'i·ness** *n.*

'tween (twēn) *prep.* [Poet.] between

tweet (twēt) *n.*, *interj.* [echoic] the thin, chirping sound of a small bird —*vi.* to make this sound

tweet·er (-ər) *n.* a small, high-fidelity loudspeaker for reproducing high-frequency sounds: cf. WOOFER

tweez·ers (twē'zərz) *n.pl.* [with sing. or pl. v.] [< obs. *tweeze*, surgical set < Fr. pl. of *étui*, a case] small pincers for plucking out hairs, handling little objects, etc.: also **pair of tweezers**

twelfth (twelfth) *adj.* [OE. *twelfta*] **1.** preceded by eleven others in a series; 12th **2.** designating any of the twelve equal parts of something —*n.* **1.** the one following the eleventh **2.** any of the twelve equal parts of something; 1/12

Twelfth Day the twelfth day (Jan. 6) after Christmas; Epiphany: the evening before, or sometimes the evening of, this day is called **Twelfth Night**

twelfth man a reserve player in a cricket team

twelve (twelv) *adj.* [OE. *twelf*] two more than ten —*n.* **1.** the cardinal number between eleven and thirteen; 12; XII **2.** any group of twelve persons or things; dozen —**the Twelve** the Twelve Apostles

Twelve Apostles the twelve disciples chosen by Jesus to go forth to teach the gospel

twelve·fold (twelv'fōld') *adj.* **1.** having twelve parts **2.** having twelve times as much or as many —*adv.* twelve times as much or as many

twelve·mo (-mō) *adj.*, *n.*, *pl.* **-mos** same as DUODECIMO

twelve·month (-munth') *n.* a year

twelve-tone (-tōn') *adj.* *Music* designating or of a system of composition in which the twelve tones of the chromatic scale are arranged into some arbitrary, fixed succession (*tone row*) as a basis for further thematic development

twen·ti·eth (twen'tē ith) *adj.* **1.** preceded by nineteen others in a series; 20th **2.** designating any of the twenty equal parts of something —*n.* **1.** the one following the nineteenth **2.** any of twenty equal parts of something; 1/20

twen·ty (twen'tē) *adj.* [OE. *twegentig*] two times ten —*n., pl.* **-ties** the cardinal number between nineteen and twenty-one; 20; XX —**the twenties** the numbers or years, as of a century, from twenty to twenty-nine

twen·ty·fold (-fōld') *adj.* **1.** having twenty parts **2.** having twenty times as much or as many —*adv.* twenty times as much or as many

'twere (twur) [Poet.] it were

twerp (twurp) *n.* [< ?] [Slang] a person regarded as insignificant, contemptible, etc.

twi- (twī) [ME. < OE.] *a prefix meaning* two, double, twice

twice (twīs) *adv.* [OE. *twiges* < *twiga*] **1.** on two occasions or in two instances **2.** two times **3.** two times as much or as many; twofold; doubly

twid·dle (twid''l) *vt.* **-dled, -dling** [prob. < TW(IST) + (D)IDDLE[1]] to twirl or play with lightly —*vi.* **1.** to toy with some object **2.** to be busy about trifles —*n.* **1.** a light, twirling motion, as with the thumbs **2.** a wavy line or mark —**twiddle one's thumbs** **1.** to twirl one's thumbs idly around one another **2.** to be idle —**twid'dler** *n.* —**twid'dly** *adj.*

twig (twig) *n.* [OE. *twigge*] a small branch or shoot of a tree or shrub —**twigged** *adj.* —**twig'gy** *adj.* **-gi·er, -gi·est**

twi·light (twī'līt') *n.* [ME. < *twi-*, two + LIGHT[1]] **1.** *a)* the soft, dim light just after sunset or, sometimes, just before sunrise *b)* the period from sunset to dark **2.** any growing darkness **3.** a condition of gradual decline **4.** a condition of imperfect comprehension —*adj.* of or like twilight

twilight of the gods *Norse Myth.* the destruction of the world in the last great conflict between the gods and the forces of evil: also **Rag'na·rok** (rag'nə rok')

twilight sleep a state of partial anaesthia induced by morphine and scopolamine, formerly used in childbirth

twilight zone **1.** an inner city area that has deteriorated **2.** any indefinite condition or area

twi·lit (twī'lit) *adj.* full of or bathed in the soft, dim light of twilight

twill (twil) *n.* [OE. *twilic*, woven of double thread, ult. < L. *bilix*, double-threaded] **1.** a cloth woven so as to have parallel diagonal lines or ribs **2.** the pattern of this weave —*vt.* to weave with a twill —**twilled** *adj.*

'twill (twil) [Poet.] it will

twin (twin) *adj.* [OE. *twinn* & ON. *tvinnr*, double] **1.** consisting of, or being one of a pair of, two separate but similar or closely related things; paired **2.** being two, or either of two, that have been born at the same birth [*twin* girls, a *twin* sister] —*n.* **1.** either of two born at the same birth: twins are either *identical* (produced from the same ovum) or *fraternal* (produced from separate ova) **2.** either of two persons or things very much alike in appearance, shape, etc. —*vi.* **twinned, twin'ning** **1.** to give birth to twins **2.** to be paired (with another) —*vt.* **1.** to give birth to as twins **2.** to pair or couple

twine (twīn) *n.* [OE. *twin*, double thread] **1.** a strong thread, string, or cord of two or more strands twisted together **2.** a twining or being twined **3.** a twined thing or part; twist —*vt.* **twined, twin'ing** **1.** *a)* to twist together; intertwine *b)* to form in this way **2.** to wreathe or wind (one thing) around or with another **3.** to enfold, embrace, etc. [a wreath *twining* his brow] —*vi.* **1.** to twist, interlace, etc. **2.** to twist and turn —**twin'ing·ly** *adv.*

twin-en·gined (twin'en'jənd) *adj.* powered by two engines: said of an aeroplane: also **twin'-en'gine**

twinge (twinj) *vt., vi.* **twinged, twing'ing** [OE. *twengan*, to squeeze] to have or cause to have a sudden, brief, darting pain or pang —*n.* **1.** a sudden, brief, darting pain or pang **2.** a sudden, brief feeling of remorse, shame, etc.; qualm

twin·kle (twin'k'l) *vi.* **-kled, -kling** [OE. *twinclian*] **1.** to shine with quick flashes of light at intervals, as some stars; sparkle **2.** to light up, as with amusement: said of the eyes **3.** to move about quickly and lightly, as a dancer's feet; flicker —*vt.* **1.** to make twinkle **2.** to emit (light) in quick flashes at intervals —*n.* **1.** a wink of the eye **2.** a quick flash of amusement, etc. in the eye **3.** a quick flash of light; sparkle **4.** the instant that it takes to wink —**twin'kler** *n.*

twin·kling (-kliŋ) *n.* **1.** the action of a thing that twinkles **2.** *a)* the winking of an eye *b)* the very brief time it takes to wink; instant

twinset (twin'set') *n.* a matching cardigan and jumper for a woman

twin towns two towns in different countries which have created social and cultural links

twirl (twurl) *vt., vi.* [prob. < Scand.] **1.** to rotate rapidly; spin **2.** to whirl in a circle **3.** to twist or coil —*n.* **1.** a twirling or being twirled **2.** something twirled; specif., a twist, coil, flourish, etc. —**twirl'er** *n.*

twirp (twurp) *n.* [Slang] *var. of* TWERP

twist (twist) *vt.* [< OE. *-twist*, a rope (in *mæst-twist*, rope to stay a mast)] **1.** to wind (strands of cotton, silk, etc.) around one another, as in spinning or in making thread, cord, etc. **2.** to wreathe; twine **3.** to wind (thread, rope, etc.) around something **4.** to make (one's or its way) by turning one way and then another **5.** to give spiral shape to **6.** *a)* to subject to torsion *b)* to wrench; sprain **7.** *a)* to contort or distort (the face, etc.) *b)* to cause to be malformed [fingers *twisted* with arthritis] **8.** to distort or pervert the meaning of **9.** to cause to turn round or rotate **10.** to break off by turning the end (often with *off*) **11.** to make (a ball) go in a curve by giving it a spinning motion —*vi.* **1.** to undergo twisting and thus take on a spiral or coiled form **2.** to spiral, coil, twine, etc. (*round* or *about* something) **3.** to revolve or rotate **4.** to turn to one side **5.** to wind or meander, as a path **6.** to squirm; writhe **7.** to move in a curved path, as a ball **8.** to dance the twist —*n.* **1.** a strong, closely twisted silk thread **2.** a twisted roll of tobacco leaves **3.** a loaf of bread or roll made of twisted pieces of dough **4.** a knot, etc. made by twisting **5.** a sliver of peel from a lemon, lime, etc. twisted and added to a drink **6.** a twisting or being twisted **7.** a spin given to a ball in throwing or striking it **8.** stress due to torsion, or the degree of this **9.** a contortion, as of the face **10.** a wrench or sprain **11.** a turning aside; turn; bend **12.** a place at which something twists **13.** a personal tendency; eccentricity; quirk **14.** distortion, as of meaning **15.** a different or unexpected meaning, method, slant, etc. **16.** a dance in which couples face each other and vigorously move the hips and arms **17.** [Slang] *a)* a drink of two mixed ingredients *b)* a hearty appetite —**round the twist** [Slang] mad —**twist a person's arm** **1.** to hurt someone by wrenching his arm **2.** to bring moral pressure to bear on someone in order to persuade or compel him to do something —**twist** (a person) **round one's little finger** to have complete dominance over (a person) —**twist'y** *adj.*

twist·er (twis'tər) *n.* **1.** a person or thing that twists; specif., a thrown or batted ball that has been given a twist **2.** a swindler; cheat **3.** [U.S.] a tornado or cyclone

twit[1] (twit) *vt.* **twit'ted, twit'ting** [< OE. *ætwitan* < *æt*, at + *witan*, to accuse] to reproach, tease, taunt, etc., esp. by reminding of a fault or mistake —*n.* a reproach or taunt

twit[2] (twit) *n.* [? < prec.] [Slang] a foolish, contemptible person

twitch (twich) *vt., vi.* [< OE. *twiccian*, to pluck] **1.** to pull (at) with a quick, slight jerk; pluck **2.** to move with a quick, slight jerk, often due to muscle spasm **3.** to ache with a sudden, sharp pain —*n.* **1.** a quick, slight jerk **2.** a sudden, quick motion, esp. one caused by muscle spasm; tic **3.** a sudden, sharp pain; twinge **4.** a noose fixed over the upper lip of a horse to control it, as during an operation

twitch-grass (-gräs') *n.* [var. of QUITCH] *same as* COUCH GRASS

twite (twīt) *n.* [of echoic origin] a small, upland, European finch, related to the linnet

twit·ter[1] (twit'ər) *vi.* [ME. *twiteren*: orig. echoic] **1.** to make a series of light, sharp vocal sounds; chirp, as birds do **2.** *a)* to talk in a rapid or agitated manner; chatter *b)* to giggle —*vt.* to say in a twittering manner —*n.* **1.** the act or sound of twittering **2.** a condition of trembling excitement; flutter —**twit'ter·er** *n.* —**twit'ter·y** *adj.*

twit·ter[2] (twit'ər) *n.* a person who twits

'twixt (twikst) *prep.* [Poet.] betwixt

two (tōō) *adj.* [OE. *twa*] totalling one more than one —*n.* **1.** the cardinal number between one and three; 2; II **2.** anything having two units or members, or numbered two —**in two** in two parts —**put two and two together** to reach an obvious conclusion by considering several facts together —**that makes two of us** [Colloq.] that applies equally to me

two-edged (-ejd') *adj.* **1.** that has two cutting edges **2.** that can have two different meanings, as a remark

two-faced (-fāst') *adj.* **1.** having two faces **2.** deceitful; hypocritical —**two'-fac'ed·ly** (-fās'id lē) *adv.*

two-fist·ed (-fis'tid) *adj.* [Colloq.] **1.** clumsy **2.** [U.S.] vigorous; virile

two·fold (-fōld') *adj.* **1.** having two parts; double **2.** having twice as much or as many —*adv.* twice as much or as many

two-hand·ed (-han'did) *adj.* **1.** that needs to be used or wielded with both hands **2.** worked by two people [a *two-handed* saw] **3.** for two people, as a card game **4.** having two hands **5.** using both hands equally well

two-leg·ged (-leg'id, -legd') *adj.* having two legs

two minutes' silence the period of quiet observed at 11 a.m. on Remembrance Sunday

two·pence (tōō'pens'; *for 3 & 4, also* tup''ns) *n.* **1.** the sum of two pennies **2.** a British coin worth one fiftieth of a pound **3.** a former British silver coin **4.** something of little value [he doesn't care *twopence* for it]

two-pen·ny (tup'ə nē) *adj.* **1.** worth or costing twopence **2.** cheap; worthless

two-piece (tōō′pēs′) *adj.* consisting of two separate parts [a *two-piece* bathing suit]

two-ply (-plī′) *adj.* 1. having two thicknesses, layers, strands, etc. 2. woven double

two-sid·ed (-sīd′id) *adj.* 1. having two sides 2. having two aspects [a *two-sided* question]

two·some (-səm) *n.* 1. two people; a couple 2. *Golf* a game involving two players

two-step (-step′) *n.* 1. a ballroom dance in 2/4 time 2. a piece of music for this dance

two-time (tōō′tīm′) *vt.* **-timed′, -tim′ing** [Slang] to deceive; esp., to be unfaithful to **—two′-tim′er** *n.*

'twould (twood) [Poet.] it would

two-way (tōō′wā′) *adj.* 1. moving, permitting movement, or operating in either of two opposite directions [*two-way* traffic, a *two-way* valve] 2. involving the same obligations, privileges, etc. towards each other by two parties, nations, etc. [a *two-way* cultural exchange] 3. used for both transmitting and receiving [a *two-way* radio]

-ty¹ (tē, ti) [< OFr. -té < L. -tas] a suffix meaning quality of, condition of [*novelty*]

-ty² (tē, ti) [OE. -tig] a suffix meaning tens, times ten [*sixty*]

ty·coon (tī kōōn′) *n.* [< Jap. < Chin. *ta*, great + *kiun*, prince] 1. a title applied by foreigners to the former shogun of Japan 2. a wealthy and powerful industrialist, financier, etc.

ty·ing (tī′iŋ) *prp. of* TIE

tyke (tīk) *n.* [ON. *tik*, a bitch] 1. [Chiefly N Dial.] a dog, esp. a mongrel or cur b) a rough, ill-mannered person; boor 2. [Slang] a Yorkshireman 3. [Chiefly U.S. Colloq.] a small child Also sp. **tike**

ty·lo·pod (tī′lo pod′, tī′lō-) *n.* [< Gr. *tylos*, a callus + *pous* (gen. *podos*), a foot] a ruminant with padded digits, as the camel [a *tylop'o·dous adj.*

tym·pan (tim′pən) *n.* [ME. < OE. < L.: see TYMPANUM] *Printing* the sheet of paper, parchment, etc. stretched over the impression cylinder of a printing press to cushion the paper being printed and equalize type pressure

tym·pa·ni (tim′pə nē) *n.pl., sing.* **-no′** (-nō′) *var. of* TIMPANI **—tym′pa·nist** *n.*

tym·pan·ic membrane (tim pan′ik) a thin membrane that separates the middle ear from the external ear and vibrates when struck by sound waves; eardrum

tym·pa·num (tim′pə nəm) *n., pl.* **-nums, -na** (-nə) [L., a drum < Gr. *tympanon*] 1. *Anat. same as:* a) MIDDLE EAR b) TYMPANIC MEMBRANE 2. a drum or drumhead 3. *Archit.* a) the recessed space, usually triangular, enclosed by the slanting cornices of a pediment b) the space enclosed by an arch and the top of the door or window below it 4. a scoop wheel for raising water **—tym·pan′ic** (-pan′ik) *adj.*

Tyn·wald (tin′wəld) [< ON. *thingvollr* < *thing*, assembly + *vollr*, field] the parliament of the Isle of Man

typ·al (tīp′'l) *adj.* of, pertaining to, or serving as a type

type (tīp) *n.* [< LL. < L. < Gr. *typos*, a figure, model < *typtein*, to strike] 1. a person, thing, or event that represents another, esp. another that it is thought will appear later; symbol; token; sign 2. the characteristic form, plan, style, etc. of a particular class or group 3. a class, group, etc. having characteristics in common [a new *type* of aircraft] 4. a person, animal, or thing that is representative or characteristic of a class or group 5. a perfect example; model; pattern 6. the device on either side of a coin 7. [Colloq.] a person, esp. of a specified kind [he's a strange *type*] 8. *Biol.* a) a specimen designated as the one serving as the basis for the original description and name of a taxon b) *same as* TYPE GENUS 9. *Printing* a) a rectangular piece of metal or, sometimes, wood, with a raised letter, figure, etc. in reverse on its upper end b) such pieces collectively c) a printed or photographically reproduced character or characters **—vt. typed, typ′ing** 1. to classify according to type [to *type* a blood sample] 2. to write with a typewriter; typewrite **—vi.** to use a typewriter **—typ′a·ble** *adj.*

-type (tīp) [< Gr. *typos:* see TYPE] a combining form meaning: 1. type, example [*prototype*] 2. stamp, print, printing type [*monotype*]

type·cast (tīp′kāst′) *vt.* **-cast′, -cast′ing** to cast (an actor) repeatedly in the same type of part, or in the part of a character whose traits are very much like his own

type-cast (tīp′kāst′) *vt., vi.* **-cast′, -cast′ing** to cast (type)

type·face (-fās′) *n.* same as FACE (*n.* 10)

type genus *Biol.* the particular genus that is theoretically most typical of a family and whose name serves as the base for the family name

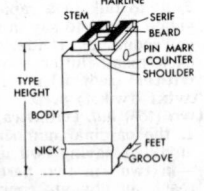

TYPE

type metal an alloy of tin, lead, and antimony, and sometimes copper, used for making type, etc.

type·script (tīp′skript′) *n.* any typed document

type·set (-set′) *vt.* **-set′, -set′ting** to set in type

type·set·ter (-set′ər) *n.* 1. a person who sets type; compositor 2. a machine for setting type **—type′set′ting** *n., adj.*

type·write (-rīt′) *vt., vi.* **-wrote′, -writ′ten, -writ′ing** to write with a typewriter: now usually shortened to *type*

type·writ·er (-rīt′ər) *n.* 1. a writing machine with a keyboard for reproducing letters, figures, etc. that resemble printed ones 2. earlier term for TYPIST

ty·phoid (tī′foid) *n.* [TYPH(US) + -OID] 1. orig., any typhuslike disorder 2. an infectious disease caused by a bacillus and acquired by eating food or drinking water contaminated by excreta: it causes fever, intestinal disorders, etc.: in full, **typhoid fever —ty·phoi′dal** *adj.*

ty·phoon (tī fōōn′) *n.* [< Chin. dial. *tai-fung*, lit., great wind; merged with earlier *tuphan, tufan,* < Port. < Ar. < Gr. *typhon,* hurricane] any violent tropical cyclone originating in the W Pacific, esp. in the South China Sea **—ty·phon′ic** (-fon′ik) *adj.*

ty·phus (tī′fəs) *n.* [ModL. < Gr. *typhos,* a fever] an acute infectious disease caused by a rickettsia transmitted to man by fleas, lice, etc., and causing fever, red spots on the skin, etc.: in full, **typhus fever —ty′phous** (-fəs) *adj.*

typ·i·cal (tip′i k'l) *adj.* 1. serving as a type; symbolic 2. having the distinguishing characteristics, qualities, etc. of a class, group, etc.; representative 3. belonging to a type; characteristic Also **typ′ic —typ′i·cal·ly** *adv.* **—typ′i·cal·ness,** typ·i·cal′i·ty (-kal′ə tē) *n.*

typ·i·fy (tip′ə fī′) *vt.* **-fied′, -fy′ing** [see TYPE & -FY] 1. to be a type or emblem of; symbolize 2. to have or show the distinctive characteristics of; be typical of **—typ′i·fi·ca′tion** *n.* **—typ′i·fi′er** *n.*

typ·ist (tīp′ist) *n.* a person whose work is typing

ty·po (tī′pō) *n., pl.* **-pos** [Colloq.] 1. a typographer 2. [U.S.] a typographical error; mechanical mistake made in setting type or in typing

ty·po- [< Gr. *typos:* see TYPE] a combining form meaning type

ty·pog·ra·pher (tī pog′rə fər) *n.* a person skilled in typography; printer, compositor, etc.

ty·po·graph·i·cal (tī′pə graf′i k'l) *adj.* of typography; having to do with the setting of type, printing, etc.: also **ty′po·graph′ic —ty′po·graph′i·cal·ly** *adv.*

ty·pog·ra·phy (tī pog′rə fē) *n.* [< Fr. < ML.: see TYPO- & -GRAPHY] 1. the art or process of printing from type 2. the art or process of setting and arranging type for printing 3. the arrangement, style, or appearance of matter printed from type

ty·ran·ni·cal (ti ran′i k'l, tī-) *adj.* 1. of or suited to a tyrant; arbitrary; despotic 2. harsh, cruel, unjust, etc. Also **ty·ran′nic —ty·ran′ni·cal·ly** *adv.*

ty·ran·ni·cide (-ə sīd′) *n.* 1. the act of killing a tyrant 2. a person who kills a tyrant

tyr·an·nize (tir′ə nīz′) *vi.* **-nized′, -niz′ing** 1. to govern as a tyrant 2. to use authority harshly or cruelly **—vt.** to treat tyrannically; oppress **—tyr′an·niz′er** *n.*

ty·ran·no·saur (ti ran′ə sôr′) *n.* [< ModL. < Gr. *tyrannos,* tyrant + -SAURUS] any of various huge, twofooted, flesh-eating dinosaurs of the Cretaceous Period in N America: also **ty·ran′no·saur′us** (-əs)

tyr·an·nous (tir′ə nəs) *adj.* tyrannical; despotic, oppressive, unjust, etc. **—tyr′an·nous·ly** *adv.*

tyr·an·ny (tir′ə nē) *n., pl.* **-nies** 1. the office, authority, government, etc. of a tyrant, or absolute ruler 2. oppressive and unjust government; despotism 3. very cruel and unjust use of power or authority 4. harshness; severity 5. a tyrannical act

ty·rant (tī′rənt) *n.* [< OFr. < L. < Gr. *tyrannos*] 1. an absolute ruler 2. a cruel, oppressive ruler; despot 3. any person who uses his authority in an oppressive manner

tyre (tīr) *n.* [prob. var. of ME. *atir,* equipment] a hoop of iron or rubber, or a rubber tube filled with air, fixed around the wheel of a vehicle to form a tread

tyre-gauge (-gāj′) *n.* a small instrument for measuring air pressure in tyres

Tyr·i·an (tir′ē ən) *adj.* designating or of Tyre, a seaport in SW Lebanon, and centre of ancient Phoenician culture **—n.** an inhabitant of Tyre

Tyrian purple (or **dye**) 1. a purple or crimson dye used by the ancient Romans and Greeks: it was made from certain molluscs, orig. at Tyre 2. bluish red

ty·ro (tī′rō) *n., pl.* **-ros** [ML. < L. *tiro,* recruit] a beginner in learning something; novice

Tyr·rhe·ni·an (ti rē′nē ən) *adj.* [< L. *Tyrrhenus*] Etruscan **—n.** an Etruscan Also **Tyr·rhene**

tzar (tsär, zär) *n. var. of* CZAR **—tzar′dom** *n.* **—tzar′ism** *n.* **—tzar′ist** *adj., n.*

tzar·e·vitch (tsär′ə vich, zär′-) *n. var. of* CZAREVITCH

tza·ri·na (tsä rē′nə, zä-) *n. var. of* CZARINA

‡tzi·gane (tsē gän′) *n.* [Fr. < Hung.] a gypsy

u

U, u (yōō) *n., pl.* **U's, u's** 1. the twenty-first letter of the English alphabet 2. a sound of *U* or *u*

U (yōō) *n.* 1. something shaped like U 2. *Cinema* [< *universal*] a film to which a person of any age may be admitted —*adj.* 1. shaped like U 2. [Colloq.] of the upper class, as supposedly characterized by behaviour, tastes, etc.

U *Chem.* uranium

U., U 1. Union 2. United 3. University

U., U, u., u unit; units

U.A.R. United Arab Republic

u·biq·ui·tous (yōō bik′wə təs) *adj.* [see ff. & -OUS] present, or seeming to be present, everywhere at the same time; omnipresent —**u·biq′ui·tous·ly** *adv.* —**u·biq′ui·tous·ness** *n.*

u·biq·ui·ty (-tē) *n.* [< Fr. < L. *ubique*, everywhere] the state, fact, or capacity of being, or seeming to be, everywhere at the same time; omnipresence

U-boat (yōō′bōt′) *n.* [< G. *U-boot*, abbrev. of *Unterseeboot*, undersea boat] a German submarine

u.c. *Printing* upper case

U.C.C.A. Universities Central Council on Admissions

U.D.C. 1. Universal Decimal Classification 2. [Obs.] Urban District Council

ud·der (ud′ər) *n.* [OE. *udr*] a mammary gland with two or more teats, as in cows

U.D.I. unilateral declaration of independence

u·dom·e·ter (yōō dom′ə tər) *n.* [< Fr. < L. *undus*, moist + -METER] an instrument for measuring rainfall

UFO (yōō′fō, yōō ef ō′) *n., pl.* **UFOs, UFO's** [*u*(*nidentified*) *f*(*lying*) *o*(*bject*)] any of a number of unidentified objects reported, esp. since 1947, to have been seen flying at varying heights and speeds and variously regarded as hallucinations, spacecraft from another planet, etc.

ugh (ōōkh, uH, ōō, ug, *etc.*) *interj.* [echoic] an exclamation of disgust, horror, etc.

ug·li (ug′lē) *n.* [altered < UGLY: from its misshapen appearance] a Jamaican citrus fruit that is a three-way cross between a grapefruit, orange, and tangerine: also called **ugli fruit**

ug·li·fy (ug′lə fī) *vt.* **-fied′, -fy′ing** to make ugly; disfigure

ug·ly (ug′lē) *adj.* **-li·er, -li·est** [< ON. *uggligr*, fearful < *uggr*, fear] 1. unpleasing to look at; unsightly 2. bad, vile, repulsive, offensive, etc. [an ugly lie] 3. ominous; dangerous [ugly storm clouds] 4. [Colloq.] ill-tempered; cross [an ugly disposition] —**ug′li·ly** *adv.* —**ug′li·ness** *n.*

ugly duckling [from a story by H. C. Andersen] a very plain child or unpromising thing that in time becomes or could become beautiful, important, etc.

U·gri·an (ōō′grē ən, yōō′-) *adj.* 1. designating or of a group of Finno-Ugric peoples of W Siberia and Hungary 2. *same as* UGRIC (*adj.* 1) —*n.* 1. a member of any of the Ugrian peoples 2. *same as* UGRIC

U·gric (-grik) *adj.* 1. designating or of a branch of the Finno-Ugric subfamily of languages including Hungarian (Magyar) 2. *same as* UGRIAN (*adj.* 1) —*n.* the Ugric languages

uh (u, un) *interj.* 1. *same as* HUH 2. a prolonged sound made in speaking, as while searching for a word

UHF, U.H.F., uhf, u.h.f. ultrahigh frequency

uh-huh (ə hu′; *for 2* un′un′) *interj.* 1. an exclamation indicating: *a)* an affirmative response *b)* that one is listening attentively 2. *var. of* UH-UH

uh·lan (ōō′län, yōō′-; -lən; ōō län′) *n.* [< G. < Pol. *ulan*, a lancer] formerly, a mounted lancer in Poland, Prussia, etc.

uh-uh (un′un′, -un′) *interj.* an exclamation indicating a negative response

uit·land·er (üt′län′dər; *E.* āt′lan′dər) *n.* [Afrik. < Du. *uit*, out + *land*, land] [*sometimes* U-] in South Africa, a foreigner; specif., one not a Boer in the Transvaal

U.K. United Kingdom

U.K.A.E.A. United Kingdom Atomic Energy Authority

u·kase (yōō kās′, -kāz′) *n.* [Russ. *ukaz*, edict] 1. in Czarist Russia, an imperial order or decree 2. any official, esp. arbitrary, decree or proclamation

U·krain·i·an (yōō krā′nē ən) *adj.* of the Ukraine, its people, their language, etc. —*n.* 1. a native or inhabitant of the Ukraine 2. the East Slavic language of the Ukrainians, very closely related to Russian

u·ku·le·le (yōō′kə lā′lē) *n.* [Haw., lit., flea] a musical instrument with four strings, like a small guitar

ul·cer (ul′sər) *n.* [L. *ulcus* (gen. *ulceris*)] 1. an open sore on the skin or some mucous membrane, that festers, damages the tissue, etc. 2. any corrupting condition or influence

UKULELE

ul·cer·ate (ul′sə rāt′) *vt., vi.* **-at′ed, -at′ing** [< L. pp. of *ulcerare*] to make or become ulcerous —**ul′cer·a′tion** *n.* —**ul′cer·a′tive** *adj.*

ul·cer·ous (-sər əs) *adj.* 1. having an ulcer or ulcers 2. of or like an ulcer or ulcers

-ule (yōōl, yool) [< Fr. < L. *-ulus, -ula, -ulum*] a suffix meaning little [*sporule*]

-u·lent (yoo lənt) [< Fr. < L. *-ulentus*] a suffix meaning full of, abounding in [*fraudulent*]

ull·age (ul′ij) *n.* [< ME. < OFr. *ouillage*, a filling to the brim] the amount by which a container, esp. of liquid, falls short of being full

ul·na (ul′nə) *n., pl.* **-nae** (-nē), **-nas** [ModL. < L., the elbow] 1. the larger of the two bones of the forearm, on the side opposite the thumb 2. a corresponding bone in the forelimb of other vertebrates —**ul′nar** (-nər) *adj.*

-u·lose (yoo lōs′) [< L. *-ulosus*] a suffix meaning characterized by, marked by [*granulose*]

u·lot·ri·chous (yoo lot′ri kəs) *adj.* [< Gr. < *oulos*, woolly + *thrix*, hair + -OUS] having woolly or tightly twisted hair

-u·lous (yoo ləs) [< L. *-ulosus*] a suffix meaning tending to, characterized by [*populous*]

ul·ster (ul′stər) *n.* [< *Ulster*, in Ireland, where the fabric was originally made] a long, loose, heavy overcoat

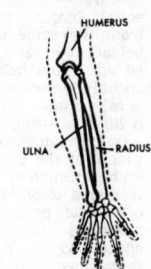

HUMERUS

ULNA — RADIUS

Ul·ster·man (ul′stər mən) *n.* a native or inhabitant of Ulster —**Ul·ster·wom·an** (-woom′ən) *n.fem.*

ult. 1. ultimate 2. ultimately 3. ultimo

ul·te·ri·or (ul tir′ē ər) *adj.* [L., compar. of hyp. *ulter*, beyond] 1. lying beyond or on the farther side 2. later, subsequent, or future 3. beyond what is openly said or made known [an *ulterior* motive] —**ul·te′ri·or·ly** *adv.*

ul·ti·ma (ul′ti mə) *n.* [L., fem. of *ultimus*, last] the last syllable of a word

ul·ti·mate (ul′tə mit) *adj.* [< LL. pp. of *ultimare*, to come to an end < L. *ultimus*, last] 1. beyond which it is impossible to go; farthest 2. final; last 3. most basic; fundamental; primary 4. greatest or highest possible; maximum —*n.* something ultimate [the *ultimate* in pleasure] —**ul′ti·ma·cy** (-mə sē), **ul′ti·mate·ness** *n.* —**ul′ti·mate·ly** *adv.*

ul·ti·ma Thu·le (ul′ti mə thōō′lē) [L.] 1. among the ancients, the northernmost region of the world 2. any far-off, unknown region

ul·ti·ma·tum (ul′tə māt′əm) *n., pl.* **-tums, -ta** (-ə) [ModL. < LL., neut. pp.: see ULTIMATE] a final offer or demand presented to another in a dispute, esp. with a threat to break off relations, use force, etc.

ul·ti·mo (ul′tə mō′) *adv.* [L. *ultimo* (*mense*), (in the) last (month)] in the preceding month: an old-fashioned usage [yours of the 13th (day) *ultimo* received]

ul·tra (ul′trə) *adj.* [L., beyond] going beyond the usual limit; extreme —*n.* an extremist, as in opinions held

ul·tra- [L.] a prefix meaning: 1. beyond [*ultraviolet*] 2. to an extreme degree [*ultramodern*] 3. beyond the range of [*ultramicroscopic*]

ul·tra·con·serv·a·tive (ul′trə kən sur′və tiv) *adj.* conservative to an extreme degree —*n.* an ultraconservative person

ul·tra·high frequency (ul′trə hī′) any radio frequency between 300 and 3000 megahertz

ul·tra·ma·rine (ul′trə mə rēn′) *adj.* [< ML.: see ULTRA- & MARINE] 1. beyond the sea 2. deep-blue —*n.* 1. a blue pigment orig. made from powdered lapis lazuli 2. any similar pigment made from other substances 3. a deep blue

ul·tra·mi·cro·scope (-mī′krə skōp′) *n.* an instrument for observing by dispersed light objects, as colloidal particles, too small to be seen with an ordinary microscope —**ul′-tra·mi·cros′co·py** (-mī kros′ka pē) *n.*

ul·tra·mi·cro·scop·ic (-mī′krə skop′ik) *adj.* 1. too small to be seen with an ordinary microscope 2. of an ultramicroscope —**ul′tra·mi′cro·scop′i·cal·ly** *adv.*

ul·tra·mod·ern (-mod′ərn) *adj.* modern to an extreme degree —**ul′tra·mod′ern·ism** *n.* —**ul′tra·mod′ern·ist** *n.*

ul·tra·mon·tane (-mon′tān) *adj.* [< ML. < L. *ultra*, beyond + *mons* (gen. *montis*), mountain] 1. beyond the mountains, specif., the Alps 2. of, or supporting, the doctrine of papal supremacy —*n.* 1. a person living south of the Alps 2. a person holding ultramontane principles —**ul′tra·mon′ta·nism** *n.*

ul·tra·mun·dane (-mun′dān) *adj.* [ULTRA- + MUNDANE] beyond the world or the solar system

ul·tra·na·tion·al·ism (-nash′ən ′l iz′m) *n.* nationalism that is excessive or extreme —**ul′tra·na′tion·al·ist** *adj., n.* —**ul′-tra·na′tion·al·is′tic** *adj.*

ul·tra·son·ic (-son′ik) *adj.* [ULTRA- + SONIC] designating or of a frequency of mechanical vibrations above the range audible to the human ear, i.e., above 20000 vibrations per second —**ul′tra·son′i·cal·ly** *adv.*

ul·tra·son·ics (-son′iks) *n.pl.* [with sing. v.] the science dealing with ultrasonic phenomena

ul·tra·sound (ul′trə sound′) *n.* ultrasonic waves, used in medical diagnosis and therapy, in surgery, etc.

ul·tra·struc·ture (-struk′chər) *n.* the minute, invisible, elemental structure of protoplasm —**ul′tra·struc′tur·al** *adj.*

ul·tra·vi·o·let (ul′trə vī′ə lit) *adj.* 1. lying just beyond the violet end of the visible spectrum and having wavelengths shorter than 4000 angstroms 2. of or producing light rays of such wavelengths —*n.* ultraviolet radiation

ul·u·late (yōōl′yoo lāt′, ul′-) *vi.* **-lat′ed, -lat′ing** [< L. pp. of *ululare*, to howl: echoic] 1. to howl or hoot 2. to wail or lament loudly —**ul′u·lant** (-lant) *adj.* —**ul′u·la′tion** *n.*

um·bel (um′b′l) *n.* [L. *umbella*: see UMBRELLA] a cluster of flowers with stalks of nearly equal length which spring from the same point —**um′-bel·late** (-it, -āt′), **um′bel·lat′-ed** *adj.* —**um′bel·late′ly** *adv.*

um·bel·lif·er·ous (um′bə lif′ər əs) *adj.* [Mod.L. *um-bellifer* < UMBEL + -FER + -OUS] having an umbel, as plants of the parsley family

um·ber (um′bər) *n.* [< Fr. < It. (*terra d′)ombra*, lit., (earth of) shade, prob. < L. *umbra*, a shade] 1. a kind of earth containing oxides of manganese and iron, used as a pigment: raw umber is yellowish-brown; burnt, or calcined, umber is reddish-brown 2. a yellowish-brown or reddish-brown colour —*adj.* of the colour of raw umber or burnt umber —*vt.* to colour with or as with umber

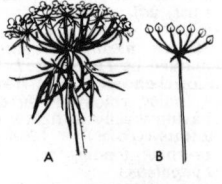

UMBEL
(A, compound;
B, simple)

um·bil·i·cal (um bil′i k′l) *adj.* 1. of or like an umbilicus or an umbilical cord 2. situated at or near the navel 3. linked together by or as if by an umbilical cord —*n.* 1. same as UMBILICAL CORD 2. any vital link or connection, as the cable supplying oxygen, etc. to an astronaut when he is outside his spacecraft

umbilical cord a cordlike structure that connects a foetus with the placenta: it is severed at birth, the navel being formed at the point where it was attached to the foetus

um·bil·i·cus (um bil′i kəs, um′bi li′kəs) *n., pl.* **-ci** (-si′, -sī) [L.] 1. same as NAVEL 2. a navellike depression, as the hilum of a seed

um·bo (um′bō) *n., pl.* **um·bo·nes** (um bō′nēz), **um′bos** [L.] 1. the boss at the centre of a shield 2. something resembling this; protuberance; knob

um·bra (um′brə) *n., pl.* **-brae** (-brē), **-bras** [L., a shade] 1. a shade or shadow 2. the dark cone of shadow projecting from a planet or satellite on the side opposite the sun: see ECLIPSE, illus. 3. the dark central part of a sunspot

um·brage (um′brij) *n.* [OFr. < L. < *umbra*, a shade] 1. [Obs.] shade; shadow 2. foliage, considered as shade-giving 3. offence or resentment [to take *umbrage* at a remark] —**um·bra′geous** (-brā′jəs) *adj.* —**um·bra′geous·ly** *adv.*

um·brel·la (um brel′ə) *n.* [< It. < L. < *umbella*, parasol, dim. of *umbra*, shade] 1. cloth, plastic, etc. stretched over a folding radial frame at the top of a stick, carried for protection against the rain or sun 2. something that looks like this or is suggestive of this, as in its overall coverage: specif., *a)* any comprehensive, protective organization, alliance, etc. [the *umbrella* of insurance] *b)* a force of aircraft sent up to screen ground or naval forces —*adj.* embracing a variety of items; comprehensive [delegates of various firms were included under the *umbrella* title "commercial"]

umbrella bush [Aust.] a small, bushy acacia

umbrella tree 1. an American magnolia with clusters of long leaves at the ends of the branches 2. any of various trees that have an umbrellalike shape

Um·bri·an (um′brē ən) *adj.* of or relating to Umbria, in C Italy —*n.* 1. a native or inhabitant of Umbria 2. the language spoken in ancient Umbria

u·mi·ak, u·mi·ack (ōō′mē ak′) *n.* [Esk.] an open Eskimo boat made of skins stretched on a wooden frame

um·laut (oom′lout) *n.* [G. < *um*, about + *Laut*, a sound] Linguis. 1. *a)* a change in sound of a vowel, caused by its assimilation to another vowel or semivowel originally in the next syllable but later generally lost *b)* a vowel resulting from such assimilation 2. the diacritical mark (¨) placed over such a vowel, esp. in German, to indicate umlaut —*vt.* to sound or write with an umlaut

um·pire (um′pīr) *n.* [ME. *oumpere* (by faulty separation of *a noumpere*) < MFr. *nomper*, uneven, hence third person < *non, not + per*, even] 1. a person chosen to give a decision in a dispute; arbiter 2. an official who administers the rules of a game, as in cricket —*vt., vi.* **-pired, -pir·ing** to act as umpire (in or of)

ump·teen (ump′tēn′) *adj.* [Colloq.] a great number of; very many —**ump′teenth′** *adj.*

'un (ən) *pron.* [Colloq.] one [that's a big *'un*]

un- (un; *unstressed, also* ən) *either of two prefixes meaning:* 1. [OE. *un-*] not, lack of, the opposite of [unhappy, untruth] 2. [OE. *un-, on-, and-*] the reverse or removal of: added to verbs to indicate a reversal of the action of the verb [unfasten] and to nouns to indicate a removal or release from the thing, state, etc. indicated by the noun [unbosom]; sometimes *un-* is merely intensive [unloosen] The list at the bottom of the following pages includes many of the more common compounds formed with *un-* (either prefix) that do not have special meanings

UN, U.N. United Nations

un·a·ble (un ā′b′l) *adj.* not able; lacking the ability, means, or power to do something

un·a·bridged (un′ə brijd′) *adj.* not abridged, or shortened: often applied to a large, extensive book that is not abridged from a larger work

un·ac·count·a·ble (un′ə koun′tə b′l) *adj.* 1. that cannot be explained or accounted for; strange 2. not responsible —**un′ac·count′a·bil′i·ty** *n.* —**un′ac·count′a·bly** *adv.*

un·ac·cus·tomed (-ə kus′təmd) *adj.* 1. not accustomed (to) 2. not usual; strange [an *unaccustomed* action]

un·a·dopt·ed (-ə dopt′id) *adj.* 1. not adopted 2. (of roads) not maintained by a local authority

un·ad·vised (-əd vīzd′) *adj.* 1. without counsel or advice 2. thoughtlessly hasty; indiscreet —**un′ad·vis′ed·ly** (-vīz′id lē) *adv.* —**un′ad·vis′ed·ness** *n.*

un·af·fect·ed (-ə fek′tid) *adj.* 1. not affected or influenced 2. without affectation; sincere and natural —**un′af·fect′ed·ly** *adv.* —**un′af·fect′ed·ness** *n.*

un-A·mer·i·can (-ə mer′i kən) *adj.* not American; esp., thought of as not conforming to the principles, policies, etc. of the U.S. —**un′-A·mer′i·can·ism** *n.*

u·nan·i·mous (yoo nan′ə məs) *adj.* [< L. < *unus*, one + *animus*, the mind] 1. agreeing completely; united in opinion 2. showing, or based on, complete agreement —**u·na·nim′i·ty** (yōō′nə nim′ə tē) *n.* —**u·nan′i·mous·ly** *adv.*

un·ap·proach·a·ble (un′ə prōch′ə b′l) *adj.* 1. not approachable or accessible, friendly, etc. 2. having no rival or equal; unmatched —**un′ap·proach′a·bil′i·ty** *n.* —**un′-ap·proach′a·bly** *adv.*

un·arm (un ärm′) *vt.* same as DISARM

unabashed	unaccounted-for	unaggressive	unamusing
unabated	unaccredited	unaided	unannounced
unabbreviated	unacknowledged	unaimed	unanswerable
unabetted	unacquainted	unalike	unanticipated
unabsolved	unadaptable	unallied	unapologetic
unabsorbed	unadjustable	unallowable	unapparent
unacademic	unadorned	unalloyed	unappealable
unaccented	unadulterated	unalterable	unappealing
unacceptable	unadventurous	unaltered	unappeasable
unacclimated	unadvertised	unambiguous	unappetizing
unaccommodating	unadvisable	unambitious	unappreciated
unaccompanied	unaffiliated	unamiable	unappreciative
unaccomplished	unafraid	unamplified	unapproached

un·armed (-ärmd′) *adj.* having no weapons, esp. firearms, or armour; defenceless

un·as·sail·a·ble (un′ə sāl′ə b'l) *adj.* not assailable; specif., *a)* that cannot be successfully attacked *b)* that cannot be successfully denied —**un′as·sail′a·ble·ness, un′as·sail′a·bil′-i·ty** *n.* —**un′as·sail′a·bly** *adv.*

un·as·sum·ing (-ə syōō′miŋ) *adj.* not assuming, pretentious, or forward; modest —**un′as·sum′ing·ly** *adv.* —**un′as·sum′-ing·ness** *n.*

un·at·tached (-ə tacht′) *adj.* **1.** not attached or fastened **2.** not connected with any organization **3.** not engaged or married **4.** *Law* not taken as security for a judgment

un·a·vail·ing (-ə vā′liŋ) *adj.* not availing; useless; futile —**un′a·vail′ing·ly** *adv.*

un·a·void·a·ble (-ə voi′də b'l) *adj.* that cannot be avoided; inevitable —**un′a·void′a·ble·ness** *n.* —**un′a·void′a·bly** *adv.*

un·a·ware (-ə wer′) *adj.* not aware or conscious [*unaware* of danger] —*adv.* same as UNAWARES —**un′a·ware′ness** *n.*

un·a·wares (-ə werz′) *adv.* **1.** without knowing or being aware **2.** unexpectedly; by surprise [to catch someone *unawares*]

un·backed (-bakt′) *adj.* **1.** without a back or backing **2.** having no backers, supporters, etc.

un·bal·ance (-bal′əns) *vt.* **-anced, -anc·ing 1.** to throw out of balance **2.** to derange (the mind) —*n.* the condition of being unbalanced

un·bal·anced (-bal′ənst) *adj.* **1.** not balanced or equal **2.** not sane or normal in mind

un·bar (-bär′) *vt.* **-barred′, -bar′ring** to unbolt or unlock

un·bear·a·ble (-ber′ə b'l) *adj.* that cannot be endured or tolerated —**un·bear′a·ble·ness** *n.* —**un·bear′a·bly** *adv.*

un·beat·a·ble (-bēt′ə b'l) *adj.* that cannot be defeated or surpassed

un·beat·en (-bēt′ən) *adj.* **1.** not struck, pounded, etc. **2.** untrodden or untravelled **3.** undefeated or unsurpassed

un·be·com·ing (un′bi kum′iŋ) *adj.* not suited to one's appearance, status, character, etc. [an *unbecoming* dress, *unbecoming* behaviour] —**un′be·com′ing·ly** *adv.* —**un′-be·com′ing·ness** *n.*

un·be·known (-bi nōn′) *adj.* unknown or unnoticed; without one's knowledge (usually with *to*): also **un′-be·knownst′** (-nōnst′)

un·be·lief (-bə lēf′) *n.* a withholding or lack of belief, esp. in religion

un·be·liev·a·ble (-bə lēv′ə b'l) *adj.* beyond belief; astounding; incredible —**un′be·liev′a·bly** *adv.*

un·be·liev·er (-bə lē′vər) *n.* **1.** a person who does not believe; doubter **2.** a person who does not accept any, or any particular, religious belief

un·be·liev·ing (-bə lē′viŋ) *adj.* doubting; sceptical; incredulous —**un′be·liev′ing·ly** *adv.*

un·bend (un bend′) *vt., vi.* **-bent′** or **-bend′ed, -bend′ing 1.** to make or become less tense, less formal, etc. **2.** to make or become straight again

un·bend·ing (-ben′diŋ) *adj.* not bending; specif., *a)* rigid; stiff *b)* firm; resolute *c)* aloof; austere —*n.* a relaxation of restraint, severity, etc. —**un·bend′ing·ly** *adv.* —**un·bend′-ing·ness** *n.*

un·bib·li·cal (-bib′li k'l) *adj.* not according to the text or authority of the Bible

un·bid·den (-bid′'n) *adj.* **1.** not commanded **2.** not invited Also **un·bid′**

un·bind (-bīnd′) *vt.* **-bound′, -bind′ing 1.** to untie; unfasten **2.** to release from restraints

un·blessed, un·blest (-blest′) *adj.* **1.** not blessed **2.** wretched; unhappy

un·blush·ing (-blush′iŋ) *adj.* **1.** not blushing **2.** shameless —**un·blush′ing·ly** *adv.*

un·bolt (-bōlt′) *vt., vi.* to draw back the bolt or bolts of (a door, etc.); unbar; open

un·bolt·ed¹ (-bōlt′id) *adj.* not fastened with a bolt

un·bolt·ed² (-bōlt′id) *adj.* not bolted or sifted, as flour

un·born (-bôrn′) *adj.* **1.** not born **2.** still within the mother's womb **3.** yet to come or be; future

un·bos·om (-booz′əm) *vt., vi.* to tell or reveal (one's feelings, secrets, etc.) —**unbosom oneself** to express (oneself) openly about one's feelings, etc.

un·bound·ed (-boun′did) *adj.* **1.** without bounds or limits **2.** not restrained; uncontrolled

un·bowed (-boud′) *adj.* **1.** not bowed or bent **2.** not yielding or giving in; unsubdued

un·bri·dled (-brī′d'ld) *adj.* **1.** having no bridle on, as a horse **2.** not controlled; unrestrained

un·bro·ken (-brō′k'n) *adj.* not broken; specif., *a)* whole; intact *b)* not tamed or subdued *c)* continuous; uninterrupted *d)* not surpassed [an *unbroken* record]

un·buck·le (-buk′'l) *vt.* **-led, -ling** to unfasten the buckle or buckles of

un·bur·den (-burd′'n) *vt.* **1.** to free from a burden **2.** to relieve (oneself or one's mind) by disclosing (something hard to bear)

un·but·ton (-but′'n) *vt., vi.* to unfasten the buttons of

un·called-for (un kôld′fôr′) *adj.* **1.** not required **2.** unnecessary and out of place; impertinent

un·can·ny (-kan′ē) *adj.* **1.** mysterious in an eerie way; weird **2.** so remarkable, acute, etc. as to seem unnatural [*uncanny* vision] —**un·can′ni·ly** *adv.* —**un·can′ni·ness** *n.*

un·cap (-kap′) *vt.* **-capped′, -cap′ping 1.** to remove the cap from the head of (a person) **2.** to remove the cap from (a bottle, etc.)

un·cared-for (-kerd′fôr′) *adj.* not cared for or looked after; neglected

un·cer·e·mo·ni·ous (un′ser ə mō′nē əs) *adj.* **1.** less ceremonious than is expected; informal **2.** so curt or abrupt as to be discourteous —**un′cer·e·mo′ni·ous·ly** *adv.* —**un′-cer·e·mo′ni·ous·ness** *n.*

un·cer·tain (un surt′'n) *adj.* **1.** *a)* not surely or certainly known; questionable *b)* not sure or certain in knowledge; doubtful **2.** not definite; vague **3.** liable to change; not dependable or reliable **4.** not steady or constant; varying —**un·cer′tain·ly** *adv.* —**un·cer′tain·ness** *n.*

un·cer·tain·ty (-tē) *n.* **1.** lack of certainty; doubt **2.** *pl.* **-ties** something uncertain

un·char·i·ta·ble (-char′i tə b'l) *adj.* harsh or severe, as in opinion; unforgiving, ungenerous, or faultfinding —**un·char′-i·ta·ble·ness** *n.* —**un·char′i·ta·bly** *adv.*

un·chris·tian (-kris′chən) *adj.* **1.** not having or practising a Christian religion **2.** not in accord with the principles of Christianity **3.** [Colloq.] outrageous; dreadful

un·church (-church′) *vt.* **1.** to deprive (a person) of membership in a given church **2.** to deprive (a congregation) of its rights as a church

un·ci·al (un′si əl, -shē əl, -shəl) *adj.* [< L. < *uncia*, an inch] designating or of a form of large, rounded letter used in the script of Greek and Latin manuscripts between 300 and 900 A.D. —*n.* **1.** an uncial letter **2.** an uncial manuscript **3.** uncial script

un·ci·nate (un′si nit, -nāt′) *adj.* [L. *uncinatus* < *uncinus*, a hook] bent like a hook; hooked

un·cir·cum·cised (un sur′kəm sīzd′) *adj.* **1.** not circumcised; specif., not Jewish; gentile **2.** [Archaic] heathen

un·civ·il (un siv′'l) *adj.* **1.** not civilized; barbarous **2.** not civil or courteous; ill-mannered —**un·civ′il·ly** *adv.*

un·civ·i·lized (-siv′ə līzd′) *adj.* **1.** not civilized; barbarous **2.** far from civilization

un·clad (-klad′) *adj.* wearing no clothes; naked

unarguable	unavailable	unbreakable	uncertified
unarmoured	unavenged	unbreathable	unchain
unartistic	unavowed	unbridgeable	unchallenged
unascertained	unawed	unbrotherly	unchangeable
unashamed	unbaked	unbruised	unchanged
unasked	unbaptized	unbrushed	unchaperoned
unaspiring	unbathed	unbudgeted	uncharacteristic
unassigned	unbefitting	unbuilt	uncharged
unassimilated	unbelted	unburied	uncharted
unassisted	unbiased	unburned	unchartered
unassociated	unbiddable	unburnt	unchaste
unassorted	unblamable	unbusinesslike	unchastened
unassured	unbleached	uncaged	unchecked
unattainable	unblemished	uncancelled	uncherished
unattempted	unblinking	uncaring	unchewed
unattended	unblock	uncarpeted	unchilled
unattested	unbought	uncatalogued	unchivalrous
unattired	unbound	uncaught	unchosen
unattractive	unbraced	unceasing	unchristened
unauthentic	unbraid	uncelebrated	unclaimed
unauthenticated	unbranched	uncensored	unclarified
unauthorized	unbranded	uncensured	unclassifiable

un·clasp (-kläsp′) *vt.* **1.** to unfasten the clasp of **2.** to release from a clasp or grasp —*vi.* **1.** to become unfastened **2.** to relax the clasp or grasp

un·cle (uŋ′k′l) *n.* [OFr. < L. *avunculus,* one's mother's brother] **1.** the brother of one's father or mother **2.** the husband of one's aunt **3.** [Colloq.] a term of address sometimes used by children for any man, esp. a friend of the parents **4.** [Old Slang] a pawnbroker

un·clean (un klēn′) *adj.* **1.** dirty; filthy; foul **2.** not pure according to religious laws **3.** morally impure; unchaste; obscene —**un·clean′ness** *n.*

un·clean·ly[1] (-klen′lē) *adj.* not cleanly; unclean; dirty —**un·clean′li·ness** *n.*

un·clean·ly[2] (-klēn′lē) *adv.* in an unclean manner

un·clench (-klench′) *vt., vi.* to open: said of something clenched, or clinched: also **un·clinch′** (-klinch′)

Uncle Sam [< abbrev. U.S.] [Colloq.] the U.S. (government or people), personified as a tall man with chin whiskers, dressed in a red, white, and blue suit

Uncle Tom [after an elderly Negro slave in H. B. Stowe's antislavery novel, *Uncle Tom's Cabin* (1852)] [U.S.] a Negro whose behaviour towards whites is regarded as fawning or servile: a term of contempt —**Uncle Tom′ism**

un·cloak (un klōk′) *vt., vi.* **1.** to remove a cloak or other covering (from) **2.** to reveal; expose

un·close (-klōz′) *vt., vi.* **-closed′, -clos′ing 1.** to open **2.** to disclose or reveal

un·clothe (-klō*th*′) *vt.* **-clothed′** or **-clad′, -cloth′ing** to strip of or as of clothes; uncover; divest

un·coil (-koil′) *vt., vi.* to unwind or release from being coiled

un·com·fort·a·ble (-kumf′tər b′l, -kum′fər tə b′l) *adj.* **1.** not comfortable; feeling discomfort **2.** not pleasant; causing discomfort **3.** ill at ease —**un·com′fort·a·ble·ness** *n.* —**un·com′fort·a·bly** *adv.*

un·com·mit·ted (un′kə mit′id) *adj.* **1.** not committed, as a crime **2.** not bound or pledged to a specific opinion, course of action, or cause **3.** not having taken a position; neutral **4.** not imprisoned

un·com·mon (-kom′ən) *adj.* **1.** not common; rare; not usual **2.** strange; remarkable; extraordinary —**un·com′mon·ly** *adv.* —**un·com′mon·ness** *n.*

un·com·mu·ni·ca·tive (un′kə myoo′ni kə tiv) *adj.* not communicative; reserved; taciturn —**un′com·mu′ni·ca′tive·ly** *adv.* —**un′com·mu′ni·ca′tive·ness** *n.*

un·com·pro·mis·ing (un kom′prə mī′ziŋ) *adj.* not yielding or giving in at all; firm; inflexible

un·con·cern (un′kən surn′) *n.* **1.** lack of interest; indifference **2.** lack of concern, or worry

un·con·cerned (-kən surnd′) *adj.* not concerned; specif., *a)* not interested *b)* not solicitous or anxious *c)* not involved —**un′con·cern′ed·ly** (-sur′nid lē) *adv.* —**un′con·cern′-ed·ness** *n.*

un·con·di·tion·al (-kən dish′ən ′l) *adj.* without conditions or stipulations; absolute —**un′con·di′tion·al·ly** *adv.*

un·con·di·tioned (-kən dish′ənd) *adj.* **1.** *same as* UNCONDITIONAL **2.** *Psychol.* natural; inborn [an *unconditioned* reflex]

un·con·scion·a·ble (un kon′shən ə b′l) *adj.* **1.** not guided or restrained by conscience; unscrupulous **2.** unreasonable, excessive, etc. —**un·con′scion·a·bly** *adv.*

un·con·scious (-kon′shəs) *adj.* **1.** deprived of consciousness [*unconscious* from a blow on the head] **2.** not aware (of) **3.** not realized or intended by the person himself [*unconscious* humour] —**the unconscious** *Psychoanalysis* the sum of all memories, thoughts, feelings, etc. of which the individual is not conscious but which influence his emotions and behaviour —**un·con′scious·ly** *adv.* —**un·con′-scious·ness** *n.*

un·con·sti·tu·tion·al (un′kon stə tyoo′shən ′l) *adj.* not in accordance with or permitted by a constitution, as of a country or state —**un′con·sti·tu′tion·al′i·ty** (-shə nal′ə tē) *n.* —**un′con·sti·tu′tion·al·ly** *adv.*

un·con·ven·tion·al (un′kən ven′shən ′l) *adj.* not conforming to customary, formal, or accepted practices, standards, etc. —**un′con·ven′tion·al′i·ty** (-shə nal′ə tē) *n.* —**un′con·ven′tion·al·ly** *adv.*

un·cork (un kôrk′) *vt.* **1.** to pull the cork out of **2.** [Colloq.] to let out, unleash, release, etc.

un·count·ed (-koun′tid) *adj.* **1.** not counted **2.** too many to be counted; innumerable

un·cou·ple (-kup′′l) *vt.* **-pled, -pling** to unfasten (things coupled); disconnect —*vi.* to become unfastened

un·couth (-kooth′) *adj.* [OE. *uncuth,* unknown < *un-,* not + *cuth,* pp. of *cunnan,* to know] **1.** awkward; clumsy; ungainly **2.** uncultured; crude; boorish —**un·couth′ly** *adv.* —**un·couth′ness** *n.*

un·cov·er (-kuv′ər) *vt.* **1.** to make known; disclose **2.** to lay bare by removing a covering **3.** to remove the cover or protection from **4.** to remove the hat, cap, etc. from (the head), as in showing respect —*vi.* to bare the head, as in showing respect

unc·tion (uŋk′shən) *n.* [L. *unctio* < *ungere,* to anoint] **1.** *a)* the act of anointing, as in medical treatment or a religious ceremony *b)* the oil, ointment, etc. used for this **2.** anything that soothes or comforts **3.** *a)* a very earnest manner of speaking or behaving, esp. about religious matters *b)* such a manner when it is pretended or seems put on

unc·tu·ous (uŋk′tyoo əs) *adj.* [< ML. < L. *unctum,* ointment < *ungere,* to anoint] **1.** of, like, or characteristic of an ointment; oily or greasy **2.** like oil, soap, or grease to the touch: said of certain minerals **3.** characterized by a smug, smooth pretence of spiritual feeling or earnestness, as in seeking to persuade; too suave or oily in speech or manner —**unc′tu·os′i·ty** (-wos′ə tē), **unc′tu·ous·ness** *n.* —**unc′-tu·ous·ly** *adv.*

un·cut (un kut′) *adj.* not cut; specif., *a)* having untrimmed margins: said of the pages of a book *b)* not ground to shape: said of a gem *c)* not abridged

un·daunt·ed (-dôn′tid) *adj.* not daunted; not afraid or discouraged —**un·daunt′ed·ly** *adv.*

un·dec·a·gon (un′dek′ə gon′) *n.* [< L. *undecim,* eleven] a figure having eleven angles and eleven sides

un·de·ceive (un′di sēv′) *vt.* **-ceived′, -ceiv′ing** to cause to be no longer deceived, mistaken, or misled

un·de·cid·ed (-di sīd′id) *adj.* **1.** that is not decided or settled **2.** not having come to a decision —**un′de·cid′ed·ly** *adv.* —**un′de·cid′ed·ness** *n.*

un·de·ni·a·ble (-di nī′ə b′l) *adj.* **1.** that cannot be denied **2.** unquestionably good or excellent —**un′de·ni′a·bly** *adv.*

un·der (un′dər) *prep.* [OE.] **1.** in, at, or to a position down from; below **2.** beneath the surface of [*under* water] **3.** below and to the other side of [to drive *under* a bridge] **4.** covered or concealed by [a jumper *under* a coat] **5.** *a)* lower in authority, position, etc. than *b)* lower in value, amount, etc. than *c)* lower than the required degree of [*under* age] **6.** *a)* subject to the control, government, direction, influence, etc. of *b)* bound by [*under* oath] *c)* subjected to; undergoing [*under* repair] **7.** with the character, disguise, etc. of [*under* an alias] **8.** in (the designated category) [spiders are classified *under*

unclassified	uncomplimentary	unconsumed	uncrystallized
uncleaned	uncomplying	uncontaminated	unculled
unclear	uncompounded	uncontemplated	uncultivated
uncleared	uncomprehending	uncontested	uncultured
unclipped	uncompressed	uncontradictable	uncurbed
unclog	unconcealed	uncontrived	uncured
unclouded	unconciliated	uncontrollable	uncurl
uncluttered	unconcluded	uncontrolled	undamaged
uncoated	uncondemned	unconverted	undated
uncocked	uncondensed	unconvinced	undebatable
uncollectable	unconfessed	unconvincing	undecayed
uncollected	unconfined	uncooked	undecipherable
uncollectible	unconfirmed	uncooperative	undeclared
uncolonized	unconformity	uncoordinated	undeclinable
uncoloured	unconfused	uncorrected	undecorated
uncombed	uncongenial	uncorroborated	undefeatable
uncombinable	unconnected	uncorrupted	undefeated
uncombined	unconquerable	uncountable	undefended
uncomely	unconquered	uncovenanted	undefiled
uncomforted	unconscientious	uncrate	undefinable
uncommissioned	unconsecrated	uncredited	undefined
uncompanionable	unconsidered	uncritical	undeliverable
uncompensated	unconsoled	uncropped	undemanding
uncomplaining	unconsolidated	uncross	undemocratic
uncompleted	unconstrained	uncrowded	undemonstrable
uncomplicated	unconstricted	uncrowned	undemonstrative

arachnids] **9.** during the rule of [France *under* Louis XV]
10. being the subject of [the question *under* discussion] **11.**
because of [*under* the circumstances] **12.** authorized or
attested by [*under* her signature] **13.** planted with [an
acre *under* barley] **14.** driven by the power of [*under* sail]
—*adv.* **1.** in or to a lower position; beneath **2.** beneath the
surface, as of water **3.** in or to a subordinate condition **4.**
so as to be covered or concealed **5.** less in amount, value,
etc. —*adj.* lower in position, authority, rank, amount,
degree, etc.

un·der- [OE.] *a prefix meaning:* **1.** in, on, to, or from a
lower place or side; beneath or below [*undershirt*] **2.** in an
inferior or subordinate position or rank [*undergraduate*] **3.**
too little, not enough, below normal [*underdeveloped*]: the
list below includes some common compounds formed with
under- that can be understood if *too little* or *insufficiently* is
added to the meaning of the base word

underactive	undermanned
underbake	underprice
undercook	undersubscribe
underemphasize	undersupply
underexercise	undertrained

un·der·a·chieve (un'dər ə chēv') *vi.* **-chieved', -chiev'ing**
to fail to do as well in school studies as might be expected
from scores made on intelligence tests —**un'der·a·chieve'-**
ment *n.* —**un'der·a·chiev'er** *n.*

un·der·act (-akt') *vt., vi.* to act (a theatrical role) with too
little emphasis or too great restraint

un·der·age (-āj') *adj.* **1.** not of full or mature age **2.** below
the age required by law

un·der·arm (un'dər ärm') *adj.* **1.** under the arm; in the
armpit **2.** *same as* UNDERHAND (sense 1) —*adv.* *same as*
UNDERHAND (sense 1)

un·der·bel·ly (-bel'ē) *n.* **1.** the lower, posterior part of an
animal's belly **2.** any vulnerable or unprotected area or part

un·der·bid (un'dər bid'; *for n.* un'dər bid') *vt., vi.* **-bid',**
-bid'ding **1.** to bid lower than (another person) **2.** to bid
less than the worth of —*n.* a lower or inadequate bid

un·der·bod·y (un'dər bod'ē) *n.* **1.** the underpart of an
animal's body **2.** the undersurface of a vehicle

un·der·buy (un'dər bī') *vt., vi.* **-bought', -buy'ing** **1.** to buy
at less than the real value **2.** to buy more cheaply than
(another or others)

un·der·cap·i·tal·ize (-kap'ə tə līz') *vt., vi.* **-ized', -iz'ing** to
provide (a business) with too little capital for successful
operation —**un'der·cap'i·tal·i·za'tion** *n.*

un·der·car·riage (un'dər kar'ij) *n.* a supporting frame or
structure, as of a motor car

un·der·charge (un'dər chärj'; *for n.* un'dər chärj') *vt., vi.*
-charged', -charg'ing **1.** to charge too low a price (to) **2.**
to provide with too little or low a charge —*n.* a charge that
is too little or low

un·der·cliff (un'dər clif') *n.* a lesser cliff beneath a higher
one, formed by debris from the latter

un·der·clothes (un'dər klōthz', -klōz') *n.pl.* *same as*
UNDERWEAR: also **un'der·cloth'ing** (-klōth'iŋ)

un·der·coat (-kōt') *n.* **1.** a coat worn under an overcoat **2.**
same as UNDERFUR **3.** a coat of paint, varnish, etc. applied
before the final coat Also **un'der·coat'ing** —*vt.* to apply
an undercoat (of paint, etc.) to

un·der·cov·er (-kuv'ər) *adj.* acting or done in secret

un·der·croft (un'dər kroft') *n.* [ME. < *under* + *croft*, a
vault] a crypt

un·der·cur·rent (-kur'ənt) *n.* **1.** a current flowing below
another or beneath the surface **2.** a hidden or underlying
tendency, opinion, etc., usually conflicting with a more
obvious one

un·der·cut (un'dər kut'; *for v.* un'dər kut') *n.* **1.** a cut made
below another so as to leave an overhang **2.** *Sports* an
undercutting —*adj.* that is undercut —*vt.* **-cut', -cut'ting**
1. to make an undercut (sense 1) in **2.** to cut out the
underpart of **3.** to undersell or work for lower wages than
4. to weaken the position of; undermine **5.** *Sports* to strike
(a ball) with an oblique downward motion, as in golf, or to
chop with an underhand stroke, as in tennis, esp. so as to
impart backspin —*vi.* to undercut someone or something

un·der·de·vel·op (un'dər di vel'əp) *vt.* **1.** to develop to a
point below what is needed **2.** *Photog.* to develop (a film,
etc.) for too short a time or with a weak developer

un·der·de·vel·oped (-əpt) *adj.* not developed to a desirable
degree; specif., inadequately developed economically and
industrially [*underdeveloped* nations]

un·der·do (-dōō') *vt.* **-did', -done', -do'ing** to do less than
is usual, needed, or desired

un·der·dog (un'dər dog') *n.* **1.** the one that is losing, as in a
contest **2.** a person who is handicapped or a victim of
injustice, discrimination, etc.

un·der·done (un'dər dun') *adj.* not cooked enough, as meat

un·der·em·ployed (-im ploid') *adj.* **1.** employed at less than
full time **2.** working at low-skilled, poorly paid jobs when
one can do more skilled work —**the underemployed**
underemployed people —**un'der·em·ploy'ment** *n.*

un·der·es·ti·mate (-es'tə māt'; *for n.* -mit) *vt., vi.* **-mat'ed,**
-mat'ing to set too low an estimate on or for —*n.* an
estimate that is too low —**un'der·es'ti·ma'tion** *n.*

un·der·ex·pose (-ik spōz') *vt.* **-posed', -pos'ing** to expose
(a photographic film, etc.) to inadequate light or for too
short a time —**un'der·ex·po'sure** (-spō'zhər) *n.*

un·der·feed (-fēd') *vt.* **-fed', -feed'ing** to feed less than is
needed

un·der·felt (un'dər felt) *n.* felt laid underneath a carpet as
an underlay

un·der·floor (-flôr) *adj.* designating something beneath the
floor, specif., a heating system

un·der·foot (un'dər foot') *adv., adj.* **1.** under the foot or
feet **2.** in the way, as of one walking

un·der·fur (un'dər fur') *n.* the softer, finer fur under the
outer coat of some animals, as beavers or seals

un·der·gar·ment (-gär'mənt) *n.* an item of underwear

un·der·gird (un'dər gurd') *vt.* **-gird'ed** or **-girt', -gird'ing**
1. to gird or strengthen from the bottom side **2.** to supply
support for

un·der·glaze (un'dər glāz') *adj.* *Ceramics* designating
colours, designs, etc. applied before the glaze is put on —*n.*
such colours, designs, etc.

un·der·go (-gō') *vt.* **-went', -gone', -go'ing** to experience;
endure; go through

un·der·grad·u·ate (-grad'yōō it) *n.* a student at a university
or college who has not yet received a bachelor's degree

un·der·ground (un'dər ground'; *for n.* -ground') *adj.* **1.**
occurring, working, etc. beneath the surface of the earth **2.**
secret; undercover **3.** designating or of noncommercial
newspapers, films, etc. that are unconventional,
experimental, radical, etc. —*adv.* **1.** beneath the surface of
the earth **2.** in or into secrecy or hiding —*n.* **1.** the entire
region beneath the surface of the earth **2.** a secret
movement organized to oppose the government in power or
enemy forces of occupation **3.** an underground electric
railway for passenger travel **4.** any radical or avant-garde
group, movement, etc. that operates outside the
establishment

Underground Railroad in the U.S. before the Civil War, a
system set up by abolitionists to help fugitive slaves to
escape to free states and Canada

un·der·growth (-grōth') *n.* small trees, shrubs, etc. that
grow beneath large trees in woods or forests

un·der·hand (un'dər hand') *adj.* **1.** performed with the
hand below the level of the elbow or shoulder **2.** *same as*
UNDERHANDED (sense 1) —*adv.* **1.** with an underhand
motion **2.** underhandedly

un·der·hand·ed (un'dər han'did) *adj.* **1.** secret, sly,
deceitful, etc. **2.** lacking workers, players, etc.;
shorthanded —**un'der·hand'ed·ly** *adv.* —**un'der·hand'-**
ed·ness *n.*

un·der·hung (-huŋ') *adj.* **1.** *a)* projecting beyond the upper
jaw: said of the lower jaw *b)* having such a lower jaw **2.**
resting or moving on a track beneath, as some sliding doors

un·der·lay (un'dər lā'; *for n.* un'dər lā') *vt.* **-laid', -lay'ing**
1. to cover the bottom of **2.** to raise or support with
something laid underneath —*n.* something laid underneath;
specif., *a)* patches of paper laid under type to raise it *b)* a
layer of felt, rubber, etc. laid under a carpet to increase
insulation and resilience

un·der·lie (-lī') *vt.* **-lay', -lain', -ly'ing** **1.** to lie under or
beneath **2.** to form the basis or foundation of

un·der·line (un'dər līn'; *also, for v.*, un'dər līn') *vt.* **-lined',**
-lin'ing **1.** to draw a line beneath; underscore **2.** to stress
or emphasize —*n.* *same as* UNDERSCORE

un·der·ling (un'dər liŋ) *n.* [OE.: see UNDER- & -LING¹] a
person who must carry out the orders of others above him;
inferior: a disparaging term

un·der·ly·ing (un'dər lī'iŋ) *adj.* **1.** lying under; placed
beneath **2.** fundamental; basic **3.** not clearly evident, but
implicit

un·der·mine (un'dər mīn') *vt.* **-mined', -min'ing** **1.** to dig
beneath, so as to form a tunnel or mine **2.** to wear away
and weaken the supports of **3.** to injure, weaken, or impair,
esp. in a slow or stealthy way

un·der·most (un'dər mōst') *adj., adv.* lowest in place,
position, rank, etc.

un·der·neath (un'dər nēth') *adv.* **1.** under; below; beneath
2. at a lower level —*prep.* under; below; beneath —*adj.*
under or lower —*n.* the underpart

un·der·nour·ish (-nur'ish) *vt.* to provide with less food
than is needed for health and growth —**un'der·nour'-**
ish·ment *n.*

un·der·pants (un'dər pants') *n.pl.* an undergarment, long
or short, for the lower part of the body, with a separate
opening for each leg, worn by men

un·der·part (-pärt') *n.* the lower part or side, as of an
animal's body or an aeroplane's fuselage

un·der·pass (-päs') *n.* a passageway under something;
esp., a road that runs under a railway or another road

un·der·pay (un'dər pā') *vt., vi.* **-paid', -pay'ing** to pay too
little, or less than is right —**un'der·pay'ment** *n.*

un·der·pin (-pin') *vt.* **-pinned'**, **-pin'ning** to support or strengthen from beneath, as with props

un·der·pin·ning (un'dər pin'iŋ) *n.* **1.** a supporting structure, esp. one placed beneath a wall **2.** a support or prop

un·der·play (un'dər plā') *vt., vi.* **1.** to act (a role or scene) with subtlety or little emphasis, in an intentionally restrained manner **2.** *same as* UNDERACT **3.** *Cards* to play a low card deliberately instead of a higher one of the same suit

un·der·priv·i·leged (-priv''l ijd, -priv'lijd) *adj.* deprived of basic social rights and security through poverty, discrimination, etc. **—the underprivileged** underprivileged people

un·der·pro·duce (-prə dyōos') *vt., vi.* **-duced'**, **-duc'ing** to produce in a quantity that is below full capacity or that fails to meet the need or demand **—un'der·pro·duc'tion** *n.*

un·der·proof (-prōōf') *adj.* containing less alcohol than proof spirit does

un·der·rate (-rāt') *vt.* **-rat'ed**, **-rat'ing** to rate, assess, or estimate too low

un·der·score (un'dər skôr'; *for n.* un'dər skôr') *vt.* **-scored'**, **-scor'ing** *same as* UNDERLINE **—n.** a line drawn under a word, passage, etc., as for emphasis

un·der·sea (-sē') *adj., adv.* beneath the surface of the sea: also **un'der·seas'** (-sēz') *adv.*

un·der·seal (-sēl') *n.* a coating of tarlike material applied to the undersurface of a car, etc. to retard rust, etc **—vt.** to apply an underseal to

un·der·sec·re·tar·y (-sek'rə tər ē, -trē) *n., pl.* **-tar·ies** an assistant secretary: specif., any of various senior civil servants in certain government departments

un·der·sell (-sel') *vt.* **-sold'**, **-sell'ing** **1.** to sell at a lower price than (another seller) **2.** to promote in a restrained or inadequate manner

un·der·sexed (-sekst') *adj.* having a weaker than normal sexual drive or interest

un·der·shirt (un'dər shurt') *n.* [Chiefly U.S.] a usually sleeveless undergarment worn under a shirt by men and boys

un·der·shoot (un'dər shōōt') *vt.* **-shot'**, **-shoot'ing** **1.** to shoot or fall short of (a target, mark, etc.) **2.** to bring an aircraft down short of (the runway, etc.) **—vi.** to shoot or go short of the mark

un·der·shot (-shot') *adj.* **1.** with the lower part jutting out past the upper [an *undershot* jaw] **2.** driven by water flowing along the lower part [an *undershot* water wheel]

un·der·side (-sīd') *n.* the side or surface underneath

un·der·sign (un'dər sīn') *vt.* to sign one's name at the end of (a letter, document, etc.) **—the undersigned** the person or persons undersigning

un·der·sized (-sīzd') *adj.* smaller in size than is usual, average, or proper: also **un'der·size'**

un·der·skirt (-skurt') *n.* a garment worn under a skirt; waist-slip

un·der·slung (-sluŋ') *adj.* attached to the underside of the axles: said of a vehicle frame

un·der·staffed (un'dər stäft') *adj.* having too small a staff; having fewer personnel than needed

un·der·stand (un'dər stand') *vt.* **-stood'**, **-stand'ing** [OE. *understandan*, lit., to stand under] **1.** to get or know the meaning of **2.** to gather or assume from what is heard, known, etc.; infer **3.** to take as meant or meaning; interpret **4.** to take for granted or as a fact **5.** to supply mentally (an idea, word, etc.), as for grammatical completeness **6.** to be informed of; learn **7.** to know clearly or fully the nature, character, etc. of **8.** to have a sympathetic rapport with [no one *understands* me] **—vi.** **1.** to have understanding, comprehension, etc., either in general or with reference to something specific **2.** to be informed; believe **—un'der·stand'a·ble** *adj.* **—un'der·stand'a·bly** *adv.*

un·der·stand·ing (-iŋ) *n.* **1.** the act, state, or feeling of a person who understands; comprehension, knowledge, sympathetic awareness, etc. **2.** the power to think, learn, judge, etc.; intelligence; sense **3.** an explanation or interpretation [one's *understanding* of the matter] **4.** *a)* mutual comprehension, as of ideas, intentions, etc. *b)* an agreement, esp. one that settles differences or is informal **—adj.** that understands; having or showing comprehension, sympathy, etc. **—un'der·stand'ing·ly** *adv.*

un·der·state (un'dər stāt') *vt.* **-stat'ed**, **-stat'ing** **1.** to make a weaker statement of than is warranted by truth, accuracy, or importance **2.** to express in a restrained style **—un'der·state'ment** *n.*

un·der·stud·y (un'dər stud'ē) *n., pl.* **-stud'ies** an actor who learns the part of another actor so that he can serve as a substitute when necessary **—vt., vi.** **-stud'ied**, **-stud'y·ing** **1.** to act as an understudy (to) **2.** to learn (a part) as an understudy

un·der·sur·face (-sur'fis) *n.* *same as* UNDERSIDE

un·der·take (un'dər tāk') *vt.* **-took'**, **-tak'en**, **-tak'ing** **1.** to enter into or upon (a task, journey, etc.); take upon oneself; agree to do **2.** to give a promise or pledge that; contract **3.** to promise; guarantee

un·der·tak·er (un'dər tā'kər; *for 2* un'dər tā'kər) *n.* **1.** a person who undertakes something **2.** a contractor who makes all the necessary arrangements for a burial

un·der·tak·ing (un'dər tā'kiŋ; *also, & for 3 always*, un'dər tā'-kiŋ) *n.* **1.** something undertaken; task; enterprise **2.** a promise; guarantee **3.** the business of an undertaker (sense 2) **4.** the act of one who undertakes a task, etc.

un·der·the·count·er (un'dər thə koun'tər) *adj.* [Colloq.] done, sold, given, etc. secretly in an unlawful or unethical way: also **un'der·the·ta'ble**

un·der·things (-thiŋz') *n.pl.* women's or girls' underwear

un·der·tone (-tōn') *n.* **1.** a low tone of sound or voice **2.** a subdued or background colour **3.** any underlying quality, factor, element, etc. [an *undertone* of horror]

un·der·tow (-tō') *n.* [UNDER- + TOW¹] a current of water moving beneath the surface water and in a different direction, as seawards under the incoming tide

un·der·trick (-trik') *n.* *Bridge* any of the tricks by which one falls short of one's contract

un·der·val·ue (un'dər val'yōō) *vt.* **-ued**, **-u·ing** **1.** to value too low, or below the real worth **2.** to regard or esteem too lightly **—un'der·val'u·a'tion** *n.*

un·der·wa·ter (un'dər wôt'ər) *adj.* **1.** being, done, etc. beneath the surface of the water **2.** used or for use under water **—adv.** beneath the surface of the water

un·der·way (un'dər wā') *adj.* *Naut.* not at anchor or moored or aground

un·der·wear (un'dər wer') *n.* clothing worn under one's outer clothes, usually next to the skin, as vests, pants, slips, bras, etc.

un·der·weight (un'dər wāt'; *also for adj.*, un'dər wāt') *adj.* below the normal, desirable, or allowed weight **—n.** less weight than is needed, desired, or allowed

un·der·went (un'dər went') *pt. of* UNDERGO

un·der·wood (-wood') *n.* *same as* UNDERGROWTH

un·der·world (un'dər wurld') *n.* **1.** the mythical world of the dead; Hades **2.** the criminal members of society, or people living by vice or crime, regarded as a group **3.** the opposite side of the earth; antipodes

un·der·write (un'dər rīt') *vt.* **-wrote'**, **-writ'ten**, **-writ'ing** **1.** to write under something written; subscribe to, as by signature **2.** to agree to buy (an issue of stocks, bonds, etc.) on a given date and at a fixed price, or to guarantee the purchase of (stocks or bonds to be made available to the public) **3.** to pledge to support (an undertaking, etc.) financially **4.** *a)* to sign one's name to (an insurance policy), thus assuming liability *b)* to insure *c)* to assume liability to the amount of (a specified sum) **—vi.** to practise insurance, esp. in shipping

un·der·writ·er (-ər) *n.* **1.** a person or enterprise that underwrites public issues of shares, bonds, etc. **2.** *a)* an official of an insurance company who determines the acceptability of risks, the premiums that should be charged, etc. *b)* an agent who underwrites insurance

un·de·sir·a·ble (un'di zīr'ə b'l) *adj.* not desirable; objectionable **—n.** an undesirable person **—un'de·sir'a·bil'-i·ty** *n.* **—un'de·sir'a·bly** *adv.*

un·dies (un'dēz) *n.pl.* [Colloq.] women's or girls' underwear

un·dine (un'dēn; un dēn') *n.* [G. < Mod.L. < *unda*, a wave] *Folklore* a female water spirit who could acquire a soul by marrying, and having a child by, a mortal

undenied	undetected
undenominational	undeterminable
undependable	undeterred
undepreciated	undeveloped
undeserving	undeviating
undesignated	undevoured
undesigning	undevout
undesired	undifferentiated
undesirous	undiffused
undestroyed	undigested
undetachable	undigestible

undignified	undiscouraged
undiluted	undiscoverable
undiminished	undiscovered
undimmed	undiscriminating
undiplomatic	undiscussed
undirected	undisguised
undiscernible	undismayed
undiscerning	undispelled
undischarged	undisposed
undisciplined	undisputed
undisclosed	undissected

UNDERSHOT WHEEL

un·do (un dōō′) *vt.* **-did′, -done′, -do′ing** **1.** *a)* to release or untie (a fastening) *b)* to open (a parcel, door, etc.) by this means **2.** to reverse or do away with (something done or its effect) **3.** to ruin or destroy —**un·do′er** *n.*

un·do·ing (-iŋ) *n.* **1.** a reversal of something done or its effect **2.** ruin or the cause of ruin

un·done¹ (un dun′) *pp.* of UNDO —*adj.* ruined, disgraced, etc.

un·done² (un dun′) *adj.* not done; not performed, accomplished, completed, etc.

un·doubt·ed (-dout′id) *adj.* not doubted or called in question; certain —**un·doubt′ed·ly** *adv.*

un·dreamed (-drēmd′) *adj.* not even dreamed (*of*) or imagined; inconceivable: also **un·dreamt′** (-dremt′)

un·dress (un dres′; *for n. usually* un′dres′) *vt.* **1.** to take off the clothing of; strip **2.** to remove the dressing from (a wound) —*vi.* to take off one's clothes; strip —*n.* **1.** the state of being naked, partly clothed, in a dressing gown, etc. **2.** ordinary or informal dress, as opposed to uniform.

un·due (un dyōō′) *adj.* **1.** not yet due or payable **2.** not suitable; improper [*undue* flippancy] **3.** too much; excessive [*undue* haste]

un·du·lant (un′dyoo lənt) *adj.* moving in or as in waves; undulating

undulant fever a form of brucellosis, transmitted to man from domestic animals or their products, and marked by recurrent fever, sweating, and pains in the joints

un·du·late (-lāt′; *for adj. usually* -lit) *vt.* **-lat′ed, -lat′ing** [< L. *undulatus*, undulated, ult. < *unda*, a wave] **1.** to cause to move in waves **2.** to give a wavy form, surface, etc. to —*vi.* **1.** to move in waves **2.** to have a wavy form, surface, etc. —*adj.* having a wavy form, margin, or surface: also **un′du·lat′ed** —**un′du·la·to·ry** *adj.*

un·du·la·tion (un′dyoo lā′shən) *n.* **1.** an undulating or undulating motion **2.** a wavy, curving form or outline, esp. one of a series **3.** *Physics* wave motion, as of light or sound, or a wave or vibration

un·du·ly (un dyōō′lē) *adv.* beyond what is proper or right; too much [*unduly* alarmed]

un·dy·ing (-dī′iŋ) *adj.* not dying; immortal or eternal

un·earned (-urnd′) *adj.* **1.** not earned by work or service; specif., obtained as a return on an investment [*unearned* income] **2.** not deserved; unmerited

un·earth (-urth′) *vt.* **1.** to dig up from out of the earth **2.** to bring to light; discover or disclose

un·earth·ly (-urth′lē) *adj.* **1.** not, or as if not, of this earth **2.** supernatural **3.** weird; mysterious **4.** [Colloq.] absurd, unreasonable, etc. —**un·earth′li·ness** *n.*

un·eas·y (-ē′zē) *adj.* **-eas′i·er, -eas′i·est** **1.** having, showing, or allowing no ease of body or mind; uncomfortable **2.** awkward; constrained **3.** worried; anxious —**un·ease′**, **un·eas′i·ness** *n.* —**un·eas′i·ly** *adv.*

un·ed·it·ed (-ed′it id) *adj.* **1.** not edited for publication **2.** not assembled for presentation [an *unedited* film]

un·em·ploy·a·ble (un′im ploi′ə b'l) *adj.* not employable; specif., that cannot be employed because of age, physical or mental deficiency, etc. —*n.* an unemployable person

un·em·ployed (-im ploid′) *adj.* **1.** not employed; without work **2.** not being used; idle —**the unemployed** people who are out of work

un·em·ploy·ment (-im ploi′mənt) *n.* **1.** the state of being unemployed; lack of employment **2.** the number or percentage of persons in the normal labour force out of work

un·e·qual (un ē′kwəl) *adj.* **1.** not equal, as in size, strength, ability, value, rank, amount, etc. **2.** *a)* not balanced or symmetrical *b)* that matches unequal contestants [an *unequal* battle] **3.** not even, regular, etc.; variable **4.** not equal or adequate [*unequal* to the task] —*n.* one that is not equal to another —**un·e′qual·ly** *adv.*

un·e·qualled (-ē′kwəld) *adj.* not equalled; unmatched; unrivalled; supreme

un·e·quiv·o·cal (un′i kwiv′ə k'l) *adj.* not equivocal; not ambiguous; plain; clear —**un′e·quiv′o·cal·ly** *adv.*

un·err·ing (un ur′iŋ) *adj.* **1.** free from error **2.** not missing or failing; sure; exact —**un·err′ing·ly** *adv.*

UNESCO (yoo nes′kō) United Nations Educational, Scientific, and Cultural Organization

un·e·ven (un ē′vən) *adj.* not even; specif., *a)* not level, smooth, or flat; rough; irregular *b)* not equal in size, amount, etc. *c)* not uniform; varying *d)* not equally balanced or matched *e) Math.* not evenly divisible by two —**un·e′ven·ly** *adv.* —**un·e′ven·ness** *n.*

un·ex·am·pled (un′ig zam′p'ld) *adj.* with nothing like it before; with no other example; unprecedented

un·ex·cep·tion·a·ble (-ik sep′shə nə b'l) *adj.* not exceptionable; without flaw or fault; not warranting even the slightest critism —**un′ex·cep′tion·a·bly** *adv.*

un·ex·cep·tion·al (-ik sep′shən 'l) *adj.* **1.** not uncommon or unusual; ordinary **2.** not admitting of any exception —**un′ex·cep′tion·al·ly** *adv.*

un·ex·pect·ed (-ik spek′tid) *adj.* not expected; unforeseen —**un′ex·pect′ed·ly** *adv.* —**un′ex·pect′ed·ness** *n.*

un·fail·ing (un fāl′iŋ) *adj.* **1.** not failing **2.** never ceasing or falling short; inexhaustible **3.** always reliable; certain —**un·fail′ing·ly** *adv.*

un·fair (-fer′) *adj.* **1.** not just or impartial; biased; inequitable **2.** dishonest or unethical in business dealings —**un·fair′ly** *adv.* —**un·fair′ness** *n.*

un·faith·ful (-fāth′fəl) *adj.* **1.** failing to stay loyal or to keep a vow, promise, etc.; faithless **2.** not true, accurate, etc.; untrustworthy **3.** guilty of adultery —**un·faith′ful·ly** *adv.* —**un·faith′ful·ness** *n.*

un·fa·mil·iar (un′fə mil′yər) *adj.* **1.** not familiar or well-known; strange [*unfamiliar* lands] **2.** not acquainted (*with* something) —**un′fa·mil′i·ar′i·ty** (-yar′ə tē, -ē ar′-) *n.* —**un′fa·mil′iar·ly** *adv.*

un·fas·ten (un fäs′'n) *vt.* to open or make loose; untie, unlock, undo, etc. —*vi.* to become unfastened

un·fa·vour·a·ble (-fā′vər ə b'l, -fāv′rə b'l) *adj.* not favourable; opposed, harmful, disadvantageous, inauspicious, etc. —**un·fa′vour·a·bly** *adv.*

un·feel·ing (-fēl′iŋ) *adj.* **1.** without feeling **2.** hardhearted; cruel —**un·feel′ing·ly** *adv.*

un·feigned (-fānd′) *adj.* genuine; real; sincere —**un·feign′ed·ly** (-fān′id lē) *adv.*

un·fin·ished (-fin′isht) *adj.* **1.** not finished or completed **2.** having no finish, or final coat, as of paint

un·fit (-fit′) *adj.* **1.** not meeting requirements; not fit or suitable **2.** not physically or mentally fit **3.** not fitted for a given purpose —*vt.* **-fit′ted, -fit′ting** to make unfit —**un·fit′ly** *adv.* —**un·fit′ness** *n.*

un·fix (-fiks′) *vt.* to unfasten; loosen

un·flap·pa·ble (-flap′ə b'l) *adj.* [see FLAP, *n.* 4] [Colloq.] not easily excited or upset; calm

un·fledged (-flejd′) *adj.* **1.** not fully fledged; unfeathered, as a young bird **2.** immature; undeveloped

un·flinch·ing (-flin′chiŋ) *adj.* steadfast; resolute; unyielding —**un·flinch′ing·ly** *adv.*

un·fold (-fōld′) *vt.* **1.** to open and spread out (something folded) **2.** to lay open to view; reveal, disclose, display, or

undissolved	uneatable	unenslaved	unexpendable
undistilled	uneaten	unentangled	unexpired
undistinguishable	uneclipsed	unenterprising	unexplainable
undistinguished	uneconomical	unentertaining	unexplained
undistorted	unedifying	unenthusiastic	unexploded
undistracted	uneducated	unentitled	unexploited
undistressed	uneffaced	unenviable	unexplored
undistributed	unemancipated	unenvious	unexposed
undisturbed	unembarrassed	unequipped	unexpressed
undiversified	unembellished	unescorted	unexpurgated
undiverted	unemotional	unessential	unextended
undivested	unemphatic	unestablished	unextinguished
undivided	unemptied	unestimated	unfading
undivulged	unenclosed	unethical	unfaltering
undocumented	unencumbered	uneventful	unfashionable
undogmatic	unending	unexacting	unfathomable
undomestic	unendorsed	unexaggerated	unfathomed
undomesticated	unendowed	unexamined	unfeared
undrained	unendurable	unexcelled	unfeasible
undramatic	unenforceable	unexchangeable	unfeathered
undraped	unengaged	unexcitable	unfed
undried	unenjoyable	unexciting	unfederated
undrinkable	unenlightened	unexcused	unfelt
undutiful	unenriched	unexecuted	unfeminine
undyed	unenrolled	unexercised	unfenced

explain **3.** to open up; unwrap —*vi.* **1.** to become unfolded **2.** to develop fully

un·for·tu·nate (-fôr'chə nit) *adj.* **1.** *a)* having bad luck; unlucky *b)* bringing, or coming by, bad luck; unfavourable **2.** not suitable or successful —*n.* an unfortunate person —**un·for'tu·nate·ly** *adv.*

un·found·ed (-foun'did) *adj.* **1.** not founded on fact or truth; baseless **2.** not established

un·freeze (-frēz') *vt.* **-froze', -froz'en, -freez'ing** **1.** to cause to thaw **2.** to remove financial controls from (prices, wages, etc.)

un·friend·ed (-fren'did) *adj.* having no friends; friendless

un·friend·ly (-frend'lē) *adj.* **1.** not friendly or kind; hostile **2.** not favourable or propitious —**un·friend'li·ness** *n.*

un·frock (-frok') *vt.* **1.** to remove a frock from **2.** to deprive of the rank or function of priest or minister

un·furl (-furl') *vt., vi.* to open or unfold from a furled state

un·gain·ly (-gān'lē) *adj.* **1.** awkward; clumsy **2.** coarse and unattractive —**un·gain'li·ness** *n.*

un·glued (-glōōd') *adj.* broken open; separated: said of things glued together

un·god·ly (-god'lē) *adj.* **1.** not godly or religious; impious **2.** sinful; wicked **3.** [Colloq.] outrageous; dreadful —**un·god'li·ness** *n.*

un·gov·ern·a·ble (-guv'ər nə b'l) *adj.* that cannot be governed or controlled; unruly —**un·gov'ern·a·bly** *adv.*

un·gra·cious (-grā'shəs) *adj.* **1.** rude; discourteous; impolite **2.** unpleasant; unattractive —**un·gra'cious·ly** *adv.* —**un·gra'cious·ness** *n.*

un·guard·ed (-gärd'id) *adj.* **1.** unprotected **2.** without guile or cunning; open **3.** careless; thoughtless; imprudent —**un·guard'ed·ly** *adv.*

un·guent (uŋ'gwənt) *n.* [L. *unguentum* < *unguere*, to anoint] a salve or ointment —**un'guen·tar·y** (-gwən tər ē) *adj.*

un·guis (uŋ'gwis) *n., pl.* **un'gues** (-gwēz) [L., a nail] **1.** *Bot.* the narrow base of certain petals **2.** *Zool.* a nail, claw, or hoof: also **un'gu·la** (-gyoo lə), *pl.* **-lae'** (-lē') —**un'gual** *adj.*

un·gu·late (-gyoo lit, -lāt') *adj.* [< L. *ungula*, a hoof] having hoofs; of or belonging to a former group of all mammals having hoofs —*n.* a mammal having hoofs

un·hal·lowed (un hal'ōd) *adj.* **1.** not hallowed or consecrated; unholy **2.** wicked; profane

un·hand (-hand') *vt.* to loose or release from the hand or hands or one's grasp; let go of

un·hand·y (-han'dē) *adj.* **-hand'i·er, -hand'i·est** **1.** not handy, convenient, or easy to reach **2.** not clever with the hands; awkward —**un·hand'i·ly** *adv.* —**un·hand'i·ness** *n.*

un·hap·py (-hap'ē) *adj.* **-pi·er, -pi·est** **1.** unlucky; unfortunate **2.** sad; wretched; sorrowful **3.** not suitable —**un·hap'pi·ly** *adv.* —**un·hap'pi·ness** *n.*

un·health·y (-hel'thē) *adj.* **-health'i·er, -health'i·est** **1.** having or showing poor health; sickly; not well **2.** harmful to health; unwholesome **3.** harmful to morals **4.** dangerous or risky [an *unhealthy* situation] —**un·health'i·ly** *adv.* —**un·health'i·ness** *n.*

un·heard (-hurd') *adj.* **1.** not perceived by the ear **2.** not given a hearing

un·heard-of (-hurd'ov') *adj.* **1.** not heard of before; unprecedented **2.** unacceptable or outrageous [*unheard-of* behaviour]

un·hinge (-hinj') *vt.* **-hinged', -hing'ing** **1.** a) to remove from the hinges *b)* to remove the hinges from **2.** to dislodge or detach **3.** to throw (the mind, etc.) into confusion; unbalance or upset

un·his·tor·ic (un'his tor'ik) *adj.* not historic or historical;

specif., *Linguis.* not having a historical basis; accidental, as the *b* in *thumb*: also **un'his·tor'i·cal**

un·hitch (un hich') *vt.* **1.** to free from a hitch **2.** to unfasten; release; detach

un·ho·ly (-hō'lē) *adj.* **-li·er, -li·est** **1.** not sacred, hallowed, or consecrated **2.** wicked; profane; impious **3.** [Colloq.] outrageous; dreadful —**un·ho'li·ness** *n.*

un·hook (-hook') *vt.* **1.** to remove or loosen from a hook **2.** to undo or unfasten the hook or hooks of —*vi.* to become unhooked

un·horse (-hôrs') *vt.* **-horsed', -hors'ing** **1.** to throw (a rider) from a horse **2.** to overthrow

un·hu·man (-hyōo'mən) *adj.* **1.** *rare var. of:* a) INHUMAN *b)* SUPERHUMAN **2.** not human in kind, quality, etc. —**un·hu'man·ly** *adv.*

u·ni- [< L. *unus*, one] a combining form meaning having or consisting of one only [*unicellular*]

U·ni·ate, U·ni·at (yōo'nē ət, -at') *n.* [< Russ. *uniyat*, ult. < L. *unus*, one: from union with the Roman Church] a member of the Eastern Church (sense 1b)

u·ni·cam·er·al (yōo'nə kam'ər əl) *adj.* [< UNI- + LL. *camera*, a chamber] of or having a single legislative chamber

UNICEF (yōo'nə sef') United Nations International Children's Emergency Fund

u·ni·cel·lu·lar (yōo'nə sel'yoo lər) *adj.* having or consisting of a single cell

u·ni·corn (yōo'nə kôrn') *n.* [< OFr. < L. < *unus*, one + *cornu*, a horn] a mythical horse-like animal with a single horn growing from the centre of its forehead

u·ni·cycle (yōo'nə sī'k'l) *n.* a riding device with only one wheel, which is straddled by the rider

UNIDO United Nations Industrial Development Organization

u·ni·fi·ca·tion (yōo'nə fi kā'shən) *n.* the act of unifying or the state of being unified

UNICORN

u·ni·form (yōo'nə fôrm') *adj.* [< MFr. < L. < *unus*, one + *-formis*, -form] **1.** always the same; not varying in form, rate, degree, manner, etc. **2.** having the same form, appearance, etc. as others of the same class **3.** consistent in action, effect, etc. —*n.* the official or distinctive clothes worn by the members of a particular group, as policemen or soldiers —*vt.* to clothe or supply with a uniform —**uniform** with having the same form, appearance, etc. as —**u'ni·form'ly** *adv.*

u·ni·form·i·ty (yōo'nə fôr'mə tē) *n., pl.* **-ties** state, quality, or instance of being uniform

u·ni·fy (yōo'nə fī') *vt., vi.* **-fied', -fy'ing** [< MFr. < LL. *unificare*: see UNI- & -FY] to combine into one; become or make united; consolidate —**u'ni·fi'a·ble** *adj.* —**u'ni·fi'er** *n.*

u·ni·lat·er·al (yōo'nə lat'ər əl) *adj.* [UNI- + LATERAL] **1.** of, occurring on, or affecting one side only **2.** involving one only of several parties; done by one only [*unilateral* disarmament] **3.** taking into account one side only of a matter; one-sided **4.** turned to, or having its parts on, one side —**u'ni·lat'er·al·ism** *n.* —**u'ni·lat'er·al·ly** *adv.*

u·ni·lin·e·ar (-lin'ē ər) *adj.* of or following a single, consistent path of development or progression

un·im·peach·a·ble (un'im pēch'ə b'l) *adj.* that cannot be doubted, questioned, or discredited; irreproachable —**un'im·peach'a·bly** *adv.*

un·im·proved (un'im prōovd') *adj.* **1.** not bettered, improved, or developed, as land by planting, building, etc. **2.** not used to good advantage **3.** not improved in health

un·in·hib·it·ed (-in hib′it id) *adj.* without inhibition; esp., free from the usual social or psychological restraints

un·ion (yōōn′yən, -ē ən) *n.* [< MFr. < LL. < L. < *unus*, one] **1.** a uniting or being united; combination; junction; specif., *a)* a grouping together of nations, political groups, etc. for some specific purpose *b)* marriage **2.** something united; a whole made up of united parts; specif., *a)* an organization or confederation uniting various individuals, political units, etc. *b) short for* TRADE UNION **3.** a device symbolizing political union, used in a flag or ensign **4.** [often U-] *a)* a facility for social recreation at a university *b)* the buildings of such an organization In full, **student union** **5.** a device for joining together parts; esp,, a coupling for linking the ends of pipes **6.** harmony; concord **7.** formerly, *a)* a combination of parishes for the administration of the poor law *b)* a workhouse under such administration **8.** a fabric made of two or more materials **9.** *Math.* a set containing all the elements of two or more given sets, with no element listed more than once —**the Union 1.** *a)* the union of the English and Scottish crowns in 1603 *b)* the union of England and Scotland in 1707 **2.** the union of Great Britain and Ireland in 1801 **3.** *a)* [U.S.] the United States of America *b)* the northern states of the U.S.A. during the American Civil War —**un′ion·ism** *n.*

un·ion·ist (-ist) *n.* **1.** *a)* a supporter of the principle of union *b)* a supporter of a specified union **2.** a member of a trade union **3.** [U-] a supporter of the union of Great Britain and Ireland, esp. N Ireland **4.** [U-] during the American Civil War, a supporter of the Federal union of the U.S. —*adj.* relating to unionism, esp. trade unionism —**un′ion·is′tic** *adj.*

un·ion·ize (-īz′) *vt.* **-ized′, -iz′ing 1.** to organize (a group of workers) into a trade union **2.** to bring into conformity with the rules, standards, etc. of a trade union —*vi.* to join or organize a trade union —**un′ion·i·za′tion** *n.*

Union Jack the national flag of the United Kingdom, consisting of the crosses of St. George, St. Andrew and St. Patrick

union shop *same as* CLOSED SHOP

u·nique (yōō nēk′) *adj.* [Fr. < L. *unicus*, single < *unus*, one] **1.** one and only; sole **2.** having no like or equal; unparalleled **3.** highly unusual, extraordinary, etc.: a common usage still objected to by many —**u·nique′ly** *adv.* —**u·nique′ness** *n.*

u·ni·sex (yōō′nə seks′) *adj.* [Colloq.] designating or of a fashion, as in garments, hair styles, etc., adopted by persons of either sex

u·ni·sex·u·al (yōō′nə sek′shoo wəl) *adj.* having one sex (male or female) only; not hermaphroditic —**u′ni·sex′u·al′- i·ty** (-shoo wal′ə tē) *n.* —**u′ni·sex′u·al·ly** *adv.*

u·ni·son (yōō′nə sən, -zən) *n.* [MFr. < ML. < L. *unus*, one + *sonus*, a sound] **1.** identity of musical pitch, as of two or more voices or tones **2.** agreement; concord; harmony —**in unison 1.** sounding the same note at the same time **2.** with all the voices or instruments performing the same part **3.** uttering the same words, or producing the same sound, at the same time **4.** in agreement

u·nit (yōō′nit) *n.* [< UNITY] **1.** *a)* the smallest whole number; one *b)* the number in the position just to the left of the decimal point **2.** any fixed quantity, amount, measure, etc. used as a standard; specif., the amount of a drug, vaccine, etc. needed to produce a given result **3.** *a)* a single person or group, esp. as distinguished from others or as part of a whole *b)* a single, distinct part, esp. one used for a specific purpose [the lens *unit* of a camera] *c)* a piece of furniture designed to form a whole with other, matching parts **4.** a subdivision of a military formation **5.** a complete system, organization, etc. that performs a specific function [a production *unit*]

U·ni·tar·i·an (yōō′nə ter′ē ən) *n.* **1.** a person who denies the doctrine of the Trinity, rejecting the divinity of Jesus and holding that God exists as one person or being **2.** a member of a Christian denomination based on these beliefs and showing tolerance of differing views —*adj.* **1.** of Unitarians or their beliefs **2.** [u-] *same as* UNITARY —**U′ni·tar′i·an·ism** *n.*

u·ni·tar·y (yōō′nə tər ē, -trē) *adj.* **1.** of a unit or units **2.** of, based on, or characterized by unity **3.** having the nature of or used as a unit

unit character *Genetics* a character or trait determined by a single gene or gene pair

u·nite (yoo nīt′) *vt., vi.* **-nit′ed, -nit′ing** [< L. pp. of *unire*, to unite < *unus*, one] **1.** to put or join together so as to make one; combine into a whole **2.** *a)* to bring or come together

in common cause, interest, action, etc.; join through fellowship, legal bonds, etc. *b)* to join in marriage

u·nit·ed (yoo nīt′id) *adj.* **1.** combined; joined **2.** of or resulting from joint action or association **3.** in agreement —**u·nit′ed·ly** *adv.* —**u·nit′ed·ness** *n.*

United Kingdom country in W Europe, consisting of England, Scotland, Wales, Northern Ireland, the Channel Isles, and the Isle of Man: in full, **United Kingdom of Great Britain and Northern Ireland**

United Nations an international organization of nations pledged to promote world peace and security under a charter signed in 1945 by 50 nations: 97 additional members had been admitted by 1977

unit holder a person who holds stock in a unit trust

u·ni·tive (yōō′nə tiv) *adj.* **1.** having unity **2.** tending to unite

unit price the price per unit, as per lb., as distinct from the total price of an item

unit trust a company formed by public subscriptions which are pooled to buy stocks and shares in a number of companies, under the supervision of a trustee

u·ni·ty (yōō′nə tē) *n., pl.* **-ties** [< OFr. < L. *unitas* < *unus*, one] **1.** the state of being one, or united; oneness **2.** a single, separate thing **3.** harmony; agreement; concord **4.** *a)* unification *b)* a unified group or body **5.** a complex that is a union of related parts **6.** *a)* an arrangement of parts that will produce a single, harmonious effect in an artistic or literary production *b)* an effect so produced **7.** constancy or continuity of purpose, action, etc. **8.** *Math.* any quantity, magnitude, etc. identified as a unit, or 1

Univ. 1. Universalist **2.** University

u·ni·va·lent (yōō′nə vā′lənt) *adj. Chem.* **1.** having one valence **2.** having a valence of one —**u′ni·va′lence,** **u′ni·va′len·cy** *n.*

u·ni·valve (yōō′nə valv′) *n.* **1.** a mollusc having a one-piece shell, as a snail **2.** such a one-piece shell —*adj.* **1.** having a one-piece shell **2.** having one valve only: also **u′ni·valved′**

u·ni·ver·sal (yōō′nə vur′s′l) *adj.* [< OFr. < L.: see UNIVERSE] **1.** of the universe; present or occurring everywhere **2.** of, for, or including all or the whole; not limited **3.** entire; whole **4.** broad in knowledge, interests, etc. **5.** that can be used for all kinds, forms, sizes, etc. **6.** used, intended to be used, or understood by all **7.** *Logic* predicating something of every member of a specified class —*n.* **1.** *short for* UNIVERSAL JOINT **2.** *Logic* a universal proposition —**u′ni·ver′sal·ness** *n.*

u·ni·ver·sal·ism (-iz′m) *n.* **1.** *same as* UNIVERSALITY **2.** [U-] the theological doctrine that all souls will eventually find salvation —**U′ni·ver′sal·ist** *adj., n.*

u·ni·ver·sal·i·ty (yōō′nə vur sal′ə tē) *n., pl.* **-ties 1.** quality, state, or instance of being universal **2.** unlimited range, application, occurrence, etc.; comprehensiveness

u·ni·ver·sal·ize (-vur′sə līz′) *vt.* **-ized′, -iz′ing** to make universal —**u′ni·ver′sal·i·za′tion** *n.*

universal joint (or **coupling**) a joint or coupling that permits a swing of limited angle in any direction, esp. one used to transmit rotary motion from one shaft to another not in line with it, as in the drive shaft of a motor car

u·ni·ver·sal·ly (-vur′s′lē) *adv.* **1.** in every instance **2.** in every part or place

universal suffrage suffrage for all adult citizens

universal time *same as* GREENWICH (MEAN) TIME

u·ni·verse (yōō′nə vurs′) *n.* [L. *universum* < *unus*, one + pp. of *vertere*, to turn] **1.** the totality of all the things that exist; the cosmos **2.** the world

UNIVERSAL JOINT

u·ni·ver·si·ty (yōō′nə vur′sə tē) *n., pl.* **-ties** [< MFr. < ML. < L. *universitas*, the whole, a society: see prec.] **1.** an educational institution of the highest level, often having one or more undergraduate colleges or similar establishments, and authorized to confer various degrees **2.** the buildings, students, faculty, or administrators of a university

un·joint (un joint′) *vt.* **1.** to separate (a joint) **2.** to separate the joints of

un·just (-just′) *adj.* not just or right; unfair —**un·just′ly** *adv.* —**un·just′ness** *n.*

un·kempt (-kempt′) *adj.* [UN- + *kempt*, pp. of dial. *kemben*,

unillustrated	unimportance
unimaginable	unimportant
unimaginably	unimposing
unimaginative	unimpregnated
unimitated	unimpressed
unimpaired	unimpressionable
unimpassioned	unimpressive
unimpeded	unimpugned
unimplemented	unincorporated

unindulged	uninhabited
unindustrialized	uninitiated
unindustrious	uninjured
uninfected	uninspired
uninfested	uninspiring
uninflected	uninstructed
uninfluenced	uninsurable
uninformed	uninsured
uninhabitable	unintegrated

to comb] 1. not combed 2. not tidy, neat, or groomed —**un·kempt′ness** *n.*

un·kind (-kīnd′) *adj.* 1. not sympathetic to or considerate of others 2. harsh, severe, cruel, etc. —**un·kind′ness** *n.*

un·kind·ly (-kīnd′lē) *adj.* *same as* UNKIND —*adv.* in an unkind manner —**un·kind′li·ness** *n.*

un·known (-nōn′) *adj.* 1. not in one's knowledge, acquaintance, etc.; unfamiliar (*to*) 2. not discovered, identified, etc. —*n.* an unknown person, thing, or quantity

unknown quantity 1. someone or something whose influence cannot be predicted; an enigma 2. *Math.* a quantity whose value is unknown

un·lace (-lās′) *vt.* -**laced′**, -**lac′ing** to undo or unfasten the laces of

un·lade (-lād′) *vt., vi.* -**lad′ed**, -**lad′ed** or -**lad′en**, -**lad′ing** 1. to unload (a ship, etc.) 2. to discharge (a cargo, etc.)

un·latch (-lach′) *vt., vi.* to open by release of a latch

un·law·ful (-lô′fəl) *adj.* 1. against the law; illegal 2. against moral or ethical standards; immoral —**un·law′ful·ly** *adv.* —**un·law′ful·ness** *n.*

un·lay (-lā′) *vt., vi.* -**laid′**, -**lay′ing** *Naut.* to untwist: said of a rope

un·learn (-lʉrn′) *vt., vi.* to forget (something learned) by a conscious effort, as in retraining

un·learn·ed (-lʉr′nid; *for 2* -lʉrnd′) *adj.* 1. *a*) not learned or educated; ignorant *b*) showing a lack of learning or education 2. known or acquired without conscious study [*unlearned* tact] —**un·learn′ed·ly** *adv.*

un·leash (-lēsh′) *vt.* to release from or as from a leash

un·less (ən les′) *conj.* [earlier *on lesse that,* at less than] in any case other than; except if [he won't go *unless* she does] —*prep.* except

un·let·tered (un let′ərd) *adj.* 1. *a*) uneducated *b*) illiterate 2. not marked with letters

un·like (-līk′) *adj.* not alike; different; dissimilar —*prep.* 1. not like; different from 2. not characteristic of [it's *unlike* her to cry] —**un·like′ness** *n.*

un·like·ly (-līk′lē) *adj.* 1. not likely to happen or be true; improbable 2. not likely to succeed —*adv.* improbably —**un·like′li·hood′**, **un·like′li·ness** *n.*

un·lim·ber (-lim′bər) *vt., vi.* 1. to prepare (a field gun) for use by detaching the limber 2. to get ready for action

un·lim·it·ed (-lim′it id) *adj.* 1. without limits or restrictions 2. without boundaries

un·load (-lōd′) *vt.* 1. *a*) to remove (a load, cargo, etc.) *b*) to take a load, etc. from 2. *a*) to express or tell (one's troubles, etc.) freely *b*) to relieve of something that troubles, burdens, etc. 3. to remove the charge from (a gun) 4. to get rid of —*vi.* to unload something

un·lock (-lok′) *vt.* 1. *a*) to open (a lock) *b*) to open the lock of (a door, etc.) 2. to let loose as if by opening a lock [to *unlock* a flood of tears] 3. to cause to separate [to *unlock* clenched jaws] 4. to lay open [to *unlock* a secret] —*vi.* to become unlocked

un·looked-for (-lookt′fôr′) *adj.* not expected or foreseen

un·loose (-lōōs′) *vt.* -**loosed′**, -**loos′ing** to make or set loose: also **un·loos′en**

un·luck·y (-luk′ē) *adj.* -**luck′i·er**, -**luck′i·est** not lucky;

having or marked by bad luck; unfortunate —**un·luck′i·ly** *adv.*

un·make (-māk′) *vt.* -**made′**, -**mak′ing** 1. to cause to be as before; make revert to original condition 2. to ruin; destroy 3. to depose from a position or authority

un·man (-man′) *vt.* -**manned′**, -**man′ning** 1. to deprive of manly courage, confidence, etc. 2. to castrate

un·man·ly (-man′lē) *adj.* -**li·er**, -**li·est** not manly; specif., cowardly, weak, effeminate, etc. —**un·man′li·ness** *n.*

un·manned (-mand′) *adj.* not manned; specif., without men aboard and operating by automatic or remote control

un·man·ner·ly (-man′ər lē) *adj.* having or showing poor manners; rude; discourteous —*adv.* rudely —**un·man′·ner·li·ness** *n.*

un·mask (-mask′) *vt., vi.* 1. to remove a mask or disguise (from) 2. to show or appear in true character

un·mean·ing (-mēn′iŋ) *adj.* 1. lacking in meaning or sense 2. showing no sense or intelligence; expressionless

un·meet (-mēt′) *adj.* not meet, or fit; unsuitable

un·men·tion·a·ble (un men′shən ə b'l) *adj.* not fit to be mentioned; not nice to talk about —*n.* [*pl.*] unmentionable things; specif., underwear: a humorous usage

un·mer·ci·ful (-mʉr′si fəl) *adj.* 1. having or showing no mercy; cruel; relentless; pitiless 2. excessive —**un·mer′·ci·ful·ly** *adv.*

un·mind·ful (-mīnd′fəl) *adj.* not mindful; heedless

un·mis·tak·a·ble (un′mis tāk′ə b'l) *adj.* that cannot be mistaken or misunderstood; clear; plain —**un′mis·tak′a·bly** *adv.*

un·mit·i·gat·ed (un mit′ə gāt′id) *adj.* 1. not lessened or eased [*unmitigated* suffering] 2. out-and-out; absolute [an *unmitigated* fool] —**un·mit′i·gat′ed·ly** *adv.*

un·mor·al (-môr′'l) *adj.* *var. of* AMORAL

un·muz·zle (-muz′'l) *vt.* -**zled**, -**zling** 1. to free (a dog, etc.) from a muzzle 2. to stop restraining or censoring

un·nat·u·ral (-nach′ər əl) *adj.* not natural; specif., *a*) abnormal; strange *b*) artificial; strained *c*) abnormally evil or cruel —**un·nat′u·ral·ly** *adv.* —**un·nat′u·ral·ness** *n.*

un·nec·es·sar·y (-nes′ə sər ē) *adj.* not necessary or required; needless —**un·nec′es·sar′i·ly** (-nes′ə ser′ə lē) *adv.*

un·nerve (-nʉrv′) *vt.* -**nerved′**, -**nerv′ing** 1. to cause to lose one's courage, confidence, etc. 2. to make nervous

un·num·bered (-num′bərd) *adj.* 1. not counted 2. *same as* INNUMERABLE 3. having no identifying number

U.N.O. United Nations Organization

un·oc·cu·pied (-ok′yə pīd′) *adj.* 1. having no occupant; vacant; empty 2. at leisure; idle

un·or·gan·ized (-ôr′gə nīzd′) *adj.* 1. having no organic structure 2. not having or following any regular order or system 3. not having or belonging to a trade union

un·pack (-pak′) *vt.* 1. to open and remove the packed contents of 2. to take from a crate, trunk, etc. 3. to remove a pack or load from —*vi.* to empty a packed trunk, etc.

un·paged (-pājd′) *adj.* having the pages unnumbered: said of a book, etc.

un·par·al·leled (-par′ə leld′) *adj.* that has no parallel, equal, or counterpart; unmatched

unintelligent	unlifelike	unmeasured	unmystified
unintelligible	unlighted	unmechanical	unnail
unintended	unlikable	unmedicated	unnamable
unintentional	unlikeable	unmeditated	unnameable
uninterested	unlined	unmelodious	unnamed
uninteresting	unlink	unmelted	unnaturalized
uninterrupted	unlisted	unmended	unnavigable
unintimidated	unlit	unmentioned	unnavigated
uninventive	unlively	unmercenary	unneeded
uninvested	unlocated	unmerited	unneedful
uninvited	unlovable	unmethodical	unneighbourly
uninviting	unloved	unmilitary	unnoted
uninvolved	unlovely	unmilled	unnoticeable
unissued	unloving	unmingled	unnoticed
unjoined	unlubricated	unmistaken	unnurtured
unjudicial	unmagnified	unmixed	unobjectionable
unjustifiable	unmalleable	unmodified	unobliged
unkept	unmanageable	unmoistened	unobliging
unkissed	unmanifested	unmolested	unobscured
unknit	unmanufacturable	unmollified	unobservant
unknot	unmanufactured	unmoor	unobserved
unknowable	unmarked	unmortgaged	unobserving
unknowing	unmarketable	unmotivated	unobstructed
unlabelled	unmarred	unmounted	unobtainable
unlaboured	unmarried	unmourned	unobtrusive
unladylike	unmastered	unmovable	unoffending
unlamented	unmatchable	unmoved	unoffensive
unlaundered	unmatched	unmoving	unoffered
unleased	unmated	unmown	unofficial
unleavened	unmatted	unmuffle	unofficious
unlevied	unmeant	unmurmuring	unoiled
unlicensed	unmeasurable	unmusical	unopen

un·par·lia·men·ta·ry (-pär′lə men′tər ē, -trē) *adj.* contrary to parliamentary law or usage

un·peg (-peg′) *vt.* **-pegged′, -peg′ging** 1. to remove a peg or pegs from 2. to unfasten or detach in this way

un·peo·ple (-pē′p'l) *vt.* **-pled, -pling** to reduce the population of; depopulate

un·per·son (un′pur′s'n) *n.* [< George Orwell's novel *1984*] a person who was formerly a public figure and who has been intentionally removed from public recognition, as for political reasons

un·pick (un′pik′) *vt.* to undo the stitches of a piece of sewing or knitting

un·pin (-pin′) *vt.* **-pinned′, -pin′ning** 1. to remove a pin or pins from 2. to unfasten or detach in this way

un·pleas·ant (-plez′'nt) *adj.* not pleasant; offensive; disagreeable —**un·pleas′ant·ly** *adv.* —**un·pleas′ant·ness** *n.*

un·plumbed (-plumd′) *adj.* 1. not sounded or measured with a plumb 2. not fully plumbed or understood

un·polled (-pōld′) *adj.* 1. *a)* not canvassed in a poll *b)* not cast or registered: said of votes 2. unshorn

un·pop·u·lar (-pop′yə lər) *adj.* not popular; not liked by the public or the majority —**un′pop·u·lar′i·ty** (-yə lar′ə tē) *n.*

un·prac·ti·cal (-prak′tə k'l) *adj. same as* IMPRACTICAL

un·prac·tised (-prak′tist) *adj.* 1. not practised; not regularly done, etc. 2. not skilled or experienced

un·prec·e·dent·ed (-pres′ə den′tid) *adj.* having no precedent or parallel; unheard-of; novel

un·prej·u·diced (-prej′ōō dist) *adj.* 1. without prejudice or bias; impartial 2. not impaired

un·prin·ci·pled (-prin′sə p'ld) *adj.* characterized by lack of moral principles; unscrupulous

un·print·a·ble (-print′ə b'l) *adj.* not printable; not fit to be printed, as because of obscenity

un·pro·fes·sion·al (un′prə fesh′ən 'l) *adj.* 1. violating the ethical code of a given profession 2. not of, typical of, or belonging to a profession —**un′pro·fes′sion·al·ly** *adv.*

un·qual·i·fied (un kwol′ə fīd′) *adj.* 1. lacking the necessary qualifications; not fit 2. not limited; absolute [an *unqualified* success] —**un·qual′i·fied′ly** *adv.*

un·ques·tion·a·ble (-kwes′chən ə b'l) *adj.* 1. not to be questioned, doubted, or disputed; certain 2. with no exception or qualification —**un·ques′tion·a·bly** *adv.*

un·ques·tioned (-kwes′chənd) *adj.* not questioned; specif., *a)* not interrogated *b)* not disputed; accepted

un·qui·et (-kwī′ət) *adj.* not quiet; restless, disturbed,

uneasy, anxious, etc. —*n.* an unquiet state —**un·qui′et·ly** *adv.* —**un·qui′et·ness** *n.*

un·quote (un′kwōt′) *interj.* I end the quotation: used in speech after a quotation —*vi.* to close (a quotation) esp. in printing

un·rav·el (un rav′'l) *vt.* **-elled, -el·ling** 1. to undo (something woven, tangled, etc.); separate the threads of 2. to make clear; solve —*vi.* to become unravelled —**un·rav′el·ment** *n.*

un·read (-red′) *adj.* 1. not read, as a book 2. having read little or nothing 3. unlearned (*in* a subject)

un·read·y (-red′ē) *adj.* 1. not ready; unprepared, as for action 2. not prompt or alert; slow —**un·read′i·ly** *adv.* —**un·read′i·ness** *n.*

un·real (-rē′əl, -rēl′) *adj.* not real; imaginary, false, etc. —**un′re·al′i·ty** (-rē al′ə tē) *n., pl.* **-ties**

un·re·al·is·tic (un′rē ə lis′tik) *adj.* not realistic; impractical; visionary —**un′re·al·is′ti·cal·ly** *adv.*

un·rea·son (un rē′z'n) *n.* lack of reason; irrationality

un·rea·son·a·ble (-ə b'l) *adj.* not reasonable; specif., *a)* having or showing little sense *b)* excessive; immoderate —**un·rea′son·a·ble·ness** *n.* —**un·rea′son·a·bly** *adv.*

un·rea·son·ing (-iŋ) *adj.* lacking reason or judgment; irrational —**un·rea′son·ing·ly** *adv.*

un·reel (un rēl′) *vt., vi.* to unwind as from a reel

un·re·gen·er·ate (un′ri jen′ər it) *adj.* 1. not spiritually reborn 2. not converted to a particular belief, etc. 3. recalcitrant or obstinate Also **un′re·gen′er·at′ed**

un·re·lent·ing (-ri len′tiŋ) *adj.* 1. refusing to yield or relent 2. without mercy or compassion 3. not relaxing, as in effort —**un′re·lent′ing·ly** *adv.*

un·re·li·gious (-ri lij′əs) *adj.* 1. *same as* IRRELIGIOUS 2. not involving religion; nonreligious

un·re·mit·ting (-ri mit′iŋ) *adj.* not stopping, relaxing, or slackening; persistent —**un′re·mit′ting·ly** *adv.*

un·re·served (-ri zurvd′) *adj.* not reserved; specif., *a)* frank; open *b)* unlimited *c)* not set aside for advance sale, as seats —**un′re·serv′ed·ly** (-zur′vid lē) *adv.*

un·rest (un rest′) *n.* a troubled or disturbed state; restlessness; specif., a state of discontent close to revolt

un·rid·dle (-rid′'l) *vt.* **-dled, -dling** to solve or explain (a riddle, mystery, etc.)

un·rig (-rig′) *vt.* **-rigged′, -rig′ging** to strip of rigging

un·right·eous (-rī′chəs) *adj.* 1. not righteous; wicked; sinful 2. not right; unjust; unfair —**un·right′eous·ly** *adv.* —**un·right′eous·ness** *n.*

unopened	unplaced	unpropitious	unreflecting
unopposed	unplanned	unproportionate	unreformed
unoppressed	unplanted	unproposed	unrefreshed
unordained	unplayable	unprosperous	unregarded
unoriginal	unplayed	unprotected	unregistered
unornamental	unpleasing	unproved	unregretted
unorthodox	unpledged	unproven	unregulated
unostentatious	unpliable	unprovided	unrehearsed
unowned	unploughed	unprovoked	unrelated
unoxidized	unplucked	unpruned	unrelaxed
unpacified	unplug	unpublished	unreliability
unpaid	unpoetic	unpunctual	unreliable
unpaid-for	unpoetical	unpunished	unrelieved
unpainful	unpointed	unpurged	unremedied
unpainted	unpoised	unpurified	unremembered
unpaired	unpolished	unquenchable	unremorseful
unpalatable	unpolitical	unquenched	unremovable
unpardonable	unpolluted	unquestioning	unremoved
unpardoned	unpopulated	unquotable	unremunerated
unparted	unposted	unquoted	unremunerative
unpasteurized	unpredictable	unransomed	unrenewed
unpatched	unpremeditated	unrated	unrenowned
unpatented	unprepared	unratified	unrentable
unpatriotic	unprepossessing	unreachable	unrented
unpaved	unprescribed	unreadable	unrepaid
unpeaceful	unpresentable	unrealized	unrepairable
unpenetrated	unpreserved	unreasoned	unrepaired
unpensioned	unpressed	unrebuked	unrepealed
unperceived	unpretending	unreceived	unrepentant
unperceiving	unpretentious	unreceptive	unrepenting
unperceptive	unpreventable	unreciprocated	unreplaceable
unperfected	unpriced	unreclaimable	unreplaced
unperformed	unprinted	unreclaimed	unreplenished
unperplexed	unprivileged	unrecognizable	unreported
unpersuadable	unprobed	unrecognized	unrepresentative
unpersuaded	unprocessed	unrecommended	unrepresented
unpersuasive	unprocurable	unrecompensed	unrepressed
unperturbed	unproductive	unreconcilable	unreprieved
unphilosophic	unprofaned	unreconciled	unreprimanded
unphilosophical	unprofessed	unreconstructed	unrequested
unpicked	unprofitable	unrecorded	unrequited
unpicturesque	unprogressive	unrecoverable	unresentful
unpierced	unpromising	unrectified	unresigned
unpile	unprompted	unredeemed	unresistant
unpitied	unpronounceable	unrefined	unresisting
unpitying	unpronounced	unreflected	unresolved

un·rip (-rip′) *vt.* **-ripped′**, **-rip′ping** to rip open; take apart or detach by ripping

un·ripe (-rīp′) *adj.* **1.** not ripe or mature; green **2.** not yet fully developed *[unripe plans]* —**un·ripe′ness** *n.*

un·ri·valled (-rī′v′ld) *adj.* having no rival, equal, or competitor; matchless; peerless

un·roll (-rōl′) *vt.* **1.** to open or extend (something rolled up) **2.** to present to view; display —*vi.* to become unrolled

un·ruf·fled (-ruf′′ld) *adj.* not ruffled, disturbed, or agitated; calm; smooth; serene

un·rul·y (-rōō′lē) *adj.* **-rul′i·er**, **-rul′i·est** [< ME. < *un-*, not + *reuly*, orderly] hard to control, restrain, or keep in order; disobedient, disorderly, etc. —**un·rul′i·ness** *n.*

un·sad·dle (-sad′′l) *vt.* **-dled**, **-dling** **1.** to take the saddle off (a horse, etc.) **2.** to throw from the saddle; unhorse —*vi.* to take the saddle off a horse, etc

un·said (-sed′) *pt. & pp.* of UNSAY —*adj.* not expressed

un·sat·u·rat·ed (-sach′ə rāt′id) *adj.* **1.** not saturated **2.** *Chem. a)* capable of dissolving more of the solute than has been dissolved *b)* designating an organic compound with a double or triple bond between carbon atoms, capable of combining with other elements or compounds by adding on at the bond

un·sa·vour·y (-sā′vər ē) *adj.* **1.** orig., tasteless **2.** unpleasant to taste or smell **3.** morally offensive —**un·sa′vour·i·ly** *adv.* —**un·sa′vour·i·ness** *n.*

un·say (-sā′) *vt.* **-said′**, **-say′ing** to take back or retract (what has been said)

un·scathed (-skāthd′) *adj.* not hurt; unharmed

un·scram·ble (-skram′b′l) *vt.* **-bled**, **-bling** to cause to be no longer scrambled, disordered, etc.; specif., *Electronics* to make (incoming scrambled signals) intelligible at the receiver —**un·scram′bler** *n.*

un·screw (-skrōō′) *vt.* **1.** to remove a screw or screws from **2.** *a)* to remove or loosen by removing a screw or screws, or by turning *b)* to remove a threaded top, cover, etc. from (a jar, etc.) —*vi.* to be or become unscrewed

un·script·ed (-skript′əd) *adj.* performed or delivered without a script, as a radio programme, speech etc.

un·scru·pu·lous (-skrōō′pyə ləs) *adj.* not scrupulous; heedless of what is right, just, etc.; unprincipled —**un·scru′pu·lous·ly** *adv.* —**un·scru′pu·lous·ness** *n.*

un·seal (-sēl′) *vt.* **1.** to break or remove the seal of **2.** to open by or as by breaking a seal

un·seam (-sēm′) *vt.* to open the seam or seams of; rip

un·search·a·ble (-surch′ə b′l) *adj.* that cannot be searched into; inscrutable —**un·search′a·bly** *adv.*

un·sea·son·a·ble (-sē′z′n ə b′l) *adj.* **1.** not usual for the season **2.** coming at the wrong time; untimely; inopportune —**un·sea′son·a·ble·ness** *n.* —**un·sea′son·a·bly** *adv.*

un·seat (-sēt′) *vt.* **1.** to throw or dislodge from a seat, saddle, etc. **2.** to remove from office, deprive of rank, etc.

un·seem·ly (-sēm′lē) *adj.* not seemly; not proper; unbecoming —*adv.* unbecomingly —**un·seem′li·ness** *n.*

un·self·ish (-sel′fish) *adj.* not selfish; altruistic; generous —**un·self′ish·ly** *adv.* —**un·self′ish·ness** *n.*

un·set·tle (-set′′l) *vt.* **-tled**, **-tling** to make unsettled, insecure, etc.; disturb, displace, disorder, etc. —*vi.* to become unsettled —**un·set′tle·ment** *n.*

un·set·tled (-set′′ld) *adj.* **1.** not settled; not in order, not stable, not decided or determined, etc. **2.** not paid or disposed of, as a debt or estate **3.** having no settlers **4.** not established in a place or abode **5.** troubled or restless —**un·set′tled·ness** *n.*

un·sex (-seks′) *vt.* to deprive of the qualities considered characteristic of one's sex

un·shack·le (-shak′′l) *vt.* **-led**, **-ling** **1.** to loosen or remove the shackles from **2.** to free

un·sheathe (-shēth′) *vt.* **-sheathed′**, **-sheath′ing** to remove (a sword, knife, etc.) from a sheath

un·ship (-ship′) *vt.* **-shipped′**, **-ship′ping** **1.** to unload from a ship **2.** to remove (an oar, etc.) from position

un·sight·ly (-sīt′lē) *adj.* not pleasant to look at; ugly —**un·sight′li·ness** *n.*

un·skil·ful (-skil′fəl) *adj.* not skilful; awkward; clumsy —**un·skil′ful·ly** *adv.* —**un·skil′ful·ness** *n.*

un·skilled (-skild′) *adj.* not skilled; specif., having, showing, or requiring no special skill or training

un·sling (-sliŋ′) *vt.* **-slung′**, **-sling′ing** **1.** to take (a rifle, etc.) from a slung position **2.** to release from slings

un·snap (-snap′) *vt.* **-snapped′**, **-snap′ping** to undo the snap or snaps of, so as to loosen or detach

un·snarl (-snärl′) *vt.* to free of snarls; untangle

un·so·cia·ble (-sō′shə b′l) *adj.* **1.** avoiding others; not sociable **2.** not conducive to sociability —**un·so′cia·bil′i·ty**, **un·so′cia·ble·ness** *n.* —**un·so′cia·bly** *adv.*

un·so·cial (-sō′shəl) *adj.* having or showing a dislike for the society of others —**un·so′cial·ly** *adv.*

un·sol·der (-sold′ər) *vt.* **1.** to take apart (things soldered together) **2.** to disunite; separate

un·so·phis·ti·cat·ed (un′sə fis′ti·kāt′id) *adj.* not sophisticated; artless, simple, unworldly, unrefined, etc. —**un′·so·phis′ti·cat′ed·ly** *adv.* —**un′so·phis′ti·ca′tion** *n.*

un·sound (-sound′) *adj.* not sound or free from defect; specif., *a)* not normal or healthy *b)* not safe or secure *c)* not safe and secure financially *d)* not accurate, sensible, etc. *e)* light: said of sleep —**un·sound′ly** *adv.* —**un·sound′ness** *n.*

un·spar·ing (-sper′iŋ) *adj.* **1.** not sparing or stinting; lavish **2.** not merciful; severe —**un·spar′ing·ly** *adv.*

un·speak·a·ble (-spēk′ə b′l) *adj.* **1.** that cannot be spoken **2.** marvellous, awesome, etc. beyond expression **3.** indescribably bad, evil, etc. —**un·speak′a·bly** *adv.*

un·sta·ble (-stā′b′l) *adj.* not stable; specif., *a)* easily upset, unbalanced, disturbed, etc. *b)* changeable *c)* unreliable; fickle *d) Chem., Physics* readily decomposing —**un·sta′ble·ness** *n.* —**un·sta′bly** *adv.*

un·stead·y (-sted′ē) *adj.* not steady; specif., *a)* not firm or stable *b)* changeable or erratic —*vt.* **-stead′ied**, **-stead′y·ing** to make unsteady —**un·stead′i·ly** *adv.* —**un·stead′i·ness** *n.*

un·stick (-stik′) *vt.* **-stuck′**, **-stick′ing** to loosen or free (something stuck)

un·stop (-stop′) *vt.* **-stopped′**, **-stop′ping** **1.** to remove the stopper from **2.** to clear (an obstructed pipe, etc.)

un·strap (-strap′) *vt.* **-strapped′**, **-strap′ping** to loosen or remove the strap or straps of

unresponsive	unsalaried	unseeded	unshorn
unrested	unsaleable	unseeing	unshortened
unrestful	unsalted	unseen	unshrinkable
unrestrainable	unsampled	unsegmented	unshrinking
unrestrained	unsanctified	unsegregated	unshriven
unrestraint	unsanctioned	unselected	unshrunk
unrestricted	unsanitary	unselective	unshuffled
unretarded	unsated	unsent	unshut
unretentive	unsatiable	unsentimental	unshuttered
unretracted	unsatiated	unseparated	unsifted
unretrieved	unsatisfactory	unserved	unsighted
unreturned	unsatisfied	unserviceable	unsigned
unrevealed	unsatisfying	unset	unsilenced
unrevenged	unsaved	unsevered	unsimplified
unreversed	unscalable	unsewn	unsingable
unreviewed	unscaled	unshaded	unsinkable
unrevised	unscanned	unshadowed	unsisterly
unrevoked	unscarred	unshakable	unsized
unrewarded	unscented	unshakeable	unslackened
unrewarding	unscheduled	unshaken	unslaked
unrhetorical	unscholarly	unshamed	unsleeping
unrhymed	unschooled	unshaped	unsliced
unrhythmic	unscientific	unshapely	unsmiling
unrhythmical	unscorched	unshared	unsmoked
unrightful	unscraped	unsharpened	unsoftened
unrobe	unscratched	unshaved	unsoiled
unromantic	unscreened	unshaven	unsold
unroof	unscriptural	unshed	unsoldierly
unrounded	unsculptured	unshelled	unsolicited
unruled	unseasoned	unsheltered	unsolidified
unsafe	unseaworthy	unshielded	unsolvable
unsaintly	unseconded	unshockable	unsolved
unsalable	unsecured	unshod	unsorted

un·string (-striŋ′) *vt.* **-strung′, -string′ing** **1.** to loosen or remove the string or strings of **2.** to remove from a string **3.** to make nervous, weak, upset, etc.

un·struc·tured (-struk′chərd) *adj.* not formally or systematically organized; loose, free, open, etc.

un·strung (-struŋ′) *adj.* **1.** nervous, upset, etc. **2.** having the string(s) loosened or detached, as a bow

un·stud·ied (-stud′ēd) *adj.* **1.** not got by study or conscious effort **2.** spontaneous; natural; unaffected **3.** not having studied; unlearned or unversed (*in*)

un·sub·stan·tial (un′səb stan′shəl) *adj.* not substantial; specif., *a)* having no material substance *b)* flimsy; light *c)* unreal; visionary **—un′sub·stan′ti·al′i·ty** (-stan′shē al′ə tē) *n.* **—un′sub·stan′tial·ly** *adv.*

un·suit·a·ble (un syōōt′ə b'l) *adj.* not suitable; unbecoming; inappropriate **—un·suit′a·bly** *adv.*

un·sung (-suŋ′) *adj.* **1.** not sung **2.** not honoured or celebrated, as in song or poetry

un·sus·pect·ed (un′sə spek′tid) *adj.* **1.** not believed guilty, bad, harmful, etc. **2.** not imagined existent, probable, etc. **—un′sus·pect′ed·ly** *adv.*

un·tan·gle (un taŋ′g'l) *vt.* **-gled, -gling** **1.** to free from a snarl or tangle; disentangle **2.** to free from confusion; clear up; put in order

un·taught (-tôt′) *adj.* **1.** not taught or educated **2.** acquired without being taught; natural

un·ten·a·ble (-ten′ə b'l) *adj.* **1.** not tenable; that cannot be defended **2.** incapable of being tenanted or occupied **—un′ten·a·bil′i·ty, un·ten′a·ble·ness** *n.*

un·thank·ful (-thaŋk′fəl) *adj.* **1.** not thankful; ungrateful **2.** thankless; unappreciated **—un·thank′ful·ly** *adv.* **—un·thank′ful·ness** *n.*

un·think·a·ble (-thiŋk′ə b'l) *adj.* **1.** beyond thought or imagination; inconceivable **2.** not to be considered; impossible **—un·think′a·bly** *adv.*

un·think·ing (-thiŋk′iŋ) *adj.* **1.** showing little or no thought or consideration; thoughtless **2.** lacking the ability to think; not rational **—un·think′ing·ly** *adv.*

un·thread (-thred′) *vt.* **1.** to draw the thread from **2.** to disentangle; unravel **3.** to find one's way through (a maze, etc.)

un·throne (-thrōn′) *vt.* **-throned′, -thron′ing** *same as* DETHRONE **—un·throne′ment** *n.*

un·ti·dy (-tī′dē) *adj.* **-di·er, -di·est** not tidy or neat; slovenly; messy **—un·ti′di·ly** *adv.* **—un·ti′di·ness** *n.*

un·tie (-tī′) *vt.* **-tied′, -ty′ing** **1.** to loosen or undo (something tied or knotted) **2.** to free, as from difficulty, restraint, etc. **3.** to untangle **—vi.** to become untied

un·til (un til′, ən-) *prep.* [ME. *untill* < *un-* (see UNTO) + *till*, *till*] **1.** up to the time of; till [*until* payday] **2.** before (a specified time) [not *until* tomorrow] **—conj.** **1.** up to the time when or that [*until* I go] **2.** to the point, degree, etc. that [heat water *until* it boils] **3.** before [don't leave *until* he does]

un·time·ly (un tīm′lē) *adj.* **1.** before the usual or expected time; premature [his *untimely* death] **2.** at the wrong time; inopportune **—adv.** **1.** prematurely **2.** inopportunely **—un·time′li·ness** *n.*

un·to (un′tōō, -too) *prep.* [ME. *un-*, until + *to*, to] *archaic or poet. var. of:* **1.** TO **2.** UNTIL

un·told (un tōld′) *adj.* **1.** not told or revealed **2.** too great, numerous, etc. to be counted, measured, or described

un·touch·a·ble (-tuch′ə b'l) *adj.* that cannot or should not be touched **—n.** **1.** an untouchable person or thing **2.** in India, formerly, one whose touch was regarded as defiling to higher-caste Hindus **—un′touch·a·bil′i·ty** *n.*

un·to·ward (un′tə wôrd′, un tō′ərd) *adj.* **1.** inappropriate, improper, unseemly, etc. [an *untoward* remark] **2.** not favourable or fortunate [*untoward* circumstances]

un·true (un trōō′) *adj.* **1.** not correct; false **2.** not agreeing with a standard or rule **3.** not faithful or loyal **—un·tru′ly** *adv.*

un·truth (-trōōth′) *n.* **1.** the quality or state of being untrue **2.** an untrue statement; falsehood; lie

un·truth·ful (-trōōth′fəl) *adj.* **1.** not in accordance with the truth **2.** telling a lie or lies, esp. habitually **—un·truth′ful·ly** *adv.* **—un·truth′ful·ness** *n.*

un·tu·tored (-tyōōt′ərd) *adj.* **1.** not tutored or taught; uneducated **2.** simple; naive; unsophisticated

un·twine (-twīn′) *vt.* **-twined′, -twin′ing** to undo (something twined or twisted); disentangle or unwind **—vi.** to become untwined

un·twist (-twist′) *vt., vi.* to turn in the opposite direction so as to loosen or separate; untwine

un·used (-yōōzd′) *adj.* **1.** not in use **2.** that has never been used **3.** unaccustomed (*to*)

un·u·su·al (-yōō′zhōō wəl) *adj.* not usual or common; rare **—un·u′su·al·ly** *adv.* **—un·u′su·al·ness** *n.*

un·ut·ter·a·ble (-ut′ər ə b'l) *adj.* that cannot be expressed or described **—un·ut′ter·a·bly** *adv.*

un·var·nished (-vär′nisht) *adj.* **1.** not varnished **2.** plain; simple; unadorned [the *unvarnished* truth]

un·veil (un vāl′) *vt.* to reveal as by removing a veil or covering from **—vi.** to take off a veil; reveal oneself

un·veil·ing (-iŋ) *n.* a formal or ceremonial removal of a covering from a new statue, tombstone, etc.

un·voiced (un voist′) *adj.* **1.** not uttered or expressed **2.** *Phonet. same as* VOICELESS

un·war·y (-wer′ē) *adj.* not wary or cautious; not alert to possible danger, trickery, etc. **—un·war′i·ly** *adv.* **—un·war′i·ness** *n.*

un·wea·ried (-wir′ēd) *adj.* **1.** not weary or tired **2.** never wearying; tireless; indefatigable

un·well (-wel′) *adj.* not well; ailing; ill; sick

un·wept (-wept′) *adj.* **1.** not shed [*unwept* tears] **2.** not wept for; unmourned

un·whole·some (-hōl′səm) *adj.* not wholesome; specif., *a)* harmful to body or mind *b)* unhealthy or unhealthy-looking *c)* morally bad **—un·whole′some·ly** *adv.* **—un·whole′some·ness** *n.*

unsought	unsupervised	untethered	unvaccinated
unsounded	unsupplied	unthanked	unvacillating
unsowed	unsupportable	untheatrical	unvalued
unsown	unsupported	unthoughtful	unvanquished
unspecialized	unsuppressed	unthought-of	unvaried
unspecific	unsure	untinged	unvarying
unspecified	unsurpassable	untired	unventilated
unspectacular	unsurpassed	untiring	unverifiable
unspent	unsurprised	untitled	unverified
unspiritual	unsusceptible	untorn	unversed
unspoiled	unsuspecting	untouched	unvisited
unspoken	unsustained	untraceable	unwakened
unsporting	unswayed	untraced	unwalled
unsportsmanlike	unsweetened	untrained	unwanted
unspotted	unswept	untrammelled	unwarlike
unsprung	unswerving	untransferable	unwarmed
unstained	unswollen	untransferred	unwarned
unstamped	unsymmetrical	untranslatable	unwarrantable
unstandardized	unsympathetic	untransmitted	unwarranted
unstarched	unsympathizing	untrapped	unwashed
unstarred	unsystematic	untravelled	unwasted
unstated	unsystematized	untraversed	unwatched
unstatesmanlike	untack	untreated	unwatchful
unsterilized	untactful	untried	unwatered
unstinted	untainted	untrimmed	unwavering
unstitched	untalented	untroubled	unwaxed
unstoppable	untalked-of	untrustworthy	unweakened
unstrained	untamable	untunable	unwearable
unstratified	untamed	untuned	unwearying
unstressed	untapped	unturned	unweathered
unsubdued	untarnished	untypical	unwed
unsubsidized	untasted	unusable	unwedded
unsubstantiated	unteachable	unutilizable	unweeded
unsuccessful	untechnical	unutilized	unweighed
unsuited	untenanted	unuttered	unwelcome
unsullied	untended		unwelded

un·wield·y (-wēl′dē) *adj.* hard to wield, manage, handle, etc. because of weight, shape, etc. —**un·wield′i·ness** *n.*

un·will·ing (-wil′iŋ) *adj.* 1. not willing; reluctant 2. done, given, etc. against one's will —**un·will′ing·ly** *adv.*

un·wind (-wīnd′) *vt.* -wound′, -wind′ing 1. to wind off or undo (something wound) 2. to uncoil 3. to untangle 4. [Colloq.] to relax —*vi.* to become unwound, relaxed, etc.

un·wis·dom (-wiz′dəm) *n.* lack of wisdom; foolishness

un·wise (-wīz′) *adj.* not wise; foolish or imprudent

un·wit·ting (-wit′iŋ) *adj.* 1. not knowing; unaware 2. not intended; unintentional —**un·wit′ting·ly** *adv.*

un·wont·ed (-wôn′tid) *adj.* not common, usual, or habitual —**un·wont′ed·ly** *adv.*

un·world·ly (-wurld′lē) *adj.* 1. unearthly or otherworldly 2. not worldly-wise; unsophisticated

un·wor·thy (-wur′thē) *adj.* -thi·er, -thi·est 1. lacking merit or value; worthless 2. not deserving (often with *of*) 3. not fit or becoming (usually with *of*) 4. not deserved —**un·wor′-thi·ly** *adv.* —**un·wor′thi·ness** *n.*

un·wrap (-rap′) *vt.* -wrapped′, -wrap′ping to take off the wrapping of; open or undo (something wrapped) —*vi.* to become unwrapped

un·writ·ten (-rit′'n) *adj.* 1. not in writing; not written or printed 2. operating only through custom or tradition [an *unwritten* rule] 3. not written on; blank

unwritten law law based on custom, usage, court decisions, etc. rather than on the action of a lawmaking body

un·yoke (-yōk′) *vt.* -yoked′, -yok′ing 1. to release from a yoke 2. to separate or disconnect —*vi.* 1. to become unyoked 2. to remove a yoke

un·zip (-zip′) *vt., vi.* -zipped′, -zip′ping 1. to open (a zip fastener) 2. to open the zip fastener of (a garment, etc.)

up (up) *adv.* [OE.] 1. to a higher place 2. in or on a higher position or level 3. in a direction or place thought of as higher or above 4. above the horizon 5. to a later period [from childhood *up*] 6. to a higher condition or rank 7. to a higher amount, degree, etc. 8. *a)* in or into a standing or upright position *b)* out of bed 9. in or into action, view, consideration, etc. [to bring a matter *up*] 10. aside; away; by [lay *up* grain] 11. so as to be even with in space, time, degree, etc. [keep *up* with the times] 12. so as to be tightly closed, bound, packed, etc. [tie it *up*] 13. completely [eat it *up*] 14. so as to stop [to rein *up* a horse] 15. *Naut.* windward 16. *Sports & Games* ahead (by a specified number of points, goals, etc.) The adverb *up* is also used with verbs *a)* to form combinations having special meanings (Ex.: show *up*) *b)* as an intensive (Ex.: dress *up*) *c)* as a virtually meaningless addition (Ex.: light *up* a cigarette) —*prep.* 1. to, towards, or at a higher place, condition, rank, etc. on or in 2. at, along, or towards a more distant part of [*up* the road] 3. towards the source or against the flow, etc. of [*up* the river] 4. in or towards the interior or more northerly part of (a country, territory, etc.) —*adj.* 1. *a)* being in or directed towards a higher position, condition, etc. *b)* going towards a more important place, as a major city, from a less important one [an *up* train] 2. *a)* above the ground *b)* above the horizon 3. higher in amount, degree, etc. [rents are *up*] 4. *a)* standing or upright *b)* out of bed 5. active, excited, etc. [her temper was *up*] 6. even with in space, time, etc. 7. in the inner; higher part of a country, etc. 8. at an end; over [time is *up*] 9. [Colloq.] happening [what's *up*?] a period or state of prosperity, good luck, etc. —*vi.* upped, up′ping [Colloq.] to get up; rise: sometimes used without inflection to emphasize a second verb [he *up* and left] —*vt.* [Colloq.] to put up, lift up, or take up —**on the up and up** [Colloq.] 1. honest 2. making steady progress; improving —**up against** [Colloq.] faced with —**up against it** [Colloq.] in difficulty, esp. financially —**up and around** (or **about**) out of bed and again active, as after an illness —**up and doing** busy; active —**up for** 1. presented or considered for (an elective office, election, sale, auction, etc.) 2. before a court for (trial) or on (a charge) —**ups and downs** good periods and bad periods —**up to** [Colloq.] 1. occupied with; doing; scheming [*up* to mischief] 2. equal to (a task, etc.) 3. capable of (doing, undertaking, etc.) 4. as many as [*up* to four] 4. as far as [*up* to here] 5. dependent upon; incumbent upon —**up with!** give or restore power, favour, etc. to! —**well up on** (or **in**) [Colloq.] well-informed about

up- *a combining form meaning* up [uphill]

up-and-com·ing (up′'n kum′iŋ) *adj.* 1. enterprising, alert, and promising 2. gaining in importance or status

up-and-down (-dɑun′) *adj.* 1. going alternately up and down, to and fro, etc. 2. variable; changing; fluctuating

U·pan·i·shad (ŏŏ pun′i shəd) *n.* [Sans.] any of a group of metaphysical treatises dealing with man in relation to the universe: part of the Veda

u·pas (yŏŏ′pəs) *n.* [short for Malay *pohon upas*, tree of poison] 1. a tall Javanese tree of the mulberry family, whose whitish bark yields a poisonous juice 2. the juice

up·beat (up′bēt′) *n.* 1. an upward trend; upswing 2. *Music* an upward stroke made by a conductor to show an unaccented beat —*adj.* lively; cheerful

up·braid (up brād′) *vt.* [< OE. < *up-*, up + *bregdan*, to pull, shake] to rebuke severely; censure sharply

up·bring·ing (up′briŋ′iŋ) *n.* the training and education received while growing up; rearing; nurture

up·cast (up′kàst′) *n.* 1. something cast up 2. *Geol.* same as UPTHROW (sense 2) 3. *Mining* a ventilating shaft through which air is returned to the surface —*adj.* thrown or directed upwards

up·coun·try (-kun′trē) *adj.* of or located in the interior of a country —*n.* the interior of a country —*adv.* in or towards the interior of a country

up·date (up dāt′) *vt.* -dat′ed, -dat′ing to bring up to date; make conform to the most recent facts, methods, ideas, etc.

up·draught (up′dràft′) *n.* an upward air current

up·end (up end′) *vt., vi.* 1. to turn or stand on end 2. to upset or topple

up·grade (up′grād′; *for v. usually* up grād′) *n.* an upward slope, esp. in a road —*adj., adv.* uphill; upwards —*vt.* -grad′ed, -grad′ing 1. to promote to a more skilled job at higher pay 2. to raise in importance, value, etc. —**on the upgrade** advancing or improving in status, influence, health, etc.

up·heav·al (up hē′v'l) *n.* 1. an upheaving, as of the earth's crust by an earthquake 2. a sudden, violent change 3. any disturbance or sudden change in a settled routine

up·heave (-hēv′) *vt.* -heaved′ or -hove′, -heav′ing to heave or lift up —*vi.* to rise as if forced up

up·hill (up′hil′) *adv.* 1. towards the top of a hill 2. with difficulty —*adj.* 1. going or sloping up 2. requiring great effort

up·hold (up hōld′) *vt.* -held′, -hold′ing 1. to hold up; raise 2. to keep from falling; support 3. to give moral support to 4. to decide in favour of; support against opposition —**up·hold′er** *n.*

up·hol·ster (up hōl′stər, ə pōl′-) *vt.* [altered < ME. *upholder*, dealer in small wares < *upholden*, to repair] to fit out (furniture, etc.) with covering, padding, springs, etc. —**up·hol′ster·er** *n.*

up·hol·ster·y (-stər ē, -strē) *n., pl.* -ster·ies 1. the materials used in upholstering 2. the business or work of upholstering

up·keep (up′kēp′) *n.* 1. the keeping up of buildings, equipment, etc.; maintenance 2. the cost of this 3. state of repair

up·land (-lənd, -land′) *n.* land elevated above other land —*adj.* of or situated in upland

up·lift (up lift′; *for n.* up′lift′) *vt.* 1. to lift up; elevate 2. to raise to a higher moral, social, or cultural level —*n.* 1. an uplifting 2. any influence, movement, etc. aimed at uplifting society —*adj.* designating a brassiere designed to lift and support the breasts —**up·lift′er** *n.* —**up·lift′ment** *n.*

up·most (up′mōst′) *adj.* *same as* UPPERMOST

up·on (ə pon′) *prep.* on, or up and on: generally interchangeable with *on*, the choice depending on idiom, sentence rhythm, etc. —*adv.* on: used only for completing a verb [a canvas not painted *upon*]

up·per (up′ər) *adj.* 1. higher in place or physical position 2. farther north or farther inland 3. higher in rank, authority, etc. 4. [U-] *Geol.* later: used of a division of a period —*n.* the part of a shoe or boot above the sole —**on one's uppers** [Colloq.] 1. wearing shoes with soles worn through 2. in need; poor

Upper Carboniferous see GEOLOGY, chart

upper case [from their being kept in the upper of two cases of type] capital-letter type used in printing, as distinguished from small letters (*lower case*) —**up′-per-case′** *adj.* —**up′per-case′** *vt.* -cased′, -cas′ing

upper class the social class above the middle class; rich, socially prominent, or aristocratic class

up·per·cut (-kut′) *n.* *Boxing* a short, swinging blow directed upwards —*vt., vi.* -cut′, -cut′ting to hit with an uppercut

upper hand the position of advantage or control

Upper House [often u- h-] the smaller and less representative branch of a legislature having two branches

up·per·most (up′ər mōst′) *adj.* highest in place, power, authority, etc.; predominant; foremost —*adv.* in the highest place, rank, etc.

up·pish (up′ish) *adj.* [Colloq.] inclined to be arrogant, snobbish, etc.: also **up′pi·ty** (-ə tē) —**up′pish·ly** *adv.* —**up′-pish·ness** *n.*

up·raise (up rāz′) *vt.* **-raised′, -rais′ing** to raise up

up·rear (-rir′) *vt.* **1.** to lift up **2.** to erect; build **3.** to exalt **4.** to bring up; rear —*vi.* to rise up

up·right (up′rīt′; *also for adv.* up rīt′) *adj.* **1.** standing or directed straight up; erect **2.** honest and just; honourable —*adv.* in an upright position —*n.* **1.** the state of being upright or vertical **2.** something having an upright position **3.** short for UPRIGHT PIANO —**up′right′ly** *adv.* —**up′right′-ness** *n.*

upright piano a piano with a vertical rectangular body

up·rise (up rīz′; *for n.* up′rīz′) *vi.* **-rose′, -ris′en, -ris′ing 1.** to rise; get up, move up, rise into view, swell, etc. **2.** to rise in revolt —*n.* a rising up

up·ris·ing (up′rīz′iŋ) *n.* a rising up; specif., a revolt

up·roar (-rôr′) *n.* [Du. *oproer,* a stirring up] **1.** a violent disturbance; tumult **2.** loud, confused noise; din

up·roar·i·ous (up rôr′ē əs) *adj.* **1.** making, or marked by, an uproar; tumultuous **2.** *a)* loud and boisterous, as laughter *b)* causing such laughter [an *uproarious* joke] —**up·roar′-i·ous·ly** *adv.* —**up·roar′i·ous·ness** *n.*

up·root (up rōōt′) *vt.* **1.** to tear up by the roots **2.** to destroy or remove utterly; eradicate

up·sa·dai·sy (up′sə dā′zē) *interj.* var. *of* UPSY-DAISY

up·set (up set′; *for n. and occas. adj.* up′set′) *vt.* **-set′, -set′-ting 1.** *a)* to tip over; overturn *b)* to defeat, esp. unexpectedly **2.** *a)* to disturb the functioning, fulfilment, or completion of *b)* to disturb mentally, emotionally, or physically **3.** *Mech.* to shorten and thicken (metal) by beating —*vi.* to become overturned —*n.* an upsetting or being upset; specif., *a)* an overturning *b)* a defeat, esp. when unexpected *c)* a disorder of mind or body: disturbance —*adj.* **1.** overturned **2.** defeated **3.** disturbed —**up·set′-ter** *n.*

upset price the price fixed as the minimum at which something will be sold at an auction

up·shot (up′shot′) *n.* [orig., the final shot in an archery match] the conclusion; result; outcome

up·side (-sīd′) *n.* the upper side or part —**to be upsides with** [Colloq.] to be on equal terms with; to be quits

upside down 1. with the top side or part underneath **2.** in disorder; topsy-turvy —**up′side′-down′** *adj.*

upside-down cake a cake baked with a bottom layer of fruit and turned upside down before serving

up·si·lon (yōōp′sə lon′, up′-; -lən) *n.* [Gr.] the twentieth letter of the Greek alphabet (Υ, υ)

up·stage (up′stāj′; *for v.* up stāj′) *adv.* towards or at the rear of a stage —*adj.* **1.** of or having to do with the rear of a stage **2.** haughty and aloof —*vt.* **-staged′, -stag′ing** to draw attention, as of an audience, to oneself at the expense of (another)

up·stairs (up′sterz′) *adv.* **1.** up the stairs **2.** on or to an upper floor or higher level —*adj.* situated on an upper floor —*n.* **1.** an upper floor or floors **2.** the masters and mistresses of a house collectively, as opposed to the servants —**kick upstairs** [Colloq.] to promote from a position of power to a higher but less powerful position

up·stand·ing (up stan′diŋ) *adj.* **1.** standing straight; erect **2.** upright in character and behaviour; honourable

up·start[1] (up′stärt′) *n.* a person who has recently come into wealth, power, etc., esp. one who is aggressive; parvenu —*adj.* of or characteristic of an upstart

up·start[2] (up stärt′) *vi., vt.* to start, or spring, up or cause to spring up

up·stream (-strēm′) *adv., adj.* in the direction against the current of a stream

up·surge (up surj′; *for n.* up′surj′) *vi.* **-surged′, -surg′ing** to surge up —*n.* a surge upwards

up·sweep (up′swēp′; *for v.* up swēp′) *n.* a sweep or curve upwards —*vt., vi.* **-swept′, -sweep′ing** to sweep or curve upwards

up·swept (up′swept′) *adj.* **1.** curved upwards **2.** designating or of a style of hairdo in which the hair is combed up in the back and piled on the top of the head

up·swing (up′swiŋ′; *for v.* up swiŋ′) *n.* a swing or trend upwards; specif., an upward trend in business —*vi.* **-swung′, -swing′ing 1.** to swing upward **2.** to advance

up·sy-dai·sy (up′sə dā′zē, up′sē-) *interj.* [baby-talk extension of UP] up you go: used playfully in lifting a baby

up·take (up′tāk′) *n.* the act of taking up; a drawing up, absorbing, etc. —**quick** (or **slow**) **on the uptake** [Colloq.] quick (or slow) to understand or comprehend

up·throw (-thrō′) *n.* **1.** a throwing up **2.** *Geol.* that side of a fault which has moved upwards relative to the other side

up·thrust (-thrust′) *n.* **1.** an upward push or thrust **2.** an upheaval of a part of the earth's crust

up·tight, up·tight (up′tīt′) *adj.* [Colloq.] **1.** very tense, nervous, anxious, etc. **2.** excessively conventional or strict in attitudes Also **up tight**

up-to-date (up′tə dāt′) *adj.* **1.** extending to the present time **2.** keeping up with what is most recent, modern, etc. —**up′-to-date′ness** *n.*

up·town (up′toun′) *adj., adv.* [Chiefly U.S.] of, in, like, to, or towards the upper part of a city or town —*n.* [Chiefly U.S.] the uptown part

up·turn (up turn′; *for n.* up′turn′) *vt., vi.* to turn up, upwards, or over —*n.* an upward turn, curve, or trend —**up′turned′** *adj.*

up·ward (up′wərd) *adv., adj.* **1.** towards a higher place, position, degree, etc. **2.** from an earlier to a later time **3.** beyond (an indicated price, amount, etc.) [tickets cost *upward* of £1] Also **up′wards** *adv.* —**upwards** (or **upward**) **of** more than —**up′ward·ly** *adv.*

upward mobility movement from a lower to a higher social and economic status

up·wind (up′wind′) *adv., adj.* in the direction from which the wind is blowing or usually blows [the ship tacked *upwind*]

u·ra·cil (yoor′ə sil) *n.* [UR(O)- + AC(ETIC) + -IL(E)] a crystalline base found in ribonucleic acid

u·rae·mi·a (yoo rē′mē ə, -rēm′yə) *n* [Mod.L. < Gr. *ouron,* urine + *haima,* blood] a toxic condition caused by the presence in the blood of waste products normally eliminated in the urine —**u·rae′mic** *adj.*

u·rae·us (yoo rē′əs) *n., pl.* **-rae′i** (-ī) [< Mod.L. < Gr. *ouraios,* a cobra] the sacred serpent on the headdress of ancient Egyptian rulers

U·ral-Al·ta·ic (yoor′əl al tā′ik) *n.* the group of languages which includes, among others, the Uralic and Altaic families —*adj.* **1.** designating or of this group of languages **2.** of the peoples speaking these languages

U·ral·ic (yoo ral′ik, -rä′lik) *adj.* designating or of the family of languages including Finno-Ugric and Samoyed —*n.* this family of languages Also **U·ra′li·an** (-rä′lē ən)

U·ra·ni·a (yoo rā′nē ə) *Gr. Myth.* the Muse of astronomy

u·ra·ni·um (yoo rā′nē əm) *n.* [ModL. < URANUS, the planet] a very hard, heavy, radioactive metallic chemical element: it is found only in combination, and its isotopes are important in work on atomic energy: symbol, U; at. wt., 238.03; at. no., 92

U·ra·nus (yoo rā′nəs, yoor′ə nəs) **1.** *Gr. Myth.* a god who personified the heavens and was the father of the Titans, Furies, and Cyclopes: he was overthrown by his son Cronus (Saturn) **2.** a planet of the solar system, seventh in distance from the sun: diameter, 47 400 km

u·rate (yoor′āt) *n.* a salt of uric acid

ur·ban (ur′bən) *adj.* [< L. < *urbs,* a city] **1.** of, in, or constituting a city or town **2.** characteristic of the city as distinguished from the country

urban district formerly, an urban division of an administrative county, with an elected council: cf. RURAL DISTRICT

ur·bane (ur bān′) *adj.* [< L.: see URBAN] polite and courteous in a smooth, polished way; refined —**ur·bane′ly** *adv.* —**ur·bane′ness** *n.*

urban guerrilla a guerrilla operating in an urban environment, using terrorist methods of intimidation

ur·ban·ism (ur′bən iz'm) *n.* **1.** *a)* the character of life in the cities *b)* the study of this **2.** concentration of the population in the cities —**ur′ban·ist** *n., adj.*

ur·ban·ite (-īt′) *n.* a person living in a city

ur·ban·i·ty (ur ban′ə tē) *n., pl.* **-ties 1.** the quality of being urbane **2.** [*pl.*] civilities, courtesies, or amenities

ur·ban·ize (ur′bə nīz′) *vt.* **-ized′, -iz′ing** to change from rural to urban —**ur′ban·i·za′tion** *n.*

ur·ban·ol·o·gist (ur′bə nol′ə jist) *n.* [URBAN + -O- + -LOG(Y) + -IST] a specialist in urban problems —**ur·ban′ol·o·gy** *n.*

urban renewal the renewal of urban areas suffering from neglect and decay, as by clearing slums and constructing new housing projects, etc.

ur·ce·o·late (ur′sē ə līt, -lāt′) *adj.* [< Mod.L. < L. *urceolus,* dim. of *urceus,* vase] shaped like a vase or urn

ur·chin (ur′chin) *n.* [< OFr. < L. *ericius,* a hedgehog < *er,* hedgehog] **1.** same as SEA URCHIN **2.** a small boy, or any youngster, esp. one who is mischievous

Ur·du (oor′dōō) *n.* [Hindi, < *zabān-i-urdū,* language of the camp] an Indic language, a variant of Hindi written with Arabic characters: an official language of Pakistan

-ure [Fr. < L. *-ura*] a suffix meaning: **1.** act or result of being [*exposure*] **2.** agent, instrument, or scope of [*legislature*] **3.** state of being [*composure*]

u·re·a (yoo rē′ə, yoor′ē ə) *n.* [ModL. < Fr. < Gr. *ouron,* urine] a soluble, crystalline solid, CO(NH₂)₂, found in the urine of mammals or produced synthetically: used in making plastics, adhesives,etc. —**u·re′al, u·re′ic** *adj.*

u·re·ter (yoo rēt′ər) *n.* [ModL. < Gr. < *ourein,* to urinate] a duct or tube that carries urine from a kidney to the bladder or cloaca —**u·re′ter·al, u·re·ter·ic** (yoor′ə ter′ik) *adj.*

u·re·thane (yoor′ə thān′) *n.* [Fr. *uréthane:* see UREA, ETHER & -ANE] a white crystalline compound, produced from urea and ethyl alcohol, used as a sedative, solvent, etc.

u·re·thra (yoo rē′thrə) *n., pl.* **-thrae** (-thrē) **, -thras** [LL. < Gr. < *ouron,* urine] the canal through which urine is discharged from the bladder in most mammals: in the male,

semen is also discharged through the urethra —**u·re′thral**
adj.

urge (ʉrj) *vt.* **urged, urg′ing** [L. *urgere,* to press hard] **1.** *a)*
to press upon the attention; speak in favour of [to *urge*
caution] *b)* to entreat or plead with; exhort **2.** to
stimulate or incite; provoke **3.** to drive or force onwards;
impel —*vi.* **1.** to make an earnest presentation of
arguments, claims, charges, etc. **2.** to exert a force that
impels, as to action —*n.* **1.** the act of urging **2.** an impulse
to do a certain thing —**urg′er** *n.*
ur·gen·cy (ʉr′jən sē) *n., pl.* **-cies 1.** an urgent quality or
state; need for action, haste, etc. **2.** insistence; importunity
3. something urgent
ur·gent (-jənt) *adj.* [MFr. < L. prp. of *urgere,* to urge] **1.**
calling for haste, immediate action, etc.; pressing **2.**
insistent —**ur′gent·ly** *adv.*
-ur·gy (ʉr′jē) [< Gr. < *-ourgos,* worker < *ergon,* work] *a*
combining form meaning a working with or by means of
(something specified) [*zymurgy*]
-u·ri·a (yoor′ē ə) [ModL. < Gr. < *ouron,* urine] *a*
combining form meaning a (diseased) condition of the urine
[*haematuria*]
u·ric (yoor′ik) *adj.* of, contained in, or derived from urine
uric acid a white, odourless, crystalline substance found in
urine
u·ri·nal (yoor′ə n'l, yoo rī′-) *n.* **1.** a portable container used
for urinating **2.** a place for urinating; specif., a fixture for
use by men in urinating
u·ri·nal·y·sis (yoor′ə nal′ə sis) *n., pl.* **-ses′** (-sēz′) chemical
or microscopic analysis of the urine
u·ri·nar·y (yoor′ə nər ē) *adj.* **1.** of urine **2.** of the organs
involved in secreting and discharging urine
u·ri·nate (yoor′ə nāt′) *vi.* **-nat′ed, -nat′ing** to discharge
urine from the body —*vt.* to discharge as or with the urine
—**u′ri·na′tion** *n.* —**u′ri·na′tive** *adj.*
u·rine (yoor′in) *n.* [OFr. < L. *urina*] in mammals, the
yellowish fluid containing urea and other waste products,
secreted from the blood by the kidneys, passed to the
bladder, and periodically discharged through the urethra
u·ri·no- [< L. *urina,* urine] *a combining form meaning*
urine, urinary tract: also, before a vowel, **urin-**
u·ri·no·gen·i·tal (yoor′ə nō jen′ə t'l) *adj.* *same as*
UROGENITAL
urn (ʉrn) *n.* [L. *urna*] **1.** *a)* a vase, esp. one with a foot or
pedestal *b)* a container for the ashes of a cremated body **2.**
a metal container with a tap, used for making or serving
coffee, tea, etc.
u·ro- [< Gr. *ouron,* urine] *a combining form meaning*
urine, urination, urinary tract: also, before a vowel, **ur-**
u·ro·gen·i·tal (yoor′ō jen′ə t'l) *adj.* designating or of the
urinary and genital organs; genitourinary
u·rol·o·gy (yoo rol′ə jē) *n.* the branch of medicine dealing
with the urogenital or urinary system and its diseases
—**u·ro·log·ic** (yoor′ə loj′ik), **u′ro·log′i·cal** *adj.* —**u·rol′o·**
gist *n.*
u·ros·co·py (yoo ros′kə pē) *n., pl.* **-pies** examination of the
urine, as for the diagnosis of disease —**u·ro·scop·ic**
(yoor′ə skop′ik) *adj.*
Ur·sa Major (ʉr′sə) [L., lit., Great Bear] the most
conspicuous constellation in the northern sky: it contains
the seven stars which form the Plough
Ursa Minor [L., lit., Little Bear] the northernmost
constellation: it contains the North Star
ur·sine (ʉr′sīn, -sin) *adj.* [< L. < *ursus,* a bear] of or like a
bear or the bear family; bearlike
Ur·su·line (ʉr′syə lin, -līn′) *n.* [< Mod.L.: after Saint
Ursula, a legendary Christian Brit. princess said to have
lived in the 4th cent.] R.C.Ch. any member of a teaching
order of nuns founded c. 1537 —*adj.* of this order
ur·ti·car·i·a (ʉr′tə ker′ē ə) *n.* [ModL. < L. *urtica,* a nettle]
same as HIVES —**ur′ti·car′i·al** *adj.*
u·rus (yoor′əs) *n.* [L. < Gmc. name] *same as* AUROCHS
(sense 1)
us (us) *pron.* [OE.] *objective case of* WE: also used
colloquially as a predicate complement with a linking verb
(Ex.: that's *us*)
U.S., US United States
USA, U.S.A. 1. United States of America **2.** United States
Army
us·a·ble, use·a·ble (yōo′zə b'l) *adj.* that can be used; fit,
convenient, or available for use —**us′a·bil′i·ty, us′a·ble·ness**
n. —**us′a·bly** *adv.*
USAF, U.S.A.F. United States Air Force
us·age (yōo′sij, -zij) *n.* **1.** the act, way, or extent of using;
treatment **2.** a long-continued or established practice;
custom; habit **3.** the way in which a word, phrase, etc. is
used in speaking or writing, or an instance of this
us·ance (yōo′z'ns) *n.* [ME. < M.Fr. *usance* < L. *usus,* see USE]
Commerce the time allowed for the payment of a foreign bill
of exchange, as established by custom
use (yōoz; *for n.* yōos) *vt.* **used** (yōozd; *for vt.* 6 & *vi.,* with
the following "to" yōos′tə *or* yōos′too), **us′ing** [< OFr., ult.
< L. *usus,* pp. of *uti,* to use] **1.** to put or bring into action

or service **2.** to practise; exercise [*use* your judgment] **3.**
to behave towards; treat [to *use* a friend badly] **4.** to do
away with by using; consume, expend, etc. [to *use* up one's
energy] **5.** *a)* to smoke or chew (tobacco) *b)* to take or
consume habitually [to *use* drugs] **6.** to accustom (used in
the passive with *to*) [to become *used* to certain ways] **7.** to
exploit (a person) —*vi.* to be accustomed (now only in the
past tense, with an infinitive, meaning "did at one time")
[he *used* to live in Oxford] —*n.* **1.** a using or being used
2. the ability to use [he lost the use of his leg] **3.** the right
or permission to use **4.** the need or opportunity to use [no
further *use* for his services] **5.** an instance or way of using
6. usefulness; utility **7.** the object or purpose for which
something is used **8.** function, service, or benefit **9.**
custom; habit; practice **10.** *Eccles.* a distinctive form of
liturgical observance, as of a diocese **11.** *Law a)* the
enjoyment of property, as from occupying or employing it *b)*
profit or benefit, esp. that of property held in trust by
another —**have no use for 1.** to have no need of **2.** to
dislike strongly —**in use** being used —**make use of** to use;
have occasion to use —**put to use** to use
used (yōozd) *pt. & pp. of* USE —*adj.* **1.** that has been used
2. *same as* SECONDHAND
use·ful (yōos′fəl) *adj.* **1.** that can be used; serviceable;
helpful **2.** [Colloq.] very good; highly capable or desirable
[he's a *useful* member of the team] —**use′ful·ly** *adv.* —**use′-**
ful·ness *n.*
use·less (-lis) *adj.* **1.** having no use; unserviceable;
worthless **2.** to no purpose; ineffectual; of no avail —**use′-**
less·ly *adv.* —**use′less·ness** *n.*
us·er (yōo′zər) *n.* **1.** a person or thing that uses; often in
combination [a road-*user*] **2.** *Law a)* the continued
exercise or enjoyment of a right *b)* presumptive right based
on long-continued use
U-shaped (yōo′shăpt′) *adj.* having the shape of a U
ush·er (ush′ər) *n.* [OFr. *uissier* < L. *ostiarius* < *ostium,*
door] **1.** an official doorkeeper **2.** a person whose duty it
is to show people to their seats in a theatre, church, etc. **3.**
any of the groom's attendants at a wedding **4.** an official
who precedes a person of rank in a procession **5.** [Obs.] an
assistant teacher —*vt.* **1.** to escort or conduct (others) to
seats, etc. **2.** to herald or bring (*in*) —*vi.* to act as an usher
ush·er·ette (ush′ə ret′) *n.* a woman or girl usher, as in a
cinema
USN, U.S.N. United States Navy
U.S.S. United States Ship, Steamer, or Steamship
U.S.S.R., USSR Union of Soviet Socialist Republics
u·su·al (yōo′zhoo wəl, -zhwəl, -zhəl) *adj.* [< MFr. < LL.
usualis < L. *usus:* see USE] such as is most often seen,
heard, used, etc.; common; ordinary; customary —**as usual**
in the usual way —**u′su·al·ly** *adv.* —**u′su·al·ness** *n.*
u·su·fruct (yōo′zyoo frukt′, -zoo-, -soo-) *n.* [< LL. < L. *usus,*
a use + *fructus,* a fruit] *Law* the right to use and enjoy the
advantages and profits of the property of another without
altering or damaging the substance —**u′su·fruc′tu·ar·y**
(-fruk′choo wər ē) *adj., n., pl.* **-ar·ies**
u·su·rer (yōo′zhoo rər) *n.* a person who engages in usury
u·su·ri·ous (yōo zhoor′ē əs) *adj.* **1.** practising usury **2.** of or
involving usury —**u·su′ri·ous·ly** *adv.* —**u·su′ri·ous·ness** *n.*
u·surp (yōo sʉrp′, -zʉrp′) *vt., vi.* [< MFr. < L. *usurpare* <
usus, a use + *rapere,* to seize] to take or assume and hold
(power, position, rights, etc.) by force or without right
—**u·surp′er** *n.* —**u·surp′ing·ly** *adv.*
u·sur·pa·tion (yōo′sʉr pā′shən, -zʉr-) *n.* unlawful or violent
seizure of a throne, power, etc.
u·su·ry (yōo′zhoo rē) *n., pl.* **-ries** [< ML. < L. *usura* <
usus: see USE] **1.** the lending of money at interest, now
specif. at a rate of interest that is excessively or unlawfully
high **2.** interest at such a high rate
usw, u.s.w. [G. *und so weiter*] and so forth
U.T. universal time
u·ten·sil (yōo ten′s'l) *n.* [< MFr. < L. < *utensilis,* fit for use
< *uti,* to use] an implement or container used for a
particular purpose, now esp. one used in a kitchen [cooking
utensils]
u·ter·ine (yōot′ər in, yōot′ə rīn′) *adj.* **1.** of the uterus **2.**
having the same mother but a different father [*uterine*
sisters]
u·ter·us (yōot′ər əs) *n., pl.* **u′ter·i** (-ī′) [L.] a hollow,
muscular organ of female mammals in which the ovum is
deposited and the embryo and foetus are developed; womb
u·til·i·tar·i·an (yoo til′ə ter′ē ən) *adj.* **1.** of or having utility;
useful **2.** stressing usefulness over beauty, etc. **3.** of or
believing in utilitarianism —*n.* a person who believes in
utilitarianism
u·til·i·tar·i·an·ism (-iz'm) *n.* **1.** the doctrine that the value
of anything is determined solely by its utility **2.** the
doctrine that the purpose of all action should be to bring
about the greatest happiness of the greatest number **3.**
utilitarian character or quality
u·til·i·ty (yoo til′ə tē) *n., pl.* **-ties** [< OFr. < L. < *utilis,*
useful < *uti,* to use] **1.** usefulness **2.** something useful **3.**
a) something useful to the public, esp. the service of

electricity, gas, water, etc. *b*) a company providing such a service: see also PUBLIC UTILITY 4. *Econ.* the power to satisfy the wants of humanity —*adj.* for practical use with little attention to beauty

utility room a room containing various household appliances and equipment, as for heating, laundry, cleaning, etc.

u·ti·lize (yōōt′əl īz′) *vt.* -lized′, -liz′ing to put to use; make practical or profitable use of: also sp. **u′ti·lise** —**u′ti·liz′-a·ble** *adj.* —**u′ti·li·za′tion** *n.* —**u′ti·liz′er** *n.*

ut·most (ut′mōst′) *adj.* [OE. *utemest*, double superl. of *ut*, out] 1. most extreme or distant; farthest 2. of or to the greatest or highest degree, amount, etc.; greatest —*n.* the most that is possible

U·to·pi·a (yōō tō′pē ə) *n.* [Mod.L. < Gr. *ou*, not + *topos*, a place: an imaginary island described in a book of the same name by Sir Thomas More (1516) as having a perfect political and social system] 1. any idealized place, state, or situation of perfection 2. any visionary scheme for an ideally perfect society

U·to·pi·an (-ən) *adj.* 1. of or like Utopia 2. [*often* u-] having or based on ideas envisioning perfection in social and political organization; idealistic; visionary —*n.* 1. an inhabitant of Utopia 2. [*often* u-] a person who believes in a utopia, esp. of a social or political nature; visionary —**u·to′pi·an·ism** *n.*

u·tri·cle (yōō′tri k′l) *n.* [< Fr. < L. dim. of *uter*, leather bag] a small sac, vesicle, or baglike part: also **u·tric·u·lus** (yōō trik′yə ləs), *pl.* -**li′** (-lī′) —**u·tric′u·lar** *adj.*

ut·ter¹ (ut′ər) *adj.* [OE. *uttera*, compar. of *ut*, out] 1. complete; total 2. unqualified; absolute; unconditional —**ut′ter·ly** *adv.* —**ut′ter·ness** *n.*

ut·ter² (ut′ər) *vt.* [< ME. < *utter*, outward < *ut*, out] 1.

orig., to give out; put forth; now esp., to pass (counterfeit money, forged cheques, etc.) 2. to make or express with the voice [to *utter* a cry, to *utter* a thought] 3. to express in any way 4. to make known; divulge —**ut′ter·a·ble** *adj.* —**ut′ter·er** *n.*

ut·ter·ance (ut′ər əns, ut′rəns) *n.* 1. the act, power, or way of uttering 2. something uttered or said

ut·ter·most (ut′ər mōst′) *adj., n.* same as UTMOST

U-turn (yōō′turn′) *n.* a turning completely around, esp. of a vehicle within the width of a street or road, so as to head in the opposite direction

UV, uv ultraviolet

u·vu·la (yōō′vyə lə) *n., pl.* -**las**, -**lae** (-lē′) [ML., dim. of L. *uva*, a grape] the small, fleshy part of the soft palate hanging down above the back of the tongue

u·vu·lar (-lər) *adj.* 1. of or having to do with the uvula 2. *Phonet.* pronounced with a vibration of the uvula, or with the back of the tongue near or touching the uvula —*n.* a uvular sound —**u′vu·lar·ly** *adv.*

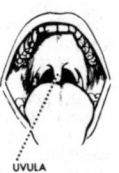

UVULA

ux·o·ri·al (ək sôr′ē əl, əg zôr′-) *adj.* [see ff.] of, befitting, or characteristic of a wife —**ux·or′i·al·ly** *adv.*

ux·o·ri·ous (-əs) *adj.* [< L. < *uxor*, wife] dotingly fond of or submissive to one's wife —**ux·o′ri·ous·ly** *adv.* —**ux·o′-ri·ous·ness** *n.*

Uz·bek (ooz′bek, uz′-) *n.* 1. a member of a Turkic people living in the region of the Uzbek S.S.R. 2. the Turkic language of the Uzbeks Also **Uz′beg** (-beg)

V

V, v (vē) *n., pl.* **V's, v's** 1. the twenty-second letter of the English alphabet 2. the sound of V or v

V (vē) *n.* 1. something shaped like V 2. a Roman numeral for 5 —*adj.* shaped like V

V 1. *Chem.* vanadium 2. *Physics* the symbol for volt

V v 1. velocity 2. victory

v. 1. [L. *vice*] in the place of 2. [G. *von*] of 3. [L. *vide*] see 4. verb 5. *pl.* vv. verse 6. version 7. versus 8. vice- 9. *pl.* vv. violin 10. voice 11. volt 12. voltage 13. volume

V1 [< G. *Vergeltungswaffe*, retaliation weapon] a robot bomb invented by the Germans in World War II: also called **doo·dle·bug** (dōō′d′l bug′)

V2 [see prec.] a rocket-powered ballistic missile invented by the Germans in World War II

VA, V.A. 1. Vicar Apostolic 2. Vice-Admiral 3. (Order of) Victoria and Albert

vac (vak) *n.* [Colloq.] vacation

va·can·cy (vā′kən sē) *n., pl.* -**cies** 1. the state of being vacant; emptiness 2. *a)* empty space *b)* a vacant space; gap, blank, opening, etc. 3. lack of intelligence, interest, or thought 4. an unoccupied position or office 5. a room, flat, etc. available for rent

va·cant (vā′kənt) *adj.* [< OFr. < L. prp. of *vacare*, to be empty] 1. having nothing in it, as a space; empty 2. not held, filled, or occupied, as a position, a seat, a house, etc. 3. free from work or activity [*vacant* hours] 4. without thought, interest, etc. [a *vacant* mind, stare, etc.] —**va′cant·ly** *adv.* —**va′cant·ness** *n.*

va·cate (vā kāt′, və-) *vt.* -**cat′ed**, -**cat′ing** [< L. pp. of *vacare*, to be empty] 1. to make vacant; specif., to leave (an office, position, etc.) or move out of (a house, room, etc.) 2. *Law* to make void; annul

va·ca·tion (və kā′shən, vā-) *n.* [< MFr. < L. *vacatio*] 1. a period of the year when law courts or universities are closed 2. [Rare] a vacating 3. [U.S.] same as HOLIDAY (sense 2) —*vi* [U.S.] to take a holiday —**va·ca′tion·er, va·ca′-tion·ist** *n.*

vac·ci·nate (vak′sə nāt′) *vt.* -**nat′ed**, -**nat′ing** to inoculate with a specific vaccine in order to prevent disease, as in immunizing against smallpox —*vi.* to practise vaccination —**vac′ci·na′tor** *n.*

vac·ci·na·tion (vak′sə nā′shən) *n.* 1. the act or practice of vaccinating 2. the scar on the skin where the vaccine has been applied

vac·cine (vak′sēn, -sin) *n.* [L. *vaccinus*, from cows < *vacca*, a cow: from use of cowpox virus in smallpox vaccine] any

preparation of killed microorganisms, living weakened organisms, etc. introduced into the body to produce immunity to a specific disease by causing antibodies to be formed —**vac′ci·nal** *adj.*

vac·il·late (vas′ə lāt′) *vi.* -**lat′ed**, -**lat′ing** [< L. pp. of *vacillare*] 1. to sway to and fro; waver 2. to fluctuate or oscillate 3. to waver in mind; show indecision —**vac′il·lat′-ing** *adj.* —**vac′il·lat′ing·ly** *adv.* —**vac′il·la′tion** *n.*

va·cu·i·ty (va kyōō′ə tē) *n., pl.* -**ties** [< L. < *vacuus*, empty] 1. the quality or state of being empty; emptiness 2. an empty space; void or vacuum 3. lack of intelligence, interest, or thought 4. something inane; inanity

vac·u·ole (vak′yoo wōl′) *n.* [Fr. < L. *vacuus*, empty] *Biol.* a fluid-filled cavity within the plasma membrane of a cell, believed to have the function of discharging excess water or wastes —**vac′u·o·lar** (-wə lər, vak′yoo wō′lər) *adj.*

vac·u·ous (vak′yoo wəs) *adj.* [L. *vacuus*] 1. empty 2. stupid; senseless; inane 3. lacking purpose; idle —**vac′-u·ous·ly** *adv.* —**vac′u·ous·ness** *n.*

vac·u·um (vak′yoo wəm; *also*, & *for adj.* & *v.* usually, vak′-yoom] *n., pl.* -**u·ums**, -**u·a** (-yoo wə) [L., neut. sing. of *vacuus*, empty] 1. a space with nothing at all in it 2. an enclosed space, as that inside a vacuum tube, out of which most of the air or gas has been taken, as by pumping 3. a space left empty as by the removal of something; void: often used figuratively 4. *short for* VACUUM CLEANER —*adj.* 1. of a vacuum 2. used to make a vacuum 3. having a vacuum 4. working by suction or the creation of a partial vacuum —*vt., vi.* to clean with a vacuum cleaner: in full, **vac′-u·um-clean′**

vacuum cleaner a machine for cleaning carpets, floors, upholstery, etc. by suction

vacuum flask (or **jug**) same as THERMOS

vacuum-packed (-pakt′) *adj.* packed in an airtight container from which most of the air was exhausted before sealing, so as to keep the contents fresh

vacuum pump a pump used to draw air or gas out of a sealed space

vacuum tube a sealed tube which has been made a partial vacuum for observing the effect of a discharge of electricity through rarefied gas, as a neon tube

V.A.D. Voluntary Aid Detachment

va·de me·cum (vā′dē mē′kəm, vä′dī mā′kəm) [L., lit., go with me] something carried about by a person for constant use, reference, etc., as a handbook

vag·a·bond (vag′ə bond′) *adj.* [< MFr. < L. *vagabundus*, strolling about < *vagari*, to wander] 1. moving from place to place; wandering **2.** of, having to do with, or living an unsettled, drifting, irresponsible life; vagrant; shiftless **3.** aimlessly following an irregular course —*n.* **1.** a person who wanders from place to place, having no fixed abode **2.** a tramp **3.** an idle, disreputable, or shiftless person —*vi.* to wander —**vag'a·bond'age, vag'a·bond'ism** *n.*

va·gar·y (vā'gər ē, və ger'ē) *n., pl.* **-gar·ies** [< L. *vagari,* to wander] **1.** an odd, eccentric, or unexpected action **2.** an odd, whimsical, or eccentric idea or notion —**va·gar'i·ous** *adj.* —**va·gar'i·ous·ly** *adv.*

va·gi·na (və jī'nə) *n., pl.* **-nas, -nae** (-nē) [L., a sheath] a sheath or sheathlike structure; specif., in female mammals, the canal leading from the vulva to the uterus —**vag·i·nal** (vaj'ə n'l, və jī'n'l) *adj.*

vag·i·nate (vaj'ə nit, -nāt') *adj.* **1.** having a vagina or sheath; sheathed **2.** like a sheath

va·got·o·my (vā got'ə mē) *n., pl.* **-mies** [VAG(US) + -TOMY] the surgical cutting of the vagus nerve

va·gran·cy (vā'grən sē) *n., pl.* **-cies** [< ff.] **1.** a wandering in thought or talk; digression **2.** a wandering from place to place **3.** shiftless or idle wandering without money or work, as of tramps, beggars, etc.

va·grant (vā'grənt) *n.* [prob. < Anglo-Fr. < OFr. *walcrer,* to wander; infl. prob. by L. *vagari,* to wander] a person who wanders from place to place; esp., one without a regular job, supporting himself by begging, etc.; vagabond, tramp, etc. —*adj.* **1.** wandering from place to place; roaming; nomadic **2.** of, characteristic of, or living the life of a vagrant **3.** following no fixed direction or course; random, wayward, etc. —**va'grant·ly** *adv.*

vague (vāg) *adj.* **va'guer, va'guest** [Fr. < L. *vagus,* wandering] **1.** not clearly or precisely expressed or stated **2.** indefinite in shape or form **3.** not sharp, certain, or precise in thought or expression **4.** not known or determined; uncertain —**vague'ly** *adv.* —**vague'ness** *n.*

va·gus (vā'gəs) *n., pl.* **va'gi** (-jī) [ModL. < L., wandering] either of a pair of cranial nerves acting upon the larynx, lungs, heart, oesophagus, and most of the abdominal organs: also **vagus nerve** —**va'gal** (-g'l) *adj.*

vail¹ (vāl) *n.* [ME. *vailen*] [Obs.] a tip; gratuity

vail² (vāl) *vt.* [ME. *valen* < OFr. *avaler,* to descend] [Archaic] **1.** to lower **2.** to take off (one's hat, etc.) as a sign of respect or submission

vain (vān) *adj.* [< OFr. < L. *vanus,* empty] **1.** having no real value or significance; worthless, empty, etc. [*vain pomp*] **2.** without force or effect; futile, fruitless, etc. [a *vain attempt*] **3.** having or showing an excessively high regard for one's self, looks, ability, etc.; conceited —**in vain 1.** unsuccessfully; fruitlessly **2.** lightly; profanely —**vain'ly** *adv.* —**vain'ness** *n.*

vain·glo·ri·ous (vān'glôr'ē əs) *adj.* [< ML.: see ff.] **1.** boastfully vain and proud of oneself **2.** characterized by boastful vanity —**vain'glo'ri·ous·ly** *adv.* —**vain'glo'ri·ous·ness** *n.*

vain·glo·ry (vān glôr'ē) *n.* [< OFr. < L. *vana gloria,* empty boasting: see VAIN & GLORY] **1.** extreme self-pride and boastfulness **2.** vain show or empty pomp

Vais·ya (vīs'ya) *n.* [< Sans.] a member of the third caste among the Hindus, the business and agricultural class

val·ance (val'əns, val'-) *n.* [< ? *Valence,* city in France] **1.** a short drapery or curtain hanging from the edge of a bed, shelf, etc., often to the floor **2.** a short drapery or facing of wood or metal across the top of a window —**val'anced** *adj.* Also **val·ence**

vale¹ (vāl) *n.* [< OFr. < L. *vallis*] [Poet.] *same as* VALLEY

va·le² (vā'lē, wä'lā) *interj., n.* [L.] farewell

val·e·dic·tion (val'ə dik'shən) *n.* [< L. pp. of *valedicere* < *vale,* farewell (imper. of *valere,* to be well) + *dicere,* to say] **1.** a bidding farewell **2.** something said in parting

val·e·dic·to·ry (val'ə dik'tər ē) *adj.* said or done at parting, by way of farewell; uttered as a valediction —*n., pl.* **-ries** a farewell speech, esp. one delivered by a U.S. student at graduation

va·lence (vā'ləns) *n.* [< ML., ult. < L. prp. of *valere,* to be strong] *Chem.* **1.** the combining capacity of an element or radical, as measured by the number of hydrogen or chlorine atoms which one radical or one atom of the element will combine with or replace **2.** same as VALENCY (sense 1)

valence electrons the mobile electrons in the outermost shell of an atom which largely determine its properties

Va·len·ci·ennes (val'ən sē en') *n.* [after *Valenciennes,* city in N France where orig. made] a flat bobbin lace with the pattern and ground worked in one operation

va·len·cy (vā'lən sē) *n.* **1.** any of the units of valence which an element may have **2.** *same as* VALENCE (sense 1)

-va·lent (vā'lənt) [< L. *valens*] *Chem. a suffix meaning:* **1.** having a specified valence **2.** having a specified number of valences

val·en·tine (val'ən tīn') *n.* **1.** a sweetheart chosen or complimented on Saint Valentine's Day **2.** a greeting card or gift sent on this day

va·le·ri·an (və lir'ē ən) *n.* [< MFr. < ML. *valeriana*] **1.** any of various plants with clusters or spikes of white, pink, red, or purplish flowers **2.** a drug made from the roots of some of these plants, formerly used as a sedative —**va·ler'ic** *adj.*

val·et (val'it, val'ā; *Fr.* vȧ lā') *n.* [Fr., a groom < OFr. *vaslet,* young man, page] **1.** a man's personal manservant who takes care of the man's clothes, helps him in dressing, etc. **2.** an employee, as of a hotel, who cleans or presses clothes, etc. —*vt., vi.* to serve (a person) as a valet

val·e·tu·di·nar·i·an (val'ə tyoo'də ner'ē ən) *n.* [< L. < *valetudo,* state of health, sickness < *valere,* to be strong] **1.** a person in poor health; invalid **2.** a person who worries constantly about his health —*adj.* **1.** in poor health; sickly **2.** anxiously concerned about one's health Also **val'e·tu'di·nar·y,** *pl.* **-nar·ies**

val·iant (val'yənt) *adj.* [< OFr. prp. of *valoir* < L. *valere,* to be strong] courageous; brave —**val'iance, val'ian·cy** *n.* —**val'iant·ly** *adv.*

val·id (val'id) *adj.* [< Fr. < L. *validus,* strong < *valere,* to be strong] **1.** having legal force; binding under law **2.** well-grounded on principles or evidence, as an argument; sound **3.** effective, cogent, etc. **4.** *Logic* correctly derived or inferred according to the rules of logic —**val'id·ly** *adv.* —**val'id·ness** *n.*

val·i·date (val'ə dāt') *vt.* **-dat'ed, -dat'ing** [< ML. pp. of *validare*] **1.** to give legal force to; declare legally valid **2.** to prove to be valid —**val'i·da'tion** *n.*

va·lid·i·ty (və lid'ə tē) *n., pl.* **-ties** the state, quality, or fact of being valid in law or in argument, proof, etc.

val·ine (văl'ēn, va'-) *n.* [(iso)val(eric acid) + -INE⁴] a white, crystalline essential amino acid, found in many proteins

va·lise (və lēs') *n.* [Fr. < It. *valigia* < ?] a piece of hand luggage: an old-fashioned term

val·ley (val'ē) *n., pl.* **-leys** [< OFr. < L. *vallis*] **1.** a stretch of low land lying between hills or mountains **2.** the land drained or watered by a great river system [the Nile *valley*] **3.** any long dip or hollow

val·lum (val'əm) *n.* [L.] *Archaeology* a Roman earthwork or rampart

val·or·i·za·tion (val'ər i zā'shən) *n.* [Port. *valorização,* ult. < LL. *valor,* VALOUR] a fixing of prices, usually by government action, as by buying up a commodity at the fixed price, etc. —**val'or·ize'** (-ə rīz') *vt., vi.* **-ized', -iz'ing**

val·our (val'ər) *n.* [< OFr. < LL. < L. *valere,* to be strong] great courage or bravery: also, U.S. sp., **val'or** —**val'or·ous** *adj.* —**val'or·ous·ly** *adv.* —**val'or·ous·ness** *n.*

‡valse (vȧls) *n.* [Fr.] a waltz

val·u·a·ble (val'yoo b'l, -yoo wə b'l) *adj.* **1.** *a)* being worth money *b)* having great value in terms of money **2.** highly regarded as precious, useful, worthy, etc. —*n.* an article of value, as a piece of jewellery —**val'u·a·ble·ness** *n.* —**val'u·a·bly** *adv.*

val·u·ate (val'yoo wāt') *vt.* **-at'ed, -at'ing** to set a value on; appraise —**val'u·a'tor** *n.*

val·u·a·tion (val'yoo wā'shən) *n.* **1.** the act of determining the value of anything, esp. the formal assessment of property, etc. by a professional valuer; evaluation **2.** determined or estimated value **3.** estimation of the worth, merit, etc. of anything —**val'u·a'tion·al** *adj.* —**val'u·a'tion·al·ly** *adv.*

val·ue (val'yoo) *n.* [< OFr. pp. of *valoir,* to be strong, to be worth < L. *valere*] **1.** a fair equivalent in money, etc. for something sold or exchanged **2.** the worth of a thing in money or goods at a certain time **3.** estimated or appraised worth **4.** purchasing power **5.** that quality of a thing that makes it more or less desirable, useful, etc. **6.** [*pl.*] the social principles, goals, or standards held by an individual class, society, etc. **7.** precise meaning, as of a word **8.** numerical order assigned to a playing card, etc. **9.** *Art* relative lightness or darkness of a colour *b)* the effect produced by the use of light and shade **10.** *Math.* the quantity for which a symbol stands **11.** *Music* the relative duration of a note, tone, or rest **12.** *Phonet.* the quality of a speech sound [the different *values* of the vowel *e* in English] —*vt.* **-ued, -u·ing 1.** to estimate the value of; appraise **2.** to place a certain estimate of worth on in a scale of values [to *value* health above wealth] **3.** to think highly of; prize [I *value* your friendship] —**val'ue·less** *adj.* —**val'u·er** *n.*

value-added tax (-ad'id) a tax levied on the difference between a commodity's pretax selling price per unit and its materials' cost per unit

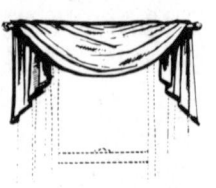

VALANCE

val·ued (-yōōd) *adj.* 1. estimated; appraised 2. highly thought of; esteemed

value judgment an estimate made of the worth, goodness, etc. of a person, action, event, etc., esp. when such a judgment is not called for or desired

va·lu·ta (va lōōt'ə, va lyōōt'ə) *n.* [It., value] the exchange value of a currency with reference to another currency

val·vate (val'vāt) *adj.* [L. *valvatus*, having folding doors < *valva*: see ff.] 1. having a valve or valves 2. *Bot. a)* meeting without overlapping, as petals, etc. *b)* opening by valves, as a pea pod

valve (valv) *n.* [L. *valva*, leaf of a folding door] 1. a sluice gate 2. *Anat.* a membranous structure which permits body fluids to flow in one direction only, or opens and closes a tube, etc. 3. *Bot.* any of the segments into which a seed capsule separates 4. *same as* THERMIONIC VALVE 5. *Mech. a)* any device in a pipe, etc. that permits a flow in one direction only, or regulates or stops the flow by means of a flap, lid, plug, etc. *b)* this flap, lid, plug, etc. 6. *Music* a device, as in the trumpet, that opens an auxiliary to the main tube, lengthening the air column and lowering the pitch 7. *Zool.* one of the parts making up the shell of a mollusc, clam, etc. —*vt., vi.* **valved, valv'ing** 1. to fit with a valve or valves 2. to regulate the flow of (a fluid) by means of a valve —**valve'less** *adj.* —**valve'like** *adj.*

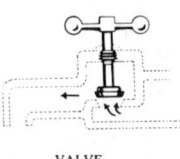

VALVE
(in a tap)

val·vu·lar (val'vyə lər) *adj.* 1. having the form or function of a valve 2. having a valve or valves 3. of a valve or valves; esp., of the valves of the heart

vam·brace (vam'brās) *n.* [ME. < OFr. *vauntbras* < *avant*, fore + *bras*, arm] a piece of armour to protect the forearm

va·moose (va mōōs') *vi., vt.* **-moosed', -moos'ing** [Sp. *vamos*, let us go] [Old Slang] to leave quickly; go away (from) hurriedly: also **va·mose'** (-mōs') **-mosed', -mos'ing**

vamp¹ (vamp) *n.* [< OFr. *avampié* < *avant*, before + *pié*, a foot] 1. the part of a boot or shoe covering the instep and, in some styles, also the toes 2. something patched up to seem new 3. *Music* a simple, improvised introduction or interlude —*vt.* 1. to put a vamp on (a shoe, etc.) 2. to patch (*up*); repair 3. to invent; fabricate 4. *Music* to improvise —*vi.* *Music* to play a vamp

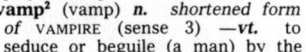

VAMP

vamp² (vamp) *n.* *shortened form of* VAMPIRE (sense 3) —*vt.* to seduce or beguile (a man) by the use of feminine charms —*vi.* to act the part of a vamp

vam·pire (vam'pīr) *n.* [Fr. < G. *Vampir*; of Slav. orig.] 1. *Folklore* a corpse that comes alive at night and sucks the blood of sleeping persons 2. a person who preys on others in a dishonest, evil, or wicked way 3. a beautiful but wicked woman who seduces men and leads them to their ruin 4. *shortened form of* VAMPIRE BAT —**vam'pir·ism** *n.*

vampire bat 1. a tropical American bat that lives on the blood of animals 2. any of various other bats mistakenly believed to be bloodsuckers

van¹ (van) *n.* [abbrev. < VANGUARD] 1. the front of an army or fleet when advancing 2. the foremost position in a line, movement, endeavour, etc., or those in this position

van² (van) *n.* [< CARAVAN] 1. a closed vehicle for carrying furniture, etc. 2. *a)* a closed railway carriage for luggage or goods, or for the guard *b)* a delivery vehicle

va·na·di·um (və nā'dē əm) *n.* [ModL. < ON. *Vanadis*, a name of Freya, goddess of love] a rare, ductile metallic chemical element: cf. VANADIUM STEEL: symbol, V; at. wt., 50.942; at. no., 23

vanadium steel a steel alloy containing 0.15 to 0.25 percent vanadium to harden and toughen it

Van Al·len (radiation) belt (van al'ən) [after J. A. *Van Allen* (1914-), U.S. physicist] either of two belts of high intensity radiation encircling the earth at varying altitudes, starting at c. 2400 km

van·dal (van'd'l) *n.* [after the *Vandals*, an E GMC. tribe that ravaged Gaul, Spain, etc. and sacked Rome (455 A.D.)] a person who destroys or spoils things on purpose, esp. works of art or public property, etc. —*adj.* 1. [V-] of the Vandals: also **Van·dal·ic** (van dal'ik) 2. like a vandal; ruthlessly destructive

van·dal·ism (-iz'm) *n.* wilful destruction of public or private property, esp. of that which is beautiful —**van'dal·is'tic** *adj.*

van·dal·ize (-īz') *vt.* **-ized', -iz'ing** to destroy or damage (public or private property) on purpose

Van·dyke beard (van dīk') [after Sir Anthony *Van Dyck* (1599-1641), Fl. painter] a closely trimmed, pointed beard, as seen in portraits by Van Dyck

Van·dyke collar a broad linen or lace collar with a deeply indented edge

vane (vān) *n.* [OE. *fana*, a flag] 1. *same as* WEATHER VANE 2. any of several flat or curved pieces set around an axle and rotated about it by moving air, water, etc. [the *vanes* of a windmill] or mechanically rotated to move the air, water, etc. [the *vanes* of a turbine] 3. a projecting plate or strip of metal fixed to a rocket, missile, etc. to give stability or guidance 4. the web or flat part of a feather 5. *Surveying a)* the sight on a quadrant or compass *b)* the movable marker on a levelling staff —**vaned** *adj.* —**vane'less** *adj.*

VANDYKE
BEARD

van·guard (van'gärd') *n.* [< OFr. < *avant*, before + *garde*, guard] 1. the front part of an army in an advance; the van 2. the leading position or persons in a movement

va·nil·la (və nil'ə) *n.* [ModL., genus name < Sp. dim. of *vaina*, a pod < L. *vagina*, a sheath] 1. any of various tropical climbing orchids with fragrant flowers 2. the podlike capsule (**vanilla bean**) of some of these plants 3. a flavouring made from these capsules —**va·nil'lic** *adj.*

va·nil·lin (və nil'in, van'ə lin) *n.* a fragrant, white, crystalline substance produced from the vanilla bean or made synthetically and used for flavouring

van·ish (van'ish) *vi.* [< OFr., ult. < L. < *vanus*, vain < *evanescere*: see EVANESCE] 1. to go or pass suddenly from sight; disappear 2. to cease to exist; come to an end —**van'ish·er** *n.*

vanishing cream a cosmetic cream which sinks into the skin leaving no trace of grease

vanishing point 1. the point where parallel lines receding from the observer seem to come together 2. a time, place, or stage at which something disappears

van·i·ty (van'ə tē) *n., pl.* **-ties** [< OFr. < L. < *vanus*, vain] 1. any thing or act that is vain, futile, or worthless 2. the fact or quality of being vain, or worthless; futility 3. the fact or quality of being vain, or excessively proud of oneself, one's possessions, etc.

vanity case a woman's small travelling case fitted for carrying cosmetics, toilet articles, etc.

vanity unit a wash basin built into a tiled, etc. surface, usually with storage space beneath it

van·quish (vaŋ'kwish, van'-) *vt.* [< OFr. < L. < *vincere*, to conquer] 1. to conquer or defeat in battle 2. *a)* to defeat in any conflict *b)* to overcome (a feeling, condition, etc.); suppress —**van'quish·er** *n.*

van·tage (vän'tij) *n.* [see ADVANTAGE] 1. a position more advantageous than that of an opponent 2. a position that allows a clear and broad view: also **vantage point** 3. *Tennis same as* ADVANTAGE (sense 4)

van·ward (van'wərd) *adj.* in the van, or front, as of an army —*adv.* towards the van

vap·id (vap'id) *adj.* [L. *vapidus*] 1. having no taste or flavour 2. lifeless; dull; boring —**vap·id·i·ty** (va pid'ə tē), *pl.* **-ties, vap'id·ness** *n.* —**vap'id·ly** *adv.*

va·por (vā'pər) *n., vi., vt.* *U.S. sp* of VAPOUR

va·por·ize (vā'pə rīz') *vt., vi.* **-ized', -iz'ing** to change into vapour, as by heating or spraying —**va'por·iz'a·ble** *adj.* —**va'por·i·za'tion** *n.* —**va'por·iz'er** *n.*

va·por·ous (vā'pər əs) *adj.* 1. giving off or forming vapour 2. full of vapour; foggy 3. like vapour 4. *a)* fleeting, fanciful, etc.: said of things, ideas, etc. *b)* given to such ideas or talk Also **va'pour·y** —**va'por·ous·ly** *adv.* —**va'por·ous·ness, va'por·os'i·ty** (-ə ros'ə tē) *n.*

va·pour (vā'pər) *n.* [< Anglo-Fr. < MFr. < L. *vapor*] 1. *a)* visible particles of moisture floating in the air, as fog, mist, or steam *b)* anything, as smoke, fumes, etc., given off in a cloud 2. the gaseous form of any substance that is usually a liquid or solid 3. [*pl.*] [Obs.] depressed spirits (often with *the*) —*vi.* 1. to rise or pass off as vapour; evaporate 2. to give off vapour 3. to brag or bluster —*vt. same as* VAPORIZE —**va'pour·er** *n.* —**va'pour·ish** *adj.* —**va'pour·like** *adj.*

va·pour·ing (vā'pər iŋ) *adj.* boastful, bombastic, etc. —*n.* boastful or extravagant talk or behaviour

va·que·ro (vä ker'ō) *n., pl.* **-ros** [Sp. < *vaca*, a cow < L. *vacca*] a herdsman; cowboy, esp. in Latin America or the SW U.S.

var. 1. variant(s) 2. variation 3. variety 4. various

va·rac·tor (və rak'tər) *n.* [VAR(IABLE) + (RE)ACT(ANCE) + -OR] *Electronics* a semiconductor diode capacitor whose capacitance varies with the voltage applied

var·ec (var'ek) *n.* [< Fr. *varech*, seaweed] impure sodium carbonate made from the calcined ashes of seaweed; kelp

var·i·a·ble (ver'ē ə b'l) *adj.* 1. apt to change or vary; changeable, inconstant, etc. 2. that can be changed or varied 3. *Biol.* tending to deviate in some way from the type **4.** *Math.* having no fixed value —*n.* **1.** anything changeable; thing that varies **2.** *Math.* a) a quantity that may have a number of different values b) a symbol for such a quantity **3.** *Naut.* a shifting wind —**var′i·a·bil′i·ty, var′- i·a·ble·ness** *n.* —**var′i·a·bly** *adv.*

variable star a star whose brightness varies from time to time as the result of causes operating outside the earth's atmosphere

var·i·ance (ver′ē əns) *n.* **1.** a varying or being variant **2.** degree of change or difference; discrepancy **3.** a quarrel; dispute **4.** *Accounting* the difference between actual costs of production and the expected costs **5.** *Law* a discrepancy between two parts of a legal proceeding, as between a statement and the evidence offered in support of it **6.** *Statistics* the square of the standard deviation —**at variance** not in agreement; conflicting

var·i·ant (-ənt) *adj.* varying; different; esp., different in some way from others of the same kind—*n.* anything that is variant, as a different spelling of the same word

var·i·a·tion (ver′ē ā′shən) *n.* **1.** a) the act, fact, or process of varying; change in form, condition, extent, etc. b) the degree or extent of such change **2.** *same as* DECLINATION (sense 3) **3.** a thing that is somewhat different from another of the same kind **4.** *Astron.* deviation from the mean orbit of a planet, satellite, etc. **5.** *Ballet* a solo dance **6.** *Biol.* a deviation from the usual or parental type in structure or form **7.** *Music* the repetition of a melody or theme with changes in harmony, rhythm, key, etc. —**var′- i·a′tion·al** *adj.*

var·i·cel·la (var′ə sel′ə) *n.* [ModL., dim. of *variola*: see VARIOLA] *same as* CHICKEN POX —**var′i·cel′loid** (-oid) *adj.*

var·i·col·oured (ver′i kul′ərd) *adj.* of several or many colours

var·i·cose (var′ə kōs′) *adj.* [L. *varicosus < varix* (gen. *varicis*), enlarged vein] **1.** abnormally and irregularly swollen [*varicose veins*] **2.** resulting from varicose veins [*varicose ulcer*] —**var′i·cos′i·ty** (-kos′ə tē) *n.*

var·ied (ver′əd) *adj.* **1.** of different kinds; various **2.** variegated **3.** changed; altered —**var′ied·ly** *adv.*

var·i·e·gate (ver′ē ə gāt′, ver′ə gāt′) *vt.* -**gat′ed, -gat′ing** [< L. pp. of *variegare < varius*, various] **1.** to make varied in appearance by differences, as in colours **2.** to give variety to; diversify —**var′i·e·gat′ed** *adj.* —**var′i·e·ga′tion** *n.*

va·ri·e·tal (və rī′ə t'l) *adj.* of or being a variety

va·ri·e·ty (və rī′ə tē) *n., pl.* **-ties** [< Fr. < L. *varietas*] **1.** a being various or varied; absence of monotony or sameness **2.** any of the various forms of something; sort; kind [*varieties of cloth*] **3.** a number of different kinds [a *variety* of fruits, a *variety* of merchandise] **4.** a subdivision of a species; subspecies or variant; specif., *Bot.* a recognized variant of a wild plant, even though brought under cultivation —*adj.* of or in a variety show

variety show a show made up of different kinds of acts, as comic skits, songs, dances, etc.

var·i·form (ver′ə fôrm′) *adj.* having various forms

va·ri·o·la (və rī′ə lə) *n.* [ModL. < ML., a pustule < L. *varius*, various, mottled] any of a group of virus diseases characterized by pustular eruptions and including smallpox, cowpox, etc.

var·i·ole (ver′ē ōl′) *n.* [Fr. < ML.: see prec.] **1.** a tiny pit or depression **2.** a spherule in variolite

var·i·o·lite (-ə līt′) *n.* [< G. *Variolit < ML. variola*: see VARIOLA] a basaltic rock which is embedded with spherules of feldspar

var·i·om·e·ter (ver′ē om′ə tər, var′-) *n.* [VARIO(US) -METER] **1.** a device for determining variations of magnetic force esp. at different places on the earth **2.** a rate-of-climb or vertical-speed indicator, used esp. in gliders **3.** *Radio* a unit consisting of a coil that can be rotated within a fixed coil to vary inductance

var·i·o·rum (ver′ē ôr′əm, var′-) *n.* [L., of various (scholars)] **1.** an edition or text, as of a literary work, with notes by various editors, scholars, etc. **2.** an edition containing variant texts —*adj.* of or being a variorum

var·i·ous (ver′ē əs) *adj.* [L. *varius*, diverse] **1.** differing one from another; of several kinds **2.** a) several or many [found in *various* parts of the country] b) individual; distinct [bequests to the *various heirs*] **3.** many-sided; versatile **4.** characterized by variety; varied in nature or appearance —**var′i·ous·ly** *adv.*

va·ris·tor (və ris′tər) *n.* [VAR(IOUS) + (RES)ISTOR] a semiconductor device whose resistance drops as the voltage is increased

var·ix (var′iks) *n., pl.* **var′i·ces′** (-ə sēz′) [L.] **1.** *Med.* a permanently swollen or dilated blood or lymph vessel; varicose vein **2.** *Zool.* a ridge across the whorls of various spiral shells

var·let (vär′lit) *n.* [OFr., var. of *vaslet*: see VALET] [Archaic] **1.** an attendant **2.** a scoundrel; knave

var·mint, var·ment (vär′mənt) *n.* [dial. var. of VERMIN]

[Dial. or Colloq.] a person or animal regarded as troublesome or objectionable

var·na (vär′nə) *n.* [Hindi *varna*, colour < Sans.] *same as* CASTE (sense 1)

var·nish (vär′nish) *n.* [< OFr. < ML. *veronix*, a resin < Gr. *Berenikē*, an ancient city] **1.** a) a preparation made of resinous substances dissolved in oil (**oil varnish**) or in alcohol, turpentine, etc. (**spirit varnish**), used to give a hard, glossy surface to wood, etc. b) any of various natural or prepared products similarly used **2.** the hard, glossy surface produced **3.** a surface gloss or smoothness, as of manner —*vt.* **1.** to cover with varnish **2.** to smooth over in a false way —**var′nish·er** *n.*

var·si·ty (vär′sə tē) *n., pl.* **-ties** [contr. & altered < UNIVERSITY] [Colloq.] university —*adj.* [Colloq.] of or designating a university

varve (värv) *n.* [Swed. *varv*, a layer] an annual layer of glacial sediment deposited in lakes and fiords

var·y (ver′ē) *vt.* **var′ied, var′y·ing** [< L. *variare < varius*, various] **1.** to change in form, nature, etc.; alter **2.** to make different from one another **3.** to give variety to —*vi.* **1.** to be or become different; differ or change **2.** to deviate or depart (*from*) —**var′i·er** *n.*

vas (vas) *n., pl.* **va·sa** (vā′sə) [L., a vessel] *Anat., Biol.* a vessel or duct —**va·sal** (vā′s'l) *adj.*

vas·cu·lar (vas′kyə lər) *adj.* [< ModL. < L. *vasculum*, dim. of *vas*, a vessel] **1.** *Anat., Zool.* of or consisting of vessels carrying blood or lymph **2.** *Bot.* of, consisting of, or having special cells, xylem, and phloem that carry water and food, as ferns and seed plants

vascular bundle a unit of the conducting system of higher plants, consisting chiefly of xylem and phloem

vas de·fe·rens (vas def′ə renz′) *pl.* **va·sa de·fe·ren·ti·a** (vā′- sə def′ə ren′shē ə) [ModL. < L. *vas*, a vessel + *deferens*, carrying down] the duct that carries sperm from the testicle to the ejaculatory duct of the penis

vase (vāz) *n.* [< Fr. < L. *vas*, a vessel, dish] an open container of metal, glass, pottery, etc. used for decoration, holding flowers, etc.

vas·ec·to·my (vas ek′tə mē) *n., pl.* **-mies** [VAS(O) + ECTOMY] the cutting, tying, and removing of part of the vas deferens for the purpose of sterilizing sexually

Vas·e·line (vas′ə lēn′) [coinage < G. *Was*(*ser*), water + Gr. *el*(*aion*), oil + -INE⁴] *a trademark for* PETROLATUM —*n.* [v-] petroleum jelly

vas·o- [< L. *vas*, a vessel] *a combining form meaning:* **1.** blood vessels [*vasomotor*] **2.** vas deferens [*vasectomy*] **3.** vasomotor [*vasoinhibitor*] Also, before a vowel, **vas-**

vas·o·con·stric·tor (vas′ō kən strik′tər, vās′-) *adj.* [prec. + CONSTRICTOR] *Physiol.* constricting the blood vessels —*n.* a nerve or drug doing this —**vas′o·con·stric′tion** *n.*

vas·o·di·la·tor (-dī lāt′ər) [VASO- + *dilator* (see DILATE)] *Physiol.* dilating the blood vessels —*n.* a nerve or drug doing this —**vas′o·dil′a·ta′tion** (-dil′ə tā′shən), **vas′o·di·la′- tion** *n.*

vas·o·in·hib·i·tor (-in hib′ə tər) *n.* [VASO- + INHIBITOR] a drug or agent inhibiting the action of the vasomotor nerves —**vas′o·in·hib′i·to·ry** (-tər ē) *adj.*

vas·o·mo·tor (-mōt′ər) *adj.* [VASO- + MOTOR] *Physiol.* regulating the diameter of blood vessels by causing contraction or dilatation, as certain nerves or nerve centres

vas·o·pres·sin (-pres′ən) *n.* [< VASO- + PRESS(URE) + -IN¹] a hormone of the pituitary gland that increases blood pressure

vas·o·pres·sor (-pres′ər) *n.* [VASO- + PRESS(URE) + -OR] a substance causing a rise in blood pressure

vas·sal (vas′'l) *n.* [OFr. < ML. *vassalus < vassus*, servant < Celt.] **1.** a person in the feudal system who held land in return for fealty, military help, etc. to an overlord **2.** a subordinate, servant, slave, etc. —*adj.* of, like, or being a vassal —**vas′sal·age** (-ij) *n.*

vast (väst) *adj.* [L. *vastus*] very great in size, extent, amount, degree, etc. —**vast′ly** *adv.* —**vast′ness** *n.*

vast·y (väs′tē) *adj.* **-i·er, -i·est** [Archaic] vast; immense

vat (vat) *n.* [< OE. *fæt*, a cask] a large tank, tub, or cask for holding liquids as for use in a manufacturing process —*vt.* **vat′ted, vat′ting** to put or store in a vat

V.A.T. value-added tax

Vat·i·can (vat′i k'n) **1.** the papal palace, a group of buildings in Vatican City **2.** the papal government or authority —*adj.* **1.** of the Vatican **2.** designating either of the Roman Catholic Ecumenical Councils held in Vatican City in 1869-70 (**Vatican I**) or 1962-65 (**Vatican II**)

vau·de·ville (vō′də vil, vô′də-) *n.* [Fr. < *Vau-de-Vire*, a valley in Normandy, famous for light convivial songs] **1.** a stage show consisting of mixed specialty acts, including songs, dances, comic skits, acrobatics, etc. **2.** such entertainment generally —**vaude·vil′li·an** (-vil′ē ən, -yən) *n., adj.*

Vau·dois (vō dwä′) **1.** *pl.* **Vau·dois′** an inhabitant of the Vaud **2.** the language spoken there

vault¹ (vôlt) *n.* [< OFr., ult. < L. *volvere*, to roll] 1. an arched roof, ceiling, etc. of masonry 2. an arched chamber or space, esp. when underground 3. a cellar room used for storage 4. *a*) a burial chamber *b*) a concrete or metal enclosure in the ground, into which the coffin is lowered at burial 5. a secure room for the safekeeping of valuables or money, as in a bank 6. the sky as a vaultlike canopy —*vt.* 1. to cover with a vault 2. to build as a vault — *vi.* to curve like a vault —**vault′ed** *adj.*

GROINED VAULT

vault² (vôlt) *vi.* [< MFr. < OIt. *voltare*, ult. < L. *volvere*, to roll] to leap as over a barrier, esp. putting the hands on the barrier or using a long pole —*vt.* to vault over —*n.* a vaulting —**vault′er** *n.*

vault·ing¹ (vôl′tiŋ) *n.* 1. the arched work forming a vault 2. a vault or vaults

vault·ing² (vôl′tiŋ) *adj.* 1. that vaults or leaps 2. reaching too far or beyond one's abilities [*vaulting* ambition]

vaunt (vônt) *vi., vt.* [< OFr. < LL. *vanitare* < L. *vanus*, vain] to boast or brag (of) —*n.* a boast or brag —**vaunt′ed** *adj.* —**vaunt′er** *n.*

vav·a·sour (vav′ə sōōr′) *n.* [ME. < OFr. < ML. *vavassor*, pron. < *vassus vassorum*, vassal of vassals] in the Middle Ages, a vassal holding lands from a superior lord and having vassals under him: also **vav′a·sor′** (-sôr′)

vb. 1. verb 2. verbal

V.C. 1. Vice Chairman 2. Vice Chancellor 3. Vice-Consul 4. Victoria Cross

VD, V.D. venereal disease

VE Victory in Europe —**V-E Day** (vē′ē′) May 8, 1945, the official date of Germany's surrender ending the European phase of World War II

've contraction of HAVE [*we've* seen it]

veal (vēl) *n.* [OFr. *veel* < L. dim. of *vitulus*, a calf] the flesh of a young calf, used as food

vec·tor (vek′tər) *n.* [ModL. < L., a carrier < pp. of *vehere*, to carry] 1. *Biol.* an animal, as an insect, that transmits a disease-producing organism from one host to another 2. *Math.* *a*) a physical quantity with both magnitude and direction, such as a force or velocity: distinguished from SCALAR *b*) a directed line segment representing such a quantity —*vt.* to guide (an aircraft, etc.) by radioed directions —**vec·to′ri·al** (-tôr′ē əl) *adj.*

Ve·da (vā′də, vē′-) *n.* [Sans. *veda*, knowledge] 1. any of four ancient sacred books of Hinduism, consisting of psalms, chants, sacred formulas, etc. 2. these books collectively —**Ve·da·ic** (vi dā′ik), **Ve′dic** *adj.*

Ve·dan·ta (vi dän′tə, -dan′-) *n.* [< Sans. < *veda*, knowledge + *anta*, an end] a system of Hindu monistic or pantheistic philosophy based on the Vedas —**Ve·dan′tic** *adj.* —**Ve·dan′-tism** *n.*

ve·dette (vi det′) *n.* [Fr. < It. *vedetta* < Sp. < L. *vigilare*, to keep watch] 1. formerly, a mounted sentry posted in advance of the outposts of an army 2. *Naval* a small patrol vessel

veer (vir) *vi.* [altered < Fr. *virer*, to turn around] 1. to change direction; turn 2. to change sides, as from one opinion to another 3. to turn clockwise: said of the wind —*vt.* to turn or swing; change the course of —*n.* a change of direction —**veer′ing·ly** *adv.*

Ve·ga (vē′gə, vā′-) *n.* [ML. < Ar.] a very bright star in the constellation Lyra

ve·gan (vē′gən) *n.* [< VEGETARIAN] a person who eats no animal products; a strict vegetarian

veg·e·ta·ble (vej′tə b'l, vej′ə tə-) *adj.* [< ML. *vegetabilis*, vegetative < LL., animating < L *vegetare*: see VEGETATE] 1. of plants in general [the *vegetable* kingdom] 2. of, like, or from vegetables [*vegetable* oil] —*n.* 1. any plant, as distinguished from something animal or inorganic 2. *a*) any plant that is eaten whole or in part, raw or cooked *b*) the edible part of such a plant, as the root (e.g., a carrot), tuber (a potato), seed (a pea), fruit (a tomato), stem (celery), leaf (lettuce), etc. 3. a person thought of as vegetablelike because living in or as in a coma

vegetable ivory the fully ripe, ivorylike seed of a S. American palm, used to make buttons, ornaments, etc.

vegetable marrow 1. a plant yielding long, green striped fruit 2. the fruit of the marrow eaten as a vegetable

vegetable oil any of various liquid fats derived from the fruits or seeds of plants, used in food products, etc.

veg·e·tal (vej′ə t'l) *adj.* *same as:* 1. VEGETABLE 2. VEGETATIVE (sense 3)

veg·e·tar·i·an (vej′ə ter′ē ən) *n.* [VEGET(ABLE) + -ARIAN] a person who eats no meat; strictly, one who believes in a diet of only vegetables, fruits, grains, and nuts as the proper one for people —*adj.* 1. of vegetarians, their principles, etc. 2. consisting only of vegetables, fruits, etc. —**veg′e·tar′-i·an·ism** *n.*

veg·e·tate (vej′ə tāt′) *vi.* -tat′ed, -tat′ing [< L. pp. of *vegetare*, to enliven < *vegetus*, lively < *vegere*, to quicken] 1. to grow as plants 2. to exist with little mental and physical activity; lead a dull, inactive life

veg·e·ta·tion (vej′ə tā′shən) *n.* 1. the act or process of vegetating 2. plant life in general 3. dull, passive, unthinking existence —**veg′e·ta′tion·al** *adj.*

veg·e·ta·tive (vej′ə tāt′iv) *adj.* 1. of plants or plant growth 2. growing as plants 3. designating or of the functions or parts of plants not related to reproduction 4. helping plant growth [*vegetative* loams] 5. dull and inactive [a *vegetative* life] 6. *Zool.* of or pertaining to asexual reproduction —**veg′e·ta′tive·ly** *adv.* —**veg′e·ta′tive·ness** *n.*

ve·he·ment (vē′ə mənt) *adj.* [< MFr. < L. *vehemens*, eager < *vehere*, to carry] 1. acting or moving with great force; violent; impetuous 2. full of or showing very strong feeling; intense, fervent, impassioned, etc. —**ve′he·mence, ve′-he·men·cy** *n.* —**ve′he·ment·ly** *adv.*

ve·hi·cle (vē′ə k'l) *n.* [< Fr. < L. *vehiculum*, carriage < *vehere*, to carry] 1. a means of carrying persons or things, esp. over land or in space, as a motor car, bicycle, spacecraft, etc. 2. a means of expressing ideas 3. *Painting* a liquid, as water or oil, with which pigments are mixed for use 4. *Pharmacy* a substance, as a syrup, in which medicines are given —**ve·hic·u·lar** (vē hik′yoo lər) *adj.*

veil (vāl) *n.* [< ONormFr. < L. *vela*, pl. of *velum*, cloth] 1. a piece of light fabric, as net or gauze, worn, esp. by women, over the face or head to hide the features or as an ornament 2. any cloth, curtain, etc. used to conceal or separate 3. anything that covers or conceals [a *veil* of mist, a *veil* of silence] 4. *a*) a part of a nun's headdress, draped along the face and over the shoulders *b*) the state or life of a nun: chiefly in **take the veil,** to become a nun 5. *Bot., Zool.* *same as* VELUM —*vt.* to cover, conceal, etc. with or as with a veil —**veil′like′** *adj.*

veiled (vāld) *adj.* 1. wearing or covered with a veil 2. concealed, disguised, obscured, etc. 3. not openly expressed [a *veiled* threat]

veil·ing (vā′liŋ) *n.* 1. a veil 2. fabric for veils

vein (vān) *n.* [< OFr. < L. *vena*] 1. any blood vessel bringing blood back to the heart from some part of the body 2. any riblike support in an insect wing 3. any of the fine lines, or ribs, in a leaf 4. a layer of mineral, rock, etc. in a fissure or zone of different rock; lode 5. a streak or marking of a colour or substance different from the surrounding material, as in marble 6. *a*) a distinctive quality or strain running through something [a *vein* of humour] *b*) course or tenor of thought, feeling, action, etc. 7. a temporary state of mind; mood [in a serious *vein*] —*vt.* 1. to mark as with veins 2. to branch out through like veins

vein·ing (-iŋ) *n.* formation or arrangement of veins

vein·let (-lit) *n.* *same as* VENULE: also **vein′ule** (-yōōl)

vein·y (-ē) *adj.* **vein′i·er, vein′i·est** full of veins or veinlike markings

ve·la·men (və lā′mən) *n.,* *pl.* **-lam′i·na** (-lam′i nə) [L., a covering] 1. *Anat.* a membrane 2. *Bot.* the corky outer layer of the aerial roots of certain orchids

ve·lar (vē′lər) *adj.* 1. of a velum; esp., of the soft palate 2. *Phonet.* pronounced with the back of the tongue touching or near the soft palate, as the sound of *k* followed by a back vowel like (ōō) —*n.* a velar sound

Vel·cro (vel′krō) [arbitrary formation < VEL(VET)] *a trademark for* a nylon material made with both a surface of tiny hooks and one of pile: matching strips are used in garments, etc. as fasteners, easily pressed together or pulled apart —*n.* this material

veld, veldt (velt) *n.* [Afrik. < MDu. *veld*, a field] in South Africa, open grassy country

ve·le·ta (və lē′tə) *n.* [Sp., a weather cock] an old-time dance in slow triple time: also **va·le′ta**

vel·lum (vel′əm) *n.* [MFr. *velin*, vellum < OFr. *veel*: see VEAL] 1. a fine parchment used for writing on or for binding books 2. a manuscript on vellum 3. a strong paper resembling vellum —*adj.* of or like vellum

ve·loc·i·pede (və los′ə pēd′) *n.* [< Fr. < L. *velox* (gen. *velocis*), swift + *pes* (gen. *pedis*), a foot] any of various early bicycles or tricycles

ve·loc·i·ty (-tē) *n.,* *pl.* **-ties** [< Fr. < L. *velox*: see prec.] 1. quickness of motion or action; speed 2. rate of change of position, or rate of motion in a particular direction, in relation to time

ve·lour, ve·lours (və loor′) *n.,* *pl.* **ve·lours′** [Fr.: see VELURE] a fabric with a soft nap like velvet, used for upholstery, hats, clothing, etc.

ve·lou·té (və loo′tā) *n.* [Fr., velvety] a rich white sauce made from fish or meat stock thickened with flour and butter

ve·lum (vē′ləm) *n.,* *pl.* **-la** (-lə) [L., a veil] *Biol.* any of various veillike membranous partitions or coverings; specif., *same as* SOFT PALATE

ve·lure (və loor′) *n.* [Fr. *velours* < OFr. < LL. *villosus*, shaggy < *villus*, shaggy hair] velvet or velvetlike fabric

ve·lu·ti·nous (və lōōt′in əs) *adj.* [< It. *velluto*, velvet + -OUS] *Bot., Zool.* covered with short, soft, velvety hairs

vel·vet (vel′vit) *n.* [< OFr. < VL. *villutus* < L. *villus*, shaggy hair] **1.** a rich fabric of silk, cotton, rayon, nylon, etc. with a soft, thick pile **2.** anything with a surface like that of velvet, as the soft, furry covering of the newly-formed antlers of a deer **3.** [Old Slang] extra or clear profit or gain —*adj.* **1.** made of or covered with velvet **2.** smooth or soft like velvet —**on velvet** in a position of ease or advantage —**vel′vet·y** *adj.*

vel·vet·een (vel′və tēn′) *n.* a velvetlike cotton cloth

Ven. Venerable

ve·na ca·va (vē′nə kā′və) *pl.* **ve′nae ca′vae** (vē′nē kā′vē) [ModL. < L. *vena*, vein + *cava*, fem. of *cavus*, hollow] *Anat.* either of two large veins carrying blood to the right atrium of the heart

ve·nal (vē′n'l) *adj.* [L. *venalis*, salable < *venum*, sale] **1.** that can readily be bribed or corrupted **2.** characterized by bribery or corruption —**ve·nal′i·ty** (-nal′ə tē) *n., pl.* -ties —**ve′nal·ly** *adv.*

ve·na·tion (vē nā′shən) *n.* [< L. *vena*, a vein] **1.** an arrangement or system of veins, as in an insect's wing or a leaf **2.** such veins collectively

vend (vend) *vt., vi.* [< Fr. < L. *vendere*, contr. < *venum dare*, to offer for sale] to sell, esp. by peddling

vend·ee (ven′dē′) *n.* the person to whom a thing is sold

ven·det·ta (ven det′ə) *n.* [It. < L. *vindicta*, vengeance] **1.** a feud in which relatives of a murdered or wronged person seek vengeance on the guilty person or his family **2.** any bitter quarrel or feud —**ven·det′tist** *n.*

vend·i·ble (ven′də b'l) *adj.* [see VEND] capable of being sold —*n.* something vendible —**vend′i·bil′i·ty** *n.* —**vend′i·bly** *adv.*

vending machine a coin-operated machine for selling certain kinds of articles, refreshments, etc.

ven·dor, vend·er (ven′dər) *n.* **1.** one who vends, or sells; seller **2.** same as VENDING MACHINE

ve·neer (və nir′) *vt.* [G. *furnieren* < Fr. *fournir*, to furnish] **1.** to cover with a thin layer of finer material; esp., to cover (wood) with wood of a finer quality **2.** to make outwardly attractive **3.** to glue (thin wood layers) together to form plywood —*n.* **1.** a thin layer used to veneer something; also, any of the layers used in making plywood **2.** a surface appearance that hides what is below [a *veneer* of culture]

ve·neer·ing (-iŋ) *n.* **1.** the act or process of veneering **2.** material used for veneer

ven·er·a·ble (ven′ər ə b'l, ven′rə b'l) *adj.* [see VENERATE] **1.** worthy of respect or reverence by reason of age, dignity, character, etc. **2.** impressively ancient, historic, or hallowed **3.** *a)* *Anglican Ch.* an archdeacon's title *b)* *R.C.Ch.* a title indicating the lowest of the three degrees of sanctity, the others being beatification and canonization —**ven′er·a·bil′i·ty** *n.* —**ven′er·a·bly** *adv.*

ven·er·ate (ven′ə rāt′) *vt.* -at′ed, -at′ing [< L. pp. of *venerari*, to worship] to feel or show deep respect for; revere —**ven′er·a′tor** *n.*

ven·er·a·tion (ven′ə rā′shən) *n.* **1.** a venerating or being venerated **2.** a feeling of deep respect and reverence **3.** an act showing this

ve·ne·re·al (və nir′ē əl) *adj.* [< L. *venereus* < *venus* (gen. *veneris*), love] **1.** *a)* relating to sexual love or intercourse *b)* arousing sexual desire **2.** *a)* transmitted only or chiefly by sexual intercourse with an infected individual, as syphilis and gonorrhoea *b)* infected with a venereal disease *c)* of or dealing with venereal disease

ven·er·y[1] (ven′ər ē) *n.* [< L. *Venus* (gen. *Veneris*), Venus, love] [Archaic] sexual intercourse

ven·er·y[2] (ven′ər ē) *n.* [< MFr. < *vener*, to hunt < L. *venari*] [Archaic] the hunting of game; the chase

Ve·ne·tian (və nē′shən) *adj.* of Venice, its people, culture, etc. —*n.* a native or inhabitant of Venice

Venetian blind [*also* v- b-] a window blind made of a number of thin, horizontal slats that can be set at any angle to regulate the light and air passing through or drawn up by cords to the window top

venge·ance (ven′jəns) *n.* [OFr. < *venger*, to avenge < L. *vindicare*; see VINDICATE] **1.** the return of an injury for an injury, in punishment; an avenging; revenge **2.** the desire to make such a return —**with a vengeance 1.** with great force or fury **2.** to an excessive or unusual extent

venge·ful (venj′fəl) *adj.* **1.** desiring or seeking vengeance; vindictive **2.** arising from a desire for vengeance: said of actions or feelings **3.** inflicting vengeance —**venge′ful·ly** *adv.* —**venge′ful·ness** *n.*

ve·ni·al (vē′nē əl, vēn′yəl) *adj.* [OFr. < LL.

VENETIAN
BLIND

venialis < L. *venia*, grace] **1.** that can be forgiven, pardoned, or excused, as an error or fault **2.** *R.C.Ch.* not causing spiritual death: said of sins not regarded as serious —**ve′ni·al·ly** *adv.*

ven·in (ven′in) *n.* [< VEN(OM) + -IN[1]] any of the specific toxic constituents of animal venoms

ven·i·son (ven′i s'n, -z'n, ven′zən) *n.* [< OFr. < L. < pp. of *venari*, to hunt] the flesh of deer, used as food

‡**ve·ni, vi·di, vi·ci** (vā′nē vē′dē vē′chē, wā′nē wē′dē wē′kē, vē′nī vī′dī vī′sī) [L.] I came, I saw, I conquered: Julius Caesar's report to the Roman Senate of a victory

Venn diagrams (ven) [after John *Venn* (1834–1923), Brit. logician] *Math.* diagrams using overlapping circles to show relationships between sets

ven·om (ven′əm) *n.* [< OFr. < L. *venenum*, a poison] **1.** the poison secreted by some snakes, spiders, insects, etc., injected into the victim by bite or sting **2.** spite; malice

ven·om·ous (-əs) *adj.* **1.** full of venom; poisonous **2.** full of spite or ill will; malicious **3.** *Zool.* able to inject venom by bite or sting —**ven′om·ous·ly** *adv.* —**ven′om·ous·ness** *n.*

ve·nous (vē′nəs) *adj.* [L. *venosus*] **1.** *Biol. a)* of a vein or veins *b)* having veins or full of veins; veiny **2.** *Physiol.* designating blood being carried in the veins back to the heart and lungs —**ve′nous·ly** *adv.*

vent[1] (vent) *n.* [OFr. *venter*, to blow, ult. < L. *ventus*, a wind] **1.** an issuing, as of air, or the means of this; outlet; passage; escape **2.** expression; release [giving *vent* to emotion] **3.** a small opening to let gas, etc. out **4.** the opening in a volcano through which it erupts **5.** *Zool.* the excretory opening in animals —*vt.* **1.** to make a vent in **2.** to let (steam, gas, etc.) out through an opening **3.** to give release or expression to **4.** to unburden by giving vent to feelings

vent[2] (vent) *n.* [< OFr., ult. < L. pp. of *findere*, to split] a vertical slit in a garment, esp. one put in the back or sides of a jacket —*vt.* to make a vent or vents in

ven·ti·duct (ven′ti dukt′) *n.* [< L. *ventus*, a wind + DUCT] an air ventilating passage

ven·ti·late (ven′təl āt′) *vt.* -lat′ed, -lat′ing [< L. pp. of *ventilare*, to fan < *ventus*, a wind] **1.** *a)* to circulate fresh air in (a room, etc.) *b)* to circulate in (a room, etc.): said of fresh air **2.** to put a vent in, to let air, gas, etc. escape **3.** to examine and discuss (a grievance, etc.) openly **4.** to aerate (blood); oxygenate —**ven′ti·la′tion** *n.*

ven·ti·la·tor (-ər) *n.* a thing that ventilates; esp., any device used to bring in fresh air and drive out foul air

ven·tral (ven′trəl) *adj.* [Fr. < L. *ventralis* < *venter*, belly] of, on, or near the belly —**ven′tral·ly** *adv.*

ven·tri·cle (ven′tri k'l) *n.* [< L. dim. of *venter*, belly] *Anat., Zool.* a cavity; specif., *a)* either of the two lower chambers of the heart which receive blood from the atria and pump it into the arteries *b)* any of the four small continuous cavities within the brain —**ven·tric′u·lar** (-trik′-yə lər) *adj.*

ven·tri·cose (-kōs′) *adj.* [ModL. *ventricosus* < *venter*: see prec.] **1.** large-bellied **2.** *Biol.* swelling out on one side

ven·tril·o·quism (ven tril′ə kwiz′m) *n.* [< L. < *venter*, belly + *loqui*, to speak + -ISM] the art or practice of speaking so that the voice seems to come from some source other than the speaker: also **ven·tril′o·quy** (-kwē) —**ven·tril′-o·quist** *n.* —**ven·tril′o·quis′tic** *adj.* —**ven·tril′o·quize′** (-kwīz′) *vi., vt.* -quized′, -quiz′ing

ven·ture (ven′chər) *n.* [< ME. *aventure*: see ADVENTURE] **1.** a risky undertaking; esp., a business enterprise in which there is danger of loss as well as chance for profit **2.** something on which a risk is taken **3.** chance; fortune: now only in **at a venture**, by mere chance —*vt.* -tured, -tur·ing **1.** to risk; hazard **2.** to take the risk of; brave **3.** to express (an opinion, etc.) at the risk of being criticized, etc. —*vi.* to do or go at some risk —**ven′tur·er** *n.*

Venture Scout a member of the senior branch of the Boy Scouts

ven·ture·some (-səm) *adj.* **1.** inclined to venture; daring **2.** risky; hazardous —**ven′ture·some·ly** *adv.* —**ven′ture·some·ness** *n.*

ven·tu·ri (**tube**) (ven tyoor′ē) [after G. B. *Venturi* (1746–1822), It. physicist] a short tube with a narrow throat that increases the velocity and lowers the pressure of a fluid flowing through it: used to measure fluid flow, to regulate the mixture in a carburettor, etc.

ven·tur·ous (ven′chər əs) *adj.* same as VENTURESOME —**ven′tur·ous·ly** *adv.* —**ven′tur·ous·ness** *n.*

ven·ue (ven′yōō) *n.* [OFr., arrival < *venir*, to come < L. *venire*] **1.** *a)* a meeting place *b)* the scene of an action **2.** *Law a)* the locality in which a cause of action or a crime occurs *b)* the locality in which a jury is drawn and a case tried —**change of venue 1.** a change of rendezvous **2.** *Law* the substitution of another place of trial, as when the jury or court is likely to be prejudiced

ven·ule (ven′yōōl) *n.* [< L. dim. of *vena*, vein] 1. *Anat.* a small vein 2. *Biol.* any small branch of a vein in a leaf or in an insect wing —**ven′u·lar** (-yoo lər) *adj.*

Ve·nus (vē′nəs) [L., lit., love] 1. *Rom. Myth.* the goddess of love and beauty: identified with the Greek goddess Aphrodite 2. a planet in the solar system, second in distance from the sun: diameter, c. 12230 km —*n.* 1. a statue or image of Venus 2. a very beautiful woman

Ve·nus′ fly·trap (vē′nəs flī′trap′) a white-flowered swamp plant native to North and South Carolina, U.S.A., having leaves with two hinged blades that snap shut and so trap insects

ve·ra·cious (və rā′shəs) *adj.* [< L. < *verus*, true] 1. habitually truthful; honest 2. true; accurate —**ve·ra′cious·ly** *adv.* —**ve·ra′cious·ness** *n.*

ve·rac·i·ty (və ras′ə tē) *n.,* pl. **-ties** [< ML. < L. *verus*, true] 1. habitual truthfulness; honesty 2. accordance with truth; accuracy of statement 3. accuracy or precision, as of perception 4. that which is true; truth

VENUS' FLYTRAP

ve·ran·da, ve·ran·dah (və ran′də) *n.* [Anglo-Ind. < Port. *varanda*, a balcony < *vara*, a pole < L., forked stick] an open gallery, usually roofed, along the outside of a building

verb (vurb) *n.* [< OFr. < L. *verbum*, a word] 1. any of a class of words expressing action, existence, or occurrence, and acting as the main part of a predicate: see also AUXILIARY VERB, LINKING VERB 2. any phrase or construction used as a verb —*adj.* of, or functioning as, a verb

ver·bal (vur′b'l) *adj.* 1. of, in, or by means of words 2. concerned merely with words rather than with facts, ideas, or actions 3. oral rather than written 4. *Gram.* of, like, or derived from a verb —*n.* *Gram.* a verbal noun or other word derived from a verb: in English, gerunds, infinitives, and participles are verbals —**ver′bal·ly** *adv.*

ver·bal·ism (-iz′m) *n.* 1. an expression in one or more words; word or word phrase 2. words only, without any real meaning 3. any virtually meaningless phrase

ver·bal·ist (-ist) *n.* 1. a person skilled in verbal expression 2. a person who gives more importance to words than to the facts or ideas they convey

ver·bal·ize (vur′bəl īz′) *vi.* **-ized′, -iz′ing** 1. to be wordy, or verbose 2. to communicate in words —*vt.* 1. to express in words 2. to change (a noun, etc.) into a verb —**ver′-bal·i·za′tion** *n.* —**ver′bal·iz′er** *n.*

verbal noun *Gram.* a noun derived from a verb and acting in some respects like a verb: in English it is either a noun ending in *-ing* (a gerund) or an infinitive (Ex.: *walking* is healthy, *to err* is human)

ver·ba·tim (vər bāt′əm) *adv.* [ML. < L. *verbum*, a word] word for word; in exactly the same words —*adj.* following the original, word for word [a *verbatim* account]

ver·be·na (vər bē′nə) *n.* [ModL., genus name < L., foliage] any of a group of ornamental plants with spikes or clusters of red, white, or purplish flowers, some being very sweet-scented

ver·bi·age (vur′bē ij) *n.* [Fr. < OFr. < L. *verbum*, a word] an excess of words beyond those needed to express concisely what is meant; wordiness

ver·bose (vər bōs′) *adj.* [L. *verbosus*, full of words < *verbum*, a word] using or containing too many words; wordy; long-winded —**ver·bose′ly** *adv.* —**ver·bos′i·ty** (-bos′ə tē), **ver·bose′ness** *n.*

‡**ver·bo·ten** (fer bō′tən) *adj.* [G.] forbidden; prohibited

ver·dant (vur′d'nt) *adj.* [prob. < VERD(URE) + -ANT] 1. green 2. covered with green vegetation 3. inexperienced; immature [*verdant* youth] —**ver′dan·cy** (-dən sē) *n.*

ver·dict (vur′dikt) *n.* [< Anglo-Fr. < ML. < L. *vere*, truly + *dictum*, a thing said < *dicere*, to say] 1. *Law* the decision reached by a jury at the end of a trial 2. any decision or judgment

ver·di·gris (vur′di grēs, -gris) *n.* [< MFr. < OFr. < *verd*, green + *de*, of + *Grece*, Greece] 1. a green or greenish-blue poisonous compound prepared by treating copper with acetic acid and used as a pigment, dye, etc. 2. a green or greenish-blue coating that forms on brass, bronze, or copper

ver·dure (vur′jər; vur′dyər) *n.* [OFr. < *verd*, green] 1. the fresh green colour of growing things 2. green vegetation —**ver′dured** *adj.* —**ver′dur·ous** *adj.*

verge[1] (vurj) *n.* [< OFr. < L. *virga*, rod] 1. *a)* the edge, brink, or margin [the *verge* of a forest, on the *verge* of hysteria] *b)* a grassy border, as along a road 2. a rod or staff symbolic of an office —*vi.* **verged, verg′ing** to be on the verge, brink, or border (usually with *on* or *upon*)

verge[2] (vurj) *vi.* **verged, verg′ing** [L. *vergere*] 1. to tend or incline (*to* or *towards*) 2. to be in the process of change into something else; pass gradually (*into*) [dawn *verging* into daylight]

verg·er (vur′jər) *n.* [see VERGE[1] & -ER] 1. a person who carries a staff of office before a bishop, etc. 2. a church caretaker or usher

Ver·gil·ian (vur jil′ē ən) *adj.* var. of VIRGILIAN

ver·glas (ver glä′) *n.* [Fr. < OFr. < *verre*, glass + *glaz* ice] a thin coating of ice on rock

ver·i·est (ver′ē ist) [superl. of VERY, *adj.*] being such to the highest degree; utter [the *veriest* nonsense]

ver·i·fi·ca·tion (ver′ə fi kā′shən) *n.* a verifying or being verified; establishment or confirmation of the truth or accuracy of a fact, theory, etc.

ver·i·fy (ver′ə fī′) *vt.* **-fied′, -fy′ing** [< MFr. < ML. < L. *verus*, true + *-ficare*, to make] 1. to prove to be true by demonstration, evidence, etc.; confirm or substantiate 2. to test the accuracy of, as by comparison with a standard 3. *Law a)* to substantiate (an oath) *b)* to add an affidavit to (a pleading) —**ver′i·fi′a·ble** *adj.* —**ver′i·fi′a·bly** *adv.* —**ver′i·fi′-er** *n.*

ver·i·ly (ver′ə lē) *adv.* [Archaic] in very truth; truly

ver·i·sim·i·lar (ver′ə sim′ə lər) *adj.* [< L. < *verus*, true + *similis*, like] seeming to be true or real; likely

ver·i·si·mil·i·tude (ver′ə si mil′ə tyōōd′) *n.* [< L.: see prec.] 1. the appearance of being true or real 2. something having the mere appearance of being true or real

ver·ism (vir′iz′m, ver′-) *n.* [< It. *verismo* < *vero*, true + -ISM] realism in the arts —**ver′ist** *adj., n.*

ver·i·ta·ble (ver′i tə b'l) *adj.* [< OFr. < L. *veritas*, truth] being such in truth or fact; actual [a *veritable* feast] —**ver′-i·ta·bly** *adv.*

ver·i·ty (ver′ə tē) *n.,* pl. **-ties** [< OFr. < L. *veritas*, truth < *verus*, true] 1. conformity to truth or fact 2. a principle, belief, etc. taken to be fundamentally and permanently true; a truth; a reality

ver·juice (vur′jōōs′) *n.* [< MFr. < *vert*, green + *jus*, juice] 1. the sour, acid juice of green, or unripe, fruit 2. sourness of temper, looks, etc.

ver·mi- [< L. *vermis*] a combining form meaning worm

ver·mi·cel·li (vur′mə sel′ē, -chel′ē) *n.* [It., little worms < L. dim. of *vermis*, a worm] pasta like spaghetti, but in thinner strings

ver·mi·cide (vur′mə sīd′) *n.* [VERMI- + -CIDE] a drug or other agent used to kill worms, esp. intestinal worms

ver·mic·u·lar (vər mik′yə lər) *adj.* [< ModL. < L. dim. of *vermis*, a worm] 1. *a)* wormlike in shape or movement *b)* having twisting lines, ridges, etc. that look like worm tracks 2. of, made by, or caused by worms Also **ver·mic′u·late** (-lit), **ver·mic′u·lat′ed** (-lāt′id)

ver·mic·u·lite (vər mik′yə līt′) *n.* [< L.: see prec. & -ITE] any of various hydrous silicate minerals, usually as mica in tiny scales that expand when heated: used for insulation, water adsorption, etc.

ver·mi·form (vur′mə fôrm′) *adj.* [VERMI- + -FORM] shaped like a worm

vermiform appendix see APPENDIX (sense 2)

ver·mi·fuge (vur′mə fyōōj′) *adj.* [VERMI- + -FUGE] serving to expel worms and other parasites from the intestinal tract —*n.* a vermifuge drug

ver·mil·ion (vər mil′yən) *n.* [< OFr. < *vermeil*, bright-red < L. dim. of *vermis*, a worm] 1. *a)* bright-red mercuric sulphide, used as a pigment *b)* any of several other red pigments resembling this 2. a bright red or scarlet —*adj.* of the colour vermilion

ver·min (vur′min) *n.,* pl. **-min** [< OFr. < L. *vermis*, a worm] 1. *a)* any of various insects, bugs, or small animals regarded as pests because they are destructive, disease-carrying, etc., as flies, lice, or rats *b)* such pests collectively 2. collectively, birds or animals that kill game on preserves 3. *a)* a vile, loathsome person *b)* such persons collectively —**ver′min·ous** *adj.*

ver·mouth (vur′məth, vər mōōth′) *n.* [Fr. < G. *Wermut*, wormwood] a sweet or dry, fortified white wine flavoured with aromatic herbs, used in cocktails and as an aperitif

ver·nac·u·lar (vər nak′yə lər) *adj.* [L. *vernaculus*, native < *verna*, a homeborn slave] 1. using the native language of a place [a *vernacular* writer] 2. commonly spoken by the people of a particular country or place [a *vernacular* dialect] 3. of or in the native language 4. native to a place [*vernacular* arts] 5. designating or of the common name, rather than the scientific Latin name, of an animal or plant —*n.* 1. the native language or dialect of a country or place 2. the common, everyday language of ordinary people in a particular locality 3. the shoptalk of a profession or trade 4. a vernacular word or term —**ver·nac′u·lar·ism** *n.* —**ver·nac′u·lar·ly** *adv.*

ver·nal (vur′n'l) *adj.* [L. *vernalis* < *vernus* < *ver*, spring]

1. of the spring **2.** springlike; fresh, warm, and mild **3.** fresh and young; youthful —**ver′nal·ly** *adv.*

ver·nal·ize (-īz′) *vt.* **-ized′, -iz′ing** to stimulate the growth and flowering of (a plant) by artificially shortening the dormant period —**ver′nal·i·za′tion** *n.*

ver·na·tion (vər nā′shən) *n.* [ModL. < pp. of L. *vernare*, to flourish] *Bot.* the arrangement of leaves in a leaf bud

ver·ni·er (vur′nē ər, -nir) *n.* [after P. *Vernier*, 17th-c. Fr. mathematician] a short, graduated scale that slides along a longer graduated instrument and is used to indicate fractional parts of divisions: also **vernier scale**

Ver·o·nal (ver′ə n'l) [G., name after *Verona*, city in Italy] *a trademark for* BARBITONE

ve·ron·i·ca (və ron′i kə) *n.* [LL. < ? the feminine name *Veronica*] **1.** *same as* SPEEDWELL **2.** *Bullfighting* a slow, pivoting movement made by a matador, with his cape held out, as the bull charges past him

ver·ru·ca (və rōō′kə) *n., pl.* **-cae** (-sē) [L., WART] **1.** *same as* WART **2.** a wartlike elevation, as on a toad's back

ver·sant (vur′sənt) *n.* [Fr. < L. *versans*, prp. of *versare*: see ff.] **1.** the shape of a mountain or mountain chain **2.** the general slope of a region

ver·sa·tile (vur′sə til′) *adj.* [Fr. < L. < pp. of *versare*, freq. of *vertere*, to turn] **1.** *a)* competent in many things; able to turn easily from one subject or occupation to another *b)* adaptable to many uses or functions **2.** *Biol.* moving freely, as the anther of a flower or the antenna of an insect —**ver′sa·tile·ly** *adv.* —**ver′sa·til′i·ty** (-til′ə tē) *n.*

verse (vurs) *n.* [< OE. & OFr. < L. *versus*, a turning, row, pp. of *vertere*, to turn] **1.** a single line of poetry **2.** *a)* poetry in general; sometimes, specif., poems of a light or amusing nature *b)* poetry of a specified kind [blank *verse*] **3.** *a)* a single poem *b)* the poetry of a particular writer, period, etc. **4.** a stanza or other short subdivision of a poem **5.** any of the single, usually numbered, short divisions of a chapter of the Bible —*vt., vi.* **versed, vers′ing** [Now Rare] *same as* VERSIFY

versed (vurst) *adj.* [< L. pp. of *versari*, to be busy] acquainted by experience and study; skilled or learned (*in* a specified subject)

ver·si·cle (vur′si k'l) *n.* [< L. *versiculus*, dim. of *versus*, a verse] a short verse or sentence, esp. one said or sung in a religious service and followed by a response

ver·si·fi·ca·tion (vur′sə fi kā′shən) *n.* **1.** the act of versifying **2.** the art, practice, or theory of poetic composition **3.** the form or metrical structure of a poem

ver·si·fy (vur′sə fī′) *vi.* **-fied′, -fy′ing** [< MFr. < L. < *versus*: see VERSE & -FY] to compose verses —*vt.* **1.** to tell about or describe in verse **2.** to put into verse form —**ver′·si·fi′er** *n.*

ver·sion (vur′zhən, -shən) *n.* [Fr. < ML. < L. *versus*: see VERSE] **1.** *a)* a translation *b)* [often V-] a translation of the Bible **2.** an account giving one point of view [two *versions* of the accident] **3.** a particular form or variation, esp. as adapted to another art form [the film *version* of the novel] —**ver′sion·al** *adj.*

‡**vers li·bre** (ver lē′br′) *French term for* FREE VERSE

ver·so (vur′sō) *n., pl.* **-sos** [ModL. (folio) *verso* < L., abl. of *versus*: see VERSE] *Printing* any left-hand page of a book; back of a leaf: opposed to RECTO

verst (vurst, verst; *Russ.* vyôrst) *n.* [< Russ. *versta*] a former Russian unit of linear measure, equal to c. 1067 m

ver·sus (vur′səs) *prep.* [ML. < L., toward < *vertere*, to turn] **1.** in contest against [our team *versus* theirs] **2.** in contrast with; as an alternative to [peace *versus* war]

ver·te·bra (vur′tə brə) *n., pl.* **-brae** (-brē′), **-bras** [L., a joint < *vertere*, to turn] any of the single bones or segments of the spinal column —**ver′te·bral** *adj.*

ver·te·brate (-brit, -brāt′) *adj.* [< L.: see prec.] **1.** having a backbone, or spinal column **2.** of or belonging to the vertebrates —*n.* any of a large group of animals, including all mammals, fishes, birds, reptiles, and amphibians, that have a backbone and a brain and cranium

ver·te·bra·tion (vur′tə brā′shən) *n.* vertebral formation; segmentation into vertebrae

ver·tex (vur′teks) *n., pl.* **-tex·es, -ti·ces** (-tə sēz′) [L., the top, the turning point < *vertere*, to turn] **1.** *a)* the highest point; top; apex *b)* *same as* ZENITH **2.** *Anat., Zool.* the top of the head **3.** *Geom. a)* the point where the two sides of an angle intersect *b)* a corner point of a triangle, square, cube, etc.

ver·ti·cal (vur′ti k'l) *adj.* **1.** of or at the vertex, or highest point; directly overhead

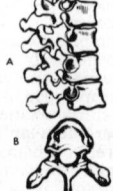

VERTEBRAE (A, section of spinal column; B, single vertebra)

2. perpendicular to the plane of the horizon or to a level surface; upright; straight up or down **3.** of or including the different levels, as in the manufacture or distribution of some product **4.** *Biol.* lengthwise —*n.* **1.** a vertical line, plane, etc. **2.** upright position —**ver′ti·cal′i·ty** (-kal′ə tē) *n.* —**ver′ti·cal·ly** *adv.*

ver·ti·cil (vur′tə sil) *n.* [L. *verticillus*, dim. of *vertex*, a whirl] *Bot.* a circle of leaves, flowers, etc. on a stem; whorl —**ver·tic·il·late** (vər tis′'l it, -āt′) *adj.*

ver·tig·i·nous (vər tij′ə nəs) *adj.* **1.** of, affected by, or causing vertigo; dizzy or dizzying **2.** whirling; spinning **3.** unstable; inconstant —**ver·tig′i·nous·ly** *adv.*

ver·ti·go (vur′ti gō′) *n., pl.* **-goes′, ver·tig·i·nes** (vər tij′ə nēz′) [L. < *vertere*, to turn] *Med.* dizziness in an individual who feels as if he is whirling or as if his surroundings are

ver·tu (vər tōō′, vur′tōō) *n. same as* VIRTU

ver·vain (vur′vān) *n.* [< OFr. < L. *verbena*, foliage] any of a number of verbenas

verve (vurv) *n.* [Fr. < OFr., caprice < L. *verba*, words] **1.** vigour and energy **2.** vivacity; spirit; dash

ver·vet (vur′vit) *n.* [Fr.] a small African monkey

ver·y (ver′ē) *adj.* **ver′i·er, ver′i·est** [< OFr., ult. < L. *verus*, true] **1.** in the fullest sense; complete; utter [the *very* opposite of the truth] **2.** same; identical [the *very* hat he lost] **3.** exactly right, suitable, etc.; precise [the *very* one I want] **4.** even (the): used as an intensive [the *very* rafters shook] **5.** actual [caught in the *very* act] —*adv.* **1.** in a high degree; exceedingly **2.** truly; really: used as an intensive [the *very* same man]

very high frequency any radio frequency between 30 and 300 megahertz

very low frequency any radio frequency between 10 and 30 kilohertz

Ver·y signal (or **light**) (ver′ē, vir′ē) [after E. W. *Very*, 19th-c. U.S. ordnance expert] a coloured flare fired from a special pistol (**Very pistol**) for signalling at night

ves·i·cant (ves′i kənt) *adj.* [< L. *vesica*, a blister] causing blisters —*n.* a vesicant agent Also **ves′i·ca·to·ry** (-kə tər ē) *adj., n., pl.* **-to·ries**

ves·i·cate (-kāt′) *vt., vi.* **-cat′ed, -cat′ing** [< L. *vesica*, a bladder, blister] to blister —**ves′i·ca′tion** *n.*

ves·i·cle (ves′i k'l) *n.* [< Fr. < L. dim. of *vesica*, bladder] **1.** a small, membranous cavity, sac, or cyst; specif., a blister **2.** *Geol.* a small, spherical cavity in volcanic rock —**ve·sic·u·lar** (və sik′yə lər), **ve·sic′u·late** (-lit) *adj.*

ves·per (ves′pər) *n.* [L.] **1.** *a)* orig., evening *b)* [Poet.] [V-] *same as* EVENING STAR **2.** an evening prayer or service; specif., [pl.] [often V-] *a)* R.C.Ch. the sixth of the seven canonical hours, recited or sung in the late afternoon *b)* Anglican Ch. *same as* EVENSONG —*adj.* **1.** of evening **2.** of vespers

ves·per·tine (ves′pər tin, -tīn′) *adj.* [< prec.] of or occurring in the evening

ves·pi·ary (ves′pē ər ē) *n.* [< L. *vespa*, a wasp + (AP)IARY] a nest or colony of wasps

ves·sel (ves′'l) *n.* [< OFr. < LL. dim. of L. *vas*, a vessel] **1.** a utensil for holding something, as a bowl, pot, tub, etc. **2.** a ship or large boat **3.** *a)* Anat., Zool. a tube or duct containing or circulating a body fluid *b)* Bot. a water-conducting tube in the xylem

vest (vest) *n.* [< Fr. < It. < L. *vestis*, a garment] **1.** an undergarment covering the body from the shoulders to the hips **2.** a piece set into a woman's bodice **3.** [Obs.] any form of dress **4.** [U.S.] a waistcoat —*vt.* **1.** to dress, as in church vestments; clothe **2.** to place (some right, power, or property) in the control of a person or group (with *in*) **3.** to provide or invest (a person or group) (*with* some right, power, or property) —*vi.* **1.** to put on garments or vestments **2.** to become vested (*in* a person), as property

ves·ta (ves′tə) *n.* [after *Vesta*, in Rom. Myth. the goddess of the hearth] a short, wooden, or, orig., wax, match

ves·tal (ves′t'l) *adj.* **1.** of or sacred to Vesta **2.** of the vestal virgins **3.** chaste; pure —*n.* **1.** *short for* VESTAL VIRGIN **2.** a chaste woman; specif., a virgin

vestal virgin in ancient Rome, any of the virgin priestesses of Vesta, who tended the sacred fire in her temple

vest·ed interest (ves′tid) **1.** an established right that cannot be done away with, as to some future benefit **2.** [pl.] the powerful persons and groups that own and control industry, business, etc.

vest·ee (ves tē′) *n. dim. of* VEST (n. 2)

ves·ti·ar·y (ves′tē ər ē) *n., pl.* **-ar·ies** [< OFr. < L. *vestiarium*: see VESTRY] a supply room for clothing, as in a monastery

ves·ti·bule (ves′tə byōōl′) *n.* [L. *vestibulum*, entrance hall] **1.** a small entrance hall, either to a building or a room **2.** Anat., Zool. any cavity or space serving as an entrance to another cavity or space [the *vestibule* of the inner ear leading into the cochlea] —**ves·tib·u·lar** (ves tib′yə lər) *adj.*

ves·tige (ves′tij) *n.* [Fr. < L. *vestigium*, a footprint] **1.** a trace or remaining bit of something once present or whole [*vestiges* of an ancient wall, not a *vestige* of hope] **2.** *Biol.* an organ or part not so fully developed or functional as it once was in the embryo or species: also **ves·tig·i·um** (ves tij′ē əm), *pl.* **-i·a** (-ə) —**ves·tig·i·al** (-tij′ē əl, -tij′əl) *adj.* —**ves·tig′i·al·ly** *adv.*

ves·ti·ture (ves′tə chər) *n.* [ME. < LL. *vestitura* < *vestire*, to clothe] **1.** an investiture **2.** clothing **3.** *Zool.* a natural covering, as hair, feathers, etc.

vest·ment (vest′mənt) *n.* [< OFr. < L. *vestimentum* < *vestire*, to clothe] **1.** a garment; esp., an official robe or gown **2.** *Eccles.* any of the garments worn by clergymen, etc. during religious services

ves·try (ves′trē) *n.*, *pl.* **-tries** [< OFr. < L. *vestiarium*, a wardrobe < L. *vestis*, a garment] **1.** a room in a church, where vestments and sacred vessels are kept **2.** a room in a church, used for meetings, Sunday school, etc. **3.** *Anglican Ch.* a group of church members who manage the business affairs of the church

ves·try·man (-mən) *n.*, *pl.* **-men** a member of a vestry

ves·ture (ves′chər) *n.* [< OFr. < VL. < L. *vestire*, to clothe] [Now Rare] **1.** clothing **2.** a covering —*vt.* **-tured, -tur·ing** [Rare or Archaic] to clothe or cover

vet (vet) *n.* shortened form of VETERINARY SURGEON —*vt.* **vet′ted, vet′ting** [Colloq.] **1.** to examine or treat as a veterinarian does **2.** to examine or evaluate thoroughly

vet. 1. veteran 2. veterinary surgeon 3. veterinary

vetch (vech) *n.* [< ONormFr. < L. *vicia*, vetch] any of a number of leafy, climbing or trailing plants of the legume family, used chiefly as fodder or fertilizer

vet·er·an (vet′ər ən, vet′rən) *adj.* [L. *veteranus* < *vetus* (gen. *veteris*), old] **1.** having had long experience in some kind of work or in military service **2.** of a veteran or veterans —*n.* **1.** a person with much experience in some kind of work, esp. in the armed forces of a country **2.** [U.S.] an ex-serviceman

veteran car a car made before 1916, or, strictly, before 1905

vet·er·i·nar·y (vet′ər ə nər ē, vet′rə-) *adj.* [< L. < *veterina*, beasts of burden] designating or of the branch of medicine dealing with the treatment of diseases and injuries in animals, esp. domestic animals —*n.*, *pl.* **-nar·ies** same as VETERINARY SURGEON

veterinary surgeon a person who practises veterinary medicine or surgery: also now chiefly U.S. **vet·er·i·nar·i·an** (vet′ər ə ner′ē ən, vet′rə ner′-)

ve·to (vē′tō) *n.*, *pl.* **-toes** [L., I forbid < *vetare*, to forbid] **1.** *a)* an order forbidding some proposed act; prohibition *b)* the power to prevent action thus **2.** the constitutional right or power of a ruler or legislature to reject bills passed by another branch of the government **3.** [U.S.] a document or message giving the reasons of the executive for rejecting a bill **4.** the power of any of the five permanent members of the Security Council of the United Nations to prevent an action by casting a negative vote —*vt.* **-toed, -to·ing** **1.** to prevent (a bill) from becoming law by veto **2.** to forbid; prohibit —**ve′to·er** *n.*

vex (veks) *vt.* [< MFr. < L. *vexare*, to agitate] **1.** to disturb, irritate, etc., esp. in a petty, nagging way **2.** to distress or afflict —**vexed question** a difficult matter which is much debated —**vex·ed·ly** (vek′sid lē) *adv.* —**vex′er** *n.*

vex·a·tion (vek sā′shən) *n.* **1.** a vexing or being vexed **2.** something that vexes; cause of annoyance or distress

vex·a·tious (-shəs) *adj.* **1.** characterized by or causing vexation; annoying, troublesome, etc. **2.** *Law* instituted without real grounds, to cause annoyance to the defendant: said of legal actions —**vex·a′tious·ly** *adv.*

vex·il·lol·o·gy (veks′ə lol′ə jē) *n.* [< L. *vexillum*, flag + -LOGY] the study of flags —**vex′il·lol′o·gist** *n.*

vex·il·lum (vek sil′əm) *n.*, *pl.* **-il′la** (-ə) [L.] **1.** in ancient Roman civilization, *a)* a square standard carried by troops *b)* a body of troops under one standard **2.** *Bot.* the large, upper petal of a butterfly-shaped flower **3.** *Zool.* the vane of a feather

vex·ing (vek′siŋ) *adj.* that vexes —**vex′ing·ly** *adv.*

VHF, V.H.F., vhf, v.h.f. very high frequency

vi., v.i. intransitive verb

v.i. [L. *vide infra*] see below

vi·a (vī′ə, vē′ə) *prep.* [L., abl. sing. of *via*, a way] **1.** by way of; passing through [from Rome to London *via* Paris] **2.** by means of [*via* airmail]

vi·a·ble (vī′ə b′l) *adj.* [< Fr. < *vie*, life < L. *vita*] **1.** *a)* able to live; specif., developed enough to be able to live outside the uterus [a premature but *viable* infant] *b)* capable of growing [*viable* seeds] **2.** workable; likely to survive [a

viable economy, *viable* ideas] —**vi′a·bil′i·ty** *n.* —**vi′a·bly** *adv.*

vi·a·duct (vī′ə dukt′) *n.* [L. *via* (see VIA) + (AQUE)DUCT] a bridge consisting of a series of short spans supported on piers or towers, usually to carry a road or railway over a valley, gorge, etc.

vi·al (vī′əl) *n.* [< OFr. < OPr., ult. < Gr. *phialē*, shallow cup] a small bottle, usually of glass, for holding medicine or other liquids; phial —*vt.* **-alled, -al·ling** to put or keep in or as in a vial

‡**vi·a me·di·a** (vī′ə mē′dē ə, vē′ə me′-) [L.] a middle way; course between two extremes

vi·and (vī′ənd) *n.* [< OFr., ult. < L. *vivenda*, neut. pl. gerundive of *vivere*, to live] **1.** an article of food **2.** [*pl.*] food; esp., choice dishes

vi·at·i·cum (vī at′i kəm) *n.*, *pl.* **-ca** (-kə), **-cums** [L. < *viaticus*, of a way or road < *via*, way] **1.** money or supplies for a journey **2.** [*often* V-] the Eucharist as given to a person dying or in danger of death

vibes (vībz) *n.pl.* **1.** [Colloq.] a vibraphone **2.** [< VIBRATION(S)] [Slang] qualities in a person or thing that produce an emotional response in one

vi·brac·u·lum (vī brak′yoo ləm) *n.*, *pl.* **-u·la** (-lə) [ModL. < *vibrare*: see VIBRATE] a flexible, threadlike appendage with which certain aquatic organisms seek food or protect themselves

vi·brant (vī′brənt) *adj.* [< L. prp. of *vibrare*, vibrate] **1.** quivering; vibrating **2.** produced by vibration; resonant: said of sound **3.** active; lively **4.** energetic, sparkling, vivacious, etc. [a *vibrant* woman] —**vi′bran·cy** *n.* —**vi′brant·ly** *adv.*

vi·bra·phone (vī′brə fōn′) *n.* [VIBRA(TE) + -PHONE] a musical instrument resembling the marimba, but with electrically operated valves in the resonators, that produce a gentle vibrato —**vi′bra·phon′ist** *n.*

vi·brate (vī′brāt′) *vt.* **-brat′ed, -brat′ing** [< L. pp. of *vibrare*, to vibrate] **1.** to give off (light or sound) by vibration **2.** to set in to-and-fro motion; oscillate **3.** to cause to quiver —*vi.* **1.** to swing back and forth, as a pendulum **2.** to move rapidly back and forth; quiver, as a plucked string **3.** to resound **4.** to feel very excited; thrill

vi·bra·tile (vī′brə til′) *adj.* **1.** of or characterized by vibration **2.** capable of vibrating or being vibrated **3.** having a vibrating motion —**vi′bra·til′i·ty** *n.*

vi·bra·tion (vī brā′shən) *n.* **1.** a vibrating; esp., rapid movement back and forth; quivering **2.** [*pl.*] same as VIBES (sense 2) **3.** *Physics a)* rapid, periodic, to-and-fro motion or oscillation of an elastic body or the particles of a fluid, as in transmitting sound *b)* a single, complete oscillation —**vi·bra′tion·al** *adj.*

vi·bra·to (vi brät′ō, vē-) *n.*, *pl.* **-tos** [It.] *Music* the pulsating effect of a rapid, hardly noticeable variation in pitch, produced by a slight oscillation of the finger on a violin string, by a slight wavering of the tone in singing, etc.

vi·bra·tor (vī′brāt′ər) *n.* something that vibrates, as an electrical device used in massage, etc.

vi·bra·to·ry (vī′brə tər ē) *adj.* **1.** of, like, or causing vibration **2.** vibrating or capable of vibration

vi·bris·sa (vī bris′ə) *n.*, *pl.* **-sae** (-ē) [ModL., akin to *vibrare*, to vibrate] **1.** any of the stiff hairs growing in or near the nostrils of certain animals, as a cat's whisker **2.** any of the bristle-like feathers growing near the mouth of certain insect-eating birds

vi·bur·num (vī bur′nəm) *n.* [ModL., genus name < L., the wayfaring tree] **1.** any of various shrubs or small trees related to the honeysuckle and bearing white flowers **2.** the bark of several species, sometimes used in medicine

vic·ar (vik′ər) *n.* [< OFr. < L. *vicarius* < *vicis*, a change] **1.** a person who acts in place of another; deputy **2.** *Anglican Ch.* a priest in charge of a parish in which, formerly, the tithes belonged to a layman, monastery, etc. **3.** *R.C.Ch.* a church officer acting as deputy of a bishop —**vi·car·i·al** (vī ker′ē əl, vi-) —**vi·car′ship** *adj.* —**vi·car′i·ate** (-it, -āt′), **vic′ar·ate** (-it, -ə rāt′) *n.*

vic·ar·age (-ij) *n.* **1.** the residence of a vicar **2.** the benefice or salary of a vicar

vicar apostolic *pl.* **vicars apostolic** *R.C.Ch.* a titular bishop in a region where no regular see has yet been organized

vic·ar-gen·er·al (vik′ər jen′ər əl) *n.*, *pl.* **vic′ars-gen′er·al** **1.** *Anglican Ch.* a layman serving as administrative deputy to an archbishop or bishop **2.** *R.C.Ch.* a priest, etc. acting as administrative deputy to a bishop or to the general superior of a religious order

vi·car·i·ous (vī ker′ē əs, vi-) *adj.* [L. *vicarius*, substituted < *vicis*, a change] **1.** *a)* taking the place of another *b)* delegated [*vicarious* powers] **2.** *a)* done or undergone by one person in place of another *b*) felt as if one were actually taking part in another's experience [a *vicarious* thrill] —**vi·car′i·ous·ly** *adv.* —**vi·car′i·ous·ness** *n.*

Vicar of Christ the Pope

vice[1] (vīs) *n.* [< OFr. < L. *vitium*] **1.** *a*) an evil or wicked action, habit, etc. *b*) depravity or corruption *c*) prostitution **2.** any fault, failing, defect, etc. —**vice′less** *adj.*

vi·ce[2] (vī′sē, -sə) *prep.* [L.: see VICE-] in the place of; as the deputy or successor of

vice[3] (vīs) *n.* [< OFr. < L. *vitis*, a vine, lit., that which winds] a device consisting of two jaws opened and closed by a screw, lever, etc., used for holding firmly an object being worked on —*vt.* **viced, vic′ing** to hold or sqeeze with or as with a vice —**vice′like′** *adj.*

vice- [< L. *vice*, in the place of another, abl. of *vicis*: see VICAR] a *prefix meaning* one who acts in the place of; subordinate; deputy [*vice*-president]

vice admiral see MILITARY RANKS, table

vice-con·sul (-kon′s'l) *n.* an officer who is subordinate to or a substitute for a consul —**vice′-con′su·lar** *adj.* —**vice′-con′su·late** (-it) *n.* —**vice′-con′sul·ship′** *n.*

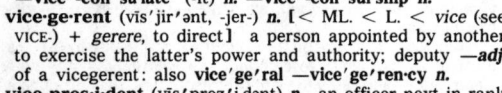

VICE

vice·ge·rent (vīs′jir′ənt, -jer-) *n.* [< ML. < L. < *vice* (see VICE-) + *gerere*, to direct] a person appointed by another to exercise the latter's power and authority; deputy —*adj.* of a vicegerent: also **vice′ge′ral** —**vice′ge′ren·cy** *n.*

vice-pres·i·dent (vīs′prez′i dənt) *n.* an officer next in rank below a president, acting in his place during his absence or incapacity —**vice′-pres′i·den·cy** *n.* —**vice′-pres′i·den′tial** *adj.*

vice-re·gal (vīs′rē′g'l) *adj.* of a viceroy

vice-re·gent (-rē′jənt) *n.* a deputy of a regent

vice-reine (vīs′rān) *n.* [Fr. < *vice*- (see VICE-) + *reine*, queen < L. *regina*] the wife of a viceroy

vice·roy (vīs′roi) *n.* [MFr. < *vice*- (see VICE-) + *roy*, a king < L. *rex*] a person ruling a country, province, etc. as the deputy of a sovereign —**vice′roy′al·ty**, *pl.* **-ties**, **vice′-roy·ship′** *n.*

vice squad a police squad assigned to the suppression or control of prostitution, gambling, etc.

vi·ce ver·sa (vī′sē vur′sə, vī′sə; vīs′) [L.] the order or relation being reversed; conversely

vi·chy·ssoise (vē′shē swäz′, vish′ē-) *n.* [Fr.] a thick cream soup of potatoes, etc., usually served cold

Vi·chy (water) (vish′ē, vē′shē; *Fr.* vē shē′) **1.** a mineral water found at Vichy, in C France **2.** a natural or processed water like this

vic·i·nage (vis′ə nij) *n.* [< MFr., ult. < L. *vicinus*: see ff.] **1.** *same as* VICINITY **2.** the people living in a particular neighbourhood

vi·cin·i·ty (və sin′ə tē) *n.*, *pl.* **-ties** [< L. < *vicinus*, near < *vicus*, village] **1.** a being near or close by; nearness **2.** nearby or surrounding region; neighbourhood

vi·cious (vish′əs) *adj.* [< OFr. < L. < *vitium*, a vice] **1.** *a*) characterized by vice or evil; depraved *b*) debasing; corrupting **2.** ruined by defects, flaws, etc. [a vicious argument] **3.** having bad or harmful habits; unruly [a vicious horse] **4.** malicious; spiteful; mean [a vicious rumour] **5.** very intense, sharp, etc. [a vicious wind] —**vi′cious·ly** *adv.* —**vi′cious·ness** *n.*

vicious circle 1. a situation in which the solution of one problem gives rise to another, but the solution of this brings back the first, etc. **2.** *Logic* an argument which is not valid because its conclusion rests on a premise which itself depends on the conclusion

vi·cis·si·tude (vi sis′ə tyood′) *n.* [Fr. < L. *vicissitudo* < *vicis*, a turn] **1.** a condition of constant change or alternation, as a natural process **2.** [*pl.*] unpredictable changes or variations that keep occurring in life, fortune, etc.; shifting circumstances; ups and downs —**vi·cis′si·tu′di·nar·y**, **vi·cis′si·tu′di·nous** *adj.*

vic·tim (vik′təm) *n.* [L, *victima*] **1.** a person or animal killed as a sacrifice to a god **2.** someone or something killed, destroyed, etc. [victims of war] **3.** a person who suffers some loss, esp. by being swindled; dupe

vic·tim·ize (vik′tə mīz′) *vt.* **-ized′, -iz′ing** to make a victim of —**vic′tim·i·za′tion** *n.* —**vic′tim·iz′er** *n.*

vic·tor (vik′tər) *n.* [L. < pp. of *vincere*, to conquer] the winner in a battle, struggle, etc. —*adj.* *same as* VICTORIOUS

vic·to·ri·a (vik tôr′ē ə) *n.* [after Queen *Victoria* (1837-1901), queen of Britain] **1.** a four-wheeled carriage for two passengers, with a folding top and a high seat for the coachman **2.** a S. American waterlily with large leaves and large, night-blooming flowers

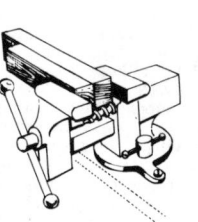

VICTORIA

Victoria Cross the highest British military decoration, given for deeds of exceptional valour

Vic·to·ri·an (-ən) *adj.* **1.** of or characteristic of the time when Victoria was queen of England **2.** showing the middle-class respectability, prudery, etc. regarded as typical of Victorians —*n.* a person, esp. a British writer, of the time of Queen Victoria —**Vic·to′ri·an·ism** *n.*

vic·to·ri·ous (vik tôr′ē əs) *adj.* **1.** having won a victory; triumphant **2.** of, typical of, or bringing about victory —**vic·to′ri·ous·ly** *adv.*

vic·to·ry (vik′tər ē, -trē) *n.*, *pl.* **-ries** [< OFr. < L. *victoria* < *victor*, VICTOR] **1.** the decisive winning of a battle or war **2.** success in any contest or struggle involving the defeat of an opponent or the overcoming of obstacles

vict·ual (vit′'l) *n.* [< MFr. < LL. < L. *victualis*, of food < *victus*, food < pp. of *vivere*, to live] **1.** [Archaic or Dial.] food or other provisions **2.** [*pl.*] [Dial. or Colloq.] articles of food —*vt.* **-ualled, -ual·ling** to supply with victuals —*vi.* to lay in a supply of food

vict·ual·ler (-ər) *n.* **1.** formerly, *a*) a person who supplied victuals, as to an army or a ship; sutler *b*) a supply ship **2.** a licensed purveyor of spirits; innkeeper

vi·cu·ña (vi koon′yə, -koon′ə; vi kyoon′-) *n.*, *pl.* **-ñas, -ña:** see PLURAL, II, D, 1 [Sp., of Quechuan origin] **1.** an animal found wild in the S American Andes, related to the llama and alpaca, with soft, shaggy wool **2.** this wool **3.** a fabric made from it or in imitation of it

VICUNA
(to 1 m high
at shoulder)

‡**vi·de** (vī′dē, vē′dā) [L.] see: used to direct attention to a particular page, book, etc.

‡**vide an·te** (an′tē) [L.] see before (in the book, etc.)

‡**vide in·fra** (in′frə) [L.] see below; see further on or (in the book, etc.)

‡**vi·de·li·cet** (vi del′ə sit) *adv.* [L. < *videre licet*, it is permitted to see] that is; namely

vid·e·o (vid′ē ō′) *adj.* [L., I see] **1.** of or used in television **2.** designating or of the picture portion of a television broadcast: cf. AUDIO —*n.* [U.S.] *same as* TELEVISION

vide·o·phone (vid′ē ō fōn′) *n.* [VIDEO + (TELE)PHONE] a telephone combined with a television receiver and transmitter so that users can see, as well as speak to, each other

vid·e·o·tape (vid′ē ō tāp′) *n.* a magnetic tape on which the video and audio portions of a television broadcast can be recorded as for later broadcasting

‡**vide su·pra** (soo′prə) [L.] see above; see earlier (in the book, etc.)

vid·i·con (vid′ə kon) *n.* [VID(EO) + ICON(OSCOPE)] a TV camera pickup tube in which optical images are scanned by an electron beam for transmission

vie (vī) *vi.* **vied, vy′ing** [< OFr. < L. *invitare*, to challenge, invite] to be a rival or rivals; compete (*with* someone) —**vi′er** *n.*

Vi·et·nam·ese (vē ət nə mēz′, vyet-) *adj.* designating or of Vietnam, a country on the E coast of the Indochinese peninsula —*n.* **1.** a native or inhabitant of Vietnam **2.** the language of Vietnam

view (vyoo) *n.* [< OFr. < *veoir*, to see < L. *videre*] **1.** a seeing or looking, as in inspection **2.** sight or vision; esp., range of vision **3.** mental examination or survey [a correct view of the situation] **4.** *a*) a scene or prospect, as of a landscape *b*) a picture of such a scene **5.** visual appearance of something **6.** manner of regarding something; opinion **7.** an object; aim; goal [with a view to helping] **8.** a general survey —*vt.* **1.** to inspect; scrutinize **2.** to see; behold **3.** to survey mentally; consider **4.** to regard in a particular way —**in view 1.** in sight **2.** under consideration **3.** as an object aimed at **4.** in expectation; as a hope —**in view of 1.** because of **2.** in a position from which one can see something, or from which one can be seen [came *in view of* the sea, was *in full view of* the

enemy *l* —**on view** displayed publicly —**with a view to** 1. with the purpose of 2. with a hope of; looking forward to
view·er (-ər) *n.* 1. a person who views something, esp. television; spectator 2. an optical device for individual viewing of slides, filmstrips, etc.
view·find·er (-fīn'dər) *n. same as* FINDER (sense 2)
view·less (-lis) *adj.* 1. affording no view, or prospect 2. [Rare] invisible 3. having or expressing no opinions
view·point (-point') *n.* the mental position from which things are viewed and judged; point of view
vi·ges·i·mal (vī jes'ə m'l) *adj.* [< L., ult. < *viginti*, twenty] 1. of or based on the number twenty 2. twentieth
vig·il (vij'əl) *n.* [< OFr. < L. < *vigil*, awake < *vigere*, to be lively] 1. *a*) a watchful staying awake during the usual hours of sleep *b*) a watch kept 2. *Eccles.* the evening or day before a festival, or the devotional services held then
vig·i·lance (vij'ə ləns) *n.* the quality or state of being vigilant; watchfulness
vigilance committee [U.S.] a group that sets itself up, without legal authority, to punish crime, etc. independently of the usual process of law-enforcement
vig·i·lant (vij'ə lant) *adj.* [Fr. < L. prp. of *vigilare*, to watch < *vigil*, awake] staying watchful and alert to danger or trouble —**vig'i·lant·ly** *adv.*
vig·i·lan·te (vij'ə lan'tē) *n.* [Sp., vigilant] [U.S.] a member of a vigilance committee
vig·i·lan·tism (vij'ə lan tiz'm) *n.* [U.S.] the lawless, violent methods, spirit, etc. of vigilantes —**vig'i·lan'tist** *adj.*
vign·er·on (vēn'yər on) *n.* [Fr.] a vine-grower
vi·gnette (vin yet') *n.* [Fr., dim. < *vigne*, a vine] 1. an ornamental design or illustration used in a book, magazine, etc., as at the beginning or end of a chapter or section 2. a picture or photograph shading off gradually at the edges 3. a short, delicate literary sketch —*vt.* -**gnet'ted**, -**gnet'ting** to make a vignette of —**vi·gnet'tist** *n.*
vig·or·ous (vig'ər əs) *adj.* 1. strong; robust 2. of, characterised by, or requiring vigour 3. forceful; energetic; powerful —**vig'or·ous·ly** *adv.* —**vig'or·ous·ness** *n.*
vig·our (vig'ər) *n.* [< OFr. < L. < *vigere*, to be strong] 1. active physical or mental force; vitality 2. active or healthy growth 3. intensity, force, or energy 4. effective legal force; validity Also, U.S. sp., **vig'or**
vik·ing (vī'kiŋ) *n.* [ON. *vikingr*] any of the Scandinavian pirates who ravaged the coasts of Europe from the 8th to the 10th centuries
vi·la·yet (vi lä'yet) *n.* [Turk., < Ar *wilāyat*, region] an administrative division of Turkey
vile (vīl) *adj.* [< OFr. < L. < *vilis*, cheap, base] 1. morally base or evil; wicked 2. repulsive; disgusting 3. degrading; low 4. most inferior; very bad [*vile* weather] —**vile'ly** *adv.* —**vile'ness** *n.*
vil·i·fy (vil'ə fī') *vt.* -**fied'**, -**fy'ing** [LL. *vilificare:* see VILE & -FY] to use abusive or slanderous language about; revile; defame —**vil'i·fi·ca'tion** *n.* —**vil'i·fi'er** *n.*
vil·la (vil'ə) *n.* [It. < L.] 1. a country house or estate, esp. when large or luxurious and used as a retreat or summer house 2. a small suburban house 3. a house, as at the seaside, which is rented to holiday makers 4. in ancient Roman civilisation, a country house, including its farm buildings and lands
vil·lage (vil'ij) *n.* [< OFr. < L. < *villa*, a country house] 1. a group of houses in the country, larger than a hamlet and smaller than a town 2. the people of a village, collectively —*adj.* of a village —**vil'lag·er** *n.*
vil·lain (vil'ən) *n.* [< OFr. < VL. *villanus*, a farm servant < L. *villa*, a farm] 1. a person guilty of great crimes; evil person; scoundrel 2. a wicked character in a novel, play, etc. who opposes the hero 3. *same as* VILLEIN 4. [Colloq.] a rogue; rascal: used humorously —**vil'lain·ess** *n.fem.*
vil·lain·ous (-əs) *adj.* 1. of or like a villain; evil; wicked 2. very bad or disagreeable [a *villainous* climate] —**vil'-lain·ous·ly** *adv.*
vil·lain·y (-ē) *n., pl.* -**lain·ies** 1. the fact or state of being villainous 2. villainous conduct 3. a villainous act; wicked, detestable, or criminal deed
vil·la·nelle (vil'ə nel') *n.* [Fr. < It. *villanella*, rustic] a poem of 19 lines, usually in five three-line stanzas and a final four-line stanza, with only two rhymes throughout
-ville (vil) [< Fr. *ville*, town, city] [Chiefly U.S.] place or condition characterized by: freely used in coining slang terms [*"dullsville"*] from its use in forming names of some U.S. towns
vil·lein (vil'ən) *n.* [see VILLAIN] in medieval times, an unfree peasant attached to a lord, to whom he paid dues and services in return for his land —**vil'lein·age, vil'len·age** *n.*
vil·lus (vil'əs) *n., pl.* **vil'li** (-ī) [L., shaggy hair] 1. *Anat.* any of numerous hairlike growths on certain mucous membranes of the body, as of the small intestines, serving to secrete mucus and absorb fats, etc. 2. *Bot.* any of the

long, soft hairs on certain plants —**vil·los·i·ty** (vi los'ə tē) *n., pl.* -**ties** —**vil'lous** (-əs) *adj.*
vim (vim) *n.* [L., acc. of *vis*, strength] [Colloq.] energy; vigour
‡**vin** (van) *n.* [Fr.] wine
vi·na (vē'nə) *n.* [< Hindi *bīnā*, < Sans.] an Indian four-stringed musical instrument
vi·na·ceous (vī nā'shəs) *adj.* [< L. < *vinum*, wine] 1. of or like wine or grapes 2. wine-coloured; red
vin·ai·grette (vin'ā gret', vin'i-) *n.* [Fr. < *vinaigre*, vinegar] a small ornamental box or bottle with a perforated lid, used for holding aromatic vinegar, smelling salts, etc.
vinaigrette sauce a savoury sauce made of vinegar, oil, herbs, etc. and used on salads, etc.
Vin·cent's angina (vin's'nts) [after J. H. *Vincent* (1862–1950), Fr. physician] an infectious disease of the mouth and throat in which the mucous membranes become ulcerated: also called **Vincent's infection**
vin·ci·ble (vin'sə b'l) *adj.* [< L. < *vincere*, to overcome] that can be overcome or defeated —**vin'ci·bil'i·ty** *n.*
vin·cu·lum (viŋ'kyoo ləm) *n., pl.* -**la** (-lə) [L. *vincere*, to bind] 1. a bond; tie 2. *Anat.* a ligament 3. *Math.* a line drawn over two or more terms of a compound quantity to show that they are to be treated together (Ex.: a - $\overline{x + y}$)
vin·di·ca·ble (vin'di kə b'l) *adj.* that can be vindicated; justifiable
vin·di·cate (vin'də kāt') *vt.* -**cat'ed**, -**cat'ing** [< L. pp. of *vindicare*, to claim < *vim*, acc. of *vis*, force + *dicere* to say] 1. to clear from criticism, blame, suspicion, etc. 2. to defend (a cause, etc.) against opposition 3. to justify [he *vindicated* their belief in him] —**vin'di·ca'tive** (-kāt'iv, vin dik'ə tiv), **vin'di·ca·to·ry** *adj.* —**vin'di·ca'tor** *n.*
vin·di·ca·tion (vin'də kā'shən) *n.* 1. a vindicating or being vindicated 2. a fact or circumstance that vindicates
vin·dic·tive (vin dik'tiv) *adj.* [< L. *vindicta*, revenge (see VINDICATE) + -IVE] 1. revengeful in spirit 2. said or done in revenge [*vindictive* punishment] —**vin·dic'tive·ly** *adv.* —**vin·dic'tive·ness** *n.*
vine (vīn) *n.* [< OFr. < L. < *vinum*, wine] 1. any of a genus of climbing or trailing perennial plants, esp. the grapevine 2. the stem of such a plant 3. [Aust. & N.Z.] any climbing or trailing plant —**vine'like** *adj.*
vin·e·gar (vin'i gər) *n.* [< MFr. < *vin*, wine + *aigre*, sour < L. *acris*, acrid] 1. a sour liquid containing acetic acid, made by fermenting cider, wine, malt, etc.: it is used as a condiment and preservative 2. ill-tempered speech, character, etc. —**vin'e·gar·y, vin'e·gar·ish** *adj.*
vin·er·y (vīn'ər ē) *n., pl.* -**er·ies** 1. an enclosed area or building in which grapevines are grown 2. vines collectively
vine·yard (vin'yərd) *n.* land devoted to cultivating grapevines
‡**vingt-et-un** (vant ā ën') *n.* [Fr., lit., twenty-one] a gambling game at cards in which each player's aim is to obtain from the dealer cards totalling twenty-one points or close to that total without exceeding it; blackjack
vin·i- [< L. *vinum*, wine] a combining form meaning wine grapes or wine [*viniculture*]
vin·i·cul·ture (vin'i kul'chər) *n.* [prec. + CULTURE] the cultivation of wine grapes —**vin'i·cul'tur·al** *adj.* —**vin'i·cul'-tur·ist** *n.*
‡**vi·no** (vē'nō) *n.* [It. & Sp.] [Colloq.] wine
vi·nous (vī'nəs) *adj.* [< L. < *vinum*, wine] 1. of, having the nature of, or characteristic of wine 2. *a*) fond of drinking wine *b*) resulting from drinking wine —**vi·nos'i·ty** (-nos'ə tē) *n.*
vin·tage (vin'tij) *n.* [< OFr. < L. *vindemia* < *vinum*, wine + *demere*, to remove] 1. *a*) the crop of grapes or the resultant wine of a vineyard or grape-growing region in a single season *b*) the wine, esp. a prized wine, of a particular region in a specified year 2. the act or season of gathering grapes or of making wine 3. the type or model of a particular year or period [a car of prewar *vintage*] —*adj.* 1. *a*) of choice vintage [*vintage* wine] *b*) representative of the best 2. dating from a period long past [*vintage* clothes]
vintage car an old car, specif., one made between 1917 and 1930
vin·tag·er (-ər) *n.* a person who harvests grapes
vint·ner (vint'nər) *n.* [< OFr. < ML. < L. *vinetum*, a vineyard] a wine merchant
vin·y (vī'nē) *adj.* **vin'i·er, vin'i·est** 1. of or like vines 2. filled or covered with vines
vi·nyl (vī'n'l) *n.* [< L. *vinum*, wine + -YL] 1. the univalent radical, CH₂:CH-, derived from ethylene 2. any of various plastics made from polymerized vinyl compounds
vi·ol (vī'əl) *n.* [MFr. *viole* < OPr. *viula* < ?] any of an early family of stringed instruments, usually with six strings, frets, and a flat back: used in sizes from the treble viol to the bass viol
vi·o·la¹ (vē ō'lə, vī-) *n.* [It. < OPr. *viula*, viol] a stringed instrument of the violin family, slightly larger than a violin and tuned a fifth lower
vi·o·la² (vī'ə lə, vī ō'lə) *n.* [< L., a violet] any of various violets developed from a pansy

vi·o·la·ble (vī′ə lə b′l) *adj.* that can be, or is likely to be, violated —**vi′o·la·bil′i·ty,** **vi′o·la·ble·ness** *n.* —**vi′o·la·bly** *adv.*

viola da gam·ba (də gäm′bə) [It., lit., viol for the leg] an early instrument of the viol family, held between the knees and comparable in range to the cello

vi·o·late (vī′ə lāt′) *vt.* **-lat′ed, -lat′ing** [< L. pp. of *violare,* to use force] 1. to break (a law, rule, promise, etc.); fail to observe; infringe on 2. to assault sexually; esp., to rape (a woman) 3. to desecrate or profane (something sacred) 4. to break in on; disturb [to *violate* one's privacy] 5. to offend, insult, etc. [to *violate* one's sense of decency] —**vi′-o·la′tive** *adj.* —**vi′o·la′tor** *n.*

vi·o·la·tion (vī′ə lā′shən) *n.* a violating or being violated; specif., a) infringement or breach b) rape c) desecration of something sacred d) disturbance

vi·o·lence (vī′ə ləns) *n.* [< MFr. < L. < *violentus,* violent] 1. physical force used so as to injure or damage 2. intense, powerful force, as of a storm, etc. 3. a) unjust or callous use of force or power, as in violating another's rights, privacy, etc. b) the harm done by this 4. vehemence; fury 5. a violent deed or act —**do violence to** 1. a) to outrage b) to act contrary to 2. to twist the sense of a phrase, text, etc. so as to distort meaning

vi·o·lent (-lənt) *adj.* 1. a) acting with or characterized by great physical force, so as to injure, etc. b) acting with or characterized by unlawful force 2. caused by violence 3. a) furious; passionate; immoderate [*violent* language] b) emotionally disturbed and uncontrollable 4. extreme; intense [a *violent* storm] —**vi′o·lent·ly** *adv.*

vi·o·let (vī′ə lit) *n.* [< OFr. < L. *viola,* a violet] 1. a) any of a number of related short plants with white, blue, purple, or yellow flowers b) the flower of any of these plants 2. any of various similar but unrelated plants, as the African violet 3. a bluish-purple colour —*adj.* bluish-purple

vi·o·lin (vī′ə lin′) *n.* [< It. dim. of *viola,* a viol] 1. an instrument having four strings and no frets, and played with a bow: the smallest and highest-pitched in the modern family of similar instruments 2. a violinist [first *violin*]

vi·o·lin·ist (-ist) *n.* a violin player

vi·o·list (vī′ə l ist; *for 2* vē ō′list) *n.* 1. a viol player 2. a viola player

vi·o·lon·cel·lo (vī′ə lən chel′ō) *n., pl.* **-los** [It., dim. of *violone,* base viol < *viola,* viol] *same as* CELLO —**vi′-o·lon·cel′list** *n.*

VIP, V.I.P. [Colloq.] very important person

vi·per (vī′pər) *n.* [OFr. < L. *vipera* < ? *vivus,* living + *parere,* to bear] 1. any of a family of venomous snakes found in Europe, Africa, and Asia, including the adder (sense 1) 2. a malicious or treacherous person —**vi′per·ine** (-in, -in′) *adj.*

vi·per·ous (-əs) *adj.* of, having the nature of, or like a viper; esp., spiteful or malicious: also **vi′per·ish** —**vi′per·ous·ly** *adv.* —**vi′per·ous-ness** *n.*

VIOLIN
(A, scroll; B, pegs; C, neck; D, finger-board; E, waist; F, tailpiece; G, chinboard)

vi·ra·go (vi rä′gō, -rā′-) *n., pl.* **-goes, -gos** [OE. < L., a manlike maiden < *vir,* a man] a quarrelsome, shrewish woman; scold

vi·ral (vī′rəl) *adj.* of, involving, or caused by a virus

vi·res·cent (vī res′ənt, vi-) *adj.* [< L. prp. of *virescere* < *virere,* to be green] 1. turning or becoming green 2. greenish —**vi·res′cence** *n.*

vir·gate[1] (vur′gāt, -git) *n.* [ME. *virgata (terrae)* < L. *virga,* a rod: used as transl. of OE. *gierdland,* yardland] an old English land measure, usually about thirty acres

vir·gate[2] (-gāt, -git) *adj.* [ModL. *virgatus* < *virga:* see prec] *Bot.* long, straight and thin: rod-like

Vir·gil·i·an (vur jil′ē ən) *adj.* of, or in the style of, Virgil (70-19 B.C.), Roman poet

vir·gin (vur′jin) *n.* [< OFr. < L. *virgo* (gen. *virginis*), a maiden] 1. a person, esp. a woman, who has not had sexual intercourse 2. an unmarried girl or woman —[V-] *Astron. same as* VIRGO —*adj.* 1. being a virgin 2. like a virgin; chaste; modest 3. untouched, pure, clean, etc. [*virgin* snow] 4. as yet unused, untrod, unexplored, etc. by man [a *virgin* forest] 5. being the first [a *virgin* effort] —**the Virgin** Mary, the mother of Jesus

vir·gin·al[1] (vur′ji n′l) *adj.* 1. of or like a virgin; maidenly 2. pure; fresh; unsullied —**vir′gin·al·ly** *adv.*

vir·gin·al[2] (vur′ji n′l) *n.* [prob. akin to prec.] [*sometimes pl.*] a harpsichord; esp., a small, rectangular harpsichord of the 16th cent., placed on a table or in the lap to be played: also **pair of virginals**

Virgin Birth *Christian Theol.* the doctrine that Jesus was born to Mary, a virgin, and that she was his only human parent

Vir·gin·ia creeper (vur jin′yə) a widely cultivated vine, native to North America, with leaves that turn bright red in autumn

vir·gin·i·ty (vər jin′ə tē) *n.* 1. the state or fact of being a virgin; maidenhood, chastity, etc. 2. the state of being virgin, pure, clean, etc.

Virgin Mary Mary, the mother of Jesus

Virgin Queen Elizabeth I of England

vir·gin's-bow·er (vur′jinz bou′ər) *n.* a white-flowered, rambling variety of clematis

virgin wool wool that has never before been processed

Vir·go (vur′gō) [L., lit., virgin] 1. a large constellation between Leo and Libra 2. the sixth sign of the zodiac: see ZODIAC, illus.

vir·gule (vur′gyōōl) *n.* [Fr. < L. dim. of *virga,* a twig] a short, diagonal line (/) placed between two words to show that either can be used (and/or), in dates or fractions (3/8), to express "per" (kilometres/hour), etc.

vir·i·des·cent (vir′ə des′ənt) *adj.* [< LL., ult. < *viridis,* green] greenish —**vir′i·des′cence** *n.*

vi·rid·i·an (və rid′ē ən) *n.* [< L. *viridis,* green] a bluish-green pigment, hydrated chromic oxide —*adj.* bluish-green

vi·rid·i·ty (-ə tē) *n.* [< ME. < MFr. < L. *viridis:* see prec.] greenness; freshness

vir·ile (vir′īl) *adj.* [< L. < *vir,* a man] 1. of or characteristic of an adult man; masculine; male 2. having manly strength or vigour 3. of or capable of copulation; sexually potent —**vir′ile·ly** *adv.* —**vi·ril·i·ty** (vi ril′ə tē) *n.*

vi·rol·o·gy (vī rol′ə jē) *n.* [< VIR(US) + *-o-* + -LOGY] the study of viruses and virus diseases —**vi·ro·log·ic** (vī′rə loj′-ik), **vi′ro·log′i·cal** *adj.* —**vi·rol′o·gist** *n.*

vir·tu (vər tōō′, vur′tōō) *n.* [It. < L. *virtus,* virtue] 1. a love of, or taste for, artistic objects 2. such objects, collectively 3. the quality of being so artistic, beautiful, rare, etc. as to interest a collector

vir·tu·al (vur′chōo wəl) *adj.* being such practically or in effect, although not in actual fact or name [a *virtual* dictator] —**vir′tu·al′i·ty** (-wal′ə tē) *n.*

virtual image an optical image formed by the apparent, rather than the actual, divergence of rays from a point

vir·tu·al·ly (-chōo wəl ē, -chōo lē) *adv.* in effect although not in fact; for all practical purposes [*virtually* identical]

vir·tue (vur′chōo, vur′tyōo) *n.* [< OFr. < L. *virtus,* manliness, worth] 1. general moral excellence; goodness of character 2. a specific moral quality regarded as good 3. chastity 4. a) excellence in general; merit b) a specific excellence; good quality 5. efficacy; potency; esp., healing power, as of a medicine —**by** (or **in**) **virtue of** because of; on the grounds of —**make a virtue of necessity** to do what has to be done as if one really wanted to

vir·tu·os·i·ty (vur′tyōo wos′ə tē) *n., pl.* **-ties** [< ff. + -ITY] great technical skill in some fine art, esp. in the performance of music

vir·tu·o·so (vur′tyōo wō′zō, -sō) *n., pl.* **-sos, -si** (-sē) [It., skilled] 1. orig., a) a person with a broad interest in the arts or sciences b) a person with highly cultivated tastes concerning art 2. a person having great technical skill in some fine art, esp. in the performance of music —*adj.* of or like that of a virtuoso: also **vir′tu·os′ic** (-wos′ik)

vir·tu·ous (vur′tyōo wəs) *adj.* 1. having, or characterized by, moral virtue 2. chaste: said of a woman —**vir′tu·ous·ly** *adv.* —**vir′tu·ous·ness** *n.*

vir·u·lent (vir′ə lənt) *adj.* [< L. *virulentus* < *virus,* a poison] 1. a) extremely poisonous or injurious; deadly b) bitterly spiteful; full of hate and enmity 2. *Med.* a) violent and rapid in its course: said of a disease b) highly infectious: said of a microorganism —**vir′u·lence, vir′u·len·cy** *n.* —**vir′-u·lent·ly** *adv.*

vi·rus (vī′rəs) *n.* [L., a poison] 1. orig., venom, as of a snake 2. a) any of a group of ultramicroscopic infective agents that cause various diseases in animals or plants: see also FILTERABLE VIRUS b) a disease caused by a virus 3. an evil or harmful influence

‡**vis** (vis) *n., pl.* **vi·res** (vī′rēz) [L.] force; strength

vi·sa (vē′zə) *n.* [Fr. < L. pp. of *videre,* see endorsement on a passport, showing that it has been examined by the proper officials of a country and granting entry into that country —*vt.* **-saed, -sa·ing** 1. to put a visa on (a passport) 2. to give a visa to (someone)

vis·age (viz′ij) *n.* [< OFr. < L. *visus,* a look < pp. of *videre,* to see] 1. the face; countenance 2. appearance; aspect —**vis′aged** *adj.*

vis-à-vis (vē′zə vē′) *adj., adv.* [Fr.] face to face; opposite —*prep.* 1. face to face with 2. in relation to —*n.* a person or thing opposite, or corresponding to, another

Visc. 1. Viscount 2. Viscountess Also **Vis., Visct.**

vis·cer·a (vis′ər ə) *n.pl., sing.* **vis′cus** (-kəs) [L.] the internal organs of the body, as the heart, lungs, liver, intestines, etc.; specif., in popular usage, the intestines

vis·cer·al (-əl) *adj.* 1. of, like, or affecting the viscera 2. intuitive, emotional, etc. rather than intellectual —**vis′-cer·al·ly** *adv.*

vis·cid (vis′id) *adj.* [< LL. < L. *viscum,* birdlime] being a

cohesive and sticky fluid; viscous —**vis·cid·i·ty** (vi sid′ə tē)
n. —**vis′cid·ly** *adv.*
vis·cose (vis′kōs) *adj.* 1. *same as* VISCOUS 2. of viscose
—*n.* a syruplike solution made by treating cellulose with
sodium hydroxide and carbon disulphide: used in making
cellophane and rayon thread and fabrics (**viscose rayon**)
vis·cos·i·ty (vis kos′ə tē) *n., pl.* **-ties** 1. a viscous quality or
state 2. *Physics* the internal friction of a fluid, caused by
molecular attraction
vis·count (vī′kount) *n.* [< OFr. < ML. *vice comes:* see
VICE- & COUNT²] a nobleman below an earl or count and
above a baron —**vis′count·cy, vis′count·y, vis′count·ship′** *n.*
vis·count·ess (vī′koun tis) *n.* 1. the wife of a viscount 2. a
peeress having the same rank as a viscount
vis·cous (vis′kəs) *adj.* [< LL. < L. *viscum,* birdlime] 1.
being a cohesive and sticky fluid; viscid 2. *Physics* having
viscosity —**vis′cous·ly** *adv.* —**vis′cous·ness** *n.*
vise (vīs) *n., vt.* Chiefly U.S. sp. of VICE³
vi·sé (vē′zā, vē zā′) *n., vt.* **-séed, -sé·ing** [Fr.] *same as* VISA
vis·i·bil·i·ty (viz′ə bil′ə tē) *n., pl.* **-ties** 1. a being visible 2.
a) the relative possibility of being seen under the conditions
of distance, light, and atmosphere that exist at a certain
time *b*) range of vision
vis·i·ble (viz′ə b'l) *adj.* [< OFr. < L. *visibilis* < pp. of
videre, to see] 1. that can be seen 2. that can be
perceived; evident; manifest 3. on hand [*visible* supply]
—**vis′i·ble·ness** *n.* —**vis′i·bly** *adv.*
vi·sion (vizh′ən) *n.* [< OFr. < L. *visio* < pp. of *videre,* to
see] 1. the act or power of seeing 2. *a*) something
supposedly seen by other than normal sight, as in a dream,
trance, etc. *b*) the experience of having seen something in
this way 3. a mental image [*visions* of power] 4. *a*) the
ability to perceive something not actually visible, as through
mental acuteness *b*) force or power of imagination [a
statesman of great *vision*] 5. something or someone of
great beauty —*vt.* to see as in a vision —**vi′sion·al** *adj.*
vi·sion·ar·y (ə r ē) *adj.* 1. of, having the nature of, or seen in
a vision 2. *a*) imaginary *b*) not realistic; impractical, as an
idea 3. seeing or disposed to see visions 4. characterized
by impractical ideas or schemes —*n., pl.* **-ar·ies** 1. a
person who sees visions 2. a person who has impractical
ideas; dreamer
vis·it (viz′it) *vt.* [< OFr. < L. *visitare,* freq. < *visere,* to go
to see < pp. of *videre,* to see] 1. to go or come to see
(someone) out of friendship or for business or professional
reasons 2. to stay with as a guest 3. to go or come to (a
place) as in order to inspect or look at 4. to occur or come
to [*visited* by an odd idea] 5. to come upon or afflict [a
drought *visited* the land] 6. to inflict (punishment,
suffering, etc.) upon (someone) —*vi.* to visit someone or
something; specif., *a*) to make a social call *b*) to stay with
someone as a guest —*n.* a visiting; specif., *a*) a social call
b) a stay as a guest *c*) an official call, as of a doctor,
inspector, etc. —**vis′it·a·ble** *adj.*
vis·i·tant (-ənt) *n.* 1. a visitor 2. a supernatural being
supposedly seen 3. a migratory bird in any of its temporary
resting places —*adj.* [Archaic] visiting
vis·it·a·tion (viz′ə tā′shən) *n.* 1. a visiting; esp., an official
visit as to inspect 2. any trouble looked on as punishment
sent by God —**the Visitation** *R.C.Ch.* 1. the visit of the
Virgin Mary to Elizabeth: Luke 1:39–56 2. a church feast
(July 2) commemorating this —**vis′it·a′tion·al** *adj.*
—**vis·it·a·to·ri·al** (viz′it ə tôr′ē əl), **vis′i·to′ri·al** *adj.*
vis·it·ing card (viz′i tiŋ) a small card with one's name, and
sometimes one's address on it, given to business or social
acquaintances
vis·i·tor (viz′it ər) *n.* a person making a visit
vis·or (vī′zər) *n.* [< Anglo-Fr. < OFr. < *vis,*
a face] 1. *a*) in armour, the movable part
of a helmet that could be lowered to cover
the upper part of the face *b*) a movable
section of safety glass, that is part of a
protective head covering 2. a mask 3. the
projecting brim of a cap, for shading the
eyes 4. an adjustable shade in a car, over
the windscreen, for shading the eyes —**vis′-
ored** *adj.*
vis·ta (vis′tə) *n.* [< It., ult. < L. *videre,* to
see] 1. a view, esp. one seen through a
long passage, as between rows of houses or
trees 2. a comprehensive mental view of a
series of events —**vis′taed** *adj.*
vis·u·al (vizh′oo wəl) *adj.* [< LL. < L. *visus,*
a sight < pp. of *videre,* to see] 1. of,
connected with, based on, or used in seeing
2. that is or can be seen; visible —**vis′u·al·ly**
adv.

VISORS

visual aids films, slides, charts, etc. (but not books) used in
teaching, illustrating lectures, etc.
vis·u·al·ize (vizh′yoo wə līz′, -yoo līz′) *vt.* **-ized, -iz′ing** to
form a mental image of (something not visible) —**vis′-
u·al·i·za′tion** *n.*
vi·tal (vīt′'l) *adj.* [< MFr. < L. < *vita,* life] 1. of or

concerned with life 2. *a*) essential to life [*vital* organs]
b) destroying life; fatal [*vital* wounds] 3. *a*) essential;
indispensable *b*) of crucial importance 4. affecting the
validity, truth, etc. of something [a *vital* error] 5. full of
life and vigour; energetic —*n.* [*pl.*] 1. the vital organs, as
the heart, brain, etc. 2. the essential parts of anything
—**vi′tal·ly** *adv.* —**vi′tal·ness** *n.*
vi·tal·ism (-iz'm) *n.* the doctrine that the life in living
organisms is caused and sustained by a basic force (**vital
force** or **principle**) that is distinct from all physical and
chemical forces —**vi′tal·ist** *n., adj.* —**vi′tal·is′tic** *adj.*
vi·tal·i·ty (vī tal′ə tē) *n., pl.* **-ties** 1. power to live or go on
living 2. power to endure or survive 3. mental or physical
energy; vigour
vi·tal·ize (vīt′əl īz′) *vt.* **-ized, -iz′ing** 1. to make vital; give
life to 2. to give vigour or animation to —**vi′tal·i·za′tion** *n.*
Vi·tal·li·um (vī tal′ē əm) *a trademark for* an alloy of cobalt,
chromium, and molybdenum, used in bone surgery, etc.
vital statistics 1. data on births, deaths, marriages, etc.
2. [Colloq.] the measurements of a woman's bust, waist, and
hips
vi·ta·min (vīt′ə min, vīt-) *n.* [< L. *vita,* life + AMINE: from
the orig. mistaken idea that these substances all contain
amino acids] any of a number of complex organic
substances found variously in foods and essential for the
normal functioning of the body —**vi′ta·min′ic** *adj.*
vitamin A a fat-soluble alcohol found in fish-liver oil, egg
yolk, butter, etc. or derived from carotene in carrots and
other vegetables: a deficiency of this vitamin results in
night blindness: it occurs in two forms, **vitamin A₁**, and
vitamin A₂
vitamin B (complex) a group of unrelated water-soluble
substances, including: *a*) **vitamin B₁** (*see* THIAMINE) *b*)
vitamin B₂ (*see* RIBOFLAVIN) *c*) **vitamin B₆** (*see* PYRIDOXINE)
d) NIACIN *e*) PANTOTHENIC ACID *f*) BIOTIN: also called **vitamin
H** *g*) INOSITOL *h*) PARA-AMINOBENZOIC ACID *i*) CHOLINE *j*)
FOLIC ACID *k*) **vitamin B₁₂** a complex vitamin, essential for
normal growth and used esp. in treating pernicious anaemia
vitamin C *same as* ASCORBIC ACID
vitamin D any of several fat-soluble vitamins occurring in
fish-liver oils, milk, egg yolk, etc.: a deficiency of this
vitamin tends to produce rickets: this group includes
vitamin D₂, vitamin D₃, vitamin D₄, and **vitamin D₅**
vitamin E the tocopherols collectively, necessary for
fertility in some animals
vitamin H *same as* BIOTIN
vitamin K a fat-soluble vitamin that promotes blood
clotting: **vitamin K₁** is found chiefly in alfalfa leaves and
vitamin K₂ chiefly in fish meal: **vitamin K₃** and **vitamin K₄**
are prepared synthetically
vi·tel·lin (vi tel′in, vī-) *n.* [< L. *vitellus,* the yolk of an egg] a
phosphoprotein occurring in the yolks of eggs
vi·tel·lus (vi tel′əs, vī-) *n.* [see prec.] the yolk of an egg
—**vi·tel′line** *adj.*
vi·ti·ate (vish′ē āt′) *vt.* **-at′ed, -at′ing** [< L. pp. of *vitiare* <
vitium, a VICE¹] 1. to make imperfect or faulty; spoil 2. to
weaken morally; debase 3. to make legally ineffective
—**vi′ti·a′tion** *n.* —**vi′ti·a′tor** *n.*
vit·i·cul·ture (vit′ə kul′chər, vīt′-) *n.* [< L. *vitis,* a vine +
CULTURE] the cultivation of grapes —**vit′i·cul′tur·al** *adj.*
—**vit′i·cul′tur·ist** *n.*
vit·re·ous (vit′rē əs) *adj.* [< L. < *vitrum,* glass] 1. *a*) of or
like glass; glassy *b*) derived from or made of glass 2. of the
vitreous humour —**vit′re·ous·ness** *n.*
vitreous body (or **humour**) the transparent, colourless,
jellylike substance that fills the eyeball between the retina
and lens
vit·ri·fy (vit′rə fī′) *vt., vi.* **-fied′, -fy′ing** [< Fr. < L. *vitrum,*
glass + Fr. *-fier,* -FY] to change into glass or a glasslike
substance by fusion due to heat —**vit′ri·fi′a·ble** *adj.* —**vit′-
ri·fi·ca′tion, vit′ri·fac′tion** *n.*
vit·rine (vi trēn′) *n.* [Fr., ult. < L. *vitrum,* glass] a
glass-panelled cabinet for art objects, curios, etc.
vit·ri·ol (vit′rē əl, -ol′) *n.* [< MFr. < ML. *vitriolum* < LL. <
L. *vitreus,* glassy] 1. *a*) any of several sulphates of metals,
as of copper (*blue vitriol*), of iron (*green vitriol*), of zinc
(*white vitriol*), etc. *b*) *same as* SULPHURIC ACID: in full, **oil of
vitriol** 2. sharpness or bitterness, as in speech or writing
vit·ri·ol·ic (vit′rē ol′ik) *adj.* 1. of, like, or derived from a
vitriol 2. extremely biting or caustic [*vitriolic* talk]
vit·ri·ol·ize (vit′rē ə līz′) *vt.* **-ized′, -iz′ing** 1. to convert
into vitriol 2. to subject to the action of vitriol
vit·tle (vit′'l) *n., v.* *obs.* or *dial.* var. of VICTUAL
vi·tu·per·ate (vi tyoo′pə rāt′, vī-) *vt.* **-at′ed, -at′ing** [< L.
pp. of *vituperare* < *vitium,* a fault + *parare,* to make ready]
to speak abusively to or about; berate —**vi·tu′per·a′tion** *n.*
—**vi·tu′per·a′tive** *adj.* —**vi·tu′per·a′tive·ly** *adv.* —**vi·tu′-
per·a′tive·ness** *n.* —**vi·tu′per·a′tor** *n.*
vi·va (vē′və) *n.* [Colloq.] *same as* VIVA VOCE
‡**vi·va** (vē′vä) *interj.* [It., Sp.] (long) live (someone or
something specified)!: an exclamation of praise
vi·va·ce (vi vä′chā) *adj., adv.* [It.] *Music* in a lively, spirited
manner: a direction to the performer

vi·va·cious (vi vā′shəs, vī-) *adj.* [< L. *vivax* (gen. *vivacis*) < *vivere*, to live] full of animation; spirited; lively —**vi·va′·cious·ly** *adv.* —**vi·va′cious·ness** *n.*

vi·vac·i·ty (vi vas′ə tē, vī-) *n.* the quality or state of being vivacious; liveliness; animation

vi·var·i·um (vī ver′ē əm) *n., pl.* **-i·ums, -i·a** (-ə) [L., ult. < *vivere*, to live] an enclosed place for animals to live as if in their natural environment

vi·va vo·ce (vī′və vō′sē, vō′chē) [ML., with living voice] by word of mouth; orally —*n.* an oral examination —**vi′·va-vo′ce** *adj.*

‡**vive** (vēv) *interj.* [Fr.] (long) live (someone or something specified)!: an exclamation of praise

viv·id (viv′id) *adj.* [< L. < *vivere*, to live] 1. full of life; lively; striking [a *vivid* personality] 2. bright; intense: said of colours, light, etc. 3. forming or suggesting clear or striking mental images [a *vivid* imagination, a *vivid* description] 4. clearly perceived, as a recollection —**viv′·id·ly** *adv.* —**viv′id·ness** *n.*

viv·i·fy (viv′ə fī′) *vt.* **-fied′, -fy′ing** [< Fr. < LL. < L. *vivus*, alive + *facere*, to make] 1. to give life to; animate 2. to make more lively, active, striking, etc. —**viv′i·fi·ca′tion** *n.* —**viv′i·fi′er** *n.*

vi·vip·a·rous (vi vip′ər əs, vī-) *adj.* [< L. < *vivus*, alive + *parere*, to produce] bearing living young (as most mammals and some other animals do) instead of laying eggs —**vi·vip′a·rous·ly** *adv.*

viv·i·sect (viv′ə sekt′) *vt., vi.* [< ff.] to practise vivisection (on) —**viv′i·sec′tor** *n.*

viv·i·sec·tion (viv′ə sek′shən) *n.* [< L. *vivus*, alive + SECTION] medical research consisting of surgical operations or other experiments done on living animals to study the living organs and to investigate the effects of diseases and therapy —**viv′i·sec′tion·al** *adj.*

viv·i·sec·tion·ist (-ist) *n.* a person who practises or favours the practice of vivisection for the good of science

vix·en (vik′s'n) *n.* [ME. *fixen* < OE. *fyxe*, she-fox] 1. a female fox 2. an ill-tempered, shrewish woman —**vix′·en·ish** *adj.* —**vix′en·ish·ly** *adv.*

viz., viz (viz; *often read* "namely") [ML., altered < contr. for L. *videlicet*] videlicet; that is; namely

viz·ard (viz′ərd) *n.* [altered < *visar*, var. of VISOR] a mask, as for disguise

vi·zier (vi zē′ər, viz′yər) *n.* [< Turk. , Ar. *wazīr*, lit., bearer of burdens < *wazara*, to bear a burden] in Moslem countries, a high officer in the government; esp., a minister of state: also sp. **vi·zir′** —**vi·zier′ate** (-it, -āt), **vi·zier′ship** *n.* —**vi·zier′i·al** *adj.*

viz·or (vī′zər) *n. alt. sp. of* VISOR

vizs·la (vēz′lə) *n.* [Hung.] a Hungarian hunting dog with a short, rusty-gold coat

VJ Victory over Japan —**V-J Day** the day on which the fighting with Japan officially ended in World War II (Aug. 15, 1945) or the day of formal surrender (Sept. 2, 1945)

VL. Vulgar Latin

vlei (flā, vlā) *n.* [< Du. dial.] in South Africa, an area of low, marshy ground

VLF, V.L.F., vlf, v.l.f. very low frequency

V-neck (vē′nek′) *n.* a neckline V-shaped in front

voc. vocative

vocab. vocabulary

vo·ca·ble (vō′kə b'l) *n.* [Fr. < L. *vocabulum* < *vocare*, to call] a word; esp., a word regarded as a unit of sounds or letters rather than as a unit of meaning

vo·cab·u·lar·y (vō kab′yə lər ē, və-) *n., pl.* **-lar·ies** [< ML. < L. *vocabulum*, a word: see prec.] 1. a list of words, usually arranged in alphabetical order and defined or otherwise identified, as in a dictionary or glossary 2. all the words of a language, 3. *a)* all the words used by a particular person, class, profession, etc. *b)* all the words recognised and understood by a particular person, even if not used by him

vo·cal (vō′k'l) *adj.* [< L. *vocalis* < *vox* (gen. *vocis*), a voice] 1. *a)* uttered by the voice; esp., spoken; oral [*vocal* sounds] *b)* sung or to be sung [*vocal* music] 2. having a voice; able to speak or make oral sounds 3. of, used in, connected with, or belonging to the voice [*vocal* organs] 4. full of voices 5. speaking freely or strongly —*n.* 1. a vocal sound 2. the part of a popular song that is sung, as distinguished from the parts played by the instruments —**vo′cal·ly** *adv.*

vocal cords either of two pairs of membranous cords or folds in the larynx, consisting of a thicker upper pair (**false vocal cords**) and a lower pair (**true vocal cords**): voice is produced when air from the lungs causes the lower (true) cords to vibrate

vo·cal·ic (vō kal′ik) *adj.* 1. *a)* of, or having the nature of, a vowel *b)* composed mainly or entirely of vowels 2. producing or involving vowel change —**vo·cal′i·cal·ly** *adv.*

vo·cal·ism (vō′k'l iz'm) *n.* 1. the use of the voice 2. the act or art of singing 3. *a)* a vowel system *b)* a vowel

vo·cal·ist (vō′k'l ist) *n.* a singer

vo·cal·ize (vō′k'l īz′) *vt.* **-ized′, -iz′ing** 1. *a)* to give utterance to; express with the voice *b)* to make capable of vocal expression 2. *Phonet. a)* to change into or use as a

vowel *b)* to voice —*vi.* to make vocal sounds; speak or sing; specif., to do a singing exercise, using various vowel sounds —**vo′cal·i·za′tion** *n.* —**vo′cal·iz′er** *n.*

vo·ca·tion (vō kā′shən) *n.* [< LL. < L. < *vocare*, to call] 1. *a)* a call or will to carry on some work or enter a certain career, esp. a religious one *b)* the work or career towards which one believes oneself to be called 2. any trade, profession, or occupation

vo·ca·tion·al (-'l) *adj.* 1. of a vocation, trade, occupation, etc. 2. designating or of education, training, etc. intended to prepare one for an occupation, sometimes specif. in a trade —**vo·ca′tion·al·ism** *n.* —**vo·ca′tion·al·ly** *adv.*

vocational guidance the work of testing and interviewing persons in order to guide them towards the choice of a suitable vocation

voc·a·tive (vok′ə tiv) *adj.* [< OFr. < L. < pp. of *vocare*, to call < *vox*, the voice] *Gram.* in certain inflected languages, designating or of the case indicating the person or things addressed —*n.* 1. the vocative case 2. a word in this case —**voc′a·tive·ly** *adv.*

vo·cif·er·ate (vō sif′ə rāt′) *vt., vi.* **-at′ed, -at′ing** [< L. pp. of *vociferari* < *vox*, voice + *ferre*, to bear] to utter or shout loudly or vehemently; bawl; clamour —**vo·cif′er·ant** (-ər ənt) *adj.* —**vo·cif′er·a′tion** *n.* —**vo·cif′er·a′tor** *n.*

vo·cif·er·ous (vō sif′ər əs) *adj.* loud, noisy, or vehement in making one's feelings known; clamorous —**vo·cif′er·ous·ly** *adv.* —**vo·cif′er·ous·ness** *n.*

vod·ka (vod′kə) *n.* [Russ., dim. of *voda*, water] a colourless spirit distilled from wheat, rye, etc.

voe (vō) *n.* [< ON. *vagr*] in Orkney and Shetland, a creek, inlet, or bay

vogue (vōg) *n.* [Fr., a fashion, lit., a rowing < *voguer*, to row < MLowG.] 1. the accepted fashion at any particular time; mode: often with *the* 2. general acceptance; popularity —*adj.* in vogue: also **vogu·ish** (vō′gish)

voice (vois) *n.* [< OFr. < L. < *vox* (gen. *vocis*)] 1. sound made through the mouth, esp. by human beings in talking, singing, etc. 2. the ability to make such sounds [to lose one's *voice*] 3. any sound, influence, etc. regarded as like vocal utterance [the *voice* of the sea, the *voice* of one's conscience] 4. a specified or distinctive quality of vocal sound [an angry *voice*] 5. *a)* an expressed wish, choice, opinion, etc. [the *voice* of the people] *b)* the right to express one's choice, opinion, etc.; vote 6. utterance or expression [giving *voice* to his joy] 7. the means by which something is expressed [a newspaper known to be the *voice* of the administration] 8. *Gram.* a form of a verb showing the connection between the subject and the verb, either as performing (**active voice**) or receiving (**passive voice**) the action 9. *Music a)* the quality of a person's singing [a good *voice*] *b)* a singer *c)* any of the individual parts sung or played together in a musical composition 10. *Phonet.* sound made by vibrating the vocal cords with air forced from the lungs, as in pronouncing all vowels and such consonants as (b), (d), (g), (m), etc. —*vt.* voiced, voic′ing 1. to utter or express in words 2. *Music* to regulate the tone of (organ pipes, etc.) 3. *Phonet.* to utter with voice —**in voice** with the voice in good condition, as for singing —**with one voice** unanimously —**voic′er** *n.*

voiced (voist) *adj.* 1. having a voice 2. having (a specified kind of) voice [deep-*voiced*] 3. expressed by the voice 4. *Phonet.* made by vibrating the vocal cords with air forced from the lungs: said of certain consonants

voice·less (vois′lis) *adj.* 1. having no voice; mute 2. not speaking or spoken 3. *Phonet.* uttered without voice [p, t, k, etc. are *voiceless* consonants] —**voice′less·ly** *adv.* —**voice′less·ness** *n.*

voice-o·ver (-ō′vər) *n.* the voice commenting or narrating off camera, as for a television commercial

voice print (-print′) *n.* a pattern of wavy lines and whorls recorded by a device actuated by the sound of a person's voice and supposedly distinctive for each individual, like a fingerprint

void (void) *adj.* [< OFr., ult. < L. *vacivus* < *vacare*, to be empty] 1. not occupied; vacant: said of a position or office 2. *a)* having nothing in it; empty *b)* lacking; devoid (*of*) [*void* of sense] 3. useless; ineffective 4. *Law* of no legal force; not binding; invalid —*n.* 1. an empty space or vacuum 2. *a)* total absence of something normally present *b)* a feeling of emptiness or loss —*vt.* 1. *a)* to empty (the contents of something) *b)* to discharge (urine or faeces) 2. to make void; annul —*vi.* to defecate or, esp., to urinate —**void′a·ble** *adj.* —**void′er** *n.*

‡**voi·là** (vwà lá′) [Fr., see there] behold; there it is: often used as an interjection

voile (voil) *n.* [Fr., a veil] a thin, sheer fabric, as of cotton

vol. 1. volcano 2. *pl.* vols. volume 3. volunteer

vo·lant (vō′lənt) *adj.* [Fr. < L. prp. of *volare*, to fly] 1. flying or capable of flying 2. nimble; quick 3. *Heraldry* represented as flying

vo·lar (vō′lər) *adj.* [< L. *vola*, the hollow of hand or foot] *Anat.* of the palm of the hand or sole of the foot

vol·a·tile (vol′ə til) *adj.* [MFr. < L. < *volare*, to fly] 1.

vaporizing or evaporating quickly, as alcohol **2.** *a*) unstable or explosive [a *volatile* social condition] *b*) moving capriciously from one idea, interest, etc. to another; fickle *c*) not lasting long; fleeting —**vol′a·til′i·ty** (-til′ə tē), **vol′a-tile·ness** *n.*

vo·lat·i·lize (vo lat′ə līz′) *vt., vi.* **-ized′, -iz′ing** to make or become volatile; evaporate —**vol′a·til·i·za′tion** *n.*

‡**vol-au-vent** (vôl ō von′) *n.* [Fr., lit., flight in the wind] a puff-pastry case with a filling of meat, fish, etc. in a thick sauce

vol·can·ic (vol kan′ik) *adj.* **1.** of, from, or produced by a volcano **2.** having volcanoes **3.** like a volcano; likely to explode; violent —**vol·can′i·cal·ly** *adv.*

vol·can·ism (vol′kə niz′m) *n.* volcanic activity or phenomena

vol·ca·no (vol kā′nō) *n., pl.* **-noes, -nos** [It. < L. *Volcanus*, Vulcan: the god of fire in Roman myth.] **1.** a vent in the earth's crust through which molten rock (*lava*), rock fragments, gases, ashes, etc. erupt or burst from the earth's interior **2.** a cone-shaped hill or mountain, chiefly of volcanic materials, built up around the vent, usually so as to form a crater

vol·can·ol·o·gy (vol′kə nol′ə jē) *n.* [VOLCANO + -LOGY] the science dealing with volcanoes and volcanic activity —**vol′-can·o·log′i·cal** *adj.* —**vol′can·ol′o·gist** *n.*

vole (vōl) *n.* [earlier *vole mouse* < Scand., as in Norw. *voll*, field + MOUSE] any of a number of small rodents with a stout body and short tail

vo·li·tion (vō lish′ən, və-) *n.* [Fr. < ML. *volitio*, ult. < L. *velle*, to will] **1.** the act or power of using the will **2.** a conscious or deliberate decision —**vo·li′tion·al** *adj.*

vol·i·tive (vol′ə tiv) *adj.* **1.** of the will **2.** *Gram.* expressing a wish, as a verb, mood, etc.

vol·ley (vol′ē) *n., pl.* **-leys** [MFr. *volee*, ult. < L. pp. of *volare*, to fly] **1.** *a*) the simultaneous discharge of a number of guns or other weapons *b*) the missiles discharged in this way **2.** a burst of words or acts suggestive of this [a *volley* of curses] **3.** *Sports a*) the flight of a ball, etc. before it touches the ground *b*) a return of a ball, etc. before it touches the ground *c*) loosely, any extended exchange of shots, as in tennis, esp. in warming up —*vt., vi.* **-leyed, -ley·ing 1.** to discharge or be discharged as in a volley **2.** *Sports* to return (the ball, etc.) as a volley; engage in a volley —**vol′ley·er** *n.*

vol·ley·ball (-bôl′) *n.* **1.** a game played on a court by two teams who hit a large, light, inflated ball back and forth over a high net with the hands, each team trying to return the ball before it touches the ground **2.** this ball

vol·plane (vol′plān′) *vi.* **-planed′, -plan′ing** [Fr. *vol plané* < *voler*, to fly + *plané*, pp. of *planer*, to glide] to glide down as or in an aircraft with the engine cut off —*n.* such a glide

vols. volumes

volt[1] (vōlt) *n.* [< Fr. < It. < L. pp. of *volvere*, to turn] **1.** a turning movement of a horse, sideways around a centre **2.** *Fencing* a leap to avoid a thrust Also **volte**

volt[2] (vōlt) *n.* [after A. Volta (1745-1827), It. physicist] the SI unit of electromotive force or difference in potential; the potential difference between two points on a conductor carrying a constant current of one ampere and dissipating one watt of power

volt·age (vōl′tij) *n.* electromotive force, or difference in electrical potential, expressed in volts

vol·ta·ic (vol tā′ik) *adj.* **1.** designating or of electricity produced by chemical action; galvanic **2.** used in so producing electricity

voltaic battery 1. a battery composed of voltaic cells **2.** same as VOLTAIC CELL

voltaic cell a device for producing an electric current by the action of two plates of different metals in an electrolyte

volt·am·e·ter (vol tam′ə tər) *n.* an electrolytic cell for measuring an electric current by the amount of gas liberated or metal deposited from an electrolyte

volt·am·me·ter (vōlt′am′mēt′ər) *n.* an instrument for measuring either voltage or amperage

volt-am·pere (-am′per) *n.* a unit of electric power equal to the product of one volt and one ampere

‡**volte-face** (vôlt fás′) *n.* [Fr. < It. *volta faccia* < *volta*, a turn & *faccia*, face] a sudden reversal of opinion or direction; about-face

volt·me·ter (vōlt′mēt′ər) *n.* an instrument for measuring voltage

vol·u·ble (vol′yoo b'l) *adj.* [Fr. < L. *volubilis* < pp. of *volvere*, to roll] talking very much and easily; talkative, glib, etc. —**vol′u·bil′i·ty** *n.* —**vol′u·bly** *adv.*

vol·ume (vol′yoom, -yəm) *n.* [MFr. < L. *volumen*, a scroll < pp. of *volvere*, to roll] **1.** orig., a roll of parchment, a scroll, etc. **2.** *a*) a collection of written or printed sheets bound together; book *b*) any of the books of a set **3.** a set of the issues of a periodical over a fixed period of time, usually a year **4.** the amount of space occupied in three dimensions; cubic contents **5.** *a*) a quantity, bulk, mass, or amount *b*) a large quantity **6.** the strength or loudness of sound **7.**

Music fullness of tone —**speak volumes** to be very meaningful

vol·u·met·ric (vol′yoo met′rik) *adj.* of or based on the measurement of volume: also **vol′u·met′ri·cal** —**vol′u·met′-ri·cal·ly** *adv.*

vo·lu·mi·nous (və loo′mə nəs; və lyoo′-) *adj.* **1.** writing, producing, or consisting of enough to fill volumes **2.** of great volume; large; bulky; full —**vo·lu′mi·nos′i·ty** (-nos′ə tē) *n.* —**vo·lu′mi·nous·ly** *adv.*

vol·un·tar·y (vol′ən tər ē, -trē) *adj.* [< L. < *voluntas*, free will, ult. < *velle*, to will] **1.** brought about by one's own free choice; given or done of one's own free will **2.** acting willingly or of one's own accord [a *voluntary* guide] **3.** controlled by the will [*voluntary* muscles] **4.** having free will or the power of free choice [man is a *voluntary* agent] **5.** *a*) supported by freewill contributions *b*) done by, or composed of, volunteers rather than people paid or conscripted [a *voluntary* organisation] **6.** *Law* acting or done without legal obligation or compulsion —*n., pl.* **-tar·ies** an organ solo played for a church service —**vol′-un·tar′i·ly** (-ə lē, vol′ən ter′-) *adv.*

Voluntary Service Overseas a British organisation which provides skilled volunteers to help in underdeveloped areas of the world

vol·un·teer (vol′ən tir′) *n.* [< obs. Fr. *volontaire*, a voluntary] **1.** a person who offers to do something of his own free will **2.** a person who enlists in the armed forces of his own free will —*adj.* **1.** of or made up of volunteers **2.** serving as a volunteer **3.** *same as* VOLUNTARY —*vt.* to offer or give of one's own free will —*vi.* to enter or offer to enter into any service of one's own free will; enlist

vo·lup·tu·ar·y (və lup′tyoo wər ē) *n., pl.* **-ar·ies** [see ff.] a person devoted to luxurious living and sensual pleasures —*adj.* of or characterized by luxury and sensual pleasures

vo·lup·tu·ous (-tyoo wəs) *adj.* [< L. < *voluptas*, pleasure] **1.** full of, producing, or characterized by sensual pleasures **2.** fond of luxury, the pleasures of the senses, etc. **3.** suggesting, or arising from, sensual pleasure **4.** sexually attractive because of a full, shapely figure —**vo·lup′tu·ous·ly** *adv.* —**vo·lup′tu·ous·ness** *n.*

vo·lute (və loot′) *n.* [< L. < pp. of *volvere*, to roll] **1.** a spiral or twisting form; whorl **2.** *Archit.* a spiral scroll, as of an Ionic capital **3.** *Zool.* any of the whorls of a spiral shell —*adj.* spiralled: also **vo·lut′ed** —**vo·lu′tion** *n.*

vo·mer (vō′mər) *n.* [L., a ploughshare] *Anat.* a thin, flat bone separating the nasal passages

vom·it (vom′it) *n.* [< L. < pp. of *vomere*] matter thrown up from the stomach —*vi., vt.* **1.** to throw up (the contents of the stomach) through the mouth **2.** to throw out or be thrown out with force; belch forth —**vom′it·er** *n.*

vom·i·tive (-ə tiv) *adj.* of or causing vomiting; emetic

vom·i·to·ry (vom′ə tər ē) *adj.* [L. *vomitorius*] [Archaic] emetic —*n.* **1.** an emetic **2.** in a Roman amphitheatre, a passage for entrance and exit

‡**von** (fôn; *E.* von) *prep.* [G.] of; from: a prefix occurring in many names of German and Austrian families, esp. of the nobility

voo·doo (voo′doo) *n., pl.* **-doos** [Creole Fr. < a WAfr. word] **1.** a primitive religion based on a belief in sorcery, fetishism, etc.: it originated in Africa and is still practised, chiefly by natives of the West Indies **2.** a person who practises voodoo **3.** a voodoo charm, fetish, etc. —*adj.* of voodoos or their practices, beliefs, etc. —*vt.* to affect by voodoo magic —**voo′doo·ism** *n.* —**voo′doo·ist** *n.* —**voo′-doo·is′tic** *adj.*

vo·ra·cious (vô rā′shəs, və-) *adj.* [L. *vorax* (gen. *voracis*) < *vorare*, to devour] **1.** greedy in eating; ravenous; gluttonous **2.** very greedy or eager in some desire or pursuit [a *voracious* reader] —**vo·ra′cious·ly** *adv.* —**vo·rac′-i·ty** (-ras′ə tē), **vo·ra′cious·ness** *n.*

-vo·rous (və rəs) [< L. < *vorare*, to devour] a combining form meaning feeding on, eating [omnivorous]

vor·tex (vôr′teks) *n., pl.* **-tex·es, vor′ti·ces′** (-tə sēz′) [L. < *vertere*, to turn] **1.** a whirling mass of water forming a vacuum at its centre, into which anything caught in the motion is drawn; whirlpool **2.** a whirl of air; whirlwind **3.** any activity, situation, etc. that is like a whirlpool in its rush, engulfing effect, catastrophic power, etc. —**vor′ti·cal** *adj.* —**vor′ti·cal·ly** *adv.*

vor·ti·cel·la (vôr′tə sel′ə) *n., pl.* **-cel′lae** (-ē) [ModL. < L. *vortex*: see prec.] any of a genus of one-celled aquatic animals, with a bell-shaped body on a thin, contractile stem

vo·ta·ry (vōt′ə rē) *n., pl.* **-ries** [< L. pp. of *vovere*, to vow + -ARY] **1.** *a*) a person bound by religious vows, as a monk *b*) a devout worshipper **2.** a devoted supporter; one who is devoted to some cause or interest Also **vo′ta·rist** —**vo′-ta·ress** (-ris) *n.fem.*

vote (vōt) *n.* [L. *votum*, a vow < pp. of *vovere*, to vow] **1.** a decision on a proposal, etc., or a choice between candidates for office **2.** *a*) the expression of such a decision or choice *b*) the ballot, voice, etc. by which it is expressed **3.** the right to exercise such a decision, etc.; suffrage **4.** *a*) votes collectively *b*) a specified group of voters, or their votes [the Scottish *vote*] **5.** [Archaic] a voter —*vi.* **vot′ed,** **vot′ing** to express preference in a matter by ballot, etc. —*vt.* **1.** *a*) to decide, choose, enact, or authorize by vote *b*) to confer by vote *c*) to support (a specified party) in voting **2.** to declare by general opinion **3.** [Colloq.] to suggest (often with *that*) —**vote down** to defeat by voting —**vote in** to elect —**vote out** to defeat (an incumbent) in an election —**vote′less** *adj.*

vot·er (vōt′ər) *n.* a person who has a right to vote; elector, esp. one who actually votes

voting machine a machine on which the votes in an election are cast, registered, and counted

vo·tive (vōt′iv) *adj.* [L. *votivus* < *votum:* see VOTE] given, done, etc. in fulfilment of a vow [*votive* offerings]

vouch (vouch) *vt.* [< OFr. < L. *vocare,* to call < *vox,* a voice] to uphold by demonstration or evidence —*vi.* **1.** to give assurance, a guarantee, etc. (with *for*) [to *vouch* for his honesty] **2.** to serve as evidence or assurance (*for*)

vouch·er (vou′chər) *n.* **1.** a person who vouches, as for the truth of a statement **2.** a paper giving evidence of or attesting to the expenditure or receipt of money, the accuracy of an account, etc. **3.** a ticket or card entitling the holder to receive goods or services of a specific value [a luncheon *voucher*]

vouch·safe (vouch sāf′) *vt.* **-safed′, -saf′ing** [< ME. *vouchen safe,* to vouch as safe] to be kind or gracious enough to give or grant —**vouch·safe′ment** *n.*

vous·soir (vōō swär′) *n.* [Fr. < OFr., ult. < L. pp. of *volvere,* to roll] *Archit.* any of the wedge-shaped stones of which an arch or vault is built

vow (vou) *n.* [< OFr. < L. *votum:* see VOTE] a solemn promise or pledge, as one made to God or with God as one's witness, binding oneself to an act, way of life, etc. [marriage *vows*] **2.** a solemn affirmation —*vt.* **1.** to promise solemnly **2.** to swear solemnly to do, get, etc. **3.** to declare in a forceful or earnest way —*vi.* to make a vow —**take vows** to enter a religious order —**vow′er** *n.*

vow·el (vou′əl, voul) *n.* [< MFr. < L. *vocalis* (*littera*), vocal (letter) < *vox,* a voice] **1.** any speech sound made by letting the voiced breath pass in a continuous stream through the pharynx and opened mouth **2.** a letter, as *a, e, i, o, u,* and sometimes *y,* representing such a sound —*adj.* of a vowel or vowels

vow·el·ize (vou′ə līz′) *vt.* **-ized′, -iz′ing** to add vowel points to [to *vowelize* a Hebrew text] —**vow′el·i·za′tion** *n.*

‡**vox** (voks) *n., pl.* **vo·ces** (vō′sēz) [L.] voice

‡**vox pop·u·li** (pop′yōō lī′) [L.] the voice of the people; public opinion or sentiment: abbrev. **vox pop.**

voy·age (voi′ij) *n.* [< OFr. < L. *viaticum,* provision for a journey < *via,* way] **1.** a relatively long journey by water or, formerly, by land **2.** a journey by aircraft or spacecraft —*vi.* **-aged, -ag·ing** to make a voyage; travel —*vt.* to sail or travel over or on —**voy′ag·er** *n.*

‡**vo·ya·geur** (vwä yä zhër′) *n., pl.* **-geurs** (-zhër′) [Fr.] in Canada, **1.** formerly, a person who transported goods and men for the fur companies **2.** any woodsman or boatman of the wilds

vo·yeur (vwä yur′) *n.* [Fr. < *voir,* to see] a person who has an exaggerated interest in viewing sexual objects or activities to obtain sexual gratification; peeping Tom —**vo·yeur′ism** *n.* —**vo′yeur·is′tic** *adj.*

V.P., VP Vice-President
V.R.D. Volunteer Reserve Decoration
V.Rev. Very Reverend
vs. versus
V.S. veterinary surgeon
v.s. [L. *vide supra*] see above
V-shaped (vē′shāpt′) *adj.* shaped like the letter V
V.S.O. Voluntary Service Overseas
V.S.O.P. very superior (or special) old pale: said of brandy
vt., v.t. transitive verb
VTOL [*v*(*ertical*) *t*(*ake*)*o*(*ff* and) *l*(*anding*)] an aircraft,

usually other than a helicopter, that can take off and land vertically

V-type engine (vē′tīp′) an internal combustion engine in which the cylinders are set at an angle in two banks forming a V

vul·can·ite (vul′kə nīt′) *n.* [< *Vulcan,* in Rom. myth. the god of fire and metalworking, & -ITE] a hard rubber made by treating crude rubber with a large amount of sulphur and subjecting it to intense heat; ebonite: used in combs, electrical insulation, etc.

vul·can·ize (-nīz′) *vt., vi.* **-ized′, -iz′ing** [see prec.] to treat (crude rubber) with sulphur and subject it to heat in order to increase its strength and elasticity —**vul′can·iz′-a·ble** *adj.* —**vul′can·i·za′tion** *n.* —**vul′can·iz′er** *n.*

Vulg. Vulgate

vul·gar (vul′gər) *adj.* [< L. *vulgaris* < *vulgus,* the common people] **1.** of the great mass of people in general; common; popular [a *vulgar* superstition] **2.** of or in the vernacular **3.** *a*) characterized by a lack of culture, refinement, taste, etc.; crude; boorish *b*) indecent or obscene —**vul′gar·ly** *adv.* —**vul′gar·ness** *n.*

vulgar fraction *same as* SIMPLE FRACTION

vul·gar·i·an (vul ger′ē ən) *n.* a vulgar person; esp., a rich person with coarse, showy manners or tastes

vul·gar·ism (vul′gər iz′m) *n.* **1.** a word, phrase, etc. that is used widely but is regarded as nonstandard, coarse, or obscene **2.** vulgar behaviour, quality, etc.; vulgarity

vul·gar·i·ty (vul gar′ə tē) *n.* **1.** the state or quality of being vulgar, crude, etc. **2.** *pl.* **-ties** a vulgar act, habit, usage in speech, etc.

vul·gar·ize (vul′gə rīz′) *vt.* **-ized′, -iz′ing** to make vulgar; specif., *a*) to make coarse, crude, etc. *b*) to popularize —**vul′gar·i·za′tion** *n.* —**vul′gar·iz′er** *n.*

Vulgar Latin the everyday speech of the Roman people, from which the Romance languages developed

Vul·gate (vul′gāt, -git) *n.* [ML. *vulgata* (*editio*), popular (edition)] **1.** a Latin version of the Bible prepared in the 4th cent., serving as an authorized version of the Roman Catholic Church **2.** [v-] *a*) any text in common acceptance *b*) the vernacular, or common speech —*adj.* **1.** of or in the Vulgate **2.** [v-] *a*) commonly accepted *b*) of or in the vernacular

vul·ner·a·ble (vul′nər ə b'l) *adj.* [< LL. < L. *vulnerare,* to wound < *vulnus* (gen. *vulneris*), a wound] **1.** that can be wounded or physically injured **2.** *a*) open to, or easily hurt by, criticism or attack *b*) affected by a specified influence, etc. [*vulnerable* to political pressure] **3.** open to attack by armed forces **4.** *Bridge* open to increased penalties or increased bonuses: said of a team which has won one game —**vul′ner·a·bil′i·ty** *n.* —**vul′ner·a·bly** *adv.*

vul·ner·ar·y (vul′nə rər ē) *adj.* [L. *vulnerarius* < *vulnus:* see prec.] used for healing wounds —*n.* any vulnerary drug, plant, etc.

vul·pine (vul′pīn, -pin) *adj.* [< L. < *vulpes,* a fox] **1.** of or like a fox or foxes **2.** clever, cunning, etc.

vul·ture (vul′chər) *n.* [L. *vultur*] **1.** a large bird related to the eagles and hawks, with a naked head: vultures feed on carrion **2.** a greedy, ruthless person who preys on others —**vul′tur·ous** *adj.*

vul·va (vul′və) *n., pl.* **-vae** (-vē), **-vas** [ModL. < L., womb] the external genital organs of the female —**vul′val, vul′var** *adj.* —**vul′vate** (-vāt, -vit) *adj.*

vv. **1.** verses **2.** violins
v.v. vice versa
vy·ing (vī′iŋ) *adj.* that vies; that competes

VULTURE
(to 80 cm long; wingspread to 1.8 m)

W

W, w (dub′'l yōō, -yə) *n., pl.* **W's, w's** **1.** the twenty-third letter of the English alphabet **2.** the sound of *W* or *w*
W **1.** *Chem.* tungsten **2.** *Physics the symbol for* watt
W, W., w, w. **1.** west **2.** western
W. **1.** Wales **2.** Welsh **3.** women's (size)
W., w. **1.** weight **2.** width **3.** won
w. **1.** week(s) **2.** wide **3.** wife **4.** with
W.A. Western Australia
Waac (wak) *n.* a member of the Women's Army Auxiliary Corps
WAAC Women's Army Auxiliary Corps

Waaf (waf) *n.* a member of the Women's Auxiliary Air Force
WAAF Women's Auxiliary Air Force
wab·ble (wob′'l) *n., vt., vi.* **-bled, -bling** *var. of* WOBBLE
wack·y (wak′ē) *adj.* **wack′i·er, wack′i·est** [< ? WHACK + -Y²] [Slang] odd, silly, or crazy —**wack′i·ly** *adv.* —**wack′i·ness** *n.*
wad (wod) *n.* [ML. *wadda,* wadding < ?] **1.** a small, soft mass or ball, as a handful of cottonwool, crumpled paper, etc. **2.** a lump or small, compact mass [a *wad* of chewing tobacco] **3.** a mass of soft material used for padding,

packing, etc. **4.** a plug stuffed against a charge to keep it firmly in place, as in a muzzleloading gun **5.** a roll or bundle, esp. of bank notes —*vt.* **wad′ded, wad′ding** **1.** to compress, or roll up, into a wad **2.** to plug or stuff with a wad **3.** to pad with wadding **4.** to hold (a charge) in place by a wad —**wad′der** *n.*

wad·ding (wod′iŋ) *n.* any soft material for use in padding, packing, stuffing, etc.; esp., cotton made up into loose, fluffy sheets

wad·dle (wod′'l) *vi.* **-dled, -dling** [freq. of WADE] to walk with short steps, swaying from side to side, as a duck —*n.* **1.** the act of waddling **2.** a waddling gait —**wad′dler** *n.*

wad·dy (wod′ē) *n.* [< Abor., ? < E. WOOD] [Aust.] **1.** a heavy wooden club used by Australian aborigines **2.** a stick

wade (wād) *vi.* **wad′ed, wad′ing** [OE. *waden*, to go] **1.** to walk through a substance, as water, mud, tall grass, etc., that slows one down **2.** to walk and splash about in shallow water in play **3.** to make one's way with difficulty [to *wade* through a book] **4.** [Colloq.] to start or attack with vigour (with *in* or *into*) —*vt.* to go across or through by wading —*n.* an act of wading —**wad′a·ble** *adj.*

wad·er (wād′ər) *n.* **1.** a person or thing that wades **2.** same as WADING BIRD **3.** *a)* [*pl.*] high waterproof boots *b)* [*usually pl.*] waterproof trousers with bootlike parts for the feet, worn by fishermen

wa·di (wod′ē) *n., pl.* **-dis, -dies** [Ar. *wādī*] in Arabia, N Africa, etc., **1.** a valley, ravine, etc. that is dry except during the rainy season **2.** the rush of water that flows through it Also sp. **wa′dy**, *pl.* **-dies**

wading bird any of various unrelated, long-legged birds that wade in shallow water and marshes for food, as the crane, heron, and flamingo

wa·fer (wā′fər) *n.* [< ONormFr. *waufre* < MDu. *wafel*] **1.** *a)* a thin, crisp sweetened biscuit *b)* anything resembling this **2.** a thin cake of unleavened bread used in the Eucharist **3.** a small disc of sticky paper, used as a seal on letters, documents, etc.

waf·fle[1] (wof′'l) *n.* [Du. *wafel*] a crisp batter cake with small, square hollows, baked in a waffle iron

waf·fle[2] (wof′'l) *vi.* **-fled, -fling** [orig., to yelp < echoic *waff*, to yelp] [Colloq.] to speak or write in a wordy, vague, or indecisive manner —*n.* [Colloq.] talk or writing of this kind —**waf′fling** *adj.*

waffle iron a utensil or appliance for cooking waffles, having two flat, studded plates pressed together so that the waffle bakes between them

waft (waft, woft) *vt.* [< obs. *wafter*, a convoy < Du. *wachter*, lit., a watcher] **1.** to carry or move (objects, sounds, etc.) lightly through the air or over water **2.** to transport as if in this manner —*vi.* **1.** to float, as in the air **2.** to blow gently: said of breezes —*n.* **1.** an odour, sound, etc. carried through the air **2.** a puff or gust of wind **3.** a wafting movement **4.** *Naut.* formerly, a flag hoisted furled as a signal —**waft′er** *n.*

wag[1] (wag) *vt.* **wagged, wag′ging** [prob. < ON. *vaga*, to rock] **1.** *a)* to cause to move rapidly back and forth, up and down, etc. [the dog *wagged* his tail] *b)* to shake (a finger) or nod (the head), as in reproving, etc. **2.** to move (the tongue) in talking, esp. in idle gossip —*vi.* **1.** to move rapidly back and forth, up and down, etc. **2.** to keep moving in talk: said of the tongue —*n.* the act or an instance of wagging —**wag′ger** *n.*

wag[2] (wag) *n.* [prob. < obs. *waghalter*, a gallows bird, rogue] a comical or humorous person; joker; wit

wage (wāj) *vt.* **waged, wag′ing** [< ONormFr. *wagier* < *wage* (OFr. *gage*), a pledge < Frank.] to engage in or carry on (a war, campaign, etc.) —*n.* **1.** [often *pl.*] money paid to an employee for work done, usually on an hourly, daily, weekly or piecework basis **2.** [*usually pl.*, *formerly with sing. v.*] what is given in return; recompense; requital ["The *wages* of sin is death"]

wage earner **1.** a person who works for wages **2.** someone who supports, or helps to support, a household by earning money

wa·ger (wā′jər) *n.* [< ONormFr.: see WAGE] same as BET (*n.* 1, 2) —*vt., vi.* same as BET —**wager of battle** a challenge by a defendant to prove his innocence by personal combat —**wa′ger·er** *n.*

wag·ger·y (wag′ər ē) *n., pl.* **-ger·ies** **1.** roguish humour or merriment **2.** a joke; esp., a practical joke

wag·gish (-ish) *adj.* **1.** of or like a wag; roguishly merry **2.** playful; jesting [a *waggish* remark] —**wag′gish·ly** *adv.*

wag·gle (wag′'l) *vt.* **-gled, -gling** [freq. of WAG[1]] to wag, esp. with short, quick movements —*vi.* to wobble —*n.* the act of waggling —**wag′gly** *adj.*

Wag·ne·ri·an (väg nir′ē ən) *adj.* **1.** of or like Richard Wagner or his music, theories, etc. **2.** designating or of a soprano, tenor, etc. specializing in Wagner's operas —*n.* an admirer of Wagner's music, theories, etc.

wag·on, wag·gon (wag′ən) *n.* [Du. *wagen*] **1.** a four-wheeled vehicle for hauling heavy loads **2.** a railway goods vehicle, esp. an open one **3.** [Colloq.] a lorry —*vt., vi.* to carry or move (goods in a wagon) —**hitch one's**

wagon to a star **1.** to set oneself an ambitious goal **2.** to attach oneself to a person of greater importance, rank, etc. —**on** (or **off**) **the wagon** [Slang] no longer (or once again) drinking alcohol

wag·on·er, wag·gon·er (-ər) *n.* a person who drives a wagon

wag·on·ette, wag·gon·ette (wag′ə net′) *n.* [dim. of WAGON] a four-wheeled carriage with two seats set lengthwise facing each other behind the driver's seat

‡**wag·on-lit** (và gôn lē′) *n., pl.* **wag·ons-lits′** (-gôn lē′) [Fr. < *wagon*, a car + *lit*, a bed] in Europe, a railway sleeping car

wag·on·load, wag·gon·load (wag′ən lōd′) *n.* the amount a wagon holds

wagon train a line of wagons travelling together, as one carrying military supplies, or one in which pioneers crossed the western plains of America

wagon vault same as BARREL VAULT

wag·tail (wag′tāl′) *n.* **1.** a small bird having a long tail that wags up and down **2.** any of various similar birds

Wah·ha·bi, Wa·ha·bi (wə hä′bē) *n.* [Ar. *Wahhabi*] a member of a strict Moslem sect in Saudi Arabia —**Wah·ha′bism, Wa·ha′bism** *n.* —**Wah·ha′bite** (-bīt) *n., adj.*

wa·hi·ne (wä hē′nä) *n.* [Maori & Haw.] a Polynesian woman, esp. of Hawaii

wa·hoo (wä′hoo, wä hoo′) *n., pl.* **-hoo, -hoos:** see PLURAL, II, D, 2 [< ?] a large game and food fish, related to the mackerels and found in warm seas

waif (wāf) *n.* [ONormFr., prob. < ON.] **1.** anything found that is without an owner **2.** a person without home or friends; esp., a homeless child **3.** a stray animal

wail (wāl) *vi.* [< ON. *væla* < *væ*, woe] **1.** to express grief or pain by long, loud cries **2.** to make a sad, crying sound [the wind *wails*] —*vt.* [Archaic] **1.** to lament; mourn **2.** to cry out in mourning —*n.* **1.** a long cry of grief or pain **2.** a sound like this **3.** the act of wailing —**wail′er** *n.* —**wail′ful** *adj.* —**wail′ful·ly** *adv.*

Wail·ing Wall a wall in Jerusalem, believed to be part of Herod's temple, where Jews traditionally gather for prayer and lamentation

wain (wān) *n.* [OE. *wægn*] [Archaic or Dial.] a wagon or cart

wain·scot (wān′skət, -skot′) *n.* [< MDu. *wagenschot*] **1.** a lining or panelling of wood, etc. on the walls of a room, often on the lower part only **2.** the lower part of the walls of a room when finished differently from the upper part —*vt.* **-scot·ed** or **-scot·ted, -scot·ing** or **-scot·ting** to line (a wall, etc.) with wainscoting

wain·scot·ing, wain·scot·ting (-iŋ) *n.* **1.** same as WAINSCOT **2.** material used to wainscot

wain·wright (wān′rīt′) *n.* [WAIN + WRIGHT] a person who builds or repairs wagons

waist (wāst) *n.* [< base of OE. *weaxan*, to grow] **1.** the part of the body between the ribs and the hips **2.** *a)* the part of a garment that covers the waist *b)* same as WAISTLINE (sense 2) **3.** the middle, narrow part of something **4.** *Naut.* the central part of a ship between the forecastle and the quarterdeck —**waist′ed** *adj.*

waist·band (wāst′band′) *n.* a band encircling the waist, esp. one at the top of a skirt, trousers, etc.

waist·coat (wāst′kōt; obs. or dial. wes′kət) *n.* **1.** a short, tight-fitting, sleeveless garment worn, esp. under a suit jacket, by men **2.** a similar, jacketlike garment worn by women —**waist′coat·ed** *adj.*

waist·line (wāst′līn′) *n.* **1.** the line of the waist, between the ribs and the hips **2.** *a)* the narrow part of a woman's dress, etc., worn at the waist or above or below it as styles change *b)* the line where the waist and skirt of a dress join **3.** the distance round the waist

wait (wāt) *vi.* [ONormFr. *waitier* < Frank.] **1.** to stay in place or remain in readiness or in anticipation (often with *until* or *for*) **2.** to be ready [dinner is *waiting* for us] **3.** to remain undone for a time [that job will have to *wait*] **4.** to serve food (with *at* or *on*) [to *wait* at table, to *wait* on a person] —*vt.* **1.** to be, remain, or delay in expectation of [to *wait* one's turn] **2.** [Colloq.] to delay serving (a meal) as in waiting for someone [to *wait* dinner] —*n.* **1.** the act or a period of waiting **2.** [*pl.*] *a)* itinerant carol singers at Christmas *b)* formerly, official bands of musicians employed by a city —**lie in wait (for)** to wait so as to catch after planning an ambush or trap (for) —**wait on** (or **upon**) **1.** to act as a servant to **2.** to call on or visit (esp. a superior) in order to pay one's respects, ask a favour, etc. **3.** to be a consequence of **4.** to serve (a customer, etc.) as a waiter, etc. **5.** [Dial.] to wait for; await —**wait out** [Chiefly U.S.] to remain inactive during the course of —**wait up 1.** to put off going to bed until someone expected arrives or something expected happens (often with *for*) **2.** [U.S. Colloq.] to stop and wait for someone to catch up —**you wait!** [Colloq.] I will have my revenge: also **just you wait!**

wait·er (wāt′ər) *n.* **1.** a person who waits or awaits **2.** a man who waits at table, as in a restaurant **3.** a tray for carrying dishes; salver

wait·ing (-iŋ) *adj.* **1.** that waits **2.** of or for a wait —*n.* **1.** the act of one that waits **2.** a period of waiting —**in waiting** in attendance, as on a king or other royal person

waiting game a delaying or postponing action until one has the advantage

waiting list a list of applicants, as for a vacancy or an item in short supply, in the order of their application

waiting room a room in which people wait, as in a railway station, at a dentist's surgery, etc.

wait·ress (wā′tris) *n.* a woman or girl who waits at table, as in a restaurant

waive (wāv) *vt.* **waived, waiv′ing** [< Anglo-Fr. *waiver*, to renounce < ON. *veifa*, to fluctuate] **1.** to give up or forgo (a right, claim, etc.) **2.** to refrain from insisting on or taking advantage of **3.** to postpone; defer

waiv·er (wā′vər) *n.* *Law* **1.** a waiving, or giving up voluntarily, of a right, claim, etc. **2.** a formal written statement of this

wake[1] (wāk) *vi.* **woke** or **waked, waked,** (**wok′en** or, occas. **woke**), **wak′ing** [< OE. *wacian*, to be awake & *wacan*, to arise] **1.** to come out of sleep or a state like sleep; awake (often with *up*) **2.** to be or stay awake **3.** to become active again (often with *up*) **4.** to become alert (*to* a danger, possibility, etc.) **5.** [Chiefly Dial.] to hold a wake —*vt.* **1.** to cause to wake from or as from sleep (often with *up*) **2.** to arouse or excite (passions, etc.) **3.** [Chiefly Dial.] *pt. & pp.* **waked** to hold a wake over (a corpse) —*n.* **1.** an all-night vigil over a corpse before burial **2.** formerly, a festival, orig. preceded by a vigil, celebrating the dedication of a parish church **3.** [*usually pl.*] [N Eng. Dial.] an annual holiday

wake[2] (wāk) *n.* [ON. *vök*, a hole in the ice] **1.** the track left in the water by a moving boat or ship **2.** any track left behind —**in the wake of** following close behind

wake·ful (-fəl) *adj.* **1.** keeping awake **2.** alert; watchful **3.** *a)* unable to sleep *b)* sleepless —**wake′ful·ly** *adv.* —**wake′ful·ness** *n.*

wake·less (-lis) *adj.* unbroken; deep: said of sleep

wak·en (wāk′'n) *vi., vt.* [OE. *wacnian*] to become awake or cause to wake; wake up; rouse —**wak′en·er** *n.*

wake-rob·in (wāk′rob′in) *n.* any of several plants of the arum family, esp. the cuckoopint

Wal·den·ses (wəl den′sēz) *n.pl.* [after Peter *Waldo*, 12th-c. Fr. founder of the sect] a sect of dissenters from the Roman Catholic Church which arose about 1170 in S France

wale (wāl) *n.* [OE. *walu*, a weal] **1.** a raised line made on the skin by a slash of a whip, etc.; welt **2.** *a)* a ridge on the surface of cloth, as corduroy *b)* texture of cloth **3.** [*pl.*] heavy planks fastened to the outside of the hull of a wooden ship —*vt.* **waled, wal′ing 1.** to mark (the skin) with wales **2.** to make (cloth, etc.) with wales

walk (wôk) *vi.* [OE. *wealcan*, to roll] **1.** to move along on foot at a moderate pace by placing one foot (or, with quadrupeds, two feet) on the ground before lifting the other (or others) **2.** to appear after death as a ghost **3.** to follow a certain course, way of life, etc. [let us *walk* in peace] —*vt.* **1.** to go along, over, etc. by walking [to *walk* the deck] **2.** to cause (a horse, dog, etc.) to walk, as for exercise **3.** to push (a bicycle, etc.) while walking alongside **4.** to go along with (a person) on a walk [I'll *walk* you home] **5.** to bring to a specified state by walking [to *walk* oneself to exhaustion] —*n.* **1.** the act of walking **2.** a stroll or hike **3.** a route taken in walking **4.** a distance to walk [an hour's *walk* from here] **5.** the pace of one who walks **6.** a way of walking [I knew her by her *walk*] **7.** a particular station in life, sphere of activity, etc. [people from all *walks* of life] **8.** a path, avenue, etc. set apart for walking **9.** an enclosure for grazing or exercising animals [sheepwalk] **10.** the route regularly taken by a tradesman, postman, etc. —**walk (all) over** [Colloq.] **1.** to defeat decisively **2.** to domineer over —**walk a person off his feet** to tire someone out by walking —**walk away from** to outdistance easily —**walk away with 1.** to steal **2.** to win easily —**walk into** [Colloq.] **1.** to become involved in an awkward situation through lack of caution —**walk off 1.** to go away, esp. without warning **2.** to get rid of (fat, etc.) by walking —**walk off with 1.** to steal **2.** to win (something), esp. easily —**walk on air** to be extremely happy —**walk out 1.** to go on strike **2.** to leave suddenly esp. in anger —**walk out on** [Colloq.] to leave; desert —**walk out with** [Obs.] to court or be courted by —**walk the plank** to be forced to walk blindfold along a plank projecting from a ship's side until one falls into the sea —**walk the streets 1.** to pace the streets aimlessly, or in search of work **2.** to be a prostitute —**walk the wards** (or **hospitals**) to be a medical student —**walk′ing** *adj., n.*

walk·a·bout (wôk′ə bout′) *n.* **1.** an Australian Aborigine's periodic nomadic excursion into the bush **2.** an occasion when members of the royal family, etc. walk among and meet the public informally

walk·er (-ər) *n.* **1.** a person or animal that walks **2.** a frame on wheels for babies learning to walk, **3.** a

somewhat similar frame used as a support in walking by convalescents, etc.

walk·ie-talk·ie (wôk′ē tôk′ē) *n.* a compact radio transmitter and receiver that can be carried by one person: also **walk′y-talk′y,** *pl.* **-talk′ies**

walk-in (-in′) *adj.* large enough for one to walk inside [a *walk-in* cupboard]

walking-on part same as WALK-ON

walking papers [Chiefly U.S. Colloq.] dismissal from a job

walking stick a stick carried when walking; cane

walk-on (wôk′on′) *n.* a minor role in which an actor has no speaking lines or just a very few

walk·out (-out′) *n.* **1.** a strike of workers **2.** an abrupt departure of people as a show of protest

walk·o·ver (-ō′vər) *n.* **1.** a race in which the one horse entered has merely to walk over the course to win **2.** an easily won victory

walk-through (-thrōō′) *n.* an early rehearsal of a play in which the actors begin to carry out actions on stage

walk·way (-wā′) *n.* a path, passage, etc. for pedestrians, esp. one that is sheltered

wall (wôl) *n.* [OE. *weall* < L. *vallum*, a rampart < *vallus*, a stake] **1.** an upright structure of wood, stone, etc., serving to enclose, divide, support, or protect [the *walls* of a room, building, garden, etc.] **2.** [usually *pl.*] a surrounding fortification **3.** anything like a wall in appearance or function [a *wall* of fire, a *wall* of silence] —*adj.* of, on, in, or along a wall —*vt.* **1.** to furnish, enclose, divide, etc. with or as with a wall (often with *off, in,* etc.) **2.** to close up (an opening) with a wall (usually with *up*) —**drive** (or **push**) **to the wall** to place in a desperate position —**drive** (or **send,** etc.) **up the wall** [Colloq.] to make frantic, tense, etc. —**go to the wall 1.** to suffer defeat **2.** to fail in business —**run** (or **bang**) **one's head against a brick wall** to try to deal with an impossibly difficult problem; —**walls have ears** [Colloq.] there may be eavesdroppers listening —**walled** *adj.* —**wall′-less** *adj.* —**wall′-like** *adj.*

wal·la·by (wol′ə bē) *n., pl.* **-bies, -by:** see PLURAL, II, D, 1 [< Abor. name] a small or medium-sized marsupial related to the kangaroo —**on the wallaby track** [Aust.] tramping the country; roaming, or searching for work

Wallace's Line (wol′i saz) [after A.R. *Wallace* (1823-1913), Brit. naturalist] the hypothetical dividing line between the typically Australian and Oriental zoogeographical regions, separating the typically Australian fauna from that of the Asian mainland

wal·lah (wol′ə) *n.* [Anglo-Ind. < Hindu *-wālā,* a suffix of agency] [Anglo-Indian] a person connected with a particular thing or function: also sp. **wal′la**

wal·la·roo (wol′ə rōō′) *n.* [< Abor. name] a large kangaroo that has a stocky body and broad, thickly padded feet

wall·board (wôl′bôrd′) *n.* fibrous material made up into thin slabs for use in making or covering walls etc.; in place of plaster, etc.

wal·let (wol′it) *n.* [ME. *walet* < ?] **1.** formerly, a knapsack **2.** a flat case, as of leather, with compartments for banknotes, cards, etc.

wall·eye (wôl′ī′) *n.* [< ff.] **1.** an eye, as of a horse, with a whitish iris or white, opaque cornea **2.** an eye that turns outwards, showing more white than is normal **3.** any of several fishes with large, staring eyes

wall·eyed (-īd′) *adj.* [< ON., ult. < *vagl,* a beam + *eygr,* having eyes] having a walleye or walleyes

wall·flow·er (-flou′ər) *n.* **1.** any of a number of garden plants having racemes of yellow, orange, etc. flowers **2.** [Colloq.] a person, esp. a girl, who merely looks on at a dance from lack of a partner

Wal·loon (wo lōōn′) *n.* [Fr. *Wallon*] **1.** a member of a people living mostly in S and SE Belgium and nearby parts of France **2.** the French dialect of the Walloons

wal·lop (wol′əp) *vi.* [< ONormFr. *waloper* (OFr. *galoper),* to gallop < Frank.] [Dial.] **1.** to move along in a rapid, reckless, awkward way **2.** to boil vigorously and noisily —*vt.* [Colloq.] **1.** to beat soundly **2.** to strike hard **3.** to defeat crushingly —*n.* [Colloq.] **1.** a hard blow **2.** the power to strike a hard blow **3.** [Slang] beer —**wal′lop·er** *n.*

wal·lop·ing (-iŋ) *adj.* [Colloq.] impressively large; enormous —*n.* **1.** a thrashing **2.** a crushing defeat

wal·low (wol′ō) *vi.* [OE. *wealwian,* to roll around] **1.** to roll about, as in mud, dust, etc. **2.** to roll and pitch, as a ship **3.** to give oneself over to, or revel in, some feeling, way of life, etc. [to *wallow* in self-pity, to *wallow* in riches] —*n.* **1.** a wallowing **2.** a place where animals wallow

wall·pa·per (wôl′pā′pər) *n.* paper for covering the walls or ceiling of a room —*vt.* to put wallpaper on or in

wall plate a horizontal timber placed along the top of a wall to support the ends of joists and distribute the load

Wall Street [after the street in New York City which is the main U.S. financial centre] U.S. financiers and their power, policies, etc., or the U.S. money market

wall-to-wall (wôl′tə wôl′) *adj.* that completely covers a floor [*wall-to-wall* carpeting]

wal·nut (wôl′nut′, -nət) *n.* [< OE. < *wealh,* foreign + *hnutu,* a nut] **1.** any of a number of related trees, valued for their nuts and wood **2.** their edible nut, having a hard, crinkled shell and a two-lobed seed **3.** their wood, used for furniture, etc.

Wal·pur·gis Night (väl poor′gis) the eve of May Day (April 30), when witches supposedly gathered for a demonic orgy: also [G.] **Wal·pur·gis·nacht** (väl poor′gis nächt′)

wal·rus (wôl′rəs, wol′-) *n.,* *pl.* **-rus·es, -rus:** see PLURAL, II, D, 1 [Du. < Dan. *hvalros,* prob. < ON. *hrosshvalr,* lit., horse whale] a massive sea mammal of the seal family, having two tusks jutting from the upper jaw, a thick moustache, a thick hide, and a heavy layer of blubber —*adj.* like that of a walrus [a *walrus* moustache]

Walter Mitty an inveterate day-dreamer, who dreams of his own triumphs

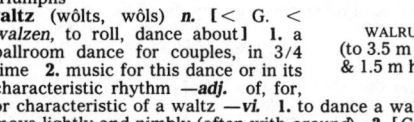

WALRUS
(to 3.5 m long
& 1.5 m high)

waltz (wôlts, wôls) *n.* [< G. < *walzen,* to roll, dance about] **1.** a ballroom dance for couples, in 3/4 time **2.** music for this dance or in its characteristic rhythm —*adj.* of, for, or characteristic of a waltz —*vi.* **1.** to dance a waltz **2.** to move lightly and nimbly (often with *around*) **3.** [Colloq.] to move, progress, etc. effortlessly and successfully (usually with *through*) —*vt.* to dance with in a waltz —**waltz′er** *n.*

wam·pum (wom′pəm) *n.* [< Algonquian] **1.** small beads made of shells and used by N American Indians as money, for ornament, etc.

wan (won) *adj.* **wan′ner, wan′nest** [OE. *wann,* dark] **1.** sickly pale; pallid [a *wan* complexion] **2.** suggestive of a sickly condition or great weariness; feeble [a *wan* smile] —**wan′ly** *adj.* —**wan′ness** *n.*

wand (wond) *n.* [ON. *vondr*] **1.** a slender, supple switch, as of a young tree· **2.** a rod carried as a symbol of authority; sceptre **3.** any rod of supposed magic power **4.** a conductor's baton

wan·der (won′dər) *vi.* [OE. *wandrian*] **1.** to move or go about aimlessly; ramble; roam **2.** to go to a place in a casual or indirect way; idle **3.** *a)* to stray (*from* a path, course, etc.) *b)* to stray from home, friends, etc. (often with *off*) **4.** to go astray in mind or purpose; specif., *a)* to drift away from a subject, as in discussion *b)* to be disordered, incoherent, etc. **5.** to meander, as a river **6.** to move idly from one object to another: said of the eyes, etc. —*vt.* to roam through, in, or over —**wan′der·er** *n.* —**wan′der·ing** *adj., n.* —**wan′der·ing·ly** *adv.*

Wandering Jew 1. in medieval folklore, a Jew condemned to wander the earth until the second coming of Christ because of his scornful attitude just before the Crucifixion **2.** [w- j-] any of several trailing plants, including tradescantia

wan·der·lust (-lust′) *n.* [G.] an impulse, longing, or urge to wander or travel

wan·der·oo (won′də roo͞′) *n.* [< Sinh. *vanduru,* monkeys] **1.** a langur of Sri Lanka **2.** a macaque of India

wan·doo (won′doo͞) *n.* [Abor.] the white gum tree of Western Australia, which yields a hard, durable wood

wane (wān) *vi.* **waned, wan′ing** [OE. *wanian*] **1.** to grow gradually less in extent: said of the moon after it has become full **2.** to grow dim or faint: said of light, etc. **3.** to decline in power, importance, etc. **4.** to approach the end [the day *wanes*] —*n.* **1.** a waning **2.** a period of waning —**on the wane** declining, decreasing, etc.

wane·y, wan·y (wān′ē) *adj.* [ult. < OE. *wan,* a prefix indicating privation] having a rounded or defective edge; not properly squared: said of a plank

wan·gle (waŋ′g'l) *vt.* **-gled, -gling** [altered < ? WAGGLE] [Colloq.] **1.** to get, make, or bring about by persuasion, influence, manipulation, etc. **2.** to falsify or juggle (accounts, etc.) —*vi.* [Colloq.] to make use of tricky and indirect methods to achieve one's aims —**wan′gler** *n.*

Wan·kel engine (väŋ′k'l, waŋ′-) [after F. *Wankel* (1902–), G. engineer] a rotary combustion engine having a spinning piston and requiring fewer parts and less fuel than a comparable turbine engine

want (wont) *vt.* [ON. *vanta*] **1.** to have too little of; lack **2.** to be short by (a specified amount) [it *wants* two minutes of noon] **3.** to feel the need of; crave [to *want* love] **4.** to desire or wish (followed by the infinitive) [to *want* to travel] **5.** *a)* to wish to see or speak with (someone) [*wanted* on the phone] *b)* to wish to apprehend, as for arrest [*wanted* by the police] **6.** to require; need *Want* is also used colloquially as an auxiliary meaning *ought* or *should* [you *want* to be careful] —*vi.* **1.** to have a need or lack (usually with *for*) **2.** to be destitute or very poor —*n.* **1.** a scarcity; shortage; lack **2.** poverty; destitution **3.** a wish for something; craving **4.** something needed; need —**want′er** *n.*

want ad [U.S. Colloq.] a classified advertisement, as in a newspaper, stating that one wants a job, an employee, etc.

want·ing (won′tiŋ) *adj.* **1.** absent; lacking [a coat with buttons *wanting*] **2.** not up to some standard [weighed and found *wanting*] **3.** [Dial.] mentally deficient —*prep.* **1.** lacking (something); without **2.** minus —**wanting in** having not enough of (some quality, etc.)

wan·ton (won′t'n) *adj.* [< OE. < *wan,* lacking + *togen,* pp. of *teon,* to bring up] **1.** orig., undisciplined [*wanton* boys] **2.** *a)* sexually loose *b)* [Poet.] frisky; playful *c)* [Poet.] capricious [*wanton* winds] **3.** senseless, unprovoked, or deliberately malicious [*wanton* cruelty] **4.** recklessly ignoring justice, decency, morality, etc. **5.** lavish, luxurious, or extravagant —*n.* a wanton person or thing; esp., a sexually loose woman —*vi.* to be wanton —**wan′ton·ly** *adv.* —**wan′ton·ness** *n.*

wap·en·take (wop′ən tāk′, wap′-) *n.* [ME. < OE. *wapentac* < ON. *vapnatak,* lit., a weapon-taking] in England, formerly, **1.** a subdivision of certain northern counties originally under Norse domination, corresponding to the hundred in other counties **2.** a law court in such a division

wap·i·ti (wop′ə tē) *n., pl.* **-tis, -ti:** see PLURAL, II, D, 1 [< Algonquian] the American elk, the largest N American deer, with large, branching antlers and a short tail

war (wôr) *n.* [ONormFr. *werre,* strife < Frank.] **1.** open armed conflict between countries or between factions within the same country **2.** any period of such conflict **3.** the conduct of a particular armed conflict, as in a number of related campaigns **4.** any active hostility, contention, or struggle [the *war* against poverty] **5.** military operations as a science —*adj.* of, used in, or resulting from war —*vi.* **warred, war′ring 1.** to carry on war **2.** to contend; strive [*warring* factions] —**at war** in a state of active armed conflict —**carry the war into the enemy's camp** (or **country**) to resort to offensive, rather than defensive, measures in any conflict —**declare war** (**on**) **1.** to make a formal declaration of being at war (with) **2.** to announce one's hostility (to) —**go to war 1.** to enter into a war **2.** to join the armed forces during a war —**to have been in the wars** to have injuries or marks of ill-treatment as the result of a struggle

War. Warwickshire

wa·ra·tah (wo′rə tä) *n.* [Abor.] any of several Australian shrubs with bright red flowers

war·ble[1] (wôr′b'l) *vt.* **-bled, -bling** [ONormFr. *werbler* < Frank.] **1.** to sing (notes, etc.) with trills, quavers, runs, etc., as a bird **2.** to express in song —*vi.* **1.** to sing melodiously, with trills, etc. **2.** to make a musical sound —*n.* **1.** an act of warbling **2.** a warbling sound; trill

war·ble[2] (wôr′b'l) *n.* [< ?] **1.** a swelling on a horse's back caused by the rubbing of a saddle **2.** a swelling under an animal's hide, caused by the presence of the larva of the **warble fly**

war·bler (wôr′blər) *n.* **1.** a bird or person that warbles **2.** any of a family of small songbirds related to the thrushes **3.** any of a family of small, brightly-coloured American birds

war correspondent a journalist who reports on a war from the scene of action

war crime any crime committed in war in violation of accepted rules of war, as ill-treatment of prisoners of war —**war criminal**

war cry 1. a name, phrase, etc. shouted in a charge or battle **2.** a phrase or slogan adopted by a party in any conflict, contest, election, etc.

ward (wôrd) *vt.* [OE. *weardian,* to protect, guard] **1.** to turn aside; fend off (usually with *off*) **2.** [Rare] to guard —*n.* **1.** a guarding: now only in **watch and ward 2.** a being under guard **3.** *a)* a child or person not able to manage his own affairs who is placed under the care of a guardian or court [*ward* in Chancery] *b)* any person under another's care **4.** each of the divisions of a jail or prison **5.** a division of a hospital [a maternity *ward*] **6.** a division of a city or town, for purposes of administration, voting, etc. **7.** a means of defence **8.** a defensive posture, as in fencing **9.** *a)* a ridge in a lock that allows only the right key to enter *b)* the notch in a key that fits this ridge

-ward (wərd) [< OE. *-weard* < base of *weorthan,* to become] *a suffix forming adjectives meaning* in a (specified) direction or course [*backward*]

war dance a ceremonial dance performed as by some American Indian tribes before battle or after victory

war·den (wôr′d'n) *n.* [< ONormFr. < OFr. *gardein*] **1.** a person who guards, or has charge of, something; keeper, or officer with supervisory powers [a game *warden,* a traffic *warden*] **2.** a governing officer in certain hospitals, colleges, etc. **3.** same as CHURCHWARDEN —**war′den·ship′** *n.*

Warden of the Cinque Ports the governor of the Cinque ports in the South of England: now an honorary title

ward·er (wôr′dər) *n.* **1.** [Obs.] a watchman; gatekeeper **2.** an official in charge of prisoners in a jail; prison officer —**ward′ress** *n.fem.*

ward maid a cleaner in a hospital ward

ward·robe (wôrd'rōb') *n.* 1. a cupboard or tall cabinet with hangers for holding clothes 2. a room where clothes are kept, as a room in a theatre for costumes 3. one's supply of clothes

wardrobe mistress the person in charge of the costumes of a theatrical company

ward·room (wôrd'rōōm') *n.* in a warship, a compartment used for eating and relaxing in by commissioned officers, except, usually, the captain

-wards (wərdz) *a suffix forming adverbs meaning* in a (specified) direction or course [*backwards*]: also sometimes **-ward**

ward·ship (wôrd'ship') *n.* 1. guardianship; custody, as of a minor 2. the condition of being a ward

ware (wer) *n.* [OE. *waru*] 1. any thing or service that one has to sell: *usually used in pl.* 2. things that are for sale, esp. a (specified) kind of merchandise [*hardware, glass-ware*] 3. pottery or a specified kind of pottery

ware·house (wer'hous'; *for v., usually* -houz') *n.* 1. a building where wares, or goods, are stored 2. a wholesale store, or, sometimes, a large retail store —*vt.* **-housed'**, **-hous'ing** to place or store in a warehouse —**ware'house'·man** (-mən) *n., pl.* **-men**

war·fare (wôr'fer') *n.* 1. the action of waging war; armed conflict 2. conflict of any kind

war·far·in (wôr'fə rin) *n.* [*W*(*isconsin*) *A*(*lumni*) *R*(*esearch*) *F*(*oundation*) + (*coum*)*arin*, a chemical] 1. a crystalline powder used as a rat poison 2. this drug neutralized and used in medicine as an anticoagulant

war game 1. training in military tactics in which maps and small figures are used to represent terrain, troops, etc. 2. [*pl.*] practice manoeuvres for troops —**war'-game'** *vt., vi.* to operate, or engage in, a scheme, strategy, etc., by means of, or in a way resembling, a war game

war hawk *same as* HAWK¹ (*n.* 2)

war·head (wôr'hed') *n.* the front section of a self-propelled projectile, etc. containing the explosive charge

war horse 1. a horse used in battle 2. [Colloq.] a person who has engaged in many struggles For 2 now usually **war'-horse'** *n.*

war·i·ly (wer'ə lē) *adv.* in a wary manner; cautiously

war·i·ness (-ē nis) *n.* the quality or state of being wary

war·like (wôr'līk') *adj.* 1. fit for, fond of, or ready for war; bellicose 2. of or appropriate to war 3. threatening war

war·lock (wôr'lok') *n.* [OE. *wærloga*, a traitor, liar] a sorcerer or wizard: male equivalent of a *witch*

war·lord (wôr'lôrd') *n.* 1. a high military officer in a warlike nation 2. a local ruler or leader with a military following, as formerly in China

warm (wôrm) *adj.* [OE. *wearm*] 1. *a)* having or giving off a moderate degree of heat [*a warm iron*] *b)* giving off pleasurable heat [*a warm fire*] *c)* hot [*a warm night*] 2. *a)* overheated, as with exercise *b)* such as to make one heated [*warm work*] 3. effective in keeping body heat in [*warm clothing*] 4. marked by lively disagreement, as an argument 5. ardent; enthusiastic [*warm encouragement*] 6. lively, vigorous, etc. 7. quick to anger; irascible 8. *a)* cordial or sincere [*a warm welcome*] *b)* sympathetic or loving 9. suggesting warmth: said of yellow, orange, or red colours 10. newly made; fresh, as a scent or trail 11. [Colloq.] close to discovering something 12. [Colloq.] disagreeable [we'll make it *warm* for him] —*vt., vi.* 1. to make or become warm 2. to make or become excited, ardent, lively, etc. 3. to make or become friendly, affectionate, etc. —*n.* [Colloq.] 1. a warming or being warmed [have a *warm* by the fire] 2. a warm place; warmth [come into the *warm*] —**warm up** 1. *a)* to make or become warm *b)* to make or become warm enough to operate efficiently 2. to reheat (cooked food, etc.) 3. to establish a suitable lively or relaxed frame of mind (in an audience) before the start of a show or a particular act 4. *Sports* to practise or exercise before going into a game —**warm'er** *n.* —**warm'ish** *adj.* —**warm'ly** *adv.* —**warm'·ness** *n.*

warm·blood·ed (-blud'id) *adj.* 1. having a relatively constant body temperature, independent of and usually warmer than that of the surroundings, as mammals and birds 2. ardent; fervent; impetuous —**warm'blood'·ed·ness** *n.*

war memorial a monument erected in a public place and bearing the names of those killed in war

warm front *Meteorol.* the edge of an advancing mass of warm air replacing colder air

warm·heart·ed (wôrm'här'tid) *adj.* kind, sympathetic, friendly, etc. —**warm'heart'ed·ly** *adv.* —**warm'heart'·ed·ness** *n.*

warming pan a long-handled, covered pan for holding live coals: formerly used to warm beds

war·mon·ger (wôr'muŋ'gər) *n.* a person or agency that advocates war or tries to bring about a war —**war'mon'·ger·ing** *adj., n.*

warmth (wôrmth) *n.* 1. *a)* the state or quality of being warm *b)* mild heat 2. *a)* excitement or vigour of feeling; enthusiasm *b)* cordial or affectionate feelings or nature *c)* slight anger 3. a glowing effect obtained by using red, yellow, or orange

warm-up (wôrm'up') *n.* the act or an instance of warming up

warn (wôrn) *vt.* [OE. *wearnian*] 1. to tell (a person) of a danger, coming evil, etc. 2. to caution about certain acts [*warned* against smoking] 3. to notify in advance 4. to give notice to (a person) to stay or keep (*off, away,* etc.) —*vi.* to give warning —**warn'er** *n.*

warn·ing (wôr'niŋ) *n.* 1. the act of one that warns, or the state of being warned 2. something that serves to warn —*adj.* that warns —**warn'ing·ly** *adv.*

warp (wôrp) *n.* [OE. *wearp*, the base of *weorpan*, to throw] 1. *a)* a distortion, as a twist or bend in wood *b)* any similar distortion 2. a mental twist, quirk, bias, etc. 3. a rope run from a ship to a dock, etc., used to haul the vessel into position 4. silt, sediment deposited as by a stream 5. *a) Weaving* the threads running lengthwise in the loom and crossed by the weft or woof *b)* foundation; base —*vt.* 1. to bend or twist out of shape 2. to distort, pervert, bias, etc. [a *warped* mind] 3. to move (a ship) by hauling on a line fastened to a dock, etc. —*vi.* 1. to become bent or twisted out of shape 2. to turn aside from the natural or right course —**warp'er** *n.*

war paint 1. a pigment applied to the face and body, as by some American Indian tribes, in preparation for war 2. [Slang] *a)* ceremonial dress *b)* women's cosmetics

war·path (wôr'päth') *n.* the path taken by American Indians on a warlike expedition —**on the warpath** 1. at war, ready for war, etc. 2. angry; ready to fight

war·plane (wôr'plān') *n.* any aeroplane for use in war

war·rant (wor'ənt) *n.* [< ONormFr. (OFr. *garant*), a warrant < Frank.] 1. *a)* authorization, as by the law *b)* justification for some act, belief, etc. 2. something that serves as a guarantee of some event or result 3. a written authorization or certification for something; specif., *a)* authorization for the payment or receipt of money *b) Law* a writ authorizing an officer to make an arrest, search, etc. *c) Mil.* the certificate of appointment to the grade of warrant officer —*vt.* 1. *a)* to give (someone) authorization to do something *b)* to authorize (the doing of something) 2. to serve as justification for (an act, belief, etc.) 3. *a)* to guarantee the quality, quantity, etc. (of goods) to a purchaser *b)* to guarantee to (the purchaser) that goods sold are as represented 4. [Colloq.] to state with confidence [I *warrant* he'll be late] —**war'rant·a·ble** *adj.*

war·ran·tee (wor'ən tē') *n. Law* a person to whom a warranty is given

warrant officer *see* MILITARY RANKS, table: in the army the rank has two classes: class 1, regimental sergeant major, & class 2, company sergeant major

war·ran·tor (wôr'ən tôr', -tər) *n. Law* a person who warrants, or gives warranty: also **war'rant·er** (-tər)

war·ran·ty (-tē) *n., pl.* **-ties** [see WARRANT] 1. official authorization 2. justification, as for an opinion or action 3. *Law* a guarantee; specif., a guarantee of something in a contract, as to a purchaser that goods sold him are as represented

war·ren (wor'ən) *n.* [< ONormFr. < OFr. *warir*, to preserve < Frank.] 1. a space or limited area in which rabbits breed or are numerous 2. any building or buildings crowded like a rabbit warren

war·rig·al (wo'rig əl) *n.* [Abor., lit., a dog] [Aust.] 1. a wild dog 2. a wild horse 3. an Aborigine —*adj.* [Aust.] wild; savage

war·ri·or (wo'rē ər) *n.* [< ONormFr. *werrier*, to make war < *werre*, WAR] a man experienced in conflict or war; soldier

war·ship (wôr'ship') *n.* any ship constructed or armed for combat use, as a battleship, destroyer, etc.

wart (wôrt) *n.* [OE. *wearte*] 1. a small, usually hard, tumorous growth on the skin 2. a small growth on a plant 3. an imperfection, failing, flaw, etc. —**warts and all** [Colloq.] with all defects and blemishes revealed [a lovable person, *warts and all*] —**wart'y** *adj.* **wart'i·er, wart'i·est**

wart hog a wild African pig with large, incurved tusks, and a number of warts below the eyes

war·time (wôr'tīm') *n.* a time of war —*adj.* of or characteristic of such a time

war whoop a loud shout or yell uttered, as by N American Indians, on going into battle, etc.

war·y (wer'ē) *adj.* **war'i·er, war'i·est** [< archaic adj. *ware*, watchful + -y²] 1. cautious; on one's guard 2. characterized by caution —**wary of** careful of

was (woz; *unstressed* wəz) [OE. *wæs*] *1st and 3rd pers. sing., pt., of* BE

wash (wosh) *vt.* [OE. *wæscan*] **1.** to clean by means of water or other liquid, often with soap, etc. **2.** to make clean in a religious or moral sense; purify **3.** to wet; moisten **4.** to cleanse by licking, as a cat does **5.** to flow over, past, or against: said of a sea, waves, etc. **6.** to soak (*out*), flush (*off*), or carry (*away*) by the action of water **7.** *a*) to make by flowing over and wearing away substance [rain *washed* gullies in the bank] *b*) to erode [the flood *washed* out the tracks] **8.** to be a cleansing agent for [soap that will *wash* silks] **9.** to cover with a thin coating of paint or metal **10.** *Mining* to pass water through or over (earth, etc.) in order to separate (ore, precious stones, etc.) —*vi.* **1.** to wash oneself or one's hands, face, etc. **2.** to wash clothes **3.** to undergo washing, esp. without fading, etc. **4.** to be removed by washing [the stain *washed* out] **5.** to be worn or carried away by the action of water [the soil *washed* away] **6.** [Colloq.] to withstand a test [his story won't *wash*] —*n.* **1.** *a*) the act or an instance of washing *b*) a place where something is washed [a car *wash*] **2.** a quantity of clothes, etc. washed, or to be washed **3.** refuse liquid food; swill **4.** *a*) the rush or surge of water or waves *b*) the sound of this *c*) the eddy of water caused by a propeller, oars, etc. *d*) a slipstream **5.** erosion caused by the action of water **6.** silt, mud, etc. carried and dropped by running water **7.** earth from which metals, ores, etc. may be washed **8.** *a*) low ground which is flooded part of the time and partly dry the rest *b*) a fen; marsh **9.** a thin coating of paint or metal **10.** any of various liquids for cosmetic or medicinal use [mouthwash] **11.** a thin, weak beverage or liquid food —**come out in the wash** [Slang] to be revealed or explained sooner or later —**wash down 1.** to clean by washing **2.** to follow (food, a drink of whisky, etc.) with a drink, as of water —**wash one's hands (of)** to disclaim all responsibility for —**wash up** to wash eating and cooking utensils after use

wash·a·ble (wosh′ə b'l) *adj.* that can be washed without damage

wash-and-wear (-′n wer′) *adj.* designating or of fabrics or garments that need little or no ironing after washing

wash·ba·sin (-bā′s'n) *n.* a basin or bowl for use in washing one's hands and face, etc., esp. a bathroom fixture fitted with taps and a drain: also **wash′bowl′** (-bōl′)

wash·board (-bôrd′) *n.* **1.** a board or frame with a ridged surface of metal, glass, etc. used for scrubbing dirt out of clothes **2.** a board above the gunwale of a boat to keep the waves from washing over

wash bottle a bottle with two tubes passing through the cork, used for washing chemical precipitates, gases, etc.

wash·day (-dā′) *n.* a day when the clothes and linens of a household are washed

wash drawing a painting done in transparent watercolours, usually in shades of black or grey

washed-out (wosht′out′) *adj.* **1.** faded in colour, specif. from washing **2.** [Colloq.] tired; spiritless **3.** [Colloq.] tired-looking; pale and wan

washed-up (-up′) *adj.* [Slang] finished; done for; having failed

wash·er (wosh′ər) *n.* **1.** a person who washes **2.** a flat disc or ring of metal, rubber, etc., used to make a seat for the head of a bolt or for a nut or tap valve, to lock a nut in place, to provide packing, etc. **3.** [Colloq.] a washing machine

wash·er·wom·an (-woom′ən) *n., pl.* **-wom′en** a woman whose work is washing clothes, etc. —**wash′er·man** (-mən) *n.masc., pl.* **-men**

wash·er·y (wosh′ər ē) *n.* a cleaning plant at a mine where dirt is removed from minerals

wash house formerly, an outbuilding for washing clothes

wash·ing (wosh′iŋ) *n.* **1.** the act of a person or thing that washes **2.** clothes, etc. washed or to be washed, esp. at one time **3.** matter obtained or removed by washing **4.** a thin coating, as of metal, put on in liquid form

washing day *same as* WASHDAY

washing machine a machine for washing clothes, linens, etc.

washing powder a powdered soap or detergent used for washing fabrics

washing soda a crystalline form of sodium carbonate

wash·ing-up (-up) *n.* **1.** the washing of dishes, cutlery, etc. after a meal **2.** the dishes, cutlery, etc. that are to be washed up

wash leather a piece of leather, usually chamois, used as a wash cloth for cars, windows, etc.

wash·out (wosh′out′) *n.* **1.** the washing away of soil, rocks, etc. by a sudden, strong flow of water **2.** a hole made by such washing away, as in a road **3.** [Colloq.] a complete failure

wash·stand (-stand′) *n.* **1.** a table holding a bowl and

pitcher, etc. for washing the face and hands: also **wash-hand stand 2.** a washbasin that is a bathroom fixture

wash·tub (-tub′) *n.* a tub for washing clothes

wash·y (-ē) *adj.* **wash′i·er, wash′i·est 1.** watery; weak **2.** weak in colour; pale **3.** without force or substance; insipid —**wash′i·ness** *n.*

was·n't (woz′'nt) was not

WASP, Wasp (wosp) *n.* [U.S.] a white Anglo-Saxon Protestant: often a derogatory term

wasp (wosp) *n.* [OE. *wæsp*] any of a large, worldwide group of winged insects with a slender body, biting mouthparts, and, in the females and workers, a sharp sting —**wasp′like′** *adj.* —**wasp′y** *adj.* **wasp′i·er, wasp′-i·est**

WASP
(c. 1.2-7 cm long)

wasp·ish (wos′pish) *adj.* **1.** of or like a wasp **2.** bad-tempered; snappish —**wasp′ish·ly** *adv.* —**wasp′ish·ness** *n.*

wasp waist a very slender or tightly corseted waist —**wasp′-waist′ed** *adj.*

was·sail (wo′səl) *n.* [< ON. *ves heill,* lit., be hearty] **1.** a toast formerly given in drinking healths **2.** the spiced ale or other drink with which such healths were drunk **3.** a celebration with much drinking, esp. at Christmas time —*vi.* **1.** to drink wassails; carouse **2.** to go from house to house carol singing at Christmas —*vt.* to drink to the health of —**was′sail·er** *n.*

Was·ser·mann test (or **reaction**) (wäs′ər mən) [after A. von *Wassermann* (1866-1925), G. bacteriologist] a test for syphilis by determining the presence of syphilitic antibodies in the blood serum

wast (wost; *unstressed* wəst) *archaic 2nd pers. sing., past indic., of* BE: *used with* thou

wast·age (wās′tij) *n.* **1.** loss by use, decay, etc. **2.** the process of wasting **3.** anything wasted, or the amount of this; waste

waste (wāst) *vt.* **wast′ed, wast′ing** [ONormFr. *waster* < L. *vastare,* to lay waste] **1.** to destroy; devastate, ruin **2.** to wear away; use up **3.** to make weak or feeble [a man *wasted* by age and disease] **4.** to use up or spend without need, gain, or purpose; squander **5.** to fail to take advantage of [to *waste* an opportunity] —*vi.* **1.** to lose strength, health, flesh, etc., as by disease (often with *away*) **2.** to be used up or worn down gradually **3.** to be wasted, or not put to full or proper use —*adj.* **1.** uncultivated or uninhabited, as a desert; wild; barren; desolate **2.** left over; no longer of use [a *waste* product] **3.** excreted from the body, as faeces or urine **4.** used to carry off or hold waste [a *waste* pipe] —*n.* **1.** uncultivated or uninhabited land, as a desert **2.** *a*) a desolate or devastated area *b*) a vast expanse, as of the sea **3.** a wasting or being wasted; specif., *a*) a squandering, as of money, time, etc. *b*) a failure to take advantage (*of* something) *c*) a gradual loss or decrease by use, wear, decay, etc. **4.** useless or discarded material, as ashes, refuse, etc. **5.** matter excreted from the body, as faeces **6.** refuse cotton fibre or yarn, used for wiping machinery, etc. —**go to waste** to be or become wasted —**lay waste (to)** to destroy; devastate —**waste breath** (or **words**) talk to no effect, as in giving advice which will not be heeded —**wast′er** *n.*

waste·ful (-fəl) *adj.* in the habit of wasting or characterized by waste; squandering; extravagant —**waste′ful·ly** *adv.* —**waste′ful·ness** *n.*

waste·land (-land′) *n.* **1.** land that is uncultivated, barren, unproductive, devastated, etc. **2.** anything which is considered spiritually, culturally or aesthetically desolate

waste·pa·per (-pā′pər) *n.* paper thrown away after use or as useless: also **waste paper**

wastepaper basket a basket or other open container for wastepaper and other dry litter

waste pipe a pipe for carrying off waste water, sink drainage, excess steam, etc.

wast·er (wās′tər) *n.* a person or thing that wastes; esp., a spendthrift or prodigal; wastrel

wast·ing (wās′tiŋ) *adj.* **1.** desolating; destructive [a *wasting* war] **2.** destructive to health, as a disease —**wast′-ing·ly** *adv.*

wast·rel (wās′trəl) *n.* **1.** a person who wastes; esp., a spendthrift **2.** a good-for-nothing

watch (woch) *n.* [OE. *wæcce* < base of *wacian,* to be awake] **1.** the act or fact of keeping awake, esp. in order to protect or guard **2.** *a*) close observation for a time, as to find out something *b*) vigilant, careful guarding **3.** a person or group on duty to protect or guard **4.** [*pl.*] hours (of the night): only in **watches of the night 5.** the period of duty of a guard **6.** a small timepiece carried in the pocket, worn on the wrist, etc. **7.** *Naut. a)* any of the periods of duty (usually four hours) into which the day is divided on board ship *b)* the part of the crew on duty during any such period —*vi.* **1.** to stay awake at night; keep vigil **2.** to be on the alert; keep guard **3.** to look; observe **4.** to be looking or waiting attentively (with *for*) [*watch* for your chance] —*vt.* **1.** to guard **2.** to observe carefully and constantly **3.** to keep informed about **4.** to wait for and look for [to *watch* one's chance] **5.** to keep watch over; tend —**on the watch** watching; on the lookout —**watch it!** [Colloq.] be careful!; look out! —**watch oneself** to be careful or cautious —**watch one's step** to be circumspect in one's behaviour —**watch out** to be alert and on one's guard —**watch over** to protect from harm —**watch'er** *n.*

watch·case (-kās') *n.* the metal case, or outer covering, of a watch

watch chain a chain used for fastening a pocket watch to the clothing

watch·dog (-dog') *n.* **1.** a dog kept to guard property **2.** a person or group that keeps watch to prevent waste, dishonest practices, etc.

watch fire a fire kept burning at night as a signal or for the use of those staying awake to guard

watch·ful (-fəl) *adj.* **1.** watching closely; alert **2.** characterized by vigilance —**watch'ful·ly** *adv.* —**watch'-ful·ness** *n.*

watching brief an instruction to observe proceedings in a law court on behalf of a client only indirectly concerned

watch·mak·er (-mā'kər) *n.* a person who makes or repairs watches —**watch'mak'ing** *n.*

watch·man (-mən) *n., pl.* **-men** a person hired to watch or guard, esp. at night

watch night a religious service held on New Year's Eve: also **watch meeting** or **watch-night service**

watch pocket a small pocket, usually in a waistcoat or trousers, for carrying a watch

watch·spring (-sprin) *n.* the mainspring of a watch

watch·strap (-strap) *n.* a band of leather, metal, cloth, etc. for holding a watch on the wrist

watch·tow·er (-tou'ər) *n.* a high tower from which a sentinel watches for enemies, forest fires, etc.; lookout

watch·word (-wurd') *n.* **1.** a password **2.** a slogan; esp., the slogan or cry of a group or party

wa·ter (wôt'ər) *n.* [OE. *wæter*] **1.** the colourless, transparent liquid occurring on earth as rivers, lakes, oceans, etc., and falling as rain: chemically a compound of hydrogen and oxygen H_2O, it freezes at $0°C$ ($32°F$) and boils at $100°C$ ($212°F$) **2.** [*often pl.*] *a)* a large body of water, as a river, lake, sea, etc. *b)* an area of a sea [international *waters*] **3.** water with reference to its depth, its surface, its level, etc. [ten feet of *water*, under *water*, high *water*] **4.** [*pl.*] the water of mineral springs **5.** any body fluid or secretion, as urine, saliva, tears, etc. **6.** a solution of any substance, often a gas, in water [ammonia *water*] **7.** *a)* the degree of transparency and lustre of a precious stone [a diamond of the first *water*] *b)* degree of quality or conformity to type [an artist of the first *water*] **8.** a wavy, lustrous finish given to linen, silk, etc., or to a metal surface **9.** *Finance* an illegal issue of watered stock —*vt.* **1.** to supply with water; specif., *a)* to give (animals) water to drink *b)* to give water to (soil, crops, etc.), as by sprinkling, irrigating, etc. *c)* to soak or moisten with water *d)* to dilute with water [often with *down*] **2.** to give a wavy lustre to the finish of (silk, etc.) **3.** *Finance* to add illegally to the total face value of (stock) without increasing assets to justify this valuation —*vi.* **1.** to fill with tears: said of the eyes **2.** to secrete or fill with saliva [his mouth *watered*] **3.** to take on a supply of water **4.** to drink water: said of animals —*adj.* **1.** of or having to do with water **2.** in or on water [*water* sports] **3.** growing in or living on or near water [*water* plants, *water* birds] **4.** *a)* operated by water [a *water* wheel] *b)* derived from running water [*water* power] —**by water** by ship or boat —**hold water** to remain sound, logical, etc. [the argument won't *hold water*] —**like water** lavishly; freely: said of money spent, etc. —**make one's mouth water** to create a desire or appetite in one —**make (or pass) water** to urinate —**water down** to weaken the power or effectiveness of —**water under the bridge** past history; irrevocable events —**wa'ter·er** *n.* —**wa'ter·less** *adj.*

Water Bearer *same as* AQUARIUS

water bed a heavy vinyl bag filled with water and used as a bed or as a mattress in a special frame

water beetle any of various beetles that live in freshwater ponds and streams

water bird a swimming or wading bird

water biscuit a thin, crisp, plain biscuit, usually served with butter or cheese

water boatman any of various water bugs that swim about by movement of their fringed, oarlike hind legs

wa·ter·borne (-bôrn') *adj.* floating on or carried by water

wa·ter·buck (-buk') *n., pl.* **-buck', -bucks'** : see PLURAL, II, D, 2 an African antelope having lyre-shaped horns, found near rivers and streams

water buffalo a slow, powerful, oxlike draught animal native to S Asia, Malaya, and the Philippine Islands

WATERBUCK
(0.8 - 1.2 m high
at shoulder)

water bus a small river or lake craft used as a form of public transport

water butt a large barrel with one end open, used for collecting and storing rainwater

water cannon a powerful hose which fires water at high pressure: used to control crowds

water chestnut **1.** a Chinese sedge, growing in clumps in water **2.** its button-shaped tuber, used in cooking

water clock a mechanism for measuring time by the fall or flow of water; clepsydra

water closet *same as* TOILET (*n.* 4)

wa·ter·col·our (-kul'ər) *n.* **1.** a pigment or colouring matter mixed with water for use as a paint **2.** a painting done with such paints **3.** the art of painting with such colours —*adj.* painted in watercolours —**wa'ter·col'our·ist** *n.*

wa·ter-cooled (-kōōld') *adj.* kept from overheating by having water circulated around or through it, as in pipes or a water jacket [a *water-cooled* engine] —**wa'ter·cool'** *vt.*

water cooler a device for cooling water, esp. by refrigeration, for drinking

wa·ter·course (-kôrs') *n.* **1.** a stream of water; river, brook, etc. **2.** a channel for water, as a canal or stream bed

wa·ter·craft (-kräft') *n.* **1.** skill in water sports, boating, etc. **2.** *pl.* **-craft'** a boat, ship, or other water vehicle

wa·ter·cress (-kres') *n.* a plant of the cabbage family, growing generally in running water: its leaves are used in salads, etc.

water cure *same as:* **1.** HYDROPATHY **2.** HYDROTHERAPY

water diviner a person able to locate the presence of water, esp. underground, with a divining rod

wa·ter·fall (-fôl') *n.* a steep fall of water, as of a stream, from a height; cascade

wa·ter·fowl (-foul') *n., pl.* **-fowls', -fowl'** : see PLURAL, II, D, 1 a bird that lives on or near the water, esp. one that swims

wa·ter·front (-frunt') *n.* the land or part of a city or town adjoining a body of water, as, a harbour, lake, etc.

water gap a break in a mountain ridge, with a stream flowing through it

water gas a fuel gas that is a poisonous mixture of hydrogen, carbon dioxide, carbon monoxide, and nitrogen, made by forcing steam through hot coke

water gate **1.** a gate controlling the flow of water; floodgate **2.** a gate giving access to a body of water

Wa·ter·gate (-gāt') *n.* **1.** the burglary, during the 1972 U.S. presidential campaign, of the Democratic Party's headquarters in the Watergate Building, Washington **2.** *a)* the ensuing political scandal, resulting in President Nixon's resignation *b)* loosely, any political scandal

water gauge **1.** a gauge for measuring the level or flow of water in a stream or channel **2.** a device, as a glass tube, that shows the water level in a tank, boiler, etc.

water glass **1.** a drinking glass; tumbler; goblet **2.** *same as* WATER GAUGE (sense 2) **3.** sodium silicate or, sometimes, potassium silicate, usually dissolved in water to form a syrupy liquid used as an adhesive, as a preservative for eggs, etc. **4.** a glass-bottomed tube for looking at things under water Also **wa'ter·glass'** *n.*

water hammer the sharp concussion produced when the flow of water in a pipe is suddenly blocked

water hole **1.** a dip or hole in the surface of the ground, in which water collects; pool; pond **2.** a hole in the ice on a body of water

water hyacinth a floating plant with showy lavender flowers, native to S America

water ice water and sugar flavoured and frozen

wa·ter·i·ness (-ē nis) *n.* the state or quality of being watery

watering can a container with a spout, often having a perforated nozzle, for watering plants

wa·ter·ing place (-in) **1.** a place at a stream, lake, etc. where animals go to drink **2.** a resort or spa with mineral springs for drinking or bathing, or with a beach for swimming, water sports, etc.

water jacket a casing for holding water that circulates, as around the cylinders of an internal-combustion engine

water jump a strip, ditch, or channel of water that a horse must jump, as in a steeplechase

water level 1. *a)* the surface of still water *b)* the height of this 2. *same as: a)* WATER TABLE (sense 1) *b)* WATERLINE (senses 1 & 2) 3. a levelling instrument containing water in a glass tube

wa·ter·lil·y (-lil′ē) *n.,* pl. **-lil′ies** 1. any of various water plants having large, flat, floating leaves and showy flowers in many colours 2. the flower of such a plant

wa·ter·line (-līn′) *n.* 1. the line to which the surface of the water comes on the side of a ship or boat 2. any of several lines parallel to this, marked on the hull of a ship, indicating how far the ship has sunk in the water when it is fully or partly loaded, or unloaded 3. a pipe, tube, etc. connected to a source of water

WATERLILY

wa·ter·logged (-logd′) *adj.* 1. soaked or filled with water so as to be heavy and sluggish in movement: said of boats or floating objects 2. soaked with water; swampy

Wa·ter·loo (wôt′ər lōō′; *occas.* wôt′ər lōō′) *n.* [after the town in C Belgium; scene of Napoleon's final defeat (1815)] any disastrous or decisive defeat

water main a main pipe in a system of water pipes

wa·ter·man (wôt′ər mən) *n.,* pl. **-men** a person who works on or with boats; esp., an oarsman —**wa′ter·man·ship′** *n.*

wa·ter·mark (-märk′) *n.* 1. a mark showing the limit to which water has risen 2. *Papermaking a)* a faint mark in paper, produced by a projecting design, as in the mould *b)* the design —*vt.* 1. to mark (paper) with a watermark 2. to impress (a design) as a watermark

water-meadow (-med′ō) *n.* a meadow which is kept fertile by periodic flooding by a stream

wa·ter·mel·on (-mel′ən) *n.* 1. a large, edible fruit with a hard, green rind and juicy, pink or red pulp having many seeds 2. the plant on which it grows

water mill a mill whose machinery is driven by water

water nymph *Gr. & Rom. Myth.* a goddess having the form of a lovely young girl, supposed to dwell in a stream, pool, lake, etc.

water of crystallization water that occurs in crystalline substances and can be removed by heat: the loss of water usually results in the loss of crystalline structure

water of hydration water which is chemically combined with a substance to form a hydrate and which can be removed, as by heating

water ouzel any of several birds of Europe, Asia, and America; esp., the dipper

water pipe 1. a pipe for carrying water 2. a smoking pipe in which the smoke is drawn through water; hookah

water pistol a toy gun that shoots water in a stream

water plant any plant living under water or with only the roots in or under water

water polo a water game played with a round, partly inflated ball by two teams of seven swimmers

water power 1. the power of running or falling water, used to drive machinery, etc. 2. a fall of water that can be so used Also **wa′ter·pow′er** *n.*

wa·ter·proof (-prōōf′) *adj.* that keeps out water completely; esp., treated with rubber, plastic, etc. so that water will not penetrate —*n.* 1. waterproof material 2. a raincoat, etc. of waterproof material —*vt.* to make waterproof —**wa′ter·proof′er** *n.*

water rail a bird which inhabits swamps, ponds, etc., in Europe and Asia

water rat any of various rodents that live on the banks of streams and ponds, esp. the water vole

water rate a charge levied for the public supplying of water

wa·ter·re·pel·lent (-ri pel′ənt) *adj.* that repels water but is not thoroughly waterproof

water seal a bend in a pipe which holds water and prevents the passage of odours or gas

wa·ter·shed (-shed′) *n.* [WATER + SHED² (n.)] 1. a ridge dividing the areas drained by different river systems 2. popularly, the area drained by a river system 3. a crucial turning point

wa·ter·side (-sīd′) *n.* land at the edge of a body of water —*adj.* of, at, or on the waterside

wa·ter·ski (-skē′) *vi.* **-skied′, -ski′ing** to be towed, as a sport, on skilike boards (**water skis**) by a line attached to a speedboat —**wa′ter·ski′er** *n.*

water snake any of numerous saltwater or freshwater snakes

water softener 1. a chemical compound added to hard water to make it soft, or free from mineral salts 2. a tank, etc. in which water is filtered through chemicals to make it soft

water spaniel a large spaniel having a curly coat and used to retrieve waterfowl

wa·ter·splash (-splash) *n.* a place where a shallow stream crosses a road

wa·ter·spout (-spout′) *n.* 1. a hole, pipe, or spout from which water runs 2. a tornado occurring over water, appearing as a rapidly rotating column of spray 3. a sudden downpour of heavy rain

water sprite in folklore, a spirit, nymph, etc. dwelling in or haunting the water

water table 1. the level below which the ground is saturated with water 2. a sloping projection designed to deflect water from a building

wa·ter·tight (-tīt′) *adj.* 1. so snugly put together that no water can get in or through 2. well thought out, with no weak points: said of an argument, plan, etc. —**wa′ter·tight′-ness** *n.*

water tower 1. an elevated tank used for water storage and for keeping equal pressure on a water system 2. a firefighting apparatus that can be used to lift high-pressure hoses, etc. to great height

water vapour water in the form of mist or tiny diffused particles, esp. when below the boiling point, as in the air: distinguished from STEAM

wa·ter·way (-wā′) *n.* 1. a channel through or along which water runs 2. any body of water wide enough and deep enough for boats, ships, etc.

wa·ter·weed (-wēd′) *n.* any of various weedy aquatic plants

water wheel 1. a wheel with paddles turned by running water, used to give power 2. a wheel with buckets on its rim, used for lifting water

water wings a device, inflated with air, used to keep one afloat while learning to swim

wa·ter·works (-wʉrks′) *n.pl.* [often with sing. v.] 1. a system of reservoirs, pumps, etc. used to bring a water supply to a city, etc. 2. a pumping station in such a system 3. [Slang] tears: usually in **turn on the waterworks,** to weep 4. [Slang] the urinary system

wa·ter·worn (-wôrn′) *adj.* worn, smoothed, or polished by the action of running water

wa·ter·y (-ē) *adj.* 1. of or like water 2. containing or full of water 3. thin, diluted, weak, etc. [watery tea] 4. tearful 5. in or consisting of water [a watery grave] 6. soft or soggy —**wa′ter·i·ness** *n.*

watt (wot) *n.* [after James *Watt* (1736-1819), Scot. engineer & inventor] the SI unit of power; equivalent to one joule per second

watt·age (wot′ij) *n.* 1. amount of electrical power, expressed in watts 2. the number of watts required to operate a given appliance or device

wat·tle (wot′'l) *n.* [OE. *watul*] 1. a woven work of sticks intertwined with twigs or branches, used for walls, roofs, etc. 2. [Dial.] *a)* a stick, twig, etc. *b)* a hurdle made of wattle 3. in Australia, any of various acacias 4. a fleshy, often brightly coloured piece of skin that hangs from the throat of a cock, turkey, etc., or of some lizards —*adj.* made of or roofed with wattle —*vt.* **-tled, -tling** 1. to intertwine (sticks, twigs, etc.) so as to form an interwoven structure 2. to construct (a fence) by intertwining twigs, etc. 3. to build of wattle

WATTLES

wattle and daub a form of wall construction consisting of a framework of interwoven twigs plastered with a mixture of clay, lime, etc.

watt·me·ter (wot′mēt′ər) *n.* an instrument for measuring in watts the power in an electric circuit

waul (wôl) *vi.,* *n.* wail, squall, or howl

wave (wāv) *vi.* **waved, wav′ing** [OE. *wafian*] 1. to move up and down or back and forth in a curving motion; sway to and fro [the flag *waves*] 2. to signal by moving a hand, arm, etc. to and fro 3. to have the form of a series of curves [hair that *waves* naturally] —*vt.* 1. to cause to wave or sway to and fro 2. to brandish (a weapon) 3. *a)* to move or swing (something) as a signal *b)* to signal (something) by doing this [to *wave* farewell] *c)* to signal to (someone) by doing this [he *waved* us on] 4. to arrange (hair, etc.) in a series of curves —*n.* 1. *a)* a ridge or swell moving along the surface of a body of water, etc. *b)* something that suggests this as when wind blows over a field of grain 2. a curve or series of curves, as in the hair, etc. 3. a motion to and fro or up and down, as that made by the hand in signalling 4. something like a wave in action or effect; specif., *a)* an upsurge or rise [a crime *wave,* a *wave* of emotion] *b)* a movement of people, etc., in groups [a *wave* of settlers] 5. [Poet.] water; esp., the sea 6. *Physics* a state of motion that periodically advances and retreats as it is transmitted progressively from one particle in a medium to the next in a given direction, as in the propagation of light, sound, etc. —**wave down** to signal to the driver of a vehicle to stop —**wave'less** *adj.* —**wave'-like'** *adj.* —**wav'er** *n.*

wave band *Radio & TV* a specific range of wave frequencies

wave-form (wāv'form') *n. Physics* the shape of the graph of a wave or oscillation obtained by plotting the value of some changing quantity against time

wave front *Physics* a surface, at right angles to a propagated disturbance, that passes at any given moment through those parts of the wave motion that are in the same phase and are moving in the same direction

wave function *Physics* a mathematical function of position and sometimes time, used in wave mechanics to describe the state of a physical system

wave-guide (-gīd') *n.* a metal tube used for the conduction or directional transmission of microwaves: also **wave guide**

wave-length (-leŋkth, -leŋth) *n. Physics* the distance, measured in the direction of the progression of a wave, from any given point to the next point characterized by the same phase **2.** the wavelength used by a particular broadcasting station —**on someone's** (or **the same**) **wavelength** [Colloq.] having similar thoughts, views, etc. as another

wave-let (-lit) *n.* a little wave; ripple

wave mechanics *Physics* the formulation of quantum mechanics in which the behaviour of systems, such as atoms or molecules, is described in terms of their wave functions

wa-ver (wā'vər) *vi.* [< ME. < *waven,* to WAVE] **1.** to sway to and fro; flutter **2.** to show indecision; vacillate **3.** to become unsteady; falter **4.** to tremble: said of the voice, etc. **5.** to flicker: said of light —*n.* a wavering —**wa'ver-er** *n.* —**wa'ver-ing-ly** *adv.*

wav-y (wā'vē) *adj.* **wav'i-er, wav'i-est 1.** having waves **2.** moving in a wavelike motion **3.** having curves; forming waves and hollows **4.** like or characteristic of waves **5.** wavering; fluctuating; unsteady —**wav'i-ly** *adv.* —**wav'-i-ness** *n.*

wax¹ (waks) *n.* [OE. *weax*] **1.** an easily moulded, dull yellow substance secreted by bees for building cells; beeswax: it is used for candles, modelling, etc. **2.** any substance like this; specif., *a)* paraffin wax *b)* earwax *c)* sealing wax —*vt.* to rub, polish, cover, or treat with wax —*adj.* made of wax —**be wax in a person's hands** to be completely under the control of another person —**wax'er** *n.* —**wax'like'** *adj.*

wax² (waks) *vi.* **waxed, waxed** or archaic **wax'en, wax'ing** [OE. *weaxan,* to grow] **1.** to increase in strength, intensity, volume, etc. **2.** to become gradually full: said of the moon **3.** to become [to *wax* angry]

wax³ (waks) *n.* [< ? WAX²] [Old Slang] a fit of rage or temper [he's in a *wax* today]

wax-ber-ry (waks'bər ē) *n., pl.* **-ries** *same as:* **1.** SNOWBERRY (senses 1 & 3) **2.** WAX MYRTLE

wax-en (wak's'n) *adj.* **1.** made of, or covered with, wax **2.** like wax, in being pale, soft, easily moulded, etc.

wax flower an Australian shrub, found in sandy or rocky areas, with waxy, usually pink, flowers

wax light a candle or wax taper

wax myrtle an evergreen shrub native to eastern N America and having greyish-white berries coated with a wax used for candles: also called **candleberry myrtle**

wax palm 1. *same as* CARNAUBA **2.** a palm of the Andes that yields a wax used to make candles, polishes, etc.

wax paper a kind of paper made moisture-proof by a wax, or paraffin, coating: also **waxed paper**

wax-wing (waks'wiŋ') *n.* any of a group of birds with silky-brown plumage, a showy crest, and scarlet spines, suggesting sealing wax, at the ends of the secondary quill feathers

wax-work (-wurk') *n.* **1.** work, as objects, figures, etc., made of wax **2.** a human figure made of wax

wax-works (-wurks') *n.pl.* [with sing. v.] an exhibition of wax figures made to look like famous or notorious persons: also **wax museum**

wax-y (wak'sē) *adj.* **wax'i-er, wax'i-est 1.** full of, covered with, or made of wax **2.** like wax in nature or appearance **3.** [Slang] angry —**wax'i-ly** *adv.* —**wax'i-ness** *n.*

way (wā) *n.* [OE. *weg*] **1.** a road, street, path, etc. **2.** room for passing; an opening, as in a crowd **3.** a course from one place to another [motorway, one-way street] **4.** a specified route or direction [on the *way* to town] **5.** course or habits of life [to fall into evil *ways*] **6.** a method of doing something **7.** a customary or characteristic manner of living, acting, etc. [to change one's *ways*] **8.** *a)* manner; style [to have a pleasant *way*] *b)* power of pleasing [he has a *way* with children] **9.** distance [a long *way* off] **10.** direction of movement, etc. [look this *way*] **11.** respect; point; particular [to be right in some *ways*] **12.** wish; will

[to get one's *way*] **13.** range, as of experience [that never came my *way*] **14.** relationship as to those taking part [a four-*way* agreement] **15.** [Colloq.] a (specified) state or condition [he is in a bad *way*] **16.** [Colloq.] a district; locality [out our *way*] **17.** [*pl.*] a timber framework on which a ship is built and along which it slides in launching **18.** *Naut.* a ship's movement or momentum through water —*adv.* [Colloq.] away; far [*way* behind] —**by the way 1.** incidentally **2.** on or beside the way —**by way of 1.** passing through; via **2.** as a way, method, or means of —**come one's way 1.** to come to one **2.** to turn out successfully for one: also **go one's way** —**give way 1.** to withdraw; yield **2.** to break down —**give way to** to yield to —**go out of the** (or **one's**) **way** to make a special effort —**in the way** in such a position as to obstruct, hinder, etc. —**lead the way** to be a guide or example —**look the other way** to feign ignorance of something which one ought to deal with —**make one's way 1.** to proceed **2.** to succeed by one's own efforts —**make way 1.** to clear a passage **2.** to make progress —**on the way out 1.** becoming unfashionable or unpopular **2.** dying —**out of the way 1.** in a position so as not to hinder, etc. **2.** disposed of **3.** not on the right or usual route **4.** *a)* improper; amiss *b)* unusual —**the way** according to the way that [with things the way they are] —**under way 1.** moving; advancing **2.** *Naut. see* UNDERWAY

way-bill (wā'bil') *n.* a paper giving a list of goods and instructions, sent with the goods being transported

way-far-er (-fer'ər) *n.* a person who travels, esp. from place to place on foot —**way'far'ing** *adj., n.*

way-lay (wā'lā', wā'lā') *vt.* **-laid', -lay'ing 1.** to lie in wait for and attack; ambush **2.** to wait for and accost (a person) on the way —**way'lay'er** *n.*

way-leave (wā'lēv) *n.* a right of way granted by a land-owner for a specific purpose in return for a payment

way-out (wā'out') *adj.* [Colloq.] very unusual, unconventional, experimental, nonconformist, esoteric, etc.

-ways (wāz) [< *way* (see WAY) + adv. gen. *-s*] a suffix meaning in a (specified) direction, position, or manner [endways]: equivalent to -WISE (sense 1)

ways and means 1. methods and resources at the disposal of a person, company, etc. **2.** methods of raising money, as for government

way-side (wā'sīd') *n.* the area close to the side of a road —*adj.* on, near, or along the side of a road —**go by the wayside** to be put aside or discarded

way-ward (-wərd) *adj.* [see AWAY & -WARD] **1.** insistent upon having one's own way; headstrong, wilful, disobedient, etc. **2.** unpredictable; erratic —**way'ward-ly** *adv.* —**way'-ward-ness** *n.*

way-worn (-wôrn') *adj.* tired from travelling

Wb *Physics the symbol for* weber

W.B., W/B waybill

w.c. 1. water closet **2.** without charge

W/Cdr. Wing Commander

we (wē) *pron. for sing. see* I [OE.] **1.** the persons speaking or writing: sometimes used by a person in referring to two or more persons including himself and often the person or persons addressed, or by a monarch, author, editor, etc. in referring to himself **2.** you: used in direct address as to a child, invalid, etc. [shall *we* take a nap now?] *We* is the nominative case form of the first personal plural pronoun

W.E.A. Workers' Educational Association

weak (wēk) *adj.* [ON. *veikr*] **1.** *a)* lacking in strength of body or muscle; not physically strong *b)* lacking vitality; feeble; infirm **2.** lacking in skill or strength for combat or competition [a *weak* team] **3.** lacking in moral strength or will power **4.** lacking in mental power, or the ability to judge, decide, etc. **5.** *a)* lacking ruling power, or authority *b)* having few resources, little wealth, etc. [a *weak* nation] **6.** lacking in force, effectiveness, or credibility [that's a bit *weak*] **7.** *a)* not strong in material or construction; easily broken, bent, etc. *b)* not sound or secure **8.** *a)* not functioning normally or well: said of a body organ or part [*weak* eyes] *b)* easily upset; queasy [a *weak* stomach] **9.** suggesting moral or physical lack of strength [*weak* features] **10.** lacking in volume, intensity, etc.; faint [a *weak* voice] **11.** lacking the usual or proper strength [*weak* tea] **12.** poor or deficient in something specified [*weak* in grammar] **13.** ineffective; faulty [a *weak* argument] **14.** *Chem.* having a low ion concentration, as certain acids and bases **15.** *Gram.* inflected by adding a suffix such as *-ed, -d* rather than by an internal vowel change: said of regular verbs **16.** *Phonet.* unstressed or lightly stressed **17.** *Prosody* designating or of a verse ending in which the stress falls on a word or syllable normally unstressed —**weak'ish** *adj.*

weak-en (-'n) *vt., vi.* to make or become weak or weaker

weak-kneed (wēk'nēd') *adj.* **1.** having weak knees **2.** lacking courage, determination, resistance, etc.

weak·ling (-liŋ) *n.* 1. a person or animal low in physical strength or vitality 2. a person of weak character or intellect —*adj.* weak; feeble

weak·ly (-lē) *adj.* -li·er, -li·est sickly; feeble; weak —*adv.* in a weak way —**weak'li·ness** *n.*

weak-mind·ed (-mīn'did) *adj.* 1. not firm of mind; indecisive 2. mentally retarded 3. showing weakness of thought —**weak'-mind'ed·ness** *n.*

weak·ness (-nis) *n.* 1. a being weak 2. a weak point; fault 3. a liking or an unreasonable fondness (*for* something) 4. something of which one is unreasonably fond

weal[1] (wēl) *n.* [var. of WALE] a mark, line, or ridge raised on the skin, as by a blow; welt

weal[2] (wēl) *n.* [OE. *wela*] a prosperous state; well-being

weald (wēld) *n.* [OE.] 1. a wooded area; forest 2. wild, open country —**The Weald** region in SE England, in Surrey, Kent, and Sussex: formerly heavily forested —**weald'en** *adj.*

wealth (welth) *n.* [see WEAL[2] & -TH[1]] 1. *a)* much money or property; riches *b)* the state of being rich; affluence 2. a large amount; abundance [*a wealth* of ideas] 3. valuable products, contents, or derivatives [the *wealth* of the oceans] 4. *Econ. a)* everything having value in money or a price *b)* any useful material thing capable of being bought and sold

wealth tax a tax on a person's assets, irrespective of whether or not they are sources of income

wealth·y (wel'thē) *adj.* **wealth'i·er**, **wealth'i·est** 1. having wealth; rich 2. of or suggestive of wealth 3. abounding (*in* something) —**wealth'i·ly** *adv.* —**wealth'i·ness** *n.*

wean[1] (wēn) *vt.* [OE. *wenian*] 1. to accustom (a child or young animal) to food other than its mother's milk; now, often, to cause to give up drinking milk from a bottle with a nipple 2. to withdraw (a person) by degrees (*from* a habit, object of affection, etc.) as by substituting something else —**wean'er** *n.*

wean[2] (wān) *n.* [contr. of Scot. *wee ane*, little one] [Scot.] a child or baby

wean·ling (wēn'liŋ) *n.* a child or young animal that has just been weaned —*adj.* recently weaned

weap·on (wep'ən) *n.* [OE. *wæpen*] 1. any instrument or device used for fighting, as specif. in warfare 2. any organ or part (of an animal or plant) used for attacking or defending 3. any means of attack or defence [the *weapon* of the law]

weap·on·ry (-rē) *n.* 1. the design and production of weapons 2. weapons collectively, esp. of a nation for use in war

wear[1] (wer) *vt.* **wore**, **worn**, **wear'ing** [OE. *werian*] 1. *a)* to have or carry (clothing, jewellery, a weapon, etc.) on the body *b)* to hold the position symbolized by [to *wear* the crown] 2. to have or show in one's expression or appearance [to *wear* a smile] 3. to damage, impair, diminish, etc. by constant use, friction, etc. (often with *away*) 4. to bring by use to a specified state [to *wear* a coat to rags] 5. to make by the friction of rubbing, flowing, etc. [to *wear* a hole in the rug] 6. to tire or exhaust 7. [Colloq.] to accept; tolerate [he won't *wear* it] —*vi.* 1. to become damaged, impaired, diminished, etc. by constant use, friction, etc. 2. to hold up in spite of use; last [a fabric that *wears* well] 3. to become in time; grow gradually [courage *wearing* thin] 4. to pass away gradually: said of time [the day *wore* on] 5. to have an irritating or exhausting effect (*on*) [noise *wearing* on his nerves] —*n.* 1. a wearing or being worn 2. things, esp. clothes, worn, or for wearing, on the body [men's *wear*]: often in combination [*sportswear*] 3. damage, impairment, loss, etc. from use, friction, etc. 4. the ability to last in spite of use [a lot of *wear* left in the tyre] —**wear down** 1. to lose or cause to lose thickness or height by use, friction, etc. 2. to tire out; exhaust 3. to overcome by constant effort —**wear off** to pass away or diminish by degrees —**wear out** 1. to make or become useless from continued wear or use 2. to waste or consume by degrees 3. to tire out; exhaust —**wear the trousers** [Colloq.] to be master of the house —**wear thin** to be almost exhausted: said of one's patience or temper —**wear'er** *n.*

wear[2] (wer) *vt.* **wore**, **worn**, **wear'ing** [altered < *veer* (to let out)] to turn (a ship) about by swinging its bow away from the wind —*vi.* to turn about by having the bow swung away from the wind

wear·a·ble (wer'ə b'l) *adj.* that can be worn; suitable for wear —**wear'a·bil'i·ty** *n.*

wear and tear loss and damage resulting from use

wear·ing (-iŋ) *adj.* 1. of or for wear [*wearing* apparel] 2. causing wear or loss 3. tiring —**wear'ing·ly** *adv.*

wea·ri·some (wir'ē səm) *adj.* causing weariness; tiring; tiresome —**wea'ri·some·ly** *adv.* —**wea'ri·some·ness** *n.*

wea·ry (wir'ē) *adj.* -ri·er, -ri·est [OE. *werig*] 1. tired; worn out 2. no longer liking, patient, etc.; bored (*with* or *of*) [*weary* of jokes] 3. tiring [*weary* work] 4. irksome;

tedious [*weary* excuses] —*vt.*, *vi.* -ried, -ry·ing to make or become weary —**wea'ri·ly** *adv.* —**wea'ri·ness** *n.*

Weary Willie [Slang] 1. a tramp 2. a person who is habitually lacking in energy

wea·sand (wē'zənd) *n.* [OE. *wæsend*] the gullet; oesophagus

wea·sel (wē'z'l) *n.*, *pl.* **-sels**, **-sel:** see PLURAL, II, D, 1 [OE. *wesle*] 1. an agile, flesh-eating mammal related to the stoat with a long, slender body, short legs, and a long, bushy tail: they feed on rats, birds, eggs, etc. 2. a sly or deceitful person —*vi.* 2. [Colloq.] to evade a commitment or responsibility (with *out*) —**wea'sel·ly** *adj.*

WEASEL
(15–35 cm long,
including tail)

wea·sel-faced (-fāst') *adj.* having a sharp, hungry-looking thin face

weasel words [Chiefly U.S.] words or remarks that are deliberately misleading because they can be understood in more than one way

weath·er (weth'ər) *n.* [OE. *weder*] 1. the general condition (as to temperature, moisture, cloudiness, etc.) of the atmosphere at a particular time and place 2. disagreeable atmospheric conditions; storm, rain, etc. [protected against the *weather*] —*vt.* 1. to expose to the weather or atmosphere, as for airing, drying, seasoning, etc. 2. to wear away, discolour, etc. by exposure to the atmosphere 3. to get through safely [to *weather* a storm] 4. to slope (sills, etc.) so as to throw off rain, etc. 5. *Naut.* to pass to the windward of (a cape, reef, etc.) —*vi.* 1. to become worn, discoloured, etc. by exposure to the weather 2. to endure such exposure in a specified way [it *weathers* well] —*adj.* 1. designating or of the side of a ship, etc. towards the wind; windward 2. exposed to the elements [*weather* deck] —**under the weather** [Colloq.] 1. not feeling well; ailing 2. somewhat drunk

weath·er-beat·en (-bēt''n) *adj.* showing the effect of weather, as *a)* stained, damaged, or worn *b)* sunburned, roughened, etc.: said of a person, his face, etc.

weath·er·board (-bôrd') *n.* 1. a sloping plank, as at the bottom of a door, to deflect rain 2. [*pl.*] feather-edged, overlapping boards fixed horizontally: used on walls, etc.: also **weath·er·board·ing** —*vt.* to put weatherboards on (a wall, etc.)

weath·er·bound (-bound') *adj.* delayed or halted by bad weather, as a ship, aircraft, etc.

weath·er·cock (-kok') *n.* 1. a weather vane in the form of a rooster 2. a fickle or changeable person or thing

weather eye 1. an eye alert to signs of changing weather 2. a close watch for any change —**keep a weather eye open** to be on the alert

weather forecast prediction of future weather for a particular period based on scientific data collected by a meteorological office

weath·er·glass (-gläs') *n. same as* BAROMETER (sense 1)

weath·er·house (-hous) *n.* an ornament with the figures of a man and a woman attached to a piece of catgut affected by moisture, so that one emerges in wet weather and the other in dry: also **weath'er-box**

weath·er·ing (-iŋ) *n. Geol.* the effects of the forces of weather on rock surfaces, as in forming soil, sand, etc.

weath·er·ly (-lē) *adj. Naut.* that can sail close to the wind with very little drift to leeward —**weath'er·li·ness** *n.*

weath·er·man (-man') *n.*, *pl.* **-men'** (-men') a person who forecasts the weather, or, esp., one who reports weather conditions and forecasts, as on television

weather map a map or chart showing weather conditions in a certain area at a given time by indicating barometric pressures, temperatures, wind direction, etc.

weath·er·proof (-proof') *adj.* that can be exposed to wind, rain, snow, etc. without being damaged —*vt.* to make weatherproof

weather station a post or office where weather conditions are recorded and studied and forecasts are made

weath·er·strip (-strip') *n.* a thin strip of metal, felt, wood, etc. used to cover the joint between a door or window and its casing, so as to keep out draughts, rain, etc.: also **weather strip** —*vt.* **-stripped'**, **-strip'ping** to provide with this: also **weath'er-strip'**

weath·er·strip·ping (-strip'iŋ) *n.* 1. *same as* WEATHERSTRIP 2. weatherstrips collectively

weather vane a shaped piece of metal, etc., set up high to swing in the wind and show which way it is blowing

weath·er-wise (-wīz') *adj.* 1. skilled in predicting the weather 2. skilled in predicting shifts of opinion, feeling, etc.

weath·er·worn (-wôrn′) *adj.* same as WEATHER-BEATEN

weave (wēv) *vt.* **wove** or, chiefly for *vt.* 6 & *vi.* 3, **weaved,** **wo′ven** or **wove** or, chiefly for *vt.* 6 & *vi.* 3, **weaved, weav′-ing** [OE. *wefan*] **1.** *a)* to make (a fabric), esp. on a loom, by interlacing threads or yarns *b)* to form (threads) into a fabric **2.** *a)* to construct in the mind *b)* to form (incidents, etc.) into a story, poem, etc. **3.** *a)* to make by interlacing twigs, straw, etc. [to *weave* baskets] *b)* to interlace (twigs, straw, etc.) so as to make something **4.** to twist (something) into, through, or among [to *weave* flowers into one's hair] **5.** to spin (a web): said of spiders, etc. **6.** *a)* to cause (a vehicle, etc.) to move from side to side or in and out *b)* to make (one's) way by moving thus —*vi.* **1.** to do weaving **2.** to become interlaced **3.** to move from side to side or in and out [*weaving* through traffic] —*n.* a method or pattern of weaving —**get weaving** [Colloq.] to get on with one's work; hurry

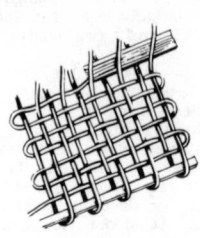

WEAVING

weav·er (wē′vər) *n.* **1.** a person who weaves; esp., one whose work is weaving **2.** same as WEAVERBIRD

weav·er·bird (-burd′) *n.* any of a number of related tropical, finchlike birds that weave elaborate domed nests of sticks, grass, and other vegetation

web (web) *n.* [OE. *webb*] **1.** any woven fabric; esp., a length of cloth being woven on a loom or just taken off **2.** the network spun by a spider or by the larvae of certain insects **3.** a carefully woven trap **4.** anything contrived in an intricate way [a *web* of lies] **5.** *Anat.* a tissue or membrane **6.** *Mech.* the plate joining the flanges of a girder, rail, etc. **7.** *Printing* a large roll of paper for continuously feeding a type of rotary press (**web press**) **8.** *Zool. a)* the vane of a feather *b)* a membrane joining the digits of various water birds, water animals, etc. —*vt.* **webbed, web′bing 1.** to join by a web **2.** to cover as with a web **3.** to snare in a web —**web′like′** *adj.*

web·bing (-iŋ) *n.* **1.** a strong, tough fabric, as of jute, woven in strips and used for belts, in upholstery, etc. **2.** a membrane joining the digits, as of a duck or frog **3.** a part like this **4.** a netlike structure of interwoven cord, etc.

web·by (-ē) *adj.* **web′bi·er, web′bi·est 1.** of or like a web **2.** webbed or web-footed

we·ber (vā′bər, wē′-) *n.* [after Wilhelm *Weber* (1804-91), G. physicist] the SI unit of magnetic flux, defined as the flux which, in a circuit of one turn, produces an electromotive force of one volt reducing to zero in one second

web·foot (web′foot′) *n., pl.* **-feet 1.** a foot with the toes webbed **2.** an animal with webfeet —**web′-foot′ed** *adj.*

web-offset (-of′set) *n.* offset printing onto a long roll of paper

web-toed (web′tōd′) *adj.* having webfeet

wed (wed) *vt.* **wed′ded, wed′ded** or **wed, wed′ding** [OE. *weddian*] **1.** to marry; specif., *a)* to take as husband or wife *b)* to join in marriage **2.** to join closely —*vi.* to get married

we'd (wed) **1.** we had **2.** we should **3.** we would

Wed. Wednesday

wed·ded (wed′id) *adj.* **1.** married **2.** devoted [*wedded* to one's work] **3.** joined [*wedded* by common interests]

wed·ding (-iŋ) *n.* [OE. *wedding*] **1.** the act or ceremony of getting married, or the festivities that go with it **2.** a marriage anniversary [Diamond *Wedding*] **3.** a joining together

wedding breakfast the meal at the reception following a marriage ceremony

wedding cake a rich iced fruit cake, usually with several tiers, served at a wedding reception

wedding ring a ring put on the bride's finger by the groom during the marriage ceremony; also, a ring sometimes given to the groom by the bride during the ceremony

wedge (wej) *n.* [OE. *wecg*] **1.** a piece of wood, metal, etc. tapering to a thin edge that can be driven into a narrow opening, as to split wood **2.** anything with a wedgelike shape or part; specif., *a) Golf* an iron with much loft, as for shots out of bunkers *b)* a shoe having a wedge-like piece under the heel so as to form a solid sole, flat from heel to toe: also **wedge heel 3.** any action or procedure used to open the way for a change —*vt.* **wedged, wedg′ing 1.** to split as with a wedge **2.** to fix in place by driving a wedge under, beside, etc. **3.** to pack (*in*) or crowd together —*vi.* to push or be forced as or like a wedge —**the thin end of the**

WEDGE

wedge the first step or concession, insignificant in itself, which may lead ultimately to momentous results or inordinate demands —**wedge′like′** *adj.* —**wedg′y** *adj.*

Wedg·wood (**ware**) (wej′wood′) [after J. *Wedgwood,* 18th-c. Brit. potter] a trademark for a fine pottery, typically with neoclassical figures applied in relief

wed·lock (wed′lok′) *n.* [< OE. < *wed,* a pledge + *-lac,* an offering] the state of being married

Wednes·day (wenz′dē, -dā) *n.* [OE. *Wodnes dæg,* Woden's day] the fourth day of the week

Wednes·days (-dēz, -dāz) *adv.* [Colloq.] on or during every Wednesday

wee[1] (wē) *adj.* **we′er, we′est** [OE. *wege*] **1.** very small; tiny **2.** very early [the *wee* hours] —*n.* [Scot. & N Eng. Dial.] a little bit; esp., a short time

wee[2] (wē) *n.* [Slang] **1.** the act of urinating **2.** urine —*vi.* [Slang] to urinate

weed (wēd) *n.* [OE. *weod*] **1.** any undesired, uncultivated plant, esp. one growing in profusion and crowding out a desired crop, spoiling a lawn, etc. **2.** [Colloq.] *a)* tobacco: with *the b)* a cigar or cigarette *c)* a marijuana cigarette **3.** something useless, specif., a horse unfit for racing or breeding **4.** [Slang] a thin, scrawny person; weakling —*vt.* **1.** to remove weeds from (a garden, etc.) **2.** to remove as useless, harmful, etc.: often with *out* **3.** to rid of useless or harmful elements —*vi.* to remove weeds, etc. —**weed′er** *n.* —**weed′like′** *adj.*

weed·kill·er (-kil′ər) *n.* a substance, usually a chemical or hormone, used for destroying weeds

weeds (wēdz) *n.pl.* [< OE. *wæde,* a garment] black mourning clothes, esp. those worn by a widow

weed·y (wēd′ē) *adj.* **weed′i·er, weed′i·est 1.** full of weeds **2.** of or like a weed, as in rapid growth **3.** [Colloq.] lean, lanky, ungainly, etc. —**weed′i·ness** *n.*

week (wēk) *n.* [OE. *wicu*] **1.** a period of seven days, esp. one beginning with Sunday and ending with Saturday **2.** the hours or days of work in a seven-day period [a 40-hour *week*] **3.** [Colloq.] weekdays, as opposed to weekends [it opens during the *week*] —**week after week** every week —**week by week** each week —**week in, week out** every week

week·day (-dā′) *n.* **1.** any day of the week except Sunday (or, as in Judaism, Saturday) **2.** any day not in the weekend —*adj.* of, for, or on a weekday

week·days (-dāz′) *adv.* [Colloq.] on or during every weekday or most weekdays

week·end, week-end (wēk′end′; wēk′end′) *n.* the period from Friday night or Saturday to Monday morning: also **week end** —*adj.* of, for, or on a weekend —*vi.* to spend the weekend (at or in a specified place)

week·end·er (-en′dər) *n.* **1.** a person who takes a holiday or goes for a visit at a weekend **2.** [Chiefly U.S.] a small piece of luggage for use on a weekend trip: also **weekend case** (or **bag**)

week·ends (-endz′) *adv.* [Colloq.] on or during every weekend or most weekends

week·ly (wēk′lē) *adj.* **1.** continuing or lasting for a week **2.** done, happening, appearing, etc. once a week or every week [a *weekly* visit] **3.** of a week, or of each week [a *weekly* wage] —*adv.* once a week; every week —*n., pl.* **-lies** a periodical published once a week

week night (-nīt) *n.* the night or evening of a weekday

ween (wēn) *vi., vt.* [OE. *wenan*] [Archaic] to think; suppose; imagine

wee·ny (wē′nē) *adj.* **-ni·er, -ni·est** [WEE[1] + (TI)NY] [Colloq.] small; tiny

weeny-bopper (wēn′ē bop′ər) *n.* [Colloq.] a very young person, esp. a girl, who follows all the latest fads, esp. in clothes and pop music: cf. TEENY-BOPPER

weep (wēp) *vi.* **wept, weep′ing** [OE. *wepan*] **1.** to show or express strong emotion, usually grief or sorrow, by crying, wailing, or, esp., shedding tears **2.** to lament or mourn (with *for*) **3.** to drip or form liquid drops, esp. of moisture condensed from the air **4.** to exude liquid —*vt.* **1.** to weep for; lament **2.** to shed (tears, etc.) —*n.* [often *pl.*] a fit of weeping —**weep′er** *n.*

weep·er (wē′pər) *n.* **1.** a person who weeps, esp. a hired mourner at a funeral **2.** a badge of mourning, as a black crêpe band **3.** same as CAPUCHIN (sense 3)

weep·ie (wēp′ē) *n.* [Colloq.] a film, play, etc. that is highly sentimental

weep·ing (wē′piŋ) *n.* the act of one who or that which weeps —*adj.* **1.** that weeps tears or other liquid **2.** having graceful, drooping branches —**weep′ing·ly** *adv.*

weeping willow a Chinese willow widely grown as an ornamental tree for its delicate, drooping branches

weep·y (wē′pē) *adj.* **weep′i·er, weep′i·est 1.** *a)* inclined to weep; tearful *b)* exuding liquid **2.** characterized by or apt to cause weeping —**weep′i·ness** *n.*

wee·ver (wē′vər) *n.* [< OFr. *wivre* < *guivre* < L. *vipera,* viper] any of a number of edible sea fishes with sharp, very poisonous spines on the gill cover and dorsal fin

wee·vil (wē′v'l) *n.* [OE. *wifel*] any of numerous beetles, esp. those with projecting beaks, including many pest species that feed, esp. as larvae, on cotton, fruits, grain, etc. —**wee′vil·y, wee′vil·ly** *adj.*

weft (weft) *n.* [OE. *weft* < base of *wefan*, to weave] **1.** in weaving, the horizontal threads crossing the warp; the woof **2.** something woven

weigh¹ (wā) *vt.* [OE. *wegan*, to carry] **1.** to determine the weight of by means of a scale or balance **2.** to have a (specified) weight [it *weighs* ten kilogrammes] : orig., and still when used with an adverb, construed as a *vi.* **3.** *same as* WEIGHT (vt. 1) **4.** to lift or balance (an object) in the hand(s) in order to estimate its heaviness **5.** to measure out as by weight (often with *out*) **6.** *a)* to consider and choose carefully [to *weigh* one's words] *b)* to consider in order to make a choice [to *weigh* one plan against another] **7.** *Naut.* to hoist, or lift (an anchor) —*vi.* **1.** to have significance, importance, or influence **2.** to be a burden (with *on* or *upon*) [his crime *weighed* on his mind] **3.** *Naut.* to hoist anchor —**weigh down 1.** to make bend down as with added weight **2.** to bear down on so as to oppress —**weigh in 1.** to weigh (a boxer, jockey, etc.) before or after a contest so as to verify his declared weight **2.** to be so weighed —**weigh in with** to contribute (to a discussion, etc.) an argument regarded as new or clinching —**weigh up** to form a judgment of; appraise —**weigh′a·ble** *adj.* —**weigh′er** *n.*

weigh² (wā) *n.* *var. of* WAY, in **under weigh,** progressing, advancing: cf. UNDERWAY

weigh·bridge (-brij) *n.* a machine with a platform onto which a vehicle can be driven to be weighed with its contents

weight (wāt) *n.* [OE. *wiht* < *wegan*: see WEIGH¹] **1.** a quantity weighing a specified amount **2.** heaviness as a quality; specif., the force of gravity acting on a body **3.** how much a thing weighs or should weigh **4.** *a)* any unit of heaviness *b)* any system of such units [troy *weight*] : see TABLES OF WEIGHTS AND MEASURES in Supplements *c)* a piece of metal, etc. of a specific standard heaviness, used on a balance or scale in weighing **5.** any block or mass used for its heaviness; specif., *a)* one used to hold light things down *b)* one used to drive a mechanism [clock *weights*] *c)* one lifted for exercise **6.** *a)* any heavy thing or load *b)* a burden of responsibility, sorrow, etc. **7.** importance or consequence **8.** influence, power, or authority **9.** the relative thickness or heaviness of a fabric or article of clothing **10.** *Printing* the relative thickness of the lines in founts **11.** *Sports a)* any of the classifications for boxers and wrestlers based on what they weigh *b)* how many pounds a horse must carry for a race, including the weight of the jockey, saddle, and, often, added lead weights —*vt.* **1.** to add weight to **2.** to load down; burden **3.** to control or manipulate so as to favour a particular side [weighted evidence] —**by weight** as determined by weighing —**carry weight** to be important, influential, etc. —**pull one's weight** to do one's share —**throw one's weight around** to act in an overauthoritarian, aggressive manner

weight·ing (-iŋ) *n.* extra money or allowances given in particular cases, as with a job located in an area of high living costs

weight·less (-lis) *adj.* having little or no apparent weight; specif., free of or offsetting the pull of gravity —**weight′-less·ly** *adv.* —**weight′less·ness** *n.*

weight lifting the athletic exercise or competitive sport of lifting barbells —**weight lifter**

weight-watch·er (-woch′ər) a person who is habitually concerned to avoid overweight; a dieter

weight·y (-ē) *adj.* **weight′i·er, weight′i·est 1.** very heavy **2.** burdensome; oppressive **3.** of great significance; serious **4.** of great importance —**weight′i·ly** *adv.* —**weight′i·ness** *n.*

Wei·ma·ra·ner (vī′mə rän′ər, wī′-) *n.* [< *Weimar,* where the breed was developed] any of a breed of lean, medium-sized hunting dog with a smooth, grey coat

weir (wir) *n.* [OE. *wer*] **1.** a low dam built in a river to back up or divert water, as for a mill **2.** a fence built in a stream or channel to catch fish

weird (wird) *adj.* [ult. < OE. *wyrd,* fate] **1.** of or suggestive of ghosts or other supernatural things; unearthly, mysterious, eerie, etc. **2.** [Colloq.] strikingly odd, strange, etc.; fantastic; bizarre —**weird′ly** *adv.* —**weird′ness** *n.*

weir·do (wir′dō) *n., pl.* **-dos** [Colloq.] a person who behaves in an eccentric or bizarre manner: also **weir′die**

Weis·mann·ism (vīs′män iz′m) *n.* [after A. *Weismann,* (1834-1914), G. biologist] a theory of heredity stating that acquired characteristics are not transmitted to offspring

Welch (welsh) *adj., n. var. of* WELSH

welch (welsh) *vt., vi.* [Slang] *var. of* WELSH

wel·come (wel′kəm) *adj.* [< OE. *wilcuma,* orig. *n.,* a welcome guest < *willa,* pleasure + *cuma,* a guest] **1.** gladly received [a *welcome* guest] **2.** agreeable or gratifying [*welcome* news] **3.** willingly permitted or invited [*welcome* to use the library] **4.** under no obligation [you're *welcome*]: used in a conventional response to thanks —*n.* an act or expression of welcoming [a hearty

welcome] —*interj.* you are welcome: an expression of cordial greeting —*vt.* **-comed, -com·ing 1.** to greet with pleasure and hospitality **2.** to receive with pleasure or satisfaction [to *welcome* criticism] **3.** to meet, receive, or acknowledge in a specified way —**bid welcome** to receive with cordial greetings —**wear out** or **outstay one's welcome** to come too often or stay too long —**wel′com·er** *n.*

weld (weld) *vt.* [altered < obs. *well,* to weld] **1.** to unite (pieces of metal, etc.) by heating until molten and fused or until soft enough to hammer or press together **2.** to unite closely —*vi.* to be welded or capable of being welded —*n.* **1.** a welding or being welded **2.** the joint formed by welding —**weld′a·bil′i·ty** *n.* —**weld′a·ble** *adj.* —**weld′er** *n.*

wel·fare (wel′fer′) *n.* [see WELL² & FARE] **1.** condition of health, happiness, and comfort; well-being **2.** financial or other assistance, esp. that given by the state for the poor, unemployed, etc. **3.** [Colloq.] the public agencies involved in giving such aid (often with *the*) **4.** *same as* WELFARE WORK —**on welfare** [Chiefly U.S.] receiving government aid because of poverty, unemployment, etc.

welfare state a nation in which the government assumes responsibility for the welfare of the citizens, with regard to employment, medical care, social security, etc.

welfare work the organized effort of a community or organization to improve the living conditions and standards of its needy members —**welfare worker**

wel·kin (wel′kin) *n.* [OE. *wolcen*] [Archaic or Poet.] the vault of heaven, the sky, or the upper air

well¹ (wel) *n.* [OE. *wella,* akin to *weallan,* to boil up] **1.** a natural spring and pool **2.** a hole sunk into the earth to get water, gas, oil, etc. **3.** an abundant source **4.** any shaft like a well; esp., *a)* an open shaft in a building for a staircase *b)* a shaft to let light and air into a building or between buildings *c)* a lift shaft *d) Naut.* an enclosure for the pumps in the hold of a ship *e)* in a fishing boat, a compartment for freshly caught fish **5.** any cavity, space or container for liquid, as an inkwell **6.** the space in a lawcourt where solicitors sit —*vi., vt.* to pour forth as from a well; gush (*up, forth, down, out,* etc.)

well² (wel) *adv.* **bet′ter, best** [OE. *wel*] **1.** in a pleasing or desirable way; satisfactorily **2.** *a)* in a proper or friendly way *b)* in a kind or favourable way [to speak *well* of someone] **3.** skilfully **4.** fittingly **5.** *a)* in comfort and plenty *b)* to one's advantage **6.** with good reason; in justice **7.** to a considerable degree, extent, etc. **8.** thoroughly **9.** with certainty; definitely [you know very *well* why] **10.** intimately; closely [to know a person *well*] **11.** in good spirit; with good grace *Well* is also used in hyphenated compounds, to mean *properly, satisfactorily, thoroughly,* etc. [*well*-defined] —*adj.* **1.** proper, right, etc. [it is *well* that he came] **2.** in good health, condition, etc. —*interj.* an exclamation used to express surprise, agreement, resignation, etc., or to introduce a remark —**as well 1.** besides; in addition **2.** with equal reason or effect —**as well as 1.** just as much or as good as **2.** in addition to —**leave** (or **let**) **well alone** refrain from interfering in a situation which appears satisfactory —**well away** [Colloq.] drunk —**well up in** [Colloq.] well acquainted with; knowing thoroughly —**wish someone well** to wish someone success or good luck

we'll (wēl, wil) **1.** we shall **2.** we will

well-ad·vised (wel′əd vīzd′) *adj.* showing or resulting from careful consideration or sound advice; wise

well-ap·point·ed (wel′ə poin′tid) *adj.* excellently furnished or equipped [a *well-appointed* office]

well·a·way (wel′ə wā′) *interj.* [ME. *wei la wei,* lit., woe! lo! woe!] [Archaic] alas!: also **well′a·day′** (-dā′)

well-bal·anced (wel′bal′ənst) *adj.* **1.** carefully balanced, adjusted, etc. [a *well-balanced* meal] **2.** sane; sensible

well-be·haved (-bi hāvd′) *adj.* behaving well; polite

well-be·ing (-bē′iŋ) *n.* the state of being well, happy, or prosperous; welfare

well-be·loved (-bi luvd′, -luv′id) *adj.* **1.** deeply loved **2.** highly respected: used on formal occasions

well·born (-bôrn′) *adj.* born into a family of high social position

well-bred (-bred′) *adj.* **1.** showing good breeding; courteous and considerate **2.** of good stock: said of animals

well-chos·en (-chō′z'n) *adj.* chosen with care; proper

well-con·nect·ed (-cə nekt′id) *adj.* having influential or well-born relatives

well-con·tent (-kən tent′) *adj.* thoroughly pleased or satisfied: also **well′-con·tent′ed**

well dressing the annual decoration of a well, and the accompanying festivity, traditional in certain areas of Britain, esp. in Derbyshire

well-dis·posed (-dis pōzd′) *adj.* **1.** suitably or properly placed or arranged **2.** inclined to be friendly, kindly, or favourable (*towards* a person) or receptive (*to* an idea, etc.)

well-done (-dun′) *adj.* **1.** performed with skill and efficiency **2.** thoroughly cooked: said esp. of meat —*interj.* an exclamation of approval of another's action

well-fa·voured (-fā′vərd) *adj.* [Now Rare] handsome; pretty

well-fed (-fed′) *adj.* showing the effect of eating much good food; specif., plump or fat

well-found·ed (-foun′did) *adj.* based on facts, good evidence, or sound judgment [a *well-founded* suspicion]

well-groomed (-grōōmd′) *adj.* 1. carefully cared for [a *well-groomed* horse] 2. clean and neat; carefully washed, combed, dressed, etc.

well-ground·ed (-groun′did) *adj.* 1. having a thorough basic knowledge of a subject 2. based on good reasons

well·head (wel′hed′) *n.* 1. the source of a spring of water; spring 2. any source; fountainhead 3. *a)* the top part of a well shaft *b)* the structure erected over it

well-heeled (wel′hēld′) *adj.* [Slang] rich; prosperous

wel·lie (wel′ē) *n.* [Colloq.] a wellington boot

well-in·formed (-in fôrmd′) *adj.* 1. having thorough knowledge of a subject 2. having considerable knowledge of many subjects, esp. those of current interest

Wel·ling·ton (boot) (wel′iŋ tən) [after 1st Duke of *Wellington* (1769-1852), Brit. general & statesman] [*also* **w-b-**] a high boot, traditionally extending just above the knee in front and just below at the back, now usually just below the knee and made from rubber

well-in·ten·tioned (-in ten′shənd) *adj.* having or showing good or kindly intentions, but often with bad results

well-knit (-nit′) *adj.* having a strong, compact, or sturdy structure

well-known (-nōn′) *adj.* 1. widely or generally known; famous 2. thoroughly known

well-made (-mād′) *adj.* 1. skilfully and strongly built 2. skilfully contrived or plotted [a *well-made* play]

well-man·nered (-man′ərd) *adj.* polite; courteous

well-mean·ing (-mē′niŋ) *adj.* 1. having good or kindly intentions 2. said or done with good intentions, but often unwisely or with bad results: also **well′-meant′** (-ment′)

well-nigh (-nī′) *adv.* very nearly; almost

well-off (-of′) *adj.* 1. in a favourable or fortunate condition or circumstance 2. prosperous; well-to-do

well-or·dered (-ôr′dərd) *adj.* properly or carefully organized

well-pre·served (-pri zurvd′) *adj.* in good condition or of good appearance, in spite of age

well-read (-red′) *adj.* 1. having read much (*in* a subject) 2. having a wide knowledge of books through having read much

well-round·ed (-roun′did) *adj.* 1. well planned for proper balance [a *well-rounded* programme] 2. showing interest, ability, etc. in many fields 3. shapely

well set up [Colloq.] well built; sturdy

well spent achieving satisfactory results; not wasted: said esp. of time or money

well-spo·ken (wel′spō′k'n) *adj.* 1. speaking fluently, graciously, etc. 2. properly or aptly spoken

well·spring (wel′spriŋ′) *n.* 1. a spring or fountainhead 2. a source of abundant supply

well-thought-of (wel′thôt′ov′, -uv′) *adj.* having a good reputation; of good repute

well-timed (-tīmd′) *adj.* timely; opportune

well-to-do (-tə dōō′) *adj.* prosperous; well-off; wealthy

well-tried (-trīd′) *adj.* proved to be satisfactory by frequent or long experience

well-turned (-turnd′) *adj.* 1. gracefully shaped 2. expressed or worded well [a *well-turned* phrase]

well-wish·er (-wish′ər) *n.* a person who wishes well to another or to a cause, etc. —**well′-wish′ing** *adj., n.*

well-worn (-wôrn′) *adj.* 1. much worn; much used 2. overused; trite [a *well-worn* joke]

Welsh (welsh) *adj.* of Wales, its people, their language, etc. —*n.* the Brythonic language spoken in Wales —**the Welsh** the people of Wales

welsh (welsh) *vt., vi.* [< ?] [Slang] 1. to cheat by failing to pay a bet or other debt 2. to evade (an obligation) Often with *on* —**welsh′er** *n.*

Welsh corgi *same as* CORGI

Welsh harp a musical instrument with three rows of strings

Welsh·man (welsh′mən) *n., pl.* **-men** a native or inhabitant of Wales

Welsh rabbit [orig., a humorous usage] a dish of melted cheese, often mixed with ale or beer, served on toast: also **Welsh rarebit**

Welsh terrier a wire-haired terrier closely resembling the Airedale but smaller, orig. from Wales

welt (welt) *n.* [ME. *welte*] 1. a strip of leather in the seam between the sole and upper of a shoe to strengthen the joining 2. a strip of material at an edge or seam of a garment, etc. to reinforce or trim it 3. *a)* a ridge raised on the skin by the blow of a whip, etc. *b)* such a blow —*vt.* 1. to furnish with a welt 2. to raise welts on (the body) 3. to beat severely; thrash

welt·er (wel′tər) *vi.* [MDu. *welteren*] 1. to roll about or wallow, as a pig in mud 2. to be deeply involved [to *welter* in sin] 3. to be soaked, stained, etc. [to *welter* in blood]

—*n.* 1. a tossing and tumbling 2. a turmoil 3. a confused mass; jumble

welt·er·weight (wel′tər wāt′) *n.* [prob. < WELT + -ER + WEIGHT] *see* TABLE OF BOXING AND WRESTLING WEIGHTS

wen[1] (wen) *n.* [OE. *wenn*] a harmless skin tumour esp. of the scalp, consisting of a sebaceous cyst

wen[2] (wen) *n.* [ME. < OE., var. of *win*, joy] an Old English rune, replaced in the 11th cent. by the letter *w*

wench (wench) *n.* [OE. *wencel*, a child] 1. a girl or young woman: now a somewhat derogatory or jocular term 2. [Archaic] *a)* a country girl *b)* a female servant *c)* a prostitute or loose woman —*vi.* to be sexually promiscuous with prostitutes or loose women —**wench′er** *n.*

Wend (wend) *n.* [G. *Wende*] *same as* SORB

wend (wend) *vt.* **wend′ed** *or archaic* **went, wend′ing** [OE. *wendan*, to turn] to proceed on (one's way)

Wen·dy house (wen′dē) a construction which is just big enough for children to enter and play in; a playhouse

Wens·ley·dale (wenz′lē dāl) *n.* [after *Wensleydale* in N Yorkshire] 1. a type of blue-veined or white cheese 2. a breed of long-haired sheep

went (went) [old pt. of WEND, used to replace missing form of GO] *pt. of* GO

wen·tle·trap (wen′t'l trap′) *n.* [Du. *wenteltrap*, lit., a winding staircase] any of a number of deep-sea gastropod molluscs enclosed in a single, usually white, spiral shell

wept (wept) *pt. & pp. of* WEEP

were (wur; *unstressed* wər) [OE. *wæron*] *pl. & 2nd pers. sing., past indic., and the past subj., of* BE

we're (wir) we are

weren't (wurnt) were not

were·wolf (wir′woolf′, wur′-, wer′-) *n., pl.* **-wolves′** (-woolvz′) [< OE. < *wer*, a man + *wulf*, a wolf] *Folklore* a person changed into a wolf or able to take the form of a wolf at will: also sp. **wer′wolf′**, *pl.* **wer′wolves′**

wert (wurt; *unstressed* wərt) *archaic 2nd pers. sing., past indic. & subj., of* BE: *used with* thou

Wes·ley·an (wez′lē ən, wes′-) *adj.* of John Wesley or the Methodist Church —*n.* a follower of John Wesley; Methodist —**Wes′ley·an·ism** *n.*

west (west) *n.* [OE.] 1. the direction to the left of a person facing north; direction in which sunset occurs (270° on the compass, opposite east) 2. a region or district in or towards this direction 3. [W-] the Western Hemisphere, or the Western Hemisphere and Europe; the Occident 4. [W-] the Western Roman Empire —*adj.* 1. in, of, to, or towards the west 2. from the west 3. [W-] designating the western part of a country, etc. —*adv.* in or towards the west —go west [Colloq.] 1. to be lost, ruined, etc. 2. to die 3. to emigrate to the U.S., esp. to seek one's fortune —the West 1. the non-communist countries of Europe and America 2. in the U.S., the region west of the Mississippi

west·bound (-bound′) *adj.* going westwards

West Country the southwest of England, esp. Cornwall, Devon, and Somerset

West End the part of London containing the main shopping and entertainment areas

west·er·ing (west′ər iŋ) *adj.* [Poet.] moving towards the west

west·er·ly (wes′tər lē) *adj., adv.* 1. towards the west 2. from the west —*n., pl.* **-lies** a wind from the west

west·ern (-tərn) *adj.* 1. in, of, or towards the west 2. from the west 3. [W-] of or characteristic of the West —*n.* a story, film, etc. about cowboys or frontiersmen in the western U.S. —**west′ern·most** (-mōst′) *adj.*

Western Church 1. that part of the Catholic Church which recognizes the Pope and follows the Latin Rite; the Roman Catholic Church 2. broadly, all the Christian churches of Europe and America

west·ern·er (wes′tər nər) *n.* a native or inhabitant of the west

Western Hemisphere that half of the earth that includes North & South America

west·ern·ize (wes′tərn īz′) *vt.* **-ized′, -iz′ing** to make western in character, etc. —**west′ern·i·za′tion** *n.*

western roll *Athletics* a technique in high jumping in which the jumper executes a half-turn of the body to clear the bar

Western Roman Empire the W part of the Roman Empire, from its separation (395 A.D.) to its overthrow (476 A.D.)

West·min·ster (west′min′stər) [after *Westminster* in London: site of the Houses of Parliament] the British parliament

west-north·west (west′nôrth′west′; *nautical* -nôr′-) *n.* the direction halfway between due west and northwest; 22°30′ north of due west —*adj., adv.* 1. in or towards this direction 2. from this direction

west-south·west (west′south′west′; *nautical* -sou′-) *n.* the direction halfway between due west and southwest; 22°30′ south of due west —*adj., adv.* 1. in or towards this direction 2. from this direction

west·ward (-wərd) *adv., adj.* towards the west: also **west'·wards** *adv.* —*n.* a westward direction, point, or region
west·ward·ly (-lē) *adv., adj.* 1. towards the west 2. from the west
wet (wet) *adj.* **wet'ter, wet'test** [OE. *wæt*] 1. covered or soaked with water or other liquid 2. rainy; misty 3. not yet dry [*wet* paint] 4. preserved in liquid 5. using, or done with or in, water or other liquid 6. permitting or favouring the sale of alcoholic liquors 7. [Slang] feeble, ineffectual —*n.* 1. water; moisture 2. rain or rainy weather 3. [Slang] a feeble, ineffectual person —*vt., vi.* **wet** or **wet'ted**, **wet'ting** 1. to make or become wet (often with *through* or *down*) 2. to make (a bed, oneself, etc.) wet by urination —**wet behind the ears** [Colloq.] young and inexperienced —**wet'ly** *adv.* —**wet'ness** *n.* —**wet'ta·ble** *adj.* —**wet'ter** *n.* —**wet'tish** *adj.*
we·ta (we'tə) *n.* [Maori] a large New Zealand grasshopper
wet blanket a person or thing that dampens or lessens the enthusiasm or gaiety of others
wet cell a voltaic cell in which the electrolyte is a liquid
wet dream an involuntary emission of semen by men during sleep, usually accompanying a sexual dream
weth·er (weth'ər) *n.* [OE.] a castrated male sheep
wet look a shiny finish given to certain clothing and footwear materials by coating them with urethane
wet nurse a woman hired to suckle another woman's child —**wet-nurse** (wet'nurs') *vt.* **-nursed'**, **-nurs'ing**
wet suit a closefitting, usually one-piece suit of rubber, worn by skin divers for warmth
we've (wēv) we have
wf, w.f. *Printing* wrong fount
Wg. Cdr. Wing Commander
WGmc. West Germanic
whack (wak, hwak) *vt., vi.* [echoic] [Colloq.] to strike or slap with a sharp, resounding blow —*n.* 1. [Colloq.] a sharp, resounding blow, or its sound 2. [Colloq.] a share; portion —**at a** (or **one**) **whack** [Colloq.] at one time and quickly or without pausing —**have** (or **take**) **a whack at** [Colloq.] 1. to aim a blow at 2. to make an attempt at —**out of whack** [Colloq.] not in proper condition —**whack'er** *n.*
whacked (wakt, hwakt) *adj.* [Colloq.] tired out, exhausted
whack·ing (wak'iŋ, hwak'-) *adj.* [Colloq.] big; great
whack·y (-ē) *adj.* **-i·er, -i·est** [Slang] same as WACKY
whale[1] (wāl, hwāl) *n., pl.* **whales, whale:** see PLURAL, II, D, 1 [OE. *hwæl*] any of various large mammals that live in the sea and have a fishlike form, with a flat, horizontal tail and with front limbs modified into flippers; esp., any of the larger mammals of this kind (up to 30 m in length), as distinguished from the porpoises and dolphins: see TOOTHED WHALE, WHALEBONE WHALE —*vi.* **whaled, whal'ing** to hunt whales —**a whale of a** [Colloq.] an exceptionally large, fine, etc. example of (a class of persons or things)
whale[2] (wāl, hwāl) *vt.* **whaled, whal'ing** [prob. var. of WALE] [U.S. Colloq.] to beat; whip; thrash
whale·back (wāl'bak', hwāl'-) *n.* something rounded on top like a whale's back
whale·boat (-bōt') *n.* 1. a long rowing boat, pointed at both ends: used formerly by whalers 2. a similar lifeboat, often motorized (**motor whaleboat**)
whale·bone (-bōn') *n.* 1. horny, elastic material hanging in fringed sheets from the upper jaw or palate of whalebone whales and straining the tiny sea animals they feed on 2. something made of this, as a corset stay
whalebone whale any of a main division of whales, as the blue whale, having whalebone in the mouth and no teeth
whal·er (wā'lər, hwā'-) *n.* 1. a ship used in whaling 2. a man whose work is whaling: also **whale'man**, *pl.* **-men**
whale shark a very large, spotted, tropical shark that feeds on plankton and small fishes
whal·ing (-liŋ) *n.* the work or trade of hunting and killing whales for their blubber, whalebone, etc.
wham (wam, hwam) *interj.* a sound imitating a heavy blow or explosion —*n.* a heavy blow or impact —*vt., vi.* **whammed, wham'ming** to strike, explode, etc. loudly
whang (waŋ, hwaŋ) *vt.* [echoic] to strike with a resounding blow —*vi.* to make a loud noise by hitting —*n.* the noise or blow so made
wha·re (wo'rē) *n.* [Maori] a house
wharf (wôrf, hwôrf) *n., pl.* **wharves** (wôrvz, hwôrvz), **wharfs** [OE. *hwerf*, a dam < base of *hweorfan*, to turn] a platform built along or out from the shore, where ships can dock and load or unload; pier; dock —*vt.* 1. to bring to a wharf 2. to unload or store on a wharf
wharf·age (-ij) *n.* 1. the use of a wharf 2. a fee charged for this 3. wharves collectively
wharf·in·ger (-fin jər) *n.* [altered < earlier *wharfoger* < prec.] a person who owns or manages a wharf
what (wot, hwot; *unstressed* wət, hwət) *pron.* [OE. *hwæt*, neut. of *hwa*, who] 1. which thing, event, etc.: used in asking questions or in asking someone to repeat, explain, specify, etc. [*what* is that object? you told him *what*?] 2. that which or those which: used as a relative pronoun [to

know *what* one wants, not *what* it once was]: also used elliptically for "what it is," "what to do," etc. [I'll tell you *what*] —*n.* the nature (*of* an event) [the *what* and why of his exile] —*adj.* 1. which or which kind of: used interrogatively or relatively [*what* man told you that? I know *what* books you like] 2. as much, or as many, as [take *what* time (or men) you need] 3. how great, surprising, etc.: in exclamations [*what* joy!] —*adv.* 1. in what respect? to what degree? how? [*what* does it matter?] 2. in some manner or degree; in part; partly (usually with *with*) [*what* with singing and joking, the time passed quickly] 3. how greatly, surprisingly, etc. [*what* sad news!] —*conj.* that: in **but what**, but that [never doubt *but what* he loves you] —*interj.* an exclamation of surprise, anger, etc. [*what*! no dinner?] —**and what not** and other things of all sorts —**what about** what do you think, know, etc. concerning? —**what for** 1. why? 2. [Slang] punishment [you'll get *what for*] —**what have you** [Colloq.] anything similar [games, toys, or *what have you*] —**what if** 1. what would happen if 2. what difference would it make if —**what's what** [Colloq.] the true state of affairs —**what's yours?** [Colloq.] what would you like to drink? —**what the** (**heck, devil,** etc.) 1. an exclamation of surprise 2. what: used emphatically —**what though** no matter if
what·ev·er (wot ev'ər, hwot-, wət-, hwət-) *pron.* 1. what: used for emphasis; specif., a) which thing, event, etc.: used in questions [*whatever* can it be?] b) anything that [tell her *whatever* you like] c) no matter what [*whatever* you do, don't rush] 2. [Colloq.] anything of the sort [use pen, pencil, or *whatever*] —*adj.* 1. of no matter what type, degree, etc. [make *whatever* repairs are needed] 2. being who it may be [*whatever* man told you that, it isn't true] 3. of any kind [no plans *whatever*] Also [Poet.] **what·e'er'** (-er')
what·not (wot'not', hwot'-) *n.* 1. a nondescript thing 2. a set of open shelves, as for bric-a-brac —**or** (or **and**) **whatnot** or (or and) any other such things
what's (wots, hwots) what is
what·so·ev·er (wot'sō ev'ər, hwot'-) *pron., adj.* whatever: used for emphasis: also [Poet.] **what'so·e'er'** (-er')
whaup (wôp, hwôp) *n.* [echoic] [Chiefly Scot.] a curlew
wheal (wēl, hwēl) *n.* same as WEAL[1]
wheat (wēt, hwēt) *n.* see PLURAL, II, D, 3 [OE. *hwæte*] 1. any of a group of cereal grasses with dense spikes that grow upright and bear grains that are threshed to remove the chaff 2. such grain, used for flour, cereals, pasta, etc.
wheat·ear (-ir') *n.* [earlier *white ears* < WHITE + *eeres, ers,* var. of ARSE] a small, upland, migratory bird of the thrush family, with a white rump, native of N Europe, Asia, and N America
wheat·en (-'n) *adj.* 1. made of wheat or wheat flour 2. of the pale-yellow colour of wheat
wheat germ 1. the wheat-kernel embryo, rich in vitamins, milled out as an oily flake 2. the milled flakes
Wheat·stone bridge (wēt'stōn, hwēt'-) [after Sir Charles *Wheatstone* (1802-75), Brit. physicist] a divided bridge circuit (see BRIDGE[1], *n.* 10) used for the measurement of electrical resistance

WHEAT

whee (wē, hwē: *with prolonged vowel*) *interj.* an exclamation expressing joy, exultation, etc.
whee·dle (wē'd'l, hwē'-) *vt., vi.* **-dled, -dling** [< ? G. *wedeln*, to wag the tail, hence to flatter] 1. to influence or persuade (a person) by flattery, soothing words, coaxing, etc. 2. to get (something) by coaxing or flattery —**whee'·dler** *n.*
wheel (wēl, hwēl) *n.* [OE. *hweol*] 1. a solid disc, or a circular frame connected by spokes to a central hub, capable of turning on a central axis 2. anything like a wheel in shape, movement, etc. 3. a device having as its main part a wheel or wheels; specif., a) a medieval torture instrument that was a circular frame on which a victim was painfully stretched b) a wheel with projecting handles, to control a ship's rudder c) short for POTTER'S WHEEL, SPINNING WHEEL, etc. 4. [*usually pl.*] the moving, propelling, or controlling forces or agencies [the *wheels* of progress] 5. a turning movement —*vt., vi.* 1. to move or roll on wheels or in a wheeled vehicle 2. to turn round; rotate, revolve, pivot, etc. 3. to turn so as to reverse direction, attitude, etc. (often with *about* or *round*) —**at the wheel** 1. steering a ship, motor vehicle, etc. 2. in charge; directing activities —**wheel and deal** [Chiefly U.S. Slang] to behave in an aggressive, flamboyant way, as in a business deal —**wheel of fortune** the changes, good and bad, that occur in life —**wheels within wheels** a series of intricately connected events, plots, etc. devolving on one another —**wheeled** *adj.*
wheel and axle a grooved wheel fixed to a shaft or drum,

used for lifting weights: the turning of the wheel by a rope in the groove winds a rope on the shaft or drum

wheel animalcule *same as* ROTIFER

wheel·bar·row (-bar′ō) *n.* a shallow, open box for moving small loads, having a single wheel in front, two legs at the back, and two shafts with handles for raising the vehicle off its legs and pushing or pulling it —*vt.* to carry in a wheelbarrow

wheel·base (-bās′) *n.* in a motor vehicle, the distance in inches from the centre of the hub of a front wheel to the centre of the hub of the corresponding back wheel

wheel·chair (-cher′) *n.* a chair mounted on large wheels, used in moving about by persons unable to walk

wheel·er (-ər) *n.* 1. a person or thing that wheels 2. *same as* WHEEL HORSE (sense 1) 3. something with a specified kind or number of wheels [two-*wheeler*]

wheel·er-deal·er (wēl′ər dēl′ər, hwēl′-) *n.* [Chiefly U.S. Slang] a person who wheels and deals: see phrase at entry WHEEL —**wheel′er-deal′ing** *n.*

wheel horse 1. the horse, or one of the horses, harnessed nearest the front wheels of a vehicle 2. [U.S.] a person who works especially hard and effectively in any enterprise

wheel·house (-hous′) *n.* an enclosed place on the upper deck of a ship, for the helmsman

wheel lock 1. an early type of gunlock in which a rough wheel is spun on a flint to throw sparks into the pan and set off the charge 2. a gun with such a lock

wheel·race (-rās′) *n.* the area of a millrace where the water wheel is fixed

wheel·spin (-spin′) *n.* the revolution of wheels without full grip of the road

wheel·wright (-rīt′) *n.* a person who makes and repairs wagon and carriage wheels

wheeze (wēz, hwēz) *vi.* **wheezed, wheez′ing** [ON. *hvaesa,* to hiss] 1. to breathe hard with a whistling, breathy sound, as in asthma 2. to make a sound like this [the old organ *wheezed*] —*vt.* to utter with a sound of wheezing —*n.* 1. an act or sound of wheezing 2. [Slang] an old, hackneyed joke or anecdote 3. [Slang] trick; clever idea or plan —**wheez′er** *n.* —**wheez′ing·ly** *adv.*

wheez·y (wē′zē, hwē′-) *adj.* **wheez′i·er, wheez′i·est** wheezing or characterized by wheezing —**wheez′i·ly** *adv.*

whelk[1] (welk, hwelk) *n.* [OE. *wioluc*] any of various large sea snails with spiral shells, esp. those species used for food

whelk[2] (welk, hwelk) *n.* [OE. *hwylca*] a pimple or pustule

whelm (welm, hwelm) *vt.* [? merging of OE. *-hwelfan,* to overwhelm, with *helmian,* to cover] to submerge or engulf

whelp (welp, hwelp) *n.* [OE. *hwelp*] 1. a young dog; puppy 2. a young lion, tiger, wolf, etc.; cub 3. a youth or child: contemptuous usage —*vt., vi.* to give birth to whelps

WHELK
(7.5 cm long)

when (wen, hwen; *unstressed* wən, hwən) *adv.* [OE. *hwænne*] 1. at what time? 2. on what occasion or under what circumstances? 3. at what point? [*when* shall I stop pouring?] —*conj.* 1. at the time or point that [he told us *when* we sat down] 2. at which [a time *when* men must speak out] 3. as soon as [come *when* I call] 4. at whatever time that [he rested *when* he could] 5. although [to object *when* there's no reason to do so] 6. if [how can he help *when* they won't let him?] —*pron.* what time or which time [until *when* will you stay?] —*n.* the time or moment (of an event) [the *when* and where of his arrest] —**say when** [Colloq.] to indicate at what point an operation should begin or stop: used esp. of the pouring of a drink

when·as (wen az′, hwen-) *conj.* [Archaic] 1. when 2. inasmuch as 3. whereas

whence (wens, hwens) *adv.* [OE. *hwanan*] from what place, source, cause, etc.; from where [*whence* do you come? *whence* did he get his facts?] —*conj.* 1. to the place from which [return *whence* you came] 2. because of which fact

whence·so·ev·er (wens′sō ev′ər, hwens′-) *adv., conj.* from whatever place, source, or cause

when·ev·er (wen ev′ər, hwen-, wən-, hwən-) *adv.* [Colloq.] when: used for emphasis [*whenever* will he learn?] —*conj.* at whatever time; on whatever occasion [visit us *whenever* you can] Also [Poet.] **when′e′er′** (-er′)

when·so·ev·er (wen′sō ev′ər, hwen′-) *adv., conj.* whenever: used for emphasis: also [Poet.] **when′so·e′er′** (-er′)

where (wer, hwer) *adv.* [OE. *hwær*] 1. in or at what place? [*where* is the car?] 2. to or towards what place? [*where* did he go?] 3. in what situation? [*where* will we be if we lose?] 4. in what respect? [*where* is she to blame?] 5. from what place or source? [*where* did you find out?] —*conj.* 1. in or at what place [he knows *where* it is] 2. in

or at which place [we came home, *where* we ate dinner] 3. in or at the place or situation in which [he is *where* he should be] 4. in whatever place, situation, or respect in which [there is never peace *where* men are greedy] 5. *a*) to or towards the place to which [he'll go *where* we go] *b*) to a place in which [send help *where* it's needed] 6. to or towards whatever place [go *where* you please] 7. [Colloq.] *same as* WHEREAS —*pron.* 1. the place or situation in, at, or to which [it is a mile from *where* he lives] 2. what or which place [*where* are you from?] —*n.* the place (of an event) [the *where* and when of the party]

where·a·bouts (wer′ə bouts′, hwer′-) *adv.* near or at what place? where? —*n.* the place where a person or thing is [do you know his *whereabouts?*]

where·as (wer az′, hwer-, wər-, hwər-) *conj.* 1. in view of the fact that: used at the beginning of a formal document 2. but on the other hand; while [she is slender, *whereas* he is stout]

where·at (-at′) *adv.* [Archaic] at what? [*whereat* was he angry?] —*conj.* [Archaic] at which point [he left, *whereat* she began to weep]

where·by (-bī′) *adv.* [Archaic] by what? how? [*whereby* did you expect to profit?] —*conj.* by which; by means of which [a plan *whereby* to make money]

where·fore (wer′fôr, hwer′-) *adv.* [Archaic] for what reason or purpose? why? [*wherefore* are you angry?] —*conj.* 1. for which [the reason *wherefore* we have met] 2. because of which; therefore [we won, *wherefore* rejoice] —*n.* the reason; cause

where·from (wer from′, hwer-) *adv., conj.* [Archaic] from which

where·in (-in′) *adv.* [Archaic] in what way? how? [*wherein* is it wrong?] —*conj.* in which [the room *wherein* he lay]

where·of (-ov′) *adv., conj.* of what, which, or whom

where·on (-on′) *adv.* [Archaic] on what? [*whereon* do you rely?] —*conj.* on which [the hill *whereon* we stand]

where·so·ev·er (wer′sō ev′ər, hwer′-) *adv., conj.* wherever: used for emphasis: also [Poet.] **where′so·e′er′** (-er′)

where·to (-tōō′) *adv.* to what? towards what place, direction, or end? —*conj.* to which

where·up·on (wer′ə pon′, hwer′-; wer′ə pon, hwer′-) *adv.* [Archaic] upon what? whereon? —*conj.* 1. upon which [the ground *whereupon* he had fallen] 2. at which [she told a joke, *whereupon* he laughed]

wher·ev·er (wer ev′ər, hwer-, wər-, hwər-) *adv.* [Colloq.] where: used for emphasis [*wherever* did you hear that?] —*conj.* in, at, or to whatever place or situation [he thinks of us, *wherever* he is] Also [Poet.] **wher′e′er′** (-er′)

where·with (wer with′, hwer-; -with′) *adv.* [Archaic] with what? [*wherewith* shall he be saved?] —*conj.* with which [lacking the money *wherewith* to pay him] —*pron.* that with which [to have *wherewith* to build]

where·with·al (wer′with ôl, hwer′-; -with) *n.* that with which something can be done; necessary means, esp. money (usually with *the*) [the *wherewithal* to continue one's education] —*adv., conj.* archaic var. of WHEREWITH

wher·ry (wer′ē, hwer′-) *n., pl.* **-ries** [< ? ME. *whirren,* to whir, with idea of fast movement] 1. a light rowing boat used on rivers 2. a large, broad, but light barge —*vt.* **-ried, -ry·ing** to transport in a wherry —**wher′ry·man** *n.*

whet (wet, hwet) *vt.* **whet′ted, whet′ting** [OE. *hwettan* < *hwæt,* keen] 1. to sharpen by rubbing or grinding (the edge of a knife or tool); hone 2. to stimulate [to *whet* the appetite] —*n.* 1. an act of whetting 2. something that whets —**whet′ter** *n.*

wheth·er (weth′ər, hweth′ər) *conj.* [OE. *hwæther*] 1. if it be the case or fact that [ask *whether* she will help] 2. in case; in either case that: used to introduce alternatives [*whether* it rains or snows] 3. either [*whether* by accident or design] —**whether or no** in any case

whet·stone (wet′stōn, hwet′-) *n.* an abrasive stone for sharpening knives or other edged tools

whew (wyōō, hyōō) *interj.* [echoic] an exclamation of relief, surprise, dismay, etc.

whey (wā, hwā) *n.* [OE. *hwæg*] the thin, watery part of milk, which separates from the thicker part (curds) after coagulation —**whey′ey** (-ē) *adj.*

whey·face (-fās′) *n.* 1. a pale or pallid face 2. a person having such a face —**whey′faced** *adj.*

which (wich, hwich) *pron.* [OE. *hwylc*] 1. what one (or ones) of the persons, things, or events mentioned or implied? [*which* do you want?] 2. the one (or ones) that [he knows *which* he wants] 3. that: used as a relative referring to the thing or event specified in the antecedent [her hat, *which* is blue; the boat *which* sank] 4. any that; whichever [take *which* you like] 5. a thing or fact that [you are late —*which* reminds me, where is Joe?] —*adj.* 1. what one or ones (of the number mentioned or implied) [*which* man (or men) came?] 2. whatever [try *which* plan you like] 3. being the one just mentioned [he is old, *which* fact is important]

which·ev·er (wich ev′ər, hwich-) *pron., adj.* 1. any one (of two or more) [he may choose *whichever* (desk) he likes] **2.** no matter which [*whichever* (desk) he chooses, they won't be pleased]

which·so·ev·er (wich'sō ev'ər, hwich'-) *pron., adj.* whichever: used for emphasis

whick·er (wik'ər, hwik'-) *vi.* [echoic] **1.** to utter a partly stifled laugh; snicker; titter **2.** to neigh or whinny

whid·ah bird (wid'ə, hwid'-) *same as* WHYDAH BIRD

whiff (wif, hwif) *n.* [echoic] **1.** a light puff or gust of air or wind; breath **2.** a slight gust of odour [a *whiff* of garlic] **3.** an inhaling or exhaling of tobacco smoke **4.** a light sculling boat —*vt.* **1.** to blow with a puff or gust; waft **2.** to smoke (a pipe, etc.) —*vi.* **1.** to blow or move in puffs **2.** to inhale or exhale whiffs, as in smoking **3.** [Slang] to smell unpleasant; stink —**whiff'er** *n.*

whif·fet (-it) *n.* [dim. of prec.] **1.** a little whiff **2.** [U.S. Colloq.] an insignificant person

whif·fle (-'l) *vi.* **-fled, -fling** [freq. of WHIFF] **1.** to blow in gusts: said of the wind **2.** to shift; veer; vacillate —*vt.* to blow or scatter with or as with a puff of wind —**whif'fler** *n.*

Whig (wig, hwig) *n.* [< *whiggamore* (applied to Scot. Presbyterians who marched on Edinburgh in 1648) < WScot. < *whig*, a cry to urge on horses < *mare*, a horse] **1.** orig. in Scotland, a Covenanter **2.** a member of the Eng. political party which supported the Hanoverian succession, and (18th-mid-19th. cent.) championed popular rights: it later became the Liberal Party **3.** [U.S.] a supporter of the War of American Independence **4.** [U.S.] a member of an American political party (c.1836–1856) opposing the Democratic Party —*adj.* of or being a Whig —**Whig'gish** *adj.* —**Whig'gism, Whig'ger·y** *n.*

while (wīl, hwīl) *n.* [OE. *hwil*] a period of time [a short *while*] —*conj.* **1.** during or throughout the time that [we talked *while* we ate] **2.** at the same time that [*while* you're up, close the door] **3.** *a)* although [*while* she isn't pretty, she is charming] *b)* whereas [the walls are green, *while* the ceiling is white] —*vt.* **whiled, whil'ing** to spend (time) in a pleasant way [to *while* away the hours] —**between whiles** at intervals —**the while** during this very time —**worth (one's) while** worth one's time; profitable

whiles (wīlz, hwīlz) *adv.* [Chiefly Scot.] *same as* SOMETIMES —*conj.* [Archaic or Dial.] *same as* WHILE

whi·lom (wī'ləm, hwī'-) *adv.* [OE. *hwilum*, dat. pl. of *hwil*, while] [Archaic] at one time; formerly —*adj.* formerly such; former [their *whilom* friends]

whilst (wīlst, hwīlst) *conj. same as* WHILE

whim (wim, hwim) *n.* [short for WHIM-WHAM] **1.** a sudden fancy; idle and passing notion; caprice **2.** a kind of winch formerly used in mines for raising ore or water

whim·brel (wim'brəl, hwim'-) *n.* [earlier *whimrel*, prob. echoic] a small European curlew

whim·per (wim'pər, hwim'-) *vi.* [? echoic: akin to WHINE] **1.** to cry with low, whining, broken sounds **2.** to complain in a whining plaintive way —*vt.* to utter with a whimper —*n.* a whimpering sound or cry —**whim'per·er** *n.* —**whim'per·ing·ly** *adv.*

whim·si·cal (wim'zi k'l, hwim'-) *adj.* **1.** full of whims or whimsy; having odd notions **2.** different in an odd way; freakish **3.** unpredictable —**whim'si·cal'i·ty** (-kal'ə tē), *pl.* **-ties, whim'si·cal·ness** *n.* —**whim'si·cal·ly** *adv.*

whim·sy (wim'zē, hwim'-) *n., pl.* **-sies** [prob. < ff.] **1.** an odd fancy; idle notion; whim **2.** quaint or fanciful humour Also sp. **whim'sey**, *pl.* **-seys**

whim-wham (wim'hwam', hwim'wam') *n.* [< ?] **1.** a bauble; trinket **2.** an odd notion; whim —**the whim-whams** [U.S. Colloq.] a nervous feeling; the jitters

whin¹ (win, hwin) *n.* [prob. < Scand.] *same as* FURZE

whin² (win, hwin) *n.* [ME. *quin* < ?] any of several hard, igneous or basaltic rocks: also **whin'stone**

whin·chat (win'chat', hwin'-) *n.* [WHIN¹ + *chat*, a warbler] a brown and buff songbird

whine (wīn, hwīn) *vi.* **whined, whin'ing** [OE. *hwinan*] **1.** *a)* to utter a peevish, high-pitched sound, as in complaint, distress, etc. *b)* to make a drawn-out, high-pitched sound **2.** to complain or beg in a childish, undignified way —*vt.* to utter with a whine —*n.* **1.** the act or sound of whining **2.** a complaint uttered in a whining tone —**whin'er** *n.* —**whin'i·ness** *n.* —**whin'ing·ly** *adv.* —**whin'y, whin'i·er, whin'i·est**

whin·ny (win'ē, hwin'ē) *vi.* **-nied, -ny·ing** [prob. < or akin to WHINE] to neigh in a low, gentle way: said of a horse —*vt.* to express with a whinny —*n., pl.* **-nies** the whinnying of a horse, or a similar sound

whip (wip, hwip) *vt.* **whipped, whip'ping** [MDu. *wippen*, to swing] **1.** to move, pull, throw, etc. suddenly (usually with *out, off, up, etc.*) [to *whip* out a knife] **2.** to strike, as with a strap, rod, etc.; lash; beat **3.** to drive, urge, etc. by or as by whipping **4.** to strike as a whip does [the rain *whipped* her face] **5.** to wind (cord or thread) round (a rope, etc.), so as to prevent fraying **6.** to fish (a stream, etc.) by making repeated casts **7.** to beat (eggs, cream, etc.) into a froth with a fork, mixer, etc. **8.** to sew (a seam, etc.) with a loose, overcasting or overhand stitch **9.** [Colloq.] to defeat

or outdo —*vi.* **1.** to move, go, etc. quickly and suddenly [he *whipped* out of the room] **2.** to flap about in a whiplike manner [flags *whip* in high wind] —*n.* **1.** an instrument for striking or flogging, consisting of a rod with a lash attached to one end **2.** a blow, cut, etc. made with or as with a whip **3.** a person who uses a whip, as a coachman **4.** *a)* an officer of a political party in parliament, etc. who enforces party discipline, attendance, etc.: also **party whip** *b)* in the Brit. Parliament a notice issued to members to be in attendance at a certain time, underlined to indicate the degree of importance [a three-line *whip*] **5.** a whipping motion **6.** a dessert made of sugar and whipped cream, beaten egg whites, etc., and often fruit **7.** something resembling a whip in its action **8.** a hoisting apparatus consisting of a single rope passing through an overhead pulley **9.** *same as* WHIPPER-IN —**whip into shape** [Colloq.] to bring by vigorous action into a desired condition —**whip up** **1.** to rouse; excite **2.** [Colloq.] to prepare quickly and efficiently —**whip'like'** *adj.* —**whip'per** *n.*

whip·cord (-kôrd') *n.* **1.** a hard, twisted or braided cord used for whiplashes, etc. **2.** a strong worsted cloth with a hard, diagonally ribbed surface

whip hand **1.** the hand in which a driver holds his whip **2.** the position of advantage or control

whip·lash (-lash') *n.* **1.** the lash of a whip **2.** a sudden, severe jolting of the neck backwards and then forwards, as caused by the impact of a rear-end motor car collision: also **whiplash injury**

whipped cream rich sweet cream stiffened as by whipping and used as a topping on desserts, etc.

whip·per-in (wip'ər in', hwip'-) *n., pl.* **-pers-in** a huntsman's assistant who keeps the hounds together

whip·per·snap·per (wip'ər snap'ər, hwip'-) *n.* [< *whip-snapper*, one who snaps whips] a young or unimportant person who does not seem to show proper respect for those older or more important than himself

whip·pet (wip'it, hwip'-) *n.* [dim. < WHIP, or < obs. *whippet*, to move fast] a swift dog resembling a small greyhound, used in racing

WHIPPET
(45–55 cm high
at shoulder)

whip·ping (-iŋ) *n.* **1.** a flogging or beating, as in punishment **2.** cord, twine, etc. used to whip, or bind

whipping boy **1.** orig., a boy brought up with a young prince and required to take punishment for the latter's misdeeds **2.** *same as* SCAPEGOAT (sense 2)

whipping cream cream with a high percentage of butterfat, that can be whipped until stiff

whipping post a post to which offenders are tied to be whipped as a legal punishment

whipping top a toy top which is kept spinning by strokes from a whip

whip·ple·tree (wip''l trē', hwip'-) *n.* [< WHIP + TREE] *same as* SWINGLETREE

whip·poor·will (wip'ər wil', hwip'-) *n., pl.* **-wills', -will'**: see PLURAL, II, D, 1 [echoic] a greyish nightjar of eastern N America,

whip-round (-round) *n.* [Colloq.] an impromptu collection of money, as to buy a present for someone

whip·saw (wip'sô', hwip'-) *n.* a long-bladed saw; esp., one with a handle at each end for use by two persons —*vt.* to cut with a whipsaw

whip·stitch (-stich') *vt., vi.* Sewing to overcast or whip —*n.* a stitch made in this way

whip·stock (-stok') *n.* the handle of a whip

whir, whirr (wur, hwur) *vi., vt.* **whirred, whir'ring** [prob. < Scand.] to fly, revolve, vibrate, etc. with a whizzing or buzzing sound —*n.* a sound like this, as of a propeller

whirl (wurl, hwurl) *vi.* [ON. *hvirfla*] **1.** to move rapidly in a circular manner or as in an orbit **2.** to rotate or spin fast; gyrate **3.** to move, go, etc. swiftly **4.** to seem to spin; reel [my head is *whirling*] —*vt.* **1.** to cause to rotate, revolve, etc. rapidly **2.** to move, carry, etc. with a rotating motion [the wind *whirled* the leaves] —*n.* **1.** the act of whirling **2.** a whirling motion **3.** something whirling or being whirled **4.** a round of parties, etc. **5.** a tumult; uproar; stir **6.** a confused or giddy condition [my head is in a *whirl*] —**give it a whirl** [Colloq.] to make an attempt —**whirl'er** *n.*

whirl·i·gig (wur'li gig', hwur'-) *n.* [see WHIRL & GIG¹] **1.** a child's toy that whirls or spins **2.** a merry-go-round **3.** a whirling motion **4.** something that seems to whirl or revolve in a cycle **5.** a water beetle which gyrates rapidly on the surface of still water

whirl·pool (wurl'pool', hwurl'-) *n.* **1.** water in rapid, violent, whirling motion tending to form a circle into which floating objects are drawn; eddy of water **2.** anything like a whirlpool, as in violent motion

whirl·wind (-wind′) *n.* **1.** a current of air whirling violently upwards in a spiral that has a forward motion **2.** anything resembling a whirlwind, as in violent or destructive force, etc.—*adj.* carried on as fast as possible [a *whirlwind* courtship]

whirl·y·bird (wur′lē burd′, hwur′-) *n.* *colloq. term for* HELICOPTER

whish (wish, hwish) *vi.* [echoic] to move with a soft, rushing sound; whiz; swish —*n.* a sound so made

whisht (wisht, hwisht) *interj.* *same as* WHIST¹

whisk (wisk, hwisk) *n.* [ON. *visk*, a brush] **1.** *a)* the act of brushing with a quick, light, sweeping motion *b)* such a motion **2.** a small bunch of straw, hair, etc. used for brushing **3.** a kitchen utensil consisting of wire loops fixed in a handle, for whipping eggs, etc. —*vt.* **1.** to move, remove, brush (*away, off, out,* etc.) with a quick, sweeping motion **2.** to wave lightly (a tail, etc.) **3.** to whip (eggs, cream, etc.) —*vi.* **1.** to move quickly, nimbly, or briskly

whisk·er (wis′kər, hwis′-) *n.* [see WHISK & -ER] **1.** [*pl.*] the hair growing on a man's face; esp., the beard on the cheeks **2.** *a)* a hair of a man's beard *b)* any of the long, bristly hairs growing on the upper lip of a cat, rat, etc. —**by a whisker** [Colloq.] by a narrow margin; only just —**whisk′ered,** **whisk′er·y** *adj.*

whis·ky (wis′kē, hwis′kē) *n.,* *pl.* **-kies** [short for *usquebaugh* < IrGael. *uisce,* water + *beathadh,* life] **1.** a strong alcoholic liquor distilled from the fermented mash of grain, esp. barley **2.** a drink of whisky —*adj.* of, for, or made with whisky *Note:* in the U.S. and Ireland, the usual spelling is **whiskey**

whis·per (wis′pər, hwis′-) *vi.* [OE. *hwisprian*] **1.** to speak very softly, esp. without vibration of the vocal cords **2.** to talk in a quiet or furtive way, as in gossiping or plotting **3.** to make a soft, rustling sound —*vt.* **1.** to say very softly, esp. by whispering **2.** to tell as a secret —*n.* **1.** a whispering; soft, low speech produced with breath but, usually, without voice **2.** something whispered; a secret, hint, rumour, etc. **3.** a soft, rustling sound —**whis′per·er** *n.* —**whis′per·ing** *adj., n.* —**whis′per·ing·ly** *adv.* —**whis′per·y** *adj.*

whispering campaign the spreading, by word of mouth, of malicious rumours intended to discredit a political candidate, cause, etc.

whispering gallery a place so shaped that any faint sound is heard at an unusually long distance

whist¹ (wist, hwist) *interj.* [echoic] [Archaic or Dial.] hush! silence! —*vt., vi.* to be or become quiet

whist² (wist, hwist) *n.* [< earlier *whisk*] a card game usually played by two pairs of players, similar to, and the forerunner of, bridge

whist drive a form of progressive whist, in which the individual winners of each hand proceed to different tables to partner the losers of the previous hand

whis·tle (wis′′l, hwis′-) *vi.* **-tled, -tling** [OE. *hwistlian*] **1.** *a)* to make a clear, shrill sound by forcing breath between the teeth or through puckered lips *b)* to make a similar sound by sending steam through a small opening **2.** to make a clear, shrill cry: said of some birds and animals **3.** to move, pass, go, etc. with a high, shrill sound, as the wind **4.** *a)* to blow a whistle *b)* to have its whistle blown, as a train —*vt.* **1.** to produce (a tune, etc.) by whistling **2.** to summon, signal, etc. by whistling —*n.* **1.** an instrument for making whistling sounds **2.** the act or sound of whistling —**wet one's whistle** to take a drink —**whistle for** to seek or expect in vain —**whistle in the dark** to pretend to be confident —**whis′tling** *adj., n.*

whis·tler (-lər) *n.* **1.** a person, animal, or thing that whistles **2.** any of various birds that whistle **3.** a type of marriot **4.** an atmospheric disturbance picked up by radio receivers, characterized by a whistling sound

whistle stop [U.S.] **1.** a small town, orig. one at which a train stopped only upon signal **2.** a brief stop in a small town as part of a tour, esp. in a political campaign —**whis′-tle-stop′** *vi.* **-stopped′, -stop′ping**

whistling kettle a kettle in which steam activates a whistling signal when the water boils

whit (wit, hwit) *n.* [Early ModE. resp. of OE. *wiht,* a wight] the least bit; jot; iota: chiefly in negative constructions [not a *whit* the wiser]

white (wit, hwit) *adj.* **whit′er, whit′est** [OE. *hwit*] **1.** having the colour of pure snow or milk; of the colour of reflected light containing all of the visible rays of the spectrum: opposite to black, or COLOUR **2.** of a light or pale colour; specif., *a)* grey; silvery *b)* very blond *c)* pale; wan [a face *white* with terror] *d)* light-yellow or amber [*white* wines] *e)* blank, as a space unmarked by printing *f)* snowy **3.** colourless [*white* creme de menthe] **4.** clothed in white [the *White* Friars] **5.** pure; innocent **6.** free from evil intent; harmless [*white* magic] **7.** *a)* having a light-coloured skin; Caucasoid *b)* of or controlled by Caucasoids **8.** [Slang] honest; fair —*n.* **1.** white colour **2.** the state of being white; specif., *a)* fairness of complexion *b)* purity; innocence **3.** a white or light-coloured part or

thing, as the albumen of an egg, the white part of the eyeball, the light-coloured part of meat, wood, etc., a white garment, white wine, white pigment, etc. **4.** a person with a light-coloured skin; Caucasoid —*vt.* **whit′ed, whit′ing** to make white; whiten —**bleed white** to drain (a person) completely of money, resources, etc. —**white′ly** *adv.* —**white′ness** *n.*

white ant *same as* TERMITE

white·bait (-bāt′) *n., pl.* **-bait′** any of various small, silvery fishes, as young herring, used as food

white bass (bas) a silvery, freshwater, food and game fish of eastern N America

white·beam (-bēm) *n.* a tree with white down on the undersides of the leaves

white blood cell *same as* LEUCOCYTE: also called **white blood corpuscle**

white bread bread of a light colour, made from finely sifted wheat flour

white·cap (-kap′) *n.* a wave with its crest broken into white foam

white clover a creeping species of clover with white flower clusters, grown as a forage plant

white coal water as a source of power

white coffee coffee made with milk or cream

white-col·lar (-kol′ər) *adj.* [from the formerly typical white shirt worn by such workers] designating or of clerical or professional workers or others, employed in work not essentially manual

whited sepulchre a hypocrite: Matt. 23:27

white dwarf any of a class of small, extremely dense stars of low luminosity

white elephant **1.** an albino elephant, regarded as sacred by the Thais, Burmese, etc. **2.** something that is of little profit or use but costs a lot to maintain **3.** any object that its owner no longer wants to keep but that others may want to own or buy

white-eye (wīt′ī, hwīt′ī) *n.* any of various small songbirds of E Asia, S Africa and Australia, usually with rings of white feathers round the eyes

white feather [from belief that a white feather in a gamecock's tail shows bad breeding, hence cowardice] an indication of cowardice: chiefly in **show the white feather**

white·fish (-fish′) *n., pl.* **-fish′, -fish′es**: see FISH **1.** any of various white or silvery freshwater food fishes of the salmon family **2.** any of various food fishes with white, non-oily flesh, as the cod, plaice, etc.

white flag a white banner or cloth hoisted as a signal of truce or surrender

white·fly (-flī′) *n., pl.* **-flies′** any of various tiny whitish insects, often harmful to plants

White Friar a Carmelite friar: so called from the white mantle worn by these friars

white gold gold alloyed with nickel, zinc, etc., to give it a white, platinumlike appearance for use in jewellery

white-haired (-herd′) *adj.* having white or very light hair

White·hall (wīt′hôl, hwīt′-) *n.* [after a street in London, site of several government offices] the British government or its central administration

white-headed boy (-hed′id-) a person who is treated with special favour

white heat **1.** the degree of intense heat (beyond red heat) at which metal, etc. glows white **2.** a state of intense emotion, excitement, etc.

white hope any person who is expected to bring honour and glory to a place, group, etc.

white horse **1.** a white-crested wave **2.** the figure of a horse on a hillside, formed by removing the turf and exposing the underlying chalk

white-hot (wīt′hot′, hwīt′-) *adj.* **1.** glowing white with heat **2.** extremely angry, excited, enthusiastic, etc.

White House, the [after the white mansion in Washington which is the official residence of the president of the U.S.] the executive branch of the U.S. government

white lead **1.** a poisonous, heavy, white powder, basic lead carbonate, used as a paint pigment, for pottery glazes, etc. **2.** any of several white pigments containing lead, as lead sulphate

white lie a lie about something unimportant, often one told to spare someone's feelings

white light *Physics* light, as sunlight, composed of rays of all the wavelengths ranging from red to violet

white-liv·ered (-liv′ərd) *adj.* cowardly; craven

white man's burden the supposed duty of the white man to bring their civilization to the non-white inhabitants of their colonies

white matter whitish nerve tissue of the brain and spinal cord, consisting chiefly of nerve fibres

white meat any light-coloured meat, as veal, pork, the breast of poultry, etc.

white monk a Cistercian

whit·en (wīt′′n, hwīt′-) *vt., vi.* to make or become white or whiter —**whit′en·er** *n.* —**whit′en·ing** *n.*

white noise a sound containing a blend of all the audible frequencies distributed equally over the range of the frequency band

white·out (-out′) *n.* a weather condition occurring in polar regions in which the snowy ground and white sky merge so that one's sense of direction and distance disappears

white paper an official government report that defines or supports the ministry's policy on a specific matter

white pepper pepper ground from the husked, dried seeds of the nearly ripe pepper berry

white race loosely, the Caucasoid group of mankind

White Russian 1. a native or inhabitant of White Russia; Byelorussian 2. any of the Russians who fought against the Bolsheviks (Reds) in the Russian civil war

white sale a sale of sheets, towels, linens, etc. held in a department store

white sauce a sauce for vegetables, meat, fish, etc., made of fat or butter, flour, milk or stock, and seasoning

white slave a woman enticed or forced into or held in prostitution for the profit of others —**white′-slave′** *adj.* —**white slaver** —**white slavery**

white-smith (-smith′) *n.* 1. a worker in white metals, esp. tin 2. a worker in iron who does finishing, polishing, or galvanizing

white spirit a light-coloured mixture of petroleum hydrocarbons used as a solvent, etc.

white-tailed deer (-tāld′) a common American deer having a tail that is white on the undersurface, a white-spotted red coat in summer, and a brownish-grey coat in winter: also **white′tail′**e

white-thorn (-thôrn′) *n.* the hawthorn

white-throat (-thrōt′) *n.* any of several warblers with a whitish throat

white tie a white bow tie, properly worn with a swallow-tailed coat 2. a swallow-tailed coat and its accessories

white·wash (-wosh′) *n.* 1. a mixture of lime, whiting, size, water, etc., for whitening walls, etc. 2. *a)* a concealing of faults or defects as in an effort to avoid blame *b)* something said or done for this purpose 3. [U.S. Colloq.] *Sports* a defeat in which the loser scores no points —*vt.* 1. to cover with whitewash 2. to conceal the faults or defects of 3. [U.S. Colloq.] *Sports* to defeat (an opponent) without permitting him to score —**white′wash′**er *n.* —**white′wash′-ing** *n.*

white whale *same as* BELUGA (sense 2)

white·wood (-wood′) *n.* 1. any of a number of trees with white or light-coloured wood 2. the wood of such a tree, esp. when prepared for painting or staining —*adj.* made of such a wood [*whitewood* furniture]

whith·er (with′ər, hwith′-) *adv.* [OE. *hwider*] to what place, condition, etc.? where? —*conj.* 1. to which place, condition, etc. 2. wherever *Where* is now almost always used in place of *whither*

whith·er·so·ev·er (with′ər sō ev′ər, hwith′-) *adv., conj.* [Archaic or Poet.] to whatever place; wheresoever

whit·ing¹ (wīt′iŋ, hwīt′-) *n., pl.* -**ings, -ing:** see PLURAL, II, D, 1 [MDu. *wijting* < *wit*, white] 1. a small, edible, European seafish 2. any of various similar fishes, as the American hake

whit·ing² (wīt′iŋ, hwīt′-) *n.* [see WHITE, *v.* + -ING] powdered chalk used in making paints, inks, etc.

whit·ish (-ish) *adj.* somewhat white —**whit′ish·ness** *n.*

whit·low (wit′lō, hwit′-) *n.* [ME. *whitflawe:* of disputed origin] *same as* FELON²

Whit·sun (wit′s'n, hwit′-) *adj.* of or observed on Whitsunday or at Whitsuntide

Whit·sun·day (wit′sun′dē, hwit′-; -dā; -s'n dā′) *n.* [OE. *Hwita Sunnandæg*, white Sunday] *same as* PENTECOST (sense 2)

Whit·sun·tide (-s'n tīd′) *n.* the week beginning with Whitsunday, esp. the first three days of that week

whit·tle (wit′'l, hwit′-) *vt.* -**tled, -tling** [OE. *thwitan*, to cut] 1. a) to cut thin shavings from (wood) with a knife *b)* to carve (an object) in this manner 2. to reduce, destroy, etc. gradually, as if by whittling: usually with *down, away,* etc. [to *whittle* down costs] —*vi.* to whittle wood —**whit′-tler** *n.*

whit·y (wīt′ē, hwīt′-) *adj.* whit′i·er, whit′i·est *same as* WHITISH

whiz, whizz (wiz, hwiz) *vi.* whizzed, whiz′zing [echoic] 1. to make the buzzing or hissing sound of something moving swiftly through the air 2. to speed by with or as with this sound [the bus *whizzed* by him] —*vt.* to cause to whiz —*n.* a whizzing sound or movement —**whiz′zing·ly** *adv.*

whiz kid, whizz kid [Colloq.] outstandingly able and successful, or potentially successful, young person

who (hoo) *pron.,* objective **whom,** poss. **whose** [OE. *hwa*] 1. what or which person or persons: used to introduce a question [*who* is he? I don't know *who* he is] 2. a) (the, or a, person or persons) that: used to introduce a relative clause [the man *who* came to dinner] *b)* any person or persons that: used as an indefinite relative [*"who* steals my purse steals nought"] The use of *who* rather than *whom* as

the object of a verb or preposition [*who* did you see? *who* was it written by?], although widespread, is objected to by some —**who's who** who the important people are

WHO World Health Organization

whoa (wō, hwō) *interj.* [for HO] stop!: used esp. in directing a horse to stand still

who·dun·it (hoo dun′it) *n.* [Colloq.] a mystery novel, play, etc.: cf. MYSTERY¹ (sense 2b)

who·ev·er (-ev′ər) *pron.* 1. any person that; whatever person 2. no matter what person [*whoever* said it, it's not so] 3. what person? who?: used for emphasis [*whoever* told you that?]

whole (hōl) *adj.* [OE. *hal*] 1. healthy; not diseased or injured 2. not broken, damaged, defective, etc.; intact 3. containing all the elements or parts; complete 4. not divided up; in a single unit 5. constituting the entire amount, extent, etc. [the *whole* week] 6. having both parents in common [a *whole* brother] 7. in all aspects of one's being [the *whole* man] 8. *Arith.* not mixed or fractional [25 is a *whole* number] —*n.* 1. the entire amount, etc.; totality 2. a complete organization of parts; unity; entirety, etc. —**as a whole** as a complete unit; altogether —**on the whole** all things considered; in general —**whole′ness** *n.*

whole·heart·ed (-här′tid) *adj.* doing or done with all one's energy, enthusiasm, etc.; sincere —**whole′heart′ed·ly** *adv.* —**whole′heart′ed·ness** *n.*

whole-hog (hōl′hog′) *adj., adv.* [Slang] without reservation; complete(ly): chiefly in **to go the whole hog**

whole-hoofed (hōl′hooft′) *adj.* having hoofs which are not divided

whole·meal (hōl′mēl′) *adj.* 1. made of the entire wheat kernel [*wholemeal* flour] 2. made of wholemeal flour [*wholemeal* bread]

whole milk [U.S.] milk from which none of the butterfat or other elements have been removed

whole note *Music* U.S. name for SEMIBREVE

whole number zero or any positive or negative multiple of 1; integer [28 is a *whole number*]

whole·sale (hōl′sāl′) *n.* the selling of goods in relatively large quantities, esp. to retailers who then sell them at higher prices to consumers —*adj.* 1. of, connected with, or engaged in such selling 2. extensive or sweeping [*wholesale* criticism] —*adv.* 1. in wholesale amounts or at wholesale prices 2. extensively or sweepingly [to reject proposals *wholesale*] —*vt., vi.* -**saled, -sal′ing** to sell wholesale —**whole′sal′er** *n.*

whole·some (-səm) *adj.* [see WHOLE & -SOME¹] 1. good for one's health or well-being; healthful [*wholesome* food] 2. tending to improve the mind or character 3. having or showing health and vigour 4. suggesting health [a *wholesome* smile] —**whole′some·ly** *adv.* —**whole′-some·ness** *n.*

whole tone *Music* an interval consisting of two adjacent semitones

who'll (hool) 1. who shall 2. who will

whol·ly (hō′lē, hōl′lē) *adv.* to the whole amount or extent; totally; entirely

whom (hoom) *pron. objective case of* WHO: see note at WHO on the use of *who* and *whom*

whom·ev·er (hoom ev′ər) *pron. objective case of* WHOEVER

whom·so·ev·er (hoom′sō ev′ər) *pron. objective case of* WHOSOEVER

whoop (hoop, hwoop, woop) *n.* [OFr. *houper,* to cry out] 1. a loud shout, cry, etc., as of excitement, joy, etc. 2. a hoot, as of an owl 3. the gasping sound made when a breath of air is taken in following a fit of coughing in whooping cough —*vi., vt.* to utter, or utter with, a whoop or whoops —**whoop it** (or **things**) **up** [Slang] 1. to create a noisy disturbance, as in celebrating 2. to create enthusiasm (for)

whoop·ee (woo′pē, hwoo′-, woo′-, hwoo′-) *interj.* [< prec.] an exclamation of great joy, gay abandonment, etc. —*n.* 1. a shout of "whoopee!" 2. noisy fun —**make whoopee** [Slang] 1. to revel or have fun in a noisy way 2. to be lightheartedly amorous

whoop·er (-ər) *n.* 1. a person or thing that whoops 2. a large swan with a noisy, whooping cry: also **whoop·ing swan**

whoop·ing cough (hoop′piŋ) an acute infectious disease, usually affecting children, in which there are repeated attacks of coughing that end in a whoop

whoops (woops, hwoops, woops, hwoops) *interj.* an exclamation uttered as in regaining one's balance after stumbling or one's composure after a slip of the tongue

whoosh (woosh, hwoosh) *vi., vt.* [echoic] to make or cause to make a hissing or rushing sound while moving swiftly through the air —*n.* this sound

whop (wop, hwop) *vt., vi.* whopped, whop′ping [prob. echoic] [Colloq.] 1. to beat, strike, etc. 2. to defeat decisively —*n.* [Colloq.] a sharp, loud blow, thump, etc.

whop·per (-ər) *n.* [< prec.] [Colloq.] 1. anything extraordinarily large 2. a great lie

whop·ping (-iŋ) *adj.* [< WHOP + -ING] [Colloq.] extraordinarily large or great; colossal

whore (hôr) *n.* [OE. *hore* < or akin to ON. *hora*] a sexually promiscuous woman; esp., a prostitute —*vi.* **whored, whor'-ing** 1. to be a whore 2. to fornicate with whores —**whor'-ish** *adj.*

who're (hōō'ər, hoor) who are

whore·house (-hous') *n.* a brothel

whore·mon·ger (hôr'muŋ'gər) *n.* a man who associates with whores; specif., a pimp or pander: also **whore'mas'ter**

whorl (wôrl, hwôrl, wurl, hwurl) *n.* [< dial. var. of WHIRL] anything with a coiled or spiral appearance; specif., *a)* any of the circular ridges that form the design of a fingerprint *b)* *Bot.* a circular growth of leaves, petals, etc. about the same point on a stem *c)* *Zool.* any of the turns in a spiral shell —**whorled** *adj.*

whor·tle·ber·ry (wur't'l bər ē, hwur'-) *n.,* pl. **-ries** [< Brit. dial. form of earlier *hurtleberry* < OE. *horta*] *same as* BILBERRY

who's (hōōz) 1. who is 2. who has

whose (hōōz) *pron.* [OE. *hwæs*] that or those belonging to whom [*whose* is this?] —*possessive pronominal adj.* of, belonging to, made, or done by whom or which [the man *whose* car was stolen]

who·so (hōō'sō) *pron.* [OE. *hwa swa*] [Archaic] whoever; whosoever

who·so·ev·er (hōō'sō ev'ər) *pron.* whoever: used for emphasis

why (wī, hwī) *adv.* [OE. *hwi,* instrumental case of *hwæt, what*] for what reason, cause, or purpose? [*why* did he go? he told her *why* he went] —*conj.* 1. because of which [there is no reason *why* you should go] 2. the reason for which [that is why he went] —*n.,* pl. **whys** the reason, cause, etc. [never mind the *why* and wherefore] —*interj.* an exclamation used to show surprise, impatience, etc. or to introduce a remark

whyd·ah (bird) (wid'ə, hwid'-) [altered < *widow bird,* by association with *Ouidah* (sometimes sp. *Whidah*) seaport in Benin] any of several chiefly brown and black West African weaverbirds

W.I. 1. West Indies 2. Women's Institute

wick[1] (wik) *n.* [OE. *weoca*] a piece of cord or tape, or a thin bundle of threads, in a candle, oil lamp, cigarette lighter, etc., that absorbs the fuel and, when lighted, burns with a steady flame —**get on a person's wick** [Colloq.] to cause extreme irritation to a person

wick[2] (wik) *n.* [ME. *wik* < OE. *wic*] a village, town, or hamlet: now archaic except as compounded in *bailiwick* and (often in the form **-wich**) in placenames, as in *Warwick, Greenwich*

wick·ed (wik'id) *adj.* [ME. < *wikke,* evil, akin to OE. *wicce, witch*] 1. morally bad or wrong; acting or done with evil intent 2. generally painful, unpleasant, etc. [a *wicked* blow on the head] 3. naughty; mischievous [a *wicked* smile] —**wick'ed·ly** *adv.* —**wick'ed·ness** *n.*

wick·er (wik'ər) *n.* [< Scand.] 1. a thin, flexible twig; withe 2. *a)* such twigs or long, woody strips woven together, as in making baskets or furniture *b)* *same as* WICKERWORK (sense 1) —*adj.* made of wicker

wick·er·work (-wurk') *n.* 1. things made of wicker 2. *same as* WICKER (sense 2a) 3. the art or craft of making wicker objects

wick·et (wik'it) *n.* [ONormFr. *wiket* < Gmc.] 1. a small door or gate, esp. one set in or near a larger one 2. a small gate for regulating the flow of water, as to a water wheel 3. *Cricket a)* either of two sets of three stumps each, with two bails resting on top of them *b)* the playing space between the two wickets, esp. with regard to its condition [a fast *wicket*] *c)* a player's turn at batting or the period during which two batsmen bat together [a third-*wicket* partnership] *d)* the instance of a batsman being got out [the bowler took three *wickets*]

wick·et·keep·er (-kē'pər) *n.* *Cricket* the fielder stationed immediately behind the wicket

wick·ing (wik'iŋ) *n.* cord, tape, etc. for wicks

wid·der·shins (wid'ər shinz') *adv.* var. of WITHERSHINS

wide (wīd) *adj.* **wid'er, wid'est** [OE. *wid*] 1. extending over a large area; esp., extending over a larger area from side to side than is usual 2. of a specified extent from side to side [two kilometres *wide*] 3. of great extent, range, etc. [a *wide* variety] 4. roomy; ample; full [*wide* trousers] 5. opened as far as possible [eyes *wide* with fear] 6. far from the point, issue, etc. aimed at [*wide* of the mark] 7. [Slang] shrewd and unscrupulous [a *wide* boy] —*adv.* 1. over a relatively large area; widely [to travel far and *wide*] 2. to a large or full extent; fully [*wide* open] 3. so as to miss the point, issue, etc. aimed at; astray [his shot went *wide*] —*n.* 1. [Rare] a wide area 2. *Cricket* a ball bowled out of the batsman's reach —**give a wide berth** (to) to steer clear of (something); shun —**wide of the mark** far afield; mistaken —**wide'ly** *adv.* —**wide'ness** *n.*

-wide (wīd) a *combining form* meaning existing or extending throughout [*nationwide*]

wide-an·gle (wīd'aŋ'g'l) *adj.* 1. designating or of a kind of camera lens covering a wide angle of view 2. designating or of any of several systems using one or more film cameras (and projectors) and a very wide, curved screen

wide-a·wake (-ə wāk') *adj.* 1. completely awake 2. alert 3. [Colloq.] knowing; wise [he's *wide-awake* to the time of day] —*n.* a low-crowned, broad-brimmed hat —**wide'-a·wake'ness** *n.*

wide-eyed (-īd') *adj.* with the eyes wide open

wid·en (wīd''n) *vt., vi.* to make or become wide or wider

wide-o·pen (wīd'ō'p'n) *adj.* 1. opened wide 2. exposed to attack; vulnerable 3. [U.S.] not having or enforcing laws against prostitution, gambling, the sale of alcohol, etc. [a *wide-open* city]

wide·spread (-spred') *adj.* spread widely; esp., *a)* widely extended [with *widespread* arms] *b)* occurring over a wide area or extent [*widespread* benefits]

widg·eon (wij'ən) *n.,* pl. **-eons, -eon:** see PLURAL, II, D,1 < MFr. *vigeon*] any of various wild, freshwater ducks

wid·get (wij'it) *n.* [altered < GADGET] a small gadget or device, esp. one without a specific description

wid·ow (wid'ō) *n.* [OE. *widewe*] 1. a woman whose husband has died and who has not remarried 2. *Cards* a group of cards dealt to the table, typically for the use of the highest bidder 3. *Printing* an incomplete line, as that ending a paragraph, carried over to the top of a new page or column 4. [Colloq.] a woman whose husband is often away indulging in a specified hobby or activity [a golf *widow*] —*vt.* to cause to become a widow [widowed by the war] —**wid'ow·hood** *n.*

widow bird *same as* WHYDAH BIRD

wid·ow·er (wid'ə wər) *n.* a man whose wife has died and who has not remarried

widow's cruse a supply that is apparently inexhaustible: I Kings 17:10-17; II Kings 4:1-7

widow's mite a small gift or contribution freely given by one who can scarcely afford it: Mark 12:41-44

widow's peak a point formed by hair growing down in the middle of a forehead

width (width, witth) *n.* [< WIDE, by analogy with LENGTH] 1. a being wide; wideness 2. the distance from side to side 3. a piece of something of a certain width [two *widths* of cloth]

wield (wēld) *vt.* [OE. *wealdan & wieldan*] 1. to handle and use (a tool or weapon), esp. with skill and control 2. to exercise (power, influence, etc.) —**wield'er** *n.*

wield·y (wēl'dē) *adj.* **wield'i·er, wield'i·est** that can be wielded easily; manageable

wie·ner (wē'nər) *n.* [short for G. *Wiener Wurst,* Vienna sausage] [U.S.] a frankfurter: also **wie'ner·wurst'**

wife (wīf) *n.,* pl. **wives** (wīvz) [OE. *wif*] 1. orig., a woman: still so used in *midwife, housewife,* etc. 2. a married woman —**take to wife** to marry (a specified woman) —**wife'hood** *n.* —**wife'less** *adj.* —**wife'ly** *adj.* **-li·er, -li·est**

wig (wig) *n.* [shortened < PERIWIG] 1. a false covering of real or synthetic hair for the head 2. *same as* TOUPEE —*vt.* **wigged, wig'ging** 1. to furnish with a wig or wigs 2. [Colloq.] to scold, rebuke, etc. —**wig'less** *adj.*

wi·geon (wij'ən) *n.* *var. of* WIDGEON

wig·ging (wig'iŋ) *n.* [Colloq.] a scolding

wig·gle (wig''l) *vt., vi.* **-gled, -gling** [prob. < MDu. & MLowG. *wiggelen,* freq. of *wiggen,* to move from side to side] to move with short, jerky or twisting motions from side to side —*n.* the act or an instance of wiggling —**wig'gler** *n.*

wig·gly (-lē) *adj.* **-gli·er, -gli·est** 1. that wiggles; wiggling 2. wavy [a *wiggly* line]

wight (wīt) *n.* [OE. *wiht*] [Archaic] a human being; person

wig·wag (wig'wag') *vt., vi.* **-wagged', -wag'ging** [< obs. *wig,* to move + WAG[1]] 1. to move back and forth; wag 2. to send (a message) by waving flags, lights, etc. back and forth in accordance with a code —*n.* 1. the sending of messages in this way 2. a message so sent

wig·wam (wig'wam) *n.* [< Algonquian] a dwelling made by the Indians of E and C N America, consisting typically of a framework of arched poles covered with bark

wil·co (wil'kō) *interj.* [*wil(l) co(mply)*] I will comply with your request: used in radio-telephony

WIGWAM

wild (wīld) *adj.* [OE. *wilde*] 1. living or growing in its original, natural state; not domesticated or cultivated [*wild* flowers, *wild* animals] 2. not lived in or cultivated; overgrown, waste, etc. [*wild* land] 3. not civilized; savage [a *wild* tribe] 4. not controlled; unruly, rough, lawless, etc. [*wild* children] 5. lacking social or moral restraint; dissolute, orgiastic, etc. [a *wild* rake, a *wild* party] 6. turbulent; stormy [*wild* seas] 7. *a)* very excited or enthusiastic [*wild* with delight, *wild* about skating] *b)* angered, frantic, crazed, etc. [*wild* with desperation*]* **8.** in a state of disorder, confusion, etc. *[wild hair]* **9.** fantastically impractical *[a wild scheme]* **10.** reckless; imprudent *[a wild wager]* **11.** missing the target *[a wild shot]* **12.** *Cards* having any value specified by the holder: said of a card **—adv.** in a wild manner *[to shoot wild]* **—n.** *[usually pl.]* a wilderness or wasteland **—out in the wilds** far from civilization; living in the country rather than a town **—run wild** to grow, exist, or behave in an uncontrolled way **—wild and woolly** rough and uncivilized **—wild horses wouldn't drag it from me** [Colloq.] I will keep the secret at all costs **—wild'ly** *adv.* **—wild'ness** *n.*

wild boar a variety of pig living wild in Europe, Asia, and Africa, from which domestic pigs have been derived

wild carrot a common biennial weed, with finely divided foliage and umbels of white flowers: the cultivated carrot is derived from it: also called **Queen Anne's lace**

wild-cat (wīld'kat') *n.,* *pl.* **-cats'**, **-cat'**: see PLURAL, II, D, 1 **1.** an undomesticated European cat, resembling the domestic tabby, but larger and having a bushy tail **2.** any of various other fierce, medium sized undomesticated animals of the cat family, as the lynx **3.** a house cat that has escaped from domestication: in this sense, usually **wild cat** **4.** a fierce, aggressive person **5.** [U.S.] an unsound or risky business scheme **6.** [Chiefly U.S.] an oil well drilled in an area not known before to have oil **—adj.** **1.** unsound or financially risky **2.** *a)* operating in an illegal or unethical way *b)* not officially authorized *[a wildcat strike]* **—vi.** **-cat'ted, -cat'ting** [Chiefly U.S.] to drill for oil in an area considered unproductive before **—wild'cat'ter** *n.*

wil·de·beest (wil'də bēst', vil')' *n.,* *pl.* **-beests'**, **-beest'**: see PLURAL, II, D, 1 *[Afrik. < Du. wild, wild + beeste, beast]* *same as* GNU

wil·der·ness (wil'dər nis) *n.* *[< ME. wilderne, wild place (< OE. < wilde, wild + deor, animal) + -nesse, -NESS]* **1.** wasteland or overgrown land with no settlers **2.** a part of a garden left in a wild state **3.** a large, confused mass or tangle of persons or things

wild-eyed (wīld'īd') *adj.* staring in a wild, distracted, or demented way

wild-fire (-fīr') *n.* **1.** a fire that spreads fast and is hard to put out *[the rumours spread like wildfire]* **2.** *same as* GREEK FIRE **3.** lightning without audible thunder; heat lightning **4.** *same as* WILL-O'-THE-WISP

wild flower any flowering plant growing without cultivation in fields, woods, etc. Also **wild'flow·er**

wild·fowl (-foul') *n.,* *pl.* **-fowls'**, **-fowl'**: see PLURAL, II, D, 1 a game bird, esp. an aquatic one

wild-goose chase (-gōōs') any search or undertaking as futile as trying to catch a wild goose by chasing it

wild·ing (wīl'diŋ) *n.* **1.** *a)* an uncultivated plant, esp. the crab apple *b)* a cultivated plant that has become wild **2.** [Rare] a wild animal

wild·life (wīld'līf') *n.* wild animals and birds, collectively

wild oats any of several wild grasses, having twisted awns: also **wild oat** **—sow one's wild oats** to be sexually promiscuous and dissolute in youth before settling down: usually said of a man

wild pansy an uncultivated pansy, esp. a European species with petals in combinations of white, yellow, and purple

wild rice **1.** a tall grass of the U.S. and Canada, found in swampy borders of lakes and streams **2.** its edible grain

wild rose any of various roses growing wild, as eglantine

wild silk silk made from wild silkworms; tussah

Wild West the western U.S. in its early frontier period of lawlessness

wild·wood (wīld'wood') *n.* a natural woodland or forest, esp. when unfrequented by man

wile (wīl) *n.* [Late OE. *wil* < OE. *wigle,* magic] **1.** a sly trick; stratagem **2.** a beguiling or coquettish trick *Usually used in pl.* **—vt.** **wiled, wil'ing** beguile; lure **—wile away** to while away (time): by confusion with *while*

wil·ful (wil'fəl) *adj.* **1.** done deliberately or intentionally **2.** always wanting one's own way; doing as one pleases; self-willed **—wil'ful·ly** *adv.* **—wil'ful·ness** *n.*

will¹ (wil) *n.* [OE. *willa*] **1.** the power of making a reasoned choice or decision or of controlling one's own actions **2.** *a)* strong and fixed purpose; determination *[where there's a will there's a way]* *b)* energy and enthusiasm *[to work with a will]* **3.** attitude towards others *[good will]* **4.** *a)* the desire, purpose, choice, etc. of a certain person or group *[what is your will?]* *b)* a compelling command or decree *[the will of the people]* **5.** *a)* the legal statement of a person's wishes concerning the disposal of his property after death *b)* the document containing this **—vt.** **1.** to have as the object of one's will **2.** to control or influence by the power of the will **3.** to bequeath by a will **—vi.** **1.** to exert one's will **2.** to choose or prefer **—at will** when one wishes **—will'a·ble** *adj.* **—will'·less** *adj.*

will² (wil; *unstressed* wəl) *v.,* *pt.* **would** [OE. *willan*] **1.** an auxiliary regularly used to express the future: in the rules of some grammarians, esp. formerly, *will* is to be used in the second and third persons for simple future and in the first person to show determination or obligation, and *shall* is to be used in the first person for simple future and in the second and third persons to show determination or obligation: in practice *will* and *shall* are used interchangeably, with *will* in more common use by all people **2.** an auxiliary used to express: *a)* willingness *[will you do me a favour?]* *b)* ability or capacity *[it will hold another quart]* *c)* habit, custom, inclination, or inevitability *[boys will be boys]* *d)* expectation, surmise, etc. *[that will be his wife with him, I suppose]* See also SHALL **—vt., vi.** to wish; desire *[do what (or as) you will]*

willed (wild) *adj.* having a will, esp. a specified kind of will: used in hyphenated compounds *[strong-willed]*

will·ful (wil'fəl) *adj.* *alt. U.S. sp.* of WILFUL

wil·lies (wil'ēz) *n.pl.* [< ?] [Slang] a state of nervousness; jitters: with *the*

will·ing (wil'iŋ) *adj.* **1.** ready or agreeing (*to* do something) *[willing* to try] **2.** doing, giving, etc. or done, given, etc. readily or gladly; voluntarily **—will'ing·ly** *adv.* **—will'ing·ness** *n.*

wil·li·waw, wil·ly·waw (wil'i wô') *n.* [< ?] **1.** a sudden squall, esp. in the Strait of Magellan **2.** [U.S.] a sudden, violent, cold wind blowing down from mountain passes towards the coast in far northern or southern latitudes

will-o'-the-wisp (wil'ə *th*ə wisp') *n.* [earlier *Will* (personal name) *with the wisp*] **1.** a light seen moving over marshes at night: see also IGNIS FATUUS **2.** any person or thing that allures and misleads; deception; delusion

wil·low (wil'ō) *n.* [OE. *welig*] **1.** *a)* any of a genus of trees and shrubs bearing catkins and usually narrow leaves: the flexible twigs of certain species are used in weaving baskets, chair seats, etc. *b)* the wood of any of these **2.** [orig. made of willow] [Colloq.] a cricket bat

willow herb any of a genus of perennial plants of the evening-primrose family, with narrow leaves and whitish or purple flowers

willow pattern a design for china picturing a river, pagoda, willow trees, etc., usually in blue on a white ground

wil·low·y (wil'ō wē) *adj.* **1.** covered or shaded with willows **2.** like a willow; specif., *a)* gracefully slender *b)* pliant, supple, lithe, etc.

will·pow·er (wil'pou'ər) *n.* strength of will, mind, or determination; self-control

wil·ly-nil·ly (wil'ē nil'ē) *adv.* [contr. < *will I, nill I: nill <* OE. *nyllan < ne,* not + *willan,* to WILL¹] whether one wishes it or not; willingly or unwillingly **—adj.** that is or happens whether one wishes it or not

willy willy [Aust.] a tropical storm or whirlwind

wilt¹ (wilt) *vi.* [var. of obs. *welk,* to wither] **1.** to become limp, as from heat or lack of water; wither; droop: said of plants **2.** to become weak or faint; languish **3.** to lose courage; quail **—vt.** to cause to wilt **—n.** **1.** the act of wilting or condition of being wilted **2.** any of various plant diseases characterized by wilting

wilt² (wilt) *archaic 2nd pers. sing., pres. indic.,* of WILL²

Wil·ton (wilt'ən) *n.* [< *Wilton,* in Wiltshire where first made] a kind of carpet with a velvety pile of cut loops: also **Wilton carpet, Wilton rug**

Wilts. Wiltshire

wil·y (wī'lē) *adj.* **wil'i·er, wil'i·est** full of wiles; crafty; sly **—wil'i·ness** *n.*

wim·ble (wim'b'l) *n.* [< Anglo-Fr. < MDu. *wimmel,* an auger] a tool for boring, as a gimlet, auger, etc. **—vt.** **-bled, -bling** to bore with a wimble

wim·ple (wim'p'l) *n.* [OE. *wimpel*] a woman's head covering of medieval times consisting of a cloth arranged about the head, cheeks, chin, and neck: now worn only by certain nuns **—vt.** **-pled, -pling** **1.** to clothe as with a wimple **2.** to lay in folds **3.** to cause to ripple **—vi.** **1.** to lie in folds **2.** to ripple

WIMPLE

Wim·py (wim'pē) *n.* [after a cartoon-strip character who ate hamburgers] a *trademark* for a hamburger in a soft bread-roll

win (win) *vi.* **won, win'ning** [OE. *winnan,* to fight] **1.** *a)* to gain a victory; be victorious; triumph *b)* to finish in first place in a race, contest, etc. **2.** to succeed in reaching or achieving a specified state or place (with various prepositions, adverbs, etc.) *[to win back to health]* **—vt.** **1.** to get by effort, struggle, etc.; specif., *a)* to gain through accomplishment *[to win distinctions]* *b)* to achieve (one's point, demands, etc.) *c)* to gain (a prize or award) in competition *d)* to earn (a livelihood, etc.) **2.** to be victorious in (a contest, dispute, etc.) **3.** to get to with effort *[they won the hilltop by noon]* **4.** to influence or persuade: often with *over [to win someone over to one's side]* **5.** *a)* to gain the sympathy, favour, etc. of [to *win* a supporter] b) to gain (someone's sympathy, etc.) **6.** to persuade to marry one **7.** to obtain ores, minerals, etc. by mining —*n.* **1.** [Colloq.] an act of winning; victory, as in a contest **2.** anything won, as a sum of money **3.** *Racing* first position at the finish

wince[1] (wins) *vi.* **winced, winc′ing** [< Anglo-Fr. var. of OFr. *guenchir* < Frank.] to draw back slightly, usually grimacing, as in pain —*n.* a wincing —**winc′er** *n.*

wince[2] (wins) *n.* [var. of WINCH] a roller used between dyeing vats to facilitate the transfer of pieces of cloth

win·cey·ette (win′sē et′) *n.* [*wincey,* a kind of fabric + -ETTE] a kind of flannelette or cotton flannel

winch (winch) *n.* [OE. *wince*] **1.** a crank with a handle for transmitting motion **2.** a hoisting or hauling apparatus consisting of a drum or cylinder on which is to be wound a rope or cable attached to the object to be lifted or moved —*vt.* to hoist or haul with a winch

Win·ches·ter (**rifle**) (win′ches′tər, -chis-) [after O. F. *Winchester* (1810–80), U.S. manufacturer] *a trademark for* a type of repeating rifle with a tubular magazine set horizontally under the barrel

wind[1] (wīnd) *vt.* **wound wind′ing** [OE. *windan*] **1.** a) to turn, or make revolve [to *wind* a crank] b) to move as by cranking **2.** a) to coil (string, ribbon, etc.) round itself or round something else [*winding* a bandage round his toe] b) to cover by encircling with something [to *wind* a spool with thread] **3.** a) to make (one's way) in a winding or twisting course b) to make move in such a course **4.** to introduce deviously; insinuate [*winding* his way into her heart] **5.** to hoist or haul as with a winch (often with *up*) **6.** to tighten the spring of (a clock, etc.) as by turning a stem (often with *up*) —*vi.* **1.** to move or go in a twisting or curving course **2.** to appear in a way that is circuitous, devious, etc. **3.** to coil or spiral (*about* or *round* something) **4.** to undergo winding [this clock *winds* easily] —*n.* **1.** the act of winding **2.** a single turn of something wound **3.** a turn; twist; bend; curve —**wind down 1.** to reduce gradually; bring, or draw, to an end **2.** to relax; unwind —**wind up 1.** to wind into a ball, etc. **2.** to entangle or involve **3.** to bring or come to an end; finish **4.** to make or become very tense, nervous, excited, etc. —**wind′er** *n.*

wind[2] (wind; *for n., also poet.* wīnd) *n.* [OE.] **1.** air that is moving **2.** a strong, fast-moving air current; gale **3.** an air current regarded as bearing a scent, as in hunting [to lose (the) *wind* of the fox] **4.** figuratively, air regarded as bearing information, indicating trends, etc. [rumours in the *wind*] **5.** [Colloq.] a hint; intimation [we got *wind* that you were coming] **6.** breath or the power of breathing [to get the *wind* knocked out of one] **7.** a) idle or empty talk b) bragging; pomposity **8.** gas in the stomach or intestines; indigestion **9.** the instruments of an orchestra, or the players of these —*vt.* **1.** to expose to the wind, as for drying; air **2.** to get or follow the scent of **3.** to put out of breath [to be *winded* by a long run] **4.** to rest (a horse, etc.) so as to allow recovery of breath —**break wind** to expel gas from the bowels —**get the wind up** [Colloq.] to become alarmed —**get** (or **have**) **wind of** to get (or have) information or a hint about —**how the wind blows** (or **lies**) what the trend of affairs, public opinion, etc. is —**in the teeth of the wind** straight against the wind: also **in the wind's eye** —**in the wind** happening or about to happen —**into the wind** in the direction from which the wind is blowing —**put the wind up** [Colloq.] to alarm —**take the wind out of one's sails** to remove one's advantage, nullify one's argument, etc. suddenly —**wind′less** *adj.* —**wind′less·ness** *n.*

wind[3] (wīnd, wind) *vt., vi.* **wound** or rarely **wind′ed, wind′ing** [< prec.] [Poet.] **1.** to blow (a horn, etc.) **2.** to sound (a signal, etc.), as on a horn

wind·age (win′dij) *n.* **1.** the disturbance of air around a moving projectile **2.** deflection of a projectile by the wind, or the degree of this

wind·bag (wind′bag′) *n.* [Colloq.] a person who talks much and pretentiously but says little of importance

wind·blown (-blōn′) *adj.* **1.** blown by the wind **2.** twisted in growth by the prevailing wind: said of a tree

wind·borne (-bôrn′) *adj.* carried by the wind, as pollen

wind·break (-brāk′) *n.* a hedge, fence, or row of trees that serves as a protection from wind

wind·burn (-burn′) *n.* a roughened, reddened, sore condition of the skin, caused by overexposure to the wind

wind·cheat·er (-chē′tər) *n.* a short, warm jacket with a closefitting elastic waistband and cuffs: also **windjammer** [U.S.] *Trademark* **Windbreaker**

wind chest a chamber on an organ in which air from the bellows is stored under pressure before being supplied to the pipes or reeds

wind cone *same as* WINDSOCK

wind-down (wīnd′doun′) *n.* a gradual reduction; the act or process of winding down

wind·fall (-fôl′) *n.* **1.** something blown down by the wind,

as fruit from a tree **2.** any money or gain that one gets without expecting it

wind·flaw (-flô′) *n.* a gust of wind: see FLAW[2]

wind·flow·er (-flou′ər) *n.* *same as* ANEMONE (sense 1)

wind gauge 1. *same as* ANEMOMETER **2.** a graduated attachment on a gun sight for indicating the degree of deflection necessary to counteract windage **3.** *Music* a device for measuring the wind pressure in the bellows of an organ

wind·hov·er (wind′hov′ər) *n.* *same as* KESTREL

wind·i·ly (win′də lē) *adv.* in a windy manner

wind·i·ness (-dē nis) *n.* a windy quality or condition

wind·ing (wīn′diŋ) *n.* **1.** the action or effect of a person or thing that winds; a coiling, twining, turn, bend, etc. **2.** something that winds or is wound round an object —*adj.* that winds, turns, coils, spirals, etc.

winding sheet a cloth in which the body of a dead person is wrapped for burial; shroud

wind instrument (wind) a musical instrument sounded by blowing air, esp. breath, through it, as an oboe

wind·jam·mer (wind′jam′ər) *n.* **1.** *same as* WINDCHEATER **2.** *Naut.* a sailing ship, esp. a large one, or one of its crew

wind·lass (wind′las) *n.* [ON. *vindass* < *vinda,* to WIND[1] + *ass,* a beam] a winch, esp. a simple one worked by a crank —*vt., vi.* to hoist, etc. with a windlass

win·dle·straw (win′d'l strô′) *n.* [< OE. *windelstreaw* < *windel,* a bundle + *streaw,* straw] [Scot.] **1.** a dried stalk of grass **2.** a slender or weak person or thing

WINDLASS

wind·mill (wind′mil′) *n.* **1.** a machine propelled by the wind blowing on vanes fixed like spokes of a wheel on a shaft at the top of a tower: it gives power for grinding grain, pumping water, etc. **2.** a toy consisting of a stick with attached coloured vanes which revolve in the wind —**fight** (or **tilt at**) **windmills** to fight imaginary opponents: from Don Quixote's mistaking windmills for giants —**throw one's cap over the windmill** to behave in a reckless or unorthodox fashion —*vt., vi.* to rotate like a windmill

win·dow (win′dō) *n.* [< ON. < *vindr,* WIND[2] + *auga,* an eye] **1.** a) an opening in a building, vehicle, etc., to let in light or air or to look through, usually having a pane or panes of glass, etc. set in a frame that is usually movable b) any such pane or frame **2.** any similar opening **3.** the transparent panel of a window envelope **4.** any portion of the frequency spectrum of the earth's atmosphere through which light, heat, or radio waves can penetrate to the earth's surface **5.** *same as* LAUNCH WINDOW —*vt.* to provide with a window or windows —**win′dow·less** *adj.*

window box a long, narrow box on or outside a window ledge, for growing plants

window dressing 1. the display of goods and decorations in a shop window to attract customers **2.** any display or attempt to make something seem better than it really is

window envelope an envelope with a transparent panel, through which the address on the enclosure can be seen

window ledge *same as* WINDOWSILL

win·dow·pane (-pān′) *n.* a pane of glass in a window

window seat a seat built in beneath a window or windows and usually containing storage space

win·dow-shop (-shop′) *vi.* **-shopped′, -shop′ping** to look at displays of goods in shop windows without entering the shops to buy —**win′dow-shop′per** *n.*

win·dow·sill (-sil′) *n.* the sill of a window

window tax a tax levied (1696-1851) on windows of inhabited buildings

wind·pipe (wind′pīp′) *n.* *same as* TRACHEA (sense 1)

wind·proof (-prōōf′) *adj.* that the wind cannot blow through, blow out, etc.

wind rose a diagram that shows for a particular place the frequency and intensity of wind from different directions

wind·row (-rō′) *n.* **1.** a row of hay or of grain, etc. raked together to dry **2.** a row of dry leaves, dust, etc. swept together by the wind —*vt.* to rake or sweep into windrows

wind·screen (-skrēn′) *n.* the sheet of flat or curved glass forming the front window of a motor vehicle: also, chiefly U.S. **wind′shield**

windscreen wiper a rubber-edged blade which can be electrically operated to clear the windscreen of a vehicle of rainwater, etc.

wind section that part of the orchestra where wind instruments, as the oboe, clarinet, etc. are situated

wind·sock (-sok′) *n.* a long, cone-shaped cloth bag, open at both ends and attached to the top of a mast, as at an airfield, to show wind direction: also called **wind sleeve**

Wind·sor chair (win′zər) a style of wooden chair, esp. popular in the 18th-cent., with spreading legs, a spindle back, and usually a saddlelike seat

Windsor knot a form of double slipknot in a necktie, resulting in a wider, bulkier knot

wind·storm (wind′stôrm′) *n.* a storm with a strong wind but little or no rain, hail, etc.

wind-swept (-swept′) *adj.* swept by or exposed to winds

wind tunnel a tunnellike chamber through which air is forced and in which scale models of aircraft, etc. are tested to determine the effects of wind pressure

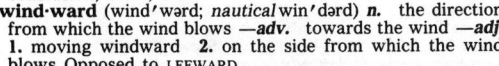

WINDSOR CHAIR

wind·up (wīnd′up′) *n.* a winding up, or conclusion; close; end

wind·ward (wind′wərd; *nautical* win′dərd) *n.* the direction from which the wind blows —*adv.* towards the wind —*adj.* 1. moving windward 2. on the side from which the wind blows Opposed to LEEWARD

wind·y (win′dē) *adj.* **wind′i·er, wind′i·est** 1. characterized by wind [*a windy day*] 2. swept by strong winds [*a windy city*] 3. violent like wind [*windy anger*] 4. *a)* without substance; empty, flimsy, etc. *b)* long-winded, pompous, boastful, etc. 5. *same as* FLATULENT 6. [Slang] frightened; cowardly

wine (wīn) *n.* [OE. *win*, ult. < L. *vinum*] 1. the fermented juice of grapes, used as an alcoholic beverage and in cooking, etc. 2. the fermented juice of other fruits or plants, used as a beverage [*dandelion wine*] 3. anything that exhilarates one 4. a dark, purplish red like that of red wine —*vt., vi.* **wined, win′ing** to provide with or drink wine: usually in **wine and dine,** to entertain with food, drink, etc.

wine·bib·ber (-bib′ər) *n.* a person given to drinking much or too much wine —**wine′bib′bing** *adj. n.*

wine cellar 1. a cellar where wine is stored 2. a stock of wine

wine-col·oured (-kul′ərd) *adj.* having the colour of red wine; dark purplish-red

wine-cooler (-kōōl′ər) *n.* a receptacle in which wine bottles are chilled with ice before being served at table

wine gallon the old English gallon of 231 cubic inches, now the standard gallon in the U.S. (c. 3.8 litres)

wine·glass (-gläs′) *n.* a small glass, usually stemmed, for serving wine —**wine′glass′ful′** *n., pl.* **-fuls′**

wine·grow·ing (-grō′iŋ) *n.* the art or process of cultivating grapes and making wine from them —**wine′grow′er** *n.*

wine press a vat in which grapes are trodden, or a machine for pressing them, to extract the juice for making wine

win·er·y (wīn′ər ē) *n., pl.* **-er·ies** an establishment where wine is made

wine·skin (wīn′skin′) *n.* in Eastern countries, a large bag for holding wine, made of the skin of an animal

wine-tast·ing (-tāst′iŋ) *n.* the assessing of the qualities of wines by tasting small samples —**wine′tast·er** *n.*

wing (wiŋ) *n.* [< ON. pl. of *vaengr*] 1. *a)* either of the two feathered forelimbs of a bird, developed in most birds for use in flying *b)* either of a pair of structures on a bat or an insect used for flying *c)* any of various winglike structures used by certain animals for gliding, as the pectoral fin of a flying fish 2. either of a pair of winglike structures that angels, dragons, etc. are thought of as having 3. something used as or like a wing; esp., a (or the) main supporting surface of an aeroplane 4. something like a wing in its position or relation to the main part; esp., *a)* a distinct part of a building, often at one side or added later or having a special use *b)* either side of a theatre stage out of sight of the audience *c)* any winglike part, as on some seeds *d)* the part of a car body that surrounds the wheels; mudguard 5. a group having a winglike relation to another group; specif., *a)* the right or left section of an army, fleet, etc. *b)* a section or faction, as of a political party, viewed as radical or conservative 6. in soccer, hockey, etc. *a)* either of the two sides of the pitch near the touchline *b)* a player stationed there; winger 7. *a)* any of various air force units; specif., R.A.F. a unit larger than a squadron *b)* [*pl.*] the insignia worn by pilots of military aircraft 8. a flying, or a means or way of flying: now chiefly in **give wing to, take wing** (see phrases below) 9. [Slang] a person's arm —*vt.* 1. to provide with wings 2. *a)* to cause to fly or speed as on wings *b)* to make (one's way) by flying *c)* to go through or over by flying 3. to transport as by flight 4. to wound, as with a bullet, in the wing, arm, etc. —*vi.* to go swiftly as on wings; fly —**give wing** (or **wings**) to enable to fly or soar on or as if on wings —**on the wing** 1. flying, or while in flight 2. in motion or while moving or travelling —**on wings of** filled with joy or rapture by [*on wings of song*] —**spread one's wings** to develop one's capabilities fully —**take wing** 1. to take flight; fly away 2. to become

joyous or enraptured —**under one's wing** under one's protection, patronage, etc. —**wing′less** *adj.*

wing chair an upholstered armchair with a high back from each side of which high sides, or wings, extend forwards

wing collar a man's stiff, stand-up collar having the top corners in front turned down

wing commander *see* MILITARY RANKS, table

winged (wiŋd; *often poet.* wiŋ′id) *adj.* 1. having wings or winglike parts 2. moving, esp. swiftly, on or as if on wings 3. lofty; sublime [*winged words*]

wing·er (-ər) *n.* Soccer, Hockey, etc. a player stationed on the wing

wing nut a nut with flared sides for turning with the thumb and forefinger

wing·span (wiŋ′span′) *n.* the distance between the tips of an aeroplane's wings

wing·spread (-spred′) *n.* 1. the distance between the tips of a pair of fully spread wings 2. *same as* WINGSPAN

wing tip the outermost end of a wing Also **wing′-tip, wing′-tip′** *n.*

wink (wiŋk) *vi.* [OE. *wincian*] 1. to close the eyelids and open them again quickly 2. *a)* to close and open an eyelid quickly so as to signal, etc. *b)* to be closed and opened thus: said of the eye 3. to shine or twinkle in flashes of light —*vt.* 1. to make (the eyes or an eye) wink 2. to move, remove, etc. by winking [*to wink back tears*] 3. to signal, etc. by winking —*n.* 1. a winking, or the instant of time it takes 2. a tiny interval (of sleep) [*didn't sleep a wink*] 3. a signal, etc. given by winking 4. a twinkle —**wink at** to pretend not to notice (some wrongdoing)

wink·er (-ər) *n.* 1. a person or thing that winks 2. a blinker (for a horse) 3. [Dial.] an eyelash or an eye

win·kle¹ (wiŋ′k'l) *n.* short for PERIWINKLE²

win·kle² (wiŋ′k'l) *vt.* **-kled, -kling** [Colloq.] to pry or rout from cover, secrecy, etc. (with *out, out of,* etc.)

win·kle-pick·er (-pik′ər) *n.* [Slang] a shoe with a narrow, sharply pointed toe

win·ner (win′ər) *n.* one that wins; esp., [Colloq.] one that seems destined to win or be successful

win·ning (-iŋ) *adj.* 1. that wins; victorious 2. attractive; charming —*n.* 1. victory 2. [*pl.*] something won, esp. money —**win′ning·ly** *adv.*

winning post a post marking the end of a racecourse

win·now (win′ō) *vt.* [OE. *windwian* < *wind,* WIND²] 1. *a)* to blow the chaff from (grain) *b)* to blow off (chaff) 2. to blow away; scatter 3. to analyse or examine carefully so as to separate the various elements; sift 4. *a)* to separate out (poor or useless parts) *b)* to sort out or extract (good or useful parts) 5. [Now Rare] to fan with or as with wings —*vi.* to winnow grain —*n.* 1. a winnowing 2. an apparatus for winnowing —**win′now·er** *n.*

win·o (wī′nō) *n., pl.* **-os** [Chiefly U.S. Slang] a person, esp. an alcoholic, who habitually gets drunk on wine, esp. cheap wine

win·some (win′səm) *adj.* [OE. *wynsum,* pleasant] attractive in a sweet, engaging way; charming —**win′-some·ly** *adv.* —**win′some·ness** *n.*

win·ter (win′tər) *n.* [OE.] 1. the coldest season of the year, following autumn 2. a year as reckoned by this season 3. any period regarded, like winter, as a time of decline, dreariness, etc. —*adj.* 1. of, typical of, or suitable for winter 2. that will keep during the winter [*winter apples*] 3. planted in the autumn to be harvested in the spring [*winter wheat*] —*vi.* 1. to pass the winter 2. to be supplied with food and shelter in the winter —*vt.* to keep or maintain during the winter —**win′ter·er** *n.*

win·ter·green (-grēn′) *n.* 1. any of several evergreen plants, esp. an American shrub with small, rounded leaves 2. an aromatic compound (**oil of wintergreen**) made from these leaves or from birch bark or synthetically, used in medicine and as a flavouring 3. its flavour

win·ter·ize (-īz′) *vt.* **-ized′, -iz′ing** [Chiefly U.S.] to put into condition for winter

win·ter·kill (-kil′) *vt., vi.* [Chiefly U.S.] to kill or die by exposure to winter cold: said of plants

winter quarters 1. a winter residence 2. a place where troops settle in for the winter

winter solstice the time in the Northern Hemisphere when the sun is farthest south of the celestial equator; December 21 or 22

winter sports open-air sports on ice or snow

win·ter·time (-tīm′) *n.* the season of winter

win·ter·weight (-wāt′) *adj.* warm or thick enough to be suitable to wear in winter: said of clothing

win·try (win′trē) *adj.* **-tri·er, -tri·est** of or like winter; cold, bleak, etc. [*a wintry day, a wintry stare*]: also **win′ter·ly** (-tər lē), **win′ter·y** (-tər ē, -trē) —**win′tri·ly** (-trə lē) *adv.* —**win′tri·ness** (-trē nis) *n.*

win·y (wī′nē) *adj.* **win′i·er, win′i·est** like wine in taste, smell, colour, etc.

wipe (wīp) *vt.* **wiped, wip′ing** [OE. *wipian*] 1. *a)* to rub with a cloth, etc., as for cleaning or drying *b)* to clean or dry in this manner 2. to rub or pass (a cloth, etc.) over something **3.** to apply by wiping **4.** to remove as by wiping (with *away, off,* etc.) —*n.* a wiping —**wipe out 1.** to remove; erase **2.** to kill off **3.** to destroy —**wipe the floor with** [Slang] to defeat utterly, as in an argument

wip·er (wī′par) *n.* **1.** a person or thing that wipes **2.** a moving electrical contact, as in a rheostat **3.** a projecting piece on a rotating or rocking part, which raises and lowers or trips another, usually reciprocating, part **4.** *same as* WINDSCREEN WIPER

wipe·out (-out′) *n.* [U.S.] **1.** a fall or jump in surfing **2.** any failure or defeat

wire (wīr) *n.* [OE. *wir*] **1.** metal that has been drawn into a long thread **2.** a length of this, used for conducting electric current, etc. **3.** wire netting or other wirework **4.** anything made of wire or wirework, as a telephone cable, a snare, etc. **5.** *a)* telegraph [reply by *wire*] *b)* a telegram [made of wire or wirework —*vt.* **wired, wir′ing 1.** to furnish, connect, bind, etc. with wire **2.** to supply with a system of wires for electric current **3.** to telegraph —*vi.* to telegraph —**wire′like′** *adj.*

wire cloth a type of fine wire netting used for strainers, etc.

wire cutter an instrument for cutting wire

wire·draw (-drô′) *vt.* **-drew′, -drawn′, -draw′ing 1.** to draw (metal) into wire **2.** to strain (a point in argument)

wire gauge a device for measuring the diameter of wire, thickness of sheet metal, etc.: it usually consists of a disc with notches of graduated sizes along its edge

wire-haired (-herd′) *adj.* having coarse, or wiry, hair

wire-haired terrier a fox terrier with a wiry coat

wire·less (-lis) *adj.* **1.** without wire or wires; specif., operating with electromagnetic waves and not with conducting wire **2.** *same as* RADIO —*n.* **1.** *same as:* **a)** WIRELESS TELEGRAPHY **b)** RADIO **2.** a message sent by wireless —*vt., vi.* to communicate (with) by wireless

wireless telegraphy (or **telegraph**) telegraphy by radio-transmitted signals

wireless telephone a telephone operating by radio-transmitted signals —**wireless telephony**

wire netting netting of woven wire, used in various sizes for fences, etc.

Wire·pho·to (-fōt′ō) *a trademark for:* **1.** a system of reproducing photographs at a distance by means of electric impulses transmitted by wire **2.** a photograph so produced

wire·pull·er (-pool′ər) *n.* a person who gets what he wants through his friends' influence, esp. in politics —**wire′pull′-ing** *n.*

wire service a business organization that sends news stories, features, etc. by direct telegraph to subscribing or member newspapers and radio and television stations

wire·tap (-tap′) *vi., vt.* **-tapped′, -tap′ping** to tap (a telephone wire, etc.) to get information secretly or underhandedly —*n.* **1.** the act or an instance of wiretapping **2.** a device used in wiretapping —*adj.* of or relating to wiretapping —**wire′tap′per** *n.*

wire wheel a wheel in which the rim is attached to the hub by wire spokes

wire wool a pad of fine wire used esp. in scrubbing cooking utensils

wire·work (-wurk′) *n.* netting, mesh, etc. made of wire

wire·worm (-wurm′) *n.* **1.** the slender, hard-bodied wormlike larva of the click beetle **2.** a millipede **3.** a roundworm infesting cattle and sheep

wir·ing (wīr′iŋ) *n.* **1.** the action of a person or thing that wires **2.** a system of wires, as to provide a house with electricity —*adj.* **1.** that wires **2.** used in wiring

wir·y (wīr′ē) *adj.* **wir′i·er, wir′i·est 1.** of wire **2.** like wire in shape and substance; stiff **3.** lean, sinewy, and strong: said of persons and animals —**wir′i·ly** *adv.* —**wir′i·ness** *n.*

wis (wis) *vt.* [< ME. *iwis,* certainly: erroneously understood as "I know"] [Archaic] to suppose; imagine; deem

wis·dom (wiz′dəm) *n.* [OE. < *wis,* WISE[1] + *-dom,* -DOM] **1.** the quality of being wise; good judgment, based on knowledge, etc.; sagacity **2.** learning; knowledge; erudition **3.** wise teaching **4.** a wise plan or course of action

wisdom tooth the back tooth on each side of each jaw in human beings, appearing usually between the ages of 17 and 25

wise[1] (wīz) *adj.* **wis′er, wis′est** [OE. *wis*] **1.** having or showing good judgment; sagacious **2.** judicious; sound [a *wise* saying] **3.** informed [none the *wiser*] **4.** learned; erudite **5.** shrewd; cunning **6.** [U.S. Slang] *a)* annoyingly self-assured, etc. *b)* impudent; fresh —**be** (or **get**) **wise to** [Slang] to be (or become) aware of —**be wise after the event** to realize what should have been done when it is too late —**put wise** (**to**) [Slang] to give (someone) information, etc. (about) —**wise′ly** *adv.* —**wise′ness** *n.*

wise[2] (wīz) *n.* [OE.] way; manner: used chiefly in phrases, as **in no wise, in this wise,** etc.

-wise (wīz) [< prec.] *a suffix meaning:* **1.** a (specified) direction, position, or manner [*lengthwise*] **2.** in the same way or direction as [*clockwise*] **3.** [Colloq.] with regard to; in connection with [*weatherwise*]

wise·a·cre (wīz′ā′kər) *n.* [< MDu. < OHG. *wizzago,* a

prophet] a person who acts as though he were much wiser than he really is

wise·crack (-krak′) *n.* [Colloq.] a flippant or joking remark, often a gibe or retort —*vi.* [Colloq.] to make wisecracks —*vt.* [Colloq.] to say as a wisecrack —**wise′-crack′er** *n.*

wise guy [Slang] a person who is brashly and annoyingly conceited, knowing, etc.; smart alec

wish (wish) *vt.* [OE. *wyscan*] **1.** to have a longing for; want; desire **2.** to have or express a desire concerning [to *wish* the day were over, to *wish* her good luck] **3.** to bid [to *wish* a person good morning] **4.** to request [he *wishes* her to leave] **5.** to impose (with *on*) [he *wished* the job on me] —*vi.* **1.** to long; yearn **2.** to make a wish —*n.* **1.** a wishing; desire for something **2.** something wished for [he got his *wish*] **3.** a polite request with some of the force of an order **4.** [*pl.*] expressed desire for a person's health, etc. [to offer one's best *wishes*] —**wish′er** *n.*

wish·bone (-bōn′) *n.* the forked bone in front of the breastbone of most birds

wish·ful (-fəl) *adj.* having or showing a wish; desirous; longing —**wish′ful·ly** *adv.* —**wish′ful·ness** *n.*

wishful thinking thinking in which one interprets facts in terms of what one would like to believe

wish·y-wash·y (wish′ē wosh′ē) *adj.* [redupl. of WASHY] [Colloq.] **1.** watery; insipid; thin **2.** not strong or decisive in character; weak —**wish′y-wash′i·ly** *adv.*

wisp (wisp) *n.* [prob. < Scand.] **1.** a small bunch or tuft [a *wisp* of straw, hair, etc.] **2.** a thin, filmy bit or puff [a *wisp* of smoke] **3.** something delicate, frail, etc. [a *wisp* of a girl] **4.** *same as* WILL-O′-THE-WISP —*vt.* to roll into a wisp —**wisp′y** *adj.* **wisp′i·er, wisp′i·est**

wist (wist) *pt. & pp. of* WIT[2]

wis·te·ri·a (wis tir′ē ə) *n.* [ModL., after C. *Wistar* (1761–1818), U.S. anatomist] a twining shrub of the legume family, with showy clusters of bluish, white, pink, or purple flowers: also **wis·tar′i·a** (-ter′-)

wist·ful (wist′fəl) *adj.* [altered (after WISHFUL) < earlier *wistly,* attentive] showing or expressing vague yearnings or pensive longing —**wist′ful·ly** *adv.* —**wist′ful·ness** *n.*

wit[1] (wit) *n.* [OE.] **1.** [*pl.*] powers of thinking and reasoning, esp. in a normal, effective way **2.** alert, practical intelligence; good sense **3.** *a)* the ability to make lively, clever remarks expressed in a surprising, epigrammatic, or ironic way *b)* a person having this ability, or speech or writing in which it is expressed —**at one's wits' end** at a loss as to what to do —**keep** (or **have**) **one's wits about one** to remain mentally alert, as in an emergency —**live by one's wits** to live by trickery or craftiness

wit[2] (wit) *vt., vi.* wist, wit′ting [OE. *witan*] [Archaic] to know or learn *Wit* is conjugated in the present indicative: (I) *wot,* (thou) *wost* or *wot(t)est, (he, she, it) wot* or *wot(t)eth, (we, ye, they) wite* or *witen* —**to wit** that is to say; namely

witch[1] (wich) *n.* [OE. *wicce,* fem. of *wicca,* sorcerer] **1.** a person, now specif. a woman, who is supposed to have magic power, esp. with the help of evil spirits: cf. WARLOCK **2.** an ugly and ill-tempered old woman **3.** [Colloq.] a bewitching or fascinating woman or girl —*vt.* **1.** to put a magic spell on **2.** to charm; fascinate

witch[2] (wich) *n., pl.* witch, witch′es: see PLURAL, II, D, 2 [< ? WITCH[1]] an edible flatfish found in N Atlantic coastal waters

witch·craft (-kräft′) *n.* **1.** *a)* the power or practices of witches; black magic; sorcery *b)* an instance of this **2.** bewitching attraction or charm

witch doctor among certain tribes, esp. in Africa, a person who practises a type of primitive medicine involving the use of magic, witchcraft, etc.

witch elm *var. of* WYCH ELM

witch·er·y (wich′ər ē) *n., pl.* **-er·ies 1.** witchcraft; sorcery **2.** bewitching charm; fascination

witch·es′-broom (wich′iz broom′) *n.* an abnormal growth of closely bunched twigs at the ends of branches of various woody plants, caused by fungi, viruses, etc.

witches′ Sabbath a midnight meeting of witches, sorcerers and demons, supposed in medieval times to have been held annually as a demonic orgy

witch·et·ty (wich′ə tē) *n.* [Abor.] the wood-boring caterpillar of an Australian moth, which is eaten by Aborigines: also **witchetty grub**

witch hazel [OE. *wice*] **1.** an American shrub with yellow flowers and woody fruit **2.** an alcoholic lotion containing an extract from the leaves and bark of this shrub

witch hunt [after the cruel treatment of persons once imagined to be witches] an investigation usually carried on with much publicity, supposedly to uncover activities aimed at overthrowing the government but really to harass and weaken political opposition —**witch hunter**

witch·ing (wich′iŋ) *n.* witchcraft —*adj.* that witches; bewitching —**witch′ing·ly** *adv.*

witching hour the time of night when witches are supposed to appear, usually midnight (preceded by *the*)

wit·e·na·ge·mot, wit·e·na·ge·mote (wit'ən ə gə mōt') *n.* [< OE. < *witena*, gen. pl. of *wita*, wise man + (*ge*)*mot*, a meeting] the king's council of the Anglo-Saxons

with (with, with) *prep.* [OE., orig., against] **1.** against [to argue *with* a friend] **2.** *a)* alongside; near to *b)* in the company of *c)* into; among [mix blue *with* red] **3.** as an associate, or companion, of [he played golf *with* me] **4.** *a)* as a member of [to sing *with* a quartet] *b)* working for [*with* the firm 20 years] **5.** in regard to; concerning [pleased *with* her gift] **6.** in the same terms as; compared to [having equal standing *with* the others] **7.** as well as [he can run *with* the best] **8.** *a)* of the same opinions as [I'm *with* you] *b)* able to understand; following the drift of someone's thoughts **9.** on the side of [he voted *with* the Tories] **10.** in the opinion of [it's all right *with* me] **11.** as a result of [faint *with* hunger] **12.** *a)* by means of; using [stir *with* a spoon] *b)* by [filled *with* air] **13.** having received [*with* your permission, he'll go] **14.** having or showing [a boy *with* red hair, to enter *with* confidence, to play *with* skill] **15.** in the keeping, care, etc. of [leave the baby *with* me] **16.** *a)* added to [the boy, *with* his friend, arrived] *b)* including [*with* the newcomers, the class is large] **17.** in spite of [*with* all her faults, I love her still] **18.** *a)* at the same time as [to rise *with* the lark] *b)* in the same direction as [to travel *with* the sun] *c)* in proportion to [wages varying *with* skills] *d)* in the course of [grief lessens *with* time] **19.** from [to part *with* money] **20.** after [*with* that remark, he left] —**with child** pregnant —**with it** [Colloq.] in the current mode; fashionable; up to date —**with that** after that

with- [OE. < prec.] *a combining form meaning:* **1.** away, back [*withdraw*] **2.** against, from [*withhold*]

with·al (with ôl', with-) *adv.* **1.** besides **2.** despite that; notwithstanding **3.** [Archaic] with that; therewith —*prep.* [Archaic] with: used following its object

with·draw (-drô') *vt.* **-drew', -drawn', -draw'ing 1.** to take back or draw back; remove **2.** to take back (something said, offered, etc.) **3.** in the British Parliament, to remove (a motion or amendment) from consideration —*vi.* **1.** to move back; go away; retreat **2.** to remove oneself (*from* an organization, activity, association with other people, etc.) —**with·draw'er** *n.*

with·draw·al (-drô'əl) *n.* **1.** the act of withdrawing **2.** a giving up the use of a narcotic drug to which one has become addicted, typically accompanied by distress of body and mind (**withdrawal symptoms**)

with·drawn (-drôn') *pp. of* WITHDRAW —*adj.* withdrawing within oneself; shy, reserved, unsociable, etc.

withe (with, with, with) *n.* [OE. *withthe*] a tough, flexible twig of willow, etc., used for binding things —*vt.* **withed, with'ing** to bind with withes

with·er (with'ər) *vi.* [< ME. var. of *wederen*, lit., to weather] **1.** to dry up; shrivel [plants *withering* in the heat, a face *withering* with age] **2.** to lose strength; weaken [our hopes soon *withered*] —*vt.* **1.** to cause to wither **2.** to make feel abashed, as by a scornful glance —**with'er·ing** *adv.*

with·ers (with'ərz) *n.pl.* [OE. *withre*, resistance < *wither*, against] the highest part of the back of a horse, etc., between the shoulder blades

with·er·shins (with'ər shinz') *adv.* [< MLowG. < MHG. *widdersinnes* < *wider*, against + *sinnes*, gen. of *sin*, direction] [Chiefly Scot.] in a direction contrary to the apparent course of the sun; anticlockwise

with·hold (with hôld', with-) *vt.* **-held', -hold'ing 1.** to hold back; restrain **2.** to keep from giving; refuse [to *withhold* approval] —*vi.* to refrain; forbear

with·in (with in', with-) *adv.* [OE. *withinnan*] **1.** on or to the inside **2.** indoors **3.** inside the body, mind, spirit, etc. —*prep.* **1.** in the inner part of; inside **2.** not more than; not beyond [*within* a mile of home] **3.** inside the limits of [*within* the law] —*n.* the inside or the interior

with·out (-out') *adv.* [OE. *withutan*] **1.** [Archaic] on or to the outside **2.** [Archaic] outdoors —*prep.* **1.** at, on, or to the outside of **2.** beyond the limits of **3.** not with; lacking [shoes *without* laces] **4.** free from [a man *without* fear] **5.** with avoidance of [to pass by *without* speaking] —*conj.* [Dial.] unless —**go** (or **do**) **without** to manage although lacking something

with·stand (with stand', with-) *vt., vi.* **-stood', -stand'ing** to oppose, resist, or endure, esp. in a successful way

with·y (with'ē, with'ē) *n., pl.* **with'ies** [OE. *withig*] a tough, flexible twig of willow, etc.; withe

wit·less (wit'lis) *adj.* lacking wit or intelligence; foolish —**wit'less·ly** *adv.* —**wit'less·ness** *n.*

wit·ling (wit'liŋ) *n.* one who fancies himself a wit

wit·ness (wit'nis) *n.* [OE. *gewitnes*, knowledge, testimony] **1.** evidence; testimony **2.** a person who saw, or can give a firsthand account of, something **3.** a person who testifies in court **4.** a person who watches a contract, will, etc. being signed and then, as proof that he did, signs it himself **5.** something serving as evidence —*vt.* **1.** to testify to **2.** to serve as evidence of **3.** to act as witness of (a contract,

will, etc.) **4.** to be present at; see personally **5.** to be the scene of [this field *witnessed* a battle] —*vi.* **1.** to give, or serve as, evidence **2.** to testify to religious beliefs or faith —**bear witness** to be or give evidence

witness box the place from which a witness gives his testimony in a law court: *U.S. name* **witness stand**

wit·ted (wit'id) *adj.* having (a specified kind of) wit: used in hyphenated compounds [slow-*witted*]

wit·ti·cism (wit'ə siz'm) *n.* [< WITTY + -*cism*, as in CRITICISM] a witty remark

wit·ting (wit'iŋ) *adj.* [ME. *wytting*] done knowingly; intentional —**wit'ting·ly** *adv.*

wit·ty (wit'ē) *adj.* **-ti·er, -ti·est** [OE. *wittig*] having or showing wit; cleverly amusing —**wit'ti·ly** *adv.* —**wit'ti·ness** *n.*

wive (wīv) *vi., vt.* **wived, wiv'ing** [OE. *wifian*] [Archaic] to marry (a woman)

wi·vern (wī'vərn) *n. same as* WYVERN

wives (wīvz) *n. pl. of* WIFE

wiz (wiz) *n. shortened form of* WIZARD (*n.* 2, *adj.* 3)

wiz·ard (wiz'ərd) *n.* [ME. *wisard*, prob. < *wis*, WISE[1] + -*ard*, -ARD] **1.** a magician; sorcerer **2.** [Colloq.] a person exceptionally gifted or clever at a specified activity —*adj.* **1.** of wizards or wizardry **2.** magic **3.** [Slang] outstanding; excellent —**wiz'ard·ly** *adv.*

wiz·ard·ry (-rē) *n.* witchcraft; magic; sorcery

wiz·en (wiz''n, wēz'-) *vt., vi.* [OE. *wisnian*] to dry up; wither; shrivel —*adj. same as* WIZENED

wiz·ened (-'nd) *adj.* dried up; withered; shrivelled

wk. *pl.* **wks. 1.** week **2.** work

WL, w.l. 1. waterline **2.** wavelength

W.M.O. World Meteorological Organization

WNW, W.N.W., w.n.w. west-northwest

WO, W.O. Warrant Officer

woad (wōd) *n.* [OE. *wad*] **1.** any of a group of plants of the mustard family, esp. a plant (**dyer's woad**) with yellow flowers and leaves that yield a blue dye **2.** this dye

wob·be·gong (wob'ə goŋ) *n.* [Abor.] [Aust.] the carpet shark

wob·ble (wob''l) *vi.* **-bled, -bling** [prob. < LowG. *wabbeln*] **1.** to move from side to side in an unsteady way **2.** to shake as jelly does **3.** to waver in mind —*vt.* to cause to wobble —*n.* an unsteady wobbling motion or sound [wheel *wobble*] —**wob'bler** *n.* —**wob'bli·ness** *n.* —**wob'bly** *adj.* **-bli·er, -bli·est**

wodge (woj) *n.* [altered < WEDGE] [Colloq.] a large, or carelessly cut, piece or lump

woe (wō) *n.* [OE. *wa*] **1.** great sorrow; grief **2.** a cause of sorrow, trouble —*interj.* alas! Also [Archaic] **wo**

woe·be·gone (wō'bi gon') *adj.* **1.** [Archaic] woeful **2.** showing woe; looking sad or mournful

woe·ful (-fəl) *adj.* **1.** full of woe; sad; mournful **2.** of, causing, or involving woe **3.** pitiful; wretched; miserable —**woe'ful·ly** *adv.* —**woe'ful·ness** *n.*

wog (wog) *n.* [< ?] [Slang] a derogatory name for a foreigner, esp. one who is not white

wog·gle (wog''l) *n.* [< ?] a ring worn, esp. formerly, by boy scouts, to fasten their neckerchiefs

wok (wok) *n.* [Chin.] a metal cooking pan with a convex bottom, often used with a ringlike stand

woke (wōk) *alt. pt. & pp. of* WAKE[1]

wok·en (wō'k'n) *pp. of* WAKE[1]

wold (wōld) *n.* [OE. *wald*] a treeless, rolling plain, esp. a high one —**the Wolds** range of chalk hills in NE England, running from north to south in Humberside and Lincolnshire

wolf (woolf) *n., pl.* **wolves** [OE. *wulf*] **1.** *a)* any of a group of wild, flesh-eating, doglike mammals, esp. the grey wolf, formerly widespread throughout the Northern Hemisphere *b)* the fur of a wolf **2.** *a)* a fierce, cruel, or greedy person *b)* [Slang] a man who boldly approaches women for sexual purposes —*vt.* to eat greedily (often with *down*) —**cry wolf** to give a false alarm —**keep the wolf from the door** to provide the necessities of life —**throw to the wolves** to sacrifice without scruples in order to further one's own ends —**wolf in sheep's clothing** a malicious person in a harmless or friendly guise —**wolf'ish** *adj.* —**wolf'ish·ly** *adv.* —**wolf'ish·ness** *n.*

Wolf Cub *former name of* CUB SCOUT

wolf·hound (woolf'hound') *n.* a large dog of any of several breeds formerly used for hunting wolves: see IRISH WOLFHOUND, BORZOI (*Russian wolfhound*)

wolf·ram (wool'frəm) *n.* [G. < *Wolf*, wolf + MHG. *ram*, dirt] *same as* TUNGSTEN

wolf·ram·ite (-frə mīt') *n.* [< G.: see prec.] a brownish or blackish mineral, a compound of tungsten (wolfram), iron, and manganese: the principal ore of tungsten

wolfs·bane (woolfs'bān') *n. same as* ACONITE (sense 1)

wolf spider any of a family of spiders that hunt their prey and do not build webs

wolf whistle a two-note whistle made by a man to express admiration of a woman and attract her attention —*vi., vi.* to give such a whistle

wol·ver·ine (wool′və rēn′, wool′və rēn′) *n.*, *pl.* **-ines′**, **-ine′**: see PLURAL, II, D, 1 [irreg. dim. < WOLF] 1. a stocky, ferocious, flesh-eating mammal with thick fur, found in the northern U.S., northern Eurasia, and Canada: the European variety is the GLUTTON (sense 3) 2. its fur Also sp. **wol′ver·ene′**

wolves (woolvz) *n. pl.* of WOLF

wom·an (woom′ən) *n.*, *pl.* **wom′en** (wim′in) [OE. *wifmann* < *wif*, a female + *mann*, a human being] 1. an adult, female human being 2. women as a group ["*Woman's* work is never done"] 3. a female servant or domestic help 4. *a)* [Dial.] a wife *b)* a sweetheart or a mistress 5. womanly qualities [it's the *woman* in her] —*adj.* female

wom·an·hood (-hood′) *n.* 1. the condition of being a woman 2. womanly qualities 3. women; womankind

wom·an·ish (-ish) *adj.* like, characteristic of, or suitable to a woman; feminine or effeminate —**wom′an·ish·ly** *adv.* —**wom′an·ish·ness** *n.*

wom·an·ize (-īz′) *vt.* **-ized′**, **-iz′ing** to make effeminate —*vi.* [Colloq.] to be sexually promiscuous with women —**wom′an·iz′er** *n.*

wom·an·kind (-kīnd′) *n.* women in general

wom·an·like (-līk′) *adj.* womanly

wom·an·ly (-lē) *adj.* 1. like a woman; womanish 2. characteristic of or fit for a woman —**wom′an·li·ness** *n.*

womb (woom) *n.* [OE. *wamb*] 1. same as UTERUS 2. any place in which something is contained, developed, etc.

wom·bat (wom′bat) *n.* [altered < Abor. name] a burrowing marsupial that looks like a small bear, found in Australia, Tasmania, and several Pacific islands

wom·en (wim′in) *n. pl.* of WOMAN

wom·en·folk (-fōk′) *n.pl.* [Dial. or Colloq.] women; womankind

Women's Institute a society for women in rural areas, with regular meetings for craft and cultural activities

Women's Liberation a movement among women to eradicate all inequalities in social and economic life that are based on the assumption that men are superior to women: also **Women's Lib**

women's rights the rights claimed by and for women of equal privileges and opportunities with men: cf. FEMINISM: also **woman's rights**

won[1] (wun) *pt.* & *pp.* of WIN

won[2] (won) *n.*, *pl.* **won** [Korean < Chin. *yüan*, round] the monetary unit of North Korea and South Korea: see MONETARY UNITS, table

won·der (wun′dər) *n.* [OE. *wundor*] 1. a person, thing, or event so unusual as to cause surprise, amazement, etc.; marvel 2. the feeling of surprise, amazement, etc. caused by something strange, remarkable, etc. 3. a miracle —*vi.* 1. to feel wonder; marvel 2. to have curiosity, sometimes mixed with doubt —*vt.* 1. to have curiosity or doubt about; want to know [I *wonder* what he meant] 2. to request politely or tentatively [I *wondered* if I might borrow it] —**do wonders for** to make a remarkable improvement in —**no wonder!** now I know why! —**won′der·er** *n.*

won·der·ful (-fəl) *adj.* 1. that causes wonder; marvellous; amazing 2. [Colloq.] very good; excellent —**won′der·ful·ly** *adv.* —**won′der·ful·ness** *n.*

won·der·land (-land′) *n.* an imaginary land or place full of wonders, or a real place like this

won·der·ment (-mənt) *n.* wonder or amazement

won·der·struck (-struk′) *adj.* struck with wonder, surprise, admiration, etc.: also **won′der·strick′en** (-strik′′n)

won·der·work (-wurk′) *n.* 1. a wonderful work; wonder 2. a miraculous act; miracle —**won′der·work′er** *n.*

won·drous (wun′drəs) *adj.* [Now Rare] wonderful —*adv.* [Now Rare] wonderfully; remarkably —**won′drous·ly** *adv.*

wong·a-wong·a (woŋ′ə woŋ′ə) *n.* [Abor.] a large Australian pigeon

wonga-wonga vine a hardy, evergreen Australian climbing plant with showy flowers

won·ky (woŋ′kē) *adj.* **-ki·er**, **-ki·est** [< ? dial. words based on OE. *wancal*, shaky] [Slang] 1. shaky; unsteady 2. unsound; unreliable

wont (wōnt) *adj.* [ult. < OE. *wunian*, to be used to] accustomed [he was *wont* to rise early] —*n.* usual practice; habit

won't (wōnt) [contr. < ME. *wol not*] will not

wont·ed (wōn′tid) *adj.* customary; accustomed

woo (woo) *vt.* [OE. *wogian*] 1. to try to get the love of; seek as a mate; court 2. to try to get; seek [to *woo* fame] 3. to entreat; coax; urge —*vi.* 1. to court a person 2. to make entreaty —**woo′er** *n.*

wood (wood) *n.* [OE. *wudu*] 1. [usually *pl.*] a thick growth

WOLVERINE
(70–106 cm long, including tail; 30–40 cm high at shoulder)

of trees; forest or grove 2. the hard, fibrous substance beneath the bark of trees and shrubs 3. timber 4. wood used as fuel; firewood 5. something made of wood; specif., *a)* a wooden cask [whisky aged in *wood*] *b)* any of the biased wooden bowls used in the game of bowls *c)* *Golf* any of a set of numbered clubs with wooden heads having various lofts —*adj.* 1. made of wood; wooden 2. for cutting, shaping, or holding wood 3. growing or living in woods —*vt.* 1. to plant trees thickly over 2. to furnish with wood, esp. for fuel —*vi.* 1. to get a supply of wood —**cannot see the wood for the trees** lose sight of larger issues in a mass of detail — **out of the wood** [Colloq.] out of difficulty, danger, etc.

wood alcohol *same as* METHANOL

wood·bine (wood′bīn′) *n.* [OE. *wudubinde*: see WOOD & BIND] 1. the wild honeysuckle 2. [U.S.] *same as* VIRGINIA CREEPER

wood block a block of wood, esp. one used in making a woodcut —**wood′block′** *adj.*

wood·carv·ing (-kär′viŋ) *n.* 1. the art or craft of carving wood by hand to make art objects, decorative mouldings, etc. 2. an object so made —**wood′carv′er** *n.*

wood·chuck (-chuk′) *n.* [altered < Algonquian name] a common N American marmot, an animal that burrows in the ground and sleeps all winter; also called **groundhog**

wood·cock (-kok′) *n.*, *pl.* **-cocks′**, **-cock′**: see PLURAL, II, D, 1 1. a widespread, European, migratory game bird with short legs and a long bill 2. a smaller, related game bird of N America

wood·craft (-kräft′) *n.* 1. matters relating to the woods, as camping, hunting, etc. 2. *same as:* *a)* WOODWORKING *b)* WOODCARVING 3. skill in any of these

wood·cut (-kut′) *n.* 1. a wooden block engraved with a design, etc. 2. a print made from this

wood·cut·ter (-kut′ər) *n.* a person who fells trees, cuts wood, etc. —**wood′cut′ting** *n.*

wood·ed (-id) *adj.* covered with trees or woods

wood·en (wood′′n) *adj.* 1. made of wood 2. stiff, clumsy, or lifeless 3. dull; insensitive —**wood′en·ly** *adv.* —**wood′en·ness** *n.*

wood engraving 1. the art or process of engraving on wood 2. *same as* WOODCUT —**wood engraver**

wood·en·head·ed (wood′′n hed′id) *adj.* [Colloq.] dull; stupid —**wood′en·head′ed·ness** *n.*

wood·land (wood′lənd) *n.* land covered with woods or trees —*adj.* of, living in, or relating to the woods —**wood′land·er** *n.*

wood louse any of several small, terrestrial crustaceans with a flat, oval body, living in damp places, as under rocks

wood·man (-mən) *n.*, *pl.* **-men** a person who lives or works in the woods, as a hunter, woodcutter, etc.

wood·note (-nōt′) *n.* a sound of a forest bird or animal

wood nymph a nymph that lives in the woods; dryad

wood·peck·er (-pek′ər) *n.* any of various tree-climbing birds that have a strong, pointed bill used to drill holes in bark to get insects

wood pigeon a common pigeon, resembling the domestic pigeon, but larger, with white patches on the wings and neck: also called **ring′dove**

wood·pile (-pīl′) *n.* a pile of wood, esp. of firewood

wood pulp pulp made from wood fibre, used in paper manufacture

wood·ruff (-ruf′) *n.* [OE. *wudurofe*] a plant with small white, sweet-scented flowers

wood screw a metal screw with a sharp point and a coarse thread, for use in wood

wood·shed (-shed′) *n.* a shed for storing firewood

woods·man (woodz′mən) *n.*, *pl.* **-men** 1. *same as* WOODMAN 2. a person at home in the woods or skilled in woodcraft

wood sorrel any of a group of plants with white, pink, or yellow, five-petalled flowers

wood spirit *same as* METHANOL

wood tar a dark, sticky, syruplike substance obtained by the dry distillation of wood

wood turning the art or process of turning, or shaping, wood on a lathe —**wood′-turn′er** *n.* —**wood′-turn′ing** *n.*

wood·wind (-wind′) *n.* 1. [*pl.*] the wind instruments of an orchestra made, esp. originally, of wood: clarinets, oboes, bassoons, flutes, and cor anglais 2. any of these instruments —*adj.* of or for such instruments

wood·work (-wurk′) *n.* 1. work done in wood 2. things made of wood, esp. the interior mouldings, doors, stairs, etc. of a house

wood·work·ing (-wur′kiŋ) *n.* the art or work of making things out of wood —*adj.* of woodworking —**wood′work′er** *n.*

WOODCHUCK
(head & body to c. 40 cm long; tail to c. 15 cm long)

wood·worm (-wurm′) *n.* any of a number of insect larvae that live on and burrow in wood
wood·y (wood′ē) *adj.* wood′i·er, wood′i·est 1. covered with trees; wooded 2. consisting of or forming wood [a *woody* plant] 3. like wood —**wood′i·ness** *n.*
woody nightshade a plant of the nightshade family with purple flowers and poisonous, red berries
woof[1] (woof) *n.* [OE. *owef* < *o-* (< *on*) + *-wef* < base of *wefan*, to weave] 1. *same as* WEFT 2. a woven fabric
woof[2] (woof) *n.* a gruff barking sound of or like that of a dog —*vi.* to make such a sound
woof·er (woof′ər) *n.* [prec. + -ER] in an assembly of two or more loudspeakers, a large speaker for reproducing low-frequency sounds: cf. TWEETER
wool (wool) *n.* see PLURAL, II, D, 3 [OE. *wull*] 1. *a)* the soft, curly hair of sheep *b)* the hair of some other animals, as the goat, llama, or alpaca 2. *a)* yarn spun from the fibres of such hair *b)* cloth, clothing, etc. made of this yarn 3. anything that looks or feels like wool 4. [Colloq.] short, thick, curly hair —*adj.* of wool or woollen goods —**lose one's wool** [Colloq.] to become angry —**pull the wool over someone's eyes** to deceive or trick someone —**wool′-like′** *adj.*
wool clip annual production of wool
wool fat 1. the natural grease found in a sheep's wool, yielding lanolin: also **wool grease** 2. *same as* LANOLIN
wool·fell (wool′fel′) *n.* [WOOL + FELL[4]] the pelt of a wool-bearing animal with the wool still on it
wool·gath·er·ing (-gath′ər iŋ) *n.* absent-mindedness or daydreaming —**wool′gath′er·er** *n.*
wool·grow·er (-grō′ər) *n.* a person who raises sheep for wool —**wool′grow′ing** *n.*
wool·len (-ən) *adj.* 1. made of wool 2. of or relating to wool or woollen cloth —*n.* [*pl.*] woollen goods or clothing: U.S. sp. **wool′en**
wool·ly (wool′ē) *adj.* -li·er, -li·est 1. of or like wool 2. bearing wool 3. covered with wool or something like wool in texture 4. confused; fuzzy [*woolly* ideas] —*n.*, *pl.* -lies a woollen garment, esp. a knitted one, as a cardigan —**wool′li·ness** *n.*
woolly bear the furry caterpillar of the tiger moth
wool·pack (wool′pak′) *n.* 1. a large bag in which to pack wool for sale 2. a bale of wool so packed 3. a cirrocumulus cloud
wool·sack (wool′sak′) *n.* 1. a sack of wool 2. a cushion stuffed with wool, on which the Lord Chancellor sits in the House of Lords 3. the office of Lord Chancellor
wool stapler 1. a person who sells wool 2. a person who sorts wool according to its staple, or fibre
woom·er·a (woom′ər ə) *n.* [Abor.] a spear-throwing device used by Australian aborigines: also **wom′er·a** (wom′ər ə)
wooz·y (woo′zē, wooz′ē) *adj.* wooz′i·er, wooz′i·est [prob. < *wooze*, var. of OOZE[1]] [Colloq.] 1. dizzy, faint, and sickish 2. befuddled, as from drink —**wooz′i·ly** *adv.* —**wooz′i·ness** *n.*
wop (wop) *n.* [< ? It. dial. *guappo*, braggart] [Slang] a derogatory term for a member of a Latin people, esp. an Italian
Worces·ter sauce (woos′tər) [orig. made in *Worcester*] a spicy sauce for meats, poultry, etc., containing soy sauce, vinegar, etc.
word (wurd) *n.* [OE.] 1. *a)* a speech sound, or series of speech sounds, serving to communicate meaning; unit of language consisting of a single morpheme or a group of morphemes *b)* a letter or group of letters, written or printed, representing such a unit of language 2. a brief expression; remark [a *word* of advice] 3. a promise [he gave his *word*] 4. news; information [no *word* from home] 5. *a)* a password or signal *b)* a command; order 6. [usually *pl.*] *a)* talk; speech *b)* lyrics; text; libretto 7. [*pl.*] a quarrel; dispute 8. an ordered combination of characters with meaning, regarded as a unit and stored in a computer —*vt.* to express in words; phrase —**a good word** a favourable comment, or commendation —**by word of mouth** by speech; orally —**have a word with** to have a brief conversation with —**have no words for** to be incapable of describing —**have words with** to argue angrily with —**in a word** in short; briefly —**in so many words** precisely; succinctly —**man** (or **woman**) **of his** (or **her**) **word** one who keeps his promises —**of many** (or **few**) **words** talkative (or untalkative) —**put words into a person's mouth** 1. to impute a statement to a person who has not said it 2. to tell a person what to say —**take a person at his word** take action in the belief that someone meant what he said —**take the words out of one's mouth** to have someone else say what one was about to say oneself —**the Word** 1. the Bible: also **Word of God** 2. the spirit of God as revealed in Jesus: John I 3. *same as* GOSPEL (sense 1) —**(upon) my word!** indeed! really! —**word for word** in precisely the same words —**word′less** *adj.* —**word′less·ly** *adv.* —**word′less·ness** *n.*
word·age (-ij) *n.* words collectively, or the number of words (of a story, novel, etc.)

word blindness *same as:* 1. ALEXIA 2. DYSLEXIA —**word′-blind′** *adj.*
word·book (-book′) *n.* a dictionary, lexicon, or vocabulary
word deafness a cerebral disorder characterized by loss of ability to understand spoken words; auditory aphasia
word-for-word (-fər wurd′) *adj.* in exactly the same words
word game any game involving the formation, discovery, or alteration of a word or words
word·ing (-iŋ) *n.* choice and arrangement of words
word of honour pledged word; solemn promise
word order the arrangement of words in a phrase, clause, or sentence
word-per·fect (-pur′fikt) *adj.* knowing one's lesson, theatrical role, etc. perfectly by heart
word·play (-plā′) *n.* 1. a subtle or clever exchange of words; repartee 2. punning or a pun
word square a square made of letters so arranged that they spell the same words in the same order horizontally and vertically
word·y (wur′dē) *adj.* word′i·er, word′i·est containing or using many or too many words; verbose —**word′i·ly** *adv.* —**word′i·ness** *n.*
wore (wôr) *pt.* of WEAR[1]
work (wurk) *n.* [OE. *weorc*] 1. physical or mental effort exerted to do or make something; labour; toil 2. *a)* employment at a job [out of *work*] *b)* one's place of employment [phone me at *work*] 3. occupation, profession, business, trade, craft, etc. 4. *a)* something one is making, doing, or acting upon; task [to take *work* home] *b)* the amount of this [a day's *work*] 5. something that has been made or done; specif., *a)* an act; deed: *usually used in* pl. [good *works*] *b)* [*pl.*] collected writings *c)* [*pl.*] engineering structures, as bridges, dams, etc. *d)* a fortification *e)* needlework; embroidery *f)* *same as* WORK OF ART 6. [*pl.*, *with sing. v.*] a place where work is done, as a factory 7. workmanship 8. the action of, or effect produced by, natural forces 9. *Mech.* transference of force from one body or system to another, measured by the product of the force and the amount of displacement in the line of force —*adj.* of, for, or used in work —*vi.* **worked** or **wrought**, **work′ing** 1. to do work; labour; toil 2. to be employed 3. *a)* to perform its function; operate; act *b)* to operate effectively 4. to undergo fermentation 5. to produce results or exert an influence [let it *work* in his mind] 6. to be manipulated, kneaded, etc. [putty that *works* easily] 7. to move, proceed, etc. slowly and with or as with difficulty 8. to move, twitch, etc. as from agitation [his face *worked* with emotion] 9. to change into a specified condition, as by repeated movement [the handle *worked* loose] —*vt.* 1. to cause; bring about [his idea *worked* wonders] 2. to mould; shape [to *work* silver] 3. to sew, embroider, etc. [to *work* a sampler] 4. to solve (a problem or a difficulty) (often with *out*) 5. to manipulate; knead [to *work* dough] 6. to bring into a specified condition, as by moving back and forth [to *work* a nail loose] 7. to cultivate (soil) 8. to cause to function; operate; use 9. to cause fermentation in 10. to cause to work [to *work* a crew hard] 11. to influence; persuade [*work* him to your ideas] 12. to make (one's way, etc.) by work or effort 13. to provoke; rouse [to *work* oneself into a rage] 14. to carry on activity in, along, etc.; cover [a salesman *working* his territory] 15. [Colloq.] to contrive or manipulate to one's own advantage —**at work** working —**get** (or **give one**) **the works** [Slang] to be (or cause one to be) the victim of an ordeal —**have one's work cut out (for one)** have difficulty in accomplishing one's task —**make short** (or **quick**) **work of** to deal with or dispose of quickly —**out of work** unemployed —**shoot the works** [Chiefly U.S. Slang] 1. to risk everything on one chance 2. to make a supreme effort —**the works** 1. the working parts (of a watch, clock, etc.) 2. everything —**work in** to insert or be inserted —**work off** 1. to get rid of, as by exertion 2. to pay (a debt or obligation) by work instead of money —**work on** (or **upon**) 1. to influence 2. to try to persuade —**work out** 1. to make its way out, as from being embedded 2. to exhaust (a mine, etc.) 3. *same as* WORK OFF (sense 2) 4. to accomplish 5. to solve 6. to result in some way 7. to calculate 8. to reach a total [it *works out* at £1 each] 9. to develop; elaborate 10. to engage in a workout —**work over** [Colloq.] to subject to harsh or cruel treatment —**work to rule** to adhere strictly to all working regulations in order to reduce the rate of working, as a form of industrial action —**work up** 1. to advance; rise 2. to develop; elaborate 3. to arouse; excite
work·a·ble (wur′kə b'l) *adj.* 1. that can be worked 2. practicable; feasible —**work′a·bil′i·ty, work′a·ble·ness** *n.*
work·a·day (wur′kə dā′) *adj.* 1. of or suitable for working days; everyday 2. commonplace; ordinary
work·bag (-bag′) *n.* a container for tools and materials, esp. sewing equipment: also called **work′bas′ket, work′box**
work·bench (wurk′bench′) *n.* a table at which work is done, as by a mechanic, carpenter, etc.
work·book (-book′) *n.* 1. a book containing questions and

exercises to be worked by students **2.** a book of operating instructions **3.** a book containing a record of work planned or done

work·day (-dā´) *n.* **1.** a day on which work is done; working day **2.** the part of a day during which work is done [a 7-hour *workday*] —*adj.* same as WORKADAY

work·er (wʉr´kər) *n.* **1.** a person, animal, or thing that works; specif., a person who works for a living **2.** a person who works for a cause, etc. [a party *worker*] **3.** any of various sterile female ants, bees, etc. that do work for the colony

work·er-priest (-prēst) *n.* a Roman Catholic priest who has a full-time or part-time secular job in order to be more closely in touch with the problems of the laity

work force the total number of workers actively employed in, or available for work in, a nation, region, plant, etc.

work·horse (wʉrk´hôrs´) *n.* **1.** a horse used for working, as for pulling a plough **2.** a steady, responsible worker with a heavy workload **3.** a durable machine, vehicle, etc.

work·house (-haus´) *n.* **1.** formerly, a poorhouse **2.** [U.S.] a kind of prison where petty offenders are confined and made to work

work·ing (wʉr´kiŋ) *adj.* **1.** that works **2.** of, for, or used in work **3.** sufficient to get work done [a *working* majority] **4.** on which further work may be based [a *working* hypothesis] —*n.* **1.** the act or process of a person or thing that works **2.** [*usually pl.*] a part of a mine, quarry, etc. where work is or has been done —**in working order** in a condition of fitness or readiness to operate

working capital the part of a company's capital that can be converted readily into cash

working class workers as a class; esp., industrial or manual workers as a class; proletariat —**work´ing-class´** *adj.*

working day 1. a day on which work is done, esp. as distinguished from a Sunday, holiday, etc. **2.** the part of a day during which work is done; specif., the number of hours each day that an employee is required to work

working drawing a scale drawing for the guidance of those doing the work illustrated by it

working lunch a meal at which business associates discuss business matters

work·ing·man (-man´) *n., pl.* **-men´** (-men´) a worker; esp., an industrial or manual worker; wage earner; labourer

working party 1. a body appointed to investigate a problem, question, etc. **2.** a group of soldiers or prisoners assigned to perform a task

working week the total number of hours or days worked in a week for the regular wage or salary

work·ing·wom·an (-woom´ən) *n., pl.* **-wom´en** a woman worker; esp., a woman industrial or manual worker

work·load (wʉrk´lōd´) *n.* the amount of work assigned to be completed within a given time

work·man (wʉrk´mən) *n., pl.* **-men 1.** same as WORKINGMAN **2.** a craftsman

work·man·like (-līk´) *adj.* characteristic of a good workman; skilful: also **work´man·ly**

work·man·ship (-ship´) *n.* **1.** skill of a workman; craftsmanship **2.** something produced by this skill

workmen's compensation compensation for death, injury, accident, or disease suffered during or in connection with employment

work of art 1. something produced in one of the fine arts, as a painting, sculpture, etc. **2.** anything made, performed, etc. with great skill and beauty

work·out (wʉrk´out´) *n.* a period of doing exercises intended to develop physical fitness or athletic skill

work·room (-room´) *n.* a room in which work is done

works council a joint council of employer and employees which discusses matters of common interest within an industrial or commercial organization

work·shop (-shop´) *n.* **1.** a room or building where work is done **2.** a seminar or series of meetings for intensive study, work, etc. in some field [a writers' *workshop*]

work·shy (-shī) *adj.* avoiding work; lazy

work song a folk song sung by labourers, as in the fields, with a marked rhythm matching the rhythm of their work

work study the examination and analysis of working methods in order to organize labour in the most efficient way possible

work·ta·ble (-tā´b'l) *n.* a table at which work is done, esp. one with drawers for tools, materials, etc.

work-to-rule (-tə·rool´) *n.* a form of industrial action in which employees adhere strictly to all working regulations, in order to reduce their rate of working and efficiency

work·wom·an (-woom´ən) *n., pl.* **-wom´en** same as WORKINGWOMAN

world (wʉrld) *n.* [OE. *werold*] **1.** *a)* the planet earth *b)* the whole universe *c)* any heavenly body imagined as being inhabited **2.** the earth and its inhabitants **3.** *a)* mankind *b)* people generally [the news startled the *world*] **4.** *a)* [also **W-**] some part of the earth [the Old *World*] *b)* some period of history, its society, etc. [the ancient *world*] *c)* any sphere or domain [the animal *world*] *d)* any sphere of human activity [the *world* of music] **5.** individual experience, outlook, etc. [his *world* is narrow] **6.** *a)* the usual social life of people, as apart from a life devoted to religious or spiritual matters *b)* people leading the usual social life **7.** [often *pl.*] a large amount; great deal [to do a *world* (or *worlds*) of good] —**bring into the world** to give birth to —**come into the world** to be born —**dead to the world** unaware of one's surroundings, esp. fast asleep or very drunk —**for all the world 1.** for any reason or consideration at all **2.** in every respect; exactly —**in the world 1.** on earth or in the universe; anywhere **2.** at all; ever —**on top of the world** very happy; cheerful; elated

World Bank an agency (officially **International Bank for Reconstruction and Development**) of the UN, established in 1945 to make loans to member nations

world·beat·er (-bēt´ər) *n.* [Colloq.] one that is, or has the qualities needed to become, a great success

World Cup an award given in a competition held every four years between football teams of various countries

world·ling (-liŋ) *n.* a worldly person

world·ly (wʉrld´lē) *adj.* **-li·er, -li·est 1.** of or limited to this world; temporal or secular **2.** devoted to or concerned with the affairs, pleasures, etc. of this world: also **world´-ly-mind´ed 3.** worldly-wise —**world´li·ness** *n.*

world·ly-wise (-wīz´) *adj.* wise in the ways or affairs of the world; sophisticated —**worldly wisdom**

world power a nation or organization large or powerful enough to have a worldwide influence

World Series [*also* **w- s-**] an annual series of games between the winning teams of the two major U.S. baseball leagues to decide the championship

world-shak·ing (wʉrld´shā´kiŋ) *adj.* of great importance, effect, or influence; momentous

World War I the war (1914–18) between the Allies (Great Britain, France, Russia, the U.S., Italy, Japan, etc.) and the Central Powers (Germany, Austria-Hungary, etc.)

World War II the war (1939–45) between the Allies (Great Britain, France, the Soviet Union, the U.S., etc.) and the Axis (Germany, Italy, Japan, etc.)

world-wea·ry (wʉrld´wir´ē) *adj.* weary of the world; bored with living

world·wide (-wīd´) *adj.* extending throughout the world

worm (wʉrm) *n.* [OE. *wyrm*, serpent] **1.** any of many long, slender, soft-bodied, creeping animals, as the annelids, roundworms, etc. **2.** popularly, *a)* an insect larva, as a grub or maggot *b)* any of several molluscs, as the shipworms *c)* any of various wormlike animals, as the glow worm **3.** a person looked down on as being too meek, wretched, etc. **4.** something that distresses one mentally, suggesting a parasitic worm **5.** something thought of as being wormlike because of its spiral shape; specif., a short, rotating screw that meshes with the teeth of a worm wheel or a rack **6.** [*pl.*] *Med.* any disease or disorder caused by parasitic worms in the intestines, etc. —*vi.* to move, proceed, etc. like a worm, in a winding, creeping, or roundabout manner —*vt.* **1.** to bring about, get, make, etc. in a winding, creeping, or roundabout manner **2.** to rid of worms; esp., to purge of intestinal worms —**the worm will turn** a hitherto meek, yielding person will suddenly assert his will if provoked too far —**worm´er** *n.* —**worm´like** *adj.*

worm·cast (-kast´) *n.* a coil of earth that has been egested by an earthworm

worm-eat·en (-ēt´'n) *adj.* **1.** eaten into by worms, termites, etc. **2.** worn-out, out-of-date, etc.

worm gear 1. same as WORM WHEEL **2.** a gear consisting of a worm and worm wheel

worm·hole (-hōl´) *n.* a hole made, as in wood, by a worm, termite, etc.

worm wheel a toothed wheel designed to gear with the thread of a worm

worm·wood (wʉrm´wood´) *n.* [altered by folk etym. < OE. *wermod*] **1.** any of various strong-smelling plants; esp., a Eurasian perennial that yields a bitter-tasting, dark-green oil (**wormwood oil**) used in making absinthe **2.** a bitter, unpleasant experience

WORM GEAR

worm·y (wʉr´mē) *adj.* **worm´i·er, worm´i·est 1.** containing a worm or worms; worm-infested **2.** same as WORM-EATEN **3.** like a worm **4.** debased; grovelling —**worm´i·ness** *n.*

worn (wôrn) *pp.* of WEAR[1] —*adj.* **1.** showing the effects of use, wear, etc. **2.** damaged by use or wear **3.** showing the effects of worry or anxiety **4.** exhausted; spent

worn-out (-out´) *adj.* **1.** used or worn until no longer effective, usable, or serviceable **2.** exhausted; tired out

wor·ri·ment (wʉr´ē mənt) *n.* [Colloq.] **1.** a worrying or being worried; mental disturbance; anxiety **2.** a cause of worry

wor·ri·some (-səm) *adj.* **1.** causing worry or anxiety **2.** having a tendency to worry —**wor´ri·some·ly** *adv.*

wor·rit (wʉr´it) *n., vt., vi.* [Dial. or Colloq.] same as WORRY

wor·ry (wʉr´ē) *vt.* **-ried, -ry·ing** [OE. *wyrgan*, to strangle] **1.** *a)* to treat roughly, as with continual biting [a dog *worrying* a bone *]* *b*) to pluck at, touch, etc. repeatedly in a nervous way *[to worry a loose tooth with the tongue]* **2.** to annoy; bother **3.** to cause to feel troubled or uneasy —*vi.* **1.** to bite, pull, or tear (*at* an object) with the teeth **2.** to be anxious, troubled, etc. **3.** to manage to get (*along* or *through*) in the face of difficulties —*n.*, *pl.* **-ries** **1.** the act of worrying **2.** a troubled state of mind; anxiety **3.** something that causes anxiety —**worry out** to discover by persistent effort —**wor′ri·er** *n.*

worry beads a string of beads that when fingered or played with supposedly relieves nervous tension

wor·ry·guts (-guts) *n.* [Colloq.] a person who tends to worry, esp. over trivial details: also [Chiefly U.S.] **wor′-ry-wart′**

worse (wʉrs) *adj.* *compar.* *of* BAD[1] & ILL [OE. *wiersa*] **1.** *a*) bad, evil, harmful, etc. in a greater degree *b*) of inferior quality or condition **2.** in poorer health; more ill **3.** in a less satisfactory situation —*adv.* *compar.* *of* BADLY & ILL in a worse manner; to a worse extent —*n.* that which is worse —**for the worse** to a worse condition —**the worse for wear** shabby or worn —**worse off** financially poorer

wors·en (wʉr′s'n) *vt.*, *vi.* [orig., a dial. word < prec. + -EN] to make or become worse

wor·ship (wʉr′ship) *n.* [< OE.: see WORTH & -SHIP] **1.** *a*) reverence or devotion for a deity; veneration *b*) a church service or other rite showing this **2.** intense love or admiration of any kind **3.** something worshipped **4.** a title of honour (preceded by *your* or *his*) used in addressing magistrates, etc. —*vt.* **-shipped, -ship·ping** **1.** to show religious reverence for **2.** to have intense love or admiration for —*vi.* to engage in worship —**wor′ship·per** *n.*

wor·ship·ful (-fəl) *adj.* **1.** honourable; respected: used as a title of respect **2.** feeling or offering great devotion or respect —**wor′ship·ful·ly** *adv.* —**wor′ship·ful·ness** *n.*

worst (wʉrst) *adj.* *superl.* *of* BAD[1] & ILL [OE. *wyrsta*] **1.** *a*) bad, evil, harmful, etc. in the greatest degree *b*) of the lowest quality or condition **2.** in the least satisfactory situation —*adv.* *superl.* *of* BADLY & ILL in the worst manner; to the worst extent —*n.* that which is worst —*vt.* to get the better of; defeat —**at worst** under the worst circumstances —**if the worst comes to the worst** if the worst possible thing happens —**make the worst of** to be pessimistic about

wor·sted (woos′tid) *n.* [after *Worsted*, now *Worstead*, Norfolk, where first made] **1.** a smooth, hard-twisted thread or yarn made from long-staple wool **2.** fabric made from this —*adj.* made of worsted

wort[1] (wʉrt) *n.* [< OE. *wyrt*- (in compounds) ult. allied with WORT[2]] a liquid prepared with malt which, after fermenting, becomes beer, ale, etc.

wort[2] (wʉrt) *n.* [OE. *wyrt*, a root] a plant or herb: now usually in compounds *[liverwort]*

worth (wʉrth) *n.* [OE. *weorth*] **1.** material value, esp. as expressed in terms of money **2.** the esteem in which a person or thing is held; importance, value, etc. **3.** the quantity of something that may be had for a given sum *[four pounds′ worth of petrol]* **4.** wealth; possessions —*adj.* [with prepositional force] **1.** deserving or worthy of; meriting **2.** equal in value to (something specified) **3.** having wealth amounting to —**for all one is worth** to the utmost

worth·less (-lis) *adj.* without worth or merit; useless, valueless, etc. —**worth′less·ly** *adv.* —**worth′less·ness** *n.*

worth·while (-wīl′, -hwīl′) *adj.* important or valuable enough to repay time or effort spent; of true value

wor·thy (wʉr′thē) *adj.* **-thi·er, -thi·est** **1.** having worth, value, or merit **2.** deserving; meriting (often with *of* or an infinitive) —*n.*, *pl.* **-thies** a person of outstanding worth or importance: often used humorously —**wor′thi·ly** *adv.* —**wor′thi·ness** *n.*

wot (wot) *1st & 3rd pers. sing., pres. indic.,* *of* WIT[2]

would (wood; *unstressed* wəd) *v.* [OE. *wolde*, pt. *of willan*, to will] **1.** *pt. of* WILL[2] **2.** an auxiliary used: *a*) to express condition *[he would go if you would]* *b*) in indirect discourse to express futurity *[he said he would come]* *c*) to express habitual action *[Sundays he would sleep late]* *d*) to soften a request *[would you please leave?]* **3.** I wish *[would that we were here]* See also SHOULD

would-be (wood′bē′) *adj.* **1.** wishing or pretending to be *[a would-be expert]* **2.** intended to be *[a would-be help]*

would·n't (wood′n't) would not

wouldst (woodst) *archaic 2nd pers. sing. of* WILL[2]: *used with* thou: also **would·est** (wood′ist)

wound[1] (woond) *n.* [OE. *wund*] **1.** an injury in which the skin or other tissue is broken, cut, torn, etc. **2.** any hurt to the feelings, honour, etc. —*vt.*, *vi.* to inflict a wound (*on* or *upon*); injure —**the wounded** persons wounded, esp. in warfare

wound[2] (wound) **1.** *pt. & pp. of* WIND[1] **2.** *pt. & pp. of* WIND[3]

wove (wōv) *pt. & alt. pp. of* WEAVE

wo·ven (-'n) *alt. pp. of* WEAVE

wove paper paper made on a mould in which the wires are

so closely woven together that the finished sheets do not readily show wire marks as on laid paper

wow[1] (wou) *interj.* an exclamation of surprise, pleasure, pain, etc. —*n.* [Chiefly U.S. Slang] a remarkable, successful, exciting, etc. person or thing —*vt.* [Chiefly U.S. Slang] to be a great success with

wow[2] (wou) *n.* [echoic] a distortion in reproduced sound, caused by variations in speed of the turntable, tape, etc. either in recording or playing

wow·ser (wouz′ər) *n.* [< ?] [Aust.] a fanatically puritanical person; killjoy

wpm words per minute

W.R. **1.** Western Region **2.** West Riding (of Yorkshire)

W.R.A.C. Women′s Royal Army Corps

wrack (rak) *n.* [< OE. *wræc*, misery & MDu. *wrak*, a wreck] **1.** ruin; destruction: now chiefly in **wrack and ruin** **2.** seaweed, etc. cast up on shore

W.R.A.F. Women′s Royal Air Force

wraith (rāth) *n.* [Scot., ult. < ? ON. *vorthr*, guardian < *vartha*, to guard] **1.** a ghost **2.** a ghostlike figure of a person supposedly seen just before his death

wran·gle[1] (raŋ′g'l) *vi.* **-gled, -gling** [< ME. freq. of *wringen*, to WRING] **1.** to quarrel angrily and noisily **2.** to argue; dispute —*vt.* to argue (a person) *into* or *out of* something —*n.* an angry, noisy dispute or quarrel

wran·gle[2] (raŋ′g'l) *vt.* **-gled, -gling** [< WRANGLER[2]] [U.S.] to herd (livestock, esp. saddle horses)

wran·gler[1] (raŋ′glər) *n.* [WRANGLE + -ER] **1.** a person who wrangles, or argues, esp. in a noisy or angry way **2.** at Cambridge University, a candidate who has obtained first-class honours in the mathematics tripos

wran·gler[2] (raŋ′glər) *n.* [< (*horse*) *wrangler*, partial transl. of AmSp. *caballerango*, a groom] [U.S.] a cowboy who herds livestock, esp. saddle horses

wrap (rap) *vt.* **wrapped** or **wrapt, wrap′ping** [ME. *wrappen*] **1.** *a*) to wind or fold (a covering) round something *b*) to cover by this means **2.** to envelop; hide; conceal *[a town wrapped in fog]* **3.** to enclose and fasten in a wrapper of paper, etc. **4.** to wind or fold *[to wrap one′s arms round someone]* —*vi.* to twine, extend, coil, etc. (usually with *over, round,* etc.) —*n.* **1.** an outer covering; esp., an outer garment worn by being wrapped around the body **2.** *[pl.]* secrecy; censorship *[plans kept under wraps]* —**wrapped up in 1.** devoted to; absorbed in (work, etc.) **2.** involved in —**wrap up 1.** to enfold in a covering **2.** to put on warm clothing **3.** [Colloq.] *a*) to bring to an end *b*) to give a concluding report, etc. *c*) to be quiet —**wrap′page** *n.*

wrap·a·round (rap′ə·round′) *adj.* **1.** that has a full-length opening and is wrapped around the body *[a wraparound skirt]* **2.** moulded, etc. so as to curve *[a wraparound windscreen]* —*n.* a wraparound garment, esp. a skirt

wrap·per (-ər) *n.* **1.** a person or thing that wraps **2.** that in which something is wrapped; covering; specif., *a*) the tobacco leaf forming the covering of a cigar *b*) the dust jacket of a book *c*) the covering of paper, polythene, etc., in which a sweet, biscuit, etc. is enclosed *d*) the paper in which a magazine, etc. is enclosed for posting **3.** a loose garment, as a woman′s dressing gown

wrap·ping (-iŋ) *n.* [often *pl.*] the material, as paper, in which something is wrapped

wrasse (ras) *n.*, *pl.* **wrass′es, wrasse:** see PLURAL, II, D, 1 [Corn. *wrach*] any of various fishes with spiny fins and bright colouring, found esp. in tropical seas

wrath (roth, rôth) *n.* [O.E. *wræththo* < *wrath*, wroth] **1.** intense anger; rage **2.** [Archaic] any action carried out in great anger, esp. for punishment or vengeance

wrath·ful (-fəl) *adj.* **1.** full of wrath **2.** resulting from or expressing wrath —**wrath′ful·ly** *adv.* —**wrath′ful·ness** *n.*

wreak (rēk) *vt.* [OE. *wrecan*, to revenge] **1.** to give vent or free play to (anger, malice, etc.) **2.** to inflict (vengeance), cause (havoc), etc. —**wreak′er** *n.*

wreath (rēth) *n.*, *pl.* **wreaths** (rēthz, rēths) [OE. *writha*, a ring < *writhan*, to twist] **1.** a twisted band or ring of leaves, flowers, etc. **2.** something suggesting this in shape *[wreaths of smoke]* —**wreath′like′** *adj.*

wreathe (rēth) *vt.* **wreathed, wreath′ing** **1.** to coil, twist, or entwine, esp. so as to form a wreath **2.** to coil, twist, or entwine round; encircle *[clouds wreathe the hills]* **3.** to decorate with wreaths **4.** to cover or envelop *[a face wreathed in smiles]* —*vi.* **1.** to have a twisting or coiling movement **2.** to form a wreath

wreck (rek) *n.* [Anglo-Fr. *wrec* < ON. *vrek*, driftwood, wreckage] **1.** goods or wreckage cast ashore after a shipwreck **2.** *a*) the disabling or destruction of a ship by a storm or other disaster; shipwreck *b*) a ship thus disabled or destroyed **3.** the remains of anything that has been destroyed or badly damaged **4.** a person in very poor health **5.** a wrecking or being wrecked; ruin —*vt.* **1.** to destroy or damage badly **2.** [Chiefly U.S.] to tear down (a building, etc.) **3.** to overthrow; thwart **4.** to destroy the health of —*vi.* **1.** to be wrecked **2.** to work as a wrecker

wreck·age (-ij) *n.* **1.** a wrecking or being wrecked **2.** the remains of something that has been wrecked

wreck·er (-ər) *n.* **1.** a person or thing that wrecks **2.** a person who causes ruin, obstruction, etc. **3.** a person employed in salvaging, or recovering cargo from, a wrecked ship **4.** formerly, a person who lured ships to destruction on rocky coasts in order to plunder the wreckage **5.** [Chiefly U.S.] a person employed to demolish buildings **6.** [U.S.] a breakdown van

wreck·ing (-iŋ) *n.* the act or work of a wrecker —*adj.* engaged or used in dismantling or salvaging wrecks

wrecking bar a crowbar with a chiselike point at one end and a curved claw at the other

Wren (ren) *n.* [< initials *W.R.N.S.*] a member of the Women's Royal Naval Service

wren (ren) *n.* [OE. *wrenna*] any of various small, insect-eating songbirds having a long bill, rounded wings, and a stubby, erect tail

wrench (rench) *n.* [OE. *wrenc*, a trick] **1.** a sudden, sharp twist or pull **2.** an injury caused by a twist or jerk, as to the back **3.** a sudden feeling of anguish, grief, etc., as at parting from someone **4.** any of a number of tools used for holding and turning nuts, bolts, pipes etc. —*vt.* **1.** to twist, pull, or jerk violently **2.** to injure (a part of the body) with a twist or wrench **3.** to distort (a meaning, statement, etc.) —*vi.* to pull or tug (*at* something) with a wrenching movement

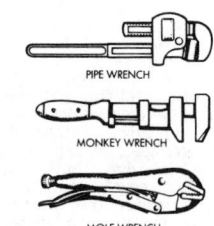

PIPE WRENCH

MONKEY WRENCH

MOLE WRENCH

TYPES OF WRENCH

wrest (rest) *vt.* [OE. *wræstan*] **1.** to pull or force away violently with a twisting motion **2.** to take by force; usurp **3.** to distort or change the true meaning, purpose, etc. of —*n.* **1.** a wresting; a twist; wrench **2.** [Now Rare] a wrenchlike key used in tuning pianos, harps, etc., for turning the pins (**wrest pins**) round which the strings are coiled —**wrest'er** *n.*

wres·tle (res''l) *vi., vt.* -tled, -tling [< OE. freq. of *wræstan*, to twist] **1.** to struggle hand to hand with (an opponent) in an attempt to throw or force him to the ground without striking blows **2.** to struggle hard (*with* a problem, etc.) or struggle to move or lift (something) —*n.* **1.** a wrestling; wrestling bout **2.** a struggle or contest —**wres'tler** *n.*

wres·tling (-liŋ) *n.* a form of sport in which the opponents wrestle, or struggle hand to hand

wretch (rech) *n.* [OE. *wrecca*, an outcast] **1.** a miserable or unhappy person **2.** a person who is despised or scorned

wretch·ed (-id) *adj.* [OE. *wræcc*] **1.** very unhappy; miserable; unfortunate **2.** causing misery [*wretched* slums] **3.** very inferior [a *wretched* meal] **4.** deserving to be despised —**wretch'ed·ly** *adv.* —**wretch'ed·ness** *n.*

wrick (rik) *vt., n.* [prob. < Scand.] a sprain or wrench

wrig·gle (rig''l) *vi.* -gled, -gling [MLowG. *wriggeln*] **1.** to twist and turn to and fro; squirm **2.** to move along with a twisting, writhing motion **3.** to make one's way by subtle or shifty means; dodge —*vt.* **1.** to cause to wriggle **2.** to bring into a specified condition by wriggling [to *wriggle* out of the difficulty] —*n.* a wriggling —**wrig'gler** *n.* —**wrig'-gly** *adj.* -gli·er, -gli·est

wright (rīt) *n.* [OE. *wyrhta* < *wyrcan*, to work] a person who makes, constructs, or repairs: used chiefly in compounds [*shipwright*]

wring (riŋ) *vt.* **wrung**, **wring'ing** [OE. *wringan*] **1.** *a)* to squeeze, press, or twist, esp. so as to force out water or other liquid *b)* to force out (water, etc.) by this means (usually with *out*) **2.** to clasp and twist (the hands) together as an expression of distress **3.** to clasp (another's hand) forcefully in greeting **4.** to wrench or twist forcibly **5.** to get or extract by force, threats, persistence, etc. **6.** to afflict with anguish, pity, etc. [the story *wrung* her heart] —*vi.* to squirm or twist with force or great effort —*n.* a wringing —**wringing wet** soaked; drenched

wring·er (-ər) *n.* **1.** a person or thing that wrings **2.** a device with two rollers close together between which wet clothes are run to squeeze out the water

wrin·kle¹ (riŋ'k'l) *n.* [prob. < OE. (*ge*)*wrinclod*, pp. of (*ge*)*wrinclian*, to wind about] **1.** a small ridge or furrow in a normally smooth surface, caused by contraction, folding, etc. **2.** a crease or pucker in the skin —*vt., vi.* -kled, -kling to contract or pucker into small ridges or creases —**wrin'-kly** *adj.* -kli·er, -kli·est

wrin·kle² (riŋ'k'l) *n.* [prob. ult. < OE. *wrenc*, a trick] [Colloq.] **1.** a clever idea or device **2.** a piece of useful information; tip

wrist (rist) *n.* [OE.] **1.** the joint or part of the arm between the hand and the forearm; carpus **2.** the corresponding part in an animal

wrist·band (rist'band') *n.* a band that goes around the wrist, as on the cuff of a sleeve

wrist pin the stud or pin by which the connecting rod is attached to a wheel, crank, etc.

wrist·watch (-woch') *n.* a watch worn on a strap or band that fits around the wrist

writ (rit) *n.* [OE. < *writan*, to write] **1.** [Rare or Archaic] something written **2.** a formal legal document ordering or prohibiting some action

write (rīt) *vt.* **wrote**, **writ'ten**, **writ'ing;** archaic pt. & pp. **writ** [OE. *writan*, to scratch, write] **1.** *a)* to form (words, letters, etc.) on a surface, esp. with a pen or pencil *b)* to form the words, letters, etc. of [*write* your name] **2.** to spell (a word, etc.) [words *written* the same are often pronounced differently] **3.** to know (a specific language, etc.) well enough to communicate in writing **4.** to be the author or composer of (literary or musical material) **5.** to fill in (a cheque, form, etc.) with the writing required **6.** to cover with writing [he *wrote* 10 pages] **7.** to communicate in writing [he *wrote* that he was ill] **8.** [Colloq. & U.S.] to communicate with in writing [*write* me every day] **9.** to record (information) in a computer's memory or on a tape, etc. for use by a computer **10.** to leave signs or evidence of [greed was *written* on his face] —*vi.* **1.** to form words, letters, etc. on a surface, esp. with a pen or pencil **2.** to write books or other literary matter **3.** to write a letter **4.** to produce writing of a specified kind [to *write* legibly] —**write down** **1.** to put into written form **2.** to discredit in writing **3.** to write in a very simple style so as to be easily understood **4.** to increase the nominal value of (an asset) —**write in** **1.** to insert entries in writing, as on a form, crossword, etc. **2.** [Colloq.] to send a letter to an organization, as a newspaper **3.** [U.S.] to vote for (someone not officially on a ballot) by inserting his name on the ballot —**write off** **1.** to cancel or remove from accounts (bad debts, etc.) **2.** to drop from consideration —**write out** **1.** to put into writing **2.** to write in full —**write up** **1.** to write an account of **2.** to praise in writing **3.** to bring a piece of writing, as a diary, up to date **4.** to increase the nominal value of (an asset) —**writ'a·ble** *adj.*

write-off (rīt'ôf') *n.* something which is damaged beyond repair, esp. a car

writ·er (rīt'ər) *n.* a person who writes, esp. as a business or occupation; author, journalist, etc.

write-up (rīt'up') *n.* [Colloq.] a written report or description, often a favourable account, as for publicity

writhe (rīth) *vt.* **writhed**, **with'ing** [OE. *writhan*, to twist] to cause to twist or turn; contort —*vi.* **1.** to make twisting or turning movements; squirm **2.** to suffer great emotional distress —*n.* a writhing movement

writ·ing (rīt'iŋ) *n.* **1.** the act of a person who writes **2.** something written, as a letter, document, etc. **3.** written form **4.** *short for* HANDWRITING **5.** a literary work **6.** the profession or occupation of a writer **7.** the art, style, etc. of literary composition —*adj.* **1.** that writes **2.** used in writing —**the writing on the wall** signs of approaching disaster

writing case a small, portable container for writing materials

writing desk a piece of furniture with a writing surface and drawers and compartments for papers, etc.

writing paper paper for writing on, esp. stationery

writ·ten (rit''n) *pp. of* WRITE —*adj.* put down in a form to be read; not spoken or oral

W.R.N.S. Women's Royal Naval Service

wrong (roŋ) *adj.* [OE. *wrang* < ON. *rangr*, twisted] **1.** not just, moral, etc.; unlawful, immoral, or improper **2.** not in accordance with an established standard, etc. [the *wrong* method] **3.** not suitable or appropriate [the *wrong* thing to say] **4.** *a)* contrary to fact, reason, etc.; incorrect *b)* acting, believing, etc. incorrectly; mistaken **5.** in an unsatisfactory or bad condition **6.** not functioning properly [what's *wrong* with the light?] **7.** designating the unfinished, inner, or under side [the *wrong* side of a fabric] —*adv.* in a wrong manner, direction, etc.; incorrectly —*n.* **1.** something wrong, esp. an unjust or immoral act **2.** *Law* a violation of a legal right —*vt.* **1.** to treat badly or unjustly; injure **2.** to think badly of without real justification —**get hold of the wrong end of the stick** to misunderstand completely —**get (someone or something) wrong** [Colloq.] to fail to understand (someone or something) properly —**go wrong** **1.** to turn out badly **2.** to change from good behaviour to bad —**in the wrong** not on the side supported by truth, justice, etc. —**wrong'er** *n.* —**wrong'ly** *adv.* —**wrong'ness** *n.*

wrong·do·ing (-dōō'iŋ) *n.* any act or behaviour that is wrong; transgression —**wrong'do'er** *n.*

wrong·ful (-fəl) *adj.* **1.** full of wrong; unjust, unfair, or injurious **2.** without legal right; unlawful [*wrongful* dismissal] —**wrong'ful·ly** *adv.* —**wrong'ful·ness** *n.*

wrong·head·ed (-hed'id) *adj.* stubborn in sticking to wrong opinions, ideas, etc.; perverse —**wrong'head'ed·ly** *adv.* —**wrong'head'ed·ness** *n.*

wrong number a telephone number reached through error, as by dialling incorrectly, or the person reached

wrong' un 1. [Colloq.] a bad character 2. *Cricket* a googly
wrote (rōt) *pt.* of WRITE
wroth (rōth, roth) *adj.* [OE. *wrath*] angry; wrathful
wrought (rôt) *alt. pt. & pp.* of WORK —*adj.* 1. formed; fashioned 2. shaped by hammering or beating: said of metals 3. elaborated with care 4. decorated; ornamented
wrought iron a kind of iron that contains some slag and very little carbon: it is tough but easy to work or shape and is used in gates, balconies, etc. —**wrought'-i'ron** *adj.*
wrought-up (rôt'up') *adj.* very disturbed or excited
wrung (rug) *pt. & pp.* of WRING
W.R.V.S. Women's Royal Voluntary Service
wry (rī) *vt., vi.* **wried, wry'ing** [OE. *wrigian*, to turn] to writhe or twist —*adj.* **wri'er, wri'est** 1. turned or bent to one side; twisted; distorted 2. made by twisting or distorting the features [a *wry* face] 3. perverse; ironic [*wry* humour] —**wry'ly** *adv.* —**wry'ness** *n.*
wry-billed plover (-bild) *n.* a New Zealand bird with a

slender bill curved to the right
wry·neck (-nek') *n.* 1. a condition in which the neck is twisted by a muscle spasm 2. a bird related to the woodpecker, noted for its habit of twisting its neck
WSW, W.S.W., w.s.w. west-southwest
wt. weight
Wun·der·kind (voon'dər kint') *n., pl.* **-kin'der** (-kin'dər) [G. < *Wunder*, wonder + *Kind*, child] a child prodigy
wurst (wurst, woorst; *G.* voorst) *n.* [G.] a large sausage, esp. a type made in Germany
wych-elm (wich'elm') *n.* [< OE. *wice*, applied to trees with pliant branches + ELM] 1. a small variety of elm native to Europe and N Asia 2. its wood
wynd (wīnd) *n.* [MScot. *wynde* < ME. *winden*, WIND[1]] [Scot.] a narrow lane or alley
wy·vern (wī'vərn) *n.* [ME. *wivere* < ONormFr. *wivre*, dragon, serpent < L. *vipera*: see VIPER] *Heraldry* a two-legged dragon with wings and a barbed tail

X, x (eks) *n., pl.* **X's, x's** 1. the twenty-fourth letter of the English alphabet 2. a sound of *X* or *x*
X (eks) *n.* 1. a mark shaped like X, used to represent the signature of a person who cannot write, to mark a particular point on a map or diagram, etc. 2. the Roman numeral for 10 3. a person or thing unknown or unrevealed 4. *Cinema* a film to which no one under the age of eighteen may be admitted —*adj.* shaped like X
x *a symbol for:* 1. *Math. a)* an unknown quantity *b)* times (in multiplication) [3 × 3 = 9] *c)* an abscissa 2. *a)* by [1 m × 2 m] *b)* power of magnification (in optical instruments) *c)* one's choice or answer (on a ballot, test, etc.)
xan·the·in (zan'thē in) *n.* [Fr. *xanthéine*] the water-soluble part of the yellow pigment in some plants
xan·thic (zan'thik) *adj.* [< Fr.: see XANTHO- & -IC] 1. yellow 2. of or having to do with xanthine
xan·thine (-thēn, -thin) *n.* [Fr.: cf. XANTHO- & -IN[1]] a white, crystalline nitrogenous compound present in blood, urine, and certain plants
Xan·thip·pe (zan thip'ē) *n.* [after the wife of Socrates] a nagging or quarrelsome wife: also **Xan·tip·pe** (zan tip'ē)
xan·tho- (zan'thō, -thə) [< Gr. *xanthos*, yellow] *a combining form meaning* yellow: also, before a vowel, **xanth-**
xan·tho·ma (zan thō'mə) *n., pl.* **-mas, -ma·ta** (-mə tə) [XANTH(O)- + -OMA] a skin disease in which yellow patches develop, esp. around the eyelids
xan·tho·phyll (zan'thō fil) *n.* [XANTHO- + -PHYLL] a yellow crystalline pigment found in plants, it is the basis of the yellow seen in autumn leaves
xan·thous (zan'thəs) *adj.* [Gr. *xanthos*] yellow
x-ax·is (eks'ak'sis) *n., pl.* **x'-ax'es** (-sēz) *Math.* the horizontal axis along which the abscissa is measured
X chromosome *Genetics* one of the sex chromosomes: see SEX CHROMOSOME
Xe *Chem.* xenon
xe·bec (zē'bek) *n.* [< Fr. *chébec*, ult. < Ar. *shabbāk*] a small, three-masted ship with overhanging bow and stern: once common in the Mediterranean
xen·o- [< Gr. *xenos*] *a combining form meaning:* 1. stranger, foreigner [*xenophobia*] 2. strange, foreign [*xenolith*] Also, before a vowel, **xen-**
xen·o·lith (zen'ə lith) *n.* [XENO- + -LITH] *Geol.* a rock fragment different in kind from the igneous rock in which it is embedded —**xen'o·lith'ic** *adj.*
xe·non (zē'non) *n.* [Gr., neut. of *xenos*, strange] a heavy, colourless, gaseous chemical element present in the air in minute quantities: used in electron tubes, lasers, etc.: symbol, Xe; at. wt., 131.30; at. no., 54
xen·o·pho·bi·a (zen'ə fō'bē ə) *n.* [ModL.: see XENO- & -PHOBIA] fear or hatred of strangers or foreigners —**xen'-o·phobe** (-fōb') *n.* —**xen'o·pho'bic** (-fō'bik) *adj.*
xe·ro- (zir'ō, -ə) [< Gr. *xēros*] *a combining form meaning* dry [*xerophyte*]: also, before a vowel, **xer-**
xe·rog·ra·phy (zi rog'rə fē) *n.* [< Gr. *xēros*, dry + -GRAPHY] a process for copying printed or written material, etc., in which an image of the material is electrically charged on a surface and attracts oppositely charged dry ink particles, which are then fused in place —**xe·ro·graph·ic** (zir'ə graf'-ik) *adj.*
xe·roph·i·lous (zi rof'ə ləs) *adj.* [< Gr. *xēros*, dry + -PHILOUS] thriving in a hot, dry climate —**xe·roph'i·ly** *n.*

xe·ro·phyte (zir'ə fīt') *n.* [< Gr. *xēros*, dry + -PHYTE] a plant adapted to grow under very dry or desert conditions —**xe'ro·phyt'ic** (-fit'ik) *adj.*
Xe·rox (zir'oks) *a trademark for* a device for copying printed or written material, etc. by xerography —*n.* a copy made by such a device —*vt., vi.* to reproduce by such a device
Xho·sa (kō'sə, -zə; *the* k *is actually a click*) *n.* 1. *pl.* **Xho'-sas, Xho'sa** any member of a people living in Cape Province, South Africa 2. their Bantu language, characterized by clicks Also sp. **Xo'sa**
xi (zī, sī; *Gr.* ksē) *n.* [Gr.] the fourteenth letter of the Greek alphabet (Ξ, ξ)
xiph·i·ster·num (zif'ə stur'nəm) *n., pl.* **-na** (-nə) [ModL. < Gr. *xyphos*, sword + STERNUM] the sword-shaped cartilage at the bottom of the breastbone
xiph·oid (zif'oid) *adj.* [Gr. *xiphoeides*, sword-shaped < *xiphos*, a sword + *eidos*, a form] *Anat., Zool.* shaped like a sword —*n.* same as XIPHISTERNUM: in full **xiphoid process**
Xmas (kris'məs; *occas.* eks'məs) *n.* [X (chi), 1st letter in Gr. *Christos*, Christ + -MAS] *same as* CHRISTMAS
X-ray (eks'rā') *n.* 1. an electromagnetic ray or radiation of very short wavelength produced by the bombardment of a metal by a stream of electrons, as in a vacuum tube: X-rays can penetrate solid substances and are widely used in medicine to study the bones, organs, etc. inside the body and to diagnose and treat certain disorders 2. a photograph made by means of X-rays —*adj.* of, by, or having to do with X-rays —*vt.* to examine, treat, or photograph with X-rays Also **X ray, x-ray, x ray**
xy·lem (zī'ləm, -lem) *n.* [G. < Gr. *xylon*, wood] the woody tissue of a plant, which gives support to the softer tissues and contains vessels or cells that conduct water, minerals, etc.
xy·lene (zī'lēn) *n.* [XYL(O)- + -ENE] any of three isomeric, colourless hydrocarbons, with the characteristics of benzene and derived from coal tar, and petroleum: used as solvents, antiseptics, etc.
xy·lo- [< Gr. *xylon*] *a combining form meaning* wood [*xylophone*]: also before a vowel, **xyl-**
xy·lo·carp (zī'lə kärp') *n.* *Bot.* a hard and woody fruit —**xy'lo·car'pous** *adj.*
xy·lo·graph (zī'lo graf', -gräf') *n.* [XYLO- + -GRAPH] [Rare] a woodcut or a wood engraving —**xy·log'ra·phy** *n.*
xy·loph·a·gous (zī lof'ə gəs) *adj.* [XYLO- + -PHAGOUS] eating, boring into, or destroying wood, as the larvae of certain insects
xy·lo·phone (zī'lə fōn') *n.* [XYLO- + -PHONE] a musical instrument consisting of a series of wooden bars graduated in length so as to sound the notes of the scale when struck with small wooden hammers —**xy·lo'phon'ist** (-fō'-nist, zī lof'ə nist) *n.*
xy·lose (zī'lōs) *n.* [XYL(O)- + -OSE[1]] a colourless sugar derived from wood, straw, etc. and used in dyeing, diabetic foods, etc.

XYLOPHONE

Y, y (wī) *n., pl.* **Y's, y's** 1. the twenty-fifth letter of the English alphabet 2. a sound of *Y* or *y*
Y (wī) *n.* something shaped like Y —*adj.* shaped like Y
Y *Chem.* yttrium
y *Math. a symbol for:* 1. the second of a set of unknown quantities, *x* usually being the first 2. an ordinate
-y¹ (ē, i) [ME. *-y, -i, -ie,* prob. < OFr.] *a suffix meaning* little, dear: used in forming diminutives, nicknames, and terms of endearment [*kitty, Billy*]
-y² (ē, i) [OE. *-ig*] *a suffix meaning:* 1. having, full of, or characterized by [*dirty*] 2. somewhat; rather [*chilly*] 3. tending to [*sticky*] 4. suggestive of, somewhat like [*wavy*] In some words, *-y* simply adds force without changing the meaning [*vasty*]
-y³ (ē, i) [< OFr. *-ie* < L. *-ia* < or akin to Gr. *-ia*] *a suffix meaning:* 1. quality or condition of (being) [*jealousy*] 2. a shop or goods of a specified kind [*bakery*] 3. a collective body of a specified kind [*soldiery*]
-y⁴ (ē, i) [< Anglo-Fr. *-ie* < L. *-ium*] *a suffix meaning* action of [*inquiry, entreaty*]
y. year(s)
yab·ber (ya′bər) *vi., n.* [Abor.] [Chiefly Aust. Colloq.] talk; jabber
yab·by (ya′bē) *n.* [Abor.] a small crayfish found in various parts of Australia
yacht (yot) *n.* [Du. *jacht,* short for *jaghtschip,* pursuit ship] a large boat or small ship for pleasure cruises, races, etc. —*vi.* to sail in a yacht —**yacht′ing** *n.*
yachts·man (yots′mən) *n., pl.* **-men** a person who owns or sails a yacht —**yachts′man·ship′** *n.*
yack, yack-yack, yackety-yack *var. of* YAK², YAK-YAK, etc.
yah (yä) *interj.* a shout of scorn, defiance, etc.
Ya·hoo (yä hōō′) *n.* 1. in Swift's *Gulliver's Travels,* any of a race of coarse, brutish creatures having the form and vices of man 2. [y-] a vicious, coarse person
Yah·weh, Yah·we (yä′wā) [Heb.: see JEHOVAH] God: a form of the Hebrew name in the Scriptures: also **Yah·ve, Yah·veh** (yä′vā)
yak¹ (yak) *n., pl.* **yaks, yak:** see PLURAL, II, D, 1 [Tibet. *gyak*] a stocky, long-haired wild ox of Tibet and C Asia, often used as a beast of burden
yak² (yak) *vi.* **yakked, yak′king** [echoic] [Slang] to talk much or idly; chatter —*n.* [Slang] idle talk or chatter Also **yak′-yak′, yak·e·ty-yak** (yak′ə tē yak′) —**yak′ker** *n.*
yak·ka (ya′kə) *n.* [Abor.] [Aust. Colloq.] work: also sp. **yack·er**
Yale (lock) [< its U.S. inventor, Linus *Yale,* 1821-68] *a trademark for* a type of cylinder lock using a flat serrated key
yam (yam) *n.* [Port. *inhame,* prob. < WAfr. name] 1. *a)* the edible, starchy root of a climbing plant grown in tropical regions *b)* this plant 2. [U.S.] the sweet potato
ya·mal·ka, ya·mul·ka (yäm′əl kə) *n. var. of* YARMULKE
yam·mer (yam′ər) *vi.* [ME. *yameren* < OE. *geomerian,* to lament < *geomor,* mournful] [Colloq. or Dial.] 1. to whine; wail 2. to talk incoherently —*n.* the act of yammering —**yam′mer·er** *n.*
yang (yaŋ) *n.* [< Chin. dial.] in Chinese philosophy, the active, positive, masculine force or principle in the universe, complementary to the *yin:* see YIN
Yank (yaŋk) *n.* [Slang] a Yankee; esp., a U.S. soldier in World Wars I and II —*adj.* of or like a Yank or Yanks
yank (yaŋk) *n.* [< ?] [Colloq.] a sudden, strong pull; jerk —*vt., vi.* [Colloq.] to jerk
Yan·kee (yaŋ′kē) *n.* [< ? Du. *Jan Kees* (taken as pl.) < *Jan,* John + *Kees* < *kaas,* cheese: a disparaging nickname applied by Dutch colonists in America to English settlers] 1. a native or inhabitant of the U.S. 2. [U.S.] a native or inhabitant of New England 3. [U.S.] *a)* a native or inhabitant of a Northern state *b)* a Union soldier in the American Civil War —*adj.* of or like Yankees —**Yan′kee·dom** *n.*
Yankee Doo·dle (dōō′d'l) 1. an old American song, popular during the War of American Independence 2. *same as* YANKEE (sense 1)
yap (yap) *vi.* **yapped, yap′ping** [echoic] 1. to make a sharp, shrill bark or yelp 2. [Colloq.] to talk noisily and stupidly —*n.* 1. a sharp, shrill bark or yelp 2. [Colloq.] *a)* noisy, stupid talk *b)* a crude, noisy person *c)* [Chiefly U.S.] the mouth —**yap′per** *n.* —**yap′ping·ly** *adv.*

ya·pok, ya·pock (yə pok′, yap′ok) *n.* [< *Oyapok,* river in Guiana] a small, water-dwelling marsupial of Central and South America, with webbed hind feet
yapp (yap) *n.* [after *Yapp,* Brit. bookseller, its inventor (c. 1860)] a style of bookbinding in limp leather in which the cover projects beyond the edges of the book
Yar·bor·ough (yär′bər ə) *n.* [said to be so named after second Earl of *Yarborough,* who would bet 1000 to 1 against its occurring] a bridge or whist hand containing no card higher than a nine
yard¹ (yärd) *n.* [OE. *gierd,* a rod] 1. *a)* a measure of length, equal to 3 feet, or 36 inches (0.914 m) *b)* a cubic yard (a *yard* of topsoil) 2. *Naut.* a slender rod or spar fastened across a mast to support a sail or to hold signal flags, lights, etc.
yard² (yärd) *n.* [OE. *geard,* enclosure] 1. a piece of enclosed ground, esp. one adjoining or surrounded by a building or buildings 2. a place in the open used for a particular purpose, work, etc. [a *shipyard*] 3. an area with a network of railway lines where trains are made up, serviced, etc.: also **railway yard** —*vt.* to put, keep, or enclose in a yard —**the Yard** *clipped form of* SCOTLAND YARD
yard·age¹ (yär′dij) *n.* 1. measurement in yards 2. the extent of something so measured
yard·age² (yar′dij) *n.* 1. the use of a yard for storage 2. the charge for this
yard·arm (yärd′ärm′) *n. Naut.* either end of a yard supporting a square sail, signal lights, etc.
yard·man (-mən) *n., pl.* **-men** a man who works in a yard, esp. a railway yard
yard·mas·ter (-mäs′tər) *n.* a man in charge of a railway yard
yard of ale 1. a long, narrow, horn-shaped drinking glass 2. the contents of such a glass
yard·stick (-stik′) *n.* 1. a measuring stick one yard long 2. any standard used in judging, comparing, etc.
yar·mul·ke (yär′məl kə) *n.* [Yid. < Pol. *yarmulka*] a skullcap often worn by Jewish men and boys at prayer or study, at meals, etc.: also **yar′mel·ke, yar′mel·ke**
yarn (yärn) *n.* [OE. *gearn*] 1. a continuous strand or thread of spun wool, silk, cotton, nylon, glass, etc., for weaving, knitting, rope-making, etc. 2. [Colloq.] a tale or story, esp. one that seems exaggerated —*vi.* [Old Colloq.] to tell yarns —**spin a yarn** [Colloq.] to tell a yarn
yar·ra·man (yar′ə man) *n.* [Abor.] [Aust.] a horse
yar·row (yar′ō) *n.* [OE. *gæruwe*] a plant of the composite family, having a strong smell, finely divided leaves, and clusters of small, pink or white flower heads
yash·mak (yash′mak) *n.* [Ar. *yashmaq*] the double veil worn by Moslem women in public
yat·a·ghan, yat·a·gan (yat′ə gan′, -gən) *n.* [Turk. *yātāghan*] a type of Turkish short sabre with a double-curved blade and a handle without a guard
yat·ter (yat′ər) *vi.* [prob. < YA(K)² + (CHA)TTER] to talk idly about trivial things —*n.* a yattering
yaw (yô) *vi.* [? ON. *jaga,* to sway] 1. to swing back and forth across its course, as a ship pushed by high waves 2. to rotate or swing about the vertical axis, as an aircraft, spacecraft, etc. —*vt.* to cause to yaw —*n.* a yawing
yawl (yôl) *n.* [< MLowG. *jolle* or Du. *jol*] 1. a ship's boat 2. a sailing boat like a ketch, but with the short mizzenmast behind the rudderpost
yawn (yôn) *vi.* [prob. merging of OE. *ginian* & *ganian,* to gape] 1. to open the mouth wide and breathe in deeply, as one often does automatically when sleepy or tired 2. to open wide; gape [a *yawning* chasm] —*vt.* to express with a yawn —*n.* 1. a yawning 2. [Colloq.] a person or thing that is boring —**yawn′er** *n.*
yaws (yôz) *n.pl.* [with *sing. v.*] [of Carib origin] a tropical infectious disease caused by a spirochete and characterized by raspberrylike skin eruptions followed by destructive lesions
y-ax·is (wī′ak′sis) *n., pl.* **y′-ax′es** (-sēz) *Math.* the vertical axis along which the ordinate is measured
Yb *Chem.* ytterbium
Y chromosome *Genetics* one of the sex chromosomes: see SEX CHROMOSOME
y·clept, y·cleped (i klept′) *pp.* [OE. *geclypod,* pp. of *clipian,* to call] [Archaic] called; named
yd. *pl.* **yd., yds.** yard

ye¹ (*thə, th*i, *thē; now often* yē) *adj.* archaic form of THE: *y* was substituted for the thorn (þ), the Old and Middle English character representing the sound (*th*)

ye² (yē; *unstressed* yi) *pron.* [OE. *ge*] [Archaic] you

yea (yā) *adv.* [OE. *gea*] 1. yes: used to express affirmation 2. indeed; truly —*n.* an answer or vote of "yes"

yean (yēn) *vt., vi.* [< OE. hyp. *ge-eanian*] to bring forth (young): said of a sheep or goat

yean·ling (-lin) *n.* a lamb or kid —*adj.* newborn

year (yir) *n.* [OE. *gear*] 1. a period of 365 days (in leap year, 366 days) divided into 12 months (from Jan. 1 to Dec. 31) 2. the period (365 days, 5 hours, 48 minutes, and 46 seconds) spent by the sun in its apparent passage from vernal equinox to vernal equinox: the year of the seasons: also **astronomical, equinoctial, tropical** or **solar year** 3. the period (365 days, 6 hours, 9 minutes, and 9.54 seconds) spent by the sun in its apparent passage from a fixed star and back to the same position again: also **sidereal year** 4. a period of 12 lunar months, as in the Jewish calendar: also **lunar year** 5. the period of time in which any planet makes its revolution around the sun 6. a period of 12 calendar months starting from any date [six *years* ago] 7. a calendar year of a specified number in an era [the *year* 500 B.C.] 8. a specific period, not necessarily corresponding with a calendar year, used for some particular activity [a school *year*] 9. the total intake of students, etc., admitted to an educational establishment in any one academic year 10. [*pl.*] a) age [old for his *years*] b) time; esp., a long time [*years* ago] —**the year dot** an extremely long time ago —**year after year** every year —**year by year** each year —**year in, year out** every year

year·book (-book') *n.* a reference book of facts and statistics, published yearly

year·ling (yir'lin, yur'-) *n.* an animal one year old or in its second year —*adj.* being a year old

year·long (yir'lon') *adj.* continuing for a full year

year·ly (-lē) *adj.* 1. lasting a year 2. done, happening, etc. once a year, or every year 3. of a year, or each year —*adv.* annually; every year

yearn (yurn) *vi.* [OE. *gyrnan* < *georn*, eager] 1. to be filled with longing or desire 2. to feel tenderness or sympathy —**yearn'er** *n.* —**yearn'ing** *n., adj.* —**yearn'ing·ly** *adv.*

year-round (yir'round') *adj.* open, in use, operating, etc. throughout the year

yeast (yēst) *n.* [OE. *gist*] 1. any of various single-celled fungi that live on sugary solutions, ferment sugars to form alcohol and carbon dioxide, and are used in making beer, whisky, etc. and as a leavening in baking Also **yeast plant** 2. *a)* the yellowish, moist mass of yeast plants occurring as a froth on fermenting solutions *b)* this substance dried in flakes or granules or compressed into cakes 3. foam; froth 4. *a)* something that agitates or causes ferment; leaven *b)* ferment; agitation —**yeast'like'** *adj.*

yeast·y (yēs'tē) *adj.* **yeast'i·er, yeast'i·est** 1. of, like, or containing yeast 2. frothy; foamy 3. light; frivolous 4. in a ferment; restless —**yeast'i·ness** *n.*

yegg (yeg) *n.* [U.S. Slang] a criminal; esp., a safecracker or burglar: also **yegg'man** (-mən), *pl.* **-men**

yell (yel) *vi.* [OE. *giellan*] to cry out loudly; shout; scream —*vt.* to utter by yelling —*n.* 1. a loud outcry or shout; scream 2. [U.S.] a rhythmic cheer given in unison, as by students at a football game —**yell'er** *n.*

yel·low (yel'ō) *adj.* [OE. *geolu*] 1. of the colour of gold, butter, or ripe lemons 2. having a yellowish skin; Mongoloid 3. [Colloq.] cowardly 4. cheaply sensational [*yellow* press] —*n.* 1. a yellow colour; colour between orange and green in the spectrum 2. a yellow pigment or dye 3. the yolk of an egg —*vt., vi.* to make or become yellow —**yel'low·ish** *adj.* —**yel'low·ness** *n.*

yel·low-bel·ly (-bel'ē) *n., pl.* **-lies** 1. [Slang] a coward 2. any of several Australian and New Zealand fish —**yel'-low-bel'lied** *adj.*

yel·low·bird (-burd') *n.* a bird yellow in colour, as the American goldfinch, etc.

yellow fever a tropical disease caused by a virus carried to man by the bite of the **yellow-fever mosquito**, and marked by fever, jaundice, vomiting, etc.

yellow flag a flag indicating that a ship is in quarantine

yel·low·ham·mer (-ham'ər) *n.* [ult. < OE. *geolu*, yellow + *amore*, kind of finch] a small European finch, having a yellow head, neck, and breast

yellow jack *same as* 1. YELLOW FEVER 2. YELLOW FLAG

yellow metal 1. gold 2. brass that is 60 parts copper and 40 parts zinc

Yellow Pages [*also* y- p-] the section or volume of a telephone directory, on yellow paper, containing classified listings of subscribers according to business, profession, etc.

yellow spot *same as* MACULA LUTEA

yellow streak a tendency to be cowardly

yel·low·wood (-wood') *n.* 1. any of several trees with yellow wood, esp. a) West Indian satinwood *b)* a white-flowered tree of the SE U.S. 2. the wood of any of these

yel·low·y (yel'ə wē) *adj.* somewhat yellow

yelp (yelp) *vi.* [OE. *gielpan*, to boast] 1. to utter a short, sharp cry or bark, as a dog 2. to cry out sharply, as in pain —*vt.* to express by yelping —*n.* a short, sharp cry or bark —**yelp'er** *n.*

yen¹ (yen) *n., pl.* **yen** [Jap. < Chin. *yüan*, round] the monetary unit of Japan: see MONETARY UNITS, table

yen² (yen) *n.* [Chin. *yán*, opium] [Colloq.] a strong longing or desire —*vi.* **yenned, yen'ning** [Colloq.] to have a yen (*for*); long; yearn

yeo·man (yō'mən) *n., pl.* **-men** [ME. *yeman*, prob. contr. < *yung man*, young man] 1. orig., a) a manservant in a royal or noble household *b)* a freeholder of a class below the gentry 2. a) a small landowner *b)* same as YEOMAN OF THE GUARD *c)* a member of the yeomanry (sense 2) 3. U.S. Navy a petty officer assigned to clerical duty —*adj.* of or like yeomen: see also YEOMAN'S SERVICE

yeo·man·ly (-lē) *adj.* 1. of, like, or befitting a yeoman 2. brave; sturdy —*adv.* in a yeomanly manner

yeoman of the (royal) guard any of the 100 men forming a ceremonial guard for the British royal family

yeo·man·ry (-rē) *n.* 1. yeomen collectively 2. a British volunteer cavalry force, organized in 1761 for home defence, but later merged with the Territorial Army

yeoman's service very good, useful, or loyal service or assistance: also **yeoman service**

yep (yep) *adv.* [Chiefly U.S. Slang] yes: an affirmative reply

-yer (yər) *same as* -IER: usually after *w*, as in *lawyer*

yer·ba (yur'bə; *Sp.* yer'bä) *n.* [Sp.] *same as* MATÉ

yes (yes) *adv.* [OE. *gese*, prob. < *gea*, yea + *si*, be it so] 1. aye; yea; it is so: the opposite of NO, used to express agreement, consent, affirmation, etc. 2. not only that, but more; moreover [ready, *yes*, eager to help] *Yes* is sometimes used alone in inquiry to signify "What is it?" or as a polite expression of interest —*n., pl.* **yes'es** 1. the act of saying *yes* 2. an affirmative vote, voter, etc. —*vt., vi.* **yessed, yes'sing** to say *yes* (to)

yes man [Colloq.] a person who indicates approval of every suggestion or opinion offered by his superior; servile sycophant

yes·ter (yes'tər) *adj.* [< ff.] 1. of yesterday 2. previous to this Usually in combination [*yestereve, yesteryear*]

yes·ter·day (yes'tər dē, -dā') *n.* [< OE. < *geostran*, yesterday + *dæg*, day] 1. the day before today 2. a recent day or time 3. [*usually pl.*] time gone by —*adv.* 1. on the day before today 2. recently

yes·ter·year (-yir') *n., adv.* [Poet.] 1. last year 2. (in) recent years

yet (yet) *adv.* [OE. *giet*] 1. up to now or to the time specified; thus far [he hasn't gone *yet*] 2. at the present time; now [we can't leave *yet*] 3. still; even now [there is *yet* a chance for peace] 4. at some future time; sooner or later [she will thank you *yet*] 5. now or at a particular time, as continuing from a preceding time [we could hear her *yet*] 6. in addition; still [he was *yet* more kind] 7. as much as; even [he did not come, nor *yet* write] 8. now, after all the time that has elapsed [hasn't he finished *yet?*] 9. nevertheless [he was rich, *yet* lonely] —*conj.* nevertheless; however [she seems happy, *yet* she is troubled] —**as yet** up to now

ye·ti (yet'ē) *n.* [Tibet.] [*often* Y-] same as ABOMINABLE SNOWMAN

yew (yōō) *n.* [OE. *iw*] 1. an evergreen shrub or tree with red, waxy cones and a fine-grained, elastic wood 2. the wood, used esp. for making archers' bows

Ygg·dra·sil (ig'drə sil) [ON.] *Norse Myth.* the great ash tree whose roots and branches hold together the universe: also *sp.* **Yg'dra·sil, Ygg'dra·sill**

Y.H.A. Youth Hostels Association

yid (yid) *n.* [see ff.] [Slang] a derogatory term for a Jew

Yid·dish (yid'ish) *n.* [Yid. *yidish* < MHG. *jüdisch*, ult. < L. *Judaeus*, a Jew] a language derived from medieval High German, spoken by East European Jews and their descendants in other countries: it is written in the Hebrew alphabet and contains elements of Hebrew, Russian, Polish, English, etc.: abbrev. **Yid.** —*adj.* of or in this language

yield (yēld) *vt.* [OE. *gieldan*, to pay] 1. to produce; specif., a) to give or furnish as a natural process [the orchard *yields* a good crop] b) to give in return; produce as a result, profit, etc. 2. to give up under pressure; surrender 3. to concede; grant —*vi.* 1. to produce or bear 2. to give up; surrender 3. to give way to physical force 4. to give place; lose precedence, etc. (often with *to*); specif., to give up willingly a right, etc. —*n.* 1. the amount yielded or produced 2. the earnings received from investment in stocks, bonds, etc. 3. the force in kilotons or megatons of a nuclear or thermonuclear explosion—**yield'er** *n.*

yield·ing (yēl'din) *adj.* 1. producing a good yield; productive 2. bending easily; flexible 3. submissive; obedient

yield point the stress at which certain materials, such as iron and steel, suffer a large plastic elongation that is independent of the applied load

yin (yin) *n.* [< Chin. dial.] in Chinese philosophy, the passive, negative, feminine force or principle in the universe, complementary to the *yang*: see YANG

yip (yip) *n.* [echoic] [Colloq.] a yelp, or bark —*vi.* **yipped, yip′ping** [Colloq.] to yelp, or bark

yip·pee (yip′ē) *interj.* an exclamation of joy, delight, etc.

-yl (il; *now rarely* ēl) [< Gr. *hylē*, wood] *Chem. a combining form meaning:* 1. a univalent hydrocarbon radical [ethyl] 2. a radical containing oxygen [hydroxyl]

y·lang-y·lang (ē′laŋ ē′laŋ) *n.* [Tagalog] 1. an East Indian tree with fragrant, greenish-yellow flowers 2. the oil obtained from these flowers, used in perfumes

YMCA, Y.M.C.A. Young Men's Christian Association

yob (yob) *n.* [back slang for BOY] [Slang] a hoodlum or lout: also **yob·bo** (yo′bō)

yo·del (yō′d'l) *vt., vi.* **-delled, -del·ling** [G. *jodeln*] to sing with sudden changes back and forth between the normal chest voice and the falsetto —*n.* 1. the act or sound of yodelling 2. a song sung in this way —**yo′del·ler** *n.*

yo·ga (yō′gə) *n.* [Sans., union] 1. *Hinduism* a discipline by which one seeks to achieve union with the universal soul through deep meditation, prescribed postures, controlled breathing, etc. 2. a system of exercising involving such postures, breathing, etc. —**yo′gic** (-gik) *adj.*

yogh (yōkh, yōk, yokh, yok) *n.* [ME.] the name of the Middle English character ȝ, representing *a*) a voiceless fricative, or guttural, similar to Modern German *ch*, as in *doch b*) a voiced palatal fricative, now represented by the *y* of *yes*

yo·gi (yō′gē) *n., pl.* **-gis** a person who practises yoga: also **yo′gin** (-gin)

yo·gurt (yō′gərt, yo′-) *n.* [Turk. *yōghurt*] a thick, semisolid food made from milk fermented by a bacterium: often prepared with various flavours: also sp. **yo′ghurt, yo′·ghourt**

yo-heave-ho (yō′hēv′hō′) *interj.* a chant formerly used by sailors while pulling or lifting together in rhythm

yoicks (yoiks) *interj.* [earlier *hoik, hike*, also *yoaks*] a cry used for urging on the hounds in fox hunting

yoke (yōk) *n., pl.* **yokes**; for 2, usually **yoke** [OE. *geoc*] 1. a wooden frame with bows at either end, fitted round the necks of a pair of oxen, etc. to harness them 2. a pair of animals harnessed together 3. the condition of being under another's power or control; bondage 4. something that binds, unites, etc. 5. something like a yoke, as a frame fitting over the shoulders for carrying pails, etc. 6. a part of a garment fitted closely round the shoulders or hips to support the gathered parts below —*vt.* **yoked, yok′ing** 1. to put a yoke on 2. to harness (an animal) to (a plough, etc.) 3. to join together —*vi.* to be joined together

YOKE
(on pair of oxen)

yo·kel (yō′k'l) *n.* [prob. < dial. *yokel*, green woodpecker] a country person; rustic: a contemptuous term

yolk (yōk) *n.* [OE. *geolca*] the yellow, principal substance of an egg —**yolked, yolk′y** *adj.*

yolk sac a sac containing yolk that is attached to and supplies nourishment for the embryos of birds, fishes, and reptiles

Yom Kip·pur (yom kip′ər; *Heb.* yōm′ kē pōor′) a Jewish holiday, the Day of Atonement, a fast day observed on the 10th day of Tishri

yon (yon) *adj., adv.* [OE. *geon*] [Archaic or Dial.] yonder —*pron.* [Archaic or Dial.] yonder person or thing [yon's a foal]

yon·der (yon′dər) *adj.* [ME.] 1. farther; more distant (with *the*) 2. being at a distance, but within, or as within, sight —*adv.* at or in that place; over there

yo·ni (yō′nē) *n.* [Sans., vulva, womb] *Hinduism* a representation of the vulva, a symbol used in the worship of Shakti

yoo-hoo (yoo′hoo′) *interj., n.* a shout or call used to attract someone's attention

yore (yôr) *adv.* [OE. *geara*] [Obs.] long ago —*n.* time long past: now only in **of yore**, formerly

york (yôrk) *vt.* [see ff.] *Cricket* to bowl or try to bowl (a batsman) with a yorker

york·er (yôrk′ər) *n.* [prob. so named after the *Yorkshire* County Cricket Club] *Cricket* a ball bowled so as to pitch just under or just beyond the bat

York·ist (yôr′kist) *n.* a member or supporter of the English royal house of York —*adj.* of or supporting the house of York, esp. in the Wars of the Roses

Yorks. Yorkshire

York·shire pudding (yôrk′shər) a batter of flour, eggs, and milk baked in the drippings of roasting meat

Yorkshire terrier a long-haired toy terrier of a breed originating in Yorkshire

Yo·ru·ba (yo′roo bə, yō′-) *n.* 1. *pl.* **-bas, -ba** any member of a large ethnic group of SW Nigeria and SE Benin 2. their language

you (yoo; *unstressed* yoo, yə) *pron.* [OE. *eow*, dat. & acc. pl. of *ge*, YE²] 1. the person or persons to whom one is speaking or writing: *you* is the nominative and objective form (sing. & pl.) of the second personal pronoun 2. a person or people generally [*you* never can tell!] —**you and yours** [Colloq.] you, your family, and your possessions

you'd (yood; *unstressed* yood, yəd) 1. you had 2. you would

you'll (yool; *unstressed* yool, yəl) 1. you will 2. you shall

young (yuŋ) *adj.* [OE. *geong*] 1. being in an early period of life or growth 2. characteristic of youth in quality, appearance, etc.; fresh; vigorous 3. representing or embodying a new tendency, social movement, etc. [the *Young* Liberals] 4. of youth or early life [in my *young* days] 5. lately begun; in an early stage 6. lacking experience or practice; immature; green 7. younger than another of the same name or family —*n.* 1. young people 2. offspring, esp. young offspring, collectively [a bear and her *young*] —**with young** pregnant —**young′ish** *adj.* —**young′ness** *n.*

young·ber·ry (yuŋ′bər ē, -brē) *n., pl.* **-ries** [after B. *Young*, 19th-c. U.S. horticulturist] 1. a large, sweet, dark-purple berry, a cross between a blackberry and a dewberry 2. the trailing bramble bearing this fruit

young blood 1. young people 2. youthful vigour, ideas, etc.

younger hand in certain card games for two people, the player who plays second

young·ling (yuŋ′liŋ) *n.* 1. a young person; youth 2. a young animal or plant —*adj.* young

young·ster (-stər) *n.* 1. a child 2. a youth 3. a young animal

Young Turk [orig., member of early 20th-c. revolutionary party in Turkey] [*also* y- T-] any of a group of younger people seeking to take control of an organization, political party, etc. from the older, usually conservative, people in power

your (yoor, yôr; *unstressed* yər) *possessive pronominal adj.* [OE. *eower*] 1. of, belonging to, or done by you: also used before some titles [*your* Honour] 2. [Colloq.] indicating all things or people of a certain type [*your* average working man]

you're (yoor, yōor, yôr; *unstressed* yər) you are

yours (yoorz, yôrz) *pron.* that or those belonging to you: the absolute form of *your*, used without a following noun [that book is *yours, yours* are better]: also used after *of* to indicate possession [a friend of *yours*]

your·self (yôr self′, yoor-, yər-) *pron., pl.* **-selves** (-selvz′) 1. a form of the 2nd pers. sing. pronoun, used: *a*) as an intensive [*you yourself* went] *b*) as a reflexive [*you* hurt *yourself*] *c*) as a quasi-noun meaning "your real or true self" [*you* are not *yourself* today] 2. *same as* ONESELF [it is best to do it *yourself*]

Yours faithfully a phrase used before the signature in ending a formal letter

Yours sincerely a phrase used before the signature in ending an informal letter

yours truly 1. a phrase used before the signature in ending a formal letter 2. [Colloq.] I or me

youth (yooth) *n., pl.* **youths** (yooths, yooth z) [OE. *geoguthe*] 1. the state or quality of being young 2. the period of life coming between childhood and maturity; adolescence 3. an early stage of growth or existence 4. young people collectively 5. a young person; esp., a young man

youth·ful (-fəl) *adj.* 1. young; possessing youth 2. of, characteristic of, or suitable for youth 3. fresh; vigorous 4. new; early; in an early stage —**youth′ful·ly** *adv.* —**youth′·ful·ness** *n.*

youth hostel any of a system of supervised shelters providing cheap lodging on a cooperative basis for young people on bicycle tours, hikes, etc.

you've (yoov; *unstressed* yoov, yəv) you have

yowl (youl) *vi.* [ME. *goulen, youlen* < ON. *gaula*] to utter a long, mournful cry; howl —*n.* such a cry

yo-yo (yō′yō′) *n.* [< Tagalog name: the toy originated in the Philippines] a spoollike toy attached to one end of a string upon which it may be made to spin up and down

yr. 1. year(s) 2. younger 3. your

yrs. 1. years 2. yours

yt·ter·bi·um (i tur′bē əm) *n.* [ModL. < *Ytterby*, Sweden] a scarce, silvery, metallic chemical element of the rare-earth group: symbol, Yb; at. wt., 173.04; at. no., 70

yt·tri·um (it′rē əm) *n.* [ModL. < *Ytterby*, Sweden] a rare, silvery, metallic chemical element: symbol, Y; at. wt., 88.905; at. no., 39

yu·an (yoo an′) *n.* [Chin. *yüan*, round] *see* MONETARY UNITS, table (China)

yuc·ca (yuk′ə) *n.* [ModL., genus name < Sp. *yuca*] 1. a plant of the U.S. and Latin America, having stiff, sword-shaped leaves and white flowers in an erect raceme 2. its flower

Yu·go·slav (yoo′gō släv′, -gə-) *adj.* of Yugoslavia or its people: also **Yu'go·slav'ic** —*n.* a member of a Slavic people, including Serbs, Croats, and Slovenes, who live in Yugoslavia Also **Yu'go·sla'vi·an**

yuk (yuk) *interj.* an exclamation indicating contempt or disgust —*n.* [U.S. Slang] a loud laugh

yuk·ky, yuck·y (yuk'ē) *adj.* [Colloq.] messy; revolting

yule (yōol) *n.* [OE. *geol*] Christmas or the Christmas season

yule log 1. a large log formerly used as a foundation for the ceremonial Christmas Eve fire 2. a swiss roll, usually chocolate flavoured, decorated to resemble a log and served at Christmas

yule·tide (-tīd') *n.* Christmas time

yum·my (yum'ē) *adj.* **-mi·er, -mi·est** [echoic] [Colloq.] very tasty; delectable; delicious

yum-yum (yum'yum') *interj.* [echoic] an expression indicating appreciation of food, or the anticipation of eating

yurt (yoort) *n.* [< Russ. *yurta*, lit., dwelling] a circular tent of felt or skins on a framework of poles, used by the nomads of Mongolia

YWCA, Y.W.C.A. Young Women's Christian Association

Z

Z, z (zed) *n., pl.* **Z's, z's** 1. the twenty-sixth and last letter of the English alphabet 2. the sound of Z or z 3. *a symbol for* the last in a sequence or group

Z (zed) *n.* an object shaped like Z —*adj.* shaped like Z

z *Math.* a symbol for: 1. the third in a set of unknown quantities, *x* and *y* usually being the first two 2. a variable

za·ba·glio·ne (zab'əl yō'nē) *n.* [It.] a frothy dessert made of eggs, sugar, and wine, typically Marsala

zaf·fer, zaf·fre (zaf'ər) *n.* [< Fr *zafre* or It. *zaffera*, prob. < Ar. *sufr*, yellow copper, brass] a blue pigment from an impure cobalt oxide, used in enamelling, etc.

za·ire (zā ir') *n., pl.* **-ire'** [Bantu, lit., river] *see* MONETARY UNITS, table (Zaire)

za·ny (zā'nē) *n., pl.* **-nies** [< Fr. < It. *zanni*, orig., an abbrev. pronun. of *Giovanni*, John] 1. a clown or buffoon 2. a silly or foolish person; simpleton —*adj.* **-ni·er, -ni·est** of or like a zany, *a*) comical in a crazy way *b*) foolish or crazy —**za'ni·ly** *adv.* —**za'ni·ness** *n.*

zap (zap) *vt., vi.* **zapped, zap'ping** [echoic] [Slang] to move, strike, stun, kill, etc. with sudden speed and force —*n.* [Slang] energy, verve, pep, etc. —*interj.* an exclamation used to express sudden, swift action

za·re·ba, za·ree·ba (zə rē'bə) *n.* [Ar. *zarība*, a pen] in the Sudan and surrounding territory, a camping place or enclosure formed by a palisade or thorn hedge

zarf (zärf) *n.* [Ar. *zarf*, a saucer] a small, cuplike holder, used in the Levant for a hot coffee cup

zeal (zēl) *n.* [< LL. *zelus* < Gr. *zēlos*] intense enthusiasm; ardent endeavour or devotion; fervour

zeal·ot (zel'ət) *n.* [< LL. < Gr. *zēlōtēs* < *zēlos*, zeal] 1. a person who is zealous, esp. to an extreme or excessive degree; fanatic 2. [Z-] among the ancient Jews, a member of a radical political and religious sect who openly resisted Roman rule in Palestine —**zeal'ot·ry** *n.*

zeal·ous (zel'əs) *adj.* full of or showing zeal; fervent; enthusiastic —**zeal'ous·ly** *adv.* —**zeal'ous·ness** *n.*

ze·bec, ze·beck (zē'bek) *n.* *same as* XEBEC

ze·bra (zeb'rə, zē'brə) *n., pl.* **-bras, -bra**: see PLURAL, II, D, 1 [Port., prob. ult. < L.] any of several swift African mammals related to the horse, with dark stripes on a white or tawny body —**ze'brine** (-brīn, -brin) *adj.*

zebra crossing a street crossing, marked with black and white bands, at which pedestrians have the right of way

zebra fish any of a number of unrelated fishes with barred, zebralike markings, often kept in aquariums

ze·bu (zē'byōo) *n., pl.* **-bus, -bu**: see PLURAL, II, D, 1 [Fr. *zébu* < ?] an oxlike domestic animal of Asia and Africa: it has a large hump and short, curving horns: see BRAHMAN (sense 2)

zed (zed) *n.* [< MFr. < LL. < Gr. *zēta*] the letter Z, z

zee (zē) *n., pl.* **zees** *U.S. name for the letter Z, z*

Zee·man effect (zā'män, zē'mən) [after Pieter *Zeeman* (1865–1943), Du. physicist] the splitting of a line in a spectrum into several closely spaced lines when the material producing the spectrum is placed in a magnetic field

ze·in (zē'in) *n.* [ModL. *Zea*, a genus of grasses] a white, tasteless, odourless protein extracted from maize, used in plastics, paints, etc.

‡Zeit·geist (tsīt'gīst') *n.* [G., time spirit] the trend of thought and feeling in a period of history

Zen (zen) *n.* [Jap. < Chin., ult. < Sans. *dhyāna*, meditation] 1. a Japanese Buddhist sect that seeks enlightenment through meditation and intuition rather than in traditional scripture 2. the beliefs and practices of this sect —**zen'-ist** *n.*

ze·na·na (zə nä'nə) *n.* [Hindi *zanāna* < Per. *zanāna* < *Zan*, woman] in India and Iran, the part of the house reserved for women

Zend (zend) *n.* [Per., interpretation] the Middle Persian translation of and commentary on the Zoroastrian Avesta —**Zend'ic** *adj.*

Zend-A·ves·ta (-ə ves'tə) *n.* the sacred writings of the Zoroastrians

ze·nith (zen'ith) *n.* [< MFr. < ML. *cenit* < Ar. *semt*, road] 1. the point in the sky directly overhead: that point of the celestial sphere directly opposite to the nadir 2. the highest point; peak

zenith distance the angular distance of a heavenly body from the zenith

ze·o·lite (zē'ə līt') *n.* [Sw. *zeolit* < Gr. *zein*, to boil: from its swelling up when heated] any of a large group of natural hydrous aluminium silicates of sodium, calcium, potassium, or barium, characterized by a ready loss or gain of water of hydration 2. a similar natural or synthetic silicate, used for softening water

zeph·yr (zef'ər) *n.* [< L. < Gr. *zephyros*] 1. the west wind 2. a soft, gentle breeze 3. a fine, soft, lightweight yarn, cloth, or garment

zep·pe·lin (zep'ə lin, zep'lin) *n.* [after F. von *Zeppelin* (1838–1917), G. inventor] [often Z-] a type of dirigible airship designed about 1900

ze·ro (zir'ō, zē'rō) *n., pl.* **-ros, -roes** [Fr. *zéro* < It. < Ar. *sifr*, CIPHER] 1. the symbol or numeral 0; cipher; nought 2. the point, marked 0, from which positive or negative quantities are reckoned on a graduated scale, as on thermometers 3. a temperature that causes a thermometer to register zero 4. nothing 5. the lowest point [his chances sank to zero] —*adj.* 1. of or at zero 2. without measurable value 3. designating or of visibility limited to very short distances, as in flying —*vt.* **-roed, -ro·ing** to adjust (an instrument, etc.) to a zero point from which all positive or negative readings are to be made —**zero in** 1. to adjust the sight settings of (a rifle) by calibrated firing on a standard range 2. to aim (a gun or guns) directly at (a target) —**zero in on** 1. to adjust gunfire so as to be aiming directly at (a target) 2. [Colloq.] to concentrate attention on

zero gravity a condition of weightlessness

zero hour 1. the time set for the beginning of an attack or other military operation 2. any critical point

zero (population) growth a condition in a given population in which the birthrate equals the death rate so that the population remains constant

zest (zest) *n.* [Fr. *zeste*, orange peel used to give flavour] 1. something that gives flavour or relish 2. stimulating or exciting quality; piquancy 3. keen enjoyment; gusto (often with *for*) [a zest for life] 4. orange or lemon peel, used as a flavouring in drinks, etc. —**zest'ful** *adj.* —**zest'ful·ly** *adv.* —**zest'ful·ness** *n.* —**zest'y** *adj.*

ze·ta (zēt'ə) *n.* [Gr.] the sixth letter of the Greek alphabet (Z, ζ)

zeug·ma (zyōog'mə) *n.* [L. < Gr. *zeugma*, lit., yoke] a figure of speech in which a word, usually a verb or an adjective, modifies two or more words, with only one of which it seems logically connected (Ex.: the room was not light, but his fingers were)

zib·et (zib'it) *n.* [< ML. *zibethum* < Ar. *zabād*, civet] a large civet of S and SE Asia

zig·gu·rat (zig'oo rat) *n.* [Assyr. *ziqquratu*, height] an ancient Assyrian or Babylonian temple built as a pyramid with steplike storeys

zig·zag (zig'zag') *n.* [Fr.] 1. a series of short, sharp angles or turns in alternate directions, as in a line or course 2. a design, path, etc. having a series of such angles or turns —*adj.* having the form of a zigzag —*adv.* in a zigzag course —*vt., vi.* **-zagged', -zag'ging** to move or form in a zigzag

zil·lah (zil′a) *n.* [< Hindi *dilah*, division] an administrative district in India: also sp. **zi·la, zil·la**

zil·lion (zil′yən) *n.* [arbitrary coinage, after MILLION] [U.S. Colloq.] a very large, indefinite number

zinc (ziŋk) *n.* [G. *Zink*] a bluish-white, metallic chemical element, used as a protective coating for iron, in electric batteries and in alloys, and, in the form of salts, in medicines: symbol, Zn; at. wt., 65.37; at. no., 30 —*vt.* **zincked** or **zinced**, **zinck′ing** or **zinc′ing** to coat or treat with zinc; galvanize —**zinc′ic** (-ik), **zinck′y, zink′y, zinc′y** *adj.*

zin·co·graph (ziŋ′kō gräf′, -graf′) *n.* 1. a printing plate made by zincography 2. a print taken from such a plate

zin·co·gra·phy (ziŋ kog′rə fē) *n.* [ZINC + -GRAPHY] the art or process of engraving or etching on zinc plates for printing —**zin·cog′ra·pher** *n.* —**zin′co·graph′ic** (-kə graf′ik) *adj.*

zinc ointment an ointment containing zinc oxide

zinc oxide a white powder, ZnO, used as a pigment and in making glass, cosmetics, ointments, etc.

zinc white zinc oxide used as a white pigment

zing (ziŋ) *n.* [echoic] [Slang] 1. a shrill, high-pitched sound, as of something moving at high speed 2. vitality, vigour, zest, etc. —*vi.* [Slang] to make, or move with, or as if with, a shrill, high-pitched sound —**zing′y** *adj.* **zing′-i·er, zing′i·est**

zin·ni·a (zin′ē·a, zin′yə) *n.* [ModL., after J. G. *Zinn*, 18th-c. G. botanist] a plant of the composite family, having colourful flowers, native to N. and S. America

Zi·on (zī′ən) *n.* 1. the hill in Jerusalem on which the Temple was built: a symbol of the centre of Jewish national life 2. *a)* Jerusalem *b)* the land of Israel 3. the Jewish people 4. heaven 5. the theocracy of God

Zi·on·ism (-iz′m) *n.* a movement formerly for reestablishing, now for supporting, the Jewish national state of Israel —**Zi′on·ist** *n., adj.* —**Zi′on·is′tic** *adj.*

zip (zip) *n.* [echoic] 1. a short, sharp hissing sound, as of a passing bullet 2. [Colloq.] energy; vim 3. *same as* ZIP FASTENER —*vi.* **zipped, zip′ping** 1. to make, or move with, a zip 2. [Colloq.] to act or move with speed or energy 3. to become fastened by means of a zip fastener —*vt.* to fasten with a zip fastener (often with *up*)

zip fastener a device used to fasten and unfasten two edges of material: it consists of two rows of interlocking teeth worked by a part that slides up or down: also **zip′per**

zip·py (-ē) *adj.* **-pi·er, -pi·est** [< ZIP + -Y²] [Colloq.] full of vim and energy; brisk

zir·con (zur′kon) *n.* [G. *zirkon*, ult. < Per. *zargūn*, gold-coloured < *zar*, gold] a crystalline silicate of zirconium, coloured yellow, brown, red, etc.: transparent varieties are used as gems

zir·co·ni·um (zər kō′nē əm) *n.* [ModL.: see prec.] a soft grey or black metallic chemical element used in alloys, ceramics, etc.: symbol, Zr; at. wt., 91.22; at. no., 40 —**zir·con′ic** (-kon′ik) *adj.*

zith·er (zith′ər, zith′-) *n.* [G. < L. < Gr. *kithara*, a lute] a musical instrument having from thirty to forty strings stretched across a flat soundboard and played with a plectrum and the fingers —**zith′er·ist** *n.*

zlo·ty (zlo′tē) *n., pl.* **-tys** [Pol., lit., golden] *see* MONETARY UNITS, table (Poland)

Zn *Chem.* zinc

zo (zō) *n.* *same as* DZO

zo- *same as* ZOO-: used before a vowel

-zo·a (zō′ə) [ModL. < Gr. *zōia*, pl. of *zōion*, an animal] a combining form used in zoology to form names of groups [Protozoa]

zo·di·ac (zō′dē ak′) *n.* [< MFr. < L. < Gr. *zōdiakos* (*kyklos*), lit., (circle) of animals < *zōidion*, dim. of *zōion*, animal] 1. an imaginary belt in the heavens extending on either side of the apparent path of the sun and including the paths of the moon and the principal planets: it is divided into twelve equal parts, or signs, each named for a different constellation 2. a diagram representing the zodiac and its signs: used in astrology —**zo·di·a·cal** (-dī′ə k'l) *adj.*

zodiacal light a faint cone of light in the sky, sometimes visible in N latitudes in the east just before sunrise in autumn, and in the west just after sunset in spring

zo·ic (zō′ik) *adj.* [< Gr. *zōon*, an animal] 1. pertaining to, or having, animal life 2. *Geol.* containing fossilized animals

‡**Zoll·ver·ein** (tsôl′fer īn′) *n.* [G. < *Zoll*, custom, toll, + *Verein*, union] a customs union formed by the German states in the 19th cent.

zom·bie (zom′bē) *n.* [of Afr. origin] 1. in West Indian superstition, a dead person supposedly brought back by magic power to a form of life in which he can be made to move or act as he is ordered 2. [Colloq.] *a)* a person like a zombie as in seeming to be half dead, to move automatically, etc. *b)* an eccentric person For sense 1, also sp. **zom′bi**

zone (zōn) *n.* [Fr. < L. < Gr. *zōnē* < *zōnnynai*, to gird] 1. *a)* an encircling band, stripe, etc. distinct in colour, structure, etc. from what surrounds it *b)* formerly, a belt or girdle 2. any of the five great divisions into which the earth's surface is marked off by imaginary lines: see TORRID ZONE, TEMPERATE ZONE, and FRIGID ZONE 3. any area or region considered with reference to its particular use, properties, features, etc. [a demilitarized *zone*, a non-parking *zone*] 4. short for TIME ZONE 5. *Sports* any of the areas into which a basketball court, etc. is divided —*vt.* **zoned, zon′ing** 1. to divide into zones, as for different uses, jurisdiction, etc. 2. to designate as a zone 3. to encircle; surround —**zon′al** *adj.*

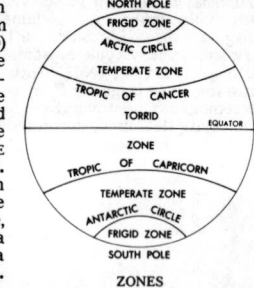

ZONES

zoo (zōō) *n.* [< *zoo(logical garden)*] a place where a collection of wild animals is kept for public showing

zo·o- [< Gr. *zōion*, an animal] a combining form meaning: 1. animal, animals 2. zoology and [zoogeography]

zo·o·ge·og·ra·phy (zō′ə jē og′rə fē) *n.* the science dealing with the geographical distribution of animals —**zo′o·ge·og′ra·pher** *n.* —**zo′o·ge′o·graph′ic** (-jē′ə graf′ik), **zo′o·ge′o·graph′i·cal** *adj.* —**zo′o·ge′o·graph′i·cal·ly** *adv.*

zo·og·ra·phy (zō og′rə fē) *n.* [ZOO- + -GRAPHY] the branch of zoology concerned with the description of animals, their habits, etc. —**zo·og′ra·pher** *n.* —**zo·o·graph·ic** (zō′ə graf′ik), **zo′o·graph′i·cal** *adj.*

zo·oid (zō′oid) *n.* [ZO(O)- + -OID] 1. a comparatively independent animal organism produced by fission, gemmation, etc. rather than by sexual means 2. any of the individual members of a compound organism, as the coral —*adj.* of, or having the nature of, an animal: also **zo·oi′dal**

zool. 1. zoological 2. zoology

zoological garden *same as* ZOO

zo·ol·o·gy (zō ol′ə jē, zōō-) *n.* [< ModL.: see ZOO- & -LOGY] 1. the branch of biology that deals with animals, their life, growth, classification, etc. 2. the animal life of an area; fauna 3. the characteristics of an animal or an animal group —**zo′o·log′i·cal** (-ə loj′i k'l), **zo′o·log′ic** *adj.* —**zo′o·log′i·cal·ly** *adv.* —**zo·ol′o·gist** *n.*

zoom (zōōm) *vi.* [echoic] 1. to make a loud, low-pitched, buzzing or humming sound 2. to move with a zooming sound 3. to climb suddenly and sharply: said of an aircraft 4. to rise rapidly [prices *zoomed*] 5. to focus a camera by using a zoom lens —*vt.* to cause to zoom —*n.* 1. a zooming or a zooming sound 2. *same as* ZOOM LENS —*adj.* equipped with a zoom lens

zoom lens a system of lenses, as in a film or TV camera, that can be rapidly adjusted for close-up shots or distance views while keeping the image in focus

zo·o·mor·phism (zō′ə môr′fiz'm) *n.* [ZOO- + -MORPH + -ISM] 1. the attributing of animal form or characteristics to a deity 2. the representation of animal forms in decorative art or symbolism —**zo′o·mor′phic** *adj.*

zo·oph·i·lism (zō of′ə liz'm) *n.* [ZOO- + PHIL(O)- + -ISM]

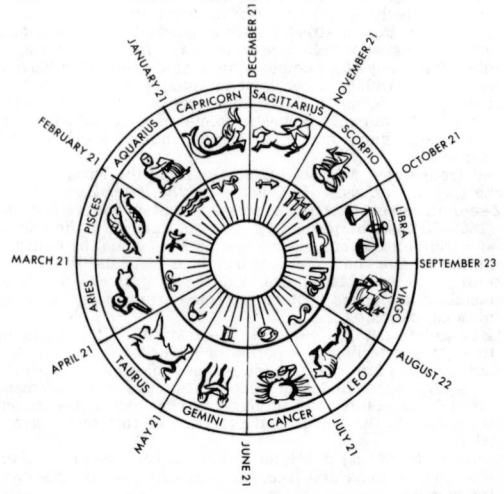

ZODIAC

extreme love for animals; specif., abnormal sexual attraction to animals: also **zo·oph′i·ly**

zo·o·phyte (zō′ə fīt′) *n.* [< ModL. < Gr.: see ZOO- & -PHYTE] any animal, as a coral, sponge, etc., that looks and grows somewhat like a plant —**zo′o·phyt′ic** (-fit′ik), **zo′o·phyt′i·cal** *adj.*

zo·o·plank·ton (zō′ə plaŋk′tən) *n.* plankton consisting of animals, as protozoans

zo·o·spore (zō′ə spôr′) *n.* *Bot.* an asexual spore, esp. of certain fungi or algae, capable of independent motion usually by means of cilia or flagella —**zo′o·spor′ic**, **zo·os′po·rous** (-os′pə rəs) *adj.*

zo·ot·o·my (zō ot′ə mē) *n.* [ModL. *zootomia*: see ZOO- & -TOMY] the anatomy or dissection of animals other than man —**zo′o·tom′ic** (-ə tom′ik), **zo′o·tom′i·cal** *adj.* —**zo·ot′o·mist** *n.*

zo·ri (zor′ē) *n.,* *pl.* **zo′ris**, **zo′ri** [Jap.] a sandal of a Japanese style, consisting of a flat sole held on the foot with a thong between the big toe and the toe next to it

zor·ille, **zor·il** (zor′il) *n.* [Fr. *zorille* < Sp. *zorilla*, *zorillo*, dim. of *zorra*, *zorro*, a fox] a small, striped, black and white African mammal, related to the weasel

Zo·ro·as·tri·an·ism (zo′rō as′trē ən iz′m) *n.* the religious system of the ancient Persians, teaching the eventual triumph of the spirit of good over the spirit of evil

Zou·ave (zoo äv′, zwäv) *n.* [Fr. < Ar. *Zwāwa*, an Algerian tribe] 1. a member of a former infantry unit in the French army that wore a colourful Oriental uniform 2. a member of any military group having a similar uniform

zounds (zoundz) *interj.* [altered < the oath (*by*) *God's wounds*] [Archaic] a mild oath expressing surprise or anger

Zr *Chem.* zirconium

zuc·chet·to (zoo ket′ō, -ə; *It.* tsoo ket′tō) *n.,* *pl.* **-tos**; *It.* **-ti** (-tē) [< It. < *zucca*, a gourd] *R.C.Ch.* a skullcap worn by clergymen: a priest's is black, a bishop's purple, a cardinal's red, and the Pope's white

zuc·chi·ni (zoo kē′nē) *n.,* *pl.* **-ni**, **-nis** [It., pl. of *zucchino*, dim. of *zucca*, a gourd] a courgette; baby marrow

zug·zwang (*G.* tsoo′ktsväŋ) *n.* [< G. < *Zug*, a pull, + *Zwang*, compulsion] *Chess* a position in which one player can move only with loss or severe disadvantage —*vt.* to manoeuvre (one's opponent) into a zugzwang

Zu·lu (zoo′loo) *n.* 1. *pl.* **-lus**,. **-lu** any member of a cattle-owning people living in Natal, South Africa 2. their Bantu language —*adj.* of the Zulus, their language, etc.

Zu·ñi (zoon′yē) *n.* [AmSp. < AmInd.] 1. *pl.* **-ñis**, **-ñi** any member of a tribe of American Indians living in a pueblo in W New Mexico, U.S. 2. their language —**Zu′ñi·an** *adj., n.*

zwie·back (zwē′bak; *G.* tsvē′bäk′) *n.* [G. < *zwie-*, twice + *backen*, to bake] a kind of rusk or biscuit that is sliced and toasted after baking

Zwing·li·an (zwiŋ′glē ən, tsviŋ′le ən) *adj.* of or relating to the doctrines of Ulrich Zwingli (1484-1531),. Swiss Protestant reformer —*n.* a follower of Zwingli

zwit·ter·i·on (tsvit′ər ī′ən) *n.* [G. < *zwitter*, hybrid + *ion*, ION] an ion carrying both a positive and a negative charge in different parts of the molecule, as in certain amino acids and protein molecules

zy·go·ma (zī gō mə, zi-) *n.,* *pl.* **-ma·ta** (-mə tə), **-mas** [ModL. < Gr. *zygōma* < *zygoun*, to yoke < *zygon*, yoke] the cheekbone —**zy·go·mat·ic** (zī′gə mat′ik, zig′ə-) *adj.*

zy·gote (zī′gōt, zig′ōt) *n.* [< Gr. *zygōtos*, yoked < *zygon*, a yoke] a cell formed by the union of male and female gametes; fertilized egg cell before cleavage —**zy·got′ic** (-got′ik) *adj.* —**zy·got′i·cal·ly** *adv.*

zy·mase (zī′mās) *n.* [Fr.: see ff. & -ASE] an enzyme, present in yeast, that promotes fermentation by breaking down glucose and some other carbohydrates into alcohol and carbon dioxide

zyme (zīm) *n.* [Gr. *zymē*, a leaven] [Obs.] a ferment or enzyme

zy·mo- [< Gr. *zymē*, a leaven] *a combining form meaning* fermentation [*zymology*]: also, before a vowel, **zym-**

zy·mo·gen (zī′mə jən) *n.* *Biochem.* an inactive form of an enzyme that can be made active

zy·mol·o·gy (zī mol′ə jē) *n.* [ZYMO- + -LOGY] the science dealing with fermentation —**zy′mo·log′ic** (-mə loj′ik), **zy′mo·log′i·cal** *adj.* —**zy·mol′o·gist** *n.*

zy·mot·ic (zī mot′ik) *adj.* [< Gr. *zymōtikos* < *zymoun*, to ferment < *zymē*, a ferment] 1. of fermentation 2. [Obs.] designating or of any infectious disease

zy·mur·gy (zī′mur jē) *n.* [ZYM(O)- + -URGY] the branch of chemistry dealing with fermentation, as applied in wine making, brewing, etc.

TABLE OF ALPHABETS

The sounds of the letters in Arabic, Hebrew, Greek, Russian, and German are shown in parentheses

ENGLISH (Upper and Lower Case)	ARABIC	HEBREW	GREEK (Print and Script)	RUSSIAN (Upper and Lower Case)	GERMAN (Upper and Lower Case)
A a	Alif 1	Aleph 4	Α α Alpha (a)	А а (a)	𝔄 a (a)
B b	Be (b)	Bet (b)	Β β Beta (b)	Б б (b)	𝔄̈ ä (e) 5
C c	Te (t)	Vet (v) 5	Γ γ Gamma (g)	В в (v)	𝔅 b (b)
D d	Se (th)	Gimel (g)	Δ δ Delta (d)	Г г (g)	ℭ c (k, ts, s)
E e	Jim (j) 2	Daled (d)	Ε ε Epsilon (e)	Д д (d)	Ch ch (H, kh)
F f	He (h) 2	He (h)	Ζ ζ Zeta (z)	Е е (ye)	D d (d)
G g	Khe (kh) 2	Vav (v)	Η η Eta (ā)	Ж ж (zh)	e (e, ā)
H h	Dal (d)	Zayin (z)	Θ θ Theta (th)	З з (z)	f (f)
I i	Zal (th)	Het (kh)	Ι ι Iota (ē)	И и (i, ē)	g (g, kh)
J j	Re (r)	Tet (t)	Κ κ Kappa (k)	Й й (ē) 7	h (h)
K k	Ze (z)	Yod (y)	Λ λ Lambda (l)	К к (k)	i (i, ē)
L l	Sin (s) 2	Kaf (k) 6	Μ μ Mu (m)	Л л (l)	j (y)
M m	Shin (sh) 2	Khaf (kh) 5, 6	Ν ν Nu (n)	М м (m)	k (k)
N n	Sad (s) 2	Lamed (l)	Ξ ξ Xi (ks)	Н н (n)	l (l)
O o	Dad (th) 2	Mem (m) 6	Ο ο Omicron (o)	О о (ŏ, o)	m (m)
P p	Ta (t)	Nun (n) 6	Π π Pi (p)	П п (p)	n (n)
Q q	Za (z)	Samekh (s)	Ρ ρ Rho (r)	Р р (r)	o (ŏ, ô)
R r	Ain 2, 3	Ayin 4	Σ σ ς Sigma (s) 6	С с (s)	ö (ö) 5
S s	Ghain (kh) 2	Pe (p)	Τ τ Tau (t)	Т т (t)	p (p)
T t	Fe (f) 2	Fe (f) 5, 6	Υ υ Upsilon (ü, ōō)	У у (ōō)	(u) q (u) (kv)
U u	Qaf (ka) 2	Tsadi (ts) 6	Φ φ Phi (f)	Ф ф (f)	r (r)
V v	Kef (k) 2	Kof (k)	Χ χ Chi (H)	Х х (kh)	ß (s, z) 6
W w	Lam (l) 2	Resh (r)	Ψ ψ Psi (ps)	Ц ц (ts)	Sch sch (sh)
X x	Mim (m) 2	Shin (sh)	Ω ω Omega (ō)	Ч ч (ch)	t (t)
Y y	Nun (n) 2	Sin (s) 5		Ш ш (sh)	(ōō)
Z z	He (h)	Tav (t)		Щ щ (shch)	ü (ü) 5
	Waw (w)	Thav (th, s) 5		Ъ ъ 8	v (f)
	Ye (y) 6			Ы ы (ē)	w (v)
				Ь ь 9	(ks)
				Э э (e)	(ē, ü)
				Ю ю (yōō)	(ts)
				Я я (yä)	

NOTES

1. A neutral letter, silent in the middle of words, but represented by ('), indicating the glottal stop, when used at the beginning of a word.
2. The first form is used at the beginning of a word; the second, in the middle; the third, at the end.
3. A neutral letter represented by ('), indicating rough breathing, when used at the beginning of a word.
4. A neutral letter, either silent or sounded according to the accompanying diacritical mark.
5. A variant of the preceding character, not counted in the alphabet.
6. The final form is used only as the last letter of a word and (in German) of some syllables.
7. Used only as the second vowel in a diphthong.
8. Indicates nonpalatalization of a preceding consonant.
9. Indicates palatalization of a preceding consonant.